BECKETT ALMANAC
OF BASEBALL CARDS & COLLECTIBLES

NUMBER 26

THE HOBBY'S MOST RELIABLE AND RELIED UPON SOURCE

Founder: Dr. James Beckett III

Edited by Brian Fleischer with the staff of Beckett Baseball

Prices in this guide reflect current retail rates determined just prior to printing. They do not reflect for-sale prices by the author, publisher, distributors, advertisers, or any card dealers associated with this guide. Every effort has been made to eliminate errors. Readers are invited to write us noting any errors which may be researched and corrected in subsequent printings. The publisher will not be held responsible for losses which may occur in the sale or purchase of cards because of information contained herein.

BECKETT is a registered trademark of BECKETT MEDIA LLC, DALLAS, TEXAS
Manufactured in the United States of America | Published by Beckett Media LLC

Beckett Media LLC
4635 McEwen Dr.
Dallas, TX 75244
(972) 991-6657
www.beckett.com

First Printing
ISBN: 978-1-953801-04-3

CONTENTS

About the Author

Based in Dallas, Beckett Media LLC is the leading publisher of sports and specialty market collectible products in the U.S. Beckett operates Beckett.com and is the premier publisher of monthly sports and entertainment collectibles magazines. Beckett, the number one authority on collectibles, currently publishes 18 magazines with a combined circulation of more than 1.1 million.

The growth of Beckett Media's sports magazines, *Beckett Baseball, Beckett Sports Card Monthly, Beckett Basketball, Beckett Football* and *Beckett Hockey,* is another indication of the unprecedented popularity of sports cards. Founded in 1984 by Dr. James Beckett, Beckett sports magazines contain the most extensive and accepted monthly Price Guide, collectible superstar covers, colorful feature articles, the Hot List, tips for beginners, Readers Write letters to and responses from the editors, information on errors and varieties, autograph collecting tips and profiles of the sport's hottest stars. Published twelve times a year, *Beckett Baseball* is the hobby's largest baseball periodical.

The *Beckett Almanac of Baseball Cards & Collectibles* is the best annual guide available to the exciting world of baseball cards and collectibles. Read it and use it, and may your enjoyment and your card collection increase in the coming months and years.

Beckett Media LLC also publishes 15 other niche magazines devoted to the homes, outdoors, automotive and action sports categories.

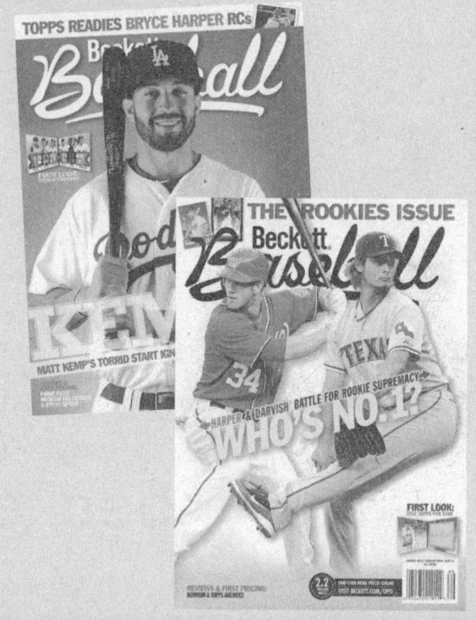

HOW TO USE AND CONDITION GUIDE

Every year, this book gets bigger and better. This edition has been enhanced and expanded from the previous volume with the addition of new releases, updated prices and changes to older listings. The *Beckett Almanac of Baseball Cards and Collectibles* has been successful where other attempts have failed because it is complete, current, and valid. The prices were added to the card lists just prior to printing and reflect not the author's opinions or desires, but the going retail prices for each card, based on the marketplace - sports memorabilia conventions and shows, sports card shops, online trading, auction results and other firsthand reports of realized sales.

What is the best price guide available on the market today? Of course sellers will prefer the price guide with the highest prices, while buyers will naturally prefer the one with the lower prices. Accuracy, however, is the true test. Compared to other price guides, The *Beckett Almanac of Baseball Cards and Collectibles* may not always have the highest or lowest values, but the accuracy of both our checklists and pricing – produced with the utmost integrity – has made it the most widely used reference book in the industry.

To facilitate your use of this book, please read the complete introductory section before going on to the pricing pages, paying special attention to the section on grading and card conditions, as the condition of the card greatly affects its value. We hope you find the book both interesting and useful in your collecting pursuits.

ADVERTISING

Within this Price Guide you will find advertisements for sports memorabilia material, mail order, and retail sports collectibles establishments. All advertisements were accepted in good faith based on the reputation of the advertiser. However, neither the author, publisher, the distributors, nor the other advertisers in this Price Guide accept any responsibility for any particular advertiser not complying with the terms of his or her ad.

HOW TO COLLECT

Each collection is personal and reflects the individuality of its owner. There are no set rules on how to collect cards. Since card collecting is a hobby or leisure pastime, what you collect, how much you collect, and how much time and money you spend collecting are entirely up to you. The funds you have available for collecting and your own personal taste should determine how you collect.

It is impossible to collect every card ever produced. Therefore, beginners as well as intermediate and advanced collectors usually specialize in some way. One of the reasons this hobby is popular is that individual collectors can define and tailor their collecting methods to match their own tastes.

Many collectors select complete sets from particular years, acquire only certain players, some collectors are only interested in the first cards or Rookie Cards of certain players, and others collect cards by team.

Remember, this is a hobby, so pick a style of collecting that appeals to you.

UNDERSTANDING CARD VALUES

Why are some cards more valuable than others? Obviously, the economic laws of supply and demand are applicable to card collecting just as they are to any other field where a commodity is bought, sold or traded in a free, unregulated market.

Supply (the number of cards available on the market) is less than the total number of cards originally produced since attrition diminishes that original quantity. Each year a percentage of cards is typically thrown away, destroyed or otherwise lost to collectors. This percentage is much, much

GLOSSARY/LEGEND

Our glossary defines terms most frequently used in the card collecting hobby. Many of these terms are common to other types of sports memorabilia collecting. Some terms may have several meanings depending on the use and context.

AU – Certified autograph.

AS – All-Star card. A card portraying an All-Star Player that says "All-Star" on its face.

ATG – All-Time Great card.

Brick – A group of 50 or more cards having common characteristics that is intended to be bought, sold or traded as a unit.

Cabinet Card – Popular and highly valuable photographs on thick card stock produced in the 19th and early 20th century.

Checklist – A list of the cards contained in a particular set. The list is always in numerical order if the cards are numbered. Some unnumbered sets are artificially numbered in alphabetical order or by team.

CL – Checklist card. A card that lists, in order, the cards and players in the set or series.

CO – Coach.

Common Card – The typical card of any set. It has no premium value accruing from the subject matter, numerical scarcity, popular demand, or anomaly.

continued on page 16

smaller today than it was in the past because more and more people have become increasingly aware of the value of their cards.

For those who collect only Mint condition cards, the supply of older cards can be quite small indeed. Until recently, collectors were not so conscious of the need to preserve the condition of their cards. For this reason, it is difficult to know exactly how many 1953 Topps are currently available, Mint or otherwise. It is generally accepted that there are fewer 1953 Topps available than 1963, 1973 or 1983 Topps cards. If demand were equal for each of these sets, the law of supply and demand would increase the price for the least available sets. Demand, however, is never equal for all sets, so price correlations can be complicated. The demand for a card is influenced by many factors. These include the age of the card, the number of cards printed, the player(s) portrayed on the card, the attractiveness and popularity of the set and the physical condition of the card.

In general, the older the card, the fewer the number of the cards printed, the more famous, popular and talented the player, the more attractive and popular the set, and the better the condition of the card, the higher the value of the card will be. There are exceptions to all but one of these factors: the condition of the card. Given two cards similar in all respects except condition, the one in the best condition will always be valued higher.

While those guidelines help to establish the value of a card, the countless exceptions and peculiarities make any simple, direct mathematical formula to determine card values impossible.

WHAT THE COLUMNS MEAN

The LO and HI columns reflect a range of current retail selling prices and are listed in U.S. dollars. The HI column represents the typical full retail selling price while the LO column represents the lowest price one could expect to find through extensive shopping. Both columns represent the same condition for the card listed. Keep in mind that market conditions can change quickly up and down based on extreme levels of demand.

PRICING PREMIUMS

Some cards can trade at premium price levels compared to values listed in this issue. Those include but are not limited to: cards of players who became hot since this book went to press, regional stars or fan favorites in high demand locally and memorabilia cards with unusually dramatic swatches or patches.

ONLY A REFERENCE

The data and pricing information contained within this publication is intended for reference only and is not to be used as an endorsement of any specific product(s) or as a recommendation to buy or sell any product(s). Beckett's goal is to provide the most accurate and verifiable information in the industry. However, Beckett cannot guarantee the accuracy of all data published. Typographical errors occasionally occur and unverifiable information may reach print from time to time. Buyers and sellers of sports collectibles should be aware of this and handle their personal transactions at their own risk. If you discover an error or misprint in this book, please notify us via email at baseballmag@beckett.com

MULTIPLIERS

Some parallel sets and lightly traded insert sets are listed with multipliers to provide values of unlisted cards. Multiplier ranges (i.e. 10X to 20X HI) apply only to the HI column. Example: If basic-issue card A or the insert card in question lists for 20 to 50 cents, and the multiplier is "20X to 40X HI", then the parallel version of card A or the insert card in question is valued at $10 to $20. Please note that the term "basic card" used in the Price Guide refers to a player's standard regular-issue card. A "basic card" cannot be an insert or parallel card.

GLOSSARY/LEGEND

Continued from page 15

Convention – A gathering of dealers and collectors at a single location with the purpose of buying, selling and trading sports memorabilia items. Conventions are open to the public and sometimes feature autograph guests, door prizes, contests, or seminars. They are frequently referred to as "shows."

COR – Corrected.

Dealer – A person who engages in the buying, selling and trading of sports collectibles or supplies. A dealer may also be a collector, but as a dealer, his main goal it to earn a profit.

Die-cut – A card with part of its stock partially cut, allowing one or more parts to be folded or removed. After removal or appropriate folding, the remaining part of the card can frequently be made to stand up.

DK – Diamond King.

DP – Draft pick or double print. A double print is a card that was printed in double the quantity compared to other cards in the same series.

Dufex- A method of manufacturing technology patented by Pinnacle Brands, Inc. It involves refractive quality to a card with a foil coating.

ERR – Error card. A card with erroneous information, spelling or depiction on either side of the card. Most errors are not corrected by the manufacturer.

EXCH – Exchange.

High Number – The cards in the last series of a set in a year in which such

continued on page 17

STATED ODDS AND PRINT RUNS

Odds of pulling insert cards are often listed as a ratio (1:12 – one in 12 packs). If the odds vary by pack type, they are generally listed separately. Stated print runs are also included in the set header lines or after the player's name for many serial numbered cards or for sets which the manufacturer has chosen to announce print runs. Stated odds and print runs are provided by the manufacturer based on the entire print run and should be considered very close estimates and not exact figures. The data provided in this book has been verified by Beckett to the best of our ability. Neither the stated odds nor print runs should be viewed as a guarantee by either Beckett or the manufacturer.

CONDITION GUIDE

Much of the value of your card is dependent on the condition or "grade" of your card. Prices in this issue reflect the highest raw condition (i.e. not professionally graded by a third party) of the card most commonly found at shows, shops, on the internet and right out of the pack for brand new releases. This generally means Near Mint-Mint condition for modern era cards. Use the chart below as a guide to estimate the value of your cards in a variety of condition using the prices found in this Annual. A complete condition guide follows.

The most widely used grades are defined on page 14. Obviously, many cards will not perfectly fit one of the definitions. Therefore, categories between the major grades known as in-between grades are used, such as Good to Very Good (G-Vg), Very Good to Excellent (VgEx), and Excellent-Mint to Near Mint (ExMt-NrMt). Such grades indicate a card with all qualities of the lower category but with at least a few qualities of the higher category.

Unopened packs, boxes and factory-collated sets are considered mint in their unknown (and presumed perfect) state. Once opened, however, each card can be graded (and valued) in its own right by taking into account any defects that may be present in spite of the fact that the card has never been handled.

GENERAL CARD FLAWS CENTERING

Current centering terminology uses numbers representing the percentage of border on either side of the main design. Obviously, centering is diminished in importance for borderless cards.

Slightly Off-Center (60/40)

A slightly off-center card is one that upon close inspection is found to have one border bigger than the opposite border. This degree once was offensive to only purists, but now some hobbyists try to avoid cards that are anything other than perfectly centered.

CONDITION CHART

	Pre-1930	1930-47	1948-59	1960-80	1981-89	1990-Present
MT	N/A	300+%	300+%	250+%	100-150%	100-125%
NRMT-MT	300+%	150-300%	150-250%	125-200%	100%	100%
NRMT	150-300%	150%	100%	100%	30-50%	30-50%
EX-MT	100%	100%	50-75%	40-60%	25-40%	20-30%
EX	50-75%	50-75%	30-50%	20-40%	15-25%	10-20%
VG	30-50%	30-50%	15-30%	10-20%	5-15%	5-10%
G/F/P	10-30%	10-30%	5-15%	5-10%	5%	5%

GLOSSARY/LEGEND

Continued from page 16

high-numbered cards were printed or distributed in significantly less amounts than the lower numbered cards. Not all years have high numbers in terms of this definition.

HOF – Hall of Fame or a card that pictures of Hall of Famer (HOFer).

HOR – Horizonal pose on a card as opposed to the standart vertical orientation found on most cards.

IA – In action.

Insert – A card or any other sports collectible contained and sold in the same package along with a card or cards from a major set. An insert card may or may not be numbered in the same sequence as the major set. Many times the inserts are randomly inserted in packs.

Issue – Synonymous with set, but usually used in conjunction with a manufacturer, e.g. a Topps issue.

JSY – Jersey.

Major Set – A set produced by a national manufacturer of cards.

Mini – A small card; for example a 1975 Topps card of identical desing but smaller dimensions than the regular 1975 Topps issue.

Multi-player Card – A single card depicting two or more players.

NNO – Unnumbered.

NNOF – No Name On Front.

Packs – A means by which cards are issued in terms of pack type (wax, cello, foil, rack, etc.) and channel of distribution (hobby, retail, etc.).

continued on page 18

Off-Center (70/30)
An off-center card has one border that is noticeably more than twice as wide as the opposite border.

Badly Off-Center (80/20 or worse)
A badly off-center card has virtually no border on one side of the card.

Miscut
A miscut card actually shows part of the adjacent card in its larger border and consequently a corresponding amount of its card is cut off.

CORNER WEAR

Corner wear is the most scrutinized grading criteria in the hobby.

Corner with a slight touch of wear
The corner still is sharp, but there is a slight touch of wear showing. On a dark-bordered card, this shows as a dot of white.

Fuzzy corner
The corner still comes to a point, but the point has just begun to fray. A slightly "dinged" corner is considered the same as a fuzzy corner.

Slightly rounded corner
The fraying of the corner has increased to where there is only a hint of a point. Mild layering may be evident. A "dinged" corner is considered the same as a slightly rounded corner.

Rounded corner
The point is completely gone. Some layering is noticeable.

Badly rounded corner
The corner is completely round and rough. Severe layering is evident.

CREASES

A third common defect is the crease. The degree of creasing in a card is difficult to show in a drawing or picture. On giving the specific condition of an expensive card for sale, the seller should note any creases additionally. Creases can be categorized as to severity according to the following scale.

Light Crease
A light crease is a crease that is barely noticeable upon close inspection. In fact, when cards are in plastic sheets or holders, a light crease may not be seen (until the card is taken out of the holder). A light crease on the front is much more serious than a light crease on the card back only.

Medium Crease
A medium crease is noticeable when held and studied at arm's length by the naked eye, but does not overly detract from the appearance of the card. It is an obvious crease, but not one that breaks the picture surface of the card.

Heavy Crease: A heavy crease is one that has torn or broken through the card's surface, e.g., puts a tear in the photo surface.

ALTERATIONS

Deceptive Trimming
This occurs when someone alters the card in order to shave off edge wear, to improve the sharpness of the corners, or to improve centering – obviously their objective is to falsely increase the perceived value of the card to an unsuspecting buyer. The shrinkage usually is evident only if the trimmed card is compared to an adjacent full-sized card or if the trimmed card is itself measured.

Obvious Trimming
Trimming is noticeable. It is usually performed by non-collectors who give no thought to the present or future value of their cards.

Deceptively Retouched Borders
This occurs when the borders (especially on those cards with dark borders) are touched up on the edges and corners with magic marker or crayons of appropriate color in order to make the card appear to be Mint.

MISCELLANEOUS CARD FLAWS

The following are common minor flaws that, depending on severity, lower a card's condition by one to

GLOSSARY/LEGEND
Continued from page 17

Parallel – A card that is similar in design to its counterpart from a basic set, but offers a distinguishing quality.

Premium – A card that is obtained in conjunction with, or redemption for, another card or product. The premium is not packaged in the same unit as the primary item.

(RC) – Rookie Logo Card. These cards feature the official MLBPA Rookie Logo. However, the player depicted on the card has already had a Rookie Card(s) issued in a previous year.

RC – Rookie Card.

Redemption – A program established by multiple card manufacturers that allows collectors to mail in a special card (usually a random insert) in return for special cards, sets, or other prizes not available through conventional channels.

Refractor – A card that features a design element that enhances its color or appearance by deflecting light.

ROY – Rookie of the Year.

Series – The entire set of cards issued by a particular manufacturer in a particular year. Within a particular set, a series can refer to a group of consecutively numbered cards printed at the same time.

Set – One of each of the entire run of cards of the same type produced by a particular manufacturer during a single year.

Skip-numbered – A set that has many unissued card numbers between the lowest and highest

continued on page 19

four grades and often render it no better than Excellent-Mint: bubbles (lumps in surface), gum and wax stains, diamond cutting (slanted borders), notching, off-centered backs, paper wrinkles, scratched-off cartoons or puzzles on back, rubber band marks, scratches, surface impressions and warping.

The following are common serious flaws that, depending on severity, lower a card's condition at least four grades and often render it no better than Good: chemical or sun fading, erasure marks, mildew, miscutting (severe off-centering), holes, bleached or retouched borders, tape marks, tears, trimming, water or coffee stains and writing.

GRADES

Mint (Mt)

A card with no flaws or wear. The card has four perfect corners, 55/45 or better centering from top to bottom and from left to right, original gloss, smooth edges and original color borders. A Mint card does not have print spots, color or focus imperfections.

Near Mint-Mint (NrMt-Mt)

A card with one minor flaw. Any one of the following would lower a Mint card to Near Mint-Mint: one corner with a slight touch of wear, barely noticeable print spots, color or focus imperfections. The card must have 60/40 or better centering in both directions, original gloss, smooth edges and original color border.

Near Mint (NrMt)

A card with one minor flaw. Any one of the following would lower a Mint card to Near Mint: one fuzzy corner or two to four corners with slight touches of wear, 70/30 to 60/40 centering, slightly rough edges, minor print spots, color or focus imperfections. The card must have original gloss and original color borders.

Excellent-Mint (ExMt)

A card with two or three fuzzy, but not rounded, corners and centering no worse than 80/20. The card may have no more than two of the following: slightly rough edges, slightly discolored borders, minor print spots, color or focus imperfections. The card must have original gloss.

Excellent (Ex)

A card with four fuzzy but definitely not rounded corners and centering no worse than 70/30. The card may have a small amount of original gloss lost, rough edges, slightly discolored borders and minor print spots, color or focus imperfections.

Very Good (Vg)

A card that has been handled but not abused: slightly rounded corners with slight layering, slight notching on edges, a significant amount of gloss lost from the surface but no scuffing and moderate discoloration of borders. The card may have a few light creases.

Good (G), Fair (F), Poor (P)

A well-worn, mishandled or abused card: badly rounded and layered corners, scuffing, most or all original gloss missing, seriously discolored borders, moderate or heavy creases, and one or more serious flaws. The grade of Good, Fair or Poor depends on the severity of wear and flaws. Good, Fair and Poor cards generally are used only as fillers.

GLOSSARY/LEGEND

Continued from page 18

number in the set. A major set in which only a few numbers were not printed is not considered to be skip-numbered.

SP – Single or Short Print. A short print is a card that was printed in less quantity compared to the other cards in the same series.

TC – Team card.

TP – Triple print. A card that was printed in triple the quantity compared to the other cards in the same series.

UER – Uncorrected error.

UNI – Uniform.

VAR – Variation card. One of two or more cards from the same series, with the same card number, that differ from one and other in some way. This sometimes occurs when the manufacture notices an error in one or more of the cards, corrects the mistake, and then resumes the printing process. In some cases, on of the variations may be relatively scarce.

XRC – Extended Rookie Card.

* – Used to denote an announced print run.

Note: Nearly all other abbreviations signify various subsets (i.e. B, G and S in 1996 Finest are short for Bronze, Gold and Silver. WS in the 1960s and 1970s Topps sets is short for World Series as examples).

MAJOR LEAGUE

1906 A's Lincoln Publishing Postcards

These ornate postcards were issued by the Philadelphia A's to honor the pennant winning team of 1905. The fronts have the words "American League Champions" on the top along with the years 1905 and 1906. The backs are blank except for the words post card. These cards were issued by the Lincoln Publishing Co. The cards are unnumbered so we have sequenced them in alphabetical order.

COMPLETE SET (20)	5000.00	10000.00
1 Chief Bender	500.00	1000.00
2 Andy Coakley	200.00	400.00
3 Lave Cross	200.00	400.00
4 Monte Cross	200.00	400.00
5 Harry Davis	200.00	400.00
6 Jimmy Dygert	200.00	400.00
7 Topsy Hartsel	200.00	400.00
8 Weldon Henley	200.00	400.00
9 Danny Hoffman	200.00	400.00
10 John Knight	200.00	400.00
11 Bris Lord	200.00	400.00
12 Connie Mack MG	800.00	1500.00
13 Danny Murphy	200.00	400.00
14 Joe Myers	200.00	400.00
15 Rube Oldring	200.00	400.00
16 Eddie Plank	600.00	1200.00
17 Mike Powers	200.00	400.00
18 Ossie Schreckengost	200.00	400.00
19 Ralph Seybold	200.00	400.00
20 Rube Waddell	600.00	1200.00

1911 A's Fireside T208

The cards in this 18-card set of color lithographs measure 1 1/2" by 2 5/8"; the cards were marketed in 1911 by Fireside Cigarettes honoring the 1910 World Champion Philadelphia Athletics. This tobacco brand was a product of the Thomas Cullivan Company of Syracuse, New York. The same front designs were also used in the D359 set by Rochester Baking. The players have been alphabetized and numbered for reference in the checklist below since the cards are unnumbered.

COMPLETE SET (18)	12500.00	25000.00
1 Frank Baker	5000.00	10000.00
2 Jack Barry	1250.00	2500.00
3 Chief Bender	5000.00	10000.00
4 Eddie Collins	6000.00	12000.00
5 Harry Davis	1250.00	2500.00
6 Jimmy Dygert	1250.00	2500.00
7 Topsy Hartsel	1250.00	2500.00
8 Harry Krause	1250.00	2500.00
9 John Lapp	1250.00	2500.00
10 Paddy Livingston	1250.00	2500.00
11 Bris Lord	1250.00	2500.00
12 Connie Mack MG	5000.00	10000.00
13 Cy Morgan	1250.00	2500.00
14 Danny Murphy	1250.00	2500.00
15 Rube Oldring	1250.00	2500.00
16 Eddie Plank	6000.00	12000.00
17 Amos Strunk	1250.00	2500.00
18 Ira Thomas	1250.00	2500.00

1911 A's Monarch Typewriter

These postcards, which measure approximately 5 3/4" x 3 5/8" feature members of the Philadelphia Athletics. The front has a small advertisement for Monarch Typewriters along with the player's photo and his name on the bottom. The back has a message from Connie Mack along with results of all the World Series from 1903 to 1910. There may be more cards in this set.

COMPLETE SET (2)	600.00	1200.00
1 Chief Bender	400.00	800.00
2 Eddie Plank	400.00	800.00

1911 A's Rochester/Williams Baking D359

This set measures approximately 1 1/2" by 2 5/8" and features members of the Philadelphia A's who had won the 1910 World Series. Over the player's photo is a "World Championship 1910" notation. Cards can be found with both Rochester and Williams backs.

1 Frank Baker	1500.00	3000.00
2 Jack Barry	1000.00	2000.00
3 Chief Bender	1500.00	3000.00
4 Eddie Collins	2000.00	4000.00
5 Harry Davis	1500.00	3000.00
6 Jimmy Dygert	750.00	1500.00
7 Topsy Hartsel	750.00	1500.00
8 Harry Krause	750.00	1500.00
9 Jack Lapp	750.00	1500.00
10 Paddy Livingston	750.00	1500.00
11 Bristol Lord	750.00	1500.00
12 Connie Mack MG	1500.00	3000.00
13 Cy Morgan	750.00	1500.00
14 Danny Murphy	750.00	1500.00
15 Rube Oldring	750.00	1500.00
16 Eddie Plank	1500.00	3000.00
17 Amos Strunk	750.00	1500.00
18 Ira Thomas	750.00	1500.00
1910 above head		
19 Ira Thomas	750.00	1500.00
1910 on side		

1911 A's Stevens Firearms

These blank-backed advertising blotters, which measure 6 1/8" by 3 1/2", feature members of the World Champion Philadelphia Athletics. The front has a photo of the player on the left and then some advertising for Stevens Firearms on the right. Since these cards are unnumbered, we have sequenced them in alphabetical order.

COMPLETE SET (10)	2500.00	5000.00
1 Frank Baker	500.00	1000.00
2 Jack Barry	250.00	500.00
3 Chief Bender	500.00	1000.00
4 Eddie Collins	500.00	1000.00
5 Harry Davis	250.00	500.00
6 Bris Lord	250.00	500.00
7 Connie Mack MG	500.00	1000.00
8 Danny Murphy	250.00	500.00
9 Rube Oldring	250.00	500.00
10 Ira Thomas	250.00	500.00

1929 A's Villa

Little is known about these postcard size cards issued in the Philadelphia area around 1929. The cards feature a portrait of the player on the front with their name and position on the bottom right. The back mentions a free Saturday matinee on October 12th. The villa logo is on the bottom. This listing may be incomplete so all additions are appreciated.

COMPLETE SET (5)	600.00	1200.00
1 Eddie Collins	300.00	600.00
2 Jimmy Dykes	100.00	200.00
3 Mule Haas	100.00	200.00
4 Bing Miller	100.00	200.00
5 Rube Walberg	100.00	200.00

1930 A's Becker

Similar to the 1929 A's Villa cards, these postcard size cards feature members of the Philadelphia A's. They were used to promote the local Becker Brothers Theatre. The front have a player photo while the back has a movie schedule. Since these cards are unnumbered we have sequenced them in alphabetical order.

COMPLETE SET (5)	500.00	1000.00
1 Max Bishop	50.00	100.00
2 Mickey Cochrane	125.00	250.00
3 Sammy Hale	50.00	100.00
4 Jimmie Foxx	200.00	400.00
5 Al Simmons	125.00	250.00

1942 A's Team Issue

This 38-card set of the 1942 Athletics features black-and-white player posted photos with white borders. The backs are blank. The cards are unnumbered and checklisted below in alphabetical order.

COMPLETE SET (38)	200.00	400.00
1 Johnnie Babich	5.00	10.00
2 Bill Beckman	5.00	10.00
3 Herman Besse	5.00	10.00
4 Lena Blackburne CO	5.00	10.00
5 Buddy Blair	5.00	10.00
6 Al Brancato	5.00	10.00
7 Earle Brucker	5.00	10.00
8 Fred Caligiuri	5.00	10.00
9 Jim Castiglia	5.00	10.00
10 Russell Christopher	5.00	10.00
11 Eddie Collins Jr.	5.00	10.00
12 Lawrence Davis	5.00	10.00
13 Richard Fowler	5.00	10.00
14 Bob Harris	5.00	10.00
15 Lum Harris	6.00	12.00
16 Frank Hayes	5.00	10.00
17 Bob Johnson	7.50	15.00
18 Bill Knickerbocker	5.00	10.00
19 Jack Knott	5.00	10.00
20 Mike Kreevich	5.00	10.00
21 Connie Mack MG	12.50	25.00
22 Earle Mack	5.00	10.00
23 Felix Mackiewicz	5.00	10.00
24 Phil Marchildon	6.00	12.00
25 Benny McCoy	5.00	10.00
26 Dee Miles	5.00	10.00
27 Tex Shirley	5.00	10.00
28 Shibe Park	5.00	10.00
29 Dick Siebert	5.00	10.00
30 Al Simmons CO	12.50	25.00
31 Pete Suder	5.00	10.00
32 Bob Swift	5.00	10.00
33 Elmer Valo	5.00	10.00
34 Porter Vaughn	5.00	10.00
35 Harold Wagner	5.00	10.00
36 Jack Wallaesa	5.00	10.00
37 Roger Wolff	5.00	10.00
38 1942 Athletics Team	6.00	12.00

1943 A's Team Issue

This 28-card set of the Philadelphia Athletics was issued by the club and features 7" by 10" black-and-white player portraits in white borders and with blank backs. The cards are unnumbered and checklisted below in alphabetical order. The team picture (card number 1) measures 7 1/2" by 10 1/2". The two Connie Mack cards also measure differently than the other cards.

COMPLETE SET (28)	150.00	300.00
1 1943 Athletics Team	15.00	30.00
2 Tal Abernathy	5.00	10.00
3 Orie Arntzen	5.00	10.00
4 Herman Besse	5.00	10.00
5 Don Black	5.00	10.00
6 James Blackburne	5.00	10.00
7 Earle Brucker	5.00	10.00
8 Russ Christopher	5.00	10.00
9 Bobby Estalella	5.00	10.00
10 Everett Fagan	5.00	10.00
11 Jesse Flores	5.00	10.00
12 Irv Hall	5.00	10.00
13 Luman Harris	6.00	12.00
14 Sam Loury	5.00	10.00
15 Connie Mack	15.00	30.00
No border; facsimile autograph		
16 Connie Mack MG	15.00	30.00
17 Earle Mack CO	5.00	10.00
18 Eddie Mayo	5.00	10.00
19 Dick Siebert	5.00	10.00
20 Frank Skaff	5.00	10.00
21 Pete Suder	5.00	10.00
22 Bob Swift	5.00	10.00
23 Jim Tyack	5.00	10.00
24 Elmer Valo	6.00	12.00
25 Hal Wagner	5.00	10.00
26 Johnny Welaj	5.00	10.00
27 Jo-Jo White	5.00	10.00
28 Roger Wolff	5.00	10.00

1945 A's Team Issue

This 30-card set of the Philadelphia Athletics was issued by the club and features 7" by 10" black-and-white player portraits in white borders and with blank backs. The cards are unnumbered and checklisted below in alphabetical order.

COMPLETE SET (30)	150.00	300.00
1 1945 Athletics Team Photo	15.00	30.00
2 Charlie Berry CO	5.00	10.00
3 Don Black	5.00	10.00
4 Earle Brucker	5.00	10.00
5 Joe Burns	5.00	10.00
6 Ed Busch	5.00	10.00
7 Russ Christopher	5.00	10.00
8 Joseph Cicero	5.00	10.00
9 Larry Drake	5.00	10.00
10 Hal Epps	5.00	10.00
11 Bobby Estalella	5.00	10.00
12 Jesse Flores	5.00	10.00
13 Mike Garbark	5.00	10.00
14 Charles Gassaway	5.00	10.00
15 Steve Gerkin	5.00	10.00
16 Irv Hall	5.00	10.00
17 Frankie Hayes	5.00	10.00
18 Dave Keefe	5.00	10.00
19 George Kell	12.50	25.00
20 Lou Knerr	5.00	10.00
21 Bill McGhee	5.00	10.00
22 Charles Metro	5.00	10.00
23 Bobo Newsom	6.00	12.00
24 Earle Mack CO	5.00	10.00
25 Hal Peck	5.00	10.00
26 Jim Pruett	5.00	10.00
27 Reidy	5.00	10.00
28 Dick Siebert	5.00	10.00
29 Al Simmons CO	12.50	25.00
30 Bobby Wilkins	5.00	10.00

1946 A's Team Issue

This 15-card set of the Philadelphia Athletics was issued by the club and features 7" by 10" black-and-white player portraits in white borders and with blank backs. The cards are unnumbered and checklisted below in alphabetical order.

COMPLETE SET (15)	100.00	200.00
1 1946 Athletics Team Picture	15.00	30.00
2 Earle Brucker	4.00	8.00
3 Sam Chapman	4.00	8.00
4 Russ Christopher	4.00	8.00
5 Jess Flores	4.00	8.00
6 Richard Fowler	4.00	8.00
7 Luman Harris	5.00	10.00
8 Luther Kaear	4.00	8.00
9 Dave Keefe	4.00	8.00
10 Connie Mack MG	15.00	30.00
11 Phil Marchildon	4.00	8.00
12 Al Simmons	12.50	25.00
13 Pete Suder	4.00	8.00
14 Elmer Valo	6.00	12.00
15 Shibe Park	15.00	30.00

1947 A's Team Issue

This 30-card set of the Philadelphia Athletics measures approximately 7" by 10" and features black-and-white player photos with white borders. The backs are blank. The cards are unnumbered and checklisted below in alphabetical order. These sets were shipped in an team-issued envelope.

COMPLETE SET (30)	125.00	250.00
1 1947 Athletics Team Picture	15.00	30.00
2 Dick Adams	3.00	6.00
3 George Binks	3.00	6.00
4 Earle Brucker	3.00	6.00
5 Sam Chapman	3.00	6.00
6 Russ Christopher	3.00	6.00
7 Joe Coleman	3.00	6.00
8 Bill Dietrich	3.00	6.00
9 Everett Fagan	3.00	6.00
10 Ferris Fain	6.00	12.00
11 Jesse Flores	3.00	6.00
12 Dick Fowler	3.00	6.00
13 Mike Guerra	3.00	6.00
14 Gene Handley	3.00	6.00
15 Eddie Joost	5.00	10.00
16 Dave Keefe	3.00	6.00
17 Bill Knickerbocker	3.00	6.00
18 Connie Mack MG	12.50	25.00
19 Hank Majeski	3.00	6.00
20 Phil Marchildon	3.00	6.00
21 Bill McCahan	3.00	6.00
22 Barney McCosky	3.00	6.00
23 Ray Poole	3.00	6.00
24 Don Richmond	3.00	6.00
25 Buddy Rosar	3.00	6.00
26 Bob Savage	3.00	6.00
27 Carl Scheib	3.00	6.00
28 Al Simmons CO	12.50	25.00
29 Pete Suder	3.00	6.00
30 Elmer Valo	6.00	12.00

1948 A's Team Issue

This 27-card set of the Philadelphia Athletics measures approximately 7" by 10" and features black-and-white player photos with white borders. The backs are blank. The cards are unnumbered and checklisted below in alphabetical order.

COMPLETE SET (27)	100.00	200.00
1 1948 Athletics Team Picture	12.50	25.00
2 Leland Brissie	3.00	6.00
3 Earle Brucker	3.00	6.00
4 Sam Chapman	5.00	10.00
5 Joe Coleman	3.00	6.00
6 Billy DeMars	3.00	6.00
7 Ferris Fain	6.00	12.00
8 Dick Fowler	3.00	6.00
9 Herman Franks	4.00	8.00
10 Mike Guerra	3.00	6.00
11 Charles Harris	3.00	6.00
12 Eddie Joost	5.00	10.00
13 David Keefe	3.00	6.00
14 Connie Mack MG	12.50	25.00
15 Hank Majeski	3.00	6.00
16 Phil Marchildon	3.00	6.00
17 Bill McCahan	3.00	6.00
18 Barney McCosky	3.00	6.00
19 Buddy Rosar	3.00	6.00
20 Bob Savage	3.00	6.00
21 Carl Scheib	3.00	6.00
22 Al Simmons CO	12.50	25.00
23 Pete Suder	3.00	6.00
24 Elmer Valo	6.00	12.00
25 Skeeter Webb	3.00	6.00
26 Don White	3.00	6.00
27 Rudy York	4.00	8.00

1949 A's Team Issue

This 33-card set of the Philadelphia Athletics features black-and-white player photos with white borders. Card number 1 measures 8" by 10" and is an actual team photograph. The backs are blank. The cards are unnumbered and checklisted below in alphabetical order. The photos were available direct from the A's for either three cents each or $1 for the set at the time of issue.

COMPLETE SET (33)	150.00	300.00
1 1949 Athletics Team	15.00	30.00
8x10		
2 1949 Athletics Team	15.00	30.00
3 Shibe Park	15.00	30.00
4 Joe Astroth	3.00	6.00
5 Henry Biasatti	3.00	6.00
6 Lou Brissie	4.00	8.00
7 Earle Brucker	3.00	6.00
8 Sam Chapman	5.00	10.00
9 Joe Coleman	3.00	6.00
10 Tom Davis	3.00	6.00
11 Jimmie Dykes CO	4.00	8.00
12 Ferris Fain	5.00	10.00
13 Dick Fowler	3.00	6.00
14 Nelson Fox	15.00	30.00
15 Mike Guerra	3.00	6.00
16 Charlie Harris	3.00	6.00
17 Eddie Joost	5.00	10.00
18 David Keefe	3.00	6.00
19 Alex Kellner	3.00	6.00
20 Connie Mack MG	12.50	25.00
21 Earl Mack	3.00	6.00
22 Hank Majeski	3.00	6.00
23 Phil Marchildon	3.00	6.00
24 Barney McCosky	3.00	6.00
25 Lester McCrabb	3.00	6.00
26 Wally Moses	4.00	8.00
27 Buddy Rosar	3.00	6.00
28 Carl Scheib	3.00	6.00
29 Bobby Shantz	6.00	12.00
30 Pete Suder	3.00	6.00
31 Elmer Valo	5.00	10.00
32 Don White	3.00	6.00
33 Taft Wright	3.00	6.00

1950 A's Team Issue

This 28-card set of the Philadelphia Athletics was issued by the club and features black-and-white player portraits that were used previously in the team sets. For a number of years, the A's did not issue new sets, but carried the same cards over several years. The backs are blank. The cards are unnumbered and checklisted below in alphabetical order.

COMPLETE SET (27)	75.00	150.00
1 Joseph Astroth	3.00	6.00
2 Leland Brissie	3.00	6.00
3 Lou Brissie	3.00	6.00
4 Samuel Chapman	4.00	8.00
5 Mickey Cochrane CO	12.50	25.00
6 Joseph Coleman	3.00	6.00
7 Bob Dillinger	3.00	6.00
8 Jimmy Dykes CO	4.00	8.00
9 Ferris Fain	4.00	8.00
10 Dick Fowler	3.00	6.00
11 Mike Guerra	3.00	6.00
12 William Hitchcock	3.00	6.00
13 Robert Hooper	3.00	6.00
14 Edwin Joost	4.00	8.00
15 Alex Kellner	3.00	6.00
16 Paul Lehner	3.00	6.00
17 Hank Majeski	3.00	6.00
18 Phil Marchildon	3.00	6.00
19 William McCoskey	3.00	6.00
20 Bing Miller CO	3.00	6.00
21 Wally Moses	4.00	8.00
22 Carl Scheib	3.00	6.00
23 Bobby Shantz	5.00	10.00
24 Pete Suder	3.00	6.00
25 Joe Tipton	3.00	6.00
26 Elmer Valo	4.00	8.00
27 Kermit Wahl	3.00	6.00
28 Henry Wyse	3.00	6.00

1951 A's Team Issue

This 35-card set of the Philadelphia Athletics was issued by the club and features the same photos as in the 1949 or 1950 Athletics team sets. The cards are unnumbered and checklisted below in alphabetical order.

COMPLETE SET (35)	125.00	250.00
1 1951 Athletics Team Photo	12.50	25.00
2 Joe Astroth	3.00	6.00
3 Chief Bender CO	6.00	12.00
4 Ed Burtschy	3.00	6.00
5 Samuel Chapman	4.00	8.00
6 Allie Clark	3.00	6.00
7 Joe Coleman	3.00	6.00
8 Jimmy Dykes MG	4.00	8.00
9 Ferris Fain	4.00	8.00
10 Richard Fowler	3.00	6.00
11 Bill Hitchcock	3.00	6.00
12 Bob Hooper	3.00	6.00
13 Eddie Joost	4.00	8.00
14 Alex Kellner	3.00	6.00
15 Lou Klein	3.00	6.00
16 John Kucab	3.00	6.00
17 Paul Lehner	3.00	6.00
18 Lou Limmer	3.00	6.00
19 Connie Mack OWN	10.00	20.00
20 Earl Mack CO	3.00	6.00
21 Hank Majeski	3.00	6.00
22 Morris Martin	3.00	6.00
23 Bing Miller CO	4.00	8.00
24 Wallace Moses	4.00	8.00
25 Ray Murray	3.00	6.00
26 Tom Oliver CO	3.00	6.00
27 Dave Philley	4.00	8.00
28 Carl Scheib	3.00	6.00
29 Bobby Shantz	5.00	10.00
30 Pete Suder	3.00	6.00
31 Joe Tipton	3.00	6.00
32 Elmer Valo	4.00	8.00
33 Kermit Wahl	3.00	6.00
34 Gus Zernial	5.00	10.00
35 Sam Zoldack	3.00	6.00

1952 A's Team Issue

This 31-card set of the Philadelphia Athletics was issued by the club and features the same photos as in the 1949 and 1951 Athletics team sets. The cards are unnumbered and checklisted below in alphabetical order.

COMPLETE SET (31)	125.00	250.00
1 1952 Athletics Team Photo	12.50	25.00
2 Shibe Park	12.50	25.00
3 Joe Astroth	3.00	6.00
4 Hal Bevan	3.00	6.00
5 Harry Byrd	3.00	6.00
6 Allie Clark	3.00	6.00
7 Jimmy Dykes MG	4.00	8.00
8 Ferris Fain	5.00	10.00
9 Dick Fowler	3.00	6.00
10 Bill Hitchcock	3.00	6.00
11 Bob Hooper	3.00	6.00
12 Eddie Joost	4.00	8.00
13 Skeeter Kell	3.00	6.00
14 Alex Kellner	3.00	6.00
15 John Kucab	3.00	6.00
16 Connie Mack OWN	10.00	20.00
17 Morris Martin	3.00	6.00
18 Bing Miller CO	4.00	8.00
19 Wally Moses CO	4.00	8.00
20 Ray Murray	3.00	6.00
21 Bobo Newsom	4.00	8.00
22 Dave Philley	4.00	8.00
23 Sherry Robertson	3.00	6.00
24 Carl Scheib	3.00	6.00
25 Bobby Shantz	5.00	10.00
26 Pete Suder	3.00	6.00
27 Keith Thomas	3.00	6.00
28 Elmer Valo	4.00	8.00
29 Ed Wright	3.00	6.00
30 Gus Zernial	5.00	10.00
31 Sam Zoldak	3.00	6.00

1953 A's Team Issue

This 31-card set of the Philadelphia Athletics was issued by the club and features the same photos as in the 1951 and 1952 Athletics team sets. The cards are unnumbered and checklisted below in alphabetical order.

COMPLETE SET (31)	125.00	250.00
1 1953 Athletics Team Photo	12.50	25.00
2 Joe Astroth	3.00	6.00
3 Loren Babe	3.00	6.00
4 Chief Bender CO	6.00	12.00
5 Charlie Bishop	3.00	6.00
6 Harry Byrd	3.00	6.00
7 Joe Coleman	4.00	8.00
8 Joe DeMaestri	3.00	6.00
9 Jimmy Dykes MG	5.00	10.00
10 Frank Fanovich	3.00	6.00
11 Marion Fricano	3.00	6.00
12 Tom Hamilton	3.00	6.00
13 Eddie Joost	5.00	10.00
14 Alex Kellner	3.00	6.00
15 Morris Martin	3.00	6.00
16 Connie Mack OWN	10.00	20.00
17 Ed McGhee	3.00	6.00
18 Cass Michaels	3.00	6.00
19 Bing Miller CO	4.00	8.00
20 Ed Monahan	3.00	6.00
21 Wally Moses	4.00	8.00
22 Ray Murray	3.00	6.00
23 Bobo Newsom	4.00	8.00
24 Tom Oliver CO	3.00	6.00
25 Dave Philley	3.00	6.00
26 Ed Robinson	3.00	6.00
27 Carl Scheib	3.00	6.00
28 Bobby Shantz	5.00	10.00
29 Pete Suder	3.00	6.00
30 Elmer Valo	4.00	8.00
31 Gus Zernial	5.00	10.00

1954 A's Team Issue

This 30-card set of the Philadelphia Athletics was issued by the club and features the same photos as in the 1953 Athletics team set. The cards are unnumbered and checklisted below in alphabetical order.

COMPLETE SET (30)	100.00	200.00
1 1954 Athletics Team Photo	12.50	25.00
2 Joe Astroth	3.00	6.00
3 Charlie Bishop	3.00	6.00
4 Don Bollweg	3.00	6.00
5 Ed Burtchy	3.00	6.00
6 Joe DeMaestri	3.00	6.00
7 Art Ditmar	3.00	6.00
8 Jim Finigan	3.00	6.00
9 Marion Fricano	3.00	6.00
10 John Gray	3.00	6.00
11 Forest Jacobs	3.00	6.00
12 Eddie Joost	4.00	8.00
13 Alex Kellner	3.00	6.00
14 Lou Limmer	3.00	6.00
15 Wally Moses	4.00	8.00
16 Ray Murray	3.00	6.00
17 Dave Philley	3.00	6.00
18 Arnold Portocarrero	3.00	6.00
19 Vic Power	5.00	10.00
20 Bill Renna	3.00	6.00
21 Al Robertson	3.00	6.00
22 Carl Scheib	3.00	6.00
23 Bill Shantz	3.00	6.00
24 Bobby Shantz	5.00	10.00
25 Pete Suder	3.00	6.00
26 Bob Trice	3.00	6.00
27 Elmer Valo	4.00	8.00
28 Ozzie Van Brabant	3.00	6.00
29 Lee Wheat	3.00	6.00
30 Gus Zernial	5.00	10.00

1955 A's Rodeo Meats

The cards in this 47-card set measure 2 1/2" by 3 1/2". The 1955 Rodeo Meats set contains unnumbered, color cards of the first Kansas City A's team. There are many background color variations noted in the checklist, and the card reverses carry a scrapbook offer. The Grimes and Kryhoski cards listed in the scrapbook album were apparently never issued. The catalog number for this set is F152-1. The cards have been arranged in alphabetical order and assigned numbers for reference.

COMPLETE SET (47)	4000.00	8000.00
1 Joe Astroth	75.00	150.00
2 Harold Bevan	125.00	250.00
3 Charles Bishop	125.00	250.00
4 Don Bollweg	125.00	250.00
5 Lou Boudreau MG	225.00	450.00
6 Cloyd Boyer Salmon	75.00	150.00
7 Cloyd Boyer Light Blue	150.00	300.00
8 Ed Burtschy	150.00	300.00
9 Art Ceccarelli	125.00	250.00
10 Joe DeMaestri Yellow	75.00	150.00
11 Joe DeMaestri Green	75.00	150.00
12 Art Ditmar	75.00	150.00
13 John Dixon	125.00	250.00
14 Jim Finigan	75.00	150.00
15 Marion Fricano	125.00	250.00
16 Tom Gorman	75.00	150.00
17 John Gray	125.00	250.00
18 Ray Herbert	75.00	150.00
19 Forrest Jacobs	150.00	300.00
20 Alex Kellner	75.00	150.00
21 Harry Kraft CO UER	75.00	150.00
Last name misspelled		
22 Jack Littrell	75.00	150.00
23 Hector Lopez	100.00	200.00
24 Oscar Melillo CO	75.00	150.00
25 Arnold Portocarrero Purple	150.00	300.00
26 Arnold Portocarrero Gray	75.00	150.00
27 Vic Power Yellow	100.00	200.00
28 Vic Power Pink	150.00	300.00
29 Vic Raschi	150.00	300.00
30 Bill Renna Lavender	75.00	150.00
31 Bill Renna Dark Pink	150.00	300.00
32 Al Robertson	125.00	250.00
33 Johnny Sain	200.00	300.00
34 Bobby Schantz ERR	225.00	450.00
Name misspelled		
35 Bobby Shantz COR	150.00	300.00
36 Wilmer Shantz Orange	75.00	150.00
37 Wilmer Shantz Lavender	75.00	150.00
38 Harry Simpson	75.00	150.00
39 Enos Slaughter	225.00	450.00
40 Lou Sleater	75.00	150.00
41 George Susce CO	125.00	250.00
42 Bob Trice	125.00	250.00
43 Elmer Valo Yellow	150.00	300.00
44 Elmer Valo Green	100.00	200.00
45 Bill Wilson Yellow	150.00	300.00
46 Bill Wilson Lavender	75.00	150.00
47 Gus Zernial	125.00	250.00

1955 A's Team Issue

This 29-card set measuring approximately 6 1/4" by 9 1/4" features borderless sepia photos of the Kansas City Athletics. The backs are blank. The cards are unnumbered and checklisted below in alphabetical order.

COMPLETE SET (29)	50.00	100.00
1 Joe Asthroth	1.50	3.00
2 Lou Boudreau MG	5.00	10.00
3 Cloyd Boyer	2.50	5.00
4 Art Cecarelli	1.50	3.00
5 Harry Craft CO	1.50	3.00
6 Joe DeMaestri	1.50	3.00
7 Art Dittmar	1.50	3.00
8 Jim Finigan	1.50	3.00
9 Tom Gorman	1.50	3.00
10 Ray Herbert	1.50	3.00
11 Alex Kellner	1.50	3.00
12 Dick Kryhoski	1.50	3.00
13 Jack Littrell	1.50	3.00
14 Hector Lopez	2.00	4.00
15 Oscar Melillo CO	1.50	3.00
16 Arnold Portocarrero	1.50	3.00
17 Vic Power	2.50	5.00
18 Vic Raschi	2.50	5.00
19 Bill Renna	1.50	3.00
20 John Sain	3.00	6.00
21 Bill Shantz	1.50	3.00
22 Bobby Shantz	3.00	6.00
23 Harry Simpson	1.50	3.00
24 Enos Slaughter	4.00	8.00
25 Lou Sleator	1.50	3.00
26 George Susce	1.50	3.00
27 Elmer Valo	2.00	4.00
28 Bill Wilson	1.50	3.00
29 Gus Zernial	2.50	5.00

1956-60 A's Postcards

This multi-year postcard set of the Kansas City Athletics features borderless black-and-white player photos measuring approximately 3 1/4" by 5 1/2". The backs are blank. These set was issued by the club at no charge and issued over a series of years. The cards are unnumbered and checklisted below in alphabetical order.

COMPLETE SET (90)	300.00	600.00
1 Jim Archer	5.00	10.00
2 Hank Bauer	7.50	15.00
3 Mike Baxes	5.00	10.00
Fielding		
4 Mike Baxes	5.00	10.00
Portrait		
5 Zeke Bella	5.00	10.00
6 Lou Boudreau MG	10.00	20.00
7 Cletis Boyer	7.50	15.00
8 George Brunet	5.00	10.00
9 Wally Burnette	5.00	10.00
10 Ed Burtschy	5.00	10.00
11 Andy Carey	6.00	12.00
12 Chico Carrasquel	6.00	12.00
13 Robert Cerv	5.00	10.00
Portrait to letters		
14 Bob Cerv	5.00	10.00
Portrait to neck		
15 Harry Chiti	5.00	10.00
16 Rip Coleman	5.00	10.00
17 Walt Craddock	5.00	10.00
18 Harry Craft	5.00	10.00
19 Jack Crimian	5.00	10.00
20 Bud Daley	5.00	10.00
21 Pete Daley	5.00	10.00
22 Bob Davis	5.00	10.00
23 Joe DeMaestri	5.00	10.00
Fielding		
24 Joe DeMaestri	5.00	10.00
With bat		
25 Art Ditmar	5.00	10.00
26 Jim Ewell TR	5.00	10.00
27 Jim Finigan	5.00	10.00
28 Mark Freeman	5.00	10.00
29 Ned Garver	5.00	10.00
30 Bob Giggie	5.00	10.00
31 Joe Ginsberg	5.00	10.00
32 Tom Gorman	5.00	10.00
To hips		
33 Tom Gorman	5.00	10.00
Pitching		
34 Tom Gorman	5.00	10.00
Standing with glove		
35 Bob Grim	5.00	10.00
36 Johnny Groth	5.00	10.00
Portrait		
37 Johnny Groth	5.00	10.00
Standing with bat		
38 Kent Hadley	5.00	10.00
39 Dick Hall	5.00	10.00
40 Ken Hamlin	5.00	10.00
41 Ray Herbert	5.00	10.00
Dark background		
42 Ray Herbert	5.00	10.00
White background		
43 Troy Herriage	5.00	10.00
44 Whitey Herzog	7.50	15.00
45 Frank House	5.00	10.00
46 Spook Jacobs	5.00	10.00
47 Bob Johnson	5.00	10.00
48 Ken Johnson	5.00	10.00

49 Alex Kellner 5.00 10.00
50 Leo Kiely 5.00 10.00
51 Lou Kretlow 5.00 10.00
52 Johnny Kucks 5.00 10.00
53 Marty Kutnya 5.00 10.00
54 Don Larsen 7.50 15.00
55 Tom Lasorda 12.50 25.00
56 Hec Lopez 5.00 10.00
Batting
57 Hector Lopez 5.00 10.00
Portrait
58 Jerry Lumpe 5.00 10.00
59 Jack McMahan 5.00 10.00
60 Roger Maris 25.00 50.00
61 Oscar Melillo CO 5.00 10.00
62 Al Pilarick 5.00 10.00
63 Rance Pless 5.00 10.00
64 Vic Power 7.50 15.00
65 Eddie Robinson 5.00 10.00
66 Jose Santiago 5.00 10.00
67 Bobby Shantz 7.50 15.00
68 Norm Siebern 5.00 10.00
69 Harry Simpson 5.00 10.00
Batting
70 Harry Simpson 5.00 10.00
Portrait
71 Harry Simpson 5.00 10.00
Fielding
72 Lou Skizas 5.00 10.00
73 Enos Slaughter 10.00 20.00
Fielding
74 Enos Slaughter 10.00 20.00
Batting
75 Hal Smith 5.00 10.00
76 Russ Snyder 5.00 10.00
77 George Susce 5.00 10.00
78 Ralph Terry 5.00 10.00
79 Wayne Terwilliger 5.00 10.00
80 Charles Thompson 5.00 10.00
81 Dick Tomanek 5.00 10.00
82 John Tsitouris 5.00 10.00
83 Marv Throneberry 7.50 15.00
84 Bob Trowbridge 5.00 10.00
85 Bill Tuttle 5.00 10.00
86 Jack Urban 5.00 10.00
87 Preston Ward 5.00 10.00
88 Dick Williams 7.50 15.00
89 Gus Zernial 7.50 15.00
Batting
90 Gus Zernial 7.50 15.00
Catching

1956 A's Rodeo Meats

The cards in this 12-card set measure 2 1/2" by 3 1/2". The unnumbered, color cards of the 1956 Rodeo baseball series are easily distinguished from their 1955 counterparts by the absence of the scrapbook offer on the reverse. They were available only in packages of Rodeo All-Meat Wieners. The catalog designation for this set is F152-2, and the cards have been assigned numbers in alphabetical order in the checklist below.

COMPLETE SET (12) 750.00 1500.00
1 Joe Astroth 75.00 150.00
2 Lou Boudreau MG 225.00 450.00
3 Joe DeMaestri 75.00 150.00
4 Art Ditmar 75.00 150.00
5 Jim Finigan 75.00 150.00
6 Hector Lopez 75.00 150.00
7 Vic Power 75.00 150.00
8 Bobby Shantz 125.00 250.00
9 Harry Simpson 75.00 150.00
10 Enos Slaughter 225.00 450.00
11 Elmer Valo 100.00 200.00
12 Gus Zernial 100.00 200.00

1957 A's Jay Publishing

This 12-card set of the Kansas City Athletics measures approximately 5" by 7" and features black-and-white player photos in a white border. These cards were packaged 12 to a packet. The backs are blank. The cards are unnumbered and checklisted below in alphabetical order. The cards have the player's name and Athletics on the bottom

COMPLETE SET (12) 20.00 50.00
1 Lou Boudreau MG 3.00 8.00
2 Bob Cerv 1.50 4.00
3 Tom Gorman 1.50 4.00
4 Milt Graff 1.50 4.00
5 Billy Hunter 1.50 4.00
6 Hector Lopez 1.50 4.00
7 Maury McDermott 1.50 4.00
8 Tom Morgan 1.50 4.00
9 Vic Power 1.50 4.00
10 Harry Simpson 1.50 4.00
11 Lou Skizas 1.50 4.00
12 Hal Smith 1.50 4.00

1958 A's Jay Publishing

This 12-card set of the Kansas City Athletics measures approximately 5" by 7" and features black-and-white player photos in a white border. These cards were packaged 12 to a packet. The backs are blank. The cards are unnumbered and checklisted below in alphabetical order.

COMPLETE SET (12) 25.00 50.00
1 Harry Craft MG 2.00 4.00
2 Joe DeMaestri 2.00 4.00
3 Ned Garver 2.00 4.00
4 Woody Held 2.00 4.00
5 Frank House 2.00 4.00
6 Hector Lopez 2.00 4.00
7 Vic Power 3.00 6.00
8 Hal Smith 2.00 4.00
9 Ralph Terry 2.50 5.00
10 Virgil Trucks 3.00 6.00
11 Bill Tuttle 2.00 4.00
12 Jack Urban 2.00 4.00

1959 A's Jay Publishing

This 12-card set of the Kansas City Athletics measures approximately 5" by 7" and features black-and-white player photos in a white border. The backs are blank. The cards are unnumbered and checklisted below in alphabetical order.

COMPLETE SET (12) 15.00 40.00
1 Bob Cerv 1.25 3.00
2 Harry Craft MG 1.25 3.00
3 Bud Daley 1.25 3.00
4 Ned Garver 1.25 3.00
5 Bob Grim 1.25 3.00
6 Ray Herbert 1.25 3.00
7 Frank House 1.25 3.00
8 Hector Lopez 1.25 3.00
9 Roger Maris 6.00 15.00
10 Hal Smith 1.25 3.00
11 Ralph Terry 1.50 4.00
12 Bill Tuttle 1.25 3.00

1960 A's Jay Publishing

This 12-card set of the Kansas City Athletics measures approximately 5" by 7" and features black-and-white player photos in a white border. The backs are blank. The cards are unnumbered and checklisted below in alphabetical order.

COMPLETE SET (11) 15.00 40.00
1 Hank Bauer 2.00 5.00
2 Bud Daley 1.25 3.00
3 Bob Elliott MG 1.25 3.00
4 Ned Garver 1.25 3.00
5 Ray Herbert 1.25 3.00
6 Johnny Kucks 1.25 3.00
7 Don Larsen 1.50 4.00
8 Jerry Lumpe 1.25 3.00
9 Norm Siebern 1.25 3.00
10 Marv Throneberry 2.00 5.00
11 Bill Tuttle 1.25 3.00
12 Dick Williams 2.00 5.00

1960 A's Team Issue

These 3 1/4" by 5 1/2" blank backed cards feature members of the 1960 A's. The fronts have fascimile autographs and we have sequenced the set in alphabetical order

COMPLETE SET (18) 20.00 50.00
1 Hank Bauer 2.00 5.00
2 Zeke Bella 1.00 2.50
3 Bob Cerv 1.00 2.50
4 Bud Daley 1.00 2.50
5 Jim Ewell 1.00 2.50
6 Ken Hamlin 1.00 2.50
7 Ray Herbert 1.00 2.50
8 Whitey Herzog 2.00 5.00
9 Bob Johnson 1.00 2.50
10 Ken Johnson 1.00 2.50
11 Johnny Kucks 1.00 2.50
12 Marty Kutnya 1.00 2.50
13 Jerry Lumpe 1.00 2.50
14 Norm Siebern 1.00 2.50
15 Russ Snyder 1.00 2.50
16 John Tsitouris 1.00 2.50
17 Bill Tuttle 1.00 2.50
18 Dick Williams 2.00 5.00

1961-62 A's Jay Publishing

This 24-card set of the Kansas City Athletics measures approximately 5" by 7". The fronts feature black-and-white posed player photos with the player's and team name printed below in the white border. These cards were packaged 12 to a packet and originally sold for 25 cents. The backs are blank. The cards are unnumbered and checklisted below in alphabetical order.

COMPLETE SET (24) 20.00 50.00
1 Jim Archer .75 2.00
2 Norm Bass .75 2.00
3 Hank Bauer 61 1.50 4.00
4 Bob Boyd 61 .75 2.00
5 Wayne Causey .75 2.00
6 Frank Cipriani .75 2.00
7 Bud Daley 61 .75 2.00
8 Joe Gordon MG 61 1.25 3.00
9 Ray Herbert 61 .75 2.00
10 Dick Howser 1.25 3.00
11 Manny Jimenez 62 .75 2.00
12 Jerry Lumpe .75 2.00
Head photo
13 Jerry Lumpe .75 2.00
At bat
14 Joe Nuxhall 61 .75 2.00
15 Joe Pignatano 61 .75 2.00
16 Leo Posada .75 2.00
17 Ed Rakow .75 2.00
18 Norm Siebern .75 2.00
At bat
19 Norm Siebern .75 2.00
Head photo
20 Haywood Sullivan .75 2.00
Waist-up photo
21 Haywood Sullivan .75 2.00
Head photo
22 Marv Throneberry 61 1.25 3.00
23 Bill Tuttle 61 .75 2.00
24 Jerry Walker .75 2.00

1961 A's Team Issue

These cards measure 3 1/4" by 5 1/2" and are blank backs. The fronts have black and white borderless photos with fascimile autographs. We have sequenced this set in alphabetical order. Often, these cards are found with a red Kansas City A's envelope. It is believed that these cards were sold as a set at the ballpark.

COMPLETE SET 30.00 60.00
1 Jim Archer .75 2.00
2 Norm Bass .75 2.00
3 Hank Bauer 1.25 3.00
4 Bob Boyd .75 2.00
5 Andy Carey .75 2.00
6 Wayne Causey .75 2.00
7 Clint Courtney .75 2.00
8 Bud Daley .75 2.00
9 Joe Gordon MG 1.25 3.00
10 Jay Hankins .75 2.00
11 Ray Herbert .75 2.00
12 Dick Howser 1.25 3.00
13 Ken Johnson .75 2.00
14 Ed Keegan .75 2.00
15 Lou Klimchock .75 2.00
16 Bill Kunkel .75 2.00
17 Frank Lane GM .75 2.00
18 Don Larsen 1.50 4.00
19 Jerry Lumpe .75 2.00
20 Joe Nuxhall .75 2.00
21 Joe Pignatano .75 2.00
22 Al Pilarcik .75 2.00
23 Leo Posada .75 2.00
24 Ed Rakow .75 2.00
25 Norm Siebern .75 2.00
26 Haywood Sullivan .75 2.00
27 Marv Throneberry 1.25 3.00
28 Bill Tuttle .75 2.00

1962 A's Team Issue

These 4" by 5" black and white cards were used by the Kansas City Athletics to deal with photo requests. These photos have the players name and position on the front surrounded by a white border. Since these cards are unnumbered, we have sequenced them in alphabetical order.

COMPLETE SET (32) 15.00 40.00
1 Jim Archer .75 2.00
2 Joe Azcue .75 2.00
3 Norm Bass .75 2.00
4 Hank Bauer MG 1.00 2.50
5 Wayne Causey .75 2.00
6 Ed Charles 1.00 2.50
7 Gino Cimoli .75 2.00
8 Bob Del Greco .75 2.00
9 Art Ditmar .75 2.00
10 Bob Grim .75 2.00
11 Dick Howser 1.00 2.50
12 Manny Jimenez .75 2.00
13 Bill Kunkel .75 2.00
14 Dario Lodigiani .75 2.00
15 Ed Lopat CO 1.25 3.00
16 Jerry Lumpe .75 2.00
17 Danny McDevitt .75 2.00
18 Gus Niarhos CO .75 2.00
19 Dan Osinski .75 2.00
20 Dan Pfister .75 2.00
21 Leo Posada .75 2.00
22 Ed Rakow .75 2.00
23 Diego Segui .75 2.00
24 Norm Siebern .75 2.00
25 Gene Stephens .75 2.00
26 Haywood Sullivan .75 2.00
27 Jose Tartabull .75 2.00
28 Jerry Walker .75 2.00
29 Jo-Jo White CO .75 2.00
30 Dave Wickersham .75 2.00
31 Gordon Windhorn .75 2.00
32 John Wyatt .75 2.00

1963 A's Jay Publishing

This 12-card set of the Kansas City Athletics measures approximately 5" by 7". The fronts feature black-and-white posed player photos with the player's and team name printed below in the white border. These cards were packaged 12 to a packet. The backs are blank. The cards are unnumbered and checklisted below in alphabetical order.

COMPLETE SET (12) 15.00 40.00
1 Jim Archer .75 2.00
2 Norm Bass .75 2.00
3 Wayne Causey .75 2.00
4 Bill Fischer .75 2.00
5 Dick Howser 1.25 3.00
6 Manny Jiminez .75 2.00
7 Ed Lopat MG 1.25 3.00
8 Jerry Lumpe 1.25 3.00
9 Norm Siebern .75 2.00
10 Haywood Sullivan .75 2.00
11 Jose Tartabull .75 2.00
12 Jerry Walker .75 2.00

1964 A's Jay Publishing

This 12-card set of the Kansas City Athletics measures approximately 5" by 7". The fronts feature black-and-white posed player photos with the player's and team name printed below in the white border. These cards were packaged 12 to a packet. The backs are blank. The cards are unnumbered and checklisted below in alphabetical order.

COMPLETE SET (12) 12.50 30.00
1 Wayne Causey 1.25 3.00
2 Ed Charles 1.25 3.00
3 Moe Drabowsky 1.25 3.00
4 Doc Edwards 1.25 3.00
5 Jim Gentile 1.25 3.00
6 Ken Harrelson 2.00 5.00
7 Manny Jimenez 1.25 3.00
8 Charlie Lau 1.25 3.00
9 Ed Lopat MG 1.25 3.00
10 Orlando Pena 1.25 3.00
11 Diego Segui 1.25 3.00
12 Jose Tartabull 1.25 3.00

1965 A's Jay Publishing

This 12-card set of the Kansas City Athletics measures approximately 5" by 7". The fronts feature black-and-white posed player photos with the player's and team name printed below in the white border. These cards were packaged 12 to a packet. The backs are blank. The cards are unnumbered and checklisted below in alphabetical order.

COMPLETE SET (12) 10.00 25.00
1 Bill Bryan .75 2.00
2 Wayne Causey .75 2.00
3 Ed Charles .75 2.00
4 Doc Edwards .75 2.00
5 Jim Gentile 1.00 2.50
6 Dick Green .75 2.00
7 Ken Harrelson 1.25 3.00
8 Mike Hershberger .75 2.00
9 Jim Landis .75 2.00
10 Mel McGaha MG .75 2.00
11 Wes Stock .75 2.00
12 Fred Talbot .75 2.00

1969 A's Black and White

This 15-card set measures approximately 2 1/16" by 3 5/8" and features black-and-white close-up player photos on a white card face. The player's name and position appears below the picture along with the team name. The backs are blank. The cards are unnumbered and checklisted below in alphabetical order. This set features a card of Joe DiMaggio as an A's coach as well as a card from Reggie Jackson's Rookie Card year. The set is dated by the fact that 1969 was the only year Tom Reynolds played for the A's. It is believed that this is a collectors issue set produced by long time collector, Mike Andersen.

COMPLETE SET (15) 50.00 100.00
1 Sal Bando 1.50 4.00
2 Hank Bauer MG 1.25 3.00
3 Bert Campaneris 1.25 3.00
4 Danny Cater .75 2.00
5 Joe DiMaggio CO 12.50 30.00
6 Chuck Dobson .75 2.00
7 Dick Green .75 2.00
8 Catfish Hunter 4.00 10.00
9 Reggie Jackson 40.00 80.00
10 Rick Monday 1.25 3.00
11 Jim Nash .75 2.00
12 Blue Moon Odom 1.25 3.00
13 Tom Reynolds .75 2.00
14 Phil Roof .75 2.00
15 Ramon Webster .75 2.00

1970 A's Black and White

Similar to the set which was issued in 1969 and some collectors call Jack in the Box, this set features members of the 1970 A's. The black and white photos take up most of the card with the players name and Oakland A logo on the bottom. The backs are blank so we have sequenced these cards in alphabetical order.

COMPLETE SET (24) 40.00 80.00
1 Felipe Alou 2.00 5.00
2 Sal Bando 1.50 4.00
3 Bert Campaneris 1.50 4.00
4 Chuck Dobson .60 1.50
5 Al Downing .60 1.50
6 Dave Duncan .60 1.50
7 Frank Fernandez .60 1.50
8 Tito Francona .60 1.50
9 Rollie Fingers 4.00 10.00
10 Jim Mudcat Grant .60 1.50
11 Dick Green .60 1.50
12 Larry Haney .60 1.50
13 Catfish Hunter 5.00 12.00
14 Reggie Jackson 10.00 25.00
15 Paul Lindblad .60 1.50
16 John McNamara MG .60 1.50
17 Don Mincher .60 1.50
18 Rick Monday .15 4.00
19 John Odom .60 1.50
20 Roberto Pena .60 1.50
21 Jim Roland .60 1.50
22 Roberto Rodriguez .60 1.50
23 Diego Segui .60 1.50
24 Jose Tartabull .60 1.50

1973 A's 1874 TCMA Postcards

These nine postcards issued feature members of the National Association Philadelphia Athletics of the 19th century. The fronts feature black and white posed photos while the backs mention these photos are reproduced from the July 25th 1874 Harpers Weekly. Interestingly, these players are from the National Association and this is one of the few sets which features players from that league which existed before the National League was formed.

COMPLETE SET (9) 4.00 10.00
1 Cap Anson 1.25 3.00
2 Joseph Battin .40 1.00
3 John Clapp .40 1.00
4 Weston Fisler .40 1.00
5 Count Gedney .40 1.00
6 Dick McBride .40 1.00
7 Mike McGeary .40 1.00
8 John (Lefty) McMullen .40 1.00
9 Ezra Sutton .60 1.50

1974 A's 1910-14 TCMA Postcards

This 12-card set features photos of the 1910-1914 Philadelphia A's players printed on postcards. The cards are numbered on the front. This postcard set had two printings - one in black and white and the other in blue and white.

COMPLETE SET (12) 10.00 25.00
501 Chief Bender 2.50 6.00
502 John Coombs .40 1.00
503 Eddie Plank 2.50 6.00
504 Amos Strunk .40 1.00
506 Ira Thomas .40 1.00
508 Stuffy McInnis .40 1.00
510 Rube Oldring .40 1.00
511 Eddie Collins 3.00 8.00
512 Frank Baker 2.50 6.00
515 Jack Barry .40 1.00
516 Jack Lapp .40 1.00
518 Danny Murphy .40 1.00

1974 A's 1929-31 TCMA

This 28-card set features photos of the 1929-31 Philadelphia Athletics team and measure approximately 2 1/2" by 4". The cards are unnumbered and checklisted below in alphabetical order.

COMPLETE SET (28) 12.50 30.00
1 Max Bishop .40 1.00
2 Joe Boley .40 1.00
3 George Burns .40 1.00
4 Mickey Cochrane 1.50 4.00
5 Eddie Collins 1.25 3.00
Lew Krausse
6 Doc Cramer .60 1.50
7 Jimmy Dykes .75 2.00
8 George Earnshaw .60 1.50
9 Howard Ehmke .40 1.00
10 Lou Finney .40 1.00
John Heving
11 Jimmie Foxx 2.00 5.00
12 Walt French .60 1.50
Waite Hoyt
13 Lefty Grove 1.50 4.00
14 Mule Haas .40 1.00
15 Sammy Hale .40 1.00
16 Pinky Higgins .40 1.00
Phil Todt
17 Connie Mack .60 1.50
Earl Mack
18 Roy Mahaffey .40 1.00
19 Eric McNair .40 1.00
20 Bing Miller .40 1.00
21 Jack Quinn .75 2.00
22 Eddie Rommel .60 1.50
23 Wally Shang .60 1.50
24 Al Simmons 1.25 3.00
25 Homer Summa .40 1.00
26 Rube Walberg .40 1.00
27 Dib Williams .40 1.00
28 Jim Moore .40 1.00
Jim Peterson
29 A's Team Card 2.00 5.00
Large photo

1974 A's 1931 BraMac

This set, which measures 3 1/2" by 5" features members of the 1931 Philadelphia A's and was issued by the Bra-Mac collaboration.

COMPLETE SET (5) 6.00 15.00
1 Jimmy Moore .20 .50
2 Mule Haas .20 .50
3 Dib Williams .20 .50
4 Jimmie Foxx 1.50 4.00
5 Al Simmons 1.00 2.50
6 Bing Miller .20 .50
7 Jimmie Dykes .40 1.00
8 Eric McNair .20 .50
9 Joe Boley .20 .50
10 Mickey Cochrane 1.00 2.50
11 Max Bishop .20 .50
12 Joe Heving .20 .50
13 Doc Cramer .40 1.00
14 Lefty Grove 1.00 2.50
15 Ed Rommel .20 .50
16 Rube Walberg .20 .50
17 Roy Mahaffey .20 .50
18 Lew Krausse .20 .50
19 Hank McDonald .20 .50

1975 A's 1913 TCMA

These unnumbered black and white cards, which measure approximately 5 1/8" by 3 1/8", feature members of the 1913 Philadelphia A's. Since these cards are unnumbered, we have sequenced them in alphabetical order.

COMPLETE SET 6.00 15.00
1 Frank Baker .75 2.00
2 Jack Barry .20 .50
3 Chief Bender .75 2.00
4 Joe Bush .30 .75
5 Eddie Collins 1.25 3.00
6 Jack Coombs .20 .50
7 Connie Mack MG 1.00 2.50
8 Stuffy McInnis .20 .50
9 Danny Murphy .20 .50
10 Eddie Murphy .20 .50
11 Rube Oldring .20 .50
12 Bill Orr .20 .50
13 Eddie Plank .75 2.00
14 Wally Schang .30 .75
15 Amos Strunk .20 .50

1976 A's Rodeo Meat Commemorative

This 30-card standard-sized set commemorates the 1955 Rodeo Meat series. The cards feature posed black-and-white player photos with white borders. The player's name appears in the lower margin. The Rodeo Meat logo is superimposed at the lower left corner of the picture. The backs carry the player's name, biographical information and a player profile. The cards are arranged in alphabetical order and numbered on the back. These cards were also issued in uncut sheet form and the set was available from the producer for $6.50 for the card set or $10 for the uncut sheet. The biographies on the back of these cards did not appear on the originals; however, those biographies did appear in the albums of the 1950's cards which were available via mail.

COMPLETE SET (30) 6.00 15.00
1 Title Card .20 .50
2 Checklist .20 .50
3 Joe Astroth .20 .50
4 Lou Boudreau MG .60 1.50
5 Cloyd Boyer .40 1.00
6 Art Ceccarelli .20 .50
7 Harry Craft CO .20 .50
8 Joe DeMaestri .20 .50
9 Art Ditmar .40 1.00
10 Jim Finigan .20 .50
11 Tom Gorman .40 1.00
12 Ray Herbert .30 .75
13 Alex Kellner .20 .50
14 Jack Littrell .20 .50
15 Hector Lopez .40 1.00
16 Oscar Melillo CO .20 .50
17 Arnold Portocarrero .20 .50
18 Vic Power .30 .75
19 Vic Raschi .40 1.00
20 Bill Renna .20 .50
21 John Sain .40 1.00
22 Bobby Shantz .40 1.00
23 Wilmer Shantz .20 .50
24 Harry Simpson .20 .50
25 Enos Slaughter .75 2.00
26 Lou Sleator .20 .50
27 George Susce CO .20 .50
28 Elmer Valo .30 .75
29 Bill Wilson .20 .50
30 Gus Zernial .30 .75

1981 A's Granny Goose

This set is the hardest to obtain of the three years Granny Goose issued cards of the Oakland A's. The Revering card was supposedly destroyed by the printer soon after he was traded away and hence is in shorter supply than the other 14 cards in the set. Wayne Gross is also supposedly available in lesser quantity compared to the other players. The standard-size cards were issued in bags of potato chips. Cards are numbered on the front and back by the player's uniform number.

COMPLETE SET (15) 60.00 120.00
1 Billy Martin MG 4.00 10.00
2 Mike Heath .60 1.50
5 Jeff Newman .60 1.50
6 Mitchell Page .60 1.50
8 Rob Picciolo .60 1.50
10 Wayne Gross SP 2.00 5.00
13 Dave Revering SP 12.50 30.00
17 Mike Norris .60 1.50
20 Tony Armas .75 2.00
21 Dwayne Murphy .60 1.50
22 Rick Langford .60 1.50
27 Matt Keough .60 1.50
35 Rickey Henderson 50.00 100.00
39 Dave McKay .60 1.50
54 Steve McCatty .60 1.50

1982 A's Granny Goose

The cards in this 15-card set measure 2 1/2" by 3 1/2". Granny Goose Foods, Inc., a California based company, repeated its successful promotional idea of 1981 by issuing a new set of Oakland A's baseball cards for 1982. Each color player picture is surrounded by white borders and has trim and lettering done in Oakland's green and yellow colors. The cards are, in a sense, numbered according to the uniform number of the player; the card numbering below is according to alphabetical order by name. The card backs carry vital statistics done in black print on a white background. The cards were distributed in packages of potato chips and were also handed out on August 15th at Oakland/Alameda stadium. Although Picciolo was traded, his card was not withdrawn (as was Revering in 1981) and, therefore, its value is no greater than other cards in the set. Blank backs exist for all players; there is no known price differential for these cards.

COMPLETE SET (15) 6.00 15.00
1 Tony Armas .30 .75
2 Wayne Gross .20 .50
3 Mike Heath .20 .50
4 Rickey Henderson 3.00 8.00
5 Cliff Johnson .30 .75
6 Matt Keough .20 .50
7 Rick Langford .20 .50
8 Davey Lopes .40 1.00
9 Billy Martin MG 1.00 2.50
10 Steve McCatty .20 .50
11 Dwayne Murphy .20 .50
12 Jeff Newman .20 .50
13 Mike Norris .20 .50
14 Rob Picciolo .20 .50
15 Fred Stanley .20 .50

1983 A's Granny Goose

The cards in this 15-card set measure 2 1/2" by 4 1/4". The 1983 Granny Goose Potato Chips set again features Oakland A's players. The cards that were issued in bags of potato chips have a tear off coupon on the bottom with a scratch off section featuring prizes. The grand prize was a World Series trip for two. In addition to their release in bags of potato chips, the Granny Goose cards were also given away (as complete sets with no tabs) to fans attending the Oakland game of July 3, 1983. Prices listed below are for cards without the detachable tabs that came on the bottom of the cards; cards with tabs intact are valued 50 percent higher than the prices below. The card numbering below is according to uniform number. According to promotional materials, more than one million cards were distributed during the promotion.

COMPLETE SET (15) 5.00 12.00
2 Mike Heath .20 .50
4 Carney Lansford .60 1.50
10 Wayne Gross .20 .50
14 Steve Boros MG .20 .50
15 Davey Lopes .40 1.00
16 Mike Davis .20 .50
17 Mike Norris .20 .50
21 Dwayne Murphy .20 .50
22 Rick Langford .20 .50
27 Matt Keough .20 .50
31 Tom Underwood .20 .50
33 Dave Beard .20 .50
35 Rickey Henderson 3.00 8.00
39 Tom Burgmeier .20 .50
54 Steve McCatty .20 .50

1983 A's Greats TCMA

This 12-card set features black-and-white photos with red borders of the Athletics franchise all-time great players. The backs carry player information.

COMPLETE SET (12) 3.00 8.00
1 Jimmie Foxx .75 2.00
2 Eddie Collins .60 1.50
3 Frank Baker .40 1.00
4 Jack Barry .08 .25
5 Al Simmons .40 1.00
6 Mule Haas .08 .25
7 Bing Miller .08 .25
8 Mickey Cochrane .50 1.25
9 Chief Bender .40 1.00
10 Lefty Grove .60 1.50
11 John Wyatt .08 .25
12 Connie Mack .20 .50

1984 A's Mother's

The cards in this 28-card set measure 2 1/2" by 3 1/2". In 1984, the Los Angeles based Mother's Cookies Co. issued five sets of cards featuring players from major league teams. Similar to the Mother's Cookies 1952 and 1953 issues, the cards have rounded corners. The backs of the cards contain the Mother's Cookies logo. The cards were distributed in partial sets to fans at the respective stadiums of the teams involved. Whereas 20 cards were given to each patron, a redemption card, redeemable for eight more cards was included. Unfortunately, the eight cards received by redeeming the coupon were not necessarily the eight needed to complete a set. Hobbyist Barry Colla was involved in the production of these sets.

COMPLETE SET (28) 5.00 12.00
1 Steve Boros MG .08 .25
2 Rickey Henderson 2.00 5.00
3 Joe Morgan 1.25 3.00
4 Dwayne Murphy .08 .25
5 Mike Davis .08 .25
6 Bruce Bochte .08 .25
7 Carney Lansford .30 .75
8 Steve McCatty .08 .25
9 Mike Heath .08 .25
10 Chris Codiroli .08 .25
11 Bill Almon .08 .25
12 Bill Caudill .08 .25
13 Donnie Hill .08 .25
14 Lary Sorensen .08 .25
15 Dave Kingman .30 .75
16 Garry Hancock .08 .25
17 Jeff Burroughs .08 .25
18 Tom Burgmeier .08 .25
19 Jim Essian .08 .25
20 Mike Warren .08 .25
21 Davey Lopes .30 .75
22 Ray Burris .08 .25
23 Tony Phillips .40 1.00
24 Tim Conroy .08 .25
25 Jeff Bettendorf .08 .25
26 Keith Atherton .08 .25
27 A's Coaches .20 .50
Ron Schueler
Billy Williams
Clete B
28 A's Checklist .08 .25
Oakland Coliseum

1984 A's Pro Arts

CARDS LISTED ALPHABETICALLY
1 Bill Almon 4.00 10.00
2 Bruce Bochte 4.00 10.00
3 Tom Burgmeier 4.00 10.00
4 Jeff Burroughs 4.00 10.00
5 Chris Codiroli 4.00 10.00
6 Mike Heath 4.00 10.00
Bill Allan
Artists
7 Mike Heath 4.00 10.00
Richard Shaw
Artists
8 Rickey Henderson 15.00 40.00
9 Donnie Hill 4.00 10.00
10 Dave Kingman 4.00 10.00
11 Carney Lansford 4.00 10.00
12 Davey Lopes 4.00 10.00
13 Joe Morgan 6.00 15.00
14 Dwayne Murphy 4.00 10.00
15 Tony Phillips 4.00 10.00
16 Checklist 4.00 10.00
17 Header Card 4.00 10.00

1985 A's Mother's

The cards in this 28-card set measure 2 1/2" by 3 1/2". In 1985, the Los Angeles based Mother's Cookies Co. again issued five sets of cards featuring players from Major League teams. The backs of the cards contain the Mother's Cookies logo. Cards were passed out at the stadium on July 6.

COMPLETE SET (28) 4.00 10.00
1 Jackie Moore MG .08 .25
2 Dave Kingman .30 .75
3 Don Sutton .60 1.50
4 Mike Heath .08 .25
5 Alfredo Griffin .08 .25
6 Dwayne Murphy .08 .25
7 Mike Davis .08 .25
8 Carney Lansford .30 .75
9 Chris Codiroli .08 .25
10 Bruce Bochte .08 .25
11 Mickey Tettleton .60 1.50
12 Donnie Hill .08 .25
13 Rob Picciolo .08 .25
14 Dave Collins .08 .25
15 Dusty Baker .40 1.00
16 Tim Conroy .08 .25
17 Keith Atherton .08 .25
18 Jay Howell .08 .25
19 Mike Warren .08 .25
20 Steve McCatty .08 .25
21 Bill Krueger .08 .25
22 Curt Young .08 .25
23 Dan Meyer .08 .25
24 Mike Gallego .08 .25
25 Jeff Kaiser .08 .25
26 Steve Henderson .08 .25
27 A's Coaches .20 .50
Clete Boyer
Bob Didier
Dave McKay/
28 A's Checklist .08 .25
Oakland Stadium

1986 A's Greats TCMA

These 12 standard-size cards feature some of the best Oakland A's ever. The fronts feature player photos while the backs have player biographies.

COMPLETE SET (12) 2.50 6.00
1 Gene Tenace .20 .50
2 Dick Green .08 .25
3 Bert Campaneris .20 .50
4 Sal Bando .20 .50
5 Joe Rudi .08 .25
6 Rick Monday .08 .25
7 Billy North .08 .25
8 Dave Duncan .08 .25
9 Jim Catfish Hunter .75 2.00
10 Ken Holtzman .20 .50
11 Rollie Fingers .60 1.50
12 Alvin Dark MG .08 .25

1986 A's Mother's

This set consists of 28 full-color, rounded-corner cards each measuring the standard size. Starter sets (only 20 cards but also including a certificate for eight more cards) were given out at the ballpark and collectors were encouraged to trade to fill in the rest of their set. The cards were originally given away on July 20th at Oakland Coliseum. Jose Canseco is featured in his rookie season.

COMPLETE SET (28) 6.00 15.00
1 Jackie Moore MG .08 .25
2 Dave Kingman .30 .75
3 Dusty Baker .40 1.00
4 Joaquin Andujar .08 .25
5 Alfredo Griffin .08 .25
6 Dwayne Murphy .08 .25
7 Mike Davis .08 .25
8 Carney Lansford .30 .75
9 Jose Canseco 4.00 10.00
10 Bruce Bochte .08 .25
11 Mickey Tettleton .40 1.00
12 Donnie Hill .08 .25
13 Jose Rijo .08 .25
14 Rick Langford .08 .25

15 Chris Codiroli	.08	.25
16 Moose Haas	.08	.25
17 Keith Atherton	.08	.25
18 Jay Howell	.08	.25
19 Tony Phillips	.30	.75
20 Steve Henderson	.08	.25
21 Bill Krueger	.08	.25
22 Steve Ontiveros	.08	.25
23 Bill Bathe	.08	.25
24 Ricky Peters	.08	.25
25 Tim Birtsas	.08	.25
26 A's Trainers and Equipment Managers Frank Ciensc	.08	.25
27 A's Coaches Bob Didier Dave McKay Jeff Newman/	.20	.50
28 A's Checklist Card Oakland Coliseum	.08	.25

1987 A's Mother's

This set consists of 28 full-color, rounded-corner cards each measuring the standard size. Starter sets (only 20 cards but also including a certificate for eight more cards) were given out at the ballpark and collectors were encouraged to trade to fill in the rest of their set. The cards were originally given away on July 5th at Oakland Coliseum during a game against the Boston Red Sox. This set is actually an All-Time All-Star set including every A's All-Star player since 1968 (when the franchise moved to Oakland). The vintage photos (each shot during the year of All-Star appearance) were taken from the collection of Doug McWilliams. The set is sequenced by what year the player first made the All-Star team. The sets were reportedly given out free to the first 25,000 paid admissions at the game.

COMPLETE SET (28)	8.00	20.00
1 Bert Campaneris	.20	.50
2 Rick Monday	.20	.50
3 John Odom	.08	.25
4 Sal Bando	.20	.50
5 Reggie Jackson	1.50	4.00
6 Jim Hunter	.60	1.50
7 Vida Blue	.30	.75
8 Dave Duncan	.20	.50
9 Joe Rudi	.30	.75
10 Rollie Fingers	.50	1.25
11 Ken Holtzman	.20	.50
12 Dick Williams MG	.08	.25
13 Alvin Dark MG	.08	.25
14 Gene Tenace	.20	.50
15 Claudell Washington	.08	.25
16 Phil Garner	.20	.50
17 Wayne Gross	.08	.25
18 Matt Keough	.08	.25
19 Jeff Newman	.08	.25
20 Rickey Henderson	1.50	4.00
21 Tony Armas	.08	.25
22 Mike Norris	.08	.25
23 Billy Martin MG	.40	1.00
24 Bill Caudill	.08	.25
25 Jay Howell	.08	.25
26 Jose Canseco	1.25	3.00
27 Jose and Reggie/(Canseco and Jackson) 1.50		.60
28 Checklist Card A's Logo	.08	.25

1987 A's Smokey Colorgrams

These cards are actually pages of a booklet featuring members of the Oakland A's and Smokey's fire safety tips. The booklet has 12 pages each containing a black and white photo card (approximately 2 1/2" by 3 3/4") and a black and white player caricature postcard measuring approximately 3 3/4" by 5 5/8". The unnumbered cards feature biographical information and a fire-prevention cartoon on the back of the card.

COMPLETE SET (12)	6.00	15.00
1 Joaquin Andujar	.20	.50
2 Jose Canseco	2.50	6.00
3 Mike Davis	.20	.50
4 Alfredo Griffin	.20	.50
5 Moose Haas	.20	.50
6 Jay Howell	.20	.50
7 Reggie Jackson	1.25	3.00
8 Carney Lansford	.60	1.50
9 Dwayne Murphy	.20	.50
10 Tony Phillips	.20	.50
11 Dave Stewart	.75	2.00
12 Curt Young	.20	.50

1988 A's Donruss Team Book

The 1988 Donruss Athletics Team Book set features 27 cards issued as three pages with nine cards on each page, plus a large full-page puzzle of Stan Musial. Cards are in full color and are standard size. The set was distributed as a four-page book and thought the puzzle page was perforated, the card pages were not. The cover of the "Team Collection" book is primarily bright red. Card fronts are very similar in design to the 1988 Donruss regular issue. The card numbers on the backs are the same for those players that are the same as in the regular Donruss set, the new players pictured are numbered on the back as "NEW." 1988 A.L. Rookie of the Year Walt Weiss makes his first Donruss appearance in this set as a "NEW" card. The book is usually sold intact. When cut from the book into individual cards, these cards are distinguishable from the regular 1988 Donruss cards since these have a 1988 copyright on the back whereas the regular issue has a 1987 copyright on the back.

COMPLETE SET (27)	3.00	8.00
97 Curt Young	.02	.10
133 Gene Nelson	.02	.10
158 Terry Steinbach	.08	.25
178 Carney Lansford	.08	.25
221 Tony Phillips	.02	.10
256 Mark McGwire	1.25	3.00
302 Jose Canseco	.75	2.00
349 Dennis Eckersley	.40	1.00
379 Mike Gallego	.02	.10
425 Luis Polonia	.02	.10
467 Steve Ontiveros	.02	.10
472 Dave Stewart	.08	.25
503 Eric Plunk	.02	.10
528 Greg Cadaret	.02	.10
590 Rick Honeycutt	.02	.10
595 Storm Davis	.02	.10
NEW Don Baylor UER Incorrect career stats	.08	.25
NEW Ron Hassey	.02	.10
NEW Dave Henderson	.08	.25
NEW Glenn Hubbard	.02	.10
NEW Stan Javier	.02	.10
NEW Doug Jennings	.02	.10
NEW Ed Jurak	.02	.10
NEW Dave Parker	.08	.25
NEW Walt Weiss	.20	.50
NEW Bob Welch	.08	.25
NEW Matt Young	.02	.10

1988 A's Mother's

This set consists of 28 full-color, rounded-corner cards each measuring the standard-size. Starter sets (only 20 cards but also including a certificate for eight more cards) were given out at the ballpark and collectors were encouraged to trade to fill in the rest of their set. The cards were originally given away on July 23rd at Oakland Coliseum during a game. Short sets (20 cards plus certificate) were reportedly given out free to the first 35,000 paid admissions at the game.

COMPLETE SET (28)	8.00	20.00
1 Tony LaRussa MG	.40	1.00
2 Mark McGwire	2.00	5.00
3 Dave Stewart	.30	.75
4 Terry Steinbach	.20	.50
5 Dave Parker.	.40	1.00
6 Carney Lansford	.30	.75
7 Jose Canseco	1.25	3.00
8 Don Baylor	.30	.75
9 Bob Welch	.20	.50
10 Dennis Eckersley	.75	2.00
11 Walt Weiss	.30	.75
12 Tony Phillips	.20	.50
13 Steve Ontiveros	.08	.25
14 Dave Henderson	.08	.25
15 Stan Javier	.08	.25
16 Ron Hassey	.08	.25
17 Curt Young	.08	.25
18 Glenn Hubbard	.08	.25
19 Storm Davis	.08	.25
20 Eric Plunk	.08	.25
21 Matt Young	.08	.25
22 Mike Gallego	.08	.25
23 Rick Honeycutt	.08	.25
24 Doug Jennings	.08	.25
25 Gene Nelson	.08	.25
26 Greg Cadaret	.08	.25
27 Athletics Coaches Dave Duncan Rene Lacheman Jim	.20	.50
28 Checklist Card Jose Canseco Mark McGwire	.60	1.50

1989 A's Mother's

The 1989 Mother's Cookies Oakland A's set contains 28 standard-size cards with rounded corners. The fronts have borderless color photos, and the horizontally oriented backs have biographical information. Starter sets containing 20 of these cards were given away at an A's home game during the 1989 season.

COMPLETE SET (28)	6.00	15.00
1 Tony LaRussa MG	.40	1.00
2 Mark McGwire	1.50	4.00
3 Terry Steinbach	.20	.50
4 Dave Parker	.40	1.00
5 Carney Lansford	.30	.75
6 Dave Stewart	.30	.75
7 Jose Canseco	1.25	3.00
8 Walt Weiss	.20	.50
9 Bob Welch	.20	.50
10 Dennis Eckersley	.60	1.50
11 Tony Phillips	.20	.50
12 Mike Moore	.08	.25
13 Dave Henderson	.08	.25
14 Curt Young	.08	.25
15 Ron Hassey	.08	.25
16 Eric Plunk	.08	.25
17 Luis Polonia	.08	.25
18 Storm Davis	.08	.25
19 Glenn Hubbard	.08	.25
20 Greg Cadaret	.08	.25
21 Stan Javier	.08	.25
22 Felix Jose	.08	.25
23 Mike Gallego	.08	.25
24 Todd Burns	.08	.25
25 Rick Honeycutt	.08	.25
26 Gene Nelson	.08	.25
27 A's Coaches Dave Duncan Rene Lachemann Art Kusn	.20	.50
28 Checklist Card Walt Weiss Mark McGwire Jose Can	.60	1.50

1989 A's Mother's ROY's

The 1989 Mother's A's ROY's set contains four standard-size cards with rounded corners. The fronts have borderless color photos, and the horizontally oriented backs have biographical information. One card was included in each specially marked box of Mother's Cookies. The words "Rookie of the Year", along with the year in which they won the award, are printed on the front of the first three cards.

COMPLETE SET (4)	4.00	10.00
1 Jose Canseco	1.25	3.00
2 Mark McGwire	1.50	4.00
3 Walt Weiss	.40	1.00
4 Walt Weiss Mark McGwire Jose Canseco	1.25	3.00

1990 A's Mother's

1990 Mother's Cookies Oakland Athletics set contains 28 standard-size cards with rounded corners. The envelope containing the cards honors the 1989 World Championship Oakland Athletics. The A's cards were released at the July 22nd game to the first 35,000 fans to walk through the gates. They were distributed in 20-card random packets at the game and eight more at the redemption booths. Both groups of cards were random and there was no guarantee of getting a complete set of cards. The promotional idea was that the only way one could finish the set was to trade for them. The redemption certificates were to be used at the Labor Day San Francisco card show.

COMPLETE SET (28)	6.00	15.00
1 Tony LaRussa MG	.40	1.00
2 Mark McGwire	1.50	4.00
3 Terry Steinbach	.20	.50
4 Rickey Henderson	1.25	3.00
5 Dave Stewart	.30	.75
6 Jose Canseco	.75	2.00
7 Dennis Eckersley	.60	1.50
8 Carney Lansford	.30	.75
9 Mike Moore	.08	.25
10 Walt Weiss	.08	.25
11 Scott Sanderson	.08	.25
12 Ron Hassey	.08	.25
13 Rick Honeycutt	.08	.25
14 Ken Phelps	.08	.25
15 Jamie Quirk	.08	.25
16 Bob Welch	.20	.50
17 Felix Jose	.08	.25
18 Dave Henderson	.08	.25
19 Mike Norris	.08	.25
20 Todd Burns	.08	.25
21 Lance Blankenship	.08	.25
22 Gene Nelson	.08	.25
23 Stan Javier	.08	.25
24 Curt Young	.08	.25
25 Mike Gallego	.08	.25
26 Joe Klink	.08	.25
27 A's Coaches Rene Lachemann Dave Duncan Merv Ret	.20	.50
28 Checklist Card A's Personnel Larry Davis& TR St	.08	.25

1991 A's Mother's

The 1991 Mother's Cookies Oakland Athletics set contains 28 standard-size cards with rounded corners. The set includes an additional card advertising a trading card collectors album.

COMPLETE SET (28)	6.00	15.00
1 Tony LaRussa MG	.40	1.00
2 Mark McGwire	1.25	3.00
3 Terry Steinbach	.20	.50
4 Rickey Henderson	1.00	2.50
5 Dave Stewart	.30	.75
6 Jose Canseco	.75	2.00
7 Dennis Eckersley	.60	1.50
8 Carney Lansford	.30	.75
9 Bob Welch	.20	.50
10 Walt Weiss	.08	.25
11 Mike Moore	.08	.25
12 Vance Law	.08	.25
13 Rick Honeycutt	.08	.25
14 Harold Baines	.30	.75
15 Jamie Quirk	.08	.25
16 Ernest Riles	.08	.25
17 Willie Wilson	.08	.25
18 Dave Henderson	.08	.25
19 Kirk Dressendorfer	.08	.25
20 Todd Burns	.08	.25
21 Lance Blankenship	.08	.25
22 Gene Nelson	.08	.25
23 Eric Show	.08	.25
24 Curt Young	.08	.25
25 Mike Gallego	.08	.25
26 Joe Klink	.08	.25
27 Steve Chitren	.08	.25
28 Checklist Card Tommie Reynolds CO Art Kusnyer CO	.20	.50

1991 A's S.F. Examiner

The fifteen 6" by 9" giant-sized cards in this set were issued on yellow cardboard sheets measuring approximately 8 1/2" by 11" and designed for storage in a three-ring binder. The cards are unnumbered and checklisted below in alphabetical order.

COMPLETE SET (15)	15.00	40.00
1 Harold Baines	.75	2.00
2 Jose Canseco	3.00	8.00
3 Dennis Eckersley	1.25	3.00
4 Mike Gallego	.40	1.00
5 Dave Henderson	.40	1.00
6 Rickey Henderson	3.00	8.00
7 Rick Honeycutt	.40	1.00
8 Mark McGwire	5.00	12.00
9 Mike Moore	.40	1.00
10 Gene Nelson	.40	1.00
11 Eric Show	.40	1.00
12 Terry Steinbach	.60	1.50
13 Dave Stewart	1.00	2.50
14 Walt Weiss	.40	1.00
15 Bob Welch	.60	1.50

1992 A's Mother's

This 28-card standard-size set, sponsored by Mother's Cookies, contains borderless posed color player photos of the Oakland Athletics team. The cards have rounded corners. The red and purple backs include biographical information. The set also includes an order-form card for a Mother's Cookies Oakland Athletics collectors album. The album was available for 3.95.

COMPLETE SET (28)	6.00	15.00
1 Tony LaRussa MG	.40	1.00
2 Mark McGwire	1.00	2.50
3 Terry Steinbach	.30	.75
4 Rickey Henderson	.75	2.00
5 Dave Stewart	.30	.75
6 Jose Canseco	.60	1.50
7 Dennis Eckersley	.60	1.50
8 Carney Lansford	.30	.75
9 Bob Welch	.20	.50
10 Walt Weiss	.20	.50
11 Mike Moore	.08	.25
12 Goose Gossage	.30	.75
13 Rick Honeycutt	.08	.25
14 Harold Baines	.30	.75
15 Jamie Quirk	.08	.25
16 Jeff Parrett	.08	.25
17 Willie Wilson	.08	.25
18 Dave Henderson	.08	.25
19 Joe Slusarski	.08	.25
20 Mike Bordick	.20	.50
21 Lance Blankenship	.08	.25
22 Gene Nelson	.08	.25
23 Vince Horsman	.08	.25
24 Ron Darling	.08	.25
25 Randy Ready	.08	.25
26 Scott Hemond	.08	.25
27 Scott Brosius	.60	1.50
28 Checklist Rene Lachemann CO Art Kusnyer CO Dave	.20	.50

1993 A's Mother's

The 1993 Mother's Cookies Athletics set consists of 28 standard-size cards with rounded corners.

COMPLETE SET (28)	5.00	12.00
1 Tony LaRussa MG	.40	1.00
2 Mark McGwire	1.25	3.00
3 Terry Steinbach	.20	.50
4 Dennis Eckersley	.60	1.50
5 Ruben Sierra	.20	.50
6 Rickey Henderson	1.00	2.50
7 Mike Bordick	.08	.25
8 Rick Honeycutt	.08	.25
9 Dave Henderson	.08	.25
10 Bob Welch	.20	.50
11 Dale Sveum	.08	.25
12 Ron Darling	.08	.25
13 Jerry Browne	.08	.25
14 Bobby Witt	.08	.25
15 Troy Neel	.08	.25
16 Goose Gossage	.30	.75
17 Brent Gates	.08	.25
18 Storm Davis	.08	.25
19 Scott Hemond	.08	.25
20 Kelly Downs	.08	.25
21 Kevin Seitzer	.08	.25
22 Lance Blankenship	.08	.25
23 Mike Mohler	.08	.25
24 Edwin Nunez	.08	.25
25 Joe Boever	.08	.25
26 Shawn Hillegas	.08	.25
27 Coaches Card Dave McKay Dave Duncan Tommie Reyn	.20	.50
28 Frank Cienscyzk EQ MG CL	.08	.25

1993 A's Smokey McGwire

This two-card set measures approximately 2" by 8" and features a small action color photo of Mark McGwire. The backs contain recommended reading from the local library.

COMPLETE SET (2)	6.00	15.00
1 Mark McGwire Catching the ball	3.00	8.00
2 Mark McGwire Batting	3.00	8.00

1993 A's Stadium Club

This 30-card standard-size set features the 1993 Oakland Athletics. The set was issued in hobby (plastic box) and retail (blister) form.

COMP. FACT SET (30)	3.00	8.00
1 Dennis Eckersley	.60	1.50
2 Lance Blankenship	.02	.10
3 Mike Mohler	.02	.10
4 Jerry Browne	.02	.10
5 Kevin Seitzer	.02	.10
6 Storm Davis	.02	.10
7 Mark McGwire	1.25	3.00
8 Rickey Henderson	1.00	2.50
9 Terry Steinbach	.08	.25
10 Ruben Sierra	.08	.25
11 Dave Henderson	.02	.10
12 Bob Welch	.08	.25
13 Rick Honeycutt	.02	.10
14 Ron Darling	.02	.10
15 Joe Boever	.02	.10
16 Bobby Witt	.02	.10
17 Izzy Molina	.02	.10
18 Mike Bordick	.02	.10
19 Brent Gates	.02	.10
20 Shawn Hillegas	.02	.10
21 Scott Hemond	.02	.10
22 Todd Van Poppel	.02	.10
23 Johnny Guzman	.02	.10
24 Scott Lydy	.02	.10
25 Scott Baker	.02	.10
26 Todd Revenig	.02	.10
27 Scott Brosius	.20	.50
28 Troy Neel	.02	.10
29 Dale Sveum	.02	.10
30 Mike Neill	.02	.10

1994 A's Mother's

The 1994 Mother's Cookies Athletics set consists of 28 standard-size cards with rounded corners.

COMPLETE SET (28)	5.00	12.00
1 Tony La Russa MG	.40	1.00
2 Mark McGwire	1.25	3.00
3 Terry Steinbach	.20	.50
4 Dennis Eckersley	.60	1.50
5 Mike Bordick	.08	.25
6 Rickey Henderson	.60	1.50
7 Ruben Sierra	.20	.50
8 Stan Javier	.08	.25
9 Todd Van Poppel	.08	.25
10 Bob Welch	.20	.50
11 Miguel Jimenez	.08	.25
12 Steve Karsay	.08	.25
13 Geronimo Berroa	.08	.25
14 Bobby Witt	.08	.25
15 Troy Neel	.08	.25
16 Ron Darling	.08	.25
17 Scott Hemond	.08	.25
18 Steve Ontiveros	.08	.25
19 Mike Aldrete	.08	.25
20 Carlos Reyes	.08	.25
21 Brent Gates	.08	.25
22 Mark Acre	.08	.25
23 Eric Helfand	.08	.25
24 Vince Horsman	.08	.25
25 Bill Taylor	.08	.25
26 Scott Brosius	.20	.50
27 John Briscoe	.08	.25
28 Checklist Coaches	.20	.50

1994 A's Pogs Target

These 30 Pogs were issued in panels of six - five of which featured a member of the A's and the sixth featuring the Oakland A's logo. Since the pogs are unnumbered we have sequenced them in alphabetical order. All the player pogs have a fascimile autograph on them.

COMPLETE SET (30)	5.00	12.00
1 Mike Aldrete	.10	.25
2 Geronino Berroa	.10	.25
3 Mike Bordick	.10	.25
4 John Briscoe	.10	.25
5 Scott Brosius	.25	.60
6 Ron Darling	.10	.25
7 Dave Duncan CO	.10	.25
8 Dennis Eckersley	1.00	2.50
9 Brent Gates	.10	.25
10 Scott Hemond	.10	.25
11 Rickey Henderson	2.00	5.00
12 Stan Javier	.10	.25
13 Steve Karsay	.10	.25
14 Carney Lansford	.25	.60
15 Jim Lefebvre	.10	.25
16 Tony LaRussa MG	.50	1.25
17 Mark McGwire	2.50	6.00
18 Dave McKay CO	.10	.25
19 Junior Noboa	.10	.25
20 Troy Neel	.10	.25
21 Edwin Nunez	.10	.25
22 Steve Ontiveros	.10	.25
23 Carlos Reyes	.10	.25
24 Tommy Reynolds CO	.10	.25
25 Ruben Sierra	.25	.60
26 Terry Steinbach	.25	.60
27 Bill Taylor	.10	.25
28 Todd Van Poppel	.10	.25
29 Bob Welch	.25	.60
30 Bobby Witt	.10	.25

1995 A's CHP

Sponsored by the California Highway Patrol, this eight-card set of the Oakland A's features borderless color action player photos. The backs carry player information and a safety message.

COMPLETE SET (8)	8.00	20.00
1 Brent Gates	.40	1.00
2 Mark McGwire	3.00	8.00
3 Geronimo Berroa	.40	1.00
4 Jason Giambi	2.50	6.00
5 Terry Steinbach	.75	2.00
6 Mike Bordick	.40	1.00
7 Todd Van Poppel	.40	1.00
8 Ariel Prieto	.40	1.00

1995 A's Mother's

The 1995 Mother's Cookies Oakland A's set consists of 30 standard-size cards with rounded corners. A special card of Ariel Prieto, as well as a special coupon card, was issued in September as part of Hispanic-American night. The complete set includes the Prieto SP card.

COMPLETE SET (30)	10.00	25.00
1 Tony La Russa	.40	1.00
2 Mark McGwire	1.25	3.00
3 Terry Steinbach	.20	.50
4 Dennis Eckersley	.60	1.50
5 Rickey Henderson	1.00	2.50
6 Ron Darling	.08	.25
7 Ruben Sierra	.20	.50
8 Mike Aldrete	.08	.25
9 Stan Javier	.08	.25
10 Mike Bordick	.08	.25
11 Dave Stewart	.30	.75
12 Geronimo Berroa	.08	.25
13 Todd Van Poppel	.08	.25
14 Todd Stottlemyre	.08	.25
15 Eric Helfand	.08	.25
16 Dave Leiper	.08	.25
17 Rick Honeycutt	.08	.25
18 Steve Ontiveros	.08	.25
19 Mike Gallego	.08	.25
20 Carlos Reyes	.08	.25
21 Brent Gates	.08	.25
22 Craig Paquette	.08	.25
23 Mike Harkey	.08	.25
24 Andy Tomberlin	.08	.25
25 Jim Corsi	.08	.25
26 Mark Acre	.08	.25
27 Scott Brosius	.20	.50
28 Coaches Checklist	.20	.50
29 Ariel Prieto SP	4.00	10.00
30 Coupon Card	.08	.25

1996 A's Mother's

This 28-card set consists of borderless posed color player portraits in stadium settings

COMPLETE SET (28)	5.00	12.00
1 Art Howe MG	.20	.50
2 Mark McGwire	1.50	4.00
3 Jason Giambi	1.00	2.50
4 Terry Steinbach	.20	.50
5 Mike Bordick	.08	.25
6 Brent Gates	.08	.25
7 Scott Brosius	.20	.50
8 Doug Johns	.08	.25
9 Jose Herrera	.08	.25
10 John Wasdin	.08	.25
11 Ernie Young	.08	.25
12 Pedro Munoz	.08	.25
13 Steve Wojciechowski	.08	.25
14 Geronimo Berroa	.08	.25
15 Phil Plantier	.08	.25
16 Bobby Chouinard	.08	.25
17 George Williams	.08	.25
18 Jim Corsi	.08	.25
19 Mike Mohler	.08	.25
20 Torey Lovullo	.08	.25
21 Carlos Reyes	.08	.25
22 Buddy Groom	.08	.25
23 Don Wengert	.08	.25
24 Bill Taylor	.08	.25
25 Todd Van Poppel	.08	.25
26 Rafael Bournigal	.08	.25
27 Damon Mashore	.08	.25
28 Coaches Card CL/	.08	.25

1996 A's Postcard Team

These postcards, featuring photographs taken by noted sports photographer Barry Colla, were issued by the Oakland A's in 1996. The full-color, borderless fronts feature color photos while the back has vital stats and biographical information.

COMPLETE SET (21)	6.00	15.00
1 Mark McGwire	1.25	3.00
2 Mark Acre	.20	.50
3 Mike Bordick	.20	.50
4 John Briscoe	.20	.50
5 Scott Brosius	.30	.75
6 Jim Corsi	.20	.50
7 Brent Gates	.20	.50
8 Jason Giambi	1.00	2.50
9 Art Howe MG	.20	.50
10 Doug Johns	.20	.50
11 Steve Karsay	.20	.50
12 Mike Mohler	.20	.50
13 Craig Paquette	.20	.50
14 Ariel Prieto	.20	.50
15 Carlos Reyes	.20	.50
16 Terry Steinbach	.30	.75
17 Dave Stewart	.30	.75
18 Todd Van Poppel	.20	.50
19 John Wasdin	.20	.50
20 George Williams	.20	.50
21 Steve Wojciehowski	.20	.50

1996 A's Postcard Volume

Some of these postcards parallel the regular A's Postcards issued in 1996 while others are new. The difference between these and the regular Postcards are that they are sponsored by Volume Services and there is a note as to a phone number one can call for A's Tickets. Please note that this set is skip numbered.

COMPLETE SET (16)	5.00	12.00
3 Mike Bordick	.20	.50
5 Scott Brosius	.30	.75
6 Jim Corsi	.20	.50
7 Brent Gates	.20	.50
8 Jason Giambi	1.00	2.50
10 Doug Johns	.20	.50
14 Ariel Prieto	.20	.50
15 Carlos Reyes	.20	.50
16 Terry Steinbach	.30	.75
18 Todd Van Poppel	.20	.50
62 Allen Battle	.20	.50
63 Gerohimo Berroa	.20	.50
64 Art Howe MG	.20	.50
65 Mark McGwire	1.25	3.00
66 Phil Plantier	.20	.50
67 Ernie Young	.20	.50

1997 A's Mother's

This 28-card set of the Oakland Athletics sponsored by Mother's Cookies consists of posed color player photos with rounded corners. The backs carry biographical information and the sponsor's logo on a white background in red and purple print. A blank slot for the player's autograph rounds out the back.

COMPLETE SET (28)	5.00	12.00
1 Art Howe MG	.20	.50
2 Mark McGwire	1.25	3.00
3 Jose Canseco	.60	1.50
4 Jason Giambi	.60	1.50
5 Geronimo Berroa	.08	.25
6 Ernie Young	.08	.25
7 Scott Brosius	.20	.50
8 Dave Magadan	.08	.25
9 Mike Mohler	.08	.25
10 George Williams	.08	.25
11 Tony Batista	.20	.50
12 Steve Karsay	.08	.25
13 Rafael Bournigal	.08	.25
14 Ariel Prieto	.08	.25
15 Buddy Groom	.08	.25
16 Matt Stairs	.08	.25
17 Brent Mayne	.08	.25
18 Bill Taylor	.08	.25
19 Scott Spiezio	.20	.50
20 Richie Lewis	.08	.25
21 Mark Acre	.08	.25
22 Dave Telgheder	.08	.25
23 Willie Adams	.08	.25
24 Izzy Molina	.08	.25
25 Don Wengert	.08	.25
26 Damon Mashore	.08	.25
27 Aaron Small	.20	.50
28 Coaches Card CL Bob Alejo Bob Cluck Duffy Dyer#	.08	.25

1997 A's Pinnacle Season Ticket McGwire

This two-card set was produced by Pinnacle for the Oakland Athletics. The cards featurea a 2 1/2" by 3 1/2" color photo of Mark McGwire running with Brent Gates ready to shake his hand. The picture is printed on a fading green or yellow background on a plastic 3" by 7" card made available to 1997 Season Ticket Holders. The backs are blank. After Brent Gates was traded, the set was pulled off the market and replaced by other passes.

COMPLETE SET (2)	12.50	30.00

1998 A's Mother's

This 28-card set of the Oakland Athletics sponsored by Mother's Cookies consists of posed color player photos with rounded corners.

COMPLETE SET (28)	5.00	12.00
1 Art Howe MG	.20	.50
2 Rickey Henderson	1.00	2.50
3 Jason Giambi	.60	1.50
4 Tom Candiotti	.08	.25
5 Matt Stairs	.08	.25
6 Kenny Rogers	.20	.50
7 Scott Spiezio	.08	.25
8 Ben Grieve	.08	.25
9 Kevin Mitchell	.08	.25
10 A.J. Hinch	.08	.25
11 Bill Taylor	.08	.25
12 Rafael Bournigal	.08	.25
13 Miguel Tejada	1.50	4.00
14 Kurt Abbott	.08	.25
15 Buddy Groom	.08	.25
16 Dave Magadan	.08	.25
17 Mike Oquist	.08	.25
18 Mike Macfarlane	.08	.25
19 Mike Fetters	.08	.25
20 Ryan Christenson	.08	.25
21 T.J. Mathews	.08	.25
22 Mike Mohler	.08	.25
23 Jason McDonald	.08	.25
24 Blake Stein	.08	.25
25 Mike Blowers	.08	.25
26 Jimmy Haynes	.08	.25
27 Aaron Small	.20	.50
28 Coaches Card CL Duffy Dyer Brad Fischer Gary Jo	.08	.25

1998-99 A's Historical Society

This 46 card set measuring slightly more than the standard size was issued by the Philadelphia A's historical society and honored great and popular players who played for the A's before they moved to Kansas City. The original cost of the set from the A's society was $18.75

COMPLETE SET (46)	12.50	30.00
1 Connie Mack MG	.75	2.00
2 Sam Chapman	.20	.50
3 Bobby Shantz	.40	1.00
4 Al Brancato	.20	.50
5 Bob Dillinger	.30	.75
6 Irv Hall	.20	.50
7 Joe Hauser	.20	.50
8 Taffy Wright	.20	.50
9 Gus Zernial	.40	1.00
10 Ray Murray	.20	.50
11 Skeeter Kell	.20	.50
12 Morrie Martin	.20	.50
13 Pete Suder	.20	.50
14 Pinky Higgins	.20	.50
15 Allie Clark	.20	.50
16 Hank Wyse	.20	.50
17 George Kell	.60	1.50
18 Hank Majeski	.20	.50
19 Jimmie Foxx	1.00	2.50
20 Crash Davis	.20	.50
21 Elmer Valo	.20	.50
22 Ray Coleman	.20	.50
23 Carl Scheib	.20	.50
24 Billy Hitchcock	.20	.50
25 Earle Brucker Jr.	.20	.50
26 Dave Philley	.20	.50
27 Joe DeMaestri	.20	.50
28 Eddie Collins Jr.	.20	.50
29 Eddie Joost	.30	.75
30 Spook Jacobs	.20	.50
31 Ferris Fain	.30	.75
32 Eddie Robinson	.20	.50
33 Vic Power	.30	.75
34 Lou Brissie	.20	.50
35 Bill Renna	.20	.50
36 Nellie Fox	.60	1.50
37 Lou Limmer	.20	.50
38 Eddie Collins	.60	1.50
39 Roger Cramer	.30	.75
40 Joe Astroth	.20	.50
41 Bill Werber Issued in 1999	1.00	2.50
42 Rube Oldring	.20	.50
43 Stuffy McInnis	.20	.50
44 Bing Miller	.20	.50
45 Bob Johnson	.30	.75
NNO Joe Jackson	2.00	5.00

1998-99 A's Ted Walker

These 48 oversize cards were drawn by artist Ted Walker and featured members of the Philadelphia A's. Ted Walker's grandfather was Tom Walker, a pitcher in the early 20th century with the A's. The cards are unnumbered so we have sequenced them in alphabetical order. The first 44 cards were issued in 1998 and the last four were issued in 1999.

COMPLETE SET (48)	15.00	40.00
1 Joe Astroth	.20	.50
2 Frank Baker	.60	1.50
3 Chief Bender	.60	1.50
4 Max Bishop	.20	.50
5 Ty Cobb	2.00	5.00
6 Mickey Cochrane	.60	1.50
7 Eddie Collins	.60	1.50
8 Doc Cramer	.30	.75
9 Joe DeMaestri	.20	.50
10 Bill Dietrich	.20	.50
11 Jimmy Dykes	.30	.75
12 George Earnshaw	.30	.75
13 Elmer Flick	.40	1.00
14 Nellie Fox	.60	1.50
15 Jimmy Foxx (Jimmie)	1.00	2.50
16 Walter French	.20	.50
17 Lefty Grove	.60	1.50
18 Mule Haas	.20	.50
19 Sammy Hale	.20	.50
20 Joe Jackson	2.00	5.00
21 Bob Johnson	.20	.50

22 Alex Kellner .20 .50
23 Nap Lajoie 1.00 2.50
24 Connie Mack MG .75 2.00
25 Hank Majeski .20 .50
26 Stuffy McInnis .20 .50
27 Bing Miller .20 .50
28 Wally Moses .20 .50
29 Dave Philley .20 .50
30 Eddie Plank .60 1.50
31 Jack Quinn .30 .75
32 Eddie Rommell .30 .75
33 Buddy Rosar .20 .50
34 Carl Scheib .20 .50
35 Wally Schang .20 .50
36 Bobby Shantz .30 .75
37 Al Simmons .60 1.50
38 Tris Speaker 1.00 2.50
39 Pete Suder .20 .50
40 Homer Summa .20 .50
41 Rude Waddell .60 1.50
42 Rube Walberg .20 .50
43 Tom Walker .20 .50
44 Gus Zernial .30 .75
45 George Burns .20 .50
46 Ferris Fain .30 .75
47 Eddie Joost .30 .75
48 Zack Wheat .60 1.50

1999 A's Plumbers Union

This 28 card standard-size set was issued and featured members of the 1999 Oakland A's. The cards have green amd gold borders and inside the borders are posed shots of the A's. The backs have biographical information and the logo of the Plumbers Steamfitters Refrigeration Local number 342.

COMPLETE SET (28) 5.00 12.00
1 Art Howe MG .25 .60
2 Ben Grieve .25 .60
3 Jason Giambi .30 .75
4 Kenny Rogers .25 .60
5 Matt Stairs .25 .60
6 Tom Candiotti .25 .60
7 Tony Phillips .25 .60
8 Eric Chavez .30 .75
9 Tim Raines .25 .60
10 A.J. Hinch .25 .60
11 Bill Taylor .25 .60
12 Miguel Tejada .30 .75
13 Tim Worrell .25 .60
14 Scott Spiezio .25 .60
15 Buddy Groom .25 .60
16 Olmedo Saenz .25 .60
17 T.J. Mathews .25 .60
18 Mike Macfarlane .25 .60
19 Brad Rigby .25 .60
20 Ryan Christenson .25 .60
21 Doug Jones .25 .60
22 Terry Clark .25 .60
23 Jorge Velandia .25 .60
24 Gil Heredia .25 .60
25 John Jaha .25 .60
26 Jimmy Haynes .25 .60
27 Jason McDonald .25 .60
28 Thad Bosley .25 .60
Brad Fischer
Dave Hudgens
Ken Macha

2000 A's AT and T Fanfest

COMPLETE SET (36) 10.00 25.00
1 Bob Alejo CO .20 .50
2 Kevin Appier .20 .50
3 Rich Becker .20 .50
4 Thad Bosley .20 .50
5 Eric Chavez 2.00
6 Rollie Fingers .80 2.00
7 Brad Fischer .20 .50
8 Jason Giambi .75 2.00
9 Ben Grieve .20 .50
10 Chad Harville .20 .50
11 Gil Heredia .20 .50
12 A.J. Hinch .20 .50
13 Ken Holtzman .30 .75
14 Art Howe MG .20 .50
15 Tim Hudson 1.00 2.50
16 Jason Isringhausen .40 1.00
17 John Jaha .20 .50
18 Doug Jones .20 .50
19 Tim Kubinski .20 .50
20 Brett Laxton .20 .50
21 Ken Macha CO .20 .50
22 Mike Magnante .20 .50
23 Ron Mahay .20 .50
24 T.J. Mathews .20 .50
25 Frank Menechino .20 .50
26 Mark Mulder 1.00 2.50
27 Billy North .20 .50
28 John Odom .20 .50
29 Adam Piatt .20 .50
30 Bo Porter .20 .50
31 Mike Quade CO .20 .50
32 Matt Stairs .20 .50
33 Gene Tenace .30 .75
34 Jorge Velendia .20 .50
35 Randy Velarde .20 .50
36 Ron Washington CO .20 .50

2000 A's Plumbers Union

COMPLETE SET (28) 5.00 12.00
1 Art Howe MG .25 .60
2 Jason Giambi .30 .75
3 Tim Hudson .30 .75
4 Matt Stairs .25 .60
5 Kevin Appier .25 .60
6 Ben Grieve .25 .60
7 Randy Velarde .25 .60
8 Eric Chavez .30 .75
9 Mark Mulder .30 .75
10 Sal Fasano .25 .60
11 Doug Jones .25 .60
12 Miguel Tejada .30 .75
13 Omar Oliveras .25 .60
14 Jeremy Giambi .25 .60
15 Gil Heredia .25 .60
16 Olmedo Saenz .25 .60
17 T.J. Mathews .25 .60
18 Ramon Hernandez .25 .60
19 Jeff Tam .25 .60
20 Ryan Christenson .25 .60
21 John Jaha .25 .60
22 Rich Saveur .25 .60
23 Terrence Long .25 .60
24 Mike Magnante .25 .60
25 Scott Service .25 .60
26 Frank Menechino .25 .60
27 Jason Isringhausen .25 .60
28 Bob Alejo CO .25 .60
Rick Peterson CO
Thad Bosley CO
Ke

2001 A's Plumbers Union

COMPLETE SET (28) 5.00 12.00
1 Art Howe .25 .60
2 Jason Giambi .30 .75
3 Tim Hudson .30 .75
4 Johnny Damon .40 1.00
5 Barry Zito .30 .75
6 John Jaha .25 .60
7 Miguel Tejada .30 .75
8 Eric Chavez .25 .60
9 Mark Mulder .30 .75
10 Frank Menechino .25 .60
11 Tom Wilson .25 .60
12 Jeremy Giambi .25 .60
13 Jason Isringhausen .25 .60
14 Olmedo Saenz .25 .60
15 Gil Heredia .25 .60
16 Terrence Long .25 .60
17 T.J. Mathews .25 .60
18 Ramon Hernandez .25 .60
19 Mark Guthrie .25 .60
20 Adam Piatt .25 .60
21 Chad Bradford .25 .60
22 Mike Magnante .25 .60
23 Jim Mecir .25 .60
24 Jeff Tam .25 .60
25 Mark Bellhorn .25 .60
26 Cory Lidle .25 .60
27 Mario Valdez .25 .60
28 Coaches .25 .60

2002 A's Plumbers Union

COMPLETE SET (28) 5.00 12.00
1 Art Howe .25 .60
2 Tim Hudson .30 .75
3 David Justice .25 .60
4 Mark Mulder .30 .75
5 Jermaine Dye .25 .60
6 Barry Zito .30 .75
7 Miguel Tejada .30 .75
8 Eric Chavez .25 .60
9 Terrence Long .25 .60
10 John Mabry .25 .60
11 Billy Koch .25 .60
12 Adam Piatt .25 .60
13 Ramon Hernandez .25 .60
14 Randy Velarde .25 .60
15 Scott Hatteberg .25 .60
16 Mike Magnante .25 .60
17 Greg Myers .25 .60
18 Cory Lidle .25 .60
19 Olmedo Saenz .25 .60
20 Jim Mecir .25 .60
21 Eric Byrnes .25 .60
22 Mark Ellis .25 .60
23 Mike Venafro .25 .60
24 Carlos Pena .25 .60
25 Mike Fyhrie .25 .60
26 Aaron Harang .25 .60
27 Chad Bradford .25 .60
28 Coaches .25 .60

2003 A's Plumbers Union

COMPLETE SET (28) 5.00 12.00
1 Ken Macha .25 .60
2 Tim Hudson .30 .75
3 Miguel Tejada .30 .75
4 Mark Mulder .30 .75
5 Ramon Hernandez .25 .60
6 Barry Zito .30 .75
7 Jose Guillen .25 .60
8 Eric Chavez .25 .60
9 Terrence Long .25 .60
10 Ricardo Rincon .25 .60
11 Erubiel Durazo .25 .60
12 Mark Ellis .25 .60
13 Keith Foulke .25 .60
14 Eric Byrnes .25 .60
15 Ted Lilly .25 .60
16 Scott Hatteberg .25 .60
17 Rich Harden .30 .75
18 Chris Singleton .25 .60
19 Chad Bradford .25 .60
20 Jermaine Dye .25 .60
21 Chad Harville .25 .60
22 Adam Melhuse .25 .60
23 Jim Mecir .25 .60
24 John Halama .25 .60
25 Mike Neu .25 .60
26 Billy McMillon .25 .60
27 Frank Menechino .25 .60
28 Coaches .25 .60

2004 A's Plumbers Union

COMPLETE SET (32) 5.00 12.00
1 Ken Macha MGR .25 .60
2 Eric Chavez .25 .60
3 Tim Hudson .30 .75
4 Mark Mulder .30 .75
5 Barry Zito .30 .75
6 Jermaine Dye .25 .60
7 Scott Hatteberg .25 .60
8 Bobby Crosby .25 .60
9 Eric Byrnes .25 .60
10 Marco Scutaro .25 .60
11 Erubiel Durazo .25 .60
12 Justin Duchscherer .25 .60
13 Chad Bradford .25 .60
14 Rich Harden .25 .60
15 Ricardo Rincon .25 .60
16 Jim Mecir .25 .60
17 Adam Melhuse .25 .60
18 Damian Miller .25 .60
19 Mark Kotsay .25 .60
20 Bobby Kielty .25 .60
21 Mark Redman .25 .60
22 Chris Hammond .25 .60
23 Arthur Rhodes .25 .60
24 Mark McLemore .25 .60
25 Billy McMillon .25 .60
26 Octavio Dotel .25 .60
27 Mark Ellis .25 .60
28 Justin Lehr .25 .60
29 Esteban German .25 .60
30 Jairo Garcia .25 .60
31 Coaches .25 .60
32 Team Card .25 .60

2004 A's Team Issue

COMPLETE SET 1.25 3.00
1 Eric Byrnes .20 .50
2 Eric Chavez .20 .50
3 Jermaine Dye .20 .50
4 Rich Harden .20 .50
5 Scott Hatteberg .20 .50
6 Ken Macha MG .20 .50
7 Damian Miller .20 .50
8 Billy McMillon .20 .50
9 Arthur Rhodes .20 .50
10 Ricardo Rincon .20 .50
11 Barry Zito .30 .75

2006 A's Dibs

COMPLETE SET (30) 12.00 30.00

2007 A's E-Loan

COMPLETE SET (2) .40 1.00
DH Dan Haren .20 .50
HS Huston Street .20 .50

2007 A's Upper Deck Mercury News

COMPLETE SET (25) 3.00 8.00
3 Eric Chavez .15 .40
6 Travis Buck .15 .40
7 Bobby Crosby .15 .40
14 Mark Ellis .15 .40
15 Dan Haren .15 .40
19 Marco Scutaro .25 .60
20 Huston Street .15 .40
21 Mark Kotsay .15 .40
24 Shannon Stewart .15 .40
25 Esteban Loaiza .15 .40
28 Kurt Suzuki .15 .40
29 Dan Johnson .15 .40
31 Mike Piazza .40 1.00
32 Jack Cust .15 .40
33 Nick Swisher .25 .60
37 Joe Kennedy .15 .40
40 Rich Harden .15 .40
41 Alan Embree .15 .40
44 Santiago Casilla .15 .40
52 Jay Marshall .15 .40
53 Bob Geren .15 .40
55 Joe Blanton .15 .40
56 Lenny DiNardo .15 .40
57 Chad Gaudin .15 .40
58 Justin Duchscherer .15 .40

2006 Athletics Topps

COMPLETE SET (14) 3.00 8.00
OAK1 Eric Chavez .12 .30
OAK2 Bobby Crosby .12 .30
OAK3 Mark Kotsay .12 .30
OAK4 Jay Payton .12 .30
OAK5 Rich Harden .12 .30
OAK6 Barry Zito .20 .50
OAK7 Huston Street .12 .30
OAK8 Joe Blanton .12 .30
OAK9 Jason Kendall .12 .30
OAK10 Mark Ellis .12 .30
OAK11 Nick Swisher .20 .50
OAK12 Dan Johnson .12 .30
OAK13 Esteban Loaiza .12 .30
OAK14 Danny Haren .12 .30

2007 Athletics Topps

COMPLETE SET (14) 3.00 8.00
OAK1 Nick Swisher .20 .50
OAK2 Mark Ellis .12 .30
OAK3 Mike Piazza .30 .75
OAK4 Rich Harden .12 .30
OAK5 Mark Kotsay .12 .30
OAK6 Eric Chavez .12 .30
OAK7 Joe Blanton .12 .30
OAK8 Huston Street .12 .30
OAK9 Milton Bradley .12 .30
OAK10 Dan Haren .12 .30
OAK11 Jason Kendall .12 .30
OAK12 Dan Johnson .12 .30
OAK13 Bobby Crosby .12 .30
OAK14 Esteban Loaiza .12 .30

2008 A's Topps

COMPLETE SET (14) 3.00 8.00
OAK1 Eric Chavez .12 .30
OAK2 Mark Ellis .12 .30
OAK3 Chad Gaudin .20 .50
OAK4 Daric Barton .12 .30
OAK5 Lenny DiNardo .20 .50
OAK6 Travis Buck .20 .50
OAK7 Joe Blanton .12 .30
OAK8 Huston Street .20 .50
OAK9 Jack Cust .12 .30
OAK10 Rich Harden .12 .30
OAK11 Kurt Suzuki .12 .30
OAK12 Dan Johnson .12 .30
OAK13 Bobby Crosby .12 .30
OAK14 Ryan Sweeney .12 .30

2009 A's Topps

COMPLETE SET (15) 5.00 12.00
OAK1 Matt Holliday .40 1.00
OAK2 Cliff Pennington .15 .40
OAK3 Kurt Suzuki .15 .40
OAK4 Justin Duchscherer .15 .40
OAK5 Jason Giambi .15 .40
OAK6 Gio Gonzalez .25 .60
OAK7 Travis Buck .15 .40
OAK8 Eric Chavez .15 .40
OAK9 Brad Ziegler .15 .40
OAK10 Dana Eveland .15 .40
OAK11 Bobby Crosby .15 .40
OAK12 Sean Gallagher .15 .40
OAK13 Mark Ellis .15 .40
OAK14 Jack Cust .15 .40
OAK15 Stomper .15 .40

2010 A's Topps

COMPLETE SET (17) 5.00 12.00
OAK1 Kurt Suzuki .15 .40
OAK2 Eric Chavez .15 .40
OAK3 Gio Gonzalez .25 .60
OAK4 Mark Ellis .15 .40
OAK5 Ryan Sweeney .15 .40
OAK6 Brett Anderson .15 .40
OAK7 Kevin Kouzmanoff .15 .40
OAK8 Andrew Bailey .15 .40
OAK9 Justin Duchscherer .15 .40
OAK10 Travis Buck .15 .40
OAK11 Trevor Cahill .15 .40
OAK12 Vin Mazzaro .15 .40
OAK13 Josh Outman .15 .40
OAK14 Rajai Davis .15 .40
OAK15 Cliff Pennington .15 .40
OAK16 Coco Crisp .15 .40
OAK17 Jack Cust .15 .40

2011 A's Topps

OAK1 Brett Anderson .15 .40
OAK2 Andrew Bailey .15 .40
OAK3 Daric Barton .15 .40
OAK4 Dallas Braden .15 .40
OAK5 Trevor Cahill .15 .40
OAK6 Chris Carter .15 .40
OAK7 Coco Crisp .15 .40
OAK8 Kurt Suzuki .15 .40
OAK9 Cliff Pennington .15 .40
OAK10 Mark Ellis .15 .40
OAK11 Gio Gonzalez .25 .60
OAK12 Ryan Sweeney .15 .40
OAK13 Josh Willingham .25 .60
OAK14 David DeJesus .15 .40
OAK15 Kevin Kouzmanoff .15 .40
OAK16 Rich Harden .15 .40
OAK17 Oakland-Alameda County Coliseum .15
.40

2012 A's Topps

COMPLETE SET (17) 3.00 8.00
OAK1 Brett Anderson .25 .60
OAK2 Cliff Pennington .25 .60
OAK3 Coco Crisp .25 .60
OAK4 Dallas Braden .25 .60
OAK5 Kurt Suzuki .25 .60
OAK6 Seth Smith .25 .60
OAK7 Scott Sizemore .25 .60
OAK8 Brandon Allen .25 .60
OAK9 Tom Milone .25 .60
OAK10 Brandon McCarthy .25 .60
OAK11 Michael Taylor .25 .60
OAK12 Jemile Weeks .25 .60
OAK13 Collin Cowgill .25 .60
OAK14 Josh Reddick .25 .60
OAK15 Brad Peacock .25 .60
OAK16 Rich Harden .15 .40
OAK17 Oakland-Alameda County Coliseum .15
.40

2013 A's Topps

COMPLETE SET (17) 3.00 8.00
OAK1 Yoenis Cespedes .25 .60
OAK2 Josh Reddick .15 .40
OAK3 Bartolo Colon .15 .40
OAK4 Ryan Cook .15 .40
OAK5 Tommy Milone .15 .40
OAK6 Jarrod Parker .15 .40
OAK7 Seth Smith .15 .40
OAK8 Josh Donaldson .20 .50
OAK9 Brett Anderson .15 .40
OAK10 Jed Lowrie .15 .40
OAK11 Grant Balfour .15 .40
OAK12 Chris Young .15 .40
OAK13 A.J. Griffin .15 .40
OAK14 Scott Sizemore .15 .40
OAK15 Derek Norris .15 .40
OAK16 Brandon Moss .15 .40
OAK17 Coco Crisp .15 .40

2014 A's Topps

COMPLETE SET (17) 3.00 8.00
OAK1 Yoenis Cespedes .25 .60
OAK2 Josh Reddick .15 .40
OAK3 Scott Kazmir .15 .40
OAK4 Sonny Gray .20 .50
OAK5 Craig Gentry .15 .40
OAK6 Jarrod Parker .15 .40
OAK7 Jim Johnson .15 .40
OAK8 Josh Donaldson .20 .50
OAK9 Sean Doolittle .15 .40
OAK10 Jed Lowrie .15 .40
OAK11 Derek Norris .15 .40
OAK12 Dan Straily .15 .40
OAK13 A.J. Griffin .15 .40
OAK14 Alberto Callaspo .15 .40
OAK15 Brandon Moss .15 .40
OAK16 Coco Crisp .15 .40
OAK17 O.co Coliseum .15 .40

2015 A's Topps

COMPLETE SET (17) 3.00 8.00
OA1 Sonny Gray .20 .50
OA2 Coco Crisp .15 .40
OA3 Brett Lawrie .20 .50
OA4 Sean Doolittle .15 .40
OA5 Sam Fuld .15 .40
OA6 Jesse Chavez .15 .40
OA7 Ben Zobrist .20 .50
OA8 Scott Kazmir .15 .40
OA9 Stephen Vogt .20 .50
OA10 Drew Pomeranz .20 .50
OA11 Josh Reddick .15 .40
OA12 Eric Sogard .15 .40
OA13 Marcus Semien .25 .60
OA14 Ike Davis .15 .40
OA15 Dan Otero .15 .40
OA16 Tyler Clippard .15 .40
OA17 Billy Butler .15 .40

2016 A's Topps

COMPLETE SET (17) 3.00 8.00
OAK1 Sonny Gray .20 .50
OAK2 Billy Burns .15 .40
OAK3 Josh Reddick .15 .40
OAK4 Coco Crisp .15 .40
OAK5 Danny Valencia .20 .50
OAK6 Marcus Semien .25 .60
OAK7 Jed Lowrie .15 .40
OAK8 Stephen Vogt .20 .50
OAK9 Yonder Alonso .15 .40
OAK10 Kendall Graveman .15 .40
OAK11 Sean Doolittle .15 .40
OAK12 Billy Butler .15 .40
OAK13 Mark Canha .15 .40
OAK14 Ryan Madson .15 .40
OAK15 John Axford .15 .40
OAK16 Rich Hill .15 .40
OAK17 Liam Hendriks .15 .40

2017 A's Topps

COMPLETE SET (17) 3.00 8.00
OAK1 Khris Davis .25 .60
OAK2 Josh Phegley .15 .40
OAK3 Sonny Gray .20 .50
OAK4 Marcus Semien .25 .60
OAK5 Kendall Graveman .15 .40
OAK6 Mark Canha .15 .40
OAK7 Sean Manaea .15 .40
OAK8 Ryon Healy .20 .50
OAK9 Jed Lowrie .15 .40
OAK10 Yonder Alonso .15 .40
OAK11 Ryan Madson .15 .40
OAK12 Stephen Vogt .20 .50
OAK13 Liam Hendriks .15 .40
OAK14 Jharel Cotton .15 .40
OAK15 Matt Joyce .15 .40
OAK16 John Axford .15 .40
OAK17 Sean Doolittle .15 .40

2018 A's Topps

COMPLETE SET (17) 2.00 5.00
OA1 Khris Davis .25 .60
OA2 Bruce Maxwell .15 .40
OA3 Jharel Cotton .15 .40
OA4 Jed Lowrie .15 .40
OA5 Marcus Semien .25 .60
OA6 Kendall Graveman .15 .40
OA7 Sean Manaea .15 .40
OA8 Matt Joyce .15 .40
OA9 Stephen Piscotty .15 .40
OA10 Matt Chapman .25 .60
OA11 Blake Treinen .15 .40
OA12 Chad Pinder .15 .40
OA13 Santiago Casilla .15 .40
OA14 Matt Olson .25 .60
OA15 Daniel Mengden .15 .40
OA16 Dustin Fowler .15 .40
OA17 Josh Phegley .15 .40

2019 Athletics Topps

COMPLETE SET (17) 2.00 5.00
OA1 Khris Davis .25 .60
OA2 Matt Chapman .25 .60
OA3 Matt Olson .25 .60
OA4 Sean Manaea .15 .40
OA5 Stephen Piscotty .15 .40
OA6 Ramon Laureano .30 .75
OA7 Mike Fiers .15 .40
OA8 Paul Blackburn .15 .40
OA9 Franklin Barreto .15 .40
OA10 Nick Martini .15 .40
OA11 Blake Treinen .15 .40
OA12 Lou Trivino .15 .40
OA13 Chad Pinder .15 .40
OA14 Andrew Triggs .15 .40
OA15 Marcus Semien .25 .60
OA16 Dustin Fowler .15 .40
OA17 Fernando Rodney .15 .40

2020 A's Topps

OAK1 Mike Fiers .15 .40
OAK2 Matt Chapman .25 .60
OAK3 Stephen Piscotty .15 .40
OAK4 Ramon Laureano .20 .50
OAK5 Matt Olson .25 .60
OAK6 Sean Manaea .15 .40
OAK7 Marcus Semien .25 .60
OAK8 Liam Hendriks .15 .40
OAK9 Khris Davis .25 .60
OAK10 Lou Trivino .15 .40
OAK11 Jesus Luzardo .30 .75
OAK12 A.J. Puk .25 .60
OAK13 Chris Bassitt .15 .40
OAK14 Daniel Mengden .15 .40
OAK15 Chad Pinder .15 .40
OAK16 Seth Brown .15 .40
OAK17 Sean Murphy .25 .60

1975 Aaron Magnavox

These promotional photos, which measures approximately 4" by 6 7/8" feature Hank Aaron in an Milwaukee Brewer uniform. The photos were issued in either black and white or in color are both types are surrounded by white borders and the bottom has the facsimile greeting "best wishes, Hank Aaron" on the bottom and the photo is courtesy of the Magnavox Company. In addition, a pin signifying membership into the Hank Aaron 715 Home Run Club was also issued by Magnavox as part of their promotional efforts

1 Hank Aaron B&W 4.00 10.00
2 Hank Aaron COL 4.00 10.00
3 Hank Aaron 4.00 10.00
Pin

1984 Aaron Rockstad Poster

This one card set features a colored painting in a white border of Hank Aaron by artist Stephen D. Rockstad. The poster-size portrait measures approximately 16" by 20". The backs are blank. Only 500 of these portraits were produced and are sequentially numbered as well as signed by the artist.

1 Hank Aaron 6.00 15.00

1974 Aaron 715 Homer

These 12 black and white postcards, which measure approximately 3" by 5" features highlights from the game where Hank Aaron hit his 715th homer.

COMPLETE SET (12) 6.00 15.00
1 Hank Aaron .75 2.00
715
2 Hank Aaron .75 2.00
Picking the bat
3 Hank Aaron .75 2.00
Crack
4 Hank Aaron .75 2.00
Watching the ball
5 Hank Aaron .75 2.00
Going, going
6 Hank Aaron .75 2.00
Gone
7 Hank Aaron .75 2.00
Tom House
Catching the HR ball
8 Hank Aaron .75 2.00
With fans running bases
9 Hank Aaron .75 2.00
A hero's welcome
10 Hank Aaron .75 2.00
Tips his cap
11 Hank Aaron .75 2.00
Atlanta loves hank
12 Hank Aaron .75 2.00
Holding 715

1997 Kyle Abbott

This one-card set was privately printed and published by Kyle Abbott. The front features a color action player photo in a green border. The back displays player information and a religious message from Kyle Abbott.

1 Kyle Abbott .40 1.00

2017 Absolute

INSERTED IN '17 CHRONICLES PACKS
STATED PRINT RUN 99 SER.#'d SETS
*BLUE: .25X TO .6X BASIC
*SPEC.RED/49: .4X TO 1X BASIC
*SPEC.GRN/25: .6X TO 1.5X BASIC
1 Aaron Judge 10.00 25.00
2 Cody Bellinger 12.00 30.00
3 Yoan Moncada 2.50 6.00
4 Andrew Benintendi 2.50 6.00
5 Christian Arroyo 1.25 3.00
6 Dansby Swanson 2.00 5.00
7 Carson Fulmer .75 2.00
8 Ryon Healy 1.00 2.50
9 Mitch Haniger 1.25 3.00
10 Antonio Senzatela .75 2.00
11 Ian Happ 1.50 4.00
12 Trey Mancini 1.50 4.00
13 Jordan Montgomery 1.25 3.00
14 Bradley Zimmer 1.00 2.50
15 Hunter Renfroe 1.00 2.50
16 Jorge Bonifacio .75 2.00
17 Lewis Brinson 1.25 3.00
18 Jacoby Jones 1.00 2.50
19 Alex Bregman 4.00 10.00
20 Josh Bell 2.00 5.00
21 Derek Fisher 1.00 2.50
22 Austin Slater .75 2.00
23 Paul DeJong 2.50 6.00
24 Franklin Barreto .75 2.00
25 Sam Travis 1.00 2.50

2017 Absolute Rookie Premiere Materials Autographs

INSERTED IN '17 CHRONICLES PACKS
PRINT RUNS B/WN 20-99 COPIES PER
EXCHANGE DEADLINE 5/22/2019
1 Aaron Judge/99 100.00 250.00
2 Cody Bellinger/49 60.00 150.00
3 Andrew Benintendi/99 20.00 50.00
4 Dansby Swanson/20 12.00 30.00
5 Alex Bregman/20 20.00 50.00
6 Franklin Barreto/99 4.00 10.00
7 Yoan Moncada/20
8 Ian Happ/99 8.00 20.00
9 Hunter Renfroe/99 5.00 12.00
10 Mitch Haniger/99 6.00 15.00
11 Josh Bell/99 8.00 20.00
12 Lewis Brinson/99 6.00 15.00
13 Sam Travis/99 5.00 12.00
14 Ryon Healy/99 5.00 12.00
15 Bradley Zimmer/99 8.00 20.00
16 Antonio Senzatela/99 4.00 10.00
17 Jorge Bonifacio/99 4.00 10.00
18 Trey Mancini/99 6.00 15.00
19 Jordan Montgomery/99 4.00 10.00
20 Dinelson Lamet/99 4.00 10.00
21 Derek Fisher/99 8.00 20.00
22 Magneuris Sierra/99 4.00 10.00
23 Francis Martes/99 4.00 10.00
24 Orlando Arcia/99 6.00 15.00
25 Jacoby Jones/99 5.00 12.00

2017 Absolute Tools of the Trade Materials Double

INSERTED IN '17 CHRONICLES PACKS
PRINT RUNS B/WN 25-99 COPIES PER
*DBL PRIME/25: .5X TO 1.2X BASIC
1 Aaron Judge/99 25.00 60.00
2 Cody Bellinger/99 8.00 20.00
3 Yoan Moncada/99 5.00 12.00
4 Dansby Swanson/99 4.00 10.00
5 Alex Bregman/99 4.00 10.00
6 Lewis Brinson/99 3.00 8.00
7 Mickey Mantle/25 30.00 80.00
8 Bradley Zimmer/99 2.50 6.00
9 Hunter Renfroe/99 2.50 6.00
10 Franklin Barreto/99 2.00 5.00
11 Ian Happ/99 4.00 10.00
12 Albert Pujols/99 4.00 10.00
13 Sam Travis/99 2.50 6.00
14 Mike Trout/25 20.00 50.00
15 Bryce Harper/25 6.00 15.00
16 Kris Bryant/25 5.00 12.00
17 Buster Posey/49 4.00 10.00
18 Tony Gwynn/25 12.00 30.00
19 Rickey Henderson/25 15.00 40.00
20 Alex Rodriguez/99 4.00 10.00
21 Nomar Garciaparra/99 2.50 6.00
22 Miguel Sano/99 2.50 6.00
23 David Ortiz/49 3.00 8.00
24 Manny Machado/99 3.00 8.00
25 Joey Votto/99 3.00 8.00

2017 Absolute Tools of the Trade Materials Quad

INSERTED IN '17 CHRONICLES PACKS
PRINT RUNS B/WN 10-25 COPIES PER
NO PRICING ON QTY 10
2 Cody Bellinger/25 12.00 30.00
3 Aaron Judge/25 30.00 80.00
5 Cal Ripken/25 12.00 30.00

2017 Absolute Tools of the Trade Materials Triple

INSERTED IN '17 CHRONICLES PACKS
PRINT RUNS B/WN 25-99 COPIES PER
1 Aaron Judge/99 25.00 60.00
2 Cody Bellinger/99 8.00 20.00
3 Dansby Swanson/99 4.00 10.00
4 Alex Bregman/99 4.00 10.00
5 Yoan Moncada/99 5.00 12.00
6 Amed Rosario/99 3.00 8.00
7 Mickey Mantle/25 30.00 80.00
8 Alex Reyes/99 2.50 6.00
9 David Dahl/99 2.50 6.00
10 Don Mattingly/25 12.00 30.00
11 Salvador Perez/99 5.00 12.00
12 Francisco Lindor/99 3.00 8.00
13 Ken Griffey Jr./49 12.00 30.00
14 Lewis Brinson/99 3.00 8.00
15 Kirby Puckett/25 50.00 120.00

2019 Absolute Rookie Autographs

RANDOM INSERTS IN PACKS
EXCHANGE DEADLINE 2/21/2021
*GOLD: .5X TO 1.2X
*RED: .6X TO 1.5X
*HOLO SLVR: .75X TO 2X
1 Adam Kolarek 2.50 6.00
2 Pablo Lopez 2.50 6.00
3 Dean Deetz 2.50 6.00
4 Thomas Pannone 4.00 10.00
5 Nick Martini 2.50 6.00
6 Isaac Galloway 2.50 6.00
7 Trevor Richards 2.50 6.00
8 Scott Barlow 2.50 6.00
9 Ryan Meisinger 2.50 6.00
10 Dawel Lugo 4.00 10.00
11 Michael Perez 2.50 6.00
12 Rosell Herrera 2.50 6.00
13 DJ Stewart 3.00 8.00
14 Austin Dean 2.50 6.00
15 Meibrys Viloria 2.50 6.00
16 Gabriel Guerrero 2.50 6.00
17 Nick Ciuffo 2.50 6.00
18 Austin Wynns 2.50 6.00
19 Richie Martin 2.50 6.00
20 C.D. Pelham 2.50 6.00
21 Harold Castro 3.00 8.00
22 James Norwood 2.50 6.00
23 Tanner Rainey 2.50 6.00
24 Heath Fillmyer 5.00 12.00
25 Jalen Beeks 2.50 6.00
26 Brett Kennedy 2.50 6.00
27 Ty Buttrey 2.50 6.00
28 Yency Almonte 2.50 6.00
29 Connor Sadzeck 2.50 6.00
30 Austin Voth 2.50 6.00
31 Edmundo Sosa 3.00 8.00
32 Jefry Rodriguez 2.50 6.00
33 Chad Sobotka 2.50 6.00
34 Victor Reyes 2.50 6.00
35 Duane Underwood 2.50 6.00
36 Justin Williams 2.50 6.00
37 Abiatal Avelino 2.50 6.00
38 Pablo Reyes 2.50 6.00
39 Andrew Velazquez 2.50 6.00
40 Eric Haase 2.50 6.00
41 Daniel Ponce de Leon 4.00 10.00
42 Josh Naylor 3.00 8.00
43 Steven Duggar 3.00 8.00
44 Jake Cave 3.00 8.00
45 Cionel Perez 2.50 6.00
46 Rowdy Tellez 4.00 10.00
47 Kyle Wright 4.00 10.00
48 Dakota Hudson 5.00 12.00

2019 Absolute Triple Memorabilia

RANDOM INSERTS IN PACKS
*GOLD/99: .5X TO 1.2X
*GOLD/50: .6X TO 1.5X
*GOLD/25: .75X TO 2X
*BLUE/25: .75X TO 2X
1 Vladimir Guerrero Jr. 10.00 25.00
2 Fernando Tatis Jr. 25.00 60.00
3 Eloy Jimenez 6.00 15.00
4 Kyle Tucker 4.00 10.00
5 Yusei Kikuchi 2.50 6.00
6 Michael Kopech 5.00 12.00
7 Touki Toussaint 2.00 5.00
8 Justus Sheffield 2.50 6.00
9 Pete Alonso 6.00 15.00
10 Ramon Laureano 3.00 8.00
11 Christin Stewart 2.00 5.00
12 Jeff McNeil 4.00 10.00
13 Mike Trout 12.00 30.00
14 Jose Altuve 2.00 5.00
15 Aaron Judge 6.00 15.00
16 Yasiel Puig 2.50 6.00
17 Marcell Ozuna 2.50 6.00
18 Gleyber Torres 5.00 12.00
19 Miguel Andujar 2.50 6.00
20 Victor Robles 3.00 8.00
21 Alex Rodriguez 3.00 8.00
22 Adrian Beltre 2.50 6.00
23 George Brett 5.00 12.00
24 Vladimir Guerrero 10.00 25.00
25 Don Mattingly 5.00 12.00

2020 Absolute

101-166 RANDOMLY INSERTED
101-166 PRINT RUN 149 SER.#'d SETS
EXCHANGE DEADLINE 1/8/2022
1 Bryce Harper .60 1.50
2 Alex Verdugo .30 .75
3 Adalberto Mondesi .30 .75

4 Yogi Berra .40 1.00
5 Gerrit Cole .60 1.50
6 Andrew Benintendi .40 1.00
7 Mickey Mantle 1.25 3.00
8 Jose Berrios .30 .75
9 Ronald Acuna Jr. 1.50 4.00
10 Manny Machado .40 1.00
11 Kris Bryant .50 1.25
12 Pete Alonso 1.00 2.50
13 Anthony Rizzo .50 1.25
14 Josh Bell .30 .75
15 Stephen Strasburg .40 1.00
16 Luis Arraez .50 1.25
17 Ramon Laureano .30 .75
18 Charlie Morton .40 1.00
19 Corey Kluber .30 .75
20 Christian Yelich .50 1.25
21 Aaron Nola .30 .75
22 Zack Greinke .40 1.00
23 Jorge Polanco .30 .75
24 Tim Anderson .40 1.00
25 Juan Soto 1.25 3.00
26 Jose Ramirez .30 .75
27 Brian Anderson .25 .60
28 Mookie Betts .75 2.00
29 Javier Baez .50 1.25
30 Marco Gonzales .25 .60
31 Ozzie Albies .40 1.00
32 Clayton Kershaw .60 1.50
33 Ketel Marte .30 .75
34 Jose Altuve .30 .75
35 Byron Buxton .40 1.00
36 Jorge Soler .40 1.00
37 Mike Soroka .40 1.00
38 Trevor Story .40 1.00
39 Nolan Arenado .60 1.50
40 Jack Flaherty .40 1.00
41 Joe DiMaggio .75 2.00
42 Josh Donaldson .30 .75
43 Nicholas Castellanos .40 1.00
44 Max Scherzer .40 1.00
45 Nick Senzel .40 1.00
46 Victor Robles .50 1.25
47 Walker Buehler .50 1.25
48 Trea Turner .30 .75
49 Alex Bregman .40 1.00
50 Jose Abreu .40 1.00
51 Ted Williams .75 2.00
52 Rhys Hoskins .50 1.25
53 Fernando Tatis Jr. 2.00 5.00
54 Xander Bogaerts .40 1.00
55 Gleyber Torres .75 2.00
56 Sandy Alcantara .25 .60
57 Giancarlo Stanton .40 1.00
58 Cavan Biggio .50 1.25
59 Jacob deGrom .75 2.00
60 Hyun-Jin Ryu .30 .75
61 Stan Musial .60 1.50
62 Yasmani Grandal .25 .60
63 Whit Merrifield .40 1.00
64 Anthony Rendon .40 1.00
65 Justin Verlander .40 1.00
66 Franmil Reyes .25 .60
67 Rafael Devers .50 1.25
68 Austin Meadows .40 1.00
69 Will Smith .25 .60
70 Eugenio Suarez .30 .75
71 Shane Bieber .40 1.00
72 Yadier Molina .50 1.25
73 Tommy Edman .40 1.00
74 Paul Goldschmidt .40 1.00
75 Cody Bellinger .75 2.00
76 Jimmie Foxx .40 1.00
77 Buster Posey .50 1.25
78 Vladimir Guerrero Jr. .60 1.50
79 Yoan Moncada .40 1.00
80 Chris Paddack .40 1.00
81 Trey Mancini .40 1.00
82 Nelson Cruz .40 1.00
83 Keston Hiura .50 1.25
84 Eloy Jimenez .75 2.00
85 Amed Rosario .30 .75
86 Aaron Judge 1.00 2.50
87 Ken Griffey Jr. 1.50 4.00
88 Roberto Clemente 2.00 5.00
89 David Dahl .25 .60
90 Babe Ruth 1.00 2.50
91 Miguel Cabrera .40 1.00
92 Marcus Semien .40 1.00
93 Freddie Freeman .50 1.25
94 Shohei Ohtani .60 1.50
95 DJ LeMahieu .40 1.00
96 Francisco Lindor .40 1.00
97 Miguel Andujar .40 1.00
98 Mike Trout 2.00 5.00
99 Joey Gallo .40 1.00
100 J.T. Realmuto .40 1.00
101 Bryan Abreu AU RC 3.00 8.00
102 Mauricio Dubon AU RC 4.00 10.00
103 Isan Diaz AU RC 8.00 20.00
104 Domingo Leyba AU RC 4.00 10.00
105 Sean Murphy AU RC 6.00 15.00
106 Kwang-Hyun Kim AU RC 20.00 50.00
107 Brock Burke AU RC 3.00 8.00
108 Adrian Morejon AU RC 3.00 8.00
109 Tony Gonsolin AU RC 10.00 25.00
110 Danny Mendick AU RC 4.00 10.00
111 Josh Rojas AU RC 3.00 8.00
112 Zac Gallen AU RC 8.00 20.00
113 Luis Robert AU RC EXCH 75.00 200.00
114 Yonathan Daza AU RC 4.00 10.00
115 Yoshitomo Tsutsugo AU RC 8.00 20.00
116 Gavin Lux AU RC 25.00 60.00
117 Jordan Yamamoto AU RC 3.00 8.00
118 Trent Grisham AU RC 10.00 25.00
119 Sheldon Neuse AU RC 4.00 10.00
120 Justin Dunn AU RC 4.00 10.00
121 Matt Thaiss AU RC 4.00 10.00
122 Logan Webb AU RC 5.00 12.00
123 Jake Fraley AU RC 4.00 10.00
124 Anthony Kay AU RC 3.00 8.00
125 Donnie Walton AU RC 8.00 20.00
126 Willi Castro AU RC 5.00 12.00
127 Jaylin Davis AU RC 5.00 12.00
128 Brendan McKay AU RC 5.00 12.00
129 Sam Hilliard AU RC 8.00 20.00
130 Deivy Grullon AU RC 3.00 8.00
131 Dustin May AU RC 15.00 40.00
132 Abraham Toro AU RC 4.00 10.00
133 Nico Hoerner AU RC 12.00 30.00
134 Joe Palumbo AU RC 3.00 8.00
135 Ronald Bolanos AU RC 3.00 8.00
136 Logan Allen AU RC 3.00 8.00
137 Michel Baez AU RC 3.00 8.00
138 Nick Solak AU RC 8.00 20.00
139 Aaron Civale AU RC 8.00 20.00
140 Jonathan Hernandez AU RC 3.00 8.00
141 Brusdar Graterol AU RC 5.00 12.00
142 Rico Garcia AU RC 5.00 12.00
143 Shogo Akiyama AU RC 15.00 40.00
144 T.J. Zeuch AU RC 3.00 8.00
145 Dylan Cease AU RC 5.00 12.00
146 Kyle Lewis AU RC 20.00 50.00
147 Randy Arozarena AU RC 25.00 60.00
148 Bobby Bradley AU RC 3.00 8.00
149 Zack Collins AU RC 4.00 10.00
150 Aristides Aquino AU RC 8.00 20.00
151 Yu Chang AU RC 12.00 30.00
152 Yordan Alvarez AU RC 30.00 80.00
153 Michael King AU RC 10.00 25.00
154 Patrick Sandoval AU RC 5.00 12.00
155 Tres Barrera AU RC 6.00 15.00
156 Jake Rogers AU RC 6.00 15.00
157 Adbert Alzolay AU RC 6.00 15.00
158 Edwin Rios AU RC 12.00 30.00
159 Tyrone Taylor AU RC 3.00 8.00
160 A.J. Puk AU RC 5.00 12.00
161 Jesus Luzardo AU RC 6.00 15.00
162 Lewis Thorpe AU RC 3.00 8.00
163 Shun Yamaguchi AU RC 6.00 15.00
164 Travis Demeritte AU RC 5.00 12.00
165 Andres Munoz AU RC 6.00 15.00
166 Bo Bichette AU RC 40.00 100.00

2020 Absolute Black

*BLACK/125: .5X TO 1.2X BASIC
RANDOM INSERTS IN PACKS
STATED PRINT RUN 125 SER.#'d SETS
EXCHANGE DEADLINE 1/8/22
146 Kyle Lewis AU 30.00 80.00

2020 Absolute Black Gold

*BLK GOLD/25: .8X TO 2X BASIC
RANDOM INSERTS IN PACKS
STATED PRINT RUN 25 SER.#'d SETS
EXCHANGE DEADLINE 1/8/22
103 Isan Diaz AU 20.00 50.00
106 Kwang-Hyun Kim AU 50.00 120.00
109 Tony Gonsolin AU 20.00 50.00
113 Luis Robert AU EXCH 150.00 400.00
126 Willi Castro AU 15.00 40.00
128 Brendan McKay AU 25.00 60.00
133 Nico Hoerner AU 40.00 100.00
139 Aaron Civale AU 20.00 50.00
146 Kyle Lewis AU 100.00 2500.00
150 Aristides Aquino AU 25.00 60.00
161 Jesus Luzardo AU 25.00 60.00
166 Bo Bichette AU 75.00 200.00

2020 Absolute Blue

*BLUE/99: .5X TO 1.2X BASIC
RANDOM INSERTS IN PACKS
STATED PRINT RUN 99 SER.#'d SETS
EXCHANGE DEADLINE 1/8/22
128 Brendan McKay AU 6.00 15.00
146 Kyle Lewis AU 30.00 80.00

2020 Absolute Light Blue

*LGHT BLUE/50: .5X TO 1.2X BASIC
*LGHT BLUE/19: .8X TO 2X BASIC
RANDOM INSERTS IN PACKS
PRINT RUNS B/WN 19-50 COPIES PER
EXCHANGE DEADLINE 1/8/22
113 Luis Robert AU/50 EXCH 100.00 250.00
126 Willi Castro AU/50 10.00 25.00
128 Brendan McKay AU/50 12.00 30.00
146 Kyle Lewis AU/50 30.00 80.00
150 Aristides Aquino AU/50 15.00 40.00
161 Jesus Luzardo AU/50 15.00 40.00
166 Bo Bichette AU/50 50.00 120.00

2020 Absolute Pink

*PINK/75: .5X TO 1.2X BASIC
RANDOM INSERTS IN PACKS
STATED PRINT RUN 99 SER.#'d SETS
EXCHANGE DEADLINE 1/8/22
113 Luis Robert AU EXCH 100.00 250.00
128 Brendan McKay AU 6.00 15.00
146 Kyle Lewis AU 30.00 80.00
150 Aristides Aquino AU 15.00 40.00
161 Jesus Luzardo AU 15.00 40.00

2020 Absolute 500 HR Club Bats

RANDOM INSERTS IN PACKS
1 Eddie Mathews 30.00 80.00
2 Rafael Palmeiro
3 Jimmie Foxx
4 Mark McGwire 20.00 50.00
6 Babe Ruth 150.00 400.00
8 Alex Rodriguez 20.00 50.00
9 Mike Schmidt 12.00 30.00

2020 Absolute Absolute Heroes

RANDOM INSERTS IN PACKS
*SP BLUE: .6X TO 1.5X BASIC
*SP SILVER/99: .8X TO 2X BASIC
*SP PURPLE/25: 1.2X TO 3X BASIC
1 Mike Trout 3.00 8.00
2 Ronald Acuna Jr. 4.00 10.00
3 Pete Alonso 1.50 4.00
4 Vladimir Guerrero Jr. 1.00 2.50
5 Cody Bellinger 1.25 3.00
6 Juan Soto 2.00 5.00
7 Christian Yelich .75 2.00
8 Mookie Betts 1.25 3.00
9 Aaron Judge 1.50 4.00
10 Fernando Tatis Jr. 3.00 8.00
11 Nolan Arenado 1.00 2.50
12 Rafael Devers .75 2.00
13 Francisco Lindor .60 1.50
14 Javier Baez .60 1.50
15 Max Scherzer .60 1.50

2020 Absolute Absolute Heroes Material Signatures

RANDOM INSERTS IN PACKS
PRINT RUNS B/WN 10-99 COPIES PER
NO PRICING ON QTY 15 OR LESS
EXCHANGE DEADLINE 1/8/22
1 Darryl Strawberry/25 15.00 40.00
4 Josh Bell/49 10.00 25.00
6 Andy Pettitte/49 10.00 25.00
7 Cliff Lee/25 10.00 25.00
9 Cavan Biggio/99 12.00 30.00
10 Chris Paddack/99 5.00 12.00
11 Dale Murphy/25 20.00 50.00
16 Juan Soto/99 EXCH 30.00 80.00
17 Paul Molitor/25 15.00 40.00
21 Keston Hiura/99 10.00 25.00
23 Ronald Acuna Jr./25 50.00 120.00
25 Michael Chavis/99 8.00 20.00
29 Fergie Jenkins/49 10.00 25.00
30 Eloy Jimenez/49 EXCH 20.00 50.00
31 Chris Sale/25 15.00 40.00
34 Adam Haseley/99 4.00 10.00
35 Bert Blyleven/25 10.00 25.00
37 Ketel Marte/49 15.00 40.00
40 Adrian Beltre/25 20.00 50.00

2020 Absolute Absolute Heroes Material Signatures Spectrum Purple

*PURPLE/25: .6X TO 1.5X p/r 49-99
RANDOM INSERTS IN PACKS
PRINT RUNS B/WN 5-25 COPIES PER
NO PRICING ON QTY 15 OR LESS
3 Paul Konerko/25 12.00 30.00
14 Goose Gossage/25 6.00 15.00
21 Keston Hiura/25 40.00 100.00
24 Pete Alonso/25 EXCH 50.00 120.00
25 Michael Chavis/25 25.00 60.00

2020 Absolute Absolute Heroes Materials

RANDOM INSERTS IN PACKS
PRINT RUNS B/WN 10-199 COPIES PER
NO PRICING ON QTY 10 OR LESS
1 Barry Larkin/99 6.00 15.00
2 Cal Ripken/99 10.00 25.00
3 Frank Thomas/99 6.00 15.00
4 George Brett/25 20.00 50.00
5 Reggie Jackson/25 6.00 15.00
6 Billy Martin/49 8.00 20.00
7 Robin Yount/99 3.00 8.00
8 Tom Seaver/49 3.00 8.00
9 Mike Trout/49 25.00 60.00
10 Ted Williams/25 20.00 50.00
11 Aaron Judge/199 6.00 15.00
12 Joe DiMaggio/10
13 Ken Griffey Jr./99 8.00 20.00
14 Ichiro/49 6.00 15.00
15 Ron Santo/49 10.00 25.00
16 Roberto Clemente/10
17 Randy Johnson/49 5.00 12.00
18 Tony Gwynn/49 10.00 25.00
19 Greg Maddux/49 5.00 12.00
20 Chipper Jones/49 8.00 20.00

2020 Absolute Absolute Heroes Materials Spectrum Purple

*PURPLE/25: .6X TO 1.5X p/r 99-199
*PURPLE/25: .5X TO 1.2X p/r 49
RANDOM INSERTS IN PACKS
STATED PRINT RUN 25 SER.#'d SETS
2 Cal Ripken/25 30.00 80.00
13 Ken Griffey Jr./25 20.00 50.00

2020 Absolute Absolute Heroes Materials Spectrum Red

RANDOM INSERTS IN PACKS
PRINT RUNS B/WN 5-49 COPIES PER
NO PRICING ON QTY 15 OR LESS
13 Ken Griffey Jr./49 12.00 30.00
14 Ichiro/25 15.00 40.00
15 Ron Santo/25 15.00 40.00
17 Randy Johnson/25 10.00 25.00

2020 Absolute Absolute Ink

RANDOM INSERTS IN PACKS
PRINT RUNS B/WN 10-199 COPIES PER
EXCHANGE DEADLINE 1/8/22
*PURPLE/25: .6X TO 1.5X p/r 49-99
*PURPLE/25: .4X TO 1X p/r 25
1 Mike Soroka/99 12.00 30.00
2 Jordan Hicks/99 4.00 10.00
3 Nathaniel Lowe/99 8.00 20.00
4 Miguel Tejada/25 5.00 12.00
5 Nomar Mazara/99 3.00 8.00
6 Josh Donaldson/25 6.00 15.00
7 Chris Paddack/99 5.00 12.00
8 Alex Verdugo/71 12.00 30.00
9 Luis Urias/99 10.00 25.00
10 Gleyber Torres/49 25.00 60.00
11 Cole Hamels/25 6.00 15.00
12 Trey Mancini/75 5.00 12.00
13 Salvador Perez/99 8.00 20.00
14 Willie Calhoun/99 3.00 8.00
16 Josh Bell/49 4.00 10.00
17 Whit Merrifield/99 5.00 12.00
18 Corey Seager/49 12.00 30.00
19 Justin Turner/99 10.00 25.00
20 Ben Zobrist/99 4.00 10.00
21 Rafael Devers/49 6.00 15.00
22 Ramon Laureano/99 4.00 10.00
23 Max Muncy/99 4.00 10.00
24 Matt Carpenter/99 8.00 20.00
25 Harold Baines/49 8.00 20.00
26 Ketel Marte/25 6.00 15.00
28 Eloy Jimenez/25 15.00 40.00
29 Bobby Bradley/99 3.00 8.00
30 Matt Thaiss/99 4.00 10.00
31 Keston Hiura/25 10.00 25.00
32 Nick Solak/99 6.00 15.00
33 Tommy Edman/99 12.00 30.00
34 Zack Collins/25 6.00 15.00
35 A.J. Puk/99 5.00 12.00
36 Kwang-Hyun Kim/49 6.00 15.00
37 Shun Yamaguchi/99 4.00 10.00
38 Yoshitomo Tsutsugo/49 12.00 30.00
39 Shogo Akiyama/99 5.00 12.00
40 Luis Robert/25 75.00 200.00
41 Evan White/99 8.00 20.00
42 Mauricio Dubon/25 6.00 15.00
43 Isan Diaz/75 8.00 20.00
44 Jesus Luzardo/25 10.00 25.00
45 Eugenio Suarez/99 12.00 30.00
46 Brendan McKay/25 8.00 20.00
48 Kyle Lewis/99 25.00 60.00
49 Aroldis Chapman/49 25.00 60.00
50 Nico Hoerner/25 20.00 50.00

2020 Absolute Absolute Jersey Signatures

RANDOM INSERTS IN PACKS
PRINT RUNS B/WN 25-199 COPIES PER
EXCHANGE DEADLINE 1/8/22
1 Jorge Posada/49 15.00 40.00
3 Andres Munoz/199 5.00 12.00
4 Bryan Abreu/140 3.00 8.00
5 Danny Mendick/140 4.00 10.00
6 Jaylin Davis/140 5.00 12.00
7 Joe Palumbo/140 3.00 8.00
8 Jonathan Hernandez/125 3.00 8.00
9 Justin Dunn/99 4.00 10.00
10 Lewis Thorpe/140 3.00 8.00
11 Logan Allen/149 3.00 8.00
13 Rico Garcia/140 5.00 12.00
14 Sheldon Neuse/140 4.00 10.00
15 T.J. Zeuch/140 3.00 8.00
16 Travis Demeritte/140 5.00 12.00
23 Dansby Swanson/109 10.00 25.00
24 Cody Bellinger/25 30.00 80.00

2020 Absolute Absolute Jersey Signatures Spectrum Purple

*PURPLE/25: .6X TO 1.5X p/r 49-199
PRINT RUNS B/WN 5-25 COPIES PER
NO PRICING ON QTY 15 OR LESS
EXCHANGE DEADLINE 1/8/22
2 Adrian Morejon/25 8.00 20.00
6 Jaylin Davis/25 12.00 30.00
14 Sheldon Neuse/25 10.00 25.00
17 Trent Grisham/25 20.00 50.00
19 Walker Buehler/25 30.00 80.00
21 Miguel Andujar/25 25.00 60.00

2020 Absolute Absolute Jersey Signatures Spectrum Red

*RED/49-99: .4X TO 1X p/r 49-199
*RED/25: .6X TO 1.5X p/r 49-199
PRINT RUNS B/WN 10-99 COPIES PER
NO PRICING ON QTY 15 OR LESS
EXCHANGE DEADLINE 1/8/22
6 Jaylin Davis/49 8.00 20.00
17 Trent Grisham/99 12.00 30.00
19 Walker Buehler/49 15.00 40.00
20 Vladimir Guerrero Jr./25 25.00 60.00
21 Miguel Andujar/49 15.00 40.00

2020 Absolute Absolute Jersey Signatures Spectrum Silver

*SLVR/43-99: .4X TO 1X p/r 49-199
*SLVR/25: .6X TO 1.5X p/r 49-199
PRINT RUNS B/WN 15-99 COPIES PER
NO PRICING ON QTY 15 OR LESS
EXCHANGE DEADLINE 1/8/22
6 Jaylin Davis/75 6.00 15.00
18 Victor Robles/43 6.00 15.00
19 Walker Buehler/99 15.00 40.00

2020 Absolute Absolute Legends

RANDOM INSERTS IN PACKS
*SP BLUE: .6X TO 1.5X BASIC
*SP SILVER/99: .8X TO 2X BASIC
*SP PURPLE/25: 1.2X TO 3X BASIC
1 Babe Ruth 1.50 4.00
2 Gil Hodges .50 1.25
3 Billy Martin .50 1.25
4 Ron Santo .50 1.25
5 Joe DiMaggio 1.25 3.00
6 Ted Williams 4.00 10.00
7 Mickey Mantle 4.00 10.00
8 Yogi Berra .60 1.50
9 Jimmie Foxx .60 1.50
10 Roberto Clemente 3.00 8.00
11 Stan Musial 1.00 2.50
12 Cal Ripken 2.00 5.00
13 George Brett 1.25 3.00
14 Nolan Ryan 2.00 5.00
15 Harmon Killebrew .60 1.50
16 Reggie Jackson 2.50 6.00
17 Tony Gwynn 2.00 5.00
18 Warren Spahn .50 1.25
19 Jim Palmer .50 1.25
20 Babe Ruth 1.50 4.00

2020 Absolute Absolute Rookie Materials

RANDOM INSERTS IN PACKS
*SP RED/99: .5X TO 1.2X BASIC
*SP PURPLE/25: .8X TO 2X BASIC
1 Brendan McKay 2.50 6.00
2 Jonathan Hernandez 1.50 4.00
3 Kyle Lewis 6.00 15.00
4 Bo Bichette 6.00 15.00
5 Jordan Yamamoto 1.50 4.00
6 Bobby Bradley 1.50 4.00
7 Domingo Leyba 2.00 5.00
8 Zac Gallen 4.00 10.00
9 Deivy Grullon 1.50 4.00
10 Matt Thaiss 2.00 5.00
11 Aaron Civale 2.50 6.00
12 Brock Burke 1.50 4.00
14 Andres Munoz 2.50 6.00
15 Jaylin Davis 2.50 6.00
16 Dylan Cease 2.50 6.00
17 Tres Barrera 3.00 8.00
18 Rico Garcia 5.00 12.00
19 Josh Rojas 1.50 4.00
20 Bryan Abreu 1.50 4.00
21 Gavin Lux 5.00 12.00
22 Ronald Bolanos 1.50 4.00
23 Logan Allen 1.50 4.00
24 Donnie Walton 4.00 10.00
25 Travis Demeritte 2.50 6.00
26 T.J. Zeuch 1.50 4.00
28 Yordan Alvarez 4.00 10.00
29 Shun Yamaguchi 2.00 5.00
30 Aristides Aquino 4.00 10.00

2020 Absolute Baseball Material Signatures

RANDOM INSERTS IN PACKS
PRINT RUNS B/WN 6-149 COPIES PER
NO PRICING ON QTY 15 OR LESS
EXCHANGE DEADLINE 1/8/22
*BLK GOLD/25: .6X TO 1.5X p/r 33-149
1 Omar Vizquel/25 20.00 50.00
2 Barry Larkin/24 25.00 60.00
3 Bobby Richardson/100 10.00 25.00
4 Ken Griffey Jr./25 125.00 300.00
5 Cal Ripken/26 40.00 100.00
6 Dave Winfield/43 8.00 20.00
7 Shohei Ohtani/20 100.00 250.00
8 Don Sutton/50 8.00 20.00
11 Pedro Martinez/25 30.00 80.00
12 Paul Konerko/25 15.00 40.00
13 Frank Robinson/57 15.00 40.00
14 Dustin Pedroia/28 20.00 50.00
15 Jeff Bagwell/38 25.00 60.00
16 Ozzie Smith/55 30.00 80.00
17 Reggie Jackson/33 25.00 60.00
18 Rickey Henderson/50 60.00 150.00
20 Don Mattingly/25 40.00 100.00
21 Dylan Carlson/149 12.00 30.00
23 Vladimir Guerrero/50 25.00 60.00
24 Wade Boggs/40 15.00 40.00
26 Chipper Jones/25 50.00 120.00
27 Rafael Palmeiro/20 6.00 15.00
28 Roger Clemens/26 25.00 60.00
29 Randy Johnson/25 30.00 80.00
30 John Smoltz/27 20.00 50.00
31 Evan White/149 10.00 25.00
32 Frank Thomas/25 30.00 80.00
33 Whitey Ford/21 30.00 80.00

2020 Absolute Baseball Material Signatures Black

*BLACK/124-125: .4X TO 1X p/r 33-149
*BLACK/20: .6X TO 1.5X p/r 33-149
*BLACK/20: .4X TO 1X p/r 20-28
RANDOM INSERTS IN PACKS
PRINT RUNS B/WN 10-125 COPIES PER
NO PRICING ON QTY 15 OR LESS
EXCHANGE DEADLINE 1/8/22
9 Dwight Gooden/124 8.00 20.00

2020 Absolute Baseball Material Signatures Blue

*BLUE/50-99: .4X TO 1X p/r 33-149
RANDOM INSERTS IN PACKS
PRINT RUNS B/WN 50-99 COPIES PER
EXCHANGE DEADLINE 1/8/22
9 Dwight Gooden/50 8.00 20.00

2020 Absolute Baseball Material Signatures Light Blue

*LGHT BLUE/20-25: .6X TO 1.5X p/r 33-149
RANDOM INSERTS IN PACKS
PRINT RUNS B/WN 10-25 COPIES PER
NO PRICING ON QTY 15 OR LESS
EXCHANGE DEADLINE 1/8/22
9 Dwight Gooden/25 12.00 30.00

2020 Absolute Baseball Material Signatures Pink

*PINK/50-75: .4X TO 1X p/r 33-149
RANDOM INSERTS IN PACKS
PRINT RUNS B/WN 50-75 COPIES PER
EXCHANGE DEADLINE 1/8/22
9 Dwight Gooden/50 8.00 20.00

2020 Absolute Grip It-N-Rip It Materials

RANDOM INSERTS IN PACKS
PRINT RUNS B/WN 49-199 COPIES PER
1 Adrian Beltre/49 6.00 15.00
3 Fernando Tatis Jr./149 10.00 25.00
4 Eloy Jimenez/149 6.00 15.00
6 Manuel Margot/199 2.00 5.00
7 Ozzie Albies/145 8.00 20.00
9 Victor Robles/99 4.00 10.00
10 Vladimir Guerrero Jr./149 5.00 12.00
11 Alex Verdugo/99 2.50 6.00
12 Andrew Benintendi/149 6.00 15.00
15 Aristides Aquino/199 5.00 12.00
18 Bo Bichette/149 8.00 20.00
20 Luis Robert/199 15.00 40.00

2020 Absolute Grip It-N-Rip It Materials Spectrum Purple

RANDOM INSERTS IN PACKS
PRINT RUNS B/WN 10-25 COPIES PER
NO PRICING ON QTY 15 OR LESS

2020 Absolute Grip It-N-Rip It Materials Spectrum Red

RANDOM INSERTS IN PACKS
PRINT RUNS B/WN 35-99 COPIES PER
14 Nico Hoerner/99 6.00 15.00
16 Yordan Alvarez/99 6.00 15.00
17 Gavin Lux/49 8.00 20.00
19 Isan Diaz/49 4.00 10.00

2020 Absolute Hall Bound Materials

RANDOM INSERTS IN PACKS
1 Larry Walker 2.00 5.00
2 Ichiro 4.00 10.00
3 Albert Pujols 3.00 8.00
4 Adrian Beltre 2.50 6.00
5 Justin Verlander 2.50 6.00
6 Clayton Kershaw 4.00 10.00
7 Mike Trout 12.00 30.00
8 Miguel Cabrera 2.50 6.00
9 Alex Rodriguez 3.00 8.00
10 Robinson Cano 2.00 5.00

2020 Absolute Hall Bound Materials Spectrum Purple

*PURPLE/25: .8X TO 2X BASIC
RANDOM INSERTS IN PACKS
STATED PRINT RUN 25 SER.#'d SETS
3 Albert Pujols 20.00 50.00

2020 Absolute Hall Bound Materials Spectrum Red

*RED/49: .6X TO 1.5X BASIC
*RED/25: .8X TO 2X BASIC
RANDOM INSERTS IN PACKS
PRINT RUNS B/WN 25-49 COPIES PER
3 Albert Pujols/49 8.00 20.00

2020 Absolute Iconic Ink

RANDOM INSERTS IN PACKS
PRINT RUNS B/WN 10-99 COPIES PER
NO PRICING ON QTY 15 OR LESS
EXCHANGE DEADLINE 1/8/22
*PURPLE/25: .6X TO 1.5X p/r 49-99
*PURPLE/25: .4X TO 1X p/r 25
1 Brooks Robinson/25 15.00 40.00
3 Jose Canseco/49 6.00 15.00
5 Robin Yount/25 20.00 50.00
6 Willie McGee/25 10.00 25.00
14 Cody Bellinger/25 20.00 50.00
17 Anthony Rendon/96 10.00 25.00
19 Matt Chapman/49 EXCH 5.00 12.00
21 Fernando Tatis Jr./99 50.00 120.00
22 Vladimir Guerrero Jr./49 20.00 50.00
24 Paul Goldschmidt/25 12.00 30.00
25 Jose Ramirez/49 8.00 20.00
26 Yoenis Cespedes/25 8.00 20.00
30 Yordan Alvarez/25 EXCH 40.00 100.00

2020 Absolute Iconic Ink Dual Materials

RANDOM INSERTS IN PACKS
PRINT RUNS B/WN 15-99 COPIES PER
NO PRICING ON QTY 15 OR LESS
EXCHANGE DEADLINE 1/8/22
*PURPLE/25: .6X TO 1.5X p/r 49
1 Jim Rice/49 12.00 30.00
3 Darryl Strawberry/49 15.00 40.00
4 Dave Concepcion/49 20.00 50.00
6 Kenny Lofton/25 30.00 80.00
10 Omar Vizquel/49 6.00 15.00
11 Tommy Lasorda/25 30.00 80.00
15 Brooks Robinson/25 25.00 60.00
19 CC Sabathia/25 25.00 60.00

2020 Absolute Iconic Ink Duals

RANDOM INSERTS IN PACKS
PRINT RUNS B/WN 15-49 COPIES PER
NO PRICING ON QTY 15 OR LESS
EXCHANGE DEADLINE 1/8/22
*PURPLE/25: .6X TO 1.5X p/r 49
*PURPLE/25: .4X TO 1X p/r 25
1 S.Akiyama/Y.Tsutsugo/25 EXCH 30.00 80.00
2 S.Yamaguchi/K.Kim/25 20.00 50.00
3 J.Adell/L.Robert/15
4 X.Bogaerts/R.Devers/15
5 R.Acuna Jr./J.Soto/15
6 E.Jimenez/F.Thomas/15
7 V.Guerrero/V.Guerrero Jr./15
8 F.Lindor/J.Ramirez/25 8.00 20.00
9 W.Franco/J.Dominguez/25 EXCH 400.00 800.00
10 T.Story/F.Tatis Jr./49 50.00 120.00

2020 Absolute Iconic Ink Materials

RANDOM INSERTS IN PACKS
PRINT RUNS B/WN 10-99 COPIES PER
NO PRICING ON QTY 15 OR LESS
EXCHANGE DEADLINE 1/8/22
*PURPLE/25: .6X TO 1.5X p/r 40-99
12 Brooks Robinson/25 10.00 25.00
14 Tony Perez/49 15.00 40.00
17 Steve Garvey/25 25.00 60.00
21 Dale Murphy/49 15.00 40.00
22 Trevor Hoffman/25 12.00 30.00
23 Harold Baines/40 10.00 25.00
25 Paul Molitor/25 15.00 40.00
29 Jose Canseco/49 20.00 50.00
30 Goose Gossage/49 8.00 20.00
33 Kerry Wood/99 10.00 25.00
34 Mark Grace/40 25.00 60.00
40 Andre Dawson/49 10.00 25.00

2020 Absolute Iconic Ink Triples

RANDOM INSERTS IN PACKS
PRINT RUNS B/WN 7-25 COPIES PER
NO PRICING ON QTY 15 OR LESS
EXCHANGE DEADLINE 1/8/22
2 Murphy/Puk/Luzardo/25 20.00 50.00
3 Rutschman/Bart/Ruiz/25 30.00 80.00
4 Vaughn/White/Mountcastle/25 30.00 80.00
6 Aquino/Bichette/Alvarez/25 EXCH 100.00 250.00
10 Cease/McKay/May/25 20.00 50.00

2020 Absolute Introductions

RANDOM INSERTS IN PACKS
*SP BLUE: .6X TO 1.5X BASIC
1 Pete Alonso 1.50 4.00
2 Vladimir Guerrero Jr. 1.00 2.50
3 Shohei Ohtani 1.00 2.50
4 Eloy Jimenez 1.25 3.00
5 Fernando Tatis Jr. 3.00 8.00
6 Luis Robert 3.00 8.00
7 Mike Soroka .60 1.50
8 Walker Buehler .75 2.00
9 Ronald Acuna Jr. 2.50 6.00
10 Juan Soto 2.00 5.00
11 Gleyber Torres 1.25 3.00
12 Jack Flaherty .60 1.50
13 Shohei Ohtani 1.00 2.50
14 Yordan Alvarez 4.00 10.00
15 Bo Bichette 3.00 8.00

2020 Absolute Introductions Spectrum Purple

1 Pete Alonso 12.00 30.00

2020 Absolute Introductions Spectrum Silver

*SP SILVER/99: .8X TO 2X BASIC
RANDOM INSERTS IN PACKS
STATED PRINT RUN 99 SER.#'d SETS
1 Pete Alonso 4.00 10.00

2020 Absolute One Two Punch

RANDOM INSERTS IN PACKS
*SP BLUE: .6X TO 1.5X BASIC
*SP SILVER/99: .8X TO 2X BASIC
*SP PURPLE/25: 1.2X TO 3X BASIC
1 M.Scherzer/S.Strasburg .60 1.50
2 Z.Greinke/J.Verlander .60 1.50
3 M.Clevinger/S.Bieber .60 1.50
4 J.deGrom/N.Syndergaard 1.25 3.00
5 W.Buehler/C.Kershaw 1.00 2.50
6 L.Castillo/S.Gray .50 1.25
7 B.Snell/C.Morton .60 1.50
8 E.Rodriguez/C.Sale .60 1.50
9 M.Tanaka/G.Cole 1.00 2.50
10 R.Johnson/C.Schilling .60 1.50

2020 Absolute Rookie Round Up

RANDOM INSERTS IN PACKS
1 Bo Bichette 3.00 8.00
2 Luis Robert 3.00 8.00
3 Brendan McKay .60 1.50
4 Yordan Alvarez 4.00 10.00
5 Gavin Lux 2.00 5.00
6 Dustin May 1.25 3.00
7 Aristides Aquino 1.00 2.50
8 Nico Hoerner 1.50 4.00
9 Jesus Luzardo .75 2.00
10 Trent Grisham 1.50 4.00
11 A.J. Puk .60 1.50
12 Yoshitomo Tsutsugo 1.00 2.50
14 Zac Gallen 1.00 2.50
15 Sean Murphy .60 1.50
16 Kwang-Hyun Kim .75 2.00
17 Shun Yamaguchi .50 1.25
18 Dylan Cease .60 1.50
19 Adbert Alzolay .50 1.25
20 Isan Diaz .60 1.50
21 Brendan McKay .60 1.50
22 Sam Hilliard .60 1.50
23 Abraham Toro .50 1.25
24 Kyle Lewis 1.50 4.00
25 Bobby Bradley .40 1.00

2020 Absolute Rookie Round Up Spectrum Blue

*SP BLUE: .6X TO 1.5X BASIC
RANDOM INSERTS IN PACKS
24 Kyle Lewis 4.00 10.00

2020 Absolute Rookie Round Up Spectrum Purple

*SP PURPLE/25: 1.2X TO 3X BASIC
RANDOM INSERTS IN PACKS
STATED PRINT RUN 25 SER.#'d SETS
24 Kyle Lewis 15.00 40.00

2020 Absolute Rookie Round Up Spectrum Silver

*SP SILVER/99: .8X TO 2X BASIC
RANDOM INSERTS IN PACKS
STATED PRINT RUN 99 SER.#'d SETS
24 Kyle Lewis 10.00 25.00

2020 Absolute Rookie Threads

RANDOM INSERTS IN PACKS
*SP RED/99: .5X TO 1.2X BASIC
*SP PURPLE/25: .8X TO 2X BASIC
1 Brendan McKay 2.50 6.00
2 Adrian Morejon 1.50 4.00
4 Michel Baez 1.50 4.00
5 Jake Rogers 1.50 4.00
6 Brusdar Graterol 2.50 6.00
7 Trent Grisham 6.00 15.00
8 Adbert Alzolay 2.00 5.00
9 Nico Hoerner 4.00 10.00
10 Zack Collins 2.00 5.00
11 Sean Murphy 2.50 6.00
12 Jesus Luzardo 3.00 8.00
13 Mauricio Dubon 2.00 5.00
14 Joe Palumbo 1.50 4.00
15 Randy Arozarena 8.00 20.00
16 Kwang-Hyun Kim 3.00 8.00
17 Sheldon Neuse 2.00 5.00
18 Nick Solak 6.00 15.00
19 A.J. Puk 2.50 6.00
20 Justin Dunn 2.00 5.00
21 Tony Gonsolin 6.00 15.00
22 Sam Hilliard 2.50 6.00
23 Yordan Alvarez 15.00 40.00
24 Logan Webb 2.50 6.00
25 Jake Fraley 2.00 5.00
26 Anthony Kay 1.50 4.00
27 Lewis Thorpe 1.50 4.00
28 Aristides Aquino 6.00 15.00
30 Danny Mendick 2.00 5.00
31 Abraham Toro 2.00 5.00
33 Yonathan Daza 2.00 5.00
34 Tyrone Taylor 1.50 4.00
35 Willi Castro 2.50 6.00
36 Dustin May 5.00 12.00
37 Edwin Rios 4.00 10.00
38 Patrick Sandoval 2.50 6.00
39 Isan Diaz 2.50 6.00
40 Michael King 2.50 6.00

2020 Absolute Rookie Threads Duals

RANDOM INSERTS IN PACKS
*SP RED/99: .5X TO 1.2X BASIC
*SP PURPLE/25: .8X TO 2X BASIC
1 Nico Hoerner 4.00 10.00
2 Aristides Aquino 4.00 10.00
3 Gavin Lux 5.00 12.00
4 Bo Bichette 6.00 15.00
5 Dylan Cease 2.50 6.00
7 Yu Chang 2.50 6.00
8 Sam Hilliard 2.50 6.00
9 Jake Fraley 2.00 5.00
10 Jordan Yamamoto 1.50 4.00

2020 Absolute Rookie Threads Duals Spectrum Purple

*SP PURPLE/25: .8X TO 2X BASIC
RANDOM INSERTS IN PACKS
STATED PRINT RUN 25 SER.#'d SETS
4 Bo Bichette 15.00 40.00

2020 Absolute Rookie Threads Duals Spectrum Red

*SP RED/99: .5X TO 1.2X BASIC
RANDOM INSERTS IN PACKS
STATED PRINT RUN 99 SER.#'d SETS
4 Bo Bichette 12.00 30.00

2020 Absolute Team Tandem Materials

RANDOM INSERTS IN PACKS
1 F.Freeman/R.Acuna Jr. 10.00 25.00
3 M.Trout/J.Adell 12.00 30.00
4 J.Ramirez/F.Lindor 2.50 6.00
5 C.Yelich/K.Hiura 3.00 8.00
6 N.Arenado/T.Story 4.00 10.00
7 T.Williams/D.DiMaggio 15.00 40.00
8 K.Bryant/A.Rizzo 5.00 12.00
9 J.Soto/V.Robles 6.00 15.00
10 M.Mantle/Y.Berra 30.00 80.00

2020 Absolute Team Tandem Materials Spectrum Purple

*PURPLE/25: .8X TO 2X BASIC

RANDOM INSERTS IN PACKS
PRINT RUNS B/WN 10-25 COPIES PER
NO PRICING ON QTY 15 OR LESS
8 Kris Bryant 12.00 30.00
Anthony Rizzo/25

2020 Absolute Team Tandem Materials Spectrum Red

*RED/99: .5X TO 1.2X BASIC
*RED/49: .6X TO 1.5X BASIC
*RED/25: .8X TO 2X BASIC
RANDOM INSERTS IN PACKS
PRINT RUNS B/WN 25-99 COPIES PER
8 Kris Bryant 8.00 20.00
Anthony Rizzo/99

2020 Absolute Tools of the Trade Dual Swatch Signatures

RANDOM INSERTS IN PACKS
PRINT RUNS B/WN 49-199 COPIES PER
EXCHANGE DEADLINE 1/8/22
2 Bo Bichette/149 25.00 60.00
8 Jake Fraley/140 4.00 10.00
10 Tony Gonsolin/149 12.00 30.00
13 Deivy Grullon/149 3.00 8.00
16 Bert Blyleven/49 4.00 10.00
17 Josh Rojas/125 3.00 8.00
18 Kyle Lewis/99 25.00 60.00
20 Michael King/140 5.00 12.00
21 Michel Baez/125 3.00 8.00
22 Patrick Sandoval/140 5.00 12.00
24 Tyrone Taylor/132 3.00 8.00
25 Willi Castro/125 5.00 12.00
26 Tres Barrera/93 6.00 15.00
28 Yu Chang/149 5.00 12.00
29 Sam Hilliard/140 5.00 12.00

2020 Absolute Tools of the Trade Dual Swatch Signatures Spectrum Purple

*PURPLE/25: .6X TO 1.5X BASIC
PRINT RUNS B/WN 5-25 COPIES PER
NO PRICING ON QTY 15 OR LESS
EXCHANGE DEADLINE 1/8/22
1 Yordan Alvarez/25 EXCH 40.00 100.00
3 Aristides Aquino/25 25.00 60.00
4 Luis Robert/25 150.00 400.00
5 Brendan McKay/20 20.00 50.00
7 Dustin May/25 40.00 100.00

2020 Absolute Tools of the Trade Dual Swatch Signatures Spectrum Red

*RED/35-49: .4X TO 1X BASIC
*RED/25: .6X TO 1.5X BASIC
PRINT RUNS B/WN 10-49 COPIES PER
NO PRICING ON QTY 15 OR LESS
EXCHANGE DEADLINE 1/8/22
1 Yordan Alvarez/49 EXCH 25.00 60.00
2 Bo Bichette/25 60.00 150.00
4 Luis Robert/49 100.00 250.00
5 Brendan McKay/35 12.00 30.00
19 Goose Gossage/25 15.00 40.00

2020 Absolute Tools of the Trade Dual Swatch Signatures Spectrum Silver

*SLVR: .4X TO 1X BASIC
PRINT RUNS B/WN 15-99 COPIES PER
NO PRICING ON QTY 15 OR LESS
EXCHANGE DEADLINE 1/8/22
2 Bo Bichette/49 40.00 100.00

2020 Absolute Tools of the Trade Quad Swatch Signatures

RANDOM INSERTS IN PACKS
PRINT RUNS B/WN 99-199 COPIES PER
EXCHANGE DEADLINE 1/8/22
6 Dylan Carlson/149 25.00 60.00
8 Royce Lewis/99 12.00 30.00
9 Brock Burke/99 3.00 8.00
10 Sean Murphy/150 6.00 15.00
11 Mauricio Dubon/149 4.00 10.00
12 Jordan Yamamoto/199 3.00 8.00
13 Aaron Civale/140
14 Dylan Cease/99 5.00 12.00
15 Donnie Walton/149 8.00 20.00

2020 Absolute Tools of the Trade Quad Swatch Signatures Spectrum Purple

*PURPLE/25: .6X TO 1.5X BASIC
PRINT RUNS B/WN 5-25 COPIES PER
NO PRICING ON QTY 15 OR LESS
EXCHANGE DEADLINE 1/8/22
4 Pete Alonso/25 75.00 200.00
6 Dylan Carlson/25 75.00 200.00
7 Hunter Greene/25 25.00 60.00

2020 Absolute Tools of the Trade Quad Swatch Signatures Spectrum Red

*RED/49-99: .4X TO 1X BASIC
*RED/25: .6X TO 1.5X BASIC
PRINT RUNS B/WN 10-99 COPIES PER
NO PRICING ON QTY 15 OR LESS
EXCHANGE DEADLINE 1/8/22
3 Phil Niekro/25 15.00 40.00
4 Pete Alonso/49 50.00 120.00
6 Dylan Carlson/49 50.00 120.00
7 Hunter Greene/49 15.00 40.00

2020 Absolute Tools of the Trade Quad Swatch Signatures Spectrum Silver

*SLVR/49-149: .4X TO 1X BASIC
*SLVR/25: .6X TO 1.5X BASIC
PRINT RUNS B/WN 25-149 COPIES PER
EXCHANGE DEADLINE 1/8/22
7 Hunter Greene/75 12.00 30.00

2020 Absolute Tools of the Trade Quad Swatches

RANDOM INSERTS IN PACKS
STATED PRINT RUN 99 SER.#'d SETS
1 Christin Stewart 2.00 5.00
2 Domingo Leyba 2.50 6.00
3 Vladimir Guerrero Jr. 6.00 15.00
4 Adbert Alzolay 2.50 6.00
5 David Fletcher 3.00 8.00
6 Ronald Acuna Jr. 12.00 30.00
7 Aaron Civale 4.00 10.00
8 Estevan Florial 3.00 8.00
9 Yu Chang 3.00 8.00
10 Taylor Ward 3.00 8.00
11 Sam Hilliard 3.00 8.00
12 Nick Williams 2.00 5.00
13 Jake Rogers 2.00 5.00
14 Orlando Arcia 2.00 5.00
15 Abraham Toro 2.50 6.00
16 Patrick Wisdom 2.00 5.00
17 Edwin Rios 5.00 12.00
18 Miguel Sano 2.50 6.00
19 Jordan Yamamoto 2.00 5.00
20 Jesus Sanchez 3.00 8.00

2020 Absolute Tools of the Trade Quad Swatches Spectrum Purple

*PURPLE/25: .6X TO 1.5X BASIC
RANDOM INSERTS IN PACKS
STATED PRINT RUN 25 SER.#'d SETS
3 Vladimir Guerrero Jr. 15.00 40.00

2020 Absolute Tools of the Trade Quad Swatches Spectrum Red

*RED/49: .5X TO 1.2X BASIC
RANDOM INSERTS IN PACKS
STATED PRINT RUN 49 SER.#'d SETS
3 Vladimir Guerrero Jr. 12.00 30.00

2020 Absolute Tools of the Trade Six Swatch Signatures

RANDOM INSERTS IN PACKS
PRINT RUNS B/WN 140-299 COPIES PER
EXCHANGE DEADLINE 1/8/22
*SLVR/75-199: .4X TO 1X BASIC
*RED/49-99: .4X TO 1X BASIC
*PURPLE/25: .6X TO 1.5X BASIC
1 Yonathan Daza/199 4.00 10.00
2 Domingo Leyba/149 4.00 10.00
3 Brandon Lowe/299 4.00 10.00
5 Tyler Mahle/149 8.00 20.00
7 Randy Arozarena/149 50.00 120.00
8 Edwin Rios/140 10.00 25.00
10 Cavan Biggio/199 15.00 40.00

2020 Absolute Tools of the Trade Six Swatches

RANDOM INSERTS IN PACKS
STATED PRINT RUN 99 SER.#'d SETS
*RED/49: .5X TO 1.2X BASIC
*PURPLE/25: .6X TO 1.5X BASIC
1 Kyle Tucker 3.00 8.00
2 Evan White 5.00 12.00
3 Aristides Aquino 5.00 12.00
4 Yordan Alvarez 12.00 30.00
5 Bo Bichette 12.00 30.00
6 Gavin Lux 10.00 25.00
7 Isan Diaz 3.00 8.00
8 Eloy Jimenez 6.00 15.00
9 Jake Bauers 4.00 10.00
10 Jeff McNeil 2.50 6.00

2020 Absolute Tools of the Trade Triple Swatch Signatures

RANDOM INSERTS IN PACKS
PRINT RUNS B/WN 49-149 COPIES PER
EXCHANGE DEADLINE 1/8/22
1 Kwang-Hyun Kim/99 15.00 40.00
2 Ronald Bolanos/140 3.00 8.00
3 Zac Gallen/99 8.00 20.00
4 Brusdar Graterol/140 5.00 12.00
9 J.D. Martinez/49 5.00 12.00
11 Adbert Alzolay/149 4.00 10.00
12 Troy Glaus/49 12.00 30.00
14 Jake Rogers/140 3.00 8.00
16 Abraham Toro/149 4.00 10.00
17 Gavin Lux/99 25.00 60.00

2020 Absolute Tools of the Trade Triple Swatch Signatures Spectrum Purple

*PURPLE/25: .6X TO 1.5X BASIC
PRINT RUNS B/WN 5-25 COPIES PER
NO PRICING ON QTY 15 OR LESS
EXCHANGE DEADLINE 1/8/22
13 Luis Robert/25 150.00 400.00
18 Nico Hoerner/25 20.00 50.00
20 Ryan Zimmerman/25 10.00 25.00

2020 Absolute Tools of the Trade Triple Swatch Signatures Spectrum Red

*RED/35-99: .4X TO 1X BASIC
*RED/25-30: .6X TO 1.5X BASIC
PRINT RUNS B/WN 10-99 COPIES PER
NO PRICING ON QTY 15 OR LESS
EXCHANGE DEADLINE 1/8/22
13 Luis Robert/49 100.00 250.00
18 Nico Hoerner/49 12.00 30.00
20 Ryan Zimmerman/30 10.00 25.00

2020 Absolute Tools of the Trade Triple Swatch Signatures Spectrum Silver

*SLVR/49-125: .4X TO 1X BASIC
*SLVR/25: .6X TO 1.5X BASIC
PRINT RUNS B/WN 15-125 COPIES PER
NO PRICING ON QTY 15 OR LESS
EXCHANGE DEADLINE 1/8/22
19 Paul Molitor/25 15.00 40.00

2020 Absolute Tools of the Trade Triple Swatches

RANDOM INSERTS IN PACKS
PRINT RUNS B/WN 49-99 COPIES PER
1 Sheldon Neuse/99 2.50 6.00
2 Dustin Pedroia/49 5.00 12.00
3 Adrian Morejon/99 2.00 5.00
4 Ryan McMahon/99 3.00 8.00
5 Jaylin Davis/99 3.00 8.00
6 Fernando Tatis Jr./99 12.00 30.00
7 Donnie Walton/99 5.00 12.00
8 Ryan O'Hearn/99 2.00 5.00
9 Willie Calhoun/99 2.00 5.00
10 Wander Franco/99 15.00 40.00
11 Nick Solak/99 8.00 20.00
12 Max Kepler/99 2.50 6.00
13 Tres Barrera/99 4.00 10.00
14 Kyle Tucker/99 3.00 8.00
15 Jake Fraley/99 2.50 6.00
16 Kevin Kramer/99 2.00 5.00
18 Kevin Newman/99 3.00 8.00

2020 Absolute Tools of the Trade Triple Swatches Spectrum Purple

*PURPLE/25: .6X TO 1.5X p/r 99
RANDOM INSERTS IN PACKS
STATED PRINT RUN 25 SER.#'d SETS
17 Stan Musial 15.00 40.00
19 Gil Hodges 10.00 25.00
20 Kirby Puckett 30.00 80.00

2020 Absolute Tools of the Trade Triple Swatches Spectrum Red

*RED/49: .5X TO 1.2X p/r 99
*RED/25: .5X TO 1.2X p/r 49
RANDOM INSERTS IN PACKS
PRINT RUNS B/WN 25-49 COPIES PER
2 Dustin Pedroia/25 12.00 30.00

2020 Absolute Unsung Heroes

RANDOM INSERTS IN PACKS
*SP.BLUE: .6X TO 1.5X BASIC
*SP.SILVER/99: .8X TO 2X BASIC
*SP.PURPLE/25: 1.2X TO 3X BASIC
1 Mike Clevinger .50 1.25
2 Jorge Soler .60 1.50
3 Andrew Benintendi .60 1.50
4 Tommy Pham .40 1.00
5 Mark Canha .40 1.00
6 Yoan Moncada .60 1.50
7 Jonathan Villar .40 1.00
8 Yuli Gurriel .50 1.25
9 Kyle Schwarber .60 1.50
10 Ozzie Albies .60 1.50
11 Elvis Andrus .50 1.25
12 Starling Marte .50 1.25
13 Eddie Rosario .50 1.25
14 Gio Urshela .60 1.50
15 Justin Turner .60 1.50

2001 Absolute Memorabilia

COMP.SET w/o SP's (150) 15.00 40.00
COMMON CARD (1-150) .30 .75
COMMON RPM (151-200) 3.00 8.00
RPM 151-200 STATED ODDS 1:18
EXCHANGE DEADLINE 06/01/03
1 Alex Rodriguez 1.00 2.50
2 Barry Bonds 2.00 5.00
3 Cal Ripken 2.50 6.00
4 Chipper Jones .75 2.00
5 Derek Jeter 2.00 5.00
6 Troy Glaus .30 .75
7 Frank Thomas .75 2.00
8 Greg Maddux 1.25 3.00
9 Ivan Rodriguez .50 1.25
10 Jeff Bagwell .50 1.25
11 Ryan Dempster .30 .75
12 Todd Helton .50 1.25
13 Ken Griffey Jr. 1.50 4.00
14 Manny Ramirez Sox .50 1.25
15 Mark McGwire 2.00 5.00
16 Mike Piazza 1.25 3.00
17 Nomar Garciaparra 1.25 3.00
18 Pedro Martinez .50 1.25
19 Randy Johnson .75 2.00
20 Rick Ankiel .30 .75
21 Rickey Henderson .75 2.00
22 Roger Clemens 1.50 4.00
23 Sammy Sosa .75 2.00
24 Tony Gwynn 1.00 2.50
25 Vladimir Guerrero .75 2.00
26 Kazuhiro Sasaki .30 .75
27 Roberto Alomar .50 1.25
28 Barry Zito .50 1.25
29 Pat Burrell .30 .75
30 Harold Baines .30 .75
31 Carlos Delgado .30 .75
32 J.D. Drew .30 .75
33 Jim Edmonds .30 .75
34 Darin Erstad .30 .75
35 Jason Giambi .30 .75
36 Tom Glavine .50 1.25
37 Juan Gonzalez .30 .75
38 Mark Grace .50 1.25
39 Shawn Green .30 .75
40 Tim Hudson .30 .75
41 Andruw Jones .50 1.25
42 David Justice .30 .75
43 Jeff Kent .30 .75
44 Barry Larkin .50 1.25
45 Rafael Furcal .30 .75
46 Mike Mussina .50 1.25
47 Hideo Nomo .75 2.00
48 Rafael Palmeiro .50 1.25
49 Adam Piatt .30 .75
50 Scott Rolen .50 1.25
51 Gary Sheffield .30 .75
52 Bernie Williams .50 1.25
53 Bob Abreu .30 .75
54 Edgardo Alfonzo .30 .75
55 Edgar Renteria .30 .75
56 Phil Nevin .30 .75
57 Craig Biggio .50 1.25
58 Andres Galarraga .30 .75
59 Edgar Martinez .50 1.25
60 Fred McGriff .50 1.25
61 Magglio Ordonez .30 .75
62 Jim Thome .50 1.25
63 Matt Williams .30 .75
64 Kerry Wood .30 .75
65 Moises Alou .30 .75
66 Brady Anderson .30 .75
67 Garret Anderson .30 .75
68 Russell Branyan .30 .75
69 Tony Batista .30 .75
70 Vernon Wells .30 .75
71 Carlos Beltran .30 .75
72 Adrian Beltre .30 .75
73 Kris Benson .30 .75
74 Lance Berkman .30 .75
75 Kevin Brown .30 .75
76 Dee Brown .30 .75
77 Jeromy Burnitz .30 .75
78 Timo Perez .30 .75
79 Sean Casey .30 .75
80 Luis Castillo .30 .75
81 Eric Chavez .30 .75
82 Jeff Cirillo .30 .75
83 Bartolo Colon .30 .75
84 David Cone .30 .75
85 Freddy Garcia .30 .75
86 Johnny Damon .50 1.25
87 Ray Durham .30 .75
88 Jermaine Dye .30 .75
89 Juan Encarnacion .30 .75
90 Terrence Long .30 .75
91 Carl Everett .30 .75
92 Steve Finley .30 .75
93 Cliff Floyd .30 .75
94 Brad Fullmer .30 .75
95 Brian Giles .30 .75
96 Luis Gonzalez .30 .75
97 Rusty Greer .30 .75
98 Jeffrey Hammonds .30 .75
99 Mike Hampton .30 .75
100 Orlando Hernandez .30 .75
101 Richard Hidalgo .30 .75
102 Geoff Jenkins .30 .75
103 Jacque Jones .30 .75
104 Brian Jordan .30 .75
105 Gabe Kapler .30 .75
106 Eric Karros .30 .75
107 Jason Kendall .30 .75
108 Adam Kennedy .30 .75
109 Deion Sanders .50 1.25
110 Ryan Klesko .30 .75
111 Chuck Knoblauch .30 .75
112 Paul Konerko .30 .75
113 Carlos Lee .30 .75
114 Kenny Lofton .30 .75
115 Javy Lopez .30 .75
116 Tino Martinez .50 1.25
117 Ruben Mateo .30 .75
118 Kevin Millwood .30 .75
119 Jimmy Rollins .30 .75
120 Raul Mondesi .30 .75
121 Trot Nixon .30 .75
122 John Olerud .30 .75
123 Paul O' Neill .50 1.25
124 Chan Ho Park .30 .75
125 Andy Pettitte .50 1.25
126 Jorge Posada .50 1.25
127 Mark Quinn .30 .75
128 Aramis Ramirez .30 .75
129 Mariano Rivera .75 2.00
130 Tim Salmon .50 1.25
131 Curt Schilling .30 .75
132 Richie Sexson .30 .75
133 John Smoltz .50 1.25
134 J.T. Snow .30 .75
135 Jay Payton .30 .75
136 Shannon Stewart .30 .75
137 B.J. Surhoff .30 .75
138 Mike Sweeney .30 .75
139 Fernando Tatis .30 .75
140 Miguel Tejada .30 .75
141 Jason Varitek .75 2.00
142 Greg Vaughn .30 .75
143 Mo Vaughn .30 .75
144 Robin Ventura .30 .75
145 Jose Vidro .30 .75
146 Omar Vizquel .50 1.25
147 Larry Walker .30 .75
148 David Wells .30 .75
149 Rondell White .30 .75
150 Preston Wilson .30 .75
151 Bud Smith RPM RC 3.00 8.00
152 Cory Aldridge RPM RC 3.00 8.00
153 Wilmy Caceres RPM RC 3.00 8.00
154 Josh Beckett RPM 4.00 10.00
155 Wilson Betemit RPM RC 4.00 10.00
156 Jason Michaels RPM RC 3.00 8.00
157 Albert Pujols RPM RC 40.00 100.00
158 Andres Torres RPM RC 3.00 8.00
159 Jack Wilson RPM RC 4.00 10.00
160 Alex Escobar RPM 3.00 8.00
161 Ben Sheets RPM 4.00 10.00
162 Rafael Soriano RPM RC 3.00 8.00
163 Nate Frese RPM RC 3.00 8.00
164 Carlos Garcia RPM 3.00 8.00
165 Brandon Larson RPM RC 3.00 8.00
166 Alexis Gomez RPM RC 3.00 8.00
167 Jason Hart RPM 3.00 8.00
168 Nick Johnson RPM 3.00 8.00
169 Donaldo Mendez RPM 3.00 8.00
170 Christian Parker RPM RC 3.00 8.00
171 Jackson Melian RPM 3.00 8.00
172 Jack Cust RPM 3.00 8.00
173 Adrian Hernandez RPM 3.00 8.00
174 Joe Crede RPM 4.00 10.00
175 Jose Mieses RPM RC 3.00 8.00
176 Roy Oswalt RPM 4.00 10.00
177 Eric Munson RPM 3.00 8.00
178 Xavier Nady RPM 3.00 8.00
179 Horacio Ramirez RPM RC 4.00 10.00
180 Abraham Nunez RPM 3.00 8.00
181 Jose Ortiz RPM 3.00 8.00
182 Jeremy Owens RPM RC 3.00 8.00
183 Claudio Vargas RPM RC 3.00 8.00
184 Marcus Giles RPM 3.00 8.00
185 Aubrey Huff RPM 3.00 8.00
186 C.C. Sabathia RPM 3.00 8.00
187 Adam Dunn RPM 4.00 10.00
188 Adam Pettyjohn RPM 3.00 8.00
189 Elpidio Guzman RPM RC 3.00 8.00
190 Jay Gibbons RPM RC 4.00 10.00
191 Wilkin Ruan RPM RC 3.00 8.00
192 Tsuyoshi Shinjo RPM RC 4.00 10.00
193 Alfonso Soriano RPM 4.00 10.00
194 Corey Patterson RPM 3.00 8.00
195 Ichiro Suzuki RPM RC 40.00 100.00
196 Billy Sylvester RPM 3.00 8.00
197 Juan Uribe RPM RC 4.00 10.00
198 Johnny Estrada RPM RC 4.00 10.00
199 Carlos Valderrama RPM RC 3.00 8.00
200 Matt White RPM 3.00 8.00

2001 Absolute Memorabilia Ball Hoggs

CARDS DISPLAY CUMULATIVE PRINT RUN
ACTUAL PRINT RUNS LISTED BELOW
12/13/32/34 ONLY AVAIL.AS BOSS HOGG'S
BH1 Vladimir Guerrero/50* 10.00 25.00
BH2 Troy Glaus/50* 6.00 15.00
BH3 Tony Gwynn/50* 10.00 25.00
BH4 Cal Ripken/150* 20.00 50.00
BH5 Todd Helton/50* 10.00 25.00
BH6 Jacque Jones/100* 6.00 15.00
BH7 Shawn Green/75* 6.00 15.00
BH8 Ichiro Suzuki/25* 60.00 150.00
BH9 Scott Rolen/75* 10.00 25.00
BH10 Roger Clemens/50* 10.00 25.00
BH14 Sammy Sosa/50* 10.00 25.00
BH15 J.D. Drew/25* 6.00 15.00
BH16 Barry Bonds/50* 15.00 40.00
BH17 Pat Burrell/50* 6.00 15.00
BH18 Mark McGwire/50* 12.50 30.00
BH19 Mike Piazza/25* 10.00 25.00
BH20 Magglio Ordonez/100* 6.00 15.00
BH21 Miguel Tejada/50* 6.00 15.00
BH22 Albert Pujols/50* 100.00 250.00
BH23 Derek Jeter/25* 20.00 50.00
BH24 Johnny Damon/100* 10.00 25.00
BH25 Mike Sweeney/50* 6.00 15.00
BH26 Ben Grieve/100* 6.00 15.00
BH27 Jeff Kent/50* 6.00 15.00
BH28 Andres Galarraga/50* 6.00 15.00
BH30 Juan Encarnacion/100* 6.00 15.00
BH31 Ruben Mateo/50* 6.00 15.00
BH33 Manny Ramirez Sox/50* 10.00 25.00
BH35 Ivan Rodriguez/50* 10.00 25.00
BH36 Darin Erstad/100* 6.00 15.00
BH37 Carlos Delgado/75* 6.00 15.00
BH38 Jeff Bagwell/100* 10.00 25.00
BH39 Jermaine Dye/50* 6.00 15.00
BH40 Jose Ortiz/25* 6.00 15.00
BH41 Gary Sheffield/50* 6.00 15.00
BH42 Eric Chavez/100* 6.00 15.00
BH43 Mark Grace/50* 10.00 25.00
BH44 Rafael Palmeiro/100* 10.00 25.00
BH45 Tsuyoshi Shinjo/50* 10.00 25.00
BH46 Terrence Long/50* 6.00 15.00
BH48 Frank Thomas/50* 10.00 25.00
BH50 Jason Giambi/50* 6.00 15.00

2001 Absolute Memorabilia Boss Hoggs

AU CL: 1-3/5/10/22/32/34/41/49

2001 Absolute Memorabilia Home Opener Souvenirs

ONE HOME OPENER PER BOX
STATED PRINT RUN 400 SERIAL #'d SETS
OD1 Barry Bonds 10.00 25.00
OD2 Cal Ripken 15.00 40.00
OD3 Pedro Martinez 4.00 10.00
OD4 Troy Glaus 3.00 8.00
OD5 Frank Thomas 4.00 10.00
OD6 Alex Rodriguez 6.00 15.00
OD7 Ivan Rodriguez 4.00 10.00
OD8 Jeff Bagwell 4.00 10.00
OD9 Mark McGwire 10.00 25.00
OD10 Todd Helton 4.00 10.00
OD11 Gary Sheffield 3.00 8.00
OD12 Manny Ramirez Sox 4.00 10.00
OD13 Mike Piazza 6.00 15.00
OD14 Sammy Sosa 4.00 10.00
OD15 Preston Wilson 3.00 8.00
OD16 Tony Gwynn 6.00 15.00
OD17 Vladimir Guerrero 4.00 10.00
OD18 Carlos Delgado 3.00 8.00
OD19 Roberto Alomar 4.00 10.00
OD20 Todd Helton 4.00 10.00
OD21 Albert Pujols UER 50.00 120.00
OD22 Jason Giambi 3.00 8.00
OD23 Sammy Sosa 4.00 10.00
OD24 Ken Griffey Jr. 6.00 15.00
OD25 Darin Erstad 3.00 8.00
OD26 Mark McGwire 15.00 40.00
OD27 Carlos Delgado 3.00 8.00
OD28 Juan Gonzalez 3.00 8.00
OD29 Mike Sweeney 3.00 8.00
OD30 Alex Rodriguez 6.00 15.00
OD31 Roger Clemens 6.00 15.00
OD32 Tsuyoshi Shinjo 4.00 10.00
OD33 Ben Grieve 3.00 8.00
OD34 Jeff Kent 3.00 8.00
OD35 Vladimir Guerrero 4.00 10.00
OD36 Shawn Green 3.00 8.00
OD37 Rafael Palmeiro 4.00 10.00
OD38 Tony Gwynn 6.00 15.00
OD39 Scott Rolen 4.00 10.00
OD40 Ken Griffey Jr. 6.00 15.00
OD41 Albert Pujols 50.00 120.00
OD42 Barry Bonds 10.00 25.00
OD43 Mark Grace 4.00 10.00
OD44 Bernie Williams 4.00 10.00
OD45 Frank Thomas 4.00 10.00
OD46 Jermaine Dye 3.00 8.00
OD47 Mike Piazza 6.00 15.00
OD48 Chipper Jones 4.00 10.00
OD49 Richie Sexson 3.00 8.00
OD50 Magglio Ordonez 3.00 8.00

2001 Absolute Memorabilia Home Opener Souvenirs Double

*DOUBLE: .6X TO 1.5X BASIC SOUV.

2001 Absolute Memorabilia Home Opener Souvenirs Triple

*TRIPLE: 1.25X TO 3X BASIC SOUV.

2001 Absolute Memorabilia Signing Bonus Baseballs

ONE PER BOX
STATED PRINT RUNS LISTED BELOW
NO PRICING ON PRINT RUNS OF 25 OR LESS
1 Al Oliver/500 10.00 25.00
2 Andre Dawson/550 10.00 25.00
4 Bill Madlock/524 10.00 25.00
6 Billy Williams/325 10.00 25.00
7 Bob Feller/550 10.00 25.00
9 Bobby Doerr/300 10.00 25.00
10 Bobby Richardson/500 15.00 40.00
11 Boog Powell/500 10.00 25.00
13 Bucky Dent/500 10.00 25.00
16 Clete Boyer/500 10.00 25.00
18 Dave Concepcion/500 10.00 25.00
19 Dave Kingman/500 10.00 25.00
20 Don Larsen/200 10.00 25.00
21 Don Newcombe/500 10.00 25.00
22 Don Zimmer/500 10.00 25.00
24 Earl Weaver/300 10.00 25.00
25 Enos Slaughter/525 15.00 40.00
26 Fergie Jenkins/1000 10.00 25.00
27 Frank Howard/500 10.00 25.00
30 Gary Carter/200 10.00 25.00
31 Gaylord Perry/1000 12.00 30.00
32 George Foster/500 10.00 25.00
33 George Kell/300 15.00 40.00
34 Goose Gossage/500 10.00 25.00
37 Hank Bauer/500 10.00 25.00
38 Harmon Killebrew/200 30.00 60.00
39 Henry Rodriguez/400 10.00 25.00
40 Herb Score/500 10.00 25.00
41 Hoyt Wilhelm/500 15.00 40.00
45 Jim Palmer/500 10.00 25.00
46 Joe Pepitone/500 10.00 25.00
48 Johnny Podres/500 10.00 25.00
49 Juan Marichal/485 10.00 25.00
51 Larry Doby/300 15.00 40.00
53 Luis Tiant/500 10.00 25.00
54 Magglio Ordonez/200 10.00 25.00
56 Maury Wills/500 10.00 25.00
58 Minnie Minoso/1000 10.00 25.00
59 Monte Irvin/500 15.00 40.00
60 Moose Skowron/500 10.00 25.00
64 Ralph Kiner/100 20.00 50.00
66 Red Schoendienst/500 10.00 25.00
69 Robin Roberts/500 20.00 50.00
71 Rollie Fingers/575 10.00 25.00
76 Steve Garvey/1000 10.00 25.00
80 Tommy John/1000 10.00 25.00
82 Tony Perez/400 10.00 25.00
84 Warren Spahn/500 40.00 80.00

2001 Absolute Memorabilia Tools of the Trade

HAT PRINT RUN 100 SERIAL #'d SETS
BAT PRINT RUN 100 SERIAL #'d SETS
JSY PRINT RUN 300 SERIAL #'d SETS
TT1 Vladimir Guerrero Jsy 6.00 15.00
TT2 Troy Glaus Jsy 4.00 10.00
TT3 Tony Gwynn Jsy 10.00 25.00
TT4 Todd Helton Jsy 6.00 15.00
TT5 Scott Rolen Jsy 6.00 15.00
TT6 Roger Clemens Jsy 15.00 40.00
TT7 Pedro Martinez Jsy 6.00 15.00
TT8 Richie Sexson Jsy 4.00 10.00
TT9 Magglio Ordonez Jsy 4.00 10.00
TT10 Ben Grieve Jsy 4.00 10.00
TT11 Jeff Bagwell Jsy 6.00 15.00
TT12 Edgar Martinez Jsy 6.00 15.00
TT13 Greg Maddux Jsy 10.00 25.00
TT14 Larry Walker Jsy 4.00 10.00
TT15 Frank Thomas Jsy 6.00 15.00
TT16 Edgardo Alfonzo Jsy 4.00 10.00
TT17 Cal Ripken Jsy 20.00 50.00
TT18 Jose Vidro Jsy 4.00 10.00
TT19 Andruw Jones Jsy 6.00 15.00
TT20 Kazuhiro Sasaki Jsy 4.00 10.00
TT21 Barry Bonds Bat 20.00 50.00
TT22 Juan Gonzalez Bat 10.00 25.00
TT23 Andruw Jones Bat 15.00 40.00
TT24 Cal Ripken Bat 40.00 100.00
TT25 Greg Maddux Bat 15.00 40.00
TT26 Manny Ramirez Sox Bat 15.00 40.00
TT27 Roberto Alomar Bat 15.00 40.00
TT28 Shawn Green Bat 10.00 25.00
TT29 Edgardo Alfonzo Bat 10.00 25.00
TT30 Rafael Palmeiro Bat 15.00 40.00
TT31 Hideo Nomo Bat 75.00 150.00
TT32 Andres Galarraga Bat 10.00 25.00
TT33 Todd Helton Bat 15.00 40.00
TT34 Darin Erstad Bat 10.00 25.00
TT35 Ivan Rodriguez Bat 15.00 40.00
TT36 Sean Casey Bat 10.00 25.00
TT37 Vladimir Guerrero Bat 15.00 40.00
TT38 David Justice Bat 10.00 25.00
TT39 Troy Glaus Bat 10.00 25.00
TT41 Barry Bonds Glove 75.00 150.00
TT42 Cal Ripken Glove 100.00 200.00
TT43 Rob Alomar Glove 15.00 40.00
TT44 Sean Casey Glove 10.00 25.00
TT46 Bernie Williams Hat 15.00 40.00
TT47 Barry Zito Hat 15.00 40.00
TT49 Tom Glavine Hat 15.00 40.00
TT50 Troy Glaus Hat 10.00 25.00

2002 Absolute Memorabilia

COMP.SET w/o SP's (150) 15.00 40.00
COMMON CARD (1-150) .30 .75
COMMON CARD (151-200) 2.00 5.00
151-200 RANDOM INSERTS IN PACKS
151-200 PR.RUN RUN 1000 SERIAL #'d SETS
1 David Eckstein .30 .75
2 Darin Erstad .30 .75
3 Troy Glaus .30 .75
4 Garret Anderson .30 .75
5 Tim Salmon .50 1.25
6 Curt Schilling .30 .75
7 Randy Johnson .75 2.00
8 Luis Gonzalez .30 .75
9 Mark Grace .50 1.25
10 Tom Glavine .50 1.25
11 Greg Maddux 1.25 3.00
12 Chipper Jones .75 2.00
13 Gary Sheffield .30 .75
14 John Smoltz .50 1.25
15 Andruw Jones .50 1.25
16 Wilson Betemit .30 .75
17 Tony Batista .30 .75
18 Javier Vazquez .30 .75
19 Scott Erickson .30 .75
20 Josh Towers .30 .75
21 Pedro Martinez .50 1.25
22 Johnny Damon Sox .50 1.25
23 Manny Ramirez .50 1.25
24 Rickey Henderson .75 2.00
25 Trot Nixon .30 .75
26 Nomar Garciaparra 1.25 3.00
27 Juan Cruz .30 .75
28 Kerry Wood .30 .75
29 Fred McGriff .50 1.25
30 Moises Alou .30 .75
31 Sammy Sosa .75 2.00
32 Corey Patterson .30 .75
33 Mark Buehrle .30 .75
34 Keith Foulke .30 .75
35 Frank Thomas .75 2.00
36 Kenny Lofton .30 .75
37 Magglio Ordonez .30 .75
38 Barry Larkin .50 1.25
39 Ken Griffey Jr. 1.50 4.00
40 Adam Dunn .30 .75
41 Juan Encarnacion .30 .75
42 Sean Casey .30 .75
43 Bartolo Colon .30 .75
44 C.C. Sabathia .30 .75
45 Travis Fryman .30 .75
46 Jim Thome .50 1.25
47 Omar Vizquel .50 1.25
48 Ellis Burks .30 .75
49 Russell Branyan .30 .75
50 Mike Hampton .30 .75
51 Todd Helton .50 1.25
52 Jose Ortiz .30 .75
53 Juan Uribe .30 .75
54 Juan Pierre .30 .75
55 Larry Walker .30 .75
56 Mike Rivera .30 .75
57 Robert Fick .30 .75
58 Bobby Higginson .30 .75
59 Josh Beckett .30 .75
60 Richard Hidalgo .30 .75
61 Cliff Floyd .30 .75
62 Mike Lowell .30 .75
63 Roy Oswalt .30 .75
64 Morgan Ensberg .30 .75
65 Jeff Bagwell .50 1.25
66 Craig Biggio .50 1.25
67 Lance Berkman .30 .75
68 Carlos Beltran .30 .75
69 Mike Sweeney .30 .75
70 Neifi Perez .30 .75
71 Kevin Brown .30 .75
72 Hideo Nomo .75 2.00
73 Paul Lo Duca .30 .75
74 Adrian Beltre .30 .75
75 Shawn Green .30 .75
76 Eric Karros .30 .75
77 Brad Radke .30 .75
78 Corey Koskie .30 .75
79 Doug Mientkiewicz .30 .75
80 Torii Hunter .30 .75
81 Jacque Jones .30 .75
82 Ben Sheets .30 .75
83 Richie Sexson .30 .75
84 Geoff Jenkins .30 .75
85 Tony Armas Jr. .30 .75
86 Michael Barrett .30 .75
87 Jose Vidro .30 .75
88 Vladimir Guerrero .75 2.00
89 Roger Clemens 1.50 4.00
90 Derek Jeter 2.00 5.00
91 Bernie Williams .50 1.25
92 Jason Giambi .30 .75
93 Jorge Posada .50 1.25
94 Mike Mussina .50 1.25
95 Andy Pettitte .50 1.25
96 Nick Johnson .30 .75
97 Alfonso Soriano .30 .75
98 Shawn Estes .30 .75
99 Al Leiter .30 .75
100 Mike Piazza 1.25 3.00
101 Roberto Alomar .50 1.25
102 Mo Vaughn .30 .75
103 Jeromy Burnitz .30 .75
104 Tim Hudson .30 .75
105 Barry Zito .30 .75
106 Mark Mulder .30 .75
107 Eric Chavez .30 .75
108 Miguel Tejada .30 .75
109 Carlos Pena .30 .75
110 Jermaine Dye .30 .75
111 Mike Lieberthal .30 .75
112 Scott Rolen .50 1.25
113 Pat Burrell .30 .75
114 Brandon Duckworth .30 .75
115 Bobby Abreu .30 .75
116 Jason Kendall .30 .75
117 Aramis Ramirez .30 .75
118 Brian Giles .30 .75
119 Pokey Reese .30 .75
120 Phil Nevin .30 .75
121 Ryan Klesko .30 .75
122 Jeremy Giambi .30 .75
123 Trevor Hoffman .30 .75
124 Barry Bonds 2.00 5.00
125 Rich Aurilia .30 .75
126 Jeff Kent .30 .75
127 Tsuyoshi Shinjo .30 .75
128 Ichiro Suzuki 1.50 4.00
129 Edgar Martinez .50 1.25
130 Freddy Garcia .30 .75
131 Bret Boone .30 .75
132 Matt Morris .30 .75
133 Tino Martinez .50 1.25

134 Albert Pujols 1.50 4.00
135 J.D. Drew .30 .75
136 Jim Edmonds .30 .75
137 Gabe Kapler .30 .75
138 Paul Wilson .30 .75
139 Ben Grieve .30 .75
140 Wade Miller .30 .75
141 Chan Ho Park .30 .75
142 Alex Rodriguez 1.00 2.50
143 Rafael Palmeiro .50 1.25
144 Juan Gonzalez .30 .75
145 Ivan Rodriguez .50 1.25
146 Carlos Delgado .30 .75
147 Jose Cruz Jr. .30 .75
148 Shannon Stewart .30 .75
149 Raul Mondesi .30 .75
150 Vernon Wells .30 .75
151 So Taguchi RP RC 3.00 8.00
152 Kazuhisa Ishii RP RC 3.00 8.00
153 Hank Blalock RP 3.00 8.00
154 Sean Burroughs RP 2.00 5.00
155 Geronimo Gil RP 2.00 5.00
156 Jon Rauch RP 2.00 5.00
157 Fernando Rodney RP 2.00 5.00
158 Miguel Asencio RP RC 2.00 5.00
159 Franklyn German RP RC 2.00 5.00
160 Luis Ugueto RP RC 2.00 5.00
161 Jorge Sosa RP RC 3.00 8.00
162 Felix Escalona RP RC 2.00 5.00
163 Colby Lewis RP 2.00 5.00
164 Mark Teixeira RP 3.00 8.00
165 Mark Prior RP 3.00 8.00
166 Francis Beltran RP RC 2.00 5.00
167 Joe Thurston RP 2.00 5.00
168 Earl Snyder RP RC 2.00 5.00
169 Takahito Nomura RP RC 2.00 5.00
170 Bill Hall RP 2.00 5.00
171 Marlon Byrd RP 2.00 5.00
172 Dave Williams RP 2.00 5.00
173 Yorvit Torrealba RP 2.00 5.00
174 Brandon Backe RP RC 3.00 8.00
175 Jorge De La Rosa RP RC 2.00 5.00
176 Brian Mallette RP RC 2.00 5.00
177 Rodrigo Rosario RP RC 2.00 5.00
178 Anderson Machado RP RC 2.00 5.00
179 Jorge Padilla RP RC 2.00 5.00
180 Allan Simpson RP RC 2.00 5.00
181 Doug Devore RP RC 2.00 5.00
182 Steve Bechler RP RC 2.00 5.00
183 Raul Chavez RP RC 2.00 5.00
184 Tom Shearn RP RC 2.00 5.00
185 Ben Howard RP RC 2.00 5.00
186 Chris Baker RP RC 2.00 5.00
187 Travis Hughes RP RC 2.00 5.00
188 Kevin Mench RP 2.00 5.00
189 Drew Henson RP 2.00 5.00
190 Mike Moriarty RP RC 2.00 5.00
191 Corey Thurman RP RC 2.00 5.00
192 Bobby Hill RP 2.00 5.00
193 Steve Kent RP RC 2.00 5.00
194 Satoru Komiyama RP RC 2.00 5.00
195 Jason Lane RP 2.00 5.00
196 Angel Berroa RP 2.00 5.00
197 Brandon Puffer RP RC 2.00 5.00
198 Brian Fitzgerald RP RC 2.00 5.00
199 Rene Reyes RP RC 2.00 5.00
200 Hee Seop Choi RP 2.00 5.00

2002 Absolute Memorabilia Spectrum

*SPECTRUM 1-150: 2.5X TO 6X BASIC
1-150 PRINT RUN 100 SERIAL #'d SETS
151-200 PRINT RUN 50 SERIAL #'d SETS
72 Hideo Nomo 5.00 12.00
151 So Taguchi RP 4.00 10.00
152 Kazuhisa Ishii RP 4.00 10.00
153 Hank Blalock RP 4.00 10.00
154 Sean Burroughs RP 3.00 8.00
155 Geronimo Gil RP 3.00 8.00
156 Jon Rauch RP 3.00 8.00
157 Fernando Rodney RP 3.00 8.00
158 Miguel Asencio RP 3.00 8.00
159 Franklyn German RP 3.00 8.00
160 Luis Ugueto RP 3.00 8.00
161 Jorge Sosa RP 4.00 10.00
162 Felix Escalona RP 3.00 8.00
163 Colby Lewis RP 3.00 8.00
164 Mark Teixeira RP 6.00 15.00
165 Mark Prior RP 4.00 10.00
166 Francis Beltran RP 3.00 8.00
167 Joe Thurston RP 3.00 8.00
168 Earl Snyder RP 3.00 8.00
169 Takahito Nomura RP 6.00 15.00
170 Bill Hall RP 3.00 8.00
171 Marlon Byrd RP 3.00 8.00
172 Dave Williams RP 3.00 8.00
173 Yorvit Torrealba RP 3.00 8.00
174 Brandon Backe RP 4.00 10.00
175 Jorge De La Rosa RP 4.00 10.00
176 Brian Mallette RP 3.00 8.00
177 Rodrigo Rosario RP 3.00 8.00
178 Anderson Machado RP 3.00 8.00
179 Jorge Padilla RP 3.00 8.00
180 Allan Simpson RP 3.00 8.00
181 Doug Devore RP 3.00 8.00
182 Steve Bechler RP 3.00 8.00
183 Raul Chavez RP 3.00 8.00
184 Tom Shearn RP 3.00 8.00
185 Ben Howard RP 3.00 8.00
186 Chris Baker RP 3.00 8.00
187 Travis Hughes RP 3.00 8.00
188 Kevin Mench RP 3.00 8.00
189 Drew Henson RP 3.00 8.00
190 Mike Moriarty RP 3.00 8.00
191 Corey Thurman RP 3.00 8.00
192 Bobby Hill RP 3.00 8.00
193 Steve Kent RP 3.00 8.00
194 Satoru Komiyama RP 3.00 8.00
195 Jason Lane RP 3.00 8.00
196 Angel Berroa RP 3.00 8.00
197 Brandon Puffer RP 3.00 8.00
198 Brian Fitzgerald RP 3.00 8.00
199 Rene Reyes RP 3.00 8.00
200 Hee Seop Choi RP 3.00 8.00

2002 Absolute Memorabilia Absolutely Ink

STATED ODDS 1:22 HOBBY, 1:36 RETAIL
SP PRINT RUNS PROVIDED BY DONRUSS
SP'S ARE NOT SERIAL-NUMBERED
CARD NUMBER 9 DOES NOT EXIST
NO PRICING ON QTY OF 25 OR LESS
GOLD RANDOM INSERTS IN PACKS
GOLD PRINT RUN 25 SERIAL #'d SETS
NO GOLD PRICING DUE TO SCARCITY
AI1 Adrian Beltre 10.00 25.00
AI2 Alex Rodriguez SP/50 * 30.00 80.00
AI3 Ben Sheets 6.00 15.00
AI5 Bobby Doerr 6.00 15.00
AI6 Blaine Neal 4.00 10.00
AI7 Carlos Beltran 10.00 25.00
AI8 Carlos Pena 4.00 10.00
AI9 Corey Patterson SP/150 * 6.00 15.00
AI11 Dave Parker 6.00 15.00
AI12 David Justice SP/65 * 10.00 25.00
AI13 Don Mattingly SP/75 * 40.00 80.00
AI15 Duaner Sanchez 4.00 10.00
AI16 Eric Chavez SP/100 * 6.00 15.00
AI17 Freddy Garcia SP/200 * 6.00 15.00
AI18 Gary Carter SP/150 * 12.50 30.00
AI22 Ivan Rodriguez SP/50 * 20.00 50.00
AI23 J.D. Drew SP/100 * 6.00 15.00
AI24 Jack Cust 4.00 10.00
AI25 Jason Michaels 4.00 10.00
AI26 Jermaine Dye SP/125 * 6.00 15.00
AI27 Jim Palmer SP/150 * 6.00 15.00
AI28 Jose Vidro 4.00 10.00
AI29 Josh Towers 4.00 10.00
AI30 Kerry Wood SP/50 * 15.00 40.00
AI31 Kirby Puckett SP/50 * 125.00 250.00
AI32 Luis Gonzalez SP/75 * 10.00 25.00
AI33 Luis Rivera 4.00 10.00
AI34 Manny Ramirez SP/50 * 20.00 50.00
AI35 Marcus Giles 6.00 15.00
AI36 Mark Prior SP/100 * 6.00 15.00
AI37 Mark Teixeira SP/100 * 15.00 40.00
AI38 Marlon Byrd SP/250 * 6.00 15.00
AI38 Matt Ginter 4.00 10.00
AI40 Moises Alou SP/150 * 6.00 15.00
AI41 Nate Frese 4.00 10.00
AI42 Nick Johnson 6.00 15.00
AI44 Pablo Ozuna 4.00 10.00
AI45 Paul Lo Duca SP/200 * 6.00 15.00
AI46 Richie Sexson 6.00 15.00
AI47 Roberto Alomar SP/100 * 10.00 25.00
AI48 Roy Oswalt SP/300 * 6.00 15.00
AI49 Ryan Klesko SP/75 * 10.00 25.00
AI50 Sean Casey SP/125 * 6.00 15.00
AI51 Shannon Stewart 6.00 15.00
AI52 So Taguchi 8.00 20.00
AI53 Terrence Long 4.00 10.00
AI54 Timo Perez 4.00 10.00
AI56 Tony Gwynn SP/50 * 40.00 80.00
AI57 Troy Glaus SP/300 * 10.00 25.00
AI58 Vladimir Guerrero SP/225 * 15.00 40.00
AI59 Wade Miller 4.00 10.00
AI60 Wilson Betemit 4.00 10.00

2002 Absolute Memorabilia Absolutely Ink Numbers

PRINT RUNS BASED ON UNIFORM NUMBER
NO PRICING ON QTY OF 25 OR LESS
SKIP-NUMBERED 50 CARD SET
AI1 Adrian Beltre/29 12.50 30.00
AI11 Dave Parker/39 10.00 25.00
AI17 Freddy Garcia/34 12.50 30.00
AI21 Greg Maddux/31 60.00 120.00
AI24 Jack Cust/67 6.00 15.00
AI29 Josh Towers/35 8.00 20.00
AI30 Kerry Wood/34 20.00 50.00
AI31 Kirby Puckett/34 150.00 300.00
AI33 Luis Rivera/60 6.00 15.00
AI42 Nick Johnson/36 12.50 30.00
AI48 Roy Oswalt/44 10.00 25.00
AI49 Ryan Klesko/30 12.50 30.00
AI52 So Taguchi/99 10.00 25.00
AI58 Vladimir Guerrero/27 40.00 100.00
AI59 Wade Miller/52 6.00 15.00

2002 Absolute Memorabilia Signing Bonus

ONE SEALED FRAME PER HOBBY BOX
STATED PRINT RUNS LISTED BELOW
N ='s NUMBER DESIGN
NO PRICING ON QTY OF 25 OR LESS
1 Bob Abreu Gray-N/53 15.00 40.00
2 Bob Abreu Stripe-N/53 15.00 40.00
5 Rob Alomar Gray-N/100 15.00 40.00
6 Rob Alomar Stripe-N/100 15.00 40.00
7 Moises Alou Blue-L/250 10.00 25.00
10 Moises Alou Stripe-L/250 10.00 25.00
17 Carlos Beltran Blue-N/50 15.00 40.00
18 Carlos Beltran Gray-N/50 15.00 40.00
20 Adrian Beltre Blue-N/150 15.00 40.00
21 Adrian Beltre Gray-N/150 15.00 40.00
22 Adrian Beltre White-N/29 30.00 60.00
27 Angel Berroa Black-N/100 8.00 20.00
28 Angel Berroa Blue-N/100 8.00 20.00
29 Angel Berroa Gray-N/50 10.00 25.00
31 Wilson Betemit Gray-N/250 6.00 15.00
32 Wilson Betemit White-N/250 6.00 15.00
38 Hank Blalock Gray-N/50 15.00 40.00
39 Hank Blalock White-N/100 12.50 30.00
43 Lou Brock Gray-N/100 30.00 60.00
44 Lou Brock White-N/200 15.00 40.00
45 Kevin Brown Blue-N/27 20.00 50.00
46 Kevin Brown Gray-N/150 10.00 25.00
47 Kevin Brown White-N/100 12.50 30.00
48 Mark Buehrle Black-N/200 15.00 40.00
49 Mark Buehrle Gray-N/200 15.00 40.00
50 Mark Buehrle Stripe-N/56 40.00 80.00
54 Marlon Byrd Gray-N/61 10.00 25.00
55 Marlon Byrd Stripe-N/61 10.00 25.00
56 Steve Carlton Gray-N/100 12.50 30.00
57 Steve Carlton Stripe-N/150 10.00 25.00
59 Sean Casey Stripe-L/100 12.50 30.00
63 Eric Chavez White-N/28 20.00 50.00
68 Juan Cruz Blue-L/51 10.00 25.00
69 Juan Cruz Blue-N/51 10.00 25.00
70 Juan Cruz Gray-N/51 10.00 25.00
71 Juan Cruz Stripe-L/51 10.00 25.00
72 Juan Cruz Stripe-N/51 10.00 25.00
73 J.D. Drew Gray-N/100 12.50 30.00
75 Bran Duckworth Gray-N/56 10.00 25.00
76 Bran Duckworth Stripe-N/150 6.00 15.00
79 Adam Dunn Stripe-N/44 30.00 60.00
80 Jermaine Dye Gray-N/250 10.00 25.00
81 Jermaine Dye Green-N/100 12.50 30.00
82 Jermaine Dye White-N/100 12.50 30.00
83 Morg Ensberg Gray-N/100 12.50 30.00
84 Morg Ensberg Red-N/100 12.50 30.00
85 Morg Ensberg Stripe-N/100 12.50 30.00
86 Morg Ensberg White-N/100 12.50 30.00
89 Cliff Floyd Gray-N/200 10.00 25.00
90 Cliff Floyd Stripe-N/200 10.00 25.00
92 Freddy Garcia Blue-N/34 20.00 50.00
93 Freddy Garcia Gray-N/34 20.00 50.00
94 Freddy Garcia White-N/125 10.00 25.00
97 Troy Glaus Gray-N/50 30.00 60.00
98 Troy Glaus White-N/100 15.00 40.00
100 Tom Glavine White-N/200 25.00 60.00
102 Luis Gonzalez Gray-N/125 10.00 25.00
103 Luis Gonzalez Purple-N/125 10.00 25.00
104 Luis Gonzalez Stripe-N/125 10.00 25.00
106 Vlad Guerrero Gray-N/27 60.00 120.00
107 Vlad Guerrero Stripe-N/150 40.00 80.00
111 Rich Hidalgo Gray-N/100 8.00 20.00
112 Rich Hidalgo Red-N/135 6.00 15.00
114 Rich Hidalgo White-N/150 6.00 15.00
116 Tim Hudson Gray-N/50 30.00 60.00
117 Tim Hudson Green-N/100 15.00 40.00
122 Reg Jackson Gray-N/44 40.00 80.00
123 Reg Jackson Stripe-N/44 50.00 100.00
124 Nick Johnson Gray-N/200 10.00 25.00
125 Nick Johnson Stripe-N/200 6.00 15.00
127 Andruw Jones Gray-N/75 30.00 60.00
132 Al Kaline White-L/250 50.00 120.00
134 Gabe Kapler Blue-N/125 10.00 25.00
136 Gabe Kapler White-N/175 10.00 25.00
137 Ryan Klesko Blue-N/30 20.00 50.00
138 Ryan Klesko Gray-N/30 20.00 50.00
139 Ryan Klesko White-N/30 20.00 50.00
141 Jason Lane Gray-N/100 12.50 30.00
142 Jason Lane Red-N/100 12.50 30.00
143 Jason Lane Stripe-N/100 12.50 30.00
144 Jason Lane White-N/100 12.50 30.00
145 Barry Larkin Gray-N/50 40.00 80.00
146 Barry Larkin Stripe-L/100 20.00 50.00
150 Paul LoDuca White-N/50 15.00 40.00
151 Fred Lynn Gray-N/250 10.00 25.00
152 Fred Lynn White-N/150 10.00 25.00
154 Greg Maddux Gray-N/31 100.00 200.00
155 Greg Maddux White-N/31 100.00 200.00
157 Edgar Martinez Blue-N/150 20.00 50.00
158 Edgar Martinez Gray-N/150 20.00 50.00
161 P.Martinez White-N/45 60.00 120.00
162 D.Mattingly Gray-N/100 60.00 120.00
163 D.Mattingly Stripe-N/100 60.00 120.00
164 W.McCovey Gray-N/190 15.00 40.00
165 W.McCovey White-N/250 15.00 40.00
166 Wade Miller Gray-N/150 6.00 15.00
167 Wade Miller Stripe-N/250 6.00 15.00
168 Wade Miller Red-N/52 10.00 25.00
169 Wade Miller White-N/52 10.00 25.00
170 Paul Molitor Blue-N/75 15.00 40.00
171 Paul Molitor Gray-N/100 15.00 40.00
172 Paul Molitor White-N/125 10.00 25.00
175 Mark Mulder White-N/40 15.00 40.00
178 Jose Ortiz Gray-N/125 6.00 15.00
179 Jose Ortiz Purple-N/125 6.00 15.00
180 Jose Ortiz Stripe-L/125 6.00 15.00
181 Jose Ortiz Stripe-N/125 6.00 15.00
182 Roy Oswalt Gray-N/44 15.00 40.00
183 Roy Oswalt Red-N/44 15.00 40.00
184 Roy Oswalt Stripe-N/100 12.50 30.00
185 Roy Oswalt White-N/100 12.50 30.00
190 Jim Palmer Gray-N/250 10.00 25.00
191 Jim Palmer White-N/150 10.00 25.00
192 Dave Parker Black-N/150 12.50 30.00
193 Dave Parker White-N/150 12.50 30.00
194 Cor Patterson Blue-L/250 10.00 25.00
196 Cor Patterson Gray-N/250 10.00 25.00
197 Cor Patterson Stripe-L/250 10.00 25.00
198 Cor Patterson Stripe-N/250 2.00 5.00
200 Carlos Pena Green-N/250 6.00 15.00
201 Carlos Pena White-N/150 6.00 15.00
203 Tony Perez Stripe-L/250 10.00 25.00
205 Juan Pierre Gray-N/75 15.00 40.00
206 Juan Pierre Purple-N/75 10.00 25.00
207 Juan Pierre White-L/75 10.00 25.00
208 Juan Pierre White-N/75 10.00 25.00
209 Mark Prior Blue-L/75 15.00 40.00
210 Mark Prior Blue-N/125 12.50 30.00
211 Mark Prior Gray-N/75 15.00 40.00
212 Mark Prior Stripe-L/50 15.00 40.00
214 Kirby Puckett Blue-N/34 60.00 120.00
216 Kirby Puckett Stripe-N/34 60.00 120.00
218 Albert Pujols White-N/100 150.00 250.00
219 Aram Ramirez Black-N/125 10.00 25.00
220 Aram Ramirez Gray-N/50 15.00 40.00
224 Phil Rizzuto Gray-N/250 40.00 80.00
226 B.Robinson Gray-N/250 12.50 30.00
227 B.Robinson White-N/150 40.00 80.00
238 N.Ryan Angel Gray-N/30 125.00 250.00
239 N.Ryan Angel White-N/30 125.00 250.00
240 N.Ryan Astro Gray-N/34 125.00 250.00
241 N.Ryan Astro White-N/34 125.00 250.00
242 N.Ryan Rgr Blue-N/34 125.00 250.00
243 N.Ryan Rgr Gray-N/34 125.00 250.00
244 N.Ryan Rgr White-N/34 125.00 250.00
248 Ryne Sandberg Blue-L/50 75.00 150.00
251 R.Sandberg Stripe-L/50 75.00 150.00
257 Mike Schmidt Gray-N/100 60.00 120.00
258 Mike Schmidt Stripe-N/100 60.00 120.00
259 Richie Sexson Blue-N/100 12.50 30.00
260 Richie Sexson Gray-N/100 12.50 30.00
261 Richie Sexson White-N/100 12.50 30.00
262 Ben Sheets Blue-N/150 10.00 25.00
263 Ben Sheets Gray-N/100 12.50 30.00
264 Ben Sheets White-N/100 12.50 30.00
269 A.Soriano Stripe-N/100 15.00 40.00
271 Shan Stewart Blue-N/150 10.00 25.00
272 Shan Stewart Gray-N/100 8.00 20.00
274 M.Sweeney Black-N/100 12.50 30.00
275 M.Sweeney Blue-N/100 12.50 30.00
276 M.Sweeney Gray-N/100 12.50 30.00
277 M.Sweeney White-N/100 12.50 30.00
278 So Taguchi Gray-N/99 20.00 50.00
279 So Taguchi White-N/99 20.00 50.00
280 Mark Teixeira Blue-N/100 20.00 50.00
282 Mark Teixeira White-N/100 20.00 50.00
283 Miguel Tejada Gray-N/50 10.00 25.00
285 Miguel Tejada White-N/40 10.00 25.00
286 Frank Thomas Black-N/35 60.00 120.00
293 Jav Vazquez Gray-N/125 10.00 25.00
294 Jav Vazquez Stripe-N/125 10.00 25.00
295 Jose Vidro Gray-N/150 6.00 15.00
296 Jose Vidro Stripe-N/150 6.00 15.00
304 Kerry Wood Blue-L/34 40.00 80.00
305 Kerry Wood Blue-N/34 40.00 80.00
306 Kerry Wood Gray-N/34 40.00 80.00
307 Kerry Wood Stripe-L/34 40.00 80.00
308 Kerry Wood Stripe-N/34 40.00 80.00
312 Barry Zito White-N/50 30.00 60.00

2002 Absolute Memorabilia Team Quads

STATED ODDS 1:18 HOBBY
*GOLD: .75X TO 2X BASIC QUADS
GOLD ODDS 1:72 HOBBY
*SPECTRUM: .6X TO 1.5X BASIC QUADS
SPECTRUM ODDS 1:36 HOBBY
TQ1 Troy Glaus .75 2.00
Darin Erstad
Garret Anderson
Troy Percival
TQ2 Curt Schilling 2.00 5.00
Randy Johnson
Luis Gonzalez
Mark Grace
TQ3 Jones/Jones/Madd/Glav 3.00 8.00
TQ4 Nomar Garciaparra 1.25 3.00
Manny Ramirez
Trot Nixon
Pedro Martinez
TQ5 Kerry Wood 2.00 5.00
Sammy Sosa
Fred McGriff
Moises Alou
TQ6 Frank Thomas 2.00 5.00
Magglio Ordonez
Mark Buehrle
Kenny Lofton
TQ7 Griffey/Lark/Dunn/Casey 4.00 10.00
TQ8 C.C Sabathia 1.25 3.00
Jim Thome
Bartolo Colon
Russell Branyan
TQ9 Todd Helton 1.25 3.00
Larry Walker
Juan Pierre
Mike Hampton
TQ10 Jeff Bagwell 1.25 3.00
Craig Biggio
Lance Berkman
Richard Hidalgo
TQ11 Shawn Green 2.00 5.00
Adrian Beltre
Hideo Nomo
Paul Lo Duca
TQ12 Piazza/Alom/Vaughn/Cedeno 2.00 5.00
TQ13 Clemens/Jeter/Giamb/Muss 5.00 12.00
TQ14 Barry Zito 1.25 3.00
Tim Hudson
Eric Chavez
Miguel Tejada
TQ15 Pat Burrell 1.25 3.00
Scott Rolen
Bobby Abreu
Marlon Byrd
TQ16 Bernie Williams 1.25 3.00
Jorge Posada
Alfonso Soriano
Andy Pettitte
TQ17 Bonds/Aur/Shinjo/Kent 3.00 8.00
TQ18 Ichiro/Sasaki/Boone/Mart 2.50 6.00
TQ19 Pujols/Drew/Edmnd/Mart 4.00 10.00
TQ20 Arod/Irod/Gonz/Palm 2.50 6.00

2002 Absolute Memorabilia Team Quads Materials

STATED PRINT RUN 100 SERIAL #'d SETS
CARD NUMBER 7 DOES NOT EXIST
GOLD PRINT RUN 25 SERIAL #'d SETS
NO GOLD PRICING DUE TO SCARCITY
TQ1 Troy Glaus Jsy 10.00 25.00
Darin Erstad Jsy
Garret Anderson Jsy
Troy Percival Jsy
TQ2 Curt Schilling Jsy 15.00 40.00
Randy Johnson Jsy
Luis Gonzalez Jsy
Mark Grace Jsy
TQ3 Chipper/Jones/Madd/Glav 20.00 50.00
TQ4 Nomar/Ramirez/Pedro/Nizon 20.00 50.00
TQ5 Kerry Wood Base 15.00 40.00
Sammy Sosa Base
Fred McGriff Base
Moises Alou Base
TQ6 Frank Thomas Jsy 15.00 40.00
Magglio Ordonez Jsy
Mark Buehrle Jsy
Kenny Lofton Bat
TQ8 C.C Sabathia Jsy 15.00 40.00
Jim Thome Jsy
Bartolo Colon Jsy
Russell Branyan Jsy
TQ9 Todd Helton Jsy 15.00 40.00
Larry Walker Jsy
Juan Pierre Jsy
Mike Hampton Jsy
TQ10 Jeff Bagwell Jsy 15.00 40.00
Craig Biggio Jsy
Lance Berkman Jsy
Richard Hidalgo Pants
TQ11 Green/Beltre/Nomo/LoDuca 30.00 60.00
TQ12 Piazza/Alom/Vaughn/Cedeno 15.00 40.00
TQ13 Clemens/Jeter/Giamb/Muss 40.00 80.00
TQ14 Barry Zito Jsy 10.00 25.00
Tim Hudson Jsy
Eric Chavez Bat
Miguel Tejada Jsy
TQ15 Pat Burrell Jsy 15.00 40.00
Scott Rolen Jsy
Bobby Abreu Jsy
Marlon Byrd Jsy
TQ16 Bernie Williams Jsy 15.00 40.00
Jorge Posada Jsy
Alfonso Soriano Bat
Andy Pettitte Jsy
TQ17 Bonds/Aur/Shinjo/Kent 10.00 25.00
TQ18 Ichiro/Sasaki/Mart/Boone 40.00 80.00
TQ19 Pujols/Drew/Edm/Mart 30.00 60.00
TQ20 Arod/Irod/Gonz/Palm 15.00 40.00

2002 Absolute Memorabilia Team Tandems

STATED ODDS 1:12 HOBBY, 1:36 RETAIL
*GOLD: .75X TO 2X BASIC TANDEMS
GOLD ODDS 1:72 HOBBY, 1:216 RETAIL
*SPECTRUM: .6X TO 1.5X BASIC TANDEMS
SPECTRUM ODDS 1:36 HOBBY
TT1 T.Glaus 1.25 3.00
D.Erstad
TT2 C.Schilling 2.00 5.00
R.Johnson
TT3 C.Jones 2.00 5.00
A.Jones
TT4 G.Maddux 3.00 8.00
T.Glavine
TT5 N.Garciaparra 3.00 8.00
M.Ramirez
TT6 P.Martinez 1.25 3.00
T.Nixon
TT7 K.Wood 2.00 5.00
S.Sosa
TT8 F.Thomas 2.00 5.00
M.Ordonez
TT9 K.Griffey Jr. 4.00 10.00
B.Larkin
TT10 C.Sabathia 1.25 3.00
J.Thome
TT11 T.Helton 1.25 3.00
L.Walker
TT12 B.Higginson 1.25 3.00
S.Halter
TT13 C.Floyd 1.25 3.00
B.Penny
TT14 J.Bagwell 1.25 3.00
C.Biggio
TT15 S.Green 1.25 3.00
A.Beltre
TT16 B.Sheets 1.25 3.00
R.Sexson
TT17 V.Guerrero 2.00 5.00
J.Vidro
TT18 M.Piazza 3.00 8.00
R.Alomar
TT19 R.Clemens 4.00 10.00
M.Mussina
TT20 D.Jeter 5.00 12.00
J.Giambi
TT21 B.Zito 1.25 3.00
T.Hudson
TT22 E.Chavez 1.25 3.00
M.Tejada
TT23 P.Burrell 1.25 3.00
S.Rolen
TT24 B.Giles 1.25 3.00
A.Ramirez
TT25 R.Klesko 1.25 3.00
P.Nevin
TT26 B.Bonds 4.00 10.00
R.Aurilia
TT27 I.Suzuki 4.00 10.00
K.Sasaki
TT28 A.Pujols 4.00 10.00
J.Drew
TT29 A.Rodriguez 2.50 6.00
I.Rodriguez
TT30 C.Delgado 1.25 3.00
S.Stewart
TT31 M.Vaughn 1.25 3.00
R.Cedeno
TT32 C.Beltran 1.25 3.00
M.Sweeney
TT33 E.Martinez 1.25 3.00
B.Boone
TT34 J.Gonzalez 1.25 3.00
R.Palmeiro
TT35 J.Damon 2.00 5.00
R.Henderson
TT36 S.Casey 1.25 3.00
A.Dunn
TT37 J.Kent 1.25 3.00
T.Shinjo
TT38 L.Berkman 1.25 3.00
R.Hidalgo
TT39 S.Taguchi 1.25 3.00
T.Martinez
TT40 H.Nomo 1.25 3.00
K.Ishii

2002 Absolute Memorabilia Team Tandems Materials

STATED ODDS 1:33 HOBBY, 1:164 RETAIL
SP PRINT RUNS PROVIDED BY DONRUSS
SP'S ARE NOT SERIAL-NUMBERED
TT1 Glaus Jsy/Erstad Bat 4.00 10.00
TT2 Schilling Jsy/Johnson Jsy 6.00 15.00
TT3 Chipper Bat/Andruw Bat 6.00 15.00
TT4 Maddux Jsy/Glavine Jsy 10.00 25.00
TT5 Nomar Bat/Manny Bat/200 * 10.00 25.00
TT6 Pedro Jsy/Nixon Bat/200 * 8.00 20.00
TT7 Wood Base/Sosa Base/250 * 8.00 20.00
TT8 Thomas Bat/Magglio Bat 6.00 15.00
TT9 Griffey Base/Larkin Base 6.00 15.00
TT10 Sabath Jsy/Thome Bat/225 * 8.00 20.00
TT11 Helton Bat/Walker Bat 6.00 15.00
TT12 Higginson Bat/Halter Bat 4.00 10.00
TT13 Floyd Bat/Penny Jsy 4.00 10.00
TT14 Bagwell Bat/Biggio Bat 6.00 15.00
TT15 Green Bat/Beltre Bat 4.00 10.00
TT16 Sheets Jsy/Sexson Bat 4.00 10.00
TT17 Guerrero Bat/Vidro Bat 6.00 15.00
TT18 Piazza Bat/Alomar Bat/250 * 8.00 20.00
TT19 Clemens Glv/Muss Glv/50 * 15.00 40.00
TT20 Jeter Base/Giam Base/200 * 8.00 20.00
TT21 Zito Jsy/Hudson Shoe/200 * 6.00 15.00
TT22 Chavez Bat/Tejada Bat/200 * 6.00 15.00
TT23 Burrell Bat/Rolen Bat 6.00 15.00
TT24 Giles Bat/A.Ramirez Bat 4.00 10.00
TT25 Klesko Bat/Nevin Jsy/250 * 6.00 15.00
TT26 Bonds Base/Aurilia Base 8.00 20.00
TT27 Ichiro Deck/Sasaki Deck SP
TT28 Pujols Base/Drew Base/150 * 8.00 20.00
TT29 A.Rod Bat/I.Rod Bat 8.00 20.00
TT30 Delgado Bat/Stewart Bat 4.00 10.00
TT31 Vaughn Bat/Cedeno Bat 4.00 10.00
TT32 Beltran Bat/Sweeney Bat 4.00 10.00
TT33 Edgar Bat/Boone Bat 6.00 15.00
TT34 J.Gonz Bat/Palmeiro Bat 6.00 15.00
TT35 Damon Bat/Henderson Bat 6.00 15.00
TT36 Casey Bat/Dunn Shoe/100 * 6.00 15.00
TT37 Kent Bat/Shinjo Bat/250 * 6.00 15.00
TT38 Berkman Bat/Hidalgo Bat 4.00 10.00
TT39 Taguchi Bat/Tino Bat/100 * 8.00 20.00
TT40 Nomo Jsy/Ishii Jsy/50 * 15.00 40.00

2002 Absolute Memorabilia Team Tandems Materials Gold

TT1 Glaus Jsy/Erstad Bat 10.00 25.00
TT2 Schilling Jsy/Johnson Jsy 15.00 40.00
TT3 Chipper Bat/Andruw Bat 15.00 40.00
TT4 Maddux Jsy/Glavine Jsy 25.00 60.00
TT5 Nomar Bat/Manny Bat 20.00 50.00
TT6 Pedro Jsy/Nixon Bat 15.00 40.00
TT7 Wood Base/Sosa Ball 15.00 40.00
TT8 Thomas Jsy/Magglio Jsy 15.00 40.00
TT9 Griffey Base/Larkin Base 15.00 40.00
TT10 Sabath Jsy/Thome Jsy 15.00 40.00
TT11 Helton Jsy/Walker Jsy 15.00 40.00
TT12 Higginson Bat/Halter Bat 10.00 25.00
TT13 Floyd Jsy/Penny Jsy 10.00 25.00
TT14 Bagwell Jsy/Biggio Jsy 15.00 40.00
TT15 Green Jsy/Beltre Jsy 10.00 25.00
TT16 Sheets Jsy/Sexson Jsy 10.00 25.00
TT17 Guerrero Jsy/Vidro Jsy 15.00 40.00
TT18 Piazza Jsy/Alomar Shoe 15.00 40.00
TT19 Clemens Jsy/Mussina Shoe 20.00 50.00
TT20 Jeter Ball/Giambi Ball 20.00 50.00
TT21 Zito Jsy/Hudson Jsy 12.50 30.00
TT22 Chavez Bat/Tejada Jsy 12.50 30.00
TT23 Burrell Jsy/Rolen Jsy 15.00 40.00
TT24 Giles Jsy/Ramirez Jsy 10.00 25.00
TT25 Klesko Glv/Nevin Jsy 12.50 30.00
TT26 Bonds Ball/Aurilia Base 20.00 50.00
TT27 Ichiro Ball/Sasaki Deck 50.00 100.00
TT28 Pujols Ball/Drew Base 15.00 40.00
TT29 A.Rod Jsy/I.Rod Jsy 20.00 50.00
TT30 Delgado Jsy/Stewart Jsy 10.00 25.00
TT31 Vaughn Bat/Cedeno Bat 10.00 25.00
TT32 Beltran Jsy/Sweeney Jsy 10.00 25.00
TT33 Edgar Jsy/Boone Jsy 15.00 40.00
TT34 J.Gonz Jsy/Palmeiro Jsy 15.00 40.00
TT35 Damon Bat/Henderson Bat 15.00 40.00
TT36 Casey Jsy/Dunn Hat 10.00 25.00
TT37 Kent Jsy/Shinjo Bat 12.50 30.00
TT38 Berkman Jsy/Hidalgo Pants 10.00 25.00
TT39 Taguchi Jsy/Tino Bat 12.50 30.00

2002 Absolute Memorabilia Tools of the Trade

STATED ODDS 1:9 HOBBY, 1:24 RETAIL
*GOLD: .75X TO 2X BASIC TOOLS
GOLD ODDS 1:45 HOBBY, 1:144 RETAIL
TT1 Mike Mussina 1.50 4.00
TT2 Rickey Henderson 2.50 6.00
TT3 Raul Mondesi 1.00 2.50
TT4 Nomar Garciaparra 4.00 10.00
TT5 Randy Johnson 2.50 6.00
TT6 Roger Clemens 5.00 12.00
TT7 Shawn Green 1.00 2.50
TT8 Todd Helton 1.50 4.00
TT9 Aramis Ramirez 1.00 2.50
TT10 Barry Larkin 1.50 4.00
TT11 Byung-Hyun Kim 1.00 2.50
TT12 C.C. Sabathia 1.00 2.50
TT13 Curt Schilling 1.00 2.50
TT14 Darin Erstad 1.00 2.50
TT15 Eric Karros 1.00 2.50
TT16 Freddy Garcia 1.00 2.50
TT17 Greg Maddux 4.00 10.00
TT18 Jason Kendall 1.00 2.50
TT19 Jim Thome 1.50 4.00
TT20 Juan Gonzalez 1.00 2.50
TT21 Kazuhiro Sasaki 1.00 2.50
TT22 Kerry Wood 1.00 2.50
TT23 Luis Gonzalez 1.00 2.50
TT24 Mark Mulder 1.00 2.50
TT25 Rich Aurilia 1.00 2.50
TT26 Ray Durham 1.00 2.50
TT27 Ben Grieve 1.00 2.50
TT28 Bret Boone 1.00 2.50
TT29 Edgar Martinez 1.50 4.00
TT30 Ivan Rodriguez 1.50 4.00
TT31 Jorge Posada 1.50 4.00
TT32 Mike Piazza 4.00 10.00
TT33 Pat Burrell 1.00 2.50
TT34 Robin Ventura 1.00 2.50
TT35 Trot Nixon 1.00 2.50
TT36 Adrian Beltre 1.00 2.50
TT37 Bernie Williams 1.50 4.00
TT38 Bobby Abreu 1.00 2.50
TT39 Carlos Delgado 1.00 2.50
TT40 Craig Biggio 1.50 4.00
TT41 Garret Anderson 1.00 2.50
TT42 Jermaine Dye 1.00 2.50
TT43 Johnny Damon Sox 1.50 4.00
TT44 Tim Salmon 1.50 4.00
TT45 Tino Martinez 1.50 4.00
TT46 Fred McGriff 1.50 4.00
TT47 Gary Sheffield 1.00 2.50
TT48 Adam Dunn 1.00 2.50
TT49 Joe Mays 1.00 2.50
TT50 Kenny Lofton 1.00 2.50
TT51 Josh Beckett 1.00 2.50
TT52 Bud Smith 1.00 2.50
TT53 Johnny Estrada 1.00 2.50
TT54 Charles Johnson 1.00 2.50
TT55 Craig Wilson 1.00 2.50
TT56 Terrence Long 1.00 2.50
TT57 Andy Pettitte 1.50 4.00
TT58 Brian Giles 1.00 2.50
TT59 Juan Pierre 1.00 2.50
TT60 Cliff Floyd 1.00 2.50
TT60 Ivan Rodriguez 1.50 4.00
TT62 Andruw Jones 1.50 4.00
TT63 Lance Berkman 1.00 2.50
TT64 Mark Buehrle 1.00 2.50
TT65 Miguel Tejada 1.00 2.50
TT66 Wade Miller 1.00 2.50
TT67 Johnny Estrada 1.00 2.50
TT68 Tsuyoshi Shinjo 1.00 2.50
TT69 Scott Rolen 1.50 4.00
TT70 Roberto Alomar 1.50 4.00
TT71 Mark Grace 1.50 4.00
TT72 Larry Walker 1.00 2.50
TT73 Jim Edmonds 1.00 2.50
TT74 Jeff Kent 1.00 2.50
TT75 Frank Thomas 2.50 6.00
TT76 Carlos Beltran 1.00 2.50
TT77 Barry Zito 1.00 2.50
TT78 Alex Rodriguez 3.00 8.00
TT79 Troy Glaus 1.00 2.50
TT80 Ryan Klesko 1.00 2.50
TT81 Tom Glavine 1.50 4.00
TT82 Ben Sheets 1.00 2.50
TT83 Manny Ramirez 1.50 4.00
TT84 Shannon Stewart 1.00 2.50
TT85 Vladimir Guerrero 2.50 6.00
TT86 Chipper Jones 2.50 6.00
TT87 Jeff Bagwell 1.50 4.00
TT88 Richie Sexson 1.00 2.50
TT89 Sean Casey 1.00 2.50
TT90 Tim Hudson 1.00 2.50
TT91 J.D. Drew 1.00 2.50
TT92 Ivan Rodriguez 1.50 4.00
TT93 Magglio Ordonez 1.00 2.50
TT94 John Buck 1.00 2.50
TT95 Paul Lo Duca 1.00 2.50

2002 Absolute Memorabilia Tools of the Trade Materials

1-32 PRINT RUN 300 SERIAL #'d SETS
33-47 PRINT RUN 250 SERIAL #'d SETS
48-55 PRINT RUN 150 SERIAL #'d SETS
56-61 PRINT RUN 125 SERIAL #'d SETS
62-66 PRINT RUN 50 SERIAL #'d SETS
67 PRINT RUN 100 SERIAL #'d CARDS
68-82 PRINT RUN 200 SERIAL #'d SETS
83-87 PRINT RUN 75 SERIAL #'d SETS
88-95 PRINT RUN 50 SERIAL #'d SETS
95 Paul Lo Duca Quad 15.00 40.00
TT1 Mike Mussina Jsy 4.00 10.00
TT2 Rickey Henderson Jsy 4.00 10.00
TT3 Raul Mondesi Jsy 3.00 8.00
TT4 Nomar Garciaparra Jsy 6.00 15.00
TT5 Randy Johnson Jsy 4.00 10.00
TT6 Roger Clemens Jsy 6.00 15.00
TT7 Shawn Green Jsy 3.00 8.00
TT8 Todd Helton Jsy 4.00 10.00
TT9 Aramis Ramirez Jsy 3.00 8.00
TT10 Barry Larkin Jsy 4.00 10.00
TT11 Byung-Hyun Kim Jsy 4.00 10.00
TT12 C.C. Sabathia Jsy 3.00 8.00
TT13 Curt Schilling Jsy 3.00 8.00
TT14 Darin Erstad Jsy 3.00 8.00
TT15 Eric Karros Jsy 3.00 8.00
TT16 Freddy Garcia Jsy 3.00 8.00
TT17 Greg Maddux Jsy 6.00 15.00
TT18 Jason Kendall Jsy 3.00 8.00
TT19 Jim Thome Jsy 4.00 10.00
TT20 Juan Gonzalez Jsy 3.00 8.00
TT21 Kazuhiro Sasaki Jsy 3.00 8.00
TT22 Kerry Wood Jsy 3.00 8.00
TT23 Luis Gonzalez Jsy 3.00 8.00
TT24 Mark Mulder Jsy 3.00 8.00
TT25 Rich Aurilia Jsy 3.00 8.00
TT26 Ray Durham Jsy 3.00 8.00
TT27 Ben Grieve Jsy 3.00 8.00
TT28 Bret Boone Jsy 3.00 8.00
TT29 Edgar Martinez Jsy 4.00 10.00
TT30 Ivan Rodriguez Jsy 4.00 10.00
TT31 Jorge Posada Jsy 4.00 10.00
TT32 Mike Piazza Jsy 6.00 15.00
TT33 Pat Burrell Bat 3.00 8.00
TT34 Robin Ventura Bat 3.00 8.00
TT35 Trot Nixon Bat 3.00 8.00
TT36 Adrian Beltre Bat 3.00 8.00
TT37 Bernie Williams Bat 4.00 10.00
TT38 Bobby Abreu Bat 3.00 8.00
TT39 Carlos Delgado Bat 3.00 8.00
TT40 Craig Biggio Bat 4.00 10.00
TT41 Garret Anderson Bat 3.00 8.00
TT42 Jermaine Dye Bat 3.00 8.00
TT43 Johnny Damon Sox Bat 4.00 10.00
TT44 Tim Salmon Bat 4.00 10.00
TT45 Tino Martinez Bat 4.00 10.00
TT46 Fred McGriff Bat 4.00 10.00
TT47 Gary Sheffield Bat 3.00 8.00
TT48 Adam Dunn Shoe 4.00 10.00
TT49 Joe Mays Shoe 4.00 10.00
TT50 Kenny Lofton Shoe 6.00 15.00
TT51 Josh Beckett Shoe 4.00 10.00
TT52 Bud Smith Shoe 4.00 10.00
TT53 Johnny Estrada Shin 4.00 10.00
TT54 Charles Johnson Shin 4.00 10.00
TT55 Craig Wilson Shin 4.00 10.00
TT56 Terrence Long Fld Glv 4.00 10.00
TT57 Andy Pettitte Fld Glv 6.00 15.00
TT58 Brian Giles Fld Glv 4.00 10.00
TT59 Juan Pierre Fld Glv 4.00 10.00
TT60 Cliff Floyd Fld Glv 4.00 10.00
TT61 Ivan Rodriguez Fld Glv 10.00 25.00
TT62 Andruw Jones Hat 10.00 25.00
TT63 Lance Berkman Hat 6.00 15.00
TT64 Mark Buehrle Hat 6.00 15.00
TT65 Miguel Tejada Hat 6.00 15.00
TT66 Wade Miller Hat 6.00 15.00
TT67 Johnny Estrada Mask 4.00 10.00
TT68 Tsuyoshi Shinjo Bat-Shoe 6.00 15.00
TT69 Scott Rolen Jsy-Bat 8.00 20.00
TT70 Roberto Alomar Bat-Shoe 8.00 20.00
TT71 Mark Grace Jsy-Fld Glv 6.00 15.00
TT72 Larry Walker Jsy-Bat 6.00 15.00
TT73 Jim Edmonds Jsy-Bat 6.00 15.00
TT74 Jeff Kent Jsy-Bat 6.00 15.00
TT75 Frank Thomas Jsy-Bat 8.00 20.00
TT76 Carlos Beltran Jsy-Bat 6.00 15.00
TT77 Barry Zito Jsy-Shoe 6.00 15.00
TT78 Alex Rodriguez Jsy-Bat 10.00 25.00
TT79 Troy Glaus Jsy-Jsy 6.00 15.00
TT80 Ryan Klesko Bat-Fld Glv 6.00 15.00
TT81 Tom Glavine Jsy-Shoe 8.00 20.00

TT82 Ben Sheets Jsy-Bat 6.00 15.00
TT83 Manny Ramirez Triple 15.00 40.00
TT84 Shannon Stewart Triple 8.00 20.00
TT85 Vladimir Guerrero Triple 20.00 50.00
TT86 Chipper Jones Triple 20.00 50.00
TT87 Jeff Bagwell Triple 15.00 40.00
TT88 Richie Sexson Quad 15.00 40.00
TT89 Sean Casey Quad 15.00 40.00
TT90 Tim Hudson Quad 15.00 40.00
TT91 J.D. Drew Quad 15.00 40.00
TT92 Ivan Rodriguez Quad 15.00 40.00
TT93 Magglio Ordonez Quad 15.00 40.00
TT94 John Buck Quad 10.00 25.00

2003 Absolute Memorabilia

COMP.LO SET w/o SP's (150) 15.00 40.00
COMMON CARD (1-150) .30 .75
COMMON CARD (151-208) .40 1.00
151-200 RANDOM INSERTS IN PACKS
151-200 PRINT RUN 1500 SERIAL #'d SETS
201-208 PRINT RUN 1000 SERIAL #'d SETS
1 Nomar Garciaparra .50 1.25
2 Barry Bonds 1.25 3.00
3 Greg Maddux 1.00 2.50
4 Roger Clemens 1.00 2.50
5 Derek Jeter 2.00 5.00
6 Alex Rodriguez 1.00 2.50
7 Chipper Jones .75 2.00
8 Sammy Sosa .75 2.00
9 Alfonso Soriano .50 1.25
10 Albert Pujols 1.00 2.50
11 Adam Dunn .50 1.25
12 Tom Glavine .50 1.25
13 Pedro Martinez .50 1.25
14 Jim Thome .50 1.25
15 Hideo Nomo .75 2.00
16 Roberto Alomar .50 1.25
17 Barry Zito .50 1.25
18 Troy Glaus .30 .75
19 Kerry Wood .30 .75
20 Magglio Ordonez .50 1.25
21 Todd Helton .50 1.25
22 Craig Biggio .50 1.25
23 Roy Oswalt .50 1.25
24 Torii Hunter .30 .75
25 Miguel Tejada .50 1.25
26 Tsuyoshi Shinjo .30 .75
27 Scott Rolen .50 1.25
28 Rafael Palmeiro .50 1.25
29 Victor Martinez .50 1.25
30 Hank Blalock .30 .75
31 Jason Lane .30 .75
32 Junior Spivey .30 .75
33 Gary Sheffield .30 .75
34 Corey Patterson .30 .75
35 Corky Miller .30 .75
36 Brian Tallet .30 .75
37 Cliff Lee 2.00 5.00
38 Jason Jennings .30 .75
39 Kirk Saarloos .30 .75
40 Wade Miller .30 .75
41 Angel Berroa .30 .75
42 Mike Sweeney .30 .75
43 Paul Lo Duca .30 .75
44 A.J. Pierzynski .30 .75
45 Drew Henson .30 .75
46 Eric Chavez .30 .75
47 Tim Hudson .50 1.25
48 Aramis Ramirez .30 .75
49 Jack Wilson .30 .75
50 Ryan Klesko .30 .75
51 Antonio Perez .30 .75
52 Dewon Brazelton .30 .75
53 Mark Teixeira .50 1.25
54 Eric Hinske .30 .75
55 Freddy Sanchez .30 .75
56 Mike Rivera .30 .75
57 Alfredo Amezaga .30 .75
58 Cliff Floyd .30 .75
59 Brandon Larson .30 .75
60 Richard Hidalgo .30 .75
61 Cesar Izturis .30 .75
62 Richie Sexson .30 .75
63 Michael Cuddyer .30 .75
64 Javier Vazquez .30 .75
65 Brandon Claussen .30 .75
66 Carlos Rivera .30 .75
67 Vernon Wells .30 .75
68 Kenny Lofton .30 .75
69 Aubrey Huff .30 .75
70 Adam LaRoche .30 .75
71 Jeff Baker .30 .75
72 Jose Castillo .30 .75
73 Joe Borchard .30 .75
74 Walter Young .30 .75
75 Jose Morban .30 .75
76 Vinnie Chulk .30 .75
77 Christian Parker .30 .75
78 Mike Piazza .75 2.00
79 Ichiro Suzuki 1.00 2.50
80 Kazuhisa Ishii .30 .75
81 Rickey Henderson .75 2.00
82 Ken Griffey Jr. 1.50 4.00
83 Jason Giambi .30 .75
84 Randy Johnson .75 2.00
85 Curt Schilling .50 1.25
86 Manny Ramirez .75 2.00
87 Barry Larkin .50 1.25
88 Jeff Bagwell .50 1.25
89 Vladimir Guerrero .50 1.25
90 Mike Mussina .50 1.25
91 Juan Gonzalez .30 .75
92 Andruw Jones .30 .75
93 Frank Thomas .75 2.00
94 Sean Casey .30 .75
95 Josh Beckett .30 .75
96 Lance Berkman .50 1.25
97 Shawn Green .30 .75
98 Bernie Williams .50 1.25
99 Pat Burrell .30 .75
100 Edgar Martinez .50 1.25
101 Ivan Rodriguez .50 1.25
102 Jeremy Guthrie .30 .75
103 Alexis Rios .30 .75
104 Nic Jackson .30 .75
105 Jason Anderson .30 .75
106 Travis Chapman .30 .75
107 Mac Suzuki .30 .75
108 Toby Hall .30 .75
109 Mark Prior .50 1.25
110 So Taguchi .30 .75
111 Marlon Byrd .30 .75
112 Garret Anderson .30 .75
113 Luis Gonzalez .30 .75
114 Jay Gibbons .30 .75
115 Mark Buehrle .50 1.25
116 Wily Mo Pena .30 .75
117 C.C. Sabathia .50 1.25
118 Ricardo Rodriguez .30 .75
119 Robert Fick .30 .75
120 Rodrigo Rosario .30 .75
121 Alexis Gomez .30 .75
122 Carlos Beltran .50 1.25
123 Joe Thurston .30 .75
124 Ben Sheets .30 .75
125 Jose Vidro .30 .75
126 Nick Johnson .30 .75
127 Mark Mulder .30 .75
128 Bobby Abreu .30 .75
129 Brian Giles .30 .75
130 Brian Lawrence .30 .75
131 Jeff Kent .30 .75
132 Chris Snelling .30 .75
133 Kevin Mench .30 .75
134 Carlos Delgado .30 .75
135 Orlando Hudson .30 .75
136 Juan Cruz .30 .75
137 Jim Edmonds .50 1.25
138 Geronimo Gil .30 .75
139 Joe Crede .30 .75
140 Wilson Valdez .30 .75
141 Runelvys Hernandez .30 .75
142 Nick Neugebauer .30 .75
143 Takahito Nomura .30 .75
144 Andres Galarraga .50 1.25
145 Mark Grace .50 1.25
146 Brandon Duckworth .30 .75
147 Oliver Perez .30 .75
148 Xavier Nady .30 .75
149 Rafael Soriano .30 .75
150 Ben Kozlowski .30 .75
151 Prentice Redman ROO RC .40 1.00
152 Craig Brazell ROO RC .40 1.00
153 Nook Logan ROO RC .40 1.00
154 Greg Aquino ROO RC .40 1.00
155 Matt Kata ROO RC .40 1.00
156 Ian Ferguson ROO RC .40 1.00
157 Chien-Ming Wang ROO RC 1.50 4.00
158 Beau Kemp ROO RC .40 1.00
159 Alejandro Machado ROO RC .40 1.00
160 Michael Hessman ROO RC .40 1.00
161 Francisco Rosario ROO RC .40 1.00
162 Pedro Liriano ROO .40 1.00
163 Rich Fischer ROO RC .40 1.00
164 Franklin Perez ROO RC .40 1.00
165 Oscar Villarreal ROO RC .40 1.00
166 Arnie Munoz ROO RC .40 1.00
167 Tim Olson ROO RC .40 1.00
168 Jose Contreras ROO RC 1.00 2.50
169 Francisco Cruceta ROO RC .40 1.00
170 Jeremy Bonderman ROO RC 1.50 4.00
171 Jeremy Griffiths ROO RC .40 1.00
172 John Webb ROO .40 1.00
173 Phil Seibel ROO RC .40 1.00
174 Aaron Looper ROO RC .40 1.00
175 Brian Stokes ROO RC .40 1.00
176 Guillermo Quiroz ROO RC .40 1.00
177 Fernando Cabrera ROO RC .40 1.00
178 Josh Hall ROO RC .40 1.00
179 Diegomar Markwell ROO RC .40 1.00
180 Andrew Brown ROO RC .40 1.00
181 Doug Waechter ROO RC .40 1.00
182 Felix Sanchez ROO RC .40 1.00
183 Gerardo Garcia ROO .40 1.00
184 Matt Bruback ROO RC .40 1.00
185 Michel Hernandez ROO RC .40 1.00
186 Rett Johnson ROO RC .40 1.00
187 Ryan Cameron ROO RC .40 1.00
188 Rob Hammock ROO RC .40 1.00
189 Clint Barmes ROO RC 1.00 2.50
190 Brandon Webb ROO RC 1.25 3.00
191 Jon Leicester ROO RC .40 1.00
192 Shane Bazzell ROO RC .40 1.00
193 Joe Valentine ROO RC .40 1.00
194 Josh Stewart ROO RC .40 1.00
195 Pete LaForest ROO RC .40 1.00
196 Shane Victorino ROO RC 1.25 3.00
197 Terrmel Sledge ROO RC .40 1.00
198 Lew Ford ROO RC .40 1.00
199 Todd Wellemeyer ROO RC .40 1.00
200 Hideki Matsui ROO RC 2.00 5.00
201 Adam Loewen ROO RC .40 1.00
202 Ramon Nivar ROO RC .40 1.00
203 Dan Haren ROO RC 2.00 5.00
204 Dontrelle Willis ROO .40 1.00
205 Chad Gaudin ROO RC .40 1.00
206 Rickie Weeks ROO RC 1.25 3.00
207 Ryan Wagner ROO RC .40 1.00
208 Delmon Young ROO RC 2.50 6.00

2003 Absolute Memorabilia Spectrum

*SPECTRUM 1-150: 2.5X TO 6X BASIC
*SPECTRUM 151-208: 1X TO 2.5X BASIC
1-200 RANDOM INSERTS IN PACKS
STATED PRINT RUN 100 SERIAL #'d SETS

2003 Absolute Memorabilia Glass Plaques

ONE PER SEALED BOX
PRINT RUNS B/WN 10-200 COPIES PER
NO PRICING ON QTY OF 25 OR LESS
3 Roberto Alomar Bat-Jsy/100 15.00 40.00
4 Roberto Alomar Jsy/150 10.00 25.00
7 Jeff Bagwell Bat-Jsy/100 15.00 40.00
12 Ernie Banks Jsy/150 10.00 25.00
15 Lance Berkman Bat-Jsy/100 10.00 25.00
16 Lance Berkman Jsy/150 6.00 15.00
21 Barry Bonds Ball-Base/50 40.00 80.00
22 Barry Bonds Ball-Base/100 30.00 60.00
23 Barry Bonds Base/200 20.00 50.00
26 George Brett Bat-Jsy/50 40.00 80.00
27 George Brett Jsy/200 40.00 80.00
30 Pat Burrell Bat-Jsy/100 10.00 25.00
31 Pat Burrell Jsy/150 6.00 15.00
32 Steve Carlton AU/50 20.00 50.00
35 Steve Carlton Jsy/150 10.00 25.00
38 R.Clemens Sox FG-J/50 40.00 80.00
39 R.Clemens Sox Jsy/150 40.00 80.00
42 Clemens Yanks Glv-Jsy/50 100.00 200.00
43 R.Clemens Yanks Jsy/200 40.00 80.00
46 Roberto Clemente Jsy/200 50.00 100.00
49 Jose Contreras Jsy-Jsy/100 15.00 40.00
53 Adam Dunn Bat-Jsy/100 10.00 25.00
54 Adam Dunn Jsy/150 6.00 15.00
55 Bob Feller AU/50 15.00 40.00
57 Bob Feller Jsy-Jsy/50 15.00 40.00
58 Bob Feller Jsy/100 6.00 15.00
59 N.Garciaparra Bat-Jsy/100 40.00 80.00
60 N.Garciaparra Jsy/200 30.00 60.00
61 Jason Giambi Bat-Jsy/100 10.00 25.00
62 Jason Giambi Jsy/150 6.00 15.00
66 Troy Glaus Jsy/150 6.00 15.00
73 Luis Gonzalez Bat-Jsy/100 10.00 25.00
74 Luis Gonzalez Jsy/150 6.00 15.00
75 Mark Grace AU/50 40.00 80.00
78 Mark Grace Jsy/150 10.00 25.00
81 Shawn Green Bat-Jsy/100 10.00 25.00
82 Shawn Green Jsy/150 6.00 15.00
84 Ken Griffey Jr. Ball-Base/100 20.00 50.00
88 Vladimir Guerrero Bat-Jsy/100 15.00 40.00
100 R.Henderson Bat-Jsy/100 15.00 40.00
101 R.Henderson Jsy/200 10.00 25.00
102 Tim Hudson AU/50 30.00 60.00
104 Tim Hudson Hat-Jsy/100 10.00 25.00
105 Tim Hudson Jsy/150 6.00 15.00
106 Torii Hunter AU/50 20.00 50.00
108 Torii Hunter Hat-Jsy/100 10.00 25.00
112 Kazuhisa Ishii Bat-Jsy/100 10.00 25.00
113 Kazuhisa Ishii Jsy/200 6.00 15.00
119 Randy Johnson Bat -Jsy/100 15.00 40.00
120 Randy Johnson Jsy/150 10.00 25.00
124 Andruw Jones Jsy/150 10.00 25.00
127 Chipper Jones Bat-Jsy/100 30.00 60.00
128 Chipper Jones Jsy/150 10.00 25.00
131 Al Kaline Bat-Jsy/100 20.00 50.00
132 Al Kaline Jsy/150 20.00 50.00
133 Barry Larkin AU/50 40.00 80.00
135 Barry Larkin Bat-Jsy/100 20.00 50.00
136 Barry Larkin Jsy/150 10.00 25.00
139 Greg Maddux Bat -Jsy/100 30.00 60.00
140 Greg Maddux Jsy/200 20.00 50.00
143 Pedro Martinez Bat-Jsy/100 15.00 40.00
144 Pedro Martinez Jsy/150 10.00 25.00
145 H.Matsui Ball-Base/50 50.00 100.00
146 H.Matsui Ball-Base/150 30.00 60.00
147 H.Matsui Base/200 15.00 40.00
150 Don Mattingly Bat-Jsy/100 30.00 60.00
152 Mark Mulder AU/50 20.00 50.00
154 Mark Mulder Jsy/150 6.00 15.00
155 Mark Mulder Jsy-Jsy/100 10.00 25.00
162 Hideo Nomo Bat-Jsy/50 60.00 120.00
163 Hideo Nomo Bat-Jsy/100 15.00 40.00
164 Hideo Nomo Jsy/200 10.00 25.00
165 Magglio Ordonez AU/50 20.00 50.00
167 M.Ordonez Bat-Jsy/100 10.00 25.00
168 Magglio Ordonez Jsy/150 6.00 15.00
169 Roy Oswalt AU/50 20.00 50.00
171 Roy Oswalt Bat-Jsy/100 10.00 25.00
172 Roy Oswalt Jsy/150 6.00 15.00
175 Rafael Palmeiro Bat-Jsy/100 15.00 40.00
176 Rafael Palmeiro Jsy/150 10.00 25.00
179 Mike Piazza Bat-Jsy/50 50.00 100.00
180 Mike Piazza Bat-Jsy/100 30.00 60.00
181 Mike Piazza Jsy/200 20.00 50.00
184 Mark Prior Bat-Jsy/100 15.00 40.00
185 Mark Prior Jsy/150 10.00 25.00
188 Albert Pujols Bat-Jsy/150 50.00 100.00
189 Albert Pujols Jsy/150 75.00 150.00
192 Manny Ramirez Bat-Jsy/100 15.00 40.00
193 Manny Ramirez Jsy/150 10.00 25.00
196 Cal Ripken Bat-Jsy/150 60.00 120.00
197 Cal Ripken Jsy/200 50.00 100.00
198 Frank Robinson AU/50 30.00 60.00
200 Frank Robinson Bat-Jsy/100 15.00 40.00
201 Frank Robinson Jsy/150 10.00 25.00
205 Alex Rodriguez Jsy/200 20.00 50.00
209 N.Ryan Angels Jsy/200 50.00 100.00
213 N.Ryan Astros Jsy/200 50.00 100.00
214 N.Ryan Astros Jsy-Jsy/100 60.00 120.00
218 N.Ryan Rgr Jsy/200 30.00 60.00
219 N.Ryan Rgr Jsy-Jsy/100 40.00 80.00
222 R.Sandberg Bat-Jsy G/50 75.00 150.00
223 R.Sandberg Bat-Jsy S/50 75.00 150.00
224 R.Sandberg Jsy/200 40.00 80.00
228 Curt Schilling Jsy/150 6.00 15.00
231 Mike Schmidt Bat-Jsy/100 50.00 100.00
232 Mike Schmidt Jsy/200 40.00 80.00
235 Ozzie Smith Bat-Jsy/100 50.00 100.00
236 Ozzie Smith Jsy/150 20.00 50.00
239 A.Soriano Bat-Jsy/150 10.00 25.00
240 A.Soriano Jsy/150 6.00 15.00
241 Sammy Sosa Bat-Jsy/150 15.00 40.00
242 Sammy Sosa Jsy/200 10.00 25.00
245 Junior Spivey Bat-Jsy/100 10.00 25.00
246 Junior Spivey Jsy/150 6.00 15.00
247 I.Suzuki Ball-Base/50 15.00 40.00
248 I.Suzuki Ball-Base/150 12.00 30.00
249 I.Suzuki Base/200 10.00 25.00
252 Mark Teixeira Bat-Jsy/100 15.00 40.00
253 Mark Teixeira Jsy/150 10.00 25.00
254 Miguel Tejada AU/50 12.50 30.00
256 Miguel Tejada Bat-Jsy/100 10.00 25.00
257 Miguel Tejada Jsy/150 6.00 15.00
260 Frank Thomas Bat-Jsy/100 15.00 40.00
261 Frank Thomas Jsy/150 10.00 25.00
264 Bernie Williams Bat-Jsy/100 15.00 40.00
265 Bernie Williams Jsy/150 10.00 25.00
266 Kerry Wood AU/50 30.00 60.00
268 Kerry Wood Bat-Jsy/100 10.00 25.00
269 Kerry Wood Jsy/150 10.00 25.00
270 Barry Zito AU/50 20.00 50.00
272 Barry Zito Hat-Jsy/100 10.00 25.00
273 Barry Zito Jsy/150 6.00 15.00

2003 Absolute Memorabilia Player Collection

*PLAY.COLL: .75X TO 2X PRESTIGE PC
STATED PRINT RUN 75 SERIAL #'d SETS
SEE 2003 PRESTIGE PLAY.COLL FOR PRICING
SPECTRUM PRINT RUN 25 SERIAL #'d SETS
NO SPECTRUM PRICING DUE TO SCARCITY

2003 Absolute Memorabilia Portraits Promos

STATED ODDS ONE PER BOX
1 Vladimir Guerrero .60 1.50
2 Luis Gonzalez .40 1.00
3 Andruw Jones .40 1.00
4 Manny Ramirez 1.00 2.50
5 Derek Jeter 2.50 6.00
6 Eric Hinske .40 1.00
7 Curt Schilling .60 1.50
8 Adam Dunn .60 1.50
9 Jason Jennings .40 1.00
10 Mike Piazza 1.00 2.50
11 Jason Giambi .40 1.00
12 Jeff Bagwell .60 1.50
13 Rickey Henderson 1.00 2.50
14 Randy Johnson 1.00 2.50
15 Roger Clemens 1.25 3.00
16 Troy Glaus .40 1.00
17 Hideo Nomo 1.00 2.50
18 Joe Borchard .40 1.00
19 Torii Hunter .40 1.00
20 Lance Berkman .60 1.50
21 Todd Helton .60 1.50
22 Mike Mussina .60 1.50
23 Vernon Wells .40 1.00
24 Pat Burrell .40 1.00
25 Ichiro Suzuki 1.25 3.00
26 Shawn Green .40 1.00
27 Frank Thomas 1.00 2.50
28 Barry Zito .60 1.50
29 Barry Bonds 1.50 4.00
30 Ken Griffey Jr. 2.00 5.00
31 Albert Pujols 1.25 3.00
32 Roberto Alomar .60 1.50
33 Barry Larkin .60 1.50
34 Tony Gwynn 1.00 2.50
35 Chipper Jones 1.00 2.50
36 Pedro Martinez .60 1.50
37 Juan Gonzalez .40 1.00
38 Greg Maddux 1.25 3.00
39 Tim Hudson .60 1.50
40 Sammy Sosa 1.00 2.50
41 Victor Martinez .60 1.50
42 Mark Buehrle .60 1.50
43 Austin Kearns .40 1.00
44 Kerry Wood .40 1.00
45 Nomar Garciaparra .60 1.50
46 Alfonso Soriano .60 1.50
47 Mark Prior .60 1.50
48 Richie Sexson .40 1.00
49 Mark Teixeira .60 1.50
50 Craig Biggio .60 1.50
51 Rafael Palmeiro .60 1.50
52 Carlos Beltran .60 1.50
53 Bernie Williams .60 1.50
54 Eric Chavez .40 1.00
55 Paul Konerko .60 1.50
56 Nolan Ryan 3.00 8.00
57 Mark Mulder .40 1.00
58 Miguel Tejada .60 1.50
59 Roy Oswalt .60 1.50
60 Jim Edmonds .60 1.50
61 Ryan Klesko .40 1.00
62 Cal Ripken 3.00 8.00
63 Josh Beckett .40 1.00
64 Kazuhisa Ishii .40 1.00
65 Alex Rodriguez 1.25 3.00
66 Mike Sweeney .40 1.00
67 C.C. Sabathia .60 1.50
68 Jose Vidro .40 1.00
69 Magglio Ordonez .60 1.50
70 Carlos Delgado .40 1.00
71 Jorge Posada .60 1.50
72 Bobby Abreu .40 1.00

2003 Absolute Memorabilia Rookie Materials Jersey Number

PRINT RUNS B/WN 5-51 COPIES PER
NO PRICING ON QTY OF 25 OR LESS
2 Yogi Berra Jsy/35 8.00 20.00
3 Vladimir Guerrero Jsy/27 20.00 50.00
4 Randy Johnson Jsy/51 20.00 50.00
10 Alfonso Soriano Jsy/33 20.00 50.00

2003 Absolute Memorabilia Rookie Materials Season

PRINT RUNS B/WN 42-101 COPIES PER
1 Stan Musial Jsy/42 50.00 120.00
2 Yogi Berra Jsy/47 10.00 25.00
3 Vladimir Guerrero Jsy/97 10.00 25.00
4 Randy Johnson Jsy/89 10.00 25.00
5 Andruw Jones Jsy/96 10.00 25.00
6 Jeff Kent Jsy/92 6.00 15.00
8 Hideo Nomo Jsy/95 8.00 20.00
9 Ivan Rodriguez Jsy/91 10.00 25.00
10 Alfonso Soriano Jsy/101 6.00 15.00
11 Scott Rolen Jsy/96 10.00 25.00
12 Juan Gonzalez Jsy/89 6.00 15.00
13 Rafael Palmeiro Bat/86 10.00 25.00
14 Mike Schmidt Bat/73 30.00 60.00
15 Cal Ripken Bat/82 15.00 40.00

2003 Absolute Memorabilia Spectrum Signatures

1-200 RANDOM INSERTS IN PACKS
PRINT RUNS B/WN 5-304 COPIES PER
NO PRICING ON QTY OF 25 OR LESS
29 Victor Martinez/100 15.00 40.00
30 Hank Blalock/50 10.00 25.00
32 Junior Spivey/50 6.00 15.00
34 Corey Patterson/50 6.00 15.00
37 Cliff Lee/100 10.00 25.00
40 Wade Miller/50 6.00 15.00
41 Angel Berroa/100 6.00 15.00
42 Mike Sweeney/50 10.00 25.00
43 Paul Lo Duca/50 10.00 25.00
44 A.J. Pierzynski/100 10.00 25.00
45 Drew Henson/50 6.00 15.00
47 Tim Hudson/50 6.00 15.00
52 Dewon Brazelton/50 6.00 15.00
53 Mark Teixeira/50 6.00 15.00
54 Eric Hinske/100 6.00 15.00
55 Freddy Sanchez/100 6.00 15.00
57 Alfredo Amezaga/100 6.00 15.00
60 Richard Hidalgo/100 6.00 15.00
63 Michael Cuddyer/100 6.00 15.00
68 Kenny Lofton/50 15.00 40.00
69 Aubrey Huff/100 10.00 25.00
70 Adam LaRoche/100 6.00 15.00
71 Jeff Baker/100 6.00 15.00
72 Jose Castillo/100 6.00 15.00
73 Joe Borchard/100 6.00 15.00
74 Walter Young/100 6.00 15.00
76 Vinnie Chulk/100 6.00 15.00
87 Barry Larkin/50 50.00 100.00
89 Vladimir Guerrero/50 10.00 25.00
95 Josh Beckett/100 6.00 15.00
100 Edgar Martinez/50 20.00 50.00
102 Jeremy Guthrie/100 6.00 15.00
103 Alexis Rios/100 10.00 25.00
104 Nic Jackson/100 6.00 15.00
106 Travis Chapman/100 6.00 15.00
107 Mac Suzuki/304 10.00 25.00
109 Mark Prior/50 6.00 15.00
111 Marlon Byrd/100 6.00 15.00
114 Jay Gibbons/100 6.00 15.00
118 Ricardo Rodriguez/100 6.00 15.00
119 Robert Fick/100 6.00 15.00
121 Alexis Gomez/100 6.00 15.00
124 Ben Sheets/50 10.00 25.00
126 Nick Johnson/50 10.00 25.00
127 Mark Mulder/50 10.00 25.00
132 Chris Snelling/100 6.00 15.00
133 Kevin Mench/100 10.00 25.00
135 Orlando Hudson/50 6.00 15.00
139 Joe Crede/100 6.00 15.00
141 Runelvys Hernandez/100 6.00 15.00
143 Takahito Nomura/47 10.00 25.00
147 Oliver Perez/50 10.00 25.00
148 Xavier Nady/100 6.00 15.00
150 Ben Kozlowski/100 6.00 15.00
151 Prentice Redman ROO/250 4.00 10.00
152 Craig Brazell ROO/250 4.00 10.00
153 Nook Logan ROO/250 6.00 15.00
154 Greg Aquino ROO/250 4.00 10.00
155 Matt Kata ROO/250 4.00 10.00
156 Ian Ferguson ROO/250 4.00 10.00
157 Chien Wang ROO/250 60.00 120.00
158 Beau Kemp ROO/250 4.00 10.00
159 Alej Machado ROO/250 4.00 10.00
160 Mike Hessman ROO/250 4.00 10.00
161 Franc Rosario ROO/250 4.00 10.00
162 Pedro Liriano ROO/250 4.00 10.00
163 Rich Fischer ROO/250 4.00 10.00
165 Oscar Villarreal ROO/250 4.00 10.00
166 Arnie Munoz ROO/250 4.00 10.00
167 Tim Olson ROO/250 4.00 10.00
168 Jose Contreras ROO/250 8.00 20.00
169 Franc Cruceta ROO/250 4.00 10.00
170 J.Bonderman ROO/250 20.00 50.00
171 Jeremy Griffiths ROO/250 4.00 10.00
174 Aaron Looper ROO/250 4.00 10.00
175 Brian Stokes ROO/250 4.00 10.00
176 Guillermo Quiroz ROO/250 4.00 10.00
177 Fernando Cabrera ROO/250 4.00 10.00
178 Josh Hall ROO/250 4.00 10.00
179 Diego Markwell ROO/250 4.00 10.00
180 Andrew Brown ROO/250 6.00 15.00
181 Doug Waechter ROO/250 6.00 15.00
182 Felix Sanchez ROO/250 4.00 10.00
184 Matt Bruback ROO/250 4.00 10.00
186 Rett Johnson ROO/250 4.00 10.00
187 Ryan Cameron ROO/250 4.00 10.00
188 Rob Hammock ROO/250 4.00 10.00
189 Clint Barmes ROO/250 6.00 15.00
190 Brandon Webb ROO/250 12.50 30.00
191 Jon Leicester ROO/250 4.00 10.00
192 Shane Bazzell ROO/250 4.00 10.00
193 Joe Valentine ROO/250 4.00 10.00
195 Pete LaForest ROO/250 4.00 10.00
196 Shane Victorino ROO/250 6.00 15.00
197 Terrmel Sledge ROO/250 4.00 10.00
198 Lew Ford ROO/250 6.00 15.00
199 Todd Wellemeyer ROO/250 4.00 10.00
201 Adam Loewen ROO/100 10.00 25.00
202 Ramon Nivar ROO/100 4.00 10.00
203 Dan Haren ROO/100 10.00 25.00
205 Chad Gaudin ROO/50 6.00 15.00
207 Ryan Wagner ROO/100 4.00 10.00

2003 Absolute Memorabilia Team Tandems

STATED ODDS 1:48
*SPECTRUM: 1.25X TO 3X BASIC
SPECTRUM PRINT RUN 100 #'d SETS
TTA1 S.Sosa M.Prior 1.50 4.00
TTA2 V.Guerrero J.Vidro 1.00 2.50
TTA3 B.Williams A.Soriano 1.00 2.50
TTA4 M.Sweeney C.Beltran 1.00 2.50
TTA5 M.Ordonez P.Konerko 1.00 2.50
TTA6 A.Dunn A.Kearns 1.00 2.50
TTA7 R.Johnson C.Schilling 1.50 4.00
TTA8 H.Nomo K.Ishii 1.50 4.00
TTA9 P.Burrell B.Abreu .60 1.50
TTA10 T.Helton L.Walker 1.00 2.50

2003 Absolute Memorabilia Team Tandems Materials

1-7/10 PRINT RUN 100 SERIAL #'d SETS
8-9 PRINT RUN 40 SERIAL #'d SETS
SPECTRUM 1-7/10 PRINT RUN 25 #'d SETS
SPECTRUM 8-9 PRINT RUN 10 #'d SETS
NO SPECTRUM PRICING DUE TO SCARCITY
ALL FEATURE DUAL JERSEY SWATCHES
TTA1 S.Sosa/M.Prior 6.00 15.00
TTA2 V.Guerrero/J.Vidro 4.00 10.00
TTA3 B.Williams/A.Soriano 4.00 10.00
TTA4 M.Sweeney/C.Beltran 4.00 10.00
TTA5 M.Ordonez/P.Konerko 4.00 10.00
TTA6 A.Dunn/A.Kearns 4.00 10.00
TTA7 R.Johnson/C.Schilling 6.00 15.00
TTA8 H.Nomo/K.Ishii/40 20.00 50.00
TTA9 P.Burrell/B.Abreu/40 10.00 25.00
TTA10 T.Helton/L.Walker 4.00 10.00

2003 Absolute Memorabilia Team Trios

STATED ODDS 1:88
*SPECTRUM: 1.2X TO 3X BASIC
SPECTRUM PRINT RUN 50 SERIAL #'d SETS
TTR1 Maddux Chipper Andruw 2.00 5.00
TTR2 Sosa/Prior/Wood 1.50 4.00
TTR3 Pedro/Nomar/Manny 1.50 4.00
TTR4 Giambi/Soriano/Clemens 2.00 5.00
TTR5 A.Rod/Palmeiro/Teixeira 2.00 5.00
TTR6 Piazza/Alomar/Shinjo 1.50 4.00
TTR7 Bagwell/Biggio/Berkman 1.00 2.50
TTR8 Glaus/Garret/Percival .60 1.50
TTR9 Tejada/Chavez/Zito 1.00 2.50
TTR10 L.Gonz/Randy/Schilling 1.50 4.00

2003 Absolute Memorabilia Team Trios Materials

1-2/4-5/7/9-10 PRINT RUN 100 #'d SETS
3/6/8 PRINT RUNS B/WN 40-50 COPIES PER
SPECTRUM 1-2/4-5/7/9-10 PRINT 25 #'d SETS
SPECTRUM 3/6/8 PRINT RUN 10 #'d SETS
NO SPECTRUM PRICING DUE TO SCARCITY
ALL FEATURE THREE JERSEY SWATCHES
TTR1 Maddux/Chipper/Andruw 15.00 40.00
TTR2 Sosa/Prior/Wood 15.00 40.00
TTR3 Pedro/Nomar/Manny/50 40.00 80.00
TTR4 Giambi/Soriano/Clemens 20.00 50.00
TTR5 A.Rod/Palmeiro/Teixeira 15.00 40.00
TTR6 Piazza/Alomar/Shinjo/40 30.00 60.00
TTR7 Bagwell/Biggio/Berkman 15.00 40.00
TTR8 Glaus/Garret/Percival/40 15.00 40.00
TTR9 Tejada/Chavez/Zito 15.00 40.00
TTR10 L.Gonz/Randy/Schilling 15.00 40.00

2003 Absolute Memorabilia Tools of the Trade

STATED ODDS 1:5
*SPECTRUM: 1X TO 2.5X BASIC
SPECTRUM PRINT RUN 100 #'d SETS
TT1 Sammy Sosa 1.00 2.50
TT2 Nomar Garciaparra .60 1.50
TT3 Andruw Jones .40 1.00
TT4 Troy Glaus .40 1.00
TT5 Greg Maddux 1.25 3.00
TT6 Rickey Henderson 1.00 2.50
TT7 Alex Rodriguez 1.25 3.00
TT8 Manny Ramirez 1.00 2.50
TT9 Lance Berkman .60 1.50
TT10 Roger Clemens 1.25 3.00
TT11 Ivan Rodriguez .60 1.50
TT12 Kazuhisa Ishii .40 1.00
TT13 Alfonso Soriano .60 1.50
TT14 Austin Kearns .40 1.00
TT15 Mike Piazza 1.00 2.50
TT16 Curt Schilling .60 1.50
TT17 Jeff Bagwell .60 1.50
TT18 Todd Helton .60 1.50
TT19 Randy Johnson 1.00 2.50
TT20 Vladimir Guerrero .60 1.50
TT21 Kerry Wood .40 1.00
TT22 Rafael Palmeiro .60 1.50
TT23 Roy Oswalt .60 1.50
TT24 Chipper Jones 1.00 2.50
TT25 Pat Burrell .40 1.00
TT26 Jason Giambi .40 1.00
TT27 Pedro Martinez .60 1.50
TT28 Roberto Alomar .60 1.50
TT29 Shawn Green .40 1.00
TT30 Adam Dunn .60 1.50
TT31 Juan Gonzalez .40 1.00
TT32 Mark Prior .60 1.50
TT33 Hideo Nomo 1.00 2.50
TT34 Torii Hunter .40 1.00
TT35 Mark Teixeira .60 1.50
TT36 Craig Biggio .60 1.50
TT37 Rafael Palmeiro .60 1.50
TT38 Jeff Bagwell .60 1.50
TT39 Albert Pujols 1.25 3.00
TT40 Richie Sexson .40 1.00
TT41 Alex Rodriguez 1.25 3.00
TT42 Carlos Delgado .40 1.00
TT43 Frank Thomas 1.00 2.50
TT44 Sammy Sosa 1.00 2.50
TT45 Marlon Byrd .40 1.00
TT46 Mark Prior .60 1.50
TT47 Adrian Beltre 1.00 2.50
TT48 Tom Glavine .60 1.50
TT49 So Taguchi .40 1.00
TT50 Jeff Bagwell .60 1.50
TT51 Mike Sweeney .40 1.00
TT52 Luis Gonzalez .40 1.00
TT53 Chipper Jones 1.00 2.50
TT54 Jason Giambi .40 1.00
TT55 Miguel Tejada .60 1.50
TT56 Todd Helton .60 1.50
TT57 Andruw Jones .40 1.00
TT58 Mike Piazza 1.00 2.50
TT59 Manny Ramirez 1.00 2.50
TT60 Randy Johnson 1.00 2.50
TT61 Carlos Beltran .60 1.50
TT62 Victor Martinez .60 1.50
TT63 Orlando Hudson .40 1.00
TT64 Jeff Kent .40 1.00
TT65 Greg Maddux 1.25 3.00
TT66 Garret Anderson .40 1.00
TT67 Joe Thurston .40 1.00
TT68 Mark Teixeira .60 1.50
TT69 Kazuhisa Ishii .40 1.00
TT70 Austin Kearns .40 1.00
TT71 Pat Burrell .40 1.00
TT72 Joe Borchard .40 1.00
TT73 Josh Phelps .40 1.00
TT74 Travis Hafner .40 1.00
TT75 So Taguchi .40 1.00
TT76 Victor Martinez .60 1.50
TT77 Paul Lo Duca .40 1.00
TT78 Bernie Williams .60 1.50
TT79 Josh Phelps .40 1.00
TT80 Marlon Byrd .40 1.00
TT81 Manny Ramirez 1.00 2.50
TT82 Jason Giambi .40 1.00
TT83 Jeff Bagwell .60 1.50
TT84 Sammy Sosa 1.00 2.50
TT85 Josh Phelps .40 1.00
TT86 Tim Hudson .60 1.50
TT87 Randy Johnson 1.00 2.50
TT88 Troy Glaus .40 1.00
TT89 Joe Thurston .40 1.00
TT90 Miguel Tejada .60 1.50
TT91 Adam Dunn .60 1.50
TT92 Magglio Ordonez .60 1.50
TT93 Mike Sweeney .40 1.00
TT94 Andruw Jones .40 1.00
TT95 Carlos Beltran .60 1.50
TT96 Joe Borchard .40 1.00
TT97 Austin Kearns .40 1.00
TT98 Richie Sexson .40 1.00
TT99 Mark Prior .60 1.50
TT100 Mark Teixeira .60 1.50
TT101 Ryan Klesko .40 1.00
TT102 Jason Jennings .40 1.00
TT103 Travis Hafner .40 1.00
TT104 Mark Buehrle .60 1.50
TT105 Eric Hinske .40 1.00
TT106 Rafael Palmeiro .60 1.50
TT107 Roy Oswalt .60 1.50
TT108 Kerry Wood .40 1.00
TT109 Brian Giles .40 1.00
TT110 Ivan Rodriguez .60 1.50

2003 Absolute Memorabilia Tools of the Trade Materials

1-74 PRINT RUNS B/WN 40-250 COPIES PER
75-90 PRINT RUNS B/WN 50-125 COPIES PER
91-97 PRINT RUN 100 SERIAL #'d SETS
98-104 PRINT RUN 50 SERIAL #'d SETS
105-110 PRINT RUN 50 SERIAL #'d SETS
TT1 Sammy Sosa Jsy/250 4.00 10.00
TT2 Nomar Garciaparra Jsy/250 6.00 15.00
TT3 Andruw Jones Jsy/250 4.00 10.00
TT4 Troy Glaus Jsy/250 3.00 8.00
TT5 Greg Maddux Jsy/250 4.00 10.00
TT6 Rickey Henderson Jsy/40 10.00 25.00
TT7 Alex Rodriguez Jsy/250 6.00 15.00
TT8 Manny Ramirez Jsy/250 4.00 10.00
TT9 Lance Berkman Jsy/250 3.00 8.00
TT10 Roger Clemens Jsy/250 6.00 15.00
TT11 Ivan Rodriguez Jsy/250 4.00 10.00
TT12 Kazuhisa Ishii Jsy/40 6.00 15.00
TT13 Alfonso Soriano Jsy/250 3.00 8.00
TT14 Austin Kearns Jsy/250 3.00 8.00
TT15 Mike Piazza Jsy/250 4.00 10.00
TT16 Curt Schilling Jsy/250 3.00 8.00
TT17 Jeff Bagwell Jsy/250 4.00 10.00
TT18 Todd Helton Jsy/250 4.00 10.00
TT19 Randy Johnson Jsy/250 4.00 10.00
TT20 Vladimir Guerrero Jsy/250 4.00 10.00
TT21 Kerry Wood Jsy/250 3.00 8.00
TT22 Rafael Palmeiro Jsy/250 4.00 10.00
TT23 Roy Oswalt Jsy/250 3.00 8.00
TT24 Chipper Jones Jsy/250 4.00 10.00
TT25 Pat Burrell Jsy/40 6.00 15.00
TT26 Jason Giambi Jsy/250 3.00 8.00
TT27 Pedro Martinez Jsy/250 4.00 10.00
TT28 Roberto Alomar Jsy/40 10.00 25.00
TT29 Shawn Green Jsy/250 3.00 8.00
TT30 Adam Dunn Jsy/250 3.00 8.00
TT31 Juan Gonzalez Jsy/40 6.00 15.00
TT32 Mark Prior Jsy/250 4.00 10.00
TT33 Hideo Nomo Jsy/250 6.00 15.00
TT34 Torii Hunter Jsy/250 3.00 8.00
TT35 Mark Teixeira Jsy/250 4.00 10.00
TT36 Craig Biggio Pants/250 4.00 10.00
TT37 Rafael Palmeiro Pants/250 4.00 10.00
TT38 Jeff Bagwell Pants/250 4.00 10.00
TT39 Albert Pujols Jsy/200 6.00 15.00
TT40 Richie Sexson Pants/250 3.00 8.00
TT41 Alex Rodriguez Bat/250 6.00 15.00
TT42 Carlos Delgado Bat/250 3.00 8.00
TT43 Frank Thomas Bat/75 6.00 15.00
TT44 Sammy Sosa Bat/250 4.00 10.00
TT45 Marlon Byrd Bat/250 3.00 8.00
TT46 Mark Prior Bat/250 4.00 10.00
TT47 Adrian Beltre Bat/250 3.00 8.00
TT48 Tom Glavine Bat/250 4.00 10.00
TT49 So Taguchi Bat/250 3.00 8.00
TT50 Jeff Bagwell Bat/250 4.00 10.00
TT51 Mike Sweeney Bat/250 3.00 8.00
TT52 Luis Gonzalez Bat/250 3.00 8.00
TT53 Chipper Jones Bat/100 6.00 15.00
TT54 Jason Giambi Bat/250 3.00 8.00
TT55 Miguel Tejada Bat/250 3.00 8.00
TT56 Todd Helton Bat/250 4.00 10.00
TT57 Andruw Jones Bat/250 4.00 10.00
TT58 Mike Piazza Bat/250 4.00 10.00
TT59 Manny Ramirez Bat/250 4.00 10.00
TT60 Randy Johnson Bat/250 4.00 10.00
TT61 Carlos Beltran Bat/250 3.00 8.00
TT62 Victor Martinez Bat/250 4.00 10.00
TT63 Orlando Hudson Bat/250 3.00 8.00
TT64 Jeff Kent Bat/250 3.00 8.00
TT65 Greg Maddux Bat/250 4.00 10.00
TT66 Garret Anderson Bat/150 3.00 8.00
TT67 Joe Thurston Bat/250 3.00 8.00
TT68 Mark Teixeira Bat/250 4.00 10.00
TT69 Kazuhisa Ishii Bat/250 3.00 8.00
TT70 Austin Kearns Bat/250 3.00 8.00
TT71 Pat Burrell Bat/100 4.00 10.00
TT72 Joe Borchard Bat/250 3.00 8.00
TT73 Josh Phelps Bat/250 3.00 8.00
TT74 Travis Hafner Bat/250 3.00 8.00

TT75 So Taguchi Shoe/125 4.00 10.00
TT76 Victor Martinez Fld Glv/125 6.00 15.00
TT77 Paul Lo Duca Shoe/125 4.00 10.00
TT78 Bernie Williams Shoe/125 6.00 15.00
TT79 Josh Phelps Shoe/125 4.00 10.00
TT80 Marlon Byrd Fld Glv/125 4.00 10.00
TT81 Manny Ramirez Hat/100 6.00 15.00
TT82 Jason Giambi Hat/125 3.00 8.00
TT84 Sammy Sosa Shoe/125 6.00 15.00
TT85 Josh Phelps Hat/125 4.00 10.00
TT86 Tim Hudson Hat/125 4.00 10.00
TT88 Troy Glaus Btg Glv/125 4.00 10.00
TT89 Joe Thurston Fld Glv/125 4.00 10.00
TT90 Miguel Tejada Hat/125 4.00 10.00
TT91 Adam Dunn Btg Glv-Fld Glv/100 6.00 15.00
TT92 Magglio Ordonez Btg Glv-Hat/100 6.00 15.00
TT93 Mike Sweeney Btg Glv-Fld Glv/100 6.00 15.00
TT94 Andruw Jones Btg-Glv-Hat/100 10.00 25.00
TT95 Carlos Beltran Hat-Shoe/100 6.00 15.00
TT96 Joe Borchard Fld Glv-Shoe/100 6.00 15.00
TT97 Austin Kearns Hat-Shoe/100 6.00 15.00
TT98 Richie Sexson Triple/50 10.00 25.00
TT99 Mark Prior Triple/50 15.00 40.00
TT100 Mark Teixeira Triple/50 15.00 40.00
TT101 Ryan Klesko Triple/50 10.00 25.00
TT103 Travis Hafner Triple/50 10.00 25.00
TT104 Mark Buehrle Triple/50 10.00 25.00
TT105 Eric Hinske Quad/50 10.00 25.00
TT106 Rafael Palmeiro Quad/50 30.00 60.00
TT107 Roy Oswalt Quad/50 15.00 40.00
TT108 Kerry Wood Quad/50 15.00 40.00
TT109 Brian Giles Quad/50 15.00 40.00
TT110 Ivan Rodriguez Quad/50 30.00 60.00

2003 Absolute Memorabilia Tools of the Trade Materials Spectrum

*SPECTRUM p/r 40-50: 1.25X TO 3X BASIC
PRINT RUNS B/WN 10-50 COPIES PER
NO PRICING ON QTY OF 25 OR LESS

2003 Absolute Memorabilia Total Bases

STATED ODDS 1:16
TB1 Albert Pujols 1.25 3.00
TB2 Nomar Garciaparra .60 1.50
TB3 Jason Giambi .40 1.00
TB4 Miguel Tejada .60 1.50
TB5 Rafael Palmeiro .60 1.50
TB6 Sammy Sosa 1.00 2.50
TB7 Pat Burrell .40 1.00
TB8 Lance Berkman .60 1.50
TB9 Bernie Williams .60 1.50
TB10 Jim Thome .60 1.50
TB11 Carlos Beltran .60 1.50
TB12 Eric Chavez .40 1.00
TB13 Alex Rodriguez 1.25 3.00
TB14 Magglio Ordonez .60 1.50
TB15 Brian Giles .40 1.00
TB16 Alfonso Soriano .60 1.50
TB17 Shawn Green .40 1.00
TB18 Vladimir Guerrero .60 1.50
TB19 Garret Anderson .40 1.00
TB20 Todd Helton .60 1.50
TB21 Barry Bonds 1.50 4.00
TB22 Jeff Kent .40 1.00
TB23 Torii Hunter .40 1.00
TB24 Ichiro Suzuki 1.25 3.00
TB25 Derek Jeter 2.50 6.00
TB26 Chipper Jones 1.00 2.50
TB27 Jeff Bagwell .60 1.50
TB28 Mike Piazza 1.00 2.50
TB29 Rickey Henderson 1.00 2.50
TB30 Ken Griffey Jr. 2.00 5.00

2003 Absolute Memorabilia Total Bases Materials 1B

PRINT RUNS B/WN 28-165 COPIES PER
TB1 Albert Pujols/109 8.00 20.00
TB2 Nomar Garciaparra/112 8.00 20.00
TB3 Jason Giambi/100 4.00 10.00
TB4 Miguel Tejada/140 4.00 10.00
TB5 Rafael Palmeiro/58 10.00 25.00
TB6 Sammy Sosa/90 6.00 15.00
TB7 Pat Burrell/87 4.00 10.00
TB8 Lance Berkman/90 4.00 10.00
TB9 Bernie Williams/146 4.00 10.00
TB10 Jim Thome/73 12.50 30.00
TB11 Carlos Beltran/94 4.00 10.00
TB12 Eric Chavez/93 4.00 10.00
TB13 Alex Rodriguez/101 8.00 20.00
TB14 Magglio Ordonez/103 4.00 10.00
TB15 Brian Giles/68 4.00 10.00
TB16 Alfonso Soriano/117 4.00 10.00
TB17 Shawn Green/92 4.00 10.00
TB18 Vladimir Guerrero/128 4.00 10.00
TB19 Garret Anderson/107 4.00 10.00
TB20 Todd Helton/109 6.00 15.00
TB21 Barry Bonds/70 12.50 30.00
TB22 Jeff Kent/114 4.00 10.00
TB23 Torii Hunter/92 4.00 10.00
TB24 Ichiro Suzuki/165 15.00 40.00
TB25 Derek Jeter/147 15.00 40.00
TB26 Chipper Jones/117 6.00 15.00
TB27 Jeff Bagwell/100 6.00 15.00
TB29 Rickey Henderson/28 15.00 40.00

2003 Absolute Memorabilia Total Bases Materials 2B

PRINT RUNS B/WN 6-56 COPIES PER
NO PRICING ON QTY OF 25 OR LESS
TB1 Albert Pujols/40 20.00 50.00
TB2 Nomar Garciaparra/56 15.00 40.00
TB7 Pat Burrell/39 6.00 15.00
TB8 Lance Berkman/35 10.00 25.00
TB11 Carlos Beltran/44 6.00 15.00
TB13 Alex Rodriguez/27 10.00 25.00
TB14 Magglio Ordonez/47 6.00 15.00
TB16 Alfonso Soriano/51 6.00 15.00
TB17 Shawn Green/31 10.00 25.00
TB18 Vladimir Guerrero/37 10.00 25.00
TB19 Garret Anderson/56 6.00 15.00
TB20 Todd Helton/39 10.00 25.00
TB21 Barry Bonds/31 25.00 60.00
TB22 Jeff Kent/42 6.00 15.00
TB23 Torii Hunter/37 6.00 15.00
TB25 Derek Jeter/26 30.00 80.00
TB26 Chipper Jones/35 10.00 25.00
TB27 Jeff Bagwell/33 15.00 40.00

2003 Absolute Memorabilia Total Bases Materials HR

PRINT RUNS B/WN 5-57 COPIES PER
NO PRICING ON QTY OF 25 OR LESS
TB1 Albert Pujols/34 25.00 60.00
TB3 Jason Giambi/41 6.00 15.00
TB4 Miguel Tejada/34 10.00 25.00
TB5 Rafael Palmeiro/43 10.00 25.00
TB6 Sammy Sosa/49 10.00 25.00
TB7 Pat Burrell/37 6.00 15.00
TB8 Lance Berkman/42 6.00 15.00
TB10 Jim Thome/52 10.00 25.00
TB11 Carlos Beltran/29 10.00 25.00
TB12 Eric Chavez/34 10.00 25.00
TB13 Alex Rodriguez/57 15.00 40.00
TB14 Magglio Ordonez/38 6.00 15.00
TB15 Brian Giles/38 6.00 15.00
TB16 Alfonso Soriano/39 6.00 15.00
TB17 Shawn Green/42 6.00 15.00
TB18 Vladimir Guerrero/39 10.00 25.00
TB19 Garret Anderson/29 10.00 25.00
TB21 Barry Bonds/46 20.00 50.00
TB22 Jeff Kent/37 6.00 15.00
TB23 Torii Hunter/29 10.00 25.00
TB26 Chipper Jones/26 15.00 40.00
TB27 Jeff Bagwell/31 15.00 40.00
TB28 Mike Piazza/33 20.00 50.00

2004 Absolute Memorabilia

COMMON ACTIVE (1-200) .50 1.25
COMMON RETIRED (1-200) .75 2.00
1-200 PRINT RUN 1349 SERIAL #'d SETS
COMMON CARD (201-250) .75 2.00
COMMON AU (201-250) 3.00 8.00
201-250 RANDOM INSERTS IN PACKS
201-250 NON AU PRINT RUNS 1000 #'d PER
201-250 AU PRINTS B/WN 500-700 #'d PER
1 Troy Glaus .50 1.25
2 Garret Anderson .50 1.25
3 Tim Salmon .50 1.25
4 Bartolo Colon .50 1.25
5 Troy Percival .50 1.25
6 Nolan Ryan Angels 4.00 10.00
7 Vladimir Guerrero .75 2.00
8 Richie Sexson .50 1.25
9 Shea Hillenbrand .50 1.25
10 Luis Gonzalez .50 1.25
11 Brandon Webb .50 1.25
12 Randy Johnson 1.25 3.00
13 Robby Hammock .50 1.25
14 Edgar Gonzalez .50 1.25
15 Roberto Alomar .75 2.00
16 Andruw Jones .50 1.25
17 Chipper Jones 1.25 3.00
18 Dale Murphy 1.25 3.00
19 Rafael Furcal .50 1.25
20 J.D. Drew .50 1.25
21 Bubba Nelson .50 1.25
22 Julio Franco .50 1.25
23 Adam LaRoche .50 1.25
24 Michael Hessman .50 1.25
25 Warren Spahn .75 2.00
26 Jay Gibbons .50 1.25
27 Cal Ripken 4.00 10.00
28 Miguel Tejada .75 2.00
29 Adam Loewen .50 1.25
30 Rafael Palmeiro .75 2.00
31 Javy Lopez .50 1.25
32 Luis Matos .50 1.25
33 Jason Varitek 1.25 3.00
34 Carl Yastrzemski 1.25 3.00
35 Manny Ramirez 1.25 3.00
36 Trot Nixon .50 1.25
37 Curt Schilling .75 2.00
38 Pedro Martinez .75 2.00
39 Nomar Garciaparra .75 2.00
40 Luis Tiant .50 1.25
41 Kevin Youkilis .50 1.25
42 Michel Hernandez .50 1.25
43 Sammy Sosa 1.25 3.00
44 Greg Maddux 1.50 4.00
45 Kerry Wood .50 1.25
46 Mark Prior .75 2.00
47 Ernie Banks 1.25 3.00
48 Aramis Ramirez .50 1.25
49 Brendan Harris .50 1.25
50 Todd Wellemeyer .50 1.25
51 Frank Thomas 1.25 3.00
52 Magglio Ordonez .75 2.00
53 Carlos Lee .50 1.25
54 Joe Crede .50 1.25
55 Joe Borchard .50 1.25
56 Mark Buehrle .75 2.00
57 Sean Casey .50 1.25
58 Adam Dunn .75 2.00
59 Austin Kearns .50 1.25
60 Ken Griffey Jr. 2.50 6.00
61 Barry Larkin .75 2.00
62 Ryan Wagner .50 1.25
63 Jody Gerut .50 1.25
64 Jeremy Guthrie .50 1.25
65 Travis Hafner .50 1.25
66 Brian Tallet .50 1.25
67 Todd Helton .75 2.00
68 Preston Wilson .50 1.25
69 Jeff Baker .50 1.25
70 Clint Barmes .75 2.00
71 Joe Kennedy .50 1.25
72 Jack Morris .75 2.00
73 George Kell .75 2.00
74 Preston Larrison .50 1.25
75 Dmitri Young .50 1.25
76 Ivan Rodriguez .75 2.00
77 Dontrelle Willis .50 1.25
78 Josh Beckett .50 1.25
79 Miguel Cabrera 1.25 3.00
80 Mike Lowell .50 1.25
81 Luis Castillo .50 1.25
82 Juan Pierre .50 1.25
83 Jeff Bagwell .75 2.00
84 Jeff Kent .50 1.25
85 Craig Biggio .75 2.00
86 Lance Berkman .75 2.00
87 Andy Pettitte .75 2.00
88 Roy Oswalt .75 2.00
89 Chris Burke .50 1.25
90 Jason Lane .50 1.25
91 Roger Clemens 1.50 4.00
92 Mike Sweeney .50 1.25
93 Carlos Beltran .75 2.00
94 Angel Berroa .50 1.25
95 Juan Gonzalez .50 1.25
96 Ken Harvey .50 1.25
97 Byron Gettis .50 1.25
98 Alexis Gomez .50 1.25
99 Ian Ferguson .50 1.25
100 Duke Snider .75 2.00
101 Shawn Green .50 1.25
102 Hideo Nomo 1.25 3.00
103 Kazuhisa Ishii .50 1.25
104 Edwin Jackson .50 1.25
105 Fred McGriff .50 1.25
106 Hong-Chih Kou .50 1.25
107 Don Sutton .75 2.00
108 Rickey Henderson 1.25 3.00
109 Cesar Izturis .50 1.25
110 Robin Ventura .50 1.25
111 Paul Lo Duca .50 1.25
112 Rickie Weeks .50 1.25
113 Scott Podsednik .50 1.25
114 Junior Spivey .50 1.25
115 Lyle Overbay .50 1.25
116 Tony Oliva .50 1.25
117 Jacque Jones .50 1.25
118 Shannon Stewart .50 1.25
119 Torii Hunter .50 1.25
120 Johan Santana .75 2.00
121 J.D. Durbin .50 1.25
122 Jason Kubel .50 1.25
123 Michael Cuddyer .50 1.25
124 Nick Johnson .50 1.25
125 Jose Vidro .50 1.25
126 Orlando Cabrera .50 1.25
127 Zach Day .50 1.25
128 Mike Piazza 1.25 3.00
129 Tom Glavine .75 2.00
130 Jae Weong Seo .50 1.25
131 Gary Carter .75 2.00
132 Phil Seibel .50 1.25
133 Edwin Almonte .50 1.25
134 Aaron Boone .50 1.25
135 Kenny Lofton .50 1.25
136 Don Mattingly 2.50 6.00
137 Jason Giambi .50 1.25
138 Alex Rodriguez Yanks 1.50 4.00
139 Jorge Posada .75 2.00
140 Bernie Williams .75 2.00
141 Hideki Matsui 2.00 5.00
142 Mike Mussina .75 2.00
143 Mariano Rivera 1.50 4.00
144 Gary Sheffield .50 1.25
145 Derek Jeter 3.00 8.00
146 Chien-Ming Wang 2.00 5.00
147 Javier Vazquez .50 1.25
148 Jose Contreras .50 1.25
149 Whitey Ford .75 2.00
150 Kevin Brown .50 1.25
151 Eric Chavez .50 1.25
152 Barry Zito .75 2.00
153 Mark Mulder .50 1.25
154 Tim Hudson .75 2.00
155 Rich Harden .50 1.25
156 Eric Byrnes .50 1.25
157 Jim Thome .75 2.00
158 Bobby Abreu .50 1.25
159 Marlon Byrd .50 1.25
160 Lenny Dykstra .50 1.25
161 Steve Carlton .75 2.00
162 Ryan Howard 1.00 2.50
163 Bobby Hill .50 1.25
164 Jose Castillo .50 1.25
165 Jay Payton .50 1.25
166 Ryan Klesko .50 1.25
167 Brian Giles .50 1.25
168 Henri Stanley .50 1.25
169 Jason Schmidt .50 1.25
170 Jerome Williams .50 1.25
171 J.T. Snow .50 1.25
172 Bret Boone .50 1.25
173 Edgar Martinez .75 2.00
174 Ichiro Suzuki 1.50 4.00
175 Jamie Moyer .50 1.25
176 Rich Aurilia .50 1.25
177 Chris Snelling .50 1.25
178 Scott Rolen .75 2.00
179 Albert Pujols 1.50 4.00
180 Jim Edmonds .75 2.00
181 Stan Musial 2.00 5.00
182 Dan Haren .50 1.25
183 Red Schoendienst .75 2.00
184 Aubrey Huff .50 1.25
185 Delmon Young .75 2.00
186 Rocco Baldelli .50 1.25
187 Dewon Brazelton .50 1.25
188 Mark Teixeira .75 2.00
189 Hank Blalock .50 1.25
190 Nolan Ryan Rgr 4.00 10.00
191 Alfonso Soriano .75 2.00
192 Michael Young .50 1.25
193 Vernon Wells .50 1.25
194 Roy Halladay .75 2.00
195 Carlos Delgado .50 1.25
196 Dustin McGowan .50 1.25
197 Josh Phelps .50 1.25
198 Alexis Rios .50 1.25
199 Eric Hinske .50 1.25
200 Josh Towers .50 1.25
201 Kazuo Matsui/1000 RC 1.25 3.00
202 Fernando Nieve AU/500 RC 3.00 8.00
203 Mike Rouse/1000 RC .75 2.00
204 Dennis Sarfate AU/500 RC 3.00 8.00
205 Josh Labandeira AU/500 RC 3.00 8.00
206 Chris Oxspring AU/500 RC 3.00 8.00
207 Alfredo Simon/1000 RC 1.25 3.00
208 Cory Sullivan AU/500 RC 3.00 8.00
209 Ruddy Yan AU/500 3.00 8.00
210 Jason Bartlett AU/500 RC 4.00 10.00
211 Akinori Otsuka/1000 RC .75 2.00
212 Lincoln Holdzkom/1000 RC .75 2.00
213 Justin Leone/1000 RC .75 2.00
214 Jorge Sequea AU/500 RC 3.00 8.00
215 John Gall/1000 RC .75 2.00
216 Jerome Gamble/1000 RC .75 2.00
217 Tim Bittner AU/500 RC 3.00 8.00
218 Ronny Cedeno AU/500 RC 6.00 15.00
219 Justin Hampson/1000 RC .75 2.00
220 Ryan Wing AU/500 RC 3.00 8.00
221 Mariano Gomez AU/500 RC 3.00 8.00
222 Carlos Vasquez/1000 RC .75 2.00
223 Casey Daigle AU/500 RC 3.00 8.00
224 Renyel Pinto AU/500 RC 3.00 8.00
225 Chris Shelton AU/500 RC 10.00 25.00
226 Mike Gosling AU/700 RC 3.00 8.00
227 Aarom Baldiris AU/700 RC 3.00 8.00
228 Ramon Ramirez AU/700 RC 3.00 8.00
229 Roberto Novoa AU/500 RC 3.00 8.00
230 Sean Henn AU/500 RC 3.00 8.00
231 Jamie Brown AU/500 RC 3.00 8.00
232 Nick Regilio AU/500 RC 3.00 8.00
233 Dave Crouthers AU/700 RC 3.00 8.00
234 Greg Dobbs AU/500 RC 3.00 8.00
235 Angel Chavez AU/500 RC 3.00 8.00
236 Willy Taveras AU/500 RC 8.00 20.00
237 Justin Knoedler AU/500 RC 3.00 8.00
238 Ian Snell AU/700 RC 6.00 15.00
239 Jason Frasor AU/500 RC 3.00 8.00
240 Jerry Gil AU/500 RC 3.00 8.00
241 Carlos Hines AU/500 RC 3.00 8.00
242 Ivan Ochoa AU/500 RC 3.00 8.00
243 Jose Capellan AU/700 RC 3.00 8.00
244 Onil Joseph AU/700 RC 3.00 8.00
245 Hector Gimenez AU/700 RC 3.00 8.00
246 Shawn Hill AU/700 RC 3.00 8.00
247 Freddy Guzman AU/700 RC 3.00 8.00
248 Graham Koonce AU/500 3.00 8.00
249 Ronald Belisario AU/500 RC 3.00 8.00
250 Merkin Valdez AU/700 RC 4.00 10.00

2004 Absolute Memorabilia Retail

*RETAIL 1-200 : .1X TO .25X BASIC
1-200 ISSUED IN RETAIL PACKS
RETAIL CARDS ARE NOT SERIAL #'d

2004 Absolute Memorabilia Spectrum Gold

*GOLD 1-200: 1.5X TO 4X BASIC ACTIVE
*GOLD 1-200: 1.5X TO 4X BASIC RETIRED
*GOLD 201-250: .6X TO 1.5X BASIC
*GOLD 201-250: .3X TO .8X BASIC AU
RANDOM INSERTS IN PACKS
STATED PRINT RUN 50 SERIAL #'d SETS

2004 Absolute Memorabilia Spectrum Silver

*SILVER 1-200: 1X TO 2.5X BASIC ACTIVE
*SILVER 1-200: 1X TO 2.5X BASIC RETIRED
*SILVER 201-250: .4X TO 1X BASIC
*SILVER 201-250: .2X TO .5X BASIC AU
RANDOM INSERTS IN PACKS
STATED PRINT RUN 100 SERIAL #'d SETS

2004 Absolute Memorabilia Signature Spectrum Gold

PRINT RUNS B/WN 1-100 COPIES PER
NO PRICING ON QTY OF 10 OR LESS
1 Troy Glaus/15 30.00 60.00
2 Garret Anderson/100 6.00 15.00
7 Vladimir Guerrero/25 30.00 60.00
8 Richie Sexson/15 15.00 40.00
9 Shea Hillenbrand/100 6.00 15.00
11 Brandon Webb/100 4.00 10.00
15 Roberto Alomar/25 20.00 50.00
18 Dale Murphy/100 10.00 25.00
19 Rafael Furcal/100 6.00 15.00
22 Julio Franco/25 12.50 30.00
23 Adam LaRoche/100 4.00 10.00
26 Jay Gibbons/100 4.00 10.00
29 Adam Loewen/100 4.00 10.00
32 Luis Matos/50 5.00 12.00
33 Jason Varitek/25 30.00 60.00
36 Trot Nixon/100 6.00 15.00
40 Luis Tiant/50 8.00 20.00
41 Kevin Youkilis/25 8.00 20.00
45 Kerry Wood/25 20.00 50.00
46 Mark Prior/100 10.00 25.00
47 Ernie Banks/100 20.00 50.00
52 Magglio Ordonez/100 6.00 15.00
53 Carlos Lee/100 6.00 15.00
54 Joe Crede/50 8.00 20.00
59 Austin Kearns/100 4.00 10.00
61 Barry Larkin/25 30.00 60.00
62 Ryan Wagner/50 5.00 12.00
63 Jody Gerut/100 4.00 10.00
64 Jeremy Guthrie/25 8.00 20.00
65 Travis Hafner/25 8.00 20.00
68 Preston Wilson/100 6.00 15.00
69 Jeff Baker/25 8.00 20.00
73 George Kell/100 10.00 25.00
79 Miguel Cabrera/100 15.00 40.00
81 Luis Castillo/25 8.00 20.00
83 Jeff Bagwell/25 40.00 80.00
87 Andy Pettitte/25 15.00 40.00
93 Carlos Beltran/100 6.00 15.00
94 Angel Berroa/100 4.00 10.00
100 Duke Snider/100 10.00 25.00
104 Edwin Jackson/50 12.50 30.00
106 Hong-Chih Kou/25 40.00 80.00
107 Don Sutton/25 12.50 30.00
112 Rickie Weeks/24 12.50 30.00
113 Scott Podsednik/100 10.00 25.00
116 Tony Oliva/50 8.00 20.00
117 Jacque Jones/100 6.00 15.00
119 Torii Hunter/100 6.00 15.00
130 Jae Weong Seo/100 6.00 15.00
131 Gary Carter/100 15.00 40.00
136 Don Mattingly/100 30.00 60.00
139 Jorge Posada/25 75.00 150.00
144 Gary Sheffield/25 20.00 50.00
146 Chien-Ming Wang/25 125.00 200.00
153 Mark Mulder/100 6.00 15.00
155 Rich Harden/50 8.00 20.00
159 Marlon Byrd/100 4.00 10.00
160 Lenny Dykstra/100 6.00 15.00
161 Steve Carlton/50 8.00 20.00
164 Jose Castillo/50 5.00 12.00
165 Jay Payton/100 4.00 10.00
170 Jerome Williams/50 5.00 12.00
178 Scott Rolen/50 12.50 30.00
181 Stan Musial/100 50.00 100.00
182 Dan Haren/25 8.00 20.00
183 Red Schoendienst/100 6.00 15.00
184 Aubrey Huff/100 6.00 15.00
185 Delmon Young/100 10.00 25.00
187 Dewon Brazelton/25 8.00 20.00
188 Mark Teixeira/50 6.00 15.00
189 Hank Blalock/25 12.50 30.00
192 Michael Young/100 10.00 25.00
194 Roy Halladay/25 20.00 50.00
198 Alexis Rios/50 8.00 20.00
202 Fernando Nieve/100 6.00 15.00
205 Josh Labandeira/100 4.00 10.00
206 Chris Oxspring/100 4.00 10.00
208 Cory Sullivan/100 4.00 10.00
209 Ruddy Yan/100 4.00 10.00
210 Jason Bartlett/100 6.00 15.00
212 Lincoln Holdzkom/100 4.00 10.00
213 Justin Leone/100 6.00 15.00
214 Jorge Sequea/100 4.00 10.00
217 Tim Bittner/100 4.00 10.00
219 Justin Hampson/100 4.00 10.00
220 Ryan Wing/100 4.00 10.00
221 Mariano Gomez/100 4.00 10.00
222 Carlos Vasquez/100 6.00 15.00
224 Renyel Pinto/100 5.00 12.00
225 Chris Shelton/100 10.00 25.00
230 Sean Henn/100 4.00 10.00
232 Nick Regilio/100 4.00 10.00
234 Greg Dobbs/50 6.00 15.00
235 Angel Chavez/100 4.00 10.00
242 Ivan Ochoa/100 4.00 10.00
248 Graham Koonce/100 4.00 10.00

2004 Absolute Memorabilia Signature Spectrum Silver

PRINT RUNS B/WN 1-250 COPIES PER
NO PRICING ON QTY OF 14 OR LESS
1 Troy Glaus/34 15.00 40.00
2 Garret Anderson/100 6.00 15.00
6 Nolan Ryan Angels/25 75.00 150.00
7 Vladimir Guerrero/100 12.50 30.00
8 Richie Sexson/34 10.00 25.00
9 Shea Hillenbrand/100 6.00 15.00
11 Brandon Webb/100 4.00 10.00
13 Robby Hammock/250 4.00 10.00
14 Edgar Gonzalez/104 4.00 10.00
15 Roberto Alomar/32 15.00 40.00
16 Andruw Jones/50 12.50 30.00
18 Dale Murphy/100 10.00 25.00
19 Rafael Furcal/100 6.00 15.00
21 Bubba Nelson/250 4.00 10.00
22 Julio Franco/100 6.00 15.00
23 Adam LaRoche/100 4.00 10.00
24 Michael Hessman/250 4.00 10.00
26 Jay Gibbons/100 4.00 10.00
29 Adam Loewen/100 4.00 10.00
32 Luis Matos/100 4.00 10.00
33 Jason Varitek/50 15.00 40.00
36 Trot Nixon/100 6.00 15.00
40 Luis Tiant/100 6.00 15.00
41 Kevin Youkilis/25 6.00 15.00
42 Michael Hernandez/190 4.00 10.00
43 Sammy Sosa/21 50.00 100.00
45 Kerry Wood/50 12.50 30.00
46 Mark Prior/100 8.00 20.00
47 Ernie Banks/100 20.00 50.00
48 Aramis Ramirez/50 8.00 20.00
49 Brendan Harris/250 4.00 10.00
50 Todd Wellemeyer/250 4.00 10.00
51 Frank Thomas/50 15.00 40.00
52 Magglio Ordonez/100 6.00 15.00
53 Carlos Lee/100 6.00 15.00
54 Joe Crede/100 6.00 15.00
55 Joe Borchard/250 4.00 10.00
57 Sean Casey/50 8.00 20.00
58 Adam Dunn/100 10.00 25.00
59 Austin Kearns/100 4.00 10.00
61 Barry Larkin/50 15.00 40.00
62 Ryan Wagner/100 4.00 10.00
63 Jody Gerut/100 4.00 10.00
64 Jeremy Guthrie/50 5.00 12.00
65 Travis Hafner/50 5.00 12.00
66 Brian Tallet/250 4.00 10.00
68 Preston Wilson/100 6.00 15.00
69 Jeff Baker/50 5.00 12.00
70 Clint Barmes/250 6.00 15.00
71 Joe Kennedy/250 4.00 10.00
73 George Kell/100 10.00 25.00
74 Preston Larrison/250 4.00 10.00
77 Dontrelle Willis/100 10.00 25.00
78 Josh Beckett/25 15.00 40.00
79 Miguel Cabrera/100 30.00 60.00
80 Mike Lowell/25 10.00 25.00
81 Luis Castillo/50 5.00 12.00
83 Jeff Bagwell/50 30.00 60.00
85 Craig Biggio/50 8.00 20.00
86 Lance Berkman/25 15.00 40.00
87 Andy Pettitte/25 15.00 40.00
88 Roy Oswalt/25 10.00 25.00
89 Chris Burke/250 6.00 15.00
90 Jason Lane/231 6.00 15.00
93 Carlos Beltran/100 6.00 15.00
94 Angel Berroa/100 4.00 10.00
95 Juan Gonzalez/25 10.00 25.00
96 Ken Harvey/200 4.00 10.00
97 Byron Gettis/250 4.00 10.00
98 Alexis Gomez/250 4.00 10.00
99 Ian Ferguson/104 4.00 10.00
100 Duke Snider/100 10.00 25.00
103 Kazuhisa Ishii/25 10.00 25.00
104 Edwin Jackson/100 10.00 25.00
105 Fred McGriff/50 12.50 30.00
106 Hong-Chih Kou/50 20.00 50.00
107 Don Sutton/100 6.00 15.00
109 Cesar Izturis/101 4.00 10.00
110 Robin Ventura/25 10.00 25.00
111 Paul Lo Duca/50 8.00 20.00
112 Rickie Weeks/21 10.00 25.00
113 Scott Podsednik/100 10.00 25.00
114 Junior Spivey/89 4.00 10.00
115 Lyle Overbay/89 4.00 10.00
116 Tony Oliva/72 6.00 15.00
117 Jacque Jones/100 6.00 15.00
118 Shannon Stewart/100 6.00 15.00
119 Torii Hunter/100 6.00 15.00
120 Johan Santana/50 12.50 30.00
121 J.D. Durbin/250 4.00 10.00
122 Jason Kubel/250 4.00 10.00
123 Michael Cuddyer/225 4.00 10.00
124 Nick Johnson/25 10.00 25.00
125 Jose Vidro/25 6.00 15.00
126 Orlando Cabrera/25 10.00 25.00
127 Zach Day/100 4.00 10.00
130 Jae Weong Seo/100 6.00 15.00
131 Gary Carter/100 15.00 40.00
132 Phil Seibel/177 4.00 10.00
133 Edwin Almonte/250 4.00 10.00
136 Don Mattingly/100 30.00 60.00
139 Jorge Posada/50 60.00 120.00
144 Gary Sheffield/100 6.00 15.00
146 Chien-Ming Wang/50 50.00 100.00
147 Javier Vazquez/25 10.00 25.00
148 Jose Contreras/25 10.00 25.00
149 Whitey Ford/50 15.00 40.00
151 Eric Chavez/50 8.00 20.00
153 Mark Mulder/100 6.00 15.00
154 Tim Hudson/50 12.50 30.00
155 Rich Harden/100 6.00 15.00
156 Eric Byrnes/250 4.00 10.00
159 Marlon Byrd/100 4.00 10.00
160 Lenny Dykstra/100 6.00 15.00
161 Steve Carlton/100 6.00 15.00
162 Ryan Howard/250 15.00 40.00
163 Bobby Hill/250 4.00 10.00
164 Jose Castillo/100 4.00 10.00
165 Jay Payton/100 4.00 10.00
168 Henri Stanley/112 4.00 10.00
170 Jerome Williams/100 4.00 10.00
171 J.T. Snow/89 6.00 15.00
173 Edgar Martinez/50 12.50 30.00
175 Jamie Moyer/19 15.00 40.00
176 Rich Aurilia/25 6.00 15.00
177 Chris Snelling/177 4.00 10.00
178 Scott Rolen/100 10.00 25.00
180 Jim Edmonds/50 12.50 30.00
181 Stan Musial/100 40.00 80.00
182 Dan Haren/200 4.00 10.00
183 Red Schoendienst/100 10.00 25.00
184 Aubrey Huff/100 6.00 15.00
185 Delmon Young/100 10.00 25.00
186 Rocco Baldelli/50 8.00 20.00
187 Dewon Brazelton/50 5.00 12.00
188 Mark Teixeira/100 5.00 12.00
189 Hank Blalock/50 8.00 20.00
190 Nolan Ryan Rgr/25 75.00 150.00
192 Michael Young/100 10.00 25.00
194 Roy Halladay/50 50.00 100.00
196 Dustin McGowan/250 4.00 10.00
197 Josh Phelps/25 6.00 15.00
198 Alexis Rios/100 6.00 15.00
200 Josh Towers/158 4.00 10.00
202 Fernando Nieve/250 5.00 12.00
203 Mike Rouse/100 4.00 10.00
204 Dennis Sarfate/100 4.00 10.00
205 Josh Labandeira/250 4.00 10.00
206 Chris Oxspring/250 4.00 10.00
207 Alfredo Simon/100 4.00 10.00
208 Cory Sullivan/250 4.00 10.00
209 Ruddy Yan/250 4.00 10.00
210 Jason Bartlett/250 6.00 15.00
211 Akinori Otsuka/100 12.50 30.00
212 Lincoln Holdzkom/250 4.00 10.00
213 Justin Leone/250 6.00 15.00
214 Jorge Sequea/250 4.00 10.00
215 John Gall/50 8.00 20.00
217 Tim Bittner/250 4.00 10.00
219 Justin Hampson/250 4.00 10.00
220 Ryan Wing/250 4.00 10.00
221 Mariano Gomez/250 4.00 10.00
222 Carlos Vasquez/250 6.00 15.00
223 Casey Daigle/150 4.00 10.00
224 Renyel Pinto/250 5.00 12.00
229 Roberto Novoa/225 5.00 12.00
230 Sean Henn/250 4.00 10.00
231 Jamie Brown/200 4.00 10.00
232 Nick Regilio/250 4.00 10.00
234 Greg Dobbs/250 4.00 10.00
235 Angel Chavez/250 4.00 10.00
237 Justin Knoedler/225 4.00 10.00
239 Jason Frasor/225 4.00 10.00
240 Jerry Gil/225 4.00 10.00
241 Carlos Hines/225 4.00 10.00
242 Ivan Ochoa/250 4.00 10.00
248 Graham Koonce/250 4.00 10.00
249 Ronald Belisario/225 4.00 10.00

2004 Absolute Memorabilia Absolutely Ink

PRINT RUNS B/WN 1-100 COPIES PER
NO PRICING ON QTY OF 10 OR LESS
*SPECTRUM p/r 25: .75X TO 2Xp/r 100
*SPECTRUM p/r 25: .6X TO 1.5X p/r 50
*SPECTRUM p/r 25: .5X TO 1.2X p/r 25
SPECTRUM PRINTS B/WN 1-25 COPIES PER
NO SPECT.PRICING ON QTY OF 10 OR LESS
AI1 Adam Dunn/100 6.00 15.00
AI2 Al Kaline/100 12.00 30.00
AI3 Alan Trammell/100 10.00 25.00
AI6 Andre Dawson Cubs/100 6.00 15.00
AI7 Andre Dawson Expos/100 6.00 15.00
AI8 Andruw Jones/50 6.00 15.00
AI9 Angel Berroa/50 5.00 12.00
AI10 Aramis Ramirez/50 8.00 20.00
AI11 Aubrey Huff/100 6.00 15.00
AI12 Austin Kearns/100 4.00 10.00
AI13 Barry Larkin/50 15.00 40.00
AI16 Bert Blyleven/100 10.00 25.00
AI17 Billy Williams/100 15.00 40.00
AI19 Bob Feller/100 10.00 25.00
AI20 Bob Gibson/25 20.00 50.00
AI21 Bobby Doerr/100 6.00 15.00
AI22 Brandon Webb/100 10.00 25.00
AI23 Brett Myers/50 8.00 20.00
AI24 Brooks Robinson/100 10.00 25.00
AI27 Carlos Beltran/100 6.00 15.00
AI28 Carlos Lee/100 6.00 15.00
AI31 Craig Biggio/50 8.00 20.00
AI33 Dale Murphy/100 10.00 25.00
AI34 Darryl Strawberry/100 6.00 15.00
AI35 Dave Concepcion/50 8.00 20.00
AI36 Dave Parker/50 8.00 20.00
AI38 Don Mattingly/100 30.00 60.00
AI39 Dontrelle Willis/100 10.00 25.00
AI40 Duke Snider/100 10.00 25.00
AI41 Dwight Gooden/100 6.00 15.00
AI42 Edgar Martinez/50 12.00 30.00
AI43 Eric Chavez/50 8.00 20.00
AI44 Ernie Banks/100 12.00 30.00
AI45 Fergie Jenkins/100 6.00 15.00
AI46 Frank Robinson/100 15.00 40.00
AI47 Frank Thomas/25 40.00 100.00
AI48 Fred Lynn/50 5.00 12.00
AI49 Fred McGriff/25 10.00 25.00
AI50 Garret Anderson/100 5.00 12.00
AI51 Gary Carter Expos/100 12.00 30.00
AI52 Gary Carter Mets/100 12.00 30.00
AI53 Gary Sheffield/50 12.00 30.00
AI54 Gaylord Perry/100 6.00 15.00
AI57 Hank Blalock/100 6.00 15.00
AI58 Harold Baines/50 8.00 20.00
AI62 Jacque Jones/100 6.00 15.00
AI63 Jae Weong Seo/100 6.00 15.00
AI64 Jamie Moyer/25 12.00 30.00
AI65 Jason Varitek/50 20.00 50.00
AI66 Jay Gibbons/50 5.00 12.00
AI67 Jim Edmonds/25 20.00 50.00
AI68 Jim Palmer/100 10.00 25.00
AI69 Jim Rice/50 8.00 20.00
AI71 Johan Santana/50 12.00 30.00
AI72 Jorge Posada/50 10.00 25.00
AI73 Josh Beckett/25 20.00 50.00
AI74 Juan Gonzalez/25 12.00 30.00
AI75 Keith Hernandez/100 6.00 15.00
AI76 Kirby Puckett/25 30.00 80.00
AI77 Luis Tiant/100 6.00 15.00
AI78 Magglio Ordonez/100 6.00 15.00
AI81 Mark Grace/25 10.00 25.00
AI82 Mark Mulder/100 6.00 15.00
AI83 Mark Prior/100 10.00 25.00
AI84 Mark Teixeira/100 10.00 25.00
AI85 Marty Marion/100 6.00 15.00
AI86 Mike Lowell/25 12.00 30.00
AI90 Nolan Ryan/25 30.00 80.00
AI91 Orel Hershiser/100 15.00 40.00
AI92 Orlando Cepeda/100 6.00 15.00
AI97 Phil Niekro/100 6.00 15.00
AI99 Ralph Kiner/100 10.00 25.00
AI101 Red Schoendienst/100 6.00 15.00
AI103 Robin Roberts/50 8.00 20.00
AI104 Robin Ventura/100 6.00 15.00
AI106 Rocco Baldelli/25 12.00 30.00
AI110 Sean Casey/23 12.00 30.00
AI111 Shannon Stewart/50 5.00 12.00
AI113 Stan Musial/100 15.00 40.00
AI114 Steve Carlton/50 8.00 20.00
AI115 Steve Garvey/100 6.00 15.00
AI117 Tommy John/100 6.00 15.00
AI118 Tony Gwynn/25 25.00 60.00
AI119 Tony Oliva/100 6.00 15.00
AI120 Torii Hunter/100 6.00 15.00
AI121 Trot Nixon/50 8.00 20.00
AI122 Troy Glaus/50 12.00 30.00
AI123 Vernon Wells/25 12.00 30.00
AI124 Vladimir Guerrero/100 10.00 25.00
AI125 Will Clark/100 10.00 25.00

2004 Absolute Memorabilia Absolutely Ink Material

PRINT RUNS B/WN 5-100 COPIES PER
NO PRICING ON QTY OF 14 OR LESS
*PRIME p/r 25: .5X TO 1.2X BASIC p/r 25
PRIME PRINT RUNS B/WN 1-25 COPIES PER
NO PRIME PRICING ON QTY OF 5 OR LESS
ADD 20% FOR NOTATED AUTOGRAPHS
AI1 Adam Dunn Jsy/100 6.00 15.00
AI2 Al Kaline Pants/50 30.00 80.00
AI3 Alan Trammell Jsy/100 12.00 30.00
AI6 Andre Dawson Cubs Jsy/100 8.00 20.00
AI7 Andre Dawson Expos Jsy/100 8.00 20.00
AI9 Angel Berroa Jsy/100 6.00 15.00
AI11 Aubrey Huff Jsy/100 8.00 20.00
AI12 Austin Kearns Jsy/100 6.00 15.00
AI16 Bert Blyleven Jsy/100 8.00 20.00
AI17 Billy Williams Jsy/100 12.50 30.00
AI19 Bob Feller Jsy/100 12.50 30.00
AI21 Bobby Doerr Jsy/100 8.00 20.00
AI22 Brandon Webb Jsy/50 15.00 40.00
AI23 Brett Myers Jsy/100 8.00 20.00
AI24 Brooks Robinson Jsy/100 12.00 30.00
AI27 Carlos Beltran Jsy/100 8.00 20.00
AI28 Carlos Lee Jsy/100 8.00 20.00
AI33 Dale Murphy Jsy/100 12.00 30.00
AI34 Darryl Strawberry Jsy/100 8.00 20.00
AI35 Dave Concepcion Jsy/50 15.00 40.00
AI36 Dave Parker Jsy/100 8.00 20.00
AI38 Don Mattingly Jsy/50 50.00 100.00
AI39 Dontrelle Willis Jsy/20 20.00 50.00
AI41 Dwight Gooden Jsy/60 10.00 25.00
AI42 Edgar Martinez Jsy/100 20.00 50.00
AI44 Ernie Banks Jsy/50 30.00 60.00
AI45 Fergie Jenkins Pants/100 8.00 20.00
AI46 Frank Robinson Jsy/50 15.00 40.00
AI48 Fred Lynn Jsy/100 6.00 15.00
AI49 Fred McGriff Jsy/20 12.00 30.00
AI50 Garret Anderson Jsy/100 8.00 20.00
AI51 Gary Carter Expos Jsy/100 12.00 30.00
AI52 Gary Carter Mets Jacket/100 12.00 30.00
AI53 Gary Sheffield Jsy/100 8.00 20.00
AI54 Gaylord Perry Jsy/100 8.00 20.00
AI57 Hank Blalock Jsy/100 8.00 20.00
AI58 Harold Baines Jsy/100 8.00 20.00
AI63 Jae Weong Seo Jsy/100 6.00 15.00
AI64 Jamie Moyer Jsy/100 8.00 20.00

AI65 Jason Varitek Jsy/100 20.00 50.00
AI66 Jay Gibbons Jsy/100 6.00 15.00
AI68 Jim Palmer Jsy/100 12.00 30.00
AI69 Jim Rice Jsy/100 8.00 20.00
AI70 Joe Carter Jsy/50 10.00 25.00
AI71 Johan Santana Jsy/100 12.00 30.00
AI72 Jorge Posada Jsy/15 75.00 150.00
AI75 Keith Hernandez Jsy/100 8.00 20.00
AI77 Luis Tiant Jsy/100 8.00 20.00
AI82 Mark Mulder Jsy/20 12.00 30.00
AI85 Marty Marion Jsy/100 8.00 20.00
AI86 Mike Lowell Jsy/60 10.00 25.00
AI92 Orlando Cepeda Bat/65 10.00 25.00
AI97 Phil Niekro Jsy/25 12.00 30.00
AI99 Ralph Kiner Bat/100 12.00 30.00
AI101 Red Schoendienst Jsy/60 10.00 25.00
AI103 Robin Roberts Hat/50 10.00 25.00
AI104 Robin Ventura Jsy/65 15.00 40.00
AI110 Sean Casey Jsy/75 8.00 20.00
AI111 Shannon Stewart Jsy/100 6.00 15.00
AI114 Steve Carlton Jsy/50 10.00 25.00
AI115 Steve Garvey Bat/100 12.00 30.00
AI117 Tommy John Jsy/100 8.00 20.00
AI119 Tony Oliva Jsy/100 8.00 20.00
AI120 Torii Hunter Jsy/50 10.00 25.00
AI121 Trot Nixon Jsy/100 8.00 20.00
AI124 Vladimir Guerrero Jsy/55 12.00 30.00
AI125 Will Clark Jsy/100 12.00 30.00

2004 Absolute Memorabilia Absolutely Ink Combo Material

*COMBO p/r 100: .5X TO 1.2X p/r 100
*COMBO p/r 50-65: .6X TO 1.5X p/r 75-100
*COMBO p/r 50-65: .5X TO 1.2X p/r 50-65
*COMBO p/r 25: .75X TO 2X p/r 100
PRINT RUNS B/WN 1-100 COPIES PER
NO PRICING ON QTY OF 10 OR LESS
PRIME PRINT RUNS B/WN 1-5 COPIES PER
NO PRIME PRICING DUE TO SCARCITY
RANDOM INSERTS IN PACKS
AI43 E.Chavez Bat-Jsy/15 15.00 40.00
AI74 J.Gonzalez Bat-Jsy/15 15.00 40.00

2004 Absolute Memorabilia Fans of the Game

RANDOM INSERTS IN RETAIL PACKS
251FG1 Landon Donovan 3.00 8.00
252FG2 Jennie Finch 2.00 5.00
253FG3 Bonnie Blair .75 2.00
254FG4 Dan Jansen .75 2.00
255FG5 Kerri Strug 1.25 3.00

2004 Absolute Memorabilia Fans of the Game Autographs

RANDOM INSERTS IN RETAIL PACKS
SP PRINT RUNS PROVIDED BY DONRUSS
SP'S ARE NOT SERIAL-NUMBERED
251FG1 Landon Donovan 30.00 60.00
252FG2 Jennie Finch 20.00 50.00
253FG3 Bonnie Blair SP/250 15.00 40.00
254FG4 Dan Jansen SP/250 6.00 15.00
255FG5 Kerri Strug SP/250 12.00 30.00

2004 Absolute Memorabilia Marks of Fame

STATED PRINT RUN 100 SERIAL #'d SETS
*SPECTRUM: .75X TO 2X BASIC
SPECTRUM PRINT RUN 25 SERIAL #'d SETS
RANDOM INSERTS IN PACKS
MOF1 Nolan Ryan 5.00 12.00
MOF2 Ernie Banks 1.50 4.00
MOF3 Bob Feller 1.00 2.50
MOF4 Duke Snider 1.00 2.50
MOF5 Sammy Sosa 1.50 4.00
MOF6 Whitey Ford 1.00 2.50
MOF7 Steve Carlton 1.00 2.50
MOF8 Tony Gwynn 1.50 4.00
MOF9 Jim Bunning 1.00 2.50
MOF10 Stan Musial 2.50 6.00
MOF11 Cal Ripken 5.00 12.00
MOF12 George Brett 3.00 8.00
MOF13 Gary Carter 1.00 2.50
MOF14 Jim Palmer 1.00 2.50
MOF15 Gaylord Perry 1.00 2.50

2004 Absolute Memorabilia Marks of Fame Signature

PRINT RUNS B/WN 10-100 COPIES PER
NO PRICING ON QTY OF 10 OR LESS
*SPECTRUM p/r 25: .6X TO 1.5X p/r 100
*SPECTRUM p/r 25: .5X TO 1.2X p/r 50
SPECTRUM PRINTS B/WN 1-25 COPIES PER
NO SPECT.PRICING ON QTY OF 10 OR LESS
RANDOM INSERTS IN PACKS
MOF1 Nolan Ryan/50 50.00 120.00
MOF2 Ernie Banks/50 20.00 50.00
MOF3 Bob Feller/100 10.00 25.00
MOF4 Duke Snider/100 10.00 25.00
MOF5 Sammy Sosa/21 50.00 100.00
MOF6 Whitey Ford/25 20.00 50.00
MOF7 Steve Carlton/100 6.00 15.00
MOF8 Tony Gwynn/25 40.00 80.00
MOF9 Jim Bunning/100 10.00 25.00
MOF10 Stan Musial/50 40.00 80.00
MOF12 George Brett/25 60.00 120.00
MOF13 Gary Carter/100 12.50 30.00
MOF14 Jim Palmer/50 8.00 20.00
MOF15 Gaylord Perry/100 6.00 15.00

2004 Absolute Memorabilia Signature Club

RANDOM INSERTS IN PACKS
PRINT RUNS B/WN 5-50 COPIES PER
NO PRICING ON QTY OF 5 OR LESS
2 Gary Sheffield Bat/50 8.00 20.00
4 Will Clark Bat/50 15.00 40.00
5 Ernie Banks Bat/50 30.00 60.00

2004 Absolute Memorabilia Signature Material

PRINT RUNS B/WN 25-50 COPIES PER
PRIME PRINT RUN 5 SERIAL #'d SETS
NO PRIME PRICING DUE TO SCARCITY
*COMBO: .5X TO 1.2X BASIC
COMBO PRINT RUNS B/WN 25-50 COPIES PER
COMBO PRIME PRINT 5 SERIAL #'d SETS
NO COMBO PRIME PRICE DUE SCARCITY
RANDOM INSERTS IN PACKS
2 Gary Carter Jsy/50 10.00 25.00
3 Dale Murphy Jsy/50 10.00 25.00
4 Don Mattingly Jsy/25 60.00 120.00
5 Stan Musial Jsy/25 60.00 120.00

2004 Absolute Memorabilia Team Quad

STATED PRINT RUN 100 SERIAL #'d SETS
*SPECTRUM: 1X TO 2.5X BASIC
SPECTRUM PRINT RUN 25 SERIAL #'d SETS
RANDOM INSERTS IN PACKS
TQ1 Biggio 1.00 2.50
Berk
Kent
Bagwell
TQ2 Nomar 1.50 4.00
Manny
Pedro
Nixon
TQ3 Koner 1.50 4.00
Lee
Maggilo
Thomas
TQ4 Smoltz 1.50 4.00
Chip
Andruw
Furcal
TQ5 Garret .60 1.50
Perc
Glaus
Erstad
TQ6 Finley 1.50 4.00
Webb
Randy
L.Gonz
TQ7 Lo Duca 1.50 4.00
Nomo
Green
Ishii
TQ8 Walker 1.00 2.50
Helton
Jen
Wilson
TQ9 Burn .60 1.50
Willis
Penny
Beckett
TQ10 Reyes 1.50 4.00
Seo
Glavine
Piazza
TQ11 Bernie 4.00 10.00
Jeter
Giambi
Soriano
TQ12 Harden 1.00 2.50
Hudson
Zito
Mulder
TQ13 Millwood 1.00 2.50
Byrd
Thome
Abreu
TQ14 Rent 2.00 5.00
Edmonds
Pujols
Rolen
TQ15 Clemens 2.00 5.00
Pett
Miller
Oswalt

2004 Absolute Memorabilia Team Quad Material

STATED PRINT RUN 100 SERIAL #'d SETS
PRIME PRINT RUN 5 SERIAL #'d SETS
NO PRIME PRICING DUE TO SCARCITY
RANDOM INSERTS IN PACKS
ALL HAVE 4 JSY SWATCHES UNLESS NOTED
CARD 15 IS BAT-BAT-JSY-JSY
TQ1 Kent/Berk/Biggio/Bagwell 10.00 25.00
TQ2 Nomar/Manny/Pedro/Nixon 15.00 40.00
TQ3 Koner/Lee/Maggilo/Thomas 10.00 25.00
TQ4 Smoltz/Chip/Andruw/Furcal 10.00 25.00
TQ5 Garret/Perc/Glaus/Erstad 6.00 15.00
TQ6 Finley/Webb/Randy/L.Gonz 10.00 25.00
TQ7 Lo Duca/Nomo/Green/Ishii 10.00 25.00
TQ8 Walker/Helton/Jen/Wilson 10.00 25.00
TQ9 Burn/Willis/Penny/Beckett 10.00 25.00
TQ10 Reyes/Seo/Glavine/Piazza 10.00 25.00
TQ11 Bernie/Jeter/Giambi/Soriano 15.00 40.00
TQ12 Harden/Hudson/Zito/Mulder 6.00 15.00
TQ13 Millwood/Byrd/Thome/Abreu 10.00 25.00
TQ14 Rent/Edmonds/Pujols/Rolen 15.00 40.00
TQ15 Clemens/Pett/Miller/Oswalt 15.00 40.00

2004 Absolute Memorabilia Team Tandem

STATED PRINT RUN 250 SERIAL #'d SETS
*SPECTRUM: 2X TO 5X BASIC
SPECTRUM PRINT RUN 25 SERIAL #'d SETS
RANDOM INSERTS IN PACKS
TAN1 V.Guerrero 1.00 2.50
R.Jackson
TAN2 D.Murphy 1.50 4.00
C.Jones
TAN3 G.Carter 1.50 4.00
M.Piazza
TAN4 M.Tejada 5.00 12.00
C.Ripken
TAN5 G.Sheffield 4.00 10.00
D.Jeter
TAN6 C.Schilling 1.00 2.50
P.Martinez
TAN7 R.Clemens 2.00 5.00
A.Pettitte
TAN8 M.Sweeney 3.00 8.00
G.Brett
TAN9 K.Ishii 1.50 4.00
H.Nomo
TAN10 A.Kearns 1.00 2.50
A.Dunn
TAN11 M.Cabrera 1.50 4.00
D.Willis
TAN12 D.Mattingly 4.00 10.00
D.Jeter
TAN13 B.Zito 1.00 2.50
E.Chavez
TAN14 J.Thome 2.50 6.00
M.Schmidt
TAN15 A.Pujols 2.50 6.00
S.Musial
TAN16 N.Ryan 5.00 12.00
A.Rodriguez
TAN17 K.Wood 1.00 2.50
M.Prior
TAN18 R.Palmeiro 1.00 2.50
J.Gibbons
TAN19 N.Garciaparra 1.50 4.00
M.Ramirez
TAN20 I.Rodriguez 1.50 4.00
M.Piazza

2004 Absolute Memorabilia Team Tandem Material

STATED PRINT RUN 250 SERIAL #'d SETS
PRIME PRINT RUN 5 SERIAL #'d SETS
NO PRIME PRICING DUE TO SCARCITY
RANDOM INSERTS IN PACKS
TAN1 Reggie Bat/Guerrero Bat 4.00 10.00
TAN2 C.Jones Jsy/D.Murphy Jsy 4.00 10.00
TAN3 G.Carter Jsy/M.Piazza Jsy 4.00 10.00
TAN4 M.Tejada Bat/C.Ripken Bat 10.00 25.00
TAN5 D.Jeter Bat/G.Sheffield Bat 10.00 25.00
TAN6 C.Schilling Bat/Pedro Bat 4.00 10.00
TAN7 Clemens Bat/Pettitte Bat 6.00 15.00
TAN8 M.Sweeney Jsy/G.Brett Jsy 6.00 15.00
TAN9 K.Ishii Jsy/H.Nomo Jsy 4.00 10.00
TAN10 A.Kearns Jsy/A.Dunn Jsy 3.00 8.00
TAN11 D.Willis Jsy/M.Cabrera Jsy 4.00 10.00
TAN12 D.Mattingly Jsy/D.Jeter Jsy 15.00 40.00
TAN13 B.Zito Jsy/E.Chavez Jsy 3.00 8.00
TAN14 J.Thome Jsy/M.Schmidt Jsy 8.00 20.00
TAN15 A.Pujols Jsy/S.Musial Jsy 10.00 25.00
TAN16 N.Ryan Jsy/A.Rod Jsy 10.00 25.00
TAN17 M.Prior Jsy/K.Wood Jsy 6.00 15.00
TAN18 Palmeiro Jsy/Gibbons Jsy 4.00 10.00
TAN19 Nomar Jsy/M.Ramirez Jsy 6.00 15.00
TAN20 I.Rod Jsy/M.Piazza Jsy 4.00 10.00

2004 Absolute Memorabilia Team Trio

STATED PRINT RUN 100 SERIAL #'d SETS
*SPECTRUM: 1X TO 2.5X BASIC
SPECTRUM PRINT RUN 25 SERIAL #'d SETS
RANDOM INSERTS IN PACKS
TTR1 Sosa 1.50 4.00
Wood
Prior
TTR2 Blalock 2.00 5.00
Teixeira
A.Rod
TTR3 Wells 1.00 2.50
Halladay
Delgado
TTR4 Mussina 2.00 5.00
Posada
Rivera
TTR5 Stewart .60 1.50
Torii
Jacque
TTR6 Beltran 1.00 2.50
Sweeney
Berroa
TTR7 Willis 1.50 4.00
Cabrera
Beckett
TTR8 Bagwell 1.00 2.50
Biggio
Berkman
TTR9 Nomar 1.50 4.00
Pedro
Manny
TTR10 Green 1.50 4.00
Ishii
Nomo
TTR11 Mulder 1.00 2.50
Zito
Hudson
TTR12 Edmonds 2.00 5.00
Rolen
Pujols
TTR13 Ripken 5.00 12.00
Gibbons
Palmeiro
TTR14 Sosa 3.00 8.00
Grace
Sandberg
TTR15 Ryan 5.00 12.00
Clemens
Randy

2004 Absolute Memorabilia Team Trio Material

STATED PRINT RUN 100 SERIAL #'d SETS
CARD 15 PRINT RUN 25 SERIAL #'d CARDS
PRIME PRINT RUN 5 SERIAL #'d SETS
NO PRIME PRICING DUE TO SCARCITY
RANDOM INSERTS IN PACKS
ALL HAVE 3 JSY SWATCHES UNLESS NOTED
CARD 15 HAS FIELD GLOVE SWATCHES
TTR1 Sosa/Wood/Prior 6.00 15.00
TTR2 Blalock/Teixeira/A.Rod 6.00 15.00
TTR3 Wells/Halladay/Delgado 4.00 10.00
TTR4 Mussina/Posada/Rivera 12.50 30.00
TTR5 Stewart/Torii/Jacque 4.00 10.00
TTR6 Beltran/Sweeney/Berroa 4.00 10.00
TTR7 Willis/Cabrera/Beckett 6.00 15.00
TTR8 Bagwell/Biggio/Berkman 10.00 25.00
TTR9 Nomar/Pedro/Manny 10.00 25.00
TTR10 Green/Ishii/Nomo 6.00 15.00
TTR11 Mulder/Zito/Hudson 4.00 10.00
TTR12 Edmonds/Rolen/Pujols 10.00 25.00
TTR13 Ripken/Gibbons/Palmeiro 20.00 50.00
TTR14 Sosa/Grace/Sandberg 6.00 15.00
TTR15 Ryan/Clemens/Randy/25 15.00 40.00

2004 Absolute Memorabilia Tools of the Trade Blue

STATED PRINT RUN 250 SERIAL #'d SETS
BLACK PRINT RUN 1 SERIAL #'d SET
NO BLACK PRICING DUE TO SCARCITY
BLACK SPECTRUM PRINT RUN 1 #'d SET
NO BLACK SPEC.PRICING DUE SCARCITY
*BLUE SPEC: .75X TO 2X BASIC
BLUE SPECTRUM PRINT RUN 125 #'d SETS
*GREEN: .6X TO 1.5X BASIC
GREEN PRINT RUN 150 SERIAL #'d SETS
*GREEN SPEC: 1.5X TO 4X BASIC
GREEN SPECTRUM PRINT RUN 50 #'d SETS
*RED: .5X TO 1.2X BASIC
RED PRINT RUN 200 SERIAL #'d SETS
*RED SPECTRUM: 1X TO 2.5X BASIC
RED SPECTRUM PRINT RUN 100 #'d SETS
TT1 Adam Dunn H .75 2.00
TT2 Adam Dunn A .75 2.00
TT3 Alan Trammell .75 2.00
TT4 Albert Pujols H 1.50 4.00
TT5 Albert Pujols A 1.50 4.00
TT6 Alex Rodriguez M's 1.50 4.00
TT7 Alex Rodriguez Rgr H 1.50 4.00
TT8 Alex Rodriguez Rgr Alt 1.50 4.00
TT9 Alfonso Soriano .75 2.00
TT10 Andre Dawson .75 2.00
TT11 Andruw Jones H .50 1.25
TT12 Andruw Jones A .50 1.25
TT13 Andy Pettitte H .75 2.00
TT14 Andy Pettitte A .75 2.00
TT15 Angel Berroa .50 1.25
TT16 Aubrey Huff .50 1.25
TT17 Austin Kearns .50 1.25
TT18 Barry Zito Alt .75 2.00
TT19 Barry Zito A .75 2.00
TT20 Bernie Williams .75 2.00
TT21 Bobby Abreu .50 1.25
TT22 Brandon Webb .50 1.25
TT23 Cal Ripken H 4.00 10.00
TT24 Cal Ripken A 4.00 10.00
TT25 Cal Ripken Alt 4.00 10.00
TT26 Carlos Beltran .75 2.00
TT27 Carlos Delgado H .50 1.25
TT28 Carlos Delgado A .50 1.25
TT29 Carlos Lee .50 1.25
TT30 Chipper Jones H 1.25 3.00
TT31 Chipper Jones A 1.25 3.00
TT32 Craig Biggio H .75 2.00
TT33 Craig Biggio A .75 2.00
TT34 Curt Schilling D'backs .75 2.00
TT35 Curt Schilling Phils .75 2.00
TT36 Dale Murphy H 1.25 3.00
TT37 Dale Murphy A 1.25 3.00
TT38 Darryl Strawberry .50 1.25
TT39 Derek Jeter H 3.00 8.00
TT40 Derek Jeter A 3.00 8.00
TT41 Don Mattingly H 2.50 6.00
TT42 Don Mattingly A 2.50 6.00
TT43 Dontrelle Willis H .50 1.25
TT44 Dontrelle Willis A .50 1.25
TT45 Dwight Gooden .50 1.25
TT46 Edgar Martinez .75 2.00
TT47 Eric Chavez .50 1.25
TT48 Frank Thomas A 1.25 3.00
TT49 Frank Thomas Alt 1.25 3.00
TT50 Garret Anderson .50 1.25
TT51 Gary Carter .75 2.00
TT52 Gary Sheffield .50 1.25
TT53 George Brett H 2.50 6.00
TT54 George Brett A 2.50 6.00
TT55 Greg Maddux 1.50 4.00
TT56 Hank Blalock .50 1.25
TT57 Hideo Nomo 1.25 3.00
TT58 Ivan Rodriguez Marlins .75 2.00
TT59 Ivan Rodriguez Rgr .75 2.00
TT60 Jacque Jones .50 1.25
TT61 Jae Weong Seo .50 1.25
TT62 Jason Giambi Yanks .50 1.25
TT63 Jason Giambi A's .50 1.25
TT64 Javy Lopez .50 1.25
TT65 Jay Gibbons .50 1.25
TT66 Jeff Bagwell A .75 2.00
TT67 Jeff Bagwell Alt .75 2.00
TT68 Jeff Kent .50 1.25
TT69 Jim Edmonds .75 2.00
TT70 Jim Thome .75 2.00
TT71 Jorge Posada .75 2.00
TT72 Jose Canseco .75 2.00
TT73 Jose Reyes .50 1.25
TT74 Josh Beckett .50 1.25
TT75 Juan Gonzalez .50 1.25
TT76 Kazuhisa Ishii .50 1.25
TT77 Kerry Wood H .50 1.25
TT78 Kerry Wood Alt .50 1.25
TT79 Kirby Puckett 1.25 3.00
TT80 Lance Berkman .75 2.00
TT81 Lou Brock .75 2.00
TT82 Luis Castillo .50 1.25
TT83 Luis Gonzalez .50 1.25
TT84 Magglio Ordonez .50 1.25
TT85 Manny Ramirez Sox 1.25 3.00
TT86 Manny Ramirez Indians 1.25 3.00
TT87 Marcus Giles .50 1.25
TT88 Mark Grace .75 2.00
TT89 Mark Mulder .50 1.25
TT90 Mark Prior H .75 2.00
TT91 Mark Prior A .75 2.00
TT92 Mark Teixeira .75 2.00
TT93 Marlon Byrd .50 1.25
TT94 Miguel Cabrera 1.25 3.00
TT95 Miguel Tejada .75 2.00
TT96 Mike Lowell .50 1.25
TT97 Mike Mussina O's .75 2.00
TT98 Mike Mussina Yanks .75 2.00
TT99 Mike Piazza Marlins 1.25 3.00
TT100 Mike Piazza Dodgers 1.25 3.00
TT101 Mike Piazza Mets 1.25 3.00
TT102 Mike Schmidt H 2.00 5.00
TT103 Mike Schmidt A 2.00 5.00
TT104 Mike Sweeney .50 1.25
TT105 Nick Johnson .50 1.25
TT106 Nolan Ryan Angels 4.00 10.00
TT107 Nolan Ryan Astros 4.00 10.00
TT108 Nolan Ryan Rangers 4.00 10.00
TT109 Nomar Garciaparra H .75 2.00
TT110 Nomar Garciaparra A .75 2.00
TT111 Pat Burrell .50 1.25
TT112 Paul Lo Duca .50 1.25
TT113 Pedro Martinez Sox .75 2.00
TT114 Pedro Martinez Expos .75 2.00
TT115 Preston Wilson .50 1.25
TT116 Rafael Palmeiro O's .75 2.00
TT117 Rafael Palmeiro Rgr .75 2.00
TT118 Randy Johnson D'backs 1.25 3.00
TT119 Randy Johnson M's 1.25 3.00
TT120 Richie Sexson .50 1.25
TT121 Rickey Henderson A's 1.25 3.00
TT122 Rickey Henderson Padres 1.25 3.00
TT123 Rickey Henderson M's 1.25 3.00
TT124 Roberto Alomar .75 2.00
TT125 Rocco Baldelli .50 1.25
TT126 Rod Carew .75 2.00
TT127 Roger Clemens Sox 1.50 4.00
TT128 Roger Clemens Yanks 1.50 4.00
TT129 Roy Halladay .75 2.00
TT130 Roy Oswalt .75 2.00
TT131 Ryne Sandberg 2.50 6.00
TT132 Sammy Sosa H 1.25 3.00
TT133 Sammy Sosa A 1.25 3.00
TT134 Sammy Sosa Sox 1.25 3.00
TT135 Scott Rolen .75 2.00
TT136 Shawn Green .50 1.25
TT137 Steve Carlton .75 2.00
TT138 Tim Hudson .75 2.00
TT139 Todd Helton H .75 2.00
TT140 Todd Helton A .75 2.00
TT141 Tom Glavine Braves .75 2.00
TT142 Tom Glavine Mets .75 2.00
TT142 Will Clark .75 2.00
TT143 Tony Gwynn A 1.25 3.00
TT144 Tony Gwynn Alt 1.25 3.00
TT146 Torii Hunter .50 1.25
TT146 Trot Nixon .50 1.25
TT147 Troy Glaus .50 1.25
TT148 Vernon Wells .50 1.25
TT149 Vladimir Guerrero .75 2.00

2004 Absolute Memorabilia Tools of the Trade Signature Blue Spectrum

PRINT RUNS B/WN 1-100 COPIES PER
NO PRICING ON QTY OF 10 OR LESS
BLACK PRINT RUN 1 SERIAL #'d SET
NO BLACK PRICING DUE TO SCARCITY
GREEN PRINT RUN B/WN 1-10 COPIES PER
NO GREEN PRICING DUE TO SCARCITY
*RED p/r 50: .5X TO 1.2X BLUE p/r 100
*RED p/r 25: .6X TO 1.5X BLUE p/r 100
*RED p/r 23-25: .5X TO 1.2X BLUE p/r 50
*RED p/r 25: .4X TO 1X BLUE p/r 25
RED PRINT RUNS B/WN 1-50 COPIES PER
NO RED PRICING ON QTY OF 11 OR LESS
TT3 Alan Trammell/100 6.00 15.00
TT10 Andre Dawson/100 6.00 15.00
TT15 Angel Berroa/100 4.00 10.00
TT16 Aubrey Huff/100 6.00 15.00
TT17 Austin Kearns/100 4.00 10.00
TT22 Brandon Webb/100 4.00 10.00
TT26 Carlos Beltran/100 6.00 15.00
TT29 Carlos Lee/100 6.00 15.00
TT36 Dale Murphy H/50 15.00 40.00
TT37 Dale Murphy A/50 15.00 40.00
TT38 Darryl Strawberry/50 10.00 25.00
TT41 Don Mattingly H/50 30.00 60.00
TT42 Don Mattingly A/50 40.00 80.00
TT43 Dontrelle Willis H/25 20.00 50.00
TT44 Dontrelle Willis A/25 20.00 50.00
TT45 Dwight Gooden/50 10.00 25.00
TT46 Edgar Martinez/25 20.00 50.00
TT48 Frank Thomas A/25 30.00 60.00
TT49 Frank Thomas Alt/25 30.00 60.00
TT50 Garret Anderson/100 6.00 15.00
TT51 Gary Carter/100 10.00 25.00
TT60 Jacque Jones/50 10.00 25.00
TT61 Jae Weong Seo/25 12.50 30.00
TT65 Jay Gibbons/50 6.00 15.00
TT69 Jim Edmonds/25 20.00 50.00
TT71 Jorge Posada/25 75.00 150.00
TT73 Jose Reyes/25 12.50 30.00
TT75 Juan Gonzalez/20 12.50 30.00
TT77 Kerry Wood H/25 20.00 50.00
TT78 Kerry Wood Alt/25 20.00 50.00
TT81 Lou Brock/100 10.00 25.00
TT84 Magglio Ordonez/50 10.00 25.00
TT87 Marcus Giles/50 10.00 25.00
TT88 Mark Grace/25 20.00 50.00
TT89 Mark Mulder/100 6.00 15.00
TT90 Mark Prior H/50 12.50 30.00
TT91 Mark Prior A/50 12.50 30.00
TT92 Mark Teixeira/50 15.00 40.00
TT93 Marlon Byrd/50 6.00 15.00
TT94 Miguel Cabrera/100 30.00 60.00
TT102 Mike Schmidt H/25 50.00 100.00
TT103 Mike Schmidt A/25 30.00 60.00
TT106 Nolan Ryan Angels/25 40.00 80.00
TT107 Nolan Ryan Astros/25 40.00 80.00
TT108 Nolan Ryan Rangers/25 40.00 80.00
TT112 Paul Lo Duca/50 10.00 25.00
TT115 Preston Wilson/100 6.00 15.00
TT129 Roy Halladay/25 12.50 30.00
TT130 Roy Oswalt/25 12.50 30.00
TT135 Scott Rolen/50 15.00 40.00
TT137 Steve Carlton/50 10.00 25.00
TT143 Tony Gwynn A/25 40.00 80.00
TT144 Tony Gwynn Alt/25 40.00 80.00
TT145 Torii Hunter/50 10.00 25.00
TT146 Trot Nixon/25 12.50 30.00
TT149 Vladimir Guerrero/25 30.00 60.00
TT150 Will Clark/50 30.00 60.00

2004 Absolute Memorabilia Tools of the Trade Material Combo

PRINT RUNS B/WN 25-250 COPIES PER
SINGLE PRINT RUNS B/WN 1-5 COPIES PER
NO SINGLE PRICING DUE TO SCARCITY
SINGLE PS PRINT RUN 1 SERIAL #'d SET
NO SINGLE PS PRICING DUE TO SCARCITY
*COMBO PS p/r 25: 1.5X TO 4X COM.p/r 250
*COMBO PS p/r 25: 1X TO 2.5X COM.p/r 100
COMBO PS PRINT RUNS B/WN 1-25 PER
NO COMBO PS PRICING ON 10 OR LESS
*TRIO p/r 100: .6X TO 1.5X COMBO p/r 250
*TRIO p/r 100: .5X TO 1.2X COMBO p/r 100
*TRIO p/r 50: 1X TO 2.5X COMBO p/r 250
*TRIO p/r 50: .6X TO 1.5X COMBO p/r 100
*TRIO p/r 25: 1.5X TO 4X COMBO p/r 250
*TRIO p/r 25: .75X TO 2X COMBO p/r 100
TRIO PRINT RUNS B/WN 5-100 COPIES PER
NO TRIO PRICING ON QTY OF 10 OR LESS
TRIO PS PRINT RUNS B/WN 1-10 PER
NO TRIO PS PRICING DUE TO SCARCITY
*QUAD p/r 50: 1.5X TO 4X COMBO p/r 250
*QUAD p/r 50: 1.25X TO 3X COMBO p/r 100
*QUAD p/r 50: .6X TO 1.5X COMBO p/r 25
*QUAD p/r 25: 2X TO 5X COMBO p/r 250
*QUAD p/r 25: 1X TO 2.5X COMBO p/r 100
QUAD PRINT RUNS B/WN 1-50 COPIES PER
NO QUAD PRICING ON QTY OF 10 OR LESS
QUAD PS PRINT RUNS B/WN 1-10 PER
NO QUAD PS PRICING DUE TO SCARCITY
*FIVE p/r 25: 2.5X TO 6X COMBO p/r 250
*FIVE p/r 25: 2X TO 5X COMBO p/r 100
*FIVE p/r 25: .75X TO 2X COMBO p/r 25
FIVE PRINT RUNS B/WN 10-25 COPIES PER
NO FIVE PRICING ON QTY OF 10 OR LESS
FIVE PS PRINT RUNS B/WN 1-5 COPIES PER
NO FIVE PS PRICING DUE TO SCARCITY
*SIX p/r 25: 3X TO 8X COMBO p/r 250
*SIX p/r 25: 2.5X TO 6X COMBO p/r 100
SIX PRINT RUNS B/WN 5-25 COPIES PER
NO SIX PRICING ON QTY OF 5 OR LESS
SIX PS PRINT RUNS B/WN 1-5 COPIES PER
NO SIX PS PRICING DUE TO SCARCITY
TT1 A.Dunn H Bat-Jsy/250 2.50 6.00
TT2 A.Dunn A Bat-Jsy/250 2.50 6.00
TT3 A.Trammell Bat-Jsy/250 2.50 6.00
TT4 A.Pujols H Bat-Jsy/250 8.00 20.00
TT5 A.Pujols A Bat-Jsy/250 8.00 20.00
TT6 A.Rod M's Bat-Jsy/250 4.00 10.00
TT7 A.Rod Rgr H Bat-Jsy/250 4.00 10.00
TT8 A.Rod Rgr Alt Bat-Jsy/250 4.00 10.00
TT9 A.Soriano Bat-Jsy/100 3.00 8.00
TT10 A.Dawson Bat-Jsy/250 2.50 6.00
TT11 A.Jones H Bat-Jsy/100 4.00 10.00
TT12 A.Jones A Bat-Jsy/250 3.00 8.00
TT13 A.Pettitte H Bat-Jsy/100 4.00 10.00
TT14 A.Pettitte A Bat-Jsy/100 4.00 10.00
TT15 A.Berroa Bat-Jsy/250 2.00 5.00
TT16 A.Huff Bat-Jsy/250 2.50 6.00
TT17 A.Kearns Bat-Jsy/250 2.00 5.00
TT18 B.Zito Alt Bat-Jsy/250 2.50 6.00
TT19 B.Zito A Bat-Jsy/250 2.50 6.00
TT20 B.Williams Bat-Jsy/250 3.00 8.00
TT21 B.Abreu Bat-Jsy/250 2.50 6.00
TT22 B.Webb Bat-Jsy/250 2.00 5.00
TT23 C.Ripken H Bat-Jsy/250 12.50 30.00
TT24 C.Ripken A Bat-Jsy/250 12.50 30.00
TT25 C.Ripken Alt Bat-Jsy/250 12.50 30.00
TT26 C.Beltran Bat-Jsy/250 2.50 6.00
TT27 C.Delgado H Bat-Jsy/250 2.50 6.00
TT28 C.Delgado A Bat-Jsy/250 2.50 6.00
TT29 C.Lee Bat-Jsy/250 2.50 6.00
TT30 C.Jones H Bat-Jsy/250 4.00 10.00
TT31 C.Jones A Bat-Jsy/250 4.00 10.00
TT32 C.Biggio H Bat-Jsy/250 2.50 6.00
TT33 C.Biggio A Bat-Jsy/100 3.00 8.00
TT34 C.Schill D'backs Bat-Jsy/250 2.50 6.00
TT35 C.Schill Phils Bat-Jsy/250 2.50 6.00
TT36 D.Murphy H Bat-Jsy/250 3.00 8.00
TT37 D.Murphy A Bat-Jsy/100 4.00 10.00
TT38 D.Strawberry Bat-Jsy/250 2.50 6.00
TT39 D.Jeter H Bat-Jsy/100 15.00 40.00
TT40 D.Jeter A Bat-Jsy/100 15.00 40.00
TT41 D.Mattingly H Bat-Jsy/100 10.00 25.00
TT42 D.Mattingly A Bat-Jsy/100 10.00 25.00
TT43 D.Willis H Bat-Jsy/250 3.00 8.00
TT44 D.Willis A Bat-Jsy/250 3.00 8.00
TT45 D.Gooden Bat-Jsy/250 2.50 6.00
TT46 E.Martinez Bat-Jsy/250 3.00 8.00
TT47 E.Chavez Bat-Jsy/250 2.50 6.00
TT48 F.Thomas A Bat-Jsy/250 4.00 10.00
TT49 F.Thomas Alt Bat-Jsy/250 4.00 10.00
TT50 G.Anderson Bat-Jsy/250 2.50 6.00
TT51 G.Carter Bat-Jsy/250 2.50 6.00
TT52 G.Sheffield Bat-Jsy/250 2.50 6.00
TT53 G.Brett H Bat-Jsy/250 8.00 20.00
TT54 G.Brett A Bat-Jsy/250 8.00 20.00
TT55 G.Maddux Bat-Jsy/250 5.00 12.00
TT56 H.Blalock Bat-Jsy/250 2.50 6.00
TT57 H.Nomo Bat-Jsy/250 5.00 12.00
TT58 I.Rod Marlins Bat-Jsy/250 3.00 8.00
TT59 I.Rod Rgr Bat-Jsy/250 3.00 8.00
TT60 J.Jones Bat-Jsy/250 2.50 6.00
TT62 J.Giambi Yanks Bat-Jsy/250 2.50 6.00
TT63 J.Giambi A's Bat-Jsy/250 2.50 6.00
TT64 J.Lopez Bat-Jsy/250 2.50 6.00
TT65 J.Gibbons Bat-Jsy/250 2.00 5.00
TT66 J.Bagwell A Bat-Jsy/250 3.00 8.00
TT67 J.Bagwell Alt Bat-Jsy/250 3.00 8.00
TT68 J.Kent Bat-Jsy/250 2.50 6.00
TT69 J.Edmonds Bat-Jsy/250 3.00 8.00
TT70 J.Thome Bat-Jsy/250 3.00 8.00
TT71 J.Posada Bat-Jsy/250 3.00 8.00
TT72 J.Canseco Bat-Jsy/250 3.00 8.00
TT73 J.Reyes Bat-Jsy/250 2.50 6.00
TT74 J.Beckett Bat-Jsy/250 2.50 6.00
TT75 J.Gonzalez Bat-Jsy/250 2.50 6.00
TT76 K.Ishii Bat-Jsy/250 2.50 6.00
TT77 K.Wood H Bat-Jsy/250 2.50 6.00
TT78 K.Wood Alt Bat-Jsy/250 2.50 6.00
TT79 K.Puckett Bat-Jsy/250 6.00 15.00
TT80 L.Berkman Bat-Jsy/250 2.50 6.00
TT81 L.Brock Bat-Jsy/250 2.50 6.00
TT82 L.Castillo Bat-Jsy/25 2.00 5.00
TT83 L.Gonzalez Bat-Jsy/250 2.50 6.00
TT84 M.Ordonez Bat-Jsy/250 2.50 6.00
TT85 M.Ramirez Sox Bat-Jsy/250 3.00 8.00
TT86 M.Ram Indians Bat-Jsy/250 3.00 8.00
TT87 M.Giles Bat-Jsy/25 6.00 15.00
TT88 M.Grace Bat-Jsy/250 3.00 8.00
TT89 M.Mulder Bat-Jsy/250 2.50 6.00
TT90 M.Prior H Bat-Jsy/250 3.00 8.00
TT91 M.Prior A Bat-Jsy/250 3.00 8.00
TT92 M.Teixeira Bat-Jsy/250 3.00 8.00
TT93 M.Byrd Bat-Jsy/250 2.00 5.00
TT94 M.Cabrera Bat-Jsy/250 3.00 8.00
TT95 M.Tejada Bat-Jsy/250 2.50 6.00
TT96 M.Lowell Bat-Jsy/250 2.50 6.00
TT97 M.Muss O's Jsy-Pants/250 3.00 8.00
TT98 M.Muss Yanks Jsy-Jsy/250 3.00 8.00
TT99 M.Piazza Marlins Bat-Jsy/250 5.00 12.00
TT100 M.Piaz Dodgers Bat-Jsy/250 5.00 12.00
TT101 M.Piazza Mets Bat-Jsy/250 5.00 12.00
TT102 M.Schmidt H Bat-Jsy/100 10.00 25.00
TT103 M.Schmidt A Bat-Jsy/100 10.00 25.00
TT104 M.Sweeney Bat-Jsy/250 2.50 6.00
TT105 N.Johnson Bat-Jsy/250 2.50 6.00
TT106 N.Ryan Angels Jkt-Jsy/250 10.00 25.00
TT107 N.Ryan Astros Jkt-Jsy/250 10.00 25.00
TT108 N.Ryan Rgr Jsy-Pants/250 10.00 25.00
TT109 N.Garciaparra H Bat-Jsy/250 5.00 12.00
TT110 N.Garciaparra A Bat-Jsy/250 5.00 12.00
TT111 P.Burrell Bat-Jsy/250 2.50 6.00
TT112 P.Lo Duca Bat-Jsy/250 2.50 6.00
TT113 P.Martinez Sox Bat-Jsy/250 3.00 8.00
TT114 P.Mart Expos Bat-Jsy/250 3.00 8.00
TT115 P.Wilson Bat-Jsy/250 2.50 6.00
TT116 R.Palmeiro O's Bat-Jsy/250 3.00 8.00
TT117 R.Palmeiro Rgr Bat-Jsy/250 3.00 8.00
TT118 R.John D'backs Bat-Jsy/250 4.00 10.00
TT119 R.Johnson M's Bat-Jsy/250 4.00 10.00
TT120 R.Sexson Bat-Jsy/250 2.50 6.00
TT121 R.Hend A's Bat-Jsy/250 4.00 10.00
TT122 R.Hend Padres Bat-Jsy/250 4.00 10.00
TT123 R.Hend M's Bat-Jsy/250 4.00 10.00
TT124 R.Alomar Bat-Jsy/250 3.00 8.00
TT125 R.Baldelli Bat-Jsy/250 2.50 6.00
TT126 R.Carew Bat-Jsy/250 3.00 8.00
TT127 R.Clemens Sox Bat-Jsy/250 6.00 15.00
TT128 R.Clem Yanks Bat-Jsy/250 6.00 15.00
TT129 R.Halladay Jsy-Jsy/250 2.50 6.00
TT130 R.Oswalt Bat-Jsy/250 2.50 6.00
TT131 R.Sandberg Bat-Jsy/250 6.00 15.00
TT132 S.Sosa H Bat-Jsy/250 4.00 10.00
TT133 S.Sosa A Bat-Jsy/250 4.00 10.00
TT134 S.Sosa Sox Bat-Jsy/250 4.00 10.00
TT135 S.Rolen Bat-Jsy/250 3.00 8.00
TT136 S.Green Bat-Jsy/250 2.50 6.00
TT137 S.Carlton Bat-Jsy/250 2.50 6.00
TT138 T.Hudson Bat-Jsy/250 2.50 6.00
TT139 T.Helton H Bat-Jsy/250 3.00 8.00
TT140 T.Helton A Bat-Jsy/250 3.00 8.00
TT141 T.Glav Braves Bat-Jsy/250 3.00 8.00
TT142 T.Glav Mets Bat-Jsy/250 3.00 8.00
TT143 T.Gwynn A Bat-Jsy/250 6.00 15.00
TT144 T.Gwynn Alt Bat-Jsy/250 6.00 15.00
TT145 T.Hunter Bat-Jsy/250 2.50 6.00
TT146 T.Nixon Bat-Jsy/250 2.50 6.00
TT147 T.Glaus Bat-Jsy/250 2.50 6.00
TT148 V.Wells Bat-Jsy/250 2.50 6.00
TT149 V.Guerrero Bat-Jsy/250 4.00 10.00
TT150 W.Clark Bat-Jsy/250 3.00 8.00

2004 Absolute Memorabilia Tools of the Trade Material Signature Single

PRINT RUNS B/WN 1-50 COPIES PER
NO PRICING ON QTY OF 11 OR LESS
SINGLE PS PRINT RUNS B/WN 1-5 PER
NO SINGLE PS PRICING DUE TO SCARCITY
*COMBO p/r 25: .5X TO 1.2X SINGLE p/r 50
COMBO PRINT RUNS B/WN 1-25 PER
NO COMBO PRICES ON QTY OF 10 OR LESS
COMBO PS PRINT RUNS B/WN 1-5 PER
NO COMBO PS PRICING DUE TO SCARCITY
TRIO PRINT RUNS B/WN 1-10 COPIES PER
NO TRIO PRICING DUE TO SCARCITY
TRIO PS PRINT RUNS B/WN 1-5 PER
NO TRIO PS PRICING DUE TO SCARCITY
QUAD PRINT RUNS B/WN 1-10 COPIES PER
NO QUAD PRICING DUE TO SCARCITY
QUAD PS PRINT RUNS B/WN 1-5 PER
NO QUAD PS PRICING DUE TO SCARCITY
TT1 Adam Dunn H Jsy/25 20.00 50.00
TT2 Adam Dunn A Jsy/25 20.00 50.00
TT3 Alan Trammell Jsy/25 20.00 50.00
TT10 Andre Dawson Jsy/25 12.50 30.00
TT15 Angel Berroa Jsy/50 6.00 15.00
TT17 Austin Kearns Jsy/28 10.00 25.00
TT21 Bobby Abreu Jsy/25 12.50 30.00
TT22 Brandon Webb Jsy/25 10.00 25.00
TT26 Carlos Beltran Jsy/15 15.00 40.00
TT29 Carlos Lee Jsy/25 12.50 30.00
TT36 Dale Murphy H Jsy/25 20.00 50.00
TT37 Dale Murphy A Jsy/25 20.00 50.00
TT38 Darryl Strawberry Jsy/39 10.00 25.00
TT43 Dontrelle Willis H Jsy/25 20.00 50.00
TT44 Dontrelle Willis A Jsy/25 20.00 50.00
TT45 Dwight Gooden Jsy/16 15.00 40.00
TT50 Garret Anderson Jsy/16 15.00 40.00
TT61 Jae Weong Seo Jsy/25 12.50 30.00
TT71 Jorge Posada Jsy/20 75.00 150.00
TT74 Josh Beckett Jsy/21 20.00 50.00
TT82 Luis Castillo Jsy/25 10.00 25.00
TT89 Mark Mulder Jsy/20 12.50 30.00
TT93 Marlon Byrd Jsy/29 10.00 25.00
TT94 Miguel Cabrera Jsy/20 30.00 60.00
TT96 Mike Lowell Jsy/19 15.00 40.00
TT112 Paul Lo Duca Jsy/50 10.00 25.00
TT115 Preston Wilson Jsy/44 10.00 25.00
TT125 Rocco Baldelli Jsy/25 12.50 30.00
TT129 Roy Halladay Jsy/32 20.00 50.00
TT137 Steve Carlton Jsy/25 12.50 30.00
TT145 Torii Hunter Jsy/25 12.50 30.00
TT146 Trot Nixon Jsy/25 12.50 30.00

2005 Absolute Memorabilia

COMMON CARD (1-200) .25 .60
1 Andruw Jones .25 .60

2 B.J. Upton .40 1.00
3 Jim Edmonds .40 1.00
4 Johan Santana .40 1.00
5 Jeff Bagwell .40 1.00
6 Derek Jeter 1.50 4.00
7 Eric Chavez .25 .60
8 Albert Pujols .75 2.00
9 Craig Biggio .40 1.00
10 Hank Blalock .25 .60
11 Chipper Jones .60 1.50
12 Jacque Jones .25 .60
13 Alfonso Soriano .40 1.00
14 Carl Crawford .40 1.00
15 Ben Sheets .25 .60
16 Garret Anderson .25 .60
17 Luis Gonzalez .25 .60
18 Andy Pettitte .40 1.00
19 Miguel Tejada .40 1.00
20 Carlos Delgado .25 .60
21 Austin Kearns .25 .60
22 Adrian Beltre .60 1.50
23 Rafael Palmeiro .40 1.00
24 Greg Maddux .75 2.00
25 Jason Bay .25 .60
26 Jason Varitek .60 1.50
27 David Ortiz .60 1.50
28 Dontrelle Willis .25 .60
29 Adam Dunn .40 1.00
30 Carlos Lee .25 .60
31 Manny Ramirez .60 1.50
32 Rocco Baldelli .25 .60
33 Jeff Kent .25 .60
34 Jake Peavy .25 .60
35 Vernon Wells .25 .60
36 Ichiro Suzuki .75 2.00
37 C.C. Sabathia .40 1.00
38 Hideki Matsui 1.00 2.50
39 Gary Sheffield .25 .60
40 Paul Lo Duca .25 .60
41 Vladimir Guerrero .40 1.00
42 Omar Vizquel .40 1.00
43 Lance Berkman .40 1.00
44 Shawn Green .25 .60
45 Josh Beckett .25 .60
46 Barry Zito .40 1.00
47 Roger Clemens .75 2.00
48 Sean Casey .25 .60
49 Edgar Renteria .25 .60
50 Mark Teixeira .40 1.00
51 Frank Thomas .60 1.50
52 Khalil Greene .25 .60
53 Bobby Abreu .25 .60
54 Rafael Furcal .25 .60
55 Jose Vidro .25 .60
56 Nomar Garciaparra .40 1.00
57 Melvin Mora .25 .60
58 Trot Nixon .25 .60
59 Magglio Ordonez .40 1.00
60 Michael Young .25 .60
61 Richie Sexson .25 .60
62 Alex Rodriguez .75 2.00
63 Tim Hudson .40 1.00
64 Todd Helton .40 1.00
65 Mike Lowell .25 .60
66 Mark Mulder .25 .60
67 Sammy Sosa .60 1.50
68 Mark Prior .40 1.00
69 Shannon Stewart .25 .60
70 Miguel Cabrera .60 1.50
71 Troy Glaus .25 .60
72 Scott Rolen .40 1.00
73 Ken Griffey Jr. 1.25 3.00
74 Mike Piazza .60 1.50
75 Roy Halladay .40 1.00
76 Larry Walker .40 1.00
77 Kerry Wood .25 .60
78 Mike Mussina .40 1.00
79 Curt Schilling .40 1.00
80 Rich Harden .25 .60
81 Victor Martinez .40 1.00
82 Roy Oswalt .40 1.00
83 Pedro Martinez .40 1.00
84 Tom Glavine .40 1.00
85 Randy Johnson .60 1.50
86 Ivan Rodriguez .40 1.00
87 Carlos Beltran .40 1.00
88 Torii Hunter .25 .60
89 Hideo Nomo .60 1.50
90 Jim Thome .40 1.00
91 Aramis Ramirez .25 .60
92 J.D. Drew .25 .60
93 Javy Lopez .25 .60
94 David Wright .50 1.25
95 Bobby Crosby .25 .60
96 Jeff Niemann RC .60 1.50
97 Yuniesky Betancourt RC 1.00 2.50
98 Tadahito Iguchi RC .40 1.00
99 Phil Humber RC .60 1.50
100 Justin Verlander RC 5.00 12.00
101 Al Kaline .60 1.50
102 Albert Pujols .75 2.00
103 Alex Rodriguez .75 2.00
104 Andruw Jones .25 .60
105 Aubrey Huff .25 .60
106 Barry Zito .40 1.00
107 Ben Sheets .25 .60
108 Chipper Jones .60 1.50
109 Curt Schilling .40 1.00
110 Dale Murphy .60 1.50
111 David Dellucci .25 .60
112 David Ortiz .60 1.50
113 Dennis Eckersley .40 1.00
114 Derek Jeter 1.50 4.00
115 Don Mattingly 1.25 3.00
116 Don Sutton .40 1.00
117 Dontrelle Willis .25 .60
118 Duke Snider .40 1.00
119 Edgar Renteria .25 .60
120 Fergie Jenkins .40 1.00
121 Frank Robinson .40 1.00
122 Frank Thomas .60 1.50
123 Garret Anderson .25 .60
124 Gary Sheffield .25 .60
125 Greg Maddux .75 2.00
126 Hideki Matsui 1.00 2.50
127 Hideo Nomo .60 1.50
128 Ichiro Suzuki .75 2.00
129 Jamie Moyer .25 .60
130 Jason Varitek .60 1.50
131 Jeff Bagwell .40 1.00
132 Stephen Drew RC .75 2.00
133 Jeff Niemann .60 1.50
134 Jeremy Bonderman .25 .60
135 Jim Bunning .40 1.00
136 Jim Leyritz .25 .60
137 Jim Thome .40 1.00
138 Johan Santana .40 1.00
139 John Kruk .25 .60
140 Johnny Podres .25 .60
141 Jose Guillen .25 .60
142 Justin Verlander 5.00 12.00
143 Keiichi Yabu RC .25 .60
144 Keith Foulke .25 .60
145 Keith Hernandez .25 .60
146 Ken Griffey Jr. 1.25 3.00
147 Kent Hrbek .25 .60
148 Anthony Lerew .25 .60
149 Larry Walker .40 1.00
150 Lew Ford .25 .60
151 Lou Brock .40 1.00
152 Luis Aparicio .40 1.00
153 Luis Tiant .25 .60
154 Manny Ramirez .60 1.50
155 Mark Mulder .25 .60
156 Mark Prior .40 1.00
157 Mark Teixeira .40 1.00
158 Marty Marion .25 .60
159 Miguel Cabrera .60 1.50
160 Miguel Tejada .40 1.00
161 Mike Lieberthal .25 .60
162 Mike Piazza .60 1.50
163 Minnie Minoso .25 .60
164 Monte Irvin .40 1.00
165 Morgan Ensberg .25 .60
166 Nolan Ryan 2.00 5.00
167 Octavio Dotel .25 .60
168 Omar Vizquel .40 1.00
169 Ozzie Smith .75 2.00
170 Pedro Martinez .40 1.00
171 Phil Humber .60 1.50
172 Phil Rizzuto .40 1.00
173 Prince Fielder RC 2.00 5.00
174 Ralph Kiner .40 1.00
175 Randy Johnson .60 1.50
176 Red Schoendienst .40 1.00
177 Rich Gossage .40 1.00
178 Rick Dempsey .25 .60
179 Rickie Weeks .25 .60
180 Robin Roberts .40 1.00
181 Rod Carew .40 1.00
182 Roger Clemens .75 2.00
183 Rollie Fingers .40 1.00
184 Ron Guidry .25 .60
185 Ron Santo .40 1.00
186 Russ Ortiz .25 .60
187 Ryne Sandberg 1.25 3.00
188 Sammy Sosa .60 1.50
189 Scott Rolen .40 1.00
190 Stan Musial 1.00 2.50
191 Steve Carlton .40 1.00
192 Steve Garvey .25 .60
193 Steve Stone .25 .60
194 Tim Salmon .25 .60
195 Todd Helton .40 1.00
196 Todd Walker .25 .60
197 Tom Gordon .25 .60
198 Trot Nixon .25 .60
199 Troy Percival .25 .60
200 Vladimir Guerrero .40 1.00

2005 Absolute Memorabilia Retail

*RETAIL: .12X TO .3X BASIC
ISSUED ONLY IN RETAIL PACKS
RETAIL CARDS LACK FOIL FRONTS

2005 Absolute Memorabilia Black

*BLACK 1-95: .75X TO 2.5X BASIC RETAIL
*BLACK 96-100: .75X TO 2.5X BASIC RETAIL
STATED ODDS 1:18 RETAIL

2005 Absolute Memorabilia Spectrum Gold

*GOLD p/r 50: 1.25X TO 3X BASIC
*GOLD p/r 50: 1.25X TO 3X BASIC RC
*GOLD p/r 25: 1.5X TO 4X BASIC
RANDOM INSERTS IN PACKS
PRINT RUNS B/WN 10-50 COPIES PER
NO PRICING ON QTY OF 10
NO RC YR PRICING ON QTY OF 25

2005 Absolute Memorabilia Spectrum Silver

*SILVER p/r 100-150: 1X TO 2.5X BASIC
*SILVER p/r 100-150 : 1X TO 2.5X BASIC RC
RANDOM INSERTS IN PACKS
1-100 PRINT RUN 100 SERIAL #'d SETS
101-200 PRINT RUN 150 SERIAL #'d SETS

2005 Absolute Memorabilia Autograph Spectrum Gold

*GOLD p/r 41-50: .5X TO 1.2X SILV p/r 74-150
*GOLD p/r 41-50: .4X TO 1X SILV p/r 40-64
*GOLD p/r 21-34: .6X TO 1.5X SILV p/r 74-150
*GOLD p/r 21-34: .5X TO 1.2X SILV p/r 40-64
*GOLD p/r 21-34: .4X TO 1X SILV p/r 22-34
OVERALL AU-GU ODDS ONE PER PACK
PRINT RUNS B/WN 1-50 COPIES PER
NO PRICING ON QTY OF 14 OR LESS
120 Fergie Jenkins/50 8.00 20.00
122 Frank Thomas/25 20.00 50.00
131 Jeff Bagwell/27 25.00 60.00

2005 Absolute Memorabilia Autograph Spectrum Silver

OVERALL AU-GU ODDS ONE PER PACK
PRINT RUNS B/WN 1-150 COPIES PER
NO PRICING ON QTY OF 13 OR LESS
101 Al Kaline/150 15.00 40.00
106 Barry Zito/74 6.00 15.00
107 Ben Sheets/93 6.00 15.00
111 David Dellucci/150 6.00 15.00
113 Dennis Eckersley/100 6.00 15.00
115 Don Mattingly/22 40.00 80.00
116 Don Sutton/137 6.00 15.00
118 Duke Snider/50 5.00 12.00
119 Edgar Renteria/148 6.00 15.00
121 Frank Robinson/150 10.00 25.00
123 Garret Anderson/64 8.00 20.00
124 Gary Sheffield/100 10.00 25.00
125 Greg Maddux/50 30.00 60.00
129 Jamie Moyer/150 6.00 15.00
133 Jeff Niemann/150 6.00 15.00
134 Jeremy Bonderman/43 8.00 20.00
135 Jim Bunning/150 6.00 15.00
136 Jim Leyritz/99 4.00 10.00
138 Johan Santana/40 15.00 40.00
140 Johnny Podres/150 12.50 30.00
141 Jose Guillen/145 4.00 10.00
142 Justin Verlander/150 30.00 80.00
143 Keiichi Yabu/150 6.00 15.00
144 Keith Foulke/150 10.00 25.00
145 Keith Hernandez/149 6.00 15.00
147 Kent Hrbek/98 6.00 15.00
150 Lew Ford/150 4.00 10.00
151 Lou Brock/126 12.50 30.00
152 Luis Aparicio/110 8.00 20.00
153 Luis Tiant/147 6.00 15.00
154 Manny Ramirez/34 30.00 60.00
155 Mark Mulder/150 6.00 15.00
157 Mark Teixeira/91 10.00 25.00
158 Marty Marion/150 6.00 15.00
159 Miguel Cabrera/146 20.00 50.00
161 Mike Lieberthal/150 6.00 15.00
163 Minnie Minoso/150 6.00 15.00
164 Monte Irvin/150 6.00 15.00
166 Nolan Ryan/50 40.00 80.00
167 Octavio Dotel/150 4.00 10.00
168 Omar Vizquel/150 10.00 25.00
169 Ozzie Smith/50 20.00 50.00
171 Phil Humber/108 6.00 15.00
172 Phil Rizzuto/109 10.00 25.00
173 Prince Fielder/45 50.00 100.00
174 Ralph Kiner/150 15.00 40.00
176 Red Schoendienst/150 8.00 20.00
177 Rich Gossage/150 10.00 25.00
178 Rick Dempsey/104 4.00 10.00
179 Rickie Weeks/148 6.00 15.00
180 Robin Roberts/148 10.00 25.00
181 Rod Carew/150 20.00 50.00
183 Rollie Fingers/120 10.00 24.00
184 Ron Guidry/150 10.00 25.00
185 Ron Santo/142 15.00 40.00
186 Russ Ortiz/150 4.00 10.00
187 Ryne Sandberg/150 20.00 50.00
188 Sammy Sosa/15 50.00 100.00
189 Scott Rolen/87 4.00 10.00
190 Stan Musial/150 40.00 80.00
191 Steve Carlton/100 6.00 15.00
192 Steve Garvey/144 12.50 30.00
193 Steve Stone/150 6.00 15.00
194 Tim Salmon/147 6.00 15.00
196 Todd Walker/150 4.00 10.00
197 Tom Gordon/150 4.00 10.00
198 Trot Nixon/43 8.00 20.00
199 Troy Percival/144 6.00 15.00

2005 Absolute Memorabilia Absolutely Ink

OVERALL AU-GU ODDS ONE PER PACK
PRINT RUNS B/WN 1-150 COPIES PER
NO PRICING ON QTY OF 14 OR LESS
AI101 Al Kaline/150 15.00 40.00
AI103 Alfonso Soriano/67 12.50 30.00
AI105 Ben Sheets/150 6.00 15.00
AI109 Cal Ripken/25 50.00 120.00
AI111 Dennis Eckersley/150 6.00 15.00
AI112 Don Sutton/150 6.00 15.00
AI113 Duke Snider/150 4.00 10.00
AI114 Fergie Jenkins/100 6.00 15.00
AI115 Frank Thomas/50 20.00 50.00
AI116 Gary Sheffield/25 15.00 40.00
AI117 Gaylord Perry/100 10.00 25.00
AI118 Jacque Jones/100 6.00 15.00
AI119 Jae Weong Seo/100 6.00 15.00
AI120 Jeremy Bonderman/100 6.00 15.00
AI122 Joe Torre/25 15.00 40.00
AI125 Junior Spivey/75 4.00 10.00
AI126 Luis Aparicio/150 8.00 20.00
AI127 Magglio Ordonez/100 6.00 15.00
AI129 Michael Young/75 4.00 10.00
AI130 Mike Schmidt/17 25.00 60.00
AI131 Morgan Ensberg/51 8.00 20.00
AI132 Orlando Cabrera/100 6.00 15.00
AI133 Paul Konerko/100 5.00 12.00
AI134 Rollie Fingers/100 6.00 15.00
AI135 Roy Oswalt/100 6.00 15.00
AI136 Scott Rolen/27 15.00 40.00
AI137 Sean Casey/63 8.00 20.00
AI139 Torii Hunter/100 6.00 15.00
AI140 Wade Boggs/50 15.00 40.00

2005 Absolute Memorabilia Absolutely Ink Spectrum

*SPEC p/r 74: .4X TO 1X INK p/r 67-150
*SPEC p/r 39-50: .5X TO 1.2X INK p/r 67-150
*SPEC p/r 25-34: .6X TO 1.5X INK p/r 67-150
*SPEC p/r 25-34: .5X TO 1.2X INK p/r 50-63
*SPEC p/r 16-19: .75X TO 2X INK p/r 67-150
OVERALL AU-GU ODDS ONE PER PACK
PRINT RUNS B/WN 1-74 COPIES PER
NO PRICING ON QTY OF 14 OR LESS
AI109 Cal Ripken/25 50.00 120.00

2005 Absolute Memorabilia Absolutely Ink Swatch Single

OVERALL AU-GU ODDS ONE PER PACK
PRINT RUNS B/WN 1-50 COPIES PER
NO PRICING ON QTY OF 10 OR LESS
AI1 Rafael Furcal Jsy/50 10.00 25.00
AI3 Dale Murphy Jsy/50 15.00 40.00
AI4 Duke Snider Pants/25 20.00 50.00
AI5 Bill Madlock Bat/50 10.00 25.00
AI7 Bobby Crosby Jsy/50 10.00 25.00
AI8 Cal Ripken Jsy/25 75.00 150.00
AI9 Hank Blalock Jsy/25 12.50 30.00
AI10 Vernon Wells Jsy/50 10.00 25.00
AI11 Lyle Overbay Jsy/50 6.00 15.00
AI13 Omar Vizquel Jsy/50 15.00 40.00
AI15 Ben Sheets Jsy/25 12.50 30.00
AI16 Aramis Ramirez Jsy/25 12.50 30.00
AI18 Travis Hafner Jsy/50 10.00 25.00
AI19 Mike Lowell Jsy/25 8.00 20.00
AI20 Frank Robinson Bat/50 15.00 40.00
AI22 Juan Gonzalez Jsy/50 10.00 25.00
AI27 Darryl Strawberry Jsy/50 10.00 25.00
AI28 Alexis Rios Bat/50 10.00 25.00
AI30 Magglio Ordonez Jsy/50 10.00 25.00
AI31 Jay Gibbons Jsy/50 6.00 15.00
AI32 Steve Carlton Jsy/25 12.50 30.00
AI34 Kerry Wood Jsy/25 20.00 50.00
AI35 Dontrelle Willis Jsy/15 30.00 60.00
AI36 Eric Chavez Jsy/25 12.50 30.00
AI37 Keith Hernandez Jsy/50 10.00 25.00
AI38 Carlos Zambrano Jsy/50 10.00 25.00
AI39 Brett Myers Jsy/50 6.00 15.00
AI40 Rich Harden Jsy/50 10.00 25.00
AI41 Danny Kolb Jsy/50 6.00 15.00
AI42 Mark Prior Jsy/25 15.00 40.00
AI43 Joey Gathright Jsy/25 8.00 20.00
AI44 David Cone Jsy/50 10.00 25.00
AI45 Carlos Lee Jsy/50 10.00 25.00
AI47 Jack Morris Jsy/50 10.00 25.00
AI48 Torii Hunter Jsy/50 10.00 25.00
AI49 Garret Anderson Jsy/50 10.00 25.00
AI51 Dave Parker Bat/50 10.00 25.00
AI52 C.C. Sabathia Jsy/50 12.50 30.00
AI53 D.Eckersley A's Jsy/50 10.00 25.00
AI54 Barry Larkin Jsy/25 30.00 60.00
AI55 Brandon Webb Pants/50 12.50 30.00
AI56 Sean Casey Jsy/50 10.00 25.00
AI57 Johan Santana Jsy/50 6.00 15.00
AI58 Miguel Cabrera Jsy/50 20.00 50.00
AI59 Bert Blyleven Jsy/50 8.00 20.00
AI60 Casey Kotchman Jsy/50 10.00 25.00
AI61 Dwight Gooden Jsy/50 10.00 25.00
AI62 Milton Bradley Jsy/50 6.00 15.00
AI63 John Kruk Jsy/50 8.00 20.00
AI64 Michael Young Jsy/50 10.00 25.00
AI66 Robin Ventura Jsy/50 10.00 25.00
AI67 Tim Hudson Jsy/25 20.00 50.00
AI68 Will Clark Bat/50 15.00 40.00
AI69 Lew Ford Jsy/50 6.00 15.00
AI70 Jody Gerut Jsy/50 6.00 15.00
AI71 Don Sutton Jsy/50 6.00 15.00
AI72 B.J. Upton Bat/25 12.50 30.00
AI73 Austin Kearns Jsy/50 6.00 15.00
AI77 Ryan Wagner Jsy/50 6.00 15.00
AI78 Jermaine Dye Jsy/50 10.00 25.00
AI80 Al Oliver Jsy/50 10.00 25.00
AI81 Angel Berroa Pants/50 6.00 15.00
AI82 Edgar Renteria Jsy/50 10.00 25.00
AI83 D.Eckersley Sox Jsy/25 12.50 30.00
AI84 Roy Oswalt Jsy/50 10.00 25.00
AI86 Dave Righetti Jsy/50 10.00 25.00
AI87 Aubrey Huff Jsy/25 12.50 30.00
AI89 Jose Vidro Jsy/50 6.00 15.00
AI90 Harold Baines Jsy/50 10.00 25.00
AI93 Ken Harvey Jsy/50 6.00 15.00
AI95 Jason Bay Jsy/50 10.00 25.00
AI96 Dwight Evans Jsy/50 15.00 40.00
AI97 Luis Tiant Pants/50 6.00 15.00
AI98 Ron Santo Bat/50 15.00 40.00
AI99 Brian Roberts Jsy/50 5.00 12.00
AI100 Marty Marion Jsy/50 10.00 25.00
AI101 Al Kaline Bat/50 20.00 50.00
AI102 Alan Trammell Jsy/63 10.00 25.00
AI103 Alfonso Soriano Bat/100 6.00 15.00
AI104 Barry Larkin Bat/150 15.00 40.00
AI105 Ben Sheets Jsy/40 10.00 25.00
AI106 Bill Madlock Bat/150 5.00 12.00
AI107 Bobby Doerr Pants/82 8.00 20.00
AI108 Brandon Webb Pants/46 12.50 30.00
AI109 Cal Ripken Jsy/50 60.00 120.00
AI110 Dale Murphy Jsy/50 15.00 40.00
AI111 Dennis Eckersley Jsy/150 8.00 20.00
AI114 Fergie Jenkins Pants/55 10.00 25.00
AI115 Frank Thomas Bat/50 30.00 60.00
AI116 Gary Sheffield Fld Glv/150 6.00 15.00
AI117 Gaylord Perry Jsy/150 6.00 15.00
AI118 Jacque Jones Bat/45 10.00 25.00
AI120 Jeremy Bonderman Jsy/15 15.00 40.00
AI121 Jim Rice Jsy/95 8.00 20.00
AI123 Johan Santana Jsy/118 15.00 40.00
AI124 Juan Gonzalez Jsy/75 8.00 20.00
AI125 Junior Spivey Jsy/75 5.00 12.00
AI127 Magglio Ordonez Bat/150 8.00 20.00
AI128 Mark Grace Fld Glv/150 8.00 20.00
AI130 Mike Schmidt Sock/75 30.00 60.00
AI132 Orlando Cabrera Jsy/45 10.00 25.00
AI133 Paul Konerko Bat/34 20.00 50.00
AI135 Roy Oswalt Bat/44 10.00 25.00
AI136 Scott Rolen Jsy/150 12.50 30.00
AI138 Tom Seaver Hat/150 20.00 50.00
AI140 Wade Boggs Bat/150 12.50 30.00

2005 Absolute Memorabilia Absolutely Ink Swatch Single Spectrum

*SPEC p/r 36-50: .5X TO 1.2X SNG p/r 75-150
*SPEC p/r 36-50: .4X TO 1X SNG p/r 40-63
*SPEC p/r 25: .6X TO 1.5X SNG p/r 75-150
*SPEC p/r 25: .5X TO 1.2X SNG p/r 40-63
*SPEC p/r 15-17: .75X TO 2X SNG p/r 75-150
*SPEC p/r 15-17: .6X TO 1.5X SNG p/r 40-63
*SPEC p/r 15-17: .5X TO 1.2X SNG p/r 25-34
OVERALL AU-GU ODDS ONE PER PACK
PRINT RUNS B/WN 1-50 COPIES PER
NO PRICING ON QTY OF 13 OR LESS
AI23 Mark Teixeira Jsy/25 20.00 50.00
AI92 Mark Mulder Jsy/25 12.50 30.00
AI109 Cal Ripken Jsy/25 75.00 150.00

2005 Absolute Memorabilia Absolutely Ink Swatch Single Spectrum Prime

*PRIMEp/r70-100: .5X TO 1.2X SNGp/r75-150
*PRIME p/r 70-100: .4X TO 1X SNG p/r 40-63
*PRIME p/r 20-35: .75X TO 2X SNG p/r 75-150
*PRIME p/r 20-35: .4X TO 1X SNG p/r 15
OVERALL AU-GU ODDS ONE PER PACK
PRINT RUNS B/WN 1-100 COPIES PER
NO PRICING ON QTY OF 10 OR LESS
AI112 Don Sutton Jsy/100 8.00 20.00
AI119 Jae Weong Seo Jsy/45 12.50 30.00
AI122 Joe Torre Jsy/70 12.50 30.00
AI126 Luis Aparicio Jsy/25 15.00 40.00
AI134 Rollie Fingers Jsy/25 15.00 40.00

2005 Absolute Memorabilia Absolutely Ink Swatch Double

*DBL p/r 70-100: .4X TO 1X SNG p/r 75-150
*DBL p/r 50: .5X TO 1.2X SNG p/r 75-150
*DBL p/r 50: .4X TO 1X SNG p/r 40-63
*DBL p/r 20-30: .6X TO 1.5X SNG p/r 75-150
*DBL p/r 20-30: .5X TO 1.2X SNG p/r 40-63
*DBL p/r 20-30: .4X TO 1X SNG p/r 25-34
*DBL p/r 15-18: .75X TO 2X SNG p/r 75-150
*DBL p/r 15-18: .6X TO 1.5X SNG p/r 40-63
*DBL p/r 15-18: .5X TO 1.2X SNG p/r 25-34
OVERALL AU-GU ODDS ONE PER PACK
PRINT RUNS B/WN 1-100 COPIES PER
NO PRICING ON QTY OF 10 OR LESS
AI23 Mark Teixeira FG-J/50 15.00 40.00
AI92 Mark Mulder J-J/20 12.50 30.00
AI122 Joe Torre B-J/70 12.50 30.00
AI129 Michael Young B-J/25 12.50 30.00
AI137 Sean Casey J-SH/100 8.00 20.00

2005 Absolute Memorabilia Absolutely Ink Swatch Double Spectrum

*SPEC p/r 40-50: .5X TO 1.2X SNG p/r 75-150
*SPEC p/r 40-50: .4X TO 1X SNG p/r 40-63
*SPEC p/r 20-30: .6X TO 1.5X SNG p/r 75-150
*SPEC p/r 20-30: .5X TO 1.2X SNG p/r 40-63
*SPEC p/r 15: .75X TO 2X SNG p/r 75-150
*SPEC p/r 15: .6X TO 1.5X SNG p/r 40-63
OVERALL AU-GU ODDS ONE PER PACK
PRINT RUNS B/WN 1-50 COPIES PER
NO PRICING ON QTY OF 10 OR LESS
AI122 Joe Torre B-J/15 30.00 60.00
AI129 Michael Young B-J/25 12.50 30.00
AI137 Sean Casey J-SH/50 10.00 25.00

2005 Absolute Memorabilia Absolutely Ink Swatch Double Spectrum Prime

*PRIME p/r 50: .6X TO 1.5X SNG p/r 75-150
*PRIME p/r 25: .75X TO 2X SNG p/r 75-150
*PRIME p/r 25: .6X TO 1.5X SNG p/r 40-63
*PRIME p/r 15: 1X TO 2.5X SNG p/r 75-150
OVERALL AU-GU ODDS ONE PER PACK
PRINT RUNS B/QN 1-50 COPIES PER
NO PRICING ON QTY OF 10 OR LESS
AI134 Rollie Fingers J-J/25 15.00 40.00

2005 Absolute Memorabilia Absolutely Ink Swatch Triple

*TRIP p/r 75: .4X TO 1X SNG p/r 40-63
*TRIP p/r 50: .6X TO 1.5X SNG p/r 75-150
*TRIP p/r 50: .5X TO 1.2X SNG p/r 40-63
*TRIP p/r 25: .75X TO 2X SNG p/r 75-150
*TRIP p/r 25: .6X TO 1.5X SNG p/r 40-63
*TRIP p/r 25: .5X TO 1.2X SNG p/r 25-34
*TRIP p/r 15: .75X TO 2X SNG p/r 40-63
OVERALL AU-GU ODDS ONE PER PACK
PRINT RUNS B/WN 1-75 COPIES PER
NO PRICING ON QTY OF 10 OR LESS
AI8 Cal Ripken B-J-P/25 90.00 180.00
AI23 Mark Teixeira B-H-J/75 15.00 40.00
AI126 Luis Aparicio B-J-P/15 20.00 50.00
AI129 Michael Young B-J-J/25 15.00 40.00

2005 Absolute Memorabilia Absolutely Ink Swatch Triple Spectrum

*SPEC p/r 25: .75X TO 2X SNG p/r 75-150
*SPEC p/r 25: .6X TO 1.5X SNG p/r 40-63
OVERALL AU-GU ODDS ONE PER PACK
PRINT RUNS B/WN 1-25 COPIES PER
NO PRICING ON QTY OF 10 OR LESS
AI23 Mark Teixeira B-H-J/25 30.00 60.00
AI129 Michael Young B-J-J/25 15.00 40.00

2005 Absolute Memorabilia Absolutely Ink Swatch Triple Spectrum Prime

*PRIME p/r 25: 1X TO 2.5X SNG p/r 75-150
*PRIME p/r 15: 1X TO 2.5X SNG p/r 40-63
OVERALL AU-GU ODDS ONE PER PACK
PRINT RUNS B/WN 1-25 COPIES PER
NO PRICING ON QTY OF 10 OR LESS

2005 Absolute Memorabilia Heroes

STATED PRINT RUN 250 SERIAL #'d SETS
*SPEC 1-50: 1X TO 2.5X BASIC
*SPEC 51-70: .75X TO 2X BASIC
SPEC 1-50 PRINT RUN 50 #'d SETS
SPEC 51-70 PRINT RUN 100 #'d SETS
*REV.SPEC: 1.5X TO 4X BASIC
REVERSE SPEC.PRINT RUN 25 #'d SETS
RANDOM INSERTS IN PACKS
AH1 Billy Martin .75 2.00
AH2 Rickey Henderson 1.25 3.00
AH3 Alan Trammell .75 2.00
AH4 Lenny Dykstra .50 1.25
AH5 Jeff Bagwell .75 2.00
AH6 Steve Garvey .50 1.25
AH7 Catfish Hunter .75 2.00
AH8 Cal Ripken 4.00 10.00
AH9 Reggie Jackson .75 2.00
AH10 Gary Sheffield .50 1.25
AH11 Edgar Martinez .75 2.00
AH12 Roberto Alomar .75 2.00
AH13 Luis Tiant .50 1.25
AH14 Jim Rice .75 2.00
AH15 Carlos Beltran .75 2.00
AH16 Hideo Nomo 1.25 3.00
AH17 Mark Grace .75 2.00
AH18 Joe Cronin .50 1.25
AH19 Tony Gwynn 1.50 4.00
AH20 Bo Jackson 1.25 3.00
AH21 Roger Clemens Sox 1.50 4.00
AH22 Roger Clemens Yanks 1.50 4.00
AH23 Don Mattingly 2.50 6.00
AH24 Willie Mays 2.50 6.00
AH25 Andruw Jones .50 1.25
AH26 Andre Dawson .75 2.00
AH27 Carlton Fisk .75 2.00
AH28 Robin Yount 1.25 3.00
AH29 Joe Carter .50 1.25
AH30 Dale Murphy 1.25 3.00
AH31 Greg Maddux 1.50 4.00
AH32 Ichiro Suzuki 1.50 4.00
AH33 Jose Canseco .75 2.00
AH34 Nolan Ryan 4.00 10.00
AH35 Frank Thomas 1.25 3.00
AH36 Fred Lynn .50 1.25
AH37 Curt Schilling Phils .75 2.00
AH38 Curt Schilling Sox .75 2.00
AH39 Dave Parker .50 1.25
AH40 Randy Johnson M's 1.25 3.00
AH41 Randy Johnson Expos 1.25 3.00
AH42 Vladimir Guerrero .75 2.00
AH43 Bernie Williams .75 2.00
AH44 Wade Boggs .75 2.00
AH45 Pedro Martinez .75 2.00
AH46 Andy Pettitte .75 2.00
AH47 Fergie Jenkins .75 2.00
AH48 Darryl Strawberry .50 1.25
AH49 Rafael Palmeiro .75 2.00
AH50 Albert Pujols 1.50 4.00
AH51 Adrian Beltre 1.25 3.00
AH52 Albert Pujols 1.50 4.00
AH53 Andre Dawson .75 2.00
AH54 Carlos Beltran .75 2.00
AH55 Don Mattingly 2.50 6.00
AH56 Greg Maddux 1.50 4.00
AH57 Ivan Rodriguez .75 2.00
AH58 John Smoltz 1.25 3.00
AH59 Manny Ramirez 1.25 3.00
AH60 Mark Grace .75 2.00
AH61 Mark Teixeira .75 2.00
AH62 Mike Mussina .75 2.00
AH63 Paul Lo Duca .50 1.25
AH64 Pedro Martinez .75 2.00
AH65 Scott Rolen .75 2.00
AH66 Shawn Green .50 1.25
AH67 Tony Gwynn 1.50 4.00
AH68 Tony Oliva .50 1.25
AH69 Torii Hunter .50 1.25
AH70 Wade Boggs .75 2.00

2005 Absolute Memorabilia Heroes Swatch Double

OVERALL AU-GU ODDS ONE PER PACK
PRINT RUNS B/WN 1-150 COPIES PER
NO PRICING ON QTY OF 1
AH1 Billy Martin J-P/50 10.00 25.00
AH2 Rickey Henderson B-J/50 5.00 12.00
AH3 Alan Trammell B-J/50 4.00 10.00
AH4 Lenny Dykstra B-J/50 4.00 10.00
AH5 Jeff Bagwell B-J/50 4.00 10.00
AH6 Steve Garvey B-J/50 4.00 10.00
AH7 Catfish Hunter J-J/25 6.00 15.00
AH8 Cal Ripken J-P/50 15.00 40.00
AH9 Reggie Jackson JK-J/50 5.00 12.00
AH10 Gary Sheffield FG-J/50 3.00 8.00
AH11 Edgar Martinez J-J/50 4.00 10.00
AH12 Roberto Alomar J-J/50 4.00 10.00
AH13 Luis Tiant H-J/25 5.00 12.00
AH14 Jim Rice J-P/50 4.00 10.00
AH15 Carlos Beltran B-J/50 3.00 8.00
AH16 Hideo Nomo B-J/50 6.00 15.00
AH17 Mark Grace FG-J/50 4.00 10.00
AH18 Joe Cronin J-P/50 10.00 25.00
AH19 Tony Gwynn B-J/50 8.00 20.00
AH20 Bo Jackson B-J/50 6.00 15.00
AH21 Roger Clemens Sox J-J/50 8.00 20.00
AH22 R.Clemens Yanks J-J/50 8.00 20.00
AH23 Don Mattingly B-J/50 10.00 25.00
AH24 Willie Mays B-J/50 20.00 50.00
AH25 Andruw Jones B-J/50 4.00 10.00
AH26 Andre Dawson J-P/50 4.00 10.00
AH28 Robin Yount H-J/50 6.00 15.00
AH29 Joe Carter B-J/50 4.00 10.00
AH30 Dale Murphy B-J/50 5.00 12.00
AH31 Greg Maddux J-J/50 8.00 20.00
AH33 Jose Canseco H-J/50 6.00 15.00
AH34 Nolan Ryan B-J/50 12.50 30.00
AH35 Frank Thomas J-P/50 5.00 12.00
AH36 Fred Lynn B-J/50 4.00 10.00
AH37 C.Schil Phils J-J/50 3.00 8.00
AH38 Curt Schilling Sox J-J/50 4.00 10.00
AH39 Dave Parker B-J/50 4.00 10.00
AH40 Randy Johnson M's J-J/50 5.00 12.00
AH41 R.Johnson Expos B-J/25 6.00 15.00
AH42 Vladimir Guerrero J-J/50 5.00 12.00
AH43 Bernie Williams J-J/50 4.00 10.00
AH44 Wade Boggs B-J/50 5.00 12.00
AH45 Pedro Martinez J-J/50 4.00 10.00
AH46 Andy Pettitte J-J/50 4.00 10.00
AH47 Fergie Jenkins H-J/50 4.00 10.00
AH48 Darryl Strawberry J-P/50 4.00 10.00
AH49 Rafael Palmeiro B-J/50 4.00 10.00
AH50 Albert Pujols J-J/50 15.00 40.00
AH51 Adrian Beltre H-S/120 2.50 6.00
AH52 Albert Pujols B-J/150 10.00 25.00
AH53 Andre Dawson J-P/35 5.00 12.00
AH53 Carlos Beltran J-J/45 3.00 8.00
AH56 Greg Maddux J-J/150 6.00 15.00
AH57 Ivan Rodriguez B-J/150 3.00 8.00
AH58 John Smoltz J-J/150 3.00 8.00
AH60 Mark Grace FG-J/25 5.00 12.00
AH62 Mike Mussina J-S/50 4.00 10.00
AH63 Paul Lo Duca B-CP/150 2.50 6.00
AH64 Pedro Martinez J-J/50 4.00 10.00
AH65 Scott Rolen J-J/50 4.00 10.00
AH66 Shawn Green B-J/150 2.50 6.00
AH67 Tony Gwynn J-P/150 6.00 15.00
AH68 Tony Oliva B-J/150 3.00 8.00
AH69 Torii Hunter B-J/71 2.50 6.00

2005 Absolute Memorabilia Heroes Swatch Double Spectrum Prime

*PRIME p/r 100: .5X TO 1.2X DBL p/r 71-150
*PRIME p/r 45: .6X TO 1.5X DBL p/r 71-150
*PRIME p/r 25: .6X TO 1.5X DBL p/r 45-50
*PRIME p/r 25: .5X TO 1.2X DBL p/r 25-35
*PRIME p/r 15: 1X TO 2.5X DBL p/r 71-150
OVERALL AU-GU ODDS ONE PER PACK
PRINT RUNS B/WN 1-100 COPIES PER
NO PRICING ON QTY OF 10 OR LESS
AH27 Carlton Fisk B-J/25 8.00 20.00
AH59 Manny Ramirez B-J/25 8.00 20.00

2005 Absolute Memorabilia Heroes Swatch Triple

*TRIP p/r 70-150: .5X TO 1.2X DBL p/r 71-150
*TRIP p/r 70-150: .3X TO .8X DBL p/r 25-35
*TRIP p/r 36-50: .6X TO 1.5X DBL p/r 71-150
*TRIP p/r 36-50: .5X TO 1.2X DBL p/r 45-50
*TRIP p/r 20-30: .75X TO 2X DBL p/r 71-150
*TRIP p/r 20-30: .6X TO 1.5X DBL p/r 45-50
*TRIP p/r 15: .75X TO 2X DBL p/r 45-50
*TRIP p/r 15: .6X TO 1.5X DBL p/r 25-35
OVERALL AU-GU ODDS ONE PER PACK
PRINT RUNS B/WN 1-150 COPIES PER
NO PRICING ON QTY OF 1
AH24 Willie Mays B-J-P/25 40.00 80.00
AH55 D.Mattingly B-BG-H/70 15.00 40.00
AH59 Manny Ramirez B-J-S/20 6.00 15.00
AH61 Mark Teixeira B-FG-S/40 5.00 12.00

2005 Absolute Memorabilia Heroes Swatch Triple Spectrum Prime

*PRIME p/r 15: 1.25X TO 3X DBL p/r 45-50
*PRIME p/r 15: 1X TO 2.5X DBL p/r 25-35
OVERALL AU-GU ODDS ONE PER PACK
PRINT RUNS B/WN 1-100 COPIES PER
NO PRICING ON QTY OF 10 OR LESS
AH27 Carlton Fisk B-J-J/15 15.00 40.00
AH53 Andre Dawson B-J-P/95 6.00 15.00
AH54 Carlos Beltran J-J-J/70 6.00 15.00
AH56 Greg Maddux J-J-J/30 20.00 50.00
AH58 John Smoltz J-J-J/100 8.00 20.00
AH59 Manny Ramirez B-J-J/25 12.50 30.00
AH64 Pedro Martinez H-J-J/25 12.50 30.00
AH66 Shawn Green B-J-J/100 6.00 15.00
AH68 Tony Oliva B-J-J/75 6.00 15.00
AH69 Torii Hunter B-H-J/50 8.00 20.00

2005 Absolute Memorabilia Heroes Autograph

OVERALL AU-GU ODDS ONE PER PACK
PRINT RUNS B/WN 1-79 COPIES PER
NO PRICING ON QTY OF 8 OR LESS
AH70 Wade Boggs/26 15.00 40.00
AH55 Don Mattingly/50 30.00 60.00
AH61 Mark Teixeira/79 10.00 25.00
AH65 Scott Rolen/27 8.00 20.00
AH67 Tony Gwynn/19 30.00 60.00
AH69 Torii Hunter/50 8.00 20.00

2005 Absolute Memorabilia Heroes Autograph Spectrum

*SPEC p/r 50: .5X TO 1.2X AUTO p/r 79
OVERALL AU-GU ODDS ONE PER PACK
PRINT RUNS B/WN 1-50 COPIES PER
NO PRICING ON QTY OF 5 OR LESS

2005 Absolute Memorabilia Heroes Autograph Swatch Double Spectrum Prime

PRINT RUNS B/WN 1-20 COPIES PER
NO PRICING ON QTY OF 8 OR LESS
TRIPLE PRINT RUN B/WN 1-5 COPIES PER
NO TRIPLE PRICING DUE TO SCARCITY
OVERALL AU-GU ODDS ONE PER PACK
AH3 Alan Trammell B-J/15 20.00 50.00
AH4 Lenny Dykstra B-J/15 20.00 50.00
AH6 Steve Garvey B-J/15 20.00 50.00
AH9 Reggie Jackson JK-J/15 40.00 80.00
AH10 Gary Sheffield FG-J/15 40.00 80.00
AH11 Edgar Martinez J-J/15 40.00 80.00
AH12 Roberto Alomar J-J/15 40.00 80.00
AH13 Luis Tiant H-J/15 12.50 30.00
AH14 Jim Rice J-P/15 20.00 50.00
AH15 Carlos Beltran B-J/15 20.00 50.00
AH17 Mark Grace FG-J/15 20.00 50.00
AH19 Tony Gwynn B-J/15 40.00 80.00
AH20 Bo Jackson B-J/15 50.00 100.00
AH23 Don Mattingly B-J/15 50.00 100.00
AH26 Andre Dawson J-P/15 20.00 50.00
AH27 Carlton Fisk B-J/15 40.00 80.00
AH28 Robin Yount H-J/15 50.00 100.00
AH30 Dale Murphy B-J/15 40.00 80.00
AH33 Jose Canseco H-J/15 50.00 100.00
AH34 Nolan Ryan B-J/15 125.00 200.00
AH35 Frank Thomas J-P/15 50.00 100.00
AH36 Fred Lynn B-J/15 20.00 50.00
AH39 Dave Parker B-J/15 20.00 50.00
AH44 Wade Boggs B-J/15 40.00 80.00
AH47 Fergie Jenkins H-J/15 12.50 30.00
AH48 Darryl Strawberry J-P/15 20.00 50.00
AH56 Greg Maddux J-J/20 75.00 150.00
AH61 Mark Teixeira B-H/20 30.00 60.00

2005 Absolute Memorabilia Marks of Fame

STATED PRINT RUN 150 SERIAL #'d SETS
*SPEC: 1.25X TO 3X BASIC
SPECTRUM PRINT RUN 25 #'d SETS
RANDOM INSERTS IN PACKS
MF1 Bobby Doerr 1.25 3.00
MF2 Reggie Jackson Yanks 1.25 3.00
MF3 Harmon Killebrew 2.00 5.00
MF4 Duke Snider 1.25 3.00
MF5 Brooks Robinson 1.25 3.00
MF6 Al Kaline 2.00 5.00
MF7 Carlton Fisk 1.25 3.00
MF8 Willie Stargell 1.25 3.00
MF9 Enos Slaughter 1.25 3.00
MF10 Nolan Ryan Rgr 6.00 15.00
MF11 Luis Aparicio R.Sox 1.25 3.00
MF12 Hoyt Wilhelm 1.25 3.00
MF13 Orlando Cepeda 1.25 3.00
MF14 Mike Schmidt 3.00 8.00
MF15 Frank Robinson 1.25 3.00
MF16 Whitey Ford 1.25 3.00
MF17 Don Sutton 1.25 3.00
MF18 Joe Morgan 1.25 3.00
MF19 Bob Feller 1.25 3.00
MF20 Lou Brock 1.25 3.00
MF21 Warren Spahn 1.25 3.00
MF22 Jim Palmer 1.25 3.00
MF23 Reggie Jackson Angels 1.25 3.00
MF24 Willie Mays 4.00 10.00
MF25 George Brett 4.00 10.00
MF26 Billy Williams 1.25 3.00
MF27 Juan Marichal 1.25 3.00
MF28 Early Wynn 1.25 3.00
MF29 Rod Carew 1.25 3.00
MF30 Maury Wills .75 2.00
MF31 Fergie Jenkins 1.25 3.00
MF32 Steve Carlton 1.25 3.00
MF33 Eddie Murray 1.25 3.00
MF34 Kirby Puckett 2.00 5.00
MF35 Johnny Bench 2.00 5.00
MF36 Gaylord Perry 1.25 3.00
MF37 Gary Carter 1.25 3.00

MF38 Tony Perez 1.25 3.00
MF39 Tony Oliva .75 2.00
MF40 Luis Aparicio W.Sox 1.25 3.00
MF41 Tom Seaver 1.25 3.00
MF42 Paul Molitor 2.00 5.00
MF43 Dennis Eckersley 1.25 3.00
MF44 Willie McCovey 1.25 3.00
MF45 Bob Gibson 1.25 3.00
MF46 Robin Roberts 1.25 3.00
MF47 Carl Yastrzemski 2.50 6.00
MF48 Ozzie Smith 2.50 6.00
MF49 Nolan Ryan Angels 6.00 15.00
MF50 Stan Musial 3.00 8.00
MF51 Bob Feller 1.25 3.00
MF52 Bob Gibson 1.25 3.00
MF53 Cal Ripken 6.00 15.00
MF54 Carl Yastrzemski 2.50 6.00
MF55 Carlton Fisk 1.25 3.00
MF56 Duke Snider Dgr 1.25 3.00
MF57 Duke Snider Mets 1.25 3.00
MF58 Gary Carter 1.25 3.00
MF59 George Brett 4.00 10.00
MF60 Johnny Bench 2.00 5.00
MF61 Juan Marichal 1.25 3.00
MF62 Kirby Puckett 2.00 5.00
MF63 Mike Schmidt 3.00 8.00
MF64 Nolan Ryan 6.00 15.00
MF65 Ozzie Smith 2.50 6.00
MF66 Paul Molitor 2.00 5.00
MF67 Phil Niekro 1.25 3.00
MF68 Ryne Sandberg 4.00 10.00
MF69 Wade Boggs 1.25 3.00
MF70 Willie McCovey 1.25 3.00

2005 Absolute Memorabilia Marks of Fame Swatch Double

OVERALL AU-GU ODDS ONE PER PACK
PRINT RUNS B/WN 1-50 COPIES PER
NO PRICING ON QTY OF 10 OR LESS
MF1 Bobby Doerr B-P/50 3.00 8.00
MF2 R.Jack Yanks B-P/50 5.00 12.00
MF3 Harmon Killebrew B-J/50 6.00 15.00
MF4 Duke Snider J-P/25 6.00 15.00
MF5 Brooks Robinson B-J/50 6.00 15.00
MF7 Carlton Fisk B-JK/50 5.00 12.00
MF8 Willie Stargell B-J/50 5.00 12.00
MF9 Enos Slaughter J-J/50 4.00 10.00
MF10 Nolan Ryan Rgr J-P/50 12.50 30.00
MF11 Luis Aparicio Bos B-J/50 4.00 10.00
MF12 Hoyt Wilhelm J-J/50 4.00 10.00
MF13 Orlando Cepeda B-P/50 4.00 10.00
MF14 Mike Schmidt B-J/50 10.00 25.00
MF15 Frank Robinson B-S/50 4.00 10.00
MF16 Whitey Ford J-J/25 6.00 15.00
MF17 Don Sutton J-J/50 4.00 10.00
MF18 Joe Morgan B-J/50 4.00 10.00
MF20 Lou Brock B-JK/50 5.00 12.00
MF21 Warren Spahn J-P/50 6.00 15.00
MF22 Jim Palmer H-P/50 4.00 10.00
MF23 R.Jackson Angels B-J/50 5.00 12.00
MF24 Willie Mays B-J/25 10.00 25.00
MF26 Billy Williams J-J/50 4.00 10.00
MF27 Juan Marichal J-P/50 4.00 10.00
MF28 Early Wynn J-J/25 6.00 15.00
MF29 Rod Carew B-J/50 5.00 12.00
MF31 Fergie Jenkins FG-P/50 4.00 10.00
MF32 Steve Carlton B-P/50 4.00 10.00
MF33 Eddie Murray B-J/50 8.00 20.00
MF34 Kirby Puckett B-J/50 6.00 15.00
MF35 Johnny Bench B-J/50 6.00 15.00
MF36 Gaylord Perry J-J/50 4.00 10.00
MF37 Gary Carter B-J/50 4.00 10.00
MF39 Tony Oliva B-J/50 4.00 10.00
MF41 Tom Seaver J-P/50 5.00 12.00
MF42 Paul Molitor B-J/50 4.00 10.00
MF43 Dennis Eckersley J-J/50 4.00 10.00
MF44 Willie McCovey J-P/50 5.00 12.00
MF47 Carl Yastrzemski B-J/50 10.00 25.00
MF48 Ozzie Smith H-P/50 8.00 20.00
MF49 Nolan Ryan Angels JK-J/50 12.50 30.00
MF50 Stan Musial B-P/50 12.50 30.00
MF53 Cal Ripken JK-P/100 10.00 25.00
MF54 Carl Yastrzemski B-H/70 10.00 25.00
MF57 Duke Snider J-P/100 4.00 10.00
MF58 Gary Carter FG-J/100 3.00 8.00
MF62 Kirby Puckett FG-S/20 8.00 20.00
MF66 Paul Molitor B-J/100 3.00 8.00

2005 Absolute Memorabilia Marks of Fame Swatch Double Spectrum Prime

*PRIME p/r 44-50: .6X TO 1.5X DBL p/r 70-100
*PRIME p/r 25: .6X TO 1.5X DBL p/r 50
*PRIME p/r 25: .5X TO 1.2X DBL p/r 20-25
*PRIME p/r 15: 1X TO 2.5X DBL p/r 70-100
OVERALL AU-GU ODDS ONE PER PACK
PRINT RUNS B/WN 1-75 COPIES PER
NO PRICING ON QTY OF 10 OR LESS
MF21 Warren Spahn J-P/25 40.00 80.00
MF30 Maury Wills J-J/25 6.00 15.00
MF52 Bob Gibson J-J/75 5.00 12.00
MF67 Phil Niekro B-J/50 5.00 12.00
MF70 Willie McCovey J-J/44 6.00 15.00

2005 Absolute Memorabilia Marks of Fame Swatch Triple

*TRIP p/r 50-55: .6X TO 1.5X DBL p/r 70-100
*TRIP p/r 50-55: .4X TO 1X DBL p/r 20-25
*TRIP p/r 25: .6X TO 1.5X DBL p/r 50
OVERALL AU-GU ODDS ONE PER PACK
PRINT RUNS B/WN 1-55 COPIES PER
NO PRICING ON QTY OF 10 OR LESS
MF21 Warren Spahn J-J-P/25 40.00 80.00
MF24 Willie Mays B-J-P/25 40.00 80.00

2005 Absolute Memorabilia Marks of Fame Swatch Triple Spectrum Prime

*PRIME p/r 15: 1.25X TO 3X DBL p/r 50
OVERALL AU-GU ODDS ONE PER PACK
PRINT RUNS B/WN 1-50 COPIES PER
NO PRICING ON QTY OF 10 OR LESS
MF21 Warren Spahn J-J-P/15 60.00 120.00
MF67 Phil Niekro B-J-J/50 6.00 15.00
MF70 Willie McCovey J-J-J/15 12.50 30.00

2005 Absolute Memorabilia Marks of Fame Autograph

OVERALL AU-GU ODDS ONE PER PACK
PRINT RUNS B/WN 2-200 COPIES PER
NO PRICING ON QTY OF 11 OR LESS
MF51 Bob Feller/150 10.00 25.00
MF52 Bob Gibson/150 10.00 25.00
MF55 Carlton Fisk/77 6.00 15.00
MF56 Duke Snider Dgr/150 12.50 30.00
MF57 Duke Snider Mets/150 10.00 25.00
MF58 Gary Carter/25 10.00 25.00
MF59 George Brett/54 40.00 80.00
MF60 Johnny Bench/200 15.00 40.00
MF61 Juan Marichal/19 12.50 30.00
MF63 Mike Schmidt/35 20.00 50.00
MF64 Nolan Ryan/100 40.00 80.00
MF65 Ozzie Smith/150 20.00 50.00
MF68 Ryne Sandberg/100 20.00 50.00
MF69 Wade Boggs/26 15.00 40.00

2005 Absolute Memorabilia Marks of Fame Autograph Spectrum

*SPEC p/r 133: .4X TO 1X AUTO p/r 77-200
*SPEC p/r 50: .5X TO 1.2X AUTO p/r 77-200
*SPEC p/r 20-23: .6X TO 1.5X AUTOp/r77-200
OVERALL AU-GU ODDS ONE PER PACK
PRINT RUNS B/WN 1-133 COPIES PER
NO PRICING ON QTY OF 10 OR LESS

2005 Absolute Memorabilia Marks of Fame Autograph Swatch Single

OVERALL AU-GU ODDS ONE PER PACK
PRINT RUNS B/WN 1-125 COPIES PER
NO PRICING ON QTY OF 10 OR LESS
MF1 Bobby Doerr Pants/125 8.00 20.00
MF3 Harmon Killebrew Jsy/50 30.00 60.00
MF4 Duke Snider Jsy/25 20.00 50.00
MF5 Brooks Robinson Jsy/125 12.50 30.00
MF6 Al Kaline Bat/125 20.00 50.00
MF7 Carlton Fisk Jkt/50 15.00 40.00
MF10 Nolan Ryan Rgr Pants/50 50.00 100.00
MF11 Luis Aparicio Bos Jsy/125 8.00 20.00
MF13 Orlando Cepeda Pants/50 10.00 25.00
MF14 Mike Schmidt Jsy/50 30.00 60.00
MF15 Frank Robinson Bat/125 15.00 40.00
MF16 Whitey Ford Jsy/50 20.00 50.00
MF17 Don Sutton Jsy/125 5.00 12.00
MF19 Bob Feller Pants/125 12.50 30.00
MF20 Lou Brock Jkt/125 12.50 30.00
MF22 Jim Palmer Pants/50 10.00 25.00
MF26 Billy Williams Jsy/50 10.00 25.00
MF27 Juan Marichal Pants/125 8.00 20.00
MF29 Rod Carew Jsy/50 15.00 40.00
MF31 Fergie Jenkins Pants/125 8.00 20.00
MF32 Steve Carlton Pants/125 8.00 20.00
MF35 Johnny Bench Pants/50 20.00 50.00
MF36 Gaylord Perry Jsy/125 8.00 20.00
MF37 Gary Carter Pants/50 12.50 30.00
MF38 Tony Perez Jsy/50 10.00 25.00
MF39 Tony Oliva Jsy/125 12.00 30.00
MF40 Luis Aparicio Chi Bat/125 8.00 20.00
MF41 Tom Seaver Pants/50 25.00 60.00
MF42 Paul Molitor Pants/50 10.00 25.00
MF43 Dennis Eckersley Jsy/125 8.00 20.00
MF44 Willie McCovey Pants/50 15.00 40.00
MF46 Robin Roberts Hat/50 10.00 25.00
MF48 Ozzie Smith Pants/50 20.00 50.00
MF49 Nolan Ryan Angels Jkt/50 50.00 100.00
MF50 Stan Musial Pants/50 40.00 80.00
MF51 Bob Feller Pants/15 30.00 60.00
MF52 Bob Gibson Jsy/113 12.50 30.00
MF53 Cal Ripken Jsy/25 75.00 150.00
MF58 Gary Carter Jsy/100 12.50 30.00
MF61 Juan Marichal Pants/50 10.00 25.00
MF63 Mike Schmidt Sock/25 30.00 60.00
MF64 Nolan Ryan Jsy/50 50.00 100.00
MF66 Paul Molitor Jsy/48 10.00 25.00
MF70 Willie McCovey Jsy/44 15.00 40.00

2005 Absolute Memorabilia Marks of Fame Autograph Swatch Double

*DBL p/r 75-100: .4X TO 1X SNG p/r 100-125
*DBL p/r 75-100: .3X TO .8X SNG p/r 44-50
*DBL p/r 50: .5X TO 1.2X SNG p/r 100-125
*DBL p/r 50: .4X TO 1X SNG p/r 44-50
*DBL p/r 25-30: .6X TO 1.5X SNG p/r 100-125
*DBL p/r 25-30: .5X TO 1.2X SNG p/r 44-50
*DBL p/r 25-30: .4X TO 1X SNG p/r 25
OVERALL AU-GU ODDS ONE PER PACK
PRINT RUNS B/WN 1-100 COPIES PER
NO PRICING ON QTY OF 10 OR LESS
MF1 Bobby Doerr B-P/50 10.00 25.00
MF12 Hoyt Wilhelm J-J/25 20.00 50.00
MF53 Cal Ripken JK-P/25 75.00 150.00
MF55 Carlton Fisk B-J/30 20.00 50.00
MF58 Gary Carter H-J/25 15.00 40.00
MF66 Paul Molitor B-J/50 15.00 40.00

2005 Absolute Memorabilia Marks of Fame Autograph Swatch Double Spectrum Prime

*PRIME p/r 20-25: .6X TO 1.5X SNG p/r 44-50
OVERALL AU-GU ODDS ONE PER PACK
PRINT RUNS B/WN 1-25 COPIES PER
NO PRICING ON QTY OF 10 OR LESS

2005 Absolute Memorabilia Marks of Fame Autograph Swatch Triple

PRINT RUNS B/WN 1-25 COPIES PER
NO PRICING ON QTY OF 10 OR LESS
PRIME PRINT RUNS B/WN 1-10 PER
NO PRIME PRICING DUE TO SCARCITY
OVERALL AU-GU ODDS ONE PER PACK
MF53 Cal Ripken JK-J-P/25 90.00 180.00
MF55 Carlton Fisk B-J-J/25 30.00 60.00

2005 Absolute Memorabilia Recollection Autographs

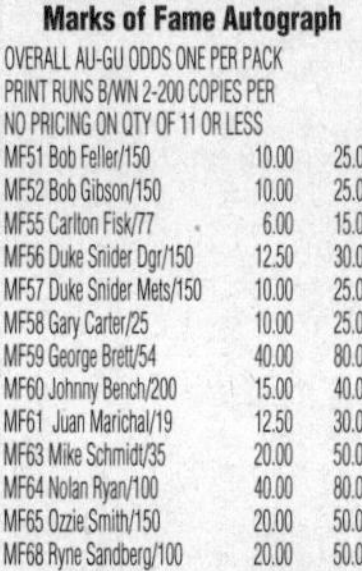

OVERALL AU-GU ODDS ONE PER PACK
NO PRICING ON QTY OF 18 OR LESS
PRINT RUNS B/WN 1-73 COPIES PER
DMU3 D.Murphy 87 Don DK/72 10.00 25.00
DMU6 D.Murphy 03 DK/73 10.00 25.00
DS1 Duke Snider 04 DK/20 15.00 40.00
DY1 Delmon Young 03 DK/46 20.00 50.00
HB1 Hank Blalock 02 DR/20 10.00 25.00
HB2 Hank Blalock 03 Don/20 10.00 25.00
KG2 Kirk Gibson 86 Don DK/20 10.00 25.00
MC2 Miguel Cabrera 04 DK/33 20.00 50.00
OS1 O.Smith 87 Don DK/30 20.00 50.00
OS8 O.Smith 03 DK/33 20.00 50.00

2005 Absolute Memorabilia Team Tandems

STATED PRINT RUN 250 SERIAL #'d SETS
*SPEC: .5X TO 1.2X BASIC
SPECTRUM PRINT RUN 150 #'d SETS
RANDOM INSERTS IN PACKS
TT1 M.Prior .75 2.00
K.Wood
TT2 B.Zito .75 2.00
T.Hudson
TT3 C.Schilling .75 2.00
P.Martinez
TT4 W.Clark .75 2.00
M.Williams
TT5 B.Williams .75 2.00
J.Giambi
TT6 V.Wells .75 2.00
R.Halladay
TT7 J.Beckett .50 1.25
A.Burnett
TT8 D.Murphy 1.25 3.00
P.Niekro
TT9 M.Schmidt 2.00 5.00
S.Carlton
TT10 T.Oliva 1.25 3.00
H.Killebrew
TT11 R.Yount 1.25 3.00
P.Molitor
TT12 F.Rodriguez .75 2.00
T.Percival
TT13 B.Sheets .50 1.25
D.Kolb
TT14 A.Jones .50 1.25
R.Furcal
TT15 T.Helton .75 2.00
P.Wilson
TT16 W.Boggs .75 2.00
F.McGriff
TT17 M.Ramirez 1.25 3.00
D.Ortiz
TT18 M.Cabrera 1.25 3.00
D.Willis
TT19 E.Renteria .75 2.00
S.Rolen
TT20 C.Beltran .75 2.00
J.Kent
TT21 E.Davis .75 2.00
D.Sanders
TT22 F.Thomas 1.25 3.00
P.Konerko
TT23 M.Piazza 1.25 3.00
A.Leiter
TT24 S.Burroughs .50 1.25
R.Klesko
TT25 K.Harvey .50 1.25
M.Sweeney
TT26 D.Sanders 2.00 5.00
H.Matsui
TT27 S.Carlton .75 2.00
M.Buehrle
TT28 G.Perry 1.25 3.00
R.Johnson
TT29 J.Morgan .75 2.00
S.Carlton
TT30 V.Guerrero .75 2.00
O.Cabrera
TT31 S.Rolen .75 2.00
J.Kruk
TT32 A.Boone .50 1.25
D.Young
TT33 R.Henderson 1.25 3.00
V.Guerrero
TT34 C.Johnson .50 1.25
C.Floyd
TT35 C.Ripken 4.00 10.00
R.Palmeiro
TT36 N.Ryan 4.00 10.00
F.Rodriguez
TT37 D.Erstad .75 2.00
J.Edmonds
TT38 T.Glaus 1.25 3.00
R.Henderson
TT39 B.Kim .50 1.25
R.Sanders
TT40 A.Galarraga .75 2.00
D.Justice
TT41 B.Jordan .50 1.25
R.Klesko
TT42 E.Bedard .50 1.25
G.Gil
TT43 B.Robinson .75 2.00
W.Clark
TT44 J.Towers .50 1.25
E.Bedard
TT45 N.Garciaparra .75 2.00
W.Boggs
TT46 J.Varitek 1.25 3.00
W.Boggs
TT47 J.Cruz .50 1.25
H.Choi
TT48 D.Lee .50 1.25
C.Patterson
TT49 J.Borchard .50 1.25
R.Durham
TT50 E.Davis .50 1.25
S.Casey
TT51 D.Young .50 1.25
W.Pena
TT52 E.Wynn .75 2.00
H.Newhouser
TT53 S.Casey .50 1.25
R.Branyan
TT54 B.Blyleven .75 2.00
J.Thome
TT55 J.Uribe .50 1.25
J.Pierre
TT56 J.Encarnacion .50 1.25
R.Fick
TT57 D.Young .50 1.25
J.Encarnacion
TT58 M.Ordonez .75 2.00
B.Higginson
TT59 C.Johnson .50 1.25
R.Dempster
TT60 C.Floyd .50 1.25
R.Dempster
TT61 M.Lowell .50 1.25
C.Floyd
TT62 D.Willis .50 1.25
C.Johnson
TT63 J.Cruz .50 1.25
K.Saarloos
TT64 J.Bagwell .75 2.00
R.Hidalgo
TT65 L.Berkman .75 2.00
R.Hidalgo
TT66 R.Hernandez .50 1.25
M.Sweeney
TT67 R.Hernandez .50 1.25
W.Wilson
TT68 J.Buck .50 1.25
R.Hernandez
TT69 A.Berroa .50 1.25
J.Affeldt
TT70 C.Park .75 2.00
K.Ishii
TT71 S.Green .50 1.25
K.Ishii
TT72 S.Green 1.25 3.00
R.Henderson
TT73 R.Sexson .50 1.25
L.Overbay
TT74 D.Ortiz 1.25 3.00
J.Romero
TT75 D.Ortiz 1.25 3.00
K.Puckett
TT76 M.Barrett .50 1.25
R.White
TT77 Z.Day .50 1.25
M.Barrett
TT78 T.Armas Jr. .50 1.25
Z.Day
TT79 R.Henderson 1.25 3.00
E.Alfonzo
TT80 H.Matsui 2.00 5.00
B.Williams
TT81 D.Mattingly 2.50 6.00
H.Matsui
TT82 M.Ellis .50 1.25
T.Long
TT83 R.Hernandez .50 1.25
E.Durazo
TT84 B.Duckworth .50 1.25
A.Machado
TT85 C.Wilson .50 1.25
F.Sanchez
TT86 B.Lawrence .50 1.25
D.Tankersley
TT87 T.Gwynn 1.50 4.00
T.Hoffman
TT88 A.Galarraga .75 2.00
P.Feliz
TT89 J.Kent .50 1.25
J.Snow
TT90 F.Garcia .50 1.25
J.Olerud
TT91 F.Garcia .75 2.00
E.Martinez
TT92 S.Taguchi .50 1.25
J.Drew
TT93 B.Grieve .50 1.25
B.Backe
TT94 D.Brazelton .50 1.25
J.Kennedy
TT95 T.Hall .50 1.25
P.LaForest
TT96 F.Francisco .50 1.25
G.Kapler
TT97 T.Hafner .50 1.25
D.Davis
TT98 J.Kent .50 1.25
R.Mondesi
TT99 S.Green .50 1.25
O.Hudson
TT100 M.Byrd .50 1.25
P.Wilson

2005 Absolute Memorabilia Team Tandems Swatch Single

OVERALL AU-GU ODDS ONE PER PACK
PRINT RUNS B/WN 5-150 COPIES PER
NO PRICING ON QTY OF 10 OR LESS
ALL ARE DUAL JERSEY UNLESS NOTED
TT1 M.Prior/K.Wood/125 3.00 8.00
TT2 B.Zito/T.Hudson125 2.50 6.00
TT3 C.Schilling/P.Martinez/125 3.00 8.00
TT4 W.Clark/M.Williams/125 3.00 8.00
TT5 B.Williams/J.Giambi/125 3.00 8.00
TT6 V.Wells/R.Halladay/125 2.50 6.00
TT7 J.Beckett/A.Burnett/125 2.50 6.00
TT8 D.Murphy/P.Niekro/125 6.00 15.00
TT9 M.Schmidt/S.Carlton/125 6.00 15.00
TT10 T.Oliva/H.Killebrew/50 10.00 25.00
TT11 R.Yount/P.Molitor/125 6.00 15.00
TT12 F.Rodriguez/T.Percival/25 4.00 10.00
TT13 B.Sheets/D.Kolb/125 2.50 6.00
TT14 A.Jones/R.Furcal/125 3.00 8.00
TT15 T.Helton/P.Wilson/125 3.00 8.00
TT16 W.Boggs/F.McGriff/50 4.00 10.00
TT17 M.Ramirez/D.Ortiz/125 5.00 12.00
TT18 M.Cabrera/D.Willis/125 3.00 8.00
TT19 E.Renteria/S.Rolen/125 3.00 8.00
TT20 C.Beltran/J.Kent Bat/125 2.50 6.00
TT21 E.Davis Bat/D.Sanders/125 3.00 8.00
TT22 F.Thomas/P.Konerko/50 5.00 12.00
TT23 M.Piazza/A.Leiter/125 4.00 10.00
TT24 S.Burroughs/R.Klesko/125 2.50 6.00
TT25 K.Harvey/M.Sweeney/125 2.50 6.00
TT26 D.Sanders/H.Matsui/125 10.00 25.00
TT27 S.Carlton/M.Buehrle/50 3.00 8.00
TT28 G.Perry/R.Johnson/125 4.00 10.00
TT29 J.Morgan/S.Carlton/25 4.00 10.00
TT31 S.Rolen/J.Kruk/125 3.00 8.00
TT32 A.Boone/D.Young/125 2.50 6.00
TT33 R.Hend Hat/V.Guerrero/25 6.00 15.00
TT34 C.Johnson/C.Floyd/125 2.50 6.00
TT35 C.Ripken/R.Palmeiro/125 10.00 25.00
TT36 N.Ryan/F.Rodriguez/75 10.00 25.00
TT37 D.Erstad/J.Edmonds Bat/25 4.00 10.00
TT38 T.Glaus/R.Hend Bat/150 4.00 10.00
TT39 B.Kim/R.Sanders/150 2.50 6.00
TT40 D.Justice/A.Galarraga/150 3.00 8.00
TT41 B.Jordan/R.Klesko/150 2.50 6.00
TT43 B.Rob Bat/W.Clark Bat/150 3.00 8.00
TT44 E.Bedard/J.Tow Pants/150 2.50 6.00
TT45 N.Garc Bat/W.Bog Bat/150 4.00 10.00
TT46 J.Var Bat/W.Boggs Bat/150 4.00 10.00
TT47 J.Cruz Hat/H.Choi/75 2.50 6.00
TT48 C.Patt Shoe/D.Lee/50 4.00 10.00
TT49 J.Borchard/R.Durham/75 2.50 6.00
TT50 E.Davis Bat/S.Casey/150 2.50 6.00
TT51 D.Young/W.Pena Bat/150 2.50 6.00
TT52 E.Wynn/H.Newhouser/150 3.00 8.00
TT53 S.Casey/R.Branyan/150 2.50 6.00
TT55 J.Uribe/J.Pierre Bat/150 2.50 6.00
TT56 J.Encar/R.Fick Bat/150 2.50 6.00
TT57 D.Young/J.Encarnacion/150 2.50 6.00
TT58 M.Ord Bat/B.Higg Bat/150 2.50 6.00
TT59 C.Johnson/R.Dempster/150 2.50 6.00
TT60 C.Floyd Bat/R.Demp/150 2.50 6.00
TT61 M.Lowell/C.Floyd Bat/150 2.50 6.00
TT62 D.Willis Bat/C.Johnson/150 2.50 6.00
TT63 J.Cruz/K.Saarloos/150 2.50 6.00
TT64 J.Bag Pants/R.Hid Bat/150 3.00 8.00
TT65 L.Berk Bat/R.Hid Pants/150 2.50 6.00
TT66 Ru.Hern/M.Sween Bat/50 3.00 8.00
TT67 Ru.Hern/W.Wils Bat/50 3.00 8.00
TT68 J.Buck Bat/Ru.Hern/50 3.00 8.00
TT69 A.Berr Bat/J.Aff Shoe/100 2.50 6.00
TT70 C.Park/K.Ishii/150 2.50 6.00
TT71 S.Green Bat/K.Ishii/150 2.50 6.00
TT72 S.Green Bat/R.Hen Bat/150 4.00 10.00
TT73 R.Sexson/L.Overbay/100 2.50 6.00
TT74 D.Ortiz/J.Romero/150 4.00 10.00
TT75 D.Ortiz/K.Puck Bat/150 4.00 10.00
TT76 M.Barrett/R.White/50 3.00 8.00
TT77 Z.Day/M.Barrett/50 3.00 8.00
TT78 T.Armas Jr./Z.Day/150 2.50 6.00
TT79 R.Hend Jkt/E.Alf Bat/150 4.00 10.00
TT80 H.Mat Bat/B.Will Bat/150 10.00 25.00
TT81 D.Matt Bat/H.Mat Bat/150 10.00 25.00
TT82 T.Long/M.Ellis/150 2.50 6.00
TT83 Ra.Hern/E.Durazo Bat/150 2.50 6.00
TT84 B.Duck/A.Machado/150 2.50 6.00
TT85 C.Wils Bat/F.San Bat/150 2.50 6.00
TT86 B.Law Bat/D.Tank Bat/150 2.50 6.00
TT87 T.Gwynn Pants/T.Hoff/150 6.00 15.00
TT88 A.Gala Bat/P.Feliz Shoe/50 4.00 10.00
TT89 J.Kent/J.Snow/150 2.50 6.00
TT90 F.Garcia/J.Olerud/50 3.00 8.00
TT91 F.Garcia/E.Martinez/100 3.00 8.00
TT92 S.Taguchi/J.Drew Bat/150 2.50 6.00
TT93 B.Grieve/B.Backe/100 2.50 6.00
TT94 D.Braz/J.Kennedy Bat/75 2.50 6.00
TT95 T.Hall/P.LaForest Bat/150 2.50 6.00
TT96 F.Francisco/G.Kapler/100 2.50 6.00
TT97 T.Hafner/D.Davis/100 2.50 6.00
TT98 J.Kent/R.Mondesi/100 2.50 6.00
TT100 M.Byrd Bat/P.Wils Bat/150 2.50 6.00

2005 Absolute Memorabilia Team Tandems Swatch Single Spectrum

*SPEC: p/r 75: .4X TO 1X SNG p/r 75-150
*SPEC: p/r 25: .6X TO 1.5X SNG p/r 75-150
*SPEC: p/r 25: .5X TO 1.2X SNG p/r 50
*SPEC: p/r 15: .6X TO 1.5X SNG p/r 50
OVERALL AU-GU ODDS ONE PER PACK
PRINT RUNS B/WN 1-75 COPIES PER
NO PRICING ON QTY OF 10 OR LESS

2005 Absolute Memorabilia Team Tandems Swatch Single Spectrum Prime Black

*PRIMEp/r70-150: .5X TO 1.2X SNGp/r75-150
*PRIME p/r 70-150: .4X TO 1X SNG p/r 50
*PRIMEp/r40-65: .6X TO 1.5X SNGp/r75-150
*PRIME p/r 25: .75X TO 2X SNG p/r 75-150
*PRIME p/r 15: 1X TO 2.5X SNG p/r 75-150
*PRIME p/r 15: .75X TO 2X SNG p/r 50
*PRIME p/r 15: .6X TO 1.5X SNG p/r 25
OVERALL AU-GU ODDS ONE PER PACK
PRINT RUNS B/WN 1-150 COPIES PER
NO PRICING ON QTY OF 1
TT30 V.Guerrero/O.Cabrera/15 10.00 25.00
TT42 G.Gil/E.Bedard/65 4.00 10.00
TT54 B.Blyleven/J.Thome/125 4.00 10.00

2005 Absolute Memorabilia Team Tandems Swatch Double

*DBL p/r 70-150: .6X TO 1.5X SNG p/r 75-150
*DBL p/r 70-150: .5X TO 1.2X SNG p/r 50
*DBL p/r 70-150: .4X TO 1X SNG p/r 25
*DBL p/r 50: .75X TO 2X SNG p/r 75-150
*DBL p/r 50: .6X TO 1.5X SNG p/r 50
*DBL p/r 50: .5X TO 1.2X SNG p/r 25
*DBL p/r 25: 1X TO 2.5X SNG p/r 75-150
*DBL p/r 25: .75X TO 2X SNG p/r 50
*DBL p/r 25: .6X TO 1.5X SNG p/r 25
OVERALL AU-GU ODDS ONE PER PACK
PRINT RUNS B/WN 1-150 COPIES PER
NO PRICING ON QTY OF 10 OR LESS
TT42 G.Gil/E.Bedard/150 4.00 10.00

2005 Absolute Memorabilia Team Tandems Swatch Double Spectrum

*SPECp/r70-100: .6X TO 1.5X SNGp/r75-150
*SPEC p/r 70-100: .5X TO 1.2X SNG p/r 50
*SPEC p/r 50-65: .75X TO 2X SNG p/r 75-150
*SPEC p/r 25: 1X TO 2.5X SNG p/r 75-150
*SPEC p/r 25: .6X TO 1.5X SNG p/r 25
OVERALL AU-GU ODDS ONE PER PACK
PRINT RUNS B/WN 1-100 COPIES PER
NO PRICING ON QTY OF 10 OR LESS
TT42 Erik Bedard Bat-Jsy 5.00 12.00
Geronimo Gil Bat-Jsy/65

2005 Absolute Memorabilia Team Tandems Swatch Double Spectrum Prime Black

*PRIME p/r 15: 1.5X TO 4X SNG p/r 125
*PRIME p/r 15: 1.25X TO 3X SNG p/r 50
*PRIME p/r 15: 1X TO 2.5X SNG p/r 25
OVERALL AU-GU ODDS ONE PER PACK
PRINT RUNS B/WN 1-15 COPIES PER
NO PRICING ON QTY OF 1
TT30 Vlad J-J/Cabrera B-J/15 15.00 40.00

2005 Absolute Memorabilia Team Trios

STATED PRINT RUN 200 SERIAL #'d SETS
*SPEC: .5X TO 1.2X BASIC
SPECTRUM PRINT RUN 125 #'d SETS
RANDOM INSERTS IN PACKS
TT1 Ripken 5.00 12.00
Palmer
Murray
TT2 Clemens/Boggs/Evans 2.00 5.00
TT3 Palmeiro/Tejada/Javy 1.00 2.50
TT4 Crawford/Baldelli/Upton 1.00 2.50
TT5 Buehrle/Magglio/C.Lee 1.00 2.50
TT6 V.Mart/Hafner/Gerut 1.00 2.50
TT7 Abreu/Myers/Millwood .60 1.50
TT8 Sosa/Aramis/Zambrano 1.50 4.00
TT9 Bo/Brett/Beltran 3.00 8.00
TT10 Nomo/Beltre/Green 1.50 4.00
TT11 Wilson/Wilson/Bay .60 1.50
TT12 Seaver/Ryan/Gooden 5.00 12.00
TT13 Dellucci/Nix/Mench .60 1.50
TT14 Trammell/Morris/Gibson 1.00 2.50
TT15 M.Will/Grace/Randy 1.50 4.00
TT16 Dawson/G.Cart/T.Perez 1.00 2.50
TT17 Murphy/Kruk/Dykstra 1.50 4.00
TT18 B.Roberts/Gibb/Bigbie .60 1.50
TT19 Lowell/I.Rod/Penny 1.00 2.50
TT20 Murray/Straw/Oliver 1.00 2.50
TT21 Straw/Rickey/Shef 1.50 4.00
TT22 Alomar/Crede/Durham 1.00 2.50
TT23 Kendall/Giles/Aramis .60 1.50
TT24 Delmon/Huff/Tino 1.50 4.00
TT25 Bagwell/Cruz/Morgan 1.00 2.50
TT26 Snow/Aurilia/Kent .60 1.50
TT27 Jenkins/Ryan/Cordero 5.00 12.00
TT28 Lofton/Thome/Alomar 1.00 2.50
TT29 Atkins/Helton/Jennings 1.00 2.50
TT30 G.Cart/Pedro/Randy 1.50 4.00
TT31 F.Rod/Glaus/Kotch 1.00 2.50
TT32 Kim/Williams/Womack 1.00 2.50
TT33 Just/Betemit/Ramirez .60 1.50
TT34 Jordan/Furcal/Helms .60 1.50
TT35 B.Rob/Matos/Lopez 1.00 2.50
TT36 Rickey/Nomar/Boggs 1.50 4.00
TT37 Choi/Alou/Lofton .60 1.50
TT38 Bo/Johnson/Borchard 1.50 4.00
TT39 Phillips/Branyan/Bard .60 1.50
TT40 Pierre/Atkins/Jennings .60 1.50
TT41 Monroe/Magg/Maroth 1.00 2.50
TT42 Pierre/Floyd/Dempster .60 1.50
TT43 Bagwell/Alou/Hidalgo 1.00 2.50
TT44 Berkman/Hidalgo/Alou 1.00 2.50
TT45 Runelvys/White/Wilson .60 1.50
TT46 Oliver/Park/Ishii 1.00 2.50
TT47 Molitor/Ginter/Sexson 1.50 4.00
TT48 Molitor/Jenk/Overbay 1.50 4.00
TT49 Ortiz/Mientk/Cuddyer 1.50 4.00
TT50 Floyd/Alfonzo/Payton .60 1.50
TT51 Alf/Cedeno/Ventura .60 1.50
TT52 Giambi/John/Lofton .60 1.50
TT53 Duck/Lofton/Byrd .60 1.50
TT54 Lofton/Sanchez/Wilson .60 1.50
TT55 Gwynn/Carter/Lawr 2.00 5.00
TT56 Snow/Alfonzo/Cruz .60 1.50
TT57 Pujols/Edmonds/Drew 2.00 5.00
TT58 Delgado/Wells/Mondesi .60 1.50
TT59 Hudson/Hinske/Halla 1.00 2.50
TT60 Byrd/Loaiza/Wilson .60 1.50

2005 Absolute Memorabilia Team Trios Swatch Single

OVERALL AU-GU ODDS ONE PER PACK
PRINT RUNS B/WN 25-150 COPIES PER
TT1 Ripken/Palmer/Murray/50 10.00 25.00
TT2 Clemens/Boggs/Evans/50 12.50 30.00
TT3 Palmeiro/Tejada/Javy/50 6.00 15.00
TT4 Crawford/Baldelli/Upton/50 5.00 12.00
TT5 Buehrle/Magglio/C.Lee/50 5.00 12.00
TT6 V.Mart/Hafner/Gerut/50 5.00 12.00
TT7 Abreu/Myers/Millwood/50 5.00 12.00
TT8 Sosa/Aramis/Zambrano/50 8.00 20.00
TT9 Bo/Brett/Beltran/50 12.50 30.00
TT10 Nomo/Beltre/Green/50 8.00 20.00
TT11 Wilson/Wilson/Bay/50 5.00 12.00
TT12 Seaver/Ryan/Gooden/50 15.00 40.00
TT13 Dellucci/Nix/Mench/50 5.00 12.00
TT14 Trammell/Morris/Gibson/50 5.00 12.00
TT15 M.Will/Grace/Randy/50 8.00 20.00
TT16 Dawson/G.Cart/T.Perez/50 5.00 12.00
TT17 Murphy/Kruk/Dykstra/50 8.00 20.00
TT18 B.Roberts/Gibb/Bigbie/50 5.00 12.00
TT19 Lowell/I.Rod/Penny/50 6.00 15.00
TT20 Murray/Straw/Oliver/50 8.00 20.00
TT21 Straw/Rickey/Shef/50 6.00 15.00
TT22 Alomar/Crede/Durham/50 6.00 15.00
TT23 Kendall/Giles/Aramis/25 6.00 15.00
TT24 Delmon/Huff/Tino/50 6.00 15.00
TT25 Bagwell/Cruz/Morgan/50 6.00 15.00
TT26 Snow/Aurilia/Kent/50 5.00 12.00
TT27 Jenkins/Ryan/Cordero/50 10.00 25.00
TT28 Lofton/Thome/Alomar/50 6.00 15.00
TT29 Atkins/Helton/Jennings/50 6.00 15.00
TT30 G.Cart/Pedro/Randy/50 8.00 20.00
TT31 F.Rod/Glaus/Kotch/150 4.00 10.00
TT32 Kim/Williams/Womack/150 5.00 12.00
TT33 Just/Betemit/Ramirez/50 5.00 12.00
TT34 Jordan/Furcal/Helms/150 4.00 10.00
TT35 B.Rob/Matos/Lopez/150 5.00 12.00
TT36 Rickey/Nomar/Boggs/150 6.00 15.00
TT37 Choi/Alou/Lofton/150 4.00 10.00
TT38 Bo/Johnson/Borchard/150 6.00 15.00
TT39 Phillips/Branyan/Bard/150 4.00 10.00
TT40 Pierre/Atkins/Jennings/150 4.00 10.00
TT41 Monroe/Magg/Maroth/150 4.00 10.00
TT42 Pierre/Floyd/Dempster/150 4.00 10.00
TT43 Bagwell/Alou/Hidalgo/150 5.00 12.00
TT44 Berkman/Hidalgo/Alou/150 4.00 10.00
TT45 R.Hern/White/Wilson/150 4.00 10.00
TT46 Oliver/Park/Ishii/150 4.00 10.00
TT47 Molitor/Ginter/Sexson/25 6.00 15.00
TT48 Molitor/Jenk/Overbay/150 4.00 10.00
TT49 Ortiz/Mientk/Cuddyer/150 5.00 12.00
TT50 Floyd/Alfonzo/Payton/150 4.00 10.00
TT51 Alf/Cedeno/Ventura/150 4.00 10.00
TT52 Giambi/John/Lofton/150 4.00 10.00
TT53 Duck/Lofton/Byrd/150 4.00 10.00
TT54 Lofton/Sanch/Wilson/150 4.00 10.00
TT55 Gwynn/Carter/Lawr/150 6.00 15.00
TT56 Snow/Alfonzo/Cruz/150 4.00 10.00
TT57 Pujols/Edmonds/Drew/100 10.00 25.00
TT59 Hudson/Hinske/Halla/150 4.00 10.00
TT60 Byrd/Loaiza/Wilson/150 4.00 10.00

2005 Absolute Memorabilia Team Trios Swatch Single Spectrum

*SPEC p/r 50: .4X TO 1X SNG p/r 50
*SPEC p/r 25: .6X TO 1.5X SNG p/r 100-150
*SPEC p/r 25: .5X TO 1.2X SNG p/r 50
*SPEC p/r 25: .4X TO 1X SNG p/r 25
OVERALL AU-GU ODDS ONE PER PACK
PRINT RUNS B/WN 10-50 COPIES PER
NO PRICING ON QTY OF 10

2005 Absolute Memorabilia Team Trios Swatch Single Spectrum Prime Black

*PRIMEp/r40-50: .6X TO 1.5X SNGp/r100-150
*PRIMEp/r100-150:.5XTO1.2XSNGp/r100-150
OVERALL AU-GU ODDS ONE PER PACK
PRINT RUNS B/WN 10-150 COPIES PER
NO PRICING ON QTY OF 10

2005 Absolute Memorabilia Team Trios Swatch Double

*DBL p/r 100: .6X TO 1.5X SNG p/r 50
*DBL p/r 50: .75X TO 2X SNG p/r 50
*DBL p/r 25: 1X TO 2.5X SNG p/r 50
OVERALL AU-GU ODDS ONE PER PACK
PRINT RUNS B/WN 25-100 COPIES PER

2005 Absolute Memorabilia Team Trios Swatch Double Spectrum

*SPEC p/r 35: .5X TO 1.2X SNG p/r 50
PRINT RUNS B/WN 5-35 COPIES PER
NO PRICING ON QTY OF 10 OR LESS
PRIME BLACK PRINT RUNS B/WN 5-10 PER
NO PRIME BLK PRICING DUE TO SCARCITY
OVERALL AU-GU ODDS ONE PER PACK

2005 Absolute Memorabilia Team Quads

STATED PRINT RUN 150 SERIAL #'d SETS
*SPEC: .5X TO 1.2X BASIC
SPECTRUM PRINT RUN 100 #'d SETS
RANDOM INSERTS IN PACKS
TQ1 St. Louis Card Active 2.00 5.00
TQ2 Cleveland Indians 1.00 2.50
TQ3 California Angels 1.00 2.50
TQ4 Boston Red Sox 1.00 2.50
TQ5 New York Yanks Active 2.50 6.00
TQ6 Atlanta Braves 2.00 5.00
TQ7 Oakland A's 1.00 2.50
TQ8 Anaheim Angels 1.00 2.50
TQ9 Texas Rangers Active 1.00 2.50
TQ10 Minnesota Twins Active 1.00 2.50
TQ11 New York Mets 1.50 4.00
TQ12 Houston Astros 5.00 12.00
TQ13 San Diego Padres 2.00 5.00
TQ14 Cincinnati Reds 1.00 2.50
TQ15 Texas Rangers Retro 5.00 12.00
TQ16 New York Yanks Retro 3.00 8.00
TQ17 St. Louis Cards Retro 2.00 5.00
TQ18 Pittsburgh Pirates 1.00 2.50
TQ19 Chicago Cubs 1.00 2.50
TQ20 Minnesota Twins Retro 1.50 4.00
TQ21 Anaheim Angels 1.50 4.00
TQ22 Arizona Diamondbacks 1.00 2.50
TQ23 Atlanta Braves 1.50 4.00
TQ24 Atlanta Braves 2.00 5.00
TQ25 Atlanta Braves 1.00 2.50
TQ26 Baltimore Orioles 1.00 2.50
TQ27 Boston Red Sox 1.50 4.00
TQ28 Boston Red Sox 2.00 5.00
TQ29 Boston Red Sox 1.50 4.00
TQ30 Chicago Cubs 1.50 4.00
TQ31 Chicago White Sox 1.50 4.00
TQ32 Chicago White Sox 1.50 4.00
TQ33 Chicago White Sox 1.50 4.00
TQ34 Cincinnati Reds 1.00 2.50
TQ35 Cincinnati Reds 1.00 2.50
TQ36 Cincinnati Reds 1.00 2.50
TQ37 Cleveland Indians 1.00 2.50
TQ38 Colorado Rockies 1.00 2.50
TQ39 Colorado Rockies .60 1.50
TQ40 Detroit Tigers .60 1.50
TQ41 Florida Marlins .60 1.50
TQ42 Florida Marlins .60 1.50
TQ43 Houston Astros 1.00 2.50
TQ44 Houston Astros 1.00 2.50
TQ45 Houston Astros 1.00 2.50
TQ46 Kansas City Royals .60 1.50
TQ47 Los Angeles Dodgers 1.50 4.00
TQ48 Los Angeles Dodgers 1.00 2.50
TQ49 Milwaukee Brewers 1.50 4.00
TQ50 Minnesota Twins 1.50 4.00
TQ51 Minnesota Twins 1.50 4.00

TQ52 Minnesota Twins 1.50 4.00
TQ53 Montreal Expos .60 1.50
TQ54 Montreal Expos .60 1.50
TQ55 New York Mets 3.00 8.00
TQ56 New York Mets 1.50 4.00
TQ57 New York Yankees 3.00 8.00
TQ58 New York Yankees 2.00 5.00
TQ59 New York Yankees 1.00 2.50
TQ60 Oakland A's .60 1.50
TQ61 Philadelphia Phillies 1.00 2.50
TQ62 Philadelphia Phillies .60 1.50
TQ63 Pittsburgh Pirates .60 1.50
TQ64 San Diego Padres 2.00 5.00
TQ65 San Francisco Giants 1.00 2.50
TQ66 San Francisco Giants 1.00 2.50
TQ67 Seattle Mariners .60 1.50
TQ68 St. Louis Cardinals 2.00 5.00
TQ69 Tampa Bay Devil Rays .60 1.50
TQ70 Tampa Bay Devil Rays 1.50 4.00
TQ71 Texas Rangers 1.00 2.50
TQ72 Texas Rangers 1.00 2.50
TQ73 Texas Rangers 1.00 2.50
TQ74 Toronto Blue Jays .60 1.50
TQ75 Toronto Blue Jays .60 1.50

2005 Absolute Memorabilia Team Quads Swatch Single

OVERALL AU-GU ODDS ONE PER PACK
PRINT RUNS B/WN 25-150 COPIES PER
TQ1 St. Louis Card Active/100 10.00 25.00
TQ2 Cleveland Indians/100 15.00 40.00
TQ3 California Angels/100 6.00 15.00
TQ4 Boston Red Sox/100 6.00 15.00
TQ5 New York Yanks Active/100 10.00 25.00
TQ6 Atlanta Braves/100 10.00 25.00
TQ7 Oakland A's/100 6.00 15.00
TQ8 Anaheim Angels/100 8.00 20.00
TQ9 Texas Rangers Active/100 6.00 15.00
TQ10 Minnesota Twins Active/25 10.00 25.00
TQ11 New York Mets/100 8.00 20.00
TQ12 Houston Astros/100 15.00 40.00
TQ13 San Diego Padres/100 10.00 25.00
TQ14 Cincinnati Reds/100 5.00 12.00
TQ15 Texas Rangers Retro/100 12.50 30.00
TQ16 New York Yanks Retro/100 20.00 50.00
TQ17 St. Louis Cards Retro/25 15.00 40.00
TQ18 Pittsburgh Pirates/100 6.00 15.00
TQ19 Chicago Cubs/100 6.00 15.00
TQ20 Minnesota Twins Retro/100 8.00 20.00
TQ21 Anaheim Angels/150 8.00 20.00
TQ22 Arizona Diamondbacks/150 5.00 12.00
TQ23 Atlanta Braves/150 8.00 20.00
TQ24 Atlanta Braves/150 10.00 25.00
TQ25 Atlanta Braves/150 6.00 15.00
TQ26 Baltimore Orioles/150 6.00 15.00
TQ27 Boston Red Sox/150 8.00 20.00
TQ28 Boston Red Sox/150 10.00 25.00
TQ29 Boston Red Sox/150 8.00 20.00
TQ30 Chicago Cubs/150 8.00 20.00
TQ31 Chicago White Sox/150 8.00 20.00
TQ32 Chicago White Sox/150 8.00 20.00
TQ33 Chicago White Sox/150 8.00 20.00
TQ34 Cincinnati Reds/100 5.00 12.00
TQ35 Cincinnati Reds/150 5.00 12.00
TQ36 Cincinnati Reds/150 5.00 12.00
TQ37 Cleveland Indians/150 5.00 12.00
TQ38 Colorado Rockies/150 5.00 12.00
TQ39 Colorado Rockies/150 5.00 12.00
TQ40 Detroit Tigers/150 5.00 12.00
TQ41 Florida Marlins/150 5.00 12.00
TQ42 Florida Marlins/150 5.00 12.00
TQ43 Houston Astros/150 6.00 15.00
TQ44 Houston Astros/150 6.00 15.00
TQ45 Houston Astros/150 5.00 12.00
TQ46 Kansas City Royals/150 5.00 12.00
TQ47 Los Angeles Dodgers/150 8.00 20.00
TQ48 Los Angeles Dodgers/150 5.00 12.00
TQ49 Milwaukee Brewers/100 5.00 12.00
TQ50 Minnesota Twins/150 8.00 20.00
TQ51 Minnesota Twins/150 8.00 20.00
TQ52 Minnesota Twins/150 8.00 20.00
TQ53 Montreal Expos/150 5.00 12.00
TQ54 Montreal Expos/150 5.00 12.00
TQ55 New York Mets/150 15.00 40.00
TQ56 New York Mets/150 8.00 20.00
TQ57 New York Yankees/150 20.00 50.00
TQ58 New York Yankees/100 8.00 20.00
TQ59 New York Yankees/150 6.00 15.00
TQ60 Oakland A's/150 5.00 12.00
TQ61 Philadelphia Phillies/75 5.00 12.00
TQ62 Philadelphia Phillies/150 5.00 12.00
TQ63 Pittsburgh Pirates/150 6.00 15.00
TQ64 San Diego Padres/150 8.00 20.00
TQ65 San Francisco Giants/150 6.00 15.00
TQ66 San Francisco Giants/150 6.00 15.00
TQ67 Seattle Mariners/150 5.00 12.00
TQ68 St. Louis Cardinals/135 10.00 25.00
TQ69 Tampa Bay Devil Rays/150 5.00 12.00
TQ71 Texas Rangers/150 6.00 15.00
TQ72 Texas Rangers/150 6.00 15.00
TQ73 Texas Rangers/150 6.00 15.00
TQ74 Toronto Blue Jays/150 5.00 12.00
TQ75 Toronto Blue Jays/150 5.00 12.00

2005 Absolute Memorabilia Team Quads Swatch Single Spectrum

*SPEC p/r 75-100: .4X TO 1X SNG p/r 75-150
*SPEC p/r 45-50: .5X TO 1.2X SNG p/r 75-150
*SPEC p/r 25-35: .6X TO 1.5X SNG p/r 75-150
OVERALL AU-GU ODDS ONE PER PACK
PRINT RUNS B/WN 10-100 COPIES PER
NO PRICING ON QTY OF 10

2005 Absolute Memorabilia Team Quads Swatch Single Spectrum Prime Black

*PRIMEp/r100-150:.6XTO1.5XSNGp/r75-150
*PRIMEp/r60-:.75XTO 2X SNGp/r75-150
OVERALL AU-GU ODDS ONE PER PACK
PRINT RUNS B/WN 10-150 COPIES PER
NO PRICING ON QTY OF 10

2005 Absolute Memorabilia Team Quads Swatch Double

*DBL p/r 75: .6X TO 1.5X SNG p/r 100
*DBL p/r 25: 1X TO 2.5X SNG p/r 100
*DBL p/r 25: .6X TO 1.5X SNG p/r 25
OVERALL AU-GU ODDS ONE PER PACK
PRINT RUNS B/WN 25-75 COPIES PER

2005 Absolute Memorabilia Team Quads Swatch Double Spectrum

*SPEC p/r 25: 1X TO 2.5X SNG p/r 100
PRINT RUNS B/WN 1-25 COPIES PER
NO PRICING ON QTY OF 10 OR LESS
PRIME BLK PRINT RUNS B/WN 1-5 PER
NO PRIME BLK PRICING DUE TO SCARCITY
OVERALL AU-GU ODDS ONE PER PACK

2005 Absolute Memorabilia Team Six

STATED PRINT RUN 100 SERIAL #'d SETS
*SPEC: .6X TO 1.5X BASIC
SPECTRUM PRINT RUN 50 #'d SETS
RANDOM INSERTS IN PACKS
TS1 San Francisco Giants 4.00 10.00
TS2 Houston Astros 2.50 6.00
TS3 Cincinnati Reds 2.00 5.00
TS4 St. Louis Cardinals 3.00 8.00
TS5 New York Yankees 4.00 10.00
TS6 Chicago Cubs 2.50 6.00
TS7 Arizona Diamondbacks 1.25 3.00
TS8 Los Angeles Dodgers 2.00 5.00
TS9 Anaheim Angels 1.25 3.00
TS10 Boston Red Sox 2.50 6.00
TS11 Seattle Mariners 2.50 6.00
TS12 Chicago White Sox 2.00 5.00
TS13 Philadelphia Phillies 3.00 8.00
TS14 New York Mets 6.00 15.00
TS15 Atlanta Braves 2.00 5.00
TS16 Anaheim Angels 2.00 5.00
TS17 Arizona Diamondbacks 1.25 3.00
TS18 Atlanta Braves 2.50 6.00
TS19 Atlanta Braves 2.00 5.00
TS20 Baltimore Orioles 1.25 3.00
TS21 Boston Red Sox 2.50 6.00
TS22 Boston Red Sox 2.50 6.00
TS23 Chicago Cubs 1.25 3.00
TS24 Chicago Cubs 2.00 5.00
TS25 Chicago White Sox 2.00 5.00
TS26 Chicago White Sox 2.00 5.00
TS27 Cincinnati Reds 1.25 3.00
TS28 Cincinnati Reds 1.25 3.00
TS29 Cleveland Indians 1.25 3.00
TS30 Cleveland Indians 1.25 3.00
TS31 Colorado Rockies 1.25 3.00
TS32 Colorado Rockies 1.25 3.00
TS33 Detroit Tigers 1.25 3.00
TS34 Florida Marlins .75 2.00
TS35 Houston Astros 1.25 3.00
TS36 Houston Astros 1.25 3.00
TS37 Houston Astros 1.25 3.00
TS38 Kansas City Royals .75 2.00
TS39 Los Angeles Dodgers 2.00 5.00
TS40 Los Angeles Dodgers 2.00 5.00
TS41 Minnesota Twins 1.25 3.00
TS42 Minnesota Twins 2.00 5.00
TS43 Minnesota Twins 2.00 5.00
TS44 Montreal Expos 1.25 3.00
TS45 New York Mets 4.00 10.00
TS46 New York Mets 2.00 5.00
TS47 New York Yankees 4.00 10.00
TS48 New York Yankees 1.25 3.00
TS49 Philadelphia Phillies 1.25 3.00
TS50 Pittsburgh Pirates .75 2.00
TS51 San Diego Padres 2.50 6.00
TS52 San Francisco Giants 4.00 10.00
TS53 St. Louis Cardinals 3.00 8.00
TS54 St. Louis Cardinals 2.50 6.00
TS55 Tampa Bay Devil Rays 2.00 5.00
TS56 Texas Rangers 1.25 3.00
TS57 Texas Rangers 6.00 15.00
TS58 Toronto Blue Jays 1.25 3.00
TS59 Toronto Blue Jays .75 2.00
TS60 Toronto Blue Jays .75 2.00

2005 Absolute Memorabilia Team Six Swatch Single

OVERALL AU-GU ODDS ONE PER PACK
PRINT RUNS B/WN 14-150 COPIES PER
NO PRICING ON QTY OF 14
TS1 San Francisco Giants/50 50.00 100.00
TS2 Houston Astros/50 15.00 40.00
TS3 Cincinnati Reds/15 20.00 50.00
TS4 St. Louis Cardinals/15 50.00 100.00
TS5 New York Yankees/50 30.00 60.00
TS6 Chicago Cubs/50 15.00 40.00
TS7 Arizona Diamondbacks/50 8.00 20.00
TS8 Los Angeles Dodgers/50 12.50 30.00
TS9 Anaheim Angels/50 12.50 30.00
TS10 Boston Red Sox/50 20.00 50.00
TS12 Chicago White Sox/50 12.50 30.00
TS13 Philadelphia Phillies/50 15.00 40.00
TS14 New York Mets/50 20.00 50.00
TS15 Atlanta Braves/50 12.50 30.00
TS16 Anaheim Angels/150 10.00 25.00
TS17 Arizona Diamondbacks/150 8.00 20.00
TS18 Atlanta Braves/150 10.00 25.00
TS19 Atlanta Braves/150 15.00 40.00
TS20 Baltimore Orioles/150 8.00 20.00
TS21 Boston Red Sox/150 15.00 40.00
TS22 Boston Red Sox/150 15.00 40.00
TS23 Chicago Cubs/150 8.00 20.00
TS24 Chicago Cubs/150 10.00 25.00
TS25 Chicago White Sox/150 10.00 25.00
TS26 Chicago White Sox/150 10.00 25.00
TS27 Cincinnati Reds/150 6.00 15.00
TS28 Cincinnati Reds/150 6.00 15.00
TS30 Cleveland Indians/150 8.00 20.00
TS31 Colorado Rockies/150 6.00 15.00
TS32 Colorado Rockies/150 6.00 15.00
TS33 Detroit Tigers/150 6.00 15.00
TS34 Florida Marlins/150 6.00 15.00
TS35 Houston Astros/150 8.00 20.00
TS36 Houston Astros/150 8.00 20.00
TS37 Houston Astros/150 8.00 20.00
TS38 Kansas City Royals/150 6.00 15.00
TS39 Los Angeles Dodgers/75 10.00 25.00
TS40 Los Angeles Dodgers/150 10.00 25.00
TS41 Minnesota Twins/150 8.00 20.00
TS42 Minnesota Twins/150 10.00 25.00
TS43 Minnesota Twins/150 10.00 25.00
TS44 Montreal Expos/150 6.00 15.00
TS45 New York Mets/150 20.00 50.00
TS46 New York Mets/150 10.00 25.00
TS47 New York Yankees/150 20.00 50.00
TS48 New York Yankees/150 8.00 20.00
TS49 Philadelphia Phillies/150 6.00 15.00
TS50 Pittsburgh Pirates/150 6.00 15.00
TS51 San Diego Padres/150 10.00 25.00
TS52 San Francisco Giants/150 20.00 50.00
TS54 St. Louis Cardinals/150 15.00 40.00
TS56 Texas Rangers/150 8.00 20.00
TS57 Texas Rangers/100 15.00 40.00
TS58 Toronto Blue Jays/150 6.00 15.00
TS59 Toronto Blue Jays/150 6.00 15.00

2005 Absolute Memorabilia Team Six Swatch Single Spectrum

*SPEC p/r 75-100: .4X TO 1X SNG p/r 75-150
*SPEC p/r 50: .5X TO 1.2X SNG p/r 75-150
*SPEC p/r 25: .6X TO 1.5X SNG p/r 75-150
*SPEC p/r 25: .5X TO 1.2X SNG p/r 50
PRINT RUNS B/WN 1-100 COPIES PER
NO PRICING ON QTY OF 10 OR LESS
PRIME BLACK PRINT RUN 5 #'d SETS
NO PRIME BLK PRICING DUE TO SC ARCITY
OVERALL AU-GU ODDS ONE PER PACK

2005 Absolute Memorabilia Tools of the Trade Red

STATED PRINT RUN 250 SERIAL #'d SETS
*BLACK: .6X TO 1.5X BASIC
BLACK PRINT RUN 100 SERIAL #'d SETS
*BLUE: .5X TO 1.2X BASIC
BLUE PRINT RUN 150 SERIAL #'d SETS
REV.SPEC.BLACK PRINT RUN 5 #'d SETS
NO REV.SPEC.BLACK PRICING AVAILABLE
REV.SPEC.BLUE PRINT RUN 10 #'d SETS
NO REV.SPEC.BLUE PRICING AVAILABLE
*REV.SPEC.RED: 1X TO 2.5X BASIC
REV.SPEC.RED PRINT RUN 50 #'d SETS
1 Ozzie Smith 1.50 4.00
2 Carlos Beltran Astros .75 2.00
3 Dale Murphy 1.25 3.00
4 Paul Molitor 1.25 3.00
5 George Brett 2.50 6.00
6 Stan Musial 2.00 5.00
7 Ivan Rodriguez FLA .75 2.00
8 Carl Yastrzemski 1.50 4.00
9 Reggie Jackson A's .75 2.00
10 Hideo Nomo 1.25 3.00
11 Gary Sheffield .50 1.25
12 Roberto Alomar .75 2.00
13 Pedro Martinez .75 2.00
14 Ernie Banks 1.25 3.00
15 Tim Hudson .75 2.00
16 Dwight Gooden .50 1.25
17 Lance Berkman .75 2.00
18 Darryl Strawberry Mets .50 1.25
19 Larry Walker .75 2.00
20 Lou Brock .75 2.00
21 Roger Clemens 1.50 4.00
22 Paul Lo Duca .50 1.25
23 Don Mattingly 2.50 6.00
24 Willie Mays 2.50 6.00
25 Rafael Palmeiro .75 2.00
26 Roy Oswalt .75 2.00
27 Vladimir Guerrero .75 2.00
28 Austin Kearns .50 1.25
29 Rod Carew .75 2.00
30 Nolan Ryan Angels 4.00 10.00
31 Richie Sexson .50 1.25
32 Steve Carlton .75 2.00
33 Eddie Murray .75 2.00
34 Nolan Ryan Rgr 4.00 10.00
35 Mike Mussina O's .75 2.00
36 Sean Casey .50 1.25
37 Juan Gonzalez Rgr .50 1.25
38 Curt Schilling Sox .75 2.00
39 Darryl Strawberry Yanks .50 1.25
40 Alfonso Soriano .75 2.00
41 Tom Seaver .75 2.00
42 Mike Schmidt 2.00 5.00
43 Todd Helton .75 2.00
44 Reggie Jackson Yanks .75 2.00
45 Shawn Green .50 1.25
46 Mike Mussina Yanks .75 2.00
47 Tom Glavine .75 2.00
48 Torii Hunter .50 1.25
49 Kerry Wood .50 1.25
50 Carlos Delgado .50 1.25
51 Randy Johnson Astros 1.25 3.00
52 David Ortiz 1.25 3.00
53 Troy Glaus .50 1.25
54 Rickey Henderson Mets 1.25 3.00
55 Craig Biggio .75 2.00
56 Brad Penny .50 1.25
57 Gary Carter Mets .75 2.00
58 Andy Pettitte .75 2.00
59 Mark Prior .75 2.00
60 Kirby Puckett 1.25 3.00
61 Willie McCovey .75 2.00
62 Andre Dawson Expos .75 2.00
63 Greg Maddux 1.50 4.00
64 Adrian Beltre 1.25 3.00
65 Andruw Jones .50 1.25
66 Juan Gonzalez Indians .50 1.25
67 Frank Thomas 1.25 3.00
68 Victor Martinez .75 2.00
69 Randy Johnson D'backs 1.25 3.00
70 Andre Dawson Cubs .75 2.00
71 Adam Dunn .75 2.00
72 Carlton Fisk .75 2.00
73 Cal Ripken 4.00 10.00
74 Kenny Lofton .50 1.25
75 Barry Zito .75 2.00
76 Sammy Sosa 1.25 3.00
77 Deion Sanders .75 2.00
78 Tony Gwynn 1.50 4.00
79 Mike Piazza 1.25 3.00
80 Jeff Bagwell .75 2.00
81 Manny Ramirez 1.25 3.00
82 Carlos Beltran Royals .75 2.00
83 Mark Grace .75 2.00
84 Robin Yount 1.25 3.00
85 Albert Pujols 1.50 4.00
86 Dontrelle Willis .50 1.25
87 Jim Thome .75 2.00
88 Magglio Ordonez .75 2.00
89 Miguel Tejada .75 2.00
90 Mark Teixeira .75 2.00
91 Gary Carter Expos .75 2.00
92 Ivan Rodriguez Rgr .75 2.00
93 Jason Giambi .50 1.25
94 Rickey Henderson A's 1.25 3.00
95 Curt Schilling D'backs .75 2.00
96 Bobby Doerr .75 2.00
97 Chipper Jones 1.25 3.00
98 Eric Chavez .50 1.25
99 Johnny Bench 1.25 3.00
100 Harmon Killebrew 1.25 3.00
101 Andre Dawson .75 2.00
102 Babe Ruth 3.00 8.00
103 Bernie Williams .75 2.00
104 Billy Wagner .50 1.25
105 Billy Williams .75 2.00
106 Bo Jackson 1.25 3.00
107 Bob Gibson .75 2.00
108 Brad Penny .50 1.25
109 Burleigh Grimes .75 2.00
110 Cal Ripken 4.00 10.00
111 Casey Fossum .50 1.25
112 Curt Schilling .75 2.00
113 Dale Murphy 1.25 3.00
114 Darryl Strawberry .50 1.25
115 Dave Concepcion .50 1.25
116 Dave Winfield .75 2.00
117 David Cone .50 1.25
118 Fergie Jenkins .75 2.00
119 Gary Carter .75 2.00
120 Gary Sheffield .50 1.25
121 Gaylord Perry .75 2.00
122 Hank Aaron 2.50 6.00
123 Harmon Killebrew 1.25 3.00
124 Harold Baines .75 2.00
125 Hideki Matsui 2.00 5.00
126 Hideo Nomo 1.25 3.00
127 Hoyt Wilhelm .75 2.00
128 Jason Giambi Yanks .50 1.25
129 Jason Giambi A's .50 1.25
130 Jeff Bagwell .75 2.00
131 Jim Palmer .75 2.00
132 Jim Thorpe 2.00 5.00
133 Joe Mays .50 1.25
134 John Buck .50 1.25
135 John Kruk .50 1.25
136 Jorge Posada .75 2.00
137 Josh Beckett .50 1.25
138 Josh Phelps .50 1.25
139 Juan Pierre .50 1.25
140 Kazuhisa Ishii .50 1.25
141 Kenny Lofton .50 1.25
142 Kevin Brown .50 1.25
143 Kevin Millwood Braves .50 1.25
144 Kevin Millwood Phils .50 1.25
145 Lance Berkman .75 2.00
146 Lenny Dykstra .75 2.00
147 Lou Boudreau .75 2.00
148 Magglio Ordonez .75 2.00
149 Marcus Giles .50 1.25
150 Mark Grace .75 2.00
151 Mark Prior .75 2.00
152 Marlon Byrd .50 1.25
153 Miguel Tejada .75 2.00
154 Mike Lowell .50 1.25
155 Mike Piazza 1.25 3.00
156 Mike Sweeney .50 1.25
157 Morgan Ensberg .50 1.25
158 Nolan Ryan 4.00 10.00
159 Orel Hershiser .50 1.25
160 Ozzie Smith 1.50 4.00
161 Pedro Martinez .75 2.00
162 Phil Rizzuto .75 2.00
163 Rafael Furcal .50 1.25
164 Rafael Palmeiro .75 2.00
165 Randy Johnson D'backs 1.25 3.00
166 Randy Johnson Astros 1.25 3.00
167 Richie Sexson .50 1.25
168 Rickey Henderson Mets 1.25 3.00
169 Rickey Henderson A's 1.25 3.00
170 Rickey Henderson M's 1.25 3.00
171 Roberto Alomar .75 2.00
172 Roberto Clemente 3.00 8.00
173 Robin Yount 1.25 3.00
174 Rod Carew .75 2.00
175 Roger Clemens 1.50 4.00
176 Roger Maris A's 1.25 3.00
177 Roger Maris Yanks 1.25 3.00
178 Ron Cey .50 1.25
179 Ryan Klesko .50 1.25
180 Ryne Sandberg 2.50 6.00
181 Sammy Sosa 1.25 3.00
182 Shawn Green .50 1.25
183 Stan Musial 2.00 5.00
184 Steve Carlton .75 2.00
185 Ted Williams 2.50 6.00
186 Ted Williams 2.50 6.00
187 Tim Hudson .75 2.00
188 Todd Helton .75 2.00
189 Tom Glavine .75 2.00
190 Tom Seaver .75 2.00
191 Tommy John .50 1.25
192 Tony Gwynn 1.50 4.00
193 Vladimir Guerrero .75 2.00
194 Wade Boggs Sox .75 2.00
195 Wade Boggs Rays .75 2.00
196 Warren Spahn .75 2.00
197 Willie Mays 2.50 6.00
198 Willie McCovey .75 2.00
199 Willie Stargell .75 2.00
200 Yogi Berra 1.25 3.00

2005 Absolute Memorabilia Tools of the Trade Bat

OVERALL AU-GU ODDS ONE PER PACK
PRINT RUNS B/WN 1-250 COPIES PER
NO PRICING ON QTY OF 1
102 Babe Ruth/250 75.00 200.00
122 Hank Aaron/250 10.00 25.00
172 Roberto Clemente/250 15.00 40.00
176 Roger Maris A's/100 12.50 30.00
177 Roger Maris Yanks/61 15.00 40.00
185 Ted Williams/250 15.00 40.00
197 Willie Mays/50 15.00 40.00

2005 Absolute Memorabilia Tools of the Trade Bat Reverse

*REV p/r 100-150: .4X TO 1X BAT p/r 100-250
*REV p/r 50: .4X TO 1X BAT p/r 50-61
*REV p/r 24-35: .6X TO 1.5X BAT p/r 100-250
*REV p/r 24-35: .5X TO 1.2X BAT p/r 50-61
OVERALL AU-GU ODDS ONE PER BOX
PRINT RUNS B/WN 1-150 COPIES PER
NO PRICING ON QTY OF 1
102 Babe Ruth/150 75.00 200.00

2005 Absolute Memorabilia Tools of the Trade Bat Red

*RED p/r 50: .5X TO 1.2X BAT p/r 100-250
*RED p/r 21-25: .6X TO 1.5X BAT p/r 100-250
PRINT RUNS B/WN 1-50 COPIES PER
NO PRICING ON QTY OF 10 OR LESS
BLACK PRINT RUN 1 SERIAL #'d SET
NO BLACK PRICING DUE TO SCARCITY
OVERALL AU-GU ODDS ONE PER PACK
102 Babe Ruth/25 100.00 250.00

2005 Absolute Memorabilia Tools of the Trade Jersey

OVERALL AU-GU ODDS ONE PER PACK
PRINT RUNS B/WN 1-250 COPIES PER
NO PRICING ON QTY OF 14 OR LESS
102 Babe Ruth/100 250.00 500.00
122 Hank Aaron/250 15.00 40.00
132 Jim Thorpe/250 50.00 100.00
177 R.Maris Yanks Pants/100 15.00 40.00
186 Ted Williams/75 30.00 60.00
197 Willie Mays/24 15.00 40.00

2005 Absolute Memorabilia Tools of the Trade Jersey Reverse

*REV p/r 150: .4X TO 1X JSY p/r 75-250
*REV p/r 41-50: .5X TO 1.2X JSY p/r 75-250
OVERALL AU-GU ODDS ONE PER PACK
PRINT RUNS B/WN 1-150 COPIES PER
NO PRICING ON QTY OF 10 OR LESS
102 Babe Ruth/50 100.00 200.00
132 Jim Thorpe/150 50.00 100.00
199 Willie Stargell/25 5.00 12.00

2005 Absolute Memorabilia Tools of the Trade Jersey Red

*RED p/r 25: .6X TO 1.5X JSY p/r 75-250
PRINT RUNS B/WN 1-25 COPIES PER
NO PRICING ON QTY OF 10 OR LESS
BLACK PRINT RUN 1 SERIAL #'d SET
NO BLACK PRICING DUE TO SCARCITY
OVERALL AU-GU ODDS ONE PER PACK
102 Babe Ruth/25 250.00 400.00
132 Jim Thorpe/25 75.00 150.00

2005 Absolute Memorabilia Tools of the Trade Swatch Single Jumbo

*SNG p/r 75-250: .6X TO 1.5X DBL p/r 70-200
*SNG p/r 75-250: .5X TO 1.2X DBL p/r 50-60
*SNG p/r 75-250: .4X TO 1X DBL p/r 20-29
*SNG p/r 45-62: .75X TO 2X DBL p/r 70-200
*SNG p/r 45-62: .6X TO 1.5X DBL p/r 50-60
*SNG p/r 45-62: .5X TO 1.2X DBL p/r 20-29
*SNG p/r 25: 1X TO 2.5X DBL p/r 70-200
*SNG p/r 25: .75X TO 2X DBL p/r 50-60
*SNG p/r 25: .6X TO 1.5X DBL p/r 20-29
OVERALL AU-GU ODDS ONE PER PACK
PRINT RUNS B/WN 1-250 COPIES PER
NO PRICING ON QTY OF 10 OR LESS
37 J.Gonzalez Rgr Jsy/25 6.00 15.00
70 A.Dawson Cubs Jsy/50 6.00 15.00
98 Eric Chavez Jsy/100 4.00 10.00
102 Babe Ruth Jsy/95 1500.00 2500.00
104 Billy Wagner Jsy/250 4.00 10.00
105 Billy Williams Jsy/85 5.00 12.00
106 Bo Jackson Jsy/250 8.00 20.00
107 Bob Gibson Jsy/50 12.50 30.00
109 B.Grimes Pants/83 75.00 150.00
111 Casey Fossum Jsy/250 3.00 8.00
114 D.Strawberry Jsy/100 5.00 12.00
118 Fergie Jenkins Jsy/95 5.00 12.00
127 Hoyt Wilhelm Jsy/225 8.00 20.00
132 Jim Thorpe Jsy/200 75.00 200.00
136 Jorge Posada Jsy/250 6.00 15.00
138 Josh Phelps Jsy/200 3.00 8.00
139 Juan Pierre Jsy/250 4.00 10.00
142 Kevin Brown Jsy/250 4.00 10.00
143 K.Millwood Braves Jsy/250 4.00 10.00
144 K.Millwood Phils Jsy/250 4.00 10.00
146 Lenny Dykstra Jsy/100 5.00 12.00
147 Lou Boudreau Jsy/75 15.00 40.00
152 Marlon Byrd Jsy/25 5.00 12.00
154 Mike Lowell Jsy/200 4.00 10.00
159 Orel Hershiser Jsy/100 5.00 12.00
161 Pedro Martinez Jsy/175 5.00 12.00
162 Phil Rizzuto Jsy/100 15.00 40.00
176 R.Maris A's Jsy/199 40.00 80.00
177 R.Maris Yanks Jsy/250 40.00 80.00
178 Ron Cey Jsy/250 5.00 12.00
179 Ryan Klesko Jsy/250 4.00 10.00
185 Ted Williams Jsy/50 90.00 150.00
186 Ted Williams Jkt/100 25.00 60.00
198 W.McCovey Pants/100 15.00 40.00

2005 Absolute Memorabilia Tools of the Trade Swatch Single Jumbo Reverse

*REV p/r 75-150: .6X TO 1.5X DBL p/r 70-200
*REV p/r 75-150: .5X TO 1.2X DBL p/r 50-60
*REV p/r 75-150: .4X TO 1X DBL p/r 20-29
*REV p/r 44-59: .75X TO 2X DBL p/r 70-200
*REV p/r 20-25: 1X TO 2.5X DBL p/r 70-200
*REV p/r 20-25: .75X TO 2X DBL p/r 50-60
*REV p/r 20-25: .6X TO 1.5X DBL p/r 20-29
*REV p/r 15-17: 1.25X TO 3X DBL p/r 70-200
OVERALL AU-GU ODDS ONE PER PACK
PRINT RUNS B/WN 1-50 COPIES PER
NO PRICING ON QTY OF 10 OR LESS
70 A.Dawson Cubs Jsy/25 8.00 20.00
98 Eric Chavez Jsy/50 5.00 12.00
102 Babe Ruth Jsy/24 1200.00 2000.00
104 Billy Wagner Jsy/100 4.00 10.00
105 Billy Williams Jsy/25 8.00 20.00
106 Bo Jackson Jsy/150 10.00 25.00
107 Bob Gibson Jsy/25 12.50 30.00
109 B.Grimes Pants/23 100.00 175.00
111 Casey Fossum Jsy/150 3.00 8.00
114 Darryl Strawberry Jsy/25 8.00 20.00
118 Fergie Jenkins Jsy/25 8.00 20.00
127 Hoyt Wilhelm Jsy/50 10.00 25.00
132 Jim Thorpe Jsy/50 200.00 400.00
135 John Kruk Jsy/20 8.00 20.00
136 Jorge Posada Jsy/150 12.50 30.00
138 Josh Phelps Jsy/50 4.00 10.00
139 Juan Pierre Jsy/150 4.00 10.00
142 Kevin Brown Jsy/150 4.00 10.00
143 K.Millwood Braves Jsy/100 4.00 10.00
144 K.Millwood Phils Jsy/150 4.00 10.00
146 Lenny Dykstra Jsy/50 6.00 15.00
147 Lou Boudreau Jsy/25 20.00 50.00
154 Mike Lowell Jsy/100 4.00 10.00
159 Orel Hershiser Jsy/25 8.00 20.00
161 Pedro Martinez Jsy/100 5.00 12.00
176 R.Maris A's Jsy/50 50.00 100.00
177 R.Maris Yanks Jsy/59 50.00 100.00
179 Ryan Klesko Jsy/100 4.00 10.00
186 Ted Williams Jkt/25 100.00 175.00
198 W.McCovey Pants/44 10.00 25.00
200 Yogi Berra Pants/100 20.00 50.00

2005 Absolute Memorabilia Tools of the Trade Swatch Single Jumbo Prime Black

*BLACK p/r 25: .6X TO 1.5X RED p/r 75
*BLACK p/r 25: .5X TO 1.2X RED p/r 40-50
OVERALL AU-GU ODDS ONE PER PACK
PRINT RUNS B/WN 1-25 COPIES PER
NO PRICING ON QTY OF 10 OR LESS

2005 Absolute Memorabilia Tools of the Trade Swatch Single Jumbo Prime Red

OVERALL AU-GU ODDS ONE PER PACK
PRINT RUNS B/WN 1-50 COPIES PER
NO PRICING ON QTY OF 10 OR LESS
*LISTED PRICES ARE FOR 3-COLOR PATCH
*ADD 20% FOR 4-COLOR+ PATCH
*REDUCE 20% FOR 2-COLOR PATCH
NO PRICING AVAIL FOR LOGO PATCHES
LOGO PATCHES COMMAND BIG PREMIUMS
7 I.Rodriguez M's Jsy/25 40.00 80.00
10 Hideo Nomo Jsy/25 75.00 150.00
12 Roberto Alomar Jsy/25 10.00 25.00
15 Tim Hudson Jsy/50 20.00 50.00
17 Lance Berkman Jsy/25 50.00 100.00
19 Larry Walker Jsy/50 20.00 50.00
22 Paul Lo Duca Jsy/50 15.00 40.00
25 Rafael Palmeiro Jsy/25 40.00 80.00
27 Vladimir Guerrero Jsy/25 50.00 100.00
31 Richie Sexson Jsy/50 15.00 40.00
36 Sean Casey Jsy/50 15.00 40.00
43 Todd Helton Jsy/15 40.00 80.00
45 Shawn Green Jsy/50 15.00 40.00
47 Tom Glavine Jsy/50 40.00 80.00
50 Carlos Delgado Jsy/25 20.00 50.00
53 Troy Glaus Jsy/50 15.00 40.00
59 Mark Prior Jsy/25 40.00 80.00
63 Greg Maddux Jsy/25 125.00 250.00
64 Adrian Beltre Jsy/50 15.00 40.00
65 Andruw Jones Jsy/50 40.00 80.00
67 Frank Thomas Jsy/50 40.00 80.00
68 Victor Martinez Jsy/15 20.00 50.00
71 Adam Dunn Jsy/25 20.00 50.00
73 Cal Ripken Jsy/25 60.00 120.00
76 Sammy Sosa Jsy/25 50.00 100.00
78 Tony Gwynn Jsy/50 15.00 40.00
79 Mike Piazza Jsy/25 100.00 200.00
80 Jeff Bagwell Jsy/25 50.00 100.00
82 C.Beltran Royal Jsy/50 15.00 40.00
85 Albert Pujols Jsy/25 175.00 300.00
88 M.Ordonez Jsy/50 12.50 30.00
89 Miguel Tejada Jsy/50 20.00 50.00
90 Mark Teixeira Jsy/25 40.00 80.00
92 I.Rodriguez Rgr Jsy/25 40.00 80.00
98 Eric Chavez Jsy/15 20.00 50.00
112 Curt Schilling Jsy/35 20.00 50.00
115 D.Concepcion Jsy/25 40.00 80.00
117 David Cone Jsy/35 8.00 20.00
128 J.Giambi Yanks Jsy/15 40.00 80.00
138 Josh Phelps Jsy/45 4.00 10.00
142 Kevin Brown Jsy/30 20.00 50.00
143 K.Millwood Braves Jsy/40 10.00 25.00
144 K.Millwood Phils Jsy/75 10.00 25.00
152 Marlon Byrd Jsy/75 6.00 15.00
159 Orel Hershiser Jsy/25 50.00 100.00
161 P.Martinez Expos Jsy/25 75.00 150.00
168 R.Hend Mets Jkt/15 75.00 150.00
169 R.Hend A's Jsy/15 75.00 150.00
170 R.Hend M's Jsy/44 20.00 50.00
173 Robin Yount Jsy/50 15.00 40.00
181 Sammy Sosa Jsy/50 30.00 60.00
187 Tim Hudson Jsy/25 20.00 50.00
189 Tom Glavine Jsy/25 50.00 100.00
191 Tommy John Jsy/15 40.00 80.00
199 Willie Stargell Jsy/50 40.00 80.00

2005 Absolute Memorabilia Tools of the Trade Swatch Double

OVERALL AU-GU ODDS ONE PER PACK
PRINT RUNS B/WN 1-200 COPIES PER
NO PRICING ON QTY OF 10 OR LESS
B = Bat, BL = Belt, BG = Batting Glove
CP = Chest Protector, FG = Fielding Glove
H = Hat, HM = Helmet, JK = Jacket
J = Jersey, P = Pants, SG = Shin Guard
S = Shoes, SO = Socks, ST = Stirrups
SW = Sweatband
1 Ozzie Smith B-P/50 8.00 20.00
2 C.Belt Astros J-S/50 8.00 20.00
3 Dale Murphy J-J/50 5.00 12.00
4 Paul Molitor J-P/150 3.00 8.00
5 George Brett B-H/25 12.50 30.00
6 Stan Musial B-P/25 15.00 40.00
7 Ivan Rodriguez M's J-J/150 3.00 8.00
8 Carl Yastrzemski B-J/25 12.50 30.00
9 Reggie Jackson A's J-J/50 5.00 12.00
10 Hideo Nomo J-P/150 5.00 12.00
11 Gary Sheffield H-J/25 4.00 10.00
12 Roberto Alomar B-J/150 3.00 8.00
13 Pedro Martinez J-P/150 3.00 8.00
15 Tim Hudson H-J/100 2.50 6.00
17 Lance Berkman B-J/150 2.50 6.00
19 Larry Walker J-J/150 3.00 8.00
20 Lou Brock B-JK/150 4.00 10.00
21 Roger Clemens B-J/150 6.00 15.00
22 Paul Lo Duca B-J/50 3.00 8.00
23 Don Mattingly BG-P/50 10.00 25.00
24 Willie Mays B-P/25 30.00 60.00
25 Rafael Palmeiro B-J/150 3.00 8.00
27 Vladimir Guerrero B-J/150 4.00 10.00
29 Rod Carew JK-JK/150 4.00 10.00
30 N.Ryan Angels B-JK/150 10.00 25.00
31 Richie Sexson H-J/150 2.50 6.00
32 Steve Carlton B-H/150 4.00 10.00
33 Eddie Murray B-J/150 6.00 15.00
34 Nolan Ryan Rgr B-J/150 10.00 25.00
35 Mike Mussina O's J-P/125 3.00 8.00
36 Sean Casey J-P/150 2.50 6.00
38 Curt Schilling Sox J-J/150 3.00 8.00
39 Darryl Strawberry Yanks B-J/150 3.00 8.00
41 Tom Seaver J-P/150 4.00 10.00
42 Mike Schmidt B-J/150 8.00 20.00
43 Todd Helton B-J/150 3.00 8.00
45 Shawn Green B-J/150 2.50 6.00
47 Tom Glavine B-J/150 3.00 8.00
49 Kerry Wood FG-J/150 2.50 6.00
50 Carlos Delgado B-J/100 2.50 6.00
51 R.John Astros J-P/150 4.00 10.00
52 David Ortiz B-J/150 4.00 10.00
53 Troy Glaus J-J/150 2.50 6.00
54 R.Hend Mets B-J/150 4.00 10.00
55 Craig Biggio B-J/150 3.00 8.00
56 Brad Penny FG-J/150 2.00 5.00
57 Gary Carter Mets J-P/150 3.00 8.00
58 Andy Pettitte J-J/150 3.00 8.00
59 Mark Prior FG-J/150 3.00 8.00
60 Kirby Puckett B-FG/100 5.00 12.00
61 Willie McCovey J-P/150 4.00 10.00
62 A.Dawson Expos B-J/20 10.00 25.00
63 Greg Maddux B-J/50 8.00 20.00
64 Adrian Beltre J-J/150 2.50 6.00
65 Andruw Jones B-J/150 3.00 8.00
67 Frank Thomas J-J/150 10.00 25.00
68 Victor Martinez CP-J/150 2.50 6.00
69 Randy Johnson D'back J-P/150 4.00 10.00
71 Adam Dunn B-J/95 2.50 6.00
72 Carlton Fisk B-J/150 4.00 10.00
73 Cal Ripken J-P/150 10.00 25.00
74 Kenny Lofton B-H/150 3.00 8.00
75 Barry Zito J-J/150 2.50 6.00
76 Sammy Sosa B-J/150 4.00 10.00
77 Deion Sanders J-P/150 8.00 20.00
78 Tony Gwynn J-P/150 6.00 15.00
79 Mike Piazza J-P/150 4.00 10.00
80 Jeff Bagwell J-P/150 3.00 8.00
81 Manny Ramirez B-J/150 3.00 8.00
83 Mark Grace B-J/50 4.00 10.00
84 Robin Yount B-J/150 5.00 12.00
85 Albert Pujols B-P/150 10.00 25.00
86 Dontrelle Willis B-J/150 2.50 6.00
88 Magglio Ordonez B-S/150 2.50 6.00
89 Miguel Tejada H-J/150 2.50 6.00
90 Mark Teixeira FG-J/150 3.00 8.00
91 Gary Carter Expos B-J/25 5.00 12.00
92 Ivan Rodriguez Rgr CP-J/150 3.00 8.00
93 Jason Giambi H-J/50 3.00 8.00
94 R.Hend A's B-P/150 4.00 10.00
95 C.Schil D'back J-J/150 2.50 6.00
96 Bobby Doerr B-P/150 3.00 8.00
97 Chipper Jones B-J/150 4.00 10.00
99 Johnny Bench B-P/150 6.00 15.00
100 H.Killebrew H-J/50 12.50 30.00
101 Andre Dawson B-J/50 4.00 10.00
102 Babe Ruth B-P/150 150.00 250.00
103 Bernie Williams B-J/85 3.00 8.00
108 Brad Penny FG-S/70 2.00 5.00
110 Cal Ripken JK-P/100 10.00 25.00
112 Curt Schilling FG-J/100 2.50 6.00
115 Dave Concepcion B-J/60 5.00 12.00
116 Dave Winfield FG-H/75 3.00 8.00
122 Hank Aaron B-J/200 20.00 50.00
124 Harold Baines J-J/75 3.00 8.00
125 Hideki Matsui B-P/150 8.00 20.00
126 Hideo Nomo J-P/125 4.00 10.00
128 J.Giambi Yanks J-J/100 2.50 6.00
130 Jeff Bagwell P-P/150 3.00 8.00
133 Joe Mays FG-J/150 2.00 5.00
134 John Buck B-CP/150 2.00 5.00
140 Kazuhisa Ishii J-J/150 2.00 5.00
141 Kenny Lofton B-FG/125 3.00 8.00
149 Marcus Giles J-S/135 2.50 6.00
153 Miguel Tejada J-J/75 2.50 6.00
155 Mike Piazza B-P/150 4.00 10.00
156 M.Sweeney B-FG/55 3.00 8.00
157 M.Ensberg FG-H/55 3.00 8.00
163 Rafael Furcal B-J/150 2.50 6.00
164 R.Palmeiro B-P/150 3.00 8.00
165 R.John D'backs J-J/75 4.00 10.00
166 R.John Astros J-P/150 4.00 10.00
167 Richie Sexson J-P/150 2.50 6.00
168 R.Hend Mets B-JK/150 5.00 12.00
169 R.Hend A's J-P/100 5.00 12.00
170 R.Hend M's B-J/150 4.00 10.00
171 Roberto Alomar B-J/25 6.00 15.00
174 Rod Carew J-J/29 6.00 15.00
175 Roger Clemens B-J/100 6.00 15.00
176 Roger Maris A's J-P/50 30.00 60.00
177 R.Maris Yanks J-P/150 20.00 50.00
181 Sammy Sosa B-J/150 4.00 10.00
182 Shawn Green B-J/150 2.50 6.00
184 Steve Carlton FG-P/150 3.00 8.00
185 Ted Williams JK-J/100 30.00 60.00
186 Ted Williams B-J/100 30.00 60.00
187 Tim Hudson H-J/150 2.50 6.00
188 Todd Helton B-J/150 3.00 8.00
189 Tom Glavine B-J/25 5.00 12.00
190 Tom Seaver J-P/150 4.00 10.00
191 Tommy John B-J/150 3.00 8.00
192 Tony Gwynn J-P/150 6.00 15.00
193 V.Guerrero B-J/100 4.00 10.00
196 Warren Spahn J-P/150 10.00 25.00
197 Willie Mays B-J/150 15.00 40.00
199 Willie Stargell B-J/25 6.00 15.00
200 Yogi Berra J-P/25 12.50 30.00

2005 Absolute Memorabilia Tools of the Trade Swatch Double Prime Black

*PRIME p/r 100: .75X TO 2X DBL p/r 20-29
*PRIME p/r 45-50: .6X TO 1.5X DBL p/r 70-200
*PRIME p/r 45-50: .5X TO 1.2X DBL p/r 50-60
*PRIME p/r 45-50: .4X TO 1X DBL p/r 20-29
*PRIME p/r 20-35: .75X TO 2X DBL p/r 70-200
*PRIME p/r 20-35: .6X TO 1.5X DBL p/r 50-60
*PRIME p/r 20-35: .5X TO 1.2X DBL p/r 20-29
*PRIME p/r 15: 1X TO 2.5X DBL p/r 70-200
*PRIME p/r 15: .6X TO 1.5X DBL p/r 20-29
OVERALL AU-GU ODDS ONE PER PACK
PRINT RUNS B/WN 1-100 COPIES PER
NO PRICING ON QTY OF 10 OR LESS
16 Dwight Gooden J-S/20 6.00 15.00
18 D.Strawberry Mets B-J/50 5.00 12.00
26 Roy Oswalt J-S/25 5.00 12.00
28 Austin Kearns B-J/25 4.00 10.00
37 Juan Gonzalez Rgr J-P/50 4.00 10.00
48 Torii Hunter B-J/50 4.00 10.00
66 J.Gonz Indians B-J/50 4.00 10.00
82 C.Belt Royal H-J/25 5.00 12.00
104 Billy Wagner J-J/25 5.00 12.00
105 Billy Williams J-J/50 5.00 12.00
107 Bob Gibson J-J/25 10.00 25.00
111 Casey Fossum J-J/50 3.00 8.00
114 D.Strawberry B-J/35 6.00 15.00
119 Gary Carter B-JK/30 6.00 15.00
136 Jorge Posada J-J/45 6.00 15.00
143 K.Millw Braves J-J/35 5.00 12.00
144 K.Millw Phils J-J/50 4.00 10.00
159 Orel Hershiser J-J/15 8.00 20.00
161 Pedro Martinez J-J/15 8.00 20.00

2005 Absolute Memorabilia Tools of the Trade Swatch Double Prime Red

*PRIMEp/r75-150: .5X TO 1.2X DBLp/r70-200
*PRIME p/r 75-150: .4X TO 1X DBL p/r 50-60
*PRIME p/r 75-150: .3X TO .8X DBL p/r 20-29
*PRIME p/r 40-55: .6X TO 1.5X DBL p/r 70-200
*PRIME p/r 40-55: .5X TO 1.2X DBL p/r 50-60
*PRIME p/r 40-55: .4X TO 1X DBL p/r 20-29
*PRIME p/r 20-35: .75X TO 2X DBL p/r 70-200
*PRIME p/r 20-35: .6X TO 1.5X DBL p/r 50-60
*PRIME p/r 20-35: .5X TO 1.2X DBL p/r 20-29
*PRIME p/r 15: 1X TO 2.5X DBL p/r 70-200
*PRIME p/r 15: .6X TO 1.5X DBL p/r 20-29
OVERALL AU-GU ODDS ONE PER PACK
PRINT RUNS B/WN 1-150 COPIES PER
NO PRICING ON QTY OF 12 OR LESS
14 Ernie Banks B-J/25 30.00 60.00
16 Dwight Gooden J-S/50 5.00 12.00
18 D.Strawberry Mets B-J/50 5.00 12.00
26 Roy Oswalt J-S/50 4.00 10.00
28 Austin Kearns B-J/50 3.00 8.00
37 Juan Gonzalez Rgr J-P/100 3.00 8.00
48 Torii Hunter B-J/100 3.00 8.00
66 J.Gonz Indians B-J/100 3.00 8.00
70 A.Dawson Cubs J-P/15 8.00 20.00
82 C.Belt Royal H-J/50 4.00 10.00
87 Jim Thome J-J/25 6.00 15.00
96 Eric Chavez B-J/25 5.00 12.00
104 Billy Wagner J-J/90 3.00 8.00
105 Billy Williams J-J/150 4.00 10.00
107 Bob Gibson J-J/50 8.00 20.00
111 Casey Fossum J-J/110 2.50 6.00
113 Dale Murphy B-J/15 10.00 25.00
114 Darryl Strawberry B-J/150 4.00 10.00
118 Fergie Jenkins J-J/15 8.00 20.00
119 Gary Carter B-JK/50 5.00 12.00
121 Gaylord Perry J-J/20 6.00 15.00
127 Hoyt Wilhelm J-J/30 10.00 25.00
129 J.Giambi A's B-H/20 5.00 12.00
142 Kevin Brown J-J/25 5.00 12.00
143 K.Millwood Braves J-J/150 3.00 8.00
144 K.Millwood Phils J-J/150 3.00 8.00
159 Orel Hershiser J-J/55 5.00 12.00
161 Pedro Martinez J-J/50 5.00 12.00

2005 Absolute Memorabilia Tools of the Trade Swatch Triple

*TRIP p/r 70-175: .5X TO 1.2X DBL p/r 70-200
*TRIP p/r 70-175: .4X TO 1X DBL p/r 50-60
*TRIP p/r 50-55: .4X TO 1X DBL p/r 20-29
*TRIP p/r 20-25: .75X TO 2X DBL p/r 70-200
*TRIP p/r 20-25: .6X TO 1.5X DBL p/r 50-60
*TRIP p/r 20-25: .5X TO 1.2X DBL p/r 20-29
*TRIP p/r 15: 1X TO 2.5X DBL p/r 70-200
*TRIP p/r 15: .75X TO 2X DBL p/r 50-60
OVERALL AU-GU ODDS ONE PER PACK
PRINT RUNS B/WN 1-175 COPIES PER
NO PRICING ON QTY OF 10 OR LESS
14 Ernie Banks B-H-J/15 20.00 50.00
18 D.Straw Mets B-FG-S/15 8.00 20.00
37 Juan Gonzalez 5.00 12.00
Rgr B-J-P/25
70 A.Dawson Cubs B-J-P/25 6.00 15.00
82 C.Belt Royal B-J-S/15 6.00 15.00
96 Eric Chavez B-J-J/25 5.00 12.00
102 Babe Ruth B-J-P/50 450.00 750.00
111 Casey Fossum FG-J-S/55 3.00 8.00
122 Hank Aaron B-H-J/75 20.00 50.00
138 Josh Phelps B-FG-J/115 2.50 6.00
139 Juan Pierre B-BG-J/100 3.00 8.00
142 Kevin Brown B-J-J/25 6.00 15.00
146 L.Dykstra B-FG-J/125 4.00 10.00
154 Mike Lowell B-J-J/175 3.00 8.00
176 R.Maris A's B-J-P/50 40.00 80.00
177 R.Maris Yanks B-J-P/100 30.00 60.00
179 Ryan Klesko FG-J-J/25 5.00 12.00
185 Ted Williams B-JK-J/50 50.00 100.00
186 Ted Williams B-JK-J/50 50.00 100.00
197 Willie Mays B-J-P/100 20.00 50.00
200 Yogi Berra J-J-P/25 20.00 50.00

2005 Absolute Memorabilia Tools of the Trade Swatch Triple Prime Black

*PRIME p/r 40-50: 1X TO 2.5X DBL p/r 70-200
*PRIME p/r 40-50: .75X TO 2X DBL p/r 50-60
*PRIMEp/r25-30: 1.25X TO 3X DBLp/r70-200
*PRIME p/r 25-30: .75X TO 2X DBL p/r 20-29
*PRIME p/r 15: 1.5X TO 4X DBL p/r 70-200
OVERALL AU-GU ODDS ONE PER PACK
PRINT RUNS B/WN 1-50 COPIES PER
NO PRICING ON QTY OF 10 OR LESS
26 Roy Oswalt BG-FG-J/15 10.00 25.00
37 J.Gonzalez Rgr B-J-P/15 10.00 25.00
48 Torii Hunter B-J-J/15 10.00 25.00
66 J.Gonz Indians B-J-J/15 10.00 25.00
111 Casey Fossum J-J-S/50 5.00 12.00
114 D.Strawberry B-J-J/50 8.00 20.00
119 Gary Carter BG-JK-S/30 10.00 25.00
127 Hoyt Wilhelm J-J-J/25 15.00 40.00
129 J.Giambi A's H-J-J/15 10.00 25.00
138 Josh Phelps FG-J-J/40 5.00 12.00
142 Kevin Brown B-J-J/50 6.00 15.00
144 K.Millw Phils J-J-J/50 6.00 15.00
151 Mark Prior B-H-H/25 10.00 25.00
152 Marlon Byrd B-J-J/50 5.00 12.00
161 Pedro Martinez B-J-J/25 10.00 25.00

2005 Absolute Memorabilia Tools of the Trade Swatch Triple Prime Red

*PRIME p/r 75-100: .75X TO 2X DBLp/r70-200
*PRIME p/r 75-100: .6X TO 1.5X DBLp/r 50-60
*PRIME p/r 40-65: 1X TO 2.5X DBL p/r 70-200
*PRIME p/r 40-65: .75X TO 2X DBL p/r 50-60
*PRIME p/r 40-65: .6X TO 1.5X DBL p/r 20-29
*PRIMEp/r24-35: 1.25X TO 3X DBLp/r70-200
*PRIMEp/r24-35: .75X TO 2X DBLp/r20-29
*PRIME p/r 15: 1.5X TO 4X DBL p/r 70-200
*PRIME p/r 15: 1.25X TO 3X DBL p/r 50-60
*PRIME p/r 15: 1X TO 2.5X DBL p/r 20-29
OVERALL AU-GU ODDS ONE PER PACK
PRINT RUNS B/WN 1-100 COPIES PER
NO PRICING ON QTY OF 10 OR LESS
26 Roy Oswalt BG-FG-J/25 8.00 20.00
28 Austin Kearns B-FG-J/15 8.00 20.00
37 J.Gonzalez Rgr B-J-P/25 8.00 20.00
40 Alfonso Soriano B-J-J/25 8.00 20.00
48 Torii Hunter B-J-J/25 8.00 20.00
66 J.Gonz Indians B-J-J/25 8.00 20.00
70 A.Dawson Cubs B-J-P/15 12.50 30.00
87 Jim Thome J-J-J/15 12.50 30.00
98 Eric Chavez B-J-J/15 10.00 25.00
111 Casey Fossum J-J-S/100 4.00 10.00
114 D.Strawberry B-J-J/100 6.00 15.00
119 Gary Carter BG-JK-S/50 8.00 20.00
122 Hank Aaron B-H-J/100 30.00 80.00
127 Hoyt Wilhelm J-J-J/75 10.00 25.00
129 J.Giambi A's H-J-J/35 8.00 20.00
138 Josh Phelps FG-J-J/75 4.00 10.00
142 Kevin Brown B-J-J/100 5.00 12.00
144 K.Millw Phils J-J-J/100 5.00 12.00
151 Mark Prior B-H-H/40 8.00 20.00
152 Marlon Byrd B-J-J/100 4.00 10.00
161 Pedro Martinez B-J-J/75 6.00 15.00
197 Willie Mays B-J-P/24 60.00 120.00

2005 Absolute Memorabilia Tools of the Trade Swatch Quad

*QUAD p/r 75-150: .75X TO 2X DBL p/r 70-200
*QUAD p/r 75-150: .6X TO 1.5X DBL p/r 50-60
*QUAD p/r 75-150: .5X TO 1.2X DBL p/r 20-29
*QUAD p/r 50-65: 1X TO 2.5X DBL p/r 70-200
*QUAD p/r 50-65: .75X TO 2X DBL p/r 50-60
*QUAD p/r 20-35: 1.25X TO 3X DBL p/r 70-200
*QUAD p/r 20-35: 1X TO 2.5X DBL p/r 50-60
*QUAD p/r 20-35: .75X TO 2X DBL p/r 20-29
*QUAD p/r 15: 1.5X TO 4X DBL p/r 70-200
*QUAD p/r 15: 1.25X TO 3X DBL p/r 50-60
OVERALL AU-GU ODDS ONE PER PACK
PRINT RUNS B/WN 1-150 COPIES PER
NO PRICING ON QTY OF 10 OR LESS
14 Ernie Banks B-H-J-J/25 15.00 40.00
24 Willie Mays B-J-P-J/25 40.00 100.00
26 Roy Oswalt BG-FG-J-S/30 8.00 20.00
37 J.Gonz Rgr B-H-J-P/15 10.00 25.00
46 M.Muss Yank H-J-J-S/25 10.00 25.00
66 J.Gonz Indians B-J-J-J/30 8.00 20.00
70 A.Daws Cubs B-J-J-P/25 10.00 25.00
82 C.Belt Royal B-H-J-S/20 8.00 20.00
98 Eric Chavez B-J-J-J/15 10.00 25.00
102 Babe Ruth B-J-J-P/20 700.00 1200.00
111 C.Fossum FG-H-J-S/150 4.00 10.00
113 Dale Murphy B-J-J-J/30 12.50 30.00
114 D.Straw B-FG-J-J/75 6.00 15.00
120 G.Sheffield B-FG-H-S/25 8.00 20.00
122 Hank Aaron B-H-J-J/150 30.00 60.00
129 J.Giam A's B-H-J-J/150 5.00 12.00
138 Josh Phelps B-FG-J-S/75 4.00 10.00
139 Juan Pierre B-H-J-S/112 5.00 12.00
151 Mark Prior B-H-J-S/50 8.00 20.00
152 Marlon Byrd B-J-J-S/35 6.00 15.00
161 P.Martinez B-J-J-P/150 6.00 15.00
173 Robin Yount H-HM-J-J/15 20.00 50.00
179 Ryan Klesko FG-H-J-J/25 8.00 20.00
186 T.Williams B-JK-J-J/50 125.00 200.00

2005 Absolute Memorabilia Tools of the Trade Swatch Quad Reverse

*REV p/r 100: .75X TO 2X DBL p/r 70-200
*REV p/r 40-65: 1X TO 2.5X DBL p/r 70-200
*REV p/r 20-35: 1.25X TO 3X DBL p/r 70-200
*REV p/r 20-35: .75X TO 2X DBL p/r 20-29
*REV p/r 15: 1.5X TO 4X DBL p/r 70-200
*REV p/r 15: 1.25X TO 3X DBL p/r 50-60
OVERALL AU-GU ODDS ONE PER PACK
PRINT RUNS B/WN 1-100 COPIES PER
NO PRICING ON QTY OF 10 OR LESS
111 C.Fossum FG-H-J-S/65 5.00 12.00
114 D.Straw B-FG-J-J/25 10.00 25.00
122 Hank Aaron B-H-J-J/100 20.00 50.00
129 J.Giambi A's B-H-J-J/50 6.00 15.00
138 Josh Phelps B-FG-J-S/25 6.00 15.00
139 Juan Pierre B-H-J-S/65 6.00 15.00
151 Mark Prior B-H-J-S/25 10.00 25.00
152 Marlon Byrd B-J-J-S/15 8.00 20.00
161 P.Martinez B-J-J-P/50 8.00 20.00

2005 Absolute Memorabilia Tools of the Trade Swatch Quad Prime Black

*PRIME p/r 25: 1.5X TO 4X DBL p/r 70-200
*PRIME p/r 25: 1.25X TO 3X DBL p/r 50-60
OVERALL AU-GU ODDS ONE PER PACK
PRINT RUNS B/WN 1-25 COPIES PER
NO PRICING ON QTY OF 5 OR LESS
119 G.Cart BG-CP-FG-JK/25 12.50 30.00
142 Kevin Brown B-J-J-J/25 10.00 25.00
148 M.Ordonez B-BG-J-S/25 10.00 25.00
154 Mike Lowell B-J-J-J/25 10.00 25.00

2005 Absolute Memorabilia Tools of the Trade Swatch Quad Prime Red

*PRIME p/r 50: 1.25X TO 3X DBL p/r 70-200
*PRIME p/r 50: 1X TO 2.5X DBL p/r 50-60
OVERALL AU-GU ODDS ONE PER PACK
PRINT RUNS B/WN 1-75 COPIES PER
NO PRICING ON QTY OF 12 OR LESS
119 G.Cart BG-CP-FG-JK/75 12.50 30.00
142 Kevin Brown B-J-J-J/50 8.00 20.00
148 M.Ordonez B-BG-J-S/50 8.00 20.00
154 Mike Lowell B-J-J-J/50 8.00 20.00
164 R.Palmeiro B-H-P-S/15 15.00 40.00
193 V.Guerrero B-FG-J-J/25 15.00 40.00

2005 Absolute Memorabilia Tools of the Trade Swatch Five

*FIVE p/r 75-150: 1X TO 2.5X DBL p/r 70-200
*FIVE p/r 75-150: .6X TO 1.5X DBL p/r 20-29
*FIVE p/r 40-50: 1.25X TO 3X DBL p/r 70-200
*FIVE p/r 40-50: 1X TO 2.5X DBL p/r 50-60
*FIVE p/r 20-35: 1.5X TO 4X DBL p/r 70-200
*FIVE p/r 20-35: 1.25X TO 3X DBL p/r 50-60
*FIVE p/r 20-35: 1X TO 2.5X DBL p/r 20-29
*FIVE p/r 15-17: 2X TO 5X DBL p/r 70-200
*FIVE p/r 15-17: 1.5X TO 4X DBL p/r 50-60
OVERALL AU-GU ODDS ONE PER PACK
PRINT RUNS B/WN 1-150 COPIES PER
NO PRICING ON QTY OF 10 OR LESS
26 R.Oswalt B-BG-FG-J-S/25 10.00 25.00
28 A.Kearns B-H-J-J-S/25 8.00 20.00
82 Carlos Beltran 10.00 25.00
Royal B-H-J-J-S/20
123 H.Kill B-H-J-J-S/25 20.00 50.00
129 J.Giam A's B-H-J-J-J/20 10.00 25.00
138 J.Phelps B-FG-H-J-S/15 10.00 25.00
145 L.Berk B-BG-FG-J-S/20 10.00 25.00
152 M.Byrd B-FG-H-J-S/25 8.00 20.00
179 R.Klesko BG-FG-H-J-J/25 10.00 25.00

2005 Absolute Memorabilia Tools of the Trade Swatch Five Reverse

*REV p/r 75-100: 1X TO 2.5X DBL p/r 70-200
*REV p/r 20-35: 1.5X TO 4X DBL p/r 70-200
*REV p/r 20-35: 1X TO 2.5X DBL p/r 20-29
*REV p/r 15: 2X TO 5X DBL p/r 70-200
*REV p/r 15: 1.5X TO 4X DBL p/r 50-60
*REV p/r 15: 1.25X TO 3X DBL p/r 20-29
OVERALL AU-GU ODDS ONE PER PACK
PRINT RUNS B/WN 1-15 COPIES PER
NO PRICING ON QTY OF 10 OR LESS
26 Roy Oswalt 12.50 30.00
Bat-Btg Glv-Fld Glv-Jsy-Shoes/15
28 Austin Kearns Bat-Hat-Jsy-Jsy-Shoes/15 10.00
25.00
123 30.00 60.00
152 10.00 25.00

2005 Absolute Memorabilia Tools of the Trade Swatch Five Prime Red

*PRIME p/r 25: 2X TO 5X DBL p/r 70-200
*PRIME p/r 15: 1.5X TO 4X DBL p/r 20-29
PRINT RUNS B/WN 1-25 COPIES PER
NO PRICING ON QTY OF 10 OR LESS
PRIME BLACK PRINT B/WN 1-10 PER
NO PRIME BLACK PRICING DUE TO SCARCITY
OVERALL AU-GU ODDS ONE PER PACK

2005 Absolute Memorabilia Tools of the Trade Swatch Six

*SIX p/r 75-150: 1.5X TO 4X DBL p/r 70-200
*SIX p/r 50: 2X TO 5X DBL p/r 70-200
*SIX p/r 50: 1.5X TO 4X DBL p/r 50-60
*SIX p/r 25-30: 2.5X TO 6X DBL p/r 70-200
*SIX p/r 15: 3X TO 8X DBL p/r 70-200
*SIX p/r 15: 2.5X TO 6X DBL p/r 50-60
*SIX p/r 15: 2X TO 5X DBL p/r 20-29
OVERALL AU-GU ODDS ONE PER PACK
PRINT RUNS B/WN 1-150 COPIES PER
NO PRICING ON QTY OF 10 OR LESS
26 R.Oswalt BG-FG-H-J-J-S/15 20.00 50.00
123 H.Kill B-H-J-J-P-S/30 30.00 80.00
138 J.Phelps B-FG-H-J-J-S/150 8.00 20.00
145 L.Berk B-BG-FG-H-J-S/25 15.00 40.00
152 M.Byrd B-BG-FG-H-J-S/150 15.00 40.00
179 R.Klesko BG-FG-H-J-J-S/100 10.00 25.00

2005 Absolute Memorabilia Tools of the Trade Swatch Six Reverse

*REV p/r 20-25: 2.5X TO 6X DBL p/r 70-200
OVERALL AU-GU ODDS ONE PER PACK
PRINT RUNS B/WN 1-100 COPIES PER
NO PRICING ON QTY OF 10 OR LESS
123 H.Kill B-H-J-J-P-S/25 50.00 100.00
138 J.Phelps B-FG-H-J-J-S/50 10.00 25.00
152 M.Byrd B-BG-FG-H-J-S/45 10.00 25.00
179 R.Klesko BG-FG-H-J-J-S/25 15.00 40.00

2005 Absolute Memorabilia Tools of the Trade Swatch Six Prime Black

*PRIME p/r 25: 3X TO 8X DBL p/r 70-200
OVERALL AU-GU ODDS ONE PER PACK
PRINT RUNS B/WN 1-25 COPIES PER
NO PRICING ON QTY OF 10 OR LESS

2005 Absolute Memorabilia Tools of the Trade Swatch Six Prime Red

*PRIME p/r 50: 2.5X TO 6X DBL p/r 70-200
*PRIME p/r 25: 3X TO 8X DBL p/r 70-200
OVERALL AU-GU ODDS ONE PER PACK
PRINT RUNS B/WN 1-50 COPIES PER
NO PRICING ON QTY OF 9 OR LESS

2005 Absolute Memorabilia Tools of the Trade Autograph

OVERALL AU-GU ODDS ONE PER PACK
PRINT RUNS B/WN 1-150 COPIES PER
NO PRICING ON QTY OF 11 OR LESS
105 Billy Williams/150 10.00 25.00
107 Bob Gibson/88 15.00 40.00
117 David Cone/75 6.00 15.00
118 Fergie Jenkins/100 6.00 15.00
119 Gary Carter/43 12.50 30.00
120 Gary Sheffield/36 12.50 30.00
121 Gaylord Perry/16 12.50 30.00
122 Hank Aaron/100 100.00 175.00
131 Jim Palmer/106 6.00 15.00
137 Josh Beckett/56 10.00 25.00
150 Mark Grace/50 12.50 30.00
158 Nolan Ryan/75 40.00 80.00
159 Orel Hershiser/21 10.00 25.00
160 Ozzie Smith/150 15.00 40.00
162 Phil Rizzuto/99 12.00 30.00
174 Rod Carew/150 10.00 25.00
178 Ron Cey/100 6.00 15.00
180 Ryne Sandberg/150 15.00 40.00
183 Stan Musial/150 25.00 60.00
184 Steve Carlton/150 6.00 15.00
188 Todd Helton/100 6.00 15.00
190 Tom Seaver/18 30.00 80.00
194 Wade Boggs Sox/70 10.00 25.00
195 Wade Boggs Rays/35 15.00 40.00

2005 Absolute Memorabilia Tools of the Trade Autograph Reverse

*REV p/r 75-100: .4X TO 1X AU p/r 70-150
*REV p/r 37-50: .5X TO 1.2X AU p/r 70-150
*REV p/r 37-50: .4X TO 1X AU p/r 36-56
*REV p/r 20-32: .6X TO 1.5X AU p/r 70-150
*REV p/r 20-32: .4X TO 1X AU p/r 21-35
*REV p/r 20-32: .3X TO .8X AU p/r 16-18
*REV p/r 15: .6X TO 1.5X AU p/r 36-56
OVERALL AU-GU ODDS ONE PER PACK
PRINT RUNS B/WN 1-100 COPIES PER
NO PRICING ON QTY OF 7 OR LESS
122 Hank Aaron/32 125.00 200.00
183 Stan Musial/100 25.00 60.00
192 Tony Gwynn/25 20.00 50.00

2005 Absolute Memorabilia Tools of the Trade Autograph Red

*RED p/r 25-30: .6X TO 1.5X AU p/r 70-150
*RED p/r 16-19: .75X TO 2X AU p/r 70-150
PRINT RUNS B/WN 1-30 COPIES PER
NO PRICING ON QTY OF 12 OR LESS
BLACK PRINT RUN 1 SERIAL #'d SET
BLACK CARD 175 PRINT RUN 4 #'d COPIES
NO BLACK PRICING DUE TO SCARCITY
OVERALL AU-GU ODDS ONE PER PACK
192 Tony Gwynn/19 20.00 50.00

2005 Absolute Memorabilia Tools of the Trade Autograph Bat

*BAT p/r 100: .3X TO .8X AU p/r 36-56
*BAT p/r 50: .5X TO 1.2X AU p/r 70-150
*BAT p/r 50: .3X TO .8X AU p/r 21-35
OVERALL AU-GU ODDS ONE PER PACK
PRINT RUNS B/WN 1-100 COPIES PER
NO PRICING ON QTY OF 7 OR LESS
113 Dale Murphy/100 10.00 25.00

2005 Absolute Memorabilia Tools of the Trade Autograph Bat Reverse

*BAT p/r 25: .6X TO 1.5X AU p/r 70-150
*BAT p/r 25: .5X TO 1.2X AU p/r 36-56
*BAT p/r 25: .4X TO 1X AU p/r 21-35
OVERALL AU-GU ODDS ONE PER PACK
PRINT RUNS B/WN 1-50 COPIES PER
NO PRICING ON QTY OF 3 OR LESS
113 Dale Murphy/50 12.50 30.00

2005 Absolute Memorabilia Tools of the Trade Autograph Jersey

*JSY p/r 75-150: .4X TO 1X AU p/r 70-150
*JSY p/r 50: .5X TO 1.2X AU p/r 70-150
*JSY p/r 25-35: .6X TO 1.5X AU p/r 70-150
*JSY p/r 25-35: .5X TO 1.2X AU p/r 36-56
*JSY p/r 25-35: .3X TO .8X AU p/r 16-18
OVERALL AU-GU ODDS ONE PER PACK
PRINT RUNS B/WN 1-150 COPIES PER
NO PRICING ON QTY OF 10 OR LESS
113 Dale Murphy/50 12.50 30.00
122 Hank Aaron/50 125.00 200.00
135 John Kruk/150 10.00 25.00
192 Tony Gwynn/100 20.00 50.00

2005 Absolute Memorabilia Tools of the Trade Autograph Jersey Reverse

*JSY p/r 97-100: .4X TO 1X AU p/r 70-150
*JSY p/r 50: .5X TO 1.2X AU p/r 70-150
*JSY p/r 25: .6X TO 1.5X AU p/r 70-150
*JSY p/r 15: .6X TO 1.5X AU p/r 36-56
OVERALL AU-GU ODDS ONE PER PACK
PRINT RUNS B/WN 1-100 COPIES PER
NO PRICING ON QTY OF 10 OR LESS
113 Dale Murphy/25 15.00 40.00
122 Hank Aaron/25 125.00 200.00
123 Harmon Killebrew/15 40.00 80.00
135 John Kruk/100 10.00 25.00
192 Tony Gwynn/50 20.00 50.00

2005 Absolute Memorabilia Tools of the Trade Autograph Jersey Red

*RED p/r 25: .6X TO 1.5X AU p/r 70-150
OVERALL AU-GU ODDS ONE PER PACK
PRINT RUNS B/WN 1-25 COPIES PER
NO PRICING ON QTY OF 10 OR LESS
135 John Kruk/25 15.00 40.00
192 Tony Gwynn/25 25.00 60.00

2005 Absolute Memorabilia Tools of the Trade Autograph Swatch Single Jumbo

*SNG p/r 100: .5X TO 1.2X DBL p/r 75-100
*SNG p/r 44-50: .6X TO 1.5X DBL p/r 75-100
*SNG p/r 44-50: .5X TO 1.2X DBL p/r 40-65
OVERALL AU-GU ODDS ONE PER PACK
PRINT RUNS B/WN 1-100 COPIES PER
NO PRICING ON QTY OF 10 OR LESS
105 Billy Williams Jsy/25 12.50 30.00
118 Fergie Jenkins Jsy/25 12.50 30.00
135 John Kruk Jsy/25 12.50 30.00
159 Orel Hershiser Jsy/25 12.50 30.00
162 Phil Rizzuto Jsy/100 20.00 50.00
198 Willie McCovey Pants/44 15.00 40.00

2005 Absolute Memorabilia Tools of the Trade Autograph Swatch Single Jumbo Prime Red

PRINT RUNS B/WN 1-30 COPIES PER
NO PRICING ON QTY OF 10 OR LESS
PRIME BLACK PRINT RUNS B/WN 1-10 PER
NO PRIME BLK PRICING DUE TO SCARCITY
OVERALL AU-GU ODDS ONE PER PACK
121 Gaylord Perry Jsy/30 12.50 30.00

2005 Absolute Memorabilia Tools of the Trade Autograph Swatch Double

OVERALL AU-GU ODDS ONE PER PACK
PRINT RUNS B/WN 1-100 COPIES PER
NO PRICING ON QTY OF 10 OR LESS
1 Ozzie Smith B-P/25 30.00 60.00
3 Dale Murphy J-J/50 15.00 40.00
4 Paul Molitor J-P/25 12.50 30.00
15 Tim Hudson H-J/15 30.00 60.00
20 Lou Brock B-JK/50 15.00 40.00
22 Paul Lo Duca B-J/25 6.00 15.00
30 Nolan Ryan Angels B-JK/15 75.00 150.00
34 Nolan Ryan Rgr B-J/15 75.00 150.00
36 Sean Casey J-P/50 10.00 25.00
37 Juan Gonzalez Rgr J-P/25 12.50 30.00
39 D.Straw Yanks B-J/50 10.00 25.00
41 Tom Seaver J-P/25 30.00 80.00
42 Mike Schmidt B-J/15 50.00 100.00
48 Torii Hunter B-J/40 10.00 25.00
56 Brad Penny FG-J/75 5.00 12.00
57 Gary Carter Mets J-P/25 20.00 50.00
61 Willie McCovey J-P/15 30.00 60.00
62 A.Dawson Expos B-J/50 10.00 25.00
64 Adrian Beltre B-J/50 10.00 25.00
66 J.Gonz Indians B-J/25 12.50 30.00
70 A.Dawson Cubs J-P/50 10.00 25.00
72 Carlton Fisk B-J/15 30.00 60.00
73 Cal Ripken J-P/25 75.00 150.00
78 Tony Gwynn J-P/15 30.00 60.00
88 Magglio Ordonez B-S/25 12.50 30.00
91 Gary Carter Expos B-J/25 15.00 40.00
96 Bobby Doerr B-P/50 6.00 15.00
98 Eric Chavez B-J/25 12.50 30.00
99 Johnny Bench B-P/15 40.00 80.00
100 Harmon Killebrew H-J/25 40.00 80.00
110 Cal Ripken J-J/25 75.00 150.00
120 Gary Sheffield FG-H/50 10.00 25.00
122 Hank Aaron B-J/25 150.00 250.00
123 Harmon Killebrew B-J/65 30.00 60.00
126 Hideo Nomo J-P/30 150.00 250.00
130 Jeff Bagwell P-P/25 30.00 60.00
131 Jim Palmer H-P/40 20.00 50.00
146 Lenny Dykstra B-J/75 8.00 20.00
151 Mark Prior H-S/25 12.50 30.00
152 Marlon Byrd B-J/100 5.00 12.00
174 Rod Carew J-J/100 12.50 30.00
184 Steve Carlton FG-P/32 12.50 30.00
187 Tim Hudson H-J/15 30.00 60.00
188 Todd Helton B-J/17 30.00 60.00
190 Tom Seaver J-P/100 20.00 50.00
192 Tony Gwynn J-P/50 15.00 40.00

2005 Absolute Memorabilia Tools of the Trade Autograph Swatch Double Reverse

*REV p/r 75: .3X TO .8X DBL p/r 40-65
*REV p/r 41-50: .5X TO 1.2X DBL p/r 75-100
*REV p/r 41-50: .4X TO 1X DBL p/r 40-65
*REV p/r 25-29: .6X TO 1.5X DBL p/r 75-100
*REV p/r 25-29: .5X TO 1.2X DBL p/r 40-65
*REV p/r 25-29: .4X TO 1X DBL p/r 20-32
*REV p/r 15: .5X TO 1.2X DBL p/r 20-32
OVERALL AU-GU ODDS ONE PER PACK
PRINT RUNS B/WN 1-75 COPIES PER
NO PRICING ON QTY OF 10 OR LESS
113 Dale Murphy B-J/25 20.00 50.00
122 Hank Aaron B-J/15 150.00 250.00

2005 Absolute Memorabilia Tools of the Trade Autograph Swatch Double Prime Black

OVERALL AU-GU ODDS ONE PER PACK
PRINT RUNS B/WN 1-15 COPIES PER
NO PRICING ON QTY OF 10 OR LESS
159 Orel Hershiser J-J/15 15.00 40.00

2005 Absolute Memorabilia Tools of the Trade Autograph Swatch Double Prime Red

*PRIME p/r 40-50: .6X TO 1.5X DBL p/r 75-100
*PRIME p/r 40-50: .5X TO 1.2X DBL p/r 40-65
*PRIME p/r 40-50: .4X TO 1X DBL p/r 20-32
*PRIME p/r 25: .75X TO 2X DBL p/r 75-100
*PRIME p/r 25: .5X TO 1.2X DBL p/r 20-32
*PRIME p/r 15: .75X TO 2X DBL p/r 40-65
*PRIME p/r 15: .6X TO 1.5X DBL p/r 20-32
OVERALL AU-GU ODDS ONE PER PACK
PRINT RUNS B/WN 1-50 COPIES PER
NO PRICING ON QTY OF 10 OR LESS
2 C.Belt Astros B-J/25 15.00 40.00
16 Dwight Gooden J-S/45 12.50 30.00
18 D.Strawberry Mets B-J/50 12.50 30.00
82 C.Belt Royal H-J/25 15.00 40.00
148 Magglio Ordonez B-J/15 20.00 50.00
159 Orel Hershiser J-J/25 15.00 40.00
163 Rafael Furcal B-J/15 20.00 50.00
198 Willie McCovey J-P/25 30.00 60.00

2005 Absolute Memorabilia Tools of the Trade Autograph Swatch Triple

*TRIP p/r 75-100: .5X TO 1.2X DBL p/r 75-100
*TRIP p/r 75-100: .4X TO 1X DBL p/r 40-65
*TRIP p/r 75-100: .3X TO .8X DBL p/r 20-32
*TRIP p/r 45-50: .6X TO 1.5X DBL p/r 75-100
*TRIP p/r 45-50: .5X TO 1.2X DBL p/r 40-65
*TRIP p/r 45-50: .4X TO 1X DBL p/r 20-32
*TRIP p/r 25-32: .75X TO 2X DBL p/r 75-100
*TRIP p/r 25-32: .6X TO 1.5X DBL p/r 40-65
*TRIP p/r 25-32: .5X TO 1.2X DBL p/r 20-32
*TRIP p/r 15: .5X TO 1.5X DBL p/r 20-32
OVERALL AU-GU ODDS ONE PER PACK
PRINT RUNS B/WN 1-100 COPIES PER
NO PRICING ON QTY OF 10 OR LESS
2 C.Belt Astros B-J-J/25 15.00 40.00
18 D.Straw Mets B-FG-S/75 10.00 25.00
73 Cal Ripken B-J-P/25 90.00 180.00
82 C.Belt Royal B-J-S/25 15.00 40.00
108 Brad Penny FG-J-S/30 10.00 25.00
110 Cal Ripken JK-J-P/25 90.00 180.00
113 Dale Murphy B-J-J/45 20.00 50.00
122 Hank Aaron B-H-J/25 175.00 300.00
126 Hideo Nomo J-J-P/25 175.00 300.00
163 Rafael Furcal B-J-J/25 15.00 40.00
165 R.John D'backs J-J-P/15 60.00 120.00
166 R.John Astros H-J-P/50 40.00 80.00

2005 Absolute Memorabilia Tools of the Trade Autograph Swatch Triple Reverse

*REV p/r 50: .6X TO 1.5X DBL p/r 75-100
*REV p/r 50: .5X TO 1.2X DBL p/r 40-65
*REV p/r 25: .75X TO 2X DBL p/r 75-100
*REV p/r 25: .6X TO 1.5X DBL p/r 40-65
*REV p/r 25: .5X TO 1.2X DBL p/r 20-32
*REV p/r 15: 1X TO 2.5X DBL p/r 75-100
*REV p/r 15: .75X TO 2X DBL p/r 40-65
*REV p/r 15: .6X TO 1.5X DBL p/r 20-32
OVERALL AU-GU ODDS ONE PER PACK
PRINT RUNS B/WN 1-50 COPIES PER
NO PRICING ON QTY OF 10 OR LESS
18 D.Straw Mets B-FG-S/50 12.50 30.00
110 Cal Ripken JK-J-P/25 90.00 180.00
113 Dale Murphy B-J-J/15 30.00 60.00
122 Hank Aaron B-H-J/15 175.00 300.00
126 Hideo Nomo J-J-P/15 175.00 300.00
166 R.John Astros H-J-P/25 50.00 100.00

2005 Absolute Memorabilia Tools of the Trade Autograph Swatch Triple Prime Red

*PRIME p/r 25: 1X TO 2.5X DBL p/r 75-100
*PRIME p/r 25: .75X TO 2X DBL p/r 40-65
PRINT RUNS B/WN 1-25 COPIES PER
NO PRICING ON QTY OF 13 OR LESS
PRIME BLACK PRINT RUNS B/WN 1-10 PER
NO PRIME BLK PRICING DUE TO SCARCITY
OVERALL AU-GU ODDS ONE PER PACK
16 Dwight Gooden B-J-J/15 30.00 60.00
28 Austin Kearns B-J-J/25 12.50 30.00

2005 Absolute Memorabilia Tools of the Trade Autograph Swatch Quad

*QUAD p/r 25: 1X TO 2.5X DBL p/r 75-100
*QUAD p/r 25: .75X TO 2X DBL p/r 40-65
*QUAD p/r 25: .6X TO 1.5X DBL p/r 20-32
*QUAD p/r 25: .5X TO 1.2X DBL p/r 15
*QUAD p/r 15: 1X TO 2.5X DBL p/r 40-65
*QUAD p/r 15: .6X TO 1.5X DBL p/r 15-17
OVERALL AU-GU ODDS ONE PER PACK
PRINT RUNS B/WN 1-25 COPIES PER
NO PRICING ON QTY OF 10 OR LESS
23 Don Mattingly B-JK-J-S/25 60.00 120.00
73 Cal Ripken B-H-JK-J/25 125.00 200.00
83 Mark Grace B-FG-J-J/15 30.00 60.00
192 Tony Gwynn FG-J-P-S/25 60.00 120.00

2005 Absolute Memorabilia Tools of the Trade Autograph Swatch Quad Reverse

*REV p/r 15: 1.25X TO 3X DBL p/r 75-100
*REV p/r 15: 1X TO 2.5X DBL p/r 40-65
*REV p/r 15: .75X TO 2X DBL p/r 20-32
*REV p/r 15: .6X TO 1.5X DBL p/r 15-17
OVERALL AU-GU ODDS ONE PER PACK
PRINT RUNS B/WN 1-15 COPIES PER
NO PRICING ON QTY OF 10 OR LESS
23 Don Mattingly B-JK-J-S/15 75.00 150.00
73 Cal Ripken B-H-JK-J/15 150.00 250.00
77 Deion Sanders B-J-J-P/15 50.00 100.00

1970-71 Action Cartridge

During the time period of 1970-71 a group of 8 mm cartridges featuring leading players with playing tips were issued. The yellow boxes which measured 2 5/8" by 6" featured the player photo as well as what the tips included. Each player photo includes a fascimile autograph. Since these are unnumbered, we have sequenced them in alphabetical order.

COMPLETE SET (12) 200.00 400.00
1 Hank Aaron 40.00 80.00
2 Glenn Beckert 6.00 15.00
Don Kessinger
3 Lou Brock 12.50 40.00
4 Rod Carew 20.00 50.00
5 Willie Davis 6.00 15.00
6 Bill Freehan 8.00 20.00
7 Reggie Jackson 20.00 50.00
8 Willie McCovey 12.50 40.00
9 Dave McNally 8.00 20.00
10 Brooks Robinson 12.50 40.00
11 Pete Rose 30.00 60.00
12 Tom Seaver 30.00 60.00

1988 Action Packed Test

The 1988 Action Packed Test set contains six standard-size cards with slightly rounded corners. This apparently was the set of cards that Action Packed produced to show their technique to Major League Baseball and the Major League Baseball Players Association in their unsuccessful attempt to seek a baseball card license in 1988. The embossed color player photos on the fronts are bordered in gold. In black lettering, the player's name appears on a gold plaque above the picture, and the team name on a gold plaque beneath the picture. The card backs have the same design as Score issues, with a color head shot, team logo, biography, and major league batting or pitching statistics, again inside a gold border. The face on the front photo of the Ozzie Smith card was apparently considered too dark and thus reportedly not submitted. The cards are unnumbered and checklisted below in alphabetical order.

COMPLETE SET (6) 10.00 25.00
1 Wade Boggs 3.00 8.00
2 Andre Dawson 2.50 6.00
3 Dwight Gooden 6.00 15.00
4 Carney Lansford 1.50 4.00
5 Don Mattingly 6.00 15.00
6 Ozzie Smith SP 6.00 15.00

1992 Action Packed ASG Prototypes

COMPLETE SET (5) 10.00 25.00
1 Yogi Berra 3.00 8.00
2 Bob Gibson 1.50 4.00
3 Willie Mays 4.00 10.00
4 Warren Spahn 1.50 4.00
5 Willie Stargell 1.50 4.00

1992 Action Packed ASG

The 1992 Action Packed All-Star Gallery consists of 84 player standard-size cards and pays tribute to former greats of baseball. With the exception of Joe Garagiola, all the players represented appeared in at least one All-Star game. The first 18 cards feature Hall of Famers, and Action Packed guaranteed one Hall of Famer card in each seven-card foil pack. Also 24K gold leaf stamped versions of these Hall of Famer cards were randomly inserted into foil packs. The fronts feature embossed action player photos framed by inner gold border stripes and a black outer border. Most of the photos are color; 13 of them, however, are sepia-toned that have been converted to black and white.

COMPLETE SET (84) 6.00 15.00
1 Yogi Berra .50 1.25
2 Lou Brock .40 1.00
3 Bob Gibson .40 1.00
4 Ferguson Jenkins .30 .75
5 Ralph Kiner .30 .75
6 Al Kaline .40 1.00
7 Lou Boudreau .20 .50
8 Bobby Doerr .20 .50
9 Billy Herman .20 .50
10 Monte Irvin .20 .50
11 George Kell .20 .50
12 Robin Roberts .30 .75
13 Johnny Mize .30 .75
14 Willie Mays 1.00 2.50
15 Enos Slaughter .20 .50
16 Warren Spahn .30 .75
17 Willie Stargell .30 .75
18 Billy Williams .08 .25
19 Vernon Law .02 .10
20 Virgil Trucks .02 .10
21 Mel Parnell .02 .10
22 Wally Moon .02 .10
23 Gene Woodling .02 .10
24 Richie Ashburn .40 1.00
25 Mark Fidrych .08 .25
26 Roy Face .02 .10
27 Larry Doby .08 .25
28 Dick Groat .02 .10
29 Cesar Cedeno .02 .10
30 Bob Horner .02 .10
31 Bobby Richardson .08 .25
32 Bobby Murcer .08 .25
33 Gil McDougald .02 .10
34 Roy White .02 .10
35 Bill Skowron .08 .25
36 Mickey Lolich .08 .25
37 Minnie Minoso .08 .25
38 Bill Pierce .08 .25
39 Ron Santo .20 .50
40 Sal Bando .08 .25
41 Ralph Branca .08 .25
42 Bert Campaneris .02 .10
43 Joe Garagiola .20 .50
44 Vida Blue .08 .25
45 Frank Crosetti .20 .50
46 Luis Tiant .02 .10
47 Maury Wills .08 .25
48 Sam McDowell .02 .10
49 Jimmy Piersall .08 .25
50 Jim Lonborg .02 .10
51 Don Newcombe .08 .25
52 Bobby Thomson .08 .25
53 Wilbur Wood .02 .10
54 Carl Erskine .08 .25
55 Chris Chambliss .02 .10
56 Dave Kingman .02 .10
57 Ken Holtzman .02 .10
58 Bud Harrelson .02 .10
59 Clem Labine .08 .25
60 Tony Oliva .08 .25
61 George Foster .02 .10
62 Bobby Bonds .08 .25
63 Harvey Haddix .02 .10
64 Steve Garvey .08 .25
65 Rocky Colavito .20 .50
66 Orlando Cepeda .20 .50
67 Ed Lopat .08 .25
68 Al Oliver .08 .25
69 Bill Mazeroski .30 .75
70 Al Rosen .08 .25
71 Bob Grich .08 .25
72 Curt Flood .08 .25
73 Willie Horton .08 .25
74 Rico Carty .02 .10
75 Davey Johnson .02 .10
76 Don Kessinger .02 .10
77 Frank Thomas .02 .10
78 Bobby Shantz .02 .10
79 Herb Score .08 .25
80 Boog Powell .08 .25
81 Rusty Staub .08 .25

82 Bill Madlock .08 .25
83 Manny Mota .02 .10
84 Bill White .08 .25

1992 Action Packed ASG 24K

COMPLETE SET (18) 150.00 300.00
1G Yogi Berra 15.00 40.00
2G Lou Brock 10.00 25.00
3G Bob Gibson 10.00 25.00
4G Ferguson Jenkins 6.00 15.00
5G Ralph Kiner 8.00 20.00
6G Al Kaline 10.00 25.00
7G Lou Boudreau 6.00 15.00
8G Bobby Doerr 6.00 15.00
9G Billy Herman 6.00 15.00
10G Monte Irvin 6.00 15.00
11G George Kell 6.00 15.00
12G Robin Roberts 8.00 20.00
13G Johnny Mize 8.00 20.00
14G Willie Mays 20.00 50.00
15G Enos Slaughter 6.00 15.00
16G Warren Spahn 8.00 20.00
17G Willie Stargell 8.00 20.00
18G Billy Williams 6.00 15.00

1993 Action Packed ASG

The second series of the Action Packed All-Star Gallery baseball set consists of 84 standard-size cards. Fifty two of the cards are in color, 31 are sepia-tone, and one is a colorized black-and-white. Action Packed included 46 Hall of Famers in the series and guaranteed one of these cards in every pack. Moreover, series II includes randomly inserted 24K cards of these Hall of Famers and contains a card honoring Bud Abbott and Lou Costello, creators of the famous "Who's on First" comedy routine. And as a special bonus for hobby dealers only, each box of cards included two free "Chiptopper" prototype cards of forthcoming Action Packed cards.

COMPLETE SET (84) 8.00 20.00
85 Cy Young .20 .50
86 Honus Wagner .30 .75
87 Christy Mathewson .30 .75
88 Ty Cobb .60 1.50
89 Eddie Collins .08 .25
90 Walter Johnson .30 .75
91 Tris Speaker .20 .50
92 Grover Alexander .20 .50
93 Edd Roush .08 .25
94 Babe Ruth .75 2.00
95 Rogers Hornsby .30 .75
96 Pie Traynor .08 .25
97 Lou Gehrig .60 1.50
98 Mickey Cochrane .20 .50
99 Lefty Grove .20 .50
100 Jimmie Foxx .40 1.00
101 Tony Lazzeri .08 .25
102 Mel Ott .20 .50
103 Carl Hubbell .08 .25
104 Al Lopez .08 .25
105 Lefty Gomez .20 .50
106 Dizzy Dean .30 .75
107 Hank Greenberg .30 .75
108 Joe Medwick .08 .25
109 Arky Vaughan .08 .25
110 Bob Feller .20 .50
111 Hal Newhouser .08 .25
112 Early Wynn .08 .25
113 Bob Lemon .08 .25
114 Red Schoendienst .08 .25
115 Satchel Paige .30 .75
116 Whitey Ford .20 .50
117 Eddie Mathews .20 .50
118 Harmon Killebrew .20 .50
119 Roberto Clemente .75 2.00
120 Brooks Robinson .20 .50
121 Don Drysdale .20 .50
122 Luis Aparicio .08 .25
123 Willie McCovey .20 .50
124 Juan Marichal .08 .25
125 Gaylord Perry .08 .25
126 Catfish Hunter .08 .25
127 Jim Palmer .20 .50
128 Rod Carew .20 .50
129 Tom Seaver .20 .50
130 Rollie Fingers .08 .25
131 Joe Jackson .60 1.50
132 Pepper Martin .08 .25
133 Joe Gordon .15 .40
134 Marty Marion .08 .25
135 Allie Reynolds .15 .40
136 Johnny Sain .15 .40
137 Gil Hodges .30 .75
138 Ted Kluszewski .15 .40
139 Nellie Fox .30 .75
140 Billy Martin .25 .60
141 Smoky Burgess .15 .40
142 Lew Burdette .15 .40
143 Joe Black .08 .25
144 Don Larsen .15 .40
145 Ken Boyer .15 .40
146 Johnny Callison .08 .25
147 Norm Cash .15 .40
148 Keith Hernandez .08 .25
149 Jim Kaat .15 .40
150 Bill Freehan .08 .25
151 Joe Torre .30 .75
152 Bob Uecker .15 .40
153 Dave McNally .08 .25
154 Denny McLain .15 .40
155 Dick Allen .15 .40
156 Jimmy Wynn .08 .25
157 Tommy John .15 .40
158 Paul Blair .08 .25
159 Reggie Smith .08 .25
160 Jerry Koosman .08 .25
161 Thurman Munson .25 .60
162 Graig Nettles .15 .40
163 Ron Cey .08 .25
164 Cecil Cooper .08 .25
165 Dave Parker .15 .40
166 Jim Rice .15 .40
167 Kent Tekulve .08 .25
168 Who's On First .30 .75

1993 Action Packed ASG 24K

19G Cy Young 4.00 10.00
20G Honus Wagner 4.00 10.00
21G Christy Mathewson 4.00 10.00
22G Ty Cobb 6.00 15.00
23G Eddie Collins 2.50 6.00
24G Walter Johnson 4.00 10.00
25G Tris Speaker 2.50 6.00
26G Grover Alexander 2.50 6.00
27G Ed Roush 2.50 6.00
28G Babe Ruth 10.00 25.00
29G Rogers Hornsby 2.50 6.00
30G Pie Traynor 2.50 6.00
31G Lou Gehrig 8.00 20.00
32G Mickey Cochrane 2.50 6.00
33G Lefty Grove 2.50 6.00
34G Jimmie Foxx 4.00 10.00
35G Tony Lazzeri 2.50 6.00
36G Mel Ott 4.00 10.00
37G Carl Hubbell 2.50 6.00
38G Al Lopez 1.50 4.00
39G Lefty Gomez 1.50 4.00
40G Dizzy Dean 1.50 4.00
41G Hank Greenberg 4.00 10.00
42G Joe Medwick 1.50 4.00
43G Arky Vaughan 1.50 4.00
44G Bob Feller 2.50 6.00
45G Hal Newhouser 1.50 4.00
46G Early Wynn 1.50 4.00
47G Bob Lemon 2.50 6.00
48G Red Schoendienst 2.50 6.00
49G Satchel Paige 4.00 10.00
50G Whitey Ford 2.50 6.00
51G Eddie Mathews 4.00 10.00
52G Harmon Killebrew 4.00 10.00
53G Roberto Clemente 10.00 25.00
54G Brooks Robinson 2.50 6.00
55G Don Drysdale 2.50 6.00
56G Luis Aparicio 2.50 6.00
57G Willie McCovey 2.50 6.00
58G Juan Marichal 2.50 6.00
59G Gaylord Perry 2.50 6.00
60G Catfish Hunter 2.50 6.00
61G Jim Palmer 2.50 6.00
62G Rod Carew 2.50 6.00
63G Tom Seaver 2.50 6.00
64G Rollie Fingers 2.50 6.00
65G Who's On First 1.50 4.00

1993 Action Packed ASG Coke/Amoco

This 18-card standard-size set pays tribute to former greats of baseball. The cards feature Hall of Fame players and were sponsored by Coca Cola and Amoco. With the purchase of four multi-packs of Coca-Cola products at participating Amoco gas stations, collectors could send in through the mail for a complete set plus a 1.00 off coupon good toward the purchase of Amoco Ultimate gasoline. There was also a pre-promotion set with a red header card, with reportedly only 3000 sets produced, which was not distributed to the public. The red header version was indistinguishable from the gray header set listed below with the exception that Ferguson Jenkins and Billy Herman were replaced in the gray set by Red Schoendienst and Gaylord Perry; Jenkins and Herman were both members of the original 1992 Action Packed ASG set.

COMPLETE SET (18) 2.00 5.00
1 Yogi Berra .30 .75
2 Lou Brock .20 .50
3 Bob Gibson .20 .50
4 Red Schoendienst .20 .50
5 Ralph Kiner .20 .50
6 Al Kaline .30 .75
7 Lou Boudreau .20 .50
8 Bobby Doerr .20 .50
9 Gaylord Perry .20 .50
10 Monte Irvin .20 .50
11 George Kell .20 .50
12 Robin Roberts .20 .50
13 Johnny Mize .20 .50
14 Willie Mays .60 1.50
15 Enos Slaughter .20 .50
16 Warren Spahn .20 .50
17 Willie Stargell .20 .50
18 Billy Williams .20 .50

1993 Action Packed Seaver Promos

This five-card standard-size promo set features embossed color player photos accented by gold foil and red borders. The player's name appears in the gold foil border at the bottom. The horizontal backs are gray and carry biographical and statistical information, and career highlights. The cards are numbered on the back with a "TS" prefix. Random insertions of these cards were also found in packs of Action Packed racing cards.

COMPLETE SET (5) 8.00 20.00
TS1 Tom Seaver 2.00 5.00
The Franchise
TS2 Tom Seaver 2.00 5.00
Amazin' Mets
TS3 Tom Seaver 2.00 5.00
A Tearful Goodbye
TS4 Tom Seaver 2.00 5.00
Tom Terrific
TS5 Tom Seaver 2.00 5.00
Dazzling the Windy City

1956 Adventure R749

The Adventure series produced by Gum Products in 1956, contains a wide variety of subject matter. Cards in the set measure the standard size. The color drawings are printed on a heavy thickness of cardboard and have large white borders. The backs contain the card number, the caption, and a short text. The most expensive cards in the series (100 are those associated with sports (Louis, Tunney, etc.). In addition, card number 86 (Schmeling) is notorious and sold at a premium price because of the Nazi symbol printed on the card. Although this set is considered by many to be a topical or non-sport set, several boxers are featured (cards 11, 22, 31-35, 41-44, 76-80, 86-90). One of the few cards of Boston-area legend Harry Agganis is in this set. The sports-related cards are in greater demand than the non-sport cards. These cards came in one-card penny packs where were packed 240 to a box.

COMPLETE SET (100) 225.00 450.00
55 Harry Agganis 10.00 20.00

1990 AGFA

This 22-card standard-size set was issued by MSA (Michael Schechter Associates) for AGFA. The promotion reportedly-consisted of a three-card pack of these cards given away with any purchase of a three-pack of AGFA film.

COMPLETE SET (22) 8.00 20.00
1 Willie Mays .75 2.00
2 Carl Yastrzemski .40 1.00
3 Harmon Killebrew .40 1.00
4 Joe Torre .30 .75
5 Al Kaline .40 1.00
6 Hank Aaron .75 2.00
7 Rod Carew .40 1.00
8 Roberto Clemente 1.00 2.50
9 Luis Aparicio .20 .50
10 Roger Maris .30 .75
11 Joe Morgan .30 .75
12 Maury Wills .20 .50
13 Brooks Robinson .40 1.00
14 Tom Seaver .40 1.00
15 Steve Carlton .30 .75
16 Whitey Ford .40 1.00
17 Jim Palmer .40 1.00
18 Rollie Fingers .20 .50
19 Bruce Sutter .08 .25
20 Willie McCovey .40 1.00
21 Mike Schmidt .40 1.00
22 Yogi Berra .40 1.00

1969 Ajman Hall of Fame Stamps

These six stamps, were issued by the little country of Ajman to commemorate the 100th anniversary of professional baseball. Six of the players who were on the all-time greatest teams were included in this set. Since these stamps were unnumbered, we have sequenced them in alphabetical order.

COMPLETE SET (6) 6.00 15.00
1 Joe DiMaggio 1.25 3.00
2 Babe Ruth 2.00 5.00
3 George Sisler .40 1.00
4 Stan Musial .75 2.00
5 Ty Cobb 1.25 3.00
6 Honus Wagner .75 2.00

1939-52 Albertype Hall of Fame PC754-2

The Albertype Company issued postcards of Hall of Fame inductees from 1936 through 1952. However, since the HOF was not officially opened until 1939, we are dating this set as 1939-52. This black and white postcard set, the cards being called plaques as they feature the Hall of Fame plaque of the player, was addended to each year by new Hall of Fame inductees. Sixty-two Albertype postcards are known and are listed in the checklist below. The set is sequenced in order of induction into the Hall of Fame.

COMPLETE SET (62) 425.00 850.00
1 Ty Cobb 25.00 50.00
2 Walter Johnson 20.00 40.00
3 Christy Mathewson 20.00 40.00
4 Babe Ruth 37.50 75.00
5 Honus Wagner 20.00 40.00
6 Morgan Bulkeley 5.00 10.00
7 Ban Johnson 5.00 10.00
8 Nap Lajoie 10.00 20.00
9 Connie Mack 10.00 20.00
10 John McGraw 10.00 20.00
11 Tris Speaker 10.00 20.00
12 George Wright 5.00 10.00
13 Cy Young 25.00 50.00
14 Grover Cleveland Alexander 10.00 20.00
15 Alexander Cartwright 7.50 15.00
16 Henry Chadwick 5.00 10.00
17 Cap Anson 12.50 25.00
18 Eddie Collins 10.00 20.00
19 Charlie Comiskey 5.00 10.00
20 Candy Cummings 5.00 10.00
21 Buck Ewing 5.00 10.00
22 Lou Gehrig 30.00 60.00
23 Willie Keeler 5.00 10.00
24 Ole Hoss Radbourne 5.00 10.00
25 George Sisler 7.50 15.00
26 Albert Spalding 5.00 10.00
27 Rogers Hornsby 12.50 25.00
28 Kenesaw Mountain Landis 5.00 10.00
29 Roger Bresnahan 5.00 10.00
30 Dan Brouthers 5.00 10.00
31 Fred Clarke 5.00 10.00
32 Jimmy Collins 5.00 10.00
33 Ed Delahanty 5.00 10.00
34 Hugh Duffy 5.00 10.00
35 Hugh Jennings 5.00 10.00
36 King Kelly 5.00 10.00
37 Jimmy O'Rourke 5.00 10.00
38 Wilbert Robinson 5.00 10.00
39 Jesse Burkett 5.00 10.00
40 Frank Chance 10.00 20.00
41 Jack Chesbro 5.00 10.00
42 Johnny Evers 10.00 20.00
43 Clark Griffith 7.50 15.00
44 Tom McCarthy 5.00 10.00
45 Joe McGinnity 5.00 10.00
46 Eddie Plank 10.00 20.00
47 Joe Tinker 10.00 20.00
48 Rube Waddell 5.00 10.00
49 Ed Walsh 7.50 15.00
50 Mickey Cochrane 10.00 20.00
51 Frankie Frisch 10.00 20.00
52 Lefty Grove 12.50 25.00
53 Carl Hubbell 12.50 25.00
54 Herb Pennock 7.50 15.00
55 Pie Traynor 10.00 20.00
56 Mordecai Brown 10.00 20.00
57 Charlie Gehringer 7.50 15.00
58 Kid Nichols 5.00 10.00
59 Jimmy Foxx 12.50 25.00
(Jimmie)
60 Mel Ott 10.00 20.00
61 Harry Heilmann 5.00 10.00
62 Paul Waner 7.50 15.00
63 Abner Doubleday 5.00 10.00
64 Christy Mathewson BUST 5.00 10.00
65 HOF Exterior 5.00 10.00
66 HOF Interior 5.00 10.00

1971 Aldana Yesterday Heroes

This crude 16 card blank-backed set was issued in the early 1970's and was presumebly issued by Carl Aldana as one of the many collector issue sets he produced around that time period. The fronts have small shots of the player with their first name on top and their last name on the bottom. The purpose of this set was to create cards for players who had never been on a card before.

COMPLETE SET (16) 125.00 250.00
1 Wally Hood 8.00 20.00
2 Jim Westlake 8.00 20.00
3 Stan McWilliams 8.00 20.00
4 Les Fleming 8.00 20.00
5 John Ritchey 8.00 20.00
6 Steve Nagy 8.00 20.00
7 Ken Gables 8.00 20.00
8 Maurice Fisher 8.00 20.00
9 Don Lang 8.00 20.00
10 Harry Malmberg 8.00 20.00
11 Jack Conway 8.00 20.00
12 Don White 8.00 20.00
13 Dick Lajeskie 8.00 20.00
14 Walt Judnich 8.00 20.00
15 Joe Kirrene 8.00 20.00
16 Ed Sauer 8.00 20.00

1990 All-American Baseball Team

This 24-card, standard-size set was issued by MSA (Michael Schechter Associates) for 7/11, Squirt, and Dr. Pepper, and other carbonated beverages (but there are no markings on the cards whatsoever to indicate who sponsored the set other than MSA). These cards were distributed and issued inside 12-packs of sodas. The 12-packs included a checklist on one panel, and the cards themselves were glued on the inside of the pack so that it was difficult to remove a card without damaging it. The fronts feature a red, white and blue design framing the players photos while the back has major league career statistics and a sentence of career highlights. The back also has a fascimile autograph of the player on the back. Like many of the sets sponsored by MSA there are no team logos on the cards as they have been airbrushed away.

COMPLETE SET (24) 10.00 25.00
1 George Brett 1.00 2.50
2 Mark McGwire 1.25 3.00
3 Wade Boggs .75 2.00
4 Cal Ripken 2.00 5.00
5 Rickey Henderson 1.00 2.50
6 Dwight Gooden .20 .50
7 Bo Jackson .40 1.00
8 Roger Clemens 1.00 2.50
9 Orel Hershiser .20 .50
10 Ozzie Smith 1.00 2.50
11 Don Mattingly 1.00 2.50
12 Kirby Puckett .60 1.50
13 Robin Yount .60 1.50
14 Tony Gwynn 1.00 2.50
15 Jose Canseco .50 1.25
16 Nolan Ryan 2.00 5.00
17 Ken Griffey Jr. 2.00 5.00
18 Will Clark .40 1.00
19 Ryne Sandberg .75 2.00
20 Kent Hrbek .08 .25
21 Carlton Fisk .75 2.00
22 Paul Molitor .75 2.00
23 Dave Winfield .60 1.50
24 Andre Dawson .40 1.00

1908 All-American Ladies Baseball Club

This extremely rare set of printed postcards by an unknown publisher features stars of the All-American Ladies Base Ball Club which toured America early in the 20th century. Although no date is listed on the cards they were produced sometime after 1907 beacuse they have a divided back. Prior to 1907 all postcards backs were undivided and all messages had to be written on the front or picture side of the card. All cards show close up action views of the players on a white background. We have listed the known versions, all additions to this checklist are appreciated.

COMPLETE SET (5) 500.00 1000.00
1 Bessie Barrett 100.00 200.00
2 May Fay 100.00 200.00
3 Harriett Murphy 100.00 200.00
4 Carrie Nation 100.00 200.00
5 Elizabeth Pull 100.00 200.00

1949 All-Star Photos

Sold as a group, these 21 photos which measure approximately 6 1/4" by 9", features players who for the most part had great seasons in either 1948 or 1949 and thus were among the leading players in the game. Since these photos are unnumbered, we have sequenced them in alphabetical order.

1 Luke Appling 12.50 25.00
2 Lou Boudreau P/MG 12.50 25.00
3 Dom DiMaggio 10.00 20.00
4 Joe DiMaggio 25.00 50.00
5 Bobby Doerr 12.50 25.00
6 Bob Feller 15.00 30.00
7 Joe Gordon 10.00 20.00
8 Tommy Henrich 10.00 20.00
9 George Kell 12.50 25.00
10 Bob Kennedy 5.00 12.00
11 Ralph Kiner 15.00 30.00
12 Bob Lemon 12.00 25.00
13 Marty Marion 6.00 15.00
14 Stan Musial 25.00 50.00
15 Don Newcombe 5.00 12.00
16 Pee Wee Reese 15.00 30.00
17 Phil Rizzuto 15.00 30.00
18 Jackie Robinson 50.00 100.00
19 Enos Slaughter 12.50 50.00
20 Vern Stephens 5.00 12.00
21 Ted Williams 50.00 100.00

1950 All-Star Pinups

These 10 pinups measure approximately 7" in diameter and feature the player photo along with a printed ID on the front. The back features instructions on how to pop out the pinup. These pinups are unnumbered and punched out from a book, which was issued with a 50 cent cover price. We have sequenced them in alphabetical order. Ted Williams is the featured player on the book cover.

COMPLETE SET (10) 700.00 1400.00
1 Joe DiMaggio 125.00 250.00
2 Jim Hegan 10.00 20.00
3 Gil Hodges 40.00 80.00
4 George Kell 30.00 60.00
5 Ralph Kiner 40.00 80.00
6 Stan Musial 100.00 200.00
7 Mel Parnell 10.00 20.00
8 Phil Rizzuto 60.00 120.00
9 Jackie Robinson 200.00 400.00
10 Ted Williams 200.00 400.00

1971 All-Star Baseball Album

The 1971 All-Star Baseball Album contains two pages of 12 perforated player pictures for a total of 24 cards. Each page has three rows of four cards measuring approximately 7 1/2 by 8 3/4". The individual cards measure 1 7/8" by 2 7/8". The cards are printed on thin paper stock. The fronts feature a posed all star color player photo with the player's autograph facsimile across the bottom of the picture. The backs carry biography, team name, and player profile superimposed over a ghosted team logo. The cards are unnumbered and checklisted below in alphabetical order. On an additional page that follows each of the player picture pages, is a page listing the player's statistics. A 1971 American and National League team schedule appears on the back of the album. The album, titled Today's All-Stars was produced by Dell and originally sold for 39 cents.

COMPLETE SET (24) 10.00 25.00
1 Hank Aaron .40 1.00
2 Luis Aparicio .15 .40
3 Ernie Banks .30 .75
4 Johnny Bench .30 .75
5 Rico Carty .08 .20
6 Roberto Clemente 1.25 3.00
7 Bob Gibson .15 .40
8 Willie Horton .08 .20
9 Frank Howard .12 .30
10 Reggie Jackson .30 .75
11 Ferguson Jenkins .15 .40
12 Alex Johnson .08 .20
13 Al Kaline .15 .40
14 Harmon Killebrew .15 .40
15 Willie Mays .40 1.00
16 Sam McDowell .08 .20
17 Denny McLain .12 .30
18 Boog Powell .12 .30
19 Brooks Robinson .15 .40
20 Frank Robinson .15 .40
21 Pete Rose .30 .75
22 Tom Seaver .30 .75
23 Rusty Staub .12 .30
24 Carl Yastrzemski .15 .40
NNO Album 2.00 5.00

1981 All-Star Game Program Inserts

This 180-card set was distributed inside the 1981 All-Star Game Official Program on foldout sheets with each sheet containing 30 cards. Each card measures approximately 1 1/4" by 2" and features color action photos of the American League (numbers 1-90) and the National League All-Star Nominees (numbers 91-181). The cards are unnumbered and checklisted below in alphabetical order by position within each player's respective league.

COMPLETE SET (180) 4.00 10.00
1 Willie Aikens .01 .05
2 Bruce Bochte .01 .05
3 Rod Carew .25 .60
4 Cecil Cooper .02 .10
5 Mike Hargrove .02 .10
6 Tony Perez .25 .60
7 John Mayberry .02 .10
8 Eddie Murray 1.00 2.50
9 Bob Watson .02 .10
10 Julio Cruz .01 .05
11 Rich Dauer .01 .05
12 Damaso Garcia .01 .05
13 Bobby Grich .02 .10
14 Duane Kuiper .01 .05
15 Willie Randolph .05 .15
16 Lou Whitaker .07 .20
17 Frank White .01 .05
18 Bump Wills .01 .05
19 Mark Belanger .01 .05
20 Rick Burleson .01 .05
21 Bucky Dent .01 .05
22 Alfredo Griffin .01 .05
23 Roy Smalley .01 .05
24 Alan Trammell .25 .60
25 Tom Veryzer .01 .05
26 Robin Yount .50 1.25
27 U.L. Washington .01 .05
28 Buddy Bell .02 .10
29 George Brett 2.00 5.00
30 John Castino .01 .05
31 Doug DeCinces .01 .05
32 Wayne Gross .01 .05
33 Toby Harrah .01 .05
34 Butch Hobson .01 .05
35 Carney Lansford .01 .05
36 Graig Nettles .05 .15
37 Rick Cerone .01 .05
38 Rick Dempsey .01 .05
39 Brian Downing .02 .10
40 Carlton Fisk .50 1.25
41 Ron Hassey .01 .05
42 Lance Parrish .02 .10
43 Ted Simmons .02 .10
44 Jim Sundberg .01 .05
45 Butch Wynegar .01 .05
46 Tony Armas .01 .05
47 Don Baylor .02 .10
48 Al Bumbry .01 .05
49 Joe Charboneau .07 .20
50 Miguel Dilone .01 .05
51 Dan Ford .01 .05
52 Rickey Henderson 1.50 4.00
53 Reggie Jackson .50 1.25
54 Steve Kemp .01 .05
55 Ron LeFlore .01 .05
56 Chet Lemon .01 .05
57 Greg Luzinski .02 .10
58 Fred Lynn .02 .10
59 Hal McRae .01 .05
60 Paul Molitor .75 2.00
61 Dwayne Murphy .01 .05
62 Ben Oglivie .01 .05
63 Al Oliver .05 .15
64 Jorge Orta .01 .05
65 Amos Otis .01 .05
66 Jim Rice .05 .15
67 Mickey Rivers .01 .05
68 Ken Singleton .01 .05
69 Gorman Thomas .01 .05
70 Willie Wilson .01 .05
71 Dave Winfield .50 1.25
72 Carl Yastrzemski .50 1.25
73 Floyd Bannister .01 .05
74 Len Barker .01 .05
75 Britt Burns .01 .05
76 Dick Dotson .01 .05
77 Dennis Eckersley .40 1.00
78 Rollie Fingers .25 .60
79 Mike Flanagan .01 .05
80 Ken Forsch .01 .05
81 Rich Gossage .05 .15
82 Ron Guidry .02 .10
83 Larry Gura .01 .05
84 Tommy John .05 .15
85 Matt Keough .01 .05
86 Dennis Leonard .01 .05
87 Scott McGregor .01 .05
88 Mike Norris .01 .05
89 Dave Stieb .02 .10
90 Milt Wilcox .01 .05
91 Bill Buckner .01 .05
92 Enos Cabell .01 .05
93 Chris Chambliss .02 .10
94 Dan Driessen .01 .05
95 Steve Garvey .25 .60
96 Keith Hernandez .02 .10
97 Willie Montanez .01 .05
98 Pete Rose 1.00 2.50
99 Willie Stargell .40 1.00
100 Doug Flynn .01 .05
101 Phil Garner .02 .10
102 Glenn Hubbard .01 .05
103 Rafael Landestoy .01 .05
104 Davey Lopes .02 .10
105 Ron Oester .01 .05
106 Rodney Scott .01 .05
107 Rennie Stennett .01 .05
108 Manny Trillo .01 .05
109 Larry Bowa .01 .05
110 Dave Concepcion .02 .10
111 Ivan DeJesus .01 .05
112 Tim Foli .01 .05
113 Bill Russell .01 .05
114 Ozzie Smith 1.25 3.00
115 Chris Speier .01 .05
116 Frank Taveras .01 .05
117 Garry Templeton .01 .05
118 Ron Cey .02 .10
119 Darrell Evans .02 .10
120 Bob Horner .01 .05
121 Ray Knight .01 .05
122 Bill Madlock .02 .10
123 Ken Oberkfell .01 .05
124 Larry Parrish .01 .05
125 Ken Reitz .01 .05
126 Mike Schmidt 1.00 2.50
127 Alan Ashby .01 .05
128 Johnny Bench .75 2.00
129 Bob Boone .02 .10
130 Gary Carter .75 2.00
131 Terry Kennedy .01 .05
132 Milt May .01 .05
133 Darrell Porter .01 .05
134 John Stearns .01 .05
135 Steve Yeager .01 .05
136 Dusty Baker .02 .10
137 Cesar Cedeno .02 .10
138 Jack Clark .01 .05
139 Dave Collins .01 .05
140 Warren Cromartie .01 .05
141 Jose Cruz .02 .10
142 Andre Dawson .40 1.00
143 Mike Easler .01 .05
144 George Foster .01 .05
145 Ken Griffey .02 .10
146 Steve Henderson .01 .05
147 George Hendrick .01 .05
148 Dave Kingman .05 .15
149 Ken Landreaux .01 .05
150 Sixto Lezcano .01 .05
151 Garry Maddox .01 .05
152 Jerry Martin .01 .05
153 Gary Matthews .01 .05
154 Lee Mazzilli .02 .10
155 Bake McBride .01 .05
156 Omar Moreno .01 .05
157 Dale Murphy .40 1.00
158 Dave Parker .02 .10
159 Terry Puhl .01 .05
160 Gene Richards .01 .05
161 Reggie Smith .01 .05
162 Ellis Valentine .01 .05
163 Doyle Alexander .01 .05
164 Neil Allen .01 .05
165 Jim Bibby .01 .05
166 Vida Blue .02 .10
167 Steve Carlton .50 1.25
168 Juan Eichelberger .01 .05
169 Burt Hooton .01 .05
170 Bob Knepper .01 .05
171 Joe Niekro .01 .05
172 Rick Rhoden .01 .05
173 Dick Ruthven .01 .05
174 Nolan Ryan 2.00 5.00
175 Scott Sanderson .01 .05
176 Tom Seaver .50 1.25
177 Lary Sorensen .01 .05
178 Bruce Sutter .20 .50
179 Don Sutton .25 .60
180 Fernando Valenzuela 1.00 2.50

1982 All-Star Game Program Inserts

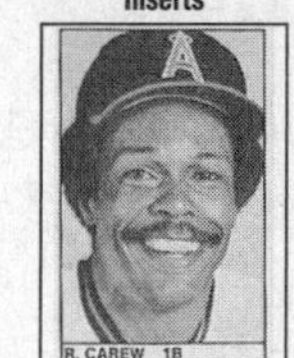

This 180-card set was distributed inside the 1982 All-Star Game Official Program on foldout sheets with each sheet containing 30 cards. Each card measures approximately 1 1/4" by 2" and features color action photos of the National League (numbers 1-90) and the Americanl League All-Star Nominees (numbers 91-181). The cards are unnumbered and checklisted below in alphabetical order by position within each player's respective league.

COMPLETE SET (180) 4.00 10.00
1 Bill Buckner .02 .10
2 Chris Chambliss .02 .10
3 Dan Driessen .01 .05
4 Steve Garvey .25 .60
5 Keith Hernandez .07 .20
6 Art Howe .02 .10
7 Dave Kingman .02 .10
8 Al Oliver .02 .10
9 Pete Rose 1.00 2.50
10 Juan Bonilla .01 .05
11 Phil Garner .02 .10
12 Tom Herr .01 .05
13 Glenn Hubbard .01 .05
14 Joe Morgan .25 .60
15 Ron Oester .01 .05
16 Steve Sax .25 .60
17 Rodney Scott .01 .05
18 Manny Trillo .01 .05
19 Larry Bowa .02 .10
20 Dave Concepcion .05 .15
21 Ivan DeJesus .01 .05
22 Johnnie LeMaster .01 .05
23 Craig Reynolds .01 .05
24 Bill Russell .01 .05
25 Ozzie Smith 1.00 2.50
26 Chris Speier .01 .05
27 Garry Templeton .01 .05
28 Johnny Bench .75 2.00
29 Hubie Brooks .02 .10
30 Ron Cey .05 .15
31 Darrell Evans .02 .10
32 Bob Horner .01 .05
33 Ray Knight .01 .05
34 Bill Madlock .02 .10
35 Ken Oberkfell .01 .05
36 Mike Schmidt .75 2.00
37 Alan Ashby .01 .05
38 Bruce Benedict .01 .05
39 Gary Carter .40 1.00
40 Bo Diaz .01 .05
41 Terry Kennedy .01 .05
42 Tony Pena .05 .15
43 Darrell Porter .01 .05
44 Mike Scioscia .05 .15
45 John Stearns .01 .05
46 Dusty Baker .02 .10
47 Cesar Cedeno .02 .10
48 Jack Clark .02 .10
49 Warren Cromartie .01 .05
50 Jose Cruz .01 .05
51 Andre Dawson .25 .60
52 Leon Durham .01 .05
53 Mike Easler .01 .05
54 George Foster .02 .10
55 Pedro Guerrero .05 .15
56 Steve Henderson .01 .05
57 George Hendrick .01 .05
58 Ken Landreaux .01 .05
59 Sixto Lezcano .01 .05
60 Garry Maddox .01 .05
61 Gary Matthews .01 .05
62 Omar Moreno .01 .05
63 Dale Murphy .25 .60
64 Dave Parker .07 .20
65 Terry Puhl .01 .05
66 Tim Raines .25 .60
67 Gene Richards .01 .05
68 Tony Scott .01 .05
69 Lonnie Smith .05 .15
70 Claudell Washington .01 .05
71 Mookie Wilson .02 .10
72 Joel Youngblood .01 .05
73 Bruce Berenyi .01 .05
74 Rick Camp .01 .05
75 Steve Carlton .50 1.25
76 Bob Forsch .01 .05
77 Alan Fowlkes .01 .05
78 Gene Garber .02 .10
79 Randy Jones .01 .05
80 Tim Lollar .01 .05
81 Randy Martz .01 .05
82 Joe Niekro .02 .10
83 Jeff Reardon .05 .15
84 Jerry Reuss .02 .10
85 Don Robinson .01 .05
86 Steve Rogers .01 .05
87 Bruce Sutter .05 .15
88 Don Sutton .25 .60
89 Kent Tekulve .01 .05
90 Fernando Valenzuela .25 .60
91 Willie Aikens .01 .05
92 Rod Carew .50 1.25
93 Dave Collins .01 .05
94 Cecil Cooper .02 .10
95 Mike Hargrove .02 .10
96 John Mayberry .01 .05
97 Eddie Murray .50 1.25
98 Tom Paciorek .01 .05
99 Carl Yastrzemski 1.00 2.50

100 Tony Bernazard .01 .05
101 Julio Cruz .01 .05
102 Rich Dauer .01 .05
103 Jim Gantner .01 .05
104 Bobby Grich .02 .10
105 Willie Randolph .05 .15
106 Jerry Remy .01 .05
107 Lou Whitaker .05 .15
108 Frank White .02 .10
109 Bill Almon .01 .05
110 Rick Burleson .01 .05
111 Bucky Dent .02 .10
112 Alfredo Griffin .01 .05
113 Glenn Hoffman .01 .05
114 Roy Smalley .01 .05
115 Alan Trammell .07 .20
116 U.L. Washington .01 .05
117 Robin Yount .25 .60
118 Buddy Bell .02 .10
119 George Brett 1.25 3.00
120 John Castino .01 .05
121 Doug DeCinces .02 .10
122 Toby Harrah .01 .05
123 Carney Lansford .02 .10
124 Paul Molitor .25 .60
125 Graig Nettles .02 .10
126 Cal Ripken Jr. 6.00 15.00
127 Rick Cerone .01 .05
128 Rick Dempsey .01 .05
129 Carlton Fisk .25 .60
130 Ron Hassey .01 .05
131 Mike Heath .01 .05
132 Lance Parrish .05 .15
133 Ted Simmons .02 .10
134 Jim Sundberg .01 .05
135 Butch Wynegar .01 .05
136 Tony Armas .01 .05
137 Harold Baines .05 .15
138 Don Baylor .02 .10
139 Bruce Bochte .01 .05
140 Al Bumbry .01 .05
141 Dwight Evans .07 .20
142 Dan Ford .01 .05
143 Kirk Gibson .25 .60
144 Ken Griffey .02 .10
145 Rickey Henderson 1.50 4.00
146 Reggie Jackson 1.00 2.50
147 Steve Kemp .01 .05
148 Ron LeFlore .01 .05
149 Chet Lemon .01 .05
150 Fred Lynn .02 .10
151 Bake McBride .01 .05
152 Jerry Mumphrey .01 .05
153 Dwayne Murphy .01 .05
154 Ben Oglivie .01 .05
155 Amos Otis .01 .05
156 Jim Rice .07 .20
157 Mickey Rivers .02 .10
158 Ken Singleton .01 .05
159 Gorman Thomas .01 .05
160 Willie Wilson .01 .05
161 Dave Winfield .40 1.00
162 Richie Zisk .01 .05
163 Floyd Bannister .01 .05
164 Len Barker .01 .05
165 Britt Burns .01 .05
166 Bill Caudill .01 .05
167 Jim Clancy .01 .05
168 Danny Darwin .01 .05
169 Ron Davis .01 .05
170 Rollie Fingers .25 .60
171 Ron Guidry .07 .20
172 Larry Gura .01 .05
173 Lamarr Hoyt .01 .05
174 Matt Keough .01 .05
175 Scott McGregor .01 .05
176 Jack Morris .05 .15
177 Dave Stieb .02 .10
178 John Tudor .01 .05
179 Pete Vuckovich .01 .05
180 Geoff Zahn .01 .05

1983 All-Star Game Program Inserts

This 180-card set was distributed inside the 1983 All-Star Game Official Program on foldout sheets with each sheet containing 30 cards. Each card measures approximately 1 1/4" by 2" and features color action photos of the American League (numbers 1-90) and the National League All-Star Nominees (numbers 91-181). The cards are unnumbered and checklisted below in alphabetical order by position within each player's respective league.

COMPLETE SET (180) 4.00 10.00
1 Willie Aikens .01 .05
2 Rod Carew .25 .60
3 Cecil Cooper .02 .10
4 Kent Hrbek .02 .10
5 Eddie Murray .75 2.00
6 Tom Paciorek .01 .05
7 Andre Thornton .01 .05
8 Willie Upshaw .01 .05
9 Carl Yastrzemski .40 1.00
10 Rich Dauer .01 .05
11 Jim Gantner .01 .05
12 Damaso Garcia .01 .05
13 Bobby Grich .02 .10
14 Willie Randolph .02 .10
15 Jerry Remy .01 .05
16 Manny Trillo .01 .05
17 Lou Whitaker .07 .20
18 Frank White .01 .05
19 Todd Cruz .01 .05
20 Tim Foli .01 .05
21 Alfredo Griffin .01 .05
22 Glenn Hoffman .01 .05
23 Cal Ripken 1.50 4.00
24 Roy Smalley .01 .05
25 Alan Trammell .25 .60
26 U.L. Washington .01 .05
27 Robin Yount .40 1.00
28 Buddy Bell .02 .10
29 Wade Boggs 3.00 8.00
30 George Brett .75 2.00
31 Doug DeCinces .01 .05
32 Gary Gaetti .40 1.00
33 Toby Harrah .01 .05
34 Carney Lansford .01 .05
35 Paul Molitor .60 1.50
36 Graig Nettles .05 .15
37 Bob Boone .02 .10
38 Rick Cerone .01 .05
39 Rick Dempsey .01 .05
40 Carlton Fisk .50 1.25
41 Mike Heath .01 .05
42 Lance Parrish .02 .10
43 Ted Simmons .02 .10
44 Jim Sundberg .01 .05
45 John Wathan .01 .05
46 Tony Armas .01 .05
47 Harold Baines .07 .20
48 Barry Bonnell .01 .05
49 Tom Brunansky .01 .05
50 Al Cowens .01 .05
51 Brian Downing .01 .05
52 Dwight Evans .02 .10
53 Kirk Gibson .07 .20
54 Rickey Henderson 1.00 2.50
55 Larry Herndon .01 .05
56 Reggie Jackson .50 1.25
57 Steve Kemp .01 .05
58 Chet Lemon .01 .05
59 Greg Luzinski .02 .10
60 Fred Lynn .02 .10
61 Rick Manning .01 .05
62 Hal McRae .01 .05
63 Jerry Mumphrey .01 .05
64 Dwayne Murphy .01 .05
65 Ben Oglivie .01 .05
66 Amos Otis .01 .05
67 Jim Rice .05 .15
68 Ken Singleton .01 .05
69 Gorman Thomas .01 .05
70 Gary Ward .01 .05
71 Willie Wilson .01 .05
72 Dave Winfield .50 1.25
73 Bert Blyleven .02 .10
74 Bill Caudill .01 .05
75 Richard Dotson .01 .05
76 Dennis Eckersley .40 1.00
77 Mike Flanagan .01 .05
78 Ken Forsch .01 .05
79 Larry Gura .01 .05
80 Rick Honeycutt .01 .05
81 Dennis Lamp .01 .05
82 Mike Norris .01 .05
83 Dan Petry .01 .05
84 Dan Quisenberry .01 .05
85 Shane Rawley .01 .05
86 Jim Slaton .01 .05
87 Bob Stanley .01 .05
88 Dave Stieb .01 .05
89 Al Williams .01 .05
90 Geoff Zahn .01 .05
91 Bill Buckner .01 .05
92 Chris Chambliss .02 .10
93 Dan Driessen .01 .05
94 Steve Garvey .07 .20
95 Keith Hernandez .02 .10
96 Ray Knight .01 .05
97 Al Oliver .02 .10
98 Pete Rose .50 1.25
99 Jason Thompson .01 .05
100 Juan Bonilla .01 .05
101 Doug Flynn .01 .05
102 Tom Herr .01 .05
103 Glenn Hubbard .01 .05
104 Joe Morgan .25 .60
105 Ron Oester .01 .05
106 Johnny Ray .01 .05
107 Ryne Sandberg 2.50 6.00
108 Steve Sax .02 .10
109 Larry Bowa .01 .05
110 Dave Concepcion .02 .10
111 Ivan DeJesus .01 .05
112 Rafael Ramirez .01 .05
113 Bill Russell .01 .05
114 Ozzie Smith 1.00 2.50
115 Chris Speier .01 .05
116 Garry Templeton .01 .05
117 Dickie Thon .01 .05
118 Hubie Brooks .01 .05
119 Ron Cey .02 .10
120 Phil Garner .02 .10
121 Pedro Guerrero .02 .10
122 Bob Horner .01 .05
123 Bill Madlock .02 .10
124 Ken Oberkfell .01 .05
125 Mike Schmidt .75 2.00
126 Tim Wallach .01 .05
127 Alan Ashby .01 .05
128 Bruce Benedict .01 .05
129 Gary Carter .40 1.00
130 Jody Davis .01 .05
131 Bo Diaz .01 .05
132 Terry Kennedy .01 .05
133 Tony Pena .02 .10
134 Darrell Porter .01 .05
135 John Stearns .01 .05
136 Dusty Baker .02 .10
137 Cesar Cedeno .01 .05
138 Jack Clark .01 .05
139 Warren Cromartie .01 .05
140 Jose Cruz .02 .10
141 Chili Davis .02 .10
142 Andre Dawson .25 .60
143 Leon Durham .01 .05
144 Mike Easler .01 .05
145 George Foster .01 .05
146 Von Hayes .01 .05
147 George Hendrick .01 .05
148 Ruppert Jones .01 .05
149 Ken Landreaux .01 .05
150 Sixto Lezcano .01 .05
151 Garry Maddox .01 .05
152 Gary Matthews .01 .05
153 Willie McGee .50 1.25
154 Omar Moreno .01 .05
155 Dale Murphy .25 .60
156 Dave Parker .02 .10
157 Terry Puhl .01 .05
158 Tim Raines .07 .20
159 Gene Richards .01 .05
160 Lonnie Smith .01 .05
161 Claudell Washington .01 .05
162 Mookie Wilson .02 .10
163 Joaquin Andujar .01 .05
164 Rick Camp .01 .05
165 Steve Carlton .40 1.00
166 Atlee Hammaker .01 .05
167 Fergie Jenkins .25 .60
168 Bob Knepper .01 .05
169 Charlie Lea .01 .05
170 Larry McWilliams .01 .05
171 Alejandro Pena .01 .05
172 Pascual Perez .01 .05
173 Jerry Reuss .02 .10
174 Steve Rogers .01 .05
175 Nolan Ryan 1.50 4.00
176 Tom Seaver .50 1.25
177 Rod Scurry .01 .05
178 Eric Show .01 .05
179 Mario Soto .01 .05
180 Bruce Sutter .20 .50

1984 All-Star Game Program Inserts

This 180-card set was distributed inside the 1984 All-Star Game Official Program on foldout sheets with each sheet containing 30 cards. Each card measures approximately 1 3/16" by 1 7/8" and features color photos of the National League (numbers 1-90) and the American League All-Star Nominees (numbers 91-181). The cards are unnumbered and checklisted below in alphabetical order by position within each player's respective league. Inserts listed above number 180 were issued as pitchers and write in candidates.

COMPLETE SET (180) 4.00 10.00
1 Bill Buckner .02 .10
2 Chris Chambliss .02 .10
3 Dan Driessen .01 .05
4 Steve Garvey .05 .15
5 David Green .01 .05
6 Keith Hernandez .05 .15
7 Ray Knight .01 .05
8 Al Oliver .02 .10
9 Jason Thompson .01 .05
10 Bill Doran .01 .05
11 Tommy Herr .01 .05
12 Glenn Hubbard .01 .05
13 Ron Oester .01 .05
14 Johnny Ray .01 .05
15 Ryne Sandberg 1.50 4.00
16 Steve Sax .01 .05
17 Manny Trillo .01 .05
18 Alan Wiggins .01 .05
19 Dale Berra .01 .05
20 Dave Concepcion .02 .10
21 Ivan DeJesus .01 .05
22 Johnnie LeMaster .01 .05
23 Rafael Ramirez .01 .05
24 Bill Russell .02 .10
25 Ozzie Smith 1.00 2.50
26 Garry Templeton .01 .05
27 Dickie Thon .01 .05
28 Ron Cey .02 .10
29 Phil Garner .02 .10
30 Pedro Guerrero .01 .05
31 Bob Horner .01 .05
32 Bill Madlock .02 .10
33 Graig Nettles .02 .10
34 Ken Oberkfell .01 .05
35 Mike Schmidt .50 1.25
36 Tim Wallach .01 .05
37 Alan Ashby .01 .05
38 Bruce Benedict .01 .05
39 Gary Carter .20 .50
40 Jody Davis .01 .05
41 Bo Diaz .01 .05
42 Terry Kennedy .01 .05
43 Tony Pena .02 .10
44 Darrell Porter .01 .05
45 Steve Yeager .01 .05
46 Jack Clark .02 .10
47 Jose Cruz .02 .10
48 Chili Davis .02 .10
49 Andre Dawson .05 .15
50 Leon Durham .07 .20
51 George Foster .01 .05
52 Tony Gwynn 1.50 4.00
53 George Hendrick .01 .05
54 Ken Landreaux .01 .05
55 Joe Lefebvre .01 .05
56 Jeff Leonard .01 .05
57 Willie McGee .07 .20
58 Mike Marshall .01 .05
59 Gary Matthews .01 .05
60 Keith Moreland .01 .05
61 Jerry Mumphrey .01 .05
62 Dale Murphy .07 .20
63 Amos Otis .01 .05
64 Dave Parker .05 .15
65 Terry Puhl .01 .05
66 Tim Raines .05 .15
67 Gary Redus .01 .05
68 Pete Rose .50 1.25
69 Darryl Strawberry .08 .25
70 Lonnie Smith .01 .05
71 Claudell Washington .01 .05
72 Mookie Wilson .02 .10
73 Joaquin Andujar .01 .05
74 Steve Bedrosian .01 .05
75 John Candelaria .01 .05
76 John Denny .01 .05
77 Dwight Gooden .50 1.25
78 Rich Gossage .05 .15
79 Al Holland .01 .05
80 Rick Honeycutt .01 .05
81 Dave LaPoint .01 .05
82 Gary Lavelle .01 .05
83 Charlie Lea .01 .05
84 Jesse Orosco .02 .10
85 Alejandro Pena .01 .05
86 Nolan Ryan 1.50 4.00
87 Eric Show .01 .05
88 Bryn Smith .01 .05
89 Lee Smith .05 .15
90 Mario Soto .01 .05
91 Rod Carew .25 .60
92 Cecil Cooper .02 .10
93 Darrell Evans .02 .10
94 Ken Griffey .02 .10
95 Kent Hrbek .01 .05
96 Eddie Murray .50 1.25
97 Tom Paciorek .01 .05
98 Andre Thornton .01 .05
99 Willie Upshaw .01 .05
100 Julio Cruz .01 .05
101 Rich Dauer .01 .05
102 Jim Gantner .01 .05
103 Damaso Garcia .01 .05
104 Bobby Grich .02 .10
105 Willie Randolph .02 .10
106 Jerry Remy .01 .05
107 Lou Whitaker .07 .20
108 Frank White .02 .10
109 Tim Foli .01 .05
110 Julio Franco .07 .20
111 Alfredo Griffin .01 .05
112 Glenn Hoffman .01 .05
113 Cal Ripken 1.50 4.00
114 Dick Schofield .01 .05
115 Alan Trammell .25 .60
116 Robin Yount .25 .60
117 U.L. Washington .01 .05
118 Buddy Bell .02 .10
119 Wade Boggs 1.50 4.00
120 George Brett 1.00 2.50
121 John Castino .01 .05
122 Doug DeCinces .01 .05
123 Toby Harrah .01 .05
124 Carney Lansford .01 .05
125 Vance Law .01 .05
126 Paul Molitor .25 .60
127 Bob Boone .02 .10
128 Rick Dempsey .01 .05
129 Carlton Fisk .25 .60
130 Mike Heath .01 .05
131 Lance Parrish .05 .15
132 Jim Sundberg .01 .05
133 Ted Simmons .02 .10
134 John Wathan .01 .05
135 Butch Wynegar .01 .05
136 Tony Armas .01 .05
137 Harold Baines .05 .15
138 Don Baylor .05 .15
139 Jesse Barfield .01 .05
140 Tom Brunansky .01 .05
141 Brian Downing .01 .05
142 Dwight Evans .02 .10
143 Rickey Henderson .75 2.00
144 Larry Herndon .01 .05
145 Reggie Jackson .40 1.00
146 Steve Kemp .01 .05
147 Ron Kittle .01 .05
148 Chet Lemon .01 .05
149 John Lowenstein .01 .05
150 Greg Luzinski .02 .10
151 Fred Lynn .02 .10
152 Hal McRae .01 .05
153 Lloyd Moseby .01 .05
154 Dwayne Murphy .01 .05
155 Larry Parrish .01 .05
156 Ben Oglivie .01 .05
157 Jim Rice .05 .15
158 Gorman Thomas .01 .05
159 Ken Singleton .01 .05
160 Gary Ward .01 .05
161 Dave Winfield .40 1.00
162 George Wright .01 .05
163 Dave Beard .01 .05
164 Bert Blyleven .05 .15
165 Mike Boddicker .01 .05
166 Mike Caldwell .01 .05
167 Bill Caudill .01 .05
168 Danny Darwin .01 .05
169 Ron Davis .01 .05
170 Richard Dotson .01 .05
171 Larry Gura .01 .05
172 Bruce Hurst .01 .05
173 Luis Leal .01 .05
174 Jack Morris .05 .15
175 Dan Petry .01 .05
176 Mike Smithson .01 .05
177 Sammy Stewart .01 .05
178 Dave Stieb .02 .10
179 Milt Wilcox .01 .05
180 Geoff Zahn .01 .05
181 Aurelio Lopez .01 .05
182 Tippy Martinez .01 .05
183 Don Mattingly 3.00 8.00
184 Pete O'Brien .01 .05
185 Tom Paciorek .01 .05
186 Dan Quisenberry .01 .05
187 Jerry Remy .01 .05
188 Luis Sanchez .01 .05
189 Pat Tabler .01 .05

1985 All-Star Game Program Inserts

This 180-card set was distributed inside the 1985 All-Star Game Official Program on foldout sheets with each sheet containing 30 cards. Each card measures approximately 1 1/4" by 2" and features color photos of the American League (numbers 1-90) and the National League All-Star Nominees (numbers 91-181). The cards are unnumbered and checklisted below in alphabetical order by position within each player's respective league.

COMPLETE SET (180) 4.00 10.00
1 Bill Buckner .01 .05
2 Rod Carew .25 .60
3 Cecil Cooper .02 .10
4 Alvin Davis .02 .10
5 Kent Hrbek .02 .10
6 Don Mattingly 1.00 2.50
7 Eddie Murray .50 1.25
8 Pete O'Brien .01 .05
9 Willie Upshaw .01 .05
10 Marty Barrett .01 .05
11 Julio Cruz .01 .05
12 Jim Gantner .01 .05
13 Damaso Garcia .01 .05
14 Bobby Grich .02 .10
15 Willie Randolph .02 .10
16 Tim Teufel .01 .05
17 Lou Whitaker .08 .25
18 Frank White .01 .05
19 Onix Concepcion .01 .05
20 Tony Fernandez .05 .15
21 Julio Franco .05 .15
22 Alfredo Griffin .01 .05
23 Jackie Gutierrez .01 .05
24 Spike Owen .01 .05
25 Cal Ripken 1.50 4.00
26 Alan Trammell .25 .60
27 Robin Yount .40 1.00
28 Buddy Bell .02 .10
29 Wade Boggs 1.00 2.50
30 George Brett .75 2.00
31 Doug DeCinces .01 .05
32 Darrell Evans .02 .10
33 Gary Gaetti .02 .10
34 Carney Lansford .02 .10
35 Paul Molitor .50 1.25
36 Rance Mulliniks .01 .05
37 Bob Boone .02 .10
38 Rick Dempsey .01 .05
39 Carlton Fisk .50 1.25
40 Rich Gedman .01 .05
41 Mike Heath .01 .05
42 Lance Parrish .02 .10
43 Jim Sundberg .01 .05
44 Ernie Whitt .01 .05
45 Butch Wynegar .01 .05
46 Tony Armas .01 .05
47 Harold Baines .05 .15
48 Jesse Barfield .01 .05
49 Don Baylor .02 .10
50 George Bell .01 .05
51 Tom Brunansky .01 .05
52 Brett Butler .02 .10
53 Dave Collins .01 .05
54 Brian Downing .01 .05
55 Mike Easler .01 .05
56 Dwight Evans .02 .10
57 Kirk Gibson .08 .25
58 Ricky Henderson .75 2.00
59 Reggie Jackson .50 1.25
60 Ron Kittle .01 .05
61 Lee Lacy .01 .05
62 Chet Lemon .01 .05
63 Fred Lynn .02 .10
64 Lloyd Moseby .01 .05
65 Dwayne Murphy .01 .05
66 Ben Oglivie .01 .05
67 Larry Parrish .01 .05
68 Kirby Puckett 2.00 5.00
69 Jim Rice .05 .15
70 Gary Ward .01 .05
71 Willie Wilson .01 .05
72 Dave Winfield .50 1.25
73 Doyle Alexander .01 .05
74 Mike Boddicker .01 .05
75 Oil Can Boyd .01 .05
76 Danny Darwin .01 .05
77 Ron Guidry .02 .10
78 Willie Hernandez .01 .05
79 Mark Langston .08 .25
80 Charlie Liebrandt .01 .05
81 Jack Morris .02 .10
82 Dickie Noles .01 .05
83 Dan Petry .01 .05
84 Dan Quisenberry .02 .10
85 Dave Righetti .02 .10
86 Don Schulze .01 .05
87 Tom Seaver .40 1.00
88 Jim Slaton .01 .05
89 Frank Viola .02 .10
90 Geoff Zahn .01 .05
91 Greg Brock .01 .05
92 Enos Cabell .01 .05
93 Dan Driessen .01 .05
94 Leon Durham .01 .05
95 Steve Garvey .08 .25
96 David Green .01 .05
97 Keith Hernandez .02 .10
98 Pete Rose .50 1.25
99 Jason Thompson .01 .05
100 Bill Doran .01 .05
101 Tommy Herr .01 .05
102 Glenn Hubbard .01 .05
103 Johnny Ray .01 .05
104 Juan Samuel .01 .05
105 Ryne Sandberg 1.00 2.50
106 Steve Sax .02 .10
107 Manny Trillo .01 .05
108 Alan Wiggins .01 .05
109 Larry Bowa .02 .10
110 Hubie Brooks .01 .05
111 Dave Concepcion .02 .10
112 Ivan DeJesus .01 .05
113 Rafael Ramirez .01 .05
114 Craig Reynolds .01 .05
115 Bill Russell .01 .05
116 Ozzie Smith .75 2.00
117 Garry Templeton .01 .05
118 Ron Cey .02 .10
119 Phil Garner .02 .10
120 Bob Horner .01 .05
121 Ray Knight .01 .05
122 Bill Madlock .02 .10
123 Graig Nettles .05 .15
124 Terry Pendleton .08 .25
125 Mike Schmidt .40 1.00
126 Tim Wallach .01 .05
127 Bob Brenly .01 .05
128 Gary Carter .25 .60
129 Jody Davis .01 .05
130 Mike Fitzgerald .01 .05
131 Terry Kennedy .01 .05
132 Tony Pena .02 .10
133 Darrell Porter .01 .05
134 Mike Scioscia .05 .15
135 Ozzie Virgil .01 .05
136 Jack Clark .01 .05
137 Jose Cruz .02 .10
138 Chili Davis .02 .10
139 Andre Dawson .15 .40
140 Bob Dernier .01 .05
141 George Foster .01 .05
142 Pedro Guerrero .02 .10
143 Tony Gwynn 1.00 2.50
144 Von Hayes .01 .05
145 George Hendrick .01 .05
146 Steve Kemp .01 .05
147 Jeff Leonard .01 .05
148 Mike Marshall .01 .05
149 Gary Mathews .01 .05
150 Willie McGee .08 .25
151 Kevin McReynolds .01 .05
152 Keith Moreland .01 .05
153 Jerry Mumphrey .01 .05
154 Dale Murphy .08 .25
155 Dave Parker .02 .10
156 Terry Puhl .01 .05
157 Tim Raines .02 .10
158 Lonnie Smith .01 .05
159 Darryl Strawberry .02 .10
160 Claudell Washington .01 .05
161 Mookie Wilson .02 .10
162 Marvell Wynne .01 .05
163 Joaquin Andujar .01 .05
164 Steve Bedrosian .01 .05
165 John Candelaria .01 .05
166 Jose DeLeon .01 .05
167 John Denny .01 .05
168 Dennis Eckersley .40 1.00
169 Dwight Gooden .50 1.25
170 Rich Gossage .05 .15
171 Mike Krukow .01 .05
172 Rick Mahler .01 .05
173 Jesse Orosco .02 .10
174 Shane Rawley .01 .05
175 Nolan Ryan 1.50 4.00
176 Bryn Smith .01 .05
177 Lee Smith .05 .15
178 Mario Soto .01 .05
179 Steve Trout .01 .05
180 Fernando Valenzuela .08 .25

2001 All-Star Game Program Promos

COMPLETE SET (5) 12.50 30.00
1 Ken Griffey Jr. 2.50 6.00
2 Derek Jeter 3.00 8.00
3 Pedro Martinez 1.50 4.00
4 Mike Piazza 2.00 5.00
5 Ichiro Suzuki 5.00 12.00

1904 Allegheny Card Company

This set, which looks like playing cards, featured National League players only. The fronts of the cards feature the player's portrait in a circle with the team name on top and the player's name and position on the bottom. Since the cards are not numbered, we have sequenced them in alphabetical order. It is important to note that only one of these sets have been discovered so far.

COMPLETE SET

1887 Allen and Ginter N28

This 50-card set of The World's Champions was marketed by Allen and Ginter in 1887. The cards feature color lithographs of champion athletes from seven categories of sport, with baseball, rowing and boxing each having 10 individuals portrayed. Cards numbered 1 to 10 depict baseball players and cards numbered 11 to 20 depict popular boxers of the era. This set is called the first series although no such title appears on the cards. All 50 cards are checklisted on the reverse, and they are unnumbered. An album (catalog: A16) and an advertising banner (catalog: G20) were also issued in conjunction with this set.

COMPLETE SET (50) 5000.00 10000.00
1 Cap Anson 2500.00 4000.00
Baseball
2 Charles Bennett 350.00 600.00
Baseball
3 Robert L. Caruthers 350.00 600.00
Baseball
4 John Clarkson 900.00 1500.00
Baseball
5 Charles Comiskey 1200.00 2000.00
Baseball
6 Captain Jack Glasscock 500.00 800.00
Baseball
7 Timothy Keefe 900.00 1500.00
Baseball
8 Mike Kelly 1200.00 2000.00
Baseball
9 Joseph Mulvey 500.00 800.00
Baseball
10 John M. Ward 900.00 1500.00
Baseball

1888 Allen and Ginter N29

The second series of The World's Champions was probably issued in 1888. Like the first series, the cards are backlisted and unnumbered. However, there are 17 distinct categories of sports represented in this set, with only six baseball players portrayed (as opposed to 10 in the first series). Each card has a color lithograph of the individual set against a white background. An album (catalog: A17) and an advertising banner (catalog: G21) were issued in conjunction with the set. The numbering below is alphabetical within sport, e.g., baseball players (1-6), boxers (7-14), and other sports (15-50).

COMPLETE SET (50) 5000.00 10000.00
1 Buck Ewing 800.00 1500.00
Baseball
2 James H. Fogarty 350.00 700.00
Baseball
3 Charles H. Getzein 350.00 700.00
Baseball
4 George F. Miller 350.00 700.00
Baseball
5 John Morrell 350.00 700.00
Baseball
6 James Ryan 375.00 750.00
Baseball

1888 Allen and Ginter N43

The primary designs of this 50-card set are identical to those of N29, but these are placed on a much larger card with extraneous background detail. The set was produced in 1888 by Allen and Ginter as inserts for a larger tobacco package than those in which sets N28 and N29 were marketed. Cards of this set, which is backlisted, are considered to be much scarcer than their counterparts in N29.

COMPLETE SET (50) 9000.00 18000.00
1 Buck Ewing 1500.00 3000.00
Baseball
2 James J. Fogarty 700.00 1400.00
Baseball
3 Charles H. Getzein 700.00 1400.00
Baseball
4 George F. Miller 700.00 1400.00
Baseball
5 John Morrell 700.00 1400.00
Baseball
6 James Ryan 750.00 1500.00
Baseball

1991 Alrak Griffey Gazette

Produced by Alrak Enterprises, these standard-size cards were issued in honor of Ken Griffey Jr. There were 3,000 promo sets distributed at the SuperBowl Sports Collectors Classic III in Bellevue, Washington (January, 1992). These promos carry the following stamp on their backs: "Promo Card, SuperBowl Sports Collectors Classic III, Bellevue, Washington, January 1992" and are valued at double the prices listed below.

COMPLETE SET (4) 2.50 6.00
1 Ken Griffey Jr. .75 2.00
Crowd Pleaser
2 Ken Griffey Jr. .75 2.00
Holdin' On
3 Ken Griffey Jr. .75 2.00
A 24ct. Gold Moment
4 Ken Griffey Jr. .75 2.00
Ken Griffey Sr.
Next of Ken

1991 Alrak Griffey Postcard

This one card set measures approximately 5 3/8" by 7 1/4" and was distributed by Alrak Enterprises to advertise their Ken Griffey Jr. Solid Brass Monthly Sportcard Series.

1 Ken Griffey Jr. 1.00 2.50

1992 Alrak Griffey Ace Auto Supply

This ten-card set, subtitled "Griffey's Golden Moments," was produced by Alrak Enterprises for Ace Auto Supply and Grand Auto Supply stores. The production run was reportedly 85,000 sets and they were sold at 145 stores in northern California, Nevada Washington and Alaska. The plastic cards measure approximately 3 3/8" by 2 1/8" and resemble plastic credit cards.

COMPLETE SET (10) 5.00 12.00
1 Ken Griffey Jr. .60 1.50
Complete Minor
Major League Batting
2 Ken Griffey Jr. .60 1.50
Career Highlights
3 Ken Griffey Jr. .60 1.50
Personal Data
4 Ken Griffey Jr. .60 1.50
Facts and Figures
5 Ken Griffey Jr. .60 1.50
Ken Griffey Sr.
Father and Son
6 Ken Griffey Jr. .60 1.50
1991 Highlights
7 Ken Griffey Jr. .60 1.50
Career Highlights
8 Ken Griffey Jr. .60 1.50
Facts About Junior
9 Ken Griffey Jr. .60 1.50
Facts About Junior
10 Ken Griffey Jr. .60 1.50
Ken Griffey Sr.
Father and Son

1992 Alrak Griffey Golden Moments

This ten-card set measures approximately 2 1/8" by 3 3/8" and is similar in design and material to credit cards. The cards feature posed and action color photos of Ken Griffey Jr. and Ken Griffey Sr. with white borders. The cards indicate "X of 20" on the back, so a second series of ten more cards was evidently planned.

COMPLETE SET (10) 6.00 15.00
1 Ken Griffey Jr. .75 2.00
Batting, horizontal shot
2 Ken Griffey Jr. .75 2.00
Fielding off wall
3 Ken Griffey Jr. .75 2.00
Sliding
4 Ken Griffey Jr. .75 2.00
Holding bat
5 Ken Griffey Jr. .75 2.00
Ken Griffey Sr.
6 Ken Griffey Jr. .75 2.00
Batting, vertical shot
7 Ken Griffey Jr. .75 2.00
With All-Star trophy
8 Ken Griffey Jr. .75 2.00
Close-up
9 Ken Griffey Jr. .75 2.00
On base
10 Ken Griffey Jr. .75 2.00
Ken Griffey Sr.
In dugout

1992 Alrak Griffey Golden Moments Sheet

This commemorative blank-backed sheet measures approximately 8 1/2" by 10 3/4" and features pictures of the Griffey's Golden Moments limited edition plastic baseball cards from Series I and II. Each sheet is individually numbered with production was limited to 1,000.

1 Ken Griffey Jr. 2.50 6.00

1992 Alrak Griffey McDonald's

This set, sponsored by McDonald's, contains three card and pin combinations. The cards are numbered on the front and measure 2 1/2" X 3 1/2". The card back describes the Ronald McDonald Children's Charities program in Western Washington. The set was produced by Alrak Enterprises with a reported production run of 100,000 for each card and pin combination. They were sold in 117 Western

McDonald's Washington restaurants.
COMPLETE SET (3) 4.00 10.00
1 Ken Griffey Jr. 2.00 5.00
Yellow background
2 Ken Griffey Jr. 2.00 5.00
Black and red background
3 Ken Griffey Jr. 2.00 5.00
Black and blue background

1993 Alrak Griffey 24 Taco Time

This six-card standard-size set was issued in the Pacific Northwest at Taco Time restaurants. Three cards have cut-out color player photos against gradated backgrounds of various colors. Color coordinated striped borders edged with gold foil frame the pictures. A gold-foil stamp at the lower right carries the words "Griffey 24" and "One of 24,000." The backs give player profile information and statistics against brightly colored backgrounds with a baseball player icon. The fourth card in the set is a 1992 All-Star MVP commemorative. It features a posed shot of Griffey with the MVP award. The horizontal back carries a color action photo with statistics in a ghosted white box on the left side. The fifth and sixth cards carry the red-foil Taco Time logo in their upper left corners and have red-foil-trimmed borders. The backs carry designs similar to the first three cards described above. The cards are unnumbered.

COMPLETE SET (6) 4.00 10.00
COMMON PLAYER (1-6) .80 2.00
1 Ken Griffey Jr. 1.00 2.50
Portrait
2 Ken Griffey Jr. 1.00 2.50
Batting
3 Ken Griffey Jr. 1.00 2.50
Throwing
4 Ken Griffey Jr. 1.00 2.50
All-Star MVP
5 Ken Griffey Jr. 1.00 2.50
Leaving batter's box
6 Ken Griffey Jr. 1.00 2.50
Head-first slide

1993 Alrak Griffey Mt. Vernon Ohio

Twenty thousand of these three-card standard-size sets were produced for the city of Mt. Vernon and all profits were to benefit the Mt. Vernon Ohio Youth Baseball League. Two different versions of the cards exist, one with and one without a gold-foil facsimile autograph inscribed across the picture. Either version is valued at the same price.

COMPLETE SET (3) 2.50 6.00
1 Ken Griffey Jr. 1.00 2.50
Portrait
2 Ken Griffey Jr. 1.00 2.50
Batting
3 Ken Griffey Jr. 1.00 2.50
Throwing

1993 Alrak Griffey Triple Play

This tri-fold card measures 7 1/2" by 3 1/2" unfolded and features a full-length color action photo of Griffey on one side with the words "Triple Play" appearing above the photo and statistics below. The production run was reportedly 24,000.

1 Ken Griffey Jr. 1.50 4.00

1993 Alrak Griffey Two-sided

This card measures the standard size and features a cut-out action shot of Griffey batting on one side and three cut-out action photos of Griffey on the other side.

1 Ken Griffey Jr. 1.50 4.00

1994 Alrak Griffey Jr. Taco Time

As part of a "Double Play" combination promotion, these 11 cards were specially offered as foil-wrapped singles to purchasers of a a 44 oz. Coke in a special Ken Griffey Jr. Collector's Cup at Taco Time Restaurants of Western Washington. Production of card numbers 1-6 was limited to 35,000 silver foil-accented sets. Additionally, 5,000 special gold foil-accented versions were created and randomly issued. The production run of the silver-foil SP2, SP4, and SP5 was 15,000, while that of the holographic foil SP1-3 was 20,000. Also, 30,000 cards were distributed to kick off the promotion to fans attending the Mariners-White Sox game of June 24. Measuring 3 1/2" by 5", the fronts feature original caricatures of Griffey by sports artist Larry Weber. The backs carry a description of a memorable moment in the career of the Mariners' star, as well as the Mariners, Alrak, and Taco Time logos.

COMPLETE SET (11) 4.00 10.00
COMMON SILVER CARD (1-6) .75 2.00
*GOLD: 3X VALUE
COMPLETE SP SET (5) 12.50 30.00
1 Ken Griffey Jr. 1.00 2.50
1990 First Gold Glove
2 Ken Griffey Jr. 1.00 2.50
1993
3 Ken Griffey Jr. 1.00 2.50
1993 AL Defensive
Player of the Year
4 Ken Griffey Jr. 1.00 2.50
1992 All-Star MVP
5 Ken Griffey Jr. 1.00 2.50
1994 All-Star
6 Ken Griffey Jr. 1.00 2.50
Mariners Care
SP1 Ken Griffey Jr. 3.00 8.00
1993 AL Defensive Record
SP2 Ken Griffey Jr. 4.00 10.00
1993 Home Run Streak
SP3 Ken Griffey Jr. 3.00 8.00
100th Home Run
SP4 Ken Griffey Jr. 4.00 10.00
1993 Off the Wall
SP5 Ken Griffey Jr. 4.00 10.00
1989 Major League Debut

2007 Americana Sports Legends

RANDOM INSERTS IN PACKS
STATED PRINT RUN 500 SERIAL #'d SETS
1 Willie Mays 3.00 8.00
2 Jackie Robinson 3.00 8.00
4 Lou Gehrig 4.00 10.00
8 Stan Musial 3.00 8.00

2007 Americana Sports Legends Material

RANDOM INSERTS IN PACKS
PRINT RUNS B/WN 25-500 COPIES PER
1 Willie Mays Jsy/100 12.50 30.00
2 Jackie Robinson Jacket/100 15.00 40.00
4 Lou Gehrig Jsy/100 50.00 100.00
8 Stan Musial Jsy/25 15.00 40.00

2007 Americana Sports Legends Signature

RANDOM INSERTS IN PACKS
PRINT RUNS B/WN 25-50 COPIES PER
1 Willie Mays/25 125.00 200.00
8 Stan Musial/25 40.00 80.00

2007 Americana Sports Legends Signature Material

*MTL: .5X TO 1.2X BASIC SIG
RANDOM INSERTS IN PACKS
PRINT RUNS B/WN 25-50 COPIES PER
1 Willie Mays Jsy/25 125.00 200.00
8 Stan Musial Jsy/25 40.00 80.00

2008 Americana II

201-270 ONE PER BOX
*RETAIL: .3X TO .8X BASIC CARDS
*SILVER 101-200: 1.5X TO 4X BASIC CARDS
SILVER 101-200 #'d TO 250
UNPRICED SILVER 201-270 #'d TO 25
*GOLD 101-200: 2X TO 5X BASIC CARDS
GOLD 101-200 #'d TO 100
UNPRICED GOLD 201-270 #'d TO 10
*PLATINUM 101-200: 3X TO 8X BASIC CARDS
PLATINUM 101-200 #'d TO 25
UNPRICED PLATINUM 201-270 #'d TO 5
185 Willie Mays 1.00 2.50

2008 Americana II Headliners

RANDOM INSERTS IN PACKS
STATED PRINT RUN 500 SERIAL #'d SETS
4 Hank Aaron 2.00 5.00
5 Willie Mays 2.00 5.00

2008 Americana II Headliners Material

RANDOM INSERTS IN PACKS
PRINT RUNS B/WN 44-100 COPIES PER
4 Hank Aaron/44 8.00 20.00
5 Willie Mays/100 12.50 30.00

2008 Americana II Headliners Signature

RANDOM INSERTS IN PACKS
PRINT RUNS B/WN 6-25 COPIES PER
NO PRICING ON QTY OF 10 OR LESS
5 Willie Mays/25 60.00 100.00

2008 Americana II Headliners Signature Material

RANDOM INSERTS IN PACKS
PRINT RUNS B/WN 10-25 COPIES PER
NO PRICING ON QTY OF 10
5 Willie Mays/25 75.00 125.00

2008 Americana II Private Signings

RANDOM INSERTS IN PACKS
PRINT RUNS B/WN 1-1200 COPIES PER
NO PRICING ON QTY OF 14 OR LESS
EXCHANGE DEADLINE 01/16/10
185 Willie Mays/25 60.00 120.00

2008 Americana II Stars Material

RANDOM INSERTS IN PACKS
PRINT RUNS B/WN 5-500 COPIES PER
NO PRICING ON QTY OF 5
185 Willie Mays/500 8.00 20.00

2008 Americana II Stars Material Gold Proofs

*GOLD: .75X TO 2X BASIC
RANDOM INSERTS IN PACKS
PRINT RUNS B/WN 5-25 COPIES PER
NO PRICING ON QTY OF 5

2008 Americana II Stars Material Silver Proofs

*SILVER: .6X TO 1.5X BASIC
RANDOM INSERTS IN PACKS
PRINT RUNS B/WN 10-100 COPIES PER
NO PRICING ON QTY OF 10

2008 Americana II Stars Signature Material

RANDOM INSERTS IN PACKS
PRINT RUNS B/WN 5-250 COPIES PER
NO PRICING ON QTY OF 10 OR LESS
185 Willie Mays/75 60.00 120.00

2009 Americana Movie Posters Triple Material

PRINT RUNS B/WN 15-500 COPIES PER

1908-10 American Caramel E91

The cards in this 99-card set measure 1 1/2" by 2 3/4". E91 encompasses three separate sets of color cards issued in 1908 and 1910. The 33 ballplayer drawings of the 1908 set were also used in the two 1910 sets. Eleven players were dropped and 11 were added for set 3. There are only 75 different players, so that, for example, there are two cards of Bender with identical fronts, but a different player is "named" in the same pose in set 3. Likewise, there can be three different players assigned to the same pose -- one from each set. The set 1 checklist lists "Athletics" first; set 3 "Pittsburgh" first.

COMPLETE SET (99) 5000.00 10000.00
1 Chief Bender 150.00 300.00
2 Roger Bresnahan 150.00 300.00
3 Al Bridwell 75.00 150.00
4 Mordecai Brown 150.00 300.00
5 Frank Chance 100.00 200.00
6 James Collins 150.00 300.00
7 Harry Davis 75.00 150.00
8 Art Devlin 75.00 150.00
9 Mike Donlin 100.00 200.00
10 Johnny Evers 100.00 200.00
11 Topsy Hartsel 75.00 150.00
12 Johnny Kling 75.00 150.00
13 Christy Mathewson 150.00 300.00
14 Joe McGinnity 150.00 300.00
15 John McGraw 100.00 200.00
16 Danny Murphy 75.00 150.00
17 Simon Nichols 75.00 150.00
18 Rube Oldring 75.00 150.00
19 Orval Overall 75.00 150.00
20 Eddie Plank 100.00 200.00
21 Ed Reulbach 75.00 150.00
22 Jimmy Scheckard 75.00 150.00
23 Ossie Schreckengost 75.00 150.00
24 Frank Schulte 100.00 200.00
25 Ralph Seybold 75.00 150.00
26 J.B. Seymore 75.00 150.00
27 Daniel Shay 75.00 150.00
28 James Slagle 75.00 150.00
29 Harry Steinfeldt 100.00 200.00
30 Luther Taylor 75.00 150.00
31 Fred Tenney 75.00 150.00
32 Joe Tinker 200.00 400.00
33 Rube Waddell 150.00 300.00
34 Jimmy Archer 75.00 150.00
35 Frank Baker 150.00 300.00
36 Jack Barry 75.00 150.00
37 Chief Bender 150.00 300.00
38 Al Bridwell 75.00 150.00
39 Mordecai Brown 150.00 300.00
40 Frank Chance 200.00 400.00
41 Eddie Collins 200.00 400.00
42 Harry Davis 75.00 150.00
43 Art Devlin 75.00 150.00
44 Mike Donlin 100.00 200.00
45 Larry Doyle 100.00 200.00
46 Johnny Evers 200.00 400.00
47 Bob Ganley 75.00 150.00
48 Fred Hartzell 75.00 150.00
49 Solly Hoffman 75.00 150.00
50 Harry Krause 75.00 150.00
51 Rube Marquard 150.00 300.00
52 Christy Mathewson 300.00 600.00
53 John McGraw 150.00 300.00
54 Chief Meyers 100.00 200.00
55 Danny Murphy 75.00 150.00
56 Red Murray 75.00 150.00
57 Orval Overall 75.00 150.00
58 Eddie Plank 200.00 400.00
59 Ed Reulbach 75.00 150.00
60 Jimmy Scheckard 75.00 150.00
61 Frank Schulte 100.00 200.00
62 J.B. Seymore 75.00 150.00
63 Harry Steinfeldt 100.00 200.00
64 Fred Tenney 75.00 150.00
65 Ira Thomas 75.00 150.00
66 Joe Tinker 200.00 400.00
67 Jap Barbeau 75.00 150.00
68 George Browne 75.00 150.00
69 Ed Carger 75.00 150.00
70 Charlie Chech 75.00 150.00
71 Fred Clarke 150.00 300.00
72 Wid Conroy 75.00 150.00
73 Jim Delehanty 75.00 150.00
74 Jiggs Donahue 75.00 150.00
75 J.A. Donohue 75.00 150.00
76 George Gibson 75.00 150.00
77 Bob Groom 75.00 150.00
78 Harry Hooper 150.00 300.00
79 Tom Hughes 75.00 150.00
80 Walter Johnson 300.00 600.00
81 Tommy Leach 100.00 200.00
82 Sam Leever 75.00 150.00
83 Harry Lord 75.00 150.00
84 George McBride 75.00 150.00
85 Amby McConnell 75.00 150.00
86 Clyde Milan 100.00 200.00
87 J.B. Miller 75.00 150.00
88 Harry Niles 75.00 150.00
89 Deacon Phillippe 100.00 200.00
90 Tris Speaker 200.00 400.00
91 Jack Stahl 100.00 200.00
92 Allen Storke 75.00 150.00
93 Gabby Street 100.00 200.00
94 Bob Unglaub 75.00 150.00
95 Charlie Wagner 75.00 150.00
96 Honus Wagner 400.00 800.00
97 Vic Willis 150.00 300.00
98 Owen Wilson 75.00 150.00
99 Joe Wood 150.00 300.00

1909-11 American Caramel E90-1

The cards in this 120-card set measure 1 1/2" by 2 3/4". The E90-1 set contains in order, the Mitchell of Cincinnati, Sweeney of Boston, and Graham cards which are more difficult to obtain than other cards in the set. In fact, there are many differential levels of scarcity in this set which was issued from 1909 through 1911. Several players exist in more than one pose or color background; these cards are noted in the checklist below. Of note, pricing for raw cards is provided in VgEx condition due to the fact that most cards from this set are found in off-grade shape.

1 William Bailey 60.00 120.00
2 Frank Baker 200.00 400.00
3 Jack Barry 60.00 120.00
4 George Bell 60.00 120.00
5 Harry Bemis 150.00 300.00
6 Chief Bender 250.00 500.00
7 Bob Bescher 150.00 250.00
8 Cliff Blankenship 75.00 150.00
9 John Bliss 60.00 120.00
10 Bill Bradley 100.00 200.00
11 Kitty Bransfield 60.00 120.00
P on Shirt
12 Kitty Bransfield 75.00 150.00
No P on Shirt
13 Roger Bresnahan 200.00 400.00
14 Al Bridwell 60.00 120.00
15 Buster Brown 150.00 250.00
16 Mordecai Brown 400.00 800.00
17 Donie Bush 60.00 120.00
18 John Butler 60.00 120.00
19 Howie Camnitz 60.00 120.00
20 Frank Chance 200.00 400.00
21 Hal Chase 175.00 350.00
22 Fred Clarke Phil 200.00 400.00
23 Fred Clarke Pitt 600.00 1000.00
24 Wallace O. Clement 75.00 150.00
25 Ty Cobb 2000.00 3000.00
26 Eddie Collins 200.00 400.00
27 Frank Corridon 60.00 120.00
28 Sam Crawford 200.00 400.00
29 Lou Criger 60.00 120.00
30 George Davis 250.00 500.00
31 Jasper Davis 60.00 120.00
32 Ray Demmitt 150.00 250.00
33 Mike Donlin 100.00 200.00
34 Wild Bill Donovan 75.00 150.00
35 Red Dooin 60.00 120.00
36 Patsy Dougherty 250.00 500.00
37 Hugh Duffy 1500.00 2000.00
38 Jimmy Dygert 60.00 120.00
39 Rube Ellis 60.00 120.00
40 Clyde Engle 100.00 200.00
41 Art Fromme 150.00 250.00
42 George Gibson Back 225.00 450.00
43 George Gibson Front 100.00 200.00
44 George Graham 1500.00 2000.00
45 Eddie Grant 75.00 150.00
46 Dolly Gray 75.00 150.00
47 Bob Groom 60.00 120.00
48 Charles Hall 75.00 150.00
49 Tippy Hartzell Green 60.00 120.00
50 Tippy Hartzell Pink 100.00 200.00
51 William Heitmuller 60.00 120.00
52 H.Howell Follow Through 60.00 120.00
53 H.Howell Wind Up 75.00 150.00
54 Tex Erwin 75.00 150.00
55 Frank Isbell 60.00 120.00
56 Joe Jackson 20000.00 30000.00
57 Hugh Jennings 100.00 200.00
58 Tim Jordan 60.00 120.00
59 Addie Joss 600.00 1000.00
Pitching
60 Addie Joss 400.00 800.00
Portrait
61 Ed Karger 400.00 800.00
62 Willie Keeler Pink Port 300.00 600.00
63 Willie Keeler Red Port 1000.00 1500.00
64 Willie Keeler 1000.00 1500.00
Throwing
65 John Knight 150.00 250.00
66 Harry Krause 75.00 150.00
67 Nap Lajoie 400.00 800.00
68 Tommy Leach 75.00 150.00
Batting
69 Tommy Leach 75.00 150.00
Throwing
70 Sam Leever 60.00 120.00
71 Hans Lobert 175.00 350.00
72 Harry Lumley 60.00 120.00
73 Rube Marquard 200.00 400.00
74 Christy Matthewson 1000.00 1500.00
75 Stuffy McInnes 75.00 150.00
76 Harry McIntyre 60.00 120.00
77 Larry McLean 225.00 450.00
78 George McQuillan 60.00 120.00
79 Dots Miller 60.00 120.00
w/o sunset in background
80 Dots Miller
Red sunset in background
81 Mike Mitchell 3000.00 5000.00
82 Fred Mitchell 100.00 200.00
83 George Mullin 75.00 150.00
84 Rebel Oakes 200.00 400.00
85 Patrick O'Connor 75.00 150.00
86 Charley O'Leary 60.00 120.00
87 Orval Overall 200.00 400.00
88 Jim Pastorius 60.00 120.00
89 Ed Phelps 60.00 120.00
90 Eddie Plank 600.00 1000.00
91 Lew Richie 60.00 120.00
92 Germany Schaefer 75.00 150.00
93 Victor Schlitzer 150.00 300.00
94 Johnny Siegle 150.00 250.00
95 Dave Shean 175.00 350.00
96 Jimmy Sheckard 75.00 150.00
97 Tris Speaker 3000.00 4000.00
98 Jake Stahl 800.00 1200.00
99 Oscar Stanage 60.00 120.00
100 George Stone 300.00 600.00
Left Hand
101 George Stone 60.00 120.00
No Hands
102 George Stovall 60.00 120.00
103 Ed Summers 60.00 120.00
104 Bill Sweeney 1000.00 1500.00
105 Jeff Sweeney 60.00 120.00
106 Jesse Tannehill 60.00 120.00
107 Lee Tannehill 60.00 120.00
108 Fred Tenney 100.00 200.00
109 Ira Thomas 75.00 150.00
110 Roy Thomas 60.00 120.00
111 Joe Tinker 200.00 400.00
112 Bob Unglaub 60.00 120.00
113 Jerry Upp 300.00 600.00
114 Honus Wagner 2000.00 3000.00
Batting
115 Honus Wagner 2000.00 3000.00
Throwing
116 Bobby Wallace 150.00 300.00
117 Ed Walsh 1500.00 2500.00
118 Vic Willis 250.00 500.00
119 Hooks Wiltse 100.00 200.00
120 Cy Young 1500.00 2000.00
Boston
121 Cy Young 1500.00 2000.00
Cleveland

1910 American Caramel E90-3

The E90-3 American Caramels "All the Star Players" set contains 20 unnumbered cards (each measuring 1 1/2" by 2 3/4") featuring the Chicago White Sox and Chicago Cubs. The eleven Cubs are listed first in the checklist below in alphabetical order (1-11), followed by the White Sox (12-20). The backs are slightly different from E90-1 cards and the fronts differ in the use of the team nicknames.

COMPLETE SET (20) 5000.00 10000.00
1 Jimmy Archer 300.00 600.00
2 Mordecai Brown 1000.00 2000.00
3 Frank Chance 1250.00 2500.00
4 King Cole 300.00 600.00
5 Johnny Evers 1000.00 2000.00
6 Solly Hoffman 300.00 600.00
7 Orval Overall 300.00 600.00
8 Frank Schulte 400.00 800.00
9 Jimmy Scheckard 300.00 600.00
10 Harry Steinfeldt 400.00 800.00
11 Joe Tinker 1000.00 2000.00
12 Lena Blackburne 300.00 600.00
13 Patsy Dougherty 300.00 600.00
14 Chick Gandil 1000.00 2000.00
15 Ed Hahn 300.00 600.00
16 Fred Payne 300.00 600.00
17 Billy Purtell 300.00 600.00
18 Frank (Nig) Smith 300.00 600.00
19 Ed Walsh 1000.00 2000.00
20 Rollie Zeider 300.00 600.00

1915 American Caramel E106

The cards in this 48-card set measure 1 1/2" by 2 3/4". The color cards in this series of "leading Baseball players in the National, American and Federal Leagues" were produced by the American Caramel Company of York, PA. The obverse surfaces appear glazed, a process used in several other sets of this vintage (T213, T216), probably as protection against stain damage. The set was issued in 1915. The cards have been alphabetized and numbered in the checklist below. The complete set price includes all variation cards listed in the checklist below. Listed pricing references raw "VG" condition.

COMPLETE SET (48) 40000.00 80000.00
1 Jack Barry 150.00 250.00
2A Chief Bender Striped Hat 350.00 600.00
2B Chief Bender White Hat 350.00 600.00
3 Bob Bescher 150.00 250.00
4 Roger Bresnahan 300.00 500.00
5 Al Bridwell 150.00 250.00
6 Donie Bush 150.00 250.00
7A Hal Chase Portrait 250.00 400.00
7B Hal Chase Catching 250.00 400.00
8A Ty Cobb Batting Front 2500.00 4000.00
8B Ty Cobb Batting Side 2500.00 4000.00
9 Eddie Collins 300.00 500.00
10 Sam Crawford 300.00 500.00
11 Ray Demmitt 150.00 250.00
12 Bill Donovan 150.00 250.00
13 Red Dooin 150.00 250.00
14 Mickey Doolan 150.00 250.00
15 Larry Doyle 150.00 250.00
16 Clyde Engle 150.00 250.00
17 Johnny Evers 300.00 500.00
18 Art Fromme 150.00 250.00
19A George Gibson Back 150.00 250.00
19B George Gibson Front 150.00 250.00
20 Topsy Hartzell 150.00 250.00
21 Fred Jacklitsch 150.00 250.00
22 Hugh Jennings MG 300.00 500.00
23 Otto Knabe 150.00 250.00
24 Nap Lajoie 600.00 1000.00
25 Hans Lobert 150.00 250.00
26 Rube Marquard 300.00 500.00
27 Christy Mathewson 1500.00 2500.00
28 John McGraw MG 300.00 500.00
29 George McQuillan 150.00 250.00
30 Dots Miller 150.00 250.00
31 Danny Murphy 150.00 250.00
32 Rebel Oakes 150.00 250.00
33 Eddie Plank 600.00 1000.00
34 Germany Schaefer 150.00 250.00
35 Tris Speaker 700.00 1200.00
36 Oscar Stanage 150.00 250.00
37 George Stovall 150.00 250.00
38 Jeff Sweeney 150.00 250.00
39A Joe Tinker Batting 350.00 600.00
39B Joe Tinker Portrait 350.00 600.00
40A Honus Wagner Batting 2500.00 4000.00
40B Honus Wagner Throwing 2500.00 4000.00
41 Hooks Wiltse 150.00 250.00
42 Heinie Zimmerman 150.00 250.00

1922 E122 American Caramel Series of 80

The cards in this 80-card set measure 2" by 3 1/2". The principal feature of this re-issue of the "80 series" of set E121 is the cross-hatch pattern or "screen" which covers the obverse of the card. The photos are black and white, and the player's name, position and team appear in a panel under his picture, all enclosed within the rectangular frame line. The set, which is unnumbered, was marketed in 1922 by the American Caramel Company. The cards have been alphabetized and numbered in the checklist below.

COMPLETE SET (80) 15000.00 30000.00
1 Grover C. Alexander 500.00 1000.00
2 Jim Bagby 100.00 200.00
3 Frank Baker 250.00 500.00
4 Dave Bancroft 250.00 500.00
5 Ping Bodie 100.00 200.00
6 George H. Burns 100.00 200.00
7 George J. Burns 100.00 200.00
8 Owen Bush 100.00 200.00
9 Max Carey 250.00 500.00
10 Red Causey 100.00 200.00
11 Ty Cobb 1250.00 2500.00
12 Eddie Collins 500.00 1000.00
13 Jake Daubert 150.00 300.00
14 Hooks Dauss 100.00 200.00
15 Charlie Deal 100.00 200.00
16 Bill Doak 100.00 200.00
17 Bill Donovan MG 100.00 200.00
18 Johnny Evers MG 250.00 500.00
19 Urban Faber 250.00 500.00
20 Eddie Foster 100.00 200.00
21 Larry Gardner 100.00 200.00
22 Kid Gleason MG 150.00 300.00
23 Hank Gowdy 150.00 300.00
24 John Graney 100.00 200.00
25 Tom Griffith 100.00 200.00
26 Harry Heilmann 250.00 500.00
27 Walter Holke 100.00 200.00
28 Charley Hollacher 100.00 200.00
29 Harry Hooper 250.00 500.00
30 Rogers Hornsby 600.00 1200.00
31 Baby Doll Jacobson 100.00 200.00
32 Walter Johnson 750.00 1500.00
33 James Johnston 100.00 200.00
34 Joe Judge 150.00 300.00
35 George Kelly 250.00 500.00
36 Dick Kerr 150.00 300.00
37 Pete Kilduff 100.00 200.00
38 Bill Killefer 100.00 200.00
39 John Lavan 100.00 200.00
40 Duffy Lewis 100.00 200.00
41 Al Mamaux 100.00 200.00
42 Rabbit Maranville 250.00 500.00
43 Carl Mays 150.00 300.00
44 John McGraw MG 250.00 500.00
45 Snuffy McInnis 150.00 300.00
46 Clyde Milan 150.00 300.00
47 Otto Miller 100.00 200.00
48 Guy Morton 100.00 200.00
49 Eddie Murphy 100.00 200.00
50 Hy Myers 100.00 200.00
51 Steve O'Neill 150.00 300.00
52 Roger Peckinpaugh 150.00 300.00
53 Jeff Pfeffer 100.00 200.00
54 Wally Pipp 150.00 300.00
55 Sam Rice 250.00 500.00
56 Eppa Rixey 250.00 500.00
57 Babe Ruth 2500.00 5000.00
58 Slim Sallee 100.00 200.00
59 Ray Schalk 250.00 500.00
60 Walter Schang 100.00 200.00
61 Ferd Schupp UER 100.00 200.00
62 Fred Schupp COR 100.00 200.00
63 Everett Scott 150.00 300.00
64 Hank Severeid 100.00 200.00
65 George Sisler 500.00 1000.00
Batting
66 George Sisler 500.00 1000.00
Throwing
67 Tris Speaker 500.00 1000.00
68 Milton Stock 100.00 200.00
69 Amos Strunk 100.00 200.00
70 Chester Thomas 100.00 200.00
71 George Tyler 100.00 200.00
72 Jim Vaughn 100.00 200.00
73 Bob Veach 100.00 200.00
74 Oscar Vitt 100.00 200.00
75 Bill Wambsganss 150.00 300.00
76 Zach Wheat 250.00 500.00
77 Fred Williams 150.00 300.00
78 Ivy Wingo 100.00 200.00
79 Joe Wood 200.00 400.00
80 Pep Young 100.00 200.00

1910 American Caramel Die Cuts E125

These cards were first discovered in 1969. Cards from this set have been found from the following teams: Philadelphia A's; Boston Red Sox; New York Giants and Pittsburgh Pirates. The best supposition about this set places it being produced during the 1910 season. The cards are black and white and range as high as 7" and as much as 4" wide. Please not that this checklist may be incomplete.

COMPLETE SET (42) 60000.00 120000.00
1 Babe Adams 1250.00 2500.00
2 Red Ames 1000.00 2000.00
3 Frank Baker 3000.00 6000.00
4 Jack Barry 1000.00 2000.00
5 Chief Bender 3000.00 6000.00
6 Al Bridwell 1000.00 2000.00
7 Bobby Byrne 1000.00 2000.00
8 Bill Carrigan 1000.00 2000.00
9 Eddie Cicotte 3000.00 6000.00
10 Fred Clarke UER 3000.00 6000.00
Name misspelled
11 Eddie Collins 4000.00 8000.00
12 Harry Davis 1000.00 2000.00
13 Art Devlin 1000.00 2000.00
14 Josh Devore 1000.00 2000.00
15 Larry Doyle 1250.00 2500.00
16 John Flynn 1000.00 2000.00
17 George Gibson 1000.00 2000.00
18 Topsy Hartsel UER 1000.00 2000.00
Name misspelled
19 Harry Hooper 2500.00 5000.00
20 Harry Krause 1000.00 2000.00
21 Tommy Leach 1000.00 2000.00
22 Harry Lord 1000.00 2000.00
23 Christy Mathewson 7500.00 15000.00
24 Ambrose McConnell 1000.00 2000.00
25 Fred Merkle 1250.00 2500.00
26 Dots Miller 1000.00 2000.00
27 Danny Murphy 1000.00 2000.00
28 Red Murray 1000.00 2000.00
29 Harry Niles 1000.00 2000.00
30 Rube Oldring 1000.00 2000.00
31 Eddie Plank 4000.00 8000.00
32 Cy Seymour 1000.00 2000.00
33 Tris Speaker 4000.00 8000.00
Batting
34 Tris Speaker 4000.00 8000.00
Fielding
35 Jake Stahl 1000.00 2000.00
36 Ira Thomas 1000.00 2000.00
37 Heinie Wagner 1000.00 2000.00
38 Honus Wagner 5000.00 10000.00
Batting
39 Honus Wagner 5000.00 10000.00
Throwing
40 Art Wilson 1000.00 2000.00
41 Owen Wilson 1250.00 2500.00
42 Hooks Wiltse 1000.00 2000.00

1927 American Caramel E126

The cards in this 60-card set measure 1 5/8" by 3 1/4". The cards contain black and white pictures, with the individual's name centered underneath, and his team and position to either side below that. This is the only numbered series of baseball cards to be issued by American Caramel. The backs contain advertising for an album designed to hold the set.

COMPLETE SET (60) 7500.00 15000.00
1 John Gooch 100.00 200.00
2 Clyde Barnhart 100.00 200.00
3 Joe Bush 125.00 250.00
4 Lee Meadows 100.00 200.00
5 Dick Cox 100.00 200.00
6 Red Faber 200.00 400.00
7 Aaron Ward 100.00 200.00
8 Ray Schalk 200.00 400.00
9 Specs Toporcer 100.00 200.00
10 Billy Southworth 125.00 250.00
11 Allen Sothoron 100.00 200.00
12 Will Sherdel 100.00 200.00
13 Grover C. Alexander 250.00 500.00
14 Jack Quinn 125.00 250.00
15 Chick Galloway 100.00 200.00
16 Eddie Collins 250.00 500.00
17 Ty Cobb 1000.00 2000.00
18 Percy Jones 100.00 200.00
19 Charlie Grimm 125.00 250.00
20 Bennie Karr 100.00 200.00
21 Charlie Jamieson 100.00 200.00
22 Sherrod Smith 100.00 200.00
23 Vergil Cheeves 100.00 200.00
24 James Ring 100.00 200.00
25 Muddy Ruel 100.00 200.00
26 Joe Judge 125.00 250.00
27 Tris Speaker 300.00 600.00
28 Walter Johnson 500.00 1000.00
29 Sam Rice 200.00 400.00
30 Hank DeBerry 100.00 200.00
31 Walter Henline 100.00 200.00
32 Max Carey 200.00 400.00
33 Arnold Statz 100.00 200.00
34 Irish Meusel 125.00 250.00
35 Pat Collins 100.00 200.00
36 Urban Shocker 125.00 250.00
37 Bob Shawkey 125.00 250.00
38 Babe Ruth 1500.00 3000.00
39 Bob Meusel 125.00 250.00
40 Alex Ferguson 100.00 200.00
41 Stuffy McInnis 125.00 250.00
42 Cy Williams 125.00 250.00
43 Russell Wrightstone 100.00 200.00
44 John Tobin UER 125.00 250.00
photo is Ed Brown
45 Baby Doll Jacobson 100.00 200.00
46 Bryan Harris 100.00 200.00
47 Elam VanGilder 100.00 200.00
48 Ken Williams 125.00 250.00
49 George Sisler 250.00 500.00
50 Ed Brown UER 125.00 250.00
photo is John Tobin
51 Jack Smith 100.00 200.00
52 Dave Bancroft 200.00 400.00
53 Larry Woodall 100.00 200.00
54 Lu Blue 100.00 200.00
55 Johnny Bassler 100.00 200.00
56 Jackie May 100.00 200.00
57 Horace Ford 100.00 200.00
58 Curt Walker 100.00 200.00
59 Art Nehf 100.00 200.00
60 George Kelly 200.00 400.00

1908 American League Publishing Co. PC770

This 1908-issued set features a large action shot or pose the player in uniform and also a small portrait of the player in street clothes in an oval at the top of the card. A short biography in a rectangular box is also featured at the base of the front, and the identifying line "American League Pub. Company, Cleveland, O." is located directly below the box.

COMPLETE SET (15) 4000.00 8000.00
1 Harry Bay 175.00 350.00
2 Charles Berger 175.00 350.00
3 Joe Birmingham 175.00 350.00
4 Bill Bradley 175.00 350.00
5 Walter Clarkson 175.00 350.00
6 Ty Cobb 900.00 1800.00
7 Elmer Flick 300.00 600.00
8 Claude Hickman 175.00 350.00
9 William Hinchman 175.00 350.00
10 Addie Joss 400.00 800.00
11 Nap Lajoie 350.00 700.00
12 Glen Liebhardt 175.00 350.00
13 George Nill 175.00 350.00
14 George Perring 175.00 350.00
15 Honus Wagner 600.00 1200.00

2011 American League All-Stars Topps

COMPLETE SET (17) 3.00 8.00
AL1 Derek Jeter 1.00 2.50
AL2 Adrian Gonzalez .30 .75
AL3 Josh Hamilton .25 .60
AL4 Miguel Cabrera .40 1.00
AL5 Joe Mauer .30 .75
AL6 Justin Morneau .25 .60
AL7 Alex Rodriguez .50 1.25
AL8 CC Sabathia .25 .60
AL9 Mark Teixeira .25 .60
AL10 Ichiro Suzuki .50 1.25
AL11 Felix Hernandez .25 .60
AL12 Evan Longoria .25 .60
AL13 Jose Bautista .25 .60
AL14 Adam Dunn .25 .60
AL15 Carl Crawford .25 .60
AL16 Jon Lester .25 .60
AL17 Elvis Andrus .25 .60

2012 American League All-Stars Topps

COMPLETE SET (17) 3.00 8.00
AL1 Albert Pujols .50 1.25
AL2 Evan Longoria .30 .75
AL3 Miguel Cabrera .40 1.00
AL4 Josh Hamilton .30 .75
AL5 Jacoby Ellsbury .30 .75
AL6 Jose Bautista .30 .75
AL7 Jered Weaver .30 .75
AL8 Felix Hernandez .30 .75
AL9 Justin Verlander .40 1.00
AL10 Ichiro Suzuki .50 1.25
AL11 Robinson Cano .30 .75
AL12 CC Sabathia .30 .75
AL13 Prince Fielder .30 .75
AL14 Dustin Pedroia .40 1.00

AL15 Adrian Gonzalez .30 .75
AL16 Derek Jeter 1.00 2.50
AL17 Alex Rodriguez .50 1.25

2013 American League All-Stars Topps

COMPLETE SET (17) 3.00 8.00
AL1 Prince Fielder .20 .50
AL2 Derek Jeter .60 1.50
AL3 Robinson Cano .20 .50
AL4 David Price .20 .50
AL5 Adrian Beltre .25 .60
AL6 Jose Bautista .20 .50
AL7 Justin Verlander .25 .60
AL8 Josh Hamilton .20 .50
AL9 Yu Darvish .25 .60
AL10 Albert Pujols .30 .75
AL11 Mike Trout 2.00 5.00
AL12 Felix Hernandez .20 .50
AL13 Jose Reyes .20 .50
AL14 Chris Sale .25 .60
AL15 Miguel Cabrera .25 .60
AL16 Evan Longoria .20 .50
AL17 Dustin Pedroia .25 .60

2014 American League All-Stars Topps

COMPLETE SET (17) 3.00 8.00
AL1 Mike Trout 1.25 3.00
AL2 Derek Jeter .60 1.50
AL3 Robinson Cano .20 .50
AL4 David Ortiz .25 .60
AL5 Adrian Beltre .25 .60
AL6 Adam Jones .20 .50
AL7 Justin Verlander .25 .60
AL8 Josh Hamilton .20 .50
AL9 Yu Darvish .25 .60
AL10 Chris Davis .15 .40
AL11 Prince Fielder .20 .50
AL12 Felix Hernandez .20 .50
AL13 Jose Reyes .20 .50
AL14 Joe Mauer .20 .50
AL15 Miguel Cabrera .25 .60
AL16 Evan Longoria .20 .50
AL17 Dustin Pedroia .25 .60

2015 American League All-Stars Topps

COMPLETE SET (17) 3.00 8.00
AL1 Mike Trout 1.25 3.00
AL2 Jose Abreu .25 .60
AL3 Miguel Cabrera .25 .60
AL4 Robinson Cano .20 .50
AL5 Jose Altuve .20 .50
AL6 Adrian Beltre .25 .60
AL7 Alexei Ramirez .20 .50
AL8 Michael Brantley .20 .50
AL9 Salvador Perez .20 .50
AL10 Adam Jones .20 .50
AL11 Jose Bautista .20 .50
AL12 Yoenis Cespedes .25 .60
AL13 David Ortiz .25 .60
AL14 Felix Hernandez .20 .50
AL15 David Price .20 .50
AL16 Greg Holland .15 .40
AL17 Corey Kluber .20 .50

2016 American League All-Stars Topps

COMPLETE SET (17) 3.00 8.00
AL1 Mike Trout 1.25 3.00
AL2 Salvador Perez .20 .50
AL3 Miguel Cabrera .25 .60
AL4 Jose Altuve .25 .60
AL5 Josh Donaldson .20 .50
AL6 Carlos Correa .25 .60
AL7 David Price .20 .50
AL8 Jose Bautista .20 .50
AL9 J.D. Martinez .25 .60
AL10 Wade Davis .15 .40
AL11 David Ortiz .25 .60
AL12 Dallas Keuchel .20 .50
AL13 Sonny Gray .20 .50
AL14 Nelson Cruz .25 .60
AL15 Manny Machado .25 .60
AL16 Francisco Lindor .25 .60
AL17 Chris Archer .15 .40

2017 American League All-Stars Topps

COMPLETE SET (17) 3.00 8.00
AL1 Mike Trout 1.25 3.00
AL2 Manny Machado .25 .60
AL3 Mookie Betts .50 1.25
AL4 Miguel Cabrera .25 .60
AL5 Eric Hosmer .20 .50
AL6 Jose Altuve .20 .50
AL7 Gary Sanchez .25 .60
AL8 Robinson Cano .20 .50
AL9 Francisco Lindor .25 .60
AL10 Nelson Cruz .25 .60
AL11 Edwin Encarnacion .25 .60
AL12 Josh Donaldson .20 .50
AL13 Salvador Perez .20 .50
AL14 Jackie Bradley Jr. .25 .60
AL15 Aroldis Chapman .25 .60
AL16 Chris Sale .25 .60
AL17 Xander Bogaerts .25 .60

2019 American League All-Stars Topps

COMPLETE SET (17) 5.00 12.00
AL1 Mookie Betts .50 1.25
AL2 Jose Altuve .20 .50
AL3 Mike Trout 1.25 3.00
AL4 J.D. Martinez .25 .60
AL5 Aaron Judge .60 1.50
AL6 Alex Bregman .25 .60
AL7 Jose Abreu .25 .60
AL8 Gleyber Torres .50 1.25
AL9 Chris Sale .25 .60
AL10 Jose Ramirez .20 .50
AL11 Francisco Lindor .25 .60
AL12 Giancarlo Stanton .25 .60
AL13 Blake Snell .20 .50
AL14 Shohei Ohtani .40 1.00
AL15 Justin Verlander .25 .60
AL16 Gerrit Cole .25 .60
AL17 Corey Kluber .20 .50

2020 American League All-Stars Topps

AL1 Mike Trout 1.25 3.00
AL2 Aaron Judge .60 1.50
AL3 Jose Altuve .20 .50
AL4 Mookie Betts .50 1.25
AL5 Alex Bregman .25 .60
AL6 Marcus Semien .25 .60
AL7 Tim Anderson .25 .60
AL8 Justin Verlander .25 .60
AL9 Francisco Lindor .25 .60
AL10 Gerrit Cole .40 1.00
AL11 Blake Snell .20 .50
AL12 Shohei Ohtani .40 1.00
AL13 Xander Bogaerts .25 .60
AL14 Whit Merrifield .25 .60
AL15 Vladimir Guerrero Jr. .40 1.00
AL16 George Springer .20 .50
AL17 Nelson Cruz .25 .60

1968 American Oil Winners Circle

This set of 12 perforated game cards measures approximately 2 5/8" by 2 1/8". There are "left side" and "right side" game cards which had to be matched to win a car or a cash prize. The "right side" game cards have a color drawing of a sports personality in a circle on the left, surrounded by laurel leaf twigs, and a short career summary on the right. There is a color bar on the bottom of the game piece carrying a dollar amount and the words "right side". The "left side" game cards carry a rectangular drawing of a sports personality or a photo of a Camaro or a Corvette. A different color bar with a dollar amount and the words "left side" are under the picture. On a dark blue background, the "right side" backs carry the rules of the game, and the "left side" cards show a "Winners Circle". The cards are unnumbered and checklisted below in alphabetical order.

COMPLETE SET (12) 75.00 150.00
7 Mickey Mantle 25.00 50.00
Left side
8 Willie Mays 15.00 30.00
Right side
10 Babe Ruth 25.00 50.00
Right side

1950 American Nut and Chocolate Co. Pennant

This 23-pennant set was distributed by the American Nut and Chocolate Co. and originally sold for 50 cents a set. The pennants measure approximately 1 7/8" by 4" and feature crude line-art drawings of the players with a facsimile autograph. The pennants are unnumbered and checklisted below in alphabetical order.

COMPLETE SET (23) 600.00 1200.00
1 Ewell Blackwell 15.00 30.00
2 Harry Brecheen 15.00 30.00
3 Phil Cavarretta 20.00 40.00
4 Bobby Doerr 25.00 50.00
5 Bob Elliott 15.00 30.00
6 Boo Ferriss 15.00 30.00
7 Joe Gordon 20.00 40.00
8 Tommy Holmes 15.00 30.00
9 Charles Keller 20.00 40.00
10 Ken Keltner 15.00 30.00
11 Whitey Kurowski 15.00 30.00
12 Ralph Kiner 40.00 80.00
13 Johnny Pesky 20.00 40.00
14 Pee Wee Reese 40.00 80.00
15 Phil Rizzuto 40.00 80.00
16 Johnny Sain 20.00 40.00
17 Enos Slaughter 25.00 50.00
18 Warren Spahn 40.00 80.00
19 Vern Stephens 15.00 30.00
20 Earl Torgeson 15.00 30.00
21 Dizzy Trout 15.00 30.00
22 Ted Williams 100.00 200.00
23 Ted Williams CL 50.00 100.00

1961-66 American Tract Society

These cards are quite attractive and feature the "pure card" concept that is always popular with collectors, i.e., no borders or anything else on the card front to detract from the color photo. The cards are numbered on the back and the skip-numbering of the cards below is actually due to the fact that these cards are part of a much larger (sport and non-sport) set with a Christian theme. The set features Christian ballplayers giving first-person testimonies on the card backs telling how their belief in Jesus has changed their lives. These cards are sometimes referred to as "Tracards." The cards measure approximately 2 3/4" X 3 1/2". The set price below refers to only one of each player, not including any variations. These cards were issued throughout the 1960's, as one of the Felipe Alou cards features him in an Atlanta Braves cap (The Braves would not move to Atlanta until 1966)

COMPLETE SET (12) 60.00 120.00
43A Bobby Richardson 8.00 20.00
Black print on back
43B Bobby Richardson 8.00 20.00
Blue print on back
43C Bobby Richardson 8.00 20.00
Black print on back
with red Play Ball
43D Bobby Richardson 8.00 20.00
Black print on back
with exclamation point
51A Jerry Kindall 3.00 8.00
Portrait from chest up
black print on back
51B Jerry Kindall 3.00 8.00
On one knee
blue print on back
52A Felipe Alou 5.00 12.00
On one knee
black print on back
52B Felipe Alou 8.00 20.00
On one knee
blue print on back
52C Felipe Alou#Batting pose 5.00 12.00
52D Felipe Alou 3.00 8.00
66 Al Worthington 3.00 8.00
Black print on back

XX Jim Kaat 8.00 20.00
Black and White

1961 Angels Jay Publishing

This 12-card set of the Los Angeles Angels measures approximately 5" by 7". The fronts feature black-and-white posed player photos with the player's and team name printed below in the white border. These cards were packaged 12 to a packet. The backs are blank. The cards are unnumbered and checklisted below in alphabetical order.

COMPLETE SET (12) 6.00 15.00
1 Ken Aspromonte .75 2.00
2 Julio Becquer .75 2.00
3 Steve Bilko .75 2.00
4 Fritz Brickell .75 2.00
5 Bob Cerv .75 2.00
6 Ned Garver .75 2.00
7 Ted Kluszewski 3.00 8.00
8 Tom Morgan .75 2.00
9 Albie Pearson .75 2.00
10 Bill Rigney MG .75 2.00
11 Faye Throneberry .75 2.00
12 Ed Yost .75 2.00

1962 Angels Jay Publishing

This 12-card set of the Los Angeles Angels measures approximately 5" by 7". The fronts feature black-and-white posed player photos with the player's and team name printed below in the white border. These cards were packaged 12 to a packet. The backs are blank. The cards are unnumbered and checklisted below in alphabetical order.

COMPLETE SET (12) 12.50 30.00
1 Earl Averill .75 2.00
2 Steve Bilko .75 2.00
3 Ryne Duren 1.25 3.00
4 Eli Grba .75 2.00
5 Ken Hunt .75 2.00
6 Ted Kluszewski 3.00 8.00
7 Tom Morgan .75 2.00
8 Albie Pearson .75 2.00
9 Bill Rigney MG .75 2.00
10 Ed Sadowski .75 2.00
11 Leon Wagner .75 2.00
12 Eddie Yost .75 2.00

1963-64 Angels Jay Publishing

This set of the Los Angeles Angels was issued over two years and measures approximately 5" by 7". The fronts feature black-and-white posed player photos with the player's and team name printed below in the white border. These cards were packaged 12 to a packet. The backs are blank. The cards are unnumbered and checklisted below in alphabetical order.

COMPLETE SET (19) 15.00 40.00
1 Bo Belinsky 64 1.25 3.00
2 Dean Chance 1.50 4.00
Head photo
3 Dean Chance 1.50 4.00
Action pose
4 Charlie Dees 64 .75 2.00
5 Jim Fregosi 1.50 4.00
6 Ken Hunt 63 .75 2.00
7 Don Lee .75 2.00
8 Ken McBride 64 .75 2.00
9 Billy Moran .75 2.00
10 Tom Morgan 63 .75 2.00
11 Dan Osinski 64 .75 2.00
12 Albie Pearson .75 2.00
Action pose
13 Albie Pearson .75 2.00
Pose with bat
14 Bill Rigney MG .75 2.00
15 Bob Rodgers .75 2.00
16 Ed Sadowski .75 2.00
17 Lee Thomas .75 2.00
Pose with bat
18 Lee Thomas .75 2.00
Closer pose with bat
19 Leon Wagner 63 .75 2.00

1964 Angels Team Issue

This 10 card blank-backed set, which measures 5" by 7" was issued by the Angels as a package with a price of 25 cents. The fronts have white borders with the player's photo and the fascimile autograph on the bottom. Since the cards are unnumbered, we have sequenced them in alphabetical order.

COMPLETE SET (10) 20.00 40.00
1 Charlie Dees 2.00 5.00
2 Jim Fregosi 3.00 8.00
3 Ed Kirkpatrick 2.00 5.00
4 Joe Koppe 2.00 5.00
5 Barry Latman 2.00 5.00
6 Bob Lee 2.00 5.00
7 Albie Pearson 2.50 6.00
8 Jimmy Piersall 3.00 8.00
9 Bill Rigney MG 2.00 5.00
10 Bob Rodgers 2.00 5.00

1965 Angels Matchbooks County National

These matchbooks were issued by County National bank and feature members of the 1965 California Angels. The checklist is incomplete so any additions to finish the set are appreciated.

COMPLETE SET (8) 20.00 50.00
1 Jim Fregosi 4.00 10.00
2 Ed Kirkpatrick 2.50 6.00
3 Bobby Knoop 2.50 6.00
4 Barry Latman 2.50 6.00
5 Fred Newman 2.50 6.00
6 Bob Rodgers 2.50 6.00
7 Tom Satriano 2.50 6.00
8 Willie Smith 2.50 6.00

1965 Angels Matchbook Santa Ana

These matchbooks were issued by Santa Ana Savings bank and feature members of the 1965 California Angels. The checklist is incomplete so any additions to finish the set are appreciated.

COMPLETE SET (8) 20.00 50.00
1 Dean Chance 3.00 8.00
2 Jim Fregosi 4.00 10.00
3 Bobby Knoop 2.50 6.00
4 Ken McBride 2.50 6.00
5 Rick Reichardt 2.50 6.00
6 Bill Rigney MG 2.50 6.00
7 Bob Rodgers 2.50 6.00
8 Willie Smith 2.50 6.00

1966 Angels Dexter Press

Produced by Dexter Press, Inc. (West Nyack, New York), this sixteen-card set measures approximately 4" by 5 7/8". The fronts feature glossy posed color player photos with white borders. The player's autograph is inscribed in black across the top of the picture. In blue print, the back has the player's name, position, and biographical information. The cards are unnumbered and checklisted below in alphabetical order.

COMPLETE SET (16) 50.00 100.00
1 George Brunet 3.00 8.00
2 Jose Cardenal 3.00 8.00
3 Dean Chance 4.00 10.00
4 Jim Fregosi 5.00 12.00
5 Ed Kirkpatrick 3.00 8.00
6 Bob Knoop 3.00 8.00
7 Bob Lee 3.00 8.00
8 Marcelino Lopez 3.00 6.00
9 Fred Newman 3.00 8.00
10 Albie Pearson 3.00 8.00
11 Jimmy Piersall 5.00 12.00
12 Rick Reichardt 3.00 8.00
13 Bob Rodgers 3.00 8.00
14 Paul Schaal 3.00 8.00
15 Norm Siebern 3.00 8.00
16 Willie Smith 4.00 10.00

1966 Angels Matchbook

These matchbooks feature members of the 1966 California Angels and were produced for the County National Bank. This checklist may be incomplete so any additions are appreciated.

COMPLETE SET (8) 15.00 40.00
1 Dean Chance 2.50 6.00
2 Ed Kirkpatrick 2.00 5.00
3 Barry Latman 2.00 5.00
4 Bob Lee 2.00 5.00
5 Fred Newman 2.00 5.00
6 Bill Rigney MG 2.00 5.00
7 Bob Rodgers 2.00 5.00
8 Willie Smith 2.00 5.00

1969 Angels Jack in the Box

This 13-card set measures approximately 2 by 3 1/2" and features black-and-white player photos on a white card face. The cards are unnumbered and checklisted below in alphabetical order.

COMPLETE SET (13) 20.00 50.00
1 Sandy Alomar 1.25 3.00
2 Joe Azcue 1.00 2.50
3 Jim Fregosi 2.00 5.00
4 Lou Johnson 1.00 2.50
5 Jay Johnstone 1.25 3.00
6 Rudy May 1.00 2.50
7 Jim McGlothlin 1.00 2.50
8 Andy Messersmith 2.00 5.00
9 Tom Murphy 1.00 2.50
10 Rick Reichardt 1.00 2.50
11 Aurelio Rodriguez 1.00 2.50
12 Jim Spencer 1.00 2.50
13 Hoyt Wilhelm 4.00 10.00

1971 Angels Jack in the Box

This 10-card set measures approximately 4 by 2 1/2" and features yellowish tone player photos printed on tan paper stock. The cards are unnumbered and checklisted below in alphabetical order.

COMPLETE SET (10) 10.00 25.00
1 Sandy Alomar 1.00 2.50
2 Ken Berry .75 2.00
3 Tony Conigliaro 2.50 6.00
4 Jim Fregosi 1.50 4.00
5 Alex Johnson .75 2.00
6 Rudy May .75 2.00
7 Andy Messersmith 1.25 3.00
8 Lefty Phillips MG .75 2.00
9 Jim Spencer .75 2.00
10 Clyde Wright .75 2.00

1972 Angels Postcards

These 30 black and white 3 1/4" by 4 3/4" blank backed postcards feature members of the 1972 California Angels. A key card in the set is Nolan Ryan, during his first season as a member of the Angels.

COMPLETE SET (30) 8.00 20.00
1 Lloyd Allen .20 .50
2 Sandy Alomar .30 .75
3 Steve Barber .20 .50
4 Ken Berry .20 .50
5 Leo Cardenas .20 .50
6 Rick Clark .20 .50
7 Eddie Fisher .20 .50
8 Art Kusnyer .20 .50
9 Winston Llenas .20 .50
10 Rudy May .20 .50
11 Ken McMullen .20 .50
12 Andy Messersmith .20 .50
13 Bob Oliver .20 .50
14 Vada Pinson .40 1.00
15 Mel Queen .20 .50
16 Mickey Rivers .60 1.50
17 Don Rose .20 .50
18 Nolan Ryan 4.00 10.00
19 Jim Spencer .20 .50
20 Lee Stanton .20 .50
21 John Stephenson .20 .50
22 Jeff Torborg .20 .50
23 Clyde Wright .20 .50
24 Del Rice MG .20 .50
25 Peanuts Lowrey CO .20 .50
26 Tom Morgan CO .20 .50
27 Jimmie Reese CO .30 .75
28 John Roseboro CO .20 .50
29 Bobby Winkles CO .20 .50
30 Gene Autry OWN .30 .75
Most of tie showing

1973 Angels Postcards

These 40 3 1/4" by 4 3/4" blank-backed, black and white, postcards feature members of the 1973 California Angels.

COMPLETE SET (40) 10.00 25.00
1 Lloyd Allen .20 .50
2 Sandy Alomar .20 .50
3 Steve Barber .20 .50
4 Ken Berry .20 .50
5 Jerry DaVanon .20 .50
6 Mike Epstein .20 .50
7 Alan Gallagher .20 .50
8 Bill Grabarkewitz .20 .50
9 Rich Hand .20 .50
10 Art Kusnyer .20 .50
11 Dick Lange .20 .50
12 Winston Llenas .20 .50
13 Rudy May .20 .50
14 Tom McCraw .20 .50
15 Rudy Meoli .20 .50
16 Aurelio Monteagudo .20 .50
17 Tom Morgan CO .20 .50
18 Bob Oliver .20 .50
19 Bill Parker .20 .50
20 Salty Parker CO .20 .50
21 Ron Perranoski .20 .50
22 Vada Pinson .40 1.00
23 Jimmie Reese CO .30 .75
24 Frank Robinson 1.50 4.00
25 John Roseboro CO .20 .50
26 Nolan Ryan 3.00 8.00
27 Richie Scheinblum .20 .50
28 Dave Sells .20 .50
29 Bill Singer .20 .50
30 Jim Spencer .20 .50
31 Lee Stanton .20 .50
32 John Stephenson .20 .50
33 Jeff Torborg .30 .75
34 Bobby Valentine .30 .75
35 Bobby Winkles MG .20 .50
36 Clyde Wright .20 .50
37 Gene Autry OWN .30 .75
Photo closely cropped
38 Harry Dalton GM .20 .50
39 Don Drysdale ANN .60 1.50
40 Dick Enberg ANN .30 .75

1974 Angels Postcards

These 39 black and white, blank-backed postcards feature members of the 1974 California Angels. They are unnumbered and we have sequenced them in alphabetical order. Dick Williams replaced Bobby Winkles as manager midway through the season which accounts for the two different manager cards in this set.

COMPLETE SET (39) 12.50 30.00
1 Sandy Alomar .30 .75
2 Dave Chalk .20 .50
3 John Doherty .20 .50
4 Denny Doyle .20 .50
5 Tom Egan .20 .50
6 Ed Figueroa .20 .50
7 Andy Hassler .20 .50
8 Whitey Herzog CO .30 .75
9 Doug Howard .20 .50
10 Joe Lahoud .20 .50
11 Dick Lange .20 .50
12 Winston Llenas .20 .50
13 Skip Lockwood .20 .50
14 Rudy May .20 .50
15 Tom McCraw .20 .50
16 Tom Morgan CO .20 .50
17 Bob Oliver .20 .50
18 Salty Parker CO .20 .50
19 Jimmie Reese CO .30 .75
20 Mickey Rivers .30 .75
21 Frank Robinson 1.50 4.00
22 Ellie Rodriguez .20 .50
23 John Roseboro CO .20 .50
24 Nolan Ryan 3.00 8.00
25 Charlie Sands .20 .50
26 Paul Schaal .20 .50
27 Dave Sells .20 .50
28 Dick Selma .20 .50
29 Bill Singer .20 .50
30 Lee Stanton .20 .50
31 Bill Stoneman .30 .75
32 Frank Tanana .40 1.00
33 Bobby Valentine .30 .75
34 Dick Williams MG .30 .75
35 Bob Winkles MG .20 .50
36 Gene Autry OWN .30 .75
37 Harry Dalton GM .20 .50
38 Don Drysdale ANN .60 1.50
39 Dick Enberg ANN .30 .75

1975 Angels Postcards

This 48-card set of the California Angels features player photos on postcard-size cards. The cards are unnumbered and checklisted in alphabetical order.

COMPLETE SET (48) 12.50 30.00
1 Jerry Adair CO .20 .50
2 Bob Allietta .20 .50
3 Gene Autry OWN .40 1.00
4 John Balaz .20 .50
5 Steve Blateric .20 .50
6 Bruce Bochte .30 .75
7 Jim Brewer .20 .50
8 Dave Chalk .20 .50
9 Dave Collins .20 .50
10 Harry Dalton GM .20 .50
11 Chuck Dobson .20 .50
12 John Doherty .20 .50
13 Denny Doyle .20 .50
14 Don Drysdale ANN .75 2.00
15 Tom Egan .20 .50
16 Dick Enberg ANN .30 .75
17 Ed Figueroa .20 .50
18 Ike Hampton .20 .50
19 Tommy Harper .20 .50
20 Andy Hassler .20 .50
21 Whitey Herzog MG .40 1.00
22 Chuck Hockenbery .20 .50
23 Don Kirkwood .20 .50
24 Joe Lahoud .20 .50
25 Dick Lange .20 .50
26 Winston Llenas .20 .50
27 Rudy Meoli .20 .50
28 Mike Miley .20 .50
29 Billy Muffett CO .20 .50
30 Morris Nettles .20 .50
31 Orlando Pena .20 .50
32 Orlando Ramirez .20 .50
33 Jimmie Reese CO .30 .75
34 Jerry Remy .20 .50
35 Grover Resinger CO .20 .50
36 Mickey Rivers .30 .75
37 Ellie Rodriguez .20 .50
38 Nolan Ryan 3.00 8.00
39 Mickey Scott .20 .50
40 Dave Sells .20 .50
41 Bill Singer .20 .50
42 Billy Smith .20 .50
43 Lee Stanton .20 .50
44 Bill Sudakis .20 .50
45 Frank Tahana .40 1.00
46 Bob Valentine .30 .75
47 Dick Williams MG .30 .75
48 Anaheim Stadium .20 .50

1976 Angels Postcards

These 39 blank-backed black and white postcards feature members of the 1976 California Angels. They measure 3 1/4" by 5 1/2" and we have sequenced them alphabetically.

COMPLETE SET (39) 10.00 25.00
1 Orlando Alvarez .20 .50
2 Bruce Bochte .20 .50
3 Bobby Bonds .40 1.00
4 Jim Brewer .20 .50
5 Dan Briggs .20 .50
6 Dave Chalk .20 .50
7 Bob Clear CO .20 .50
8 Dave Collins .20 .50
9 Paul Dade .20 .50
10 Dick Drago .20 .50
11 Andy Etchebarren .20 .50
12 Adrian Garrett .20 .50
13 Mario Guerrero .20 .50
14 Ike Hampton .20 .50
15 Paul Hartzell .20 .50
16 Ed Herrmann .20 .50
17 Vern Hoscheit CO .20 .50
18 Terry Humphrey .20 .50
19 Ron Jackson .20 .50
20 Bob Jones .20 .50
21 Bill Melton .20 .50
22 Sid Monge .20 .50
23 Billy Muffett CO .20 .50
24 Mike Overy .20 .50
25 Orlando Ramirez .20 .50
26 Jimmie Reese CO .30 .75
27 Jerry Remy .20 .50
Position listed as 2B
28 Jerry Remy .20 .50
Position listed as IF
29 Grover Resinger CO .20 .50
30 Gary Ross .20 .50
31 Nolan Ryan 2.00 5.00
Entire collar on jersey
32 Nolan Ryan 2.00 5.00
Collar cut off
33 Mickey Scott .20 .50
34 Norm Sherry CO .20 .50
35 Lee Stanton .20 .50
36 Frank Tanana .30 .75
37 Rusty Torres .20 .50
38 John Verhoeven .20 .50
39 Dick Williams MG .30 .75

1977 Angels Postcards

These 49 blank backed postcards measure 3 1/4" by 5 1/2" and feature members of the 1977 California Angels. These cards are unnumbered so we have sequenced them alphabetically.

COMPLETE SET (49) 12.50 30.00
1 Willie Aikens .20 .50
2 Mike Barlow .20 .50
3 Don Baylor .60 1.50
4 Bruce Bochte .20 .50
5 Bobby Bonds .40 1.00
6 Thad Bosley .20 .50
7 Ken Brett .20 .50
8 Dan Briggs .20 .50
9 John Caneira .20 .50
10 Dave Chalk .20 .50
11 Bob Clear CO .20 .50
12 Del Crandall CO .20 .50
13 Mike Cuellar .30 .75
14 Dick Drago .20 .50
15 Andy Etchebarren .20 .50
16 Gil Flores .20 .50
17 Dave Garcia MG .20 .50
18 Dan Goodwin .20 .50
19 Marv Grissom CO .20 .50
20 Bobby Grich .30 .75
21 Mario Guerrero .20 .50
22 Ike Hampton .20 .50
23 Paul Hartzell .20 .50
24 Terry Humphrey .20 .50
25 Ron Jackson .20 .50
26 Bob Jones .20 .50
27 Don Kirkwood .20 .50
28 Fred Kuhaulua .20 .50
29 Ken Landreaux .30 .75
30 Dave LaRoche .20 .50
31 Carlos May .20 .50
32 Billy Muffett CO .20 .50
33 Rance Mulliniks .20 .50
34 Dyar Miller .20 .50
35 Gary Nolan .20 .50
36 Jimmie Reese CO .30 .75
37 Jerry Remy .20 .50
38 Frank Robinson CO 1.00 2.50
39 Gary Ross .20 .50
40 Joe Rudi .20 .50
41 Nolan Ryan 2.00 5.00
42 Mickey Scott .20 .50
43 Norm Sherry MG .20 .50
44 Wayne Simpson .20 .50
45 Tony Soliata .20 .50
46 Frank Tanana .30 .75
47 Rusty Torres .20 .50
48 John Verhoeven .20 .50
49 Dick Enberg ANN .30 .75

1978 Angels Family Fun Centers

This 37-card set features members of the 1978 California Angels. These large cards measure approximately 3 1/2" by 5 1/2" and display sepia tone player photos. The cards are unnumbered and checklisted below in alphabetical order. This set was also available in uncut sheet form.

COMPLETE SET (37) 20.00 50.00
1 Don Aase .20 .50
2 Mike Barlow .60 1.50
3 Don Baylor 1.00 2.50
4 Lyman Bostock 2.00 5.00
5 Ken Brett .75 2.00
6 Dave Chalk .60 1.50
7 Bob Clear .60 1.50
8 Brian Downing 1.00 2.50
9 Ron Fairly .75 2.00
10 Gil Flores .60 1.50
11 Dave Frost .60 1.50
12 Dave Garcia .60 1.50
13 Bobby Grich 1.00 2.50
14 Tom Griffin .60 1.50
15 Marv Grissom CO .60 1.50
16 Ike Hampton .60 1.50
17 Paul Hartzell .60 1.50
18 Terry Humphrey .60 1.50
19 Ron Jackson .60 1.50
20 Chris Knapp .60 1.50
21 Ken Landreaux .75 2.00
22 Carney Lansford 1.25 3.00
23 Dave LaRoche .60 1.50
24 John McNamara MG .75 2.00
25 Dyar Miller .60 1.50
26 Rick Miller .60 1.50
27 Balor Moore .60 1.50
28 Rance Mulliniks .75 2.00
29 Floyd Rayford .60 1.50
30 Jimmie Reese CO 1.00 2.50
31 Merv Rettenmund .60 1.50
32 Joe Rudi .75 2.00
33 Nolan Ryan 6.00 15.00
34 Bob Skinner CO .60 1.50
35 Tony Solaita .60 1.50
36 Frank Tanana 1.00 2.50
37 Dickie Thon .75 2.00

1984 Angels Postcards

These 29 postcards, which measure 3 1/2" by 5 1/2", feature members of the 1984 California Angels. The fronts have the player photo, while the backs have the players name, the Angels logo and the year of issue. Since these cards are unnumbered, we have sequenced them in alphabetical order.

COMPLETE SET (29) 8.00 20.00
1 Don Aase .20 .50
2 Mike Barlow .20 .50
3 Juan Beniquez .20 .50
4 Bob Boone .30 .75
5 Rick Burleson .20 .50
6 Rod Carew .75 2.00
7 Doug Corbett .20 .50
8 John Curtis .20 .50
9 Doug DeCinces .30 .75
10 Brian Downing .30 .75
11 Ken Forsch .20 .50
12 Bobby Grich .30 .75
13 Reggie Jackson 1.25 3.00
14 Ron Jackson .20 .50
15 Tommy John .60 1.50
16 Curt Kaufman .20 .50
17 Bruce Kison .20 .50
18 Frank LaCorte .20 .50
19 Fred Lynn .40 1.00
20 John McNamara MG .20 .50
21 Jerry Narron .30 .75
22 Gary Pettis .20 .50
23 Rob Picciolo .20 .50
24 Dick Schofield .20 .50
25 Jim Slaton .20 .50
26 Rob Wilfong .20 .50
27 Ellis Valentine .20 .50
28 Mike Witt .20 .50
29 Geoff Zahn .20 .50

1984 Angels Smokey

The cards in this 32-card set measure approximately 2 1/2" by 3 3/4" and feature the California Angels in full color. Sets were given out to persons 15 and under attending the June 16th game against the Indians. The player's photo, the Angels' logo, and the Smokey the Bear logo appear on the front, in addition to the California Department of Forestry and the U.S. Forest Service logos. The abbreviated backs contain short biographical data, career statistics, and an anti-wildfire hint from the player on the front. Since the cards are unnumbered, they are ordered and numbered below alphabetically by the player's name.

COMPLETE SET (32) 4.00 10.00
1 Don Aase .08 .25
2 Juan Beniquez .08 .25
3 Bob Boone .40 1.00
4 Rick Burleson .08 .25
5 Rod Carew 1.00 2.50
6 John Curtis .08 .25
7 Doug DeCinces .30 .75
8 Brian Downing .30 .75
9 Ken Forsch .08 .25
10 Bobby Grich .30 .75
11 Reggie Jackson 1.25 3.00
12 Ron Jackson .08 .25
13 Tommy John .40 1.00
14 Curt Kaufman .08 .25
15 Bruce Kison .08 .25
16 Frank LaCorte .08 .25
17 Logo Card/Forestry Dept. .08 .25
18 Fred Lynn .20 .50
19 John McNamara MG .08 .25
20 Jerry Narron .08 .25
21 Gary Pettis .08 .25
22 Rob Picciolo .08 .25
23 Ron Romanick .08 .25
24 Luis Sanchez .08 .25
25 Dick Schofield .08 .25
26 Daryl Sconiers .08 .25

27 Jim Slaton .08 .25
28 Smokey the Bear .08 .25
29 Ellis Valentine .08 .25
30 Rob Wilfong .08 .25
31 Mike Witt .08 .25
32 Geoff Zahn .08 .25

1985 Angels Smokey

The cards in this 24-card set measure approximately 4 1/4" by 6" and feature the California Angels in full color. The player's photo, the Angels' logo, and the Smokey the Bear logo appear on the front, in addition to the California Department of Forestry and the U.S. Forest Service logos. The abbreviated backs contain short biographical data and an anti-wildfire message.

COMPLETE SET (24) 3.00 8.00
1 Mike Witt .08 .25
2 Reggie Jackson 1.00 2.50
3 Bob Boone .40 1.00
4 Mike Brown .08 .25
5 Rod Carew .75 2.00
6 Doug DeCinces .30 .75
7 Brian Downing .30 .75
8 Ken Forsch .08 .25
9 Gary Pettis .08 .25
10 Jerry Narron .20 .50
11 Ron Romanick .08 .25
12 Bobby Grich .30 .75
13 Dick Schofield .08 .25
14 Juan Beniquez .08 .25
15 Geoff Zahn .08 .25
16 Luis Sanchez .08 .25
17 Jim Slaton .08 .25
18 Doug Corbett .08 .25
19 Ruppert Jones .08 .25
20 Rob Wilfong .08 .25
21 Donnie Moore .08 .25
22 Pat Clements .08 .25
23 Tommy John .40 1.00
24 Gene Mauch MG .20 .50

1985 Angels Straw Hat

This 13-card set was distributed by Straw Hat Pizza Restaurants and measures approximately 11" by 16". The fronts feature color player drawings with a white border. The bottom part of the card contains a coupon for pizza and a Silver Anniversary Sweepstakes form. The backs are blank. The cards are unnumbered and checklisted below in alphabetical order.

COMPLETE SET (13) 15.00 40.00
1 Gene Autry OWN 1.25 3.00
2 Don Baylor 1.25 3.00
3 Bo Belinsky .75 2.00
4 Rod Carew 2.00 5.00
5 Dean Chance .75 2.00
6 Jim Fregosi .75 2.00
7 Bobby Grich .75 2.00
Bobby Knoop
8 Reggie Jackson 3.00 8.00
9 Alex Johnson .75 2.00
10 Ted Kluszewski 1.25 3.00
Albie Pearson
11 Nolan Ryan 4.00 10.00
12 Frank Tanana 1.25 3.00
13 Mike Witt .75 2.00

1986 Angels Greats TCMA

This 12-card standard-size set features some of the leading all-time members of the California Angels. The fronts feature a player photo while the backs have a player biography.

COMPLETE SET (12) 2.00 5.00
1 Rod Carew 1.00 2.50
2 Sandy Alomar .08 .25
3 Jim Fregosi .30 .75
4 Dave Chalk .08 .25
5 Leon Wagner .08 .25
6 Albie Pearson .08 .25
7 Rick Reichardt .08 .25
8 Bob Rodgers .08 .25
9 Dean Chance .20 .50
10 Clyde Wright .08 .25
11 Bob Lee .08 .25
12 Bill Rigney MG .08 .25

1986 Angels Postcards

These 28 black and white postcards feature members of the division-winning California Angels. These cards measure 3 1/2" by 5 1/2" and are in black and white. The backs have a postcard back, the Angels logo, the player's name and a team logo. Since these cards are unnumbered we have sequenced them in alphabetical order.

COMPLETE SET (28) 8.00 20.00
1 Bob Boone .30 .75
2 Rick Burleson .20 .50
3 John Candelaria .20 .50
4 Bob Clear CO .20 .50
5 Doug Corbett .20 .50
6 Doug DeCinces .30 .75
7 Brian Downing .30 .75
8 Terry Forster .20 .50
9 Bobby Grich .30 .75
10 George Hendrick .30 .75
11 Reggie Jackson 1.25 3.00
12 Ruppert Jones .20 .50
13 Wally Joyner .75 2.00
14 Bobby Knoop CO .20 .50
15 Marcel Lachemann CO .20 .50
16 Gary Lucas .20 .50
17 Gene Mauch MG .20 .50
18 Kirk McCaskill .20 .50
19 Donnie Moore .20 .50
20 Jerry Narron .30 .75
21 Gary Pettis .20 .50
22 Jimmie Reese CO .30 .75
23 Ron Romanick .20 .50
24 Dick Schofield .20 .50
25 Moose Stubing CO .20 .50
26 Don Sutton .75 2.00
27 Rob Wilfong .20 .50
28 Mike Witt .20 .50

1986 Angels Smokey

The Forestry Service (in conjunction with the California Angels) produced this 24-card set. The cards feature Smokey the Bear pictured in the upper right corner of the card. The card backs give a fire safety tip. The set was given out free at Anaheim Stadium on August 9th. The cards measure approximately 4 1/4" by 6" and are subtitled "Wildfire Prevention" on the front.

COMPLETE SET (24) 3.00 8.00
1 Mike Witt .08 .25
2 Reggie Jackson 1.00 2.50
3 Bob Boone .40 1.00
4 Don Sutton .60 1.50
5 Kirk McCaskill .08 .25
6 Doug DeCinces .30 .75
7 Brian Downing .30 .75
8 Doug Corbett .08 .25
9 Gary Pettis .08 .25
10 Jerry Narron .20 .50
11 Ron Romanick .08 .25
12 Bobby Grich .30 .75
13 Dick Schofield .08 .25
14 George Hendrick .08 .25
15 Rick Burleson .08 .25
16 John Candelaria .08 .25
17 Jim Slaton .08 .25
18 Darrell Miller .08 .25
19 Ruppert Jones .08 .25
20 Rob Wilfong .08 .25
21 Donnie Moore .08 .25
22 Wally Joyner .60 1.50
23 Terry Forster .08 .25
24 Gene Mauch MG .20 .50

1987 Angels Grich Sheet

ssued to pay tribute to Bobby Grich's last season, this sheet was issued to fans at Bobby Grich Night, May 1, 1987. The perforated sheet measures approximately 10" by 17 1/2" and features 17 different Topps cards of Grich, from his 1971 Rookie Card (number 193) through his 1987 Topps card (number 677). When perforated, each card measured the standard size. This sheet was sponsored by the Sheraton Hotel chain and the top perforated card mentions that.

COMPLETE SET (17) 3.00 8.00

1987 Angels Promotional Photo Sheet

This 40-card set was distributed on four 8" by 10" sheets with ten photos on each sheet. The photos are black-and-white portraits of the California Angels measuring approximately 1 1/2" by 2 1/4" each. The backs are blank. The cards are unnumbered and checklisted below in alphabetical order.

COMPLETE SET (40) 6.00 15.00
1 Gene Autry OWN .20 .50
2 DeWayne Buice .08 .25
3 John Candelaria .08 .25
4 Ray Chadwick .08 .25
5 Bob Clear CO .08 .25
6 Stu Cliburn .08 .25
7 Mike Cook .08 .25
8 Sherman Corbett .08 .25
9 Doug DeCinces .20 .50
10 Rick Down CO .08 .25
11 Brian Downing .20 .50
12 Jack Fimple .08 .25
13 Chuck Finley .60 1.50
14 Todd Fischer .08 .25
15 Willie Fraser .08 .25
16 George Hendrick .08 .25
17 Jack Howell .08 .25
18 Ruppert Jones .08 .25
19 Wally Joyner .60 1.50
20 Bobby Knoop CO .08 .25
21 Marcel Lachemann CO .08 .25
22 Gary Lucas .08 .25
23 Urbano Lugo .08 .25
24 Gene Mauch MG .20 .50
25 Kirk McCaskill .08 .25
26 Mark McLemore .40 1.00
27 Darrell Miller .08 .25
28 Donnie Moore .08 .25
29 Gary Pettis .08 .25
30 Gus Polidor .08 .25
31 Mike Port GM .08 .25
32 Jimmie Reese CO .30 .75
33 Vern Ruhle .08 .25
34 Mark Ryal .08 .25
35 Dick Schofield .08 .25
36 Moose Stubing CO .08 .25
37 Don Sutton .60 1.50
38 Devon White .40 1.00
39 Mike Witt .08 .25
40 Butch Wynegar .08 .25

1987 Angels Smokey

The U.S. Forestry Service (in conjunction with the California Angels) produced 24-card set to commemorate the 43rd birthday of Smokey. The cards feature Smokey the Bear pictured at the bottom of every card. The card backs give a cartoon fire safety tip. The cards measure approximately 4" by 6" and are subtitled "Wildfire Prevention" on the front.

COMPLETE SET (24) 3.00 8.00
1 John Candelaria .08 .25
2 Don Sutton .60 1.50
3 Mike Witt .08 .25
4 Gary Lucas .08 .25
5 Kirk McCaskill .08 .25
6 Chuck Finley .60 1.50
7 Willie Fraser .08 .25
8 Donnie Moore .08 .25
9 Urbano Lugo .08 .25
10 Butch Wynegar .08 .25
11 Darrell Miller .08 .25
12 Wally Joyner .60 1.50
13 Mark McLemore .40 1.00
14 Mark Ryal .08 .25
15 Dick Schofield .08 .25
16 Jack Howell .08 .25
17 Doug DeCinces .30 .75
18 Gus Polidor .08 .25
19 Brian Downing .30 .75
20 Gary Pettis .08 .25
21 Ruppert Jones .08 .25
22 George Hendrick .08 .25
23 Devon White .40 1.00
24 Checklist Card .08 .25

1988 Angels Smokey

The U.S. Forestry Service (in conjunction with the California Angels) produced this 25-card set. The cards feature Smokey the Bear pictured at the bottom of every card. The card backs give a cartoon fire safety tip. The cards measure approximately 2 1/2" by 3 1/2" and are in full color. The cards are numbered on the back. They were distributed during promotions on August 28, September 4, and September 18.

COMPLETE SET (25) 3.00 8.00
1 Cookie Rojas MG .08 .25
2 Johnny Ray .08 .25
3 Jack Howell .08 .25
4 Mike Witt .08 .25
5 Tony Armas .08 .25
6 Gus Polidor .08 .25
7 DeWayne Buice .08 .25
8 Dan Petry .08 .25
9 Bob Boone .40 1.00
10 Chili Davis .40 1.00
11 Greg Minton .08 .25
12 Kirk McCaskill .08 .25
13 Devon White .20 .50
14 Willie Fraser .08 .25
15 Chuck Finley .40 1.00
16 Dick Schofield .08 .25
17 Wally Joyner .40 1.00
18 Brian Downing .30 .75
19 Stu Cliburn .08 .25
20 Donnie Moore .08 .25
21 Bryan Harvey .20 .50
22 Mark McLemore .20 .50
23 Butch Wynegar .08 .25
24 George Hendrick .08 .25
NNO Checklist .08 .25
Logo Card

1989 Angels Smokey

The 1989 Smokey Angels All-Stars set contains 20 standard-size cards. The fronts have red and white borders. The backs are blue and red and feature career highlights. This set, which depicts current and former Angels who appeared in the All-Star game, was given away at the June 25, 1989 Angels home game. The set numbering is ordered chronologically according to when each subject participated in the respective All-Star Game as an Angel representative.

COMPLETE SET (20) 5.00 12.00
1 Bill Rigney MG .08 .25
2 Dean Chance .20 .50
3 Jim Fregosi .20 .50
4 Bobby Knoop .08 .25
5 Don Mincher .08 .25
6 Clyde Wright .08 .25
7 Nolan Ryan 2.50 6.00
8 Frank Robinson .75 2.00
9 Frank Tanana .20 .50
10 Rod Carew .75 2.00
11 Bobby Grich .30 .75
12 Brian Downing .20 .50
13 Don Baylor .40 1.00
14 Fred Lynn .20 .50
15 Reggie Jackson .75 2.00
16 Doug DeCinces .30 .75
17 Bob Boone .40 1.00
18 Wally Joyner .40 1.00
19 Mike Witt .08 .25
20 Johnny Ray .08 .25

1990 Angels Smokey

The 1990 Smokey Angels set contains standard-size cards which were produced by the U.S. Forest Service and Bureau of Land Management in conjunction with the California Department of Forestry. The first 18 cards in the set are alphabetically arranged. Bailes and McClure were apparently added to the checklist later than these 18, after they were acquired by the Angels.

COMPLETE SET (20) 2.50 6.00
1 Jim Abbott .20 .50
2 Bert Blyleven .30 .75
3 Chili Davis .40 1.00
4 Brian Downing .20 .50
5 Chuck Finley .30 .75
6 Willie Fraser .08 .25
7 Bryan Harvey .08 .25
8 Jack Howell .08 .25
9 Wally Joyner .30 .75
10 Mark Langston .20 .50
11 Kirk McCaskill .08 .25
12 Mark McLemore .08 .25
13 Lance Parrish .20 .50
14 Johnny Ray .08 .25
15 Dick Schofield .08 .25
16 Mike Witt .08 .25
17 Claudell Washington .08 .25
18 Devon White .20 .50
19 Scott Bailes .08 .25
20 Bob McClure .08 .25

1991 Angels Smokey

This 20-card standard-size set was sponsored by the USDA Forest Service and USDI Bureau of Land Management in cooperation with the California Department of Forestry.

COMPLETE SET (20) 2.50 6.00
1 Luis Polonia .08 .25
2 Junior Felix .08 .25
3 Dave Winfield .50 1.25
4 Dave Parker .30 .75
5 Lance Parrish .20 .50
6 Wally Joyner .30 .75
7 Jim Abbott .20 .50
8 Mark Langston .20 .50
9 Chuck Finley .30 .75
10 Kirk McCaskill .08 .25
11 Jack Howell .08 .25
12 Donnie Hill .08 .25
13 Gary Gaetti .20 .50
14 Dick Schofield .08 .25
15 Luis Sojo .08 .25
16 Mark Eichhorn .08 .25
17 Bryan Harvey .08 .25
18 Jeff D. Robinson .08 .25
19 Scott Lewis .08 .25
20 John Orton .08 .25

1992 Angels Police

This 18-card standard-size set was co-sponsored by the Orange County Sheriff's Department and Carl's Jr. Restaurants in Orange County, California. Deputies and police officers distributed the cards to children in grades K through 6, and 15,000 sets were given out at the September 19 Angel home game. The total number of cards produced was 870,000 individual cards.

COMPLETE SET (18) 2.50 6.00
1 Jim Abbott .20 .50
2 Gene Autry OWN .60 1.50
3 Bert Blyleven .30 .75
4 Hubie Brooks .08 .25
5 Chad Curtis .20 .50
6 Alvin Davis .08 .25
7 Gary DiSarcina .08 .25
8 Junior Felix .08 .25
9 Chuck Finley .30 .75
10 Gary Gaetti .20 .50
11 Rene Gonzales .08 .25
12 Von Hayes .08 .25
13 Carl Karcher .08 .25
Founder of Carl's Jr.
14 Mark Langston .20 .50
15 Luis Polonia .08 .25
16 Bobby Rose .08 .25
17 Lee Stevens .08 .25
18 Happy Star .08 .25
Title Card

1993 Angels Adohr Farms

Adohr Dairy of Santa Ana, Calif., produced a four-milk carton set featuring California Angels players. Each carton includes a headshot of Tim Salmon, Chad Curtis, J.T. Snow and Damion Easley, along with the player's name, the Angel's logo and a safety tip on the front of the carton. The cartons were issued during the later half of the 1993 season at schools and hospitals in Los Angeles and Orange Counties. It was not available to the general public. According to one collector two million cartons were filled with milk, while 1,500 were left flat and undistributed. This is the first year that Adohr has highlighted Angels players. Previously the company produced cartons with Raiders, Rams and Clippers players.

COMPLETE SET (4) 6.00 15.00
1 Chad Curtis 1.25 3.00
2 Damion Easley 1.25 3.00
3 Tim Salmon 2.00 5.00
4 J.T. Snow 2.50 6.00

1993 Angels Mother's

The 1993 Mother's Cookies Angels set consists of 28 standard-size cards with rounded corners.

COMPLETE SET (28) 5.00 12.00
1 Buck Rodgers MG .08 .25
2 Gary DiSarcina .08 .25
3 Chuck Finley .30 .75
4 J.T. Snow .60 1.50
5 Gary Gaetti .20 .50
6 Chili Davis .20 .50
7 Tim Salmon 1.25 3.00
8 Mark Langston .20 .50
9 Scott Sanderson .08 .25
10 John Orton .08 .25
11 Julio Valera .08 .25
12 Chad Curtis .08 .25
13 Kelly Gruber .08 .25
14 Rene Gonzales .08 .25
15 Luis Polonia .08 .25
16 Greg Myers .08 .25
17 Gene Nelson .08 .25
18 Torey Lovullo .08 .25
19 Scott Lewis .08 .25
20 Chuck Crim .08 .25
21 John Farrell .08 .25
22 Steve Frey .08 .25
23 Stan Javier .08 .25
24 Ken Patterson .08 .25
25 Ron Tingley .08 .25
26 Damion Easley .20 .50
27 Joe Grahe .08 .25
28 Checklist .30 .75
Coaches
Chuck Hernandez
Jimmie Reese/

1993 Angels Police

This 21-card standard-size set was sponsored by Carl's Jr. restaurants. The first 11 cards included a paper insert urging the collector to visit any participating Orange Country Carl's Jr. restaurant to receive the rest of the set. Reportedly only 20,000 sets were produced. Card number 21 comes in two different colors, there is no differenation for pricing for either version.

COMPLETE SET (21) 10.00 25.00
1 Gene Autry OWN 2.00 5.00
2 Carl Karcher .40 1.00
Chairman and Founder
Carl's Jr.
3 Buck Rodgers MG .40 1.00
4 Rod Carew CO 2.00 5.00
5 Kelly Gruber .40 1.00
6 Chili Davis .50 1.25
7 Chad Curtis .40 1.00
8 Mark Langston .50 1.25
9 Scott Sanderson .40 1.00
10 J.T. Snow 2.00 5.00
11 Rene Gonzales .40 1.00
12 Jimmie Reese CO .60 1.50
13 Damion Easley .50 1.25
14 Julio Valera .40 1.00
15 Luis Polonia .40 1.00
16 John Orton .40 1.00
17 Gary DiSarcina .40 1.00
18 Greg Myers .40 1.00
19 Chuck Finley .60 1.50
20 Tim Salmon 2.00 5.00
21 Happy Star .40 1.00
Carl's Jr. mascot

1993 Angels Stadium Club

This 30-card standard-size set features the 1993 California Angels. The set was issued in hobby (plastic box) and retail (blister) form.

COMP.FACT SET (30) 2.00 5.00
1 J.T. Snow .60 1.50
2 Chuck Crim .02 .10
3 Chili Davis .08 .25
4 Mark Langston .08 .25
5 Ron Tingley .02 .10
6 Eduardo Perez .02 .10
7 Scott Sanderson .02 .10
8 Jorge Fabregas .02 .10
9 Troy Percival .20 .50
10 Rod Correia .02 .10
11 Greg Myers .02 .10
12 Steve Frey .02 .10
13 Tim Salmon .75 2.00
14 Scott Lewis .02 .10
15 Rene Gonzales .02 .10
16 Chuck Finley .08 .25
17 John Orton .02 .10
18 Joe Grahe .02 .10
19 Luis Polonia .02 .10
20 John Farrell .02 .10
21 Damion Easley .08 .25
22 Gene Nelson .02 .10
23 Chad Curtis .02 .10
24 Russ Springer .02 .10
25 DeShawn Warren .02 .10
26 Darryl Scott .02 .10
27 Gary DiSarcina .02 .10
28 Jerry Nielsen .02 .10
29 Torey Lovullo .02 .10
30 Julio Valera .02 .10

1994 Angels Adohr Farms

For the second year, Adohr farms produced a set of milk cartons featuring members of the California Angels.

COMPLETE SET (4) 4.00 10.00
1 Gary DiSarcina 1.00 2.50
2 Phil Leftwich 1.00 2.50
3 Joe Magrane 1.00 2.50
4 Greg Myers 1.00 2.50

1994 Angels L.A. Times

These 26 collector sheets were issued by the Orange County edition of the Los Angeles Times, were printed on semigloss paper, and measure 7 1/2" by 8 3/4". The sheets are numbered on the front as "X of 26."

COMPLETE SET (26) 6.00 15.00
1 Chili Davis .40 1.00
2 Chad Curtis .20 .50
3 John Dopson .20 .50
4 Gary DiSarcina .20 .50
5 Jim Edmonds .75 2.00
6 Joe Grahe .20 .50
7 Bo Jackson .60 1.50
8 Joe Magrane .20 .50
9 Phil Leftwich .20 .50
10 Bill Sampen .20 .50
11 Chuck Finley .40 1.00
12 Dwight Smith .20 .50
13 Mark Leiter .20 .50
14 Mark Langston .30 .75
15 Mike Butcher .20 .50
16 Rex Hudler .30 .75
17 Craig Lefferts .20 .50
18 Damion Easley .20 .50
19 Greg Myers .20 .50
20 Chris Turner .20 .50
21 Tim Salmon .75 2.00
22 Harold Reynolds .40 1.00
23 Bob Patterson .20 .50
24 Spike Owen .20 .50
25 Eduardo Perez .20 .50
26 Marcel Lachemann MG .20 .50

1994 Angels Mother's

The 1994 Mother's Cookies Angels set consists of 28 standard-size cards with rounded corners.

COMPLETE SET (28) 5.00 12.00
1 Marcel Lachemann MG .08 .25
2 Mark Langston .20 .50
3 J.T. Snow .40 1.00
4 Chad Curtis .08 .25
5 Tim Salmon 1.25 3.00
6 Gary DiSarcina .08 .25
7 Bo Jackson .40 1.00
8 Dwight Smith .08 .25
9 Chuck Finley .30 .75
10- Rod Correia .08 .25
11 Spike Owen .08 .25
12 Harold Reynolds .30 .75
13 Chris Turner .08 .25
14 Chili Davis .30 .75
15 Bob Patterson .08 .25
16 Jim Edmonds 1.25 3.00
17 Joe Magrane .08 .25
18 Craig Lefferts .08 .25
19 Scott Lewis .08 .25
20 Rex Hudler .20 .50
21 Mike Butcher .08 .25
22 Brian Anderson .20 .50
23 Greg Myers .08 .25
24 Mark Leiter .08 .25
25 Joe Grahe .08 .25
26 Jorge Fabregas .08 .25
27 John Dopson .08 .25
28 Checklist .20 .50
Coaches
Chuck Hernandez
Ken Macha
Bob

1995 Angels CHP

Sponsored by the California Highway Patrol and commemorating the 35th anniversary of the California Angels, this 16-card set features color action player photos in a silver frame. The backs carry player information and a safety message.

COMPLETE SET (16) 8.00 20.00
1 Tim Salmon 1.50 4.00
2 Chuck Finley .75 2.00
3 Mark Langston .60 1.50
4 Gary Disarcina .40 1.00
5 Damion Easley .40 1.00
6 Spike Owen .40 1.00
7 Troy Percival .75 2.00
8 Chili Davis .75 2.00
9 Jim Edmonds 1.50 4.00
10 Rex Hudler .60 1.50
11 Greg Myers .40 1.00
12 Brian Anderson .60 1.50
13 J.T. Snow .60 1.50
14 Tony Phillips .40 1.00
15 Lee Smith .60 1.50
16 Marcel Lachemann MG .40 1.00
Chief Don Watkins

1995 Angels Mother's

This 1995 Mother's Cookies California Angels set consists of 28 standard-size cards with rounded corners.

COMPLETE SET (28) 5.00 12.00
1 Marcel Lachemann MG .08 .25
2 Mark Langston .20 .50
3 J.T. Snow .40 1.00
4 Tim Salmon .75 2.00
5 Chili Davis .20 .50
6 Gary DiSarcina .08 .25
7 Tony Phillips .08 .25
8 Jim Edmonds .75 2.00
9 Chuck Finley .30 .75
10 Mark Dalesandro .08 .25
11 Greg Myers .08 .25
12 Spike Owen .08 .25
13 Lee Smith .20 .50
14 Eduardo Perez .08 .25
15 Bob Patterson .08 .25
16 Mitch Williams .20 .50
17 Garret Anderson .40 1.00
18 Mike Bielecki .08 .25
19 Shawn Boskie .08 .25
20 Damion Easley .08 .25
21 Mike Butcher .08 .25
22 Brian Anderson .08 .25
23 Andy Allanson .08 .25
24 Scott Sanderson .08 .25
25 Troy Percival .30 .75
26 Rex Hudler .20 .50
27 Mike James .08 .25
28 Coaches .30 .75
Checklist
Rod Carew
Chuck Hernandez
Ric

1995 Angels Team Issue

This three-card set features a color player photo on the front with a black-and-white elongated photo, player information, statistics and a facsimile autograph on the back. The cards are unnumbered and checklisted below in alphabetical order.

COMPLETE SET (3) 2.00 5.00
1 Jim Abbott .75 2.00
2 Chili Davis .75 2.00
3 J.T. Snow .75 2.00

1996 Angels Mother's

This 28-card set consists of borderless posed color player portraits in stadium settings.

COMPLETE SET (28) 4.00 10.00
1 Marcel Lachemann MG .08 .25
2 Chili Davis .20 .50
3 Mark Langston .20 .50
4 Tim Salmon .60 1.50
5 Jim Abbott .20 .50
6 Jim Edmonds .60 1.50
7 Gary DiSarcina .08 .25
8 J.T. Snow .30 .75
9 Chuck Finley .30 .75
10 Tim Wallach .08 .25
11 Lee Smith .20 .50
12 George Arias .08 .25
13 Troy Percival .30 .75
14 Randy Velarde .08 .25
15 Garret Anderson .60 1.50
16 Jorge Fabregas .08 .25
17 Shawn Boskie .08 .25
18 Mark Eichhorn .08 .25
19 Jack Howell .08 .25
20 Jason Grimsley .08 .25
21 Rex Hudler .20 .50
22 Mike Aldrete .08 .25
23 Mike James .08 .25
24 Scott Sanderson .08 .25
25 Don Slaught .08 .25
26 Mark Holzemer .08 .25
27 Dick Schofield .08 .25
28 Coaches Card CL/ .30 .75

1997 Angels Mother's

This 28-card set of the Anaheim Angels sponsored by Mother's Cookies consists of posed color player photos with rounded corners.

COMPLETE SET (28) 5.00 12.00
1 Terry Collins MG .08 .25
2 Tim Salmon .60 1.50
3 Eddie Murray .40 1.00
4 Mark Langston .20 .50
5 Jim Edmonds .60 1.50
6 Tony Phillips .08 .25
7 Gary DiSarcina .08 .25
8 Garret Anderson .50 1.25
9 Chuck Finley .30 .75
10 Darin Erstad 1.25 3.00
11 Jim Leyritz .08 .25
12 Shigetoshi Hasegawa .40 1.00
13 Luis Alicea .08 .25
14 Troy Percival .30 .75
15 Allen Watson .08 .25
16 Craig Grebeck .08 .25
17 Mike Holtz .08 .25
18 Chad Kreuter .08 .25
19 Dennis Springer .08 .25
20 Jason Dickson .08 .25
21 Mike James .08 .25
22 Orlando Palmeiro .08 .25
23 Dave Hollins .08 .25
24 Mark Gubicza .08 .25
25 Pep Harris .08 .25
26 Jack Howell .08 .25
27 Rich DeLucia .08 .25
28 Coaches Card CL .30 .75
Larry Bowa
Rod Carew
Joe Colema

1998 Angels Postcards

These 30 blank backed postcards measure 5" by 7" and feature members of the 1998 Anaheim Angels. They are black and white and since they are unnumbered except for a uniform notation on the bottom we have sequenced them in alphabetical order

COMPLETE SET (30) 8.00 20.00
1 Garret Anderson .75 2.00
2 Mike Billmeyer .20 .50
3 Larry Bowa CO .30 .75
4 Greg Cadaret .20 .50
5 Rod Carew CO .60 1.50
6 Joe Coleman CO .20 .50
7 Terry Collins MG .20 .50
8 Jason Dickson .20 .50
9 Gary DiSarcina .20 .50
10 Jim Edmonds .75 2.00
11 Cecil Fielder .30 .75
12 Chuck Finley .40 1.00
13 Troy Glaus 1.50 4.00
14 Todd Greene .20 .50
15 Pep Harris .20 .50
16 George Hendrick CO .20 .50
17 Dave Hollins .20 .50
18 Ken Hill .20 .50
19 Marcel Lachemann CO .20 .50
20 Joe Maddon CO .30 .75
21 Jack McDowell .20 .50
22 Orlando Palmeiro .20 .50
23 Troy Percival .40 1.00
24 Tim Salmon .60 1.50
25 Craig Shipley .20 .50
26 Steve Sparks .20 .50
27 Randy Velarde .20 .50
28 Matt Walbeck .20 .50
29 Jarrod Washburn .60 1.50
30 Allen Watson .20 .50

1998 Angels Score

This 15-card set was issued in special retail packs and features color photos of the Anaheim Angels team. The backs carry player information. A special platinum parallel set was also issued and randomly inserted in packs.

COMPLETE SET (15) 2.50 6.00
*PLATINUM: 5X BASIC CARDS
1 Rickey Henderson .75 2.00
2 Todd Greene .08 .25
3 Shigetoshi Hasegawa .40 1.00
4 Darin Erstad .75 2.00
5 Jason Dickson .08 .25
6 Tim Salmon .40 1.00
7 Ken Hill .08 .25
8 Dave Hollins .08 .25
9 Gary DiSarcina .08 .25
10 Mike James .08 .25
11 Jim Edmonds .60 1.50
12 Troy Percival .40 1.00
13 Chuck Finley .20 .50
14 Tony Phillips .08 .25
15 Garret Anderson .60 1.50

1999 Angels CHP

This 10 card standard-size set was issued by the California Highway Patrol and featured members of the Angels. Some of the players are posed with officers and some of the players have action shots.

COMPLETE SET (10) 15.00 40.00
1 Chuck Finley 1.00 2.50
2 Shigetosi Hasegawa 1.00 2.50
3 Gary DiSarcina .60 1.50
4 Darin Erstad 5.00 12.00
5 Mo Vaughn 1.00 2.50
6 Tim Salmon 2.50 6.00
With Angel Johnson
and JoAnn O'Hair
7 Troy Percival 1.00 2.50
With Ana Burson
and Mike Lundqui
8 Jim Edmonds 2.50 6.00
With Tony Lassos
and Galen Burson
9 Troy Glaus 4.00 10.00
With Keith Bauer
and Ed Exley
10 Santa Ana CHP .60 1.50
Mike Lundquist
Ana Burson
Galen B

1999 Angels Magnets

These four magnets were sold directly at Edison Field and featured members of the Anaheim Angels. The fronts have the player's last name printed down the side along with a photo and the Angels logo. The backs, are obviously, blank. Since these are unnumbered we have sequenced them in alphabetical order. Please note that Jim Edmonds and Chuck Finley were only available in 1999 so they are slightly tougher than Darin Erstad and Tim Salmon. The magnets are sequenced in alphabetical order.

COMPLETE SET (4) 10.00 25.00
1 Jim Edmonds 3.00 8.00
2 Darin Erstad 3.00 8.00
3 Chuck Finley 2.50 6.00
4 Tim Salmon 2.00 5.00

2002 Angels Topps '82 Commemorative

COMPLETE SET (10) 3.00 8.00
1 Don Baylor .40 1.00
2 Rod Carew .75 2.00
3 Doug DeCinces .20 .50
4 Brian Downing .40 1.00
5 Reggie Jackson .75 2.00
6 Fred Lynn .20 .50
7 Geoff Zahn .08 .25
8 Bob Boone .20 .50
9 Bobby Grich .30 .75
NNO Header Card .08 .25
Fox Sports Net

2004 Angels Playing Cards

COMP.FACT SET (53) 5.00 10.00
1C Mike Scioscia MG .03 .10

2C Adam Kennedy .05 .15
3C Garret Anderson .10 .25
4C Bartolo Colon .10 .25
5C David Eckstein .05 .15
6C Jose Guillen .05 .15
7C Darin Erstad .07 .20
8C Kelvim Escobar .03 .10
9C Tim Salmon .05 .15
10C Bengie Molina .03 .10
11C Troy Percival .05 .15
12C Troy Glaus .10 .25
13C Vladimir Guerrero .20 .50
JK Rally Monkey .03 .10

2006 Angels Topps

COMPLETE SET (14) 3.00 8.00
ANG1 Vladimir Guerrero .20 .50
ANG2 Bartolo Colon .12 .30
ANG3 Garret Anderson .12 .30
ANG4 Edgardo Alfonzo .12 .30
ANG5 Orlando Cabrera .12 .30
ANG6 Francisco Rodriguez .20 .50
ANG7 Ervin Santana .12 .30
ANG8 John Lackey .20 .50
ANG9 Kelvim Escobar .12 .30
ANG10 Darin Erstad .12 .30
ANG11 Chone Figgins .12 .30
ANG12 Dallas McPherson .12 .30
ANG13 Adam Kennedy .12 .30
ANG14 Casey Kotchman .12 .30

2007 Angels Topps

COMPLETE SET (14) 3.00 8.00
LAA1 Vladimir Guerrero .20 .50
LAA2 Ervin Santana .12 .30
LAA3 Jered Weaver .20 .50
LAA4 Mike Napoli .12 .30
LAA5 Gary Matthews .12 .30
LAA6 Chone Figgins .12 .30
LAA7 Garret Anderson .12 .30
LAA8 Shea Hillenbrand .12 .30
LAA9 Orlando Cabrera .12 .30
LAA10 John Lackey .20 .50
LAA11 Kelvim Escobar .12 .30
LAA12 Bartolo Colon .12 .30
LAA13 Howie Kendrick .12 .30
LAA14 Francisco Rodriguez .20 .50

2008 Angels Topps

COMPLETE SET (14) 3.00 8.00
LAA1 Vladimir Guerrero .20 .50
LAA2 Jon Garland .12 .30
LAA3 Jered Weaver .20 .50
LAA4 Jeff Mathis .12 .30
LAA5 Gary Matthews .12 .30
LAA6 Chone Figgins .12 .30
LAA7 Garret Anderson .12 .30
LAA8 Torii Hunter .12 .30
LAA9 Casey Kotchman .12 .30
LAA10 John Lackey .20 .50
LAA11 Kelvim Escobar .20 .50
LAA12 Bartolo Colon .12 .30
LAA13 Howie Kendrick .12 .30
LAA14 Francisco Rodriguez .20 .50

2009 Angels Topps

COMPLETE SET (15) 3.00 8.00
LAA1 Torii Hunter .15 .40
LAA2 Chone Figgins .15 .40
LAA3 Jered Weaver .25 .60
LAA4 Mike Napoli .15 .40
LAA5 Brian Fuentes .15 .40
LAA6 Joe Saunders .15 .40
LAA7 Juan Rivera .15 .40
LAA8 Ervin Santana .15 .40
LAA9 Gary Matthews .15 .40
LAA10 John Lackey .25 .60
LAA11 Vladimir Guerrero .25 .60
LAA12 Erick Aybar .15 .40
LAA13 Howie Kendrick .15 .40
LAA14 Brandon Wood .15 .40
LAA15 Mike Scioscia .15 .40

2010 Angels Topps

COMPLETE SET (17) 3.00 8.00
LAA1 Torii Hunter .15 .40
LAA2 Joe Saunders .15 .40
LAA3 Howie Kendrick .15 .40
LAA4 Bobby Abreu .15 .40
LAA5 Kendry Morales .15 .40
LAA6 Gary Matthews Jr. .15 .40
LAA7 Brandon Wood .15 .40
LAA8 Juan Rivera .15 .40
LAA9 Scott Kazmir .15 .40
LAA10 Erick Aybar .15 .40
LAA11 Mike Napoli .15 .40
LAA12 Ervin Santana .15 .40
LAA13 Jered Weaver .25 .60
LAA14 Brian Fuentes .15 .40
LAA15 Hideki Matsui .40 1.00
LAA16 Matt Palmer .15 .40
LAA17 Jeff Mathis .15 .40

2011 Angels Topps

COMPLETE SET (17) 3.00 8.00
ANG1 Kendry Morales .15 .40
ANG2 Dan Haren .15 .40
ANG3 Torii Hunter .15 .40
ANG4 Maicer Izturis .15 .40
ANG5 Jeff Mathis .15 .40
ANG6 Joel Pineiro .15 .40
ANG7 Vernon Wells .15 .40
ANG8 Fernando Rodney .15 .40
ANG9 Howie Kendrick .15 .40
ANG10 Ervin Santana .15 .40
ANG11 Jered Weaver .25 .60
ANG12 Bobby Abreu .15 .40
ANG13 Erick Aybar .15 .40
ANG14 Peter Bourjos .25 .60
ANG15 Hank Conger .25 .60
ANG16 Scott Kazmir .15 .40
ANG17 Angel Stadium of Anaheim .15 .40

2012 Angels Topps

COMPLETE SET (17) 3.00 8.00
ANG1 Albert Pujols .50 1.25
ANG2 Peter Bourjos .25 .60
ANG3 Vernon Wells .25 .60
ANG4 Mark Trumbo .25 .60
ANG5 Alberto Callaspo .25 .60
ANG6 Ervin Santana .25 .60
ANG7 Mike Trout 12.00 30.00
ANG8 Bobby Abreu .25 .60
ANG9 Howie Kendrick .25 .60
ANG10 Dan Haren .25 .60
ANG11 Jered Weaver .30 .75
ANG12 Torii Hunter .30 .75
ANG13 C.J. Wilson .25 .60
ANG14 Chris Iannetta .25 .60
ANG15 Erick Aybar .25 .60
ANG16 Jordan Walden .25 .60
ANG17 Angel Stadium of Anaheim .15 .40

2013 Angels Topps

COMPLETE SET (17) 3.00 8.00
LAA1 Josh Hamilton .20 .50
LAA2 Mike Trout 2.00 5.00
LAA3 Albert Pujols .30 .75
LAA4 Jered Weaver .20 .50
LAA5 Mark Trumbo .15 .40
LAA6 Tommy Hanson .15 .40
LAA7 C.J. Wilson .15 .40
LAA8 Joe Blanton .15 .40
LAA9 Ryan Madson .15 .40
LAA10 Ernesto Frieri .15 .40
LAA11 Jason Vargas .15 .40
LAA12 Chris Iannetta .15 .40
LAA13 Howie Kendrick .15 .40
LAA14 Erick Aybar .15 .40
LAA15 Peter Bourjos .15 .40
LAA16 Alberto Callaspo .15 .40
LAA17 Angel Stadium of Anaheim .15 .40

2014 Angels Topps

COMPLETE SET (17) 3.00 8.00
LAA1 Mike Trout 1.25 3.00
LAA2 Josh Hamilton .20 .50
LAA3 Albert Pujols .30 .75
LAA4 Jered Weaver .20 .50
LAA5 Tyler Skaggs .15 .40
LAA6 Hank Conger .15 .40
LAA7 C.J. Wilson .15 .40
LAA8 Kole Calhoun .15 .40
LAA9 Garrett Richards .20 .50
LAA10 Ernesto Frieri .15 .40
LAA11 Raul Ibanez .20 .50
LAA12 Chris Iannetta .15 .40
LAA13 Howie Kendrick .15 .40
LAA14 Erick Aybar .15 .40
LAA15 David Freese .15 .40
LAA16 Hector Santiago .15 .40
LAA17 Angel Stadium of Anaheim .15 .40

2015 Angels Topps

COMPLETE SET (17) 3.00 8.00
A1 Mike Trout 1.25 3.00
A2 Josh Rutledge .15 .40
A3 Josh Hamilton .20 .50
A4 Chris Iannetta .15 .40
A5 Garrett Richards .20 .50
A6 Matt Shoemaker .20 .50
A7 Erick Aybar .15 .40
A8 Jered Weaver .20 .50
A9 C.J. Wilson .15 .40
A10 Albert Pujols .30 .75
A11 Kole Calhoun .15 .40
A12 David Freese .15 .40
A13 Matt Joyce .15 .40
A14 Hector Santiago .15 .40
A15 Huston Street .15 .40
A16 C.J. Cron .15 .40
A17 Andrew Heaney .15 .40

2016 Angels Topps

COMPLETE SET (17) 3.00 8.00
LAA1 Mike Trout 1.25 3.00
LAA2 Kole Calhoun .15 .40
LAA3 C.J. Cron .15 .40
LAA4 Andrelton Simmons .15 .40
LAA5 Johnny Giavotella .15 .40
LAA6 Albert Pujols .30 .75
LAA7 Garrett Richards .20 .50
LAA8 Andrew Heaney .15 .40
LAA9 Jered Weaver .20 .50
LAA10 Hector Santiago .15 .40
LAA11 Matt Shoemaker .20 .50
LAA12 Huston Street .15 .40
LAA13 C.J. Wilson .15 .40
LAA14 Yunel Escobar .15 .40
LAA15 Joe Smith .15 .40
LAA16 Carlos Perez .15 .40
LAA17 Cliff Pennington .15 .40

2017 Angels Topps

COMPLETE SET (17) 3.00 8.00
ANG1 Mike Trout 1.25 3.00
ANG2 Albert Pujols .30 .75
ANG3 C.J. Cron .15 .40
ANG4 Garrett Richards .20 .50
ANG5 Danny Espinosa .15 .40
ANG6 J.C. Ramirez .15 .40
ANG7 Angel Stadium of Anaheim .15 .40
ANG8 Yunel Escobar .15 .40
ANG9 Nick Tropeano .15 .40
ANG10 Kole Calhoun .15 .40
ANG11 Ricky Nolasco .15 .40
ANG12 Johnny Giavotella .15 .40
ANG13 Matt Shoemaker .20 .50
ANG14 Andrew Heaney .15 .40
ANG15 Cameron Maybin .15 .40
ANG16 Huston Street .15 .40
ANG17 Martin Maldonado .15 .40

2018 Angels Topps

COMPLETE SET (17) 4.00 10.00
A1 Mike Trout 1.25 3.00
A2 Andrelton Simmons .15 .40
A3 Yunel Escobar .15 .40
A4 J.C. Ramirez .15 .40
A5 Matt Shoemaker .20 .50
A6 Albert Pujols .30 .75
A7 Kole Calhoun .15 .40
A8 Martin Maldonado .15 .40
A9 C.J. Cron .15 .40
A10 Luis Valbuena .15 .40
A11 Brandon Phillips .15 .40
A12 Justin Upton .20 .50
A13 Parker Bridwell .15 .40
A14 Zack Cozart .15 .40
A15 Garrett Richards .20 .50
A16 Ian Kinsler .20 .50
A17 Shohei Ohtani 4.00 10.00

2019 Angels Topps

COMPLETE SET (17) 3.00 8.00
A1 Mike Trout 1.25 3.00
A2 Shohei Ohtani .40 1.00
A3 Albert Pujols .30 .75
A4 Justin Upton .20 .50
A5 Andrelton Simmons .15 .40
A6 Kole Calhoun .15 .40
A7 Zack Cozart .15 .40
A8 Andrew Heaney .15 .40
A9 Tyler Skaggs .15 .40
A10 Nick Tropeano .15 .40
A11 Jose Briceno .15 .40
A12 David Fletcher .50 1.25
A13 Taylor Ward .15 .40
A14 Justin Bour .15 .40
A15 Matt Harvey .20 .50
A16 Keynan Middleton .15 .40
A17 Jaime Barria .15 .40

2020 Angels Topps

A1 Mike Trout 1.25 3.00
A2 Shohei Ohtani .40 1.00
A3 Albert Pujols .30 .75
A4 Dylan Bundy .20 .50
A5 Andrelton Simmons .15 .40
A6 Matt Thaiss .20 .50
A7 Andrew Heaney .15 .40
A8 Jaime Barria .15 .40
A9 David Fletcher .25 .60
A10 Hansel Robles .15 .40
A11 Anthony Rendon .25 .60
A12 Tommy La Stella .15 .40
A13 Brian Goodwin .15 .40
A14 Justin Upton .20 .50
A15 Max Stassi .15 .40
A16 Griffin Canning .25 .60
A17 Taylor Ward .25 .60

1993 Anti-Gambling Postcards

COMPLETE SET (13) 6.00 15.00
1 Will Clark BB .75 2.00
2 Glenn Davis BB .50 1.25
3 Dennis Eckersley BB .60 1.50
4 Dave Stewart BB .50 1.25
5 Bob Welch BB .40 1.00

2000 APBA Superstars

COMPLETE SET (30) 5.00 12.00
1 Roberto Alomar .15 .40
2 Jeff Bagwell .15 .40
3 Barry Bonds .40 1.00
4 Jeromy Burnitz .10 .25
5 Carlos Delgado .10 .25
6 Jermaine Dye .10 .25
7 Cliff Floyd .10 .25
8 Jason Giambi .10 .25
9 Juan Gonzalez .10 .25
10 Shawn Green .10 .25
11 Ken Griffey Jr. .50 1.25
12 Vladimir Guerrero .15 .40
13 Tony Gwynn .25 .60
14 Todd Helton .15 .40
15 Derek Jeter .60 1.50
16 Randy Johnson .25 .60
17 Chipper Jones .25 .60
18 Jason Kendall .10 .25
19 Matt Lawton .10 .25
20 Pedro Martinez .15 .40
21 Mark McGwire .40 1.00
22 Mike Piazza .25 .60
23 Cal Ripken .75 2.00
24 Alex Rodriguez .30 .75
25 Ivan Rodriguez .15 .40
26 Scott Rolen .15 .40
27 Sammy Sosa .25 .60
28 Frank Thomas .25 .60
29 Greg Vaughn .10 .25
30 Mo Vaughn .10 .25

2000 APBA Superstars Cut-outs

COMPLETE SET (6) 3.00 8.00
1 Barry Bonds .75 2.00
2 Nomar Garciaparra .30 .75
3 Ken Griffey Jr. 1.00 2.50
4 Mark McGwire .75 2.00
5 Mike Piazza .50 1.25
6 Alex Rodriguez .60 1.50

1987 A Question of Sport UK

These cards are part of a British board game "A Question of Sport" in which participants attempt to name an athlete by seeing a picture of them. These white bordered, full color cards measure 2 1/4" by 3 1/2" and have a back that contains only the player's name on a green background. The copyright on the box is 1986, but the game was released in early 1987. We've arranged the unnumbered cards alphabetically below.

COMPLETE SET (240) 20.00 40.00
227 Fernando Valenzuela .60 1.50

1991 Arena Holograms

The 1991 Arena Hologram cards were distributed through hobby dealers and feature famous athletes. According to Arena, production quantities were limited to 250,000 of each card. The standard-size hologram cards have on the horozontially oriented backs a color photo of the player in a tuxedo. Ken Griffey Jr. Frank Thomas, David Robinson, Joe Montana and Barry Sanders all signed cards with each being serial numbered by hand. A card-sized certificate of authenticity was also issued with each signed card.

COMPLETE SET (5) 3.20 8.00
2 Ken Griffey Jr. 1.00 2.50
3A Frank Thomas Silver 1.25 3.00
3B Frank Thomas Gold 1.25 3.00
AU2 Ken Griffey Jr. AU/2500 20.00 50.00
AU3 Frank Thomas AU/1250 12.50 30.00

1991 Arena Holograms 12th National

These standard-size cards have on their fronts a 3-D silver-colored emblem on a white background with orange borders. Though the back of each card salutes a different superstar, the players themselves are not pictured; instead, one finds pictures of a football; hockey stick and puck; basketball; and baseball in glove respectively. The cards are numbered on the front.

COMPLETE SET (4) 4.00 10.00
4 Nolan Ryan 1.50 4.00

1996 Arizona Lottery

This three-card set features black-and-white action player photos with black borders. The backs carry player information and career highlights as well as information on what the collector can win playing the lottery scratch-off game, "Diamond Bucks." The cards are unnumbered and checklisted below in alphabetical order.

COMPLETE SET (3) 3.00 8.00
1 Ernie Banks 1.25 3.00
2 Gaylord Perry .75 2.00
3 Brooks Robinson 1.25 3.00

1979 Arizona Sports Collectors Show

COMPLETE SET (10) 7.50 15.00
1 Jim Colborn .30 .75
2 Jocko Conlon 1.25 3.00
3 Gary Gentry .30 .75
4 Charlie Grimm .60 1.50
6 Ken Rudolph .30 .75
7 Mike Sadek .30 .75
10 George Zuverink .30 .75

2005 Artifacts

COMP.SET w/o SP's (100) 15.00 40.00
COMMON CARD (1-100) .20 .50
COMMON CARD (101-150) .30 .75
101-150 STATED ODDS 1:5
101-150 PRINT RUN 1350 SERIAL #'d SETS
COMMON CARD (151-200) .30 .75
151-200 STATED ODDS 1:3
151-200 PRINT RUN 1999 SERIAL #'d SETS
COMMON CARD (201-285) .30 .75
201-285 ISSUED IN 05 UD UPDATE PACKS
201-285: ONE #'d CARD OR AU PER PACK
201-285 PRINT RUN 799 SERIAL #'d SETS
1 Adam Dunn .30 .75
2 Adrian Beltre .50 1.25
3 Albert Pujols .60 1.50
4 Alex Rodriguez .60 1.50
5 Alfonso Soriano .30 .75
6 Andruw Jones .20 .50
7 Andy Pettitte .30 .75
8 Aramis Ramirez .20 .50
9 Aubrey Huff .20 .50
10 Barry Larkin .30 .75
11 Ben Sheets .20 .50
12 Bernie Williams .30 .75
13 Bobby Abreu .20 .50
14 Brad Penny .20 .50
15 Bret Boone .20 .50
16 Brian Giles .20 .50
17 Carl Crawford .30 .75
18 Carl Pavano .20 .50
19 Carlos Beltran .30 .75
20 Carlos Delgado .20 .50
21 Carlos Guillen .20 .50
22 Carlos Lee .20 .50
23 Carlos Zambrano .30 .75
24 Chipper Jones .50 1.25
25 Craig Biggio .30 .75
26 Craig Wilson .20 .50
27 Curt Schilling .30 .75
28 David Ortiz .50 1.25
29 Derek Jeter 1.25 3.00
30 Eric Chavez .20 .50
31 Eric Gagne .20 .50
32 Frank Thomas .50 1.25
33 Garret Anderson .20 .50
34 Gary Sheffield .20 .50
35 Greg Maddux .60 1.50
36 Hank Blalock .20 .50
37 Hideki Matsui .75 2.00
38 Ichiro Suzuki .60 1.50
39 Ivan Rodriguez .30 .75
40 J.D. Drew .20 .50
41 Jake Peavy .20 .50
42 Jason Kendall .20 .50
43 Jason Schmidt .20 .50
44 Jeff Bagwell .30 .75
45 Jeff Kent .20 .50
46 Jim Edmonds .30 .75
47 Jim Thome .30 .75
48 Joe Mauer .40 1.00
49 Johan Santana .30 .75
50 John Smoltz .50 1.25
51 Jose Reyes .30 .75
52 Jose Vidro .20 .50
53 Josh Beckett .20 .50
54 Ken Griffey Jr. 1.00 2.50
55 Kerry Wood .20 .50
56 Kevin Brown .20 .50
57 Lance Berkman .30 .75
58 Larry Walker .30 .75
59 Livan Hernandez .20 .50
60 Luis Gonzalez .20 .50
61 Lyle Overbay .20 .50
62 Magglio Ordonez .30 .75
63 Manny Ramirez .50 1.25
64 Mark Mulder .20 .50
65 Mark Prior .30 .75
66 Mark Teixeira .30 .75
67 Melvin Mora .20 .50
68 Michael Young .20 .50
69 Miguel Cabrera .50 1.25
70 Miguel Tejada .30 .75
71 Mike Lowell .20 .50
72 Mike Mussina .30 .75
73 Mike Piazza .50 1.25
74 Mike Sweeney .20 .50
75 Nomar Garciaparra .30 .75
76 Oliver Perez .20 .50
77 Paul Konerko .30 .75
78 Pedro Martinez .30 .75
79 Preston Wilson .20 .50
80 Rafael Furcal .20 .50
81 Rafael Palmeiro .30 .75
82 Randy Johnson .50 1.25
83 Richie Sexson .20 .50
84 Roger Clemens .60 1.50
85 Roy Halladay .30 .75
86 Roy Oswalt .30 .75
87 Sammy Sosa .50 1.25
88 Scott Podsednik .20 .50
89 Scott Rolen .30 .75
90 Shawn Green .20 .50
91 Steve Finley .20 .50
92 Tim Hudson .30 .75
93 Todd Helton .30 .75
94 Tom Glavine .30 .75
95 Torii Hunter .20 .50
96 Travis Hafner .20 .50
97 Troy Glaus .20 .50
98 Vernon Wells .20 .50
99 Victor Martinez .30 .75
100 Vladimir Guerrero .30 .75
101 Aaron Rowand FS .30 .75
102 Adam LaRoche FS .30 .75
103 Adrian Gonzalez FS .60 1.50
104 Alexis Rios FS .30 .75
105 Angel Guzman FS .30 .75
106 B.J. Upton FS .50 1.25
107 Bobby Crosby FS .30 .75
108 Bobby Madritsch FS .30 .75
109 Brandon Claussen FS .30 .75
110 Bucky Jacobsen FS .30 .75
111 Casey Kotchman FS .30 .75
112 Chad Cordero FS .30 .75
113 Chase Utley FS .50 1.25
114 Chris Burke FS .30 .75
115 Dallas McPherson FS .30 .75
116 Daniel Cabrera FS .30 .75
117 David DeJesus FS .30 .75
118 David Wright FS .60 1.50
119 Eddy Rodriguez FS .30 .75
120 Edwin Jackson FS .30 .75
121 Gabe Gross FS .30 .75
122 Garrett Atkins FS .30 .75
123 Gavin Floyd FS .30 .75
124 Gerald Laird FS .30 .75
125 Guillermo Quiroz FS .30 .75
126 J.D. Closser FS .30 .75
127 Jason Bay FS .30 .75
128 Jason DuBois FS .30 .75
129 Jason Lane FS .30 .75
130 Jayson Werth FS .50 1.25
131 Jeff Francis FS .30 .75
132 Jesse Crain FS .30 .75
133 Joe Blanton FS .30 .75
134 Joe Mauer FS .60 1.50
135 Jose Capellan FS .30 .75
136 Kevin Youkilis FS .30 .75
137 Khalil Greene FS .30 .75
138 Laynce Nix FS .30 .75
139 Nick Swisher FS .50 1.25
140 Oliver Perez FS .30 .75
141 Rickie Weeks FS .30 .75
142 Robb Quinlan FS .30 .75
143 Roman Colon FS .30 .75
144 Ryan Howard FS .60 1.50
145 Ryan Wagner FS .30 .75
146 Scott Kazmir FS .75 2.00
147 Scott Proctor FS .30 .75
148 Wily Mo Pena FS .30 .75
149 Yhency Brazoban FS .30 .75
150 Zack Greinke FS 1.00 2.50
151 Al Kaline LGD .75 2.00
152 Babe Ruth LGD 2.00 5.00
153 Billy Williams LGD .50 1.25
154 Bob Feller LGD .50 1.25
155 Bob Gibson LGD .50 1.25
156 Bob Lemon LGD .50 1.25
157 Bobby Doerr LGD .50 1.25
158 Brooks Robinson LGD .50 1.25
159 Cal Ripken LGD 2.50 6.00
160 Christy Mathewson LGD .75 2.00
161 Cy Young LGD .50 1.25
162 Dizzy Dean LGD .50 1.25
163 Don Drysdale LGD .50 1.25
164 Eddie Mathews LGD .75 2.00
165 Enos Slaughter LGD .50 1.25
166 Ernie Banks LGD .75 2.00
167 Fergie Jenkins LGD .50 1.25
168 George Sisler LGD .50 1.25
169 Harmon Killebrew LGD .75 2.00
170 Honus Wagner LGD .50 1.25
171 Jackie Robinson LGD .50 1.25
172 Jimmie Foxx LGD .50 1.25
173 Joe DiMaggio LGD 1.50 4.00
174 Joe Morgan LGD .50 1.25
175 Juan Marichal LGD .50 1.25
176 Lou Brock LGD .50 1.25
177 Lou Gehrig LGD 1.50 4.00
178 Luis Aparicio LGD .50 1.25
179 Mel Ott LGD .75 2.00
180 Mickey Cochrane LGD .50 1.25
181 Mickey Mantle LGD 2.50 6.00
182 Mike Schmidt LGD 1.25 3.00
183 Nolan Ryan LGD 2.50 6.00
184 Pee Wee Reese LGD .50 1.25
185 Phil Rizzuto LGD .50 1.25
186 Ralph Kiner LGD .50 1.25
187 Rogers Hornsby LGD .30 .75
188 Roy Campanella LGD .50 1.25
189 Satchel Paige LGD .75 2.00
190 Stan Musial LGD 1.25 3.00
191 Rick Ferrell LGD .30 .75
192 Thurman Munson LGD .50 1.25
193 Tom Seaver LGD .50 1.25
194 Ty Cobb LGD 1.25 3.00
195 Walter Johnson LGD .50 1.25
196 Warren Spahn LGD .50 1.25
197 Whitey Ford LGD .50 1.25
198 Willie McCovey LGD .50 1.25
199 Willie Stargell LGD .50 1.25
200 Yogi Berra LGD .75 2.00
201 Adam Shabala FS RC .30 .75
202 Ambiorix Burgos FS RC .30 .75
203 Ambiorix Concepcion FS RC .30 .75
204 Anibal Sanchez FS RC 1.25 3.00
205 Bill McCarthy FS RC .30 .75
206 Brandon McCarthy FS RC .50 1.25
207 Brian Burres FS RC .30 .75
208 Carlos Ruiz FS RC .50 1.25
209 Casey Rogowski FS RC .50 1.25
210 Chad Orvella FS RC .30 .75
211 Chris Resop FS RC .30 .75
212 Chris Roberson FS RC .30 .75
213 Chris Seddon FS RC .30 .75
214 Colter Bean FS RC .30 .75
215 Dae-Sung Koo FS RC .30 .75
216 Dave Gassner FS RC .30 .75
217 Brian Anderson FS RC .50 1.25
218 D.J. Houlton FS RC .30 .75
219 Derek Wathan FS RC .30 .75
220 Devon Lowery FS RC .30 .75
221 Enrique Gonzalez FS RC .30 .75
222 Eude Brito FS RC .30 .75
223 Francisco Butto FS RC .30 .75
224 Franquelis Osoria FS RC .30 .75
225 Garrett Jones FS RC .50 1.25
226 Geovany Soto FS RC 1.50 4.00
227 Hayden Penn FS RC .30 .75
228 Ismael Ramirez FS RC .30 .75
229 Jared Gothreaux FS RC .30 .75
230 Jason Hammel FS RC .75 2.00
231 Jeff Miller FS RC .30 .75
232 Jeff Niemann FS RC .75 2.00
233 Joel Peralta FS RC .30 .75
234 John Hattig FS RC .30 .75
235 Jorge Campillo FS RC .30 .75
236 Juan Morillo FS RC .30 .75
237 Justin Verlander FS RC 6.00 15.00
238 Ryan Garko FS RC .30 .75
239 Keiichi Yabu FS RC .30 .75
240 Kendry Morales FS RC .75 2.00
241 Luis Hernandez FS RC .30 .75
242 Luis Pena FS RC .30 .75
243 Luis O.Rodriguez FS RC .30 .75
244 Luke Scott FS RC .75 2.00
245 Marcos Carvajal FS RC .30 .75
246 Mark Woodyard FS RC .30 .75
247 Matt A.Smith FS RC .30 .75
248 Matthew Lindstrom FS RC .30 .75
249 Miguel Negron FS RC .50 1.25
250 Mike Morse FS RC 1.00 2.50
251 Nate McLouth FS RC .50 1.25
252 Nelson Cruz FS RC 4.00 10.00
253 Nick Masset FS RC .30 .75
254 Oscar Robles FS RC .30 .75
255 Paulino Reynoso FS RC .30 .75
256 Pedro Lopez FS RC .30 .75
257 Pete Orr FS RC .50 1.25
258 Philip Humber FS RC .75 2.00
259 Prince Fielder FS RC 1.50 4.00
260 Randy Messenger FS RC .30 .75
261 Randy Williams FS RC .30 .75
262 Raul Tablado FS RC .30 .75
263 Ronny Paulino FS RC .50 1.25
264 Russ Rohlicek FS RC .30 .75
265 Russell Martin FS RC 1.00 2.50
266 Scott Baker FS RC .50 1.25
267 Scott Munter FS RC .30 .75
268 Sean Thompson FS RC .30 .75
269 Sean Tracey FS RC .30 .75
270 Shane Costa FS RC .30 .75
271 Stephen Drew FS RC 1.00 2.50
272 Steve Schmoll FS RC .30 .75
273 Tadahito Iguchi FS RC .50 1.25
274 Tony Giarratano FS RC .30 .75
275 Tony Pena FS RC .30 .75
276 Travis Bowyer FS RC .30 .75
277 Ubaldo Jimenez FS RC .75 2.00
278 Wladimir Balentien FS RC .50 1.25
279 Yorman Bazardo FS RC .30 .75
280 Yuniesky Betancourt FS RC 1.25 3.00
281 Ryan Zimmerman FS RC 1.50 4.00
282 Chris Denorfia FS RC .30 .75
283 Dana Eveland FS RC .30 .75
284 Jermaine Van Buren FS .30 .75
285 Mark McLemore FS RC .30 .75

2005 Artifacts Rainbow Blue

*BLUE 1-100: 2.5X TO 6X BASIC
*BLUE 101-150: .6X TO 1.5X BASIC
*BLUE POST-WAR 151-200: 1.5X TO 4X
*BLUE PRE-WAR 151-200: .6X TO 1.5X
1-200 OVERALL PARALLEL ODDS 1:10
*BLUE 201-285: .6X TO 1.5X BASIC
201-285 ISSUED IN '05 UD UPDATE PACKS
201-285 ONE #'d CARD OR AU PER PACK
STATED PRINT RUN 100 SERIAL #'d SETS

2005 Artifacts Rainbow Gold

*GOLD 1-100: 6X TO 15X BASIC
*GOLD 101-150: 1.5X TO 4X BASIC
*GOLD POST-WAR 151-200: 4X TO 10X
*GOLD PRE-WAR 151-200: 1.5X TO 4X
1-200 OVERALL PARALLEL ODDS 1:10
201-285 ISSUED IN '05 UD UPDATE PACKS
201-285 ONE #'d CARD OR AU PER PACK
STATED PRINT RUN 25 SERIAL #'d SETS
201-285 NO PRICING DUE TO SCARCITY

2005 Artifacts Rainbow Red

*RED 1-100: 4X TO 10X BASIC
*RED 101-150: 1X TO 2.5X BASIC
*RED POST-WAR 151-200: 1.25X TO 3X
*RED PRE-WAR 151-200: 1X TO 2.5X
1-200 OVERALL PARALLEL ODDS 1:10
*RED 201-285: 1X TO 2.5X BASIC
201-285 ISSUED IN '05 UD UPDATE PACKS
201-285 ONE #'d CARD OR AU PER PACK
STATED PRINT RUN 50 SERIAL #'d SETS

2005 Artifacts UD Promos

*PROMO: .6X TO 1.5X BASIC

2005 Artifacts AL/NL Artifacts

OVERALL GAME-USED ODDS 1:3
PRINT RUNS B/WN 100-325 COPIES PER
AB Adrian Beltre Jsy/325 3.00 8.00
AD Andre Dawson Jsy/325 3.00 8.00
AH Aubrey Huff Jsy/325 3.00 8.00
AK Al Kaline Jsy/325 5.00 12.00
AO Akinori Otsuka Jsy/325 3.00 8.00
AP Albert Pujols Jsy/325 6.00 15.00
BA Bobby Abreu Jsy/325 3.00 8.00
BB Bert Blyleven Jsy/325 3.00 8.00
BC Bobby Crosby Jsy/325 3.00 8.00
BD Bobby Doerr Bat/325 3.00 8.00
BE Johnny Bench Jsy/325 5.00 12.00
BF Bob Feller Pants/325 4.00 10.00
BG Bob Gibson Pants/325 4.00 10.00
BPA Boog Powell Jsy/325 3.00 8.00
BPN Brad Penny Jsy/325 3.00 8.00
BR Brooks Robinson Jsy/325 4.00 10.00
BS Ben Sheets Jsy/325 3.00 8.00
BU B.J. Upton Jsy/325 3.00 8.00
CA Steve Carlton Jsy/325 3.00 8.00
CB Carlos Beltran Jsy/325 3.00 8.00
CK Casey Kotchman Jsy/325 3.00 8.00
CP Corey Patterson Jsy/325 3.00 8.00
CR Cal Ripken Jsy/325 10.00 25.00
CY Carl Yastrzemski Jsy/325 6.00 15.00
CZ Carlos Zambrano Jsy/325 3.00 8.00
DG Dwight Gooden Pants/325 3.00 8.00
DJ Derek Jeter Jsy/325 8.00 20.00
DK Dave Kingman Bat/325 3.00 8.00
DL Derrek Lee Jsy/325 3.00 8.00
DMA Dallas McPherson Jsy/325 3.00 8.00
DMN Dale Murphy Jsy/150 4.00 10.00
DO David Ortiz Jsy/325 3.00 8.00
DW David Wright Jsy/325 6.00 15.00
EC Eric Chavez Jsy/325 3.00 8.00
EG Eric Gagne Jsy/325 3.00 8.00
FL Fred Lynn Bat/325 3.00 8.00
FR Frank Robinson Jsy/325 3.00 8.00
GB George Brett Jsy/325 6.00 15.00
GI Brian Giles Jsy/325 3.00 8.00
GK George Kell Bat/325 3.00 8.00
GM Greg Maddux Jsy/275 6.00 15.00
GN Graig Nettles Jsy/325 3.00 8.00
GR Ken Griffey Sr. Jsy/325 3.00 8.00
HB Hank Blalock Jsy/325 3.00 8.00
HK Harmon Killebrew Jsy/325 5.00 12.00
JB Jason Bay Jsy/325 3.00 8.00
JK Jim Kaat Jsy/325 3.00 8.00
JM Joe Mauer Jsy/325 3.00 8.00
JPA Jim Palmer Jsy/325 3.00 8.00
JPN Jake Peavy Jsy/325 3.00 8.00
JRA Jim Rice Jsy/325 3.00 8.00
JRN Jose Reyes Jsy/250 3.00 8.00
JSA Johan Santana Jsy/325 4.00 10.00
JSN Jason Schmidt Jsy/325 3.00 8.00
KG Ken Griffey Jr. Jsy/325 6.00 15.00
KHA Kent Hrbek Jsy/325 3.00 8.00
KHN Keith Hernandez Bat/325 3.00 8.00
KL Khalil Greene Jsy/325 3.00 8.00
KW Kerry Wood Jsy/325 3.00 8.00
LN Laynce Nix Jsy/325 3.00 8.00
MA Don Mattingly Jsy/325 6.00 15.00
MC Miguel Cabrera Jsy/325 3.00 8.00
MG Marcus Giles Jsy/325 3.00 8.00
MK Mark Grace Jsy/175 4.00 10.00
ML Mike Lowell Jsy/325 3.00 8.00
MM Mark Mulder Jsy/325 3.00 8.00
MP Mark Prior Jsy/325 3.00 8.00
MS Mike Schmidt Jsy/325 6.00 15.00
MT Mark Teixeira Jsy/325 3.00 8.00
MW Maury Wills Jsy/325 3.00 8.00
MY Michael Young Jsy/325 3.00 8.00
NR Nolan Ryan Jsy/325 8.00 20.00
OC Orlando Cepeda Jsy/185 3.00 8.00
PM Paul Molitor Jsy/325 3.00 8.00
PN Phil Niekro Jsy/325 3.00 8.00
RCA Rod Carew Jsy/325 4.00 10.00
RCN Roger Clemens Jsy/325 4.00 10.00
RH Rich Harden Jsy/325 3.00 8.00
RJ Randy Johnson Jsy/325 4.00 10.00
RK Ralph Kiner Bat/325 4.00 10.00
RO Roy Oswalt Jsy/325 3.00 8.00
RP Rico Petrocelli Pants/325 3.00 8.00
RW Rickie Weeks Jsy/325 3.00 8.00
RY Robin Yount Jsy/325 5.00 12.00
SC Sean Casey Jsy/325 3.00 8.00
SL Sparky Lyle Pants/325 3.00 8.00
SM John Smoltz Jsy/325 3.00 8.00
SP Scott Podsednik Jsy/325 3.00 8.00
SR Scott Rolen Jsy/325 3.00 8.00
ST Shingo Takatsu Jsy/325 3.00 8.00
SU Bruce Sutter Jsy/325 3.00 8.00
TG Tony Gwynn Jsy/325 5.00 12.00
TH Travis Hafner Jsy/325 3.00 8.00
TS Tom Seaver Jsy/325 4.00 10.00
VM Victor Martinez Jsy/325 3.00 8.00
WB Wade Boggs Jsy/325 4.00 10.00
WC Will Clark Jsy/100 5.00 12.00
WM Willie McCovey Jsy/325 4.00 10.00
YB Yogi Berra Pants/325 6.00 15.00

2005 Artifacts AL/NL Artifacts Rainbow

*RAINBOW p/r 99: .5X TO 1.2X p/r 150-325
*RAINBOW p/r 50: .5X TO 1.2X p/r 100
OVERALL GAME-USED ODDS 1:3
PRINT RUNS B/WN 50-99 COPIES PER

2005 Artifacts AL/NL Artifacts Signatures

STATED PRINT RUN 30 SERIAL #'d SETS
RARE PRINT RUN 1 SERIAL #'d SET
NO RARE PRICING DUE TO SCARCITY
OVERALL AUTO ODDS 1:10
EXCHANGE DEADLINE 04/11/08
AB Adrian Beltre Jsy 10.00 25.00
AD Andre Dawson Jsy 10.00 25.00
AH Aubrey Huff Jsy 10.00 25.00
AK Al Kaline Jsy 30.00 80.00
AO Akinori Otsuka Jsy 15.00 40.00
BB Bert Blyleven Jsy 10.00 25.00
BD Bobby Doerr Bat 10.00 25.00
BE Johnny Bench Jsy 30.00 60.00
BF Bob Feller Pants 15.00 40.00
BG Bob Gibson Pants 15.00 40.00
BPA Boog Powell Jsy 15.00 40.00
BPN Brad Penny Jsy 10.00 25.00
BR Brooks Robinson Jsy 30.00 60.00
BU B.J. Upton Jsy 10.00 25.00
CA Steve Carlton Jsy 10.00 25.00
CK Casey Kotchman Jsy 10.00 25.00
CR Cal Ripken Jsy 100.00 200.00
CY Carl Yastrzemski Jsy 40.00 80.00
CZ Carlos Zambrano Jsy 15.00 40.00
DG Dwight Gooden Pants 10.00 25.00
DJ Derek Jeter Jsy 125.00 200.00
DK Dave Kingman Bat 10.00 25.00
DL Derrek Lee Jsy 15.00 40.00
DMN Dale Murphy Jsy 15.00 40.00
DO David Ortiz Jsy 30.00 60.00
DW David Wright Jsy 40.00 80.00
EC Eric Chavez Jsy 10.00 25.00
FL Fred Lynn Bat 10.00 25.00
FR Frank Robinson Jsy 15.00 40.00

GB George Brett Jsy 50.00 100.00
GI Brian Giles Jsy 10.00 25.00
GK George Kell Bat 15.00 40.00
GN Graig Nettles Jsy 15.00 40.00
GR Ken Griffey Sr. Jsy 10.00 25.00
HB Hank Blalock Jsy 10.00 25.00
HK Harmon Killebrew Jsy 40.00 80.00
JB Jason Bay Jsy 10.00 25.00
JK Jim Kaat Jsy 10.00 25.00
JPA Jim Palmer Jsy 15.00 40.00
JPN Jake Peavy Jsy 15.00 40.00
JRA Jim Rice Jsy 10.00 25.00
JSN Jason Schmidt Jsy 10.00 25.00
KG Ken Griffey Jr. Jsy 75.00 150.00
KHA Kent Hrbek Jsy 30.00 60.00
KHN Keith Hernandez Bat 10.00 25.00
KL Khalil Greene Jsy 15.00 40.00
KW Kerry Wood Jsy 10.00 25.00
LN Laynce Nix Jsy 6.00 15.00
MA Don Mattingly Jsy 50.00 100.00
MC Miguel Cabrera Jsy 20.00 50.00
MG Marcus Giles Jsy 10.00 25.00
MK Mark Grace Jsy 15.00 40.00
ML Mike Lowell Jsy 10.00 25.00
MM Mark Mulder Jsy 10.00 25.00
MP Mark Prior Jsy 15.00 40.00
MS Mike Schmidt Jsy 40.00 80.00
MT Mark Teixeira Jsy 15.00 40.00
MW Maury Wills Jsy 10.00 25.00
NR Nolan Ryan Jsy 75.00 150.00
OC Orlando Cepeda Jsy 10.00 25.00
PM Paul Molitor Jsy 10.00 25.00
PN Phil Niekro Jsy 10.00 25.00
RCA Rod Carew Jsy 15.00 40.00
RH Rich Harden Jsy 10.00 25.00
RK Ralph Kiner Bat 15.00 40.00
RO Roy Oswalt Jsy 10.00 25.00
RP Rico Petrocelli Pants 10.00 25.00
RW Rickie Weeks Jsy 10.00 25.00
RY Robin Yount Jsy 30.00 60.00
SC Sean Casey Jsy 10.00 25.00
SL Sparky Lyle Pants 10.00 25.00
SP Scott Podsednik Jsy 15.00 40.00
ST Shingo Takatsu Jsy 10.00 25.00
SU Bruce Sutter Jsy 10.00 25.00
TG Tony Gwynn Jsy 40.00 80.00
TH Travis Hafner Jsy 10.00 25.00
TS Tom Seaver Jsy 30.00 80.00
VM Victor Martinez Jsy 10.00 25.00
WB Wade Boggs Jsy 20.00 50.00
WC Will Clark Jsy 30.00 60.00
WM Willie McCovey Jsy 30.00 60.00
YB Yogi Berra Pants 30.00 80.00

2005 Artifacts Autofacts

PRINT RUNS B/WN 15-699 COPIES PER
NO PRICING ON QTY OF 15
RAINBOW PRINT RUN 1 SERIAL #'d SET
NO RAINBOW PRICING DUE TO SCARCITY
OVERALL AUTO ODDS 1:10
EXCHANGE DEADLINE 04/11/08
AD Andre Dawson/25 10.00 25.00
AH Aubrey Huff/350 6.00 15.00
AO Akinori Otsuka/599 10.00 25.00
BF Bob Feller/25 15.00 40.00
BH Burt Hooton/599 4.00 10.00
BP Brad Penny/599 4.00 10.00
BR Brooks Robinson/25 20.00 50.00
BU B.J. Upton/599 6.00 15.00
CK Casey Kotchman/599 6.00 15.00
DG1 Dwight Gooden Mets/350 6.00 15.00
DG2 Dwight Gooden Yanks/350 6.00 15.00
DJ Derek Jeter/350 125.00 250.00
DK Dave Kingman/75 10.00 25.00
DM Dale Murphy/75 10.00 25.00
DW David Wright/599 12.50 30.00
EC Eric Chavez/25 10.00 25.00
EK Ed Kranepool/599 6.00 15.00
FL Fred Lynn/25 10.00 25.00
GI Marcus Giles/350 6.00 15.00
GN Graig Nettles/75 6.00 15.00
GR Khalil Greene/599 10.00 25.00
HB Hank Blalock/25 10.00 25.00
HO Ken Holtzman/599 4.00 10.00
HR Kent Hrbek/599 6.00 15.00
JA Jake Peavy/75 10.00 25.00
JB Jason Bay/599 6.00 15.00
JK1 Jim Kaat Cards/458 6.00 15.00
JK2 Jim Kaat Twins/458 6.00 15.00
JL Jim Lonborg/599 4.00 10.00
JP Jim Palmer/25 15.00 40.00
JR Ken Griffey Jr./699 40.00 80.00
JS Johan Santana/350 6.00 15.00
KG1 Ken Griffey Sr. Reds/699 6.00 15.00
KG2 Ken Griffey Sr. Yanks/699 6.00 15.00
KH1 Keith Hernandez Mets/350 6.00 15.00
KH2 Keith Hernandez Cards/350 6.00 15.00
LD1 Lenny Dykstra Mets/599 6.00 15.00
LD2 Lenny Dykstra Phils/599 6.00 15.00
LN Laynce Nix/599 4.00 10.00
LT Luis Tiant/75 6.00 15.00
MG Mark Grace/25 15.00 40.00
MI Miguel Cabrera/25 20.00 50.00
ML Mike Lowell/75 6.00 15.00
MT Mark Teixeira/25 15.00 40.00
MY Michael Young/599 6.00 15.00
OC Orlando Cepeda/25 15.00 40.00
OP Oliver Perez/350 4.00 10.00
PE Jim Perry/599 4.00 10.00
PN1 Phil Niekro Braves/75 6.00 15.00
PN2 Phil Niekro Yanks/75 6.00 15.00
PO Boog Powell/350 10.00 25.00
RC Rocky Colavito/75 40.00 80.00
RH Rich Harden/599 6.00 15.00
RI Jim Rice/25 10.00 25.00
RK Ralph Kiner/25 15.00 40.00
RO Roy Oswalt/350 6.00 15.00
RP Rico Petrocelli/599 6.00 15.00
RW Rickie Weeks/75 6.00 15.00
SF Sid Fernandez/599 6.00 15.00
SL1 Sparky Lyle Sox/599 6.00 15.00
SL2 Sparky Lyle Yanks/599 6.00 15.00
SP Scott Podsednik/75 10.00 25.00
ST Shingo Takatsu/599 6.00 15.00
SU Bruce Sutter/350 10.00 25.00
TH Travis Hafner/599 6.00 15.00
VM Victor Martinez/599 6.00 15.00

2005 Artifacts Dual Artifacts

OVERALL GAME-USED ODDS 1:3
STATED PRINT RUN 99 SERIAL #'d SETS
CLARK/MCCOVEY PRINT RUN 56 #'d CARDS
KILLEB/MCCOVEY PRINT RUN 44 #'d CARDS
AB B.Abreu Jsy/C.Beltran Jsy 4.00 10.00
AD A.Beltre Jsy/D.McPher Jsy 4.00 10.00
AG B.Abreu Jsy/K.Griffey Jr. Jsy 8.00 20.00
BB G.Brett Jsy/W.Boggs Jsy 10.00 25.00
BC A.Beltre Jsy/E.Chavez Jsy 4.00 10.00
BD B.Gibs Pants/Gooden Pants 8.00 20.00
BE B.Crosby Jsy/E.Chavez Jsy 4.00 10.00
BJ B.Rob Jsy/J.Palmer Jsy 8.00 20.00
BK J.Bay Jsy/R.Kiner Bat 8.00 20.00
BM B.Giles Jsy/M.Giles Jsy 4.00 10.00
BN H.Blalock Jsy/L.Nix Jsy 4.00 10.00
BP C.Beltran Jsy/C.Patterson Jsy 4.00 10.00
BR E.Banks Pants/F.Rob Jsy 8.00 20.00
BS B.Sheets Jsy/S.Podsed Jsy 4.00 10.00
BY H.Blalock Jsy/M.Young Jsy 4.00 10.00
CB J.Bay Jsy/B.Crosby Jsy 4.00 10.00
CC M.Cabrera Jsy/O.Cep Jsy 6.00 15.00
CG D.Gooden Pants/G.Cart Jsy 6.00 15.00
CH S.Casey Jsy/T.Hafner Jsy 4.00 10.00
CK H.Kill Jsy/R.Carew Jsy 8.00 20.00
CL M.Cabrera Jsy/M.Lowell Jsy 6.00 15.00
CM W.Clark Jsy/McCov Jsy/56 12.50 30.00
CN E.Chavez Jsy/G.Nettles Jsy 6.00 15.00
CO R.Clemens Jsy/R.Osw Jsy 6.00 15.00
CR B.Crosby Jsy/C.Ripken Jsy 15.00 40.00
DC A.Dawson Jsy/O.Cep Jsy 6.00 15.00
DK B.Doerr Bat/G.Kell Bat 10.00 25.00
FB C.Fisk Jsy/J.Bench Jsy 8.00 20.00
FW B.Feller Pants/K.Wood Jsy 8.00 20.00
GB B.Giles Jsy/J.Bay Jsy 4.00 10.00
GC K.Grif Jr. Jsy/S.Casey Jsy 8.00 20.00
GG K.Grif Sr. Jsy/K.Grif Jr. Jsy 10.00 25.00
GK K.Griffey Jr. Jsy/R.Kiner Bat 8.00 20.00
GL E.Gagne Jsy/S.Lyle Pants 6.00 15.00
GS D.Good Pants/T.Seav Jsy 8.00 20.00
HC B.Crosby Jsy/R.Harden Jsy 4.00 10.00
HG K.Hern Bat/M.Grace Jsy 8.00 20.00
HH A.Huff Jsy/T.Hafner Jsy 4.00 10.00
HM T.Hafner Jsy/V.Martinez Jsy 4.00 10.00
HU A.Huff Jsy/B.J.Upton Jsy 4.00 10.00
HW H.Kill Jsy/W.McCov Jsy/44 12.50 30.00
JG D.Jeter Jsy/K.Greene Jsy 12.50 30.00
JJ J.Mauer Jsy/J.Santana Jsy 6.00 15.00
JR J.Rice Jsy/R.Petro Pants 6.00 15.00
JW D.Jeter Jsy/M.Wills Jsy 12.50 30.00
JY J.Bench Jsy/Y.Berra Pants 12.50 30.00
KB J.Kaat Jsy/B.Blyleven Jsy 6.00 15.00
KC J.Kaat Jsy/S.Carlton Jsy 6.00 15.00
KD K.Hern Bat/D.Mattingly Jsy 10.00 25.00
KK A.Kaline Jsy/R.Kiner Bat 8.00 20.00
KM A.Kaline Jsy/D.Murphy Jsy 8.00 20.00
KN J.Kaat Jsy/P.Niekro Jsy 6.00 15.00
LC D.Lee Jsy/S.Casey Jsy 6.00 15.00
LG D.Lee Jsy/M.Grace Jsy 8.00 20.00
LP F.Lynn Bat/R.Petro Pants 6.00 15.00
LR F.Lynn Bat/J.Rice Jsy 6.00 15.00
MC D.Mattingly Jsy/W.Clark Jsy 10.00 25.00
MD B.Maz Jsy/B.Doerr Bat 8.00 20.00
MH M.Mulder Jsy/R.Harden Jsy 4.00 10.00
MK B.Maz Jsy/R.Kiner Bat 8.00 20.00
MM J.Mauer Jsy/V.Martinez Jsy 4.00 10.00
MS D.Murph Jsy/M.Schmidt Jsy 12.50 30.00
MW P.Molitor Jsy/R.Weeks Jsy 6.00 15.00
NL G.Nettles Jsy/S.Lyle Pants 6.00 15.00
NT L.Nix Jsy/M.Teixeira Jsy 8.00 20.00
NY L.Nix Jsy/M.Young Jsy 6.00 15.00
OF D.Ortiz Jsy/C.Fisk Jsy 8.00 20.00
OG A.Otsuka Jsy/K.Greene Jsy 6.00 15.00
OP A.Otsuka Jsy/J.Peavy Jsy 6.00 15.00
OT A.Otsuka Jsy/S.Takatsu Jsy 6.00 15.00
PD A.Dawson Jsy/C.Patt Jsy 6.00 15.00
PG B.Penny Jsy/E.Gagne Jsy 4.00 10.00
PH J.Peavy Jsy/R.Harden Jsy 4.00 10.00
PP B.Powell Jsy/J.Palmer Jsy 6.00 15.00
PR B.Powell Jsy/B.Rob Jsy 10.00 25.00
PS B.Penny Jsy/J.Schmidt Jsy 4.00 10.00
RB E.Banks Pants/C.Rip Jsy 20.00 50.00
RC N.Ryan Jsy/S.Carlton Jsy 12.50 30.00
RJ J.Reyes Jsy/R.Weeks Jsy 4.00 10.00
RP F.Rob Jsy/B.Powell Jsy 6.00 15.00
RR F.Rob Jsy/B.Robinson Jsy 10.00 25.00
RW D.Wright Jsy/S.Rolen Jsy 6.00 15.00
SB B.Blylev Jsy/J.Santana Jsy 8.00 20.00
SC J.Sant Jsy/R.Clemens Jsy 8.00 20.00
SF B.Sheets Jsy/B.Feller Pants 8.00 20.00
SG B.Sutter Jsy/E.Gagne Jsy 6.00 15.00
SM J.Schmidt Jsy/M.Mulder Jsy 4.00 10.00
SO B.Sheets Jsy/R.Oswalt Jsy 4.00 10.00
SP B.Sheets Jsy/B.Penny Jsy 4.00 10.00
TH M.Teixeira Jsy/T.Hafner Jsy 6.00 15.00
TL S.Takatsu Jsy/S.Lyle Pants 6.00 15.00
TY M.Teixeira Jsy/M.Young Jsy 6.00 15.00
UJ B.Upton Jsy/D.Jeter Jsy 12.50 30.00
WL D.Wright Jsy/M.Lowell Jsy 6.00 15.00
WR D.Wright Jsy/J.Reyes Jsy 8.00 20.00
YM R.Yount Jsy/P.Molitor Jsy 12.50 30.00
YP C.Yaz Jsy/R.Petro Pants 10.00 25.00
ZM C.Zamb Jsy/G.Maddux Jsy 8.00 20.00
ZP C.Zamb Jsy/M.Prior Jsy 6.00 15.00
ZW C.Zamb Jsy/K.Wood Jsy 4.00 10.00

2005 Artifacts Dual Artifacts Rainbow

*RAINBOW: .6X TO 1.5X p/r 99
*RAINBOW: .5X TO 1.2X p/r 44-56
OVERALL GAME-USED ODDS 1:3
STATED PRINT RUN 25 SERIAL #'d SETS

2005 Artifacts Dual Artifacts Bat

OVERALL GAME-USED ODDS 1:3
STATED PRINT RUN 25 SERIAL #'d SETS
BC J.Beckett/M.Cabrera 10.00 25.00
BW J.Beckett/K.Wood 6.00 15.00
DR C.Delgado/M.Ramirez 10.00 25.00
GC K.Griffey Jr./M.Cabrera 15.00 40.00
GS K.Griffey Jr./I.Suzuki 60.00 120.00
JP D.Jeter/M.Piazza 20.00 50.00
JR D.Jeter/M.Ramirez 20.00 50.00
RG M.Ramirez/V.Guerrero 10.00 25.00
RJ C.Ripken/D.Jeter 50.00 100.00
RT C.Ripken/M.Tejada 40.00 80.00
WP K.Wood/M.Prior 10.00 25.00

2005 Artifacts MLB Apparel

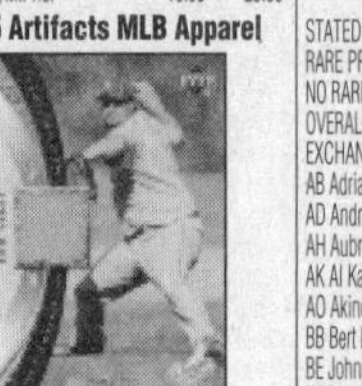

OVERALL GAME-USED ODDS 1:3
PRINT RUNS B/WN 100-325 COPIES PER
AB Adrian Beltre Jsy/325 3.00 8.00
AD Andre Dawson Jsy/325 3.00 8.00
AH Aubrey Huff Jsy/325 3.00 8.00
AK Al Kaline Jsy/325 5.00 12.00
AO Akinori Otsuka Jsy/325 3.00 8.00
BA Bobby Abreu Jsy/325 3.00 8.00
BB Bert Blyleven Jsy/150 3.00 8.00
BC Bobby Crosby Jsy/325 3.00 8.00
BE Johnny Bench Jsy/325 5.00 12.00
BF Bob Feller Pants/325 6.00 15.00
BG Bob Gibson Pants/325 4.00 10.00
BM Bill Mazeroski Jsy/100 5.00 12.00
BO Bret Boone Jsy/325 3.00 8.00
BP Boog Powell Jsy/325 3.00 8.00
BR Brooks Robinson Jsy/325 4.00 10.00
BS Ben Sheets Jsy/325 3.00 8.00
BU B.J. Upton Jsy/325 3.00 8.00
CA Steve Carlton Jsy/325 3.00 8.00
CB Carlos Beltran Jsy/325 3.00 8.00
CF Carlton Fisk R.Sox Jsy/175 4.00 10.00
CF1 Carlton Fisk W.Sox Jsy/175 4.00 10.00
CK Casey Kotchman Jsy/325 3.00 8.00
CL Roger Clemens Jsy/325 4.00 10.00
CP Corey Patterson Jsy/325 3.00 8.00
CR Cal Ripken Jsy/325 10.00 25.00
CY Carl Yastrzemski Jsy/325 6.00 15.00
CZ Carlos Zambrano Jsy/325 3.00 8.00
DG Dwight Gooden Pants/325 3.00 8.00
DJ Derek Jeter Jsy/325 8.00 20.00
DL Derrek Lee Jsy/325 3.00 8.00
DM Dale Murphy Jsy/150 4.00 10.00
DO David Ortiz Jsy/325 3.00 8.00
DW David Wright Jsy/325 6.00 15.00
EC Eric Chavez Jsy/325 3.00 8.00
EG Eric Gagne Jsy/325 3.00 8.00
FR Frank Robinson Jsy/325 3.00 8.00
GA Garret Anderson Jsy/325 3.00 8.00
GB George Brett Jsy/325 6.00 15.00
GC Gary Carter Jsy/325 3.00 8.00
GI Brian Giles Jsy/325 3.00 8.00
GN Graig Nettles Jsy/325 3.00 8.00
GR Ken Griffey Sr. Jsy/325 3.00 8.00
GS Marcus Giles Jsy/325 3.00 8.00
HB Hank Blalock Jsy/325 3.00 8.00
HK Harmon Killebrew Jsy/325 4.00 10.00
HU Tim Hudson Jsy/325 3.00 8.00
JB Jason Bay Jsy/325 3.00 8.00
JJ Jacque Jones Jsy/325 3.00 8.00
JK Jim Kaat Jsy/325 3.00 8.00
JM Joe Mauer Jsy/325 3.00 8.00
JP Jake Peavy Jsy/325 3.00 8.00
JR Jim Rice Jsy/325 3.00 8.00
JS Jason Schmidt Jsy/325 3.00 8.00
JV Jose Vidro Jsy/325 3.00 8.00
KG Ken Griffey Jr. Jsy/325 6.00 15.00
KH Kent Hrbek Jsy/325 3.00 8.00
KL Khalil Greene Jsy/325 3.00 8.00
KW Kerry Wood Jsy/325 3.00 8.00
LN Laynce Nix Jsy/325 3.00 8.00
MA Don Mattingly Jsy/325 12.50 30.00
MC Dallas McPherson Jsy/325 3.00 8.00
MI Miguel Cabrera Jsy/325 3.00 8.00
MK Mark Grace Jsy/175 4.00 10.00
ML Mike Lowell Jsy/325 3.00 8.00
MM Mark Mulder Jsy/325 3.00 8.00
MP Mark Prior Jsy/325 3.00 8.00
MS Mike Schmidt Jsy/325 6.00 15.00
MT Mark Teixeira Jsy/325 3.00 8.00
MW Maury Wills Jsy/325 3.00 8.00
MY Michael Young Jsy/325 3.00 8.00
NR Nolan Ryan Jsy/325 8.00 20.00
OC Orlando Cepeda Jsy/325 3.00 8.00
PA Jim Palmer Jsy/325 10.00 25.00
PE Brad Penny Jsy/325 3.00 8.00
PM Paul Molitor Jsy/325 3.00 8.00
PN Phil Niekro Jsy/325 3.00 8.00
RC Rod Carew Jsy/325 4.00 10.00
RE Jose Reyes Jsy/325 3.00 8.00
RH Rich Harden Jsy/325 3.00 8.00
RO Roy Oswalt Jsy/325 3.00 8.00
RP Rico Petrocelli Pants/325 3.00 8.00
RW Rickie Weeks Jsy/325 3.00 8.00
RY Robin Yount Jsy/325 5.00 12.00
SA Johan Santana Jsy/325 3.00 8.00
SC Sean Casey Jsy/325 3.00 8.00
SL Sparky Lyle Pants/325 3.00 8.00
SM John Smoltz Jsy/325 3.00 8.00
SP Scott Podsednik Jsy/325 3.00 8.00
SR Scott Rolen Jsy/325 3.00 8.00
ST Shingo Takatsu Jsy/325 3.00 8.00
SU Bruce Sutter Jsy/325 3.00 8.00
TG Tony Gwynn Jsy/325 5.00 12.00
TH Travis Hafner Jsy/325 3.00 8.00
TO Torii Hunter Jsy/325 3.00 8.00
TS Tom Seaver Jsy/300 4.00 10.00
VM Victor Martinez Jsy/325 3.00 8.00
WB Wade Boggs Jsy/325 4.00 10.00
WC Will Clark Jsy/100 4.00 10.00
WM Willie McCovey Jsy/325 4.00 10.00
YB Yogi Berra Pants/325 5.00 12.00

2005 Artifacts MLB Apparel Rainbow

*RAINBOW p/r 75-99: .5X TO 1.2X p/r 150-325
*RAINBOW p/r 75: .4X TO 1X p/r 100
*RAINBOW p/r 50: .5X TO 1.2X p/r 100
OVERALL GAME-USED ODDS 1:3
PRINT RUNS B/WN 50-99 COPIES PER

2005 Artifacts MLB Apparel Autographs

STATED PRINT RUN 30 SERIAL #'d SETS
RARE PRINT RUN 1 SERIAL #'d SET
NO RARE PRICING DUE TO SCARCITY
OVERALL AUTO ODDS 1:10
EXCHANGE DEADLINE 04/11/08
AB Adrian Beltre Jsy 10.00 25.00
AD Andre Dawson Jsy 15.00 40.00
AH Aubrey Huff Jsy 10.00 25.00
AK Al Kaline Jsy 30.00 80.00
AO Akinori Otsuka Jsy 10.00 25.00
BB Bert Blyleven Jsy 10.00 25.00
BE Johnny Bench Jsy 30.00 60.00
BF Bob Feller Pants 15.00 40.00
BG Bob Gibson Pants 15.00 40.00
BM Bill Mazeroski Jsy 20.00 50.00
BO Bret Boone Jsy 10.00 25.00
BP Boog Powell Jsy 15.00 40.00
BR Brooks Robinson Jsy 10.00 25.00
BU B.J. Upton Jsy 10.00 25.00
CA Steve Carlton Jsy 10.00 25.00
CF Carlton Fisk R.Sox Jsy 15.00 40.00
CF1 Carlton Fisk W.Sox Jsy 15.00 40.00
CK Casey Kotchman Jsy 10.00 25.00
CR Cal Ripken Jsy 75.00 200.00
CY Carl Yastrzemski Jsy 40.00 80.00
CZ Carlos Zambrano Jsy 15.00 40.00
DG Dwight Gooden Pants 10.00 25.00
DJ Derek Jeter Jsy 125.00 200.00
DL Derrek Lee Jsy 15.00 40.00
DM Dale Murphy Jsy 10.00 25.00
DO David Ortiz Jsy 30.00 60.00
DW David Wright Jsy 40.00 80.00
EG Eric Gagne Jsy 15.00 40.00
FR Frank Robinson Jsy 15.00 40.00
GA Garret Anderson Jsy 10.00 25.00
GB George Brett Jsy 50.00 100.00
GC Gary Carter Jsy 20.00 50.00
GI Brian Giles Jsy 10.00 25.00
GN Graig Nettles Jsy 15.00 40.00
GR Ken Griffey Sr. Jsy 10.00 25.00
GS Marcus Giles Jsy 10.00 25.00
HB Hank Blalock Jsy 10.00 25.00
HK Harmon Killebrew Jsy 40.00 80.00
HU Tim Hudson Jsy 15.00 40.00
JB Jason Bay Jsy 10.00 25.00
JJ Jacque Jones Jsy 10.00 25.00
JK Jim Kaat Jsy 10.00 25.00
JP Jake Peavy Jsy 15.00 40.00
JR Jim Rice Jsy 10.00 25.00
JS Jason Schmidt Jsy 10.00 25.00
JV Jose Vidro Jsy 10.00 25.00
KG Ken Griffey Jr. Jsy 75.00 150.00
KH Kent Hrbek Jsy 30.00 60.00
KL Khalil Greene Jsy 15.00 40.00
KW Kerry Wood Jsy 15.00 40.00
LN Laynce Nix Jsy 6.00 15.00
MA Don Mattingly Jsy 50.00 100.00
MI Miguel Cabrera Jsy 20.00 50.00
MK Mark Grace Jsy 15.00 40.00
ML Mike Lowell Jsy 10.00 25.00
MM Mark Mulder Jsy 10.00 25.00
MP Mark Prior Jsy 15.00 40.00
MS Mike Schmidt Jsy 25.00 60.00
MT Mark Teixeira Jsy 15.00 40.00
MW Maury Wills Jsy 10.00 25.00
NR Nolan Ryan Jsy 75.00 150.00
OC Orlando Cepeda Jsy 15.00 40.00
PA Jim Palmer Jsy 15.00 40.00
PE Brad Penny Jsy 10.00 25.00
PM Paul Molitor Jsy 10.00 25.00
PN Phil Niekro Jsy 10.00 25.00
RC Rod Carew Jsy 15.00 40.00
RH Rich Harden Jsy 10.00 25.00
RO Roy Oswalt Jsy 10.00 25.00
RP Rico Petrocelli Pants 10.00 25.00
RW Rickie Weeks Jsy 10.00 25.00
RY Robin Yount Jsy 30.00 60.00
SC Sean Casey Jsy 10.00 25.00
SL Sparky Lyle Pants 10.00 25.00
SP Scott Podsednik Jsy 15.00 40.00
ST Shingo Takatsu Jsy 10.00 25.00
SU Bruce Sutter Jsy 15.00 40.00
TG Tony Gwynn Jsy 40.00 80.00
TH Travis Hafner Jsy 10.00 25.00
TO Torii Hunter Jsy 10.00 25.00
TS Tom Seaver Jsy 30.00 80.00
VM Victor Martinez Jsy 10.00 25.00
WB Wade Boggs Jsy 20.00 50.00
WC Will Clark Jsy 30.00 60.00
WM Willie McCovey Jsy 30.00 80.00
YB Yogi Berra Pants 30.00 80.00

2005 Artifacts Patches

PRINT RUNS B/WN 3-50 COPIES PER
NO PRICING ON QTY OF 11 OR LESS
ACTIVE PRICES ARE 1 OR 2 COLOR PATCH
ADD 20% FOR ACTIVE 3-COLOR
ADD 50% OR MORE FOR ACTIVE 4-COLOR+
RETIRED PRICES ARE 1 COLOR PATCH
ADD 20% FOR RETIRED 2-COLOR+
ADD 50% OR MORE FOR RETIRED 3-COLOR+
SIG PATCH PRINT RUN B/WN 4-10 PER
NO SIG PATCH PRICING DUE TO SCARCITY
OVERALL GAME-USED ODDS 1:3
AB Adrian Beltre/50 6.00 15.00
AD Andre Dawson/50 6.00 15.00
AH Aubrey Huff/50 6.00 15.00
AO Akinori Otsuka/50 10.00 25.00
BA Bobby Abreu/50 6.00 15.00
BB Bert Blyleven/50 6.00 15.00
BC Bobby Crosby/50 6.00 15.00
BE Johnny Bench/50 10.00 25.00
BO Bret Boone/50 6.00 15.00
BP Boog Powell/50 10.00 25.00
BR Brooks Robinson/35 15.00 40.00
BS Ben Sheets/50 6.00 15.00
BU B.J. Upton/50 6.00 15.00
CA Steve Carlton/30 10.00 25.00
CB Carlos Beltran/50 6.00 15.00
CK Casey Kotchman/50 6.00 15.00
CL Roger Clemens/50 15.00 40.00
CP Corey Patterson/50 4.00 10.00
CR Cal Ripken/50 20.00 50.00
CY Carl Yastrzemski/50 15.00 40.00
CZ Carlos Zambrano/50 6.00 15.00
DG Dwight Gooden/50 6.00 15.00
DJ Derek Jeter/50 20.00 50.00
DL Derrek Lee/50 10.00 25.00
DM Dale Murphy/50 15.00 40.00
DO David Ortiz/50 10.00 25.00
DW David Wright/50 15.00 40.00
EC Eric Chavez/50 6.00 15.00
EG Eric Gagne/50 6.00 15.00
FR Frank Robinson/50 10.00 25.00
GA Garret Anderson/50 6.00 15.00
GB George Brett/50 15.00 40.00
GC Gary Carter/50 6.00 15.00
GI Brian Giles/50 6.00 15.00
GM Greg Maddux/50 15.00 40.00
GN Graig Nettles/50 10.00 25.00
GR Ken Griffey Sr./50 6.00 15.00
GS Marcus Giles/50 6.00 15.00
HB Hank Blalock/50 6.00 15.00
HK Harmon Killebrew/50 10.00 25.00
HU Tim Hudson/50 6.00 15.00
JJ Jacque Jones/50 6.00 15.00
JK Jim Kaat/50 6.00 15.00
JM Joe Mauer/50 6.00 15.00
JP Jake Peavy/50 6.00 15.00
JS Jason Schmidt/50 10.00 25.00
JV Jose Vidro/50 6.00 15.00
KG Ken Griffey Jr./50 10.00 25.00
KH Kent Hrbek/50 10.00 25.00
KL Khalil Greene/50 10.00 25.00
KW Kerry Wood/50 6.00 15.00
LN Laynce Nix/50 4.00 10.00
MA Don Mattingly/50 15.00 40.00
MC Dallas McPherson/50 4.00 10.00
MI Miguel Cabrera/50 10.00 25.00
MK Mark Grace/50 6.00 15.00
ML Mike Lowell/50 6.00 15.00
MM Mark Mulder/50 6.00 15.00
MP Mark Prior/50 6.00 15.00
MS Mike Schmidt/50 15.00 40.00
MT Mark Teixeira/50 6.00 15.00
MW Maury Wills/20 10.00 25.00
MY Michael Young/50 6.00 15.00
NR Nolan Ryan/50 20.00 50.00
PA Jim Palmer/50 6.00 15.00
PE Brad Penny/50 6.00 15.00
PN Phil Niekro/50 6.00 15.00
RC Rod Carew/50 10.00 25.00
RE Jose Reyes/50 6.00 15.00
RH Rich Harden/50 6.00 15.00
RJ Randy Johnson/50 10.00 25.00
RO Roy Oswalt/50 6.00 15.00
RW Rickie Weeks/50 6.00 15.00
RY Robin Yount/50 10.00 25.00
SA Johan Santana/50 10.00 25.00
SC Sean Casey/50 6.00 15.00
SM John Smoltz/50 10.00 25.00
SP Scott Podsednik/50 6.00 15.00
SR Scott Rolen/50 6.00 15.00
ST Shingo Takatsu/50 6.00 15.00
SU Bruce Sutter/50 6.00 15.00
TG Tony Gwynn/50 10.00 25.00
TH Travis Hafner/50 6.00 15.00
TO Torii Hunter/50 6.00 15.00
VM Victor Martinez/50 6.00 15.00
WB Wade Boggs/50 10.00 25.00
WC Will Clark/20 15.00 40.00
WM Willie McCovey/50 10.00 25.00

2006 Artifacts

COMPLETE SET (100) 15.00 40.00
1 Luis Gonzalez .20 .50
2 Conor Jackson (RC) .50 1.25
3 Joey Devine RC .30 .75
4 Andruw Jones .20 .50
5 Chipper Jones .50 1.25
6 John Smoltz .50 1.25
7 Jeff Francoeur .50 1.25
8 Brian Roberts .20 .50
9 Miguel Tejada .30 .75
10 Nick Markakis (RC) .60 1.50
11 Curt Schilling .30 .75
12 David Ortiz .50 1.25
13 Johnny Damon .30 .75
14 Manny Ramirez .50 1.25
15 Jonathan Papelbon (RC) 1.50 4.00
16 Aramis Ramirez .20 .50
17 Carlos Zambrano .30 .75
18 Derrek Lee .20 .50
19 Greg Maddux .60 1.50
20 Mark Prior .30 .75
21 Mark Buehrle .30 .75
22 Paul Konerko .30 .75
23 Adam Dunn .30 .75
24 Ken Griffey Jr. 1.00 2.50
25 Travis Hafner .20 .50
26 Victor Martinez .30 .75
27 Todd Helton .30 .75
28 Ivan Rodriguez .30 .75
29 Jeremy Bonderman .20 .50
30 Jeremy Hermida (RC) .30 .75
31 Carlos Delgado .20 .50
32 Dontrelle Willis .20 .50
33 Josh Beckett .20 .50
34 Miguel Cabrera .50 1.25
35 Craig Biggio .30 .75
36 Lance Berkman .30 .75
37 Roger Clemens .60 1.50
38 Roy Oswalt .30 .75
39 Josh Willingham (RC) .50 1.25
40 Hanley Ramirez (RC) .50 1.25
41 Prince Fielder (RC) 1.50 4.00
42 Zack Greinke .50 1.25
43 Francisco Rodriguez .30 .75
44 Vladimir Guerrero .30 .75
45 Tim Hamulack (RC) .30 .75
46 Jeff Kent .20 .50
47 Ben Sheets .20 .50
48 Rickie Weeks .20 .50
49 Francisco Liriano (RC) .75 2.00
50 Joe Mauer .30 .75
51 Johan Santana .30 .75
52 Justin Morneau .30 .75
53 Torii Hunter .20 .50
54 Carlos Beltran .30 .75
55 David Wright .40 1.00
56 Jose Reyes .30 .75
57 Mike Piazza .50 1.25
58 Pedro Martinez .30 .75
59 Alex Rodriguez .60 1.50
60 Derek Jeter 1.25 3.00
61 Hideki Matsui .50 1.25
62 Randy Johnson .50 1.25
63 Justin Verlander (RC) 2.50 6.00
64 Bobby Crosby .20 .50
65 Eric Chavez .20 .50
66 Brian Anderson (RC) .30 .75
67 Bobby Abreu .20 .50
68 Pat Burrell .20 .50
69 Jason Bay .20 .50
70 Oliver Perez .20 .50
71 Chuck James (RC) .30 .75
72 Brian Giles .20 .50
73 Jake Peavy .20 .50
74 Khalil Greene .20 .50
75 Jason Schmidt .20 .50
76 Kenji Johjima RC .75 2.00
77 Jeremy Accardo RC .30 .75
78 Adrian Beltre .50 1.25
79 Ichiro Suzuki .60 1.50
80 Jeff Harris RC .30 .75
81 Felix Hernandez .30 .75
82 Albert Pujols .60 1.50
83 Chris Carpenter .30 .75
84 Jim Edmonds .30 .75
85 Scott Rolen .30 .75
86 Mike Jacobs (RC) .30 .75
87 Carl Crawford .30 .75
88 Anderson Hernandez (RC) .30 .75
89 Scott Kazmir .30 .75
90 Josh Rupe (RC) .30 .75
91 Scott Feldman RC .30 .75
92 Alfonso Soriano .30 .75
93 Hank Blalock .20 .50
94 Mark Teixeira .30 .75
95 Michael Young .20 .50
96 Roy Halladay .30 .75
97 Vernon Wells .20 .50
98 Jason Bergmann RC .30 .75
99 Ryan Zimmerman (RC) 1.00 2.50
100 Jose Vidro .20 .50

2006 Artifacts AL/NL Artifacts Blue

OVERALL GU ODDS 3:10
PRINT RUNS B/WN 200-325 COPIES PER
ADN Adam Dunn Jsy/250 5.00 12.00
AHN Aaron Harang Jsy/325 3.00 8.00
APN Albert Pujols Jsy/250 8.00 20.00
ASN Alfonso Soriano Jsy/325 5.00 12.00
BBA Ben Broussard Jsy/325 3.00 8.00
BHN Bill Hall Jsy/235 3.00 8.00
BLA Joe Blanton Jsy/325 3.00 8.00
BLN Brad Lidge Jsy/325 3.00 8.00
BMA B.McCarthy Jsy/325 3.00 8.00
BMN Brian McCann Jsy/325 4.00 10.00
CAN Chris Capuano Jsy/325 3.00 8.00
CBN Chris Burke Jsy/325 3.00 8.00
CCA Carl Crawford Jsy/325 5.00 12.00
CCN Chris Carpenter Jsy/325 4.00 10.00
CHN Chad Cordero Jsy/325 3.00 8.00
CJN Chipper Jones Jsy/325 4.00 10.00
CLA Cliff Lee Jsy/325 5.00 12.00
CLN Clint Barmes Jsy/325 3.00 8.00
COA Coco Crisp Jsy/325 3.00 8.00
CRA Joe Crede Jsy/325 3.00 8.00
CSA Chris Shelton Jsy/325 3.00 8.00
CUN Chase Utley Jsy/325 6.00 15.00
DAA Dan Johnson Jsy/325 3.00 8.00
DHA Dan Haren Jsy/325 3.00 8.00
DJA Derek Jeter Jsy/325 10.00 25.00
DLN Derrek Lee Jsy/325 3.00 8.00
DOA David Ortiz Jsy/325 4.00 10.00
DWN Dontrelle Willis Jsy/325 3.00 8.00
DYA Dmitri Young Jsy/325 3.00 8.00
ECA Eric Chavez Jsy/325 3.00 8.00
EGN Eric Gagne Jsy/325 3.00 8.00
ESA Ervin Santana Jsy/325 3.00 8.00
FHA Felix Hernandez Jsy/325 4.00 10.00
FLN Felipe Lopez Jsy/325 3.00 8.00
GAA Jon Garland Jsy/325 3.00 8.00
GAN Garrett Atkins Jsy/325 3.00 8.00
GCA Gustavo Chacin Jsy/325 3.00 8.00
GSA Grady Sizemore Jsy/325 4.00 10.00
HBA Hank Blalock Jsy/325 3.00 8.00
HSA Huston Street Jsy/325 3.00 8.00
JAN Jason Bay Jsy/325 3.00 8.00
JBA J.Bonderman Jsy/325 3.00 8.00
JCA Jorge Cantu Jsy/325 3.00 8.00
JFN Jeff Francoeur Jsy/325 6.00 15.00
JGA Jonny Gomes Jsy/325 3.00 8.00
JMA Joe Mauer Jsy/325 4.00 10.00
JNA Joe Nathan Jsy/325 3.00 8.00
JPA Joel Pineiro Jsy/325 3.00 8.00
JPN Jake Peavy Jsy/325 3.00 8.00
JSN John Smoltz Jsy/250 3.00 8.00
JUA Justin Morneau Jsy/325 5.00 12.00
JVA Jason Varitek Jsy/325 4.00 10.00
JWA Jake Westbrook Jsy/325 3.00 8.00
JWN Jack Wilson Jsy/200 3.00 8.00
KGN Ken Griffey Jr. Jsy/325 6.00 15.00
LEN Carlos Lee Jsy/325 3.00 8.00
MBA Mark Buehrle Jsy/325 5.00 12.00
MCN Miguel Cabrera Jsy/325 4.00 10.00
MEN Morgan Ensberg Jsy/325 3.00 8.00
MGN Marcus Giles Jsy/325 3.00 8.00
MHN Matt Holliday Jsy/325 4.00 10.00
MLA Mark Loretta Jsy/325 3.00 8.00
MTA Miguel Tejada Jsy/325 5.00 12.00
MYA Michael Young Jsy/325 3.00 8.00
NJN Nick Johnson Jsy/325 3.00 8.00
NLN Noah Lowry Jsy/325 3.00 8.00
NSA Nick Swisher Jsy/325 5.00 12.00
PEA Jhonny Peralta Jsy/325 3.00 8.00
PFN Prince Fielder Jsy/325 4.00 10.00
PMN Pedro Martinez Jsy/325 4.00 10.00
RBA Rocco Baldelli Jsy/325 3.00 8.00
RCN Ryan Church Jsy/325 3.00 8.00
RHN R.Hernandez Jsy/325 3.00 8.00
RJA R.Johnson Pants/235 4.00 10.00
RON Roy Oswalt Jsy/325 5.00 12.00
RWN Rickie Weeks Jsy/325 3.00 8.00
RYN Ryan Howard Jsy/325 10.00 25.00
RZN R.Zimmerman Jsy/325 4.00 10.00
SBA Scott Baker Jsy/325 3.00 8.00
SPA Scott Podsednik Jsy/325 3.00 8.00
THA Travis Hafner Jsy/325 3.00 8.00
TIA Tadahito Iguchi Jsy/325 3.00 8.00
TRN Trevor Hoffman Jsy/325 5.00 12.00
VGA V.Guerrero Jsy/325 4.00 10.00
VMA Victor Martinez Jsy/325 5.00 12.00
WRN David Wright Jsy/325 6.00 15.00
YMN Yadier Molina Jsy/325 4.00 10.00
ZDN Zach Duke Jsy/325 3.00 8.00

2006 Artifacts AL/NL Artifacts Green

*GREEN p/r 150: .5X TO 1.2X BLUE p/r 325
*GRN p/r 75-85: .5X TO 1.2X BLUEp/r200-250
*GRNp/r50-55: .6X TO 1.5X BLUEp/r200-250
OVERALL GU ODDS 3:10
PRINT RUNS B/WN 50-150 COPIES PER
FGA Freddy Garcia Jsy/75 5.00 12.00
JDA Jermaine Dye Jsy/150 4.00 10.00
JSN John Smoltz Jsy/55 10.00 25.00

2006 Artifacts AL/NL Artifacts Red

*RED p/r 150-250: .5X TO 1.2X BLUE p/r 325
*REDp/r150-250: .4X TO 1X BLUEp/r200-250
*REDp/r100-125:.5X TO 1.2XBLUEp/r200-250
OVERALL GU ODDS 3:10
PRINT RUNS B/WN 100-250 COPIES PER
FGA Freddy Garcia Jsy/175 4.00 10.00

2006 Artifacts Auto-Facts Signatures

OVERALL AU ODDS 1:10
PRINT RUNS B/WN 5-800 COPIES PER
NO DUFFY PRICING DUE TO SCARCITY
AD Andre Dawson/300 6.00 15.00
AH Aaron Harang/800 4.00 10.00
AJ Andruw Jones/150 10.00 25.00
AM Aaron Miles/494 4.00 10.00
AR Aaron Rowand/520 6.00 15.00
AV Andy Van Slyke/800 5.00 12.00
BE Jason Bergmann/800 4.00 10.00
BI Bill Madlock/300 4.00 10.00
BL Barry Larkin/300 15.00 40.00
BO Bo Jackson/250 20.00 50.00
BR Brian Roberts/200 6.00 15.00
BY Clete Boyer/484 6.00 15.00
CA Chris Capuano/800 6.00 15.00
CB Clint Barmes/800 4.00 10.00
CC Chris Chambliss/400 4.00 10.00
CD Chris Demaria/800 4.00 10.00
CH Chris Carpenter/51 15.00 40.00
CJ Conor Jackson/800 6.00 15.00
CK Jack Clark/800 4.00 10.00
CL Cliff Lee/800 5.00 12.00
CO Coco Crisp/800 5.00 12.00
CP Jose Capellan/800 4.00 10.00
CR Cal Ripken/100 60.00 120.00
CS Chris Shelton/750 6.00 15.00
CU Chase Utley/200 12.50 30.00
CY Chris Young/700 10.00 25.00
CZ Carlos Zambrano/300 10.00 25.00
DA Chris Denorfia/659 4.00 10.00
DE Joey Devine/350 4.00 10.00
DH Dan Haren/800 4.00 10.00
DJ Derek Jeter/100 75.00 150.00
DL Derrek Lee/300 4.00 10.00
DW David Wright/300 6.00 15.00
DY Dmitri Young/300 4.00 10.00
ED Eric Davis/487 12.50 30.00
FH Felix Hernandez/300 15.00 40.00
GA Garrett Atkins/800 4.00 10.00
GB George Bell/715 6.00 15.00
GC Gustavo Chacin/800 4.00 10.00
GF George Foster/300 4.00 10.00
GG Goose Gossage/300 6.00 15.00
GN Graig Nettles/300 6.00 15.00
GO Jonny Gomes/700 4.00 10.00
HR Hanley Ramirez/800 5.00 12.00
HS Huston Street/500 6.00 15.00
IK Ian Kinsler/800 5.00 12.00
JA Jeremy Accardo/800 4.00 10.00
JB Jason Bay/200 6.00 15.00
JC Joe Carter/400 8.00 20.00
JD Jermaine Dye/652 6.00 15.00
JE Jeff Harris/800 4.00 10.00
JK Jason Kubel/400 4.00 10.00
JL Jason Lane/800 4.00 10.00
JM Joe Mauer/400 12.00 30.00
JN Joe Nathan/800 6.00 15.00
JP Jhonny Peralta/700 4.00 10.00
JR Jim Rice/200 6.00 15.00
JS Johan Santana/150 10.00 25.00
JV Justin Verlander/700 10.00 25.00
JW Jake Westbrook/650 4.00 10.00
KG Ken Griffey Jr./800 30.00 80.00
KH Kent Hrbek/239 8.00 20.00
LA Luis Aparicio/250 6.00 15.00
LD Lenny Dykstra/412 4.00 10.00
MA Matt Cain/700 8.00 20.00
MC Miguel Cabrera/250 30.00 60.00
MG Marcus Giles/350 6.00 15.00
MO Magglio Ordonez/437 6.00 15.00
MW Maury Wills/150 6.00 15.00
MY Michael Young/600 8.00 20.00
NS Nick Swisher/700 6.00 15.00
PF Prince Fielder/200 10.00 25.00
PM Pedro Martinez/100 30.00 80.00
RC Ryan Church/800 4.00 10.00
RE Chris Resop/800 4.00 10.00
RJ Reggie Jackson/200 20.00 50.00
RW Rickie Weeks/91 6.00 15.00
RZ Ryan Zimmerman/800 6.00 15.00
SF Scott Feldman/800 4.00 10.00
SG Steve Garvey/300 6.00 15.00
TH Travis Hafner/400 6.00 15.00
TI Tadahito Iguchi/700 6.00 15.00
TM Tim Hamulack/742 4.00 10.00
TO Tony Oliva/300 10.00 25.00
TP Tony Perez/251 6.00 15.00
WI Dontrelle Willis/50 10.00 25.00
WT Willy Taveras/500 4.00 10.00
YM Yadier Molina/800 40.00 80.00

2006 Artifacts Awesome Artifacts Jumbos

OVERALL GU ODDS 3:10
PRINT RUNS B/WN 21-45 COPIES PER
NO PRICING ON QTY OF 25 OR LESS
AD Adam Dunn Jsy/45 6.00 15.00
AH Aaron Harang Jsy/45 6.00 15.00
AP Albert Pujols Jsy/45 15.00 40.00
AR Aaron Rowand Jsy/45 6.00 15.00
AS Alfonso Soriano Jsy/45 6.00 15.00
AV Andy Van Slyke Jsy/45 10.00 25.00
BA Jeff Bagwell Jsy/45 10.00 25.00
BH Bill Hall Jsy/45 6.00 15.00
BL Joe Blanton Jsy/45 6.00 15.00
BM Brandon McCarthy Jsy/45 6.00 15.00
BO Bo Jackson Jsy/45 15.00 40.00
BR Brian McCann Jsy/45 10.00 25.00
BU Chris Burke Jsy/45 6.00 15.00
CA Matt Cain Jsy/45 6.00 15.00
CB Clint Barmes Jsy/45 6.00 15.00
CC Carl Crawford Jsy/45 6.00 15.00
CF Carlton Fisk Jsy/45 10.00 25.00
CH Chris Carpenter Jsy/45 6.00 15.00
CJ Chipper Jones Jsy/45 15.00 40.00
CL Cliff Lee Jsy/45 6.00 15.00
CO Conor Jackson Jsy/45 8.00 20.00
CR Cal Ripken Jsy/45 12.00 30.00
CS Chris Shelton Jsy/45 6.00 15.00
CU Chase Utley Jsy/45 6.00 40.00
DA Dan Johnson Jsy/45 6.00 15.00
DE Derrek Lee Jsy/45 6.00 15.00
DH Dan Haren Jsy/45 6.00 15.00
DJ Derek Jeter Jsy/45 40.00 80.00
DO David Ortiz Jsy/45 10.00 25.00
DP Dave Parker Jsy/45 6.00 15.00
DW David Wells Jsy/45 6.00 15.00
EC Eric Chavez Jsy/45 6.00 15.00
EG Eric Gagne Jsy/45 6.00 15.00
EM Eddie Mathews Pants/45 10.00 25.00
ES Ervin Santana Jsy/45 6.00 15.00
FH Felix Hernandez Jsy/45 10.00 25.00
FT Frank Thomas Jsy/45 10.00 25.00
GA Jon Garland Jsy/45 6.00 15.00
GC Gustavo Chacin Jsy/45 6.00 15.00
GF Gavin Floyd Jsy/45 6.00 15.00
GP Gaylord Perry Jsy/45 6.00 15.00
GS Grady Sizemore Jsy/45 10.00 25.00
HA Hank Blalock Jsy/45 6.00 15.00
HB Harold Baines Jsy/45 6.00 15.00
HS Huston Street Jsy/45 6.00 15.00
IR Ivan Rodriguez Jsy/45 10.00 25.00
JA Jason Schmidt Jsy/45 6.00 15.00
JB Jason Bay Jsy/45 6.00 15.00
JE Jim Edmonds Jsy/45 6.00 15.00
JF Jeff Francoeur Jsy/45 15.00 40.00
JG Jonny Gomes Jsy/45 6.00 15.00
JL Jason Lane Jsy/45 6.00 15.00
JO Joel Pineiro Jsy/45 6.00 15.00
JP Jake Peavy Jsy/45 6.00 15.00
JS John Smoltz Jsy/45 15.00 40.00
JU Justin Morneau Jsy/45 6.00 15.00
JV Jason Varitek Jsy/45 10.00 25.00
JW Jack Wilson Jsy/45 6.00 15.00
KG Ken Griffey Jr. Jsy/45 15.00 40.00
MB Mark Buehrle Jsy/45 6.00 15.00
MC Miguel Cabrera Jsy/45 10.00 25.00
ME Morgan Ensberg Jsy/45 6.00 15.00
MI Miguel Tejada Jsy/45 6.00 15.00
MP Mark Prior Jsy/45 6.00 15.00
MR Manny Ramirez Jsy/45 10.00 25.00
NJ Nick Johnson Jsy/45 6.00 15.00
NL Noah Lowry Jsy/45 10.00 25.00
NS Nick Swisher Jsy/45 6.00 15.00
PE Jhonny Peralta Jsy/45 6.00 15.00
PF Prince Fielder Jsy/45 10.00 25.00
PM Pedro Martinez Jsy/45 10.00 25.00
RA Randy Johnson Pants/45 12.00 30.00
RB Rocco Baldelli Jsy/45 6.00 15.00
RO Roy Oswalt Jsy/45 6.00 15.00
RS Ron Santo Jsy/45 10.00 25.00
RW Rickie Weeks Jsy/45 6.00 15.00
RY Ryan Howard Jsy/45 20.00 50.00
RZ Ryan Zimmerman Jsy/45 10.00 25.00
SB Scott Baker Jsy/45 6.00 15.00
SG Steve Garvey Pants/45 6.00 15.00
SP Satchel Paige Pants/45 75.00 150.00
TH Todd Helton Jsy/45 10.00 25.00
TR Trevor Hoffman Jsy/45 6.00 15.00
VG Vladimir Guerrero Jsy/45 10.00 25.00
WC Will Clark Pants/45 10.00 25.00
WE Jake Westbrook Jsy/45 6.00 15.00
WI Dontrelle Willis Jsy/45 6.00 15.00
WR David Wright Jsy/45 15.00 40.00
YM Yadier Molina Jsy/45 10.00 25.00
ZD Zach Duke Jsy/45 6.00 15.00

2006 Artifacts MLB Game-Used Apparel

OVERALL GU ODDS 3:10
STATED PRINT RUN 325 SERIAL #'d SETS
M.SCHMIDT PRINT RUN 85 #'d CARDS
AH Aaron Harang Jsy/325 3.00 8.00
AR Aaron Rowand Jsy/325 3.00 8.00
AT Garrett Atkins Jsy/325 3.00 8.00
AV Andy Van Slyke Jsy/325 3.00 8.00
BA Clint Barmes Jsy/325 3.00 8.00
BB Ben Broussard Jsy/325 3.00 8.00
BC Brian McCann Jsy/325 4.00 10.00
BI Bill Madlock Jsy/325 3.00 8.00
BL Brad Lidge Jsy/325 3.00 8.00
BM Brandon McCarthy Jsy/325 3.00 8.00
BO Bo Jackson Jsy/325 4.00 10.00
BP Boog Powell Jsy/325 3.00 8.00
BR Brian Roberts Jsy/325 3.00 8.00
BY Jason Bay Jsy/325 3.00 8.00
CA Carl Crawford Jsy/325 3.00 8.00
CB Chris Burke Jsy/325 3.00 8.00
CD Chad Cordero Jsy/325 3.00 8.00
CF Carlton Fisk Jsy/325 4.00 10.00
CH Chris Carpenter Jsy/325 4.00 10.00
CJ Conor Jackson Jsy/325 4.00 10.00
CK Casey Kotchman Jsy/325 3.00 8.00
CL Cliff Lee Jsy/325 3.00 8.00
CO Coco Crisp Jsy/325 3.00 8.00
CR Cal Ripken Jsy/325 10.00 25.00
CS Chris Capuano Jsy/325 3.00 8.00
CU Chase Utley Jsy/325 6.00 15.00
CY Carl Yastrzemski Pants/325 6.00 15.00
DA Dan Johnson Jsy/325 3.00 8.00
DH Dan Haren Jsy/325 3.00 8.00
DJ Derek Jeter Jsy/325 10.00 25.00
DL Derrek Lee Jsy/325 3.00 8.00
DO Don Larsen Pants/325 4.00 10.00
DW Dontrelle Willis Jsy/325 3.00 8.00
DY Dmitri Young Jsy/325 3.00 8.00
ES Ervin Santana Jsy/325 3.00 8.00
FH Felix Hernandez Jsy/325 4.00 10.00
FL Felipe Lopez Jsy/325 3.00 8.00
FM Fred McGriff Jsy/325 4.00 10.00
GA Jon Garland Jsy/325 3.00 8.00
GC Gustavo Chacin Jsy/325 3.00 8.00
GF Gavin Floyd Jsy/325 3.00 8.00
GG Goose Gossage Jsy/325 3.00 8.00
GN Graig Nettles Jsy/325 3.00 8.00
GO Adrian Gonzalez Jsy/325 3.00 8.00
GP Gaylord Perry Jsy/325 3.00 8.00
GS Grady Sizemore Jsy/325 4.00 10.00
HB Harold Baines Jsy/325 3.00 8.00
HO Ryan Howard Jsy/325 10.00 25.00
HS Huston Street Jsy/325 3.00 8.00
JE Jeremy Bonderman Jsy/325 3.00 8.00
JG Jonny Gomes Jsy/325 3.00 8.00
JH Jeremy Hermida Jsy/325 4.00 10.00
JK John Kruk Jsy/325 3.00 8.00
JL Jason Lane Jsy/325 3.00 8.00
JM Joe Mauer Jsy/325 4.00 10.00
JN Joe Nathan Jsy/325 3.00 8.00
JO Joe Blanton Jsy/325 3.00 8.00
JP Jhonny Peralta Jsy/325 3.00 8.00
JR Jose Reyes Jsy/325 3.00 8.00
JU Jorge Cantu Jsy/325 3.00 8.00
JW Jake Westbrook Jsy/325 3.00 8.00
JY Jeremy Reed Jsy/325 3.00 8.00
KE Jason Kendall Jsy/325 3.00 8.00
KG Ken Griffey Jr. Jsy/325 6.00 15.00
LE Carlos Lee Jsy/325 3.00 8.00
MA Matt Cain Jsy/325 3.00 8.00
MC Miguel Cabrera Jsy/325 4.00 10.00
MG Marcus Giles Jsy/325 3.00 8.00
MH Matt Holliday Jsy/325 4.00 10.00
ML Mark Loretta Jsy/325 3.00 8.00
MO Justin Morneau Jsy/325 3.00 8.00
MS Mike Schmidt Jsy/85 10.00 25.00
MY Michael Young Jsy/325 3.00 8.00
NL Noah Lowry Jsy/325 3.00 8.00
NS Nick Swisher Jsy/325 3.00 8.00
OR Magglio Ordonez Jsy/325 3.00 8.00
PE Jake Peavy Jsy/325 3.00 8.00
PF Prince Fielder Jsy/325 5.00 12.00
PI Joel Pineiro Jsy/325 3.00 8.00
RB Rocco Baldelli Jsy/325 3.00 8.00
RC Ryan Church Jsy/325 3.00 8.00
RH Ramon Hernandez Jsy/325 3.00 8.00
RO Roy Oswalt Jsy/325 5.00 12.00
RS Ron Santo Jsy/325 6.00 15.00
RW Rickie Weeks Jsy/325 3.00 8.00
RZ Ryan Zimmerman Jsy/325 4.00 10.00
SB Scott Baker Jsy/325 3.00 8.00
SG Steve Garvey Pants/325 3.00 8.00
SH Chris Shelton Jsy/325 3.00 8.00
SK Scott Kazmir Jsy/325 3.00 8.00
SP Scott Podsednik Jsy/325 3.00 8.00
ST So Taguchi Jsy/325 3.00 8.00
TI Tadahito Iguchi Jsy/325 3.00 8.00
WC Will Clark Pants/325 4.00 10.00
WR David Wright Jsy/325 6.00 15.00
YB Yuniesky Betancourt Jsy/325 3.00 8.00
YM Yadier Molina Jsy/325 6.00 15.00

2006 Artifacts MLB Game-Used Apparel Gold Limited

*GOLD p/r 150: .5X TO 1.2X BASIC p/r 325
*GOLD p/r 30: .6X TO 1.5X BASIC p/r 85
OVERALL GU ODDS 3:10
STATED PRINT RUN 150 SERIAL #'d SETS
M.SCHMIDT PRINT RUN 30 #'d SETS
JD Jermaine Dye Jsy/150 4.00 10.00

2006 Artifacts MLB Game-Used Apparel Silver Limited

*SILVER p/r 250: .5X TO 1.2X BASIC p/r 325
*SILVER p/r 50: .5X TO 1.2X BASIC p/r 85
OVERALL GU ODDS 3:10
STATED PRINT RUN 250 SERIAL #'d SETS
M.SCHMIDT PRINT RUN 50 #'d SETS

2006 Artifacts MLB Game-Used Apparel Autographs

OVERALL AU ODDS 1:10
STATED PRINT RUN 30 SERIAL #'d SETS
R.SANTO PRINT RUN 28 SERIAL #'d CARDS
HOWARD PRINT RUN 23 SERIAL #'d CARDS
NO HOWARD PRICING DUE TO SCARCITY
AH Aaron Harang Jsy/30 6.00 15.00
AR Aaron Rowand Jsy/30 10.00 25.00
AT Garrett Atkins Jsy/30 6.00 15.00
AV Andy Van Slyke Jsy/30 12.50 30.00
BA Clint Barmes Jsy/30 6.00 15.00
BB Ben Broussard Jsy/30 6.00 15.00
BI Bill Madlock Jsy/30 6.00 15.00
BL Brad Lidge Jsy/30 10.00 25.00
BM B.McCarthy Jsy/30 6.00 15.00
BO Bo Jackson Jsy/30 60.00 120.00
BP Boog Powell Jsy/30 10.00 25.00
BY Jason Bay Jsy/30 10.00 25.00
CA Carl Crawford Jsy/30 10.00 25.00
CB Chris Burke Jsy/30 6.00 15.00
CD Chad Cordero Jsy/30 6.00 15.00
CF Carlton Fisk Jsy/30 15.00 40.00
CH Chris Carpenter Jsy/30 15.00 40.00
CJ Conor Jackson Jsy/30 15.00 40.00
CK Casey Kotchman Jsy/30 10.00 25.00
CL Cliff Lee Jsy/30 10.00 25.00
CO Coco Crisp Jsy/30 15.00 40.00
CR Cal Ripken Jsy/30 50.00 120.00
CS Chris Capuano Jsy/30 10.00 25.00
CU Chase Utley Jsy/30 40.00 80.00
CY C.Yastrzemski Pants/30 40.00 80.00
DA Dan Johnson Jsy/30 6.00 15.00
DH Dan Haren Jsy/30 6.00 15.00
DJ Derek Jeter Jsy/30 125.00 200.00
DL Derrek Lee Jsy/30 15.00 40.00
DO Don Larsen Pants/30 10.00 25.00
DW Dontrelle Willis Jsy/30 6.00 20.00
DY Dmitri Young Jsy/30 6.00 15.00
FH Felix Hernandez Jsy/30 10.00 25.00
FL Felipe Lopez Jsy/30 6.00 15.00
GC Gustavo Chacin Jsy/30 6.00 15.00
GG Goose Gossage Jsy/30 6.00 15.00
GN Graig Nettles Jsy/30 10.00 25.00
GO Adrian Gonzalez Jsy/30 10.00 25.00
GP Gaylord Perry Jsy/30 10.00 25.00
HB Harold Baines Jsy/30 10.00 25.00
HS Huston Street Jsy/30 10.00 25.00
JD Jermaine Dye Jsy/30 10.00 25.00
JE J.Bonderman Jsy/30 10.00 25.00
JG Jonny Gomes Jsy/30 10.00 25.00
JH Jeremy Hermida Jsy/30 15.00 40.00
JK John Kruk Jsy/30 8.00 20.00
JM Joe Mauer Jsy/30 50.00 100.00
JN Joe Nathan Jsy/30 10.00 25.00
JO Joe Blanton Jsy/30 6.00 15.00
JP Jhonny Peralta Jsy/30 6.00 15.00
JR Jose Reyes Jsy/30 15.00 40.00
JW Jake Westbrook Jsy/30 6.00 15.00
KG Ken Griffey Jr. Jsy/30 75.00 150.00
LE Carlos Lee Jsy/30 10.00 25.00
MA Matt Cain Jsy/30 30.00 60.00
MC Miguel Cabrera Jsy/30 20.00 50.00
MG Marcus Giles Jsy/30 10.00 25.00
MO Justin Morneau Jsy/30 6.00 15.00
MS Mike Schmidt Jsy/30 40.00 80.00
MY Michael Young Jsy/30 10.00 25.00
NL Noah Lowry Jsy/30 15.00 40.00
NS Nick Swisher Jsy/30 10.00 25.00
OR Magglio Ordonez Jsy/30 15.00 40.00
PE Jake Peavy Jsy/30 15.00 40.00
PF Prince Fielder Jsy/30 30.00 60.00
PI Joel Pineiro Jsy/30 6.00 15.00
RC Ryan Church Jsy/30 6.00 15.00
RH Ramon Hernandez Jsy/30 6.00 15.00
RO Roy Oswalt Jsy/30 10.00 25.00
RS Ron Santo Jsy/28 40.00 80.00
RW Rickie Weeks Jsy/30 10.00 25.00
RZ R.Zimmerman Jsy/30 15.00 40.00
SB Scott Baker Jsy/30 6.00 15.00
SG Steve Garvey Pants/30 20.00 50.00
SH Chris Shelton Jsy/30 6.00 15.00
SK Scott Kazmir Jsy/30 15.00 40.00
SP Scott Podsednik Jsy/30 15.00 40.00
TI Tadahito Iguchi Jsy/30 30.00 60.00
WC Will Clark Pants/30 20.00 50.00
WR David Wright Jsy/30 20.00 50.00
YB Y.Betancourt Jsy/30 10.00 25.00
YM Yadier Molina Jsy/30 50.00 100.00

2007 Artifacts

COMPLETE SET (100) 15.00 40.00
COMMON CARD (1-70) .15 .40
COMMON ROOKIE (71-100) .30 .75
1 Miguel Tejada .25 .60
2 David Ortiz .40 1.00
3 Manny Ramirez .40 1.00
4 Curt Schilling .25 .60
5 Jim Thome .25 .60
6 Paul Konerko .25 .60
7 Jermaine Dye .15 .40
8 Travis Hafner .15 .40
9 Victor Martinez .25 .60
10 Grady Sizemore .25 .60
11 Ivan Rodriguez .25 .60
12 Magglio Ordonez .25 .60
13 Justin Verlander .40 1.00
14 Mark Teahen .15 .40
15 Vladimir Guerrero .25 .60
16 Jered Weaver .25 .60
17 Justin Morneau .25 .60
18 Joe Mauer .30 .75
19 Torii Hunter .15 .40
20 Johan Santana .25 .60
21 Derek Jeter 1.00 2.50
22 Alex Rodriguez .50 1.25
23 Johnny Damon .25 .60
24 Huston Street .15 .40
25 Nick Swisher .25 .60
26 Ichiro Suzuki .50 1.25
27 Richie Sexson .15 .40
28 Carl Crawford .25 .60
29 Scott Kazmir .25 .60
30 Michael Young .15 .40
31 Mark Teixeira .25 .60
32 Vernon Wells .15 .40
33 Roy Halladay .25 .60
34 Brandon Webb .25 .60
35 Stephen Drew .15 .40
36 Chipper Jones .40 1.00
37 Andruw Jones .15 .40
38 Derrek Lee .15 .40
39 Aramis Ramirez .15 .40
40 Ken Griffey Jr. .75 2.00
41 Adam Dunn .25 .60
42 Todd Helton .25 .60
43 Matt Holliday .40 1.00
44 Miguel Cabrera .40 1.00
45 Hanley Ramirez .25 .60
46 Dontrelle Willis .15 .40
47 Lance Berkman .25 .60
48 Roy Oswalt .25 .60
49 Craig Biggio .25 .60
50 Nomar Garciaparra .25 .60
51 Derek Lowe .15 .40
52 Prince Fielder .25 .60
53 Rickie Weeks .15 .40
54 Jose Reyes .25 .60
55 David Wright .30 .75
56 Carlos Beltran .25 .60
57 Ryan Howard .30 .75
58 Chase Utley .25 .60
59 Jimmy Rollins .25 .60
60 Jason Bay .25 .60
61 Freddy Sanchez .15 .40
62 Trevor Hoffman .25 .60
63 Adrian Gonzalez .30 .75
64 Omar Vizquel .25 .60
65 Matt Cain .25 .60
66 Albert Pujols .50 1.25
67 Jim Edmonds .25 .60
68 Chris Carpenter .25 .60
69 David Eckstein .15 .40
70 Ryan Zimmerman .25 .60
71 Alexi Casilla RC .50 1.25
72 Andrew Miller RC 1.25 3.00
73 Andy Cannizaro RC .30 .75
74 Brian Stokes (RC) .30 .75
75 Carlos Maldonado (RC) .30 .75
76 Cesar Jimenez RC .30 .75
77 Daisuke Matsuzaka RC 1.25 3.00
78 Delmon Young (RC) .50 1.25
79 Delwyn Young (RC) .30 .75
80 Fred Lewis (RC) .50 1.25
81 Glen Perkins (RC) .30 .75
82 Jeff Baker (RC) .30 .75
83 Jeff Fiorentino (RC) .30 .75
84 Jeff Salazar (RC) .30 .75
85 Jerry Owens (RC) .30 .75
86 Josh Fields (RC) .30 .75
87 Juan Perez RC .30 .75
88 Juan Salas (RC) .30 .75
89 Justin Hampson (RC) .30 .75
90 Kevin Kouzmanoff (RC) .30 .75
91 Michael Bourn (RC) .50 1.25
92 Miguel Montero (RC) .30 .75
93 Mike Rabelo RC .30 .75
94 Oswaldo Navarro RC .30 .75
95 Philip Humber (RC) .30 .75
96 Ryan Braun RC .30 .75
97 Ryan Sweeney (RC) .30 .75
98 Sean Henn (RC) .30 .75
99 Jose Reyes RC .30 .75
100 Troy Tulowitzki (RC) 1.00 2.50

2007 Artifacts Antiquity Artifacts

RANDOM INSERTS IN PACKS
STATED PRINT RUN 199 SER.#'d SETS
GOLD ISSUED IN RETAIL PACKS
GOLD ARE NOT SERIAL NUMBERED
PATCHES RANDOMLY INSERTED
PATCH PRINT RUN 50 SER.#'d SETS
AB Adrian Beltre 3.00 8.00
AJ Andruw Jones 3.00 8.00
AL Adam LaRoche 3.00 8.00
AP Albert Pujols 6.00 15.00
AR Aramis Ramirez 3.00 8.00
AT Garrett Atkins 3.00 8.00
BA Bobby Abreu 3.00 8.00
BC Bartolo Colon 3.00 8.00
BE Carlos Beltran 3.00 8.00
BG Brian Giles 3.00 8.00
BO Jeremy Bonderman 3.00 8.00
BR Brian Roberts 3.00 8.00
BU B.J. Upton 3.00 8.00
BW Billy Wagner 3.00 8.00
BZ Barry Zito 3.00 8.00
CA Miguel Cabrera 3.00 8.00
CB Craig Biggio 3.00 8.00
CC Carl Crawford 3.00 8.00
CF Chone Figgins 3.00 8.00
CH Chris Carpenter 3.00 8.00
CJ Chipper Jones 5.00 12.00
CL Carlos Lee 3.00 8.00
CR Cal Ripken Jr. 10.00 25.00
CS Curt Schilling 3.00 8.00
CU Chase Utley 4.00 10.00
DJ Derek Jeter 8.00 20.00
DO David Ortiz 4.00 10.00
DR J.D. Drew 3.00 8.00
DU Dan Uggla 3.00 8.00
DW Dontrelle Willis 3.00 8.00
EC Eric Chavez 3.00 8.00
ED Jim Edmonds 3.00 8.00
FG Freddy Garcia 3.00 8.00
FH Felix Hernandez 3.00 8.00
FL Francisco Liriano 3.00 8.00
FT Frank Thomas 4.00 10.00
GA Garret Anderson 3.00 8.00
GJ Geoff Jenkins 3.00 8.00
GM Greg Maddux 5.00 12.00
GR Ken Griffey Jr. 6.00 15.00
GS Grady Sizemore 3.00 8.00
HA Rich Harden 3.00 8.00
HB Hank Blalock 3.00 8.00
HO Trevor Hoffman 3.00 8.00
HR Hanley Ramirez 3.00 8.00
HS Huston Street 3.00 8.00
HU Torii Hunter 3.00 8.00
IR Ivan Rodriguez 3.00 8.00
JA Jason Bay 3.00 8.00
JC Jorge Cantu 3.00 8.00
JD Jermaine Dye 3.00 8.00
JE Johnny Estrada 3.00 8.00
JF Jeff Francoeur 4.00 10.00
JG Jason Giambi 3.00 8.00
JJ Josh Johnson 3.00 8.00
JK Jeff Kent 3.00 8.00
JM Joe Mauer 3.00 8.00
JP Jake Peavy 3.00 8.00
JR Jimmy Rollins 3.00 8.00
JS Jason Schmidt 3.00 8.00
JT Jim Thome 3.00 8.00
JV Justin Verlander 4.00 10.00
JZ Joel Zumaya 3.00 8.00
KG Khalil Greene 3.00 8.00
LB Lance Berkman 3.00 8.00
LG Luis Gonzalez 3.00 8.00
MO Justin Morneau 3.00 8.00
MR Manny Ramirez 3.00 8.00
MT Mark Teixeira 3.00 8.00
MY Michael Young 3.00 8.00
NS Nick Swisher 3.00 8.00
OR Magglio Ordonez 3.00 8.00
PA Jonathan Papelbon 4.00 10.00
PB Pat Burrell 3.00 8.00
PE Jhonny Peralta 3.00 8.00
PF Prince Fielder 4.00 10.00
PK Paul Konerko 3.00 8.00
PM Pedro Martinez 3.00 8.00
PO Jorge Posada 3.00 8.00
RC Roger Clemens 6.00 15.00
RE Jose Reyes 4.00 10.00
RH Roy Halladay 3.00 8.00
RJ Randy Johnson 4.00 10.00
RO Roy Oswalt 3.00 8.00
RW Rickie Weeks 3.00 8.00
RZ Ryan Zimmerman 4.00 10.00
SA Johan Santana 3.00 8.00
SK Scott Kazmir 3.00 8.00
SM John Smoltz 3.00 8.00
SR Scott Rolen 3.00 8.00
TE Miguel Tejada 3.00 8.00
TG Tom Glavine 3.00 8.00
TH Todd Helton 3.00 8.00
TI Tim Hudson 3.00 8.00
VA Jason Varitek 4.00 10.00
VG Vladimir Guerrero 4.00 10.00
VM Victor Martinez 3.00 8.00
VW Vernon Wells 3.00 8.00

2007 Artifacts Antiquity Artifacts Gold

*GOLD: .3X TO .75X BASIC
GOLD NOT SERIAL NUMBERED
RANDOM INSERTS IN RETAIL PACKS
TR Travis Hafner 2.50 6.00

2007 Artifacts Antiquity Artifacts Patch

*PATCH: .75X TO 2X BASIC
RANDOM INSERTS IN PACKS
STATED PRINT RUN 50 SER.#'d SETS
JB Josh Beckett 6.00 15.00
TR Travis Hafner 6.00 15.00
VA Jason Varitek 12.50 30.00

2007 Artifacts Autofacts

RANDOM INSERTS IN PACKS
EXCHANGE DEADLINE 6/14/2010
AD Adam Dunn 6.00 15.00
AK Austin Kearns 3.00 8.00
AL Adam LaRoche 4.00 10.00
AM Andrew Miller 15.00 40.00
AS Angel Sanchez 3.00 8.00
BB Boof Bonser 3.00 8.00
BC Bobby Crosby 3.00 8.00
BE Josh Beckett 15.00 40.00
BO Jeremy Bonderman 12.50 30.00
BT Jason Bartlett 3.00 8.00
BU Ambiorix Burgos 3.00 8.00
CH Cole Hamels 8.00 20.00
CJ Cesar Jimenez 3.00 8.00
CL Carlos Lee 6.00 15.00
CR Cal Ripken Jr. 40.00 80.00
CY Chris Young 6.00 15.00
CZ Carlos Zambrano 6.00 15.00
DJ Derek Jeter 100.00 200.00
DO David Ortiz 20.00 50.00
DW Dontrelle Willis 4.00 10.00
DY Delmon Young 6.00 15.00
EC Eric Chavez 4.00 10.00
GA Garrett Atkins 4.00 10.00
HA Rich Harden 4.00 10.00
HG Hector Gimenez 3.00 8.00
HK Hong-Chih Kuo 6.00 15.00
HR Hanley Ramirez 6.00 15.00
IK Ian Kinsler 5.00 12.00
JA Joaquin Arias 3.00 8.00
JB Jason Bay 3.00 8.00
JC Jesse Crain 3.00 8.00
JE Johnny Estrada 4.00 10.00
JG Jonny Gomes 3.00 8.00
JJ Josh Johnson 5.00 12.00
JS John Smoltz 20.00 50.00
JW Jered Weaver 8.00 20.00
KE Howie Kendrick 4.00 10.00
KG Ken Griffey Jr. 30.00 80.00
KM Kendry Morales 3.00 8.00
KN Jon Knott 3.00 8.00
KW Kerry Wood 4.00 10.00
MJ Mike Jacobs 6.00 15.00
MM Miguel Montero 3.00 8.00
MO Justin Morneau 6.00 15.00
PA Jonathan Papelbon 5.00 12.00
PE Jhonny Peralta 3.00 8.00
PH Philip Humber 3.00 8.00
PM Pedro Martinez 15.00 40.00
RA Chris Ray 3.00 8.00
RC Roger Clemens 20.00 50.00
RH Rich Hill 6.00 15.00
RW Rickie Weeks 3.00 8.00
SB Scott Baker 3.00 8.00
SD Stephen Drew 6.00 15.00
SK Scott Kazmir 5.00 12.00
SO Jeremy Sowers 3.00 8.00
SR Scott Rolen 6.00 15.00
TI Tadahito Iguchi 6.00 15.00
TT Troy Tulowitzki 6.00 15.00
UP B.J. Upton 5.00 12.00
VE Justin Verlander 10.00 25.00
VG Vladimir Guerrero 15.00 40.00
VM Victor Martinez 4.00 10.00
WI Josh Willingham 3.00 8.00
YB Yuniesky Betancourt 6.00 15.00
ZG Zack Greinke 10.00 25.00
ZS Zack Segovia 4.00 10.00

2007 Artifacts Awesome Artifacts

RANDOM INSERTS IN PACKS
PRINT RUNS B/WN 29-50 SER.#'d SETS
AD Adam Dunn 5.00 12.00
AG Adrian Gonzalez 5.00 12.00
AP Albert Pujols 15.00 40.00
AR Aramis Ramirez 5.00 12.00
AS Alfonso Soriano 5.00 12.00
BA Bobby Abreu 5.00 12.00
BC Bartolo Colon 5.00 12.00
BG Brian Giles 5.00 12.00
BI Craig Biggio 6.00 15.00
BR Brian Roberts 5.00 12.00
BW Billy Wagner 5.00 12.00
BZ Barry Zito 5.00 12.00
CA Carl Crawford 5.00 12.00
CB Carlos Beltran 5.00 12.00
CC Carl Crawford 5.00 12.00
CC Chris Carpenter 5.00 12.00
CD Carlos Delgado 5.00 12.00
CF Chone Figgins 5.00 12.00
CJ Chipper Jones 8.00 20.00
CL Carlos Lee 5.00 12.00
CR Cal Ripken Jr. 20.00 50.00
CS Curt Schilling 6.00 15.00
CU Chase Utley 8.00 20.00
DJ Derek Jeter 40.00 80.00
DO David Ortiz 8.00 20.00
DU Dan Uggla 6.00 15.00
DW Dontrelle Willis 5.00 12.00
EC Eric Chavez 5.00 12.00
FG Freddy Garcia 5.00 12.00
FH Felix Hernandez 6.00 15.00
FL Francisco Liriano 8.00 20.00
FT Frank Thomas 12.50 30.00
GA Garret Anderson 5.00 12.00
GM Greg Maddux 12.50 30.00
GR Khalil Greene 6.00 15.00
GS Grady Sizemore 6.00 15.00
HA Roy Halladay 5.00 12.00
HB Hank Blalock 5.00 12.00
HE Todd Helton 6.00 15.00
HR Hanley Ramirez 6.00 15.00
HS Huston Street 5.00 12.00
HU Torii Hunter 5.00 12.00
IK Ian Kinsler 5.00 12.00
IR Ivan Rodriguez 6.00 15.00
JA Jason Bay 5.00 12.00
JB Jeremy Bonderman 5.00 12.00
JC Jorge Cantu 5.00 12.00
JD Jermaine Dye 5.00 12.00
JE Jim Edmonds 6.00 15.00
JF Jeff Francoeur 12.50 30.00
JG Jason Giambi 5.00 12.00
JH Johnny Damon 6.00 15.00
JJ Josh Johnson 5.00 12.00
JK Jeff Kent 5.00 12.00
JM Joe Mauer 6.00 15.00
JO Josh Barfield 5.00 12.00
JP Jake Peavy 5.00 12.00
JR Jimmy Rollins 5.00 12.00
JS Jason Schmidt 5.00 12.00
JT Jim Thome 6.00 15.00
JV Justin Verlander 8.00 20.00
JW Jered Weaver 6.00 15.00
JZ Joel Zumaya 6.00 15.00
KG Ken Griffey Jr. 12.50 30.00
KM Kendry Morales 6.00 15.00
MC Miguel Cabrera 6.00 15.00
MO Justin Morneau 5.00 12.00
MR Manny Ramirez 6.00 15.00
MT Mark Teixeira 6.00 15.00
MY Michael Young 5.00 12.00
OR Magglio Ordonez 5.00 12.00
OS Roy Oswalt 5.00 12.00
PA Jonathan Papelbon 8.00 20.00
PB Pat Burrell 5.00 12.00
PE Jhonny Peralta 5.00 12.00
PF Prince Fielder 8.00 20.00
PO Jorge Posada 6.00 15.00
RC Robinson Cano 6.00 15.00
RE Jose Reyes 10.00 25.00
RF Rafael Furcal 5.00 12.00
RH Rich Harden 5.00 12.00
RJ Randy Johnson 8.00 20.00
RO Roger Clemens 15.00 40.00
RW Rickie Weeks 5.00 12.00
RZ Ryan Zimmerman 8.00 20.00
SK Scott Kazmir 6.00 15.00
SM John Smoltz 6.00 15.00
SR Scott Rolen 6.00 15.00
TG Tom Glavine 6.00 15.00
TH Trevor Hoffman 5.00 12.00
TI Tim Hudson 5.00 12.00
TR Travis Hafner 5.00 12.00
VA Jason Varitek 8.00 20.00
VG Vladimir Guerrero 8.00 20.00
VM Victor Martinez 5.00 12.00
VW Vernon Wells 5.00 12.00

2007 Artifacts Divisional Artifacts

RANDOM INSERTS IN PACKS
PRINT RUNS B/WN 117-199 COPIES PER
GOLD RANDOMLY INSERTED IN RETAIL PACKS
GOLD RANDOMLY INSERTED IN PACKS
LIMITED STATED PRINT RUN 130 SER.#'d SETS
AA Aaron Rowand 3.00 8.00
AD Adam Dunn 3.00 8.00
AJ Andruw Jones 4.00 10.00
AL Adam LaRoche 3.00 8.00
AR Aramis Ramirez 3.00 8.00
BA Bobby Abreu 3.00 8.00
BC Bartolo Colon 3.00 8.00
BE Carlos Beltran 3.00 8.00
BG Brian Giles 3.00 8.00
BO Jeremy Bonderman 3.00 8.00
BR Brian Roberts 3.00 8.00
BW Billy Wagner 3.00 8.00
BZ Barry Zito 3.00 8.00
CA Robinson Cano 4.00 10.00
CB Craig Biggio 3.00 8.00
CC Carl Crawford 3.00 8.00
CD Carlos Delgado 3.00 8.00
CH Chris Carpenter 3.00 8.00
CJ Chipper Jones 4.00 10.00
CL Carlos Lee 3.00 8.00
CR Cal Ripken Jr. 10.00 25.00
CS Curt Schilling 3.00 8.00
CU Chase Utley 4.00 10.00
DJ Derek Jeter 8.00 20.00
DL Derrek Lee 3.00 8.00
DO David Ortiz 4.00 10.00
DU Dan Uggla 3.00 8.00
DW Dontrelle Willis 3.00 8.00
EC Eric Chavez 3.00 8.00
FG Freddy Garcia 3.00 8.00
FH Felix Hernandez 3.00 8.00
FL Francisco Liriano 3.00 8.00
FT Frank Thomas 4.00 10.00
GA Garret Anderson 3.00 8.00
GM Greg Maddux 5.00 12.00
GR Ken Griffey Jr. 6.00 15.00
GS Grady Sizemore 3.00 8.00
HA Rich Harden 3.00 8.00
HB Hank Blalock 3.00 8.00
HO Trevor Hoffman 3.00 8.00
HR Hanley Ramirez 3.00 8.00
HU Torii Hunter 3.00 8.00
IK Ian Kinsler 3.00 8.00
IR Ivan Rodriguez 3.00 8.00
JA Jason Bay 3.00 8.00
JC Jorge Cantu 3.00 8.00
JD Jermaine Dye 3.00 8.00
JE Jim Edmonds 3.00 8.00
JF Jeff Francoeur 4.00 10.00
JG Jason Giambi 3.00 8.00
JJ Josh Johnson 3.00 8.00
JK Jeff Kent 3.00 8.00
JM Joe Mauer 3.00 8.00
JN Joe Nathan 3.00 8.00
JO Josh Barfield 3.00 8.00
JP Jake Peavy 3.00 8.00
JR Jimmy Rollins 3.00 8.00
JS Jason Schmidt 3.00 8.00
JT Jim Thome 3.00 8.00
JV Justin Verlander 4.00 10.00
JW Jered Weaver 3.00 8.00
JZ Joel Zumaya 3.00 8.00
KG Khalil Greene 3.00 8.00
KM Kendry Morales 3.00 8.00
LB Lance Berkman 3.00 8.00
MC Miguel Cabrera 4.00 10.00
ME Melky Cabrera 3.00 8.00
MO Justin Morneau 3.00 8.00
MR Manny Ramirez 3.00 8.00
MT Mark Teixeira 3.00 8.00
MY Michael Young 3.00 8.00
NS Nick Swisher 3.00 8.00
OR Magglio Ordonez 3.00 8.00
PA Jonathan Papelbon 4.00 10.00
PB Pat Burrell 3.00 8.00
PE Jhonny Peralta 3.00 8.00
PF Prince Fielder 4.00 10.00
PK Paul Konerko 3.00 8.00
PO Jorge Posada 3.00 8.00
RC Roger Clemens 6.00 15.00
RE Jose Reyes 4.00 10.00
RH Roy Halladay 3.00 8.00
RJ Randy Johnson 3.00 8.00
RO Roy Oswalt 3.00 8.00
RW Rickie Weeks 3.00 8.00
RZ Ryan Zimmerman 4.00 10.00
SK Scott Kazmir 3.00 8.00
SM John Smoltz 3.00 8.00
SR Scott Rolen 3.00 8.00
TG Tom Glavine 3.00 8.00
TH Todd Helton 3.00 8.00
TI Tim Hudson 3.00 8.00
TR Travis Hafner 3.00 8.00
VA Jason Varitek 4.00 10.00
VG Vladimir Guerrero 4.00 10.00
VM Victor Martinez 3.00 8.00
VW Vernon Wells 3.00 8.00

2007 Artifacts Divisional Artifacts Gold

*GOLD: .3X TO .75X BASIC
RANDOMLY INSERTED IN RETAIL PACKS
GOLD NOT SERIAL NUMBERED
AP Albert Pujols 5.00 12.00
PM Pedro Martinez 2.50 6.00
TE Miguel Tejada 2.50 6.00

2007 Artifacts Divisional Artifacts Limited

*LIMITED: .4X TO 1X BASIC
RANDOM INSERTS IN PACKS
STATED PRINT RUN 130 SER.#'d SETS
AP Albert Pujols 6.00 15.00
PM Pedro Martinez 3.00 8.00
TE Miguel Tejada 3.00 8.00

2007 Artifacts MLB Apparel

RANDOM INSERTS IN PACKS
PRINT RUNS B/WN 25-199 COPIES PER
GOLD RANDOMLY INSERTS IN RETAIL PACKS
LIMITED RANDOM INSERTS IN PACKS
LIMITED PRINT RUN 75-130 COPIES PER
AD Adam Dunn 3.00 8.00
AJ Andruw Jones/25 4.00 10.00
AL Adam LaRoche 3.00 8.00
AP Albert Pujols 6.00 15.00
AR Aramis Ramirez 3.00 8.00
AT Garrett Atkins 3.00 8.00
BA Bobby Abreu 3.00 8.00
BC Bartolo Colon 3.00 8.00
BG Brian Giles 3.00 8.00
BI Craig Biggio 3.00 8.00
BO Jeremy Bonderman 3.00 8.00
BR Brian Roberts 3.00 8.00
BU B.J. Upton 3.00 8.00
BW Billy Wagner 3.00 8.00
BZ Barry Zito 3.00 8.00
CB Carlos Beltran 3.00 8.00
CC Carl Crawford 3.00 8.00
CH Cole Hamels 3.00 8.00
CJ Chipper Jones 4.00 10.00
CL Carlos Lee 3.00 8.00
CR Cal Ripken Jr. 10.00 25.00
CS Curt Schilling 3.00 8.00
CU Chase Utley 4.00 10.00
DJ Derek Jeter 8.00 20.00
DO David Ortiz 4.00 10.00
DU Dan Uggla 3.00 8.00
DW Dontrelle Willis 3.00 8.00
DY Jermaine Dye 3.00 8.00
EC Eric Chavez 3.00 8.00
ES Johnny Estrada 3.00 8.00
FG Freddy Garcia 3.00 8.00
FH Felix Hernandez 3.00 8.00
FL Francisco Liriano 3.00 8.00
FT Frank Thomas 4.00 10.00
GA Garret Anderson 3.00 8.00
GJ Geoff Jenkins 3.00 8.00
GM Greg Maddux 5.00 12.00
GR Khalil Greene 3.00 8.00
GS Grady Sizemore/168 3.00 8.00
HA Roy Halladay 3.00 8.00
HB Hank Blalock 3.00 8.00

HE Todd Helton 3.00 8.00
HO Trevor Hoffman 3.00 8.00
HR Hanley Ramirez 3.00 8.00
HU Torii Hunter 3.00 8.00
IR Ivan Rodriguez 3.00 8.00
JB Jason Bay 3.00 8.00
JC Jorge Cantu 3.00 8.00
JD J.D. Drew 3.00 8.00
JE Jim Edmonds 3.00 8.00
JF Jeff Francoeur 4.00 10.00
JG Jason Giambi 3.00 8.00
JJ Josh Johnson 3.00 8.00
JK Jeff Kent 3.00 8.00
JM Joe Mauer 3.00 8.00
JN Joe Nathan 3.00 8.00
JO Johnny Damon 3.00 8.00
JP Jake Peavy 3.00 8.00
JR Jimmy Rollins 3.00 8.00
JS Jason Schmidt 3.00 8.00
JT Jim Thome 3.00 8.00
JV Justin Verlander 4.00 10.00
JZ Joel Zumaya 3.00 8.00
KG Ken Griffey Jr. 6.00 15.00
LB Lance Berkman 3.00 8.00
LG Luis Gonzalez 3.00 8.00
MC Miguel Cabrera/67 4.00 10.00
MO Justin Morneau 3.00 8.00
MR Manny Ramirez 3.00 8.00
MT Mark Teixeira 3.00 8.00
MY Michael Young 3.00 8.00
OR Magglio Ordonez 3.00 8.00
PA Jonathan Papelbon 4.00 10.00
PB Pat Burrell 3.00 8.00
PE Jhonny Peralta 3.00 8.00
PF Prince Fielder 4.00 10.00
PM Pedro Martinez 3.00 8.00
PO Jorge Posada 3.00 8.00
RC Roger Clemens 6.00 15.00
RE Jose Reyes 4.00 10.00
RH Rich Harden 3.00 8.00
RI Mariano Rivera 4.00 10.00
RJ Randy Johnson 3.00 8.00
RO Roy Oswalt 3.00 8.00
RW Rickie Weeks 3.00 8.00
RZ Ryan Zimmerman 4.00 10.00
SA Johan Santana 3.00 8.00
SK Scott Kazmir/31 4.00 10.00
SM John Smoltz 3.00 8.00
SR Scott Rolen 3.00 8.00
TG Tom Glavine 3.00 8.00
TH Tim Hudson 3.00 8.00
TR Travis Hafner 3.00 8.00
VA Jason Varitek 4.00 10.00
VG Vladimir Guerrero/99 4.00 10.00
VM Victor Martinez 3.00 8.00
VW Vernon Wells 3.00 8.00

2007 Artifacts MLB Apparel Gold

*GOLD: .3X TO .75X BASIC
RANDOM INSERTS IN RETAIL PACKS
GOLD NOT SERIAL NUMBERED
AB Adrian Beltre 2.50 6.00

2007 Artifacts MLB Apparel Limited

*LIMITED: .4X TO 1X BASIC
RANDOM INSERTS IN PACKS
PRINT RUNS B/WN 75-130 COPIES PER
AB Adrian Beltre 3.00 8.00
MT Miguel Tejada 3.00 8.00

1953-63 Artvue Hall of Fame Postcards

This 91-card set features photos of the members of the Baseball Hall of Fame printed on postcard-size cards. The cards are unnumbered and checklisted below in alphabetical order.

COMPLETE SET (91) 300.00 600.00
1 Grover Alexander 5.00 12.00
2 Cap Anson 5.00 12.00
3 Frank Baker 4.00 10.00
4 Ed Barrow 2.00 5.00
5 Chief Bender 2.50 6.00
6 Roger Bresnahan 2.00 5.00
7 Modecai Brown 4.00 10.00
8 Morgan Bulkeley 2.00 5.00
9 Jesse Burkett 2.00 5.00
10 Max Carey 2.00 5.00
11 Alexander Cartwright 2.00 5.00
12 Henry Chadwick 2.00 5.00
13 Frank Chance 2.50 6.00
14 Jack Chesbro 2.00 5.00
15 Fred Clarke 2.00 5.00
16 John Clarkson 2.00 5.00
17 Ty Cobb 10.00 25.00
18 Mickey Cochrane 2.50 6.00
19 Eddie Collins 4.00 10.00
20 Jimmy Collins 2.00 5.00
21 Charlie Comiskey 2.00 5.00
22 Tom Connolly 2.00 5.00
23 Sam Crawford 3.00 8.00
24 Joe Cronin 2.50 6.00
25 Candy Cummings 2.00 5.00
26 Dizzy Dean 2.50 6.00
27 Ed Delehanty 2.00 5.00
28 Bill Dickey 2.50 6.00
29 Joe DiMaggio 15.00 40.00
30 Hugh Duffy 2.00 5.00
31 Johnny Evers 2.00 5.00
32 Buck Ewing 2.00 5.00
33 Bob Feller 40.00 80.00
34 Elmer Flick 2.00 5.00
35 Jimmy Foxx 3.00 8.00
(Jimmie)
36 Frankie Frisch 2.50 6.00
37 Lou Gehrig 12.50 30.00
38 Charlie Gehringer 4.00 10.00
39 Hank Greenberg 4.00 10.00
40 Clark Griffith 2.50 6.00
41 Lefty Grove 6.00 15.00
42 Billy Hamilton 2.50 6.00
43 Gabby Hartnett 2.00 5.00
44 Harry Heilmann 2.00 5.00
45 Rogers Hornsby 6.00 12.00
46 Carl Hubbell 5.00 12.50
47 Hugh Jennings 2.00 5.00
48 Ban Johnson 2.00 5.00
49 Walter Johnson 7.50 20.00
50 Willie Keeler 2.50 6.00
51 King Kelly 2.50 6.00
52 Bill Klem 2.00 5.00
53 Nap Lajoie 7.50 20.00
54 Kenesaw Mountain Landis 2.00 5.00
55 Ted Lyons 2.00 5.00
56 Connie Mack 4.00 10.00
57 Rabbit Maranville 2.00 5.00
58 Christy Mathewson 6.00 15.00
59 Joe McCarthy 2.00 5.00
60 Tom McCarthy 2.00 5.00
61 Joe McGinnity 2.00 5.00
62 John McGraw 4.00 10.00
63 Bill McKechnie 2.00 5.00
64 Kid Nichols 2.00 5.00
65 Jimmy O'Rourke 2.00 5.00
66 Mel Ott 3.00 8.00
67 Herb Pennock 2.00 5.00
68 Eddie Plank 2.00 5.00
69 Sam Rice 2.00 5.00
70 Eppa Rixey 2.00 5.00
71 Jackie Robinson 10.00 25.00
72 Wilbert Robinson 2.00 5.00
73 Edd Roush 2.00 5.00
74 Babe Ruth 20.00 50.00
75 Ray Schalk 2.00 5.00
76 Al Simmons 2.50 6.00
77 George Sisler 4.00 10.00
78 Albert Spalding 2.50 6.00
79 Tris Speaker 4.00 10.00
80 Bill Terry 2.50 6.00
81 Joe Tinker 2.50 6.00
82 Dazzy Vance 2.50 6.00
83 Rube Waddell 3.00 8.00
84 Honus Wagner 8.00 20.00
85 Bobby Wallace 2.00 5.00
86 Ed Walsh 2.00 5.00
87 Paul Waner 2.50 6.00
88 Zach Wheat 2.00 5.00
89 George Wright 2.00 5.00
90 Harry Wright 2.00 5.00
91 Cy Young 8.00 20.00

1982 ASA Mickey Mantle

This seventy-two card standard-size set was the first issued by ASA to honor past greats of the game. The first card in this set comes either signed or unsigned. We have priced the set both ways. There were 5,000 numbered sets issued with Mantle autographed cards which were originally issued at $24.99 each and 15,000 unnumbered sets issued with no signed cards at $12.99 each.

COMPLETE SET/w AU (72) 150.00 300.00
COMPLETE SET/w AU (72) 60.00 125.00
1 Mickey Mantle 1.25 3.00
1AU Mickey Mantle/Autographed 150.00 250.00
2 Mickey Mantle .50 1.25
Merlyn Mantle, 1951
3 Mickey Mantle .75 2.00
Spring Training 1951
4 Mickey Mantle .75 2.00
Spring Training 1951
5 Mickey Mantle .50 1.25
Merlyn Mantle
6 Mickey Mantle .75 2.00
First HR in NY 4/15/51
7 Mickey Mantle 1.50 4.00
Joe DiMaggio
Ted Williams
8 Mickey Mantle .50 1.25
Signs his 1951 contract
9 Mickey Mantle .50 1.25
Billy Mantle
Mickey Jr.
10 Mickey Mantle .50 1.25
Roy Mantle
Ray Mantle
11 Mickey Mantle .75 2.00
Spring Training 1952
12 Mickey Mantle .50 1.25
Hank Bauer
Johnny Hopp
13 Mickey Mantle .75 2.00
1952 Season
14 Mickey Mantle .75 2.00
Billy Martin
on to 1952 Series
15 Mickey Mantle .75 2.00
Billy Martin 1953
16 Mickey Mantle .75 2.00
Knee Injury 1953
17 Mickey Mantle .75 2.00
Before knee surgery 1953
18 Mickey Mantle .75 2.00
New Business 1953
19 Mickey Mantle .75 2.00
1953 World Series Power
20 Mickey Mantle .75 2.00
The Long Homerun 1953
21 Mickey Mantle .75 2.00
1955 Hall of Fame Game
22 Mickey Mantle .75 2.00
1955
23 Mickey Mantle 1.00 2.50
Billy Skowron
Phil Rizzuto 1955
24 Mickey Mantle 1.25 3.00
Jackie Robinson 1954
25 Mickey Mantle 1.25 3.00
Ted Williams 1956
26 Mickey Mantle 1.00 2.50
Bill Skowron
Yogi Berra 1955
27 Mickey Mantle .75 2.00
Bob Lemon
Safe at first 1956
28 Mickey Mantle 1.00 2.50
Yogi Berra
Elston Howard
Hank Bauer
1956 World Series
29 Mickey Mantle 1.00 2.50
Yogi Berra
Whitey Ford 1957
30 Mickey Mantle .50 1.25
Roy Sievers 1957
31 Mickey Mantle .75 2.00
1957 World Series
32 Mickey Mantle .75 2.00
1957 Hitchcock Award
33 Mickey Mantle .50 1.25
Cardinal Spellman 1957
34 Mickey Mantle .50 1.25
Teresa Brewer 1957
35 Mickey Mantle .75 2.00
Brooks Robinson 1957
36 Mickey Mantle .75 2.00
1958 World Series
37 Mickey Mantle 1.00 2.50
Ernie Banks
1958 All-Star Game
38 Mickey Mantle 1.00 2.50
Casey Stengel 1959
39 Mickey Mantle 1.00 2.50
Roger Maris 1960
40 Mickey Mantle .75 2.00
1960 World Series
41 Mickey Mantle .75 2.00
1961 All-Star Game
42 Mickey Mantle 1.00 2.50
Roger Maris
Yogi Berra
Elston Howard
Bill Skowron
John Blanchard 1961
43 Mickey Mantle 1.00 2.50
Roger Maris
Mrs. Babe Ruth 1961
44 Mickey Mantle 1.00 2.50
Roger Maris 1961
45 Mickey Mantle 54 HRs 1.00 2.50
Roger Maris 61 HRs 1961
46 Mickey Mantle .75 2.00
400th Career Homerun 1962
47 Mickey Mantle .75 2.00
1962 World Series
48 Mickey Mantle .75 2.00
1963 Season
49 Mickey Mantle .75 2.00
1963 World Series
50 Mickey Mantle .75 2.00
1964 World Series
51 Mickey Mantle .75 2.00
Joe Pepitone
Whitey Ford
1964 Banner Year
52 Mickey Mantle .75 2.00
1964 Season
53 Mickey Mantle 1.25 3.00
Robert F. Kennedy
1965
54 Mickey Mantle .75 2.00
1965 Season
55 Mickey Mantle 1.25 3.00
Joe DiMaggio 1966
56 Billy Mantle .50 1.25
Merlyn Mantle
Mickey Mantle Jr.
Danny Mantle
David Mantle
57 Mickey Mantle .75 2.00
1967 Season
58 Mickey Mantle .75 2.00
Hits Homerun No. 529 1968
59 Mickey Mantle .75 2.00
1968 Retirement
60 Mickey Mantle .75 2.00
His Farewell 1968
61 Mickey Mantle .75 2.00
Trophy Room
62 Mickey Mantle .75 2.00
Welcome Back Coach 1970
63 Mickey Mantle .75 2.00
TV Commercial 1973
64 Mickey Mantle .75 2.00
1974 Visit
65 Mickey Mantle .75 2.00
1974 Visit
66 Mickey Mantle 1.25 3.00
Whitey Ford
Casey Stengel
1974 Hall of Fame Inductees
67 Mickey Mantle 1.25 3.00
Billy Martin
Joe DiMaggio
Whitey Ford
1979 Old Timers Game
68 Mickey Mantle .75 2.00
Don Larsen
1981 Old Timers Game
69 Mickey Mantle .50 1.25
Butch Mantle
Roy Mantle
Barbara Mantle
Mrs. Mantle
Ray Mantle
Family Day
70 Mickey Mantle .75 2.00
The Mantle Swing
71 Mickey Mantle .75 2.00
The Mantle Swing
72 Mickey Mantle .75 2.00
The Mantle Swing

1983 ASA Bob Feller

This 12-card standard-size set honors the career of Bob Feller and features fronts of white-bordered and red-trimmed black-and-white photos of him during his career. The backs are red-bordered, trimmed by a black line and carry a story that is continuous from card to card. Card number 1 carries an authentic autograph and is numbered sequentially out of 2,000.

COMPLETE SET (12) 10.00 25.00
1 Bob Feller AU 8.00 20.00
2 Bob Feller .40 1.00
Steve O'Neill MG 1937
3 Bob Feller .60 1.50
Gene Tunney
1942 Navy Induction
4 Bob Feller .40 1.00
Rollie Hemsley
Tommy Bridges
Bucky Walters
1946 Bob Owens Baseball School
5 Bob Feller 1.00 2.50
Satchel Paige 1946
6 Bob Feller .40 1.00
Bill Veeck OWN 1947
7 Bob Feller .60 1.50
Hal Newhouser 1947
8 Bob Feller .40 1.00
Joe Gordon
Kenny Keltner 1947
9 Bob Feller .60 1.50
Bob Lemon 1950
10 Bob Feller .40 1.00
Jim Hegan
Al Rosen
Luke Easter
200th Victory 1951
11 Bob Feller .60 1.50
1954 Indians Pitching Staff
12 Bob Feller .60 1.50
The Feller Style

1983 ASA Brooks Robinson

This 12-card standard-size set honors the career of Brooks Robinson and features fronts of white-bordered and red-trimmed black-and-white photos of him during his career. The backs are red-bordered, trimmed by a black line and carry a story that is continuous from card to card. Card number 1 carries an authentic autograph and is numbered sequentially out of 2,000.

COMPLETE SET (12) 12.50 30.00
1 Brooks Robinson .40 1.00
Header Card
1AU Brooks Robinson AU 8.00 20.00
2 Brooks Robinson .40 1.00
Tito Francona
Bob Hale
1956 Spring Training
3 Brooks Robinson .40 1.00
The Best Fielding 3rd Baseman Ever
4 Brooks Robinson .40 1.00
Yankee Stadium
5 Brooks Robinson .40 1.00
1969 World Series
6 Brooks Robinson .75 2.00
Thurman Munson
Luis Aparicio
Mickey Lolich
Harmon Killebrew
1971 All-Star Game
7 Brooks Robinson .40 1.00
Spring Training
Follow-Through
Orange Name on Uniform
8 Brooks Robinson .40 1.00
J. Roy Stockton Award
9 Brooks Robinson .40 1.00
Spring Training
Back Facing Camera
10 Brooks Robinson .40 1.00
Spring Training
Facing Camera
11 Brooks Robinson .40 1.00
1972 All-Star for the 16th time
12 Brooks Robinson .40 1.00
1974

1983 ASA Duke Snider

This 12-card standard-size set honors the career of Duke Snider and features fronts of white-bordered and red-trimmed black-and-white photos of him during his career. The backs are red-bordered, trimmed by a black line and carry a story that is continuous from card to card. Card number 1 carries an authentic autograph and is numbered sequentially out of 2,000.

COMPLETE SET (12) 12.50 30.00
1 Duke Snider AU 8.00 20.00
2 Duke Snider .40 1.00
1948
3 Duke Snider .40 1.00
1950 Sliding Home
4 Duke Snider .40 1.00
Billy Cox
Pee Wee Reese
Jackie Robinson
Roy Campanella
Andy Pafko
Gil Hodges
Carl Furillo
Joe Black
5 Duke Snider .75 2.00
Gil Hodges
Carl Furillo
Roy Campanella
Jackie Robinson
Pee Wee Reese
Chuck Dressen MG
Dick Williams
Wes Westrum
Hoyt Wilhelm
6 Duke Snider .75 2.00
Gil Hodges
Don Hoak
Pee Wee Reese
7 Duke Snider .40 1.00
Joe Black
Chuck Dressen MG
8 Duke Snider .40 1.00
Jumping for Joy
9 Duke Snider .75 2.00
Gil Hodges
Johnny Podres
Clem Labine
10 Duke Snider .40 1.00
L.A. Dodger
11 Duke Snider .40 1.00
N.Y. Met
12 Duke Snider .40 1.00
S.F. Giant

1983 ASA Frank Robinson

This 12-card standard-size set honors the career of Frank Robinson and features fronts of white-bordered and red-trimmed black-and-white photos of him during his career. The backs are red-bordered, trimmed by a black line and carry a story that is continuous from card to card. Card number 1 carries an authentic autograph and is numbered sequentially out of 2,000.

COMPLETE SET (12) 12.50 30.00
1 Frank Robinson .40 1.00
Header Card
1AU Frank Robinson AU 8.00 20.00
2 Frank Robinson .40 1.00
1962 Reds
3 Frank Robinson .40 1.00
1959 Reds
4 Frank Robinson .40 1.00
1961 Reds
5 Frank Robinson .40 1.00
Traded to the Orioles
6 Frank Robinson .40 1.00
A Great Year 1966
7 Frank Robinson .40 1.00
1969 World Series
8 Frank Robinson .40 1.00
1969 Orioles
9 Frank Robinson .40 1.00
Home Run 521
10 Frank Robinson .40 1.00
Mike Strahler
1972 Santurce
11 Frank Robinson .40 1.00
1978 Rochester
12 Frank Robinson .40 1.00
1982 Giants

1983 ASA Hank Aaron

This 12-card standard-size set honors the career of Hank Aaron and features fronts of white-bordered and red-trimmed black-and-white photos of him during his career. The backs are red-bordered, trimmed by a black line and carry a story that is continuous from card to card. Card number 1 carries an authentic autograph and is numbered sequentially out of 2,000.

COMPLETE SET (12) 40.00 100.00
1 Hank Aaron AU 50.00 100.00
2 Hank Aaron .40 1.00
Ben Geraghty MGR
1953 Jacksonville
3 Hank Aaron .40 1.00
1954 Milwaukee
4 Hank Aaron .40 1.00
Wes Covington
Bob Hazle
1957 Braves
5 Hank Aaron .40 1.00
Red Schoendienst
Fred Haney MG
1958 Braves
6 Hank Aaron 1.00 2.50
Mickey Mantle
1958 World Series
7 Hank Aaron .60 1.50
Eddie Mathews
1965 Braves
8 Hank Aaron .40 1.00
1969 Braves
9 Hank Aaron .40 1.00
Rico Carty
1970 Braves
10 Hank Aaron .40 1.00
Home Run #700
11 Hank Aaron .40 1.00
Home Run #712
12 Hank Aaron .40 1.00
Darrell Evans
Dave Johnson
1973 Braves

1983 ASA Joe DiMaggio

This 12-card standard-size set honors the career of Joe DiMaggio and features fronts of white-bordered and red-trimmed black-and-white photos of him during his career. The backs are red-bordered, trimmed by a black line and carry a story that is continuous from card to card. Card number 1 carries an authentic autograph and is numbered sequentially out of 2,000.

COMPLETE SET (12) 100.00 200.00
1 Joe DiMaggio AU 75.00 200.00
2 Joe DiMaggio 1.00 2.50
Dom DiMaggio
San Francisco 1935
3 Joe DiMaggio 1.00 2.50
Joe McCarthy MG
Jacob Ruppert OWN
Tony Lazzeri
1936 World Series
4 Joe DiMaggio 1.50 4.00
Lou Gehrig
George Selkirk
Bill Dickey
1936
5 Joe DiMaggio 1.00 2.50
That Classic Stance 1947
6 Joe DiMaggio 1.50 4.00
Ted Williams 1942
7 Joe DiMaggio 1.00 2.50
Charlie Keller
Tommy Henrich 1946
8 Joe DiMaggio 1.00 2.50
1950 Spring Training
9 Joe DiMaggio 1.50 4.00
Mickey Mantle 1951
10 Joe DiMaggio 1.00 2.50
Mel Allen ANN 1951
11 Joe DiMaggio 1.00 2.50
A's 1968
12 Joe DiMaggio 1.00 2.50
Billy Martin
Mickey Mantle
Whitey Ford 1978

1983 ASA Johnny Mize

This 12-card standard-size set honors the career of Johnny Mize and features fronts of white-bordered and red-trimmed black-and-white photos of him during his career. The backs are red-bordered, trimmed by a black line and carry a story that is continuous from card No. 2 to card No. 9. The backs of cards 10, 11, and 12 carry his lifetime career and World Series records, respectively. Card number 1 carries an authentic autograph and is numbered sequentially out of 2,000.

COMPLETE SET (12) 10.00 25.00
1 Johnny Mize AU 8.00 20.00
2 Johnny Mize .20 .50
1933-35 with Rochester
3 Johnny Mize .20 .50
1936 Home run in Chicago
4 Johnny Mize .20 .50
1939 With teammates
5 Johnny Mize .20 .50
1943 Traded to the Giants
6 Johnny Mize .20 .50
1948 New York Giants
7 Johnny Mize .20 .50
1949 Traded to the Yankees
8 Johnny Mize .20 .50
1949 World Series Game Heroes
9 Johnny Mize .20 .50
1951 World Series
10 Johnny Mize .20 .50
Duke of Windsor
Duchess of Windsor
11 Johnny Mize .40 1.00
Yogi Berra
Ed Lopat
Playing Cards
12 Johnny Mize .20 .50
1973 Recreation Director

1983 ASA Juan Marichal

This 12-card standard-size set honors the career of Juan Marichal and features fronts of white-bordered and red-trimmed black-and-white photos of him during his career. The backs are red-bordered, trimmed by a black line and carry a story that is continuous from card to card. Card number 1 carries an authentic autograph and is numbered sequentially out of 2,000.

COMPLETE SET (12) 8.00 20.00
1 Juan Marichal AU 6.00 15.00
2 Juan Marichal .40 1.00
Giants 1960
3 Juan Marichal .40 1.00
Giants 1962
4 Juan Marichal .40 1.00
Giants 1966
5 Juan Marichal .75 2.00
Willie Mays 1971
6 Juan Marichal .40 1.00
Giants 1972
7 Juan Marichal .60 1.50
Willie McCovey 1973
8 Juan Marichal .40 1.00
Giants 1973
9 Juan Marichal .40 1.00
Walt Alston MG 1975
10 Juan Marichal .40 1.00
Walt Alston MG
April 17, 1975
11 Juan Marichal .40 1.00
1983 HOF Induction
12 Juan Marichal .40 1.00
1983 Cracker Jack All-Star Game

1983 ASA Warren Spahn

This 12-card standard-size set honors the career of Warren Spahn and features fronts of white-bordered and green-trimmed black-and-white photos of him during his career. The backs are green-bordered, trimmed by a black line and carry a story that is continuous from card No. 2 to card No. 9. The backs of cards 10, 11, and 12 carry his lifetime career and World Series records, respectively.

COMPLETE SET (12) 2.00 5.00
1 Warren Spahn .20 .50
Title card
1A Warren Spahn AU 8.00 20.00
2 Warren Spahn .20 .50
1947-High Kick
3 Warren Spahn .20 .50
1948 World Series
Pitching to Dale Mitchell
4 Warren Spahn UER .30 .75
Vern Bickford
Johnny Sain
Misspelled upon on card back
5 Warren Spahn .20 .50
1951 Spring Training
6 Warren Spahn .30 .75
Fred Haney MG
Bobby Thomson
Lew Burdette
7 Warren Spahn UER .20 .50
Misspelled Burxette on back
8 Warren Spahn .20 .50
On to '58 World Series
9 Warren Spahn .20 .50
Warren beats Pirates
10 Warren Spahn .20 .50
1959 Strikeout 2,382
11 Warren Spahn .20 .50
1965 With the Mets
12 Warren Spahn .20 .50
1973 Indians Coach-HOF

1983 ASA Willie Mays 12

This 12-card standard-size set honors the career of Willie Mays and features fronts of white-bordered and red-trimmed black-and-white photos of him during his career. The backs are red-bordered, trimmed by a black line and carry a story that is continuous from card to card. Card number 1 carries an authentic autograph and is numbered sequentially out of 2,000.

COMPLETE SET (12) 40.00 100.00
1 Willie Mays AU 40.00 80.00
2 Willie Mays .75 2.00
1951 Minneapolis
3 Willie Mays 1.50 4.00
Mickey Mantle 1951
4 Willie Mays .75 2.00
1953 Army Induction
5 Willie Mays .75 2.00
Say-Hey Day 1954
6 Willie Mays 1.25 3.00
Stan Musial 1956
7 Willie Mays .75 2.00
1958 Giants
8 Willie Mays 1.25 3.00
Roberto Clemente
Hank Aaron
1969
9 Willie Mays .75 2.00
1972 Mets
10 Willie Mays .75 2.00
22-Jul-72
11 Willie Mays 1.25 3.00
Roberto Clemente
Sept. 30, 1972
12 Willie Mays .75 2.00
Ralph Kiner
1982

1983 ASA Yogi Berra

This 12-card standard-size set honors the career of Yogi Berra and features fronts of white-bordered and red-trimmed black-and-white photos of him during his career. The backs are red-bordered, trimmed by a black line and carry a story that is continuous from card to card. Card number 1 carries an authentic autograph and is numbered sequentially out of 2,000.

COMPLETE SET (12) 15.00 40.00
1 Yogi Berra AU 15.00 30.00
2 Yogi Berra .40 1.00
Youthful Yogi
3 Yogi Berra 1.00 2.50
Mickey Mantle
Joe Collins
Hank Bauer
Gene Woodling
1953 Yankees
4 Yogi Berra .40 1.00
Sal Maglie
Don Larsen 1958
5 Yogi Berra 1.00 2.50
Roger Maris
Mickey Mantle
Bobby Richardson
Bill Skowron
Tony Kubek
Art Ditmar
Hector Lopez
Clete Boyer
Casey Stengel MG 1960
6 Yogi Berra 1.00 2.50
Roger Maris
Mickey Mantle
Elston Howard
Bill Skowron
John Blanchard 1961
7 Yogi Berra MG 1.00 2.50
Casey Stengel MG 1964
8 Yogi Berra 1.00 2.50
Joe DiMaggio
Red Ruffing
Whitey Ford
Charlie Keller
Don Larsen
Bobby Richardson
Tommy Henrich
Old Timers Day 1967
9 Yogi Berra .75 2.00
Bill Dickey
Elston Howard
Thurman Munson
Yankee Catching Tradition
10 Yogi Berra CO .40 1.00
Gil Hodges MG
Eddie Yost
Rube Walker
Joe Pignatano
11 Yogi Berra MG .40 1.00
Walter Alston MG 1973
12 Yogi Berra CO .40 1.00
1978 Yankees

1984 ASA Willie Mays 90

This ninety-card standard-size set was issued by ASA and printed by Renata Galasso Inc. to honor the life and career of Willie Mays. These cards were issued in set form only. Sets were issued with and without the number one card being signed by Mays. The complete set does not include the autograph card which is valued seperately. Cards 1-45 contain biographical information about Mays while cards 46-90 have a puzzle back. The puzzle when put together features a collage of all Willie Mays baseball cards.

COMPLETE SET (90) 15.00 40.00
1A Willie Mays AU 40.00 80.00
1B Willie Mays .10 .25
Say Hey
2 Willie Mays .10 .25
Tearing up the Minor Leagues
3 Willie Mays .10 .25
Called up to the Majors
4 Willie Mays .30 .75
Leo Durocher
Hank Thompson
Monte Irvin
1951 Rookie Season
5 Willie Mays .10 .25
Joins the Army
6 Willie Mays .10 .25
MVP Season
7 Willie Mays .40 1.00
The Catch
8 Willie Mays .10 .25
Winter Ball
9 Willie Mays .10 .25
Billiards for Willie
10 Willie Mays .10 .25
Endorsements
11 Willie Mays .10 .25
Honors for Willie
12 Willie Mays .20 .50
Horace Stoneham OWN
A Sportsman and A Gentleman

13 Willie Mays	.30	.75
Duke Snider		
The Toast of New York		
14 Willie Mays	.10	.25
A Superb Fielder		
15 Willie Mays	.10	.25
Giants Move to San Francisco		
16 Willie Mays	.10	.25
A Favorite with Fans		
17 Willie Mays	.10	.25
Making Adjustments		
18 Willie Mays	.10	.25
Coming Home		
19 Willie Mays	.30	.75
Roberto Clemente		
3,000 Hitters		
20 Willie Mays	.10	.25
4 Homers in One Game		
21 Willie Mays	.10	.25
Always Hustling		
22 Willie Mays	.10	.25
Concentration		
23 Willie Mays	.10	.25
San Francisco Wins 1st Pennant		
24 Willie Mays	.30	.75
Whitey Ford		
Tom Tresh		
Friendly Foes UER		
Tresh misspelled		
25 Willie Mays	.10	.25
The One That Didn't		
Get Away		
26 Willie Mays	.20	.50
Dick Stuart		
Earl Wilson		
Spring Training		
27 Willie Mays	.20	.50
Warren Giles PRES		
Another MVP Season		
28 Willie Mays	.10	.25
N.L. Home Run King		
29 Willie Mays	.40	1.00
Mickey Mantle		
30 Willie Mays	.40	1.00
Stan Musial		
Pride of the N.L.		
31 Willie Mays	.20	.50
Roy Hofheinz OWN		
The Birthday Boy		
32 Willie Mays	.20	.50
Ernie Banks		
500 Home Run Hitters		
33 Willie Mays	.30	.75
#600		
34 Willie Mays	.10	.25
Returns to New York		
35 Willie Mays	.30	.75
Don Drysdale		
All-Stars		
36 Willie Mays	.10	.25
Retirement		
37 Willie Mays	.10	.25
Cover Boy		
38 Willie Mays	.20	.50
John Lindsay MAYOR		
Willie Mays Day		
39 Willie Mays	.40	1.00
Queen Elizabeth		
Ronald Reagan		
Holding Court		
40 Willie Mays	.40	1.00
Hank Aaron		
Home Run Kings		
41 Willie Mays	.10	.25
Hall of Fame		
42 Willie Mays	.10	.25
Santa		
43 Willie Mays	.20	.50
Mae Mays		
The Exhibit		
44 Willie Mays	.40	1.00
Joe DiMaggio		
Baseball Immortals		
45 Willie Mays	.10	.25
Greatest of Them All		
46 Willie Mays	.40	1.00
Mrs. Willie Mays		
Bill Cosby		
47 Willie Mays	.10	.25
Head shot		
48 Willie Mays	.10	.25
Batting stance		
stadium background		
49 Willie Mays	.10	.25
Follow-through		
50 Willie Mays	.10	.25
Crouching, two bats on ground		
51 Willie Mays	.10	.25
Posed, bat on right shoulder		
52 Willie Mays	.40	1.00
Hank Aaron		
53 Willie Mays	.10	.25
On one knee		
resting knee on bat		
54 Willie Mays	.10	.25
Looking over left shoulder		
55 Willie Mays	.10	.25
Head shot, no hat		
56 Willie Mays	.10	.25
Head shot, hat on		
57 Willie Mays	.10	.25
Head shot, looking right		
58 Willie Mays	.10	.25
Posed batting stance		
59 Willie Mays	.10	.25
On one knee, frowning		
60 Willie Mays	.10	.25
Bat in air over		
left shoulder		
61 Willie Mays	.10	.25
Posed, bat over left shoulder		
62 Willie Mays	.10	.25
Posed, looking left		
bat held straight up		
63 Willie Mays	.10	.25
Side view		
bat on right shoulder		
64 Willie Mays	.10	.25
Smiling, no hat		
65 Willie Mays	.10	.25
Two bats		
resting on right shoulder		
66 Willie Mays	.10	.25
Mets uniform		
bat in air		
67 Willie Mays	.10	.25
Posed		
bat on right shoulder		
smiling		
68 Willie Mays	.10	.25
Portrait, frown on face		
69 Willie Mays	.10	.25
Right shoulder to camera		
looking serious		
70 Willie Mays	.10	.25
Posed, bat on right shoulder		
Giants' player		
30 in background		
71 Willie Mays	.10	.25
Running with		
sunglasses flipped up		
72 Willie Mays	.10	.25
Holding right hand		
in glove with a		
stadium background		
73 Willie Mays	.10	.25
Swinging		
74 Willie Mays	.10	.25
Portrait		
wearing black turtleneck		
under uniform		
75 Willie Mays	.10	.25
Head shot		
hands gripping bat on left		
76 Willie Mays	.10	.25
Portrait, Mets uniform		
batting cage		
77 Willie Mays	.10	.25
Head shot, faded color		
78 Willie Mays	.10	.25
Posed, swinging		
79 Willie Mays	.10	.25
Head shot, no bat		
80 Willie Mays	.10	.25
Preparing to field		
81 Willie Mays	.10	.25
Side view		
bat in air		
over right shoulder		
82 Willie Mays	.10	.25
Head shot, serious look		
83 Willie Mays	.10	.25
Posed, batting stance		
84 Willie Mays	.10	.25
Autographing fan's baseball		
85 Willie Mays	.10	.25
Holding bat across chest		
86 Willie Mays	.10	.25
Smiling, head shot		
87 Willie Mays	.10	.25
Faded color		
posed batting stance		
88 Willie Mays	.10	.25
Side portrait		
89 Willie Mays	.10	.25
In batting cage		
wearing Mets uniform		
90 Willie Mays	.10	.25
Horizontal view		
holding bat extended		
straight out		

1967 Ashland Oil

This 12 card set measures 2" by 7 1/2" and the cards are unnumbered. Therefore, we have sequenced the cards in alphabetical order. Jim Maloney is considered tougher and is notated as a SP in the listings below.

COMPLETE SET (9)	150.00	300.00
1 Jim Bunning	10.00	25.00
2 Elston Howard	6.00	15.00
3 Al Kaline	20.00	40.00
4 Harmon Killebrew	12.50	30.00
5 Ed Kranepool	4.00	10.00
6 Jim Maloney SP	30.00	60.00
7 Bill Mazeroski	10.00	25.00
8 Frank Robinson	10.00	25.00
9 Ron Santo	20.00	40.00
10 Joe Torre	8.00	20.00
11 Leon Wagner	4.00	10.00
12 Pete Ward	4.00	10.00

1965 Astros Jay Publishing

This 12-card set of the Houston Astros measures approximately 5" by 7". The fronts feature black-and-white posed player photos with the player's and team name printed below in the white border. These cards were packaged 12 to a packet. The backs are blank. The cards are unnumbered and checklisted below in alphabetical order. This was the debut season for Houston to be named the Astros.

COMPLETE SET (12)	20.00	50.00
1 Dave Adlesh	2.00	5.00
2 Bob Aspromonte	2.00	5.00
3 John Bateman	2.00	5.00
4 Walt Bond	2.00	5.00
5 Ron Brand	2.00	5.00
6 Nellie Fox	4.00	10.00
7 Jerry Grote	2.00	5.00
8 Sonny Jackson	2.00	5.00
9 Eddie Kasko	2.00	5.00
10 Bob Lillis	2.00	5.00
11 Mike White	2.00	5.00
12 Lum Harris MG	2.00	5.00

1965 Astros Team Issue

These blank-back black and white photos measure 3 1/4" by 5 1/2". The photos are facsimile autographs on the bottom and we have sequenced them in alphabetical order.

COMPLETE SET (25)	50.00	100.00
1 Jimmie Adair CO	1.25	3.00
2 Bob Aspromonte	1.50	4.00
3 John Bateman	1.25	3.00
4 Walt Bond	1.25	3.00
5 Bob Bruce	1.25	3.00
6 Jim Busby CO	1.25	3.00
7 Danny Coombs	1.25	3.00
8 Larry Dierker	2.50	6.00
9 Dick Farrell	1.25	3.00
10 Nellie Fox CO	6.00	15.00
11 Joe Gaines	1.25	3.00
12 Dave Giusti	1.50	4.00
13 Luman Harris MG	1.25	3.00
14 Eddie Kasko	1.25	3.00
15 Bob Lillis	1.25	3.00
16 Ken Mackenzie	1.25	3.00
17 Joe Morgan	4.00	10.00
18 Don Nottebart	1.25	3.00
19 Jim Owens	1.25	3.00
20 Howie Pollet CO	1.25	3.00
21 Gene Ratliff	1.25	3.00
22 Claude Raymond	1.25	3.00
23 Rusty Staub	3.00	8.00
24 Jim Wynn	2.50	6.00
25 Hal Woodeshick	1.25	3.00

1967 Astros

These 30 blank-backed cards are irregularly cut, but most measure approximately 1 1/4" by 2". They feature white bordered black-and-white posed player photos and carry the player's name and position in black lettering within the lower white margin. The backs are blank. The cards are unnumbered and checklisted below in alphabetical order.

COMPLETE SET (30)	30.00	60.00
1 Dave Adlesh	.75	2.00
2 Bob Aspromonte	1.00	2.50
3 John Bateman	.75	2.00
4 Wade Blasingame	.75	2.00
5 John Buzhardt	.75	2.00
6 Danny Coombs	.75	2.00
7 Mike Cuellar	1.25	3.00
8 Ron Davis	.75	2.00
9 Larry Dierker	1.50	4.00
10 Dave Giusti	1.00	2.50
11 Fred Gladding	.75	2.00
12 Julio Gotay	.75	2.00
13 Buddy Hancken CO	.75	2.00
14 Grady Hatton MG	.75	2.00
15 Hal King	.75	2.00
16 Denny Lemaster	.75	2.00
17 Mel McGaha CO	.75	2.00
18 Denis Menke	.75	2.00
19 Norm Miller	.75	2.00
20 Joe Morgan	4.00	10.00
21 Ivan Murrell	.75	2.00
22 Jim Owens CO	.75	2.00
23 Salty Parker CO	.75	2.00
24 Doug Rader	1.25	3.00
25 Jim Ray	.75	2.00
26 Rusty Staub	2.50	6.00
27 Lee Thomas	.75	2.00
28 Hector Torres	.75	2.00
29 Don Wilson	1.25	3.00
30 Jimmy Wynn	1.50	4.00

1967 Astros Team Issue Postcards

These cards, which measure just slightly shorter than standard postcards, feature members of the 1967 Houston Astros. These cards have the player's name , position and Houston Astros (in all caps) at the bottom of the white borders. Since these cards are unnumbered, we have sequenced them in alphabetical order.

COMPLETE SET (27)	15.00	40.00
1 Bob Aspromonte	.60	1.50
2 Lee Bales	.40	1.00
3 John Bateman	.40	1.00
4 Ron Brand	.40	1.00
5 Bo Belinsky	.60	1.50
6 Mike Cuellar	.75	2.00
7 Ron Davis	.40	1.00
8 Larry Dierker	1.00	2.50
9 Dick Farrell	.40	1.00
10 Dave Giusti	.40	1.00
11 Chuck Harrison	.40	1.00
12 Grady Hatton MG	.40	1.00
13 Bill Heath	.40	1.00
14 Sonny Jackson	.40	1.00
15 Jim Landis	.40	1.00
16 Bob Lillis	.40	1.00
17 Barry Latman	.40	1.00
18 Ed Mathews	2.00	5.00
19 Joe Morgan	3.00	8.00
20 Aaron Pointer	.40	1.00
21 Claude Raymond	.40	1.00
22 Carroll Sembera	.40	1.00
23 Dan Schneider	.40	1.00
24 Rusty Staub	1.25	3.00
25 Don Wilson	.75	2.00
26 Jim Wynn	.60	1.50
27 Chris Zachary	.40	1.00

1967 Astros Team Issue

This 12-card team-issued set features the 1967 Houston Astros. The cards measure approximately 2 1/2" by 3" and show signs of perforation on their sides. The reason for the perforations were that the they were issued as a perforated sheet and sold at Astrodome souvenir stands. The posed color player photos have white borders and a facsimile autograph inscribed across them. The horizontally oriented backs have biography and career summary information on a yellow background, and complete statistics. The cards are unnumbered and checklisted below in alphabetical order. This set was available for $1 direct from the Astros.

COMPLETE SET (12)	50.00	100.00
1 Bob Aspromonte	2.00	5.00
2 John Bateman	1.25	3.00
3 Mike Cuellar	2.50	6.00
4 Larry Dierker	3.00	8.00
5 Dave Giusti	2.00	5.00
6 Grady Hatton MG	1.25	3.00
7 Bill Heath	1.25	3.00
8 Sonny Jackson	1.25	3.00
9 Eddie Mathews	10.00	25.00
10 Joe Morgan	10.00	25.00
11 Rusty Staub	3.00	8.00
12 Jim Wynn	3.00	8.00

1970 Astros Photos

These photos feature members of the 1970 Houston Astros. The photos are unnumbered and we have sequenced them in alphabetical order. A photo of Cesar Cedeno in his rookie season is included in this set.

COMPLETE SET	8.00	20.00
1 Jack Billingham	.20	.50
2 Cesar Cedeno	.60	1.50
3 Ron Cook	.20	.50
4 George Culver	.20	.50
5 Larry Dierker	.40	1.00
6 Jack DiLauro	.20	.50
7 John Edwards	.20	.50
8 Ken Forsch	.30	.75
9 Fred Gladding	.20	.50
10 Larry Howard	.20	.50
11 Keith Lampard	.20	.50
12 Denny LeMaster	.20	.50
13 Marty Martinez	.20	.50
14 John Mayberry	.30	.75
15 Denis Menke	.20	.50
16 Roger Metzger	.20	.50
17 Jesus Alou	.30	.75
18 Norm Miller	.20	.50
19 Joe Morgan	1.50	4.00
20 Doug Rader	.40	1.00
21 Jim Ray	.20	.50
22 Hector Torres	.20	.50
23 Harry Walker MG	.20	.50
24 Bob Watson	.40	1.00
25 Bob Watson	.40	1.00
26 Don Wilson	.20	.50
27 Jim Wynn	.40	1.00
28 Jim York	.20	.50

1970 Astros Team Issue

This 12-card set of the Houston Astros measures approximately 4 1/4" by 7". The fronts display black-and-white player portraits bordered in white. The player's name and team are printed in the top margin. The backs are blank. The cards are unnumbered and checklisted below in alphabetical order.

COMPLETE SET (10)	8.00	20.00
1 Tommy Davis	.75	2.00
2 Larry Dierker	.75	2.00
3 John Edwards	.40	1.00
4 Fred Gladding	.40	1.00
5 Tom Griffin	.40	1.00
6 Denny Lemaster	.40	1.00
7 Denis Menke	.40	1.00
8 Joe Morgan	2.00	5.00
9 Joe Pepitone	.60	1.50
10 Doug Rader	.60	1.50
11 Don Wilson	.60	1.50
12 Jim Wynn	.75	2.00

1971 Astros Coke

Sponsored by the Houston Coca-Cola Bottling Company, these twelve photos measure approximately 8" by 11" and feature artwork depicting Houston Astro players against stadium backgrounds. The pictures have white borders. A facsimile autograph is printed in black on the picture. The horizontal backs show a pale blue tinted photo of the Astrodome, with player biographical information, statistics and career highlights printed in darker blue over the photo. At the top are the Coca-Cola emblem and slogan. The photos are unnumbered and checklisted below in alphabetical order. Wade Blasingame and Jimmy Wynn are considered to be in shorter supply than the other cards and have been marked with SP in the checklist.

COMPLETE SET (12)	20.00	50.00
1 Jesus Alou	1.00	2.50
2 Wade Blasingame SP	4.00	10.00
3 Cesar Cedeno	1.50	4.00
4 Larry Dierker	1.25	3.00
5 John Edwards	.75	2.00
6 Denis Menke	.75	2.00
7 Roger Metzger	.75	2.00
8 Joe Morgan	4.00	10.00
9 Doug Rader	1.00	2.50
10 Bob Watson	1.25	3.00
11 Don Wilson	.75	2.00
12 Jim Wynn SP	6.00	15.00

1971 Astros Team Issue

This 24-card set measures approximately 3 1/2" by 5 3/8" and features black-and-white player portraits in a white border. A facsimile autograph is printed across the bottom of the picture. The backs are blank. The cards are unnumbered and checklisted below in alphabetical order.

COMPLETE SET (24)	6.00	15.00
1 Wade Blasingame	.20	.50
2 Cesar Cedeno	.60	1.50
3 Rich Chiles	.20	.50
4 George Culver	.20	.50
5 Larry Dierker	.40	1.00
6 John Edwards	.20	.50
7 Ken Forsch	.30	.75
8 Fred Gladding	.20	.50
9 Tom Griffin	.20	.50
10 Buddy Harris	.20	.50
11 Buddy Hancken CO	.20	.50
12 Jack Hiatt	.20	.50
13 Larry Howard	.20	.50
14 Hub Kittle CO	.20	.50
15 Roger Metzger	.30	.75
16 Joe Morgan	1.25	3.00
17 Jim Owens CO	.20	.50
18 Salty Parker CO	.20	.50
19 Doug Rader	.30	.75
20 Jim Ray	.20	.50
21 Harry Walker MG	.30	.75
22 Bob Watson	.40	1.00
23 Don Wilson	.30	.75
24 Jim Wynn	.40	1.00

1972 Astros Team Issue

This 30-card set of the 1972 Houston Astros measures approximately 3 1/2" by 5" and features black-and-white player portraits with white borders. A facsimile autographed is printed across the bottom of the photo. The backs are blank. The cards are unnumbered and checklisted below in alphabetical order.

COMPLETE SET (30)	6.00	15.00
1 Jesus Alou	.30	.75
2 Wade Blasingame	.20	.50
3 Cesar Cedeno	.60	1.50
4 George Culver	.20	.50
5 Larry Dierker	.40	1.00
6 John Edwards	.20	.50
7 Robert Fenwick	.20	.50
8 Ken Forsch	.20	.50
9 Fred Gladding	.20	.50
10 Tom Griffin	.20	.50
11 Buddy Hancken CO	.20	.50
12 Tommy Helms	.20	.50
13 Jack Hiatt	.20	.50
14 Hub Kittle CO	.20	.50
15 Lee May	.30	.75
16 Roger Metzger	.20	.50
17 Norm Miller	.20	.50
18 Jim Owens CO	.20	.50
19 Salty Parker CO	.20	.50
20 Doug Rader	.30	.75
21 Jim Ray	.20	.50
22 Jerry Reuss	.40	1.00
23 Dave Roberts	.20	.50
24 Jim Stewart	.20	.50
25 Bob Stinson	.20	.50
26 Harry Walker	.20	.50
27 Bob Watson	.40	1.00
28 Don Wilson	.30	.75
29 Jim Wynn	.40	1.00
30 Jim York	.20	.50

1975 Astros Postcards

These photos were issued and featured members of the 1975 Houston Astros. They are unnumbered and we have sequenced them in alphabetical order.

COMPLETE SET (30)	6.00	15.00
1 Rob Andrews	.20	.50
2 Rafael Batista	.20	.50
3 Ken Boswell	.20	.50
4 Enos Cabell	.20	.50
5 Cesar Cedeno	.60	1.50
6 Jose Cruz	.30	.75
7 Larry Dierker	.40	1.00
8 Mike Easler	.30	.75
9 Ken Forsch	.20	.50
10 Preston Gomez MG	.20	.50
11 Wayne Granger	.20	.50
12 Tom Griffin	.20	.50
13 Greg Gross	.20	.50
14 Tommy Helms	.20	.50
15 Wilbur Howard	.20	.50
16 Cliff Johnson	.20	.50
17 Skip Jutze	.20	.50
18 Hub Kittle CO	.20	.50
19 Doug Konieczny	.20	.50
20 Bob Lillis CO	.20	.50
21 Milt May	.20	.50
22 Roger Metzger	.20	.50
23 Larry Milbourne	.20	.50
24 Doug Rader	.20	.50
25 J.R. Richard	.40	1.00
26 Dave Roberts	.20	.50
27 Fred Scherman	.20	.50
28 Bob Watson	.40	1.00
29 Jim Williams	.20	.50
30 Jim York	.20	.50

1976 Astros Postcards

This 32-card set of the Houston Astros features player photos on postcard-size cards. The cards are unnumbered and checklisted below in alphabetical order.

COMPLETE SET (32)	6.00	15.00
1 Joaquin Andujar	.30	.75
2 Mike Barlow	.20	.50
3 Ken Boswell	.20	.50
4 Enos Cabell	.20	.50
5 Cesar Cedeno	.30	.75
6 Mike Cosgrove	.20	.50
7 Jose Cruz	.40	1.00
8 Larry Dierker	.40	1.00
9 Jerry DaVanon	.20	.50
10 Ken Forsch	.20	.50
11 Tom Griffin	.20	.50
12 Greg Gross	.20	.50
13 Larry Hardy	.20	.50
14 Wilbur Howard	.20	.50
15 Art Howe	.60	1.50
16 Cliff Johnson	.30	.75
17 Deacon Jones CO	.20	.50
18 Skip Jutze	.20	.50
19 Bob Lillis CO	.20	.50
20 Joe McIntosh	.20	.50
21 Roger Metzger	.20	.50
22 Larry Milbourne	.20	.50
23 Joe Niekro	.40	1.00
24 Tony Pacheco	.20	.50
25 Gene Pentz	.20	.50
26 J.R. Richard	.40	1.00
27 Leon Roberts	.20	.50
28 Gil Rondon	.20	.50
29 Jose Sosa	.20	.50
30 Bill Virdon MG	.20	.50
31 Bob Watson	.40	1.00
32 Mel Wright CO	.20	.50

1978 Astros Burger King

The cards in this 23-card set measure 2 1/2" by 3 1/2". Released in local Houston Burger King outlets during the 1978 season, this Houston Astros series contains the standard 22 numbered player cards and one unnumbered checklist. The player poses found to differ from the regular Topps issue are marked with asterisks.

COMPLETE SET (23)	6.00	15.00
1 Bill Virdon MG	.40	1.00
2 Joe Ferguson	.20	.50
3 Ed Herrmann	.20	.50
4 J.R. Richard	.60	1.50
5 Joe Niekro	.40	1.00
6 Floyd Bannister	.30	.75
7 Joaquin Andujar	.60	1.50
8 Ken Forsch	.20	.50
9 Mark Lemongello	.20	.50
10 Joe Sambito	.20	.50
11 Gene Pentz	.20	.50
12 Bob Watson	.60	1.50
13 Julio Gonzalez	.20	.50
14 Enos Cabell	.30	.75
15 Roger Metzger	.20	.50
16 Art Howe	.40	1.00
17 Jose Cruz	.60	1.50
18 Cesar Cedeno	.60	1.50
19 Terry Puhl	.30	.75
20 Wilbur Howard	.20	.50
21 Dave Bergman *	.30	.75
22 Jesus Alou *	.30	.75
NNO Checklist Card TP	.10	.25

1978 Astros Postcards

These postcards feature members of the 1978 Houston Astros. They are unnumbered and we have ordered them alphabetically.

COMPLETE SET (28)	6.00	15.00
1 Jesus Alou	.20	.50
2 Joaquin Andujar	.20	.50
3 Floyd Bannister	.20	.50
4 Dave Bergman	.20	.50
5 Enos Cabell	.20	.50
6 Cesar Cedeno	.40	1.00
7 Jose Cruz	.30	.75
8 Tom Dixon	.20	.50
9 Ken Forsch	.20	.50
10 Julio Gonzalez	.20	.50
11 Wilbur Howard	.20	.50
12 Art Howe	.40	1.00
13 Deacon Jones CO	.20	.50
14 Rafael Landestoy	.20	.50
15 Mark Lemongello	.20	.50
16 Bob Lillis CO	.20	.50
17 Tony Pacheco CO	.20	.50
18 Terry Puhl	.20	.50
19 Luis Pujois	.20	.50
20 Joe Niekro	.30	.75
21 J. R. Richard	.40	1.00
22 Joe Sambito	.30	.75
23 Jimmy Sexton	.30	.75
24 Bill Virdon MG	.20	.50
25 Dennis Walling	.20	.50
26 Bob Watson	.40	1.00
27 Rick Williams	.20	.50
28 Mel Wright CO	.20	.50

1979 Astros Postcards

These 4" by 5" postcards feature members of the 1979 Houston Astros. They are unnumbered and sequenced them in alphabetical order.

COMPLETE SET (28)	6.00	15.00
1 Jesus Alou	.20	.50
2 Joaquin Andujar	.20	.50
3 Alan Ashby	.20	.50
4 Bruce Bochy	.60	1.50
5 Enos Cabell	.20	.50
6 Cedar Cedeno	.30	.75
7 Jose Cruz	.30	.75
8 Tom Dixon	.20	.50
9 Ken Forsch	.20	.50
10 Julio Gonzalez	.20	.50
11 Art Howe	.20	.50
12 Rafael Landestoy	.20	.50
13 Jeff Leonard	.20	.50
14 Bo McLaughlin	.20	.50
15 Joe Niekro	.30	.75
16 Randy Niemann	.20	.50
17 Terry Puhl	.20	.50
18 Craig Reynolds	.20	.50
19 Frank Riccelli	.20	.50
20 J.R. Richard	.40	1.00
21 Bert Roberge	.20	.50
22 Vern Ruhle	.20	.50
23 Joe Sambito	.20	.50
24 Jimmy Sexton	.30	.75
25 Bill Virdon MG	.20	.50
26 Denny Walling	.20	.50
27 Bob Watson	.40	1.00
28 Gary Wilson	.20	.50

1980 Astros Team Issue

Measuring 4" by 5", these dull finish cards had a limited distribution. Since they are unnumbered we have sequenced them in alphabetical order.

COMPLETE SET (29)	8.00	20.00
1 Joaquin Andujar	.20	.50
2 Alan Ashby	.20	.50
3 Dave Bergman	.20	.50
4 Bruce Bochy	.30	.75
5 Enos Cabell	.20	.50
6 Cesar Cedeno	.40	1.00
7 Jose Cruz	.30	.75
8 Ken Forsch	.20	.50
9 Julio Gonzalez	.20	.50
10 Danny Heep	.20	.50
11 Art Howe	.20	.50
12 Deacon Jones CO	.20	.50
13 Frank LaCorte	.20	.50
14 Rafael Landestoy	.20	.50
15 Bob Lillis CO	.20	.50
16 Don Leppert CO	.20	.50
17 Joe Morgan	.75	2.00
18 Joe Niekro	.30	.75
19 Gordon Pladson	.20	.50
20 Terry Puhl	.20	.50
21 Craig Reynolds	.20	.50
22 J.R. Richard	.40	1.00
23 Bert Roberge	.20	.50
24 Nolan Ryan	1.50	4.00
25 Joe Sambito	.20	.50
26 Dave Smith	.40	1.00
27 Bill Virdon MG	.20	.50
28 Denny Walling	.20	.50
29 Mel Wright CO	.20	.50

1981 Astros Postcards

These 30 postcards were issued and featured members of the playoff bound 1981 Houston Astros. They are unnumbered and we have sequenced them in alphabetical order.

COMPLETE SET (30)	8.00	20.00
1 Alan Ashby	.20	.50
2 Cesar Cedeno	.30	.75
3 Jose Cruz	.30	.75
4 Kiko Garcia	.20	.50
5 Danny Heep	.20	.50
6 Art Howe	.20	.50
7 Mike Ivie	.20	.50
8 Deacon Jones CO	.20	.50
9 Bob Knepper	.20	.50
10 Frank LaCorte	.20	.50
11 Don Leppert CO	.20	.50
12 Bob Lillis CO	.20	.50
13 Joe Niekro	.30	.75
14 Joe Pittman	.20	.50
15 Terry Puhl	.20	.50
16 Luis Pujols	.20	.50
17 Craig Reynolds	.20	.50
18 J.R. Richard	.40	1.00
19 Dave Roberts	.20	.50
20 Vern Ruhle	.20	.50
21 Nolan Ryan	2.00	5.00
22 Joe Sambito	.20	.50
23 Dave Smith	.30	.75
24 Bobby Sprowl	.20	.50
25 Don Sutton	.60	1.50
26 Dickie Thon	.20	.50
27 Denny Walling	.20	.50
28 Gary Woods	.20	.50
29 Mel Wright	.20	.50
30 Mel Wright CO	.20	.50

1982 Astros Postcards

These postcards feature members of the 1982 Houston Astros. They are unnumbered and we have sequenced them in alphabetical order.

COMPLETE SET (29)	6.00	15.00
1 Alan Ashby	.20	.50
2 Jose Cruz	.30	.75
3 Kiko Garcia	.20	.50
4 Phil Garner	.30	.75
5 Danny Heep	.20	.50
6 Art Howe	.20	.50
7 Deacon Jones CO	.20	.50
8 Bob Knepper	.20	.50
9 Alan Knicely	.20	.50
10 Ray Knight	.20	.50
11 Mike LaCoss	.20	.50
12 Frank LaCorte	.20	.50
13 Don Leppert CO	.20	.50
14 Bob Lillis MG	.20	.50
15 Randy Moffitt	.20	.50
16 Joe Niekro	.30	.75
17 Terry Puhl	.20	.50
18 Luis Pujols	.20	.50
19 Craig Reynolds	.20	.50
20 J.R. Richard	.30	.75
21 Vern Ruhle	.20	.50
22 Nolan Ryan	2.00	5.00
23 Joe Sambito	.20	.50
24 Tony Scott	.20	.50
25 Harry Spilman	.20	.50
26 Dave Smith	.20	.50
27 Dickie Thon	.20	.50
28 Denny Walling	.20	.50
29 Mel Wright CO	.20	.50

1983 Astros Postcards

These postcards feature members of the 1983 Houston Astros. They are unnumbered and we have sequenced them in alphabetical order.

COMPLETE SET (35)	8.00	20.00
1 Alan Ashby	.20	.50
2 Kevin Bass	.20	.50
3 Jose Cruz	.30	.75
4 Bill Dawley	.20	.50
5 Cot Deal CO	.20	.50
6 Frank DiPino	.20	.50
7 Bill Doran	.30	.75
8 Phil Garner	.30	.75
9 Art Howe	.20	.50
10 Bob Knepper	.20	.50
11 Ray Knight	.20	.50
12 Frank LaCorte	.20	.50
13 Mike LaCoss	.20	.50
14 Don Leppert CO	.20	.50
15 Bob Lillis MG	.20	.50
16 Mike Madden	.20	.50
17 Denis Menke	.20	.50
18 Omar Moreno	.20	.50
19 Les Moss CO	.20	.50
20 Joe Niekro	.30	.75
21 Terry Puhl	.20	.50
22 Luis Pujols	.20	.50
23 Craig Reynolds	.20	.50
24 Vern Ruhle	.20	.50
25 Nolan Ryan	2.00	5.00
26 Joe Sambito	.20	.50
27 Mike Scott	.40	1.00
28 Tony Scott	.20	.50
29 Dave Smith	.20	.50
30 Julio Solano	.20	.50
31 Harry Spillman	.20	.50
32 Dickie Thon	.20	.50
33 Tim Tolman	.20	.50
34 Jerry Walker CO	.20	.50
35 Denny Walling	.20	.50

1984 Astros Mother's

The cards in this 28-card set measure 2 1/2" by 3 1/2". In 1984, the Los Angeles based Mother's Cookies Co. issued five sets of cards featuring players from Major League teams. Similar to their 1952 and 1953 issues, the cards have rounded corners. The backs of the cards contain the Mother's Cookies logo. The cards were distributed in partial sets to fans at the respective stadiums of the teams involved. Whereas 20 cards were given to each patron, a redemption card - redeemable for eight more cards - was included. Unfortunately, the eight cards received by redeeming the coupon were not necessarily the eight needed to complete a set. Hobbyist Barry Colla was involved in the production of these sets.

COMPLETE SET (28)	8.00	20.00

1 Nolan Ryan 4.00 10.00
2 Joe Niekro .30 .75
3 Alan Ashby .08 .25
4 Bill Doran .30 .75
5 Phil Garner .20 .50
6 Ray Knight . .08 .25
7 Dickie Thon .08 .25
8 Jose Cruz .40 1.00
9 Jerry Mumphrey .08 .25
10 Terry Puhl .20 .50
11 Enos Cabell .08 .25
12 Harry Spilman .08 .25
13 Dave Smith .20 .50
14 Mike Scott .40 1.00
15 Bob Lillis MG .08 .25
16 Bob Knepper .08 .25
17 Frank DiPino .08 .25
18 Tom Wieghaus .08 .25
19 Denny Walling .08 .25
20 Tony Scott .08 .25
21 Alan Bannister .08 .25
22 Bill Dawley .08 .25
23 Vern Ruhle .08 .25
24 Mike LaCoss .08 .25
25 Mike Madden .08 .25
26 Craig Reynolds .08 .25
27 Astros' Coaches .20 .50
 Cot Deal
 Don Leppert
 Denis Menk
28 Astros' Checklist .08 .25
 Astros Logo

1984 Astros Postcards

These postcards feature members of the 1984 Astros. They are unnumbered so we have sequenced them in alphabetical order.

COMPLETE SET (5) 8.00 20.00
1 Alan Ashby .20 .50
2 Mark Bailey .20 .50
3 Kevin Bass .20 .50
4 Enos Cabell .20 .50
5 Jose Cruz .30 .75
6 Bill Dawley .20 .50
7 Cot Deal CO .20 .50
8 Frank DiPino .20 .50
9 Bill Doran .30 .75
10 Phil Garner .30 .75
11 Bob Knepper .20 .50
12 Ray Knight .20 .50
13 Mike LaCoss .20 .50
14 Don Leppert CO .20 .50
15 Bob Lillis MG .20 .50
16 Mike Madden .20 .50
17 Denis Menke CO .20 .50
18 Les Moss CO .20 .50
19 Jerry Mumphrey .20 .50
20 Joe Niekro .30 .75
21 Terry Puhl .20 .50
22 Craig Reynolds .20 .50
23 Vern Ruhle .20 .50
24 Nolan Ryan 2.00 5.00
25 Joe Sambito .20 .50
26 Mike Scott .40 1.00
27 Dave Smith .20 .50
28 Julio Solano .20 .50
29 Harry Spilman .20 .50
30 Dickie Thon .20 .50
31 Jerry Walker CO .20 .50
32 Denny Walling .20 .50

1985 Astros Mother's

The cards in this 28-card set measure 2 1/2" by 3 1/2". In 1985, the Los Angeles-based Mother's Cookies Co. again issued five sets of cards featuring players from Major League teams. The backs of the cards contain the Mother's Cookies logo. Cards were passed out at the stadium on July 13. The checklist card features the Astros logo on the obverse.

COMPLETE SET (28) 5.00 12.00
1 Bob Lillis MG .08 .25
2 Nolan Ryan 3.00 8.00
3 Phil Garner .20 .50
4 Jose Cruz .40 1.00
5 Denny Walling .08 .25
6 Joe Niekro .30 .75
7 Terry Puhl .20 .50
8 Bill Doran .08 .25
9 Dickie Thon .08 .25
10 Enos Cabell .08 .25
11 Frank DiPino .08 .25
12 Julio Solano .08 .25
13 Alan Ashby .08 .25
14 Craig Reynolds .08 .25
15 Jerry Mumphrey .08 .25
16 Bill Dawley .08 .25
17 Mark Bailey .08 .25
18 Mike Scott .40 1.00
19 Harry Spilman .08 .25
20 Bob Knepper .08 .25
21 Dave Smith .20 .50
22 Kevin Bass .08 .25
23 Tim Tolman .08 .25
24 Jeff Calhoun .08 .25
25 Jim Pankovits .08 .25
26 Ron Mathis .08 .25
27 Astros' Coaches .20 .50
 Cot Deal
 Matt Galante
 Don Leppe
28 Astros' Checklist .08 .25
 Astros Logo

1985 Astros Postcards

These black and white blank-backed postcards were issued by the Houston Astros and feature members of the 1985 Astros. Since these photos are unnumbered, we have sequenced them in alphabetical order.

COMPLETE SET (32) 8.00 20.00
1 Alan Ashby .20 .50
2 Mark Bailey .20 .50
3 Kevin Bass .20 .50
4 Jeff Calhoun .20 .50
5 Jose Cruz .30 .75
6 Bill Dawley .20 .50
7 Cot Deal CO .20 .50
8 Frank DiPino .20 .50
9 Bill Doran .20 .50
10 Matt Galante CO .20 .50
11 Phil Garner .30 .75
12 Chris Jones .20 .50
13 Bob Knepper .20 .50
14 Bob Lillis MG .20 .50
15 Mike Madden .20 .50
16 Ron Mathis .20 .50
17 Denis Menke CO .20 .50
18 Les Moss CO .20 .50
19 Jerry Mumphrey .20 .50
20 Joe Niekro .30 .75
21 Jim Pankovits .20 .50
22 Bert Pena .20 .50
23 Terry Puhl .20 .50
24 Craig Reynolds .20 .50
25 Mike Richardt .20 .50
26 Nolan Ryan 2.00 5.00
27 Mike Scott .40 1.00
28 Dave Smith .30 .75
29 Harry Spilman .20 .50
30 Dickie Thon .20 .50
31 Jerry Walker CO .20 .50
32 Denny Walling .20 .50

1986 Astros Greats TCMA

This 12-card standard-size set features some of the best Astros players since their inception in 1962. The cards feature a player photo on the front. Player information as well as statistics are on the back.

COMPLETE SET (12) 2.00 5.00
1 Bob Watson .30 .75
2 Joe Morgan .75 2.00
3 Roger Metzger .08 .25
4 Doug Rader .08 .25
5 Jimmy Wynn .30 .75
6 Cesar Cedeno .30 .75
7 Rusty Staub .40 1.00
8 Johnny Edwards .08 .25
9 J.R. Richard .20 .50
10 Dave Roberts .08 .25
11 Fred Gladding .08 .25
12 Bill Virdon MG .08 .25

1986 Astros Miller Lite

This 22 card set measures 4 1/2" by 6 3/4" and was issued at Astros games. The Nolan Ryan card was not issued at games and is considered a short print as supplies of the card are very limited. The complete set price does include the Ryan card.

COMPLETE SET (21) 10.00 25.00
1 Alan Ashby .40 1.00
2 Mark Bailey .40 1.00
3 Kevin Bass .40 1.00
4 Jose Cruz 1.00 2.50
5 Glenn Davis .60 1.50
6 Jim Deshaies .40 1.00
7 Frank DiPino .40 1.00
8 Bill Doran .40 1.00
9 Phil Garner .60 1.50
10 Billy Hatcher .40 1.00
11 Charlie Kerfeld .40 1.00
12 Bob Knepper .40 1.00
13 Hal Lanier .40 1.00
14 Mike Madden .40 1.00
15 Jim Pankovits .40 1.00
16 Terry Puhl .60 1.50
17 Craig Reynolds .40 1.00
18 Nolan Ryan SP 100.00 200.00
19 Mike Scott 1.00 2.50
20 Dave Smith .60 1.50
21 Dickie Thon .40 1.00
22 Denny Walling .40 1.00

1986 Astros Mother's

This set consists of 28 full-color, rounded-corner standard-size cards. Starter sets (only 20 cards but also including a certificate for eight more cards) were given out at the ballpark and collectors were encouraged to trade to fill in the rest of their set. Cards were originally given out at the Astrodome on July 10th. Since the 1986 All-Star Game was held in Houston, the set features Astro All-Stars since 1962 as painted by artist Richard Wallich. The set numbering is essentially chronological according to when each player was selected for the All-Star Game as an Astro.

COMPLETE SET (28) 5.00 12.00
1 Dick Farrell .08 .25
2 Hal Woodeshick .08 .25
3 Joe Morgan .75 2.00
4 Claude Raymond .08 .25
5 Mike Cuellar .20 .50
6 Rusty Staub .40 1.00
7 Jimmy Wynn .30 .75
8 Larry Dierker .30 .75
9 Denis Menke .08 .25
10 Don Wilson .08 .25
11 Cesar Cedeno .20 .50
12 Lee May .20 .50
13 Bob Watson .40 1.00
14 Ken Forsch .08 .25
15 Joaquin Andujar .08 .25
16 Terry Puhl .20 .50
17 Joe Niekro .30 .75
18 Craig Reynolds .08 .25
19 Joe Sambito .08 .25
20 Jose Cruz .40 1.00
21 J.R. Richard .30 .75
22 Bob Knepper .08 .25
23 Nolan Ryan 3.00 8.00
24 Ray Knight .08 .25
25 Bill Dawley .08 .25
26 Dickie Thon .08 .25
27 Jerry Mumphrey .08 .25
28 Checklist Card .08 .25
 Astros' A-S Logo

1986 Astros Police

This 26-card safety set was also sponsored by Kool-Aid. The backs contain a biographical paragraph above a "Tip from the Dugout". The front features a full-color photo of the player, his name, and uniform number. The cards are numbered on the back and measure approximately 2 5/8" by 4 1/8". The backs are printed in orange and blue on white card stock. Sets were distributed at the Astrodome on June 14th as well as given away throughout the summer by the Houston Police.

COMPLETE SET (26) 3.00 8.00
1 Jim Pankovits .08 .25
2 Nolan Ryan 1.50 4.00
3 Mike Scott .40 1.00
4 Kevin Bass .08 .25
5 Bill Doran .08 .25
6 Hal Lanier MG .08 .25
7 Denny Walling .08 .25
8 Alan Ashby .08 .25
9 Phil Garner .20 .50
10 Charlie Kerfeld .08 .25
11 Dave Smith .20 .50
12 Jose Cruz .40 1.00
13 Craig Reynolds .08 .25
14 Mark Bailey .08 .25
15 Bob Knepper .08 .25
16 Julio Solano .08 .25
17 Dickie Thon .08 .25
18 Mike Madden .08 .25
19 Jeff Calhoun .08 .25
20 Tony Walker .08 .25
21 Terry Puhl .20 .50
22 Glenn Davis .30 .75
23 Billy Hatcher .08 .25
24 Jim Deshaies .08 .25
25 Frank DiPino .08 .25
26 Coaching Staff .30 .75
 Gene Tenace
 Matt Galante
 Denis M

1986 Astros Postcards

These blank-backed black and white postcards feature members of the division champion 1986 Houston Astros. The fronts have a posed portrait with the players name at the bottom. Since these are unnumbered, we have sequenced them in alphabetical order.

COMPLETE SET (32) 8.00 20.00
1 Larry Andersen .20 .50
2 Alan Ashby .20 .50
3 Kevin Bass .20 .50
4 Yogi Berra CO .75 2.00
5 Jeff Calhoun .20 .50
6 Jose Cruz .30 .75
7 Danny Darwin .20 .50
8 Jim Deshaies .20 .50
9 Glenn Davis .30 .75
10 Bill Doran .20 .50
11 Dan Driessen .20 .50
12 Ty Gainey .20 .50
13 Matt Galante CO .20 .50
14 Phil Garner .30 .75
15 Billy Hatcher .20 .50
16 Charlie Kerfeld .20 .50
17 Bob Knepper .20 .50
18 Hal Lanier MG .20 .50
19 Davey Lopes .30 .75
20 Aurelio Lopez .20 .50
21 Denis Menke CO .20 .50
22 Les Moss CO .20 .50
23 Jim Pankovits .20 .50
24 Terry Puhl .20 .50
25 Craig Reynolds .20 .50
26 Nolan Ryan 2.00 5.00
27 Mike Scott .40 1.00
28 Dave Smith .30 .75
29 Dickie Thon .20 .50
30 Gene Tenace .30 .75
31 Tony Walker .20 .50
32 Denny Walling .20 .50

1986 Astros Team Issue

These 16 blank-backed photos feature members of the Division Winner '86 Astros. These photos measure 6" by 9" and have full-color photos and a facsimile signature. The photos are unnumbered and we have checklisted them in alphabetical order.

COMPLETE SET (16) 4.00 10.00
1 Alan Ashby .08 .25
2 Kevin Bass .08 .25
3 Jose Cruz .40 1.00
4 Glenn Davis .30 .75
5 Bill Doran .08 .25
6 Phil Garner .20 .50
7 Billy Hatcher .08 .25
8 Charlie Kerfeld .08 .25
9 Bob Knepper .08 .25
10 Aurelio Lopez .08 .25
11 Terry Puhl .20 .50
12 Craig Reynolds .08 .25
13 Nolan Ryan 2.50 6.00
14 Mike Scott .30 .75
15 Dickie Thon .08 .25
16 Denny Walling .08 .25

1987 Astros Inaugural Season

This set features members of the 1965 Houston Astros. The cards are unnumbered, therefore we have sequenced them in alphabetical order.

COMPLETE SET (32) 5.00 12.00
1 Bob Aspromonte .08 .25
2 John Bateman .08 .25
3 Jim Beauchamp .08 .25
4 Walt Bond .08 .25
5 Ron Brand .08 .25
6 Hal Brown .08 .25
7 Bob Bruce .08 .25
8 Larry Dierker .30 .75
9 Dick (Turk) Farrell .08 .25
10 Nellie Fox .75 2.00
11 Dave Giusti .08 .25
12 Sonny Jackson .08 .25
13 Ken Johnson .08 .25
14 Eddie Kasko .08 .25
15 Don Larsen .20 .50
16 Bob Lillis .08 .25
17 Joe Morgan 1.25 3.00
18 Don Nottebart .08 .25
19 Claude Raymond .08 .25
20 Al Spangler .08 .25
21 Rusty Staub .40 1.00
22 Hal Woodeshick .08 .25
23 Jim Wynn .20 .50
24 Don Larsen .20 .50
 Bob Turley
25 Joe Morgan .75 2.00
 Nellie Fox
26 Doug Rader .08 .25
 Norm Miller
27 Jim Owens .30 .75
 Nellie Fox
 Turk Farrell
28 Al Spangler .20 .50
 Rusty Staub
 Jim Wynn
29 Bob Aspromonte .40 1.00
 Eddie Kasko
 Joe Morgan
 Walt Bond
30 Lum Harris .08 .25
 Clint Courtney
 Jim Busby
 Jimmy Adair
31 1965 Team Photo .08 .25
32 Hats Photo .08 .25

1987 Astros Mother's

This set consists of 28 full-color, rounded-corner standard-size cards. Starter sets (only 20 cards but also including a certificate for eight more cards) were given out at the ballpark and collectors were encouraged to trade to fill in the rest of their set. Cards were originally given out at the Astrodome on July 17th during a game against the Phillies. Photos were taken by Barry Colla. The sets were reportedly given out free to the first 25,000 paid admissions at the game.

COMPLETE SET (28) 5.00 12.00
1 Hal Lanier MG .08 .25
2 Mike Scott .30 .75
3 Jose Cruz .40 1.00
4 Bill Doran .08 .25
5 Bob Knepper .08 .25
6 Phil Garner .20 .50
7 Terry Puhl .20 .50
8 Nolan Ryan 2.50 6.00
9 Kevin Bass .08 .25
10 Glenn Davis .20 .50
11 Alan Ashby .08 .25
12 Charlie Kerfeld .08 .25
13 Denny Walling .08 .25
14 Danny Darwin .08 .25
15 Mark Bailey .08 .25
16 Davey Lopes .30 .75
17 Dave Meads .08 .25
18 Aurelio Lopez .08 .25
19 Craig Reynolds .08 .25
20 Dave Smith .20 .50
21 Larry Andersen .08 .25
22 Jim Pankovits .08 .25
23 Jim Deshaies .08 .25
24 Bert Pena .08 .25
25 Dickie Thon .08 .25
26 Billy Hatcher .08 .25
27 Astros' Coaches .40 1.00
 Yogi Berra
 Denis Menke
 Gene Ten
28 Checklist Card .08 .25
 Astrodome

1987 Astros 1983-85 Postcard Rerelease

Issued in 1987, these black and white blank-backed postcards feature members of the 1983-85 Houston Astros. For some reason, these cards were rereleased in 1987. Since the cards are unnumbered, we have sequenced them in alphabetical order.

COMPLETE SET (42) 10.00 25.00
1 Alan Ashby .20 .50
2 Mark Bailey .20 .50
3 George Bjorkman .20 .50
4 Enos Cabell .20 .50
5 Jose Cruz .30 .75
6 Glenn Davis .30 .75
7 Bill Dawley .20 .50
8 Frank DiPino .20 .50
9 Bill Doran .20 .50
10 Ty Gainey .20 .50
11 Phil Garner .30 .75
12 Art Howe .20 .50
13 Chris Jones .20 .50
14 Bob Knepper .20 .50
15 Ray Knight .20 .50
16 Frank Lacorte .20 .50
17 Mike LaCoss .20 .50
18 Don Leppert CO .20 .50
19 Bob Lillis MG .20 .50
20 Mike Madden .20 .50
21 Omar Moreno .20 .50
22 Jerry Mumphrey .20 .50
23 Jim Pankovits .20 .50
24 Terry Puhl .20 .50
25 Joe Niekro .30 .75
26 Bert Pena .20 .50
27 Luis Pujols .20 .50
28 Craig Reynolds .20 .50
29 J.R. Richard .40 1.00
30 Mike Richardt .20 .50
31 Mark Ross .20 .50
32 Vern Ruhle .20 .50
33 Nolan Ryan 2.00 5.00
34 Joe Sambito .20 .50
35 Mike Scott .40 1.00
36 Tony Scott .20 .50
37 Dave Smith .30 .75
39 Julio Solano .20 .50
39 Harry Spilman .20 .50
40 Stretch Suba .20 .50
41 Dickie Thon .20 .50
42 Denny Walling .20 .50

1987 Astros Police

This 26-card safety set was sponsored by the Astros, Deer Park Hospital, and Sportsmedia Presentations. The backs contain a biographical paragraph above a "Tip from the Dugout". The front features a full-color photo of the player, his name, position, and uniform number. The cards are numbered on the back and measure 2 5/8" by 4 1/8". The first twelve cards were distributed at the Astrodome on July 14th and the rest were given away later in the summer by the Deer Park Hospital.

COMPLETE SET (26) 3.00 8.00
1 Larry Andersen .08 .25
2 Mark Bailey .08 .25
3 Jose Cruz .40 1.00
4 Danny Darwin .08 .25
5 Bill Doran .08 .25
6 Billy Hatcher .08 .25
7 Hal Lanier MG .08 .25
8 Davey Lopes .20 .50
9 Dave Meads .08 .25
10 Craig Reynolds .08 .25
11 Mike Scott .30 .75
12 Denny Walling .08 .25
13 Aurelio Lopez .08 .25
14 Dickie Thon .08 .25
15 Terry Puhl .20 .50
16 Nolan Ryan 1.50 4.00
17 Dave Smith .20 .50
18 Julio Solano .08 .25
19 Jim Deshaies .08 .25
20 Bob Knepper .08 .25
21 Alan Ashby .08 .25
22 Kevin Bass .08 .25
23 Glenn Davis .20 .50
24 Phil Garner .20 .50
25 Jim Pankovits .08 .25
26 Coaching Staff .20 .50
 Gene Tenace
 Matt Galante
 Denis M

1987 Astros Postcards

These blank-backed black and white postcards feature members of the 1987 Houston Astros. The fronts have a posed portrait with the players name at the bottom. Since these are unnumbered, we have sequenced them in alphabetical order.

COMPLETE SET (33) 8.00 20.00
1 Larry Andersen .20 .50
2 Alan Ashby .20 .50
3 Mark Bailey .20 .50
4 Kevin Bass .20 .50
5 Yogi Berra CO .75 2.00
6 Jose Cruz .30 .75
7 Danny Darwin .20 .50
8 Glenn Davis .30 .75
9 Jim Deshaies .20 .50
10 Bill Doran .20 .50
11 Ty Gainey .20 .50
12 Matt Galante CO .20 .50
13 Phil Garner .30 .75
14 Billy Hatcher .20 .50
15 Charlie Kerfeld .20 .50
16 Bob Knepper .20 .50
17 Hal Lanier MG .20 .50
18 Dave Lopes .30 .75
19 Aurelio Lopez .20 .50
20 Dave Meads .20 .50
21 Denis Menke CO .20 .50
22 Les Moss CO .20 .50
23 Jim Pankovits .20 .50
24 Bert Pena .20 .50
25 Terry Puhl .20 .50
26 Craig Reynolds .20 .50
27 Nolan Ryan 2.00 5.00
28 Mike Scott .40 1.00
29 Dave Smith .20 .50
30 Julio Solano .20 .50
31 Gene Tenace CO .20 .50
32 Dickie Thon .20 .50
33 Denny Walling .20 .50

1987 Astros Shooting Stars-Series One

This set features all-time Houston Astros players. "Shooting Stars" refers to the uniform worn by the Astros in the late 60's and early 70's.These cards were issued in three different series. The cards are unnumbered so we have sequenced them in alphabetical order.

COMPLETE SET (32) 4.00 10.00
1 Cesar Cedeno .20 .50
2 Danny Coombs .08 .25
3 Mike Cuellar .20 .50
4 Larry Dierker .30 .75
5 John Edwards .08 .25
6 Dick Farrell .08 .25
7 Ken Forsch .08 .25
8 Dave Giusti .08 .25
9 Fred Gladding .08 .25
10 Tom Griffin .08 .25
11 Chuck Harrison .08 .25
12 Tommy Helms .08 .25
13 Sonny Jackson .08 .25
14 Denny Lemaster .08 .25
15 Lee May .20 .50
16 Denis Menke .08 .25
17 Norm Miller .08 .25
18 Joe Morgan 1.00 2.50
19 Doug Rader .08 .25
20 J.R. Richard .20 .50
21 Al Spangler .08 .25
22 Rusty Staub .40 1.00
23 Bob Watson .30 .75
24 Don Wilson .08 .25
25 Jim Wynn .20 .50
26 Mickey Mantle 1.25 3.00
 Don Drysdale
 Rusty Staub
27 1969 Pitching Staff .08 .25
28 Don Wilson .08 .25
 Harry Walker MG
29 Astro Bullpen Car .08 .25
30 1966 Team Photo .08 .25
31 1967 Team Photo .08 .25
32 1968 Team Photo .08 .25

1987 Astros Shooting Stars-Series Two

COMPLETE SET (32) 5.00 12.00
1 Jesus Alou .08 .25
2 Jack Billingham .08 .25
3 Jim Bouton .40 1.00
4 George Culver .08 .25
5 Ron Davis .08 .25
6 Nellie Fox .60 1.50
7 Cesar Geronimo .08 .25
8 Julio Gotay .08 .25
9 Greg Gross .08 .25
10 Cliff Johnson .20 .50
11 Dave Nicholson .08 .25
12 Claude Osteen .08 .25
13 Claude Raymond .08 .25
14 Dave Roberts .08 .25
15 Fred Scherman .08 .25
16 Hector Torres .08 .25
17 Bob Stinson .08 .25
18 Sandy Valdespino .08 .25
19 Jim York .08 .25
20 Chris Zachary .08 .25
21 Willie Mays 1.25 3.00
 Leo Durocher MG
 Cesar Cedeno
22 John Mayberry .40 1.00
 Joe Morgan
23 Eddie Mathews .30 .75
 Chuck Harrison
24 Doug Rader .08 .25
 Harry Walker
 Curt Blefary
 Joe Morgan
25 Rusty Staub 1.25 3.00
 Willie Mays
26 1973 Outfield Stars .08 .25
 Norm Miller
 Jesus Alou
 Jimm
27 1971 Starters .40 1.00
 Cesar Cedeno
 Joe Morgan
 Jim Wynn#
28 Don Wilson .20 .50
 Don Larsen
 Bo Belinsky
29 Danny Coombs .20 .50
 Dan Schneider
 Bo Belinsky
 Mike Cue
30 1969 Team Photo .08 .25
31 1970 Team Photo .08 .25
32 1971 Team Photo .08 .25

1987 Astros Shooting Stars-Series Three

COMPLETE SET (32) 3.00 8.00
1 Dave Adlesh .08 .25
2 John Bateman .08 .25
3 Bo Belinsky .30 .75
4 Nate Colbert .08 .25
5 Tommy Davis .20 .50
6 Jack DiLauro .08 .25
7 Mike Easler .08 .25
8 Jim Gentile .08 .25
9 Preston Gomez MG .08 .25
10 Jim Landis .08 .25
11 Barry Latman .08 .25
12 Mike Marshall .20 .50
13 Marty Martinez .08 .25
14 Milt May .08 .25
15 John Mayberry .20 .50
16 Larry Milbourne .08 .25
17 Jim Owens .08 .25
18 Joe Pepitone .20 .50
19 Jim Ray .08 .25
20 Jerry Reuss .20 .50
21 Larry Sherry .08 .25
22 Dick Simpson .08 .25
23 Jimmy Stewart .08 .25
24 Robin Roberts .30 .75
 Larry Dierker
25 Doug Rader .08 .25
 Roger Metzger
 Tommy Helms
 Lee May
26 Jerry Reuss .08 .25
 J.R. Richard
 Tom Griffin
 Jim Owens CO
 Don Wilson
 Dave Roberts
 Ken Forsch
 Larry Dierker
27 John Bateman .08 .25
 Dave Adlesh
 Ron Brand
 Bill Heath
28 Don Wilson .08 .25
 Tom Griffin
 Larry Dierker
 Denny LeMaster
29 Bob Watson .08 .25
 Larry Howard
 John Edwards
 Bob Stinson
 Skip Jutze
30 1972 Team Photo .08 .25
31 1973 Team Photo .08 .25
32 1974 Team Photo .08 .25

1987 Astros Rainbow Postcards-Series One

This 32-card set features photos of Houston Astros printed on commemorative postcards. These cards were issued in three different series. Tha backs are blank and the cards are unnumbered, so we have sequenced them in alphabetical order.

COMPLETE SET (32) 8.00 20.00
1 Jesus Alou .20 .50
2 Joaquin Andujar .20 .50
3 Dave Bergman .20 .50
4 Enos Cabell .20 .50
5 Cesar Cedeno .30 .75
6 Ken Forsch .20 .50
7 Tom Griffin .20 .50
8 Greg Gross .20 .50
9 Wilbur Howard .20 .50
10 Art Howe .30 .75
11 Alan Knicely .20 .50
12 Ray Knight .20 .50
13 Frank Lacorte .20 .50
14 Mike Lacoss .20 .50
15 Rafael Landestoy .20 .50
16 Jeff Leonard .20 .50
17 Bob Lillis .20 .50
18 Milt May .20 .50
19 Larry Milbourne .20 .50
20 Roger Metzger .20 .50
21 Joe Morgan 1.00 2.50
22 Joe Niekro .40 1.00
23 Phil Niekro .60 1.50
 Donald Davidson FO
 Joe Niekro
24 Luis Pujols .20 .50
25 Doug Radar .20 .50
26 J.R. Richard .30 .75
27 Vern Ruhle .20 .50
28 Joe Sambito .20 .50
29 Don Sutton 1.00 2.50
30 Bob Watson .40 1.00
31 Bob Lillis CO .20 .50
 Jesus Alou CO
 Bill Virdon MG
 Deacon Jones CO
 Mel Wright CO
32 1980 Championship Award .20 .50

1987 Astros Rainbow Postcards-Series Two

COMPLETE SET (32) 8.00 20.00
1 Floyd Bannister .20 .50
2 Bruce Bochy .30 .75
3 Ken Boswell .20 .50
4 Tom Dixon .20 .50
5 Joe Ferguson .20 .50
6 Joe Ferguson .20 .50
 Deacon Jones
 Cesar Cedeno
 Bob Watson
 Jose Cruz
 Leon Roberts
7 Jim Fuller .20 .50
8 Kiko Garcia .20 .50
9 Julio Gonzalez .20 .50
10 Larry Hardy .20 .50
11 Danny Heep .20 .50
12 Ed Hermann .20 .50
13 Wilbur Howard .20 .50
14 Mike Ivie .20 .50
15 Cliff Johnson .30 .75
16 Skip Jutze .20 .50
17 Doug Konieczny .20 .50
18 Pete Ladd .20 .50
19 Mark Lemongello .20 .50
20 Joe Niekro .40 1.00
21 Randy Niemann .20 .50
22 Johnny Ray .20 .50
23 Nolan Ryan 4.00 10.00
24 Dave Roberts C .20 .50
25 Dave Roberts P .20 .50
26 Tony Scott .20 .50
27 Harry Spilman .20 .50
28 Bill Virdon .30 .75
29 Bob Watson .30 .75
 Millionth Run
30 Gary Woods .20 .50
31 Jim York .20 .50
32 Cot Deal CO .20 .50
 Don Leppert CO
 Matt Galante CO
 Jerry Walker CO
 Denis Menke CO
 Bob Lillis MG

1987 Astros Rainbow Postcards-Series Three

COMPLETE SET (32) 10.00 25.00
1 Alan Ashby .20 .50
2 Reggie Baldwin .20 .50
3 Mike Cosgrove .20 .50
4 Jose Cruz .60 1.50
5 Phil Garner .30 .75
6 Bob Knepper .20 .50
7 Dan Larson .20 .50
8 Scott Loucks .20 .50
9 Bo McLaughlin .20 .50
10 Joe Niekro .30 .75
 Joe Sambito
11 Joe Pittman .20 .50
12 Terry Puhl .20 .50
13 Craig Reynolds .20 .50
14 J.R. Richard .40 1.00
15 Nolan Ryan 4.00 10.00
16 Nolan Ryan 4000th K 2.50 6.00
17 Jimmy Sexton .30 .75
18 Paul Siebert .20 .50
19 Dave Smith .30 .75
20 Rob Sperring .20 .50
21 Dickie Thon .20 .50
22 Denny Walling .20 .50
23 Danny Walton .20 .50
24 Rick Williams .20 .50
25 1975 Astros Team Picture .20 .50
26 1976 Astros Team Picture .20 .50
27 1977 Astros Team Picture .20 .50
28 1978 Astros Team Picture .20 .50
29 1979 Astros Team Picture .20 .50
30 1980 Astros Team Picture .20 .50
31 1981 Astros Team Picture .20 .50
32 1982 Astros Team Picture .20 .50

1988 Astros Mother's

This set consists of 28 full-color, rounded-corner standard-size cards. Starter sets (only 20 cards but also including a certificate for eight more cards) were given out at the ballpark and collectors were encouraged to trade to fill in the rest of their set. Cards were originally given out at the Astrodome on August 26th during a game. The sets were reportedly given out free to the first 25,000 paid admissions at the game.

COMPLETE SET (28) 5.00 12.00
1 Hal Lanier MG .08 .25
2 Mike Scott .30 .75
3 Gerald Young .08 .25
4 Bill Doran .08 .25
5 Bob Knepper .08 .25
6 Billy Hatcher .08 .25
7 Terry Puhl .20 .50
8 Nolan Ryan 2.50 6.00
9 Kevin Bass .08 .25
10 Glenn Davis .20 .50
11 Alan Ashby .08 .25
12 Steve Henderson .08 .25
13 Denny Walling .08 .25
14 Danny Darwin .08 .25
15 Mark Bailey .08 .25
16 Ernie Camacho .08 .25
17 Rafael Ramirez .08 .25

18 Jeff Heathcock .08 .25
19 Craig Reynolds .08 .25
20 Dave Smith .20 .50
21 Larry Andersen .08 .25
22 Jim Pankovits .08 .25
23 Jim Deshaies .08 .25
24 Juan Agosto .08 .25
25 Chuck Jackson .08 .25
26 Joaquin Andujar .08 .25
27 Astros' Coaches .40 1.00
Yogi Berra
Gene Clines
Matt Gal
28 Checklist Card .08 .25
Dave Labossiere TR
Dennis Liborio

1988 Astros Police

This 26-card safety set was sponsored by the Astros, Deer Park Hospital, and Sportsmedia Presentations. The backs contain a biographical paragraph above "Tips from the Dugout". The front features a full-color photo of the player, his name, position, and uniform number. The cards are numbered on the back and measure 2 5/8" by 4 1/8". The sets were supposedly distributed to the first 15,000 youngsters attending the New York Mets game against the Astros at the Astrodome on July 9th.

COMPLETE SET (26) 4.00 10.00
1 Juan Agosto .08 .25
2 Larry Andersen .08 .25
3 Joaquin Andujar .08 .25
4 Alan Ashby .08 .25
5 Mark Bailey .08 .25
6 Kevin Bass .08 .25
7 Danny Darwin .08 .25
8 Glenn Davis .20 .50
9 Jim Deshaies .08 .25
10 Bill Doran .08 .25
11 Billy Hatcher .08 .25
12 Jeff Heathcock .08 .25
13 Steve Henderson .08 .25
14 Chuck Jackson .08 .25
15 Bob Knepper .08 .25
16 Jim Pankovits .08 .25
17 Terry Puhl .20 .50
18 Rafael Ramirez .08 .25
19 Craig Reynolds .08 .25
20 Nolan Ryan 2.50 6.00
21 Mike Scott .20 .50
22 Dave Smith .20 .50
23 Denny Walling .08 .25
24 Gerald Young .08 .25
25 Hal Lanier MG .08 .25
26 Coaching Staff .20 .50

1989 Astros Colt .45s Smokey

The 1989 Smokey Houston Colt .45s set contains 29 standard-size cards. The Houston Astros were originally called the Houston Colt .45s. The card fronts have black and white photos with white and light blue borders. This set depicts Houston Colt .45s' players from their inaugural 1962 season.

COMPLETE SET (29) 2.50 6.00
1 Bob Bruce .08 .25
2 Al Cicotte .08 .25
3 Dave Giusti .20 .50
4 Jim Golden .08 .25
5 Ken Johnson .08 .25
6 Tom Borland .08 .25
7 Bobby Shantz .20 .50
8 Dick Farrell .20 .50
9 Jim Umbricht .08 .25
10 Hal Woodeshick .08 .25
11 Merritt Ranew .08 .25
12 Hal Smith .08 .25
13 Jim Campbell .08 .25
14 Norm Larker .08 .25
15 Joe Amalfitano .08 .25
16 Bob Aspromonte .20 .50
17 Bob Lillis .08 .25
18 Dick Gernert .08 .25
19 Don Buddin .08 .25
20 Pidge Browne .08 .25
21 Von McDaniel .08 .25
22 Don Taussig .08 .25
23 Al Spangler .08 .25
24 Al Heist .08 .25
25 Jim Pendleton .08 .25
26 Johnny Weekly .08 .25
27 Harry Craft MG .08 .25
28 Colt Coaches .08 .25
29 1962 Houston Colt 45s .30 .75

1989 Astros Lennox HSE

The 1989 Lennox HSE Astros set contains 26 cards measuring approximately 2 5/8" by 4 1/8". The fronts have color photos with burnt orange and white borders. The backs feature biographical information and career highlights. The set looks very much like the Astros Police sets of previous years, but is missing both the police sponsorship and saftey tip.

COMPLETE SET (26) 3.00 8.00
1 Billy Hatcher .08 .25
2 Greg Gross .08 .25
3 Rick Rhoden .08 .25
4 Mike Scott .20 .50
5 Kevin Bass .08 .25
6 Alex Trevino .08 .25
7 Jim Clancy .08 .25
8 Bill Doran .08 .25
9 Dan Schatzeder .08 .25
10 Bob Knepper .08 .25
11 Jim Deshaies .08 .25
12 Eric Yelding .08 .25
13 Danny Darwin .08 .25
14 Matt Galante CO .20 .50
Yogi Berra CO
Ed Napoleon CO
Ed Ott CO
Phil Garner CO
Les Moss CO
15 Craig Reynolds .08 .25
16 Rafael Ramirez .08 .25
17 Juan Agosto .08 .25
18 Larry Andersen .08 .25
19 Dave Smith .20 .50
20 Gerald Young .08 .25
21 Ken Caminiti .60 1.50
22 Terry Puhl .20 .50
23 Bob Forsch .08 .25
24 Craig Biggio 1.00 2.50
25 Art Howe MG .08 .25
26 Glenn Davis .20 .50

1989 Astros Mother's

The 1989 Mother's Cookies Houston Astros set contains 28 standard-size cards with rounded corners. The fronts have borderless color photos, and the horizontally oriented backs have biographical information. Starter sets containing 20 of these cards were given away at an Astros home game during the 1989 season.

COMPLETE SET (28) 4.00 10.00
1 Art Howe MG .08 .25
2 Mike Scott .30 .75
3 Gerald Young .08 .25
4 Bill Doran .08 .25
5 Billy Hatcher .08 .25
6 Terry Puhl .20 .50
7 Bob Knepper .08 .25
8 Kevin Bass .08 .25
9 Glenn Davis .20 .50
10 Alan Ashby .08 .25
11 Bob Forsch .08 .25
12 Greg Gross .08 .25
13 Danny Darwin .08 .25
14 Craig Biggio 1.50 4.00
15 Jim Clancy .08 .25
16 Rafael Ramirez .08 .25
17 Alex Trevino .08 .25
18 Craig Reynolds .08 .25
19 Dave Smith .20 .50
20 Larry Andersen .08 .25
21 Eric Yelding .08 .25
22 Jim Deshaies .08 .25
23 Juan Agosto .08 .25
24 Rick Rhoden .08 .25
25 Ken Caminiti .60 1.50
26 Dave Meads .08 .25
27 Astros Coaches .40 1.00
Yogi Berra
Ed Napoleon
Matt Gala
28 Checklist Card .08 .25
Dave Labossiere TR
Doc Ewell TR/

1989 Astros Smokey

These 4" by 6" cards feature members of the Houston Astros. These cards feature player photos on the front and various safety tips on the back. We have sequenced this set in alphabetical order.

COMPLETE SET (40) 4.00 10.00
1 Juan Agosto .08 .25
2 Larry Andersen .08 .25
3 Alan Ashby .08 .25
4 Kevin Bass .08 .25
5 Yogi Berra CO .40 1.00
6 Craig Biggio 1.00 2.50
7 Ken Caminiti .60 1.50
8 Casey Candaele .08 .25
9 Jim Clancy .08 .25
10 Danny Darwin .08 .25
11 Glenn Davis .20 .50
12 Jim Deshaies .08 .25
13 Bill Doran .08 .25
14 Bob Forsch .08 .25
15 Matt Galante CO .08 .25
16 Phil Garner CO .20 .50
17 Greg Gross .08 .25
18 Billy Hatcher .08 .25
19 Art Howe MG .08 .25
20 Chuck Jackson .08 .25
21 Charley Kerfeld .08 .25
22 Bob Knepper .08 .25
23 Steve Lombardozzi .08 .25
24 Roger Mason .08 .25
25 Louie Meadows .08 .25
26 Dave Meads .08 .25
27 Brian Meyer .08 .25
28 Les Moss CO .08 .25
29 Ed Napoleon CO .08 .25
30 Ed Ott CO .08 .25
31 Terry Puhl .20 .50
32 Rafael Ramirez .08 .25
33 Craig Reynolds .08 .25
34 Rick Rhoden .08 .25
35 Dan Schatzeder .08 .25
36 Mike Scott .20 .50
37 Dave Smith .20 .50
38 Alex Trevino .08 .25
39 Eric Yelding .08 .25
40 Gerald Young .08 .25

1990 Astros Lennox HSE

This 28-card, approximately 3 1/2" by 5", set was issued in conjunction with HSE Cable Network and Lennox Heating and Air Conditioning as indicated on both the front and back of the cards. The front of the cards have full color portraits of the player while the back gives brief information about the player. The set has been checklisted below in alphabetical order.

COMPLETE SET (28) 5.00 12.00
1 Juan Agosto .20 .50
2 Larry Andersen .20 .50
3 Eric Anthony .20 .50
4 Craig Biggio 1.00 2.50
5 Ken Caminiti .60 1.50
6 Casey Candaele .20 .50
7 Jose Cano .20 .50
8 Jim Clancy .20 .50
9 Danny Darwin .20 .50
10 Mark Davidson .20 .50
11 Glenn Davis .30 .75
12 Jim Deshaies .20 .50
13 Bill Doran .20 .50
14 Bill Gullickson .20 .50
15 Xavier Hernandez .20 .50
16 Art Howe MG .20 .50
17 Mark Portugal .20 .50
18 Terry Puhl .30 .75
19 Rafael Ramirez .20 .50
20 David Rohde .20 .50
21 Dan Schatzeder .20 .50
22 Mike Scott .30 .75
23 Dave Smith .30 .75
24 Franklin Stubbs .20 .50
25 Alex Trevino .20 .50
26 Glenn Wilson .20 .50
27 Eric Yelding .20 .50
28 Gerald Young .20 .50

1990 Astros Mother's

This 28-card standard-size set features members of the 1990 Houston Astros. This set features the traditional rounded corners and has biographical information about each player on the back. These Astros cards were given away on July 15th to the first 25,000 fans at the Astrodome. They were distributed in 20 card random packets at the game and eight more at the redemption booths. However, both groups of cards were random and there was no guarantee of getting a complete set in the cards. The promotional idea was that the only way one could finish the set was to trade for them. The certificates of redemption for eight were redeemable at the major card show at the AstroArena on August 24-26, 1990.

COMPLETE SET (28) 3.00 8.00
1 Art Howe MG .08 .25
2 Glenn Davis .20 .50
3 Eric Anthony .08 .25
4 Mike Scott .30 .75
5 Craig Biggio .75 2.00
6 Ken Caminiti .40 1.00
7 Bill Doran .08 .25
8 Gerald Young .08 .25
9 Terry Puhl .20 .50
10 Mark Portugal .08 .25
11 Mark Davidson .08 .25
12 Jim Deshaies .08 .25
13 Bill Gullickson .08 .25
14 Franklin Stubbs .08 .25
15 Danny Darwin .08 .25
16 Ken Oberkfell .08 .25
17 Dave Smith .20 .50
18 Dan Schatzeder .08 .25
19 Rafael Ramirez .08 .25
20 Larry Andersen .08 .25
21 Alex Trevino .08 .25
22 Glenn Wilson .08 .25
23 Jim Clancy .08 .25
24 Eric Yelding .08 .25
25 Casey Candaele .08 .25
26 Juan Agosto .08 .25
27 Coaches Card .20 .50
Billy Bowman
Bob Cluck
Phil Garner
28 Personnel Card .08 .25
Dave Labossiere TR
Dennis Liborio

1991 Astros Mother's

The 1991 Mother's Cookies Houston Astros set contains 28 standard-size cards with rounded corners.

COMPLETE SET (28) 4.00 10.00
1 Art Howe MG .08 .25
2 Steve Finley .60 1.50
3 Pete Harnisch .08 .25
4 Mike Scott .30 .75
5 Craig Biggio .60 1.50
6 Ken Caminiti .30 .75
7 Eric Yelding .08 .25
8 Jeff Bagwell 2.00 5.00
9 Jim Deshaies .08 .25
10 Mark Portugal .08 .25
11 Mark Davidson .08 .25
12 Jimmy Jones .08 .25
13 Luis Gonzalez .75 2.00
14 Karl Rhodes .08 .25
15 Curt Schilling 1.00 2.50
16 Ken Oberkfell .08 .25
17 Mark McLemore .08 .25
18 Dave Rohde .08 .25
19 Rafael Ramirez .08 .25
20 Al Osuna .08 .25
21 Jim Corsi .08 .25
22 Carl Nichols .08 .25
23 Jim Clancy .08 .25
24 Dwayne Henry .08 .25
25 Casey Candaele .08 .25
26 Xavier Hernandez .08 .25
27 Darryl Kile .60 1.50
28 Checklist Card .20 .50
Phil Garner CO
Bob Cluck CO
Ed O

1992 Astros Mother's

The 1992 Mother's Cookies Astros set contains 28 standard-size cards with rounded corners.

COMPLETE SET (28) 4.00 10.00
1 Art Howe MG .08 .25
2 Steve Finley .40 1.00
3 Pete Harnisch .08 .25
4 Pete Incaviglia .08 .25
5 Craig Biggio .60 1.50
6 Ken Caminiti .30 .75
7 Eric Anthony .08 .25
8 Jeff Bagwell 1.50 4.00
9 Andujar Cedeno .08 .25
10 Mark Portugal .08 .25
11 Eddie Taubensee .08 .25
12 Jimmy Jones .08 .25
13 Joe Boever .08 .25
14 Benny Distefano .08 .25
15 Juan Guerrero .08 .25
16 Doug Jones .08 .25
17 Scott Servais .08 .25
18 Butch Henry .08 .25
19 Rafael Ramirez .08 .25
20 Al Osuna .08 .25
21 Rob Murphy .08 .25
22 Chris Jones .08 .25
23 Rob Mallicoat .08 .25
24 Darryl Kile .40 1.00
25 Casey Candaele .08 .25
26 Xavier Hernandez .08 .25
27 Coaches .20 .50
Rudy Jaramillo
Ed Ott
Matt Galante
Bob
28 Checklist .08 .25
Dennis Liborio EQMG
Dave Labossiere TR

1993 Astros Mother's

The 1993 Mother's Cookies Astros set consists of 28 standard-size cards with rounded corners.

COMPLETE SET (28) 4.00 10.00
1 Art Howe MG .08 .25
2 Steve Finley .40 1.00
3 Pete Harnisch .08 .25
4 Craig Biggio .75 2.00
5 Doug Drabek .08 .25
6 Scott Servais .08 .25
7 Jeff Bagwell 1.25 3.00
8 Eric Anthony .08 .25
9 Ken Caminiti .30 .75
10 Andujar Cedeno .08 .25
11 Mark Portugal .08 .25
12 Jose Uribe .08 .25
13 Rick Parker .08 .25
14 Doug Jones .08 .25
15 Luis Gonzalez .60 1.50
16 Kevin Bass .08 .25
17 Greg Swindell .08 .25
18 Eddie Taubensee .08 .25
19 Darryl Kile .40 1.00
20 Brian Williams .08 .25
21 Chris James .08 .25
22 Chris Donnels .08 .25
23 Xavier Hernandez .08 .25
24 Casey Candaele .08 .25
25 Eric Bell .08 .25
26 Mark Grant .08 .25
27 Tom Edens .08 .25
28 Checklist .20 .50
Coaches
Ed Ott
Bob Cluck
Matt Galante

1993 Astros Stadium Club

This 30-card standard-size set features the 1993 Houston Astros. The set was issued in hobby (plastic box) and retail (blister) form.

COMP. FACT SET (30) 2.00 5.00
1 Doug Drabek .02 .10
2 Eddie Taubensee .02 .10
3 James Mouton .02 .10
4 Ken Caminiti .20 .50
5 Chris James .02 .10
6 Jeff Juden .02 .10
7 Eric Anthony .02 .10
8 Jeff Bagwell .60 1.50
9 Greg Swindell .02 .10
10 Steve Finley .30 .75
11 Al Osuna .02 .10
12 Gary Mota .02 .10
13 Scott Servais .02 .10
14 Craig Biggio .50 1.25
15 Doug Jones .02 .10
16 Rob Mallicoat .02 .10
17 Darryl Kile .30 .75
18 Kevin Bass .02 .10
19 Pete Harnisch .02 .10
20 Andujar Cedeno .02 .10
21 Brian L.Hunter .02 .10
22 Brian Williams .02 .10
23 Chris Donnels .02 .10
24 Xavier Hernandez .02 .10
25 Todd Jones .08 .25
26 Luis Gonzalez .40 1.00
27 Rick Parker .02 .10
28 Casey Candaele .02 .10
29 Tony Eusebio .02 .10
30 Mark Portugal .02 .10

1994 Astros Mother's

The 1994 Mother's Cookies Astros set consists of 28 standard-size cards with rounded corners.

COMPLETE SET (28) 4.00 10.00
1 Terry Collins MG .08 .25
2 Mitch Williams .20 .50
3 Jeff Bagwell 1.00 2.50
4 Luis Gonzalez .50 1.25
5 Craig Biggio .60 1.50
6 Darryl Kile .40 1.00
7 Ken Caminiti .30 .75
8 Steve Finley .40 1.00
9 Pete Harnisch .08 .25
10 Sid Bream .08 .25
11 Mike Felder .08 .25
12 Tom Edens .08 .25
13 James Mouton .08 .25
14 Doug Drabek .08 .25
15 Greg Swindell .08 .25
16 Chris Donnels .08 .25
17 John Hudek .08 .25
18 Andujar Cedeno .08 .25
19 Scott Servais .08 .25
20 Todd Jones .20 .50
21 Kevin Bass .08 .25
22 Shane Reynolds .08 .25
23 Brian Williams .08 .25
24 Tony Eusebio .08 .25
25 Mike Hampton .40 1.00
26 Andy Stankiewicz .08 .25
27 Astros Coaches .20 .50
28 Checklist .08 .25

1995 Astros Mother's

This 1995 Mother's Cookies Houston Astros set consists of 28 standard-size cards with rounded corners.

COMPLETE SET (28) 4.00 10.00
1 Terry Collins MG .08 .25
2 Jeff Bagwell 1.00 2.50
3 Luis Gonzalez .50 1.25
4 Darryl Kile .20 .50
5 Derek Bell .08 .25
6 Scott Servais .08 .25
7 Craig Biggio .60 1.50
8 Dave Magadan .08 .25
9 Milt Thompson .08 .25
10 Derrick May .08 .25
11 Doug Drabek .08 .25
12 Tony Eusebio .08 .25
13 Phil Nevin .20 .50
14 James Mouton .08 .25
15 Phil Plantier .08 .25
16 Pedro Martinez .08 .25
17 Orlando Miller .08 .25
18 John Hudek .08 .25
19 Doug Brocail .08 .25
20 Craig Shipley .08 .25
21 Shane Reynolds .08 .25
22 Mike Hampton .20 .50
23 Todd Jones .20 .50
24 Greg Swindell .08 .25
25 Jim Dougherty .08 .25
26 Brian L. Hunter .08 .25
27 Dave Veres .08 .25
28 Coaches .20 .50
Checklist

1996 Astros Mother's

This 28-card set consists of borderless posed color player portraits in stadium settings.

COMPLETE SET (28) 3.00 8.00
1 Terry Collins MG .08 .25
2 Jeff Bagwell 1.00 2.50
3 Craig Biggio .60 1.50
4 Derek Bell .08 .25
5 Darryl Kile .20 .50
6 Sean Berry .08 .25
7 Doug Drabek .08 .25
8 Derrick May .08 .25
9 Orlando Miller .08 .25
10 Mike Hampton .30 .75
11 Rick Wilkins .08 .25
12 Brian Hunter .08 .25
13 Shane Reynolds .08 .25
14 James Mouton .08 .25
15 Greg Swindell .08 .25
16 Bill Spiers .08 .25
17 Alvin Morman .08 .25
18 Tony Eusebio .08 .25
19 John Hudek .08 .25
20 Doug Brocail .08 .25
21 Anthony Young .08 .25
22 John Cangelosi .08 .25
23 Jeff Tabaka .08 .25
24 Mike Simms .08 .25
25 Todd Jones .20 .50
26 Ricky Gutierrez .08 .25
27 Mark Small .08 .25
28 Coaches Card CL .08 .25
Matt Galante
Julio Linares
Rick

1997 Astros Mother's

This 28-card set of the Houston Astros sponsored by Mother's Cookies consists of posed color player photos with rounded corners.

COMPLETE SET (28) 5.00 12.00
1 Larry Dierker MG .20 .50
2 Jeff Bagwell 1.25 3.00
3 Craig Biggio .75 2.00
4 Darryl Kile .40 1.00
5 Luis Gonzalez .50 1.25
6 Shane Reynolds .08 .25
7 James Mouton .08 .25
8 Sean Berry .08 .25
9 Billy Wagner .60 1.50
10 Ricky Gutierrez .08 .25
11 Mike Hampton .30 .75
12 Tony Eusebio .08 .25
13 Derek Bell .08 .25
14 Ray Montgomery .08 .25
15 Bill Spiers .08 .25
16 Sid Fernandez .20 .50
17 Brad Ausmus .08 .25
18 John Hudek .08 .25
19 Bob Abreu .75 2.00
20 Russ Springer .08 .25
21 Chris Holt .08 .25
22 Tom Martin .08 .25
23 Donne Wall .08 .25
24 Thomas Howard .08 .25
25 Jose Lima .08 .25
26 Pat Listach .08 .25
27 Ramon Garcia .08 .25
28 Coaches Card CL .20 .50
Alan Ashby
Jose Cruz
Mike Cubba

1998 Astros Mother's

This 28-card set of the Houston Astros sponsored by Mother's Cookies consists of posed color player photos with rounded corners.

COMPLETE SET (28) 4.00 10.00
1 Larry Dierker MG .20 .50
2 Jeff Bagwell .75 2.00
3 Craig Biggio .60 1.50
4 Derek Bell .08 .25
5 Shane Reynolds .08 .25
6 Sean Berry .08 .25
7 Moises Alou .40 1.00
8 Carl Everett .08 .25
9 Billy Wagner .30 .75
10 Tony Eusebio .08 .25
11 Mike Hampton .20 .50
12 Ricky Gutierrez .08 .25
13 Jose Lima .08 .25
14 Brad Ausmus .08 .25
15 Bill Spiers .08 .25
16 C.J. Nitkowski .08 .25
17 Randy Johnson 1.00 2.50
18 Mike Magnante .08 .25
19 Dave Clark .08 .25
20 Sean Bergman .08 .25
21 Richard Hidalgo .20 .50
22 Pete Schourek .08 .25
23 Jay Powell .08 .25
24 Trever Miller .08 .25
25 Tim Bogar .08 .25
26 Doug Henry .08 .25
27 Scott Elarton .08 .25
28 Jose Cruz CO .08 .25
Mike Cubbage CO
Dave Engle CO
Matt

1999 Astros Albertsons

This 34 card standard-size set features members of the 1999 Houson Astros, the last team to play in the Astrodome. The cards have rounded corners and the upper left corner features a Nabisco logo while the lower right corner has the 1999 Astros logo. The cards are unnumbered except for the uniform numbers so we have sequenced them in alphabetical order.

COMPLETE SET (34) 5.00 12.00
1 Moises Alou .40 1.00
2 Jeff Bagwell .75 2.00
3 Paul Bako .08 .25
4 Glen Barker .08 .25
5 Derek Bell .08 .25
6 Sean Bergman .08 .25
7 Craig Biggio .50 1.25
8 Tim Bogar .08 .25
9 Ken Caminiti .30 .75
10 Mike Cubbage CO .08 .25
11 Jose Cruz CO .20 .50
12 Larry Dierker MG .20 .50
13 Scott Elarton .08 .25
14 Tony Eusebio .08 .25
15 Carl Everett .08 .25
16 Matt Galante CO .08 .25
17 Ricky Gutierrez .08 .25
18 Mike Hampton .30 .75
19 Doug Henry .08 .25
20 Richard Hidalgo .30 .75
21 Chris Holt .08 .25
22 Jack Howell .08 .25
23 Russ Johnson .08 .25
24 Jose Lima .08 .25
25 Tom McCraw CO .08 .25
26 Mitch Meluskey .08 .25
27 Trever Miller .08 .25
28 Jay Powell .08 .25
29 Shane Reynolds .08 .25
30 Vern Ruhle CO .08 .25
31 Bill Spiers .08 .25
32 John Tamargo CO .08 .25
33 Billy Wagner .40 1.00
34 Brian Wiliams .08 .25

1999 Astros Buddies

This five card standard-size set features people involved with the 1999 Houston Astros, either as a player or as a coach/manager. The fronts feature a player photo with the words "Exclusive Edition" on top, the "Astros Buddies Logo" on the upper left and the players name on the bottom.

COMPLETE SET (5) 3.00 8.00
1 Larry Dierker .40 1.00
2 Jose Cruz .40 1.00
3 Craig Biggio 1.25 3.00
4 Jeff Bagwell 1.50 4.00
5 Houston Astrodome .20 .50

2001 Astros Team Issue

COMPLETE SET (30) 4.00 10.00
1 Larry Dierker .10 .25
2 Moises Alou .20 .50
3 Brad Ausmus .10 .25
4 Jeff Bagwell .60 1.50
5 Lance Berkman .60 1.50
6 Craig Biggio .60 1.25
7 Scott Elarton .10 .25
8 Tony Eusebio .10 .25
9 Richard Hidalgo .10 .25
10 Jose Lima .10 .25
11 Julio Lugo .10 .25
12 Shane Reynolds .10 .25
13 Billy Spiers .10 .25
14 Chris Truby .10 .25
15 Jose Vizcaino .10 .25
16 Billy Wagner .40 1.00
17 Glen Barker .10 .25
18 Kent Bottenfield .10 .25
19 Nelson Cruz .10 .25
20 Octavio Dotel .20 .50
21 Morgan Ensberg .75 2.00
22 Adam Everett .60 1.50
23 Keith Ginter .10 .25
24 Mike Jackson .10 .25
25 Brad Lidge .60 1.50
26 Tony McKnight .10 .25
27 Wade Miller .30 .75
28 Roy Oswalt 1.25 3.00
29 Jay Powell .10 .25
30 Daryle Ward .10 .25

2002 Astros Postcards

COMPLETE SET (5) 10.00 20.00
1 Brad Ausmus .20 .50
2 Jeff Bagwell 1.00 2.50
3 Lance Berkman .60 1.50
4 Craig Biggio .75 2.00
5 Doug Brocail .20 .50
6 Nelson Cruz .20 .50
7 Richard Hidalgo .20 .50
8 Julio Lugo .20 .50
9 Orlando Merced .20 .50
10 Wade Miller .20 .50
11 Roy Oswalt 1.25 3.00
12 Shane Reynolds .20 .50
13 Jose Vizcaino .20 .50
14 Billy Wagner .75 2.00
15 Daryle Ward .20 .50
16 Jimy Williams MG .20 .50
70 Octavio Dotel .20 .50
71 Morgan Ensberg .75 2.00
72 Adam Everett .60 1.50
73 Carlos Hernandez .20 .50
74 Brian L. Hunter .20 .50
75 T.J. Mathews .20 .50
76 Dave Mlicki .20 .50
77 Ricky Stone .20 .50
78 Greg Zaun .20 .50
79 Jose Cruz CO .30 .75
80 Burt Hooton CO .20 .50
81 Gene Lamont CO .20 .50
82 Tony Pena CO .20 .50
83 Harry Spilman CO .20 .50
84 John Tamargo CO .20 .50

2003 Astros Team Issue

COMPLETE SET (33) 10.00 20.00
1 Brad Ausmus .20 .50
2 Jeff Bagwell 1.00 2.50
3 Lance Berkman .60 1.50
4 Craig Biggio .75 2.00
5 Octavio Dotel .20 .50
6 Richard Hidalgo .20 .50
7 Brian L. Hunter .20 .50
8 Jeff Kent .60 1.50
9 Julio Lugo .20 .50
10 Orlando Merced .20 .50
11 Wade Miller .20 .50
12 Roy Oswalt 1.00 2.50
13 Shane Reynolds .20 .50
14 Jose Vizcaino .20 .50
15 Billy Wagner .75 2.00
16 Jimy Williams MG .20 .50
17 Geoff Blum .20 .50
18 Raul Chavez .20 .50
19 Bruce Chen .20 .50
20 Morgan Ensberg .60 1.50
21 Brad Lidge .60 1.50
22 Brian Moehler .20 .50
23 Pete Munro .20 .50
24 Tim Redding .20 .50
25 Jeriome Robertson .20 .50
26 Ricky Stone .20 .50
27 Gregg Zaun .20 .50
28 Mark Bailey .20 .50
29 Jose Cruz CO .30 .75
30 Burt Hooton CO .20 .50
31 Gene Lamont CO .20 .50
32 Harry Spilman CO .20 .50
33 John Tamargo CO .20 .50

2004 Astros Fanfest

COMPLETE SET 40.00 80.00
1 Roger Clemens Jsy 10.00 25.00
Fleer
2 Andy Pettitte Jsy 5.00 12.00
Upper Deck
3 Jeff Bagwell Jsy 6.00 15.00
Playoff
4 Lance Berkman Jsy 5.00 12.00
Topps
5 Roy Oswalt 1.25 3.00
Topps
6 Craig Biggio 1.00 2.50
Playoff
7 Jeff Kent .60 1.50
Upper Deck
8 Adam Everett .40 1.00
Fleer
9 Nolan Ryan 2.00 5.00
Roger Clemens
Fleer
10 Nolan Ryan 2.00 5.00
Roger Clemens
Upper Deck
11 Nolan Ryan 2.00 5.00
Roger Clemens
Playoff
12 Nolan Ryan 2.00 5.00
Roger Clemens
Topps

2004 Astros Team Issue

COMPLETE SET (32) 8.00 20.00
1 Brad Ausmus .20 .50
2 Jeff Bagwell .75 2.00
3 Lance Berkman .60 1.50
4 Craig Biggio .75 2.00
5 Roger Clemens 1.25 3.00
6 Octavio Dotel .20 .50
7 Morgan Ensberg .60 1.50
8 Adam Everett .40 1.00
9 Richard Hidalgo .20 .50
10 Jeff Kent .60 1.50
11 Brad Lidge .60 1.50
12 Wade Miller .20 .50
13 Roy Oswalt .75 2.00
14 Andy Pettitte .60 1.50
15 Tim Redding .20 .50
16 Jose Vizcaino .20 .50
17 Jimy Williams MG .20 .50
18 Mark Bailey CO .20 .50
19 Jose Cruz CO .20 .50
20 Burt Hooton CO .20 .50
21 Gene Lamont CO .20 .50
22 Harry Spilman CO .20 .50
23 John Tamargo CO .20 .50
24 Brandon Backe .40 1.00
25 Eric Bruntlett .30 .75
26 Raul Chavez .20 .50
27 Brandon Duckworth .20 .50
28 Mike Gallo .20 .50
29 Jason Lane .60 1.50
30 Dan Miceli .20 .50
31 Orlando Palmeiro .20 .50
32 Ricky Stone .20 .50

2006 Astros Topps

COMPLETE SET (14) 3.00 8.00
HOU1 Roy Oswalt .20 .50
HOU2 Andy Pettitte .20 .50

HOU3 Brad Lidge .12 .30
HOU4 Brandon Backe .12 .30
HOU5 Mike Lamb .12 .30
HOU6 Jeff Bagwell .20 .50
HOU7 Craig Biggio .20 .50
HOU8 Lance Berkman .20 .50
HOU9 Chris Burke .12 .30
HOU10 Adam Everett .12 .30
HOU11 Morgan Ensberg .12 .30
HOU12 Jason Lane .12 .30
HOU13 Willy Taveras .12 .30
HOU14 Brad Ausmus .12 .30

2007 Astros Topps

COMPLETE SET (14) 3.00 8.00
HOU1 Lance Berkman .20 .50
HOU2 Brad Ausmus .12 .30
HOU3 Brad Lidge .12 .30
HOU4 Dan Wheeler .12 .30
HOU5 Roy Oswalt .20 .50
HOU6 Chris Burke .12 .30
HOU7 Craig Biggio .20 .50
HOU8 Woody Williams .12 .30
HOU9 Carlos Lee .12 .30
HOU10 Luke Scott .12 .30
HOU11 Morgan Ensberg .12 .30
HOU12 Jason Jennings .12 .30
HOU13 Adam Everett .12 .30
HOU14 Roger Clemens .40 1.00

2008 Astros Topps

COMPLETE SET (14) 3.00 8.00
HOU1 Hunter Pence .20 .50
HOU2 Brad Ausmus .12 .30
HOU3 Michael Bourn .12 .30
HOU4 Jose Valverde .12 .30
HOU5 Roy Oswalt .20 .50
HOU6 Ty Wigginton .20 .50
HOU7 Woody Williams .20 .50
HOU8 Wandy Rodriguez .12 .30
HOU9 Carlos Lee .12 .30
HOU10 Kazuo Matsui .12 .30
HOU11 Miguel Tejada .20 .50
HOU12 Geoff Blum .12 .30
HOU13 Brandon Backe .12 .30
HOU14 Lance Berkman .20 .50

2009 Astros Topps

COMPLETE SET (15) 3.00 8.00
HOU1 Lance Berkman .25 .60
HOU2 Roy Oswalt .25 .60
HOU3 Carlos Lee .15 .40
HOU4 Brandon Backe .15 .40
HOU5 Hunter Pence .25 .60
HOU6 J.R. Towles .15 .40
HOU7 Miguel Tejada .25 .60
HOU8 Jose Valverde .15 .40
HOU9 Kazuo Matsui .15 .40
HOU10 Wandy Rodriguez .15 .40
HOU11 Mike Hampton .15 .40
HOU12 Darin Erstad .15 .40
HOU13 Geoff Blum .15 .40
HOU14 Michael Bourn .15 .40
HOU15 Minute Maid Park .15 .40

2010 Astros Topps

HOU1 Lance Berkman .25 .60
HOU2 Pedro Feliz .15 .40
HOU3 Jeff Keppinger .15 .40
HOU4 Tommy Manzella .15 .40
HOU5 Brett Meyers .15 .40
HOU6 J.R. Towles .15 .40
HOU7 Yorman Bazardo .15 .40
HOU8 Michael Bourn .15 .40
HOU9 Kazuo Matsui .15 .40
HOU10 Roy Oswalt .25 .60
HOU11 Wandy Rodriguez .15 .40
HOU12 Bud Norris .15 .40
HOU13 Carlos Lee .15 .40
HOU14 Hunter Pence .25 .60
HOU15 Jason Michaels .15 .40
HOU16 Brandon Lyon .15 .40
HOU17 Matt Lindstrom .15 .40

2011 Astros Topps

COMPLETE SET (17) 3.00 8.00
HOU1 Hunter Pence .25 .60
HOU2 Jason Castro .15 .40
HOU3 J.A. Happ .25 .60
HOU4 Chris Johnson .15 .40
HOU5 Carlos Lee .15 .40
HOU6 Brett Myers .15 .40
HOU7 Wandy Rodriguez .15 .40
HOU8 Bud Norris .15 .40
HOU9 Brett Wallace .15 .40
HOU10 Jeff Keppinger .15 .40
HOU11 Michael Bourn .15 .40
HOU12 Jason Michaels .15 .40
HOU13 Brandon Lyon .15 .40
HOU14 Bill Hall .15 .40
HOU15 Clint Barmes .15 .40
HOU16 Nelson Figueroa .15 .40
HOU17 Minute Maid Park .15 .40

2012 Astros Topps

COMPLETE SET (17) 3.00 8.00
HOU1 Jed Lowrie .25 .60
HOU2 Jordan Schafer .25 .60
HOU3 J.D. Martinez .40 1.00
HOU4 Brett Wallace .25 .60
HOU5 Chris Johnson .25 .60
HOU6 Wandy Rodriguez .25 .60
HOU7 Jason Bourgeois .25 .60
HOU8 Jimmy Paredes .25 .60
HOU9 Humberto Quintero .25 .60
HOU10 Brett Myers .25 .60
HOU11 Carlos Lee .25 .60
HOU12 Brian Bogusevic .25 .60
HOU13 Jose Altuve .30 .75
HOU14 Bud Norris .25 .60
HOU15 J.A. Happ .30 .75
HOU16 Matt Downs .25 .60
HOU17 Minute Maid Park .15 .40

2013 Astros Topps

COMPLETE SET (17) 3.00 8.00
HOU1 Jose Altuve .20 .50
HOU2 Chris Carter .15 .40
HOU3 Brett Wallace .15 .40
HOU4 Brandon Barnes .15 .40
HOU5 Carlos Pena .20 .50
HOU6 Lucas Harrell .15 .40
HOU7 Bud Norris .15 .40
HOU8 Jordan Lyles .15 .40
HOU9 Philip Humber .15 .40
HOU10 Matt Dominguez .15 .40
HOU11 Jason Castro .15 .40
HOU12 Alex White .10 .25
HOU13 Justin Maxwell .15 .40
HOU14 J.D. Martinez .25 .60
HOU15 Dallas Keuchel .20 .50
HOU16 Fernando Martinez .15 .40
HOU17 Minute Maid Park .15 .40

2014 Astros Topps

COMPLETE SET (17) 3.00 8.00
HOU1 Jose Altuve .20 .50
HOU2 Chris Carter .15 .40
HOU3 Brett Wallace .15 .40
HOU4 Dexter Fowler .20 .50
HOU5 Robbie Grossman .15 .40
HOU6 Scott Feldman .15 .40
HOU7 Lucas Harrell .15 .40
HOU8 Jesse Crain .15 .40
HOU9 Jarred Cosart .15 .40
HOU10 Matt Dominguez .15 .40
HOU11 Jason Castro .15 .40
HOU12 Brad Peacock .15 .40
HOU13 L.J. Hoes .15 .40
HOU14 Brett Oberholtzer .15 .40
HOU15 Dallas Keuchel .20 .50
HOU16 Jonathan Villar .15 .40
HOU17 Minute Maid Park .15 .40

2015 Astros Topps

COMPLETE SET (17) 3.00 8.00
HA1 Jose Altuve .20 .50
HA2 Jason Castro .15 .40
HA3 Matt Dominguez .15 .40
HA4 Brett Oberholtzer .15 .40
HA5 Evan Gattis .15 .40
HA6 Jon Singleton .20 .50
HA7 Colby Rasmus .20 .50
HA8 Marwin Gonzalez .15 .40
HA9 Chris Carter .15 .40
HA10 Jed Lowrie .15 .40
HA11 Jake Marisnick .15 .40
HA12 George Springer .20 .50
HA13 Luke Gregerson .15 .40
HA14 L.J. Hoes .15 .40
HA15 Scott Feldman .15 .40
HA16 Dallas Keuchel .20 .50
HA17 Collin McHugh .15 .40

2016 Astros Topps

COMPLETE SET (17) 3.00 8.00
HA1 Carlos Correa .25 .60
HA2 Dallas Keuchel .20 .50
HA3 Colby Rasmus .20 .50
HA4 Carlos Gomez .15 .40
HA5 George Springer .20 .50
HA6 Ken Giles .15 .40
HA7 Jose Altuve .20 .50
HA8 Luis Valbuena .15 .40
HA9 Jason Castro .15 .40
HA10 Evan Gattis .15 .40
HA11 Collin McHugh .15 .40
HA12 Mike Fiers .15 .40
HA13 Luke Gregerson .15 .40
HA14 Lance McCullers .15 .40
HA15 Jake Marisnick .15 .40
HA16 Preston Tucker .15 .40
HA17 Marwin Gonzalez .15 .40

2017 Astros Topps

COMPLETE SET (17) 3.00 8.00
HOU1 Jose Altuve .20 .50
HOU2 Mike Fiers .15 .40
HOU3 Alex Bregman .75 2.00
HOU4 Evan Gattis .15 .40
HOU5 Brian McCann .20 .50
HOU6 Dallas Keuchel .20 .50
HOU7 Josh Reddick .15 .40
HOU8 Marwin Gonzalez .15 .40
HOU9 Yulieski Gurriel .25 .60
HOU10 Lance McCullers .15 .40
HOU11 A.J. Reed .15 .40
HOU12 Ken Giles .15 .40
HOU13 Collin McHugh .15 .40
HOU14 Carlos Beltran .20 .50
HOU15 Jake Marisnick .15 .40
HOU16 Carlos Correa .25 .60
HOU17 George Springer .20 .50

2018 Astros Topps

COMPLETE SET (17) 2.50 6.00
HA1 Jose Altuve .20 .50
HA2 Jake Marisnick .15 .40
HA3 Josh Reddick .15 .40
HA4 Carlos Correa .25 .60
HA5 Brad Peacock .15 .40
HA6 Charlie Morton .25 .60
HA7 Alex Bregman .25 .60
HA8 Yulieski Gurriel .20 .50
HA9 Justin Verlander .25 .60
HA10 Dallas Keuchel .20 .50
HA11 Marwin Gonzalez .15 .40
HA12 Brian McCann .20 .50
HA13 Lance McCullers .15 .40
HA14 George Springer .20 .50
HA15 Ken Giles .15 .40
HA16 Evan Gattis .15 .40
HA17 Derek Fisher .15 .40

2019 Astros Topps

COMPLETE SET (17) 2.50 6.00
HA1 Alex Bregman .25 .60
HA2 Jose Altuve .20 .50
HA3 Justin Verlander .25 .60
HA4 George Springer .20 .50
HA5 Carlos Correa .25 .60
HA6 Gerrit Cole .25 .60
HA7 Yuli Gurriel .20 .50
HA8 Hector Rondon .15 .40
HA9 Jake Marisnick .15 .40
HA10 Max Stassi .15 .40
HA11 Josh Reddick .15 .40
HA12 Tony Kemp .15 .40
HA13 Robinson Chirinos .15 .40
HA14 Josh James .25 .60
HA15 Tyler White .15 .40
HA16 Roberto Osuna .15 .40
HA17 Michael Brantley .20 .50

2020 Astros Topps

HOU1 Jose Altuve .20 .50
HOU2 Carlos Correa .25 .60
HOU3 Jose Urquidy .20 .50
HOU4 Justin Verlander .25 .60
HOU5 Michael Brantley .20 .50
HOU6 George Springer .20 .50
HOU7 Josh Reddick .15 .40
HOU8 Alex Bregman .25 .60
HOU9 Yordan Alvarez 1.50 4.00
HOU10 Zack Greinke .25 .60
HOU11 Kyle Tucker .25 .60
HOU12 Yuli Gurriel .20 .50
HOU13 Minute Maid Park .15 .40
HOU14 Roberto Osuna .15 .40
HOU15 Rogelio Armenteros .20 .50
HOU16 Ryan Pressly .15 .40
HOU17 Josh James .15 .40

2017 Astros Topps National Baseball Card Day

COMPLETE SET (10) 6.00 15.00
HOU1 Jose Altuve .75 2.00
HOU2 Carlos Correa 1.00 2.50
HOU3 Alex Bregman 3.00 8.00
HOU4 Dallas Keuchel .75 2.00
HOU5 George Springer .75 2.00
HOU6 Brian McCann .75 2.00
HOU7 Carlos Beltran .75 2.00
HOU8 Josh Reddick .60 1.50
HOU9 Lance McCullers Jr. .60 1.50
HOU10 Jeff Bagwell .75 2.00

1997 AT and T Ambassadors of Baseball

These four standard-size cards were issued by AT and T featured retired ballplayers whose trips were arranged by the Major League Baseball Players Alumni. The cards have the AT and T logo in the upper right corner and the Ambassadors of Baseball Logo on the lower left corner. The cards are not numbered so we have sequenced them in alphabetical order.

COMPLETE SET (4) 8.00 20.00
1 Jesse Barfield 2.50 6.00
2 Darrell Evans 2.50 6.00
3 Al Hrabosky 2.00 5.00
4 Jerry Koosman 2.50 6.00

1988 Athletes in Action

The set features six Texas Rangers (1-6) and six Dallas Cowboys (7-12). The cards are standard size, 2 1/2" by 3 1/2". The fronts display color action player photos bordered in white. The words "Athletes in Action" are printed in black across the lower edge of the picture. The backs carry a player quote, a salvation message, and the player's favorite Scripture.

COMPLETE SET (12) 5.00 12.00
1 Pete O'Brien .50 1.25
2 Scott Fletcher .50 1.25
3 Oddibe McDowell .50 1.25
4 Steve Buechele .50 1.25
5 Jerry Browne .50 1.25
6 Larry Parrish .50 1.25

1978 Atlanta Convention

This 24-card standard-size set features circular black-and-white player photos framed in light green and bordered in white. The player's name is printed in black across the top with his position, team name, and logo at the bottom. The white backs carry the player's name and career information. The cards are unnumbered and checklisted below in alphabetical order. Almost all of the players in this set played for the Braves at one time.

COMPLETE SET (24) 7.50 15.00
1 Hank Aaron 2.50 5.00
2 Joe Adcock .25 .50
3 Felipe Alou .50 1.00
4 Frank Bolling .13 .25
5 Orlando Cepeda .75 1.50
6 Ty Cline .13 .25
7 Tony Cloninger .13 .25
8 Del Crandall .13 .25
9 Fred Haney MG .13 .25
10 Pat Jarvis .13 .25
11 Ernie Johnson .25 .50
12 Ken Johnson .13 .25
13 Denver Lemaster .13 .25
14 Eddie Mathews .75 1.50
15 Lee Maye .13 .25
16 Denis Menke .13 .25
17 Felix Millan .13 .25
18 Johnny Mize .75 1.50
20 Gene Oliver .13 .25
21 Johnny Sain .25 .50
22 Warren Spahn .75 1.50
23 Joe Torre .50 1.00
24 Bob Turley .25 .50

1968 Atlantic Oil Play Ball Contest Cards

These fifty cards were issued in two-card panels which when split, become standard-size cards. For easier reference we have sequenced the set in alphabetical order and listed the player number and prize (when applicable) next to the player's name. Winning cards of more than $1 are not priced and not included in the complete set price. "Clean" cards - cards without glue underneath - may sell for a premium.

COMPLETE SET (50) 125.00 250.00
1 Hank Aaron-4 10.00 25.00
2 Tommy Agee-2 ($2500)
3 Felipe Alou-3 1.25 3.00
4 Max Alvis-2 .60 1.50
5 Bob Aspromonte-1 .60 1.50
6 Ernie Banks-5 ($100)
7 Lou Brock-1 6.00 15.00
8 Jim Bunning-9 1.50 4.00
9 Johnny Callison-1 .75 2.00
10 Bert Campaneris-2 .75 2.00
11 Norm Cash-5 1.25 3.00
12 Orlando Cepeda-4 1.50 4.00
13 Dean Chance-9 .60 1.50
14 Roberto Clemente-7 15.00 40.00
15 Tommy Davis-4 ($100)
16 Andy Etchebarren-8 ($5)
17 Ron Fairly-6 ($10)
18 Bill Freehan-3 ($2500)
19 Jim Fregosi-2 .75 2.00
20 Bob Gibson-9 6.00 15.00
21 Jim Hart-3 .60 1.50
22 Joe Horlen-9 .60 1.50
23 Al Kaline-2 8.00 20.00
24 Jim Lonborg-9 .75 2.00
25 Jim Maloney-9 .75 2.00
26 Roger Maris-7 6.00 15.00
27 Mike McCormick-9 .60 1.50
28 Willie McCovey-4 6.00 15.00
29 Sam McDowell-9 .75 2.00
30 Tug McGraw-7 ($10)
31 Tony Oliva-1 1.25 3.00
32 Claude Osteen-11 ($1) 1.50 4.00
33 Milt Pappas-10 .75 2.00
34 Joe Pepitone-6 .75 2.00
35 Vada Pinson-3 .75 2.00
36 Boog Powell-6 .75 2.00
37 Brooks Robinson-1 6.00 15.00
38 Frank Robinson-5 6.00 15.00
39 Pete Rose-1 15.00 40.00
40 Jose Santiago-11 .60 1.50
41 Ron Santo-4 1.25 3.00
42 George Scott-6 .60 1.50
43 Ron Swoboda-7 .60 1.50
44 Tom Tresh-2 .60 1.50
45 Fred Valentine-6 .60 1.50
46 Pete Ward-1 .60 1.50
47 Billy Williams-8 ($5)
48 Maury Wills-1 .75 2.00
49 Earl Wilson-10 ($1) 1.50 4.00
50 Carl Yastrzemski-5 6.00 15.00

1888 August Beck N403

The tobacco brand with the unusual name of Yum Yum was marketed by the August Beck Company of Chicago. The cards are blank-backed with sepia fronts and are not numbered. There are ballplayers known, and the series was released to the public in 1887 or 1888. We have sequenced this set in alphabetical order. There are new additions added to this checklist and more may be out there so any information would be greatly appreciated. The Cap Anson card actually features a photo of Ned Wiliamson which depresses its value slightly.

COMPLETE SET (51) 125000.00 250000.00
1 Cap Anson UER 6000.00 12000.00
Ned Williamson pictured
2 Lady Baldwin 2500.00 5000.00
3 Dan Brouthers 4000.00 8000.00
4 Bill Brown 2500.00 5000.00
5 Charlie Buffington 2500.00 5000.00
6A Tommy Burns 2500.00 5000.00
(Chicago Portrait
6B Tommy Burns 2500.00 5000.00
Chicago With bat
7A John Clarkson 4000.00 8000.00
Portrait
7B John Clarkson 4000.00 8000.00
Throwing
8 John Coleman 2500.00 5000.00
9 Roger Connor 4000.00 8000.00
10 Larry Corcoran 2500.00 5000.00
11 Tom Daly UER 2500.00 5000.00
Billy Sunday pictured
12 Tom Deasley 2500.00 5000.00
13 Mike Dorgan 2500.00 5000.00
14 Buck Ewing 4000.00 8000.00
15 Silver Flint 2500.00 5000.00
16 Pud Galvin 4000.00 8000.00
17 Joe Gerhardt 2500.00 5000.00
18 Charlie Getzien 2500.00 5000.00
19 Pete Gillespie 2500.00 5000.00
20 Jack Glasscock 2500.00 5000.00
21 George Gore 2500.00 5000.00
22 Ed Greer 2500.00 5000.00
23 Tim Keefe 4000.00 8000.00
24 Mike King Kelly 6000.00 12000.00
25 Gus Krock 2500.00 5000.00
26 Connie Mack 6000.00 12000.00
27 Kid Madden 2500.00 5000.00
28 George Miller 2500.00 5000.00
29 John Morrill 2500.00 5000.00
30 James Mutrie 5000.00 10000.00
31 Bill Nash: Boston 2500.00 5000.00
32A Jim O'Rourke 4000.00 8000.00
New York Portrait
32B Jim O'Rourke 4000.00 8000.00
No team; with bat
33 Danny Richardson 2500.00 5000.00
34 James (Chief) Roseman 2500.00 5000.00
35 Jimmy Ryan 3000.00 6000.00
36 Bill Sowders 2500.00 5000.00
37 Marty Sullivan 2500.00 5000.00
38A Billy Sunday 5000.00 10000.00
Fielding
38B Billy Sunday UER 4000.00 8000.00
Mark Baldwin pictured
39 Ezra Sutton 2500.00 5000.00
40 Mike Tiernan 2500.00 5000.00
41 George Van Haltren 2500.00 5000.00
42 John Montgomery Ward 5000.00 10000.00
43A Mickey Welch 4000.00 8000.00
New York Portrait *
43B Mickey Welch 4000.00 8000.00
New York Pitching
43C Mickey Welch 4000.00 8000.00
New York Portrait
Righ arm extended
44 Jim Whitney 2500.00 5000.00
45 George Wood 2500.00 5000.00

1998 Aurora

The 1998 Aurora set (produced by Pacific) was issued in one series totalling 200 cards. The cards were issued in six card packs with a SRP of $2.99. In addition, a Tony Gwynn sample card was issued prior to the product's release. The card was distributed to dealers and hobby media to preview the product. It's identical in design to a standard Aurora card except for the word "SAMPLE" printed on the card back in the area typically designated for a card number. A Maggio Ordonez Rookie Card is the key card in this set.

COMPLETE SET (200) 15.00 40.00
1 Garret Anderson .15 .40
2 Jim Edmonds .15 .40
3 Darin Erstad .15 .40
4 Cecil Fielder .15 .40
5 Chuck Finley .15 .40
6 Todd Greene .15 .40
7 Ken Hill .15 .40
8 Tim Salmon .25 .60
9 Roberto Alomar .25 .60
10 Brady Anderson .15 .40
11 Joe Carter .15 .40
12 Mike Mussina .25 .60
13 Rafael Palmeiro .25 .60
14 Cal Ripken 1.25 3.00
15 B.J. Surhoff .15 .40
16 Steve Avery .15 .40
17 Nomar Garciaparra .60 1.50
18 Pedro Martinez .25 .60
19 John Valentin .15 .40
20 Jason Varitek .40 1.00
21 Mo Vaughn .15 .40
22 Albert Belle .15 .40
23 Ray Durham .15 .40
24 Magglio Ordonez RC .75 2.00
25 Frank Thomas .40 1.00
26 Robin Ventura .15 .40
27 Sandy Alomar Jr. .15 .40
28 Travis Fryman .15 .40
29 Dwight Gooden .15 .40
30 David Justice .15 .40
31 Kenny Lofton .15 .40
32 Manny Ramirez .25 .60
33 Jim Thome .25 .60
34 Omar Vizquel .25 .60
35 Enrique Wilson .15 .40
36 Jaret Wright .15 .40
37 Tony Clark .15 .40
38 Bobby Higginson .15 .40
39 Brian Hunter .15 .40
40 Bip Roberts .15 .40
41 Justin Thompson .15 .40
42 Jeff Conine .15 .40
43 Johnny Damon .25 .60
44 Jermaine Dye .15 .40
45 Jeff King .15 .40
46 Jeff Montgomery .15 .40
47 Hal Morris .15 .40
48 Dean Palmer .15 .40
49 Terry Pendleton .15 .40
50 Rick Aguilera .15 .40
51 Marty Cordova .15 .40
52 Paul Molitor .15 .40
53 Otis Nixon .15 .40
54 Brad Radke .15 .40
55 Terry Steinbach .15 .40
56 Todd Walker .15 .40
57 Chili Davis .15 .40
58 Derek Jeter 1.00 2.50
59 Chuck Knoblauch .15 .40
60 Tino Martinez .25 .60
61 Paul O'Neill .25 .60
62 Andy Pettitte .25 .60
63 Mariano Rivera .40 1.00
64 Bernie Williams .25 .60
65 Jason Giambi .15 .40
66 Ben Grieve .15 .40
67 Rickey Henderson .40 1.00
68 A.J. Hinch .15 .40
69 Kenny Rogers .15 .40
70 Jay Buhner .15 .40
71 Joey Cora .15 .40
72 Ken Griffey Jr. .75 2.00
73 Randy Johnson .40 1.00
74 Edgar Martinez .25 .60
75 Jamie Moyer .15 .40
76 Alex Rodriguez .60 1.50
77 David Segui .15 .40
78 Rolando Arrojo RC .15 .40
79 Wade Boggs .25 .60
80 Roberto Hernandez .15 .40
81 Dave Martinez .15 .40
82 Fred McGriff .25 .60
83 Paul Sorrento .15 .40
84 Kevin Stocker .15 .40
85 Will Clark .25 .60
86 Juan Gonzalez .15 .40
87 Tom Goodwin .15 .40
88 Rusty Greer .15 .40
89 Ivan Rodriguez .25 .60
90 John Wetteland .15 .40
91 Jose Canseco .25 .60
92 Roger Clemens .75 2.00
93 Jose Cruz Jr. .15 .40
94 Carlos Delgado .15 .40
95 Pat Hentgen .15 .40
96 Jay Bell .15 .40
97 Andy Benes .15 .40
98 Karim Garcia .15 .40
99 Travis Lee .15 .40
100 Devon White .15 .40
101 Matt Williams .15 .40
102 Andres Galarraga .15 .40
103 Tom Glavine .25 .60
104 Andruw Jones .25 .60
105 Chipper Jones .40 1.00
106 Ryan Klesko .15 .40
107 Javy Lopez .15 .40
108 Greg Maddux .60 1.50
109 Walt Weiss .15 .40
110 Rod Beck .15 .40
111 Jeff Blauser .15 .40
112 Mark Grace .25 .60
113 Lance Johnson .15 .40
114 Mickey Morandini .15 .40
115 Henry Rodriguez .15 .40
116 Sammy Sosa .40 1.00
117 Kerry Wood .20 .50
118 Lenny Harris .15 .40
119 Damian Jackson .15 .40
120 Barry Larkin .25 .60
121 Reggie Sanders .15 .40
122 Brett Tomko .15 .40
123 Dante Bichette .15 .40
124 Ellis Burks .15 .40
125 Vinny Castilla .15 .40
126 Todd Helton .25 .60
127 Darryl Kile .15 .40
128 Larry Walker .15 .40
129 Bobby Bonilla .15 .40
130 Livan Hernandez .15 .40
131 Charles Johnson .15 .40
132 Derrek Lee .25 .60
133 Edgar Renteria .15 .40
134 Gary Sheffield .15 .40
135 Moises Alou .15 .40
136 Jeff Bagwell .25 .60
137 Derek Bell .15 .40
138 Craig Biggio .25 .60
139 John Halama RC .15 .40
140 Mike Hampton .15 .40
141 Richard Hidalgo .15 .40
142 Wilton Guerrero .15 .40
143 Todd Hollandsworth .15 .40
144 Eric Karros .15 .40
145 Paul Konerko .15 .40
146 Raul Mondesi .15 .40
147 Hideo Nomo .40 1.00
148 Chan Ho Park .15 .40
149 Mike Piazza .60 1.50
150 Jeromy Burnitz .15 .40
151 Todd Dunn .15 .40
152 Marquis Grissom .15 .40
153 John Jaha .15 .40
154 Dave Nilsson .15 .40
155 Fernando Vina .15 .40
156 Mark Grudzielanek .15 .40
157 Vladimir Guerrero .40 1.00
158 F.P. Santangelo .15 .40
159 Jose Vidro .15 .40
160 Rondell White .15 .40
161 Edgardo Alfonzo .15 .40
162 Carlos Baerga .15 .40
163 John Franco .15 .40
164 Todd Hundley .15 .40
165 Brian McRae .15 .40
166 John Olerud .15 .40
167 Rey Ordonez .15 .40
168 Masato Yoshii RC .15 .40
169 Ricky Bottalico .15 .40
170 Doug Glanville .15 .40
171 Gregg Jefferies .15 .40
172 Desi Relaford .15 .40
173 Scott Rolen .25 .60
174 Curt Schilling .15 .40
175 Jose Guillen .15 .40
176 Jason Kendall .15 .40
177 Al Martin .15 .40
178 Doug Strange .15 .40
179 Kevin Young .15 .40
180 Royce Clayton .15 .40
181 Delino DeShields .15 .40
182 Gary Gaetti .15 .40
183 Ron Gant .15 .40
184 Brian Jordan .15 .40
185 Ray Lankford .15 .40
186 Willie McGee .15 .40
187 Mark McGwire 1.00 2.50
188 Kevin Brown .25 .60
189 Ken Caminiti .15 .40
190 Steve Finley .15 .40
191 Tony Gwynn .50 1.25
192 Wally Joyner .15 .40
193 Ruben Rivera .15 .40
194 Quilvio Veras .15 .40
195 Barry Bonds 1.00 2.50
196 Shawn Estes .15 .40
197 Orel Hershiser .15 .40
198 Jeff Kent .15 .40
199 Robb Nen .15 .40
200 J.T. Snow .15 .40
NNO Tony Gwynn Sample 1.25 3.00

1998 Aurora Cubes

COMPLETE SET (20) 60.00 120.00
1 Travis Lee .75 2.00
2 Chipper Jones 2.00 5.00
3 Greg Maddux 3.00 8.00
4 Cal Ripken 6.00 15.00
5 Nomar Garciaparra 3.00 8.00
6 Frank Thomas 2.00 5.00
7 Manny Ramirez 1.25 3.00
8 Larry Walker .75 2.00
9 Hideo Nomo 2.00 5.00
10 Mike Piazza 3.00 8.00
11 Derek Jeter 5.00 12.00
12 Ben Grieve .75 2.00
13 Mark McGwire 5.00 12.00
14 Tony Gwynn 2.50 6.00
15 Barry Bonds 5.00 12.00
16 Ken Griffey Jr. 4.00 10.00
17 Alex Rodriguez 3.00 8.00
18 Wade Boggs 1.25 3.00
19 Juan Gonzalez .75 2.00
20 Jose Cruz Jr. .75 2.00

1998 Aurora Hardball Cel-Fusions

COMPLETE SET (20) 40.00 80.00
STATED ODDS 1:73
1 Travis Lee 1.00 2.50
2 Chipper Jones 2.50 6.00
3 Greg Maddux 3.00 8.00
4 Cal Ripken 8.00 20.00
5 Nomar Garciaparra 1.50 4.00
6 Frank Thomas 2.50 6.00
7 David Justice 1.00 2.50
8 Jeff Bagwell 1.50 4.00
9 Hideo Nomo 2.50 6.00
10 Mike Piazza 2.50 6.00
11 Derek Jeter 6.00 15.00
12 Ben Grieve 1.00 2.50
13 Scott Rolen 1.50 4.00
14 Mark McGwire 4.00 10.00
15 Tony Gwynn 2.50 6.00
16 Ken Griffey Jr. 5.00 12.00
17 Alex Rodriguez 3.00 8.00
18 Ivan Rodriguez 1.50 4.00
19 Roger Clemens 3.00 8.00
20 Jose Cruz Jr. 1.00 2.50

1998 Aurora Kings of the Major Leagues

COMPLETE SET (10) 50.00 100.00
STATED ODDS 1:361
1 Chipper Jones 4.00 10.00
2 Greg Maddux 5.00 12.00
3 Cal Ripken 12.00 30.00
4 Nomar Garciaparra 2.50 6.00
5 Frank Thomas 4.00 10.00
6 Mike Piazza 4.00 10.00
7 Mark McGwire 6.00 15.00
8 Tony Gwynn 4.00 10.00
9 Ken Griffey Jr. 8.00 20.00
10 Alex Rodriguez 5.00 12.00

1998 Aurora On Deck Laser Cuts

COMPLETE SET (20) 30.00 80.00
STATED ODDS 4:37 HOBBY
1 Travis Lee .50 1.25
2 Chipper Jones 1.25 3.00
3 Greg Maddux 2.00 5.00
4 Cal Ripken 4.00 10.00
5 Nomar Garciaparra 2.00 5.00
6 Frank Thomas 1.25 3.00
7 Manny Ramirez .75 2.00
8 Larry Walker .50 1.25
9 Hideo Nomo 1.25 3.00
10 Mike Piazza 2.00 5.00
11 Derek Jeter 3.00 8.00
12 Ben Grieve .50 1.25
13 Mark McGwire 3.00 8.00
14 Tony Gwynn 1.50 4.00
15 Barry Bonds 3.00 8.00
16 Ken Griffey Jr. 2.50 6.00
17 Alex Rodriguez 2.00 5.00
18 Wade Boggs .75 2.00
19 Juan Gonzalez .50 1.25
20 Jose Cruz Jr. .50 1.25

1998 Aurora Pennant Fever

COMPLETE SET (50) 10.00 25.00
*RED: 1.5X TO 4X BASIC PENNANT
RED STATED ODDS 1:4 RETAIL
*SILVER: 8X TO 20X BASIC PENNANT
SILVER: RANDOM INSERTS IN RETAIL PACKS
SILVER PRINT RUN 250 SERIAL #'d SETS
*PLAT.BLUE: 15X TO 40X BASIC PENNANT
PLAT.BLUE: RANDOM INSERTS IN ALL PACKS
PLAT.BLUE PRINT RUN 100 SERIAL #'d SETS
*COPPER: 40X TO 100X BASIC PENNANT
COPPER: RANDOM INSERTS IN HOBBY PACKS
COPPER PRINT RUN 20 SERIAL #'d SETS
1 Tony Gwynn .50 1.25
2 Derek Jeter 1.00 2.50
3 Alex Rodriguez .60 1.50
4 Paul Molitor .15 .40
5 Nomar Garciaparra .60 1.50
6 Jeff Bagwell .25 .60
7 Ivan Rodriguez .25 .60
8 Cal Ripken 1.25 3.00
9 Matt Williams .15 .40
10 Chipper Jones .40 1.00
11 Edgar Martinez .25 .60
12 Wade Boggs .25 .60
13 Paul Konerko .15 .40
14 Ben Grieve .15 .40
15 Sandy Alomar Jr. .15 .40
16 Travis Lee .15 .40
17 Scott Rolen .25 .60
18 Ryan Klesko .15 .40
19 Juan Gonzalez .15 .40
20 Albert Belle .15 .40
21 Roger Clemens .75 2.00
22 Javy Lopez .15 .40
23 Jose Cruz Jr. .15 .40
24 Ken Griffey Jr. .75 2.00
25 Mark McGwire 1.00 2.50
26 Brady Anderson .15 .40
27 Jaret Wright .15 .40
28 Roberto Alomar .25 .60
29 Joe Carter .15 .40
30 Hideo Nomo .40 1.00
31 Mike Piazza .60 1.50
32 Andres Galarraga .15 .40
33 Larry Walker .15 .40
34 Tim Salmon .25 .60
35 Frank Thomas .40 1.00
36 Moises Alou .15 .40
37 David Justice .15 .40
38 Manny Ramirez .25 .60
39 Jim Edmonds .15 .40
40 Barry Bonds 1.00 2.50
41 Jim Thome .25 .60
42 Mo Vaughn .15 .40
43 Rafael Palmeiro .25 .60
44 Darin Erstad .15 .40
45 Pedro Martinez .25 .60
46 Greg Maddux .60 1.50
47 Jose Canseco .25 .60
48 Vladimir Guerrero .40 1.00
49 Bernie Williams .25 .60
50 Randy Johnson .40 1.00

1999 Aurora

The 1999 Aurora set (produced by Pacific) was issued in April, 1999 in one series totalling 200 cards and was distributed in six-card packs with a SRP of $2.99. Each card features a total of three color photos (two on the front and one on the back) of some of baseball's most popular players.

COMPLETE SET (200) 10.00 25.00
1 Garret Anderson .15 .40
2 Jim Edmonds .25 .60
3 Darin Erstad .15 .40
4 Matt Luke .15 .40
5 Tim Salmon .15 .40
6 Mo Vaughn .15 .40
7 Jay Bell .15 .40
8 David Dellucci .15 .40

Card	Low	High
9 Steve Finley	.15	.40
10 Bernard Gilkey	.15	.40
11 Randy Johnson	.40	1.00
12 Travis Lee	.15	.40
13 Matt Williams	.15	.40
14 Andres Galarraga	.25	.60
15 Tom Glavine	.25	.60
16 Andruw Jones	.15	.40
17 Chipper Jones	.40	1.00
18 Brian Jordan	.15	.40
19 Javy Lopez	.15	.40
20 Greg Maddux	.50	1.25
21 Albert Belle	.15	.40
22 Will Clark	.25	.60
23 Scott Erickson	.15	.40
24 Mike Mussina	.25	.60
25 Cal Ripken	1.25	3.00
26 B.J. Surhoff	.15	.40
27 Nomar Garciaparra	.25	.60
28 Reggie Jefferson	.15	.40
29 Darren Lewis	.15	.40
30 Pedro Martinez	.25	.60
31 John Valentin	.15	.40
32 Rod Beck	.15	.40
33 Mark Grace	.25	.60
34 Lance Johnson	.15	.40
35 Mickey Morandini	.15	.40
36 Sammy Sosa	.40	1.00
37 Kerry Wood	.15	.40
38 James Baldwin	.15	.40
39 Mike Caruso	.15	.40
40 Ray Durham	.15	.40
41 Magglio Ordonez	.25	.60
42 Frank Thomas	.40	1.00
43 Aaron Boone	.15	.40
44 Sean Casey	.15	.40
45 Barry Larkin	.25	.60
46 Hal Morris	.15	.40
47 Denny Neagle	.15	.40
48 Greg Vaughn	.15	.40
49 Pat Watkins	.15	.40
50 Roberto Alomar	.25	.60
51 Sandy Alomar Jr.	.15	.40
52 David Justice	.15	.40
53 Kenny Lofton	.15	.40
54 Manny Ramirez	.40	1.00
55 Richie Sexson	.15	.40
56 Jim Thome	.25	.60
57 Omar Vizquel	.25	.60
58 Dante Bichette	.15	.40
59 Vinny Castilla	.15	.40
60 Edgard Clemente	.15	.40
61 Derrick Gibson	.15	.40
62 Todd Helton	.25	.60
63 Darryl Kile	.15	.40
64 Larry Walker	.25	.60
65 Tony Clark	.15	.40
66 Damion Easley	.15	.40
67 Bob Higginson	.15	.40
68 Brian Hunter	.15	.40
69 Dean Palmer	.15	.40
70 Justin Thompson	.15	.40
71 Craig Counsell	.15	.40
72 Todd Dunwoody	.15	.40
73 Cliff Floyd	.15	.40
74 Alex Gonzalez	.15	.40
75 Livan Hernandez	.15	.40
76 Mark Kotsay	.15	.40
77 Derrek Lee	.15	.40
78 Moises Alou	.15	.40
79 Jeff Bagwell	.25	.60
80 Derek Bell	.15	.40
81 Craig Biggio	.25	.60
82 Ken Caminiti	.15	.40
83 Richard Hidalgo	.15	.40
84 Shane Reynolds	.15	.40
85 Jeff Conine	.15	.40
86 Johnny Damon	.25	.60
87 Jermaine Dye	.15	.40
88 Jeff King	.15	.40
89 Jeff Montgomery	.15	.40
90 Mike Sweeney	.15	.40
91 Kevin Brown	.15	.40
92 Mark Grudzielanek	.15	.40
93 Eric Karros	.15	.40
94 Raul Mondesi	.15	.40
95 Chan Ho Park	.25	.60
96 Gary Sheffield	.15	.40
97 Jeromy Burnitz	.15	.40
98 Jeff Cirillo	.15	.40
99 Marquis Grissom	.15	.40
100 Geoff Jenkins	.15	.40
101 Dave Nilsson	.15	.40
102 Jose Valetin	.15	.40
103 Fernando Vina	.15	.40
104 Marty Cordova	.15	.40
105 Matt Lawton	.15	.40
106 David Ortiz	.40	1.00
107 Brad Radke	.15	.40
108 Todd Walker	.15	.40
109 Shane Andrews	.15	.40
110 Orlando Cabrera	.15	.40
111 Brad Fullmer	.15	.40
112 Vladimir Guerrero	.25	.60
113 Wilton Guerrero	.15	.40
114 Carl Pavano	.15	.40
115 Fernando Seguignol	.15	.40
116 Ugueth Urbina	.15	.40
117 Edgardo Alfonzo	.15	.40
118 Bobby Bonilla	.15	.40
119 Rickey Henderson	.40	1.00
120 Hideo Nomo	.40	1.00
121 John Olerud	.15	.40
122 Rey Ordonez	.15	.40
123 Mike Piazza	.40	1.00
124 Masato Yoshii	.15	.40
125 Scott Brosius	.15	.40
126 Orlando Hernandez	.15	.40
127 Hideki Irabu	.15	.40
128 Derek Jeter	1.00	2.50
129 Chuck Knoblauch	.15	.40
130 Tino Martinez	.15	.40
131 Jorge Posada	.25	.60
132 Bernie Williams	.25	.60
133 Eric Chavez	.15	.40
134 Ryan Christenson	.15	.40
135 Jason Giambi	.15	.40
136 Ben Grieve	.15	.40
137 A.J. Hinch	.15	.40
138 Matt Stairs	.15	.40
139 Miguel Tejada	.25	.60
140 Bob Abreu	.15	.40
141 Gary Bennett RC	.15	.40
142 Desi Relaford	.15	.40
143 Scott Rolen	.25	.60
144 Curt Schilling	.15	.40
145 Kevin Sefcik	.15	.40
146 Brian Giles	.15	.40
147 Jose Guillen	.15	.40
148 Jason Kendall	.15	.40
149 Aramis Ramirez	.15	.40
150 Tony Womack	.15	.40
151 Kevin Young	.15	.40
152 Eric Davis	.15	.40
153 J.D. Drew	.15	.40
154 Ray Lankford	.15	.40
155 Eli Marrero	.15	.40
156 Mark McGwire	.60	1.50
157 Luis Ordaz	.15	.40
158 Edgar Renteria	.15	.40
159 Andy Ashby	.15	.40
160 Tony Gwynn	.40	1.00
161 Trevor Hoffman	.25	.60
162 Wally Joyner	.15	.40
163 Jim Leyritz	.15	.40
164 Ruben Rivera	.15	.40
165 Reggie Sanders	.15	.40
166 Quilvio Veras	.15	.40
167 Rich Aurilia	.15	.40
168 Marvin Benard	.15	.40
169 Barry Bonds	.60	1.50
170 Ellis Burks	.15	.40
171 Jeff Kent	.15	.40
172 Bill Mueller	.15	.40
173 J.T. Snow	.15	.40
174 Jay Buhner	.15	.40
175 Jeff Fassero	.15	.40
176 Ken Griffey Jr.	.75	2.00
177 Carlos Guillen	.15	.40
178 Edgar Martinez	.25	.60
179 Alex Rodriguez	.50	1.25
180 David Segui	.15	.40
181 Dan Wilson	.15	.40
182 Rolando Arrojo	.15	.40
183 Wade Boggs	.25	.60
184 Jose Canseco	.25	.60
185 Aaron Ledesma	.15	.40
186 Dave Martinez	.15	.40
187 Quinton McCracken	.15	.40
188 Fred McGriff	.25	.60
189 Juan Gonzalez	.15	.40
190 Tom Goodwin	.15	.40
191 Rusty Greer	.15	.40
192 Roberto Kelly	.15	.40
193 Rafael Palmeiro	.25	.60
194 Ivan Rodriguez	.25	.60
195 Roger Clemens	.50	1.25
196 Jose Cruz Jr.	.15	.40
197 Carlos Delgado	.15	.40
198 Alex Gonzalez	.15	.40
199 Roy Halladay	.25	.60
200 Pat Hentgen	.15	.40

1999 Aurora Opening Day

*OPENING DAY: 20X TO 50X BASIC
STATED ODDS ONE PER 24 CT.HOBBY BOX
STATED PRINT RUN 31 SERIAL #'d SETS

1999 Aurora Red

*RED: 3X TO 8X BASIC
STATED ODDS 4:25 TREAT RETAIL

1999 Aurora Complete Players

STATED PRINT RUN 299 SER.#'d SETS
A AND B CARDS ARE EQUALLY VALUED

Card	Low	High
1A Cal Ripken	6.00	15.00
1B Cal Ripken	6.00	15.00
2A Nomar Garciaparra	1.25	3.00
2B Nomar Garciaparra	1.25	3.00
3A Sammy Sosa	2.00	5.00
3B Sammy Sosa	2.00	5.00
4A Kerry Wood	.75	2.00
4B Kerry Wood	.75	2.00
5A Frank Thomas	2.00	5.00
5B Frank Thomas	2.00	5.00
6A Mike Piazza	2.00	5.00
6B Mike Piazza	2.00	5.00
7A Mark McGwire	3.00	8.00
7B Mark McGwire	3.00	8.00
8A Tony Gwynn	2.00	5.00
8B Tony Gwynn	2.00	5.00
9A Ken Griffey Jr.	4.00	10.00
9B Ken Griffey Jr.	4.00	10.00
10A Alex Rodriguez	2.50	6.00
10B Alex Rodriguez	2.50	6.00

1999 Aurora Kings of the Major Leagues

STATED ODDS 1:361 HOB/RET

Card	Low	High
1 Cal Ripken	15.00	40.00
2 Nomar Garciaparra	3.00	8.00
3 Sammy Sosa	5.00	12.00
4 Kerry Wood	2.00	5.00
5 Frank Thomas	5.00	12.00
6 Mike Piazza	5.00	12.00
7 Mark McGwire	8.00	20.00
8 Tony Gwynn	5.00	12.00
9 Ken Griffey Jr.	10.00	25.00
10 Alex Rodriguez	6.00	15.00

1999 Aurora On Deck Laser-Cuts

Card	Low	High
COMPLETE SET (20)	15.00	40.00
STATED ODDS 4:37 HOBBY		
1 Chipper Jones	1.00	2.50
2 Cal Ripken	3.00	8.00
3 Nomar Garciaparra	.60	1.50
4 Sammy Sosa	1.00	2.50
5 Frank Thomas	1.00	2.50
6 Manny Ramirez	1.00	2.50
7 Todd Helton	.60	1.50
8 Larry Walker	.60	1.50
9 Jeff Bagwell	.60	1.50
10 Vladimir Guerrero	.60	1.50
11 Mike Piazza	1.00	2.50
12 Derek Jeter	2.50	6.00
13 Bernie Williams	.60	1.50
14 J.D. Drew	.40	1.00
15 Mark McGwire	1.50	4.00
16 Tony Gwynn	1.00	2.50
17 Ken Griffey Jr.	2.00	5.00
18 Alex Rodriguez	1.25	3.00
19 Juan Gonzalez	.40	1.00
20 Ivan Rodriguez	.60	1.50

1999 Aurora Pennant Fever

Card	Low	High
COMPLETE SET (20)	15.00	40.00
*SINGLES: 1X TO 2.5X BASE CARD HI		
STATED ODDS 4:37 HOB/RET		
*SILVER: 1.5X TO 4X BASIC PEN.FEVER		
SILVER: RANDOM INSERTS IN RETAIL PACKS		
SILVER PRINT RUN 250 SERIAL #d SETS		
*PLAT.BLUE: 3X TO 8X BASIC PEN.FEVER		
PLAT.BLUE: RANDOM INS.IN HOB/RET.PACKS		
PLAT.BLUE PRINT RUN 100 SERIAL #d SETS		
*COPPER: 10X TO 25X BASIC PEN.FEVER		
COPPER: RANDOM INSERTS IN HOBBY PACKS		
COPPER PRINT RUN 20 SERIAL #d SETS		
GWYNN AU'S RANDOM IN PACKS		
GWYNN SIGNED 97 P.FEVER BASIC CARDS		
GWYNN SIGNED 1 P.FEVER COPPER CARD		
GWYNN SIGNED 1 P.FEVER P.BLUE CARD		
GWYNN SIGNED 1 P.FEVER SILVER CARD		
NO GWYNN 1 OF 1 PRICING AVAILABLE		
1 Chipper Jones	.50	1.25
2 Greg Maddux	.60	1.50
3 Cal Ripken	1.50	4.00
4 Nomar Garciaparra	.30	.75
5 Sammy Sosa	.50	1.25
6 Kerry Wood	.20	.50
7 Frank Thomas	.50	1.25
8 Manny Ramirez	.50	1.25
9 Todd Helton	.30	.75
10 Jeff Bagwell	.30	.75
11 Mike Piazza	.50	1.25
12 Derek Jeter	1.25	3.00
13 Bernie Williams	.30	.75
14 J.D. Drew	.20	.50
15 Mark McGwire	.75	2.00
16 Tony Gwynn	.50	1.25
17 Ken Griffey Jr.	1.00	2.50
18 Alex Rodriguez	.60	1.50
19 Juan Gonzalez	.20	.50
20 Ivan Rodriguez	.30	.75
S16 Tony Gwynn AU/97	20.00	50.00

1999 Aurora Styrotechs

Card	Low	High
COMPLETE SET (20)	12.50	30.00
STATED ODDS 1:37 HOB/RET		
1 Chipper Jones	1.00	2.50
2 Greg Maddux	1.25	3.00
3 Cal Ripken	3.00	8.00
4 Nomar Garciaparra	.60	1.50
5 Sammy Sosa	1.00	2.50
6 Kerry Wood	.40	1.00
7 Frank Thomas	1.00	2.50
8 Manny Ramirez	1.00	2.50
9 Larry Walker	.60	1.50
10 Jeff Bagwell	.60	1.50
11 Mike Piazza	1.00	2.50
12 Derek Jeter	2.50	6.00
13 Bernie Williams	.60	1.50
14 J.D. Drew	.40	1.00
15 Mark McGwire	1.50	4.00
16 Tony Gwynn	1.00	2.50
17 Ken Griffey Jr.	2.00	5.00
18 Alex Rodriguez	1.25	3.00
19 Juan Gonzalez	.40	1.00
20 Ivan Rodriguez	.60	1.50

1999 Aurora Players Choice

These cards which parallel the regular Aurora cards were given out at the Players Choice award ceremony. The cards have a special "Players Choice" stamp on them but otherwise parallel the regular Aurora cards. We have skip-numbered this set to match the regular card numbers. Varying amounts of each card were issued so we have put the print run next to the players name.

Card	Low	High
13 Matt Williams/109	5.00	12.00
20 Greg Maddux/79	15.00	40.00
36 Sammy Sosa/82	12.00	30.00
54 Manny Ramirez/100	12.00	30.00
79 Jeff Bagwell/109	8.00	20.00
119 R.Henderson/108	12.00	30.00

2000 Aurora

Card	Low	High
COMPLETE SET (151)	15.00	40.00
COMPLETE SET INCLUDES GRIFFEY REDS		
1 Darin Erstad	.15	.40
2 Troy Glaus	.15	.40
3 Tim Salmon	.15	.40
4 Mo Vaughn	.15	.40
5 Jay Bell	.15	.40
6 Erubiel Durazo	.15	.40
7 Luis Gonzalez	.15	.40
8 Randy Johnson	.40	1.00
9 Matt Williams	.15	.40
10 Tom Glavine	.25	.60
11 Andruw Jones	.15	.40
12 Chipper Jones	.40	1.00
13 Brian Jordan	.15	.40
14 Greg Maddux	.50	1.25
15 Kevin Millwood	.15	.40
16 Albert Belle	.15	.40
17 Will Clark	.25	.60
18 Mike Mussina	.25	.60
19 Cal Ripken	1.25	3.00
20 B.J. Surhoff	.15	.40
21 Nomar Garciaparra	.25	.60
22 Pedro Martinez	.25	.60
23 Troy O'Leary	.15	.40
24 Wilton Veras	.15	.40
25 Mark Grace	.25	.60
26 Henry Rodriguez	.15	.40
27 Sammy Sosa	.40	1.00
28 Kerry Wood	.15	.40
29 Ray Durham	.15	.40
30 Paul Konerko	.15	.40
31 Carlos Lee	.15	.40
32 Magglio Ordonez	.25	.60
33 Chris Singleton	.15	.40
34 Frank Thomas	.40	1.00
35 Mike Cameron	.15	.40
36 Sean Casey	.15	.40
37 Barry Larkin	.25	.60
38 Pokey Reese	.15	.40
39 Eddie Taubensee	.15	.40
40 Roberto Alomar	.25	.60
41 David Justice	.15	.40
42 Kenny Lofton	.15	.40
43 Manny Ramirez	.40	1.00
44 Richie Sexson	.15	.40
45 Jim Thome	.25	.60
46 Omar Vizquel	.25	.60
47 Todd Helton	.25	.60
48 Mike Lansing	.15	.40
49 Neifi Perez	.15	.40
50 Ben Petrick	.15	.40
51 Larry Walker	.25	.60
52 Tony Clark	.15	.40
53 Damion Easley	.15	.40
54 Juan Encarnacion	.15	.40
55 Juan Gonzalez	.15	.40
56 Dean Palmer	.15	.40
57 Luis Castillo	.15	.40
58 Cliff Floyd	.15	.40
59 Alex Gonzalez	.15	.40
60 Mike Lowell	.15	.40
61 Preston Wilson	.15	.40
62 Jeff Bagwell	.25	.60
63 Craig Biggio	.25	.60
64 Ken Caminiti	.15	.40
65 Jose Lima	.15	.40
66 Billy Wagner	.15	.40
67 Carlos Beltran	.25	.60
68 Johnny Damon	.25	.60
69 Jermaine Dye	.15	.40
70 Mark Quinn	.15	.40
71 Mike Sweeney	.15	.40
72 Kevin Brown	.15	.40
73 Shawn Green	.15	.40
74 Eric Karros	.15	.40
75 Chan Ho Park	.25	.60
76 Gary Sheffield	.15	.40
77 Ron Belliard	.15	.40
78 Jeromy Burnitz	.15	.40
79 Marquis Grissom	.15	.40
80 Geoff Jenkins	.15	.40
81 David Nilsson	.15	.40
82 Ron Coomer	.15	.40
83 Jacque Jones	.15	.40
84 Brad Radke	.15	.40
85 Todd Walker	.15	.40
86 Michael Barrett	.15	.40
87 Peter Bergeron	.15	.40
88 Vladimir Guerrero	.25	.60
89 Jose Vidro	.15	.40
90 Rondell White	.15	.40
91 Edgardo Alfonzo	.15	.40
92 Darryl Hamilton	.15	.40
93 Rey Ordonez	.15	.40
94 Mike Piazza	.40	1.00
95 Robin Ventura	.15	.40
96 Roger Clemens	.50	1.25
97 Orlando Hernandez	.15	.40
98 Derek Jeter	1.00	2.50
99 Tino Martinez	.15	.40
100 Mariano Rivera	.50	1.25
101 Bernie Williams	.25	.60
102 Eric Chavez	.15	.40
103 Jason Giambi	.15	.40
104 Ben Grieve	.15	.40
105 Tim Hudson	.25	.60
106 John Jaha	.15	.40
107 Matt Stairs	.15	.40
108 Bob Abreu	.15	.40
109 Doug Glanville	.15	.40
110 Mike Lieberthal	.15	.40
111 Scott Rolen	.25	.60
112 Curt Schilling	.25	.60
113 Brian Giles	.15	.40
114 Chad Hermansen	.15	.40
115 Jason Kendall	.15	.40
116 Warren Morris	.15	.40
117 Kevin Young	.15	.40
118 Rick Ankiel	.25	.60
119 J.D. Drew	.15	.40
120 Ray Lankford	.15	.40
121 Mark McGwire	.60	1.50
122 Edgar Renteria	.15	.40
123 Fernando Tatis	.15	.40
124 Ben Davis	.15	.40
125 Tony Gwynn	.40	1.00
126 Trevor Hoffman	.25	.60
127 Phil Nevin	.15	.40
128 Barry Bonds	.60	1.50
129 Ellis Burks	.15	.40
130 Jeff Kent	.15	.40
131 J.T. Snow	.15	.40
132 Freddy Garcia	.15	.40
133 Ken Griffey Jr.	.75	2.00
133R Ken Griffey Jr. Reds	.75	2.00
134 Edgar Martinez	.25	.60
135 Alex Rodriguez	.50	1.25
136 Dan Wilson	.15	.40
137 Jose Canseco	.25	.60
138 Roberto Hernandez	.15	.40
139 Dave Martinez	.15	.40
140 Fred McGriff	.25	.60
141 Rusty Greer	.15	.40
142 Ruben Mateo	.15	.40
143 Rafael Palmeiro	.25	.60
144 Ivan Rodriguez	.25	.60
145 Jeff Zimmerman	.15	.40
146 Homer Bush	.15	.40
147 Carlos Delgado	.15	.40
148 Raul Mondesi	.15	.40
149 Shannon Stewart	.15	.40
150 Vernon Wells	.15	.40
SAMP Tony Gwynn Samp.	.40	1.00

2000 Aurora Pinstripes

Card	Low	High
COMPLETE SET (50)	30.00	60.00
4 Mo Vaughn	.40	1.00
8 Randy Johnson	1.00	2.50
9 Matt Williams	.40	1.00
11 Andruw Jones	.40	1.00
12 Chipper Jones	1.00	2.50
14 Greg Maddux	1.25	3.00
19 Cal Ripken	3.00	8.00
21 Nomar Garciaparra	.60	1.50
22 Pedro Martinez	.60	1.50
27 Sammy Sosa	1.00	2.50
32 Magglio Ordonez	.60	1.50
34 Frank Thomas	1.00	2.50
36 Sean Casey	.40	1.00
37 Barry Larkin	.60	1.50
42 Kenny Lofton	.40	1.00
43 Manny Ramirez	1.00	2.50
45 Jim Thome	.60	1.50
47 Todd Helton	.60	1.50
51 Larry Walker	.60	1.50
55 Juan Gonzalez	.40	1.00
62 Jeff Bagwell	.60	1.50
63 Craig Biggio	.60	1.50
67 Carlos Beltran	.60	1.50
73 Shawn Green	.40	1.00
76 Gary Sheffield	.40	1.00
78 Jeromy Burnitz	.40	1.00
88 Vladimir Guerrero	.60	1.50
91 Edgardo Alfonzo	.40	1.00
94 Mike Piazza	1.00	2.50
96 Roger Clemens	1.25	3.00
97 Orlando Hernandez	.40	1.00
98 Derek Jeter	2.50	6.00
101 Bernie Williams	.60	1.50
102 Eric Chavez	.40	1.00
105 Tim Hudson	.60	1.50
111 Scott Rolen	.60	1.50
112 Curt Schilling	.60	1.50
113 Brian Giles	.40	1.00
118 Rick Ankiel	.60	1.50
121 Mark McGwire	1.50	4.00
125 Tony Gwynn	1.00	2.50
128 Barry Bonds	1.50	4.00
130 Jeff Kent	.40	1.00
133 Ken Griffey Jr.	2.00	5.00
135 Alex Rodriguez	1.25	3.00
137 Jose Canseco	.60	1.50
140 Fred McGriff	.60	1.50
143 Rafael Palmeiro	.60	1.50
144 Ivan Rodriguez	.60	1.50
147 Carlos Delgado	.40	1.00

2000 Aurora Pinstripes Premiere Date

Card	Low	High
4 Mo Vaughn	4.00	10.00
8 Randy Johnson	10.00	25.00
9 Matt Williams	4.00	10.00
11 Andruw Jones	4.00	10.00
12 Chipper Jones	10.00	25.00
14 Greg Maddux	12.00	30.00
19 Cal Ripken	30.00	80.00
21 Nomar Garciaparra	6.00	15.00
22 Pedro Martinez	6.00	15.00
27 Sammy Sosa	10.00	25.00
32 Magglio Ordonez	6.00	15.00
34 Frank Thomas	10.00	25.00
36 Sean Casey	4.00	10.00
37 Barry Larkin	6.00	15.00
42 Kenny Lofton	4.00	10.00
43 Manny Ramirez	10.00	25.00
45 Jim Thome	6.00	15.00
47 Todd Helton	6.00	15.00
51 Larry Walker	6.00	15.00
55 Juan Gonzalez	4.00	10.00
62 Jeff Bagwell	6.00	15.00
63 Craig Biggio	6.00	15.00
67 Carlos Beltran	6.00	15.00
73 Shawn Green	4.00	10.00
76 Gary Sheffield	4.00	10.00
78 Jeromy Burnitz	4.00	10.00
88 Vladimir Guerrero	6.00	15.00
91 Edgardo Alfonzo	4.00	10.00
94 Mike Piazza	10.00	25.00
96 Roger Clemens	12.00	30.00
97 Orlando Hernandez	4.00	10.00
98 Derek Jeter	25.00	60.00
101 Bernie Williams	6.00	15.00
102 Eric Chavez	4.00	10.00
105 Tim Hudson	6.00	15.00
111 Scott Rolen	6.00	15.00
112 Curt Schilling	6.00	15.00
113 Brian Giles	4.00	10.00
118 Rick Ankiel	6.00	15.00
121 Mark McGwire	15.00	40.00
125 Tony Gwynn	10.00	25.00
128 Barry Bonds	15.00	40.00
130 Jeff Kent	4.00	10.00
133 Ken Griffey Jr.	20.00	50.00
135 Alex Rodriguez	12.00	30.00
137 Jose Canseco	6.00	15.00
140 Fred McGriff	6.00	15.00
143 Rafael Palmeiro	6.00	15.00
144 Ivan Rodriguez	6.00	15.00
147 Carlos Delgado	4.00	10.00

2000 Aurora Premiere Date

*PREMIERE: 10X TO 25X BASIC
ONE PREM.DATE PER HOBBY BOX
STATED PRINT RUN 52 SERIAL #'d SETS

2000 Aurora Dugout View Net Fusions

Card	Low	High
COMPLETE SET (20)	30.00	60.00
1 Mo Vaughn	.60	1.50
2 Chipper Jones	1.50	4.00
3 Cal Ripken	5.00	12.00
4 Nomar Garciaparra	1.00	2.50
5 Sammy Sosa	1.50	4.00
6 Manny Ramirez	1.50	4.00
7 Larry Walker	1.00	2.50
8 Juan Gonzalez	.60	1.50
9 Jeff Bagwell	1.00	2.50
10 Craig Biggio	1.00	2.50
11 Shawn Green	.60	1.50
12 Vladimir Guerrero	1.00	2.50
13 Mike Piazza	1.50	4.00
14 Derek Jeter	6.00	15.00
15 Scott Rolen	1.00	2.50
16 Mark McGwire	2.50	6.00
17 Tony Gwynn	1.50	4.00
18 Ken Griffey Jr.	3.00	8.00
19 Alex Rodriguez	2.00	5.00
20 Rafael Palmeiro	1.00	2.50

2000 Aurora Pennant Fever

Card	Low	High
COMPLETE SET (20)	20.00	50.00
STATED ODDS 4:37		
*COPPER: 1.5X TO 4X BASIC PEN.FEVER		
1 Andruw Jones	.40	1.00
2 Chipper Jones	1.00	2.50
3 Greg Maddux	1.25	3.00
4 Cal Ripken	3.00	8.00
5 Nomar Garciaparra	.60	1.50
6 Pedro Martinez	.60	1.50
7 Sammy Sosa	1.00	2.50
8 Manny Ramirez	1.00	2.50
9 Jim Thome	.60	1.50
10 Jeff Bagwell	.60	1.50
11 Mike Piazza	1.00	2.50
12 Roger Clemens	1.25	3.00
13 Derek Jeter	2.50	6.00
14 Bernie Williams	.60	1.50
15 Mark McGwire	1.50	4.00
16 Tony Gwynn	1.00	2.50
17 Ken Griffey Jr.	2.00	5.00
18 Alex Rodriguez	1.25	3.00
19 Rafael Palmeiro	.60	1.50
20 Ivan Rodriguez	.60	1.50
AU16 Tony Gwynn AU/147	15.00	40.00

2000 Aurora Scouting Report

Card	Low	High
COMPLETE SET (20)	12.50	30.00
1 Randy Johnson	1.00	2.50
2 Andruw Jones	.40	1.00
3 Chipper Jones	1.00	2.50
4 Cal Ripken	3.00	8.00
5 Nomar Garciaparra	.60	1.50
6 Pedro Martinez	.60	1.50
7 Sammy Sosa	1.00	2.50
8 Sean Casey	.40	1.00
9 Carlos Beltran	.60	1.50
10 Shawn Green	.40	1.00
11 Vladimir Guerrero	.60	1.50
12 Roger Clemens	1.25	3.00
13 Derek Jeter	2.50	6.00
14 Scott Rolen	.60	1.50
15 Rick Ankiel	.60	1.50
16 Mark McGwire	1.50	4.00
17 Ken Griffey Jr.	2.00	5.00
18 Alex Rodriguez	1.25	3.00
19 Ruben Mateo	.40	1.00
20 Ivan Rodriguez	.60	1.50

2000 Aurora Star Factor

Card	Low	High
COMPLETE SET (10)	30.00	60.00
1 Chipper Jones	2.00	5.00
2 Cal Ripken	6.00	15.00
3 Nomar Garciaparra	1.25	3.00
4 Sammy Sosa	2.00	5.00
5 Mike Piazza	2.00	5.00
6 Derek Jeter	5.00	12.00
7 Mark McGwire	3.00	8.00
8 Tony Gwynn	2.00	5.00
9 Ken Griffey Jr.	4.00	10.00
10 Alex Rodriguez	2.50	6.00

2000 Aurora Styrotechs

Card	Low	High
COMPLETE SET (20)	50.00	100.00
1 Chipper Jones	2.50	6.00
2 Cal Ripken	8.00	20.00
3 Nomar Garciaparra	1.50	4.00
4 Sammy Sosa	2.50	6.00
5 Frank Thomas	20.00	50.00
6 Manny Ramirez	2.50	6.00
7 Larry Walker	1.50	4.00
8 Jeff Bagwell	1.50	4.00
9 Carlos Beltran	1.50	4.00
10 Vladimir Guerrero	1.50	4.00
11 Mike Piazza	2.50	6.00
12 Derek Jeter	10.00	25.00
13 Bernie Williams	1.50	4.00
14 Mark McGwire	4.00	10.00
15 Tony Gwynn	2.50	6.00
16 Barry Bonds	4.00	10.00
17 Ken Griffey Jr.	40.00	100.00
18 Alex Rodriguez	3.00	8.00
19 Jose Canseco	1.50	4.00
20 Ivan Rodriguez	1.50	4.00

1998 Authentic Images

Issued by Authentic Images, these standard-sized metallic cards honor some of the leading players in baseball history. The fronts have ghosted photos of the featured player with the player's name on top, the team logo and a fascimile signature. The back has biographical information, a picture, a write-up and career statistics.

Card	Low	High
COMPLETE SET (4)	15.00	40.00
1 Roger Maris/10000	6.00	15.00
2 Mickey Mantle/536	10.00	25.00
3 Mark McGwire/62000	6.00	15.00
4 Sammy Sosa/25000	6.00	15.00

1945 Autographs Playing Cards

Cards from this set are part of a playing card game released in 1945 by Leister Game Co. of Toledo Ohio. The cards feature a photo of a famous person, such as an actor or writer, or athlete on the top half of the card with his signature across the middle. A photo appears in the upper left hand corner along with some biographical information about him printed in orange in the center. The bottom half of the cardfront features a drawing along with information about a second personality in the same field or vocation. Those two characters are featured on another card with the positions reversed top and bottom. Note that a card number was also used in the upper left corner with each pair being featured on two of the same card number. We've listed the player who's photo appears on the card first, followed by the personality featured at the bottom of the card.

Card	Low	High
COMPLETE SET (55)	200.00	400.00
9A Joe DiMaggio Babe Ruth	25.00	50.00
9A Babe Ruth Joe DiMaggio	25.00	50.00

1992 Avery Police

Sponsored by the Atlanta Police Athletic League, this card measures the standard-size. One card was given out with each paid admission to a charity auction and autograph session on June 20, 1992. A total of 5,000 cards were produced and each card bears a serial number on the back. The front features a color action photo; the top border is white, while the borders on the other three sides are turquoise. A neon yellow bar at the bottom contains the words "Help Steve Strike Out Drugs." The back has biography, professional pitching record, career highlights and an anti-drug and alcohol quote by Avery. The card is unnumbered.

Card	Low	High
1 Steve Avery	1.25	3.00

1914 B18 Blankets

This set of felt-type cloth squares was issued in 1914 with several brands of cigarettes. Each blanket is a 5 1/4" square. Each player exists with two different color combinations based on his team; however, only those variations reflecting price differentials are listed in the checklist below. Cleveland players have either yellow or purple bases; New York Yankees players have either blue or green infields; St. Louis Browns players have either red or purple paths; Washington players have either brown or green bases; Brooklyn players have either blue or green infields; New York Giants players have either brown or green paths; Pittsburgh players have either red or purple bases; and St. Louis Cardinals players have either purple or yellow paths. Some blankets are known to exist in a (third) different color scheme -- those with red infields. These blankets are quite scarce and are listed in the checklist below. The complete set price below reflects a set including all variations listed below. The blankets are unnumbered and are ordered below alphabetically within team, i.e., Cleveland Indians (1-9), Detroit Tigers (10-19), New York Yankees (20-28), St. Louis Browns (29-37), Washington Senators (38-46), Boston Bees NL (47-55), Brooklyn Dodgers (56-64), New York Giants (65-73), Pittsburgh Pirates (74-82) and St. Louis Cardinals (83-91).

Card	Low	High
1A Babe Adams Purple bases	25.00	50.00
1B Babe Adams Red bases	25.00	50.00
2A Sam Agnew Purple paths	25.00	50.00
2B Sam Agnew Red paths	25.00	50.00
3A Eddie Ainsmith Brown bases	12.50	25.00
3B Eddie Ainsmith Green bases	12.50	25.00
4A Jimmy Austin Purple paths	25.00	50.00
4B Jimmy Austin Red paths	25.00	50.00
5A Del Baker Brown infield	30.00	60.00
5B Del Baker Red infield	1500.00	3000.00
5C Del Baker White infield	12.50	25.00
6A Johnny Bassler Purple bases	20.00	40.00
6B Johnny Bassler Yellow bases	25.00	50.00
7A Paddy Bauman UER Name misspelled Brown infield	30.00	60.00
7B Paddy Bauman UER Name misspelled Red infield	1500.00	3000.00
7C Paddy Bauman white infield	12.50	25.00
8A Luke Boone Blue infield	12.50	25.00
8B Luke Boone Green infield	12.50	25.00
9A George Burns Brown infield	12.50	25.00
9B George Burns Red infield	1500.00	3000.00
9C George Burns White infield	12.50	25.00
10A George Burns Brown infield	12.50	25.00
10B George Burns White infield	30.00	60.00
11A Max Carey Purple bases	75.00	150.00
11B Max Carey Red bases	75.00	150.00
12A Marty Cavanaugh UER Name misspelled Brown infield	30.00	60.00
12B Marty Cavanaugh UER Name misspelled Red infield	1500.00	3000.00
12C Marty Cavanaugh UER Name misspelled White infield	12.50	25.00
12D Marty Kavanaugh UER Name misspelled White infield	12.50	25.00
13A Frank Chance Brown pennants	50.00	100.00
13B Frank Chance Green infield	50.00	100.00
13C Frank Chance Yellow pennants	250.00	500.00
14A Ray Chapman Purple bases	20.00	40.00
14B Ray Chapman Yellow bases	25.00	50.00
15A Ty Cobb Brown infield	300.00	600.00
15B Ty Cobb Red infield	7000.00	14000.00

15C Ty Cobb 250.00 500.00
White infield
16A King Cole 12.50 25.00
Blue infield
16B King Cole 12.50 25.00
Green infield
17A Joe Connolly 30.00 60.00
Brown infield
17B Joe Connolly 1500.00 3000.00
Red infield
17C Joe Connolly 12.50 25.00
White infield
18A Harry Coveleski 30.00 60.00
Brown infield
18B Harry Coveleski 1500.00 3000.00
Red infield
18C Harry Coveleski 12.50 25.00
White infield
19A George Cutshaw 12.50 25.00
Blue infield
19B George Cutshaw 12.50 25.00
Green infield
20A Jake Daubert 15.00 30.00
Green infield
20B Jake Daubert#Blue infield 15.00 30.00
21A Ray Demmitt 30.00 60.00
Brown infield
21B Ray Demmitt 1500.00 3000.00
Red infield
21C Ray Demmitt 12.50 25.00
White infield
22A Bill Doak 20.00 40.00
Purple paths
22B Bill Doak 25.00 50.00
Yellow paths
23A Cozy Dolan 15.00 30.00
Purple paths
23B Cozy Dolan 25.00 50.00
Yellow paths
24A Larry Doyle 15.00 30.00
Brown paths
24B Larry Doyle 15.00 30.00
Geen paths
25A Art Fletcher 12.50 25.00
Brown paths
25B Art Fletcher 12.50 25.00
Green paths
26A Eddie Foster 12.50 25.00
Brown pennants
26B Eddie Foster 12.50 25.00
Green pennants
27A Del Gainor 30.00 60.00
Brown infield
27B Del Gainor 12.50 25.00
White infield
28A Chick Gandil 40.00 80.00
Brown infield
28B Chick Gandil#Brown pennants 40.00 80.00
29A George Gibson 25.00 50.00
Purple bases
29B George Gibson 25.00 50.00
Red bases
30A Hank Gowdy 30.00 60.00
Brown infield
30B Hank Gowdy 1500.00 3000.00
Red infield
30C Hank Gowdy 12.50 25.00
White infield
31A Jack Graney 20.00 40.00
Purple bases
31B Jack Graney 25.00 50.00
Yellow bases
32A Eddie Grant 15.00 30.00
Brown paths
32B Eddie Grant 15.00 30.00
Green paths
33A Tommy Griffith 30.00 60.00
Brown infield
33B Tommy Griffith 1500.00 3000.00
Red infield
33C Tommy Griffith 12.50 25.00
White infield
34A Earl Hamilton 25.00 50.00
Purple paths
34B Earl Hamilton 25.00 50.00
Red paths
35A Topsy Hartzell 12.50 25.00
Blue infield
35B Topsy Hartzell 12.50 25.00
Green infield
36A Miller Huggins 25.00 50.00
Purple paths
36B Miller Huggins 100.00 200.00
Yellow paths
37A John Hummel 12.50 25.00
Blue infield
37B John Hummel 12.50 25.00
Green infield
38A Ham Hyatt 25.00 50.00
Purple bases
38B Ham Hyatt 25.00 50.00
Red bases
39A Joe Jackson 400.00 800.00
Purple bases
39B Joe Jackson 600.00 1200.00
Yellow bases
40A Bill James 30.00 60.00
Brown infield
40B Bill James 1500.00 3000.00
Red infield
40C Bill James 12.50 25.00
White infield
41A Walter Johnson 75.00 150.00
Brown pennants
41B Walter Johnson 75.00 150.00
Green pennants
42A Ray Keating 12.50 25.00
Blue infield
42B Ray Keating 12.50 25.00
Green infield
43A Joe Kelley UER 25.00 50.00
Name misspelled
Purple bases
43B Joe Kelley UER 25.00 50.00
Name misspelled
Red bases
44A Ed Konetchy 25.00 50.00
Purple bases
44B Ed Konetchy 25.00 50.00
Red bases
45A Nemo Leibold 20.00 40.00
Purple bases
45B Nemo Leibold 25.00 50.00
Yellow bases
46A Fritz Maisel 12.50 25.00
Blue infield
46B Fritz Maisel 12.50 25.00
Green infield
47A Les Mann 30.00 60.00
Brown infield
47B Les Mann 1500.00 3000.00
Red infield
47C Les Mann 12.50 25.00
White infield
48A Rabbit Maranville 50.00 100.00
Brown infield
48B Rabbit Maranville 1500.00 3000.00
Red infield
48C Rabbit Maranville 20.00 40.00
White infield
49A Bill McAllister UER 25.00 50.00
Name misspelled
Purple paths
49B Bill McAllister UER 25.00 50.00
Name misspelled
Red paths
50A George McBride 12.50 25.00
Brown pennants
50B George McBride 12.50 25.00
Green pennants
51A Chief Meyers 12.50 25.00
Brown paths
51B Chief Meyers 12.50 25.00
Green paths
52A Clyde Milan 15.00 30.00
Brown pennants
52B Clyde Milan 15.00 30.00
Green pennants
53A Dots Miller 20.00 40.00
Purple paths
53B Dots Miller 25.00 50.00
Yellow paths
54A Otto Miller 12.50 25.00
Brown infield
54B Otto Miller 12.50 25.00
Green infield
55A Willie Mitchell 25.00 50.00
Purple bases
55B Willie Mitchell 25.00 50.00
Yellow bases
56A Danney Moeller 12.50 25.00
Brown pennants
56B Danney Moeller 12.50 25.00
Green pennants
57A Ray Morgan 12.50 25.00
Brown pennants
57B Ray Morgan 12.50 25.00
Green pennants
58A George Moriarty 30.00 60.00
Brown infield
58B George Moriarty 1500.00 3000.00
Red infield
58C George Moriarty 12.50 25.00
White infield
59A Mike Mowrey 25.00 50.00
Purple bases
59B Mike Mowrey 25.00 50.00
Red bases
60A Red Murray 12.50 25.00
Brown paths
60B Red Murray 12.50 25.00
Green paths
61A Ivy Olson 20.00 40.00
Purple bases
61B Ivy Olson 25.00 50.00
Yellow bases
62A Steve O'Neil 20.00 40.00
Purple pennants
62B Steve O'Neil 25.00 50.00
Red pennants
62C Steve O'Neil 25.00 50.00
Yellow bases
63A Marty O'Toole 25.00 50.00
Purple bases
63B Marty O'Toole 25.00 50.00
Red bases
64A Roger Peckinpaugh 15.00 30.00
Blue infield
64B Roger Peckinpaugh 15.00 30.00
Green infield
65A Hub Perdue 30.00 60.00
Brown infield
65B Hub Perdue 1500.00 3000.00
Red infield
65C Hub Perdue 12.50 25.00
White infield
66A Del Pratt 25.00 50.00
Purple paths
66B Del Pratt 25.00 50.00
Red paths
67A Hank Robinson 20.00 40.00
Purple paths
67B Hank Robinson 25.00 50.00
Yellow paths
68A Nap Rucker 15.00 30.00
Blue infield
68B Nap Rucker 15.00 30.00
Green infield
69A Slim Sallee 20.00 40.00
Purple paths
69B Slim Sallee 25.00 50.00
Yellow paths
70A Howard Shanks 12.50 25.00
Brown pennants
70B Howard Shanks 12.50 25.00
Green pennants
70C Howard Shanks 12.50 25.00
White infield
71A Burt Shotton 25.00 50.00
Purple paths
71B Burt Shotton 25.00 50.00
Red paths
72A Red Smith 12.50 25.00
Blue infield
72B Red Smith 12.50 25.00
Green infield
73A Fred Snodgrass 12.50 25.00
Brown paths
73B Fred Snodgrass 12.50 25.00
Green paths
74A Bill Steele 20.00 40.00
Purple paths
74B Bill Steele 25.00 50.00
Yellow paths
75A Casey Stengel 50.00 100.00
Blue infield
75B Casey Stengel 50.00 100.00
Green infield
76A Jeff Sweeney 12.50 25.00
Blue infield
76B Jeff Sweeney 12.50 25.00
Green infield
77A Jeff Tesreau 12.50 25.00
Brown paths
77B Jeff Tesreau 12.50 25.00
Green paths
78A Terry Turner 20.00 40.00
Purple bases
78B Terry Turner 25.00 50.00
Yellow bases
79A Lefty Tyler 30.00 60.00
Brown infield
79B Lefty Tyler 1500.00 3000.00
Red infield
79C Lefty Tyler 12.50 25.00
White infield
80A Jim Viox 25.00 50.00
Purple bases
80B Jim Viox 25.00 50.00
Red bases
81A Bull Wagner 12.50 25.00
Blue infield
81B Bull Wagner 12.50 25.00
Green infield
82A Bobby Wallace 30.00 60.00
Purple paths
82B Bobby Wallace 30.00 60.00
Red paths
83A Dee Walsh 12.50 25.00
Purple paths
83B Dee Walsh 12.50 25.00
Red paths
84A Jimmy Walsh 25.00 50.00
Purple paths
84B Jimmy Walsh 25.00 50.00
Red paths
85A Bart Whaling 30.00 60.00
Brown infield
85B Bart Whaling 1500.00 3000.00
Red infield
85C Bart Whaling 12.50 25.00
White infield
86A Zach Wheat 20.00 40.00
Blue infield
86B Zach Wheat 20.00 40.00
Green infield
87A Possum Whitted 20.00 40.00
Purple paths
87B Possum Whitted 25.00 50.00
Yellow paths
88A Gus Williams 25.00 50.00
Purple bases
88B Gus Williams 25.00 50.00
Red bases
89A Owen Wilson 20.00 40.00
Purple paths
89B Owen Wilson 25.00 50.00
Yellow paths
90A Hooks Wiltse 12.50 25.00
Brown paths
90B Hooks Wiltse 12.50 25.00
Green paths

1928 Babe Ruth Candy Company E-Unc.

This six-card set is one of the more obscure candy sets and features cards picturing Babe Ruth which measure approximately 1 7/8" by 4". The cards are sepia in color and depict scenes from either a movie, "Babe Comes Home" (numbers 1, 2 and 4), or scenes from the Yankee Post Season West Coast Exhibition Tour in 1924 (numbers 3 and 6). Each card has "Babe Ruth" below the photo followed by a caption. The backs contain instructions on how to exchange all six cards for a baseball with Babe Ruth's genuine signature on it. Compared to the others in the set, card number six seems to be considerably tougher to find.

COMPLETE SET (6) 1250.00 2500.00
1 Babe Ruth 500.00 1000.00
In uniform of Los Angeles
2 Babe Ruth 500.00 1000.00
Swinging, follow thru
3 Babe Ruth 600.00 1200.00
In uniform with a young boy
4 Babe Ruth 500.00 1000.00
In civilian dress with Anna Q. Nilsson
5 Babe Ruth 500.00 1000.00
In uniform kissing a small girl
6 Babe Ruth 1000.00 2000.00
Autographing a ball

1948 Swell Babe Ruth Story

The 1948 Babe Ruth Story set of 28 black and white numbered cards (measuring approximately 2" by 2 1/2") was issued by the Philadelphia Chewing Gum Company to commemorate the 1949 movie of the same name starring William Bendix, Claire Trevor, and Charles Bickford. Babe Ruth himself appears on several cards. The last 12 cards (17 to 28) are more difficult to obtain than other cards in the set and are also more desirable in that most picture actual players as well as actors from the movie. Supposedly these last 12 cards were issued much later after the first 16 cards had already been released and distributed. The last seven cards (22-28) in the set are subtitled "The Babe Ruth Story in the Making" at the top of every reverse. The bottom of every card says "Swell Bubble Gum, Philadelphia Chewing Gum Corporation." The catalog designation for this set is R421.

COMPLETE SET (28) 750.00 1500.00
1 The Babe Ruth Story 75.00 150.00
In the Making
Babe Ruth and William Bendix
2 Bat Boy Becomes the Babe 12.50 25.00
Facsimile autograph by Bendix
3 Claire Hodgson 10.00 20.00
played by Claire Trevor
4 Babe Ruth played by 10.00 20.00
William Bendix
Claire Hodgson played by
Claire Trevor
5 Brother Matthias 10.00 20.00
played by Charles Bickford
6 Phil Conrad 10.00 20.00
played by Sam Levene
7 Night Club Singer 10.00 20.00
played by
Gertrude Niesen
8 Baseball's Famous Deal 10.00 20.00
9 Babe Ruth played by 10.00 20.00
William Bendix
Mrs.Babe Ruth played by
Claire Trevor
10 Actors for Babe Ruth 10.00 20.00
Mrs. Babe Ruth
Brother Matthias
11 Babe Ruth played by 10.00 20.00
William Bendix
Miller Huggins played by
Fred Lightner
12 Babe Ruth played by 10.00 20.00
William Bendix
Johnny Sylvester played by
George Marshall
13 Actors for Mr. and Mrs. 10.00 20.00
and Johnny Sylvester
14 When A Feller 10.00 20.00
Needs A Friend
15 Dramatic Home Run 10.00 20.00
16 The Homer That Set 10.00 20.00
the Record
17 The Slap That Started 25.00 50.00
Baseball's Most
Famous Career
18 The Babe Plays 25.00 50.00
Santa Claus
19 Matt Briggs 25.00 50.00
Fred Lightner
Actors for Ed Barrow
Jacob Ruppert
Miller Huggins
20 Broken Window 25.00 50.00
Paid Off
21 Regardless of the 25.00 50.00
Generation
Babe Ruth
Bendix shown getting
mobbed by crowd
22 Ted Lyons 30.00 60.00
William Bendix
23 Charley Grimm 25.00 50.00
William Bendix
24 Lefty Gomez 37.50 75.00
William Bendix
Bucky Harris
25 Babe Ruth 100.00 200.00
William Bendix
Babe Ruth
pictured with ball
26 Babe Ruth 100.00 200.00
William Bendix
Babe Ruth
pictured with bat
27 Babe Ruth 100.00 200.00
Claire Trevor
28 William Bendix 100.00 200.00
Babe Ruth
Claire Trevor
Babe Ruth pictured
autographing ball

1948 Swell Babe Ruth Story Premium

This 8" by 9 1/2" sepia photo was given away at the movie theatre premiere of the "Babe Ruth Story" movie. The front shows long-time teammates Lou Gehrig and Ruth in a posed shot. The back has Babe Ruth's career information.

1 Babe Ruth 2500.00 5000.00
Lou Gehrig

1994 Ball Park Franks Will Clark

Measuring the standard-size, this card was sponsored by Ball Park Franks. The front features a full-bleed color action player photo. The player's name and the sponsor name appear at the upper left corner. On a black panel outlined in red, the back carries career highlights. The card is unnumbered.

1 Will Clark .40 1.00

1995 Ball Park Franks

Measuring the standard size, these two autograph cards were produced for Ball Park Franks by Collector's Edge. Collectors could receive the two cards through a mail-in offer for 8 UPC codes from any Ball Park product; for 4 UPC codes and $2.50; or for 2 UPC codes and $5.00. The offer expired on May 31, 1995 or while supplies lasted. The fronts display color action photos that fade to marbleized borders. The player's signature is inscribed across the picture. The cards are unnumbered and checklisted below in alphabetical order. Each card was accompanied by a second card, featuring a ghosted photo and certifying that the signature is authentic.

COMPLETE SET (2) 8.00 20.00
1 Yogi Berra AU 15.00 40.00
2 Frank Robinson AU 8.00 20.00

1997 Bally's Mays Chips

These four $5 chips feature Hall of Famer and one time Bally's spokesperson, Willie Mays. Since they are unnumbered, we have sequenced them in order of playing career

COMPLETE SET (4) 15.00 40.00
1 Willie Mays 4.00 10.00
1954 WS Catch
2 Willie Mays 4.00 10.00
NL Home Run Champ
3 Willie Mays 4.00 10.00
1965 NL MVP
4 Willie Mays 4.00 10.00
1979 HOF

1995 Baltimore Sun Ripken Vending Card

This card appears to be one of a set of eight commemorative cards produced for the Baltimore Sun and measuring approximately 11" by 17". The white-bordered front features a black-and-white player picture on the left half with a commemorative statement on the right. The Baltimore Sun's logo is printed at the bottom. The back is blank.

1 Cal Ripken 2.00 5.00

1911 Baseball Bats E-Unc.

This 44-card set was distributed on candy boxes with the player panel on one side and the name "Baseball Bats" printed on crossed bats and a ball on the opposite side. The two side panels indicate "All Leading Players" and an end flap displays "One Cent." The cards measure approximately 1 3/8" by 2 3/8" and feature a player picture surrounded by either a white or orange border and a thin black line.

COMPLETE SET (44) 2500.00 5000.00
1 Frank Baker 300.00 600.00
2 Jack Baker 125.00 250.00
3 Chief Bender 200.00 400.00
4 Al Bridwell 125.00 250.00
5 Mordecai Brown 200.00 400.00
6 Bill Corrigan UER 125.00 250.00
Name misspelled
7 Frank Chance 250.00 500.00
8 Hal Chase 250.00 500.00
9 Eddie Cicotte 250.00 500.00
10 Fred Clarke UER 200.00 400.00
Name misspelled
11 Ty Cobb 1500.00 3000.00
12 King Cole 125.00 250.00
13 Shano Collins 125.00 250.00
14 Sam Crawford 250.00 500.00
15 Lou Criger 125.00 250.00
16 Harry Davis 125.00 250.00
17 Jim Delehanty 125.00 250.00
18 Art Devlin 125.00 250.00
19 Josh Devore 125.00 250.00
20 Patsy Donovan 125.00 250.00
21 Larry Doyle 150.00 300.00
22 Johnny Evers 250.00 500.00
23 John Flynn 125.00 250.00
24 Solly Hofman 125.00 250.00
25 Walter Johnson 750.00 1500.00
26 Johnny Kling 125.00 250.00
27 Nap Lajoie 400.00 800.00
28 Matthew McIntyre 125.00 250.00
29 Fred Merkle 150.00 300.00
30 Tom Needham 125.00 250.00
31 Rube Oldring 125.00 250.00
32 Frank Schulte 125.00 250.00
33 Cy Seymour 125.00 250.00
34 James Sheckard 125.00 250.00
35 Tris Speaker 250.00 500.00
36 Oscar Stanage 125.00 250.00
Batting; side
37 Oscar Stanage 125.00 250.00
Batting, front
38 Ira Thomas 125.00 250.00
39 Joe Tinker 250.00 500.00
40 Heinie Wagner 125.00 250.00
41 Honus Wagner 500.00 1000.00
42 Ed Walsh 200.00 400.00
43 Chief Wilson 150.00 300.00
44 Art Wilson 125.00 250.00

1910 Baseball Comics T203

This 25-card set was issued by Winner Cut Plug and Mayo Cut Plug. Measuring 2 1/16" by 3 1/8", each card features a color comic picture relating to a baseball phrase or slogan. The back carries an advertisement inside a picture frame. The cards are unnumbered.

COMPLETE SET (25) 250.00 500.00
1 A Crack Outfielder 20.00 40.00
2 A Fancy Twirler 20.00 40.00
3 A Fine Slide 20.00 40.00
4 A Fowl Bawl 20.00 40.00
5 A Great Game 20.00 40.00
6 A Home Run 20.00 40.00
7 An All Star Battery 20.00 40.00
8 A Short Stop 20.00 40.00
9 A Star Catcher 20.00 40.00
10 A White Wash 20.00 40.00
11 A Tie Game 20.00 40.00
12 A Two Bagger 20.00 40.00
13 A Wild Pitch 20.00 40.00
14 Caught Napping 20.00 40.00
15 On to the Curves 20.00 40.00
16 Out 20.00 40.00
17 Put Out on 1st 20.00 40.00
18 Right over the Plate 20.00 40.00
19 Rooting for the Home Team 20.00 40.00
20 Stealing a Base 20.00 40.00
21 Stealing Home 20.00 40.00
22 Strike One 20.00 40.00
23 The Bleachers 20.00 40.00
24 The Naps 20.00 40.00
25 The Red Sox 20.00 40.00

1979 Baseball Greats

These 2 1/2" by 3 3/4" cards were issued in 1979 by Carl Berg. They have the same design as 53 Bowman Black and White and use photos from that era as well. The cards are numbered 65 through 80 as if they were a continuation of the 53 Bowman Black and White set.

COMPLETE SET (16) 10.00 25.00
65 Monte Irvin .20 .50
66 Early Wynn .20 .50
67 Robin Roberts .20 .50
68 Stan Musial 1.25 3.00
69 Ernie Banks .75 2.00
70 Willie Mays 2.00 5.00
71 Yogi Berra .75 2.00
72 Mickey Mantle 3.00 8.00
73 Whitey Ford .75 2.00
74 Bob Feller .75 2.00
75 Ted Williams 2.00 5.00
76 Satchel Paige 1.25 3.00
77 Jackie Robinson 2.00 5.00
78 Ed Mathews .20 .50
79 Warren Spahn .20 .50
80 Ralph Kiner .20 .50

1982 Baseball Card News

This 20-card standard-size set features glossy, black-and-white posed player photos with rounded corners. Backs display the player's name at the top and below the heading "Baseball Card News," each card carries a portion of a 20-part history of baseball cards by Ken Cicalo. The cards are numbered on the back with Roman numerals. These cards were also issued with subscription offer backs.

COMPLETE SET (20) 15.00 40.00
1 Mickey Mantle 1.50 4.00
2 Ted Williams 1.25 3.00
3 Stan Musial .75 2.00
4 Yogi Berra .40 1.00
5 Roger Maris .40 1.00
6 Hank Aaron 1.00 2.50
7 Willie Mays 1.00 2.50
8 Joe DiMaggio .60 1.50
Bob Feller
9 Lou Brock .20 .50
Portrait
10 Roberto Clemente 1.25 3.00
11 Ernie Banks .40 1.00
12 Lou Brock .20 .50
Holding bat
13 Jackie Robinson .60 1.50
Roy Campanella
14 Maury Wills .08 .25
15 Bob Feller .20 .50
16 Roy Campanella .40 1.00
17 Sandy Koufax .40 1.00
18 Joe DiMaggio 1.25 3.00
19 Satchel Paige .75 2.00
20 Babe Ruth 1.50 4.00

1910 Baseball Fans

These four fans which measure 7 1/2" in diameter and 5 1/4" in length of handles features some of the leading players of the time. On the top of the fan is the expression "A fan for a fan:". The players photo and a fascimile signature is underneath that expression. Since these fans are unnumbered, we have sequenced them in alphabetical order.

COMPLETE SET (4) 3000.00 6000.00
1 Hal Chase 500.00 1000.00
2 Ty Cobb 1500.00 3000.00
3 Larry Doyle 250.00 500.00
4 Christy Mathewson 1000.00 2000.00

1910 Baseball Magazine Premium Posters

Measuring approximately 11 1/2" by 19 1/2" this poster was probably an redemption issued by Baseball Magazine. Little is known about these posters and all future information and additions to our checklist would be appreciated.

1 Frank Chance 500.00 1000.00
2 Ty Cobb 1250.00 2500.00
3 Walter Johnson 1000.00 2000.00
4 Honus Wagner 750.00 1500.00

1963 Baseball Magazine M118

These 8 1/2" by 11" photos feature a player portrait surrounded by white borders. The backs are blank

COMPLETE SET (88) 400.00 800.00
1 Hank Aaron 8.00 20.00
2 Joe Adcock 2.50 6.00
3 Grover Alexander 4.00 10.00
4 Bob Allison 2.00 5.00
5 George Altman 2.00 5.00
6 Luis Aparicio 4.00 10.00
7 Richie Ashburn 4.00 10.00
8 Ernie Banks 5.00 12.00
9 Steve Barber 2.00 5.00
10 Earl Battey 2.00 5.00
11 Yogi Berra 6.00 15.00
12 Jim Bunning 4.00 10.00
13 Roy Campanella 6.00 15.00
14 Norm Cash 3.00 8.00
15 Orlando Cepeda 4.00 10.00
16 Ty Cobb 8.00 20.00
17 Rocky Colavito 3.00 8.00
18 Bennie Daniels 2.00 5.00
19 Dizzy Dean 4.00 10.00
20 Joe DiMaggio 12.50 30.00
21 Don Drysdale 4.00 10.00
22 Ryne Duren 2.00 5.00
23 Roy Face 2.50 6.00
24 Bob Feller 4.00 10.00
25 Whitey Ford 5.00 12.00
26 Nelson Fox 4.00 10.00
27 Tito Francona 2.00 5.00
28 Bob Friend 2.00 5.00
29 Lou Gehrig 10.00 25.00
30 Jim Gentile 2.00 5.00
31 Hank Greenberg 5.00 12.00
32 Dick Groat 2.50 6.00
33 Lefty Grove 4.00 10.00
34 Ron Hansen 2.00 5.00
35 Woody Held 2.00 5.00
36 Gil Hodges 4.00 10.00
37 Rogers Hornsby 4.00 10.00
38 Elston Howard 3.00 8.00
39 Dick Howser 2.00 5.00
40 Joe Jay 2.00 5.00
41 Jack Jensen 2.50 6.00
42 Walter Johnson 6.00 15.00
43 Al Kaline 4.00 10.00
44 Harmon Killebrew 4.00 10.00
45 Willie Kirkland 2.00 5.00
46 Sandy Koufax 8.00 20.00
47 Ted Kluszewski 3.00 8.00
48 Jim Landis 2.00 5.00
49 Dale Long 2.00 5.00
50 Jerry Lumpe 2.00 5.00
51 Connie Mack 4.00 10.00
52 Art Mahaffey 2.00 5.00
53 Frank Malzone 2.00 5.00
54 Mickey Mantle 12.50 30.00
55 Roger Maris 6.00 15.00
56 Eddie Mathews 4.00 10.00
57 Christy Mathewson 4.00 10.00
58 Willie Mays 8.00 20.00
59 Minnie Minoso 2.50 6.00
60 Wally Moon 2.00 5.00
61 Stan Musial 5.00 12.00
62 Charley Neal 2.00 5.00
63 Mel Ott 4.00 10.00
64 Camilo Pascual 2.00 5.00
65 Albie Pearson 2.00 5.00
66 Jim Piersall 2.50 6.00
67 Vada Pinson 2.50 6.00
68 Paul Richards 2.00 5.00
69 Robin Roberts
70 Brooks Robinson 4.00 10.00
71 Frank Robinson 4.00 10.00
72 Jackie Robinson 8.00 20.00
73 Pete Runnels 2.00 5.00
74 Babe Ruth 12.50 30.00
75 Ron Santo 3.00 8.00
76 Norm Siebern 2.00 5.00
77 Roy Sievers 2.00 5.00
78 Duke Snider 5.00 12.00
79 Warren Spahn 4.00 10.00
80 Tris Speaker 4.00 10.00
81 Casey Stengel 4.00 10.00
82 Dick Stuart 2.00 5.00
83 Lee Thomas 2.00 5.00
84 Honus Wagner 4.00 10.00
85 Bill White 2.50 6.00
86 Ted Williams 10.00 25.00
87 Gene Woodling 2.00 5.00
88 Early Wynn 4.00 10.00
89 Cy Young 4.00 10.00

1975 Baseball Royalty

These eight cards were created for and given away to the 1st 500 attendees at the 1975 Mid-Atlantic Sports Collectors Association show. The fronts have the words "Baseball Royalty" on top with the players photo underneath and then the information about the show. These players were selected since each player had a "royal" nickname. Since these cards are unnumbered we have sequenced them in alphabetical order.

COMPLETE SET (5) 8.00 20.00
1 Paul Derringer .40 1.00
2 Roy Face .40 1.00
3 Rogers Hornsby 1.50 4.00
4 Carl Hubbell 1.00 2.50
5 Charlie Keller .60 1.50
6 Babe Ruth 3.00 8.00
7 Hal Schumacher .40 1.00
8 Duke Snider 1.25 3.00

1990 Baseball Wit

The 1990 Baseball Wit set was issued in complete set form only. This set was dedicated to and featured several ex-members of the Little Leagues. This 108-card, standard-size set was available primarily in retail and chain outlets. Most of the older (retired) players in the set are shown in black and white. The card backs typically give three trivia questions with answers following. The object of the game is to collect points by correctly answering any one of the questions on the back of each card or identifying the picture on the front. The first printing of 10,000 sets had several errors, and the cards were not numbered. The second printing corrected these errors and numbered the cards. The number on the front of the card is used when playing the game and is not to be confused with the card number, which is found on the back of all cards.

COMP. FACT SET (108) 3.00 8.00
1 Orel Hershiser .02 .10
2 Tony Gwynn .40 1.00
3 Mickey Mantle .75 2.00
4 Willie Stargell .05 .15
5 Don Baylor .02 .10
6 Hank Aaron .40 1.00
7 Don Larsen .02 .10
8 Lee Mazzilli .01 .05
9 Boog Powell .02 .10
10 Little League .01 .05
World Series
11 Jose Canseco .20 .50
12 Mike Scott .01 .05
13 Bob Feller .05 .15
14 Ron Santo .08 .25
15A Mel Stottlemyer ERR .02 .10
Name misspelled
15B Mel Stottlemyre COR .02 .10
16 Shea Stadium .01 .05
17 Brooks Robinson .08 .25
18 Willie Mays .40 1.00
19 Ernie Banks .08 .25
20 Keith Hernandez .02 .10
21 Bret Saberhagen .02 .10
22 Baseball Hall of Fame .01 .05
23 Luis Aparicio .05 .15
24 Yogi Berra .08 .25
25 Manny Mota .02 .10
26 Steve Garvey .02 .10
27 Bill Shea .01 .05
28 Fred Lynn .01 .05
29 Todd Worrell .01 .05
30 Roy Campanella .08 .25
31 Bob Gibson .05 .15
32 Gary Carter .08 .25
33 Jim Palmer .05 .15
34 Carl Yastrzemski .05 .15
35 Dwight Gooden .02 .10
36 Stan Musial .20 .50
37 Rickey Henderson .20 .50
38 Dale Murphy .05 .15
39 Mike Schmidt .08 .25
40 Gaylord Perry .05 .15
41 Ozzie Smith .40 1.00
42 Reggie Jackson .08 .25
43 Steve Carlton .05 .15
44 Jim Perry .01 .05
45 Vince Coleman .01 .05
46 Tom Seaver .08 .25
47 Marty Marion .01 .05
48 Frank Robinson .05 .15
49 Joe DiMaggio .60 1.50
50 Ted Williams .60 1.50
51 Rollie Fingers .02 .10
52 Jackie Robinson .40 1.00
53 Vic Raschi .01 .05

54 Johnny Bench .08 .25
55 Nolan Ryan .75 2.00
56 Ty Cobb .40 1.00
57 Harry Steinfeldt .01 .05
58 James O'Rourke .01 .05
59 John McGraw .05 .15
60 Candy Cummings .02 .10
61 Jimmie Foxx .05 .15
62 Walter Johnson .05 .15
63 1903 World Series .01 .05
64 Satchel Paige .08 .25
65 Bobby Wallace .02 .10
66 Cap Anson .05 .15
67 Hugh Duffy .02 .10
68 William (Buck) Ewing .02 .10
69 Bobo Holloman .01 .05
70 Ed Delahanty .02 .10
71 Dizzy Dean .05 .15
72 Tris Speaker .05 .15
73 Lou Gehrig .50 1.25
74 Wee Willie Keeler .02 .10
75 Cal Hubbard .02 .10
76 Eddie Collins .05 .15
77 Chris Von Der Ahe .01 .05
78 Sam Crawford .05 .15
79 Cy Young .05 .15
80 Johnny Vander Meer .02 .10
81 Joey Jay .01 .05
82 Zack Wheat .02 .10
83 Jim Bottomley .02 .10
84 Honus Wagner .08 .25
85 Casey Stengel .08 .25
86 Babe Ruth .75 2.00
87 John Lindemuth .01 .05
Carl Stotz
88 Max Carey .02 .10
89 Mordecai Brown .02 .10
90 Cincinnati Red Stockings 1869 .01 .05
91 Rube Marquard .02 .10
92 Charles Radbourne .02 .10
93 Hack Wilson .02 .10
94 Lefty Grove .05 .15
95 Carl Hubbell .05 .15
96 A.J. Cartwright .02 .10
97 Rogers Hornsby .05 .15
98 Ernest Thayer .01 .05
99 Connie Mack .02 .10
100 Cent. Celebration 1939 .20 .50
101 Branch Rickey .02 .10
102 Dan Brouthers .02 .10
103 1st Baseball Uniform .01 .05
104 Christy Mathewson .05 .15
105 Joe Nuxhall .01 .05
106 Cent. Celebration 1939 .01 .05
107 William H. Taft PRES .05 .15
108 Abner Doubleday .01 .05

1990 Baseball Wit Unnumbered

*UNNUMBERED: 2X TO 5X BASIC

1991 Baseball's Best Aces of the Mound

This 8" by 8" sticker album is 24 pages in length and features 18 of MLB's outstanding pitchers. One page is devoted to each player and includes player profile, a black and white photo, and a slot for the sticker. The stickers measure 2 1/2" square and feature glossy color action player photos with white borders. They appear on two insert sheets in the middle of the album and are arranged alphabetically, with the number appearing on the front.

COMPLETE SET (18) 3.00 8.00
1 Rick Aguilera .08 .25
2 Jack Armstrong .08 .25
3 Tim Belcher .08 .25
4 Roger Clemens 1.25 3.00
5 Doug Drabek .08 .25
6 Dennis Eckersley .75 2.00
7 Chuck Finley .30 .75
8 Dwight Gooden .20 .50
9 Neal Heaton .08 .25
10 Teddy Higuera .08 .25
11 Dennis Martinez .30 .75
12 Randy Myers .08 .25
13 Gregg Olson .08 .25
14 Bret Saberhagen .20 .50
15 Mike Scott .08 .25
16 Dave Stewart .20 .50
17 Dave Stieb .08 .25
18 Frank Viola .08 .25

1991 Baseball's Best Hit Men

This 8" by 8" sticker album is 24 pages in length and features 18 of MLB's outstanding hitters. One page is devoted to each player and includes player profile, a black and white photo, and a slot for the sticker. The stickers measure 2 1/2" square and feature glossy color action player photos with white borders. They appear on two insert sheets in the middle of the album and are arranged alphabetically, with the number appearing on the front.

COMPLETE SET (18) 6.00 15.00
1 George Bell .08 .25
2 Wade Boggs .50 1.25
3 George Brett 1.00 2.50
4 Hubie Brooks .08 .25
5 Will Clark .40 1.00
6 Len Dykstra .20 .50
7 Ken Griffey Jr. 1.50 4.00
8 Pedro Guerrero .20 .50
9 Ozzie Guillen .20 .50
10 Tony Gwynn 1.00 2.50
11 Gregg Jefferies .08 .25
12 Carney Lansford .08 .25
13 Barry Larkin .50 1.25
14 Don Mattingly 1.00 2.50
15 Kirby Puckett .60 1.50
16 Tim Raines .20 .50
17 Ryne Sandberg 1.00 2.50
18 Robin Yount .50 1.25

1991 Baseball's Best Home Run Kings

This 8" by 8" sticker album is 24 pages in length and features 18 of MLB's home run kings. One page is devoted to each player and includes player profile, a black and white photo, and a slot for the sticker. The stickers measure 2 1/2" square and feature glossy color action player photos with white borders. The stickers are unnumbered and checklisted below in alphabetical order.

COMPLETE SET (18) 4.00 10.00
1 Jesse Barfield .08 .25
2 Jose Canseco .75 2.00
3 Eric Davis .20 .50
4 Glenn Davis .08 .25
5 Andre Dawson .40 1.00
6 Dwight Evans .20 .50
7 Cecil Fielder .20 .50
8 Kelly Gruber .08 .25
9 Von Hayes .08 .25
10 Kent Hrbek .08 .25
11 Bo Jackson .40 1.00
12 Howard Johnson .08 .25
13 Mark McGwire 1.25 3.00
14 Kevin Mitchell .08 .25
15 Eddie Murray .60 1.50
16 Ruben Sierra .20 .50
17 Darryl Strawberry .20 .50
18 Tim Wallach .08 .25

1991 Baseball's Best Record Breakers

This 8" by 8" sticker album is 24 pages in length and features 18 of MLB's outstanding players. One page is devoted to each player and includes player profile, a black and white photo, and a slot for the sticker. The stickers measure 2 1/2" square and feature glossy color action player photos with white borders. They appear on two insert sheets in the middle of the album and are arranged alphabetically, with the number appearing on the front.

COMPLETE SET (18) 6.00 15.00
1 Bert Blyleven .20 .50
2 Jose Canseco .60 1.50
3 Gary Carter .40 1.00
4 Vince Coleman .08 .25
5 Mark Davis .08 .25
6 Carlton Fisk .50 1.25
7 Rickey Henderson .60 1.50
8 Reggie Jackson .50 1.25
9 Howard Johnson .08 .25
10 Ramon Martinez .08 .25
11 Don Mattingly 1.00 2.50
12 Dave Righetti .08 .25
13 Cal Ripken Jr. 2.00 5.00
14 Nolan Ryan 2.00 5.00
15 Ryne Sandberg .75 2.00
16 Mike Schmidt .50 1.25
17 Ozzie Smith 1.00 2.50
18 Fernando Valenzuela .20 .50

1934-36 Batter-Up

The 1934-36 Batter-Up set, issued by National Chicle, contains 192 blank-backed die-cut cards. Numbers 1 to 80 are approximately 2 3/8" by 3 1/4" in size while 81 to 192 are 2 3/8" by 3". The latter are more difficult to find than the former. The pictures come in basic black and white or in tints of blue, brown, green, purple, red, or sepia. There are three combination cards (each featuring two players per card) in the high series (98, 111, and 115). Cards with the die-cut backing removed are graded fair at best.

COMPLETE SET (192) 10000.00 20000.00
WRAP.(1-CENT, CATCH) 150.00 200.00
WRAP.(1-CENT, BAT) 500.00 600.00
1 Wally Berger 60.00 120.00
2 Ed Brandt 25.00 50.00
3 Al Lopez XRC 60.00 120.00
4 Dick Bartell 30.00 60.00
5 Carl Hubbell 75.00 150.00
6 Bill Terry 100.00 175.00
7 Pepper Martin 40.00 80.00
8 Jim Bottomley 60.00 120.00
9 Tommy Bridges 30.00 60.00
10 Rick Ferrell 60.00 120.00
11 Ray Benge 25.00 50.00
12 Wes Ferrell 30.00 60.00
13 Chalmer Cissell 25.00 50.00
14 Pie Traynor 75.00 150.00
15 Leroy Mahaffey 25.00 50.00
16 Chick Hafey XRC 60.00 120.00
17 Lloyd Waner 60.00 120.00
18 Jack Burns 25.00 50.00
19 Buddy Myer 30.00 60.00
20 Bob Johnson XRC 30.00 60.00
21 Arky Vaughan 60.00 120.00
22 Red Rolfe XRC 30.00 60.00
23 Lefty Gomez 100.00 175.00
24 Earl Averill 75.00 150.00
25 Mickey Cochrane 100.00 175.00
26 Van Lingle Mungo XRC 40.00 80.00
27 Mel Ott 150.00 250.00
28 Jimmie Foxx 200.00 300.00
29 Jimmy Dykes 30.00 60.00
30 Bill Dickey 150.00 250.00
31 Lefty Grove 150.00 250.00
32 Joe Cronin 100.00 175.00
33 Frankie Frisch 75.00 150.00
34 Al Simmons 75.00 150.00
35 Rogers Hornsby 200.00 300.00
36 Ted Lyons 60.00 120.00
37 Rabbit Maranville 60.00 120.00
38 Jimmy Wilson 30.00 60.00
39 Willie Kamm 25.00 50.00
40 Bill Hallahan 25.00 50.00
41 Gus Suhr 25.00 50.00
42 Charley Gehringer 75.00 150.00
43 Joe Heving XRC 25.00 50.00
44 Adam Comorosky 25.00 50.00
45 Tony Lazzeri 125.00 200.00
46 Sam Leslie XRC 25.00 50.00
47 Bob Smith 25.00 50.00
48 Willis Hudlin 25.00 50.00
49 Carl Reynolds 25.00 50.00
50 Fred Schulte 25.00 50.00
51 Cookie Lavagetto XRC 40.00 80.00
52 Hal Schumacher 30.00 60.00
53 Roger Cramer XRC 30.00 60.00
54 Sylvester Johnson XRC 25.00 50.00
55 Ollie Bejma XRC 25.00 50.00
56 Sam Byrd 25.00 50.00
57 Hank Greenberg XRC 200.00 300.00
58 Bill Knickerbocker XRC 25.00 50.00
59 Bill Urbanski 25.00 50.00
60 Eddie Morgan 25.00 50.00
61 Rabbit McNair XRC 25.00 50.00
62 Ben Chapman 30.00 60.00
63 Roy Johnson 25.00 50.00
64 Dizzy Dean 300.00 450.00
65 Zeke Bonura XRC 25.00 50.00
66 Fred Marberry 25.00 50.00
67 Gus Mancuso 25.00 50.00
68 Joe Vosmik XRC 25.00 50.00
69 Earl Grace RC 25.00 50.00
70 Tony Piet 25.00 50.00
71 Rollie Hemsley XRC 25.00 50.00
72 Fred Fitzsimmons 30.00 60.00
73 Hack Wilson 100.00 175.00
74 Chick Fullis XRC 25.00 50.00
75 Fred Frankhouse 25.00 50.00
76 Ethan Allen 25.00 50.00
77 Heinie Manush 60.00 120.00
78 Rip Collins XRC 25.00 50.00
79 Tony Cuccinello 25.00 50.00
80 Joe Kuhel 25.00 50.00
81 Tommy Bridges 60.00 120.00
82 Clint Brown XRC 50.00 100.00
83 Albert Blanche XRC 50.00 100.00
84 Boze Berger XRC 50.00 100.00
85 Goose Goslin 125.00 200.00
86 Lefty Gomez 150.00 250.00
87 Joe Glenn XRC 50.00 100.00
88 Cy Blanton XRC 50.00 100.00
89 Tom Carey XRC 50.00 100.00
90 Ralph Birkofer XRC 50.00 100.00
91 Fred Gabler XRC 50.00 100.00
92 Dick Coffman 50.00 100.00
93 Ollie Bejma XRC 50.00 100.00
94 Leroy Parmelee 50.00 100.00
95 Carl Reynolds 50.00 100.00
96 Ben Cantwell 50.00 100.00
97 Curtis Davis XRC 50.00 100.00
98 E. Webb XRC/W. Moses XRC 75.00 150.00
99 Ray Benge 50.00 100.00
100 Pie Traynor 150.00 250.00
101 Phil Cavarretta XRC 60.00 120.00
102 Pep Young XRC 50.00 100.00
103 Willis Hudlin 50.00 100.00
104 Mickey Haslin XRC 50.00 100.00
105 Ossie Bluege 60.00 120.00
106 Paul Andrews XRC 50.00 100.00
107 Ed Brandt 50.00 100.00
108 Don Taylor XRC 50.00 100.00
109 Thornton Lee XRC 60.00 120.00
110 Hal Schumacher 60.00 120.00
111 F.Hayes XRC/T.Lyons 75.00 150.00
112 Odell Hale XRC 50.00 100.00
113 Earl Averill 125.00 200.00
114 Italo Chelini XRC 50.00 100.00
115 I.Andrews/J.Bottomley 75.00 150.00
116 Bill Walker 50.00 100.00
117 Bill Dickey 250.00 350.00
118 Gerald Walker XRC 50.00 100.00
119 Ted Lyons 125.00 200.00
120 Eldon Auker XRC 50.00 100.00
121 Bill Hallahan 60.00 120.00
122 Fred Lindstrom 125.00 200.00
123 Oral Hildebrand XRC 50.00 100.00
124 Luke Appling XRC 150.00 250.00
125 Pepper Martin 60.00 120.00
126 Rick Ferrell 125.00 200.00
127 Ival Goodman XRC 50.00 100.00
128 Joe Kuhel 50.00 100.00
129 Ernie Lombardi XRC 125.00 200.00
130 Charley Gehringer 150.00 250.00
131 Van Lingle Mungo XRC 60.00 120.00
132 Larry French XRC 50.00 100.00
133 Buddy Myer 60.00 120.00
134 Mel Harder XRC 60.00 120.00
135 Augie Galan XRC 50.00 100.00
136 Gabby Hartnett 125.00 200.00
137 Stan Hack XRC 60.00 120.00
138 Billy Herman 125.00 200.00
139 Bill Jurges 50.00 100.00
140 Bill Lee XRC 60.00 120.00
141 Zeke Bonura XRC 50.00 100.00
142 Tony Piet 50.00 100.00
143 Paul Dean XRC 60.00 120.00
144 Jimmie Foxx 300.00 450.00
145 Joe Medwick XRC 150.00 250.00
146 Rip Collins XRC 50.00 100.00
147 Mel Almada XRC 50.00 100.00
148 Allan Cooke XRC 50.00 100.00
149 Moe Berg 300.00 450.00
150 Dolph Camilli XRC 60.00 120.00
151 Oscar Melillo XRC 50.00 100.00
152 Bruce Campbell XRC 50.00 100.00
153 Lefty Grove 250.00 350.00
154 Johnny Murphy XRC 60.00 120.00
155 Luke Sewell 60.00 120.00
156 Leo Durocher 200.00 300.00
157 Lloyd Waner 125.00 200.00
158 Guy Bush 50.00 100.00
159 Jimmy Dykes 60.00 120.00
160 Steve O'Neill XRC 60.00 120.00
161 General Crowder 60.00 120.00
162 Joe Cascarella XRC 60.00 120.00
163 Daniel Hafey XRC 60.00 120.00
164 Gilly Campbell XRC 50.00 100.00
165 Ray Hayworth XRC 50.00 100.00
166 Frank Demaree 50.00 100.00
167 John Babich XRC 50.00 100.00
168 Marvin Owen XRC 50.00 100.00
169 Ralph Kress 50.00 100.00
170 Mule Haas 50.00 100.00
171 Frank Higgins XRC 60.00 120.00
172 Wally Berger 60.00 120.00
173 Frankie Frisch 200.00 300.00
174 Wes Ferrell 60.00 120.00
175 Pete Fox XRC 50.00 100.00
176 John Vergez 50.00 100.00
177 Billy Rogell 50.00 100.00
178 Don Brennan XRC 50.00 100.00
179 Jim Bottomley 125.00 200.00
180 Travis Jackson 125.00 200.00
181 Red Rolfe XRC 60.00 120.00
182 Frank Crosetti 75.00 150.00
183 Joe Cronin 125.00 200.00
184 Schoolboy Rowe XRC 60.00 120.00
185 Chuck Klein 150.00 250.00
186 Lon Warneke 60.00 120.00
187 Gus Suhr 50.00 100.00
188 Ben Chapman 60.00 120.00
189 Clint Brown XRC 50.00 100.00
190 Paul Derringer XRC 60.00 120.00
191 John Burns XRC 50.00 100.00
192 John Broaca XRC 75.00 150.00

1959 Bauer Hayes Company PC750

The 1959 Hayes Company postacrd consists of but one card. The Dexter Press printed Hank Bauer card is in full color and features a facsimile autograph of Bauer at the bottom of the card.

1 Hank Bauer 7.50 15.00

1959 Bazooka

The 23 full-color, unnumbered cards comprising the 1959 Bazooka set were cut from the bottom of the boxes of gum marketed nationally that year by Topps. Bazooka was the brand name which Topps had been using to sell its one cent bubblegum. This year, Topps decided to distribute 25 dual pieces of Bazooka gum in a box. The cards themselves measure 2 13/16" by 4 15/16". Only nine cards were originally issued; 14 more were added to the set at a later date (these are marked with SP in the checklist). The latter are less plentiful and hence more valuable than the original nine. All the cards are blank backed and the catalog designation is R414-15. The prices below are for the cards cut from the box; complete boxes intact would command a premium. Hank Aaron's card can be found with his name in either white or yellow print.

COMPLETE SET (23) 4000.00 8000.00
1 Hank Aaron White 250.00 500.00
1 Hank Aaron Yellow 250.00 500.00
2 Richie Ashburn SP 200.00 400.00
3 Ernie Banks SP 300.00 600.00
4 Ken Boyer SP 150.00 300.00
5 Orlando Cepeda 100.00 200.00
6 Bob Cerv SP 100.00 200.00
7 Rocky Colavito SP 200.00 400.00
8 Del Crandall 25.00 50.00
9 Jim Davenport 25.00 50.00
10 Don Drysdale SP 250.00 500.00
11 Nellie Fox SP 200.00 400.00
12 Jackie Jensen SP 150.00 300.00
13 Harvey Kuenn SP 125.00 250.00
14 Mickey Mantle 800.00 1600.00
15 Willie Mays 300.00 600.00
16 Bill Mazeroski 100.00 200.00
17 Roy McMillan 25.00 50.00
18 Billy Pierce SP 125.00 250.00
19 Roy Sievers SP 100.00 200.00
20 Duke Snider SP 400.00 800.00
21 Gus Triandos SP 100.00 200.00
22 Bob Turley 50.00 100.00
23 Vic Wertz SP 100.00 200.00

1960 Bazooka

In 1960, Topps introduced a 36-card baseball player set in three card panels on the bottom of Bazooka gum boxes. The cards measure 1 13/16" by 2 3/4" and the panels measure 2 3/4" by 5 1/2". The cards carried full color pictures and were numbered at the bottom underneath the team position. The checklist below contains prices for individual cards. Complete panels or complete boxes would command a premium above these prices.

COMPLETE INDIV.SET (36) 600.00 1200.00
1 Ernie Banks 20.00 50.00
2 Bud Daley 8.00 20.00
3 Wally Moon 8.00 20.00
4 Hank Aaron 50.00 100.00
5 Milt Pappas 8.00 20.00
6 Dick Stuart 8.00 20.00
7 Roberto Clemente 125.00 250.00
8 Yogi Berra 40.00 80.00
9 Ken Boyer 8.00 20.00
10 Orlando Cepeda 12.50 30.00
11 Gus Triandos 8.00 20.00
12 Frank Malzone 8.00 20.00
13 Willie Mays 60.00 120.00
14 Camilo Pascual 8.00 20.00
15 Bob Cerv 8.00 20.00
16 Vic Power 8.00 20.00
17 Larry Sherry 8.00 20.00
18 Al Kaline 20.00 50.00
19 Warren Spahn 20.00 50.00
20 Harmon Killebrew 20.00 50.00
21 Jackie Jensen 8.00 20.00
22 Luis Aparicio 12.50 30.00
23 Gil Hodges 12.50 30.00
24 Richie Ashburn 15.00 40.00
25 Nellie Fox 15.00 40.00
26 Robin Roberts 15.00 40.00
27 Joe Cunningham 8.00 20.00
28 Early Wynn 12.50 30.00
29 Frank Robinson 20.00 50.00
30 Rocky Colavito 12.50 30.00
31 Mickey Mantle 175.00 350.00
32 Glen Hobbie 8.00 20.00
33 Roy McMillan 8.00 20.00
34 Harvey Kuenn 8.00 20.00
35 Johnny Antonelli 8.00 20.00
36 Del Crandall 8.00 20.00

1961 Bazooka

The 36 card set issued by Bazooka in 1961 follows the format established in 1960; three full color, numbered cards to each panel found on a Bazooka gum box. The individual cards measure 1 13/16" by 2 3/4" whereas the panels measure 2 3/4" by 5 1/2". The cards of 1960 and 1961 are similar in design but are easily distinguished from one another by their numbers. Complete panels or complete boxes would command a premium above these prices.

COMPLETE INDIV. SET (36) 750.00 1500.00
1 Art Mahaffey 8.00 20.00
2 Mickey Mantle 400.00 800.00
3 Ron Santo 10.00 25.00
4 Bud Daley 8.00 20.00
5 Roger Maris 50.00 100.00
6 Eddie Yost 8.00 20.00
7 Minnie Minoso 10.00 25.00
8 Dick Groat 8.00 20.00
9 Frank Malzone 8.00 20.00
10 Dick Donovan 8.00 20.00
11 Eddie Mathews 40.00 80.00
12 Jim Lemon 8.00 20.00
13 Chuck Estrada 8.00 20.00
14 Ken Boyer 10.00 25.00
15 Harvey Kuenn 8.00 20.00
16 Ernie Broglio 8.00 20.00
17 Rocky Colavito 20.00 50.00
18 Ted Kluszewski 20.00 50.00
19 Ernie Banks 40.00 80.00
20 Al Kaline 40.00 80.00
21 Ed Bailey 8.00 20.00
22 Jim Perry 8.00 20.00
23 Willie Mays 75.00 150.00
24 Bill Mazeroski 20.00 50.00
25 Gus Triandos 8.00 20.00
26 Don Drysdale 30.00 60.00
27 Frank Herrera 8.00 20.00
28 Earl Battey 8.00 20.00
29 Warren Spahn 40.00 80.00
30 Gene Woodling 8.00 20.00
31 Frank Robinson 40.00 80.00
32 Pete Runnels 8.00 20.00
33 Woodie Held 8.00 20.00
34 Norm Larker 8.00 20.00
35 Luis Aparicio 20.00 50.00
36 Bill Tuttle 8.00 20.00

1962 Bazooka

The 1962 Bazooka set of 45 full color, blank backed, unnumbered cards was issued in panels of three on Bazooka bubble gum. The individual cards measure 1 13/16" by 2 3/4" whereas the panels measure 2 3/4" by 5 1/2". The cards below are numbered by panel alphabetically based on the last name of the player pictured on the far left card of the panel. The cards with SP in the checklist below are more difficult to obtain. Complete panels or complete boxes would command a premium above these prices.

COMPLETE INDIV. SET (9) 1700.00 3400.00
1 Bob Allison SP 100.00 200.00
2 Eddie Mathews SP 250.00 500.00
3 Vada Pinson SP 125.00 250.00
4 Earl Battey 6.00 15.00
5 Warren Spahn 20.00 50.00
6 Lee Thomas 6.00 15.00
7 Orlando Cepeda 12.50 30.00
8 Woodie Held 6.00 15.00
9 Bob Aspromonte 6.00 15.00
10 Dick Howser 6.00 15.00
11 Roberto Clemente 125.00 250.00
12 Al Kaline 20.00 50.00
13 Joe Jay 6.00 15.00
14 Roger Maris 40.00 80.00
15 Frank Howard 8.00 20.00
16 Sandy Koufax 40.00 80.00
17 Jim Gentile 6.00 15.00
18 Johnny Callison 6.00 15.00
19 Jim Landis 6.00 15.00
20 Ken Boyer 8.00 20.00
21 Chuck Schilling 6.00 15.00
22 Art Mahaffey 6.00 15.00
23 Mickey Mantle 175.00 350.00
24 Dick Stuart 6.00 15.00
25 Ken McBride 6.00 15.00
26 Frank Robinson 20.00 50.00
27 Gil Hodges 15.00 40.00
28 Milt Pappas 6.00 15.00
29 Hank Aaron 50.00 100.00
30 Luis Aparicio 12.50 30.00
31 Johnny Romano SP 100.00 200.00
32 Ernie Banks SP 350.00 700.00
33 Norm Siebern SP 100.00 200.00
34 Ron Santo 10.00 25.00
35 Norm Cash 8.00 20.00
36 Jim Piersall 8.00 20.00
37 Don Schwall 6.00 15.00
38 Willie Mays 60.00 120.00
39 Norm Larker 6.00 15.00
40 Bill White 8.00 20.00
41 Whitey Ford 20.00 50.00
42 Rocky Colavito 12.50 30.00
43 Don Zimmer SP 50.00 100.00
44 Harmon Killebrew SP 350.00 700.00
45 Gene Woodling SP 100.00 200.00

1963 Bazooka

The 1963 Bazooka set of 36 full color, blank backed numbered cards was issued on Bazooka bubble gum boxes. This year marked a change in format from previous Bazooka issues with a smaller sized card being issued. The individual cards measure 1 9/16" by 2 1/2" whereas the panels measure 2 1/2" by 4 11/16". The card features a white strip with the player's name printed in black on the card. The number appears in the white border on the bottom of the card. Three cards were issued per panel. Complete panels or complete boxes would command a premium above these prices.

COMPLETE INDIV.SET (36) 400.00 800.00
1 Mickey Mantle 125.00 250.00
2 Bob Rodgers 3.00 8.00
3 Ernie Banks 20.00 50.00
4 Norm Siebern 3.00 8.00
5 Warren Spahn 15.00 40.00
6 Bill Mazeroski 8.00 20.00
7 Harmon Killebrew 15.00 40.00
8 Dick Farrell 3.00 8.00
9 Hank Aaron 40.00 80.00
10 Dick Donovan 3.00 8.00
11 Jim Gentile 3.00 8.00
12 Willie Mays 40.00 80.00
13 Camilo Pascual 3.00 8.00
14 Roberto Clemente 50.00 100.00
15 Johnny Callison 3.00 8.00
16 Carl Yastrzemski 20.00 50.00
17 Don Drysdale 12.50 30.00
18 Johnny Romano 3.00 8.00
19 Al Jackson 3.00 8.00
20 Ralph Terry 3.00 8.00
21 Bill Monbouquette 3.00 8.00
22 Orlando Cepeda 8.00 20.00
23 Stan Musial 20.00 50.00
24 Floyd Robinson 3.00 8.00
25 Chuck Hinton 3.00 8.00
26 Bob Purkey 3.00 8.00
27 Ken Hubbs 4.00 10.00
28 Bill White 4.00 10.00
29 Ray Herbert 3.00 8.00
30 Brooks Robinson 20.00 50.00
31 Frank Robinson 20.00 50.00
32 Lee Thomas 3.00 8.00
33 Rocky Colavito 8.00 20.00
34 Al Kaline 20.00 50.00
35 Art Mahaffey 3.00 8.00
36 Tommy Davis 3.00 8.00

1963 Bazooka ATG Silver

*SILVER: .75X TO 2X BASIC

1963 Bazooka ATG

The 1963 Bazooka All Time Greats set contains 41 black and white numbered cards issued as inserts in boxes of Bazooka Bubble gum. The cards feature bust shots with gold trim and measure 1 9/16" by 2 1/2". The backs are yellow with black print containing vital information and a biography of the player. Many of the players are pictured not as they looked during their playing careers but as they looked many years after their playing days were through. The cards also exist in a scarcer variety with silver trim instead of gold.

COMPLETE SET (41) 175.00 350.00
1 Joe Tinker 2.50 6.00
2 Harry Heilmann 2.50 6.00
3 Jack Chesbro 1.50 4.00
4 Christy Mathewson 6.00 15.00
5 Herb Pennock 2.50 6.00
6 Cy Young 4.00 10.00
7 Ed Walsh 2.50 6.00
8 Nap Lajoie 4.00 10.00
9 Eddie Plank 2.50 6.00
10 Honus Wagner 8.00 20.00
11 Chief Bender 2.50 6.00
12 Walter Johnson 6.00 15.00
13 Mordecai Brown 2.50 6.00
14 Rabbit Maranville 2.50 6.00
15 Lou Gehrig 20.00 50.00
16 Ban Johnson 1.50 4.00
17 Babe Ruth 40.00 80.00
18 Connie Mack 2.50 6.00
19 Hank Greenberg 2.50 6.00
20 John McGraw 2.50 6.00
21 Johnny Evers 2.50 6.00
22 Al Simmons 2.50 6.00
23 Jimmy Collins 2.50 6.00
24 Tris Speaker 3.00 8.00
25 Frank Chance 2.50 6.00
26 Fred Clarke 2.50 6.00
27 Wilbert Robinson 2.50 6.00
28 Dazzy Vance 2.50 6.00
29 Pete Alexander 3.00 8.00
30 Judge Landis 2.50 6.00
31 Willie Keeler 2.50 6.00
32 Rogers Hornsby 4.00 10.00
33 Hugh Duffy 2.50 6.00
34 Mickey Cochrane 2.50 6.00
35 Ty Cobb 20.00 50.00
36 Mel Ott 4.00 10.00
37 Clark Griffith 2.50 6.00
38 Ted Lyons 2.50 6.00
39 Cap Anson 2.50 6.00
40 Bill Dickey 2.50 6.00
41 Eddie Collins 2.50 6.00

1964 Bazooka

The 1964 Bazooka set of 36 full color, blank backed, numbered cards were issued in panels of three on the backs of Bazooka bubble gum boxes. The individual cards measure 1 9/16" by 2 1/2" whereas the panels measure 2 1/2" by 4 11/16". Many players who were in the 1963 set have the same number in this set; however, the pictures are different. Complete panels or complete boxes would command a premium above these prices.

COMPLETE INDIV. SET (36) 500.00 1000.00
1 Mickey Mantle 125.00 250.00
2 Dick Groat 3.00 8.00
3 Steve Barber 3.00 8.00
4 Ken McBride 3.00 8.00
5 Warren Spahn 15.00 40.00
6 Bob Friend 3.00 8.00
7 Harmon Killebrew 15.00 40.00
8 Dick Farrell 3.00 8.00
9 Hank Aaron 40.00 80.00
10 Rich Rollins 3.00 8.00
11 Jim Gentile 3.00 8.00
12 Willie Mays 40.00 80.00
13 Camilo Pascual 3.00 8.00
14 Roberto Clemente 60.00 120.00
15 Johnny Callison 3.00 8.00
16 Carl Yastrzemski 30.00 60.00
17 Billy Williams 8.00 20.00
18 Johnny Romano 3.00 8.00
19 Jim Maloney 3.00 8.00
20 Norm Cash 4.00 10.00
21 Willie McCovey 8.00 20.00
22 Jim Fregosi 3.00 8.00
23 George Altman 3.00 8.00
24 Floyd Robinson 3.00 8.00
25 Chuck Hinton 3.00 8.00
26 Ron Hunt 3.00 8.00
27 Gary Peters 3.00 8.00
28 Dick Ellsworth 3.00 8.00
29 Elston Howard 4.00 10.00
30 Brooks Robinson 20.00 50.00
31 Frank Robinson 20.00 50.00
32 Sandy Koufax 40.00 80.00
33 Rocky Colavito 8.00 20.00
34 Al Kaline 20.00 50.00
35 Ken Boyer 4.00 10.00
36 Tommy Davis 3.00 8.00

1964 Bazooka Stamps

Each small stamp is 1" by 1 1/2". The subject's name, team and position are found in a colored rectangle beneath the picture area. Each sheet is numbered in the upper left hand corner outside the picture area. The sheet number is given after the player's name in the checklist below with the prefix S. The stamps were issued in sheets of 10 but an album to hold this particular set has not yet been seen.

COMPLETE SET (100) 400.00 800.00
1 Ed Charles .75 2.00
2 Vada Pinson 1.25 3.00
3 Jimmy Hall .75 2.00
4 Milt Pappas 1.00 2.50
5 Dick Ellsworth .75 2.00
6 Frank Malzone 1.00 2.50
7 Max Alvis .75 2.00
8 Pete Ward .75 2.00
9 Tony Taylor 1.00 2.50
10 Bill White 1.50 4.00
11 Don Zimmer 1.25 3.00
12 Bobby Richardson 4.00 10.00
13 Larry Jackson .75 2.00
14 Norm Siebern .75 2.00
15 Frank Robinson 12.50 30.00
16 Bob Aspromonte .75 2.00
17 Al McBean .75 2.00
18 Floyd Robinson .75 2.00
19 Bill Monbouquette .75 2.00
20 Willie Mays 40.00 80.00
21 Brooks Robinson S3 10.00 25.00
22 Joe Pepitone S3 1.50 4.00
23 Carl Yastrzemski S3 12.50 30.00
24 Don Lock S3 .75 2.00
25 Ernie Banks S3 10.00 25.00
26 Dave Nicholson S3 .75 2.00
27 Roberto Clemente S3 60.00 120.00
28 Curt Flood S3 1.50 4.00
29 Woody Held S3 .75 2.00
30 Jesse Gonder S3 .75 2.00
31 Juan Pizarro .75 2.00
32 Jim Maloney S4 1.00 2.50
33 Ron Santo 1.50 4.00
34 Harmon Killebrew 8.00 20.00
35 Ed Roebuck S4 .75 2.00
36 Boog Powell 1.50 4.00
37 Jim Grant S4 .75 2.00
38 Hank Aguirre S4 .75 2.00
39 Juan Marichal 8.00 20.00
40 Bill Mazeroski 2.50 6.00
41 Dick Radatz S5 .75 2.00
42 Albie Pearson S5 .75 2.00
43 Tommy Harper S5 1.00 2.50
44 Carl Willey S5 .75 2.00
45 Jim Bouton 1.50 4.00
46 Ron Perranoski S5 .75 2.00
47 Chuck Hinton S5 .75 2.00
48 John Romano S5 .75 2.00
49 Norm Cash 1.50 4.00
50 Orlando Cepeda 4.00 10.00
51 Dick Stuart S6 .75 2.00
52 Rich Rollins S6 .75 2.00
53 Mickey Mantle S6 100.00 200.00
54 Steve Barber S6 .75 2.00
55 Jim O'Toole S6 .75 2.00
56 Gary Peters S6 .75 2.00
57 Warren Spahn S6 10.00 25.00
58 Tony Gonzalez S6 .75 2.00
59 Joe Torre S6 1.50 4.00
60 Jim Fregosi S6 1.25 3.00
61 Ken Boyer 1.50 4.00
62 Felipe Alou 1.00 2.50
63 Jim Davenport S7 .75 2.00
64 Tommy Davis 1.25 3.00
65 Rocky Colavito 3.00 8.00
66 Bob Friend S7 1.00 2.50
67 Billy Moran S7 .75 2.00
68 Bill Freehan 1.25 3.00
69 George Altman S7 .75 2.00
70 Ken Johnson S7 .75 2.00
71 Earl Battey S8 .75 2.00
72 Elston Howard 1.50 4.00
73 Billy Williams 8.00 20.00
74 Claude Osteen 1.00 2.50
75 Jim Gentile 1.00 2.50
76 Donn Clendenon 1.00 2.50
77 Ernie Broglio .75 2.00
78 Hal Woodeshick .75 2.00
79 Don Drysdale 8.00 20.00
80 John Callison 1.00 2.50
81 Dick Groat 1.00 2.50
82 Moe Drabowsky .75 2.00
83 Frank Howard 1.00 2.50
84 Hank Aaron 40.00 80.00
85 Al Jackson .75 2.00
86 Jerry Lumpe .75 2.00
87 Wayne Causey .75 2.00
88 Rusty Staub 1.50 4.00
89 Ken McBride .75 2.00
90 Jack Baldschun .75 2.00
91 Sandy Koufax S10 20.00 50.00
92 Camilo Pascual S10 .75 2.00
93 Ron Hunt S10 .75 2.00
94 Willie McCovey S10 10.00 25.00
95 Al Kaline S10 12.50 30.00
96 Ray Culp S10 .75 2.00
97 Ed Mathews S10 10.00 25.00
98 Dick Farrell S10 .75 2.00
99 Lee Thomas S10 1.00 2.50
100 Vic Davalillo S10 .75 2.00

1965 Bazooka

The 1965 Bazooka set of 36 full color, blank backed, numbered cards was issued in panels of three on the backs of Bazooka bubble gum boxes. The individual cards measure 1 9/16" by 2 1/2" whereas the panels measure 2 1/2" by 4 11/16". As in the previous two years some of the players have the same numbers on their cards; however all pictures are different from the previous two years. Complete panels or complete boxes would command a premium above these prices.

COMPLETE INDIV. SET (36) 400.00 800.00
1 Mickey Mantle 125.00 250.00
2 Larry Jackson 3.00 8.00
3 Chuck Hinton 3.00 8.00
4 Tony Oliva 6.00 15.00
5 Dean Chance 3.00 8.00
6 Jim O'Toole 3.00 8.00
7 Harmon Killebrew 12.50 30.00
8 Pete Ward 3.00 8.00
9 Hank Aaron 40.00 80.00
10 Dick Radatz 3.00 8.00
11 Boog Powell 4.00 10.00
12 Willie Mays 40.00 80.00
13 Bob Veale 3.00 8.00
14 Roberto Clemente 60.00 120.00
15 Johnny Callison 3.00 8.00
16 Joe Torre 6.00 15.00
17 Billy Williams 10.00 25.00
18 Bob Chance 3.00 8.00
19 Bob Aspromonte 3.00 8.00
20 Joe Christopher 3.00 8.00
21 Jim Bunning 8.00 20.00
22 Jim Fregosi 3.00 8.00
23 Bob Gibson 12.50 30.00
24 Juan Marichal 12.50 30.00
25 Dave Wickersham 3.00 8.00
26 Ron Hunt 3.00 8.00
27 Gary Peters 3.00 8.00
28 Ron Santo 6.00 15.00
29 Elston Howard 4.00 10.00
30 Brooks Robinson 15.00 40.00
31 Frank Robinson 15.00 40.00
32 Sandy Koufax 20.00 50.00
33 Rocky Colavito 8.00 20.00
34 Al Kaline 15.00 40.00
35 Ken Boyer 4.00 10.00
36 Tommy Davis 3.00 8.00

1966 Bazooka

The 1966 Bazooka set of 48 full color, blank backed, numbered cards was issued in panels of three on the backs of Bazooka bubble gum boxes. The individual cardsd measure 1 9/16" by 2 1/2" whereas the complete panels measure 2 1/2" by 4 11/16". The set is distinguishable from the previous years by mention of "48 card set" at the bottom of the card. Complete panels or complete boxes would command a premium above these prices.

COMPLETE INDIV. SET (48) 500.00 1000.00
1 Sandy Koufax 20.00 50.00
2 Willie Horton 3.00 8.00
3 Frank Howard 4.00 10.00
4 Richie Allen 4.00 10.00
5 Mel Stottlemyre 4.00 10.00
6 Tony Conigliaro 5.00 12.00
7 Mickey Mantle 125.00 250.00
8 Leon Wagner 3.00 8.00
9 Ed Kranepool 3.00 8.00
10 Juan Marichal 10.00 25.00
11 Harmon Killebrew 10.00 25.00
12 Johnny Callison 3.00 8.00
13 Roy McMillan 3.00 8.00
14 Willie McCovey 10.00 25.00
15 Rocky Colavito 6.00 15.00
16 Willie Mays 40.00 80.00
17 Sam McDowell 3.00 8.00
18 Vern Law 3.00 8.00
19 Jim Fregosi 3.00 8.00
20 Ron Fairly 3.00 8.00
21 Bob Gibson 10.00 25.00
22 Carl Yastrzemski 15.00 40.00
23 Bill White 4.00 10.00
24 Bob Aspromonte 3.00 8.00
25 Dean Chance 3.00 8.00
26 Roberto Clemente 60.00 120.00
27 Tony Cloninger 3.00 8.00
28 Curt Blefary 3.00 8.00
29 Milt Pappas 3.00 8.00
30 Hank Aaron 40.00 80.00
31 Jim Bunning 6.00 15.00
32 Frank Robinson 12.50 30.00
33 Bill Skowron 4.00 10.00
34 Brooks Robinson 12.50 30.00
35 Jim Wynn 3.00 8.00
36 Joe Torre 5.00 12.00
37 Jim Grant 3.00 8.00
38 Pete Rose 30.00 60.00
39 Ron Santo 5.00 12.00
40 Tom Tresh 4.00 10.00
41 Tony Oliva 5.00 12.00
42 Don Drysdale 10.00 25.00
43 Pete Richert 3.00 8.00
44 Bert Campaneris 3.00 8.00
45 Jim Maloney 3.00 8.00
46 Al Kaline 12.50 30.00
47 Eddie Fisher 3.00 8.00
48 Billy Williams 8.00 20.00

1967 Bazooka

The 1967 Bazooka set of 48 full color, blank backed, numbered cards was issued in panels of three on the backs of Bazooka bubble gum boxes. The individual cards measure 1 9/16" by 2 1/2" whereas the complete panels measure 2 1/2" by 4 11/16". This set is virtually identical to the 1966 set with the exception of ten new cards as replacements for ten 1966 cards. The remaining 38 cards are identical in pose and number. Complete panels or complete boxes would command a premium above these prices.

COMPLETE INDIV. SET (48) 500.00 1000.00
1 Rick Reichardt 3.00 8.00
2 Tommie Agee 3.00 8.00
3 Frank Howard 4.00 10.00
4 Richie Allen 4.00 10.00
5 Mel Stottlemyre 4.00 10.00
6 Tony Conigliaro 5.00 12.00
7 Mickey Mantle 125.00 250.00
8 Leon Wagner 3.00 8.00
9 Gary Peters 3.00 8.00
10 Juan Marichal 10.00 25.00
11 Harmon Killebrew 10.00 25.00
12 Johnny Callison 3.00 8.00
13 Denny McLain 5.00 12.00
14 Willie McCovey 10.00 25.00
15 Rocky Colavito 6.00 15.00
16 Willie Mays 40.00 80.00
17 Sam McDowell 3.00 8.00
18 Jim Kaat 5.00 12.00
19 Jim Fregosi 3.00 8.00
20 Ron Fairly 3.00 8.00
21 Bob Gibson 10.00 25.00
22 Carl Yastrzemski 15.00 40.00
23 Bill White 4.00 10.00
24 Bob Aspromonte 3.00 8.00
25 Dean Chance 3.00 8.00
26 Roberto Clemente 60.00 120.00
27 Tony Cloninger 3.00 8.00
28 Curt Blefary 3.00 8.00
29 Phil Regan 3.00 8.00
30 Hank Aaron 40.00 80.00
31 Jim Bunning 6.00 15.00
32 Frank Robinson 12.50 30.00
33 Ken Boyer 4.00 10.00
34 Brooks Robinson 12.50 30.00
35 Jim Wynn 3.00 8.00
36 Joe Torre 5.00 12.00
37 Tommy Davis 3.00 8.00
38 Pete Rose 30.00 60.00
39 Ron Santo 5.00 12.00
40 Tom Tresh 4.00 10.00
41 Tony Oliva 5.00 12.00
42 Don Drysdale 10.00 25.00
43 Pete Richert 3.00 8.00
44 Bert Campaneris 3.00 8.00
45 Jim Maloney 3.00 8.00
46 Al Kaline 12.50 30.00
47 Matty Alou 3.00 8.00
48 Billy Williams 8.00 20.00

1968 Bazooka Panels

The 1968 Bazooka Tipps from the Topps is a set of 15 numbered boxes (measuring 5 1/2" by 6 1/4" when detached). each containing on the back panel (measuring 3" by 6 1/4") a baseball playing tip from a star, and on the side panels four mini cards, two per side, in full color, measuring 1 1/4" by 3 1/8". Although the set contains a total of 60 of these small cards, 4 are repeated; therefore there are only 56 different small cards. Some collectors cut the panels into individual card; however most collectors retain entire panels or boxes. The prices in the checklist therfore reflect only the values of the complete boxes.

COMPLETE BOX SET (15) 450.00 900.00
1 Maury Wills 60.00 120.00
Clete Boyer
Paul Casanova
Al Kaline
Tom Seaver
2 Carl Yastrzemski 50.00 100.00
Matty Alou
Bill Freehan
Jim Hunter
Jim Lefebvre
3 Bert Campaneris 20.00 50.00
Bobby Knoop
Tim McCarver
Frank Robinson
Bob Veale
4 Maury Wills 20.00 50.00
Jose Azcue
Tony Conigliaro
Ken Holtzman
Bill White
5 Julian Javier 60.00 120.00
Hank Aaron
Juan Marichal
Joe Pepitone
Rico Petrocelli
6 Orlando Cepeda 50.00 100.00
Tommie Agee
Don Drysdale
Pete Rose
Ron Santo
7 Bill Mazeroski 20.00 50.00
Jim Bunning
Frank Howard
John Roseboro
George Scott
8 Brooks Robinson 30.00 60.00
Tony Gonzalez
Wille Horton
Harmon Killebrew
Jim McGlothlin
9 Jim Fregosi 20.00 50.00
Max Alvis
Bob Gibson
Tony Oliva
Vada Pinson
10 Joe Torre 20.00 50.00
Dean Chance
Tommy Davis
Fergie Jenkins
Rick Monday
11 Jim Lonborg 125.00 250.00
Curt Flood
Joel Horlen
Mickey Mantle
Jim Wynn
12 Mike McCormick 30.00 60.00
Roberto Clemente
Al Downing
Don Mincher
Tony Perez
13 Frank Crosetti 20.00 50.00
Rod Carew
Willie McCovey
Ron Swoboda
Don Wilson
14 Willie Mays 60.00 120.00
Richie Allen
Gary Peters
Rusty Staub
Billy Williams
15 Lou Brock 75.00 150.00
Tommie Agee
Don Drysdale
Pete Rose
Ron Santo

1969-70 Bazooka Panels

The 1969-70 Bazooka Baseball Extra News set contains 12 complete panels, each comprising a large action shot of a significant event in baseball history and four small cards, comparable to those in the Tipps from the Topps set of 1968, of Hall of Famers. Although some collectors cut the panels into individual cards (measuring 3" by 6 1/4" or 1 1/4" by 3 1/8"), most collectors retain the entire panel, or box (measuring 5 1/2" by 6 1/4"). The prices in the checklist below reflect the value for the entire box, as these cards are more widely seen and collected as complete panels or boxes.

COMPLETE PANEL SET (12) 200.00 400.00
1 No Hit Duel - Brown/Cobb/Keeler/Plank 15.00 40.00
2 Alexander Conquers - Hornsby/Johnson/Johnson/Simmons 12.50 30.00
3 Yanks Lazzeri - Duffy/Gehrig Speaker/Tinker 12.50 30.00
4 Home Run Almost - Alexander/Bender/Mathewson/Young 15.00 40.00
5 Four Consecutive - Chance Cochrane/McGraw/Ruth 50.00 100.00
6 No-Hit Game - Evers/Johnson McGraw/Young 12.50 30.00
7 Twelve RBIs - Cobb/Collins Evers/Gehrig 20.00 50.00
8 Ty Ties Record - Cochrane Collins/Ott/Wagner 15.00 40.00
9 Babe Ruth Hits - Anson/Chesbro Simmons/Speaker 20.00 50.00
10 Calls Shot - Lajoie Mack.Maranville/Walsh 20.00 50.00
11 Ruth's 60th - Chance/Lajoie/Ott Tinker 20.00 50.00
12 Double Shutout - Hornsby/Maranville Mathewson/Wagner 12.50 30.00

1971 Bazooka Numbered Test

This was supposedly a test issue which was different from the more common unnumbered set and much more difficult to find. There are 48 cards (16 panels) in this numbered set whereas the unnumbered set had only 12 panels or 36 individual cards. Individual cards measure approximately 2" by 2 5/8" whereas the panels measure 2 5/8" by 5 15/16". Complete panels or complete boxes would command a premium above these prices. Cards #46-48 (Hundley,Mays and Hunter) are not priced due to scarcity.

COMPLETE SET (48) 900.00 1800.00
1 Tim McCarver 8.00 20.00
2 Frank Robinson 40.00 80.00
3 Bill Mazeroski 30.00 60.00
4 Willie McCovey 30.00 60.00
5 Carl Yastrzemski 60.00 120.00
6 Clyde Wright 6.00 15.00
7 Jim Merritt 6.00 15.00
8 Luis Aparicio 30.00 60.00
9 Bobby Murcer 8.00 20.00
10 Rico Petrocelli 6.00 15.00
11 Sam McDowell 6.00 15.00
12 Clarence Gaston 6.00 15.00
13 Fergie Jenkins 30.00 60.00
14 Al Kaline 40.00 80.00
15 Ken Harrelson 6.00 15.00
16 Tommie Agee 6.00 15.00
17 Harmon Killebrew 30.00 60.00
18 Reggie Jackson 40.00 80.00
19 Juan Marichal 30.00 60.00
20 Frank Howard 8.00 20.00
21 Bill Melton 6.00 15.00
22 Brooks Robinson 40.00 80.00
23 Hank Aaron 50.00 100.00
24 Larry Dierker 6.00 15.00
25 Jim Fregosi 6.00 15.00
26 Billy Williams 30.00 60.00
27 Dave McNally 8.00 20.00
28 Rico Carty 6.00 15.00
29 Johnny Bench 75.00 150.00
30 Tommy Harper 6.00 15.00
31 Bert Campaneris 6.00 15.00
32 Pete Rose 125.00 250.00
33 Orlando Cepeda 30.00 60.00
34 Maury Wills 8.00 20.00
35 Tom Seaver 40.00 80.00
36 Tony Oliva 20.00 50.00
37 Bill Freehan 6.00 15.00
38 Roberto Clemente 200.00 400.00
39 Claude Osteen 6.00 15.00
40 Rusty Staub 8.00 20.00
41 Bob Gibson 30.00 60.00
42 Amos Otis 6.00 15.00
43 Jim Wynn 8.00 20.00
44 Rich Allen 20.00 50.00
45 Tony Conigliaro 20.00 50.00
46 Randy Hundley
47 Willie Mays
48 Jim Hunter

1971 Bazooka Unnumbered

The 1971 Bazooka set of 36 full-color, unnumbered cards was issued in 12 panels of three cards each on the backs of boxes containing one cent Bazooka bubble gum. Individual cards measure approximately 2" by 2 5/8" whereas the panels measure 2 5/8" by 5 15/16". The panels are numbered in the checklist alphabetically by the player's last name on the left most card of the panel. Complete panels or complete boxes would command a premium above these prices

COMPLETE INDIV.SET (36) 200.00 400.00
1 Tommie Agee 1.25 3.00
2 Harmon Killebrew 6.00 15.00
3 Reggie Jackson 12.50 30.00
4 Bert Campaneris 1.25 3.00
5 Pete Rose 15.00 40.00
6 Orlando Cepeda 6.00 15.00
7 Rico Carty 1.25 3.00
8 Johnny Bench 10.00 25.00
9 Tommy Harper 1.25 3.00
10 Bill Freehan 1.25 3.00
11 Roberto Clemente 30.00 60.00
12 Claude Osteen 1.25 3.00
13 Jim Fregosi 1.25 3.00
14 Billy Williams 6.00 15.00
15 Dave McNally 1.25 3.00
16 Randy Hundley 1.25 3.00
17 Willie Mays 12.50 35.00
18 Jim Hunter 6.00 15.00
19 Juan Marichal 6.00 15.00
20 Frank Howard 2.00 5.00
21 Bill Melton 1.25 3.00
22 Willie McCovey 6.00 15.00
23 Carl Yastrzemski 10.00 25.00
24 Clyde Wright 1.25 3.00
25 Jim Merritt 1.25 3.00
26 Luis Aparicio 6.00 15.00
27 Bobby Murcer 2.00 5.00
28 Rico Petrocelli 1.25 3.00
29 Sam McDowell 1.25 3.00
30 Clarence Gaston 1.25 3.00
31 Brooks Robinson 8.00 20.00
32 Hank Aaron 12.50 30.00
33 Larry Dierker 1.25 3.00
34 Rusty Staub 2.00 5.00
35 Bob Gibson 6.00 15.00
36 Amos Otis 1.25 3.00

1988 Bazooka

There are 22 standard-size cards in the set. The cards have extra thick white borders. Card backs are printed in blue and red on white card stock. Some sets can also be found with gray backs; these gray backs carry no additional value premium. Cards are numbered on the back; they were numbered by Topps alphabetically. The word "Bazooka" only appears faintly as background for the statistics on the back of the card. Cards were available inside specially marked boxes of Bazooka gum retailing between 59 cents and 99 cents. The emphasis in the player selection for this set is on young stars of baseball.

COMPLETE SET (22) 3.00 8.00
1 George Bell .02 .10
2 Wade Boggs .30 .75
3 Jose Canseco .40 1.00
4 Roger Clemens .50 1.25
5 Vince Coleman .02 .10
6 Eric Davis .08 .25
7 Tony Fernandez .02 .10
8 Dwight Gooden .08 .25
9 Tony Gwynn .50 1.25
10 Wally Joyner .02 .10
11 Don Mattingly .50 1.25
12 Willie McGee .08 .25
13 Mark McGwire .60 1.50
14 Kirby Puckett .30 .75
15 Tim Raines .08 .25
16 Dave Righetti .02 .10
17 Cal Ripken 1.00 2.50
18 Juan Samuel .02 .10
19 Ryne Sandberg .30 .75
20 Benito Santiago .08 .25
21 Darryl Strawberry .08 .25
22 Todd Worrell .02 .10

1989 Bazooka

The 1989 Bazooka Shining Stars set contains 22 standard-size cards. The fronts have white borders and a large yellow stripe; the vertically oriented backs are pink, red and white and have career stats. The cards were inserted one per box of Bazooka Gum. The set is sequenced in alphabetical order.

COMPLETE SET (22) 2.00 5.00
1 Tim Belcher .02 .10
2 Damon Berryhill .02 .10
3 Wade Boggs .40 1.00
4 Jay Buhner .08 .25
5 Jose Canseco .60 1.50
6 Vince Coleman .02 .10
7 Cecil Espy .02 .10
8 Dave Gallagher .02 .10
9 Ron Gant .08 .25
10 Kirk Gibson .08 .25
11 Paul Gibson .02 .10
12 Mark Grace .40 1.00
13 Tony Gwynn .50 1.25
14 Rickey Henderson .50 1.25
15 Orel Hershiser .08 .25
16 Gregg Jefferies .02 .10
17 Ricky Jordan .02 .10
18 Chris Sabo .02 .10
19 Gary Sheffield .60 1.50
20 Darryl Strawberry .08 .25
21 Frank Viola .02 .10
22 Walt Weiss .02 .10

1990 Bazooka

The 1990 Bazooka Shining Stars set contains 22 standard-size cards with a mix of award winners, league leaders, and young stars. This set was issued by Topps using the Bazooka name. Card backs were printed in blue and red on white card stock. The word "Bazooka" appears faintly as background for the statistics on the back of the card as well as appearing prominently on the front of each card.

COMPLETE SET (22) 2.50 6.00
1 Kevin Mitchell .02 .10
2 Robin Yount .30 .75
3 Mark Davis .02 .10
4 Bret Saberhagen .08 .25
5 Fred McGriff .20 .50
6 Tony Gwynn .60 1.50
7 Kirby Puckett .30 .75
8 Vince Coleman .02 .10
9 Rickey Henderson .50 1.25
10 Ben McDonald .02 .10
11 Gregg Olson .02 .10
12 Todd Zeile .08 .25
13 Carlos Martinez .02 .10
14 Gregg Jefferies .02 .10
15 Craig Worthington .02 .10
16 Gary Sheffield .40 1.00
17 Greg Briley .02 .10
18 Ken Griffey Jr. 1.25 3.00
19 Jerome Walton .02 .10
20 Bob Geren .02 .10
21 Tom Gordon .20 .50
22 Jim Abbott .08 .25

1991 Bazooka

The 1991 Bazooka Shining Stars set contains 22 standard-size cards featuring league leaders and rookie sensations. The set was produced by Topps for Bazooka. One card was inserted in each box of Bazooka Bubble Gum. The fronts are similar to the Topps regular issue, only that the "Shining Star" emblem appears at the card top and the Bazooka logo overlays the lower right corner of the picture. In a blue and red design on white card stock, the backs have statistics and biography.

COMPLETE SET (22) 2.50 6.00
1 Barry Bonds .75 2.00
2 Rickey Henderson .50 1.25
3 Bob Welch .02 .10
4 Doug Drabek .02 .10
5 Alex Fernandez .02 .10
6 Jose Offerman .02 .10
7 Frank Thomas .40 1.00
8 Cecil Fielder .08 .25
9 Ryne Sandberg .40 1.00
10 George Brett .40 1.00
11 Willie McGee .08 .25
12 Vince Coleman .02 .10
13 Hal Morris .02 .10
14 Delino DeShields .02 .10
15 Robin Ventura .20 .50
16 Jeff Huson .02 .10
17 Felix Jose .02 .10
18 Dave Justice .20 .50
19 Larry Walker .30 .75
20 Sandy Alomar Jr. .08 .25
21 Kevin Appier .02 .10
22 Scott Radinsky .02 .10

1992 Bazooka Quadracard '53 Archives

This 22-card set was produced by Topps for Bazooka, and the set is subtitled "Topps Archives Quadracard" on the top of the backs. Each standard-size card features four micro-reproductions of 1953 Topps baseball cards. These front and back borders of the cards are blue.

COMPLETE SET (22) 6.00 15.00
1 Joe Adcock .50 1.25
Bob Lemon
Willie Mays
Vic Wertz
2 Carl Furillo .30 .75
Don Newcombe
Phil Rizzuto
Hank Sau
3 Ferris Fain .30 .75
John Logan
Ed Mathews
Bobby Shantz
4 Yogi Berra .40 1.00
Del Crandall
Howie Pollet
Gene Woodl
5 Richie Ashburn .50 1.25
Leo Durocher MG
Allie Reynolds
E
6 Hank Aaron .75 2.00
Ray Boone
Luke Easter
Dick Williams
7 Ralph Branca .40 1.00
Bob Feller
Rogers Hornsby
Bobby Th
8 Jim Gilliam .30 .75
Billy Martin
Minnie Minoso
Hal Newh
9 Smoky Burgess .30 .75
John Mize
Preacher Roe
Warren Spa
10 Monte Irvin .40 1.00
Bobo Newsom
Duke Snider
Wes Westrum
11 Carl Erskine .30 .75
Jackie Jensen
George Kell
Red Scho
12 Bill Bruton .30 .75
Whitey Ford
Ed Lopat
Mickey Vernon
13 Joe Black .20 .50
Lew Burdette
Johnny Pesky
Enos Slaugh
14 Gus Bell .40 1.00
Mike Garia
Mel Parnell
Jackie Robinson
15 Alvin Dark .30 .75
Dick Groat
Pee Wee Reese
John Sain
16 Gil Hodges .30 .75
Sal Maglie
Wilmer Mizell
Billy Pierc
17 Nellie Fox .30 .75
Ralph Kiner
Ted Kluszewski
Eddie Sta
18 Ewell Blackwell .30 .75
Vern Law
Satchel Paige
Jim Wils
19 Lou Boudreau MG .20 .50
Roy Face
Harvey Haddix
Bill Rig
20 Roy Campanella .30 .75
Walt Dropo
Harvey Kuenn
Al Rosen
21 Joe Garagiola .50 1.25
Robin Roberts
Casey Stengel MG
Ho
22 John Antonelli .50 1.25
Bob Friend
Dixie Walker CO
Ted W

1993 Bazooka Team USA

Originally available only in a special Bazooka collector's box, these 22 standard-size cards were produced by Topps and feature the 1993 Team USA players. The card design is similar to that of the '93 Topps series. The white-bordered fronts feature posed color player photos. The player's name appears in a blue stripe near the bottom; the Bazooka logo appears at the upper right. The colorful white-bordered backs carry a color head shot, biography, statistics, and career highlights. The cards are numbered on the back as "X of 22." Todd Helton has a very early card in this set. The full box this set came in also contained 50 pieces of Bazooka gum.

COMP.FACT. SET (22) 20.00 50.00
1 Terry Harvey .02 .10
2 Dante Powell .02 .10
3 Andy Barkett .02 .10
4 Steve Reich .02 .10
5 Charlie Nelson .02 .10
6 Todd Walker 3.00 8.00
7 Dustin Hermanson .75 2.00
8 Pat Clougherty .02 .10
9 Danny Graves 3.00 8.00
10 Paul Wilson .75 2.00
11 Todd Helton 30.00 60.00
12 Russ Johnson .08 .25
13 Darren Grass .02 .10
14 A.J. Hinch .08 .25
15 Mark Merila .02 .10
16 John Powell .02 .10
17 Bob Scafa .02 .10
18 Matt Beaumont .02 .10
19 Todd Dunn .02 .10
20 Mike Martin .02 .10
21 Carlton Loewer .20 .50
22 Bret Wagner .02 .10

1995 Bazooka

This 132-card standard-size set was issued by Topps. For the previous 35 years, Topps had used the Bazooka label to issue various cards, but this was the first time a mainstream set was issued in pack form. The five-card packs, with a suggested retail price of 50 cents, included an info card as well as a piece of bubble gum. The fronts have an action photo surrounded by white borders. The "Bazooka" label is in the upper left corner, while the player's name and team are on the bottom of the card. The player's position is identified on the right. The backs have a game as well as his previous season and career stats. There are no Rookie Cards in this set. Factory sets included five Red Hot inserts.

COMPLETE SET (132) 4.00 10.00
COMP.FACT.SET (137) 4.00 10.00
1 Greg Maddux .30 .75
2 Cal Ripken .60 1.50
3 Lee Smith .07 .20
4 Sammy Sosa .20 .50
5 Jason Bere .02 .10
6 David Justice .07 .20
7 Kevin Mitchell .02 .10
8 Ozzie Guillen .07 .20
9 Roger Clemens .40 1.00
10 Mike Mussina .10 .30
11 Sandy Alomar Jr. .02 .10
12 Cecil Fielder .07 .20
13 Dennis Martinez .07 .20
14 Randy Myers .07 .20
15 Jay Buhner .07 .20
16 Ivan Rodriguez .10 .30
17 Mo Vaughn .07 .20
18 Ryan Klesko .07 .20
19 Chuck Finley .07 .20
20 Barry Bonds .60 1.50
21 Dennis Eckersley .07 .20
22 Kenny Lofton .07 .20
23 Rafael Palmeiro .10 .30
24 Mike Stanley .02 .10
25 Gregg Jefferies .02 .10
26 Robin Ventura .07 .20
27 Mark McGwire .50 1.25
28 Ozzie Smith .30 .75
29 Troy Neel .02 .10
30 Tony Gwynn .25 .60
31 Ken Griffey Jr. .40 1.00
32 Will Clark .10 .30
33 Craig Biggio .10 .30
34 Shawon Dunston .02 .10
35 Wilson Alvarez .02 .10
36 Bobby Bonilla .07 .20
37 Marquis Grissom .07 .20
38 Ben McDonald .02 .10
39 Delino DeShields .02 .10
40 Barry Larkin .10 .30
41 John Olerud .07 .20
42 Jose Canseco .10 .30
43 Greg Vaughn .02 .10
44 Gary Sheffield .07 .20
45 Paul O'Neill .10 .30
46 Bob Hamelin .02 .10
47 Don Mattingly .50 1.25
48 John Franco .07 .20
49 Bret Boone .07 .20
50 Rick Aguilera .07 .20
51 Tim Wallach .02 .10
52 Roberto Kelly .02 .10
53 Danny Tartabull .02 .10
54 Randy Johnson .20 .50
55 Greg McMichael .02 .10
56 Bip Roberts .02 .10
57 David Cone .07 .20
58 Raul Mondesi .07 .20
59 Travis Fryman .07 .20
60 Jeff Conine .07 .20
61 Jeff Bagwell .10 .30
62 Rickey Henderson .20 .50
63 Fred McGriff .10 .30
64 Matt Williams .07 .20
65 Rick Wilkins .02 .10
66 Eric Karros .07 .20
67 Mel Rojas .02 .10
68 Juan Gonzalez .07 .20
69 Chuck Carr .02 .10
70 Moises Alou .07 .20
71 Mark Grace .10 .30
72 Alex Fernandez .02 .10
73 Rod Beck .02 .10
74 Ray Lankford .07 .20
75 Dean Palmer .07 .20
76 Joe Carter .07 .20
77 Mike Piazza .30 .75
78 Eddie Murray .20 .50
79 Dave Nilsson .02 .10
80 Brett Butler .07 .20
81 Roberto Alomar .10 .30
82 Jeff Kent .07 .20
83 Andres Galarraga .07 .20
84 Brady Anderson .07 .20
85 Jimmy Key .07 .20
86 Bret Saberhagen .07 .20
87 Chili Davis .07 .20
88 Jose Rijo .02 .10
89 Wade Boggs .10 .30
90 Len Dykstra .07 .20
91 Steve Howe .02 .10
92 Hal Morris .02 .10
93 Larry Walker .07 .20
94 Jeff Montgomery .02 .10
95 Wil Cordero .02 .10
96 Jay Bell .07 .20
97 Tom Glavine .10 .30
98 Chris Hoiles .02 .10
99 Steve Avery .02 .10
100 Ruben Sierra .07 .20
101 Mickey Tettleton .02 .10
102 Paul Molitor .07 .20
103 Carlos Baerga .02 .10
104 Walt Weiss .02 .10
105 Darren Daulton .07 .20
106 Jack McDowell .02 .10
107 Doug Drabek .02 .10
108 Mark Langston .02 .10
109 Manny Ramirez .10 .30
110 Kevin Appier .07 .20
111 Andy Benes .02 .10
112 Chuck Knoblauch .07 .20
113 Kirby Puckett .20 .50
114 Dante Bichette .07 .20
115 Deion Sanders .10 .30
116 Albert Belle .07 .20
117 Todd Zeile .07 .20
118 Devon White .07 .20
119 Tim Salmon .10 .30
120 Frank Thomas .20 .50
121 John Wetteland .07 .20
122 James Mouton .02 .10
123 Javier Lopez .07 .20
124 Carlos Delgado .07 .20
125 Cliff Floyd .07 .20
126 Alex Gonzalez .02 .10
127 Billy Ashley .02 .10
128 Rondell White .07 .20
129 Rico Brogna .02 .10
130 Melvin Nieves .02 .10
131 Jose Oliva .02 .10
132 J.R. Phillips .02 .10

1995 Bazooka Red Hot

COMPLETE SET (22) 8.00 20.00
STATED ODDS 1:6
FIVE PER FACTORY SET
RH1 Greg Maddux .60 1.50
RH2 Cal Ripken 1.25 3.00
RH3 Barry Bonds 1.00 2.50
RH4 Kenny Lofton .15 .40
RH5 Mike Stanley .15 .40
RH6 Tony Gwynn .50 1.25
RH7 Ken Griffey Jr. .75 2.00
RH8 Barry Larkin .20 .50
RH9 Jose Canseco .20 .50
RH10 Paul O'Neill .20 .50
RH11 Randy Johnson .30 .75
RH12 David Cone .15 .40
RH13 Jeff Bagwell .20 .50
RH14 Matt Williams .15 .40
RH15 Mike Piazza .60 1.50
RH16 Roberto Alomar .20 .50
RH17 Jimmy Key .15 .40
RH18 Wade Boggs .20 .50
RH19 Paul Molitor .15 .40
RH20 Carlos Baerga .15 .40
RH21 Albert Belle .15 .40
RH22 Frank Thomas .30 .75

1996 Bazooka

The 1996 Bazooka standard-size set was issued in one series totalling 132 cards. The five-card packs retailed for $.50 each. The set contains baseball's best rookies, rising stars and veterans. The card fronts feature an exciting full-color photo of the player. The back of each card contains one of five different Bazooka Joe characters, along with the Bazooka Ball flipping game, the player's biographical data and 1995 career statistics. Additionally, every card contains a Funny Fortune, which predicts the fate of each player on a particular date. Packs contain five cards plus one chunk of Bazooka gum. Finally, each factory set also included a reprint of Mickey Mantle's 1959 Bazooka card.

COMP.FACT.SET (133) 5.00 12.00
COMPLETE SET (132) 4.00 10.00
ONE 59 MANTLE PER FACT.SET
PRODUCED BY TOPPS
1 Ken Griffey Jr. .40 1.00
2 J.T. Snow .07 .20
3 Rondell White .07 .20
4 Reggie Sanders .07 .20
5 Jeff Montgomery .07 .20
6 Mike Stanley .07 .20
7 Bernie Williams .10 .30
8 Mike Piazza .30 .75

9 Brian L.Hunter .07 .20
10 Len Dykstra .07 .20
11 Ray Lankford .07 .20
12 Kenny Lofton .07 .20
13 Robin Ventura .07 .20
14 Devon White .07 .20
15 Cal Ripken .60 1.50
16 Heathcliff Slocumb .07 .20
17 Ryan Klesko .07 .20
18 Terry Steinbach .07 .20
19 Travis Fryman .07 .20
20 Sammy Sosa .20 .50
21 Jim Thome .10 .30
22 Kenny Rogers .07 .20
23 Don Mattingly .50 1.25
24 Kirby Puckett .20 .50
25 Matt Williams .07 .20
26 Larry Walker .07 .20
27 Tim Wakefield .07 .20
28 Greg Vaughn .07 .20
29 Denny Neagle .07 .20
30 Ken Caminiti .07 .20
31 Garret Anderson .07 .20
32 Brady Anderson .07 .20
33 Carlos Baerga .07 .20
34 Wade Boggs .10 .30
35 Roberto Alomar .10 .30
36 Eric Karros .07 .20
37 Jay Buhner .07 .20
38 Dante Bichette .07 .20
39 Darren Daulton .07 .20
40 Jeff Bagwell .10 .30
41 Jay Bell .07 .20
42 Dennis Eckersley .07 .20
43 Will Clark .10 .30
44 Tom Glavine .10 .30
45 Rick Aguilera .07 .20
46 Kevin Seitzer .07 .20
47 Bret Boone .07 .20
48 Mark Grace .10 .30
49 Ray Durham .07 .20
50 Rico Brogna .07 .20
51 Kevin Appier .07 .20
52 Moises Alou .07 .20
53 Jeff Conine .07 .20
54 Marty Cordova .07 .20
55 Jose Mesa .07 .20
56 Rod Beck .07 .20
57 Marquis Grissom .07 .20
58 David Cone .07 .20
59 Albert Belle .07 .20
60 Lee Smith .07 .20
61 Frank Thomas .20 .50
62 Roger Clemens .40 1.00
63 Bobby Bonilla .07 .20
64 Paul Molitor .07 .20
65 Chuck Knoblauch .07 .20
66 Steve Finley .07 .20
67 Craig Biggio .10 .30
68 Ramon Martinez .07 .20
69 Jason Isringhausen .07 .20
70 Mark Wohlers .07 .20
71 Vinny Castilla .07 .20
72 Ron Gant .07 .20
73 Juan Gonzalez .07 .20
74 Mark McGwire .50 1.25
75 Jeff King .07 .20
76 Pedro Martinez .10 .30
77 Chad Curtis .07 .20
78 John Olerud .07 .20
79 Greg Maddux .30 .75
80 Derek Jeter .50 1.25
81 Mike Mussina .10 .30
82 Gregg Jefferies .07 .20
83 Jim Edmonds .07 .20
84 Carlos Perez .07 .20
85 Mo Vaughn .07 .20
86 Todd Hundley .07 .20
87 Roberto Hernandez .07 .20
88 Derek Bell .07 .20
89 Andres Galarraga .07 .20
90 Brian McRae .07 .20
91 Joe Carter .07 .20
92 Orlando Merced .07 .20
93 Cecil Fielder .07 .20
94 Dean Palmer .07 .20
95 Randy Johnson .20 .50
96 Chipper Jones .20 .50
97 Barry Larkin .10 .30
98 Hideo Nomo .20 .50
99 Gary Gaetti .07 .20
00 Edgar Martinez .10 .30
01 John Wetteland .07 .20
02 Rafael Palmeiro .10 .30
03 Chuck Finley .07 .20
04 Ivan Rodriguez .10 .30
05 Shawn Green .07 .20
06 Manny Ramirez .10 .30
07 Lance Johnson .07 .20
08 Jose Canseco .10 .30
09 Fred McGriff .10 .30
10 David Segui .07 .20
1 Tim Salmon .10 .30
2 Hal Morris .07 .20
3 Tino Martinez .10 .30
4 Bret Saberhagen .07 .20
5 Brian Jordan .07 .20
6 David Justice .07 .20
7 Jack McDowell .07 .20
8 Barry Bonds .60 1.50
9 Mark Langston .07 .20
0 John Valentin .07 .20
1 Raul Mondesi .07 .20
2 Quilvio Veras .07 .20
3 Randy Myers .07 .20
4 Tony Gwynn .25 .60
5 Johnny Damon .10 .30
5 Doug Drabek .07 .20
Bill Pulsipher .07 .20
Paul O'Neill .10 .30
Rickey Henderson .20 .50
Deion Sanders .10 .30
Orel Hershiser .07 .20
Gary Sheffield .07 .20
0 Mickey Mantle 4.00 10.00
59 Bazooka

2003 Bazooka

COMP.SET w/LOGO's (330) 40.00 80.00
COMPLETE SET (310) 30.00 60.00
COMP.SET w/o JOE's (280) 25.00 50.00
LOGO:122/131/133/140/151/210/229/250/280
LOGO:122/131/133/140/151/210/229/250/280
JOE'S AND LOGO'S ARE NOT SP'S
1 Luis Castillo .15 .40
2 Randy Winn .15 .40
3 Orlando Hudson .15 .40
3A Orlando Hudson Logo .15 .40
4 Fernando Vina .15 .40
5 Pat Burrell .15 .40
6 Brad Wilkerson .15 .40
7 Bazooka Joe .15 .40
7AN Bazooka Joe Angels .15 .40
7AS Bazooka Joe A's .15 .40
7AT Bazooka Joe Astros .15 .40
7BL Bazooka Joe Blue Jays .15 .40
7BR Bazooka Joe Braves .15 .40
7BW Bazooka Joe Brewers .15 .40
7CA Bazooka Joe Cardinals .15 .40
7CU Bazooka Joe Cubs .15 .40
7DE Bazooka Joe Devil Rays .15 .40
7DI Bazooka Joe Diamondbacks .15 .40
7DO Bazooka Joe Dodgers .15 .40
7EX Bazooka Joe Expos .15 .40
7GI Bazooka Joe Giants .15 .40
7IN Bazooka Joe Indians .15 .40
7MA Bazooka Joe Mariners .15 .40
7ME Bazooka Joe Mets .15 .40
7MR Bazooka Joe Marlins .15 .40
7OR Bazooka Joe Orioles .15 .40
7PA Bazooka Joe Padres .15 .40
7PH Bazooka Joe Phillies .15 .40
7PI Bazooka Joe Pirates .15 .40
7RA Bazooka Joe Rangers .15 .40
7RC Bazooka Joe Rockies .15 .40
7RD Bazooka Joe Reds .15 .40
7RS Bazooka Joe Red Sox .15 .40
7RY Bazooka Joe Royals .15 .40
7TI Bazooka Joe Tigers .15 .40
7TW Bazooka Joe Twins .15 .40
7WS Bazooka Joe White Sox .15 .40
7YA Bazooka Joe Yankees .15 .40
8 Javy Lopez .15 .40
9 Juan Pierre .15 .40
10 Hideo Nomo .40 1.00
11 Barry Larkin .25 .60
12 Alfonso Soriano .25 .60
12A Alfonso Soriano Logo .25 .60
13 Rodrigo Lopez .15 .40
14 Mark Ellis .15 .40
15 Tim Salmon .15 .40
16 Garret Anderson .15 .40
16A Garret Anderson Logo .15 .40
17 Aaron Boone .15 .40
18 Jason Kendall .15 .40
19 Hee Seop Choi .15 .40
20 Jorge Posada .25 .60
21 Sammy Sosa .40 1.00
22 Mark Prior .25 .60
22A Mark Prior Logo .25 .60
23 Mark Teixeira .25 .60
24 Manny Ramirez .40 1.00
25 Jim Thome .25 .60
26 A.J. Pierzynski .15 .40
27 Scott Rolen .25 .60
28 Austin Kearns .15 .40
29 Bret Boone .15 .40
30 Ken Griffey Jr. .75 2.00
31 Greg Maddux .50 1.25
32 Derek Lowe .15 .40
33 David Wells .15 .40
34 A.J. Burnett .15 .40
35 Randall Simon .15 .40
36 Nick Johnson .15 .40
37 Junior Spivey .15 .40
38 Eric Gagne .15 .40
39 Darin Erstad .15 .40
40 Marty Cordova .15 .40
41 Brett Myers .15 .40
42 Mo Vaughn .15 .40
43 Randy Wolf .15 .40
44 Vicente Padilla .15 .40
45 Elmer Dessens .15 .40
46 Jason Simontacchi .15 .40
47 John Mabry .15 .40
48 Torii Hunter .15 .40
48A Torii Hunter Logo .15 .40
49 Lyle Overbay .15 .40
50 Kirk Saarloos .15 .40
51 Bernie Williams .25 .60
52 Wade Miller .15 .40
53 Bobby Abreu .15 .40
54 Wilson Betemit .15 .40
55 Edwin Almonte .15 .40
56 Jarrod Washburn .15 .40
57 Drew Henson .15 .40
58 Tony Batista .15 .40
59 Juan Rivera .15 .40
60 Larry Walker .25 .60
61 Brandon Phillips .15 .40
62 Franklyn German .15 .40
63 Victor Martinez .25 .60
63A Victor Martinez Logo .25 .60
64 Moises Alou .15 .40
65 Nomar Garciaparra .25 .60
66 Willie Harris .15 .40
67 Sean Casey .15 .40
68 Omar Vizquel .25 .60
69 Robert Fick .15 .40
70 Curt Schilling .25 .60
70A Curt Schilling Logo .25 .60
71 Adam Kennedy .15 .40
72 Scott Hairston .15 .40
73 Jimmy Journell .15 .40
74 Rafael Furcal .15 .40
75 Barry Zito .25 .60
76 Ed Rogers .15 .40
77 Cliff Floyd .15 .40
78 Matt Clement .15 .40
79 Mike Lowell .15 .40
80 Randy Johnson .40 1.00
81 Craig Biggio .25 .60
82 Carlos Beltran .25 .60
83 Paul Lo Duca .15 .40
84 Jose Vidro .15 .40
85 Gary Sheffield .15 .40
86 Jacque Jones .15 .40
87 Corey Hart .15 .40
88 Roberto Alomar .25 .60
89 Robin Ventura .15 .40
90 Pedro Martinez .25 .60
91 Scott Hatteberg .15 .40
92 Marlon Byrd .15 .40
93 Pokey Reese .15 .40
94 Sean Burroughs .15 .40
95 Magglio Ordonez .25 .60
96 Mariano Rivera .50 1.25
97 John Olerud .15 .40
98 Edgar Renteria .15 .40
99 Ben Grieve .15 .40
100 Barry Bonds .60 1.50
100A Barry Bonds Logo .60 1.50
101 Ivan Rodriguez .25 .60
102 Josh Phelps .15 .40
103 Nobuaki Yoshida RC .15 .40
103A Nobuaki Yoshida Logo .15 .40
104 Roy Halladay .25 .60
105 Mark Buehrle .25 .60
106 Chan Ho Park .25 .60
107 Joe Kennedy .15 .40
108 Shin-Soo Choo .25 .60
108A Shin-Soo Choo Logo .25 .60
109 Ryan Jensen .15 .40
110 Todd Helton .25 .60
111 Chris Duncan RC .50 1.25
112 Taggert Bozied .15 .40
113 Sean Burnett .15 .40
114 Mike Lieberthal .15 .40
115 Josh Beckett .15 .40
116 Andy Pettitte .25 .60
117 Jose Reyes .40 1.00
117A Jose Reyes Logo .40 1.00
118 Bartolo Colon .15 .40
119 Justin Morneau .25 .60
120 Lance Berkman .25 .60
121 Mike Wodnicki RC .15 .40
122 Craig Brazell RC .15 .40
122A Craig Brazell Logo .15 .40
123 Troy Glaus .15 .40
124 John Smoltz .40 1.00
125 Mike Sweeney .15 .40
126 Jay Gibbons .15 .40
127 Kerry Wood .15 .40
128 Ellis Burks .15 .40
129 Carlos Pena .25 .60
130 Shawn Green .15 .40
131 Jason Stokes .15 .40
131A Jason Stokes Logo .15 .40
132 Raul Ibanez .25 .60
133 Francisco Rodriguez .25 .60
133A Francisco Rodriguez Logo .25 .60
134 Adrian Beltre .40 1.00
135 Richie Sexson .15 .40
136 Paul Byrd .15 .40
137 Bobby Kielty .15 .40
138 Dewon Brazelton .15 .40
139 Jeremy Griffiths RC .15 .40
140 Vladimir Guerrero .25 .60
140A Vladimir Guerrero Logo .25 .60
141 Jake Peavy .15 .40
142 Bryan Bullington RC .15 .40
143 Orlando Cabrera .15 .40
144 Scott Erickson .15 .40
145 Doug Mientkiewicz .15 .40
146 Derrek Lee .15 .40
147 Daryl Clark RC .15 .40
148 Trevor Hoffman .25 .60
149 Gabe Gross .15 .40
150 Roger Clemens .50 1.25
151 Khalil Greene .25 .60
151A Khalil Greene Logo .25 .60
152 Cory Doyne RC .15 .40
153 Brandon Roberson RC .15 .40
154 Josh Fogg .15 .40
155 Eric Chavez .15 .40
156 Kris Benson .15 .40
157 Billy Koch .15 .40
158 Jermaine Dye .15 .40
159 Kip Bouknight RC .15 .40
160 Brian Giles .15 .40
161 Justin Huber .15 .40
162 Mike Restovich .15 .40
163 Brandon Webb RC .50 1.25
164 Odalis Perez .15 .40
165 Phil Nevin .15 .40
166 Dontrelle Willis .15 .40
167 Aaron Heilman .15 .40
168 Dustin Moseley RC .15 .40
169 Rylan Reed RC .15 .40
170 Miguel Tejada .25 .60
171 Nic Jackson .15 .40
172 Anthony Webster RC .15 .40
173 Jorge Julio .15 .40
174 Kevin Millwood .15 .40
175 Brian Jordan .15 .40
176 Terry Tiffee RC .15 .40
177 Dallas McPherson .15 .40
178 Freddy Garcia .15 .40
179 Jaime Moyer .15 .40
180 Rafael Palmeiro .25 .60
181 Mike O'Keefe RC .15 .40
182 Kevin Youkilis RC 1.00 2.50
183 Kip Wells .15 .40
184 Joe Mauer .40 1.00
185 Edgar Martinez .25 .60
186 Jamie Bubela RC .15 .40
187 Jose Hernandez .15 .40
188 Josh Hamilton .25 .60
189 Matt Diaz RC .25 .60
190 Chipper Jones .40 1.00
191 Kevin Mench .15 .40
192 Joey Gomes RC .15 .40
193 Shannon Stewart .15 .40
194 David Eckstein .15 .40
195 Mike Piazza .40 1.00
196 Damian Moss .15 .40
197 Mike Fontenot .15 .40
198 Shea Hillenbrand .15 .40
199 Evel Bastida-Martinez RC .15 .40
200 Jason Giambi .15 .40
201 Aron Weston RC .15 .40
202 Frank Thomas .40 1.00
203 Carlos Lee .15 .40
204 C.C. Sabathia .25 .60
205 Jim Edmonds .25 .60
206 Jemel Spearman RC .15 .40
207 Jason Jennings .15 .40
208 Jeremy Bonderman RC .60 1.50
209 Preston Wilson .15 .40
210 Eric Hinske .15 .40
210A Eric Hinske Logo .15 .40
211 Will Smith .15 .40
212 Matthew Hagen RC .15 .40
213 Joe Randa .15 .40
214 James Loney .25 .60
215 Carlos Delgado .15 .40
216 Chris Kroski RC .15 .40
217 Cristian Guzman .15 .40
218 Tomo Ohka .15 .40
219 Al Leiter .15 .40
220 Adam Dunn .25 .60
221 Raul Mondesi .15 .40
222 Donald Hood RC .15 .40
223 Mark Mulder .15 .40
224 Mike Williams .15 .40
225 Ryan Klesko .15 .40
226 Rich Aurilia .15 .40
227 Chris Snelling .15 .40
228 Gary Schneidmiller RC .15 .40
229 Ichiro Suzuki .50 1.25
229A Ichiro Suzuki Logo .50 1.25
230 Luis Gonzalez .15 .40
231 Rocco Baldelli .15 .40
232 Callix Crabbe RC .15 .40
233 Adrian Gonzalez .30 .75
234 Corey Koskie .15 .40
235 Tom Glavine .25 .60
236 Kevin Beavers RC .15 .40
237 Frank Catalanotto .15 .40
238 Kevin Cash .15 .40
239 Nick Trzesniak RC .15 .40
240 Paul Konerko .25 .60
241 Jose Cruz Jr. .15 .40
242 Hank Blalock .15 .40
243 J.D. Drew .15 .40
244 Kazuhiro Sasaki .15 .40
245 Jeff Bagwell .25 .60
246 Jason Schmidt .15 .40
247 Xavier Nady .15 .40
248 Aramis Ramirez .15 .40
249 Jimmy Rollins .25 .60
250 Alex Rodriguez .50 1.25
250A Alex Rodriguez Logo .50 1.25
251 Terrence Long .15 .40
252 Derek Jeter 1.00 2.50
253 Edgardo Alfonzo .15 .40
254 Toby Hall .15 .40
255 Kazuhisa Ishii .15 .40
256 Brad Nelson .15 .40
257 Kevin Brown .15 .40
258 Roy Oswalt .25 .60
259 Mike Cameron .15 .40
260 Juan Gonzalez .15 .40
261 Dmitri Young .15 .40
262 Jose Jimenez .15 .40
263 Wily Mo Pena .15 .40
264 Joe Borchard .15 .40
265 Mike Mussina .25 .60
266 Fred McGriff .25 .60
267 Johnny Damon .25 .60
268 Joel Pineiro .15 .40
269 Andruw Jones .15 .40
270 Tim Hudson .25 .60
271 Chad Tracy .15 .40
272 Brad Fullmer .15 .40
273 Boof Bonser .15 .40
274 Clint Nageotte .15 .40
275 Jeff Kent .15 .40
276 Tino Martinez .15 .40
277 Matt Morris .15 .40
278 Jonny Gomes .15 .40
279 Benito Santiago .15 .40
280 Albert Pujols .50 1.25
280A Albert Pujols Logo .50 1.25

2003 Bazooka Minis

*MINIS: .75X TO 2X BASIC
*MINIS JOE'S: .75X TO 2X BASIC JOE'S
*MINIS LOGO'S: .75X TO 2X BASIC LOGO'S
*MINI'S RC'S: .75X TO 2X BASIC RC'S
STATED ODDS 1:1

2003 Bazooka Silver

*SILVER: .75X TO 2X BASIC
*SILVER JOE'S: .75X TO 2X BASIC JOE'S
*SILVER LOGO'S: .75X TO 2X BASIC LOGO'S
*SILVER RC'S: .75X TO 2X BASIC
ONE SILVER OR RELIC PER PACK

2003 Bazooka 4 on 1 Sticker

STATED ODDS 1:4 HOBBY, 1:6 RETAIL
1 Prior .60 1.50
Oswalt
Wash
Zito
2 Glaus .40 1.00
Shea
Chavez
Hinske
3 Hud .60 1.50
Soriano
Alomar
Vidro
4 Nomar 2.50 6.00
Jeter
Tejada
A.Rod
5 Giambi .60 1.50
Thome
Helton
Raffy
6 Will 1.00 2.50
Hoffman
Koch
Smoltz
7 Posada 1.00 2.50
Piazza
Pierz
I.Rod
8 Vlad 1.00 2.50
Edmonds
Manny
Wilk
9 Green 1.00 2.50
Sosa
Torii
Walker
10 Bernie 2.00 5.00
Griffey
Ichiro
Dunn
11 Olerud .40 1.00
Lieb
Long
Henson
12 Edgar .60 1.50
Boone
Mo
Fick
13 Randy 1.25 3.00
Clemens
Pedro
Madd
14 Schill .60 1.50
Hudson
Glav
Wood
15 Koner .60 1.50
Sween
C.Guz
Rolen
16 Phelps .40 1.00
Phillips
Choi
Blalock
17 Benito .60 1.50
Larkin
Sheff
Delgado
18 Rivera 1.00 2.50
J.Reyes
Burr
Pena
19 Batista .60 1.50
Salmon
Bagwell
Iban
20 Alfonzo .40 1.00
N.Jac
Castillo
Eck
21 Wells .40 1.00
Klesko
Nevin
Kent
22 Lowe .40 1.00
Pad
Millwood
Pineiro
23 Vina .60 1.50
Erstad
Rollins
Mient
24 Mauer 1.00 2.50
Huber
Stokes
Tracy
25 Kearns .60 1.50
Spivey
Myers
V.Mart
26 Khalil .60 1.50
Gross
Cash
Loney
27 Pujols 1.25 3.00
Buehrle
Chipper
Berk
28 Kennedy .60 1.50
Biggio
Damon
Winn
29 B.Giles .40 1.00
Drew
Byrd
Borchard
30 Leiter .60 1.50
Mussina
Colon
F.Garc
31 Kend .40 1.00
Sexson
Lowell
LoDuca
32 Burrell .40 1.00
Garret
Floyd
Andruw
33 Nady 1.00 2.50
Abreu
Bozied
Beltre
34 Baldelli .60 1.50
Willis
Snell
Teixeira
35 Harris .40 1.00
N.John
Jennings
Ishii
36 Mulder .40 1.00
Burnett
Byrd
Beckett
37 Koskie .40 1.00
Aramis
Tino
Alou
38 Cruz .60 1.50
Halladay
Braz
Gomes
39 Odalis .40 1.00
Brown
Clement
Wolf
40 Gagne .40 1.00
Jimen
German
Almon
41 L.Gonz .40 1.00
Stew
Jordan
J.Gonz
42 Hall .40 1.00
J.Kenn
Lopez
Moss
43 Magglio .60 1.50
C.Lee
Simon
Dmitri
44 Casey .40 1.00
Boone
Jacque
Rest
45 A.Gonz 1.00 2.50
Hart
McGriff
Thomas
46 Sabathia .60 1.50
Vizq
Pettitte
Vent
47 Schmidt .40 1.00
Burks
Randa
Bens
48 Cameron .40 1.00
Pokey
Dye
Wilson
49 Park 1.00 2.50
Sasaki
Ohka
Nomo
50 Simont .40 1.00
Wells
Morris
Rodrigo
51 Dallas McPherson 1.50 4.00
Josh Hamilton
Jeremy Bonderman
Aaron Heilman
52 Yosh 1.25 3.00
Dunc
Braz
Bullington
53 D.Clark 1.25 3.00
Webb
Mose
O'Keefe
54 Youkilis 2.50 6.00
Bubela
Diaz
Gomes
55 Kroski .40 1.00
Hood
Schn
Crabbe

2003 Bazooka Blasts Relics

GROUP A STATED ODDS 1:1666
GROUP B STATED ODDS 1:306
GROUP C STATED ODDS 1:197
GROUP D STATED ODDS 1:95
GROUP E STATED ODDS 1:52
GROUP F STATED ODDS 1:76
GROUP G STATED ODDS 1:326
GROUP H STATED ODDS 1:48
PARALLEL 25 ODDS 1:524
PARALLEL 25 PRINT RUN 25 #'d SETS
NO PARALLEL 25 PRICING DUE TO SCARCITY
AG Andres Galarraga C 3.00 8.00
ANR Aramis Ramirez E 3.00 8.00
AR Alex Rodriguez F 6.00 15.00
AS Alfonso Soriano D 3.00 8.00
BB Barry Bonds F 8.00 20.00
BW Bernie Williams D 4.00 10.00
CD Carlos Delgado D 3.00 8.00
CI Cesar Izturis B 4.00 10.00
CJ Chipper Jones E 4.00 10.00
DE Darin Erstad F 3.00 8.00
DH Drew Henson H 3.00 8.00
EM Edgar Martinez D 4.00 10.00
GS Gary Sheffield H 3.00 8.00
IR Ivan Rodriguez G 4.00 10.00
JD Johnny Damon H 4.00 10.00
JDD J.D. Drew B 4.00 10.00
JP Jorge Posada D 4.00 10.00
LB Lance Berkman E 3.00 8.00
LG Luis Gonzalez B 4.00 10.00
MP Mike Piazza H 6.00 15.00
MR Manny Ramirez F 4.00 10.00
MS Mike Sweeney C 3.00 8.00
NJ Nick Johnson B 4.00 10.00
PL Paul Lo Duca A 4.00 10.00
RA Roberto Alomar E 4.00 10.00
RH Rickey Henderson H 4.00 10.00
RK Ryan Klesko E 3.00 8.00
RM Raul Mondesi C 3.00 8.00
RP Rafael Palmeiro E 4.00 10.00
RV Robin Ventura F 3.00 8.00
SG Shawn Green D 3.00 8.00
TG Tony Gwynn H 6.00 15.00
TM Tino Martinez E 4.00 10.00
TS Tsuyoshi Shinjo E 3.00 8.00
WB Wilson Betemit E 3.00 8.00

2003 Bazooka Comics

COMPLETE SET (24) 10.00 25.00
STATED ODDS 1:4
1 Albert Pujols 1.25 3.00
2 Alex Rodriguez 1.25 3.00
3 Alfonso Soriano .60 1.50
4 Barry Zito .60 1.50
5 Chipper Jones 1.00 2.50
6 Derek Jeter 2.50 6.00
7 Greg Maddux 1.25 3.00
8 Ichiro Suzuki 1.25 3.00
9 Jason Giambi .40 1.00
10 Jim Thome .60 1.50
11 John Smoltz 1.00 2.50
12 Mike Piazza 1.00 2.50
13 Randy Johnson 1.00 2.50
14 Roger Clemens 1.25 3.00
15 Sammy Sosa 1.00 2.50
16 Shawn Green .40 1.00
17 Pedro Martinez .60 1.50
18 Manny Ramirez 1.00 2.50
19 Torii Hunter .40 1.00
20 Ivan Rodriguez .60 1.50
21 Miguel Tejada .60 1.50
22 Troy Glaus .40 1.00
23 Ken Griffey Jr. 2.00 5.00
24 Nomar Garciaparra .60 1.50

2003 Bazooka Piece of Americana Relics

GROUP A STATED ODDS 1:1666
GROUP B STATED ODDS 1:611
GROUP C STATED ODDS 1:226
GROUP D STATED ODDS 1:118
GROUP E STATED ODDS 1:36
GROUP F STATED ODDS 1:73
GROUP G STATED ODDS 1:190
PARALLEL 25 ODDS 1:611
PARALLEL 25 PRINT RUN 25 #'d SETS
NO PARALLEL 25 PRICING DUE TO SCARCITY
ALL CARDS FEATURE JSERSEY SWATCHES
AD Adam Dunn G 3.00 8.00
AH Aubrey Huff F 3.00 8.00
AJ Andruw Jones E 4.00 10.00
AL Al Leiter D 3.00 8.00
BB Bret Boone E 3.00 8.00
CB Craig Biggio E 4.00 10.00
CD Carlos Delgado E 3.00 8.00
CG Cristian Guzman E 3.00 8.00
CJ Chipper Jones E 4.00 10.00
CS Curt Schilling D 3.00 8.00
DB Dewon Brazelton F 3.00 8.00
FT Frank Thomas F 4.00 10.00
IR Ivan Rodriguez D 4.00 10.00
JB Jeff Bagwell A 6.00 15.00
JE Jim Edmonds E 3.00 8.00
JK Jeff Kent D 3.00 8.00
LW Larry Walker D 3.00 8.00
MM Mike Mussina C 4.00 10.00
MO Magglio Ordonez E 3.00 8.00
MP Mike Piazza E 6.00 15.00
NG Nomar Garciaparra B 8.00 20.00
PA Albert Pujols E 6.00 15.00
PL Paul Lo Duca B 4.00 10.00
PW Preston Wilson C 3.00 8.00
RF Rafael Furcal C 3.00 8.00
RP Rafael Palmeiro E 4.00 10.00
SG Shawn Green E 3.00 8.00
TG Tony Gwynn G 6.00 15.00
TH Todd Helton E 4.00 10.00
THA Toby Hall F 3.00 8.00

2003 Bazooka Stand-Ups

STATED ODDS 1:8 HOBBY, 1:24 RETAIL
1 Albert Pujols 1.25 3.00
2 Alfonso Soriano .60 1.50
3 Ichiro Suzuki 1.25 3.00
4 Sammy Sosa 1.00 2.50
5 Randy Johnson 1.00 2.50
6 Barry Bonds 1.50 4.00
7 Vladimir Guerrero .60 1.50
8 Nomar Garciaparra .60 1.50
9 Alex Rodriguez 1.25 3.00
10 Troy Glaus .40 1.00
11 Barry Zito .60 1.50
12 Derek Jeter 2.50 6.00
13 Lance Berkman .60 1.50
14 Larry Walker .60 1.50
15 Adam Dunn .60 1.50
16 Shawn Green .40 1.00
17 Curt Schilling .60 1.50
18 Todd Helton .60 1.50
19 Pedro Martinez .60 1.50
20 Pat Burrell .40 1.00
21 Miguel Tejada .60 1.50
22 Manny Ramirez 1.00 2.50
23 Mike Piazza 1.00 2.50
24 Jim Thome .60 1.50
25 Jason Giambi .40 1.00

2003 Bazooka Stand-Ups Red

COMPLETE SET (4) 3.00 8.00
1 Barry Bonds 1.50 4.00
2 Albert Pujols 1.25 3.00
3 Jim Thome .60 1.50
4 Barry Zito .60 1.50

2004 Bazooka

COMPLETE SET (330) 35.00 60.00
1 Bobby Abreu .15 .40
2 Jesse Foppert .15 .40
3 Shea Hillenbrand .15 .40
4 Jose Lima .15 .40
5 Manny Ramirez .40 1.00
6 Denny Neagle .15 .40
7 Frank Thomas .40 1.00
8 A.J. Burnett .15 .40
9 Carl Everett .15 .40
10A Scott Podsednik Blue Jsy .15 .40
10B Scott Podsednik White Jsy .15 .40
11 Travis Lee .15 .40
12 Mike Mussina .25 .60
13 Runelvys Hernandez .15 .40
14 Shannon Stewart .15 .40
15 Miguel Cabrera .40 1.00
16 Edgardo Alfonzo .15 .40

17 Victor Zambrano .15 .40
18 Rafael Furcal .15 .40
19 Eric Hinske .15 .40
20 Paul Lo Duca .15 .40
21 Phil Nevin .15 .40
22 Aramis Ramirez .15 .40
23 Jim Thome .25 .60
24 Jeromy Burnitz .15 .40
25A Mark Prior Glove Chest .25 .60
25B Mark Prior Glove Face .25 .60
26 Ramon Hernandez .15 .40
27 Cliff Lee .25 .60
28 Greg Myers .15 .40
29 Robert Fick .15 .40
30 Mike Sweeney .15 .40
31 Carlos Zambrano .25 .60
32 Roberto Alomar .25 .60
33 Orlando Cabrera .15 .40
34 Orlando Hudson .15 .40
35A Nomar Garciaparra Batting .25 .60
35B Nomar Garciaparra Fielding .25 .60
36 Esteban Loaiza .15 .40
37 Laynce Nix .15 .40
38 Joe Randa .15 .40
39 Juan Uribe .15 .40
40 Pat Burrell .15 .40
41 Steve Finley .15 .40
42 Livan Hernandez .15 .40
43 Al Leiter .15 .40
44 Brett Myers .15 .40
45 Jody Gerut .15 .40
46 Mark Teixeira .25 .60
47 Barry Zito .25 .60
48 Moises Alou .15 .40
49 Mike Cameron .15 .40
50A Albert Pujols One Hand .50 1.25
50B Albert Pujols Two Hands .50 1.25
51 Tim Hudson .25 .60
52 Kenny Lofton .15 .40
53 Trot Nixon .15 .40
54 Tim Redding .15 .40
55 Marlon Byrd .15 .40
56 Javier Vazquez .15 .40
57 Sean Burroughs .15 .40
58 Cliff Floyd .15 .40
59 Juan Rivera .15 .40
60 Mike Lieberthal .15 .40
61 Xavier Nady .15 .40
62 Brad Radke .15 .40
63 Miguel Tejada .25 .60
64A Ichiro Suzuki Running .50 1.25
64B Ichiro Suzuki Throwing .50 1.25
65 Garret Anderson .15 .40
66 Sean Casey .15 .40
67A Jason Giambi Fielding .15 .40
67B Jason Giambi Hitting .15 .40
68 Aubrey Huff .15 .40
69 Javy Lopez .15 .40
70 Hideo Nomo .40 1.00
71 Mark Redman .15 .40
72 Jose Vidro .15 .40
73 Rich Aurilia .15 .40
74 Luis Castillo .15 .40
75 Jay Gibbons .15 .40
76 Torii Hunter .15 .40
77 Derek Lowe .15 .40
78 Wes Obermueller .15 .40
79 Edgar Renteria .15 .40
80 Jeff Bagwell .25 .60
81 Fernando Vina .15 .40
82 Frank Catalanotto .15 .40
83 Marcus Giles .15 .40
84 Raul Ibanez .25 .60
85 Mike Lowell .15 .40
86 Tomo Ohka .15 .40
87A Jose Reyes w/Bat .25 .60
87B Jose Reyes w/o Bat .25 .60
88 Omar Vizquel .25 .60
89 Shawn Chacon .15 .40
90 Rocco Baldelli .15 .40
91A Brian Giles w/Bat .15 .40
91B Brian Giles w/o Bat .15 .40
92 Kazuhisa Ishii .15 .40
93 Greg Maddux .50 1.25
94 John Olerud .15 .40
95 Eric Chavez .15 .40
96 Doug Waechter .15 .40
97 Tony Batista .15 .40
98 Jerome Robertson .15 .40
99 Troy Glaus .15 .40
100A Eric Gagne Hand Out .15 .40
100B Eric Gagne Hand Up .15 .40
101A Pedro Martinez Leg Down .25 .60
101B Pedro Martinez Leg Up .25 .60
102 Magglio Ordonez .25 .60
103A Alex Rodriguez w/Bat .50 1.25
103B Alex Rodriguez w/o Bat .50 1.25
104 Jason Bay .25 .60
105 Larry Walker .25 .60
106 Matt Clement .15 .40
107 Tom Glavine .25 .60
108 Geoff Jenkins .15 .40
109 Victor Martinez .25 .60
110 David Ortiz .40 1.00
111 Ivan Rodriguez .25 .60
112 Jarrod Washburn .15 .40
113 Josh Beckett .15 .40
114 Bartolo Colon .15 .40
115 Juan Gonzalez .15 .40
116A Derek Jeter Fielding 1.00 2.50
116B Derek Jeter Hitting 1.00 2.50
117 Edgar Martinez .25 .60
118 Ramon Ortiz .15 .40
119 Scott Rolen .25 .60
120A Brandon Webb w/Ball .15 .40
120B Brandon Webb w/o Ball .15 .40
121 Carlos Beltran .25 .60
122 Jose Contreras .15 .40
123 Luis Gonzalez .15 .40
124 Jason Johnson .15 .40
125 Luis Matos .15 .40
126 Russ Ortiz .15 .40
127 Damian Rolls .15 .40
128 David Wells .15 .40
129 Adrian Beltre .40 1.00
130 Shawn Green .15 .40
131 Nate Cornejo .15 .40
132 Nick Johnson .15 .40
133 Joe Mays .15 .40
134 Roy Oswalt .25 .60
135 C.C. Sabathia .25 .60
136A Vernon Wells Fielding .15 .40
136B Vernon Wells Hitting .15 .40
137 Kris Benson .15 .40
138 Carl Crawford .25 .60
139A Ken Griffey Jr. Fielding .75 2.00
139B Ken Griffey Jr. Hitting .75 2.00
140A Randy Johnson Black Jsy .40 1.00
140B Randy Johnson White Jsy .40 1.00
141 Fred McGriff .15 .40
142 Vicente Padilla .15 .40
143 Tim Salmon .15 .40
144 Kip Wells .15 .40
145 Lance Berkman .25 .60
146 Jose Cruz Jr. .15 .40
147 Marquis Grissom .15 .40
148 Jacque Jones .15 .40
149 Gil Meche .15 .40
150A Vladimir Guerrero Fielding .25 .60
150B Vladimir Guerrero Hitting .25 .60
151 Reggie Sanders .15 .40
152 Ty Wigginton .15 .40
153 Angel Berroa .15 .40
154 Johnny Damon .25 .60
155 Rafael Palmeiro .25 .60
156A Chipper Jones w/Bat .40 1.00
156B Chipper Jones w/o Bat .40 1.00
157 Kevin Millar .15 .40
158 Corey Patterson .15 .40
159A Johan Santana Both Feet .25 .60
159B Johan Santana One Foot .25 .60
160 Bernie Williams .25 .60
161 Craig Biggio .25 .60
162A Carlos Delgado Blue Jsy .15 .40
162B Carlos Delgado White Jsy .15 .40
163 Aaron Guiel .15 .40
164 Wade Miller .15 .40
165 Andruw Jones .15 .40
166 Jay Payton .15 .40
167 Benito Santiago .15 .40
168 Woody Williams .15 .40
169 Casey Blake .15 .40
170 Adam Dunn .25 .60
171 Jose Guillen .15 .40
172 Brian Jordan .15 .40
173 Kevin Millwood .15 .40
174 Carlos Pena .25 .60
175 Curt Schilling .25 .60
176 Jerome Williams .15 .40
177A Hank Blalock Grey Jsy .15 .40
177B Hank Blalock White Jsy .15 .40
178 Erubiel Durazo .15 .40
179 Cristian Guzman .15 .40
180 Austin Kearns .15 .40
181 Raul Mondesi .15 .40
182 Andy Pettitte .25 .60
183 Jason Schmidt .15 .40
184 Jeremy Bonderman .15 .40
185A Dontrelle Willis w/Ball .15 .40
185B Dontrelle Willis w/o Ball .15 .40
186 Ray Durham .15 .40
187 Jerry Hairston Jr. .15 .40
188 Jason Kendall .15 .40
189 Melvin Mora .15 .40
190 Jeff Kent .15 .40
191 Jae Weong Seo .15 .40
192 Jack Wilson .15 .40
193 Cesar Izturis .15 .40
194 Jermaine Dye .15 .40
195A Roy Halladay w/Ball .25 .60
195B Roy Halladay w/o Ball .25 .60
196 Jason Phillips .15 .40
197 Matt Morris .15 .40
198A Mike Piazza Fielding .40 1.00
198B Mike Piazza Running .40 1.00
199 Richie Sexson .15 .40
200 Alfonso Soriano .25 .60
201 Mark Mulder .15 .40
202 David Eckstein .15 .40
203 Mike Hampton .15 .40
204 Ryan Klesko .15 .40
205 Damian Moss .15 .40
206 Juan Pierre .15 .40
207 Ben Sheets .15 .40
208 Randy Winn .15 .40
209 Bret Boone .15 .40
210 Jim Edmonds .25 .60
211 Rich Harden .15 .40
212 Paul Konerko .25 .60
213 Jamie Moyer .15 .40
214 A.J. Pierzynski .15 .40
215 Gary Sheffield .15 .40
216 Randy Wolf .15 .40
217 Kevin Brown .15 .40
218 Morgan Ensberg .15 .40
219 Bo Hart .15 .40
220 Bill Mueller .15 .40
221 Corey Koskie .15 .40
222 Joel Pineiro .15 .40
223 Preston Wilson .15 .40
224 Aaron Boone .15 .40
225 Kerry Wood .15 .40
226 Darin Erstad .15 .40
227 Wes Helms .15 .40
228 Brian Lawrence .15 .40
229 Mark Buehrle .25 .60
230A Sammy Sosa w/Ball .40 1.00
230B Sammy Sosa w/Bat .40 1.00
231 Sidney Ponson .15 .40
232 Dmitri Young .15 .40
233 Ellis Burks .15 .40
234 Kelvim Escobar .15 .40
235 Todd Helton .25 .60
236 Matt Lawton .15 .40
237 Eric Munson .15 .40
238 Jorge Posada .25 .60
239 Mariano Rivera .50 1.25
240 Michael Young .15 .40
241 Ramon Nivar .15 .40
242 Edwin Jackson .15 .40
243 Felix Pie .15 .40
244 Joe Mauer .30 .75
245 Grady Sizemore .25 .60
246 Bobby Jenks .15 .40
247 Chad Billingsley .25 .60
248 Casey Kotchman .15 .40
249 Bobby Crosby .25 .60
250 Khalil Greene .25 .60
251 Danny Garcia .15 .40
252 Nick Markakis .30 .75
253 Bernie Castro .15 .40
254 Aaron Hill .15 .40
255 Josh Barfield .15 .40
256 Ryan Wagner .15 .40
257 Ryan Harvey .15 .40
258 Jimmy Gobble .15 .40
259 Ryan Madson .15 .40
260 Zack Greinke .60 1.50
261 Rene Reyes .15 .40
262 Eric Duncan .15 .40
263 Chris Lubanski .15 .40
264 Jeff Mathis .15 .40
265 Rickie Weeks .15 .40
266 Justin Morneau .25 .60
267 Brian Snyder .15 .40
268 Neal Cotts .15 .40
269 Joe Borchard .15 .40
270 Larry Bigbie .15 .40
271 Marcus McBeth FY RC .15 .40
272 Tydus Meadows FY RC .15 .40
273 Zach Miner FY RC .25 .60
274A A.Lerew w/Ball FY RC .15 .40
274B A.Lerew w/o Ball FY RC .15 .40
275A Y.Molina w/Bat FY RC 15.00 40.00
275B Y.Molina w/o Bat FY RC 15.00 40.00
276A Jon Knott Bat Up FY RC .15 .40
276B Jon Knott Bat Down FY RC .15 .40
277 Matthew Moses FY RC .25 .60
278 Sung Jung FY RC .15 .40
279 Mike Gosling FY RC .15 .40
280 David Murphy FY RC .25 .60
281 Tim Frend FY RC .15 .40
282 Casey Myers FY RC .15 .40
283 Brayan Pena FY RC .15 .40
284 Omar Falcon FY RC .15 .40
285 Blake Hawksworth FY RC .15 .40
286 Jesse Roman FY RC .15 .40
287 Kyle Davies FY RC .15 .40
288 Matt Creighton FY RC .15 .40
289 Rodney Choy Foo FY RC .15 .40
290 Kyle Sleeth FY RC .15 .40
291 Carlos Quentin FY RC .60 1.50
292 Khalid Ballouli FY RC .15 .40
293A Tim Stauffer w/Ball FY RC .25 .60
293B Tim Stauffer w/o Ball FY RC .25 .60
294 Craig Ansman FY RC .15 .40
295 Dioner Navarro FY RC .25 .60
296A Josh Labandeira w/Ball FY RC .15 .40
296B Josh Labandeira w/o Ball FY RC .15 .40
297 Jeffrey Allison FY RC .15 .40
298 Anthony Acevedo FY RC .15 .40
299 Brad Sullivan FY RC .15 .40
300 Conor Jackson FY RC .50 1.25

2004 Bazooka Red Chunks

*CHUNKS 1-270: .75X TO 2X BASIC
*CHUNKS 271-300: .75X TO 2X BASIC
ONE PER PACK

2004 Bazooka Minis

*MINIS 1-270: .75X TO 2X BASIC
*MINIS 271-300: .75X TO 2X BASIC
ONE PER PACK

2004 Bazooka 4 on 1 Sticker

STATED ODDS 1:4 H, 1:6 R
1 Harden .40 1.00
Willis
Jerome
Webb
2 Duncan 2.50 6.00
Jeter
A.Sor
Giambi
3 Sizemore 1.25 3.00
Baldelli
Ichiro
Vlad
4 Halladay .60 1.50
Pedro
Schill
Myers
5 A.Rod 1.25 3.00
Berroa
Reyes
Greene
6 Wood .60 1.50
Dunn
Kent
Rolen
7 M.Cab 1.00 2.50
Podsednik
Hart
Teix
8 Weeks 1.25 3.00
Barfield
Pujols
Wells
9 Torii 2.00 5.00
Garret
Abreu
Griffey
10 Gibbons 1.00 2.50
Chip
Piaz
Sweeney
11 D.Ortiz 1.00 2.50
N.John
Delg
Thomas
12 Helton .60 1.50
Vidro
Lowell
Tejada
13 Wolf 1.00 2.50
Mulder
Santana
Randy
14 B.Boone .40 1.00
Huff
Chavez
Javy
15 Schmidt .60 1.50
Oswalt
Pineiro
Prior
16 Millw .60 1.50
Pettitte
Morris
T.Hud
17 Vazq .60 1.50
Loaiza
O.Cab
Alomar
18 Leiter .40 1.00
Wells
Hamp
Wash
19 LoDuca .40 1.00
Lieb
B.Giles
Andruw
20 Maggio .60 1.50
Corey
A.Boone
Bag
21 Glaus 1.00 2.50
Edgar
Manny
Ibanez
22 Sosa 1.00 2.50
Zito
Colon
Kearns
23 Edmonds .60 1.50
Sheff
Wils
Green
24 Bernie .60 1.50
Pierre
Beckett
Muss
25 R.Hern .40 1.00
Kendall
Phill
Pierz
26 Burrell .40 1.00
Nix
Cameron
Floyd
27 Gagne .60 1.50
Crawf
Guillen
Finley
28 Burks .40 1.00
Livan
Lowe
Ishii
29 Posada .60 1.50
Mathis
V.Mart
I.Rod
30 Thome .60 1.50
Giles
Nomar
Blalock
31 Renteria .40 1.00
Crosby
Cotts
R.Ortiz
32 Greinke 1.50 4.00
C.Guz
Iztur
K.Brown
33 Jenks .40 1.00
Nivar
Sexson
Klesko
34 Vizquel .60 1.50
Pena
Furcal
Meche
35 Lofton .60 1.50
Salmon
Griss
Biggio
36 Davies .40 1.00
Lerew
B.Pena
Jung
37 C.Foo .60 1.50
Ansman
Murphy
Moses
38 Quent 1.50 4.00
Navarro
McBeth
Laba
39 Sleeth 1.25 3.00
Conor
Sullivan
Allison
40 Molina 15.00 40.00
Knott
Hawk
Stauffer

2004 Bazooka Adventures Relics

GROUP A ODDS 1:134 H, 1:187 R
GROUP B ODDS 1:207 H, 1:289 R
GROUP C ODDS 1:74 H, 1:104 R
GROUP D ODDS 1:57 H, 1:80 R
GROUP E ODDS 1:86 H, 1:119 R
OVERALL PARALLEL 25 ODDS 1:94
PARALLEL 25 PRINT RUN 25 #'d SETS
NO PARALLEL 25 PRICING DUE TO SCARCITY
AD1 Adam Dunn Stripe Jsy A 3.00 8.00
AD2 Adam Dunn Grey Jsy A 3.00 8.00
AJ Andruw Jones Jsy D 4.00 10.00
AP Albert Pujols Uni D 8.00 20.00
AR1 Alex Rodriguez Blue Jsy E 4.00 10.00
AR2 Alex Rodriguez White Jsy D 4.00 10.00
AS Alfonso Soriano Uni C 3.00 8.00
BG Ben Grieve Jsy A 3.00 8.00
BP Brad Penny Jsy A 3.00 8.00
BW Bernie Williams Jsy B 4.00 10.00
BZ Barry Zito Jsy B 3.00 8.00
CB Craig Biggio Uni A 4.00 10.00
CE Carl Everett Uni D 3.00 8.00
CF Cliff Floyd Jsy B 3.00 8.00
CG Cristian Guzman Jsy C 3.00 8.00
CJ Chipper Jones Jsy D 4.00 10.00
CS Curt Schilling Jsy A 4.00 10.00
DW Dontrelle Willis Uni D 4.00 10.00
EA Edgardo Alfonzo Uni D 3.00 8.00
EC Eric Chavez Uni A 3.00 8.00
GJ Geoff Jenkins Jsy E 3.00 8.00
GM Greg Maddux Jsy D 6.00 15.00
HN Hideo Nomo Jsy C 4.00 10.00
JB Jeff Bagwell Uni A 4.00 10.00
JDG Jeremy Giambi Jsy E 3.00 8.00
JG Jason Giambi Jsy D 3.00 8.00
JK Jason Kendall Jsy B 3.00 8.00
JO John Olerud Jsy E 3.00 8.00
JT Jim Thome Jsy C 4.00 10.00
JW Jarrod Washburn Uni C 3.00 8.00
KB Kevin Brown Jsy A 3.00 8.00
KM Kevin Millwood Jsy E 3.00 8.00
KW Kerry Wood Jsy A 3.00 8.00
LB Lance Berkman Jsy D 3.00 8.00
LC Luis Castillo Jsy D 3.00 8.00
LG Luis Gonzalez Uni A 3.00 8.00
LW Larry Walker Jsy A 3.00 8.00
MB Marlon Byrd Jsy C 3.00 8.00
MCM Mike Mussina Uni C 4.00 10.00
ML Mike Lowell Jsy D 3.00 8.00
MM Mark Mulder Uni A 3.00 8.00
MP1 M.Piazza 2nd Most Jsy C 6.00 15.00
MP2 M.Piazza 10 Straight Jsy D 6.00 15.00
MR Manny Ramirez Uni C 4.00 10.00
MT Miguel Tejada Uni E 3.00 8.00
MV Mo Vaughn Jsy A 3.00 8.00
NG Nomar Garciaparra Uni C 6.00 15.00
PB Pat Burrell Jsy E 3.00 8.00
PK Paul Konerko Jsy B 3.00 8.00
PL Paul Lo Duca Jsy C 3.00 8.00
PW Preston Wilson Jsy E 3.00 8.00
RJ Randy Johnson Jsy C 4.00 10.00
RP1 R.Palmeiro 500th HR Jsy D 4.00 10.00
RP2 R.Palmeiro 9 Straight Jsy D 4.00 10.00
SC Sean Casey Jsy D 3.00 8.00
SG Shawn Green Jsy C 3.00 8.00
TAH1 T.Hudson Most Wins Jsy B 3.00 8.00
TAH2 T.Hudson 3rd Best Uni D 3.00 8.00
TEG Troy Glaus Uni A 3.00 8.00
TG Tom Glavine Jsy A 4.00 10.00
TH Toby Hall Jsy A 3.00 8.00
TJS Tim Salmon Uni B 4.00 10.00
VG Vladimir Guerrero Jsy C 4.00 10.00

2004 Bazooka Blasts Bat Relics

GROUP A ODDS 1:62 H, 1:86 R
GROUP B ODDS 1:29 H, 1:40 R
OVERALL PARALLEL 25 ODDS 1:94
PARALLEL 25 PRINT RUN 25 #'d SETS
NO PARALLEL 25 PRICING DUE TO SCARCITY
AD Adam Dunn A 3.00 8.00
AG Adrian Gonzalez B 3.00 8.00
AH Aubrey Huff A 3.00 8.00
AJG Andres Galarraga A 3.00 8.00
ANR Aramis Ramirez B 3.00 8.00
AP Albert Pujols B 8.00 20.00
AR Alex Rodriguez B 4.00 10.00
AS Alfonso Soriano A 3.00 8.00
BB Bret Boone B 3.00 8.00
BF Brad Fullmer A 3.00 8.00
BW Bernie Williams A 4.00 10.00
CB Craig Biggio A 4.00 10.00
CC Carl Crawford A 3.00 8.00
CE Carl Everett B 3.00 8.00
CG Cristian Guzman A 3.00 8.00
CIB Carlos Beltran A 3.00 8.00
CJ Chipper Jones B 4.00 10.00
CL Carlos Lee A 3.00 8.00
CP Corey Patterson A 3.00 8.00
DM Doug Mientkiewicz A 3.00 8.00
EM Edgar Martinez B 4.00 10.00
FM Fred McGriff A 4.00 10.00
FT Frank Thomas B 4.00 10.00
GS Gary Sheffield B 3.00 8.00
HB Hank Blalock A 3.00 8.00
IR Ivan Rodriguez B 4.00 10.00
JAG Juan Gonzalez B 3.00 8.00
JB Jeff Bagwell A 4.00 10.00
JG Jason Giambi A 3.00 8.00
JNB Jeromy Burnitz A 3.00 8.00
JO John Olerud A 3.00 8.00
JP Jorge Posada A 4.00 10.00
JR Juan Rivera B 3.00 8.00
LB Lance Berkman B 3.00 8.00
LG Luis Gonzalez A 3.00 8.00
LW Larry Walker B 3.00 8.00
MA Moises Alou A 3.00 8.00
MAT Michael Tucker A 3.00 8.00
MCT Mark Teixeira A 4.00 10.00
MG Marquis Grissom B 3.00 8.00
ML Matt Lawton B 3.00 8.00
MO Magglio Ordonez B 3.00 8.00
MP Mike Piazza A 6.00 15.00
MR Manny Ramirez B 4.00 10.00
MT Miguel Tejada A 3.00 8.00
MV Mo Vaughn B 3.00 8.00
NG Nomar Garciaparra A 6.00 15.00
NH Nathan Haynes B 3.00 8.00
OV Omar Vizquel B 4.00 10.00
PK Paul Konerko A 3.00 8.00
PL Paul Lo Duca A 3.00 8.00
RA Roberto Alomar B 4.00 10.00
RB Rocco Baldelli A 3.00 8.00
RF Rafael Furcal B 3.00 8.00
RP Rafael Palmeiro B 4.00 10.00
RS Ruben Sierra B 3.00 8.00
RSA Rich Aurilia B 3.00 8.00
RW Rondell White B 3.00 8.00
SB Sean Burroughs B 3.00 8.00
SG Shawn Green B 3.00 8.00
SR Scott Rolen A 4.00 10.00
SS Shannon Stewart A 3.00 8.00
ST So Taguchi B 3.00 8.00
TB Tony Batista B 3.00 8.00
TG Troy Glaus A 3.00 8.00
TH Torii Hunter A 3.00 8.00
TJS Tim Salmon A 4.00 10.00
TKH Todd Helton B 4.00 10.00
TM Tino Martinez A 4.00 10.00
VG Vladimir Guerrero B 4.00 10.00
VW Vernon Wells A 3.00 8.00

2004 Bazooka Comics

COMPLETE SET (24) 10.00 25.00
STATED ODDS 1:4
BC1 Garret Anderson .40 1.00
BC2 Jeff Bagwell .60 1.50
BC3 Hank Blalock .40 1.00
BC4 Roy Halladay .60 1.50
BC5 Dontrelle Willis .40 1.00
BC6 Roger Clemens 1.25 3.00
BC7 Carlos Delgado .40 1.00
BC8 Rafael Furcal .40 1.00
BC9 Eric Gagne .40 1.00
BC10 Nomar Garciaparra .60 1.50
BC11 Derek Jeter 2.50 6.00
BC12 Esteban Loaiza .40 1.00
BC13 Kevin Millwood UER .40 1.00
No-hitter date incorrect
BC14 Bill Mueller .40 1.00
BC15 Rafael Palmeiro .60 1.50
BC16 Albert Pujols 1.25 3.00
BC17 Jose Reyes .60 1.50
BC18 Alex Rodriguez 1.25 3.00
BC19 Alfonso Soriano .60 1.50
BC20 Sammy Sosa 1.00 2.50
BC21 Ichiro Suzuki 1.25 3.00
BC22 Frank Thomas 1.00 2.50
BC23 Brad Wilkerson .40 1.00
BC24 Roy Oswalt .60 1.50
Pete Munro
Kirk Saarloos
Brad Lidge
Octavio Dotel
Billy Wagner

2004 Bazooka One-Liners Relics

GROUP A ODDS 1:62 H, 1:86 R
GROUP B ODDS 1:98 H, 1:136 R
OVERALL PARALLEL 25 ODDS 1:94
PARALLEL 25 PRINT RUN 25 #'d SETS
NO PARALLEL 25 PRICING DUE TO SCARCITY
AD Andre Dawson Bat A 4.00 10.00
BB Bert Blyleven Jsy A 4.00 10.00
BC Bert Campaneris Jsy A 4.00 10.00
BM Bill Madlock Bat A 4.00 10.00
BS Bret Saberhagen Jsy A 4.00 10.00
CS Chris Sabo Bat A 4.00 10.00
CY Carl Yastrzemski Uni A 12.50 30.00
DA Dick Allen Bat A 4.00 10.00
DE Dennis Eckersley Jsy A 4.00 10.00
DJ1 David Justice Bat A 4.00 10.00
DJ2 David Justice Uni A 4.00 10.00
DM Dale Murphy Bat A 6.00 15.00
DP Dave Parker Jsy A 4.00 10.00
DW Dwight Gooden Jsy A 4.00 10.00
EM Eddie Murray Uni A 10.00 25.00
FR Frank Robinson Uni A 4.00 10.00
GB George Brett Jsy B 8.00 20.00
GC Gary Carter Bat A 4.00 10.00
GP Gaylord Perry Uni A 4.00 10.00
HK Harmon Killebrew Jsy A 6.00 15.00
JB Johnny Bench Bat B 6.00 15.00
JC Jose Canseco Bat B 6.00 15.00
JCA Joe Carter Jsy A 4.00 10.00
JK Jerry Koosman Jsy A 4.00 10.00
JM Joe Morgan Jsy A 4.00 10.00
KG1 Kirk Gibson Bat A 4.00 10.00
KG2 Kirk Gibson Jsy A 4.00 10.00
KH Keith Hernandez Bat B 4.00 10.00
KP1 Kirby Puckett Bat B 6.00 15.00
KP2 Kirby Puckett Jsy B 6.00 15.00
MS Mike Schmidt Jsy B 8.00 20.00
NR Nolan Ryan Jsy A 30.00 60.00
OC Orlando Cepeda Bat A 4.00 10.00
PN Phil Niekro Uni A 4.00 10.00
RC Rod Carew Bat B 6.00 15.00
RD Ron Darling Jsy A 4.00 10.00
RJ Reggie Jackson Jsy A 6.00 15.00
RS Red Schoendienst Bat B 4.00 10.00
RSA Ron Santo Bat A 6.00 15.00
RY Robin Yount Bat A 6.00 15.00
TM Tug McGraw Jsy A 6.00 15.00
TS Tom Seaver Uni A 6.00 15.00
WB1 Wade Boggs Bat B 6.00 15.00
WB2 Wade Boggs Jsy B 6.00 15.00
WM Willie Mays Uni A 30.00 60.00
WMC Willie McGee Bat A 6.00 15.00
WS Willie Stargell Bat A 6.00 15.00

2004 Bazooka Stand-Ups

STATED ODDS 1:8 H, 1:24 R
1 Jose Reyes .60 1.50
2 Jim Thome .60 1.50
3 Roy Halladay .60 1.50
4 Jason Giambi .40 1.00
5 Dontrelle Willis .40 1.00
6 Mike Piazza 1.00 2.50
7 Chipper Jones 1.00 2.50
8 Mark Prior .60 1.50
9 Todd Helton .60 1.50
10 Miguel Cabrera 1.00 2.50
11 Derek Jeter 2.50 6.00
12 Nomar Garciaparra .60 1.50
13 Alex Rodriguez 1.25 3.00
14 Miguel Tejada .60 1.50
15 Carlos Delgado .40 1.00
16 Pedro Martinez .60 1.50
17 Sammy Sosa 1.00 2.50
18 Ichiro Suzuki 1.25 3.00
19 Vladimir Guerrero .60 1.50
20 Alfonso Soriano .60 1.50
21 Eric Chavez .40 1.00
22 Albert Pujols 1.25 3.00
23 Ivan Rodriguez .60 1.50
24 Vernon Wells .40 1.00
25 Eric Gagne .40 1.00

2004 Bazooka Tattoos

STATED ODDS 1:4 H, 1:6 R
AD Adam Dunn .60 1.50
AJ Andruw Jones .40 1.00
AP Albert Pujols 1.25 3.00
AR Alex Rodriguez 1.25 3.00
AS Alfonso Soriano .60 1.50
BAZ Bazooka Logo .40 1.00
BP Brad Penny .40 1.00
BW Bernie Williams .60 1.50
BZ Barry Zito .60 1.50
CB Craig Biggio .60 1.50
CF Cliff Floyd .40 1.00
CG Cristian Guzman .40 1.00
CJ Chipper Jones 1.00 2.50
CS Curt Schilling .60 1.50
DW Dontrelle Willis .40 1.00
EC Eric Chavez .40 1.00
GJ Geoff Jenkins .40 1.00
GM Greg Maddux 1.25 3.00
HN Hideo Nomo 1.00 2.50
JB Jeff Bagwell .60 1.50
JG Jason Giambi .40 1.00
JK Jason Kendall .40 1.00
JO John Olerud .40 1.00
JT Jim Thome .60 1.50
JW Jarrod Washburn .40 1.00
KB Kevin Brown .40 1.00
KM Kevin Millwood .40 1.00
KW Kerry Wood .40 1.00
LB Lance Berkman .60 1.50
LC Luis Castillo .40 1.00
LG Luis Gonzalez .40 1.00
LW Larry Walker .60 1.50
MB Marlon Byrd .40 1.00
MCM Mike Mussina .60 1.50
ML Mike Lowell .40 1.00
MM Mark Mulder .40 1.00
MP Mike Piazza 1.00 2.50
MR Manny Ramirez 1.00 2.50
MT Miguel Tejada .60 1.50
NG Nomar Garciaparra .60 1.50
PB Pat Burrell .40 1.00
PK Paul Konerko .60 1.50
PL Paul Lo Duca .40 1.00
PW Preston Wilson .40 1.00
RJ Randy Johnson 1.00 2.50
RP Rafael Palmeiro .60 1.50
SC Sean Casey .40 1.00
SG Shawn Green .40 1.00
TAH Tim Hudson .60 1.50
TEG Troy Glaus .40 1.00
TG Tom Glavine .60 1.50
TH Toby Hall .40 1.00
TJS Tim Salmon .40 1.00
TOP Topps Logo .40 1.00
VG Vladimir Guerrero .60 1.50

2005 Bazooka

COMPLETE SET (220) 30.00 60.00
1 Eric Gagne .15 .40
2 Aramis Ramirez .15 .40
3 Hank Blalock .15 .40
4 Jason Kendall .15 .40
5 Jeromy Burnitz .15 .40
6 Jose Guillen .15 .40
7 Tom Glavine .25 .60
8 Adrian Beltre .40 1.00
9 Jason Bay .15 .40
10 Mark Teixeira .25 .60
11 Moises Alou .15 .40
12 Ronnie Belliard .15 .40
13 Aaron Guiel .15 .40
14 Vladimir Guerrero .25 .60
15 Scott Podsednik .15 .40
16 Alfonso Soriano .25 .60
17 Craig Wilson .15 .40
18 Jose Reyes .25 .60
19 Mark Prior .25 .60
20 Preston Wilson .15 .40
21 Shawn Green .15 .40
22 Troy Glaus .15 .40
23 Dmitri Young .15 .40
24 Garret Anderson .15 .40
25 Kazuo Matsui .15 .40
26 Kerry Wood .15 .40
27 Michael Young .15 .40
28 Oliver Perez .15 .40
29 Bartolo Colon .15 .40
30 Richie Sexson .15 .40
31 Brad Penny .15 .40
32 Carlos Guillen .15 .40
33 Carlos Zambrano .25 .60
34 David Wright .30 .75
35 Al Leiter .15 .40
36 Jack Wilson .15 .40
37 Ryan Drese .15 .40
38 Darin Erstad .15 .40
39 Derrek Lee .15 .40
40 Ivan Rodriguez .25 .60
41 Kenny Rogers .15 .40
42 Mike Piazza .40 1.00
43 Phil Nevin .15 .40
44 Geoff Jenkins .15 .40
45 Jorge Posada .25 .60
46 Khalil Greene .15 .40
47 Randy Johnson .40 1.00
48 Rondell White .15 .40
49 Sammy Sosa .40 1.00
50 Vernon Wells .15 .40
51 Ben Sheets .15 .40
52 Brian Giles .15 .40
53 Carlos Delgado .15 .40
54 Derek Jeter 1.00 2.50
55 Jeremy Bonderman .15 .40
56 Magglio Ordonez .25 .60
57 Chad Tracy .15 .40
58 Kevin Brown .15 .40
59 Luis Castillo .15 .40
60 Lyle Overbay .15 .40

61 Mark Buehrle .25 .60
62 Mark Loretta .15 .40
63 Orlando Hudson .15 .40
64 Adam Dunn .25 .60
65 Frank Thomas .40 1.00
66 Jake Peavy .15 .40
67 Jason Giambi .15 .40
68 Joe Mauer .30 .75
69 Marcus Giles .15 .40
70 Mike Lowell .15 .40
71 Roy Halladay .25 .60
72 Aaron Rowand .15 .40
73 Alex Rodriguez .50 1.25
74 Brian Lawrence .15 .40
75 Gabe Gross .15 .40
76 Johnny Estrada .15 .40
77 Justin Morneau .25 .60
78 Miguel Cabrera .40 1.00
79 Alex Rios .15 .40
80 Gary Sheffield .15 .40
81 Jason Schmidt .15 .40
82 Juan Pierre .15 .40
83 Paul Konerko .25 .60
84 Jermaine Dye .15 .40
85 Rafael Furcal .15 .40
86 Torii Hunter .15 .40
87 A.J. Pierzynski .15 .40
88 Carl Pavano .15 .40
89 Carlos Lee .15 .40
90 J.D. Drew .15 .40
91 Javier Vazquez .15 .40
92 Lew Ford .15 .40
93 Ted Lilly .15 .40
94 Austin Kearns .15 .40
95 Chipper Jones .40 1.00
96 Erubiel Durazo .15 .40
97 Johan Santana .25 .60
98 Josh Beckett .15 .40
99 Mariano Rivera .50 1.25
100 Mark Mulder .15 .40
101 Andruw Jones .15 .40
102 Barry Zito .25 .60
103 Bret Boone .15 .40
104 Paul LoDuca .15 .40
105 Shannon Stewart .15 .40
106 Wily Mo Pena .15 .40
107 Dontrelle Willis .15 .40
108 Eric Chavez .15 .40
109 Jamie Moyer .15 .40
110 Joe Nathan .15 .40
111 Sidney Ponson .15 .40
112 John Smoltz .40 1.00
113 Ichiro Suzuki .50 1.25
114 Javy Lopez .15 .40
115 Victor Martinez .25 .60
116 Ken Griffey Jr. .75 2.00
117 Lance Berkman .25 .60
118 Scott Hatteberg .15 .40
119 Jim Edmonds .25 .60
120 Kazuhisa Ishii .15 .40
121 Miguel Tejada .25 .60
122 Roger Clemens .50 1.25
123 Ryan Freel .15 .40
124 Albert Pujols .50 1.25
125 Hideo Nomo .40 1.00
126 Mark Kotsay .15 .40
127 Melvin Mora .15 .40
128 Roy Oswalt .25 .60
129 Sean Casey .15 .40
130 Casey Blake .15 .40
131 Edgar Renteria .15 .40
132 Jeff Kent .15 .40
133 Rafael Palmeiro .25 .60
134 Tim Hudson .25 .60
135 Barry Bonds .60 1.50
136 Andy Pettitte .25 .60
137 Brian Roberts .15 .40
138 Jose Vidro .15 .40
139 Omar Vizquel .25 .60
40 Rich Harden .15 .40
41 Scott Rolen .25 .60
42 Carlos Beltran .25 .60
43 Chris Carpenter .25 .60
44 Manny Ramirez .40 1.00
45 Nick Johnson .15 .40
46 Pat Burrell .15 .40
47 C.C. Sabathia .25 .60
48 Johnny Damon .25 .60
49 Juan Rivera .15 .40
50 Ken Harvey .15 .40
51 Kevin Millwood .15 .40
52 Larry Walker .25 .60
53 Aubrey Huff .15 .40
54 Curt Schilling .25 .60
5 Jake Westbrook .15 .40
6 Randy Wolf .15 .40
7 Zach Day .15 .40
8 Zack Greinke .50 1.25
9 Brad Wilkerson .15 .40
0 Carl Crawford .25 .60
1 Jim Thome .25 .60
2 Mike Sweeney .15 .40
3 Pedro Martinez .25 .60
4 Travis Hafner .15 .40
5 Bobby Abreu .15 .40
6 Cliff Floyd .15 .40
7 David DeJesus .15 .40
3 David Ortiz .40 1.00
9 Rocco Baldelli .15 .40
0 Todd Helton .25 .60
Dallas McPherson PROS .20 .50
Kevin Youkilis PROS .20 .50
Val Majewski PROS .20 .50
Grady Sizemore PROS .30 .75
Joey Gathright PROS .20 .50
Rickie Weeks PROS .20 .50
Jason Kubel PROS .20 .50
Robinson Cano PROS .60 1.50
Nick Swisher PROS .30 .75
Ryan Howard PROS .40 1.00
Tim Stauffer PROS .20 .50
Merkin Valdez PROS .20 .50
B.J. Upton PROS .30 .75
Scott Kazmir PROS .50 1.25
Chris Burke PROS .20 .50
Felix Hernandez PROS .60 1.50
187 Freddy Guzman PROS .20 .50
188 Josh Labandeira PROS .20 .50
189 Willy Taveras PROS .20 .50
190 Casey Kotchman PROS .20 .50
191 Steve Doetsch FY RC .20 .50
192 Melky Cabrera FY RC .60 1.50
193 Luis Ramirez FY RC .20 .50
194 Chris Seddon FY RC .20 .50
195 Chad Orvella FY RC .20 .50
196 Ian Kinsler FY RC 1.00 2.50
197 Brandon Moss FY RC .75 2.00
198 Chadd Blasko FY RC .30 .75
199 Jeremy West FY RC .20 .50
200 Sean Marshall FY RC .50 1.25
201 Matt DeSalvo FY RC .20 .50
202 Ryan Sweeney FY RC .30 .75
203 Matthew Lindstrom FY RC .20 .50
204 Ryan Goleski FY RC .20 .50
205 Brett Harper FY RC .20 .50
206 Chris Roberson FY RC .20 .50
207 Andre Ethier FY RC 1.50 4.00
208 Chris Denorfia FY RC .20 .50
209 Darren Fenster FY RC .20 .50
210 Elvys Quezada FY RC .20 .50
211 Kevin West FY RC .20 .50
212 Chaz Lytle FY RC .30 .75
213 James Jurries FY RC .20 .50
214 Matt Rogelstad FY RC .20 .50
215 Wade Robinson FY RC .20 .50
216 Ian Bladergroen FY RC .20 .50
217 Jake Dittler FY .20 .50
218 Nate McLouth FY RC .30 .75
219 Kole Strayhorn FY RC .20 .50
220 Jose Vaquedano FY RC .20 .50

2005 Bazooka Gold Chunks

*GOLD 1-170: .75X TO 2X BASIC
*GOLD 171-190: .75X TO 2X BASIC
*GOLD 191-220: .75X TO 2X BASIC
ONE PER PACK

2005 Bazooka Minis

*MINIS 1-170: .75X TO 2X BASIC
*MINIS 171-190: .75X TO 2X BASIC
*MINIS 191-220: .75X TO 2X BASIC
ONE PER PACK

2005 Bazooka 4 on 1 Stickers

STATED ODDS 1:3 HOBBY, 1:6 RETAIL
ONE STICKER ALBUM PER HOBBY BOX
1 A.Rod 1.25 3.00
Blal
Rolen
Lowell
2 Posa .75 2.00
I.Rod
Mauer
Estrada
3 Ichiro 1.50 4.00
Beltran
Edm
Giles
4 Thome .50 1.25
Teix
Konerko
Over
5 Reyes .40 1.00
Loretta
Vidro
Castillo
6 Teja 1.50 4.00
Jeter
M.Young
Rent
7 Oswalt .75 2.00
Harden
Johan
Prior
8 Rivera .75 2.00
Gagne
Nath
Smoltz
9 L.Walk .50 1.25
Craw
P.Wils
Garret
10 Wily Mo .40 1.00
Kotsay
Rios
Jenk
11 V.Mart 1.25 3.00
Wright
Morn
Bay
12 C.Lee .50 1.25
Andruw
R.Bell
Chav
13 Vlad .75 2.00
Wells
Cabrera
Beltre
14 D.Ortiz .50 1.25
M.Giles
Kent
Abreu
15 Pierre .40 1.00
Torii
Drew
Kearns
16 Colon 1.50 4.00
Manny
Griffey
Willis
17 Pett .75 2.00
Hudson
Schil
Randy
18 Moyer .40 1.00
Day
Leiter
O.Perez
19 Kaz 1.25 3.00
Clemens
Khalil
Vazq
20 Pedro .75 2.00
Baldelli
Piazza
Mora
21 Nomo .75 2.00
Ishii
K.Harv
Sween
22 Blake .40 1.00
Freel
Boone
Javy
23 C.Wils .40 1.00
Green
Aramis
Erstad
24 Glaus .40 1.00
Berkman
Pods
Dunn
25 Pujols 1.50 4.00
Sheff
Chip
Magglio
26 Damon .50 1.25
Zamb
Schmidt
Lilly
27 Ponson .40 1.00
Carp
Sabath
Millw
28 Pavano .40 1.00
Mulder
Furc
J.Wils
29 Bonder .50 1.25
Westb
Greink
Glav
30 Vizq .50 1.25
C.Guil
Hallad
Sheets
31 Wood .40 1.00
K.Brown
Alou
Hafn
32 N.John .40 1.00
Duraz
A.Sori
Giam
33 Tracy .40 1.00
Sexson
Huff
Roberts
34 Helton .50 1.25
Dmitri
Burnitz
J.Guil
35 J.Riv .75 2.00
Stewart
Sosa
Floyd
36 Burrell .40 1.00
Gross
Guiel
LoDuca
37 Pierz .40 1.00
O.Hud
DeJes
B.Lawr
38 Beckett .40 1.00
Zito
Buehrle
Wolf
39 Penny .40 1.00
Peavy
Rondell
Wilk
40 Drese .40 1.00
K.Rogers
Dye
Ford
41 A.Row 2.00 5.00
Kend
Bonds
D.Lee
42 Nevin .75 2.00
Casey
Raffy
Thomas
43 Hatte .50 1.25
Laban
Kubel
Swish
44 F.Guz 1.50 4.00
Stauf
Merkin
F.Hern
45 Taver .50 1.25
Size
Gath
Delgado
46 Kazmir .40 1.00
Weeks
McPh
Youk
47 Majew .40 1.00
Kotch
R.How
Burke
48 Cano .50 1.25
Upton
Dittler
I.Blad
49 B.Harp .50 1.25
Jurr
J.West
Rogel
50 Fenst 1.00 2.50
Orv
Moss
R.Sween
51 Rober 3.00 8.00
Doet
Ethier
K.West
52 Melky 1.50 4.00
Goleski
Denorf
Lytle
53 L.Ram 1.00 2.50
DeSalvo
S.Mar
Vaq
54 Seddon .40 1.00
Blasko
Quez
Rob
55 McLouth 2.00 5.00
Lind
Stray
Kinsler
NNO Sticker Album .75 2.00

2005 Bazooka Blasts Bat Relics

GROUP A ODDS 1:649 H, 1:1205 R
GROUP B ODDS 1:47 H, 1:65 R
GROUP C ODDS 1:29 H, 1:45 R
GROUP D ODDS 1:93 H, 1:140 R
GROUP E ODDS 1:104 H, 1:158 R
GROUP A PRINT RUN 100 SETS
GROUP A ARE NOT SERIAL-NUMBERED
GROUP A PRINT RUN PROVIDED BY TOPPS
AB Angel Berroa C 3.00 8.00
AD Adam Dunn B 3.00 8.00
AGO Adrian Gonzalez B 3.00 8.00
AG1 Alex Gonzalez C 3.00 8.00
AR Aramis Ramirez B 3.00 8.00
AR1 Alex Rodriguez A/100 * 10.00 25.00
BU B.J. Upton A/100 * 6.00 15.00
CB Craig Biggio A/100 * 6.00 15.00
CE Carl Everett C 3.00 8.00
CF Chone Figgins B 3.00 8.00
CG Cristian Guzman B 3.00 8.00
CGU Carlos Guillen B 3.00 8.00
CS Curt Schilling B 4.00 10.00
DL Derrek Lee B 4.00 10.00
DO David Ortiz A/100 * 6.00 15.00
DW David Wright A/100 * 6.00 15.00
GS Gary Sheffield E 3.00 8.00
HB Hank Blalock A/100 * 4.00 10.00
JB Jeromy Burnitz B 3.00 8.00
JC Jeff Conine D 3.00 8.00
JF Julio Franco C 3.00 8.00
JK Jeff Kent B 3.00 8.00
JV Jose Valentin C 3.00 8.00
JV1 Jose Vidro C 3.00 8.00
JW Jayson Werth B 3.00 8.00
KM Kaz Matsui A/100 * 6.00 15.00
LG Luis Gonzalez B 3.00 8.00
LH Livan Hernandez C 3.00 8.00
LW Larry Walker E 4.00 10.00
MC Miguel Cabrera A/100 * 6.00 15.00
ML Mike Lowell A/100 * 4.00 10.00
MO Magglio Ordonez C 3.00 8.00
MR Manny Ramirez C 4.00 10.00
MT Miguel Tejada B 3.00 8.00
MY Michael Young B 3.00 8.00
NG Nomar Garciaparra B 4.00 10.00
PK Paul Konerko D 3.00 8.00
PM Pedro Martinez B 4.00 10.00
PW Preston Wilson B 3.00 8.00
RA Roberto Alomar C 4.00 10.00
RB Ron Belliard C 3.00 8.00
RH Richard Hidalgo C 3.00 8.00
RS Ruben Sierra C 3.00 8.00
TC Tony Clark B 3.00 8.00
TH Todd Helton C 4.00 10.00
TM Tino Martinez B 4.00 10.00
VC Vinny Castilla D 3.00 8.00
VG Vladimir Guerrero A/100 * 4.00 10.00
VM Victor Martinez A/100 * 3.00 8.00

2005 Bazooka Comics

COMPLETE SET (24) 10.00 25.00
STATED ODDS 1:4 H
1 Randy Johnson 1.00 2.50
2 Gary Sheffield .40 1.00
3 Ken Griffey Jr. 2.00 5.00
4 Alex Rodriguez 1.25 3.00
5 Vladimir Guerrero .60 1.50
6 David Bell .40 1.00
7 Carlos Pena .60 1.50
8 Eric Gagne .40 1.00
9 Jim Thome .60 1.50
10 Cleveland Indians .40 1.00
11 Greg Maddux 1.25 3.00
12 Miguel Tejada .60 1.50
13 Ichiro Suzuki 1.25 3.00
14 Mariano Rivera 1.25 3.00
15 Juan Pierre .40 1.00
16 Carl Crawford .60 1.50
17 Mike Mussina .60 1.50
18 Vladimir Guerrero .60 1.50
19 Oliver Perez .40 1.00
20 Ichiro Suzuki 1.25 3.00
21 Johan Santana .60 1.50
22 Kevin Brown .40 1.00
23 Mike Piazza 1.00 2.50
24 Randy Johnson 1.00 2.50

2005 Bazooka Fun Facts Relics

GROUP A ODDS 1:3949 H, 1:6012 R
GROUP B ODDS 1:71 H, 1:108 R
GROUP C ODDS 1:330 H, 1:500 R
GROUP D ODDS 1:83 H, 1:126 R
GROUP E ODDS 1:278 H, 1:423 R
GROUP F ODDS 1:209 H, 1:316 R
GROUP A PRINT RUN 100 SETS
GROUP A ARE NOT SERIAL-NUMBERED
GROUP A PRINT RUN PROVIDED BY TOPPS
CF Cecil Fielder Bat D 6.00 15.00
CS Cory Snyder Bat B 3.00 8.00
DD Darren Daulton Bat D 3.00 8.00
DE Darrell Evans Bat E 3.00 8.00
DJ1 Dave Justice Jsy C 3.00 8.00
DJ2 Dave Justice Bat D 3.00 8.00
DP Dave Parker Bat B 3.00 8.00
DS Darryl Strawberry Bat B 3.00 8.00
GB George Brett Bat B 6.00 15.00
GC Gary Carter Bat B 3.00 8.00
HB Harold Baines Bat D 3.00 8.00
HR Harold Reynolds Bat D 3.00 8.00
JC Jose Canseco Jsy C 6.00 15.00
JL Jim Leyritz Bat B 3.00 8.00
MR Mickey Rivers Bat B 3.00 8.00
MS Mike Schmidt Bat B 6.00 15.00
OS Ozzie Smith Bat A/100 * 15.00 40.00
RC Rod Carew Bat A/100 * 10.00 25.00
RK Ron Kittle Bat B 3.00 8.00
WB Wade Boggs Bat B 4.00 10.00
WH Willie Horton Bat B 3.00 8.00
WJ Wally Joyner Bat F 3.00 8.00
WW Walt Weiss Bat B 3.00 8.00

2005 Bazooka Moments Relics

GROUP A ODDS 1:1132 H, 1:1718 R
GROUP B ODDS 1:110 H, 1:167 R
GROUP A PRINT RUN 100 SETS
GROUP A ARE NOT SERIAL-NUMBERED
GROUP A PRINT RUN PROVIDED BY TOPPS
AP Albert Pujols Cap A/100 * 15.00 40.00
AR Alex Rodriguez Uni A/100 * 10.00 25.00
AS Alfonso Soriano Uni A/100 * 4.00 10.00
FT Frank Thomas Uni B 4.00 10.00
IR Ivan Rodriguez Uni A/100 * 6.00 15.00
JP Jorge Posada Uni A/100 * 6.00 15.00
KR Kenny Rogers Uni B 3.00 8.00
MB Matt Bush Jsy B 3.00 8.00
MM Mark Mulder Uni A/100 * 4.00 10.00
MP Mike Piazza Uni A/100 * 6.00 15.00
MT Mark Teixeira Uni B 4.00 10.00
RH Ramon Hernandez Uni B 3.00 8.00
TL Terrence Long Uni B 3.00 8.00

2005 Bazooka Tattoos

COMPLETE SET (25) 3.00 8.00
COMMON CARD (1-25) .10 .25
SEMISTARS .15 .40
UNLISTED STARS .25 .60
STATED ODDS 1:4 HOBBY/RETAIL
1 Alex Rodriguez .30 .75
2 Randy Johnson .25 .60
3 Jim Thome .15 .40
4 Pedro Martinez .15 .40
5 Roger Clemens .30 .75
6 Troy Glaus .10 .25
7 Todd Helton .15 .40
8 Albert Pujols .30 .75
9 Sammy Sosa .25 .60
10 David Wright .20 .50
11 Mike Piazza .25 .60
12 Gary Sheffield .10 .25
13 David Ortiz .25 .60
14 Hank Blalock .10 .25
15 Miguel Tejada .15 .40
16 Dontrelle Willis .10 .25
17 Ivan Rodriguez .15 .40
18 Nomar Garciaparra .15 .40
19 Alfonso Soriano .15 .40
20 Adrian Beltre .25 .60
21 Torii Hunter .10 .25
22 Brian Giles .10 .25
23 Chipper Jones .25 .60
24 Carlos Beltran .15 .40
25 Manny Ramirez .25 .60

2006 Bazooka

COMPLETE SET (220) 15.00 40.00
1 Josh Gibson .40 1.00
2 Scott Podsednik .15 .40
3 Sammy Sosa .40 1.00
4 Ivan Rodriguez .25 .60
5 Derek Jeter 1.00 2.50
6 Manny Ramirez .40 1.00
7 Nook Logan .15 .40
8 Adam Dunn .25 .60
9 Travis Hafner .15 .40
10 Felix Hernandez .25 .60
11 Larry Bigbie .15 .40
12 Magglio Ordonez .25 .60
13 Josh Beckett .15 .40
14 Mike Sweeney .15 .40
15 Mickey Mantle 1.25 3.00
16 Grady Sizemore .25 .60
17 Brian Fuentes .15 .40
18 Wily Mo Pena .15 .40
19 Morgan Ensberg .15 .40
20 Tim Hudson .25 .60
21 Justin Verlander 1.25 3.00
22 Jermaine Dye .15 .40
23 Miguel Cabrera .40 1.00
24 Greg Maddux .50 1.25
25 Jason Giambi .15 .40
26 Ben Sheets .15 .40
27 Brad Radke .15 .40
28 Torii Hunter .15 .40
29 Mike Piazza .40 1.00
30 Jason Kendall .15 .40
31 Pat Burrell .15 .40
32 Khalil Greene .15 .40
33 Brian Roberts .15 .40
34 C.C. Sabathia .25 .60
35 Mike Mussina .25 .60
36 Bob Wickman .15 .40
37 Dmitri Young .15 .40
38 Dontrelle Willis .15 .40
39 David DeJesus .15 .40
40 J.D. Drew .15 .40
41 Chad Tracy .15 .40
42 Joe Mauer .25 .60
43 Melvin Mora .15 .40
44 Carlos Zambrano .25 .60
45 Mariano Rivera .50 1.25
46 Coco Crisp .15 .40
47 Derrek Lee .15 .40
48 Cliff Floyd .15 .40
49 Willy Taveras .15 .40
50 Albert Pujols .50 1.25
51 Aaron Boone .15 .40
52 Mark Mulder .15 .40
53 Brad Wilkerson .15 .40
54 Hank Blalock .15 .40
55 Hideki Matsui .40 1.00
56 Victor Martinez .25 .60
57 Jeremy Bonderman .15 .40
58 Felipe Lopez .15 .40
59 Paul Lo Duca .15 .40
60 Derek Lowe .15 .40
61 Luis Gonzalez .15 .40
62 Paul Konerko .25 .60
63 Miguel Tejada .25 .60
64 Jeromy Burnitz .15 .40
65 Orlando Hernandez .15 .40
66 Curt Schilling .25 .60
67 Joe Nathan .15 .40
68 Jose Reyes .25 .60
69 David Wright .30 .75
70 Eric Chavez .15 .40
71 Rich Harden .15 .40
72 A.J. Pierzynski .15 .40
73 Trevor Hoffman .25 .60
74 Adrian Beltre .40 1.00
75 Alex Rodriguez .50 1.25
76 Jonathan Papelbon .75 2.00
77 Jorge Cantu .15 .40
78 Mark Teixeira .25 .60
79 Chien-Ming Wang .25 .60
80 Jeff Francoeur .40 1.00
81 Ichiro Suzuki .50 1.25
82 Jhonny Peralta .15 .40
83 Todd Helton .25 .60
84 Brad Penny .15 .40
85 Shawn Chacon .15 .40
86 Billy Wagner .15 .40
87 Jason Schmidt .15 .40
88 Austin Kearns .15 .40
89 Chris Carpenter .25 .60
90 Chipper Jones .40 1.00
91 Shawn Green .15 .40
92 A.J. Burnett .15 .40
93 Joe Crede UER .15 .40
Back comic refers to Rafael Palmeiro
94 Mark Prior .25 .60
95 Andy Pettitte .25 .60
96 Edgar Renteria .15 .40
97 Roy Halladay .25 .60
98 Eric Milton .15 .40
99 Craig Biggio .25 .60
100 Barry Bonds .60 1.50
101 Troy Glaus .15 .40
102 Aaron Rowand .15 .40
103 Aramis Ramirez .15 .40
104 Nomar Garciaparra .25 .60
105 Randy Johnson .40 1.00
106 David Ortiz .40 1.00
107 Vinny Castilla .15 .40
108 Carl Crawford .25 .60
109 Zach Duke .15 .40
110 Barry Zito .25 .60
111 Darin Erstad .15 .40
112 Chris Capuano .15 .40
113 Javy Lopez .15 .40
114 Lew Ford .15 .40
115 Robinson Cano .25 .60
116 Ronnie Belliard .15 .40
117 Placido Polanco .15 .40
118 Rickie Weeks .15 .40
119 Brad Lidge .15 .40
120 Andruw Jones .15 .40
121 Nick Swisher .25 .60
122 Bartolo Colon .15 .40
123 Juan Pierre .15 .40
124 Johan Santana .25 .60
125 Jorge Posada .25 .60
126 Jeff Francis .15 .40
127 Matt Holliday .40 1.00
128 Carlos Delgado .15 .40
129 Zack Greinke .40 1.00
130 Lyle Overbay .15 .40
131 Conor Jackson .25 .60
132 Mark Buehrle .25 .60
133 Chone Figgins .15 .40
134 Pedro Martinez .25 .60
135 Roger Clemens .50 1.25
136 Raul Ibanez .25 .60
137 Jim Edmonds .25 .60
138 Michael Young .15 .40
139 Preston Wilson .15 .40
140 Rafael Furcal .15 .40
141 Bobby Abreu .15 .40
142 Tadahito Iguchi .15 .40
143 B.J. Ryan .15 .40
144 Francisco Rodriguez UER .25 .60
Ervin Santana pictured
145 J.T. Snow .15 .40
146 Aubrey Huff .15 .40
147 Mike Morse .15 .40
148 Jason Bay .15 .40
149 Roy Oswalt .25 .60
150 Carlos Beltran .25 .60
151 Carlos Lee .15 .40
152 Emil Brown .15 .40
153 Craig Monroe .15 .40
154 Kris Benson .15 .40
155 Gary Sheffield .15 .40
156 Jake Peavy .15 .40
157 David Eckstein .15 .40
158 Tom Glavine .25 .60
159 Jeff Kent .15 .40
160 Livan Hernandez .15 .40
161 Orlando Hudson .15 .40
162 Randy Winn .15 .40
163 Jimmy Rollins .25 .60
164 Luis Castillo .15 .40
165 Nick Johnson .15 .40
166 Johnny Damon .25 .60
167 Eric Gagne .15 .40
168 Geoff Jenkins .15 .40
169 Mike Cameron .15 .40
170 Marcus Giles .15 .40
171 Huston Street .15 .40
172 Moises Alou .15 .40
173 Scott Rolen .25 .60
174 Jose Vidro .15 .40
175 Alfonso Soriano .25 .60
176 Toby Hall .15 .40
177 Orlando Cabrera .15 .40
178 Brian Giles .15 .40
179 Erubiel Durazo .15 .40
180 Matt Morris .15 .40
181 Jack Wilson .15 .40
182 Brady Clark .15 .40
183 Shannon Stewart .15 .40
184 Kerry Wood .15 .40
185 Carl Pavano .15 .40
186 Chase Utley .25 .60
187 Omar Vizquel .25 .60
188 Vladimir Guerrero .25 .60
189 Richie Sexson .15 .40
190 John Smoltz .40 1.00
191 Garret Anderson UER .15 .40
Name misspelled
192 Jon Garland .15 .40
193 Julio Lugo .15 .40
194 Rocco Baldelli .15 .40
195 Jaret Wright .15 .40
196 Matt Clement .15 .40
197 Vernon Wells .15 .40
198 Sean Casey .15 .40
199 Lance Berkman .25 .60
200 Justin Morneau .25 .60
201 Shaun Marcum (RC) .15 .40
202 Chuck James (RC) .15 .40
203 Hong-Chih Kuo (RC) .40 1.00
204 Darrell Rasner (RC) .15 .40
205 Anthony Reyes (RC) .15 .40
206 Francisco Liriano (RC) .40 1.00
207 Joe Saunders (RC) .15 .40
208 Fausto Carmona (RC) .15 .40
209 Charlton Jimerson (RC) .15 .40
210 Bryan Bullington (RC) .15 .40
211 Tom Gorzelanny (RC) .15 .40
212 Anderson Hernandez (RC) .15 .40
213 Ryan Garko (RC) .15 .40
214 John Koronka (RC) .15 .40
215 Chris Denorfia (RC) .15 .40
216 Jeff Mathis (RC) .15 .40
217 Jose Bautista (RC) .40 1.00
218 Danny Sandoval RC .15 .40
219 Robert Andino RC .15 .40
220 Justin Huber (RC) .15 .40

2006 Bazooka Blue Fortune

*BLUE 1-200: .75X TO 2X BASIC
*BLUE 201-220: .75X TO 2X BASIC
ONE PER PACK

2006 Bazooka Gold Chunks

*GOLD 1-200: .75X TO 2X BASIC
*GOLD 201-220: .75X TO 2X BASIC
ONE CHUNK OR GU PER PACK

2006 Bazooka 4 on 1 Stickers

COMPLETE SET (55) 15.00 40.00
STATED ODDS 1:3 HOBBY, 1:6 RETAIL
1 A-Rod 3.00 8.00
Bonds
Gibs
Mantle
2 Delgado 1.00 2.50
Ortiz
Giambi
Wang
3 Craw .60 1.50
Stewart
Torii
Wells
4 Kend .60 1.50
Lopez
Mauer
Posada
5 Pett 1.25 3.00
Muss
El Duque
Clem
6 Soriano .60 1.50
Hank
Pudge
Raffy
7 Schill .60 1.50
Lowe
Clement
Pedro
8 Andruw .60 1.50
Sheff
Drew
Vlad
9 Maddux 1.25 3.00
Smoltz
Hud
Glav
10 Pujols 1.25 3.00
Lee
Morneau
Teix
11 Ryan 1.25 3.00
Wick
Rivera
Hoff
12 Cam 1.00 2.50
Morse
Piazza
Sween
13 Eck .60 1.50
Rollins
Young
Cabrera
14 Burnett .60 1.50
Pier
Sabathia
Snow
15 Utley 1.25 3.00
Matsui
Ichiro
Iguchi
16 Zito 1.00 2.50
Fran
Duke
Greinke
17 Giles .60 1.50
Buehrle
Mulder
Prior
18 Abreu 1.00 2.50
Manny
Sosa
Pena
19 Belt .60 1.50
Pierre
Wilson
Pod
20 Wag .60 1.50
K-Rod
Street
Nathan

21 Chavez .60 1.50
Mora
Ens
Rolen
22 Garret .60 1.50
Edm
Damon
Alou
23 Jeter 2.50 6.00
Renteria
Lugo
Tejada
24 Fuentes .60 1.50
Willis
Felix
Harden
25 Colon .60 1.50
Zam
Schm
Bonder
26 Carp 1.00 2.50
Santana
Randy
Hall
27 Beck .60 1.50
Bens
Oswalt
Chacon
28 Lopez .60 1.50
Peralta
Reyes
Furcal
29 Verl 3.00 8.00
Wood
Livan
Morris
30 Wilson .60 1.50
Khalil
Nomar
Vizq
31 Bay .40 1.00
Burrell
Baldelli
Green
32 Lidge .40 1.00
Penny
Radke
Rob
33 Franc 1.00 2.50
Weeks
Cano
Tav
34 Jenk 1.00 2.50
Berk
Bigbie
Holliday
35 C.Lee .60 1.50
LoDu
Hall
V-Mart
36 Aramis 1.00 2.50
Chip
Wright
Glaus
37 Rowand .40 1.00
Wilk
Monroe
Winn
38 Boone 1.00 2.50
Beltre
Figg
Castilla
39 Dunn .60 1.50
Floyd
Walker
Gonz
40 Kent .40 1.00
Cantu
Polanco
Bell
41 Biggio .60 1.50
Vidro
Castillo
Hudson
42 Giles .60 1.50
Sizemore
Ford
Swish
43 Crisp .40 1.00
DeJesus
Brown
Burn
44 Gagne .40 1.00
Milton
Peavy
Wright
45 Huff .40 1.00
Kearns
Clark
Logan
46 Sheets .40 1.00
Pavano
Cap
Garl
47 Erstad .40 1.00
Young
Durazo
Haf
48 Conor 1.00 2.50
Dye
Magg
M.Cab
49 Tracy .40 1.00
Over
Sexson
Casey
50 John .60 1.50
Konerko
Iban
Helton
51 James 1.00 2.50
Rasner
Kuo
Marcum
52 Reyes 1.00 2.50
Fausto
Lir
Saund
53 Hern .40 1.00
Bull
Jimerson
Gorz
54 Denorfia .40 1.00
Mathis
Kor
Garko
55 Baut 1.00 2.50
Sand
Andino
Huber

2006 Bazooka Basics Relics

GROUP A ODDS 1:285 H, 1:465 R
GROUP B ODDS 1:124 H, 1:204 R
GROUP C ODDS 1:95 H, 1:155 R
GROUP D ODDS 1:124 H, 1:204 R
AJ Andruw Jones Jsy B 4.00 10.00
AP Albert Pujols Jsy A 6.00 15.00
BA Bobby Abreu Jsy C 3.00 8.00
BR Brian Roberts Jsy C 3.00 8.00
BW Bernie Williams Uni C 4.00 10.00
CB Craig Biggio Jsy B 4.00 10.00
CD Carlos Delgado Jsy B 3.00 8.00
CJ Chipper Jones Jsy A 4.00 10.00
CS Curt Schilling Jsy B 4.00 10.00
DW Dontrelle Willis Jsy D 3.00 8.00
EG Eric Gagne Jsy A 3.00 8.00
HB Hank Blalock Jsy D 3.00 8.00
JD Johnny Damon Jsy B 4.00 10.00
JR Jose Reyes Jsy A 3.00 8.00
LB Lance Berkman Jsy C 3.00 8.00
MC Miguel Cabrera Uni C 4.00 10.00
MG Marcus Giles Jsy D 3.00 8.00
MH Matt Holliday Jsy A 4.00 10.00
ML Mike Lowell Uni C 3.00 8.00
MM Mark Mulder Uni B 3.00 8.00
MMU Mike Mussina Uni D 4.00 10.00
MR Manny Ramirez Jsy B 4.00 10.00
MT Mark Teixeira Jsy A 4.00 10.00
PM Pedro Martinez Uni B 4.00 10.00
SB Sean Burroughs Uni C 3.00 8.00
TH Tim Hudson Uni A 3.00 8.00

2006 Bazooka Blasts Bat Relics

GROUP A ODDS 1:4020 H, 1:6370 R
GROUP B ODDS 1:67 H, 1:108 R
GROUP C ODDS 1:29 H, 1:48 R
GROUP A PRINT RUN 100 SETS
GROUP A ARE NOT SERIAL-NUMBERED
GROUP A PRINT RUN PROVIDED BY TOPPS
AD Adam Dunn B 3.00 8.00
AJ Andruw Jones C 4.00 10.00
AR Alex Rodriguez B 4.00 10.00
ARA Aramis Ramirez C 3.00 8.00
BA Bobby Abreu C 3.00 8.00
BB Barry Bonds A/100 * 15.00 40.00
CB Carlos Beltran C 3.00 8.00
CC Coco Crisp B 3.00 8.00
CF Cliff Floyd C 3.00 8.00
CJ Chipper Jones C 4.00 10.00
CP Corey Patterson B 3.00 8.00
DL Derrek Lee C 4.00 10.00
DO David Ortiz B 4.00 10.00
DW David Wright C 4.00 10.00
GJ Geoff Jenkins B 3.00 8.00
GS Gary Sheffield C 3.00 8.00
HB Hank Blalock B 3.00 8.00
JB Jason Bay B 3.00 8.00
JD Johnny Damon C 4.00 10.00
JDD J.D. Drew B 3.00 8.00
JT Jim Thome B 4.00 10.00
MA Moises Alou C 3.00 8.00
ML Mark Loretta B 3.00 8.00
MM Mickey Mantle A/100 * 125.00 200.00
MP Mike Piazza B 4.00 10.00
MT Miguel Tejada B 3.00 8.00
PK Paul Konerko C 3.00 8.00
PL Paul LoDuca C 3.00 8.00
PW Preston Wilson C 3.00 8.00
SS Sammy Sosa B 4.00 10.00
TG Troy Glaus C 3.00 8.00
TN Trot Nixon B 3.00 8.00
VG Vladimir Guerrero C 4.00 10.00
VM Victor Martinez C 3.00 8.00

2006 Bazooka Comics

COMPLETE SET (24) 6.00 15.00
STATED ODDS 1:4 HOBBY
1 Greg Maddux 1.25 3.00
2 Alex Rodriguez 1.25 3.00
3 Trevor Hoffman .60 1.50
4 Rafael Palmeiro .60 1.50
5 Roy Oswalt .60 1.50
6 Bobby Abreu .40 1.00
7 Miguel Tejada .60 1.50
8 Vladimir Guerrero .60 1.50
9 Mark Teixeira .60 1.50
10 Zach Duke .40 1.00
11 Xavier Nady .40 1.00
12 Alex Rodriguez 1.25 3.00
13 Jeremy Hermida .40 1.00
14 Craig Biggio .60 1.50
15 Manny Ramirez 1.00 2.50
16 Texas Rangers .40 1.00
17 Oakland Athletics .40 1.00
18 Alex Rodriguez 1.25 3.00
19 Jason Giambi .40 1.00
20 Aaron Small .40 1.00
21 Jimmy Rollins .60 1.50
22 Roger Clemens 1.25 3.00
23 White Sox .40 1.00
Mariners
24 Andruw Jones .40 1.00

2006 Bazooka Mickey Mantle Jumbo Reprints

COMPLETE SET (16) 200.00 300.00
ONE PER SEALED HOBBY BOX
1952 Mickey Mantle 1952 15.00 40.00
1953 Mickey Mantle 1953 8.00 20.00
1956 Mickey Mantle 1956 8.00 20.00
1957 Mickey Mantle 1957 8.00 20.00
1958 Mickey Mantle 1958 8.00 20.00
1959 Mickey Mantle 1959 8.00 20.00
1960 Mickey Mantle 1960 8.00 20.00
1961 Mickey Mantle 1961 8.00 20.00
1962 Mickey Mantle 1962 8.00 20.00
1963 Mickey Mantle 1963 8.00 20.00
1964 Mickey Mantle 1964 8.00 20.00
1965 Mickey Mantle 1965 8.00 20.00
1966 Mickey Mantle 1966 8.00 20.00
1967 Mickey Mantle 1967 8.00 20.00
1968 Mickey Mantle 1968 8.00 20.00
1969 Mickey Mantle 1969 8.00 20.00

2006 Bazooka Rewind Relics

GROUP A ODDS 1:2680 H, 1:4250 R
GROUP B ODDS 1:1066 H, 1:1700 R
GROUP C ODDS 1:400 H, 1:653 R
GROUP D ODDS 1:45 H, 1:74 R
GROUP E ODDS 1:56 H, 1:89 R
GROUP F ODDS 1:200 H, 1:324 R
GROUP G ODDS 1:251 H, 1:147 R
GROUP A PRINT RUN 100 SETS
GROUP A ARE NOT SERIAL-NUMBERED
GROUP A PRINT RUN PROVIDED BY TOPPS
NO GROUP A PRICING DUE TO SCARCITY
AJ Andruw Jones Uni C 4.00 10.00
AK Adam Kennedy Bat D 3.00 8.00
AML Adam LaRoche Jsy G 3.00 8.00
AP A.J. Pierzynski Bat D 3.00 8.00
AR Alex Rodriguez Bat F 6.00 15.00
ARO Aaron Rowand Bat E 3.00 8.00
BR Brian Roberts Bat C 3.00 8.00
CB Clint Barmes Bat D 3.00 8.00
CBI Craig Biggio Jsy D 4.00 10.00
CC Carl Crawford Bat C 3.00 8.00
CE Carl Everett Uni C 3.00 8.00
CG Cristian Guzman Bat E 3.00 8.00
CL Carlos Lee Bat E 3.00 8.00
CU Chase Utley Bat D 4.00 10.00
DW Dontrelle Willis Jsy D 3.00 8.00
ER Edgar Renteria Bat E 3.00 8.00
FL Francisco Liriano Jsy B 6.00 15.00
FT Frank Thomas Bat D 4.00 10.00
HR Hanley Ramirez Jsy G 4.00 10.00
JB Jason Botts Bat D 3.00 8.00
JD Jermaine Dye Bat E 3.00 8.00
JDA Johnny Damon Bat E 4.00 10.00
JG Jon Garland Uni C 3.00 8.00
JGU Jose Guillen Bat D 3.00 8.00
JH Justin Huber Jsy F 3.00 8.00
JR Jimmy Rollins Bat D 3.00 8.00
JV Justin Verlander Jsy B 4.00 10.00
KT Kevin Thompson Jsy G 3.00 8.00
LB Lance Berkman Jsy D 3.00 8.00
MG Mark Grudzielanek Bat D 3.00 8.00
MJ Mike Jacobs Bat D 3.00 8.00
MR Manny Ramirez Uni E 4.00 10.00
NC Nelson Cruz Jsy G 3.00 8.00
NJ Nick Johnson Bat D 3.00 8.00
PB Pat Burrell Bat D 3.00 8.00
PK Paul Konerko Bat E 3.00 8.00
RC Robinson Cano Bat E 4.00 10.00
RG Ryan Garko Jsy B 3.00 8.00
RW Rickie Weeks Bat D 3.00 8.00
RWA Ryan Wagner Jsy D 3.00 8.00
SC Shin-Soo Choo Jsy F 3.00 8.00
SP Scott Podsednik Bat D 3.00 8.00
TS Termel Sledge Bat D 3.00 8.00
WB2 William Bergolla Jsy D 3.00 8.00
WT Willy Taveras Jsy D 3.00 8.00

2006 Bazooka Signature Line

GROUP A ODDS 1:21,250 H
GROUP B ODDS 1:3165 H
GROUP C ODDS 1:1261 H
GROUP D ODDS 1:314 H
GROUP A PRINT RUN 15 CARDS
GROUP B PRINT RUN 100 SETS
GROUP A-B ARE NOT SERIAL-NUMBERED
GROUP A-B PRINTS PROVIDED BY TOPPS
NO GROUP A PRICING DUE TO SCARCITY
BM Brandon McCarthy D 6.00 15.00
KM Kevin Millar C 10.00 25.00
ML Victor Zambrano D 10.00 25.00
MM Mike Morse B/100 * 6.00 15.00

2006 Bazooka Stamps

COMPLETE SET (30) 12.50 30.00
STATED ODDS 1:3 HOBBY, 1:6 RETAIL
1 Bobby Abreu .40 1.00
2 Lance Berkman .60 1.50
3 Hank Blalock .40 1.00
4 Barry Bonds 1.50 4.00
5 Mark Buehrle .60 1.50
6 Miguel Cabrera 1.00 2.50
7 Jim Edmonds .60 1.50
8 Morgan Ensberg .40 1.00
9 Jeff Francoeur 1.00 2.50
10 Roy Halladay .60 1.50
11 Tim Hudson .60 1.50
12 Derek Jeter 2.50 6.00
13 Andruw Jones .40 1.00
14 Chipper Jones 1.00 2.50
15 Derrek Lee .40 1.00
16 Mickey Mantle 3.00 8.00
17 Victor Martinez .60 1.50
18 Justin Morneau .60 1.50
19 Manny Ramirez 1.00 2.50
20 Brian Roberts .40 1.00
21 Alex Rodriguez 1.25 3.00
22 Ivan Rodriguez .60 1.50
23 Johan Santana .60 1.50
24 Alfonso Soriano .60 1.50
25 Huston Street .40 1.00
26 Ichiro Suzuki 1.25 3.00
27 Mark Teixeira .60 1.50
28 Miguel Tejada .60 1.50
29 Rickie Weeks .40 1.00
30 Dontrelle Willis .40 1.00

1976 Cool Papa Bell

This set features highlights in the career of Negro League great Cool Papa Bell. The set was issued soon after his induction into the Hall of Fame. We have received reports that this was actually a 20 card set. However, we have only 13 cards checklisted. Collectors with checklist additions are encouraged to contact Beckett. This set was available from the producer for $2.50 at the time of issue.

COMPLETE SET (13) 6.00 15.00
1 Cool Papa Bell .60 1.50
Amazing Speed
2 Cool Papa Bell .40 1.00
Lou Brock
Sets SB Record
3 Cool Papa Bell .60 1.50
4 Cool Papa Bell .60 1.50
Cuba 1928
5 Cool Papa Bell .40 1.00
Great Fielder, Too
6 Cool Papa Bell .60 1.50
HOF, Cooperstown
7 Cool Papa Bell .60 1.50
HOF Favorite
8 Cool Papa Bell .40 1.00
Induction Day, 1974
9 Cool Papa Bell .40 1.00
The Mexican Leagues
10 Cool Papa Bell .60 1.50
On Deck in Cuba
11 Cool Papa Bell .40 1.00
On Deck In Cuba
12 Cool Papa Bell .60 1.50
Touring Havana
13 Cool Papa Bell .75 2.00
Josh Gibson
NNO Header Card .20 .50

1951 Berk Ross

The 1951 Berk Ross set consists of 72 cards (each measuring approximately 2 1/16" by 2 1/2") with tinted photographs, divided evenly into four series (designated in the checklist as 1, 2, 3 and 4). The cards were marketed in boxes containing two card panels, without gum, and the set includes stars of other sports as well as baseball players. The set is sometimes still found in the original packaging. Intact panels command a premium over the listed prices. The catalog designation for this set is W532-1. In every series the first ten cards are baseball players; the set has a heavy emphasis on Yankees and Phillies players as they were in the World Series the year before. The set includes the first card of Bob Cousy as well as a card of Whitey Ford in his Rookie Card year.

COMPLETE SET (72) 900.00 1500.00
1-Jan Al Rosen 6.00 12.00
2-Jan Bob Lemon 12.50 25.00
3-Jan Phil Rizzuto 12.50 25.00
4-Jan Hank Bauer 10.00 20.00
5-Jan Billy Johnson 5.00 10.00
6-Jan Jerry Coleman 5.00 10.00
7-Jan Johnny Mize 12.50 25.00
8-Jan Dom DiMaggio 10.00 20.00
9-Jan Richie Ashburn 20.00 50.00
10-Jan Del Ennis 5.00 10.00
1-Feb Stan Musial 60.00 120.00
2-Feb Warren Spahn 15.00 30.00
3-Feb Tom Henrich 6.00 12.00
4-Feb Yogi Berra 40.00 80.00
5-Feb Joe DiMaggio 200.00 400.00
6-Feb Bobby Brown 6.00 12.00
7-Feb Granny Hamner 5.00 10.00
8-Feb Willie Jones 5.00 10.00
9-Feb Stan Lopata 5.00 10.00
10-Feb Mike Goliat 5.00 10.00
1-Mar Ralph Kiner 12.50 25.00
2-Mar Bill Goodman 5.00 10.00
3-Mar Allie Reynolds 10.00 20.00
4-Mar Vic Raschi 7.50 15.00
5-Mar Joe Page 7.50 15.00
6-Mar Eddie Lopat 10.00 20.00
7-Mar Andy Seminick 5.00 10.00
8-Mar Dick Sisler 5.00 10.00
9-Mar Eddie Waitkus 5.00 10.00
10-Mar Ken Heintzelman 5.00 10.00
1-Apr Gene Woodling 7.50 15.00
2-Apr Cliff Mapes 5.00 10.00
3-Apr Fred Sanford 5.00 10.00
4-Apr Tommy Byrne 5.00 10.00
5-Apr Whitey Ford 50.00 100.00
6-Apr Jim Konstanty 5.00 10.00
7-Apr Russ Meyer 6.00 12.00
8-Apr Robin Roberts 15.00 30.00
9-Apr Curt Simmons 6.00 12.00
10-Apr Sam Jethroe 6.00 12.00

1952 Berk Ross

The 1952 Berk Ross set of 72 unnumbered, tinted photocards, each measuring approximately 2" by 3", seems to have been patterned after the highly successful 1951 Bowman set. The reverses of Ewell Blackwell and Nellie Fox are transposed while Phil Rizzuto comes with two different poses. The complete set below includes both poses of Rizzuto. There is a card of Joe DiMaggio even though he retired after the 1951 season. The catalog designation for this set is W532-2, and the cards have been assigned numbers in the alphabetical checklist below.

COMPLETE SET (72) 2500.00 5000.00
WRAPPER 30.00 60.00
1 Richie Ashburn 25.00 50.00
2 Hank Bauer 7.50 15.00
3 Yogi Berra 60.00 120.00
4 Ewell Blackwell UER 10.00 20.00
Nellie Fox pictured
5 Bobby Brown 7.50 15.00
6 Jim Busby 5.00 10.00
7 Roy Campanella 60.00 120.00
8 Chico Carrasquel 7.50 15.00
9 Jerry Coleman 7.50 15.00
10 Joe Collins 5.00 10.00
11 Alvin Dark 7.50 15.00
12 Dom DiMaggio 10.00 20.00
13 Joe DiMaggio 250.00 500.00
14 Larry Doby 12.50 25.00
15 Bobby Doerr 12.50 25.00
16 Bob Elliott 5.00 10.00
17 Del Ennis 5.00 10.00
18 Ferris Fain 5.00 10.00
19 Bob Feller 30.00 60.00
20 Nellie Fox UER 20.00 40.00
Ewell Blackwell pictured
21 Ned Garver 5.00 10.00
22 Clint Hartung 5.00 10.00
23 Jim Hearn 5.00 10.00
24 Gil Hodges 25.00 50.00
25 Monte Irvin 12.50 25.00
26 Larry Jansen 5.00 10.00
27 Sheldon Jones 5.00 10.00
28 George Kell 12.50 25.00
29 Monte Kennedy 5.00 10.00
30 Ralph Kiner 25.00 50.00
31 Dave Koslo 5.00 10.00
32 Bob Kuzava 5.00 10.00
33 Bob Lemon 12.50 25.00
34 Whitey Lockman 5.00 10.00
35 Ed Lopat 7.50 15.00
36 Sal Maglie 7.50 15.00
37 Mickey Mantle 1500.00 3000.00
38 Billy Martin 25.00 50.00
39 Willie Mays 250.00 500.00
40 Gil McDougald 7.50 15.00
41 Minnie Minoso 10.00 20.00
42 Johnny Mize 25.00 50.00
43 Tom Morgan 5.00 10.00
44 Don Mueller 5.00 10.00
45 Stan Musial 125.00 250.00
46 Don Newcombe 10.00 20.00
47 Ray Noble 5.00 10.00
48 Joe Ostrowski 5.00 10.00
49 Mel Parnell 7.50 15.00
50 Vic Raschi 7.50 15.00
51 Pee Wee Reese 25.00 50.00
52 Allie Reynolds 7.50 15.00
53 Bill Rigney 5.00 10.00
54A Phil Rizzuto 25.00 50.00
Bunting
54B Phil Rizzuto 25.00 50.00
Swinging
55 Robin Roberts 20.00 40.00
56 Eddie Robinson UER 5.00 10.00
White Cox on back
57 Jackie Robinson 300.00 600.00
58 Preacher Roe 7.50 15.00
59 Johnny Sain 7.50 15.00
60 Red Schoendienst 12.50 25.00
61 Duke Snider 60.00 120.00
62 George Spencer 5.00 10.00
63 Eddie Stanky 7.50 15.00
64 Hank Thompson 7.50 15.00
65 Bobby Thomson 10.00 20.00
66 Vic Wertz 5.00 10.00
67 Wally Westlake 5.00 10.00
68 Wes Westrum 5.00 10.00
69 Ted Williams 250.00 500.00
70 Gene Woodling 10.00 20.00
71 Gus Zernial 7.50 15.00

1916 Ferguson Bakery Felt Pennants BF2

These small triangular felt pennants were issued around 1916. The pennants themselves are 8 1/4" in length, whereas the unnumbered paper photos (glued on to the felt pennant) are 1 3/4" by 1 1/4". The photos are black and white and appear to have been taken from Sporting News issues of the same era. These unnumbered pennants are ordered below in alphabetical order within team. The teams themselves are ordered alphabetically within league beginning with the American League.

COMPLETE SET (97) 4500.00 9000.00
1 Jack Barry 50.00 100.00
2 Hick Cady 50.00 100.00
3 Del Gainer 50.00 100.00
4 Harry Hooper 100.00 200.00
5 Dutch Leonard 50.00 100.00
6 Duffy Lewis 50.00 100.00
7 Joe Wood 75.00 150.00
8 Joe Benz 50.00 100.00
9 Eddie Collins 100.00 200.00
10 Shano Collins 50.00 100.00
11 Charles Comiskey OWN 100.00 200.00
12 Red Faber 100.00 200.00
13 Joe Jackson 1500.00 3000.00
14 Jack Lapp 50.00 100.00
15 Eddie Murphy 50.00 100.00
16 Pants Rowland MG 50.00 100.00
17 Reb Russell 50.00 100.00
18 Ray Schalk 100.00 200.00
19 Jim Scott 50.00 100.00
20 Ed Walsh 100.00 200.00
21 Buck Weaver 150.00 300.00
22 Ray Chapman 60.00 120.00
23 Chick Gandil 75.00 150.00
24 Guy Morton 50.00 100.00
25 Donie Bush 50.00 100.00
26 Ty Cobb 1250.00 2500.00
27 Harry Coveleski 50.00 100.00
28 Sam Crawford 100.00 200.00
29 Jean Dubuc 50.00 100.00
30 Hugh Jennings MG 100.00 200.00
31 Oscar Stanage 50.00 100.00
32 Bobby Veach 50.00 100.00
33 Ralph Young 50.00 100.00
34 Frank Baker 100.00 200.00
35 Joe Gideon 50.00 100.00
36 Wally Pipp 60.00 120.00
37 Napoleon Lajoie 200.00 400.00
38 Connie Mack MG 200.00 400.00
39 Stuffy McInnis 60.00 120.00
40 Rube Oldring 50.00 100.00
41 Wally Schang 60.00 120.00
42 Earl Hamilton 50.00 100.00
43 Fielder Jones 50.00 100.00
44 Doc Lavan 50.00 100.00
45 George Sisler 100.00 200.00
46 Eddie Foster 50.00 100.00
47 Walter Johnson 400.00 800.00
48 Joe Judge 50.00 100.00
49 George McBride 50.00 100.00
50 Clyde Milan 60.00 120.00
51 Ray Morgan 50.00 100.00
52 Johnny Evers 100.00 200.00
53 Hank Gowdy 50.00 100.00
54 Bill James 50.00 100.00
55 Sherry Magee 60.00 120.00
56 Rabbit Maranville 100.00 200.00
57 Dick Rudolph 50.00 100.00
58 George Stallings MG 50.00 100.00
59 Lefty Tyler 50.00 100.00
60 Jake Daubert 50.00 100.00
61 Rube Marquard 100.00 200.00
62 Chief Meyers 60.00 120.00
63 Otto Miller 50.00 100.00
64 Nap Rucker 50.00 100.00
65 Jimmy Archer 50.00 100.00
66 Mordecai Brown 100.00 200.00
67 Claude Hendrix 50.00 100.00
68 Jimmy Lavender 50.00 100.00
69 Vic Saier 50.00 100.00
70 Wildfire Schulte 50.00 100.00
71 Joe Tinker 100.00 200.00
72 Hippo Vaughn 50.00 100.00
73 Heine Zimmerman 50.00 100.00
74 Buck Herzog 50.00 100.00
75 Ivy Wingo 50.00 100.00
76 George Burns 50.00 100.00
77 Red Dooin 50.00 100.00
78 Larry Doyle 60.00 120.00
79 Bennie Kauff 50.00 100.00
80 Hans Lobert 50.00 100.00
81 John McGraw MG 150.00 300.00
82 Fred Merkle 50.00 100.00
83 Jeff Tesreau 50.00 100.00
84 Grover C. Alexander 150.00 300.00
85 Dave Bancroft 100.00 200.00
86 Chief Bender 100.00 200.00
87 Gavvy Cravath 60.00 120.00
88 Josh Devore 50.00 100.00
89 Bill Killefer 50.00 100.00
90 Fred Luderus 50.00 100.00
91 Pat Moran 50.00 100.00
92 Dode Paskert 50.00 100.00
93 Max Carey 100.00 200.00
94 Al Mamaux 50.00 100.00
95 Honus Wagner 400.00 800.00
96 Miller Huggins 100.00 200.00
97 Slim Sallee 50.00 100.00

1937 BF104 Blanket

These blankets, which measure approximately 3 1/2" feature some of the leading players of the late 1930's. The fronts have the player's name on top with his team and league in separate "flags". The player's photo takes up the rest of the blanket. Since these are unnumbered, we have sequenced them in alphabetical order. It is possible this list is incomplete, so all additions are appreciated.

COMPLETE SET (23) 1500.00 3000.00
1 Luke Appling 125.00 250.00
2 Moe Berg 150.00 300.00
3 Cy Blanton 50.00 100.00
4 Mickey Cochrane 125.00 250.00
5 Joe Cronin 125.00 250.00
6 Tony Cuccinello 50.00 100.00
7 Dizzy Dean 200.00 400.00
8 Jimmie Dykes 60.00 120.00
9 Jimmie Foxx 200.00 400.00
10 Frankie Frisch 125.00 250.00
11 Woody Jensen 50.00 100.00
12 Harry Kelly 50.00 100.00
13 Thornton Lee 50.00 100.00
14 Connie Mack MG 150.00 300.00
16 Stu Martin 50.00 100.00
17 Joe Medwick 125.00 250.00
18 Ray Mueller 50.00 100.00
19 Bobo Newsome 60.00 120.00
20 Monty Stratton 75.00 150.00
21 Pie Traynor 125.00 250.00
22 Jim Turner 60.00 120.00
23 Bill Werber 60.00 120.00
24 Rudy York 60.00 120.00
15 Danny MacFayden 60.00 120.00

1916-20 Big Head Strip Cards W-UNC

These cards, which feature a player drawing with an enlarged head and the players name in an upper corner, were issued between 1916 and 1920. Since these cards are unnumbered, we have sequenced them in alphabetical order.

COMPLETE SET (20) 4000.00 8000.00
1 Jim Bagby 100.00 200.00
2 Frank Baker 300.00 600.00
3 Dave Bancroft 250.00 500.00
4 Ping Bodie 100.00 200.00
5 George Burns 100.00 200.00
6 Leon Cadore 125.00 250.00
7 Ty Cobb 1000.00 2000.00
8 Larry Doyle 125.00 250.00
9 Heinie Groh 100.00 200.00
10 Rogers Hornsby 800.00 1600.00
11 Walter Johnson 800.00 1600.00
12 Joe Judge 100.00 200.00
13 Ed Konetchy 100.00 200.00
14 Carl Mays 125.00 250.00
15 Clyde Milan 100.00 200.00
16 Sam Rice 250.00 500.00
17 Babe Ruth 1200.00 2400.00
18 Ray Schalk 250.00 500.00
19 Wally Schang 125.00 250.00
20 George Sisler 250.00 500.00

1986 Big League Chew

This 12-card standard-size set was produced by Big League Chew and was inserted in with their packages of Big League Chew gum, which were shaped and styled after a pouch of chewing tobacco. The cards were found one per pouch of shredded gum or were available through a mail-in offer of two coupons and $2.00 for a complete set. The cards in the packs often were damaged in the packaging process. The players featured are members of the 500 career home run club. The backs are printed in blue ink on white card stock. The set is subtitled "Home Run Legends". The front of each card shows a year inside a small flag; the year is the year that player passed 500 homers.

COMPLETE SET (12) 2.50 6.00
1 Hank Aaron .60 1.50
2 Babe Ruth .75 2.00
3 Willie Mays .60 1.50
4 Frank Robinson .20 .50
5 Harmon Killebrew .20 .50
6 Mickey Mantle .75 2.00
7 Jimmie Foxx .20 .50
8 Ted Williams .60 1.50
9 Ernie Banks .20 .50
10 Eddie Mathews .20 .50
11 Mel Ott .20 .50
12 500 HR Members .08 .25

1983 Big League Collectibles Original All-Stars

This 40-card set measures approximately 2 1/2" by 3 3/4" and features colorized individual player pictures of the original 1933 All-Star teams of both the American and National leagues. The backs carry player information and either their 1933 batting or pitching record. The set was issued in honor of the 50th Anniversary of the first All-Star Game (popularly known as The Game of the Century) that was played at Comiskey Park in Chicago, Illinois, on July 6, 1933. Only 10,000 of each set were produced and were sequentially numbered on the back of card number 1 which carried the AL All-Star Team photo. The set was originally available from the producer for $8 each.

COMP. FACT. SET (40) 10.00 25.00
1 AL All-Star Team .08 .25
2 Connie Mack MG .20 .50
3 Alvin Crowder .08 .25
4 Lefty Gomez .40 1.00
5 Jimmy Dykes .08 .25
6 Earl Averill .40 1.00
7 Charlie Gehringer .40 1.00
8 Lefty Grove .40 1.00
9 Lou Gehrig 1.25 3.00
10 Al Simmons .40 1.00
11 Ben Chapman .08 .25
12 Jimmie Foxx .60 1.50
13 Oral Hildebrand .08 .25
14 Joe Cronin .40 1.00
15 Bill Dickey .40 1.00
16 Sam West .08 .25
17 Rick Ferrell .20 .50
18 Tony Lazzeri .40 1.00
19 Wes Ferrell .08 .25
20 Babe Ruth 2.00 5.00
21 NL All-Star Team CL .08 .25
22 John McGraw MG .20 .50
23 Pepper Martin .08 .25
24 Woody English .08 .25
25 Paul Waner .40 1.00
26 Lefty O'Doul .08 .25
27 Chuck Klein .40 1.00
28 Tony Cuccinello .08 .25
29 Frankie Frisch .40 1.00
30 Gabby Hartnett .40 1.00
31 Carl Hubbell .40 1.00
32 Chick Hafey .20 .50
33 Dick Bartell .08 .25
34 Bill Hallahan .08 .25
35 Hal Schumacher .08 .25
36 Lon Warneke .08 .25
37 Wally Berger .08 .25
38 Bill Terry .40 1.00
39 Jimmy Wilson .08 .25
40 Pie Traynor .40 1.00

1985 Big League Collectibles 30s

This 90-card limited edition set features white-bordered color portraits of players who played during the 1930's. The cards measure approximately 2 1/8" by 3 1/8". The backs carry a paragraph about the player and either his pitching or batting record. Only 5,000 sets were produced and are sequentially numbered on the title card.

COMP. FACT. SET (90) 15.00 40.00
1 Title Card .08 .25
2 Bucky Walters .20 .50
3 Monte Pearson .08 .25
4 Stan Hack .20 .50
5 Joe Cronin .40 1.00
6 Leo Durocher .30 .75
7 Max Bishop .08 .25
8 Don Hurst .08 .25
9 Barney McCosky .08 .25
10 Remy Ray Kremer .08 .25
11 Julius Moose Solters .08 .25
12 Danny MacFayden .08 .25
13 Mickey Cochrane .40 1.00
14 Ethan Allen .08 .25
15 Lu Blue .08 .25
16 Johnny Mize .40 1.00
17 Joe DiMaggio 1.25 3.00
18 George Grantham .08 .25
19 Willie Kamm .08 .25
20 Charlie Root .08 .25
21 Moe Berg .75 2.0
22 Floyd Babe Herman .20 .50
23 Heinie Manush .40 1.0
24 Dolf Camilli .20 .5
25 Rudy York .20 .5
26 Truett Rip Sewell .08 .2
27 Rick Ferrell .20 .5
28 Arthur Pinky Whitney .08 .2
29 Edmund Bing Miller .08 .2
30 Gus Mancuso .08 .2
31 John Jocko Conlan .20 .5
32 Joe Medwick .40 1.0
33 Johnny Allen .08 .2
34 Johnny Vander Meer .20 .5
35 Earl Averill .40 1.0
36 Taylor Douthit .08 .2
37 Charles Buddy Myer .08 .2
38 Van Lingle Mungo .20 .5

39 Smead Jolley .08 .25
40 Flint Rhem .08 .25
41 Leon Goose Goslin .40 1.00
42 Adam Comorsky .08 .25
43 Jack Burns .08 .25
44 Ed Brandt .08 .25
45 Bob Johnson .08 .25
46 Mel Ott .40 1.00
47 Monty Stratton .20 .50
48 Paul Daffy Dean .20 .50
49 Lou Gehrig 1.25 3.00
50 Frank Buck McCormick .08 .25
51 Jeff Heath .08 .25
52 Charles Gabby Hartnett .08 .25
53 Ossie Bluege .08 .25
54 Babe Ruth 2.00 5.00
55 Bobby Doerr .40 1.00
56 Virgil Spud Davis .08 .25
57 Dale Alexander .08 .25
58 Jim Tobin .08 .25
59 Joseph Vosmik .08 .25
60 Al Lopez .40 1.00
61 Jimmie Foxx .75 2.00
62 Fred Fitzsimmons .20 .50
63 Bob Fothergill .08 .25
64 Mort Cooper .08 .25
65 George Twinkletoes Selkirk .08 .25
66 Burton Shotton .08 .25
67 Bob Feller .60 1.50
68 Larry French .08 .25
69 Joseph Judge .08 .25
70 Clyde Sukeforth .08 .25
71 Jim Tabor .08 .25
72 Silas Johnson .08 .25
73 Earl Webb .08 .25
74 Charles Red Lucas .08 .25
75 Ralph Kress .08 .25
76 Casey Stengel .50 1.25
77 George Mule Haas .08 .25
78 Joe Jo-Jo Moore .08 .25
79 Carl Reynolds .08 .25
80 James Tex Carleton .08 .25
81 Johnny Murphy .08 .25
82 Paul Derringer .08 .25
83 Harold Trosky .20 .50
84 Fred Lindstrom .40 1.00
85 Jack Russell .08 .25
86 Stan Frenchy Bordagaray .08 .25
87 Roy Johnson .08 .25
88 Sylvester Johnson .08 .25
89 Mike Pinky Higgins .08 .25
90 Arky Vaughan .40 1.00

1989 Bimbo Bread Discs

The 1989 Bimbo Bread set is a 12-disc set issued in Puerto Rico which measured 2 3/4" in diameter. This set features only Puerto Rican players. The top center of the the front of the disk has the Bimbo Bear logo. The previous years stats are on the back.

COMPLETE SET (12) 6.00 15.00
1 Carmelo Martinez .20 .50
2 Candy Maldonado .20 .50
3 Benito Santiago .30 .75
4 Rey Quinones .20 .50
5 Jose Oquendo .20 .50
6 Ruben Sierra .30 .75
7 Jose Lind .20 .50
8 Juan Beniquez .20 .50
9 Willie Hernandez .30 .75
10 Juan Nieves .20 .50
11 Jose Guzman .20 .50
12 Roberto Alomar 4.00 10.00

2005 Biography Hank Aaron HR

COMMON CARD 3.00 8.00
OVERALL LCM ODDS 1:40
OVERALL LEAF LIMITED FOIL ODDS 1:5
OVERALL PRIME CUTS FOIL ODDS APPX 1:1
1-16 ISSUED IN '05 LEAF CERT.MATERIALS
17-45 ISSUED IN '05 LEAF LIMITED
46-110 ISSUED IN '05 PRIME CUTS III

2005 Biography Hank Aaron HR Autograph

COMMON CARD 125.00 200.00
OVERALL LCM ODDS 1:40
OVERALL LEAF LIMITED AU ODDS 1:147
1-5 ISSUED IN '05 LEAF CERT.MATERIALS
6-32 ISSUED IN '05 LEAF LIMITED
33-110 ISSUED IN '05 PRIME CUT III
1 AND 44 NO PRICING DUE TO SCARCITY

2005 Biography Hank Aaron HR Materials

COMMON 1-2 PIECE JSY 20.00 50.00
COMMON 2-PIECE BAT 15.00 40.00
COMMON 3-PIECE BAT 20.00 50.00
OVERALL LCM ODDS 1:40
OVERALL LTD AU-GU ODDS 1:10
1-17 ISSUED IN '05 LEAF CERT.MATERIALS
18-40 ISSUED IN '05 LEAF LIMITED
41-110 ISSUED IN '05 PRIME CUTS III
CARD 44 NOT PRICED DUE TO SCARCITY

2005 Biography George Brett HR

COMMON CARD 4.00 10.00
OVERALL LCM ODDS 1:40
OVERALL LEAF LIMITED FOIL ODDS 1:5
1-38 ISSUED IN '05 LEAF CERT.MATERIALS
39-51 ISSUED IN '05 LEAF LIMITED

2005 Biography George Brett HR Materials

COMMON JERSEY 10.00 25.00
OVERALL LCM ODDS 1:40
OVERALL LEAF LIMITED GU ODDS 1:52
1-45 ISSUED IN '05 LEAF CERT.MATERIALS
46-51 ISSUED IN '05 LEAF LIMITED
CARD 5 NOT PRICED DUE TO SCARCITY
1 George Brett Jsy 15.00 40.00

2005 Biography Roberto Clemente Gold Glove

COMMON CARD 6.00 15.00
OVERALL LCM ODDS 1:40
OVERALL LEAF LIMITED FOIL ODDS 1:5
OVERALL PRIME CUTS FOIL ODDS APPX 1:1
1961-62 ISSUED IN '05 LEAF CERT.MAT'L
1963-1966 ISSUED IN '05 LEAF LIMITED
1967-1972 ISSUED IN '05 PRIME CUTS III

2005 Biography Roberto Clemente Gold Glove Materials

COMMON BAT 30.00 60.00
OVERALL LCM ODDS 1:40
OVERALL LEAF LIMITED GU ODDS 1:52
1961-62 ISSUED IN '05 LEAF CERT.MAT'L
1963-1966 ISSUED IN '05 LEAF LIMITED
1967-1972 ISSUED IN '05 PRIME CUTS III

2005 Biography Roberto Clemente HR

COMMON CARD 6.00 15.00
OVERALL LCM ODDS 1:40
OVERALL LEAF LIMITED FOIL ODDS 1:5
OVERALL PRIME CUTS FOIL ODDS APPX 1:1
1-8 ISSUED IN '05 LEAF CERT.MATERIALS
9-28 ISSUED IN '05 LEAF LIMITED
29-75 ISSUED IN '05 PRIME CUTS III

2005 Biography Roberto Clemente HR Materials

COMMON BAT 30.00 60.00
OVERALL LCM ODDS 1:40
OVERALL LEAF LIMITED GU ODDS 1:52
1-18 ISSUED IN '05 LEAF CERT.MATERIALS
19-28 ISSUED IN '05 LEAF LIMITED
29-75 ISSUED IN '05 PRIME CUTS III
CARD 21 NOT PRICED DUE TO SCARCITY

2005 Biography Sandy Koufax Wins

COMMON CARD 6.00 15.00
OVERALL LCM ODDS 1:40
OVERALL LEAF LIMITED FOIL ODDS 1:5
OVERALL PRIME CUTS FOIL ODDS APPX 1:1
1-40 ISSUED IN '05 LEAF CERT.MATERIALS
41-80 ISSUED IN '05 LEAF LIMITED
81-165 ISSUED IN '05 PRIME CUTS III
1-9 ARE BROOKLYN CARDS
10-165 ARE LOS ANGELES CARDS

2005 Biography Sandy Koufax Wins Autograph

COMMON CARD 300.00 400.00
OVERALL LCM ODDS 1:40
OVERALL LEAF LIMITED AU ODDS 1:147
CARD 72 ISSUED IN '05 LEAF CERT.MAT'L
CARDS 72 & 134 ISSUED IN '05 LEAF LTD
CARDS 67 & 99 ISSUED IN '05 PR.CUTS III
CL: 67/72/99/134

2005 Biography Sandy Koufax Wins Materials

COMMON 1-2 PIECE JSY 20.00 50.00
COMMON 3-PIECE JSY 20.00 50.00
OVERALL LCM ODDS 1:40
OVERALL LEAF LIMITED GU ODDS 1:52
1-22 ISSUED IN '05 LEAF CERT.MATERIALS
23-50 ISSUED IN '05 LEAF LIMITED
51-165 ISSUED IN '05 PRIME CUTS III
1-9 ARE BROOKLYN CARDS
10-165 ARE LOS ANGELES CARDS
CARD 32 NOT PRICED DUE TO SCARCITY

2005 Biography Roger Maris HR 1961 Season

COMMON CARD 3.00 8.00
OVERALL LCM ODDS 1:40
OVERALL LEAF LIMITED FOIL ODDS 1:5
OVERALL PRIME CUTS FOIL ODDS APPX 1:1
1-20 ISSUED IN '05 LEAF CERT.MATERIALS
21-41 ISSUED IN '05 LEAF LIMITED
42-61 ISSUED IN '05 PRIME CUTS III

2005 Biography Roger Maris HR 1961 Season Materials

COMMON BAT 30.00 60.00
OVERALL LCM ODDS 1:40
OVERALL LEAF LIMITED GU ODDS 1:52
1-50 ISSUED IN '05 LEAF CERT.MATERIALS
51-61 ISSUED IN '05 LEAF LIMITED
9 AND 61 NOT PRICED DUE TO SCARCITY

2005 Biography Willie Mays HR Gold Glove

COMMON CARD 3.00 8.00
OVERALL LCM ODDS 1:40
OVERALL LEAF LIMITED FOIL ODDS 1:5
OVERALL PRIME CUTS FOIL ODDS APPX 1:1
1957-58 ISSUED IN '05 LEAF CERT.MAT'L
1959-64 ISSUED IN '05 LEAF LIMITED
1965-68 ISSUEDC IN '05 PRIME CUTS III
1957 CARD IS NY GIANTS
1958-68 CARDS ARE SF GIANTS

2005 Biography Willie Mays Gold Glove Autograph

COMMON CARD 75.00 150.00
OVERALL LEAF LIMITED AU ODDS 1:147
1957-58 ISSUED IN '05 LEAF LIMITED
1959-68 ISSUED IN '05 PRIME CUTS III
*ADD 25% FOR NOTATION AUTOS

2005 Biography Willie Mays Gold Glove Materials

COMMON JERSEY (1957) 15.00 40.00
COMMON PANTS (1958-68) 15.00 40.00
OVERALL LCM ODDS 1:40
OVERALL LTD AU-GU ODDS 1:10
1957-58 ISSUED IN '05 LEAF CERT.MAT'L
1959-61 ISSUED IN '05 LEAF LIMITED
1962-68 ISSUED IN '05 PRIME CUTS III

2005 Biography Willie Mays HR

COMMON CARD 3.00 8.00
OVERALL LCM ODDS 1:40
OVERALL LEAF LIMITED FOIL ODDS 1:5
OVERALL PRIME CUTS FOIL ODDS APPX 1:1
1-10 ISSUED IN '05 LEAF CERT.MATERIALS
10-30 ISSUED IN '05 LEAF LIMITED
31-68 ISSUED IN '05 PRIME CUTS III

2005 Biography Willie Mays HR Autograph

COMMON CARD 75.00 150.00
OVERALL LCM ODDS 1:40
OVERALL LEAF LIMITED AU ODDS 1:147
1-5 ISSUED IN '05 LEAF CERT.MATERIALS
6-28 ISSUED IN '05 LEAF LIMITED
29-68 ISSUED IN '05 PRIME CUTS III
*ADD 25% FOR NOTATION AUTOS
1 AND 24 PRICING DUE TO SCARCITY

2005 Biography Willie Mays HR Materials

COMMON JERSEY 15.00 40.00
OVERALL LCM ODDS 1:40
OVERALL LEAF LIMITED GU ODDS 1:52
1-17 ISSUED IN '05 LEAF CERT.MATERIALS
18-29 ISSUED IN '05 LEAF LIMITED
30-68 ISSUED IN '05 PRIME CUTS III
CARD 24 NOT PRICED DUE TO SCARCITY

2005 Biography Cal Ripken HR

COMMON CARD 6.00 15.00
OVERALL LCM ODDS 1:40
OVERALL LEAF LIMITED FOIL ODDS 1:5
OVERALL PRIME CUTS FOIL ODDS APPX 1:1
1-27 ISSUED IN '05 LEAF CERT.MATERIALS
28-54 ISSUED IN '05 LEAF LIMITED
55-82 ISSUED IN '05 PRIME CUTS III

2005 Biography Cal Ripken HR Autograph

COMMON CARD 75.00 150.00
OVERALL LCM ODDS 1:40
OVERALL LEAF LIMITED AU ODDS 1:147
1-58 ISSUED IN '05 LEAF CERT.MATERIALS
59-68 ISSUED IN '05 LEAF LIMITED
69-82 ISSUED IN '05 PRIME CUTS III
1 AND 8 NOT PRICED DUE TO SCARCITY

2005 Biography Cal Ripken HR Materials

COMMON JERSEY 15.00 40.00
OVERALL LCM ODDS 1:40
OVERALL LEAF LIMITED GU ODDS 1:52
1-41 ISSUED IN '05 LEAF CERT.MATERIALS
42-54 ISSUED IN '05 LEAF LIMITED
55-82 ISSUED IN '05 PRIME CUTS III
CARD 8 NOT PRICED DUE TO SCARCITY

2005 Biography Babe Ruth HR

COMMON CARD (1-49) 4.00 10.00
COMMON CARD (50-162) 4.00 10.00
OVERALL LCM ODDS 1:40
OVERALL LEAF LIMITED FOIL ODDS 1:5
OVERALL PRIME CUTS FOIL ODDS APPX 1:1
1-40 ISSUED IN '05 LEAF CERT.MATERIALS
41-80 ISSUED IN '05 LEAF LIMITED
81-162 ISSUED IN '05 PRIME CUTS III
1-49 ARE RED SOX CARDS
50-162 ARE YANKEES CARDS

2005 Biography Babe Ruth HR Materials

COMMON R.SOX BAT 100.00 200.00
COM.YANK.1-2 PIECE BAT 100.00 200.00
COM.YANK.3-PIECE BAT 125.00 250.00
OVERALL LCM ODDS 1:40
OVERALL LTD AU-GU ODDS 1:10
1-28 ISSUED IN '05 LEAF CERT.MATERIALS
29-47 ISSUED IN '05 LEAF LIMITED
48-162 ISSUED IN '05 PRIME CUTS III
1-49 ARE RED SOX CARDS
50-162 ARE YANKEES CARDS
1/3/60 NO PRICING DUE TO SCARCITY

2005 Biography Nolan Ryan Wins

COMMON CARD (1-29) 4.00 10.00
COMMON CARD (30-91) 4.00 10.00
OVERALL LCM ODDS 1:40
OVERALL LEAF LIMITED FOIL ODDS 1:5
OVERALL PRIME CUTS FOIL ODDS APPX 1:1
1-23 ISSUED IN '05 LEAF CERT.MATERIALS
24-53 ISSUED IN '05 LEAF LIMITED
54-91 ISSUED IN '05 PRIME CUTS III
1-29 ARE METS CARDS
30-91 ARE ANGELS CARDS

2005 Biography Nolan Ryan Wins Autograph

COMMON METS 100.00 200.00
COMMON ANGELS 100.00 200.00
OVERALL LCM ODDS 1:40
OVERALL LTD AU-GU ODDS 1:10
1-9 ISSUED IN '05 LEAF CERT.MATERIALS
10-26 ISSUED IN '05 LEAF LIMITED
27-91 ISSUED IN '05 PRIME CUTS III
1-29 ARE METS CARDS
30-91 ARE ANGELS CARDS
1 AND 30 NOT PRICED DUE TO SCARCITY

2005 Biography Nolan Ryan Wins Materials

COMMON JERSEY (1-29) 15.00 40.00
COMMON JACKET (31-91) 15.00 40.00
OVERALL LCM ODDS 1:40
OVERALL LTD AU-GU ODDS 1:10
1-15 ISSUED IN '05 PRIME CUTS III
16-30 ISSUED IN '05 LEAF LIMITED
31-91 ISSUED IN '05 LEAF CERT.MATERIALS
1-29 ARE METS JERSEY FABRIC CARDS
30-91 ARE ANGELS JACKET FABRIC CARDS
CARD 30 NOT PRICED DUE TO SCARCITY

2005 Biography Mike Schmidt HR

COMMON CARD 3.00 8.00
OVERALL LCM ODDS 1:40
OVERALL LEAF LIMITED FOIL ODDS 1:5
1-41 ISSUED IN '05 LEAF CERT.MATERIALS
42-55 ISSUED IN '05 LEAF LIMITED

2005 Biography Mike Schmidt HR Autograph

COMMON CARD 30.00 60.00
OVERALL LCM ODDS 1:40
OVERALL LEAF LIMITED AU ODDS 1:147
1-45 ISSUED IN '05 LEAF CERT.MATERIALS
46-55 ISSUED IN '05 LEAF LIMITED
1 AND 20 NOT PRICED DUE TO SCARCITY

2005 Biography Mike Schmidt HR Materials

COMMON JERSEY 6.00 15.00
OVERALL LCM ODDS 1:40
OVERALL LEAF LIMITED GU ODDS 1:52
1-45 ISSUED IN '05 LEAF CERT.MATERIALS
46-55 ISSUED IN '05 LEAF LIMITED
CARD 20 NOT PRICED DUE TO SCARCITY
1 Mike Schmidt Jsy 10.00 25.00

2005 Biography Ted Williams HR

COMMON CARD 5.00 12.00
OVERALL LCM ODDS 1:40
OVERALL LEAF LIMITED FOIL ODDS 1:5
OVERALL PRIME CUTS FOIL ODDS APPX 1:1
1-20 ISSUED IN '05 LEAF CERT.MATERIALS
21-51 ISSUED IN '05 LEAF LIMITED
52-91 ISSUED IN '05 PRIME CUTS III

2005 Biography Ted Williams HR Materials

COMMON BAT 20.00 50.00
OVERALL LCM ODDS 1:40
OVERALL LEAF LIMITED GU ODDS 1:52
1-34 ISSUED IN '05 LEAF CERT.MATERIALS
35-48 ISSUED IN '05 LEAF LIMITED
49-91 ISSUED IN '05 PRIME CUTS III
CARD 9 NOT PRICED DUE TO SCARCITY

1999 Black Diamond

This 120-card set, produced by Upper Deck, was released in December, 1998 in six-card packs with a SRP of $3.99. This set features color player photos of 90 of Baseball's top collectible stars and photos of 30 star rookies and most promising prospects called Diamond Debut. The Diamond Debut cards were seeded into packs at a rate on one in four.

COMPLETE SET (120) 30.00 80.00
COMP.SET w/o DD's (90) 10.00 25.00
DIAMOND DEBUT STATED ODDS 1:4
1 Darin Erstad .15 .40
2 Tim Salmon .15 .40
3 Jim Edmonds .25 .60
4 Matt Williams .15 .40
5 David Dellucci .15 .40
6 Jay Bell .15 .40
7 Andres Galarraga .25 .60
8 Chipper Jones .40 1.00
9 Greg Maddux .50 1.25
10 Andruw Jones .15 .40
11 Cal Ripken 1.25 3.00
12 Rafael Palmeiro .25 .60
13 Brady Anderson .15 .40
14 Mike Mussina .25 .60
15 Nomar Garciaparra .25 .60
16 Mo Vaughn .15 .40
17 Pedro Martinez .25 .60
18 Sammy Sosa .40 1.00
19 Henry Rodriguez .15 .40
20 Frank Thomas .40 1.00
21 Magglio Ordonez .25 .60
22 Albert Belle .15 .40
23 Paul Konerko .15 .40
24 Sean Casey .15 .40
25 Jim Thome .25 .60
26 Kenny Lofton .15 .40
27 Sandy Alomar Jr. .15 .40
28 Jaret Wright .15 .40
29 Larry Walker .25 .60
30 Todd Helton .25 .60
31 Vinny Castilla .15 .40
32 Tony Clark .15 .40
33 Damion Easley .15 .40
34 Mark Kotsay .15 .40
35 Derrek Lee .15 .40
36 Moises Alou .15 .40
37 Jeff Bagwell .25 .60
38 Craig Biggio .25 .60
39 Randy Johnson .40 1.00
40 Dean Palmer .15 .40
41 Johnny Damon .25 .60
42 Chan Ho Park .25 .60
43 Raul Mondesi .15 .40
44 Gary Sheffield .15 .40
45 Jeromy Burnitz .15 .40
46 Marquis Grissom .15 .40
47 Jeff Cirillo .15 .40
48 Paul Molitor .40 1.00
49 Todd Walker .15 .40
50 Vladimir Guerrero .25 .60
51 Brad Fullmer .15 .40
52 Mike Piazza .40 1.00
53 Hideo Nomo .40 1.00
54 Carlos Baerga .15 .40
55 John Olerud .15 .40
56 Derek Jeter 1.00 2.50
57 Hideki Irabu .15 .40
58 Tino Martinez .15 .40
59 Bernie Williams .25 .60
60 Miguel Tejada .25 .60
61 Ben Grieve .15 .40
62 Jason Giambi .15 .40
63 Scott Rolen .25 .60
64 Doug Glanville .15 .40
65 Desi Relaford .15 .40
66 Tony Womack .15 .40
67 Jason Kendall .15 .40
68 Jose Guillen .15 .40
69 Tony Gwynn .40 1.00
70 Ken Caminiti .15 .40
71 Greg Vaughn .15 .40
72 Kevin Brown .15 .40
73 Barry Bonds .60 1.50
74 J.T. Snow .15 .40
75 Jeff Kent .15 .40
76 Ken Griffey Jr. .75 2.00
77 Alex Rodriguez .50 1.25
78 Edgar Martinez .25 .60
79 Jay Buhner .15 .40
80 Mark McGwire .60 1.50
81 Delino DeShields .15 .40
82 Brian Jordan .15 .40
83 Quinton McCracken .15 .40
84 Fred McGriff .25 .60
85 Juan Gonzalez .15 .40
86 Ivan Rodriguez .25 .60
87 Will Clark .25 .60
88 Roger Clemens .50 1.25
89 Jose Cruz Jr. .15 .40
90 Babe Ruth 1.00 2.50
91 Troy Glaus DD .60 1.50
92 Jarrod Washburn DD .60 1.50
93 Travis Lee DD .60 1.50
94 Bruce Chen DD .60 1.50
95 Mike Caruso DD .60 1.50
96 Jim Parque DD .60 1.50
97 Kerry Wood DD .60 1.50
98 Jeremy Giambi DD .60 1.50
99 Matt Anderson DD .60 1.50
100 Seth Greisinger DD .60 1.50
101 Gabe Alvarez DD .60 1.50
102 Rafael Medina DD .60 1.50
103 Daryle Ward DD .60 1.50
104 Alex Cora DD 1.00 2.50
105 Adrian Beltre DD 1.50 4.00
106 Geoff Jenkins DD .60 1.50
107 Eric Milton DD .60 1.50
108 Carl Pavano DD .60 1.50
109 Eric Chavez DD .60 1.50
110 Orlando Hernandez DD .60 1.50
111 A.J. Hinch DD .60 1.50
112 Carlton Loewer DD .60 1.50
113 Aramis Ramirez DD .60 1.50
114 Cliff Politte DD .60 1.50
115 Matt Clement DD .60 1.50
116 Alex Gonzalez DD .60 1.50
117 J.D. Drew DD .60 1.50
118 Shane Monahan DD .60 1.50
119 Rolando Arrojo DD .60 1.50
120 George Lombard DD .60 1.50

1999 Black Diamond Double

COMPLETE SET (120) 150.00 300.00
*DOUBLE: 2.5X TO 6X BASIC
*DOUBLE.DEB: .6X TO 1.5X BASIC DEB
RANDOM INSERTS IN PACKS
1-90 PRINT RUN 3000 SERIAL #'d SETS
91-120 PRINT RUN 2500 SERIAL #'d SETS
GRIFFEY/MAC/SOSA 1998 #'D OF EACH

1999 Black Diamond Triple

COMPLETE SET (120) 250.00 500.00
*TRIPLE: 4X TO 10X BASIC
*TRIPLE.DEB: 1X TO 2.5X BASIC DEB
RANDOM INSERTS IN PACKS
1-90 PRINT RUN 1500 SERIAL #'d SETS
91-120 PRINT RUN 1000 SERIAL #'d SETS
GRIF/MAC/SOSA PRINTS=CAREER TOTAL
18 Sammy Sosa/273 6.00 15.00
76 Ken Griffey Jr./350 12.00 30.00
80 Mark McGwire/457 10.00 25.00

1999 Black Diamond Quadruple

*QUAD: 12.5X TO 25X BASIC
*QUAD.DEB: 2.5X TO 6X BASIC DEB.
RANDOM INSERTS IN PACKS
1-90 PRINT RUN 150 SERIAL #'d SETS
91-120 PRINT RUN 100 SERIAL #'D SETS
GRIFFEY/MAC/SOSA PRINTS=98 HR TOTAL

1999 Black Diamond A Piece of History

RANDOM INSERTS IN PACKS
STATED PRINT RUN 350 SETS
BW Bernie Williams 6.00 15.00
JG Juan Gonzalez 4.00 10.00
MM Mark McGwire 40.00 80.00
MV Mo Vaughn 4.00 10.00
SS Sammy Sosa 10.00 25.00
TG Tony Gwynn 6.00 15.00

1999 Black Diamond Dominance

COMPLETE SET (30) 25.00 60.00
STATED PRINT RUN 1500 SERIAL #'d SETS
EMERALD PRINT RUN 1 SERIAL #'d SET
NO EMERALD PRICING DUE TO SCARCITY
RANDOM INSERTS IN PACKS
D1 Kerry Wood .50 1.25
D2 Derek Jeter 3.00 8.00
D3 Alex Rodriguez 1.50 4.00
D4 Frank Thomas 1.25 3.00
D5 Jeff Bagwell .75 2.00
D6 Mo Vaughn .50 1.25
D7 Ivan Rodriguez .75 2.00
D8 Cal Ripken 4.00 10.00
D9 Rolando Arrojo .50 1.25
D10 Chipper Jones 1.25 3.00
D11 Kenny Lofton .50 1.25
D12 Paul Konerko .50 1.25
D13 Mike Piazza 1.25 3.00
D14 Ben Grieve .50 1.25
D15 Nomar Garciaparra .75 2.00
D16 Travis Lee .50 1.25
D17 Scott Rolen .75 2.00
D18 Juan Gonzalez .50 1.25
D19 Tony Gwynn 1.25 3.00
D20 Tony Clark .50 1.25
D21 Roger Clemens 1.50 4.00
D22 Sammy Sosa 1.25 3.00
D23 Larry Walker .75 2.00
D24 Ken Griffey Jr. 2.50 6.00
D25 Mark McGwire 2.00 5.00
D26 Barry Bonds 2.00 5.00
D27 Vladimir Guerrero .75 2.00
D28 Tino Martinez .50 1.25
D29 Greg Maddux 1.50 4.00
D30 Babe Ruth 3.00 8.00

1999 Black Diamond Mystery Numbers

MPLETE SET (30) 150.00 300.00
EMERALD PRINT 1% OF BASIC MYST.NUM.
PRINT RUNS B/WN 100-3000 COPIES PER
NO EMERALD PRICING DUE TO SCARCITY
RANDOM INSERTS IN HOBBY PACKS
M1 Babe Ruth/100 25.00 60.00
M2 Ken Griffey Jr./200 20.00 50.00
M3 Kerry Wood/300 4.00 10.00
M4 Mark McGwire/400 15.00 40.00
M5 Alex Rodriguez/500 12.00 30.00
M6 Chipper Jones/600 10.00 25.00
M7 Nomar Garciaparra/700 6.00 15.00
M8 Derek Jeter/800 25.00 60.00
M9 Mike Piazza/900 10.00 25.00
M10 Roger Clemens/1000 2.50 6.00
M11 Greg Maddux/1100 2.50 6.00
M12 Scott Rolen/1200 1.25 3.00
M13 Cal Ripken/1300 6.00 15.00
M14 Ben Grieve/1400 .75 2.00
M15 Troy Glaus/1500 .75 2.00
M16 Sammy Sosa/1600 2.00 5.00
M17 Darin Erstad/1700 .75 2.00
M18 Juan Gonzalez/1800 .75 2.00
M19 Pedro Martinez/1900 1.25 3.00
M20 Larry Walker/2000 1.25 3.00
M21 Vladimir Guerrero/2100 1.25 3.00
M22 Jeff Bagwell/2200 1.25 3.00
M23 Jaret Wright/2300 .75 2.00
M24 Travis Lee/2400 .75 2.00
M25 Barry Bonds/2500 3.00 8.00
M26 Orlando Hernandez/2600 .75 2.00
M27 Frank Thomas/2700 2.00 5.00
M28 Tony Gwynn/2800 2.00 5.00
M29 Andres Galarraga/2900 1.25 3.00
M30 Craig Biggio/3000 1.25 3.00

2000 Black Diamond

COMPLETE SET (120) 20.00 50.00
COMP.SET w/o SP's (90) 5.00 12.00
DD STATED ODDS 1:4
REGGIE BAT LIST.W/1999 UD APH 500 CLUB
1 Darin Erstad .15 .40
2 Tim Salmon .15 .40
3 Mo Vaughn .15 .40
4 Matt Williams .15 .40
5 Travis Lee .15 .40
6 Randy Johnson .40 1.00
7 Tom Glavine .25 .60
8 Chipper Jones .40 1.00
9 Greg Maddux .50 1.25
10 Andruw Jones .15 .40
11 Brian Jordan .15 .40
12 Cal Ripken 1.25 3.00
13 Albert Belle .15 .40
14 Mike Mussina .25 .60
15 Nomar Garciaparra .25 .60
16 Troy O'Leary .15 .40
17 Pedro Martinez .25 .60
18 Sammy Sosa .40 1.00
19 Henry Rodriguez .15 .40
20 Frank Thomas .40 1.00
21 Magglio Ordonez .25 .60
22 Greg Vaughn .15 .40
23 Barry Larkin .25 .60
24 Sean Casey .15 .40
25 Jim Thome .25 .60
26 Kenny Lofton .15 .40
27 Roberto Alomar .25 .60
28 Manny Ramirez .40 1.00
29 Larry Walker .25 .60
30 Todd Helton .25 .60
31 Gabe Kapler .15 .40
32 Tony Clark .15 .40
33 Dean Palmer .15 .40
34 Cliff Floyd .15 .40
35 Alex Gonzalez .15 .40
36 Moises Alou .15 .40
37 Jeff Bagwell .25 .60
38 Craig Biggio .25 .60
39 Richard Hidalgo .15 .40
40 Carlos Beltran .25 .60
41 Johnny Damon .25 .60
42 Adrian Beltre .40 1.00
43 Gary Sheffield .15 .40
44 Kevin Brown UER .15 .40
Incorrect career strikeouts
45 Jeromy Burnitz .15 .40
46 Jeff Cirillo .15 .40
47 Joe Mays .15 .40
48 Todd Walker .15 .40
49 Vladimir Guerrero .25 .60
50 Michael Barrett .15 .40
51 Rickey Henderson .40 1.00
52 Mike Piazza .40 1.00
53 Robin Ventura .15 .40
54 John Olerud .15 .40
55 Edgardo Alfonzo .15 .40
56 Derek Jeter 1.00 2.50
57 Orlando Hernandez .15 .40
58 Tino Martinez .15 .40
59 Bernie Williams .25 .60
60 Roger Clemens .50 1.25
61 Eric Chavez .15 .40
62 Ben Grieve .15 .40
63 Jason Giambi .15 .40
64 Scott Rolen .25 .60
65 Bob Abreu .15 .40
66 Curt Schilling .25 .60
67 Mike Lieberthal .15 .40
68 Warren Morris .15 .40
69 Brian Giles .15 .40
70 Eric Owens .15 .40
71 Tony Gwynn .40 1.00
72 Reggie Sanders .15 .40
73 Barry Bonds .60 1.50
74 J.T. Snow .15 .40
75 Jeff Kent .15 .40
76 Ken Griffey Jr. .75 2.00
77 Alex Rodriguez .50 1.25
78 Edgar Martinez .25 .60
79 Jay Buhner .15 .40
80 Mark McGwire .60 1.50
81 J.D. Drew .15 .40
82 Eric Davis .15 .40
83 Fernando Tatis .15 .40
84 Wade Boggs .25 .60
85 Fred McGriff .25 .60
86 Juan Gonzalez .15 .40
87 Ivan Rodriguez .25 .60
88 Rafael Palmeiro .25 .60
89 Shawn Green .15 .40
90 Carlos Delgado .15 .40
91 Pat Burrell DD .40 1.00
92 Eric Munson DD .40 1.00
93 Jorge Toca DD .40 1.00
94 Rick Ankiel DD .60 1.50
95 Tony Armas Jr. DD .40 1.00
96 Byung-Hyun Kim DD .40 1.00
97 Alfonso Soriano DD 1.00 2.50
98 Mark Quinn DD .40 1.00
99 Ryan Rupe DD .40 1.00
100 Adam Kennedy DD .40 1.00
101 Jeff Weaver DD .40 1.00
102 Ramon Ortiz DD .40 1.00
103 Eugene Kingsale DD .40 1.00
104 Josh Beckett DD .75 2.00
105 Eric Gagne DD .40 1.00
106 Peter Bergeron DD .40 1.00
107 Erubiel Durazo DD .40 1.00
108 Chad Meyers DD .40 1.00
109 Kip Wells DD .40 1.00
110 Chad Harville DD .40 1.00
111 Matt Riley DD .40 1.00
112 Ben Petrick DD .40 1.00
113 Ed Yarnall DD .40 1.00
114 Calvin Murray DD .40 1.00
115 Vernon Wells DD .40 1.00
116 A.J. Burnett DD .40 1.00
117 Jacque Jones DD .40 1.00
118 Francisco Cordero DD .40 1.00
119 Tomo Ohka DD RC .40 1.00
120 Julio Ramirez DD .40 1.00

2000 Black Diamond Final Cut

*STARS 1-90: 10X TO 25X BASIC
*DIAM.DEB 91-120: 4X TO 10X BASIC
STATED PRINT RUN 100 SERIAL #'d SETS

2000 Black Diamond Reciprocal Cut

*STARS 1-90: 2X TO 5X BASIC CARDS
CARDS 1-90 STATED ODDS 1:7
*DIAM.DEB 91-120: .75X TO 2X BASIC DD
DD 91-120 STATED ODDS 1:12

2000 Black Diamond A Piece of History

STATED ODDS 1:179 HOBBY, 1:359 RETAIL
*DOUBLE: .6X TO 1.5X BASIC APH
DOUBLE STATED ODDS 1:1079 HOBBY
TRIPLE PRINT RUN 1 SERIAL #'d SET
NO TRIPLE PRICING DUE TO SCARCITY
AB Albert Belle 4.00 10.00
AJ Andruw Jones 6.00 15.00
AR Alex Rodriguez 6.00 15.00
BB Barry Bonds 6.00 15.00
CAL Cal Ripken 10.00 25.00
CJ Chipper Jones 6.00 15.00
DE Darin Erstad 4.00 10.00
DJ Derek Jeter 10.00 25.00
IR Ivan Rodriguez 6.00 15.00
JC Jose Canseco 6.00 15.00
JR Ken Griffey Jr. 6.00 15.00
MP Mike Piazza 6.00 15.00
MV Mo Vaughn 4.00 10.00
RM Raul Mondesi 4.00 10.00
SR Scott Rolen 6.00 15.00
TG Tony Gwynn 6.00 15.00
TH Todd Helton 6.00 15.00
TL Travis Lee 4.00 10.00
VG Vladimir Guerrero 6.00 15.00

2000 Black Diamond Barrage

COMPLETE SET (10) 8.00 20.00
STATED ODDS 1:29
B1 Mark McGwire 1.50 4.00
B2 Ken Griffey Jr. 2.00 5.00
B3 Sammy Sosa 1.00 2.50
B4 Jeff Bagwell .60 1.50
B5 Juan Gonzalez .40 1.00
B6 Alex Rodriguez 1.25 3.00
B7 Manny Ramirez 1.00 2.50
B8 Ivan Rodriguez .60 1.50
B9 Chipper Jones 1.00 2.50
B10 Mike Piazza 1.00 2.50

2000 Black Diamond Constant Threat

COMPLETE SET (10) 8.00 20.00
STATED ODDS 1:29
T1 Ken Griffey Jr. 2.00 5.00
T2 Vladimir Guerrero .60 1.50
T3 Alex Rodriguez 1.25 3.00
T4 Sammy Sosa 1.00 2.50
T5 Juan Gonzalez .40 1.00
T6 Derek Jeter 2.50 6.00
T7 Nomar Garciaparra .60 1.50
T8 Barry Bonds 1.50 4.00
T9 Chipper Jones 1.00 2.50
T10 Mike Piazza 1.00 2.50

2000 Black Diamond Diamonation

COMPLETE SET (10) 6.00 15.00
STATED ODDS 1:4
D1 Ken Griffey Jr. 2.00 5.00
D2 Randy Johnson 1.00 2.50
D3 Mark McGwire 1.50 4.00
D4 Manny Ramirez 1.00 2.50
D5 Scott Rolen .60 1.50
D6 Bernie Williams .60 1.50
D7 Roger Clemens 1.25 3.00
D8 Mo Vaughn .40 1.00
D9 Frank Thomas 1.00 2.50
D10 Sean Casey .40 1.00

2000 Black Diamond Diamonds in the Rough

COMPLETE SET (10) 2.50 6.00
STATED ODDS 1:9
R1 Pat Burrell .40 1.00
R2 Eric Munson .40 1.00
R3 Alfonso Soriano 1.00 2.50
R4 Ruben Mateo .40 1.00
R5 A.J. Burnett .40 1.00
R6 Ben Davis .40 1.00
R7 Lance Berkman .60 1.50
R8 Ed Yarnall .40 1.00
R9 Rick Ankiel .60 1.50
R10 Ryan Bradley .40 1.00

2000 Black Diamond Gallery

COMPLETE SET (10) 10.00 25.00
STATED ODDS 1:14
G1 Derek Jeter 2.50 6.00
G2 Alex Rodriguez 1.25 3.00
G3 Nomar Garciaparra .60 1.50
G4 Cal Ripken 3.00 8.00
G5 Sammy Sosa 1.00 2.50
G6 Tony Gwynn 1.00 2.50

G7 Mark McGwire 1.50 4.00
G8 Roger Clemens 1.25 3.00
G9 Greg Maddux 1.25 3.00
G10 Pedro Martinez .60 1.50

2000 Black Diamond Might

COMPLETE SET (10) 8.00 20.00
STATED ODDS 1:14
M1 Ken Griffey Jr. 2.00 5.00
M2 Mark McGwire 1.50 4.00
M3 Sammy Sosa 1.00 2.50
M4 Manny Ramirez 1.00 2.50
M5 Jeff Bagwell .60 1.50
M6 Frank Thomas 1.00 2.50
M7 Mike Piazza 1.00 2.50
M8 Juan Gonzalez .40 1.00
M9 Barry Bonds 1.50 4.00
M10 Alex Rodriguez 1.25 3.00

2000 Black Diamond Rookie Edition

COMP.SET w/o SP's (90) 10.00 25.00
GEMS PRINT RUN 1000 SERIAL #'d SETS
JERSEY RC STATED ODDS 1:24
JERSEY USA RC STATED ODDS 1:24
JERSEY USA STATED ODDS 1:96
1 Troy Glaus .15 .40
2 Mo Vaughn .15 .40
3 Darin Erstad .15 .40
4 Jason Giambi .15 .40
5 Tim Hudson .25 .60
6 Ben Grieve .15 .40
7 Eric Chavez .15 .40
8 Tony Batista .15 .40
9 Carlos Delgado .15 .40
10 David Wells .15 .40
11 Greg Vaughn .15 .40
12 Fred McGriff .25 .60
13 Manny Ramirez .40 1.00
14 Roberto Alomar .25 .60
15 Jim Thome .25 .60
16 Alex Rodriguez .50 1.25
17 Edgar Martinez .25 .60
18 John Olerud .15 .40
19 Albert Belle .15 .40
20 Mike Mussina .25 .60
21 Cal Ripken 1.25 3.00
22 Ivan Rodriguez .25 .60
23 Rafael Palmeiro .25 .60
24 Pedro Martinez .25 .60
25 Nomar Garciaparra .25 .60
26 Carl Everett .15 .40
27 Jermaine Dye .15 .40
28 Mike Sweeney .15 .40
29 Juan Gonzalez .15 .40
30 Bobby Higginson .15 .40
31 Dean Palmer .15 .40
32 Jacque Jones .15 .40
33 Eric Milton .15 .40
34 Matt Lawton .15 .40
35 Magglio Ordonez .25 .60
36 Paul Konerko .15 .40
37 Frank Thomas .40 1.00
38 Ray Durham .15 .40
39 Roger Clemens .50 1.25
40 Derek Jeter 1.00 2.50
41 Bernie Williams .25 .60
42 Jose Canseco .25 .60
43 Craig Biggio .25 .60
44 Richard Hidalgo .15 .40
45 Jeff Bagwell .25 .60
46 Greg Maddux .50 1.25
47 Chipper Jones .40 1.00
48 Rafael Furcal .25 .60
49 Andruw Jones .15 .40
50 Geoff Jenkins .15 .40
51 Jeromy Burnitz .15 .40
52 Mark McGwire .60 1.50
53 Rick Ankiel .25 .60
54 Jim Edmonds .15 .40
55 Kerry Wood .15 .40
56 Sammy Sosa .40 1.00
57 Matt Williams .15 .40
58 Randy Johnson .40 1.00
59 Steve Finley .15 .40
60 Curt Schilling .25 .60
61 Kevin Brown .15 .40
62 Gary Sheffield .15 .40
63 Shawn Green .15 .40
64 Jose Vidro .15 .40
65 Vladimir Guerrero .25 .60
66 Jeff Kent .15 .40
67 Barry Bonds .60 1.50
68 Ryan Dempster .15 .40
69 Cliff Floyd .15 .40
70 Preston Wilson .15 .40
71 Mike Piazza .40 1.00
72 Al Leiter .15 .40
73 Edgardo Alfonzo .15 .40
74 Derek Bell .15 .40
75 Ryan Klesko .15 .40
76 Tony Gwynn .40 1.00
77 Bob Abreu .15 .40
78 Pat Burrell .15 .40
79 Scott Rolen .25 .60
80 Mike Lieberthal .15 .40
81 Jason Kendall .15 .40
82 Brian Giles .15 .40
83 Ken Griffey Jr. .75 2.00
84 Pokey Reese .15 .40
85 Dmitri Young .15 .40
86 Sean Casey .15 .40
87 Jeff Cirillo .15 .40
88 Todd Helton .25 .60
89 Jeffrey Hammonds .15 .40
90 Larry Walker .25 .60
91 Barry Zito RC 3.00 8.00
92 Keith Ginter RC .40 1.00
93 Dane Sardinha RC .40 1.00
94 Kenny Kelly RC .40 1.00
95 Ryan Kohlmeier RC .40 1.00
96 Leo Estrella RC .40 1.00
97 Danys Baez RC .40 1.00
98 Paul Rigdon RC .40 1.00
99 Mike Lamb RC .40 1.00
100 Aaron McNeal RC .40 1.00
101 Juan Pierre RC 2.00 5.00
102 Rico Washington RC .40 1.00
103 Luis Matos RC .40 1.00
104 Adam Bernero RC .40 1.00
105 Wascar Serrano RC .40 1.00
106 Chris Richard RC .40 1.00
107 Justin Miller RC .40 1.00
108 Julio Zuleta RC .40 1.00
109 Alex Cabrera RC .40 1.00
110 Gene Stechschulte RC .40 1.00
111 Tony Mota RC .40 1.00
112 Tomo Ohka RC .40 1.00
113 Geraldo Guzman RC .40 1.00
114 Scott Downs RC .40 1.00
115 Timo Perez RC .60 1.50
116 Chad Durbin RC .40 1.00
117 Sun-Woo Kim RC .40 1.00
118 Tomas De la Rosa RC .40 1.00
119 Javier Cardona RC .40 1.00
120 Kazuhiro Sasaki RC 1.00 2.50
121 Brad Cresse JSY RC 2.00 5.00
122 Matt Wheatland JSY RC 2.00 5.00
123 Joe Torres JSY RC 2.00 5.00
124 Dave Krynzel JSY RC 2.00 5.00
125 Ben Diggins JSY RC 2.00 5.00
126 Sean Burnett JSY RC 2.00 5.00
127 David Espinosa JSY RC 2.00 5.00
128 Scott Heard JSY RC 2.00 5.00
129 Daylan Holt JSY RC 2.00 5.00
130 Koyie Hill JSY RC 2.00 5.00
131 Mark Buehrle JSY RC 10.00 25.00
132 Xavier Nady JSY RC 4.00 10.00
133 Mike Tonis JSY RC 2.00 5.00
134 Matt Ginter JSY RC 2.00 5.00
135 Lorenzo Barcelo JSY RC 2.00 5.00
136 Cory Vance JSY RC 2.00 5.00
137 Sean Burroughs USA 2.00 5.00
138 Todd Williams USA 2.00 5.00
139 Brad Wilkerson USA RC 3.00 8.00
140 Ben Sheets USA RC 5.00 12.00
141 Kurt Ainsworth USA RC 2.00 5.00
142 Anthony Sanders USA 2.00 5.00
143 Ryan Franklin USA RC 2.00 5.00
144 Shane Heams USA RC 2.00 5.00
145 Roy Oswalt USA RC 3.00 8.00
146 Jon Rauch USA RC 2.00 5.00
147 Brent Abernathy USA RC 2.00 5.00
148 Ernie Young USA 2.00 5.00
149 Chris George USA 2.00 5.00
150 Gookie Dawkins USA 2.00 5.00
151 Adam Everett USA 2.00 5.00
152 John Cotton USA RC 2.00 5.00
153 Pat Borders USA 2.00 5.00
154 Doug Mientkiewicz USA 2.00 5.00

2000 Black Diamond Rookie Edition Gold

*STARS 1-90: 3X TO 8X BASIC CARDS
1-90 PRINT RUN 1000 SERIAL #'d SETS
*GEMS 91-120: .5X TO 1.2X BASIC CARDS
91-120 PRINT RUN 500 SERIAL #'d SETS
*JSY 121-136: 1.25X TO 3X BASIC CARDS
121-136 PRINT RUN 100 SERIAL #'d SETS
131 Mark Buehrle JSY 40.00 80.00

2000 Black Diamond Rookie Edition Authentic Pinstripes

PRINT RUNS LISTED BELOW
NO PRICING ON QTY OF 25 OR LESS
APB Derek Jeter Bat/1000 8.00 20.00
APC Derek Jeter Cap/200 12.50 30.00
APG Derek Jeter Glove/200 20.00 50.00
APJ Derek Jeter Jsy/1000 10.00 25.00
JWOJ Jeter J/Will J/O'Neill J/100 75.00 150.00

2000 Black Diamond Rookie Edition Diamonation

COMPLETE SET (9) 6.00 15.00
STATED ODDS 1:12
D1 Pedro Martinez .60 1.50
D2 Derek Jeter 2.50 6.00
D3 Jason Giambi .40 1.00
D4 Todd Helton .60 1.50
D5 Nomar Garciaparra .60 1.50
D6 Randy Johnson 1.00 2.50
D7 Jeff Bagwell .60 1.50
D8 Cal Ripken 3.00 8.00
D9 Ivan Rodriguez .60 1.50

2000 Black Diamond Rookie Edition Gallery

COMPLETE SET (6) 8.00 20.00
STATED ODDS 1:20
G1 Sammy Sosa 1.00 2.50
G2 Barry Bonds 1.50 4.00
G3 Vladimir Guerrero .60 1.50
G4 Cal Ripken 3.00 8.00
G5 Mike Piazza 1.00 2.50
G6 Mark McGwire 1.50 4.00

2000 Black Diamond Rookie Edition Might

COMPLETE SET (9) 8.00 20.00
STATED ODDS 1:12
M1 Mark McGwire 1.50 4.00
M2 Mike Piazza 1.00 2.50
M3 Frank Thomas 1.00 2.50
M4 Ken Griffey Jr. 2.00 5.00
M5 Sammy Sosa 1.00 2.50
M6 Alex Rodriguez 1.25 3.00
M7 Carlos Delgado .40 1.00
M8 Vladimir Guerrero .60 1.50
M9 Barry Bonds 1.50 4.00

2000 Black Diamond Rookie Edition Skills

COMPLETE SET (6) 5.00 12.00
STATED ODDS 1:20
S1 Alex Rodriguez 1.25 3.00
S2 Chipper Jones 1.00 2.50
S3 Ken Griffey Jr. 2.00 5.00
S4 Pedro Martinez .60 1.50
S5 Ivan Rodriguez .60 1.50
S6 Derek Jeter 2.50 6.00

1975 Blankback Discs

This six-disc baseball-designed set measures approximately 3 3/8" in diameter. The fronts feature a black-and-white player head photo on a white background in the center with the player's name, position, and team name below. The blue and red sides contain biographical information. The backs are blank. The discs are unnumbered and checklisted below in alphabetical order. Bench and Seaver are available in lesser quantities than other players so they are labeled as SP's in the checklist below

COMPLETE SET (6) 250.00 500.00
1 Henry Aaron 12.50 30.00
2 Johnny Bench SP 75.00 150.00
3 Catfish Hunter 10.00 25.00
4 Fred Lynn 2.00 5.00
5 Pete Rose 40.00 80.00
6 Tom Seaver SP 125.00 250.00

1991 Bleachers 23K Griffey Jr.

These three 23-karat gold standard-size cards were issued by Bleachers. The production run was reported to be 10,000 numbered sets and 1,500 uncut numbered strips. On white, green, yellow and blue bars, the backs carry the player's name, biography, statistics, highlights and a serial number ("X of 10,000") inside a black border.

COMPLETE SET (3) 12.50 30.00
STATED PRINT RUN 10000 SER.#'d SETS
1 Ken Griffey Jr. 5.00 12.00
Moeller High
2 Ken Griffey Jr. 5.00 12.00
Bellingham Mariners
3 Ken Griffey Jr. 5.00 12.00
San Bernardino Spirit

1991 Bleachers 23K Thomas

These three 23-karat gold standard-size cards were produced by Bleachers. On gray, yellow, white and red stripes, the back has the player's name, biography, statistics, highlights and the serial number (1 of 10,000), inside a black border. It was reported that the production run was limited to 10,000 sets and 1,500 uncut numbered strips.

COMPLETE SET (3) 8.00 20.00
STATED PRINT RUN 10,000 SER.#'d SETS
1 Frank Thomas 4.00 10.00
Auburn Tigers
2 Frank Thomas 4.00 10.00
Sarasota White Sox
3 Frank Thomas 4.00 10.00
Birmingham Barons

1991-92 Bleachers Promos

These promo standard-size cards were distributed to dealers to promote the new forthcoming Bleachers 23K card sets. The card backs contain order information as well as information about Bleachers upcoming releases.

COMPLETE SET (7) 8.00 20.00
1 Ken Griffey Jr. 1.50 4.00
Spirit jersey
1991copyright
2 Dave Justice .75 2.00
1992 copyright
Wearing Bleachers shirt
3 Nolan Ryan 1.25 3.00
1992 copyright
Wearing tuxedo
no 800 number in border
4 Nolan Ryan 1.25 3.00
1992 copyright
Wearing tuxedo
800 number in border
5 Nolan Ryan 1.25 3.00
1992 copyright
Wearing tuxedo
East Coast National
6 Nolan Ryan 1.25 3.00
1992 copyright
Wearing tuxedo
SF Sports Collectors Expo
7 Nolan Ryan 1.25 3.00
1992 copyright
Wearing tuxedo
Tri-Star St. Louis

1992 Bleachers 23K Justice

These three 23-karat gold standard-size cards were issued by Bleachers. The production run was reported to be 10,000 numbered sets and 1,500 uncut numbered strips. On white, pink, and orange bars, the backs carry the player's name, biography, statistics, highlights, and a serial number ("X of 10,000") inside a black border. Prism cards (silver prism border instead of gold) were randomly inserted in sets on a limited basis. These prism versions are valued at double the prices listed in our checklist.

COMPLETE SET (3) 6.00 15.00
STATED PRINT RUN 10,000 SER.#'d SETS
1 Dave Justice 2.00 5.00
Durham Bulls
2 Dave Justice 2.00 5.00
Greenville Braves
3 Dave Justice 2.00 5.00
Richmond Braves

1992 Bleachers 23K Ryan

These three 23-karat gold standard-size standard-size cards were issued by Bleachers. The sets were packaged in a cardboard sleeve and shrink wrapped; promo cards and prism cards were randomly inserted. The production run is reported to be 10,000 numbered sets and 1,500 uncut numbered strips. On white, purple, and orange bars, the backs carry the player's name, biography, statistics, highlights, and a serial number ("X of 10,000") inside a black border. Prism cards (silver prism border instead of gold) were randomly inserted in sets on a limited basis. These prism versions are valued at double the prices listed in our checklist.

COMPLETE SET (3) 12.50 30.00
1 Nolan Ryan 4.00 10.00
Marion Mets
2 Nolan Ryan 4.00 10.00
Greenville Mets
3 Nolan Ryan 4.00 10.00
Jacksonville Suns
P2 Nolan Ryan PROMO 4.00 10.00

1993 Bleachers Promos

These thirteen promo standard-size cards were distributed to dealers to promote the new upcoming Bleachers 23K card sets. The card backs contain order information as well as information about Bleachers upcoming releases.

COMPLETE SET (13) 15.00 40.00
1 Barry Bonds 1.25 3.00
1993 copyright
2 Barry Bonds 1.25 3.00
1993 copyright
Tuff Stuff Buyers Club
3 Barry Bonds 1.25 3.00
1993 copyright
Tri-Star Phoenix '93
4 Nolan Ryan 2.00 5.00
1992 copyright
Tri-Star Houston '93
5 Nolan Ryan 2.00 5.00
1993 copyright
Sitting, western gear
6 Nolan Ryan 2.00 5.00
1993 copyright
Sitting; western gear
Tuff Stuff Buyers Club
7 Nolan Ryan 2.00 5.00
1993 copyright
Wearing tuxedo
Gold speckled background
8 Nolan Ryan 2.00 5.00
1993 copyright
Wearing tuxedo
Silver-speckled background
9 Nolan Ryan 2.00 5.00
1993 copyright
Wearing tuxedo
Silver wavy background
10 Ryne Sandberg 1.25 3.00
1993 copyright
Baseball, basketball and football
11 Ryne Sandberg 1.25 3.00
1993 copyright
Baseball, basketball and football
Tri-Star Phoenix '93
12 Ryne Sandberg 1.25 3.00
1993 copyright
Baseball, basketball and football
East Coast National
13 Ryne Sandberg 1.25 3.00
1993 copyright
Baseball, basketball and football
Tuff Stuff Buyers Club

1993 Bleachers Ryan 6

This six-card standard-size set of 1993 Bleachers Nolan Ryan is the premier edition of the holographic prism border cards. Production of this set was limited to 10,000 sets.

COMPLETE SET (6) 12.50 30.00
STATED PRINT RUN 10,000 SER.#'d SETS
1 Nolan Ryan 2.00 5.00
Little League Highlights
2 Nolan Ryan 2.00 5.00
High School Highlights
3 Nolan Ryan 2.00 5.00
Minor League Highlights
4 Nolan Ryan 2.00 5.00
Minor League Statistics
5 Nolan Ryan 2.00 5.00
International Strikeout King
6 Nolan Ryan 2.00 5.00
Career Highlights

1993-00 Bleachers

These cards feature embossed player images on 23 Karat all-gold sculptured cards. Each card was sold individually and packaged in a clear acrylic holder along with a Certificate of Authenticity inside a collectible foil-stamped box. The set is unnumbered and checklisted below in alphabetical order. Each card is serially numbered. The continuation line includes: year, brand, and number of cards issued.

1 Hank Aaron 12.50 30.00
1995 Classic/2297
2 Hank Aaron 4.00 10.00
1995 Classic/10000
3 Hank Aaron 4.00 10.00
1996 Diamond Star/10000
4 Hank Aaron/755 Homers 15.00 40.00
Game Used/1000
5 Roberto Alomar
Reno Padres
6 Barry Bonds 2.50 6.00
1993 Arizona State/10000
7 Barry Bonds 2.50 6.00
1993 Prince William Pirates/10000
8 Barry Bonds 2.50 6.00
1993 Hawaii Islanders/10000
9 Barry Bonds 6.00 15.00
1996 Classic/4995
10 Roberto Clemente 4.00 10.00
1997 Diamond Star10000
11 Whitey Ford/1996/25000 2.50 6.00
12 Ken Griffey Jr. 3.00 8.00
1993 Mega Star Sculptured/10000
13 Ken Griffey Jr. 3.00 8.00
1993 Mega Star Sculptured/10000
14 Ken Griffey Jr.#1995 Silver/10000 8.00 20.00
15 Ken Griffey Jr. 8.00 20.00
1996 Triple Image/10000
16 Ken Griffey Jr. 8.00 20.00
1996 Diamond Star/10000
17 Ken Griffey Jr. 15.00 40.00
1997 #1/4997
18 Ken Griffey Jr. 15.00 40.00
1997 #2/4997
19 Ken Griffey Jr. 15.00 40.00
1997 #3/4997
20 Ken Griffey Jr. 3.00 8.00
1998 Chasing 61/9861
21 Derek Jeter/1997/10000 4.00 10.00
22 Mickey Mantle 4.00 10.00
1996 #1/25000
23 Mickey Mantle 6.00 15.00
1996 #2/10000
24 Mickey Mantle 6.00 15.00
1996 #3/10000
25 Mickey Mantle 6.00 15.00
1996 #4/10000
26 Mickey Mantle 6.00 15.00
1996 #5/10000
27 Mickey Mantle 6.00 15.00
1996 Diamond Star/10000
28 Roger Maris 12.50 30.00
1998 61 Homers w/Gemstone/1000
29 Don Mattingly/1997/10000 2.50 6.00
30 Mark McGwire 2.50 6.00
1998 Chasing 61/9861
31 Mark McGwire 8.00 20.00
Sammy Sosa
Breaking History
32 Mark McGwire/1998 70 Homers w/Gemstone/9870
20.00 50.00
33 Mark McGwire/2000 70 homers Game Used/1000
40.00 100.00
34 Mark McGwire 8.00 20.00
Record Setting 70th Homer
35 Eddie Murray 4.00 10.00
1996 #1/10000
36 Eddie Murray 6.00 15.00
1996 #2/5000
37 Cal Ripken 2.50 6.00
1995 #1/75000
38 Cal Ripken 6.00 15.00
1996 #2/10000
39 Cal Ripken 2.50 6.00
1995 Ironman
40 Cal Ripken 12.50 30.00
1996 Japanese/10000
41 Cal Ripken 6.00 15.00
1996 Diamond Star/21310
42 Cal Ripken 12.50 30.00
Lou Gehrig
1995/10000
43 Cal Ripken 6.00 15.00
Lou Gehrig
1995 Iron Men/20000
44 Cal Ripken 20.00 50.00
2000 2,131 Games Game Used/1000
45 Jackie Robinson 4.00 10.00
1997 Gold Performance Mint/25000
46 Alex Rodriguez 5.00 12.00
1996 Black Autograph/5000
47 Alex Rodriguez 10.00 25.00
1996 Pearl Autograph/5000
48 Pete Rose 12.50 30.00
2000 4,256 Hits Game Used/1000
49 Babe Ruth 12.50 30.00
1997 Diamond Star/10000
50 Nolan Ryan 2.50 6.00
1993 Little League Highlights/10000
51 Nolan Ryan 2.50 6.00
1993 High School Highlights/10000
52 Nolan Ryan 2.50 6.00
1993 Minor League Highlights/10000
53 Nolan Ryan 2.50 6.00
1993 Minor League Statistics/10000
54 Nolan Ryan 2.50 6.00
1993 International Strikeout King/10000
55 Nolan Ryan 2.50 6.00
1993 Career Highlights/10000
56 Nolan Ryan 6.00 15.00
1993 #1/10000
57 Nolan Ryan 6.00 15.00
1993 #2/5714
58 Nolan Ryan 6.00 15.00
1996 All-Time Strikeout King/50000
59 Nolan Ryan 6.00 15.00
1996 Diamond Star/10000
60 Nolan Ryan 8.00 18.00
1996 Laser Cut Diamond Star/10000
61 Nolan Ryan 20.00 50.00
2000 5,714 K's Game Used/1000
62 Ryne Sandberg 2.50 6.00
1993 North Central High School/10000
63 Ryne Sandberg 2.50 6.00
1993 Helena Phillies
10000
64 Ryne Sandberg 2.50 6.00
1993 Reading Phillies
10000
65 Sammy Sosa 2.50 6.00
1998 Chasing 61/9862
66 Frank Thomas 6.00 15.00
1995/10000
67 Frank Thomas 6.00 15.00
1996 Diamond Star/10000
68 Ted Williams 6.00 15.00
1996/25000
69 Ted Williams 12.50 30.00
1996 Diamond Star/10000
P1 Ken Griffey Jr. 3.00 8.00
Promo Card
Moeller High School

1995 Bleachers 23K Cal Ripken Jr.

NNO Cal Ripken Jr. 2.00 5.00

1982 Cy Block

This one card standard-size set features insurance agent Cy Block who had a brief major leaguer career in the 1940's. The black and white card has a photo of Block on the front and complete career statistics on the back. The card, although it does not say on it, was produced by Topps for Block who used it as a buisness card during his prosperous post-playing career in insurance.

1 Cy Block .40 1.00

1978 Blue Jays Postcards

1 Alan Ashby 2.50 6.00
2 Doug Ault 2.00 5.00
3 Bob Bailor 2.00 5.00
4 Rick Bosetti 2.00 5.00
5 Rico Carty 2.50 6.00
6 Rick Cerone 2.50 6.00
7 Jim Clancy 2.00 5.00
8 Joe Coleman 2.00 5.00
9 Hector Cruz 2.00 5.00
10 Sam Ewing 2.00 5.00
11 Ron Fairly 2.50 6.00
12 Jerry Garvin 2.00 5.00
13 Luis Gomez 2.00 5.00
14 Roy Hartsfield MG 2.00 5.00
15 Roy Howell 2.00 5.00
16 Jesse Jefferson 2.00 5.00
17 Tim Johnson 2.00 5.00
18 Don Kirkwood 2.00 5.00
19 Dave Lemanczyk 2.00 5.00
20 Don Leppert CO 2.00 5.00
21 John Mayberry 2.50 6.00
22 Dave McKay 2.00 5.00
23 Bob Miller CO 2.00 5.00
24 Brian Milner 2.00 5.00
25 Balor Moore 2.00 5.00
26 Jackie Moore 2.00 5.00
27 Tom Murphy 2.00 5.00
28 Phil Roof 2.00 5.00
29 Bill Singer 2.00 5.00
30 Hector Torres 2.00 5.00
31 Tom Underwood 2.00 5.00
32 Willie Upshaw 2.50 6.00
33 Otto Velez 2.00 5.00
34 Harry Warner CO 2.00 5.00
35 Mike Willis 2.00 5.00
36 Alvis Woods 2.00 5.00

1979 Blue Jays Bubble Yum

These 20 white-bordered posed black-and-white player photographs measure approximately 5 1/2" by 8 1/2". The player's name and position along with the Blue Jays logo and a picture of a pack of Bubble Yum, appear within the wide lower white margin. The white back carries the player's name and position at the top, followed below by his uniform number, biography and statistics. The photos are unnumbered and checklisted below in alphabetical order.

COMPLETE SET (20) 20.00 50.00
1 Bob Bailor 1.50 4.00
2 Rick Bosetti 1.00 2.50
3 Tom Buskey 1.00 2.50
4 Rico Carty 2.00 5.00
5 Rick Cerone 1.25 3.00
6 Jim Clancy 1.00 2.50
7 Bobby Doerr CO 2.50 6.00
8 Dave Freisleben 1.00 2.50
9 Luis Gomez 1.00 2.50
10 Alfredo Griffin 1.50 4.00
11 Roy Hartsfield MG 1.00 2.50
12 Roy Howell 1.00 2.50
13 Phil Huffman 1.00 2.50
14 Jesse Jefferson 1.00 2.50
15 Dave Lemanczyk 1.00 2.50
16 John Mayberry 2.00 5.00
17 Balor Moore 1.00 2.50
18 Tom Underwood 1.00 2.50
19 Otto Velez 1.25 3.00
20 Al Woods 1.00 2.50

1979 Blue Jays McCarthy Postcards

In the early days of the Blue Jays, they used postcards of sports photographer J.D. McCarthy as promotional team issues. These were the new photos issued in 1979, since they are unnumbered we have sequenced them in alphabetical order. The Dave Stieb postcard predates his Rookie Card by one year while the Danny Ainge predates his Rookie Card by two years.

COMPLETE SET (28) 10.00 25.00
1 Danny Ainge 2.50 6.00
2 Bob Bailor .30 .75
3 Rick Bosetti .30 .75
4 Bobby Brown .30 .75
5 Tom Buskey .30 .75
6 Joe Cannon .30 .75
7 Rico Carty .40 1.00
8 Rick Cerone .40 1.00
9 Jim Clancy .30 .75
10 Bob Davis .30 .75
11 Dave Freisleben .30 .75
12 Luis Gomez .30 .75
13 Alfredo Griffin .30 .75
14 Roy Lee Howell .30 .75
15 Phil Huffman .30 .75
16 Tim Johnson .30 .75
17 Craig Kusick .30 .75
18 Dave Lemanczyk .30 .75
19 Mark Lemongello .30 .75
20 Dave McKay .30 .75
21 John Mayberry .40 1.00
22 Balor Moore .30 .75
23 Tom Murphy .30 .75
24 Dave Stieb 2.50 6.00
25 Tom Underwood .30 .75
26 Otto Velez .30 .75
27 Ted Wilborn .30 .75
28 Al Woods .30 .75

1982 Blue Jays Sun

This 18-card set features blue-bordered color player photos of the 1982 Toronto Blue Jays. The set was inserted for several weeks into the newspaper and could be cut out of the sports section of the Sunday Sun. The cards are unnumbered and checklisted below in alphabetical order.

COMPLETE SET (18) 6.00 15.00
1 Jesse Barfield .75 2.00
2 Barry Bonnell .40 1.00
3 Jim Clancy .40 1.00
4 Damaso Garcia .40 1.00
5 Jerry Garvin .40 1.00
6 Jim Gott .40 1.00
7 Alfredo Griffin .40 1.00
8 Garth Iorg .40 1.00
9 Roy Lee Jackson .40 1.00
10 Buck Martinez .60 1.50
11 John Mayberry .60 1.50
12 Joey McLaughlin .40 1.00
13 Lloyd Moseby .40 1.00
14 Rance Mullinks .40 1.00
15 Dale Murray .40 1.00
16 Dave Stieb .75 2.00
17 Willie Upshaw .40 1.00
18 Ernie Whitt .60 1.50

1984 Blue Jays Fire Safety

The 35 standard-size cards comprising this 1984 Blue Jays Fire Safety set feature on their fronts blue-bordered, color player action shots. The player's name, position, and uniform number appear in black lettering within the lower blue margin. The circular Blue Jays' logo rests at the bottom right. The horizontal white back carries the player's name and uniform number at the top, followed below by biography and a fire safety tip. The logos at the bottom for the Ontario Association of Fire Chiefs and The Toronto Sun round out the card. The cards are unnumbered and checklisted below in alphabetical order.

COMPLETE SET (35) 6.00 15.00
1 Jim Acker .20 .50
2 Willie Aikens .20 .50
3 Doyle Alexander .30 .75
4 Jesse Barfield .40 1.00
5 George Bell .30 .75
6 Jim Clancy .20 .50
7 Bryan Clark .20 .50
8 Stan Clarke .20 .50
9 Dave Collins .30 .75
10 Bobby Cox MG .40 1.00
11 Tony Fernandez .60 1.50
12 Damaso Garcia .30 .75
13 Cito Gaston CO .20 .50
14 Jim Gott .20 .50
15 Alfredo Griffin .30 .75
16 Kelly Gruber .40 1.00
17 Garth Iorg .20 .50
18 Roy Lee Jackson .20 .50
19 Cliff Johnson .30 .75
20 Jimmy Key 1.25 3.00
21 Dennis Lamp .20 .50
22 Rick Leach .20 .50
23 Luis Leal .20 .50
24 Buck Martinez .30 .75
25 Lloyd Moseby .40 1.00
26 Rance Mulliniks .30 .75
27 Billy Smith CO .20 .50
28 Dave Stieb .40 1.00
29 John Sullivan CO .20 .50
30 Willie Upshaw .30 .75
31 Mitch Webster .20 .50
32 Ernie Whitt .30 .75
33 Al Widmar CO .20 .50
34 Jimmy Williams CO .20 .50
35 Blue Jays Logo .20 .50

1985 Blue Jays Fire Safety

The 36 standard-size cards comprising this 1985 Blue Jays Fire Safety set feature on their fronts blue-bordered posed color player photos. The player's name, position, and uniform number appear in black lettering within the lower blue margin. The circular Blue Jays' logo rests at the bottom right. The horizontal white back carries the player's name and uniform number at the top, followed below by biography, statistics, and a fire safety tip. The logos at the bottom for the Ontario Association of Fire Chiefs, the Ontario Ministry of the Solicitor General, The Toronto Star, and Midas round out the card. The cards are unnumbered and checklisted below in alphabetical order.

COMPLETE SET (36) 4.00 10.00
1 Jim Acker .08 .25
2 Willie Aikens .08 .25
3 Doyle Alexander .20 .50
4 Jesse Barfield .30 .75
5 George Bell .20 .50
6 Jeff Burroughs .20 .50
7 Bill Caudill .08 .25
8 Jim Clancy .08 .25
9 Bobby Cox MG .40 1.00
10 Tony Fernandez .40 1.00
11 Damaso Garcia .20 .50
12 Cito Gaston CO .20 .50
13 Kelly Gruber .30 .75
14 Tom Henke .40 1.00
15 Garth Iorg .08 .25
16 Jimmy Key .60 1.50
17 Dennis Lamp .08 .25
18 Gary Lavelle .08 .25
19 Luis Leal .08 .25
20 Manny Lee .08 .25
21 Buck Martinez .20 .50
22 Len Matuszek .08 .25
23 Lloyd Moseby .20 .50
24 Rance Mulliniks .08 .25
25 Ron Musselman .08 .25
26 Billy Smith CO .08 .25
27 Dave Stieb .30 .75
28 John Sullivan CO .08 .25
29 Lou Thornton .08 .25
30 Willie Upshaw .20 .50
31 Mitch Webster .08 .25
32 Ernie Whitt .20 .50
33 Al Widmar CO .08 .25
34 Jimmy Williams CO .08 .25
35 Blue Jays Logo .08 .25
36 Blue Jays Team Photo .20 .50

1985 Blue Jays Pepsi/Frito Lay Pennants

This five-pennant set was produced by Pepsi Cola and Frito Lay and measures approximately 9 1/2" by 26". The fronts display a color drawing of the player's head alongside a full player image with the player's name and jersey number and a facsimile autograph. The cards are unnumbered and checklisted below in alphabetical order.

COMPLETE SET (5) 4.00 10.00
1 Jesse Barfield 1.25 3.00
2 Bill Caudill .75 2.00
3 Dave Stieb 1.50 4.00
4 Willie Upshaw .75 2.00
5 Ernie Whitt .75 2.00

1986 Blue Jays Ault Foods

The 24 stickers in this set, featuring members of the Toronto Blue Jays, measure approximately 2" by 3" and were to be pasted in a 9" by 12", 20-page album. Ault Foods were sold under several brands, including Sealtest, Silverwood, Royal Oak, and Copper Cliff. The stickers are unnumbered and checklisted below in alphabetical order. The set is also noteworthy in that it contains Cecil Fielder appearing in his Rookie Card year.

COMPLETE SET (24) 8.00 20.00
1 Jim Acker .20 .50
2 Doyle Alexander .20 .50
3 Jesse Barfield .60 1.50
4 George Bell .60 1.50
5 Bill Caudill .20 .50
6 Jim Clancy .20 .50
7 Steve Davis .20 .50
8 Tony Fernandez .60 1.50
9 Cecil Fielder 1.50 4.00
10 Damaso Garcia .40 1.00
11 Don Gordon .20 .50
12 Kelly Gruber .60 1.50
13 Tom Henke .60 1.50
14 Garth Iorg .20 .50
15 Cliff Johnson .40 1.00
16 Jimmy Key .75 2.00
17 Dennis Lamp .20 .50
18 Gary Lavelle .20 .50
19 Buck Martinez .40 1.00
20 Lloyd Moseby .40 1.00
21 Rance Mulliniks .40 1.00
22 Dave Stieb .60 1.50
23 Willie Upshaw .40 1.00
24 Ernie Whitt .40 1.00
NNO Ault Album 1.00 2.50

1986 Blue Jays Fire Safety

The 36 standard-size cards comprising this 1986 Toronto Blue Jays Fire set feature on their fronts blue-bordered, posed color player photos. The cards are unnumbered and checklisted below in alphabetical order. The set is also noteworthy in that it contains Cecil Fielder appearing in his Rookie Card year.

COMPLETE SET (36) 5.00 12.00
1 Jim Acker .08 .25
2 Doyle Alexander .20 .50
3 Jesse Barfield .30 .75
4 George Bell .30 .75
5 Bill Caudill .08 .25
6 Jim Clancy .08 .25
7 Steve Davis .08 .25
8 Mark Eichhorn .20 .50
9 Tony Fernandez .30 .75
10 Cecil Fielder 1.25 3.00
11 Tom Filer .08 .25
12 Damaso Garcia .20 .50
13 Cito Gaston CO .08 .25
14 Don Gordon .08 .25
15 Kelly Gruber .20 .50
16 Jeff Hearron .08 .25
17 Tom Henke .30 .75
18 Garth Iorg .08 .25
19 Cliff Johnson .20 .50
20 Jimmy Key .40 1.00
21 Dennis Lamp .08 .25
22 Gary Lavelle .08 .25
23 Rick Leach .08 .25
24 Buck Martinez .20 .50
25 John McLaren CO .08 .25
26 Lloyd Moseby .20 .50
27 Rance Mulliniks .08 .25
28 Billy Smith CO .08 .25
29 Dave Stieb .30 .75
30 John Sullivan CO .08 .25
31 Willie Upshaw .20 .50
32 Ernie Whitt .20 .50
33 Al Widmar CO .08 .25
34 Jimy Williams MG .08 .25
35 Blue Jays LOGO/(Won-Lost Record).08 .25
36 Blue Jays Team Photo/(Checklist back).08 .25

1986 Blue Jays Greats TCMA

These 12 standard-size cards honor the best players of the Toronto Blue Jays first decade. The players are pictured on the front. The backs have a biography and career statistics.

COMPLETE SET (12) 1.25 3.00
1 John Mayberry .20 .50
2 Bob Bailor .08 .25
3 Luis Gomez .08 .25
4 Roy Howell .08 .25
5 Otto Velez .08 .25
6 Rick Bosetti .08 .25
7 Al Woods .08 .25
8 Rick Cerone .20 .50
9 Dave Lemanczyk .08 .25
10 Tom Underwood .08 .25
11 Joey McLaughlin .08 .25
12 Bobby Cox MG .30 .75

1987 Blue Jays Fire Safety

The 36 standard-size cards comprising this 1987 Toronto Blue Jays Fire Safety set feature on their fronts white-bordered, posed color player photos. The cards are unnumbered and checklisted below in alphabetical order.

COMPLETE SET (36) 3.00 8.00
1 Jesse Barfield .30 .75
2 George Bell .30 .75
3 John Cerutti .08 .25
4 Checklist Card .20 .50
5 Jim Clancy .08 .25
6 Rob Ducey .08 .25
7 Mark Eichhorn .20 .50
8 Tony Fernandez .30 .75
9 Cecil Fielder .50 1.25
10 Cito Gaston CO .08 .25
11 Kelly Gruber .20 .50
12 Tom Henke .30 .75
13 Jeff Hearron .08 .25
14 Garth Iorg .08 .25
15 Joe Johnson .08 .25
16 Jimmy Key .40 1.00
17 Gary Lavelle .08 .25
18 Rick Leach .08 .25
19 Logo Card .08 .25
20 Fred McGriff 1.50 4.00
21 John McLaren CO .08 .25
22 Craig McMurtry .08 .25
23 Lloyd Moseby .20 .50
24 Rance Mulliniks .20 .50
25 Jeff Musselman .08 .25
26 Jose Nunez .08 .25
27 Mike Sharperson .08 .25
28 Billy Smith CO .08 .25
29 Matt Stark .08 .25
30 Dave Stieb .30 .75
31 John Sullivan CO .08 .25
32 Willie Upshaw .20 .50
33 Duane Ward .20 .50
34 Ernie Whitt .20 .50
35 Al Widmar CO .08 .25
36 Jimy Williams MG .08 .25

1988 Blue Jays 5x7

These 14 oversized cards measure approximately 5" by 7" and feature turquoise-bordered retouched posed color player photos. The cards are unnumbered and checklisted below in alphabetical order. This set was issued in a folder.

COMPLETE SET (14) 6.00 15.00
1 Jesse Barfield .60 1.50
2 George Bell .60 1.50
3 Jim Clancy .20 .50
4 Mark Eichhorn .20 .50
5 Tony Fernandez .60 1.50
6 Tom Henke .60 1.50
7 Jimmy Key .75 2.00
8 Nelson Liriano .20 .50
9 Lloyd Moseby .60 1.50
10 Dave Stieb .60 1.50
11 Willie Upshaw .40 1.00
12 Ernie Whitt
13 Jimy Williams MG .20 .50
14 1988 Schedule .20 .50
15 1988 Season Ticket Info .20 .50

1988 Blue Jays Fire Safety

This white-bordered, 36-card set features Toronto Blue Jays, their coaches and manager. The cards (measuring 3 1/2" by 5") are over-sized. The cards are unnumbered and checklisted below in alphabetical order.

COMPLETE SET (36) 4.00 10.00
*FRENCH: 1.5X BASIC CARDS
1 Jesse Barfield .30 .75
2 George Bell .30 .75
3 Juan Beniquez .08 .25
4 Pat Borders .20 .50
5 Sil Campusano .08 .25
6 John Cerutti .08 .25
7 Jim Clancy .08 .25
8 Rob Ducey .08 .25
9 Mark Eichhorn .08 .25
10 Tony Fernandez .30 .75
11 Cecil Fielder .40 1.00
12 Mike Flanagan .20 .50
13 Cito Gaston CO .08 .25
14 Kelly Gruber .20 .50
15 Tom Henke .30 .75
16 Jimmy Key .40 1.00
17 Rick Leach .08 .25
18 Manny Lee .08 .25
19 Nelson Liriano .08 .25
20 Winston Llenas CO .08 .25
21 Fred McGriff 1.25 3.00
22 John McLaren CO .08 .25
23 Lloyd Moseby .20 .50
24 Rance Mulliniks .20 .50
25 Jeff Musselman .08 .25
26 Billy Smith CO .08 .25
27 Dave Stieb .30 .75
28 Todd Stottlemyre .50 1.25
29 John Sullivan CO .08 .25
30 Duane Ward .08 .25
31 David Wells .40 1.00
32 Ernie Whitt .20 .50
33 Al Widmar CO .08 .25
34 Jimy Williams MG .08 .25
35 Team Card .20 .50
36 Logo Card .20 .50

1989 Blue Jays Fire Safety

The 36 standard-size cards comprising this 1989 Toronto Blue Jays Fire Safety set feature on their fronts white-bordered, color player action shots. The cards are unnumbered and checklisted below in alphabetical order.

COMPLETE SET (36) 3.00 8.00
1 Jesse Barfield .30 .75
2 George Bell .30 .75
3 Pat Borders .20 .50
4 Bob Brenly .08 .25
5 Sal Butera .08 .25
6 Sil Campusano .08 .25
7 John Cerutti .08 .25
8 Rob Ducey .08 .25
9 Tony Fernandez .30 .75
10 Mike Flanagan .20 .50
11 Cito Gaston CO .30 .75
12 Kelly Gruber .20 .50
13 Tom Henke .30 .75
14 Jimmy Key .40 1.00
15 Tom Lawless .08 .25
16 Manny Lee .08 .25
17 Nelson Liriano .08 .25
18 Fred McGriff .75 2.00
19 John McLaren CO .08 .25
20 Lloyd Moseby .20 .50
21 Rance Mulliniks .08 .25
22 Jeff Musselman .08 .25
23 Greg Myers .08 .25
24 Jose Nunez .08 .25
25 Mike Squires CO .08 .25
26 Dave Stieb .30 .75
27 Todd Stottlemyre .40 1.00
28 John Sullivan CO .08 .25
29 Duane Ward .08 .25
30 David Wells .30 .75
31 Ernie Whitt .20 .50
32 Al Widmar CO .08 .25
33 Jimy Williams MG .08 .25
34 Frank Wills .08 .25
35 Team Logo .08 .25
36 Team Photo CL .20 .50

1990 Blue Jays Fire Safety

The 36 standard-size cards comprising this 1990 Blue Jays Fan Club set feature on their fronts white-bordered color player action shots. The cards are unnumbered and checklisted below in alphabetical order. The set is also noteworthy in that it contains John Olerud appearing in his Rookie Card year.

COMPLETE SET (36) 3.00 8.00
1 Jim Acker .08 .25
2 George Bell .30 .75
3 Willie Blair .08 .25
4 Pat Borders .08 .25
5 John Cerutti .08 .25
6 Galen Cisco CO .08 .25
7 Junior Felix .08 .25
8 Tony Fernandez .30 .75
9 Cito Gaston MG .08 .25
10 Kelly Gruber .20 .50
11 Tom Henke .30 .75
12 Glenallen Hill .08 .25
13 Jimmy Key .40 1.00
14 Paul Kilgus .08 .25
15 Tom Lawless .08 .25
16 Manny Lee .08 .25
17 Al Leiter .40 1.00
18 Nelson Liriano .08 .25
19 Fred McGriff .60 1.50
20 John McLaren CO .08 .25
21 Rance Mulliniks .08 .25
22 Greg Myers .08 .25
23 John Olerud 1.00 2.50
24 Alex Sanchez .08 .25
25 Mike Squires CO .08 .25
26 Dave Stieb .30 .75
27 Todd Stottlemyre .20 .50
28 John Sullivan CO .08 .25
29 Gene Tenace CO .20 .50
30 Ozzie Virgil .08 .25
31 Duane Ward .08 .25
32 David Wells .60 1.50
33 Frank Wills .08 .25
34 Mookie Wilson .20 .50
35 Schedule Card .08 .25
36 Skydome CL .20 .50

1990 Blue Jays Hostess Stickers

These six strips of three stickers each feature color player action shots depicting great moments for the Blue Jays. Each strip measures approximately 7" by 3 1/4"; each sticker measures approximately 2 1/4" by 3 1/4". A brief description in English of the great moment, along with the Blue Jays logo, appears within the blue stripe across the top. The same description, in French, appears within the blue stripe at the bottom, along with the Hostess logo. The stickers are unnumbered and checklisted below by strip.

COMPLETE SET (6) 8.00 20.00
1 Most Double Plays: 1.50 4.00
Damaso Garcia
MVP: George Bel
2 First AL East Pennant: 1.50 4.00
Blue Jays Clinch Division#
3 First Homer in Skydome: 2.50 6.00
Fred McGriff
Club Save L
4 First 100 Wins: 1.50 4.00
Jim Clancy
ML Home Run Record:/
5 Stolen Bases: 2.00 5.00
Dave Collins
Gold Glove Winners:/
6 Home Run On First 1.50 4.00
Pitch: Junior Felix
Almost Per

1991 Blue Jays Fire Safety

This 36-card standard-size set was jointly sponsored by the Ontario Association of Fire Chiefs, the Ministry of the Solicitor General, A and P/Dominion, Oh Henry, and the Toronto Blue Jays. The cards are unnumbered and checklisted below in alphabetical order.

COMPLETE SET (36) 4.00 10.00
1 Jim Acker .08 .25
2 Roberto Alomar .75 2.00
3 Pat Borders .08 .25
4 Denis Boucher .08 .25
5 Joe Carter .60 1.50
6 Galen Cisco CO .08 .25
7 Ken Dayley .08 .25
8 Rob Ducey .08 .25
9 Cito Gaston MG .08 .25
10 Rene Gonzales .08 .25
11 Kelly Gruber .20 .50
12 Rich Hacker CO .08 .25
13 Tom Henke .30 .75
14 Glenallen Hill .08 .25
15 Jimmy Key .40 1.00
16 Manny Lee .08 .25
17 Al Leiter .40 1.00
18 Rance Mulliniks .08 .25
19 Greg Myers .08 .25
20 John Olerud .40 1.00
21 Mike Squires CO .08 .25
22 Dave Stieb .30 .75
23 Todd Stottlemyre .20 .50
24 John Sullivan CO .08 .25
25 Pat Tabler .08 .25
26 Gene Tenace CO .08 .25
27 Hector Torres CO .08 .25
28 Duane Ward .08 .25
29 David Wells .40 1.00
30 Devon White .20 .50
31 Mark Whiten .08 .25
32 Kenny Williams .30 .75
33 Frank Wills .08 .25
34 Mookie Wilson .20 .50
35 B.J. Burdy MASCOT .08 .25
36 Checklist Card .20 .50

1991 Blue Jays Score

The 1991 Score Toronto Blue Jays set contains 40 player cards plus five magic motion trivia cards. The standard-size cards feature on the fronts glossy color action photos with white borders.

COMPLETE SET (40) 5.00 12.00
1 Joe Carter .60 1.50
2 Tom Henke .30 .75
3 Jimmy Key .40 1.00
4 Al Leiter .40 1.00
5 Dave Stieb .40 1.00
6 Todd Stottlemyre .20 .50
7 Mike Timlin .20 .50
8 Duane Ward .08 .25
9 David Wells .40 1.00
10 Frank Wills .08 .25
11 Pat Borders .08 .25
12 Greg Myers .08 .25
13 Roberto Alomar .75 2.00
14 Rene Gonzales .08 .25
15 Kelly Gruber .20 .50
16 Manny Lee .08 .25
17 Rance Mulliniks .08 .25
18 John Olerud .40 1.00
19 Pat Tabler .08 .25
20 Derek Bell .20 .50
21 Jim Acker .08 .25
22 Rob Ducey .08 .25
23 Devon White .20 .50
24 Mookie Wilson .20 .50
25 Juan Guzman .20 .50
26 Ed Sprague .20 .50
27 Ken Dayley .08 .25
28 Tom Candiotti .08 .25
29 Candy Maldonado .08 .25
30 Eddie Zosky .08 .25
31 Steve Karsay .20 .50
32 Bob MacDonald .08 .25
33 Ray Giannelli .08 .25
34 Jerry Schunk .08 .25
35 Dave Weathers .08 .25
36 Cito Gaston MG .20 .50
37 Joe Carter AS .20 .50
38 Jimmy Key AS .20 .50
39 Roberto Alomar AS .40 1.00
40 1991 All-Star Game .08 .25

1992 Blue Jays Fire Safety

This 36-card standard-size set was jointly sponsored by the Ontario Association of Fire Chiefs, The Ministry of the Solicitor General, Mac's Milk, Mike's Mart, and Oh Henry. The cards are printed on recycled paper and are thinner than most sports cards. The cards are unnumbered and checklisted below in alphabetical order.

COMPLETE SET (36) 5.00 12.00
1 Roberto Alomar .75 2.00
2 Bob Bailor CO .08 .25
3 Derek Bell .08 .25
4 Pat Borders .08 .25
5 Joe Carter .50 1.25
6 Galen Cisco CO .08 .25
7 Ken Dayley .08 .25
8 Rob Ducey .08 .25
9 Cito Gaston MG .08 .25
10 Alfredo Griffin .08 .25
11 Kelly Gruber .20 .50
12 Juan Guzman .08 .25
13 Rich Hacker CO .08 .25
14 Tom Henke .30 .75
15 Larry Hisle CO .08 .25
16 Jimmy Key .40 1.00
17 Manny Lee .08 .25
18 Bob MacDonald .08 .25
19 Candy Maldonado .08 .25
20 Jack Morris .40 1.00
21 Rance Mulliniks .20 .50
22 Greg Myers .08 .25
23 John Olerud .40 1.00
24 Dave Stieb .30 .75
25 Todd Stottlemyre .20 .50
26 John Sullivan CO .08 .25
27 Pat Tabler .08 .25
28 Gene Tenace CO .08 .25
29 Mike Timlin .08 .25
30 Duane Ward .08 .25
31 Turner Ward .08 .25
32 David Wells .40 1.00
33 Devon White .20 .50
34 Dave Winfield .60 1.50
35 Eddie Zosky .08 .25
36 Checklist Card .08 .25

1992 Blue Jays Maxwell House

Sponsored by Maxwell House Coffee, this 18-card standard-size set celebrates the first fifteen years of the Toronto Blue Jays. The set includes a mail-in offer for a commemorative team card album. The cards are unnumbered and checklisted below in year order.

COMPLETE SET (18) 6.00 15.00
1 1977 Team Photo .60 1.50
9 1985 Team Photo .60 1.50
16 1992 Team Photo .60 1.50
17 Title Card .40 1.00
18 Album Offer Card .40 1.00

1993 Blue Jays Colla Postcards 15

This 15-card set is borderless, without the player's name on the front. Eight cards are marked "WC" for "World Champions", in a border across the front corner. Backs contain the player's name and the Blue Jays logo. We have checklisted the cards alphabetically.

COMPLETE SET (15) 3.00 8.00
1 Roberto Alomar .75 2.00
2 Pat Borders .20 .50
3 Joe Carter .60 1.50
4 Roberto Alomar WC .60 1.50
5 Pat Borders WC .20 .50
6 Joe Carter WC .30 .75
7 Juan Guzman WC .20 .50
8 Jack Morris WC .40 1.00
9 John Olerud WC .30 .75
10 Todd Stottlemyre WC .30 .75
11 Devon White WC .20 .50
12 Juan Guzman .20 .50
13 Paul Molitor .75 2.00
14 Dave Stewart .30 .75
15 Devon White .30 .75

1993 Blue Jays Dempster's

This 25-card standard-size set commemorates the 1992 World Series Champion Toronto Blue Jays and was sponsored by Dempster's. The cards are numbered on the front.

COMPLETE SET (25) 6.00 15.00
1 Juan Guzman .20 .50
2 Roberto Alomar .75 2.00
3 Danny Cox .20 .50
4 Paul Molitor .75 2.00
5 Todd Stottlemyre .30 .75
6 Joe Carter .60 1.50
7 Jack Morris .40 1.00
8 Ed Sprague .20 .50
9 Turner Ward .20 .50
10 John Olerud .60 1.50
11 Duane Ward .20 .50
12 Alfredo Griffin .20 .50
13 Cito Gaston MG .20 .50
14 Dave Stewart .40 1.00
15 Mark Eichhorn .20 .50
16 Darnell Coles .20 .50
17 Randy Knorr .20 .50
18 Al Leiter .60 1.50
19 Pat Hentgen .60 1.50
20 Devon White .30 .75
21 Pat Borders .20 .50
22 Darrin Jackson .20 .50
23 Dick Schofield .20 .50
24 Luis Sojo .20 .50
25 Mike Timlin .30 .75

1993 Blue Jays Donruss 45

This standard-size 45-card gold-boxed set showcases the 1992 Blue Jays with full-bleed action color photos.

COMP.FACT SET (45) 6.00 15.00
1 Checklist Card .08 .25
2 Roberto Alomar .60 1.50
3 Derek Bell .08 .25
4 Pat Borders .08 .25
5 Joe Carter .50 1.25
6 Alfredo Griffin .08 .25
7 Kelly Gruber .08 .25
8 Manny Lee .08 .25
9 Candy Maldonado .08 .25
10 John Olerud .40 1.00
11 Ed Sprague .08 .25
12 Pat Tabler .08 .25
13 Devon White .20 .50
14 Dave Winfield .60 1.50
15 David Cone .40 1.00
16 Mark Eichhorn .08 .25
17 Juan Guzman .08 .25
18 Tom Henke .08 .25
19 Jimmy Key .20 .50
20 Jack Morris .30 .75
21 Todd Stottlemyre .20 .50
22 Mike Timlin .20 .50
23 Duane Ward .08 .25
24 David Wells .40 1.00
25 Randy Knorr .08 .25
26 Rance Mulliniks .08 .25
27 Tom Quinlan .08 .25
28 Cito Gaston MG .20 .50
29 Dave Stieb .30 .75
30 Ken Dayley .08 .25
31 Turner Ward .08 .25
32 Eddie Zosky .08 .25
33 Pat Hentgen .60 1.50
34 Al Leiter .40 1.00
35 Doug Linton .08 .25
36 Bob MacDonald .08 .25
37 Rick Trlicek .08 .25
38 Domingo Martinez .08 .25
39 Mike Maksudian .08 .25
40 Rob Ducey .08 .25
41 Jeff Kent 1.50 4.00
42 Greg Myers .08 .25
43 Dave Weathers .08 .25
44 Skydome .08 .25
45 Trophy Presentation .08 .25

1993 Blue Jays Donruss McDonald's

This 36-card standard-size set was produced by Donruss for McDonald's and recognizes "Great Moments" of the Blue Jays. Foil packs sold for 45 cents Canadian with purchase of fries or hash browns. In terms of design, the set subdivides into three sections: 1985-92 Team Highlights (1-13); 1992 World Series (14-26); and regular-issue player cards (27-35). The cards have fronts depicting significant plays and players from 1985 to 1992 in action photos. The McDonald's logo is located in the top left. On cards 1-26, the gold-foil stamped "Great Moments" appears near the bottom with the name of the great moment listed below, while the back describes the event pictured on the front and is superimposed on a ghosted logo of the Blue Jays, with the date in gold lettering across the top.

COMPLETE SET (39) 8.00 20.00
1 Willie Upshaw .20 .50
2 Jesse Barfield .30 .75
3 Fred McGriff 1.00 2.50
4 George Bell .30 .75
5 Kelly Gruber .20 .50
6 Ernie Whitt .08 .25
7 Tom Henke .08 .25
8 Dave Stieb .20 .50
9 Jack Morris .30 .75
10 Team salutes fans .08 .25
11 Pat Borders .75 2.00
Mark McGwire
12 Roberto Alomar .75 2.00
13 Candy Maldonado .08 .25
14 Ed Sprague .20 .50
15 Bobby Cox MG .08 .25
Cito Gaston MG
16 Devon White .30 .75
17 Kelly Gruber .75 2.00
Deion Sanders
18A Roberto Alomar ERR .75 2.00
Kelly Gruber
No Winning Welcome
18B Roberto Alomar COR .75 2.00
Kelly Gruber
1992 Winning Welcome
19 Kelly Gruber .08 .25
Damon Berryhill
20 Jimmy Key .20 .50
21 Devon White .20 .50
Candy Maldonado
22 Joe Carter .30 .75
Otis Nixon
23 Blue Jays COR .30 .75
1992 World Champions
23 Blue Jays Celebrate .20 .50
1992 WS Champions
23A Blue Jays ERR .30 .75
1992World Champions
Jimmy Key pictured
24 Paul Beeston PR .08 .25
Cito Gaston MG
1992 WS Trophy
25 Pat Borders MVP .08 .25
26 SkyDome victory parade .08 .25
1992 WS Heroes
27 John Olerud .30 .75
28 Roberto Alomar .75 2.00
29 Ed Sprague .08 .25
30 Dick Schofield .08 .25
31 Devon White .20 .50
32 Joe Carter .60 1.50
33 Darrin Jackson .08 .25
34 Pat Borders .08 .25
35 Paul Molitor .75 2.00
36 Checklist 1-36 .08 .25

1993 Blue Jays Donruss World Series

This nine-card horizontally oriented set captures highlights from the 1992 World Series. The cards are numbered on the back with a "WS" prefix.

COMPLETE SET (9) 2.50 6.00
1 Series Opener .20 .50
Blue Jays-Braves
2 Joe Carter .40 1.00
3 Ed Sprague .20 .50
Derek Bell
4 Candy Maldonado .20 .50
5 Jimmy Key .30 .75
6 John Olerud .40 1.00
7 Dave Winfield .60 1.50
Derek Bell
8 Pat Borders .30 .75
9 Blue Jays celebrate .30 .75

1993 Blue Jays Fire Safety

This 36-card standard-size set commemorates the 1992 World Series Champion Toronto Blue Jays. The set was jointly sponsored by the Ontario Association of Fire Chiefs, The Office of the Fire Marshal, Becker's, Oh Henry, and the Blue Jays. The cards are unnumbered and checklisted below in alphabetical order.

COMPLETE SET (36) 4.00 10.00
1 Roberto Alomar .60 1.50
2 Bob Bailor CO .08 .25
3 Pat Borders .08 .25
4 Joe Carter .40 1.00
5 Galen Cisco CO .08 .25
6 Darnell Coles .08 .25
7 Danny Cox .08 .25
8 Ken Dayley .08 .25
9 Mark Eichhorn .08 .25
10 Cito Gaston MG .08 .25
11 Alfredo Griffin .08 .25
12 Juan Guzman .08 .25
13 Rich Hacker CO .08 .25
14 Pat Hentgen .20 .50
15 Larry Hisle CO .08 .25
16 Darrin Jackson .08 .25
17 Randy Knorr .08 .25
18 Al Leiter .40 1.00
19 Domingo Martinez .08 .25
20 Paul Molitor .60 1.50
21 Jack Morris .30 .75
22 John Olerud .40 1.00
23 Tom Quinlan .08 .25
24 Dick Schofield .08 .25
25 Luis Sojo .08 .25
26 Ed Sprague .08 .25
27 Dave Stewart .30 .75
28 Todd Stottlemyre .20 .50
29 John Sullivan CO .08 .25
30 Gene Tenace CO .08 .25
31 Mike Timlin .20 .50
32 Duane Ward .08 .25
33 Turner Ward .08 .25
34 Devon White .20 .50
35 Eddie Zosky .08 .25
36 Checklist 1-36 .08 .25

1994 Blue Jays Postcards

This 12-postcard set of Toronto Blue Jays was issued in a cardboard sleeve. Each postcard measures 4" by 6". The postcards are unnumbered and checklisted below in alphabetical order.

COMPLETE SET (10) 3.00 8.00
1 Roberto Alomar .75 2.00
2 Pat Borders .20 .50
3 Joe Carter .60 1.50
4 Carlos Delgado 1.25 3.00
5 Juan Guzman .20 .50
6 Paul Molitor 1.00 2.50
7 John Olerud .60 1.50
8 Ed Sprague .20 .50
9 Devon White .40 1.00
10 1992, 1993 WS Trophies .20 .50
11 World Series Rings .20 .50
12 1993 WS Champions Logo .20 .50

1994 Blue Jays U.S. Playing Cards

These 56 playing standard-size cards have rounded corners, and feature borderless color posed and action player photos on their fronts. The player's name and position appear near the bottom. The two-tone blue backs carry logos for the Blue Jays, MLB, MLBPA, and Bicycle Sports Collection. The set is checklisted below in playing card order by suits and assigned numbers to aces (1), jacks (11), queens (12), and kings (13).

COMP. FACT SET (56) 1.50 4.00
1C John Olerud .08 .25
1D Roberto Alomar .15 .40
1H Joe Carter .10 .30
1S Paul Molitor .15 .40
2C Al Leiter .08 .25
2D Eddie Zosky .01 .05
2H Woody Williams .02 .10
2S Michael Timlin .01 .05
3C Dave Stewart .02 .10
3D Rob Butler .01 .05
3H Danny Cox .01 .05
3S Randy Knorr .01 .05
4C Pat Borders .01 .05
4D Tony Castillo .01 .05
4H Todd Stottlemyre .02 .10
4S Pat Hentgen .08 .25
5C Devon White .02 .10
5D Duane Ward .01 .05
5H Ed Sprague .01 .05
5S Darnell Coles .01 .05
6C Joe Carter .10 .30
6D Paul Molitor .15 .40
6H John Olerud .08 .25
6S Juan Guzman .01 .05
7C Roberto Alomar .15 .40
7D John Olerud .08 .25
7H Paul Molitor .15 .40
7S Roberto Alomar .15 .40
8C Woody Williams .02 .10
8D Carlos Delgado .30 .75
8H Scott Brow .01 .05
8S Joe Carter .10 .30
9C Eddie Zosky .01 .05
9D Michael Timlin .02 .10
9H Pat Hentgen .08 .25
9S Scott Brow .01 .05
10C Willie Canate .01 .05
10D Randy Knorr .01 .05
10H Al Leiter .05 .15
10S Dick Schofield .01 .05
11C Danny Cox .01 .05
11D Pat Hentgen .08 .25
11H Dave Stewart .02 .10
11S Rob Butler .01 .05
12C Todd Stottlemyre .02 .10
12D Darnell Coles .01 .05
12H Pat Borders .01 .05
12S Tony Castillo .01 .05
13C Ed Sprague .01 .05
13D Juan Guzman .01 .05
13H Devon White .02 .10
13S Duane Ward .01 .05
NNO Featured Players .01 .05

1995 Blue Jays Becker

This five-card set features borderless color player photos distributed in a booklet and sponsored by Becker's stores. The backs display a postcard format and player information. The top portion of each page displays a perforated coupon redeemable for a certain food item at participating Becker's stores. The cards are unnumbered and checklisted below according to where they appear in the booklet.

COMPLETE SET (5) 4.00 10.00
1 Roberto Alomar 1.25 3.00
2 Juan Guzman .40 1.00
3 Paul Molitor 1.25 3.00
4 John Olerud .60 1.50
5 Joe Carter 1.00 2.50

1995 Blue Jays Oh Henry!

This 36-card set of the Toronto Blue Jays was sponsored by Oh Henry Candy Bars and features color player action photos. The backs carry player information and career statistics. The cards are unnumbered and checklisted below in alphabetical order.

COMPLETE SET (36) 5.00 12.00
1 Roberto Alomar .60 1.50
2 Bob Bailor CO .08 .25
3 Howard Battle .08 .25
4 Joe Carter .40 1.00
5 Tony Castillo .08 .25
6 Domingo Cedeno .08 .25
7 Galen Cisco CO .08 .25
8 David Cone .40 1.00
9 Brad Cornett .08 .25
10 Danny Cox .08 .25
11 Tim Crabtree .08 .25
12 Carlos Delgado .60 1.50
13 Cito Gaston MG .30 .75
14 Alex Gonzalez .20 .50
15 Shawn Green .75 2.00
16 Juan Guzman .08 .25
17 Darren Hall .08 .25
18 Pat Hentgen .20 .50
19 Larry Hisle CO .08 .25
20 Dennis Holmberg CO .08 .25
21 Michael Huff .08 .25
22 Randy Knorr .08 .25
23 Al Leiter .40 1.00
24 Nick Leyva CO .08 .25
25 Angel Martinez .08 .25
26 Paul Molitor .60 1.50
27 John Olerud .30 .75
28 Tomas Perez .08 .25
29 Aaron Small .30 .75
30 Paul Spoljaric .08 .25
31 Ed Sprague .08 .25
32 Gene Tenace CO .08 .25
33 Mike Timlin .20 .50
34 Duane Ward .08 .25
35 Devon White .20 .50
36 Woody Williams .20 .50

1995 Blue Jays Postcards

This five-card set of collector postcards comes in a stapled booklet which measures 4" by 8 1/2". The fronts feature borderless color player photos attached by perforation to a sponsor's coupon at the top. After perforation, the postcards measure 4" by 5 1/2".

COMPLETE SET (5) 2.00 5.00
1 Roberto Alomar .75 2.00
2 Joe Carter .60 1.50
3 Juan Guzman .40 1.00
4 Paul Molitor .75 2.00
5 John Olerud .60 1.50

1995 Blue Jays U.S. Playing Cards

These 56 standard-size playing cards have rounded corners, and feature color player photos on their white-bordered fronts. The player's name and position appear in a red bar near the bottom. The blue and gray backs carry the logos for the Toronto Blue Jays, MLBPA, and Bicycle Sports Collection. The set is checklisted below in playing card order by suits and assigned numbers to aces (1), jacks (11), queens (12), and kings (13).

COMPLETE SET (56) 2.00 5.00
1C John Olerud .08 .25
1D Joe Carter .10 .30
1H Roberto Alomar .15 .40
1S Paul Molitor .15 .40
2C Pat Hentgen .02 .10
2D Duane Ward .01 .05

2H Candy Maldonado .01 .05
2S Todd Stottlemyre .02 .10
3C Juan Guzman .01 .05
3D Dave Stewart .02 .10
3H Mike Timlin .01 .05
3S Rickey Henderson .30 .75
4C Cecil Fielder .05 .15
4D Tony Fernandez .02 .10
4H Ed Sprague .01 .05
4S Tom Henke .02 .10
5C Roberto Alomar .15 .40
5D Jack Morris .02 .10
5H Pat Borders .01 .05
5S Fred McGriff .15 .40
6C Joe Carter .10 .30
6D Dave Winfield .20 .50
6H Jimmy Key .02 .10
6S Devon White .01 .05
7C Mark Eichhorn .01 .05
7D John Olerud .08 .25
7H Paul Molitor .15 .40
7S Duane Ward .01 .05
8C Carlos Delgado .25 .60
8D Manny Lee .01 .05
8H Candy Maldonado .01 .05
8S David Wells .05 .15
9C Tom Candiotti .01 .05
9D Pat Hentgen .08 .25
9H Danny Cox .01 .05
9S David Cone .08 .25
10C Dave Stewart .02 .10
10D Randy Knorr .01 .05
10H Todd Stottlemyre .02 .10
10S Mike Timlin .02 .10
11C Tony Fernandez .05 .15
11D Juan Guzman .01 .05
11H Rickey Henderson .30 .75
11S Ed Sprague .01 .05
12C Pat Borders .01 .05
12D Fred McGriff .15 .40
12H Tom Henke .02 .10
12S Jack Morris .10 .30
13C Dave Winfield .20 .50
13D Devon White .01 .05
13H Cecil Fielder .08 .25
13S Jimmy Key .08 .25
NNO Title Card .01 .05
NNO Team Logo .01 .05
NNO Team Name .01 .05
NNO Featured players .01 .05

1996 Blue Jays Becker

This five-card set features borderless color action player photos distributed in a booklet and sponsored by Becker's stores. The backs display a postcard format and player information. The last two pages of the booklet carry perforated coupons redeemable for certain food items at participating Becker's stores. The cards are unnumbered and checklisted below according to where they appear in the booklet.

COMPLETE SET (5) 3.00 8.00
1 Alfredo Griffin .40 1.00
2 Jesse Barfield .75 2.00
3 George Bell .75 2.00
4 Kelly Gruber .60 1.50
5 Dave Stieb .60 1.50

1996 Blue Jays Bookmarks

This six-card set of the Toronto Blue Jays measures approximately 2 1/2" by 6 1/4". One side features a color player portrait with personal statistics in English and a facsimile autograph. The other side displays color action player photos with personal statistics in French and a facsimile autograph. The cards are unnumbered and checklisted below in alphabetical order.

COMPLETE SET (6) 2.00 5.00
1 Joe Carter .60 1.50
2 Pat Hentgen .40 1.00
3 Otis Nixon .08 .25
4 John Olerud .30 .75
5 Ed Sprague .08 .25
6 Woody Williams .20 .50

1996 Blue Jays Oh Henry!

This 36-card set commemorates the 20th anniversary of the Toronto Blue Jays and features color player photos with player information and statistics on the backs.

COMPLETE SET (36) 5.00 12.00
1 George Bell .30 .75
2 Brian Bohanon .08 .25
3 Joe Carter .50 1.25
4 Tony Castillo .08 .25
5 Domingo Cedeno .08 .25
6 Tim Crabtree .08 .25
7 Felipe Crespo .08 .25
8 Carlos Delgado .60 1.50
9 Cito Gaston MG .08 .25
10 Alex Gonzalez .20 .50
11 Shawn Green .75 2.00
12 Alfredo Griffin CO .08 .25
13 Kelly Gruber .20 .50
14 Juan Guzman .08 .25
15 Erik Hanson .08 .25
16 Pat Hentgen .20 .50
17 Marty Janzen .08 .25
18 Nick Leyva CO .08 .25
19 Sandy Martinez .08 .25
20 Lloyd Moseby .20 .50
21 Otis Nixon .08 .25
22 Charlie O'Brien .08 .25
23 John Olerud .40 1.00
24 Robert Perez .08 .25
25 Mel Queen CO .08 .25
26 Paul Quantrill .30 .75
27 Bill Risley .08 .25
28 Juan Samuel .08 .25
29 Ed Sprague .08 .25
30 Dave Stieb .30 .75
31 Gene Tenace CO .08 .25
32 Mike Timlin .20 .50
33 Willie Upshaw CO .08 .25
34 Jeff Ware .08 .25
35 Ernie Whitt .20 .50
36 Woody Williams .20 .50

1997 Blue Jays Bookmarks

This 12-card set of the Toronto Blue Jays measures approximately 2 7/16" by 6 1/4". One side features a color player portrait with personal statistics in English and a facsimile autograph. The other side displays the same color portrait with personal statistics in French and a facsimile autograph. The cards are unnumbered and checklisted below in alphabetical order.

COMPLETE SET (12) 6.00 15.00
1 Joe Carter .75 2.00
2 Roger Clemens 2.00 5.00
3 Tim Crabtree .40 1.00
4 Cito Gaston .60 1.50
5 Alex Gonzalez .60 1.50
6 Shawn Green 1.25 3.00
7 Juan Guzman .40 1.00
8 Pat Hentgen .60 1.50
9 Otis Nixon .40 1.00
10 Charlie O'Brien .40 1.00
11 Benito Santiago .75 2.00
12 Mike Timlin .60 1.50

1997 Blue Jays Cash Converters

This one-card set was distributed by the Toronto Blue Jays and displays color photos of four Blue Jays pitchers on a blue "K" and solid red background. The back displays an advertisement for the "K for Kids" program sponsored by Cash Converters.

1 Juan Guzman 1.25 3.00
Erik Hansen
Roger Clemens
Pat Hentg

1997 Blue Jays Copi Quik Interleague

This one-card set was sponsored by Copi Quik and commemorates the Inaugural interleague play games between the Toronoto Blue Jays and the Philadelphia Phillies at Veterans Stadium on June 13-15, 1997. The front features an action image of Roger Clemens on a blue background. The back displays information about the player and the interleague games. Only 7,000 of this card were printed and are sequentially numbered.

1 Roger Clemens 2.00 5.00

1997 Blue Jays Jackie Robinson

This one-card set commemorates the 50th anniversary of Jackie Robinson becoming the first man to cross Major League Baseball's race barrier. The front features a sepia tone player portrait with a thin black inner border and a wider blue outer border. The back displays player information below a statement by Brooklyn Dodgers owner Branch Rickey about Jackie Robinson.

1 Jackie Robinson 2.00 5.00

1997 Blue Jays Oh Henry!

This 36-card set of the Toronto Blue Jays was sponsored by Oh Henry Candy Bars and features color player action photos. The backs carry player information and career statistics.

COMPLETE SET (36) 5.00 12.00
1 Luis Andujar .08 .25
2 Tilson Brito .08 .25
3 Jacob Brumfield .08 .25
4 Joe Carter .40 1.00
5 Roger Clemens 1.00 2.50
6 Tim Crabtree .08 .25
7 Felipe Crespo .08 .25
8 Carlos Delgado .50 1.25
9 Carlos Garcia .08 .25
10 Cito Gaston MG .08 .25
11 Alex Gonzalez .20 .50
12 Shawn Green .60 1.50
13 Alfredo Griffin CO .08 .25
14 Juan Guzman .08 .25
15 Erik Hanson .08 .25
16 Pat Hentgen .40 1.00
17 Jim Lett CO .08 .25
18 Nick Leyva CO .08 .25
19 Orlando Merced .08 .25
20 Otis Nixon .08 .25
21 Charlie O'Brien .08 .25
22 Robert Perez .08 .25
23 Robert Person .08 .25
24 Dan Plesac .08 .25
25 Paul Quantrill .20 .50
26 Mel Queen CO .08 .25
27 Bill Risley .08 .25
28 Juan Samuel .08 .25
29 Benito Santiago .20 .50
30 Paul Spoljaric .08 .25
31 Ed Sprague .08 .25
32 Shannon Stewart .40 1.00
33 Gene Tenace CO .08 .25
34 Mike Timlin .20 .50
35 Willie Upshaw Co .08 .25
36 Woody Williams .20 .50

1997 Blue Jays Sizzler

This 60-card set features color player images on various colored borderless backgrounds with faint baseball images. A facsimile gold autograph is printed across the bottom of the front. The backs carry a small player photo with player information and statistics. Cards numbered 32-50 display "Magic Moments" in the team's history. For $19.95, the collector could obtain a black "Pleather" album with archival-approved sleeves to keep the cards in.

COMPLETE SET (60) 10.00 25.00
1 Alex Gonzalez .20 .50
2 Pat Hentgen .40 1.00
3 Joe Carter .40 1.00
4 Ed Sprague .08 .25
5 Benito Santiago .30 .75
6 Roger Clemens 2.00 5.00
7 Carlos Garcia .08 .25
8 Juan Guzman .08 .25
9 Dan Plesac .08 .25
10 Carlos Delgado .60 1.50
11 Orlando Merced .08 .25
12 Woody Williams .20 .50
13 Shawn Green .75 2.00
14 Erik Hanson .08 .25
15 Charlie O'Brien .08 .25
16 Otis Nixon .08 .25
17 Paul Spoljaric .08 .25
18 Jacob Brumfield .08 .25
19 Mike Timlin .20 .50
20 Tilson Brito .08 .25
21 Paul Quantrill .20 .50
22 Tim Crabtree .08 .25
23 Jim Lett .08 .25
24 Cito Gaston MG .08 .25
25 Alfredo Griffin CO .08 .25
26 Nick Leyva CO .08 .25
27 Mel Queen CO .08 .25
28 Gene Tenace CO .08 .25
29 Willie Upshaw CO .08 .25
30 Pat Hentgen .20 .50
31 Roger Clemens 1.00 2.50
32 First Pitch '77 .08 .25
33 Dave Stieb's No Hitter .08 .25
34 George Bell .08 .25
Lloyd Moseby
Jesse Barfield
35 1992 World Series .08 .25
36 1985 Pennant Win .08 .25
37 Paul Molitor .60 1.50
38 Tom Henke .08 .25
Duane Ward
39 Ernie Whitt .20 .50
40 Joe Carte .40 1.00
Home Run, 1993
41 Jack Morris .30 .75
42 Pat Borders .08 .25
43 Dave Winfield .50 1.25
44 Damaso Garcia .08 .25
45 Tony Fernandez .20 .50
46 Roberto Alomar .50 1.25
47 Dave Stewart .20 .50
48 John Olerud .30 .75
Paul Molitor
Roberto Alomar
49 Fred McGriff .50 1.25
50 Kelly Gruber .08 .25
51 Alex Gonzalez .20 .50
52 Huck Flener .08 .25
53 Marty Janzen .08 .25
54 Sandy Martinez .08 .25
55 Felipe Crespo .08 .25
56 Tomas Perez .08 .25
57 Shannon Stewart .50 1.25
58 Billy Koch .20 .50
59 Roy Halladay 1.50 4.00
60 Chris Carpenter .75 2.00

1997 Blue Jays Sun

This nine-card set was used to commemorate "Designated Driver Day at SkyDome." The fronts feature color action player photos printed on cards measuring approximately 3" by 8". The top section of the card is perforated and contains sponsor advertisements. A contest entry card was enclosed to be returned with a new slogan for the next "Designated Driver Day" and a chance to win two tickets to the Toronto Blue Jays Skybox for that day. The cards are unnumbered and checklisted below in alphabetical order.

COMPLETE SET (8) 6.00 15.00
1 Title Card .40 1.00
2 Joe Carter .75 2.00
3 Roger Clemens 1.50 4.00
4 Carlos Delgado 1.25 3.00
5 Alex Gonzalez .60 1.50
6 Pat Hentgen 1.00 2.50
7 Otis Nixon .40 1.00
8 Charlie O'Brien .40 1.00
9 Ed Sprague .40 1.00

1998 Blue Jays Labatt

These five color 4" by 6" cards feature members of the Toronto Blue Jays. The backs feature a post card back along with a safety tip

COMPLETE SET (5) 4.00 10.00
1 Jose Cruz Jr. .75 2.00
Shawn Green
Shannon Stewart
2 Carlos Delgado 1.25 3.00
3 Alex Gonzalez .40 1.00
4 Roger Clemens 1.25 3.00
Pat Hentgen
5 Set Montage .60 1.50

1998 Blue Jays Oh Henry!

COMPLETE SET (36) 4.00 10.00
1 Carlos Almanzar .20 .50
2 Kevin Brown .20 .50
3 Sal Butera .20 .50
4 Jose Canseco .30 .75
5 Chris Carpenter .30 .75
6 Roger Clemens .60 1.50
7 Felipe Crespo .20 .50
8 Jose Cruz Jr .20 .50
9 Mark Dalesandro .20 .50
10 Carlos Delgado .20 .50
11 Kelvim Escobar .20 .50
12 Tony Fernandez .20 .50
13 Darrin Fletcher .20 .50
14 Alex Gonzalez .20 .50
15 Craig Grebeck .20 .50
16 Shawn Green .20 .50
17 Juan Guzman .20 .50
18 Erik Hanson .20 .50
19 Pat Hentgen .20 .50
20 Jack Hubbard .20 .50
21 Tim Johnson .20 .50
22 Jim Lett .20 .50
23 Gary Matthews .20 .50
24 Randy Myers .20 .50
25 Paul Quantrill .20 .50
26 Mel Queen .20 .50
27 Robert Person .20 .50
28 Dan Plesac .20 .50
29 Bill Risley .20 .50
30 Eddie Rodriguez .20 .50
31 Juan Samuel .20 .50
32 Benito Santiago .20 .50
33 Ed Sprague .20 .50
34 Mike Stanley .20 .50
35 Shannon Stewart .20 .50
36 Woody Williams .20 .50

2002 Blue Jays Team Issue

COMPLETE SET (34) 4.00 10.00
1 Mike Barnett CO .08 .25
2 Dave Berg .08 .25
3 Brian Butterfield CO .08 .25
4 Chris Carpenter .40 1.00
5 Scott Cassidy .08 .25
6 Jose Cruz Jr. .20 .50
7 Carlos Delgado .60 1.50
8 Kelvim Escobar .20 .50
9 Scott Eyre .08 .25
10 Darrin Fletcher .08 .25
11 Cito Gaston ALUM MG .20 .50
12 John Gibbons CO .08 .25
13 Roy Halladay .50 1.25
14 Tom Henke .30 .75
15 Felix Heredia .08 .25
16 Eric Hinske .50 1.25
17 Ken Huckaby .08 .25
18 Joe Lawrence .08 .25
19 Esteban Loaiza .20 .50
20 Felipe Lopez .08 .25
21 Jack Morris .30 .75
22 Steve Parris .08 .25
23 Gil Patterson .08 .25
24 Cliff Politte .08 .25
25 Luke Prokopec .08 .25
26 Shannon Stewart .40 1.00
27 Corey Thurman .20 .50
28 Carlos Tosca .08 .25
29 Pete Walker .08 .25
30 Bruce Walton .08 .25
31 Vernon Wells .40 1.00
32 Devon White .20 .50
33 Tom Wilson .08 .25
34 Chris Woodward .08 .25

2006 Blue Jays Topps

COMPLETE SET (14) 3.00 8.00
TOR1 Roy Halladay .20 .50
TOR2 Vernon Wells .12 .30
TOR3 Russ Adams .12 .30
TOR4 Shea Hillenbrand .12 .30
TOR5 Gustavo Chacin .12 .30
TOR6 B.J. Ryan .12 .30
TOR7 Ted Lilly .12 .30
TOR8 Aaron Hill .12 .30
TOR9 Troy Glaus .12 .30
TOR10 Frank Catalanotto .12 .30
TOR11 Alex Rios .12 .30
TOR12 Reed Johnson .12 .30
TOR13 A.J. Burnett .12 .30
TOR14 Lyle Overbay .12 .30

2007 Blue Jays Topps

COMPLETE SET (14) 3.00 8.00
TOR1 Roy Halladay .20 .50
TOR2 Frank Thomas .30 .75
TOR3 Gregg Zaun .12 .30
TOR4 Lyle Overbay .12 .30
TOR5 Royce Clayton .12 .30
TOR6 A.J. Burnett .12 .30
TOR7 Adam Lind .12 .30
TOR8 Vernon Wells .12 .30
TOR9 Reed Johnson .12 .30
TOR10 Troy Glaus .12 .30
TOR11 Aaron Hill .12 .30
TOR12 Alex Rios .12 .30
TOR13 Gustavo Chacin .12 .30
TOR14 B.J. Ryan .12 .30

2008 Blue Jays Topps

COMPLETE SET (14) 3.00 8.00
TOR1 Roy Halladay .20 .50
TOR2 Frank Thomas .30 .75
TOR3 Gregg Zaun .12 .30
TOR4 Lyle Overbay .12 .30
TOR5 Shaun Marcum .12 .30
TOR6 A.J. Burnett .12 .30
TOR7 David Eckstein .12 .30
TOR8 Vernon Wells .12 .30
TOR9 Matt Stairs .12 .30
TOR10 Scott Rolen .20 .50
TOR11 Aaron Hill .12 .30
TOR12 Alex Rios .12 .30
TOR13 Dustin McGowan .12 .30
TOR14 B.J. Ryan .12 .30

2009 Blue Jays Topps

COMPLETE SET (15) 3.00 8.00
TOR1 Roy Halladay .25 .60
TOR2 Alex Rios .15 .40
TOR3 Vernon Wells .15 .40
TOR4 Rod Barajas .15 .40
TOR5 Lyle Overbay .15 .40
TOR6 Shaun Marcum .15 .40
TOR7 Travis Snider .25 .60
TOR8 Dustin McGowan .15 .40
TOR9 B.J. Ryan .15 .40
TOR10 Aaron Hill .15 .40
TOR11 Adam Lind .15 .40
TOR12 Scott Rolen .25 .60
TOR13 David Purcey .15 .40
TOR14 Marco Scutaro .25 .60
TOR15 Cito Gaston MG .15 .40

2010 Blue Jays Topps

COMPLETE SET (17) 3.00 8.00
TOR1 Aaron Hill .15 .40
TOR2 Lyle Overbay .15 .40
TOR3 John McDonald .15 .40
TOR4 Ricky Romero .15 .40
TOR5 Edwin Encarnacion .40 1.00
TOR6 Scott Downs .15 .40
TOR7 Alex Gonzalez .15 .40
TOR8 Vernon Wells .15 .40
TOR9 Brett Cecil .15 .40
TOR10 Brandon Morrow .15 .40
TOR11 Dustin McGowan .15 .40
TOR12 David Purcey .15 .40
TOR13 Marc Rzepczynski .15 .40
TOR14 Adam Lind .25 .60
TOR15 Jose Bautista .25 .60
TOR16 Travis Snider .15 .40
TOR17 Scott Richmond .15 .40

2011 Blue Jays Topps

COMPLETE SET (17) 3.00 8.00
TOR1 Jose Bautista .25 .60
TOR2 J.P. Arencibia .15 .40
TOR3 Rajai Davis .15 .40
TOR4 Brett Cecil .15 .40
TOR5 Kyle Drabek .25 .60
TOR6 Edwin Encarnacion .40 1.00
TOR7 Yunel Escobar .15 .40
TOR8 Aaron Hill .15 .40
TOR9 Jason Frasor .15 .40
TOR10 Adam Lind .25 .60
TOR11 Jose Molina .15 .40
TOR12 Brandon Morrow .15 .40
TOR13 Octavio Dotel .15 .40
TOR14 Travis Snider .15 .40
TOR15 Juan Rivera .15 .40
TOR16 Ricky Romero .15 .40
TOR17 Rogers Centre .15 .40

2012 Blue Jays Topps

COMPLETE SET (17) 3.00 8.00
TOR1 Jose Bautista .30 .75
TOR2 Travis Snider .25 .60
TOR3 Eric Thames .30 .75
TOR4 Yunel Escobar .25 .60
TOR5 Kelly Johnson .25 .60
TOR6 Brett Cecil .25 .60
TOR7 Colby Rasmus .30 .75
TOR8 Ricky Romero .25 .60
TOR9 J.P. Arencibia .25 .60
TOR10 Brandon Morrow .25 .60
TOR11 Henderson Alvarez .25 .60
TOR12 Edwin Encarnacion .40 1.00
TOR13 Adam Lind .30 .75
TOR14 Rajai Davis .25 .60
TOR15 Sergio Santos .25 .60
TOR16 Brett Lawrie .30 .75
TOR17 Rogers Centre .15 .40

2013 Blue Jays Topps

COMPLETE SET (17) 3.00 8.00
TOR1 Brett Lawrie .20 .50
TOR2 Jose Bautista .20 .50
TOR3 Brandon Morrow .15 .40
TOR4 Edwin Encarnacion .25 .60
TOR5 Colby Rasmus .20 .50
TOR6 Ricky Romero .15 .40
TOR7 R.A. Dickey .20 .50
TOR8 Casey Janssen .15 .40
TOR9 Adam Lind .20 .50
TOR10 Rajai Davis .15 .40
TOR11 Jose Reyes .20 .50
TOR12 Melky Cabrera .15 .40
TOR13 Josh Johnson .20 .50
TOR14 Mark Buehrle .20 .50
TOR15 J.P. Arencibia .15 .40
TOR16 Maicer Izturis .15 .40
TOR17 Rogers Centre .15 .40

2014 Blue Jays Topps

COMPLETE SET (17) 3.00 8.00
TOR1 Jose Reyes .20 .50
TOR2 Jose Bautista .20 .50
TOR3 Brandon Morrow .15 .40
TOR4 Edwin Encarnacion .25 .60
TOR5 Colby Rasmus .20 .50
TOR6 Steve Delabar .15 .40
TOR7 R.A. Dickey .20 .50
TOR8 Casey Janssen .15 .40
TOR9 Adam Lind .20 .50
TOR10 Dioner Navarro .15 .40
TOR11 Brett Lawrie .20 .50
TOR12 Melky Cabrera .15 .40
TOR13 Anthony Gose .15 .40
TOR14 Mark Buehrle .20 .50
TOR15 Moises Sierra .15 .40
TOR16 Maicer Izturis .15 .40
TOR17 Rogers Centre .15 .40

2015 Blue Jays Topps

COMPLETE SET (17) 3.00 8.00
TBJ1 Jose Bautista .20 .50
TBJ2 R.A. Dickey .20 .50
TBJ3 Edwin Encarnacion .25 .60
TBJ4 Russell Martin .15 .40
TBJ5 Dioner Navarro .15 .40
TBJ6 Jose Reyes .20 .50
TBJ7 Marco Estrada .15 .40
TBJ8 Justin Smoak .15 .40
TBJ9 Aaron Loup .15 .40
TBJ10 Dalton Pompey .20 .50
TBJ11 Drew Hutchison .15 .40
TBJ12 Josh Donaldson .20 .50
TBJ13 Michael Saunders .20 .50
TBJ14 Mark Buehrle .20 .50
TBJ15 Brett Cecil .15 .40
TBJ16 Marcus Stroman .20 .50
TBJ17 Aaron Sanchez .20 .50

2016 Blue Jays Topps

COMPLETE SET (17) 3.00 8.00
TOR1 Josh Donaldson .20 .50
TOR2 Kevin Pillar .15 .40
TOR3 Jose Bautista .20 .50
TOR4 Troy Tulowitzki .25 .60
TOR5 Justin Smoak .15 .40
TOR6 Devon Travis .15 .40
TOR7 Edwin Encarnacion .25 .60
TOR8 Brett Cecil .15 .40
TOR9 R.A. Dickey .20 .50
TOR10 J.A. Happ .20 .50
TOR11 Roberto Osuna .15 .40
TOR12 Aaron Sanchez .20 .50
TOR13 Jesse Chavez .15 .40
TOR14 Marcus Stroman .20 .50
TOR15 Russell Martin .15 .40
TOR16 Ryan Goins .15 .40
TOR17 Marco Estrada .15 .40

2017 Blue Jays Topps

COMPLETE SET (17) 3.00 8.00
TOR1 Josh Donaldson .20 .50
TOR2 Russell Martin .15 .40
TOR3 Kevin Pillar .15 .40
TOR4 J.A. Happ .20 .50
TOR5 Jason Grilli .15 .40
TOR6 Marco Estrada .15 .40
TOR7 Devon Travis .15 .40
TOR8 Roberto Osuna .15 .40
TOR9 Marcus Stroman .20 .50
TOR10 Troy Tulowitzki .25 .60
TOR11 Steve Pearce .25 .60
TOR12 Ryan Goins .15 .40
TOR13 Kendrys Morales .15 .40
TOR14 Aaron Sanchez .20 .50
TOR15 Francisco Liriano .15 .40
TOR16 Melvin Upton Jr. .20 .50
TOR17 Justin Smoak .15 .40

2018 Blue Jays Topps

COMPLETE SET (17) 2.00 5.00
TJ1 Josh Donaldson .20 .50
TJ2 Kendrys Morales .15 .40
TJ3 Kevin Pillar .15 .40
TJ4 Justin Smoak .15 .40
TJ5 Ryan Tepera .15 .40
TJ6 Teoscar Hernandez .25 .60
TJ7 Aaron Sanchez .20 .50
TJ8 Roberto Osuna .15 .40
TJ9 Joe Biagini .15 .40
TJ10 Devon Travis .15 .40
TJ11 Troy Tulowitzki .25 .60
TJ12 Steve Pearce .25 .60
TJ13 Russell Martin .15 .40
TJ14 Marcus Stroman .20 .50
TJ15 J.A. Happ .20 .50
TJ16 Aaron Loup .15 .40
TJ17 Marco Estrada .15 .40

2019 Blue Jays Topps

COMPLETE SET (17) 2.00 5.00
TJ1 Kevin Pillar .15 .40
TJ2 Randal Grichuk .15 .40
TJ3 Marcus Stroman .20 .50
TJ4 Justin Smoak .15 .40
TJ5 Brandon Drury .15 .40
TJ6 Lourdes Gurriel Jr. .20 .50
TJ7 Ken Giles .15 .40
TJ8 Kendrys Morales .15 .40
TJ9 Billy McKinney .15 .40
TJ10 Richard Urena .15 .40
TJ11 Devon Travis .15 .40
TJ12 Aaron Sanchez .20 .50
TJ13 Ryan Borucki .15 .40
TJ14 Sean Reid-Foley .15 .40
TJ15 Rowdy Tellez .25 .60
TJ16 Danny Jansen .15 .40
TJ17 Russell Martin .15 .40

2017 Blue Jays Topps National Baseball Card Day

COMPLETE SET (10) 5.00 12.00
TBJ1 Marco Estrada .60 1.50
TBJ2 Jose Bautista .75 2.00
TBJ3 Troy Tulowitzki 1.00 2.50
TBJ4 Marcus Stroman .75 2.00
TBJ5 Josh Donaldson .75 2.00
TBJ6 Aaron Sanchez .75 2.00
TBJ7 J.A. Happ .75 2.00
TBJ8 Roberto Osuna .60 1.50
TBJ9 Kevin Pillar .60 1.50
TBJ10 Roy Halladay .75 2.00

1931 Blue Ribbon Malt

These photos were issued to promote both Blue Ribbon Malt as well as Hack Wilson. The fronts have posed action shots with the words "Compliments of Blue Ribbon Malt" on the bottom. This checklist may be incomplete and additional information would be greatly appreciated.

1 Lu Blue 40.00 80.00
2 Lew Fonseca 40.00 80.00
3 Vic Frasier 40.00 80.00
4 Johnny Kerr 40.00 80.00
5 Bobby Smith 40.00 80.00
6 Billy Sullivan 40.00 80.00
7 Hack Wilson 75.00 150.00

1948-49 Blue Tint R346

The cards in this 48-card set measure 2" by 2 5/8". The "Blue Tint" set derives its name from its distinctive coloration. Collector Ralph Triplette has pointed out in his research that the set was issued during 1948 and 1949, not in 1947 as had been previously commonly thought. The cards are blank-backed and unnumbered, and were issued in strips of six or eight. The set was probably produced in Brooklyn and hence has a heavy emphasis on New York teams, especially the Yankees. Known variations are No. 2, Durocher, listed with Brooklyn or New York Giants, and No. 18, Ott, listed with Giants or no team designation. The set was initially listed in the catalog as R346 as well as being listed as W518. Although the W categorization is undoubtedly the more correct, nevertheless, the R listing has become the popularly referenced designation for the set. The complete set price below includes all listed variations. Numbers 41 through 48 exist with or without numbers on the front.

COMPLETE SET 600.00 1200.00
1 Bill Johnson 5.00 10.00
2A Leo Durocher 10.00 20.00
Brooklyn Dodgers
2B Leo Durocher 10.00 20.00
New York Giants
3 Marty Marion 6.00 12.00
4 Ewell Blackwell 6.00 12.00
5 John Lindell 5.00 10.00
6 Larry Jansen 5.00 10.00
7 Ralph Kiner 10.00 20.00
8 Chuck Dressen CO 6.00 12.00
9 Bobby Brown 6.00 12.00
10 Luke Appling 10.00 20.00
11 Bill Nicholson 6.00 12.00
12 Phil Masi 5.00 10.00
13 Frank Shea 5.00 10.00
14 Bob Dillinger 5.00 10.00
15 Pete Suder 5.00 10.00
16 Joe DiMaggio 100.00 200.00
17 John Corriden CO 5.00 10.00
18A Mel Ott MG 20.00 40.00
New York Giants
18B Mel Ott MG 20.00 40.00
No team designation
19 Buddy Rosar 5.00 10.00
20 Warren Spahn 12.50 25.00
21 Allie Reynolds 6.00 12.00
22 Lou Boudreau 10.00 20.00
23 Hank Majeski UER 5.00 10.00
Randy Gumpert pictured
24 Frank Crosetti 7.50 15.00
25 Gus Niarhos 5.00 10.00
26 Bruce Edwards 5.00 10.00
27 Rudy York 5.00 10.00
28 Don Black 5.00 10.00
29 Lou Gehrig 100.00 200.00
30 Johnny Mize 10.00 20.00
31 Ed Stanky 6.00 12.00
32 Vic Raschi 6.00 12.00
33 Cliff Mapes 5.00 10.00
34 Enos Slaughter 10.00 20.00
35 Hank Greenberg 10.00 20.00
36 Jackie Robinson 60.00 120.00
37 Frank Hiller 5.00 10.00
38 Bob Elliott 6.00 12.00
39 Harry Walker 5.00 10.00
40 Ed Lopat 7.50 15.00
41 Bobby Thomson 7.50 15.00
42 Tommy Henrich 6.00 12.00
43 Bobby Feller 25.00 50.00
44 Ted Williams 75.00 150.00
45 Dixie Walker 6.00 12.00
46 Johnny Vander Meer 6.00 12.00
47 Clint Hartung 5.00 10.00
48 Charlie Keller 6.00 12.00

1933 Blum's Baseball Bulletin

These black-backed photos, which measure 9 1/2" by 13 5/8" or 11 1/2" by 13 3/4" feature leading players of the past and present. The player's photo is on the top with his name and a biography on the bottom. Since these are unnumbered, we have sequenced them in alphabetical order.

COMPLETE SET 3000.00 6000.00
1 Grover C. Alexander 300.00 600.00
2 Eddie Collins 300.00 600.00
3 Jake Daubert 100.00 200.00
4 Bill Donovan 100.00 200.00
5 John Evers 250.00 500.00
6 Lou Gehrig 600.00 1200.00
7 Heinie Groh 100.00 200.00
8 Lefty Grove 400.00 800.00
9 Walter Johnson 500.00 1000.00
10 Nap Lajoie 300.00 600.00
11 Rabbit Maranville 200.00 400.00
12 James McAvoy 100.00 200.00
13 Tris Speaker 300.00 600.00
14 George Toporcer 100.00 200.00

1987 Boardwalk and Baseball

This 33-card standard-size set was produced by Topps for distribution by the "Boardwalk and Baseball" Theme Park which was located in Haines City, Florida. The set comes in a custom blue collector box. The full-color fronts are surrounded by a pink and black frame border. The card backs are printed in pink and black on white card stock. The set is subtitled "Top Run Makers." Hence no pitchers are included in the set. The checklist for the set is given on the back panel of the box. There are unconfirmed reports that a parallel version of this set exists without the line between the B's on the front. Any help in verifying this would be appreciated.

COMP. FACT. SET (33) 2.00 5.00
1 Mike Schmidt .30 .75
2 Eddie Murray .20 .50
3 Dale Murphy .15 .40
4 Dave Winfield .20 .50
5 Jim Rice .02 .10
6 Cecil Cooper .01 .05
7 Dwight Evans .01 .05
8 Rickey Henderson .30 1.00
9 Robin Yount .20 .50
10 Andre Dawson .10 .30
11 Gary Carter .20 .50
12 Keith Hernandez .02 .10
13 George Brett .50 1.25
14 Bill Buckner .01 .05
15 Tony Armas .01 .05
16 Harold Baines .07 .20
17 Don Baylor .02 .10
18 Steve Garvey .07 .20
19 Lance Parrish .02 .10
20 Dave Parker .02 .10
21 Buddy Bell .01 .05
22 Cal Ripken 1.00 2.50
23 Bob Horner .01 .05
24 Tim Raines .02 .10
25 Jack Clark .01 .05
26 Leon Durham .01 .05
27 Pedro Guerrero .01 .05
28 Kent Hrbek .01 .05
29 Kirk Gibson .02 .10
30 Ryne Sandberg .40 1.00
31 Wade Boggs .30 .75
32 Don Mattingly .40 1.25
33 Darryl Strawberry .02 .10

1984 Boggs Dental Group

This one card set, which measures 8 1/2" by 5 1/2" features on the front information about two dentists four offices in Connecticut as well as a color photo of Wade Boggs. The back of this card is a promotion for a fourth office opened by the dentists.

1 Wade Boggs 2.00 5.00

2003 Bonds SBC

1 Barry Bonds 2.00 5.00

1973-06 Book Promotional Cards

This set features various cards used to promote baseball books. We have sequenced them in year order. Cards number two through number 13 all were used to promote "Who was Harry Steinfeldt? And other baseball trivia.". All of these cards measure the standard size. We are not using a complete set price for this set because of the wide variance in years and availability of how these cards were released. According to information at the time, four thousand copies of the Jim Bouton 1979 card was issued.

1 Bo Belinsky 1973 6.00 15.00
Pitching and Wooing

Card		
2 Frank Baumholtz	1.25	3.00
3 Jim Bouton	2.00	5.00
4 Tony Conigliaro	2.00	5.00
5 Don Drysdale	4.00	10.00
6 Hank Greenberg	4.00	10.00
7 Walter Johnson	6.00	15.00
8 Billy Loes	1.25	3.00
9 Johnny Mize	4.00	10.00
10 Lefty O'Doul	2.00	5.00
11 Babe Ruth	10.00	25.00
12 Johnny Sain	2.00	5.00
13 Jim Thorpe	8.00	20.00
14 Jim Bouton 1979	1.25	3.00
Ball Four Plus Ball Five		
15 Billy Martin 1980	2.00	5.00
Number One		
16 Mickey Mantle 1986	4.00	10.00
The Mick		
17 Gary Carter 1987	1.50	4.00
A Dream Season		
17 Babe Ruth 1988	2.00	5.00
Babe Ruth's Book of Baseball Audio Cassette		
18 Nolan Ryan 1988	4.00	10.00
Throwing Heat		
19 Orel Hershiser 1989	1.25	3.00
Out of the Blue		
20 Gil Hodges 1992	2.00	5.00
The Quiet Man		
21 Joe Morgan 1993	1.25	3.00
A Life in Baseball		
22 Jim Bouton 1994	.75	2.00
Strike Zone		
23 Eliot Asinof 1994	.75	2.00
Strike Zone		
24 Charles Lupica 1997	.40	1.00
The Cleveland Indians Flagpole Sitter		
25 Joe Dittmar 1999	.75	2.00
Baseball Records Registry		
Postcard features Randy Johnson		
26 Sandy Koufax 2001	.40	1.00
Big Book of Jewish Baseball		
27 The Big Book of Jewish Baseball	4.00	10.00
Uncut Sheet		
Sandy Koufax		
Lipman Pike		
Moe Berg		
Jesse Levis		
Harry Shuman		
Hank Greenberg		
Harry Danning		
Cy Malis		
Hy Cohen		
28 Lou Gehrig 2002	.40	1.00
Breaking the Slump		
29 Babe Ruth 2002	.40	1.00
Breaking the Slump		
30 Hack Wilson	.40	1.00
Rogers Hornsby 2002		
Breaking the Slump		

1912 Boston Garter Color

These oversize gorgeous full color cards from the early part of the 20th century feature some of the leading players in the game. The front shows a drawing of the player along with a suitcase showing who they are. The Back lists details about how to use these cards to promote a storefront as well as a checklist on the back. According to advertising for these pieces, the cost of these photos from the manufacturer (George Frost Company in Boston) was 10 cents for a group of eight photos or 20 cents for all 16 photos.

Card		
COMPLETE SET (16)	100000.00	200000.00
1 Bob Bescher	7500.00	15000.00
2 Roger Breshnahan	12500.00	25000.00
3 Frank Chance	15000.00	30000.00
4 Hal Chase	10000.00	20000.00
5 Fred Clarke	15000.00	30000.00
6 Eddie Collins	20000.00	40000.00
7 Red Dooin	7500.00	15000.00
8 Hugh Jennings MG	12500.00	25000.00
9 Walter Johnson	25000.00	50000.00
10 Johnny Kling	7500.00	15000.00
11 Larry Lajoie	15000.00	30000.00
12 Frank LaPorte	7500.00	15000.00
13 Christy Mathewson	25000.00	50000.00
14 Nap Rucker	10000.00	20000.00
15 Tris Speaker	20000.00	40000.00
16 Ed Walsh	15000.00	30000.00

1914 Boston Garter Color

This 12 card oversize set features some of the leading players of the 1910's. These cards were issued free to retailers who sold the "Boston Garter" products. The front of the cards have a player photo in a "diamond" with the words "Boston Garter" written on baseballs located at the top. On the bottom are the words 25 and 50 cents as well as the design of the Boston Garter. The back gives career information about the player as well as has a checklist of the cards.

1 Tris Speaker
2 Ty Cobb
3 Burt Shotton UER
Name misspelled
4 Joe Tinker
5 Johnny Evers
6 Joe Jackson
7 Rabbit Maranville
8 Larry Doyle
9 Frank Baker
10 Ed Konetchy
11 Walter Johnson
12 Buck Herzog

1914 Boston Garter Sepia

This ten card white bordered set has a black and white portrait on the front with the players name and the Boston Garter logo in a baseball on the bottom. The back has information about the Boston Garter product along with a checklist and information on how to acquire these photos.

1 Christy Mathewson
2 Red Murray
3 Eddie Collins
4 Hugh Jennings MG
5 Hal Chase
6 Bob Bescher
7 Red Dooin
8 Nap Lajoie

9 Tris Speaker
10 Henie Zimmerman

1909 Boston Herald Supplements

These supplements, which feature only one player, and usually were cut from the newspaper at a 9" by 7" size, were issued in 1909 by the Boston Herald. Since these are unnumbered, we have sequenced them in alphabetical order by team.

Card		
COMPLETE SET (24)	2500.00	5000.00
1 Bill Carrigan	100.00	200.00
2 Charlie Chech	100.00	200.00
3 Ed Cicotte	300.00	600.00
4 Pat Donahue	100.00	200.00
5 Doc Gessler	100.00	200.00
6 Harry Hooper	200.00	400.00
7 Harry Lord	100.00	200.00
8 Ambrose McConnell	100.00	200.00
9 Harry Niles	100.00	200.00
10 Tris Speaker	400.00	800.00
11 Jake Stahl	100.00	200.00
12 Heinie Wagner	100.00	200.00
13 Chick Autry	100.00	200.00
14 Johnny Bates	100.00	200.00
15 Ginger Beaumont	100.00	200.00
16 Beals Becker	100.00	200.00
17 Frank Bowerman MG	100.00	200.00
18 Jack Coffey	100.00	200.00
19 Bill Dahlen	125.00	250.00
20 Peaches Graham	100.00	200.00
21 Al Mattern	100.00	200.00
22 Harry Smith	100.00	200.00
23 Bill Sweeney	100.00	200.00
24 Tom Tuckey	100.00	200.00

1909 Boston Herald Supplements Pairs

Issued in 1909, these double-sided newspaper supplements feature a member of the Boston Braves as well as the Boston Red Sox. Since these are not numbered, we have sequenced them in alphabetical order of the Red Sox player who appears. It is possible that there are more supplements to this set.

Card		
COMPLETE SET (9)	1250.00	2500.00
1 Eddie Cicotte	250.00	500.00
Tom Tuckey		
2 Pat Donahue	100.00	200.00
Harry Smith		
3 Doc Gessler	100.00	200.00
Frank Bowerman		
4 Harry Hooper	150.00	300.00
Johnny Bates		
5 Harry Lord	100.00	200.00
Unknown Player		
6 Amby McConnell	100.00	200.00
Jack Coffey		
7 Tris Speaker	250.00	500.00
Ginger Beaumont		
8 Jake Stahl	100.00	200.00
Chick Autry		
9 Heinie Wagner	100.00	200.00
Bill Dahlen		

1871 Boston Red Stockings Wright Cabinets

These cabinets, which measure approximately 4 1/4" by 6 1/2" feature members of the 1871 Boston Red Stockings. The fronts feature a posed portrait of the player in their uniforms while the back is an advertisment for the photo studio in which these photos were taken. Since these photos are unnumbered, we have sequenced them in alphabetical order.

Card		
1 Ross Barnes	7500.00	15000.00
2 David Birdsall	6000.00	12000.00
3 Andy Leonard	6000.00	12000.00
4 Cal McVey	12500.00	25000.00
5 John Ryan	6000.00	12000.00
6 Harry Schafer	6000.00	12000.00
7 Al Spalding	15000.00	30000.00
8 Harry Wright	12500.00	25000.00

1909 Boston Sunday Post Supplements

These supplements, each of which feature two players, were issued as supplements in the Sunday Papers in Boston in 1909.

Card		
COMPLETE SET (6)	750.00	1500.00
1 Ambrose McConnell	100.00	200.00
2 Harry Lord	250.00	500.00
Tris Speaker		
3 Harry Wolter	150.00	300.00
Harry Hooper		
4 Jake Stahl	100.00	200.00
Bill Carrigan		
5 Ed Cicotte	200.00	400.00
Harry Niles		
6 Heinie Wagner	100.00	200.00
Frank Arellanes		

1948 Bowman

The 48-card Bowman set of 1948 was the first major set of the post-war period. Each 2 1/16" by 2 1/2" card had a black and white photo of a current player, with his biographical information printed in black ink on a gray back. Due to the printing process and the 36-card sheet size upon which Bowman was then printing, the 12 cards marked with an SP in the checklist are scarcer numerically, as they were removed from the printing sheet in order to make room for the 12 high numbers (37-48). Cards were issued in one-card penny packs. Many cards are found with over-printed, transposed, or blank backs. The set features the Rookie Cards of Hall of Famers Yogi Berra, Ralph Kiner, Stan Musial, Red Schoendienst, and Warren Spahn. Half of the cards in the set feature New York Yankees or Giants players.

Card		
COMPLETE SET (48)	1500.00	4000.00
WRAPPER (5-CENT)	600.00	700.00
CARDS PRICED IN NM CONDITION !		
1 Bob Elliott RC	50.00	125.00
2 Ewell Blackwell RC	25.00	60.00
3 Ralph Kiner RC	100.00	250.00
4 Johnny Mize RC	50.00	120.00
5 Bob Feller RC	100.00	250.00
6 Yogi Berra RC	400.00	1000.00
7 Pete Reiser SP RC	50.00	120.00
8 Phil Rizzuto SP RC	125.00	300.00
9 Walker Cooper RC	8.00	20.00
10 Buddy Rosar RC	8.00	20.00
11 Johnny Lindell RC	10.00	25.00
12 Johnny Sain RC	20.00	50.00
13 Willard Marshall SP RC	15.00	40.00
14 Allie Reynolds RC	30.00	80.00
15 Eddie Joost	8.00	20.00
16 Jack Lohrke SP RC	15.00	40.00
17 Enos Slaughter RC	60.00	150.00
18 Warren Spahn RC	200.00	500.00
19 Tommy Henrich	20.00	50.00
20 Buddy Kerr SP RC	15.00	40.00
21 Ferris Fain RC	20.00	50.00
22 Floyd Bevens SP RC	20.00	50.00
23 Larry Jansen RC	10.00	25.00
24 Dutch Leonard SP	15.00	40.00
25 Barney McCosky	8.00	20.00
26 Frank Shea SP RC	20.00	50.00
27 Sid Gordon RC	20.00	50.00
28 Emil Verban SP RC	15.00	40.00
29 Joe Page SP RC	25.00	60.00
30 Whitey Lockman SP RC	20.00	50.00
31 Bill McCahan RC	8.00	20.00
32 Bill Rigney RC	8.00	20.00
33 Bill Johnson RC	10.00	25.00
34 Sheldon Jones SP RC	15.00	40.00
35 Snuffy Stirnweiss RC	15.00	40.00
36 Stan Musial RC	750.00	2000.00
37 Clint Hartung RC	12.00	30.00
38 Red Schoendienst RC	150.00	400.00
39 Augie Galan RC	12.00	30.00
40 Marty Marion RC	30.00	80.00
41 Rex Barney RC	25.00	60.00
42 Ray Poat RC	12.00	30.00
43 Bruce Edwards RC	15.00	40.00
44 Johnny Wyrostek RC	12.00	30.00
45 Hank Sauer RC	25.00	60.00
46 Herman Wehmeier RC	12.00	30.00
47 Bobby Thomson RC	40.00	100.00
48 Dave Koslo RC	30.00	80.00

1949 Bowman

The cards in this 240-card set measure approximately 2 1/16" by 2 1/2". In 1949 Bowman took an intermediate step between black and white and full color with this set of tinted photos on colored backgrounds. Collectors should note the series price variations, which reflect some inconsistencies in the printing process. There are four major varieties in name printing, which are noted in the checklist below: NOF: name on front; NNOF: no name on front; PR: printed name on back; and SCR: script name on back. Cards were issued in five card nickel packs which came 24 packs to a box. These variations resulted when Bowman used twelve of the lower numbers to fill out the last press sheet of 36 cards, adding to numbers 217-240. Cards 1-3 and 5-73 can be found with either gray or white backs. Certain cards have been seen with a "gray" or "slate" background on the front. These cards are a result of a color printing error and are rarely seen on the secondary market so no value is established for them. Not all numbers are known to exist in this fashion. However, within the numbers between 75 and 107, slightly more of these cards have appeared on the market. Within the high numbers series (145-240), these cards have been seen but the appearance of these cards are very rare. Other cards are known to be extant with double printed backs. The set features the Rookie Cards of Hall of Famers Richie Ashburn, Roy Campanella, Bob Lemon, Robin Roberts, Duke Snider, and Early Wynn as well as Rookie Card of Gil Hodges.

Card		
COMP. MASTER SET (252)	10000.00	16000.00
COMPLETE SET (240)	10000.00	15000.00
WRAPPER (5-CENT, GR.)	200.00	250.00
WRAPPER (5-CENT, BL.)	150.00	200.00
CARDS PRICED IN NM CONDITION		
1 Vern Bickford RC	75.00	125.00
2 Whitey Lockman	20.00	40.00
3 Bob Porterfield RC	7.50	15.00
4A Jerry Priddy NNOF RC	7.50	15.00
4B Jerry Priddy NOF	30.00	50.00
5 Hank Sauer	20.00	40.00
6 Phil Cavarretta RC	20.00	40.00
7 Joe Dobson RC	7.50	15.00
8 Murry Dickson RC	7.50	15.00
9 Ferris Fain	20.00	40.00
10 Ted Gray RC	7.50	15.00
11 Lou Boudreau MG RC	25.00	60.00
12 Cass Michaels RC	7.50	15.00
13 Bob Chesnes RC	7.50	15.00
14 Curt Simmons RC	20.00	40.00
15 Ned Garver RC	7.50	15.00
16 Al Kozar RC	7.50	15.00
17 Earl Torgeson RC	7.50	15.00
18 Bobby Thomson	20.00	40.00
19 Bobby Brown RC	35.00	60.00
20 Gene Hermanski RC	7.50	15.00
21 Frank Baumholtz RC	12.50	25.00
22 Peanuts Lowrey RC	7.50	15.00
23 Bobby Doerr	50.00	80.00
24 Stan Musial	300.00	600.00
25 Carl Scheib RC	7.50	15.00
26 George Kell RC	50.00	80.00
27 Bob Feller	200.00	300.00
28 Don Kolloway RC	7.50	15.00
29 Ralph Kiner	75.00	125.00
30 Andy Seminick RC	20.00	40.00
31 Dick Kokos RC	7.50	15.00
32 Eddie Yost RC	35.00	60.00
33 Warren Spahn	100.00	250.00
34 Dave Koslo	7.50	15.00
35 Vic Raschi RC	35.00	60.00
36 Pee Wee Reese	125.00	200.00
37 Johnny Wyrostek	7.50	15.00
38 Emil Verban	7.50	15.00
39 Billy Goodman RC	12.50	25.00
40 George Munger RC	7.50	15.00
41 Lou Brissie RC	7.50	15.00
42 Hoot Evers RC	7.50	15.00
43 Dale Mitchell RC	20.00	40.00
44 Dave Philley RC	7.50	15.00
45 Wally Westlake RC	7.50	15.00
46 Robin Roberts RC	250.00	500.00
47 Johnny Sain	35.00	60.00
48 Willard Marshall	7.50	15.00
49 Frank Shea	12.50	25.00
50 Jackie Robinson RC	2000.00	4000.00
51 Herman Wehmeier	7.50	15.00
52 Johnny Schmitz RC	7.50	15.00
53 Jack Kramer RC	7.50	15.00
54 Marty Marion	35.00	60.00
55 Eddie Joost	7.50	15.00
56 Pat Mullin RC	7.50	15.00
57 Gene Bearden RC	20.00	40.00
58 Bob Elliott	20.00	40.00
59 Jack Lohrke	7.50	15.00
60 Yogi Berra	250.00	500.00
61 Rex Barney	20.00	40.00
62 Grady Hatton RC	7.50	15.00
63 Andy Pafko RC	20.00	40.00
64 Dom DiMaggio	40.00	100.00
65 Enos Slaughter	50.00	80.00
66 Elmer Valo RC	7.50	15.00
67 Alvin Dark RC	20.00	40.00
68 Sheldon Jones	7.50	15.00
69 Tommy Henrich	20.00	40.00
70 Carl Furillo RC	90.00	150.00
71 Vern Stephens RC	7.50	15.00
72 Tommy Holmes RC	20.00	40.00
73 Billy Cox RC	20.00	40.00
74 Tom McBride RC	7.50	15.00
75 Eddie Mayo RC	7.50	15.00
76 Bill Nicholson RC	12.50	25.00
77 Ernie Bonham RC	7.50	15.00
78A Sam Zoldak NNOF RC	7.50	15.00
78B Sam Zoldak NOF	30.00	50.00
79 Ron Northey RC	7.50	15.00
80 Bill McCahan	7.50	15.00
81 Virgil Stallcup RC	7.50	15.00
82 Joe Page	35.00	60.00
83A Bob Scheffing NNOF RC	7.50	15.00
83B Bob Scheffing NOF	30.00	50.00
84 Roy Campanella RC	400.00	1000.00
85A Johnny Mize NNOF	60.00	100.00
85B Johnny Mize NOF	90.00	150.00
86 Johnny Pesky RC	35.00	60.00
87 Randy Gumpert RC	7.50	15.00
88A Bill Salkeld NNOF RC	7.50	15.00
88B Bill Salkeld NOF	30.00	50.00
89 Mizell Platt RC	7.50	15.00
90 Gil Coan RC	7.50	15.00
91 Dick Wakefield RC	7.50	15.00
92 Willie Jones RC	20.00	40.00
93 Ed Stevens RC	7.50	15.00
94 Mickey Vernon RC	20.00	40.00
95 Howie Pollet RC	7.50	15.00
96 Taft Wright	7.50	15.00
97 Danny Litwhiler RC	7.50	15.00
98A Phil Rizzuto NNOF	125.00	200.00
98B Phil Rizzuto NOF	150.00	250.00
99 Frank Gustine RC	7.50	15.00
100 Gil Hodges RC	150.00	250.00
101 Sid Gordon	7.50	15.00
102 Stan Spence RC	7.50	15.00
103 Joe Tipton RC	7.50	15.00
104 Eddie Stanky RC	20.00	40.00
105 Bill Kennedy RC	7.50	15.00
106 Jake Early RC	7.50	15.00
107 Eddie Lake RC	7.50	15.00
108 Ken Heintzelman RC	7.50	15.00
109A Ed Fitzgerald Script RC	7.50	15.00
109B Ed Fitzgerald Print	35.00	60.00
110 Early Wynn RC	100.00	250.00
111 Red Schoendienst	60.00	100.00
112 Sam Chapman	20.00	40.00
113 Ray LaManno RC	7.50	15.00
114 Allie Reynolds	35.00	60.00
115 Dutch Leonard	7.50	15.00
116 Joe Hatten RC	7.50	15.00
117 Walker Cooper	7.50	15.00
118 Sam Mele RC	7.50	15.00
119 Floyd Baker RC	7.50	15.00
120 Cliff Fannin RC	7.50	15.00
121 Mark Christman RC	7.50	15.00
122 George Vico RC	7.50	15.00
123 Johnny Blatnik UER	7.50	15.00
Name misspelled		
124A D.Murtaugh Script RC	20.00	40.00
124B D.Murtaugh Print	35.00	60.00
125 Ken Keltner RC	12.50	25.00
126A Al Brazle Script RC	7.50	15.00
126B Al Brazle Print	35.00	60.00
127A Hank Majeski Script RC	7.50	15.00
127B Hank Majeski Print	35.00	60.00
128 Johnny VanderMeer	35.00	60.00
129 Bill Johnson	20.00	40.00
130 Harry Walker RC	7.50	15.00
131 Paul Lehner RC	7.50	15.00
132A Al Evans Script RC	7.50	15.00
132B Al Evans Pint	35.00	60.00
133 Aaron Robinson RC	7.50	15.00
134 Hank Borowy RC	7.50	15.00
135 Stan Rojek RC	7.50	15.00
136 Hank Edwards RC	7.50	15.00
137 Ted Wilks RC	7.50	15.00
138 Buddy Rosar	7.50	15.00
139 Hank Arft RC	7.50	15.00
140 Ray Scarborough RC	7.50	15.00
141 Tony Lupien RC	7.50	15.00
142 Eddie Waitkus RC	20.00	40.00
143A Bob Dillinger Script RC	12.50	25.00
143B Bob Dillinger Print	35.00	60.00
144 Mickey Haefner RC	7.50	15.00
145 Sylvester Donnelly RC	30.00	50.00
146 Mike McCormick RC	30.00	50.00
147 Bert Singleton RC	30.00	50.00
148 Bob Swift RC	30.00	50.00
149 Roy Partee RC	30.00	50.00
150 Allie Clark RC	30.00	50.00
151 Mickey Harris RC	30.00	50.00
152 Clarence Maddern RC	30.00	50.00
153 Phil Masi RC	30.00	50.00
154 Clint Hartung	35.00	60.00
155 Mickey Guerra RC	30.00	50.00
156 Al Zarilla RC	30.00	50.00
157 Walt Masterson RC	30.00	50.00
158 Harry Brecheen RC	35.00	60.00
159 Glen Moulder RC	30.00	50.00
160 Jim Blackburn RC	30.00	50.00
161 Jocko Thompson RC	30.00	50.00
162 Preacher Roe RC	75.00	125.00
163 Clyde McCullough RC	30.00	50.00
164 Vic Wertz RC	50.00	80.00
165 Snuffy Stirnweiss	50.00	80.00
166 Mike Tresh RC	30.00	50.00
167 Babe Martin RC	30.00	50.00
168 Doyle Lade RC	30.00	50.00
169 Jeff Heath RC	35.00	60.00
170 Bill Rigney	35.00	60.00
171 Dick Fowler RC	30.00	50.00
172 Eddie Pellagrini RC	30.00	50.00
173 Eddie Stewart RC	30.00	50.00
174 Terry Moore RC	50.00	80.00
175 Luke Appling	75.00	200.00
176 Ken Raffensberger RC	30.00	50.00
177 Stan Lopata RC	35.00	60.00
178 Tom Brown RC	35.00	60.00
179 Hugh Casey	50.00	80.00
180 Connie Berry	30.00	50.00
181 Gus Niarhos RC	30.00	50.00
182 Hal Peck RC	30.00	50.00
183 Lou Stringer RC	30.00	50.00
184 Bob Chipman RC	30.00	50.00
185 Pete Reiser	50.00	80.00
186 Buddy Kerr	30.00	50.00
187 Phil Marchildon RC	30.00	50.00
188 Karl Drews RC	30.00	50.00
189 Earl Wooten RC	30.00	50.00
190 Jim Hearn RC	30.00	50.00
191 Joe Haynes RC	30.00	50.00
192 Harry Gumbert	30.00	50.00
193 Ken Trinkle RC	30.00	50.00
194 Ralph Branca RC	50.00	120.00
195 Eddie Bockman RC	30.00	50.00
196 Fred Hutchinson RC	35.00	60.00
197 Johnny Lindell	35.00	60.00
198 Steve Gromek RC	30.00	50.00
199 Tex Hughson RC	30.00	50.00
200 Jess Dobernic RC	30.00	50.00
201 Sibby Sisti RC	30.00	50.00
202 Larry Jansen	35.00	60.00
203 Barney McCosky	30.00	50.00
204 Bob Savage RC	30.00	50.00
205 Dick Sisler RC	35.00	60.00
206 Bruce Edwards	30.00	50.00
207 Johnny Hopp RC	30.00	50.00
208 Dizzy Trout	35.00	60.00
209 Charlie Keller	40.00	100.00
210 Joe Gordon RC	50.00	80.00
211 Boo Ferriss RC	30.00	50.00
212 Ralph Hamner RC	30.00	50.00
213 Red Barrett RC	30.00	50.00
214 Richie Ashburn RC	400.00	800.00
215 Kirby Higbe	30.00	50.00
216 Schoolboy Rowe	35.00	60.00
217 Marino Pieretti RC	30.00	50.00
218 Dick Kryhoski RC	30.00	50.00
219 Virgil Trucks RC	35.00	60.00
220 Johnny McCarthy	30.00	50.00
221 Bob Muncrief RC	30.00	50.00
222 Alex Kellner RC	30.00	50.00
223 Bobby Hofman RC	30.00	50.00
224 Satchel Paige RC	2000.00	4000.00
225 Jerry Coleman RC	50.00	80.00
226 Duke Snider RC	600.00	1200.00
227 Fritz Ostermueller	30.00	50.00
228 Jackie Mayo RC	30.00	50.00
229 Ed Lopat RC	90.00	150.00
230 Augie Galan	35.00	60.00
231 Earl Johnson RC	30.00	50.00
232 George McQuinn	35.00	60.00
233 Larry Doby RC	400.00	800.00
234 Rip Sewell RC	30.00	50.00
235 Jim Russell RC	30.00	50.00
236 Fred Sanford RC	30.00	50.00
237 Monte Kennedy RC	30.00	50.00
238 Bob Lemon RC	250.00	500.00
239 Frank McCormick	30.00	50.00
240 Babe Young UER	60.00	100.00

1950 Bowman

The cards in this 252-card set measure approximately 2 1/16" by 2 1/2". This set, marketed in 1950 by Bowman, represented a major improvement in terms of quality over their previous efforts. Each card was a beautifully colored line drawing developed from a simple photograph. The first 72 cards are the scarcest in the set, while the final 72 cards may be found with or without the copyright line. This was the only Bowman sports set to carry the famous "5-Star" logo. Cards were issued in five-card nickel packs. Key rookies in this set are Hank Bauer, Don Newcombe, and Al Rosen.

Card		
COMPLETE SET (252)	5000.00	12000.00
COMMON CARD (1-72)	30.00	50.00
WRAPPER (1-CENT)	200.00	250.00
WRAPPER (5-CENT)	200.00	250.00
CARDS PRICED IN NM CONDITION		
1 Mel Parnell RC	150.00	400.00
2 Vern Stephens	25.00	60.00
3 Dom DiMaggio	60.00	150.00
4 Gus Zernial RC	20.00	50.00
5 Bob Kuzava RC	20.00	50.00
6 Bob Feller	100.00	250.00
7 Jim Hegan	25.00	60.00
8 George Kell	30.00	80.00
9 Vic Wertz	25.00	60.00
10 Tommy Henrich	40.00	100.00
11 Phil Rizzuto	125.00	300.00
12 Joe Page	20.00	50.00
13 Ferris Fain	25.00	60.00
14 Alex Kellner	20.00	50.00
15 Al Kozar	20.00	50.00
16 Roy Sievers RC	40.00	100.00
17 Sid Hudson	20.00	50.00
18 Eddie Robinson RC	20.00	50.00
19 Warren Spahn	100.00	250.00
20 Bob Elliott	25.00	60.00
21 Pee Wee Reese	100.00	250.00
22 Jackie Robinson	1250.00	3000.00
23 Don Newcombe RC	100.00	250.00
24 Johnny Schmitz	20.00	50.00
25 Hank Sauer	25.00	60.00
26 Grady Hatton	20.00	50.00
27 Herman Wehmeier	20.00	50.00
28 Bobby Thomson	30.00	80.00
29 Eddie Stanky	25.00	60.00
30 Eddie Waitkus	25.00	60.00
31 Del Ennis	30.00	80.00
32 Robin Roberts	75.00	200.00
33 Ralph Kiner	60.00	150.00
34 Murry Dickson	20.00	50.00
35 Enos Slaughter	30.00	80.00
36 Eddie Kazak RC	25.00	60.00
37 Luke Appling	40.00	100.00
38 Bill Wight RC	20.00	50.00
39 Larry Doby	60.00	150.00
40 Bob Lemon	30.00	80.00
41 Hoot Evers	20.00	50.00
42 Art Houtteman RC	20.00	50.00
43 Bobby Doerr	30.00	80.00
44 Joe Dobson	20.00	50.00
45 Al Zarilla	20.00	50.00
46 Yogi Berra	300.00	600.00
47 Jerry Coleman	20.00	50.00
48 Lou Brissie	20.00	50.00
49 Elmer Valo	15.00	40.00
50 Dick Kokos	20.00	50.00
51 Ned Garver	25.00	60.00
52 Sam Mele	20.00	50.00
53 Clyde Vollmer RC	20.00	50.00
54 Gil Coan	20.00	50.00
55 Buddy Kerr	20.00	50.00
56 Del Crandall RC	25.00	60.00
57 Vern Bickford	20.00	50.00
58 Carl Furillo	30.00	80.00
59 Ralph Branca	30.00	80.00
60 Andy Pafko	25.00	60.00
61 Bob Rush RC	20.00	50.00
62 Ted Kluszewski	30.00	80.00
63 Ewell Blackwell	25.00	60.00
64 Alvin Dark	20.00	50.00
65 Dave Koslo	20.00	50.00
66 Larry Jansen	25.00	60.00
67 Willie Jones	25.00	60.00
68 Curt Simmons	25.00	60.00
69 Wally Westlake	20.00	50.00
70 Bob Chesnes	20.00	50.00
71 Red Schoendienst	30.00	80.00
72 Howie Pollet	20.00	50.00
73 Willard Marshall	6.00	15.00
74 Johnny Antonelli RC	25.00	60.00
75 Roy Campanella	150.00	400.00
76 Rex Barney	15.00	40.00
77 Duke Snider	100.00	250.00
78 Mickey Owen	10.00	25.00
79 Johnny VanderMeer	20.00	50.00
80 Howard Fox RC	6.00	15.00
81 Ron Northey	6.00	15.00
82 Whitey Lockman	10.00	25.00
83 Sheldon Jones	6.00	15.00
84 Richie Ashburn	50.00	120.00
85 Ken Heintzelman	6.00	15.00
86 Stan Rojek	6.00	15.00
87 Bill Werle RC	6.00	15.00
88 Marty Marion	20.00	50.00
89 George Munger	6.00	15.00
90 Harry Brecheen	15.00	40.00
91 Cass Michaels	6.00	15.00
92 Hank Majeski	6.00	15.00
93 Gene Bearden	15.00	40.00
94 Lou Boudreau MG	25.00	60.00
95 Aaron Robinson	6.00	15.00
96 Virgil Trucks	10.00	25.00
97 Maurice McDermott RC	6.00	15.00
98 Ted Williams	400.00	800.00
99 Billy Goodman	10.00	25.00
100 Vic Raschi	25.00	60.00
101 Bobby Brown	15.00	40.00
102 Billy Johnson	10.00	25.00
103 Eddie Joost	6.00	15.00
104 Sam Chapman	6.00	15.00
105 Bob Dillinger	6.00	15.00
106 Cliff Fannin	6.00	15.00
107 Sam Dente RC	6.00	15.00
108 Ray Scarborough	10.00	25.00
109 Sid Gordon	6.00	15.00
110 Tommy Holmes	10.00	25.00
111 Walker Cooper	6.00	15.00
112 Gil Hodges	50.00	120.00
113 Gene Hermanski	6.00	15.00
114 Wayne Terwilliger RC	6.00	15.00
115 Roy Smalley	6.00	15.00
116 Virgil Stallcup	6.00	15.00
117 Bill Rigney	6.00	15.00
118 Clint Hartung	6.00	15.00
119 Dick Sisler	10.00	25.00
120 John Thompson	6.00	15.00
121 Andy Seminick	10.00	25.00
122 Johnny Hopp	10.00	25.00
123 Dino Restelli RC	6.00	15.00
124 Clyde McCullough	6.00	15.00
125 Del Rice RC	6.00	15.00
126 Al Brazle	6.00	15.00
127 Dave Philley	6.00	15.00
128 Phil Masi	6.00	15.00
129 Joe Gordon	20.00	50.00
130 Dale Mitchell	10.00	25.00
131 Steve Gromek	6.00	15.00
132 Mickey Vernon	10.00	25.00
133 Don Kolloway	6.00	15.00
134 Paul Trout	6.00	15.00
135 Pat Mullin	6.00	15.00
136 Buddy Rosar	6.00	15.00
137 Johnny Pesky	10.00	25.00
138 Allie Reynolds	20.00	50.00
139 Johnny Mize	40.00	100.00
140 Pete Suder RC	6.00	15.00
141 Joe Coleman RC	10.00	25.00
142 Sherman Lollar RC	15.00	40.00
143 Eddie Stewart	6.00	15.00
144 Al Evans	6.00	15.00
145 Jack Graham RC	6.00	15.00
146 Floyd Baker	6.00	15.00
147 Mike Garcia RC	15.00	40.00
148 Early Wynn	40.00	100.00
149 Bob Swift	6.00	15.00
150 George Vico	6.00	15.00
151 Fred Hutchinson	10.00	25.00
152 Ellis Kinder RC	6.00	15.00
153 Walt Masterson	10.00	25.00
154 Gus Niarhos	6.00	15.00
155 Frank Shea	10.00	25.00
156 Fred Sanford	10.00	25.00
157 Mike Guerra	6.00	15.00
158 Paul Lehner	6.00	15.00
159 Joe Tipton	6.00	15.00
160 Mickey Harris	6.00	15.00
161 Sherry Robertson RC	6.00	15.00
162 Eddie Yost	10.00	25.00
163 Earl Torgeson	6.00	15.00
164 Sibby Sisti	6.00	15.00
165 Bruce Edwards	6.00	15.00
166 Joe Hatten	6.00	15.00
167 Preacher Roe	15.00	40.00
168 Bob Scheffing	6.00	15.00
169 Hank Edwards	6.00	15.00
170 Dutch Leonard	6.00	15.00
171 Harry Gumbert	6.00	15.00
172 Peanuts Lowrey	6.00	15.00
173 Lloyd Merriman RC	6.00	15.00
174 Hank Thompson RC	15.00	40.00
175 Monte Kennedy	6.00	15.00
176 Sylvester Donnelly	6.00	15.00
177 Hank Borowy	10.00	25.00
178 Ed Fitzgerald	6.00	15.00
179 Chuck Diering RC	6.00	15.00
180 Harry Walker	10.00	25.00
181 Marino Pieretti	6.00	15.00
182 Sam Zoldak	6.00	15.00
183 Mickey Haefner	6.00	15.00
184 Randy Gumpert	6.00	15.00
185 Howie Judson RC	6.00	15.00
186 Ken Keltner	10.00	25.00
187 Lou Stringer	6.00	15.00
188 Earl Johnson	6.00	15.00
189 Owen Friend RC	12.00	30.00
190 Ken Wood RC	6.00	15.00
191 Dick Starr RC	6.00	15.00
192 Bob Chipman	6.00	15.00
193 Pete Reiser	15.00	40.00
194 Billy Cox	25.00	60.00
195 Phil Cavarretta	15.00	40.00
196 Doyle Lade	6.00	15.00
197 Johnny Wyrostek	6.00	15.00
198 Danny Litwhiler	6.00	15.00
199 Jack Kramer	6.00	15.00
200 Kirby Higbe	10.00	25.00
201 Pete Castiglione RC	6.00	15.00
202 Cliff Chambers RC	6.00	15.00
203 Danny Murtaugh	10.00	25.00
204 Granny Hamner RC	15.00	40.00
205 Mike Goliat RC	6.00	15.00
206 Stan Lopata	10.00	25.00
207 Max Lanier RC	6.00	15.00
208 Jim Hearn	6.00	15.00
209 Johnny Lindell	6.00	15.00
210 Ted Gray	6.00	15.00
211 Charlie Keller	15.00	40.00
212 Jerry Priddy	6.00	15.00
213 Carl Scheib	6.00	15.00
214 Dick Fowler	6.00	15.00
215 Ed Lopat	25.00	60.00
216 Bob Porterfield	10.00	25.00
217 Casey Stengel MG	40.00	100.00
218 Cliff Mapes RC	10.00	25.00
219 Hank Bauer RC	25.00	60.00
220 Leo Durocher MG	25.00	60.00
221 Don Mueller RC	15.00	40.00
222 Bobby Morgan RC	6.00	15.00
223 Jim Russell	6.00	15.00
224 Jack Banta RC	6.00	15.00
225 Eddie Sawyer MG RC	10.00	25.00
226 Jim Konstanty RC	25.00	60.00
227 Bob Miller RC	10.00	25.00
228 Bill Nicholson	12.00	30.00
229 Frankie Frisch MG	25.00	60.00
230 Bill Serena RC	6.00	15.00
231 Preston Ward RC	6.00	15.00
232 Al Rosen RC	25.00	60.00
233 Allie Clark	6.00	15.00
234 Bobby Shantz RC	25.00	60.00
235 Harold Gilbert RC	6.00	15.00
236 Bob Cain RC	6.00	15.00
237 Bill Salkeld	6.00	15.00
238 Nippy Jones RC	6.00	15.00
239 Bill Howerton RC	6.00	15.00
240 Eddie Lake	6.00	15.00
241 Neil Berry RC	6.00	15.00
242 Dick Kryhoski	6.00	15.00
243 Johnny Groth RC	6.00	15.00
244 Dale Coogan RC	6.00	15.00
245 Al Papai RC	6.00	15.00
246 Walt Dropo RC	15.00	40.00
247 Irv Noren RC	10.00	25.00
248 Sam Jethroe RC	20.00	50.00
249 Snuffy Stirnweiss	10.00	25.00
250 Ray Coleman RC	6.00	15.00
251 Les Moss RC	6.00	15.00
252 Billy DeMars RC	25.00	60.00

1951 Bowman

The cards in this 324-card set measure approximately 2 1/16" by 3 1/8". Many of the obverses of the cards appearing in the 1951 Bowman set are enlargements of those appearing in the previous year. The high number series (253-324) is highly valued and contains the true Rookie Cards of Mickey Mantle and Willie Mays. Card number 195 depicts Paul Richards in caricature. George Kell's card (number 46) incorrectly lists him as being in the "1941" Bowman series. Cards were issued either in one card penny packs which came 120 to a box or in six-card nickel packs which came 24 to a box. Player names are found printed in a panel on the front of the card. These cards were supposedly also sold in sheets in variety stores in the Philadelphia area.

Card		
COMPLETE SET (324)	40000.00	100000.00
COMMON CARD (1-252)	10.00	25.00
WRAPPER (1-CENT)	150.00	200.00
WRAPPER (5-CENT)	200.00	250.00
CARDS PRICED IN NM CONDITION		

1 Whitey Ford RC 1250.00 3000.00
2 Yogi Berra 250.00 600.00
3 Robin Roberts 40.00 100.00
4 Del Ennis 20.00 50.00
5 Dale Mitchell 10.00 25.00
6 Don Newcombe 30.00 80.00
7 Gil Hodges 50.00 120.00
8 Paul Lehner 8.00 20.00
9 Sam Chapman 8.00 20.00
10 Red Schoendienst 25.00 60.00
11 George Munger 8.00 20.00
12 Hank Majeski 8.00 20.00
13 Eddie Stanky 10.00 25.00
14 Alvin Dark 15.00 40.00
15 Johnny Pesky 10.00 25.00
16 Maurice McDermott 8.00 20.00
17 Pete Castiglione 8.00 20.00
18 Gil Coan 8.00 20.00
19 Sid Gordon 8.00 20.00
20 Del Crandall UER 10.00 25.00
21 Snuffy Stirnweiss 10.00 25.00
22 Hank Sauer 15.00 40.00
23 Hoot Evers 8.00 20.00
24 Ewell Blackwell 15.00 40.00
25 Vic Raschi 25.00 60.00
26 Phil Rizzuto 75.00 200.00
27 Jim Konstanty 10.00 25.00
28 Eddie Waitkus 8.00 20.00
29 Allie Clark 8.00 20.00
30 Bob Feller 75.00 200.00
31 Roy Campanella 125.00 300.00
32 Duke Snider 150.00 400.00
33 Bob Hooper RC 8.00 20.00
34 Marty Marion MG 15.00 40.00
35 Al Zarilla 8.00 20.00
36 Joe Dobson 8.00 20.00
37 Whitey Lockman 15.00 40.00
38 Al Evans 8.00 20.00
39 Ray Scarborough 8.00 20.00
40 Gus Bell RC 25.00 60.00
41 Eddie Yost 10.00 25.00
42 Vern Bickford 10.00 25.00
43 Billy DeMars 8.00 20.00
44 Roy Smalley 8.00 20.00
45 Art Houtteman 8.00 20.00
46 George Kell UER 25.00 60.00
47 Grady Hatton 8.00 20.00
48 Ken Raffensberger 8.00 20.00
49 Jerry Coleman 10.00 25.00
50 Johnny Mize 30.00 80.00
51 Andy Seminick 10.00 25.00
52 Dick Sisler 15.00 40.00
53 Bob Lemon 30.00 80.00
54 Ray Boone RC 15.00 40.00
55 Gene Hermanski 8.00 20.00
56 Ralph Branca 25.00 60.00
57 Alex Kellner 8.00 20.00
58 Enos Slaughter 30.00 80.00
59 Randy Gumpert 10.00 25.00
60 Chico Carrasquel RC 25.00 60.00
61 Jim Hearn 12.00 30.00
62 Lou Boudreau MG 25.00 60.00
63 Bob Dillinger 8.00 20.00
64 Bill Werle 8.00 20.00
65 Mickey Vernon 15.00 40.00
66 Bob Elliott 10.00 25.00
67 Roy Sievers 15.00 30.00
68 Dick Kokos 8.00 20.00
69 Johnny Schmitz 8.00 20.00
70 Ron Northey 8.00 20.00
71 Jerry Priddy 8.00 20.00
72 Lloyd Merriman 8.00 20.00
73 Tommy Byrne RC 8.00 20.00
74 Billy Johnson 10.00 25.00
75 Russ Meyer RC 10.00 25.00
76 Stan Lopata 10.00 25.00
77 Mike Goliat 8.00 20.00
78 Early Wynn 25.00 60.00
79 Jim Hegan 10.00 25.00
80 Pee Wee Reese 75.00 200.00
81 Carl Furillo 30.00 80.00
82 Joe Tipton 8.00 20.00
83 Carl Scheib 12.00 30.00
84 Barney McCosky 8.00 20.00
85 Eddie Kazak 8.00 20.00
86 Harry Brecheen 10.00 25.00
87 Floyd Baker 8.00 20.00
88 Eddie Robinson 8.00 20.00
89 Hank Thompson 10.00 25.00
90 Dave Koslo 15.00 40.00
91 Clyde Vollmer 15.00 30.00
92 Vern Stephens 15.00 25.00
93 Danny O'Connell RC 10.00 25.00
94 Clyde McCullough 8.00 20.00
95 Sherry Robertson 8.00 20.00
96 Sandy Consuegra RC 8.00 20.00
97 Bob Kuzava 8.00 20.00
98 Willard Marshall 8.00 20.00
99 Earl Torgeson 8.00 20.00
100 Sherm Lollar 10.00 25.00
101 Owen Friend 8.00 20.00
102 Dutch Leonard 15.00 40.00
103 Andy Pafko 15.00 40.00
104 Virgil Trucks 10.00 25.00
105 Don Kolloway 8.00 20.00
106 Pat Mullin 8.00 20.00
107 Johnny Wyrostek 8.00 20.00
108 Virgil Stallcup 8.00 20.00
109 Allie Reynolds 25.00 60.00
110 Bobby Brown 15.00 40.00
111 Curt Simmons 15.00 40.00
112 Willie Jones 8.00 20.00
113 Bill Nicholson 8.00 20.00
114 Sam Zoldak 8.00 20.00
115 Steve Gromek 8.00 20.00
116 Bruce Edwards 8.00 20.00
117 Eddie Miksis RC 8.00 20.00
118 Preacher Roe 25.00 60.00
119 Eddie Joost 8.00 20.00
120 Joe Coleman 10.00 25.00
121 Gerry Staley RC 8.00 20.00
122 Joe Garagiola RC 30.00 80.00
123 Howie Judson 8.00 20.00
124 Gus Niarhos 8.00 20.00
125 Bill Rigney 10.00 25.00
126 Bobby Thomson 40.00 100.00
127 Sal Maglie RC 20.00 50.00
128 Ellis Kinder 8.00 20.00
129 Matt Batts 8.00 20.00
130 Tom Saffell RC 8.00 20.00
131 Cliff Chambers 8.00 20.00
132 Cass Michaels 8.00 20.00
133 Sam Dente 8.00 20.00
134 Warren Spahn 60.00 150.00
135 Walker Cooper 8.00 20.00
136 Ray Coleman 8.00 20.00
137 Dick Starr 8.00 20.00
138 Phil Cavarretta 10.00 25.00
139 Doyle Lade 8.00 20.00
140 Eddie Lake 8.00 20.00
141 Fred Hutchinson 10.00 25.00
142 Aaron Robinson 8.00 20.00
143 Ted Kluszewski 40.00 100.00
144 Herman Wehmeier 8.00 20.00
145 Fred Sanford 10.00 25.00
146 Johnny Hopp 12.00 30.00
147 Ken Heintzelman 8.00 20.00
148 Granny Hamner 8.00 20.00
149 Bubba Church RC 8.00 20.00
150 Mike Garcia 10.00 25.00
151 Larry Doby 125.00 300.00
152 Cal Abrams RC 8.00 20.00
153 Rex Barney 15.00 40.00
154 Pete Suder 8.00 20.00
155 Lou Brissie 8.00 20.00
156 Del Rice 8.00 20.00
157 Al Brazle 12.00 30.00
158 Chuck Diering 8.00 20.00
159 Eddie Stewart 8.00 20.00
160 Phil Masi 8.00 20.00
161 Wes Westrum RC 10.00 25.00
162 Larry Jansen 10.00 25.00
163 Monte Kennedy 8.00 20.00
164 Bill Wight 8.00 20.00
165 Ted Williams UER 600.00 1500.00
166 Stan Rojek 8.00 20.00
167 Murry Dickson 8.00 20.00
168 Sam Mele 8.00 20.00
169 Sid Hudson 8.00 20.00
170 Sibby Sisti 8.00 20.00
171 Buddy Kerr 8.00 20.00
172 Ned Garver 8.00 20.00
173 Hank Arft 10.00 25.00
174 Mickey Owen 10.00 25.00
175 Wayne Terwilliger 8.00 20.00
176 Vic Wertz 15.00 40.00
177 Charlie Keller 10.00 25.00
178 Ted Gray 8.00 20.00
179 Danny Litwhiler 8.00 20.00
180 Howie Fox 12.00 30.00
181 Casey Stengel MG 50.00 120.00
182 Tom Ferrick RC 8.00 20.00
183 Hank Bauer 20.00 50.00
184 Eddie Sawyer MG 15.00 40.00
185 Jimmy Bloodworth 8.00 20.00
186 Richie Ashburn 40.00 100.00
187 Al Rosen 15.00 40.00
188 Bobby Avila RC 10.00 25.00
189 Erv Palica RC 8.00 20.00
190 Joe Hatten 8.00 20.00
191 Billy Hitchcock RC 8.00 20.00
192 Hank Wyse RC 8.00 20.00
193 Ted Wilks 8.00 20.00
194 Peanuts Lowrey 8.00 20.00
195 Paul Richards MG 10.00 25.00
196 Billy Pierce RC 25.00 60.00
197 Bob Cain 8.00 20.00
198 Monte Irvin RC 100.00 250.00
199 Sheldon Jones 8.00 20.00
200 Jack Kramer 8.00 20.00
201 Steve O'Neill MG RC 8.00 20.00
202 Mike Guerra 8.00 20.00
203 Vernon Law RC 25.00 60.00
204 Vic Lombardi RC 8.00 20.00
205 Mickey Grasso RC 8.00 20.00
206 Conrado Marrero RC 8.00 20.00
207 Billy Southworth MG RC 20.00 50.00
208 Blix Donnelly 8.00 20.00
209 Ken Wood 8.00 20.00
210 Les Moss 12.00 30.00
211 Hal Jeffcoat RC 8.00 20.00
212 Bob Rush 8.00 20.00
213 Neil Berry 10.00 25.00
214 Bob Swift 8.00 20.00
215 Ken Peterson 8.00 20.00
216 Connie Ryan RC 8.00 20.00
217 Joe Page 10.00 25.00
218 Ed Lopat 25.00 60.00
219 Gene Woodling RC 15.00 40.00
220 Bob Miller 8.00 20.00
221 Dick Whitman RC 8.00 20.00
222 Thurman Tucker RC 10.00 25.00
223 Johnny VanderMeer 15.00 40.00
224 Billy Cox 12.00 30.00
225 Dan Bankhead RC 15.00 40.00
226 Jimmy Dykes MG 12.00 30.00
227 Bobby Shantz UER 10.00 25.00
228 Cloyd Boyer RC 10.00 25.00
229 Bill Howerton 8.00 20.00
230 Max Lanier 8.00 20.00
231 Luis Aloma RC 8.00 20.00
232 Nellie Fox RC 150.00 400.00
233 Leo Durocher MG 25.00 60.00
234 Clint Hartung 10.00 25.00
235 Jack Lohrke 8.00 20.00
236 Buddy Rosar 8.00 20.00
237 Billy Goodman 10.00 25.00
238 Pete Reiser 15.00 40.00
239 Bill MacDonald RC 8.00 20.00
240 Joe Haynes 8.00 20.00
241 Irv Noren 8.00 20.00
242 Sam Jethroe 8.00 20.00
243 Johnny Antonelli 12.00 30.00
244 Cliff Fannin 8.00 20.00
245 John Berardino RC 8.00 20.00
246 Bill Serena 8.00 20.00
247 Bob Ramazzotti RC 8.00 20.00
248 Johnny Klippstein RC 8.00 20.00
249 Johnny Groth 8.00 20.00
250 Hank Borowy 8.00 20.00
251 Willard Ramsdell RC 15.00 40.00
252 Dixie Howell RC 8.00 20.00
253 Mickey Mantle RC 30000.00 80000.00
254 Jackie Jensen RC 40.00 100.00
255 Milo Candini RC 20.00 50.00
256 Ken Silvestri RC 20.00 50.00
257 Birdie Tebbetts RC 25.00 60.00
258 Luke Easter RC 25.00 60.00
259 Chuck Dressen MG 25.00 60.00
260 Carl Erskine RC 40.00 100.00
261 Wally Moses 25.00 60.00
262 Gus Zernial 25.00 60.00
263 Howie Pollet 20.00 50.00
264 Don Richmond RC 20.00 50.00
265 Steve Bilko RC 20.00 50.00
266 Harry Dorish RC 20.00 50.00
267 Ken Holcombe RC 20.00 50.00
268 Don Mueller 25.00 60.00
269 Ray Noble RC 20.00 50.00
270 Willard Nixon RC 15.00 40.00
271 Tommy Wright RC 20.00 50.00
272 Billy Meyer MG RC 20.00 50.00
273 Danny Murtaugh 25.00 60.00
274 George Metkovich RC 20.00 50.00
275 Bucky Harris MG 30.00 80.00
276 Frank Quinn RC 20.00 50.00
277 Roy Hartsfield RC 20.00 50.00
278 Norman Roy RC 20.00 50.00
279 Jim Delsing RC 20.00 50.00
280 Frank Overmire 20.00 50.00
281 Al Widmar RC 20.00 50.00
282 Frank Frisch MG 30.00 80.00
283 Walt Dubiel RC 20.00 50.00
284 Gene Bearden 25.00 60.00
285 Johnny Lipon RC 20.00 50.00
286 Bob Usher RC 20.00 50.00
287 Jim Blackburn 20.00 50.00
288 Bobby Adams 20.00 50.00
289 Cliff Mapes 25.00 60.00
290 Bill Dickey CO 50.00 120.00
291 Tommy Henrich CO 30.00 80.00
292 Eddie Pellagrini 20.00 50.00
293 Ken Johnson RC 20.00 50.00
294 Jocko Thompson 20.00 50.00
295 Al Lopez MG RC 50.00 120.00
296 Bob Kennedy RC 25.00 60.00
297 Dave Philley 25.00 60.00
298 Joe Astroth RC 15.00 30.00
299 Clyde King RC 25.00 60.00
300 Hal Rice RC 15.00 40.00
301 Tommy Glaviano RC 20.00 50.00
302 Jim Busby RC 20.00 50.00
303 Marv Rotblatt RC 20.00 50.00
304 Al Gettell RC 20.00 50.00
305 Willie Mays RC 12000.00 30000.00
306 Jim Piersall RC 30.00 80.00
307 Walt Masterson 20.00 50.00
308 Ted Beard RC 20.00 50.00
309 Mel Queen RC 20.00 50.00
310 Erv Dusak RC 20.00 50.00
311 Mickey Harris 20.00 50.00
312 Gene Mauch RC 25.00 60.00
313 Ray Mueller RC 20.00 50.00
314 Johnny Sain 25.00 60.00
315 Zack Taylor MG 20.00 50.00
316 Duane Pillette RC 20.00 50.00
317 Smoky Burgess RC 30.00 80.00
318 Warren Hacker RC 20.00 50.00
319 Red Rolfe MG 25.00 60.00
320 Hal White RC 20.00 50.00
321 Earl Johnson 20.00 50.00
322 Luke Sewell MG 25.00 60.00
323 Joe Adcock RC 30.00 80.00
324 Johnny Pramesa RC 50.00 120.00

1952 Bowman

The cards in this 252-card set measure approximately 2 1/16" by 3 1/8". While the Bowman set of 1952 retained the card size introduced in 1951, it employed a modification of color tones from the two preceding years. The cards also appeared with a facsimile autograph on the front and, for the first time since 1949, premium advertising on the back. The 1952 set was apparently sold in sheets as well as in gum packs. Artwork for 15 cards that were never issued was discovered in the early 1980s. Cards were issued in one cent penny packs or five card nickel packs. The five cent packs came 24 to a box. Notable Rookie Cards in this set are Lew Burdette, Gil McDougald, and Minnie Minoso.

COMPLETE SET (252) 8000.00 20000.00
WRAPPER (1-CENT) 150.00 200.00
WRAPPER (5-CENT) 75.00 100.00
CARDS PRICED IN NM CONDITION
1 Yogi Berra 300.00 800.00
2 Bobby Thomson 15.00 40.00
3 Fred Hutchinson 10.00 25.00
4 Robin Roberts 50.00 120.00
5 Minnie Minoso RC 125.00 300.00
6 Virgil Stallcup 6.00 15.00
7 Mike Garcia 10.00 25.00
8 Pee Wee Reese 75.00 200.00
9 Vern Stephens 10.00 25.00
10 Bob Hooper 6.00 15.00
11 Ralph Kiner 30.00 80.00
12 Max Surkont RC 6.00 15.00
13 Cliff Mapes 6.00 15.00
14 Cliff Chambers 6.00 15.00
15 Sam Mele 6.00 15.00
16 Turk Lown RC 6.00 15.00
17 Ed Lopat 15.00 40.00
18 Don Mueller 10.00 25.00
19 Bob Cain 6.00 15.00
20 Willie Jones 6.00 15.00
21 Nellie Fox 40.00 100.00
22 Willard Ramsdell 6.00 15.00
23 Bob Lemon 25.00 60.00
24 Carl Furillo 25.00 60.00
25 Mickey McDermott 6.00 15.00
26 Eddie Joost 6.00 15.00
27 Joe Garagiola 15.00 40.00
28 Roy Hartsfield 6.00 15.00
29 Ned Garver 6.00 15.00
30 Red Schoendienst 25.00 60.00
31 Eddie Yost 10.00 25.00
32 Eddie Miksis 6.00 15.00
33 Gil McDougald RC 30.00 80.00
34 Alvin Dark 10.00 25.00
35 Granny Hamner 6.00 15.00
36 Cass Michaels 6.00 15.00
37 Vic Raschi 10.00 25.00
38 Whitey Lockman 10.00 25.00
39 Vic Wertz 10.00 25.00
40 Bubba Church 6.00 15.00
41 Chico Carrasquel 6.00 15.00
42 Johnny Wyrostek 6.00 15.00
43 Bob Feller 75.00 200.00
44 Roy Campanella 75.00 200.00
45 Johnny Pesky 10.00 25.00
46 Carl Scheib 6.00 15.00
47 Pete Castiglione 6.00 15.00
48 Vern Bickford 6.00 15.00
49 Jim Hearn 6.00 15.00
50 Gerry Staley 6.00 15.00
51 Gil Coan 6.00 15.00
52 Phil Rizzuto 60.00 150.00
53 Richie Ashburn 30.00 80.00
54 Billy Pierce 10.00 25.00
55 Ken Raffensberger 6.00 15.00
56 Clyde King 6.00 15.00
57 Clyde Vollmer 6.00 15.00
58 Hank Majeski 6.00 15.00
59 Murry Dickson 6.00 15.00
60 Sid Gordon 6.00 15.00
61 Tommy Byrne 6.00 15.00
62 Joe Presko RC 6.00 15.00
63 Irv Noren 6.00 15.00
64 Roy Smalley 6.00 15.00
65 Hank Bauer 15.00 40.00
66 Sal Maglie 10.00 25.00
67 Johnny Groth 6.00 15.00
68 Jim Busby 6.00 15.00
69 Joe Adcock 10.00 25.00
70 Carl Erskine 25.00 60.00
71 Vern Law 10.00 25.00
72 Earl Torgeson 6.00 15.00
73 Jerry Coleman 10.00 25.00
74 Wes Westrum 10.00 25.00
75 George Kell 25.00 60.00
76 Del Ennis 10.00 25.00
77 Eddie Robinson 6.00 15.00
78 Lloyd Merriman 6.00 15.00
79 Lou Brissie 6.00 15.00
80 Gil Hodges 40.00 100.00
81 Billy Goodman 10.00 25.00
82 Gus Zernial 10.00 25.00
83 Howie Pollet 6.00 15.00
84 Sam Jethroe 10.00 25.00
85 Marty Marion CO 10.00 25.00
86 Cal Abrams 6.00 15.00
87 Mickey Vernon 10.00 25.00
88 Bruce Edwards 6.00 15.00
89 Billy Hitchcock 6.00 15.00
90 Larry Jansen 12.00 30.00
91 Don Kolloway 6.00 15.00
92 Eddie Waitkus 10.00 25.00
93 Paul Richards MG 10.00 25.00
94 Luke Sewell MG 10.00 25.00
95 Luke Easter 10.00 25.00
96 Ralph Branca 15.00 30.00
97 Willard Marshall 6.00 15.00
98 Jimmie Dykes MG 10.00 25.00
99 Clyde McCullough 6.00 15.00
100 Sibby Sisti 6.00 15.00
101 Mickey Mantle 4000.00 10000.00
102 Peanuts Lowrey 6.00 15.00
103 Joe Haynes 6.00 15.00
104 Hal Jeffcoat 6.00 15.00
105 Bobby Brown 10.00 25.00
106 Randy Gumpert 6.00 15.00
107 Del Rice 6.00 15.00
108 George Metkovich 6.00 15.00
109 Tom Morgan RC 15.00 40.00
110 Max Lanier 6.00 15.00
111 Hoot Evers 6.00 15.00
112 Smoky Burgess 10.00 25.00
113 Al Zarilla 6.00 15.00
114 Frank Hiller RC 6.00 15.00
115 Larry Doby 25.00 60.00
116 Duke Snider 100.00 250.00
117 Bill Wight 6.00 15.00
118 Ray Murray RC 6.00 15.00
119 Bill Howerton 6.00 15.00
120 Chet Nichols RC 6.00 15.00
121 Al Corwin RC 6.00 15.00
122 Billy Johnson 6.00 15.00
123 Sid Hudson 6.00 15.00
124 Birdie Tebbetts 6.00 15.00
125 Howie Fox 6.00 15.00
126 Phil Cavarretta 25.00 50.00
127 Dick Sisler 6.00 15.00
128 Don Newcombe 25.00 60.00
129 Gus Niarhos 6.00 15.00
130 Allie Clark 6.00 15.00
131 Bob Swift 6.00 15.00
132 Dave Cole RC 6.00 15.00
133 Dick Kryhoski 6.00 15.00
134 Al Brazle 6.00 15.00
135 Mickey Harris 6.00 15.00
136 Gene Hermanski 6.00 15.00
137 Stan Rojek 6.00 15.00
138 Ted Wilks 6.00 15.00
139 Jerry Priddy 6.00 15.00
140 Ray Scarborough 6.00 15.00
141 Hank Edwards 6.00 15.00
142 Early Wynn 25.00 60.00
143 Sandy Consuegra 6.00 15.00
144 Joe Hatten 6.00 15.00
145 Johnny Mize 25.00 60.00
146 Leo Durocher MG 25.00 50.00
147 Marlin Stuart RC 6.00 15.00
148 Ken Heintzelman 6.00 15.00
149 Howie Judson 6.00 15.00
150 Herman Wehmeier 6.00 15.00
151 Al Rosen 10.00 25.00
152 Billy Cox 6.00 15.00
153 Fred Hatfield RC 15.00 40.00
154 Ferris Fain 6.00 15.00
155 Billy Meyer MG 6.00 15.00
156 Warren Spahn 25.00 60.00
157 Jim Delsing 10.00 25.00
158 Bucky Harris MG 15.00 30.00
159 Dutch Leonard 6.00 15.00
160 Eddie Stanky 10.00 25.00
161 Jackie Jensen 6.00 15.00
162 Monte Irvin 10.00 25.00
163 Johnny Lipon 6.00 15.00
164 Connie Ryan 10.00 25.00
165 Saul Rogovin RC 6.00 15.00
166 Bobby Adams 6.00 15.00
167 Bobby Avila 10.00 25.00
168 Preacher Roe 10.00 25.00
169 Walt Dropo 10.00 25.00
170 Joe Astroth 6.00 15.00
171 Mel Queen 6.00 15.00
172 Ebba St.Claire RC 6.00 15.00
173 Gene Bearden 6.00 15.00
174 Mickey Grasso 6.00 15.00
175 Randy Jackson RC 6.00 15.00
176 Harry Brecheen 10.00 25.00
177 Gene Woodling 20.00 50.00
178 Dave Williams RC 10.00 25.00
179 Pete Suder 6.00 15.00
180 Ed Fitzgerald 6.00 15.00
181 Joe Collins RC 10.00 25.00
182 Dave Koslo 6.00 15.00
183 Pat Mullin 6.00 15.00
184 Curt Simmons 10.00 25.00
185 Eddie Stewart 6.00 15.00
186 Frank Smith RC 10.00 25.00
187 Jim Hegan 10.00 25.00
188 Chuck Dressen MG 10.00 25.00
189 Jimmy Piersall 15.00 40.00
190 Dick Fowler 6.00 15.00
191 Bob Friend RC 10.00 25.00
192 John Cusick RC 6.00 15.00
193 Bobby Young RC 6.00 15.00
194 Bob Porterfield 10.00 25.00
195 Frank Baumholtz 6.00 15.00
196 Stan Musial 300.00 800.00
197 Charlie Silvera RC 6.00 15.00
198 Chuck Diering 6.00 15.00
199 Ted Gray 6.00 15.00
200 Ken Silvestri 6.00 15.00
201 Ray Coleman 6.00 15.00
202 Harry Perkowski RC 6.00 15.00
203 Steve Gromek 6.00 15.00
204 Andy Pafko 15.00 40.00
205 Walt Masterson 6.00 15.00
206 Elmer Valo 6.00 15.00
207 George Strickland RC 6.00 15.00
208 Walker Cooper 6.00 15.00
209 Dick Littlefield RC 6.00 15.00
210 Archie Wilson RC 6.00 15.00
211 Paul Minner RC 6.00 15.00
212 Solly Hemus RC 15.00 40.00
213 Monte Kennedy 6.00 15.00
214 Ray Boone 15.00 40.00
215 Sheldon Jones 6.00 15.00
216 Matt Batts 6.00 15.00
217 Casey Stengel MG 50.00 120.00
218 Willie Mays 2500.00 6000.00
219 Neil Berry 25.00 60.00
220 Russ Meyer 25.00 60.00
221 Lou Kretlow RC 25.00 60.00
222 Dixie Howell 25.00 60.00
223 Harry Simpson RC 25.00 60.00
224 Johnny Schmitz 25.00 60.00
225 Del Wilber RC 25.00 60.00
226 Alex Kellner 25.00 60.00
227 Clyde Sukeforth CO RC 25.00 60.00
228 Bob Chipman 25.00 60.00
229 Hank Arft 25.00 60.00
230 Frank Shea 25.00 60.00
231 Dee Fondy RC 25.00 60.00
232 Enos Slaughter 40.00 100.00
233 Bob Kuzava 25.00 60.00
234 Fred Fitzsimmons CO 25.00 60.00
235 Steve Souchock RC 25.00 60.00
236 Tommy Brown 25.00 60.00
237 Sherm Lollar 25.00 60.00
238 Roy McMillan RC 25.00 60.00
239 Dale Mitchell 25.00 60.00
240 Billy Loes RC 25.00 60.00
241 Mel Parnell 25.00 60.00
242 Everett Kell RC 25.00 60.00
243 George Munger 25.00 60.00
244 Lew Burdette RC 40.00 100.00
245 George Schmees RC 25.00 60.00
246 Jerry Snyder RC 25.00 60.00
247 Johnny Pramesa 25.00 60.00
248 Bill Werle Full Name 25.00 60.00
248A Bill Werle No W 25.00 60.00
249 Hank Thompson 25.00 60.00
250 Ike Delock RC 25.00 60.00
251 Jack Lohrke 25.00 60.00
252 Frank Crosetti CO 60.00 150.00

1953 Bowman Black and White

The cards in this 64-card set measure approximately 2 1/2" by 3 3/4". Some collectors believe that the high cost of producing the 1953 color series forced Bowman to issue this set in black and white, since the two sets are identical in design except for the element of color. This set was also produced in fewer numbers than its color counterpart, and is popular among collectors for the challenge involved in completing it and the lack of short prints. Cards were issued in one-card penny packs which came 120 to a box and five-card nickel packs. There are no key Rookie Cards in this set. Card #43, Hal Bevan, exists with him being born in either 1930 or 1950. The 1950 version seems to be is much more difficult to find.

COMPLETE SET (64) 1000.00 2500.00
WRAPPER (1-CENT) 300.00 350.00
CARDS PRICED IN NM CONDITION !
1 Gus Bell 60.00 120.00
2 Willard Nixon 25.00 40.00
3 Bill Rigney 25.00 40.00
4 Pat Mullin 25.00 40.00
5 Dee Fondy 25.00 40.00
6 Ray Murray 25.00 40.00
7 Andy Seminick 25.00 40.00
8 Pete Suder 25.00 40.00
9 Walt Masterson 25.00 40.00
10 Dick Sisler 35.00 60.00
11 Dick Gernert 25.00 40.00
12 Randy Jackson 25.00 40.00
13 Joe Tipton 25.00 40.00
14 Bill Nicholson 35.00 60.00
15 Johnny Mize 75.00 125.00
16 Stu Miller RC 35.00 60.00
17 Virgil Trucks 35.00 60.00
18 Billy Hoeft 25.00 40.00
19 Paul LaPalme 25.00 40.00
20 Eddie Robinson 25.00 40.00
21 Clarence Podbielan 25.00 40.00
22 Matt Batts 25.00 40.00
23 Wilmer Mizell 35.00 60.00
24 Del Wilber 25.00 40.00
25 Johnny Sain 50.00 80.00
26 Preacher Roe 50.00 80.00
27 Bob Lemon 50.00 120.00
28 Hoyt Wilhelm 60.00 150.00
29 Sid Hudson 25.00 40.00
30 Walker Cooper 25.00 40.00
31 Gene Woodling 50.00 80.00
32 Rocky Bridges 25.00 40.00
33 Bob Kuzava 25.00 40.00
34 Ebba St.Claire 25.00 40.00
35 Johnny Wyrostek 25.00 40.00
36 Jimmy Piersall 50.00 80.00
37 Hal Jeffcoat 25.00 40.00
38 Dave Cole 25.00 40.00
39 Casey Stengel MG 200.00 350.00
40 Larry Jansen 35.00 60.00
41 Bob Ramazzotti 25.00 40.00
42 Howie Judson 25.00 40.00
43 Hal Bevan ERR RC 25.00 40.00
43A Hal Bevan COR 25.00 40.00
44 Jim Delsing 25.00 40.00
45 Irv Noren 35.00 60.00
46 Bucky Harris MG 50.00 80.00
47 Jack Lohrke 25.00 40.00
48 Steve Ridzik RC 25.00 40.00
49 Floyd Baker 25.00 40.00
50 Dutch Leonard 25.00 40.00
51 Lou Burdette 50.00 80.00
52 Ralph Branca 50.00 80.00
53 Morrie Martin 25.00 40.00
54 Bill Miller 25.00 40.00
55 Don Johnson 25.00 40.00
56 Roy Smalley 25.00 40.00
57 Andy Pafko 35.00 60.00
58 Jim Konstanty 35.00 60.00
59 Duane Pillette 25.00 40.00
60 Billy Cox 50.00 80.00
61 Tom Gorman RC 25.00 40.00
62 Keith Thomas RC 25.00 40.00
63 Steve Gromek 25.00 40.00
64 Andy Hansen 50.00 80.00

1953 Bowman Color

The cards in this 160-card set measure approximately 2 1/2" by 3 3/4". The 1953 Bowman Color set features Kodachrome photographs with no names or facsimile autographs on the face. Cards were issued in five-card nickel packs in a 24 pack box with each pack having gum in it. The entire low number run were also printed in three card strips; it is believed that these three card strips in numerical order were box toppers to retailers. The box features an endorsement from Joe DiMaggio. Numbers 113 to 160 are somewhat more difficult to obtain, with numbers 113 to 128 being the most difficult. There are two cards of Al Corwin (126 and 149). There are no key Rookie Cards in this set.

COMPLETE SET (160) 6000.00 15000.00
WRAPPER (1-CENT) 300.00 400.00
WRAPPER (5-CENT) 250.00 300.00
CARDS PRICED IN NM CONDITION !
1 Davey Williams 50.00 120.00
2 Vic Wertz 12.00 30.00
3 Sam Jethroe 30.00 80.00
4 Art Houtteman 15.00 40.00
5 Sid Gordon 15.00 40.00
6 Joe Ginsberg 20.00 50.00
7 Harry Chiti RC 15.00 40.00
8 Al Rosen 25.00 60.00
9 Phil Rizzuto 60.00 150.00
10 Richie Ashburn 60.00 150.00
11 Bobby Shantz 20.00 50.00
12 Carl Erskine 30.00 80.00
13 Gus Zernial 15.00 40.00
14 Billy Loes 15.00 40.00
15 Jim Busby 15.00 40.00
16 Bob Friend 12.00 30.00
17 Gerry Staley 12.00 30.00
18 Nellie Fox 40.00 100.00
19 Alvin Dark 12.00 30.00
20 Don Lenhardt 12.00 30.00
21 Joe Garagiola 15.00 40.00
22 Bob Porterfield 15.00 40.00
23 Herman Wehmeier 15.00 40.00
24 Jackie Jensen 15.00 40.00
25 Hoot Evers 15.00 40.00
26 Roy McMillan 15.00 40.00
27 Vic Raschi 20.00 50.00
28 Smoky Burgess 15.00 40.00
29 Bobby Avila 15.00 40.00
30 Phil Cavarretta 15.00 40.00
31 Jimmy Dykes MG 12.00 30.00
32 Stan Musial 400.00 1000.00
33 Pee Wee Reese 500.00 1200.00
34 Gil Coan 12.00 30.00
35 Maurice McDermott 12.00 30.00
36 Minnie Minoso 30.00 80.00
37 Jim Wilson 12.00 30.00
38 Harry Byrd RC 12.00 30.00
39 Paul Richards MG 20.00 50.00
40 Larry Doby 75.00 200.00
41 Sammy White 15.00 40.00
42 Tommy Brown 12.00 30.00
43 Mike Garcia 15.00 40.00
44 Bauer/Berra/Mantle 400.00 1000.00
45 Walt Dropo 20.00 50.00
46 Roy Campanella 150.00 400.00
47 Ned Garver 20.00 50.00
48 Hank Sauer 20.00 50.00
49 Eddie Stanky MG 15.00 40.00
50 Lou Kretlow 15.00 40.00
51 Monte Irvin 40.00 100.00
52 Marty Marion MG 20.00 50.00
53 Del Rice 15.00 40.00
54 Chico Carrasquel 12.00 30.00
55 Leo Durocher MG 30.00 80.00
56 Bob Cain 15.00 40.00
57 Lou Boudreau MG 25.00 60.00
58 Willard Marshall 15.00 40.00
59 Mickey Mantle 2500.00 6000.00
60 Granny Hamner 15.00 40.00
61 George Kell 40.00 100.00
62 Ted Kluszewski 30.00 80.00
63 Gil McDougald 40.00 100.00
64 Curt Simmons 25.00 60.00
65 Robin Roberts 75.00 200.00
66 Mel Parnell 15.00 40.00
67 Mel Clark RC 12.00 30.00
68 Allie Reynolds 40.00 100.00
69 Charlie Grimm MG 20.00 50.00
70 Clint Courtney RC 15.00 40.00
71 Paul Minner 15.00 40.00
72 Ted Gray 15.00 40.00
73 Billy Pierce 15.00 40.00
74 Don Mueller 15.00 40.00
75 Saul Rogovin 12.00 30.00
76 Jim Hearn 12.00 30.00
77 Mickey Grasso 15.00 40.00
78 Carl Furillo 30.00 80.00
79 Ray Boone 20.00 50.00
80 Ralph Kiner 30.00 80.00
81 Enos Slaughter 50.00 120.00
82 Joe Astroth 20.00 50.00
83 Jack Daniels RC 20.00 50.00
84 Hank Bauer 25.00 60.00
85 Solly Hemus 20.00 50.00
86 Harry Simpson 20.00 50.00
87 Harry Perkowski 20.00 50.00
88 Joe Dobson 12.00 30.00
89 Sandy Consuegra 20.00 50.00
90 Joe Nuxhall 25.00 60.00
91 Steve Souchock 20.00 50.00
92 Gil Hodges 100.00 250.00
93 P.Rizzuto/B.Martin 100.00 250.00
94 Bob Addis 15.00 40.00
95 Wally Moses CO 15.00 40.00
96 Sal Maglie 25.00 60.00
97 Eddie Mathews 100.00 250.00
98 Hector Rodriguez RC 25.00 60.00
99 Warren Spahn 100.00 250.00
100 Bill Wight 25.00 60.00
101 Red Schoendienst 60.00 150.00
102 Jim Hegan 25.00 60.00
103 Del Ennis 30.00 80.00
104 Luke Easter 40.00 100.00
105 Eddie Joost 15.00 40.00
106 Ken Raffensberger 12.00 30.00
107 Alex Kellner 15.00 40.00
108 Bobby Adams 15.00 40.00
109 Ken Wood 15.00 40.00
110 Bob Rush 12.00 30.00
111 Jim Dyck RC 20.00 50.00
112 Toby Atwell 25.00 60.00
113 Karl Drews 40.00 100.00
114 Bob Feller 150.00 400.00
115 Cloyd Boyer 30.00 80.00
116 Eddie Yost 40.00 100.00
117 Duke Snider 200.00 500.00
118 Billy Martin 125.00 300.00
119 Dale Mitchell 30.00 80.00
120 Marlin Stuart 60.00 150.00
121 Yogi Berra 300.00 800.00
122 Bill Serena 25.00 60.00
123 Johnny Lipon 40.00 100.00
124 Charlie Dressen MG 60.00 150.00
125 Fred Hatfield 30.00 80.00
126 Al Corwin 25.00 60.00
127 Dick Kryhoski 30.00 80.00
128 Whitey Lockman 60.00 150.00
129 Russ Meyer 40.00 100.00
130 Cass Michaels 25.00 60.00
131 Connie Ryan 25.00 60.00
132 Fred Hutchinson 40.00 100.00
133 Willie Jones 25.00 60.00
134 Johnny Pesky 50.00 120.00
135 Bobby Morgan 40.00 100.00
136 Jim Brideweser RC 40.00 100.00
137 Sam Dente 20.00 50.00
138 Bubba Church 25.00 60.00
139 Pete Runnels 25.00 60.00
140 Al Brazle 25.00 60.00
141 Frank Shea 30.00 80.00
142 Larry Miggins RC 25.00 60.00
143 Al Lopez MG 40.00 100.00
144 Warren Hacker 20.00 50.00
145 George Shuba 60.00 150.00
146 Early Wynn 50.00 120.00
147 Clem Koshorek 25.00 60.00
148 Billy Goodman 50.00 120.00
149 Al Corwin 25.00 60.00
150 Carl Scheib 25.00 60.00
151 Joe Adcock 40.00 100.00
152 Clyde Vollmer 20.00 50.00
153 Whitey Ford 200.00 500.00
154 Turk Lown 30.00 80.00
155 Allie Clark 25.00 60.00
156 Max Surkont 25.00 60.00
157 Sherm Lollar 30.00 80.00
158 Howard Fox 25.00 60.00
159 Mickey Vernon UER 40.00 100.00
160 Cal Abrams 100.00 250.00

1954 Bowman

The cards in this 224-card set measure approximately 2 1/2" by 3 3/4". The set was distributed in two separate series: 1-128 in first series and 129-224 in second series. A contractual problem apparently resulted in the deletion of the number 66 Ted Williams card from this Bowman set, thereby creating a scarcity that is highly valued among collectors. The set price below does NOT include number 66 Williams but does include number 66 Jim Piersall, the apparent replacement for Williams in spite of the fact that Piersall was already number 210 to appear later in the set. Many errors in players' statistics exist (and some were corrected) while a few players' names were printed on the front, instead of appearing as a facsimile autograph. Most of these differences are so minor that there is no price differential for either card. The cards which changes were made on are numbers 12, 22,25,26,35,38,41,43,47,53,61,67,80,81,82,85,93,94, 99,103,105,124,138,139, 140,145,153,156,174,179,185,212,216 and 217. The set was issued in seven-card nickel packs and one-card penny packs. The penny packs were issued 120 to a box while the nickel packs were issued 24 to a box. The notable Rookie Cards in this set are Harvey Kuenn and Don Larsen.

COMPLETE SET (224) 5000.00 12000.00
WRAP.(1-CENT, DATED) 100.00 150.00
WRAP.(1-CENT, UNDAT) 150.00 200.00
WRAP.(5-CENT, DATED) 100.00 150.00
WRAP.(5-CENT, UNDAT) 50.00 60.00
1 Phil Rizzuto 50.00 120.00
2 Jackie Jensen 10.00 25.00
3 Marion Fricano 5.00 12.00
4 Bob Hooper 5.00 12.00
5 Billy Hunter 5.00 12.00
6 Nellie Fox 25.00 60.00
7 Walt Dropo 6.00 15.00
8 Jim Busby 5.00 12.00
9 Dave Williams 5.00 12.00
10 Carl Erskine 12.00 30.00
11 Sid Gordon 5.00 12.00
12A Roy McMillan 5.00 12.00
551/1290 At Bat
12B Roy McMillan 6.00 15.00
557/1296 At Bat
13 Paul Minner 5.00 12.00
14 Gerry Staley 5.00 12.00
15 Richie Ashburn 40.00 100.00
16 Jim Wilson 5.00 12.00
17 Tom Gorman 5.00 12.00
18 Hoot Evers 5.00 12.00
19 Bobby Shantz 5.00 12.00
20 Art Houtteman 5.00 12.00
21 Vic Wertz 5.00 12.00
22A Sam Mele 5.00 12.00
213/1661 Putouts
22B Sam Mele 6.00 15.00
217/1665 Putouts
23 Harvey Kuenn RC 15.00 40.00
24 Bob Porterfield 5.00 12.00
25A Wes Westrum 6.00 15.00
1.000/.987 Fielding Avg.
25B Wes Westrum 8.00 20.00
.982/.986 Fielding Avg.
26A Billy Cox 6.00 15.00
1.000/.960 Fielding Avg.
26B Billy Cox 8.00 20.00
.972/.960 Fielding Avg.
27 Dick Cole RC 5.00 12.00
28A Jim Greengrass Birthplace Addison, NJ 5.00 12.00
28B Jim Greengrass Birthplace Addison, NY 5.00 12.00
29 Johnny Klippstein 6.00 15.00
30 Del Rice 5.00 12.00
31 Smoky Burgess 8.00 20.00
32 Del Crandall 5.00 12.00
33A Vic Raschi No Trade 8.00 20.00
33B Vic Raschi Traded to St.Louis 10.00 25.00
34 Sammy White 5.00 12.00
35A Eddie Joost Quiz Answer is 8 5.00 12.00
35B Eddie Joost Quiz Answer is 33 6.00 15.00
36 George Strickland 6.00 15.00
37 Dick Kokos 5.00 12.00
38A Minnie Minoso 8.00 20.00
.895/.961 Fielding Avg.
38B Minnie Minoso 10.00 25.00
.963/.963 Fielding Avg.
39 Ned Garver 5.00 12.00
40 Gil Coan 5.00 12.00
41A Alvin Dark 5.00 12.00
.986/.960 Fielding Avg.
41B Alvin Dark 6.00 15.00
.968/.960 Fielding Avg.
42 Billy Loes 5.00 12.00
43A Bob Friend 20 Shutouts in Quiz 5.00 12.00
43B Bob Friend 16 Shutouts in Quiz 6.00 15.00
44 Harry Perkowski 5.00 12.00
45 Ralph Kiner 25.00 60.00
46 Rip Repulski 8.00 20.00
47A Granny Hamner 5.00 12.00
.970/.953 Fielding Avg.
47B Granny Hamner 8.00 20.00
.953/.951 Fielding Avg.
48 Jack Dittmer 5.00 12.00
49 Harry Byrd 10.00 25.00
50 George Kell 15.00 40.00
51 Alex Kellner 5.00 12.00
52 Joe Ginsberg 5.00 12.00
53A Don Lenhardt 5.00 12.00
.969/.984 Fielding Avg.
53B Don Lenhardt 5.00 12.00
.966/.983 Fielding Avg.
54 Chico Carrasquel 5.00 12.00
55 Jim Delsing 5.00 12.00
56 Maurice McDermott 5.00 12.00
57 Hoyt Wilhelm 20.00 50.00
58 Pee Wee Reese 60.00 150.00
59 Bob Schultz 5.00 12.00
60 Fred Baczewski RC 6.00 15.00
61A Eddie Miksis 5.00 12.00
.954/.962 Fielding Avg.
61B Eddie Miksis 6.00 15.00
.954/.961 Fielding Avg.
62 Enos Slaughter 20.00 50.00
63 Earl Torgeson 5.00 12.00
64 Eddie Mathews 75.00 200.00
65 Mickey Mantle 2000.00 5000.00
66A Ted Williams 1500.00 4000.00
66B Jimmy Piersall 25.00 60.00
67A Carl Scheib .306 Pct. Two Lines under Bio 5.00 12.00
67B Carl Scheib .306 Pct. One Line under Bio 6.00 15.00
67C Carl Scheib .300 Pct. 6.00 15.00
68 Bobby Avila 5.00 12.00
69 Clint Courtney 5.00 12.00
70 Willard Marshall 6.00 15.00
71 Ted Gray 6.00 15.00
72 Eddie Yost 5.00 12.00
73 Don Mueller 5.00 12.00
74 Jim Gilliam 10.00 25.00
75 Max Surkont 5.00 12.00
76 Joe Nuxhall 5.00 12.00
77 Bob Rush 5.00 12.00
78 Sal Yvars 5.00 12.00
79 Curt Simmons 5.00 12.00
80A Johnny Logan 106 Runs 5.00 12.00
80B Johnny Logan 100 Runs 6.00 15.00
81A Jerry Coleman 8.00 20.00
1.000/.975 Fielding Avg.
81B Jerry Coleman 10.00 25.00
.952/.975 Fielding Avg.
82A Bill Goodman 6.00 15.00
.965/.986 Fielding Avg.
82B Bill Goodman 8.00 20.00
.972/.985 Fielding Avg.
83 Ray Murray 5.00 12.00
84 Larry Doby 20.00 50.00
85A Jim Dyck 5.00 12.00
.926/.956 Fielding Avg.
85B Jim Dyck 6.00 15.00
.947/.960 Fielding Avg.
86 Harry Dorish 5.00 12.00
87 Don Lund 5.00 12.00
88 Tom Umphlett RC 5.00 12.00
89 Willie Mays 1250.00 3000.00
90 Roy Campanella 60.00 150.00
91 Cal Abrams 5.00 12.00
92 Ken Raffensberger 5.00 12.00
93A Bill Serena 5.00 12.00
.983/.966 Fielding Avg.
93B Bill Serena 6.00 15.00
.977/.966 Fielding Avg.
94A Solly Hemus 5.00 12.00
476/1343 Assists
94B Solly Hemus 6.00 15.00
477/1343 Assists
95 Robin Roberts 25.00 60.00
96 Joe Adcock 8.00 20.00
97 Gil McDougald 12.00 30.00
98 Ellis Kinder 8.00 20.00
99A Peter Suder 5.00 12.00
.985/.974 Fielding Avg.
99B Peter Suder 6.00 15.00
.978/.974 Fielding Avg.
100 Mike Garcia 8.00 20.00
101 Don Larsen RC 40.00 100.00
102 Billy Pierce 8.00 20.00
103A Stephen Souchock 5.00 12.00
144/1192 Putouts
103B Stephen Souchock 6.00 15.00
147/1195 Putouts
104 Frank Shea 5.00 12.00
105A Sal Maglie Quiz Answer is 8 5.00 12.00
105B Sal Maglie Quiz Answer is 1904 8.00 20.00
106 Clem Labine 10.00 25.00
107 Paul LaPalme 5.00 12.00
108 Bobby Adams 5.00 12.00
109 Roy Smalley 6.00 15.00
110 Red Schoendienst 12.00 30.00
111 Murry Dickson 8.00 20.00
112 Andy Pafko 8.00 20.00
113 Allie Reynolds 20.00 50.00
114 Willard Nixon 5.00 12.00
115 Don Bollweg 5.00 12.00
116 Luke Easter 5.00 12.00
117 Dick Kryhoski 6.00 15.00
118 Bob Boyd 5.00 12.00
119 Fred Hatfield 6.00 15.00
120 Mel Hoderlein RC 5.00 12.00
121 Ray Katt RC 5.00 12.00
122 Carl Furillo 12.00 30.00
123 Toby Atwell 5.00 12.00
124A Gus Bell 5.00 12.00
15/27 Errors
124B Gus Bell 6.00 15.00
11/26 Errors
125 Warren Hacker 5.00 12.00
126 Cliff Chambers 5.00 12.00
127 Del Ennis 8.00 20.00
128 Ebba St.Claire 5.00 12.00
129 Hank Bauer 20.00 50.00
130 Milt Bolling 5.00 12.00
131 Joe Astroth 5.00 12.00
132 Bob Feller 75.00 200.00
133 Duane Pillette 5.00 12.00
134 Luis Aloma 5.00 12.00
135 Johnny Pesky 5.00 12.00
136 Clyde Vollmer 5.00 12.00
137 Al Corwin 5.00 12.00
138A Hodges .993/.991 Field.Avg. 25.00 60.00
138B Hodges .992/.991 Field.Avg. 25.00 60.00
139A Preston Ward 5.00 12.00
.961/.992 Fielding Avg.
139B Preston Ward 6.00 15.00
.990/.992 Fielding Avg.
140A Saul Rogovin 12.00 30.00
7-12 W-L 2 Strikeouts
140B Saul Rogovin 12.00 30.00
7-12 W-L 62 Strikeouts
140C Saul Rogovin 8-12 W-L 12.00 30.00
141 Joe Garagiola 20.00 50.00
142 Al Brazle 5.00 12.00
143 Willie Jones 5.00 12.00
144 Ernie Johnson RC 8.00 20.00
145A Martin .985/.983 Field.Avg. 25.00 60.00
145B Martin .983/.982 Field.Avg. 25.00 60.00
146 Dick Gernert 5.00 12.00
147 Joe DeMaestri 5.00 12.00
148 Dale Mitchell 6.00 15.00
149 Bob Young 5.00 12.00
150 Cass Michaels 5.00 12.00
151 Pat Mullin 5.00 12.00
152 Mickey Vernon 10.00 25.00
153A Whitey Lockman 10.00 25.00
100/331 Assists
153B Whitey Lockman 12.00 30.00
102/333 Assists
154 Don Newcombe 20.00 50.00
155 Frank Thomas RC 6.00 15.00
156A Rocky Bridges 5.00 12.00
320/467 Assists
156B Rocky Bridges 6.00 15.00
328/475 Assists
157 Turk Lown 5.00 12.00
158 Stu Miller 5.00 12.00
159 Johnny Lindell 5.00 12.00
160 Danny O'Connell 6.00 15.00
161 Yogi Berra 75.00 300.00
162 Ted Lepcio 8.00 20.00
163A Dave Philley No Trade 152 Games 6.00 15.00
163B Dave Philley Traded to Cleveland 152 Games 8.00 20.00
163C Dave Philley Traded to Cleveland 157 Games 10.00 25.00
164 Early Wynn 20.00 50.00
165 Johnny Groth 5.00 12.00
166 Sandy Consuegra 5.00 12.00
167 Billy Hoeft 5.00 12.00
168 Ed Fitzgerald 5.00 12.00
169 Larry Jansen 5.00 12.00
170 Duke Snider 60.00 150.00
171 Carlos Bernier 5.00 12.00
172 Andy Seminick 5.00 12.00
173 Dee Fondy 5.00 12.00
174A Pete Castiglione 5.00 12.00
.966/.959 Fielding Avg.
174B Pete Castiglione 5.00 12.00
.970/.959 Fielding Avg.
175 Mel Clark 5.00 12.00
176 Vern Bickford 5.00 12.00
177 Whitey Ford 60.00 150.00
178 Del Wilber 6.00 15.00
179A Morris Martin 44 ERA 5.00 12.00
179B Morris Martin 4.44 ERA 5.00 12.00
180 Joe Tipton 5.00 12.00
181 Les Moss 5.00 12.00
182 Sherm Lollar 6.00 15.00
183 Matt Batts 5.00 12.00
184 Mickey Grasso 8.00 20.00
185A Daryl Spencer 5.00 12.00
.941/.944 Fielding Avg. RC
185B Daryl Spencer .933
.936 Fielding Avg. 6.00 15.00
186 Russ Meyer 8.00 20.00
187 Vern Law 10.00 25.00
188 Frank Smith 6.00 15.00
189 Randy Jackson 5.00 12.00
190 Joe Presko 5.00 12.00
191 Karl Drews 5.00 12.00
192 Lew Burdette 8.00 20.00
193 Eddie Robinson 10.00 25.00
194 Sid Hudson 8.00 20.00
195 Bob Cain 8.00 20.00
196 Bob Lemon 12.00 30.00
197 Lou Kretlow 5.00 12.00
198 Virgil Trucks 8.00 20.00
199 Steve Gromek 5.00 12.00
200 Conrado Marrero 5.00 12.00
201 Bobby Thomson 8.00 20.00
202 George Shuba 6.00 15.00
203 Vic Janowicz 5.00 12.00
204 Jack Collum RC 5.00 12.00
205 Hal Jeffcoat 5.00 12.00
206 Steve Bilko 8.00 20.00
207 Stan Lopata 5.00 12.00
208 Johnny Antonelli 5.00 12.00
209 Gene Woodling UER Reversed Photo 10.00 25.00
210 Jimmy Piersall 15.00 40.00
211 Al Robertson RC 5.00 12.00
212A Owen Friend 5.00 12.00
.964/.957 Fielding Avg.
212B Owen Friend 6.00 15.00
.967/.958 Fielding Avg.
213 Dick Littlefield 5.00 12.00
214 Ferris Fain 5.00 12.00
215 Johnny Bucha 5.00 12.00
216A Jerry Snyder 5.00 12.00
.988/.988 Fielding Avg.
216B Jerry Snyder 5.00 12.00
.968/.968 Fielding Avg.
217A Henry Thompson 10.00 25.00
.956/.951 Fielding Avg.
217B Henry Thompson 12.00 30.00
.958/.952 Fielding Avg.
218 Preacher Roe 10.00 25.00
219 Hal Rice 5.00 12.00
220 Hobie Landrith RC 5.00 12.00
221 Frank Baumholtz 5.00 12.00
222 Memo Luna RC 5.00 12.00
223 Steve Ridzik 5.00 12.00
224 Bill Bruton 10.00 25.00

1955 Bowman

The cards in this 320-card set measure approximately 2 1/2" by 3 3/4". The Bowman set of 1955 is known as the "TV set" because each player photograph is cleverly shown within a television set design. The set contains umpire cards, some transposed pictures (e.g., Johnsons and Bollings), an incorrect spelling for Harvey Kuenn, and a traded line for Palica (all of which are noted in the checklist below). Some three-card advertising strips exist, the backs of these panels contain advertising for Bowman products. Print advertisements for these cards featured Willie Mays along with publicizing the great value in nine cards for a nickel. Advertising panels seen include Nellie Fox/Carl Furillo/Carl Erskine; Hank Aaron/Johnny Logan/Eddie Miksis; Bob Rush/Ray Katt/Willie Mays; Steve Gromek/Milt Bolling/Vern Stephens, Russ Kemmerer/ Hal Jeffcoat/Dee Fondy and a Bob Darnell/Early Wynn/Pee Wee Reese. Cards were issued either in nine-card nickel packs or one card penny packs. Cello packs containing approximately 20 cards have also been seen, albeit on a very limited basis. The notable Rookie Cards in this set are Elston Howard and Don Zimmer. Hall of Fame umpires pictured in the set are Al Barlick, Jocko Conlon and Cal Hubbard. Undated five cent wrappers are also known to exist for this set.

COMPLETE SET (320) 4000.00 10000.00
COMMON CARD (1-96) 6.00 12.00
COM. CARD (97-224) 5.00 10.00
COM. CARD (225-320) 7.50 15.00
COM. UMPIRE (225-320) 18.00 30.00
WRAPPER (1-CENT) 50.00 60.00
WRAPPER (5-CENT) 50.00 60.00
1 Hoyt Wilhelm 60.00 150.00
2 Alvin Dark 8.00 20.00
3 Joe Coleman 7.50 20.00
4 Eddie Waitkus 7.50 20.00
5 Jim Robertson 6.00 15.00
6 Pete Suder 6.00 15.00
7 Gene Baker RC 6.00 15.00
8 Warren Hacker 6.00 15.00
9 Gil McDougald 20.00 50.00
10 Phil Rizzuto 40.00 100.00
11 Bill Bruton 7.50 20.00
12 Andy Pafko 7.50 20.00
13 Clyde Vollmer 6.00 15.00
14 Gus Keriazakos RC 6.00 15.00
15 Frank Sullivan RC 6.00 15.00
16 Jimmy Piersall 12.00 30.00
17 Del Ennis 7.50 20.00
18 Stan Lopata 6.00 15.00
19 Bobby Avila 7.50 20.00
20 Al Smith 7.50 20.00
21 Don Hoak 8.00 20.00
22 Roy Campanella 50.00 120.00
23 Al Kaline 60.00 150.00
24 Al Aber 6.00 15.00
25 Minnie Minoso 12.00 30.00
26 Virgil Trucks 8.00 20.00
27 Preston Ward 6.00 15.00
28 Dick Cole 6.00 15.00
29 Red Schoendienst 12.00 30.00
30 Bill Sarni 6.00 15.00
31 Johnny Temple RC 7.50 20.00
32 Wally Post 7.50 20.00
33 Nellie Fox 25.00 60.00
34 Clint Courtney 6.00 15.00
35 Bill Tuttle RC 6.00 15.00
36 Wayne Belardi RC 6.00 15.00
37 Pee Wee Reese 40.00 100.00
38 Early Wynn 20.00 50.00
39 Bob Darnell RC 7.50 20.00
40 Vic Wertz 7.50 20.00
41 Mel Clark 6.00 15.00
42 Bob Greenwood RC 10.00 25.00
43 Bob Buhl 7.50 20.00
44 Danny O'Connell 6.00 15.00
45 Tom Umphlett 8.00 20.00
46 Mickey Vernon 7.50 20.00
47 Sammy White 6.00 15.00
48A Milt Bolling ERR 10.00 25.00
48B Milt Bolling COR 10.00 25.00
49 Jim Greengrass 6.00 15.00
50 Hobie Landrith 6.00 15.00
51 Elvin Tappe RC 6.00 15.00
52 Hal Rice 6.00 15.00
53 Alex Kellner 6.00 15.00
54 Don Bollweg 6.00 15.00
55 Cal Abrams 6.00 15.00
56 Billy Cox 7.50 20.00
57 Bob Friend 7.50 20.00
58 Frank Thomas 7.50 20.00
59 Whitey Ford 50.00 120.00
60 Enos Slaughter 12.00 30.00
61 Paul LaPalme 6.00 15.00
62 Royce Lint RC 6.00 15.00
63 Irv Noren 7.50 20.00
64 Curt Simmons 7.50 20.00
65 Don Zimmer RC 20.00 50.00
66 George Shuba 10.00 25.00
67 Don Larsen 25.00 60.00
68 Elston Howard RC 40.00 100.00
69 Billy Hunter 6.00 15.00
70 Lew Burdette 10.00 25.00
71 Dave Jolly 6.00 15.00
72 Chet Nichols 6.00 15.00
73 Eddie Yost 7.50 20.00
74 Jerry Snyder 6.00 15.00
75 Brooks Lawrence RC 6.00 15.00
76 Tom Poholsky 6.00 15.00
77 Jim McDonald RC 6.00 15.00
78 Gil Coan 8.00 20.00
79 Willie Miranda 6.00 15.00
80 Lou Limmer 6.00 15.00
81 Bobby Morgan 6.00 15.00
82 Lee Walls RC 6.00 15.00
83 Max Surkont 6.00 15.00
84 George Freese RC 6.00 15.00
85 Cass Michaels 6.00 15.00
86 Ted Gray 6.00 15.00
87 Randy Jackson 6.00 15.00
88 Steve Bilko 6.00 15.00
89 Lou Boudreau MG 12.00 30.00
90 Art Ditmar RC 6.00 15.00
91 Dick Marlowe RC 6.00 15.00
92 George Zuverink 6.00 15.00
93 Andy Seminick 6.00 15.00
94 Hank Thompson 7.50 20.00
95 Sal Maglie 7.50 20.00
96 Ray Narleski RC 6.00 15.00
97 Johnny Podres 20.00 50.00
98 Jim Gilliam 10.00 25.00
99 Jerry Coleman 7.50 20.00
100 Tom Morgan 5.00 12.00
101A Don Johnson ERR 10.00 25.00
101B Don Johnson COR 10.00 25.00
102 Bobby Thomson 7.50 20.00
103 Eddie Mathews 50.00 120.00
104 Bob Porterfield 5.00 12.00
105 Johnny Schmitz 5.00 12.00
106 Del Rice 5.00 12.00
107 Solly Hemus 5.00 12.00
108 Lou Kretlow 5.00 12.00
109 Vern Stephens 7.50 20.00
110 Bob Miller 5.00 12.00
111 Steve Ridzik 5.00 12.00
112 Granny Hamner 5.00 12.00
113 Bob Hall RC 5.00 12.00
114 Vic Janowicz 7.50 20.00
115 Roger Bowman RC 5.00 12.00
116 Sandy Consuegra 5.00 12.00
117 Johnny Groth 5.00 12.00
118 Bobby Adams 5.00 12.00
119 Joe Astroth 5.00 12.00
120 Ed Burtschy RC 5.00 12.00
121 Rufus Crawford RC 5.00 12.00
122 Al Corwin 5.00 12.00
123 Marv Grissom RC 5.00 12.00
124 Johnny Antonelli 12.00 30.00
125 Paul Giel RC 7.50 20.00
126 Billy Goodman 7.50 20.00
127 Hank Majeski 5.00 12.00
128 Mike Garcia 7.50 20.00
129 Hal Naragon RC 5.00 12.00
130 Richie Ashburn 30.00 80.00
131 Willard Marshall 6.00 15.00
132A Harvey Kueen ERR 25.00 60.00
132B Harvey Kuenn COR 12.00 30.00
133 Charles King RC 5.00 12.00
134 Bob Feller 50.00 120.00
135 Lloyd Merriman 5.00 12.00
136 Rocky Bridges 5.00 12.00
137 Bob Talbot 5.00 12.00
138 Davey Williams 7.50 20.00
139 W.Shantz/B.Shantz 7.50 20.00
140 Bobby Shantz 7.50 20.00
141 Wes Westrum 7.50 20.00
142 Rudy Regalado RC 7.50 20.00
143 Don Newcombe 20.00 50.00
144 Art Houtteman 5.00 12.00
145 Bob Nieman RC 5.00 12.00
146 Don Liddle 5.00 12.00
147 Sam Mele 5.00 12.00
148 Bob Chakales 5.00 12.00
149 Cloyd Boyer 5.00 12.00
150 Billy Klaus RC 5.00 12.00
151 Jim Brideweser 5.00 12.00
152 Johnny Klippstein 5.00 12.00
153 Eddie Robinson 5.00 12.00
154 Frank Lary RC 7.50 20.00
155 Gerry Staley 5.00 12.00
156 Jim Hughes 7.50 20.00
157A Ernie Johnson ERR 10.00 25.00
157B Ernie Johnson COR 10.00 25.00
158 Gil Hodges 30.00 80.00
159 Harry Byrd 5.00 12.00
160 Bill Skowron 20.00 50.00
161 Matt Batts 5.00 12.00
162 Charlie Maxwell 5.00 12.00
163 Sid Gordon 7.50 20.00
164 Toby Atwell 5.00 12.00
165 Maurice McDermott 8.00 20.00
166 Jim Busby 10.00 25.00
167 Bob Grim RC 10.00 25.00
168 Yogi Berra 100.00 250.00
169 Carl Furillo 12.00 30.00
170 Carl Erskine 12.00 30.00
171 Robin Roberts 30.00 80.00
172 Willie Jones 5.00 12.00
173 Chico Carrasquel 5.00 12.00
174 Sherm Lollar 7.50 20.00
175 Wilmer Shantz RC 5.00 12.00
176 Joe DeMaestri 5.00 12.00
177 Willard Nixon 5.00 12.00
178 Tom Brewer RC 5.00 12.00
179 Hank Aaron 400.00 1000.00
180 Johnny Logan 8.00 20.00
181 Eddie Miksis 5.00 12.00
182 Bob Rush 5.00 12.00
183 Ray Katt 5.00 12.00
184 Willie Mays 250.00 600.00
185 Vic Raschi 5.00 12.00
186 Alex Grammas 5.00 12.00
187 Fred Hatfield 5.00 12.00
188 Ned Garver 5.00 12.00
189 Jack Collum 5.00 12.00
190 Fred Baczewski 5.00 12.00
191 Bob Lemon 20.00 50.00
192 George Strickland 5.00 12.00
193 Howie Judson 5.00 12.00
194 Joe Nuxhall 7.50 20.00
195A Erv Palica 7.50 20.00
195B Erv Palica TR 20.00 50.00
196 Russ Meyer 8.00 20.00
197 Ralph Kiner 25.00 60.00
198 Dave Pope RC 7.50 20.00
199 Vern Law 8.00 20.00
200 Dick Littlefield 8.00 20.00
201 Allie Reynolds 12.00 30.00
202 Mickey Mantle UER 750.00 2000.00
203 Steve Gromek 5.00 12.00
204A Frank Bolling ERR RC 10.00 25.00
204B Frank Bolling COR 10.00 25.00
205 Rip Repulski 5.00 12.00
206 Ralph Beard RC 5.00 12.00
207 Frank Shea 8.00 20.00
208 Ed Fitzgerald 5.00 12.00
209 Smoky Burgess 7.50 20.00
210 Earl Torgeson 5.00 12.00
211 Sonny Dixon RC 5.00 12.00
212 Jack Dittmer 5.00 12.00
213 George Kell 12.00 30.00
214 Billy Pierce 7.50 20.00
215 Bob Kuzava 5.00 12.00
216 Preacher Roe 10.00 25.00
217 Del Crandall 7.50 20.00
218 Joe Adcock 7.50 20.00
219 Whitey Lockman 8.00 20.00
220 Jim Hearn 5.00 12.00
221 Hector Brown 5.00 12.00
222 Russ Kemmerer RC 5.00 12.00
223 Hal Jeffcoat 5.00 12.00
224 Dee Fondy 5.00 12.00
225 Paul Richards MG 7.50 20.00
226 Bill McKinley UMP 15.00 40.00
227 Frank Baumholtz 7.50 20.00
228 John Phillips RC 7.50 20.00
229 Jim Brosnan RC 10.00 25.00
230 Al Brazle 7.50 20.00
231 Jim Konstanty 10.00 25.00
232 Birdie Tebbetts MG 10.00 25.00
233 Bill Serena 7.50 20.00
234 Dick Bartell CO 10.00 25.00
235 Joe Paparella UMP 15.00 40.00
236 Murry Dickson 7.50 20.00
237 Johnny Wyrostek 7.50 20.00
238 Eddie Stanky MG 10.00 25.00
239 Edwin Rommel UMP 20.00 50.00
240 Billy Loes 10.00 25.00
241 Johnny Pesky 10.00 25.00
242 Ernie Banks 200.00 500.00
243 Gus Bell 10.00 25.00
244 Duane Pillette 7.50 20.00
245 Bill Miller 7.50 20.00
246 Hank Bauer 12.00 30.00
247 Dutch Leonard CO 20.00 50.00
248 Harry Dorish 7.50 20.00
249 Billy Gardner RC 10.00 25.00
250 Larry Napp UMP 15.00 40.00
251 Stan Jok 7.50 20.00
252 Roy Smalley 7.50 20.00
253 Jim Wilson 7.50 20.00
254 Bennett Flowers RC 7.50 20.00
255 Pete Runnels 10.00 25.00
256 Owen Friend 7.50 20.00
257 Tom Alston RC 7.50 20.00
258 John Stevens UMP 15.00 40.00
259 Don Mossi RC 12.00 30.00
260 Edwin Hurley UMP 15.00 40.00
261 Walt Moryn RC 10.00 25.00
262 Jim Lemon FBC 7.50 20.00
263 Eddie Joost 7.50 20.00
264 Bill Henry RC 8.00 20.00
265 Al Barlick UMP 30.00 80.00
266 Mike Fornieles 7.50 20.00
267 J.Honochick UMP 12.00 30.00
268 Roy Lee Hawes RC 7.50 20.00
269 Joe Amalfitano RC 10.00 25.00
270 Chico Fernandez RC 10.00 25.00
271 Bob Hooper 7.50 20.00
272 John Flaherty UMP 15.00 40.00
273 Bubba Church 7.50 20.00
274 Jim Delsing 7.50 20.00
275 William Grieve UMP 15.00 40.00
276 Ike Delock 7.50 20.00
277 Ed Runge UMP 15.00 40.00
278 Charlie Neal RC 20.00 50.00
279 Hank Soar UMP 20.00 50.00
280 Clyde McCullough 7.50 20.00
281 Charles Berry UMP 20.00 50.00
282 Phil Cavarretta MG 10.00 25.00
283 Nestor Chylak UMP 50.00 120.00
284 Bill Jackowski UMP 15.00 40.00
285 Walt Dropo 10.00 25.00
286 Frank Secory UMP 15.00 40.00
287 Ron Mrozinski RC 7.50 20.00
288 Dick Smith RC 7.50 20.00
289 Arthur Gore UMP 15.00 40.00
290 Hershell Freeman RC 7.50 20.00
291 Frank Dascoli UMP 15.00 40.00
292 Marv Blaylock RC 7.50 20.00
293 Thomas Gorman UMP 20.00 50.00
294 Wally Moses CO 7.50 20.00
295 Lee Ballanfant UMP 15.00 40.00
296 Bill Virdon RC 12.00 30.00
297 Dusty Boggess UMP 15.00 40.00
298 Charlie Grimm 10.00 25.00
299 Lon Warneke UMP 12.00 30.00
300 Tommy Byrne 10.00 25.00
301 William Engeln UMP 15.00 40.00
302 Frank Malzone RC 12.00 30.00
303 Jocko Conlan UMP 50.00 120.00
304 Harry Chiti 7.50 20.00
305 Frank Umont UMP 15.00 40.00
306 Bob Cerv 10.00 25.00
307 Babe Pinelli UMP 15.00 40.00
308 Al Lopez MG 25.00 60.00
309 Hal Dixon UMP 15.00 40.00
310 Ken Lehman RC 7.50 20.00
311 Lawrence Goetz UMP 15.00 40.00
312 Bill Wight 8.00 20.00
313 Augie Donatelli UMP 25.00 60.00
314 Dale Mitchell 10.00 25.00
315 Cal Hubbard UMP 30.00 80.00
316 Marion Fricano 7.50 20.00
317 William Summers UMP 10.00 25.00
318 Sid Hudson 7.50 20.00
319 Al Schroll RC 7.50 20.00
320 George Susce RC 25.00 60.00

1954 Bowman Advertising Strips

These strips were issued in four card salesman's sample and feature the actual card along with a diamond advertising in the back middle which notates these cards as 1954 Bowman's Advertising Samples.

COMPLETE SET 500.00 1000.00
1 Martin Fricano 300.00 600.00
Bob Hooper
Sid Gordon
Roy McMillan
2 Harvey Kuenn 300.00 600.00
Bob Porterfield
Smoky Burgess
Del Crandall

1955 Bowman Advertising Strips

For Bowman's final set; these advertising panels have been seen. The fronts are standard 1955 Bowman cards while the backs have advertising information. More sheets have been recently discovered so please keep us informed on any additions to this list.

COMPLETE SET 6000.00 12000.00
1 Hank Aaron 750.00 1500.00
Johnny Logan
Eddie Miksis
2 Don Bollweg 250.00 500.00
Cal Abrams
Billy Cox
3 Bob Darnell 600.00 1200.00
Early Wynn
Pee Wee Reese
4 Del Ennis 250.00 500.00
Del Crandell
Joe Adcock
5 Whitey Ford 500.00 1000.00
Enos Slaughter
Paul LaPalme
6 Nellie Fox 500.00 1000.00
Carl Furillo
Carl Erskine
7 Bob Friend 250.00 500.00
Williard Nixon
Tom Brewer
8 Steve Gromek 250.00 500.00
Milt Bolling
Vern Stephens
9 Russ Kemmerer 250.00 500.00
Hal Jeffcoat
Dee Fondy
10 Paul LaPalme 250.00 500.00
Royce Lint
Irv Noren
11 Stan Lopata 250.00 500.00
Bobby Avila
Al Smith
12 Mickey Mantle 2500.00 5000.00
Steve Gromek
Milt Bolling
13 Bob Rush 750.00 1500.00
Ray Katt
Willie Mays
14 Virgil Trucks 250.00 500.00
Preston Ward
Dick Cole

1982 Bowman 1952 Extension

In 1980, 15 unissued pieces of artwork initially intended to be used by Bowman Gum in their 1952 baseball card set were discovered. This set consists of 15 cards made from this original artwork. The backs have been created to resemble the original 1952 series, and the set has been numbered 253-267 (the next 15 cards in the 1952 Bowman sequence). The facsimile autograph on the original 1952 Bowmans has been omitted from the cards in this set. This set was originally available from the producer for $3 per set.

COMPLETE SET (15) 2.00 5.00
253 Bob Kennedy .08 .25
254 Barney McCosky .08 .25
255 Chris Van Cuyk .08 .25
256 Morrie Martin .08 .25
257 Jim Wilson .08 .25
258 Bob Thorpe .08 .25
259 Bill Henry .08 .25
260 Bob Addis .08 .25
261 Terry Moore .30 .75
262 Joe Dobson .08 .25
263 John Merson .08 .25
264 Virgil Trucks .20 .50
265 Johnny Hopp .08 .25
267 George Shuba .20 .50

1989 Bowman

The 1989 Bowman set, produced by Topps, contains 484 slightly oversized cards (measuring 2 1/2" by 3 3/4"). The cards were released in midseason 1989 in wax, rack, cello and factory set formats. The fronts have white-bordered color photos with facsimile autographs and small Bowman logos. The backs feature charts detailing 1988 player performances vs. each team. The cards are ordered alphabetically according to teams in the AL and NL. Cards 258-261 form a father/son subset. Rookie Cards in this set include Sandy Alomar Jr., Steve Finley, Ken Griffey Jr., Tino Martinez, Gary Sheffield, John Smoltz and Robin Ventura.

COMPLETE SET (484) 10.00 25.00
COMP.FACT.SET (484) 10.00 25.00
1 Oswald Peraza RC .01 .05
2 Brian Holton .01 .05
3 Jose Bautista RC .02 .10
4 Pete Harnisch RC .08 .25
5 Dave Schmidt .01 .05
6 Gregg Olson RC .08 .25
7 Jeff Ballard .01 .05
8 Bob Melvin .01 .05
9 Cal Ripken .30 .75
10 Randy Milligan .01 .05
11 Juan Bell RC .02 .10
12 Billy Ripken .01 .05
13 Jim Traber .01 .05
14 Pete Stanicek .01 .05
15 Steve Finley RC .30 .75
16 Larry Sheets .01 .05
17 Phil Bradley .01 .05
18 Brady Anderson RC .15 .40
19 Lee Smith .02 .10
20 Tom Fischer .01 .05
21 Mike Boddicker .01 .05
22 Rob Murphy .01 .05
23 Wes Gardner .01 .05
24 John Dopson .01 .05
25 Bob Stanley .01 .05
26 Roger Clemens .40 1.00
27 Rich Gedman .01 .05
28 Marty Barrett .01 .05
29 Luis Rivera .01 .05
30 Jody Reed .01 .05
31 Nick Esasky .01 .05
32 Wade Boggs .05 .15
33 Jim Rice .02 .10
34 Mike Greenwell .01 .05
35 Dwight Evans .05 .15
36 Ellis Burks .02 .10

37 Chuck Finley .02 .10
38 Kirk McCaskill .01 .05
39 Jim Abbott RC .40 1.00
40 Bryan Harvey RC * .08 .25
41 Bert Blyleven .02 .10
42 Mike Witt .01 .05
43 Bob McClure .01 .05
44 Bill Schroeder .01 .05
45 Lance Parrish .02 .10
46 Dick Schofield .01 .05
47 Wally Joyner .02 .10
48 Jack Howell .01 .05
49 Johnny Ray .01 .05
50 Chili Davis .02 .10
51 Tony Armas .02 .10
52 Claudell Washington .01 .05
53 Brian Downing .02 .10
54 Devon White .02 .10
55 Bobby Thigpen .01 .05
56 Bill Long .01 .05
57 Jerry Reuss .01 .05
58 Shawn Hillegas .01 .05
59 Melido Perez .01 .05
60 Jeff Bittiger .01 .05
61 Jack McDowell .02 .10
62 Carlton Fisk .05 .15
63 Steve Lyons .01 .05
64 Ozzie Guillen .02 .10
65 Robin Ventura RC .30 .75
66 Fred Manrique .01 .05
67 Dan Pasqua .01 .05
68 Ivan Calderon .01 .05
69 Ron Kittle .01 .05
70 Daryl Boston .01 .05
71 Dave Gallagher .01 .05
72 Harold Baines .02 .10
73 Charles Nagy RC .08 .25
74 John Farrell .01 .05
75 Kevin Wickander .01 .05
76 Greg Swindell .01 .05
77 Mike Walker .01 .05
78 Doug Jones .01 .05
79 Rich Yett .01 .05
80 Tom Candiotti .01 .05
81 Jesse Orosco .01 .05
82 Bud Black .01 .05
83 Andy Allanson .01 .05
84 Pete O'Brien .01 .05
85 Jerry Browne .01 .05
86 Brook Jacoby .01 .05
87 Mark Lewis RC .08 .25
88 Luis Aguayo .01 .05
89 Cory Snyder .01 .05
90 Oddibe McDowell .01 .05
91 Joe Carter .02 .10
92 Frank Tanana .02 .10
93 Jack Morris .02 .10
94 Doyle Alexander .01 .05
95 Steve Searcy .01 .05
96 Randy Bockus .01 .05
97 Jeff M. Robinson .01 .05
98 Mike Henneman .01 .05
99 Paul Gibson .01 .05
100 Frank Williams .01 .05
101 Matt Nokes .01 .05
102 Rico Brogna RC .15 .40
103 Lou Whitaker .02 .10
104 Al Pedrique .01 .05
105 Alan Trammell .02 .10
106 Chris Brown .01 .05
107 Pat Sheridan .01 .05
108 Chet Lemon .02 .10
109 Keith Moreland .01 .05
110 Mel Stottlemyre Jr. .01 .05
111 Bret Saberhagen .02 .10
112 Floyd Bannister .01 .05
113 Jeff Montgomery .01 .05
114 Steve Farr .01 .05
115 Tom Gordon UER RC .15 .40
116 Charlie Leibrandt .01 .05
117 Mark Gubicza .01 .05
118 Mike Macfarlane RC * .08 .25
119 Bob Boone .02 .10
120 Kurt Stillwell .01 .05
121 George Brett .25 .60
122 Frank White .02 .10
123 Kevin Seitzer .01 .05
124 Willie Wilson .02 .10
125 Pat Tabler .01 .05
126 Bo Jackson .08 .25
127 Hugh Walker RC .02 .10
128 Danny Tartabull .01 .05
129 Teddy Higuera .01 .05
130 Don August .01 .05
131 Juan Nieves .01 .05
132 Mike Birkbeck .01 .05
133 Dan Plesac .01 .05
134 Chris Bosio .01 .05
135 Bill Wegman .01 .05
136 Chuck Crim .01 .05
137 B.J. Surhoff .02 .10
138 Joey Meyer .01 .05
139 Dale Sveum .01 .05
140 Paul Molitor .02 .10
141 Jim Gantner .01 .05
142 Gary Sheffield RC .60 1.50
143 Greg Brock .01 .05
144 Robin Yount .15 .40
145 Glenn Braggs .01 .05
146 Rob Deer .01 .05
147 Fred Toliver .01 .05
148 Jeff Reardon .02 .10
149 Allan Anderson .01 .05
150 Frank Viola .02 .10
151 Shane Rawley .01 .05
152 Juan Berenguer .01 .05
153 Johnny Ard .01 .05
154 Tim Laudner .01 .05
155 Brian Harper .01 .05
156 Al Newman .01 .05
157 Kent Hrbek .02 .10
158 Gary Gaetti .02 .10
159 Wally Backman .01 .05
160 Gene Larkin .01 .05
161 Greg Gagne .01 .05
162 Kirby Puckett .08 .25
163 Dan Gladden .01 .05
164 Randy Bush .01 .05
165 Dave LaPoint .01 .05
166 Andy Hawkins .01 .05
167 Dave Righetti .02 .10
168 Lance McCullers .01 .05
169 Jimmy Jones .01 .05
170 Al Leiter .08 .25
171 John Candelaria .01 .05
172 Don Slaught .01 .05
173 Jamie Quirk .01 .05
174 Rafael Santana .01 .05
175 Mike Pagliarulo .01 .05
176 Don Mattingly .25 .60
177 Ken Phelps .01 .05
178 Steve Sax .01 .05
179 Dave Winfield .02 .10
180 Stan Jefferson .01 .05
181 Rickey Henderson .08 .25
182 Bob Brower .01 .05
183 Roberto Kelly .01 .05
184 Curt Young .01 .05
185 Gene Nelson .01 .05
186 Bob Welch .02 .10
187 Rick Honeycutt .01 .05
188 Dave Stewart .02 .10
189 Mike Moore .01 .05
190 Dennis Eckersley .05 .15
191 Eric Plunk .01 .05
192 Storm Davis .01 .05
193 Terry Steinbach .02 .10
194 Ron Hassey .01 .05
195 Stan Royer RC .02 .10
196 Walt Weiss .01 .05
197 Mark McGwire .40 1.00
198 Carney Lansford .02 .10
199 Glenn Hubbard .01 .05
200 Dave Henderson .01 .05
201 Jose Canseco .08 .25
202 Dave Parker .02 .10
203 Scott Bankhead .01 .05
204 Tom Niedenfuer .01 .05
205 Mark Langston .01 .05
206 Erik Hanson RC .08 .25
207 Mike Jackson .01 .05
208 Dave Valle .01 .05
209 Scott Bradley .01 .05
210 Harold Reynolds .02 .10
211 Tino Martinez RC .75 2.00
212 Rich Renteria .01 .05
213 Rey Quinones .01 .05
214 Jim Presley .01 .05
215 Alvin Davis .01 .05
216 Edgar Martinez .08 .25
217 Darnell Coles .01 .05
218 Jeffrey Leonard .01 .05
219 Jay Buhner .02 .10
220 Ken Griffey Jr. RC 3.00 8.00
221 Drew Hall .01 .05
222 Bobby Witt .01 .05
223 Jamie Moyer .02 .10
224 Charlie Hough .02 .10
225 Nolan Ryan .40 1.00
226 Jeff Russell .01 .05
227 Jim Sundberg .02 .10
228 Julio Franco .02 .10
229 Buddy Bell .02 .10
230 Scott Fletcher .01 .05
231 Jeff Kunkel .01 .05
232 Steve Buechele .01 .05
233 Monty Fariss .01 .05
234 Rick Leach .01 .05
235 Ruben Sierra .02 .10
236 Cecil Espy .01 .05
237 Rafael Palmeiro .08 .25
238 Pete Incaviglia .01 .05
239 Dave Stieb .02 .10
240 Jeff Musselman .01 .05
241 Mike Flanagan .01 .05
242 Todd Stottlemyre .01 .05
243 Jimmy Key .02 .10
244 Tony Castillo RC .02 .10
245 Alex Sanchez RC .01 .05
246 Tom Henke .01 .05
247 John Cerutti .01 .05
248 Ernie Whitt .01 .05
249 Bob Brenly .01 .05
250 Rance Mulliniks .01 .05
251 Kelly Gruber .01 .05
252 Ed Sprague RC .08 .25
253 Fred McGriff .05 .15
254 Tony Fernandez .01 .05
255 Tom Lawless .01 .05
256 George Bell .02 .10
257 Jesse Barfield .02 .10
258 Roberto Alomar w Dad .05 .15
259 Ken Griffey Sr. Jr. .50 1.25
260 Cal Ripken Sr. Jr. .08 .25
261 M.Stottlemyre Jr. Sr. .01 .05
262 Zane Smith .01 .05
263 Charlie Puleo .01 .05
264 Derek Lilliquist RC .02 .10
265 Paul Assenmacher .01 .05
266 John Smoltz RC .60 1.50
267 Tom Glavine .08 .25
268 Steve Avery RC .08 .25
269 Pete Smith .01 .05
270 Jody Davis .01 .05
271 Bruce Benedict .01 .05
272 Andres Thomas .01 .05
273 Gerald Perry .01 .05
274 Ron Gant .02 .10
275 Darrell Evans .02 .10
276 Dale Murphy .05 .15
277 Dion James .01 .05
278 Lonnie Smith .01 .05
279 Geronimo Berroa .01 .05
280 Steve Wilson RC .02 .10
281 Rick Sutcliffe .02 .10
282 Kevin Coffman .01 .05
283 Mitch Williams .01 .05
284 Greg Maddux .20 .50
285 Paul Kilgus .01 .05
286 Mike Harkey RC .02 .10
287 Lloyd McClendon .01 .05
288 Damon Berryhill .01 .05
289 Ty Griffin .01 .05
290 Ryne Sandberg .15 .40
291 Mark Grace .08 .25
292 Curt Wilkerson .01 .05
293 Vance Law .01 .05
294 Shawon Dunston .01 .05
295 Jerome Walton RC .08 .25
296 Mitch Webster .01 .05
297 Dwight Smith RC .08 .25
298 Andre Dawson .02 .10
299 Jeff Sellers .01 .05
300 Jose Rijo .02 .10
301 John Franco .02 .10
302 Rick Mahler .01 .05
303 Ron Robinson .01 .05
304 Danny Jackson .01 .05
305 Rob Dibble RC .15 .40
306 Tom Browning .01 .05
307 Bo Diaz .01 .05
308 Manny Trillo .01 .05
309 Chris Sabo RC .15 .40
310 Ron Oester .01 .05
311 Barry Larkin .05 .15
312 Todd Benzinger .01 .05
313 Paul O'Neill .05 .15
314 Kal Daniels .01 .05
315 Joel Youngblood .01 .05
316 Eric Davis .02 .10
317 Dave Smith .01 .05
318 Mark Portugal .01 .05
319 Brian Meyer .01 .05
320 Jim Deshaies .01 .05
321 Juan Agosto .01 .05
322 Mike Scott .02 .10
323 Rick Rhoden .01 .05
324 Jim Clancy .01 .05
325 Larry Andersen .01 .05
326 Alex Trevino .01 .05
327 Alan Ashby .01 .05
328 Craig Reynolds .01 .05
329 Bill Doran .01 .05
330 Rafael Ramirez .01 .05
331 Glenn Davis .01 .05
332 Willie Ansley RC .02 .10
333 Gerald Young .01 .05
334 Cameron Drew .01 .05
335 Jay Howell .01 .05
336 Tim Belcher .01 .05
337 Fernando Valenzuela .02 .10
338 Ricky Horton .01 .05
339 Tim Leary .01 .05
340 Bill Bene .01 .05
341 Orel Hershiser .02 .10
342 Mike Scioscia .02 .10
343 Rick Dempsey .01 .05
344 Willie Randolph .02 .10
345 Alfredo Griffin .01 .05
346 Eddie Murray .08 .25
347 Mickey Hatcher .01 .05
348 Mike Sharperson .01 .05
349 John Shelby .01 .05
350 Mike Marshall .01 .05
351 Kirk Gibson .02 .10
352 Mike Davis .01 .05
353 Bryn Smith .01 .05
354 Pascual Perez .01 .05
355 Kevin Gross .01 .05
356 Andy McGaffigan .01 .05
357 Brian Holman RC * .02 .10
358 Dave Wainhouse RC .02 .10
359 Dennis Martinez .02 .10
360 Tim Burke .01 .05
361 Nelson Santovenia .01 .05
362 Tim Wallach .01 .05
363 Spike Owen .01 .05
364 Rex Hudler .01 .05
365 Andres Galarraga .02 .10
366 Otis Nixon .01 .05
367 Hubie Brooks .01 .05
368 Mike Aldrete .01 .05
369 Tim Raines .02 .10
370 Dave Martinez .01 .05
371 Bob Ojeda .01 .05
372 Ron Darling .02 .10
373 Wally Whitehurst RC .02 .10
374 Randy Myers .02 .10
375 David Cone .02 .10
376 Dwight Gooden .02 .10
377 Sid Fernandez .01 .05
378 Dave Proctor .01 .05
379 Gary Carter .02 .10
380 Keith Miller .01 .05
381 Gregg Jefferies .01 .05
382 Tim Teufel .01 .05
383 Kevin Elster .01 .05
384 Dave Magadan .01 .05
385 Keith Hernandez .02 .10
386 Mookie Wilson .02 .10
387 Darryl Strawberry .02 .10
388 Kevin McReynolds .01 .05
389 Mark Carreon .01 .05
390 Jeff Parrett .01 .05
391 Mike Maddux .01 .05
392 Don Carman .01 .05
393 Bruce Ruffin .01 .05
394 Ken Howell .01 .05
395 Steve Bedrosian .01 .05
396 Floyd Youmans .01 .05
397 Larry McWilliams .01 .05
398 Pat Combs RC * .02 .10
399 Steve Lake .01 .05
400 Dickie Thon .01 .05
401 Ricky Jordan RC * .08 .25
402 Mike Schmidt .20 .50
403 Tom Herr .01 .05
404 Chris James .01 .05
405 Juan Samuel .01 .05
406 Von Hayes .01 .05
407 Ron Jones .02 .10
408 Curt Ford .01 .05
409 Bob Walk .01 .05
410 Jeff D. Robinson .01 .05
411 Jim Gott .01 .05
412 Scott Medvin .01 .05
413 John Smiley .01 .05
414 Bob Kipper .01 .05
415 Brian Fisher .01 .05
416 Doug Drabek .01 .05
417 Mike LaValliere .01 .05
418 Ken Oberkfell .01 .05
419 Sid Bream .01 .05
420 Austin Manahan .01 .05
421 Jose Lind .01 .05
422 Bobby Bonilla .02 .10
423 Glenn Wilson .01 .05
424 Andy Van Slyke .05 .15
425 Gary Redus .01 .05
426 Barry Bonds .60 1.50
427 Don Heinkel .01 .05
428 Ken Dayley .01 .05
429 Todd Worrell .01 .05
430 Brad DuVall .01 .05
431 Jose DeLeon .01 .05
432 Joe Magrane .01 .05
433 John Ericks .01 .05
434 Frank DiPino .01 .05
435 Tony Pena .01 .05
436 Ozzie Smith .15 .40
437 Terry Pendleton .02 .10
438 Jose Oquendo .01 .05
439 Tim Jones .01 .05
440 Pedro Guerrero .02 .10
441 Milt Thompson .01 .05
442 Willie McGee .02 .10
443 Vince Coleman .01 .05
444 Tom Brunansky .01 .05
445 Walt Terrell .01 .05
446 Eric Show .01 .05
447 Mark Davis .01 .05
448 Andy Benes RC .15 .40
449 Ed Whitson .01 .05
450 Dennis Rasmussen .01 .05
451 Bruce Hurst .01 .05
452 Pat Clements .01 .05
453 Benito Santiago .02 .10
454 Sandy Alomar Jr. RC .15 .40
455 Garry Templeton .02 .10
456 Jack Clark .02 .10
457 Tim Flannery .01 .05
458 Roberto Alomar .08 .25
459 Carmelo Martinez .01 .05
460 John Kruk .02 .10
461 Tony Gwynn .10 .30
462 Jerald Clark RC .02 .10
463 Don Robinson .01 .05
464 Craig Lefferts .01 .05
465 Kelly Downs .01 .05
466 Rick Reuschel .02 .10
467 Scott Garrelts .01 .05
468 Wil Tejada .01 .05
469 Kirt Manwaring .01 .05
470 Terry Kennedy .01 .05
471 Jose Uribe .01 .05
472 Royce Clayton RC .15 .40
473 Robby Thompson .01 .05
474 Kevin Mitchell .02 .10
475 Ernie Riles .01 .05
476 Will Clark .05 .15
477 Donell Nixon .01 .05
478 Candy Maldonado .01 .05
479 Tracy Jones .01 .05
480 Brett Butler .02 .10
481 Checklist 1-121 .01 .05
482 Checklist 122-242 .01 .05
483 Checklist 243-363 .01 .05
484 Checklist 364-484 .01 .05

1989 Bowman Tiffany

COMP.FACT.SET (495) 200.00 400.00
*STARS: 6X TO 15X BASIC CARDS
*ROOKIES: 6X TO 15X BASIC CARDS
DISTRIBUTED ONLY IN FACTORY SET FORM
211 Tino Martinez 6.00 15.00
220 Ken Griffey Jr. 100.00 250.00
266 John Smoltz 10.00 25.00

1989 Bowman Reprint Inserts

COMPLETE SET (11) .75 2.00
ONE PER PACK
*TIFFANY: 10X TO 20X HI COLUMN
ONE TIFF.REP.SET PER TIFF.FACT.SET
1 Richie Ashburn 49 .15 .40
2 Yogi Berra 48 .08 .25
3 Whitey Ford 51 .15 .40
4 Gil Hodges 49 .20 .50
5 Mickey Mantle 51 .40 1.00
6 Mickey Mantle 53 .40 1.00
7 Willie Mays 51 .20 .50
8 Satchel Paige 49 .20 .50
9 Jackie Robinson 50 .20 .50
10 Duke Snider 49 .08 .25
11 Ted Williams 54 .20 .50

1990 Bowman

The 1990 Bowman set (produced by Topps) consists of 528 standard-size cards. The cards were issued in wax packs and factory sets. Each wax pack contained one of 11 different 1950's retro art cards. Unlike most sets, player selection focused primarily on rookies instead of proven major leaguers. The cards feature a white border with the player's photo inside and the Bowman logo on top. The card numbering is in team order with the teams themselves being ordered alphabetically within each league. Notable Rookie Cards include Moises Alou, Travis Fryman, Juan Gonzalez, Chuck Knoblauch, Ray Lankford, Sammy Sosa, Frank Thomas, Mo Vaughn, Larry Walker, and Bernie Williams.

COMPLETE SET (528) 10.00 25.00
COMP.FACT.SET (528) 10.00 25.00
ART CARDS: RANDOM INSERTS IN PACKS
1 Tommy Greene RC .02 .10
2 Tom Glavine .05 .15
3 Andy Nezelek .01 .05
4 Mike Stanton RC .08 .25
5 Rick Luecken RC .01 .05
6 Kent Mercker RC .08 .25
7 Derek Lilliquist .01 .05
8 Charlie Leibrandt .01 .05
9 Steve Avery .01 .05
10 John Smoltz .08 .25
11 Mark Lemke .01 .05
12 Lonnie Smith .01 .05
13 Oddibe McDowell .01 .05
14 Tyler Houston RC .08 .25
15 Jeff Blauser .01 .05
16 Ernie Whitt .01 .05
17 Alexis Infante .01 .05
18 Jim Presley .01 .05
19 Dale Murphy .05 .15
20 Nick Esasky .01 .05
21 Rick Sutcliffe .02 .10
22 Mike Bielecki .01 .05
23 Steve Wilson .01 .05
24 Kevin Blankenship .01 .05
25 Mitch Williams .01 .05
26 Dean Wilkins RC .01 .05
27 Greg Maddux .15 .40
28 Mike Harkey .01 .05
29 Mark Grace .05 .15
30 Ryne Sandberg .15 .40
31 Greg Smith RC .01 .05
32 Dwight Smith .01 .05
33 Damon Berryhill .01 .05
34 Earl Cunningham UER RC .02 .10
35 Jerome Walton .01 .05
36 Lloyd McClendon .01 .05
37 Ty Griffin .01 .05
38 Shawon Dunston .01 .05
39 Andre Dawson .02 .10
40 Luis Salazar .01 .05
41 Tim Layana RC .01 .05
42 Rob Dibble .02 .10
43 Tom Browning .01 .05
44 Danny Jackson .01 .05
45 Jose Rijo .01 .05
46 Scott Scudder .01 .05
47 Randy Myers UER .02 .10
(Career ERA .274,
should be 2.74
48 Brian Lane RC .02 .10
49 Paul O'Neill .05 .15
50 Barry Larkin .05 .15
51 Reggie Jefferson RC .08 .25
52 Jeff Branson RC .02 .10
53 Chris Sabo .01 .05
54 Joe Oliver .01 .05
55 Todd Benzinger .01 .05
56 Rolando Roomes .01 .05
57 Hal Morris .01 .05
58 Eric Davis .02 .10
59 Scott Bryant RC .01 .05
60 Ken Griffey Sr. .02 .10
61 Darryl Kile RC .20 .50
62 Dave Smith .01 .05
63 Mark Portugal .01 .05
64 Jeff Juden RC .02 .10
65 Bill Gullickson .01 .05
66 Danny Darwin .01 .05
67 Larry Andersen .01 .05
68 Jose Cano RC .01 .05
69 Dan Schatzeder .01 .05
70 Jim Deshaies .01 .05
71 Mike Scott .01 .05
72 Gerald Young .01 .05
73 Ken Caminiti .02 .10
74 Ken Oberkfell .01 .05
75 Dave Rohde RC .01 .05
76 Bill Doran .01 .05
77 Andujar Cedeno RC .02 .10
78 Craig Biggio .08 .25
79 Karl Rhodes RC .08 .25
80 Glenn Davis .01 .05
81 Eric Anthony RC .02 .10
82 John Wetteland .08 .25
83 Jay Howell .01 .05
84 Orel Hershiser .02 .10
85 Tim Belcher .01 .05
86 Kiki Jones RC .01 .05
87 Mike Hartley RC .01 .05
88 Ramon Martinez .01 .05
89 Mike Scioscia .01 .05
90 Willie Randolph .02 .10
91 Juan Samuel .01 .05
92 Jose Offerman RC .08 .25
93 Dave Hansen RC .08 .25
94 Jeff Hamilton .01 .05
95 Alfredo Griffin .01 .05
96 Tom Goodwin RC .08 .25
97 Kirk Gibson .02 .10
98 Jose Vizcaino RC .08 .25
99 Kal Daniels .01 .05
100 Hubie Brooks .01 .05
101 Eddie Murray .08 .25
102 Dennis Boyd .01 .05
103 Tim Burke .01 .05
104 Bill Sampen RC .01 .05
105 Brett Gideon .01 .05
106 Mark Gardner RC .02 .10
107 Howard Farmer RC .01 .05
108 Mel Rojas RC .02 .10
109 Kevin Gross .01 .05
110 Dave Schmidt .01 .05
111 Dennis Martinez .02 .10
112 Jerry Goff RC .01 .05
113 Andres Galarraga .02 .10
114 Tim Wallach .01 .05
115 Marquis Grissom RC .20 .50
116 Spike Owen .01 .05
117 Larry Walker RC .40 1.00
118 Tim Raines .02 .10
119 Delino DeShields RC .08 .25
120 Tom Foley .01 .05
121 Dave Martinez .01 .05
122 Frank Viola UER .01 .05
(Career ERA .384
should be 3.84
123 Julio Valera RC .01 .05
124 Alejandro Pena .01 .05
125 David Cone .02 .10
126 Dwight Gooden .02 .10
127 Kevin D. Brown RC .01 .05
128 John Franco .02 .10
129 Terry Bross RC .01 .05
130 Blaine Beatty RC .01 .05
131 Sid Fernandez .01 .05
132 Mike Marshall .01 .05
133 Howard Johnson .01 .05
134 Jaime Roseboro RC .01 .05
135 Alan Zinter RC .02 .10
136 Keith Miller .01 .05
137 Kevin Elster .01 .05
138 Kevin McReynolds .01 .05
139 Barry Lyons .01 .05
140 Gregg Jefferies .02 .10
141 Darryl Strawberry .02 .10
142 Todd Hundley RC .08 .25
143 Scott Service .01 .05
144 Chuck Malone RC .01 .05
145 Steve Ontiveros .01 .05
146 Roger McDowell .01 .05
147 Ken Howell .01 .05
148 Pat Combs .01 .05
149 Jeff Parrett .01 .05
150 Chuck McElroy RC .02 .10
151 Jason Grimsley RC .02 .10
152 Len Dykstra .02 .10
153 Mickey Morandini RC .08 .25
154 John Kruk .02 .10
155 Dickie Thon .01 .05
156 Ricky Jordan .01 .05
157 Jeff Jackson RC .02 .10
158 Darren Daulton .02 .10
159 Tom Herr .01 .05
160 Von Hayes .01 .05
161 Dave Hollins RC .08 .25
162 Carmelo Martinez .01 .05
163 Bob Walk .01 .05
164 Doug Drabek .01 .05
165 Walt Terrell .01 .05
166 Bill Landrum .01 .05
167 Scott Ruskin RC .01 .05
168 Bob Patterson .01 .05
169 Bobby Bonilla .02 .10
170 Jose Lind .01 .05
171 Andy Van Slyke .05 .15
172 Mike LaValliere .01 .05
173 Willie Greene RC .02 .10
174 Jay Bell .02 .10
175 Sid Bream .01 .05
176 Tom Prince .01 .05
177 Wally Backman .01 .05
178 Moises Alou RC .30 .75
179 Steve Carter .01 .05
180 Gary Redus .01 .05
181 Barry Bonds .40 1.00
182 Don Slaught UER .01 .05
(Card back shows
headings for a pitcher
183 Joe Magrane .01 .05
184 Bryn Smith .01 .05
185 Todd Worrell .01 .05
186 Jose DeLeon .01 .05
187 Frank DiPino .01 .05
188 John Tudor .01 .05
189 Howard Hilton RC .01 .05
190 John Ericks .01 .05
191 Ken Dayley .01 .05
192 Ray Lankford RC .20 .50
193 Todd Zeile .02 .10
194 Willie McGee .02 .10
195 Ozzie Smith .15 .40
196 Milt Thompson .01 .05
197 Terry Pendleton .02 .10
198 Vince Coleman .01 .05
199 Paul Coleman RC .02 .10
200 Jose Oquendo .01 .05
201 Pedro Guerrero .01 .05
202 Tom Brunansky .01 .05
203 Roger Smithberg RC .01 .05
204 Eddie Whitson .01 .05
205 Dennis Rasmussen .01 .05
206 Craig Lefferts .01 .05
207 Andy Benes .02 .10
208 Bruce Hurst .01 .05
209 Eric Show .01 .05
210 Rafael Valdez RC .01 .05
211 Joey Cora .02 .10
212 Thomas Howard .01 .05
213 Rob Nelson .01 .05
214 Jack Clark .02 .10
215 Garry Templeton .01 .05
216 Fred Lynn .01 .05
217 Tony Gwynn .10 .30
218 Benito Santiago .02 .10
219 Mike Pagliarulo .01 .05
220 Joe Carter .02 .10
221 Roberto Alomar .05 .15
222 Bip Roberts .01 .05
223 Rick Reuschel .01 .05
224 Russ Swan RC .01 .05
225 Eric Gunderson RC .01 .05
226 Steve Bedrosian .01 .05
227 Mike Remlinger RC .01 .05
228 Scott Garrelts .01 .05
229 Ernie Camacho .01 .05
230 Andres Santana RC .02 .10
231 Will Clark .05 .15
232 Kevin Mitchell .01 .05
233 Robby Thompson .01 .05
234 Bill Bathe .01 .05
235 Tony Perezchica .01 .05
236 Gary Carter .02 .10
237 Brett Butler .02 .10
238 Matt Williams .02 .10
239 Earnie Riles .01 .05
240 Kevin Bass .01 .05
241 Terry Kennedy .01 .05
242 Steve Hosey RC .02 .10
243 Ben McDonald RC .08 .25
244 Jeff Ballard .01 .05
245 Joe Price .01 .05
246 Curt Schilling .40 1.00
247 Pete Harnisch .01 .05
248 Mark Williamson .01 .05
249 Gregg Olson .02 .10
250 Chris Myers RC .01 .05
251A David Segui ERR .20 .50
Missing vital stats
at top of card back
under name)
251B David Segui COR RC .20 .50
252 Joe Orsulak .01 .05
253 Craig Worthington .01 .05
254 Mickey Tettleton .01 .05
255 Cal Ripken .30 .75
256 Bill Ripken .01 .05
257 Randy Milligan .01 .05
258 Brady Anderson .02 .10
259 Chris Hoiles RC UER .08 .25
Baltimore is spelled Balitmore
260 Mike Devereaux .01 .05
261 Phil Bradley .01 .05
262 Leo Gomez RC .02 .10
263 Lee Smith .02 .10
264 Mike Rochford .01 .05
265 Jeff Reardon .02 .10
266 Wes Gardner .01 .05
267 Mike Boddicker .01 .05
268 Roger Clemens .40 1.00
269 Rob Murphy .01 .05
270 Mickey Pina RC .01 .05
271 Tony Pena .01 .05
272 Jody Reed .01 .05
273 Kevin Romine .01 .05
274 Mike Greenwell .01 .05
275 Mo Vaughn RC .40 1.00
276 Danny Heep .01 .05
277 Scott Cooper RC .02 .10
278 Greg Blosser RC .02 .10
279 Dwight Evans UER .05 .15
(* by 1990 Team Breakdown)
280 Ellis Burks .05 .15
281 Wade Boggs .05 .15
282 Marty Barrett .01 .05
283 Kirk McCaskill .01 .05
284 Mark Langston .01 .05
285 Bert Blyleven .02 .10
286 Mike Fetters RC .08 .25
287 Kyle Abbott RC .01 .05
288 Jim Abbott .05 .15
289 Chuck Finley .02 .10
290 Gary DiSarcina RC .08 .25
291 Dick Schofield .01 .05
292 Devon White .02 .10
293 Bobby Rose .01 .05
294 Brian Downing .01 .05
295 Lance Parrish .01 .05
296 Jack Howell .01 .05
297 Claudell Washington .01 .05
298 John Orton RC .02 .10
299 Wally Joyner .02 .10
300 Lee Stevens .02 .10
301 Chili Davis .02 .10
302 Johnny Ray .01 .05
303 Greg Hibbard RC .02 .10
304 Eric King .01 .05
305 Jack McDowell .01 .05
306 Bobby Thigpen .01 .05
307 Adam Peterson .01 .05
308 Scott Radinsky RC .08 .25
309 Wayne Edwards RC .01 .05
310 Melido Perez .01 .05
311 Robin Ventura .08 .25
312 Sammy Sosa RC 1.25 3.00
313 Dan Pasqua .01 .05
314 Carlton Fisk .05 .15
315 Ozzie Guillen .02 .10
316 Ivan Calderon .01 .05
317 Daryl Boston .01 .05
318 Craig Grebeck RC .08 .25
319 Scott Fletcher .01 .05
320 Frank Thomas RC 1.00 2.50
321 Steve Lyons .01 .05
322 Carlos Martinez .01 .05
323 Joe Skalski .01 .05
324 Tom Candiotti .01 .05
325 Greg Swindell .01 .05
326 Steve Olin RC .08 .25
327 Kevin Wickander .01 .05
328 Doug Jones .01 .05
329 Jeff Shaw .01 .05
330 Kevin Bearse RC .01 .05
331 Dion James .01 .05
332 Jerry Browne .01 .05
333 Albert Belle .08 .25
334 Felix Fermin .01 .05
335 Candy Maldonado .01 .05
336 Cory Snyder .01 .05
337 Sandy Alomar Jr. .02 .10
338 Mark Lewis .01 .05
339 Carlos Baerga RC .08 .25
340 Chris James .01 .05
341 Brook Jacoby .01 .05
342 Keith Hernandez .02 .10
343 Frank Tanana .01 .05
344 Scott Aldred RC .01 .05
345 Mike Henneman .01 .05
346 Steve Wapnick RC .01 .05
347 Greg Gohr RC .02 .10
348 Eric Stone RC .01 .05
349 Brian DuBois RC .01 .05
350 Kevin Ritz RC .01 .05
351 Rico Brogna .08 .25
352 Mike Heath .01 .05
353 Alan Trammell .02 .10
354 Chet Lemon .01 .05
355 Dave Bergman .01 .05
356 Lou Whitaker .02 .10
357 Cecil Fielder UER .02 .10
* by 1990 Team Breakdown
358 Milt Cuyler RC .02 .10
359 Tony Phillips .01 .05
360 Travis Fryman RC .20 .50
361 Ed Romero .01 .05
362 Lloyd Moseby .01 .05
363 Mark Gubicza .01 .05
364 Bret Saberhagen .02 .10
365 Tom Gordon .02 .10
366 Steve Farr .01 .05
367 Kevin Appier .02 .10
368 Storm Davis .01 .05
369 Mark Davis .01 .05
370 Jeff Montgomery .02 .10
371 Frank White .02 .10
372 Brent Mayne RC .08 .25
373 Bob Boone .02 .10
374 Jim Eisenreich .01 .05

375 Danny Tartabull .01 .05
376 Kurt Stillwell .01 .05
377 Bill Pecota .01 .05
378 Bo Jackson .08 .25
379 Bob Hamelin RC .08 .25
380 Kevin Seitzer .01 .05
381 Rey Palacios .01 .05
382 George Brett .25 .60
383 Gerald Perry .01 .05
384 Teddy Higuera .01 .05
385 Tom Filer .01 .05
386 Dan Plesac .01 .05
387 Cal Eldred RC .08 .25
388 Jaime Navarro .01 .05
389 Chris Bosio .01 .05
390 Randy Veres .01 .05
391 Gary Sheffield .08 .25
392 George Canale RC .01 .05
393 B.J. Surhoff .02 .10
394 Tim McIntosh RC .01 .05
395 Greg Brock .01 .05
396 Greg Vaughn .01 .05
397 Darryl Hamilton .01 .05
398 Dave Parker .02 .10
399 Paul Molitor .02 .10
400 Jim Gantner .01 .05
401 Rob Deer .01 .05
402 Billy Spiers .01 .05
403 Glenn Braggs .01 .05
404 Robin Yount .15 .40
405 Rick Aguilera .02 .10
406 Johnny Ard .01 .05
407 Kevin Tapani RC .08 .25
408 Park Pittman RC .01 .05
409 Allan Anderson .01 .05
410 Juan Berenguer .01 .05
411 Willie Banks RC .02 .10
412 Rich Yett .01 .05
413 Dave West .01 .05
414 Greg Gagne .01 .05
415 Chuck Knoblauch RC .20 .50
416 Randy Bush .01 .05
417 Gary Gaetti .02 .10
418 Kent Hrbek .02 .10
419 Al Newman .01 .05
420 Danny Gladden .01 .05
421 Paul Sorrento RC .08 .25
422 Derek Parks RC .02 .10
423 Scott Leius RC .02 .10
424 Kirby Puckett .08 .25
425 Willie Smith .01 .05
426 Dave Righetti .01 .05
427 Jeff D. Robinson .01 .05
428 Alan Mills RC .02 .10
429 Tim Leary .01 .05
430 Pascual Perez .01 .05
431 Alvaro Espinoza .01 .05
432 Dave Winfield .02 .10
433 Jesse Barfield .01 .05
434 Randy Velarde .01 .05
435 Rick Cerone .01 .05
436 Steve Balboni .01 .05
437 Mel Hall .01 .05
438 Bob Geren .01 .05
439 Bernie Williams RC .60 1.50
440 Kevin Maas RC .08 .25
441 Mike Blowers RC .02 .10
442 Steve Sax .01 .05
443 Don Mattingly .25 .60
444 Roberto Kelly .01 .05
445 Mike Moore .01 .05
446 Reggie Harris RC .02 .10
447 Scott Sanderson .01 .05
448 Dave Otto .01 .05
449 Dave Stewart .02 .10
450 Rick Honeycutt .01 .05
451 Dennis Eckersley .02 .10
452 Carney Lansford .02 .10
453 Scott Hemond RC .02 .10
454 Mark McGwire .40 1.00
455 Felix Jose .01 .05
456 Terry Steinbach .01 .05
457 Rickey Henderson .08 .25
458 Dave Henderson .01 .05
459 Mike Gallego .01 .05
460 Jose Canseco .05 .15
461 Walt Weiss .01 .05
462 Ken Phelps .01 .05
463 Darren Lewis RC .02 .10
464 Ron Hassey .01 .05
465 Roger Salkeld RC .02 .10
466 Scott Bankhead .01 .05
467 Keith Comstock .01 .05
468 Randy Johnson .20 .50
469 Erik Hanson .01 .05
470 Mike Schooler .01 .05
471 Gary Eave RC .01 .05
472 Jeffrey Leonard .01 .05
473 Dave Valle .01 .05
474 Omar Vizquel .08 .25
475 Pete O'Brien .01 .05
476 Henry Cotto .01 .05
477 Jay Buhner .02 .10
478 Harold Reynolds .02 .10
479 Alvin Davis .01 .05
480 Darnell Coles .01 .05
481 Ken Griffey Jr. .40 1.00
482 Greg Briley .01 .05
483 Scott Bradley .01 .05
484 Tino Martinez .20 .50
485 Jeff Russell .01 .05
486 Nolan Ryan .40 1.00
487 Robb Nen RC .20 .50
488 Kevin Brown .02 .10
489 Brian Bohanon RC .02 .10
490 Ruben Sierra .02 .10
491 Pete Incaviglia .01 .05
492 Juan Gonzalez RC .40 1.00
493 Steve Buechele .01 .05
494 Scott Coolbaugh .01 .05
495 Geno Petralli .01 .05
496 Rafael Palmeiro .05 .15
497 Julio Franco .02 .10
498 Gary Pettis .01 .05
499 Donald Harris RC .01 .05
500 Monty Fariss .01 .05
501 Harold Baines .02 .10
502 Cecil Espy .01 .05
503 Jack Daugherty RC .01 .05
504 Willie Blair RC .02 .10
505 Dave Stieb .02 .10
506 Tom Henke .01 .05
507 John Cerutti .01 .05
508 Paul Kilgus .01 .05
509 Jimmy Key .02 .10
510 John Olerud RC .40 1.00
511 Ed Sprague .02 .10
512 Manuel Lee .01 .05
513 Fred McGriff .08 .25
514 Glenallen Hill .01 .05
515 George Bell .01 .05
516 Mookie Wilson .02 .10
517 Luis Sojo RC .08 .25
518 Nelson Liriano .01 .05
519 Kelly Gruber .01 .05
520 Greg Myers .01 .05
521 Pat Borders .01 .05
522 Junior Felix .01 .05
523 Eddie Zosky RC .02 .10
524 Tony Fernandez .01 .05
525 Checklist 1-132 UER .01 .05
(No copyright mark on the back)
526 Checklist 133-264 .01 .05
527 Checklist 265-396 .01 .05
528 Checklist 397-528 .01 .05

1990 Bowman Tiffany

COMP.FACT.SET (539) 100.00 200.00
*STARS: 6X TO 15X BASIC CARDS
*ROOKIES: 4X TO 10X BASIC CARDS

1990 Bowman Art Inserts

COMPLETE SET (11) .75 2.00
ONE PER PACK
*TIFFANY: 8X TO 20X BASIC ART INSERT
ONE TIFF.REP.SET PER TIFF.FACT.SET
1 Will Clark .05 .15
2 Mark Davis .01 .05
3 Dwight Gooden .02 .10
4 Bo Jackson .08 .25
5 Don Mattingly .25 .60
6 Kevin Mitchell .01 .05
7 Gregg Olson .02 .10
8 Nolan Ryan .40 1.00
9 Bret Saberhagen .02 .10
10 Jerome Walton .01 .05
11 Robin Yount .15 .40

1990 Bowman Insert Lithographs

COMPLETE SET (11) 300.00 600.00
1 Will Clark 20.00 50.00
2 Mark Davis 10.00 25.00
3 Dwight Gooden 12.50 30.00
4 Bo Jackson 20.00 50.00
5 Don Mattingly 40.00 100.00
6 Kevin Mitchell 10.00 25.00
7 Gregg Olson 10.00 25.00
8 Nolan Ryan 100.00 250.00
9 Bret Saberhagen 12.50 30.00
10 Jerome Walton 10.00 25.00
11 Robin Yount 25.00 60.00

1991 Bowman

This single-series 704-card standard-size set marked the third straight year that Topps issued a set weighted towards prospects using the Bowman name. Cards were issued in wax packs and factory sets. The cards share a design very similar to the 1990 Bowman set with white borders enframing a color photo. The player name, however, is more prominent than in the previous year set. The cards are arranged in team order by division as follows: AL East, AL West, NL East, and NL West. Subsets include Rod Carew Tribute (1-5), Minor League MVP's (180-185/693-698), AL Silver Sluggers (367-375), NL Silver Sluggers (376-384) and checklists (699-704). Rookie Cards in this set include Jeff Bagwell, Jeromy Burnitz, Carl Everett, Chipper Jones, Eric Karros, Ryan Klesko, Kenny Lofton, Javier Lopez, Raul Mondesi, Mike Mussina, Ivan "Pudge" Rodriguez, Tim Salmon, Jim Thome, and Rondell White. There are two instances of misnumbering in the set; Ken Griffey (should be 255) and Ken Griffey Jr. are both numbered 246 and Donovan Osborne (should be 406) and Thomson/Branca share number 410.

COMPLETE SET (704) 15.00 40.00
COMP.FACT.SET (704) 15.00 40.00
1 Rod Carew I .05 .15
2 Rod Carew II .05 .15
3 Rod Carew III .05 .15
4 Rod Carew IV .05 .15
5 Rod Carew V .05 .15
6 Willie Fraser .01 .05
7 John Olerud .02 .10
8 William Suero RC .01 .05
9 Roberto Alomar .05 .15
10 Todd Stottlemyre .01 .05
11 Joe Carter .02 .10
12 Steve Karsay RC .20 .50
13 Mark Whiten .01 .05
14 Pat Borders .01 .05
15 Mike Timlin RC .20 .50
16 Tom Henke .01 .05
17 Eddie Zosky .01 .05
18 Kelly Gruber .01 .05
19 Jimmy Key .02 .10
20 Jerry Schunk RC .01 .05
21 Manuel Lee .01 .05
22 Dave Stieb .01 .05
23 Pat Hentgen RC .20 .50
24 Glenallen Hill .01 .05
25 Rene Gonzales .01 .05
26 Ed Sprague .01 .05
27 Ken Dayley .01 .05
28 Pat Tabler .01 .05
29 Denis Boucher RC .05 .15
30 Devon White .02 .10
31 Dante Bichette .02 .10
32 Paul Molitor .02 .10
33 Greg Vaughn .01 .05
34 Dan Plesac .01 .05
35 Chris George RC .05 .15
36 Tim McIntosh .01 .05
37 Franklin Stubbs .01 .05
38 Bo Dodson RC .05 .15
39 Ron Robinson .01 .05
40 Ed Nunez .01 .05
41 Greg Brock .01 .05
42 Jaime Navarro .01 .05
43 Chris Bosio .01 .05
44 B.J. Surhoff .02 .10
45 Chris Johnson RC .01 .05
46 Willie Randolph .02 .10
47 Narciso Elvira RC .01 .05
48 Jim Gantner .01 .05
49 Kevin Brown .01 .05
50 Julio Machado .01 .05
51 Chuck Crim .01 .05
52 Gary Sheffield .02 .10
53 Angel Miranda RC .05 .15
54 Ted Higuera .01 .05
55 Robin Yount .15 .40
56 Cal Eldred .01 .05
57 Sandy Alomar Jr. .01 .05
58 Greg Swindell .01 .05
59 Brook Jacoby .01 .05
60 Efrain Valdez RC .01 .05
61 Ever Magallanes RC .01 .05
62 Tom Candiotti .01 .05
63 Eric King .01 .05
64 Alex Cole .01 .05
65 Charles Nagy .01 .05
66 Mitch Webster .01 .05
67 Chris James .01 .05
68 Jim Thome RC 5.00 12.00
69 Carlos Baerga .01 .05
70 Mark Lewis .01 .05
71 Jerry Browne .01 .05
72 Jesse Orosco .01 .05
73 Mike Huff .01 .05
74 Jose Escobar RC .01 .05
75 Jeff Manto .01 .05
76 Turner Ward RC .05 .15
77 Doug Jones .01 .05
78 Bruce Egloff RC .01 .05
79 Tim Costo RC .05 .15
80 Beau Allred .01 .05
81 Albert Belle .02 .10
82 John Farrell .01 .05
83 Glenn Davis .01 .05
84 Joe Orsulak .01 .05
85 Mark Williamson .01 .05
86 Ben McDonald .01 .05
87 Billy Ripken .01 .05
88 Leo Gomez UER .01 .05
Baltimore is spelled Balitmore
89 Bob Melvin .01 .05
90 Jeff M. Robinson .01 .05
91 Jose Mesa .01 .05
92 Gregg Olson .01 .05
93 Mike Devereaux .01 .05
94 Luis Mercedes RC .05 .15
95 Arthur Rhodes RC .20 .50
96 Juan Bell .01 .05
97 Mike Mussina RC 2.00 5.00
98 Jeff Ballard .01 .05
99 Chris Hoiles .01 .05
100 Brady Anderson .02 .10
101 Bob Milacki .01 .05
102 David Segui .01 .05
103 Dwight Evans .05 .15
104 Cal Ripken .30 .75
105 Mike Linskey RC .01 .05
106 Jeff Tackett RC .05 .15
107 Jeff Reardon .02 .10
108 Dana Kiecker .01 .05
109 Ellis Burks .02 .10
110 Dave Owen .01 .05
111 Danny Darwin .01 .05
112 Mo Vaughn .02 .10
113 Jeff McNeely RC .05 .15
114 Tom Bolton .01 .05
115 Greg Blosser .01 .05
116 Mike Greenwell .01 .05
117 Phil Plantier RC .05 .15
118 Roger Clemens .30 .75
119 John Marzano .01 .05
120 Jody Reed .01 .05
121 Scott Taylor RC .05 .15
122 Jack Clark .02 .10
123 Derek Livernois RC .01 .05
124 Tony Pena .01 .05
125 Tom Brunansky .01 .05
126 Carlos Quintana .01 .05
127 Tim Naehring .01 .05
128 Matt Young .01 .05
129 Wade Boggs .05 .15
130 Kevin Morton RC .01 .05
131 Pete Incaviglia .01 .05
132 Rob Deer .01 .05
133 Bill Gullickson .01 .05
134 Rico Brogna .01 .05
135 Lloyd Moseby .01 .05
136 Cecil Fielder .02 .10
137 Tony Phillips .01 .05
138 Mark Leiter RC .05 .15
139 John Cerutti .01 .05
140 Mickey Tettleton .01 .05
141 Milt Cuyler .01 .05
142 Greg Gohr .01 .05
143 Tony Bernazard .01 .05
144 Dan Gakeler RC .01 .05
145 Travis Fryman .02 .10
146 Dan Petry .01 .05
147 Scott Aldred .01 .05
148 John DeSilva RC .01 .05
149 Rusty Meacham RC .05 .15
150 Lou Whitaker .02 .10
151 Dave Haas RC .01 .05
152 Luis de los Santos .01 .05
153 Ivan Cruz RC .01 .05
154 Alan Trammell .02 .10
155 Pat Kelly RC .01 .05
156 Carl Everett RC .60 1.50
157 Greg Cadaret .01 .05
158 Kevin Maas .01 .05
159 Jeff Johnson RC .01 .05
160 Willie Smith .01 .05
161 Gerald Williams RC .20 .50
162 Mike Humphreys RC .05 .15
163 Alvaro Espinoza .01 .05
164 Matt Nokes .01 .05
165 Wade Taylor RC .01 .05
166 Roberto Kelly .01 .05
167 John Habyan .01 .05
168 Steve Farr .01 .05
169 Jesse Barfield .01 .05
170 Steve Sax .01 .05
171 Jim Leyritz .01 .05
172 Robert Eenhoorn RC .05 .15
173 Bernie Williams .08 .25
174 Scott Lusader .01 .05
175 Torey Lovullo .01 .05
176 Chuck Cary .01 .05
177 Scott Sanderson .01 .05
178 Don Mattingly .25 .60
179 Mel Hall .01 .05
180 Juan Gonzalez .08 .25
181 Hensley Meulens .01 .05
182 Jose Offerman .01 .05
183 Jeff Bagwell RC 1.25 3.00
184 Jeff Conine RC .40 1.00
185 Henry Rodriguez RC .20 .50
186 Jimmy Reese CO .02 .10
187 Kyle Abbott .01 .05
188 Lance Parrish .02 .10
189 Rafael Montalvo RC .01 .05
190 Floyd Bannister .01 .05
191 Dick Schofield .01 .05
192 Scott Lewis RC .01 .05
193 Jeff D. Robinson .01 .05
194 Kent Anderson .01 .05
195 Wally Joyner .02 .10
196 Chuck Finley .02 .10
197 Luis Sojo .01 .05
198 Jeff Richardson RC .01 .05
199 Dave Parker .02 .10
200 Jim Abbott .05 .15
201 Junior Felix .01 .05
202 Mark Langston .01 .05
203 Tim Salmon RC .60 1.50
204 Cliff Young .01 .05
205 Scott Bailes .01 .05
206 Bobby Rose .01 .05
207 Gary Gaetti .02 .10
208 Ruben Amaro RC .05 .15
209 Luis Polonia .01 .05
210 Dave Winfield .02 .10
211 Bryan Harvey .01 .05
212 Mike Moore .01 .05
213 Rickey Henderson .08 .25
214 Steve Chitren RC .01 .05
215 Bob Welch .01 .05
216 Terry Steinbach .01 .05
217 Earnest Riles .01 .05
218 Todd Van Poppel RC .20 .50
219 Mike Gallego .01 .05
220 Curt Young .01 .05
221 Todd Burns .01 .05
222 Vance Law .01 .05
223 Eric Show .01 .05
224 Don Peters RC .01 .05
225 Dave Stewart .02 .10
226 Dave Henderson .01 .05
227 Jose Canseco .05 .15
228 Walt Weiss .01 .05
229 Dann Howitt .01 .05
230 Willie Wilson .01 .05
231 Harold Baines .02 .10
232 Scott Hemond .01 .05
233 Joe Slusarski RC .01 .05
234 Mark McGwire .30 .75
235 Kirk Dressendorfer RC .05 .15
236 Craig Paquette RC .20 .50
237 Dennis Eckersley .02 .10
238 Dana Allison RC .01 .05
239 Scott Bradley .01 .05
240 Brian Holman .01 .05
241 Mike Schooler .01 .05
242 Rich DeLucia RC .01 .05
243 Edgar Martinez .05 .15
244 Henry Cotto .01 .05
245 Omar Vizquel .05 .15
246 Ken Griffey Jr. .25 .60
(See also 255)
247 Jay Buhner .02 .10
248 Bill Krueger .01 .05
249 Dave Fleming RC .05 .15
250 Patrick Lennon RC .01 .05
251 Dave Valle .01 .05
252 Harold Reynolds .02 .10
253 Randy Johnson .10 .30
254 Scott Bankhead .01 .05
255 Ken Griffey Sr. UER .01 .05
(Card number is 246)
256 Greg Briley .01 .05
257 Tino Martinez .08 .25
258 Alvin Davis .01 .05
259 Pete O'Brien .01 .05
260 Erik Hanson .01 .05
261 Bret Boone RC .60 1.50
262 Roger Salkeld .01 .05
263 Dave Burba RC .20 .50
264 Kerry Woodson RC .05 .15
265 Julio Franco .02 .10
266 Dan Peltier RC .05 .15
267 Jeff Russell .01 .05
268 Steve Buechele .01 .05
269 Donald Harris .01 .05
270 Robb Nen .05 .15
271 Rich Gossage .02 .10
272 Ivan Rodriguez RC 1.50 4.00
273 Jeff Huson .01 .05
274 Kevin Brown .02 .10
275 Dan Smith RC .05 .15
276 Gary Pettis .01 .05
277 Jack Daugherty .01 .05
278 Mike Jeffcoat .01 .05
279 Brad Arnsberg .01 .05
280 Nolan Ryan .40 1.00
281 Eric McCray RC .01 .05
282 Scott Chiamparino .01 .05
283 Ruben Sierra .02 .10
284 Geno Petralli .01 .05
285 Monty Fariss .01 .05
286 Rafael Palmeiro .05 .15
287 Bobby Witt .01 .05
288 Dean Palmer UER .02 .10
Photo is Dan Peltier
289 Tony Scruggs RC .01 .05
290 Kenny Rogers .02 .10
291 Bret Saberhagen .02 .10
292 Brian McRae RC .20 .50
293 Storm Davis .01 .05
294 Danny Tartabull .01 .05
295 David Howard RC .01 .05
296 Mike Boddicker .01 .05
297 Joel Johnston RC .05 .15
298 Tim Spehr RC .01 .05
299 Hector Wagner RC .01 .05
300 George Brett .25 .60
301 Mike Macfarlane .01 .05
302 Kirk Gibson .02 .10
303 Harvey Pulliam RC .05 .15
304 Jim Eisenreich .01 .05
305 Kevin Seitzer .01 .05
306 Mark Davis .01 .05
307 Kurt Stillwell .01 .05
308 Jeff Montgomery .01 .05
309 Kevin Appier .02 .10
310 Bob Hamelin .01 .05
311 Tom Gordon .01 .05
312 Kerwin Moore RC .05 .15
313 Hugh Walker .01 .05
314 Terry Shumpert .01 .05
315 Warren Cromartie .01 .05
316 Gary Thurman .01 .05
317 Steve Bedrosian .01 .05
318 Danny Gladden .01 .05
319 Jack Morris .02 .10
320 Kirby Puckett .08 .25
321 Kent Hrbek .02 .10
322 Kevin Tapani .01 .05
323 Denny Neagle RC .20 .50
324 Rich Garces RC .05 .15
325 Larry Casian RC .01 .05
326 Shane Mack .01 .05
327 Allan Anderson .01 .05
328 Junior Ortiz .01 .05
329 Paul Abbott RC .05 .15
330 Chuck Knoblauch .02 .10
331 Chili Davis .02 .10
332 Todd Ritchie RC .20 .50
333 Brian Harper .01 .05
334 Rick Aguilera .02 .10
335 Scott Erickson .01 .05
336 Pedro Munoz RC .05 .15
337 Scott Leius .01 .05
338 Greg Gagne .01 .05
339 Mike Pagliarulo .01 .05
340 Terry Leach .01 .05
341 Willie Banks .01 .05
342 Bobby Thigpen .01 .05
343 Roberto Hernandez RC .20 .50
344 Melido Perez .01 .05
345 Carlton Fisk .05 .15
346 Norberto Martin RC .01 .05
347 Johnny Ruffin RC .05 .15
348 Jeff Carter .01 .05
349 Lance Johnson .01 .05
350 Sammy Sosa .08 .25
351 Alex Fernandez .01 .05
352 Jack McDowell .01 .05
353 Bob Wickman RC .60 1.50
354 Wilson Alvarez .01 .05
355 Charlie Hough .02 .10
356 Ozzie Guillen .02 .10
357 Cory Snyder .01 .05
358 Robin Ventura .02 .10
359 Scott Fletcher .01 .05
360 Cesar Bernhardt RC .01 .05
361 Dan Pasqua .01 .05
362 Tim Raines .02 .10
363 Brian Drahman RC .01 .05
364 Wayne Edwards .01 .05
365 Scott Radinsky .01 .05
366 Frank Thomas .08 .25
367 Cecil Fielder SLUG .01 .05
368 Julio Franco SLUG .01 .05
369 Kelly Gruber SLUG .01 .05
370 Alan Trammell SLUG .02 .10
371 Rickey Henderson SLUG .05 .15
372 Jose Canseco SLUG .02 .10
373 Ellis Burks SLUG .01 .05
374 Lance Parrish SLUG .01 .05
375 Dave Parker SLUG .01 .05
376 Eddie Murray SLUG .05 .15
377 Ryne Sandberg SLUG .08 .25
378 Matt Williams SLUG .01 .05
379 Barry Larkin SLUG .02 .10
380 Barry Bonds SLUG .20 .50
381 Bobby Bonilla SLUG .01 .05
382 Darryl Strawberry SLUG .01 .05
383 Benny Santiago SLUG .01 .05
384 Don Robinson SLUG .01 .05
385 Paul Coleman .01 .05
386 Milt Thompson .01 .05
387 Lee Smith .02 .10
388 Ray Lankford .02 .10
389 Tom Pagnozzi .01 .05
390 Ken Hill .01 .05
391 Jamie Moyer .02 .10
392 Greg Carmona RC .01 .05
393 John Ericks .01 .05
394 Bob Tewksbury .01 .05
395 Jose Oquendo .01 .05
396 Rheal Cormier RC .05 .15
397 Mike Milchin RC .01 .05
398 Ozzie Smith .15 .40
399 Aaron Holbert RC .05 .15
400 Jose DeLeon .01 .05
401 Felix Jose .01 .05
402 Juan Agosto .01 .05
403 Pedro Guerrero .02 .10
404 Todd Zeile .01 .05
405 Gerald Perry .01 .05
406 Donovan Osborne UER RC .05 .15
407 Bryn Smith .01 .05
408 Bernard Gilkey .01 .05
409 Rex Hudler .01 .05
410 Bobby Thomson .08 .25
Ralph Branca
Shot Heard Round the World
See also 406
411 Lance Dickson RC .05 .15
412 Danny Jackson .01 .05
413 Jerome Walton .01 .05
414 Sean Cheetham RC .01 .05
415 Joe Girardi .01 .05
416 Ryne Sandberg .15 .40
417 Mike Harkey .01 .05
418 George Bell .01 .05
419 Rick Wilkins RC .05 .15
420 Earl Cunningham .01 .05
421 Heathcliff Slocumb RC .05 .15
422 Mike Bielecki .01 .05
423 Jessie Hollins RC .05 .15
424 Shawon Dunston .01 .05
425 Dave Smith .01 .05
426 Greg Maddux .15 .40
427 Jose Vizcaino .01 .05
428 Luis Salazar .01 .05
429 Andre Dawson .02 .10
430 Rick Sutcliffe .02 .10
431 Paul Assenmacher .01 .05
432 Erik Pappas RC .01 .05
433 Mark Grace .05 .15
434 Dennis Martinez .02 .10
435 Marquis Grissom .02 .10
436 Wil Cordero RC .20 .50
437 Tim Wallach .01 .05
438 Brian Barnes RC .01 .05
439 Barry Jones .01 .05
440 Ivan Calderon .01 .05
441 Stan Spencer RC .01 .05
442 Larry Walker .08 .25
443 Chris Haney RC .05 .15
444 Hector Rivera RC .01 .05
445 Delino DeShields .02 .10
446 Andres Galarraga .02 .10
447 Gilberto Reyes .01 .05
448 Willie Greene .01 .05
449 Greg Colbrunn RC .20 .50
450 Rondell White RC .40 1.00
451 Steve Frey .01 .05
452 Shane Andrews RC .05 .15
453 Mike Fitzgerald .01 .05
454 Spike Owen .01 .05
455 Dave Martinez .01 .05
456 Dennis Boyd .01 .05
457 Eric Bullock .01 .05
458 Reid Cornelius RC .05 .15
459 Chris Nabholz .01 .05
460 David Cone .02 .10
461 Hubie Brooks .01 .05
462 Sid Fernandez .01 .05
463 Doug Simons RC .01 .05
464 Howard Johnson .01 .05
465 Chris Donnels RC .01 .05
466 Anthony Young RC .05 .15
467 Todd Hundley .01 .05
468 Rick Cerone .01 .05
469 Kevin Elster .01 .05
470 Wally Whitehurst .01 .05
471 Vince Coleman .01 .05
472 Dwight Gooden .02 .10
473 Charlie O'Brien .01 .05
474 Jeromy Burnitz RC .40 1.00
475 John Franco .02 .10
476 Daryl Boston .01 .05
477 Frank Viola .02 .10
478 D.J. Dozier .01 .05
479 Kevin McReynolds .01 .05
480 Tom Herr .01 .05
481 Gregg Jefferies .01 .05
482 Pete Schourek RC .05 .15
483 Ron Darling .01 .05
484 Dave Magadan .01 .05
485 Andy Ashby RC .20 .50
486 Dale Murphy .05 .15
487 Von Hayes .01 .05
488 Kim Batiste RC .05 .15
489 Tony Longmire RC .05 .15
490 Wally Backman .01 .05
491 Jeff Jackson .01 .05
492 Mickey Morandini .01 .05
493 Darrel Akerfelds .01 .05
494 Ricky Jordan .01 .05
495 Randy Ready .01 .05
496 Darrin Fletcher .01 .05
497 Chuck Malone .01 .05
498 Pat Combs .01 .05
499 Dickie Thon .01 .05
500 Roger McDowell .01 .05
501 Len Dykstra .02 .10
502 Joe Boever .01 .05
503 John Kruk .02 .10
504 Terry Mulholland .01 .05
505 Wes Chamberlain RC .05 .15
506 Mike Lieberthal RC .40 1.00
507 Darren Daulton .02 .10
508 Charlie Hayes .01 .05
509 John Smiley .01 .05
510 Gary Varsho .01 .05
511 Curt Wilkerson .01 .05
512 Orlando Merced RC .05 .15
513 Barry Bonds .40 1.00
514 Mike LaValliere .01 .05
515 Doug Drabek .01 .05
516 Gary Redus .01 .05
517 William Pennyfeather RC .05 .15
518 Randy Tomlin RC .01 .05
519 Mike Zimmerman RC .05 .15
520 Jeff King .01 .05
521 Kurt Miller RC .05 .15
522 Jay Bell .02 .10
523 Bill Landrum .01 .05
524 Zane Smith .01 .05
525 Bobby Bonilla .02 .10
526 Bob Walk .01 .05
527 Austin Manahan .01 .05
528 Joe Ausanio RC .01 .05
529 Andy Van Slyke .05 .15
530 Jose Lind .01 .05
531 Carlos Garcia RC .05 .15
532 Don Slaught .01 .05
533 Gen.Colin Powell .20 .50
534 Frank Bolick RC .05 .15
535 Gary Scott RC .01 .05
536 Nikco Riesgo RC .01 .05
537 Reggie Sanders RC .60 1.50
538 Tim Howard RC .05 .15
539 Ryan Bowen RC .05 .15
540 Eric Anthony .01 .05
541 Jim Deshaies .01 .05
542 Tom Nevers RC .05 .15
543 Ken Caminiti .02 .10
544 Karl Rhodes .01 .05
545 Xavier Hernandez .01 .05
546 Mike Scott .01 .05
547 Jeff Juden .01 .05
548 Darryl Kile .02 .10
549 Willie Ansley .01 .05
550 Luis Gonzalez RC .60 1.50
551 Mike Simms RC .01 .05
552 Mark Portugal .01 .05
553 Jimmy Jones .01 .05
554 Jim Clancy .01 .05
555 Pete Harnisch .01 .05
556 Craig Biggio .05 .15
557 Eric Yelding .01 .05
558 Dave Rohde .01 .05
559 Casey Candaele .01 .05
560 Curt Schilling .08 .25
561 Steve Finley .02 .10
562 Javier Ortiz .01 .05
563 Andujar Cedeno .01 .05
564 Rafael Ramirez .01 .05
565 Kenny Lofton RC .60 1.50
566 Steve Avery .01 .05
567 Lonnie Smith .01 .05
568 Kent Mercker .01 .05
569 Chipper Jones RC 5.00 12.00
570 Terry Pendleton .02 .10
571 Otis Nixon .01 .05
572 Juan Berenguer .01 .05
573 Charlie Leibrandt .01 .05
574 David Justice .02 .10
575 Keith Mitchell RC .05 .15
576 Tom Glavine .05 .15
577 Greg Olson .01 .05
578 Rafael Belliard .01 .05
579 Ben Rivera RC .05 .15
580 John Smoltz .05 .15
581 Tyler Houston .01 .05
582 Mark Wohlers RC .20 .50
583 Ron Gant .02 .10
584 Ramon Caraballo RC .05 .15
585 Sid Bream .01 .05
586 Jeff Treadway .01 .05
587 Javy Lopez RC 1.25 3.00
588 Deion Sanders .05 .15
589 Mike Heath .01 .05
590 Ryan Klesko RC .40 1.00
591 Bob Ojeda .01 .05
592 Alfredo Griffin .01 .05
593 Raul Mondesi RC .40 1.00
594 Greg Smith .01 .05
595 Orel Hershiser .02 .10
596 Juan Samuel .01 .05
597 Brett Butler .02 .10
598 Gary Carter .02 .10
599 Stan Javier .01 .05
600 Kal Daniels .01 .05
601 Jamie McAndrew RC .05 .15
602 Mike Sharperson .01 .05
603 Jay Howell .01 .05
604 Eric Karros RC .60 1.50
605 Tim Belcher .01 .05
606 Dan Opperman RC .01 .05
607 Lenny Harris .01 .05
608 Tom Goodwin .01 .05
609 Darryl Strawberry .02 .10
610 Ramon Martinez .01 .05
611 Kevin Gross .01 .05
612 Zakary Shinall RC .01 .05
613 Mike Scioscia .01 .05
614 Eddie Murray .08 .25
615 Ronnie Walden RC .05 .15
616 Will Clark .05 .15
617 Adam Hyzdu RC .20 .50
618 Matt Williams .02 .10
619 Don Robinson .01 .05
620 Jeff Brantley .01 .05
621 Greg Litton .01 .05
622 Steve Decker RC .01 .05
623 Robby Thompson .01 .05
624 Mark Leonard RC .01 .05
625 Kevin Bass .01 .05
626 Scott Garrelts .01 .05
627 Jose Uribe .01 .05
628 Eric Gunderson .01 .05
629 Steve Hosey .01 .05
630 Trevor Wilson .01 .05
631 Terry Kennedy .01 .05
632 Dave Righetti .02 .10
633 Kelly Downs .01 .05
634 Johnny Ard .01 .05
635 Eric Christopherson RC .05 .15
636 Kevin Mitchell .01 .05
637 John Burkett .01 .05
638 Kevin Rogers RC .05 .15
639 Bud Black .01 .05
640 Willie McGee .02 .10
641 Royce Clayton .01 .05
642 Tony Fernandez .01 .05
643 Ricky Bones RC .05 .15
644 Thomas Howard .01 .05
645 Dave Staton RC .05 .15
646 Jim Presley .01 .05
647 Tony Gwynn .10 .30
648 Marty Barrett .01 .05

1992 Bowman

649 Scott Coolbaugh .01 .05
650 Craig Lefferts .01 .05
651 Eddie Whitson .01 .05
652 Oscar Azocar .01 .05
653 Wes Gardner .01 .05
654 Bip Roberts .01 .05
655 Robbie Beckett RC .05 .15
656 Benito Santiago .02 .10
657 Greg W.Harris .01 .05
658 Jerald Clark .01 .05
659 Fred McGriff .05 .15
660 Larry Andersen .01 .05
661 Bruce Hurst .01 .05
662 Steve Martin UER RC .05 .15
663 Rafael Valdez .01 .05
664 Paul Faries RC .01 .05
665 Andy Benes .01 .05
666 Randy Myers .01 .05
667 Rob Dibble .02 .10
668 Glenn Sutko RC .01 .05
669 Glenn Braggs .01 .05
670 Billy Hatcher .01 .05
671 Joe Oliver .01 .05
672 Freddie Benavides RC .05 .15
673 Barry Larkin .05 .15
674 Chris Sabo .01 .05
675 Mariano Duncan .01 .05
676 Chris Jones RC .01 .05
677 Gino Minutelli RC .01 .05
678 Reggie Jefferson .01 .05
679 Jack Armstrong .01 .05
680 Chris Hammond .01 .05
681 Jose Rijo .01 .05
682 Bill Doran .01 .05
683 Terry Lee RC .01 .05
684 Tom Browning .01 .05
685 Paul O'Neill .05 .15
686 Eric Davis .02 .10
687 Dan Wilson RC .20 .50
688 Ted Power .01 .05
689 Tim Layana .01 .05
690 Norm Charlton .01 .05
691 Hal Morris .01 .05
692 Rickey Henderson RB .05 .15
693 Sam Militello RC .05 .15
694 Matt Mieske RC .05 .15
695 Paul Russo RC .05 .15
696 Domingo Mota MVP .01 .05
697 Todd Guggiana RC .05 .15
698 Marc Newfield RC .05 .15
699 Checklist 1-122 .01 .05
700 Checklist 123-244 .01 .05
701 Checklist 245-366 .01 .05
702 Checklist 367-471 .01 .05
703 Checklist 472-593 .01 .05
704 Checklist 594-704 .01 .05

1992 Bowman

This 705-card standard-size set was issued in one comprehensive series. Unlike the previous Bowman issues, the 1992 set was radically upgraded to slick stock with gold foil subset cards in an attempt to reposition the brand as a premium level product. It initially stumbled out of the gate, but its superior selection of prospects enabled it to eventually gain acceptance in the hobby and now stands as one of the more important issues of the 1990's. Cards were distributed in plastic wrap packs, retail jumbo packs and special 80-card retail carton packs. Card fronts feature posed and action color player photos on a UV-coated white card face. . Forty-five foil cards inserted at a stated rate of one per wax pack and two per jumbo (23 regular cards) pack. These foil cards feature past and present Team USA players and minor league POY Award winners. Each foil card has an extremely slight variation in that the photos are cropped differently. There is no additional value to either version. Some of the regular and special cards picture prospects in civilian clothing who were still in the farm system. Rookie Cards in this set include Garret Anderson, Carlos Delgado, Mike Hampton, Brian Jordan, Mike Piazza, Manny Ramirez and Mariano Rivera.

COMPLETE SET (705) 60.00 120.00
ONE FOIL PER PACK/TWO PER JUMBO
FIVE FOILS PER 80-CARD CARTON
1 Ivan Rodriguez .50 1.25
2 Kirk McCaskill .20 .50
3 Scott Livingstone .20 .50
4 Salomon Torres RC .20 .50
5 Carlos Hernandez .20 .50
6 Dave Hollins .20 .50
7 Scott Fletcher .20 .50
8 Jorge Fabregas RC .20 .50
9 Andujar Cedeno .20 .50
10 Howard Johnson .20 .50
11 Trevor Hoffman RC 10.00 25.00
12 Roberto Kelly .20 .50
13 Gregg Jefferies .20 .50
14 Marquis Grissom .20 .50
15 Mike Ignasiak .20 .50
16 Jack Morris .20 .50
17 William Pennyfeather .20 .50
18 Todd Stottlemyre .20 .50
19 Chito Martinez .20 .50
20 Roberto Alomar .30 .75
21 Sam Militello .20 .50
22 Hector Fajardo RC .20 .50
23 Paul Quantrill RC .20 .50
24 Chuck Knoblauch .20 .50
25 Reggie Jefferson .20 .50
26 Jeremy McGarity RC .20 .50
27 Jerome Walton .20 .50
28 Chipper Jones 6.00 15.00
29 Brian Barber RC .20 .50
30 Ron Darling .20 .50
31 Roberto Petagine RC .20 .50
32 Chuck Finley .20 .50
33 Edgar Martinez .30 .75
34 Napoleon Robinson .20 .50
35 Andy Van Slyke .30 .75
36 Bobby Thigpen .20 .50
37 Travis Fryman .20 .50
38 Eric Christopherson .20 .50
39 Terry Mulholland .20 .50
40 Darryl Strawberry .20 .50
41 Manny Alexander RC .20 .50
42 Tracy Sanders RC .20 .50
43 Pete Incaviglia .20 .50
44 Kim Batiste .20 .50
45 Frank Rodriguez .20 .50
46 Greg Swindell .20 .50
47 Delino DeShields .20 .50
48 John Ericks .20 .50
49 Franklin Stubbs .20 .50
50 Tony Gwynn .60 1.50
51 Clifton Garrett RC .20 .50
52 Mike Gardella .20 .50
53 Scott Erickson .20 .50
54 Gary Caraballo RC .20 .50
55 Jose Oliva RC .20 .50
56 Brook Fordyce .20 .50
57 Mark Whiten .20 .50
58 Joe Slusarski .20 .50
59 J.R. Phillips RC .20 .50
60 Barry Bonds 1.50 4.00
61 Bob Milacki .20 .50
62 Keith Mitchell .20 .50
63 Angel Miranda .20 .50
64 Raul Mondesi .20 .50
65 Brian Koelling RC .20 .50
66 Brian McRae .20 .50
67 John Patterson RC .20 .50
68 John Wetteland .20 .50
69 Wilson Alvarez .20 .50
70 Wade Boggs .30 .75
71 Darryl Ratliff RC .20 .50
72 Jeff Jackson .20 .50
73 Jeremy Hernandez RC .20 .50
74 Darryl Hamilton .20 .50
75 Rafael Belliard .20 .50
76 Rick Trlicek RC .20 .50
77 Felipe Crespo RC .20 .50
78 Carney Lansford .20 .50
79 Ryan Long RC .20 .50
80 Kirby Puckett .50 1.25
81 Earl Cunningham .20 .50
82 Pedro Martinez 8.00 20.00
83 Scott Hatteberg RC .40 1.00
84 Juan Gonzalez UER .30 .75
65 doubles vs. Tigers
85 Robert Nutting RC .20 .50
86 Pokey Reese RC .40 1.00
87 Dave Silvestri .20 .50
88 Scott Ruffcorn RC .20 .50
89 Rick Aguilera .20 .50
90 Cecil Fielder .20 .50
91 Kirk Dressendorfer .20 .50
92 Jerry DiPoto RC .20 .50
93 Mike Felder .20 .50
94 Craig Paquette .20 .50
95 Elvin Paulino RC .20 .50
96 Donovan Osborne .20 .50
97 Hubie Brooks .20 .50
98 Derek Lowe RC 1.50 4.00
99 David Zancanaro .20 .50
100 Ken Griffey Jr. 1.00 2.50
101 Todd Hundley .20 .50
102 Mike Trombley RC .20 .50
103 Ricky Gutierrez RC .40 1.00
104 Braulio Castillo .20 .50
105 Craig Lefferts .20 .50
106 Rick Sutcliffe .20 .50
107 Dean Palmer .20 .50
108 Henry Rodriguez .20 .50
109 Mark Clark RC .40 1.00
110 Kenny Lofton .30 .75
111 Mark Carreon .20 .50
112 J.T. Bruett .20 .50
113 Gerald Williams .20 .50
114 Frank Thomas .50 1.25
115 Kevin Reimer .20 .50
116 Sammy Sosa .50 1.25
117 Mickey Tettleton .20 .50
118 Reggie Sanders .20 .50
119 Trevor Wilson .20 .50
120 Cliff Brantley .20 .50
121 Spike Owen .20 .50
122 Jeff Montgomery .20 .50
123 Alex Sutherland .20 .50
124 Brien Taylor RC .40 1.00
125 Brian Williams RC .20 .50
126 Kevin Seitzer .20 .50
127 Carlos Delgado RC 3.00 8.00
128 Gary Scott .20 .50
129 Scott Cooper .20 .50
130 Domingo Jean RC .20 .50
131 Pat Mahomes RC .40 1.00
132 Mike Boddicker .20 .50
133 Roberto Hernandez .20 .50
134 Dave Valle .20 .50
135 Kurt Stillwell .20 .50
136 Brad Pennington RC .20 .50
137 Jermaine Swinton RC .20 .50
138 Ryan Hawblitzel RC .20 .50
139 Tito Navarro RC .20 .50
140 Sandy Alomar Jr. .20 .50
141 Todd Benzinger .20 .50
142 Danny Jackson .20 .50
143 Melvin Nieves RC .20 .50
144 Jim Campanis .20 .50
145 Luis Gonzalez .20 .50
146 Dave Doorneweerd RC .20 .50
147 Charlie Hayes .20 .50
148 Greg Maddux .75 2.00
149 Brian Harper .20 .50
150 Brent Miller RC .20 .50
151 Shawn Estes RC .40 1.00
152 Mike Williams RC .40 1.00
153 Charlie Hough .20 .50
154 Randy Myers .20 .50
155 Kevin Young RC .40 1.00
156 Rick Wilkins .20 .50
157 Terry Shumpert .20 .50
158 Steve Karsay .20 .50
159 Gary DiSarcina .20 .50
160 Deion Sanders .30 .75
161 Tom Browning .20 .50
162 Dickie Thon .20 .50
163 Luis Mercedes .20 .50
164 Riccardo Ingram .20 .50
165 Tavo Alvarez RC .20 .50
166 Rickey Henderson .50 1.25
167 Jaime Navarro .20 .50
168 Billy Ashley RC .20 .50
169 Phil Dauphin RC .20 .50
170 Ivan Cruz .20 .50
171 Harold Baines .20 .50
172 Bryan Harvey .20 .50
173 Alex Cole .20 .50
174 Curtis Shaw RC .20 .50
175 Matt Williams .20 .50
176 Felix Jose .20 .50
177 Sam Horn .20 .50
178 Randy Johnson .50 1.25
179 Ivan Calderon .20 .50
180 Steve Avery .20 .50
181 William Suero .20 .50
182 Bill Swift .20 .50
183 Howard Battle RC .20 .50
184 Ruben Amaro .20 .50
185 Jim Abbott .30 .75
186 Mike Fitzgerald .20 .50
187 Bruce Hurst .20 .50
188 Jeff Juden .20 .50
189 Jeromy Burnitz .20 .50
190 Dave Burba .20 .50
191 Kevin Brown .20 .50
192 Patrick Lennon .20 .50
193 Jeff McNeely .20 .50
194 Wil Cordero .20 .50
195 Chili Davis .20 .50
196 Milt Cuyler .20 .50
197 Von Hayes .20 .50
198 Todd Revenig RC .20 .50
199 Joel Johnston .20 .50
200 Jeff Bagwell .50 1.25
201 Alex Fernandez .20 .50
202 Todd Jones RC 1.00 2.50
203 Charles Nagy .20 .50
204 Tim Raines .20 .50
205 Kevin Maas .20 .50
206 Julio Franco .20 .50
207 Randy Velarde .20 .50
208 Lance Johnson .20 .50
209 Scott Leius .20 .50
210 Derek Lee .20 .50
211 Joe Sondrini RC .20 .50
212 Royce Clayton .20 .50
213 Chris George .20 .50
214 Gary Sheffield .20 .50
215 Mark Gubicza .20 .50
216 Mike Moore .20 .50
217 Rick Huisman RC .20 .50
218 Jeff Russell .20 .50
219 D.J. Dozier .20 .50
220 Dave Martinez .20 .50
221 Alan Newman RC .20 .50
222 Nolan Ryan 1.50 4.00
223 Teddy Higuera .20 .50
224 Damon Buford RC .20 .50
225 Ruben Sierra .20 .50
226 Tom Nevers .20 .50
227 Tommy Greene .20 .50
228 Nigel Wilson RC .20 .50
229 John DeSilva .20 .50
230 Bobby Witt .20 .50
231 Greg Cadaret .20 .50
232 John Vander Wal RC .40 1.00
233 Jack Clark .20 .50
234 Bill Doran .20 .50
235 Bobby Bonilla .20 .50
236 Steve Olin .20 .50
237 Derek Bell .20 .50
238 David Cone .20 .50
239 Victor Cole RC .20 .50
240 Rod Bolton RC .20 .50
241 Tom Pagnozzi .20 .50
242 Rob Dibble .20 .50
243 Michael Carter RC .20 .50
244 Don Peters .20 .50
245 Mike LaValliere .20 .50
246 Joe Perona RC .20 .50
247 Mitch Williams .20 .50
248 Jay Buhner .20 .50
249 Andy Benes .20 .50
250 Alex Ochoa RC .20 .50
251 Greg Blosser .20 .50
252 Jack Armstrong .20 .50
253 Juan Samuel .20 .50
254 Terry Pendleton .20 .50
255 Ramon Martinez .20 .50
256 Rico Brogna .20 .50
257 John Smiley .20 .50
258 Carl Everett .30 .75
259 Tim Salmon .30 .75
260 Will Clark .30 .75
261 Ugueth Urbina RC .40 1.00
262 Jason Wood RC .20 .50
263 Dave Magadan .20 .50
264 Dante Bichette .20 .50
265 Jose DeLeon .20 .50
266 Mike Neill RC .40 1.00
267 Paul O'Neill .30 .75
268 Anthony Young .20 .50
269 Greg W. Harris .20 .50
270 Todd Van Poppel .20 .50
271 Pedro Castellano RC .20 .50
272 Tony Phillips .20 .50
273 Mike Gallego .20 .50
274 Steve Cooke RC .20 .50
275 Robin Ventura .20 .50
276 Kevin Mitchell .20 .50
277 Doug Linton RC .40 1.00
278 Robert Eenhoorn .40 1.00
279 Gabe White RC .20 .50
280 Dave Stewart .20 .50
281 Mo Sanford .20 .50
282 Greg Perschke .20 .50
283 Kevin Flora RC .20 .50
284 Jeff Williams RC .40 1.00
285 Keith Miller .20 .50
286 Andy Ashby .20 .50
287 Doug Dascenzo .20 .50
288 Eric Karros .20 .50
289 Glenn Murray RC .20 .50
290 Troy Percival RC 1.25 3.00
291 Orlando Merced .20 .50
292 Peter Hoy .20 .50
293 Tony Fernandez .20 .50
294 Juan Guzman .20 .50
295 Jesse Barfield .20 .50
296 Sid Fernandez .20 .50
297 Scott Cepicky .20 .50
298 Garret Anderson RC 2.00 5.00
299 Cal Eldred .20 .50
300 Ryne Sandberg 1.00 2.50
301 Jim Gantner .20 .50
302 Mariano Rivera RC 60.00 150.00
303 Ron Lockett RC .20 .50
304 Jose Offerman .20 .50
305 Dennis Martinez .20 .50
306 Luis Ortiz RC .20 .50
307 David Howard .20 .50
308 Russ Springer RC .40 1.00
309 Chris Howard .20 .50
310 Kyle Abbott .20 .50
311 Aaron Sele RC .40 1.00
312 David Justice .20 .50
313 Pete O'Brien .20 .50
314 Greg Hansell RC .20 .50
315 Dave Winfield .20 .50
316 Lance Dickson .20 .50
317 Eric King .20 .50
318 Vaughn Eshelman RC .20 .50
319 Tim Belcher .20 .50
320 Andres Galarraga .20 .50
321 Scott Bullett RC .20 .50
322 Doug Strange .20 .50
323 Jerald Clark .20 .50
324 Dave Righetti .20 .50
325 Greg Hibbard .20 .50
326 Eric Hillman RC .20 .50
327 Shane Reynolds RC .40 1.00
328 Chris Hammond .20 .50
329 Albert Belle .20 .50
330 Rich Becker RC .20 .50
331 Ed Williams .20 .50
332 Donald Harris .20 .50
333 Dave Smith .20 .50
334 Steve Fireovid .20 .50
335 Steve Buechele .20 .50
336 Mike Schooler .20 .50
337 Kevin McReynolds .20 .50
338 Hensley Meulens .20 .50
339 Benji Gil RC .40 1.00
340 Don Mattingly 1.25 3.00
341 Alvin Davis .20 .50
342 Alan Mills .20 .50
343 Kelly Downs .20 .50
344 Leo Gomez .20 .50
345 Tarrik Brock RC .20 .50
346 Ryan Turner RC .20 .50
347 John Smoltz .30 .75
348 Bill Sampen .20 .50
349 Paul Byrd RC 1.25 3.00
350 Mike Bordick .20 .50
351 Jose Lind .20 .50
352 David Wells .20 .50
353 Barry Larkin .30 .75
354 Bruce Ruffin .20 .50
355 Luis Rivera .20 .50
356 Sid Bream .20 .50
357 Julian Vasquez RC .20 .50
358 Jason Bere RC .40 1.00
359 Ben McDonald .20 .50
360 Scott Stahoviak RC .20 .50
361 Kirt Manwaring .20 .50
362 Jeff Johnson .20 .50
363 Rob Deer .20 .50
364 Tony Pena .20 .50
365 Melido Perez .20 .50
366 Clay Parker .20 .50
367 Dale Sveum .20 .50
368 Mike Scioscia .20 .50
369 Roger Salkeld .20 .50
370 Mike Stanley .20 .50
371 Jack McDowell .20 .50
372 Tim Wallach .20 .50
373 Billy Ripken .20 .50
374 Mike Christopher .20 .50
375 Paul Molitor .20 .50
376 Dave Stieb .20 .50
377 Pedro Guerrero .20 .50
378 Russ Swan .20 .50
379 Bob Ojeda .20 .50
380 Donn Pall .20 .50
381 Eddie Zosky .20 .50
382 Darnell Coles .20 .50
383 Tom Smith RC .20 .50
384 Mark McGwire 1.25 3.00
385 Gary Carter .20 .50
386 Rich Amaral RC .20 .50
387 Alan Embree RC .40 1.00
388 Jonathan Hurst RC .20 .50
389 Bobby Jones RC .40 1.00
390 Rico Rossy .20 .50
391 Dan Smith .20 .50
392 Terry Steinbach .20 .50
393 Jon Farrell RC .30 .75
394 Dave Anderson .20 .50
395 Benny Santiago .20 .50
396 Mark Wohlers .20 .50
397 Mo Vaughn .20 .50
398 Randy Kramer .20 .50
399 John Jaha RC .40 1.00
400 Cal Ripken 1.50 4.00
401 Ryan Bowen .20 .50
402 Tim McIntosh .20 .50
403 Bernard Gilkey .20 .50
404 Junior Felix .20 .50
405 Cris Colon RC .20 .50
406 Marc Newfield .20 .50
407 Bernie Williams .30 .75
408 Jay Howell .20 .50
409 Zane Smith .20 .50
410 Jeff Shaw .20 .50
411 Kerry Woodson .20 .50
412 Wes Chamberlain .20 .50
413 Dave Mlicki RC .40 1.00
414 Benny Distefano .20 .50
415 Kevin Rogers .20 .50
416 Tim Naehring .20 .50
417 Clemente Nunez RC .20 .50
418 Luis Sojo .20 .50
419 Kevin Ritz .20 .50
420 Omar Olivares .20 .50
421 Manuel Lee .20 .50
422 Julio Valera .20 .50
423 Omar Vizquel .30 .75
424 Darren Burton RC .20 .50
425 Mel Hall .20 .50
426 Dennis Powell .20 .50
427 Lee Stevens .20 .50
428 Glenn Davis .20 .50
429 Willie Greene .20 .50
430 Kevin Wickander .20 .50
431 Dennis Eckersley .20 .50
432 Joe Orsulak .20 .50
433 Eddie Murray .50 1.25
434 Matt Stairs RC .40 1.00
435 Wally Joyner .20 .50
436 Rondell White .20 .50
437 Rob Maurer RC .20 .50
438 Joe Redfield .20 .50
439 Mark Lewis .20 .50
440 Darren Daulton .20 .50
441 Mike Henneman .20 .50
442 John Cangelosi .20 .50
443 Vince Moore RC .20 .50
444 John Wehner .20 .50
445 Kent Hrbek .20 .50
446 Mark McLemore .20 .50
447 Bill Wegman .20 .50
448 Robby Thompson .20 .50
449 Mark Anthony RC .20 .50
450 Archi Cianfrocco RC .20 .50
451 Johnny Ruffin .20 .50
452 Javy Lopez .75 2.00
453 Greg Gohr .20 .50
454 Tim Scott .20 .50
455 Stan Belinda .20 .50
456 Darrin Jackson .20 .50
457 Chris Gardner .20 .50
458 Esteban Beltre .20 .50
459 Phil Plantier .20 .50
460 Jim Thome 3.00 8.00
461 Mike Piazza RC 15.00 40.00
462 Matt Sinatro .20 .50
463 Scott Servais .20 .50
464 Brian Jordan RC .75 2.00
465 Doug Drabek .20 .50
466 Carl Willis .20 .50
467 Bret Barberie .20 .50
468 Hal Morris .20 .50
469 Steve Sax .20 .50
470 Jerry Willard .20 .50
471 Dan Wilson .20 .50
472 Chris Hoiles .20 .50
473 Rheal Cormier .30 .75
474 John Morris .20 .50
475 Jeff Reardon .20 .50
476 Mark Leiter .20 .50
477 Tom Gordon .20 .50
478 Kent Bottenfield RC .40 1.00
479 Gene Larkin .20 .50
480 Dwight Gooden .20 .50
481 B.J. Surhoff .20 .50
482 Andy Stankiewicz .20 .50
483 Tino Martinez .30 .75
484 Craig Biggio .30 .75
485 Denny Neagle .20 .50
486 Rusty Meacham .20 .50
487 Kal Daniels .20 .50
488 Dave Henderson .20 .50
489 Tim Costo .20 .50
490 Doug Davis .20 .50
491 Frank Viola .20 .50
492 Cory Snyder .20 .50
493 Chris Martin RC .20 .50
494 Dion James .20 .50
495 Randy Tomlin .20 .50
496 Greg Vaughn .20 .50
497 Dennis Cook .20 .50
498 Rosario Rodriguez .20 .50
499 Dave Staton .20 .50
500 George Brett 1.25 3.00
501 Brian Barnes .20 .50
502 Butch Henry RC .20 .50
503 Harold Reynolds .20 .50
504 David Nied RC .20 .50
505 Lee Smith .20 .50
506 Steve Chitren .20 .50
507 Ken Hill .20 .50
508 Robbie Beckett .20 .50
509 Troy Afenir .20 .50
510 Kelly Gruber .20 .50
511 Bret Boone .30 .75
512 Jeff Branson .20 .50
513 Mike Jackson .40 1.00
514 Pete Harnisch .20 .50
515 Chad Kreuter .40 1.00
516 Joe Vitko RC .20 .50
517 Orel Hershiser .20 .50
518 John Doherty RC .20 .50
519 Jay Bell .20 .50
520 Mark Langston .20 .50
521 Dann Howitt .20 .50
522 Bobby Reed RC .20 .50
523 Bobby Munoz RC .20 .50
524 Todd Ritchie .20 .50
525 Bip Roberts .20 .50
526 Pat Listach RC .40 1.00
527 Scott Brosius RC .75 2.00
528 John Roper RC .20 .50
529 Phil Hiatt RC .20 .50
530 Denny Walling .20 .50
531 Carlos Baerga .20 .50
532 Manny Ramirez RC 3.00 8.00
533 Pat Clements UER .20 .50
Mistakenly numbered 553
534 Ron Gant .20 .50
535 Pat Kelly .20 .50
536 Bill Spiers .20 .50
537 Darren Reed .20 .50
538 Ken Caminiti .20 .50
539 Butch Huskey RC .20 .50
540 Matt Nokes .20 .50
541 John Kruk .20 .50
542 John Jaha FOIL .20 .50
543 Justin Thompson RC .20 .50
544 Steve Hosey .20 .50
545 Joe Kmak .20 .50
546 John Franco .20 .50
547 Devon White .20 .50
548 Elston Hansen FOIL SP RC .20 .50
549 Ryan Klesko .20 .50
550 Danny Tartabull .20 .50
551 Frank Thomas FOIL .50 1.25
552 Kevin Tapani .20 .50
553 Willie Banks .20 .50
See also 533
554 B.J.Wallace FOIL RC .20 .50
555 Orlando Miller RC .20 .50
556 Mark Smith RC .20 .50
557 Tim Wallach FOIL .20 .50
558 Bill Gullickson .20 .50
559 Derek Bell FOIL .20 .50
560 Joe Randa FOIL RC 1.25 3.00
561 Frank Seminara RC .20 .50
562 Mark Gardner .20 .50
563 Rick Greene FOIL RC .20 .50
564 Gary Gaetti .20 .50
565 Ozzie Guillen .20 .50
566 Charles Nagy FOIL .20 .50
567 Mike Milchin .20 .50
568 Ben Shelton RC .20 .50
569 Chris Roberts FOIL .20 .50
570 Ellis Burks .20 .50
571 Scott Scudder .20 .50
572 Jim Abbott FOIL .30 .75
573 Joe Carter .20 .50
574 Steve Finley .20 .50
575 Jim Olander FOIL .20 .50
576 Carlos Garcia .20 .50
577 Gregg Olson .20 .50
578 Greg Swindell FOIL .20 .50
579 Matt Williams FOIL .20 .50
580 Mark Grace .30 .75
581 Howard House FOIL RC .20 .50
582 Luis Polonia .20 .50
583 Erik Hanson .20 .50
584 Salomon Torres FOIL .20 .50
585 Carlton Fisk .30 .75
586 Bret Saberhagen .20 .50
587 Chad McConnell FOIL RC .20 .50
588 Jimmy Key .20 .50
589 Mike Macfarlane .20 .50
590 Barry Bonds FOIL 1.50 4.00
591 Jamie McAndrew .20 .50
592 Shane Mack .20 .50
593 Kerwin Moore .20 .50
594 Joe Oliver .20 .50
595 Chris Sabo .20 .50
596 Alex Gonzalez RC .40 1.00
597 Brett Butler .20 .50
598 Mark Hutton RC .20 .50
599 Andy Benes FOIL .20 .50
600 Jose Canseco .30 .75
601 Darryl Kile .20 .50
602 Matt Stairs FOIL .20 .50
603 Rob Butler FOIL RC .20 .50
604 Willie McGee .20 .50
605 Jack McDowell FOIL .20 .50
606 Tom Candiotti .20 .50
607 Ed Martel RC .20 .50
608 Matt Mieske FOIL .20 .50
609 Darrin Fletcher .20 .50
610 Rafael Palmeiro .30 .75
611 Bill Swift FOIL .20 .50
612 Mike Mussina .50 1.25
613 Vince Coleman .20 .50
614A Scott Cepicky
FOIL ERR(BATS LEFLT on back .20 .50
614B Scott Cepicky COR .20 .50
615 Mike Greenwell .20 .50
616 Kevin McGehee RC .20 .50
617 Jeffrey Hammonds FOIL .20 .50
618 Scott Taylor .20 .50
619 Dave Otto .20 .50
620 Mark McGwire FOIL 1.25 3.00
621 Kevin Tatar RC .20 .50
622 Steve Farr .20 .50
623 Ryan Klesko FOIL .20 .50
624 Dave Fleming .20 .50
625 Andre Dawson .20 .50
626 Tino Martinez FOIL SP .30 .75
627 Chad Curtis RC .40 1.00
628 Mickey Morandini .20 .50
629 Gregg Olson FOIL SP .20 .50
630 Lou Whitaker .20 .50
631 Arthur Rhodes .20 .50
632 Brandon Wilson RC .20 .50
633 Lance Jennings RC .20 .50
634 Allen Watson RC .20 .50
635 Len Dykstra .20 .50
636 Joe Girardi .20 .50
637 Kiki Hernandez FOIL RC .20 .50
638 Mike Hampton RC .75 2.00
639 Al Osuna .20 .50
640 Kevin Appier .20 .50
641 Rick Helling FOIL .20 .50
642 Jody Reed .20 .50
643 Ray Lankford .20 .50
644 John Olerud .20 .50
645 Paul Molitor FOIL .20 .50
646 Pat Borders .20 .50
647 Mike Morgan .20 .50
648 Larry Walker .30 .75
649 Pedro Castellano FOIL .20 .50
650 Fred McGriff .30 .75
651 Walt Weiss .20 .50
652 Calvin Murray FOIL RC .40 1.00
653 Dave Nilsson .20 .50
654 Greg Pirkl RC .20 .50
655 Robin Ventura FOIL .20 .50
656 Mark Portugal .20 .50
657 Roger McDowell .20 .50
658 Rick Hirtensteiner FOIL RC .20 .50
659 Glenallen Hill .20 .50
660 Greg Gagne .20 .50
661 Charles Johnson FOIL .20 .50
662 Brian Hunter .20 .50
663 Mark Lemke .20 .50
664 Tim Belcher FOIL SP .20 .50
665 Rich DeLucia .20 .50
666 Bob Walk .20 .50
667 Joe Carter FOIL .20 .50
668 Jose Guzman .20 .50
669 Otis Nixon .20 .50
670 Phil Nevin FOIL .20 .50
671 Eric Davis .20 .50
672 Damion Easley RC .40 1.00
673 Will Clark FOIL .30 .75
674 Mark Kiefer RC .20 .50
675 Ozzie Smith .75 2.00
676 Manny Ramirez FOIL 3.00 8.00
677 Gregg Olson .20 .50
678 Cliff Floyd RC 1.25 3.00
679 Duane Singleton RC .20 .50
680 Jose Rijo .20 .50
681 Willie Randolph .20 .50
682 Michael Tucker FOIL RC .40 1.00
683 Darren Lewis .20 .50
684 Dale Murphy .30 .75
685 Mike Pagliarulo .20 .50
686 Paul Miller RC .20 .50
687 Mike Robertson RC .20 .50
688 Mike Devereaux .20 .50
689 Pedro Astacio RC .40 1.00
690 Alan Trammell .20 .50
691 Roger Clemens 1.00 2.50
692 Bud Black .20 .50
693 Turk Wendell RC .40 1.00
694 Barry Larkin FOIL .30 .75
695 Todd Zeile .20 .50
696 Pat Hentgen .20 .50
697 Eddie Taubensee RC .40 1.00
698 Guillermo Velasquez RC .20 .50
699 Tom Glavine .30 .75
700 Robin Yount .75 2.00
701 Checklist 1-141 .20 .50
702 Checklist 142-282 .20 .50
703 Checklist 283-423 .20 .50
704 Checklist 424-564 .20 .50
705 Checklist 565-705 .20 .50

1993 Bowman

This 708-card standard-size set (produced by Topps) was issued in one series and features one of the more comprehensive selection of prospects and rookies available that year. Cards were distributed in 14-card plastic wrapped packs and jumbo packs. Each 14-card pack contained one silver foil bordered subset card. The basic issue card fronts feature white-bordered color action player photos. The 48 foil subset cards (339-374 and 693-704) feature sixteen 1992 MVPs of the Minor Leagues, top prospects and a few father/son combinations. Rookie Cards in this set include James Baldwin, Roger Cedeno, Derek Jeter, Jason Kendall, Andy Pettitte, Jose Vidro and Preston Wilson.

COMPLETE SET (708) 15.00 40.00
ONE FOIL PER PACK/2 PER JUMBO
1 Glenn Davis .05 .15
2 Hector Roa RC .08 .25
3 Ken Ryan RC .08 .25
4 Derek Wallace RC .08 .25
5 Jorge Fabregas .05 .15
6 Joe Oliver .05 .15
7 Brandon Wilson .05 .15
8 Mark Thompson RC .08 .25
9 Tracy Sanders .05 .15
10 Rich Renteria .05 .15
11 Lou Whitaker .10 .30
12 Brian L. Hunter RC .20 .50
13 Joe Vitiello .05 .15
14 Eric Karros .10 .30
15 Joe Kmak .05 .15
16 Tavo Alvarez .05 .15
17 Steve Dunn RC .08 .25
18 Tony Fernandez .05 .15
19 Melido Perez .05 .15
20 Mike Lieberthal .10 .30
21 Terry Steinbach .05 .15
22 Stan Belinda .05 .15
23 Jay Buhner .10 .30
24 Allen Watson .05 .15
25 Daryl Henderson RC .08 .25
26 Ray McDavid RC .08 .25
27 Shawn Green .40 1.00
28 Bud Black .05 .15
29 Sherman Obando RC .08 .25
30 Mike Hostetler RC .08 .25
31 Nate Minchey RC .08 .25
32 Randy Myers .05 .15
33 Brian Grebeck .05 .15
34 John Roper .05 .15
35 Larry Thomas .05 .15
36 Alex Cole .05 .15
37 Tom Kramer RC .08 .25
38 Matt Whisenant RC .08 .25
39 Chris Gomez RC .20 .50
40 Luis Gonzalez .10 .30
41 Kevin Appier .10 .30
42 Omar Daal RC .08 .25
43 Duane Singleton .05 .15
44 Bill Risley .05 .15
45 Pat Meares RC .20 .50
46 Butch Huskey .05 .15

Card	Low	High
47 Bobby Munoz	.05	.15
48 Juan Bell	.05	.15
49 Scott Lydy RC	.08	.25
50 Dennis Moeller	.05	.15
51 Marc Newfield	.05	.15
52 Tripp Cromer RC	.08	.25
53 Kurt Miller	.05	.15
54 Jim Pena	.05	.15
55 Juan Guzman	.05	.15
56 Matt Williams	.10	.30
57 Harold Reynolds	.10	.30
58 Donnie Elliott RC	.08	.25
59 Jon Shave RC	.08	.25
60 Kevin Roberson RC	.08	.25
61 Hilly Hathaway RC	.08	.25
62 Jose Rijo	.05	.15
63 Kerry Taylor RC	.05	.15
64 Ryan Hawblitzel	.05	.15
65 Glenallen Hill	.05	.15
66 Ramon Martinez RC	.08	.25
67 Travis Fryman	.10	.30
68 Tom Nevers	.05	.15
69 Phil Hiatt	.05	.15
70 Tim Wallach	.05	.15
71 B.J. Surhoff	.10	.30
72 Rondell White	.10	.30
73 Denny Hocking RC	.20	.50
74 Mike Oquist RC	.08	.25
75 Paul O'Neill	.20	.50
76 Willie Banks	.05	.15
77 Bob Welch	.05	.15
78 Jose Sandoval RC	.08	.25
79 Bill Haselman	.05	.15
80 Rheal Cormier	.05	.15
81 Dean Palmer	.10	.30
82 Pat Gomez RC	.08	.25
83 Steve Karsay	.05	.15
84 Carl Hanselman RC	.08	.25
85 T.R. Lewis RC	.08	.25
86 Chipper Jones	.30	.75
87 Scott Hatteberg	.05	.15
88 Greg Hibbard	.05	.15
89 Lance Painter RC	.08	.25
90 Chad Mottola RC	.20	.50
91 Jason Bere	.05	.15
92 Dante Bichette	.10	.30
93 Sandy Alomar Jr.	.05	.15
94 Carl Everett	.10	.30
95 Danny Bautista RC	.20	.50
96 Steve Finley	.10	.30
97 David Cone	.10	.30
98 Todd Hollandsworth	.05	.15
99 Matt Mieske	.05	.15
100 Larry Walker	.10	.30
101 Shane Mack	.05	.15
102 Aaron Ledesma RC	.08	.25
103 Andy Pettitte RC	4.00	10.00
104 Kevin Stocker	.05	.15
105 Mike Mohler RC	.08	.25
106 Tony Menendez	.05	.15
107 Derek Lowe	.10	.30
108 Basil Shabazz	.05	.15
109 Dan Smith	.05	.15
110 Scott Sanders RC	.20	.50
111 Todd Stottlemyre	.05	.15
112 Benji Simonton RC	.08	.25
113 Rick Sutcliffe	.10	.30
114 Lee Heath RC	.08	.25
115 Jeff Russell	.05	.15
116 Dave Stevens RC	.08	.25
117 Mark Holzemer RC	.08	.25
118 Tim Belcher	.05	.15
119 Bobby Thigpen	.05	.15
120 Roger Bailey RC	.08	.25
121 Tony Mitchell RC	.08	.25
122 Junior Felix	.05	.15
123 Rich Robertson RC	.08	.25
124 Andy Cook RC	.08	.25
125 Brian Bevil RC	.08	.25
126 Darryl Strawberry	.10	.30
127 Cal Eldred	.05	.15
128 Cliff Floyd	.10	.30
129 Alan Newman	.05	.15
130 Howard Johnson	.05	.15
131 Jim Abbott	.20	.50
132 Chad McConnell	.05	.15
133 Miguel Jimenez RC	.08	.25
134 Brett Backlund RC	.08	.25
135 John Cummings RC	.08	.25
136 Brian Barber	.05	.15
137 Rafael Palmeiro	.20	.50
138 Tim Worrell RC	.08	.25
139 Jose Pett RC	.08	.25
140 Barry Bonds	.75	2.00
141 Damon Buford	.05	.15
142 Jeff Blauser	.05	.15
143 Frankie Rodriguez	.05	.15
144 Mike Morgan	.05	.15
145 Gary DiSarcina	.05	.15
146 Pokey Reese	.05	.15
147 Johnny Ruffin	.05	.15
148 David Nied	.05	.15
149 Charles Nagy	.05	.15
150 Mike Myers RC	.08	.25
151 Kenny Carlyle RC	.08	.25
152 Eric Anthony	.05	.15
153 Jose Lind	.05	.15
154 Pedro Martinez	.60	1.50
155 Mark Kiefer	.05	.15
156 Tim Laker RC	.08	.25
157 Pat Mahomes	.05	.15
158 Bobby Bonilla	.10	.30
159 Domingo Jean	.05	.15
160 Darren Daulton	.10	.30
161 Mark McGwire	.75	2.00
162 Jason Kendall RC	.75	2.00
163 Desi Relaford	.05	.15
164 Ozzie Canseco	.05	.15
165 Rick Helling	.05	.15
166 Steve Pegues RC	.08	.25
167 Paul Molitor	.10	.30
168 Larry Carter RC	.05	.15
169 Arthur Rhodes	.05	.15
170 Damon Hollins RC	.20	.50
171 Frank Viola	.10	.30
172 Steve Trachsel RC	.40	1.00
173 J.T.Snow RC	.40	1.00
174 Keith Gordon RC	.08	.25
175 Carlton Fisk	.20	.50
176 Jason Bates RC	.08	.25
177 Mike Crosby RC	.08	.25
178 Benny Santiago	.10	.30
179 Mike Moore	.05	.15
180 Jeff Juden	.05	.15
181 Darren Burton	.05	.15
182 Todd Williams RC	.20	.50
183 John Jaha	.05	.15
184 Mike Lansing RC	.20	.50
185 Pedro Grifol RC	.08	.25
186 Vince Coleman	.05	.15
187 Pat Kelly	.05	.15
188 Clemente Alvarez RC	.08	.25
189 Ron Darling	.05	.15
190 Orlando Merced	.05	.15
191 Chris Bosio	.05	.15
192 Steve Dixon RC	.08	.25
193 Doug Dascenzo	.05	.15
194 Ray Holbert RC	.08	.25
195 Howard Battle	.05	.15
196 Willie McGee	.10	.30
197 John O'Donoghue RC	.08	.25
198 Steve Avery	.05	.15
199 Greg Blosser	.05	.15
200 Ryne Sandberg	.50	1.25
201 Joe Grahe	.05	.15
202 Dan Wilson	.10	.30
203 Domingo Martinez RC	.08	.25
204 Andres Galarraga	.10	.30
205 Jamie Taylor RC	.08	.25
206 Darrell Whitmore RC	.08	.25
207 Ben Blomdahl RC	.08	.25
208 Doug Drabek	.05	.15
209 Keith Miller	.05	.15
210 Billy Ashley	.05	.15
211 Mike Farrell RC	.08	.25
212 John Wetteland	.10	.30
213 Randy Tomlin	.05	.15
214 Sid Fernandez	.05	.15
215 Quilvio Veras RC	.20	.50
216 Dave Hollins	.05	.15
217 Mike Neill	.05	.15
218 Andy Van Slyke	.20	.50
219 Bret Boone	.10	.30
220 Tom Pagnozzi	.05	.15
221 Mike Welch RC	.08	.25
222 Frank Seminara	.05	.15
223 Ron Villone	.05	.15
224 D.J.Thielen RC	.08	.25
225 Cal Ripken	1.00	2.50
226 Pedro Borbon Jr. RC	.08	.25
227 Carlos Quintana	.05	.15
228 Tommy Shields	.05	.15
229 Tim Salmon	.20	.50
230 John Smiley	.05	.15
231 Ellis Burks	.10	.30
232 Pedro Castellano	.05	.15
233 Paul Byrd	.10	.30
234 Bryan Harvey	.05	.15
235 Scott Livingstone	.05	.15
236 James Mouton RC	.08	.25
237 Joe Randa	.10	.30
238 Pedro Astacio	.05	.15
239 Darryl Hamilton	.05	.15
240 Joey Eischen RC	.08	.25
241 Edgar Herrera RC	.08	.25
242 Dwight Gooden	.10	.30
243 Sam Militello	.05	.15
244 Ron Blazier RC	.08	.25
245 Ruben Sierra	.10	.30
246 Al Martin	.05	.15
247 Mike Felder	.05	.15
248 Bob Tewksbury	.05	.15
249 Craig Lefferts	.05	.15
250 Luis Lopez RC	.08	.25
251 Devon White	.10	.30
252 Will Clark	.20	.50
253 Mark Smith	.05	.15
254 Terry Pendleton	.10	.30
255 Aaron Sele	.05	.15
256 Jose Viera RC	.08	.25
257 Damion Easley	.05	.15
258 Rod Lofton RC	.08	.25
259 Chris Snopek RC	.08	.25
260 Quinton McCracken RC	.20	.50
261 Mike Matthews RC	.08	.25
262 Hector Carrasco RC	.08	.25
263 Rick Greene	.05	.15
264 Chris Holt RC	.20	.50
265 George Brett	.75	2.00
266 Rick Gorecki RC	.08	.25
267 Francisco Gamez RC	.08	.25
268 Marquis Grissom	.10	.30
269 Kevin Tapani UER	.05	.15
Misspelled Tapan on card front		
270 Ryan Thompson	.05	.15
271 Gerald Williams	.05	.15
272 Paul Fletcher RC	.08	.25
273 Lance Blankenship	.05	.15
274 Marty Neff RC	.08	.25
275 Shawn Estes	.05	.15
276 Rene Arocha RC	.20	.50
277 Scott Eyre RC	.08	.25
278 Phil Plantier	.05	.15
279 Paul Spoljaric RC	.08	.25
280 Chris Gambs	.05	.15
281 Harold Baines	.10	.30
282 Jose Oliva	.05	.15
283 Matt Whiteside RC	.08	.25
284 Brant Brown RC	.20	.50
285 Russ Springer	.05	.15
286 Chris Sabo	.05	.15
287 Ozzie Guillen	.10	.30
288 Marcus Moore RC	.08	.25
289 Chad Ogea	.05	.15
290 Walt Weiss	.05	.15
291 Brian Edmondson	.05	.15
292 Jimmy Gonzalez	.05	.15
293 Danny Miceli RC	.20	.50
294 Jose Offerman	.05	.15
295 Greg Vaughn	.05	.15
296 Frank Bolick	.05	.15
297 Mike Maksudian RC	.08	.25
298 John Franco	.10	.30
299 Danny Tartabull	.05	.15
300 Len Dykstra	.10	.30
301 Bobby Witt	.05	.15
302 Trey Beamon RC	.08	.25
303 Tino Martinez	.20	.50
304 Aaron Holbert	.05	.15
305 Juan Gonzalez	.10	.30
306 Billy Hall RC	.08	.25
307 Duane Ward	.05	.15
308 Rod Beck	.05	.15
309 Jose Mercedes RC	.08	.25
310 Otis Nixon	.05	.15
311 Gettys Glaze RC	.08	.25
312 Candy Maldonado	.05	.15
313 Chad Curtis	.05	.15
314 Tim Costo	.05	.15
315 Mike Robertson	.05	.15
316 Nigel Wilson	.05	.15
317 Greg McMichael RC	.20	.50
318 Scott Pose RC	.08	.25
319 Ivan Cruz	.05	.15
320 Greg Swindell	.05	.15
321 Kevin McReynolds	.05	.15
322 Tom Candiotti	.05	.15
323 Rob Wishnevski RC	.08	.25
324 Ken Hill	.05	.15
325 Kirby Puckett	.30	.75
326 Tim Bogar RC	.08	.25
327 Mariano Rivera	5.00	12.00
328 Mitch Williams	.05	.15
329 Craig Paquette	.05	.15
330 Jay Bell	.10	.30
331 Jose Martinez RC	.08	.25
332 Rob Deer	.05	.15
333 Brook Fordyce	.05	.15
334 Matt Nokes	.05	.15
335 Derek Lee	.05	.15
336 Paul Ellis RC	.08	.25
337 Desi Wilson RC	.08	.25
338 Roberto Alomar	.20	.50
339 Jim Tatum FOIL RC	.08	.25
340 J.T.Snow FOIL	.40	1.00
341 Tim Salmon FOIL	.20	.50
342 Russ Davis FOIL RC	.20	.50
343 Javy Lopez FOIL	.20	.50
344 Troy O'Leary FOIL RC	.20	.50
345 Marty Cordova FOIL RC	.20	.50
346 Bubba Smith RC FOIL	.08	.25
347 Chipper Jones FOIL	.30	.75
348 Jessie Hollins FOIL	.05	.15
349 Willie Greene FOIL	.05	.15
350 Mark Thompson FOIL	.05	.15
351 Nigel Wilson FOIL	.05	.15
352 Todd Jones FOIL	.10	.30
353 Raul Mondesi FOIL	.10	.30
354 Cliff Floyd FOIL	.10	.30
355 Bobby Jones FOIL	.10	.30
356 Kevin Stocker FOIL	.05	.15
357 Midre Cummings FOIL	.05	.15
358 Allen Watson FOIL	.05	.15
359 Ray McDavid FOIL	.05	.15
360 Steve Hosey FOIL	.05	.15
361 Brad Pennington FOIL	.05	.15
362 Frankie Rodriguez FOIL	.05	.15
363 Troy Percival FOIL	.20	.50
364 Jason Bere FOIL	.05	.15
365 Manny Ramirez FOIL	.50	1.25
366 Justin Thompson FOIL	.05	.15
367 Joe Vitiello FOIL	.05	.15
368 Tyrone Hill FOIL	.05	.15
369 David McCarty FOIL	.05	.15
370 Brien Taylor FOIL	.05	.15
371 Todd Van Poppel FOIL	.05	.15
372 Marc Newfield FOIL	.05	.15
373 Terrell Lowery FOIL RC	.20	.50
374 Alex Gonzalez FOIL	.05	.15
375 Ken Griffey Jr.	.60	1.50
376 Donovan Osborne	.05	.15
377 Ritchie Moody RC	.08	.25
378 Shane Andrews	.05	.15
379 Carlos Delgado	.30	.75
380 Bill Swift	.05	.15
381 Leo Gomez	.05	.15
382 Ron Gant	.10	.30
383 Scott Fletcher	.05	.15
384 Matt Walbeck RC	.20	.50
385 Chuck Finley	.10	.30
386 Kevin Mitchell	.05	.15
387 Wilson Alvarez UER	.05	.15
Misspelled Alverez on card front		
388 John Burke RC	.08	.25
389 Alan Embree	.05	.15
390 Trevor Hoffman	.30	.75
391 Alan Trammell	.10	.30
392 Todd Jones	.10	.30
393 Felix Jose	.05	.15
394 Orel Hershiser	.10	.30
395 Pat Listach	.05	.15
396 Gabe White	.05	.15
397 Dan Serafini RC	.08	.25
398 Todd Hundley	.05	.15
399 Wade Boggs	.20	.50
400 Tyler Green	.05	.15
401 Mike Bordick	.05	.15
402 Scott Bullett	.05	.15
403 LaGrande Russell RC	.08	.25
404 Ray Lankford	.10	.30
405 Nolan Ryan	1.25	3.00
406 Robbie Beckett	.05	.15
407 Brent Bowers RC	.08	.25
408 Adell Davenport RC	.08	.25
409 Brady Anderson	.10	.30
410 Tom Glavine	.20	.50
411 Doug Hecker RC	.08	.25
412 Jose Guzman	.05	.15
413 Luis Polonia	.05	.15
414 Brian Williams	.05	.15
415 Bo Jackson	.30	.75
416 Eric Young	.05	.15
417 Kenny Lofton	.10	.30
418 Orestes Destrade	.05	.15
419 Tony Phillips	.05	.15
420 Jeff Bagwell	.20	.50
421 Mark Gardner	.05	.15
422 Brett Butler	.10	.30
423 Graeme Lloyd RC	.20	.50
424 Delino DeShields	.05	.15
425 Scott Erickson	.05	.15
426 Jeff Kent	.30	.75
427 Jimmy Key	.10	.30
428 Mickey Morandini	.05	.15
429 Marcos Armas RC	.08	.25
430 Don Slaught	.05	.15
431 Randy Johnson	.30	.75
432 Omar Olivares	.05	.15
433 Charlie Leibrandt	.05	.15
434 Kurt Stillwell	.05	.15
435 Scott Brow RC	.08	.25
436 Robby Thompson	.05	.15
437 Ben McDonald	.05	.15
438 Deion Sanders	.20	.50
439 Tony Pena	.05	.15
440 Mark Grace	.20	.50
441 Eduardo Perez	.05	.15
442 Tim Pugh RC	.08	.25
443 Scott Ruffcorn	.05	.15
444 Jay Gainer RC	.08	.25
445 Albert Belle	.10	.30
446 Bret Barberie	.05	.15
447 Justin Mashore	.05	.15
448 Pete Harnisch	.05	.15
449 Greg Gagne	.05	.15
450 Eric Davis	.10	.30
451 Dave Mlicki	.05	.15
452 Moises Alou	.10	.30
453 Rick Aguilera	.05	.15
454 Eddie Murray	.30	.75
455 Bob Wickman	.05	.15
456 Wes Chamberlain	.05	.15
457 Brent Gates	.05	.15
458 Paul Wagner	.05	.15
459 Mike Hampton	.10	.30
460 Ozzie Smith	.50	1.25
461 Tom Henke	.05	.15
462 Ricky Gutierrez	.05	.15
463 Jack Morris	.10	.30
464 Joel Chimelis	.05	.15
465 Gregg Olson	.05	.15
466 Javy Lopez	.20	.50
467 Scott Cooper	.05	.15
468 Willie Wilson	.05	.15
469 Mark Langston	.05	.15
470 Barry Larkin	.20	.50
471 Rod Bolton	.05	.15
472 Freddie Benavides	.05	.15
473 Ken Ramos RC	.08	.25
474 Chuck Carr	.05	.15
475 Cecil Fielder	.10	.30
476 Eddie Taubensee	.05	.15
477 Chris Eddy RC	.08	.25
478 Greg Hansell	.05	.15
479 Kevin Reimer	.05	.15
480 Dennis Martinez	.10	.30
481 Chuck Knoblauch	.10	.30
482 Mike Draper	.05	.15
483 Spike Owen	.05	.15
484 Terry Mulholland	.05	.15
485 Dennis Eckersley	.10	.30
486 Blas Minor	.05	.15
487 Dave Fleming	.05	.15
488 Dan Cholowsky	.05	.15
489 Ivan Rodriguez	.20	.50
490 Gary Sheffield	.10	.30
491 Ed Sprague	.05	.15
492 Steve Hosey	.05	.15
493 Jimmy Haynes RC	.20	.50
494 John Smoltz	.20	.50
495 Andre Dawson	.10	.30
496 Rey Sanchez	.05	.15
497 Ty Van Burkleo	.05	.15
498 Bobby Ayala RC	.08	.25
499 Tim Raines	.10	.30
500 Charlie Hayes	.05	.15
501 Paul Sorrento	.05	.15
502 Richie Lewis RC	.08	.25
503 Jason Pfaff RC	.08	.25
504 Ken Caminiti	.10	.30
505 Mike Macfarlane	.05	.15
506 Jody Reed	.05	.15
507 Bobby Hughes RC	.08	.25
508 Wil Cordero	.05	.15
509 George Tsamis RC	.08	.25
510 Bret Saberhagen	.10	.30
511 Derek Jeter RC	15.00	40.00
512 Gene Schall	.05	.15
513 Curtis Shaw	.05	.15
514 Steve Cooke	.05	.15
515 Edgar Martinez	.20	.50
516 Mike Milchin	.05	.15
517 Billy Ripken	.05	.15
518 Andy Benes	.05	.15
519 Juan de la Rosa RC	.08	.25
520 John Burkett	.05	.15
521 Alex Ochoa	.05	.15
522 Tony Tarasco RC	.20	.50
523 Luis Ortiz	.05	.15
524 Rick Wilkins	.05	.15
525 Chris Turner RC	.08	.25
526 Rob Dibble	.10	.30
527 Jack McDowell	.05	.15
528 Daryl Boston	.05	.15
529 Bill Wertz RC	.08	.25
530 Charlie Hough	.10	.30
531 Sean Bergman	.05	.15
532 Doug Jones	.05	.15
533 Jeff Montgomery	.05	.15
534 Roger Cedeno RC	.20	.50
535 Robin Yount	.50	1.25
536 Mo Vaughn	.10	.30
537 Brian Harper	.05	.15
538 Juan Castillo RC	.05	.15
539 Steve Farr	.05	.15
540 John Kruk	.10	.30
541 Troy Neel	.05	.15
542 Danny Clyburn RC	.08	.25
543 Jim Converse RC	.08	.25
544 Gregg Jefferies	.05	.15
545 Jose Canseco	.20	.50
546 Julio Bruno RC	.08	.25
547 Rob Butler	.05	.15
548 Royce Clayton	.05	.15
549 Chris Hoiles	.05	.15
550 Greg Maddux	.50	1.25
551 Joe Ciccarella RC	.08	.25
552 Ozzie Timmons	.05	.15
553 Chili Davis	.10	.30
554 Brian Koelling	.05	.15
555 Frank Thomas	.30	.75
556 Vinny Castilla	.30	.75
557 Reggie Jefferson	.05	.15
558 Rob Natal	.05	.15
559 Mike Henneman	.05	.15
560 Craig Biggio	.20	.50
561 Billy Brewer	.05	.15
562 Dan Melendez	.05	.15
563 Kenny Felder RC	.08	.25
564 Miguel Batista RC	.40	1.00
565 Dave Winfield	.10	.30
566 Al Shirley	.05	.15
567 Robert Eenhoorn	.05	.15
568 Mike Williams	.05	.15
569 Tanyon Sturtze RC	.20	.50
570 Tim Wakefield	.30	.75
571 Greg Pirkl	.05	.15
572 Sean Lowe RC	.08	.25
573 Terry Burrows RC	.08	.25
574 Kevin Higgins	.05	.15
575 Joe Carter	.10	.30
576 Kevin Rogers	.05	.15
577 Manny Alexander	.05	.15
578 David Justice	.10	.30
579 Brian Conroy RC	.08	.25
580 Jessie Hollins	.05	.15
581 Ron Watson RC	.08	.25
582 Bip Roberts	.05	.15
583 Tom Urbani RC	.08	.25
584 Jason Hutchins RC	.08	.25
585 Carlos Baerga	.05	.15
586 Jeff Mutis	.05	.15
587 Justin Thompson	.05	.15
588 Orlando Miller	.05	.15
589 Brian McRae	.05	.15
590 Ramon Martinez	.05	.15
591 Dave Nilsson	.05	.15
592 Jose Vidro RC	.75	2.00
593 Rich Becker	.05	.15
594 Preston Wilson RC	.60	1.50
595 Don Mattingly	.75	2.00
596 Tony Longmire	.05	.15
597 Kevin Seitzer	.05	.15
598 Midre Cummings RC	.08	.25
599 Omar Vizquel	.20	.50
600 Lee Smith	.10	.30
601 David Hulse RC	.08	.25
602 Darrell Sherman RC	.08	.25
603 Alex Gonzalez	.05	.15
604 Geronimo Pena	.05	.15
605 Mike Devereaux	.05	.15
606 Sterling Hitchcock RC	.20	.50
607 Mike Greenwell	.05	.15
608 Steve Buechele	.05	.15
609 Troy Percival	.20	.50
610 Roberto Kelly	.05	.15
611 James Baldwin RC	.20	.50
612 Jerald Clark	.05	.15
613 Albie Lopez RC	.08	.25
614 Dave Magadan	.05	.15
615 Mickey Tettleton	.05	.15
616 Sean Runyan RC	.08	.25
617 Bob Hamelin	.05	.15
618 Raul Mondesi	.10	.30
619 Tyrone Hill	.05	.15
620 Darrin Fletcher	.05	.15
621 Mike Trombley	.05	.15
622 Jeromy Burnitz	.10	.30
623 Bernie Williams	.20	.50
624 Mike Farmer RC	.08	.25
625 Rickey Henderson	.30	.75
626 Carlos Garcia	.05	.15
627 Jeff Darwin RC	.08	.25
628 Todd Zeile	.05	.15
629 Benji Gil	.05	.15
630 Tony Gwynn	.40	1.00
631 Aaron Small RC	.40	1.00
632 Joe Rosselli RC	.08	.25
633 Mike Mussina	.20	.50
634 Ryan Klesko	.10	.30
635 Roger Clemens	.60	1.50
636 Sammy Sosa	.30	.75
637 Orlando Palmeiro RC	.08	.25
638 Willie Greene	.05	.15
639 George Bell	.05	.15
640 Garvin Alston RC	.08	.25
641 Pete Janicki RC	.08	.25
642 Chris Sheff RC	.08	.25
643 Felipe Lira RC	.08	.25
644 Roberto Petagine	.05	.15
645 Wally Joyner	.10	.30
646 Mike Piazza	1.25	3.00
647 Jaime Navarro	.05	.15
648 Jeff Hartsock	.05	.15
649 David McCarty	.05	.15
650 Bobby Jones	.10	.30
651 Mark Hutton	.05	.15
652 Kyle Abbott	.05	.15
653 Steve Cox RC	.08	.25
654 Jeff King	.05	.15
655 Norm Charlton	.05	.15
656 Mike Gulan RC	.08	.25
657 Julio Franco	.10	.30
658 Cameron Cairncross RC	.08	.25
659 John Olerud	.10	.30
660 Salomon Torres	.05	.15
661 Brad Pennington	.05	.15
662 Melvin Nieves	.05	.15
663 Ivan Calderon	.05	.15
664 Turk Wendell	.05	.15
665 Chris Pritchett	.05	.15
666 Reggie Sanders	.10	.30
667 Robin Ventura	.10	.30
668 Joe Girardi	.05	.15
669 Manny Ramirez	.50	1.25
670 Jeff Conine	.10	.30
671 Greg Gohr	.05	.15
672 Andujar Cedeno	.05	.15
673 Les Norman RC	.08	.25
674 Mike James RC	.08	.25
675 Marshall Boze RC	.08	.25
676 B.J.Wallace	.05	.15
677 Kent Hrbek	.10	.30
678 Jack Voigt RC	.08	.25
679 Brien Taylor	.05	.15
680 Curt Schilling	.10	.30
681 Todd Van Poppel	.05	.15
682 Kevin Young	.10	.30
683 Tommy Adams	.05	.15
684 Bernard Gilkey	.05	.15
685 Kevin Brown	.10	.30
686 Fred McGriff	.20	.50
687 Pat Borders	.05	.15
688 Kirt Manwaring	.05	.15
689 Sid Bream	.05	.15
690 John Valentin	.05	.15
691 Steve Olsen RC	.08	.25
692 Roberto Mejia RC	.08	.25
693 Carlos Delgado FOIL	.30	.75
694 Steve Gibralter FOIL RC	.08	.25
695 Gary Mota FOIL RC	.08	.25
696 Jose Malave FOIL RC	.08	.25
697 Larry Sutton FOIL RC	.08	.25
698 Dan Frye FOIL RC	.08	.25
699 Tim Clark FOIL RC	.08	.25
700 Brian Rupp FOIL RC	.08	.25
701 Felipe Alou FOIL	.10	.30
Moises Alou		
702 Barry Bonds FOIL	.40	1.00
Bobby Bonds		
703 Ken Griffey Sr. FOIL	.40	1.00
Ken Griffey Jr.		
704 Brian McRae FOIL	.05	.15
Hal McRae		
705 Checklist 1	.05	.15
706 Checklist 2	.05	.15
707 Checklist 3	.05	.15
708 Checklist 4	.05	.15

1994 Bowman Previews

Card	Low	High
COMPLETE SET (10)	10.00	25.00
STATED ODDS 1:24 SER.2 STADIUM CLUB		
1 Frank Thomas	2.00	5.00
2 Mike Piazza	4.00	10.00
3 Albert Belle	.75	2.00
4 Javier Lopez	.75	2.00
5 Cliff Floyd	.75	2.00
6 Alex Gonzalez	.50	1.25
7 Ricky Bottalico	.30	.75
8 Tony Clark	1.25	3.00
9 Mac Suzuki	.75	2.00
10 James Mouton FOIL	.50	1.25

1994 Bowman

The 1994 Bowman set consists of 682 standard-size, full-bleed cards primarily distributed in plastic wrap packs and jumbo packs. There are 52 Foil cards (337-388) that include a number of top young stars and prospects. These foil cards were issued one per foil pack and two per jumbo. Rookie Cards of note include Edgardo Alfonzo, Tony Clark, Jermaine Dye, Brad Fullmer, Richard Hidalgo, Derrek Lee, Chan Ho Park, Jorge Posada, Edgar Renteria and Billy Wagner.

Card	Low	High
COMPLETE SET (682)	20.00	50.00
1 Joe Carter	.15	.40
2 Marcus Moore	.08	.25
3 Doug Creek RC	.15	.40
4 Pedro Martinez	.40	1.00
5 Ken Griffey Jr.	.75	2.00
6 Greg Swindell	.08	.25
7 J.J. Johnson	.08	.25
8 Homer Bush RC	.15	.40
9 Arquimedez Pozo RC	.15	.40
10 Bryan Harvey	.08	.25
11 J.T. Snow	.15	.40
12 Alan Benes RC	.40	1.00
13 Chad Kreuter	.08	.25
14 Eric Karros	.15	.40
15 Frank Thomas	.40	1.00
16 Bret Saberhagen	.15	.40
17 Terrell Lowery	.08	.25
18 Rod Bolton	.08	.25
19 Harold Baines	.15	.40
20 Matt Walbeck	.08	.25
21 Tom Glavine	.25	.60
22 Todd Jones	.08	.25
23 Alberto Castillo RC	.15	.40
24 Ruben Sierra	.15	.40
25 Don Mattingly	1.00	2.50
26 Mike Morgan	.08	.25
27 Jim Musselwhite RC	.15	.40
28 Matt Brunson RC	.15	.40
29 Adam Meinershagen RC	.15	.40
30 Joe Girardi	.08	.25
31 Shane Halter	.08	.25
32 Jose Paniagua RC	.40	1.00
33 Paul Perkins RC	.15	.40
34 John Hudek RC	.15	.40
35 Frank Viola	.15	.40
36 David Lamb RC	.15	.40
37 Marshall Boze	.08	.25
38 Jorge Posada RC	5.00	12.00
39 Brian Anderson RC	.40	1.00
40 Mark Whiten	.08	.25
41 Sean Bergman	.08	.25
42 Jose Parra RC	.15	.40
43 Mike Robertson	.08	.25
44 Pete Walker RC	.15	.40
45 Juan Gonzalez	.15	.40
46 Cleveland Ladell RC	.15	.40
47 Mark Smith	.08	.25
48 Kevin Jarvis UER	.15	.40
team listed as Yankees on back		
49 Amaury Telemaco RC	.15	.40
50 Andy Van Slyke	.25	.60
51 Rikkert Faneyte RC	.15	.40
52 Curtis Shaw	.08	.25
53 Matt Drews RC	.15	.40
54 Wilson Alvarez	.08	.25
55 Manny Ramirez	.40	1.00
56 Bobby Munoz	.08	.25
57 Ed Sprague	.08	.25
58 Jamey Wright RC	.40	1.00
59 Jeff Montgomery	.08	.25
60 Kirk Rueter	.08	.25
61 Edgar Martinez	.25	.60
62 Luis Gonzalez	.15	.40
63 Tim Vanegmond RC	.15	.40
64 Bip Roberts	.08	.25
65 John Jaha	.08	.25
66 Chuck Carr	.08	.25
67 Chuck Finley	.15	.40
68 Aaron Holbert	.08	.25
69 Cecil Fielder	.15	.40
70 Tom Engle RC	.15	.40
71 Ron Karkovice	.08	.25
72 Joe Orsulak	.08	.25
73 Duff Brumley RC	.15	.40
74 Craig Clayton RC	.15	.40
75 Cal Ripken	1.25	3.00
76 Brad Fullmer RC	.40	1.00
77 Tony Tarasco	.08	.25
78 Terry Farrar RC	.15	.40
79 Matt Williams	.15	.40
80 Rickey Henderson	.40	1.00
81 Terry Mulholland	.08	.25
82 Sammy Sosa	.40	1.00
83 Paul Sorrento	.08	.25
84 Pete Incaviglia	.08	.25
85 Darren Hall RC	.15	.40
86 Scott Klingenbeck	.08	.25
87 Dario Perez RC	.15	.40
88 Ugueth Urbina	.08	.25
89 Dave Vanhof RC	.15	.40
90 Domingo Jean	.08	.25
91 Otis Nixon	.08	.25
92 Andres Berumen	.08	.25
93 Jose Valentin	.08	.25
94 Edgar Renteria RC	2.50	6.00
95 Chris Turner	.08	.25
96 Ray Lankford	.15	.40
97 Danny Bautista	.08	.25
98 Chan Ho Park RC	.60	1.50
99 Glenn DiSarcina RC	.15	.40
100 Butch Huskey	.08	.25
101 Ivan Rodriguez	.25	.60
102 Johnny Ruffin	.08	.25
103 Alex Ochoa	.08	.25
104 Torii Hunter RC	2.00	5.00
105 Ryan Klesko	.15	.40
106 Jay Bell	.15	.40
107 Kurt Peltzer RC	.15	.40
108 Miguel Jimenez	.08	.25
109 Russ Davis	.08	.25
110 Derek Wallace	.08	.25
111 Keith Lockhart RC	.40	1.00
112 Mike Lieberthal	.15	.40
113 Dave Stewart	.15	.40
114 Tom Schmidt	.08	.25
115 Brian McRae	.08	.25
116 Moises Alou	.15	.40
117 Dave Fleming	.08	.25
118 Jeff Bagwell	.25	.60
119 Luis Ortiz	.08	.25
120 Tony Gwynn	.50	1.25
121 Jaime Navarro	.08	.25
122 Benito Santiago	.15	.40
123 Darrell Whitmore	.08	.25
124 John Mabry RC	.40	1.00
125 Mickey Tettleton	.08	.25
126 Tom Candiotti	.08	.25
127 Tim Raines	.15	.40
128 Bobby Bonilla	.15	.40
129 John Dettmer	.08	.25
130 Hector Carrasco	.08	.25
131 Chris Hoiles	.08	.25
132 Rick Aguilera	.08	.25
133 David Justice	.15	.40
134 Esteban Loaiza RC	.60	1.50
135 Barry Bonds	1.00	2.50
136 Bob Welch	.08	.25
137 Mike Stanley	.08	.25
138 Roberto Hernandez	.08	.25
139 Sandy Alomar Jr.	.08	.25
140 Darren Daulton	.15	.40
141 Angel Martinez RC	.15	.40
142 Howard Johnson	.08	.25
143 Bob Hamelin UER	.08	.25
(name and card number colors don't match		
144 J.J.Thobe RC	.15	.40
145 Roger Salkeld	.08	.25
146 Orlando Miller	.08	.25
147 Dmitri Young	.15	.40
148 Tim Hyers RC	.15	.40
149 Mark Loretta RC	2.00	5.00
150 Chris Hammond	.08	.25
151 Joel Moore RC	.15	.40
152 Todd Zeile	.08	.25
153 Wil Cordero	.08	.25
154 Chris Smith	.08	.25
155 James Baldwin	.08	.25
156 Edgardo Alfonzo RC	.40	1.00
157 Kym Ashworth RC	.15	.40
158 Paul Bako RC	.15	.40
159 Rick Krivda RC	.15	.40
160 Pat Mahomes	.08	.25
161 Damon Hollins	.08	.25
162 Felix Martinez RC	.15	.40
163 Jason Myers RC	.15	.40
164 Izzy Molina RC	.15	.40
165 Brien Taylor	.08	.25
166 Kevin Orie RC	.15	.40
167 Casey Whitten RC	.15	.40
168 Tony Longmire	.08	.25
169 John Olerud	.15	.40
170 Mark Thompson	.08	.25
171 Jorge Fabregas	.08	.25
172 John Wetteland	.15	.40
173 Dan Wilson	.08	.25

174 Doug Drabek .08 .25
175 Jeff McNeely .08 .25
176 Melvin Nieves .08 .25
177 Doug Glanville RC .40 1.00
178 Javier De La Hoya RC .15 .40
179 Chad Curtis .08 .25
180 Brian Barber .08 .25
181 Mike Henneman .08 .25
182 Jose Offerman .08 .25
183 Robert Ellis RC .15 .40
184 John Franco .15 .40
185 Benji Gil .08 .25
186 Hal Morris .08 .25
187 Chris Sabo .08 .25
188 Blaise Ilsley RC .15 .40
189 Steve Avery .08 .25
190 Rick White RC .15 .40
191 Rod Beck .08 .25
192 Mark McGwire UER 1.00 2.50
No card number on back
193 Jim Abbott .25 .60
194 Randy Myers .08 .25
195 Kenny Lofton .15 .40
196 Mariano Duncan .08 .25
197 Lee Daniels RC .15 .40
198 Armando Reynoso .08 .25
199 Joe Randa .15 .40
200 Cliff Floyd .15 .40
201 Tim Harkrider RC .15 .40
202 Kevin Gallaher RC .15 .40
203 Scott Cooper .08 .25
204 Phil Stidham RC .15 .40
205 Jeff D'Amico RC .15 .40
206 Matt Whisenant .08 .25
207 De Shawn Warren .08 .25
208 Rene Arocha .08 .25
209 Tony Clark RC .60 1.50
210 Jason Jacome RC .15 .40
211 Scott Christman RC .15 .40
212 Bill Pulsipher .15 .40
213 Dean Palmer .15 .40
214 Chad Mottola .08 .25
215 Manny Alexander .08 .25
216 Rich Becker .08 .25
217 Andre King RC .15 .40
218 Carlos Garcia .08 .25
219 Ron Pezzoni RC .15 .40
220 Steve Karsay .08 .25
221 Jose Musset RC .15 .40
222 Karl Rhodes .08 .25
223 Frank Cimorelli RC .15 .40
224 Kevin Jordan RC .15 .40
225 Duane Ward .08 .25
226 John Burke .08 .25
227 Mike Macfarlane .08 .25
228 Mike Lansing .08 .25
229 Chuck Knoblauch .15 .40
230 Ken Caminiti .15 .40
231 Gar Finnvold RC .15 .40
232 Derrek Lee RC 3.00 8.00
233 Brady Anderson .15 .40
234 Vic Darensbourg RC .15 .40
235 Mark Langston .08 .25
236 T.J.Mathews RC .15 .40
237 Lou Whitaker .15 .40
238 Roger Cedeno .08 .25
239 Alex Fernandez .08 .25
240 Ryan Thompson .08 .25
241 Kerry Lacy RC .15 .40
242 Reggie Sanders .15 .40
243 Brad Pennington .08 .25
244 Bryan Eversgerd RC .15 .40
245 Greg Maddux .60 1.50
246 Jason Kendall .15 .40
247 J.R. Phillips .08 .25
248 Bobby Witt .08 .25
249 Paul O'Neill .25 .60
250 Ryne Sandberg .60 1.50
251 Charles Nagy .08 .25
252 Kevin Stocker .08 .25
253 Shawn Green .40 1.00
254 Charlie Hayes .08 .25
255 Donnie Elliott .08 .25
256 Rob Fitzpatrick RC .15 .40
257 Tim Davis .08 .25
258 James Mouton .08 .25
259 Mike Greenwell .08 .25
260 Ray McDavid .08 .25
261 Mike Kelly .08 .25
262 Andy Larkin RC .15 .40
263 Marquis Riley UER .08 .25
No card number on back
264 Bob Tewksbury .08 .25
265 Brian Edmondson .08 .25
266 Eduardo Lantigua RC .15 .40
267 Brandon Wilson .08 .25
268 Mike Welch .08 .25
269 Tom Henke .08 .25
270 Pokey Reese .08 .25
271 Gregg Zaun RC .40 1.00
272 Todd Ritchie .08 .25
273 Javier Lopez .15 .40
274 Kevin Young .08 .25
275 Kirt Manwaring .08 .25
276 Bill Taylor RC .15 .40
277 Robert Eenhoorn .08 .25
278 Jessie Hollins .08 .25
279 Julian Tavarez RC .40 1.00
280 Gene Schall .08 .25
281 Paul Molitor .15 .40
282 Neifi Perez RC .40 1.00
283 Greg Gagne .08 .25
284 Marquis Grissom .15 .40
285 Randy Johnson .40 1.00
286 Pete Harnisch .08 .25
287 Joel Bennett RC .15 .40
288 Derek Bell .08 .25
289 Darryl Hamilton .08 .25
290 Gary Sheffield .15 .40
291 Eduardo Perez .08 .25
292 Basil Shabazz .08 .25
293 Eric Davis .15 .40
294 Pedro Astacio .08 .25
295 Robin Ventura .15 .40
296 Jeff Kent .25 .60
297 Rick Helling .08 .25
298 Joe Oliver .08 .25
299 Lee Smith .15 .40
300 Dave Winfield .15 .40
301 Deion Sanders .25 .60
302 Ravelo Manzanillo RC .15 .40
303 Mark Portugal .08 .25
304 Brent Gates .08 .25
305 Wade Boggs .25 .60
306 Rick Wilkins .08 .25
307 Carlos Baerga .08 .25
308 Curt Schilling .15 .40
309 Shannon Stewart .40 1.00
310 Darren Holmes .08 .25
311 Robert Toth RC .15 .40
312 Gabe White .08 .25
313 Mac Suzuki RC .40 1.00
314 Alvin Morman RC .15 .40
315 Mo Vaughn .15 .40
316 Bryce Florie RC .15 .40
317 Gabby Martinez RC .15 .40
318 Carl Everett .15 .40
319 Kerwin Moore .08 .25
320 Tom Pagnozzi .08 .25
321 Chris Gomez .08 .25
322 Todd Williams .08 .25
323 Pat Hentgen .08 .25
324 Kirk Presley RC .15 .40
325 Kevin Brown .15 .40
326 Jason Isringhausen RC 1.25 3.00
327 Rick Forney RC .15 .40
328 Carlos Pulido RC .15 .40
329 Terrell Wade RC .15 .40
330 Al Martin .08 .25
331 Dan Carlson RC .15 .40
332 Mark Acre RC .15 .40
333 Sterling Hitchcock .08 .25
334 Jon Ratliff RC .15 .40
335 Alex Ramirez RC .15 .40
336 Phil Geisler RC .08 .25
337 Eddie Zambrano FOIL RC .15 .40
338 Jim Thome FOIL .25 .60
339 James Mouton FOIL .08 .25
340 Cliff Floyd FOIL .15 .40
341 Carlos Delgado FOIL .25 .60
342 Roberto Petagine FOIL .08 .25
343 Tim Clark FOIL .08 .25
344 Bubba Smith FOIL .08 .25
345 Randy Curtis FOIL RC .15 .40
346 Joe Biasucci FOIL RC .15 .40
347 D.J. Boston FOIL RC .15 .40
348 Ruben Rivera FOIL RC .15 .40
349 Bryan Link FOIL RC .15 .40
350 Mike Bell FOIL RC .15 .40
351 Marty Watson FOIL RC .15 .40
352 Jason Myers FOIL .08 .25
353 Chipper Jones FOIL .40 1.00
354 Brooks Kieschnick FOIL .15 .40
355 Pokey Reese FOIL .08 .25
356 John Burke FOIL .08 .25
357 Kurt Miller FOIL .08 .25
358 Orlando Miller FOIL .08 .25
359 Todd Hollandsworth FOIL .08 .25
360 Rondell White FOIL .15 .40
361 Bill Pulsipher FOIL .15 .40
362 Tyler Green FOIL .08 .25
363 Midre Cummings FOIL .08 .25
364 Brian Barber FOIL .08 .25
365 Melvin Nieves FOIL .08 .25
366 Salomon Torres FOIL .08 .25
367 Alex Ochoa FOIL .08 .25
368 Frankie Rodriguez FOIL .08 .25
369 Brian Anderson FOIL .15 .40
370 James Baldwin FOIL .08 .25
371 Manny Ramirez FOIL .40 1.00
372 Justin Thompson FOIL .08 .25
373 Johnny Damon FOIL .25 .60
374 Jeff D'Amico FOIL .15 .40
375 Rich Becker FOIL .08 .25
376 Derek Jeter FOIL 1.25 3.00
377 Steve Karsay FOIL .08 .25
378 Mac Suzuki FOIL .15 .40
379 Benji Gil FOIL .08 .25
380 Alex Gonzalez FOIL .08 .25
381 Jason Bere FOIL .08 .25
382 Brett Butler FOIL .15 .40
383 Jeff Conine FOIL .15 .40
384 Darren Daulton FOIL .15 .40
385 Jeff Kent FOIL .25 .60
386 Don Mattingly FOIL 1.00 2.50
387 Mike Piazza FOIL .75 2.00
388 Ryne Sandberg FOIL .60 1.50
389 Rich Amaral .08 .25
390 Craig Biggio .25 .60
391 Jeff Suppan RC .75 2.00
392 Andy Benes .08 .25
393 Cal Eldred .08 .25
394 Jeff Conine .15 .40
395 Tim Salmon .25 .60
396 Ray Suplee RC .15 .40
397 Tony Phillips .08 .25
398 Ramon Martinez .08 .25
399 Julio Franco .15 .40
400 Dwight Gooden .15 .40
401 Kevin Loman RC .15 .40
402 Jose Rijo .08 .25
403 Mike Devereaux .08 .25
404 Mike Zolecki RC .15 .40
405 Fred McGriff .25 .60
406 Danny Clyburn .08 .25
407 Robby Thompson .08 .25
408 Terry Steinbach .08 .25
409 Luis Polonia .08 .25
410 Mark Grace .25 .60
411 Albert Belle .15 .40
412 John Kruk .15 .40
413 Scott Spiezio RC .40 1.00
414 Ellis Burks UER .15 .40
Name spelled Elkis on front
415 Joe Vitiello .08 .25
416 Tim Costo .08 .25
417 Marc Newfield .08 .25
418 Oscar Henriquez RC .15 .40
419 Matt Perisho RC .15 .40
420 Julio Bruno .08 .25
421 Kenny Felder .08 .25
422 Tyler Green .08 .25
423 Jim Edmonds .40 1.00
424 Ozzie Smith .60 1.50
425 Rick Greene .08 .25
426 Todd Hollandsworth .08 .25
427 Eddie Pearson RC .15 .40
428 Quilvio Veras .08 .25
429 Kenny Rogers .15 .40
430 Willie Greene .08 .25
431 Vaughn Eshelman .08 .25
432 Pat Meares .08 .25
433 Jermaine Dye RC 2.50 6.00
434 Steve Cooke .08 .25
435 Bill Swift .08 .25
436 Fausto Cruz RC .15 .40
437 Mark Hutton .08 .25
438 Brooks Kieschnick RC .15 .40
439 Yorkis Perez .08 .25
440 Len Dykstra .15 .40
441 Pat Borders .08 .25
442 Doug Walls RC .15 .40
443 Wally Joyner .15 .40
444 Ken Hill .08 .25
445 Eric Anthony .08 .25
446 Mitch Williams .08 .25
447 Cory Bailey RC .15 .40
448 Dave Staton .08 .25
449 Greg Vaughn .08 .25
450 Dave Magadan .08 .25
451 Chili Davis .15 .40
452 Gerald Santos RC .15 .40
453 Joe Perona .08 .25
454 Delino DeShields .08 .25
455 Jack McDowell .08 .25
456 Todd Hundley .08 .25
457 Ritchie Moody .08 .25
458 Bret Boone .15 .40
459 Ben McDonald .08 .25
460 Kirby Puckett .40 1.00
461 Gregg Olson .08 .25
462 Rich Aude RC .15 .40
463 John Burkett .08 .25
464 Troy Neel .08 .25
465 Jimmy Key .15 .40
466 Ozzie Timmons .08 .25
467 Eddie Murray .40 1.00
468 Mark Tranberg RC .15 .40
469 Alex Gonzalez .08 .25
470 David Nied .08 .25
471 Barry Larkin .25 .60
472 Brian Looney RC .15 .40
473 Shawn Estes .08 .25
474 A.J.Sager RC .15 .40
475 Roger Clemens .75 2.00
476 Vince Moore .08 .25
477 Scott Karl RC .15 .40
478 Kurt Miller .08 .25
479 Garret Anderson .40 1.00
480 Allen Watson .08 .25
481 Jose Lima RC .40 1.00
482 Rick Gorecki .08 .25
483 Jimmy Hurst RC .15 .40
484 Preston Wilson .15 .40
485 Will Clark .25 .60
486 Mike Ferry RC .15 .40
487 Curtis Goodwin RC .15 .40
488 Mike Myers .08 .25
489 Chipper Jones .40 1.00
490 Jeff King .08 .25
491 W.VanLandingham RC .15 .40
492 Carlos Reyes RC .15 .40
493 Andy Pettitte .40 1.00
494 Brant Brown .08 .25
495 Daron Kirkreit .08 .25
496 Ricky Bottalico RC .15 .40
497 Devon White .15 .40
498 Jason Johnson RC .40 1.00
499 Vince Coleman .08 .25
500 Larry Walker .15 .40
501 Bobby Ayala .08 .25
502 Steve Finley .15 .40
503 Scott Fletcher .08 .25
504 Brad Ausmus .25 .60
505 Scott Talanoa RC .15 .40
506 Orestes Destrade .08 .25
507 Gary DiSarcina .08 .25
508 Willie Smith RC .15 .40
509 Alan Trammell .15 .40
510 Mike Piazza .75 2.00
511 Ozzie Guillen .15 .40
512 Jeromy Burnitz .15 .40
513 Darren Oliver RC .40 1.00
514 Kevin Mitchell .08 .25
515 Rafael Palmeiro .25 .60
516 David McCarty .08 .25
517 Jeff Blauser .08 .25
518 Trey Beamon .08 .25
519 Royce Clayton .08 .25
520 Dennis Eckersley .15 .40
521 Bernie Williams .25 .60
522 Steve Buechele .08 .25
523 Dennis Martinez .15 .40
524 Dave Hollins .08 .25
525 Joey Hamilton .08 .25
526 Andres Galarraga .15 .40
527 Jeff Granger .08 .25
528 Joey Eischen .08 .25
529 Desi Relaford .08 .25
530 Roberto Petagine .08 .25
531 Andre Dawson .15 .40
532 Ray Holbert .08 .25
533 Duane Singleton .08 .25
534 Kurt Abbott RC .15 .40
535 Bo Jackson .40 1.00
536 Gregg Jefferies .08 .25
537 David Mysel .08 .25
538 Raul Mondesi .15 .40
539 Chris Snopek .08 .25
540 Brook Fordyce .08 .25
541 Ron Frazier RC .15 .40
542 Brian Koelling .08 .25
543 Jimmy Haynes .08 .25
544 Marty Cordova .08 .25
545 Jason Green RC .15 .40
546 Orlando Merced .08 .25
547 Lou Pote RC .15 .40
548 Todd Van Poppel .08 .25
549 Pat Kelly .08 .25
550 Turk Wendell .08 .25
551 Herbert Perry RC .15 .40
552 Ryan Karp RC .15 .40
553 Juan Guzman .08 .25
554 Bryan Rekar RC .15 .40
555 Kevin Appier .15 .40
556 Chris Schwab RC .15 .40
557 Jay Buhner .15 .40
558 Andujar Cedeno .08 .25
559 Ryan McGuire RC .15 .40
560 Ricky Gutierrez .08 .25
561 Keith Kimsey RC .15 .40
562 Tim Clark .08 .25
563 Damion Easley .08 .25
564 Clint Davis RC .15 .40
565 Mike Moore .08 .25
566 Orel Hershiser .15 .40
567 Jason Bere .08 .25
568 Kevin McReynolds .08 .25
569 Leland Macon RC .15 .40
570 John Courtright RC .15 .40
571 Sid Fernandez .08 .25
572 Chad Roper .08 .25
573 Terry Pendleton .15 .40
574 Danny Miceli .08 .25
575 Joe Rosselli .08 .25
576 Mike Bordick .08 .25
577 Danny Tartabull .08 .25
578 Jose Guzman .08 .25
579 Omar Vizquel .25 .60
580 Tommy Greene .08 .25
581 Paul Spoljaric .08 .25
582 Walt Weiss .08 .25
583 Oscar Jimenez RC .15 .40
584 Rod Henderson .08 .25
585 Derek Lowe .15 .40
586 Richard Hidalgo RC .40 1.00
587 Shayne Bennett RC .15 .40
588 Tim Belk RC .15 .40
589 Matt Mieske .08 .25
590 Nigel Wilson .08 .25
591 Jeff Knox RC .15 .40
592 Bernard Gilkey .08 .25
593 David Cone .15 .40
594 Paul LoDuca RC 2.00 5.00
595 Scott Ruffcorn .08 .25
596 Chris Roberts .08 .25
597 Oscar Munoz RC .15 .40
598 Scott Sullivan RC .15 .40
599 Matt Jarvis RC .15 .40
600 Jose Canseco .25 .60
601 Tony Graffanino RC .60 1.50
602 Don Slaught .08 .25
603 Brett King RC .15 .40
604 Jose Herrera RC .15 .40
605 Melido Perez .08 .25
606 Mike Hubbard RC .15 .40
607 Chad Ogea .08 .25
608 Wayne Gomes RC .40 1.00
609 Roberto Alomar .25 .60
610 Angel Echevarria RC .15 .40
611 Jose Lind .08 .25
612 Darrin Fletcher .08 .25
613 Chris Bosio .08 .25
614 Darryl Kile .15 .40
615 Frankie Rodriguez .08 .25
616 Phil Plantier .08 .25
617 Pat Listach .08 .25
618 Charlie Hough .15 .40
619 Ryan Hancock RC .15 .40
620 Darrel Deak RC .15 .40
621 Travis Fryman .15 .40
622 Brett Butler .15 .40
623 Lance Johnson .08 .25
624 Pete Smith .08 .25
625 James Hurst RC .15 .40
626 Roberto Kelly .08 .25
627 Mike Mussina .25 .60
628 Kevin Tapani .08 .25
629 John Smoltz .25 .60
630 Midre Cummings .08 .25
631 Salomon Torres .08 .25
632 Willie Adams .08 .25
633 Derek Jeter 1.25 3.00
634 Steve Trachsel .08 .25
635 Albie Lopez .08 .25
636 Jason Moler .08 .25
637 Carlos Delgado .25 .60
638 Roberto Mejia .08 .25
639 Darren Burton .08 .25
640 B.J. Wallace .08 .25
641 Brad Clontz RC .15 .40
642 Billy Wagner RC 1.50 4.00
643 Aaron Sele .08 .25
644 Cameron Cairncross .08 .25
645 Brian Harper .08 .25
646 Marc Valdes UER .08 .25
No card number on back
647 Mark Ratekin .08 .25
648 Terry Bradshaw RC .15 .40
649 Justin Thompson .08 .25
650 Mike Busch RC .15 .40
651 Joe Hall RC .15 .40
652 Bobby Jones .08 .25
653 Kelly Stinnett RC .40 1.00
654 Rod Steph RC .15 .40
655 Jay Powell RC .40 1.00
656 Keith Garagozzo RC UER .15 .40
No card number on back
657 Todd Dunn .08 .25
658 Charles Peterson RC .15 .40
659 Darren Lewis .08 .25
660 John Wasdin RC .15 .40
661 Tate Seefried RC .15 .40
662 Hector Trinidad RC .15 .40
663 John Carter RC .08 .25
664 Larry Mitchell .08 .25
665 David Catlett RC .15 .40
666 Dante Bichette .15 .40
667 Felix Jose .08 .25
668 Rondell White .15 .40
669 Tino Martinez .25 .60
670 Brian L.Hunter .08 .25
671 Jose Malave .08 .25
672 Archi Cianfrocco .08 .25
673 Mike Matheny RC .60 1.50
674 Bret Barberie .08 .25
675 Andrew Lorraine RC .15 .40
676 Brian Jordan .15 .40
677 Tim Belcher .08 .25
678 Antonio Osuna RC .15 .40
679 Checklist .08 .25
680 Checklist .08 .25
681 Checklist .08 .25
682 Checklist .08 .25

1994 Bowman Superstar Samplers

1 Joe Carter .60 1.50
5 Ken Griffey Jr. 4.00 10.00
15 Frank Thomas 2.00 5.00
21 Tom Glavine 1.50 4.00
25 Don Mattingly 1.50 4.00
45 Juan Gonzalez 1.25 3.00
50 Andy Van Slyke .40 1.00
55 Manny Ramirez 2.00 5.00
69 Cecil Fielder .60 1.50
75 Cal Ripken 6.00 15.00
79 Matt Williams 1.00 2.50
118 Jeff Bagwell 2.00 5.00
120 Tony Gwynn 3.00 8.00
128 Bobby Bonilla .60 1.50
133 David Justice 1.25 3.00
135 Barry Bonds 3.00 8.00
140 Darren Daulton .60 1.50
169 John Olerud .60 1.50
200 Cliff Floyd 1.00 2.50
245 Greg Maddux 4.00 10.00
250 Ryne Sandberg 2.50 6.00
281 Paul Molitor 1.50 4.00
284 Marquis Grissom .60 1.50
285 Randy Johnson 2.50 6.00
290 Gary Sheffield 2.00 5.00
307 Carlos Baerga .40 1.00
315 Mo Vaughn .60 1.50
395 Tim Salmon .60 1.50
405 Fred McGriff 1.00 2.50
410 Mark Grace 1.00 2.50
411 Albert Belle .60 1.50
440 Len Dykstra .40 1.00
455 Jack McDowell .40 1.00
460 Kirby Puckett 2.00 5.00
471 Barry Larkin 1.25 3.00
475 Roger Clemens 3.00 8.00
485 Will Clark 1.25 3.00
500 Larry Walker 1.50 4.00
510 Mike Piazza 3.00 8.00
515 Rafael Palmeiro 1.50 4.00
526 Andres Galarraga 1.25 3.00
536 Gregg Jefferies .40 1.00
538 Raul Mondesi .60 1.50
600 Jose Canseco 2.00 5.00
609 Roberto Alomar 1.25 3.00

1995 Bowman

Cards from this 439-card standard-size prospect-oriented set were primarily issued in plastic wrapped packs and jumbo packs. Card fronts feature white borders enframing full color photos. The left border is a reversed negative of the photo. The set includes 54 silver foil subset cards (221-274). The foil subset, largely comprising of minor league stars, have embossed borders and are found one per pack and two per jumbo pack. Rookie Cards of note include Bob Abreu, Bartolo Colon, Vladmir Guerrero, Andruw Jones, Hideo Nomo and Scott Rolen.

COMPLETE SET (439) 30.00 60.00
ONE SILVER FOIL PER PACK/TWO PER JUMBO
1 Billy Wagner .30 .75
2 Chris Widger .08 .25
3 Brent Bowers .08 .25
4 Bob Abreu RC 3.00 8.00
5 Lou Collier RC .40 1.00
6 Juan Acevedo RC .20 .50
7 Jason Kelley RC .20 .50
8 Brian Sackinsky .08 .25
9 Scott Christman .08 .25
10 Damon Hollins .08 .25
11 Willis Otanez RC .20 .50
12 Jason Ryan RC .20 .50
13 Jason Giambi .30 .75
14 Andy Taulbee RC .20 .50
15 Mark Thompson .08 .25
16 Hugo Pivaral RC .20 .50
17 Brien Taylor .08 .25
18 Antonio Osuna .08 .25
19 Edgardo Alfonzo .08 .25
20 Carl Everett .20 .50
21 Matt Drews .08 .25
22 Bartolo Colon RC 1.25 3.00
23 Andruw Jones RC 12.00 30.00
24 Robert Person RC .40 1.00
25 Derrek Lee .50 1.25
26 John Ambrose RC .20 .50
27 Eric Knowles RC .20 .50
28 Chris Roberts .08 .25
29 Don Wengert .08 .25
30 Marcus Jensen RC .40 1.00
31 Brian Barber .08 .25
32 Kevin Brown C .20 .50
33 Benji Gil .08 .25
34 Mike Hubbard .08 .25
35 Bart Evans RC .20 .50
36 Enrique Wilson RC .20 .50
37 Brian Buchanan RC .20 .50
38 Ken Ray RC .20 .50
39 Micah Franklin RC .20 .50
40 Ricky Otero RC .20 .50
41 Jason Kendall .20 .50
42 Jimmy Hurst .08 .25
43 Jerry Wolak RC .20 .50
44 Jayson Peterson RC .20 .50
45 Allen Battle RC .20 .50
46 Scott Stahoviak .08 .25
47 Steve Schrenk RC .20 .50
48 Travis Miller RC .20 .50
49 Eddie Rios RC .20 .50
50 Mike Hampton .20 .50
51 Chad Frontera RC .20 .50
52 Tom Evans .08 .25
53 C.J. Nitkowski .08 .25
54 Clay Caruthers RC .20 .50
55 Shannon Stewart .20 .50
56 Jorge Posada .50 1.25
57 Aaron Holbert .08 .25
58 Harry Berrios RC .20 .50
59 Steve Rodriguez .08 .25
60 Shane Andrews .08 .25
61 Will Cunnane RC .20 .50
62 Richard Hidalgo .08 .25
63 Bill Selby RC .20 .50
64 Jay Cranford RC .20 .50
65 Jeff Suppan .20 .50
66 Curtis Goodwin .08 .25
67 John Thomson RC .40 1.00
68 Justin Thompson .08 .25
69 Troy Percival .20 .50
70 Matt Wagner RC .20 .50
71 Terry Bradshaw .08 .25
72 Greg Hansell .08 .25
73 John Burke .08 .25
74 Jeff D'Amico .08 .25
75 Ernie Young .08 .25
76 Jason Bates .08 .25
77 Chris Stynes .08 .25
78 Cade Gaspar RC .20 .50
79 Melvin Nieves .08 .25
80 Rick Gorecki .08 .25
81 Felix Rodriguez RC .20 .50
82 Ryan Hancock .08 .25
83 Chris Carpenter RC 3.00 8.00
84 Ray McDavid .08 .25
85 Chris Wimmer .08 .25
86 Doug Glanville .08 .25
87 DeShawn Warren .08 .25
88 Damian Moss RC .20 .50
89 Rafael Orellano RC .20 .50
90 Vladimir Guerrero RC ! 12.00 30.00
91 Raul Casanova RC .20 .50
92 Karim Garcia RC .20 .50
93 Bryce Florie .08 .25
94 Kevin Orie .08 .25
95 Ryan Nye RC .20 .50
96 Matt Sachse RC .20 .50
97 Ivan Arteaga RC .20 .50
98 Glenn Murray .08 .25
99 Stacy Hollins RC .20 .50
100 Jim Pittsley .08 .25
101 Craig Mattson RC .20 .50
102 Neifi Perez .08 .25
103 Keith Williams .08 .25
104 Roger Cedeno .08 .25
105 Tony Terry RC .20 .50
106 Jose Malave .08 .25
107 Joe Rosselli .08 .25
108 Kevin Jordan .08 .25
109 Sid Roberson RC .20 .50
110 Alan Embree .08 .25
111 Terrell Wade .08 .25
112 Bob Wolcott .08 .25
113 Carlos Perez RC .40 1.00
114 Mike Bovee RC .20 .50
115 Tommy Davis RC .20 .50
116 Jeremey Kendall RC .20 .50
117 Rich Aude .08 .25
118 Rick Huisman .08 .25
119 Tim Belk .08 .25
120 Edgar Renteria .20 .50
121 Calvin Maduro RC .20 .50
122 Jerry Martin RC .20 .50
123 Ramon Fermin RC .20 .50
124 Kimera Bartee RC .20 .50
125 Mark Farris .08 .25
126 Frank Rodriguez .08 .25
127 Bob Higginson RC .75 2.00
128 Bret Wagner .08 .25
129 Edwin Diaz RC .20 .50
130 Jimmy Haynes .08 .25
131 Chris Weinke RC QB .40 1.00
132 Damian Jackson RC .20 .50
133 Felix Martinez .08 .25
134 Edwin Hurtado RC .20 .50
135 Matt Raleigh RC .20 .50
136 Paul Wilson .08 .25
137 Ron Villone .08 .25
138 Eric Stuckenschneider RC .20 .50
139 Tate Seefried .08 .25
140 Rey Ordonez RC .75 2.00
141 Eddie Pearson .08 .25
142 Kevin Gallaher .08 .25
143 Torii Hunter .30 .75
144 Daron Kirkreit .08 .25
145 Craig Wilson .08 .25
146 Ugueth Urbina .08 .25
147 Chris Snopek .08 .25
148 Kym Ashworth .08 .25
149 Wayne Gomes .08 .25
150 Mark Loretta .20 .50
151 Ramon Morel RC .20 .50
152 Trot Nixon .20 .50
153 Desi Relaford .08 .25
154 Scott Sullivan .08 .25
155 Marc Barcelo .08 .25
156 Willie Adams .08 .25
157 Derrick Gibson RC .20 .50
158 Brian Meadows RC .20 .50
159 Julian Tavarez .08 .25
160 Bryan Rekar .08 .25
161 Steve Gibralter .08 .25
162 Esteban Loaiza .08 .25
163 John Wasdin .08 .25
164 Kirk Presley .08 .25
165 Mariano Rivera 1.25 3.00
166 Andy Larkin .08 .25
167 Sean Whiteside RC .20 .50
168 Matt Apana RC .20 .50
169 Shawn Senior RC .20 .50
170 Scott Gentile .08 .25
171 Quilvio Veras .08 .25
172 Eli Marrero RC .60 1.50
173 Mendy Lopez RC .20 .50
174 Homer Bush .08 .25
175 Brian Stephenson RC .20 .50
176 Jon Nunnally .08 .25
177 Jose Herrera .08 .25
178 Corey Avrard RC .20 .50
179 David Bell .08 .25
180 Jason Isringhausen .20 .50
181 Jamey Wright .08 .25
182 Lonell Roberts RC .08 .25
183 Marty Cordova .08 .25
184 Amaury Telemaco .08 .25
185 John Mabry .08 .25
186 Andrew Vessel RC .20 .50
187 Jim Cole RC .20 .50
188 Marquis Riley .08 .25
189 Todd Dunn .08 .25
190 John Carter .08 .25
191 Donnie Sadler RC .40 1.00
192 Mike Bell .08 .25
193 Chris Cumberland RC .20 .50
194 Jason Schmidt .50 1.25
195 Matt Brunson .08 .25
196 James Baldwin .08 .25
197 Bill Simas RC .20 .50
198 Gus Gandarillas .08 .25
199 Mac Suzuki .08 .25
200 Rick Holifield RC .20 .50
201 Fernando Lunar RC .20 .50
202 Kevin Jarvis .08 .25
203 Everett Stull .08 .25
204 Steve Wojciechowski .08 .25
205 Shawn Estes .08 .25
206 Jermaine Dye .20 .50
207 Marc Kroon .08 .25
208 Peter Munro RC .40 1.00
209 Pat Watkins .08 .25
210 Matt Smith .08 .25
211 Joe Vitiello .08 .25
212 Gerald Witasick Jr. .08 .25
213 Freddy Adrian Garcia RC .20 .50
214 Glenn Dishman RC .20 .50
215 Jay Canizaro RC .20 .50
216 Angel Martinez .08 .25
217 Yamil Benitez RC .20 .50
218 Fausto Macey RC .20 .50
219 Eric Owens .08 .25
220 Checklist .08 .25
221 Dwayne Hosey FOIL RC .20 .50
222 Brad Woodall FOIL RC .20 .50
223 Billy Ashley FOIL .08 .25
224 Mark Grudzielanek FOIL RC .75 2.00
225 Mark Johnson FOIL RC .40 1.00
226 Tim Unroe FOIL RC .20 .50
227 Todd Greene FOIL .08 .25
228 Larry Sutton FOIL .08 .25
229 Derek Jeter FOIL 1.50 4.00
230 Sal Fasano FOIL RC .20 .50
231 Ruben Rivera FOIL .08 .25
232 Chris Truby FOIL RC .20 .50
233 John Donati FOIL .08 .25
234 Decomba Conner FOIL RC .20 .50
235 Sergio Nunez FOIL RC .20 .50
236 Ray Brown FOIL RC .20 .50
237 Juan Melo FOIL RC .20 .50
238 Hideo Nomo FOIL RC 2.00 5.00
239 Jaime Bluma RC FOIL .20 .50
240 Jay Payton FOIL RC .75 2.00
241 Paul Konerko FOIL 1.50 4.00
242 Scott Elarton FOIL RC .40 1.00
243 Jeff Abbott FOIL RC .40 1.00
244 Jim Brower FOIL RC .20 .50
245 Geoff Blum FOIL RC .75 2.00
246 Aaron Boone FOIL RC .75 2.00
247 J.R. Phillips FOIL .08 .25
248 Alex Ochoa FOIL .08 .25
249 Nomar Garciaparra FOIL 1.50 4.00
250 Garret Anderson FOIL .20 .50
251 Ray Durham FOIL .20 .50
252 Paul Shuey FOIL .08 .25
253 Tony Clark FOIL .08 .25
254 Johnny Damon FOIL .30 .75
255 Duane Singleton FOIL .08 .25
256 LaTroy Hawkins FOIL .08 .25
257 Andy Pettitte FOIL .30 .75
258 Ben Grieve FOIL .08 .25
259 Marc Newfield FOIL .08 .25
260 Terrell Lowery FOIL .08 .25
261 Shawn Green FOIL .20 .50
262 Chipper Jones FOIL .50 1.25
263 Brooks Kieschnick FOIL .08 .25
264 Pokey Reese FOIL .08 .25
265 Doug Million FOIL .08 .25
266 Marc Valdes FOIL .08 .25
267 Brian L.Hunter FOIL .08 .25
268 Todd Hollandsworth FOIL .08 .25
269 Rod Henderson FOIL .08 .25
270 Bill Pulsipher FOIL .08 .25
271 Scott Rolen FOIL RC 5.00 12.00
272 Trey Beamon FOIL .08 .25
273 Alan Benes FOIL .08 .25
274 Dustin Hermanson FOIL .08 .25
275 Ricky Bottalico .08 .25
276 Albert Belle .20 .50
277 Deion Sanders .30 .75
278 Matt Williams .20 .50
279 Jeff Bagwell .30 .75
280 Kirby Puckett .50 1.25
281 Dave Hollins .08 .25
282 Don Mattingly 1.25 3.00
283 Joey Hamilton .08 .25
284 Bobby Bonilla .20 .50
285 Moises Alou .20 .50
286 Tom Glavine .30 .75
287 Brett Butler .20 .50
288 Chris Hoiles .08 .25
289 Kenny Rogers .20 .50
290 Larry Walker .20 .50
291 Tim Raines .20 .50
292 Kevin Appier .20 .50
293 Roger Clemens 1.00 2.50
294 Chuck Carr .08 .25
295 Randy Myers .08 .25
296 Dave Nilsson .08 .25
297 Joe Carter .20 .50
298 Chuck Finley .20 .50
299 Ray Lankford .20 .50
300 Roberto Kelly .08 .25
301 Jon Lieber .08 .25
302 Travis Fryman .20 .50
303 Mark McGwire 1.25 3.00
304 Tony Gwynn .60 1.50
305 Kenny Lofton .20 .50
306 Mark Whiten .08 .25

307 Doug Drabek .08 .25
308 Terry Steinbach .08 .25
309 Ryan Klesko .20 .50
310 Mike Piazza .75 2.00
311 Ben McDonald .08 .25
312 Reggie Sanders .20 .50
313 Alex Fernandez .08 .25
314 Aaron Sele .08 .25
315 Gregg Jefferies .08 .25
316 Rickey Henderson .50 1.25
317 Brian Anderson .08 .25
318 Jose Valentin .08 .25
319 Rod Beck .08 .25
320 Marquis Grissom .20 .50
321 Ken Griffey Jr. 1.00 2.50
322 Bret Saberhagen .20 .50
323 Juan Gonzalez .20 .50
324 Paul Molitor .20 .50
325 Gary Sheffield .20 .50
326 Darren Daulton .20 .50
327 Bill Swift .08 .25
328 Brian McRae .08 .25
329 Robin Ventura .20 .50
330 Lee Smith .20 .50
331 Fred McGriff .30 .75
332 Delino DeShields .08 .25
333 Edgar Martinez .30 .75
334 Mike Mussina .30 .75
335 Orlando Merced .08 .25
336 Carlos Baerga .08 .25
337 Wil Cordero .08 .25
338 Tom Pagnozzi .08 .25
339 Pat Hentgen .08 .25
340 Chad Curtis .08 .25
341 Darren Lewis .08 .25
342 Jeff Kent .20 .50
343 Bip Roberts .08 .25
344 Ivan Rodriguez .30 .75
345 Jeff Montgomery .08 .25
346 Hal Morris .08 .25
347 Danny Tartabull .08 .25
348 Raul Mondesi .20 .50
349 Ken Hill .08 .25
350 Pedro Martinez .30 .75
351 Frank Thomas .50 1.25
352 Manny Ramirez .30 .75
353 Tim Salmon .30 .75
354 W. VanLandingham .08 .25
355 Andres Galarraga .20 .50
356 Paul O'Neill .30 .75
357 Brady Anderson .20 .50
358 Ramon Martinez .08 .25
359 John Olerud .20 .50
360 Ruben Sierra .20 .50
361 Cal Eldred .08 .25
362 Jay Buhner .20 .50
363 Jay Bell .20 .50
364 Wally Joyner .20 .50
365 Chuck Knoblauch .20 .50
366 Len Dykstra .20 .50
367 John Wetteland .20 .50
368 Roberto Alomar .30 .75
369 Craig Biggio .30 .75
370 Ozzie Smith .75 2.00
371 Terry Pendleton .20 .50
372 Sammy Sosa .50 1.25
373 Carlos Garcia .08 .25
374 Jose Rijo .08 .25
375 Chris Gomez .08 .25
376 Barry Bonds 1.25 3.00
377 Steve Avery .08 .25
378 Rick Wilkins .08 .25
379 Pete Harnisch .08 .25
380 Dean Palmer .20 .50
381 Bob Hamelin .08 .25
382 Jason Bere .08 .25
383 Jimmy Key .20 .50
384 Dante Bichette .20 .50
385 Rafael Palmeiro .30 .75
386 David Justice .20 .50
387 Chili Davis .20 .50
388 Mike Greenwell .08 .25
389 Todd Zeile .08 .25
390 Jeff Conine .20 .50
391 Rick Aguilera .08 .25
392 Eddie Murray .50 1.25
393 Mike Stanley .08 .25
394 Cliff Floyd UER .20 .50
395 Randy Johnson .50 1.25
396 David Nied .08 .25
397 Devon White .20 .50
398 Royce Clayton .08 .25
399 Andy Benes .08 .25
400 John Hudek .08 .25
401 Bobby Jones .08 .25
402 Eric Karros .20 .50
403 Will Clark .30 .75
404 Mark Langston .08 .25
405 Kevin Brown .20 .50
406 Greg Maddux .75 2.00
407 David Cone .20 .50
408 Wade Boggs .30 .75
409 Steve Trachsel .08 .25
410 Greg Vaughn .08 .25
411 Mo Vaughn .20 .50
412 Wilson Alvarez .08 .25
413 Cal Ripken 1.50 4.00
414 Rico Brogna .08 .25
415 Barry Larkin .30 .75
416 Cecil Fielder .20 .50
417 Jose Canseco .30 .75
418 Jack McDowell .08 .25
419 Mike Lieberthal .20 .50
420 Andrew Lorraine .08 .25
421 Rich Becker .08 .25
422 Tony Phillips .08 .25
423 Scott Ruffcorn .08 .25
424 Jeff Granger .08 .25
425 Greg Pirkl .08 .25
426 Dennis Eckersley .20 .50
427 Jose Lima .08 .25
428 Russ Davis .08 .25
429 Armando Benitez .08 .25
430 Alex Gonzalez .08 .25
431 Carlos Delgado .20 .50
432 Chan Ho Park .20 .50
433 Mickey Tettleton .08 .25
434 Dave Winfield .20 .50
435 John Burkett .08 .25
436 Orlando Miller .08 .25
437 Rondell White .20 .50
438 Jose Oliva .08 .25
439 Checklist .08 .25

1995 Bowman Gold Foil

COMPLETE SET (54) 75.00 150.00
*STARS: .6X TO 1.5X BASIC CARDS
*ROOKIES: .5X TO 1.2X BASIC
STATED ODDS 1:6
229 Derek Jeter 12.00 30.00

1996 Bowman

The 1996 Bowman set was issued in one series totalling 385 cards. The 11-card packs retailed for $2.50 each. The fronts feature color action player photos in a tan-checkered frame with the player's name printed in silver foil at the bottom. The backs carry another color player photo with player information, 1995 and career player statistics. Each pack contained 10 regular issue cards plus either one foil parallel or an insert card. In a special promotional program, Topps offered collector's a $100 guarantee on complete sets. To get the guarantee, collectors had to mail in a Guaranteed Value Certificate request form, found in packs, along with a $5 processing and registration fee before the December 31st, 1996 deadline. Collectors would then receive a $100 Guaranteed Value Certificate, of which they could mail back to Topps between August 31st, 1999 and December 31st, 1999, along with their complete set, to receive $100. A reprint version of the 1952 Bowman Mickey Mantle card was randomly inserted into packs. Rookie Cards in this set include Russell Branyan, Mike Cameron, Luis Castillo, Ryan Dempster, Livan Hernandez, Geoff Jenkins, Ben Petrick and Mike Sweeney

COMPLETE SET (385) 20.00 50.00
MANTLE STATED ODDS 1:48
1 Cal Ripken 1.00 2.50
2 Ray Durham .10 .30
3 Ivan Rodriguez .20 .50
4 Fred McGriff .20 .50
5 Hideo Nomo .30 .75
6 Troy Percival .10 .30
7 Moises Alou .10 .30
8 Mike Stanley .10 .30
9 Jay Buhner .10 .30
10 Shawn Green .10 .30
11 Ryan Klesko .10 .30
12 Andres Galarraga .10 .30
13 Dean Palmer .10 .30
14 Jeff Conine .10 .30
15 Brian L.Hunter .10 .30
16 J.T. Snow .10 .30
17 Larry Walker .10 .30
18 Barry Larkin .20 .50
19 Alex Gonzalez .10 .30
20 Edgar Martinez .20 .50
21 Mo Vaughn .10 .30
22 Mark McGwire .75 2.00
23 Jose Canseco .20 .50
24 Jack McDowell .10 .30
25 Dante Bichette .10 .30
26 Wade Boggs .20 .50
27 Mike Piazza .50 1.25
28 Ray Lankford .10 .30
29 Craig Biggio .20 .50
30 Rafael Palmeiro .20 .50
31 Ron Gant .10 .30
32 Javy Lopez .10 .30
33 Brian Jordan .10 .30
34 Paul O'Neill .20 .50
35 Mark Grace .20 .50
36 Matt Williams .10 .30
37 Pedro Martinez .20 .50
38 Rickey Henderson .30 .75
39 Bobby Bonilla .10 .30
40 Todd Hollandsworth .10 .30
41 Jim Thome .20 .50
42 Gary Sheffield .30 .75
43 Tim Salmon .20 .50
44 Gregg Jefferies .10 .30
45 Roberto Alomar .20 .50
46 Carlos Baerga .10 .30
47 Mark Grudzielanek .10 .30
48 Randy Johnson .30 .75
49 Tino Martinez .20 .50
50 Robin Ventura .10 .30
51 Ryne Sandberg .50 1.25
52 Jay Bell .10 .30
53 Jason Schmidt .20 .50
54 Frank Thomas .30 .75
55 Kenny Lofton .10 .30
56 Ariel Prieto .10 .30
57 David Cone .10 .30
58 Reggie Sanders .10 .30
59 Michael Tucker .10 .30
60 Vinny Castilla .10 .30
61 Len Dykstra .10 .30
62 Todd Hundley .10 .30
63 Brian McRae .10 .30
64 Dennis Eckersley .10 .30
65 Rondell White .10 .30
66 Eric Karros .10 .30
67 Greg Maddux .50 1.25
68 Kevin Appier .10 .30
69 Eddie Murray .30 .75
70 John Olerud .10 .30
71 Tony Gwynn .40 1.00
72 David Justice .10 .30
73 Ken Caminiti .10 .30
74 Terry Steinbach .10 .30
75 Alan Benes .10 .30
76 Chipper Jones .30 .75
77 Jeff Bagwell .20 .50
78 Barry Bonds .75 2.00
79 Ken Griffey Jr. .75 2.00
80 Roger Cedeno .10 .30
81 Joe Carter .10 .30
82 Henry Rodriguez .10 .30
83 Jason Isringhausen .10 .30
84 Chuck Knoblauch .10 .30
85 Manny Ramirez .20 .50
86 Tom Glavine .20 .50
87 Jeffrey Hammonds .10 .30
88 Paul Molitor .10 .30
89 Roger Clemens .60 1.50
90 Greg Vaughn .10 .30
91 Marty Cordova .10 .30
92 Albert Belle .10 .30
93 Mike Mussina .20 .50
94 Garret Anderson .10 .30
95 Juan Gonzalez .10 .30
96 John Valentin .10 .30
97 Jason Giambi .10 .30
98 Kirby Puckett .30 .75
99 Jim Edmonds .10 .30
100 Cecil Fielder .10 .30
101 Mike Aldrete .10 .30
102 Marquis Grissom .10 .30
103 Derek Bell .10 .30
104 Raul Mondesi .10 .30
105 Sammy Sosa .30 .75
106 Travis Fryman .10 .30
107 Rico Brogna .10 .30
108 Will Clark .20 .50
109 Bernie Williams .20 .50
110 Brady Anderson .10 .30
111 Torii Hunter .10 .30
112 Derek Jeter .75 2.00
113 Mike Kusiewicz RC .20 .50
114 Scott Rolen .30 .75
115 Ramon Castro .10 .30
116 Jose Guillen RC 1.25 3.00
117 Wade Walker RC .20 .50
118 Shawn Senior .10 .30
119 Onan Masaoka RC .40 1.00
120 Marlon Anderson RC .40 1.00
121 Katsuhiro Maeda RC .40 1.00
122 Garrett Stephenson RC .20 .50
123 Butch Huskey .10 .30
124 D'Angelo Jimenez RC .40 1.00
125 Tony Mounce RC .20 .50
126 Jay Canizaro .10 .30
127 Juan Melo .10 .30
128 Steve Gibralter .10 .30
129 Freddy Adrian Garcia .10 .30
130 Julio Santana .10 .30
131 Richard Hidalgo .10 .30
132 Jermaine Dye .10 .30
133 Willie Adams .10 .30
134 Everett Stull .10 .30
135 Ramon Morel .10 .30
136 Chan Ho Park .10 .30
137 Jamey Wright .10 .30
138 Luis R.Garcia RC .20 .50
139 Dan Serafini .10 .30
140 Ryan Dempster RC .75 2.00
141 Tate Seefried .10 .30
142 Jimmy Hurst .10 .30
143 Travis Miller .10 .30
144 Curtis Goodwin .10 .30
145 Rocky Coppinger RC .20 .50
146 Enrique Wilson .10 .30
147 Jaime Bluma .10 .30
148 Andrew Vessel .10 .30
149 Damian Moss .10 .30
150 Shawn Gallagher RC .20 .50
151 Pat Watkins .10 .30
152 Jose Paniagua .10 .30
153 Danny Graves .10 .30
154 Bryon Gainey RC .20 .50
155 Steve Soderstrom .10 .30
156 Cliff Brumbaugh RC .20 .50
157 Eugene Kingsale RC .20 .50
158 Lou Collier .10 .30
159 Todd Walker .10 .30
160 Kris Detmers RC .20 .50
161 Josh Booty RC .20 .50
162 Greg Whiteman RC .20 .50
163 Damian Jackson .10 .30
164 Tony Clark .10 .30
165 Jeff D'Amico .10 .30
166 Johnny Damon .20 .50
167 Rafael Orellano .10 .30
168 Ruben Rivera .10 .30
169 Alex Ochoa .10 .30
170 Jay Powell .10 .30
171 Tom Evans .10 .30
172 Ron Villone .10 .30
173 Shawn Estes .10 .30
174 John Wasdin .10 .30
175 Bill Simas .10 .30
176 Kevin Brown .10 .30
177 Shannon Stewart .10 .30
178 Todd Greene .10 .30
179 Bob Wolcott .10 .30
180 Chris Snopek .10 .30
181 Nomar Garciaparra .60 1.50
182 Cameron Smith RC .20 .50
183 Matt Drews .10 .30
184 Jimmy Haynes .10 .30
185 Chris Carpenter .20 .50
186 Desi Relaford .10 .30
187 Ben Grieve .10 .30
188 Mike Bell .10 .30
189 Luis Castillo RC .60 1.50
190 Ugueth Urbina .10 .30
191 Paul Wilson .10 .30
192 Andruw Jones .50 1.25
193 Wayne Gomes .10 .30
194 Craig Counsell RC .60 1.50
195 Jim Cole .10 .30
196 Brooks Kieschnick .10 .30
197 Trey Beamon .10 .30
198 Marino Santana RC .20 .50
199 Bob Abreu .30 .75
200 Pokey Reese .10 .30
201 Dante Powell .10 .30
202 George Arias .10 .30
203 Jorge Velandia RC .20 .50
204 George Lombard RC .20 .50
205 Byron Browne RC .20 .50
206 John Frascatore .10 .30
207 Terry Adams .10 .30
208 Wilson Delgado RC .20 .50
209 Billy McMillon .10 .30
210 Jeff Abbott .10 .30
211 Trot Nixon .10 .30
212 Amaury Telemaco .10 .30
213 Scott Sullivan .10 .30
214 Justin Thompson .10 .30
215 Decomba Conner .10 .30
216 Ryan McGuire .10 .30
217 Matt Luke .10 .30
218 Doug Million .10 .30
219 Jason Dickson RC .20 .50
220 Ramon Hernandez RC .75 2.00
221 Mark Bellhorn RC .75 2.00
222 Eric Ludwick RC .20 .50
223 Luke Wilcox RC .20 .50
224 Marty Malloy RC .20 .50
225 Gary Coffee RC .20 .50
226 Wendell Magee RC .20 .50
227 Brett Tomko RC .40 1.00
228 Derek Lowe .10 .30
229 Jose Rosado RC .20 .50
230 Steve Bourgeois RC .20 .50
231 Neil Weber RC .20 .50
232 Jeff Ware .10 .30
233 Edwin Diaz .10 .30
234 Greg Norton .10 .30
235 Aaron Boone .10 .30
236 Jeff Suppan .10 .30
237 Bret Wagner .10 .30
238 Elieser Marrero .10 .30
239 Will Cunnane .10 .30
240 Brian Barkley RC .20 .50
241 Jay Payton .10 .30
242 Marcus Jensen .10 .30
243 Ryan Nye .10 .30
244 Chad Mottola .10 .30
245 Scott McClain RC .20 .50
246 Jesse Ibarra RC .20 .50
247 Mike Darr RC .20 .50
248 Bobby Estalella RC .20 .50
249 Michael Barrett .10 .30
250 Jamie Lopiccolo RC .20 .50
251 Shane Spencer RC .40 1.00
252 Ben Petrick RC .20 .50
253 Jason Bell RC .20 .50
254 Arnold Gooch RC .20 .50
255 T.J. Mathews .10 .30
256 Jason Ryan .10 .30
257 Pat Cline RC .20 .50
258 Rafael Carmona RC .20 .50
259 Carl Pavano RC .75 2.00
260 Ben Davis .10 .30
261 Matt Lawton RC .40 1.00
262 Kevin Sefcik RC .20 .50
263 Chris Fussell RC .20 .50
264 Mike Cameron RC .60 1.50
265 Marty Janzen RC .20 .50
266 Livan Hernandez RC .75 2.00
267 Raul Ibanez RC 2.00 5.00
268 Juan Encarnacion .10 .30
269 David Yocum RC .20 .50
270 Jonathan Johnson RC .20 .50
271 Reggie Taylor .10 .30
272 Danny Buxbaum RC .20 .50
273 Jacob Cruz .10 .30
274 Bobby Morris RC .20 .50
275 Andy Fox RC .20 .50
276 Greg Keagle .10 .30
277 Charles Peterson .10 .30
278 Derrek Lee .20 .50
279 Bryant Nelson RC .20 .50
280 Antone Williamson .10 .30
281 Scott Elarton .10 .30
282 Shad Williams RC .20 .50
283 Rich Hunter RC .20 .50
284 Chris Sheff .10 .30
285 Derrick Gibson .10 .30
286 Felix Rodriguez .10 .30
287 Brian Banks RC .20 .50
288 Jason McDonald .10 .30
289 Glendon Rusch RC .40 1.00
290 Gary Rath .10 .30
291 Peter Munro .10 .30
292 Tom Fordham .10 .30
293 Jason Kendall .10 .30
294 Russ Johnson .10 .30
295 Joe Long .10 .30
296 Robert Smith RC .20 .50
297 Jarrod Washburn RC .60 1.50
298 Dave Coggin RC .20 .50
299 Jeff Yoder RC .20 .50
300 Jed Hansen RC .20 .50
301 Matt Morris RC 1.00 2.50
302 Josh Bishop RC .20 .50
303 Dustin Hermanson .10 .30
304 Mike Gulan .10 .30
305 Felipe Crespo .10 .30
306 Quinton McCracken .10 .30
307 Jim Bonnici RC .20 .50
308 Sal Fasano .10 .30
309 Gabe Alvarez RC .20 .50
310 Heath Murray RC .20 .50
311 Javier Valentin RC .20 .50
312 Bartolo Colon .30 .75
313 Olmedo Saenz .10 .30
314 Norm Hutchins RC .20 .50
315 Chris Holt .10 .30
316 David Doster RC .20 .50
317 Robert Person .10 .30
318 Donne Wall RC .20 .50
319 Adam Riggs RC .20 .50
320 Homer Bush .10 .30
321 Brad Rigby RC .20 .50
322 Lou Merloni RC .20 .50
323 Neifi Perez .10 .30
324 Chris Cumberland .10 .30
325 Alvie Shepherd RC .20 .50
326 Jarrod Patterson RC .20 .50
327 Ray Ricken RC .20 .50
328 Danny Klassen RC .20 .50
329 David Miller RC .20 .50
330 Chad Alexander RC .20 .50
331 Matt Beaumont .10 .30
332 Damon Hollins .10 .30
333 Todd Dunn .10 .30
334 Mike Sweeney RC .75 2.00
335 Richie Sexson .20 .50
336 Billy Wagner .10 .30
337 Ron Wright RC .20 .50
338 Paul Konerko .30 .75
339 Tommy Phelps RC .20 .50
340 Karim Garcia .10 .30
341 Mike Grace RC .20 .50
342 Russell Branyan RC .40 1.00
343 Randy Winn RC .60 1.50
344 A.J. Pierzynski RC 1.50 4.00
345 Mike Busby RC .20 .50
346 Matt Beech RC .20 .50
347 Jose Cepeda RC .20 .50
348 Brian Stephenson .10 .30
349 Rey Ordonez .10 .30
350 Rich Aurilia RC .40 1.00
351 Edgard Velazquez RC .20 .50
352 Raul Casanova .10 .30
353 Carlos Guillen RC .75 2.00
354 Bruce Aven RC .20 .50
355 Ryan Jones RC .20 .50
356 Derek Aucoin RC .20 .50
357 Brian Rose RC .20 .50
358 Richard Almanzar RC .20 .50
359 Fletcher Bates RC .20 .50
360 Russ Ortiz RC .60 1.50
361 Wilton Guerrero RC .20 .50
362 Geoff Jenkins RC .60 1.50
363 Pete Janicki .10 .30
364 Yamil Benitez .10 .30
365 Aaron Holbert .10 .30
366 Tim Belk .10 .30
367 Terrell Wade .10 .30
368 Terrence Long .10 .30
369 Brad Fullmer .10 .30
370 Matt Wagner .10 .30
371 Craig Wilson RC .20 .50
372 Mark Loretta .10 .30
373 Eric Owens .10 .30
374 Vladimir Guerrero .60 1.50
375 Tommy Davis .10 .30
376 Donnie Sadler .10 .30
377 Edgar Renteria .10 .30
378 Todd Helton .60 1.50
379 Ralph Milliard RC .20 .50
380 Darin Blood RC .20 .50
381 Shayne Bennett .10 .30
382 Mark Redman .10 .30
383 Felix Martinez .10 .30
384 Sean Watkins RC .20 .50
385 Oscar Henriquez .10 .30
M20 52 Bowman Mantle 2.00 5.00
NNO Unnumbered Checklists .10 .30

1996 Bowman Foil

COMPLETE SET (385) 150.00 300.00
*STARS: 1X TO 2.5X BASIC CARDS
*ROOKIES: .6X TO 1.5X BASIC CARDS
ONE FOIL OR INSERT CARD PER HOBBY PACK
TWO FOILS PER RETAIL PACK
267 Raul Ibanez 4.00 10.00

1996 Bowman Minor League POY

COMPLETE SET (15) 10.00 25.00
STATED ODDS 1:12
1 Andruw Jones 1.25 3.00
2 Derrick Gibson .30 .75
3 Bob Abreu .75 2.00
4 Todd Walker .30 .75
5 Jamey Wright .30 .75
6 Wes Helms .60 1.50
7 Karim Garcia .30 .75
8 Bartolo Colon .75 2.00
9 Alex Ochoa .30 .75
10 Mike Sweeney .75 2.00
11 Ruben Rivera .30 .75
12 Gabe Alvarez .20 .50
13 Billy Wagner .30 .75
14 Vladimir Guerrero 1.50 4.00
15 Edgard Velazquez .20 .50

1997 Bowman

The 1997 Bowman set was issued in two series (series one numbers 1-221, series two numbers 222-441) and was distributed in 10 card packs with a suggested retail price of $2.50. The 441-card set features color photos of 300 top prospects with silver and blue foil stamping and 140 veteran stars designated by silver and red foil stamping. An unannounced Hideki Irabu red bordered card (number 441) was also included in series two packs. Players that were featured for the first time on a Bowman card also carried a blue foil "1st Bowman Card" logo on the card front. Topps offered collectors a $125 guarantee on complete sets. To get the guarantee, collectors had to mail in the Guaranteed Certificate Request Form which was found in every three packs of either series along with a $5 registration and processing fee. To redeem the guarantee, collectors had to send a complete set of Bowman regular cards (441 cards in both series) along with the certificate to Topps between August 31 and December 31 in the year 2000. Rookie Cards in this set include Adrian Beltre, Kris Benson, Eric Chavez, Jose Cruz Jr, Travis Lee, Aramis Ramirez, Miguel Tejada and Kerry Wood. Please note that cards 155 and 158 don't exist. Calvin "Pokey" Reese and George Arias are both numbered 156 (Reese is an uncorrected error - should be numbered 155). Chris Carpenter and Eric Milton are both numbered 159 (Carpenter is an uncorrected error - should be numbered 158).

COMPLETE SET (441) 10.00 25.00
COMPLETE SERIES 1 (221) 5.00 12.00
COMPLETE SERIES 2 (220) 5.00 12.00
CARDS 155 AND 158 DON'T EXIST
REESE AND ARIAS BOTH NUMBERED 156
CARPENTER 'N MILTON BOTH NUMBER 159
CONDITION SENSITIVE SET
1 Derek Jeter .75 2.00
2 Edgar Renteria .10 .30
3 Chipper Jones .30 .75
4 Hideo Nomo .30 .75
5 Tim Salmon .20 .50
6 Jason Giambi .10 .30
7 Robin Ventura .10 .30
8 Tony Clark .10 .30
9 Barry Larkin .20 .50
10 Paul Molitor .10 .30
11 Bernard Gilkey .10 .30
12 Jack McDowell .10 .30
13 Andy Benes .10 .30
14 Ryan Klesko .10 .30
15 Mark McGwire .75 2.00
16 Ken Griffey Jr. .60 1.50
17 Robb Nen .10 .30
18 Cal Ripken 1.00 2.50
19 John Valentin .10 .30
20 Ricky Bottalico .10 .30
21 Mike Lansing .10 .30
22 Ryne Sandberg .50 1.25
23 Carlos Delgado .10 .30
24 Craig Biggio .20 .50
25 Eric Karros .10 .30
26 Kevin Appier .10 .30
27 Mariano Rivera .30 .75
28 Vinny Castilla .10 .30
29 Juan Gonzalez .10 .30
30 Al Martin .10 .30
31 Jeff Cirillo .10 .30
32 Eddie Murray .30 .75
33 Ray Lankford .10 .30
34 Manny Ramirez .20 .50
35 Roberto Alomar .20 .50
36 Will Clark .20 .50
37 Chuck Knoblauch .10 .30
38 Harold Baines .10 .30
39 Trevor Hoffman .10 .30
40 Edgar Martinez .20 .50
41 Geronimo Berroa .10 .30
42 Rey Ordonez .10 .30
43 Mike Stanley .10 .30
44 Mike Mussina .20 .50
45 Kevin Brown .10 .30
46 Dennis Eckersley .10 .30
47 Henry Rodriguez .10 .30
48 Tino Martinez .20 .50
49 Eric Young .10 .30
50 Bret Boone .10 .30
51 Raul Mondesi .10 .30
52 Sammy Sosa .30 .75
53 John Smoltz .20 .50
54 Billy Wagner .10 .30
55 Jeff D'Amico .10 .30
56 Ken Caminiti .10 .30
57 Jason Kendall .10 .30
58 Wade Boggs .20 .50
59 Andres Galarraga .10 .30
60 Jeff Brantley .10 .30
61 Mel Rojas .10 .30
62 Brian L. Hunter .10 .30
63 Bobby Bonilla .10 .30
64 Roger Clemens .60 1.50
65 Jeff Kent .10 .30
66 Matt Williams .10 .30
67 Albert Belle .10 .30
68 Jeff King .10 .30
69 John Wetteland .10 .30
70 Deion Sanders .20 .50
71 Bubba Trammell RC .25 .60
72 Felix Heredia RC .15 .40
73 Billy Koch RC .40 1.00
74 Sidney Ponson RC .40 1.00
75 Ricky Ledee RC .25 .60
76 Brett Tomko .10 .30
77 Braden Looper RC .15 .40
78 Damian Jackson .10 .30
79 Jason Dickson .10 .30
80 Chad Green RC .15 .40
81 R.A. Dickey RC 1.25 3.00
82 Jeff Liefer .10 .30
83 Matt Wagner .10 .30
84 Richard Hidalgo .10 .30
85 Adam Riggs .10 .30
86 Robert Smith .10 .30
87 Chad Hermansen RC .15 .40
88 Felix Martinez .10 .30
89 J.J. Johnson .10 .30
90 Todd Dunwoody .10 .30
91 Katsuhiro Maeda .10 .30
92 Darin Erstad .10 .30
93 Elieser Marrero .10 .30
94 Bartolo Colon .10 .30
95 Chris Fussell .10 .30
96 Ugueth Urbina .10 .30
97 Josh Paul RC .15 .40
98 Jaime Bluma .10 .30
99 Seth Greisinger RC .15 .40
100 Jose Cruz Jr. RC .25 .60
101 Todd Dunn .10 .30
102 Joe Young RC .15 .40
103 Jonathan Johnson .10 .30
104 Justin Towle RC .15 .40
105 Brian Rose .10 .30
106 Jose Guillen .10 .30
107 Andruw Jones .20 .50
108 Mark Kotsay RC .60 1.50
109 Wilton Guerrero .10 .30
110 Jacob Cruz .10 .30
111 Mike Sweeney .10 .30
112 Julio Mosquera .10 .30
113 Matt Morris .10 .30
114 Wendell Magee .10 .30
115 John Thomson .10 .30
116 Javier Valentin .10 .30
117 Tom Fordham .10 .30
118 Ruben Rivera .10 .30
119 Mike Drumright RC .15 .40
120 Chris Holt .10 .30
121 Sean Maloney .10 .30
122 Michael Barrett .10 .30
123 Tony Saunders RC .15 .40
124 Kevin Brown C .10 .30
125 Richard Almanzar .10 .30
126 Mark Redman .10 .30
127 Anthony Sanders RC .15 .40
128 Jeff Abbott .10 .30
129 Eugene Kingsale .10 .30
130 Paul Konerko .20 .50
131 Randall Simon RC .25 .60
132 Andy Larkin .10 .30
133 Rafael Medina .10 .30
134 Mendy Lopez .10 .30
135 Freddy Adrian Garcia .10 .30
136 Karim Garcia .10 .30
137 Larry Rodriguez RC .15 .40
138 Carlos Guillen .10 .30
139 Aaron Boone .10 .30
140 Donnie Sadler .10 .30
141 Brooks Kieschnick .10 .30
142 Scott Spiezio .10 .30
143 Everett Stull .10 .30
144 Enrique Wilson .10 .30
145 Milton Bradley RC .75 2.00
146 Kevin Orie .10 .30
147 Derek Wallace .10 .30
148 Russ Johnson .10 .30
149 Joe Lagarde RC .15 .40
150 Luis Castillo .10 .30
151 Jay Payton .10 .30
152 Joe Long .10 .30
153 Livan Hernandez .10 .30
154 Vladimir Nunez RC .25 .60
155 Pokey Reese UER .10 .30
156 George Arias .10 .30
157 Homer Bush .10 .30
158 Chris Carpenter UER .10 .30
159 Eric Milton RC .25 .60
160 Richie Sexson .10 .30
161 Carl Pavano .10 .30
162 Chris Gissell RC .15 .40
163 Mac Suzuki .10 .30
164 Pat Cline .10 .30
165 Ron Wright .10 .30
166 Dante Powell .10 .30
167 Mark Bellhorn .10 .30
168 George Lombard .10 .30
169 Pee Wee Lopez RC .15 .40
170 Paul Wilder RC .15 .40
171 Brad Fullmer .10 .30
172 Willie Martinez RC .15 .40
173 Dario Veras RC .15 .40
174 Dave Coggin .10 .30
175 Kris Benson RC .40 1.00
176 Torii Hunter .10 .30
177 D.T. Cromer .10 .30
178 Nelson Figueroa RC .15 .40
179 Hiram Bocachica RC .15 .40
180 Shane Monahan .10 .30
181 Jimmy Anderson RC .15 .40
182 Juan Melo .10 .30
183 Pablo Ortega RC .15 .40
184 Calvin Pickering RC .15 .40
185 Reggie Taylor .10 .30
186 Jeff Farnsworth RC .15 .40
187 Terrence Long .10 .30
188 Geoff Jenkins .10 .30
189 Steve Rain RC .15 .40
190 Nerio Rodriguez RC .15 .40
191 Derrick Gibson .10 .30
192 Darin Blood .10 .30
193 Ben Davis .10 .30
194 Adrian Beltre RC 12.00 30.00
195 Damian Sapp RC UER .15 .40
196 Kerry Wood RC 2.00 5.00
197 Nate Rolison RC .15 .40
198 Fernando Tatis RC .15 .40
199 Brad Penny RC 1.25 3.00
200 Jake Westbrook RC .40 1.00
201 Edwin Diaz .10 .30
202 Joe Fontenot RC .25 .60
203 Matt Halloran RC .15 .40
204 Blake Stein RC .15 .40
205 Onan Masaoka .10 .30
206 Ben Petrick .10 .30
207 Matt Clement RC .40 1.00
208 Todd Greene .10 .30
209 Ray Ricken .10 .30
210 Eric Chavez RC 1.50 4.00
211 Edgard Velazquez .10 .30
212 Bruce Chen RC .40 1.00
213 Danny Patterson .10 .30
214 Jeff Yoder .10 .30
215 Luis Ordaz RC .15 .40
216 Chris Widger .10 .30
217 Jason Brester .10 .30
218 Carlton Loewer .10 .30
219 Chris Reitsma RC .25 .60
220 Neifi Perez .10 .30
221 Hideki Irabu RC .25 .60
222 Ellis Burks .10 .30
223 Pedro Martinez .20 .50
224 Kenny Lofton .10 .30
225 Randy Johnson .30 .75
226 Terry Steinbach .10 .30
227 Bernie Williams .20 .50
228 Dean Palmer .10 .30
229 Alan Benes .10 .30
230 Marquis Grissom .10 .30
231 Gary Sheffield .10 .30
232 Curt Schilling .10 .30
233 Reggie Sanders .10 .30
234 Bobby Higginson .10 .30
235 Moises Alou .10 .30
236 Tom Glavine .20 .50
237 Mark Grace .20 .50
238 Ramon Martinez .10 .30
239 Rafael Palmeiro .20 .50
240 John Olerud .10 .30
241 Dante Bichette .10 .30
242 Greg Vaughn .10 .30
243 Jeff Bagwell .20 .50
244 Barry Bonds .75 2.00
245 Pat Hentgen .10 .30
246 Jim Thome .20 .50
247 Jermaine Allensworth .10 .30
248 Andy Pettitte .20 .50
249 Jay Bell .10 .30
250 John Jaha .10 .30
251 Jim Edmonds .10 .30
252 Ron Gant .10 .30
253 David Cone .10 .30
254 Jose Canseco .20 .50

255 Jay Buhner .10 .30
256 Greg Maddux .50 1.25
257 Brian McRae .10 .30
258 Lance Johnson .10 .30
259 Travis Fryman .10 .30
260 Paul O'Neill .20 .50
261 Ivan Rodriguez .20 .50
262 Gregg Jefferies .10 .30
263 Fred McGriff .20 .50
264 Derek Bell .10 .30
265 Jeff Conine .10 .30
266 Mike Piazza .50 1.25
267 Mark Grudzielanek .10 .30
268 Brady Anderson .10 .30
269 Marty Cordova .10 .30
270 Ray Durham .10 .30
271 Joe Carter .10 .30
272 Brian Jordan .10 .30
273 David Justice .10 .30
274 Tony Gwynn .40 1.00
275 Larry Walker .10 .30
276 Cecil Fielder .10 .30
277 Mo Vaughn .10 .30
278 Alex Fernandez .10 .30
279 Michael Tucker .10 .30
280 Jose Valentin .10 .30
281 Sandy Alomar Jr. .10 .30
282 Todd Hollandsworth .10 .30
283 Rico Brogna .10 .30
284 Rusty Greer .10 .30
285 Roberto Hernandez .10 .30
286 Hal Morris .10 .30
287 Johnny Damon .20 .50
288 Todd Hundley .10 .30
289 Rondell White .10 .30
290 Frank Thomas .30 .75
291 Don Denbow RC .15 .40
292 Derrek Lee .20 .50
293 Todd Walker .10 .30
294 Scott Rolen .20 .50
295 Wes Helms .10 .30
296 Bob Abreu .20 .50
297 John Patterson RC .60 1.50
298 Alex Gonzalez RC .40 1.00
299 Grant Roberts RC .15 .40
300 Jeff Suppan .10 .30
301 Luke Wilcox .10 .30
302 Marlon Anderson .10 .30
303 Ray Brown .10 .30
304 Mike Caruso RC .15 .40
305 Sam Marsonek RC .15 .40
306 Brady Raggio RC .15 .40
307 Kevin McGlinchy RC .25 .60
308 Roy Halladay RC 8.00 20.00
309 Jeremi Gonzalez RC .15 .40
310 Aramis Ramirez RC 1.50 4.00
311 Dee Brown RC .15 .40
312 Justin Thompson .10 .30
313 Jay Tessmer RC .15 .40
314 Mike Johnson RC .15 .40
315 Danny Clyburn .10 .30
316 Bruce Aven .10 .30
317 Keith Foulke RC .60 1.50
318 Jimmy Osting RC .25 .60
319 Valerio De Los Santos RC .15 .40
320 Shannon Stewart .10 .30
321 Willie Adams .10 .30
322 Larry Barnes RC .15 .40
323 Mark Johnson RC .15 .40
324 Chris Stowers RC .15 .40
325 Brandon Reed .10 .30
326 Randy Winn .10 .30
327 Steve Chavez RC .15 .40
328 Nomar Garciaparra .50 1.25
329 Jacque Jones RC .60 1.50
330 Chris Clemons .10 .30
331 Todd Helton .30 .75
332 Ryan Brannan RC .15 .40
333 Alex Sanchez RC .25 .60
334 Arnold Gooch .10 .30
335 Russell Branyan .10 .30
336 Daryle Ward .15 .40
337 John LeRoy RC .15 .40
338 Steve Cox .10 .30
339 Kevin Witt .10 .30
340 Norm Hutchins .10 .30
341 Gabby Martinez .10 .30
342 Kris Detmers .10 .30
343 Mike Villano RC .15 .40
344 Preston Wilson .10 .30
345 James Manias RC .15 .40
346 Deivi Cruz RC .25 .60
347 Donzell McDonald RC .15 .40
348 Rod Myers RC .15 .40
349 Shawn Chacon RC .40 1.00
350 Elvin Hernandez RC .25 .60
351 Orlando Cabrera RC .60 1.50
352 Brian Banks .10 .30
353 Robbie Bell .15 .40
354 Brad Rigby .10 .30
355 Scott Elarton .10 .30
356 Kevin Sweeney RC .15 .40
357 Steve Soderstrom .10 .30
358 Ryan Nye .10 .30
359 Marlon Allen RC .15 .40
360 Donny Leon RC .15 .40
361 Garrett Neubart RC .25 .60
362 Abraham Nunez RC .25 .60
363 Adam Eaton RC .40 1.00
364 Octavio Dotel RC .25 .60
365 Dean Crow RC .15 .40
366 Jason Baker RC .15 .40
367 Sean Casey .40 1.00
368 Joe Lawrence RC .15 .40
369 Adam Johnson RC .15 .40
370 Scott Schoeneweis RC .25 .60
371 Gerald Witasick Jr. .10 .30
372 Ronnie Belliard RC .50 1.25
373 Russ Ortiz .10 .30
374 Robert Stratton RC .25 .60
375 Bobby Estalella .10 .30
376 Corey Lee RC .15 .40
377 Carlos Beltran .75 2.00
378 Mike Cameron .10 .30
379 Scott Randall RC .15 .40
380 Corey Erickson RC .15 .40
381 Jay Canizaro .10 .30
382 Kerry Robinson RC .15 .40
383 Todd Noel RC .15 .40
384 A.J. Zapp RC .15 .40
385 Jarrod Washburn .10 .30
386 Ben Grieve .10 .30
387 Javier Vazquez RC .60 1.50
388 Tony Graffanino .10 .30
389 Travis Lee RC .25 .60
390 DaRond Stovall .10 .30
391 Dennis Reyes RC .25 .60
392 Danny Buxbaum .10 .30
393 Marc Lewis RC .15 .40
394 Kelvim Escobar RC .40 1.00
395 Danny Klassen .10 .30
396 Ken Cloude RC .15 .40
397 Gabe Alvarez .10 .30
398 Jaret Wright RC .25 .60
399 Raul Casanova .10 .30
400 Clayton Bruner RC .15 .40
401 Jason Marquis RC .60 1.50
402 Marc Kroon .10 .30
403 Jamey Wright .10 .30
404 Matt Snyder RC .15 .40
405 Josh Garrett RC .15 .40
406 Juan Encarnacion .10 .30
407 Heath Murray .10 .30
408 Brett Herbison RC .25 .60
409 Brent Butler RC .15 .40
410 Danny Peoples RC .15 .40
411 Miguel Tejada RC 2.00 5.00
412 Damian Moss .10 .30
413 Jim Pittsley .10 .30
414 Dmitri Young .10 .30
415 Glendon Rusch .10 .30
416 Vladimir Guerrero .30 .75
417 Cole Liniak RC .25 .60
418 Ramon Hernandez .10 .30
419 Cliff Politte RC .15 .40
420 Mel Rosario RC .15 .40
421 Jorge Carrion RC .15 .40
422 John Barnes RC .15 .40
423 Chris Stowe RC .15 .40
424 Vernon Wells RC 2.00 5.00
425 Brett Caradonna RC .15 .40
426 Scott Hodges RC .25 .60
427 Jon Garland RC 1.00 2.50
428 Nathan Haynes RC .15 .40
429 Geoff Goetz RC .15 .40
430 Adam Kennedy RC .40 1.00
431 T.J. Tucker RC .15 .40
432 Aaron Akin RC .15 .40
433 Jayson Werth RC 2.00 5.00
434 Glenn Davis RC .15 .40
435 Mark Mangum RC .15 .40
436 Troy Cameron RC .15 .40
437 J.J. Davis RC .15 .40
438 Lance Berkman RC 4.00 10.00
439 Jason Standridge RC .15 .40
440 Jason Dellaero RC .25 .60
441 Hideki Irabu .25 .60

1997 Bowman International

COMPLETE SET (441) 75.00 150.00
COMPLETE SERIES 1 (221) 30.00 80.00
COMPLETE SERIES 2 (220) 30.00 80.00
*STARS: 1X TO 2.5X BASIC CARDS
*ROOKIES: .5X TO 1.2X BASIC CARDS
ONE INT'L OR INSERT PER PACK

1997 Bowman 1998 ROY Favorites

COMPLETE SET (15) 6.00 15.00
SER.2 STATED ODDS 1:12
ROY1 Jeff Abbott .40 1.00
ROY2 Karim Garcia .40 1.00
ROY3 Todd Helton 1.00 2.50
ROY4 Richard Hidalgo .40 1.00
ROY5 Geoff Jenkins .40 1.00
ROY6 Russ Johnson .40 1.00
ROY7 Paul Konerko .60 1.50
ROY8 Mark Kotsay .75 2.00
ROY9 Ricky Ledee .30 .75
ROY10 Travis Lee .30 .75
ROY11 Derrek Lee .60 1.50
ROY12 Elieser Marrero .40 1.00
ROY13 Juan Melo .40 1.00
ROY14 Brian Rose .40 1.00
ROY15 Fernando Tatis .20 .50

1997 Bowman Certified Blue Ink Autographs

STATED ODDS 1:96, ANCO 1:115
*BLACK INK: .5X TO 1.2X BLUE INK
BLACK STATED ODDS 1:503, ANCO 1:600
*GOLD INK: 1X TO 2.5X BLUE INK
GOLD: STATED ODDS 1:1509, ANCO 1:1795
*GREEN JETER: SAME VALUE AS BLUE INK
D.JETER BLUE SER.1 ODDS 1:1928
D.JETER GREEN SER.2 ODDS 1:1928
SKIP-NUMBERED SET
CA1 Jeff Abbott 5.00 12.00
CA2 Bob Abreu 6.00 15.00
CA3 Willie Adams 3.00 8.00
CA4 Brian Banks 3.00 8.00
CA5 Kris Benson 5.00 12.00
CA6 Darin Blood 3.00 8.00
CA7 Jaime Bluma 3.00 8.00
CA8 Kevin L. Brown 3.00 8.00
CA9 Ray Brown 3.00 8.00
CA10 Homer Bush 3.00 8.00
CA11 Mike Cameron 3.00 8.00
CA12 Jay Canizaro 3.00 8.00
CA13 Luis Castillo 5.00 12.00
CA14 Dave Coggin 5.00 12.00
CA15 Bartolo Colon 3.00 8.00
CA16 Rocky Coppinger 3.00 8.00
CA17 Jacob Cruz 3.00 8.00
CA18 Jose Cruz Jr. 3.00 8.00
CA19 Jeff D'Amico 3.00 8.00
CA20 Ben Davis 3.00 8.00
CA21 Mike Drumright 3.00 8.00
CA22 Scott Elarton 3.00 8.00
CA23 Darin Erstad 5.00 12.00
CA24 Bobby Estalella 3.00 8.00
CA25 Joe Fontenot 3.00 8.00
CA26 Tom Fordham 3.00 8.00
CA27 Brad Fullmer 3.00 8.00
CA28 Chris Fussell 3.00 8.00
CA29 Karim Garcia 3.00 8.00
CA30 Kris Detmers 3.00 8.00
CA31 Todd Greene 3.00 8.00
CA32 Ben Grieve 3.00 8.00
CA33 Vladimir Guerrero 15.00 40.00
CA34 Jose Guillen 5.00 12.00
CA36 Wes Helms 3.00 8.00
CA37 Chad Hermansen 3.00 8.00
CA38 Richard Hidalgo 5.00 12.00
CA39 Todd Hollandsworth 3.00 8.00
CA40 Damian Jackson 3.00 8.00
CA41 Derek Jeter 125.00 300.00
CA42 Andruw Jones 5.00 12.00
CA43 Brooks Kieschnick 3.00 8.00
CA44 Eugene Kingsale 3.00 8.00
CA45 Paul Konerko 8.00 20.00
CA46 Marc Kroon 5.00 12.00
CA47 Derrek Lee 6.00 15.00
CA48 Travis Lee 3.00 8.00
CA49 Terrence Long 3.00 8.00
CA50 Curt Lyons 5.00 12.00
CA51 Eli Marrero 3.00 8.00
CA52 Rafael Medina 3.00 8.00
CA53 Juan Melo 3.00 8.00
CA54 Shane Monahan 3.00 8.00
CA55 Julio Mosquera 3.00 8.00
CA56 Heath Murray 3.00 8.00
CA57 Ryan Nye 3.00 8.00
CA58 Kevin Orie 3.00 8.00
CA59 Russ Ortiz 5.00 12.00
CA60 Carl Pavano 5.00 12.00
CA61 Jay Payton 3.00 8.00
CA62 Neifi Perez 3.00 8.00
CA63 Sidney Ponson 5.00 12.00
CA64 Pokey Reese 5.00 12.00
CA65 Ray Ricken 3.00 8.00
CA66 Brad Rigby 3.00 8.00
CA67 Adam Riggs 3.00 8.00
CA68 Ruben Rivera 5.00 10.00
CA69 J.J. Johnson 3.00 8.00
CA70 Scott Rolen 6.00 15.00
CA71 Tony Saunders 3.00 8.00
CA72 Donnie Sadler 3.00 8.00
CA73 Richie Sexson 5.00 12.00
CA74 Scott Spiezio 3.00 8.00
CA75 Everett Stull 3.00 8.00
CA76 Mike Sweeney 5.00 12.00
CA77 Fernando Tatis 5.00 12.00
CA78 Miguel Tejada 6.00 15.00
CA79 Justin Thompson 3.00 8.00
CA80 Justin Towle 3.00 8.00
CA81 Billy Wagner 5.00 12.00
CA82 Todd Walker 5.00 12.00
CA83 Luke Wilcox 3.00 8.00
CA84 Paul Wilder 3.00 8.00
CA85 Enrique Wilson 3.00 8.00
CA86 Kerry Wood 10.00 25.00
CA87 Jamey Wright 3.00 8.00
CA88 Ron Wright 5.00 10.00
CA89 Dmitri Young 4.00 10.00
CA90 Nelson Figueroa 3.00 8.00

1997 Bowman International Best

COMPLETE SET (20) 20.00 50.00
SER.2 STATED ODDS 1:12
*ATOMIC: 1.5X TO 4X BASIC INT.BEST
ATOMIC SER.2 STATED ODDS 1:96
*REFRACTORS: .75X TO 2X BASIC INT.BEST
REFRACTOR SER.2 STATED ODDS 1:48
BBI1 Frank Thomas 1.25 3.00
BBI2 Ken Griffey Jr. 2.50 6.00
BBI3 Juan Gonzalez .50 1.25
BBI4 Bernie Williams .75 2.00
BBI5 Hideo Nomo 1.25 3.00
BBI6 Sammy Sosa 1.25 3.00
BBI7 Larry Walker .50 1.25
BBI8 Vinny Castilla .50 1.25
BBI9 Mariano Rivera 1.25 3.00
BBI10 Rafael Palmeiro .75 2.00
BBI11 Nomar Garciaparra 2.00 5.00
BBI12 Todd Walker .50 1.25
BBI13 Andruw Jones .75 2.00
BBI14 Vladimir Guerrero 1.25 3.00
BBI15 Ruben Rivera .50 1.25
BBI16 Bob Abreu .75 2.00
BBI17 Karim Garcia .50 1.25
BBI18 Katsuhiro Maeda .50 1.25
BBI19 Jose Cruz Jr. .50 1.25
BBI20 Damian Moss .50 1.25

1997 Bowman Scout's Honor Roll

COMPLETE SET (15) 10.00 25.00
SER.1 STATED ODDS 1:12
1 Dmitri Young .30 .75
2 Bob Abreu .50 1.25
3 Vladimir Guerrero .75 2.00
4 Paul Konerko .50 1.25
5 Kevin Orie .30 .75
6 Todd Walker .30 .75
7 Ben Grieve .30 .75
8 Darin Erstad .30 .75
9 Derrek Lee .50 1.25
10 Jose Cruz Jr. .30 .75
11 Scott Rolen .50 1.25
12 Travis Lee .30 .75
13 Andruw Jones .50 1.25
14 Wilton Guerrero .30 .75
15 Nomar Garciaparra 1.25 3.00

1998 Bowman Previews

COMPLETE SET (10) 10.00 25.00
SER.1 STATED ODDS 1:12 H/R, 1:4 HTA
BP1 Nomar Garciaparra 1.50 4.00
BP2 Scott Rolen .60 1.50
BP3 Ken Griffey Jr. 2.00 5.00
BP4 Frank Thomas 1.00 2.50
BP5 Larry Walker .40 1.00
BP6 Mike Piazza 1.50 4.00
BP7 Chipper Jones 1.00 2.50
BP8 Tino Martinez .60 1.50
BP9 Mark McGwire 2.50 6.00
BP10 Barry Bonds 2.50 6.00

1998 Bowman Prospect Previews

COMPLETE SET (10) 4.00 10.00
SER.2 STATED ODDS 1:12 H/R, 1:4 HTA
BP1 Ben Grieve .40 1.00
BP2 Brad Fullmer .40 1.00
BP3 Ryan Anderson .40 1.00
BP4 Mark Kotsay .50 1.25
BP5 Bobby Estalella .40 1.00
BP6 Juan Encarnacion .40 1.00
BP7 Todd Helton .60 1.50
BP8 Mike Lowell 2.00 5.00
BP9 A.J. Hinch .40 1.00
BP10 Richard Hidalgo .40 1.00

1998 Bowman

The complete 1998 Bowman set was distributed amongst two series with a total of 441 cards. The 10-card packs retailed for $2.50 each. Series one contains 221 cards while series two contains 220 cards. Each player's facsimile signature taken from the contract they signed with Topps is also on the left border. Players new to Bowman are marked with the new Bowman Rookie Card stamp. Notable Rookie Cards include Ryan Anderson. Jack Cust, Troy Glaus, Orlando Hernandez, Gabe Kapler, Ruben Mateo, Kevin Millwood and Magglio Ordonez. The 1991 BBM (Major Japanese Card set) cards of Shigetoshi Hasegawa, Hideki Irabu and Hideo Nomo (All of which are considered Japanese Rookie Cards) were randomly inserted into these packs.

COMPLETE SET (441) 20.00 50.00
COMPLETE SERIES 1 (221) 10.00 25.00
COMPLETE SERIES 2 (220) 10.00 25.00
91 BBM'S RANDOM INSERTS IN PACKS
1 Nomar Garciaparra .50 1.25
2 Scott Rolen .20 .50
3 Andy Pettitte .20 .50
4 Ivan Rodriguez .20 .50
5 Mark McGwire .75 2.00
6 Jason Dickson .10 .30
7 Jose Cruz Jr. .10 .30
8 Jeff Kent .10 .30
9 Mike Mussina .20 .50
10 Jason Kendall .10 .30
11 Brett Tomko .10 .30
12 Jeff King .10 .30
13 Brad Radke .10 .30
14 Robin Ventura .10 .30
15 Jeff Bagwell .20 .50
16 Greg Maddux .50 1.25
17 John Jaha .10 .30
18 Mike Piazza .50 1.25
19 Edgar Martinez .20 .50
20 David Justice .10 .30
21 Todd Hundley .10 .30
22 Tony Gwynn .40 1.00
23 Larry Walker .10 .30
24 Bernie Williams .20 .50
25 Edgar Renteria .10 .30
26 Rafael Palmeiro .20 .50
27 Tim Salmon .20 .50
28 Matt Morris .10 .30
29 Shawn Estes .10 .30
30 Vladimir Guerrero .30 .75
31 Fernando Tatis .10 .30
32 Justin Thompson .10 .30
33 Ken Griffey Jr. .60 1.50
34 Edgardo Alfonzo .10 .30
35 Mo Vaughn .10 .30
36 Marty Cordova .10 .30
37 Craig Biggio .20 .50
38 Roger Clemens .60 1.50
39 Mark Grace .20 .50
40 Ken Caminiti .10 .30
41 Tony Womack .10 .30
42 Albert Belle .10 .30
43 Tino Martinez .20 .50
44 Sandy Alomar Jr. .10 .30
45 Jeff Cirillo .10 .30
46 Jason Giambi .10 .30
47 Darin Erstad .10 .30
48 Livan Hernandez .10 .30
49 Mark Grudzielanek .10 .30
50 Sammy Sosa .30 .75
51 Curt Schilling .10 .30
52 Brian Hunter .10 .30
53 Neifi Perez .10 .30
54 Todd Walker .10 .30
55 Jose Guillen .10 .30
56 Jim Thome .20 .50
57 Tom Glavine .20 .50
58 Todd Greene .10 .30
59 Rondell White .10 .30
60 Roberto Alomar .20 .50
61 Tony Clark .10 .30
62 Vinny Castilla .10 .30
63 Barry Larkin .20 .50
64 Hideki Irabu .10 .30
65 Johnny Damon .20 .50
66 Juan Gonzalez .10 .30
67 John Olerud .10 .30
68 Gary Sheffield .10 .30
69 Raul Mondesi .10 .30
70 Chipper Jones .30 .75
71 David Ortiz 1.00 2.50
72 Warren Morris RC .15 .40
73 Alex Gonzalez .10 .30
74 Nick Bierbrodt .10 .30
75 Roy Halladay .60 1.50
76 Danny Buxbaum .10 .30
77 Adam Kennedy .10 .30
78 Jared Sandberg .10 .30
79 Michael Barrett .10 .30
80 Gil Meche .25 .60
81 Jayson Werth .10 .30
82 Abraham Nunez .10 .30
83 Ben Petrick .10 .30
84 Brett Caradonna .10 .30
85 Mike Lowell RC 1.25 3.00
86 Clayton Bruner .10 .30
87 John Curtice RC .25 .60
88 Bobby Estalella .10 .30
89 Juan Melo .10 .30
90 Arnold Gooch .10 .30
91 Kevin Millwood RC .60 1.50
92 Richie Sexson .10 .30
93 Orlando Cabrera .10 .30
94 Pat Cline .10 .30
95 Anthony Sanders .10 .30
96 Russ Johnson .10 .30
97 Ben Grieve .10 .30
98 Kevin McGlinchy .10 .30
99 Paul Wilder .10 .30
100 Russ Ortiz .10 .30
101 Ryan Jackson RC .15 .40
102 Heath Murray .10 .30
103 Brian Rose .10 .30
104 Ryan Radmanovich RC .15 .40
105 Ricky Ledee .10 .30
106 Jeff Wallace RC .15 .40
107 Ryan Minor RC .15 .40
108 Dennis Reyes .10 .30
109 James Manias .10 .30
110 Chris Carpenter .10 .30
111 Daryle Ward .10 .30
112 Vernon Wells .10 .30
113 Chad Green .10 .30
114 Mike Stoner RC .15 .40
115 Brad Fullmer .10 .30
116 Adam Eaton .10 .30
117 Jeff Liefer .10 .30
118 Corey Koskie RC .40 1.00
119 Todd Helton .20 .50
120 Jaime Jones RC .15 .40
121 Mel Rosario .10 .30
122 Geoff Goetz .10 .30
123 Adrian Beltre .10 .30
124 Jason Dellaero .10 .30
125 Gabe Kapler RC .40 1.00
126 Scott Schoeneweis .10 .30
127 Ryan Brannan .10 .30
128 Aaron Akin .10 .30
129 Ryan Anderson RC .15 .40
130 Brad Penny .10 .30
131 Bruce Chen .10 .30
132 Eli Marrero .10 .30
133 Eric Chavez .10 .30
134 Troy Glaus RC 1.50 4.00
135 Troy Cameron .10 .30
136 Brian Sikorski RC .15 .40
137 Mike Kinkade RC .15 .40
138 Braden Looper .10 .30
139 Mark Mangum .10 .30
140 Danny Peoples .10 .30
141 J.J. Davis .10 .30
142 Ben Davis .10 .30
143 Jacque Jones .10 .30
144 Derrick Gibson .10 .30
145 Bronson Arroyo .60 1.50
146 Luis De Los Santos RC .15 .40
147 Jeff Abbott .10 .30
148 Mike Cuddyer RC .60 1.50
149 Jason Romano .10 .30
150 Shane Monahan .10 .30
151 Ntema Ndungidi RC .15 .40
152 Alex Sanchez .10 .30
153 Jack Cust RC .75 2.00
154 Brent Butler .10 .30
155 Ramon Hernandez .10 .30
156 Norm Hutchins .10 .30
157 Jason Marquis .10 .30
158 Jacob Cruz .10 .30
159 Rob Burger RC .15 .40
160 Dave Coggin .10 .30
161 Preston Wilson .10 .30
162 Jason Fitzgerald RC .15 .40
163 Dan Serafini .10 .30
164 Peter Munro .10 .30
165 Trot Nixon .10 .30
166 Homer Bush .10 .30
167 Dermal Brown .10 .30
168 Chad Hermansen .10 .30
169 Julio Moreno RC .15 .40
170 John Roskos RC .15 .40
171 Grant Roberts .10 .30
172 Ken Cloude .10 .30
173 Jason Brester .10 .30
174 Jason Conti .10 .30
175 Jon Garland .10 .30
176 Robbie Bell .10 .30
177 Nathan Haynes .10 .30
178 Ramon Ortiz RC .25 .60
179 Shannon Stewart .10 .30
180 Pablo Ortega .10 .30
181 Jimmy Rollins RC 2.00 5.00
182 Sean Casey .10 .30
183 Ted Lilly RC .40 1.00
184 Chris Enochs RC .15 .40
185 Magglio Ordonez UER RC 2.00 5.00
186 Mike Drumright .10 .30
187 Aaron Boone .10 .30
188 Matt Clement .10 .30
189 Todd Dunwoody .10 .30
190 Larry Rodriguez .10 .30
191 Todd Noel .10 .30
192 Geoff Jenkins .10 .30
193 George Lombard .10 .30
194 Lance Berkman .10 .30
195 Marcus McCain .10 .30
196 Ryan McGuire .10 .30
197 Jhensy Sandoval .10 .30
198 Corey Lee .10 .30
199 Mario Valdez .10 .30
200 Robert Fick RC .25 .60
201 Donnie Sadler .10 .30
202 Marc Kroon .10 .30
203 David Miller .10 .30
204 Jarrod Washburn .10 .30
205 Miguel Tejada .30 .75
206 Raul Ibanez .10 .30
207 John Patterson .10 .30
208 Calvin Pickering .10 .30
209 Felix Martinez .10 .30
210 Mark Redman .10 .30
211 Scott Elarton .10 .30
212 Jose Amado RC .15 .40
213 Kerry Wood .10 .30
214 Dante Powell .10 .30
215 Aramis Ramirez .10 .30
216 A.J. Hinch .10 .30
217 Dustin Carr RC .15 .40
218 Mark Kotsay .10 .30
219 Jason Standridge .10 .30
220 Luis Ordaz .10 .30
221 Orlando Hernandez RC .75 2.00
222 Cal Ripken 1.00 2.50
223 Paul Molitor .10 .30
224 Derek Jeter .75 2.00
225 Barry Bonds .75 2.00
226 Jim Edmonds .10 .30
227 John Smoltz .20 .50
228 Eric Karros .10 .30
229 Ray Lankford .10 .30
230 Rey Ordonez .10 .30
231 Kenny Lofton .10 .30
232 Alex Rodriguez .50 1.25
233 Dante Bichette .10 .30
234 Pedro Martinez .20 .50
235 Carlos Delgado .10 .30
236 Rod Beck .10 .30
237 Matt Williams .10 .30
238 Charles Johnson .10 .30
239 Rico Brogna .10 .30
240 Frank Thomas .30 .75
241 Paul O'Neill .20 .50
242 Jaret Wright .10 .30
243 Brant Brown .10 .30
244 Ryan Klesko .10 .30
245 Chuck Finley .10 .30
246 Derek Bell .10 .30
247 Delino DeShields .10 .30
248 Chan Ho Park .10 .30
249 Wade Boggs .20 .50
250 Jay Buhner .10 .30
251 Butch Huskey .10 .30
252 Steve Finley .10 .30
253 Will Clark .20 .50
254 John Valentin .10 .30
255 Bobby Higginson .10 .30
256 Darryl Strawberry .10 .30
257 Randy Johnson .30 .75
258 Al Martin .10 .30
259 Travis Fryman .10 .30
260 Fred McGriff .20 .50
261 Jose Valentin .10 .30
262 Andruw Jones .20 .50
263 Kenny Rogers .10 .30
264 Moises Alou .10 .30
265 Denny Neagle .10 .30
266 Ugueth Urbina .10 .30
267 Derrek Lee .20 .50
268 Ellis Burks .10 .30
269 Mariano Rivera .30 .75
270 Dean Palmer .10 .30
271 Eddie Taubensee .10 .30
272 Brady Anderson .10 .30
273 Brian Giles .10 .30
274 Quinton McCracken .10 .30
275 Henry Rodriguez .10 .30
276 Andres Galarraga .10 .30
277 Jose Canseco .20 .50
278 David Segui .10 .30
279 Bret Saberhagen .10 .30
280 Kevin Brown .20 .50
281 Chuck Knoblauch .10 .30
282 Jeromy Burnitz .10 .30
283 Jay Bell .10 .30
284 Manny Ramirez .20 .50
285 Rick Helling .10 .30
286 Francisco Cordova .10 .30
287 Bob Abreu .10 .30
288 J.T. Snow .10 .30
289 Hideo Nomo .30 .75
290 Brian Jordan .10 .30
291 Javy Lopez .10 .30
292 Travis Lee .10 .30
293 Russell Branyan .10 .30
294 Paul Konerko .10 .30
295 Masato Yoshii RC .25 .60
296 Kris Benson .10 .30
297 Juan Encarnacion .10 .30
298 Eric Milton .10 .30
299 Mike Caruso .10 .30
300 Ricardo Aramboles RC .15 .40
301 Bobby Smith .10 .30
302 Billy Koch .10 .30
303 Richard Hidalgo .10 .30
304 Justin Baughman RC .15 .40
305 Chris Gissell .10 .30
306 Donnie Bridges RC .15 .40
307 Nelson Lara RC .15 .40
308 Randy Wolf RC .25 .60
309 Jason LaRue RC .25 .60
310 Jason Gooding RC .15 .40
311 Edgard Clemente .10 .30
312 Andrew Vessel .10 .30
313 Chris Reitsma .10 .30
314 Jesus Sanchez RC .15 .40
315 Buddy Carlyle RC .15 .40
316 Randy Winn .10 .30
317 Luis Rivera RC .15 .40
318 Marcus Thames RC 1.00 2.50
319 A.J. Pierzynski .10 .30
320 Scott Randall .10 .30
321 Damian Sapp .10 .30
322 Ed Yarnall RC .15 .40
323 Luke Allen RC .15 .40
324 J.D. Smart .10 .30
325 Willie Martinez .10 .30
326 Alex Ramirez .10 .30
327 Eric DuBose RC .15 .40
328 Kevin Witt .10 .30
329 Dan McKinley RC .15 .40
330 Cliff Politte .10 .30
331 Vladimir Nunez .10 .30
332 John Halama RC .15 .40
333 Nerio Rodriguez .10 .30
334 Desi Relaford .10 .30
335 Robinson Checo .10 .30
336 John Nicholson .20 .50
337 Tom LaRosa RC .15 .40
338 Kevin Nicholson RC .15 .40
339 Javier Vazquez .10 .30
340 A.J. Zapp .10 .30
341 Tom Evans .10 .30
342 Kerry Robinson .10 .30
343 Gabe Gonzalez RC .15 .40
344 Ralph Milliard .10 .30
345 Enrique Wilson .10 .30
346 Elvin Hernandez .10 .30
347 Mike Lincoln RC .15 .40
348 Cesar King RC .15 .40
349 Cristian Guzman RC .25 .60
350 Donzell McDonald .10 .30
351 Jim Parque RC .15 .40
352 Mike Saipe RC .15 .40
353 Carlos Febles RC .25 .60
354 Dernell Stenson RC .15 .40
355 Mark Osborne RC .15 .40
356 Odalis Perez RC .60 1.50
357 Jason Dewey RC .15 .40
358 Joe Fontenot .10 .30
359 Jason Grilli RC .15 .40
360 Kevin Haverbusch RC .15 .40
361 Jay Yennaco RC .15 .40
362 Brian Buchanan .10 .30
363 John Barnes .10 .30
364 Chris Fussell .10 .30
365 Kevin Gibbs RC .15 .40
366 Joe Lawrence .10 .30
367 DaRond Stovall .10 .30
368 Brian Fuentes RC .15 .40
369 Jimmy Anderson .10 .30
370 Lariel Gonzalez RC .15 .40
371 Scott Williamson RC .15 .40
372 Milton Bradley .10 .30
373 Jason Halper RC .15 .40
374 Brent Billingsley RC .15 .40
375 Joe DePastino RC .15 .40
376 Jake Westbrook .10 .30
377 Octavio Dotel .10 .30
378 Jason Williams RC .15 .40
379 Julio Ramirez RC .15 .40
380 Seth Greisinger .10 .30
381 Mike Judd RC .15 .40
382 Ben Ford RC .15 .40
383 Tom Bennett RC .15 .40
384 Adam Butler RC .15 .40
385 Wade Miller RC .40 1.00
386 Kyle Peterson RC .15 .40
387 Tommy Peterman RC .15 .40
388 Onan Masaoka .10 .30
389 Jason Rakers RC .15 .40
390 Rafael Medina .10 .30
391 Luis Lopez RC .15 .40
392 Jeff Yoder .10 .30
393 Vance Wilson RC .15 .40
394 Fernando Seguignol RC .15 .40
395 Ron Wright .10 .30
396 Ruben Mateo RC .15 .40
397 Steve Lomasney RC .25 .60
398 Damian Jackson .10 .30
399 Mike Jerzembeck RC .15 .40
400 Luis Rivas RC .40 1.00
401 Kevin Burford RC .15 .40
402 Glenn Davis .10 .30
403 Robert Luce RC .15 .40
404 Cole Liniak .10 .30
405 Matt LeCroy RC .25 .60
406 Jeremy Giambi RC .25 .60
407 Shawn Chacon .10 .30
408 Dewayne Wise RC .15 .40
409 Steve Woodard .10 .30
410 Francisco Cordero RC .40 1.00
411 Damon Minor RC .15 .40
412 Lou Collier .10 .30
413 Justin Towle .10 .30
414 Juan LeBron .10 .30
415 Michael Coleman .10 .30
416 Felix Rodriguez .10 .30
417 Paul Ah Yat RC .15 .40
418 Kevin Barker RC .15 .40
419 Brian Meadows .10 .30
420 Darnell McDonald RC .15 .40
421 Matt Kinney RC .15 .40
422 Mike Vavrek RC .15 .40
423 Courtney Duncan RC .15 .40
424 Kevin Millar RC .60 1.50
425 Ruben Rivera .10 .30
426 Steve Shoemaker RC .15 .40
427 Dan Reichert RC .15 .40
428 Carlos Lee RC 1.25 3.00
429 Rod Barajas .40 1.00
430 Pablo Ozuna RC .25 .60
431 Todd Belitz RC .15 .40
432 Sidney Ponson .10 .30
433 Steve Carver RC .15 .40
434 Esteban Yan RC .25 .60
435 Cedrick Bowers .10 .30
436 Marlon Anderson .10 .30
437 Carl Pavano .10 .30
438 Jae Weong Seo RC .25 .60
439 Jose Taveras RC .15 .40
440 Matt Anderson RC .15 .40
441 Darron Ingram RC .15 .40
CL1 Series 1 CL 1 .10 .30
CL2 Series 1 CL 2 .10 .30
CL3 Series 2 CL 1 .10 .30
CL4 Series 2 CL 2 .10 .30
NNO S.Hasegawa '91 BBM 4.00 10.00
NNO H.Irabu '91 BBM 4.00 10.00
NNO H.Nomo '91 BBM 10.00 25.00

1998 Bowman Golden Anniversary

*STARS: 12.5X TO 30X BASIC CARDS
*ROOKIES: 10X TO 20X BASIC CARDS
SER.1 STATED ODDS 1:237
SER.2 STATED ODDS 1:194
STATED PRINT RUN 50 SERIAL #'d SETS
424 Kevin Millar 15.00 30.00

1998 Bowman International

COMPLETE SET (441) 75.00 150.00
COMPLETE SERIES 1 (221) 30.00 80.00
COMPLETE SERIES 2 (220) 30.00 80.00
*STARS: 1.25X TO 3X BASIC CARDS
*ROOKIES: .6X TO 1.5X BASIC CARDS
ONE PER PACK

1998 Bowman 1999 ROY Favorites

COMPLETE SET (10) 8.00 20.00
SER.2 STATED ODDS 1:12
ROY1 Adrian Beltre .50 1.25
ROY2 Troy Glaus 1.50 4.00
ROY3 Chad Hermansen .50 1.25
ROY4 Matt Clement .50 1.25
ROY5 Eric Chavez .50 1.25
ROY6 Kris Benson .50 1.25
ROY7 Richie Sexson .50 1.25
ROY8 Randy Wolf 1.00 2.50
ROY9 Ryan Minor .60 1.50
ROY10 Alex Gonzalez .50 1.25

1998 Bowman Certified Blue Autographs

SER.1 STATED ODDS 1:149
SER.2 STATED ODDS 1:122
*GOLD FOIL: 1.5X TO 4X BLUE AU'S
SER.1 GOLD FOIL STATED ODDS 1:2976
SER.2 GOLD FOIL STATED ODDS 1:2445
*SILVER FOIL: .75X TO 2X BLUE AU'S
SER.1 SILVER FOIL STATED ODDS 1:992
SER.2 SILVER FOIL STATED ODDS 1:815
1 Adrian Beltre 100.00 250.00
2 Brad Fullmer 4.00 10.00
3 Ricky Ledee 4.00 10.00
4 David Ortiz 15.00 40.00
5 Fernando Tatis 4.00 10.00
6 Kerry Wood 4.00 10.00
7 Mel Rosario 4.00 10.00
8 Cole Liniak 4.00 10.00
9 A.J. Hinch 4.00 10.00
10 Jhensy Sandoval 4.00 10.00
11 Jose Cruz Jr. 4.00 10.00
12 Richard Hidalgo 4.00 10.00
13 Geoff Jenkins 6.00 15.00
14 Carl Pavano 8.00 20.00
15 Richie Sexson 6.00 15.00
16 Tony Womack 4.00 10.00
17 Scott Rolen 4.00 10.00
18 Ryan Minor 4.00 10.00
19 Eli Marrero 4.00 10.00
20 Jason Marquis 6.00 15.00
21 Mike Lowell 6.00 15.00
22 Todd Helton 5.00 12.00
23 Chad Green 4.00 10.00
24 Scott Elarton 4.00 10.00
25 Russell Branyan 4.00 10.00
26 Mike Drumright 4.00 10.00
27 Ben Grieve 4.00 10.00
28 Jacque Jones 6.00 15.00
29 Jared Sandberg 4.00 10.00
30 Grant Roberts 4.00 10.00
31 Mike Stoner 4.00 10.00
32 Brian Rose 4.00 10.00
33 Randy Winn 4.00 10.00
34 Justin Towle 4.00 10.00
35 Anthony Sanders 4.00 10.00
36 Rafael Medina 4.00 10.00
37 Corey Lee 4.00 10.00
38 Mike Kinkade 4.00 10.00
39 Norm Hutchins 4.00 10.00
40 Jason Brester 4.00 10.00
41 Ben Davis 4.00 10.00
42 Nomar Garciaparra 10.00 25.00
43 Jeff Liefer 4.00 10.00
44 Eric Milton 4.00 10.00
45 Preston Wilson 6.00 15.00
46 Miguel Tejada 15.00 40.00
47 Luis Ordaz 4.00 10.00
48 Travis Lee 4.00 10.00
49 Kris Benson 6.00 15.00
50 Jacob Cruz 4.00 10.00
51 Dermal Brown 4.00 10.00
52 Marc Kroon 4.00 10.00
53 Chad Hermansen 4.00 10.00
54 Roy Halladay 40.00 100.00
55 Eric Chavez 4.00 10.00
56 Jason Conti 4.00 10.00
57 Juan Encarnacion 6.00 15.00
58 Paul Wilder 4.00 10.00
59 Aramis Ramirez 8.00 20.00
60 Cliff Politte 4.00 10.00
61 Todd Dunwoody 4.00 10.00
62 Paul Konerko 10.00 25.00
63 Shane Monahan 4.00 10.00
64 Alex Sanchez 4.00 10.00
65 Jeff Abbott 4.00 10.00
66 John Patterson 6.00 15.00
67 Peter Munro 4.00 10.00
68 Jarrod Washburn 4.00 10.00
69 Derrek Lee 10.00 25.00
70 Ramon Hernandez 4.00 10.00

1998 Bowman Minor League MVP's

COMPLETE SET (11) 10.00 25.00
SER.2 STATED ODDS 1:12
MVP1 Jeff Bagwell .60 1.50
MVP2 Andres Galarraga .40 1.00
MVP3 Juan Gonzalez .40 1.00
MVP4 Tony Gwynn 1.25 3.00
MVP5 Vladimir Guerrero 1.00 2.50
MVP6 Derek Jeter 2.50 6.00
MVP7 Andruw Jones .60 1.50
MVP8 Tino Martinez .60 1.50
MVP9 Manny Ramirez .60 1.50
MVP10 Gary Sheffield .40 1.00
MVP11 Jim Thome .60 1.50

1998 Bowman Scout's Choice

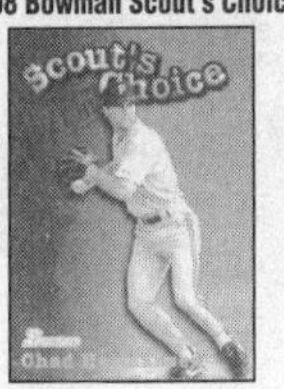

COMPLETE SET (21) 10.00 25.00
SER.1 STATED ODDS 1:12
SC1 Paul Konerko .75 2.00
SC2 Richard Hidalgo .75 2.00
SC3 Mark Kotsay .75 2.00
SC4 Ben Grieve .75 2.00
SC5 Chad Hermansen .75 2.00
SC6 Matt Clement .75 2.00
SC7 Brad Fullmer .75 2.00
SC8 Eli Marrero .75 2.00
SC9 Kerry Wood 1.00 2.50
SC10 Adrian Beltre .75 2.00
SC11 Ricky Ledee .75 2.00
SC12 Travis Lee .75 2.00
SC13 Abraham Nunez .75 2.00
SC14 Brian Rose .75 2.00
SC15 Dermal Brown .75 2.00
SC16 Juan Encarnacion .75 2.00
SC17 Aramis Ramirez .75 2.00
SC18 Todd Helton 1.25 3.00
SC19 Kris Benson .75 2.00
SC20 Russell Branyan .75 2.00
SC21 Mike Stoner 1.00 2.50

1999 Bowman Pre-Production

COMPLETE SET (6) 1.50 4.00
PP1 Andres Galarraga .60 1.50
PP2 Raul Mondesi .40 1.00
PP3 Vinny Castilla .40 1.00
PP4 Corey Koskie UER .40 1.00
PP5 Octavio Dotel .40 1.00
PP6 Dernell Stenson .40 1.00

1999 Bowman

The 1999 Bowman set was issued in two series and was distributed in 10 card packs with a suggested retail price of $3.00. The 440-card set featured the newest faces and potential talent that would carry Major League Baseball into the next millennium. This set features 300 top prospects and and 140 veterans. Prospect cards are designated with a silver and blue design while the veteran cards are shown with a silver and red design. Prospects making their debut on a Bowman card each featured a "Bowman Rookie Card" stamp on front. Notable Rookie Cards include Pat Burrell, Sean Burroughs, Carl Crawford, Adam Dunn, Rafael Furcal, Tim Hudson, Nick Johnson, Austin Kearns, Corey Patterson, Wily Mo Pena, Adam Piatt and Alfonso Soriano.

COMPLETE SET (440) 20.00 50.00
COMPLETE SERIES 1 (220) 8.00 20.00
COMPLETE SERIES 2 (220) 12.50 30.00
COMMON CARD (1-440) .10 .30
COMMON RC .15 .40
1 Ben Grieve .12 .30
2 Kerry Wood .12 .30
3 Ruben Rivera .12 .30
4 Sandy Alomar Jr. .12 .30
5 Cal Ripken 1.00 2.50
6 Mark McGwire .50 1.25
7 Vladimir Guerrero .20 .50
8 Moises Alou .12 .30
9 Jim Edmonds .20 .50
10 Greg Maddux .40 1.00
11 Gary Sheffield .12 .30
12 John Valentin .12 .30
13 Chuck Knoblauch .12 .30
14 Tony Clark .12 .30
15 Rusty Greer .12 .30
16 Al Leiter .12 .30
17 Travis Lee .12 .30
18 Jose Cruz Jr. .12 .30
19 Pedro Martinez .20 .50
20 Paul O'Neill .20 .50
21 Todd Walker .12 .30
22 Vinny Castilla .12 .30
23 Barry Larkin .20 .50
24 Curt Schilling .12 .30
25 Jason Kendall .12 .30
26 Scott Erickson .12 .30
27 Andres Galarraga .20 .50
28 Jeff Shaw .12 .30
29 John Olerud .12 .30
30 Orlando Hernandez .12 .30
31 Larry Walker .20 .50
32 Andruw Jones .12 .30
33 Jeff Cirillo .12 .30
34 Barry Bonds .50 1.25
35 Manny Ramirez .30 .75
36 Mark Kotsay .12 .30
37 Ivan Rodriguez .20 .50
38 Jeff King .12 .30
39 Brian Hunter .12 .30
40 Ray Durham .12 .30
41 Bernie Williams .20 .50
42 Darin Erstad .12 .30
43 Chipper Jones .30 .75
44 Pat Hentgen .12 .30
45 Eric Young .12 .30
46 Jaret Wright .12 .30
47 Juan Guzman .12 .30
48 Jorge Posada .20 .50
49 Bobby Higginson .12 .30
50 Jose Guillen .12 .30
51 Trevor Hoffman .20 .50
52 Ken Griffey Jr. .60 1.50
53 David Justice .12 .30
54 Matt Williams .12 .30
55 Eric Karros .12 .30
56 Derek Bell .12 .30
57 Ray Lankford .12 .30
58 Mariano Rivera .40 1.00
59 Brett Tomko .12 .30
60 Mike Mussina .20 .50
61 Kenny Lofton .12 .30
62 Chuck Finley .12 .30
63 Alex Gonzalez .12 .30
64 Mark Grace .20 .50
65 Raul Mondesi .12 .30
66 David Cone .12 .30
67 Brad Fullmer .12 .30
68 Andy Benes .12 .30
69 John Smoltz .20 .50
70 Shane Reynolds .12 .30
71 Bruce Chen .12 .30
72 Adam Kennedy .12 .30
73 Jack Cust .12 .30
74 Matt Clement .12 .30
75 Derrick Gibson .12 .30
76 Darnell McDonald .12 .30
77 Adam Everett RC .25 .60
78 Ricardo Aramboles .12 .30
79 Mark Quinn RC .15 .40
80 Jason Rakers .12 .30
81 Seth Etherton RC .15 .40
82 Jeff Urban RC .15 .40
83 Manny Aybar .12 .30
84 Mike Nannini RC .15 .40
85 Onan Masaoka .12 .30
86 Rod Barajas .12 .30
87 Mike Frank .12 .30
88 Scott Randall .12 .30
89 Justin Bowles RC .15 .40
90 Chris Haas .12 .30
91 Arturo McDowell RC .15 .40
92 Matt Belisle RC .15 .40
93 Scott Elarton .12 .30
94 Vernon Wells .12 .30
95 Pat Cline .12 .30
96 Ryan Anderson .12 .30
97 Kevin Barker .12 .30
98 Ruben Mateo .12 .30
99 Robert Fick .12 .30
100 Corey Koskie .12 .30
101 Ricky Ledee .12 .30
102 Rick Elder RC .15 .40
103 Jack Cressend RC .15 .40
104 Joe Lawrence .12 .30
105 Mike Lincoln .12 .30
106 Kit Pellow RC .15 .40
107 Matt Burch RC .15 .40
108 Cole Liniak .12 .30
109 Jason Dewey .12 .30
110 Cesar King .12 .30
111 Julio Ramirez .12 .30
112 Jake Westbrook .12 .30
113 Eric Valent RC .15 .40
114 Roosevelt Brown RC .15 .40
115 Choo Freeman RC .15 .40
116 Juan Melo .12 .30
117 Jason Grilli .12 .30
118 Jared Sandberg .12 .30
119 Glenn Davis .12 .30
120 David Riske RC .15 .40
121 Jacque Jones .12 .30
122 Corey Lee .12 .30
123 Michael Barrett .12 .30
124 Lariel Gonzalez .12 .30
125 Mitch Meluskey .12 .30
126 F.Adrian Garcia .12 .30
127 Tony Torcato RC .15 .40
128 Jeff Liefer .12 .30
129 Ntema Ndungidi .12 .30
130 Andy Brown RC .15 .40
131 Ryan Mills RC .15 .40
132 Andy Abad RC .15 .40
133 Carlos Febles .12 .30
134 Jason Tyner RC .15 .40
135 Mark Osborne .12 .30
136 Phil Norton RC .15 .40
137 Nathan Haynes .12 .30
138 Roy Halladay .20 .50
139 Juan Encarnacion .12 .30
140 Brad Penny .12 .30
141 Grant Roberts .12 .30
142 Aramis Ramirez .12 .30
143 Cristian Guzman .12 .30
144 Mamon Tucker RC .15 .40
145 Ryan Bradley .12 .30
146 Brian Simmons .12 .30
147 Dan Reichert .12 .30
148 Russ Branyan .12 .30
149 Victor Valencia RC .15 .40
150 Scott Schoeneweis .12 .30
151 Sean Spencer RC .15 .40
152 Odalis Perez .12 .30
153 Joe Fontenot .12 .30
154 Milton Bradley .12 .30
155 Josh McKinley RC .15 .40
156 Terrence Long .12 .30
157 Danny Klassen .12 .30
158 Paul Hoover RC .15 .40
159 Ron Belliard .12 .30
160 Armando Rios .12 .30
161 Ramon Hernandez .12 .30
162 Jason Conti .12 .30
163 Chad Hermansen .12 .30
164 Jason Standridge .12 .30
165 Jason Dellaero .12 .30
166 John Curtice .12 .30
167 Clayton Andrews RC .15 .40
168 Jeremy Giambi .12 .30
169 Alex Ramirez .12 .30
170 Gabe Molina RC .15 .40
171 Mario Encarnacion RC .15 .40
172 Mike Zywica RC .15 .40
173 Chip Ambres RC .15 .40
174 Trot Nixon .12 .30
175 Pat Burrell RC .60 1.50
176 Jeff Yoder .12 .30
177 Chris Jones RC .15 .40
178 Kevin Witt .12 .30
179 Keith Luuloa RC .15 .40
180 Billy Koch .12 .30
181 Damaso Marte RC .15 .40
182 Ryan Glynn RC .15 .40
183 Calvin Pickering .12 .30
184 Michael Cuddyer .12 .30
185 Nick Johnson RC .40 1.00
186 Doug Mientkiewicz RC .25 .60
187 Nate Cornejo RC .15 .40
188 Octavio Dotel .12 .30
189 Wes Helms .12 .30
190 Nelson Lara .12 .30
191 Chuck Abbott RC .15 .40
192 Tony Armas Jr. .12 .30
193 Gil Meche .12 .30
194 Ben Petrick .12 .30
195 Chris George RC .15 .40
196 Scott Hunter RC .15 .40
197 Ryan Brannan .12 .30
198 Amaury Garcia RC .15 .40
199 Chris Gissell .12 .30
200 Austin Kearns RC .60 1.50
201 Alex Gonzalez .12 .30
202 Wade Miller .12 .30
203 Scott Williamson .12 .30
204 Chris Enochs .12 .30
205 Fernando Seguignol .12 .30
206 Marlon Anderson .12 .30
207 Todd Sears RC .15 .40
208 Nate Bump RC .15 .40
209 J.M. Gold RC .15 .40
210 Matt LeCroy .12 .30
211 Alex Hernandez .12 .30
212 Luis Rivera .12 .30
213 Troy Cameron .12 .30
214 Alex Escobar RC .15 .40
215 Jason LaRue .12 .30
216 Kyle Peterson .12 .30
217 Brent Butler .12 .30
218 Dernell Stenson .12 .30
219 Adrian Beltre .30 .75
220 Daryle Ward .12 .30
221 Jim Thome .20 .50
222 Cliff Floyd .12 .30
223 Rickey Henderson .30 .75
224 Garret Anderson .12 .30
225 Ken Caminiti .12 .30
226 Bret Boone .12 .30
227 Jeromy Burnitz .12 .30
228 Steve Finley .12 .30
229 Miguel Tejada .20 .50
230 Greg Vaughn .12 .30
231 Jose Offerman .12 .30
232 Andy Ashby .12 .30
233 Albert Belle .12 .30
234 Fernando Tatis .12 .30
235 Todd Helton .20 .50
236 Sean Casey .12 .30
237 Brian Giles .12 .30
238 Andy Pettitte .20 .50
239 Fred McGriff .20 .50
240 Roberto Alomar .20 .50
241 Edgar Martinez .20 .50
242 Lee Stevens .12 .30
243 Shawn Green .12 .30
244 Ryan Klesko .12 .30
245 Sammy Sosa .30 .75
246 Todd Hundley .12 .30
247 Shannon Stewart .12 .30
248 Randy Johnson .30 .75
249 Rondell White .12 .30
250 Mike Piazza .30 .75
251 Craig Biggio .20 .50
252 David Wells .12 .30
253 Brian Jordan .12 .30
254 Edgar Renteria .12 .30
255 Bartolo Colon .12 .30
256 Frank Thomas .30 .75
257 Will Clark .20 .50
258 Dean Palmer .12 .30
259 Dmitri Young .12 .30
260 Scott Rolen .20 .50
261 Jeff Kent .12 .30
262 Dante Bichette .12 .30
263 Nomar Garciaparra .20 .50
264 Tony Gwynn .30 .75
265 Alex Rodriguez .40 1.00
266 Jose Canseco .20 .50
267 Jason Giambi .12 .30
268 Jeff Bagwell .20 .50
269 Carlos Delgado .12 .30
270 Tom Glavine .20 .50
271 Eric Davis .12 .30
272 Edgardo Alfonzo .12 .30
273 Tim Salmon .12 .30
274 Johnny Damon .20 .50
275 Rafael Palmeiro .20 .50
276 Denny Neagle .12 .30
277 Neifi Perez .12 .30
278 Roger Clemens .40 1.00
279 Brant Brown .12 .30
280 Kevin Brown .12 .30
281 Jay Bell .12 .30
282 Jay Buhner .12 .30
283 Matt Lawton .12 .30
284 Robin Ventura .12 .30
285 Juan Gonzalez .12 .30
286 Mo Vaughn .12 .30
287 Kevin Millwood .12 .30
288 Tino Martinez .12 .30
289 Justin Thompson .12 .30
290 Derek Jeter .75 2.00
291 Ben Davis .12 .30
292 Mike Lowell .12 .30
293 Calvin Murray .12 .30
294 Micah Bowie RC .15 .40
295 Lance Berkman .20 .50
296 Jason Marquis .12 .30
297 Chad Green .12 .30
298 Dee Brown .12 .30
299 Jerry Hairston Jr. .12 .30
300 Gabe Kapler .12 .30
301 Brent Stentz RC .15 .40
302 Scott Mullen RC .15 .40
303 Brandon Reed .12 .30
304 Shea Hillenbrand RC .25 .60
305 J.D. Closser RC .15 .40
306 Gary Matthews Jr. .12 .30
307 Toby Hall RC .15 .40
308 Jason Phillips RC .15 .40
309 Jose Macias RC .15 .40
310 Jung Bong RC .15 .40
311 Ramon Soler RC .15 .40
312 Kelly Dransfeldt RC .15 .40
313 Carlos E. Hernandez RC .15 .40
314 Kevin Haverbusch .12 .30
315 Aaron Myette RC .15 .40
316 Chad Harville RC .15 .40
317 Kyle Farnsworth RC .15 .40
318 Gookie Dawkins RC .15 .40
319 Willie Martinez .12 .30
320 Carlos Lee .12 .30
321 Carlos Pena RC .50 1.25
322 Peter Bergeron RC .15 .40
323 A.J. Burnett RC .25 .60
324 Bucky Jacobsen RC .15 .40
325 Mo Bruce RC .15 .40
326 Reggie Taylor .12 .30
327 Jackie Rexrode .12 .30
328 Alvin Morrow RC .15 .40
329 Carlos Beltran .20 .50
330 Eric Chavez .12 .30
331 John Patterson .12 .30
332 Jayson Werth .20 .50
333 Richie Sexson .12 .30
334 Randy Wolf .12 .30
335 Eli Marrero .12 .30
336 Paul LoDuca .12 .30
337 J.D Smart .12 .30
338 Ryan Minor .12 .30
339 Kris Benson .12 .30
340 George Lombard .12 .30
341 Troy Glaus .12 .30
342 Eddie Yarnall .12 .30
343 Kip Wells RC .15 .40
344 C.C. Sabathia RC 1.25 3.00
345 Sean Burroughs RC .15 .40
346 Felipe Lopez RC .25 .60
347 Ryan Rupe RC .15 .40
348 Orber Moreno RC .15 .40
349 Rafael Roque RC .15 .40
350 Alfonso Soriano RC 1.50 4.00
351 Pablo Ozuna .12 .30
352 Corey Patterson RC .40 1.00
353 Braden Looper .12 .30
354 Robbie Bell .12 .30
355 Mark Mulder RC .50 1.25
356 Angel Pena .12 .30
357 Kevin McGlinchy .12 .30
358 Michael Restovich RC .15 .40
359 Eric DuBose .12 .30
360 Geoff Jenkins .12 .30
361 Mark Harriger RC .15 .40
362 Junior Herndon RC .15 .40
363 Tim Raines Jr. RC .15 .40
364 Rafael Furcal RC .50 1.25
365 Marcus Giles RC .40 1.00
366 Ted Lilly .12 .30
367 Jorge Toca RC .15 .40
368 David Kelton RC .15 .40
369 Adam Dunn RC .60 1.50
370 Guillermo Mota RC .15 .40
371 Brett Laxton RC .15 .40
372 Travis Harper RC .15 .40
373 Tom Davey RC .15 .40
374 Darren Blakely RC .15 .40
375 Tim Hudson RC .60 1.50
376 Jason Romano .12 .30
377 Dan Reichert .12 .30
378 Julio Lugo RC .25 .60
379 Jose Garcia RC .15 .40
380 Erubiel Durazo RC .15 .40
381 Jose Jimenez .12 .30
382 Chris Fussell .12 .30
383 Steve Lomasney .12 .30
384 Juan Pena RC .15 .40
385 Allen Levrault RC .15 .40
386 Juan Rivera RC .40 1.00
387 Steve Colyer RC .15 .40
388 Joe Nathan RC .40 1.00
389 Ron Walker RC .15 .40
390 Nick Bierbrodt .12 .30
391 Luke Prokopec RC .15 .40
392 Dave Roberts RC .40 1.00
393 Mike Darr .12 .30
394 Abraham Nunez RC .15 .40
395 Giuseppe Chiaramonte RC .15 .40
396 Jermaine Van Buren RC .15 .40
397 Mike Kusiewicz .12 .30
398 Matt Wise RC .15 .40
399 Joe McEwing RC .15 .40
400 Matt Holliday RC .75 2.00
401 Willi Mo Pena RC .50 1.25
402 Ruben Quevedo RC .15 .40
403 Rob Ryan RC .15 .40
404 Freddy Garcia RC .40 1.00
405 Kevin Eberwein RC .15 .40
406 Jesus Colome RC .15 .40
407 Chris Singleton .12 .30
408 Bubba Crosby RC .15 .40
409 Jesus Cordero RC .15 .40
410 Donny Leon .12 .30
411 Goefrey Tomlinson RC .15 .40
412 Jeff Winchester RC .15 .40
413 Adam Piatt RC .15 .40
414 Robert Stratton .12 .30
415 T.J. Tucker .12 .30
416 Ryan Langerhans RC .25 .60
417 Anthony Shumaker RC .15 .40
418 Matt Miller RC .15 .40
419 Doug Clark RC .15 .40
420 Kory DeHaan RC .15 .40
421 David Eckstein RC .50 1.25
422 Brian Cooper RC .15 .40
423 Brady Clark RC .15 .40
424 Chris Magruder RC .15 .40
425 Bobby Seay RC .15 .40
426 Aubrey Huff RC .40 1.00
427 Mike Jerzembeck .12 .30
428 Matt Blank RC .15 .40
429 Benny Agbayani RC .15 .40
430 Kevin Beirne RC .15 .40
431 Josh Hamilton RC 1.25 3.00
432 Josh Girdley RC .15 .40
433 Kyle Snyder RC .15 .40
434 Mike Paradis RC .15 .40
435 Jason Jennings RC .25 .60
436 David Walling RC .15 .40
437 Omar Ortiz RC .15 .40
438 Jay Gehrke RC .15 .40
439 Casey Burns RC .15 .40
440 Carl Crawford RC .75 2.00

1999 Bowman Gold

*GOLD: 10X TO 25X BASIC
*GOLD RC: 8X TO 20X BASIC RC
SER.1 STATED ODDS 1:111
SER.2 STATED ODDS 1:59
STATED PRINT RUN 99 SERIAL #'d SETS

1999 Bowman International

*INT: 1X TO 2.5X BASIC
*INT RC: .75X TO 2X BASIC RC
ONE PER PACK

1999 Bowman Autographs

BLUE FOIL SER.1 ODDS 1:162
BLUE FOIL SER.2 ODDS 1:85
SILVER FOIL SER.1 ODDS 1:485
SILVER FOIL SER.2 ODDS 1:256
GOLD FOIL SER.1 ODDS 1:1941
GOLD FOIL SER.2 ODDS 1:1024
BA1 Ruben Mateo B 4.00 10.00
BA2 Troy Glaus G 6.00 15.00
BA3 Ben Davis G 6.00 15.00
BA4 Jayson Werth B 6.00 15.00
BA5 Jerry Hairston Jr. S 4.00 10.00
BA6 Darnell McDonald B 4.00 10.00
BA7 Calvin Pickering S 6.00 15.00
BA8 Ryan Minor S 6.00 15.00
BA9 Alex Escobar B 4.00 10.00
BA10 Grant Roberts B 4.00 10.00
BA11 Carlos Guillen B 6.00 15.00
BA12 Ryan Anderson S 6.00 15.00
BA13 Gil Meche S 6.00 15.00
BA14 Russell Branyan S 6.00 15.00
BA15 Alex Ramirez S 6.00 15.00
BA16 Jason Rakers S 6.00 15.00
BA17 Eddie Yarnall B 4.00 10.00
BA18 Freddy Garcia B 4.00 10.00
BA19 Jason Conti B 4.00 10.00
BA20 Corey Koskie B 6.00 15.00
BA21 Roosevelt Brown B 4.00 10.00
BA22 Willie Martinez B 4.00 10.00
BA23 Mike Jerzembeck B 4.00 10.00
BA24 Lariel Gonzalez B 4.00 10.00
BA25 Fernando Seguignol B 6.00 15.00
BA26 Robert Fick S 6.00 15.00
BA27 J.D. Smart B 4.00 10.00
BA28 Ryan Mills B 4.00 10.00
BA29 Chad Hermansen G 6.00 15.00
BA30 Jason Grilli B 4.00 10.00
BA31 Michael Cuddyer B 6.00 15.00
BA32 Jacque Jones S 10.00 25.00
BA33 Reggie Taylor B 4.00 10.00
BA34 Richie Sexson G 6.00 15.00
BA35 Michael Barrett B 4.00 10.00
BA36 Paul LoDuca B 6.00 15.00
BA37 Adrian Beltre G 15.00 40.00
BA38 Peter Bergeron B 4.00 10.00
BA39 Joe Fontenot B 4.00 10.00
BA40 Randy Wolf B 6.00 15.00
BA41 Nick Johnson B 4.00 10.00
BA42 Ryan Bradley B 4.00 10.00
BA43 Mike Lowell S 4.00 10.00
BA44 Ricky Ledee G 4.00 10.00
BA45 Mike Lincoln S 6.00 15.00
BA46 Jeremy Giambi B 4.00 10.00
BA47 Dermal Brown S 6.00 15.00
BA48 Derrick Gibson B 4.00 10.00
BA49 Scott Randall B 4.00 10.00
BA50 Ben Petrick S 6.00 15.00
BA51 Jason LaRue B 6.00 15.00
BA52 Cole Liniak B 4.00 10.00
BA53 John Curtice B 4.00 10.00
BA54 Jackie Rexrode B 4.00 10.00
BA55 John Patterson B 6.00 15.00
BA56 Brad Penny S 10.00 25.00
BA57 Jared Sandberg B 6.00 15.00
BA58 Kerry Wood G 10.00 25.00
BA59 Eli Marrero S 6.00 15.00
BA60 Jason Marquis B 6.00 15.00
BA61 George Lombard S 6.00 15.00
BA62 Bruce Chen S 6.00 15.00
BA63 Kevin Witt S 6.00 15.00
BA64 Vernon Wells B 6.00 15.00
BA65 Billy Koch B 6.00 15.00
BA66 Roy Halladay G 20.00 50.00
BA67 Nathan Haynes B 4.00 10.00
BA68 Ben Grieve G 4.00 10.00
BA69 Eric Chavez G 6.00 15.00
BA70 Lance Berkman S 15.00 40.00

1999 Bowman 2000 ROY Favorites

COMPLETE SET (10) 2.50 6.00
SER.2 STATED ODDS 1:12
ROY1 Ryan Anderson .20 .50
ROY2 Pat Burrell .75 2.00
ROY3 A.J. Burnett .30 .75
ROY4 Ruben Mateo .20 .50
ROY5 Alex Escobar .20 .50
ROY6 Pablo Ozuna .20 .50
ROY7 Mark Mulder .60 1.50
ROY8 Corey Patterson .50 1.25
ROY9 George Lombard .20 .50
ROY10 Nick Johnson .50 1.25

1999 Bowman Early Risers

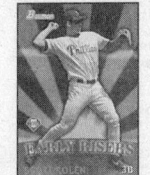

COMPLETE SET (11) 5.00 12.00
SER.2 STATED ODDS 1:12
ER1 Mike Piazza .60 1.50
ER2 Cal Ripken 2.00 5.00
ER3 Jeff Bagwell .40 1.00
ER4 Ben Grieve .25 .60
ER5 Kerry Wood .25 .60
ER6 Mark McGwire 1.00 2.50
ER7 Nomar Garciaparra .40 1.00
ER8 Derek Jeter 1.50 4.00
ER9 Scott Rolen .40 1.00
ER10 Jose Canseco .40 1.00
ER11 Raul Mondesi .25 .60

1999 Bowman Late Bloomers

COMPLETE SET (10) 2.50 6.00
SER.1 STATED ODDS 1:12
LB1 Mike Piazza .60 1.50
LB2 Jim Thome .40 1.00
LB3 Larry Walker .40 1.00
LB4 Vinny Castilla .25 .60
LB5 Andy Pettitte .40 1.00
LB6 Jim Edmonds .40 1.00
LB7 Kenny Lofton .25 .60
LB8 John Smoltz .40 1.00
LB9 Mark Grace .40 1.00
LB10 Trevor Hoffman .40 1.00

1999 Bowman Scout's Choice

COMPLETE SET (21) 6.00 15.00
SER.1 STATED ODDS 1:12
SC1 Ruben Mateo .40 1.00
SC2 Ryan Anderson .40 1.00
SC3 Pat Burrell 1.50 4.00
SC4 Troy Glaus .40 1.00
SC5 Eric Chavez .40 1.00
SC6 Adrian Beltre 1.00 2.50
SC7 Bruce Chen .40 1.00
SC8 Carlos Beltran .60 1.50
SC9 Alex Gonzalez .40 1.00
SC10 Carlos Lee .40 1.00
SC11 George Lombard .40 1.00
SC12 Matt Clement .40 1.00
SC13 Calvin Pickering .40 1.00
SC14 Marlon Anderson .40 1.00
SC15 Chad Hermansen .40 1.00
SC16 Russell Branyan .40 1.00
SC17 Jeremy Giambi .40 1.00
SC18 Ricky Ledee .40 1.00
SC19 John Patterson .40 1.00
SC20 Roy Halladay .60 1.50
SC21 Michael Barrett .40 1.00

2000 Bowman Pre-Production

COMPLETE SET (3) 1.50 4.00
PP1 Chipper Jones 1.00 2.50
PP2 Adam Piatt .40 1.00
PP3 Josh Hamilton 1.25 3.00

2000 Bowman

COMPLETE SET (440) 20.00 50.00
COMMON CARD (1-440) .12 .30
COMMON RC .15 .40
1 Vladimir Guerrero .20 .50
2 Chipper Jones .30 .75
3 Todd Walker .12 .30
4 Barry Larkin .20 .50
5 Bernie Williams .20 .50
6 Todd Helton .20 .50
7 Jermaine Dye .12 .30
8 Brian Giles .12 .30
9 Freddy Garcia .12 .30
10 Greg Vaughn .12 .30
11 Alex Gonzalez .12 .30
12 Luis Gonzalez .12 .30
13 Ron Belliard .12 .30
14 Ben Grieve .12 .30
15 Carlos Delgado .12 .30
16 Brian Jordan .12 .30
17 Fernando Tatis .12 .30
18 Ryan Rupe .12 .30
19 Miguel Tejada .20 .50
20 Mark Grace .20 .50
21 Kenny Lofton .12 .30
22 Eric Karros .12 .30
23 Cliff Floyd .12 .30
24 John Halama .12 .30
25 Cristian Guzman .12 .30
26 Scott Williamson .12 .30
27 Mike Lieberthal .12 .30
28 Tim Hudson .20 .50
29 Warren Morris .12 .30
30 Pedro Martinez .20 .50
31 John Smoltz .30 .75
32 Ray Durham .12 .30
33 Chad Allen .12 .30
34 Tony Clark .12 .30
35 Tino Martinez .20 .50
36 J.T. Snow .12 .30
37 Kevin Brown .12 .30
38 Bartolo Colon .12 .30
39 Rey Ordonez .12 .30
40 Jeff Bagwell .20 .50
41 Ivan Rodriguez .20 .50
42 Eric Chavez .12 .30
43 Eric Milton .12 .30
44 Jose Canseco .20 .50
45 Shawn Green .12 .30
46 Rich Aurilia .12 .30
47 Roberto Alomar .20 .50
48 Brian Daubach .12 .30
49 Magglio Ordonez .20 .50
50 Derek Jeter .75 2.00
51 Kris Benson .12 .30
52 Albert Belle .12 .30
53 Rondell White .12 .30
54 Justin Thompson .12 .30
55 Nomar Garciaparra .20 .50
56 Chuck Finley .12 .30
57 Omar Vizquel .20 .50
58 Luis Castillo .12 .30
59 Richard Hidalgo .12 .30
60 Barry Bonds .50 1.25
61 Craig Biggio .20 .50
62 Doug Glanville .12 .30
63 Gabe Kapler .12 .30
64 Johnny Damon .20 .50
65 Pokey Reese .12 .30
66 Andy Pettitte .20 .50
67 B.J. Surhoff .12 .30
68 Richie Sexson .12 .30
69 Javy Lopez .12 .30
70 Raul Mondesi .12 .30
71 Darin Erstad .12 .30

2000 Bowman

72 Kevin Millwood .12 .30
73 Ricky Ledee .12 .30
74 John Olerud .12 .30
75 Sean Casey .12 .30
76 Carlos Febles .12 .30
77 Paul O'Neill .20 .50
78 Bob Abreu .12 .30
79 Neifi Perez .12 .30
80 Tony Gwynn .30 .75
81 Russ Ortiz .12 .30
82 Matt Williams .12 .30
83 Chris Carpenter .20 .50
84 Roger Cedeno .12 .30
85 Tim Salmon .12 .30
86 Billy Koch .12 .30
87 Jeromy Burnitz .12 .30
88 Edgardo Alfonzo .12 .30
89 Jay Bell .12 .30
90 Manny Ramirez .30 .75
91 Frank Thomas .30 .75
92 Mike Mussina .20 .50
93 J.D. Drew .12 .30
94 Adrian Beltre .30 .75
95 Alex Rodriguez .40 1.00
96 Larry Walker .20 .50
97 Juan Encarnacion .12 .30
98 Mike Sweeney .12 .30
99 Rusty Greer .12 .30
100 Randy Johnson .30 .75
101 Jose Vidro .12 .30
102 Preston Wilson .12 .30
103 Greg Maddux .40 1.00
104 Jason Giambi .12 .30
105 Cal Ripken 1.00 2.50
106 Carlos Beltran .20 .50
107 Vinny Castilla .12 .30
108 Mariano Rivera .40 1.00
109 Mo Vaughn .12 .30
110 Rafael Palmeiro .20 .50
111 Shannon Stewart .12 .30
112 Mike Hampton .12 .30
113 Joe Nathan .12 .30
114 Ben Davis .12 .30
115 Andruw Jones .12 .30
116 Robin Ventura .12 .30
117 Damion Easley .12 .30
118 Jeff Cirillo .12 .30
119 Kerry Wood .12 .30
120 Scott Rolen .20 .50
121 Sammy Sosa .30 .75
122 Ken Griffey Jr. .60 1.50
123 Shane Reynolds .12 .30
124 Troy Glaus .12 .30
125 Tom Glavine .20 .50
126 Michael Barrett .12 .30
127 Al Leiter .12 .30
128 Jason Kendall .12 .30
129 Roger Clemens .40 1.00
130 Juan Gonzalez .12 .30
131 Corey Koskie .12 .30
132 Curt Schilling .20 .50
133 Mike Piazza .30 .75
134 Gary Sheffield .12 .30
135 Jim Thome .20 .50
136 Orlando Hernandez .12 .30
137 Ray Lankford .12 .30
138 Geoff Jenkins .12 .30
139 Jose Lima .12 .30
140 Mark McGwire .50 1.25
141 Adam Piatt .12 .30
142 Pat Manning RC .12 .30
143 Marcos Castillo RC .12 .30
144 Lesli Brea RC .12 .30
145 Humberto Cota RC .12 .30
146 Ben Petrick .12 .30
147 Kip Wells .12 .30
148 Wily Pena .12 .30
149 Chris Wakeland RC .12 .30
150 Brad Baker RC .12 .30
151 Robbie Morrison RC .12 .30
152 Reggie Taylor .12 .30
153 Matt Ginter RC .12 .30
154 Peter Bergeron .12 .30
155 Roosevelt Brown .12 .30
156 Matt Cepicky RC .12 .30
157 Ramon Castro .12 .30
158 Brad Baisley RC .12 .30
159 Jeff Goldbach RC .12 .30
160 Mitch Meluskey .12 .30
161 Chad Harville .12 .30
162 Brian Cooper .12 .30
163 Marcus Giles .12 .30
164 Jim Morris 1.50 4.00
165 Geoff Goetz .12 .30
166 Bobby Bradley RC .12 .30
167 Rob Bell .12 .30
168 Joe Crede .12 .30
169 Michael Restovich .12 .30
170 Quincy Foster RC .12 .30
171 Enrique Cruz RC .12 .30
172 Mark Quinn .12 .30
173 Nick Johnson .12 .30
174 Jeff Liefer .12 .30
175 Kevin Mench RC .30 .75
176 Steve Lomasney .12 .30
177 Jayson Werth .20 .50
178 Tim Drew .12 .30
179 Chip Ambres .12 .30
180 Ryan Anderson .12 .30
181 Matt Blank .12 .30
182 Giuseppe Chiaramonte .12 .30
183 Corey Myers RC .12 .30
184 Jeff Yoder .12 .30
185 Craig Dingman RC .12 .30
186 Jon Hamilton RC .12 .30
187 Toby Hall .12 .30
188 Russell Branyan .12 .30
189 Brian Falkenborg RC .12 .30
190 Aaron Harang RC .75 2.00
191 Juan Pena .12 .30
192 Travis Thompson RC .12 .30
193 Alfonso Soriano .30 .75
194 Alejandro Diaz RC .12 .30
195 Carlos Pena .20 .50
196 Kevin Nicholson .12 .30
197 Mo Bruce .12 .30
198 C.C. Sabathia .20 .50
199 Carl Crawford .20 .50
200 Rafael Furcal .20 .50
201 Andrew Beinbrink RC .12 .30
202 Jimmy Osting .12 .30
203 Aaron McNeal RC .12 .30
204 Brett Laxton .12 .30
205 Chris George .12 .30
206 Felipe Lopez .12 .30
207 Ben Sheets RC .30 .75
208 Mike Meyers RC .20 .50
209 Jason Conti .12 .30
210 Milton Bradley .12 .30
211 Chris Mears RC .12 .30
212 Carlos Hernandez RC .12 .30
213 Jason Romano .12 .30
214 Geofrey Tomlinson .12 .30
215 Jimmy Rollins .20 .50
216 Pablo Ozuna .12 .30
217 Steve Cox .12 .30
218 Terrence Long .12 .30
219 Jeff DaVanon RC .12 .30
220 Rick Ankiel .20 .50
221 Jason Standridge .12 .30
222 Tony Armas Jr. .12 .30
223 Jason Tyner .12 .30
224 Ramon Ortiz .12 .30
225 Daryle Ward .12 .30
226 Enger Veras RC .12 .30
227 Chris Jones .12 .30
228 Eric Cammack RC .12 .30
229 Ruben Mateo .12 .30
230 Ken Harvey RC .12 .30
231 Jake Westbrook .12 .30
232 Rob Purvis RC .12 .30
233 Choo Freeman .12 .30
234 Aramis Ramirez .12 .30
235 A.J. Burnett .12 .30
236 Kevin Barker .12 .30
237 Chance Caple RC .12 .30
238 Jarrod Washburn .12 .30
239 Lance Berkman .20 .50
240 Michael Wenner RC .12 .30
241 Alex Sanchez .12 .30
242 Pat Daneker .12 .30
243 Grant Roberts .12 .30
244 Mark Ellis RC .20 .50
245 Donny Leon .12 .30
246 David Eckstein .12 .30
247 Dicky Gonzalez RC .12 .30
248 John Patterson .12 .30
249 Chad Green .12 .30
250 Scot Shields RC .12 .30
251 Troy Cameron .12 .30
252 Jose Molina .12 .30
253 Rob Pugmire RC .12 .30
254 Rick Elder .12 .30
255 Sean Burroughs .12 .30
256 Josh Kalinowski RC .12 .30
257 Matt LeCroy .12 .30
258 Alex Graman RC .12 .30
259 Tomo Ohka RC .12 .30
260 Brady Clark .12 .30
261 Rico Washington RC .12 .30
262 Gary Matthews Jr. .12 .30
263 Matt Wise .12 .30
264 Keith Reed RC .12 .30
265 Santiago Ramirez RC .12 .30
266 Ben Broussard RC .20 .50
267 Ryan Langerhans .12 .30
268 Juan Rivera .12 .30
269 Shawn Gallagher .12 .30
270 Jorge Toca .12 .30
271 Brad Lidge .12 .30
272 Leoncio Estrella RC .12 .30
273 Ruben Quevedo .12 .30
274 Jack Cust .12 .30
275 T.J. Tucker .12 .30
276 Mike Colangelo .12 .30
277 Brian Schneider .12 .30
278 Calvin Murray .12 .30
279 Josh Girdley .12 .30
280 Mike Paradis .12 .30
281 Chad Hermansen .12 .30
282 Ty Howington RC .12 .30
283 Aaron Myette .12 .30
284 D'Angelo Jimenez .12 .30
285 Dernell Stenson .12 .30
286 Jerry Hairston Jr. .12 .30
287 Gary Majewski RC .12 .30
288 Derrin Ebert .12 .30
289 Steve Fish RC .12 .30
290 Carlos E. Hernandez .12 .30
291 Allen Levrault .12 .30
292 Sean McNally RC .12 .30
293 Randey Dorame RC .12 .30
294 Wes Anderson RC .12 .30
295 B.J. Ryan .12 .30
296 Alan Webb RC .12 .30
297 Brandon Inge RC .75 2.00
298 David Walling .12 .30
299 Sun Woo Kim RC .12 .30
300 Pat Burrell .12 .30
301 Rick Guttormson RC .12 .30
302 Gil Meche .12 .30
303 Carlos Zambrano RC .75 2.00
304 Eric Byrnes UER RC .12 .30
305 Robb Quinlan RC .12 .30
306 Jackie Rexrode .12 .30
307 Nate Bump .12 .30
308 Sean DePaula RC .12 .30
309 Matt Riley .12 .30
310 Ryan Minor .12 .30
311 J.J. Davis .12 .30
312 Randy Wolf .12 .30
313 Jason Jennings .12 .30
314 Scott Seabol RC .12 .30
315 Doug Davis .12 .30
316 Todd Moser RC .12 .30
317 Rob Ryan .12 .30
318 Bubba Crosby .12 .30
319 Lyle Overbay RC .20 .50
320 Mario Encarnacion .12 .30
321 Francisco Rodriguez RC .75 2.00
322 Michael Cuddyer .12 .30
323 Ed Yarnall .12 .30
324 Cesar Saba RC .12 .30
325 Gookie Dawkins .12 .30
326 Alex Escobar .12 .30
327 Julio Zuleta RC .12 .30
328 Josh Hamilton .40 1.00
329 Nick Neugebauer RC .12 .30
330 Matt Belisle .12 .30
331 Kurt Ainsworth RC .12 .30
332 Tim Raines Jr. .12 .30
333 Eric Munson .12 .30
334 Donzell McDonald .12 .30
335 Larry Bigbie RC .12 .30
336 Matt Watson RC .12 .30
337 Aubrey Huff .12 .30
338 Julio Ramirez .12 .30
339 Jason Grabowski RC .12 .30
340 Jon Garland .12 .30
341 Austin Kearns .12 .30
342 Josh Pressley RC .12 .30
343 Miguel Olivo RC .20 .50
344 Julio Lugo .12 .30
345 Roberto Vaz .12 .30
346 Ramon Soler .12 .30
347 Brandon Phillips RC .50 1.25
348 Vince Faison RC .12 .30
349 Mike Venafro .12 .30
350 Rick Asadoorian RC .12 .30
351 B.J. Garbe RC .12 .30
352 Dan Reichert .12 .30
353 Jason Stumm RC .12 .30
354 Ruben Salazar RC .12 .30
355 Francisco Cordero .12 .30
356 Juan Guzman RC .12 .30
357 Mike Bacsik RC .12 .30
358 Jared Sandberg .12 .30
359 Rod Barajas .12 .30
360 Junior Brignac RC .12 .30
361 J.M. Gold .12 .30
362 Octavio Dotel .12 .30
363 David Kelton .12 .30
364 Scott Morgan .12 .30
365 Wascar Serrano RC .12 .30
366 Wilton Veras .12 .30
367 Eugene Kingsale .12 .30
368 Ted Lilly .12 .30
369 George Lombard .12 .30
370 Chris Haas .12 .30
371 Wilton Pena RC .12 .30
372 Vernon Wells .12 .30
373 Jason Royer RC .12 .30
374 Jeff Heaverlo RC .12 .30
375 Calvin Pickering .12 .30
376 Mike Lamb RC .12 .30
377 Kyle Snyder .12 .30
378 Javier Cardona RC .12 .30
379 Aaron Rowand RC .60 1.50
380 Dee Brown .12 .30
381 Brett Myers RC .40 1.00
382 Abraham Nunez .12 .30
383 Eric Valent .12 .30
384 Jody Gerut RC .12 .30
385 Adam Dunn .20 .50
386 Jay Gehrke .12 .30
387 Omar Ortiz .12 .30
388 Darnell McDonald .12 .30
389 Tony Schrager RC .12 .30
390 J.D. Closser .12 .30
391 Ben Christensen RC .12 .30
392 Adam Kennedy .12 .30
393 Nick Green RC .12 .30
394 Ramon Hernandez .12 .30
395 Roy Oswalt RC 2.00 5.00
396 Andy Tracy RC .12 .30
397 Eric Gagne .12 .30
398 Michael Tejera RC .12 .30
399 Adam Everett .12 .30
400 Corey Patterson .12 .30
401 Gary Knotts RC .12 .30
402 Ryan Christianson RC .12 .30
403 Eric Ireland RC .12 .30
404 Andrew Good RC .12 .30
405 Brad Penny .12 .30
406 Jason LaRue .12 .30
407 Kit Pellow .12 .30
408 Kevin Beirne .12 .30
409 Kelly Dransfeldt .12 .30
410 Jason Grilli .12 .30
411 Scott Downs RC .12 .30
412 Jesus Colome .12 .30
413 John Sneed RC .12 .30
414 Tony McKnight .12 .30
415 Luis Rivera .12 .30
416 Adam Eaton .12 .30
417 Mike MacDougal RC .20 .50
418 Mike Nannini .12 .30
419 Barry Zito RC 1.00 2.50
420 DeWayne Wise .12 .30
421 Jason Dellaero .12 .30
422 Chad Moeller .12 .30
423 Jason Marquis .12 .30
424 Tim Redding RC .20 .50
425 Mark Mulder .12 .30
426 Josh Paul .12 .30
427 Chris Enochs .12 .30
428 Wilfredo Rodriguez RC .12 .30
429 Kevin Witt .12 .30
430 Scott Sobkowiak RC .12 .30
431 McKay Christensen .12 .30
432 Jung Bong .12 .30
433 Keith Evans RC .12 .30
434 Garry Maddox Jr. RC .12 .30
435 Ramon Santiago RC .12 .30
436 Alex Cora .20 .50
437 Carlos Lee .12 .30
438 Jason Repko RC .12 .30
439 Matt Burch .12 .30
440 Shawn Sonnier RC .12 .30

2000 Bowman Gold

*GOLD: 10X TO 25X BASIC
STATED ODDS 1:64 HOB/RET, 1:31 HTC
STATED PRINT RUN 99 SERIAL #'d SETS

2000 Bowman Retro/Future

COMPLETE SET (440) 75.00 200.00
*RETRO: 1X TO 2.5X BASIC
ONE PER PACK

2000 Bowman Autographs

BLUE ODDS 1:144 HOB/RET, 1:69 HTC
BLUE: ONE CHIP-TOPPER PER HTC BOX
SILVER ODDS 1:312 HOB/RET, 1:148 HTC
GOLD ODDS 1:1604 HOB/RET, 1:762 HTC
AD Adam Dunn B 3.00 8.00
AH Aubrey Huff B 2.00 5.00
AK Austin Kearns B 2.00 5.00
AP Adam Piatt S 2.50 6.00
AS Alfonso Soriano S 6.00 15.00
BP Ben Petrick G 3.00 8.00
BS Ben Sheets B 5.00 12.00
BWP Brad Penny B 2.00 5.00
CA Chip Ambres B 2.00 5.00
CB Carlos Beltran G 20.00 50.00
CF Choo Freeman B 2.00 5.00
CP Corey Patterson S 2.50 6.00
DB Dee Brown S 2.50 6.00
DK David Kelton B 2.00 5.00
EV Eric Valent B 2.00 5.00
EY Ed Yarnall S 2.50 6.00
JC Jack Cust S 2.50 6.00
JDC J.D. Closser B 2.00 5.00
JDD J.D. Drew G 3.00 8.00
JJ Jason Jennings B 2.00 5.00
JR Jason Romano B 2.00 5.00
JV Jose Vidro S 2.50 6.00
JZ Julio Zuleta B 2.00 5.00
KJW Kevin Witt S 2.50 6.00
KLW Kerry Wood S 2.50 6.00
LB Lance Berkman S 4.00 10.00
MC Michael Cuddyer S 2.50 6.00
MJR Mike Restovich B 2.00 5.00
MM Mike Meyers B 3.00 8.00
MQ Mark Quinn S 2.50 6.00
MR Matt Riley S 2.50 6.00
NJ Nick Johnson S 2.50 6.00
RA Rick Ankiel G 5.00 12.00
RF Rafael Furcal S 4.00 10.00
RM Ruben Mateo G 3.00 8.00
SB Sean Burroughs S 2.50 6.00
SC Steve Cox B 2.00 5.00
SD Scott Downs S 2.50 6.00
SW Scott Williamson G 3.00 8.00
VW Vernon Wells G 3.00 8.00

2000 Bowman Early Indications

COMPLETE SET (10) 10.00 25.00
STATED ODDS 1:24 HOB/RET, 1:9 HTC
E1 Nomar Garciaparra .60 1.50
E2 Cal Ripken 3.00 8.00
E3 Derek Jeter 2.50 6.00
E4 Mark McGwire 1.50 4.00
E5 Alex Rodriguez 1.25 3.00
E6 Chipper Jones 1.00 2.50
E7 Todd Helton .60 1.50
E8 Vladimir Guerrero .60 1.50
E9 Mike Piazza 1.00 2.50
E10 Jose Canseco .60 1.50

2000 Bowman Major Power

COMPLETE SET (10) 8.00 20.00
STATED ODDS 1:24 HOB/RET, 1:9 HTC
MP1 Mark McGwire 1.50 4.00
MP2 Chipper Jones 1.00 2.50
MP3 Alex Rodriguez 1.25 3.00
MP4 Sammy Sosa 1.00 2.50
MP5 Rafael Palmeiro .60 1.50
MP6 Ken Griffey Jr. 2.00 5.00
MP7 Nomar Garciaparra .60 1.50
MP8 Barry Bonds 1.50 4.00
MP9 Derek Jeter 2.50 6.00
MP10 Jeff Bagwell .60 1.50

2000 Bowman Tool Time

COMPLETE SET (20) 6.00 15.00
STATED ODDS 1:8 HOB/RET, 1:3 HTC
TT1 Pat Burrell .40 1.00
TT2 Aaron Rowand 2.00 5.00
TT3 Chris Wakeland .40 1.00
TT4 Ruben Mateo .40 1.00
TT5 Pat Burrell .40 1.00
TT6 Adam Piatt .40 1.00
TT7 Nick Johnson .40 1.00
TT8 Jack Cust .40 1.00
TT9 Rafael Furcal .60 1.50
TT10 Julio Ramirez .40 1.00
TT11 Gookie Dawkins .40 1.00
TT12 Corey Patterson .40 1.00
TT13 Ruben Mateo .40 1.00
TT14 Jason Dellaero .40 1.00
TT15 Sean Burroughs .40 1.00
TT16 Ryan Langerhans .40 1.00
TT17 D'Angelo Jimenez .40 1.00
TT18 Corey Patterson .40 1.00
TT19 Troy Cameron .40 1.00
TT20 Michael Cuddyer .40 1.00

2000 Bowman Draft

COMP.FACT.SET (111) 12.50 30.00
COMPLETE SET (110) 8.00 20.00
COMMON CARD (1-110) .12 .30
COMMON RC .12 .30
1 Pat Burrell .12 .30
2 Rafael Furcal .20 .50
3 Grant Roberts .12 .30
4 Barry Zito 1.00 2.50
5 Julio Zuleta .12 .30
6 Mark Mulder .12 .30
7 Rob Bell .12 .30
8 Adam Piatt .12 .30
9 Mike Lamb .12 .30
10 Pablo Ozuna .12 .30
11 Jason Tyner .12 .30
12 Jason Marquis .12 .30
13 Eric Munson .12 .30
14 Seth Etherton .12 .30
15 Milton Bradley .12 .30
16 Nick Green .12 .30
17 Chin-Feng Chen RC .40 1.00
18 Matt Boone RC .12 .30
19 Kevin Gregg RC .12 .30
20 Eddy Garabito RC .12 .30
21 Aaron Capista RC .12 .30
22 Esteban German RC .12 .30
23 Derek Thompson RC .12 .30
24 Phil Merrell RC .12 .30
25 Brian O'Connor RC .12 .30
26 Yamid Haad .12 .30
27 Hector Mercado RC .12 .30
28 Jason Woolf RC .12 .30
29 Eddy Furniss RC .12 .30
30 Cha Sueng Baek RC .12 .30
31 Colby Lewis RC .30 .75
32 Pasqual Coco RC .12 .30
33 Jorge Cantu RC .20 .50
34 Erasmo Ramirez RC .12 .30
35 Bobby Kielty RC .12 .30
36 Joaquin Benoit RC .12 .30
37 Brian Esposito RC .12 .30
38 Michael Wenner .12 .30
39 Juan Rincon RC .12 .30
40 Yorvit Torrealba RC .20 .50
41 Chad Durham RC .12 .30
42 Jim Mann RC .12 .30
43 Shane Loux RC .12 .30
44 Luis Rivas .12 .30
45 Ken Chenard RC .12 .30
46 Mike Lockwood RC .12 .30
47 Yovanny Lara RC .12 .30
48 Bubba Carpenter RC .12 .30
49 Ryan Dittfurth RC .12 .30
50 John Stephens RC .12 .30
51 Pedro Feliz RC .30 .75
52 Kenny Kelly RC .12 .30
53 Neil Jenkins RC .12 .30
54 Mike Glendenning RC .12 .30
55 Bo Porter .12 .30
56 Eric Byrnes .12 .30
57 Tony Alvarez RC .12 .30
58 Kazuhiro Sasaki RC .30 .75
59 Chad Durbin RC .12 .30
60 Mike Bynum RC .12 .30
61 Travis Wilson RC .12 .30
62 Jose Leon RC .12 .30
63 Ryan Vogelsong RC 1.25 3.00
64 Geraldo Guzman RC .12 .30
65 Craig Anderson RC .12 .30
66 Carlos Silva RC .12 .30
67 Brad Thomas RC .12 .30
68 Chin-Hui Tsao RC .30 .75
69 Mark Buehrle RC 2.00 5.00
70 Juan Salas RC .12 .30
71 Denny Abreu RC .12 .30
72 Keith McDonald RC .12 .30
73 Chris Richard RC .12 .30
74 Tomas De la Rosa RC .12 .30
75 Vicente Padilla RC .30 .75
76 Justin Brunette RC .12 .30
77 Scott Linebrink RC .12 .30
78 Jeff Sparks RC .12 .30
79 Tike Redman RC .12 .30
80 John Lackey RC .75 2.00
81 Joe Strong RC .12 .30
82 Brian Tollberg RC .12 .30
83 Steve Sisco RC .12 .30
84 Chris Clapinski RC .12 .30
85 Augie Ojeda RC .12 .30
86 Adrian Gonzalez RC 4.00 10.00
87 Mike Stodolka RC .12 .30
88 Adam Johnson RC .12 .30
89 Matt Wheatland RC .12 .30
90 Corey Smith RC .12 .30
91 Rocco Baldelli RC .30 .75
92 Keith Bucktrot RC .12 .30
93 Adam Wainwright RC 1.25 3.00
94 Blaine Boyer RC .12 .30
95 Aaron Herr RC .20 .50
96 Scott Thorman RC .20 .50
97 Bryan Digby RC .12 .30
98 Josh Shortslef RC .12 .30
99 Sean Smith RC .12 .30
100 Alex Cruz RC .12 .30
101 Marc Love RC .12 .30
102 Kevin Lee RC .12 .30
103 Victor Ramos RC .12 .30
104 Jason Kaanoi RC .12 .30
105 Luis Escobar RC .12 .30
106 Tripper Johnson RC .12 .30
107 Phil Dumatrait RC .12 .30
108 Bryan Edwards RC .12 .30
109 Grady Sizemore RC 2.50 6.00
110 Thomas Mitchell RC .12 .30

2000 Bowman Draft Autographs

ONE AUTOGRAPH PER FACTORY SET
CARDS 16, 32, 34, 45 AND 56 DO NOT EXIST
BDPA1 Pat Burrell 3.00 8.00
BDPA2 Rafael Furcal 5.00 12.00
BDPA3 Grant Roberts 3.00 8.00
BDPA4 Barry Zito 8.00 20.00
BDPA5 Julio Zuleta 3.00 8.00
BDPA6 Mark Mulder 3.00 8.00
BDPA7 Rob Bell 3.00 8.00
BDPA8 Adam Piatt 3.00 8.00
BDPA9 Mike Lamb 3.00 8.00
BDPA10 Pablo Ozuna 3.00 8.00
BDPA11 Jason Tyner 3.00 8.00
BDPA12 Jason Marquis 3.00 8.00
BDPA13 Eric Munson 3.00 8.00
BDPA14 Seth Etherton 3.00 8.00
BDPA15 Milton Bradley 3.00 8.00
BDPA17 Michael Wenner 3.00 8.00
BDPA18 Mike Glendenning 3.00 8.00
BDPA19 Tony Alvarez 3.00 8.00
BDPA20 Adrian Gonzalez 20.00 50.00
BDPA21 Corey Smith 3.00 8.00
BDPA22 Matt Wheatland 3.00 8.00
BDPA23 Adam Johnson 3.00 8.00
BDPA24 Mike Stodolka 3.00 8.00
BDPA25 Rocco Baldelli 8.00 20.00
BDPA26 Juan Rincon 3.00 8.00
BDPA27 Chad Durbin 3.00 8.00
BDPA28 Yorvit Torrealba 5.00 12.00
BDPA29 Nick Green 3.00 8.00
BDPA30 Derek Thompson 3.00 8.00
BDPA31 John Lackey 8.00 20.00
BDPA33 Kevin Gregg 3.00 8.00
BDPA35 Denny Abreu 3.00 8.00
BDPA36 Brian Tollberg 3.00 8.00
BDPA37 Yamid Haad 3.00 8.00
BDPA38 Grady Sizemore 12.00 30.00
BDPA39 Carlos Silva 3.00 8.00
BDPA40 Jorge Cantu 5.00 12.00
BDPA41 Bobby Kielty 3.00 8.00
BDPA42 Scott Thorman 5.00 12.00
BDPA43 Juan Salas 3.00 8.00
BDPA44 Phil Dumatrait 3.00 8.00
BDPA46 Mike Lockwood 3.00 8.00
BDPA47 Yovanny Lara 3.00 8.00
BDPA48 Tripper Johnson 3.00 8.00
BDPA49 Colby Lewis 8.00 20.00
BDPA50 Neil Jenkins 3.00 8.00
BDPA51 Keith Bucktrot 3.00 8.00
BDPA52 Eric Byrnes 3.00 8.00
BDPA53 Aaron Herr 5.00 12.00
BDPA54 Erasmo Ramirez 3.00 8.00
BDPA55 Chris Richard 3.00 8.00
BDPA57 Mike Bynum 3.00 8.00
BDPA58 Brian Esposito 3.00 8.00
BDPA59 Chris Clapinski 3.00 8.00
BDPA60 Augie Ojeda 3.00 8.00

2001 Bowman Promos

COMPLETE SET (3) 2.40 6.00
PP1 Barry Bonds .80 2.00
PP2 Roger Clemens 1.20 3.00
PP3 Adrian Gonzalez 4.00 10.00

2001 Bowman

COMPLETE SET (440) 40.00 100.00
COMMON CARD (1-440) .10 .30
COMMON RC .15 .40
SASAKI/FURCAL JSY ODDS 1:2202 HOB
SASAKI/FURCAL JSY ODDS 1:1045 HTA
BURROUGHS BALL EXCH ODDS 1:30,432
1 Jason Giambi .10 .30
2 Rafael Furcal .10 .30
3 Rick Ankiel .10 .30
4 Freddy Garcia .10 .30
5 Magglio Ordonez .10 .30
6 Bernie Williams .20 .50
7 Kenny Lofton .10 .30
8 Al Leiter .10 .30
9 Albert Belle .10 .30
10 Craig Biggio .20 .50
11 Mark Mulder .10 .30
12 Carlos Delgado .10 .30
13 Darin Erstad .10 .30
14 Richie Sexson .10 .30
15 Randy Johnson .30 .75
16 Greg Maddux .50 1.25
17 Cliff Floyd .10 .30
18 Mark Buehrle .20 .50
19 Chris Singleton .10 .30
20 Orlando Hernandez .10 .30
21 Javier Vazquez .10 .30
22 Jeff Kent .10 .30
23 Jim Thome .20 .50
24 John Olerud .10 .30
25 Jason Kendall .10 .30
26 Scott Rolen .20 .50
27 Tony Gwynn .40 1.00
28 Edgardo Alfonzo .10 .30
29 Pokey Reese .10 .30
30 Todd Helton .20 .50
31 Mark Quinn .10 .30
32 Dan Tosca RC .15 .40
33 Dean Palmer .10 .30
34 Jacque Jones .10 .30
35 Ray Durham .10 .30
36 Rafael Palmeiro .20 .50
37 Carl Everett .10 .30
38 Ryan Dempster .10 .30
39 Randy Wolf .10 .30
40 Vladimir Guerrero .30 .75
41 Livan Hernandez .10 .30
42 Mo Vaughn .10 .30
43 Shannon Stewart .10 .30
44 Preston Wilson .10 .30
45 Jose Vidro .10 .30
46 Fred McGriff .20 .50
47 Kevin Brown .10 .30
48 Peter Bergeron .10 .30
49 Miguel Tejada .10 .30
50 Chipper Jones .30 .75
51 Edgar Martinez .20 .50
52 Tony Batista .10 .30
53 Jorge Posada .20 .50
54 Ricky Ledee .10 .30
55 Sammy Sosa .30 .75
56 Steve Cox .10 .30
57 Tony Armas Jr. .10 .30
58 Gary Sheffield .10 .30
59 Bartolo Colon .10 .30
60 Pat Burrell .10 .30
61 Jay Payton .10 .30
62 Sean Casey .10 .30
63 Larry Walker .10 .30
64 Mike Mussina .20 .50
65 Nomar Garciaparra .50 1.25
66 Darren Dreifort .10 .30
67 Richard Hidalgo .10 .30
68 Troy Glaus .10 .30
69 Ben Grieve .10 .30
70 Jim Edmonds .10 .30
71 Raul Mondesi .10 .30
72 Andruw Jones .20 .50
73 Luis Castillo .10 .30
74 Mike Sweeney .10 .30
75 Derek Jeter .75 2.00
76 Ruben Mateo .10 .30
77 Carlos Lee .10 .30
78 Cristian Guzman .10 .30
79 Mike Hampton .10 .30
80 J.D. Drew .10 .30
81 Matt Lawton .10 .30
82 Moises Alou .10 .30
83 Terrence Long .10 .30
84 Geoff Jenkins .10 .30
85 Manny Ramirez Sox .20 .50
86 Johnny Damon .20 .50
87 Barry Larkin .20 .50
88 Pedro Martinez .20 .50
89 Juan Gonzalez .10 .30
90 Roger Clemens .60 1.50
91 Carlos Beltran .10 .30
92 Brad Radke .10 .30
93 Orlando Cabrera .10 .30
94 Roberto Alomar .20 .50
95 Barry Bonds .75 2.00
96 Tim Hudson .10 .30
97 Tom Glavine .20 .50
98 Jeromy Burnitz .10 .30
99 Adrian Beltre .10 .30
100 Mike Piazza .50 1.25
101 Kerry Wood .10 .30
102 Steve Finley .10 .30
103 Alex Cora .10 .30
104 Bob Abreu .10 .30
105 Neifi Perez .10 .30
106 Mark Redman .10 .30
107 Paul Konerko .10 .30
108 Jermaine Dye .10 .30
109 Brian Giles .10 .30
110 Ivan Rodriguez .20 .50
111 Vinny Castilla .10 .30
112 Adam Kennedy .10 .30
113 Eric Chavez .10 .30
114 Billy Koch .10 .30
115 Shawn Green .10 .30
116 Matt Williams .10 .30
117 Greg Vaughn .10 .30
118 Gabe Kapler .10 .30
119 Jeff Cirillo .10 .30
120 Frank Thomas .30 .75
121 David Justice .10 .30
122 Cal Ripken 1.00 2.50
123 Rich Aurilia .10 .30
124 Curt Schilling .10 .30
125 Barry Zito .20 .50
126 Brian Jordan .10 .30
127 Chan Ho Park .10 .30
128 J.T. Snow .10 .30
129 Kazuhiro Sasaki .10 .30
130 Alex Rodriguez .40 1.00
131 Mariano Rivera .30 .75
132 Eric Milton .10 .30
133 Andy Pettitte .20 .50
134 Scott Elarton .10 .30
135 Ken Griffey Jr. .60 1.50
136 Bengie Molina .10 .30
137 Jeff Bagwell .20 .50
138 Kevin Millwood .10 .30
139 Tino Martinez .20 .50
140 Mark McGwire .75 2.00
141 Larry Barnes .10 .30
142 John Buck RC 1.50 4.00
143 Freddie Bynum RC .15 .40
144 Abraham Nunez .10 .30
145 Felix Diaz RC .15 .40
146 Horacio Estrada .10 .30
147 Ben Diggins .10 .30
148 Tsuyoshi Shinjo RC .40 1.00
149 Rocco Baldelli .10 .30
150 Rod Barajas .10 .30
151 Luis Terrero .10 .30
152 Milton Bradley .10 .30
153 Kurt Ainsworth .10 .30
154 Russell Branyan .10 .30
155 Ryan Anderson .10 .30
156 Mitch Jones RC .25 .60
157 Chip Ambres .10 .30
158 Steve Bennett RC .15 .40
159 Ivanon Coffie .10 .30
160 Sean Burroughs .10 .30
161 Keith Bucktrot .10 .30
162 Tony Alvarez .10 .30
163 Joaquin Benoit .10 .30
164 Rick Asadoorian .10 .30
165 Ben Broussard .10 .30
166 Ryan Madson RC .50 1.25
167 Dee Brown .10 .30
168 Sergio Contreras RC .25 .60
169 John Barnes .10 .30
170 Ben Washburn RC .15 .40
171 Erick Almonte RC .15 .40
172 Shawn Fagan RC .15 .40
173 Gary Johnson RC .15 .40
174 Brady Clark .10 .30
175 Grant Roberts .10 .30
176 Tony Torcato .10 .30
177 Ramon Castro .10 .30
178 Esteban German .10 .30
179 Joe Hamer RC .25 .60
180 Nick Neugebauer .10 .30
181 Dernell Stenson .10 .30
182 Yhency Brazoban RC .40 1.00
183 Aaron Myette .10 .30
184 Juan Sosa .10 .30
185 Brandon Inge .10 .30
186 Domingo Guante RC .15 .40
187 Adrian Brown .10 .30
188 Deivi Mendez RC .15 .40
189 Luis Matos .10 .30
190 Pedro Liriano RC .25 .60
191 Donnie Bridges .10 .30
192 Alex Cintron .10 .30
193 Jace Brewer .10 .30
194 Ron Davenport RC .25 .60
195 Jason Belcher RC .15 .40
196 Adrian Hernandez RC .15 .40
197 Bobby Kielty .10 .30
198 Reggie Griggs RC .25 .60
199 Reggie Abercrombie RC .40 1.00
200 Troy Farnsworth RC .25 .60
201 Matt Belisle .10 .30
202 Miguel Villilo RC .25 .60
203 Adam Everett .10 .30
204 John Lackey .10 .30
205 Pasqual Coco .10 .30
206 Adam Wainwright .25 .60
207 Matt White RC .25 .60
208 Chin-Feng Chen .10 .30
209 Jeff Andra RC .15 .40
210 Willie Bloomquist .10 .30

Card	Low	High
211 Wes Anderson	.10	.30
212 Enrique Cruz	.10	.30
213 Jerry Hairston Jr.	.10	.30
214 Mike Bynum	.10	.30
215 Brian Hitchcox RC	.15	.40
216 Ryan Christianson	.10	.30
217 J.J. Davis	.10	.30
218 Jovanny Cedeno	.10	.30
219 Elvin Nina	.10	.30
220 Alex Graman	.10	.30
221 Arturo McDowell	.10	.30
222 Deivis Santos RC	.15	.40
223 Jody Gerut	.10	.30
224 Sun Woo Kim	.10	.30
225 Jimmy Rollins	.10	.30
226 Ntema Ndungidi	.10	.30
227 Ruben Salazar	.10	.30
228 Josh Girdley	.10	.30
229 Carl Crawford	.10	.30
230 Luis Montanez RC	.30	.75
231 Ramon Carvajal RC	.25	.60
232 Matt Riley	.10	.30
233 Ben Davis	.10	.30
234 Jason Grabowski	.10	.30
235 Chris George	.10	.30
236 Hank Blalock RC	1.00	2.50
237 Roy Oswalt	.30	.75
238 Eric Reynolds RC	.15	.40
239 Brian Cole	.10	.30
240 Denny Bautista RC	.40	1.00
241 Hector Garcia RC	.15	.40
242 Joe Thurston RC	.25	.60
243 Brad Cresse	.10	.30
244 Corey Patterson	.10	.30
245 Brett Evert RC	.15	.40
246 Elpidio Guzman RC	.15	.40
247 Vernon Wells	.10	.30
248 Roberto Miniel RC	.25	.60
249 Brian Bass RC	.15	.40
250 Mark Burnett RC	.25	.60
251 Juan Silvestre	.10	.30
252 Pablo Ozuna	.10	.30
253 Jayson Werth	.10	.30
254 Russ Jacobson	.10	.30
255 Chad Hermansen	.10	.30
256 Travis Hafner RC	4.00	10.00
257 Brad Baker	.10	.30
258 Gookie Dawkins	.10	.30
259 Michael Cuddyer	.10	.30
260 Mark Buehrle	.20	.50
261 Ricardo Aramboles	.10	.30
262 Esix Snead RC	.15	.40
263 Wilson Betemit RC	1.25	3.00
264 Albert Pujols RC	50.00	120.00
265 Joe Lawrence	.10	.30
266 Ramon Ortiz	.10	.30
267 Ben Sheets	.20	.50
268 Luke Lockwood RC	.25	.60
269 Toby Hall	.10	.30
270 Jack Cust	.10	.30
271 Pedro Feliz	.10	.30
272 Noel Devarez RC	.25	.60
273 Josh Beckett	.20	.50
274 Alex Escobar	.10	.30
275 Doug Gredvig RC	.15	.40
276 Marcus Giles	.10	.30
277 Jon Rauch	.10	.30
278 Brian Schmitt RC	.15	.40
279 Seung Song RC	.25	.60
280 Kevin Mench	.10	.30
281 Adam Eaton	.10	.30
282 Shawn Sonnier	.10	.30
283 Andy Van Hekken RC	.15	.40
284 Aaron Rowand	.10	.30
285 Tony Blanco RC	.25	.60
286 Ryan Kohlmeier	.10	.30
287 C.C. Sabathia	.10	.30
288 Bubba Crosby	.10	.30
289 Josh Hamilton	.25	.60
290 Dee Haynes RC	.15	.40
291 Jason Marquis	.10	.30
292 Julio Zuleta	.10	.30
293 Carlos Hernandez	.10	.30
294 Matt Lecroy	.10	.30
295 Andy Beal RC	.15	.40
296 Carlos Pena	.10	.30
297 Reggie Taylor	.10	.30
298 Bob Keppel RC	.15	.40
299 Miguel Cabrera UER	4.00	10.00
300 Ryan Franklin	.10	.30
301 Brandon Phillips	.10	.30
302 Victor Hall RC	.25	.60
303 Tony Pena Jr.	.10	.30
304 Jim Journell RC	.25	.60
305 Cristian Guerrero	.10	.30
306 Miguel Olivo	.10	.30
307 Jin Ho Cho	.10	.30
308 Choo Freeman	.10	.30
309 Danny Borrell RC	.15	.40
310 Doug Mientkiewicz	.10	.30
311 Aaron Herr	.10	.30
312 Keith Ginter	.10	.30
313 Felipe Lopez	.10	.30
314 Jeff Goldbach	.10	.30
315 Travis Harper	.10	.30
316 Paul LoDuca	.10	.30
317 Joe Torres	.10	.30
318 Eric Byrnes	.10	.30
319 George Lombard	.10	.30
320 Dave Krynzel	.10	.30
321 Ben Christensen	.10	.30
322 Aubrey Huff	.10	.30
323 Lyle Overbay	.10	.30
324 Sean McGowan	.10	.30
325 Jeff Heaverlo	.10	.30
326 Timo Perez	.10	.30
327 Octavio Martinez RC	.25	.60
328 Vince Faison	.10	.30
329 David Parrish RC	.15	.40
330 Bobby Bradley	.10	.30
331 Jason Miller RC	.15	.40
332 Corey Spencer RC	.15	.40
333 Craig House	.10	.30
334 Maxim St. Pierre RC	.25	.60
335 Adam Johnson	.10	.30
336 Joe Crede	.30	.75
337 Greg Nash RC	.15	.40
338 Chad Durbin	.10	.30
339 Pat Magness RC	.25	.60
340 Matt Wheatland	.10	.30
341 Julio Lugo	.10	.30
342 Grady Sizemore	.60	1.50
343 Adrian Gonzalez	.75	2.00
344 Tim Raines Jr.	.10	.30
345 Ranier Olmedo RC	.25	.60
346 Phil Dumatrait	.10	.30
347 Brandon Mims RC	.15	.40
348 Jason Jennings	.10	.30
349 Phil Wilson RC	.25	.60
350 Jason Hart	.10	.30
351 Cesar Izturis	.10	.30
352 Matt Butler RC	.25	.60
353 David Kelton	.10	.30
354 Luke Prokopec	.10	.30
355 Corey Smith	.10	.30
356 Joel Pineiro	.25	.60
357 Ken Chenard	.10	.30
358 Keith Reed	.10	.30
359 David Walling	.10	.30
360 Alexis Gomez RC	.15	.40
361 Justin Morneau RC	4.00	10.00
362 Josh Fogg RC	.25	.60
363 J.R. House	.10	.30
364 Andy Tracy	.10	.30
365 Kenny Kelly	.10	.30
366 Aaron McNeal	.10	.30
367 Nick Johnson	.10	.30
368 Brian Esposito	.10	.30
369 Charles Frazier RC	.15	.40
370 Scott Heard	.10	.30
371 Pat Strange	.10	.30
372 Mike Meyers	.10	.30
373 Ryan Ludwick RC	3.00	8.00
374 Brad Wilkerson	.10	.30
375 Allen Levrault	.10	.30
376 Seth McClung RC	.25	.60
377 Joe Nathan	.10	.30
378 Rafael Soriano RC	.25	.60
379 Chris Richard	.10	.30
380 Jared Sandberg	.10	.30
381 Tike Redman	.10	.30
382 Adam Dunn	.20	.50
383 Jared Abruzzo RC	.15	.40
384 Jason Richardson RC	.15	.40
385 Matt Holliday	.15	.40
386 Darwin Cubillan RC	.15	.40
387 Mike Nannini	.10	.30
388 Blake Williams RC	.15	.40
389 Valentino Pascucci RC	.25	.60
390 Jon Garland	.10	.30
391 Josh Pressley	.10	.30
392 Jose Ortiz	.10	.30
393 Ryan Hannaman RC	.25	.60
394 Steve Smyth RC	.25	.60
395 John Patterson	.10	.30
396 Chad Petty RC	.15	.40
397 Jake Peavy UER RC	1.25	3.00
398 Onix Mercado RC	.25	.60
399 Jason Romano	.10	.30
400 Luis Torres RC	.25	.60
401 Casey Fossum RC	.15	.40
402 Eduardo Figueroa RC	.15	.40
403 Bryan Barnowski RC	.15	.40
404 Tim Redding	.10	.30
405 Jason Standridge	.10	.30
406 Marvin Seale RC	.25	.60
407 Todd Moser	.10	.30
408 Alex Gordon	.10	.30
409 Steve Smitherman RC	.25	.60
410 Ben Petrick	.10	.30
411 Eric Munson	.10	.30
412 Luis Rivas	.10	.30
413 Matt Ginter	.10	.30
414 Alfonso Soriano	.20	.50
415 Rafael Boitel RC	.15	.40
416 Dany Morban RC	.15	.40
417 Justin Woodrow RC	.25	.60
418 Wilfredo Rodriguez	.10	.30
419 Derrick Van Dusen RC	.15	.40
420 Josh Spoerl RC	.25	.60
421 Juan Pierre	.10	.30
422 J.C. Romero	.10	.30
423 Ed Rogers RC	.15	.40
424 Tomo Ohka	.10	.30
425 Ben Hendrickson RC	.15	.40
426 Carlos Zambrano	.20	.50
427 Brett Myers	.10	.30
428 Scott Seabol	.10	.30
429 Thomas Mitchell	.10	.30
430 Jose Reyes RC	5.00	12.00
431 Kip Wells	.10	.30
432 Donzell McDonald	.10	.30
433 Adam Pettyjohn RC	.15	.40
434 Austin Kearns	.10	.30
435 Rico Washington	.10	.30
436 Doug Nickle RC	.15	.40
437 Steve Lomasney	.10	.30
438 Jason Jones RC	.15	.40
439 Bobby Seay	.10	.30
440 Justin Wayne RC	.25	.60
ROYR Sasaki/Furcal ROY Jsy	6.00	15.00
NNO Sean Burroughs Ball/80	6.00	15.00

2001 Bowman Gold

*STARS: 1.25X TO 3X BASIC CARDS
*ROOKIES: .6X TO 1.5X BASIC
ONE PER PACK

Card	Low	High
430 Jose Reyes	6.00	15.00

2001 Bowman Autographs

STATED ODDS 1:74 HOBBY, 1:35 HTA

Card	Low	High
BAAE Alex Escobar	3.00	8.00
BAAG Adrian Gonzalez	10.00	25.00
BAAJ Adam Johnson	3.00	8.00
BAAP Albert Pujols	200.00	500.00
BAADP Adam Piatt	3.00	8.00
BAAJG Alex Graman	3.00	8.00
BAAKG Alex Gordon	3.00	8.00
BABB Brian Barnowski	3.00	8.00
BABD Ben Diggins	3.00	8.00
BABS Ben Sheets	3.00	8.00
BABW Brad Wilkerson	3.00	8.00
BABZ Barry Zito	5.00	12.00
BACG Cristian Guerrero	3.00	8.00
BADK Dave Krynzel	3.00	8.00
BADM Dustin McGowan	3.00	8.00
BADWK David Kelton	3.00	8.00
BAFB Freddie Bynum	3.00	8.00
BAJB Jason Botts	3.00	8.00
BAJD Jose Diaz	3.00	8.00
BAJH Josh Hamilton	6.00	15.00
BAJM Justin Morneau	3.00	8.00
BAJP Josh Pressley	3.00	8.00
BAJRH J.R. House	3.00	8.00
BAJWH Jason Hart	3.00	8.00
BAKM Kevin Mench	3.00	8.00
BALM Luis Montanez	3.00	8.00
BALO Lyle Overbay	3.00	8.00
BAMV Miguel Villilo	3.00	8.00
BAND Noel Devarez	3.00	8.00
BAPL Pedro Liriano	3.00	8.00
BARF Rafael Furcal	3.00	8.00
BARJ Russ Jacobson	3.00	8.00
BASB Sean Burroughs	3.00	8.00
BASM Sean McGowan	3.00	8.00
BASS Shawn Sonnier	3.00	8.00
BASU Sixto Urena	3.00	8.00
BASDS Steve Smyth	3.00	8.00
BATH Travis Hafner	5.00	12.00
BATJ Tripper Johnson	3.00	8.00
BAWB Wilson Betemit	5.00	12.00

2001 Bowman Futures Game Relics

GROUP A ODDS 1:293 HOB, 1:139 HTA
GROUP B ODDS 1:365 HOB, 1:174 HTA
GROUP C ODDS 1:418 HOB, 1:199 HTA
GROUP D ODDS 1:274 HOB, 1:130 HTA
OVERALL ODDS 1:82 HOBBY, 1:39 HTA

Card	Low	High
FGRAE Alex Escobar A	2.00	5.00
FGRAM Aaron Myette B	2.00	5.00
FGRBB Bobby Bradley B	2.00	5.00
FGRBP Ben Petrick C	2.00	5.00
FGRBS Ben Sheets B	2.00	5.00
FGRBW Brad Wilkerson C	2.00	5.00
FGRBZ Barry Zito B	3.00	8.00
FGRCA Craig Anderson B	2.00	5.00
FGRCC Chin-Feng Chen A	6.00	15.00
FGRCG Chris George D	2.00	5.00
FGRCH Carlos Hernandez D	2.00	5.00
FGRCP Corey Patterson A	2.00	5.00
FGRCP Carlos Pena A	2.00	5.00
FGRCT Chin-Hui Tsao D	6.00	15.00
FGREM Eric Munson A	2.00	5.00
FGRFL Felipe Lopez A	2.00	5.00
FGRGR Grant Roberts D	2.00	5.00
FGRJC Jack Cust A	2.00	5.00
FGRJH Josh Hamilton	3.00	8.00
FGRJR Jason Romano C	2.00	5.00
FGRJZ Julio Zuleta A	2.00	5.00
FGRKA Kurt Ainsworth B	2.00	5.00
FGRMB Mike Bynum D	2.00	5.00
FGRMG Marcus Giles A	2.00	5.00
FGRNN Ntema Ndungidi A	2.00	5.00
FGRRA Ryan Anderson B	2.00	5.00
FGRRC Ramon Castro C	2.00	5.00
FGRRD Randey Dorame D	2.00	5.00
FGRRO Ramon Ortiz D	2.00	5.00
FGRSK Sun Woo Kim D	2.00	5.00
FGRTD Travis Dawkins C	2.00	5.00
FGRTO Tomokazu Ohka B	2.00	5.00
FGRTW Travis Wilson A	2.00	5.00
FGRVW Vernon Wells C	2.00	5.00

2001 Bowman Multiple Game Relics

GROUP A ODDS 1:1883 HOB, 1:895 HTA
GROUP B ODDS 1:6842 HOB, 1:3230 HTA
OVERALL ODDS 1:1476 HOBBY, 1:701 HTA

Card	Low	High
MGRAE Alex Escobar B	10.00	25.00
MGRBP Ben Petrick A	10.00	25.00
MGRBW Brad Wilkerson B	10.00	25.00
MGRCC Chin-Feng Chen A	75.00	150.00
MGRCP Carlos Pena A	10.00	25.00
MGREM Eric Munson B	10.00	25.00
MGRFL Felipe Lopez A	12.00	30.00
MGRJC Jack Cust A	10.00	25.00
MGRJH Josh Hamilton	20.00	50.00
MGRJR Jason Romano A	10.00	25.00
MGRJZ Julio Zuleta A	10.00	25.00
MGRMG Marcus Giles A	12.00	30.00
MGRNN Ntema Ndungidi A	10.00	25.00
MGRRC Ramon Castro A	10.00	25.00
MGRTD Travis Dawkins A	10.00	25.00
MGRTW Travis Wilson A	10.00	25.00
MGRVW Vernon Wells A	12.50	30.00
MGRDCP Corey Patterson B	10.00	25.00

2001 Bowman Rookie Reprints

Card	Low	High
COMPLETE SET (25)	25.00	60.00
STATED ODDS 1:12		
1 Yogi Berra	2.00	5.00
2 Ralph Kiner	1.25	3.00
3 Stan Musial	4.00	10.00
4 Warren Spahn	1.25	3.00
5 Roy Campanella	2.00	5.00
6 Bob Lemon	1.25	3.00
7 Robin Roberts	1.25	3.00
8 Duke Snider	1.25	3.00
9 Early Wynn	1.25	3.00
10 Richie Ashburn	1.25	3.00
11 Gil Hodges	2.00	5.00
12 Hank Bauer	1.25	3.00
13 Don Newcombe	1.25	3.00
14 Al Rosen	1.25	3.00
15 Willie Mays	5.00	12.00
16 Joe Garagiola	1.25	3.00
17 Whitey Ford	1.25	3.00
18 Lew Burdette	1.25	3.00
19 Gil McDougald	1.25	3.00
20 Minnie Minoso	1.25	3.00
21 Eddie Mathews	2.00	5.00
22 Harvey Kuenn	1.25	3.00
23 Don Larsen	1.25	3.00
24 Elston Howard	1.25	3.00
25 Don Zimmer	1.25	3.00

2001 Bowman Rookie Reprints Autographs

Card	Low	High
1 Yogi Berra	40.00	100.00
2 Willie Mays	175.00	350.00
3 Stan Musial	75.00	150.00
4 Duke Snider	30.00	60.00
5 Warren Spahn	20.00	50.00
6 Ralph Kiner	20.00	50.00
8 Don Larsen	10.00	25.00
9 Don Zimmer	10.00	25.00
10 Minnie Minoso	10.00	25.00

2001 Bowman Rookie Reprints Relic Bat

STATED ODDS 1:1954 HOBBY, 1:928 HTA

Card	Low	High
1 Willie Mays	10.00	25.00
2 Duke Snider	10.00	25.00
3 Minnie Minoso	6.00	15.00
4 Hank Bauer	6.00	15.00
5 Gil McDougald	6.00	15.00

2001 Bowman Draft

Card	Low	High
COMP.FACT.SET (112)	12.00	30.00
COMPLETE SET (110)	8.00	20.00
CARDS 51 AND 71 HAVE SWITCHED BACKS		
BDP1 Alfredo Amezaga RC	.10	.30
BDP2 Andrew Good	.10	.30
BDP3 Kelly Johnson RC	1.25	3.00
BDP4 Larry Bigbie	.10	.30
BDP5 Matt Thompson RC	.15	.40
BDP6 Wilton Chavez RC	.15	.40
BDP7 Joe Borchard RC	.15	.40
BDP8 David Espinosa	.10	.30
BDP9 Zach Day RC	.15	.40
BDP10 Brad Hawpe RC	1.00	2.50
BDP11 Nate Cornejo	.10	.30
BDP12 Matt Cooper RC	.15	.40
BDP13 Brad Lidge	.10	.30
BDP14 Angel Berroa RC	.25	.60
BDP15 Lamont Matthews RC	.15	.40
BDP16 Jose Garcia	.10	.30
BDP17 Grant Balfour RC	.10	.30
BDP18 Ron Chiavacci RC	.10	.30
BDP19 Jae Seo	.10	.30
BDP20 Juan Rivera	.10	.30
BDP21 D'Angelo Jimenez	.10	.30
BDP22 Juan A.Pena RC	.15	.40
BDP23 Marlon Byrd RC	.15	.40
BDP24 Sean Burnett	.10	.30
BDP25 Josh Pearce RC	.15	.40
BDP26 Brandon Duckworth RC	.10	.30
BDP27 Jack Taschner RC	.10	.30
BDP28 Marcus Thames	.10	.30
BDP29 Brent Abernathy	.10	.30
BDP30 David Elder RC	.10	.30
BDP31 Scott Cassidy RC	.15	.40
BDP32 Dennis Tankersley RC	.10	.30
BDP33 Denny Stark	.10	.30
BDP34 Dave Williams RC	.10	.30
BDP35 Boof Bonser RC	.10	.30
BDP36 Kris Foster RC	.10	.30
BDP37 Luis Garcia RC	.15	.40
BDP38 Shawn Chacon	.10	.30
BDP39 Mike Rivera RC	.15	.40
BDP40 Will Smith RC	.15	.40
BDP41 Morgan Ensberg RC	.75	2.00
BDP42 Ken Harvey	.10	.30
BDP43 Ricardo Rodriguez RC	.15	.40
BDP44 Jose Mieses RC	.15	.40
BDP45 Luis Maza RC	.10	.30
BDP46 Julio Perez RC	.15	.40
BDP47 Dustan Mohr RC	.15	.40
BDP48 Randy Flores RC	.10	.30
BDP49 Covelli Crisp RC	2.00	5.00
BDP50 Kevin Reese RC	.15	.40
BDP51 Brad Thomas UER	.10	.30
BDP52 Xavier Nady	.10	.30
BDP53 Ryan Vogelsong	.10	.30
BDP54 Carlos Silva	.10	.30
BDP55 Dan Wright	.10	.30
BDP56 Brent Butler	.10	.30
BDP57 Brandon Knight RC	.10	.30
BDP58 Brian Reith RC	.10	.30
BDP59 Mario Valenzuela RC	.15	.40
BDP60 Bobby Hill RC	.15	.40
BDP61 Rich Rundles RC	.15	.40
BDP62 Rick Elder	.10	.30
BDP63 J.D. Closser	.10	.30
BDP64 Scot Shields	.10	.30
BDP65 Miguel Olivo	.10	.30
BDP66 Stubby Clapp RC	.10	.30
BDP67 Jerome Williams RC	.25	.60
BDP68 Jason Lane RC	.25	.60
BDP69 Chase Utley RC	8.00	20.00
BDP70 Erik Bedard RC	2.00	5.00
BDP71 Alex Herrera UER RC	.10	.30
BDP72 Juan Cruz RC	.15	.40
BDP73 Billy Martin RC	.10	.30
BDP74 Ronnie Merrill RC	.15	.40
BDP75 Jason Kinchen RC	.10	.30
BDP76 Wilkin Ruan RC	.15	.40
BDP77 Cody Ransom RC	.10	.30
BDP78 Bud Smith RC	.10	.30
BDP79 Wily Mo Pena	.10	.30
BDP80 Jeff Nettles RC	.15	.40
BDP81 Jamal Strong RC	.10	.30
BDP82 Bill Ortega RC	.10	.30
BDP83 Mike Bell	.10	.30
BDP84 Ichiro Suzuki RC	5.00	12.00
BDP85 Fernando Rodney RC	.10	.30
BDP86 Chris Smith RC	.10	.30
BDP87 John VanBenschoten RC	.15	.40
BDP88 Bobby Crosby RC	1.50	4.00
BDP89 Kenny Baugh RC	.10	.30
BDP90 Jake Gautreau RC	.10	.30
BDP91 Gabe Gross RC	.25	.60
BDP92 Kris Honel RC	.15	.40
BDP93 Dan Denham RC	.10	.30
BDP94 Aaron Heilman RC	.15	.40
BDP95 Irvin Guzman RC	1.50	4.00
BDP96 Mike Jones RC	.25	.60
BDP97 John-Ford Griffin RC	.15	.40
BDP98 Macay McBride RC	.40	1.00
BDP99 John Rheinecker RC	.40	1.00
BDP100 Bronson Sardinha RC	.10	.30
BDP101 Jason Weintraub RC	.10	.30
BDP102 J.D. Martin RC	.10	.30
BDP103 Jayson Nix RC	.15	.40
BDP104 Noah Lowry RC	1.00	2.50
BDP105 Richard Lewis RC	.15	.40
BDP106 Brad Hennessey RC	.25	.60
BDP107 Jeff Mathis RC	.25	.60
BDP108 Jon Skaggs RC	.15	.40
BDP109 Justin Pope RC	.15	.40
BDP110 Josh Burrus RC	.15	.40

2001 Bowman Draft Autographs

ONE PER SEALED FACTORY SET

Card	Low	High
BDPAAA Alfredo Amezaga	4.00	10.00
BDPAAC Alex Cintron	4.00	10.00
BDPAAE Adam Everett	4.00	10.00
BDPAAF Alex Fernandez	4.00	10.00
BDPAAG Alexis Gomez	4.00	10.00
BDPAAH Aaron Herr	4.00	10.00
BDPAAK Austin Kearns	6.00	15.00
BDPABB Bobby Bradley	4.00	10.00
BDPABH Beau Hale	4.00	10.00
BDPABP Brandon Phillips	4.00	10.00
BDPABS Bud Smith	4.00	10.00
BDPACG Cristian Guerrero	4.00	10.00
BDPACI Cesar Izturis	4.00	10.00
BDPACP Christian Parra	4.00	10.00
BDPAER Ed Rogers	4.00	10.00
BDPAFL Felipe Lopez	4.00	15.00
BDPAGA Garrett Atkins	4.00	10.00
BDPAGJ Gary Johnson	4.00	10.00
BDPAJA Jared Abruzzo	4.00	10.00
BDPAJK Joe Kennedy	4.00	15.00
BDPAJL John Lackey	8.00	20.00
BDPAJP Joel Pineiro	6.00	15.00
BDPAJT Joe Torres	4.00	10.00
BDPANJ Nick Johnson	6.00	15.00
BDPANR Nick Regilio	4.00	10.00
BDPARC Ryan Church	6.00	15.00
BDPARD Ryan Dittfurth	4.00	10.00
BDPARL Ryan Ludwick	4.00	10.00
BDPARO Roy Oswalt	6.00	15.00
BDPASH Scott Heard	4.00	10.00
BDPASS Scott Seabol	4.00	10.00
BDPATO Tomo Ohka	6.00	15.00
BDPAANC Antoine Cameron	4.00	10.00
BDPABJS Brian Specht	4.00	10.00
BDPAJMW Justin Wayne	4.00	10.00
BDPARMM Ryan Madson	4.00	15.00
BDPAROC Ramon Carvajal	4.00	10.00

2001 Bowman Draft Futures Game Relics

ONE RELIC PER FACTORY SET

Card	Low	High
FGRAA Alfredo Amezaga	2.00	5.00
FGRAD Adam Dunn	3.00	8.00
FGRAG Adrian Gonzalez	6.00	15.00
FGRAH Alex Herrera	2.00	5.00
FGRBM Brett Myers	2.00	5.00
FGRCD Cody Ransom	2.00	5.00
FGRCG Chris George	2.00	5.00
FGRCH Carlos Hernandez	2.00	5.00
FGRCU Chase Utley	10.00	25.00
FGREB Erik Bedard	2.00	5.00
FGRGB Grant Balfour	2.00	5.00
FGRHB Hank Blalock	3.00	8.00
FGRJB Joe Borchard	2.00	5.00
FGRJC Juan Cruz	2.00	5.00
FGRJP Josh Pearce	2.00	5.00
FGRJR Juan Rivera	2.00	5.00
FGRJAP Juan A.Pena	2.00	5.00
FGRLG Luis Garcia	2.00	5.00
FGRMC Miguel Cabrera	10.00	25.00
FGRMR Mike Rivera	2.00	5.00
FGRRR Ricardo Rodriguez	2.00	5.00
FGRSC Scott Chiasson	2.00	5.00
FGRSS Seung Song	2.00	5.00
FGRTB Toby Hall	2.00	5.00
FGRWB Wilson Betemit	3.00	8.00
FGRWP Wily Mo Pena	2.00	5.00

2001 Bowman Draft Relics

ONE RELIC PER FACTORY SET

Card	Low	High
BDPRCI Cesar Izturis	2.00	5.00
BDPRGJ Gary Johnson	2.00	5.00
BDPRNR Nick Regilio	2.00	5.00
BDPRRC Ryan Church	2.00	5.00
BDPRBJS Brian Specht	2.00	5.00
BDPRJRH J.R. House	2.00	5.00

2002 Bowman

Card	Low	High
COMPLETE SET (440)	20.00	50.00
1 Adam Dunn	.20	.50
2 Derek Jeter	.75	2.00
3 Alex Rodriguez	.40	1.00
4 Miguel Tejada	.20	.50
5 Nomar Garciaparra	.20	.50
6 Toby Hall	.12	.30
7 Brandon Duckworth	.12	.30
8 Paul LoDuca	.12	.30
9 Brian Giles	.12	.30
10 C.C. Sabathia	.20	.50
11 Curt Schilling	.20	.50
12 Tsuyoshi Shinjo	.12	.30
13 Ramon Hernandez	.12	.30
14 Jose Cruz Jr.	.12	.30
15 Albert Pujols	.60	1.50
16 Joe Mays	.12	.30
17 Javy Lopez	.12	.30
18 J.T. Snow	.12	.30
19 David Segui	.12	.30
20 Jorge Posada	.20	.50
21 Doug Mientkiewicz	.12	.30
22 Jerry Hairston Jr.	.12	.30
23 Bernie Williams	.20	.50
24 Mike Sweeney	.12	.30
25 Jason Giambi	.12	.30
26 Ryan Dempster	.12	.30
27 Ryan Klesko	.12	.30
28 Mark Quinn	.12	.30
29 Jeff Kent	.12	.30
30 Eric Chavez	.12	.30
31 Adrian Beltre	.30	.75
32 Andruw Jones	.12	.30
33 Alfonso Soriano	.20	.50
34 Aramis Ramirez	.12	.30
35 Greg Maddux	.50	1.25
36 Andy Pettitte	.20	.50
37 Bartolo Colon	.12	.30
38 Ben Sheets	.12	.30
39 Bobby Higginson	.12	.30
40 Ivan Rodriguez	.20	.50
41 Brad Penny	.12	.30
42 Carlos Lee	.12	.30
43 Damion Easley	.12	.30
44 Preston Wilson	.12	.30
45 Jeff Bagwell	.20	.50
46 Eric Milton	.12	.30
47 Rafael Palmeiro	.20	.50
48 Gary Sheffield	.12	.30
49 J.D. Drew	.12	.30
50 Jim Thome	.20	.50
51 Ichiro Suzuki	.40	1.00
52 Bud Smith	.12	.30
53 Chan Ho Park	.20	.50
54 D'Angelo Jimenez	.12	.30
55 Ken Griffey Jr.	.60	1.50
56 Wade Miller	.12	.30
57 Vladimir Guerrero	.20	.50
58 Troy Glaus	.12	.30
59 Shawn Green	.12	.30
60 Kerry Wood	.12	.30
61 Jack Wilson	.12	.30
62 Kevin Brown	.12	.30
63 Marcus Giles	.12	.30
64 Pat Burrell	.12	.30
65 Larry Walker	.20	.50
66 Sammy Sosa	.30	.75
67 Raul Mondesi	.12	.30
68 Tim Hudson	.20	.50
69 Lance Berkman	.20	.50
70 Mike Mussina	.20	.50
71 Barry Zito	.12	.30
72 Jimmy Rollins	.20	.50
73 Barry Bonds	.50	1.25
74 Craig Biggio	.20	.50
75 Todd Helton	.20	.50
76 Roger Clemens	.40	1.00
77 Frank Catalanotto	.12	.30
78 Josh Towers	.12	.30
79 Roy Oswalt	.20	.50
80 Chipper Jones	.30	.75
81 Cristian Guzman	.12	.30
82 Darin Erstad	.12	.30
83 Freddy Garcia	.12	.30
84 Jason Tyner	.12	.30
85 Carlos Delgado	.12	.30
86 Jon Lieber	.12	.30
87 Juan Pierre	.12	.30
88 Matt Morris	.12	.30
89 Phil Nevin	.12	.30
90 Jim Edmonds	.20	.50
91 Magglio Ordonez	.20	.50
92 Mike Hampton	.12	.30
93 Rafael Furcal	.12	.30
94 Richie Sexson	.12	.30
95 Luis Gonzalez	.12	.30
96 Scott Rolen	.20	.50
97 Tim Redding	.12	.30
98 Moises Alou	.12	.30
99 Jose Vidro	.12	.30
100 Mike Piazza	.30	.75
101 Pedro Martinez	.20	.50
102 Geoff Jenkins	.12	.30
103 Johnny Damon Sox	.20	.50
104 Mike Cameron	.12	.30
105 Randy Johnson	.30	.75
106 David Eckstein	.12	.30
107 Javier Vazquez	.12	.30
108 Mark Mulder	.12	.30
109 Robert Fick	.12	.30
110 Roberto Alomar	.20	.50
111 Wilson Betemit	.12	.30
112 Chris Tritle RC	.25	.60
113 Ed Rogers	.12	.30
114 Juan Pena	.12	.30
115 Josh Beckett	.12	.30
116 Juan Cruz	.12	.30
117 Noochie Varner RC	.25	.60
118 Taylor Buchholz RC	.25	.60
119 Mike Rivera	.12	.30
120 Hank Blalock	.12	.30
121 Hansel Izquierdo RC	.25	.60
122 Orlando Hudson	.12	.30
123 Bill Hall	.12	.30
124 Jose Reyes	.30	.75
125 Juan Rivera	.12	.30
126 Eric Valent	.12	.30
127 Scotty Layfield RC	.25	.60
128 Austin Kearns	.12	.30
129 Nic Jackson RC	.25	.60
130 Chris Baker RC	.25	.60
131 Chad Qualls RC	.40	1.00
132 Marcus Thames	.12	.30
133 Nathan Haynes	.12	.30
134 Brett Evert	.12	.30
135 Joe Borchard	.12	.30
136 Ryan Christianson	.12	.30
137 Josh Hamilton	.20	.50
138 Corey Patterson	.12	.30
139 Travis Wilson	.12	.30
140 Alex Escobar	.12	.30
141 Alexis Gomez	.12	.30
142 Nick Johnson	.12	.30
143 Kenny Kelly	.12	.30
144 Marlon Byrd	.12	.30
145 Kory DeHaan	.12	.30
146 Matt Belisle	.12	.30
147 Carlos Hernandez	.12	.30
148 Sean Burroughs	.12	.30
149 Angel Berroa	.12	.30
150 Aubrey Huff	.12	.30
151 Travis Hafner	.12	.30
152 Brandon Berger	.12	.30
153 David Krynzel	.12	.30
154 Ruben Salazar	.12	.30
155 J.R. House	.12	.30
156 Juan Silvestre	.12	.30
157 Dewon Brazelton	.12	.30
158 Jayson Werth	.20	.50
159 Larry Barnes	.12	.30
160 Elvis Pena	.12	.30
161 Ruben Gotay RC	.25	.60
162 Tommy Marx RC	.25	.60
163 John Suomi RC	.25	.60
164 Javier Colina	.12	.30
165 Greg Sain RC	.25	.60
166 Robert Cosby RC	.25	.60
167 Angel Pagan RC	.60	1.50
168 Ralph Santana RC	.25	.60
169 Joe Orloski RC	.25	.60
170 Shayne Wright RC	.25	.60
171 Jay Caligiuri RC	.25	.60
172 Greg Montalbano RC	.25	.60
173 Rich Harden RC	.75	2.00
174 Rich Thompson RC	.25	.60
175 Fred Bastardo RC	.25	.60
176 Alejandro Giron RC	.25	.60
177 Jesus Medrano RC	.25	.60
178 Kevin Deaton RC	.25	.60
179 Mike Rosamond RC	.25	.60
180 Jon Guzman RC	.25	.60
181 Gerard Oakes RC	.25	.60
182 Francisco Liriano RC	1.25	3.00
183 Matt Allegra RC	.25	.60
184 Mike Snyder RC	.25	.60
185 James Shanks RC	.25	.60
186 Anderson Hernandez RC	.25	.60
187 Dan Trumble RC	.25	.60
188 Luis DePaula RC	.25	.60
189 Randall Shelley RC	.25	.60
190 Richard Lane RC	.25	.60
191 Antwon Rollins RC	.25	.60
192 Ryan Bukvich RC	.25	.60
193 Derrick Lewis	.12	.30
194 Eric Miller RC	.25	.60
195 Justin Schuda RC	.25	.60
196 Brian West RC	.25	.60
197 Adam Roller RC	.25	.60
198 Neal Frendling RC	.25	.60
199 Jeremy Hill RC	.25	.60
200 James Barrett RC	.25	.60
201 Brett Kay RC	.25	.60
202 Ryan Mottl RC	.25	.60
203 Brad Nelson RC	.25	.60
204 Juan M. Gonzalez RC	.25	.60
205 Curtis Legendre RC	.25	.60
206 Ronald Acuna RC	.25	.60
207 Chris Flinn RC	.25	.60
208 Nick Alvarez RC	.25	.60
209 Jason Ellison RC	.25	.60
210 Blake McGinley RC	.25	.60
211 Dan Phillips RC	.25	.60
212 Demetrius Heath RC	.25	.60
213 Eric Bruntlett RC	.25	.60
214 Joe Jiannetti RC	.25	.60
215 Mike Hill RC	.25	.60
216 Ricardo Cordova RC	.25	.60
217 Mark Hamilton RC	.25	.60
218 David Mattox RC	.25	.60
219 Jose Morban RC	.25	.60
220 Scott Wiggins RC	.25	.60
221 Steve Green	.12	.30
222 Brian Rogers	.12	.30
223 Chin-Hui Tsao	.12	.30
224 Kenny Baugh	.12	.30
225 Nate Teut	.12	.30
226 Josh Wilson RC	.25	.60
227 Christian Parker	.12	.30
228 Tim Raines Jr.	.12	.30
229 Anastacio Martinez RC	.25	.60
230 Richard Lewis	.12	.30
231 Tim Kalita RC	.25	.60
232 Edwin Almonte RC	.25	.60
233 Hee-Seop Choi	.12	.30
234 Ty Howington	.12	.30
235 Victor Alvarez RC	.25	.60
236 Morgan Ensberg	.12	.30
237 Jeff Austin RC	.12	.30
238 Luis Terrero	.12	.30
239 Adam Wainwright	.20	.50
240 Clint Weibl RC	.25	.60
241 Eric Cyr	.12	.30
242 Marlyn Tisdale RC	.25	.60
243 John VanBenschoten	.12	.30
244 Ryan Raburn RC	.40	1.00
245 Miguel Cabrera	4.00	10.00
246 Jung Bong	.12	.30
247 Raul Chavez RC	.25	.60
248 Erik Bedard	.12	.30
249 Chris Snelling RC	.25	.60
250 Joe Rogers RC	.25	.60
251 Nate Field RC	.25	.60
252 Matt Herges RC	.25	.60
253 Matt Childers RC	.25	.60
254 Erick Almonte	.12	.30
255 Nick Neugebauer	.12	.30
256 Ron Calloway RC	.25	.60
257 Seung Song	.12	.30
258 Brandon Phillips	.12	.30
259 Cole Barthel RC	.25	.60
260 Jason Lane	.12	.30
261 Jae Seo	.12	.30
262 Randy Flores	.12	.30
263 Scott Chiasson	.12	.30
264 Chase Utley	.50	1.25
265 Tony Alvarez	.12	.30
266 Ben Howard RC	.25	.60
267 Nelson Castro RC	.25	.60
268 Mark Lukasiewicz	.12	.30
269 Eric Glaser RC	.25	.60
270 Rob Henkel RC	.25	.60
271 Jose Valverde RC	.40	1.00
272 Ricardo Rodriguez	.12	.30
273 Chris Smith	.12	.30
274 Mark Prior	.20	.50
275 Miguel Olivo	.12	.30
276 Ben Broussard	.12	.30
277 Zach Sorensen	.12	.30

278 Brian Mallette RC .25 .60
279 Brad Wilkerson .12 .30
280 Carl Crawford .20 .50
281 Chone Figgins RC .40 1.00
282 Jimmy Alvarez RC .25 .60
283 Gavin Floyd RC .60 1.50
284 Josh Bonifay RC .25 .60
285 Garrett Guzman RC .25 .60
286 Blake Williams .12 .30
287 Matt Holliday .30 .75
288 Ryan Madson .12 .30
289 Luis Torres .12 .30
290 Jeff Verplancke RC .25 .60
291 Nate Espy RC .25 .60
292 Jeff Lincoln RC .25 .60
293 Ryan Snare RC .25 .60
294 Jose Ortiz .12 .30
295 Eric Munson .12 .30
296 Denny Bautista .12 .30
297 Willy Aybar .12 .30
298 Kelly Johnson .30 .75
299 Justin Morneau .30 .75
300 Derrick Van Dusen .12 .30
301 Chad Petty .12 .30
302 Mike Restovich .12 .30
303 Shawn Fagan .12 .30
304 Yurendell DeCaster RC .25 .60
305 Justin Wayne .12 .30
306 Mike Peeples RC .25 .60
307 Joel Guzman .12 .30
308 Ryan Vogelsong .60 1.50
309 Jorge Padilla RC .25 .60
310 Grady Sizemore .20 .50
311 Joe Jester RC .25 .60
312 Jim Journell .12 .30
313 Bobby Seay .12 .30
314 Ryan Church RC .25 .60
315 Grant Balfour .12 .30
316 Mitch Jones .12 .30
317 Travis Foley RC .25 .60
318 Bobby Crosby .30 .75
319 Adrian Gonzalez .30 .75
320 Ronnie Merrill .12 .30
321 Joel Pineiro .12 .30
322 John-Ford Griffin .12 .30
323 Brian Forystek RC .25 .60
324 Sean Douglass .12 .30
325 Manny Delcarmen RC .25 .60
326 Donnie Bridges .12 .30
327 Jim Kavourias RC .25 .60
328 Gabe Gross .12 .30
329 Jon Rauch .12 .30
330 Bill Ortega .12 .30
331 Joey Hammond RC .25 .60
332 Ramon Moreta RC .25 .60
333 Ron Davenport .12 .30
334 Brett Myers .12 .30
335 Carlos Pena .20 .50
336 Ezequiel Astacio RC .25 .60
337 Edwin Yan RC .25 .60
338 Josh Girdley .12 .30
339 Shaun Boyd .12 .30
340 Juan Rincon .12 .30
341 Chris Duffy RC .25 .60
342 Jason Kinchen .12 .30
343 Brad Thomas .12 .30
344 David Kelton .12 .30
345 Rafael Soriano .12 .30
346 Colin Young RC .25 .60
347 Eric Byrnes .12 .30
348 Chris Narveson RC .25 .60
349 John Rheinecker .12 .30
350 Mike Wilson RC .25 .60
351 Justin Sherrod RC .25 .60
352 Deivi Mendez .12 .30
353 Wily Mo Pena .12 .30
354 Brett Roneberg RC .25 .60
355 Trey Lunsford RC .25 .60
356 Jimmy Gobble RC .25 .60
357 Brent Butler .12 .30
358 Aaron Heilman .12 .30
359 Wilkin Ruan .12 .30
360 Brian Wolfe RC .25 .60
361 Cody Ransom .12 .30
362 Koyie Hill .12 .30
363 Scott Cassidy .12 .30
364 Tony Fontana RC .25 .60
365 Mark Teixeira .20 .50
366 Doug Sessions RC .25 .60
367 Victor Hall .12 .30
368 Josh Cisneros RC .25 .60
369 Kevin Mench .12 .30
370 Tike Redman .12 .30
371 Jeff Heaverlo .12 .30
372 Carlos Brackley RC .25 .60
373 Brad Hawpe .12 .30
374 Jesus Colome .12 .30
375 David Espinosa .12 .30
376 Jesse Foppert RC .25 .60
377 Ross Peeples RC .25 .60
378 Alex Requena RC .25 .60
379 Joe Mauer RC 6.00 15.00
380 Carlos Silva .12 .30
381 David Wright RC 4.00 10.00
382 Craig Kuzmic RC .25 .60
383 Pete Zamora RC .25 .60
384 Matt Parker RC .25 .60
385 Keith Ginter .12 .30
386 Gary Cates Jr. RC .25 .60
387 Justin Reid RC .25 .60
388 Jake Mauer RC .25 .60
389 Dennis Tankersley .12 .30
390 Josh Barfield RC .40 1.00
391 Luis Maza .12 .30
392 Henry Pichardo RC .25 .60
393 Michael Floyd RC .25 .60
394 Clint Nageotte RC .25 .60
395 Raymond Cabrera RC .25 .60
396 Mauricio Lara RC .25 .60
397 Alejandro Cadena RC .25 .60
398 Jonny Gomes RC .75 2.00
399 Jason Bulger RC .25 .60
400 Bobby Jenks RC .40 1.00
401 David Gil RC .25 .60
402 Joel Crump RC .25 .60
403 Kazuhisa Ishii RC .25 .60
404 So Taguchi RC .40 1.00
405 Ryan Doumit RC .40 1.00
406 Macay McBride .12 .30
407 Brandon Claussen .12 .30
408 Chin-Feng Chen .12 .30
409 Josh Phelps .12 .30
410 Freddie Money RC .25 .60
411 Cliff Bartosh RC .25 .60
412 Josh Pearce .12 .30
413 Lyle Overbay .12 .30
414 Ryan Anderson .12 .30
415 Terrance Hill RC .25 .60
416 John Rodriguez RC .25 .60
417 Richard Stahl .12 .30
418 Brian Specht .12 .30
419 Chris Latham RC .25 .60
420 Carlos Cabrera RC .25 .60
421 Jose Bautista RC 2.00 5.00
422 Kevin Frederick RC .25 .60
423 Jerome Williams .12 .30
424 Napoleon Calzado RC .25 .60
425 Benito Baez .12 .30
426 Xavier Nady .12 .30
427 Jason Botts RC .25 .60
428 Steve Bechler RC .25 .60
429 Reed Johnson RC .40 1.00
430 Mark Outlaw RC .25 .60
431 Billy Sylvester .12 .30
432 Luke Lockwood .12 .30
433 Jake Peavy .12 .30
434 Alfredo Amezaga .12 .30
435 Aaron Cook RC .25 .60
436 Josh Shaffer RC .25 .60
437 Dan Wright .12 .30
438 Ryan Gripp RC .25 .60
439 Alex Herrera .12 .30
440 Jason Bay RC 1.25 3.00

2002 Bowman Gold

COMPLETE SET (440) 75.00 200.00
*GOLD VET: 1.2X TO 3X BASIC
*GOLD RC: .6X TO 1.5X BASIC
ONE PER PACK
245 Miguel Cabrera 6.00 15.00

2002 Bowman Uncirculated

ONE EXCHANGE CARD PER BOX
STATED PRINT RUN 672 SETS
EXCHANGE DEADLINE 12/31/02
CARD DELIVERY OPTION AVAIL. 07/07/02
112 Chris Tritle .40 1.00
117 Noochie Varner .40 1.00
118 Taylor Buchholz .40 1.00
121 Hansel Izquierdo .40 1.00
123 Bill Hall .40 1.00
127 Scotty Layfield .40 1.00
129 Nic Jackson .40 1.00
130 Chris Baker .40 1.00
131 Chad Qualls .60 1.50
161 Ruben Gotay .40 1.00
162 Tommy Marx .40 1.00
163 John Suomi .40 1.00
164 Javier Colina .40 1.00
165 Greg Sain .40 1.00
222 Brian Rogers .40 1.00
229 Anastacio Martinez .40 1.00
230 Richard Lewis .40 1.00
231 Tim Kalita .40 1.00
232 Edwin Almonte .40 1.00
235 Victor Alvarez .40 1.00
237 Jeff Austin .40 1.00
240 Clint Weibl .40 1.00
244 Ryan Raburn .60 1.50
249 Chris Snelling .40 1.00
250 Joe Rogers .40 1.00
251 Nate Field .40 1.00
253 Matt Childers .40 1.00
256 Ron Calloway .40 1.00
259 Cole Barthel .40 1.00
266 Ben Howard .40 1.00
267 Nelson Castro .40 1.00
269 Eric Glaser .40 1.00
270 Rob Henkel .40 1.00
271 Jose Valverde .60 1.50
278 Brian Mallette .40 1.00
281 Chone Figgins .60 1.50
282 Jimmy Alvarez .40 1.00
283 Gavin Floyd 1.00 2.50
284 Josh Bonifay .40 1.00
285 Garrett Guzman .40 1.00
290 Jeff Verplancke .40 1.00
291 Nate Espy .40 1.00
293 Ryan Snare .40 1.00
304 Yurendell De Caster .40 1.00
306 Mike Peeples .40 1.00
309 Jorge Padilla .40 1.00
311 Joe Jester .40 1.00
314 Ryan Church .40 1.00
317 Travis Foley .40 1.00
323 Brian Forystek .40 1.00
325 Manny Delcarmen .40 1.00
327 Jim Kavourias .40 1.00
331 Joey Hammond .40 1.00
336 Ezequiel Astacio .40 1.00
337 Edwin Yan .40 1.00
341 Chris Duffy .40 1.00
348 Chris Narveson .40 1.00
351 Justin Sherrod .40 1.00
354 Brett Roneberg .40 1.00
355 Trey Lunsford .40 1.00
356 Jimmy Gobble .40 1.00
360 Brian Wolfe .40 1.00
362 Koyie Hill .40 1.00
364 Tony Fontana .40 1.00
366 Doug Sessions .40 1.00
368 Josh Cisneros .40 1.00
372 Carlos Brackley .40 1.00
376 Jesse Foppert .40 1.00
377 Ross Peeples .40 1.00
378 Alex Requena .40 1.00
379 Joe Mauer 5.00 12.00
381 David Wright 3.00 8.00
382 Craig Kuzmic .40 1.00
383 Pete Zamora .40 1.00
384 Matt Parker .40 1.00
386 Gary Cates Jr .40 1.00
387 Justin Reid .40 1.00
388 Jake Mauer .40 1.00
390 Josh Barfield .60 1.50
392 Henry Pichardo .40 1.00
393 Michael Floyd .40 1.00
394 Clint Nageotte .40 1.00
395 Raymond Cabrera .40 1.00
396 Mauricio Lara .40 1.00
397 Alejandro Cadena .40 1.00
398 Jonny Gomes 1.25 3.00
399 Jason Bulger .40 1.00
400 Bobby Jenks .60 1.50
401 David Gil .40 1.00
402 Joel Crump .40 1.00
403 Kazuhisa Ishii .60 1.50
404 So Taguchi .60 1.50
405 Ryan Doumit .60 1.50
410 Freddie Money .40 1.00
411 Cliff Bartosh .40 1.00
415 Terrance Hill .40 1.00
416 John Rodriguez .40 1.00
419 Chris Latham .40 1.00
420 Carlos Cabrera .40 1.00
421 Jose Bautista 3.00 8.00
422 Kevin Frederick .40 1.00
424 Napoleon Calzado .40 1.00
425 Benito Baez .40 1.00
427 Jason Botts .40 1.00
428 Steve Bechler .40 1.00
429 Reed Johnson .60 1.50
430 Mark Outlaw .40 1.00
436 Josh Shaffer .40 1.00
437 Dan Wright .40 1.00
438 Ryan Gripp .40 1.00
440 Jason Bay 2.00 5.00

2002 Bowman Autographs

GROUP A 1:67 H, 1:39 HTA, 1:89 R
GROUP B 1:129 H, 1:74 HTA, 1:170 R
GROUP C 1:881 H, 1:507 HTA, 1:1165 R
GROUP D 1:1558 H, 1:896 HTA, 1:2060 R
GROUP E 1:1685 H, 1:968 HTA, 1:2238 R
OVERALL ODDS 1:40 H, 1:24 HTA, 1:53 R
ONE ADD'L AUTO PER SEALED HTA BOX
BAAA Alfredo Amezaga A 4.00 10.00
BAAH Aubrey Huff A 4.00 10.00
BABA Brandon Claussen A 4.00 10.00
BABC Ben Christensen A 4.00 10.00
BABD Brian Cardwell A 4.00 10.00
BABBC Boof Bonser A 4.00 10.00
BABJC Brian Specht C 4.00 10.00
BABSS Bud Smith B 4.00 10.00
BACK Charles Kegley A 4.00 10.00
BACR Cody Ransom B 4.00 10.00
BACS Chris Smith B 4.00 10.00
BACT Chris Tritle B 4.00 10.00
BACU Chase Utley A 40.00 100.00
BADV Domingo Valdez A 4.00 10.00
BADW Dan Wright B 4.00 10.00
BAGA Garrett Atkins A 8.00 20.00
BAGJ Gary Johnson C 4.00 10.00
BAHB Hank Blalock B 6.00 15.00
BAJB Josh Beckett B 6.00 15.00
BAJD Jeff Davanon A 4.00 10.00
BAJL Jason Lane A 6.00 15.00
BAJP Juan Pena A 4.00 10.00
BAJS Juan Silvestre A 4.00 10.00
BAJAB Jason Botts B 6.00 15.00
BAJLW Jerome Williams A 4.00 10.00
BAKG Keith Ginter B 4.00 10.00
BALB Larry Bigbie A 6.00 15.00
BAMB Marlon Byrd B 4.00 10.00
BAMC Matt Cooper A 4.00 10.00
BAMD Manny Delcarmen A 4.00 10.00
BAME Morgan Ensberg A 6.00 15.00
BAMP Mark Prior B 6.00 15.00
BANJ Nick Johnson B 6.00 15.00
BANN Nick Neugebauer E 4.00 10.00
BANV Noochie Varner B 4.00 10.00
BARF Randy Flores D 4.00 10.00
BARH Ryan Hannaman A 4.00 10.00
BARO Roy Oswalt B 6.00 15.00
BARV Ryan Vogelsong B 6.00 15.00
BATB Tony Blanco A 4.00 10.00
BATH Toby Hall B 4.00 10.00
BATS Termel Sledge B 4.00 10.00
BAWB Wilson Betemit B 4.00 10.00
BAWS Will Smith A 4.00 10.00

2002 Bowman Futures Game Autograph Relics

GROUP A JSY 1:2193 H, 1:1262 HTA, 1:2898 R
GROUP B JSY 1:1599 H, 1:923 HTA, 1:2125 R
GROUP C JSY 1:522 H, 1:301 HTA, 1:688 R
GROUP D JSY 1:1533 H, 1:882 HTA, 1:2028 R
GROUP E JSY 1:1425 H, 1:822 HTA, 1:1882 R
GROUP F JSY 1:1316 H, 1:759 HTA, 1:1738 R
OVERALL JSY 1:196 H, 1:113 HTA, 1:259 R
BASE ODDS 1:126 HTA
CH Carlos Hernandez Jsy B 5.00 12.00
CP Carlos Pena Jsy D 5.00 12.00
DT Dennis Tankersley Jsy E 5.00 12.00
JRH J.R. House Jsy C 5.00 12.00
JW Jerome Williams Jsy F 5.00 12.00
NJ Nick Johnson Jsy C 5.00 12.00
RL Ryan Ludwick Jsy C 8.00 20.00
TH Toby Hall Base 5.00 12.00
WB Wilson Betemit Jsy A 5.00 12.00

2002 Bowman Game Used Relics

GROUP A BAT 1:3236 H, 1:1866 HTA, 1:4331 R
GROUP B BAT 1:1472 H, 1:849 HTA, 1:1949 R
GROUP C BAT 1:1647 H, 1:948 HTA, 1:2180 R
GROUP D BAT 1:894 H, 1:515 HTA, 1:1180 R
GROUP E BAT 1:375 H, 1:216 HTA, 1:496 R
GROUP F BAT 1:1042 H, 1:601 HTA, 1:1381 R
GROUP G BAT 1:939 H, 1:541 HTA, 1:1237 R
OVERALL BAT 1:135 H, 1:78 HTA, 1:179 R
GROUP A JSY 1:2085 H, 1:1202 HTA, 1:2762 R
GROUP B JSY 1:1916 H, 1:528 HTA, 1:1213 R
GROUP C JSY 1:223 H, 1:129 HTA, 1:295 R
OVERALL JSY 1:165 H, 1:95 HTA, 1:219 R
OVERALL RELIC 1:74 H, 1:43 HTA, 1:99 R
BRAB Angel Berroa Bat B 4.00 10.00
BRAC Antoine Cameron Bat C 4.00 10.00
BRAE Adam Everett Bat E 3.00 8.00
BRAF Alex Fernandez Bat B 4.00 10.00
BRAF Alex Fernandez Jsy C 3.00 8.00
BRAG Alexis Gomez Bat A 4.00 10.00
BRAK Austin Kearns Bat E 3.00 8.00
BRALC Alex Cintron Bat E 3.00 8.00
BRCG Cristian Guerrero Bat E 3.00 8.00
BRCI Cesar Izturis Bat D 3.00 8.00
BRCP Corey Patterson Bat B 4.00 10.00
BRCY Colin Young Jsy C 3.00 8.00
BRDJ D'Angelo Jimenez Bat C 4.00 10.00
BRFJ Forrest Johnson Bat G 3.00 8.00
BRGA Garrett Atkins Bat F 4.00 10.00
BRJA Jared Abruzzo Bat D 3.00 8.00
BRJA Jared Abruzzo Jsy C 3.00 8.00
BRJL Jason Lane Jsy B 3.00 8.00
BRJS Jamal Strong Jsy A 3.00 8.00
BRNC Nate Cornejo Jsy C 3.00 8.00
BRNN Nick Neugebauer Jsy C 3.00 8.00
BRRC Ryan Church Bat D 3.00 8.00
BRRD Ryan Dittfurth Jsy C 3.00 8.00
BRRM Ryan Madson Bat E 3.00 8.00
BRRS Ruben Salazar Bat A 4.00 10.00
BRRST Richard Stahl Jsy B 3.00 8.00

2002 Bowman Draft

COMPLETE SET (165) 15.00 40.00
BDP1 Clint Everts RC .12 .30
BDP2 Fred Lewis RC .12 .30
BDP3 Jon Broxton RC .30 .75
BDP4 Jason Anderson RC .12 .30
BDP5 Mike Eusebio RC .12 .30
BDP6 Zack Greinke RC 10.00 25.00
BDP7 Joe Blanton RC .20 .50
BDP8 Sergio Santos RC .12 .30
BDP9 Jason Cooper RC .12 .30
BDP10 Delwyn Young RC .12 .30
BDP11 Jeremy Hermida RC .20 .50
BDP12 Dan Ortmeier RC .12 .30
BDP13 Kevin Jepsen RC .12 .30
BDP14 Russ Adams RC .12 .30
BDP15 Mike Nixon RC .12 .30
BDP16 Nick Swisher RC .75 2.00
BDP17 Cole Hamels RC 1.50 4.00
BDP18 Brian Dopirak RC .12 .30
BDP19 James Loney RC .30 .75
BDP20 Denard Span RC .20 .50
BDP21 Billy Petrick RC .12 .30
BDP22 Jared Doyle RC .12 .30
BDP23 Jeff Francoeur RC .75 2.00
BDP24 Nick Bourgeois RC .12 .30
BDP25 Matt Cain RC .75 2.00
BDP26 John McCurdy RC .12 .30
BDP27 Mark Kiger RC .12 .30
BDP28 Bill Murphy RC .12 .30
BDP29 Matt Craig RC .12 .30
BDP30 Mike Megrew RC .12 .30
BDP31 Ben Crockett RC .12 .30
BDP32 Luke Hagerty RC .12 .30
BDP33 Matt Whitney RC .12 .30
BDP34 Dan Meyer RC .12 .30
BDP35 Jeremy Brown RC .12 .30
BDP36 Doug Johnson RC .12 .30
BDP37 Steve Obenchain RC .12 .30
BDP38 Matt Clanton RC .12 .30
BDP39 Mark Teahen RC .12 .30
BDP40 Tom Carrow RC .12 .30
BDP41 Micah Schilling RC .12 .30
BDP42 Blair Johnson RC .12 .30
BDP43 Jason Pridie RC .12 .30
BDP44 Joey Votto RC 12.00 30.00
BDP45 Taber Lee RC .12 .30
BDP46 Adam Peterson RC .12 .30
BDP47 Adam Donachie RC .12 .30
BDP48 Josh Murray RC .12 .30
BDP49 Brent Clevlen RC .12 .30
BDP50 Chad Pleiness RC .12 .30
BDP51 Zach Hammes RC .12 .30
BDP52 Chris Snyder RC .12 .30
BDP53 Chris Smith RC .12 .30
BDP54 Justin Maureau RC .12 .30
BDP55 David Bush RC .12 .30
BDP56 Tim Gilhooly RC .12 .30
BDP57 Blair Barbier RC .12 .30
BDP58 Zach Segovia RC .12 .30
BDP59 Jeremy Reed RC .12 .30
BDP60 Matt Pender RC .12 .30
BDP61 Eric Thomas RC .12 .30
BDP62 Justin Jones RC .12 .30
BDP63 Brian Slocum RC .12 .30
BDP64 Larry Broadway RC .12 .30
BDP65 Bo Flowers RC .12 .30
BDP66 Scott White RC .12 .30
BDP67 Steve Stanley RC .12 .30
BDP68 Alex Merricks RC .12 .30
BDP69 Josh Womack RC .12 .30
BDP70 Dave Jensen RC .12 .30
BDP71 Curtis Granderson RC 1.50 4.00
BDP72 Pat Osborn RC .12 .30
BDP73 Nic Carter RC .12 .30
BDP74 Mitch Talbot RC .12 .30
BDP75 Don Murphy RC .12 .30
BDP76 Val Majewski RC .12 .30
BDP77 Javy Rodriguez RC .12 .30
BDP78 Fernando Pacheco RC .12 .30
BDP79 Steve Russell RC .12 .30
BDP80 Jon Slack RC .12 .30
BDP81 John Baker RC .12 .30
BDP82 Aaron Coonrod RC .12 .30
BDP83 Josh Johnson RC .75 2.00
BDP84 Jake Blalock RC .12 .30
BDP85 Alex Hart RC .12 .30
BDP86 Wes Bankston RC .12 .30
BDP87 Josh Rupe RC .12 .30
BDP88 Dan Cevette RC .12 .30
BDP89 Kiel Fisher RC .12 .30
BDP90 Alan Rick RC .12 .30
BDP91 Charlie Morton RC 1.00 2.50
BDP92 Chad Spann RC .12 .30
BDP93 Kyle Boyer RC .12 .30
BDP94 Bob Malek RC .12 .30
BDP95 Ryan Rodriguez RC .12 .30
BDP96 Jordan Renz RC .12 .30
BDP97 Randy Frye RC .12 .30
BDP98 Rich Hill RC .30 .75
BDP99 B.J. Upton RC .60 1.50
BDP100 Dan Christensen RC .12 .30
BDP101 Casey Kotchman RC .20 .50
BDP102 Eric Good RC .12 .30
BDP103 Mike Fontenot RC .12 .30
BDP104 John Webb RC .12 .30
BDP105 Jason Dubois RC .12 .30
BDP106 Ryan Kibler RC .12 .30
BDP107 Jhonny Peralta RC .20 .50
BDP108 Kirk Saarloos RC .12 .30
BDP109 Rhett Parrott RC .12 .30
BDP110 Jason Grove RC .12 .30
BDP111 Colt Griffin RC .12 .30
BDP112 Dallas McPherson RC .12 .30
BDP113 Oliver Perez RC .30 .75
BDP114 Marshall McDougall RC .12 .30
BDP115 Mike Wood RC .12 .30
BDP116 Scott Hairston RC .12 .30
BDP117 Jason Simontacchi RC .12 .30
BDP118 Taggert Bozied RC .12 .30
BDP119 Shelley Duncan RC .30 .75
BDP120 Dontrelle Willis RC .30 .75
BDP121 Sean Burnett .12 .30
BDP122 Aaron Cook .12 .30
BDP123 Brett Evert .12 .30
BDP124 Jimmy Journell .12 .30
BDP125 Brett Myers .12 .30
BDP126 Brad Baker .12 .30
BDP127 Billy Traber RC .12 .30
BDP128 Adam Wainwright .20 .50
BDP129 Jason Young RC .12 .30
BDP130 John Buck .30 .75
BDP131 Kevin Cash RC .12 .30
BDP132 Jason Stokes RC .12 .30
BDP133 Drew Henson .12 .30
BDP134 Chad Tracy RC .20 .50
BDP135 Orlando Hudson .12 .30
BDP136 Brandon Phillips .12 .30
BDP137 Joe Borchard .12 .30
BDP138 Marlon Byrd .12 .30
BDP139 Carl Crawford .20 .50
BDP140 Michael Restovich .12 .30
BDP141 Corey Hart RC .60 1.50
BDP142 Edwin Almonte .12 .30
BDP143 Francis Beltran RC .12 .30
BDP144 Jorge De La Rosa RC .12 .30
BDP145 Gerardo Garcia RC .12 .30
BDP146 Franklyn German RC .12 .30
BDP147 Francisco Liriano .60 1.50
BDP148 Francisco Rodriguez .20 .50
BDP149 Ricardo Rodriguez .12 .30
BDP150 Seung Song .12 .30
BDP151 John Stephens .12 .30
BDP152 Justin Huber RC .12 .30
BDP153 Victor Martinez .20 .50
BDP154 Hee Seop Choi .12 .30
BDP155 Justin Morneau .30 .75
BDP156 Miguel Cabrera 4.00 10.00
BDP157 Victor Diaz RC .12 .30
BDP158 Jose Reyes .30 .75
BDP159 Omar Infante .30 .75
BDP160 Angel Berroa .12 .30
BDP161 Tony Alvarez .12 .30
BDP162 Shin Soo Choo RC 1.00 2.50
BDP163 Wily Mo Pena .12 .30
BDP164 Andres Torres .12 .30
BDP165 Jose Lopez RC .20 .50

2002 Bowman Draft Gold

COMPLETE SET (165) 30.00 80.00
*GOLD: 1.2X TO 3X BASIC
*GOLD RC'S: 1.2X TO 3X BASIC
ONE PER PACK
BDP156 Miguel Cabrera 6.00 15.00

2002 Bowman Draft Fabric of the Future Relics

STATED ODDS 1:55
ALL CARDS FEATURE JERSEY SWATCHES
AB Angel Berroa 3.00 8.00
AT Andres Torres 3.00 8.00
AW Adam Wainwright 5.00 12.00
BM Brett Myers 3.00 8.00
BT Billy Traber 2.00 5.00
CC Carl Crawford 4.00 10.00
CH Corey Hart 4.00 10.00
CT Chad Tracy 3.00 8.00
DH Drew Henson 3.00 8.00
EA Edwin Almonte 2.00 5.00
FB Francis Beltran 2.00 5.00
FG Franklyn German 2.00 5.00
FL Francisco Liriano 4.00 10.00
GG Gerardo Garcia 2.00 5.00
HC Hee Seop Choi 4.00 10.00
JH Justin Huber 3.00 8.00
JK Josh Karp 2.00 5.00
JL Jose Lopez 3.00 8.00
JR Jorge De La Rosa 2.00 5.00
JS1 Jason Stokes 2.00 5.00
JS2 John Stephens 3.00 8.00
KC Kevin Cash 2.00 5.00
MR Michael Restovich 3.00 8.00
SB Sean Burnett 3.00 8.00
SC Shin Soo Choo 6.00 15.00
TA Tony Alvarez 3.00 8.00
VD Victor Diaz 3.00 8.00
WP Wily Mo Pena 4.00 10.00

2002 Bowman Draft Freshman Fiber

BAT STATED ODDS 1:605
JERSEY STATED ODDS 1:45
AH Aubrey Huff Jsy 2.00 5.00
AK Austin Kearns Bat 3.00 8.00
BA Brent Abernathy Jsy 2.00 5.00
DB Dewon Brazelton Jsy 2.00 5.00
JH Josh Hamilton 6.00 15.00
JK Joe Kennedy Jsy 2.00 5.00
JS Jared Sandberg Jsy 2.00 5.00
JV John VanBenschoten Jsy 2.00 5.00
JWS Jason Standridge Jsy 2.00 5.00
MB Marlon Byrd Bat 3.00 8.00
MT Mark Teixeira Bat 6.00 15.00
NB Nick Bierbrodt Jsy 2.00 5.00
TH Toby Hall Jsy 2.00 5.00

2002 Bowman Draft Signs of the Future

GROUP A ODDS 1:100
GROUP B ODDS 1:110
GROUP C ODDS 1:1028
GROUP D ODDS 1:1103
GROUP E ODDS 1:386
GROUP F ODDS 1:2807
BI Brandon Inge E 5.00 12.00
BK Bob Keppel C 4.00 10.00
BP Brandon Phillips B 4.00 10.00
BS Bud Smith E 4.00 10.00
CP Christian Parra D 4.00 10.00
CT Chad Tracy A 6.00 15.00
DD Dan Denham A 4.00 10.00
EB Erik Bedard A 6.00 15.00
JEM Justin Morneau B 6.00 15.00
JM Jake Mauer B 4.00 10.00
JR Juan Rivera B 4.00 10.00
JW Jerome Williams F 4.00 10.00
KH Kris Honel A 4.00 10.00
LB Larry Bigbie E 4.00 10.00
LN Lance Niekro A 6.00 15.00
ME Morgan Ensberg E 4.00 10.00
MF Mike Fontenot A 4.00 10.00
MJ Mitch Jones A 4.00 10.00
NJ Nic Jackson B 4.00 10.00
TB Taylor Buchholz B 4.00 10.00
TL Todd Linden B 6.00 15.00

2003 Bowman

COMPLETE SET (330) 15.00 40.00
HINSKE/JENNINGS 1:765 H,1:246 HTA,1:1416 R
1 Garret Anderson .12 .30
2 Derek Jeter .75 2.00
3 Gary Sheffield .12 .30
4 Matt Morris .12 .30
5 Derek Lowe .12 .30
6 Andy Van Hekken .12 .30
7 Sammy Sosa .30 .75
8 Ken Griffey Jr. .60 1.50
9 Omar Vizquel .20 .50
10 Jorge Posada .20 .50
11 Lance Berkman .20 .50
12 Mike Sweeney .12 .30
13 Adrian Beltre .30 .75
14 Richie Sexson .12 .30
15 A.J. Pierzynski .12 .30
16 Bartolo Colon .12 .30
17 Mike Mussina .20 .50
18 Paul Byrd .12 .30
19 Bobby Abreu .12 .30
20 Miguel Tejada .20 .50
21 Aramis Ramirez .12 .30
22 Edgardo Alfonzo .12 .30
23 Edgar Martinez .20 .50
24 Albert Pujols .40 1.00
25 Carl Crawford .20 .50
26 Eric Hinske .12 .30
27 Tim Salmon .12 .30
28 Luis Gonzalez .12 .30
29 Jay Gibbons .12 .30
30 John Smoltz .30 .75
31 Tim Wakefield .20 .50
32 Mark Prior .20 .50
33 Magglio Ordonez .20 .50
34 Adam Dunn .20 .50
35 Larry Walker .20 .50
36 Luis Castillo .12 .30
37 Wade Miller .12 .30
38 Carlos Beltran .20 .50
39 Odalis Perez .12 .30
40 Alex Sanchez .12 .30
41 Torii Hunter .12 .30
42 Cliff Floyd .12 .30
43 Andy Pettitte .20 .50
44 Francisco Rodriguez .20 .50
45 Eric Chavez .12 .30
46 Kevin Millwood .12 .30
47 Dennis Tankersley .12 .30
48 Hideo Nomo .30 .75
49 Freddy Garcia .12 .30
50 Randy Johnson .30 .75
51 Aubrey Huff .12 .30
52 Carlos Delgado .12 .30
53 Troy Glaus .12 .30
54 Junior Spivey .12 .30
55 Mike Hampton .12 .30
56 Sidney Ponson .12 .30
57 Aaron Boone .12 .30
58 Kerry Wood .12 .30
59 Runelvys Hernandez .12 .30
60 Nomar Garciaparra .20 .50
61 Todd Helton .20 .50
62 Mike Lowell .12 .30
63 Roy Oswalt .20 .50
64 Raul Ibanez .20 .50
65 Brian Jordan .12 .30
66 Geoff Jenkins .12 .30
67 Jermaine Dye .12 .30
68 Tom Glavine .20 .50
69 Bernie Williams .20 .50
70 Vladimir Guerrero .20 .50
71 Mark Mulder .12 .30
72 Jimmy Rollins .20 .50
73 Oliver Perez .12 .30
74 Rich Aurilia .12 .30
75 Joel Pineiro .12 .30
76 J.D. Drew .12 .30
77 Ivan Rodriguez .20 .50
78 Josh Phelps .12 .30
79 Darin Erstad .12 .30
80 Curt Schilling .20 .50
81 Paul Lo Duca .12 .30
82 Marty Cordova .12 .30
83 Manny Ramirez .30 .75
84 Bobby Hill .12 .30
85 Paul Konerko .20 .50
86 Austin Kearns .12 .30
87 Jason Jennings .12 .30
88 Brad Penny .12 .30
89 Jeff Bagwell .20 .50
90 Shawn Green .12 .30
91 Jason Schmidt .12 .30
92 Doug Mientkiewicz .12 .30
93 Jose Vidro .12 .30
94 Bret Boone .12 .30
95 Jason Giambi .12 .30
96 Barry Zito .20 .50
97 Roy Halladay .20 .50
98 Pat Burrell .12 .30
99 Sean Burroughs .12 .30
100 Barry Bonds .50 1.25
101 Kazuhiro Sasaki .12 .30
102 Fernando Vina .12 .30
103 Chan Ho Park .20 .50
104 Andruw Jones .12 .30
105 Adam Kennedy .12 .30
106 Shea Hillenbrand .12 .30
107 Greg Maddux .40 1.00
108 Jim Edmonds .20 .50
109 Pedro Martinez .20 .50
110 Moises Alou .12 .30
111 Jeff Weaver .12 .30
112 C.C. Sabathia .20 .50
113 Robert Fick .12 .30
114 A.J. Burnett .12 .30
115 Jeff Kent .12 .30
116 Kevin Brown .12 .30
117 Rafael Furcal .12 .30
118 Cristian Guzman .12 .30
119 Brad Wilkerson .12 .30
120 Mike Piazza .30 .75
121 Alfonso Soriano .20 .50
122 Mark Ellis .12 .30
123 Vicente Padilla .12 .30
124 Eric Gagne .12 .30
125 Ryan Klesko .12 .30
126 Ichiro Suzuki .40 1.00
127 Tony Batista .12 .30
128 Roberto Alomar .20 .50
129 Alex Rodriguez .40 1.00
130 Jim Thome .20 .50
131 Jarrod Washburn .12 .30
132 Orlando Hudson .12 .30
133 Chipper Jones .30 .75
134 Rodrigo Lopez .12 .30
135 Johnny Damon .20 .50
136 Matt Clement .12 .30
137 Frank Thomas .30 .75
138 Ellis Burks .12 .30
139 Carlos Pena .20 .50
140 Josh Beckett .12 .30
141 Joe Randa .12 .30
142 Brian Giles .12 .30
143 Kazuhisa Ishii .12 .30
144 Corey Koskie .12 .30
145 Orlando Cabrera .12 .30
146 Mark Buehrle .20 .50
147 Roger Clemens .40 1.00
148 Tim Hudson .20 .50
149 Randy Wolf .12 .30
150 Josh Fogg .12 .30
151 Phil Nevin .12 .30
152 John Olerud .12 .30
153 Scott Rolen .20 .50
154 Joe Kennedy .12 .30
155 Rafael Palmeiro .20 .50
156 Chad Hutchinson .12 .30
157 Quincy Carter XRC .12 .30
158 Hee Seop Choi .12 .30
159 Joe Borchard .12 .30
160 Brandon Phillips .12 .30
161 Wily Mo Pena .12 .30
162 Victor Martinez .20 .50
163 Jason Stokes .12 .30
164 Ken Harvey .12 .30
165 Juan Rivera .12 .30
166 Jose Contreras RC .30 .75
167 Dan Haren RC .60 1.50
168 Michel Hernandez RC .12 .30
169 Eider Torres RC .12 .30
170 Chris De La Cruz RC .12 .30
171 Ramon Nivar-Martinez RC .12 .30
172 Mike Adams RC .20 .50
173 Justin Arneson RC .12 .30
174 Jamie Athas RC .12 .30
175 Dwaine Bacon RC .12 .30
176 Clint Barmes RC .30 .75
177 B.J. Barns RC .12 .30
178 Tyler Johnson RC .12 .30
179 Bobby Basham RC .12 .30
180 T.J. Bohn RC .12 .30
181 J.D. Durbin RC .12 .30
182 Brandon Bowe RC .12 .30
183 Craig Brazell RC .12 .30
184 Dusty Brown RC .12 .30
185 Brian Bruney RC .12 .30
186 Greg Bruso RC .12 .30
187 Jaime Bubela RC .12 .30
188 Bryan Bullington RC .12 .30
189 Brian Burgamy RC .12 .30
190 Eny Cabreja RC .50 1.25
191 Daniel Cabrera RC .20 .50
192 Ryan Cameron RC .12 .30
193 Lance Caraccioli RC .12 .30
194 David Cash RC .12 .30
195 Bernie Castro RC .12 .30
196 Ismael Castro RC .12 .30
197 Daryl Clark RC .12 .30
198 Jeff Clark RC .12 .30
199 Chris Colton RC .12 .30
200 Dexter Cooper RC .12 .30
201 Callix Crabbe RC .12 .30
202 Chien-Ming Wang RC .50 1.25
203 Eric Crozier RC .12 .30
204 Nook Logan RC .12 .30
205 David DeJesus RC .30 .75
206 Matt DeMarco RC .20 .50
207 Chris Duncan RC .40 1.00
208 Eric Eckenstahler .12 .30
209 Willie Eyre RC .12 .30
210 Evel Bastida-Martinez RC .12 .30
211 Chris Fallon RC .12 .30
212 Mike Flannery RC .12 .30
213 Mike O'Keefe RC .12 .30
214 Ben Francisco RC .12 .30
215 Kason Gabbard RC .12 .30

216 Mike Gallo RC .12 .30
217 Jairo Garcia RC .12 .30
218 Angel Garcia RC .12 .30
219 Michael Garciaparra RC .12 .30
220 Joey Gomes RC .12 .30
221 Dusty Gomon RC .12 .30
222 Bryan Grace RC .12 .30
223 Tyson Graham RC .12 .30
224 Henry Guerrero RC .12 .30
225 Franklin Gutierrez RC .30 .75
226 Carlos Guzman RC .12 .30
227 Matthew Hagen RC .12 .30
228 Josh Hall RC .12 .30
229 Rob Hammock RC .12 .30
230 Brendan Harris RC .12 .30
231 Gary Harris RC .12 .30
232 Clay Hensley RC .12 .30
233 Michael Hinckley RC .12 .30
234 Luis Hodge RC .12 .30
235 Donnie Hood RC .12 .30
236 Travis Ishikawa RC .30 .75
237 Edwin Jackson RC .20 .50
238 Ardley Jansen RC .12 .30
239 Ferenc Jongejan RC .12 .30
240 Matt Kata RC .12 .30
241 Kazuhiro Takeoka RC .12 .30
242 Beau Kemp RC .12 .30
243 Il Kim RC .12 .30
244 Brennan King RC .12 .30
245 Chris Kroski RC .12 .30
246 Jason Kubel RC .40 1.00
247 Pete LaForest RC .12 .30
248 Wil Ledezma RC .12 .30
249 Jeremy Bonderman RC .50 1.25
250 Gonzalo Lopez RC .12 .30
251 Brian Luderer RC .12 .30
252 Ruddy Lugo RC .12 .30
253 Wayne Lydon RC .12 .30
254 Mark Malaska RC .12 .30
255 Andy Marte RC .12 .30
256 Tyler Martin RC .12 .30
257 Branden Florence RC .12 .30
258 Aneudis Mateo RC .12 .30
259 Derell McCall RC .12 .30
260 Brian McCann RC 1.00 2.50
261 Mike McNutt RC .12 .30
262 Jacabo Meque RC .12 .30
263 Derek Michaelis RC .12 .30
264 Aaron Miles RC .12 .30
265 Jose Morales RC .12 .30
266 Dustin Moseley RC .12 .30
267 Adrian Myers RC .12 .30
268 Dan Neil RC .12 .30
269 Jon Nelson RC .12 .30
270 Mike Neu RC .12 .30
271 Leigh Neuage RC .12 .30
272 Wes O'Brien RC .12 .30
273 Trent Oeltjen RC .12 .30
274 Tim Olson RC .12 .30
275 David Pahucki RC .12 .30
276 Nathan Panther RC .12 .30
277 Arnie Munoz RC .12 .30
278 Dave Pember RC .12 .30
279 Jason Perry RC .12 .30
280 Matthew Peterson RC .12 .30
281 Ryan Shealy RC .12 .30
282 Jorge Piedra RC .12 .30
283 Simon Pond RC .12 .30
284 Aaron Rakers RC .12 .30
285 Hanley Ramirez RC 1.00 2.50
286 Manuel Ramirez RC .12 .30
287 Kevin Randel RC .12 .30
288 Darrell Rasner RC .12 .30
289 Prentice Redman RC .12 .30
290 Eric Reed RC .12 .30
291 Wilton Reynolds RC .12 .30
292 Eric Riggs RC .12 .30
293 Carlos Rijo RC .12 .30
294 Rajai Davis RC .12 .30
295 Aron Weston RC .12 .30
296 Arturo Rivas RC .12 .30
297 Kyle Roat RC .12 .30
298 Bubba Nelson RC .12 .30
299 Levi Robinson RC .12 .30
300 Ray Sadler RC .12 .30
301 Gary Schneidmiller RC .12 .30
302 Jon Schuerholz RC .12 .30
303 Corey Shafer RC .12 .30
304 Brian Shackelford RC .12 .30
305 Bill Simon RC .12 .30
306 Haj Turay RC .12 .30
307 Sean Smith RC .12 .30
308 Ryan Spataro RC .12 .30
309 Jemel Spearman RC .12 .30
310 Keith Stamler RC .12 .30
311 Luke Steidlmayer RC .12 .30
312 Adam Stern RC .12 .30
313 Jay Sitzman RC .12 .30
314 Thomari Story-Harden RC .12 .30
315 Terry Tiffee RC .12 .30
316 Nick Trzesniak RC .12 .30
317 Denny Tussen RC .12 .30
318 Scott Tyler RC .12 .30
319 Shane Victorino RC .40 1.00
320 Doug Waechter RC .12 .30
321 Brandon Watson RC .12 .30
322 Todd Wellemeyer RC .12 .30
323 Eli Whiteside RC .12 .30
324 Josh Willingham RC .40 1.00
325 Travis Wong RC .12 .30
326 Brian Wright RC .12 .30
327 Kevin Youkilis RC .75 2.00
328 Andy Sisco RC .12 .30
329 Dustin Yount RC .12 .30
330 Andrew Dominique RC .12 .30
NNO Hinske/Jennings ROY Relic 6.00 15.00

2003 Bowman Gold

COMPLETE SET (330) 75.00 150.00
*RED 1-155: 1.25X TO 3X BASIC
*BLUE 156-330: 1.25X TO 3X BASIC
*BLUE ROOKIES: 1.25X TO 3X BASIC
ONE PER PACK

2003 Bowman Uncirculated Metallic Gold

*UNC.GOLD 1-155: 2.5X TO 6X BASIC
*UNC.GOLD 156-330: 2.5X TO 6X BASIC
*UNC.GOLD ROOKIES: 2.5X TO 6X BASIC
ONE EXCH.CARD PER SEALED SILVER PACK
ONE SILVER PACK PER SEALED HOBBY BOX
STATED ODDS 1:49 RETAIL
STATED PRINT RUN 230 SETS
EXCHANGE DEADLINE 04/30/04

2003 Bowman Uncirculated Silver

*UNC.SILVER 1-155: 2.5X TO 6X BASIC
*UNC.SILVER 156-330: 2.5X TO 6X BASIC
*UNC.SILVER ROOKIES: 2.5X TO 6X BASIC
ONE PER SEALED SILVER PACK
ONE SILVER PACK PER SEALED HOBBY BOX
STATED PRINT RUN 250 SERIAL #'d SETS
SET EXCH.CARD ODDS 1:8589 H, 1:5576 HTA
SET EXCHANGE CARD DEADLINE 04/30/04
202 Chien-Ming Wang 5.00 12.00

2003 Bowman Future Fiber Bats

GROUP A ODDS 1:96 H, 1:34 HTA, 1:196 R
GROUP B ODDS 1:393 H, 1:140 HTA, 1:803 R
AG Adrian Gonzalez A 3.00 8.00
AH Aubrey Huff A 3.00 8.00
AK Austin Kearns A 3.00 8.00
BS Bud Smith B 3.00 8.00
CD Chris Duffy B 3.00 8.00
CK Casey Kotchman A 3.00 8.00
DH Drew Henson A 3.00 8.00
DW David Wright A 10.00 25.00
ES Esix Snead A 3.00 8.00
EY Edwin Yan B 3.00 8.00
FS Freddy Sanchez A 3.00 8.00
HB Hank Blalock A 3.00 8.00
JB Jason Botts A 2.00 5.00
JDM Jake Mauer A 3.00 8.00
JG Jason Grove A 3.00 8.00
JH Josh Hamilton 6.00 15.00
JM Joe Mauer A 6.00 15.00
JW Justin Wayne B 3.00 8.00
KC Kevin Cash B 3.00 8.00
KD Kory DeHaan A 3.00 8.00
MR Michael Restovich A 3.00 8.00
NH Nathan Haynes A 3.00 8.00
PF Pedro Feliz A 3.00 8.00
RB Rocco Baldelli B 3.00 8.00
RJ Reed Johnson A 3.00 8.00
RK Ryan Langerhans A 3.00 8.00
RS Randall Shelley A 3.00 8.00
SB Sean Burroughs A 3.00 8.00
ST So Taguchi A 3.00 8.00
TW Travis Wilson A 3.00 8.00
WB Wilson Betemit A 3.00 8.00
WR Wilkin Ruan B 3.00 8.00
XN Xavier Nady A 3.00 8.00

2003 Bowman Futures Game Base Autograph

STATED ODDS 1:141 HTA
JR Jose Reyes 8.00 20.00

2003 Bowman Futures Game Gear Jersey Relics

STATED ODDS 1:26 H, 1:9 HTA, 1:52 R
AC Aaron Cook 3.00 8.00
AW Adam Wainwright 3.00 8.00
BB Brad Baker 3.00 8.00
BE Brett Evert 3.00 8.00
BH Bill Hall 3.00 8.00
BM Brett Myers 3.00 8.00
BP Brandon Phillips 3.00 8.00
BT Billy Traber 3.00 8.00
CC Carl Crawford 3.00 8.00
CH Corey Hart 3.00 8.00
CT Chad Tracy 3.00 8.00
DH Drew Henson 3.00 8.00
EA Edwin Almonte 3.00 8.00
FB Francis Beltran 3.00 8.00
FL Francisco Liriano 6.00 15.00
FR Francisco Rodriguez 3.00 8.00
GG Gerardo Garcia 3.00 8.00
HC Hee Seop Choi 3.00 8.00
JB John Buck 3.00 8.00
JDR Jorge De La Rosa 3.00 8.00
JEB Joe Borchard 3.00 8.00
JH Justin Huber 3.00 8.00
JJ Jimmy Journell 3.00 8.00
JK Josh Karp 3.00 8.00
JL Jose Lopez 4.00 10.00
JM Justin Morneau 3.00 8.00
JMS John Stephens 3.00 8.00
JR Jose Reyes 3.00 8.00
JS Jason Stokes 3.00 8.00
JY Jason Young 3.00 8.00
KC Kevin Cash 3.00 8.00
LO Lyle Overbay 3.00 8.00
MB Marlon Byrd 3.00 8.00
MC Miguel Cabrera 10.00 25.00
MR Michael Restovich 3.00 8.00
OH Orlando Hudson 3.00 8.00
OI Omar Infante 3.00 8.00
RD Ryan Dittfurth 3.00 8.00
RR Ricardo Rodriguez 3.00 8.00
SB Sean Burnett 3.00 8.00
SC Shin Soo Choo 3.00 8.00
SS Seung Song 3.00 8.00
TA Tony Alvarez 3.00 8.00
VD Victor Diaz 3.00 8.00
VM Victor Martinez 4.00 10.00
WP Wily Mo Pena 3.00 8.00

2003 Bowman Signs of the Future

GROUP A ODDS 1:39 H, 1:13 HTA, 1:79 R
GROUP B ODDS 1:183 H, 1:65 HTA, 1:374 R
GROUP C ODDS 1:2288 H,1:816 HTA,1:4720 R
*RED INK: 1.25X TO 3X GROUP A
*RED INK: 1.25X TO 3X GROUP B
*RED INK: .75X TO 2X GROUP C
RED INK ODDS 1:687 H, 1:245 HTA, 1:1402 R
AV Andy Van Hekken A 4.00 10.00
BB Bryan Bullington A 3.00 8.00
BJ Bobby Jenks B 6.00 15.00
BK Ben Kozlowski A 4.00 10.00
BL Brandon League B 4.00 10.00
BS Brian Slocum A 4.00 10.00
CH Cole Hamels A 15.00 40.00
CJH Corey Hart A 6.00 15.00
CMH Chad Hutchinson C 4.00 10.00
CP Chris Piersoll B 4.00 10.00
DG Doug Gredvig A 4.00 10.00
DHM Dustin McGowan A 4.00 10.00
DL Donald Levinski A 3.00 8.00
DS Doug Sessions B 4.00 10.00
FL Fred Lewis A 4.00 10.00
FS Freddy Sanchez B 6.00 15.00
HR Hanley Ramirez A 4.00 10.00
JA Jason Arnold B 4.00 10.00
JB John Buck A 4.00 10.00
JC Jesus Cota B 4.00 10.00
JG Jason Grove B 4.00 10.00
JGU Jeremy Guthrie A 3.00 8.00
JL James Loney A 6.00 15.00
JOG Jonny Gomes B 6.00 15.00
JR Jose Reyes A 6.00 15.00
JRH Joel Hanrahan A 4.00 10.00
JSC Jason St. Clair B 4.00 10.00
KG Khalil Greene A 4.00 10.00
KH Koyie Hill B 4.00 10.00
MT Mitch Talbot A 4.00 10.00
NC Nelson Castro B 4.00 10.00
OV Oscar Villareal A 3.00 8.00
PR Prentice Redman A 3.00 8.00
QC Quincy Carter C 6.00 15.00
RC Ryan Church B 6.00 15.00
RS Ryan Snare B 4.00 10.00
TL Todd Linden B 4.00 10.00
VM Val Majewski A 4.00 10.00
ZG Zack Greinke A 15.00 40.00
ZS Zach Segovia A 4.00 10.00

2003 Bowman Signs of the Future Dual

STAT.ODDS 1:9220 H,1:3264 HTA,1:20,390 R
CH Q.Carter/C.Hutchinson 20.00 50.00

2003 Bowman Draft

COMPLETE SET (165) 20.00 50.00
1 Dontrelle Willis .12 .30
2 Freddy Sanchez .12 .30
3 Miguel Cabrera 1.50 4.00
4 Ryan Ludwick .12 .30
5 Ty Wigginton .12 .30
6 Mark Teixeira .20 .50
7 Trey Hodges .12 .30
8 Laynce Nix .12 .30
9 Antonio Perez .12 .30
10 Jody Gerut .12 .30
11 Jae Weong Seo .12 .30
12 Erick Almonte .12 .30
13 Lyle Overbay .12 .30
14 Billy Traber .12 .30
15 Andres Torres .12 .30
16 Jose Valverde .12 .30
17 Aaron Heilman .12 .30
18 Brandon Larson .12 .30
19 Jung Bong .12 .30
20 Jesse Foppert .12 .30
21 Angel Berroa .12 .30
22 Jeff DaVanon .12 .30
23 Kurt Ainsworth .12 .30
24 Brandon Claussen .12 .30
25 Xavier Nady .12 .30
26 Travis Hafner .12 .30
27 Jerome Williams .12 .30
28 Jose Reyes .30 .75
29 Sergio Mitre RC .12 .30
30 Bo Hart RC .12 .30
31 Adam Miller RC .50 1.25
32 Brian Finch RC .12 .30
33 Taylor Mattingly RC .12 .30
34 Daric Barton RC .20 .50
35 Chris Ray RC .20 .50
36 Jarrod Saltalamacchia RC .60 1.50
37 Dennis Dove RC .12 .30
38 James Houser RC .12 .30
39 Clint King RC .12 .30
40 Lou Palmisano RC .12 .30
41 Dan Moore RC .12 .30
42 Craig Stansberry RC .12 .30
43 Jo Jo Reyes RC .12 .30
44 Jake Stevens RC .12 .30
45 Tom Gorzelanny RC .20 .50
46 Brian Marshall RC .12 .30
47 Scott Beerer RC .12 .30
48 Javi Herrera RC .12 .30
49 Steve LeRud RC .12 .30
50 Josh Banks RC .12 .30
51 Jon Papelbon RC 1.25 3.00
52 Juan Valdes RC .12 .30
53 Beau Vaughan RC .12 .30
54 Matt Chico RC .12 .30
55 Todd Jennings RC .12 .30
56 Anthony Gwynn RC .12 .30
57 Matt Harrison RC .50 1.25
58 Aaron Marsden RC .12 .30
59 Casey Abrams RC .12 .30
60 Cory Stuart RC .12 .30
61 Mike Wagner RC .12 .30
62 Jordan Pratt RC .12 .30
63 Andre Randolph RC .12 .30
64 Blake Balkcom RC .12 .30
65 Josh Muecke RC .12 .30
66 Jamie D'Antona RC .12 .30
67 Cole Seifrig RC .12 .30
68 Josh Anderson RC .12 .30
69 Matt Lorenzo RC .12 .30
70 Nate Spears RC .12 .30
71 Chris Goodman RC .12 .30
72 Brian McFall RC .12 .30
73 Billy Hogan RC .12 .30
74 Jamie Romak RC .12 .30
75 Jeff Cook RC .12 .30
76 Brooks McNiven RC .12 .30
77 Xavier Paul RC .12 .30
78 Bob Zimmerman RC .12 .30
79 Mickey Hall RC .12 .30
80 Shaun Marcum RC .12 .30
81 Matt Nachreiner RC .12 .30
82 Chris Kinsey RC .12 .30
83 Jonathan Fulton RC .12 .30
84 Edgardo Baez RC .12 .30
85 Robert Valido RC .12 .30
86 Kenny Lewis RC .12 .30
87 Trent Peterson RC .12 .30
88 Johnny Woodard RC .12 .30
89 Wes Littleton RC .12 .30
90 Sean Rodriguez RC .20 .50
91 Kyle Pearson RC .12 .30
92 Josh Rainwater RC .12 .30
93 Travis Schlichting RC .12 .30
94 Tim Battle RC .12 .30
95 Aaron Hill RC .40 1.00
96 Bob McCrory RC .12 .30
97 Rick Guarno RC .12 .30
98 Brandon Yarbrough RC .12 .30
99 Peter Stonard RC .12 .30
100 Darin Downs RC .12 .30
101 Matt Bruback RC .12 .30
102 Danny Garcia RC .12 .30
103 Cory Stewart RC .12 .30
104 Ferdin Tejeda RC .12 .30
105 Kade Johnson RC .12 .30
106 Andrew Brown RC .12 .30
107 Aquilino Lopez RC .12 .30
108 Stephen Randolph RC .12 .30
109 Dave Matranga RC .12 .30
110 Dustin McGowan RC .12 .30
111 Juan Camacho RC .12 .30
112 Cliff Lee .75 2.00
113 Jeff Duncan RC .12 .30
114 C.J. Wilson 1.00 2.50
115 Brandon Roberson RC .12 .30
116 David Corrente RC .12 .30
117 Kevin Beavers RC .12 .30
118 Anthony Webster RC .12 .30
119 Oscar Villarreal RC .12 .30
120 Hong-Chih Kuo RC .60 1.50
121 Josh Barfield .12 .30
122 Denny Bautista .12 .30
123 Chris Burke RC .12 .30
124 Robinson Cano RC 5.00 12.00
125 Jose Castillo .12 .30
126 Neal Cotts .12 .30
127 Jorge De La Rosa .12 .30
128 J.D. Durbin .12 .30
129 Edwin Encarnacion 1.00 2.50
130 Gavin Floyd .12 .30
131 Alexis Gomez .12 .30
132 Edgar Gonzalez RC .12 .30
133 Khalil Greene .20 .50
134 Zack Greinke 4.00 10.00
135 Franklin Gutierrez .30 .75
136 Rich Harden .20 .50
137 J.J. Hardy RC 1.00 2.50
138 Ryan Howard RC 1.00 2.50
139 Justin Huber .12 .30
140 David Kelton .12 .30
141 Dave Krynzel .12 .30
142 Pete LaForest .12 .30
143 Adam LaRoche .12 .30
144 Preston Larrison RC .12 .30
145 John Maine RC .20 .50
146 Andy Marte .12 .30
147 Jeff Mathis .12 .30
148 Joe Mauer .30 .75
149 Clint Nageotte .12 .30
150 Chris Narveson .12 .30
151 Ramon Nivar .12 .30
152 Felix Pie RC .20 .50
153 Guillermo Quiroz RC .12 .30
154 Rene Reyes .12 .30
155 Royce Ring .12 .30
156 Alexis Rios .12 .30
157 Grady Sizemore .20 .50
158 Stephen Smitherman .12 .30
159 Seung Song .12 .30
160 Scott Thorman .12 .30
161 Chad Tracy .12 .30
162 Chin-Hui Tsao .12 .30
163 John VanBenschoten .12 .30
164 Kevin Youkilis .75 2.00
165 Chien-Ming Wang .50 1.25

2003 Bowman Draft Gold

COMPLETE SET (165) 50.00 100.00
*GOLD: 1.25X TO 3X BASIC
*GOLD RC'S: 1.25X TO 3X BASIC
*GOLD RC YR: 1.25X TO 3X BASIC
ONE PER PACK
124 Robinson Cano 6.00 15.00

2003 Bowman Draft Fabric of the Future Jersey Relics

GROUP A ODDS 1:721 H, 1:720 R
GROUP B ODDS 1:315 H/R
GROUP C ODDS 1:98 H/R
GROUP D ODDS 1:81 H, 1:82 R
GROUP E ODDS 1:263 H/R
GROUP F ODDS 1:241 H, 1:240 R
AL Adam LaRoche D 2.00 5.00
AM Andy Marte D 4.00 10.00
CN Chris Narveson C 2.00 5.00
EG Edgar Gonzalez D 2.00 5.00
FG Franklin Gutierrez C 3.00 8.00
FP Felix Pie A 4.00 10.00
GF Gavin Floyd E 2.00 5.00
GS Grady Sizemore D 4.00 10.00
JB Josh Barfield B 3.00 8.00
JD J.D. Durbin D 2.00 5.00
JH Justin Huber D 2.00 5.00
JM Joe Mauer C 8.00 20.00
JSM Jeff Mathis B 2.00 5.00
KG Khalil Greene D 4.00 10.00
RC Robinson Cano C 10.00 25.00
RH Rich Harden C 4.00 10.00
RJH Ryan Howard F 4.00 10.00
RR Rene Reyes E 2.00 5.00
RRR Royce Ring F 2.00 5.00
ZG Zack Greinke C 5.00 12.00

2003 Bowman Draft Prospect Premiums Relics

GROUP A ODDS 1:216 H/R
GROUP B ODDS 1:470 H, 1:469 R
AK Austin Kearns Jsy B 2.00 5.00
BH Brendan Harris Bat A 3.00 8.00
BM Brett Myers Jsy B 2.00 5.00
CC Carl Crawford Bat A 3.00 8.00
CS Chris Snelling Bat A 3.00 8.00
CU Chase Utley Bat A 8.00 20.00
HB Hank Blalock Bat A 3.00 8.00
JM Justin Morneau Bat A 3.00 8.00
JT Joe Thurston Bat A 3.00 8.00
NH Nathan Haynes Bat A 3.00 8.00
RB Rocco Baldelli Bat A 3.00 8.00
TH Travis Hafner Bat A 3.00 8.00

2003 Bowman Draft Signs of the Future

GROUP A ODDS 1:385 H, 1:720 R
GROUP B ODDS 1:491 H, 1:491 R
GROUP C ODDS 1:2160 H, 1:12,185 R
AT Andres Torres A 4.00 10.00
CS Cory Stewart B 4.00 10.00
DT Dennis Tankersley A 4.00 10.00
JA Jason Arnold B 4.00 10.00
ZG Zack Greinke C 25.00 60.00

2004 Bowman

COMPLETE SET (330) 20.00 50.00
COMMON CARD (1-165) .10 .30
COMMON CARD (166-330) .10 .30
ROY ODDS 1:829 H, 1:284 HTA, 1:1632 R
1 Garret Anderson .12 .30
2 Larry Walker .20 .50
3 Derek Jeter .75 2.00
4 Curt Schilling .20 .50
5 Carlos Zambrano .20 .50
6 Shawn Green .12 .30
7 Manny Ramirez .30 .75
8 Randy Johnson .30 .75
9 Jeremy Bonderman .12 .30
10 Alfonso Soriano .20 .50
11 Scott Rolen .20 .50
12 Kerry Wood .12 .30
13 Eric Gagne .12 .30
14 Ryan Klesko .12 .30
15 Kevin Millar .12 .30
16 Ty Wigginton .12 .30
17 David Ortiz .30 .75
18 Luis Castillo .12 .30
19 Bernie Williams .20 .50
20 Edgar Renteria .12 .30
21 Matt Kata .12 .30
22 Bartolo Colon .12 .30
23 Derrek Lee .12 .30
24 Gary Sheffield .12 .30
25 Nomar Garciaparra .20 .50
26 Kevin Millwood .12 .30
27 Corey Patterson .12 .30
28 Carlos Beltran .20 .50
29 Mike Lieberthal .12 .30
30 Troy Glaus .12 .30
31 Preston Wilson .12 .30
32 Jorge Posada .20 .50
33 Bo Hart .12 .30
34 Mark Prior .20 .50
35 Hideo Nomo .30 .75
36 Jason Kendall .12 .30
37 Roger Clemens .40 1.00
38 Dmitri Young .12 .30
39 Jason Giambi .12 .30
40 Jim Edmonds .20 .50
41 Ryan Ludwick .12 .30
42 Brandon Webb .12 .30
43 Todd Helton .20 .50
44 Jacque Jones .12 .30
45 Jamie Moyer .12 .30
46 Tim Salmon .12 .30
47 Kelvim Escobar .12 .30
48 Tony Batista .12 .30
49 Nick Johnson .12 .30
50 Jim Thome .20 .50
51 Casey Blake .12 .30
52 Trot Nixon .12 .30
53 Luis Gonzalez .12 .30
54 Dontrelle Willis .12 .30
55 Mike Mussina .20 .50
56 Carl Crawford .20 .50
57 Mark Buehrle .20 .50
58 Scott Podsednik .12 .30
59 Brian Giles .12 .30
60 Rafael Furcal .12 .30
61 Miguel Cabrera .30 .75
62 Rich Harden .12 .30
63 Mark Teixeira .20 .50
64 Frank Thomas .30 .75
65 Johan Santana .20 .50
66 Jason Schmidt .12 .30
67 Aramis Ramirez .12 .30
68 Jose Reyes .20 .50
69 Magglio Ordonez .20 .50
70 Mike Sweeney .12 .30
71 Eric Chavez .12 .30
72 Rocco Baldelli .12 .30
73 Sammy Sosa .30 .75
74 Javy Lopez .12 .30
75 Roy Oswalt .20 .50
76 Raul Ibanez .20 .50
77 Ivan Rodriguez .20 .50
78 Jerome Williams .12 .30
79 Carlos Lee .12 .30
80 Geoff Jenkins .12 .30
81 Sean Burroughs .12 .30
82 Marcus Giles .12 .30
83 Mike Lowell .12 .30
84 Barry Zito .20 .50
85 Aubrey Huff .12 .30
86 Esteban Loaiza .12 .30
87 Torii Hunter .12 .30
88 Phil Nevin .12 .30
89 Andruw Jones .12 .30
90 Josh Beckett .12 .30
91 Mark Mulder .12 .30
92 Hank Blalock .12 .30
93 Jason Phillips .12 .30
94 Russ Ortiz .12 .30
95 Juan Pierre .12 .30
96 Tom Glavine .20 .50
97 Gil Meche .12 .30
98 Ramon Ortiz .12 .30
99 Richie Sexson .12 .30
100 Albert Pujols .40 1.00
101 Javier Vazquez .12 .30
102 Johnny Damon .20 .50
103 Alex Rodriguez Yanks .40 1.00
104 Omar Vizquel .20 .50
105 Chipper Jones .30 .75
106 Lance Berkman .20 .50
107 Tim Hudson .20 .50
108 Carlos Delgado .12 .30
109 Austin Kearns .12 .30
110 Orlando Cabrera .12 .30
111 Edgar Martinez .20 .50
112 Melvin Mora .12 .30
113 Jeff Bagwell .20 .50
114 Marlon Byrd .12 .30
115 Vernon Wells .12 .30
116 C.C. Sabathia .20 .50
117 Cliff Floyd .12 .30
118 Ichiro Suzuki .40 1.00
119 Miguel Olivo .12 .30
120 Mike Piazza .30 .75
121 Adam Dunn .20 .50
122 Paul Lo Duca .12 .30
123 Brett Myers .12 .30
124 Michael Young .12 .30
125 Sidney Ponson .12 .30
126 Greg Maddux .40 1.00
127 Vladimir Guerrero .20 .50
128 Miguel Tejada .20 .50
129 Andy Pettitte .20 .50
130 Rafael Palmeiro .20 .50
131 Ken Griffey Jr. .60 1.50
132 Shannon Stewart .12 .30
133 Joel Pineiro .12 .30
134 Luis Matos .12 .30
135 Jeff Kent .12 .30
136 Randy Wolf .12 .30
137 Chris Woodward .12 .30
138 Jody Gerut .12 .30
139 Jose Vidro .12 .30
140 Bret Boone .12 .30
141 Bill Mueller .12 .30
142 Angel Berroa .12 .30
143 Bobby Abreu .12 .30
144 Roy Halladay .20 .50
145 Delmon Young .20 .50
146 Jonny Gomes .12 .30
147 Rickie Weeks .12 .30
148 Edwin Jackson .12 .30
149 Neal Cotts .12 .30
150 Jason Bay .20 .50
151 Khalil Greene .20 .50
152 Joe Mauer .25 .60
153 Bobby Jenks .12 .30
154 Chin-Feng Chen .12 .30
155 Chien-Ming Wang .50 1.25
156 Mickey Hall .12 .30
157 James Houser .12 .30
158 Jay Sborz .12 .30
159 Jonathan Fulton .12 .30
160 Steven Lerud .12 .30
161 Grady Sizemore .20 .50
162 Felix Pie .12 .30
163 Dustin McGowan .12 .30
164 Chris Lubanski .12 .30
165 Tom Gorzelanny .12 .30
166 Rudy Guillen FY RC .12 .30
167 Bobby Brownlie FY RC .12 .30
168 Conor Jackson FY RC .40 1.00
169 Matt Moses FY RC .20 .50
170 Ervin Santana FY RC .30 .75
171 Merkin Valdez FY RC .12 .30
172 Erick Aybar FY RC .30 .75
173 Brad Sullivan FY RC .12 .30
174 David Aardsma FY RC .12 .30
175 Brad Snyder FY RC .12 .30
176 Alberto Callaspo FY RC .30 .75
177 Brandon Medders FY RC .12 .30
178 Zach Miner FY RC .20 .50
179 Charlie Zink FY RC .12 .30
180 Adam Greenberg FY RC .60 1.50
181 Kevin Howard FY RC .12 .30
182 Wanell Severino FY RC .12 .30
183 Kevin Kouzmanoff FY RC .75 2.00
184 Joel Zumaya FY RC .50 1.25
185 Skip Schumaker FY RC .20 .50
186 Nic Ungs FY RC .12 .30
187 Todd Self FY RC .12 .30
188 Brian Steffek FY RC .12 .30
189 Brock Peterson FY RC .12 .30
190 Greg Thissen FY RC .12 .30
191 Frank Brooks FY RC .12 .30
192 Estee Harris FY RC .12 .30
193 Chris Mabeus FY RC .12 .30
194 Dan Giese FY RC .12 .30
195 Jared Wells FY RC .12 .30
196 Carlos Sosa FY RC .12 .30
197 Bobby Madritsch FY .12 .30
198 Calvin Hayes FY RC .12 .30
199 Omar Quintanilla FY RC .12 .30
200 Chris O'Riordan FY RC .12 .30
201 Tim Hutting FY RC .12 .30
202 Carlos Quentin FY RC .50 1.25
203 Brayan Pena FY RC .12 .30
204 Jeff Salazar FY RC .12 .30
205 David Murphy FY RC .20 .50
206 Alberto Garcia FY RC .12 .30
207 Ramon Ramirez FY RC .12 .30
208 Luis Bolivar FY RC .12 .30
209 Rodney Choy Foo FY RC .12 .30
210 Kyle Sleeth FY RC .12 .30
211 Anthony Acevedo FY RC .12 .30
212 Chad Santos FY RC .12 .30
213 Jason Frasor FY RC .12 .30
214 Jesse Roman FY RC .12 .30
215 James Tomlin FY RC .12 .30
216 Josh Labandeira FY RC .12 .30
217 Joaquin Arias FY RC .30 .75
218 Don Sutton FY UER RC .12 .30
219 Danny Gonzalez FY RC .12 .30
220 Javier Guzman FY RC .12 .30
221 Anthony Lerew FY RC .12 .30
222 Jon Knott FY RC .12 .30
223 Jesse English FY RC .12 .30
224 Felix Hernandez FY RC 2.00 5.00
225 Travis Hanson FY RC .12 .30
226 Jesse Floyd FY RC .12 .30
227 Nick Gorneault FY RC .12 .30
228 Craig Ansman FY RC .12 .30
229 Wardell Starling FY RC .12 .30
230 Carl Loadenthal FY RC .12 .30
231 Dave Crouthers FY RC .12 .30
232 Harvey Garcia FY RC .12 .30
233 Casey Kopitzke FY RC .12 .30
234 Ricky Nolasco FY RC .20 .50
235 Miguel Perez FY RC .12 .30
236 Ryan Mulhern FY RC .12 .30
237 Chris Aguila FY RC .12 .30
238 Brooks Conrad FY RC .12 .30
239 Damaso Espino FY RC .12 .30
240 Jereme Milons FY RC .12 .30
241 Luke Hughes FY RC .30 .75
242 Kory Casto FY RC .12 .30
243 Jose Valdez FY RC .12 .30
244 J.T. Stotts FY RC .12 .30
245 Lee Gwaltney FY RC .12 .30
246 Yoann Torrealba FY RC .12 .30
247 Omar Falcon FY RC .12 .30
248 Jon Coutlangus FY RC .12 .30
249 George Sherrill FY RC .12 .30
250 John Santor FY RC .12 .30
251 Tony Richie FY RC .12 .30
252 Kevin Richardson FY RC .12 .30
253 Tim Bittner FY RC .12 .30
254 Dustin Nippert FY RC .12 .30
255 Jose Capellan FY RC .12 .30
256 Donald Levinski FY RC .12 .30
257 Jerome Gamble FY RC .12 .30
258 Jeff Keppinger FY RC .20 .50
259 Jason Szuminski FY RC .12 .30
260 Akinori Otsuka FY RC .12 .30
261 Ryan Budde FY RC .12 .30
262 Shingo Takatsu FY RC .12 .30
263 Jeff Allison FY RC .12 .30
264 Hector Gimenez FY RC .12 .30
265 Tim Frend FY RC .12 .30
266 Tom Farmer FY RC .12 .30
267 Shawn Hill FY RC .12 .30
268 Lastings Milledge FY RC .20 .50
269 Scott Proctor FY RC .12 .30
270 Jorge Mejia FY RC .12 .30
271 Terry Jones FY RC .12 .30
272 Zach Duke FY RC .20 .50
273 Tim Stauffer FY RC .20 .50
274 Luke Anderson FY RC .12 .30
275 Hunter Brown FY RC .12 .30
276 Matt Lemanczyk FY RC .12 .30
277 Fernando Cortez FY RC .12 .30
278 Vince Perkins FY RC .12 .30
279 Tommy Murphy FY RC .12 .30
280 Mike Gosling FY RC .12 .30
281 Paul Bacot FY RC .12 .30
282 Matt Capps FY RC .12 .30
283 Juan Gutierrez FY RC .12 .30
284 Teodoro Encarnacion FY RC .12 .30
285 Juan Cedeno FY RC .12 .30
286 Matt Creighton FY RC .12 .30
287 Ryan Hankins FY RC .12 .30
288 Leo Nunez FY RC .12 .30
289 Dave Wallace FY RC .12 .30
290 Rob Tejeda FY RC .12 .30
291 Lincoln Holdzkom FY RC .12 .30
292 Jason Hirsh FY RC .12 .30
293 Tydus Meadows FY RC .12 .30
294 Khalid Ballouli FY RC .12 .30
295 Benji DeQuin FY RC .12 .30
296 Tyler Davidson FY RC .12 .30
297 Brant Colamarino FY RC .12 .30
298 Marcus McBeth FY RC .12 .30
299 Brad Eldred FY RC .12 .30
300 David Pauley FY RC .20 .50
301 Yadier Molina FY RC 20.00 50.00
302 Chris Shelton FY RC .12 .30
303 Travis Blackley FY RC .12 .30
304 Jon DeVries FY RC .12 .30
305 Sheldon Fulse FY RC .12 .30
306 Vito Chiaravalloti FY RC .12 .30
307 Warner Madrigal FY RC .12 .30
308 Reid Gorecki FY RC .12 .30
309 Sung Jung FY RC .12 .30
310 Pete Shier FY RC .12 .30
311 Michael Mooney FY RC .12 .30
312 Kenny Perez FY RC .12 .30
313 Michael Mallory FY RC .12 .30
314 Ben Himes FY RC .12 .30
315 Ivan Ochoa FY RC .12 .30
316 Donald Kelly FY RC .20 .50
317 Logan Kensing FY RC .12 .30
318 Kevin Davidson FY RC .12 .30
319 Brian Pilkington FY RC .12 .30
320 Alex Romero FY RC .12 .30
321 Chad Chop FY RC .12 .30
322 Dioner Navarro FY RC .20 .50
323 Casey Myers FY RC .12 .30
324 Mike Rouse FY RC .12 .30
325 Sergio Silva FY RC .12 .30
326 J.J. Furmaniak FY RC .12 .30
327 Brad Vericker FY RC .12 .30
328 Blake Hawksworth FY RC .12 .30
329 Brock Jacobsen FY RC .12 .30
330 Alec Zumwalt FY RC .12 .30
BW Berroa Bat/Willis Jsy ROY 6.00 15.00

2004 Bowman 1st Edition

*1ST EDITION 1-165: .75X TO 2X BASIC
*1ST EDITION 166-330: .75X TO 2X BASIC
ISSUED IN FIRST EDITION PACKS

2004 Bowman Gold

COMPLETE SET (330) 60.00 150.00
*GOLD 1-165: 1.25X TO 3X BASIC
*GOLD 166-330: 1X TO 2.5X BASIC
ONE PER HOBBY PACK
ONE PER HTA PACK
ONE PER RETAIL PACK

2004 Bowman Uncirculated Gold

ONE EXCH.CARD PER SILVER PACK

ONE SILVER PACK PER SEALED HOBBY BOX
ONE SILVER PACK PER SEALED HTA BOX
STATED ODDS 1:44 RETAIL
STATED PRINT RUN 210 SETS
SEE WWW.THEPIT.COM FOR PRICING
NNO Exchange Card 2.00 5.00

2004 Bowman Uncirculated Silver

*UNC.SILVER 1-165: 4X TO 10X BASIC
*UNC.SILVER 166-330: 3X TO 8X BASIC
ONE PER SILVER PACK
ONE SILVER PACK PER SEALED HOBBY BOX
ONE SILVER PACK PER SEALED HTA BOX
SET EXCH.CARD ODDS 1:9159 H, 1:3718 HTA
STATED PRINT RUN 245 SERIAL #'d SETS
1ST 100 SETS PRINTED HELD FOR EXCH.
LAST 145 SETS PRINTED DIST.IN BOXES
EXCHANGE DEADLINE 05/31/06

2004 Bowman Autographs

STATED ODDS 1:72 H, 1:24 HTA, 1:139 R
RED INK ODDS 1:1466 H,1:501 HTA,1:2901 R
RED INK PRINT RUN 25 SETS
RED INK ARE NOT SERIAL-NUMBERED
RED INK PRINT RUN PROVIDED BY TOPPS
NO RED INK PRICING DUE TO SCARCITY
161 Grady Sizemore 4.00 10.00
162 Felix Pie 4.00 10.00
163 Dustin McGowan 3.00 8.00
164 Chris Lubanski 4.00 10.00
165 Tom Gorzelanny 3.00 8.00
166 Rudy Guillen 4.00 10.00
167 Bobby Brownlie 4.00 10.00
168 Conor Jackson 4.00 10.00
169 Matt Moses 4.00 10.00
170 Ervin Santana 4.00 10.00
171 Merkin Valdez 4.00 10.00
172 Erick Aybar 4.00 10.00
173 Brad Sullivan 4.00 10.00
174 David Aardsma 4.00 10.00
175 Brad Snyder 4.00 10.00

2004 Bowman Relics

GROUP A 1:346 H, 1:118 HTA, 1:1685 R
GROUP B 1:133 H, 1:44 HTA, 1:269 R
HS JSY MEANS HIGH SCHOOL JERSEY
154 Chin-Feng Chen Jsy B 6.00 15.00
155 Chien-Ming Wang Uni B 6.00 15.00
156 Mickey Hall HS Jsy B 3.00 8.00
157 James Houser HS Jsy A 3.00 8.00
158 Jay Sborz HS Jsy B 3.00 8.00
159 Jonathan Fulton HS Jsy B 3.00 8.00
160 Steve Lerud HS Jsy A 3.00 8.00
164 Chris Lubanski HS Jsy B 3.00 8.00
192 Estee Harris HS Jsy A 3.00 8.00
221 Anthony Lerew Jsy B 3.00 8.00

2004 Bowman Base of the Future Autograph

STATED ODDS 1:110 HTA
RED INK ODDS 1:5112 HTA
RED INK PRINT RUN 25 SERIAL #'d CARDS
NO RED INK PRICING DUE TO SCARCITY
GS Grady Sizemore 6.00 15.00

2004 Bowman Futures Game Gear Jersey Relics

GROUP A 1:167 H, 1:58 HTA, 1:333 R
GROUP B 1:71 H, 1:23 HTA, 1:148 R
GROUP C 1:181 H, 1:63 HTA, 1:362 R
GROUP D 1:173 H, 1:59 HTA, 1:341 R
GROUP E 1:145 H, 1:70 HTA, 1:318 R
AR Alexis Rios A 3.00 8.00
CB Chris Burke B 3.00 8.00
CN Clint Nageotte B 3.00 8.00
CT Chad Tracy B 3.00 8.00
CW Chien-Ming Wang C 15.00 40.00
DB Denny Bautista D 3.00 8.00
DBK Dave Krynzel B 3.00 8.00
DK David Kelton E 3.00 8.00
EE Edwin Encarnacion A 3.00 8.00
EJ Edwin Jackson C 3.00 8.00
ES Ervin Santana D 4.00 10.00
GQ Guillermo Quiroz A 3.00 8.00
JC Jose Castillo E 3.00 8.00
JD Jorge De La Rosa C 3.00 8.00
JH J.J. Hardy A 3.00 8.00
JM John Maine B 4.00 10.00
JV John VanBenschoten B 3.00 8.00
KY Kevin Youkilis E 3.00 8.00
MV Merkin Valdez E 3.00 8.00
NC Neal Cotts D 3.00 8.00
PL Pete LaForest B 3.00 8.00
PWL Preston Larrison B 3.00 8.00
RN Ramon Nivar A 3.00 8.00
SH Shawn Hill D 3.00 8.00
SJS Seung Song B 3.00 8.00
SS Stephen Smitherman B 3.00 8.00
ST Scott Thorman C 3.00 8.00
TB Travis Blackley B 3.00 8.00

2004 Bowman Signs of the Future

GROUP A 1:75 H, 1:25 HTA, 1:147 R
GROUP B 1:847 H, 1:289 HTA, 1:1675 R
GROUP C 1:582 H, 1:198 HTA, 1:1148 R
GROUP D 1:315 H, 1:105 HTA, 1:605 R
RED INK ODDS 1:1466 H,1:501 HTA,1:2901 R
RED INK PRINT RUN 25 SETS
RED INK CARDS ARE NOT SERIAL #'d
RED INK PRINT RUN PROVIDED BY TOPPS
NO RED INK PRICING DUE TO SCARCITY
AH Aaron Hill A 5.00 12.00
BC Brent Clevlen A 8.00 20.00
BF Brian Finch D 4.00 10.00
BM Brandon Medders A 3.00 8.00
BS Brian Snyder D 4.00 10.00
BW Brandon Wood B 8.00 20.00
CS Corey Shafer A 3.00 8.00
DS Denard Span A 4.00 10.00
ED Eric Duncan D 6.00 15.00
GS Grady Sizemore D 6.00 15.00
IC Ismael Castro A 3.00 8.00
JB Justin Backsmeyer D 4.00 10.00
JH James Houser A 3.00 8.00
JV Joey Votto A 60.00 150.00
MM Matt Murton D 6.00 15.00
NM Nick Markakis C 3.00 8.00
RH Ryan Harvey C 4.00 10.00
TJ Tyler Johnson A 3.00 8.00
TL Todd Linden A 3.00 8.00

2004 Bowman Draft

COMPLETE SET (165) 15.00 40.00
COMMON CARD (1-165) .12 .30
COMMON RC (1-165) .12 .30
COMMON RC YR .12 .30
PLATES ODDS 1:559 HOBBY
PLATES PRINT RUN 1 SERIAL #'d SET
BLACK-CYAN-MAGENTA-YELLOW EXIST
NO PLATES PRICING DUE TO SCARCITY
1 Lyle Overbay .12 .30
2 David Newhan .12 .30
3 J.R. House .12 .30
4 Chad Tracy .12 .30
5 Humberto Quintero .12 .30
6 Dave Bush .12 .30
7 Scott Hairston .12 .30
8 Mike Wood .12 .30
9 Alexis Rios .12 .30
10 Sean Burnett .12 .30
11 Wilson Valdez .12 .30
12 Lew Ford .12 .30
13 Freddy Thon RC .12 .30
14 Zack Greinke .50 1.25
15 Bucky Jacobsen .12 .30
16 Kevin Youkilis .12 .30
17 Grady Sizemore .20 .50
18 Denny Bautista .12 .30
19 David DeJesus .12 .30
20 Casey Kotchman .12 .30
21 David Kelton .12 .30
22 Charles Thomas RC .12 .30
23 Kazuhito Tadano RC .12 .30
24 Justin Leone RC .12 .30
25 Eduardo Villacis RC .12 .30
26 Brian Dallimore RC .12 .30
27 Nick Green .12 .30
28 Sam McConnell RC .12 .30
29 Brad Halsey RC .12 .30
30 Roman Colon RC .12 .30
31 Josh Fields RC .20 .50
32 Cody Bunkelman RC .12 .30
33 Jay Rainville RC .12 .30
34 Richie Robnett RC .12 .30
35 Jon Poterson RC .12 .30
36 Huston Street RC .20 .50
37 Erick San Pedro RC .12 .30
38 Cory Dunlap RC .12 .30
39 Kurt Suzuki RC .20 .50
40 Anthony Swarzak RC .20 .50
41 Ian Desmond RC .20 .50
42 Chris Covington RC .12 .30
43 Christian Garcia RC .20 .50
44 Gaby Hernandez RC .20 .50
45 Steven Register RC .12 .30
46 Eduardo Morlan RC .20 .50
47 Collin Balester RC .12 .30
48 Nathan Phillips RC .12 .30
49 Dan Schwartzbauer RC .12 .30
50 Rafael Gonzalez RC .12 .30
51 K.C. Herren RC .12 .30
52 William Susdorf RC .12 .30
53 Rob Johnson RC .12 .30
54 Louis Marson RC .20 .50
55 Joe Koshansky RC .12 .30
56 Jamar Walton RC .12 .30
57 Mark Lowe RC .20 .50
58 Matt Macri RC .20 .50
59 Donny Lucy RC .12 .30
60 Mike Ferris RC .12 .30
61 Mike Nickeas RC .12 .30
62 Eric Hurley RC .12 .30
63 Scott Elbert RC .12 .30
64 Blake DeWitt RC .20 .50
65 Danny Putnam RC .12 .30
66 J.P. Howell RC .12 .30
67 John Wiggins RC .12 .30
68 Justin Orenduff RC .20 .50
69 Ray Liotta RC .12 .30
70 Billy Buckner RC .12 .30
71 Eric Campbell RC .12 .30
72 Olin Wick RC .12 .30
73 Sean Gamble RC .12 .30
74 Seth Smith RC .20 .50
75 Wade Davis RC .30 .75
76 Joe Jacobitz RC .12 .30
77 J.A. Happ RC .30 .75
78 Eric Ridener RC .12 .30
79 Matt Tuiasosopo RC .30 .75
80 Brad Bergesen RC .12 .30
81 Javy Guerra RC .30 .75
82 Buck Shaw RC .12 .30
83 Paul Janish RC .20 .50
84 Sean Kazmar RC .12 .30
85 Josh Johnson RC .12 .30
86 Angel Salome RC .12 .30
87 Jordan Parraz RC .20 .50
88 Kelvin Vazquez RC .12 .30
89 Grant Hansen RC .12 .30
90 Matt Fox RC .12 .30
91 Trevor Plouffe RC .30 .75
92 Wes Whisler RC .12 .30
93 Curtis Thigpen RC .12 .30
94 Donnie Smith RC .12 .30
95 Luis Rivera RC .12 .30
96 Jesse Hoover RC .12 .30
97 Jason Vargas RC .20 .50
98 Clary Carlsen RC .12 .30
99 Mark Robinson RC .12 .30
100 J.C. Holt RC .12 .30
101 Chad Blackwell RC .12 .30
102 Daryl Jones RC .12 .30
103 Jonathan Tierce RC .12 .30
104 Patrick Bryant RC .12 .30
105 Eddie Prasch RC .12 .30
106 Mitch Einertson RC .12 .30
107 Kyle Waldrop RC .12 .30
108 Jeff Marquez RC .12 .30
109 Zach Jackson RC .12 .30
110 Josh Wahpepah RC .12 .30
111 Adam Lind RC .20 .50
112 Kyle Bloom RC .12 .30
113 Ben Harrison RC .12 .30
114 Taylor Tankersley RC .12 .30
115 Steven Jackson RC .12 .30
116 David Purcey RC .20 .50
117 Jacob McGee RC .30 .75
118 Lucas Harrell RC .12 .30
119 Brandon Allen RC .12 .30
120 Van Pope RC .12 .30
121 Jeff Francis .12 .30
122 Joe Blanton .12 .30
123 Wil Ledezma .12 .30
124 Bryan Bullington .12 .30
125 Jairo Garcia .12 .30
126 Matt Cain .75 2.00
127 Arnie Munoz .12 .30
128 Clint Everts .12 .30
129 Jesus Cota .12 .30
130 Gavin Floyd .12 .30
131 Edwin Encarnacion .30 .75
132 Koyie Hill .12 .30
133 Ruben Gotay .12 .30
134 Jeff Mathis .12 .30
135 Andy Marte .12 .30
136 Dallas McPherson .12 .30
137 Justin Morneau .20 .50
138 Rickie Weeks .12 .30
139 Joel Guzman .12 .30
140 Shin Soo Choo .20 .50
141 Yusmeiro Petit RC .30 .75
142 Jorge Cortes RC .12 .30
143 Val Majewski .12 .30
144 Felix Pie .12 .30
145 Aaron Hill .12 .30
146 Jose Capellan .12 .30
147 Dioner Navarro .20 .50
148 Fausto Carmona RC .20 .50
149 Robinzon Diaz RC .12 .30
150 Felix Hernandez . 2.00 5.00
151 Andres Blanco RC .12 .30
152 Jason Kubel .12 .30
153 Willy Taveras RC .30 .75
154 Merkin Valdez .12 .30
155 Robinson Cano .40 1.00
156 Bill Murphy .12 .30
157 Chris Burke .12 .30
158 Kyle Sleeth .12 .30
159 B.J. Upton .20 .50
160 Tim Stauffer .20 .50
161 David Wright .25 .60
162 Conor Jackson .40 1.00
163 Brad Thompson RC .20 .50
164 Delmon Young .20 .50
165 Jeremy Reed .12 .30

2004 Bowman Draft Gold

COMPLETE SET (165) 25.00 60.00
*GOLD RC's: .6X TO 1.5X BASIC
*GOLD RC YR: .6X TO 1.5X BASIC
ONE PER PACK

2004 Bowman Draft Red

STATED ODDS 1:4471 HOBBY
STATED PRINT RUN 1 SERIAL #'d SET
NO PRICING DUE TO SCARCITY

2004 Bowman Draft AFLAC Promos

DISTRIBUTED TO DEALERS
11 Cameron Maybin
15 Ryan DeLaughter
17 Jeremy Hellickson
18 Austin Jackson
19 Ryan Mitchell
30 Ralphie Henriquez
38 Kent Matthes

2004 Bowman Draft AFLAC

COMP.FACT.SET (12) 8.00 20.00
ONE SET VIA MAIL PER AFLAC EXCH.CARD
ONE EXCH.PER '04 BOW.DRAFT HOBBY BOX
EXCH.CARD DEADLINE WAS 11/30/05
SETS ACTUALLY SENT OUT JANUARY, 2006
RED PRINT RUN 1 SERIAL #'d SET
NO RED PRICING DUE TO SCARCITY
1 C.J. Henry .20 .50
2 John Drennen .20 .50
3 Beau Jones .20 .50
4 Jeff Lyman .20 .50
5 Andrew McCutchen 3.00 8.00
6 Chris Volstad .30 .75
7 Jonathan Egan .20 .50
8 P.J. Phillips .20 .50
9 Steve Johnson .20 .50
10 Ryan Tucker .20 .50
11 Cameron Maybin .60 1.50
12 Shane Funk .20 .50

2004 Bowman Draft Futures Game Jersey Relics

STATED ODDS 1:31 HOBBY, 1:30 RETAIL
146 Jose Capellan 3.00 8.00
147 Dioner Navarro 3.00 8.00
148 Fausto Carmona 2.00 5.00
149 Robinzon Diaz 2.00 5.00
150 Felix Hernandez 10.00 25.00
151 Andres Blanco 2.00 5.00
152 Jason Kubel 2.00 5.00
153 Willy Taveras 3.00 8.00
154 Merkin Valdez 3.00 8.00
155 Robinson Cano 6.00 15.00
156 Bill Murphy 2.00 5.00
157 Chris Burke 2.00 5.00
158 Kyle Sleeth 3.00 8.00
159 B.J. Upton 3.00 8.00
160 Tim Stauffer 3.00 8.00
161 David Wright 8.00 20.00
162 Conor Jackson 3.00 8.00
163 Brad Thompson 3.00 8.00
164 Delmon Young 3.00 8.00
165 Jeremy Reed 2.00 5.00

2004 Bowman Draft Prospect Premiums Relics

GROUP A ODDS 1:145 H, 1:153 R
GROUP B ODDS 1:387 H, 1:411 R
AB Angel Berroa Bat A 2.00 5.00
BU B.J. Upton Bat B 3.00 8.00
CJ Conor Jackson Bat B 3.00 8.00
CQ Carlos Quentin Bat B 3.00 8.00
DN Dioner Navarro Bat A 2.00 5.00
DY Delmon Young Bat A 3.00 8.00
EJ Edwin Jackson Jsy A 2.00 5.00
JR Jeremy Reed Bat A 2.00 5.00
KC Kevin Cash Bat B 2.00 5.00
LM Lastings Milledge Bat A 4.00 10.00
NS Nick Swisher Bat B 2.00 5.00
RH Ryan Harvey Bat A 2.00 5.00

2004 Bowman Draft Signs of the Future

GROUP A ODDS 1:127 H, 1:127 R
GROUP B ODDS 1:509 H, 1:511 R
EXCHANGE DEADLINE 11/30/05
AL Adam Loewen A 6.00 15.00
CC Chad Cordero B 6.00 15.00
JH James Houser B 4.00 10.00
PM Paul Maholm A 4.00 10.00
TP Tyler Pelland A 4.00 10.00
TT Terry Tiffee A 4.00 10.00

2005 Bowman

COMPLETE SET (330) 20.00 50.00
COMMON CARD (1-140) .10 .30
COMMON CARD (141-165) .15 .40
COMMON CARD (166-330) .15 .40
PLATE ODDS 1:695 HOBBY, 1:177 HTA
PLATE PRINT RUN 1 SET PER COLOR
BLACK-CYAN-MAGENTA-YELLOW ISSUED
NO PLATE PRICING DUE TO SCARCITY
ROY ODDS 1:668 H, 1:248 HTA, 1:1535 R
1 Gavin Floyd .12 .30
2 Eric Chavez .12 .30
3 Miguel Tejada .20 .50
4 Dmitri Young .12 .30
5 Hank Blalock .12 .30
6 Kerry Wood .12 .30
7 Andy Pettitte .20 .50
8 Pat Burrell .12 .30
9 Johnny Estrada .12 .30
10 Frank Thomas .30 .75
11 Juan Pierre .12 .30
12 Tom Glavine .20 .50
13 Lyle Overbay .12 .30
14 Jim Edmonds .20 .50
15 Steve Finley .12 .30
16 Jermaine Dye .12 .30
17 Omar Vizquel .20 .50
18 Nick Johnson .12 .30
19 Brian Giles .12 .30
20 Justin Morneau .20 .50
21 Preston Wilson .12 .30
22 Wily Mo Pena .12 .30
23 Rafael Palmeiro .20 .50
24 Scott Kazmir .30 .75
25 Derek Jeter .75 2.00
26 Barry Zito .20 .50
27 Mike Lowell .12 .30
28 Jason Bay .12 .30
29 Ken Harvey .12 .30
30 Nomar Garciaparra .20 .50
31 Roy Halladay .20 .50
32 Todd Helton .20 .50
33 Mark Kotsay .12 .30
34 Jake Peavy .12 .30
35 David Wright .25 .60
36 Dontrelle Willis .12 .30
37 Marcus Giles .12 .30
38 Chone Figgins .12 .30
39 Sidney Ponson .12 .30
40 Randy Johnson .30 .75
41 John Smoltz .30 .75
42 Kevin Millar .12 .30
43 Mark Teixeira .20 .50
44 Alex Rios .12 .30
45 Mike Piazza .30 .75
46 Victor Martinez .20 .50
47 Jeff Bagwell .20 .50
48 Shawn Green .12 .30
49 Ivan Rodriguez .20 .50
50 Alex Rodriguez .40 1.00
51 Kazuo Matsui .12 .30
52 Mark Mulder .12 .30
53 Michael Young .12 .30
54 Javy Lopez .12 .30
55 Johnny Damon .20 .50
56 Jeff Francis .12 .30
57 Rich Harden .12 .30
58 Bobby Abreu .12 .30
59 Mark Loretta .12 .30
60 Gary Sheffield .12 .30
61 Jamie Moyer .12 .30
62 Garret Anderson .12 .30
63 Vernon Wells .12 .30
64 Orlando Cabrera .12 .30
65 Magglio Ordonez .20 .50
66 Ronnie Belliard .12 .30
67 Carlos Lee .12 .30
68 Carl Pavano .12 .30
69 Jon Lieber .12 .30
70 Aubrey Huff .12 .30
71 Rocco Baldelli .12 .30
72 Jason Schmidt .12 .30
73 Bernie Williams .20 .50
74 Hideki Matsui .50 1.25
75 Ken Griffey Jr. .60 1.50
76 Josh Beckett .12 .30
77 Mark Buehrle .20 .50
78 David Ortiz .30 .75
79 Luis Gonzalez .12 .30
80 Scott Rolen .20 .50
81 Joe Mauer .25 .60
82 Jose Reyes .20 .50
83 Adam Dunn .20 .50
84 Greg Maddux .40 1.00
85 Bartolo Colon .12 .30
86 Bret Boone .12 .30
87 Mike Mussina .20 .50
88 Ben Sheets .12 .30
89 Lance Berkman .20 .50
90 Miguel Cabrera .30 .75
91 C.C. Sabathia .20 .50
92 Mike Maroth .12 .30
93 Andruw Jones .12 .30
94 Jack Wilson .12 .30
95 Ichiro Suzuki .40 1.00
96 Geoff Jenkins .12 .30
97 Zack Greinke .40 1.00
98 Jorge Posada .20 .50
99 Travis Hafner .12 .30
100 Barry Bonds .50 1.25
101 Aaron Rowand .12 .30
102 Aramis Ramirez .12 .30
103 Curt Schilling .20 .50
104 Melvin Mora .12 .30
105 Albert Pujols .40 1.00
106 Austin Kearns .12 .30
107 Shannon Stewart .12 .30
108 Carl Crawford .20 .50
109 Carlos Zambrano .20 .50
110 Roger Clemens .40 1.00
111 Javier Vazquez .12 .30
112 Randy Wolf .12 .30
113 Chipper Jones .30 .75
114 Larry Walker .20 .50
115 Alfonso Soriano .20 .50
116 Brad Wilkerson .12 .30
117 Bobby Crosby .12 .30
118 Jim Thome .20 .50
119 Oliver Perez .12 .30
120 Vladimir Guerrero .20 .50
121 Roy Oswalt .20 .50
122 Torii Hunter .12 .30
123 Rafael Furcal .12 .30
124 Luis Castillo .12 .30
125 Carlos Beltran .20 .50
126 Mike Sweeney .12 .30
127 Johan Santana .20 .50
128 Tim Hudson .20 .50
129 Troy Glaus .12 .30
130 Manny Ramirez .30 .75
131 Jeff Kent .12 .30
132 Jose Vidro .12 .30
133 Edgar Renteria .12 .30
134 Russ Ortiz .12 .30
135 Sammy Sosa .30 .75
136 Carlos Delgado .12 .30
137 Richie Sexson .12 .30
138 Pedro Martinez .20 .50
139 Adrian Beltre .30 .75
140 Mark Prior .20 .50
141 Omar Quintanilla .15 .40
142 Carlos Quentin .25 .60
143 Dan Johnson .15 .40
144 Jake Stevens .15 .40
145 Nate Schierholtz .15 .40
146 Neil Walker .25 .60
147 Bill Bray .15 .40
148 Taylor Tankersley .15 .40
149 Trevor Plouffe .40 1.00
150 Felix Hernandez .50 1.25
151 Philip Hughes .40 1.00
152 James Houser .15 .40
153 David Murphy .25 .60
154 Ervin Santana .15 .40
155 Anthony Whittington .15 .40
156 Chris Lambert .15 .40
157 Jeremy Sowers .15 .40
158 Giovanny Gonzalez .25 .60
159 Blake DeWitt .25 .60
160 Thomas Diamond .15 .40
161 Greg Golson .15 .40
162 David Aardsma .15 .40
163 Paul Maholm .15 .40
164 Mark Rogers .15 .40
165 Homer Bailey .15 .40
166 Chip Cannon FY RC .15 .40
167 Tony Giarratano FY RC .15 .40
168 Darren Fenster FY RC .15 .40
169 Elvys Quezada FY RC .15 .40
170 Glen Perkins FY RC .15 .40
171 Ian Kinsler FY RC .75 2.00
172 Mike Bourn FY RC .40 1.00
173 Jeremy West FY RC .15 .40
174 Justin Verlander FY RC 3.00 8.00
175 Kevin West FY RC .15 .40
176 Luis Hernandez FY RC .15 .40
177 Matt Campbell FY RC .15 .40
178 Nate McLouth FY RC .25 .60
179 Ryan Goleski FY RC .15 .40
180 Matthew Lindstrom FY RC .15 .40
181 Matt DeSalvo FY RC .15 .40
182 Kole Strayhorn FY RC .15 .40
183 Jose Vaquedano FY RC .15 .40
184 James Jurries FY RC .15 .40
185 Ian Bladergroen FY RC .15 .40
186 Eric Nielsen FY RC .15 .40
187 Chris Vines FY RC .15 .40
188 Chris Denorfia FY RC .15 .40
189 Kevin Melillo FY RC .15 .40
190 Melky Cabrera FY RC .50 1.25
191 Ryan Sweeney FY RC .25 .60
192 Sean Marshall FY RC .40 1.00
193 Andy LaRoche FY RC .15 .40
194 Tyler Pelland FY RC .15 .40
195 Mike Morse FY RC .50 1.25
196 Wes Swackhamer FY RC .15 .40
197 Wade Robinson FY RC .15 .40
198 Dan Santin FY RC .15 .40
199 Steve Doetsch FY RC .15 .40
200 Shane Costa FY RC .15 .40
201 Scott Mathieson FY RC .15 .40
202 Ben Jones FY RC .15 .40
203 Michael Rogers FY RC .15 .40
204 Matt Rogelstad FY RC .15 .40
205 Luis Ramirez FY RC .15 .40
206 Landon Powell FY RC .15 .40
207 Erik Cordier FY RC .15 .40
208 Chris Seddon FY RC .15 .40
209 Chris Roberson FY RC .15 .40
210 Thomas Oldham FY RC .15 .40
211 Dana Eveland FY RC .15 .40
212 Cody Haerther FY RC .15 .40
213 Danny Core FY RC .15 .40
214 Craig Tatum FY RC .15 .40
215 Elliot Johnson FY RC .15 .40
216 Ender Chavez FY RC .15 .40
217 Errol Simonitsch FY RC .15 .40
218 Matt Van Der Bosch FY RC .15 .40
219 Eulogio de la Cruz FY RC .15 .40
220 C.J. Smith FY RC .15 .40
221 Adam Boeve FY RC .15 .40
222 Adam Harben FY RC .15 .40
223 Baltazar Lopez FY RC .15 .40
224 Russ Martin FY RC .50 1.25
225 Brian Bannister FY RC .25 .60
226 Brian Miller FY RC .15 .40
227 Casey McGehee FY RC .25 .60
228 Humberto Sanchez FY RC .25 .60
229 Javon Moran FY RC .15 .40
230 Brandon McCarthy FY RC .25 .60
231 Danny Zell FY RC .15 .40
232 Jake Postlewait FY RC .15 .40
233 Juan Tejeda FY RC .15 .40
234 Keith Ramsey FY RC .15 .40
235 Lorenzo Scott FY RC .15 .40
236 Wladimir Balentien FY RC .25 .60
237 Martin Prado FY RC 1.00 2.50
238 Matt Albers FY RC .15 .40
239 Brian Schweiger FY RC .15 .40
240 Brian Stavisky FY RC .15 .40
241 Pat Misch FY RC .15 .40
242 Pat Osborn FY .15 .40
243 Ryan Feierabend FY RC .15 .40
244 Shaun Marcum FY .40 1.00
245 Kevin Collins FY RC .15 .40
246 Stuart Pomeranz FY RC .15 .40
247 Tetsu Yofu FY RC .15 .40
248 Hernan Iribarren FY RC .15 .40
249 Mike Spidale FY RC .15 .40
250 Tony Arnerich FY RC .15 .40
251 Manny Parra FY RC .40 1.00
252 Drew Anderson FY RC .15 .40
253 T.J. Beam FY RC .15 .40
254 Pedro Lopez FY RC .15 .40
255 Andy Sides FY RC .15 .40
256 Bear Bay FY RC .15 .40
257 Bill McCarthy FY RC .15 .40
258 Daniel Haigwood FY RC .15 .40
259 Brian Sprout FY RC .15 .40
260 Bryan Triplett FY RC .15 .40
261 Steven Bondurant FY RC .15 .40
262 Darwinson Salazar FY RC .15 .40
263 David Shepard FY RC .15 .40
264 Johan Silva FY RC .15 .40
265 J.B. Thurmond FY RC .15 .40
266 Brandon Moorhead FY RC .15 .40
267 Kyle Nichols FY RC .15 .40
268 Jonathan Sanchez FY RC .60 1.50
269 Mike Esposito FY RC .15 .40
270 Erik Schindewolf FY RC .15 .40
271 Peeter Ramos FY RC .15 .40
272 Juan Senreiso FY RC .15 .40
273 Matthew Kemp FY RC .75 2.00
274 Vinny Rottino FY RC .15 .40
275 Micah Furtado FY RC .15 .40
276 George Kottaras FY RC .25 .60
277 Billy Butler FY RC .75 2.00
278 Buck Coats FY RC .15 .40
279 Kenny Durost FY RC .15 .40
280 Nick Touchstone FY RC .15 .40
281 Jerry Owens FY RC .15 .40
282 Stefan Bailie FY RC .15 .40
283 Jesse Gutierrez FY RC .15 .40
284 Chuck Tiffany FY RC .40 1.00
285 Brendan Ryan FY RC .15 .40
286 Hayden Penn FY RC .15 .40
287 Shawn Bowman FY RC .15 .40
288 Alexander Smit FY RC .15 .40
289 Micah Schnurstein FY RC .15 .40
290 Jared Gothreaux FY RC .15 .40
291 Jair Jurrjens FY RC .75 2.00
292 Bobby Livingston FY RC .15 .40
293 Ryan Speier FY RC .15 .40
294 Zach Parker FY RC .15 .40
295 Christian Colonel FY RC .15 .40
296 Scott Mitchinson FY RC .15 .40
297 Neil Wilson FY RC .15 .40
298 Chuck James FY RC .40 1.00
299 Heath Totten FY RC .15 .40
300 Sean Tracey FY RC .15 .40
301 Ismael Ramirez FY RC .15 .40
302 Matt Brown FY RC .15 .40
303 Franklin Morales FY RC .25 .60
304 Brandon Sing FY RC .15 .40
305 D.J. Houlton FY RC .15 .40
306 Jayce Tingler FY RC .15 .40
307 Mitchell Arnold FY RC .15 .40
308 Jim Burt FY RC .15 .40
309 Jason Motte FY RC .25 .60
310 David Gassner FY RC .15 .40
311 Andy Santana FY RC .15 .40
312 Kelvin Pichardo FY RC .15 .40
313 Carlos Carrasco FY RC .40 1.00
314 Willy Mota FY RC .15 .40
315 Frank Mata FY RC .15 .40
316 Carlos Gonzalez FY RC 1.25 3.00
317 Jeff Niemann FY RC .40 1.00
318 Chris B.Young FY RC .50 1.25
319 Billy Sadler FY RC .15 .40
320 Ricky Barrett FY RC .15 .40
321 Ben Harrison FY .15 .40
322 Steve Nelson FY RC .15 .40
323 Daryl Thompson FY RC .15 .40
324 Philip Humber FY RC .40 1.00
325 Jeremy Harts FY RC .15 .40
326 Nick Masset FY RC .15 .40
327 Mike Rodriguez FY RC .15 .40
328 Mike Garber FY RC .15 .40
329 Kennard Bibbs FY RC .15 .40
330 Ryan Garko FY RC .15 .40
BC Bay Bat 6.00 15.00
Crosby Bat ROY

2005 Bowman 1st Edition

*1ST EDITION 1-165: .75X TO 2X BASIC
*1ST EDITION 166-330: .75X TO 2X BASIC
ISSUED IN 1ST EDITION PACKS

2005 Bowman Gold

COMPLETE SET (330) 75.00 150.00
*GOLD 1-165: 1.25X TO 3X BASIC
*GOLD 166-330: .75X TO 2X BASIC
ONE PER HOBBY PACK
ONE PER HTA PACK
ONE PER RETAIL PACK

2005 Bowman Red

STATED ODDS 1:2768 H, 1:708 HTA
STATED PRINT RUN 1 SERIAL #'d SET
NO PRICING DUE TO SCARCITY

2005 Bowman White

*WHITE 1-165: 4X TO 10X BASIC
*WHITE 166-330: 3X TO 8X BASIC
STATED ODDS 1:23 HOBBY, 1:6 HTA
STATED PRINT RUN 240 SERIAL #'d SETS
UNCIRCULATED EXCH.ODDS 1:94 H, 1:23 R
FOUR PIT.COM CARDS PER UNCIRC.EXCH
UNCIRCULATED EXCH DEADLINE 12/31/05
50% OF PRINT SEEDED INTO PACKS
50% OF PRINT AVAIL VIA PIT.COM EXCH

2005 Bowman Autographs

GROUP A ODDS 1:74 H, 1:26 HTA, 1:118 R
GROUP B ODDS 1:95 H, 1:33 HTA, 1:212 R
RED INK ODDS 1:1599 H, 1:599 HTA, 1:3672 R
RED INK PRINT RUN 25 SETS
RED INK ARE NOT SERIAL-NUMBERED
RED INK PRINT RUN PROVIDED BY TOPPS
NO RED INK PRICING DUE TO SCARCITY
GROUP A IS CARDS 141-151
GROUP B IS CARDS 152-165
EXCHANGE DEADLINE 05/31/07
141 Omar Quintanilla A 4.00 10.00
142 Carlos Quentin A 6.00 15.00
143 Dan Johnson A 4.00 10.00
144 Jake Stevens A 4.00 10.00
145 Nate Schierholtz A 4.00 10.00
146 Neil Walker A 4.00 10.00
147 Bill Bray A 4.00 10.00
148 Taylor Tankersley A 4.00 10.00
149 Trevor Plouffe A 4.00 10.00
150 Felix Hernandez A 20.00 50.00
151 Philip Hughes A 6.00 15.00
152 James Houser B 4.00 10.00
153 David Murphy B 4.00 10.00
154 Ervin Santana B 4.00 10.00
155 Anthony Whittington B 4.00 10.00
156 Chris Lambert B 4.00 10.00
157 Jeremy Sowers B 6.00 15.00
158 Giovanny Gonzalez B 6.00 15.00
159 Blake DeWitt B 6.00 15.00
160 Thomas Diamond B 6.00 15.00
161 Greg Golson B 4.00 10.00
163 Paul Maholm B 4.00 10.00
164 Mark Rogers B 6.00 15.00
165 Homer Bailey B 6.00 15.00

2005 Bowman Relics

STATED ODDS 1:50 H, 1:19 HTA, 1:114 R
2 Eric Chavez Jsy 3.00 8.00
5 Hank Blalock Bat 3.00 8.00
23 Rafael Palmeiro Bat 4.00 10.00
43 Mark Teixeira Bat 4.00 10.00
49 Ivan Rodriguez Bat 4.00 10.00
50 Alex Rodriguez Bat 6.00 15.00
60 Gary Sheffield Bat 3.00 8.00
65 Magglio Ordonez Bat 3.00 8.00
78 David Ortiz Bat 4.00 10.00
83 Adam Dunn Jsy 3.00 8.00
90 Miguel Cabrera Bat 4.00 10.00
93 Andruw Jones Bat 4.00 10.00
100 Barry Bonds Jsy 10.00 25.00
104 Melvin Mora Jsy 3.00 8.00
105 Albert Pujols Bat 6.00 15.00
115 Alfonso Soriano Bat 3.00 8.00
120 Vladimir Guerrero Bat 4.00 10.00
125 Carlos Beltran Bat 3.00 8.00
130 Manny Ramirez Bat 4.00 10.00
135 Sammy Sosa Bat 4.00 10.00

2005 Bowman A-Rod Throwback

COMPLETE SET (4) 3.00 8.00
STATED ODDS 1:12 HOBBY
94 Alex Rodriguez 1994 .60 1.50
95 Alex Rodriguez 1995 .60 1.50
96 Alex Rodriguez 1996 .60 1.50
97 Alex Rodriguez 1997 .60 1.50

2005 Bowman A-Rod Throwback Autographs

1994 BOW ODDS 1:108,288 HTA
1995 BOW ODDS 1:27,684 H, 1:13,536 HTA
1996 BOW ODDS 1:9039 H, 1:4922 HTA
1996 BOW.DRAFT ODDS 1:44,837 H
1997 BOW ODDS 1:6815 H, 1:3734 HTA
1997 BOW.DRAFT ODDS 1:8664 H
1994 PRINT RUN 1 SERIAL #'d CARD
1995 PRINT RUN 25 SERIAL #'d CARDS
1996 PRINT RUN 75 SERIAL #'d CARDS
1997 PRINT RUN 225 SERIAL #'d CARDS
NO PRICING ON QTY OF 25 OR LESS
75 OF 99 1996 CARDS ARE IN BOWMAN
25 OF 99 1996 CARDS ARE IN BOW.DRAFT
100 OF 225 1997 CARDS ARE IN BOWMAN
125 OF 225 1997 CARDS ARE IN BOW.DRAFT
96A Alex Rodriguez 1996/99 100.00 175.00
97A Alex Rodriguez 1997/225 50.00 100.00

2005 Bowman A-Rod Throwback Jersey Relics

1994 ODDS 1:108,288 HTA
1995 ODDS 1:27,684 H, 1:13,536 HTA
1996 ODDS 1:6815 H, 1:3734 HTA
1997 ODDS 1:849 H, 1:461 HTA
1994 PRINT RUN 1 SERIAL #'d CARD
1995 PRINT RUN 25 SERIAL #'d CARDS
1996 PRINT RUN 99 SERIAL #'d CARDS
1997 PRINT RUN 800 SERIAL #'d CARDS
NO PRICING ON QTY OF 25 OR LESS
96R Alex Rodriguez 1996/99 15.00 40.00
97R Alex Rodriguez 1997/800 6.00 15.00

2005 Bowman A-Rod Throwback Posters

ONE PER SEALED HOBBY BOX
05 POSTER ISSUED IN BECKETT MONTHLY
1994 Alex Rodriguez 1994 .30 .75

1995 Alex Rodriguez 1995 .30 .75
1996 Alex Rodriguez 1996 .30 .75
1997 Alex Rodriguez 1997 .30 .75
2005 Alex Rodriguez 2005 .30 .75

2005 Bowman Base of the Future Autograph Relic

STATED ODDS 1:106 HTA
RED INK ODDS 1:4708 HTA
RED INK PRINT RUN 25 CARDS
RED INK IS NOT SERIAL-NUMBERED
RED INK PRINT RUN PROVIDED BY TOPPS
NO RED INK PRICING DUE TO SCARCITY
AH Aaron Hill 6.00 15.00

2005 Bowman Futures Game Gear Jersey Relics

STATED ODDS 1:36 H, 1:14 HTA, 1:83 R
AH Aaron Hill 2.00 5.00
AM Arnie Munoz 2.00 5.00
AMA Andy Marte 3.00 8.00
BB Bryan Bullington 2.00 5.00
CE Clint Everts 2.00 5.00
DM Dallas McPherson 2.00 5.00
EE Edwin Encarnacion 3.00 8.00
FP Felix Pie 3.00 8.00
GF Gavin Floyd 2.00 5.00
JB Joe Blanton 2.00 5.00
JC Jesus Cota 2.00 5.00
JCO Jorge Cortes 2.00 5.00
JF Jeff Francis 2.00 5.00
JG Jairo Garcia 2.00 5.00
JGU Joel Guzman 3.00 8.00
JM Jeff Mathis 2.00 5.00
JMO Justin Morneau 3.00 8.00
KH Koyie Hill 2.00 5.00
MC Matt Cain 4.00 10.00
RG Ruben Gotay 2.00 5.00
RW Rickie Weeks 3.00 8.00
SC Shin Soo Choo 2.00 5.00
VM Val Majewski 2.00 5.00
WL Wilfredo Ledezma 2.00 5.00
YP Yusmeiro Petit 3.00 8.00

2005 Bowman Signs of the Future

GROUP A ODDS 1:252 H, 1:93 HTA, 1:571 R
GROUP B ODDS 1:219 H, 1:82 HTA, 1:502 R
GROUP C ODDS 1:167 H, 1:63 HTA,1:382 R
GROUP D ODDS 1:636 H, 1:239 HTA, 1:1448 R
D.WRIGHT PRINT RUN 100 CARDS
D.WRIGHT IS NOT SERIAL-NUMBERED
D.WRIGHT PRINT RUN GIVEN BY TOPPS
EXCHANGE DEADLINE 05/31/07
AL Adam Loewen C 4.00 10.00
AW Anthony Whittington B 4.00 10.00
BB Brian Bixler B 4.00 10.00
BC Bobby Crosby B 6.00 15.00
BD Blake DeWitt C 6.00 15.00
BS Brad Sullivan C 4.00 10.00
CC Chad Cordero D 4.00 10.00
CG Christian Garcia C 4.00 10.00
DM Dallas McPherson B 4.00 10.00
DP Dan Putnam B 4.00 10.00
DW David Wright D/100 * 30.00 60.00
ES Ervin Santana D 4.00 10.00
HS Huston Street C 8.00 20.00
JR Jay Rainville C 4.00 10.00
JS Jay Sborz C 4.00 10.00
KW Kyle Waldrop B 4.00 10.00
MC Melky Cabrera C 6.00 15.00
PH Philip Hughes C 6.00 15.00
PM Paul Maholm C 4.00 10.00
RC Robinson Cano D 12.00 30.00
RR Richie Robnett A 4.00 10.00
RW Ryan Wagner C 4.00 10.00
SK Scott Kazmir D 8.00 20.00
SO Scott Olson D 4.00 10.00
TG Tom Gorzelanny C 4.00 10.00
TH Tim Hutting A 3.00 8.00
TP Trevor Plouffe D 8.00 20.00
TT Taylor Tankersley D 4.00 10.00

2005 Bowman Two of a Kind Autographs

STATED ODDS 1:55,368 H, 1:21,658 HTA
STATED PRINT RUN 13 SERIAL #'d CARDS
NO PRICING DUE TO SCARCITY

2005 Bowman Draft

COMPLETE SET (165) 15.00 40.00
COMMON CARD (1-165) .10 .30
COMMON RC .10 .30
COMMON RC YR .10 .30
OVERALL PLATE ODDS 1:826 HOBBY
PLATE PRINT RUN 1 SET PER COLOR
BLACK-CYAN-MAGENTA-YELLOW ISSUED
NO PLATE PRICING DUE TO SCARCITY
1 Rickie Weeks .12 .30
2 Kyle Davies .12 .30
3 Garrett Atkins .12 .30
4 Chien-Ming Wang .50 1.25
5 Dallas McPherson .12 .30
6 Dan Johnson .12 .30
7 Andy Sisco .12 .30
8 Ryan Doumit .12 .30
9 J.P. Howell .12 .30
10 Tim Stauffer .12 .30
12 Aaron Hill .20 .50
13 Victor Diaz .12 .30
14 Wilson Betemit .12 .30
15 Ervin Santana .12 .30
16 Mike Morse .40 1.00
17 Yadier Molina 3.00 8.00
18 Kelly Johnson .12 .30
19 Clint Barmes .12 .30
20 Robinson Cano .40 1.00
21 Brad Thompson .12 .30
22 Jorge Cantu .12 .30
23 Brad Halsey .12 .30
24 Lance Niekro .12 .30
25 D.J. Houlton .12 .30
26 Ryan Church .12 .30
27 Hayden Penn .12 .30
28 Chris Young .20 .50
29 Chad Orvella RC .12 .30
30 Mark Teahen .12 .30
31 Mark McCormick FY RC .12 .30
32 Jay Bruce FY RC 1.00 2.50
33 Beau Jones FY RC .30 .75
34 Tyler Greene FY RC .12 .30
35 Zach Ward FY RC .12 .30
36 Josh Bell FY RC .20 .50
37 Josh Wall FY RC .20 .50
38 Nick Webber FY RC .12 .30
39 Travis Buck FY RC .12 .30
40 Kyle Winters FY RC .12 .30
41 Mitch Boggs FY RC .12 .30
42 Tommy Mendoza FY RC .12 .30
43 Brad Corley FY RC .12 .30
44 Drew Butera FY RC .12 .30
45 Ryan Mount FY RC .12 .30
46 Tyler Herron FY RC .12 .30
47 Nick Weglarz FY RC .12 .30
48 Brandon Erbe FY RC .40 1.00
49 Cody Allen FY RC .12 .30
50 Eric Fowler FY RC .12 .30
51 James Boone FY RC .12 .30
52 Josh Flores FY RC .12 .30
53 Brandon Monk FY RC .12 .30
54 Kieron Pope FY RC .12 .30
55 Kyle Cofield FY RC .12 .30
56 Brent Lillibridge FY RC .12 .30
57 Daryl Jones FY RC .12 .30
58 Eli Iorg FY RC .12 .30
59 Brett Hayes FY RC .12 .30
60 Mike Durant FY RC .12 .30
61 Michael Bowden FY RC .20 .50
62 Paul Kelly FY RC .12 .30
63 Andrew McCutchen FY RC 1.50 4.00
64 Travis Wood FY RC .30 .75
65 Cesar Ramos FY RC .12 .30
66 Chaz Roe FY RC .12 .30
67 Matt Torra FY RC .12 .30
68 Kevin Slowey FY RC .60 1.50
69 Trayvon Robinson FY RC .30 .75
70 Reid Engel FY RC .12 .30
71 Kris Harvey FY RC .12 .30
72 Craig Italiano FY RC .12 .30
73 Matt Maloney FY RC .12 .30
74 Sean West FY RC .20 .50
75 Henry Sanchez FY RC .20 .50
76 Scott Blue FY RC .12 .30
77 Jordan Schafer FY RC .60 1.50
78 Chris Robinson FY RC .12 .30
79 Chris Hobdy FY RC .12 .30
80 Brandon Durden FY RC .12 .30
81 Clay Buchholz FY RC .60 1.50
82 Josh Geer FY RC .12 .30
83 Sam LeCure FY RC .12 .30
84 Justin Thomas FY RC .12 .30
85 Brett Gardner FY RC .40 1.00
86 Tommy Manzella FY RC .12 .30
87 Matt Green FY RC .12 .30
88 Yunel Escobar FY RC .50 1.25
89 Mike Costanzo FY RC .12 .30
90 Nick Hundley FY RC .12 .30
91 Zach Simons FY RC .12 .30
92 Jacob Marceaux FY RC .12 .30
93 Jed Lowrie FY RC .12 .30
94 Brandon Snyder FY RC .30 .75
95 Matt Goyen FY RC .12 .30
96 Jon Egan FY RC .12 .30
97 Drew Thompson FY RC .12 .30
98 Bryan Anderson FY RC .12 .30
99 Clayton Richard FY RC .12 .30
100 Jimmy Shull FY RC .12 .30
101 Mark Pawelek FY RC .12 .30
102 P.J. Phillips FY RC .12 .30
103 John Drennen FY RC .12 .30
104 Nolan Reimold FY RC .50 1.25
105 Troy Tulowitzki FY RC 1.25 3.00
106 Kevin Whelan FY RC .12 .30
107 Wade Townsend FY RC .12 .30
108 Micah Owings FY RC .12 .30
109 Ryan Tucker FY RC .12 .30
110 Jeff Clement FY RC .12 .30
111 Josh Sullivan FY RC .12 .30
112 Jeff Lyman FY RC .12 .30
113 Brian Bogusevic FY RC .12 .30
114 Trevor Bell FY RC .12 .30
115 Brent Cox FY RC .12 .30
116 Michael Billek FY RC .12 .30
117 Garrett Olson FY RC .12 .30
118 Steven Johnson FY RC .12 .30
119 Chase Headley FY RC .20 .50
120 Daniel Carte FY RC .12 .30
121 Francisco Liriano PROS .30 .75
122 Fausto Carmona PROS .12 .30
123 Zach Jackson PROS .12 .30
124 Adam Loewen PROS .12 .30
125 Chris Lambert PROS .12 .30
126 Scott Mathieson FY .12 .30
127 Paul Maholm PROS .12 .30
128 Fernando Nieve PROS .12 .30
129 Justin Verlander FY 2.50 6.00
130 Yusmeiro Petit PROS .12 .30
131 Joel Zumaya PROS .30 .75
132 Merkin Valdez PROS .12 .30
133 Ryan Garko FY .12 .30
134 Edison Volquez FY RC .40 1.00
135 Russ Martin FY .40 1.00
136 Conor Jackson PROS .20 .50
137 Miguel Montero FY RC .40 1.00
138 Josh Barfield PROS .20 .50
139 Delmon Young PROS .30 .75
140 Andy LaRoche FY .12 .30
141 William Bergolla PROS .12 .30
142 B.J. Upton PROS .20 .50
143 Hernan Iribarren FY .12 .30
144 Brandon Wood PROS .20 .50
145 Jose Bautista PROS .50 1.25
146 Edwin Encarnacion PROS .30 .75
147 Javier Herrera FY RC .12 .30
148 Jeremy Hermida PROS .20 .50
149 Frank Diaz PROS RC .12 .30
150 Chris B.Young FY .40 1.00
151 Shin-Soo Choo PROS .20 .50
152 Kevin Thompson PROS RC .12 .30
153 Hanley Ramirez PROS .20 .50
154 Lastings Milledge PROS .12 .30
155 Luis Montanez PROS .12 .30
156 Justin Huber PROS .12 .30
157 Zach Duke PROS .12 .30
158 Jeff Francoeur PROS .30 .75
159 Melky Cabrera FY .40 1.00
160 Bobby Jenks PROS .12 .30
161 Ian Snell PROS .12 .30
162 Fernando Cabrera PROS .12 .30
163 Troy Patton PROS .12 .30
164 Anthony Lerew PROS .12 .30
165 Nelson Cruz FY RC 1.50 4.00

2005 Bowman Draft Gold

COMPLETE SET (165) 25.00 60.00
*GOLD: 1.25X TO 3X BASIC
*GOLD: .6X TO 1.5X BASIC RC
*GOLD: .6X TO 1.5X BASIC RC YR
ONE PER PACK

2005 Bowman Draft Red

STATED ODDS 1:6609 HOBBY
STATED PRINT RUN 1 SERIAL #'d SET
NO PRICING DUE TO SCARCITY

2005 Bowman Draft White

*WHITE: 4X TO 10X BASIC
*WHITE: 3X TO 8X BASIC RC
*WHITE: 2.5X TO 6X BASIC RC YR
STATED ODDS 1:35 HOBBY, 1:72 RETAIL
STATED PRINT RUN 225 SERIAL #'d SETS

2005 Bowman Draft Futures Game Jersey Relics

STATED ODDS 1:24 HOBBY
121 Francisco Liriano 3.00 8.00
122 Fausto Carmona 1.25 3.00
123 Zach Jackson 1.25 3.00
124 Adam Loewen 1.50 4.00
125 Chris Lambert 1.25 3.00
126 Scott Mathieson 1.25 3.00
127 Paul Maholm 1.25 3.00
128 Fernando Nieve 1.25 3.00
129 Justin Verlander 6.00 15.00
130 Yusmeiro Petit 1.25 3.00
131 Joel Zumaya 3.00 8.00
132 Merkin Valdez 1.25 3.00
133 Ryan Garko 1.25 3.00
134 Edison Volquez 4.00 10.00
135 Russ Martin 4.00 10.00
136 Conor Jackson 2.00 5.00
137 Miguel Montero 4.00 10.00
138 Josh Barfield 2.00 5.00
139 Delmon Young 3.00 8.00
140 Andy LaRoche 1.25 3.00
141 William Bergolla 1.25 3.00
142 B.J. Upton 2.00 5.00
143 Hernan Iribarren 1.25 3.00
144 Brandon Wood 2.00 5.00
145 Jose Bautista 5.00 12.00
146 Edwin Encarnacion 4.00 10.00
147 Javier Herrera 1.25 3.00
148 Jeremy Hermida 2.00 5.00
149 Frank Diaz 1.25 3.00
150 Chris B.Young 4.00 10.00

2005 Bowman Draft A-Rod Throwback Autograph

SEE 2005 BOWMAN A-ROD AU'S FOR INFO

2005 Bowman Draft Signs of the Future

GROUP A ODDS 1:232 H, 1:232 R
GROUP B ODDS 1:823 H, 1:819 R
GROUP C ODDS 1:232 H, 1:232 R
GROUP D ODDS 1:1157 H, 1:1166 R
GROUP E ODDS 1:348 H, 1:349 R
GROUP F ODDS 1:1746 H, 1:1749 R
AG Angel Guzman E 3.00 8.00
BB Bill Bray E 3.00 8.00
DL Donald Lucey F 3.00 8.00
DM David Murphy E 3.00 8.00
DP David Purcey C 3.00 8.00
GG Greg Golson C 3.00 8.00
HB Homer Bailey D 3.00 8.00
JF Jeff Frazier C 3.00 8.00
JH Justin Hoyman A 3.00 8.00
JJ Justin Jones B 3.00 8.00
JP Jonathan Poterson C 3.00 8.00
JS Jeremy Sowers E 3.00 8.00
RR Richie Robnett A 3.00 8.00
TL Tyler Lumsden A 3.00 8.00

2005 Bowman Draft AFLAC Exchange Cards

STATED ODDS 1:32 HOBBY
PLATES PRINT RUN 1 SET PER COLOR
NO PLATES PRICING DUE TO SCARCITY
EXCHANGE DEADLINE 12/25/06
1 Basic Set 3.00 8.00

2005 Bowman Draft AFLAC

COMP.FACT.SET (14) 4.00 10.00
STATED ODDS 1:32 '05 BOW.DRAFT HOB.
EXCHANGE DEADLINE 12/26/06
ONE SET VIA MAIL PER AFLAC EXCH.CARD
SETS ACTUALLY SENT OUT JANUARY, 2007
PLATE PRINT RUN 1 SET PER COLOR
BLACK-CYAN-MAGENTA-YELLOW ISSUED
NO PLATE PRICING DUE TO SCARCITY
1 Billy Rowell .75 2.00
2 Kasey Kiker .50 1.25
3 Chris Marrero 1.00 2.50
4 Jeremy Jeffress .30 .75
5 Kyle Drabek .50 1.25
6 Chris Parmelee .50 1.25
7 Colton Willems .30 .75
8 Cody Johnson .30 .75
9 Hank Conger .50 1.25
10 Cory Rasmus .30 .75
11 David Christensen .30 .75
12 Chris Tillman .50 1.25
13 Torre Langley .30 .75
14 Robby Alcombrack .30 .75

2006 Bowman

COMP.SET w/o AU's (220) 15.00 40.00
COMP.SET w/PROS (330) 40.00 80.00
COMMON CARD (1-200) .10 .30
COMMON ROOKIE (201-220) .15 .40
219-220 AU ODDS 1:1150 HOBBY, 1:699 HTA
COMMON AUTO (221-231) 4.00 10.00
221-231 AU ODDS 1:82 HOBBY, 1:40 HTA
1-220 PLATE ODDS 1:588 HOBBY, 1:575 HTA
221-231 AU PLATES 1:15,700 H, 1:4100 HTA
PLATE PRINT RUN 1 SET PER COLOR
BLACK-CYAN-MAGENTA-YELLOW ISSUED
NO PLATE PRICING DUE TO SCARCITY
1 Nick Swisher .20 .50
2 Ted Lilly .12 .30
3 John Smoltz .30 .75
4 Lyle Overbay .12 .30
5 Alfonso Soriano .20 .50
6 Javier Vazquez .12 .30
7 Ronnie Belliard .12 .30
8 Jose Reyes .20 .50
9 Brian Roberts .12 .30
10 Curt Schilling .20 .50
11 Adam Dunn .20 .50
12 Zack Greinke .30 .75
13 Carlos Guillen .12 .30
14 Jon Garland .12 .30
15 Robinson Cano .20 .50
16 Chris Burke .12 .30
17 Barry Zito .20 .50
18 Russ Adams .12 .30
19 Chris Capuano .12 .30
20 Scott Rolen .20 .50
21 Kerry Wood .12 .30
22 Scott Kazmir .20 .50
23 Brandon Webb .20 .50
24 Jeff Kent .12 .30
25 Albert Pujols .40 1.00
26 C.C. Sabathia .20 .50
27 Adrian Beltre .30 .75
28 Brad Wilkerson .12 .30
29 Randy Wolf .12 .30
30 Jason Bay .12 .30
31 Austin Kearns .12 .30
32 Clint Barmes .12 .30
33 Mike Sweeney .12 .30
34 Justin Verlander 1.00 2.50
35 Justin Morneau .20 .50
36 Scott Podsednik .12 .30
37 Jason Giambi .12 .30
38 Steve Finley .12 .30
39 Morgan Ensberg .12 .30
40 Eric Chavez .12 .30
41 Roy Halladay .20 .50
42 Horacio Ramirez .12 .30
43 Ben Sheets .12 .30
44 Chris Carpenter .20 .50
45 Andruw Jones .12 .30
46 Carlos Zambrano .20 .50
47 Jonny Gomes .12 .30
48 Shawn Green .12 .30
49 Moises Alou .12 .30
50 Ichiro Suzuki .40 1.00
51 Juan Pierre .12 .30
52 Grady Sizemore .20 .50
53 Kazuo Matsui .12 .30
54 Jose Vidro .12 .30
55 Jake Peavy .12 .30
56 Dallas Mcpherson .12 .30
57 Ryan Howard .25 .60
58 Zach Duke .12 .30
59 Michael Young .12 .30
60 Todd Helton .20 .50
61 David Dejesus .12 .30
62 Ivan Rodriguez .20 .50
63 Johan Santana .20 .50
64 Danny Haren .12 .30
65 Derek Jeter .75 2.00
66 Greg Maddux .40 1.00
67 Jorge Cantu .12 .30
68 Conor Jackson .20 .50
69 Victor Martinez .20 .50
70 David Wright .25 .60
71 Ryan Church .12 .30
72 Khalil Greene .12 .30
73 Jimmy Rollins .20 .50
74 Hank Blalock .12 .30
75 Pedro Martinez .20 .50
76 Jon Papelbon .75 2.00
77 Felipe Lopez .12 .30
78 Jeff Francis .12 .30
79 Andy Sisco .12 .30
80 Hideki Matsui .30 .75
81 Ken Griffey Jr. .60 1.50
82 Nomar Garciaparra .20 .50
83 Kevin Millwood .12 .30
84 Paul Konerko .20 .50
85 A.J. Burnett .12 .30
86 Mike Piazza .30 .75
87 Brian Giles .12 .30
88 Johnny Damon .20 .50
89 Jim Thome .20 .50
90 Roger Clemens .40 1.00
91 Aaron Rowand .12 .30
92 Rafael Furcal .12 .30
93 Gary Sheffield .12 .30
94 Mike Cameron .12 .30
95 Carlos Delgado .12 .30
96 Jorge Posada .20 .50
97 Denny Bautista .12 .30
98 Mike Maroth .12 .30
99 Brad Radke .12 .30
100 Alex Rodriguez .40 1.00
101 Freddy Garcia .12 .30
102 Oliver Perez .12 .30
103 Jon Lieber .12 .30
104 Melvin Mora .12 .30
105 Travis Hafner .12 .30
106 Matt Cain .75 2.00
107 Derek Lowe .12 .30
108 Luis Castillo .12 .30
109 Livan Hernandez .12 .30
110 Tadahito Iguchi .12 .30
111 Shawn Chacon .12 .30
112 Frank Thomas .30 .75
113 Josh Beckett .12 .30
114 Aubrey Huff .12 .30
115 Derrek Lee .12 .30
116 Chien-Ming Wang .20 .50
117 Joe Crede .12 .30
118 Torii Hunter .12 .30
119 J.D. Drew .12 .30
120 Troy Glaus .12 .30
121 Sean Casey .12 .30
122 Edgar Renteria .12 .30
123 Craig Wilson .12 .30
124 Adam Eaton .12 .30
125 Jeff Francoeur .30 .75
126 Bruce Chen .12 .30
127 Cliff Floyd .12 .30
128 Jeremy Reed .12 .30
129 Jake Westbrook .12 .30
130 Wily Mo Pena .12 .30
131 Toby Hall .12 .30
132 David Ortiz .30 .75
133 David Eckstein .12 .30
134 Brady Clark .12 .30
135 Marcus Giles .12 .30
136 Aaron Hill .12 .30
137 Mark Kotsay .12 .30
138 Carlos Lee .12 .30
139 Roy Oswalt .20 .50
140 Chone Figgins .12 .30
141 Mike Mussina .20 .50
142 Orlando Hernandez .12 .30
143 Magglio Ordonez .20 .50
144 Jim Edmonds .20 .50
145 Bobby Abreu .12 .30
146 Nick Johnson .12 .30
147 Carlos Beltran .20 .50
148 Jhonny Peralta .12 .30
149 Pedro Feliz .12 .30
150 Miguel Tejada .20 .50
151 Luis Gonzalez .12 .30
152 Carl Crawford .20 .50
153 Yadier Molina .40 1.00
154 Rich Harden .12 .30
155 Tim Wakefield .20 .50
156 Rickie Weeks .12 .30
157 Johnny Estrada .12 .30
158 Gustavo Chacin .12 .30
159 Dan Johnson .12 .30
160 Willy Taveras .12 .30
161 Garret Anderson .12 .30
162 Randy Johnson .30 .75
163 Jermaine Dye .12 .30
164 Joe Mauer .20 .50
165 Ervin Santana .12 .30
166 Jeremy Bonderman .12 .30
167 Garrett Atkins .12 .30
168 Manny Ramirez .30 .75
169 Brad Eldred .12 .30
170 Chase Utley .20 .50
171 Mark Loretta .12 .30
172 John Patterson .12 .30
173 Tom Glavine .20 .50
174 Dontrelle Willis .12 .30
175 Mark Teixeira .20 .50
176 Felix Hernandez .20 .50
177 Cliff Lee .20 .50
178 Jason Schmidt .12 .30
179 Chad Tracy .12 .30
180 Rocco Baldelli .12 .30
181 Aramis Ramirez .12 .30
182 Andy Pettitte .20 .50
183 Mark Mulder .12 .30
184 Geoff Jenkins .12 .30
185 Chipper Jones .30 .75
186 Vernon Wells .12 .30
187 Bobby Crosby .12 .30
188 Lance Berkman .20 .50
189 Vladimir Guerrero .20 .50
190 Jose Capellan .12 .30
191 Brad Penny .12 .30
192 Jose Guillen .12 .30
193 Brett Myers .12 .30
194 Miguel Cabrera .30 .75
195 Bartolo Colon .12 .30
196 Craig Biggio .20 .50
197 Tim Hudson .20 .50
198 Mark Prior .20 .50
199 Mark Buehrle .20 .50
200 Barry Bonds .50 1.25
201 Anderson Hernandez (RC) .15 .40
202 Charlton Jimerson (RC) .15 .40
203 Jeremy Accardo RC .15 .40
204 Hanley Ramirez (RC) .25 .60
205 Matt Capps (RC) .15 .40
206 John-Ford Griffin (RC) .15 .40
207 Chuck James (RC) .15 .40
208 Jaime Bubela (RC) .15 .40
209 Mark Woodyard (RC) .15 .40
210 Jason Botts (RC) .15 .40
211 Chris Demaria RC .15 .40
212 Miguel Perez (RC) .15 .40
213 Tom Gorzelanny (RC) .15 .40
214 Adam Wainwright (RC) .25 .60
215 Ryan Garko (RC) .15 .40
216 Jason Bergmann RC .15 .40
217 J.J. Furmaniak (RC) .15 .40
218 Francisco Liriano (RC) .40 1.00
219 Kenji Johjima RC .40 1.00
219a Kenji Johjima AU 6.00 15.00
220 Craig Hansen RC .40 1.00
220a Craig Hansen AU 4.00 10.00
221 Ryan Zimmerman AU (RC) 8.00 20.00
222 Joey Devine AU RC 4.00 10.00
223 Scott Olsen AU (RC) 4.00 10.00
224 Darrel Rasner AU (RC) 4.00 10.00
225 Craig Breslow AU RC 4.00 10.00
226 Reggie Abercrombie AU (RC) 4.00 10.00
227 Dan Uggla AU (RC) 4.00 10.00
228 Willie Eyre AU (RC) 4.00 10.00
229 Joel Zumaya AU (RC) 4.00 10.00
230 Ricky Nolasco AU (RC) 4.00 10.00
231 Ian Kinsler AU (RC) 5.00 12.00

2006 Bowman Blue

*BLUE 1-200: 2X TO 5X BASIC
*BLUE 76/201-220: 2X TO 5X BASIC
*BLUE 221-231: 4.X TO 1X BASIC AU
1-220 ODDS 1:8 HOBBY, 1:4 HTA
221-231 AU ODDS 1:225 HOBBY, 1:115 HTA
STATED PRINT RUN 500 SERIAL #'d SETS
227 Dan Uggla AU 4.00 10.00

2006 Bowman Gold

*GOLD 1-200: 1.25X TO 3X BASIC
*GOLD 201-220: 1X TO 2.5X BASIC
ONE PER HOBBY PACK
ONE PER HTA PACK

2006 Bowman Red

STATED ODDS 1:3750 HOBBY, 1:1754 HTA
221-231 AU ODDS 1:114,583 H, 1:58,464 HTA
STATED PRINT RUN 1 SERIAL #'d SET
NO PRICING DUE TO SCARCITY

2006 Bowman White

*WHITE 1-200: 3X TO 8X BASIC
*WHITE 76/201-220: 3X TO 8X BASIC
*WHITE 221-231: .6X TO 1.5X BASIC AU
1-220 ODDS 1:32 HOBBY, 1:15 HTA
221-231 AU ODDS 1:1020 HOBBY, 1:500 HTA
STATED PRINT RUN 120 SERIAL #'d SETS
227 Dan Uggla AU 30.00 80.00

2006 Bowman Prospects

COMP.SET w/o AU's (110) 25.00 50.00
COMMON CARD (B1-B110) .15 .40
B1-B110 STATED ODDS 2:1 HOBBY, 4:1 HTA
B111-B124 AU ODDS 1:62 HOBBY, 1:35 HTA
B1-B110 PLATE ODDS 1:588 H, 1:575 HTA
B111-B124 AU PLATE 1:15,700 H, 1:4100 HTA
PLATE PRINT RUN 1 PER COLOR
BLACK-CYAN-MAGENTA-YELLOW ISSUED
NO PLATE PRICING DUE TO SCARCITY
B1 Alex Gordon .50 1.25
B2 Jonathan George .15 .40
B3 Scott Walter .15 .40
B4 Brian Holliday .15 .40
B5 Ben Copeland .15 .40
B6 Bobby Wilson .15 .40
B7 Mayker Sandoval .15 .40
B8 Alejandro de Aza .25 .60
B9 David Munoz .15 .40
B10 Josh LeBlanc .15 .40
B11 Philippe Valiquette .15 .40
B12 Edwin Bellorin .15 .40
B13 Jason Quarles .15 .40
B14 Mark Trumbo .40 1.00
B15 Steve Kelly .15 .40
B16 Jamie Hoffman .15 .40
B17 Joe Bauserman .15 .40
B18 Nick Adenhart .15 .40
B19 Mike Butia .15 .40
B20 Jon Weber .15 .40
B21 Luis Valdez .15 .40
B22 Rafael Rodriguez .15 .40
B23 Wyatt Toregas .15 .40
B24 John Vanden Berg .15 .40
B25 Mike Connolly .15 .40
B26 Mike O'Connor .15 .40
B27 Garrett Mock .15 .40
B28 Bill Layman .15 .40
B29 Luis Pena .15 .40
B30 Billy Killian .15 .40
B31 Ross Ohlendorf .15 .40
B32 Mark Kaiser .15 .40
B33 Ryan Costello .15 .40
B34 Dale Thayer .15 .40
B35 Steve Garrabrants .15 .40
B36 Samuel Deduno .15 .40
B37 Juan Portes .15 .40
B38 Javier Martinez .15 .40
B39 Clint Sammons .15 .40
B40 Andrew Kown .15 .40
B41 Matt Tolbert .15 .40
B42 Michael Ekstrom .15 .40
B43 Shawn Norris .15 .40
B44 Diory Hernandez .15 .40
B45 Chris Maples .15 .40
B46 Aaron Hathaway .15 .40
B47 Steven Baker .15 .40
B48 Greg Creek .15 .40
B49 Collin Mahoney .15 .40
B50 Corey Ragsdale .15 .40
B51 Ariel Nunez .15 .40
B52 Max Ramirez .25 .60
B53 Eric Rodland .15 .40
B54 Dante Brinkley .15 .40
B55 Casey Craig .15 .40
B56 Ryan Spilborghs .15 .40
B57 Fredy Deza .15 .40
B58 Jeff Frazier .15 .40
B59 Vince Cordova .15 .40
B60 Oswaldo Navarro .15 .40
B61 Jarod Rine .15 .40
B62 Jordan Tata .15 .40
B63 Ben Julianel .15 .40
B64 Yung-Chi Chen .25 .60
B65 Carlos Torres .15 .40
B66 Juan Francia .15 .40
B67 Brett Smith .15 .40
B68 Francisco Leandro .15 .40
B69 Chris Turner .15 .40
B70 Matt Joyce .75 2.00
B71 Jason Jones .15 .40
B72 Jose Diaz .15 .40
B73 Kevin Ool .15 .40
B74 Nate Bumstead .15 .40
B75 Omir Santos .15 .40
B76 Shawn Riggans .15 .40
B77 Ofilio Castro .15 .40
B78 Mike Rozier .15 .40
B79 Wilkin Ramirez .25 .60
B80 Yobal Duenas .15 .40
B81 Adam Bourassa .15 .40
B82 Tony Granadillo .15 .40
B83 Brad McCann .15 .40
B84 Dustin Majewski .15 .40
B85 Kelvin Jimenez .15 .40
B86 Mark Reed .15 .40
B87 Asdrubal Cabrera .75 2.00
B88 James Barthmaier .15 .40
B89 Brandon Boggs .15 .40
B90 Raul Valdez .15 .40
B91 Jose Campusano .15 .40
B92 Henry Owens .15 .40
B93 Tug Hulett .15 .40
B94 Nate Gold .15 .40
B95 Lee Mitchell .15 .40
B96 John Hardy .15 .40
B97 Aaron Wideman .15 .40
B98 Brandon Roberts .15 .40
B99 Lou Santangelo .15 .40
B100 Kyle Kendrick .40 1.00
B101 Michael Collins .15 .40
B102 Camilo Vazquez .15 .40
B103 Mark McLemore .15 .40
B104 Alexander Peralta .15 .40
B105 Josh Whitesell .15 .40
B106 Carlos Guevara .15 .40
B107 Michael Aubrey .25 .60
B108 Brandon Chaves .15 .40
B109 Leonard Davis .15 .40
B110 Kendry Morales .40 1.00
B111 Koby Clemens AU 4.00 10.00
B112 Lance Broadway AU 6.00 15.00
B113 Cameron Maybin AU 4.00 10.00
B114 Mike Aviles AU 6.00 15.00
B115 Kyle Blanks AU 10.00 25.00
B116 Chris Dickerson AU 6.00 15.00
B117 Sean Gallagher AU 10.00 25.00
B118 Jamar Hill AU 4.00 10.00
B119 Garrett Mock AU 4.00 10.00
B120 Kendry Morales AU 6.00 15.00
B121 Russ Rohlicek AU 4.00 10.00
B122 Clete Thomas AU 4.00 10.00
B123 Josh Kinney AU 4.00 10.00
B124 Justin Huber AU 4.00 10.00

2006 Bowman Prospects Blue

*BLUE B1-B110: 1.5X TO 4X BASIC
*BLUE B111-B124: .4X TO 1X BASIC
B1-B110 ODDS 1:8 HOBBY, 1:4 HTA
B111-B124 AU ODDS 1:170 H, 1:100 HTA
STATED PRINT RUN 500 SERIAL #'d SETS

2006 Bowman Prospects Gold

*GOLD B1-B110: .75X TO 2X BASIC
ONE PER HOBBY PACK
ONE PER HTA PACK

2006 Bowman Prospects Red

B1-B110 ODDS 1:3750 HOBBY, 1:1754 HTA
111-124 AU ODDS 1:80,208 H, 1:56,464 HTA
STATED PRINT RUN 1 SERIAL #'d SET
NO PRICING DUE TO SCARCITY

2006 Bowman Prospects White

*WHITE B1-B110: 2.5X TO 6X BASIC
*WHITE B111-B124: .6X TO 1.5X BASIC
B1-B110 ODDS 1:32 HOBBY, 1:15 HTA
B111-B124 AU ODDS 1:750 H, 1:450 HTA
STATED PRINT RUN 120 SERIAL #'d SETS

2006 Bowman Base of the Future

STATED ODDS 1:173 HTA
RED INK ODDS 1:7800 HTA
NO RED INK PRICING DUE TO SCARCITY
JH Justin Huber 4.00 10.00

2006 Bowman Signs of the Future

ONE PER SEALED HTA BOX
GROUP A ODDS 1:5 HTA BOXES, 1:150 RETAIL
GROUP B ODDS 1:4 HTA BOXES, 1:105 RETAIL
GROUP C-D ODDS 1:6 HTA BOXES, 1:200 R
GROUP E ODDS 1:19 HTA BOXES, 1:1050 R
AT Aaron Thompson D 4.00 10.00
BB Brian Bogusevic A 4.00 10.00
BC Ben Copeland C 4.00 10.00
CR Cesar Ramos E 4.00 10.00
DS Denard Span B 6.00 15.00
GO Garrett Olson C 6.00 15.00
HS Henry Sanchez D 4.00 10.00
JC Jeff Clement B 4.00 10.00
JD John Drennen C 4.00 10.00
JE Jacoby Ellsbury D 5.00 12.00
JM John Mayberry Jr. E 4.00 10.00
MB Michael Bowden B 6.00 15.00
MC Mike Costanzo D 4.00 10.00
RB Ryan Braun E 6.00 15.00
RR Ricky Romero B 6.00 15.00
RT Ryan Tucker C 4.00 10.00
SW Sean West D 4.00 10.00
TB Travis Buck D 6.00 15.00
TC Trevor Crowe B 4.00 10.00
TT Troy Tulowitzki A 4.00 10.00
YE Yunel Escobar A 4.00 10.00

2006 Bowman Draft

COMPLETE SET (55) 6.00 15.00
COMMON RC (1-55) .15 .40
APPX. TWO PER HOBBY/RETAL PACK
ODDS INFO PROVIDED BY BECKETT
OVERALL PLATE ODDS 1:990 HOBBY
PLATE PRINT RUN 1 SET PER COLOR
BLACK-CYAN-MAGENTA-YELLOW ISSUED
NO PLATE PRICING DUE TO SCARCITY
1 Matt Kemp (RC) .40 1.00
2 Taylor Tankersley (RC) .15 .40
3 Mike Napoli RC .25 .60
4 Brian Bannister (RC) .15 .40
5 Melky Cabrera (RC) .25 .60
6 Bill Bray (RC) .15 .40
7 Brian Anderson (RC) .15 .40
8 Jered Weaver (RC) .50 1.25
9 Chris Duncan (RC) .25 .60
10 Boof Bonser (RC) .25 .60
11 Mike Rouse (RC) .15 .40
12 David Pauley (RC) .15 .40
13 Russ Martin (RC) .25 .60
14 Jeremy Sowers (RC) .15 .40
15 Kevin Reese (RC) .15 .40
16 John Rheinecker (RC) .15 .40
17 Tommy Murphy (RC) .15 .40
18 Sean Marshall (RC) .15 .40
19 Jason Kubel (RC) .15 .40
20 Chad Billingsley (RC) .25 .60
21 Kendry Morales (RC) .40 1.00
22 Jon Lester RC .60 1.50
23 Brandon Fahey RC .15 .40
24 Josh Johnson (RC) .40 1.00
25 Kevin Frandsen (RC) .15 .40
26 Casey Janssen RC .15 .40
27 Scott Thorman (RC) .15 .40

28 Scott Mathieson (RC) .15 .40
29 Jeremy Hermida (RC) .15 .40
30 Dustin Nippert (RC) .15 .40
31 Kevin Thompson (RC) .15 .40
32 Bobby Livingston (RC) .15 .40
33 Travis Ishikawa (RC) .25 .60
34 Jeff Mathis (RC) .15 .40
35 Charlie Haeger RC .25 .60
36 Josh Willingham (RC) .25 .60
37 Taylor Buchholz (RC) .15 .40
38 Joel Guzman (RC) .15 .40
39 Zach Jackson (RC) .15 .40
40 Howie Kendrick (RC) .30 .75
41 T.J. Beam (RC) .15 .40
42 Ty Taubenheim RC .25 .60
43 Erick Aybar (RC) .15 .40
44 Anibal Sanchez (RC) .15 .40
45 Michael Pelfrey RC .40 1.00
46 Shawn Hill (RC) .15 .40
47 Chris Roberson (RC) .15 .40
48 Carlos Villanueva RC .15 .40
49 Andre Ethier (RC) .50 1.25
50 Anthony Reyes (RC) .15 .40
51 Franklin Gutierrez (RC) .15 .40
52 Angel Guzman (RC) .15 .40
53 Michael O'Connor RC .15 .40
54 James Shields RC .50 1.25
55 Nate McLouth (RC) .15 .40

2006 Bowman Draft Gold

COMPLETE SET (55) 8.00 20.00
*GOLD: .75X TO 2X BASIC
APPX. ODDS 1:3 HOBBY, 1:3 RETAIL
ODDS INFO PROVIDED BY BECKETT

2006 Bowman Draft Red

STATED ODDS 1:7934 HOBBY
STATED PRINT RUN 1 SERIAL #'d SET
NO PRICING DUE TO SCARCITY

2006 Bowman Draft White

*WHITE: 2.5X TO 6X BASIC
STATED ODDS 1:43 H,1:93 R
STATED PRINT RUN 225 SER.#'d SETS

2006 Bowman Draft Draft Picks

COMPLETE SET (65) 8.00 20.00
APPX. ODDS 1:1 HOBBY, 1:1 RETAIL
ODDS INFO PROVIDED BY BECKETT
OVERALL PLATE ODDS 1:990 HOBBY
PLATE PRINT RUN 1 SET PER COLOR
BLACK-CYAN-MAGENTA-YELLOW ISSUED
NO PLATE PRICING DUE TO SCARCITY
1 Tyler Colvin .25 .60
2 Chris Marrero .25 .60
3 Hank Conger .25 .60
4 Chris Parmelee .25 .60
5 Jason Place .15 .40
6 Billy Rowell .40 1.00
7 Travis Snider .50 1.25
8 Colton Willems .15 .40
9 Chase Fontaine .15 .40
10 Jon Jay .25 .60
11 Wade Leblanc .25 .60
12 Justin Masterson .25 .60
13 Gary Daley .15 .40
14 Justin Edwards .15 .40
15 Charlie Yarbrough .15 .40
16 Cyle Hankerd .15 .40
17 Zach McAllister .15 .40
18 Tyler Robertson .15 .40
19 Joe Smith .15 .40
20 Nate Culp .15 .40
21 John Holdzkom .15 .40
22 Patrick Bresnehan .15 .40
23 Chad Lee .15 .40
24 Ryan Morris .15 .40
25 D'Arby Myers .15 .40
26 Garrett Olson .15 .40
27 Jon Still .15 .40
28 Brandon Rice .15 .40
29 Chris Davis .30 .75
30 Zack Daeges .15 .40
31 Bobby Henson .15 .40
32 George Kontos .15 .40
33 Jermaine Mitchell .15 .40
34 Adam Coe .15 .40
35 Dustin Richardson .15 .40
36 Allen Craig .40 1.00
37 Austin McClune .15 .40
38 Doug Fister .25 .60
39 Corey Madden .15 .40
40 Justin Jacobs .15 .40
41 Jim Negrych .15 .40
42 Tyler Norrick .15 .40
43 Adam Davis .15 .40
44 Brett Logan .15 .40
45 Brian Omogrosso .15 .40
46 Kyle Drabek .25 .60
47 Jamie Ortiz .15 .40
48 Alex Presley .25 .60
49 Terrance Warren .15 .40
50 David Christensen .15 .40
51 Helder Velazquez .15 .40
52 Matt McBride .15 .40
53 Quintin Berry .40 1.00
54 Michael Eisenberg .15 .40
55 Dan Garcia .15 .40
56 Scott Cousins .15 .40
57 Sean Land .15 .40
58 Kristopher Medlen .75 2.00
59 Tyler Reves .15 .40
60 John Shelby .15 .40
61 Jordan Newton .15 .40
62 Ricky Orta .15 .40
63 Jason Donald .15 .40
64 David Huff .15 .40
65 Brett Sinkbeil .15 .40

2006 Bowman Draft Draft Picks Gold

*GOLD: .75X TO 2X BASIC
APPX. ODDS 1:2 HOBBY, 1:2 RETAIL
ODDS INFO PROVIDED BY BECKETT

2006 Bowman Draft Draft Picks Red

STATED ODDS 1:7934 HOBBY
STATED PRINT RUN 1 SERIAL #'d SET
NO PRICING DUE TO SCARCITY

2006 Bowman Draft Draft Picks White

*WHITE: 2.5X TO 6X BASIC
STATED ODDS 1:43 H,1:93 R
STATED PRINT RUN 225 SER.#'d SETS

2006 Bowman Draft Future's Game Prospects

COMPLETE SET (45) 6.00 15.00
APPX. ODDS 1:1 HOBBY, 1:1 RETAIL
ODDS INFO PROVIDED BY BECKETT
OVERALL PLATE ODDS 1:990 HOBBY
PLATE PRINT RUN 1 SET PER COLOR
BLACK-CYAN-MAGENTA-YELLOW ISSUED
NO PLATE PRICING DUE TO SCARCITY
1 Nick Adenhart .15 .40
2 Joel Guzman .15 .40
3 Ryan Braun .75 2.00
4 Carlos Carrasco .25 .60
5 Neil Walker .25 .60
6 Pablo Sandoval .60 1.50
7 Gio Gonzalez .25 .60
8 Joey Votto 1.25 3.00
9 Luis Cruz .15 .40
10 Nolan Reimold .25 .60
11 Juan Salas .15 .40
12 Josh Fields .15 .40
13 Yovani Gallardo .50 1.25
14 Radhames Liz .15 .40
15 Eric Patterson .15 .40
16 Cameron Maybin .50 1.25
17 Edgar Martinez .15 .40
18 Hunter Pence .60 1.50
19 Philip Hughes .40 1.00
20 Trent Oeltjen .15 .40
21 Nick Pereira .15 .40
22 Wladimir Balentien .15 .40
23 Stephen Drew .30 .75
24 Davis Romero .15 .40
25 Joe Koshansky .15 .40
26 Chin Lung Hu .15 .40
27 Jason Hirsh .15 .40
28 Jose Tabata .25 .60
29 Eric Hurley .15 .40
30 Yung Chi Chen .25 .60
31 Howie Kendrick .30 .75
32 Humberto Sanchez .15 .40
33 Alex Gordon .50 1.25
34 Yunel Escobar .15 .40
35 Travis Buck .15 .40
36 Billy Butler .40 1.00
37 Homer Bailey .40 1.00
38 George Kottaras .15 .40
39 Kurt Suzuki .15 .40
40 Joaquin Arias .15 .40
41 Matt Lindstrom .15 .40
42 Sean Smith .15 .40
43 Carlos Gonzalez .40 1.00
44 Jaime Garcia .75 2.00
45 Jose Garcia .15 .40

2006 Bowman Draft Future's Game Prospects Gold

*GOLD: 1X TO 2.5X BASIC
APPX. ODDS 1:6 HOBBY, 1:6 RETAIL
ODDS INFO PROVIDED BY BECKETT

2006 Bowman Draft Future's Game Prospects Red

STATED ODDS 1:7934 HOBBY
STATED PRINT RUN 1 SERIAL #'d SET
NO PRICING DUE TO SCARCITY

2006 Bowman Draft Future's Game Prospects White

*WHITE: 2.5X TO 6X BASIC
STATED ODDS 1:43 H,1:93 R
STATED PRINT RUN 225 SER.#'d SETS

2006 Bowman Draft Future's Game Prospects Relics

GROUP A ODDS 1:285 H,1:285 R
GROUP B ODDS 1:26 H,1:25 R
PRICES LISTED FOR JSY SWATCHES
PRIME SWATCHES MAY SELL FOR A PREMIUM
1 Nick Adenhart Jsy B 4.00 10.00
2 Joel Guzman Jsy B 2.50 6.00
3 Ryan Braun Jsy B 5.00 12.00
4 Carlos Carrasco Jsy B 2.50 6.00
6 Pablo Sandoval Jsy B 8.00 20.00
7 Gio Gonzalez Jsy B 2.50 6.00
8 Joey Votto Jsy B 6.00 15.00
9 Luis Cruz Jsy B 2.50 6.00
10 Nolan Reimold Jsy B 3.00 8.00
11 Juan Salas Jsy B 2.50 6.00
12 Josh Fields Jsy B 2.50 6.00
13 Yovani Gallardo Jsy B 6.00 15.00
14 Radhames Liz Jsy B 2.50 6.00
15 Eric Patterson Jsy A 2.50 6.00
16 Cameron Maybin Jsy B 3.00 8.00
17 Edgar Martinez Jsy B 2.50 6.00
18 Hunter Pence Jsy B 3.00 8.00
19 Philip Hughes Jsy B 4.00 10.00
20 Trent Oeltjen Jsy B 2.50 6.00
21 Nick Pereira Jsy B 2.50 6.00
22 Wladimir Balentien Jsy B 2.50 6.00
23 Stephen Drew Jsy B 3.00 8.00
24 Davis Romero Jsy A 2.50 6.00
25 Joe Koshansky Jsy B 2.50 6.00
26 Chin-Lung Hu Jsy Black B 10.00 25.00
26b Chin-Lung Hu Jsy Red 60.00 120.00
26c Chin-Lung Hu Jsy Yellow 50.00 100.00
27 Jason Hirsh Jsy B 2.50 6.00
28 Jose Tabata Jsy B 3.00 8.00
29 Eric Hurley Jsy B 2.50 6.00
30 Yung-Chi Chen Jsy Black B 10.00 25.00
30b Yung-Chi Chen Jsy Red 60.00 120.00
30c Yung-Chi Chen Jsy Yellow 50.00 100.00
31 Howie Kendrick Jsy A 3.00 8.00
32 Humberto Sanchez Jsy B 2.50 6.00
33 Alex Gordon Jsy B 3.00 8.00
34 Yunel Escobar Jsy A 6.00 15.00
35 Travis Buck Jsy B 6.00 15.00
36 Billy Butler Jsy B 4.00 10.00
37 Homer Bailey Jsy B 4.00 10.00
38 George Kottaras Jsy B 2.50 6.00
39 Kurt Suzuki Jsy B 2.50 6.00
40 Joaquin Arias Jsy B 2.50 6.00
43 Carlos Gonzalez Jsy B 4.00 10.00
44 Jaime Garcia Jsy B 3.00 8.00
45 Jose Garcia Jsy B 2.50 6.00

2006 Bowman Draft Head of the Class Dual Autograph

STATED ODDS 1:7640 HOBBY
STATED PRINT RUN 174 SER.#'d SETS
GOLD REF. ODDS 1:56,000 HOBBY
GOLD REF. PRINT RUN 25 SER.#'d SETS
NO GOLD PRICING DUE TO SCARCITY
SUPERFRAC. ODDS 1:261,680 HOBBY
SUPERFRAC. PRINT RUN 1 SER.#'d SET
NO SUPERFRAC.PRICING DUE TO SCARCITY
RU A.Rodriguez/J.Upton 100.00 200.00

2006 Bowman Draft Head of the Class Dual Autograph Refractor

STATED ODDS 1:27,000 HOBBY
STATED PRINT RUN 50 SERIAL #'d SETS
RU A.Rodriguez/J.Upton 125.00 250.00

2006 Bowman Draft Signs of the Future

GROUP A ODDS 1:973 H, 1:973 R
GROUP B ODDS 1:324 H, 1:323 R
GROUP C ODDS 1:430 H, 1:431 R
GROUP D ODDS 1:1140 H, 1:1140 R
GROUP E ODDS 1:322 H, 1:323 R
GROUP F ODDS 1:387 H, 1:388 R
AG Alex Gordon A 6.00 15.00
BJ Beau Jones B 3.00 8.00
BS Brandon Snyder A 3.00 8.00
CDR Chaz Roe C 3.00 8.00
CI Chris Iannetta A 4.00 10.00
CR Clayton Richard B 3.00 8.00
CRA Cesar Ramos F 3.00 8.00
CTI Craig Italiano C 3.00 8.00
DJ Daryl Jones B 6.00 15.00
HS Henry Sanchez E 3.00 8.00
JB Jay Bruce D 6.00 15.00
JC Jeff Clement B 6.00 15.00
JM Jacob Marceaux C 3.00 8.00
KC Koby Clemens A 8.00 20.00
MC Mike Costanzo F 3.00 8.00
MM Mark McCormick E 3.00 8.00
MO Micah Owings B 6.00 15.00
TB Travis Buck B 4.00 10.00
WT Wade Townsend E 3.00 8.00

2007 Bowman

COMP.SET w/o AU's (221) 20.00 50.00
COMMON CARD (1-200) .12 .30
COMMON ROOKIE (201-220) .15 .40
COMMON AUTO (221-236) 4.00 10.00
219/221-236 AU ODDS 1:98 HOBBY, 1:25 HTA
BONDS ODDS 1:51 HTA, 1:610 RETAIL
1-220 PLATE ODDS 1:1468 H, 1:212 HTA
221-231 AU PLATES 1:8200 H, 1:1150 HTA
BONDS PLATE ODDS 1:106,000 HTA
PLATE PRINT RUN 1 SET PER COLOR
BLACK-CYAN-MAGENTA-YELLOW ISSUED
NO PLATE PRICING DUE TO SCARCITY
1 Hanley Ramirez .20 .50
2 Justin Verlander .30 .75
3 Ryan Zimmerman .20 .50
4 Jered Weaver .20 .50
5 Stephen Drew .12 .30
6 Jonathan Papelbon .30 .75
7 Melky Cabrera .12 .30
8 Francisco Liriano .12 .30
9 Prince Fielder .20 .50
10 Dan Uggla .12 .30
11 Jeremy Sowers .12 .30
12 Carlos Quentin .12 .30
13 Chuck James .12 .30
14 Andre Ethier .20 .50
15 Cole Hamels UER .25 .60
16 Kenji Johjima .30 .75
17 Chad Billingsley .20 .50
18 Ian Kinsler .20 .50
19 Jason Hirsh .12 .30
20 Nick Markakis .25 .60
21 Jeremy Hermida .12 .30
22 Ryan Shealy .12 .30
23 Scott Olsen .12 .30
24 Russell Martin .12 .30
25 Conor Jackson .12 .30
26 Erik Bedard .12 .30
27 Brian McCann .12 .30
28 Michael Barrett .12 .30
29 Brandon Phillips .12 .30
30 Garrett Atkins .12 .30
31 Freddy Garcia .12 .30
32 Mark Loretta .12 .30
33 Craig Biggio .20 .50
34 Jeremy Bonderman .12 .30
35 Johan Santana .20 .50
36 Jorge Posada .20 .50
37 Brian Bannister .12 .30
38 Carlos Delgado .12 .30
39 Gary Matthews Jr. .12 .30
40 Mike Cameron .12 .30
41 Adrian Beltre .30 .75
42 Freddy Sanchez .12 .30
43 Austin Kearns .12 .30
44 Mark Buehrle .20 .50
45 Miguel Cabrera .30 .75
46 Josh Beckett .12 .30
47 Chone Figgins .12 .30
48 Edgar Renteria .12 .30
49 Derek Lowe .12 .30
50 Ryan Howard .25 .60
51 Shawn Green .12 .30
52 Jason Giambi .12 .30
53 Ervin Santana .12 .30
54 Jack Wilson .12 .30
55 Roy Oswalt .20 .50
56 Dan Haren .12 .30
57 Jose Vidro .12 .30
58 Kevin Millwood .12 .30
59 Jim Edmonds .20 .50
60 Carl Crawford .20 .50
61 Randy Wolf .12 .30
62 Paul LoDuca .12 .30
63 Johnny Estrada .12 .30
64 Brian Roberts .12 .30
65 Manny Ramirez .30 .75
66 Jose Contreras .12 .30
67 Josh Barfield .12 .30
68 Juan Pierre .12 .30
69 David DeJesus .12 .30
70 Gary Sheffield .12 .30
71 Jon Lieber .12 .30
72 Randy Johnson .30 .75
73 Rickie Weeks .12 .30
74 Brian Giles .12 .30
75 Ichiro Suzuki .40 1.00
76 Nick Swisher .20 .50
77 Justin Morneau .20 .50
78 Scott Kazmir .20 .50
79 Lyle Overbay .12 .30
80 Alfonso Soriano .20 .50
81 Brandon Webb .20 .50
82 Joe Crede .12 .30
83 Corey Patterson .12 .30
84 Kenny Rogers .12 .30
85 Ken Griffey Jr .60 1.50
86 Cliff Lee .20 .50
87 Mike Lowell .12 .30
88 Marcus Giles .12 .30
89 Orlando Cabrera .12 .30
90 Derek Jeter .75 2.00
91 Josh Johnson .30 .75
92 Carlos Guillen .12 .30
93 Bill Hall .12 .30
94 Michael Cuddyer .12 .30
95 Miguel Tejada .20 .50
96 Todd Helton .20 .50
97 C.C. Sabathia .20 .50
98 Tadahito Iguchi .12 .30
99 Jose Reyes .20 .50
100 David Wright .25 .60
101 Barry Zito .20 .50
102 Jake Peavy .12 .30
103 Richie Sexson .12 .30
104 A.J. Burnett .12 .30
105 Eric Chavez .12 .30
106 Jorge Cantu .12 .30
107 Grady Sizemore .20 .50
108 Bronson Arroyo .12 .30
109 Mike Mussina .20 .50
110 Magglio Ordonez .20 .50
111 Anibal Sanchez .12 .30
112 Jeff Francoeur .30 .75
113 Kevin Youkilis .12 .30
114 Aubrey Huff .12 .30
115 Carlos Zambrano .20 .50
116 Mark Teahen .12 .30
117 Carlos Silva .12 .30
118 Pedro Martinez .20 .50
119 Hideki Matsui .30 .75
120 Mike Piazza .30 .75
121 Jason Schmidt .12 .30
122 Greg Maddux .40 1.00
123 Joe Blanton .12 .30
124 Chris Carpenter .20 .50
125 David Ortiz .30 .75
126 Alex Rios .12 .30
127 Nick Johnson .12 .30
128 Carlos Lee .12 .30
129 Pat Burrell .12 .30
130 Ben Sheets .12 .30
131 Kazuo Matsui .12 .30
132 Adam Dunn .20 .50
133 Jermaine Dye .12 .30
134 Curt Schilling .20 .50
135 Chad Tracy .12 .30
136 Vladimir Guerrero .20 .50
137 Melvin Mora .12 .30
138 John Smoltz .30 .75
139 Craig Monroe .12 .30
140 Dontrelle Willis .12 .30
141 Jeff Francis .12 .30
142 Chipper Jones .30 .75
143 Frank Thomas .30 .75
144 Brett Myers .12 .30
145 Xavier Nady .12 .30
146 Robinson Cano .20 .50
147 Jeff Kent .12 .30
148 Scott Rolen .20 .50
149 Roy Halladay .20 .50
150 Joe Mauer .25 .60
151 Bobby Abreu .12 .30
152 Matt Cain .20 .50
153 Hank Blalock .12 .30
154 Chris Capuano .12 .30
155 Jake Westbrook .12 .30
156 Javier Vazquez .12 .30
157 Garret Anderson .12 .30
158 Aramis Ramirez .12 .30
159 Mark Kotsay .12 .30
160 Matt Kemp .25 .60
161 Adrian Gonzalez .25 .60
162 Felix Hernandez .20 .50
163 David Eckstein .12 .30
164 Curtis Granderson .25 .60
165 Paul Konerko .20 .50
166 Orlando Hudson .12 .30
167 Tim Hudson .20 .50
168 J.D. Drew .12 .30
169 Chien-Ming Wang .20 .50
170 Jimmy Rollins .20 .50
171 Matt Morris .12 .30
172 Raul Ibanez .20 .50
173 Mark Teixeira .20 .50
174 Ted Lilly .12 .30
175 Albert Pujols .40 1.00
176 Carlos Beltran .20 .50
177 Lance Berkman .20 .50
178 Ivan Rodriguez .20 .50
179 Torii Hunter .12 .30
180 Johnny Damon .20 .50
181 Chase Utley .20 .50
182 Jason Bay .20 .50
183 Jeff Weaver .12 .30
184 Troy Glaus .12 .30
185 Rocco Baldelli .12 .30
186 Rafael Furcal .12 .30
187 Jim Thome .20 .50
188 Travis Hafner .12 .30
189 Matt Holliday .30 .75
190 Andruw Jones .12 .30
191 Ramon Hernandez .12 .30
192 Victor Martinez .20 .50
193 Aaron Hill .12 .30
194 Michael Young .12 .30
195 Vernon Wells .12 .30
196 Mark Mulder .12 .30
197 Derrek Lee .12 .30
198 Tom Glavine .20 .50
199 Chris Young .12 .30
200 Alex Rodriguez .40 1.00
201 Delmon Young (RC) .25 .60
202 Alexi Casilla RC .25 .60
203 Shawn Riggans (RC) .15 .40
204 Jeff Baker (RC) .15 .40
205 Hector Gimenez (RC) .15 .40
206 Ubaldo Jimenez (RC) .50 1.25
207 Adam Lind (RC) .15 .40
208 Joaquin Arias (RC) .15 .40
209 David Murphy (RC) .15 .40
210 Daisuke Matsuzaka RC 2.00 5.00
211 Jerry Owens (RC) .15 .40
212 Ryan Sweeney (RC) .15 .40
213 Kei Igawa RC .60 1.50
214 Fred Lewis (RC) .25 .60
215 Philip Humber (RC) .15 .40
216 Kevin Hooper (RC) .15 .40
217 Jeff Fiorentino (RC) .15 .40
218 Michael Bourn (RC) .25 .60
219 Hideki Okajima RC .75 2.00
219b H.Okajima English AU 4.00 10.00
219c H.Okajima Japan AU 10.00 25.00
220 Josh Fields (RC) .15 .40
221 Andrew Miller AU RC 6.00 15.00
222 Troy Tulowitzki AU (RC) 6.00 15.00
223 Ryan Braun AU RC 4.00 10.00
224 Oswaldo Navarro AU RC 4.00 10.00
225 Philip Humber AU (RC) 4.00 10.00
226 Mitch Maier AU RC 4.00 10.00
227 Jerry Owens AU (RC) 4.00 10.00
228 Mike Rabelo AU RC 4.00 10.00
229 Delwyn Young AU (RC) 4.00 10.00
230 Miguel Montero AU (RC) 4.00 10.00
231 Akinori Iwamura AU RC 4.00 10.00
232 Matt Lindstrom AU (RC) 4.00 10.00
233 Josh Hamilton AU (RC) 6.00 15.00
235 Elijah Dukes AU RC 4.00 10.00
236 Sean Henn AU (RC) 4.00 10.00
237 Barry Bonds .50 1.25

2007 Bowman Blue

*BLUE 1-200: 2X TO 5X BASIC
*BLUE 201-220: 2X TO 5X BASIC
*BLUE 219 AU/221-236: .4X TO 1X BASIC AU
1-220 ODDS 1:17 HOB, 1:3 HTA, 1:30 RET
221-236 AU ODDS 1:241 HOBBY, 1:60 HTA
BONDS ODDS 1:1261 HTA, 1:15,500 RETAIL
STATED PRINT RUN 500 SERIAL #'d SETS
221 Andrew Miller AU 6.00 15.00

2007 Bowman Gold

*GOLD 1-200: 1.2X TO 3X BASIC
*GOLD 201-220: 1.2X TO 3X BASIC
OVERALL GOLD ODDS 1 PER PACK

2007 Bowman Orange

*ORANGE 1-200: 3X TO 8X BASIC
*ORANGE 201-220: 3X TO 8X BASIC
*ORANGE 219 AU/221-236: .5X TO 1.2X BASIC AU
1-220 ODDS 1:33 HOB, 1:6 HTA, 1:65 RET
221-236 AU ODDS 1:486 HOBBY, 1:119 HTA
BONDS ODDS 1:2521 HTA, 1:30,000 RETAIL
STATED PRINT RUN 250 SERIAL #'d SETS
219b H.Okajima English AU 15.00 40.00
221 Andrew Miller AU 8.00 20.00

2007 Bowman Red

1-220 ODDS 1:6036 HOBBY, 1:1400 HTA
221-236 AU ODDS 1:222,220 H, 1:27,000 HTA
BONDS ODDS 1:211,776 HTA
STATED PRINT RUN 1 SER.#'d SET
NO PRICING DUE TO SCARCITY

2007 Bowman Prospects

COMP.SET w/o AU's (110) 20.00 50.00
111-135 AU ODDS 1:64 HOBBY, 1:16 HTA
1-110 PLATE ODDS 1:1468 H, 1:212 HTA
111-135 AU PLATES 1:8200 H, 1:1150 HTA
PLATE PRINT RUN 1 SET PER COLOR
BLACK-CYAN-MAGENTA-YELLOW ISSUED
NO PLATE PRICING DUE TO SCARCITY
BP1 Cooper Brannon .20 .50
BP2 Jason Taylor .20 .50
BP3 Shawn O'Malley .20 .50
BP4 Robert Alcombrack .20 .50
BP5 Dellin Betances .60 1.50
BP6 Jeremy Papelbon .20 .50
BP7 Adam Carr .20 .50
BP8 Matthew Clarkson .20 .50
BP9 Darin McDonald .20 .50
BP10 Brandon Rice .20 .50
BP11 Matthew Sweeney .60 1.50
BP12 Scott Deal .20 .50
BP13 Brennan Boesch .30 .75
BP14 Scott Taylor .20 .50
BP15 Michael Brantley .50 1.25
BP16 Yahmed Yema .20 .50
BP17 Brandon Morrow 1.00 2.50
BP18 Cole Garner .20 .50
BP19 Erik Lis .30 .75
BP20 Lucas French .20 .50
BP21 Aaron Cunningham .30 .75
BP22 Ryan Schreppel .20 .50
BP23 Kevin Russo .20 .50
BP24 Yohan Pino .30 .75
BP25 Michael Sullivan .20 .50
BP26 Trey Shields .20 .50
BP27 Daniel Matienzo .20 .50
BP28 Chuck Lofgren .50 1.25
BP29 Gerrit Simpson .20 .50
BP30 David Haehnel .20 .50
BP31 Marvin Lowrance .20 .50
BP32 Kevin Ardoin .20 .50
BP33 Edwin Maysonet .20 .50
BP34 Derek Griffith .20 .50
BP35 Sam Fuld .60 1.50
BP36 Chase Wright .50 1.25
BP37 Brandon Roberts .20 .50
BP38 Kyle Aselton .20 .50
BP39 Steven Sollmann .20 .50
BP40 Mike Devaney .20 .50
BP41 Charlie Fermaint .20 .50
BP42 Jesse Litsch .30 .75
BP43 Bryan Hansen .20 .50
BP44 Ramon Garcia .20 .50
BP45 John Otness .20 .50
BP46 Trey Hearne .20 .50
BP47 Habelito Hernandez .20 .50
BP48 Edgar Garcia .20 .50
BP49 Seth Fortenberry .20 .50
BP50 Reid Brignac .30 .75
BP51 Derek Rodriguez .20 .50
BP52 Ervin Alcantara .20 .50
BP53 Thomas Hottovy .20 .50
BP54 Jesus Flores .20 .50
BP55 Matt Palmer .20 .50
BP56 Brian Henderson .20 .50
BP57 John Gragg .20 .50
BP58 Jay Garthwaite .20 .50
BP59 Esmerling Vasquez .20 .50
BP60 Gilberto Mejia .20 .50
BP61 Aaron Jensen .20 .50
BP62 Cedric Brooks .20 .50
BP63 Brandon Mann .20 .50
BP64 Myron Leslie .20 .50
BP65 Ray Aguilar .20 .50
BP66 Jesus Guzman .30 .75
BP67 Sean Thompson .20 .50
BP68 Jarrett Hoffpauir .20 .50
BP69 Matt Goodson .20 .50
BP70 Neal Musser .20 .50
BP71 Tony Abreu .50 1.25
BP72 Tony Peguero .20 .50
BP73 Michael Bertram .20 .50
BP74 Randy Wells .50 1.25
BP75 Bradley Davis .20 .50
BP76 Jay Sawatski .20 .50
BP77 Vic Buttler .20 .50
BP78 Jose Oyervidez .20 .50
BP79 Doug Deeds .20 .50
BP80 Dan Dement .20 .50
BP81 Spike Lundberg .20 .50
BP82 Ricardo Nanita .20 .50
BP83 Brad Knox .20 .50
BP84 Will Venable .30 .75
BP85 Greg Smith .30 .75
BP86 Pedro Powell .20 .50
BP87 Gabriel Medina .20 .50
BP88 Duke Sardinha .20 .50
BP89 Mike Madsen .20 .50
BP90 Rayner Bautista .20 .50
BP91 T.J. Nall .20 .50
BP92 Neil Sellers .20 .50
BP93 Andrew Dobies .20 .50
BP94 Leo Daigle .20 .50
BP95 Brian Duensing .30 .75
BP96 Vincent Blue .20 .50
BP97 Fernando Rodriguez .20 .50
BP98 Derin McMains .20 .50
BP99 Adam Bass .20 .50
BP100 Justin Ruggiano .30 .75
BP101 Jared Burton .20 .50
BP102 Mike Parisi .20 .50
BP103 Aaron Peel .20 .50
BP104 Evan Englebrook .20 .50
BP105 Sendy Vasquez .20 .50
BP106 Desmond Jennings .75 2.00
BP107 Clay Harris .20 .50
BP108 Cody Strait .20 .50
BP109 Ryan Mullins .20 .50
BP110 Ryan Webb .20 .50
BP111 Kyle Drabek AU 4.00 10.00
BP112 Evan Longoria AU 8.00 20.00
BP113 Tyler Colvin AU 6.00 15.00
BP114 Matt Long AU 4.00 10.00
BP115 Jeremy Jeffress AU 3.00 8.00
BP116 Kasey Kiker AU 4.00 10.00
BP117 Hank Conger AU 5.00 12.00
BP118 Cody Johnson AU 4.00 10.00
BP119 David Huff AU 4.00 10.00
BP120 Tommy Hickman AU 4.00 10.00
BP121 Chris Parmelee AU 4.00 10.00
BP122 Dustin Evans AU 4.00 10.00
BP123 Brett Sinkbeil AU 4.00 10.00
BP124 Andrew Carpenter AU 4.00 10.00
BP125 Colten Willems AU 4.00 10.00
BP126 Matt Antonelli AU 4.00 10.00
BP127 Marcus Sanders AU 4.00 10.00
BP128 Joshua Rodriguez AU 4.00 10.00
BP129 Keith Weiser AU 4.00 10.00
BP130 Chad Tracy AU 4.00 10.00
BP131 Matthew Sulentic AU 6.00 15.00
BP132 Adam Ottavino AU 4.00 10.00
BP133 Jarrod Saltalamacchia AU 4.00 10.00
BP134 Kyle Blanks AU 5.00 12.00
BP135 Brad Eldred AU 4.00 10.00

2007 Bowman Prospects Blue

*BLUE 1-110: 2X TO 5X BASIC
*BLUE 111-135: .4X TO 1X BASIC AU
1-110 ODDS 1:17 HOB, 1:3 HTA, 1:30 RET
111-135 AU ODDS 1:156 HOBBY, 1:38 HTA
STATED PRINT RUN 500 SERIAL #'d SETS

2007 Bowman Prospects Gold

*GOLD 1-110: .75X TO 2X BASIC
OVERALL GOLD ODDS 1 PER PACK

2007 Bowman Prospects Orange

*ORANGE 1-110: 2.5X TO 6X BASIC
*ORANGE 111-135: .5X TO 1.2X BASIC AU
1-110 ODDS 1:33 HOB, 1:6 HTA, 1:65 RET
111-135 AU ODDS 1:311 HOBBY, 1:77 HTA
STATED PRINT RUN 250 SERIAL #'d SETS
BP111 Kyle Drabek AU 10.00 25.00
BP115 Jeremy Jeffress AU 5.00 12.00
BP121 Chris Parmelee AU 10.00 25.00
BP131 Matthew Sulentic AU 10.00 25.00

2007 Bowman Prospects Red

1-110 ODDS 1:6036 HOBBY, 1:1400 HTA
111-135 AU ODDS 80,000 H, 1:19,252 HTA
STATED PRINT RUN 1 SER.#'d SET
NO PRICING DUE TO SCARCITY

2007 Bowman Signs of the Future

GROUP A ODDS 1:2725 RETAIL
GROUP B ODDS 1:385 RETAIL
GROUP C ODDS 1:268 RETAIL
GROUP D ODDS 1:82 RETAIL
GROUP E ODDS 1:83 RETAIL
GROUP F ODDS 1:89 RETAIL
PRINTING PLATE ODDS 1:8200 H, 1:1150 HTA
PLATE PRINT RUN 1 SET PER COLOR
BLACK-CYAN-MAGENTA-YELLOW ISSUED
NO PLATE PRICING DUE TO SCARCITY
AM Andrew McCutchen 15.00 40.00
AR Adam Russell 3.00 8.00
BB Brian Bixler 3.00 8.00
BM Brandon Moss 3.00 8.00
CG Chris Getz 3.00 8.00
CJS Chris Seddon 3.00 8.00
CL Chris Lubanski 3.00 8.00
CM Chris McConnell 3.00 8.00
JW Jared Wells 3.00 8.00
CS Chad Santos 3.00 8.00
DB Dellin Betances 12.00 30.00
DS Denard Span 3.00 8.00
EH Estee Harris 3.00 8.00
ER Eric Reed 3.00 8.00
FP Felix Pie 3.00 8.00
JB John Baker 3.00 8.00
CR Chris Robinson 3.00 8.00
JBC J. Brent Cox 3.00 8.00
JC Jesus Cota 3.00 8.00
JCB Jordan Brown 3.00 8.00
JD John Drennen 3.00 8.00
JBB John Bowker 3.00 8.00
JJ Jair Jurrjens 5.00 12.00
MM Matt Merricks 3.00 8.00
BF Ben Fritz 3.00 8.00
KC Koby Clemens 5.00 12.00
KD Kyle Drabek 5.00 12.00
KS Kurt Suzuki 3.00 8.00
MA Mike Aviles 3.00 8.00
ME Mike Edwards 3.00 8.00
JDA Jaime D'Antona 3.00 8.00
MN Mike Neu 3.00 8.00
MR Michael Rogers 3.00 8.00
RB Reid Brignac 5.00 12.00
RG Richie Gardner 3.00 8.00
RO Ross Ohlendorf 5.00 12.00
SG Sean Gallagher 3.00 8.00
SK Shane Komine 3.00 8.00
TT Taylor Teagarden 5.00 12.00

2007 Bowman Draft

COMMON RC (1-54) .15 .40
SEE 07 BOWMAN FOR BONDS PRICING
OVERALL PLATE ODDS 1:1294 HOBBY
PLATE PRINT RUN 1 SET PER COLOR
BLACK-CYAN-MAGENTA-YELLOW ISSUED
NO PLATE PRICING DUE TO SCARCITY
BDP1 Travis Buck (RC) .15 .40
BDP2 Matt Chico (RC) .15 .40
BDP3 Justin Upton RC .50 1.25
BDP4 Chase Wright RC .40 1.00
BDP5 Kevin Kouzmanoff (RC) .15 .40
BDP6 John Danks RC .25 .60
BDP7 Alejandro De Aza RC .25 .60
BDP8 Jamie Vermilyea RC .15 .40
BDP9 Jesus Flores RC .15 .40
BDP10 Glen Perkins (RC) .15 .40
BDP11 Tim Lincecum RC .75 2.00
BDP12 Cameron Maybin RC .25 .60
BDP13 Brandon Morrow RC .75 2.00
BDP14 Mike Rabelo RC .15 .40
BDP15 Alex Gordon RC .50 1.25
BDP16 Zack Segovia (RC) .15 .40
BDP17 Jon Knott (RC) .15 .40
BDP18 Joba Chamberlain RC .25 .60
BDP19 Danny Putnam (RC) .15 .40
BDP20 Matt DeSalvo (RC) .15 .40
BDP21 Fred Lewis (RC) .25 .60
BDP22 Sean Gallagher (RC) .15 .40
BDP23 Brandon Wood (RC) .15 .40
BDP24 Dennis Dove (RC) .15 .40
BDP25 Hunter Pence (RC) .50 1.25
BDP26 Jarrod Saltalamacchia (RC) .25 .60
BDP27 Ben Francisco (RC) .15 .40
BDP28 Doug Slaten RC .15 .40
BDP29 Tony Abreu RC .40 1.00
BDP30 Billy Butler (RC) .25 .60
BDP31 Jesse Litsch RC .25 .60
BDP32 Nate Schierholtz (RC) .15 .40
BDP33 Jared Burton RC .15 .40
BDP34 Matt Brown (RC) .15 .40
BDP35 Dallas Braden RC .25 .60
BDP36 Carlos Gomez RC .30 .75
BDP37 Brian Stokes (RC) .15 .40
BDP38 Kory Casto (RC) .15 .40
BDP39 Mark McLemore (RC) .15 .40
BDP40 Andy LaRoche (RC) .15 .40
BDP41 Tyler Clippard (RC) .25 .60
BDP42 Curtis Thigpen (RC) .15 .40
BDP43 Yunel Escobar (RC) .15 .40
BDP44 Andy Sonnanstine RC .15 .40
BDP45 Felix Pie (RC) .15 .40
BDP46 Homer Bailey (RC) .25 .60
BDP47 Kyle Kendrick RC .40 1.00
BDP48 Angel Sanchez RC .15 .40
BDP49 Phil Hughes (RC) .40 1.00
BDP50 Ryan Braun (RC) .75 2.00
BDP51 Kevin Slowey (RC) .40 1.00
BDP52 Brendan Ryan (RC) .15 .40
BDP53 Yovani Gallardo (RC) .40 1.00
BDP54 Mark Reynolds RC .50 1.25

2007 Bowman Draft Blue

*BLUE: 1.2X TO 3X BASIC
STATED ODDS 1:29 HOBBY,1:84 RETAIL
STATED PRINT RUN 399 SER.#'d SETS

2007 Bowman Draft Gold

*GOLD: .6X TO 1.5X BASIC
APPX.GOLD ODDS ONE PER PACK

2007 Bowman Draft Red

STATED ODDS 1:10,377 HOBBY
STATED PRINT RUN ONE SER.#'d SET
NO PRICING DUE TO SCARCITY

2007 Bowman Draft Draft Picks

OVERALL PLATE ODDS 1:1294 HOBBY
PLATE PRINT RUN 1 SET PER COLOR
BLACK-CYAN-MAGENTA-YELLOW ISSUED
NO PLATE PRICING DUE TO SCARCITY
BDPP1 Cody Crowell .15 .40
BDPP2 Karl Bolt .25 .60
BDPP3 Corey Brown .25 .60
BDPP4 Tyler Mach .25 .60
BDPP5 Trevor Pippin .25 .60
BDPP6 Ed Easley .15 .40
BDPP7 Cory Luebke .15 .40
BDPP8 Darin Mastroianni .15 .40
BDPP9 Ryan Zink .25 .60
BDPP10 Brandon Hamilton .15 .40
BDPP11 Kyle Lotzkar .25 .60
BDPP12 Freddie Freeman 2.50 6.00
BDPP13 Nicholas Barnese .25 .60
BDPP14 Travis d'Arnaud .25 .60
BDPP15 Eric Eiland .15 .40
BDPP16 John Ely .15 .40
BDPP17 Oliver Marmol .15 .40
BDPP18 Eric Sogard .15 .40
BDPP19 Lars Davis .15 .40
BDPP20 Sam Runion .15 .40
BDPP21 Austin Gallagher .25 .60
BDPP22 Matt West .25 .60
BDPP23 Derek Norris .40 1.00
BDPP24 Taylor Holiday .25 .60
BDPP25 Dustin Biell .15 .40
BDPP26 Julio Borbon .25 .60
BDPP27 Brant Rustich .25 .60
BDPP28 Andrew Lambo .25 .60
BDPP29 Cory Kluber .75 2.00
BDPP30 Justin Jackson .25 .60
BDPP31 Scott Carroll .15 .40
BDPP32 Danny Rams .15 .40
BDPP33 Thomas Eager .15 .40
BDPP34 Matt Dominguez .40 1.00
BDPP35 Steven Souza .50 1.25
BDPP36 Craig Heyer .15 .40
BDPP37 Michael Taylor .60 1.50
BDPP38 Drew Bowman .15 .40
BDPP39 Frank Gailey .15 .40
BDPP40 Jeremy Hefner .15 .40
BDPP41 Reynaldo Navarro .25 .60
BDPP42 Daniel Descalso .25 .60
BDPP43 Leroy Hunt .15 .40
BDPP44 Jason Kiley .15 .40
BDPP45 Ryan Pope .40 1.00
BDPP46 Josh Horton .15 .40
BDPP47 Jason Monti .15 .40
BDPP48 Richard Lucas .15 .40
BDPP49 Jonathan Lucroy .40 1.00
BDPP50 Sean Doolittle .15 .40
BDPP51 Mike McDade .25 .60
BDPP52 Charlie Culberson .25 .60
BDPP53 Michael Moustakas .40 1.00
BDPP54 Jason Heyward 1.00 2.50
BDPP55 David Price .50 1.25
BDPP56 Brad Mills .15 .40
BDPP57 John Tolisano .50 1.25
BDPP58 Jarrod Parker .40 1.00
BDPP59 Wendell Fairley .25 .60
BDPP60 Gary Gattis .15 .40
BDPP61 Madison Bumgarner 3.00 8.00
BDPP62 Danny Payne .15 .40
BDPP63 Jake Smolinski .50 1.25
BDPP64 Matt LaPorta .50 1.25
BDPP65 Jackson Williams .15 .40

2007 Bowman Draft Draft Picks Blue

*BLUE: 2X TO 5X BASIC
STATED ODDS 1:29 HOBBY,1:84 RETAIL
STATED PRINT RUN 399 SER.#'d SETS
BDPP61 Madison Bumgarner 10.00 25.00

2007 Bowman Draft Draft Picks Gold

*GOLD: .75X TO 2X BASIC
APPX.GOLD ODDS ONE PER PACK
BDPP61 Madison Bumgarner 5.00 12.00

2007 Bowman Draft Draft Picks Red

STATED ODDS 1:10,377 HOBBY
STATED PRINT RUN ONE SER.#'d SET
NO PRICING DUE TO SCARCITY

2007 Bowman Draft Future's Game Prospects

COMPLETE SET (45) 8.00 20.00
OVERALL PLATE ODDS 1:1294 HOBBY
PLATE PRINT RUN 1 SET PER COLOR
BLACK-CYAN-MAGENTA-YELLOW ISSUED
NO PLATE PRICING DUE TO SCARCITY
BDPP66 Pedro Beato .12 .30
BDPP67 Collin Balester .12 .30
BDPP68 Carlos Carrasco .20 .50
BDPP69 Clay Buchholz .40 1.00
BDPP70 Emiliano Fruto .12 .30
BDPP71 Joba Chamberlain .20 .50
BDPP72 Deolis Guerra .25 .60
BDPP73 Kevin Mulvey .30 .75
BDPP74 Franklin Morales .20 .50
BDPP75 Luke Hochevar .40 1.00
BDPP76 Henry Sosa .20 .50
BDPP77 Clayton Kershaw 3.00 8.00
BDPP78 Rich Thompson .12 .30
BDPP79 Chuck Lofgren .30 .75
BDPP80 Rick VandenHurk .12 .30
BDPP81 Michael Madsen .12 .30
BDPP82 Robinzon Diaz .12 .30
BDPP83 Jeff Niemann .20 .50
BDPP84 Max Ramirez .12 .30
BDPP85 Geovany Soto .50 1.25
BDPP86 Elvis Andrus .30 .75
BDPP87 Bryan Anderson .12 .30
BDPP88 German Duran .50 1.25
BDPP89 J.R. Towles .40 1.00
BDPP90 Alcides Escobar .30 .75
BDPP91 Brian Bocock .12 .30
BDPP92 Chin-Lung Hu .12 .30
BDPP93 Adrian Cardenas .12 .30
BDPP94 Freddy Sandoval .12 .30
BDPP95 Chris Coghlan .40 1.00
BDPP96 Craig Stansberry .12 .30
BDPP97 Brent Lillibridge .12 .30
BDPP98 Joey Votto .75 2.00
BDPP99 Evan Longoria 1.25 3.00
BDPP100 Wladimir Balentien .12 .30
BDPP101 Johnny Whittleman .12 .30
BDPP102 Gorkys Hernandez .30 .75
BDPP103 Jay Bruce .75 2.00
BDPP104 Matt Tolbert .12 .30
BDPP105 Jacoby Ellsbury .75 2.00
BDPP106 Michael Saunders .40 1.00
BDPP107 Cameron Maybin .20 .50
BDPP108 Carlos Gonzalez .30 .75
BDPP109 Colby Rasmus .30 .75
BDPP110 Justin Upton .40 1.00

2007 Bowman Draft Future's Game Prospects Blue

*BLUE: 1.2X TO 3X BASIC
STATED ODDS 1:29 HOBBY,1:84 RETAIL
STATED PRINT RUN 399 SER.#'d SETS

2007 Bowman Draft Future's Game Prospects Gold

*GOLD: .6X TO 1.5X BASIC
APPX.GOLD ODDS ONE PER PACK

2007 Bowman Draft Future's Game Prospects Red

STATED ODDS 1:10,377 HOBBY
STATED PRINT RUN ONE SER.#'d SET
NO PRICING DUE TO SCARCITY

2007 Bowman Draft Future's Game Prospects Jerseys

STATED ODDS 1:24 RETAIL
BDPP68 Carlos Carrasco 3.00 8.00
BDPP69 Clay Buchholz 5.00 12.00
BDPP71 Joba Chamberlain 10.00 25.00
BDPP73 Kevin Mulvey 3.00 8.00
BDPP74 Franklin Morales 3.00 8.00
BDPP75 Luke Hochevar 3.00 8.00
BDPP78 Rich Thompson 3.00 8.00
BDPP83 Jeff Niemann 3.00 8.00
BDPP84 Max Ramirez 3.00 8.00
BDPP89 J.R. Towles 3.00 8.00
BDPP95 Chris Coghlan 3.00 8.00
BDPP96 Craig Stansberry 3.00 8.00
BDPP97 Brent Lillibridge 3.00 8.00
BDPP98 Joey Votto 8.00 20.00
BDPP102 Gorkys Hernandez 3.00 8.00
BDPP105 Jacoby Ellsbury 8.00 20.00
BDPP106 Michael Saunders 3.00 8.00
BDPP107 Cameron Maybin 5.00 12.00
BDPP108 Carlos Gonzalez 4.00 10.00
BDPP110 Justin Upton 6.00 15.00

2007 Bowman Draft Future's Game Prospects Patches

STATED ODDS 1:384 HOBBY
STATED PRINT RUN 99 SER.#'d SETS
BDPP66 Pedro Beato 10.00 25.00
BDPP67 Collin Balester 10.00 25.00
BDPP68 Carlos Carrasco 12.50 30.00
BDPP69 Clay Buchholz 15.00 40.00
BDPP70 Emiliano Fruto 4.00 10.00
BDPP71 Joba Chamberlain 20.00 50.00
BDPP72 Deolis Guerra 12.50 30.00
BDPP73 Kevin Mulvey 6.00 15.00
BDPP74 Franklin Morales 6.00 15.00
BDPP75 Luke Hochevar 10.00 25.00
BDPP76 Henry Sosa 6.00 15.00
BDPP77 Clayton Kershaw 10.00 25.00
BDPP78 Rich Thompson 6.00 15.00
BDPP79 Chuck Lofgren 6.00 15.00
BDPP80 Rick VandenHurk 6.00 15.00
BDPP81 Michael Madsen 4.00 10.00
BDPP82 Robinzon Diaz 4.00 10.00
BDPP83 Jeff Niemann 6.00 15.00
BDPP84 Max Ramirez 10.00 25.00
BDPP85 Geovany Soto 15.00 40.00
BDPP86 Elvis Andrus 10.00 25.00
BDPP87 Bryan Anderson 10.00 25.00
BDPP88 German Duran 6.00 15.00
BDPP89 J.R. Towles 6.00 15.00
BDPP90 Alcides Escobar 6.00 15.00
BDPP91 Brian Bocock 6.00 15.00
BDPP92 Chin-Lung Hu 20.00 50.00
BDPP93 Adrian Cardenas 15.00 40.00
BDPP94 Freddy Sandoval 6.00 15.00
BDPP95 Chris Coghlan 6.00 15.00
BDPP96 Craig Stansberry 4.00 10.00
BDPP97 Brent Lillibridge 6.00 15.00
BDPP98 Joey Votto 10.00 25.00
BDPP99 Evan Longoria 10.00 25.00
BDPP100 Wladimir Balentien 6.00 15.00
BDPP101 Johnny Whittleman 6.00 15.00
BDPP102 Gorkys Hernandez 10.00 25.00
BDPP103 Jay Bruce 15.00 40.00
BDPP104 Matt Tolbert 15.00 40.00
BDPP105 Jacoby Ellsbury 15.00 40.00
BDPP106 Michael Saunders 10.00 25.00
BDPP107 Cameron Maybin 12.50 30.00
BDPP108 Carlos Gonzalez 10.00 25.00
BDPP109 Colby Rasmus 10.00 25.00
BDPP110 Justin Upton 15.00 40.00

2007 Bowman Draft Head of the Class Dual Autograph

STATED ODDS 1:4965 HOBBY
STATED PRINT RUN 174 SER.#'d SETS
EXCHANGE DEADLINE 12/31/2009
GH J.Gilmore/J.Heyward 12.50 30.00

2007 Bowman Draft Head of the Class Dual Autograph Refractors

*REF: .6X TO 1.5X BASIC
STATED ODDS 1:18,000 HOBBY
STATED PRINT RUN 50 SER.#'d SETS
EXCHANGE DEADLINE 12/31/2009
GH J.Gilmore/J.Heyward 40.00 80.00

2007 Bowman Draft Head of the Class Dual Autograph Gold Refractors

STATED ODDS 1:34,500 HOBBY
STATED PRINT RUN 25 SER.#'d SETS
NO PRICING DUE TO SCARCITY
EXCHANGE DEADLINE 12/31/2009

2007 Bowman Draft Signs of the Future

GROUP A ODDS 1:233 RETAIL
GROUP B ODDS 1:30 RETAIL
GROUP C ODDS 1:194 RETAIL
GROUP D ODDS 1:146 RETAIL
GROUP E ODDS 1:2945 RETAIL
AL Anthony Lerew 6.00 15.00
AM Adam Miller 5.00 12.00
BA Brandon Allen 4.00 10.00
CD Chris Dickerson 3.00 8.00
CM Casey McGehee 8.00 20.00
CMC Chris McConnell 4.00 10.00
CMM Carlos Marmol 6.00 15.00
CV Carlos Villanueva 3.00 8.00
FM Fernando Martinez 3.00 8.00
JGA Jaime Garcia 10.00 25.00
JK John Koronka 3.00 8.00
JR John Rheinecker 3.00 8.00
JV Jonathan Van Every 3.00 8.00
PH Philp Humber 4.00 10.00
RD Ryan Delaughter 3.00 8.00
SM Sergio Mitre 3.00 8.00
TC Trevor Crowe 3.00 8.00

2008 Bowman

COMP.SET w/o AU's (220) 8.00 20.00
COMMON CARD (1-200) .12 .30
COMMON ROOKIE (201-220) .15 .40
COMMON AUTO (221-230) 4.00 10.00
AU RC ODDS 1:233 HOBBY
1-220 PLATE ODDS 1:732 HOBBY
221-231 AU PLATES 1:4700 HOBBY
PLATE PRINT RUN 1 SET PER COLOR
BLACK-CYAN-MAGENTA-YELLOW ISSUED
NO PLATE PRICING DUE TO SCARCITY
1 Ryan Braun .20 .50
2 David DeJesus .12 .30
3 Brandon Phillips .12 .30
4 Mark Teixeira .20 .50
5 Daisuke Matsuzaka .20 .50
6 Justin Upton .20 .50
7 Jered Weaver .20 .50
8 Todd Helton .20 .50
9 Cameron Maybin .12 .30
10 Erik Bedard .12 .30
11 Jason Bay .20 .50
12 Cole Hamels .25 .60
13 Bobby Abreu .12 .30
14 Carlos Zambrano .20 .50
15 Vladimir Guerrero .20 .50
16 Joe Blanton .12 .30
17 Bengie Molina .12 .30
18 Paul Maholm .12 .30
19 Adrian Gonzalez .20 .50
20 Brandon Webb .20 .50
21 Carl Crawford .20 .50
22 A.J. Burnett .12 .30
23 Dmitri Young .12 .30
24 Jeremy Hermida .12 .30
25 C.C. Sabathia .20 .50
26 Adam Dunn .20 .50
27 Matt Garza .12 .30
28 Adrian Beltre .30 .75
29 Kevin Millwood .12 .30
30 Manny Ramirez .30 .75
31 Javier Vazquez .12 .30
32 Carlos Delgado .12 .30
33 Jason Schmidt .12 .30
34 Torii Hunter .12 .30
35 Ivan Rodriguez .20 .50
36 Nick Markakis .25 .60
37 Gil Meche .12 .30
38 Garrett Atkins .12 .30
39 Fausto Carmona .12 .30
40 Joe Mauer .25 .60
41 Tom Glavine .20 .50
42 Hideki Matsui .30 .75
43 Scott Rolen .20 .50
44 Tim Lincecum .20 .50
45 Prince Fielder .20 .50
46 Ted Lilly .12 .30
47 Frank Thomas .30 .75
48 Tom Gorzelanny .12 .30
49 Lance Berkman .20 .50
50 David Ortiz .30 .75
51 Dontrelle Willis .12 .30
52 Travis Hafner .12 .30
53 Aaron Harang .12 .30
54 Chris Young .12 .30
55 Vernon Wells .12 .30
56 Francisco Liriano .12 .30
57 Eric Chavez .12 .30
58 Phil Hughes .12 .30
59 Melvin Mora .12 .30
60 Johan Santana .20 .50
61 Brian McCann .20 .50
62 Pat Burrell .12 .30
63 Chris Carpenter .20 .50
64 Brian Giles .12 .30
65 Jose Reyes .20 .50
66 Hanley Ramirez .20 .50
67 Ubaldo Jimenez .12 .30
68 Felix Pie .12 .30
69 Jeremy Bonderman .12 .30
70 Jimmy Rollins .20 .50
71 Miguel Tejada .20 .50
72 Derek Lowe .12 .30
73 Alex Gordon .20 .50
74 John Maine .12 .30
75 Alfonso Soriano .20 .50
76 Richie Sexson .12 .30
77 Ben Sheets .12 .30
78 Hunter Pence .20 .50
79 Maggio Ordonez .20 .50
80 Josh Beckett .12 .30
81 Victor Martinez .20 .50
82 Mark Buehrle .20 .50
83 Jason Varitek .30 .75
84 Chien-Ming Wang .20 .50
85 Ken Griffey Jr. .60 1.50
86 Billy Butler .12 .30
87 Brad Penny .12 .30
88 Carlos Beltran .20 .50
89 Curt Schilling .20 .50
90 Jorge Posada .20 .50
91 Andruw Jones .12 .30
92 Bobby Crosby .12 .30
93 Freddy Sanchez .12 .30
94 Barry Zito .20 .50
95 Miguel Cabrera .30 .75
96 B.J. Upton .20 .50
97 Matt Cain .20 .50
98 Lyle Overbay .12 .30
99 Austin Kearns .12 .30
100 Alex Rodriguez .40 1.00
101 Rich Harden .12 .30
102 Justin Morneau .20 .50
103 Oliver Perez .12 .30
104 Gary Matthews .12 .30
105 Matt Holliday .30 .75
106 Justin Verlander .30 .75
107 Orlando Cabrera .20 .50
108 Rich Hill .12 .30
109 Tim Hudson .20 .50
110 Ryan Zimmerman .20 .50
111 Roy Oswalt .20 .50
112 Nick Swisher .20 .50
113 Raul Ibanez .20 .50
114 Kelly Johnson .12 .30
115 Alex Rios .12 .30
116 John Lackey .20 .50
117 Robinson Cano .20 .50
118 Michael Young .12 .30
119 Jeff Francis .12 .30
120 Grady Sizemore .20 .50
121 Mike Lowell .12 .30
122 Aramis Ramirez .12 .30
123 Stephen Drew .12 .30
124 Yovani Gallardo .12 .30
125 Chase Utley .20 .50
126 Dan Haren .12 .30
127 Jose Vidro .12 .30
128 Ronnie Belliard .12 .30
129 Yunel Escobar .12 .30
130 Greg Maddux .40 1.00
131 Garret Anderson .12 .30
132 Aubrey Huff .12 .30
133 Paul Konerko .20 .50
134 Dan Uggla .12 .30
135 Roy Halladay .20 .50
136 Andre Ethier .20 .50
137 Orlando Hernandez .12 .30
138 Troy Tulowitzki .30 .75
139 Carlos Guillen .12 .30
140 Scott Kazmir .20 .50
141 Aaron Rowand .12 .30
142 Jim Edmonds .20 .50
143 Jermaine Dye .12 .30
144 Orlando Hudson .12 .30
145 Derrek Lee .12 .30
146 Travis Buck .20 .50
147 Zack Greinke .30 .75
148 Jeff Kent .12 .30
149 John Smoltz .30 .75
150 David Wright .20 .50
151 Joba Chamberlain .12 .30
152 Adam LaRoche .12 .30
153 Kevin Youkilis .12 .30
154 Troy Glaus .20 .50
155 Nick Johnson .12 .30
156 J.J. Hardy .12 .30
157 Felix Hernandez .20 .50
158 Khalil Greene .12 .30
159 Gary Sheffield .12 .30
160 Albert Pujols .40 1.00
161 Chuck James .12 .30
162 Rocco Baldelli .12 .30
163 Eric Byrnes .12 .30
164 Brad Hawpe .12 .30
165 Delmon Young .20 .50
166 Chris Young .12 .30
167 Brian Roberts .12 .30
168 Russell Martin .12 .30
169 Hank Blalock .12 .30
170 Yadier Molina .40 1.00
171 Jeremy Guthrie .12 .30
172 Chipper Jones .30 .75
173 Johnny Damon .20 .50
174 Ryan Garko .12 .30
175 Jake Peavy .12 .30
176 Chone Figgins .12 .30
177 Edgar Renteria .12 .30
178 Jim Thome .20 .50
179 Carlos Pena .20 .50
180 Corey Patterson .12 .30
181 Dustin Pedroia .30 .75
182 Brett Myers .12 .30
183 Josh Hamilton .20 .50
184 Randy Johnson .30 .75
185 Ichiro Suzuki .40 1.00
186 Aaron Hill .12 .30
187 Jarrod Saltalamacchia .12 .30
188 Michael Cuddyer .12 .30
189 Jeff Francoeur .20 .50
190 Derek Jeter .75 2.00
191 Curtis Granderson .20 .50
192 James Loney .12 .30
193 Brian Bannister .12 .30
194 Carlos Lee .12 .30
195 Pedro Martinez .20 .50
196 Asdrubal Cabrera .20 .50
197 Kenji johjima .12 .30
198 Bartolo Colon .12 .30
199 Jacoby Ellsbury .25 .60
200 Ryan Howard .20 .50
201 Radhames Liz RC .25 .60
202 Justin Ruggiano RC .25 .60
203 Lance Broadway (RC) .15 .40
204 Joey Votto (RC) 1.25 3.00
205 Billy Buckner (RC) .15 .40
206 Joe Koshansky (RC) .15 .40
207 Ross Detwiler RC .25 .60
208 Chin-Lung Hu (RC) .15 .40
209 Luke Hochevar RC .25 .60
210 Jeff Clement (RC) .25 .60
211 Troy Patton (RC) .15 .40
212 Hiroki Kuroda RC .40 1.00
213 Emilio Bonifacio RC .40 1.00
214 Armando Galarraga RC .25 .60
215 Josh Anderson (RC) .15 .40
216 Nick Blackburn RC .25 .60
217 Seth Smith (RC) .15 .40
218 Jonathan Meloan RC .25 .60
219 Alberto Gonzalez RC .25 .60
220 Josh Banks (RC) .15 .40
221 Clay Buchholz AU (RC) 5.00 12.00
222 Nyjer Morgan AU (RC) 4.00 10.00
223 Brandon Jones AU RC 4.00 10.00
224 Sam Fuld AU RC 5.00 12.00
225 Daric Barton AU (RC) 4.00 10.00
226 Chris Seddon AU (RC) 4.00 10.00
227 J.R. Towles AU RC 4.00 10.00
228 Steve Pearce AU RC 15.00 40.00
229 Ross Ohlendorf AU RC 4.00 10.00
230 Clint Sammons AU (RC) 4.00 10.00

2008 Bowman Blue

*BLUE 1-200: 2X TO 5X BASIC
*BLUE 201-220: 2X TO 5X BASIC
*BLUE AU 221-230: .4X TO 1X BASIC AU
1-220 ODDS 1:14 HOBBY,1:32 RETAIL
221-230 AU ODDS 1:620 HOBBY
STATED PRINT RUN 500 SERIAL #'d SETS

2008 Bowman Gold

*GOLD 1-200: 1.2X TO 3X BASIC
*GOLD 201-220: 1.2X TO 3X BASIC
OVERALL GOLD ODDS 1 PER PACK

2008 Bowman Orange

*ORANGE 1-200: 2.5X TO 6X BASIC
*ORANGE 201-220: 2.5X TO 6X BASIC
*ORANGE AU 221-230: .5X TO 1.2X BASIC AU
1-220 ODDS 1:26 HOBBY,1:65 RETAIL
221-230 AU ODDS 1:1160 HOBBY
STATED PRINT RUN 250 SERIAL #'d SETS

2008 Bowman Red

1-220 ODDS 1:4512 HOBBY
221-230 AU ODDS 1:243,648 HOBBY
STATED PRINT RUN 1 SER.#'d SET
NO PRICING DUE TO SCARCITY

2008 Bowman Prospects

COMPLETE SET (110) 12.50 30.00
PRINTING PLATE ODDS 1:732 HOBBY
PLATE PRINT RUN 1 SET PER COLOR
BLACK-CYAN-MAGENTA-YELLOW ISSUED
NO PLATE PRICING DUE TO SCARCITY
BP1 Max Sapp .15 .40
BP2 Jamie Richmond .15 .40
BP3 Darren Ford .15 .40
BP4 Sergio Romo .75 2.00
BP5 Jacob Butler .15 .40
BP6 Glenn Gibson .15 .40
BP7 Tom Hagan .15 .40
BP8 Michael McCormick .15 .40
BP9 Gregorio Petit .25 .60
BP10 Bobby Parnell .15 .40
BP11 Jeff Kindel .25 .60
BP12 Anthony Claggett .25 .60
BP13 Christopher Frey .15 .40
BP14 Jonah Nickerson .25 .60
BP15 Anthony Martinez .15 .40
BP16 Rusty Ryal .25 .60
BP17 Justin Berg .25 .60
BP18 Gerardo Parra .15 .40
BP19 Wesley Wright .15 .40
BP20 Stephen Chapman .15 .40
BP21 Chance Chapman .15 .40
BP22 Brett Pill .50 1.25
BP23 Zachary Phillips .25 .60
BP24 John Raynor .40 1.00
BP25 Danny Duffy .40 1.00
BP26 Brian Finegan .15 .40
BP27 Jonathan Venters .15 .40
BP28 Steve Tolleson .15 .40
BP29 Ben Jukich .25 .60
BP30 Matthew Weston .15 .40
BP31 Kyle Mura .15 .40
BP32 Luke Hetherington .15 .40
BP33 Michael Daniel .25 .60
BP34 Jake Renshaw .15 .40
BP35 Greg Halman .25 .60
BP36 Ryan Khoury .15 .40
BP37 Ryan Ouellette .15 .40
BP38 Mike Brantley .40 1.00
BP39 Eric Brown .15 .40
BP40 Jose Duarte .15 .40
BP41 Eli Tintor .15 .40
BP42 Kent Sakamoto .15 .40
BP43 Luke Montz .15 .40
BP44 Alex Cobb .15 .40
BP45 Michael McKenry .15 .40
BP46 Javier Castillo .15 .40
BP47 Jeffrey Stevens .15 .40
BP48 Greg Burns .15 .40
BP49 Blake Johnson .15 .40
BP50 Austin Jackson .75 2.00
BP51 Anthony Recker .15 .40
BP52 Luis Durango .15 .40
BP53 Engel Beltre .50 1.25
BP54 Seth Bynum .15 .40
BP55 Ryan Strieby .25 .60
BP56 Iggy Suarez .15 .40
BP57 Ryan Morris .25 .60
BP58 Scott Van Slyke .50 1.25
BP59 Tyler Kolodny .50 1.25
BP60 Joseph Martinez .15 .40
BP61 Aaron Mathews .15 .40
BP62 Phillip Cuadrado .15 .40
BP63 Alex Liddi .25 .60
BP64 Alex Burnett .25 .60
BP65 Brian Barton .25 .60
BP66 David Welch .15 .40
BP67 Kyle Reynolds .15 .40
BP68 Francisco Hernandez .15 .40
BP69 Logan Morrison .75 2.00
BP70 Ronald Ramirez .15 .40
BP71 Brad Miller .15 .40
BP72 Braedyn Pruitt .25 .60
BP73 Jason Fernandez .25 .60
BP74 Joseph Mahoney .15 .40
BP75 Quentin Davis .25 .60
BP76 P.J. Walters .15 .40
BP77 Jordan Czarniecki .15 .40
BP78 Jonathan Mota .15 .40
BP79 Michael Hernandez .15 .40
BP80 James Guerrero .15 .40
BP81 Chris Johnson .25 .60
BP82 Daniel Cortes .40 1.00
BP83 Sal Sanchez .25 .60
BP84 Sean Henry .15 .40
BP85 Caleb Gindl .15 .40
BP86 Tommy Everidge .15 .40
BP87 Matt Rizzotti .15 .40
BP88 Luis Munoz .15 .40
BP89 Matthew Klimas .15 .40
BP90 Angel Reyes .15 .40
BP91 Sean Danielson .15 .40
BP92 Omar Poveda .15 .40
BP93 Mario Lisson .15 .40
BP94 Brian Mathews .15 .40
BP95 Matthew Buschmann .15 .40
BP96 Greg Thomson .15 .40
BP97 Matt Inouye .15 .40
BP98 Aneury Rodriguez .25 .60
BP99 Brad Harman .25 .60
BP100 Aaron Bates .40 1.00
BP101 Graham Taylor .15 .40
BP102 Ken Holmberg .15 .40
BP103 Greg Dowling .15 .40
BP104 Ronnie Ray .15 .40
BP105 Michael Wlodarczyk .15 .40
BP106 Jose Martinez .25 .60
BP107 Jason Stephens .25 .60
BP108 Will Rhymes .15 .40
BP109 Joey Side .15 .40
BP110 Brandon Waring .25 .60

2008 Bowman Prospects Blue

*BLUE 1-110: 1.2X TO 3X BASIC
1-110 ODDS 1:14 HOBBY,1:32 RETAIL
STATED PRINT RUN 500 SER.#'d SETS

2008 Bowman Prospects Gold

*GOLD 1-110: .75X TO 2X BASIC
OVERALL GOLD ODDS 1 PER PACK

2008 Bowman Prospects Orange

*ORANGE 1-110: 2X TO 5X BASIC
1-110 ODDS 1:26 HOBBY,1:65 RETAIL
STATED PRINT RUN 250 SER.#'d SETS

2008 Bowman Prospects Red

STATED ODDS 1:4512 HOBBY
STATED PRINT RUN 1 SER.#'d SET
NO PRICING DUE TO SCARCITY

2008 Bowman Scouts Autographs

GROUP A ODDS 1:176 HOB,1:410 RET
GROUP B ODDS 1:390 HOB,1:910 RET
EXCHANGE DEADLINE 5/31/2010
AS Alex Smith B 3.00 8.00
BB Bill Buck B 3.00 8.00
BE Bob Engle B 3.00 8.00
BF Bob Fontaine Jr. A 3.00 8.00
BS Bowman Scout A 3.00 8.00
CB Chris Bourjos A 3.00 8.00
DJ Dave Jennings B 3.00 8.00
DL Don Lyle B 3.00 8.00
DO Dan Ontiveros B 3.00 8.00
JC Jerome Cochran B EXCH 3.00 8.00
JD Jon Deeble A EXCH 3.00 8.00
JH Josue Herrera B 3.00 8.00
JL Jerry Lafferty A 3.00 8.00
JM Joe Mason B 3.00 8.00
LW Leon Wurth A 3.00 8.00
MR Mike Rizzo A 3.00 8.00
RA Ralph Avila A 3.00 8.00
TC Ty Coslow A 3.00 8.00
TCU Tom Couston A 3.00 8.00
TD Tony DeMacio A 3.00 8.00
TK Tim Kelly B 3.00 8.00

2008 Bowman Signs of the Future

GROUP A ODDS 1:26 RETAIL
GROUP B ODDS 1:305 RETAIL
EXCHANGE DEADLINE 5/31/2010
PLATE PRINT RUN 1 SET PER COLOR
BLACK-CYAN-MAGENTA-YELLOW ISSUED
NO PLATE PRICING DUE TO SCARCITY
AC Adam Carr 3.00 8.00
BK Brad Knox 3.00 8.00
BO Brian Omogrosso 3.00 8.00
BW Brian Wilson 10.00 25.00
CN Chris Nowak 4.00 10.00
CR Colby Rasmus 3.00 8.00
CT Clayton Tanner 3.00 8.00
CTI Chris Tillman 4.00 10.00
DS David Shafer 3.00 8.00
EJ Elliot Johnson 3.00 8.00
GM Garrett Mock 3.00 8.00
GP Gerardo Parra 8.00 20.00
GS Greg Smith 4.00 10.00
JE Jack Egbert 3.00 8.00
JG Jaime Garcia 6.00 15.00
JH Joel Hanrahan 5.00 12.00
JHI Jamar Hill 3.00 8.00
JHU Jon Huber 3.00 8.00
JJ Jason Jaramillo 3.00 8.00
JK Josh Kroeger 3.00 8.00
JL Jeff Locke 6.00 15.00
JM Jose Mijares EXCH 3.00 8.00
JV Jonathan Van Every 3.00 8.00
KB Kyle Bloom 3.00 8.00
LM Lou Marson 3.00 8.00
MC Mike Costanzo 3.00 8.00
ME Mitch Einertson 4.00 10.00
MP Matt Peterson 3.00 8.00
RK Ryan Kalish 6.00 15.00
RS Ryan Speier 3.00 8.00
SR Steven Register 3.00 8.00
TC Tyler Colvin 8.00 20.00
TM Tommy Manzella 3.00 8.00
TO Tim Olson 3.00 8.00
WI Will Inman 4.00 10.00

2008 Bowman Draft

COMPLETE SET (55) 10.00 25.00
COMMON CARD (1-55) .20 .50
OVERALL PLATE ODDS 1:750 HOBBY
PLATE PRINT RUN 1 SET PER COLOR
BLACK-CYAN-MAGENTA-YELLOW ISSUED
NO PLATE PRICING DUE TO SCARCITY
BDP1 Nick Adenhart (RC) .20 .50
BDP2 Michael Aubrey RC .30 .75
BDP3 Mike Aviles RC .30 .75
BDP4 Burke Badenhop RC .30 .75
BDP5 Wladimir Balentien (RC) .20 .50
BDP6 Collin Balester (RC) .20 .50
BDP7 Josh Banks (RC) .20 .50
BDP8 Wes Bankston (RC) .20 .50
BDP9 Joey Votto (RC) 1.50 4.00
BDP10 Mitch Boggs (RC) .20 .50
BDP11 Jay Bruce (RC) .60 1.50
BDP12 Chris Carter (RC) .30 .75
BDP13 Justin Christian RC .30 .75
BDP14 Chris Davis RC .40 1.00
BDP15 Blake DeWitt (RC) .30 .75
BDP16 Nick Evans RC .20 .50
BDP17 Jaime Garcia RC .75 2.00
BDP18 Brett Gardner (RC) .50 1.25
BDP19 Carlos Gonzalez (RC) .50 1.25
BDP20 Matt Harrison (RC) .30 .75
BDP21 Micah Hoffpauir RC .60 1.50
BDP22 Nick Hundley (RC) .20 .50
BDP23 Eric Hurley (RC) .20 .50
BDP24 Elliot Johnson (RC) .20 .50
BDP25 Matt Joyce RC .50 1.25
BDP26 Clayton Kershaw RC 6.00 15.00
BDP27 Evan Longoria RC 1.00 2.50
BDP28 Matt Macri (RC) .20 .50
BDP29 Chris Perez RC .30 .75
BDP30 Max Ramirez RC .20 .50
BDP31 Greg Reynolds RC .30 .75
BDP32 Brooks Conrad (RC) .20 .50
BDP33 Max Scherzer RC 2.00 5.00
BDP34 Daryl Thompson (RC) .20 .50
BDP35 Taylor Teagarden RC .30 .75
BDP36 Rich Thompson RC .30 .75
BDP37 Ryan Tucker (RC) .20 .50
BDP38 Jonathan Van Every RC .20 .50
BDP39 Chris Volstad (RC) .20 .50
BDP40 Michael Hollimon RC .20 .50
BDP41 Brad Ziegler RC 1.00 2.50
BDP42 Jamie D'Antona (RC) .20 .50
BDP43 Clayton Richard (RC) .20 .50
BDP44 Edgar Gonzalez (RC) .20 .50
BDP45 Bryan LaHair RC 1.50 4.00
BDP46 Warner Madrigal (RC) .20 .50
BDP47 Reid Brignac (RC) .30 .75
BDP48 David Robertson RC .50 1.25
BDP49 Nick Stavinoha RC .30 .75
BDP50 Jai Miller (RC) .20 .50
BDP51 Charlie Morton (RC) .60 1.50
BDP52 Brandon Boggs (RC) .30 .75
BDP53 Joe Mather RC .30 .75
BDP54 Gregorio Petit RC .30 .75
BDP55 Jeff Samardzija RC .60 1.50

2008 Bowman Draft Blue

*BLUE: 1X TO 2.5X BASIC
STATED ODDS 1:19 HOBBY
STATED PRINT RUN 399 SER.#'d SETS

2008 Bowman Draft Gold

*GOLD: .6X TO 1.5X BASIC
APPX.GOLD ODDS ONE PER PACK

2008 Bowman Draft Red

STATED ODDS 1:6025 HOBBY
STATED PRINT RUN 1 SER.#'d SET
NO PRICING DUE TO SCARCITY

2008 Bowman Draft Prospects

COMPLETE SET (110) 12.50 30.00
COMMON CARD (1-65) .20 .50
OVERALL PLATE ODDS 1:750 HOBBY
PLATE PRINT RUN 1 SET PER COLOR
BLACK-CYAN-MAGENTA-YELLOW ISSUED
NO PLATE PRICING DUE TO SCARCITY
BDPP1 Rick Porcello DP .60 1.50
BDPP2 Braeden Schlehuber DP .20 .50
BDPP3 Kenny Wilson DP .20 .50
BDPP4 Jeff Lanning DP .20 .50
BDPP5 Kevin Dubler DP .20 .50
BDPP6 Eric Campbell DP .30 .75
BDPP7 Tyler Chatwood DP .30 .75
BDPP8 Tyreace House DP .20 .50
BDPP9 Adrian Nieto DP .20 .50
BDPP10 Robbie Grossman DP .30 .75
BDPP11 Jordan Danks DP .50 1.25
BDPP12 Jay Austin DP .20 .50
BDPP13 Ryan Perry DP .30 .75
BDPP14 Ryan Chaffee DP .30 .75
BDPP15 Niko Vasquez DP .50 1.25
BDPP16 Shane Dyer DP .20 .50
BDPP17 Benji Gonzalez DP .20 .50
BDPP18 Miles Reagan DP .20 .50
BDPP19 Anthony Ferrara DP .20 .50
BDPP20 Markus Brisker DP .20 .50
BDPP21 Justin Bristow DP .20 .50
BDPP22 Richard Bleier DP .30 .75
BDPP23 Jeremy Beckham DP .30 .75
BDPP24 Xavier Avery DP .50 1.25
BDPP25 Christian Vazquez DP .75 2.00
BDPP26 Nick Romero DP .20 .50
BDPP27 Trey Watten DP .20 .50
BDPP28 Brett Jacobson DP .20 .50
BDPP29 Tyler Sample DP .20 .50
BDPP30 T.J. Steele DP .30 .75
BDPP31 Christian Friedrich DP .50 1.25
BDPP32 Graham Hicks DP .30 .75
BDPP33 Shane Peterson DP .30 .75
BDPP34 Brett Hunter DP .20 .50

BDPP35 Tim Federowicz DP .30 .75
BDPP36 Isaac Galloway DP .30 .75
BDPP37 Logan Schafer DP .20 .50
BDPP38 Paul Demny DP .20 .50
BDPP39 Clayton Shunick DP .20 .50
BDPP40 Andrew Liebel DP .20 .50
BDPP41 Brandon Crawford DP .50 1.25
BDPP42 Blake Tekotte DP .30 .75
BDPP43 Jason Corder DP .20 .50
BDPP44 Bryan Shaw DP .20 .50
BDPP45 Edgar Olmos DP .20 .50
BDPP46 Dusty Coleman DP .20 .50
BDPP47 Johnny Giavotella DP .60 1.50
BDPP48 Tyson Ross DP .30 .75
BDPP49 Brent Morel DP .30 .75
BDPP50 Dennis Raben DP .30 .75
BDPP51 Jake Odorizzi DP .60 1.50
BDPP52 Ryne White DP .30 .75
BDPP53 Devaris Strange-Gordon DP .60 1.50
BDPP54 Tim Murphy DP .20 .50
BDPP55 Jake Jefferies DP .20 .50
BDPP56 Anthony Capra DP .20 .50
BDPP57 Kyle Weiland DP .50 1.25
BDPP58 Anthony Bass DP .30 .75
BDPP59 Scott Green DP .20 .50
BDPP60 Zeke Spruill DP .50 1.25
BDPP61 L.J. Hoes DP .20 .50
BDPP62 Tyler Cline DP .20 .50
BDPP63 Matt Cerda DP .20 .50
BDPP64 Bobby Lanigan DP .20 .50
BDPP65 Mike Sheridan DP .20 .50
BDPP66 Carlos Carrasco FG .30 .75
BDPP67 Nate Schierholtz FG .20 .50
BDPP68 Jesus Delgado FG .20 .50
BDPP70 Shairon Martis FG .30 .75
BDPP71 Matt LaPorta FG .30 .75
BDPP72 Eddie Morlan FG .20 .50
BDPP73 Greg Golson FG .20 .50
BDPP74 Julio Pimentel FG .20 .50
BDPP75 Dexter Fowler FG .30 .75
BDPP76 Henry Rodriguez FG .20 .50
BDPP77 Cliff Pennington FG .20 .50
BDPP78 Hector Rondon FG .30 .75
BDPP79 Wes Hodges FG .20 .50
BDPP80 Polin Trinidad FG .20 .50
BDPP81 Chris Getz FG .20 .50
BDPP82 Wellington Castillo FG .20 .50
BDPP83 Mat Gamel FG .50 1.25
BDPP84 Pablo Sandoval FG .75 2.00
BDPP85 Jason Donald FG .20 .50
BDPP86 Jesus Montero FG .30 .75
BDPP87 Jamie D'Antona FG .20 .50
BDPP88 Will Inman FG .20 .50
BDPP89 Elvis Andrus FG .50 1.25
BDPP90 Taylor Teagarden FG .30 .75
BDPP91 Scott Campbell FG .20 .50
BDPP92 Jake Arrieta FG .50 1.25
BDPP93 Juan Francisco FG .50 1.25
BDPP94 Lou Marson FG .20 .50
BDPP95 Luke Hughes FG .20 .50
BDPP96 Bryan Anderson FG .20 .50
BDPP97 Ramiro Pena FG .20 .50
BDPP98 Jesse Todd FG .20 .50
BDPP99 Gorkys Hernandez FG .20 .50
BDPP100 Casey Weathers FG .20 .50
BDPP101 Fernando Martinez FG .30 .75
BDPP102 Clayton Richard FG .20 .50
BDPP103 Gerardo Parra FG .20 .50
BDPP104 Kevin Pucetas FG .30 .75
BDPP105 Wilkin Ramirez FG .20 .50
BDPP106 Ryan Mattheus FG .20 .50
BDPP107 Angel Villalona FG .50 1.25
BDPP108 Brett Anderson FG .30 .75
BDPP109 Chris Valaika FG .20 .50
BDPP110 Trevor Cahill FG .50 1.25

2008 Bowman Draft Prospects Blue

*BLUE: 1.5X TO 4X BASIC
STATED ODDS 1:19 HOBBY
STATED PRINT RUN 399 SER.#'d SETS

2008 Bowman Draft Prospects Gold

*GOLD: .75X TO 2X BASIC
APPX.GOLD ODDS ONE PER PACK

2008 Bowman Draft Prospects Red

STATED ODDS 1:6025 HOBBY
STATED PRINT RUN 1 SER.#'d SET
NO PRICING DUE TO SCARCITY

2008 Bowman Draft Prospects Jerseys

RANDOM INSERTS IN RETAIL PACKS
NO PRICING DUE TO LACK OF MARKET INFO
BDPP71 Matt LaPorta FG 3.00 8.00
BDPP75 Dexter Fowler FG 3.00 8.00

2008 Bowman Draft Signs of the Future

RANDOM INSERTS IN RETAIL PACKS
AC Adrain Cardenas 4.00 10.00
BP Billy Petrick 3.00 8.00
BS Brad Salmon 3.00 8.00
CW Corey Wimberly 6.00 15.00
DM Daniel Murphy 20.00 50.00
DS David Shafer 3.00 8.00
EM Evan MaClane 3.00 8.00
FG Freddy Galvis 3.00 8.00
GK George Kontos 3.00 8.00
JW Johnny Whittleman 3.00 8.00
KD Kyle Drabek 6.00 15.00
OP Omar Poveda 3.00 8.00
OS Oswaldo Sosa 3.00 8.00
TD Travis D'Arnaud 4.00 10.00
TS Travis Snider 5.00 12.00

2009 Bowman

COMP.SET w/o AU's (220) 12.50 30.00
COMMON CARD (1-190) .12 .30
COMMON ROOKE (66/191-220) .25 .60
COMMON AU RC (221-230) 4.00 10.00
PLATE PRINT RUN 1 SET PER COLOR
BLACK-CYAN-MAGENTA-YELLOW ISSUED
NO PLATE PRICING DUE TO SCARCITY
1 David Wright .25 .60
2 Albert Pujols .40 1.00
3 Alex Rodriguez .40 1.00
4 Chase Utley .20 .50
5 Chien-Ming Wang .20 .50
6 Jimmy Rollins .20 .50
7 Ken Griffey Jr. .60 1.50
8 Manny Ramirez .30 .75
9 Chipper Jones .30 .75
10 Ichiro Suzuki .40 1.00
11 Justin Morneau .20 .50
12 Hanley Ramirez .20 .50
13 Cliff Lee .20 .50
14 Ryan Howard .25 .60
15 Ian Kinsler .20 .50
16 Jose Reyes .20 .50
17 Ted Lilly .12 .30
18 Miguel Cabrera .30 .75
19 Nate McLouth .12 .30
20 Josh Beckett .12 .30
21 John Lackey .20 .50
22 David Ortiz .30 .75
23 Carlos Lee .12 .30
24 Adam Dunn .20 .50
25 B.J. Upton .20 .50
26 Curtis Granderson .25 .60
27 David DeJesus .12 .30
28 CC Sabathia .20 .50
29 Russell Martin .12 .30
30 Torii Hunter .12 .30
31 Rich Harden .12 .30
32 Johnny Damon .20 .50
33 Cristian Guzman .12 .30
34 Grady Sizemore .20 .50
35 Jorge Posada .20 .50
36 Placido Polanco .12 .30
37 Ryan Ludwick .20 .50
38 Dustin Pedroia .30 .75
39 Matt Garza .12 .30
40 Prince Fielder .20 .50
41 Rick Ankiel .12 .30
42 Jonathan Sanchez .12 .30
43 Erik Bedard .12 .30
44 Ryan Braun .20 .50
45 Ervin Santana .12 .30
46 Brian Roberts .12 .30
47 Mike Jacobs .12 .30
48 Phil Hughes .12 .30
49 Justin Masterson .12 .30
50 Felix Hernandez .20 .50
51 Stephen Drew .12 .30
52 Bobby Abreu .12 .30
53 Jay Bruce .20 .50
54 Josh Hamilton .20 .50
55 Garrett Atkins .12 .30
56 Jacoby Ellsbury .25 .60
57 Johan Santana .20 .50
58 James Shields .12 .30
59 Armando Galarraga .12 .30
60 Carlos Pena .20 .50
61 Matt Kemp .25 .60
62 Joey Votto .30 .75
63 Raul Ibanez .20 .50
64 Casey Kotchman .12 .30
65 Hunter Pence .20 .50
66 Daniel Murphy RC 1.00 2.50
67 Carlos Beltran .20 .50
68 Evan Longoria .20 .50
69 Daisuke Matsuzaka .20 .50
70 Cole Hamels .25 .60
71 Robinson Cano .20 .50
72 Clayton Kershaw .50 1.25
73 Kenji Johjima .20 .50
74 Kazuo Matsui .12 .30
75 Jayson Werth .20 .50
76 Brian McCann .20 .50
77 Barry Zito .20 .50
78 Glen Perkins .12 .30
79 Jeff Francoeur .20 .50
80 Derek Jeter .75 2.00
81 Ryan Doumit .12 .30
82 Dan Haren .12 .30
83 Justin Duchscherer .12 .30
84 Marlon Byrd .12 .30
85 Derek Lowe .12 .30
86 Pat Burrell .12 .30
87 Jair Jurrjens .12 .30
88 Zack Greinke .30 .75
89 Jon Lester .20 .50
90 Justin Verlander .30 .75
91 Jorge Cantu .12 .30
92 John Maine .12 .30
93 Brad Hawpe .12 .30
94 Mike Aviles .12 .30
95 Victor Martinez .20 .50
96 Ryan Dempster .12 .30
97 Miguel Tejada .20 .50
98 Joe Mauer .25 .60
99 Scott Olsen .12 .30
100 Tim Lincecum .20 .50
101 Francisco Liriano .12 .30
102 Chris Iannetta .12 .30
103 Jamie Moyer .12 .30
104 Milton Bradley .12 .30
105 John Lannan .12 .30
106 Yovani Gallardo .12 .30
107 Xavier Nady .12 .30
108 Jermaine Dye .12 .30
109 Dioner Navarro .12 .30
110 Joba Chamberlain .12 .30
111 Nelson Cruz .30 .75
112 Johnny Cueto .20 .50
113 Adam LaRoche .12 .30
114 Aaron Rowand .12 .30
115 Jason Bay .20 .50
116 Aaron Cook .12 .30
117 Mark Teixeira .20 .50
118 Gavin Floyd .12 .30
119 Magglio Ordonez .20 .50
120 Rafael Furcal .12 .30
121 Mark Buehrle .20 .50
122 Alexi Casilla .12 .30
123 Scott Kazmir .12 .30
124 Nick Swisher .20 .50
125 Carlos Gomez .12 .30
126 Javier Vazquez .12 .30
127 Paul Konerko .20 .50
128 Ronnie Belliard .12 .30
129 Pat Neshek .20 .50
130 Josh Johnson .20 .50
131 Carlos Zambrano .20 .50
132 Chris Davis .20 .50
133 Bobby Crosby .12 .30
134 Alex Gordon .20 .50
135 Chris Young .12 .30
136 Carlos Delgado .12 .30
137 Adam Wainwright .20 .50
138 Justin Upton .20 .50
139 Tim Hudson .20 .50
140 J.D. Drew .12 .30
141 Adam Lind .12 .30
142 Mike Lowell .12 .30
143 Lance Berkman .20 .50
144 J.J. Hardy .12 .30
145 A.J. Burnett .12 .30
146 Jake Peavy .12 .30
147 Blake DeWitt .12 .30
148 Matt Holliday .30 .75
149 Carl Crawford .20 .50
150 Andre Ethier .20 .50
151 Howie Kendrick .12 .30
152 Ryan Zimmerman .20 .50
153 Troy Tulowitzki .30 .75
154 Brett Myers .12 .30
155 Chris Young .12 .30
156 Jered Weaver .20 .50
157 Jeff Clement .12 .30
158 Alex Rios .12 .30
159 Shane Victorino .12 .30
160 Jeremy Hermida .12 .30
161 James Loney .12 .30
162 Michael Young .12 .30
163 Aramis Ramirez .12 .30
164 Geovany Soto .20 .50
165 Aubrey Huff .12 .30
166 Delmon Young .20 .50
167 Vernon Wells .12 .30
168 Chone Figgins .12 .30
169 Carlos Quentin .12 .30
170 Chad Billingsley .20 .50
171 Matt Cain .20 .50
172 Derrek Lee .12 .30
173 A.J. Pierzynski .12 .30
174 Collin Balester .12 .30
175 Greg Smith .12 .30
176 Alfonso Soriano .20 .50
177 Adrian Gonzalez .25 .60
178 George Sherrill .12 .30
179 Nick Markakis .25 .60
180 Brandon Webb .20 .50
181 Vladimir Guerrero .20 .50
182 Roy Oswalt .20 .50
183 Adam Jones .20 .50
184 Edinson Volquez .12 .30
185 Yunel Escobar .12 .30
186 Joe Saunders .12 .30
187 Yadier Molina .40 1.00
188 Kevin Youkilis .12 .30
189 Dan Uggla .12 .30
190 Kosuke Fukudome .20 .50
191 Matt Antonelli RC .40 1.00
192 Jeff Baisley RC .25 .60
193 Jason Bourgeois (RC) .25 .60
194 Michael Bowden (RC) .25 .60
195 Andrew Carpenter RC .40 1.00
196 Phil Coke RC .40 1.00
197 Aaron Cunningham RC .25 .60
198 Alcides Escobar RC .40 1.00
199 Dexter Fowler (RC) .40 1.00
200 Mat Gamel RC .60 1.50
201 Josh Geer (RC) .25 .60
202 Greg Golson (RC) .25 .60
203 John Jaso RC .25 .60
204 Kila Ka'aihue (RC) .40 1.00
205 George Kottaras (RC) .25 .60
206 Lou Marson (RC) .25 .60
207 Shairon Martis RC .40 1.00
208 Juan Miranda RC .40 1.00
209 Luke Montz RC .25 .60
210 Jonathon Niese RC .40 1.00
211 Bobby Parnell RC .40 1.00
212 Fernando Perez (RC) .25 .60
213 David Price RC .50 1.25
214 Angel Salome (RC) .25 .60
215 Gaby Sanchez RC .40 1.00
216 Freddy Sandoval (RC) .25 .60
217 Travis Snider RC .40 1.00
218 Will Venable RC .25 .60
219 Edwin Maysonet RC .25 .60
220 Josh Outman RC .40 1.00
221 Luke Montz AU 4.00 10.00
222 Kila Ka'aihue AU 4.00 10.00
223 Conor Gillaspie AU RC 4.00 10.00
224 Aaron Cunningham AU 4.00 10.00
225 Mat Gamel AU 6.00 15.00
226 Matt Antonelli AU 4.00 10.00
227 Robert Parnell AU 4.00 10.00
228 Jose Mijares AU RC 4.00 10.00
229 Josh Geer AU 4.00 10.00
230 Shairon Martis AU 6.00 15.00

2009 Bowman Blue

*BLUE 1-190: 2X TO 5X BASIC
*BLUE 66/191-220: 1.5X TO 4X BASIC
*BLUE AU 221-230: .4X TO 1X BASIC AU
1-220 ODDS 1:12 HOBBY
STATED PRINT RUN 500 SER.#'d SETS

2009 Bowman Gold

*GOLD 1-190: 1.2X TO 3X BASIC
*GOLD 66/191-220: 1X TO 2.5X BASIC
OVERALL GOLD ODDS 1 PER PACK

2009 Bowman Orange

*ORANGE 1-190: 2.5X TO 6X BASIC
*ORANGE 66/191-220: 2X TO 5X BASIC
*ORANGE AU 221-230: .5X TO 1.2X BASIC AU
1-220 ODDS 1:24 HOBBY
STATED PRINT RUN 250 SER.#'d SETS

2009 Bowman Checklists

RANDOM INSERTS IN PACKS
1 Checklist 1 .12 .30
2 Checklist 2 .12 .30
3 Checklist 3 .12 .30

2009 Bowman Major League Scout Autographs

SCBB Billy Blitzer 3.00 8.00
SCCJ Clarence Johns 3.00 8.00
SCDC Darrell Conner 3.00 8.00
SCFR Fred Repke 3.00 8.00
SCLP Larry Pardo 3.00 8.00
SCMW Mark Wilson 3.00 8.00
SCPC Paul Cogan 3.00 8.00
SCPD Pat Daugherty 3.00 8.00

2009 Bowman Prospects

COMPLETE SET (90) 15.00 40.00
PLATE PRINT RUN 1 SET PER COLOR
BLACK-CYAN-MAGENTA-YELLOW ISSUED
NO PLATE PRICING DUE TO SCARCITY
BP1 Neftali Feliz .25 .60
BP2 Oscar Tejeda .50 1.25
BP3 Greg Veloz .15 .40
BP4 Julio Teheran .50 1.25
BP5 Michael Almanzar .25 .60
BP6 Stolmy Pimentel .25 .60
BP7 Matthew Moore 1.25 3.00
BP8 Jericho Jones .15 .40
BP9 Kelvin de la Cruz .40 1.00
BP10 Jose Ceda .15 .40
BP11 Jesse Darcy .15 .40
BP12 Kenneth Gilbert .15 .40
BP13 Will Smith .25 .60
BP14 Samuel Freeman .15 .40
BP15 Adam Reifer .15 .40
BP16 Ehire Adrianza .40 1.00
BP17 Michael Pineda .40 1.00
BP18 Jordan Walden .25 .60
BP19 Angel Morales .25 .60
BP20 Neil Ramirez .15 .40
BP21 Kyeong Kang .25 .60
BP22 Luis Jimenez .15 .40
BP23 Tyler Flowers .40 1.00
BP24 Petey Paramore .25 .60
BP25 Jeremy Hamilton .15 .40
BP26 Tyler Yockey .25 .60
BP27 Sawyer Carroll .25 .60
BP28 Jeremy Farrell .15 .40
BP29 Tyson Brummett .15 .40
BP30 Alex Buchholz .25 .60
BP31 Luis Sumoza .25 .60
BP32 Jonathan Waltenbury .25 .60
BP33 Edgar Osuna .15 .40
BP34 Curt Smith .15 .40
BP35 Evan Bigley .25 .60
BP36 Miguel Fermin .15 .40
BP37 Ben Lasater .15 .40
BP38 David Freese .50 1.25
BP39 Jon Kibler .25 .60
BP40 Cristian Beltre .25 .60
BP41 Alfredo Figaro .15 .40
BP42 Marc Rzepczynski .25 .60
BP43 Joshua Collmenter .25 .60
BP44 Adam Mills .15 .40
BP45 Wilson Ramos .50 1.25
BP46 Esmil Rogers .15 .40
BP47 Jon Mark Owings .15 .40
BP48 Chris Johnson .25 .60
BP49 Abraham Almonte .15 .40
BP50 Patrick Ryan .15 .40
BP51 Yefri Carvajal .40 1.00
BP52 Ruben Tejada .15 .40
BP53 Edilio Colina .25 .60
BP54 Wilber Bucardo .25 .60
BP55 Nelson Perez .25 .60
BP56 Andrew Rundle .25 .60
BP57 Anthony Ortega .15 .40
BP58 Wilin Rosario .25 .60
BP59 Parker Frazier .15 .40
BP60 Kyle Farrell .15 .40
BP61 Erik Komatsu .25 .60
BP62 Michael Stutes .15 .40
BP63 David Genao .25 .60
BP64 Jack Cawley .15 .40
BP65 Jacob Goldberg .15 .40
BP66 Jarred Bogany .15 .40
BP67 Jason McEachern .15 .40
BP68 Matt Rigoli .15 .40
BP69 Jose Duran .25 .60
BP70 Justin Greene .25 .60
BP71 Nino Leyja .25 .60
BP72 Michael Swinson .25 .60
BP73 Miguel Flores .25 .60
BP74 Nick Buss .15 .40
BP75 Brett Oberholtzer .25 .60
BP76 Pat McAnaney .25 .60
BP77 Sean Conner .15 .40
BP78 Ryan Verdugo .25 .60
BP79 Will Atwood .15 .40
BP80 Tommy Johnson .40 1.00
BP81 Rene Garcia .25 .60
BP82 Robert Brooks .25 .60
BP83 Seth Garrison .15 .40
BP84 Steven Upchurch .15 .40
BP85 Zach Moore .15 .40
BP86 Derrick Phillips .15 .40
BP87 Dominic De La Osa .40 1.00
BP88 Jose Barajas .15 .40
BP89 Bryan Petersen .15 .40
BP90 Michael Cisco .25 .60

2009 Bowman Prospects Blue

*BLUE: 1.2X TO 3X BASIC
STATED ODDS 1:12 HOBBY
STATED PRINT RUN 500 SER.#'d SETS
BP17 Michael Pineda 10.00 25.00

2009 Bowman Prospects Gold

*GOLD: 1X TO 2.5X BASIC
OVERALL GOLD ODDS 1 PER PACK

2009 Bowman Prospects Orange

*ORANGE: 2X TO 5X BASIC
STATED ODDS 1:24 HOBBY
STATED PRINT RUN 250 SER.#'d SETS

2009 Bowman Prospects Autographs

BPAAH Anthony Hewitt 5.00 12.00
BPABH Brad Hand 5.00 12.00
BPADG Deolis Guerra 5.00 12.00
BPAGB Gordon Beckham 5.00 12.00
BPAGK George Kontos 5.00 12.00
BPAJK Jason Knapp 5.00 12.00
BPANG Nick Gorneault 5.00 12.00
BPABP Buster Posey 30.00 80.00
BPARK Ryan Kalish 5.00 12.00
BPATD Travis D'Arnaud 5.00 12.00

2009 Bowman WBC Prospects

COMPLETE SET (20) 6.00 15.00
PLATE PRINT RUN 1 SET PER COLOR
BLACK-CYAN-MAGENTA-YELLOW ISSUED
NO PLATE PRICING DUE TO SCARCITY
BW1 Yu Darvish 1.50 4.00
BW2 Phillippe Aumont .60 1.50
BW3 Concepcion Rodriguez .40 1.00
BW4 Michel Enriquez .40 1.00
BW5 Yulieski Gourriel 1.25 3.00
BW6 Shinnosuke Abe .60 1.50
BW7 Gift Ngoepe .40 1.00
BW8 Dylan Lindsay .60 1.50
BW9 Nick Weglarz .40 1.00
BW10 Mitch Dening .40 1.00
BW11 Justin Erasmus .40 1.00
BW12 Aroldis Chapman 2.00 5.00
BW13 Alex Liddi .60 1.50
BW14 Alexander Smit .40 1.00
BW15 Juan Carlos Sulbaran .40 1.00
BW16 Cheng-Min Peng .60 1.50
BW17 Chenhao Li .40 1.00
BW18 Tao Bu .40 1.00
BW19 Gregory Halman .60 1.50
BW20 Fu-Te Ni .60 1.50

2009 Bowman WBC Prospects Blue

*BLUE: 1.2X TO 3X BASIC
STATED ODDS 1:12 HOBBY
BW1 Yu Darvish 8.00 20.00

2009 Bowman WBC Prospects Gold

*GOLD: .75X TO 2X BASIC
OVERALL GOLD ODDS ONE PER PACK

2009 Bowman WBC Prospects Orange

*ORANGE: 1.5X TO 4X BASIC
STATED ODDS 1:24 HOBBY
BW1 Yu Darvish 15.00 40.00

2009 Bowman WBC Prospects Red

STATED ODDS 1:2720 HOBBY
STATED PRINT RUN 1 SER.#'d SETS
NO PRICING DUE TO SCARCITY

2009 Bowman Draft

COMPLETE SET (55) 6.00 15.00
COMMON CARD (1-55) .20 .50
OVERALL PLATE ODDS 1:1531 HOBBY
PLATE PRINT RUN 1 SET PER COLOR
BLACK-CYAN-MAGENTA-YELLOW ISSUED
NO PLATE PRICING DUE TO SCARCITY
BDP1 Tommy Hanson RC .50 1.25
BDP2 Jeff Manship RC .20 .50
BDP3 Trevor Bell (RC) .20 .50
BDP4 Trevor Cahill RC .50 1.25
BDP5 Trent Oeltjen (RC) .20 .50
BDP6 Wyatt Toregas RC .20 .50
BDP7 Kevin Mulvey RC .20 .50
BDP8 Rusty Ryal RC .20 .50
BDP9 Mike Carp (RC) .30 .75
BDP10 Jorge Padilla (RC) .20 .50
BDP11 J.D. Martin (RC) .20 .50
BDP12 Dusty Ryan RC .20 .50
BDP13 Alex Avila RC .60 1.50
BDP14 Brandon Allen (RC) .20 .50
BDP15 Tommy Everidge (RC) .30 .75
BDP16 Bud Norris RC .20 .50
BDP17 Neftali Feliz RC .30 .75
BDP18 Mat Latos RC .60 1.50
BDP19 Ryan Perry RC .50 1.25
BDP20 Craig Tatum (RC) .20 .50
BDP21 Chris Tillman RC .30 .75
BDP22 Jhoulys Chacin RC .30 .75
BDP23 Michael Saunders RC .50 1.25
BDP24 Jeff Stevens RC .20 .50
BDP25 Luis Valdez RC .20 .50
BDP26 Robert Manuel RC .20 .50
BDP27 Ryan Webb (RC) .20 .50
BDP28 Marc Rzepczynski RC .30 .75
BDP29 Travis Schlichting (RC) .30 .75
BDP30 Barbaro Canizares RC .20 .50
BDP31 Brad Mills RC .20 .50
BDP32 Dusty Brown (RC) .20 .50
BDP33 Tim Wood RC .20 .50
BDP34 Drew Sutton RC .30 .75
BDP35 Jarrett Hoffpauir (RC) .20 .50
BDP36 Jose Lobaton RC .20 .50
BDP37 Aaron Bates RC .20 .50
BDP38 Clayton Mortensen RC .20 .50
BDP39 Ryan Sadowski RC .20 .50
BDP40 Fu-Te Ni RC .30 .75
BDP41 Casey McGehee (RC) .20 .50
BDP42 Omir Santos RC .20 .50
BDP43 Brent Leach RC .30 .75
BDP44 Diory Hernandez RC .20 .50
BDP45 Wilkin Castillo RC .20 .50
BDP46 Trevor Crowe RC .20 .50
BDP47 Sean West (RC) .30 .75
BDP48 Clayton Richard (RC) .20 .50
BDP49 Julio Borbon RC .20 .50
BDP50 Kyle Blanks RC .30 .75
BDP51 Jeff Gray RC .20 .50
BDP52 Gio Gonzalez (RC) .30 .75
BDP53 Vin Mazzaro RC .20 .50
BDP54 Josh Reddick RC .30 .75
BDP55 Fernando Martinez RC .50 1.25

2009 Bowman Draft Blue

*BLUE: 1.5X TO 4X BASIC
STATED ODDS 1:12 HOBBY
STATED PRINT RUN 399 SER.#'d SETS

2009 Bowman Draft Gold

*GOLD: .75X TO 2X BASIC
APPX.GOLD ODDS ONE PER PACK

2009 Bowman Draft Prospect Autographs

RANDOM INSERTS IN RETAIL PACKS
AH Anthony Hewitt 5.00 12.00
BH Brad Hand 3.00 8.00
BP Buster Posey 60.00 120.00
JK Jason Knapp 3.00 8.00
LC Lonnie Chisenhall 3.00 8.00
LM Logan Morrison 5.00 12.00
MI Michael Inoa 3.00 8.00
MM Michael Moustakas 8.00 20.00
ZC Zach Collier 5.00 12.00

2009 Bowman Draft Prospects

COMPLETE SET (75) 8.00 20.00
OVERALL PLATE ODDS 1:1531 HOBBY
PLATE PRINT RUN 1 SET PER COLOR
BLACK-CYAN-MAGENTA-YELLOW ISSUED
NO PLATE PRICING DUE TO SCARCITY
BDPP1 Tanner Bushue .30 .75
BDPP2 Billy Hamilton .60 1.50
BDPP3 Enrique Hernandez 2.50 6.00
BDPP4 Virgil Hill .20 .50
BDPP5 Josh Hodges .30 .75
BDPP6 Christopher Lovett .20 .50
BDPP7 Michael Belfiore .20 .50
BDPP8 Jobduan Morales .20 .50
BDPP9 Anthony Morris .20 .50
BDPP10 Telvin Nash .60 1.50
BDPP11 Brooks Pounders .30 .75
BDPP12 Kyle Rose .20 .50
BDPP13 Seth Schwindenhammer .30 .75
BDPP14 Patrick Lehman .30 .75
BDPP15 Mathew Weaver .30 .75
BDPP16 Brian Dozier 1.00 2.50
BDPP17 Sequoyah Stonecipher .30 .75
BDPP18 Shannon Wilkerson .20 .50
BDPP19 Jerry Sullivan .20 .50
BDPP20 Jamie Johnson .20 .50
BDPP21 Kent Matthes .20 .50
BDPP22 Ben Paulsen .20 .50
BDPP23 Matthew Davidson .60 1.50
BDPP24 Benjamin Carlson .20 .50
BDPP25 Brock Holt .30 .75
BDPP26 Ben Orloff .20 .50
BDPP27 D.J. LeMahieu 3.00 8.00
BDPP28 Erik Castro .30 .75
BDPP29 James Jones .20 .50
BDPP30 Cory Burns .20 .50
BDPP31 Chris Wade .20 .50
BDPP32 Jaff Decker .30 .75
BDPP33 Naoya Washiya .20 .50
BDPP34 Brandt Walker .20 .50
BDPP35 Jordan Henry .30 .75
BDPP36 Austin Adams .20 .50
BDPP37 Andrew Bellatti .30 .75
BDPP38 Paul Applebee .30 .75
BDPP39 Robert Stock .30 .75
BDPP40 Michael Flacco .20 .50
BDPP41 Jonathan Meyer .20 .50
BDPP42 Cody Rogers .30 .75
BDPP43 Matt Heidenreich .20 .50
BDPP44 David Holmberg .50 1.25
BDPP45 Mycal Jones .20 .50
BDPP46 David Hale .50 1.25
BDPP47 Dusty Odenbach .20 .50
BDPP48 Robert Hefflinger .20 .50
BDPP49 Buddy Baumann .20 .50
BDPP50 Thomas Berryhill .20 .50
BDPP51 Darrell Ceciliani .20 .50
BDPP52 Derek McCallum .20 .50
BDPP53 Taylor Freeman .20 .50
BDPP54 Tyler Townsend .30 .75
BDPP55 Tobias Streich .30 .75
BDPP56 Ryan Jackson .20 .50
BDPP57 Chris Herrmann .30 .75
BDPP58 Robert Shields .20 .50
BDPP59 Devin Fuller .20 .50
BDPP60 Brad Stillings .20 .50
BDPP61 Ryan Goins .30 .75
BDPP62 Chase Austin .20 .50
BDPP63 Brett Nommensen .20 .50
BDPP64 Egan Smith .20 .50
BDPP65 Daniel Mahoney .20 .50
BDPP66 Darin Gorski .20 .50
BDPP67 Dustin Dickerson .30 .75
BDPP68 Victor Black .30 .75
BDPP69 Dallas Keuchel 1.50 4.00
BDPP70 Nate Baker .20 .50
BDPP71 David Nick .30 .75
BDPP72 Brian Moran .20 .50
BDPP73 Mark Fleury .20 .50
BDPP74 Brett Wallach .30 .75
BDPP75 Adam Buschini .20 .50

2009 Bowman Draft Prospects Blue

*BLUE: 1.5X TO 4X BASIC
STATED ODDS 1:12 HOBBY
STATED PRINT RUN 399 SER.#'d SETS

2009 Bowman Draft Prospects Gold

*GOLD: .75X TO 2X BASIC
APPX.GOLD ODDS ONE PER PACK

2009 Bowman Draft WBC Prospects

COMPLETE SET (35) 6.00 15.00
OVERALL PLATE ODDS 1:1531 HOBBY
PLATE PRINT RUN 1 SET PER COLOR
BLACK-CYAN-MAGENTA-YELLOW ISSUED
NO PLATE PRICING DUE TO SCARCITY
BDPW1 Ichiro Suzuki .60 1.50
BDPW2 Yu Darvish .75 2.00
BDPW3 Phillippe Aumont .30 .75
BDPW4 Derek Jeter 1.25 3.00
BDPW5 Dustin Pedroia .50 1.25
BDPW6 Earl Agnoly .20 .50
BDPW7 Jose Reyes .30 .75
BDPW8 Michel Enriquez .20 .50
BDPW9 David Ortiz .50 1.25
BDPW10 Chunhua Dong .30 .75
BDPW11 Munenori Kawasaki 1.00 2.50
BDPW12 Arquimedes Nieto .20 .50
BDPW13 Bernie Williams .30 .75
BDPW14 Pedro Lazo .20 .50
BDPW15 Jing-Chao Wang .30 .75
BDPW16 Chris Barnwell .20 .50
BDPW17 Elmer Dessens .20 .50
BDPW18 Russell Martin .20 .50
BDPW19 Luca Panerati .20 .50
BDPW20 Adam Dunn .30 .75
BDPW21 Andy Gonzalez .20 .50
BDPW22 Daisuke Matsuzaka .30 .75
BDPW23 Daniel Berg .20 .50
BDPW24 Aroldis Chapman 1.00 2.50
BDPW25 Justin Morneau .30 .75
BDPW26 Miguel Cabrera .50 1.25
BDPW27 Magglio Ordonez .30 .75
BDPW28 Shawn Bowman .20 .50
BDPW29 Robbie Cordemans .20 .50
BDPW30 Paolo Espino .20 .50
BDPW31 Chipper Jones .50 1.25
BDPW32 Frederich Cepeda .30 .75
BDPW33 Ubaldo Jimenez .20 .50
BDPW34 Seiichi Uchikawa .30 .75
BDPW35 Norichika Aoki .30 .75

2009 Bowman Draft WBC Prospects Blue

*BLUE: 1.5X TO 4X BASIC
STATED ODDS 1:12 HOBBY
STATED PRINT RUN 399 SER.#'d SETS
BDPW2 Yu Darvish 6.00 15.00

2009 Bowman Draft WBC Prospects Gold

*GOLD: .75X TO 2X BASIC
APPX.GOLD ODDS ONE PER PACK

2009 Bowman Draft WBC Prospects Red

STATED ODDS 1:4266 HOBBY
STATED PRINT RUN 1 SER.#'d SET
NO PRICING DUE TO SCARCITY

2010 Bowman

COMPLETE SET (220) 12.50 30.00
COMMON CARD (1-190) .12 .30
COMMON RC (191-220) .40 1.00
1 Ryan Braun .20 .50
2 Kevin Youkilis .12 .30
3 Jay Bruce .20 .50
4 Will Venable .12 .30
5 Zack Greinke .30 .75
6 Adrian Gonzalez .25 .60
7 Carl Crawford .20 .50
8 Scott Baker .12 .30
9 Matt Kemp .25 .60
10 Stephen Drew .12 .30
11 Jair Jurrjens .12 .30
12 Jose Reyes .20 .50
13 Josh Hamilton .20 .50
14 Carlos Pena .20 .50
15 Ubaldo Jimenez .12 .30
16 Jason Kubel .12 .30
17 Josh Beckett .12 .30
18 Martin Prado .12 .30
19 Jake Peavy .12 .30
20 Shin-Soo Choo .20 .50
21 Luke Hochever .12 .30
22 Alcides Escobar .20 .50
23 Brandon Webb .20 .50
24 Raul Ibanez .20 .50
25 Ryan Zimmerman .20 .50
26 Jeff Niemann .12 .30
27 Adam Dunn .20 .50
28 Matt Cain .20 .50
29 Robinson Cano .20 .50
30 Andre Ethier .20 .50
31 Jhoulys Chacin .12 .30
32 Mark Buehrle .20 .50
33 Magglio Ordonez .20 .50
34 Michael Cuddyer .12 .30
35 Andrew Bailey .12 .30
36 Akinori Iwamura .12 .30
37 Brian Roberts .12 .30
38 Howie Kendrick .12 .30
39 Derek Holland .12 .30
40 Ken Griffey Jr. .60 1.50
41 A.J. Burnett .12 .30
42 Scott Rolen .20 .50
43 Kenshin Kawakami .20 .50
44 Carlos Lee .12 .30
45 Chris Carpenter .20 .50
46 Adam Lind .20 .50
47 Jered Weaver .20 .50
48 Chris Coghlan .12 .30
49 Clayton Kershaw .50 1.25
50 Prince Fielder .20 .50
51 Freddy Sanchez .12 .30
52 CC Sabathia .20 .50
53 Jayson Werth .20 .50
54 David Price .25 .60
55 Matt Holliday .30 .75
56 Brett Anderson .12 .30
57 Alexei Ramirez .20 .50
58 Johnny Cueto .20 .50
59 Bobby Abreu .12 .30
60 Ian Kinsler .20 .50
61 Ricky Romero .12 .30
62 Cristian Guzman .12 .30
63 Ryan Doumit .12 .30
64 Mat Latos .20 .50
65 Andrew McCutchen .30 .75
66 John Maine .12 .30
67 Kurt Suzuki .12 .30
68 Carlos Beltran .20 .50
69 Chad Billingsley .20 .50
70 Nick Markakis .25 .60
71 Yovani Gallardo .12 .30
72 Dexter Fowler .20 .50
73 David Ortiz .30 .75
74 Kosuke Fukudome .20 .50
75 Daisuke Matsuzaka .20 .50
76 Michael Young .12 .30
77 Rajai Davis .12 .30

78 Yadier Molina .40 1.00
79 Francisco Liriano .12 .30
80 Evan Longoria .20 .50
81 Trevor Cahill .12 .30
82 Aramis Ramirez .12 .30
83 Jimmy Rollins .20 .50
84 Russell Martin .12 .30
85 Dan Haren .12 .30
86 Billy Butler .12 .30
87 James Shields .12 .30
88 Dan Uggla .12 .30
89 Wandy Rodriguez .12 .30
90 Chase Utley .20 .50
91 Ryan Dempster .12 .30
92 Ben Zobrist .20 .50
93 Jeff Francoeur .20 .50
94 Koji Uehara .12 .30
95 Victor Martinez .20 .50
96 Tim Hudson .20 .50
97 Carlos Gonzalez .20 .50
98 David DeJesus .12 .30
99 Brad Hawpe .12 .30
100 Justin Upton .20 .50
101 Jorge Posada .20 .50
102 Cole Hamels .25 .60
103 Elvis Andrus .20 .50
104 Adam Wainwright .20 .50
105 Alfonso Soriano .20 .50
106 James Loney .12 .30
107 Vernon Wells .12 .30
108 Lance Berkman .20 .50
109 Matt Garza .12 .30
110 Gordon Beckham .12 .30
111 Torii Hunter .12 .30
112 Brandon Phillips .12 .30
113 Nelson Cruz .30 .75
114 Chris Tillman .12 .30
115 Miguel Cabrera .30 .75
116 Kevin Slowey .12 .30
117 Shane Victorino .20 .50
118 Paul Maholm .12 .30
119 Kyle Blanks .12 .30
120 Johan Santana .20 .50
121 Nate McLouth .12 .30
122 Kazuo Matsui .12 .30
123 Troy Tulowitzki .30 .75
124 Jon Lester .20 .50
125 Chipper Jones .30 .75
126 Clay Buchholz .12 .30
127 Todd Helton .20 .50
128 Alex Gordon .20 .50
129 Derrek Lee .12 .30
130 Justin Morneau .20 .50
131 Michael Bourn .12 .30
132 B.J. Upton .20 .50
133 Jose Lopez .12 .30
134 Justin Verlander .30 .75
135 Hunter Pence .20 .50
136 Daniel Murphy .25 .60
137 Delmon Young .20 .50
138 Carlos Quentin .12 .30
139 Edinson Volquez .12 .30
140 Dustin Pedroia .30 .75
141 Justin Masterson .12 .30
142 Josh Willingham .20 .50
143 Miguel Montero .12 .30
144 Alex Rios .12 .30
145 David Wright .25 .60
146 Curtis Granderson .25 .60
147 Rich Harden .12 .30
148 Hideki Matsui .30 .75
149 Edwin Jackson .12 .30
150 Miguel Tejada .20 .50
151 John Lackey .20 .50
152 Vladimir Guerrero .20 .50
153 Max Scherzer .30 .75
154 Jason Bay .20 .50
155 Javier Vasquez .12 .30
156 Johnny Damon .20 .50
157 Cliff Lee .20 .50
158 Chone Figgins .12 .30
159 Kevin Millwood .12 .30
160 Roy Halladay .20 .50
161 Alex Rodriguez .40 1.00
162 Pablo Sandoval .20 .50
163 Ryan Howard .25 .60
164 Rick Porcello .20 .50
165 Hanley Ramirez .20 .50
166 Brian McCann .20 .50
167 Kendry Morales .12 .30
168 Josh Johnson .20 .50
169 Joe Mauer .25 .60
170 Grady Sizemore .20 .50
171 J.A. Happ .20 .50
172 Ichiro Suzuki .40 1.00
173 Aaron Hill .12 .30
174 Mark Teixeira .20 .50
175 Tim Lincecum .20 .50
176 Denard Span .12 .30
177 Roy Oswalt .20 .50
178 Manny Ramirez .30 .75
179 Jorge De La Rosa .12 .30
180 Joey Votto .30 .75
181 Neftali Feliz .12 .30
182 Yunel Escobar .12 .30
183 Carlos Zambrano .20 .50
184 Erick Aybar .12 .30
185 Albert Pujols .40 1.00
186 Felix Hernandez .20 .50
187 Adam Jones .20 .50
188 Jacoby Ellsbury .25 .60
189 Mark Reynolds .12 .30
190 Derek Jeter .75 2.00
191 John Raynor RC .40 1.00
192 Carlos Monasterios RC .60 1.50
193 Kanekoa Texeira RC .40 1.00
194 David Herndon RC .40 1.00
195 Ruben Tejada RC .60 1.50
196 Mike Leake RC 1.25 3.00
197 Jenrry Mejia RC .60 1.50
198 Austin Jackson RC .60 1.50
199 Scott Sizemore RC .60 1.50
200 Jason Heyward RC 1.50 4.00
201 Neil Walker (RC) .60 1.50
202 Tommy Manzella (RC) .40 1.00
203 Wade Davis (RC) .60 1.50
204 Eric Young Jr. (RC) .40 1.00
205 Luis Durango RC .40 1.00
206 Madison Bumgarner RC 4.00 10.00
207 Brent Dlugach (RC) .40 1.00
208 Buster Posey RC 3.00 8.00
209 Henry Rodriguez RC .40 1.00
210 Tyler Flowers RC .60 1.50
211 Michael Dunn RC .40 1.00
212 Drew Stubbs RC 1.00 2.50
213 Brandon Allen (RC) .40 1.00
214 Daniel McCutchen RC .60 1.50
215 Juan Francisco RC .60 1.50
216 Eric Hacker RC .60 1.50
217 Michael Brantley RC .60 1.50
218 Dustin Richardson RC .40 1.00
219 Josh Thole RC .60 1.50
220 Daniel Hudson RC .60 1.50

2010 Bowman Blue

*BLUE 1-190: 1.5X TO 4X BASIC
*BLUE: 191-220: .75X TO 2X BASIC
STATED ODDS 1:17 HOBBY
STATED PRINT RUN 520 SER.#'d SETS
200 Jason Heyward 8.00 20.00

2010 Bowman Gold

COMPLETE SET (220) 20.00 50.00
*GOLD 1-190: .75X TO 2X BASIC
*GOLD: 191-220: .6X TO 1.5X BASIC

2010 Bowman Orange

*ORANGE 1-190: 2.5X TO 6X BASIC
*ORAGE: 191-220: 1.2X TO 3X BASIC
STATED ODDS 1:35 HOBBY
STATED PRINT RUN 250 SER.#'d SETS

2010 Bowman 1992 Bowman Throwbacks

COMPLETE SET (110) 15.00 40.00
STATED ODDS 1:2 HOBBY
BT1 Jimmy Rollins .50 1.25
BT2 Ryan Zimmerman .50 1.25
BT3 Alex Rodriguez 1.00 2.50
BT4 Andrew McCutchen .75 2.00
BT5 Mark Reynolds .30 .75
BT6 Jason Bay .50 1.25
BT7 Hideki Matsui .75 2.00
BT8 Carlos Beltran .50 1.25
BT9 Justin Morneau .50 1.25
BT10 Matt Cain .50 1.25
BT11 Russell Martin .30 .75
BT12 Alfonso Soriano .50 1.25
BT13 Joe Mauer .60 1.50
BT14 Troy Tulowitzki .75 2.00
BT15 Miguel Tejada .50 1.25
BT16 Adrian Gonzalez .60 1.50
BT17 Carlos Zambrano .50 1.25
BT18 Hunter Pence .50 1.25
BT19 Torii Hunter .30 .75
BT20 Michael Young .30 .75
BT21 Pablo Sandoval .50 1.25
BT22 Manny Ramirez .75 2.00
BT23 Jose Reyes .50 1.25
BT24 Carl Crawford .50 1.25
BT25 CC Sabathia .50 1.25
BT26 Josh Beckett .30 .75
BT27 Dan Uggla .30 .75
BT28 Josh Johnson .50 1.25
BT29 Raul Ibanez .50 1.25
BT30 Grady Sizemore .50 1.25
BT31 Nate McLouth .30 .75
BT32 Robinson Cano .50 1.25
BT33 Carlos Lee .30 .75
BT34 Jorge Posada .50 1.25
BT35 B.J. Upton .50 1.25
BT36 Ubaldo Jimenez .30 .75
BT37 Ryan Braun .50 1.25
BT38 Aaron Hill .30 .75
BT39 Rick Porcello .50 1.25
BT40 Nick Markakis .60 1.50
BT41 Felix Hernandez .50 1.25
BT42 Matt Holliday .75 2.00
BT43 Prince Fielder .50 1.25
BT44 Yadier Molina 1.00 2.50
BT45 Justin Upton .50 1.25
BT46 Carlos Pena .50 1.25
BT47 Miguel Cabrera .75 2.00
BT48 Dan Haren .30 .75
BT49 Cliff Lee .50 1.25
BT50 Victor Martinez .50 1.25
BT51 Josh Hamilton .50 1.25
BT52 Evan Longoria .50 1.25
BT53 Johan Santana .50 1.25
BT54 Ryan Howard .60 1.50
BT55 Jon Lester .50 1.25
BT56 Mark Buehrle .50 1.25
BT57 Lance Berkman .50 1.25
BT58 Roy Oswalt .50 1.25
BT59 Dustin Pedroia .75 2.00
BT60 Daisuke Matsuzaka .50 1.25
BT61 Joey Votto .75 2.00
BT62 Ken Griffey Jr. 1.50 4.00
BT63 Jacoby Ellsbury .60 1.50
BT64 David Wright .60 1.50
BT65 Derek Jeter 2.00 5.00
BT66 Chase Utley .50 1.25
BT67 Mark Teixeira .50 1.25
BT68 Justin Verlander .75 2.00
BT69 Kendry Morales .30 .75
BT70 Adam Jones .50 1.25
BT71 Vladimir Guerrero .50 1.25
BT72 Albert Pujols 1.00 2.50
BT73 Roy Halladay .50 1.25
BT74 Matt Kemp .60 1.50
BT75 Kevin Youkilis .30 .75
BT76 Jake Peavy .30 .75
BT77 Hanley Ramirez .50 1.25
BT78 Ian Kinsler .50 1.25
BT79 Ichiro Suzuki 1.00 2.50
BT80 Curtis Granderson .60 1.50
BT81 Gordon Beckham .30 .75
BT82 Jayson Werth .50 1.25
BT83 Brandon Webb .50 1.25
BT84 Adam Dunn .50 1.25
BT85 David Ortiz .75 2.00
BT86 Cole Hamels .60 1.50
BT87 Brian McCann .50 1.25
BT88 Zack Greinke .75 2.00
BT89 Tim Lincecum .50 1.25
BT90 Andre Ethier .50 1.25
BT91 Matt Garza .30 .75
BT92 Billy Butler .30 .75
BT93 Yovani Gallardo .30 .75
BT94 Chone Figgins .30 .75
BT95 Yunel Escobar .30 .75
BT96 Alexei Ramirez .50 1.25
BT97 Clayton Kershaw 1.25 3.00
BT98 Chris Coghlan .30 .75
BT99 Denard Span .30 .75
BT100 A.J. Burnett .30 .75
BT101 Ivan Rodriguez .50 1.25
BT102 Chipper Jones .75 2.00
BT103 Carlos Delgado .30 .75
BT104 Gary Sheffield .30 .75
BT105 Garret Anderson .30 .75
BT106 Mariano Rivera 1.00 2.50
BT107 John Smoltz .75 2.00
BT108 Omar Vizquel .50 1.25
BT109 Jim Thome .50 1.25
BT110 Manny Ramirez .75 2.00

2010 Bowman Expectations

COMPLETE SET (50) 15.00 40.00
STATED ODDS 1:3 HOBBY
BE1 J.Posada/J.Montero .60 1.50
BE2 R.Howard/D.Brown 1.50 4.00
BE3 Ramirez/Stanton 3.00 8.00
BE4 C.Jones/F.Freeman 5.00 12.00
BE5 Lincecum/Strasburg 3.00 8.00
BE6 Jose Reyes/Wilmer Flores .60 1.50
BE7 D.Wright/I.Davis .75 2.00
BE8 A.Soriano/S.Castro 1.00 2.50
BE9 J.Bruce/T.Frazier 1.00 2.50
BE10 R.Braun/M.Gamel .60 1.50
BE11 Lester/BumgarN 4.00 10.00
BE12 Ubaldo Jimenez/Tyler Matzek 1.00 2.50
BE13 J.Mauer/B.Posey 3.00 8.00
BE14 Carl Crawford/Desmond Jennings .60 1.50
BE15 E.Longoria/A.Liddi .60 1.50
BE16 A.McCutchen/J.Tabata 1.00 2.50
BE17 C.Jones/J.Heyward 1.50 4.00
BE18 Aramis Ramirez/Josh Vitters .40 1.00
BE19 Ryan Zimmerman/Ian Desmond .60 1.50
BE20 A.Gordon/M.Moustakas 1.00 2.50
BE21 Adam Dunn/Chris Marrero .60 1.50
BE22 Mike Napoli/Hank Conger .40 1.00
BE23 Pablo Sandoval/Thomas Neal .60 1.50
BE24 Carlos Quentin/Tyler Flowers .60 1.50
BE25 V.Martinez/C.Santana 1.25 3.00
BE26 Zambrano/Cashner .60 1.50
BE27 J.Lopez/D.Ackley 1.50 4.00
BE28 Rich Harden/Neftali Feliz .40 1.00
BE29 J.Damon/S.Heathcott 1.25 3.00
BE30 Kevin Youkilis/Lars Anderson .60 1.50
BE31 Dan Haren/Jarrod Parker 1.00 2.50
BE32 Matt Kemp/Jared Mitchell .75 2.00
BE33 W.Venable/D.Tate .40 1.00
BE34 Andre Ethier/Andrew Lambo .60 1.50
BE35 Brian McCann/Tony Sanchez 1.00 2.50
BE36 Josh Beckett/Chris Withrow .40 1.00
BE37 Matt Cain/Zack Wheeler 1.25 3.00
BE38 Johnny Cueto/Jenrry Mejia .60 1.50
BE39 David Price/Jake McGee .75 2.00
BE40 M.Garza/J.Hellickson 1.00 2.50
BE41 Nick Markakis/Josh Bell .75 2.00
BE42 Ivan Rodriguez/Derek Norris .60 1.50
BE43 Elvis Andrus/Jiovanni Mier .60 1.50
BE44 Mark Reynolds/Bobby Borchering .60 1.50
BE45 Prince Fielder/Chris Carter .60 1.50
BE46 Grady Sizemore/Jordan Brown .60 1.50
BE47 S.Drew/P.Ciriaco 1.25 3.00
BE48 Chad Billingsley/John Ely .60 1.50
BE49 Justin Morneau
Christopher Parmelee .60 1.50
BE50 R.Halladay/K.Drabek .60 1.50

2010 Bowman Futures Game Triple Relic

STATED ODDS 1:402 HOBBY
STATED PRINT RUN 99 SER.#'d SETS
AE Alcides Escobar 5.00 12.00
AL Alex Liddi 4.00 10.00
BC Barbaro Canizares 4.00 10.00
BL Brad Lincoln 4.00 10.00
CC Chris Carter 6.00 15.00
CH Chris Heisey 10.00 25.00
CS Carlos Santana 10.00 25.00
CT Chris Tillman 4.00 10.00
DD Danny Duffy 10.00 25.00
DJ Daryl Jones 4.00 10.00
DJE Desmond Jennings 8.00 20.00
DV Dayan Viciedo 4.00 10.00
EY Eric Young Jr. 4.00 10.00
FS Francisco Samuel 4.00 10.00
JC Jhoulys Chacin 4.00 10.00
JH Jason Heyward 12.50 30.00
JM Jesus Montero 10.00 25.00
JP Jarrod Parker 20.00 50.00
JV Josh Vitters 8.00 20.00
KD Kyle Drabek 5.00 12.00
KK Kyeong Kang 4.00 10.00
LD Luis Durango 5.00 12.00
LS Leyson Septimo 4.00 10.00
MB Madison Bumgarner 20.00 50.00
ML Mat Latos 12.50 30.00
MS Mike Stanton 15.00 40.00
NF Neftali Feliz 5.00 12.00
NW Nick Weglarz 8.00 20.00
PB Pedro Baez 4.00 10.00
RT Rene Tosoni 5.00 12.00
SC Starlin Castro 20.00 50.00
SS Scott Sizemore 5.00 12.00
TF Tyler Flowers 4.00 10.00
TG Tyson Gillies 6.00 15.00
TR Trevor Reckling 5.00 12.00
WF Wilmer Flores 5.00 12.00
YF Yohan Flande 8.00 20.00

2010 Bowman Prospects

COMP.SET w/o AU (110) 15.00 40.00
STRASBURG AU ODDS 1:2013 HOBBY
BP1a Stephen Strasburg 1.50 4.00
BP1b Stephen Strasburg AU 40.00 100.00
BP2 Melky Mesa .30 .75
BP3 Cole McCurry .20 .50
BP4 Tyler Henley .20 .50
BP5 Andrew Cashner .20 .50
BP6 Konrad Schmidt .20 .50
BP7 Jean Segura 1.00 2.50
BP8 Jon Gaston .30 .75
BP9 Nick Santomauro .20 .50
BP10 Aroldis Chapman .75 2.00
BP11 Logan Watkins .20 .50
BP12 Bo Bowman .20 .50
BP13 Jeff Antigua .20 .50
BP14 Matt Adams .60 1.50
BP15 Joseph Cruz .30 .75
BP16 Sebastian Valle .30 .75
BP17 Stefan Gartrell .20 .50
BP18 Pedro Ciriaco .60 1.50
BP19 Tyson Gillies .50 1.25
BP20 Casey Crosby .20 .50
BP21 Luis Exposito .20 .50
BP22 Welington Dotel .20 .50
BP23 Alexander Torres .20 .50
BP24 Byron Wiley .20 .50
BP25 Pedro Florimon .20 .50
BP26 Cody Satterwhite .30 .75
BP27 Craig Clark .75 2.00
BP28 Jason Christian .20 .50
BP29 Tommy Mendonca .20 .50
BP30 Ryan Dent .20 .50
BP31 Jhan Marinez .20 .50
BP32 Eric Niesen .20 .50
BP33 Gustavo Nunez .20 .50
BP34 Scott Shaw .20 .50
BP35 Welinton Ramirez .20 .50
BP36 Trevor May .75 2.00
BP37 Mitch Moreland .30 .75
BP38 Nick Czyz .20 .50
BP39 Edinson Rincon .20 .50
BP40 Domingo Santana .60 1.50
BP41 Carson Blair .20 .50
BP42 Rashun Dixon .20 .50
BP43 Alexander Colome .50 1.25
BP44 Allan Dykstra .20 .50
BP45 J.J. Hoover .20 .50
BP46 Abner Abreu .30 .75
BP47 Daniel Nava .20 .50
BP48 Simon Castro .20 .50
BP49 Brian Baisley .20 .50
BP50 Tony Delmonico .20 .50
BP51 Chase D'Arnaud .20 .50
BP52 Sheng-An Kuo .20 .50
BP53 Leandro Castro .20 .50
BP54 Charlie Leesman .20 .50
BP55 Caleb Joseph .20 .50
BP56 Rolando Gomez .20 .50
BP57 John Lamb .50 1.25
BP58 Adam Wilk .30 .75
BP59 Randall Delgado .30 .75
BP60 Neil Medchill .30 .75
BP61 Josh Donaldson 1.00 2.50
BP62 Zach Gentile .20 .50
BP63 Kiel Roling .20 .50
BP64 Wes Freeman .20 .50
BP65 Brian Pellegrini .30 .75
BP66 Kyle Jensen .20 .50
BP67 Evan Anundsen .20 .50
BP68 Hak-Ju Lee .30 .75
BP69 C.J. Retherford .20 .50
BP70 Dillon Gee .50 1.25
BP71 Bo Greenwell .20 .50
BP72 Matt Tucker .30 .75
BP73 Joe Serafin .20 .50
BP74 Matt Brown .20 .50
BP75 Alexis Oliveras .20 .50
BP76 James Beresford .20 .50
BP77 Steve Lombardozzi .30 .75
BP78 Curtis Petersen .20 .50
BP79 Eric Farris .20 .50
BP80 Yen-Wen Kuo .20 .50
BP81 Caleb Brewer .20 .50
BP82 Jacob Elmore .30 .75
BP83 Jared Clark .30 .75
BP84 Yowill Espinal .30 .75
BP85 Jae-Hoon Ha .20 .50
BP86 Michael Wing .20 .50
BP87 Wilmer Font .20 .50
BP88 Jake Kahaulelio .20 .50
BP89 Dustin Ackley .30 .75
BP90 Donavan Tate .20 .50
BP91 Nolan Arenado 6.00 15.00
BP92 Rex Brothers .20 .50
BP93 Brett Jackson .60 1.50
BP94 Chad Jenkins .20 .50
BP95 Slade Heathcott .60 1.50
BP96 J.R. Murphy .30 .75
BP97 Patrick Schuster .20 .50
BP98 Alexia Amarista .20 .50
BP99 Thomas Neal .30 .75
BP100 Starlin Castro .50 1.25
BP101 Anthony Rizzo 2.50 6.00
BP102 Felix Doubront .20 .50
BP103 Nick Franklin .50 1.25
BP104 Anthony Gose .30 .75
BP105 Julio Teheran .30 .75
BP106 Grant Green .20 .50
BP107 David Lough .20 .50
BP108 Jose Iglesias .60 1.50
BP109 Jaff Decker .50 1.25
BP110 D.J. LeMahieu 2.00 5.00

2010 Bowman Prospects Black

COMPLETE SET (110) 20.00 50.00
*BLACK: .75X TO 2X BASIC
ISSUED VIA WRAPPER REDEMPTION PROGRAM

2010 Bowman Prospects Blue

*BLUE: 1.2X TO 3X BASIC
STATED ODDS 1:17 HOBBY
STATED PRINT RUN 520 SER.#'d SETS
STRASBURG AU ODDS 1:5700 HOBBY
STRASBURG PRINT RUN 250 SER.#'d SETS
BP1b Stephen Strasburg AU 50.00 120.00

2010 Bowman Prospects Orange

*ORANGE: 2X TO 5X BASIC
STATED ODDS 1:35 HOBBY
STATED PRINT RUN 250 SER.#'d SETS
STRASBURG AU ODDS 1:56,500 HOBBY
STRASBURG PRINT RUN 25 SER.#'d SETS

2010 Bowman Prospect Autographs

BM Brent Morel 5.00 12.00
CV Cesar Valdez 3.00 8.00
DC Dusty Coleman 3.00 8.00
DH Darin Holcomb 3.00 8.00
DT Donavan Tate 6.00 15.00
EB Eric Berger 3.00 8.00
JB Justin Bristow 3.00 8.00
JF Jeremy Farrell 3.00 8.00
LF Logan Forsythe 3.00 8.00
MH Matt Hobgood 3.00 8.00
TS Tony Sanchez 3.00 8.00
ZS Zach Simons 3.00 8.00

2010 Bowman Topps 100 Prospects

COMPLETE SET (100) 30.00 60.00
STATED ODDS 1:3 HOBBY
TP1 Stephen Strasburg 5.00 12.00
TP2 Aroldis Chapman 1.50 4.00
TP3 Jason Heyward 1.50 4.00
TP4 Jesus Montero .40 1.00
TP5 Mike Stanton 3.00 8.00
TP6 Mike Moustakas 1.00 2.50
TP7 Kyle Drabek .60 1.50
TP8 Tyler Matzek 1.00 2.50
TP9 Austin Jackson .60 1.50
TP10 Starlin Castro 1.00 2.50
TP11 Todd Frazier 1.00 2.50
TP12 Carlos Santana 1.25 3.00
TP13 Josh Vitters .40 1.00
TP14 Neftali Feliz .40 1.00
TP15 Tyler Flowers .60 1.50
TP16 Alcides Escobar .60 1.50
TP17 Ike Davis .75 2.00
TP18 Domonic Brown 1.50 4.00
TP19 Donavan Tate .40 1.00
TP20 Buster Posey 3.00 8.00
TP21 Dustin Ackley .60 1.50
TP22 Desmond Jennings .60 1.50
TP23 Brandon Allen .40 1.00
TP24 Freddie Freeman 5.00 12.00
TP25 Jake Arrieta 1.00 2.50
TP26 Bobby Borchering .60 1.50
TP27 Logan Morrison .60 1.50
TP28 Christian Friederich .60 1.50
TP29 Wilmer Flores .60 1.50
TP30 Austin Romine .60 1.50
TP31 Tony Sanchez 1.00 2.50
TP32 Madison Bumgarner 4.00 10.00
TP33 Mike Montgomery .60 1.50
TP34 Andrew Lambo .40 1.00
TP35 Derek Norris .60 1.50
TP36 Chris Withrow .40 1.00
TP37 Thomas Neal .60 1.50
TP38 Trevor Reckling .40 1.00
TP39 Andrew Cashner .40 1.00
TP40 Daniel Hudson .60 1.50
TP41 Jiovanni Mier .60 1.50
TP42 Grant Green .40 1.00
TP43 Jeremy Hellickson 1.00 2.50
TP44 Felix Doubront .40 1.00
TP45 Martin Perez 1.00 2.50
TP46 Jenrry Mejia .60 1.50
TP47 Adrian Cardenas .40 1.00
TP48 Ivan DeJesus Jr. .40 1.00
TP49 Nolan Arenado 6.00 15.00
TP50 Slade Heathcott 1.25 3.00
TP51 Ian Desmond .60 1.50
TP52 Michael Taylor .60 1.50
TP53 Jaime Garcia .60 1.50
TP54 Jose Tabata .60 1.50
TP55 Josh Bell .40 1.00
TP56 Jarrod Parker 1.00 2.50
TP57 Matt Dominguez 1.00 2.50
TP58 Koby Clemens .60 1.50
TP59 Angel Morales .40 1.00
TP60 Juan Francisco .60 1.50
TP61 John Ely .40 1.00
TP62 Brett Jackson 1.25 3.00
TP63 Chad Jenkins .40 1.00
TP64 Jose Iglesias 1.25 3.00
TP65 Logan Forsythe .40 1.00
TP66 Alex Liddi .60 1.50
TP67 Eric Arnett .40 1.00
TP68 Wilkin Ramirez .40 1.00
TP69 Lars Anderson .60 1.50
TP70 Jared Mitchell .60 1.50
TP71 Mike Leake 1.25 3.00
TP72 D.J. LeMahieu 4.00 10.00
TP73 Chris Marrero .40 1.00
TP74 Matt Moore 3.00 8.00
TP75 Jordan Brown .40 1.00
TP76 Christopher Parmelee .40 1.00
TP77 Ryan Kalish .60 1.50
TP78 A.J. Pollock 1.00 2.50
TP79 Alex White .60 1.50
TP80 Scott Sizemore .60 1.50
TP81 Jay Austin .40 1.00
TP82 Zach McAllister .60 1.50
TP83 Max Stassi .60 1.50
TP84 Robert Stock .40 1.00
TP85 Jake McGee .40 1.00
TP86 Zack Wheeler 1.25 3.00
TP87 Chase D'Arnaud .40 1.00
TP88 Danny Duffy .40 1.00
TP89 Josh Lindblom .40 1.00
TP90 Anthony Gose .60 1.50
TP91 Simon Castro .40 1.00
TP92 Chris Carter .60 1.50
TP93 Matt Hobgood 1.00 2.50
TP94 Ben Revere .60 1.50
TP95 Mat Gamel .40 1.00
TP96 Anthony Hewitt .40 1.00
TP97 Julio Teheran .60 1.50
TP98 Josh Reddick .40 1.00
TP99 Hank Conger .40 1.00
TP100 Jordan Walden .40 1.00

2010 Bowman Draft

COMPLETE SET (110) 8.00 20.00
COMMON CARD (1-110) .20 .50
BDP1 Stephen Strasburg RC 1.50 4.00
BDP2 Josh Bell (RC) .20 .50
BDP3 Ivan Nova RC 1.00 2.50
BDP4 Starlin Castro RC .50 1.25
BDP5 John Axford RC .20 .50
BDP6 Colin Curtis RC .20 .50
BDP7 Brennan Boesch RC .50 1.25
BDP8 Ike Davis RC .40 1.00
BDP9 Madison Bumgarner RC 2.00 5.00
BDP10 Austin Jackson RC .30 .75
BDP11 Andrew Cashner RC .20 .50
BDP12 Jose Tabata RC .30 .75
BDP13 Wade Davis (RC) .30 .75
BDP14 Ian Desmond (RC) .30 .75
BDP15 Felix Doubront RC .20 .50
BDP16 Danny Worth RC .20 .50
BDP17 John Ely RC .20 .50
BDP18 Jon Jay RC .30 .75
BDP19 Mike Leake RC .60 1.50
BDP20 Daniel Nava RC .20 .50
BDP21 Brad Lincoln RC .30 .75
BDP22 Jonathan Lucroy RC .50 1.25
BDP23 Brian Matusz RC .50 1.25
BDP24 Chris Nelson (RC) .30 .75
BDP25 Andy Oliver RC .20 .50
BDP26 Adam Ottavino RC .20 .50
BDP27 Trevor Plouffe (RC) .50 1.25
BDP28 Vance Worley RC .75 2.00
BDP29 Daniel McCutchen RC .30 .75
BDP30 Mike Stanton RC 1.50 4.00
BDP31 Drew Storen RC .30 .75
BDP32 Tyler Colvin RC .30 .75
BDP33 Travis Wood (RC) .30 .75
BDP34 Eric Young Jr. (RC) .20 .50
BDP35 Sam Demel RC .20 .50
BDP36 Wellington Castillo RC .20 .50
BDP37 Sam LeCure (RC) .20 .50
BDP38 Danny Valencia RC 1.25 3.00
BDP39 Fernando Salas RC .20 .50
BDP40 Jason Heyward RC .75 2.00
BDP41 Jake Arrieta RC .50 1.25
BDP42 Kevin Russo RC .20 .50
BDP43 Josh Donaldson RC 1.00 2.50
BDP44 Luis Atilano RC .20 .50
BDP45 Jason Donald RC .20 .50
BDP46 Jonny Venters RC .20 .50
BDP47 Bryan Anderson (RC) .20 .50
BDP48 Jay Sborz (RC) .20 .50
BDP49 Chris Heisey RC .30 .75
BDP50 Daniel Hudson RC .30 .75
BDP51 Ruben Tejada RC .30 .75
BDP52 Jeffrey Marquez RC .30 .75
BDP53 Brandon Hicks RC .30 .75
BDP54 Jeanmar Gomez RC .30 .75
BDP55 Erik Kratz RC .30 .75
BDP56 Lorenzo Cain RC .50 1.25
BDP57 Jhan Marinez RC .20 .50
BDP58 Omar Beltre (RC) .20 .50
BDP59 Drew Stubbs RC .50 1.25
BDP60 Alex Sanabia RC .20 .50
BDP61 Buster Posey RC 1.50 4.00
BDP62 Anthony Slama RC .20 .50
BDP63 Brad Davis RC .20 .50
BDP64 Logan Morrison RC .30 .75
BDP65 Luke Hughes (RC) .20 .50
BDP66 Thomas Diamond (RC) .20 .50
BDP67 Tommy Manzella (RC) .20 .50
BDP68 Jordan Smith RC .20 .50
BDP69 Carlos Santana RC .60 1.50
BDP70 Domonic Brown RC .75 2.00
BDP71 Scott Sizemore RC .30 .75
BDP72 Jordan Brown RC .20 .50
BDP73 Josh Thole RC .30 .75
BDP74 Jordan Norberto RC .20 .50
BDP75 Dayan Viciedo RC .30 .75
BDP76 Josh Tomlin RC .50 1.25
BDP77 Adam Moore RC .20 .50
BDP78 Kenley Jansen RC .60 1.50
BDP79 Juan Francisco RC .30 .75
BDP80 Blake Wood RC .20 .50
BDP81 John Hester RC .20 .50
BDP82 Lucas Harrell (RC) .20 .50
BDP83 Neil Walker (RC) .30 .75
BDP84 Cesar Valdez RC .20 .50
BDP85 Lance Zawadzki RC .20 .50
BDP86 Rommie Lewis RC .20 .50
BDP87 Steve Tolleson RC .20 .50
BDP88 Jeff Frazier (RC) .20 .50
BDP89 Drew Butera (RC) .20 .50
BDP90 Michael Brantley RC .30 .75
BDP91 Mitch Moreland RC .30 .75
BDP92 Alex Burnett RC .20 .50
BDP93 Allen Craig RC .50 1.25
BDP94 Sergio Santos (RC) .20 .50
BDP95 Matt Carson (RC) .20 .50
BDP96 Jenrry Mejia RC .30 .75
BDP97 Rhyne Hughes RC .20 .50
BDP98 Tyson Ross RC .20 .50
BDP99 Argenis Diaz RC .30 .75
BDP100 Hisanori Takahashi RC .30 .75
BDP101 Cole Gillespie RC .20 .50
BDP102 Ryan Kalish RC .30 .75
BDP103 J.P. Arencibia RC .40 1.00
BDP104 Peter Bourjos RC .30 .75
BDP105 Justin Turner RC 1.50 4.00
BDP106 Michael Dunn RC .20 .50
BDP107 Mike McCoy RC .20 .50
BDP108 Will Rhymes RC .20 .50
BDP109 Wilson Ramos RC .50 1.25
BDP110 Josh Butler RC .20 .50

2010 Bowman Draft Blue

*BLUE: 1.5X TO 4X BASIC
STATED PRINT RUN 399 SER.#'d SETS

2010 Bowman Draft Gold

*GOLD: 1X TO 2.5X BASIC

2010 Bowman Draft Red

STATED PRINT RUN 1 SER.#'d SET

2010 Bowman Draft Prospect Autographs

AL Andrew Liebel 3.00 8.00
AR Anthony Rizzo 15.00 40.00
BS Bryan Shaw 3.00 8.00
CG Conor Graham 3.00 8.00
DT Donavan Tate 6.00 15.00
EK Eddie Kunz 3.00 8.00
GH Graham Hicks 3.00 8.00
JJ Jake Jefferies 6.00 15.00
JM Jiovanni Mier 3.00 8.00
JP Jason Place 4.00 10.00
MH Matt Hobgood 3.00 8.00
MM Mike Montgomery 4.00 10.00
MY Michael Ynoa 3.00 8.00
NC Nick Carr 3.00 8.00
RC Ryan Chaffee 3.00 8.00
RG Randal Grichuk 10.00 25.00
RM Ryan Mattheus 3.00 8.00
SG Steve Garrison 3.00 8.00
SH Slade Heathcott 3.00 8.00
SP Shane Peterson 3.00 8.00
ZM Zach McAllister 3.00 8.00
JPI Julio Pimentel 3.00 8.00

2010 Bowman Draft Prospect Autographs Blue

*BLUE: .75X TO 2X BASIC
STATED PRINT RUN 199 SER.#'d SETS

2010 Bowman Draft Prospect Autographs Red

*RED: 1.2X TO 3X BASIC
STATED PRINT RUN 50 SER.#'d SETS

2010 Bowman Draft Prospects

BDPP1 Sam Tuivailala .25 .60
BDPP2 Alex Burgos .25 .60
BDPP3 Henry Ramos .40 1.00
BDPP4 Pat Dean .15 .40
BDPP5 Ryan Brett .25 .60
BDPP6 Jesse Biddle .25 .60
BDPP7 Leon Landry .40 1.00
BDPP8 Ryan LaMarre .25 .60
BDPP9 Josh Rutledge 1.00 2.50
BDPP10 Tyler Thornburg .40 1.00
BDPP11 Carter Jurica .15 .40
BDPP12 J.R. Bradley .15 .40
BDPP13 Devin Lohman .15 .40
BDPP14 Addison Reed .40 1.00
BDPP15 Micah Gibbs .25 .60
BDPP16 Derek Dietrich .40 1.00
BDPP18 Stephen Pryor .15 .40
BDPP19 Eddie Rosario 1.25 3.00
BDPP20 Blake Forsythe .15 .40
BDPP21 Rangel Ravelo .15 .40
BDPP22 Nick Longmire .25 .60
BDPP23 Andrelton Simmons .60 1.50
BDPP24 Chad Bettis .15 .40
BDPP25 Peter Tago .25 .60
BDPP26 Tyrell Jenkins .50 1.25
BDPP27 Marcus Knecht .15 .40
BDPP28 Seth Blair .25 .60
BDPP29 Brodie Greene .15 .40
BDPP30 Jason Martinson .15 .40
BDPP31 Bryan Morgado .25 .60
BDPP32 Eric Cantrell .15 .40
BDPP33 Niko Goodrum .50 1.25
BDPP34 Bobby Doran .15 .40
BDPP35 Cody Wheeler .15 .40
BDPP36 Cole Leonida .15 .40
BDPP37 Nate Roberts .15 .40
BDPP38 Dave Filak .15 .40
BDPP39 Taijuan Walker .40 1.00
BDPP40 Hayden Simpson .25 .60
BDPP41 Cameron Rupp .25 .60
BDPP42 Ben Heath .15 .40
BDPP43 Tyler Waldron .15 .40
BDPP44 Greg Garcia .15 .40
BDPP45 Vincent Velasquez .60 1.50
BDPP46 Jake Lemmerman .50 1.25
BDPP47 Russell Wilson 5.00 12.00
BDPP48 Cody Stanley .15 .40
BDPP49 Matt Suschak .15 .40
BDPP50 Logan Darnell .15 .40
BDPP51 Kevin Keyes .15 .40
BDPP52 Thomas Royse .15 .40
BDPP53 Scott Alexander .15 .40
BDPP54 Tony Thompson .15 .40
BDPP55 Seth Rosin .25 .60
BDPP56 Mickey Wiswall .15 .40
BDPP57 Albert Almora .50 1.25
BDPP58 Cole Billingsley .25 .60
BDPP58 Cody Hawn .25 .60
BDPP59 Drew Vettleson .25 .60
BDPP60 Matt Lipka .60 1.50
BDPP61 Michael Choice .25 .60
BDPP62 Zack Cox .50 1.25
BDPP63 Bryce Brentz .40 1.00
BDPP64 Chance Ruffin .15 .40
BDPP65 Mike Olt .50 1.25
BDPP66 Kellin Deglan .15 .40
BDPP67 Yasmani Grandal .25 .60
BDPP68 Kolbrin Vitek .40 1.00
BDPP69 Justin O'Conner .15 .40
BDPP70 Gary Brown .75 2.00
BDPP71 Mike Foltynewicz .40 1.00
BDPP72 Chevez Clarke .25 .60
BDPP73 Cito Culver .25 .60
BDPP74 Aaron Sanchez .60 1.50
BDPP75 Noah Syndergaard .60 1.50
BDPP76 Taylor Lindsey .25 .60
BDPP77 Josh Sale .50 1.25
BDPP78 Christian Yelich 3.00 8.00
BDPP79 Jameson Taillon .25 .60
BDPP80 Manny Machado 5.00 12.00
BDPP81 Christian Colon .25 .60
BDPP82 Drew Pomeranz .40 1.00
BDPP83 Delino DeShields .25 .60
BDPP84 Matt Harvey 1.00 2.50
BDPP85 Ryan Bolden .15 .40
BDPP86 Deck McGuire .25 .60
BDPP87 Zach Lee .40 1.00
BDPP88 Alex Wimmers .25 .60
BDPP89 Kaleb Cowart .25 .60
BDPP90 Mike Kvansnicka .15 .40
BDPP91 Jake Skole .25 .60

BDPP92 Chris Sale 2.50 6.00
BDPP93 Sean Brady .15 .40
BDPP94 Marc Brakeman .15 .40
BDPP95 Alex Bregman 2.50 6.00
BDPP96 Ryan Burr .40 1.00
BDPP97 Chris Chinea .25 .60
BDPP98 Troy Conyers .15 .40
BDPP99 Zach Green .15 .40
BDPP100 Carson Kelly .50 1.25
BDPP101 Timmy Lopes .15 .40
BDPP102 Adrian Marin .25 .60
BDPP103 Chris Okey .15 .40
BDPP104 Matt Olson 2.00 5.00
BDPP105 Ivan Pelaez .15 .40
BDPP106 Felipe Perez .15 .40
BDPP107 Nelson Rodriguez .25 .60
BDPP108 Corey Seager 6.00 15.00
BDPP109 Lucas Sims .40 1.00
BDPP110 Nick Travieso .25 .60

2010 Bowman Draft Prospects Blue

*BLUE: 2X TO 5X BASIC
STATED PRINT RUN 399 SER.#'d SETS

2010 Bowman Draft Prospects Gold

*GOLD: 1X TO 2.5X BASIC

2010 Bowman Draft USA Baseball Jerseys

STATED PRINT RUN 949 SER.#'d SETS
USAR1 Albert Almora 3.00 8.00
USAR2 Cole Billingsley 3.00 8.00
USAR3 Sean Brady 4.00 10.00
USAR4 Marc Brakeman 3.00 8.00
USAR5 Alex Bregman 4.00 10.00
USAR6 Ryan Burr 3.00 8.00
USAR7 Chris Chinea 4.00 10.00
USAR8 Troy Conyers 3.00 8.00
USAR9 Zach Green 3.00 8.00
USAR10 Carson Kelly 3.00 8.00
USAR11 Timmy Lopes 3.00 8.00
USAR12 Adrian Marin 3.00 8.00
USAR13 Chris Okey 3.00 8.00
USAR14 Matt Olson 6.00 15.00
USAR15 Ivan Pelaez 3.00 8.00
USAR16 Felipe Perez 3.00 8.00
USAR17 Nelson Rodriguez 3.00 8.00
USAR18 Corey Seager 4.00 10.00
USAR19 Lucas Sims 3.00 8.00
USAR20 Sheldon Neuse 3.00 8.00

2010 Bowman Draft USA Baseball Jerseys Blue

*BLUE: .5X TO 1.2X BASIC
STATED PRINT RUN 199 SER.#'d SETS

2010 Bowman Draft USA Baseball Jerseys Red

*RED: .6X TO 1.5X BASIC
STATED PRINT RUN 50 SER.#'d SETS

2011 Bowman

COMPLETE SET (220) 12.50 30.00
COMMON CARD (1-190) .12 .30
COMMON RC (191-220) .40 1.00
PLATE PRINT RUN 1 SET PER COLOR
BLACK-CYAN-MAGENTA-YELLOW ISSUED
NO PLATE PRICING DUE TO SCARCITY
1 Buster Posey .40 1.00
2 Alex Avila .20 .50
3 Edwin Jackson .12 .30
4 Miguel Montero .12 .30
5 Ryan Dempster .12 .30
6 Albert Pujols .40 1.00
7 Carlos Santana .30 .75
8 Ted Lilly .12 .30
9 Marlon Byrd .12 .30
10 Hanley Ramirez .20 .50
11 Josh Hamilton .20 .50
12 Orlando Hudson .12 .30
13 Matt Kemp .25 .60
14 Shane Victorino .20 .50
15 Domonic Brown .25 .60
16 Jeff Niemann .12 .30
17 Chipper Jones .30 .75
18 Joey Votto .30 .75
19 Brandon Phillips .12 .30
20 Michael Bourn .12 .30
21 Jason Heyward .25 .60
22 Curtis Granderson .25 .60
23 Brian McCann .20 .50
24 Mike Pelfrey .12 .30
25 Grady Sizemore .20 .50
26 Dustin Pedroia .30 .75
27 Chris Johnson .12 .30
28 Brian Matusz .12 .30
29 Jason Bay .20 .50
30 Mark Teixeira .20 .50
31 Carlos Quentin .12 .30
32 Miguel Tejada .20 .50
33 Ryan Howard .25 .60
34 Adrian Beltre .30 .75
35 Joe Mauer .25 .60
36 Johan Santana .20 .50
37 Logan Morrison .12 .30
38 C.J. Wilson .12 .30
39 Carlos Lee .12 .30
40 Ian Kinsler .20 .50
41 Shin-Soo Choo .20 .50
42 Adam Wainwright .20 .50
43 Derek Lowe .12 .30
44 Carlos Gonzalez .20 .50
45 Lance Berkman .20 .50
46 Jon Lester .20 .50
47 Miguel Cabrera .30 .75
48 Justin Verlander .30 .75
49 Tyler Colvin .12 .30
50 Matt Cain .20 .50
51 Brett Anderson .12 .30
52 Gordon Beckham .12 .30
53 David DeJesus .12 .30
54 Jonathan Sanchez .12 .30
55 Jorge Posada .20 .50
56 Neil Walker .20 .50
57 Jorge De La Rosa .12 .30
58 Torii Hunter .12 .30
59 Andrew McCutchen .30 .75
60 Mat Latos .20 .50
61 CC Sabathia .20 .50
62 Brett Myers .12 .30
63 Ryan Zimmerman .20 .50
64 Trevor Cahill .12 .30
65 Clayton Kershaw .50 1.25
66 Andre Ethier .20 .50
67 Kosuke Fukudome .20 .50
68 Justin Upton .20 .50
69 B.J. Upton .20 .50
70 J.P. Arencibia .12 .30
71 Phil Hughes .12 .30
72 Tim Hudson .20 .50
73 Francisco Liriano .12 .30
74 Ike Davis .12 .30
75 Delmon Young .20 .50
76 Paul Konerko .20 .50
77 Carlos Beltran .20 .50
78 Mike Stanton .30 .75
79 Adam Jones .20 .50
80 Jimmy Rollins .20 .50
81 Alex Rios .12 .30
82 Chad Billingsley .20 .50
83 Tommy Hanson .12 .30
84 Travis Wood .12 .30
85 Magglio Ordonez .20 .50
86 Jake Peavy .12 .30
87 Adrian Gonzalez .25 .60
88 Aaron Hill .12 .30
89 Kendry Morales .12 .30
90 Manny Ramirez .30 .75
91 Hunter Pence .20 .50
92 Josh Beckett .12 .30
93 Mark Reynolds .12 .30
94 Drew Stubbs .12 .30
95 Dan Haren .12 .30
96 Chris Carpenter .20 .50
97 Mitch Moreland .12 .30
98 Starlin Castro .20 .50
99 Roy Halladay .20 .50
100 Stephen Drew .12 .30
101 Aramis Ramirez .12 .30
102 Daniel Hudson .12 .30
103 Alexei Ramirez .20 .50
104 Rickie Weeks .12 .30
105 Will Venable .12 .30
106 David Price .25 .60
107 Dan Uggla .12 .30
108 Austin Jackson .12 .30
109 Evan Longoria .20 .50
110 Ryan Ludwick .12 .30
111 Chase Utley .20 .50
112 Johnny Cueto .20 .50
113 Billy Butler .12 .30
114 David Wright .25 .60
115 Jose Reyes .20 .50
116 Robinson Cano .20 .50
117 Josh Johnson .20 .50
118 Chris Coghlan .12 .30
119 David Ortiz .30 .75
120 Jay Bruce .20 .50
121 Jayson Werth .20 .50
122 Matt Holliday .30 .75
123 John Danks .12 .30
124 Franklin Gutierrez .12 .30
125 Zack Greinke .30 .75
126 Jacoby Ellsbury .25 .60
127 Madison Bumgarner .25 .60
128 Mike Leake .20 .50
129 Carl Crawford .20 .50
130 Clay Buchholz .12 .30
131 Gavin Floyd .12 .30
132 Mike Minor .12 .30
133 Jose Tabata .12 .30
134 Jason Castro .12 .30
135 Chris Young .12 .30
136 Jose Bautista .20 .50
137 Felix Hernandez .20 .50
138 Koji Uehara .12 .30
139 Dexter Fowler .20 .50
140 J.A. Happ .20 .50
141 Tim Lincecum .20 .50
142 Todd Helton .20 .50
143 Ubaldo Jimenez .12 .30
144 Yovani Gallardo .12 .30
145 Derek Jeter .75 2.00
146 Wade Davis .12 .30
147 Hiroki Kuroda .12 .30
148 Nelson Cruz .30 .75
149 Martin Prado .12 .30
150 Michael Cuddyer .12 .30
151 Mark Buehrle .20 .50
152 Danny Valencia .20 .50
153 Ichiro Suzuki .40 1.00
154 Brett Wallace .12 .30
155 Troy Tulowitzki .30 .75
156 Pedro Alvarez .75 2.00
157 Brandon Morrow .12 .30
158 Jered Weaver .20 .50
159 Michael Young .12 .30
160 Wandy Rodriguez .12 .30
161 Alfonso Soriano .20 .50
162 Kelly Johnson .12 .30
163 Roy Oswalt .20 .50
164 Brian Roberts .12 .30
165 Jaime Garcia .20 .50
166 Edinson Volquez .12 .30
167 Vladimir Guerrero .20 .50
168 Cliff Lee .20 .50
169 Johnny Damon .20 .50
170 Alex Rodriguez .40 1.00
171 Nick Markakis .25 .60
172 Cole Hamels .25 .60
173 Prince Fielder .20 .50
174 Kurt Suzuki .12 .30
175 Ryan Braun .20 .50
176 Justin Morneau .20 .50
177 Denard Span .12 .30
178 Elvis Andrus .20 .50
179 Stephen Strasburg .30 .75
180 Adam Lind .20 .50
181 Corey Hart .12 .30
182 Adam Dunn .20 .50
183 Bobby Abreu .12 .30
184 Gaby Sanchez .12 .30
185 Ian Kennedy .12 .30
186 Kevin Youkilis .12 .30
187 Vernon Wells .12 .30
188 Matt Garza .12 .30
189 Victor Martinez .20 .50
190 Casey McGehee .12 .30
191 Jake McGee (RC) .75 2.00
192 Lars Anderson RC .60 1.50
193 Mark Trumbo (RC) 1.00 2.50
194 Konrad Schmidt RC .40 1.00
195 Jeremy Jeffress RC .40 1.00
196 Brent Morel RC .40 1.00
197 Aroldis Chapman RC 1.25 3.00
198 Greg Halman RC .60 1.50
199 Jeremy Hellickson RC 1.00 2.50
200 Yunesky Maya RC .40 1.00
201 Kyle Drabek RC .60 1.50
202 Ben Revere RC .60 1.50
203 Desmond Jennings RC .60 1.50
204 Brandon Beachy RC 1.00 2.50
205 Freddie Freeman RC 6.00 15.00
206 Andrew Romine RC .40 1.00
207 John Lindsey RC .40 1.00
208 Mark Rogers (RC) .40 1.00
209 Brian Bogusevic (RC) .40 1.00
210 Yonder Alonso RC .60 1.50
211 Gregory Infante RC .40 1.00
212 Dillon Gee RC .60 1.50
213 Ozzie Martinez RC .40 1.00
214 Brandon Snyder (RC) .40 1.00
215 Daniel Descalso RC .40 1.00
216 Brett Sinkbeil RC .40 1.00
217 Lucas Duda RC 1.00 2.50
218 Cory Luebke RC .40 1.00
219 Hank Conger RC .60 1.50
220 Chris Sale RC 3.00 8.00

2011 Bowman Blue

*BLUE 1-190: 1.5X TO 4X BASIC
*BLUE: 191-220: .75X TO 2X BASIC
STATED PRINT RUN 500 SER.#'d SETS

2011 Bowman Gold

COMPLETE SET (220) 40.00 80.00
*GOLD 1-190: .75X TO 2X BASIC
*GOLD: 191-220: .5X TO 1.2X BASIC

2011 Bowman Green

*GREEN 1-190: 2X TO 5X BASIC
*GREEN: 191-220: .75X TO 2X BASIC
STATED PRINT RUN 450 SER.#'d SETS

2011 Bowman International

*INTER 1-190: 1.2X TO 3X BASIC
*INTER 191-220: .6X TO 1.5X BASIC
INT.PLATE PRINT RUN 1 SET PER COLOR
BLACK-CYAN-MAGENTA-YELLOW ISSUED
NO PLATE PRICING DUE TO SCARCITY

2011 Bowman Orange

*ORANGE 1-190: 2.5X TO 6X BASIC
*ORANGE 191-220: .75X TO 2X BASIC
STATED PRINT RUN 250 SER.#'d SETS

2011 Bowman Red

STATED PRINT RUN 1 SER.#'d SET
NO PRICING DUE TO SCARCITY

2011 Bowman Bowman's Best

COMPLETE SET (25) 8.00 20.00
*REF: 3X TO 8X BASIC
REF PRINT RUN 99 SER.#'d SETS
ATOMIC PRINT RUN 1 SER.#'d SET
NO ATOMIC PRICING AVAILABLE
XF PRINT RUN 25 SER.#'d SETS
NO XF PRICING DUE TO SCARCITY
BB1 Buster Posey 1.00 2.50
BB2 Roy Halladay .50 1.25
BB3 Miguel Cabrera .75 2.00
BB4 Mark Teixeira .50 1.25
BB5 Robinson Cano .50 1.25
BB6 Chase Utley .50 1.25
BB7 Ichiro Suzuki 1.00 2.50
BB8 Ryan Braun .50 1.25
BB9 Josh Hamilton .50 1.25
BB10 Mike Stanton .75 2.00
BB11 Derek Jeter 2.00 5.00
BB12 Joey Votto .75 2.00
BB13 Alex Rodriguez 1.00 2.50
BB14 Albert Pujols 1.00 2.50
BB15 Jason Heyward .60 1.50
BB16 Adrian Gonzalez .60 1.50
BB17 Troy Tulowitzki .75 2.00
BB18 Stephen Strasburg .75 2.00
BB19 Tim Lincecum .50 1.25
BB20 Felix Hernandez .50 1.25
BB21 Kevin Youkilis .30 .75
BB22 Joe Mauer .60 1.50
BB23 Ubaldo Jimenez .30 .75
BB24 Ryan Howard .60 1.50
BB25 Carl Crawford .50 1.25

2011 Bowman Bowman's Best Prospects

COMPLETE SET (50) 30.00 80.00
51-75 ODDS 1:8 HOBBY
51-75 REF.ODDS 1:256 HOBBY
REF PRINT RUN 99 SER.#'d SETS
51-75 ATOMIC ODDS 1:25,343 HOBBY
ATOMIC PRINT RUN 1 SER.#'d SET
NO ATOMIC PRICING AVAILABLE
51-75 XF ODDS 1:1013 HOBBY
XF PRINT RUN 25 SER.#'d SETS
NO XF PRICING DUE TO SCARCITY
BBP1 Bryce Harper 4.00 10.00
BBP2 Grant Green .30 .75
BBP3 Nick Franklin .50 1.25
BBP4 Simon Castro .30 .75
BBP5 Manny Machado 3.00 8.00
BBP6 Dustin Ackley .50 1.25
BBP7 Mike Moustakas .75 2.00
BBP8 Michael Pineda .75 2.00
BBP9 Mike Trout 75.00 200.00
BBP10 Jerry Sands .75 2.00
BBP11 Brett Jackson .50 1.25
BBP12 Jesus Montero .30 .75
BBP13 Jameson Taillon .50 1.25
BBP14 Julio Teheran .50 1.25
BBP15 Dee Gordon .50 1.25
BBP16 Shelby Miller 1.50 4.00
BBP17 Jacob Turner 1.25 3.00
BBP18 Brandon Belt .75 2.00
BBP19 Gary Sanchez 1.50 4.00
BBP20 Miguel Sano .60 1.50
BBP21 Devin Mesoraco .75 2.00
BBP22 Zach Britton .75 2.00
BBP23 Tyler Matzek .50 1.25
BBP24 Matt Dominguez .50 1.25
BBP25 Wil Myers .75 2.00
BBP51 Bryce Harper 4.00 10.00
BBP52 Shelby Miller 1.50 4.00
BBP53 Arodys Vizcaino .50 1.25
BBP54 Jonathan Singleton .50 1.25
BBP55 Manny Machado 3.00 8.00
BBP56 Matt Moore .75 2.00
BBP57 Devin Mesoraco .75 2.00
BBP58 Christian Colon .30 .75
BBP59 Chris Archer .60 1.50
BBP60 Martin Perez .75 2.00
BBP61 Aaron Hicks .50 1.25
BBP62 Jean Segura 1.25 3.00
BBP63 Delino DeShields Jr. .30 .75
BBP64 Wil Myers .75 2.00
BBP65 Jacob Turner 1.25 3.00
BBP66 Josh Sale .50 1.25
BBP67 Miguel Sano .60 1.50
BBP68 Jason Kipnis 1.00 2.50
BBP69 Luis Heredia .30 .75
BBP70 Anthony Ranaudo .75 2.00
BBP71 Stetson Allie .50 1.25
BBP72 Joe Benson .30 .75
BBP73 Nick Castellanos 1.50 4.00
BBP74 Billy Hamilton .60 1.50
BBP75 Manny Banuelos .75 2.00

2011 Bowman Bowman's Best Prospects Refractors

*REF: 3X TO 8X BASIC
51-75 STATED ODDS 1:256 HOBBY
STATED PRINT RUN 99 SER.#'d SETS
BBP1 Bryce Harper 20.00 50.00
BBP9 Mike Trout 600.00 1500.00
BBP51 Bryce Harper 20.00 50.00

2011 Bowman Bowman's Brightest

COMPLETE SET (25) 15.00 40.00
BBR1 Bryce Harper 4.00 10.00
BBR2 Mike Moustakas .75 2.00
BBR3 Mark Trumbo .75 2.00
BBR4 Paul Goldschmidt 4.00 10.00
BBR5 Rich Poythress .30 .75
BBR6 Mike Trout 30.00 80.00
BBR7 Dee Gordon .50 1.25
BBR8 Tyson Auer .30 .75
BBR9 Jay Austin .30 .75
BBR10 Eury Perez .30 .75
BBR11 Slade Heathcott .75 2.00
BBR12 Michael Taylor .30 .75
BBR13 Johermyn Chavez .30 .75
BBR14 Engel Beltre .30 .75
BBR15 Wilin Rosario .30 .75
BBR16 Freddie Freeman 5.00 12.00
BBR17 Wilmer Flores .50 1.25
BBR18 Domonic Brown .60 1.50
BBR19 Manny Machado 3.00 8.00
BBR20 Lonnie Chisenhall .50 1.25
BBR21 Jose Iglesias .50 1.25
BBR22 Desmond Jennings .50 1.25
BBR23 Jurickson Profar .75 2.00
BBR24 Tony Sanchez .50 1.25
BBR25 Jedd Gyorko .75 2.00

2011 Bowman Checklists

COMPLETE SET (5) .40 1.00
RED: 4X TO 10X BASIC
RED PRINT RUN 500 SER.#'d SETS

2011 Bowman Finest Futures

COMPLETE SET (25) 8.00 20.00
FF1 Jason Heyward .50 1.25
FF2 Buster Posey .75 2.00
FF3 Gordon Beckham .25 .60
FF4 Brian Matusz .25 .60
FF5 Mike Stanton .60 1.50
FF6 Starlin Castro .40 1.00
FF7 Carlos Santana .60 1.50
FF8 Aroldis Chapman .75 2.00
FF9 Pedro Alvarez .50 1.25
FF10 Freddie Freeman 4.00 10.00
FF11 Troy Tulowitzki .60 1.50
FF12 Domonic Brown .50 1.25
FF13 Chris Carter .25 .60
FF14 Ubaldo Jimenez .25 .60
FF15 Ike Davis .25 .60
FF16 Austin Jackson .25 .60
FF17 J.P. Arencibia .25 .60
FF18 Ryan Braun .40 1.00
FF19 Justin Upton .40 1.00
FF20 Mat Latos .40 1.00
FF21 Clayton Kershaw 1.00 2.50
FF22 Carlos Gonzalez .40 1.00
FF23 Stephen Strasburg .60 1.50
FF24 Andrew McCutchen .60 1.50
FF25 Madison Bumgarner .50 1.25

2011 Bowman Future's Game Triple Relics

STATED PRINT RUN 99 SER.#'d SETS
AL Alex Liddi 5.00 12.00
AR Austin Romine 5.00 12.00
AS Anthony Slama 4.00 10.00
AT Alex Torres 5.00 12.00
BJ Brett Jackson 10.00 25.00
BM Bryan Morris 5.00 12.00
BR Ben Revere 5.00 12.00
CC Chun-Hsiu Chen 10.00 25.00
CF Christian Friedrich 4.00 10.00
CP Carlos Peguero 4.00 10.00
DB Domonic Brown 12.50 30.00
DE Danny Espinosa 5.00 12.00
DG Dee Gordon 6.00 15.00
DJ Desmond Jennings 5.00 12.00
EP Eury Perez 4.00 10.00
ES Eduardo Sanchez 8.00 20.00
FP Francisco Peguero 4.00 10.00
GG Grant Green 4.00 10.00
GH Gorkys Hernandez 4.00 10.00
HA Henderson Alvarez 4.00 10.00
HC Hank Conger 5.00 12.00
HL Hak-Ju Lee 8.00 20.00
HN Hector Noesi 5.00 12.00
JF Jeurys Familia 4.00 10.00
JH Jeremy Hellickson 6.00 15.00
JT Julio Teheran 6.00 15.00
LC Lonnie Chisenhall 6.00 15.00
LJ Luis Jimenez 8.00 20.00
LM Logan Morrison 4.00 10.00
MM Mike Minor 6.00 15.00
MMO Mike Moustakas 4.00 10.00
MT Mike Trout 40.00 100.00
OM Ozzie Martinez 4.00 10.00
PB Pedro Baez 4.00 10.00
PC Pedro Ciriaco 6.00 15.00
PV Philippe Valiquette 8.00 20.00
SC Simon Castro 4.00 10.00
SM Shelby Miller 12.50 30.00
SP Stolmy Pimentel 4.00 10.00
TM Trystan Magnuson 4.00 10.00
WR Wilin Rosario 5.00 12.00
WRA Wilkin Ramirez 4.00 10.00
ZB Zach Britton 5.00 12.00
ZW Zack Wheeler 10.00 25.00

2011 Bowman Prospect Autographs

EXCHANGE DEADLINE 4/30/2014
BB Bryce Brentz 4.00 10.00
BBR Brett Brach 4.00 10.00
BC Brandon Crawford 8.00 20.00
CC Chevez Clarke 4.00 10.00
DD Daniel Descalso 4.00 10.00
DS Domingo Santana 10.00 25.00
JD Justin De Fratus 4.00 10.00
JG Joe Gardner 4.00 10.00
JO Justin O'Conner 4.00 10.00
JS Josh Sale 4.00 10.00
KC Kaleb Cowart 4.00 10.00
KV Kolbrin Vitek 4.00 10.00
MC Michael Choice 4.00 10.00
MM Manny Machado 40.00 100.00
MP Michael Pineda 6.00 15.00
TB Tim Beckham 8.00 20.00
YR Yorman Rodriguez 4.00 10.00
ZC Zack Cox 4.00 10.00
ZW Zack Wheeler 5.00 12.00

2011 Bowman Prospects

COMP.SET w/o AU (110) 20.00 50.00
PLATE PRINT RUN 1 SET PER COLOR
BLACK-CYAN-MAGENTA-YELLOW ISSUED
NO PLATE PRICING DUE TO SCARCITY
EXCHANGE DEADLINE 4/30/2014
BP1A Bryce Harper 6.00 15.00
BP1B Bryce Harper AU 100.00 250.00
BP2 Chris Dennis .15 .40
BP3 Jeremy Barfield .15 .40
BP4 Nate Freiman .15 .40
BP5 Tyler Moore .40 1.00
BP6 Anthony Carter .15 .40
BP7 Ryan Cavan .15 .40
BP8 Stephen Vogt .25 .60
BP9 Carlo Testa .15 .40
BP10 Erik Davis .15 .40
BP11 Jack Shuck .40 1.00
BP12 Charles Brewer .15 .40
BP13 Alex Castellanos .25 .60
BP14 Anthony Vasquez .15 .40
BP15 Michael Brenly .15 .40
BP16 Kody Hinze .25 .60
BP17 Hector Noesi .25 .60
BP18 Tyler Bortnick .15 .40
BP19 Thomas Layne .15 .40
BP20 Everett Teaford .15 .40
BP21 Jose Pirela .25 .60
BP22 Joel Carreno .15 .40
BP23 Vinnie Catricala .50 1.25
BP24 Tom Koehler .15 .40
BP25 Jonathan Schoop .25 .60
BP26 Chun-Hsiu Chen .40 1.00
BP27 Amaury Rivas .15 .40
BP28 Oswaldo Arcia .15 .40
BP29 Johermyn Chavez .15 .40
BP30 Michael Spina .15 .40
BP31 Kyle McPherson .25 .60
BP32 Albert Cartwright .15 .40
BP33 Joseph Wieland .40 1.00
BP34 Ben Paulsen .15 .40
BP35 Jason Hagerty .15 .40
BP36 Marcell Ozuna .60 1.50
BP37 Dave Sappelt .50 1.25
BP38 Eduardo Escobar .15 .40
BP39 Aaron Baker .15 .40
BP40 Deryk Hooker .15 .40
BP41 Ty Morrison .15 .40
BP42 Keon Broxton .15 .40
BP43 Corey Jones .15 .40
BP44 Manny Banuelos .40 1.00
BP45 Brandon Guyer .25 .60
BP46 Juan Nicasio .15 .40
BP47 Sean Ochinko .15 .40
BP48 Adam Warren .25 .60
BP49 Phillip Cerreto .15 .40
BP50 Mychal Givens .15 .40
BP51 James Fuller .15 .40
BP52 Ronnie Welty .15 .40
BP53 Dan Straily .75 2.00
BP54 Gabriel Jacobo .15 .40
BP55 David Rubinstein .15 .40
BP56 Kevin Mailloux .15 .40
BP57 Angel Castillo .15 .40
BP58 Adrian Salcedo .25 .60
BP59 Ronald Bermudez .15 .40
BP60 Jarek Cunningham .25 .60
BP61 Matt Magill .25 .60
BP62 Willie Cabrera .15 .40
BP63 Austin Hyatt .25 .60
BP64 Cody Puckett .25 .60
BP65 Jacob Goebbert .25 .60
BP66 Matt Carpenter 1.25 3.00
BP67 Dan Klein .25 .60
BP68 Sean Ratliff .15 .40
BP69 Elih Villanueva .15 .40
BP70 Wade Gaynor .15 .40
BP71 Evan Crawford .15 .40
BP72 Avisail Garcia .30 .75
BP73 Kevin Rivers .15 .40
BP74 Jim Gallagher .15 .40
BP75 Brian Broderick .15 .40
BP76 Tyson Auer .15 .40
BP77 Matt Klinker .15 .40
BP78 Cole Figueroa .15 .40
BP79 Rafael Ynoa .15 .40
BP80 Dee Gordon .25 .60
BP81 Blake Forsythe .15 .40
BP82 Jurickson Profar .40 1.00
BP83 Jedd Gyorko .40 1.00
BP84 Matt Hague .25 .60
BP85 Mason Williams .40 1.00
BP86 Stetson Allie .25 .60
BP87 Jarred Cosart .25 .60
BP88 Wagner Mateo .40 1.00
BP89 Allen Webster .25 .60
BP90 Adron Chambers .15 .40
BP91 Blake Smith .15 .40
BP92 J.D. Martinez 1.25 3.00
BP93 Brandon Belt .40 1.00
BP94 Drake Britton .15 .40
BP95 Addison Reed .15 .40
BP96 Adonis Cardona .25 .60
BP97 Yordy Cabrera .15 .40
BP98 Tony Wolters .15 .40
BP99 Paul Goldschmidt 2.00 5.00
BP100 Sean Coyle .25 .60
BP101 Rymer Liriano .40 1.00
BP102 Eric Thames .75 2.00
BP103 Brian Fletcher .15 .40
BP104 Ben Gamel .25 .60
BP105 Kyle Russell .25 .60
BP106 Sammy Solis .15 .40
BP107 Garin Cecchini .40 1.00
BP108 Carlos Perez .15 .40
BP109 Darin Mastroianni .15 .40
BP110 Jonathan Villar .40 1.00

2011 Bowman Prospects Blue

*BLUE: 1.5X TO 4X BASIC
STATED PRINT RUN 500 SER.#'d SETS
HARPER AU PRINT RUN 250 SER.#'d SETS
EXCHANGE DEADLINE 4/30/2014
BP1A Bryce Harper 15.00 40.00
BP1B Bryce Harper AU 150.00 400.00

2011 Bowman Prospects Green

*GREEN: 1.5X TO 4X BASIC
STATED PRINT RUN 450 SER.#'d SETS
BP1 Bryce Harper 12.00 30.00

2011 Bowman Prospects International

*INTERNATIONAL : 1.5X TO 4X BASIC
BP1 Bryce Harper 8.00 20.00

2011 Bowman Prospects Orange

*ORANGE: 3X TO 8X BASIC
STATED PRINT RUN 250 SER.#'d SETS
HARPER AU PRINT RUN 25 SER.#'d SETS
NO HARPER AU PRICING DUE TO SCARCITY
EXCHANGE DEADLINE 4/30/2014
BP1A Bryce Harper 25.00 60.00

2011 Bowman Prospects Purple

*PURPLE: 1.5X TO 4X BASIC
HARPER AU PRINT RUN 55 SER.#'d SETS
EXCHANGE DEADLINE 4/30/2014
BP1A Bryce Harper 20.00 50.00
BP1B Bryce Harper AU 500.00 1000.00

2011 Bowman Prospects Red

STATED PRINT RUN 1 SER.#'d SET
NO PRICING DUE TO SCARCITY

2011 Bowman Topps 100

COMPLETE SET (100) 40.00 80.00
TP1 Bryce Harper 6.00 15.00
TP2 Jonathan Singleton .50 1.25
TP3 Tony Sanchez .50 1.25
TP4 Ryan Larvarnway 1.25 3.00
TP5 Rex Brothers .30 .75
TP6 Brandon Belt .75 2.00
TP7 Christian Colon .30 .75
TP8 Reymond Fuentes .30 .75
TP9 Alex Liddi .30 .75
TP10 Zack Cox .50 1.25
TP11 Derek Norris .30 .75
TP12 Hayden Simpson .30 .75
TP13 Alex Colome .30 .75
TP14 Lonnie Chisenhall .50 1.25
TP15 Mike Montgomery .50 1.25
TP16 Gary Sanchez 1.50 4.00
TP17 Shelby Miller 1.50 4.00
TP18 Matt Moore .75 2.00
TP19 Austin Romine .30 .75
TP20 Delino DeShields .30 .75
TP21 Drew Pomeranz .50 1.25
TP22 Michael Pineda .75 2.00
TP23 Thomas Neal .30 .75
TP24 Chun-Hsiu Chen .75 2.00
TP25 Arodys Vizcaino .50 1.25
TP26 Grant Green .30 .75
TP27 Eric Thames 1.50 4.00
TP28 Matt Davidson .50 1.25
TP29 Deck McGuire .30 .75
TP30 Adeiny Hechavarria .30 .75
TP31 Jean Segura 1.25 3.00
TP32 Paul Goldschmidt 4.00 10.00
TP33 Simon Castro .30 .75
TP34 Garin Cecchini .75 2.00
TP35 Julio Teheran .50 1.25
TP36 Hak-Ju Lee .30 .75
TP37 Randall Delgado .50 1.25
TP38 Sammy Solis .30 .75
TP39 Wil Myers .75 2.00
TP40 Miguel Sano .60 1.50
TP41 Michael Taylor .30 .75
TP42 Nolan Arenado 2.00 5.00
TP43 John Lamb .30 .75
TP44 Jurickson Profar .75 2.00
TP45 Jacob Turner 1.25 3.00
TP46 Anthony Rizzo 3.00 8.00
TP47 Slade Heathcott .75 2.00
TP48 Brody Colvin .30 .75
TP49 Yasmani Grandal .50 1.25
TP50 Dellin Betances .75 2.00
TP51 Charles Brewer .30 .75
TP52 Jared Mitchell .50 1.25
TP53 Nick Franklin .50 1.25
TP54 Manny Machado 3.00 8.00
TP55 Manny Banuelos .75 2.00
TP56 Allen Webster .50 1.25
TP57 Kolbrin Vitek .50 1.25
TP58 Jesus Montero .30 .75
TP59 Wilmer Flores .50 1.25
TP60 Jarrod Parker .75 2.00
TP61 Zach Lee .50 1.25
TP62 Alex Torres .30 .75
TP63 Adron Chambers .30 .75
TP64 Tyler Skaggs .75 2.00
TP65 Kyle Seager .75 2.00
TP66 Josh Vitters .50 1.25
TP67 Matt Harvey 2.00 5.00
TP68 Rudy Owens .30 .75
TP69 Donavan Tate .50 1.25
TP70 Jose Iglesias .50 1.25
TP71 Alex White .30 .75
TP72 Robbie Erlin .50 1.25
TP73 Johermyn Chavez .30 .75
TP74 Mauricio Robles .30 .75
TP75 Matt Dominguez .50 1.25
TP76 Jason Kipnis 1.00 2.50
TP77 Aaron Sanchez .50 1.25
TP78 Tyler Matzek .50 1.25
TP79 Chance Ruffin .30 .75
TP80 Jarred Cosart .50 1.25
TP81 Chris Withrow .30 .75
TP82 Drake Britton .30 .75
TP83 Michael Choice .50 1.25
TP84 Freddie Freeman 5.00 12.00
TP85 Jameson Taillon .50 1.25
TP86 Devin Mesoraco .75 2.00
TP87 Brandon Laird .50 1.25
TP88 Keon Broxton .30 .75
TP89 Mike Moustakas .75 2.00
TP90 Mike Trout 60.00 150.00
TP91 Danny Duffy .50 1.25
TP92 Brett Jackson .50 1.25
TP93 Dustin Ackley .50 1.25
TP94 Jerry Sands .75 2.00
TP95 Jake Skole .30 .75
TP96 Kyle Gibson .50 1.25
TP97 Martin Perez .75 2.00
TP98 Zach Britton .75 2.00
TP99 Xavier Avery .30 .75
TP100 Dee Gordon .50 1.25

2011 Bowman Topps of the Class

COMPLETE SET (25) 10.00 25.00
TC1 Jerry Sands .75 2.00
TC2 Mike Olt .50 1.25
TC3 Jared Clark .30 .75
TC4 Nick Franklin .50 1.25
TC5 Paul Goldschmidt 4.00 10.00
TC6 Mike Moustakas .75 2.00
TC7 Greg Halman .50 1.25
TC8 Chris Carter .30 .75
TC9 Rich Poythress .30 .75
TC10 Mark Trumbo .75 2.00
TC11 Johermyn Chavez .30 .75
TC12 Brandon Allen .30 .75
TC13 Brandon Laird .50 1.25
TC14 J.P. Arencibia .30 .75
TC15 Marcell Ozuna 1.25 3.00
TC16 Kevin Mailloux .30 .75
TC17 Clint Robinson .30 .75
TC18 Tyler Moore .75 2.00
TC19 Joe Benson .30 .75
TC20 Anthony Rizzo 3.00 8.00
TC21 Jesus Montero .30 .75
TC22 Tim Pahuta .30 .75
TC23 Grant Green .30 .75
TC24 Lucas Duda .75 2.00
TC25 Michael Spina .30 .75

2011 Bowman Draft

COMPLETE SET (110) 8.00 20.00
COMMON CARD (1-110) .20 .50
STATED PLATE ODDS 1:928 HOBBY
PLATE PRINT RUN 1 SET PER COLOR
BLACK-CYAN-MAGENTA-YELLOW ISSUED
NO PLATE PRICING DUE TO SCARCITY
1 Mike Moustakas RC .50 1.25
2 Ryan Adams RC .20 .50
3 Alexi Amarista RC .20 .50
4 Anthony Bass RC .20 .50
5 Pedro Beato RC .20 .50
6 Bruce Billings RC .20 .50
7 Charlie Blackmon RC 4.00 10.00
8 Brian Broderick RC .20 .50
9 Rex Brothers RC .20 .50
10 Tyler Chatwood RC .20 .50
11 Jose Altuve RC 2.00 5.00
12 Salvador Perez RC .75 2.00
13 Mark Hamburger RC .20 .50
14 Matt Carpenter RC 1.50 4.00
15 Ezequiel Carrera RC .20 .50
16 Jose Ceda RC .20 .50
17 Andrew Brown RC .30 .75
18 Maikel Cleto RC .20 .50
19 Steve Cishek RC .20 .50
20 Lonnie Chisenhall RC .30 .75
21 Henry Sosa RC .20 .50
22 Tim Collins RC .20 .50
23 Josh Collmenter RC .20 .50
24 David Cooper RC .20 .50
25 Brandon Crawford RC .30 .75
26 Brandon Laird RC .30 .75
27 Tony Cruz RC .50 1.25
28 Chase d'Arnaud RC .20 .50
29 Fautino De Los Santos RC .20 .50
30 Rubby De La Rosa RC .50 1.25
31 Andy Dirks RC .50 1.25

32 Jarrod Dyson RC .30 .75
33 Cody Eppley RC .20 .50
34 Logan Forsythe RC .20 .50
35 Todd Frazier RC .50 1.25
36 Eric Fryer RC .30 .75
37 Charlie Furbush RC .20 .50
38 Cory Gearrin RC .20 .50
39 Graham Godfrey RC .20 .50
40 Dee Gordon RC .30 .75
41 Brandon Gomes RC .20 .50
42 Bryan Shaw RC .20 .50
43 Brandon Guyer RC .30 .75
44 Mark Hamilton RC .30 .75
45 Brad Hand RC .20 .50
46 Anthony Recker RC .20 .50
47 Jeremy Horst RC .30 .75
48 Tommy Hottovy (RC) .30 .75
49 Jose Iglesias RC .30 .75
50 Craig Kimbrel RC .50 1.25
51 Josh Judy RC .20 .50
52 Cole Kimball RC .20 .50
53 Alan Johnson RC .20 .50
54 Brandon Kintzler RC .20 .50
55 Pete Kozma RC .50 1.25
56 D.J. LeMahieu RC 2.50 6.00
57 Duane Below RC .30 .75
58 Josh Lindblom RC .30 .75
59 Zack Cozart RC .50 1.25
60 Al Alburquerque RC .20 .50
61 Trystan Magnuson RC .20 .50
62 Michael Martinez RC .30 .75
63 Michael McKenry RC .30 .75
64 Daniel Moskos RC .20 .50
65 Lance Lynn RC .50 1.25
66 Juan Nicasio RC .20 .50
67 Joe Paterson RC .30 .75
68 Lance Pendleton RC .20 .50
69 Luis Perez RC .20 .50
70 Anthony Rizzo RC 2.00 5.00
71 Joel Carreno RC .20 .50
72 Alex Presley RC .30 .75
73 Vinnie Pestano RC .20 .50
74 Aneury Rodriguez RC .20 .50
75 Josh Rodriguez RC .20 .50
76 Eduardo Sanchez RC .30 .75
77 Matt Young RC .20 .50
78 Amauri Sanit RC .20 .50
79 Nathan Eovaldi RC .50 1.25
80 Javy Guerra (RC) .30 .75
81 Eric Sogard RC .20 .50
82 Henderson Alvarez RC .20 .50
83 Ryan Lavarnway RC .75 2.00
84 Michael Stutes RC .30 .75
85 Everett Teaford RC .20 .50
86 Blake Tekotte RC .20 .50
87 Eric Thames RC 1.00 2.50
88 Arodys Vizcaino RC .30 .75
89 Rene Tosoni RC .20 .50
90 Alex White RC .20 .50
91 Brayan Villarreal RC .20 .50
92 Tony Watson RC .20 .50
93 Johnny Giavotella RC .20 .50
94 Kevin Whelan (RC) .20 .50
95 Mike Nickeas (RC) .20 .50
96 Elih Villanueva RC .20 .50
97 Tom Wilhelmsen RC .20 .50
98 Adam Wilk RC .30 .75
99 Mike Wilson (RC) .20 .50
100 Jerry Sands RC .50 1.25
101 Mike Trout RC 125.00 300.00
102 Kyle Weiland RC .20 .50
103 Kyle Seager RC .50 1.25
104 Jason Kipnis RC .60 1.50
105 Chance Ruffin RC .20 .50
106 J.B. Shuck RC .50 1.25
107 Jacob Turner RC .75 2.00
108 Paul Goldschmidt RC 2.50 6.00
109 Justin Sellers RC .30 .75
110 Trayvon Robinson (RC) .30 .75

2011 Bowman Draft Blue

*BLUE: 1.5X TO 4X BASIC
STATED ODDS 1:17 HOBBY
STATED PRINT RUN 499 SER.#'d SETS

2011 Bowman Draft Gold

*GOLD: 1X TO 2.5X BASIC

2011 Bowman Draft Red

STATED ODDS 1:7410 HOBBY
STATED PRINT RUN 1 SER.#'d SET
NO PRICING DUE TO SCARCITY

2011 Bowman Draft Bryce Harper Green Border Autograph

STATED ODDS 1:6500 HOBBY
EXCHANGE DEADLINE 11/30/2014
BH Bryce Harper 200.00 400.00

2011 Bowman Draft Bryce Harper Relic Autographs

STATED BASE ODDS 1:23,660 HOBBY
STATED BLUE ODDS 1:32,500 HOBBY
STATED GOLD ODDS 1:65,000 HOBBY
STATED GREEN ODDS 1:312,000 HOBBY
STATED RED ODDS 1:1,560,000 HOBBY
BASE PRINT RUN 69 SER.#'d SETS
BLUE PRINT RUN 50 SER.#'d SETS
GOLD PRINT RUN 25 SER.#'d SETS
GREEN PRINT RUN 5 SER.#'d SETS
RED PRINT RUN 1 SER.#'d SET
NO PRICING ON QTY 25 OR LESS
BHAR1A Bryce Harper/69 150.00 300.00
BHAR1B Bryce Harper Blue/50 150.00 300.00

2011 Bowman Draft Future's Game Relics

AL Alex Liddi 3.00 8.00
AR Austin Romine 3.00 8.00
AS Alfredo Silverio 4.00 10.00
AV Arodys Vizcaino 3.00 8.00
BH Bryce Harper 12.50 30.00
BP Brad Peacock 3.00 8.00
DM Devin Mesoraco 4.00 10.00
DP Drew Pomeranz 4.00 10.00
DV Dayan Viciedo 4.00 10.00
GB Gary Brown 4.00 10.00
GG Grant Green 3.00 8.00
GI Gregory Infante 4.00 10.00
HA Henderson Alvarez 5.00 12.00
HL Hak-Ju Lee 3.00 8.00
JA Jose Altuve 5.00 12.00
JC Jarred Cosart 3.00 8.00
JD James Darnell 3.00 8.00
JK Jason Kipnis 6.00 15.00
JM Jhan Marinez 3.00 8.00
JMA Jefry Marte 3.00 8.00
JPR Jurickson Profar 10.00 25.00
JS Jonathan Schoop 5.00 12.00
JTU Jacob Turner 3.00 8.00
KG Kyle Gibson 5.00 12.00
KH Kelvin Herrera 4.00 10.00
LH Liam Hendriks 4.00 10.00
MH Matt Harvey 12.50 30.00
MM Manny Machado 8.00 20.00
MMO Matt Moore 5.00 12.00
MP Martin Perez 3.00 8.00
NA Nolan Arenado 5.00 12.00
PG Paul Goldschmidt 8.00 20.00
RF Reymond Fuentes 3.00 8.00
SM Starling Marte 4.00 10.00
SMI Shelby Miller 4.00 10.00
SV Sebastian Valle 3.00 8.00
TS Tyler Skaggs 3.00 8.00
TT Tyler Thornburg 4.00 10.00
WM Wil Myers 4.00 10.00
WMI Will Middlebrooks 6.00 15.00
WR Wilin Rosario 3.00 8.00
YA Yonder Alonso 4.00 10.00

2011 Bowman Draft Future's Game Relics Blue

*BLUE: .4X TO 1X BASIC
STATED PRINT RUN 199 SER.#'d SETS
NO PRICING DUE TO SCARCITY

2011 Bowman Draft Future's Game Relics Gold

*GOLD: .5X TO 1.2X BASIC
STATED PRINT RUN 50 SER.#'d SETS
NO PRICING DUE TO SCARCITY

2011 Bowman Draft Future's Game Relics Green

STATED PRINT RUN 25 SER.#'d SETS
NO PRICING DUE TO SCARCITY

2011 Bowman Draft Prospects

COMPLETE SET (110) 12.50 30.00
STATED PLATE ODDS 1:928 HOBBY
PLATE PRINT RUN 1 SET PER COLOR
BLACK-CYAN-MAGENTA-YELLOW ISSUED
NO PLATE PRICING DUE TO SCARCITY
BDPP1 John Hicks UER .25 .60
BDPP2 Cody Asche .40 1.00
BDPP3 Tyler Anderson .15 .40
BDPP4 Jack Armstrong .25 .60
BDPP5 Pratt Maynard .15 .40
BDPP6 Javier Baez 2.00 5.00
BDPP7 Kenneth Peoples-Walls .15 .40
BDPP8 Matt Barnes .25 .60
BDPP9 Trevor Bauer 1.50 4.00
BDPP10 Daniel Vogelbach .50 1.25
BDPP11 Mike Wright UER .15 .40
BDPP12 Dante Bichette .25 .60
BDPP13 Hudson Boyd .15 .40
BDPP14 Archie Bradley .50 1.25
BDPP15 Matthew Skole .25 .60
BDPP16 Jed Bradley .25 .60
BDPP17 Tyler Pill .15 .40
BDPP18 Dylan Bundy .50 1.25
BDPP19 Harold Martinez .25 .60
BDPP20 Will Lamb .15 .40
BDPP21 Harold Riggins .15 .40
BDPP22 Zach Cone .25 .60
BDPP23 Kyle Gaedele .15 .40
BDPP24 Kyle Crick .40 1.00
BDPP25 C.J. Cron .50 1.25
BDPP26 Nicholas Delmonico .15 .40
BDPP27 Alex Dickerson .25 .60
BDPP28 Tony Cingrani .75 2.00
BDPP29 Jose Fernandez .60 1.50
BDPP30 Michael Fulmer .40 1.00
BDPP31 Carl Thomore .15 .40
BDPP32 Sean Gilmartin .15 .40
BDPP33 Tyler Goeddel .15 .40
BDPP34 Drew Gagnon .15 .40
BDPP35 Sonny Gray .40 1.00
BDPP36 Larry Greene .25 .60
BDPP37 Nick Martini .15 .40
BDPP38 Taylor Guerrieri .15 .40
BDPP39 Jake Hager .15 .40
BDPP40 James Harris .15 .40
BDPP41 Travis Harrison .25 .60
BDPP42 Nick DeSantiago .25 .60
BDPP43 Chase Larsson .15 .40
BDPP44 Logan Moore .15 .40
BDPP45 Mason Hope .15 .40
BDPP46 Adrian Houser .25 .60
BDPP47 Sean Buckley .15 .40
BDPP48 Rick Anton .15 .40
BDPP49 Scott Woodward .25 .60
BDPP50 David Goforth .15 .40
BDPP51 Taylor Jungmann .25 .60
BDPP52 Blake Snell .60 1.50
BDPP53 Francisco Lindor 2.00 5.00
BDPP54 Mikie Mahtook .40 1.00
BDPP55 Brandon Martin .25 .60
BDPP56 Kevin Quackenbush .25 .60
BDPP57 Kevin Matthews .15 .40
BDPP58 C.J. McElroy .15 .40
BDPP59 Anthony Meo .15 .40
BDPP60 Justin James .25 .60
BDPP61 Levi Michael UER .25 .60
BDPP62 Joseph Musgrove .75 2.00
BDPP63 Brandon Nimmo .75 2.00
BDPP64 Brandon Culbreth .15 .40
BDPP65 Javaris Reynolds .15 .40
BDPP66 Adam Ehrlich .15 .40
BDPP67 Henry Owens .25 .60
BDPP68 Joe Panik .40 1.00
BDPP69 Jace Peterson .15 .40
BDPP70 Lance Jeffries .15 .40
BDPP71 Matthew Budgell .15 .40
BDPP72 Dan Gamache .15 .40
BDPP73 Christopher Lee .15 .40
BDPP74 Kyle Kubitza .15 .40
BDPP75 Nick Ahmed .15 .40
BDPP76 Josh Parr .15 .40
BDPP77 Dwight Smith .15 .40
BDPP78 Steven Gruver .15 .40
BDPP79 Jeffrey Soptic .15 .40
BDPP80 Cory Spangenberg .25 .60
BDPP81 George Springer 1.00 2.50
BDPP82 Bubba Starling .25 .60
BDPP83 Robert Stephenson .30 .75
BDPP84 Trevor Story 5.00 12.00
BDPP85 Madison Boer .15 .40
BDPP86 Blake Swihart .25 .60
BDPP87 Kellen Moen .15 .40
BDPP88 Joe Tuschak .15 .40
BDPP89 Keenyn Walker .15 .40
BDPP91A William Abreu .25 .60
BDPP91B Kolten Wong .25 .60
BDPP92 Tyler Alamo .15 .40
BDPP93 Bryson Brigman .15 .40
BDPP94 Nick Ciuffo .15 .40
BDPP95 Trevor Clifton .15 .40
BDPP96 Zach Collins .25 .60
BDPP97 Joe DeMers .15 .40
BDPP98 Steven Farinaro .15 .40
BDPP99 Jake Jarvis .15 .40
BDPP100 Austin Meadows 4.00 10.00
BDPP101 Hunter Mercado-Hood .15 .40
BDPP102 Dom Nunez .15 .40
BDPP103 Arden Pabst .15 .40
BDPP104 Christian Pelaez .15 .40
BDPP105 Carson Sands .15 .40
BDPP106 Jordan Sheffield .15 .40
BDPP107 Keegan Thompson .15 .40
BDPP108 Dany Toussaint .25 .60
BDPP109 Riley Unroe .15 .40
BDPP110 Matt Vogel .15 .40

2011 Bowman Draft Prospects Blue

*BLUE: 1.5X TO 4X BASIC
STATED ODDS 1:17 HOBBY
STATED PRINT RUN 499 SER.#'d SETS

2011 Bowman Draft Prospects Gold

*GOLD: 1.2X TO 3X BASIC

2011 Bowman Draft Prospects Red

STATED ODDS 1:7410 HOBBY
STATED PRINT RUN 1 SER.#'d SET
NO PRICING DUE TO SCARCITY

2011 Bowman Draft Prospect Autographs

FOUND IN RETAIL PACKS
PLATE PRINT RUN 1 SET PER COLOR
BLACK-CYAN-MAGENTA-YELLOW ISSUED
NO PLATE PRICING DUE TO SCARCITY
AK Aaron Kurcz 3.00 8.00
AT Alex Torres 3.00 8.00
AW Alex Wimmers 3.00 8.00
CS Cody Scarpetta 3.00 8.00
EG Erik Goeddel 3.00 8.00
HA Henderson Alvarez 10.00 25.00
JC Jarek Cunningham 3.00 8.00
JK Joe Kelly 6.00 15.00
JW Joe Wieland 3.00 8.00
ML Matt Lollis 4.00 10.00
RP Rich Poythress 3.00 8.00
SV Sebastian Valle 4.00 10.00
TT Tyler Thornburg 6.00 15.00
BHO Bryan Holaday 4.00 10.00
CBM Chris Balcolm-Miller 3.00 8.00

2011 Bowman Draft Prospect Autographs Blue

*BLUE: .75X TO 2X BASIC
FOUND IN RETAIL PACKS
STATED PRINT RUN 199 SER.#'d SETS

2011 Bowman Draft Prospect Autographs Gold

*GOLD: 1.2X TO 3X BASIC
FOUND IN RETAIL PACKS
STATED PRINT RUN 50 SER.#'d SETS

2011 Bowman Draft Prospect Autographs Red

FOUND IN RETAIL PACKS
STATED PRINT RUN 25 SER.#'d SETS
NO PRICING DUE TO SCARCITY

2012 Bowman

COMP.SET w/o AU (220) 10.00 25.00
COMMON CARD (1-190) .12 .30
COMMON RC (191-220) .40 1.00
PLATE PRINT RUN 1 SET PER COLOR
BLACK-CYAN-MAGENTA-YELLOW ISSUED
NO PLATE PRICING DUE TO SCARCITY
1 Derek Jeter .75 2.00
2 Nick Swisher .25 .60
3 Jered Weaver .25 .60
4 Corey Hart .20 .50
5 Brennan Boesch .20 .50
6 Matt Garza .20 .50
7 Dan Uggla .25 .60
8 Paul Goldschmidt .30 .75
9 Cole Hamels .25 .60
10 Nelson Cruz .30 .75
11 Brett Gardner .25 .60
12 Matt Kemp .25 .60
13 Curtis Granderson .25 .60
14 Pablo Sandoval .25 .60
15 Brandon McCarthy .20 .50
16 Mark Teixeira .25 .60
17 J.J. Hardy .20 .50
18 Yadier Molina .40 1.00
19 Daniel Hudson .20 .50
20 Jacoby Ellsbury .25 .60
21 Yunel Escobar .20 .50
22 Robinson Cano .25 .60
23 Colby Rasmus .25 .60
24 Neil Walker .20 .50
25 John Danks .20 .50
26 Brandon Morrow .20 .50
27 Brandon Beachy .20 .50
28 Mat Latos .25 .60
29 Jeremy Hellickson .20 .50
30 Anibal Sanchez .20 .50
31 Dexter Fowler .25 .60
32 Ryan Braun .20 .50
33 Chris Young .20 .50
34 Mike Trout 10.00 25.00
35 Aroldis Chapman .30 .75
36 Lance Berkman .25 .60
37 Dan Haren .20 .50
38 Paul Konerko .20 .50
39 Carl Crawford .25 .60
40 Melky Cabrera .20 .50
41 B.J. Upton .25 .60
42 Madison Bumgarner .25 .60
43 Casey Kotchman .20 .50
44 Michael Bourn .20 .50
45 Adam Jones .25 .60
46 Jon Lester .20 .50
47 Jaime Garcia .25 .60
48 Zack Greinke .30 .75
49 Albert Pujols .40 1.00
50 Jose Valverde .25 .60
51 Billy Butler .20 .50
52 Mark Reynolds .20 .50
53 Adam Lind .25 .60
54 Jordan Zimmermann .25 .60
55 Geovany Soto .25 .60
56 Ted Lilly .20 .50
57 Allen Craig .25 .60
58 Justin Masterson .20 .50
59 Adam Wainwright .25 .60
60 Jordan Walden .20 .50
61 Jemile Weeks RC .60 1.50
62 Justin Upton .25 .60
63 Alex Rodriguez .40 1.00
64 Josh Beckett .20 .50
65 Ben Revere .25 .60
66 Mariano Rivera .40 1.00
67 Hunter Pence .25 .60
68 Tommy Hanson .20 .50
69 Alexi Ogando .20 .50
70 Brian McCann .25 .60
71 Hanley Ramirez .25 .60
72 Tim Hudson .25 .60
73 Justin Morneau .25 .60
74 Derek Holland .20 .50
75 Roy Halladay .25 .60
76 Andrew McCutchen .30 .75
77 Justin Verlander .30 .75
78 Drew Storen .20 .50
79 Ryan Zimmerman .25 .60
80 Jimmy Rollins .25 .60
81 Eric Hosmer .25 .60
82 Joey Votto .30 .75
83 Shane Victorino .25 .60
84 Ian Kinsler .25 .60
85 Troy Tulowitzki .30 .75
86 David Wright .25 .60
87 Joe Mauer .25 .60
88 James Shields .20 .50
89 Brian Wilson .30 .75
90 Matt Cain .25 .60
91 Chipper Jones .30 .75
92 Miguel Montero .20 .50
93 Ervin Santana .20 .50
94 Shaun Marcum .20 .50
95 Adrian Beltre .30 .75
96 Jose Reyes .20 .50
97 Craig Kimbrel .25 .60
98 Nyjer Morgan .20 .50
99 Matt Holliday .30 .75
100 Chris Sale .30 .75
101 Miguel Cabrera .30 .75
102 Clay Buchholz .20 .50
103 Mike Moustakas .25 .60
104 Ike Davis .20 .50
105 Vance Worley .25 .60
106 Pedro Alvarez .20 .50
107 Ian Kennedy .20 .50
108 Torii Hunter .25 .60
109 Michael Cuddyer .20 .50
110 Dee Gordon .20 .50
111 Ricky Romero .20 .50
112 J.P. Arencibia .20 .50
113 Yovani Gallardo .25 .60
114 Adrian Gonzalez .25 .60
115 Ian Desmond .20 .50
116 Trevor Cahill .20 .50
117 Carlos Ruiz .20 .50
118 Alex Gordon .25 .60
119 Josh Johnson .25 .60
120 Cliff Lee .25 .60
121 Neftali Feliz .20 .50
122 Howie Kendrick .20 .50
123 Todd Helton .25 .60
124 Michael Pineda .20 .50
125 John Axford .20 .50
126 Carlos Santana .25 .60
127 Jose Bautista .25 .60
128 Doug Fister .20 .50
129 Ryan Howard .25 .60
130 Cory Luebke .20 .50
131 Nick Markakis .25 .60
132 Jason Motte .20 .50
133 Gio Gonzalez .25 .60
134 Alex Avila .20 .50
135 Josh Hamilton .25 .60
136 Desmond Jennings .25 .60
137 Roy Oswalt .25 .60
138 Heath Bell .20 .50
139 Tim Lincecum .25 .60
140 Michael Morse .20 .50
141 Dustin Pedroia .30 .75
142 Ryan Vogelsong .20 .50
143 Dustin Ackley .20 .50
144 Salvador Perez .25 .60
145 Brandon Phillips .20 .50
146 Martin Prado .20 .50
147 David Freese .20 .50
148 Rickie Weeks .20 .50
149 Evan Longoria .25 .60
150 Shin-Soo Choo .25 .60
151 Clayton Kershaw .50 1.25
152 Giancarlo Stanton .30 .75
153 Elvis Andrus .25 .60
154 Scott Rolen .25 .60
155 Ben Zobrist .25 .60
156 Mark Trumbo .20 .50
157 Chris Carpenter .25 .60
158 Mike Napoli .20 .50
159 David Ortiz .30 .75
160 R.A. Dickey .25 .60
161 Jason Heyward .25 .60
162 C.J. Wilson .20 .50
163 Buster Posey .40 1.00
164 Max Scherzer .30 .75
165 Ivan Nova .25 .60
166 Victor Martinez .25 .60
167 Asdrubal Cabrera .25 .60
168 Freddie Freeman .40 1.00
169 Stephen Strasburg .30 .75
170 Johnny Cueto .25 .60
171 Lucas Duda .25 .60
172 Bud Norris .20 .50
173 Matt Joyce .20 .50
174 Felix Hernandez .25 .60
175 Starlin Castro .25 .60
176 Ichiro Suzuki .40 1.00
177 Ubaldo Jimenez .20 .50
178 Jhonny Peralta .20 .50
179 Carlos Gonzalez .25 .60
180 Michael Young .20 .50
181 David Price .25 .60
182 Prince Fielder .25 .60
183 James Loney .20 .50
184 Chase Utley .25 .60
185 Jayson Werth .25 .60
186 Aramis Ramirez .20 .50
187 Kevin Youkilis .30 .75
188 Jay Bruce .25 .60
189 Delmon Young .25 .60
190 CC Sabathia .25 .60
191 Brett Lawrie RC .75 2.00
192 Alex Liddi RC .60 1.50
193 Yoenis Cespedes RC 1.50 4.00
194 James Darnell RC .60 1.50
195 Jordan Pacheco RC .60 1.50
196 Tom Milone RC .60 1.50
197 Michael Fiers RC .40 1.00
198 Brett Pill RC 1.00 2.50
199 Taylor Green RC .60 1.50
200 Eric Surkamp RC 1.00 2.50
201 Collin Cowgill RC .60 1.50
202 Tyler Pastornicky RC .60 1.50
203 Leonys Martin RC .60 1.50
204 Jeff Locke RC 1.00 2.50
205 Matt Dominguez RC .75 2.00
206 Michael Taylor RC .60 1.50
207 Adron Chambers RC 1.00 2.50
208 Liam Hendriks RC .60 1.50
209A Yu Darvish RC 1.50 4.00
209B Yu Darvish AU 100.00 200.00
210 Jesus Montero RC .60 1.50
211 Matt Moore RC 1.00 2.50
212 Drew Pomeranz RC .60 1.50
213 Jarrod Parker RC .75 2.00
214 Devin Mesoraco RC .60 1.50
215 Joe Benson RC .60 1.50
216 Brad Peacock RC .60 1.50
217 Dellin Betances RC 1.00 2.50
218 Wilin Rosario RC .60 1.50
219 Chris Parmelee RC .60 1.50
220 Addison Reed RC .60 1.50

2012 Bowman Blue

*BLUE 1-190: 1.5X TO 4X BASIC
*BLUE: 191-220: .6X TO 1.5X BASIC
STATED ODDS 1:16 HOBBY
STATED PRINT RUN 500 SER.#'d SETS

2012 Bowman Gold

*GOLD 1-190: .75X TO 2X BASIC
*GOLD: 191-220: .5X TO 1.2X BASIC

2012 Bowman International

*INT 1-190: 1.5X TO 4X BASIC
*INT 191-220: .6X TO 1.5X BASIC
STATED ODDS 1:8 HOBBY

2012 Bowman Orange

*ORANGE 1-190: 2.5X TO 6X BASIC
*ORANGE 191-220: 1X TO 2.5X BASIC
STATED ODDS 1:32 HOBBY
STATED PRINT RUN 250 SER.#'d SETS

2012 Bowman Red

STATED ODDS 1:4150 HOBBY
STATED PRINT RUN 1 SER.#'d SET
NO PRICING DUE TO SCARCITY

2012 Bowman Silver Ice

*SILVER ICE 1-190: 2X TO 5X BASIC
*SILVER ICE 191-220: .75X TO 2X BASIC
STATED ODDS 1:24 HOBBY

2012 Bowman Silver Ice Red

STATED ODDS 1:173 HOBBY
STATED PRINT RUN 25 SER.#'d SETS
NO PRICING DUE TO SCARCITY

2012 Bowman Bowman's Best

COMPLETE SET (25) 6.00 15.00
STATED ODDS 1:6 HOBBY
PLATE PRINT RUN 1 SET PER COLOR
BLACK-CYAN-MAGENTA-YELLOW ISSUED
NO PLATE PRICING DUE TO SCARCITY
BB1 CC Sabathia .40 1.00
BB2 Dellin Betances .50 1.25
BB3 Jesus Montero .30 .75
BB4 Matt Moore .50 1.25
BB5 Drew Pomeranz .30 .75
BB6 Jarrod Parker .40 1.00
BB7 Devin Mesoraco .30 .75
BB8 Matt Dominguez .40 1.00
BB9 Joe Benson .30 .75
BB10 Brad Peacock .30 .75
BB11 Miguel Cabrera .50 1.25
BB12 Evan Longoria .40 1.00
BB13 Jacob Turner .40 1.00
BB14 Jose Bautista .40 1.00
BB15 Troy Tulowitzki .50 1.25
BB16 Justin Verlander .50 1.25
BB17 Roy Halladay .40 1.00
BB18 Tim Lincecum .40 1.00
BB19 Matt Kemp .40 1.00
BB20 Clayton Kershaw .75 2.00
BB21 Ryan Braun .30 .75
BB22 Albert Pujols .60 1.50
BB23 Josh Hamilton .40 1.00
BB24 Robinson Cano .40 1.00
BB25 Jacoby Ellsbury .40 1.00

2012 Bowman Bowman's Best Die Cut Atomic Refractors

STATED ODDS 1:34,200 HOBBY
STATED PRINT RUN 1 SER.#'d SET
NO PRICING DUE TO SCARCITY

2012 Bowman Bowman's Best Die Cut Refractors

*REF: 1.5X TO 4X BASIC
STATED ODDS 1:496 HOBBY
STATED PRINT RUN 99 SER.#'d SETS

2012 Bowman Bowman's Best Die Cut X-Fractors

STATED ODDS 1:1975 HOBBY
STATED PRINT RUN 25 SER.#'d SETS
NO PRICING DUE TO SCARCITY

2012 Bowman Bowman's Best Prospects

COMPLETE SET (25) 8.00 20.00
STATED ODDS 1:6 HOBBY
PLATE PRINT RUN 1 SET PER COLOR
BLACK-CYAN-MAGENTA-YELLOW ISSUED
NO PLATE PRICING DUE TO SCARCITY
BBP1 Trevor Bauer 2.00 5.00
BBP2 Manny Machado 2.50 6.00
BBP3 Manny Banuelos .50 1.25
BBP4 Bryce Harper 6.00 15.00
BBP5 Shelby Miller .75 2.00
BBP6 Jonathan Singleton .50 1.25
BBP7 Brett Jackson .60 1.50
BBP8 Billy Hamilton .50 1.25
BBP9 Jurickson Profar .50 1.25
BBP10 Matt Harvey 2.50 6.00
BBP11 Travis d'Arnaud .50 1.25
BBP12 Miguel Sano .50 1.25
BBP13 Jameson Taillon .50 1.25
BBP14 Bubba Starling .50 1.25
BBP15 Gerrit Cole 2.50 6.00
BBP16 Wilmer Flores .50 1.25
BBP17 Gary Sanchez 1.25 3.00
BBP18 Zack Wheeler .75 2.00
BBP19 Rymer Liriano .40 1.00
BBP20 Anthony Gose .50 1.25
BBP21 Joe Panik .60 1.50
BBP22 Will Middlebrooks .50 1.25
BBP23 Starling Marte .50 1.25
BBP24 Tyler Skaggs .60 1.50
BBP25 Gary Brown .40 1.00

2012 Bowman Bowman's Best Prospects Die Cut Refractors

*REF: 1.5X TO 4X BASIC
STATED ODDS 1:496 HOBBY
STATED PRINT RUN 99 SER.#'d SETS

2012 Bowman Lucky Redemption Autographs

LUCKY 1 ODDS 1:48,000 HOBBY
LUCKY 2 ODDS 1:30,000 HOBBY
LUCKY 3 ODDS 1:24,000 HOBBY
ANNCD PRINT RUN OF 100
EXCHANGE DEADLINE 04/30/2013
L3YC Yoenis Cespedes 125.00 250.00
L3BH Bryce Harper 150.00 300.00
L3WM Will Middlebrooks 60.00 120.00

2012 Bowman Prospect Autographs

AW Allen Webster 3.00 8.00
BH Bryce Harper 100.00 200.00
CH Chad Huffman 3.00 8.00
CP Carlos Perez 3.00 8.00
DS Dwight Smith 3.00 8.00
JF Jose Fernandez 10.00 25.00
JG Jedd Gyorko 3.00 8.00
JK Joe Kelly 3.00 8.00
JV Jordany Valdespin 5.00 12.00
KK Kyle Kubitza 3.00 8.00
KW Kolten Wong 3.00 8.00
MA Matt Adams 3.00 8.00
ML Matt Lipka 3.00 8.00
MO Mike Olt 3.00 8.00
RG Robbie Grossman 3.00 8.00
SB Sean Buckley 3.00 8.00
SG Sonny Gray 5.00 12.00
TA Tyler Anderson 3.00 8.00
TG Taylor Guerrieri 3.00 8.00
TT Trayce Thompson 3.00 8.00

2012 Bowman Prospect Autographs Blue

*BLUE: .5X TO 1.2X BASIC
STATED PRINT RUN 500 SER.#'d SETS
BH Bryce Harper 200.00 300.00

2012 Bowman Prospect Autographs Orange

*ORANGE: .75X TO 2X BASIC
PRINT RUNS B/WN 15-250 COPIES PER
NO HARPER PRICING DUE TO SCARCITY

2012 Bowman Prospects

PLATE PRINT RUN 1 SET PER COLOR
BLACK-CYAN-MAGENTA-YELLOW ISSUED
NO PLATE PRICING DUE TO SCARCITY
BP1 Justin Nicolino .30 .75
BP2 Myrio Richard .25 .60
BP3 Francisco Lindor 2.00 5.00
BP4 Nathan Freiman .25 .60
BP5 A.J. Jimenez .25 .60
BP6 Noah Perio .25 .60
BP7 Adonys Cardona .25 .60
BP8 Nick Kingham .25 .60
BP9A Eddie Rosario .50 1.25
BP9B Paul Hoilman .25 .60
BP10 Bryce Harper 4.00 10.00
BP11 Philip Wunderlich .25 .60
BP12 Rafael Ortega .25 .60
BP13 Tyler Gagnon .25 .60
BP14 Brenny Paulino .25 .60
BP15 Jose Campos .30 .75
BP16 Jesus Galindo .25 .60
BP17 Tyler Austin .40 1.00
BP18 Brandon Drury .40 1.00
BP19 Richard Jones .25 .60
BP20A Robby Price .25 .60
BP20B Jeimer Candelario .30 .75
BP21 Jose Osuna .25 .60
BP22 Claudio Custodio .30 .75
BP23 Jake Marisnick .30 .75
BP24 J.R. Graham .25 .60
BP25 Raul Alcantara .25 .60
BP26 Joseph Staley .25 .60
BP27 Josh Bowman .25 .60
BP28 Josh Edgin .25 .60
BP29 Keith Couch .25 .60
BP30 Kyrell Hudson .25 .60
BP31 Nick Maronde .30 .75
BP32 Mario Yepez .25 .60
BP33 Matthew West .25 .60
BP34 Matthew Szczur .30 .75
BP35 Devon Ethier .25 .60
BP36 Michael Brady .25 .60
BP37 Michael Crouse .25 .60
BP38 Michael Gonzales .25 .60
BP39 Mike Murray .25 .60
BP41 Zach Walters .30 .75
BP42 Tim Crabbe .25 .60
BP43 Rookie Davis .25 .60
BP44 Adam Duvall 2.50 6.00
BP45 Angelys Nina .25 .60
BP46 Anthony Fernandez .25 .60
BP47 Ariel Peña .25 .60
BP48 Boone Whiting .25 .60
BP49 Brandon Brown .25 .60
BP50 Brennan Smith .25 .60
BP51 Brett Krill .30 .75
BP52 Dean Green .25 .60
BP53 Casey Haerther .25 .60
BP54 Casey Lawrence .25 .60
BP55 Jose Vinicio .30 .75
BP56 Kyle Simon .25 .60
BP57 Chris Rearick .25 .60
BP58 Cheslor Cuthbert .25 .60
BP59 Daniel Corcino .30 .75
BP60 Danny Barnes .25 .60
BP61 David Medina .25 .60
BP62A Kes Carter .25 .60
BP62B Dayan Diaz .30 .75
BP63 Todd McInnis .25 .60
BP64 Edwar Cabrera .25 .60
BP65 Emilio King .25 .60
BP66 Jackie Bradley .60 1.50
BP67 J.T. Wise .25 .60
BP68 Jeff Malm .25 .60
BP69 Jonathan Galvez .25 .60
BP70 Luis Heredia .25 .60
BP71 Jonathon Berti .25 .60
BP72 Jabari Blash .25 .60
BP73 Will Swanner .25 .60
BP74 Eric Arce .25 .60
BP75 Dillon Maples .25 .60
BP76 Ian Gac .25 .60
BP77 Clay Holmes .25 .60
BP78 Nick Castellanos .75 2.00
BP79 Josh Bell 1.00 2.50
BP80 Matt Purke .25 .60
BP81 Taylor Whitenton .25 .60
BP83 Jacob Anderson .30 .75
BP84 Bryan Brickhouse .25 .60
BP85 Levi Michael .25 .60
BP86 Gerrit Cole 1.50 4.00
BP87 Danny Hultzen .40 1.00
BP88 Anthony Rendon 1.50 4.00
BP89 Austin Hedges .25 .60
BP91 Dillon Howard .30 .75
BP92 Nick Delmonico .25 .60
BP93 Brandon Jacobs .30 .75
BP94 Charlie Tilson .25 .60
BP96 Greg Billo .25 .60
BP97 Andrew Susac .30 .75
BP98 Greg Bird .30 .75
BP99 Dante Bichette .30 .75
BP100 Tommy Joseph .50 1.25
BP101 Julio Rodriguez .25 .60
BP102 Oscar Taveras .40 1.00
BP103 Drew Hutchison .30 .75
BP104 Joc Pederson 2.00 5.00
BP105 Xander Bogaerts 1.00 2.50
BP106 Tyler Collins .30 .75
BP107 Joe Ross .25 .60
BP108A Carlos Martinez .40 1.00
BP108B Luis Angel .25 .60
BP109 Andrelton Simmons .40 1.00
BP110 Daniel Norris .30 .75

2012 Bowman Prospects Blue

*BLUE: 2X TO 5X BASIC
STATED ODDS 1:16 HOBBY
STATED PRINT RUN 500 SER.#'d SETS

2012 Bowman Prospects International

*INT: 1.25X TO 3X BASIC
STATED ODDS 1:8 HOBBY
BP10 Bryce Harper 8.00 20.00

2012 Bowman Prospects Orange

*ORANGE: 3X TO 8X BASIC
STATED ODDS 1:32 HOBBY
STATED PRINT RUN 250 SER.#'d SETS
BP10 Bryce Harper 15.00 40.00

2012 Bowman Prospects Purple

*PURPLE: 1.5X TO 4X BASIC

2012 Bowman Prospects Red

STATED ODDS 1:4150 HOBBY
STATED PRINT RUN 1 SER.#'d SET
NO PRICING DUE TO SCARCITY

2012 Bowman Prospects Silver Ice

*SILVER ICE: 2.5X TO 6X BASIC
STATED ODDS 1:24 HOBBY

2012 Bowman Draft

COMPLETE SET (55) 6.00 15.00
STATED PLATE ODDS 1:1600 HOBBY
PLATE PRINT RUN 1 SET PER COLOR
NO PLATE PRICING DUE TO SCARCITY
1 Trevor Bauer RC 1.50 4.00
2 Tyler Pastornicky RC .30 .75
3 A.J. Griffin RC .40 1.00
4 Yoenis Cespedes RC .75 2.00
5 Drew Smyly RC .30 .75

6 Jose Quintana RC .30 .75
7 Yasmani Grandal RC .30 .75
8 Tyler Thornburg RC .40 1.00
9 A.J. Pollock RC .50 1.25
10 Bryce Harper RC 5.00 12.00
11 Joe Kelly RC .50 1.25
12 Steve Clevenger RC .20 .50
13 Tanner Scheppers RC .20 .50
14 Casey Crosby RC .40 1.00
15 Wade Miley RC .40 1.00
16 Quintin Berry RC .50 1.25
17 Martin Perez RC .50 1.25
18 Addison Reed RC .30 .75
19 Liam Hendriks RC .30 .75
20 Matt Moore RC .50 1.25
21 Wilin Rosario RC .30 .75
22 Jarrod Parker RC .40 1.00
23 Matt Adams RC .40 1.00
24 Devin Mesoraco RC .30 .75
25 Jordan Pacheco RC .30 .75
26 Irving Falu RC .30 .75
27 Edwar Cabrera RC .30 .75
28 Stephen Pryor RC .20 .50
29 Norichika Aoki RC .40 1.00
30 Jesus Montero RC .30 .75
31 Drew Pomeranz RC .30 .75
32 Jordany Valdespin RC .40 1.00
33 Andrelton Simmons RC .50 1.25
34 Xavier Avery RC .30 .75
35 Chris Archer RC .30 .75
36 Drew Hutchison RC .40 1.00
37 Dallas Keuchel RC 1.50 4.00
38 Leonys Martin RC .30 .75
39 Brian Dozier RC 1.00 2.50
40 Will Middlebrooks RC .40 1.00
41 Kirk Nieuwenhuis RC .30 .75
42 Jeremy Hefner RC .30 .75
43 Derek Norris RC .30 .75
44 Tom Milone RC .30 .75
45 Wei-Yin Chen RC .75 2.00
46 Christian Friedrich RC .30 .75
47 Kole Calhoun RC .40 1.00
48 Wily Peralta RC .30 .75
49 Hisashi Iwakuma RC .60 1.50
50 Yu Darvish RC .75 2.00
51 Elian Herrera RC .50 1.25
52 Anthony Gose RC .40 1.00
53 Brett Jackson RC .50 1.25
54 Alex Liddi RC .30 .75
55 Matt Hague RC .30 .75

2012 Bowman Draft Blue

*BLUE: 1.2X TO 3X BASIC
STATED ODDS 1:13 HOBBY
STATED PRINT RUN 500 SER.#'d SETS
10 Bryce Harper 8.00 20.00

2012 Bowman Draft Orange

*ORANGE: 1.5X TO 4X BASIC
STATED ODDS 1:26 HOBBY
STATED PRINT RUN 250 SER.#'d SETS
10 Bryce Harper 10.00 25.00

2012 Bowman Draft Silver Ice

*SILVER: 2X TO 5X BASIC
10 Bryce Harper 12.50 30.00

2012 Bowman Draft Bowman's Best Die Cut Refractors

STATED ODDS 1:288 HOBBY
STATED PRINT RUN 99 SER.#'d SETS
BB1 Mike Zunino 6.00 15.00
BB2 Kevin Gausman 12.00 30.00
BB3 Max Fried 15.00 40.00
BB4 Kyle Zimmer 5.00 12.00
BB5 Andrew Heaney 5.00 12.00
BB6 David Dahl 12.00 30.00
BB7 Gavin Cecchini 5.00 12.00
BB8 Courtney Hawkins 4.00 10.00
BB9 Nick Travieso 5.00 12.00
BB10 Tyler Naquin 6.00 15.00
BB11 D.J. Davis 5.00 12.00
BB12 Michael Wacha 8.00 20.00
BB13 Lucas Sims 5.00 12.00
BB14 Marcus Stroman 6.00 15.00
BB15 James Ramsey 4.00 10.00
BB16 Richie Shaffer 5.00 12.00
BB17 Lewis Brinson 12.00 30.00
BB18 Ty Hensley 5.00 12.00
BB19 Brian Johnson 4.00 10.00
BB20 Joey Gallo 12.00 30.00
BB21 Keon Barnum 4.00 10.00
BB22 Anthony Alford 4.00 10.00
BB23 Austin Aune 5.00 12.00
BB24 Nick Williams 4.00 10.00
BB25 Stryker Trahan 4.00 10.00
BB26 Tyler Austin 6.00 15.00
BB27 Jackie Bradley Jr. 10.00 25.00
BB28 Cody Buckel 4.00 10.00
BB29 Nick Castellanos 12.00 30.00
BB30 Alen Hanson 5.00 12.00
BB31 George Springer 15.00 40.00
BB32 Oscar Taveras 6.00 15.00
BB33 Taijuan Walker 5.00 12.00
BB34 Miles Head 4.00 10.00
BB35 Archie Bradley 2.50 6.00
BB36 Jose Fernandez 10.00 25.00
BB37 Dylan Bundy 8.00 20.00
BB38 Daniel Vogelbach 6.00 15.00
BB39 Tony Cingrani 8.00 20.00
BB40 Matt Barnes 4.00 10.00
BB41 Christian Yelich 30.00 80.00
BB42 Mason Williams 6.00 15.00
BB43 Brad Miller 4.00 10.00
BB44 Eddie Rosario 8.00 20.00
BB45 Kolten Wong 4.00 10.00
BB46 Sean Nolin 4.00 10.00
BB47 Javier Baez 15.00 40.00
BB48 Nolan Arenado 15.00 40.00
BB49 Anthony Rendon 25.00 60.00
BB50 Danny Hultzen 6.00 15.00

2012 Bowman Draft Draft Picks

COMPLETE SET (165) 12.50 30.00
STATED PLATE ODDS 1:1600 HOBBY
PLATE PRINT RUN 1 SET PER COLOR
NO PLATE PRICING DUE TO SCARCITY
BDPP1 Lucas Sims .40 1.00
BDPP2 Kevin Gausman 1.00 2.50
BDPP3 Brian Johnson .30 .75
BDPP4 Pierce Johnson .40 1.00
BDPP5 Keon Barnum .30 .75
BDPP6 Paul Blackburn .30 .75
BDPP7 Nick Travieso .40 1.00
BDPP8 Jesse Winker 2.00 5.00
BDPP9 Tyler Naquin .50 1.25
BDPP10 Kyle Zimmer .40 1.00
BDPP11 Jesmuel Valentin .40 1.00
BDPP12 Andrew Heaney .40 1.00
BDPP13 Victor Roache .60 1.50
BDPP14 Mitch Haniger .75 2.00
BDPP15 Luke Bard .30 .75
BDPP16 Jose Berrios 2.50 6.00
BDPP17 Gavin Cecchini .40 1.00
BDPP18 Kevin Plawecki .40 1.00
BDPP19 Ty Hensley .40 1.00
BDPP20 Matt Olson 1.50 4.00
BDPP21 Mitch Gueller .30 .75
BDPP22 Shane Watson .40 1.00
BDPP23 Barrett Barnes .40 1.00
BDPP24 Travis Jankowski .40 1.00
BDPP25 Mike Zunino .50 1.25
BDPP26 Michael Wacha .60 1.50
BDPP27 James Ramsey .30 .75
BDPP28 Patrick Wisdom .30 .75
BDPP29 Steve Bean .40 1.00
BDPP30 Richie Shaffer .40 1.00
BDPP31 Lewis Brinson 1.00 2.50
BDPP32 Joey Gallo 1.00 2.50
BDPP33 D.J. Davis .40 1.00
BDPP34 Tyler Gonzalez .40 1.00
BDPP35 Marcus Stroman .50 1.25
BDPP36 Matt Smoral .30 .75
BDPP37 Branden Kline .30 .75
BDPP38 Jacob Thompson .40 1.00
BDPP39 Austin Aune .40 1.00
BDPP40 Peter O'Brien .50 1.25
BDPP41 Bruce Maxwell .30 .75
BDPP42 Dylan Cozens .50 1.25
BDPP43 Wyatt Mathisen .30 .75
BDPP44 Spencer Edwards .30 .75
BDPP45 Jamie Jarmon .30 .75
BDPP46 R.J. Alvarez .30 .75
BDPP47 Bryan De La Rosa .30 .75
BDPP48 Adrian Marin .30 .75
BDPP49 Austin Maddox .30 .75
BDPP50 Fernando Perez .30 .75
BDPP51 Austin Schotts .30 .75
BDPP52 Avery Romero .30 .75
BDPP53 Kolby Copeland .30 .75
BDPP54 Jonathan Sandfort .30 .75
BDPP55 Alex Yarbrough .30 .75
BDPP56 Justin Black .30 .75
BDPP57 Ty Buttrey .30 .75
BDPP58 Austin Dean .30 .75
BDPP59 Andrew Pullin .40 1.00
BDPP60 Bralin Jackson .30 .75
BDPP61 Lex Rutledge .30 .75
BDPP62 Jordan John .30 .75
BDPP63 Andre Martinez .30 .75
BDPP64 Eric Wood .40 1.00
BDPP65 Derek Self .30 .75
BDPP66 Jacob Wilson .30 .75
BDPP67 Joe Bircher .30 .75
BDPP68 Matthew Price .30 .75
BDPP69 Hudson Randall .30 .75
BDPP70 Jorge Fernandez .30 .75
BDPP71 Nathan Minnich .30 .75
BDPP72 Yoenny Gonzalez .30 .75
BDPP73 Steven Schils .30 .75
BDPP74 Thomas Coyle .30 .75
BDPP75 Ron Miller .30 .75
BDPP76 Rowan Wick .30 .75
BDPP77 Mike Dodig .30 .75
BDPP78 John Kuchno .30 .75
BDPP79 Caleb Frare .40 1.00
BDPP80 William Carmona .30 .75
BDPP81 Clayton Henning .30 .75
BDPP82 Connor Lien .30 .75
BDPP83 Michael Meyers .30 .75
BDPP84 Julio Felix .30 .75
BDPP85 Alexander Muren .30 .75
BDPP86 Jacob Stallings .40 1.00
BDPP87 Max Foody .30 .75
BDPP88 Taylor Hawkins .30 .75
BDPP89 Jeffrey Wendelken .30 .75
BDPP90 Steven Golden .30 .75
BDPP91 Brett Wiley .30 .75
BDPP92 John Silviano .30 .75
BDPP93 Tyler Tewell .30 .75
BDPP94 Sean McAdams .40 1.00
BDPP95 Michael Vaughn .30 .75
BDPP96 Jake Proctor .30 .75
BDPP97 Richard Bielski .30 .75
BDPP98 Charles Gillies .30 .75
BDPP99 Erick Gonzalez .30 .75
BDPP100 Bennett Pickar .30 .75
BDPP101 Christopher Beck .30 .75
BDPP102 Brandon Brennan .30 .75
BDPP103 Eddie Butler .30 .75
BDPP104 David Dahl 1.00 2.50
BDPP105 Ryan Gibbard .30 .75
BDPP106 Hunter Scantling .30 .75
BDPP107 Zach Isler .30 .75
BDPP108 Joshua Turley .30 .75
BDPP109 Johendi Jiminian .30 .75
BDPP110 Jake Lamb .50 1.25
BDPP111 Mike Morin .30 .75
BDPP112 Parker Morin .30 .75
BDPP113 Scott Oberg .30 .75
BDPP114 Correlle Prime .30 .75
BDPP115 Mark Sappington .30 .75
BDPP116 Sam Selman .40 1.00
BDPP117 Paul Sewald .30 .75
BDPP118 Matt Wessinger .30 .75
BDPP119 Max White .30 .75
BDPP120 Adam Giacalone .40 1.00
BDPP121 Jeffrey Popick .30 .75
BDPP122 Alfredo Rodriguez .30 .75
BDPP123 Nick Routt .30 .75
BDPP124 Abe Ruiz .30 .75
BDPP125 Jason Stolz .30 .75
BDPP126 Ben Waldrip .30 .75
BDPP127 Eric Stamets .30 .75
BDPP128 Chris Cowell .30 .75
BDPP129 Fernelys Sanchez .30 .75
BDPP130 Kevin McKague .40 1.00
BDPP131 Rashad Brown .30 .75
BDPP132 Jorge Saez .30 .75
BDPP133 Shaun Valeriote .30 .75
BDPP134 Will Hurt .30 .75
BDPP135 Nicholas Grim .40 1.00
BDPP136 Patrick Merkling .30 .75
BDPP137 Jonathan Murphy .30 .75
BDPP138 Bryan Lippincott .30 .75
BDPP139 Austin Chubb .30 .75
BDPP140 Joseph Almaraz .30 .75
BDPP141 Robert Ravago .30 .75
BDPP142 Will Hudgins .30 .75
BDPP143 Tommy Richards .30 .75
BDPP144 Chad Carman .50 1.25
BDPP145 Joel Licon .30 .75
BDPP146 Jimmy Rider .30 .75
BDPP147 Jason Wilson .30 .75
BDPP148 Justin Jackson .30 .75
BDPP149 Casey McCarthy .30 .75
BDPP150 Hunter Bailey .30 .75
BDPP151 Jake Pintar .30 .75
BDPP152 David Cruz .30 .75
BDPP153 Mike Mudron .30 .75
BDPP154 Benjamin Kline .30 .75
BDPP155 Bryan Haar .30 .75
BDPP156 Patrick Claussen .30 .75
BDPP157 Derrick Bleeker .30 .75
BDPP158 Edward Sappelt .30 .75
BDPP159 Jeremy Lucas .30 .75
BDPP160 Josh Martin .30 .75
BDPP161 Robert Benincasa .30 .75
BDPP162 Craig Manuel .30 .75
BDPP163 Taylor Ard .30 .75
BDPP164 Dominic Leone .30 .75
BDPP165 Kevin Brady .30 .75

2012 Bowman Draft Draft Picks Blue

*BLUE: 1.5X TO 4X BASIC
STATED ODDS 1:13 HOBBY
STATED PRINT RUN 500 SER.#'d SETS

2012 Bowman Draft Draft Picks Orange

*ORANGE: 2X TO 5X BASIC
STATED ODDS 1:26 HOBBY
STATED PRINT RUN 250 SER.#'d SETS

2012 Bowman Draft Draft Picks Silver Ice

*SILVER: 2.5X TO 6X BASIC

2012 Bowman Draft Dual Top 10 Picks

COMPLETE SET (15)
STATED ODDS 1:6 HOBBY
BC Gavin Cecchini/Jay Bruce .50 1.25
BG D.Bundy/K.Gausman 1.25 3.00
BS R.Braun/B.Starling .50 1.25
CT M.Cain/M.Trout 8.00 20.00
ER James Ramsey/Jacoby Ellsbury .50 1.25
FL M.Fried/C.Kershaw 1.50 4.00
FT Prince Fielder/Troy Tulowitzki .60 1.50
HH J.Hamilton/B.Harper 6.00 15.00
JA A.Almora/D.Jeter 1.50 4.00
KH Courtney Hawkins/Paul Konerko .40 1.00
LZ E.Longoria/M.Zunino .60 1.50
MS A.McCutchen/G.Springer 1.50 4.00
PH Andrew Heaney/Jarrod Parker .50 1.25
UN Tyler Naquin/Chase Utley .60 1.50
VH J.Verlander/D.Hultzen .60 1.50

2012 Bowman Draft Future's Game Relics

STATED ODDS 1:345 HOBBY
STATED PRINT RUN 199 SER.#'d SETS
AG Anthony Gose 4.00 10.00
AM Alfredo Marte 3.00 8.00
AP Ariel Pena 3.00 8.00
AS Ali Solis 4.00 10.00
BH Billy Hamilton 10.00 25.00
BR Bruce Rondon 5.00 12.00
CB Christian Bethancourt 4.00 10.00
CY Christian Yelich 4.00 10.00
DB Dylan Bundy 12.50 30.00
DH Danny Hultzen 5.00 12.00
ER Enny Romero 3.00 8.00
FL Francisco Lindor 4.00 10.00
FR Felipe Rivero 6.00 15.00
GC Gerrit Cole 5.00 12.00
JF Jose Fernandez 10.00 25.00
JH Jae-Hoon Ha 3.00 8.00
JO Jake Odorizzi 5.00 12.00
JP Jurickson Profar 8.00 20.00
JR Julio Rodriguez 4.00 10.00
JS Jonathan Singleton 5.00 12.00
JSE Jean Segura 3.00 8.00
JT Jameson Taillon 4.00 10.00
KL Kyle Lotzkar 4.00 10.00
KW Kolten Wong 6.00 15.00
MB Matt Barnes 4.00 10.00
MC Michael Choice 3.00 8.00
MM Manny Machado 10.00 25.00
MO Mike Olt 4.00 10.00
NA Nolan Arenado 4.00 10.00
NC Nick Castellanos 6.00 15.00
OA Oswaldo Arcia 4.00 10.00
OT Oscar Taveras 12.50 30.00
RB Rob Brantly 6.00 15.00
RL Rymer Liriano 4.00 10.00
SG Scooter Gennett 6.00 15.00
TJ Tommy Joseph 4.00 10.00
TS Tyler Skaggs 3.00 8.00
TW Taijuan Walker 4.00 10.00
WF Wilmer Flores 3.00 8.00
WM Wil Myers 8.00 20.00
XB Xander Bogaerts 20.00 50.00
ZW Zack Wheeler 4.00 10.00

2013 Bowman

COMPLETE SET (220) 10.00 25.00
PRINTING PLATE ODDS 1:1881
PLATE PRINT RUN 1 SET PER COLOR
BLACK-CYAN-MAGENTA-YELLOW ISSUED
NO PLATE PRICING DUE TO SCARCITY
1 Adam Jones .25 .60
2 Jon Niese .20 .50
3 Aroldis Chapman .30 .75
4 Brett Jackson .20 .50
5 CC Sabathia .25 .60
6 David Freese .20 .50
7 Dustin Pedroia .30 .75
8 Hanley Ramirez .25 .60
9 Jered Weaver .25 .60
10 Johnny Cueto .25 .60
11 Justin Upton .25 .60
12 Mark Trumbo .20 .50
13 Melky Cabrera .20 .50
14 Allen Craig .25 .60
15 Torii Hunter .20 .50
16 Ryan Vogelsong .20 .50
17 Starlin Castro .20 .50
18 Trevor Bauer .40 1.00
19 Will Middlebrooks .20 .50
20 Yonder Alonso .20 .50
21 A.J. Pierzynski .20 .50
22 Marco Scutaro .25 .60
23 Justin Morneau .25 .60
24 Jose Reyes .25 .60
25 Dan Uggla .20 .50
26 Darwin Barney .20 .50
27 Jeff Samardzija .20 .50
28 Josh Johnson .25 .60
29 Coco Crisp .20 .50
30 Ian Kennedy .20 .50
31 Michael Young .20 .50
32 Craig Kimbrel .25 .60
33 Brandon Morrow .20 .50
34 Ben Revere .20 .50
35 Tim Lincecum .25 .60
36 Alex Rios .25 .60
37 Curtis Granderson .25 .60
38 Gio Gonzalez .25 .60
39 Dylan Bundy RC 1.00 2.50
40 Adam Eaton RC .60 1.50
41 Casey Kelly RC .50 1.25
42 A.J. Ramos RC .50 1.25
43 Ryan Wheeler RC .40 1.00
44 Henry Rodriguez RC .40 1.00
45 Alex Rodriguez .40 1.00
46 Wei-Yin Chen .20 .50
47 Brian McCann .25 .60
48 Chris Sale .30 .75
49 David Price .25 .60
50 Albert Pujols .40 1.00
51 Evan Longoria .25 .60
52 Jacoby Ellsbury .25 .60
53 Jesus Montero .20 .50
54 Jon Jay .20 .50
55 Lance Lynn .20 .50
56 Matt Cain .25 .60
57 Michael Bourn .20 .50
58 Nelson Cruz .30 .75
59 Robinson Cano .25 .60
60 Ryan Zimmerman .25 .60
61 Starling Marte .25 .60
62 Raul Ibanez .25 .60
63 Austin Jackson .20 .50
64 Yovani Gallardo .20 .50
65 Chris Davis .25 .60
66 Chase Headley .20 .50
67 Alfonso Soriano .25 .60
68 Zack Cozart .20 .50
69 Kevin Youkilis .20 .50
70 Jake Peavy .20 .50
71 C.J. Wilson .20 .50
72 Ike Davis .20 .50
73 Angel Pagan .20 .50
74 Derek Holland .20 .50
75 Doug Fister .20 .50
76 Tim Hudson .25 .60
77 Jaime Garcia .25 .60
78 Miguel Cabrera .30 .75
79 Troy Tulowitzki .30 .75
80 Elvis Andrus .25 .60
81 Cliff Lee .25 .60
82 Kris Medlen .25 .60
83 Jurickson Profar RC .50 1.25
84 Avisail Garcia RC .50 1.25
85 Trevor Rosenthal (RC) .75 2.00
86 Jeurys Familia RC .60 1.50
87 Rob Brantly RC .40 1.00
88 Didi Gregorius RC 1.50 4.00
89 Joe Nathan .20 .50
90 Billy Butler .20 .50
91 Clayton Kershaw .50 1.25
92 David Wright .25 .60
93 Felix Hernandez .25 .60
94 Jason Heyward .25 .60
95 Joe Mauer .25 .60
96 Jordan Zimmermann .25 .60
97 Madison Bumgarner .25 .60
98 Matt Holliday .30 .75
99 Miguel Montero .20 .50
100 Andrew McCutchen .30 .75
101 Paul Goldschmidt .30 .75
102 Roy Halladay .25 .60
103 Salvador Perez .25 .60
104 Stephen Strasburg .30 .75
105 Cody Ross .20 .50
106 Yadier Molina .40 1.00
107 David Murphy .20 .50
108 Jose Altuve .25 .60
109 Brandon Phillips .20 .50
110 Dayan Viciedo .20 .50
111 Desmond Jennings .25 .60
112 Mark Reynolds .20 .50
113 Mat Latos .25 .60
114 Homer Bailey .20 .50
115 Corey Hart .20 .50
116 B.J. Upton .25 .60
117 Mike Minor .20 .50
118 Tommy Milone .20 .50
119 Barry Zito .25 .60
120 Josh Beckett .20 .50
121 Mike Trout 2.50 6.00
122 Yu Darvish .30 .75
123 Edwin Encarnacion .30 .75
124 James Shields .20 .50
125 Adam Wainwright .25 .60
126 Shelby Miller RC 1.00 2.50
127 Jake Odorizzi RC .50 1.25
128 L.J. Hoes RC .50 1.25
129 Nick Maronde RC .50 1.25
130 Tyler Cloyd RC .50 1.25
131 Adeiny Hechavarria (RC) .50 1.25
132 Adrian Beltre .30 .75
133 Anthony Gose .20 .50
134 Brandon Beachy .20 .50
135 Cole Hamels .25 .60
136 Derek Jeter .75 2.00
137 Freddie Freeman .40 1.00
138 Jayson Werth .25 .60
139 Joey Votto .30 .75
140 Jose Bautista .25 .60
141 Mariano Rivera .40 1.00
142 Matt Kemp .25 .60
143 Mike Morse .20 .50
144 Pedro Alvarez .20 .50
145 Jason Motte .20 .50
146 Shaun Marcum .20 .50
147 David Ortiz .30 .75
148 Wade Miley .20 .50
149 Yasmani Grandal .20 .50
150 Bryce Harper .50 1.25
151 Carlos Santana .25 .60
152 Shin-Soo Choo .25 .60
153 Carlos Beltran .25 .60
154 Hunter Pence .25 .60
155 Mike Moustakas .25 .60
156 Colby Rasmus .25 .60
157 Jason Kipnis .25 .60
158 Jon Lester .25 .60
159 Ben Zobrist .25 .60
160 Asdrubal Cabrera .25 .60
161 Kyle Lohse .20 .50
162 Bronson Arroyo .20 .50
163 Vance Worley .25 .60
164 Fernando Rodney .20 .50
165 R.A. Dickey .25 .60
166 Alcides Escobar .25 .60
167 Adam Dunn .25 .60
168 Ian Kinsler .25 .60
169 Josh Reddick .20 .50
170 Mike Olt RC .50 1.25
171 Paco Rodriguez RC .60 1.50
172 Darin Ruf RC .75 2.00
173 Tony Cingrani RC .75 2.00
174 Kyuji Fujikawa RC .60 1.50
175 Ali Solis RC .40 1.00
176 Adrian Gonzalez .25 .60
177 Anthony Rizzo .40 1.00
178 Brandon Belt .25 .60
179 Carlos Gonzalez .25 .60
180 Josh Willingham .25 .60
181 Dexter Fowler .25 .60
182 Giancarlo Stanton .30 .75
183 Jean Segura .25 .60
184 Johan Santana .25 .60
185 Josh Hamilton .25 .60
186 Mark Teixeira .25 .60
187 Matt Moore .25 .60
188 Howard Kendrick .20 .50
189 Prince Fielder .25 .60
190 Ryan Howard .25 .60
191 Alex Gordon .25 .60
192 Todd Frazier .20 .50
193 Wilin Rosario .20 .50
194 Yoenis Cespedes .30 .75
195 Aaron Hill .20 .50
196 Ian Desmond .20 .50
197 Delmon Young .25 .60
198 Jay Bruce .25 .60
199 Rickie Weeks .20 .50
200 Buster Posey .40 1.00
201 Neil Walker .20 .50
202 A.J. Burnett .20 .50
203 Hiroki Kuroda .20 .50
204 Kendrys Morales .20 .50
205 Brett Lawrie .25 .60
206 Dan Haren .20 .50
207 Eric Hosmer .25 .60
208 Hisashi Iwakuma .25 .60
209 Jim Johnson .20 .50
210 Ryan Braun .25 .60
211 Carlos Ruiz .20 .50
212 Nick Swisher .25 .60
213 Andre Ethier .25 .60
214 Matt Harrison .20 .50
215 Manny Machado RC 2.50 6.00
216 Tyler Skaggs RC .60 1.50
217 Brock Holt RC .50 1.25
218 Hyun-Jin Ryu RC 1.00 2.50
219 Eury Perez RC .50 1.25
220 Melky Mesa RC .50 1.25
MB Marcel Bilak SP 6.00 15.00

2013 Bowman Blue

*BLUE VET: 1.5X TO 4X BASIC
*BLUE RC: .75X TO 2X BASIC
STATED ODDS 1:34 HOBBY
STATED PRINT RUN 500 SER.#'d SETS

2013 Bowman Gold

*GOLD VET: 1.5X TO 4X BASIC
*GOLD RC: .75X TO 2X BASIC

2013 Bowman Hometown

*HOME.VET: 2X TO 5X BASIC
*HOM.RC: 1X TO 2.5X BASIC
STATED ODDS 1:8 HOBBY

2013 Bowman Orange

*ORANGE VET: 4X TO 10X BASIC
*ORANGE RC: 2X TO 5X BASIC
STATED ODDS 1:67 HOBBY
STATED PRINT RUN 250 SER.#'d SETS

2013 Bowman Silver Ice

*SILVER.VET: 3X TO 8X BASIC
*SILVER.RC: 1.5X TO 4X BASIC
STATED ODDS 1:24 HOBBY

2013 Bowman Lucky Redemption Autographs

STATED ODDS 1:35,745 HOBBY
EXCHANGE DEADLINE 3/31/2016
1 Hyun-Jin Ryu 125.00 250.00
2 Jurickson Profar 20.00 50.00
3 Kevin Gausman 20.00 50.00
4 Yasiel Puig 300.00 600.00
5 Wil Myers 20.00 50.00

2013 Bowman Prospect Autographs

EXCHANGE DEADLINE 5/31/2016
AM Anthony Meo 3.00 8.00
AW Aaron West 3.00 8.00
BB Byron Buxton 15.00 40.00
BL Barret Loux 3.00 8.00
BR Ben Rowen 3.00 8.00
CC Carlos Correa 50.00 120.00
CK Carson Kelly 3.00 8.00
CW Collin Wiles 4.00 10.00
DP Dane Phillips 3.00 8.00
DS Danny Salazar 3.00 8.00
JB Josh Bowman 3.00 8.00
JC Ji-Man Choi 5.00 12.00
JCA Jamie Callahan 4.00 10.00
JG Jeff Gelalich 4.00 10.00
JH Jesse Hahn 3.00 8.00
KD Khris Davis 8.00 20.00
KM Kurtis Muller 5.00 12.00
LL Lenny Linsky 3.00 8.00
MM Matt Magill 3.00 8.00
MMQ Mike McQuillan 3.00 8.00
MW Max White 3.00 8.00
OC Orlando Calixte 3.00 8.00
TG Tyler Gonzales 3.00 8.00
TR Tanner Rahier 5.00 12.00
TS Tayler Scott 3.00 8.00

2013 Bowman Prospect Autographs Blue

*BLUE: .5X TO 1.2X BASIC
PRINT RUNS B/WN 25-500 COPIES PER
NO PRICING ON QTY 25 OR LESS
EXCHANGE DEADLINE 5/31/2016

2013 Bowman Prospect Autographs Orange

*ORANGE: .75X TO 2X BASIC
PRINT RUNS B/WN 10-250 COPIES PER
NO PRICING DUE TO SCARCITY
EXCHANGE DEADLINE 5/31/2016

2013 Bowman Prospects

COMPLETE SET (110) 10.00 25.00
PRINTING PLATE ODDS 1:1881
PLATE PRINT RUN 1 SET PER COLOR
BLACK-CYAN-MAGENTA-YELLOW ISSUED
NO PLATE PRICING DUE TO SCARCITY
BP1 Byron Buxton .75 2.00
BP2 Jonathan Griffin .15 .40
BP3 Mark Montgomery .25 .60
BP4 Gioskar Amaya .15 .40
BP5 Lucas Giolito .25 .60
BP6 Danny Salazar .30 .75
BP7 Jesse Hahn .15 .40
BP8 Tayler Scott .15 .40
BP9 Ji-Man Choi .20 .50
BP10 Tony Renda .15 .40
BP11 Jamie Callahan .15 .40
BP12 Collin Wiles .15 .40
BP13 Tanner Rahier .20 .50
BP14 Max White .15 .40
BP15 Jeff Gelalich .15 .40
BP16 Tyler Gonzales .15 .40
BP17 Mitch Nay .15 .40
BP18 Dane Phillips .15 .40
BP19 Carson Kelly .20 .50
BP20 Darwin Rivera .15 .40
BP21 Arismendy Alcantara .25 .60
BP22 Brandon Maurer .20 .50
BP23 Jin-De Jhang .15 .40
BP24 Bruce Rondon .15 .40
BP25 Jonathan Schoop .15 .40
BP26 Cory Hall .15 .40
BP27 Cory Vaughn .15 .40
BP28 Danny Muno .15 .40
BP29 Edwin Diaz .30 .75
BP30 Willians Astudillo .15 .40
BP31 Hansel Robles .15 .40
BP32 Harold Castro .15 .40
BP33 Ismael Guillon .15 .40
BP34 Jeremy Moore .15 .40
BP35 Jose Cisnero .15 .40
BP36 Jose Peraza .15 .40
BP37 Jose Ramirez .20 .50
BP38 Christian Villanueva .15 .40
BP39 Brett Gerritse .15 .40
BP40 Kris Hall .15 .40
BP41 Matt Stites .15 .40
BP42 Matt Wisler .15 .40
BP43 Matthew Koch .15 .40
BP44 Micah Johnson .20 .50
BP45 Michael Reed .15 .40
BP46 Michael Snyder .15 .40
BP47 Michael Taylor .15 .40
BP48 Nolan Sanburn .15 .40
BP49 Patrick Leonard .15 .40
BP50 Rafael Montero .15 .40
BP51 Ronnie Freeman .15 .40
BP52 Stephen Piscotty .30 .75
BP53 Steven Moya .25 .60
BP54 Chris McFarland .15 .40
BP55 Todd Kibby .15 .40
BP56 Tyler Heineman .15 .40
BP57 Wade Hinkle .15 .40
BP58 Wilfredo Rodriguez .15 .40
BP59 William Cuevas .15 .40
BP60 Yordano Ventura .20 .50
BP61 Zach Bird .15 .40
BP62 Socrates Brito .25 .60
BP63 Ben Rowen .15 .40
BP64 Seth Maness .15 .40
BP65 Corey Dickerson .20 .50
BP66 Travis Witherspoon .15 .40
BP67 Travis Shaw .15 .40
BP68 Lenny Linsky .15 .40
BP69 Anderson Feliz .15 .40
BP70 Casey Stevenson .15 .40
BP71 Pedro Ruiz .15 .40
BP72 Christian Bethancourt .25 .60
BP73 Pedro Guerra .15 .40
BP74 Ronald Guzman .25 .60
BP75 Jake Thompson .15 .40
BP76 Brian Goodwin .20 .50
BP77 Jorge Bonifacio .20 .50
BP78 Dilson Herrera .50 1.25
BP79 Gregory Polanco .30 .75
BP80 Alex Meyer .15 .40
BP81 Gabriel Encinas .15 .40
BP82 Yeicok Calderon .15 .40
BP83 Rio Ruiz .15 .40
BP84 Luis Sardinas .15 .40
BP85 Fu-Lin Kuo .20 .50
BP86 Kelvin De Leon .15 .40
BP87 Wyatt Mathisen .15 .40
BP88 Dorssys Paulino .20 .50
BP89 William Oliver .15 .40
BP90 Rony Bautista .15 .40
BP91 Gabriel Guerrero .20 .50
BP92 Patrick Kivlehan .15 .40
BP93 Ericson Leonora .15 .40
BP94 Mikeson Oliberto .15 .40
BP95 Roman Quinn .25 .60
BP96 Shane Broyles .15 .40
BP97 Cody Buckel .15 .40
BP98 Clayton Blackburn .25 .60
BP99 Evan Rutckyj .15 .40
BP100 Carlos Correa 2.00 5.00
BP101 Ronny Rodriguez .15 .40
BP102 Jayson Aquino .15 .40
BP103 Adalberto Mondesi .25 .60
BP104 Victor Sanchez .20 .50
BP105 Jairo Beras .25 .60
BP106 Stefen Romero .15 .40
BP107 Alfredo Escalera-Maldonado .20 .50
BP108 Kevin Medrano .15 .40
BP109 Carlos Sanchez .15 .40
BP110 Sam Selman .15 .40

2013 Bowman Prospects Blue

*BLUE: 2X TO 5X BASIC
STATED ODDS 1:67 HOBBY
STATED PRINT RUN 500 SER.#'d SETS

2013 Bowman Prospects Hometown

*HOMETOWN: 1.5X TO 4X BASIC
STATED ODDS 1:8 HOBBY

2013 Bowman Prospects Orange

*ORANGE: 2.5X TO 6X BASIC
STATED ODDS 1:134 HOBBY
STATED PRINT RUN 250 SER.#'d SETS

2013 Bowman Prospects Purple

*PURPLE: 1.2X TO 3X BASIC

2013 Bowman Prospects Silver Ice

*SILVER: 2X TO 5X BASIC
BP1 Byron Buxton 10.00 25.00

2013 Bowman Top 100 Prospects

STATED ODDS 1:12 HOBBY
BTP1 Dylan Bundy .60 1.50
BTP2 Jurickson Profar .30 .75
BTP3 Oscar Taveras .30 .75
BTP4 Travis d'Arnaud .30 .75
BTP5 Jose Fernandez .60 1.50
BTP6 Gerrit Cole 1.50 4.00
BTP7 Zack Wheeler .50 1.25
BTP8 Wil Myers .40 1.00
BTP9 Miguel Sano .30 .75
BTP10 Trevor Bauer .50 1.25
BTP11 Xander Bogaerts .75 2.00
BTP12 Tyler Skaggs .40 1.00
BTP13 Billy Hamilton .30 .75
BTP14 Javier Baez 1.00 2.50
BTP15 Mike Zunino .40 1.00
BTP16 Christian Yelich 2.00 5.00
BTP17 Taijuan Walker .30 .75
BTP18 Shelby Miller .60 1.50
BTP19 Jameson Taillon .30 .75
BTP20 Nick Castellanos .75 2.00
BTP21 Archie Bradley .25 .60
BTP22 Danny Hultzen .30 .75
BTP23 Taylor Guerrieri .25 .60
BTP24 Byron Buxton 1.25 3.00
BTP25 David Dahl .30 .75
BTP26 Francisco Lindor 2.00 5.00
BTP27 Bubba Starling .30 .75
BTP28 Carlos Correa 3.00 8.00
BTP29 Mike Olt .30 .75
BTP30 Jonathan Singleton .30 .75
BTP31 Anthony Rendon 1.50 4.00
BTP32 Gregory Polanco .50 1.25
BTP33 Carlos Martinez .40 1.00
BTP34 Jorge Soler .50 1.25
BTP35 Matt Barnes .30 .75
BTP36 Kevin Gausman .75 2.00
BTP37 Albert Almora .50 1.25
BTP38 Alen Hanson .30 .75
BTP39 Addison Russell .40 1.00
BTP40 Jedd Gyorko .30 .75
BTP41 Gary Sanchez .75 2.00
BTP42 Noah Syndergaard .30 .75
BTP43 Jackie Bradley .60 1.50
BTP44 Mason Williams .30 .75
BTP45 George Springer 1.00 2.50
BTP46 Aaron Sanchez .30 .75
BTP47 Nolan Arenado 2.50 6.00
BTP48 Corey Seager 1.25 3.00
BTP49 Kyle Zimmer .30 .75
BTP50 Tyler Austin .40 1.00
BTP51 Kyle Crick .40 1.00
BTP52 Robert Stephenson .25 .60
BTP53 Joc Pederson .60 1.50
BTP54 Julio Teheran .30 .75
BTP55 Brian Goodwin .30 .75
BTP56 Kaleb Cowart .30 .75
BTP57 Tony Cingrani .50 1.25
BTP58 Yasiel Puig 10.00 25.00
BTP59 Oswaldo Arcia .25 .60
BTP60 Trevor Rosenthal .50 1.25
BTP61 Alex Meyer .25 .60
BTP62 Jake Odorizzi .30 .75
BTP63 Jake Marisnick .30 .75
BTP64 Adam Eaton .40 1.00
BTP65 Rymer Liriano .25 .60
BTP66 Brad Miller .30 .75
BTP67 Max Fried 1.00 2.50
BTP68 Eddie Rosario .50 1.25
BTP69 Justin Nicolino .25 .60
BTP70 Cody Buckel .25 .60

BTP71 Jesse Biddle .30 .75
BTP72 James Paxton .30 .75
BTP73 Allen Webster .30 .75
BTP74 Kyle Gibson .40 1.00
BTP75 Nick Franklin .30 .75
BTP76 Dorssys Paulino .30 .75
BTP77 Hyun-Jin Ryu .60 1.50
BTP78 Courtney Hawkins .25 .60
BTP79 Delino DeShields .25 .60
BTP80 Joey Gallo .75 2.00
BTP81 Hak-Ju Lee .25 .60
BTP82 Kolten Wong .25 .60
BTP83 Aaron Hicks .40 1.00
BTP84 Michael Choice .25 .60
BTP85 Luis Heredia .30 .75
BTP86 C.J. Cron .30 .75
BTP87 Lucas Giolito .40 1.00
BTP88 Daniel Vogelbach .40 1.00
BTP89 Austin Hedges .30 .75
BTP90 Matt Davidson .30 .75
BTP91 Gary Brown .25 .60
BTP92 Daniel Corcino .25 .60
BTP93 Adalberto Mondesi .40 1.00
BTP94 Victor Sanchez .30 .75
BTP95 A.J. Cole .30 .75
BTP96 Joe Panik .40 1.00
BTP97 J.O. Berrios .40 1.00
BTP98 Trevor Story 1.25 3.00
BTP99 Stefen Romero .25 .60
BTP100 Andrew Heaney .30 .75

2013 Bowman Top 100 Prospects Die Cut Refractors

*REF: 5X TO 12X BASIC
STATED ODDS 1:372 HOBBY
STATED PRINT RUN 99 SER.#'d SETS

2013 Bowman Draft

STATED PLATE ODDS 1:2320 HOBBY
PLATE PRINT RUN 1 SET PER COLOR
BLACK-CYAN-MAGENTA-YELLOW ISSUED
NO PLATE PRICING DUE TO SCARCITY
1 Yasiel Puig RC 1.25 3.00
2 Tyler Skaggs RC .50 1.25
3 Nathan Karns RC .30 .75
4 Manny Machado RC 2.00 5.00
5 Anthony Rendon RC 2.00 5.00
6 Gerrit Cole RC 2.00 5.00
7 Sonny Gray RC .50 1.25
8 Henry Urrutia RC .40 1.00
9 Zoilo Almonte RC .40 1.00
10 Jose Fernandez RC .75 2.00
11 Danny Salazar RC .60 1.50
12 Nick Franklin RC .40 1.00
13 Mike Kickham RC .30 .75
14 Alex Colome RC .30 .75
15 Josh Phegley RC .30 .75
16 Drake Britton RC .40 1.00
17 Marcell Ozuna RC .75 2.00
18 Oswaldo Arcia RC .30 .75
19 Didi Gregorius RC 1.25 3.00
20 Zack Wheeler RC .60 1.50
21 Michael Wacha RC .40 1.00
22 Kyle Gibson RC .50 1.25
23 Johnny Hellweg RC .30 .75
24 Dylan Bundy RC .75 2.00
25 Tony Cingrani RC .60 1.50
26 Jurickson Profar RC .40 1.00
27 Scooter Gennett RC .50 1.25
28 Grant Green RC .50 1.25
29 Brad Miller RC .40 1.00
30 Hyun-Jin Ryu RC .75 2.00
31 Jedd Gyorko RC .40 1.00
32 Shelby Miller RC .75 2.00
33 Sean Nolin RC .40 1.00
34 Allen Webster RC .40 1.00
35 Corey Dickerson RC .40 1.00
36 Jarred Cosart RC .40 1.00
37 Evan Gattis RC .60 1.50
38 Kevin Gausman RC 1.00 2.50
39 Alex Wood RC .40 1.00
40 Christian Yelich RC 2.50 6.00
41 Nolan Arenado RC 3.00 8.00
42 Matt Magill RC .30 .75
43 Jackie Bradley Jr. RC .75 2.00
44 Mike Zunino RC .50 1.25
45 Wil Myers RC .50 1.25

2013 Bowman Draft Blue

*BLUE: 1X TO 2.5X BASIC
STATED ODDS 1:19 HOBBY
STATED PRINT RUN 500 SER.#'d SETS

2013 Bowman Draft Orange

*ORANGE: 1.2X TO 3X BASIC
STATED ODDS 1:37 HOBBY
STATED PRINT RUN 250 SER.#'d SETS

2013 Bowman Draft Red Ice

*RED ICE: 6X TO 15X BASIC
STATED ODDS 1:372 HOBBY
STATED PRINT RUN 25 SER.#'d SETS
1 Yasiel Puig 75.00 150.00

2013 Bowman Draft Silver Ice

*SILVER ICE: 1.2X TO 3X BASIC
STATED ODDS 1:24 HOBBY
1 Yasiel Puig 10.00 25.00

2013 Bowman Draft Draft Picks

BDPP1 Dominic Smith .50 1.25
BDPP2 Kohl Stewart .40 1.00
BDPP3 Josh Hart .30 .75
BDPP4 Nick Ciuffo .30 .75
BDPP5 Austin Meadows .75 2.00
BDPP6 Marco Gonzales .50 1.25
BDPP7 Jonathon Crawford .30 .75
BDPP8 D.J. Peterson .30 .75
BDPP9 Aaron Blair .30 .75
BDPP10 Dustin Peterson .30 .75
BDPP11 Billy Mckinney .40 1.00
BDPP12 Braden Shipley .30 .75
BDPP13 Tim Anderson 1.25 3.00
BDPP14 Chris Anderson .40 1.00
BDPP15 Clint Frazier 1.50 4.00
BDPP16 Hunter Renfroe .50 1.25
BDPP17 Andrew Knapp .30 .75
BDPP18 Corey Knebel .30 .75
BDPP19 Aaron Judge 8.00 20.00
BDPP20 Colin Moran .40 1.00
BDPP21 Ian Clarkin .30 .75
BDPP22 Teddy Stankiewicz .40 1.00
BDPP23 Blake Taylor .30 .75
BDPP24 Hunter Green .30 .75
BDPP25 Kevin Franklin .30 .75
BDPP26 Jonathan Gray .40 1.00
BDPP27 Reese McGuire .40 1.00
BDPP28 Travis Demeritte .40 1.00
BDPP29 Kevin Ziomek .30 .75
BDPP30 Tom Windle .30 .75
BDPP31 Ryan McMahon .75 2.00
BDPP32 J.P. Crawford .50 1.25
BDPP33 Hunter Harvey .40 1.00
BDPP34 Chance Sisco .60 1.50
BDPP35 Riley Unroe .30 .75
BDPP36 Oscar Mercado .50 1.25
BDPP37 Gosuke Katoh .40 1.00
BDPP38 Andrew Church .30 .75
BDPP39 Casey Meisner .30 .75
BDPP40 Ivan Wilson .30 .75
BDPP41 Drew Ward .40 1.00
BDPP42 Thomas Milone .30 .75
BDPP43 Jon Denney .40 1.00
BDPP44 Jan Hernandez .30 .75
BDPP45 Cord Sandberg .40 1.00
BDPP46 Jake Sweaney .30 .75
BDPP47 Patrick Murphy .30 .75
BDPP48 Carlos Salazar .30 .75
BDPP49 Stephen Gonsalves .30 .75
BDPP50 Jonah Heim .30 .75
BDPP51 Kean Wong .30 .75
BDPP52 Tyler Wade .50 1.25
BDPP53 Austin Kubitza .30 .75
BDPP54 Trevor Williams .30 .75
BDPP55 Trae Arbet .30 .75
BDPP56 Ian Mckinney .30 .75
BDPP57 Robert Kaminsky .40 1.00
BDPP58 Brian Navarreto .30 .75
BDPP59 Alex Murphy .30 .75
BDPP60 Jordon Austin .40 1.00
BDPP61 Jacob Nottingham .30 .75
BDPP62 Chris Rivera .30 .75
BDPP63 Trey Williams .50 1.25
BDPP64 Conner Greene .30 .75
BDPP65 Ian Stiffler .30 .75
BDPP66 Phil Ervin .30 .75
BDPP67 Roel Ramirez .30 .75
BDPP68 Michael Lorenzen .40 1.00
BDPP69 Jason Martin .30 .75
BDPP70 Aaron Blanton .30 .75
BDPP71 Dylan Manwaring .30 .75
BDPP72 Luis Guillorme .40 1.00
BDPP73 Brennan Middleton .30 .75
BDPP74 Austin Nicely .30 .75
BDPP75 Ian Hagenmiller .30 .75
BDPP76 Nelson Molina .30 .75
BDPP77 Denton Keys .40 1.00
BDPP78 Kendall Coleman .30 .75
BDPP79 Alec Grosser .30 .75
BDPP80 Ricardo Bautista .30 .75
BDPP81 John Costa .30 .75
BDPP82 Joseph Odom .30 .75
BDPP83 Elier Rodriguez .30 .75
BDPP84 Miles Williams .30 .75
BDPP85 Derrick Penilla .30 .75
BDPP86 Bryan Hudson .30 .75
BDPP87 Jordan Barnes .30 .75
BDPP88 Tyler Kinley .30 .75
BDPP89 Randolph Gassaway .30 .75
BDPP90 Blake Higgins .40 1.00
BDPP91 Caleb Kellogg .30 .75
BDPP92 Joseph Monge .30 .75
BDPP93 Steven Negron .30 .75
BDPP94 Justin Williams .40 1.00
BDPP95 William White .30 .75
BDPP96 Jared Wilson .30 .75
BDPP97 Niko Spezial .30 .75
BDPP98 Gabe Speier .30 .75
BDPP99 Juan Avila .30 .75
BDPP100 Jason Kanzler .30 .75
BDPP101 Tyler Brosius .30 .75
BDPP102 Tyler Vail .30 .75
BDPP103 Adam Landecker .30 .75
BDPP104 Ethan Carnes .30 .75
BDPP105 Austin Wilson .40 1.00
BDPP106 Jon Keller .30 .75
BDPP107 Gaither Bumgardner .30 .75
BDPP108 Garrett Gordon .30 .75
BDPP109 Connor Oliver .30 .75
BDPP110 Cody Harris .30 .75
BDPP111 Brandon Easton .30 .75
BDPP112 Matt Derosier .30 .75
BDPP113 Jeremy Hadley .30 .75
BDPP114 Will Morris .30 .75
BDPP115 Sean Hurley .30 .75
BDPP116 Orrin Sears .30 .75
BDPP117 Sean Townsley .30 .75
BDPP118 Chad Christensen .30 .75
BDPP119 Travis Ott .30 .75
BDPP120 Justin Maffei .30 .75
BDPP121 Reed Harper .30 .75
BDPP122 Adam Westmoreland .30 .75
BDPP123 Adrian Castano .30 .75
BDPP124 Hyrum Formo .30 .75
BDPP125 Jake Stone .40 1.00
BDPP126 Joel Effertz .30 .75
BDPP127 Matt Southard .30 .75
BDPP128 Jorge Perez .30 .75
BDPP129 Willie Medina .30 .75
BDPP130 Ty Afenir .30 .75

2013 Bowman Draft Draft Picks Blue

*BLUE: 1X TO 2.5X BASIC
STATED ODDS 1:19 HOBBY
STATED PRINT RUN 500 SER.#'d SETS
BDPP19 Aaron Judge 30.00 80.00

2013 Bowman Draft Draft Picks Orange

*ORANGE: 1.2X TO 3X BASIC INSERTS
STATED ODDS 1:37 HOBBY
STATED PRINT RUN 250 SER.#'d SETS
BDPP19 Aaron Judge 40.00 100.00

2013 Bowman Draft Draft Picks Red Ice

*RED ICE: 1.5X TO 4X BASIC
STATED PRINT RUN 25 SER.#'d SETS
BDPP5 Austin Meadows 40.00 100.00
BDPP15 Clint Frazier 40.00 100.00
BDPP19 Aaron Judge 150.00 400.00
BDPP26 Jonathan Gray 25.00 60.00

2013 Bowman Draft Draft Picks Silver Ice

*SILVER ICE: 1.2X TO 3X BASIC
STATED ODDS 1:24 HOBBY
BDPP19 Aaron Judge 40.00 100.00

2013 Bowman Draft Dual Draftee

COMPLETE SET (10) 5.00 12.00
STATED ODDS 1:18 HOBBY
AG M.Appel/J.Gray .30 .75
BD T.Ball/J.Denney .30 .75
BM K.Bryant/C.Moran 1.25 3.00
CJ I.Clarkin/E.Jagielo .25 .60
CS R.Stanek/N.Ciuffo .40 1.00
FM A.Meadows/C.Frazier 1.00 2.50
GK M.Gonzales/R.Kaminsky .30 .75
JC A.Judge/I.Clarkin 2.00 5.00
JJ E.Jagielo/A.Judge 2.00 5.00
MM A.Meadows/R.McGuire .50 1.25

2013 Bowman Draft Dual Draftee Autographs

STATED ODDS 1:11,700 HOBBY
STATED PRINT RUN 25 SER.#'d SETS
EXCHANGE DEADLINE 11/30/2016
AG Appel/Gray EXCH 20.00 50.00
BD Ball/Denney EXCH 15.00 40.00
BM K.Bryant/C.Moran 150.00 250.00
CJ I.Clarkin/E.Jagielo 40.00 80.00
FM Meadows/Frazier EXCH 200.00 400.00
GK M.Gonzales/R.Kaminsky 30.00 60.00
JC A.Judge/I.Clarkin 60.00 150.00
JJ E.Jagielo/A.Judge 60.00 150.00
MM Meadows/McGuire EXCH 125.00 250.00

2013 Bowman Draft Future of the Franchise

COMPLETE SET (30) 12.50 30.00
STATED ODDS 1:18 HOBBY
AR Addison Russell .40 1.00
AS Aaron Sanchez .30 .75
BB Byron Buxton 1.25 3.00
BH Billy Hamilton .30 .75
BHA Bryce Harper .60 1.50
CC Carlos Correa 3.00 8.00
CH Courtney Hawkins .25 .60
CY Christian Yelich 2.00 5.00
FL Francisco Lindor 2.00 5.00
GC Gerrit Cole 1.50 4.00
GS Gary Sanchez .75 2.00
HD Hunter Dozier .25 .60
JB Javier Baez 1.00 2.50
JC J.P. Crawford .40 1.00
JG Jonathan Gray .30 .75
JGY Jedd Gyorko .30 .75
JP Jurickson Profar .30 .75
JS Jean Segura .30 .75
JT Julio Teheran .30 .75
KC Kyle Crick .40 1.00
MH Matt Harvey .30 .75
MM Manny Machado 1.50 4.00
MT Mike Trout 3.00 8.00
MZ Mike Zunino .40 1.00
NC Nick Castellanos .75 2.00
OT Oscar Taveras .30 .75
PG Paul Goldschmidt .40 1.00
WM Wil Myers .40 1.00
XB Xander Bogaerts .75 2.00
YP Yasiel Puig 1.00 2.50

2013 Bowman Draft Future of the Franchise Blue

*BLUE: 1.5X TO 4X BASIC
STATED ODDS 1:272 HOBBY
STATED PRINT RUN 250 SER.#'d SETS
YP Yasiel Puig 12.50 30.00

2013 Bowman Draft Future's Game Relics

STATED ODDS 1:589 HOBBY
STATED PRINT RUN 99 SER.#'d SETS
AA Arismendy Alcantara 4.00 10.00
AC A.J. Cole 6.00 15.00
AH Austin Hedges 4.00 10.00
AJ A.J. Jimenez 5.00 12.00
AR Andre Rienzo 4.00 10.00
ARA Anthony Ranaudo 4.00 10.00
ARU Addison Russell 4.00 10.00
BN Brandon Nimmo 8.00 20.00
CB Christian Bethancourt 5.00 12.00
CC C.J. Cron 5.00 12.00
CCO Carlos Contreras 10.00 25.00
CO Chris Owings 4.00 10.00
CR C.J. Riefenhauser 4.00 10.00
DD Delino DeShields 4.00 10.00
DH Dilson Herrera 5.00 12.00
EB Eddie Butler 4.00 10.00
ER Eduardo Rodriguez 5.00 12.00
ERO Enny Romero 4.00 10.00
FL Francisco Lindor 8.00 20.00
JB Jesse Biddle 5.00 12.00
JC Ji-Man Choi 4.00 10.00
JGA Jesus Galindo 4.00 10.00
JL Jordan Lennerton 5.00 12.00
JM James McCann 5.00 12.00
KC Kyle Crick 4.00 10.00
KW Kolten Wong 5.00 12.00
MA Miguel Almonte 5.00 12.00
MD Matt Davidson 5.00 12.00
MF Maikel Franco 10.00 25.00
MY Michael Ynoa 4.00 10.00
RD Rafael De Paula 4.00 10.00
RF Reymond Fuentes 4.00 10.00
RM Rafael Montero 5.00 12.00
YA Yeison Asencio 4.00 10.00
YV Yordano Ventura 4.00 10.00

2013 Bowman Draft Scout Autographs

STATED ODDS 1:27,081 HOBBY
STATED PRINT RUN 25 SER.#'d SETS
FB Freddy Berowski 12.50 30.00
JK Jeff Katofsky 20.00 50.00
JS J.P. Schwartz 20.00 50.00

2013 Bowman Draft Scout Breakouts

COMPLETE SET (50) 15.00 40.00
STATED ODDS 1:18 HOBBY
AA Andrew Aplin .40 1.00
AAL Aaron Altherr .40 1.00
AB Andy Burns .40 1.00
AR Alexis Rivera .40 1.00
AT Andrew Toles .40 1.00
AW Adam Walker .50 1.25
BB B.J. Boyd .40 1.00
BBR Bryan Brickhouse .40 1.00
BD Brandon Drury .40 1.00
CB Christian Binford .40 1.00
CBO Chris Bostick .40 1.00
CE C.J. Edwards .60 1.50
CT Chris Taylor .60 1.50
DW Daniel Winkler .40 1.00
GC Garin Cecchini .40 1.00
GE Gabriel Encinas .40 1.00
JH Josh Hader .75 2.00
JL Jake Lamb .60 1.50
JP Jeffrey Popick .40 1.00
JPO Jorge Polanco 1.00 2.50
JT Jake Thompson .40 1.00
JW Jacob Wilson .40 1.00
KF Kendry Flores .75 2.00
KP Kevin Plawecki .40 1.00
LJ Luke Jackson .40 1.00
MJ Micah Johnson .50 1.25
MS Mark Sappington .40 1.00
MW Mac Williamson .60 1.50
NF Nolan Fontana .50 1.25
NK Nick Kingham .40 1.00
NW Nick Williams .50 1.25
OC Orlando Castro .40 1.00
PJ Pierce Johnson .50 1.25
PK Patrick Kivlehan .40 1.00
PO Peter O'Brien .50 1.25
PT Preston Tucker .60 1.50
RA R.J. Alvarez .40 1.00
RC Ryan Casteel .50 1.25
RD Rafael De Paula .40 1.00
RM Raul Mondesi .60 1.50
RMO Rafael Montero .40 1.00
RS Rock Shoulders .40 1.00
SA Stetson Allie .60 1.50
SS Sam Selman .40 1.00
TD Taylor Dugas .50 1.25
TH Tyler Heineman .40 1.00
TM Tom Murphy .40 1.00
TP Tyler Pike .40 1.00
WR Wilfredo Rodriguez .40 1.00
YP Yasiel Puig 1.50 4.00

2013 Bowman Draft Scout Breakouts Die-Cuts

*DIE CUT: 1.2X TO 3X BASIC

2013 Bowman Draft Scout Breakouts Die-Cuts X-Fractors

*X-FRACTOR: 2X TO 5X BASIC
STATED ODDS 1:349 HOBBY
STATED PRINT RUN 99 SER.#'d SETS

2013 Bowman Draft Scout Breakouts Autographs

STATED ODDS 1:12,220 HOBBY
STATED PRINT RUN 24 SER.#'d SETS
EXCHANGE DEADLINE 11/30/2016
AA Andrew Aplin 15.00 40.00
AW Adam Walker 20.00 50.00
JT Jake Thompson EXCH 12.50 30.00
MW Mac Williamson EXCH 40.00 80.00
NW Nick Williams EXCH 15.00 40.00
PK Patrick Kivlehan 12.50 30.00
TM Tom Murphy EXCH 6.00 15.00
TP Tyler Pike 20.00 50.00

2013 Bowman Draft Top Prospects

STATED PLATE ODDS 1:2320 HOBBY
PLATE PRINT RUN 1 SET PER COLOR
BLACK-CYAN-MAGENTA-YELLOW ISSUED
NO PLATE PRICING DUE TO SCARCITY
TP1 Byron Buxton .75 2.00
TP2 Tyler Austin .25 .60
TP3 Mason Williams .20 .50
TP4 Albert Almora .30 .75
TP5 Joey Gallo .50 1.25
TP6 Jesse Biddle .20 .50
TP7 David Dahl .20 .50
TP8 Kevin Gausman .50 1.25
TP9 Jorge Soler .30 .75
TP10 Carlos Correa 2.00 5.00
TP11 Preston Tucker .25 .60
TP12 Jameson Taillon .20 .50
TP13 Joc Pederson .40 1.00
TP14 Max Fried .60 1.50
TP15 Taijuan Walker .20 .50
TP16 Chris Bostick .15 .40
TP17 Francisco Lindor 1.25 3.00
TP18 Daniel Vogelbach .25 .60
TP19 Kaleb Cowart .20 .50
TP20 George Springer .60 1.50
TP21 Yordano Ventura .20 .50
TP22 Noah Syndergaard .20 .50
TP23 Ty Hensley .20 .50
TP24 C.J. Cron .20 .50
TP25 Addison Russell .25 .60
TP26 Kyle Crick .25 .60
TP27 Javier Baez .60 1.50
TP28 Kolten Wong .15 .40
TP29 Taylor Guerrieri .15 .40
TP30 Archie Bradley .15 .40
TP31 Gary Sanchez .50 1.25
TP32 Billy Hamilton .20 .50
TP33 Alen Hanson .20 .50
TP34 Jonathan Singleton .20 .50
TP35 Mark Montgomery .25 .60
TP36 Nick Castellanos .50 1.25
TP37 Courtney Hawkins .15 .40
TP38 Gregory Polanco .30 .75
TP39 Matt Barnes .20 .50
TP40 Xander Bogaerts .50 1.25
TP41 Dorssys Paulino .20 .50
TP42 Corey Seager .75 2.00
TP43 Alex Meyer .15 .40
TP44 Aaron Sanchez .20 .50
TP45 Miguel Sano .20 .50

2013 Bowman Draft Top Prospects Blue

*BLUE: 1.5X TO 4X BASIC
STATED ODDS 1:19 HOBBY
STATED PRINT RUN 500 SER.#'d SETS

2013 Bowman Draft Top Prospects Orange

*ORANGE: 2X TO 5X BASIC
STATED ODDS 1:37 HOBBY
STATED PRINT RUN 250 SER.#'d SETS

2013 Bowman Draft Top Prospects Red Ice

*RED ICE: 12X TO 30X BASIC
STATED ODDS 1:372 HOBBY
STATED PRINT RUN 25 SER.#'d SETS

2013 Bowman Draft Top Prospects Silver Ice

*SILVER ICE: 2X TO 5X BASIC
STATED ODDS 1:24 HOBBY

2014 Bowman

COMPLETE SET (220) 10.00 25.00
PLATE PRINT RUN 1 SET PER COLOR
BLACK-CYAN-MAGENTA-YELLOW ISSUED
NO PLATE PRICING DUE TO SCARCITY
1 Derek Jeter .60 1.50
2 Gerrit Cole .25 .60
3 Derek Holland .15 .40
4 Brandon Beachy .15 .40
5 Jay Bruce .20 .50
6 Oswaldo Arcia .15 .40
7 Ian Kennedy .15 .40
8 Joe Nathan .15 .40
9 Chris Johnson .15 .40
10 Mike Leake .15 .40
11 Andrelton Simmons .15 .40
12 Trevor Rosenthal .20 .50
13 Evan Gattis .15 .40
14 Starling Marte .20 .50
15 Coco Crisp .15 .40
16 Starlin Castro .15 .40
17 Desmond Jennings .20 .50
18 Austin Jackson .15 .40
19 Giancarlo Stanton .25 .60
20 Nolan Arenado .40 1.00
21 Jordan Zimmermann .20 .50
22 Johnny Cueto .20 .50
23 R.A. Dickey .20 .50
24 Bartolo Colon .15 .40
25 Carlos Gomez .15 .40
26 Jason Grilli .15 .40
27 Craig Kimbrel .20 .50
28 Salvador Perez .20 .50
29 Matt Cain .20 .50
30 Yu Darvish .25 .60
31 Adrian Beltre .25 .60
32 Sonny Gray .20 .50
33 Zack Wheeler .20 .50
34 Paul Goldschmidt .25 .60
35 Ivan Nova .20 .50
36 Matt Harvey .20 .50
37 Will Middlebrooks .15 .40
38 Torii Hunter .15 .40
39 Andrew Lambo RC .25 .60
40 Marcus Semien RC 1.25 3.00
41 Wilmer Flores RC .30 .75
42 Kolten Wong RC .30 .75
43 James Paxton RC .40 1.00
44 Abraham Almonte RC .25 .60
45 Avisail Garcia .20 .50
46 Francisco Liriano .15 .40
47 Jayson Werth .20 .50
48 James Shields .15 .40
49 Josh Reddick .15 .40
50 Miguel Cabrera .25 .60
51 CC Sabathia .20 .50
52 Tony Cingrani .20 .50
53 Edwin Encarnacion .25 .60
54 Chase Headley .15 .40
55 Ian Desmond .15 .40
56 Carlos Gonzalez .20 .50
57 Mat Latos .20 .50
58 Curtis Granderson .20 .50
59 Alex Gordon .20 .50
60 Anibal Sanchez .15 .40
61 Ubaldo Jimenez .15 .40
62 Aroldis Chapman .25 .60
63 Jean Segura .20 .50
64 Yovani Gallardo .15 .40
65 Domonic Brown .20 .50
66 Dustin Pedroia .25 .60
67 Cole Hamels .20 .50
68 Jarrod Parker .15 .40
69 John Lackey .20 .50
70 Hiroki Kuroda .15 .40
71 Kendrys Morales .15 .40
72 Anthony Rizzo .30 .75
73 Tim Lincecum .20 .50
74 David Freese .15 .40
75 Hanley Ramirez .20 .50
76 Albert Pujols .30 .75
77 Carlos Beltran .20 .50
78 Evan Longoria .20 .50
79 Jose Fernandez .25 .60
80 Matt Moore .20 .50
81 Jarred Cosart .15 .40
82 Hunter Pence .20 .50
83 Kevin Pillar RC .25 .60
84 Xander Bogaerts RC .75 2.00
85 Yordano Ventura RC .30 .75
86 Taijuan Walker RC .25 .60
87 Jake Marisnick RC .25 .60
88 Masahiro Tanaka RC .75 2.00
89 Alex Rios .20 .50
90 Jose Reyes .20 .50
91 Jeff Samardzija .15 .40
92 Jed Lowrie .15 .40
93 Adam Wainwright .20 .50
94 Max Scherzer .25 .60
95 Daniel Nava .15 .40
96 Anthony Rendon .25 .60
97 Adam Lind .20 .50
98 Jon Lester .20 .50
99 Adrian Gonzalez .20 .50
100 Clayton Kershaw .40 1.00
101 Matt Holliday .25 .60
102 Felix Hernandez .20 .50
103 Hisashi Iwakuma .20 .50
104 J.J. Hardy .15 .40
105 Yoenis Cespedes .25 .60
106 Christian Yelich .30 .75
107 Robinson Cano .20 .50
108 Alex Cobb .15 .40
109 Aaron Hill .15 .40
110 Manny Machado .25 .60
111 Wei-Yin Chen .15 .40
112 Allen Craig .20 .50
113 Joe Kelly .15 .40
114 Joey Votto .25 .60
115 Troy Tulowitzki .25 .60
116 Billy Butler .15 .40
117 Brian McCann .20 .50
118 Koji Uehara .15 .40
119 Jorge De La Rosa .15 .40
120 Alfonso Soriano .20 .50
121 Chris Sale .25 .60
122 Michael Cuddyer .15 .40
123 Josh Hamilton .20 .50
124 Mike Napoli .15 .40
125 Jose Bautista .20 .50
126 Josh Donaldson .20 .50
127 Nick Castellanos RC .75 2.00
128 Jonathan Schoop RC .25 .60
129 Jimmy Nelson RC .25 .60
130 Matt Davidson RC .30 .75
131 Andre Rienzo RC .25 .60
132 Billy Hamilton RC .30 .75
133 Homer Bailey .15 .40
134 Yadier Molina .30 .75
135 Michael Wacha .20 .50
136 Prince Fielder .20 .50
137 Mike Minor .15 .40
138 Wade Miley .15 .40
139 Carl Crawford .20 .50
140 Chris Davis .15 .40
141 Gio Gonzalez .20 .50
142 Brandon Moss .15 .40
143 Jonny Gomes .15 .40
144 Elvis Andrus .20 .50
145 Buster Posey .30 .75
146 Justin Verlander .25 .60
147 C.J. Wilson .15 .40
148 Pablo Sandoval .20 .50
149 Asdrubal Cabrera .20 .50
150 Andrew McCutchen .25 .60
151 Andre Ethier .20 .50
152 Kris Medlen .20 .50
153 Freddie Freeman .30 .75
154 Martin Prado .15 .40
155 A.J. Burnett .15 .40
156 Nick Swisher .20 .50
157 Brad Ziegler .15 .40
158 Mike Zunino .15 .40
159 Wil Myers .15 .40
160 Jason Kipnis .20 .50
161 Jered Weaver .20 .50
162 Trevor Bauer .30 .75
163 Zack Greinke .25 .60
164 David Wright .20 .50
165 Cliff Lee .20 .50
166 Matt Carpenter .25 .60
167 Justin Upton .20 .50
168 Mike Trout 1.25 3.00
169 Shelby Miller .20 .50
170 Jurickson Profar .20 .50
171 Christian Bethancourt RC .25 .60
172 J.R. Murphy RC .25 .60
173 Josmil Pinto RC .25 .60
174 Michael Choice RC .25 .60
175 Erik Johnson RC .25 .60
176 Jose Ramirez RC 2.00 5.00
177 Adam Jones .20 .50
178 Brett Lawrie .20 .50
179 Kevin Gausman .25 .60
180 Roy Halladay .20 .50
181 Ian Kinsler .20 .50
182 Andrew Cashner .15 .40
183 Chase Utley .20 .50
184 Patrick Corbin .20 .50
185 Marco Scutaro .20 .50
186 Ryan Zimmerman .20 .50
187 Jose Iglesias .20 .50
188 Eric Hosmer .20 .50
189 Joe Mauer .20 .50
190 Jedd Gyorko .15 .40
191 Mark Trumbo .15 .40
192 Tim Hudson .20 .50
193 Pedro Alvarez .15 .40
194 Tyler Skaggs .15 .40
195 Nick Franklin .15 .40
196 Chris Archer .15 .40
197 Carlos Santana .20 .50
198 Julio Teheran .20 .50
199 Fernando Rodney .15 .40
200 Bryce Harper .40 1.00
201 Matt Kemp .20 .50
202 Jason Heyward .20 .50
203 Brandon Phillips .15 .40
204 Carlos Ruiz .15 .40
205 Shane Victorino .20 .50
206 Jonathan Lucroy .20 .50
207 Hyun-Jin Ryu .20 .50
208 David Ortiz .25 .60
209 David Price .20 .50
210 Jacoby Ellsbury .20 .50
211 Madison Bumgarner .20 .50
212 Wilin Rosario .15 .40
213 Stephen Strasburg .25 .60
214 Yasiel Puig .25 .60
215 Tim Beckham RC .40 1.00
216 Travis d'Arnaud RC .30 .75
217 Enny Romero RC .25 .60
218 David Holmberg RC .25 .60
219 Chris Owings RC .25 .60
220 Onelki Garcia RC .25 .60

2014 Bowman Black

*BLK VET: 10X TO 25X BASIC VET
*BLK RC: 15X TO 40X BASIC RC
STATED ODDS 1:547 HOBBY
STATED PRINT RUN 25 SER.#'d SETS
1 Derek Jeter 60.00 120.00

2014 Bowman Blue

*BLUE VET: 2X TO 5X BASIC VET
*BLUE RC: 1.2X TO 3X BASIC RC
STATED ODDS 1:27 HOBBY
STATED PRINT RUN 500 SER.#'d SETS

2014 Bowman Gold

*GOLD VET: 6X TO 15X BASIC VET
*GOLD RC: 4X TO 10X BASIC RC
STATED ODDS 1:273 HOBBY
STATED PRINT RUN 50 SER.#'d SETS
1 Derek Jeter 40.00 80.00
168 Mike Trout 30.00 60.00

2014 Bowman Green

*GREEN VET: 4X TO 10X BASIC VET
*GREEN RC: 2.5X TO 6X BASIC RC
STATED ODDS 1:91 HOBBY
STATED PRINT RUN 150 SER.#'d SETS

2014 Bowman Hometown

*HOMETOWN VET: 1.5X TO 4X BASIC VET
*HOMETOWN RC: 1X TO 2.5X BASIC RC
STATED ODDS 1:8 HOBBY

2014 Bowman Orange

*ORANGE VET: 3X TO 8X BASIC VET
*ORANGE RC: 2X TO 5X BASIC RC
STATED ODDS 1:55 HOBBY
STATED PRINT RUN 250 SER.#'d SETS

2014 Bowman Red Ice

*RED ICE VET: 10X TO 25X BASIC VET
*RED ICE RC: 10X TO 25X BASIC RC
STATED ODDS 1:275 HOBBY
STATED PRINT RUN 25 SER.#'d SETS
1 Derek Jeter 60.00 120.00

2014 Bowman Silver

*SILVER VET: 6X TO 15X BASIC VET
*SILVER RC: 4X TO 10X BASIC RC
STATED ODDS 1:182 HOBBY
STATED PRINT RUN 75 SER.#'d SETS

2014 Bowman Silver Ice

*SILVER ICE VET: 2X TO 5X BASIC VET
*SILVER ICE RC: 1.2X TO 3X BASIC RC
STATED ODDS 1:24 HOBBY

2014 Bowman Yellow

*YEL VET: 6X TO 15X BASIC VET
*YEL RC: 4X TO 10X BASIC RC
STATED ODDS 1:138 HOBBY
STATED PRINT RUN 99 SER.#'d SETS

2014 Bowman '89 Bowman is Back Silver Diamond Refractors

COMPLETE SET (145)
BOWMAN ODDS 1:24 HOBBY
STERLING ODDS 1:6 HOBBY
89BIBAC A.J. Cole BS .60 1.50
89BIBAJ Adam Jones BI 1.25 3.00
89BIBAJ Alex Jackson BD .50 1.25
89BIBAM Austin Meadows BD 1.00 2.50
89BIBAM Andrew McCutchen BP 1.25 3.00
89BIBAM Alex Meyer BS .60 1.50
89BIBAN Aaron Nola BD 2.50 6.00
89BIBAR Addison Russell BS 1.00 2.50
89BIBAS Aaron Sanchez BS .60 1.50
89BIBBB Byron Buxton B 2.00 5.00
89BIBBH Billy Hamilton B .50 1.25
89BIBBH Bryce Harper BI 2.50 6.00
89BIBBJ Bo Jackson B .60 1.50
89BIBBL Ben Lively BD .40 1.00
89BIBBP Buster Posey BS 1.25 3.00
89BIBBS Braden Shipley BD .40 1.00
89BIBCB Christian Binford BD .40 1.00
89BIBCB Craig Biggio B .50 1.25
89BIBCC Carlos Correa BP 4.00 10.00
89BIBCD Chris Davis BP .75 2.00
89BIBCE C.J. Edwards BS .75 2.00
89BIBCF Clint Frazier BI 4.00 10.00
89BIBCFI Carlton Fisk BI 1.25 3.00
89BIBCK Clayton Kershaw BI 2.50 6.00
89BIBCM Colin Moran BI 1.00 2.50
89BIBCR Cal Ripken B 2.00 5.00
89BIBCS Corey Seager BD 2.00 5.00
89BIBDD David Dahl BD .50 1.25
89BIBDE Dennis Eckersley BI 1.25 3.00
89BIBDJ Derek Jeter B 1.50 4.00
89BIBDO David Ortiz BI 1.50 4.00
89BIBDP Dustin Pedroia BP 1.25 3.00
89BIBDR Daniel Robertson BP 1.00 2.50
89BIBDS Deion Sanders BI 1.25 3.00
89BIBDS Dominic Smith BS .60 1.50
89BIBDT Devon Travis BP .75 2.00
89BIBDW David Wright B .50 1.25
89BIBEB Eddie Butler BI 1.00 2.50
89BIBEL Evan Longoria BP 1.00 2.50
89BIBER Eddie Rosario BS 1.25 3.00
89BIBFF Freddie Freeman BS 1.25 3.00
89BIBFH Felix Hernandez BI 1.25 3.00
89BIBFL Francisco Lindor B 3.00 8.00
89BIBGB George Brett B 1.25 3.00
89BIBGM Greg Maddux B .75 2.00
89BIBGP Gregory Polanco BI 1.50 4.00
89BIBGS Gary Sanchez BI 3.00 8.00
89BIBGS Giancarlo Stanton BP 1.25 3.00
89BIBHH Hunter Harvey BD .40 1.00
89BIBHJR Hyun-Jin Ryu BP 1.00 2.50
89BIBHO Henry Owens BS .75 2.00
89BIBHR Hunter Renfroe BP 1.00 2.50
89BIBJA Jose Abreu BP 6.00 15.00
89BIBJA Jorge Alfaro BS .75 2.00
89BIBJB Javier Baez BP 3.00 8.00
89BIBJB Josh Bell BD .75 2.00
89BIBJB Jesse Biddle BI 1.25 3.00
89BIBJE Jacoby Ellsbury B .50 1.25
89BIBJG Jonathan Gray BP 1.00 2.50
89BIBJG Joey Gallo BS 1.25 3.00
89BIBJH Jeff Hoffman BD .60 1.50
89BIBJP Joc Pederson BS 1.50 4.00
89BIBJS Jorge Soler BI 2.00 5.00
89BIBJSM John Smoltz BI 1.50 4.00
89BIBJT Jameson Taillon BD .50 1.25

89BIBJT Julio Teheran BS .75 2.00
89BIBJU Julio Urias BD 2.00 5.00
89BIBJV Justin Verlander BP 1.25 3.00
89BIBJV Joey Votto BS 1.00 2.50
89BIBKB Kris Bryant B 4.00 10.00
89BIBKF Kyle Freeland BD .75 2.00
89BIBKG Ken Griffey Jr. B 1.25 3.00
89BIBKM Kodi Medeiros BD .40 1.00
89BIBKS Kohl Stewart BP .75 2.00
89BIBKS Kyle Schwarber BS 2.50 6.00
89BIBLG Lucas Giolito BD .60 1.50
89BIBLS Luis Severino BD .60 1.50
89BIBMA Mark Appel B .50 1.25
89BIBMB Mookie Betts BS 12.00 30.00
89BIBMC Michael Conforto BD .75 2.00
89BIBMC Matt Carpenter BP 1.25 3.00
89BIBMF Maikel Franco B .50 1.25
89BIBMM Manny Machado BI 1.50 4.00
89BIBMM Mark McGwire BP 2.50 6.00
89BIBMP Max Pentecost BD .40 1.00
89BIBMS Miguel Sano BI 1.25 3.00
89BIBMS Max Scherzer BS 1.00 2.50
89BIBMT Mike Trout BP 6.00 15.00
89BIBMTA Masahiro Tanaka BP 2.50 6.00
89BIBMW Michael Wacha BI 1.25 3.00
89BIBNC Nick Castellanos BI 3.00 8.00
89BIBNG Nick Gordon BS .75 2.00
89BIBNS Noah Syndergaard BS .75 2.00
89BIBOS Ozzie Smith BP 1.50 4.00
89BIBOT Oscar Taveras B .50 1.25
89BIBPG Paul Goldschmidt BI 1.50 4.00
89BIBPM Paul Molitor B .60 1.50
89BIBPS Pablo Sandoval BP 1.00 2.50
89BIBRB Ryan Braun BS .75 2.00
89BIBRC Robinson Cano BS .75 2.00
89BIBRH Rosell Herrera BP 1.25 3.00
89BIBRM Raul Mondesi BI 1.50 4.00
89BIBRS Robert Stephenson BI 1.00 2.50
89BIBRY Robin Yount BP 1.25 3.00
89BIBTB Tyler Beede BD .60 1.50
89BIBTD Travis d'Arnaud B .50 1.25
89BIBTG Tom Glavine B .50 1.25
89BIBTG Tony Gwynn BP 1.25 3.00
89BIBTG Tyler Glasnow BS 2.50 6.00
89BIBTK Tyler Kolek BS .60 1.50
89BIBTK Trea Turner BD 1.25 3.00
89BIBTT Troy Tulowitzki B .60 1.50
89BIBTW Taijuan Walker BI 1.00 2.50
89BIBWB Wade Boggs BP 1.00 2.50
89BIBWF Wilmer Flores B .50 1.25
89BIBWM Wil Myers B .40 1.00
89BIBXB Xander Bogaerts B 1.25 3.00
89BIBYD Yu Darvish BI 1.50 4.00
89BIBYM Yadier Molina B .75 2.00
89BIBYP Yasiel Puig B .60 1.50
BIB89AG Alexander Guerrero BC .50 1.25
BIB89BH Bryce Harper BC 1.00 2.50
BIB89CS Chris Sale BC .60 1.50
BIB89DP David Price BC .50 1.25
BIB89FT Frank Thomas BC .60 1.50
BIB89GC Gary Carter BC .50 1.25
BIB89GK Gosuke Katoh BC .60 1.50
BIB89JF Jose Fernandez BC .60 1.50
BIB89JK Jason Kipnis BC .50 1.25
BIB89JS Jean Segura BC .50 1.25
BIB89KC Kyle Crick BC .40 1.00
BIB89MC Miguel Cabrera BC .60 1.50
BIB89MP Mike Piazza BC .60 1.50
BIB89MR Mariano Rivera BC .75 2.00
BIB89MT Masahiro Tanaka BC 1.25 3.00
BIB89RT Rowdy Tellez BC .40 1.00
BIB89SG Sonny Gray BC .50 1.25
BIB89SS Shae Simmons BC .40 1.00
BIB89YC Yoenis Cespedes BC .60 1.50
BIB89BLI Brandon Nimmo BD .60 1.50
BIB89BSW Blake Swihart BD .50 1.25
BIB89JBE Jose Berrios BD .60 1.50
BIB89JHA Josh Hader BD .75 2.00
BIB89BMBU Madison Bumgarner BS .75 2.00
BIB89SST Stephen Strasburg BC .60 1.50

2014 Bowman '89 Bowman is Back Autographs Black Refractors

STATED ODDS 1:16,200 HOBBY
STERLING ODDS 1:302 HOBBY
PRINT RUNS B/WN 15-25 COPIES PER
EXCHANGE DEADLINE 4/30/2017
STERLING EXCHANGE 12/31/2017
89BIBCC Carlos Correa/25 150.00 300.00
89BIBDP Dustin Pedroia/25 30.00 80.00
89BIBDR Daniel Robertson/25 40.00 100.00
89BIBEL Evan Longoria/25 30.00 80.00
89BIBJA Jose Abreu/25 300.00 500.00
89BIBJG Jonathan Gray/25 30.00 80.00
89BIBMT Mike Trout/25 300.00 500.00
89BIBOS Ozzie Smith/25 40.00 100.00
89BIBWB Wade Boggs/25 30.00 60.00
89BIBACB Craig Biggio/25 50.00 100.00
89BIBACR Ripken Jr. EXCH 75.00 200.00
89BIBAJT Julio Teheran/25 15.00 40.00
89BIBAKB Kris Bryant/25 900.00 1200.00
89BIBAKG Griffey Jr. 250.00 350.00
89BIBAMA Mark Appel/25 75.00 200.00
89BIBANG Nick Gordon/25 50.00 100.00
89BIBAPM Paul Molitor EXCH/25 20.00 50.00
89BIBARB Ryan Braun/25 12.00 30.00
89BIBARC Robinson Cano/25 25.00 60.00
89BIBATG Glavine EXCH 75.00 150.00
89BIBATT Tulowitzki EXCH 50.00 100.00
89BIBAWM Wil Myers/25 75.00 150.00
89BIBAXB Xander Bogaerts/25 75.00 150.00

2014 Bowman Black Collection Autographs

BOWMAN ODDS 1:6500 HOBBY
BOW.CHROME ODDS 1:3667 HOBBY
BOW.DRAFT ODDS 1:7350 HOBBY
STERLING ODDS 1:226 HOBBY
STATED PRINT RUN 25 SER.#'d SETS
BOWMAN EXCH DEADLINE 4/30/2017
INCEPTION EXCH DEADLINE 6/30/2017
PLATINUM EXCH DEADLINE 7/31/2017
BOW.CHR.EXCH DEADLINE 9/30/2017
BOW.DRAFT EXCH DEADLINE 11/30/2017
STERLING EXCH DEADLINE 12/31/2017
BBAB Akeem Bostick BP 12.00 30.00
BBBB Byron Buxton 75.00 150.00
BBCF Chris Flexen BP 10.00 25.00
BBCS Cord Sandberg BP 12.00 30.00
BBCV Cory Vaughn BP 10.00 25.00
BBDR Daniel Robertson BP 12.00 30.00
BBDT Devon Travis BP 12.00 30.00
BBJA Jose Abreu BP 200.00 300.00
BBJB Javier Baez BP 25.00 200.00
BBJBA Jake Barrett BP 25.00 60.00
BBKB Kris Bryant BP 300.00 500.00
BBLT Lewis Thorpe BP 10.00 25.00
BBMA Mark Appel BP 60.00 120.00
BBOT Oscar Taveras BP 50.00 100.00
BBRH Rosell Herrera BP 6.00 15.00
BBRT Raimel Tapia BP 20.00 50.00
BBSS Shae Simmons BP 40.00 80.00
BBWR Wendell Rijo BP 15.00 40.00
BBYG Yimi Garcia BP 10.00 25.00
BBZB Zach Borenstein BP 10.00 25.00
BBCAA Arismendy Alcantara BI 20.00 50.00
BBCAB Archie Bradley BI 12.00 30.00
BBCAB Akeem Bostick BC 10.00 25.00
BBCAB Alex Blandino BD 15.00 40.00
BBCABU Andy Burns BC EXCH 20.00 50.00
BBCAG Alexander Guerrero BI 30.00 80.00
BBCAJ Alex Jackson BD 75.00 150.00
BBCAM Adalberto Mejia BI 12.00 30.00
BBCAN Aaron Nola BD 60.00 150.00
BBCAS Aaron Sanchez BS EXCH 12.00 30.00
BBCAT Alberto Tirado BC EXCH 20.00 50.00
BBCAT Andrew Toles 10.00 25.00
BBCAW Adam Walker BI 12.00 30.00
BBCBAN Blake Anderson BD 10.00 25.00
BBCBD Braxton Davidson BD 25.00 60.00
BBCBL Ben Lively BC 10.00 25.00
BBCBT Brandon Trinkwon EXCH 10.00 25.00
BBCBZ Bradley Zimmer BS 20.00 50.00
BBCCA Cody Anderson BC 10.00 25.00
BBCCB Chris Bostick 10.00 25.00
BBCCBI Christian Binford 15.00 40.00
BBCCC Carlos Contreras BC 10.00 25.00
BBCCJ Connor Joe BD 10.00 25.00
BBCCM Casey Meisner 10.00 25.00
BBCCP Cesar Puello 20.00 50.00
BBCCT Chris Taylor 12.00 30.00
BBCDH Derek Hill BD 10.00 25.00
BBCDM Daniel McGrath 30.00 60.00
BBCDP Daniel Palka BI 6.00 15.00
BBCDW Kean Wong BC 10.00 25.00
BBCDW Daniel Winkler BC 10.00 25.00
BBCEE Edwin Escobar BI 10.00 25.00
BBCEF Erick Fedde BD 25.00 60.00
BBCFB Franklin Barreto BC EXCH 50.00 100.00
BBCFC Franchy Cordero 15.00 40.00
BBCFG Foster Griffin BD 10.00 25.00
BBCFL Francisco Lindor BI 20.00 50.00
BBCFR Franmil Reyes BC 12.00 30.00
BBCFW Forrest Wall BD 10.00 25.00
BBCGE Gabriel Encinas EXCH 10.00 25.00
BBCGH Grant Holmes BS 40.00 100.00
BBCGS Gary Sanchez BI 15.00 40.00
BBCIK Isiah Kiner-Falefa BC 20.00 50.00
BBCJF Jack Flaherty BD 15.00 40.00
BBCJG Jonathan Gray BI 12.00 30.00
BBCJG Joan Gregorio 10.00 25.00
BBCJGA Jacob Gatewood BS EXCH 20.00 50.00
BBCJH Jason Hursh 20.00 50.00
BBCJH Jeff Hoffman BD 25.00 60.00
BBCJHA Josh Hader 10.00 25.00
BBCJL Jake Lamb BI EXCH 25.00 60.00
BBCJR Jose Rondon BC 6.00 15.00
BBCJS Justus Sheffield BD 10.00 25.00
BBCJS Jonathan Schoop BI 15.00 40.00
BBCJU Julio Urias BI EXCH 50.00 100.00
BBCJU Jose Urena BC 10.00 25.00
BBCJW Jamie Westbrook BC 10.00 25.00
BBCJWI Jacob Wilson BC EXCH 15.00 40.00
BBCKD Kelly Dugan BC 10.00 25.00
BBCKF Kendry Flores EXCH 10.00 25.00
BBCKG Kevin Garcia EXCH 15.00 40.00
BBCKS Kyle Schwarber BC 60.00 150.00
BBCLR Luigi Rodriguez BC 10.00 25.00
BBCLW LeVon Washington BC 10.00 25.00
BBCLW Luke Weaver BD 20.00 50.00
BBCMA Mark Appel BI EXCH 30.00 60.00
BBCMCH Matt Chapman BD 10.00 25.00
BBCMF Maikel Franco 50.00 100.00
BBCMJ Micah Johnson EXCH 10.00 25.00
BBCMM Mike Mayers EXCH 10.00 25.00
BBCMP Max Pentecost BD 15.00 40.00
BBCMS Marcus Semien BI 10.00 25.00
BBCMSA Miguel Sano BI 20.00 50.00
BBCNG Nick Gordon BD 60.00 120.00
BBCNH Nick Howard BD 20.00 50.00
BBCNS Noah Syndergaard BI 20.00 50.00
BBCPT Preston Tucker 6.00 15.00
BBCRB Rony Bautista 10.00 25.00
BBCRM Rafael Montero BI 12.00 30.00
BBCRO Roberto Osuna BI EXCH 20.00 50.00
BBCRS Robert Stephenson BS 60.00 150.00
BBCRU Richard Urena BC 10.00 25.00
BBCSG Severino Gonzalez 10.00 25.00
BBCSS Shae Simmons BC EXCH 20.00 50.00
BBCTB Tyler Beede BS EXCH 20.00 50.00
BBCTK Tyler Kolek BD 12.00 30.00
BBCTT Trea Turner BD 30.00 80.00
BBCTW Tyler Wade 10.00 25.00
BBCTW Taijuan Walker BI 12.00 30.00
BBCWG Willy Garcia BC 15.00 40.00
BBCZL Zech Lemond BD 10.00 25.00

2014 Bowman Future's Game Relics

STATED ODDS 1:3700 HOBBY
STATED PRINT RUN 25 SER.#'d SETS
FGRAA Arismendy Alcantara 6.00 15.00
FGRAB Archie Bradley 10.00 25.00
FGRAC A.J. Cole 15.00 40.00
FGRAH Austin Hedges 6.00 15.00
FGRAR Addison Russell 12.00 30.00
FGRARA Anthony Ranaudo 8.00 20.00
FGRBB Byron Buxton 100.00 200.00
FGRBN Brandon Nimmo 8.00 20.00
FGRCC C.J. Cron 8.00 20.00
FGRDD Delino DeShields 4.00 10.00
FGRDH Dilson Herrera 4.00 10.00
FGREB Eddie Butler 15.00 40.00
FGRER Eduardo Rodriguez 4.00 10.00
FGRFL Francisco Lindor 12.00 30.00
FGRGP Gregory Polanco 100.00 200.00
FGRJB Jesse Biddle 10.00 25.00
FGRJG Joey Gallo 15.00 40.00
FGRJP Joc Pederson 12.00 30.00
FGRKC Kyle Crick 6.00 15.00
FGRMA Miguel Almonte 12.00 30.00
FGRMF Maikel Franco 15.00 40.00
FGRMY Michael Ynoa 4.00 10.00
FGRNS Noah Syndergaard 4.00 80.00
FGRRM Rafael Montero 15.00 40.00

2014 Bowman Golden Debut Contract Winner

BGCAF Adriano Fieramosca 5.00 12.00

2014 Bowman Lucky Redemption Autographs

EXCH 1 ODDS 1:24,300 HOBBY
EXCH 2 ODDS 1:24,300 HOBBY
EXCH 3 ODDS 1:24,300 HOBBY
EXCH 4 ODDS 1:24,300 HOBBY
EXCH 5 ODDS 1:24,300 HOBBY
EXCHANGE DEADLINE 4/30/2017
1 Kris Bryant EXCH 300.00 600.00
2 Kris Bryant EXCH 300.00 600.00
3 Kris Bryant EXCH 300.00 600.00
4 Kris Bryant EXCH 300.00 600.00
5 Kris Bryant EXCH 300.00 600.00

2014 Bowman Oversized Purple Ice Autographs

STATED PRINT RUN 25 SER.#'d SETS
EXCHANGE DEADLINE 4/30/2017
OIBM Billy McKinney EXCH 15.00 40.00
OICF Clint Frazier EXCH 50.00 100.00
OIDT Devon Travis 30.00 60.00
OIJA Jose Abreu 75.00 200.00
OIJU Julio Urias EXCH 60.00 120.00
OIMA Mark Appel 60.00 120.00
OIMF Maikel Franco 30.00 60.00
OIMJ Micah Johnson EXCH 20.00 50.00
OIOT Oscar Taveras 60.00 120.00

2014 Bowman Oversized Silver Ice

STATED PRINT RUN 99 SER.#'d SETS
OIAR Anthony Ranaudo 4.00 10.00
OIBM Billy McKinney 5.00 12.00
OICF Clint Frazier 15.00 40.00
OIDT Devon Travis 4.00 10.00
OIJA Jose Abreu 20.00 50.00
OIJU Julio Urias 20.00 50.00
OIMF Maikel Franco 5.00 12.00
OIMJ Micah Johnson 4.00 10.00
OIOT Oscar Taveras 5.00 12.00

2014 Bowman Prospect Autographs

EXCHANGE DEADLINE 4/30/2017
PAAR Alex Reyes 15.00 40.00
PAGS Gus Schlosser 3.00 8.00
PAIK Isiah Kiner-Falefa 3.00 8.00
PAJW Jamie Westbrook 3.00 8.00
PAKB Kris Bryant 50.00 120.00
PAKW Kyle Waldrop 3.00 8.00
PALV Logan Vick 3.00 8.00
PALW Levon Washington 3.00 8.00
PAMA Mark Appel 8.00 20.00
PAMF Michael Feliz 3.00 8.00
PAMT Michael Taylor 4.00 10.00
PANK Nick Kingham 3.00 8.00
PARH Robert Refflinger 3.00 8.00
PASM Sam Moll 3.00 8.00
PASP Shawn Pleffner 3.00 8.00
PATC Tim Cooney 3.00 8.00
PATCO Thomas Coyle 3.00 8.00
PATG Trevor Gretzky 3.00 8.00
PATK Tommy Kahnle 3.00 8.00
PATM Tommy Murphy 3.00 8.00
PAWM Wyatt Mathisen 3.00 8.00
PAZP Zach Petrick 3.00 8.00

2014 Bowman Prospect Autographs Blue

*BLUE: .5X TO 1.2X BASIC
STATED PRINT RUN 500 SER.#'d SETS
EXCHANGE DEADLINE 4/30/2017

2014 Bowman Prospect Autographs Gold

*GOLD: 1X TO 2.5X BASIC
STATED PRINT RUN 50 SER.#'d SETS
EXCHANGE DEADLINE 4/30/2017

2014 Bowman Prospect Autographs Green

*GREEN: .75X TO 2X BASIC
STATED PRINT RUN 100 SER.#'d SETS
EXCHANGE DEADLINE 4/30/2017

2014 Bowman Prospect Autographs Orange

*ORANGE: .6X TO 1.5X BASIC
STATED PRINT RUN 250 SER.#'d SETS
EXCHANGE DEADLINE 4/30/2017

2014 Bowman Prospect Autographs Silver

*SILVER: 1X TO 2.5X BASIC
STATED PRINT RUN 35 SER.#'d SETS
EXCHANGE DEADLINE 4/30/2017
PAKB Kris Bryant 125.00 300.00

2014 Bowman Prospects

COMPLETE SET (111) 10.00 25.00
R.WILSON ODDS 1:9300 HOBBY
PLATE PRINT RUN 1 SET PER COLOR
BLACK-CYAN-MAGENTA-YELLOW ISSUED
NO PLATE PRICING DUE TO SCARCITY
BP1 Jason Hursh .15 .40
BP2 Trey Ball .15 .40
BP3 Jacob May .20 .50
BP4 Rosell Herrera .25 .60
BP5 Mark Appel .20 .50
BP6 Julio Urias .75 2.00
BP7 Devin Williams .40 1.00
BP8 Ryan Eades .15 .40
BP9 Eric Jagielo .15 .40
BP10 Zach Borenstein .20 .50
BP11 Jake Barrett .20 .50
BP12 Wendell Rijo .15 .40
BP13 Armando Rivero .15 .40
BP14 Chris Taylor .75 2.00
BP15 Edwin Diaz .30 .75
BP16 Dylan Floro .20 .50
BP17 Jose Abreu 1.25 3.00
BP18 Luke Jackson .15 .40
BP19 Billy Burns .15 .40
BP20 Leonardo Molina .15 .40
BP21 Billy McKinney .20 .50
BP22 Chris Flexen .20 .50
BP23 Kyle Parker .20 .50
BP24 Pierce Johnson .20 .50
BP25 Kris Bryant 4.00 10.00
BP26 Micah Johnson .15 .40
BP27 Raimel Tapia .20 .50
BP28 Preston Tucker .20 .50
BP29 Christian Binford .15 .40
BP30 Ty Buttrey .15 .40
BP31 Brandon Trinkwon .15 .40
BP32 Lewis Thorpe .15 .40
BP33 Devon Travis .15 .40
BP34 Cesar Puello .15 .40
BP35 Tyler Wade .25 .60
BP36 Daniel Robertson .15 .40
BP37 Maikel Franco .20 .50
BP38 Cody Reed .15 .40
BP39 Sam Moll .15 .40
BP40 Logan Vick .15 .40
BP41 Gus Schlosser .15 .40
BP42 Levon Washington .15 .40
BP43 Chris Beck .15 .40
BP44 Tim Cooney .15 .40
BP45 Michael Feliz .20 .50
BP46 Jamie Westbrook .15 .40
BP47 Alex Reyes .25 .60
BP48 Trevor Gretzky .15 .40
BP49 Isiah Kiner-Falefa .25 .60
BP50 Shawn Pleffner .15 .40
BP51 Hunter Dozier .20 .50
BP52 Hunter Renfroe .20 .50
BP53 Ryder Jones .15 .40
BP54 Tyler Danish .15 .40
BP55 Matt McPhearson .15 .40
BP56 Gosuke Katoh .25 .60
BP57 Andrew Thurman .15 .40
BP58 Jordan Paroubeck .15 .40
BP59 Tucker Neuhaus .15 .40
BP60 Dillon Overton .15 .40
BP61 Ryon Healy .25 .60
BP62 Chase Anderson .15 .40
BP63 Daniel Palka .15 .40
BP64 Duane Underwood .15 .40
BP65 Carlos Contreras .15 .40
BP66 Ben Lively .15 .40
BP67 Anthony Santander .20 .50
BP68 Melvin Mercedes .15 .40
BP69 Josh Hader .30 .75
BP70 Yimi Garcia .15 .40
BP71 Orlando Arcia .25 .60
BP72 Matthew Bowman .15 .40
BP73 Jacob deGrom 15.00 40.00
BP74 John Gant .15 .40
BP75 Robert Gsellman .20 .50
BP76 Gabriel Ynoa .20 .50
BP77 Anthony Aliotti .15 .40
BP78 Chris Bostick .20 .50
BP79 Drew Granier .15 .40
BP80 Austin Wright .15 .40
BP81 Brandon Cumpton .15 .40
BP82 Kendry Flores .15 .40
BP83 Jason Rogers .15 .40
BP84 Ryne Stanek .15 .40
BP85 Nomar Mazara .40 1.00
BP86 Victor Payano .15 .40
BP87 Franklin Barreto .20 .50
BP88 Santiago Nessy .15 .40
BP89 Michael Ratterree .15 .40
BP90 Manuel Margot .25 .60
BP91 Gabriel Rosa .15 .40
BP92 Nelson Rodriguez .20 .50
BP93 Yency Almonte .15 .40
BP94 Bobby Coyle .15 .40
BP95 Pat Stover .15 .40
BP96 Wuilmer Becerra .15 .40
BP97 Miller Diaz .15 .40
BP98 Akeel Morris .15 .40
BP99 Kenny Giles .20 .50
BP100 Brian Ragira .15 .40
BP101 Victor De Leon .15 .40
BP102 Steven Ramos .15 .40
BP103 Chris Kohler .15 .40
BP104 Seth Mejias-Brean .15 .40
BP105 Miguel Alfredo Gonzalez .15 .40
BP106 Alexander Guerrero .20 .50
BP107 Jose Herrera .15 .40
BP108 Tyler Marlette .15 .40
BP109 Mookie Betts 3.00 8.00
BP110 Joe Wendle .30 .75
BPRW Russell Wilson SP 60.00 120.00

2014 Bowman Prospects Black

*BLACK: 6X TO 15X BASIC
STATED PRINT RUN 99 SER.#'d SETS

2014 Bowman Prospects Blue

*BLUE: 1.5X TO 4X BASIC
STATED ODDS 1:79 HOBBY
STATED PRINT RUN 500 SER.#'d SETS

2014 Bowman Prospects Green

*GREEN: 3X TO 8X BASIC
STATED PRINT RUN 199 SER.#'d SETS

2014 Bowman Prospects Hometown

*HOMETOWN: 1.2X TO 3X BASIC
STATED ODDS 1:8 HOBBY

2014 Bowman Prospects Orange

*ORANGE: 2.5X TO 6X BASIC
STATED ODDS 1:150 HOBBY
STATED PRINT RUN 250 SER.#'d SETS

2014 Bowman Prospects Purple

*PURPLE: 1X TO 2.5X BASIC

2014 Bowman Prospects Red Ice

*RED ICE: 15X TO 40X BASIC
STATED ODDS 1:24 HOBBY
STATED PRINT RUN 25 SER.#'d SETS
BP6 Julio Urias 25.00 60.00
BP17 Jose Abreu 80.00 200.00
BP37 Maikel Franco 15.00 40.00
BP47 Alex Reyes 15.00 40.00
BP90 Manuel Margot 20.00 50.00
BP106 Alexander Guerrero 15.00 40.00
BP109 Mookie Betts 20.00 50.00

2014 Bowman Prospects Silver Ice

*SILVER ICE: 1.5X TO 4X BASIC
STATED ODDS 1:24 HOBBY
BP17 Jose Abreu 10.00 25.00

2014 Bowman Draft

STATED PLATE ODDS 1:5225 HOBBY
PLATE PRINT RUN 1 SET PER COLOR
BLACK-CYAN-MAGENTA-YELLOW ISSUED
NO PLATE PRICING DUE TO SCARCITY
DP1 Tyler Kolek .20 .50
DP2 Kyle Schwarber .75 2.00
DP3 Alex Jackson .25 .60
DP4 Aaron Nola 1.25 3.00
DP5 Kyle Freeland .40 1.00
DP6 Jeff Hoffman .30 .75
DP7 Michael Conforto .40 1.00
DP8 Max Pentecost .20 .50
DP9 Kodi Medeiros .20 .50
DP10 Trea Turner .60 1.50
DP11 Tyler Beede .30 .75
DP12 Sean Newcomb .30 .75
DP14 Erick Fedde .20 .50
DP15 Nick Howard .20 .50
DP16 Casey Gillaspie .30 .75
DP17 Bradley Zimmer .30 .75
DP18 Grant Holmes .20 .50
DP19 Derek Hill .20 .50
DP20 Cole Tucker .20 .50
DP21 Matt Chapman 2.00 5.00
DP22 Michael Chavis 1.00 2.50
DP23 Luke Weaver .60 1.50
DP24 Foster Griffin .20 .50
DP25 Alex Blandino .25 .60
DP26 Luis Ortiz .20 .50
DP27 Justus Sheffield .40 1.00
DP28 Braxton Davidson .20 .50
DP29 Michael Kopech 1.25 3.00
DP30 Jack Flaherty 1.25 3.00
DP32 Ryan Ripken .25 .60
DP33 Forrest Wall .30 .75
DP34 Blake Anderson .20 .50
DP35 Derek Fisher .30 .75
DP36 Mike Papi .20 .50
DP37 Connor Joe .20 .50
DP38 Chase Vallot .20 .50
DP39 Jacob Gatewood .30 .75
DP40 A.J. Reed .40 1.00
DP41 Justin Twine .20 .50
DP42 Spencer Adams .25 .60
DP43 Jake Stinnett .20 .50
DP44 Nick Burdi .20 .50
DP45 Matt Imhof .20 .50
DP46 Ryan Castellani .20 .50
DP47 Sean Reid-Foley .20 .50
DP48 Monte Harrison .40 1.00
DP49 Michael Gettys .25 .60
DP50 Aramis Garcia .20 .50
DP51 Joe Gatto .20 .50
DP52 Cody Reed .20 .50
DP53 Jacob Lindgren .25 .60
DP54 Scott Blewett .20 .50
DP55 Taylor Sparks .20 .50
DP56 Ti'Quan Forbes .20 .50
DP57 Cameron Varga .20 .50
DP58 Grant Hockin .20 .50
DP59 Alex Verdugo .40 1.00
DP60 Austin DeCarr .20 .50
DP61 Sam Travis .25 .60
DP62 Trey Supak .20 .50
DP63 Marcus Wilson .20 .50
DP64 Zech Lemond .20 .50
DP65 Jakson Reetz .20 .50
DP66 Jeff Brigham .20 .50
DP67 Chris Ellis .20 .50
DP68 Gareth Morgan .20 .50
DP69 Mitch Keller .30 .75
DP70 Spencer Turnbull .20 .50
DP71 Daniel Gossett .20 .50
DP72 Garrett Fulenchek .20 .50
DP73 Brett Graves .20 .50
DP74 Ronnie Williams .20 .50
DP75 Isan Diaz .50 1.25
DP76 Andrew Morales .20 .50
DP77 Brent Honeywell .30 .75
DP78 Carson Sands .20 .50
DP79 Dylan Cease .50 1.25
DP80 Jace Fry .20 .50
DP81 J.D. Davis .30 .75
DP82 Austin Cousino .20 .50
DP83 Aaron Brown .20 .50
DP84 Milton Ramos .20 .50
DP85 Brian Gonzalez .20 .50
DP86 Bobby Bradley .25 .60
DP87 Chad Sobotka .20 .50
DP88 Jonathan Holder .20 .50
DP89 Nick Wells .20 .50
DP90 Josh Morgan .20 .50
DP91 Brian Anderson .20 .50
DP92 Mark Zagunis .20 .50
DP93 Michael Cederoth .25 .60
DP94 Dylan Davis .25 .60
DP95 Matt Railey .20 .50
DP96 Eric Skoglund .20 .50
DP97 Wyatt Strahan .20 .50
DP98 John Richy .20 .50
DP99 Grayson Greiner .20 .50
DP100 Jordan Luplow .20 .50
DP101 Jake Cosart .25 .60
DP102 Michael Mader .20 .50
DP103 Brian Schales .20 .50
DP104 Brett Austin .20 .50
DP105 Ryan Yarbrough .30 .75
DP106 Chris Oliver .20 .50
DP107 Matt Morgan .20 .50
DP108 Trace Loehr .20 .50
DP109 Austin Gomber .25 .60
DP110 Casey Soltis .20 .50
DP111 Troy Stokes .20 .50
DP112 Nick Torres .20 .50
DP113 Jeremy Rhoades .20 .50
DP114 Jordan Montgomery .40 1.00
DP115 Gavin LaValley .20 .50
DP116 Brett Martin .20 .50
DP117 Sam Hentges .20 .50
DP118 Taylor Gushue .20 .50
DP119 Jordan Schwartz .20 .50
DP120 Justin Steele .20 .50
DP121 Jake Reed .20 .50
DP122 Rhys Hoskins 2.00 5.00
DP123 Kevin Padlo .20 .50
DP124 Lane Thomas .30 .75
DP125 Dustin DeMuth .20 .50
DP126 Nick Gordon .25 .60
DP127 Auston Bousfield .20 .50
DP128 Jordan Foley .20 .50
DP129 Corey Ray .20 .50
DP130 Jared Walker .20 .50
DP131 Tejay Antone .20 .50
DP132 Shane Zeile .20 .50

2014 Bowman Draft Blue

*BLUE: 1.2X TO 3X BASIC
STATED ODDS 1:52 HOBBY
STATED PRINT RUN 399 SER.#'d SETS

2014 Bowman Draft Green

*GREEN: 5X TO 12X BASIC
RANDOM INSERTS IN PACKS
STATED PRINT RUN 75 SER.#'d SETS

2014 Bowman Draft Orange Ice

*ORANGE ICE: 8X TO 20X BASIC
RANDOM INSERTS IN PACKS
STATED PRINT RUN 25 SER.#'d SETS

2014 Bowman Draft Purple Ice

*PURPLE ICE: 5X TO 12X BASIC
STATED ODDS 1:211 HOBBY
STATED PRINT RUN 99 SER.#'d SETS

2014 Bowman Draft Red Ice

*RED ICE: 4X TO 10X BASIC
STATED ODDS 1:137 HOBBY
STATED PRINT RUN 150 SER.#'d SETS

2014 Bowman Draft Silver Ice

*SILVER ICE: 1.2X TO 3X BASIC
STATED ODDS 1:12 HOBBY

2014 Bowman Draft Draft Night

COMPLETE SET (7) 3.00 8.00
STATED ODDS 1:12 HOBBY
DNDH Derek Hill .25 .60
DNGH Grant Holmes .25 .60
DNJG Jacob Gatewood .25 .60
DNKM Kodi Medeiros .25 .60
DNMC Michael Chavis 1.25 3.00
DNMH Monte Harrison .50 1.25
DNNG Nick Gordon .30 .75

2014 Bowman Draft Dual Draftees

COMPLETE SET (10) 3.00 8.00
STATED ODDS 1:18 HOBBY
DDCK Chavis/Kopech 1.50 4.00
DDHB Nick Howard .25 .60
Alex Blandino
DDHP Jeff Hoffman .40 1.00
Max Pentecost
DDJC A.Jackson/M.Conforto .50 1.25
DDKA Blake Anderson .25 .60
Tyler Kolek
DDKN A.Nola/T.Kolek 1.50 4.00
DDNH Grant Holmes .40 1.00
Sean Newcomb
DDSG K.Schwarber/N.Gordon 1.00 2.50
DDSS J.Stinnett/K.Schwarber 1.00 2.50
DDWF Flaherty/Luke Weaver 1.50 4.00

2014 Bowman Draft Dual Draftees Autographs

STATED ODDS 1:23,000 HOBBY
STATED PRINT RUN 25 SER.#'d SETS
EXCHANGE DEADLINE 11/30/2017
DDHB Nick Howard 10.00 25.00
Alex Blandino EXCH
DDHP Hoffman/Pentecost 50.00 100.00
DDKA Anderson/Kolek EXCH 50.00 100.00
DDKN Nola/Kolek EXCH 15.00 40.00
DDSG Schwarber/Gordon EXCH 100.00 200.00
DDSS Stinnett/Schwarber EXCH 75.00 150.00
DDWF Flaherty/Weaver EXCH 20.00 50.00

2014 Bowman Draft Future's Game Relics

RANDOM INSERTS IN PACKS
STATED PRINT RUN 50 SER.#'d SETS
FGRBS Braden Shipley 4.00 10.00
FGRCB Christian Binford 4.00 10.00
FGRCS Corey Seager 25.00 60.00
FGRHH Hunter Harvey 4.00 10.00
FGRHO Henry Owens 5.00 12.00
FGRJA Jorge Alfaro 5.00 12.00
FGRJB Josh Bell 8.00 20.00
FGRJBE Jose Berrios 6.00 15.00
FGRJC J.P. Crawford 4.00 10.00
FGRJP Jose Peraza 10.00 25.00
FGRJT Jake Thompson 4.00 10.00
FGRJW Jesse Winker 8.00 20.00
FGRLG Lucas Giolito 6.00 15.00
FGRLS Luis Severino 6.00 15.00
FGRMF Michael Feliz 5.00 12.00
FGRPO Peter O'Brien 5.00 12.00
FGRRH Rosell Herrera 6.00 15.00
FGRRN Renato Nunez 8.00 20.00

2014 Bowman Draft Initiation

STATED 1:552 HOBBY
STATED PRINT RUN 99 SER.#'d SETS
BIAB Alex Blandino 2.00 5.00
BIAJ Alex Jackson 2.50 6.00
BIAN Aaron Nola 12.00 30.00
BIBD Braxton Davidson 2.00 5.00
BIBZ Bradley Zimmer 3.00 8.00
BICG Casey Gillaspie 3.00 8.00
BICT Cole Tucker 2.00 5.00
BIDH Derek Hill 2.00 5.00
BIEF Erick Fedde 2.00 5.00
BIFG Foster Griffin 2.00 5.00
BIFW Forrest Wall 3.00 8.00
BIGH Grant Holmes 2.00 5.00
BIJF Jack Flaherty 12.00 30.00
BIJG Jacob Gatewood 2.00 5.00
BIJH Jeff Hoffman 3.00 8.00
BIJL Jacob Lindgren 2.50 6.00
BIJS Justus Sheffield 4.00 10.00
BIKF Kyle Freeland 4.00 10.00
BIKM Kodi Medeiros 2.00 5.00
BIKS Kyle Schwarber 8.00 20.00
BILO Luis Ortiz 2.00 5.00
BILW Luke Weaver 6.00 15.00
BIMC Michael Conforto 4.00 10.00
BIMCH Matt Chapman 12.00 30.00
BIMCHA Michael Chavis 10.00 25.00
BIMK Michael Kopech 12.00 30.00
BIMP Max Pentecost 2.00 5.00
BING Nick Gordon 2.50 6.00
BINH Nick Howard 2.00 5.00
BISN Sean Newcomb 3.00 8.00
BITB Tyler Beede 3.00 8.00
BITK Tyler Kolek 2.00 5.00
BITS Trey Supak 2.00 5.00
BITT Trea Turner 6.00 15.00
BIZL Zech Lemond 2.00 5.00

2014 Bowman Draft Scouts Breakout

COMPLETE SET (35) 10.00 25.00
STATED ODDS 1:18 HOBBY
BSBAB Aaron Blair .40 1.00
BSBAJ Aaron Judge 6.00 15.00
BSBAR Alex Reyes .60 1.50
BSBBJ Brian Johnson .40 1.00
BSBBL Ben Lively .40 1.00
BSBBP Brett Phillips .50 1.25
BSBCP Chad Pinder .40 1.00
BSBCS Chance Sisco .75 2.00
BSBCW Chad Wallach .60 1.50
BSBDR Daniel Robertson .50 1.25
BSBES Edmundo Sosa .40 1.00
BSBFM Francellis Montas .40 1.00
BSBGG Gabriel Guerrero .40 1.00
BSBJB Jake Bauers .60 1.50
BSBJD Jose De Leon .60 1.50
BSBJH Jabari Henry .75 2.00
BSBJJ JaCoby Jones .60 1.50
BSBJL Jordy Lara .40 1.00
BSBJP Jose Peraza .40 1.00
BSBJW Justin Williams .50 1.25
BSBKW Kyle Waldrop .40 1.00
BSBKZ Kevin Ziomek .40 1.00
BSBLS Luis Severino .60 1.50
BSBLW LeVon Washington .40 1.00
BSBMM Marcos Molina .50 1.25
BSBMO Matt Olson 2.00 5.00
BSBNL Nick Longhi .60 1.50
BSBNM Nomar Mazara 1.00 2.50
BSBRM Ryan McMahon .60 1.50
BSBRN Renato Nunez .75 2.00
BSBSC Sean Coyle .40 1.00
BSBSM Steven Matz .50 1.25
BSBTD Tyler Danish .40 1.00
BSBTG Tayron Guerrero .40 1.00
BSBWL Will Locante .40 1.00

2014 Bowman Draft Top Prospects

STATED PLATE ODDS 1:5225 HOBBY
PLATE PRINT RUN 1 SET PER COLOR
BLACK-CYAN-MAGENTA-YELLOW ISSUED
NO PLATE PRICING DUE TO SCARCITY
TP1 Kohl Stewart .20 .50
TP2 Miguel Sano .25 .60
TP3 Carlos Correa 1.00 2.50
TP4 Mark Appel .25 .60
TP5 Jameson Taillon .25 .60
TP6 Raul Mondesi .30 .75
TP7 Jorge Alfaro .25 .60
TP8 Max Fried .75 2.00
TP9 Lucas Giolito .30 .75
TP10 Austin Meadows .50 1.25
TP11 Clint Frazier .75 2.00
TP12 Colin Moran .20 .50
TP13 Lucas Sims .20 .50
TP14 Julio Urias 1.00 2.50
TP15 David Dahl .25 .60
TP16 Josh Bell .40 1.00
TP17 Braden Shipley .20 .50
TP18 D.J. Peterson .20 .50
TP19 Jose Berrios .30 .75
TP20 Trey Ball .20 .50
TP21 Rosell Herrera .30 .75
TP22 J.P. Crawford .20 .50
TP23 Reese McGuire .20 .50
TP24 Phil Ervin .20 .50
TP25 Jesse Winker .75 2.00
TP26 Dominic Smith .20 .50
TP27 Hunter Harvey .20 .50
TP28 Vincent Velasquez .30 .75
TP29 Gabriel Guerrero .20 .50
TP30 Brandon Nimmo .30 .75
TP31 Jose Peraza .20 .50
TP32 Hunter Renfroe .25 .60
TP33 Eloy Jimenez 2.50 6.00
TP34 Alen Hanson .20 .50
TP35 Albert Almora .30 .75
TP36 Lance McCullers .20 .50
TP37 Rafael Devers 2.00 5.00
TP38 Luis Severino .30 .75
TP39 Aaron Judge 3.00 8.00
TP40 Peter O'Brien .25 .60
TP41 Corey Seager 1.00 2.50
TP42 Aaron Blair .20 .50
TP43 Ben Lively .20 .50
TP44 Daniel Robertson .25 .60
TP45 Josh Hader .40 1.00
TP46 Hunter Dozier .20 .50
TP47 Tim Anderson .40 1.00
TP48 Tyler Danish .20 .50
TP49 Alex Gonzalez .30 .75
TP50 JaCoby Jones .30 .75

TP51 Eric Jagielo .20 .50
TP52 Rob Kaminsky .20 .50
TP53 Lewis Brinson .30 .75
TP54 Travis Demeritte .25 .60
TP55 Luis Torrens .20 .50
TP56 Ian Clarkin .20 .50
TP57 Josh Hart .20 .50
TP58 Michael Lorenzen .20 .50
TP59 Robert Stephenson .20 .50
TP60 Ryan McMahon .30 .75
TP61 Tyler Glasnow .75 2.00
TP62 Kris Bryant 2.00 5.00
TP63 Kyle Crick .20 .50
TP64 Mason Williams .20 .50
TP65 Christian Binford .20 .50
TP66 Jake Thompson .20 .50
TP67 Sean Coyle .20 .50
TP68 James Ramsey .20 .50
TP69 Byron Buxton 1.00 2.50
TP70 Nick Williams .25 .60
TP71 Miguel Almonte .20 .50
TP72 C.J. Edwards .25 .60
TP73 Delino DeShields .20 .50
TP74 Trevor Story 1.00 2.50
TP75 Raimel Tapia .25 .60
TP76 Michael Feliz .25 .60
TP77 Brandon Drury .20 .50
TP78 Franklin Barreto .30 .75
TP79 Chris Stratton .20 .50
TP80 Joey Gallo .40 1.00
TP81 Christian Arroyo 1.25 3.00
TP82 Mac Williamson .25 .60
TP83 Clayton Blackburn .30 .75
TP84 Blake Swihart .25 .60
TP85 Gosuke Katoh .30 .75
TP86 Roberto Osuna .20 .50
TP87 Courtney Hawkins .20 .50
TP88 Tyler Naquin .30 .75
TP89 Devon Travis .20 .50
TP90 Nomar Mazara .50 1.25

2014 Bowman Draft Top Prospects Blue

*BLUE: 1X TO 2.5X BASIC
STATED ODDS 1:52 HOBBY
STATED PRINT RUN 399 SER.#'d SETS

2014 Bowman Draft Top Prospects Green

*GREEN: 4X TO 10X BASIC
RANDOM INSERTS IN PACKS
STATED PRINT RUN 75 SER.#'d SETS

2014 Bowman Draft Top Prospects Orange Ice

*ORANGE ICE: 5X TO 12X BASIC
RANDOM INSERTS IN PACKS
STATED PRINT RUN 25 SER.#'d SETS

2014 Bowman Draft Top Prospects Purple Ice

*PURPLE ICE: 4X TO 10X BASIC
STATED ODDS 1:211 HOBBY
STATED PRINT RUN 99 SER.#'d SETS

2014 Bowman Draft Top Prospects Red Ice

*RED ICE: 3X TO 8X BASIC
STATED ODDS 1:137 HOBBY
STATED PRINT RUN 150 SER.#'d SETS

2014 Bowman Draft Top Prospects Silver Ice

*SILVER ICE: 1X TO 2.5X BASIC
STATED ODDS 1:12 HOBBY

2015 Bowman

COMPLETE SET (150) 8.00 20.00
PRINTING PLATES RANDOMLY INSERTS
PLATE PRINT RUN 1 SET PER COLOR
BLACK-CYAN-MAGENTA-YELLOW ISSUED
NO PLATE PRICING DUE TO SCARCITY
1 Clayton Kershaw .40 1.00
2 Eric Hosmer .20 .50
3 Alex Gordon .20 .50
4 Jay Bruce .20 .50
5 Anthony Rizzo .30 .75
6 Brad Ziegler .15 .40
7 Ken Giles .15 .40
8 Shin-Soo Choo .20 .50
9 Brandon Crawford .20 .50
10 Danny Salazar .20 .50
11 Ian Desmond .15 .40
12 Adam Eaton .15 .40
13 Jonathan Lucroy .20 .50
14 Zack Wheeler .20 .50
15 Zack Greinke .25 .60
16 Matt Holliday .25 .60
17 Jose Reyes .20 .50
18 Jarrod Saltalamacchia .15 .40
19 Manny Machado .25 .60
20 Paul Goldschmidt .25 .60
21 Garrett Richards .20 .50
22 Christian Yelich .30 .75
23 Josh Harrison .15 .40
24 Alex Cobb .15 .40
25 Yasiel Puig .25 .60
26 Anthony Rendon .25 .60
27 Mookie Betts .50 1.25
28 Craig Kimbrel .20 .50
29 Ian Kinsler .20 .50
30 Jose Altuve .20 .50
31 Charlie Blackmon .25 .60
32 Michael Pineda .15 .40
33 Kyle Seager .15 .40
34 Kennys Vargas .15 .40
35 Joaquin Benoit .15 .40
36 Mike Zunino .15 .40
37 Josh Reddick .15 .40
38 Jason Kipnis .20 .50
39 Chris Sale .25 .60
40 Oswaldo Arcia .15 .40
41 Matt Shoemaker .20 .50
42 J.J. Hardy .15 .40
43 Matt Carpenter .25 .60
44 Dellin Betances .20 .50
45 Joey Votto .25 .60
46 Ben Revere .15 .40
47 Tanner Roark .15 .40
48 Justin Morneau .20 .50
49 Jake Arrieta .20 .50
50 Mike Trout 1.25 3.00
51 Chris Owings .15 .40
52 David Wright .20 .50
53 Kevin Kiermaier .20 .50
54 Domonic Brown .20 .50
55 Justin Turner .25 .60
56 Mark Trumbo .15 .40
57 Carlos Gomez .15 .40
58 Hisashi Iwakuma .20 .50
59 Gregor Blanco .15 .40
60 Adeiny Hechavarria .15 .40
61 Starlin Castro .15 .40
62 Josh Hamilton .20 .50
63 Chase Headley .15 .40
64 Edwin Encarnacion .25 .60
65 Coco Crisp .15 .40
66 Jon Singleton .20 .50
67 Troy Tulowitzki .25 .60
68 Andre Ethier .20 .50
69 Victor Martinez .20 .50
70 Austin Jackson .15 .40
71 Evan Gattis .15 .40
72 Kole Calhoun .15 .40
73 Adrian Gonzalez .20 .50
74 Corey Dickerson .15 .40
75 Jacob deGrom .50 1.25
76 David Ortiz .25 .60
77 Evan Longoria .20 .50
78 R.A. Dickey .20 .50
79 Chris Davis .15 .40
80 Corey Kluber .20 .50
81 Xander Bogaerts .25 .60
82 Jose Quintana .15 .40
83 Lorenzo Cain .15 .40
84 Henderson Alvarez .15 .40
85 Kurt Suzuki .15 .40
86 Cliff Lee .20 .50
87 Jedd Gyorko .15 .40
88 Yusmeiro Petit .15 .40
89 Matt Garza .15 .40
90 Nick Castellanos .25 .60
91 Marcell Ozuna .25 .60
92 Phil Hughes .15 .40
93 CC Sabathia .20 .50
94 Jhonny Peralta .15 .40
95 Bryce Harper .40 1.00
96 Devin Mesoraco .15 .40
97 Alcides Escobar .20 .50
98 Travis d'Arnaud .20 .50
99 Ian Kennedy .15 .40
100 Madison Bumgarner .20 .50
101 Greg Holland .15 .40
102 Johnny Cueto .20 .50
103 Dexter Fowler .20 .50
104 Billy Hamilton .20 .50
105 Lonnie Chisenhall .15 .40
106 Sonny Gray .20 .50
107 David Price .20 .50
108 Aramis Ramirez .15 .40
109 Doug Fister .15 .40
110 Elvis Andrus .20 .50
111 Adam Wainwright .20 .50
112 Yu Darvish .25 .60
113 Aaron Sanchez .20 .50
114 Brandon Belt .20 .50
115 Andrew McCutchen .25 .60
116 Jake McGee .20 .50
117 Mike Napoli .15 .40
118 Yan Gomes .15 .40
119 Andrelton Simmons .15 .40
120 Jose Abreu .25 .60
121 Jorge Soler RC .40 1.00
122 Anthony Ranaudo RC .25 .60
123 Rymer Liriano RC .25 .60
124 Daniel Corcino RC .25 .60
125 Rusney Castillo RC .30 .75
126 Bryce Brentz RC .25 .60
127 Bryan Mitchell RC .25 .60
128 Cory Spangenberg RC .25 .60
129 Dilson Herrera RC .30 .75
130 Joc Pederson RC 1.00 2.50
131 Brandon Finnegan RC .25 .60
132 Yimi Garcia RC .25 .60
133 Edwin Escobar RC .25 .60
134 Mike Foltynewicz RC .25 .60
135 Jason Rogers RC .25 .60
136 R.J. Alvarez RC .25 .60
137 Maikel Franco RC .30 .75
138 Buck Farmer RC .25 .60
139 Michael Taylor RC .25 .60
140 Trevor May RC .25 .60
141 Nick Tropeano RC .25 .60
142 Gary Brown RC .25 .60
143 Matt Barnes RC .25 .60
144 Christian Walker RC .50 1.25
145 Xavier Scruggs RC .25 .60
146 Daniel Norris RC .25 .60
147 Dalton Pompey RC .30 .75
148 Steven Moya RC .30 .75
149 Jake Lamb RC .40 1.00
150 Javier Baez RC 2.00 5.00

2015 Bowman Blue

*BLUE: 2.5X TO 6X BASIC
*BLUE RC: 1.5X TO 4X BASIC RC
STATED ODDS 1:175 HOBBY
STATED PRINT RUN 150 SER.#'d SETS

2015 Bowman Gold

*GOLD: 8X TO 20X BASIC
*GOLD RC: 5X TO 12X BASIC RC
STATED ODDS 1:525 HOBBY
STATED PRINT RUN 50 SER.#'d SETS

2015 Bowman Green

*GREEN: 4X TO 10X BASIC
*GREEN RC: 2.5X TO 6X BASIC RC
STATED ODDS 1:47 RETAIL
STATED PRINT RUN 99 SER.#'d SETS

2015 Bowman Orange

*ORANGE: 10X TO 25X BASIC
*ORANGE RC: 6X TO 15X BASIC RC
STATED ODDS 1:243 HOBBY
STATED PRINT RUN 25 SER.#'d SETS

2015 Bowman Purple

*PURPLE: 2X TO 5X BASIC
*PURPLE RC: 1.2X TO 3X BASIC RC
STATED ODDS 1:105 HOBBY
STATED PRINT RUN 250 SER.#'d SETS

2015 Bowman Purple Ice

*PURPLE ICE: 8X TO 20X BASIC
*PURPLE ICE RC: 5X TO 12X BASIC RC
STATED ODDS 1:525 HOBBY
STATED PRINT RUN 50 SER.#'d SETS

2015 Bowman Silver

*SILVER: 1.5X TO 4X BASIC
*SILVER RC: 1X TO 2.5X BASIC RC
STATED ODDS 1:53 HOBBY
STATED PRINT RUN 499 SER.#'d SETS

2015 Bowman Silver Ice

*SILVER ICE: 1.2X TO 3X BASIC
*SILVER ICE RC: .75X TO 2X BASIC
STATED ODDS 1:24 HOBBY

2015 Bowman Black Collection Autographs

BOW.ODDS 1:6153 HOBBY
BI.ODDS 1:75 HOBBY
BB ODDS 1:313 MINI BOX
STATED PRINT RUN 25 SER.#'d SETS
BOW.EXCH DEADLINE 4/30/2018
BI EXCH.DEADLINE 6/30/2018
BB EXCH.DEADLINE 12/21/2017
BBCAB Andrew Benintendi BB 150.00 250.00
BBCAJ Aaron Judge BI 100.00 250.00
BBCAK Austin Kubitza BC 6.00 15.00
BBCAR Adrian Rondon BC 10.00 25.00
BBCARO Avery Romero BC 6.00 15.00
BBCBF Brandon Finnegan BC 10.00 25.00
BBCBL Ben Lively BI 20.00 50.00
BBCBP Brett Phillips BC 50.00 100.00
BBCBS Blake Swihart BI 20.00 50.00
BBCCF Carson Fulmer BD 15.00 40.00
BBCCG Casey Gillaspie BC 12.00 30.00
BBCCR Carlos Rodon BC 25.00 60.00
BBCDG Domingo German BC 30.00 80.00
BBCDG Dermis Garcia BC 20.00 50.00
BBCDH Dilson Herrera BI 15.00 40.00
BBCDT Dillon Tate BB 8.00 20.00
BBCDW Drew Ward BC 15.00 40.00
BBCEJ Eric Jagielo BI 6.00 15.00
BBCFM Francellis Montas BC 8.00 20.00
BBCGG Gabby Guerrero BI 60.00 150.00
BBCGG Grayson Greiner BC 6.00 15.00
BBCGT Gleyber Torres BC 60.00 150.00
BBCGW Garrett Whitley BD 15.00 40.00
BBCHR Harold Ramirez BC 15.00 40.00
BBCJC Jake Cave BC 15.00 40.00
BBCJH Josh Hader BI 8.00 20.00
BBCJHK Jung Ho Kang BC 60.00 150.00
BBCJK James Kaprielian BB 20.00 50.00
BBCJN Josh Naylor BB 8.00 20.00
BBCJW Jesse Winker BI 25.00 60.00
BBCKM Keury Mella BC 6.00 15.00
BBCKT Kyle Tucker BD 40.00 100.00
BBCLM Logan Moon BC 10.00 25.00
BBCLS Luis Severino BC 30.00 80.00
BBCMF Michael Feliz BI 6.00 15.00
BBCMH Monte Harrison BI 10.00 25.00
BBCMM Manuel Margot BI 20.00 50.00
BBCMO Matt Olson BI 40.00 100.00
BBCNS Nolan Sanburn BC 6.00 15.00
BBCOA Orlando Arcia BC 30.00 80.00
BBCPB Phil Bickford BD 6.00 15.00
BBCPS Pedro Severino BC 15.00 40.00
BBCRC Rusney Castillo BC 8.00 20.00
BBCRD Rafael Devers BC 125.00 300.00
BBCRI Raisel Iglesias BC 30.00 80.00
BBCRM Ryan Merritt BC 10.00 25.00
BBCRM Richie Martin BB 12.00 30.00
BBCRR Robert Refsnyder BC 25.00 60.00
BBCSC Sean Coyle BI 6.00 15.00
BBCTC Trent Clark BD 6.00 15.00
BBCTH Teoscar Hernandez BC 25.00 60.00
BBCTJ Tyler Jay BB 6.00 15.00
BBCTS Tyler Stephenson BB 12.00 30.00
BBCTT Touki Toussaint BC 25.00 60.00
BBCVC Victor Caratini BC 10.00 25.00
BBCYT Yasmany Tomas BI 15.00 40.00

2015 Bowman Dual Autographs

STATED ODDS 1:3872 HOBBY
STATED PRINT RUN 99 SER.#'d SETS
EXCHANGE DEADLINE 4/30/2018
*ORANGE/25: .5X TO 1.2X BASIC
BDABS Schwarber/Bryant 100.00 250.00
BDAGA Gallo/Alfaro 20.00 50.00
BDAGB Gordon/Buxton 40.00 100.00
BDAGF K.Freeland/J.Gray 8.00 20.00
BDAJP Jackson/Peterson 40.00 100.00
BDARK Kolek/Rodon 30.00 80.00
BDASO Owens/Swihart EXCH 25.00 60.00
BDASS Severino/Sanchez 40.00 100.00
BDATS Toussaint/Shipley 8.00 20.00

2015 Bowman Future's Game Relics

STATED ODDS 1:3595 RETAIL
STATED PRINT RUN 25 SER.#'d SETS
FGRAM Alex Meyer 10.00 25.00
FGRBS Braden Shipley 15.00 40.00
FGRCS Corey Seager 30.00 80.00
FGRFL Francisco Lindor 80.00 200.00
FGRHO Henry Owens 10.00 25.00
FGRJC J.P. Crawford 50.00 120.00
FGRJW Jesse Winker 15.00 40.00
FGRKB Kris Bryant 150.00 300.00
FGRSM Steven Moya 12.00 30.00
FGRJBE Josh Bell 20.00 50.00

2015 Bowman Golden Debut Contract Winner

STATED ODDS 1:7544 HOBBY
BGCJB Jim Boyle SP 4.00 10.00

2015 Bowman Prospects

COMPLETE SET (150) 10.00 25.00
PRINTING PLATES RANDOMLY INSERTED
PLATE PRINT RUN 1 SET PER COLOR
NO PLATE PRICING DUE TO SCARCITY
BP1 Tyler Kolek .15 .40
BP2 Jose Queliz .15 .40
BP3 Kevin Plawecki .15 .40
BP4 Jen-Ho Tseng .15 .40
BP5 Dixon Machado .20 .50
BP6 Pedro Severino .15 .40
BP7 Roman Quinn .25 .60
BP8 A.J. Cole .15 .40
BP9 Fernando Perez .15 .40
BP10 Logan Moon .15 .40
BP11 Giovanny Urshela 1.00 2.50
BP12 Emerson Jimenez .15 .40
BP13 Dermis Garcia .25 .60
BP14 Marco Gonzales .25 .60
BP15 Jeremy Rhoades .15 .40
BP16 Joe Ross .15 .40
BP17 Trevor Gott .15 .40
BP18 Forrest Wall .15 .40
BP19 David Dahl .20 .50
BP20 Adrian Sampson .15 .40
BP21 Alex Verdugo .25 .60
BP22 Williams Perez .20 .50
BP23 Alex Reyes .20 .50
BP24 Ty Blach .20 .50
BP25 Yasmany Tomas .20 .50
BP26 Hunter Harvey .15 .40
BP27 Touki Toussaint .20 .50
BP28 Austin Voth .15 .40
BP29 Luis Lugo .15 .40
BP30 Teoscar Hernandez .60 1.50
BP31 Jimmy Reed .15 .40
BP32 Austin Kubitza .15 .40
BP33 Miguel Sano .20 .50
BP34 Rafael Devers 1.00 2.50
BP35 Harold Ramirez .20 .50
BP36 Alex Meyer .15 .40
BP37 Archie Bradley .15 .40
BP38 Tim Cooney .15 .40
BP39 Jorge Lopez .15 .40
BP40 Ryan Merritt .25 .60
BP41 Carlos Correa .75 2.00
BP42 Rafael Bautista .15 .40
BP43 Francisco Mejia .40 1.00
BP44 Robert Stephenson .15 .40
BP45 James Dykstra .15 .40
BP46 Tyler DeLoach .15 .40
BP47 Kyle Lloyd .15 .40
BP48 Erik Gonzalez .15 .40
BP49 Sal Romano .15 .40
BP50 Julio Urias .50 1.25
BP51 Juan Herrera .15 .40
BP52 Jon Gray .15 .40
BP53 Corey Littrell .15 .40
BP54 Chris Stratton .15 .40
BP55 Conrad Gregor .15 .40
BP56 Hunter Dozier .15 .40
BP57 Jantzen Witte .25 .60
BP58 Kyle Schwarber .60 1.50
BP59 Champ Stuart .15 .40
BP60 James Needy .15 .40
BP61 Willy Adames .25 .60
BP62 Jose De Leon .25 .60
BP63 Buddy Borden .15 .40
BP64 Jordan Betts .15 .40
BP65 Gabriel Quintana .15 .40
BP66 Gareth Morgan .15 .40
BP67 Matt Andriese .15 .40
BP68 Raimel Tapia .25 .60
BP69 Drew Ward .15 .40
BP70 Carlos Asuaje .15 .40
BP71 Ozhaino Albies 1.50 4.00
BP72 Josh Bell .30 .75
BP73 Kyle Zimmer .15 .40
BP74 Greg Bird .20 .50
BP75 Nick Gordon .20 .50
BP76 Aaron Blair .15 .40
BP77 T.J. Chism .15 .40
BP78 Marcos Molina .15 .40
BP79 Avery Romero .15 .40
BP80 Jose Peraza .15 .40
BP81 Tim Anderson .30 .75
BP82 Nick Travieso .15 .40
BP83 Matt Wisler .15 .40
BP84 Nick Petree .15 .40
BP85 Mark Appel .15 .40
BP86 Frank Schwindel .20 .50
BP87 Jorge Mateo .50 1.25
BP88 Reese McGuire .15 .40
BP89 Tyler Naquin .25 .60
BP90 Nate Smith .15 .40
BP91 Jose Berrios .25 .60
BP92 Henry Owens .15 .40
BP93 Justin Nicolino .15 .40
BP94 Jairo Labourt .15 .40
BP95 Edmundo Sosa .20 .50
BP96 Seth Streich .15 .40
BP97 Victor Reyes .15 .40
BP98 Jhoan Urena .15 .40
BP99 Adam Engel .15 .40
BP100 Kris Bryant 1.50 4.00
BP101 Rio Ruiz .15 .40
BP102 Wes Parsons .15 .40
BP103 Raisel Iglesias .20 .50
BP104 Robert Refsnyder .20 .50
BP105 Aaron Slegers .15 .40
BP106 Tim Berry .15 .40
BP107 Nick Williams .20 .50
BP108 Jack Reinheimer .20 .50
BP109 Domingo Santana .20 .50
BP110 Chad Pinder .20 .50
BP111 Andre Wheeler .15 .40
BP112 Chih-Wei Hu .25 .60
BP113 Gary Sanchez .50 1.25
BP114 Ryan McMahon .25 .60
BP115 Taylor Williams .15 .40
BP116 Nelson Gomez .20 .50
BP117 Addison Russell .50 1.25
BP118 Domingo German .25 .60
BP119 Scott Schebler .25 .60
BP120 Joe Jackson .15 .40
BP121 Gilbert Lara .20 .50
BP122 Hunter Renfroe .25 .60
BP123 Rob Kaminsky .15 .40
BP124 Steven Matz .20 .50
BP125 Luis Severino .20 .50
BP126 Austin Meadows .40 1.00
BP127 Luis Heredia .15 .40
BP128 Victor Alcantara .15 .40
BP129 Trevor Frank .15 .40
BP130 Jake Johansen .15 .40
BP131 JaCoby Jones .20 .50
BP132 Jake Bauers .25 .60
BP133 Trey Ball .15 .40
BP134 Aaron Nola .25 .60
BP135 Orlando Arcia .20 .50
BP136 Keury Mella .15 .40
BP137 Brett Phillips .15 .40
BP138 Mike Yastrzemski 3.00 8.00
BP139 Jose Valdez .15 .40
BP140 Eric Haase .15 .40
BP141 Jaycob Brugman .20 .50
BP142 Albert Almora .20 .50
BP143 Tyler Wagner .15 .40
BP144 Francellis Montas .20 .50
BP145 Dariel Alvarez .15 .40
BP146 Raul Alcantara .15 .40
BP147 Ricardo Sanchez .15 .40
BP148 Jarlin Garcia .20 .50
BP149 Colin Moran .15 .40
BP150 Carlos Rodon .40 1.00

2015 Bowman Prospects Blue

*BLUE: 2X TO 5X BASIC
STATED ODDS 1:175 HOBBY
STATED PRINT RUN 150 SER.#'d SETS

2015 Bowman Prospects Gold

*GOLD: 5X TO 12X BASIC
STATED ODDS 1:525 HOBBY
STATED PRINT RUN 50 SER.#'d SETS

2015 Bowman Prospects Green

*GREEN: 2.5X TO 6X BASIC
STATED ODDS 1:47 RETAIL
STATED PRINT RUN 99 SER.#'d SETS

2015 Bowman Prospects Orange

*ORANGE: 8X TO 20X BASIC
STATED ODDS 1:243 HOBBY
STATED PRINT RUN 25 SER.#'d SETS

2015 Bowman Prospects Purple

*PURPLE: 1.5X TO 4X BASIC
STATED ODDS 1:105 HOBBY
STATED PRINT RUN 250 SER.#'d SETS

2015 Bowman Prospects Purple Ice

*PURPLE ICE: 5X TO 12X BASIC
STATED ODDS 1:525 HOBBY
STATED PRINT RUN 50 SER.#'d SETS

2015 Bowman Prospects Silver

*SILVER: 1.2X TO 3X BASIC
STATED ODDS 1:53 HOBBY
STATED PRINT RUN 499 SER.#'d SETS

2015 Bowman Prospects Silver Ice

*SILVER ICE: 1X TO 2.5X BASIC
STATED ODDS 1:24 HOBBY

2015 Bowman Prospects Yellow

*YELLOW: 1.2X TO 3X BASIC
RANDOM INSERTS IN PACKS

2015 Bowman Prospects Autographs

STATED ODDS 1:18 RETAIL
EXCHANGE DEADLINE 4/30/2018
PAAB Alex Balog 2.50 6.00
PAABA Anthony Banda 2.50 6.00
PAAP Adam Plutko 2.50 6.00
PAAT Andrew Triggs 2.50 6.00
PAAW Adam Walker 2.50 6.00
PABA Beau Amaral 3.00 8.00
PABB Bobby Bundy 2.50 6.00
PACH Connor Harrell 2.50 6.00
PACJ Chris Jensen 2.50 6.00
PACR Carlos Rodon 12.00 30.00
PAFM Francisco Mejia 8.00 20.00
PAJC Jason Coats 2.50 6.00
PAJH Josh Hader 3.00 8.00
PAJU Jose Urena 2.50 6.00
PAJW Jason Wheeler 2.50 6.00
PALG Luis Guillorme 2.50 6.00
PAMO Mike O'Neill 3.00 8.00
PANL Nick Longhi 3.00 8.00
PARS Rob Segedin 2.50 6.00
PASF Steven Farinaro 2.50 6.00
PATD Taylor Dugas 2.50 6.00
PATF Taylor Featherston 2.50 6.00
PAWL Will Locante 2.50 6.00
PAZJ Zack Jones 2.50 6.00

2015 Bowman Prospects Autographs Blue

*BLUE: .6X TO 1.5X BASIC
STATED ODDS 1:376 RETAIL
STATED PRINT RUN 150 SER.#'d SETS
EXCHANGE DEADLINE 4/30/2018

2015 Bowman Prospects Autographs Gold

*GOLD: 1X TO 2.5X BASIC
STATED ODDS 1:572 RETAIL
STATED PRINT RUN 50 SER.#'d SETS
EXCHANGE DEADLINE 3/31/2018

2015 Bowman Prospects Autographs Green

*GREEN: .75X TO 2X BASIC
STATED ODDS 1:572 RETAIL
STATED PRINT RUN 99 SER.#'d SETS
EXCHANGE DEADLINE 4/30/2018

2015 Bowman Prospects Autographs Orange

*ORANGE: 1.2X TO 3X BASIC
STATED ODDS 1:2288 RETAIL
STATED PRINT RUN 25 SER.#'d SETS
EXCHANGE DEADLINE 4/30/2018

2015 Bowman Prospects Autographs Purple

*PURPLE: .5X TO 1.2X BASIC
STATED ODDS 1:227 RETAIL
STATED PRINT RUN 250 SER.#'d SETS
EXCHANGE DEADLINE 4/30/2018

2015 Bowman Prospects Autographs Silver

*SILVER: .5X TO 1.2X BASIC
STATED ODDS 1:114 RETAIL
STATED PRINT RUN 499 SER.#'d SETS
EXCHANGE DEADLINE 4/30/2018

2015 Bowman Sophomore Standouts Autographs

STATED ODDS 1:3872 HOBBY
STATED PRINT RUN 99 SER.#'d SETS
EXCHANGE DEADLINE 4/30/2018
*GOLD/50: .6X TO 1.5X BASIC
SSAAA Arismendy Alcantara 4.00 10.00
SSAAS Aaron Sanchez 6.00 15.00
SSACC C.J. Cron 4.00 10.00
SSAGP Gregory Polanco 5.00 12.00
SSAGS George Springer 15.00 40.00
SSAJA Jose Abreu 10.00 25.00
SSAJD Jacob deGrom 50.00 120.00
SSAJP Joe Panik 15.00 40.00
SSAJS Jon Singleton 5.00 12.00
SSAKV Kennys Vargas 6.00 15.00
SSANC Nick Castellanos 6.00 15.00
SSARM Rafael Montero 4.00 10.00
SSATL Tommy La Stella 4.00 10.00
SSAYV Yordano Ventura 8.00 20.00

2015 Bowman Draft

COMPLETE SET (200) 12.00 30.00
STATED PLATE ODDS 1:5000 HOBBY
PLATE PRINT RUN 1 SET PER COLOR
NO PLATE PRICING DUE TO SCARCITY
1 Dansby Swanson 1.00 2.50
2 Yoan Lopez .15 .40
3 Bailey Falter .15 .40
4 Casey Gillaspie .25 .60
5 Demi Orimoloye .20 .50
6 Steven Duggar .15 .40
7 Tyler Alexander .15 .40
8 Courtney Hawkins .15 .40
9 Casey Hughston .15 .40
10 Kolby Allard .15 .40
11 Austin Meadows .40 1.00
12 Joe McCarthy .15 .40
13 Tyler Stephenson .40 1.00
14 Ashe Russell .15 .40
15 Dylan Moore .15 .40
16 Donnie Dewees .25 .60
17 Beau Burrows .15 .40
18 Greg Pickett .15 .40
19 Parker French .15 .40
20 Cam Gibson .20 .50
21 Braden Bishop .15 .40
22 Ryan Kellogg .15 .40
23 Monte Harrison .25 .60
24 Zack Erwin .15 .40
25 J.P. Crawford .15 .40
26 Ryan McMahon .25 .60
27 Kyle Holder .20 .50
28 Ian Happ .60 1.50
29 Anthony Hermelyn .15 .40
30 Jimmy Herget .15 .40
31 Mike Nikorak .15 .40
32 Alex Young .15 .40
33 Tyler Mark .15 .40
34 Trent Clark .15 .40
35 Benton Moss .15 .40
36 Matt Withrow .15 .40
37 Chris Shaw .15 .40
38 Manuel Margot .15 .40
39 Lucas Giolito .30 .75
40 Chase Ingram .15 .40
41 Lucas Herbert .15 .40
42 Trey Supak .15 .40
43 Blake Trahan .15 .40
44 Jeff Degano .20 .50
45 Desmond Lindsay .25 .60
46 Walker Buehler 1.00 2.50
47 Cody Ponce .15 .40
48 Adam Brett Walker .15 .40
49 Tyler Danish .15 .40
50 Dillon Tate .20 .50
51 Thomas Szapucki .15 .40
52 Spencer Adams .15 .40
53 Kevin Duchene .15 .40
54 Blake Perkins .15 .40
55 Thomas Eshelman .15 .40
56 Lucas Williams .15 .40
57 David Fletcher 1.50 4.00
58 James Kaprielian .15 .40
59 Preston Morrison .15 .40
60 Ryan Burr .15 .40
61 Brett Lilek .15 .40
62 Trevor Megill .15 .40
63 Jordy Lara .15 .40
64 Kevin Newman .40 1.00
65 Luis Ortiz .15 .40
66 Cornelius Randolph .15 .40
67 Domingo Leyba .15 .40
68 Sean Reid-Foley .20 .50
69 Josh Naylor .20 .50
70 Michael Matuella .20 .50
71 Cole Tucker .15 .40
72 Kyle Wilcox .15 .40
73 Forrest Wall .15 .40
74 Alex Jackson .20 .50
75 Kyle Tucker 1.25 3.00
76 Hunter Harvey .15 .40
77 Brandon Waddell .15 .40
78 Travis Neubeck .15 .40
79 Ronnie Jebavy .15 .40
80 Ryan Mountcastle 1.50 4.00
81 Kyle Zimmer .15 .40
82 A.J. Reed .20 .50
83 Alex Reyes .20 .50
84 Garrett Whitley .25 .60
85 Derek Hill .20 .50
86 Ryan Clark .15 .40
87 Andrew Sopko .15 .40
88 Breckin Williams .15 .40
89 Tate Matheny .15 .40
90 Kyle Crick .20 .50
91 Andrew Moore .20 .50
92 Hutton Moyer .15 .40
93 Jordan Ramsey .15 .40
94 Javier Medina .15 .40
95 Jack Wynkoop .15 .40
96 Triston McKenzie .50 1.25
97 Jose De Leon .25 .60
98 Justin Cohen .15 .40
99 Mark Mathias .20 .50
100 Julio Urias .50 1.25
101 Jared Foster .15 .40
102 Roman Quinn .25 .60
103 Max Wotell .15 .40
104 Jake Gatewood .15 .40
105 Willy Adames .25 .60
106 Rafael Devers 1.00 2.50
107 Blake Snell .20 .50
108 Cody Poteet .15 .40
109 Bryce Denton .25 .60
110 Nolan Watson .15 .40
111 Tyler Nevin .25 .60
112 Antonio Santillan .20 .50
113 Mac Marshall .15 .40
114 Mariano Rivera .25 .60
115 Grant Hockin .15 .40
116 Raul Mondesi .25 .60
117 Richie Martin .15 .40
118 Carson Fulmer .15 .40
119 Mikey White .20 .50
120 Lucas Sims .15 .40
121 Peter Lambert .15 .40
122 Roman Collins .15 .40
123 Austin Allen .20 .50
124 David Thompson .20 .50
125 Ka'ai Tom .15 .40
126 Renato Nunez .30 .75
127 Zech Lemond .15 .40
128 Nick Gordon .20 .50
129 Phil Bickford .15 .40
130 Taylor Ward .25 .60
131 Corey Taylor .15 .40
132 Chris Ellis .15 .40
133 Michael Chavis .40 1.00
134 Cody Jones .15 .40
135 Tyrone Taylor .15 .40
136 Tyler Jay .15 .40
137 Ke'Bryan Hayes 4.00 10.00
138 Scott Kingery .25 .60
139 Carl Wise .20 .50
140 Juan Hillman .15 .40
141 Bowdien Derby .15 .40
142 D.J. Peterson .15 .40
143 Jacob Nix .15 .40
144 Josh Staumont .20 .50
145 Nathan Kirby .20 .50
146 D.J. Stewart .15 .40
147 Matt Hall .15 .40
148 Kohl Stewart .15 .40
149 Drew Jackson .20 .50
150 Aaron Judge 2.50 6.00
151 Nick Plummer .20 .50
152 David Dahl .20 .50
153 Brian Mundell .15 .40
154 Bradley Zimmer .25 .60
155 Tanner Rainey .15 .40
156 JC Cardenas .15 .40
157 Austin Riley 2.00 5.00
158 Kevin Kramer .20 .50
159 Hunter Renfroe .25 .60
160 Grant Holmes .20 .50
161 Isaiah White .20 .50
162 Justin Jacome .15 .40
163 Amed Rosario .25 .60
164 Josh Bell .30 .75
165 Eric Jenkins .15 .40
166 Reese McGuire .15 .40
167 Sean Newcomb .20 .50
168 Reynaldo Lopez .20 .50
169 Conor Biggio .15 .40
170 Andrew Suarez .20 .50
171 Trey Ball .15 .40
172 Austin Rei .20 .50
173 Drew Finley .15 .40
174 Skye Bolt .20 .50
175 Daniel Robertson .15 .40
176 Avery Romero .15 .40
177 Jon Harris .20 .50
178 Christin Stewart .20 .50
179 Nelson Rodriguez .20 .50
180 Austin Smith .15 .40
181 Michael Soroka 1.00 2.50
182 Andrew Benintendi .75 2.00
183 Matt Crownover .15 .40
184 Franklin Barreto .20 .50
185 Willie Calhoun .25 .60
186 Braxton Davidson .15 .40
187 Jake Woodford .15 .40
188 Ryan McKenna .15 .40
189 Ryan Helsley .20 .50
190 Carson Sands .15 .40
191 Tyler Beede .20 .50
192 Jeff Hendrix .20 .50
193 Nick Howard .25 .60
194 Chris Betts .20 .50
195 Jagger Rusconi .15 .40
196 Matt Olson .75 2.00
197 Jake Cronenworth 2.00 5.00
198 Alex Robinson .15 .40
199 Albert Almora .20 .50
200 Brendan Rodgers .60 1.50

2015 Bowman Draft Blue

*BLUE: 2X TO 5X BASIC
STATED ODDS 1:134 HOBBY
STATED PRINT RUN 150 SER.#'d SETS
1 Dansby Swanson 5.00 12.00
182 Andrew Benintendi 12.00 30.00

2015 Bowman Draft Gold

*GOLD: 4X TO 10X BASIC
STATED ODDS 1:401 HOBBY
STATED PRINT RUN 50 SER.#'d SETS
1 Dansby Swanson 10.00 25.00
182 Andrew Benintendi 25.00 60.00

2015 Bowman Draft Green

*GREEN: 2.5X TO 6X BASIC
STATED ODDS 1:203 HOBBY
STATED PRINT RUN 99 SER.#'d SETS
1 Dansby Swanson 6.00 15.00
182 Andrew Benintendi 15.00 40.00

2015 Bowman Draft Orange

*ORANGE: 5X TO 12X BASIC
STATED ODDS 1:283 HOBBY
STATED PRINT RUN 25 SER.#'d SETS

1 Dansby Swanson 12.00 30.00
182 Andrew Benintendi 30.00 80.00

2015 Bowman Draft Silver

*SILVER: 1.2X TO 3X BASIC
STATED ODDS 1:41 HOBBY
STATED PRINT RUN 499 SER.#'d SETS
182 Andrew Benintendi 8.00 20.00

2015 Bowman Draft Draft Dividends

STATED ODDS 1:12 HOBBY
DDAB Andrew Benintendi 2.50 6.00
DDBZ Bradley Zimmer .60 1.50
DDCA Chris Anderson .40 1.00
DDDS Dansby Swanson 2.50 6.00
DDEF Erick Fedde .40 1.00
DDEJ Eric Jagielo .40 1.00
DDHR Hunter Renfroe .60 1.50
DDJH Jon Harris .50 1.25
DDJK James Kaprielian .40 1.00
DDLW Luke Weaver .60 1.50
DDMP Mike Papi .40 1.00
DDRM Richie Martin .40 1.00
DDTW Taylor Ward .60 1.50
DDABL Alex Blandino .40 1.00
DDDST D.J. Stewart .40 1.00

2015 Bowman Draft Draft Dividends Autographs

STATED ODDS 1:5649 HOBBY
*ORANGE/25: .6X TO 1.5X BASIC
DDAB Andrew Benintendi 60.00 150.00
DDBZ Bradley Zimmer 12.00 30.00
DDDS Dansby Swanson 30.00 80.00
DDJK James Kaprielian 12.00 30.00
DDLW Luke Weaver 12.00 30.00
DDRM Richie Martin 8.00 20.00
DDTW Taylor Ward 12.00 30.00
DDDST D.J. Stewart 8.00 20.00

2015 Bowman Draft Draft Night

STATED ODDS 1:12 HOBBY
*ORANGE/25: 1.5X TO 4X BASIC
DN1 Brendan Rodgers 1.50 4.00
DN2 Mike Nikorak .40 1.00
DN3 Ashe Russell .40 1.00
DN4 Garrett Whitley .60 1.50

2015 Bowman Draft Initiation

STATED ODDS 1:288 HOBBY
*GOLD/25: .6X TO 1.5X BASIC
BI1 Dansby Swanson 6.00 15.00
BI2 Brendan Rodgers 5.00 12.00
BI3 Dillon Tate 2.00 5.00
BI4 Kyle Tucker 12.00 30.00
BI5 Tyler Jay 1.50 4.00
BI6 Andrew Benintendi 6.00 15.00
BI7 Carson Fulmer 1.50 4.00
BI8 Ian Happ 4.00 10.00
BI9 Cornelius Randolph 1.50 4.00
BI10 Tyler Stephenson 4.00 10.00
BI11 Josh Naylor 2.00 5.00
BI12 Garrett Whitley 2.50 6.00
BI13 Kolby Allard 1.50 4.00
BI14 Trent Clark 1.50 4.00
BI15 James Kaprielian 1.50 4.00
BI16 Phil Bickford 1.50 4.00
BI17 Kevin Newman 4.00 10.00
BI18 Richie Martin 1.50 4.00
BI19 Ashe Russell 1.50 4.00
BI20 Beau Burrows 1.50 4.00

2016 Bowman

PRINTING PLATE ODDS 1:5355 HOBBY
PLATE PRINT RUN 1 SET PER COLOR
BLACK-CYAN-MAGENTA-YELLOW ISSUED
NO PLATE PRICING DUE TO SCARCITY
1 Mike Trout 1.25 3.00
2 Josh Donaldson .20 .50
3 Albert Pujols .30 .75
4 A.J. Pollock .15 .40
5 Paul Goldschmidt .25 .60
6 Yasmany Tomas .15 .40
7 Freddie Freeman .30 .75
8 Andrelton Simmons .15 .40
9 Shelby Miller .20 .50
10 David Ortiz .25 .60
11 Manny Machado .25 .60
12 Chris Davis .15 .40
13 Mookie Betts .50 1.25
14 Adam Jones .20 .50
15 Dustin Pedroia .25 .60
16 Xander Bogaerts .25 .60
17 Jon Lester .20 .50
18 Jake Arrieta .20 .50
19 Jorge Soler .25 .60
20 Kris Bryant .30 .75
21 Anthony Rizzo .30 .75
22 Jose Abreu .25 .60
23 Chris Sale .25 .60
24 Carlos Rodon .25 .60
25 Aroldis Chapman .25 .60
26 Brandon Phillips .15 .40
27 Joey Votto .25 .60
28 Francisco Lindor .25 .60
29 Corey Kluber .20 .50
30 Carlos Correa .25 .60
31 Charlie Blackmon .25 .60
32 Nolan Arenado .40 1.00
33 Miguel Cabrera .25 .60
34 Ian Kinsler .20 .50
35 Justin Verlander .25 .60
36 George Springer .20 .50
37 Carlos Santana .20 .50
38 Dallas Keuchel .20 .50
39 Jose Altuve .20 .50
40 Clayton Kershaw .40 1.00
41 Lorenzo Cain .15 .40
42 Salvador Perez .20 .50
43 Eric Hosmer .20 .50
44 Evan Gattis .15 .40
45 Zack Greinke .25 .60
46 Adrian Gonzalez .20 .50
47 Yasiel Puig .25 .60
48 Giancarlo Stanton .25 .60
49 Jose Fernandez .25 .60
50 Ichiro Suzuki .30 .75
51 Ryan Braun .20 .50
52 Byron Buxton .25 .60
53 Brian Dozier .20 .50
54 Joe Mauer .20 .50
55 Yoenis Cespedes .25 .60
56 Matt Harvey .20 .50
57 Jacob deGrom .50 1.25
58 Noah Syndergaard .20 .50
59 Dellin Betances .20 .50
60 Masahiro Tanaka .20 .50
61 Alex Rodriguez .30 .75
62 Sonny Gray .20 .50
63 Billy Butler .15 .40
64 Stephen Vogt .20 .50
65 Maikel Franco .20 .50
66 Ryan Howard .20 .50
67 Odubel Herrera .20 .50
68 Andrew McCutchen .25 .60
69 Josh Harrison .15 .40
70 Buster Posey .30 .75
71 Gregory Polanco .20 .50
72 Justin Upton .20 .50
73 Tyson Ross .15 .40
74 James Shields .15 .40
75 Jung Ho Kang .15 .40
76 Madison Bumgarner .20 .50
77 Brandon Crawford .20 .50
78 Brandon Belt .20 .50
79 Robinson Cano .20 .50
80 Felix Hernandez .20 .50
81 Nelson Cruz .25 .60
82 Jason Heyward .20 .50
83 Yadier Molina .30 .75
84 Evan Longoria .20 .50
85 Chris Archer .15 .40
86 Kevin Kiermaier .20 .50
87 Prince Fielder .20 .50
88 Cole Hamels .20 .50
89 Adrian Beltre .25 .60
90 Yu Darvish .25 .60
91 Jose Bautista .20 .50
92 David Price .20 .50
93 Edwin Encarnacion .25 .60
94 Wei-Yin Chen .15 .40
95 Max Scherzer .25 .60
96 Stephen Strasburg .25 .60
97 Garrett Richards .20 .50
98 David Peralta .15 .40
99 Julio Teheran .20 .50
100 Bryce Harper .40 1.00
101 Adam Eaton .15 .40
102 Todd Frazier .15 .40
103 Jay Bruce .20 .50
104 Carlos Gonzalez .20 .50
105 J.D. Martinez .25 .60
106 Andrew Miller .20 .50
107 Brian McCann .20 .50
108 Jacoby Ellsbury .20 .50
109 Josh Reddick .15 .40
110 Matt Kemp .20 .50
111 Craig Kimbrel .20 .50
112 Kyle Seager .15 .40
113 Marcus Stroman .20 .50
114 Mark Melancon .15 .40
115 Trevor Rosenthal .20 .50
116 Hunter Pence .20 .50
117 Michael Brantley .20 .50
118 Adam Wainwright .20 .50
119 Wade Davis .15 .40
120 Troy Tulowitzki .25 .60
121 Matt Reynolds RC .25 .60
122 Kyle Schwarber RC .75 2.00
123 Stephen Piscotty RC .40 1.00
124 Carl Edwards Jr. RC .30 .75
125 Aaron Nola RC .50 1.25
126 Hector Olivera RC .30 .75
127 Rob Refsnyder RC .30 .75
128 Jose Peraza RC .30 .75
129 Henry Owens RC .30 .75
130 Trea Turner RC .75 2.00
131 Michael Conforto RC .30 .75
132 Greg Bird RC .30 .75
133 Richie Shaffer RC .25 .60
134 Jon Gray RC .25 .60
135 Luis Severino RC .30 .75
136 Miguel Almonte RC .25 .60
137 Brandon Drury RC .40 1.00
138 Zach Lee RC .25 .60
139 Kyle Waldrop RC .30 .75
140 Miguel Sano RC .40 1.00
141 Peter O'Brien RC .25 .60
142 Frankie Montas RC .30 .75
143 Gary Sanchez RC .75 2.00
144 Ketel Marte RC .50 1.25
145 Trayce Thompson RC .40 1.00
146 Jorge Lopez RC .25 .60
147 Max Kepler RC .40 1.00
148 Tom Murphy RC .25 .60
149 Raul Mondesi RC .50 1.25
150 Corey Seager RC 2.50 6.00

2016 Bowman Blue

*BLUE: 2.5X TO 6X BASIC
*BLUE RC: 1.5X TO 4X BASIC RC
STATED ODDS 1:143 HOBBY
STATED PRINT RUN 150 SER.#'d SETS

2016 Bowman Gold

*GOLD: 6X TO 15X BASIC
*GOLD RC: 4X TO 10X BASIC RC
STATED ODDS 1:429 HOBBY
STATED PRINT RUN 50 SER.#'d SETS

2016 Bowman Green

*GREEN: 4X TO 10X BASIC
*GREEN RC: 2.5X TO 6X BASIC RC
RANDOM INSERTS IN PACKS
STATED PRINT RUN 99 SER.#'d SETS

2016 Bowman Orange

*ORANGE: 8X TO 20X BASIC
*ORANGE RC: 5X TO 12X BASIC RC
STATED ODDS 1:165 HOBBY
STATED PRINT RUN 25 SER.#'d SETS
143 Gary Sanchez 25.00 60.00

2016 Bowman Purple

*PURPLE: 2X TO 5X BASIC
*PURPLE RC: 1.2X TO 3X BASIC RC
STATED ODDS 1:86 HOBBY
STATED PRINT RUN 250 SER.#'d SETS

2016 Bowman Silver

*SILVER: 1.5X TO 4X BASIC
*SILVER RC: 1X TO 2.5X BASIC RC
STATED ODDS 1:43 HOBBY

2016 Bowman Family Tree

COMPLETE SET (7) 2.00 5.00
STATED ODDS 1:24 HOBBY
*BLUE/150: 2X TO 5X BASIC
*GREEN/99: 2.5X TO 6X BASIC
*ORANGE/25: 5X TO 12X BASIC
FTB C.Biggio/C.Biggio .40 1.00
FTH K.Hayes/C.Hayes 1.50 4.00
FTM T.Matheny/M.Matheny .40 1.00
FTN P.Nevin/T.Nevin .50 1.25
FTR M.Rivera/M.Rivera .60 1.50
FTT Tatis Jr./Tatis 5.00 12.00
FTGU Guerrero/Guerrero Jr. 2.50 6.00

2016 Bowman Family Tree Autographs

STATED ODDS 1:20,311 HOBBY
STATED PRINT RUN 25 SER.#'d SETS
EXCHANGE DEADLINE 3/31/2018
FTB C.Biggio/C.Biggio 20.00 50.00
FTH K.Hayes/C.Hayes 25.00 60.00
FTN P.Nevin/T.Nevin 20.00 50.00
FTR M.Rivera/M.Rivera 100.00 250.00

2016 Bowman International Ink

COMPLETE SET (9) 2.00 5.00
STATED ODDS 1:12 HOBBY
*BLUE/150: 1.2X TO 3X BASIC
*GREEN/99: 1.5X TO 4X BASIC
*ORANGE/25: 4X TO 10X BASIC
IICV Carlos Vargas .40 1.00
IIFR Franklin Reyes .30 .75
IIFT Fernando Tatis Jr. 10.00 25.00
IIJG Jeison Guzman .30 .75
IIJS Juan Soto 10.00 25.00
IILT Leody Taveras 1.25 3.00
IIOC Oneal Cruz 2.00 5.00
IIRO Raffy Ozuna .30 .75
IIWJ Wander Javier .50 1.25

2016 Bowman International Ink Autographs Gold

STATED ODDS 1:3202 HOBBY
STATED PRINT RUN 25 SER.#'d SETS
EXCHANGE DEADLINE 3/31/2018
IIFR Franklin Reyes EXCH 20.00 50.00
IIFT Fernando Tatis Jr. 150.00 400.00
IIJG Jeison Guzman 20.00 50.00
IIJS Juan Soto 400.00 800.00
IIWJ Wander Javier EXCH 30.00 80.00

2016 Bowman Lucky Redemption Autograph

STATED ODDS 1:25,609 HOBBY
EXCHANGE DEADLINE 3/31/2018
NNO Exchange Card EXCH 250.00 400.00

2016 Bowman Prospects

COMPLETE SET (150) 12.00 30.00
PRINTING PLATE ODDS 1:5355 HOBBY
PLATE PRINT RUN 1 SET PER COLOR
BLACK-CYAN-MAGENTA-YELLOW ISSUED
NO PLATE PRICING DUE TO SCARCITY
BP1 Daz Cameron .15 .40
BP2 Orlando Arcia .20 .50
BP3 Domingo Leyba .15 .40
BP4 Alex Bregman .75 2.00
BP5 Yadier Alvarez .20 .50
BP6 Touki Toussaint .20 .50
BP7 Brady Aiken .40 1.00
BP8 Billy McKinney .20 .50
BP9 Stone Garrett .15 .40
BP10 Victor Robles .60 1.50
BP11 Wei-Chieh Huang .15 .40
BP12 Jomar Reyes .25 .60
BP13 Lucius Fox .25 .60
BP14 Samuel Coonrod .15 .40
BP15 Seuly Matias 1.25 3.00
BP16 Willson Contreras 1.00 2.50
BP17 Fernando Tatis Jr. 25.00 60.00
BP18 Starling Heredia .25 .60
BP19 Drew Jackson .15 .40
BP20 Ruddy Giron .15 .40
BP21 Anfernee Seymour .15 .40
BP22 Iolana Akau .25 .60
BP23 Kevin Padlo .15 .40
BP24 Brady Lail .15 .40
BP25 Dillon Tate .20 .50
BP26 Jharel Cotton .15 .40
BP27 John Norwood .15 .40
BP28 Manny Sanchez .20 .50
BP29 Juan Yepez .15 .40
BP30 David Denson .15 .40
BP31 Jhailyn Ortiz .30 .75
BP32 Wander Javier .25 .60
BP33 Sal Romano .15 .40
BP34 Francis Martes .15 .40
BP35 Domingo Acevedo .25 .60
BP36 Mark Zagunis .15 .40
BP37 Franklyn Kilome .20 .50
BP38 Trey Mancini .50 1.25
BP39 Corey Black .15 .40
BP40 Anderson Espinoza .20 .50
BP41 Jordan Guerrero .15 .40
BP42 Mauricio Dubon .20 .50
BP43 Paul DeJong 1.00 2.50
BP44 Mikey White .15 .40
BP45 Andrew Suarez .20 .50
BP46 Kevin Kramer .20 .50
BP47 Nate Smith .15 .40
BP48 Ariel Jurado .15 .40
BP49 Rafael Bautista .15 .40
BP50 Dansby Swanson .60 1.50
BP51 Anthony Banda .15 .40
BP52 Mike Clevinger .30 .75
BP53 Daniel Poncedeleon .20 .50
BP54 Ian Kahaloa .15 .40
BP55 Vladimir Guerrero Jr. 10.00 25.00
BP56 Logan Allen .15 .40
BP57 Kyle Survance Jr. .15 .40
BP58 Omar Carrizales .15 .40
BP59 Anthony Alford .15 .40
BP60 Kyle Tucker .75 2.00
BP61 Tyler Jay .15 .40
BP62 Andrew Benintendi .50 1.25
BP63 Carson Fulmer .15 .40
BP64 Ian Happ .30 .75
BP65 Sean Newcomb .20 .50
BP66 Tyler Stephenson .40 1.00
BP67 Josh Naylor .20 .50
BP68 Garrett Whitley .20 .50
BP69 Kolby Allard .15 .40
BP70 Trent Clark .15 .40
BP71 James Kaprielian .15 .40
BP72 Phil Bickford .15 .40
BP73 Kevin Newman .25 .60
BP74 Richie Martin .15 .40
BP75 Ashe Russell .15 .40
BP76 Beau Burrows .15 .40
BP77 Nick Plummer .20 .50
BP78 Walker Buehler .50 1.25
BP79 D.J. Stewart .15 .40
BP80 Taylor Ward .20 .50
BP81 Mike Nikorak .15 .40
BP82 Michael Soroka .50 1.25
BP83 Kyle Holder .20 .50
BP84 Chris Shaw .15 .40
BP85 Ke'Bryan Hayes 1.50 4.00
BP86 Nolan Watson .15 .40
BP87 Christin Stewart .20 .50
BP88 Ryan Mountcastle .75 2.00
BP89 Jack Flaherty 1.00 2.50
BP90 Raimel Tapia .20 .50
BP91 Michael Fulmer .25 .60
BP92 A.J. Reed .15 .40
BP93 Gavin Cecchini .15 .40
BP94 Jorge Mateo .20 .50
BP95 Amed Rosario .25 .60
BP96 Daniel Robertson .15 .40
BP97 Nick Gordon .15 .40
BP98 Rob Kaminsky .15 .40
BP99 Amir Garrett .15 .40
BP100 Brendan Rodgers .25 .60
BP101 Duane Underwood .15 .40
BP102 Alen Hanson .20 .50
BP103 Jorge Alfaro .25 .60
BP104 Grant Holmes .20 .50
BP105 Nick Williams .20 .50
BP106 Tyler Wade .25 .60
BP107 Jake Thompson .15 .40
BP108 Alex Reyes .20 .50
BP109 Rafael Devers .50 1.25
BP110 Ozzie Albies .75 2.00
BP111 Alex Young .20 .50
BP112 Tyrell Jenkins .15 .40
BP113 Max Fried .25 .60
BP114 Chance Sisco .30 .75
BP115 Michael Kopech .50 1.25
BP116 Pierce Johnson .15 .40
BP117 Tyler Danish .15 .40
BP118 Keury Mella .15 .40
BP119 Alex Blandino .15 .40
BP120 Justus Sheffield .30 .75
BP121 Jeff Hoffman .20 .50
BP122 Ryan McMahon .25 .60
BP123 JaCoby Jones .20 .50
BP124 Colin Moran .15 .40
BP125 Derek Fisher .15 .40
BP126 Scott Blewett .15 .40
BP127 Jeimer Candelario .20 .50
BP128 Fernando Perez .15 .40
BP129 Andrew Knapp .15 .40
BP130 Sean Manaea .15 .40
BP131 Jake Bauers .25 .60
BP132 Rowdy Tellez .25 .60
BP133 Gabby Guerrero .15 .40
BP134 Christian Arroyo .30 .75
BP135 Adam Brett Walker II .15 .40
BP136 Brett Phillips .15 .40
BP137 Lewis Brinson .25 .60
BP138 Bubba Starling .20 .50
BP139 Chad Pinder .15 .40
BP140 Chris Bostick .15 .40
BP141 Luke Weaver .25 .60
BP142 Kenta Maeda .30 .75
BP143 Luiz Gohara .15 .40
BP144 Yoan Lopez .15 .40
BP145 Courtney Hawkins .15 .40
BP146 Austin Dean .15 .40
BP147 Matt Chapman .50 1.25
BP148 Yoan Moncada 1.25 3.00
BP149 Nick Travieso .15 .40
BP150 Lucas Giolito .25 .60

2016 Bowman Prospects Blue

*BLUE: 2X TO 5X BASIC
STATED ODDS 1:143 HOBBY
STATED PRINT RUN 150 SER.#'d SETS

2016 Bowman Prospects Gold

*GOLD: 5X TO 12X BASIC
STATED ODDS 1:429 HOBBY
STATED PRINT RUN 50 SER.#'d SETS

2016 Bowman Prospects Green

*GREEN: 2.5X TO 6X BASIC
INSERTED IN RETAIL PACKS
STATED PRINT RUN 99 SER.#'d SETS

2016 Bowman Prospects Orange

*ORANGE: 8X TO 20X BASIC
STATED ODDS 1:165 HOBBY
STATED PRINT RUN 25 SER.#'d SETS

2016 Bowman Prospects Purple

*PURPLE: 1.5X TO 4X BASIC
STATED ODDS 1:86 HOBBY
STATED PRINT RUN 250 SER.#'d SETS

2016 Bowman Prospects Silver

*SILVER: 1.2X TO 3X BASIC
STATED ODDS 1:43 HOBBY

2016 Bowman Prospects Yellow

*YELLOW: 1.2X TO 3X BASIC
INSERTED IN RETAIL PACKS

2016 Bowman Prospects Autographs

INSERTED IN RETAIL PACKS
EXCHANGE DEADLINE 3/31/2018
PAAN Aaron Northcraft 2.50 6.00
PAAR Adam Ravenelle 3.00 8.00
PABA Blake Anderson 2.50 6.00
PABB B.J. Boyd 2.50 6.00
PABD Brady Dragmire 2.50 6.00
PACG Conner Greene 2.50 6.00
PACM Casey Meisner 2.50 6.00
PACS Connor Sadzeck 2.50 6.00
PADM Daniel Mengden 10.00 25.00
PADS Dansby Swanson 40.00 100.00
PADW Drew Weeks 2.50 6.00
PAEW Erich Weiss 4.00 10.00
PAFM Francisco Mejia 4.00 10.00
PAIK Ian Kahaloa 2.50 6.00
PAJO John Omahen 2.50 6.00
PAJS Joe Sclafani 2.50 6.00
PALS Lucas Sims 2.50 6.00
PAMG Mike Gerber 2.50 6.00
PANG Nick Gordon 2.50 6.00
PAOA Orlando Arcia 3.00 8.00
PAPB Phil Bickford 2.50 6.00
PAPR Pierce Romero 4.00 10.00
PARM Reese McGuire 2.50 6.00
PARP Ricardo Pinto 3.00 8.00
PARW Ryan Williams 5.00 12.00
PATM Thomas Milone 2.50 6.00
PATT Touki Toussaint 4.00 10.00
PAYG Yeudy Garcia 2.50 6.00
PAJST Josh Staumont 3.00 8.00

2016 Bowman Prospects Autographs Gold

*GOLD: 1X TO 2.5X BASIC
INSERTED IN RETAIL PACKS
STATED PRINT RUN 50 SER.#'d SETS
EXCHANGE DEADLINE 3/31/2018
PADT Dillon Tate 8.00 20.00
PAIH Ian Happ 40.00 100.00

2016 Bowman Prospects Autographs Green

*GREEN: .75X TO 2X BASIC
INSERTED IN RETAIL PACKS
STATED PRINT RUN 99 SER.#'d SETS
EXCHANGE DEADLINE 3/31/2018
PADT Dillon Tate 6.00 15.00
PAIH Ian Happ 30.00 80.00

2016 Bowman Prospects Autographs Orange

*ORANGE: 1.2X TO 3X BASIC
INSERTED IN RETAIL PACKS
STATED PRINT RUN 25 SER.#'d SETS
EXCHANGE DEADLINE 3/31/2018
PADS Dansby Swanson 100.00 250.00
PADT Dillon Tate 10.00 25.00
PAIH Ian Happ 50.00 120.00

2016 Bowman Prospects Autographs Purple

*PURPLE: .5X TO 1.2X BASIC
INSERTED IN RETAIL PACKS
STATED PRINT RUN 250 SER.#'d SETS
EXCHANGE DEADLINE 3/31/2018
PADT Dillon Tate 4.00 10.00
PAIH Ian Happ 20.00 50.00

2016 Bowman Sophomore Standouts

COMPLETE SET (15) 4.00 10.00
STATED ODDS 1:8 HOBBY
*BLUE/150: 1.2X TO 3X BASIC
*GREEN/99: 1.5X TO 4X BASIC
*ORANGE/25: 4X TO 10X BASIC
SS1 Kris Bryant .60 1.50
SS2 Byron Buxton .50 1.25
SS3 Carlos Correa .50 1.25
SS4 Francisco Lindor .50 1.25
SS5 Blake Swihart .40 1.00
SS6 Jorge Soler .50 1.25
SS7 Steven Matz .30 .75
SS8 Rusney Castillo .30 .75
SS9 Noah Syndergaard .40 1.00
SS10 Joc Pederson .40 1.00
SS11 Addison Russell .50 1.25
SS12 Yasmany Tomas .30 .75
SS13 Jung Ho Kang .30 .75
SS14 Daniel Norris .30 .75
SS15 Maikel Franco .40 1.00

2016 Bowman Draft

COMPLETE SET (200) 12.00 30.00
STATED PLATE ODDS 1:947 HOBBY
PLATE PRINT RUN 1 SET PER COLOR
NO PLATE PRICING DUE TO SCARCITY
BD1 Mickey Moniak 1.00 2.50
BD2 Thomas Jones .15 .40
BD3 Dylan Carlson 5.00 12.00
BD4 Cole Irvin .40 1.00
BD5 Kevin Gowdy .25 .60
BD6 Dakota Hudson .25 .60
BD7 Walker Robbins .15 .40
BD8 Khalil Lee .25 .60
BD9 Logan Ice .15 .40
BD10 Braxton Garrett .20 .50
BD11 Anfernee Grier .20 .50
BD12 Kyle Hart .15 .40
BD13 Taylor Trammell 1.50 4.00
BD14 Brian Serven .15 .40
BD15 Buddy Reed .20 .50
BD16 Carter Kieboom 1.00 2.50
BD17 Jimmy Lambert .20 .50
BD18 Nick Solak 1.25 3.00
BD19 Alexis Torres .20 .50
BD20 Cal Quantrill .15 .40
BD21 JaVon Shelby .15 .40
BD22 Kyle Funkhouser .20 .50
BD23 Dom Thompson-Williams .25 .60
BD24 Jeremy Martinez .40 1.00
BD25 A.J. Puk .25 .60
BD26 Brett Cumberland .25 .60
BD27 Mason Thompson .15 .40
BD28 Easton McGee .15 .40
BD29 Justin Dunn .15 .40
BD30 Matt Manning .25 .60
BD31 Delvin Perez .50 1.25
BD32 Nolan Jones .25 .60
BD33 Matt Krook .15 .40
BD34 Stephen Alemais .25 .60
BD35 Joey Wentz .25 .60
BD36 Ben Bowden .15 .40
BD37 Drew Harrington .15 .40
BD38 C.J. Chatham .20 .50
BD39 Will Craig .15 .40
BD40 Zack Collins .20 .50
BD41 Skylar Szynski .15 .40
BD42 Sheldon Neuse .20 .50
BD43 Nicholas Lopez .25 .60
BD44 Heath Quinn .30 .75
BD45 Alex Speas .20 .50
BD46 Cody Sedlock .15 .40
BD47 Blake Tiberi .20 .50
BD48 Mario Feliciano .20 .50
BD49 Brett Adcock .15 .40
BD50 Riley Pint .15 .40
BD51 Jacob Heyward .15 .40
BD52 Hudson Potts .20 .50
BD53 Ronnie Dawson .15 .40
BD54 Nick Hanson .15 .40
BD55 Forrest Whitley .60 1.50
BD56 Ryan Hendrix .15 .40
BD57 Eric Lauer .20 .50
BD58 Tyson Miller .20 .50
BD59 Jesus Luzardo 1.00 2.50
BD60 Kyle Lewis 3.00 8.00
BD61 Connor Justus .15 .40
BD62 Cole Stobbe .15 .40
BD63 Garrett Hampson .30 .75
BD64 Cole Ragans .20 .50
BD65 Kyle Muller .20 .50
BD66 Logan Shore .20 .50
BD67 Gavin Lux 1.00 2.50
BD68 Shane Bieber 5.00 12.00
BD69 T.J. Zeuch .20 .50
BD70 Joshua Lowe .15 .40
BD71 Justin Alleman .15 .40
BD72 Ryan Howard .15 .40
BD73 Jake Fraley .20 .50
BD74 Bo Bichette 6.00 15.00
BD75 D.J. Peters .75 2.00
BD76 Jake Rogers .75 2.00
BD77 Bryan Reynolds .50 1.25
BD78 Colton Welker .25 .60
BD79 Nick Banks .15 .40
BD80 Will Benson .25 .60
BD81 Cavan Biggio 1.50 4.00
BD82 Braden Webb .15 .40
BD83 Chris Okey .15 .40
BD84 Will Smith 1.50 4.00
BD85 A.J. Puckett .20 .50
BD86 Colby Woodmansee .20 .50
BD87 Andy Yerzy .15 .40
BD88 J.B. Woodman .25 .60
BD89 Corbin Burnes 2.50 6.00
BD90 Alex Kirilloff 1.50 4.00
BD91 Robert Tyler .15 .40
BD92 Pete Alonso 3.00 8.00
BD93 Alec Hansen .20 .50
BD94 Daniel Johnson .15 .40
BD95 Mike Shawaryn .20 .50
BD96 Daulton Jefferies .20 .50
BD97 Jordan Sheffield .15 .40
BD98 Conner Capel .15 .40
BD99 Bobby Dalbec 4.00 10.00
BD100 Corey Ray .20 .50
BD101 Ben Rortvedt .20 .50
BD102 Tim Lynch .25 .60
BD103 Charles Leblanc .15 .40
BD104 Dane Dunning .50 1.25
BD105 Bryson Brigman .15 .40
BD106 Nolan Martinez .20 .50
BD107 Connor Jones .20 .50
BD108 Alex Call .15 .40
BD109 Reggie Lawson .15 .40
BD110 Matt Thaiss .15 .40
BD111 Bryse Wilson .50 1.25
BD112 Zack Burdi .20 .50
BD113 Nolan Williams .15 .40
BD114 Mark Ecker .15 .40
BD115 Michael Paez .25 .60
BD116 Zach Jackson .15 .40
BD117 Joe Rizzo .15 .40
BD118 Ryan Boldt .20 .50
BD119 Mikey York .15 .40
BD120 Ian Anderson 2.50 6.00
BD121 Austin Meadows .40 1.00
BD122 Nick Gordon .15 .40
BD123 Forrest Wall .15 .40
BD124 Antonio Senzatela .15 .40
BD125 Justus Sheffield .30 .75
BD126 Christian Arroyo .30 .75
BD127 Dylan Cease .25 .60
BD128 Scott Kingery .25 .60
BD129 Daniel Palka .15 .40
BD130 Bradley Zimmer .25 .60
BD131 Amir Garrett .15 .40
BD132 Dillon Tate .20 .50
BD133 Domingo Leyba .15 .40
BD134 Tyler Jay .15 .40
BD135 Sean Reid-Foley .20 .50
BD136 James Kaprielian .15 .40
BD137 Kyle Tucker .75 2.00
BD138 Derek Fisher .15 .40
BD139 Tyler O'Neill .20 .50
BD140 Anderson Espinoza .20 .50
BD141 Christin Stewart .20 .50
BD142 Grant Holmes .20 .50
BD143 Rafael Devers .50 1.25
BD144 Mitch Keller .20 .50
BD145 Francis Martes .15 .40
BD146 Nellie Rodriguez .15 .40
BD147 Chih-Wei Hu .20 .50
BD148 Anthony Banda .15 .40
BD149 Trent Clark .15 .40
BD150 Brendan Rodgers .25 .60
BD151 Ryan Cordell .15 .40
BD152 Daz Cameron .15 .40
BD153 Billy McKinney .20 .50
BD154 Jomar Reyes .25 .60
BD155 Jake Bauers .25 .60
BD156 Willy Adames .25 .60
BD157 Josh Hader .20 .50
BD158 Luis Ortiz .15 .40
BD159 Erick Fedde .15 .40
BD160 Gleyber Torres 2.50 6.00
BD161 Francisco Mejia .25 .60
BD162 Kolby Allard .15 .40
BD163 Ronnie Williams .15 .40
BD164 Matt Chapman .50 1.25
BD165 Austin Riley .50 1.25
BD166 Austin Dean .15 .40
BD167 Ryan McMahon .25 .60
BD168 Anfernee Seymour .15 .40
BD169 Marcos Diplan .15 .40
BD170 Anthony Alford .15 .40
BD171 Nick Neidert .15 .40
BD172 Bobby Bradley .20 .50
BD173 Tyler Wade .25 .60
BD174 Chase De Jong .20 .50
BD175 Brett Phillips .15 .40
BD176 Dominic Smith .15 .40
BD177 Touki Toussaint .20 .50
BD178 Reese McGuire .15 .40
BD179 Franklin Barreto .15 .40
BD180 Ian Happ .30 .75
BD181 Javier Guerra .15 .40
BD182 Tyler Beede .20 .50
BD183 Drew Jackson .15 .40
BD184 Brent Honeywell .25 .60
BD185 Michael Gettys .15 .40
BD186 Rhys Hoskins .60 1.50
BD187 Dylan Cozens .15 .40
BD188 Jon Harris .20 .50
BD189 Phil Bickford .15 .40
BD190 Amed Rosario .25 .60
BD191 Eloy Jimenez .60 1.50
BD192 Jack Flaherty 1.00 2.50
BD193 Alex Young .20 .50
BD194 Andrew Sopko .15 .40
BD195 Rafael Bautista .15 .40
BD196 Chris Shaw .15 .40
BD197 Mike Gerber .15 .40
BD198 Kevin Newman .25 .60
BD199 Ryan Mountcastle .75 2.00
BD200 Lucius Fox .25 .60

2016 Bowman Draft Blue

*BLUE: 2X TO 5X BASIC
STATED ODDS 1:26 HOBBY
STATED PRINT RUN 150 SER.#'d SETS

2016 Bowman Draft Gold

*GOLD: 4X TO 10X BASIC
STATED ODDS 1:76 HOBBY
STATED PRINT RUN 50 SER.#'d SETS

2016 Bowman Draft Green

*GREEN: 2.5X TO 6X BASIC
STATED ODDS 1:39 HOBBY
STATED PRINT RUN 99 SER.#'d SETS

2016 Bowman Draft Orange

*ORANGE: 5X TO 12X BASIC
STATED ODDS 1:152 HOBBY
STATED PRINT RUN 25 SER.#'d SETS

2016 Bowman Draft Silver

*SILVER: 1X TO 2.5X BASIC
STATED ODDS 1:8 HOBBY
STATED PRINT RUN 499 SER.#'d SETS

2016 Bowman Draft Golden Debut Contract Winner

STATED ODDS 1:1520 HOBBY
GDWFP Francis Pablo 6.00 15.00

2017 Bowman

COMPLETE SET (100) 6.00 15.00
PRINTING PLATE ODDS 1:8827 HOBBY
PLATE PRINT RUN 1 SET PER COLOR
BLACK-CYAN-MAGENTA-YELLOW ISSUED
NO PLATE PRICING DUE TO SCARCITY
1 Kris Bryant .30 .75
2 Kenta Maeda .20 .50
3 Bryce Harper .40 1.00
4 Jeff Hoffman RC .25 .60
5 Trevor Story .25 .60
6 Mookie Betts .50 1.25
7 Cole Hamels .20 .50
8 Matt Carpenter .25 .60
9 Carlos Correa .25 .60
10 Jose Bautista .20 .50
11 Ryan Braun .20 .50
12 Trea Turner .20 .50
13 Stephen Piscotty .20 .50
14 Stephen Strasburg .25 .60
15 Buster Posey .30 .75
16 Joey Votto .25 .60
17 Yoenis Cespedes .25 .60
18 Andrew McCutchen .25 .60
19 Jose Altuve .20 .50
20 Manny Margot RC .25 .60
21 Giancarlo Stanton .25 .60
22 Carson Fulmer RC .25 .60
23 Andrew Benintendi RC .75 2.00
24 Craig Kimbrel .20 .50
25 Yoan Moncada RC .75 2.00
26 Teoscar Hernandez RC 1.00 2.50
27 Reynaldo Lopez RC .25 .60
28 Miguel Cabrera .25 .60
29 Yulieski Gurriel RC .40 1.00
30 Nomar Mazara .15 .40
31 Josh Donaldson .20 .50
32 Aaron Judge RC 3.00 8.00
33 Ichiro .30 .75
34 Robert Gsellman RC .25 .60
35 Ryon Healy RC .30 .75
36 Anthony Rizzo .30 .75
37 Evan Longoria .20 .50
38 Andrew Miller .20 .50
39 Noah Syndergaard .20 .50
40 Manny Machado .25 .60
41 Orlando Arcia RC .40 1.00
42 Jose De Leon RC .25 .60
43 Max Scherzer .25 .60
44 Freddie Freeman .30 .75
45 Kyle Schwarber .25 .60
46 Willson Contreras .25 .60
47 Tim Anderson .25 .60
48 Gregory Polanco .20 .50
49 Nolan Arenado .40 1.00
50 Corey Seager .25 .60
51 Troy Tulowitzki .25 .60
52 David Ortiz .25 .60
53 Odubel Herrera .20 .50
54 David Dahl RC .30 .75
55 Rob Segedin RC .25 .60

56 Tyler Glasnow RC 1.00 2.50
57 Dansby Swanson RC .60 1.50
58 Francisco Lindor .25 .60
59 Nelson Cruz .25 .60
60 Jorge Alfaro RC .30 .75
61 Jameson Taillon .20 .50
62 Jake Thompson RC .25 .60
63 Hunter Dozier RC .25 .60
64 Matt Strahm RC .25 .60
65 Ben Zobrist .20 .50
66 Gavin Cecchini RC .25 .60
67 Aledmys Diaz .20 .50
68 Mark Trumbo .15 .40
69 Wil Myers .20 .50
70 Felix Hernandez .20 .50
71 Jake Lamb .20 .50
72 Dellin Betances .20 .50
73 Jacob deGrom .50 1.25
74 Robinson Cano .20 .50
75 Alex Bregman RC 1.25 3.00
76 Xander Bogaerts .25 .60
77 Julio Urias .25 .60
78 Raimel Tapia RC .30 .75
79 Jon Lester .20 .50
80 Clayton Kershaw .40 1.00
81 Yu Darvish .25 .60
82 Jackie Bradley Jr. .25 .60
83 Braden Shipley RC .25 .60
84 Starling Marte .20 .50
85 Gary Sanchez .25 .60
86 Tyler Austin RC .30 .75
87 George Springer .20 .50
88 Paul Goldschmidt .25 .60
89 Jharel Cotton RC .25 .60
90 Brandon Belt .20 .50
91 Chris Sale .25 .60
92 Joe Musgrove RC .75 2.00
93 Danny Salazar .20 .50
94 Michael Fulmer .15 .40
95 Justin Bour .20 .50
96 Jake Arrieta .20 .50
97 Daniel Murphy .20 .50
98 Alex Reyes RC .30 .75
99 Hunter Renfroe RC .30 .75
100 Mike Trout 1.25 3.00

2017 Bowman Blue

*BLUE: 2.5X TO 6X BASIC
*BLUE RC: 1.5X TO 4X BASIC RC
STATED ODDS 1:235 HOBBY
STATED PRINT RUN 150 SER.#'d SETS

2017 Bowman Gold

*GOLD: 6X TO 15X BASIC
*GOLD RC: 4X TO 10X BASIC RC
STATED ODDS 1:703 HOBBY
STATED PRINT RUN 50 SER.#'d SETS

2017 Bowman Green

*GREEN: 4X TO 10X BASIC
*GREEN RC: 2.5X TO 6X BASIC RC
RANDOM INSERTS IN RETAIL PACKS
STATED PRINT RUN 99 SER.#'d SETS

2017 Bowman Orange

*ORANGE: 8X TO 20X BASIC
*ORANGE RC: 5X TO 12X BASIC RC
STATED ODDS 1:304 HOBBY
STATED PRINT RUN 25 SER.#'d SETS

2017 Bowman Purple

*PURPLE: 2X TO 5X BASIC
*PURPLE RC: 1.2X TO 3X BASIC RC
STATED ODDS 1:141 HOBBY
STATED PRINT RUN 250 SER.#'d SETS

2017 Bowman Silver

*SILVER: 1.5X TO 4X BASIC
*SILVER RC: 1X TO 2.5X BASIC RC
STATED ODDS 1:71 HOBBY
STATED PRINT RUN 499 SER.#'d SETS

2017 Bowman Buyback Autographs

STATED ODDS 1:14,772 HOBBY
STATED PRINT RUN 20 SER.#'d SETS
EXCHANGE DEADLINE 3/31/2019
20 Roberto Alomar EXCH 30.00 80.00
82 Pedro Martinez 75.00 200.00
148 Greg Maddux 75.00 200.00
197 Mark McGwire EXCH 60.00 150.00
253 Randy Johnson
266 John Smoltz EXCH 40.00 100.00
320 Frank Thomas 125.00 250.00
461 Mike Piazza 150.00 300.00
569 Chipper Jones 250.00 500.00

2017 Bowman Prospect Autographs

RANDOMLY INSERTED IN RETAIL PACKS
EXCHANGE DEADLINE 3/31/2019
PAAP A.J. Puk 4.00 10.00
PADE Dietrich Enns 3.00 8.00
PADL Dinelson Lamet 10.00 25.00
PADLU Dawel Lugo 2.50 6.00
PADW Devin Williams 8.00 20.00
PAEA Eddy Alvarez 3.00 8.00
PAER Edwin Rios 8.00 20.00
PAGA Greg Allen 4.00 10.00
PAIA Ian Anderson
PAIW Isaiah White 2.50 6.00
PAJDP Juan De Paula 3.00 8.00
PAJG Jason Groome 8.00 20.00
PAJM Jorge Mateo 8.00 20.00
PAJR Josh Rogers 3.00 8.00
PAJS Jackson Stephens 3.00 8.00
PAKG Kelvin Gutierrez 2.50 6.00
PAKL Kyle Lewis
PALT Leody Taveras 10.00 25.00
PAMM Mickey Moniak 12.00 30.00
PAMMA Matt Manning
PAMS Miguelangel Sierra 5.00 12.00
PAMW Mitchell White 2.50 6.00
PANN Nick Neidert 2.50 6.00
PANS Nick Senzel 40.00 100.00
PAPW Patrick Weigel 2.50 6.00
PARR Raudy Read 3.00 8.00
PASM Scott Moss 4.00 10.00
PASN Sean Newcomb 4.00 10.00
PATM Tyson Miller 3.00 8.00
PATS Tanner Scott 2.50 6.00
PAZR Zach Rice 3.00 8.00

2017 Bowman Prospect Autographs Gold

*GOLD: 1X TO 2.5X BASIC
INSERTED IN RETAIL PACKS
STATED PRINT RUN 50 SER.#'d SETS
EXCHANGE DEADLINE 3/31/2019

2017 Bowman Prospect Autographs Green

*GREEN: .75X TO 2X BASIC
INSERTED IN RETAIL PACKS
STATED PRINT RUN 99 SER.#'d SETS
EXCHANGE DEADLINE 3/31/2019

2017 Bowman Prospect Autographs Orange

*ORANGE: 1.2X TO 3X BASIC
INSERTED IN RETAIL PACKS
STATED PRINT RUN 25 SER.#'d SETS
EXCHANGE DEADLINE 3/31/2019

2017 Bowman Prospect Autographs Purple

*PURPLE: .5X TO 1.2X BASIC
INSERTED IN RETAIL PACKS
STATED PRINT RUN 250 SER.#'d SETS
EXCHANGE DEADLINE 3/31/2019

2017 Bowman Prospects

COMPLETE SET (150) 40.00 100.00
PRINTING PLATE ODDS 1:5838 HOBBY
PLATE PRINT RUN 1 SET PER COLOR
NO PLATE PRICING DUE TO SCARCITY
BP1 Nick Senzel .50 1.25
BP2 Gavin Lux .60 1.50
BP3 Ronald Guzman .20 .50
BP4 A.J. Puckett .15 .40
BP5 Mike Soroka .50 1.25
BP6 Roniel Raudes .15 .40
BP7 Lucas Erceg .15 .40
BP8 Luis Almanzar .15 .40
BP9 Beau Burrows .15 .40
BP10 Chase Vallot .15 .40
BP11 P.J. Conlon .15 .40
BP12 Erick Fedde .15 .40
BP13 Rookie Davis .15 .40
BP14 Chris Shaw .15 .40
BP15 Nick Burdi .15 .40
BP16 Clint Frazier .30 .75
BP17 Luiz Gohara .15 .40
BP18 Lourdes Gurriel Jr. .25 .60
BP19 Eric Jenkins .15 .40
BP20 Angel Perdomo .15 .40
BP21 Dustin May .75 2.00
BP22 Freddy Peralta .25 .60
BP23 Jarlin Garcia .15 .40
BP24 Tyler O'Neill .20 .50
BP25 Lazarito Armenteros .30 .75
BP26 Paul DeJong .50 1.25
BP27 Antonio Senzatela .15 .40
BP28 Kyle Tucker .40 1.00
BP29 Aramis Garcia .15 .40
BP30 Willie Calhoun .25 .60
BP31 Chance Adams .20 .50
BP32 Vladimir Guerrero Jr. 2.00 5.00
BP33 Braxton Garrett .15 .40
BP34 Yeudy Garcia .15 .40
BP35 Dane Dunning .50 1.25
BP36 Andy Ibanez .15 .40
BP37 Francisco Rios .15 .40
BP38 Joe Jimenez .20 .50
BP39 Dylan Cozens .15 .40
BP40 Mauricio Dubon .20 .50
BP41 Franklyn Kilome .20 .50
BP42 Chance Sisco .30 .75
BP43 Sandy Alcantara .20 .50
BP44 Stephen Gonsalves .15 .40
BP45 Grant Holmes .15 .40
BP46 Dakota Chalmers .15 .40
BP47 Kolby Allard .15 .40
BP48 Tyler Alexander .15 .40
BP49 Phil Bickford .15 .40
BP50 Eloy Jimenez .60 1.50
BP51 Francisco Mejia .25 .60
BP52 Kohl Stewart .15 .40
BP53 Garrett Whitley .15 .40
BP54 Anderson Espinoza .15 .40
BP55 Cal Quantrill .15 .40
BP56 Tetsuto Yamada .30 .75
BP57 Tyler Beede .15 .40
BP58 Jake Bauers .20 .50
BP59 Ariel Jurado .15 .40
BP60 Austin Voth .15 .40
BP61 Tyler Stephenson .40 1.00
BP62 Yoshitomo Tsutsugo .40 1.00
BP63 Dominic Smith .15 .40
BP64 Matt Thaiss .15 .40
BP65 Austin Meadows .40 1.00
BP66 Mitch Keller .20 .50
BP67 Jahmai Jones .15 .40
BP68 Alex Speas .15 .40
BP69 Nolan Jones .25 .60
BP70 Kevin Newman .25 .60
BP71 T.J. Friedl .15 .40
BP72 Oscar De La Cruz .15 .40
BP73 Victor Robles .40 1.00
BP74 Patrick Weigel .15 .40
BP75 Ryan Mountcastle .75 2.00
BP76 Amed Rosario .25 .60
BP77 Nick Solak .60 1.50
BP78 Abrahan Gutierrez .25 .60
BP79 Yu-Cheng Chang .25 .60
BP80 Gleyber Torres 2.50 6.00
BP81 J.D. Davis .20 .50
BP82 Walker Buehler .40 1.00
BP83 Andrew Sopko .15 .40
BP84 Brent Honeywell .20 .50
BP85 Kyle Funkhouser .20 .50
BP86 Brian Mundell .15 .40
BP87 Brian Anderson .20 .50
BP88 Brendan Rodgers .20 .50
BP89 Josh Staumont .15 .40
BP90 Cody Sedlock .15 .40
BP91 D.J. Stewart .15 .40
BP92 Wuilmer Becerra .15 .40
BP93 Nate Smith .15 .40
BP94 Alfredo Rodriguez .20 .50
BP95 Daz Cameron .15 .40
BP96 Taylor Ward .20 .50
BP97 Takahiro Norimoto .15 .40
BP98 Tomoyuki Sugano .25 .60
BP99 Drew Jackson .15 .40
BP100 Kevin Maitan .25 .60
BP101 Rafael Devers .30 .75
BP102 Alex Kirilloff .40 1.00
BP103 Jack Flaherty 1.00 2.50
BP104 Adonis Medina .25 .60
BP105 Ke'Bryan Hayes .75 2.00
BP106 Josh Hader .20 .50
BP107 Luis Urias .60 1.50
BP108 Donnie Dewees .15 .40
BP109 Kyle Freeland .20 .50
BP110 Matt Chapman .50 1.25
BP111 Sam Coonrod .15 .40
BP112 Andrew Suarez .15 .40
BP113 David Fletcher .50 1.25
BP114 Tyler Jay .15 .40
BP115 Franklin Barreto .15 .40
BP116 Michael Kopech .50 1.25
BP117 Rhys Hoskins .60 1.50
BP118 Triston McKenzie .50 1.25
BP119 Luis Garcia 1.25 3.00
BP120 Harold Ramirez .20 .50
BP121 Blake Rutherford .25 .60
BP122 Matt Manning .25 .60
BP123 Josh Morgan .15 .40
BP124 Dylan Cease .25 .60
BP125 Kyle Lewis .30 .75
BP126 Nick Neidert .15 .40
BP127 Ronald Acuna 20.00 50.00
BP128 Luis Ortiz .15 .40
BP129 Isael Soto .15 .40
BP130 Adrian Morejon .25 .60
BP131 Mark Zagunis .15 .40
BP132 Justus Sheffield .25 .60
BP133 Jaime Schultz .15 .40
BP134 Fernando Romero .15 .40
BP135 Mickey Moniak .30 .75
BP136 Jorge Bonifacio .15 .40
BP137 Jomar Reyes .15 .40
BP138 Thomas Szapucki .20 .50
BP139 Sean Reid-Foley .15 .40
BP140 Willy Adames .20 .50
BP141 Yang Hyeon-Jong .20 .50
BP142 Bo Bichette .60 1.50
BP143 Harrison Bader .25 .60
BP144 Travis Demeritte .15 .40
BP145 Juan Hillman .15 .40
BP146 Francis Martes .15 .40
BP147 Wilkerman Garcia .20 .50
BP148 Christin Stewart .20 .50
BP149 Cody Bellinger 2.50 6.00
BP150 Jason Groome .30 .75

2017 Bowman Prospects 70th Red

*70TH RED: 1.5X TO 4X BASIC
STATED ODDS 1:94 HOBBY

2017 Bowman Prospects Blue

*BLUE: 2X TO 5X BASIC
STATED ODDS 1:157 HOBBY
STATED PRINT RUN 150 SER.#'d SETS
BP149 Cody Bellinger 25.00 60.00

2017 Bowman Prospects Gold

*GOLD: 5X TO 12X BASIC
STATED ODDS 1:469 HOBBY
STATED PRINT RUN 50 SER.#'d SETS
BP121 Blake Rutherford 15.00 40.00
BP149 Cody Bellinger 60.00 150.00

2017 Bowman Prospects Green

*GREEN: 2.5X TO 6X BASIC
RANDOMLY INSERTED IN RETAIL PACKS
STATED PRINT RUN 99 SER.#'d SETS
BP121 Blake Rutherford 8.00 20.00
BP149 Cody Bellinger 30.00 80.00

2017 Bowman Prospects Orange

*ORANGE: 8X TO 20X BASIC
STATED ODDS 1:203 HOBBY
STATED PRINT RUN 25 SER.#'d SETS
BP121 Blake Rutherford 25.00 60.00
BP149 Cody Bellinger 100.00 250.00

2017 Bowman Prospects Purple

*PURPLE: 1.5X TO 4X BASIC
STATED ODDS 1:94 HOBBY
STATED PRINT RUN 250 SER.#'d SETS
BP149 Cody Bellinger 20.00 50.00

2017 Bowman Prospects Silver

*SILVER: 1.2X TO 3X BASIC
STATED ODDS 1:47 HOBBY
STATED PRINT RUN 499 SER.#'d SETS

2017 Bowman Prospects Yellow

*YELLOW: 1.2X TO 3X BASIC
RANDOMLY INSERTED IN RETAIL PACKS

2017 Bowman Draft

COMPLETE SET (200) 12.00 30.00
STATED PLATE ODDS 1:1136 HOBBY
PLATE PRINT RUN 1 SET PER COLOR
BLACK-CYAN-MAGENTA-YELLOW ISSUED
NO PLATE PRICING DUE TO SCARCITY
BD1 Royce Lewis 1.25 3.00
BD2 Jacob Gonzalez .50 1.25
BD3 Seth Elledge .15 .40
BD4 Stuart Fairchild .20 .50
BD5 Franklin Perez .25 .60
BD6 Jeter Downs .30 .75
BD7 Yu-Cheng Chang .25 .60
BD8 T.J. Friedl .15 .40
BD9 Alex Scherff .25 .60
BD10 Nick Solak .60 1.50
BD11 Lincoln Henzman .15 .40
BD12 Heliot Ramos 1.50 4.00
BD13 Riley Adams .20 .50
BD14 Wyatt Mills .15 .40
BD15 Alex Faedo .25 .60
BD16 Marcos Diplan .15 .40
BD17 Daulton Varsho .25 .60
BD18 Jacob Heatherly .15 .40
BD19 Lourdes Gurriel Jr. .25 .60
BD20 Zach Kirtley .20 .50
BD21 Cal Quantrill .15 .40
BD22 Jacob Heyward .15 .40
BD23 Alec Hansen .15 .40
BD24 Quinn Brodey .15 .40
BD25 MacKenzie Gore 1.25 3.00
BD26 Mitch Keller .20 .50
BD27 Joey Morgan .20 .50
BD28 Juan Hillman .15 .40
BD29 Freddy Peralta .25 .60
BD30 Morgan Cooper .20 .50
BD31 Brett Netzer .20 .50
BD32 Alex Lange .25 .60
BD33 Hans Crouse .40 1.00
BD34 Michael Kopech .50 1.25
BD35 Cole Ragans .15 .40
BD36 Kolby Allard .15 .40
BD37 Matt Manning .25 .60
BD38 Bo Bichette .60 1.50
BD39 Ronald Acuna 5.00 12.00
BD40 Cristian Pache .75 2.00
BD41 Ryan Vilade .25 .60
BD42 Tyler Freeman .15 .40
BD43 Cory Abbott .15 .40
BD44 Shane Baz .25 .60
BD45 Brian Miller .20 .50
BD46 Luis Campusano .20 .50
BD47 A.J. Puk .25 .60
BD48 Griffin Canning .25 .60
BD49 Justin Dunn .15 .40
BD50 Jorge Mateo .15 .40
BD51 Trevor Clifton .15 .40
BD52 Carter Kieboom .25 .60
BD53 Trevor Rogers 2.00 5.00
BD54 Tommy Doyle .15 .40
BD55 Adam Hall .25 .60
BD56 Will Benson .15 .40
BD57 Ariel Jurado .15 .40
BD58 Forrest Whitley .40 1.00
BD59 Daniel Tillo .25 .60
BD60 Austin Beck .60 1.50
BD61 Jahmai Jones .15 .40
BD62 Adonis Medina .25 .60
BD63 Blayne Enlow .20 .50
BD64 Ryley Widell .25 .60
BD65 Tanner Houck .75 2.00
BD66 Caden Lemons .15 .40
BD67 Buddy Reed .15 .40
BD68 T.J. Zeuch .15 .40
BD69 Vladimir Gutierrez .15 .40
BD70 Anderson Espinoza .15 .40
BD71 Fernando Tatis Jr. 1.50 4.00
BD72 Eloy Jimenez .60 1.50
BD73 Jose Taveras .20 .50
BD74 Christopher Seise .25 .60
BD75 Keston Hiura 1.25 3.00
BD76 Charlie Barnes .15 .40
BD77 Connor Seabold .15 .40
BD78 David Peterson .30 .75
BD79 Seth Corry .15 .40
BD80 Blake Rutherford .25 .60
BD81 Conner Uselton .25 .60
BD82 D.L. Hall .20 .50
BD83 Peter Alonso 1.50 4.00
BD84 Glenn Otto .15 .40
BD85 Gavin Sheets .25 .60
BD86 Luis Gonzalez .20 .50
BD87 Taylor Walls .15 .40
BD88 Ernie Clement .20 .50
BD89 Dylan Carlson 1.00 2.50
BD90 Drew Waters 1.00 2.50
BD91 Christin Stewart .20 .50
BD92 Cal Mitchell .30 .75
BD93 Troy Bacon .25 .60
BD94 Zac Lowther .20 .50
BD95 Jo Adell 2.00 5.00
BD96 Francisco Rios .15 .40
BD97 Mason House .25 .60
BD98 Corey Ray .20 .50
BD99 Anfernee Grier .15 .40
BD100 Brendan McKay .60 1.50
BD101 Kacy Clemens .20 .50
BD102 Isan Diaz .40 1.00
BD103 Drew Strotman .15 .40
BD104 Will Gaddis .15 .40
BD105 Jacob Pearson .15 .40
BD106 Tyler Ivey .15 .40
BD107 Nick Allen .20 .50
BD108 Andy Ibanez .15 .40
BD109 J.J. Matijevic .20 .50
BD110 KJ Harrison .25 .60
BD111 Riley Pint .15 .40
BD112 Franklyn Kilome .20 .50
BD113 Peyton Remy .25 .60
BD114 Scott Kingery .25 .60
BD115 Adam Haseley .30 .75
BD116 Will Smith .40 1.00
BD117 Anderson Tejeda .25 .60
BD118 Quentin Holmes .20 .50
BD119 Nate Pearson 1.00 2.50
BD120 Kyle Wright .50 1.25
BD121 Matthew Whatley .15 .40
BD122 Brent Rooker .40 1.00
BD123 Daulton Jefferies .20 .50
BD124 Taylor Ward .20 .50
Missing card number
BD125 Triston McKenzie .50 1.25
BD126 Scott Hurst .20 .50
BD127 Noah Bremer .15 .40
BD128 Angel Perdomo .15 .40
BD129 Touki Toussaint .20 .50
BD130 A.J. Puckett .15 .40
BD131 Lucas Erceg .15 .40
BD132 Riley Mahan .15 .40
BD133 Corbin Martin .15 .40
BD134 Jordan Sheffield .15 .40
BD135 Lazarito Armenteros .30 .75
BD136 Dylan Cease .25 .60
BD137 Kevin Newman .25 .60
BD138 Hagen Danner .20 .50
BD139 Mark Vientos .25 .60
BD140 Justus Sheffield .25 .60
BD141 Bubba Thompson .25 .60
BD142 Desmond Lindsay .15 .40
BD143 J.B. Bukauskas .25 .60
BD144 Freddy Tarnok .20 .50
BD145 Blake Hunt .15 .40
BD146 David Thompson .20 .50
BD147 Delvin Perez .25 .60
BD148 Peter Solomon .20 .50
BD149 Brendan Murphy .15 .40
BD150 Vladimir Guerrero Jr. 2.00 5.00
BD151 Yusniel Diaz .50 1.25
BD152 Dillon Tate .15 .40
BD153 Nonie Williams .15 .40
BD154 Kyle Lewis .30 .75
BD155 Bobby Dalbec 1.00 2.50
BD156 Ian Anderson .50 1.25
BD157 Brendan Rodgers .20 .50
BD158 Drew Ellis .25 .60
BD159 Joseph Dunand .30 .75
BD160 Kevin Maitan .25 .60
BD161 Kramer Robertson .30 .75
BD162 Juan Soto 6.00 15.00
BD163 Chris Okey .15 .40
BD164 Tristen Lutz .25 .60
BD165 Wil Crowe .25 .60
BD166 Taylor Trammell 1.00 2.50
BD167 Trevor Stephan .25 .60
BD168 Matt Tabor .15 .40
BD169 James Marinan .25 .60
BD170 Cody Sedlock .15 .40
BD171 Gavin Lux .60 1.50
BD172 MJ Melendez .25 .60
BD173 Kade McClure .15 .40
BD174 Dylan Busby .15 .40
BD175 Kevin Merrell .20 .50
BD176 Dawel Lugo .15 .40
BD177 Jake Burger .30 .75
BD178 Evan White 1.25 3.00
BD179 Carl Stajduhar .15 .40
BD180 Connor Wong .25 .60
BD181 Canaan Smith .50 1.25
BD182 Nick Raquet .15 .40
BD183 Kyle Tucker .40 1.00
BD184 Sam Carlson .20 .50
BD185 Wuilmer Becerra .15 .40
Missing card number
BD186 Dane Dunning .50 1.25
BD187 Joe Perez .20 .50
BD188 Brendon Little .20 .50
BD189 Will Craig .15 .40
BD190 Ricardo De La Torre .15 .40
BD191 Nick Gordon .15 .40
BD192 Kevin Smith .15 .40
BD193 Cole Brannen .25 .60
BD194 Logan Warmoth .25 .60
BD195 Pavin Smith .25 .60
BD196 Colton Hock .20 .50
BD197 Clarke Schmidt .25 .60
BD198 Cash Case .25 .60
BD199 Luis Ortiz .15 .40
BD200 Gleyber Torres 2.50 6.00

2017 Bowman Draft Blue

*BLUE: 2X TO 5X BASIC
STATED ODDS 1:31 HOBBY
STATED PRINT RUN 150 SER.#'d SETS

2017 Bowman Draft Gold

*GOLD: 4X TO 10X BASIC
STATED ODDS 1:91 HOBBY
STATED PRINT RUN 50 SER.#'d SETS

2017 Bowman Draft Green

*GREEN: 2.5X TO 6X BASIC
STATED ODDS 1:46 HOBBY
STATED PRINT RUN 99 SER.#'d SETS

2017 Bowman Draft Orange

*ORANGE: 5X TO 12X BASIC
STATED ODDS 1:127 HOBBY
STATED PRINT RUN 25 SER.#'d SETS

2017 Bowman Draft Purple

*PURPLE: 2X TO 5X BASIC
STATED ODDS 1:19 HOBBY
STATED PRINT RUN 250 SER.#'d SETS

2017 Bowman Draft Silver

*SILVER: 1X TO 2.5X BASIC
STATED ODDS 1:10 HOBBY
STATED PRINT RUN 499 SER.#'d SETS

2018 Bowman

COMPLETE SET (100) 10.00 25.00
PRINTING PLATE ODDS 1:11,757 HOBBY
PLATE PRINT RUN 1 SET PER COLOR
BLACK-CYAN-MAGENTA-YELLOW ISSUED
NO PLATE PRICING DUE TO SCARCITY
1 Mike Trout 1.25 3.00
2 Francisco Mejia RC .30 .75
3 Corey Kluber .20 .50
4 Zack Greinke .25 .60
5 Paul Goldschmidt .25 .60
6 Victor Robles RC .60 1.50
7 Keon Broxton .15 .40
8 Hunter Renfroe .15 .40
9 Zack Granite RC .25 .60
10 Rhys Hoskins RC 1.00 2.50
11 Jen-Ho Tseng RC .15 .40
12 Chance Sisco RC .30 .75
13 Maikel Franco .20 .50
14 George Springer .20 .50
15 Corey Knebel .15 .40
16 Matt Olson .25 .60
17 Nicholas Castellanos .25 .60
18 Salvador Perez .20 .50
19 Yoan Moncada .25 .60
20 Raudy Read RC .25 .60
21 Noah Syndergaard .20 .50
22 Albert Pujols .30 .75
23 Richard Urena RC .25 .60
24 Aaron Judge .60 1.50
25 Rafael Devers RC .75 2.00
26 Clint Frazier RC .50 1.25
27 Wil Myers .20 .50
28 Manny Machado .25 .60
29 Miguel Cabrera .25 .60
30 Stephen Strasburg .25 .60
31 Willie Calhoun RC .40 1.00
32 Tyler Mahle RC .30 .75
33 Anthony Rizzo .30 .75
34 Amed Rosario RC .30 .75
35 Erick Fedde RC .25 .60
36 Dustin Fowler RC .25 .60
37 Sandy Alcantara RC .25 .60
38 Andrew Benintendi .25 .60
39 Jose Berrios .20 .50
40 Francisco Lindor .25 .60
41 Freddie Freeman .30 .75
42 Harrison Bader RC .40 1.00
43 Joey Votto .25 .60
44 Chris Archer .15 .40
45 Khris Davis .25 .60
46 Austin Hays RC .40 1.00
47 Cody Bellinger .50 1.25
48 Jackson Stephens RC .25 .60
49 Shohei Ohtani RC 6.00 15.00
50 Carlos Correa .25 .60
51 Marcell Ozuna .25 .60
52 J.D. Davis RC .30 .75
53 Charlie Blackmon .25 .60
54 Byron Buxton .25 .60
55 Dominic Smith RC .30 .75
56 Nomar Mazara .15 .40
57 Anthony Banda RC .25 .60
58 Josh Donaldson .20 .50
59 Walker Buehler RC 1.25 3.00
60 Aaron Altherr .15 .40
61 Dansby Swanson .25 .60
62 Ozzie Albies RC .75 2.00
63 Robinson Cano .20 .50
64 Clayton Kershaw .40 1.00
65 Marcus Stroman .20 .50
66 Victor Arano RC .25 .60
67 Giancarlo Stanton .25 .60
68 Andrew McCutchen .25 .60
69 Bryce Harper .40 1.00
70 Parker Bridwell RC .25 .60
71 J.P. Crawford RC .25 .60
72 Alex Verdugo RC .40 1.00
73 Nick Williams RC .30 .75
74 Garrett Cooper RC .25 .60
75 Miguel Andujar RC 1.00 2.50
76 Tomas Nido RC .25 .60
77 Avisail Garcia .20 .50
78 Jack Flaherty RC 1.00 2.50
79 Buster Posey .30 .75
80 Evan Longoria .20 .50
81 Nolan Arenado .40 1.00
82 Lucas Sims RC .25 .60
83 Nicky Delmonico RC .25 .60
84 Paul DeJong .25 .60
85 Andrew Stevenson RC .25 .60
86 Rougned Odor .20 .50
87 Tommy Pham .15 .40
88 Felix Hernandez .20 .50
89 Brandon Crawford .20 .50
90 Max Fried RC 1.00 2.50
91 Luiz Gohara RC .25 .60
92 Josh Bell .20 .50
93 Michael Conforto .20 .50
94 Chris Sale .25 .60
95 Jonathan Schoop .15 .40
96 Raisel Iglesias .20 .50
97 Gary Sanchez .25 .60
98 Whit Merrifield .25 .60
99 Ryan McMahon RC .60 1.50
100 Kris Bryant .30 .75

2018 Bowman Blue

*BLUE: 3X TO 8X BASIC
*BLUE RC: 2X TO 5X BASIC
STATED ODDS 1:313 HOBBY
STATED PRINT RUN 150 SER.#'d SETS
49 Shohei Ohtani 40.00 100.00

2018 Bowman Gold

*GOLD: 6X TO 15X BASIC
*GOLD RC: 4X TO 10X BASIC
STATED ODDS 1:939 HOBBY
STATED PRINT RUN 50 SER.#'d SETS
49 Shohei Ohtani 75.00 200.00

2018 Bowman Green

*GREEN: 4X TO 10X BASIC
*GREEN RC: 2.5X TO 6X BASIC
STATED ODDS 1:XX RETAIL
STATED PRINT RUN 99 SER.#'d SETS
49 Shohei Ohtani 50.00 120.00

2018 Bowman Orange

*ORANGE: 10X TO 25X BASIC
*ORANGE RC: 6X TO 15X BASIC
STATED ODDS 1:438 HOBBY
STATED PRINT RUN 25 SER.#'d SETS
49 Shohei Ohtani 125.00 300.00

2018 Bowman Purple

*PURPLE: 2.5X TO 6X BASIC
*PURPLE RC: 1.5X TO 4X BASIC
STATED ODDS 1:188 HOBBY
STATED PRINT RUN 250 SER.#'d SETS
49 Shohei Ohtani 30.00 80.00

2018 Bowman Sky Blue

*SKY BLUE: 1.5X TO 4X BASIC
*SKY BLUE RC: 1X TO 2.5X BASIC
STATED ODDS 1:95 HOBBY
STATED PRINT RUN 499 SER.#'d SETS
49 Shohei Ohtani 20.00 50.00

2018 Bowman Big League Breakthrough Redemptions

RANDOM INSERTS IN PACKS
EXCHANGE DEADLINE 9/31/2018
BLAB Austin Beck 4.00 10.00
BLAG Andres Gimenez 8.00 20.00
BLAM Austin Meadows 20.00 50.00
BLAR Austin Riley 15.00 40.00
BLBH Brent Honeywell 5.00 12.00
BLBM Brendan McKay 5.00 12.00
BLCA Chance Adams 10.00 25.00
BLCB Casey Gillaspie 6.00 15.00
BLCR Corey Ray 6.00 15.00
BLDC Dylan Cozens 12.00 30.00
BLEJ Eloy Jimenez 30.00 80.00
BLGT Gleyber Torres 75.00 200.00
BLHG Hunter Greene 12.00 30.00
BLJB Jake Bauers 10.00 25.00
BLJG Jay Groome 4.00 10.00
BLJS Justus Sheffield 12.00 30.00
BLKH Keston Hiura 15.00 40.00
BLKW Kyle Wright 8.00 20.00
BLLR Luis Robert 25.00 60.00
BLLT Leody Taveras 5.00 12.00
BLMC Michael Chavis 5.00 12.00
BLMG MacKenzie Gore 6.00 15.00
BLMK Michael Kopech 15.00 40.00
BLMM Mickey Moniak 8.00 20.00
BLNG Nick Gordon 12.00 30.00
BLNS Nick Senzel 10.00 25.00
BLPS Pavin Smith 5.00 12.00
BLRA Ronald Acuna 100.00 250.00
BLRL Royce Lewis 10.00 25.00
BLRM Ryan Mountcastle 10.00 25.00
BLSB Shane Baz 8.00 20.00
BLSK Scott Kingery 25.00 60.00
BLSS Sixto Sanchez 8.00 20.00
BLTO Tyler O'Neill 25.00 60.00
BLTT Taylor Trammell 8.00 20.00
BLWA Willy Adames 20.00 50.00
BLFTJ Fernando Tatis Jr. 20.00 50.00
BLJSA Jesus Sanchez 5.00 12.00
BLJSO Juan Soto 80.00 200.00
BLVGJ Vladimir Guerrero Jr. 50.00 120.00

2018 Bowman Prospect Autographs

RANDOMLY INSERTED IN RETAIL PACKS
EXCHANGE DEADLINE 3/31/2020
*PURPLE/250: .5X TO 1.2X BASE
*BLUE/150: .6X TO 1.5X BASE
*GREEN/99: .75X TO 2X BASE
*GOLD/50: 1X TO 2.5X BASE
*ORANGE/25: 1.2X TO 3X BASE
PAAK Aaron Knapp 2.50 6.00
PABB Brock Burke 2.50 6.00
PABK Brad Keller 2.50 6.00
PABM Brendan McKay 10.00 25.00
PABMU Brian Mundell 2.50 6.00
PACB Charcer Burks 2.50 6.00
PACC Carl Chester 2.50 6.00
PACF Colby Fitch 2.50 6.00
PADB David Bote 8.00 20.00
PADD Dean Deetz 2.50 6.00
PADM Dustin May 10.00 25.00
PADS Dennis Santana 4.00 10.00
PAEC Edgar Cabral 3.00 8.00
PAEU Erich Uelman 3.00 8.00
PAGT Gleyber Torres 30.00 80.00
PAHF Heath Fillmyer 2.50 6.00
PAHG Hunter Greene 60.00 150.00
PAJG Jose Gomez 2.50 6.00
PAJK Jeren Kendall 3.00 8.00
PAJR JoJo Romero 5.00 12.00
PAMB Matt Beaty 3.00 8.00
PAMD Matthias Dietz 2.50 6.00
PAMG Matt Givin 2.50 6.00
PAMK Mitch Keller 3.00 8.00
PANL Nicky Lopez 6.00 15.00
PANS Nick Solak 5.00 12.00
PAPA Peter Alonso 40.00 100.00
PARL Royce Lewis 12.00 30.00
PASH Sam Hilliard 3.00 8.00
PASS Shea Spitzbarth 3.00 8.00
PATB Trevor Bettencourt 3.00 8.00
PATE Thairo Estrada 10.00 25.00
PAWS Will Smith 20.00 50.00

2018 Bowman Prospects

PRINTING PLATE ODDS 1:7838 HOBBY
PLATE PRINT RUN 1 SET PER COLOR
BLACK-CYAN-MAGENTA-YELLOW ISSUED
NO PLATE PRICING DUE TO SCARCITY
BP1 Ronald Acuna 5.00 12.00
BP2 Bryan Mata .20 .50
BP3 Daniel Johnson .15 .40
BP4 Hunter Harvey .15 .40
BP5 Aaron Knapp .15 .40
BP6 Austin Beck .20 .50
BP7 Carter Kieboom .25 .60
BP8 Cole Ragans .15 .40
BP9 Alex Jackson .15 .40
BP10 Justin Williams .15 .40
BP11 Rowdy Tellez .15 .40
BP12 Thomas Hatch .20 .50
BP13 Sam Hilliard .30 .75
BP14 Kyle Wright .40 1.00
BP15 Tyler O'Neill .25 .60
BP16 Michael Mercado .20 .50
BP17 Kevin Newman .25 .60
BP18 Eric Lauer .20 .50
BP19 Johan Mieses .25 .60
BP20 Will Smith .40 1.00
BP21 Luis Robert 10.00 25.00
BP22 Yadier Alvarez .20 .50
BP23 Jeren Kendall .20 .50
BP24 Bobby Bradley .20 .50
BP25 Drew Ellis .20 .50
BP26 Alfredro Rodriguez .15 .40
BP27 Jose Trevino .15 .40
BP28 Kolby Allard .15 .40
BP29 Taylor Ward .20 .50
BP30 Cornelius Randolph .15 .40
BP31 DJ Peters .40 1.00
BP32 Domingo Acevedo .15 .40
BP33 James Nelson .15 .40
BP34 Josh Ockimey .15 .40
BP35 Marcos Molina .15 .40
BP36 Dennis Santana .15 .40
BP37 Jake Burger .15 .40
BP38 Mitch Keller .20 .50
BP39 Colton Welker .15 .40
BP40 Pedro Avila .15 .40
BP41 Jason Martin .15 .40
BP42 Braxton Garrett .15 .40
BP43 Brendan Rodgers .20 .50
BP44 James Kaprielian .15 .40
BP45 Greg Deichmann .20 .50
BP46 Cristian Pache .75 2.00
BP47 Ibandel Isabel .25 .60
BP48 Hunter Greene .50 1.25
BP49 Nick Gordon .15 .40
BP50 Eloy Jimenez .60 1.50
BP51 Adonis Medina .25 .60
BP52 Juan Soto 4.00 10.00
BP53 Miguelangel Sierra .15 .40
BP54 Alex Lange .15 .40
BP55 Kyle Tucker .40 1.00
BP56 TJ Zeuch .15 .40
BP57 Luis Urias .30 .75
BP58 Sean Murphy .25 .60

BP59 Oscar De La Cruz .15 .40
BP60 Brian Miller .15 .40
BP61 Matt Thaiss .15 .40
BP62 Kyle Cody .15 .40
BP63 Dylan Cozens .15 .40
BP64 MJ Melendez .15 .40
BP65 Scott Kingery .25 .60
BP66 Jordan Humphreys .15 .40
BP67 Michel Baez .15 .40
BP68 Brendan McKay .25 .60
BP69 Justus Sheffield .20 .50
BP70 Merandy Gonzalez .15 .40
BP71 Touki Toussaint .20 .50
BP72 Andres Gimenez .40 1.00
BP73 Adrian Morejon .15 .40
BP74 Austin Voth .15 .40
BP75 Luis Garcia .25 .60
BP76 Isaac Paredes .75 2.00
BP77 Jake Kalish .15 .40
BP78 Shed Long .20 .50
BP79 Keibert Ruiz .75 2.00
BP80 Matt Hall .15 .40
BP81 Nick Pratto .20 .50
BP82 Justin Dunn .20 .50
BP83 Ian Anderson .50 1.25
BP84 Franklyn Kilome .20 .50
BP85 Dane Dunning .50 1.25
BP86 Michael Kopech .60 1.50
BP87 McKenzie Mills .15 .40
BP88 Quentin Holmes .15 .40
BP89 Mike Soroka .50 1.25
BP90 Stephen Gonsalves .15 .40
BP91 Spencer Howard .50 1.25
BP92 Ryan Vilade .15 .40
BP93 Royce Lewis .60 1.50
BP94 Adam Haseley .25 .60
BP95 Jorge Mateo .15 .40
BP96 Junior Fernandez .25 .60
BP97 Corey Ray .20 .50
BP98 Evan White .40 1.00
BP99 Logan Allen .15 .40
BP100 Gleyber Torres 1.50 4.00
BP101 Zack Littell .15 .40
BP102 Matt Sauer .15 .40
BP103 Mitchell White .15 .40
BP104 Nick Solak .60 1.50
BP105 Jorge Ona .15 .40
BP106 D.J. Stewart .15 .40
BP107 D.L. Hall .15 .40
BP108 Chris Rodriguez .15 .40
BP109 Sam Howard .15 .40
BP111 JoJo Romero .20 .50
BP112 Aramis Garcia .15 .40
BP113 Taylor Clarke .15 .40
BP114 Fernando Tatis Jr. 1.50 4.00
BP115 Cal Quantrill .15 .40
BP116 Khalil Lee .15 .40
BP117 C.J. Chatham .20 .50
BP118 Lazaro Armenteros .30 .75
BP119 Gavin LaValley .15 .40
BP120 Nick Senzel .50 1.25
BP121 Jose Adolis Garcia 4.00 10.00
BP122 Ronald Guzman .15 .40
BP123 Jordan Hicks .30 .75
BP124 Alex Faedo .25 .60
BP125 J.B. Bukauskas .15 .40
BP126 Jesus Luzardo .25 .60
BP127 Josh Lowe .15 .40
BP128 Yu-Cheng Chang .20 .50
BP129 Kyle Young .20 .50
BP130 Christin Stewart .20 .50
BP131 MacKenzie Gore .30 .75
BP132 Corbin Burnes 1.25 3.00
BP133 Tyler Stephenson .40 1.00
BP134 Wander Javier .25 .60
BP135 Bryse Wilson .25 .60
BP136 Jo Adell .60 1.50
BP137 Pete Alonso 1.50 4.00
BP138 Delvin Perez .15 .40
BP139 Travis Lakins .15 .40
BP140 Blake Rutherford .20 .50
BP141 Blayne Enlow .15 .40
BP142 A.J. Puk .25 .60
BP143 Heliot Ramos .25 .60
BP144 Jahmai Jones .15 .40
BP145 Adbert Alzolay .20 .50
BP146 Will Craig .15 .40
BP147 Forrest Whitley .25 .60
BP148 Trevor Rogers .40 1.00
BP149 Steven Duggar .15 .40
BP150 Vladimir Guerrero Jr. 1.50 4.00

2018 Bowman Prospects Blue

*BLUE: 1.5X TO 4X BASIC
STATED ODDS 1:209 HOBBY
STATED PRINT RUN 150 SER.#'d SETS

2018 Bowman Prospects Camo

*CAMO: .6X TO 1.5X BASIC
THREE PER RETAIL VALUE PACK

2018 Bowman Prospects Gold

*GOLD: 4X TO 10X BASIC
STATED ODDS 1:711 HOBBY
STATED PRINT RUN 50 SER.#'d SETS

2018 Bowman Prospects Green

GREEN: 2X TO 5X BASIC
STATED ODDS 1:150 RETAIL
STATED PRINT RUN 99 SER.#'d SETS

2018 Bowman Prospects Orange

*ORANGE: 8X TO 20X BASIC
STATED ODDS 1:292 HOBBY
STATED PRINT RUN 25 SER.#'d SETS

2018 Bowman Prospects Purple

*PURPLE: 1.5X TO 4X BASIC
STATED ODDS 1:126 HOBBY
STATED PRINT RUN 250 SER.#'d SETS

2018 Bowman Prospects Sky Blue

*SKY BLUE: 1.2X TO 3X BASIC
STATED ODDS 1:63 HOBBY
STATED PRINT RUN 499 SER.#'d SETS

2018 Bowman Draft

COMPLETE SET (200) 12.00 30.00
STATED PLATE ODDS 1:1198 HOBBY
PLATE PRINT RUN 1 SET PER COLOR
BLACK-CYAN-MAGENTA-YELLOW ISSUED
NO PLATE PRICING DUE TO SCARCITY
BD1 Casey Mize 1.25 3.00
BD2 Matt Vierling .30 .75
BD3 Brusdar Graterol .30 .75
BD4 Lawrence Butler .25 .60
BD5 Terrin Vavra .30 .75
BD6 Jarred Kelenic 6.00 15.00
BD7 Yusniel Diaz .50 1.25
BD8 Lenny Torres .20 .50
BD9 Shane McClanahan .25 .60
BD10 Blayne Enlow .15 .40
BD11 Brice Turang .50 1.25
BD12 Tim Cate .25 .60
BD13 Pedro Avila .15 .40
BD14 Kyle Isbel .40 1.00
BD15 Devin Mann .25 .60
BD16 Jazz Chisholm .60 1.50
BD17 Luis Medina .25 .60
BD18 Adrian Morejon .15 .40
BD19 Arbert Cipion .15 .40
BD20 Trevor Stephan .15 .40
BD21 Drew Ellis .20 .50
BD22 Taylor Trammell .25 .60
BD23 Jayson Schroeder .15 .40
BD24 Joe Jacques .15 .40
BD25 Alec Bohm 4.00 10.00
BD26 Beau Burrows .20 .50
BD27 Jonathan Stiever .15 .40
BD28 Parker Meadows .30 .75
BD29 Jonathan Ornelas .40 1.00
BD30 Matthew Liberatore .20 .50
BD31 Greyson Jenista .25 .60
BD32 Bo Bichette .60 1.50
BD33 Durbin Feltman .25 .60
BD34 Nick Sandlin .15 .40
BD35 Jahmai Jones .15 .40
BD36 Brandon Marsh .25 .60
BD37 Lency Delgado .30 .75
BD38 Nick Madrigal 2.00 5.00
BD39 Kris Bubic .25 .60
BD40 Oneil Cruz .25 .60
BD41 Alex Faedo .25 .60
BD42 Thomas Ponticelli .15 .40
BD43 Bryan Lavastida .15 .40
BD44 Nick Schnell .15 .40
BD45 Cal Mitchell .25 .60
BD46 Nick Solak .60 1.50
BD47 Brennen Davis 1.25 3.00
BD48 Ethan Hankins .20 .50
BD49 Keston Hiura .40 1.00
BD50 Ke'Bryan Hayes .75 2.00
BD51 Jeremiah Jackson .25 .60
BD52 Lolo Sanchez .20 .50
BD53 Gregory Soto .15 .40
BD54 Nicky Lopez .25 .60
BD55 Jake Wong .15 .40
BD56 Jordan Groshans .75 2.00
BD57 Josh Breaux .20 .50
BD58 Hunter Greene .50 1.25
BD59 Dylan Cease .25 .60
BD60 Carlos Cortes .20 .50
BD61 Korry Howell .15 .40
BD62 Joey Wentz .20 .50
BD63 Logan Gilbert .25 .60
BD64 Ryan Rolison .30 .75
BD65 Anthony Seigler .40 1.00
BD66 Jorge Guzman .15 .40
BD67 Mark Vientos .25 .60
BD68 Chris Paddack .40 1.00
BD69 Kole Cottam .20 .50
BD70 Trevor Larnach 1.00 2.50
BD71 Monte Harrison .25 .60
BD72 Aramis Ademan .20 .50
BD73 Grayson Rodriguez .30 .75
BD74 Nick Gordon .15 .40
BD75 Sixto Sanchez .50 1.25
BD76 Joe Gray .25 .60
BD77 Drevian Williams-Nelson .15 .40
BD78 Tanner Dodson .20 .50
BD79 Ryan Vilade .15 .40
BD80 Blake Rivera .15 .40
BD81 Adam Haseley .25 .60
BD82 Braydon Fisher .60 1.50
BD83 Kevon Jackson .15 .40
BD84 Ryder Green .20 .50
BD85 Jawuan Harris .15 .40
BD86 Mitch Keller .20 .50
BD87 Royce Lewis .60 1.50
BD88 Jordyn Adams 2.00 5.00
BD89 Korey Holland .15 .40
BD90 Thad Ward .15 .40
BD91 Sean Murphy .25 .60
BD92 Calvin Coker .15 .40
BD93 Carter Kieboom .25 .60
BD94 Jake McCarthy .25 .60
BD95 Braxton Ashcraft .20 .50
BD96 Colton Eastman .40 1.00
BD97 Mitchell White .15 .40
BD98 Nick Pratto .20 .50
BD99 Alex McKenna .20 .50
BD100 Brendan McKay .25 .60
BD101 Mike Shawaryn .15 .40
BD102 Levi Kelly .15 .40
BD103 Osiris Johnson .20 .50
BD104 Justin Jarvis .15 .40
BD105 Ford Proctor .20 .50
BD106 Ezequiel Pagan .20 .50
BD107 Jo Adell .60 1.50
BD108 Jon Duplantier .15 .40
BD109 Luken Baker .25 .60
BD110 Grant Little .15 .40
BD111 Micah Bello .25 .60
BD112 Jonathan India 2.00 5.00
BD113 Will Banfield .20 .50
BD114 Keibert Ruiz .75 2.00
BD115 Grant Koch .15 .40
BD116 Jeren Kendall .20 .50
BD117 Nolan Gorman 1.00 2.50
BD118 Nate Pearson .50 1.25
BD119 Corbin Martin .15 .40
BD120 Shed Long .20 .50
BD121 Kody Clemens .25 .60
BD122 Josh Naylor .20 .50
BD123 Sheldon Neuse .15 .40
BD124 Nick Decker .30 .75
BD125 Cole Roederer .50 1.25
BD126 Albert Abreu .15 .40
BD127 Dallas Woolfolk .15 .40
BD128 Adonis Medina .25 .60
BD129 Tristan Pompey .15 .40
BD130 Michel Baez .15 .40
BD131 Pavin Smith .25 .60
BD132 Brian Miller .15 .40
BD133 Heliot Ramos .25 .60
BD134 Cadyn Grenier .20 .50
BD135 Brady Singer .75 2.00
BD136 Andres Gimenez .40 1.00
BD137 Griffin Roberts .15 .40
BD138 Greg Deichmann .20 .50
BD139 Sean Hjelle .20 .50
BD140 Kenen Irizarry .25 .60
BD141 Alfonso Rivas .15 .40
BD142 Daniel Lynch .20 .50
BD143 Matt Mercer .15 .40
BD144 Sean Guilbe .20 .50
BD145 Matt Manning .25 .60
BD146 Alec Hansen .15 .40
BD147 Jackson Goddard .15 .40
BD148 Jesus Luzardo .25 .60
BD149 Nick Dunn .50 1.25
BD150 MacKenzie Gore .30 .75
BD151 Jeter Downs .25 .60
BD152 Grant Witherspoon .20 .50
BD153 Griffin Conine .30 .75
BD154 Adam Hill .15 .40
BD155 Alek Thomas .60 1.50
BD156 Tyler Frank .15 .40
BD157 Sean Wymer .15 .40
BD158 Connor Scott .20 .50
BD159 Owen White .25 .60
BD160 Jameson Hannah .25 .60
BD161 Mike Siani .20 .50
BD162 Triston McKenzie .50 1.25
BD163 Bobby Bradley .20 .50
BD164 Mason Denaburg .20 .50
BD165 Nico Hoerner .75 2.00
BD166 Matt Thaiss .15 .40
BD167 Ryan Mountcastle .75 2.00
BD168 Eloy Jimenez .60 1.50
BD169 Logan Allen .15 .40
BD170 Dane Dunning .50 1.25
BD171 Triston Casas 2.00 5.00
BD172 Bryan Mata .20 .50
BD173 Cole Winn .25 .60
BD174 Leury Tejada .15 .40
BD175 Sam Carlson .20 .50
BD176 Raynel Delgado .40 1.00
BD177 Leody Taveras .25 .60
BD178 Justin Dunn .20 .50
BD179 Jeremy Eierman .15 .40
BD180 Jesus Sanchez .25 .60
BD181 Simeon Woods-Richardson .20 .50
BD182 Ryan Weathers .20 .50
BD183 Ian Anderson .50 1.25
BD184 Matt Sauer .15 .40
BD185 Adam Wolf .20 .50
BD186 Grant Lavigne .75 2.00
BD187 Estevan Florial .25 .60
BD188 Luis Robert 5.00 12.00
BD189 J.B. Bukauskas .15 .40
BD190 Josh Stowers .40 1.00
BD191 Brent Rooker .20 .50
BD192 Ryan Jeffers .30 .75
BD193 Noah Naylor .25 .60
BD194 Cody Deason .15 .40
BD195 Cal Quantrill .15 .40
BD196 Jackson Kowar 1.00 2.50
BD197 Griffin Canning .15 .40
BD198 Travis Swaggerty .50 1.25
BD199 Alex Kirilloff .25 .60
BD200 Lazaro Armenteros .30 .75

2018 Bowman Draft Blue

*BLUE: 2X TO 5X BASIC
STATED ODDS 1:32 HOBBY
STATED PRINT RUN 150 SER.#'d SETS
BD117 Nolan Gorman 15.00 40.00

2018 Bowman Draft Gold

*GOLD: 4X TO 10X BASIC
STATED ODDS 1:96 HOBBY
STATED PRINT RUN 50 SER.#'d SETS
BD117 Nolan Gorman 30.00 80.00

2018 Bowman Draft Green

*GREEN: 2.5X TO 6X BASIC
STATED ODDS 1:49 HOBBY
STATED PRINT RUN 99 SER.#'d SETS
BD117 Nolan Gorman 20.00 50.00

2018 Bowman Draft Orange

*ORANGE: 5X TO 12X BASIC
STATED ODDS 1:130 HOBBY
STATED PRINT RUN 25 SER.#'d SETS
BD117 Nolan Gorman 40.00 100.00

2018 Bowman Draft Purple

*PURPLE: 2X TO 5X BASIC
STATED ODDS 1:20 HOBBY
STATED PRINT RUN 250 SER.#'d SETS
BD117 Nolan Gorman 12.00 30.00

2018 Bowman Draft Sky Blue

*SKY BLUE: 1X TO 2.5X BASIC
STATED ODDS 1:10 HOBBY
STATED PRINT RUN 499 SER.#'d SETS
BD117 Nolan Gorman 8.00 20.00

2019 Bowman

COMP.SET w/o SP (100) 10.00 25.00
PRINTING PLATE ODDS 1:13,380 HOBBY
PLATE PRINT RUN 1 SET PER COLOR
BLACK-CYAN-MAGENTA-YELLOW ISSUED
NO PLATE PRICING DUE TO SCARCITY
1 Mike Trout 1.25 3.00
2 Cody Bellinger .50 1.25
3A Joey Wendle .20 .50
3B Bryce Harper SP 12.00 30.00
4 Cedric Mullins RC .50 1.25
5 Kyle Freeland .20 .50
6 Brad Keller RC .25 .60
7 Jonathan Loaisiga RC .30 .75
8 Scooter Gennett .20 .50
9 Khris Davis .25 .60
10 Willy Adames .15 .40
11 Matt Chapman .25 .60
12 Justus Sheffield RC .40 1.00
13 Aaron Nola .20 .50
14 Christian Yelich .30 .75
15 Clayton Kershaw .40 1.00
16 Aaron Judge .60 1.50
17 Trey Mancini .20 .50
18 Anthony Rizzo .30 .75
19 Touki Toussaint RC .30 .75
20 Bryse Wilson RC .30 .75
21 Miguel Cabrera .25 .60
22 Nolan Arenado .40 1.00
23 Salvador Perez .20 .50
24 Willians Astudillo RC .25 .60
25 Luis Urias RC .40 1.00
26 Edwin Diaz .20 .50
27 Yoan Moncada .25 .60
28 Rowdy Tellez RC .40 1.00
29 Taylor Ward RC .25 .60
30 Steven Duggar RC .30 .75
31 Francisco Arcia RC .40 1.00
32 Eugenio Suarez .20 .50
33 Christin Stewart RC .30 .75
34 Shohei Ohtani .40 1.00
35 J.D. Martinez .25 .60
36 Yadier Molina .30 .75
37 Jose Berrios .20 .50
38 Ramon Laureano RC .50 1.25
39 Luis Guillorme RC .25 .60
40 Marcus Stroman .20 .50
41 Zack Greinke .25 .60
42 Chris Shaw RC .25 .60
43 Giancarlo Stanton .25 .60
44 Ryan Borucki RC .25 .60
45 Whit Merrifield .25 .60
46 Chris Archer .15 .40
47 Maikel Franco .20 .50
48 Danny Jansen RC .25 .60
49 David Fletcher RC .75 2.00
50 Mookie Betts .50 1.25
51 Kris Bryant .30 .75
52 Kyle Wright RC .40 1.00
53 Aramis Garcia RC .25 .60
54 Kevin Newman RC .40 1.00
55 Jose Abreu .25 .60
56 Mychal Givens .15 .40
57 Brandon Crawford .20 .50
58 Sean Reid-Foley RC .25 .60
59 Evan Longoria .20 .50
60 Kevin Kramer RC .30 .75
61 Jake Cave RC .30 .75
62 Jose Altuve .20 .50
63 Eddie Rosario .20 .50
64 Justin Verlander .25 .60
65 Corbin Burnes RC 2.00 5.00
66 Jose Ramirez .20 .50
67 DJ Stewart RC .30 .75
68 Starling Marte .20 .50
69 Chance Adams RC .25 .60
70 Enyel De Los Santos RC .25 .60
71 Max Scherzer .25 .60
72 Kolby Allard RC .40 1.00
73 Dakota Hudson RC .30 .75
74 Matt Carpenter .25 .60
75 Michael Kopech RC .75 2.00
76 Jake Bauers RC .40 1.00
77 Rougned Odor .20 .50
78 Ronald Acuna Jr. 1.25 3.00
79 J.T. Realmuto .25 .60
80 Mitch Haniger .20 .50
81 Nicholas Castellanos .25 .60
82 Dawel Lugo RC .40 1.00
83 Amed Rosario .20 .50
84 Adolis Garcia RC 1.50 4.00
85 Paul Goldschmidt .25 .60
86 Eric Hosmer .20 .50
87 Josh James RC .40 1.00
88 Ronald Guzman .15 .40
89 Francisco Lindor .25 .60
90 Jeff McNeil RC .60 1.50
91 Brian Anderson .15 .40
92 Juan Soto .75 2.00
93 Ryan O'Hearn RC .25 .60
94 Kyle Tucker RC .60 1.50
95 Kevin Pillar .15 .40
96 Ozzie Albies .25 .60
97 Josh Hader .20 .50
98 Brandon Lowe RC .40 1.00
99 Wil Myers .20 .50
100 Jacob deGrom .50 1.25

2019 Bowman Gold

*GOLD: 6X TO 15X BASIC
*GOLD RC: 4X TO 10X BASIC
STATED ODDS 1:1067 HOBBY
STATED PRINT RUN 50 SER.#'d SETS
3B Bryce Harper 60.00 150.00

2019 Bowman Green

*GREEN: 4X TO 10X BASIC
*GREEN RC: 2.5X TO 6X BASIC
STATED ODDS 1:212 BLASTER
STATED PRINT RUN 99 SER.#'d SETS
3B Bryce Harper 40.00 100.00

2019 Bowman Orange

*ORANGE: 10X TO 25X BASIC
*ORANGE RC: 6X TO 15X BASIC
STATED ODDS 1:493 HOBBY
STATED PRINT RUN 25 SER.#'d SETS
3B Bryce Harper 100.00 250.00

2019 Bowman Purple

*PURPLE: 2.5X TO 6X BASIC
*PURPLE RC: 1.5X TO 4X BASIC
STATED ODDS 1:214 HOBBY
STATED PRINT RUN 250 SER.#'d SETS
3B Bryce Harper 25.00 60.00

2019 Bowman Sky Blue

*SKY BLUE: 1.5X TO 4X BASIC
*SKY BLUE RC: 1X TO 2.5X BASIC
STATED ODDS 1:107 HOBBY
STATED PRINT RUN 499 SER.#'d SETS
3B Bryce Harper 15.00 40.00

2019 Bowman '89 Bowman Buyback Autographs

STATED ODDS 1:3,299 HOBBY
EXCHANGE DEADLINE 3/31/2021
9 Cal Ripken Jr. 60.00 150.00
26 Roger Clemens 30.00 80.00
41 Bert Blyleven 10.00 25.00
62 Carlton Fisk 25.00 60.00
190 Dennis Eckersley 15.00 40.00
197 Mark McGwire 40.00 100.00
211 Tino Martinez 20.00 50.00
216 Edgar Martinez 50.00 120.00
220 Ken Griffey Jr. 500.00 1000.00
266 John Smoltz 25.00 60.00
276 Dale Murphy 40.00 100.00
290 Ryne Sandberg 20.00 50.00
298 Andre Dawson 25.00 60.00

2019 Bowman Prospect Autographs

STATED ODDS 1:67 BLASTER
EXCHANGE DEADLINE 3/31/2021
*PURPLE/250: .5X TO 1.2X BASE
*BLUE/150: .6X TO 1.5X BASE
*GREEN/99: .75X TO 2X BASE
*GOLD/50: 1X TO 2.5X BASE
*ORANGE/25: 1.2X TO 3X BASE
PAAI Andrew Istler 2.50 6.00
PAAM Alex McKenna 4.00 10.00
PAAR Alex Royalty 2.50 6.00
PAAW Adam Wolf 4.00 10.00
PABB Braden Bishop 3.00 8.00
PABD Brett Daniels 2.50 6.00
PABH Brigham Hill 3.00 8.00
PABT Bo Takahashi 2.50 6.00
PACM Casey Mize 12.00 30.00
PAEJ Eduardo Jimenez 3.00 8.00
PAJB Joey Bart 40.00 100.00
PAJK Jarred Kelenic 30.00 80.00
PAJM James Marvel 4.00 10.00
PAJO James Outman 2.50 6.00
PAJS Jesus Sanchez 4.00 10.00
PAJYC Jing-Yu Chang 6.00 15.00
PALJC Li-Jen Chu 3.00 8.00
PAMK Matt Krook 2.50 6.00
PANA Nick Allen 2.50 6.00
PANH Nolan Hoffman 2.50 6.00
PANM Nick Meyer 2.50 6.00
PAOM Owen Miller 3.00 8.00
PAPO Pablo Olivares 4.00 10.00
PASE Santiago Espinal 4.00 10.00
PASL Shed Long 4.00 10.00
PASS Sterling Sharp 4.00 10.00
PATM Tobias Myers 2.50 6.00
PAYA Yadier Alvarez 2.50 6.00

2019 Bowman Prospects

PRINTING PLATE ODDS 1:8920 HOBBY
PLATE PRINT RUN 1 SET PER COLOR
BLACK-CYAN-MAGENTA-YELLOW ISSUED
NO PLATE PRICING DUE TO SCARCITY
BP1 Vladimir Guerrero Jr. 1.00 2.50
BP2 Alec Bohm 1.00 2.50
BP3 Justin Dunn .15 .40
BP4 Jo Adell .60 1.50
BP5 Victor Victor Mesa .30 .75
BP6 Brusdar Graterol .20 .50
BP7 Tirso Ornelas .15 .40
BP8 Nick Neidert .15 .40
BP9 Taylor Widener .15 .40
BP10 Adrian Morejon .15 .40
BP11 Derian Cruz .15 .40
BP12 Corey Ray .15 .40
BP13 Jarred Kelenic .75 2.00
BP14 Seth Beer 1.00 2.50
BP15 Ethan Hankins .20 .50
BP16 Cole Tucker .25 .60
BP17 A.J. Puk .25 .60
BP18 Leody Taveras .25 .60
BP19 Logan Allen .15 .40
BP20 Blake Rutherford .15 .40
BP21 Freudis Nova .25 .60
BP22 Daniel Johnson .15 .40
BP23 Rylan Bannon .20 .50
BP24 Taylor Trammell .25 .60
BP25 Fernando Tatis Jr. 2.50 6.00
BP26 Beau Burrows .15 .40
BP27 Jay Groome .15 .40
BP28 Adam Haseley .25 .60
BP29 Adonis Medina .25 .60
BP30 Julio Pablo Martinez .15 .40
BP31 Evan White .40 1.00
BP32 Cristian Javier .20 .50
BP33 Julio Rodriguez 3.00 8.00
BP34 Domingo Acevedo .15 .40
BP35 Miguel Amaya .25 .60
BP36 Ryan Vilade .15 .40
BP37 JoJo Romero .15 .40
BP38 Sandro Fabian .15 .40
BP39 Franklyn Kilome .15 .40
BP40 Triston McKenzie .50 1.25
BP41 Ryan Mountcastle .75 2.00
BP42 Jordyn Adams .25 .60
BP43 Nick Senzel .50 1.25
BP44 Luis Robert 1.25 3.00
BP45 Brent Rooker .20 .50
BP46 Anthony Seigler .25 .60
BP47 Ian Anderson .50 1.25
BP48 Griffin Canning .25 .60
BP49 Casey Mize .40 1.00
BP50 Joey Bart .50 1.25
BP51 Hunter Greene .25 .60
BP52 Forrest Whitley .25 .60
BP53 Blaze Alexander .15 .40
BP54 Keston Hiura .50 1.25
BP55 Chris Paddack .30 .75
BP56 Franklin Perez .15 .40
BP57 Joey Wentz .15 .40
BP58 Kevin Smith .15 .40
BP59 Nico Hoerner .50 1.25
BP60 Nolan Gorman .50 1.25
BP61 Jazz Chisholm .60 1.50
BP62 Cristian Pache .40 1.00
BP63 Nick Madrigal .60 1.50
BP64 Luis Garcia .60 1.50
BP65 Colton Welker .15 .40
BP66 Ryan Weathers .15 .40
BP67 Jonathan Duplantier .15 .40
BP68 Reggie Lawson .15 .40
BP69 Orelvis Martinez 1.25 3.00
BP70 Sixto Sanchez .50 1.25
BP71 Ke'Bryan Hayes .75 2.00
BP72 Brewer Hicklen .25 .60
BP73 MacKenzie Gore .30 .75
BP74 Estevan Florial .25 .60
BP75 Cole Winn .15 .40
BP76 Zack Collins .20 .50
BP77 Andres Gimenez .40 1.00
BP78 Alex Faedo .20 .50
BP79 Logan Webb .25 .60
BP80 Dustin May .50 1.25
BP81 Ryan McKenna .15 .40
BP82 Marco Luciano 1.50 4.00
BP83 Heliot Ramos .25 .60
BP84 Aramis Ademan .15 .40
BP85 Matt Manning .25 .60
BP86 Daz Cameron .15 .40
BP87 Chad Spanberger .15 .40
BP88 Brent Honeywell .20 .50
BP89 Esteury Ruiz .20 .50
BP90 Keegan Thompson .15 .40
BP91 Will Smith .40 1.00
BP92 Michael Chavis .25 .60
BP93 Travis Swaggerty .25 .60
BP94 Dane Dunning .50 1.25
BP95 Lyon Richardson .20 .50
BP96 Jesus Luzardo .25 .60
BP97 Noelvi Marte 1.50 4.00
BP98 Carter Kieboom .25 .60
BP99 Nate Pearson .50 1.25
BP100 Wander Franco 10.00 25.00
BP101 Ryan Costello .20 .50
BP102 Jonathan India 1.00 2.50
BP103 Royce Lewis .30 .75
BP104 Victor Mesa Jr. .30 .75
BP105 Brendan McKay .25 .60
BP106 Michel Baez .15 .40
BP107 Ronny Mauricio 1.50 4.00
BP108 Anthony Kay .15 .40
BP109 Yusniel Diaz .25 .60
BP110 Brady Singer .75 2.00
BP111 Bo Bichette .50 1.25
BP112 Matthew Liberatore .15 .40
BP113 Dylan Cease .25 .60
BP114 Edward Cabrera .25 .60
BP115 Jeter Downs .25 .60
BP116 Luken Baker .20 .50
BP117 Shane Baz .15 .40
BP118 Keibert Ruiz .75 2.00
BP119 Jonathan Hernandez .15 .40
BP120 Matt Mercer .15 .40
BP121 Ryan Helsley .20 .50
BP122 Cole Ragans .15 .40
BP123 Yordan Alvarez .75 2.00
BP124 DJ Peters .25 .60
BP125 Cal Quantrill .15 .40
BP126 Drew Waters .50 1.25
BP127 Peter Alonso 1.25 3.00
BP128 MJ Melendez .25 .60
BP129 Austin Riley .75 2.00
BP130 Gavin Lux .60 1.50
BP131 Brandon Marsh .25 .60
BP132 Andrew Knizner .25 .60
BP133 Mitch Keller .20 .50
BP134 Cristian Santana .60 1.50
BP135 Jesus Sanchez .25 .60
BP136 Peter Lambert .25 .60
BP137 Brock Burke .15 .40
BP138 Alex Kirilloff .25 .60
BP139 DL Hall .15 .40
BP140 Bryan Mata .15 .40
BP141 Austin Beck .15 .40
BP142 Genesis Cabrera .25 .60
BP143 Brendan Rodgers .25 .60
BP144 Sean Murphy .20 .50
BP145 Roberto Ramos .20 .50
BP146 Ronaldo Hernandez .15 .40
BP147 Albert Abreu .15 .40
BP148 William Contreras .20 .50
BP149 Jose de la Cruz .50 1.25
BP150 Eloy Jimenez .60 1.50

2019 Bowman Prospects Blue

*BLUE: 1.5X TO 4X BASIC
STATED ODDS 1:238 HOBBY
STATED PRINT RUN 150 SER.#'d SETS

2019 Bowman Prospects Camo

*CAMO: .6X TO 1.5X BASIC
THREE PER RETAIL VALUE PACK

2019 Bowman Prospects Gold

*GOLD: 4X TO 10X BASIC
STATED ODDS 1:626 HOBBY
STATED PRINT RUN 50 SER.#'d SETS
BP1 Vladimir Guerrero Jr. 30.00 80.00
BP50 Joey Bart 50.00 120.00

2019 Bowman Prospects Green

*GREEN: 2X TO 5X BASIC
STATED ODDS 1:141 BLASTER
STATED PRINT RUN 99 SER.#'d SETS
BP1 Vladimir Guerrero Jr. 15.00 40.00

2019 Bowman Prospects Orange

*ORANGE: 8X TO 20X BASIC
STATED ODDS 1:329 HOBBY
STATED PRINT RUN 25 SER.#'d SETS
BP1 Vladimir Guerrero Jr. 60.00 150.00
BP50 Joey Bart 100.00 250.00

2019 Bowman Prospects Purple

*PURPLE: 1.5X TO 4X BASIC
STATED ODDS 1:143 HOBBY
STATED PRINT RUN 250 SER.#'d SETS

2019 Bowman Prospects Sky Blue

*SKY BLUE: 1.2X TO 3X BASIC
STATED ODDS 1:72 HOBBY
STATED PRINT RUN 499 SER.#'d SETS

2019 Bowman Draft

COMPLETE SET (200) 12.00 30.00
STATED PLATE ODDS 1:1241 HOBBY
PLATE PRINT RUN 1 SET PER COLOR
BLACK-CYAN-MAGENTA-YELLOW ISSUED
NO PLATE PRICING DUE TO SCARCITY
BD1 Adley Rutschman 3.00 8.00
BD2 Jarred Kelenic .75 2.00
BD3 Alek Manoah .30 .75
BD4 Grant McCray .25 .60
BD5 Brock Deatherage .15 .40
BD6 Matt Wallner .30 .75
BD7 Josh Jung 1.50 4.00
BD8 Andres Gimenez .40 1.00
BD9 Jackson Kowar .50 1.25
BD10 Logan Davidson .15 .40
BD11 Isaiah Campbell .30 .75
BD12 Blake Walston .25 .60
BD13 Izzy Wilson .15 .40
BD14 Yordys Valdes .30 .75
BD15 Alec Marsh .20 .50
BD16 Ryan Zeferjahn .20 .50
BD17 Brady McConnell .25 .60
BD18 Jordan Groshans .30 .75
BD19 Sammy Siani .20 .50
BD20 Kristian Robinson .75 2.00
BD21 Eric Pardinho .20 .50
BD22 Gunnar Henderson .30 .75
BD23 Joseph Ortiz .20 .50
BD24 Justin Slaten .15 .40
BD25 Drew Waters .50 1.25
BD26 Cal Mitchell .25 .60
BD27 Daniel Espino .20 .50
BD28 Ethan Small .20 .50
BD29 Logan Wyatt .25 .60
BD30 Estevan Florial .25 .60
BD31 Hunter Bishop 1.50 4.00
BD32 Thomas Dillard .30 .75
BD33 DL Hall .15 .40
BD34 T.J. Sikkema .25 .60
BD35 Dominic Fletcher .15 .40
BD36 Antoine Kelly .30 .75
BD37 Albert Abreu .15 .40
BD38 Mateo Gil .20 .50
BD39 Brett Baty 1.25 3.00
BD40 Brandon Lewis .25 .60
BD41 Jamari Baylor .40 1.00
BD42 Nolan Gorman .50 1.25
BD43 Jack Little .25 .60
BD44 Quinn Priester .20 .50
BD45 Freudis Nova .25 .60
BD46 Royce Lewis .30 .75
BD47 Tyler Callihan .20 .50
BD48 Matthew Allan 1.25 3.00
BD49 Will Stewart .15 .40
BD50 Riley Greene 2.00 5.00
BD51 Ethan Hankins .20 .50
BD52 Derian Cruz .15 .40
BD53 Andre Pallante .20 .50
BD54 Dane Dunning .50 1.25
BD55 Matt Mercer .15 .40
BD56 Chris Murphy .15 .40
BD57 Michael Busch .50 1.25
BD58 James Beard .50 1.25
BD59 Braden Shewmake .50 1.25
BD60 Julio Rodriguez 1.25 3.00
BD61 JJ Goss .20 .50
BD62 Ronny Mauricio .40 1.00
BD63 Dasan Brown .40 1.00
BD64 Michael Toglia .75 2.00
BD65 Keoni Cavaco .40 1.00
BD66 Greg Jones .75 2.00
BD67 Shea Langeliers 1.00 2.50
BD68 Evan Fitterer .40 1.00
BD69 Hudson Head .75 2.00
BD70 Tony Locey .20 .50
BD71 Julio Pablo Martinez .15 .40
BD72 Jake Agnos .25 .60
BD73 Matt Gorski .25 .60
BD74 Peyton Burdick .60 1.50
BD75 Brewer Hicklen .25 .60
BD76 Kyle Stowers .25 .60
BD77 Erik Rivera .30 .75
BD78 Leonardo Jimenez .25 .60
BD79 Bryson Stott 1.50 4.00
BD80 Cristian Santana .25 .60
BD81 Davis Wendzel .25 .60
BD82 Jake Sanford .30 .75
BD83 Casey Golden .25 .60
BD84 Tirso Ornelas .15 .40
BD85 CJ Abrams 3.00 8.00
BD86 Josh Smith .30 .75
BD87 Triston Casas .60 1.50
BD88 Victor Victor Mesa .30 .75
BD89 Sixto Sanchez .50 1.25
BD90 Seth Johnson .15 .40
BD91 Ryan Jensen .25 .60
BD92 Tim Tebow .75 2.00
BD93 Wander Franco 3.00 8.00
BD94 Matthew Thompson .20 .50
BD95 Jake Mangum .60 1.50
BD96 Jake Guenther .20 .50
BD97 Jonathan India 1.00 2.50
BD98 Jack Kochanowicz .20 .50
BD99 Noah Song .50 1.25
BD100 Andrew Vaughn 2.50 6.00
BD101 Anthony Prato .15 .40
BD102 Domingo Acevedo .15 .40
BD103 MacKenzie Gore .30 .75
BD104 Zack Thompson .25 .60
BD105 Nick Quintana .30 .75
BD106 Kyle Isbel .20 .50
BD107 Ryan Weathers .15 .40
BD108 Andre Lipcius .20 .50
BD109 Tyler Baum .20 .50
BD110 Conner Capel .20 .50
BD111 Michael Massey .20 .50
BD112 Diosbel Arias .15 .40
BD113 Brandon Williamson .25 .60
BD114 Jeter Downs .25 .60
BD115 George Kirby .25 .60
BD116 Graeme Stinson .15 .40
BD117 Brent Rooker .20 .50
BD118 Eric Yang .20 .50
BD119 Josh Wolf .20 .50
BD120 Andrew Schultz .15 .40
BD121 Grayson Rodriguez .30 .75
BD122 MJ Melendez .25 .60
BD123 Bryant Packard .25 .60
BD124 Aramis Ademan .15 .40
BD125 Corbin Carroll 1.25 3.00
BD126 Kyle McCann .20 .50
BD127 Matthew Liberatore .15 .40
BD128 Beau Philip .25 .60
BD129 Aaron Schunk .30 .75

BD130 Brice Turang .20 .50
BD131 Rece Hinds 1.00 2.50
BD132 Jimmy Lewis .15 .40
BD133 Will Robertson .25 .60
BD134 Joey Bart .50 1.25
BD135 Miguel Amaya .25 .60
BD136 Jonathan Ornelas .20 .50
BD137 Vince Fernandez .20 .50
BD138 Grant Gambrell .20 .50
BD139 Matthew Lugo .25 .60
BD140 Korey Lee .30 .75
BD141 Nasim Nunez .15 .40
BD142 Denyi Reyes .20 .50
BD143 Moises Gomez .25 .60
BD144 John Rave .15 .40
BD145 Grae Kessinger .25 .60
BD146 Isiah Gilliam .20 .50
BD147 Ryne Nelson .20 .50
BD148 Ryan Garcia .15 .40
BD149 Matt Canterino .20 .50
BD150 J.J. Bleday 2.00 5.00
BD151 Ryan Costello .20 .50
BD152 Tyler Fitzgerald .20 .50
BD153 Spencer Steer .15 .40
BD154 Jose Devers .25 .60
BD155 Blaze Alexander .15 .40
BD156 John Doxakis .20 .50
BD157 Armani Smith .50 1.25
BD158 Jordyn Adams .25 .60
BD159 Sean Hjelle .20 .50
BD160 Cristian Javier .20 .50
BD161 Jared Triolo .25 .60
BD162 Alec Bohm 1.00 2.50
BD163 Jahmai Jones .15 .40
BD164 Deivi Garcia 1.50 4.00
BD165 Brennan Malone .15 .40
BD166 Cameron Cannon .30 .75
BD167 Glenallen Hill Jr. .25 .60
BD168 Evan Edwards .15 .40
BD169 Shervyen Newton .25 .60
BD170 Travis Swaggerty .25 .60
BD171 Anthony Seigler .25 .60
BD172 Evan White .40 1.00
BD173 Luken Baker .20 .50
BD174 Trejyn Fletcher .25 .60
BD175 Spencer Brickhouse .40 1.00
BD176 Daulton Varsho .25 .60
BD177 Hayden Wesneski .20 .50
BD178 Chase Strumpf .75 2.00
BD179 Logan Gilbert .25 .60
BD180 Joshua Mears .75 2.00
BD181 Matt Vierling .25 .60
BD182 Will Wilson .75 2.00
BD183 Logan Driscoll .25 .60
BD184 Tyler Freeman .15 .40
BD185 Ian Anderson .50 1.25
BD186 Owen Miller .20 .50
BD187 Kody Hoese 1.00 2.50
BD188 Grant Lavigne .20 .50
BD189 Nick Lodolo .30 .75
BD190 Clarke Schmidt .25 .60
BD191 Erik Miller .40 1.00
BD192 Seth Beer .40 1.00
BD193 Alejandro Kirk .60 1.50
BD194 Drey Jameson .15 .40
BD195 Christian Cairo .25 .60
BD196 Kameron Misner .40 1.00
BD197 Tommy Henry .20 .50
BD198 Lazaro Armenteros .20 .50
BD199 Kendall Williams .25 .60
BD200 Cooper Johnson .25 .60

2019 Bowman Draft Blue

*BLUE: 2X TO 5X BASIC
STATED ODDS 1:34 HOBBY
STATED PRINT RUN 150 SER.#'d SETS

2019 Bowman Draft Gold

*GOLD: 4X TO 10X BASIC
STATED ODDS 1:100 HOBBY
STATED PRINT RUN 50 SER.#'d SETS

2019 Bowman Draft Green

*GREEN: 2.5X TO 6X BASIC
STATED ODDS 1:51 HOBBY
STATED PRINT RUN 99 SER.#'d SETS

2019 Bowman Draft Orange

*ORANGE: 5X TO 12X BASIC
STATED ODDS 1:134 HOBBY
STATED PRINT RUN 25 SER.#'d SETS

2019 Bowman Draft Purple

*PURPLE: 2X TO 5X BASIC
STATED ODDS 1:20 HOBBY
STATED PRINT RUN 250 SER.#'d SETS

2019 Bowman Draft Sky Blue

*SKY BLUE: 1X TO 2.5X BASIC
STATED ODDS 1:10 HOBBY
STATED PRINT RUN 499 SER.#'d SETS

2020 Bowman

COMPLETE SET (100) 10.00 25.00
PRINTING PLATE ODDS 1:17,308 HOBBY
PLATE PRINT RUN 1 SET PER COLOR
BLACK-CYAN-MAGENTA-YELLOW ISSUED
NO PLATE PRICING DUE TO SCARCITY
1 Mike Trout 1.25 3.00
2 Aaron Judge .60 1.50
3 Ketel Marte .20 .50
4 Francisco Lindor .25 .60
5 Isan Diaz RC .40 1.00
6 Jordan Yamamoto RC .25 .60
7 Mike Soroka .25 .60
8 Cavan Biggio .30 .75
9 Max Muncy .20 .50
10 Juan Soto .75 2.00
11 Sean Murphy RC .40 1.00
12 Rhys Hoskins .30 .75
13 Shane Bieber .25 .60
14 Willie Calhoun .15 .40
15 Justin Dunn RC .30 .75
16 Travis Demeritte RC .40 1.00
17 Anthony Kay RC .25 .60
18 Luis Robert RC 2.00 5.00
19 Adbert Alzolay RC .30 .75
20 Bobby Bradley RC .25 .60
21 Ramon Laureano .20 .50
22 Kris Bryant .30 .75
23 Abraham Toro RC .30 .75
24 Randy Arozarena RC 2.50 6.00
25 Yordan Alvarez RC 2.50 6.00
26 Shohei Ohtani .40 1.00
27 Ronald Acuna Jr. 1.00 2.50
28 Lorenzo Cain .15 .40
29 Eduardo Escobar .15 .40
30 Matthew Boyd .15 .40
31 Bryan Reynolds .20 .50
32 Jose Berrios .20 .50
33 Nolan Arenado .40 1.00
34 John Means .25 .60
35 Logan Allen RC .25 .60
36 Robel Garcia RC .25 .60
37 Whit Merrifield .25 .60
38 Dustin May RC .75 2.00
39 Junior Fernandez RC .25 .60
40 Aaron Civale RC .50 1.25
41 George Springer .20 .50
42 Michel Baez RC .25 .60
43 Joey Votto .25 .60
44 Seth Brown RC .25 .60
45 Mookie Betts .50 1.25
46 Austin Nola RC .40 1.00
47 Fernando Tatis Jr. 1.25 3.00
48 Zack Collins RC .30 .75
49 Eddie Rosario .20 .50
50 Vladimir Guerrero Jr. .40 1.00
51 Dan Vogelbach .15 .40
52 Bo Bichette RC 3.00 8.00
53 Max Scherzer .25 .60
54 Bryce Harper .40 1.00
55 Paul DeJong .25 .60
56 Luis Castillo .20 .50
57 Francisco Mejia .20 .50
58 Dylan Cease RC .40 1.00
59 Lucas Giolito .20 .50
60 Jose Urena .15 .40
61 Jesus Luzardo RC .50 1.25
62 Kevin Newman .25 .60
63 Tony Gonsolin RC 1.00 2.50
64 A.J. Puk RC .40 1.00
65 Adrian Morejon RC .25 .60
66 Yu Chang RC .40 1.00
67 Sheldon Neuse RC .30 .75
68 Blake Snell .20 .50
69 Alex Young RC .25 .60
70 Nomar Mazara .15 .40
71 Gavin Lux RC 2.50 6.00
72 Nico Hoerner RC 1.00 2.50
73 Matt Chapman .25 .60
74 Gleyber Torres .50 1.25
75 Zac Gallen RC .60 1.50
76 Mauricio Dubon RC .30 .75
77 Jeff McNeil .20 .50
78 Kyle Lewis RC 2.50 6.00
79 Aristides Aquino RC .60 1.50
80 Yusei Kikuchi .20 .50
81 Willy Adames .15 .40
82 Trevor Story .25 .60
83 Trent Grisham RC 1.00 2.50
84 Starlin Castro .15 .40
85 Cody Bellinger .50 1.25
86 Buster Posey .30 .75
87 Hanser Alberto .15 .40
88 Jose Altuve .20 .50
89 Brusdar Graterol RC .40 1.00
90 Andres Munoz RC .40 1.00
91 Hunter Dozier .15 .40
92 Mike Yastrzemski .40 1.00
93 Miguel Cabrera .25 .60
94 Jack Flaherty .25 .60
95 Xander Bogaerts .25 .60
96 Nick Solak RC 1.00 2.50
97 Tim Anderson .25 .60
98 Pete Alonso .60 1.50
99 Javier Baez .30 .75
100 Christian Yelich .30 .75

2020 Bowman '90 Bowman Buyback Autographs

STATED ODDS 1:3499 HOBBY
PRINT RUNS B/WN 20-50 COPIES PER
EXCHANGE DEADLINE 3/31/2022
268 Roger Clemens/20 30.00 80.00
320 Frank Thomas/50 75.00 200.00
404 Robin Yount/50 25.00 60.00

2020 Bowman 1st Edition

BFE1 Wander Franco 3.00 8.00
BFE2 Drew Waters .50 1.25
BFE3 Jacob Amaya .75 2.00
BFE4 Kody Hoese .60 1.50
BFE5 Cristian Pache .60 1.50
BFE6 Zack Thompson .20 .50
BFE7 Briam Campusano .20 .50
BFE8 Jasson Dominguez 100.00 250.00
BFE9 Aaron Shortridge .25 .60
BFE10 Xavier Edwards .75 2.00
BFE11 Jesus Sanchez .30 .75
BFE12 Ronaldo Hernandez .20 .50
BFE13 Blake Rutherford .20 .50
BFE14 Ulrich Bojarski .30 .75
BFE15 Jordyn Adams .25 .60
BFE16 Austin Beck .25 .60
BFE17 Niko Hulsizer .50 1.25
BFE18 Triston Casas .50 1.25
BFE19 Julio Rodriguez 1.25 3.00
BFE20 Shane Baz .20 .50
BFE21 Shea Langeliers .40 1.00
BFE22 Grayson Rodriguez .30 .75
BFE23 Ruben Cardenas .25 .60
BFE24 Mason Denaburg .20 .50
BFE25 Bobby Witt Jr. 10.00 25.00
BFE26 Andrew Vaughn .75 2.00
BFE27 Kristian Robinson .60 1.50
BFE28 Ronny Mauricio .50 1.25
BFE29 Alec Bohm 1.25 3.00
BFE30 Jhon Diaz .60 1.50
BFE31 Estevan Florial .30 .75
BFE32 Elehuris Montero .25 .60
BFE33 Sam Huff .40 1.00
BFE34 Zack Brown .20 .50
BFE35 Brice Turang .20 .50
BFE36 Ryan Mountcastle 1.00 2.50
BFE37 Wilfred Astudillo .25 .60
BFE38 Gus Varland .25 .60
BFE39 Nick Lodolo .30 .75
BFE40 Tyler Freeman .25 .60
BFE41 Rece Hinds .25 .60
BFE42 Brady Singer 1.00 2.50
BFE43 Cal Mitchell .20 .50
BFE44 Ethan Hankins .25 .60
BFE45 Daz Cameron .20 .50
BFE46 Sherten Apostel 1.00 2.50
BFE47 Hunter Greene .30 .75
BFE48 Josiah Gray .30 .75
BFE49 Brailyn Marquez .50 1.25
BFE50 Adley Rutschman 1.25 3.00
BFE51 Everson Pereira .50 1.25
BFE52 Bayron Lora 8.00 20.00
BFE53 Clarke Schmidt .30 .75
BFE54 Brady McConnell .25 .60
BFE55 Spencer Howard .60 1.50
BFE56 Cristian Javier .25 .60
BFE57 Aaron Ashby .20 .50
BFE58 Logan Gilbert .25 .60
BFE59 Glenallen Hill Jr. .30 .75
BFE60 Alvaro Seijas .20 .50
BFE61 Jeremy Pena .50 1.25
BFE62 CJ Abrams .60 1.50
BFE63 Franklin Perez .20 .50
BFE64 Tanner Houck .50 1.25
BFE65 Damon Jones .25 .60
BFE66 Nolan Gorman .40 1.00
BFE67 Ke'Bryan Hayes 1.00 2.50
BFE68 Bryson Stott .50 1.25
BFE69 Canaan Smith .30 .75
BFE70 Forrest Whitley .30 .75
BFE71 Drew Mendoza .50 1.25
BFE72 Jazz Chisholm .75 2.00
BFE73 Jonathan India 1.25 3.00
BFE74 MacKenzie Gore .40 1.00
BFE75 Seth Beer .40 1.00
BFE76 Joey Cantillo .20 .50
BFE77 Evan White .50 1.25
BFE78 Chris Vallimont .20 .50
BFE79 Sixto Sanchez .60 1.50
BFE80 Alex Kirilloff .40 1.00
BFE81 Tristen Lutz .25 .60
BFE82 Freudis Nova .20 .50
BFE83 Tim Cate .20 .50
BFE84 Daniel Lynch .20 .50
BFE85 Antonio Cabello .60 1.50
BFE86 Bobby Dalbec 1.25 3.00
BFE87 Colton Welker .20 .50
BFE88 Logan Davidson .25 .60
BFE89 Matthew Liberatore .25 .60
BFE90 Adam Hall .25 .60
BFE91 Jackson Rutledge .30 .75
BFE92 Dane Dunning .60 1.50
BFE93 Royce Lewis .50 1.25
BFE94 Jarred Kelenic 1.00 2.50
BFE95 Nolan Jones .30 .75
BFE96 Jerar Encarnacion .60 1.50
BFE97 Ian Anderson .60 1.50
BFE98 Alek Thomas .25 .60
BFE99 Matt Manning .25 .60
BFE100 Jo Adell .75 2.00
BFE101 Nick Madrigal .75 2.00
BFE102 Owen Miller .20 .50
BFE103 Marco Luciano .75 2.00
BFE104 Jordan Groshans .40 1.00
BFE105 Nick Allen .20 .50
BFE106 Dylan Carlson .75 2.00
BFE107 Cole Winn .20 .50
BFE108 Tarik Skubal 1.00 2.50
BFE109 Oscar Gonzalez .40 1.00
BFE110 Aramis Ademan .20 .50
BFE111 Oneil Cruz .25 .60
BFE112 Joey Bart .60 1.50
BFE113 Josh Jung .50 1.25
BFE114 Luis Garcia .75 2.00
BFE115 Jasseel De La Cruz .30 .75
BFE116 J.J. Bleday .60 1.50
BFE117 Joe Ryan .25 .60
BFE118 Keoni Cavaco .20 .50
BFE119 Hans Crouse .20 .50
BFE120 Isaac Paredes .60 1.50
BFE121 Grant Lavigne .20 .50
BFE122 Riley Greene .75 2.00
BFE123 Jordan Balazovic .40 1.00
BFE124 Nate Pearson .60 1.50
BFE125 Deivi Garcia 1.00 2.50
BFE126 Luis Garcia .75 2.00
BFE127 Leody Taveras .30 .75
BFE128 Bryan Mata .20 .50
BFE129 Hunter Bishop .40 1.00
BFE130 Taylor Trammell .30 .75
BFE131 Miguel Vargas .50 1.25
BFE132 Luis Gil .25 .60
BFE133 Grant Little .25 .60
BFE134 Gunnar Henderson .25 .60
BFE135 Eric Pardinho .25 .60
BFE136 Miguel Amaya .20 .50
BFE137 Ryan Rolison .25 .60
BFE138 Jorge Mateo .25 .60
BFE139 Anthony Volpe .75 2.00
BFE140 Nick Bennett .25 .60
BFE141 Brennen Davis .40 1.00
BFE142 Casey Mize .60 1.50
BFE143 Keibert Ruiz 1.00 2.50
BFE144 Jarren Duran .75 2.00
BFE145 Robert Puason 8.00 20.00
BFE146 Travis Swaggerty .25 .60
BFE147 Will Wilson .25 .60
BFE148 Heliot Ramos .30 .75
BFE149 Alek Manoah .25 .60
BFE150 Luis Robert 5.00 12.00

2020 Bowman 1st Edition Blue Foil

*BLUE FOIL: 3X TO 8X BASIC
STATED ODDS 1:10 PACKS
STATED PRINT RUN 150 SER.#'d SETS
BFE8 Jasson Dominguez 600.00 1500.00
BFE25 Bobby Witt Jr. 100.00 250.00
BFE50 Adley Rutschman 20.00 50.00
BFE52 Bayron Lora 60.00 120.00

2020 Bowman 1st Edition Gold Foil

*GOLD FOIL: X TO X BASIC
STATED ODDS 1:28 PACKS
STATED PRINT RUN 50 SER.#'d SETS
BFE8 Jasson Dominguez 1250.00 3000.00
BFE25 Bobby Witt Jr. 200.00 500.00
BFE50 Adley Rutschman 60.00 150.00
BFE52 Bayron Lora 100.00 250.00

2020 Bowman 1st Edition Orange Foil

*ORANGE FOIL: X TO X BASIC
STATED ODDS 1:56 PACKS
STATED PRINT RUN 25 SER.#'d SETS
BFE8 Jasson Dominguez 1500.00 4000.00
BFE25 Bobby Witt Jr. 400.00 1000.00
BFE50 Adley Rutschman 75.00 200.00
BFE52 Bayron Lora 125.00 300.00

2020 Bowman 1st Edition Sky Blue Foil

*SKY BLUE FOIL: X TO X BASIC
STATED ODDS 1:2 PACKS
BFE8 Jasson Dominguez 300.00 800.00
BFE25 Bobby Witt Jr. 60.00 150.00

2020 Bowman 1st Edition Yellow Foil

*YELLOW FOIL: X TO X BASIC
STATED ODDS 1:19 PACKS
STATED PRINT RUN 75 SER.#'d SETS
BFE8 Jasson Dominguez 800.00 2000.00
BFE25 Bobby Witt Jr. 150.00 400.00
BFE50 Adley Rutschman 40.00 100.00
BFE52 Bayron Lora 60.00 150.00

2020 Bowman Blue

*BLUE: 3X TO 8X BASIC
*BLUE RC: 2X TO 5X BASIC
STATED ODDS 1:460 HOBBY
STATED PRINT RUN 150 SER.#'d SETS
1 Mike Trout 12.00 30.00
18 Luis Robert 20.00 50.00
25 Yordan Alvarez 15.00 40.00
52 Bo Bichette 20.00 50.00

2020 Bowman Gold

*GOLD: 6X TO 15X BASIC
*GOLD RC: 4X TO 10X BASIC
STATED ODDS 1:1378 HOBBY
STATED PRINT RUN 50 SER.#'d SETS
1 Mike Trout 25.00 60.00
18 Luis Robert 40.00 100.00
25 Yordan Alvarez 30.00 80.00
52 Bo Bichette 40.00 100.00

2020 Bowman Green

*GREEN: 4X TO 10X BASIC
*GREEN RC: 2.5X TO 6X BASIC
STATED ODDS 1:326 BLASTER
STATED PRINT RUN 99 SER.#'d SETS
1 Mike Trout 15.00 40.00
18 Luis Robert 25.00 60.00
25 Yordan Alvarez 20.00 50.00
52 Bo Bichette 25.00 60.00

2020 Bowman Orange

*ORANGE: 10X TO 25X BASIC
*ORANGE RC: 6X TO 15X BASIC
STATED ODDS 1:551 HOBBY
STATED PRINT RUN 25 SER.#'d SETS
1 Mike Trout 40.00 100.00
18 Luis Robert 60.00 150.00
25 Yordan Alvarez 50.00 120.00
52 Bo Bichette 60.00 150.00

2020 Bowman Purple

*PURPLE: 2.5X TO 6X BASIC
*PURPLE RC: 1.5X TO 4X BASIC
STATED ODDS 1:276 HOBBY
STATED PRINT RUN 250 SER.#'d SETS
1 Mike Trout 10.00 25.00
18 Luis Robert 15.00 40.00
25 Yordan Alvarez 12.00 30.00
52 Bo Bichette 15.00 40.00

2020 Bowman Sky Blue

*SKY BLUE: 1.5X TO 4X BASIC
*SKY BLUE RC: 1X TO 2.5X BASIC
STATED ODDS 1:138 HOBBY
STATED PRINT RUN 499 SER.#'d SETS
1 Mike Trout 6.00 15.00
18 Luis Robert 10.00 25.00
25 Yordan Alvarez 8.00 20.00
52 Bo Bichette 10.00 25.00

2020 Bowman Yellow

*YELLOW: 5X TO 12X BASIC
*YELLOW RC: 3X TO 8X BASIC
STATED ODDS 1:326 BLASTER
STATED PRINT RUN 99 SER.#'d SETS
1 Mike Trout 20.00 50.00
18 Luis Robert 30.00 80.00
25 Yordan Alvarez 25.00 60.00
52 Bo Bichette 30.00 80.00

2020 Bowman Prospect Autographs

STATED ODDS 1:62 BLASTER
EXCHANGE DEADLINE 3/31/2022
*PURPLE/250: .5X TO 1.2X BASE
*BLUE/150: .6X TO 1.5X BASE
*GREEN/99: .75X TO 2X BASE
*GOLD/50: 1X TO 2.5X BASE
*ORANGE/25: 1.2X TO 3X BASE
PAAB Andrew Bechtold 2.50 6.00
PAAR Adley Rutschman 30.00 80.00
PAASH Avery Short 2.50 6.00
PABC Briam Campusano 2.50 6.00
PABWJ Bobby Witt Jr. 75.00 200.00
PACB Colin Barber 8.00 20.00
PACM Casey Mize 30.00 80.00
PACS Cole Stobbe 2.50 6.00
PAEW Eli White 3.00 8.00
PAIM Ian McKinney 2.50 6.00
PAJC Joey Cantillo 5.00 12.00
PAJCB Jacob Condra-Bogan 2.50 6.00
PAJD Jhoan Duran 4.00 10.00
PAJJ Joe Jacques 2.50 6.00
PAJR John Rave 2.50 6.00
PAKB Kris Bubic 4.00 10.00
PAKH Kody Hoese 8.00 20.00
PAKP Konnor Pilkington 2.50 6.00
PAKR Kristian Robinson 15.00 40.00
PAKW Ken Waldichuk 6.00 15.00
PALI Logan Ice 2.50 6.00
PALJ Liam Jenkins 2.50 6.00
PAMIM Michael Mercado 3.00 8.00
PAMM Matt Manning 3.00 8.00
PAMME MJ Melendez 2.50 6.00
PAMS Mitch Stallings 2.50 6.00
PANP Nick Pratto 2.50 6.00
PAOM Orelvis Martinez 6.00 15.00
PAPC Pedro Castellanos 3.00 8.00
PARH Rece Hinds 3.00 8.00
PARK Ryan Kreidler 3.00 8.00
PASC Sam Carlson 5.00 12.00
PASH Spencer Howard 8.00 20.00
PASHE Sam Hentges 2.50 6.00
PATB Tyler Baum 2.50 6.00
PATF Tyler Fitzgerald 3.00 8.00
PATM Trevor McDonald 2.50 6.00
PAWF Wander Franco 75.00 200.00
PAWS Will Stewart 2.50 6.00
PAWT Will Toffey 2.50 6.00
PAZB Zack Brown 2.50 6.00

2020 Bowman Prospects

PRINTING PLATE ODDS 1:11,389 HOBBY
PLATE PRINT RUN 1 SET PER COLOR
BLACK-CYAN-MAGENTA-YELLOW ISSUED
NO PLATE PRICING DUE TO SCARCITY
BP1 Wander Franco 1.50 4.00
BP2 Drew Waters .40 1.00
BP3 Jacob Amaya .60 1.50
BP4 Kody Hoese .50 1.25
BP5 Cristian Pache .50 1.25
BP6 Zack Thompson .15 .40
BP7 Briam Campusano .15 .40
BP8 Jasson Dominguez 12.00 30.00
BP9 Aaron Shortridge .20 .50
BP10 Xavier Edwards .60 1.50
BP11 Jesus Sanchez .25 .60
BP12 Ronaldo Hernandez .15 .40
BP13 Blake Rutherford .15 .40
BP14 Ulrich Bojarski .25 .60
BP15 Jordyn Adams .20 .50
BP16 Austin Beck .20 .50
BP17 Niko Hulsizer .40 1.00
BP18 Triston Casas .40 1.00
BP19 Julio Rodriguez 1.00 2.50
BP20 Shane Baz .15 .40
BP21 Shea Langeliers .30 .75
BP22 Grayson Rodriguez .25 .60
BP23 Ruben Cardenas .20 .50
BP24 Mason Denaburg .15 .40
BP25 Bobby Witt Jr. 8.00 20.00
BP26 Andrew Vaughn .60 1.50
BP27 Kristian Robinson .50 1.25
BP28 Ronny Mauricio .40 1.00
BP29 Alec Bohm 1.00 2.50
BP30 Jhon Diaz .50 1.25
BP31 Estevan Florial .25 .60
BP32 Elehuris Montero .20 .50
BP33 Sam Huff .30 .75
BP34 Zack Brown .15 .40
BP35 Brice Turang .15 .40
BP36 Ryan Mountcastle .75 2.00
BP37 Wilfred Astudillo .20 .50
BP38 Gus Varland .20 .50
BP39 Nick Lodolo .25 .60
BP40 Tyler Freeman .20 .50
BP41 Rece Hinds .20 .50
BP42 Brady Singer .75 2.00
BP43 Cal Mitchell .15 .40
BP44 Ethan Hankins .20 .50
BP45 Daz Cameron .15 .40
BP46 Sherten Apostel .75 2.00
BP47 Hunter Greene .25 .60
BP48 Josiah Gray .25 .60
BP49 Brailyn Marquez .40 1.00
BP50 Adley Rutschman 1.00 2.50
BP51 Everson Pereira .40 1.00
BP52 Bayron Lora 2.50 6.00
BP53 Clarke Schmidt .25 .60
BP54 Brady McConnell .20 .50
BP55 Spencer Howard .50 1.25
BP56 Cristian Javier .20 .50
BP57 Aaron Ashby .15 .40
BP58 Logan Gilbert .20 .50
BP59 Glenallen Hill Jr. .60 1.50
BP60 Alvaro Seijas .15 .40
BP61 Jeremy Pena .40 1.00
BP62 CJ Abrams .50 1.25
BP63 Franklin Perez .15 .40
BP64 Tanner Houck .40 1.00
BP65 Damon Jones .20 .50
BP66 Nolan Gorman .30 .75
BP67 Ke'Bryan Hayes .75 2.00
BP68 Bryson Stott .40 1.00
BP69 Canaan Smith .25 .60
BP70 Forrest Whitley .25 .60
BP71 Drew Mendoza .40 1.00
BP72 Jazz Chisholm .60 1.50
BP73 Jonathan India 1.00 2.50
BP74 MacKenzie Gore .30 .75
BP75 Seth Beer .30 .75
BP76 Joey Cantillo .15 .40
BP77 Evan White .40 1.00
BP78 Chris Vallimont .15 .40
BP79 Sixto Sanchez .50 1.25
BP80 Alex Kirilloff .30 .75
BP81 Tristen Lutz .20 .50
BP82 Freudis Nova .15 .40
BP83 Tim Cate .15 .40
BP84 Daniel Lynch .15 .40
BP85 Antonio Cabello .50 1.25
BP86 Bobby Dalbec 1.00 2.50
BP87 Colton Welker .15 .40
BP88 Logan Davidson .20 .50
BP89 Matthew Liberatore .20 .50
BP90 Adam Hall .20 .50
BP91 Jackson Rutledge .25 .60
BP92 Dane Dunning .50 1.25
BP93 Royce Lewis .40 1.00
BP94 Jarred Kelenic .75 2.00
BP95 Nolan Jones .25 .60
BP96 Jerar Encarnacion 2.00 5.00
BP97 Ian Anderson .50 1.25
BP98 Alek Thomas .20 .50
BP99 Matt Manning .20 .50
BP100 Jo Adell .60 1.50
BP101 Nick Madrigal .60 1.50
BP102 Owen Miller .15 .40
BP103 Marco Luciano .60 1.50
BP104 Jordan Groshans .30 .75
BP105 Nick Allen .15 .40
BP106 Dylan Carlson .60 1.50
BP107 Cole Winn .15 .40
BP108 Tarik Skubal .75 2.00
BP109 Oscar Gonzalez .30 .75
BP110 Aramis Ademan .15 .40
BP111 Oneil Cruz .20 .50
BP112 Joey Bart .50 1.25
BP113 Josh Jung .40 1.00
BP114 Luis Garcia .60 1.50
BP115 Jasseel De La Cruz .25 .60
BP116 J.J. Bleday .50 1.25
BP117 Joe Ryan .20 .50
BP118 Keoni Cavaco .15 .40
BP119 Hans Crouse .15 .40
BP120 Isaac Paredes .50 1.25
BP121 Grant Lavigne .15 .40
BP122 Riley Greene .60 1.50
BP123 Jordan Balazovic .30 .75
BP124 Nate Pearson .50 1.25
BP125 Deivi Garcia .75 2.00
BP126 Luis Garcia .60 1.50
BP127 Leody Taveras .25 .60
BP128 Bryan Mata .15 .40
BP129 Hunter Bishop .30 .75
BP130 Taylor Trammell .25 .60
BP131 Miguel Vargas .40 1.00
BP132 Luis Gil .20 .50
BP133 Grant Little .20 .50
BP134 Gunnar Henderson .20 .50
BP135 Eric Pardinho .20 .50
BP136 Miguel Amaya .15 .40
BP137 Ryan Rolison .20 .50
BP138 Jorge Mateo .20 .50
BP139 Anthony Volpe 1.50 4.00
BP140 Nick Bennett .20 .50
BP141 Brennen Davis .30 .75
BP142 Casey Mize .50 1.25
BP143 Keibert Ruiz .75 2.00
BP144 Jarren Duran .60 1.50
BP145 Robert Puason 5.00 12.00
BP146 Travis Swaggerty .20 .50
BP147 Will Wilson .20 .50
BP148 Heliot Ramos .25 .60
BP149 Alek Manoah .20 .50
BP150 Luis Robert 1.25 3.00

2020 Bowman Prospects Blue

*BLUE: 1.5X TO 4X BASIC
STATED ODDS 1:307 HOBBY
STATED PRINT RUN 150 SER.#'d SETS
BP8 Jasson Dominguez 60.00 150.00
BP25 Bobby Witt Jr. 40.00 100.00

2020 Bowman Prospects Camo

*CAMO: .6X TO 1.5X BASIC
FIVE PER RETAIL VALUE PACK
BP25 Bobby Witt Jr. 15.00 40.00

2020 Bowman Prospects Gold

*GOLD: 4X TO 10X BASIC
STATED ODDS 1:919 HOBBY
STATED PRINT RUN 50 SER.#'d SETS
BP8 Jasson Dominguez 150.00 400.00
BP25 Bobby Witt Jr. 100.00 250.00

2020 Bowman Prospects Green

*GREEN: 2X TO 5X BASIC
STATED ODDS 1:218 BLASTER
STATED PRINT RUN 99 SER.#'d SETS
BP8 Jasson Dominguez 75.00 200.00
BP25 Bobby Witt Jr. 50.00 120.00

2020 Bowman Prospects Orange

*ORANGE: 8X TO 20X BASIC
STATED ODDS 1:367 HOBBY
STATED PRINT RUN 25 SER.#'d SETS
BP8 Jasson Dominguez 300.00 800.00
BP25 Bobby Witt Jr. 200.00 500.00

2020 Bowman Prospects Purple

*PURPLE: 1.5X TO 4X BASIC
STATED ODDS 1:185 HOBBY
STATED PRINT RUN 250 SER.#'d SETS
BP8 Jasson Dominguez 60.00 150.00
BP25 Bobby Witt Jr. 40.00 100.00

2020 Bowman Prospects Sky Blue

2019 Bowman Prospects Sky Blue
2019 Bowman Prospects Sky Blue
2019 Bowman Prospects Sky Blue
BP8 Jasson Dominguez 50.00 120.00
BP25 Bobby Witt Jr. 30.00 80.00

2020 Bowman Prospects Yellow

*YELLOW: 2.5X TO 6X BASIC
STATED ODDS 1:613 HOBBY
STATED PRINT RUN 75 SER.#'d SETS
BP8 Jasson Dominguez 100.00 250.00
BP25 Bobby Witt Jr. 60.00 150.00

2020 Bowman Draft

STATED PLATE ODDS 1:XXX HOBBY
PLATE PRINT RUN 1 SET PER COLOR
BLACK-CYAN-MAGENTA-YELLOW ISSUED
NO PLATE PRICING DUE TO SCARCITY
BD1 Niko Hulsizer .40 1.00
BD2 Jackson Kowar .50 1.25
BD3 Korey Lee .20 .50
BD4 Milan Tolentino .25 .60
BD5 Jeter Downs .25 .60
BD6 Hans Crouse .15 .40
BD7 Mike Siani .15 .40
BD8 Dane Acker .25 .60
BD9 Ryan Jensen .20 .50
BD10 Shane Baz .15 .40
BD11 Trei Cruz .60 1.50
BD12 Emerson Hancock .60 1.50
BD13 Joey Cantillo .15 .40
BD14 Nick Loftin .25 .60
BD15 Rece Hinds .20 .50
BD16 Jared Shuster .30 .75
BD17 Jesse Franklin V .60 1.50
BD18 Kaden Polcovich .25 .60
BD19 Ben Hernandez .25 .60
BD20 Spencer Strider .25 .60
BD21 Tyler Brown .25 .60
BD22 Keoni Cavaco .15 .40
BD23 Case Williams .20 .50
BD24 Cade Cavalli .30 .75
BD25 Burl Carraway .30 .75
BD26 Daniel Espino .20 .50
BD27 Oswald Peraza .40 1.00
BD28 Zach DeLoach .60 1.50
BD29 Nick Yorke .75 2.00
BD30 Clayton Beeter .40 1.00
BD31 Joe Ryan .20 .50
BD32 Jordan Groshans .30 .75
BD33 Gage Workman .60 1.50
BD34 Austin Hendrick 1.50 4.00
BD35 Jimmy Glowenke .30 .75
BD36 Ryan Rolison .20 .50
BD37 Logan Gilbert .20 .50
BD38 Bobby Miller .60 1.50
BD39 Robert Hassell 1.25 3.00
BD40 JJ Goss .15 .40
BD41 Reid Detmers .40 1.00
BD42 Michael Busch .40 1.00
BD43 Chris McMahon .25 .60
BD44 Xavier Edwards .60 1.50
BD45 Alec Burleson .25 .60
BD46 Freddy Zamora .25 .60
BD47 Travis Swaggerty .20 .50
BD48 Sammy Infante .60 1.50
BD49 Owen Caissie .30 .75
BD50 Max Meyer .60 1.50
BD51 Logan Allen .15 .40
BD52 Landon Knack .40 1.00
BD53 Quinn Priester .20 .50
BD54 Colt Keith .75 2.00
BD55 Jarren Duran .60 1.50
BD56 Austin Wells 1.50 4.00
BD57 Jordan Walker 8.00 20.00
BD58 Jordan Balazovic .30 .75
BD59 Masyn Winn .60 1.50
BD60 Carson Tucker 1.25 3.00
BD61 Nick Bitsko 1.00 2.50
BD62 Daniel Cabrera .60 1.50
BD63 Marco Raya .30 .75
BD64 Kyle Nicolas .25 .60
BD65 Oneil Cruz .20 .50
BD66 Hunter Barnhart .15 .40
BD67 Cole Henry .20 .50
BD68 Tristen Lutz .20 .50
BD69 Petey Halpin .40 1.00
BD70 Jared Jones .25 .60
BD71 Connor Phillips .25 .60
BD72 Pete Crow-Armstrong 3.00 8.00
BD73 Casey Martin 1.50 4.00
BD74 Bryce Bonnin .25 .60
BD75 Daniel Lynch .15 .40
BD76 Tekoah Roby .15 .40
BD77 Isaiah Greene .60 1.50
BD78 Tyler Freeman .20 .50
BD79 Heliot Ramos .25 .60
BD80 Miguel Amaya .15 .40
BD81 Nick Gonzales 8.00 20.00
BD82 DL Hall .15 .40
BD83 Triston Casas .40 1.00
BD84 Christian Chamberlain .25 .60
BD85 Slade Cecconi .20 .50
BD86 Tink Hence .25 .60
BD87 Adisyn Coffey .15 .40
BD88 Asa Lacy 1.00 2.50
BD89 Geraldo Perdomo .15 .40
BD90 Nick Garcia .25 .60
BD91 Nick Swiney .30 .75
BD92 Matthew Dyer .25 .60
BD93 CJ Van Eyk .25 .60
BD94 Alerick Soularie .20 .50
BD95 Garrett Crochet 1.50 4.00
BD96 Ian Seymour .15 .40
BD97 Zavier Warren .15 .40
BD98 Ed Howard 3.00 8.00
BD99 Justin Lange .15 .40
BD100 Ian Bedell .20 .50
BD101 Aaron Shortridge .20 .50
BD102 Trevor Larnach .30 .75
BD103 David Calabrese .30 .75
BD104 Quin Cotton .15 .40
BD105 Luke Little .25 .60
BD106 Drew Romo .40 1.00
BD107 Zac Veen 2.50 6.00
BD108 Brady McConnell .20 .50
BD109 Sam Weatherly .15 .40
BD110 Jordan Nwogu .60 1.50
BD111 Jordan Westburg .40 1.00
BD112 Zach McCambley .15 .40
BD113 Trevor Hauver .25 .60
BD114 Corbin Carroll .25 .60
BD115 Tanner Burns .25 .60
BD116 Jackson Miller .40 1.00
BD117 Carter Baumler .25 .60
BD118 Garrett Mitchell 1.25 3.00
BD119 Tyler Soderstrom .60 1.50
BD120 Holden Powell .20 .50
BD121 Spencer Torkelson 5.00 12.00
BD122 Heston Kjerstad 2.50 6.00
BD123 Alexander Canario .15 .40
BD124 Justin Foscue .60 1.50
BD125 Levi Prater .20 .50
BD126 Evan Carter .40 1.00
BD127 Bryce Jarvis .20 .50
BD128 Werner Blakely .20 .50
BD129 Casey Schmitt .40 1.00
BD130 Hudson Haskin .60 1.50
BD131 Daxton Fulton .25 .60
BD132 Luis Gil .20 .50
BD133 Zach Daniels .25 .60
BD134 Jeff Criswell .20 .50
BD135 Shane McClanahan .20 .50
BD136 Alika Williams .20 .50
BD137 Gilberto Jimenez .75 2.00
BD138 Trent Palmer .20 .50
BD139 Alex Santos .50 1.25
BD140 Bryson Stott .40 1.00
BD141 Ethan Hankins .20 .50
BD142 Kody Hoese .50 1.25
BD143 Francisco Alvarez .50 1.25
BD144 Dillon Dingler .50 1.25
BD145 Carson Ragsdale .25 .60
BD146 Patrick Bailey .50 1.25

BD147 Liam Norris .15 .40
BD148 RJ Dabovich .15 .40
BD149 Carmen Mlodzinski .20 .50
BD150 AJ Vukovich 1.00 2.50
BD151 Jasson Dominguez 4.00 10.00
BD152 Bobby Witt Jr. 1.00 2.50
BD153 Andrew Vaughn .60 1.50
BD154 Adley Rutschman 1.00 2.50
BD155 Robert Puason .50 1.25
BD156 Jay Groome .15 .40
BD157 Will Klein .20 .50
BD158 Zach Britton .20 .50
BD159 Owen Miller .15 .40
BD160 Logan Hofmann .15 .40
BD161 Ronaldo Hernandez .15 .40
BD162 Jack Blomgren .25 .60
BD163 Adam Seminaris .20 .50
BD164 Bailey Horn .20 .50
BD165 Joe Boyle .25 .60
BD166 Ryan Murphy .20 .50
BD167 Thomas Saggese .15 .40
BD168 George Kirby .25 .60
BD169 Jeremiah Jackson .15 .40
BD170 Shane Drohan .20 .50
BD171 Brandon Pfaadt .15 .40
BD172 Blake Rutherford .15 .40
BD173 Hayden Cantrelle .15 .40
BD174 Mark Vientos .15 .40
BD175 Michael Toglia .15 .40
BD176 Mitchell Parker .15 .40
BD177 Jackson Rutledge .25 .60
BD178 Anthony Volpe .60 1.50
BD179 Nick Lodolo .25 .60
BD180 Riley Greene .60 1.50
BD181 JJ Bleday .50 1.25
BD182 Kyle Isbel .15 .40
BD183 Shea Langeliers .30 .75
BD184 Brett Baty .50 1.25
BD185 Jerar Encarnacion .50 1.25
BD186 Aaron Ashby .15 .40
BD187 Brennen Davis .30 .75
BD188 Julio Rodriguez 1.00 2.50
BD189 CJ Abrams .50 1.25
BD190 Marco Luciano .60 1.50
BD191 Grayson Rodriguez .25 .60
BD192 Kristian Robinson .50 1.25
BD193 Jordyn Adams .20 .50
BD194 Nolan Gorman .30 .75
BD195 Alek Thomas .20 .50
BD196 Hunter Greene .25 .60
BD197 Josh Jung .40 1.00
BD198 Matthew Liberatore .20 .50
BD199 Ronny Mauricio .40 1.00
BD200 Hunter Bishop .30 .75

2020 Bowman Draft Blue

*BLUE: 2X TO 5X BASIC
STATED ODDS 1:XXX HOBBY
STATED PRINT RUN 150 SER.#'d SETS
BD62 Daniel Cabrera 8.00 20.00

2020 Bowman Draft Gold

*GOLD: 4X TO 10X BASIC
STATED ODDS 1:XXX HOBBY
STATED PRINT RUN 50 SER.#'d SETS
BD62 Daniel Cabrera 15.00 40.00

2020 Bowman Draft Green

*GREEN: 2.5X TO 6X BASIC
STATED ODDS 1:XXX HOBBY
STATED PRINT RUN 99 SER.#'d SETS
BD62 Daniel Cabrera 10.00 25.00

2020 Bowman Draft Orange

*ORANGE: 5X TO 12X BASIC
STATED ODDS 1:XXX HOBBY
STATED PRINT RUN 25 SER.#'d SETS
BD62 Daniel Cabrera 20.00 50.00

2020 Bowman Draft Purple

*PURPLE: 2X TO 5X BASIC
STATED ODDS 1:XXX HOBBY
STATED PRINT RUN 250 SER.#'d SETS
BD62 Daniel Cabrera 6.00 15.00

2020 Bowman Draft Sky Blue

*SKY BLUE: 1X TO 2.5X BASIC
STATED ODDS 1:XXX HOBBY
STATED PRINT RUN 499 SER.#'d SETS
BD62 Daniel Cabrera 4.00 10.00

2020 Bowman Draft 1st Edition

BD1 Niko Hulsizer .50 1.25
BD2 Jackson Kowar .60 1.50
BD3 Korey Lee .25 .60
BD4 Milan Tolentino .30 .75
BD5 Jeter Downs .30 .75
BD6 Hans Crouse .20 .50
BD7 Mike Siani .20 .50
BD8 Dane Acker .30 .75
BD9 Ryan Jensen .25 .60
BD10 Shane Baz .20 .50
BD11 Trei Cruz .75 2.00
BD12 Emerson Hancock .75 2.00
BD13 Joey Cantillo .20 .50
BD14 Nick Loftin .30 .75
BD15 Rece Hinds .25 .60
BD16 Jared Shuster .40 1.00
BD17 Jesse Franklin V .75 2.00
BD18 Kaden Polcovich .30 .75
BD19 Ben Hernandez .30 .75
BD20 Spencer Strider .30 .75
BD21 Tyler Brown .30 .75
BD22 Keoni Cavaco .20 .50
BD23 Case Williams .25 .60
BD24 Cade Cavalli .40 1.00
BD25 Burl Carraway .40 1.00
BD26 Daniel Espino .25 .60
BD27 Oswald Peraza .50 1.25
BD28 Zach DeLoach .75 2.00
BD29 Nick Yorke 1.00 2.50
BD30 Clayton Beeter .50 1.25
BD31 Joe Ryan .25 .60
BD32 Jordan Groshans .40 1.00
BD33 Gage Workman .75 2.00
BD34 Austin Hendrick 10.00 25.00
BD35 Jimmy Glowenke .40 1.00
BD36 Ryan Rolison .25 .60
BD37 Logan Gilbert .25 .60
BD38 Bobby Miller .75 2.00
BD39 Robert Hassell 4.00 10.00
BD40 JJ Goss .20 .50
BD41 Reid Detmers .50 1.25
BD42 Michael Busch .50 1.25
BD43 Chris McMahon .30 .75
BD44 Xavier Edwards .75 2.00
BD45 Alec Burleson .30 .75
BD46 Freddy Zamora .30 .75
BD47 Travis Swaggerty .25 .60
BD48 Sammy Infante .75 2.00
BD49 Owen Caissie .40 1.00
BD50 Max Meyer .75 2.00
BD51 Logan Allen .20 .50
BD52 Landon Knack .50 1.25
BD53 Quinn Priester .25 .60
BD54 Colt Keith 1.00 2.50
BD55 Jarren Duran .75 2.00
BD56 Austin Wells 2.00 5.00
BD57 Jordan Walker 3.00 10.00
BD58 Jordan Balazovic .40 1.00
BD59 Masyn Winn .75 2.00
BD60 Carson Tucker 1.50 4.00
BD61 Nick Bitsko 1.25 3.00
BD62 Daniel Cabrera .75 2.00
BD63 Marco Raya .40 1.00
BD64 Kyle Nicolas .30 .75
BD65 Oneil Cruz .25 .60
BD66 Hunter Barnhart .20 .50
BD67 Cole Henry .25 .60
BD68 Tristen Lutz .25 .60
BD69 Petey Halpin .50 1.25
BD70 Jared Jones .30 .75
BD71 Connor Phillips .30 .75
BD72 Pete Crow-Armstrong 2.50 6.00
BD73 Casey Martin 2.00 5.00
BD74 Bryce Bonnin .30 .75
BD75 Daniel Lynch .20 .50
BD76 Tekoah Roby .20 .50
BD77 Isaiah Greene 1.00 2.50
BD78 Tyler Freeman .25 .60
BD79 Heliot Ramos .30 .75
BD80 Miguel Amaya .20 .50
BD81 Nick Gonzales 8.00 20.00
BD82 DL Hall .20 .50
BD83 Triston Casas .50 1.25
BD84 Christian Chamberlain .30 .75
BD85 Slade Cecconi .25 .60
BD86 Tink Hence .30 .75
BD87 Adisyn Coffey .20 .50
BD88 Asa Lacy 3.00 8.00
BD89 Geraldo Perdomo .20 .50
BD90 Nick Garcia .30 .75
BD91 Nick Swiney .40 1.00
BD92 Matthew Dyer .30 .75
BD93 CJ Van Eyk .30 .75
BD94 Alerick Soularie .25 .60
BD95 Garrett Crochet 4.00 10.00
BD96 Ian Seymour .20 .50
BD97 Zavier Warren .20 .50
BD98 Ed Howard 8.00 20.00
BD99 Justin Lange .20 .50
BD100 Ian Bedell .25 .60
BD101 Aaron Shortridge .25 .60
BD102 Trevor Larnach .40 1.00
BD103 David Calabrese .40 1.00
BD104 Quin Cotton .20 .50
BD105 Luke Little .30 .75
BD106 Drew Romo .50 1.25
BD107 Zac Veen 6.00 15.00
BD108 Brady McConnell .25 .60
BD109 Sam Weatherly .20 .50
BD110 Jordan Nwogu .75 2.00
BD111 Jordan Westburg .50 1.25
BD112 Zach McCambley .20 .50
BD113 Trevor Hauver .30 .75
BD114 Corbin Carroll .30 .75
BD115 Tanner Burns .30 .75
BD116 Jackson Miller .50 1.25
BD117 Carter Baumler .30 .75
BD118 Garrett Mitchell 2.50 6.00
BD119 Tyler Soderstrom 2.50 6.00
BD120 Holden Powell .25 .60
BD121 Spencer Torkelson 25.00 60.00
BD122 Heston Kjerstad 6.00 15.00
BD123 Alexander Canario .20 .50
BD124 Justin Foscue .75 2.00
BD125 Levi Prater .25 .60
BD126 Evan Carter .50 1.25
BD127 Bryce Jarvis .25 .60
BD128 Werner Blakely .25 .60
BD129 Casey Schmitt .50 1.25
BD130 Hudson Haskin .75 2.00
BD131 Daxton Fulton .30 .75
BD132 Luis Gil .25 .60
BD133 Zach Daniels .30 .75
BD134 Jeff Criswell .25 .60
BD135 Shane McClanahan .25 .60
BD136 Alika Williams .25 .60
BD137 Gilberto Jimenez 1.00 2.50
BD138 Trent Palmer .25 .60
BD139 Alex Santos .60 1.50
BD140 Bryson Stott .50 1.25
BD141 Ethan Hankins .25 .60
BD142 Kody Hoese .60 1.50
BD143 Francisco Alvarez .60 1.50
BD144 Dillon Dingler 1.00 2.50
BD145 Carson Ragsdale .30 .75
BD146 Patrick Bailey 2.00 5.00
BD147 Liam Norris .20 .50
BD148 RJ Dabovich .20 .50
BD149 Carmen Mlodzinski .25 .60
BD150 AJ Vukovich 1.25 3.00
BD151 Jasson Dominguez 20.00 50.00
BD152 Bobby Witt Jr. 1.25 3.00
BD153 Andrew Vaughn .75 2.00
BD154 Adley Rutschman 1.25 3.00
BD155 Robert Puason .60 1.50
BD156 Jay Groome .20 .50
BD157 Will Klein .25 .60
BD158 Zach Britton .25 .60
BD159 Owen Miller .20 .50
BD160 Logan Hofmann .20 .50
BD161 Ronaldo Hernandez .20 .50
BD162 Jack Blomgren .30 .75
BD163 Adam Seminaris .25 .60
BD164 Bailey Horn .25 .60
BD165 Joe Boyle .30 .75
BD166 Ryan Murphy .25 .60
BD167 Thomas Saggese .20 .50
BD168 George Kirby .30 .75
BD169 Jeremiah Jackson .20 .50
BD170 Shane Drohan .25 .60
BD171 Brandon Pfaadt .20 .50
BD172 Blake Rutherford .20 .50
BD173 Hayden Cantrelle .20 .50
BD174 Mark Vientos .20 .50
BD175 Michael Toglia .20 .50
BD176 Mitchell Parker .20 .50
BD177 Jackson Rutledge .30 .75
BD178 Anthony Volpe .75 2.00
BD179 Nick Lodolo .30 .75
BD180 Riley Greene .75 2.00
BD181 JJ Bleday .60 1.50
BD182 Kyle Isbel .20 .50
BD183 Shea Langeliers .40 1.00
BD184 Brett Baty .60 1.50
BD185 Jerar Encarnacion .60 1.50
BD186 Aaron Ashby .20 .50
BD187 Brennen Davis .40 1.00
BD188 Julio Rodriguez 1.25 3.00
BD189 CJ Abrams .60 1.50
BD190 Marco Luciano .75 2.00
BD191 Grayson Rodriguez .30 .75
BD192 Kristian Robinson .60 1.50
BD193 Jordyn Adams .25 .60
BD194 Nolan Gorman .40 1.00
BD195 Alek Thomas .25 .60
BD196 Hunter Greene .30 .75
BD197 Josh Jung .50 1.25
BD198 Matthew Liberatore .25 .60
BD199 Ronny Mauricio .50 1.25
BD200 Hunter Bishop .40 1.00

2020 Bowman Draft 1st Edition Blue Foil

*BLUE FOIL: 3X TO 8X BASIC
STATED ODDS 1:XXX HOBBY
STATED PRINT RUN 150 SER.#'d SETS
BD39 Robert Hassell 30.00 80.00
BD57 Jordan Walker 30.00 80.00
BD59 Masyn Winn 12.00 30.00
BD62 Daniel Cabrera 15.00 40.00
BD72 Pete Crow-Armstrong 25.00 60.00
BD88 Asa Lacy 25.00 60.00
BD121 Spencer Torkelson 300.00 800.00

2020 Bowman Draft 1st Edition Gold Foil

*GOLD FOIL: 10X TO 25X BASIC
STATED ODDS 1:XXX HOBBY
STATED PRINT RUN 50 SER.#'d SETS
BD39 Robert Hassell 100.00 250.00
BD57 Jordan Walker 100.00 250.00
BD59 Masyn Winn 40.00 100.00
BD62 Daniel Cabrera 50.00 120.00
BD72 Pete Crow-Armstrong 75.00 200.00
BD88 Asa Lacy 75.00 200.00
BD121 Spencer Torkelson 500.00 1200.00

2020 Bowman Draft 1st Edition Orange Foil

*ORANGE FOIL: 12X TO 30X BASIC
STATED ODDS 1:XXX HOBBY
STATED PRINT RUN 25 SER.#'d SETS
BD39 Robert Hassell 125.00 300.00
BD57 Jordan Walker 125.00 300.00
BD59 Masyn Winn 50.00 120.00
BD62 Daniel Cabrera 60.00 150.00
BD72 Pete Crow-Armstrong 100.00 250.00
BD88 Asa Lacy 100.00 250.00
BD121 Spencer Torkelson 600.00 1500.00

2020 Bowman Draft 1st Edition Sky Blue Foil

*SKY BLUE FOIL: 1X TO 2.5X BASIC
STATED ODDS 1:XXX HOBBY
BD39 Robert Hassell 12.00 30.00
BD62 Daniel Cabrera 6.00 15.00
BD72 Pete Crow-Armstrong 10.00 25.00
BD88 Asa Lacy 10.00 25.00
BD121 Spencer Torkelson 125.00 300.00

2020 Bowman Draft 1st Edition Yellow Foil

*YELLOW FOIL: 6X TO 15X BASIC
STATED ODDS 1:XXX HOBBY
STATED PRINT RUN 75 SER.#'d SETS
BD39 Robert Hassell 60.00 150.00
BD57 Jordan Walker 60.00 150.00
BD59 Masyn Winn 25.00 60.00
BD62 Daniel Cabrera 30.00 80.00
BD72 Pete Crow-Armstrong 50.00 120.00
BD88 Asa Lacy 50.00 120.00
BD121 Spencer Torkelson 400.00 1000.00

2021 Bowman

1 Whit Merrifield .25 .60
2 Alec Bohm RC 2.50 6.00
3 Anthony Santander .15 .40
4 Charlie Blackmon .25 .60
5 Luis Garcia RC 1.25 3.00
6 Buster Posey .30 .75
7 Bo Bichette .60 1.50
8 Andres Gimenez RC .60 1.50
9 Trevor Bauer .30 .75
10 Jo Adell RC 1.50 4.00
11 Tarik Skubal RC 1.25 3.00
12 Brian Anderson .15 .40
13 Sixto Sanchez RC 1.25 3.00
14 Freddie Freeman .30 .75
15 Josh Bell .20 .50
16 Spencer Howard RC .75 2.00
17 Mike Trout 1.25 3.00
18 Leody Taveras RC .75 2.00
19 Miguel Cabrera .25 .60
20 Tyler Stephenson RC 1.25 3.00
21 Tanner Houck RC .40 1.00
22 Max Kepler .20 .50
23 Sam Huff RC .50 1.25
24 Christian Yelich .30 .75
25 Alex Bregman .25 .60
26 Bobby Dalbec RC 2.00 5.00
27 Ian Anderson RC 1.50 4.00
28 Shane Bieber .25 .60
29 Brady Singer RC 1.25 3.00
30 Francisco Lindor .25 .60
31 Casey Mize RC 2.00 5.00
32 Joey Gallo .25 .60
33 Anderson Tejeda RC .60 1.50
34 Xander Bogaerts .25 .60
35 Dylan Carlson RC 2.00 5.00
36 Cristian Pache RC 2.50 6.00
37 Matt Chapman .25 .60
38 Keibert Ruiz RC .75 2.00
39 Max Scherzer .25 .60
40 Aaron Nola .20 .50
41 Ryan Mountcastle RC 2.50 6.00
42 Yadier Molina .30 .75
43 Brailyn Marquez RC 1.25 3.00
44 Luis Patino RC 1.00 2.50
45 Jake Cronenworth RC 1.50 4.00
46 Jacob deGrom .50 1.25
47 Garrett Crochet RC .40 1.00
48 Kyle Lewis .60 1.50
49 Joey Votto .25 .60
50 Austin Hays .25 .60
51 Joey Bart RC .75 2.00
52 Manny Machado .25 .60
53 Mike Clevinger .20 .50
54 Jorge Soler .25 .60
55 Luis Castillo .20 .50
56 Jose Garcia RC 1.00 2.50
57 Kris Bubic RC .40 1.00
58 Kris Bryant .30 .75
59 Nate Pearson RC 1.25 3.00
60 J.D. Martinez .25 .60
61 Mookie Betts .50 1.25
62 Ronald Acuna Jr. 1.00 2.50
63 Ketel Marte .20 .50
64 Mike Yastrzemski .40 1.00
65 Gerrit Cole .40 1.00
66 Ke'Bryan Hayes RC 2.50 6.00
67 Juan Soto .75 2.00
68 Luis Campusano RC .25 .60
69 Keston Hiura .30 .75
70 Yu Darvish .25 .60
71 Jazz Chisholm RC 1.00 2.50
72 Deivi Garcia RC 2.00 5.00
73 Vladimir Guerrero Jr. .40 1.00
74 Aaron Judge .60 1.50
75 Alex Kirilloff RC 1.00 2.50
76 Sean Murphy .15 .40
77 Nick Madrigal RC 2.00 5.00
78 Yordan Alvarez .60 1.50
79 Triston McKenzie RC .75 2.00
80 Cody Bellinger .50 1.25
81 Daulton Varsho RC .60 1.50
82 Blake Snell .20 .50
83 Cristian Javier RC .60 1.50
84 Jose Altuve .20 .50
85 Shohei Ohtani .40 1.00
86 Pete Alonso .60 1.50
87 Fernando Tatis Jr. 1.25 3.00
88 Javier Baez .30 .75
89 Evan White RC 1.50 4.00
90 Bryce Harper .40 1.00
91 Nolan Arenado .40 1.00
92 Jose Abreu .25 .60
93 Anthony Rendon .25 .60
94 Luis Robert .75 2.00
95 Paul Goldschmidt .25 .60
96 Josh Donaldson .20 .50
97 Gleyber Torres .50 1.25
98 Clarke Schmidt RC .40 1.00
99 Austin Meadows .25 .60
100 Jesus Sanchez RC .75 2.00

2021 Bowman Blue

*BLUE: 3X TO 8X BASIC
*BLUE RC: 2X TO 5X BASIC RC
STATED ODDS 1:551 HOBBY
STATED PRINT RUN 150 SER.#'d SETS
17 Mike Trout 15.00 40.00
26 Bobby Dalbec 20.00 50.00
35 Dylan Carlson 30.00 80.00
66 Ke'Bryan Hayes 25.00 60.00

2021 Bowman Fuchsia

*FUCHSIA: 2.5X TO 6X BASIC
*FUCHSIA RC: 1.5X TO 4X BASIC RC
STATED ODDS 1:277 HOBBY
STATED PRINT RUN 299 SER.#'d SETS
17 Mike Trout 12.00 30.00
26 Bobby Dalbec 12.00 30.00
35 Dylan Carlson 25.00 60.00
66 Ke'Bryan Hayes 20.00 50.00

2021 Bowman Gold

*GOLD: 6X TO 15X BASIC
*GOLD RC: 4X TO 10X BASIC RC
STATED ODDS 1:XX HOBBY
STATED PRINT RUN 50 SER.#'d SETS
17 Mike Trout 30.00 80.00
26 Bobby Dalbec 40.00 100.00
35 Dylan Carlson 60.00 150.00
66 Ke'Bryan Hayes 50.00 120.00

2021 Bowman Green

*GREEN: 4X TO 10X BASIC
*GREEN RC: 2.5X TO 6X BASIC RC
STATED ODDS 1:XX RETAIL
STATED PRINT RUN 99 SER.#'d SETS
17 Mike Trout 20.00 50.00
26 Bobby Dalbec 25.00 60.00
35 Dylan Carlson 40.00 100.00
66 Ke'Bryan Hayes 30.00 80.00

2021 Bowman Neon Green

*NEON GRN: 2X TO 5X BASIC
*NEON GRN RC: 1.2X TO 3X BASIC RC
STATED ODDS 1:207 HOBBY
STATED PRINT RUN 399 SER.#'d SETS
17 Mike Trout 10.00 25.00
26 Bobby Dalbec 10.00 25.00
35 Dylan Carlson 20.00 50.00
66 Ke'Bryan Hayes 15.00 40.00

2021 Bowman Orange

*ORANGE: 10X TO 25X BASIC
*ORANGE RC: 6X TO 15X BASIC RC
STATED ODDS 1:XX HOBBY
STATED PRINT RUN 25 SER.#'d SETS
17 Mike Trout 50.00 120.00
26 Bobby Dalbec 60.00 150.00
35 Dylan Carlson 100.00 250.00
66 Ke'Bryan Hayes 75.00 200.00

2021 Bowman Purple

*PURPLE: 2.5X TO 6X BASIC
*PURPLE RC: 1.5X TO 4X BASIC RC
STATED ODDS 1:331 HOBBY
STATED PRINT RUN 250 SER.#'d SETS
17 Mike Trout 12.00 30.00
26 Bobby Dalbec 12.00 30.00
35 Dylan Carlson 25.00 60.00
66 Ke'Bryan Hayes 20.00 50.00

2021 Bowman Sky Blue

*SKY BLUE: 1.5X TO 4X BASIC
*SKY BLUE RC: 1X TO 2.5X BASIC RC
STATED ODDS 1:165 HOBBY
STATED PRINT RUN 499 SER.#'d SETS
35 Dylan Carlson 15.00 40.00
66 Ke'Bryan Hayes 12.00 30.00

2021 Bowman Yellow

*YELLOW: 5X TO 12X BASIC
*YELLOW RC: 3X TO 8X BASIC RC
STATED ODDS 1:1111 HOBBY
STATED PRINT RUN 75 SER.#'d SETS
17 Mike Trout 25.00 60.00
26 Bobby Dalbec 30.00 80.00
35 Dylan Carlson 50.00 120.00
66 Ke'Bryan Hayes 40.00 100.00

2021 Bowman 1st Edition

BFE1 Bobby Witt Jr. 4.00 10.00
BFE2 Freddy Zamora .30 .75
BFE3 Zac Veen .60 1.50
BFE4 Riley Greene .75 2.00
BFE5 Nick Maton .20 .50
BFE6 James Beard .30 .75
BFE7 Maximo Acosta 6.00 15.00
BFE8 Marco Luciano .75 2.00
BFE9 Forrest Whitley .30 .75
BFE10 Brice Turang .20 .50
BFE11 Jeremy Pena .50 1.25
BFE12 Ed Howard 2.00 5.00
BFE13 Jasson Dominguez 10.00 25.00
BFE14 CJ Abrams .60 1.50
BFE15 Colton Welker .20 .50
BFE16 Clayton Beeter .50 1.25
BFE17 Bryson Stott .60 1.50
BFE18 Hunter Bishop .40 1.00
BFE19 Vidal Brujan 1.50 4.00
BFE20 Nick Lodolo .30 .75
BFE21 Adinso Reyes 2.00 5.00
BFE22 Pete Crow-Armstrong .60 1.50
BFE23 Ronny Mauricio .50 1.25
BFE24 Oneil Cruz .25 .60
BFE25 Jeremy De La Rosa 5.00 12.00
BFE26 Reid Detmers .50 1.25
BFE27 Alek Manoah .25 .60
BFE28 Shea Langeliers .40 1.00
BFE29 Matthew Liberatore .25 .60
BFE30 Jordyn Adams .25 .60
BFE31 Alek Thomas .25 .60
BFE32 Dax Fulton .30 .75
BFE33 Eddy Diaz .20 .50
BFE34 Nick Gonzales .60 1.50
BFE35 Nolan Jones .30 .75
BFE36 Ismael Mena .30 .75
BFE37 Jeisson Rosario .30 .75
BFE38 Josh Jung .50 1.25
BFE39 Kody Hoese .60 1.50
BFE40 Yolbert Sanchez .40 1.00
BFE41 Justin Foscue .50 1.25
BFE42 Mick Abel .30 .75
BFE43 Jackson Kowar .60 1.50
BFE44 Bryce Jarvis .25 .60
BFE45 Robert Puason .50 1.25
BFE46 Jonathan India 1.25 3.00
BFE47 Austin Wells .75 2.00
BFE48 Braden Shewmake .30 .75
BFE49 Gunnar Henderson .25 .60
BFE50 Oswald Peraza .50 1.25
BFE51 Tyler Soderstrom .50 1.25
BFE52 Liover Peguero .30 .75
BFE53 Francisco Alvarez .50 1.25
BFE54 Daniel Lynch .20 .50
BFE55 Austin Hendrick 1.50 4.00
BFE56 Freudis Nova .20 .50
BFE57 Wander Franco 2.00 5.00
BFE58 Logan Gilbert .25 .60
BFE59 Jake Vogel .25 .60
BFE60 Seth Beer .40 1.00
BFE61 Jordan Balazovic .20 .50
BFE62 Isaiah Greene .60 1.50
BFE63 Royce Lewis .50 1.25
BFE64 Andrew Dalquist .20 .50
BFE65 Brennen Davis .40 1.00
BFE66 Max Meyer .50 1.25
BFE67 Brett Baty .60 1.50
BFE68 Ryan Vilade .20 .50
BFE69 Heliot Ramos .30 .75
BFE70 Jordan Groshans .40 1.00
BFE71 Blaze Jordan 12.00 30.00
BFE72 Dillon Dingler .40 1.00
BFE73 Keoni Cavaco .20 .50
BFE74 Matthew Thompson .25 .60
BFE75 Bobby Miller .75 2.00
BFE76 Yusniel Diaz .30 .75
BFE77 Carson Tucker .60 1.50
BFE78 Emerson Hancock .50 1.25
BFE79 Luis Garcia .75 2.00
BFE80 Trevor Larnach .40 1.00
BFE81 Drew Waters .50 1.25
BFE82 Antonio Gomez .30 .75
BFE83 Asa Lacy 1.00 2.50
BFE84 Triston Casas .50 1.25
BFE85 Anthony Volpe .75 2.00
BFE86 Julio Rodriguez 3.00 8.00
BFE87 Austin Martin 20.00 50.00
BFE88 Andrew Vaughn 1.50 4.00
BFE89 Gabriel Arias 4.00 10.00
BFE90 Nolan Gorman .40 1.00
BFE91 Tyler Callihan .25 .60
BFE92 Casey Martin .60 1.50
BFE93 JJ Bleday .60 1.50
BFE94 Trent Deveaux .25 .60
BFE95 Simeon Woods Richardson .30 .75
BFE96 Spencer Torkelson 5.00 12.00
BFE97 Kevin Alcantara 8.00 20.00
BFE98 Jordan Westburg .50 1.25
BFE99 Cade Cavalli .40 1.00
BFE100 Terrin Vavra .40 1.00
BFE101 Xavier Edwards .60 1.50
BFE102 Jarred Kelenic 3.00 8.00
BFE103 Jackson Rutledge .30 .75
BFE104 Blake Walston .30 .75
BFE105 MacKenzie Gore .40 1.00
BFE106 Jared Kelley .20 .50
BFE107 Jeter Downs .30 .75
BFE108 Patrick Bailey .40 1.00
BFE109 Geraldo Perdomo .20 .50
BFE110 Jose Salas .20 .50
BFE111 Matt Manning .25 .60
BFE112 Brandon Marsh .30 .75
BFE113 C.J. Chatham .25 .60
BFE114 Nick Yorke .75 2.00
BFE115 Logan Davidson .25 .60
BFE116 Elehuris Montero .25 .60
BFE117 George Kirby .30 .75
BFE118 Grayson Rodriguez .30 .75
BFE119 Tyler Freeman .20 .50
BFE120 Robert Hassell 1.25 3.00
BFE121 Adley Rutschman 2.00 5.00
BFE122 DL Hall .20 .50
BFE123 Daniel Espino .25 .60
BFE124 Bo Naylor .25 .60
BFE125 Aaron Sabato 5.00 12.00
BFE126 Drew Romo .50 1.25
BFE127 Hunter Greene .30 .75
BFE128 Jose Tena .50 1.25
BFE129 Garrett Mitchell 1.25 3.00
BFE130 Hyun-il Choi .30 .75
BFE131 Christopher Morel .20 .50
BFE132 Taylor Trammell .30 .75
BFE133 Mario Feliciano .30 .75
BFE134 Shane Baz .20 .50
BFE135 Jarren Duran .75 2.00
BFE136 Kristian Robinson .60 1.50
BFE137 Michael Toglia .20 .50
BFE138 Heston Kjerstad 1.00 2.50
BFE139 Bayron Lora 1.00 2.50
BFE140 Yunior Severino .25 .60
BFE141 Edward Cabrera .30 .75
BFE142 Corbin Carroll .30 .75
BFE143 Nick Bitsko .60 1.50
BFE144 Nick Loftin .30 .75
BFE145 Alexander Ramirez 2.00 5.00
BFE146 Jordan Walker .60 1.50
BFE147 Nick Allen .20 .50
BFE148 Miguel Amaya .20 .50
BFE149 Ivan Johnson .30 .75
BFE150 Josiah Gray .30 .75

2021 Bowman 1st Edition Blue Foil

*BLUE/150: 3X TO 8X BASIC
STATED ODDS 1:12 HOBBY
STATED PRINT RUN 150 SER.#'d SETS
BFE1 Bobby Witt Jr. 50.00 120.00
BFE57 Wander Franco 25.00 60.00
BFE87 Austin Martin 200.00 500.00
BFE125 Aaron Sabato 50.00 120.00

2021 Bowman 1st Edition Gold Foil

*GOLD/50: 10X TO 25X BASIC
STATED ODDS 1:35 HOBBY
STATED PRINT RUN 50 SER.#'d SETS
BFE1 Bobby Witt Jr. 150.00 400.00
BFE4 Riley Greene 30.00 80.00
BFE57 Wander Franco 75.00 200.00
BFE87 Austin Martin 600.00 1500.00
BFE125 Aaron Sabato 150.00 400.00

2021 Bowman 1st Edition Orange Foil

*ORANGE/25: 12X TO 30X BASIC
STATED ODDS 1:70 HOBBY
STATED PRINT RUN 25 SER.#'d SETS
BFE1 Bobby Witt Jr. 200.00 500.00
BFE4 Riley Greene 40.00 100.00
BFE7 Maximo Acosta 200.00 500.00
BFE57 Wander Franco 100.00 250.00
BFE87 Austin Martin 800.00 2000.00
BFE125 Aaron Sabato 200.00 500.00

2021 Bowman 1st Edition Sky Blue Foil

*SKY BLUE: 1.2X TO 3X BASIC
STATED ODDS 1:2 HOBBY
BFE1 Bobby Witt Jr. 20.00 50.00
BFE57 Wander Franco 10.00 25.00
BFE87 Austin Martin 75.00 200.00
BFE125 Aaron Sabato 20.00 50.00

2021 Bowman Prospects

STATED ODDS 1:XX HOBBY
*CAMO: .75X TO 2X BASIC
BP1 Bobby Witt Jr. 1.00 2.50
BP2 Freddy Zamora .25 .60
BP3 Zac Veen .50 1.25
BP4 Riley Greene .60 1.50
BP5 Nick Maton .15 .40
BP6 James Beard .25 .60
BP7 Maximo Acosta 2.50 6.00
BP8 Marco Luciano .60 1.50
BP9 Forrest Whitley .25 .60
BP10 Brice Turang .15 .40
BP11 Jeremy Pena .40 1.00
BP12 Ed Howard .75 2.00
BP13 Jasson Dominguez 2.00 5.00
BP14 CJ Abrams .50 1.25
BP15 Colton Welker .15 .40
BP16 Clayton Beeter .40 1.00
BP17 Bryson Stott .50 1.25
BP18 Hunter Bishop .30 .75
BP19 Vidal Brujan 1.25 3.00
BP20 Nick Lodolo .25 .60
BP21 Adinso Reyes .60 1.50
BP22 Pete Crow-Armstrong .50 1.25
BP23 Ronny Mauricio .40 1.00
BP24 Oneil Cruz .20 .50
BP25 Jeremy De La Rosa 2.50 6.00
BP26 Reid Detmers .40 1.00
BP27 Alek Manoah .20 .50
BP28 Shea Langeliers .30 .75
BP29 Matthew Liberatore .20 .50
BP30 Jordyn Adams .20 .50
BP31 Alek Thomas .20 .50
BP32 Dax Fulton .25 .60
BP33 Eddy Diaz .15 .40
BP34 Nick Gonzales .50 1.25
BP35 Nolan Jones .25 .60
BP36 Ismael Mena .25 .60
BP37 Jeisson Rosario .25 .60
BP38 Josh Jung .40 1.00
BP39 Kody Hoese .50 1.25
BP40 Yolbert Sanchez .30 .75
BP41 Justin Foscue .40 1.00
BP42 Mick Abel .25 .60
BP43 Jackson Kowar .50 1.25
BP44 Bryce Jarvis .20 .50
BP45 Robert Puason .40 1.00
BP46 Jonathan India 1.00 2.50
BP47 Austin Wells .60 1.50
BP48 Braden Shewmake .25 .60
BP49 Gunnar Henderson .20 .50
BP50 Oswald Peraza .40 1.00
BP51 Tyler Soderstrom .40 1.00
BP52 Liover Peguero .25 .60
BP53 Francisco Alvarez .40 1.00
BP54 Daniel Lynch .15 .40
BP55 Austin Hendrick 1.25 3.00
BP56 Freudis Nova .15 .40
BP57 Wander Franco 1.50 4.00
BP58 Logan Gilbert .20 .50
BP59 Jake Vogel .20 .50
BP60 Seth Beer .30 .75
BP61 Jordan Balazovic .15 .40
BP62 Isaiah Greene .50 1.25
BP63 Royce Lewis .40 1.00
BP64 Andrew Dalquist .15 .40
BP65 Brennen Davis .30 .75
BP66 Max Meyer .40 1.00
BP67 Brett Baty .50 1.25
BP68 Ryan Vilade .15 .40
BP69 Heliot Ramos .25 .60
BP70 Jordan Groshans .30 .75
BP71 Blaze Jordan 6.00 15.00
BP72 Dillon Dingler .30 .75
BP73 Keoni Cavaco .15 .40
BP74 Matthew Thompson .20 .50
BP75 Bobby Miller .60 1.50
BP76 Yusniel Diaz .25 .60
BP77 Carson Tucker .50 1.25
BP78 Emerson Hancock .40 1.00
BP79 Luis Garcia .60 1.50
BP80 Trevor Larnach .30 .75
BP81 Drew Waters .40 1.00
BP82 Antonio Gomez .25 .60
BP83 Asa Lacy .75 2.00
BP84 Triston Casas .40 1.00
BP85 Anthony Volpe .60 1.50
BP86 Julio Rodriguez 1.00 2.50
BP87 Austin Martin 5.00 12.00
BP88 Andrew Vaughn .60 1.50
BP89 Gabriel Arias 2.00 5.00
BP90 Nolan Gorman .30 .75
BP91 Tyler Callihan .20 .50
BP92 Casey Martin .50 1.25
BP93 JJ Bleday .50 1.25
BP94 Trent Deveaux .20 .50
BP95 Simeon Woods Richardson .25 .60
BP96 Spencer Torkelson 1.00 2.50
BP97 Kevin Alcantara 4.00 10.00
BP98 Jordan Westburg .40 1.00
BP99 Cade Cavalli .30 .75
BP100 Terrin Vavra .30 .75
BP101 Xavier Edwards .50 1.25
BP102 Jarred Kelenic .75 2.00
BP103 Jackson Rutledge .25 .60
BP104 Blake Walston .25 .60
BP105 MacKenzie Gore .30 .75
BP106 Jared Kelley .15 .40
BP107 Jeter Downs .25 .60
BP108 Patrick Bailey .30 .75
BP109 Geraldo Perdomo .15 .40
BP110 Jose Salas .15 .40
BP111 Matt Manning .20 .50
BP112 Brandon Marsh .25 .60
BP113 CJ Chatham .20 .50
BP114 Nick Yorke .60 1.50
BP115 Logan Davidson .20 .50
BP116 Elehuris Montero .20 .50
BP117 George Kirby .25 .60
BP118 Grayson Rodriguez .25 .60
BP119 Tyler Freeman .15 .40
BP120 Robert Hassell 1.00 2.50
BP121 Adley Rutschman 1.00 2.50
BP122 DL Hall .15 .40
BP123 Daniel Espino .20 .50
BP124 Bo Naylor .20 .50
BP125 Aaron Sabato .60 1.50
BP126 Drew Romo .40 1.00
BP127 Hunter Greene .25 .60
BP128 Jose Tena .40 1.00
BP129 Garrett Mitchell 1.00 2.50
BP130 Hyun-il Choi .25 .60
BP131 Christopher Morel .15 .40
BP132 Taylor Trammell .25 .60
BP133 Mario Feliciano .25 .60
BP134 Shane Baz .15 .40
BP135 Jarren Duran .60 1.50
BP136 Kristian Robinson .50 1.25
BP137 Michael Toglia .15 .40
BP138 Heston Kjerstad .75 2.00
BP139 Bayron Lora .75 2.00
BP140 Yunior Severino .20 .50
BP141 Edward Cabrera .25 .60
BP142 Corbin Carroll .25 .60
BP143 Nick Bitsko .50 1.25
BP144 Nick Loftin .25 .60
BP145 Alexander Ramirez .40 1.00
BP146 Jordan Walker .50 1.25
BP147 Nick Allen .15 .40
BP148 Miguel Amaya .15 .40
BP149 Ivan Johnson .25 .60
BP150 Josiah Gray .25 .60

2021 Bowman Prospects Blue

*BLUE: 1.5X TO 4X BASIC
STATED ODDS 1:XX HOBBY
STATED PRINT RUN 150 SER.#'d SETS
BP1 Bobby Witt Jr. 12.00 30.00

BP21 Adinso Reyes	5.00	12.00
BP57 Wander Franco	15.00	40.00
BP96 Spencer Torkelson	8.00	20.00
BP125 Aaron Sabato	12.00	30.00

2021 Bowman Prospects Fuchsia

*FUCHSIA: 1.5X TO 4X BASIC
STATED ODDS 1:XX HOBBY
STATED PRINT RUN 299 SER.#'d SETS

BP1 Bobby Witt Jr.	12.00	30.00
BP21 Adinso Reyes	5.00	12.00
BP57 Wander Franco	15.00	40.00
BP96 Spencer Torkelson	8.00	20.00
BP125 Aaron Sabato	12.00	30.00

2021 Bowman Prospects Gold

*GOLD: 4X TO 10X BASIC
STATED ODDS 1:XX HOBBY
STATED PRINT RUN 50 SER.#'d SETS

BP1 Bobby Witt Jr.	30.00	80.00
BP21 Adinso Reyes	12.00	30.00
BP57 Wander Franco	40.00	100.00
BP96 Spencer Torkelson	20.00	50.00
BP125 Aaron Sabato	30.00	80.00

2021 Bowman Prospects Green

*GREEN: 2X TO 5X BASIC
STATED ODDS 1:XX RETAIL
STATED PRINT RUN 99 SER.#'d SETS

BP1 Bobby Witt Jr.	15.00	40.00
BP21 Adinso Reyes	6.00	15.00
BP57 Wander Franco	20.00	50.00
BP96 Spencer Torkelson	10.00	25.00
BP125 Aaron Sabato	15.00	40.00

2021 Bowman Prospects Neon Green

*NEON GRN: 1.2X TO 3X BASIC
STATED ODDS 1:XX HOBBY
STATED PRINT RUN 399 SER.#'d SETS

BP1 Bobby Witt Jr.	10.00	25.00
BP21 Adinso Reyes	4.00	10.00
BP57 Wander Franco	10.00	25.00
BP125 Aaron Sabato	10.00	25.00

2021 Bowman Prospects Orange

*ORANGE: 8X TO 20X BASIC
STATED ODDS 1:XX HOBBY
STATED PRINT RUN 25 SER.#'d SETS

BP1 Bobby Witt Jr.	60.00	150.00
BP21 Adinso Reyes	25.00	60.00
BP57 Wander Franco	75.00	200.00
BP96 Spencer Torkelson	40.00	100.00
BP125 Aaron Sabato	60.00	150.00

2021 Bowman Prospects Purple

*PURPLE: 1.5X TO 4X BASIC
STATED ODDS 1:XX HOBBY
STATED PRINT RUN 250 SER.#'d SETS

BP1 Bobby Witt Jr.	12.00	30.00
BP21 Adinso Reyes	5.00	12.00
BP57 Wander Franco	15.00	40.00
BP96 Spencer Torkelson	8.00	20.00
BP125 Aaron Sabato	12.00	30.00

2021 Bowman Prospects Sky Blue

*SKY BLUE: 1.2X TO 3X BASIC
STATED ODDS 1:XX HOBBY
STATED PRINT RUN 499 SER.#'d SETS

BP21 Adinso Reyes	4.00	10.00
BP57 Wander Franco	10.00	25.00
BP125 Aaron Sabato	10.00	25.00

2021 Bowman Prospects Yellow

*YELLOW: 2.5X TO 6X BASIC
STATED ODDS 1:XX HOBBY
STATED PRINT RUN 75 SER.#'d SETS

BP1 Bobby Witt Jr.	20.00	50.00
BP21 Adinso Reyes	8.00	20.00
BP57 Wander Franco	25.00	60.00
BP96 Spencer Torkelson	12.00	30.00
BP125 Aaron Sabato	20.00	50.00

2008 Bowman AFLAC Autographs

09 BOW.DFT.ODDS 1:238 HOBBY
12 BOW.ODDS 1:703 HOBBY
PRINT RUNS B/WN 22-245 COPIES PER

AS Andrew Susac/210	6.00	15.00
BP Brooks Pounders/240	4.00	10.00
DN David Nick/243	8.00	20.00
DT Daniel Tuttle/102	8.00	20.00
DT Donavan Tate/244	12.00	30.00
EW Everett Williams/127	10.00	25.00
IK Ian Krol/127	8.00	20.00
JM Jiovanni Mier/245	5.00	12.00
JS Jonathan Singleton/127	50.00	100.00
JT Jacob Turner/22		
KS Keyvius Sampson/127	4.00	10.00
LB Luke Bailey/230	4.00	10.00
MD Matthew Davidson/206	12.00	30.00
MG Mychal Givens/230	4.00	10.00
MP Matthew Purke/230	8.00	20.00
MS Max Stassi/174	6.00	15.00
MZ Michael Zunino/225	25.00	60.00
SG Scooter Gennett/230	25.00	60.00
SH Slade Heathcott/81	40.00	80.00
TM Tyler Matzek/244	4.00	10.00
ZW Zack Wheeler/244	75.00	150.00

2009 Bowman AFLAC

DISTRIBUTED AT 2009 AFLAC GAME

AC Andrew Cole	4.00	10.00
AS Aaron Sanchez	3.00	8.00
AV A.J. Vanegas	2.00	5.00
AW Austin Wilson	4.00	10.00
BH Bryce Harper	25.00	60.00
BR Brian Ragira	2.00	5.00
BS Brandon Stephens	2.00	5.00
CB Cameron Bedrosian	5.00	12.00
CC Chevez Clarke	3.00	8.00
CG Conrad Gregor	2.00	5.00
CN Connor Narron	2.00	5.00
DC Dylan Covey	4.00	10.00
DS DeAndre Smelter	4.00	10.00
JJ Jacoby Jones	3.00	8.00
JL Jared Lakind	2.00	5.00
JO Justin O'Conner	5.00	12.00
JS Josh Sale	4.00	10.00
JT Jameson Taillon	5.00	12.00
KB1 Krey Bratsen	4.00	10.00
KB2 Kris Bryant	50.00	120.00
KC Kaleb Cowart	4.00	10.00
KG Kevin Gausman	4.00	10.00
KS Kellen Sweeney	2.00	5.00
KW Karsten Whitson	4.00	10.00
MA Michael Arencibia	2.00	5.00
ML1 Matt Lipka	2.00	5.00
ML2 Marcus Littlewood	4.00	10.00
ML3 Michael Lorenzen	2.00	5.00
PT Peter Tago	4.00	10.00
RA Robert Aviles	2.00	5.00
RG Reggie Golden	4.00	10.00
SA Stetson Allie	4.00	10.00
SR Shane Rowland	2.00	5.00
SS Stefan Sabol	4.00	10.00
TA Tyler Austin	3.00	8.00
TG Trey Griffin	4.00	10.00
TS Tyler Shreve	2.00	5.00
TW Tony Wolters	3.00	8.00
YC Yordy Cabrera	5.00	12.00
ZA Zach Alvord	2.00	5.00

2009 Bowman AFLAC Autographs

12 BOW.ODDS 1:703 HOBBY
13 BOW.DFT.ODDS 1:619 HOBBY
14 BOW.ODDS 1:1150 HOBBY
14 BOW.CHR.ODDS 1:1020 HOBBY
PRINT RUNS B/WN 35-235 COPIES PER

AS Aaron Sanchez/38	40.00	80.00
AW Austin Wilson/225	10.00	25.00
BH Bryce Harper/230	300.00	500.00
CC Chevez Clarke/35	60.00	120.00
JJ Jacoby Jones/225	15.00	40.00
JO Justin O'Conner/230	6.00	15.00
JS Josh Sale/230	15.00	40.00
JT Jameson Taillon/230	15.00	40.00
KB Kris Bryant/235	400.00	600.00
KC Kaleb Cowart/230	8.00	20.00
KG Kevin Gausman/225	12.00	30.00
PT Peter Tago/230	4.00	10.00
SA Stetson Allie/230	6.00	15.00
ML1 Matt Lipka/37	60.00	120.00
ML3 Michael Lorenzen/235	10.00	25.00

2010 Bowman AFLAC

COMPLETE SET (38)	50.00	120.00
AB Archie Bradley	5.00	12.00
AH Austin Hedges	1.50	4.00
AS Austin Slater	1.50	4.00
ASU Andrew Suarez	1.50	4.00
BS Brandon Sedell	1.50	4.00
BSW Blake Swihart	4.00	10.00
CE Cecil Espy CO	1.50	4.00
CG Cameron Gallagher	4.00	10.00
CL Christian Lopes	2.50	6.00
CM Christian Montgomery	1.50	4.00
DB Dylan Bundy	5.00	12.00
DD Dylan Davis	1.50	4.00
DH Dillon Howard	2.50	6.00
DL Deshorn Lake	1.50	4.00
DM Daniel Camarena	1.50	4.00
DMA Dillon Maples	1.50	4.00
DME Daniel Mengden	1.50	4.00
DN Daniel Norris	5.00	12.00
FL Francisco Lindor	20.00	50.00
HO Henry Owens	2.50	6.00
JB Javier Baez	20.00	50.00
JC Jake Cave	4.00	10.00
JF Jose Fernandez	15.00	30.00
JM John Magliozzi	1.50	4.00
JR Joe Ross	1.50	4.00
JT Josh Tobias	1.50	4.00
LG Larry Greene	2.50	6.00
MD Matthew Dean	2.50	6.00
MK Michael Kelly	1.50	4.00
PE Phillip Evans	1.50	4.00
PP Philip Pfeifer	1.50	4.00
RJ Ricky Jacquez	1.50	4.00
RS Robert Stephenson	4.00	10.00
SD Shawon Dunston Jr.		
ST Sean Trent	1.50	4.00
TB Tyler Beede	3.00	8.00
TH Travis Harrison	2.50	6.00
TM Tyler Marlette	1.50	4.00
WF William Flamion	1.50	4.00

2010 Bowman AFLAC Autographs

12 BOW.ODDS 1:703 HOBBY
14 BOW.ODDS 1:1150 HOBBY
14 BOW.CHR.ODDS 1:1020 HOBBY
PRINT RUNS B/WN 200-240 COPIES PER
11 BOW.DFT CARDS NOT NUMBERED

AB Archie Bradley	10.00	25.00
AH Austin Hedges/240	6.00	15.00
BS Blake Swihart	20.00	50.00
DB Dylan Bundy	12.00	30.00
DH Dillon Howard/225	10.00	25.00
DM Dillon Maples/230	6.00	15.00
DN Daniel Norris/240	15.00	40.00
FL Francisco Lindor	60.00	150.00
HO Henry Owens/235	12.00	30.00
JB Javier Baez/200	75.00	200.00
JF Jose Fernandez/240	75.00	150.00
LG Larry Greene	6.00	15.00
RS Robert Stephenson	12.00	30.00
TB Tyler Beede/225	12.00	30.00
TH Travis Harrison	8.00	20.00

1997 Bowman Chrome

The 1997 Bowman Chrome set was issued in one series totalling 300 cards and was distributed in four-card packs with a suggested retail price of $3.00. The cards parallel the 1997 Bowman brand and the 300 card set represents a selection of top cards taken from the 441-card 1997 Bowman set. The product was released in the Winter, after the end of the 1997 season. The fronts feature color action player photos printed on dazzling chromium stock. The backs carry player information. Rookie Cards in this set include Adrian Beltre, Kris Benson, Lance Berkman, Kris Benson, Eric Chavez, Jose Cruz Jr., Travis Lee, Aramis Ramirez, Miguel Tejada, Vernon Wells and Kerry Wood.

COMPLETE SET (300)	40.00	80.00
1 Derek Jeter	1.25	3.00
2 Chipper Jones	.50	1.25
3 Hideo Nomo	.50	1.25
4 Tim Salmon	.30	.75
5 Robin Ventura	.20	.50
6 Tony Clark	.20	.50
7 Barry Larkin	.30	.75
8 Paul Molitor	.20	.50
9 Andy Benes	.20	.50
10 Ryan Klesko	.20	.50
11 Mark McGwire	1.25	3.00
12 Ken Griffey Jr.	1.00	2.50
13 Robb Nen	.20	.50
14 Cal Ripken	1.50	4.00
15 John Valentin	.20	.50
16 Ricky Bottalico	.20	.50
17 Mike Lansing	.20	.50
18 Ryne Sandberg	.75	2.00
19 Carlos Delgado	.20	.50
20 Craig Biggio	.30	.75
21 Eric Karros	.20	.50
22 Kevin Appier	.20	.50
23 Mariano Rivera	.50	1.25
24 Vinny Castilla	.20	.50
25 Juan Gonzalez	.20	.50
26 Al Martin	.20	.50
27 Jeff Cirillo	.20	.50
28 Ray Lankford	.20	.50
29 Manny Ramirez	.30	.75
30 Roberto Alomar	.30	.75
31 Will Clark	.30	.75
32 Chuck Knoblauch	.20	.50
33 Harold Baines	.20	.50
34 Edgar Martinez	.30	.75
35 Mike Mussina	.30	.75
36 Kevin Brown	.20	.50
37 Dennis Eckersley	.20	.50
38 Tino Martinez	.30	.75
39 Raul Mondesi	.20	.50
40 Sammy Sosa	.50	1.25
41 John Smoltz	.30	.75
42 Billy Wagner	.20	.50
43 Ken Caminiti	.20	.50
44 Wade Boggs	.30	.75
45 Andres Galarraga	.20	.50
46 Roger Clemens	1.00	2.50
47 Matt Williams	.20	.50
48 Albert Belle	.20	.50
49 Jeff King	.20	.50
50 John Wetteland	.20	.50
51 Deion Sanders	.30	.75
52 Ellis Burks	.20	.50
53 Pedro Martinez	.30	.75
54 Kenny Lofton	.20	.50
55 Randy Johnson	.50	1.25
56 Bernie Williams	.30	.75
57 Marquis Grissom	.20	.50
58 Gary Sheffield	.20	.50
59 Curt Schilling	.20	.50
60 Reggie Sanders	.20	.50
61 Bobby Higginson	.20	.50
62 Moises Alou	.20	.50
63 Tom Glavine	.30	.75
64 Mark Grace	.30	.75
65 Rafael Palmeiro	.30	.75
66 John Olerud	.20	.50
67 Dante Bichette	.20	.50
68 Jeff Bagwell	.30	.75
69 Barry Bonds	1.25	3.00
70 Pat Hentgen	.20	.50
71 Jim Thome	.30	.75
72 Andy Pettitte	.30	.75
73 Jay Bell	.20	.50
74 Jim Edmonds	.20	.50
75 Ron Gant	.20	.50
76 David Cone	.20	.50
77 Jose Canseco	.30	.75
78 Jay Buhner	.20	.50
79 Greg Maddux	.75	2.00
80 Lance Johnson	.20	.50
81 Travis Fryman	.20	.50
82 Paul O'Neill	.30	.75
83 Ivan Rodriguez	.30	.75
84 Fred McGriff	.30	.75
85 Mike Piazza	.75	2.00
86 Brady Anderson	.20	.50
87 Marty Cordova	.20	.50
88 Joe Carter	.20	.50
89 Brian Jordan	.20	.50
90 David Justice	.20	.50
91 Tony Gwynn	.60	1.50
92 Larry Walker	.20	.50
93 Mo Vaughn	.20	.50
94 Sandy Alomar Jr.	.20	.50
95 Rusty Greer	.20	.50
96 Roberto Hernandez	.20	.50
97 Hal Morris	.20	.50
98 Todd Hundley	.20	.50
99 Rondell White	.20	.50
100 Frank Thomas	.50	1.25
101 Bubba Trammell RC	.60	1.50
102 Sidney Ponson RC	1.00	2.50
103 Ricky Ledee RC	.60	1.50
104 Brett Tomko	.20	.50
105 Braden Looper RC	.40	1.00
106 Jason Dickson	.20	.50
107 Chad Green RC	.40	1.00
108 R.A. Dickey RC	4.00	10.00
109 Jeff Liefer	.20	.50
110 Richard Hidalgo	.20	.50
111 Chad Hermansen RC	.40	1.00
112 Felix Martinez	.20	.50
113 J.J. Johnson	.20	.50
114 Todd Dunwoody	.20	.50
115 Katsuhiro Maeda	.20	.50
116 Darin Erstad	.20	.50
117 Elieser Marrero	.20	.50
118 Bartolo Colon	.20	.50
119 Ugueth Urbina	.20	.50
120 Jaime Bluma	.20	.50
121 Seth Greisinger RC	.40	1.00
122 Jose Cruz Jr. RC	.60	1.50
123 Todd Dunn	.20	.50
124 Justin Towle RC	.40	1.00
125 Brian Rose	.20	.50
126 Jose Guillen	.20	.50
127 Andruw Jones	.30	.75
128 Mark Kotsay RC	1.50	4.00
129 Wilton Guerrero	.20	.50
130 Jacob Cruz	.20	.50
131 Mike Sweeney	.20	.50
132 Matt Morris	.20	.50
133 John Thomson	.20	.50
134 Javier Valentin	.20	.50
135 Mike Drumright RC	.40	1.00
136 Michael Barrett	.20	.50
137 Tony Saunders RC	.40	1.00
138 Kevin Brown	.20	.50
139 Anthony Sanders RC	.40	1.00
140 Jeff Abbott	.20	.50
141 Eugene Kingsale	.20	.50
142 Paul Konerko	.30	.75
143 Randall Simon RC	.60	1.50
144 Freddy Adrian Garcia	.20	.50
145 Karim Garcia	.20	.50
146 Carlos Guillen	.20	.50
147 Aaron Boone	.20	.50
148 Donnie Sadler	.20	.50
149 Brooks Kieschnick	.20	.50
150 Scott Spiezio	.20	.50
151 Kevin Orie	.20	.50
152 Russ Johnson	.20	.50
153 Livan Hernandez	.20	.50
154 Vladimir Nunez RC	.40	1.00
155 Pokey Reese	.20	.50
156 Chris Carpenter	.20	.50
157 Eric Milton RC	.60	1.50
158 Richie Sexson	.20	.50
159 Carl Pavano	.20	.50
160 Pat Cline	.20	.50
161 Ron Wright	.20	.50
162 Dante Powell	.20	.50
163 Mark Bellhorn	.20	.50
164 George Lombard	.20	.50
165 Paul Wilder RC	.40	1.00
166 Brad Fullmer	.20	.50
167 Kris Benson RC	1.00	2.50
168 Torii Hunter	.20	.50
169 D.T. Cromer RC	.40	1.00
170 Nelson Figueroa RC	.40	1.00
171 Hiram Bocachica RC	.40	1.00
172 Shane Monahan	.20	.50
173 Juan Melo	.20	.50
174 Calvin Pickering RC	.40	1.00
175 Reggie Taylor	.20	.50
176 Geoff Jenkins	.20	.50
177 Steve Rain RC	.40	1.00
178 Nerio Rodriguez RC	.40	1.00
179 Derrick Gibson	.20	.50
180 Darin Blood	.20	.50
181 Ben Davis	.20	.50
182 Adrian Beltre RC	25.00	60.00
183 Kerry Wood RC	3.00	8.00
184 Nate Rolison RC	.40	1.00
185 Fernando Tatis RC	.40	1.00
186 Jake Westbrook RC	1.00	2.50
187 Edwin Diaz	.20	.50
188 Joe Fontenot RC	.40	1.00
189 Matt Halloran RC	.40	1.00
190 Matt Clement RC	1.00	2.50
191 Todd Greene	.20	.50
192 Eric Chavez RC	4.00	10.00
193 Edgard Velazquez	.20	.50
194 Bruce Chen RC	1.00	2.50
195 Jason Brester	.20	.50
196 Chris Reitsma RC	.60	1.50
197 Neifi Perez	.20	.50
198 Hideki Irabu RC	.60	1.50
199 Don Denbow RC	.40	1.00
200 Derrek Lee	.30	.75
201 Todd Walker	.20	.50
202 Scott Rolen	.30	.75
203 Wes Helms	.20	.50
204 Bob Abreu	.30	.75
205 John Patterson RC	1.50	4.00
206 Alex Gonzalez RC	1.00	2.50
207 Grant Roberts RC	.40	1.00
208 Jeff Suppan	.20	.50
209 Luke Wilcox	.20	.50
210 Marlon Anderson	.20	.50
211 Mike Caruso RC	.40	1.00
212 Roy Halladay RC	12.00	30.00
213 Jeremi Gonzalez RC	.40	1.00
214 Aramis Ramirez RC	4.00	10.00
215 Dee Brown RC	.40	1.00
216 Justin Thompson	.20	.50
217 Danny Clyburn	.20	.50
218 Bruce Aven	.20	.50
219 Keith Foulke RC	1.50	4.00
220 Shannon Stewart	.20	.50
221 Larry Barnes RC	.40	1.00
222 Mark Johnson RC	.40	1.00
223 Randy Winn	.20	.50
224 Nomar Garciaparra	.75	2.00
225 Jacque Jones RC	1.50	4.00
226 Chris Clemons	.20	.50
227 Todd Helton	.50	1.25
228 Ryan Brannan RC	.40	1.00
229 Alex Sanchez RC	.60	1.50
230 Russell Branyan	.20	.50
231 Daryle Ward	.40	1.00
232 Kevin Witt	.20	.50
233 Gabby Martinez	.20	.50
234 Preston Wilson	.20	.50
235 Donzell McDonald RC	.40	1.00
236 Orlando Cabrera RC	1.50	4.00
237 Brian Banks	.20	.50
238 Robbie Bell	.40	1.00
239 Brad Rigby	.20	.50
240 Scott Elarton	.20	.50
241 Donny Leon RC	.40	1.00
242 Abraham Nunez RC	.40	1.00
243 Adam Eaton RC	1.00	2.50
244 Octavio Dotel RC	.60	1.50
245 Sean Casey	1.00	2.50
246 Joe Lawrence RC	.40	1.00
247 Adam Johnson RC	.40	1.00
248 Ronnie Belliard RC	1.25	3.00
249 Bobby Estalella	.20	.50
250 Corey Lee RC	.40	1.00
251 Mike Cameron	.20	.50
252 Kerry Robinson RC	.40	1.00
253 A.J. Zapp RC	.40	1.00
254 Jarrod Washburn	.20	.50
255 Ben Grieve	.20	.50
256 Javier Vazquez RC	1.50	4.00
257 Travis Lee RC	.60	1.50
258 Dennis Reyes RC	.40	1.00
259 Danny Buxbaum	.20	.50
260 Kelvim Escobar RC	1.00	2.50
261 Danny Klassen	.20	.50
262 Ken Cloude RC	.40	1.00
263 Gabe Alvarez	.20	.50
264 Clayton Bruner RC	.40	1.00
265 Jason Marquis RC	1.50	4.00
266 Jamey Wright	.20	.50
267 Matt Snyder RC	.40	1.00
268 Josh Garrett RC	.40	1.00
269 Juan Encarnacion	.20	.50
270 Heath Murray	.20	.50
271 Brent Butler RC	.40	1.00
272 Danny Peoples RC	.40	1.00
273 Miguel Tejada RC	4.00	10.00
274 Jim Pittsley	.20	.50
275 Dmitri Young	.20	.50
276 Vladimir Guerrero	.50	1.25
277 Cole Liniak RC	.40	1.00
278 Ramon Hernandez	.20	.50
279 Cliff Politte RC	.40	1.00
280 Mel Rosario RC	.40	1.00
281 Jorge Carrion RC	.40	1.00
282 John Barnes RC	.40	1.00
283 Chris Stowe RC	.40	1.00
284 Vernon Wells RC	3.00	8.00
285 Brett Caradonna RC	.40	1.00
286 Scott Hodges RC	.40	1.00
287 Jon Garland RC	2.50	6.00
288 Nathan Haynes RC	.40	1.00
289 Geoff Goetz RC	.40	1.00
290 Adam Kennedy RC	1.00	2.50
291 T.J. Tucker RC	.40	1.00
292 Aaron Akin RC	.40	1.00
293 Jayson Werth RC	3.00	8.00
294 Glenn Davis RC	.40	1.00
295 Mark Mangum RC	.40	1.00
296 Troy Cameron RC	.40	1.00
297 J.J. Davis RC	.40	1.00
298 Lance Berkman RC	4.00	10.00
299 Jason Standridge RC	.40	1.00
300 Jason Dellaero RC	.40	1.00

1997 Bowman Chrome International

*STARS: 1.25X TO 3X BASIC CARDS
*ROOKIES: .4X TO 1X BASIC CARDS
STATED ODDS 1:4

108 R.A. Dickey	8.00	20.00

1997 Bowman Chrome International Refractors

*STARS: 6X TO 15X BASIC CARDS
*ROOKIES: 2X TO 5X BASIC CARDS
STATED ODDS 1:24

108 R.A. Dickey	15.00	40.00
182 Adrian Beltre	150.00	400.00
212 Roy Halladay	100.00	250.00
273 Miguel Tejada	20.00	50.00
284 Vernon Wells	15.00	40.00
293 Jayson Werth	30.00	60.00

1997 Bowman Chrome Refractors

*STARS: 3X TO 8X BASIC CARDS
*ROOKIES: 1.5X TO 4X BASIC CARDS
STATED ODDS 1:12
INT'L REF.STATED ODDS 1:24

212 Roy Halladay	60.00	150.00
273 Miguel Tejada	15.00	40.00
284 Vernon Wells	12.50	30.00

1997 Bowman Chrome 1998 ROY Favorites

COMPLETE SET (15)	10.00	25.00

STATED ODDS 1:24
*REFRACTORS: .75X TO 2X BASIC ROY
REFRACTOR STATED ODDS 1:72

ROY1 Jeff Abbott	.60	1.50
ROY2 Karim Garcia	.60	1.50
ROY3 Todd Helton	1.50	4.00
ROY4 Richard Hidalgo	.60	1.50
ROY5 Geoff Jenkins	.60	1.50
ROY6 Russ Johnson	.60	1.50
ROY7 Paul Konerko	1.00	2.50
ROY8 Mark Kotsay	1.00	2.50
ROY9 Ricky Ledee	.40	1.00
ROY10 Travis Lee	.40	1.00
ROY11 Derrek Lee	1.00	2.50
ROY12 Elieser Marrero	.60	1.50
ROY13 Juan Melo	.60	1.50
ROY14 Brian Rose	.60	1.50
ROY15 Fernando Tatis	.25	.60

1997 Bowman Chrome Scout's Honor Roll

COMPLETE SET (15)	12.50	30.00

STATED ODDS 1:12
*REF: .75X TO 2X BASIC CHR.HONOR
REFRACTOR STATED ODDS 1:36

SHR1 Dmitri Young	.50	1.25
SHR2 Bob Abreu	.75	2.00
SHR3 Vladimir Guerrero	1.25	3.00
SHR4 Paul Konerko	.75	2.00
SHR5 Kevin Orie	.50	1.25
SHR6 Todd Walker	.50	1.25
SHR7 Ben Grieve	.50	1.25
SHR8 Darin Erstad	.50	1.25
SHR9 Derrek Lee	.75	2.00
SHR10 Jose Cruz Jr.	.50	1.25
SHR11 Scott Rolen	.75	2.00
SHR12 Travis Lee	.50	1.25
SHR13 Andruw Jones	.75	2.00
SHR14 Wilton Guerrero	.50	1.25
SHR15 Nomar Garciaparra	2.00	5.00

1998 Bowman Chrome

The 1998 Bowman Chrome set was issued in two separate series with a total of 441 cards. The four-card packs retailed for $3.00 each. These cards are parallel to the regular Bowman set but with a premium Chrome finish. Unlike the 1997 brand, the 1998 issue parallels the entire Bowman brand. Rookie Cards include Ryan Anderson, Jack Cust, Troy Glaus, Orlando Hernandez, Gabe Kapler, Carlos Lee, Ted Lilly, Ruben Mateo, Kevin Millwood, Magglio Ordonez and Jimmy Rollins.

COMPLETE SET (441)	20.00	50.00
COMPLETE SERIES 1 (221)	10.00	25.00
COMPLETE SERIES 2 (220)	10.00	25.00
1 Nomar Garciaparra	.75	2.00
2 Scott Rolen	.30	.75
3 Andy Pettitte	.30	.75
4 Ivan Rodriguez	.30	.75
5 Mark McGwire	1.25	3.00
6 Jason Dickson	.20	.50
7 Jose Cruz Jr.	.20	.50
8 Jeff Kent	.20	.50
9 Mike Mussina	.30	.75
10 Jason Kendall	.20	.50
11 Brett Tomko	.20	.50
12 Jeff King	.20	.50
13 Brad Radke	.20	.50
14 Robin Ventura	.20	.50
15 Jeff Bagwell	.30	.75
16 Greg Maddux	.75	2.00
17 John Jaha	.20	.50
18 Mike Piazza	.75	2.00
19 Edgar Martinez	.30	.75
20 David Justice	.20	.50
21 Todd Hundley	.20	.50
22 Tony Gwynn	.60	1.50
23 Larry Walker	.20	.50
24 Bernie Williams	.30	.75
25 Edgar Renteria	.20	.50
26 Rafael Palmeiro	.30	.75
27 Tim Salmon	.30	.75
28 Matt Morris	.20	.50
29 Shawn Estes	.20	.50
30 Vladimir Guerrero	.50	1.25
31 Fernando Tatis	.20	.50
32 Justin Thompson	.20	.50
33 Ken Griffey Jr.	1.00	2.50
34 Edgardo Alfonzo	.20	.50
35 Mo Vaughn	.20	.50
36 Marty Cordova	.20	.50
37 Craig Biggio	.30	.75
38 Roger Clemens	1.00	2.50
39 Mark Grace	.30	.75
40 Ken Caminiti	.20	.50
41 Tony Womack	.20	.50
42 Albert Belle	.20	.50
43 Tino Martinez	.30	.75
44 Sandy Alomar Jr.	.20	.50
45 Jeff Cirillo	.20	.50
46 Jason Giambi	.20	.50
47 Darin Erstad	.20	.50
48 Livan Hernandez	.20	.50
49 Mark Grudzielanek	.20	.50
50 Sammy Sosa	.50	1.25
51 Curt Schilling	.20	.50
52 Brian Hunter	.20	.50
53 Neifi Perez	.20	.50
54 Todd Walker	.20	.50
55 Jose Guillen	.20	.50
56 Jim Thome	.30	.75
57 Tom Glavine	.30	.75
58 Todd Greene	.20	.50
59 Rondell White	.20	.50
60 Roberto Alomar	.30	.75
61 Tony Clark	.20	.50
62 Vinny Castilla	.20	.50
63 Barry Larkin	.30	.75
64 Hideki Irabu	.20	.50
65 Johnny Damon	.30	.75
66 Juan Gonzalez	.20	.50
67 John Olerud	.20	.50
68 Gary Sheffield	.20	.50
69 Raul Mondesi	.20	.50
70 Chipper Jones	.50	1.25
71 David Ortiz	2.50	6.00
72 Warren Morris RC	.40	1.00
73 Alex Gonzalez	.20	.50
74 Nick Bierbrodt	.20	.50
75 Roy Halladay	1.00	2.50
76 Danny Buxbaum	.20	.50
77 Adam Kennedy	.20	.50
78 Jared Sandberg	.20	.50
79 Michael Barrett	.20	.50
80 Gil Meche	.60	1.50
81 Jayson Werth	.20	.50
82 Abraham Nunez	.20	.50
83 Ben Petrick	.20	.50
84 Brett Caradonna	.20	.50
85 Mike Lowell RC	2.50	6.00
86 Clay Bruner	.20	.50
87 John Curtice RC	.60	1.50
88 Bobby Estalella	.20	.50
89 Juan Melo	.20	.50
90 Arnold Gooch	.20	.50
91 Kevin Millwood RC	1.50	4.00
92 Richie Sexson	.20	.50
93 Orlando Cabrera	.20	.50
94 Pat Cline	.20	.50
95 Anthony Sanders	.20	.50
96 Russ Johnson	.20	.50
97 Ben Grieve	.20	.50
98 Kevin McGlinchy	.20	.50
99 Paul Wilder	.20	.50
100 Russ Ortiz	.20	.50
101 Ryan Jackson RC	.40	1.00
102 Heath Murray	.20	.50
103 Brian Rose	.20	.50
104 Ryan Radmanovich RC	.40	1.00
105 Ricky Ledee	.20	.50
106 Jeff Wallace RC	.40	1.00
107 Ryan Minor RC	.40	1.00
108 Dennis Reyes	.20	.50
109 James Manias	.20	.50
110 Chris Carpenter	.20	.50
111 Daryle Ward	.20	.50
112 Vernon Wells	.20	.50
113 Chad Green	.20	.50
114 Mike Stoner RC	.40	1.00
115 Brad Fullmer	.20	.50
116 Adam Eaton	.20	.50
117 Jeff Liefer	.20	.50
118 Corey Koskie RC	1.00	2.50
119 Todd Helton	.30	.75
120 Jaime Jones RC	.40	1.00
121 Mel Rosario	.20	.50
122 Geoff Goetz	.20	.50
123 Adrian Beltre	.20	.50
124 Jason Dellaero	.20	.50
125 Gabe Kapler RC	1.00	2.50
126 Scott Schoeneweis	.20	.50
127 Ryan Brannan	.20	.50
128 Aaron Akin	.20	.50
129 Ryan Anderson RC	.40	1.00
130 Brad Penny	.20	.50
131 Bruce Chen	.20	.50
132 Eli Marrero	.20	.50
133 Eric Chavez	.20	.50
134 Troy Glaus RC	3.00	8.00
135 Troy Cameron	.20	.50
136 Brian Sikorski RC	.40	1.00
137 Mike Kinkade RC	.40	1.00
138 Braden Looper	.20	.50
139 Mark Mangum	.20	.50
140 Danny Peoples	.20	.50
141 J.J. Davis	.20	.50
142 Ben Davis	.20	.50
143 Jacque Jones	.20	.50
144 Derrick Gibson	.20	.50
145 Bronson Arroyo	1.50	4.00
146 Luis De Los Santos RC	.40	1.00
147 Jeff Abbott	.20	.50
148 Mike Cuddyer RC	1.50	4.00
149 Jason Romano	.20	.50
150 Shane Monahan	.20	.50
151 Ntema Ndungidi RC	.40	1.00
152 Alex Sanchez	.20	.50
153 Jack Cust RC	3.00	8.00
154 Brent Butler	.20	.50
155 Ramon Hernandez	.20	.50
156 Norm Hutchins	.20	.50
157 Jason Marquis	.20	.50
158 Jacob Cruz	.20	.50
159 Rob Burger RC	.40	1.00
160 Dave Coggin	.20	.50
161 Preston Wilson	.20	.50
162 Jason Fitzgerald RC	.40	1.00
163 Dan Serafini	.20	.50
164 Pete Munro	.20	.50
165 Trot Nixon	.20	.50
166 Homer Bush	.20	.50
167 Dermal Brown	.20	.50
168 Chad Hermansen	.20	.50
169 Julio Moreno RC	.40	1.00
170 John Roskos RC	.40	1.00
171 Grant Roberts	.20	.50
172 Ken Cloude	.20	.50
173 Jason Brester	.20	.50
174 Jason Conti	.20	.50
175 Jon Garland	.20	.50
176 Robbie Bell	.20	.50
177 Nathan Haynes	.20	.50
178 Ramon Ortiz RC	.60	1.50
179 Shannon Stewart	.20	.50
180 Pablo Ortega	.20	.50
181 Jimmy Rollins RC	4.00	10.00
182 Sean Casey	.20	.50
183 Ted Lilly RC	1.00	2.50
184 Chris Enochs RC	.40	1.00
185 Magglio Ordonez UER RC	4.00	10.00
186 Mike Drumright	.20	.50
187 Aaron Boone	.20	.50
188 Matt Clement	.20	.50
189 Todd Dunwoody	.20	.50
190 Larry Rodriguez	.20	.50
191 Todd Noel	.20	.50
192 Geoff Jenkins	.20	.50
193 George Lombard	.20	.50
194 Lance Berkman	.20	.50
195 Marcus McCain	.20	.50
196 Ryan McGuire	.20	.50
197 Jhensy Sandoval	.20	.50
198 Corey Lee	.20	.50
199 Mario Valdez	.20	.50
200 Robert Fick RC	.60	1.50
201 Donnie Sadler	.20	.50
202 Marc Kroon	.20	.50
203 David Miller	.20	.50
204 Jarrod Washburn	.20	.50
205 Miguel Tejada	.50	1.25
206 Raul Ibanez	.20	.50
207 John Patterson	.20	.50
208 Calvin Pickering	.20	.50
209 Felix Martinez	.20	.50
210 Mark Redman	.20	.50
211 Scott Elarton	.20	.50
212 Jose Amado RC	.40	1.00
213 Kerry Wood	.20	.50
214 Dante Powell	.20	.50
215 Aramis Ramirez	.20	.50
216 A.J. Hinch	.20	.50
217 Dustin Carr RC	.40	1.00
218 Mark Kotsay	.20	.50
219 Jason Standridge	.20	.50
220 Luis Ordaz	.20	.50
221 Orlando Hernandez RC	2.00	5.00
222 Cal Ripken	1.50	4.00
223 Paul Molitor	.20	.50
224 Derek Jeter	1.25	3.00
225 Barry Bonds	1.25	3.00
226 Jim Edmonds	.20	.50

227 John Smoltz .30 .75
228 Eric Karros .20 .50
229 Ray Lankford .20 .50
230 Rey Ordonez .20 .50
231 Kenny Lofton .20 .50
232 Alex Rodriguez .75 2.00
233 Dante Bichette .20 .50
234 Pedro Martinez .30 .75
235 Carlos Delgado .20 .50
236 Rod Beck .20 .50
237 Matt Williams .20 .50
238 Charles Johnson .20 .50
239 Rico Brogna .20 .50
240 Frank Thomas .50 1.25
241 Paul O'Neill .30 .75
242 Jaret Wright .20 .50
243 Brant Brown .20 .50
244 Ryan Klesko .20 .50
245 Chuck Finley .20 .50
246 Derek Bell .20 .50
247 Delino DeShields .20 .50
248 Chan Ho Park .20 .50
249 Wade Boggs .30 .75
250 Jay Buhner .20 .50
251 Butch Huskey .20 .50
252 Steve Finley .20 .50
253 Will Clark .30 .75
254 John Valentin .20 .50
255 Bobby Higginson .20 .50
256 Darryl Strawberry .20 .50
257 Randy Johnson .50 1.25
258 Al Martin .20 .50
259 Travis Fryman .20 .50
260 Fred McGriff .30 .75
261 Jose Valentin .20 .50
262 Andruw Jones .30 .75
263 Kenny Rogers .20 .50
264 Moises Alou .20 .50
265 Denny Neagle .20 .50
266 Ugueth Urbina .20 .50
267 Derrek Lee .30 .75
268 Ellis Burks .20 .50
269 Mariano Rivera .50 1.25
270 Dean Palmer .20 .50
271 Eddie Taubensee .20 .50
272 Brady Anderson .20 .50
273 Brian Giles .20 .50
274 Quinton McCracken .20 .50
275 Henry Rodriguez .20 .50
276 Andres Galarraga .20 .50
277 Jose Canseco .30 .75
278 David Segui .20 .50
279 Bret Saberhagen .20 .50
280 Kevin Brown .30 .75
281 Chuck Knoblauch .20 .50
282 Jeromy Burnitz .20 .50
283 Jay Bell .20 .50
284 Manny Ramirez .30 .75
285 Rick Helling .20 .50
286 Francisco Cordova .20 .50
287 Bob Abreu .20 .50
288 J.T. Snow .20 .50
289 Hideo Nomo .50 1.25
290 Brian Jordan .20 .50
291 Javy Lopez .20 .50
292 Travis Lee .20 .50
293 Russell Branyan .20 .50
294 Paul Konerko .20 .50
295 Masato Yoshii RC .60 1.50
296 Kris Benson .20 .50
297 Juan Encarnacion .20 .50
298 Eric Milton .20 .50
299 Mike Caruso .20 .50
300 Ricardo Aramboles RC .40 1.00
301 Bobby Smith .20 .50
302 Billy Koch .20 .50
303 Richard Hidalgo .20 .50
304 Justin Baughman RC .40 1.00
305 Chris Gissell .20 .50
306 Donnie Bridges RC .40 1.00
307 Nelson Lara RC .40 1.00
308 Randy Wolf RC .60 1.50
309A Jason LaRue COR RC .60 1.50
Reds logo
309B Jason LaRue ERR RC .60 1.50
Red Sox logo
310 Jason Gooding RC .40 1.00
311 Edgard Clemente .20 .50
312 Andrew Vessel .20 .50
313 Chris Reitsma .20 .50
314 Jesus Sanchez RC .40 1.00
315 Buddy Carlyle RC .40 1.00
316 Randy Winn .20 .50
317 Luis Rivera RC .40 1.00
318 Marcus Thames RC 2.50 6.00
319 A.J. Pierzynski .20 .50
320 Scott Randall .20 .50
321 Damian Sapp .20 .50
322 Ed Yarnall RC .40 1.00
323 Luke Allen RC .40 1.00
324 J.D. Smart .20 .50
325 Willie Martinez .20 .50
326 Alex Ramirez .20 .50
327 Eric DuBose RC .40 1.00
328 Kevin Witt .20 .50
329 Dan McKinley RC .40 1.00
330 Cliff Politte .20 .50
331 Vladimir Nunez .20 .50
332 John Halama RC .40 1.00
333 Nerio Rodriguez .20 .50
334 Desi Relaford .20 .50
335 Robinson Checo .20 .50
336 John Nicholson .30 .75
337 Tom LaRosa RC .40 1.00
338 Kevin Nicholson RC .40 1.00
339 Javier Vazquez .20 .50
340 A.J. Zapp .20 .50
341 Tom Evans .20 .50
342 Kerry Robinson .20 .50
343 Gabe Gonzalez RC .40 1.00
344 Ralph Milliard .20 .50
345 Enrique Wilson .20 .50
346 Elvin Hernandez .20 .50
347 Mike Lincoln RC .40 1.00
348 Cesar King RC .40 1.00
349 Cristian Guzman RC .60 1.50
350 Donzell McDonald .20 .50
351 Jim Parque RC .40 1.00
352 Mike Saipe RC .40 1.00
353 Carlos Febles RC .60 1.50
354 Dernell Stenson RC .40 1.00
355 Mark Osborne RC .40 1.00
356 Odalis Perez RC 1.50 4.00
357 Jason Dewey RC .40 1.00
358 Joe Fontenot .20 .50
359 Jason Grilli RC .40 1.00
360 Kevin Haverbusch RC .40 1.00
361 Jay Yennaco RC .40 1.00
362 Brian Buchanan .20 .50
363 John Barnes .20 .50
364 Chris Fussell .20 .50
365 Kevin Gibbs RC .40 1.00
366 Joe Lawrence .20 .50
367 DaRond Stovall .20 .50
368 Brian Fuentes RC .40 1.00
369 Jimmy Anderson .20 .50
370 Lariel Gonzalez RC .40 1.00
371 Scott Williamson RC .40 1.00
372 Milton Bradley .20 .50
373 Jason Halper RC .40 1.00
374 Brent Billingsley RC .40 1.00
375 Joe DePastino RC .40 1.00
376 Jake Westbrook .20 .50
377 Octavio Dotel .20 .50
378 Jason Williams RC .40 1.00
379 Julio Ramirez RC .40 1.00
380 Seth Greisinger .20 .50
381 Mike Judd RC .40 1.00
382 Ben Ford RC .40 1.00
383 Tom Bennett RC .40 1.00
384 Adam Butler RC .40 1.00
385 Wade Miller RC 1.00 2.50
386 Kyle Peterson RC .40 1.00
387 Tommy Peterman RC .40 1.00
388 Onan Masaoka .20 .50
389 Jason Rakers RC .40 1.00
390 Rafael Medina .20 .50
391 Luis Lopez RC .40 1.00
392 Jeff Yoder .20 .50
393 Vance Wilson RC .40 1.00
394 Fernando Seguignol RC .40 1.00
395 Ron Wright .20 .50
396 Ruben Mateo RC .40 1.00
397 Steve Lomasney RC .60 1.50
398 Damian Jackson .20 .50
399 Mike Jerzembeck RC .40 1.00
400 Luis Rivas RC 1.00 2.50
401 Kevin Burford RC .40 1.00
402 Glenn Davis .20 .50
403 Robert Luce RC .40 1.00
404 Cole Liniak .20 .50
405 Matt LeCroy RC .60 1.50
406 Jeremy Giambi RC .60 1.50
407 Shawn Chacon .20 .50
408 Dewayne Wise RC .40 1.00
409 Steve Woodard .20 .50
410 Francisco Cordero RC 1.00 2.50
411 Damon Minor RC .40 1.00
412 Lou Collier .20 .50
413 Justin Towle .20 .50
414 Juan LeBron .20 .50
415 Michael Coleman .20 .50
416 Felix Rodriguez .20 .50
417 Paul Ah Yat RC .40 1.00
418 Kevin Barker RC .40 1.00
419 Brian Meadows .20 .50
420 Darnell McDonald RC .40 1.00
421 Matt Kinney RC .40 1.00
422 Mike Vavrek RC .40 1.00
423 Courtney Duncan RC .40 1.00
424 Kevin Millar RC 1.50 4.00
425 Ruben Rivera .20 .50
426 Steve Shoemaker RC .40 1.00
427 Dan Reichert RC .40 1.00
428 Carlos Lee RC 2.50 6.00
429 Rod Barajas 1.00 2.50
430 Pablo Ozuna RC .60 1.50
431 Todd Belitz RC .40 1.00
432 Sidney Ponson .20 .50
433 Steve Carver RC .40 1.00
434 Esteban Yan RC .60 1.50
435 Cedrick Bowers .20 .50
436 Marlon Anderson .20 .50
437 Carl Pavano .20 .50
438 Jae Weong Seo RC .60 1.50
439 Jose Taveras RC .40 1.00
440 Matt Anderson RC .40 1.00
441 Darron Ingram RC .40 1.00

1998 Bowman Chrome Golden Anniversary

*STARS: 6X TO 15X BASIC CARDS
*ROOKIES: 3X TO 8X BASIC CARDS
SER.1 STATED ODDS 1:164
SER.2 STATED ODDS 1:133
STATED PRINT RUN 50 SERIAL #'d SETS

1998 Bowman Chrome Golden Anniversary Refractors

SER.1 STATED ODDS 1:1279
SER.2 STATED ODDS 1:1022
STATED PRINT RUN 5 SERIAL #'d SETS
NO PRICING DUE TO SCARCITY

1998 Bowman Chrome International

*STARS: 1.5X TO 4X BASIC CARDS
*ROOKIES: .4X TO 1X BASIC
STATED ODDS 1:4

1998 Bowman Chrome International Refractors

COMPLETE SET (441) 2500.00 5000.00
*STARS: 5X TO 12X BASIC CARDS
*ROOKIES: 2X TO 5X BASIC CARDS
STATED ODDS 1:24

1998 Bowman Chrome Refractors

COMPLETE SET (441) 1500.00 2500.00
*STARS: 3X TO 8X BASIC CARDS
*ROOKIES: 1.5X TO 4X BASIC CARDS
STATED ODDS 1:12

1998 Bowman Chrome Reprints

COMPLETE SET (50) 75.00 150.00
COMPLETE SERIES 1 (25) 30.00 80.00
COMPLETE SERIES 2 (25) 30.00 80.00
STATED ODDS 1:12
*REFRACTORS: 1X TO 2.5X BASIC REPRINTS
REFRACTOR STATED ODDS 1:36
ODD NUMBER CARDS DIST.IN SER.1
EVEN NUMBER CARDS DIST.IN SER.2
1 Yogi Berra 1.50 4.00
2 Jackie Robinson 1.50 4.00
3 Don Newcombe .60 1.50
4 Satchell Paige 1.50 4.00
5 Willie Mays 4.00 10.00
6 Gil McDougald .60 1.50
7 Don Larsen .60 1.50
8 Elston Howard 1.00 2.50
9 Robin Ventura .60 1.50
10 Brady Anderson .60 1.50
11 Gary Sheffield .60 1.50
12 Tino Martinez 1.00 2.50
13 Ken Griffey Jr. 3.00 8.00
14 John Smoltz 1.00 2.50
15 Sandy Alomar Jr. .40 1.00
16 Larry Walker .60 1.50
17 Todd Hundley .40 1.00
18 Mo Vaughn .60 1.50
19 Sammy Sosa 1.50 4.00
20 Frank Thomas 1.50 4.00
21 Chuck Knoblauch .60 1.50
22 Bernie Williams 1.00 2.50
23 Juan Gonzalez .60 1.50
24 Mike Mussina 1.00 2.50
25 Jeff Bagwell 1.00 2.50
26 Tim Salmon 1.00 2.50
27 Ivan Rodriguez 1.00 2.50
28 Kenny Lofton .60 1.50
29 Chipper Jones 1.50 4.00
30 Javy Lopez .60 1.50
31 Ryan Klesko .60 1.50
32 Raul Mondesi .60 1.50
33 Jim Thome 1.00 2.50
34 Carlos Delgado .60 1.50
35 Mike Piazza 2.50 6.00
36 Manny Ramirez 1.00 2.50
37 Andy Pettitte 1.00 2.50
38 Derek Jeter 4.00 10.00
39 Brad Fullmer .40 1.00
40 Richard Hidalgo .40 1.00
41 Tony Clark .40 1.00
42 Andruw Jones 1.00 2.50
43 Vladimir Guerrero 1.50 4.00
44 Nomar Garciaparra 2.50 6.00
45 Paul Konerko .60 1.50
46 Ben Grieve .40 1.00
47 Hideo Nomo 1.50 4.00
48 Scott Rolen 1.00 2.50
49 Jose Guillen .60 1.50
50 Livan Hernandez .60 1.50

1999 Bowman Chrome

The 1999 Bowman Chrome set was issued in two distinct series and were distributed in four card packs with a suggested retail price of $3.00. The set contains 440 regular cards printed on brilliant chromium 18-pt. Stock. Within the set are 300 top prospects that are designated with silver and blue foil. Each player's facsimile rookie signature are featured on these cards. There are also 140 vereran stars designated with a red and silver foil stamp. The backs contain information on each player's rookie and most recent season, career statistics and a scouting report from early league days Rookie Cards include Pat Burrell, Carl Crawford, Adam Dunn, Rafael Furcal, Freddy Garcia, Tim Hudson, Nick Johnson, Austin Kearns, Willy Mo Pena, Adam Piatt, Corey Patterson and Alfonso Soriano.

COMPLETE SET (440) 60.00 120.00
COMPLETE SERIES 1 (220) 20.00 50.00
COMPLETE SERIES 2 (220) 30.00 80.00
COMMON CARD (1-440) .20 .50
COMMON RC .40 1.00
1 Ben Grieve .20 .50
2 Kerry Wood .20 .50
3 Ruben Rivera .20 .50
4 Sandy Alomar Jr. .20 .50
5 Cal Ripken 1.50 4.00
6 Mark McGwire .75 2.00
7 Vladimir Guerrero .30 .75
8 Moises Alou .20 .50
9 Jim Edmonds .30 .75
10 Greg Maddux .60 1.50
11 Gary Sheffield .20 .50
12 John Valentin .20 .50
13 Chuck Knoblauch .20 .50
14 Tony Clark .20 .50
15 Rusty Greer .20 .50
16 Al Leiter .20 .50
17 Travis Lee .20 .50
18 Jose Cruz Jr. .20 .50
19 Pedro Martinez .30 .75
20 Paul O'Neill .30 .75
21 Todd Walker .20 .50
22 Vinny Castilla .20 .50
23 Barry Larkin .30 .75
24 Curt Schilling .20 .50
25 Jason Kendall .20 .50
26 Scott Erickson .20 .50
27 Andres Galarraga .30 .75
28 Jeff Shaw .20 .50
29 John Olerud .20 .50
30 Orlando Hernandez .20 .50
31 Larry Walker .30 .75
32 Andruw Jones .20 .50
33 Jeff Cirillo .20 .50
34 Barry Bonds .75 2.00
35 Manny Ramirez .50 1.25
36 Mark Kotsay .20 .50
37 Ivan Rodriguez .30 .75
38 Jeff King .20 .50
39 Brian Hunter .20 .50
40 Ray Durham .20 .50
41 Bernie Williams .30 .75
42 Darin Erstad .20 .50
43 Chipper Jones .50 1.25
44 Pat Hentgen .20 .50
45 Eric Young .20 .50
46 Jaret Wright .20 .50
47 Juan Guzman .20 .50
48 Jorge Posada .30 .75
49 Bobby Higginson .20 .50
50 Jose Guillen .20 .50
51 Trevor Hoffman .30 .75
52 Ken Griffey Jr. 1.00 2.50
53 David Justice .20 .50
54 Matt Williams .20 .50
55 Eric Karros .20 .50
56 Derek Bell .20 .50
57 Ray Lankford .20 .50
58 Mariano Rivera .60 1.50
59 Brett Tomko .20 .50
60 Mike Mussina .30 .75
61 Kenny Lofton .20 .50
62 Chuck Finley .20 .50
63 Alex Gonzalez .20 .50
64 Mark Grace .30 .75
65 Raul Mondesi .20 .50
66 David Cone .20 .50
67 Brad Fullmer .20 .50
68 Andy Benes .20 .50
69 John Smoltz .30 .75
70 Shane Reynolds .20 .50
71 Bruce Chen .20 .50
72 Adam Kennedy .20 .50
73 Jack Cust .20 .50
74 Matt Clement .20 .50
75 Derrick Gibson .20 .50
76 Darnell McDonald .20 .50
77 Adam Everett RC .60 1.50
78 Ricardo Aramboles .20 .50
79 Mark Quinn RC .40 1.00
80 Jason Rakers .20 .50
81 Seth Etherton RC .40 1.00
82 Jeff Urban RC .40 1.00
83 Manny Aybar .20 .50
84 Mike Nannini RC .40 1.00
85 Onan Masaoka .20 .50
86 Rod Barajas .20 .50
87 Mike Frank .20 .50
88 Scott Randall .20 .50
89 Justin Bowles RC .40 1.00
90 Chris Haas .20 .50
91 Arturo McDowell RC .40 1.00
92 Matt Belisle RC .40 1.00
93 Scott Elarton .20 .50
94 Vernon Wells .20 .50
95 Pat Cline .20 .50
96 Ryan Anderson .20 .50
97 Kevin Barker .20 .50
98 Ruben Mateo .20 .50
99 Robert Fick .20 .50
100 Corey Koskie .20 .50
101 Ricky Ledee .20 .50
102 Rick Elder RC .40 1.00
103 Jack Cressend RC .40 1.00
104 Joe Lawrence .20 .50
105 Mike Lincoln .20 .50
106 Kit Pellow RC .40 1.00
107 Matt Burch RC .40 1.00
108 Cole Liniak .20 .50
109 Jason Dewey .20 .50
110 Cesar King .20 .50
111 Julio Ramirez .20 .50
112 Jake Westbrook .20 .50
113 Eric Valent RC .40 1.00
114 Roosevelt Brown RC .40 1.00
115 Choo Freeman RC .40 1.00
116 Juan Melo .20 .50
117 Jason Grilli .20 .50
118 Jared Sandberg .20 .50
119 Glenn Davis .20 .50
120 David Riske RC .40 1.00
121 Jacque Jones .20 .50
122 Corey Lee .20 .50
123 Michael Barrett .20 .50
124 Lariel Gonzalez .20 .50
125 Mitch Meluskey .20 .50
126 F.Adrian Garcia .20 .50
127 Tony Torcato RC .40 1.00
128 Jeff Liefer .20 .50
129 Ntema Ndungidi .20 .50
130 Andy Brown RC .40 1.00
131 Ryan Mills RC .40 1.00
132 Andy Abad RC .40 1.00
133 Carlos Febles .20 .50
134 Jason Tyner RC .40 1.00
135 Mark Osborne .20 .50
136 Phil Norton RC .40 1.00
137 Nathan Haynes .20 .50
138 Roy Halladay .30 .75
139 Juan Encarnacion .20 .50
140 Brad Penny .20 .50
141 Grant Roberts .20 .50
142 Aramis Ramirez .20 .50
143 Cristian Guzman .20 .50
144 Mamon Tucker RC .40 1.00
145 Ryan Bradley .20 .50
146 Brian Simmons .20 .50
147 Dan Reichert .20 .50
148 Russell Branyan .20 .50
149 Victor Valencia RC .40 1.00
150 Scott Schoeneweis .20 .50
151 Sean Spencer RC .40 1.00
152 Odalis Perez .20 .50
153 Joe Fontenot .20 .50
154 Milton Bradley .20 .50
155 Josh McKinley RC .40 1.00
156 Terrence Long .20 .50
157 Danny Klassen .20 .50
158 Paul Hoover RC .40 1.00
159 Ron Belliard .20 .50
160 Armando Rios .20 .50
161 Ramon Hernandez .20 .50
162 Jason Conti .20 .50
163 Chad Hermansen .20 .50
164 Jason Standridge .20 .50
165 Jason Dellaero .20 .50
166 John Curtice .20 .50
167 Clayton Andrews RC .40 1.00
168 Jeremy Giambi .20 .50
169 Alex Ramirez .20 .50
170 Gabe Molina RC .40 1.00
171 Mario Encarnacion RC .40 1.00
172 Mike Zywica RC .40 1.00
173 Chip Ambres RC .40 1.00
174 Trot Nixon .20 .50
175 Pat Burrell RC 1.50 4.00
176 Jeff Yoder .20 .50
177 Chris Jones RC .40 1.00
178 Kevin Witt .20 .50
179 Keith Luuloa RC .40 1.00
180 Billy Koch .20 .50
181 Damaso Marte RC .40 1.00
182 Ryan Glynn RC .40 1.00
183 Calvin Pickering .20 .50
184 Michael Cuddyer .20 .50
185 Nick Johnson RC 1.00 2.50
186 Doug Mientkiewicz RC .60 1.50
187 Nate Cornejo RC .40 1.00
188 Octavio Dotel .20 .50
189 Wes Helms .20 .50
190 Nelson Lara .20 .50
191 Chuck Abbott RC .40 1.00
192 Tony Armas Jr. .20 .50
193 Gil Meche .20 .50
194 Ben Petrick .20 .50
195 Chris George RC .40 1.00
196 Scott Hunter RC .40 1.00
197 Ryan Brannan .20 .50
198 Amaury Garcia RC .40 1.00
199 Chris Gissell .20 .50
200 Austin Kearns RC 1.50 4.00
201 Alex Gonzalez .20 .50
202 Wade Miller .20 .50
203 Scott Williamson .20 .50
204 Chris Enochs .20 .50
205 Fernando Seguignol .20 .50
206 Marlon Anderson .20 .50
207 Todd Sears RC .40 1.00
208 Nate Bump RC .40 1.00
209 J.M. Gold RC .40 1.00
210 Matt LeCroy .20 .50
211 Alex Hernandez .20 .50
212 Luis Rivera .20 .50
213 Troy Cameron .20 .50
214 Alex Escobar RC .40 1.00
215 Jason LaRue .20 .50
216 Kyle Peterson .20 .50
217 Brent Butler .20 .50
218 Dernell Stenson .20 .50
219 Adrian Beltre .50 1.25
220 Daryle Ward .20 .50
221 Jim Thome .30 .75
222 Cliff Floyd .20 .50
223 Rickey Henderson .50 1.25
224 Garret Anderson .20 .50
225 Ken Caminiti .20 .50
226 Bret Boone .20 .50
227 Jeromy Burnitz .20 .50
228 Steve Finley .20 .50
229 Miguel Tejada .30 .75
230 Greg Vaughn .20 .50
231 Jose Offerman .20 .50
232 Andy Ashby .20 .50
233 Albert Belle .20 .50
234 Fernando Tatis .20 .50
235 Todd Helton .30 .75
236 Sean Casey .20 .50
237 Brian Giles .20 .50
238 Andy Pettitte .30 .75
239 Fred McGriff .30 .75
240 Roberto Alomar .30 .75
241 Edgar Martinez .30 .75
242 Lee Stevens .20 .50
243 Shawn Green .20 .50
244 Ryan Klesko .20 .50
245 Sammy Sosa .50 1.25
246 Todd Hundley .20 .50
247 Shannon Stewart .20 .50
248 Randy Johnson .50 1.25
249 Rondell White .20 .50
250 Mike Piazza .50 1.25
251 Craig Biggio .30 .75
252 David Wells .20 .50
253 Brian Jordan .20 .50
254 Edgar Renteria .20 .50
255 Bartolo Colon .20 .50
256 Frank Thomas .50 1.25
257 Will Clark .30 .75
258 Dean Palmer .20 .50
259 Dmitri Young .20 .50
260 Scott Rolen .30 .75
261 Jeff Kent .20 .50
262 Dante Bichette .20 .50
263 Nomar Garciaparra .30 .75
264 Tony Gwynn .50 1.25
265 Alex Rodriguez .60 1.50
266 Jose Canseco .30 .75
267 Jason Giambi .20 .50
268 Jeff Bagwell .30 .75
269 Carlos Delgado .20 .50
270 Tom Glavine .30 .75
271 Eric Davis .20 .50
272 Edgardo Alfonzo .20 .50
273 Tim Salmon .30 .75
274 Johnny Damon .30 .75
275 Rafael Palmeiro .30 .75
276 Denny Neagle .20 .50
277 Neifi Perez .20 .50
278 Roger Clemens .60 1.50
279 Brant Brown .20 .50
280 Kevin Brown .20 .50
281 Jay Bell .20 .50
282 Jay Buhner .20 .50
283 Matt Lawton .20 .50
284 Robin Ventura .20 .50
285 Juan Gonzalez .20 .50
286 Mo Vaughn .20 .50
287 Kevin Millwood .20 .50
288 Tino Martinez .20 .50
289 Justin Thompson .20 .50
290 Derek Jeter 1.25 3.00
291 Ben Davis .20 .50
292 Mike Lowell .20 .50
293 Calvin Murray .20 .50
294 Micah Bowie RC .40 1.00
295 Lance Berkman .30 .75
296 Jason Marquis .20 .50
297 Chad Green .20 .50
298 Dee Brown .20 .50
299 Jerry Hairston Jr. .20 .50
300 Gabe Kapler .20 .50
301 Brent Stentz RC .40 1.00
302 Scott Mullen RC .40 1.00
303 Brandon Reed .20 .50
304 Shea Hillenbrand RC .60 1.50
305 J.D. Closser RC .40 1.00
306 Gary Matthews Jr. .20 .50
307 Toby Hall RC .40 1.00
308 Jason Phillips RC .40 1.00
309 Jose Macias RC .40 1.00
310 Jung Bong RC .40 1.00
311 Ramon Soler RC .40 1.00
312 Kelly Dransfeldt RC .40 1.00
313 Carlos E. Hernandez RC .40 1.00
314 Kevin Haverbusch .20 .50
315 Aaron Myette RC .40 1.00
316 Chad Harville RC .40 1.00
317 Kyle Farnsworth RC .40 1.00
318 Gookie Dawkins RC .40 1.00
319 Willie Martinez .20 .50
320 Carlos Lee .20 .50
321 Carlos Pena RC 1.25 3.00
322 Peter Bergeron RC .40 1.00
323 A.J. Burnett RC .60 1.50
324 Bucky Jacobsen RC .40 1.00
325 Mo Bruce RC .40 1.00
326 Reggie Taylor .20 .50
327 Jackie Rexrode .20 .50
328 Alvin Morrow RC .40 1.00
329 Carlos Beltran .30 .75
330 Eric Chavez .20 .50
331 John Patterson .20 .50
332 Jayson Werth .30 .75
333 Richie Sexson .20 .50
334 Randy Wolf .20 .50
335 Eli Marrero .20 .50
336 Paul LoDuca .20 .50
337 J.D Smart .20 .50
338 Ryan Minor .20 .50
339 Kris Benson .20 .50
340 George Lombard .20 .50
341 Troy Glaus .20 .50
342 Eddie Yarnall .20 .50
343 Kip Wells RC .40 1.00
344 C.C. Sabathia RC 3.00 8.00
345 Sean Burroughs RC .40 1.00
346 Felipe Lopez RC .60 1.50
347 Ryan Rupe RC .40 1.00
348 Orber Moreno RC .40 1.00
349 Rafael Roque RC .40 1.00
350 Alfonso Soriano RC 4.00 10.00
351 Pablo Ozuna .20 .50
352 Corey Patterson RC 1.00 2.50
353 Braden Looper .20 .50
354 Robbie Bell .20 .50
355 Mark Mulder RC 1.25 3.00
356 Angel Pena .20 .50
357 Kevin McGlinchy .20 .50
358 Michael Restovich RC .40 1.00
359 Eric DuBose .20 .50
360 Geoff Jenkins .20 .50
361 Mark Harriger RC .40 1.00
362 Junior Herndon RC .40 1.00
363 Tim Raines Jr. RC .40 1.00
364 Rafael Furcal RC 1.25 3.00
365 Marcus Giles RC 1.00 2.50
366 Ted Lilly .20 .50
367 Jorge Toca RC .40 1.00
368 David Kelton RC .40 1.00
369 Adam Dunn RC 1.50 4.00
370 Guillermo Mota RC .40 1.00
371 Brett Laxton RC .40 1.00
372 Travis Harper RC .40 1.00
373 Tom Davey RC .40 1.00
374 Darren Blakely RC .40 1.00
375 Tim Hudson RC 1.50 4.00
376 Jason Romano .20 .50
377 Dan Reichert .20 .50
378 Julio Lugo RC .60 1.50
379 Jose Garcia RC .40 1.00
380 Erubiel Durazo RC .40 1.00
381 Jose Jimenez .20 .50
382 Chris Fussell .20 .50
383 Steve Lomasney .20 .50
384 Juan Pena RC .40 1.00
385 Allen Levrault RC .40 1.00
386 Juan Rivera RC 1.00 2.50
387 Steve Colyer RC .40 1.00
388 Joe Nathan RC 1.00 2.50
389 Ron Walker RC .40 1.00
390 Nick Bierbrodt .20 .50
391 Luke Prokopec RC .40 1.00
392 Dave Roberts RC 1.00 2.50
393 Mike Darr .20 .50
394 Abraham Nunez RC .40 1.00
395 Giuseppe Chiaramonte RC .40 1.00
396 Jermaine Van Buren RC .40 1.00
397 Mike Kusiewicz .20 .50
398 Matt Wise RC .40 1.00
399 Joe McEwing RC .40 1.00
400 Matt Holliday RC 2.00 5.00
401 Willi Mo Pena RC 1.25 3.00
402 Ruben Quevedo RC .40 1.00
403 Rob Ryan RC .40 1.00
404 Freddy Garcia RC 1.00 2.50
405 Kevin Eberwein RC .40 1.00
406 Jesus Colome RC .40 1.00
407 Chris Singleton .20 .50
408 Bubba Crosby RC .40 1.00
409 Jesus Cordero RC .40 1.00
410 Donny Leon .20 .50
411 Goefrey Tomlinson RC .40 1.00
412 Jeff Winchester RC .40 1.00
413 Adam Piatt RC .40 1.00
414 Robert Stratton .20 .50
415 T.J. Tucker .20 .50
416 Ryan Langerhans RC .60 1.50
417 Anthony Shumaker RC .40 1.00
418 Matt Miller RC .40 1.00
419 Doug Clark RC .40 1.00
420 Kory DeHaan RC .40 1.00
421 David Eckstein RC 1.25 3.00
422 Brian Cooper RC .40 1.00
423 Brady Clark RC .40 1.00
424 Chris Magruder RC .40 1.00
425 Bobby Seay RC .40 1.00
426 Aubrey Huff RC 1.00 2.50
427 Mike Jerzembeck .20 .50
428 Matt Blank RC .40 1.00
429 Benny Agbayani RC .40 1.00
430 Kevin Beirne RC .40 1.00
431 Josh Hamilton RC 3.00 8.00
432 Josh Girdley RC .40 1.00
433 Kyle Snyder RC .40 1.00
434 Mike Paradis RC .40 1.00
435 Jason Jennings RC .60 1.50
436 David Walling RC .40 1.00
437 Omar Ortiz RC .40 1.00
438 Jay Gehrke RC .40 1.00
439 Casey Burns RC .40 1.00
440 Carl Crawford RC 2.00 5.00

1999 Bowman Chrome Gold

*GOLD: 2.5X TO 6X BASIC
*GOLD RC: 1.25X TO 3X BASIC RC
SER.1 STATED ODDS 1:12
SER.2 STATED ODDS 1:24

1999 Bowman Chrome Gold Refractors

*GOLD REF: 20X TO 50X BASIC
SER.1 STATED ODDS 1:305
SER.2 STATED ODDS 1:200
STATED PRINT RUN 25 SERIAL #'d SETS
NO RC PRICING DUE TO SCARCITY

1999 Bowman Chrome International

*INT: 1.25X TO 3X BASIC
*INT.RC: .6X TO 1.5X BASIC
SER.1 STATED ODDS 1:4
SER.2 STATED ODDS 1:12

1999 Bowman Chrome International Refractors

*INT REF: 6X TO 15X BASIC
*INT RC: 4X TO 8X BASIC RC
SER.1 STATED ODDS 1:76
SER.2 STATED ODDS 1:50
STATED PRINT RUN 100 SERIAL #'d SETS
369 Adam Dunn 75.00 150.00

1999 Bowman Chrome Refractors

*REF: 4X TO 10X BASIC
*REF RC: 2X TO 5X BASIC RC
SER.1 AND SER.2 STATED ODDS 1:12

1999 Bowman Chrome 2000 ROY Favorites

COMPLETE SET (10) 5.00 12.00
SER.2 STATED ODDS 1:20
*REF: .75X TO 2X BASIC CHR.2000 ROY
REFRACTOR SER.2 STATED ODDS 1:100
ROY1 Ryan Anderson .40 1.00
ROY2 Pat Burrell 1.50 4.00
ROY3 A.J. Burnett .60 1.50
ROY4 Ruben Mateo .40 1.00
ROY5 Alex Escobar .40 1.00
ROY6 Pablo Ozuna .40 1.00
ROY7 Mark Mulder 1.25 3.00
ROY8 Corey Patterson 1.00 2.50
ROY9 George Lombard .40 1.00
ROY10 Nick Johnson 1.00 2.50

1999 Bowman Chrome Diamond Aces

COMPLETE SET (18) 12.50 30.00
SER.1 STATED ODDS 1:21
*REF: .75X TO 2X BASIC CHR.ACES
REFRACTOR SER.1 ODDS 1:84
DA1 Troy Glaus .40 1.00
DA2 Eric Chavez .40 1.00
DA3 Fernando Seguignol .40 1.00
DA4 Ryan Anderson .40 1.00
DA5 Ruben Mateo .40 1.00
DA6 Carlos Beltran .60 1.50
DA7 Adrian Beltre 1.00 2.50
DA8 Bruce Chen .40 1.00
DA9 Pat Burrell 1.50 4.00
DA10 Mike Piazza 1.00 2.50
DA11 Ken Griffey Jr. 2.00 5.00
DA12 Chipper Jones 1.00 2.50
DA13 Derek Jeter 2.50 6.00
DA14 Mark McGwire 1.50 4.00
DA15 Nomar Garciaparra .60 1.50
DA16 Sammy Sosa 1.00 2.50
DA17 Juan Gonzalez .40 1.00
DA18 Alex Rodriguez 1.25 3.00

1999 Bowman Chrome Impact

COMPLETE SET (20) 15.00 40.00
SER.2 STATED ODDS 1:15
*REF: .75X TO 2X BASIC IMPACT
REFRACTOR SER.2 STATED ODDS 1:75
I1 Alfonso Soriano 4.00 10.00
I2 Pat Burrell 1.50 4.00
I3 Ruben Mateo .40 1.00
I4 A.J. Burnett .60 1.50
I5 Corey Patterson 1.00 2.50
I6 Daryle Ward .40 1.00
I7 Eric Chavez .40 1.00
I8 Troy Glaus .40 1.00
I9 Sean Casey .40 1.00
I10 Joe McEwing .40 1.00
I11 Gabe Kapler .40 1.00
I12 Michael Barrett .40 1.00
I13 Sammy Sosa 1.00 2.50
I14 Alex Rodriguez 1.25 3.00
I15 Mark McGwire 1.50 4.00
I16 Derek Jeter 2.50 6.00
I17 Nomar Garciaparra .60 1.50
I18 Mike Piazza 1.00 2.50
I19 Chipper Jones 1.00 2.50
I20 Ken Griffey Jr. 2.00 5.00

1999 Bowman Chrome Scout's Choice

COMPLETE SET (21) 10.00 25.00
SER.1 STATED ODDS 1:12
*REF: .75X TO 2X BASIC
REFRACTOR SER.1 ODDS 1:48
SC1 Ruben Mateo .40 1.00
SC2 Ryan Anderson .40 1.00
SC3 Pat Burrell 1.50 4.00
SC4 Troy Glaus .40 1.00
SC5 Eric Chavez .40 1.00
SC6 Adrian Beltre 1.00 2.50
SC7 Bruce Chen .40 1.00
SC8 Carlos Beltran .60 1.50
SC9 Alex Gonzalez .40 1.00
SC10 Carlos Lee .40 1.00
SC11 George Lombard .40 1.00
SC12 Matt Clement .40 1.00
SC13 Calvin Pickering .40 1.00
SC14 Marlon Anderson .40 1.00
SC15 Chad Hermansen .40 1.00
SC16 Russell Branyan .40 1.00
SC17 Jeremy Giambi .40 1.00
SC18 Ricky Ledee .40 1.00
SC19 John Patterson .40 1.00
SC20 Roy Halladay .60 1.50
SC21 Michael Barrett .40 1.00

2000 Bowman Chrome

COMPLETE SET (440) 40.00 80.00
COMMON CARD (1-440) .20 .50
COMMON RC .20 .50
1 Vladimir Guerrero .30 .75
2 Chipper Jones .50 1.25
3 Todd Walker .20 .50
4 Barry Larkin .30 .75
5 Bernie Williams .30 .75
6 Todd Helton .30 .75
7 Jermaine Dye .20 .50
8 Brian Giles .20 .50
9 Freddy Garcia .20 .50
10 Greg Vaughn .20 .50
11 Alex Gonzalez .20 .50
12 Luis Gonzalez .20 .50
13 Ron Belliard .20 .50
14 Ben Grieve .20 .50
15 Carlos Delgado .20 .50
16 Brian Jordan .20 .50
17 Fernando Tatis .20 .50
18 Ryan Rupe .20 .50
19 Miguel Tejada .30 .75
20 Mark Grace .30 .75
21 Kenny Lofton .20 .50
22 Eric Karros .20 .50
23 Cliff Floyd .20 .50
24 John Halama .20 .50
25 Cristian Guzman .20 .50
26 Scott Williamson .20 .50
27 Mike Lieberthal .20 .50
28 Tim Hudson .30 .75
29 Warren Morris .20 .50
30 Pedro Martinez .30 .75
31 John Smoltz .50 1.25
32 Ray Durham .20 .50
33 Chad Allen .20 .50
34 Tony Clark .20 .50
35 Tino Martinez .20 .50
36 J.T. Snow .20 .50
37 Kevin Brown .20 .50
38 Bartolo Colon .20 .50
39 Rey Ordonez .20 .50
40 Jeff Bagwell .30 .75
41 Ivan Rodriguez .30 .75
42 Eric Chavez .20 .50
43 Eric Milton .20 .50
44 Jose Canseco .30 .75
45 Shawn Green .20 .50
46 Rich Aurilia .20 .50
47 Roberto Alomar .30 .75
48 Brian Daubach .20 .50
49 Magglio Ordonez .30 .75
50 Derek Jeter 1.25 3.00
51 Kris Benson .20 .50
52 Albert Belle .20 .50
53 Rondell White .20 .50
54 Justin Thompson .20 .50
55 Nomar Garciaparra .30 .75
56 Chuck Finley .20 .50
57 Omar Vizquel .30 .75
58 Luis Castillo .20 .50
59 Richard Hidalgo .20 .50
60 Barry Bonds .75 2.00
61 Craig Biggio .30 .75
62 Doug Glanville .20 .50
63 Gabe Kapler .20 .50
64 Johnny Damon .30 .75
65 Pokey Reese .20 .50
66 Andy Pettitte .30 .75
67 B.J. Surhoff .20 .50
68 Richie Sexson .20 .50
69 Javy Lopez .20 .50
70 Raul Mondesi .20 .50
71 Darin Erstad .20 .50
72 Kevin Millwood .20 .50
73 Ricky Ledee .20 .50
74 John Olerud .20 .50
75 Sean Casey .20 .50
76 Carlos Febles .20 .50
77 Paul O'Neill .30 .75
78 Bob Abreu .20 .50
79 Neifi Perez .20 .50
80 Tony Gwynn .50 1.25
81 Russ Ortiz .20 .50
82 Matt Williams .20 .50
83 Chris Carpenter .30 .75
84 Roger Cedeno .20 .50
85 Tim Salmon .20 .50
86 Billy Koch .20 .50
87 Jeromy Burnitz .20 .50
88 Edgardo Alfonzo .20 .50
89 Jay Bell .20 .50
90 Manny Ramirez .50 1.25
91 Frank Thomas .50 1.25
92 Mike Mussina .30 .75
93 J.D. Drew .20 .50
94 Adrian Beltre .50 1.25
95 Alex Rodriguez .60 1.50
96 Larry Walker .30 .75
97 Juan Encarnacion .20 .50
98 Mike Sweeney .20 .50
99 Rusty Greer .20 .50
100 Randy Johnson .50 1.25
101 Jose Vidro .20 .50
102 Preston Wilson .20 .50
103 Greg Maddux .60 1.50
104 Jason Giambi .20 .50
105 Cal Ripken 1.50 4.00
106 Carlos Beltran .30 .75
107 Vinny Castilla .20 .50
108 Mariano Rivera .60 1.50
109 Mo Vaughn .20 .50
110 Rafael Palmeiro .30 .75
111 Shannon Stewart .20 .50
112 Mike Hampton .20 .50
113 Joe Nathan .20 .50
114 Ben Davis .20 .50
115 Andruw Jones .20 .50
116 Robin Ventura .20 .50
117 Damion Easley .20 .50
118 Jeff Cirillo .20 .50
119 Kerry Wood .20 .50
120 Scott Rolen .30 .75
121 Sammy Sosa .50 1.25
122 Ken Griffey Jr. 1.00 2.50
123 Shane Reynolds .20 .50
124 Troy Glaus .20 .50
125 Tom Glavine .30 .75
126 Michael Barrett .20 .50
127 Al Leiter .20 .50
128 Jason Kendall .20 .50
129 Roger Clemens .60 1.50
130 Juan Gonzalez .20 .50
131 Corey Koskie .20 .50
132 Curt Schilling .30 .75
133 Mike Piazza .50 1.25
134 Gary Sheffield .20 .50
135 Jim Thome .30 .75
136 Orlando Hernandez .20 .50
137 Ray Lankford .20 .50
138 Geoff Jenkins .20 .50
139 Jose Lima .20 .50
140 Mark McGwire .75 2.00
141 Adam Piatt .20 .50
142 Pat Manning RC .20 .50
143 Marcos Castillo RC .20 .50
144 Lesli Brea RC .20 .50
145 Humberto Cota RC .20 .50
146 Ben Petrick .20 .50
147 Kip Wells .20 .50
148 Wily Pena .20 .50
149 Chris Wakeland RC .20 .50
150 Brad Baker RC .20 .50
151 Robbie Morrison RC .20 .50
152 Reggie Taylor .20 .50
153 Matt Ginter RC .20 .50
154 Peter Bergeron .20 .50
155 Roosevelt Brown .20 .50
156 Matt Cepicky RC .20 .50
157 Ramon Castro .20 .50
158 Brad Baisley RC .20 .50
159 Jason Hart RC .20 .50
160 Mitch Meluskey .20 .50
161 Chad Harville .20 .50
162 Brian Cooper .20 .50
163 Marcus Giles .20 .50
164 Jim Morris 2.50 6.00
165 Geoff Goetz .20 .50
166 Bobby Bradley RC .20 .50
167 Rob Bell .20 .50
168 Joe Crede .20 .50
169 Michael Restovich .20 .50
170 Quincy Foster RC .20 .50
171 Enrique Cruz RC .20 .50
172 Mark Quinn .20 .50
173 Nick Johnson .20 .50
174 Jeff Liefer .20 .50
175 Kevin Mench RC .50 1.25
176 Steve Lomasney .20 .50
177 Jayson Werth .30 .75
178 Tim Drew .20 .50
179 Chip Ambres .20 .50
180 Ryan Anderson .20 .50
181 Matt Blank .20 .50
182 Giuseppe Chiaramonte .20 .50
183 Corey Myers RC .20 .50
184 Jeff Yoder .20 .50
185 Craig Dingman RC .20 .50
186 Jon Hamilton RC .20 .50
187 Toby Hall .20 .50
188 Russell Branyan .20 .50
189 Brian Falkenborg RC .20 .50
190 Aaron Harang RC 1.25 3.00
191 Juan Pena .20 .50
192 Chin-Hui Tsao RC .50 1.25
193 Alfonso Soriano .50 1.25
194 Alejandro Diaz RC .20 .50
195 Carlos Pena .30 .75
196 Kevin Nicholson .20 .50
197 Mo Bruce .20 .50
198 C.C. Sabathia .30 .75
199 Carl Crawford .30 .75
200 Rafael Furcal .30 .75
201 Andrew Beinbrink RC .20 .50
202 Jimmy Osting .20 .50
203 Aaron McNeal RC .20 .50
204 Brett Laxton .20 .50
205 Chris George .20 .50
206 Felipe Lopez .20 .50
207 Ben Sheets RC .50 1.25
208 Mike Meyers RC .30 .75
209 Jason Conti .20 .50
210 Milton Bradley .20 .50
211 Chris Mears RC .20 .50
212 Carlos Hernandez RC .20 .50
213 Jason Romano .20 .50
214 Geofrey Tomlinson .20 .50
215 Jimmy Rollins .30 .75
216 Pablo Ozuna .20 .50
217 Steve Cox .20 .50
218 Terrence Long .20 .50
219 Jeff DaVanon RC .20 .50
220 Rick Ankiel .30 .75
221 Jason Standridge .20 .50
222 Tony Armas Jr. .20 .50
223 Jason Tyner .20 .50
224 Ramon Ortiz .20 .50
225 Daryle Ward .20 .50
226 Enger Veras RC .20 .50
227 Chris Jones .20 .50
228 Eric Cammack RC .20 .50
229 Ruben Mateo .20 .50
230 Ken Harvey RC .20 .50
231 Jake Westbrook .20 .50
232 Rob Purvis RC .20 .50
233 Choo Freeman .20 .50
234 Aramis Ramirez .20 .50
235 A.J. Burnett .20 .50
236 Kevin Barker .20 .50
237 Chance Caple RC .20 .50
238 Jarrod Washburn .20 .50
239 Lance Berkman .30 .75
240 Michael Wenner RC .20 .50
241 Alex Sanchez .20 .50
242 Pat Daneker .20 .50
243 Grant Roberts .20 .50
244 Mark Ellis RC .30 .75
245 Donny Leon .20 .50
246 David Eckstein .20 .50
247 Dicky Gonzalez RC .20 .50
248 John Patterson .20 .50
249 Chad Green .20 .50
250 Scot Shields RC .20 .50
251 Troy Cameron .20 .50
252 Jose Molina .20 .50
253 Rob Pugmire RC .20 .50
254 Rick Elder .20 .50
255 Sean Burroughs .20 .50
256 Josh Kalinowski RC .20 .50
257 Matt LeCroy .20 .50
258 Alex Graman RC .20 .50
259 Juan Silvestre RC .20 .50
260 Brady Clark .20 .50
261 Rico Washington RC .20 .50
262 Gary Matthews Jr. .20 .50
263 Matt Wise .20 .50
264 Keith Reed RC .20 .50
265 Santiago Ramirez RC .20 .50
266 Ben Broussard RC .30 .75
267 Ryan Langerhans .20 .50
268 Juan Rivera .20 .50
269 Shawn Gallagher .20 .50
270 Jorge Toca .20 .50
271 Brad Lidge .20 .50
272 Leoncio Estrella RC .20 .50
273 Ruben Quevedo .20 .50
274 Jack Cust .20 .50
275 T.J. Tucker .20 .50
276 Mike Colangelo .20 .50
277 Brian Schneider .20 .50
278 Calvin Murray .20 .50
279 Josh Girdley .20 .50
280 Mike Paradis .20 .50
281 Chad Hermansen .20 .50
282 Ty Howington RC .20 .50
283 Aaron Myette .20 .50
284 D'Angelo Jimenez .20 .50
285 Dernell Stenson .20 .50
286 Jerry Hairston Jr. .20 .50
287 Gary Majewski RC .20 .50
288 Derrin Ebert .20 .50
289 Steve Fish RC .20 .50
290 Carlos E. Hernandez .20 .50
291 Allen Levrault .20 .50
292 Sean McNally RC .20 .50
293 Randey Dorame RC .20 .50
294 Wes Anderson RC .20 .50
295 B.J. Ryan .20 .50
296 Alan Webb RC .20 .50
297 Brandon Inge RC 1.25 3.00
298 David Walling .20 .50
299 Sun Woo Kim RC .20 .50
300 Pat Burrell .20 .50
301 Rick Guttormson RC .20 .50
302 Gil Meche .20 .50
303 Carlos Zambrano RC 1.25 3.00
304 Eric Byrnes UER RC .20 .50
305 Robb Quinlan RC .20 .50
306 Jackie Rexrode .20 .50
307 Nate Bump .20 .50
308 Sean DePaula RC .20 .50
309 Matt Riley .20 .50
310 Ryan Minor .20 .50
311 J.J. Davis .20 .50
312 Randy Wolf .20 .50
313 Jason Jennings .20 .50
314 Scott Seabol RC .20 .50
315 Doug Davis .20 .50
316 Todd Moser RC .20 .50
317 Rob Ryan .20 .50
318 Bubba Crosby .20 .50
319 Lyle Overbay RC .30 .75
320 Mario Encarnacion .20 .50
321 Francisco Rodriguez RC 1.25 3.00
322 Michael Cuddyer .20 .50
323 Ed Yarnall .20 .50
324 Cesar Saba RC .20 .50
325 Gookie Dawkins .20 .50
326 Alex Escobar .20 .50
327 Julio Zuleta RC .20 .50
328 Josh Hamilton .60 1.50
329 Carlos Urquiola RC .20 .50
330 Matt Belisle .20 .50
331 Kurt Ainsworth RC .20 .50
332 Tim Raines Jr. .20 .50
333 Eric Munson .20 .50
334 Donzell McDonald .20 .50
335 Larry Bigbie RC .20 .50
336 Matt Watson RC .20 .50
337 Aubrey Huff .20 .50
338 Julio Ramirez .20 .50
339 Jason Grabowski RC .20 .50
340 Jon Garland .20 .50
341 Austin Kearns .20 .50
342 Josh Pressley RC .20 .50
343 Miguel Olivo RC .30 .75
344 Julio Lugo .20 .50
345 Roberto Vaz .20 .50
346 Ramon Soler .20 .50
347 Brandon Phillips RC .75 2.00
348 Vince Faison RC .20 .50
349 Mike Venafro .20 .50
350 Rick Asadoorian RC .20 .50
351 B.J. Garbe RC .20 .50
352 Dan Reichert .20 .50
353 Jason Stumm RC .20 .50
354 Ruben Salazar RC .20 .50
355 Francisco Cordero .20 .50
356 Juan Guzman RC .20 .50
357 Mike Bacsik RC .20 .50
358 Jared Sandberg .20 .50
359 Rod Barajas .20 .50
360 Junior Brignac RC .20 .50
361 J.M. Gold .20 .50
362 Octavio Dotel .20 .50
363 David Kelton .20 .50
364 Scott Morgan .20 .50
365 Wascar Serrano RC .20 .50
366 Wilton Veras .20 .50
367 Eugene Kingsale .20 .50
368 Ted Lilly .20 .50
369 George Lombard .20 .50
370 Chris Haas .20 .50
371 Wilton Pena RC .20 .50
372 Vernon Wells .20 .50
373 Keith Ginter RC .20 .50
374 Jeff Heaverlo RC .20 .50
375 Calvin Pickering .20 .50
376 Mike Lamb RC .20 .50
377 Kyle Snyder .20 .50
378 Javier Cardona RC .20 .50
379 Aaron Rowand RC 1.00 2.50
380 Dee Brown .20 .50
381 Brett Myers RC .60 1.50
382 Abraham Nunez .20 .50
383 Eric Valent .20 .50
384 Jody Gerut RC .20 .50
385 Adam Dunn .30 .75
386 Jay Gehrke .20 .50
387 Omar Ortiz .20 .50
388 Darnell McDonald .20 .50
389 Tony Schrager RC .20 .50
390 J.D. Closser .20 .50
391 Ben Christensen RC .20 .50
392 Adam Kennedy .20 .50
393 Nick Green RC .20 .50
394 Ramon Hernandez .20 .50
395 Roy Oswalt RC 3.00 8.00
396 Andy Tracy RC .20 .50
397 Eric Gagne .20 .50
398 Michael Tejera RC .20 .50
399 Adam Everett .20 .50
400 Corey Patterson .20 .50
401 Gary Knotts RC .20 .50
402 Ryan Christianson RC .20 .50
403 Eric Ireland RC .20 .50
404 Andrew Good RC .20 .50
405 Brad Penny .20 .50
406 Jason LaRue .20 .50
407 Kit Pellow .20 .50
408 Kevin Beirne .20 .50
409 Kelly Dransfeldt .20 .50
410 Jason Grilli .20 .50
411 Scott Downs RC .20 .50
412 Jesus Colome .20 .50
413 John Sneed RC .20 .50
414 Tony McKnight .20 .50
415 Luis Rivera .20 .50
416 Adam Eaton .20 .50
417 Mike MacDougal RC .30 .75
418 Mike Nannini .20 .50
419 Barry Zito RC 1.50 4.00
420 DeWayne Wise .20 .50
421 Jason Dellaero .20 .50
422 Chad Moeller .20 .50
423 Jason Marquis .20 .50
424 Tim Redding RC .30 .75
425 Mark Mulder .20 .50
426 Josh Paul .20 .50
427 Chris Enochs .20 .50
428 Wilfredo Rodriguez RC .20 .50
429 Kevin Witt .20 .50
430 Scott Sobkowiak RC .20 .50
431 McKay Christensen .20 .50
432 Jung Bong .20 .50
433 Keith Evans RC .20 .50
434 Garry Maddox Jr. RC .20 .50
435 Ramon Santiago RC .20 .50
436 Alex Cora .30 .75
437 Carlos Lee .20 .50
438 Jason Repko RC .20 .50
439 Matt Burch .20 .50
440 Shawn Sonnier RC .20 .50

2000 Bowman Chrome Oversiz

COMPLETE SET (8) 2.50 6.00
ONE PER HOBBY BOX CHIP-TOPPER
1 Pat Burrell .40 1.00
2 Josh Hamilton 1.25 3.00
3 Rafael Furcal .60 1.50
4 Corey Patterson .40 1.00
5 A.J. Burnett .40 1.00
6 Eric Munson .40 1.00
7 Nick Johnson .40 1.00
8 Alfonso Soriano 1.00 2.50

2000 Bowman Chrome Refractors

*STARS: 3X TO 8X BASIC CARDS
*ROOKIES: 3X TO 8X BASIC CARDS
STATED ODDS 1:12

2000 Bowman Chrome Retro/Future

*RETRO: 1.5X TO 4X BASIC
STATED ODDS 1:6

2000 Bowman Chrome Retro/Future Refractors

*RETRO REF.: 6X TO 15X BASIC CARDS
STATED ODDS 1:60

2000 Bowman Chrome Bidding for the Call

COMPLETE SET (15) 5.00 12.00
STATED ODDS 1:16
*REFRACTORS: 1.25X TO 3X BASIC BID
REFRACTOR STATED ODDS 1:160
BC1 Adam Piatt .40 1.00
BC2 Pat Burrell .40 1.00
BC3 Mark Mulder .40 1.00
BC4 Nick Johnson .40 1.00
BC5 Alfonso Soriano 1.00 2.50
BC6 Chin-Feng Chen 1.25 3.00
BC7 Scott Sobkowiak .40 1.00
BC8 Corey Patterson .40 1.00
BC9 Jack Cust .40 1.00
BC10 Sean Burroughs .40 1.00
BC11 Josh Hamilton 1.25 3.00
BC12 Corey Myers .40 1.00
BC13 Eric Munson .40 1.00
BC14 Wes Anderson .40 1.00
BC15 Lyle Overbay .60 1.50

2000 Bowman Chrome Meteoric Rise

COMPLETE SET (10) 10.00 25.00
STATED ODDS 1:24
*REF: 1.25X TO 3X BASIC METEORIC
REFRACTOR STATED ODDS 1:240
MR1 Nomar Garciaparra .60 1.50
MR2 Mark McGwire 1.50 4.00
MR3 Ken Griffey Jr. 2.00 5.00
MR4 Chipper Jones 1.00 2.50
MR5 Manny Ramirez 1.00 2.50
MR6 Mike Piazza 1.00 2.50
MR7 Cal Ripken 3.00 8.00
MR8 Ivan Rodriguez .60 1.50
MR9 Greg Maddux 1.25 3.00
MR10 Randy Johnson 1.00 2.50

2000 Bowman Chrome Rookie Class 2000

COMPLETE SET (10) 2.50 6.00
STATED ODDS 1:24
*REF: 1.25X TO 3X BASIC ROOKIE CLASS
REFRACTOR STATED ODDS 1:240
RC1 Pat Burrell .40 1.00
RC2 Rick Ankiel .60 1.50
RC3 Ruben Mateo .40 1.00
RC4 Vernon Wells .40 1.00
RC5 Mark Mulder .40 1.00
RC6 A.J. Burnett .40 1.00
RC7 Chad Hermansen .40 1.00
RC8 Corey Patterson .40 1.00
RC9 Rafael Furcal .60 1.50
RC10 Mike Lamb .40 1.00

2000 Bowman Chrome Teen Idols

COMPLETE SET (15) 8.00 20.00
*SINGLES: 1X TO 2.5X BASIC CARDS
STATED ODDS 1:16
*REFRACTORS: 1.25X TO 3X BASIC TEEN
REFRACTOR STATED ODDS 1:160
TI1 Alex Rodriguez 1.25 3.00
TI2 Andruw Jones .40 1.00
TI3 Juan Gonzalez .40 1.00
TI4 Ivan Rodriguez .60 1.50
TI5 Ken Griffey Jr. 2.00 5.00
TI6 Bobby Bradley .40 1.00
TI7 Brett Myers 1.25 3.00
TI8 C.C. Sabathia .60 1.50
TI9 Ty Howington .40 1.00
TI10 Brandon Phillips 1.50 4.00
TI11 Rick Asadoorian .40 1.00
TI12 Wily Mo Pena .40 1.00
TI13 Sean Burroughs .40 1.00
TI14 Josh Hamilton 1.25 3.00
TI15 Rafael Furcal .60 1.50

2000 Bowman Chrome Draft

COMP.FACT.SET (110) 15.00 40.00
COMMON CARD (1-110) .20 .50
COMMON RC .20 .50
1 Pat Burrell .20 .50
2 Rafael Furcal .30 .75
3 Grant Roberts .30 .75
4 Barry Zito 1.50 4.00
5 Julio Zuleta .20 .50
6 Mark Mulder .20 .50
7 Rob Bell .20 .50
8 Adam Piatt .20 .50
9 Mike Lamb .20 .50
10 Pablo Ozuna .20 .50
11 Jason Tyner .20 .50
12 Jason Marquis .20 .50
13 Eric Munson .20 .50
14 Seth Etherton .20 .50
15 Milton Bradley .20 .50
16 Nick Green .20 .50
17 Chin-Feng Chen RC .60 1.50
18 Matt Boone RC .20 .50
19 Kevin Gregg RC .20 .50
20 Eddy Garabito RC .20 .50
21 Aaron Capista RC .20 .50
22 Esteban German RC .20 .50
23 Derek Thompson RC .20 .50
24 Phil Merrell RC .20 .50
25 Brian O'Connor RC .20 .50
26 Yamid Haad .20 .50
27 Hector Mercado RC .20 .50
28 Jason Woolf RC .20 .50
29 Eddy Furniss RC .20 .50
30 Cha Sueng Baek RC .20 .50
31 Colby Lewis RC .50 1.25
32 Pasqual Coco RC .20 .50
33 Jorge Cantu RC .30 .75
34 Erasmo Ramirez RC .20 .50
35 Bobby Kielty RC .20 .50
36 Joaquin Benoit RC .20 .50
37 Brian Esposito RC .20 .50
38 Michael Wenner .20 .50
39 Juan Rincon RC .20 .50
40 Yorvit Torrealba RC .30 .75
41 Chad Durham RC .20 .50
42 Jim Mann RC .20 .50
43 Shane Loux RC .20 .50
44 Luis Rivas .20 .50
45 Ken Chenard RC .20 .50
46 Mike Lockwood RC .20 .50
47 Yovanny Lara RC .20 .50
48 Bubba Carpenter RC .20 .50
49 Ryan Dittfurth RC .20 .50
50 John Stephens RC .20 .50
51 Pedro Feliz RC .50 1.25
52 Kenny Kelly RC .20 .50
53 Neil Jenkins RC .20 .50
54 Mike Glendenning RC .20 .50
55 Bo Porter .20 .50
56 Eric Byrnes .20 .50
57 Tony Alvarez RC .20 .50
58 Kazuhiro Sasaki RC .50 1.25
59 Chad Durbin RC .20 .50
60 Mike Bynum RC .20 .50
61 Travis Wilson RC .20 .50
62 Jose Leon RC .20 .50
63 Ryan Vogelsong RC 2.00 5.00
64 Geraldo Guzman RC .20 .50
65 Craig Anderson RC .20 .50
66 Carlos Silva RC .20 .50
67 Brad Thomas RC .20 .50
68 Chin-Hui Tsao .50 1.25
69 Mark Buehrle RC 3.00 8.00
70 Juan Salas RC .20 .50
71 Denny Abreu RC .20 .50
72 Keith McDonald RC .20 .50
73 Chris Richard RC .20 .50
74 Tomas De la Rosa RC .20 .50
75 Vicente Padilla RC .50 1.25
76 Justin Brunette RC .20 .50
77 Scott Linebrink RC .20 .50
78 Jeff Sparks RC .20 .50
79 Tike Redman RC .20 .50
80 John Lackey RC 1.25 3.00
81 Joe Strong RC .20 .50
82 Brian Tollberg RC .20 .50
83 Steve Sisco RC .20 .50
84 Chris Clapinski RC .20 .50
85 Augie Ojeda RC .20 .50
86 Adrian Gonzalez RC 6.00 15.00
87 Mike Stodolka RC .20 .50
88 Adam Johnson RC .20 .50
89 Matt Wheatland RC .20 .50
90 Corey Smith RC .20 .50
91 Rocco Baldelli RC .50 1.25
92 Keith Bucktrot RC .20 .50
93 Adam Wainwright RC 2.00 5.00
94 Blaine Boyer RC .20 .50
95 Aaron Herr RC .30 .75
96 Scott Thorman RC .30 .75
97 Bryan Digby RC .20 .50
98 Josh Shortslef RC .20 .50
99 Sean Smith RC .20 .50
100 Alex Cruz RC .20 .50
101 Marc Love RC .20 .50
102 Kevin Lee RC .20 .50
103 Timo Perez RC .30 .75
104 Alex Cabrera RC .20 .50
105 Shane Heams RC .20 .50
106 Tripper Johnson RC .20 .50
107 Brent Abernathy RC .20 .50
108 John Cotton RC .20 .50
109 Brad Wilkerson RC .50 1.25
110 Jon Rauch RC .20 .50

2001 Bowman Chrome

COMP.SET w/o SP's (220) 30.00 80.00
COMMON (1-110/201-310) .20 .50
COM.REF (111-200/311-330) 2.00 5.00
111-200/311-330 STATED ODDS 1:4
COMMON AU REF (331-350) 6.00 15.00
331-350 STATED ODDS 1:147
331-350 PRINT RUN 500 SERIAL #'d SETS
CARDS 111-200/311-350 ARE REFRACTORS
ICHIRO EXCH ODDS SAME AS OTHER REF.
ICHIRO PRINT RUN: 50% ENGL.-50% JAPAN
EXCHANGE DEADLINE 06/30/03
1 Jason Giambi .20 .50
2 Rafael Furcal .20 .50
3 Bernie Williams .30 .75
4 Kenny Lofton .20 .50
5 Al Leiter .20 .50
6 Albert Belle .20 .50
7 Craig Biggio .30 .75
8 Mark Mulder .20 .50
9 Carlos Delgado .20 .50
10 Darin Erstad .20 .50
11 Richie Sexson .20 .50
12 Randy Johnson .50 1.25
13 Greg Maddux .75 2.00
14 Orlando Hernandez .20 .50
15 Javier Vazquez .20 .50
16 Jeff Kent .20 .50
17 Jim Thome .30 .75
18 John Olerud .20 .50
19 Jason Kendall .20 .50
20 Scott Rolen .30 .75
21 Tony Gwynn .60 1.50
22 Edgardo Alfonzo .20 .50
23 Pokey Reese .20 .50
24 Todd Helton .30 .75
25 Mark Quinn .20 .50
26 Dean Palmer .20 .50
27 Ray Durham .20 .50
28 Rafael Palmeiro .30 .75
29 Carl Everett .20 .50
30 Vladimir Guerrero .50 1.25
31 Livan Hernandez .20 .50
32 Preston Wilson .20 .50
33 Jose Vidro .20 .50
34 Fred McGriff .30 .75
35 Kevin Brown .20 .50
36 Miguel Tejada .20 .50
37 Chipper Jones .50 1.25
38 Edgar Martinez .30 .75
39 Tony Batista .20 .50
40 Jorge Posada .30 .75
41 Sammy Sosa .50 1.25
42 Gary Sheffield .20 .50
43 Bartolo Colon .20 .50
44 Pat Burrell .20 .50
45 Jay Payton .20 .50
46 Mike Mussina .30 .75
47 Nomar Garciaparra .75 2.00
48 Darren Dreifort .20 .50
49 Richard Hidalgo .20 .50
50 Troy Glaus .20 .50
51 Ben Grieve .20 .50
52 Jim Edmonds .20 .50
53 Raul Mondesi .20 .50
54 Andruw Jones .30 .75
55 Mike Sweeney .20 .50
56 Derek Jeter 1.25 3.00
57 Ruben Mateo .20 .50
58 Cristian Guzman .20 .50
59 Mike Hampton .20 .50
60 J.D. Drew .20 .50
61 Matt Lawton .20 .50
62 Moises Alou .20 .50
63 Terrence Long .20 .50
64 Geoff Jenkins .20 .50
65 Manny Ramirez Sox .30 .75
66 Johnny Damon .30 .75
67 Pedro Martinez .30 .75
68 Juan Gonzalez .20 .50
69 Roger Clemens 1.00 2.50
70 Carlos Beltran .20 .50
71 Roberto Alomar .30 .75
72 Barry Bonds 1.25 3.00
73 Tim Hudson .20 .50
74 Tom Glavine .30 .75
75 Jeromy Burnitz .20 .50
76 Adrian Beltre .20 .50
77 Mike Piazza .75 2.00
78 Kerry Wood .20 .50
79 Steve Finley .20 .50
80 Bob Abreu .20 .50
81 Neifi Perez .20 .50
82 Mark Redman .20 .50
83 Paul Konerko .20 .50
84 Jermaine Dye .20 .50
85 Brian Giles .20 .50
86 Ivan Rodriguez .30 .75
87 Adam Kennedy .20 .50
88 Eric Chavez .20 .50
89 Billy Koch .20 .50
90 Shawn Green .20 .50
91 Matt Williams .20 .50
92 Greg Vaughn .20 .50
93 Jeff Cirillo .20 .50
94 Frank Thomas .50 1.25
95 David Justice .20 .50
96 Cal Ripken 1.50 4.00
97 Curt Schilling .20 .50
98 Barry Zito .30 .75
99 Brian Jordan .20 .50
100 Chan Ho Park .20 .50
101 J.T. Snow .20 .50
102 Kazuhiro Sasaki .20 .50
103 Alex Rodriguez .60 1.50
104 Mariano Rivera .50 1.25
105 Eric Milton .20 .50
106 Andy Pettitte .30 .75
107 Ken Griffey Jr. 1.00 2.50
108 Bengie Molina .20 .50
109 Jeff Bagwell .30 .75
110 Mark McGwire 1.25 3.00
111 Dan Tosca RC 2.00 5.00
112 Sergio Contreras RC 3.00 8.00
113 Mitch Jones RC 3.00 8.00
114 Ramon Carvajal RC 3.00 8.00
115 Ryan Madson RC 4.00 10.00
116 Hank Blalock RC 6.00 15.00
117 Ben Washburn RC 2.00 5.00
118 Erick Almonte RC 2.00 5.00
119 Shawn Fagan RC 3.00 8.00
120 Gary Johnson RC 2.00 5.00
121 Brett Evert RC 2.00 5.00
122 Joe Hamer RC 3.00 8.00
123 Yhency Brazoban RC 4.00 10.00
124 Domingo Guante RC 2.00 5.00
125 Delvi Mendez RC 2.00 5.00
126 Adrian Hernandez RC 2.00 5.00
127 Reggie Abercrombie RC 4.00 10.00
128 Steve Bennett RC 2.00 5.00
129 Matt White RC 3.00 8.00
130 Brian Hitchcox RC 2.00 5.00
131 Deivis Santos RC 2.00 5.00
132 Luis Montanez RC 4.00 10.00
133 Eric Reynolds RC 2.00 5.00
134 Denny Bautista RC 4.00 10.00
135 Hector Garcia RC 2.00 5.00
136 Joe Thurston RC 3.00 8.00
137 Tsuyoshi Shinjo RC 4.00 10.00
138 Elpidio Guzman RC 2.00 5.00
139 Brian Bass RC 2.00 5.00
140 Mark Burnett RC 3.00 8.00
141 Russ Jacobson UER 2.00 5.00
142 Travis Hafner RC 5.00 12.00
143 Wilson Betemit RC 6.00 15.00
144 Luke Lockwood RC 3.00 8.00
145 Noel Devarez RC 3.00 8.00
146 Doug Gredvig RC 2.00 5.00
147 Seung Song RC 3.00 8.00
148 Andy Van Hekken RC 2.00 5.00
149 Ryan Kohlmeier 2.00 5.00
150 Dee Haynes RC 2.00 5.00
151 Jim Journell RC 3.00 8.00
152 Chad Petty RC 2.00 5.00
153 Danny Borrell RC 2.00 5.00
154 Dave Krynzel 2.00 5.00
155 Octavio Martinez RC 3.00 8.00
156 David Parrish RC 2.00 5.00
157 Jason Miller RC 2.00 5.00
158 Corey Spencer RC 2.00 5.00

159 Maxim St. Pierre RC 3.00 8.00
160 Pat Magness RC 3.00 8.00
161 Ranier Olmedo RC 3.00 8.00
162 Brandon Mims RC 2.00 5.00
163 Phil Wilson RC 3.00 8.00
164 Jose Reyes RC 12.00 30.00
165 Matt Butler RC 3.00 8.00
166 Joel Pineiro 3.00 8.00
167 Ken Chenard 2.00 5.00
168 Alexis Gomez RC 2.00 5.00
169 Justin Morneau RC 6.00 15.00
170 Josh Fogg RC 3.00 8.00
171 Charles Frazier RC 2.00 5.00
172 Ryan Ludwick RC 3.00 8.00
173 Seth McClung RC 3.00 8.00
174 Justin Wayne RC 3.00 8.00
175 Rafael Soriano RC 4.00 10.00
176 Jared Abruzzo RC 2.00 5.00
177 Jason Richardson RC 2.00 5.00
178 Darwin Cubillan RC 2.00 5.00
179 Blake Williams RC 2.00 5.00
180 Valentino Pascucci RC 3.00 8.00
181 Ryan Hannaman RC 3.00 8.00
182 Steve Smyth RC 3.00 8.00
183 Jake Peavy RC 5.00 12.00
184 Onix Mercado RC 3.00 8.00
185 Luis Torres RC 3.00 8.00
186 Casey Fossum RC 2.00 5.00
187 Eduardo Figueroa RC 2.00 5.00
188 Bryan Barnowski RC 2.00 5.00
189 Jason Standridge 2.00 5.00
190 Marvin Seale RC 3.00 8.00
191 Steve Smitherman RC 3.00 8.00
192 Rafael Boitel RC 2.00 5.00
193 Dany Morban RC 2.00 5.00
194 Justin Woodrow RC 3.00 8.00
195 Ed Rogers RC 2.00 5.00
196 Ben Hendrickson RC 2.00 5.00
197 Thomas Mitchell 2.00 5.00
198 Adam Pettyjohn RC 2.00 5.00
199 Doug Nickle RC 2.00 5.00
200 Jason Jones RC 2.00 5.00
201 Larry Barnes .20 .50
202 Ben Diggins .20 .50
203 Dee Brown .20 .50
204 Rocco Baldelli .20 .50
205 Luis Terrero .20 .50
206 Milton Bradley .20 .50
207 Kurt Ainsworth .20 .50
208 Sean Burroughs .20 .50
209 Rick Asadoorian .20 .50
210 Ramon Castro .20 .50
211 Nick Neugebauer .20 .50
212 Aaron Myette .20 .50
213 Luis Matos .20 .50
214 Donnie Bridges .20 .50
215 Alex Cintron .20 .50
216 Bobby Kielty .20 .50
217 Matt Belisle .20 .50
218 Adam Everett .20 .50
219 John Lackey .20 .50
220 Adam Wainwright .75 2.00
221 Jerry Hairston Jr. .20 .50
222 Mike Bynum .20 .50
223 Ryan Christianson .20 .50
224 J.J. Davis .20 .50
225 Alex Graman .20 .50
226 Abraham Nunez .20 .50
227 Sun Woo Kim .20 .50
228 Jimmy Rollins .20 .50
229 Ruben Salazar .20 .50
230 Josh Girdley .20 .50
231 Carl Crawford .20 .50
232 Ben Davis .20 .50
233 Jason Grabowski .20 .50
234 Chris George .20 .50
235 Roy Oswalt .50 1.25
236 Brian Cole .20 .50
237 Corey Patterson .20 .50
238 Vernon Wells .20 .50
239 Brad Baker .20 .50
240 Gookie Dawkins .20 .50
241 Michael Cuddyer .20 .50
242 Ricardo Aramboles .20 .50
243 Ben Sheets .30 .75
244 Toby Hall .20 .50
245 Jack Cust .20 .50
246 Pedro Feliz .20 .50
247 Josh Beckett .30 .75
248 Alex Escobar .20 .50
249 Marcus Giles .20 .50
250 Jon Rauch .20 .50
251 Kevin Mench .20 .50
252 Shawn Sonnier .20 .50
253 Aaron Rowand .20 .50
254 C.C. Sabathia .20 .50
255 Bubba Crosby .20 .50
256 Josh Hamilton .40 1.00
257 Carlos Hernandez .20 .50
258 Carlos Pena .20 .50
259 Miguel Cabrera UER 6.00 15.00
260 Brandon Phillips .20 .50
261 Tony Pena Jr. .20 .50
262 Cristian Guerrero .20 .50
263 Jin Ho Cho .20 .50
264 Aaron Herr .20 .50
265 Keith Ginter .20 .50
266 Felipe Lopez .20 .50
267 Travis Harper .20 .50
268 Joe Torres .20 .50
269 Eric Byrnes .20 .50
270 Ben Christensen .20 .50
271 Aubrey Huff .20 .50
272 Lyle Overbay .20 .50
273 Vince Faison .20 .50
274 Bobby Bradley .20 .50
275 Joe Crede .50 1.25
276 Matt Wheatland .20 .50
277 Grady Sizemore .75 2.00
278 Adrian Gonzalez .60 1.50
279 Tim Raines Jr. .20 .50
280 Phil Dumatrait .20 .50
281 Jason Hart .20 .50
282 David Kelton .20 .50
283 David Walling .20 .50
284 J.R. House .20 .50
285 Kenny Kelly .20 .50
286 Aaron McNeal .20 .50
287 Nick Johnson .20 .50
288 Scott Heard .20 .50
289 Brad Wilkerson .20 .50
290 Allen Levrault .20 .50
291 Chris Richard .20 .50
292 Jared Sandberg .20 .50
293 Tike Redman .20 .50
294 Adam Dunn .30 .75
295 Josh Pressley .20 .50
296 Jose Ortiz .20 .50
297 Jason Romano .20 .50
298 Tim Redding .20 .50
299 Alex Gordon .20 .50
300 Ben Petrick .20 .50
301 Eric Munson .20 .50
302 Luis Rivas .20 .50
303 Matt Ginter .20 .50
304 Alfonso Soriano .30 .75
305 Wilfredo Rodriguez .20 .50
306 Brett Myers .20 .50
307 Scott Seabol .20 .50
308 Tony Alvarez .20 .50
309 Donzell McDonald .20 .50
310 Austin Kearns .20 .50
311 Will Ohman RC 3.00 8.00
312 Ryan Soules RC 2.00 5.00
313 Cody Ross RC 6.00 15.00
314 Bill Whitecotton RC 2.00 5.00
315 Mike Burns RC 3.00 8.00
316 Manuel Acosta RC 2.00 5.00
317 Lance Niekro RC 4.00 10.00
318 Travis Thompson RC 3.00 8.00
319 Zach Sorensen RC 3.00 8.00
320 Austin Evans RC 2.00 5.00
321 Brad Stiles RC 2.00 5.00
322 Joe Kennedy RC 4.00 10.00
323 Luke Martin RC 3.00 8.00
324 Juan Diaz RC 3.00 8.00
325 Pat Hallmark RC 2.00 5.00
326 Christian Parker RC 2.00 5.00
327 Ronny Corona RC 3.00 8.00
328 Jermaine Clark RC 2.00 5.00
329 Scott Dunn RC 3.00 8.00
330 Scott Chiasson RC 3.00 8.00
331 Greg Nash AU RC 6.00 15.00
332 Brad Cresse AU 6.00 15.00
333 John Buck AU RC 6.00 15.00
334 Freddie Bynum AU RC 6.00 15.00
335 Felix Diaz AU RC 6.00 15.00
336 Jason Belcher AU RC 6.00 15.00
337 Troy Farnsworth AU RC 6.00 15.00
338 Roberto Miniel AU RC 6.00 15.00
339 Esix Snead AU RC 6.00 15.00
340 Albert Pujols AU RC 4000.00 8000.00
341 Jeff Andra AU RC 6.00 15.00
342 Victor Hall AU RC 6.00 15.00
343 Pedro Liriano AU RC 6.00 15.00
344 Andy Beal AU RC 6.00 15.00
345 Bob Keppel AU RC 6.00 15.00
346 Brian Schmitt AU RC 6.00 15.00
347 Ron Davenport AU RC 6.00 15.00
348 Tony Blanco AU RC 6.00 15.00
349 Reggie Griggs AU RC 6.00 15.00
350 Derrick Van Dusen AU RC 6.00 15.00
351A Ichiro Suzuki English RC 75.00 200.00
351B Ichiro Suzuki Japan RC 75.00 200.00

2001 Bowman Chrome Gold Refractors

*STARS: 8X TO 20X BASIC CARDS
*ROOKIES: 1.5X TO 4X BASIC CARDS
STATED ODDS 1:47
STATED PRINT RUN 99 SERIAL #'d SETS
ICHIRO ENGLISH PRINT RUN 50 #'d CARDS
ICHIRO JAPAN PRINT RUN 49 #'d CARDS
ICHIRO ENGLISH ARE EVEN SERIAL #'d
ICHIRO ENGLISH ARE ODD SERIAL #'d
ICHIRO EXCHANGE DEADLINE 06/30/03
56 Derek Jeter 40.00 80.00
NNOA Ichiro English/50 400.00 1000.00
NNOB Ichiro Japan/49 400.00 1000.00

2001 Bowman Chrome X-Fractors

*STARS: 4X TO 10X BASIC CARDS
*ROOKIES: .75X TO 2X BASIC CARDS
STATED ODDS 1:23
ICHIRO PRINT RUN: 50% ENGL.-50% JAPAN
EXCHANGE DEADLINE 06/30/03

2001 Bowman Chrome Futures Game Relics

STATED ODDS 1:460
FGRAE Alex Escobar 3.00 8.00
FGRAM Aaron Myette 3.00 8.00
FGRBB Bobby Bradley 3.00 8.00
FGRBP Ben Petrick 3.00 8.00
FGRBS Ben Sheets 6.00 15.00
FGRBW Brad Wilkerson 3.00 8.00
FGRBZ Barry Zito 6.00 15.00
FGRCA Craig Anderson 3.00 8.00
FGRCC Chin-Feng Chen 30.00 60.00
FGRCG Chris George 3.00 8.00
FGRCH Carlos Hernandez 4.00 10.00
FGRCP Carlos Pena 10.00 25.00
FGRCT Chin-Hui Tsao 40.00 80.00
FGREM Eric Munson 3.00 8.00
FGRFL Felipe Lopez 4.00 10.00
FGRJC Jack Cust 3.00 8.00
FGRJH Josh Hamilton 6.00 15.00
FGRJR Jason Romano 3.00 8.00
FGRJZ Julio Zuleta 3.00 8.00
FGRKA Kurt Ainsworth 3.00 8.00
FGRMB Mike Bynum 3.00 8.00
FGRMG Marcus Giles 4.00 10.00
FGRNN Ntema Ndungidi 3.00 8.00
FGRRA Ryan Anderson 3.00 8.00
FGRRC Ramon Castro 3.00 8.00
FGRRD Randey Dorame 3.00 8.00
FGRSK Sun Woo Kim 3.00 8.00
FGRTO Tomo Ohka 3.00 8.00
FGRTW Travis Wilson 3.00 8.00
FGRDCP Corey Patterson 3.00 8.00

2001 Bowman Chrome Rookie Reprints

COMPLETE SET (25) 20.00 50.00
STATED ODDS 1:12
*REFRACTORS: .75X TO 2X BASIC REPRINT
REFRACTOR STATED ODDS 1:203
REF.PRINT RUN 299 SERIAL #'d SETS
1 Yogi Berra 3.00 8.00
2 Ralph Kiner 1.50 4.00
3 Stan Musial 5.00 12.00
4 Warren Spahn 1.50 4.00
5 Roy Campanella 3.00 8.00
6 Bob Lemon 1.50 4.00
7 Robin Roberts 1.50 4.00
8 Duke Snider 1.50 4.00
9 Early Wynn 1.50 4.00
10 Richie Ashburn 1.50 4.00
11 Gil Hodges 2.50 6.00
12 Hank Bauer 1.50 4.00
13 Don Newcombe 1.50 4.00
14 Al Rosen 1.50 4.00
15 Willie Mays 6.00 15.00
16 Joe Garagiola 1.50 4.00
17 Whitey Ford 1.50 4.00
18 Lew Burdette 1.50 4.00
19 Gil McDougald 1.50 4.00
20 Minnie Minoso 1.50 4.00
21 Eddie Mathews 2.50 6.00
22 Harvey Kuenn 1.50 4.00
23 Don Larsen 1.50 4.00
24 Elston Howard 1.50 4.00
25 Don Zimmer 1.50 4.00

2001 Bowman Chrome Rookie Reprints Relics

STATED BAT ODDS 1:3674
STATED JSY ODDS 1:244
1 David Justice Jsy 4.00 10.00
2 Richie Sexson Jsy 4.00 10.00
3 Sean Casey Jsy 4.00 10.00
4 Mike Piazza Bat 15.00 40.00
5 Carlos Delgado Jsy 4.00 10.00
6 Chipper Jones Jsy 6.00 15.00

2002 Bowman Chrome

COMP.RED SET (110) 15.00 40.00
COMP.BLUE w/o SP's (110) 15.00 40.00
SP STATED ODDS 1:3
324B/384-405 GROUP A AUTO ODDS 1:28
403-404 GROUP B AUTO ODDS 1:290
324B/384-405 OVERALL AUTO ODDS 1:27
FULL SET INCLUDES ISHII/TAGUCHI RC'S
FULL SET EXCLUDES ISHII/TAGUCHI AU'S
BROUSSARD/MAUER ARE BOTH CARD 324
CARD 388 DOES NOT EXIST
1 Adam Dunn .30 .75
2 Derek Jeter 1.25 3.00
3 Alex Rodriguez .60 1.50
4 Miguel Tejada .30 .75
5 Nomar Garciaparra .30 .75
6 Toby Hall .20 .50
7 Brandon Duckworth .20 .50
8 Paul LoDuca .20 .50
9 Brian Giles .20 .50
10 C.C. Sabathia .30 .75
11 Curt Schilling .30 .75
12 Tsuyoshi Shinjo .20 .50
13 Ramon Hernandez .20 .50
14 Jose Cruz Jr. .20 .50
15 Albert Pujols 1.00 2.50
16 Joe Mays .20 .50
17 Javy Lopez .20 .50
18 J.T. Snow .20 .50
19 David Segui .20 .50
20 Jorge Posada .30 .75
21 Doug Mientkiewicz .20 .50
22 Jerry Hairston Jr. .20 .50
23 Bernie Williams .30 .75
24 Mike Sweeney .20 .50
25 Jason Giambi .20 .50
26 Ryan Dempster .20 .50
27 Ryan Klesko .20 .50
28 Mark Quinn .20 .50
29 Jeff Kent .20 .50
30 Eric Chavez .20 .50
31 Adrian Beltre .50 1.25
32 Andruw Jones .20 .50
33 Alfonso Soriano .30 .75
34 Aramis Ramirez .20 .50
35 Greg Maddux .75 2.00
36 Andy Pettitte .30 .75
37 Bartolo Colon .20 .50
38 Ben Sheets .20 .50
39 Bobby Higginson .20 .50
40 Ivan Rodriguez .30 .75
41 Brad Penny .20 .50
42 Carlos Lee .20 .50
43 Damion Easley .20 .50
44 Preston Wilson .20 .50
45 Jeff Bagwell .30 .75
46 Eric Milton .20 .50
47 Rafael Palmeiro .30 .75
48 Gary Sheffield .20 .50
49 J.D. Drew .20 .50
50 Jim Thome .30 .75
51 Ichiro Suzuki .60 1.50
52 Bud Smith .20 .50
53 Chan Ho Park .30 .75
54 D'Angelo Jimenez .20 .50
55 Ken Griffey Jr. 1.00 2.50
56 Wade Miller .20 .50
57 Vladimir Guerrero .30 .75
58 Troy Glaus .20 .50
59 Shawn Green .20 .50
60 Kerry Wood .20 .50
61 Jack Wilson .20 .50
62 Kevin Brown .20 .50
63 Marcus Giles .20 .50
64 Pat Burrell .20 .50
65 Larry Walker .30 .75
66 Sammy Sosa .50 1.25
67 Raul Mondesi .20 .50
68 Tim Hudson .20 .50
69 Lance Berkman .30 .75
70 Mike Mussina .30 .75
71 Barry Zito .30 .75
72 Jimmy Rollins .30 .75
73 Barry Bonds .75 2.00
74 Craig Biggio .30 .75
75 Todd Helton .30 .75
76 Roger Clemens .60 1.50
77 Frank Catalanotto .20 .50
78 Josh Towers .20 .50
79 Roy Oswalt .20 .50
80 Chipper Jones .50 1.25
81 Cristian Guzman .20 .50
82 Darin Erstad .20 .50
83 Freddy Garcia .20 .50
84 Jason Tyner .20 .50
85 Carlos Delgado .20 .50
86 Jon Lieber .20 .50
87 Juan Pierre .20 .50
88 Matt Morris .20 .50
89 Phil Nevin .20 .50
90 Jim Edmonds .30 .75
91 Magglio Ordonez .30 .75
92 Mike Hampton .20 .50
93 Rafael Furcal .20 .50
94 Richie Sexson .20 .50
95 Luis Gonzalez .20 .50
96 Scott Rolen .30 .75
97 Tim Redding .20 .50
98 Moises Alou .20 .50
99 Jose Vidro .20 .50
100 Mike Piazza .50 1.25
101 Pedro Martinez .30 .75
102 Geoff Jenkins .20 .50
103 Johnny Damon Sox .30 .75
104 Mike Cameron .20 .50
105 Randy Johnson .50 1.25
106 David Eckstein .20 .50
107 Javier Vazquez .20 .50
108 Mark Mulder .20 .50
109 Robert Fick .20 .50
110 Roberto Alomar .30 .75
111 Wilson Betemit .30 .75
112 Chris Tritle SP RC 1.25 3.00
113 Ed Rogers .30 .75
114 Juan Pena .30 .75
115 Josh Beckett .30 .75
116 Juan Cruz .30 .75
117 Noochie Varner SP RC 1.25 3.00
118 Blake Williams .30 .75
119 Mike Rivera .30 .75
120 Hank Blalock .30 .75
121 Hansel Izquierdo SP RC 1.25 3.00
122 Orlando Hudson .30 .75
123 Bill Hall SP 1.25 3.00
124 Jose Reyes .75 2.00
125 Juan Rivera .30 .75
126 Eric Valent .30 .75
127 Scotty Layfield SP RC 1.25 3.00
128 Austin Kearns .30 .75
129 Nic Jackson SP RC 1.25 3.00
130 Scott Chiasson .30 .75
131 Chad Qualls SP RC 2.00 5.00
132 Marcus Thames .30 .75
133 Nathan Haynes .30 .75
134 Joe Borchard .30 .75
135 Josh Hamilton .50 1.25
136 Corey Patterson .30 .75
137 Travis Wilson .30 .75
138 Alex Escobar .30 .75
139 Alexis Gomez .30 .75
140 Nick Johnson .30 .75
141 Marlon Byrd .30 .75
142 Kory DeHaan .30 .75
143 Carlos Hernandez .30 .75
144 Sean Burroughs .30 .75
145 Angel Berroa .30 .75
146 Aubrey Huff .30 .75
147 Travis Hafner .30 .75
148 Brandon Berger .30 .75
149 J.R. House .30 .75
150 Dewon Brazelton .30 .75
151 Jayson Werth .50 1.25
152 Larry Barnes .30 .75
153 Ruben Gotay SP RC 1.25 3.00
154 Tommy Marx SP RC 1.25 3.00
155 John Suomi SP RC 1.25 3.00
156 Javier Colina SP 1.25 3.00
157 Greg Sain SP RC 1.25 3.00
158 Robert Cosby SP RC 1.25 3.00
159 Angel Pagan SP RC 3.00 8.00
160 Ralph Santana RC .30 .75
161 Joe Orloski RC .30 .75
162 Shayne Wright SP RC 1.25 3.00
163 Jay Caligiuri SP RC 1.25 3.00
164 Greg Montalbano SP RC 1.25 3.00
165 Rich Harden SP RC 4.00 10.00
166 Rich Thompson SP RC 1.25 3.00
167 Fred Bastardo SP RC 1.25 3.00
168 Alejandro Giron SP RC 1.25 3.00
169 Jesus Medrano SP RC 1.25 3.00
170 Kevin Deaton SP RC 1.25 3.00
171 Mike Rosamond RC .30 .75
172 Jon Guzman SP RC 1.25 3.00
173 Gerard Oakes SP RC 1.25 3.00
174 Francisco Liriano SP RC 6.00 15.00
175 Matt Allegra SP RC 1.25 3.00
176 Mike Snyder SP RC 1.25 3.00
177 James Shanks SP RC 1.25 3.00
178 Anderson Hernandez SP RC 1.25 3.00
179 Dan Trumble SP RC 1.25 3.00
180 Luis DePaula SP RC 1.25 3.00
181 Randall Shelley SP RC 1.25 3.00
182 Richard Lane SP RC 1.25 3.00
183 Antwon Rollins SP RC 1.25 3.00
184 Ryan Bukvich SP RC 1.25 3.00
185 Derrick Lewis SP 1.25 3.00
186 Eric Miller SP RC 1.25 3.00
187 Justin Schuda SP RC 1.25 3.00
188 Brian West SP RC 1.25 3.00
189 Brad Wilkerson .30 .75
190 Neal Frendling SP RC 1.25 3.00
191 Jeremy Hill SP RC 1.25 3.00
192 James Barrett SP RC 1.25 3.00
193 Brett Kay SP RC 1.25 3.00
194 Ryan Mottl SP RC 1.25 3.00
195 Brad Nelson SP RC 1.25 3.00
196 Juan M. Gonzalez SP RC 1.25 3.00
197 Curtis Legendre SP RC 1.25 3.00
198 Ronald Acuna SP RC 1.25 3.00
199 Chris Flinn SP RC 1.25 3.00
200 Nick Alvarez SP RC 1.25 3.00
201 Jason Ellison SP RC 1.25 3.00
202 Blake McGinley SP RC 1.25 3.00
203 Dan Phillips SP RC 1.25 3.00
204 Demetrius Heath SP RC 1.25 3.00
205 Eric Bruntlett SP RC 1.25 3.00
206 Joe Jiannetti SP RC 1.25 3.00
207 Mike Hill SP RC 1.25 3.00
208 Ricardo Cordova SP RC 1.25 3.00
209 Mark Hamilton SP RC 1.25 3.00
210 David Mattox SP RC 1.25 3.00
211 Jose Morban SP RC 1.25 3.00
212 Scott Wiggins SP RC 1.25 3.00
213 Steve Green .30 .75
214 Brian Rogers SP 1.25 3.00
215 Kenny Baugh .30 .75
216 Anastacio Martinez SP RC 1.25 3.00
217 Richard Lewis .30 .75
218 Tim Kalita SP RC 1.25 3.00
219 Edwin Almonte SP RC 1.25 3.00
220 Hee Seop Choi .30 .75
221 Ty Howington .30 .75
222 Victor Alvarez SP RC 1.25 3.00
223 Morgan Ensberg .30 .75
224 Jeff Austin SP RC 1.25 3.00
225 Clint Weibl SP RC 1.25 3.00
226 Eric Cyr .30 .75
227 Marlyn Tisdale SP RC 1.25 3.00
228 John VanBenschoten .30 .75
229 David Krynzel .30 .75
230 Raul Chavez SP RC 1.25 3.00
231 Brett Evert .30 .75
232 Joe Rogers SP RC 1.25 3.00
233 Adam Wainwright .50 1.25
234 Matt Herges RC .30 .75
235 Matt Childers SP RC 1.25 3.00
236 Nick Neugebauer .30 .75
237 Carl Crawford .50 1.25
238 Seung Song .30 .75
239 Randy Flores .30 .75
240 Jason Lane .30 .75
241 Chase Utley 1.25 3.00
242 Ben Howard SP RC 1.25 3.00
243 Eric Glaser SP RC 1.25 3.00
244 Josh Wilson RC .30 .75
245 Jose Valverde SP RC 2.00 5.00
246 Chris Smith .30 .75
247 Mark Prior .50 1.25
248 Brian Mallette SP RC 1.25 3.00
249 Chone Figgins SP RC 2.00 5.00
250 Jimmy Alvarez SP RC 1.25 3.00
251 Luis Terrero .30 .75
252 Josh Bonifay SP RC 1.25 3.00
253 Garrett Guzman SP RC 1.25 3.00
254 Jeff Verplancke SP RC 1.25 3.00
255 Nate Espy SP RC 1.25 3.00
256 Jeff Lincoln SP RC 1.25 3.00
257 Ryan Snare SP RC 1.25 3.00
258 Jose Ortiz .30 .75
259 Denny Bautista .30 .75
260 Willy Aybar .30 .75
261 Kelly Johnson .75 2.00
262 Shawn Fagan .30 .75
263 Yurendell DeCaster SP RC 1.25 3.00
264 Mike Peeples SP RC 1.25 3.00
265 Joel Guzman .30 .75
266 Ryan Vogelsong 1.50 4.00
267 Jorge Padilla SP RC 1.25 3.00
268 Joe Jester SP RC 1.25 3.00
269 Ryan Church SP RC 1.25 3.00
270 Mitch Jones .30 .75
271 Travis Foley SP RC 1.25 3.00
272 Bobby Crosby .75 2.00
273 Adrian Gonzalez .75 2.00
274 Ronnie Merrill .30 .75
275 Joel Pineiro .30 .75
276 John-Ford Griffin .30 .75
277 Brian Forystek SP RC 1.25 3.00
278 Sean Douglass .30 .75
279 Manny Delcarmen SP RC 1.25 3.00
280 Jim Kavourias SP RC 1.25 3.00
281 Gabe Gross .30 .75
282 Bill Ortega .30 .75
283 Joey Hammond SP RC 1.25 3.00
284 Brett Myers .30 .75
285 Carlos Pena .50 1.25
286 Ezequiel Astacio SP RC 1.25 3.00
287 Edwin Yan SP RC 1.25 3.00
288 Chris Duffy SP RC 1.25 3.00
289 Jason Kinchen .30 .75
290 Rafael Soriano .30 .75
291 Colin Young RC .30 .75
292 Eric Byrnes .30 .75
293 Chris Narveson SP RC 1.25 3.00
294 John Rheinecker .30 .75
295 Mike Wilson SP RC 1.25 3.00
296 Justin Sherrod SP RC 1.25 3.00
297 Deivi Mendez .30 .75
298 Wily Mo Pena .30 .75
299 Brett Roneberg SP RC 1.25 3.00
300 Trey Lunsford SP RC 1.25 3.00
301 Christian Parker .30 .75
302 Brent Butler .30 .75
303 Aaron Heilman .30 .75
304 Wilkin Ruan .30 .75
305 Kenny Kelly .30 .75
306 Cody Ransom .30 .75
307 Koyie Hill SP 1.25 3.00
308 Tony Fontana SP RC 1.25 3.00
309 Mark Teixeira .50 1.25
310 Doug Sessions SP RC 1.25 3.00
311 Josh Cisneros SP RC 1.25 3.00
312 Carlos Brackley SP RC 1.25 3.00
313 Tim Raines Jr. .30 .75
314 Ross Peeples SP RC 1.25 3.00
315 Alex Requena SP RC 1.25 3.00
316 Chin-Hui Tsao .30 .75
317 Tony Alvarez .30 .75
318 Craig Kuzmic SP RC 1.25 3.00
319 Pete Zamora SP RC 1.25 3.00
320 Matt Parker SP RC 1.25 3.00
321 Keith Ginter .30 .75
322 Gary Cates Jr. SP RC 1.25 3.00
323 Matt Belisle .30 .75
324A Ben Broussard .30 .75
324B Jake Mauer AU A RC 4.00 10.00
325 Dennis Tankersley .30 .75
326 Juan Silvestre .30 .75
327 Henry Pichardo SP RC 1.25 3.00
328 Michael Floyd SP RC 1.25 3.00
329 Clint Nageotte SP RC 1.25 3.00
330 Raymond Cabrera SP RC 1.25 3.00
331 Mauricio Lara SP RC 1.25 3.00
332 Alejandro Cadena SP RC 1.25 3.00
333 Jonny Gomes SP RC 4.00 10.00
334 Jason Bulger SP RC 1.25 3.00
335 Nate Teut .30 .75
336 David Gil SP RC 1.25 3.00
337 Joel Crump SP RC 1.25 3.00
338 Brandon Phillips .30 .75
339 Macay McBride .30 .75
340 Brandon Claussen .30 .75
341 Josh Phelps .30 .75
342 Freddie Money SP RC 1.25 3.00
343 Cliff Bartosh SP RC 1.25 3.00
344 Terrance Hill SP RC 1.25 3.00
345 John Rodriguez SP RC 1.25 3.00
346 Chris Latham SP RC 1.25 3.00
347 Carlos Cabrera SP RC 1.25 3.00
348 Jose Bautista SP RC 10.00 25.00
349 Kevin Frederick SP RC 1.25 3.00
350 Jerome Williams .30 .75
351 Napoleon Calzado SP RC 1.25 3.00
352 Benito Baez SP 1.25 3.00
353 Xavier Nady .30 .75
354 Jason Botts SP RC 1.25 3.00
355 Steve Bechler SP RC 1.25 3.00
356 Reed Johnson SP RC 2.00 5.00
357 Mark Outlaw SP RC 1.25 3.00
358 Jake Peavy .30 .75
359 Josh Shaffer SP RC 1.25 3.00
360 Dan Wright SP 1.25 3.00
361 Ryan Gripp SP RC 1.25 3.00
362 Nelson Castro SP RC 1.25 3.00
363 Jason Bay SP RC 6.00 15.00
364 Franklyn German SP RC 1.25 3.00
365 Corwin Malone SP RC 1.25 3.00
366 Kelly Ramos SP RC 1.25 3.00
367 John Ennis SP RC 1.25 3.00
368 George Perez SP 1.25 3.00
369 Rene Reyes SP RC 1.25 3.00
370 Rolando Viera SP RC 1.25 3.00
371 Earl Snyder SP RC 1.25 3.00
372 Kyle Kane SP RC 1.25 3.00
373 Mario Ramos SP RC 1.25 3.00
374 Tyler Yates SP RC 1.25 3.00
375 Jason Young SP RC 1.25 3.00
376 Chris Bootcheck SP RC 1.25 3.00
377 Jesus Cota SP RC 1.25 3.00
378 Corky Miller SP 1.25 3.00
379 Matt Erickson SP RC 1.25 3.00
380 Justin Huber SP RC 1.25 3.00
381 Felix Escalona SP RC 1.25 3.00
382 Kevin Cash SP RC 1.25 3.00
383 J.J. Putz SP RC 2.00 5.00
384 Chris Snelling AU A RC 4.00 10.00
385 David Wright AU A RC 30.00 80.00
386 Brian Wolfe AU A RC 4.00 10.00
387 Justin Reid AU A RC 4.00 10.00
389 Ryan Raburn AU A RC 4.00 10.00
390 Josh Barfield AU A RC 4.00 10.00
391 Joe Mauer AU A RC 75.00 200.00
392 Bobby Jenks AU A RC 4.00 10.00
393 Rob Henkel AU A RC 4.00 10.00
394 Jimmy Gobble AU A RC 4.00 10.00
395 Jesse Foppert AU A RC 4.00 10.00
396 Gavin Floyd AU A RC 4.00 10.00
397 Nate Field AU A RC 4.00 10.00
398 Ryan Doumit AU A RC 4.00 10.00
399 Ron Calloway AU A RC 4.00 10.00
400 Taylor Buchholz AU A RC 4.00 10.00
401 Adam Roller AU A RC 4.00 10.00
402 Cole Barthel AU A RC 4.00 10.00
403 Kazuhisa Ishii SP RC 2.00 5.00
403A Kazuhisa Ishii AU B 30.00 50.00
404 So Taguchi SP RC 2.00 5.00
404A So Taguchi AU B 30.00 50.00
405 Chris Baker AU A RC 4.00 10.00

2002 Bowman Chrome Facsimile Autograph Variations

118 Taylor Buchholz 4.00 10.00
130 Chris Baker 4.00 10.00
189 Adam Roller 4.00 10.00
229 Ryan Raburn 6.00 15.00
231 Chris Snelling 4.00 10.00
233 Nate Field 4.00 10.00
237 Ron Calloway 4.00 10.00
239 Cole Barthel 4.00 10.00
244 Rob Henkel 4.00 10.00
251 Gavin Floyd 10.00 25.00
301 Jimmy Gobble 4.00 10.00
305 Brian Wolfe 4.00 10.00
313 Jesse Foppert 4.00 10.00
316 Joe Mauer 100.00 250.00
317 David Wright 60.00 150.00
323 Justin Reid 4.00 10.00
324 Jake Mauer 4.00 10.00
326 Josh Barfield 6.00 15.00
335 Bobby Jenks 6.00 15.00
338 Ryan Doumit 6.00 15.00

2002 Bowman Chrome Uncirculated

ONE EXCHANGE CARD PER BOX
AU EXCHANGE CARDS ARE HOBBY-ONLY
STATED PRINT RUN 350 SETS
AU STATED PRINT RUN 10 SETS
EXCHANGE DEADLINE 12/31/02

112 Chris Tritle 1.00 2.50
117 Noochie Varner 1.00 2.50
121 Hansel Izquierdo 1.00 2.50
123 Bill Hall 1.00 2.50
127 Scotty Layfield 1.00 2.50
129 Nic Jackson 1.00 2.50
131 Chad Qualls 1.50 4.00
153 Ruben Gotay 1.00 2.50
154 Tommy Marx 1.00 2.50
155 John Suomi 1.00 2.50
156 Javier Colina 1.00 2.50
157 Greg Sain 1.00 2.50
158 Robert Crosby 1.00 2.50
159 Angel Pagan 2.50 6.00
162 Shayne Wright 1.00 2.50
163 Jay Caligiuri 1.00 2.50
164 Greg Montalbano 1.00 2.50
165 Rich Harden 3.00 8.00
166 Rich Thompson 1.00 2.50
167 Fred Bastardo 1.00 2.50
168 Alejandro Giron 1.00 2.50
169 Jesus Medrano 1.00 2.50
170 Kevin Deaton 1.00 2.50
172 Jon Guzman 1.00 2.50
173 Gerard Oakes 1.00 2.50
174 Francisco Liriano 5.00 12.00
175 Matt Allegra 1.00 2.50
176 Mike Snyder 1.00 2.50
178 Anderson Hernandez 1.00 2.50
179 Dan Trumble 1.00 2.50
180 Luis DePaula 1.00 2.50
181 Randall Shelley 1.00 2.50
182 Richard Lane 1.00 2.50
183 Antwon Rollins 1.00 2.50
184 Ryan Bukvich 1.00 2.50
185 Derrick Lewis 1.00 2.50
186 Eric Miller 1.00 2.50
187 Justin Schuda 1.00 2.50
188 Brian West 1.00 2.50
190 Neal Frendling 1.00 2.50
191 Jeremy Hill 1.00 2.50
192 James Barrett 1.00 2.50
193 Brett Kay 1.00 2.50
194 Ryan Mottl 1.00 2.50
195 Brad Nelson 1.00 2.50
196 Juan M. Gonzalez 1.00 2.50
197 Curtis Legendre 1.00 2.50
198 Ronald Acuna 1.00 2.50
199 Chris Flinn 1.00 2.50
200 Nick Alvarez 1.00 2.50
201 Jason Ellison 1.00 2.50
202 Blake McGinley 1.00 2.50
203 Dan Phillips 1.00 2.50
204 Demetrius Heath 1.00 2.50
205 Eric Bruntlett 1.00 2.50
206 Joe Jiannetti 1.00 2.50
207 Mike Hill 1.00 2.50
208 Ricardo Cordova 1.00 2.50
209 Mark Hamilton 1.00 2.50
210 David Mattox 1.00 2.50
211 Jose Morban 1.00 2.50
212 Scott Wiggins 1.00 2.50
214 Brian Rogers 1.00 2.50
216 Anastacio Martinez 1.00 2.50
218 Tim Kalita 1.00 2.50
219 Edwin Almonte 1.00 2.50
222 Victor Alvarez 1.00 2.50
224 Jeff Austin 1.00 2.50
225 Clint Weibl 1.00 2.50
227 Marlyn Tisdale 1.00 2.50
230 Raul Chavez 1.00 2.50
232 Joe Rogers 1.00 2.50
235 Matt Childers 1.00 2.50
242 Ben Howard 1.00 2.50
243 Eric Glaser 1.00 2.50
245 Jose Valverde 1.50 4.00
248 Brian Mallette 1.00 2.50
249 Chone Figgins 1.50 4.00
250 Jimmy Alvarez 1.00 2.50
252 Josh Bonifay 1.00 2.50
253 Garrett Guzman 1.00 2.50
254 Jeff Verplancke 1.00 2.50
255 Nate Espy 1.00 2.50
256 Jeff Lincoln 1.00 2.50
257 Ryan Snare 1.00 2.50
263 Yurendell DeCaster 1.00 2.50
264 Mike Peeples 1.00 2.50
267 Jorge Padilla 1.00 2.50
268 Joe Jester 1.00 2.50
269 Ryan Church 1.00 2.50
271 Travis Foley 1.00 2.50
277 Brian Forystek 1.00 2.50
279 Manny Delcarmen 1.00 2.50
280 Jim Kavourias 1.00 2.50
283 Joey Hammond 1.00 2.50
286 Ezequiel Astacio 1.00 2.50
287 Edwin Yan 1.00 2.50
288 Chris Duffy 1.00 2.50
293 Chris Narveson 1.00 2.50
295 Mike Wilson 1.00 2.50
296 Justin Sherrod 1.00 2.50
299 Brett Roneberg 1.00 2.50
300 Trey Lunsford 1.00 2.50
307 Koyie Hill 1.00 2.50
308 Tony Fontana 1.00 2.50
310 Doug Sessions 1.00 2.50
311 Josh Cisneros 1.00 2.50
312 Carlos Brackley 1.00 2.50
314 Ross Peeples 1.00 2.50
315 Alex Requena 1.00 2.50
318 Craig Kuzmic 1.00 2.50
319 Pete Zamora 1.00 2.50
320 Matt Parker 1.00 2.50
322 Gary Cates Jr. 1.00 2.50
327 Henry Pichardo 1.00 2.50
328 Michael Floyd 1.00 2.50
329 Clint Nageotte 1.00 2.50
330 Raymond Cabrera 1.00 2.50
331 Mauricio Lara 1.00 2.50
332 Alejandro Cadena 1.00 2.50
333 Jonny Gomes 3.00 8.00
334 Jason Bulger 1.00 2.50
336 David Gil 1.00 2.50
337 Joel Crump 1.00 2.50
342 Freddie Money 1.00 2.50
343 Cliff Bartosh 1.00 2.50

344 Terrance Hill 1.00 2.50
345 John Rodriguez 1.00 2.50
346 Chris Latham 1.00 2.50
347 Carlos Cabrera 1.00 2.50
348 Jose Bautista 8.00 20.00
349 Kevin Frederick 1.00 2.50
351 Napolean Calzado 1.00 2.50
352 Benito Baez 1.00 2.50
354 Jason Botts 1.00 2.50
355 Steve Bechler 1.00 2.50
356 Reed Johnson 1.50 4.00
357 Mark Outlaw 1.00 2.50
359 Josh Shaffer 1.00 2.50
360 Dan Wright 1.00 2.50
361 Ryan Gripp 1.00 2.50
362 Nelson Castro 1.00 2.50
363 Jason Bay 5.00 12.00
364 Franklyn German 1.00 2.50
365 Corwin Malone 1.00 2.50
366 Kelly Ramos 1.00 2.50
367 John Ennis 1.00 2.50
368 George Perez 1.00 2.50
369 Rene Reyes 1.00 2.50
370 Rolando Viera 1.00 2.50
371 Earl Snyder 1.00 2.50
372 Kyle Kane 1.00 2.50
373 Mario Ramos 1.00 2.50
374 Tyler Yates 1.00 2.50
375 Jason Young 1.00 2.50
376 Chris Bootcheck 1.00 2.50
377 Jesus Cota 1.00 2.50
378 Corky Miller 1.00 2.50
379 Matt Erickson 1.00 2.50
380 Justin Huber 1.00 2.50
381 Felix Escalona 1.00 2.50
382 Kevin Cash 1.00 2.50
383 J.J. Putz 1.50 4.00
403 Kazuhisa Ishii 1.50 4.00
404 So Taguchi 1.50 4.00

2002 Bowman Chrome Refractors

*REF RED: 1.5X TO 4X BASIC
*REF BLUE: 2.5X TO 6X BASIC
*REF BLUE SP: .6X TO 1.5X BASIC
*REF AU: .5X TO 1.2X BASIC AU'S
1-383/403-404 ODDS 1:6
324B/384-405 GROUP A AUTO ODDS 1:88
403-404 GROUP B AUTO ODDS 1:4392
324B/384-405 OVERALL AUTO ODDS 1:86
1-383/403-404 PRINT 500 SERIAL #'d SETS
324B/384-405 GROUP A PRINT RUN 500 SETS
403-404 GROUP B PRINT RUN 100 SETS
403 Kazuhisa Ishii AU B 40.00 80.00
404 So Taguchi AU B 30.00 60.00

2002 Bowman Chrome Gold Refractors

*GOLD REF RED: 5X TO 12X BASIC
*GOLD REF BLUE: 5X TO 12X BASIC
*GOLD REF BLUE SP: 1.2X TO 3X BASIC
*GOLD REF AU: 1.5X TO 4X BASIC
1-383/403-404 ODDS 1:56
384-405 GROUP A AUTO ODDS 1:879
403-404 GROUP B AUTO ODDS 1:59,616
324B/384-405 OVERALL AUTO ODDS 1:866
1-383/403-404 PRINT 50 SERIAL #'d SETS
324B/384-405 GROUP A AU PRINT 50 SETS
403-404 GROUP B AU PRINT RUN 10 SETS
NO GROUP B AU PRICING DUE TO SCARCITY
174 Francisco Liriano 100.00 200.00
241 Chase Utley 60.00 120.00
348 Jose Bautista 100.00 200.00
363 Jason Bay 100.00 200.00
391 Joe Mauer AU A 400.00 1000.00

2002 Bowman Chrome X-Fractors

*XFRACT RED: 3X TO 8X BASIC
*XFRACT BLUE: 3X TO 8X BASIC
*XFRACT BLUE SP: .75X TO 2X BASIC
*XFRACT AU: .75X TO 2X BASIC
1-383/403-404 ODDS 1:10
324B/384-405 GROUP A AUTO ODDS 1:176
403-404 GROUP B AUTO ODDS 1:9072
324B/384-405 OVERALL AUTO ODDS 1:173
1-383/403-404 PRINT 250 SERIAL #'d SETS
324B/384-405 GROUP A PRINT RUN 250 SETS
403-404 GROUP B PRINT RUN 50 SETS
403 Kazuhisa Ishii AU B 60.00 100.00
404 So Taguchi AU B 60.00 100.00

2002 Bowman Chrome Reprints

COMPLETE SET (20) 10.00 25.00
STATED ODDS 1:6
*BLACK REF: .6X TO 1.5X BASIC REPRINTS
BLACK REFRACTOR ODDS 1:18
BCRAJ Andruw Jones 95 .75 2.00
BCRBC Bartolo Colon 95 .75 2.00
BCRBW Bernie Williams 90 .75 2.00
BCRCD Carlos Delgado 92 .75 2.00
BCRCJ Chipper Jones 91 1.00 2.50
BCRDJ Derek Jeter 93 3.00 8.00
BCRFT Frank Thomas 90 1.00 2.50
BCRGS Gary Sheffield 89 .75 2.00
BCRIR Ivan Rodriguez 91 .75 2.00
BCRJB Jeff Bagwell 91 .75 2.00
BCRJG Juan Gonzalez 90 .75 2.00
BCRJK Jason Kendall 93 .75 2.00
BCRJP Jorge Posada 94 .75 2.00
BCRKG Ken Griffey Jr. 89 2.50 6.00
BCRLG Luis Gonzalez 91 .75 2.00
BCRLW Larry Walker 90 .75 2.00
BCRMP Mike Piazza 92 2.00 5.00
BCRMS Mike Sweeney 96 .75 2.00
BCRSR Scott Rolen 95 .75 2.00
BCRVG Vladimir Guerrero 95 1.00 2.50

2002 Bowman Chrome Draft

COMPLETE SET (175) 125.00 300.00
COMP.SET w/o AU's (165) 40.00 100.00
1-165 TWO PER BOWMAN DRAFT PACK
166-175 AU ODDS 1:45 BOWMAN DRAFT
1 Clint Everts RC .40 1.00
2 Fred Lewis RC .40 1.00
3 Jon Broxton RC 1.00 2.50
4 Jason Anderson RC .40 1.00
5 Mike Eusebio RC .40 1.00
6 Zack Greinke RC 40.00 100.00
7 Joe Blanton RC .60 1.50
8 Sergio Santos RC .40 1.00
9 Jason Cooper RC .40 1.00
10 Delwyn Young RC .40 1.00
11 Jeremy Hermida RC .60 1.50
12 Dan Ortmeier RC .40 1.00
13 Kevin Jepsen RC .40 1.00
14 Russ Adams RC .40 1.00
15 Mike Nixon RC .40 1.00
16 Nick Swisher RC 2.50 6.00
17 Cole Hamels RC 5.00 12.00
18 Brian Dopirak RC .40 1.00
19 James Loney RC 1.00 2.50
20 Denard Span RC .60 1.50
21 Billy Petrick RC .40 1.00
22 Jared Doyle RC .40 1.00
23 Jeff Francoeur RC 2.50 6.00
24 Nick Bourgeois RC .40 1.00
25 Matt Cain RC 2.50 6.00
26 John McCurdy RC .40 1.00
27 Mark Kiger RC .40 1.00
28 Bill Murphy RC .40 1.00
29 Matt Craig RC .40 1.00
30 Mike Megrew RC .40 1.00
31 Ben Crockett RC .40 1.00
32 Luke Hagerty RC .40 1.00
33 Matt Whitney RC .40 1.00
34 Dan Meyer RC .40 1.00
35 Jeremy Brown RC .40 1.00
36 Doug Johnson RC .40 1.00
37 Steve Obenchain RC .40 1.00
38 Matt Clanton RC .40 1.00
39 Mark Teahen RC .40 1.00
40 Tom Carrow RC .40 1.00
41 Micah Schilling RC .40 1.00
42 Blair Johnson RC .40 1.00
43 Jason Pridie RC .40 1.00
44 Joey Votto RC 30.00 80.00
45 Taber Lee RC .40 1.00
46 Adam Peterson RC .40 1.00
47 Adam Donachie RC .40 1.00
48 Josh Murray RC .40 1.00
49 Brent Clevlen RC .40 1.00
50 Chad Pleiness RC .40 1.00
51 Zach Hammes RC .40 1.00
52 Chris Snyder RC .40 1.00
53 Chris Smith RC .40 1.00
54 Justin Maureau RC .40 1.00
55 David Bush RC .40 1.00
56 Tim Gilhooly RC .40 1.00
57 Blair Barbier RC .40 1.00
58 Zach Segovia RC .40 1.00
59 Jeremy Reed RC .40 1.00
60 Matt Pender RC .40 1.00
61 Eric Thomas RC .40 1.00
62 Justin Jones RC .40 1.00
63 Brian Slocum RC .40 1.00
64 Larry Broadway RC .40 1.00
65 Bo Flowers RC .40 1.00
66 Scott White RC .40 1.00
67 Steve Stanley RC .40 1.00
68 Alex Merricks RC .40 1.00
69 Josh Womack RC .40 1.00
70 Dave Jensen RC .40 1.00
71 Curtis Granderson RC 5.00 12.00
72 Pat Osborn RC .40 1.00
73 Nic Carter RC .40 1.00
74 Mitch Talbot RC .40 1.00
75 Don Murphy RC .40 1.00
76 Val Majewski RC .40 1.00
77 Javy Rodriguez RC .40 1.00
78 Fernando Pacheco RC .40 1.00
79 Steve Russell RC .40 1.00
80 Jon Slack RC .40 1.00
81 John Baker RC .40 1.00
82 Aaron Coonrod RC .40 1.00
83 Josh Johnson RC 2.50 6.00
84 Jake Blalock RC .40 1.00
85 Alex Hart RC .40 1.00
86 Wes Bankston RC .40 1.00
87 Josh Rupe RC .40 1.00
88 Dan Cevette RC .40 1.00
89 Kiel Fisher RC .40 1.00
90 Alan Rick RC .40 1.00
91 Charlie Morton RC 3.00 8.00
92 Chad Spann RC .40 1.00
93 Kyle Boyer RC .40 1.00
94 Bob Malek RC .40 1.00
95 Ryan Rodriguez RC .40 1.00
96 Jordan Renz RC .40 1.00
97 Randy Frye RC .40 1.00
98 Rich Hill RC 1.00 2.50
99 B.J. Upton RC 2.00 5.00
100 Dan Christensen RC .40 1.00
101 Casey Kotchman RC .60 1.50
102 Eric Good RC .40 1.00
103 Mike Fontenot RC .40 1.00
104 John Webb RC .40 1.00
105 Jason Dubois RC .40 1.00
106 Ryan Kibler RC .40 1.00
107 Jhonny Peralta RC .60 1.50
108 Kirk Saarloos RC .40 1.00
109 Rhett Parrott RC .40 1.00
110 Jason Grove RC .40 1.00
111 Colt Griffin RC .40 1.00
112 Dallas McPherson RC .40 1.00
113 Oliver Perez RC 1.00 2.50
114 Marshall McDougall RC .40 1.00
115 Mike Wood RC .40 1.00
116 Scott Hairston RC .40 1.00
117 Jason Simontacchi RC .40 1.00
118 Taggert Bozied RC .40 1.00
119 Shelley Duncan RC 1.00 2.50
120 Dontrelle Willis RC 1.00 2.50
121 Sean Burnett .15 .40
122 Aaron Cook .15 .40
123 Brett Evert .15 .40
124 Jimmy Journell .15 .40
125 Brett Myers .15 .40
126 Brad Baker .15 .40
127 Billy Traber RC .40 1.00
128 Adam Wainwright .25 .60
129 Jason Young .15 .40
130 John Buck .40 1.00
131 Kevin Cash .15 .40
132 Jason Stokes RC .40 1.00
133 Drew Henson .15 .40
134 Chad Tracy RC .60 1.50
135 Orlando Hudson .15 .40
136 Brandon Phillips .15 .40
137 Joe Borchard .15 .40
138 Marlon Byrd .15 .40
139 Carl Crawford .25 .60
140 Michael Restovich .15 .40
141 Corey Hart RC 2.00 5.00
142 Edwin Almonte .15 .40
143 Francis Beltran RC .40 1.00
144 Jorge De La Rosa RC .40 1.00
145 Gerardo Garcia RC .40 1.00
146 Franklyn German RC .40 1.00
147 Francisco Liriano .75 2.00
148 Francisco Rodriguez .25 .60
149 Ricardo Rodriguez .15 .40
150 Seung Song .15 .40
151 John Stephens .15 .40
152 Justin Huber RC .40 1.00
153 Victor Martinez .25 .60
154 Hee Seop Choi .15 .40
155 Justin Morneau .40 1.00
156 Miguel Cabrera 5.00 12.00
157 Victor Diaz RC .40 1.00
158 Jose Reyes .40 1.00
159 Omar Infante .40 1.00
160 Angel Berroa .15 .40
161 Tony Alvarez .15 .40
162 Shin Soo Choo RC 3.00 8.00
163 Wily Mo Pena .15 .40
164 Andres Torres .15 .40
165 Jose Lopez RC .60 1.50
166 Scott Moore AU RC 4.00 10.00
167 Chris Gruler AU RC 4.00 10.00
168 Joe Saunders AU RC 4.00 10.00
169 Jeff Francis AU RC 4.00 10.00
170 Royce Ring AU RC 4.00 10.00
171 Greg Miller AU RC 4.00 10.00
172 Brandon Weeden AU RC 6.00 15.00
173 Drew Meyer AU RC 4.00 10.00
174 Khalil Greene AU RC 4.00 10.00
175 Mark Schramek AU RC 4.00 10.00

2002 Bowman Chrome Draft Refractors

*REFRACTOR 1-165: 4X TO 10X BASIC
*REFRACTOR RC 1-165: 1.5X TO 4X BASIC
*REFRACTOR 166-175: .5X TO 1.2X BASIC
1-165 ODDS 1:11 BOWMAN DRAFT
166-175 AU ODDS 1:154 BOWMAN DRAFT
1-165 PRINT RUN 300 SERIAL #'d SETS
166-175 ARE NOT SERIAL NUMBERED

2002 Bowman Chrome Draft Gold Refractors

*GOLD REF 1-165: 10X TO 25X BASIC
*GOLD REF RC 1-165: 4X TO 10X BASIC
1-165 ODDS 1:67 BOWMAN DRAFT
166-175 AU ODDS 1:1546 BOWMAN DRAFT
1-165 PRINT RUN 50 SERIAL #'d SETS
166-175 ARE NOT SERIAL-NUMBERED
166-175 NO PRICING DUE TO SCARCITY
23 Jeff Francoeur 75.00 150.00
25 Matt Cain 250.00 500.00
156 Miguel Cabrera 60.00 150.00

2002 Bowman Chrome Draft X-Fractors

*X-FRACTOR 1-165: 6X TO 15X BASIC
*X-FRACTOR RC 1-165: 3X TO 6X BASIC
*X-FRACTOR 166-175: .75X TO 1.5X BASIC
1-165 ODDS 1:22 BOWMAN DRAFT
166-175 AU ODDS 1:309 BOWMAN DRAFT
1-165 PRINT RUN 150 SERIAL #'d SETS
166-175 ARE NOT SERIAL-NUMBERED
156 Miguel Cabrera 40.00 100.00

2003 Bowman Chrome

COMPLETE SET (351) 300.00 500.00
COMP.SET w/o AU's (331) 75.00 150.00
COMMON CARD (1-165) .20 .50
COMMON CARD (166-330) .20 .50
COMMON RC (156-330) .40 1.00
331/333-350 AU A STATED ODDS 1:26
331/333-350 AU A PRINT RUN 1700 SETS
AU A CARDS ARE NOT SERIAL-NUMBERED
AU A EXCH.DEADLINE 07/31/05
332 AU B STATED ODDS 1:3351
332 AU B PRINT RUN 340 CARDS
AU B IS NOT SERIAL-NUMBERED
COMP.SET w/o AU'S INCLUDES 351 MAYS
MAYS ODDS ONE PER BOX LOADER PACK
MAYS AU ODDS 1:384 BOX LOADER PACKS
MAYS AU PRINT RUN 150 CARDS
MAYS AU IS NOT-SERIAL-NUMBERED
MAYS AU IS NOT PART OF 351-CARD SET
1 Garret Anderson .20 .50
2 Derek Jeter 1.25 3.00
3 Gary Sheffield .20 .50
4 Matt Morris .20 .50
5 Derek Lowe .20 .50
6 Andy Van Hekken .20 .50
7 Sammy Sosa .50 1.25
8 Ken Griffey Jr. 1.00 2.50
9 Omar Vizquel .30 .75
10 Jorge Posada .30 .75
11 Lance Berkman .30 .75
12 Mike Sweeney .20 .50
13 Adrian Beltre .50 1.25
14 Richie Sexson .20 .50
15 A.J. Pierzynski .20 .50
16 Bartolo Colon .20 .50
17 Mike Mussina .30 .75
18 Paul Byrd .20 .50
19 Bobby Abreu .20 .50
20 Miguel Tejada .30 .75
21 Aramis Ramirez .20 .50
22 Edgardo Alfonzo .20 .50
23 Edgar Martinez .30 .75
24 Albert Pujols .60 1.50
25 Carl Crawford .30 .75
26 Eric Hinske .20 .50
27 Tim Salmon .20 .50
28 Luis Gonzalez .20 .50
29 Jay Gibbons .20 .50
30 John Smoltz .50 1.25
31 Tim Wakefield .30 .75
32 Mark Prior .30 .75
33 Magglio Ordonez .30 .75
34 Adam Dunn .30 .75
35 Larry Walker .30 .75
36 Luis Castillo .20 .50
37 Wade Miller .20 .50
38 Carlos Beltran .30 .75
39 Odalis Perez .20 .50
40 Alex Sanchez .20 .50
41 Torii Hunter .20 .50
42 Cliff Floyd .20 .50
43 Andy Pettitte .30 .75
44 Francisco Rodriguez .30 .75
45 Eric Chavez .20 .50
46 Kevin Millwood .20 .50
47 Dennis Tankersley .20 .50
48 Hideo Nomo .50 1.25
49 Freddy Garcia .20 .50
50 Randy Johnson .50 1.25
51 Aubrey Huff .20 .50
52 Carlos Delgado .20 .50
53 Troy Glaus .20 .50
54 Junior Spivey .20 .50
55 Mike Hampton .20 .50
56 Sidney Ponson .20 .50
57 Aaron Boone .20 .50
58 Kerry Wood .20 .50
59 Willie Harris .20 .50
60 Nomar Garciaparra .30 .75
61 Todd Helton .30 .75
62 Mike Lowell .20 .50
63 Roy Oswalt .30 .75
64 Raul Ibanez .30 .75
65 Brian Jordan .20 .50
66 Geoff Jenkins .20 .50
67 Jermaine Dye .20 .50
68 Tom Glavine .30 .75
69 Bernie Williams .30 .75
70 Vladimir Guerrero .30 .75
71 Mark Mulder .20 .50
72 Jimmy Rollins .30 .75
73 Oliver Perez .20 .50
74 Rich Aurilia .20 .50
75 Joel Pineiro .20 .50
76 J.D. Drew .20 .50
77 Ivan Rodriguez .30 .75
78 Josh Phelps .20 .50
79 Darin Erstad .20 .50
80 Curt Schilling .30 .75
81 Paul Lo Duca .20 .50
82 Marty Cordova .20 .50
83 Manny Ramirez .50 1.25
84 Bobby Hill .20 .50
85 Paul Konerko .30 .75
86 Austin Kearns .20 .50
87 Jason Jennings .20 .50
88 Brad Penny .20 .50
89 Jeff Bagwell .30 .75
90 Shawn Green .20 .50
91 Jason Schmidt .20 .50
92 Doug Mientkiewicz .20 .50
93 Jose Vidro .20 .50
94 Bret Boone .20 .50
95 Jason Giambi .20 .50
96 Barry Zito .30 .75
97 Roy Halladay .30 .75
98 Pat Burrell .20 .50
99 Sean Burroughs .20 .50
100 Barry Bonds .75 2.00
101 Kazuhiro Sasaki .20 .50
102 Fernando Vina .20 .50
103 Chan Ho Park .30 .75
104 Andruw Jones .20 .50
105 Adam Kennedy .20 .50
106 Shea Hillenbrand .20 .50
107 Greg Maddux .60 1.50
108 Jim Edmonds .30 .75
109 Pedro Martinez .30 .75
110 Moises Alou .20 .50
111 Jeff Weaver .20 .50
112 C.C. Sabathia .30 .75
113 Robert Fick .20 .50
114 A.J. Burnett .20 .50
115 Jeff Kent .20 .50
116 Kevin Brown .20 .50
117 Rafael Furcal .20 .50
118 Cristian Guzman .20 .50
119 Brad Wilkerson .20 .50
120 Mike Piazza .50 1.25
121 Alfonso Soriano .30 .75
122 Mark Ellis .20 .50
123 Vicente Padilla .20 .50
124 Eric Gagne .20 .50
125 Ryan Klesko .20 .50
126 Ichiro Suzuki .60 1.50
127 Tony Batista .20 .50
128 Roberto Alomar .30 .75
129 Alex Rodriguez .60 1.50
130 Jim Thome .30 .75
131 Jarrod Washburn .20 .50
132 Orlando Hudson .20 .50
133 Chipper Jones .50 1.25
134 Rodrigo Lopez .20 .50
135 Johnny Damon .30 .75
136 Matt Clement .20 .50
137 Frank Thomas .50 1.25
138 Ellis Burks .20 .50
139 Carlos Pena .30 .75
140 Josh Beckett .20 .50
141 Joe Randa .20 .50
142 Brian Giles .20 .50
143 Kazuhisa Ishii .20 .50
144 Corey Koskie .20 .50
145 Orlando Cabrera .20 .50
146 Mark Buehrle .30 .75
147 Roger Clemens .60 1.50
148 Tim Hudson .30 .75
149 Randy Wolf .20 .50
150 Josh Fogg .20 .50
151 Phil Nevin .20 .50
152 John Olerud .20 .50
153 Scott Rolen .30 .75
154 Joe Kennedy .20 .50
155 Rafael Palmeiro .30 .75
156 Chad Hutchinson .20 .50
157 Quincy Carter XRC .40 1.00
158 Hee Seop Choi .20 .50
159 Joe Borchard .20 .50
160 Brandon Phillips .20 .50
161 Wily Mo Pena .20 .50
162 Victor Martinez .30 .75
163 Jason Stokes .20 .50
164 Ken Harvey .20 .50
165 Juan Rivera .20 .50
166 Joe Valentine RC .40 1.00
167 Dan Haren RC 2.00 5.00
168 Michel Hernandez RC .40 1.00
169 Eider Torres RC .40 1.00
170 Chris De La Cruz RC .40 1.00
171 Ramon Nivar-Martinez RC .40 1.00
172 Mike Adams RC .60 1.50
173 Justin Arneson RC .40 1.00
174 Jamie Athas RC .40 1.00
175 Dwaine Bacon RC .40 1.00
176 Clint Barmes RC 1.00 2.50
177 B.J. Barns RC .40 1.00
178 Tyler Johnson RC .40 1.00
179 Brandon Webb RC 1.25 3.00
180 T.J. Bohn RC .40 1.00
181 Ozzie Chavez RC .40 1.00
182 Brandon Bowe RC .40 1.00
183 Craig Brazell RC .40 1.00
184 Dusty Brown RC .40 1.00
185 Brian Bruney RC .40 1.00
186 Greg Bruso RC .40 1.00
187 Jaime Bubela RC .40 1.00
188 Matt Diaz RC .60 1.50
189 Brian Burgamy RC .40 1.00
190 Eny Cabreja RC 1.50 4.00
191 Daniel Cabrera RC .60 1.50
192 Ryan Cameron RC .40 1.00
193 Lance Caraccioli RC .40 1.00
194 David Cash RC .40 1.00
195 Bernie Castro RC .40 1.00
196 Ismael Castro RC .40 1.00
197 Cory Doyne RC .40 1.00
198 Jeff Clark RC .40 1.00
199 Chris Colton RC .40 1.00
200 Dexter Cooper RC .40 1.00
201 Callix Crabbe RC .40 1.00
202 Chien-Ming Wang RC 1.50 4.00
203 Eric Crozier RC .40 1.00
204 Nook Logan RC .40 1.00
205 David DeJesus RC 1.00 2.50
206 Matt DeMarco RC .40 1.00
207 Chris Duncan RC 1.25 3.00
208 Eric Eckenstahler .20 .50
209 Willie Eyre RC .40 1.00
210 Evel Bastida-Martinez RC .40 1.00
211 Chris Fallon RC .40 1.00
212 Mike Flannery RC .40 1.00
213 Mike O'Keefe RC .40 1.00
214 Lew Ford RC .40 1.00
215 Kason Gabbard RC .40 1.00
216 Mike Gallo RC .40 1.00
217 Jairo Garcia RC .40 1.00
218 Angel Garcia RC .40 1.00
219 Michael Garciaparra RC .40 1.00
220 Jeremy Griffiths RC .40 1.00
221 Dusty Gomon RC .40 1.00
222 Bryan Grace RC .40 1.00
223 Tyson Graham RC .40 1.00
224 Henry Guerrero RC .40 1.00
225 Franklin Gutierrez RC 1.00 2.50
226 Carlos Guzman RC .40 1.00
227 Matthew Hagen RC .40 1.00
228 Josh Hall RC .40 1.00
229 Rob Hammock RC .40 1.00
230 Brendan Harris RC .40 1.00
231 Gary Harris RC .40 1.00
232 Clay Hensley RC .40 1.00
233 Michael Hinckley RC .40 1.00
234 Luis Hodge RC .40 1.00
235 Donnie Hood RC .40 1.00
236 Matt Hensley RC .40 1.00
237 Edwin Jackson RC .60 1.50
238 Ardley Jansen RC .40 1.00
239 Ferenc Jongejan RC .40 1.00
240 Matt Kata RC .40 1.00
241 Kazuhiro Takeoka RC .40 1.00
242 Charlie Manning RC .40 1.00
243 Il Kim RC .40 1.00
244 Brennan King RC .40 1.00
245 Chris Kroski RC .40 1.00
246 David Martinez RC .40 1.00
247 Pete LaForest RC .40 1.00
248 Wil Ledezma RC .40 1.00
249 Jeremy Bonderman RC 1.50 4.00
250 Gonzalo Lopez RC .40 1.00
251 Brian Luderer RC .40 1.00
252 Ruddy Lugo RC .40 1.00
253 Wayne Lydon RC .40 1.00
254 Mark Malaska RC .40 1.00
255 Andy Marte RC .40 1.00
256 Tyler Martin RC .40 1.00
257 Branden Florence RC .40 1.00
258 Aneudis Mateo RC .40 1.00
259 Derell McCall RC .40 1.00
260 Elizardo Ramirez RC .40 1.00
261 Mike McNutt RC .40 1.00
262 Jacobo Meque RC .40 1.00
263 Derek Michaelis RC .40 1.00
264 Aaron Miles RC .40 1.00
265 Jose Morales RC .40 1.00
266 Dustin Moseley RC .40 1.00
267 Adrian Myers RC .40 1.00
268 Dan Neil RC .40 1.00
269 Jon Nelson RC .40 1.00
270 Mike Neu RC .40 1.00
271 Leigh Neuage RC .40 1.00
272 Wes O'Brien RC .40 1.00
273 Trent Oeltjen RC .40 1.00
274 Tim Olson RC .40 1.00
275 David Pahucki RC .40 1.00
276 Nathan Panther RC .40 1.00
277 Arnie Munoz RC .40 1.00
278 Dave Pember RC .40 1.00
279 Jason Perry RC .40 1.00
280 Matthew Peterson RC .40 1.00
281 Greg Aquino RC .40 1.00
282 Jorge Piedra RC .40 1.00
283 Simon Pond RC .40 1.00
284 Aaron Rakers RC .40 1.00
285 Felix Sanchez RC .40 1.00
286 Manuel Ramirez RC .40 1.00
287 Kevin Randel RC .40 1.00
288 Kelly Shoppach RC .60 1.50
289 Prentice Redman RC .40 1.00
290 Eric Reed RC .40 1.00
291 Wilton Reynolds RC .40 1.00
292 Eric Riggs RC .40 1.00
293 Carlos Rijo RC .40 1.00
294 Tyler Adamczyk RC .40 1.00
295 Jon-Mark Sprowl RC .40 1.00
296 Arturo Rivas RC .40 1.00
297 Kyle Roat RC .40 1.00
298 Bubba Nelson RC .40 1.00
299 Levi Robinson RC .40 1.00
300 Ray Sadler RC .40 1.00
301 Rylan Reed RC .40 1.00
302 Jon Schuerholz RC .40 1.00
303 Nobuaki Yoshida RC .40 1.00
304 Brian Shackelford RC .40 1.00
305 Bill Simon RC .40 1.00
306 Haj Turay RC .40 1.00
307 Sean Smith RC .40 1.00
308 Ryan Spataro RC .40 1.00
309 Jemel Spearman RC .40 1.00
310 Keith Stamler RC .40 1.00
311 Luke Steidlmayer RC .40 1.00
312 Adam Stern RC .40 1.00
313 Jay Sitzman RC .40 1.00
314 Mike Wodnicki RC .40 1.00
315 Terry Tiffee RC .40 1.00
316 Nick Trzesniak RC .40 1.00
317 Denny Tussen RC .40 1.00
318 Scott Tyler RC .40 1.00
319 Shane Victorino RC 1.25 3.00
320 Doug Waechter RC .40 1.00
321 Brandon Watson RC .40 1.00
322 Todd Wellemeyer RC .40 1.00
323 Eli Whiteside RC .40 1.00
324 Josh Willingham RC 1.25 3.00
325 Travis Wong RC .40 1.00
326 Brian Wright RC .40 1.00
327 Felix Pie RC .60 1.50
328 Andy Sisco RC .40 1.00
329 Dustin Yount RC .40 1.00
330 Andrew Dominique RC .40 1.00
331 Brian McCann AU A RC 8.00 20.00
332 Jose Contreras AU B RC 12.50 30.00
333 Corey Shafer AU A RC 4.00 10.00
334 Hanley Ramirez AU A RC 10.00 25.00
335 Ryan Shealy AU A RC 4.00 10.00
336 Kevin Youkilis AU A RC 6.00 15.00
337 Jason Kubel AU A RC 4.00 10.00
338 Aron Weston AU A RC 4.00 10.00
339 J.D. Durbin AU A RC 4.00 10.00
340 Gary Schneidmiller AU A RC 4.00 10.00
341 Travis Ishikawa AU A RC 4.00 10.00
342 Ben Francisco AU A RC 4.00 10.00
343 Bobby Basham AU A RC 4.00 10.00
344 Joey Gomes AU A RC 4.00 10.00
345 Beau Kemp AU A RC 4.00 10.00
346 T.Story-Harden AU A RC 4.00 10.00
347 Daryl Clark AU A RC 4.00 10.00
348 Bryan Bullington AU A RC 4.00 10.00
349 Rajai Davis AU A RC 4.00 10.00
350 Darrell Rasner AU A RC 4.00 10.00
351 Willie Mays 1.00 2.50
351AU Willie Mays AU 150.00 300.00

2003 Bowman Chrome Refractors

*REF 1-155: 1.5X TO 4X BASIC
*REF 156-330: 1.5X TO 4X BASIC
*REF 156-330 RC'S: 1.5X TO 4X BASIC
1-330 STATED ODDS 1:4 HOBBY
*REF AU A 331/333-350: .5X TO 1.2X BASIC
AU A ODDS 1:92 HOBBY
AU A STATED PRINT RUN 500 SETS
AU A CARDS ARE NOT SERIAL-NUMBERED
AU A EXCH.DEADLINE 07/31/05
AU B ODDS 1:11,479 HOBBY
AU B STATED PRINT RUN 100 CARDS
AU B CARDS ARE NOT SERIAL-NUMBERED
*REF.MAYS: 2X TO 5X BASIC
REF.MAYS ODDS 1:12 BOX LOADER PACKS
332 Jose Contreras AU B 30.00 60.00

2003 Bowman Chrome Blue Refractors

*BLUE: 1.5X TO 4X BASIC
ONE EXCH.CARD PER BOX LOADER PACK
ONE BOX LOADER PACK PER HOBBY BOX
EXCHANGE DEADLINE 11/30/05
SEE WWW.THEPIT.COM FOR PRICING

2003 Bowman Chrome Gold Refractors

*GOLD REF 1-155: 3X TO 8X BASIC
*GOLD REF 156-330: 3X TO 8X BASIC
*GOLD REF RC'S 156-330: 3X TO 8X BASIC
1-330 ODDS ONE PER BOX LOADER PACK
1-330 PRINT RUN 170 SERIAL #'d SETS
AU A ODDS 1:1202 HOBBY
AU A STATED PRINT RUN 50 SETS
AU A CARDS ARE NOT SERIAL-NUMBERED
AU A EXCH.DEADLINE 07/31/05
AU B ODDS 1:177,606 HOBBY
AU B PRINT RUN 10 CARDS
AU B CARD IS NOT SERIAL-NUMBERED
NO AU B PRICING DUE TO SCARCITY
*GOLD MAYS: 6X TO 15X BASIC
GOLD MAYS ODDS 1:116 BOX LDR PACKS
SET EXCH.CARDS ODDS 1:78,936 HOBBY
SET EXCH.CARD PRINT RUN 10 CARDS
SET EXCHANGE CARD DEADLINE 11/30/05
331 Brian McCann AU A 100.00 250.00
333 Corey Shafer AU A 30.00 60.00
334 Hanley Ramirez AU A 100.00 250.00
335 Ryan Shealy AU A 30.00 60.00
337 Jason Kubel AU A 30.00 60.00
338 Aron Weston AU A 30.00 60.00
339 J.D. Durbin AU A 30.00 60.00
340 Gary Schneidmiller AU A 30.00 60.00
341 Travis Ishikawa AU A 30.00 60.00
342 Ben Francisco AU A 30.00 60.00
343 Bobby Basham AU A 30.00 60.00
344 Joey Gomes AU A 30.00 60.00
345 Beau Kemp AU A 30.00 60.00
346 Thomari Story-Harden AU A 30.00 60.00
347 Daryl Clark AU A 30.00 60.00
348 Bryan Bullington AU A 30.00 60.00
349 Rajai Davis AU A 30.00 60.00
350 Darrell Rasner AU A 30.00 60.00

2003 Bowman Chrome X-Fractors

*X-FR 1-155: 2.5X TO 6X BASIC
*X-FR 156-330: 2.5X TO 6X BASIC
*X-FR RC'S 156-330: 1.25X TO 3X BASIC
1-330 STATED ODDS 1:9 HOBBY
*X-FR AU A 331/333-350: .6X TO 1.5X BASIC
AU A ODDS 1:199 HOBBY
AU A STATED PRINT RUN 250 SETS
AU A CARDS ARE NOT SERIAL-NUMBERED
AU A EXCH.DEADLINE 07/31/05
AU B ODDS 1:22,959 HOBBY
AU B STATED PRINT RUN 50 CARDS
AU B CARD IS NOT SERIAL-NUMBERED
*X-FR MAYS: 4X TO 10X BASIC
X-FR MAYS ODDS 1:58 BOX LOADER PACKS
332 Jose Contreras AU B 40.00 80.00

2003 Bowman Chrome Draft

COMPLETE SET (176) 400.00 550.00
COMP.SET w/o AU's (165) 30.00 60.00
COMMON CARD (1-165) .20 .50
COMMON RC .40 1.00
COMMON RC YR .20 .50
1-165 TWO PER BOWMAN DRAFT PACK
COMMON CARD (166-176) 4.00 10.00
166-176 STATED ODDS 1:41 H/R
168-176 ARE ALL PARTIAL LIVE/EXCH DIST.
168-176 EXCH.DEADLINE 11/30/05
LUBANSKI IS AN SP BY 1000 COPIES
1 Dontrelle Willis .20 .50
2 Freddy Sanchez .20 .50
3 Miguel Cabrera 2.50 6.00
4 Ryan Ludwick .20 .50
5 Ty Wigginton .20 .50
6 Mark Teixeira .30 .75
7 Trey Hodges .20 .50
8 Laynce Nix .20 .50
9 Antonio Perez .20 .50
10 Jody Gerut .20 .50
11 Jae Weong Seo .20 .50
12 Erick Almonte .20 .50
13 Lyle Overbay .20 .50
14 Billy Traber .20 .50
15 Andres Torres .20 .50
16 Jose Valverde .20 .50
17 Aaron Heilman .20 .50
18 Brandon Larson .20 .50
19 Jung Bong .20 .50
20 Jesse Foppert .20 .50
21 Angel Berroa .20 .50
22 Jeff DaVanon .20 .50
23 Kurt Ainsworth .20 .50
24 Brandon Claussen .20 .50
25 Xavier Nady .20 .50
26 Travis Hafner .20 .50
27 Jerome Williams .20 .50
28 Jose Reyes .50 1.25
29 Sergio Mitre RC .40 1.00
30 Bo Hart RC .40 1.00
31 Adam Miller RC 1.50 4.00
32 Brian Finch RC .40 1.00
33 Taylor Mattingly RC .40 1.00
34 Daric Barton RC .60 1.50
35 Chris Ray RC .60 1.50
36 Jarrod Saltalamacchia RC 2.00 5.00
37 Dennis Dove RC .40 1.00
38 James Houser RC .40 1.00
39 Clint King RC .40 1.00
40 Lou Palmisano RC .40 1.00
41 Dan Moore RC .40 1.00
42 Craig Stansberry RC .40 1.00
43 Jo Jo Reyes RC .40 1.00
44 Jake Stevens RC .40 1.00
45 Tom Gorzelanny RC .60 1.50
46 Brian Marshall RC .40 1.00
47 Scott Beerer RC .40 1.00
48 Javi Herrera RC .40 1.00
49 Steve LeRud RC .40 1.00
50 Josh Banks RC .40 1.00
51 Jon Papelbon RC 4.00 10.00
52 Juan Valdes RC .40 1.00
53 Beau Vaughan RC .40 1.00
54 Matt Chico RC .40 1.00
55 Todd Jennings RC .40 1.00
56 Anthony Gwynn RC .40 1.00
57 Matt Harrison RC 1.50 4.00
58 Aaron Marsden RC .40 1.00
59 Casey Abrams RC .40 1.00
60 Cory Stuart RC .40 1.00
61 Mike Wagner RC .40 1.00
62 Jordan Pratt RC .40 1.00
63 Andre Randolph RC .40 1.00
64 Blake Balkcom RC .40 1.00
65 Josh Muecke RC .40 1.00
66 Jamie D'Antona RC .40 1.00
67 Cole Seifrig RC .40 1.00
68 Josh Anderson RC .40 1.00
69 Matt Lorenzo RC .40 1.00
70 Nate Spears RC .40 1.00
71 Chris Goodman RC .40 1.00
72 Brian McFall RC .40 1.00
73 Billy Hogan RC .40 1.00
74 Jamie Romak RC .40 1.00
75 Jeff Cook RC .40 1.00
76 Brooks McNiven RC .40 1.00
77 Xavier Paul RC .40 1.00
78 Bob Zimmerman RC .40 1.00

79 Mickey Hall RC .40 1.00
80 Shaun Marcum RC .40 1.00
81 Matt Nachreiner RC .40 1.00
82 Chris Kinsey RC .40 1.00
83 Jonathan Fulton RC .40 1.00
84 Edgardo Baez RC .40 1.00
85 Robert Valido RC .40 1.00
86 Kenny Lewis RC .40 1.00
87 Trent Peterson RC .40 1.00
88 Johnny Woodard RC .40 1.00
89 Wes Littleton RC .40 1.00
90 Sean Rodriguez RC .60 1.50
91 Kyle Pearson RC .40 1.00
92 Josh Rainwater RC .40 1.00
93 Travis Schlichting RC .40 1.00
94 Tim Battle RC .40 1.00
95 Aaron Hill RC 1.25 3.00
96 Bob McCrory RC .40 1.00
97 Rick Guarno RC .40 1.00
98 Brandon Yarbrough RC .40 1.00
99 Peter Stonard RC .40 1.00
100 Darin Downs RC .40 1.00
101 Matt Bruback RC .40 1.00
102 Danny Garcia RC .40 1.00
103 Cory Stewart RC .40 1.00
104 Ferdin Tejeda RC .40 1.00
105 Kade Johnson RC .40 1.00
106 Andrew Brown RC .40 1.00
107 Aquilino Lopez RC .40 1.00
108 Stephen Randolph RC .40 1.00
109 Dave Matranga RC .40 1.00
110 Dustin McGowan RC .40 1.00
111 Juan Camacho RC .40 1.00
112 Cliff Lee 1.25 3.00
113 Jeff Duncan RC .40 1.00
114 C.J. Wilson 1.50 4.00
115 Brandon Roberson RC .40 1.00
116 David Corrente RC .40 1.00
117 Kevin Beavers RC .40 1.00
118 Anthony Webster RC .40 1.00
119 Oscar Villarreal RC .40 1.00
120 Hong-Chih Kuo RC 2.00 5.00
121 Josh Barfield .20 .50
122 Denny Bautista .20 .50
123 Chris Burke RC .40 1.00
124 Robinson Cano RC 6.00 15.00
125 Jose Castillo .20 .50
126 Neal Cotts .20 .50
127 Jorge De La Rosa .20 .50
128 J.D. Durbin .20 .50
129 Edwin Encarnacion 1.50 4.00
130 Gavin Floyd .20 .50
131 Alexis Gomez .20 .50
132 Edgar Gonzalez RC .40 1.00
133 Khalil Greene .30 .75
134 Zack Greinke 6.00 15.00
135 Franklin Gutierrez .50 1.25
136 Rich Harden .30 .75
137 J.J. Hardy RC 3.00 8.00
138 Ryan Howard RC 3.00 8.00
139 Justin Huber .20 .50
140 David Kelton .20 .50
141 Dave Krynzel .20 .50
142 Pete LaForest .20 .50
143 Adam LaRoche .20 .50
144 Preston Larrison RC .40 1.00
145 John Maine RC .60 1.50
146 Andy Marte .20 .50
147 Jeff Mathis .20 .50
148 Joe Mauer .50 1.25
149 Clint Nageotte .20 .50
150 Chris Narveson .20 .50
151 Ramon Nivar .20 .50
152 Felix Pie .30 .75
153 Guillermo Quiroz RC .40 1.00
154 Rene Reyes .20 .50
155 Royce Ring .20 .50
156 Alexis Rios .20 .50
157 Grady Sizemore .30 .75
158 Stephen Smitherman .20 .50
159 Seung Song .20 .50
160 Scott Thorman .20 .50
161 Chad Tracy .20 .50
162 Chin-Hui Tsao .20 .50
163 John VanBenschoten .20 .50
164 Kevin Youkilis 1.25 3.00
165 Chien-Ming Wang .75 2.00
166 Chris Lubanski AU SP RC 4.00 10.00
167 Ryan Harvey AU RC 4.00 10.00
168 Matt Murton AU RC 4.00 10.00
169 Jay Sborz AU RC 4.00 10.00
170 Brandon Wood AU RC 5.00 12.00
171 Nick Markakis AU RC 25.00 60.00
172 Rickie Weeks AU RC 4.00 10.00
173 Eric Duncan AU RC 4.00 10.00
174 Chad Billingsley AU RC 4.00 10.00
175 Ryan Wagner AU RC 4.00 10.00
176 Delmon Young AU RC 4.00 10.00

2003 Bowman Chrome Draft Refractors

*REFRACTOR 1-165: 1.25X TO 3X BASIC
*REFRACTOR RC 1-165: .6X TO 1.5X BASIC
*REFRACTOR RC YR 1-165: .6X TO 1.5X BASIC
*REFRACTOR AU 166-176: .6X TO 1.5X BASIC
1-165 ODDS 1:11 BOWMAN DRAFT H/R
166-176 AU ODDS 1:196 BOW.DRAFT HOBBY
166-176 AU ODDS 1:197 BOW.DRAFT RETAIL
166-176 AU PRINT RUN 500 SETS
166-176 AU PRINT RUN PROVIDED BY TOPPS
166-176 AU'S ARE NOT SERIAL-NUMBERED
51 Jon Papelbon 15.00 40.00

2003 Bowman Chrome Draft Gold Refractors

*GOLD REF 1-165: 6X TO 15X BASIC
*GOLD REF RC 1-165: 3X TO 8X BASIC
*GOLD REF RC YR 1-165: 3X TO 8X BASIC
1-165 ODDS 1:98 BOWMAN DRAFT HOBBY
166-176 AU ODDS 1:1479 BOW.DRAFT HOBBY
1-165 PRINT RUN 50 SERIAL #'d SETS
166-176 AU PRINT RUN 50 SETS
166-176 AU PRINT RUN PROVIDED BY TOPPS
166-176 AU'S ARE NOT SERIAL-NUMBERED
GOLD REF ARE HOBBY-ONLY DISTRIBUTION
51 Jon Papelbon 125.00 250.00
124 Robinson Cano 75.00 200.00
138 Ryan Howard 100.00 200.00

2003 Bowman Chrome Draft X-Fractors

*X-FRACTOR 1-165: 2.5X TO 6X BASIC
*X-FRACTOR RC 1-165: 1.25X TO 3X BASIC
*X-FRACTOR RC YR 1-165: 1.25X TO 3X BASIC
*X-FRACTOR AU 166-176: .75X TO 2X BASIC
1-165 ODDS 1:50 BOWMAN DRAFT HOBBY
1-165 ODDS 1:52 BOWMAN DRAFT RETAIL
166-176 AU ODDS 1:393 BOW.DRAFT HOBBY
166-176 AU ODDS 1:394 BOW.DRAFT RETAIL
1-165 PRINT RUN 130 SERIAL #'d SETS
166-176 AU PRINT RUN 250 SETS
166-176 AU PRINT RUN PROVIDED BY TOPPS
166-176 AU'S ARE NOT SERIAL-NUMBERED

2004 Bowman Chrome

COMPLETE SET (350) 150.00 300.00
COMP.SET w/o AU's (330) 30.00 60.00
COMMON CARD (1-150) .20 .50
COMMON CARD (151-165) .20 .50
COMMON CARD (166-330) .40 1.00
COMMON AUTO (331-350) 4.00 10.00
331-350 AU STATED ODDS 1:25
331-350 AU PRINT RUN 2000 SETS
331-350 AU'S ARE NOT SERIAL-NUMBERED
331-350 PRINT RUN PROVIDED BY TOPPS
EXCHANGE DEADLINE 08/31/06
1 Garret Anderson .20 .50
2 Larry Walker .30 .75
3 Derek Jeter 1.25 3.00
4 Curt Schilling .30 .75
5 Carlos Zambrano .30 .75
6 Shawn Green .20 .50
7 Manny Ramirez .50 1.25
8 Randy Johnson .50 1.25
9 Jeremy Bonderman .20 .50
10 Alfonso Soriano .30 .75
11 Scott Rolen .30 .75
12 Kerry Wood .20 .50
13 Eric Gagne .20 .50
14 Ryan Klesko .20 .50
15 Kevin Millar .20 .50
16 Ty Wigginton .20 .50
17 David Ortiz .50 1.25
18 Luis Castillo .20 .50
19 Bernie Williams .30 .75
20 Edgar Renteria .20 .50
21 Matt Kata .20 .50
22 Bartolo Colon .20 .50
23 Derrek Lee .20 .50
24 Gary Sheffield .20 .50
25 Nomar Garciaparra .30 .75
26 Kevin Millwood .20 .50
27 Corey Patterson .20 .50
28 Carlos Beltran .30 .75
29 Mike Lieberthal .20 .50
30 Troy Glaus .20 .50
31 Preston Wilson .20 .50
32 Jorge Posada .30 .75
33 Bo Hart .20 .50
34 Mark Prior .30 .75
35 Hideo Nomo .50 1.25
36 Jason Kendall .20 .50
37 Roger Clemens .60 1.50
38 Dmitri Young .20 .50
39 Jason Giambi .20 .50
40 Jim Edmonds .30 .75
41 Ryan Ludwick .20 .50
42 Brandon Webb .20 .50
43 Todd Helton .30 .75
44 Jacque Jones .20 .50
45 Jamie Moyer .20 .50
46 Tim Salmon .20 .50
47 Kelvim Escobar .20 .50
48 Tony Batista .20 .50
49 Nick Johnson .20 .50
50 Jim Thome .30 .75
51 Casey Blake .20 .50
52 Trot Nixon .20 .50
53 Luis Gonzalez .20 .50
54 Dontrelle Willis .20 .50
55 Mike Mussina .30 .75
56 Carl Crawford .30 .75
57 Mark Buehrle .30 .75
58 Scott Podsednik .20 .50
59 Brian Giles .20 .50
60 Rafael Furcal .20 .50
61 Miguel Cabrera .50 1.25
62 Rich Harden .20 .50
63 Mark Teixeira .30 .75
64 Frank Thomas .50 1.25
65 Johan Santana .30 .75
66 Jason Schmidt .20 .50
67 Aramis Ramirez .20 .50
68 Jose Reyes .30 .75
69 Magglio Ordonez .30 .75
70 Mike Sweeney .20 .50
71 Eric Chavez .20 .50
72 Rocco Baldelli .20 .50
73 Sammy Sosa .50 1.25
74 Javy Lopez .20 .50
75 Roy Oswalt .30 .75
76 Raul Ibanez .30 .75
77 Ivan Rodriguez .30 .75
78 Jerome Williams .20 .50
79 Carlos Lee .20 .50
80 Geoff Jenkins .20 .50
81 Sean Burroughs .20 .50
82 Marcus Giles .20 .50
83 Mike Lowell .20 .50
84 Barry Zito .30 .75
85 Aubrey Huff .20 .50
86 Esteban Loaiza .20 .50
87 Torii Hunter .20 .50
88 Phil Nevin .20 .50
89 Andruw Jones .20 .50
90 Josh Beckett .20 .50
91 Mark Mulder .20 .50
92 Hank Blalock .20 .50
93 Jason Phillips .20 .50
94 Russ Ortiz .20 .50
95 Juan Pierre .20 .50
96 Tom Glavine .30 .75
97 Gil Meche .20 .50
98 Ramon Ortiz .20 .50
99 Richie Sexson .20 .50
100 Albert Pujols .60 1.50
101 Javier Vazquez .20 .50
102 Johnny Damon .30 .75
103 Alex Rodriguez .60 1.50
104 Omar Vizquel .30 .75
105 Chipper Jones .50 1.25
106 Lance Berkman .30 .75
107 Tim Hudson .30 .75
108 Carlos Delgado .20 .50
109 Austin Kearns .20 .50
110 Orlando Cabrera .20 .50
111 Edgar Martinez .30 .75
112 Melvin Mora .20 .50
113 Jeff Bagwell .30 .75
114 Marlon Byrd .20 .50
115 Vernon Wells .20 .50
116 C.C. Sabathia .30 .75
117 Cliff Floyd .20 .50
118 Ichiro Suzuki .60 1.50
119 Miguel Olivo .20 .50
120 Mike Piazza .50 1.25
121 Adam Dunn .30 .75
122 Paul Lo Duca .20 .50
123 Brett Myers .20 .50
124 Michael Young .20 .50
125 Sidney Ponson .20 .50
126 Greg Maddux .60 1.50
127 Vladimir Guerrero .30 .75
128 Miguel Tejada .30 .75
129 Andy Pettitte .30 .75
130 Rafael Palmeiro .30 .75
131 Ken Griffey Jr. 1.00 2.50
132 Shannon Stewart .20 .50
133 Joel Pineiro .20 .50
134 Luis Matos .20 .50
135 Jeff Kent .20 .50
136 Randy Wolf .20 .50
137 Chris Woodward .20 .50
138 Jody Gerut .20 .50
139 Jose Vidro .20 .50
140 Bret Boone .20 .50
141 Bill Mueller .20 .50
142 Angel Berroa .20 .50
143 Bobby Abreu .20 .50
144 Roy Halladay .30 .75
145 Delmon Young .30 .75
146 Jonny Gomes .20 .50
147 Rickie Weeks .20 .50
148 Edwin Jackson .20 .50
149 Neal Cotts .20 .50
150 Jason Bay .30 .75
151 Khalil Greene .30 .75
152 Joe Mauer .40 1.00
153 Bobby Jenks .20 .50
154 Chin-Feng Chen .20 .50
155 Chien-Ming Wang .75 2.00
156 Mickey Hall .20 .50
157 James Houser .20 .50
158 Jay Sborz .20 .50
159 Jonathan Fulton .20 .50
160 Steven Lerud .20 .50
161 Grady Sizemore .30 .75
162 Felix Pie .20 .50
163 Dustin McGowan .20 .50
164 Chris Lubanski .20 .50
165 Tom Gorzelanny .20 .50
166 Rudy Guillen RC .40 1.00
167 Aarom Baldiris RC .40 1.00
168 Conor Jackson RC 1.25 3.00
169 Matt Moses RC .60 1.50
170 Ervin Santana RC 1.00 2.50
171 Merkin Valdez RC .40 1.00
172 Erick Aybar RC 1.00 2.50
173 Brad Sullivan RC .40 1.00
174 Joey Gathright RC .40 1.00
175 Brad Snyder RC .40 1.00
176 Alberto Callaspo RC 1.00 2.50
177 Brandon Medders RC .40 1.00
178 Zach Miner RC .60 1.50
179 Charlie Zink RC .40 1.00
180 Adam Greenberg RC 2.00 5.00
181 Kevin Howard RC .40 1.00
182 Wanell Severino RC .40 1.00
183 Chin-Lung Hu RC .40 1.00
184 Joel Zumaya RC 1.50 4.00
185 Skip Schumaker RC .60 1.50
186 Nic Ungs RC .40 1.00
187 Todd Self RC .40 1.00
188 Brian Steffek RC .40 1.00
189 Brock Peterson RC .40 1.00
190 Greg Thissen RC .40 1.00
191 Frank Brooks RC .40 1.00
192 Scott Olsen RC .40 1.00
193 Chris Mabeus RC .40 1.00
194 Dan Giese RC .40 1.00
195 Jared Wells RC .40 1.00
196 Carlos Sosa RC .40 1.00
197 Bobby Madritsch .40 1.00
198 Calvin Hayes RC .40 1.00
199 Omar Quintanilla RC .40 1.00
200 Chris O'Riordan RC .40 1.00
201 Tim Hutting RC .40 1.00
202 Carlos Quentin RC 1.50 4.00
203 Brayan Pena RC .40 1.00
204 Jeff Salazar RC .40 1.00
205 David Murphy RC .60 1.50
206 Alberto Garcia RC .40 1.00
207 Ramon Ramirez RC .40 1.00
208 Luis Bolivar RC .40 1.00
209 Rodney Choy Foo RC .40 1.00
210 Fausto Carmona RC .60 1.50
211 Anthony Acevedo RC .40 1.00
212 Chad Santos RC .40 1.00
213 Jason Frasor RC .40 1.00
214 Jesse Roman RC .40 1.00
215 James Tomlin RC .40 1.00
216 Josh Labandeira RC .40 1.00
217 Ryan Meaux RC .40 1.00
218 Don Sutton RC .40 1.00
219 Danny Gonzalez RC .40 1.00
220 Javier Guzman RC .40 1.00
221 Anthony Lerew RC .40 1.00
222 Jon Connolly RC .40 1.00
223 Jesse English RC .40 1.00
224 Hector Made RC .40 1.00
225 Travis Hanson RC .40 1.00
226 Jesse Floyd RC .40 1.00
227 Nick Gorneault RC .40 1.00
228 Craig Ansman RC .40 1.00
229 Paul McAnulty RC .40 1.00
230 Carl Loadenthal RC .40 1.00
231 Dave Crouthers RC .40 1.00
232 Harvey Garcia RC .40 1.00
233 Casey Kopitzke RC .40 1.00
234 Ricky Nolasco RC .60 1.50
235 Miguel Perez RC .40 1.00
236 Ryan Mulhern RC .40 1.00
237 Chris Aguila RC .40 1.00
238 Brooks Conrad RC .40 1.00
239 Damaso Espino RC .40 1.00
240 Jereme Milons RC .40 1.00
241 Luke Hughes RC 1.00 2.50
242 Kory Casto RC .40 1.00
243 Jose Valdez RC .40 1.00
244 J.T. Stotts RC .40 1.00
245 Lee Gwaltney RC .40 1.00
246 Yoann Torrealba RC .40 1.00
247 Omar Falcon RC .40 1.00
248 Jon Coutlangus RC .40 1.00
249 George Sherrill RC .40 1.00
250 John Santor RC .40 1.00
251 Tony Richie RC .40 1.00
252 Kevin Richardson RC .40 1.00
253 Tim Bittner RC .40 1.00
254 Chris Saenz RC .40 1.00
255 Jose Capellan RC .40 1.00
256 Donald Levinski RC .40 1.00
257 Jerome Gamble RC .40 1.00
258 Jeff Keppinger RC .60 1.50
259 Jason Szuminski RC .40 1.00
260 Akinori Otsuka RC .40 1.00
261 Ryan Budde RC .40 1.00
262 Marland Williams RC .40 1.00
263 Jeff Allison RC .40 1.00
264 Hector Gimenez RC .40 1.00
265 Tim Frend RC .40 1.00
266 Tom Farmer RC .40 1.00
267 Shawn Hill RC .40 1.00
268 Mike Huggins RC .40 1.00
269 Scott Proctor RC .40 1.00
270 Jorge Mejia RC .40 1.00
271 Terry Jones RC .40 1.00
272 Zach Duke RC .60 1.50
273 Jesse Crain RC .60 1.50
274 Luke Anderson RC .40 1.00
275 Hunter Brown RC .40 1.00
276 Matt Lemanczyk RC .40 1.00
277 Fernando Cortez RC .40 1.00
278 Vince Perkins RC .40 1.00
279 Tommy Murphy RC .40 1.00
280 Mike Gosling RC .40 1.00
281 Paul Bacot RC .40 1.00
282 Matt Capps RC .40 1.00
283 Juan Gutierrez RC .40 1.00
284 Teodoro Encarnacion RC .40 1.00
285 Chad Bentz RC .40 1.00
286 Kazuo Matsui RC .60 1.50
287 Ryan Hankins RC .40 1.00
288 Leo Nunez RC .40 1.00
289 Dave Wallace RC .40 1.00
290 Rob Tejeda RC .40 1.00
291 Paul Maholm RC .60 1.50
292 Casey Daigle RC .40 1.00
293 Tydus Meadows RC .40 1.00
294 Khalid Ballouli RC .40 1.00
295 Benji DeQuin RC .40 1.00
296 Tyler Davidson RC .40 1.00
297 Brant Colamarino RC .40 1.00
298 Marcus McBeth RC .40 1.00
299 Brad Eldred RC .40 1.00
300 David Pauley RC .60 1.50
301 Yadier Molina RC 50.00 120.00
302 Chris Shelton RC .40 1.00
303 Nyjer Morgan RC .40 1.00
304 Jon DeVries RC .40 1.00
305 Sheldon Fulse RC .40 1.00
306 Vito Chiaravalloti RC .40 1.00
307 Warner Madrigal RC .40 1.00
308 Reid Gorecki RC .40 1.00
309 Sung Jung RC .40 1.00
310 Pete Shier RC .40 1.00
311 Michael Mooney RC .40 1.00
312 Kenny Perez RC .40 1.00
313 Michael Mallory RC .40 1.00
314 Ben Himes RC .40 1.00
315 Ivan Ochoa RC .40 1.00
316 Donald Kelly RC .60 1.50
317 Tom Mastny RC .40 1.00
318 Kevin Davidson RC .40 1.00
319 Brian Pilkington RC .40 1.00
320 Alex Romero RC .40 1.00
321 Chad Chop RC .40 1.00
322 Kody Kirkland RC .40 1.00
323 Casey Myers RC .40 1.00
324 Mike Rouse RC .40 1.00
325 Sergio Silva RC .40 1.00
326 J.J. Furmaniak RC .40 1.00
327 Brad Vericker RC .40 1.00
328 Blake Hawksworth RC .40 1.00
329 Brock Jacobsen RC .40 1.00
330 Alec Zumwalt RC .40 1.00
331 Wardell Starling AU RC 4.00 10.00
332 Estee Harris AU RC 4.00 10.00
333 Kyle Sleeth AU RC 4.00 10.00
334 Dioner Navarro AU RC 4.00 10.00
335 Logan Kensing AU RC 4.00 10.00
336 Travis Blackley AU RC 4.00 10.00
337 Lincoln Holdzkom AU RC 4.00 10.00
338 Jason Hirsh AU RC 4.00 10.00
339 Juan Cedeno AU RC 4.00 10.00
340 Matt Creighton AU RC 4.00 10.00
341 Tim Stauffer AU RC 4.00 10.00
342 Shingo Takatsu AU RC 4.00 10.00
343 Lastings Milledge AU RC 4.00 10.00
344 Dustin Nippert AU RC 4.00 10.00
345 Felix Hernandez AU RC 25.00 60.00
346 Joaquin Arias AU RC 4.00 10.00
347 Kevin Kouzmanoff AU RC 4.00 10.00
348 Bobby Brownlie AU RC 4.00 10.00
349 David Aardsma AU RC 4.00 10.00
350 Jon Knott AU RC 6.00 15.00

2004 Bowman Chrome Refractors

*REF 1-150: 1.5X TO 4X BASIC
*REF 151-165: 2X TO 5X BASIC
*REF 166-330: 1X TO 2.5X BASIC
1-330 STATED ODDS 1:4 HOBBY
*REF AU 331-350: .5X TO 1.2X BASIC
331-350 AU ODDS 1:100 HOBBY
331-350 AU PRINT RUN 500 SETS
331-350 AU'S ARE NOT SERIAL-NUMBERED
331-350 PRINT RUN PROVIDED BY TOPPS
EXCHANGE DEADLINE 08/31/06

2004 Bowman Chrome Blue Refractors

*BLUE REF 166-330: 1.25X TO 3X BASIC
EXCH.CARDS AVAIL VIA PIT.COM WEBSITE
ONE EXCH.CARD PER BOX-LOADER PACK
ONE BOX-LOADER PACK PER HOBBY BOX
STATED PRINT RUN 290 SETS
EXCHANGE DEADLINE 12/31/04
NNO Exchange Card

2004 Bowman Chrome Gold Refractors

*GOLD REF 1-150: 5X TO 12X BASIC
*GOLD REF 151-165: 8X TO 20X BASIC
*GOLD REF 166-330: 6X TO 15X BASIC
1-330 STATED ODDS 1:60 HOBBY
1-330 PRINT RUN 50 SERIAL #'d SETS
*GOLD REF 331-350: 2X TO 4X BASIC
331-350 AU ODDS 1:1003 HOBBY
331-350 AU STATED PRINT RUN 50 SETS
331-350 AU'S ARE NOT SERIAL-NUMBERED
331-350 PRINT RUN PROVIDED BY TOPPS
EXCHANGE DEADLINE 08/31/06

2004 Bowman Chrome X-Fractors

*X-FR 1-150: 3X TO 8X BASIC
*X-FR 151-165: 4X TO 10X BASIC
*X-FR 166-330: 2X TO 5X BASIC
1-330 ODDS ONE PER BOX LOADER PACK
ONE BOX LOADER PACK PER HOBY BOX
INSTANT WIN 1-330 ODDS 1:103,968 H
1-330 PRINT RUN 172 SERIAL #'d SETS
SETS 1-10 AVAIL.VIA INSTANT WIN CARD
SETS 11-172 ISSUED IN BOX-LOADER PACKS
*X-FR AU 331-350: .6X TO 1.5X BASIC
331-350 AU ODDS 1:200 HOBBY
331-350 AU STATED PRINT RUN 250 SETS
331-350 AU'S ARE NOT SERIAL-NUMBERED
331-350 PRINT RUNS PROVIDED BY TOPPS
EXCHANGE DEADLINE 08/31/06
NNO Complete 1-330 Instant Win/10

2004 Bowman Chrome Stars of the Future

STATED ODDS 1:600 HOBBY
STATED PRINT RUN 500 SETS
CARDS ARE NOT SERIAL-NUMBERED
PRINT RUN INFO PROVIDED BY TOPPS
REFRACTORS RANDOM INSERTS IN PACKS
NO REFRACTOR PRICING DUE TO SCARCITY
EXCHANGE DEADLINE 08/31/06
LHC Luban/Harvey/Cord 10.00 25.00
MHD Markakis/Hill/Duncan 10.00 25.00
YSS Delmon/Sleeth/Stauffer 10.00 25.00

2004 Bowman Chrome Draft

COMPLETE SET (175) 175.00 300.00
COMP.SET w/o SP's (165) 50.00 100.00
COMMON CARD (1-165) .15 .40
COMMON RC .40 1.00
COMMON RC YR .15 .40
1-165 TWO PER BOWMAN DRAFT PACK
COMMON CARD (166-175) 4.00 10.00
166-175 ODDS 1:60 BOWMAN DRAFT HOBBY
166-175 ODDS 1:60 BOWMAN DRAFT RETAIL
166-175 STATED PRINT RUN 1695 SETS
166-175 ARE NOT SERIAL-NUMBERED
166-175 PRINT RUN PROVIDED BY TOPPS
PLATES 1-165 ODDS 1:559 HOBBY
PLATES 166-175 ODDS 1:18,354 HOBBY
PLATES PRINT RUN 1 SERIAL #'d SET
BLACK-CYAN-MAGENTA-YELLOW EXIST
NO PLATES PRICING DUE TO SCARCITY
1 Lyle Overbay .15 .40
2 David Newhan .15 .40
3 J.R. House .15 .40
4 Chad Tracy .15 .40
5 Humberto Quintero .15 .40
6 Dave Bush .15 .40
7 Scott Hairston .15 .40
8 Mike Wood .15 .40
9 Alexis Rios .15 .40
10 Sean Burnett .15 .40
11 Wilson Valdez .15 .40
12 Lew Ford .15 .40
13 Freddy Thon RC .40 1.00
14 Zack Greinke .60 1.50
15 Bucky Jacobsen .15 .40
16 Kevin Youkilis .15 .40
17 Grady Sizemore .25 .60
18 Denny Bautista .15 .40
19 David DeJesus .15 .40
20 Casey Kotchman .15 .40
21 David Kelton .15 .40
22 Charles Thomas RC .40 1.00
23 Kazuhito Tadano RC .40 1.00
24 Justin Leone RC .40 1.00
25 Eduardo Villacis RC .40 1.00
26 Brian Dallimore RC .40 1.00
27 Nick Green .15 .40
28 Sam McConnell RC .40 1.00
29 Brad Halsey RC .40 1.00
30 Roman Colon RC .40 1.00
31 Josh Fields RC .60 1.50
32 Cody Bunkelman RC .40 1.00
33 Jay Rainville RC .40 1.00
34 Richie Robnett RC .40 1.00
35 Jon Poterson RC .40 1.00
36 Huston Street RC .60 1.50
37 Erick San Pedro RC .40 1.00
38 Cory Dunlap RC .40 1.00
39 Kurt Suzuki RC .60 1.50
40 Anthony Swarzak RC .60 1.50
41 Ian Desmond RC .60 1.50
42 Chris Covington RC .40 1.00
43 Christian Garcia RC .60 1.50
44 Gaby Hernandez RC .60 1.50
45 Steven Register RC .40 1.00
46 Eduardo Morlan RC .60 1.50
47 Collin Balester RC .40 1.00
48 Nathan Phillips RC .40 1.00
49 Dan Schwartzbauer RC .40 1.00
50 Rafael Gonzalez RC .40 1.00
51 K.C. Herren RC .40 1.00
52 William Susdorf RC .40 1.00
53 Rob Johnson RC .40 1.00
54 Louis Marson RC .60 1.50
55 Joe Koshansky RC .40 1.00
56 Jamar Walton RC .40 1.00
57 Mark Lowe RC .60 1.50
58 Matt Macri RC .60 1.50
59 Donny Lucy RC .40 1.00
60 Mike Ferris RC .40 1.00
61 Mike Nickeas RC .40 1.00
62 Eric Hurley RC .40 1.00
63 Scott Elbert RC .40 1.00
64 Blake DeWitt RC .60 1.50
65 Danny Putnam RC .40 1.00
66 J.P. Howell RC .40 1.00
67 John Wiggins RC .40 1.00
68 Justin Orenduff RC .60 1.50
69 Ray Liotta RC .40 1.00
70 Billy Buckner RC .40 1.00
71 Eric Campbell RC .40 1.00
72 Olin Wick RC .40 1.00
73 Sean Gamble RC .40 1.00
74 Seth Smith RC .40 1.00
75 Wade Davis RC 1.00 2.50
76 Joe Jacobitz RC .40 1.00
77 J.A. Happ RC 1.00 2.50
78 Eric Ridener RC .40 1.00
79 Matt Tuiasosopo RC 1.00 2.50
80 Brad Bergesen RC .40 1.00
81 Javy Guerra RC 1.00 2.50
82 Buck Shaw RC .40 1.00
83 Paul Janish RC .60 1.50
84 Sean Kazmar RC .40 1.00
85 Josh Johnson RC .40 1.00
86 Angel Salome RC .40 1.00
87 Jordan Parraz RC .60 1.50
88 Kelvin Vazquez RC .40 1.00
89 Grant Hansen RC .40 1.00
90 Matt Fox RC .40 1.00
91 Trevor Plouffe RC 1.00 2.50
92 Wes Whisler RC .40 1.00
93 Curtis Thigpen RC .40 1.00
94 Donnie Smith RC .40 1.00
95 Luis Rivera RC .40 1.00
96 Jesse Hoover RC .40 1.00
97 Jason Vargas RC .60 1.50
98 Clary Carlsen RC .40 1.00
99 Mark Robinson RC .40 1.00
100 J.C. Holt RC .40 1.00
101 Chad Blackwell RC .40 1.00
102 Daryl Jones RC .40 1.00
103 Jonathan Tierce RC .40 1.00
104 Patrick Bryant RC .40 1.00
105 Eddie Prasch RC .40 1.00
106 Mitch Einertson RC .40 1.00
107 Kyle Waldrop RC .40 1.00
108 Jeff Marquez RC .40 1.00
109 Zach Jackson RC .40 1.00
110 Josh Wahpepah RC .40 1.00
111 Adam Lind RC .60 1.50
112 Kyle Bloom RC .40 1.00
113 Ben Harrison RC .40 1.00
114 Taylor Tankersley RC .40 1.00
115 Steven Jackson RC .40 1.00
116 David Purcey RC .60 1.50
117 Jacob McGee RC 1.00 2.50
118 Lucas Harrell RC .40 1.00
119 Brandon Allen RC .40 1.00
120 Van Pope RC .40 1.00
121 Jeff Francis .15 .40
122 Joe Blanton .15 .40
123 Wil Ledezma .15 .40
124 Bryan Bullington .15 .40
125 Jairo Garcia .15 .40
126 Matt Cain 1.00 2.50
127 Arnie Munoz .15 .40
128 Clint Everts .15 .40
129 Jesus Cota .15 .40
130 Gavin Floyd .15 .40
131 Edwin Encarnacion .40 1.00
132 Koyie Hill .15 .40
133 Ruben Gotay .15 .40
134 Jeff Mathis .15 .40
135 Andy Marte .15 .40
136 Dallas McPherson .15 .40
137 Justin Morneau .25 .60
138 Rickie Weeks .15 .40
139 Joel Guzman .15 .40
140 Shin Soo Choo .25 .60
141 Yusmeiro Petit RC 1.00 2.50
142 Jorge Cortes RC .40 1.00
143 Val Majewski .15 .40
144 Felix Pie .15 .40
145 Aaron Hill .15 .40
146 Jose Capellan .15 .40
147 Dioner Navarro .25 .60
148 Fausto Carmona .25 .60
149 Robinzon Diaz RC .40 1.00
150 Felix Hernandez 2.50 6.00
151 Andres Blanco RC .40 1.00
152 Jason Kubel .15 .40
153 Willy Taveras RC 1.00 2.50
154 Merkin Valdez .15 .40
155 Robinson Cano .50 1.25
156 Bill Murphy .15 .40
157 Chris Burke .15 .40
158 Kyle Sleeth .15 .40
159 B.J. Upton .25 .60
160 Tim Stauffer .25 .60
161 David Wright .30 .75
162 Conor Jackson .50 1.25
163 Brad Thompson RC .60 1.50
164 Delmon Young .25 .60
165 Jeremy Reed .15 .40
166 Matt Bush AU RC 6.00 15.00
167 Mark Rogers AU RC 4.00 10.00
168 Thomas Diamond AU RC 4.00 10.00
169 Greg Golson AU RC 4.00 10.00
170 Homer Bailey AU RC 5.00 12.00
171 Chris Lambert AU RC 4.00 10.00
172 Neil Walker AU RC 4.00 10.00
173 Bill Bray AU RC 4.00 10.00
174 Philip Hughes AU RC 5.00 12.00
175 Gio Gonzalez AU RC 4.00 10.00

2004 Bowman Chrome Draft Refractors

*REF 1-165: 1.5X TO 4X BASIC
*REF RC 1-165: 1.25X TO 3X BASIC
*REF RC YR 1-165: 1.5X TO 4X BASIC
1-165 ODDS 1:11 BOWMAN DRAFT HOBBY
1-165 ODDS 1:11 BOWMAN DRAFT RETAIL
*REF AU 166-175: .6X TO 1.5X BASIC
166-175 AU ODDS BOW.DRAFT 1:204 HOB
166-175 AU ODDS BOW.DRAFT 1:204 RET
166-175 STATED PRINT RUN 500 SETS
166-175 ARE NOT SERIAL-NUMBERED
166-175 PRINT RUN PROVIDED BY TOPPS

2004 Bowman Chrome Draft Gold Refractors

*GOLD REF 1-165: 8X TO 20X BASIC
*GOLD REF RC 1-165: 8X TO 20X BASIC
*GOLD REF RC YR 1-165: 6X TO 15X BASIC
1-165 ODDS 1:119 BOWMAN DRAFT HOBBY
1-165 ODDS 1:205 BOWMAN DRAFT RETAIL
1-165 PRINT RUN 50 SERIAL #'d SETS
*GOLD REF 166-175: 4X TO 8X BASIC
166-175 AU ODDS 1:2045 BOW.DRAFT HOB
166-175 AU ODDS 1:2055 BOW.DRAFT RET
166-175 STATED PRINT RUN 50 SETS
166-175 ARE NOT SERIAL-NUMBERED
166-175 PRINT RUN PROVIDED BY TOPPS

2004 Bowman Chrome Draft X-Fractors

*XF 1-165: 3X TO 8X BASIC
*XF RC 1-165: 2.5X TO 6X BASIC
*XF RC YR 1-165: 2.5X TO 6X BASIC
1-165 ODDS 1:48 BOWMAN DRAFT HOBBY
1-165 ODDS 1:80 BOWMAN DRAFT RETAIL
1-165 PRINT RUN 125 SERIAL #'d SETS
*XF AU 166-175: .75X TO 2X BASIC
166-175 AU ODDS 1:407 BOW.DRAFT HOB
166-175 AU ODDS 1:407 BOW.DRAFT RET
166-175 STATED PRINT RUN 250 SETS
166-175 ARE NOT SERIAL-NUMBERED
166-175 PRINT RUN PROVIDED BY TOPPS

2004 Bowman Chrome Draft AFLAC

COMP.FACT.SET (12) 12.50 30.00
ONE SET VIA MAIL PER AFLAC EXCH.CARD
ONE EXCH.PER '04 BOW.DRAFT HOBBY BOX
EXCH.CARD DEADLINE WAS 11/30/05
SETS ACTUALLY SENT OUT JANUARY, 2006
RED REF PRINT RUN 1 SERIAL #'d SET
NO RED REF PRICING DUE TO SCARCITY
1 C.J. Henry .60 1.50
2 John Drennen .60 1.50
3 Beau Jones .60 1.50
4 Jeff Lyman .60 1.50
5 Andrew McCutchen 10.00 25.00
6 Chris Volstad 1.00 2.50
7 Jonathan Egan .60 1.50
8 P.J. Phillips .60 1.50
9 Steve Johnson .60 1.50
10 Ryan Tucker .60 1.50
11 Cameron Maybin 2.00 5.00
12 Shane Funk .60 1.50

2004 Bowman Chrome Draft AFLAC Refractors

COMP.FACT.SET (12) 40.00 80.00
*REF: 1.5X TO 4X BASIC
ONE SET VIA MAIL PER AFLAC EXCH.CARD
ONE EXCH.PER '04 BOW.DRAFT HOBBY BOX
STATED PRINT RUN 550 SERIAL #'d SETS
EXCH.CARD DEADLINE WAS 11/30/05
SETS ACTUALLY SENT OUT JANUARY, 2006

2004 Bowman Chrome Draft AFLAC Gold Refractors

COMP.FACT.SET (12) 200.00 400.00
*GOLD REF: X TO X BASIC
ONE SET VIA MAIL PER AFLAC EXCH.CARD
ONE EXCH.PER '04 BOW.DRAFT HOBBY BOX
STATED PRINT RUN 50 SERIAL #'d SETS
EXCH.CARD DEADLINE WAS 11/30/05
SETS ACTUALLY SENT OUT JANUARY, 2006

2004 Bowman Chrome Draft AFLAC X-Fractors

COMP.FACT.SET (12) 100.00 200.0
*X-FRAC: 4X TO 10X BASIC
ONE SET VIA MAIL PER AFLAC EXCH.CARD
ONE EXCH.PER '04 BOW.DRAFT HOBBY BOX
STATED PRINT RUN 125 SERIAL #'d SETS
EXCH.CARD DEADLINE WAS 11/30/05
SETS ACTUALLY SENT OUT JANUARY, 2006

2004 Bowman Chrome Draft AFLAC Autograph Refractors

ONE SET VIA MAIL PER GOLD EXCH.CARD
STATED PRINT RUN 125 SERIAL #'d SETS
SETS ACTUALLY SENT OUT JUNE, 2006
AM Andrew McCutchen 40.00 100.
CH C.J. Henry 15.00 40.
CM Cameron Maybin 25.00 60.
JU Justin Upton 100.00 250.

2005 Bowman Chrome

COMP.SET w/o AU's (330) 20.00 50.
COMMON CARD (1-140) .20
COMMON CARD (141-165) .20

COMMON CARD (166-330) .40 1.00
COMMON AUTO (331-353) 4.00 10.00
331-353 AU ODDS 1:28 HOBBY, 1:83 RETAIL
1-330 PLATE ODDS 1:779 HOBBY
331-353 AU PLATE ODDS 1:10,996 HOBBY
PLATE PRINT RUN 1 SET PER COLOR
BLACK-CYAN-MAGENTA-YELLOW ISSUED
NO PLATE PRICING DUE TO SCARCITY
1 Gavin Floyd .20 .50
2 Eric Chavez .20 .50
3 Miguel Tejada .30 .75
4 Dmitri Young .20 .50
5 Hank Blalock .20 .50
6 Kerry Wood .20 .50
7 Andy Pettitte .30 .75
8 Pat Burrell .20 .50
9 Johnny Estrada .20 .50
10 Frank Thomas .50 1.25
11 Juan Pierre .20 .50
12 Tom Glavine .30 .75
13 Lyle Overbay .20 .50
14 Jim Edmonds .30 .75
15 Steve Finley .20 .50
16 Jermaine Dye .20 .50
17 Omar Vizquel .30 .75
18 Nick Johnson .20 .50
19 Brian Giles .20 .50
20 Justin Morneau .30 .75
21 Preston Wilson .20 .50
22 Wily Mo Pena .20 .50
23 Rafael Palmeiro .30 .75
24 Scott Kazmir .50 1.25
25 Derek Jeter 1.25 3.00
26 Barry Zito .30 .75
27 Mike Lowell .20 .50
28 Jason Bay .20 .50
29 Ken Harvey .20 .50
30 Nomar Garciaparra .30 .75
31 Roy Halladay .30 .75
32 Todd Helton .30 .75
33 Mark Kotsay .20 .50
34 Jake Peavy .20 .50
35 David Wright .40 1.00
36 Dontrelle Willis .20 .50
37 Marcus Giles .20 .50
38 Chone Figgins .20 .50
39 Sidney Ponson .20 .50
40 Randy Johnson .50 1.25
41 John Smoltz .50 1.25
42 Kevin Millar .20 .50
43 Mark Teixeira .30 .75
44 Alex Rios .20 .50
45 Mike Piazza .50 1.25
46 Victor Martinez .30 .75
47 Jeff Bagwell .30 .75
48 Shawn Green .20 .50
49 Ivan Rodriguez .30 .75
50 Alex Rodriguez .60 1.50
51 Kazuo Matsui .20 .50
52 Mark Mulder .20 .50
53 Michael Young .20 .50
54 Javy Lopez .20 .50
55 Johnny Damon .30 .75
56 Jeff Francis .20 .50
57 Rich Harden .20 .50
58 Bobby Abreu .20 .50
59 Mark Loretta .20 .50
60 Gary Sheffield .20 .50
61 Jamie Moyer .20 .50
62 Garret Anderson .20 .50
63 Vernon Wells .20 .50
64 Orlando Cabrera .20 .50
65 Magglio Ordonez .30 .75
66 Ronnie Belliard .20 .50
67 Carlos Lee .20 .50
68 Carl Pavano .20 .50
69 Jon Lieber .20 .50
70 Aubrey Huff .20 .50
71 Rocco Baldelli .20 .50
72 Jason Schmidt .20 .50
73 Bernie Williams .30 .75
74 Hideki Matsui .75 2.00
75 Ken Griffey Jr. 1.00 2.50
76 Josh Beckett .20 .50
77 Mark Buehrle .30 .75
78 David Ortiz .50 1.25
79 Luis Gonzalez .20 .50
80 Scott Rolen .30 .75
81 Joe Mauer .40 1.00
82 Jose Reyes .30 .75
83 Adam Dunn .30 .75
84 Greg Maddux .60 1.50
85 Bartolo Colon .20 .50
86 Bret Boone .20 .50
87 Mike Mussina .30 .75
88 Ben Sheets .20 .50
89 Lance Berkman .30 .75
90 Miguel Cabrera .50 1.25
91 C.C. Sabathia .30 .75
92 Mike Maroth .20 .50
93 Andruw Jones .20 .50
94 Jack Wilson .20 .50
95 Ichiro Suzuki .60 1.50
96 Geoff Jenkins .20 .50
97 Zack Greinke .60 1.50
98 Jorge Posada .30 .75
99 Travis Hafner .20 .50
100 Barry Bonds .75 2.00
101 Aaron Rowand .20 .50
102 Aramis Ramirez .20 .50
103 Curt Schilling .30 .75
104 Melvin Mora .20 .50
105 Albert Pujols .60 1.50
106 Austin Kearns .20 .50
107 Shannon Stewart .20 .50
108 Carl Crawford .30 .75
109 Carlos Zambrano .30 .75
110 Roger Clemens .60 1.50
111 Javier Vazquez .20 .50
112 Randy Wolf .20 .50
113 Chipper Jones .50 1.25
114 Larry Walker .30 .75
115 Alfonso Soriano .30 .75
116 Brad Wilkerson .20 .50
117 Bobby Crosby .20 .50
118 Jim Thome .30 .75
119 Oliver Perez .20 .50
120 Vladimir Guerrero .30 .75
121 Roy Oswalt .30 .75
122 Torii Hunter .20 .50
123 Rafael Furcal .20 .50
124 Luis Castillo .20 .50
125 Carlos Beltran .30 .75
126 Mike Sweeney .20 .50
127 Johan Santana .30 .75
128 Tim Hudson .30 .75
129 Troy Glaus .20 .50
130 Manny Ramirez .50 1.25
131 Jeff Kent .20 .50
132 Jose Vidro .20 .50
133 Edgar Renteria .20 .50
134 Russ Ortiz .20 .50
135 Sammy Sosa .50 1.25
136 Carlos Delgado .20 .50
137 Richie Sexson .20 .50
138 Pedro Martinez .30 .75
139 Adrian Beltre .50 1.25
140 Mark Prior .30 .75
141 Omar Quintanilla .20 .50
142 Carlos Quentin .30 .75
143 Dan Johnson .20 .50
144 Jake Stevens .20 .50
145 Nate Schierholtz .20 .50
146 Neil Walker .30 .75
147 Bill Bray .20 .50
148 Taylor Tankersley .20 .50
149 Trevor Plouffe .50 1.25
150 Felix Hernandez .60 1.50
151 Philip Hughes .50 1.25
152 James Houser .20 .50
153 David Murphy .30 .75
154 Ervin Santana .20 .50
155 Anthony Whittington .20 .50
156 Chris Lambert .20 .50
157 Jeremy Sowers .20 .50
158 Giovanny Gonzalez .30 .75
159 Blake DeWitt .30 .75
160 Thomas Diamond .20 .50
161 Greg Golson .20 .50
162 David Aardsma .20 .50
163 Paul Maholm .20 .50
164 Mark Rogers .20 .50
165 Homer Bailey .20 .50
166 Elvin Puello RC .40 1.00
167 Tony Giarratano RC .40 1.00
168 Darren Fenster RC .40 1.00
169 Elvys Quezada RC .40 1.00
170 Glen Perkins RC .40 1.00
171 Ian Kinsler RC 2.00 5.00
172 Adam Bostick RC .40 1.00
173 Jeremy West RC .40 1.00
174 Brett Harper RC .40 1.00
175 Kevin West RC .40 1.00
176 Luis Hernandez RC .40 1.00
177 Matt Campbell RC .40 1.00
178 Nate McLouth RC .60 1.50
179 Ryan Goleski RC .40 1.00
180 Matthew Lindstrom RC .40 1.00
181 Matt DeSalvo RC .40 1.00
182 Kole Strayhorn RC .40 1.00
183 Jose Vaquedano RC .40 1.00
184 James Jurries RC .40 1.00
185 Ian Bladergroen RC .40 1.00
186 Kila Kaaihue RC 1.00 2.50
187 Luke Scott RC 1.00 2.50
188 Chris Denorfia RC .40 1.00
189 Jai Miller RC .40 1.00
190 Melky Cabrera RC 1.25 3.00
191 Ryan Sweeney RC .60 1.50
192 Sean Marshall RC 1.00 2.50
193 Erick Abreu RC .40 1.00
194 Tyler Pelland RC .40 1.00
195 Cole Armstrong RC .40 1.00
196 John Hudgins RC .40 1.00
197 Wade Robinson RC .40 1.00
198 Dan Santin RC .40 1.00
199 Steve Doetsch RC .40 1.00
200 Shane Costa RC .40 1.00
201 Scott Mathieson RC .40 1.00
202 Ben Jones RC .40 1.00
203 Michael Rogers RC .40 1.00
204 Matt Rogelstad RC .40 1.00
205 Luis Ramirez RC .40 1.00
206 Landon Powell RC .40 1.00
207 Erik Cordier RC .40 1.00
208 Chris Seddon RC .40 1.00
209 Chris Roberson RC .40 1.00
210 Thomas Oldham RC .40 1.00
211 Dana Eveland RC .40 1.00
212 Cody Haerther RC .40 1.00
213 Danny Core RC .40 1.00
214 Craig Tatum RC .40 1.00
215 Elliot Johnson RC .40 1.00
216 Ender Chavez RC .40 1.00
217 Errol Simonitsch RC .40 1.00
218 Matt Van Der Bosch RC .40 1.00
219 Eulogio de la Cruz RC .40 1.00
220 Drew Toussaint RC .40 1.00
221 Adam Boeve RC .40 1.00
222 Adam Harben RC .40 1.00
223 Baltazar Lopez RC .40 1.00
224 Russ Martin RC 1.25 3.00
225 Brian Bannister RC .60 1.50
226 Chris Walker RC .40 1.00
227 Casey McGehee RC .60 1.50
228 Humberto Sanchez RC .60 1.50
229 Javon Moran RC .40 1.00
230 Brandon McCarthy RC .60 1.50
231 Danny Zell RC .40 1.00
232 Kevin Barry RC .40 1.00
233 Juan Tejeda RC .40 1.00
234 Keith Ramsey RC .40 1.00
235 Lorenzo Scott RC .40 1.00
236 Jon Barratt RC .40 1.00
237 Martin Prado RC 2.50 6.00
238 Matt Albers RC .40 1.00
239 Brian Schweiger RC .40 1.00
240 Raul Tablado RC .40 1.00
241 Pat Misch RC .40 1.00
242 Pat Osborn .40 1.00
243 Ryan Feierabend RC .40 1.00
244 Shaun Marcum 1.00 2.50
245 Kevin Collins RC .40 1.00
246 Stuart Pomeranz RC .40 1.00
247 Tetsu Yofu RC .40 1.00
248 Hernan Iribarren RC .40 1.00
249 Mike Spidale RC .40 1.00
250 Tony Arnerich RC .40 1.00
251 Manny Parra RC 1.00 2.50
252 Drew Anderson RC .40 1.00
253 T.J. Beam RC .40 1.00
254 Claudio Arias RC .40 1.00
255 Andy Sides RC .40 1.00
256 Bear Bay RC .40 1.00
257 Bill McCarthy RC .40 1.00
258 Daniel Haigwood RC .40 1.00
259 Brian Sprout RC .40 1.00
260 Bryan Triplett RC .40 1.00
261 Steven Bondurant RC .40 1.00
262 Darwinson Salazar RC .40 1.00
263 David Shepard RC .40 1.00
264 Johan Silva RC .40 1.00
265 J.B. Thurmond RC .40 1.00
266 Brandon Moorhead RC .40 1.00
267 Kyle Nichols RC .40 1.00
268 Jonathan Sanchez RC 1.50 4.00
269 Mike Esposito RC .40 1.00
270 Erik Schindewolf RC .40 1.00
271 Peeter Ramos RC .40 1.00
272 Juan Senreiso RC .40 1.00
273 Travis Chick RC .40 1.00
274 Vinny Rottino RC .40 1.00
275 Micah Furtado RC .40 1.00
276 George Kottaras RC .60 1.50
277 Abel Gomez RC .40 1.00
278 Buck Coats RC .40 1.00
279 Kenny Durost RC .40 1.00
280 Nick Touchstone RC .40 1.00
281 Jerry Owens RC .40 1.00
282 Stefan Bailie RC .40 1.00
283 Jesse Gutierrez RC .40 1.00
284 Chuck Tiffany RC 1.00 2.50
285 Brendan Ryan RC .40 1.00
286 Julio Pimentel RC .40 1.00
287 Shawn Bowman RC .40 1.00
288 Alexander Smit RC .40 1.00
289 Micah Schnurstein RC .40 1.00
290 Jared Gothreaux RC .40 1.00
291 Jair Jurrjens RC 2.00 5.00
292 Bobby Livingston RC .40 1.00
293 Ryan Speier RC .40 1.00
294 Zach Parker RC .40 1.00
295 Christian Colonel RC .40 1.00
296 Scott Mitchinson RC .40 1.00
297 Neil Wilson RC .40 1.00
298 Chuck James RC 1.00 2.50
299 Heath Totten RC .40 1.00
300 Sean Tracey RC .40 1.00
301 Tadahito Iguchi RC .60 1.50
302 Matt Brown RC .40 1.00
303 Franklin Morales RC .60 1.50
304 Brandon Sing RC .40 1.00
305 D.J. Houlton RC .40 1.00
306 Jayce Tingler RC .40 1.00
307 Mitchell Arnold RC .40 1.00
308 Jim Burt RC .40 1.00
309 Jason Motte RC .60 1.50
310 David Gassner RC .40 1.00
311 Andy Santana RC .40 1.00
312 Kelvin Pichardo RC .40 1.00
313 Carlos Carrasco RC 1.00 2.50
314 Willy Mota RC .40 1.00
315 Frank Mata RC .40 1.00
316 Carlos Gonzalez RC 3.00 8.00
317 Jesse Floyd .40 1.00
318 Chris B.Young RC 1.25 3.00
319 Billy Sadler RC .40 1.00
320 Ricky Barrett RC .40 1.00
321 Ben Harrison .40 1.00
322 Steve Nelson RC .40 1.00
323 Daryl Thompson RC .40 1.00
324 Davis Romero RC .40 1.00
325 Jeremy Harts RC .40 1.00
326 Nick Masset RC .40 1.00
327 Thomas Pauly RC .40 1.00
328 Mike Garber RC .40 1.00
329 Kennard Bibbs RC .40 1.00
330 Colter Bean RC .40 1.00
331 Justin Verlander AU RC 125.00 300.00
332 Chip Cannon AU RC 4.00 10.00
333 Kevin Melillo AU RC 4.00 10.00
334 Jake Postlewait AU RC 4.00 10.00
335 Wes Swackhamer AU RC 4.00 10.00
336 Mike Rodriguez AU RC 4.00 10.00
337 Philip Humber AU RC 4.00 10.00
338 Jeff Niemann AU RC 4.00 10.00
339 Brian Miller AU RC 4.00 10.00
340 Chris Vines AU RC 4.00 10.00
341 Andy LaRoche AU RC 4.00 10.00
342 Mike Bourn AU RC 4.00 10.00
343 Eric Nielsen AU RC 4.00 10.00
344 Wladimir Balentien AU RC 4.00 10.00
345 Ismael Ramirez AU RC 4.00 10.00
346 Pedro Lopez AU RC 4.00 10.00
347 Shawn Bowman AU 4.00 10.00
348 Hayden Penn AU RC 4.00 10.00
349 Matthew Kemp AU RC 25.00 60.00
350 Brian Stavisky AU RC 4.00 10.00
351 C.J. Smith AU RC 4.00 10.00
352 Mike Morse AU RC 4.00 10.00
353 Billy Butler AU RC 5.00 12.00

2005 Bowman Chrome Refractors

*REF 1-165: 1.5X TO 4X BASIC
*REF 166-330: .75X TO 2X BASIC
1-330 ODDS 1:4 HOBBY, 1: 6 RETAIL
*REF AU 331-353: .5X TO 1.2X BASIC AU
331-353 AU ODDS 1:88 HOB, 1:259 RET
331-353 PRINT RUN 500 SERIAL #'d SETS

2005 Bowman Chrome Blue Refractors

*BLUE REF 1-165: 2.5X TO 6X BASIC
*BLUE REF 166-330: 1.2X TO 3X BASIC
1-330 ODDS 1:20 HOBBY, 1:69 RETAIL
*BLUE REF AU 331-353: 1.25X TO 2.5X BASIC
331-353 AU ODDS 1:294 HOB, 1:866 RET
STATED PRINT RUN 150 SERIAL #'d SETS
331 Justin Verlander AU 600.00 1200.00

2005 Bowman Chrome Gold Refractors

*GOLD REF 1-165: 4X TO 10X BASIC
*GOLD REF 166-330: 2X TO 5X BASIC
1-330 ODDS 1:61 HOBBY, 1:206 RETAIL
*GOLD REF AU 331-353: 1.5X TO 4X BASIC
331-353 AU ODDS 1:880 HOB, 1:2612 RET
STATED PRINT RUN 50 SERIAL #'d SETS
331 Justin Verlander AU 2000.00 4000.00
349 Matthew Kemp AU 150.00 400.00

2005 Bowman Chrome Green Refractors

*GREEN: 1.5X TO 4X BASIC
ISSUED VIA THE PIT.COM
STATED PRINT RUN 225 SERIAL #'d SETS

2005 Bowman Chrome Super-Fractors

1-330 STATED ODDS 1:3117 H
331-353 AU STATED ODDS 1:47,238 H
STATED PRINT RUN 1 SERIAL #'d SET
NO PRICING DUE TO SCARCITY

2005 Bowman Chrome X-Fractors

*X-FRACTOR 1-165: 2X TO 5X BASIC
*X-FRACTOR 166-330: 1X TO 2.5X BASIC
1-330 ODDS 1:13 HOBBY, 1:61 RETAIL
*X-FRACT AU 331-353: .6X TO 1.5X BASIC AU
331-353 AU ODDS 1:196 HOB, 1:573 RET
STATED PRINT RUN 225 SERIAL #'d SETS

2005 Bowman Chrome A-Rod Throwback

COMPLETE SET (4) 4.00 10.00
COMMON CARD (94-97) 1.25 3.00
STATED ODDS 1:9 HOBBY, 1:12 RETAIL
*REF: 1X TO 2.5X BASIC
REFRACTOR ODDS 1:445 HOBBY
REFRACTOR PRINT RUN 499 #'d SETS
SUPER-FRACTOR ODDS 1:226,044 HOBBY
SUPER-FRACTOR PRINT RUN 1 #'d SET
NO SUPER-FRACTOR PRICING AVAILABLE
*X-FRACTOR: 1.5X TO 4X BASIC
X-FRACTOR ODDS 1:2241 HOBBY
X-FRACTOR PRINT RUN 99 #'d SETS
94AR Alex Rodriguez 1994 1.00 2.50
95AR Alex Rodriguez 1995 1.00 2.50
96AR Alex Rodriguez 1996 1.00 2.50
97AR Alex Rodriguez 1997 1.00 2.50

2005 Bowman Chrome A-Rod Throwback Autographs

1994 CARD STATED ODDS 1:614,088 H
1995 CARD STATED ODDS 1:36,122 H
1996 CARD STATED ODDS 1:18,061 H
1997 CARD STATED ODDS 1:9042 H
1994 CARD PRINT RUN 1 #'d CARD
1995 CARD PRINT RUN 25 #'d CARDS
1996 CARD PRINT RUN 50 #'d CARDS
1997 CARD PRINT RUN 99 #'d CARDS
NO PRICING ON 1994 CARD AVAILABLE
96AR A.Rodriguez 1996 RF/50 100.00 175.00
97AR A.Rodriguez 1997 CH/99 60.00 120.00

2005 Bowman Chrome Two of a Kind Autographs

STATED ODDS 1:76,761 HOBBY
STATED PRINT RUN 13 SERIAL #'d CARDS
NO PRICING DUE TO SCARCITY

2005 Bowman Chrome Draft

COMP.SET w/o SP's (165) 15.00 40.00
COMMON CARD (1-165) .15 .40
COMMON RC .40 1.00
COMMON RC YR .15 .40
1-165 TWO PER BOWMAN DRAFT PACK
166-180 GROUP A ODDS 1:671 H, 1:643 R
166-180 GROUP B ODDS 1:69 H, 1:69 R
1-165 PLATE ODDS 1:826 HOBBY
166-180 AU PLATE ODDS 1:18,411 HOBBY
PLATE PRINT RUN 1 SET PER COLOR
BLACK-CYAN-MAGENTA-YELLOW ISSUED
NO PLATE PRICING DUE TO SCARCITY
1 Rickie Weeks .15 .40
2 Kyle Davies .15 .40
3 Garrett Atkins .15 .40
4 Chien-Ming Wang .60 1.50
5 Dallas McPherson .15 .40
6 Dan Johnson .15 .40
7 Andy Sisco .15 .40
8 Ryan Doumit .15 .40
9 J.P. Howell .15 .40
10 Tim Stauffer .15 .40
11 Willy Taveras .15 .40
12 Aaron Hill .25 .60
13 Victor Diaz .15 .40
14 Wilson Betemit .15 .40
15 Ervin Santana .15 .40
16 Mike Morse .50 1.25
17 Yadier Molina 6.00 15.00
18 Kelly Johnson .15 .40
19 Clint Barmes .15 .40
20 Robinson Cano .50 1.25
21 Brad Thompson .15 .40
22 Jorge Cantu .15 .40
23 Brad Halsey .15 .40
24 Lance Niekro .15 .40
25 D.J. Houlton .15 .40
26 Ryan Church .15 .40
27 Hayden Penn .15 .40
28 Chris Young .25 .60
29 Chad Orvella RC .40 1.00
30 Mark Teahen .15 .40
31 Mark McCormick FY RC .40 1.00
32 Jay Bruce FY RC 3.00 8.00
33 Beau Jones FY RC 1.00 2.50
34 Tyler Greene FY RC .40 1.00
35 Zach Ward FY RC .40 1.00
36 Josh Bell FY RC .60 1.50
37 Josh Wall FY RC .60 1.50
38 Nick Webber FY RC .40 1.00
39 Travis Buck FY RC .40 1.00
40 Kyle Winters FY RC .40 1.00
41 Mitch Boggs FY RC .40 1.00
42 Tommy Mendoza FY RC .40 1.00
43 Brad Corley FY RC .40 1.00
44 Drew Butera FY RC .40 1.00
45 Ryan Mount FY RC .40 1.00
46 Tyler Herron FY RC .40 1.00
47 Nick Weglarz FY RC .40 1.00
48 Brandon Erbe FY RC 1.25 3.00
49 Cody Allen FY RC .40 1.00
50 Eric Fowler FY RC .40 1.00
51 James Boone FY RC .40 1.00
52 Josh Flores FY RC .40 1.00
53 Brandon Monk FY RC .40 1.00
54 Kieron Pope FY RC .40 1.00
55 Kyle Cofield FY RC .40 1.00
56 Brent Lillibridge FY RC .40 1.00
57 Daryl Jones FY RC .40 1.00
58 Eli Iorg FY RC .40 1.00
59 Brett Hayes FY RC .40 1.00
60 Mike Durant FY RC .40 1.00
61 Michael Bowden FY RC .60 1.50
62 Paul Kelly FY RC .40 1.00
63 Andrew McCutchen FY RC 5.00 12.00
64 Travis Wood FY RC 1.00 2.50
65 Cesar Ramos FY RC .40 1.00
66 Chaz Roe FY RC .40 1.00
67 Matt Torra FY RC .40 1.00
68 Kevin Slowey FY RC 2.00 5.00
69 Trayvon Robinson FY RC 1.00 2.50
70 Reid Engel FY RC .40 1.00
71 Kris Harvey FY RC .40 1.00
72 Craig Italiano FY RC .40 1.00
73 Matt Maloney FY RC .40 1.00
74 Sean West FY RC .60 1.50
75 Henry Sanchez FY RC .60 1.50
76 Scott Blue FY RC .40 1.00
77 Jordan Schafer FY RC 2.00 5.00
78 Chris Robinson FY RC .40 1.00
79 Chris Hobdy FY RC .40 1.00
80 Brandon Durden FY RC .40 1.00
81 Clay Buchholz FY RC 2.00 5.00
82 Josh Geer FY RC .40 1.00
83 Sam LeCure FY RC .40 1.00
84 Justin Thomas FY RC .40 1.00
85 Brett Gardner FY RC 1.25 3.00
86 Tommy Manzella FY RC .40 1.00
87 Matt Green FY RC .40 1.00
88 Yunel Escobar FY RC 1.50 4.00
89 Mike Costanzo FY RC .40 1.00
90 Nick Hundley FY RC .40 1.00
91 Zach Simons FY RC .40 1.00
92 Jacob Marceaux FY RC .40 1.00
93 Jed Lowrie FY RC .40 1.00
94 Brandon Snyder FY RC 1.00 2.50
95 Matt Goyen FY RC .40 1.00
96 Jon Egan FY RC .40 1.00
97 Drew Thompson FY RC .40 1.00
98 Bryan Anderson FY RC .40 1.00
99 Clayton Richard FY RC .40 1.00
100 Jimmy Shull FY RC .40 1.00
101 Mark Pawelek FY RC .40 1.00
102 P.J. Phillips FY RC .40 1.00
103 John Drennen FY RC .40 1.00
104 Nolan Reimold FY RC 1.50 4.00
105 Troy Tulowitzki FY RC 4.00 10.00
106 Kevin Whelan FY RC .40 1.00
107 Wade Townsend FY RC .40 1.00
108 Micah Owings FY RC .40 1.00
109 Ryan Tucker FY RC .40 1.00
110 Jeff Clement FY RC .40 1.00
111 Josh Sullivan FY RC .40 1.00
112 Jeff Lyman FY RC .40 1.00
113 Brian Bogusevic FY RC .40 1.00
114 Trevor Bell FY RC .40 1.00
115 Brent Cox FY RC .40 1.00
116 Michael Billek FY RC .40 1.00
117 Garrett Olson FY RC .40 1.00
118 Steven Johnson FY RC .40 1.00
119 Chase Headley FY RC .60 1.50
120 Daniel Carte FY RC .40 1.00
121 Francisco Liriano PROS .40 1.00
122 Fausto Carmona PROS .15 .40
123 Zach Jackson PROS .15 .40
124 Adam Loewen PROS .15 .40
125 Chris Lambert PROS .15 .40
126 Scott Mathieson FY .15 .40
127 Paul Maholm PROS .15 .40
128 Fernando Nieve PROS .15 .40
129 Justin Verlander FY 15.00 40.00
130 Yusmeiro Petit PROS .15 .40
131 Joel Zumaya PROS .40 1.00
132 Merkin Valdez PROS .15 .40
133 Ryan Garko FY RC .40 1.00
134 Edison Volquez FY RC 1.25 3.00
135 Russ Martin FY .50 1.25
136 Conor Jackson PROS .25 .60
137 Miguel Montero FY RC 1.25 3.00
138 Josh Barfield PROS .25 .60
139 Delmon Young PROS .40 1.00
140 Andy LaRoche FY .15 .40
141 William Bergolla PROS .15 .40
142 B.J. Upton PROS .25 .60
143 Hernan Iribarren FY .15 .40
144 Brandon Wood PROS .25 .60
145 Jose Bautista PROS .60 1.50
146 Edwin Encarnacion PROS .40 1.00
147 Javier Herrera FY RC .40 1.00
148 Jeremy Hermida PROS .25 .60
149 Frank Diaz PROS RC .40 1.00
150 Chris B.Young FY .50 1.25
151 Shin-Soo Choo PROS .25 .60
152 Kevin Thompson PROS RC .40 1.00
153 Hanley Ramirez PROS .25 .60
154 Lastings Milledge PROS .15 .40
155 Luis Montanez PROS .15 .40
156 Justin Huber PROS .15 .40
157 Zach Duke PROS .15 .40
158 Jeff Francoeur PROS .40 1.00
159 Melky Cabrera FY .50 1.25
160 Bobby Jenks PROS .15 .40
161 Ian Snell PROS .15 .40
162 Fernando Cabrera PROS .15 .40
163 Troy Patton PROS .15 .40
164 Anthony Lerew PROS .15 .40
165 Nelson Cruz FY RC 5.00 12.00
166 Stephen Drew AU A RC 4.00 10.00
167 Jered Weaver AU A RC 10.00 25.00
168 Ryan Braun AU B RC 20.00 50.00
169 John Mayberry Jr. AU B RC 4.00 10.00
170 Aaron Thompson AU B RC 4.00 10.00
171 Cesar Carrillo AU B RC 4.00 10.00
172 Jacoby Ellsbury AU B RC 8.00 20.00
173 Matt Garza AU B RC 5.00 12.00
174 Cliff Pennington AU B RC 4.00 10.00
175 Colby Rasmus AU B RC 5.00 12.00
176 Chris Volstad AU B RC 4.00 10.00
177 Ricky Romero AU B RC 4.00 10.00
178 Ryan Zimmerman AU B RC 20.00 50.00
179 C.J. Henry AU B RC 4.00 10.00
180 Eddy Martinez AU B RC 4.00 10.00

2005 Bowman Chrome Draft Refractors

*REF 1-165: 2X TO 5X BASIC
*REF 1-165: .75X TO 2X BASIC RC
1-165 ODDS 1:11 BOWMAN DRAFT HOBBY
1-165 ODDS 1:11 BOWMAN DRAFT RETAIL
*REF AU 166-180: .6X TO 1.5X BASIC
166-180 AU ODDS 1:186 BOW.DRAFT HOB
166-180 AU ODDS 1:186 BOW.DRAFT RET
166-180 PRINT RUN 500 SERIAL #'d SETS
129 Justin Verlander FY 50.00 120.00

2005 Bowman Chrome Draft Blue Refractors

*BLUE 1-165: 4X TO 10X BASIC
*BLUE 1-165: 3X TO 8X BASIC RC
1-165 ODDS 1:52 BOWMAN DRAFT HOBBY
1-165 ODDS 1:107 BOWMAN DRAFT RETAIL
*BLUE AU 166-180: 1.25X TO 2.5X BASIC
166-180 AU ODDS 1:619 BOW.DRAFT HOB
166-180 AU ODDS 1:619 BOW.DRAFT RET
STATED PRINT RUN 150 SERIAL #'d SETS
129 Justin Verlander FY 200.00 500.00

2005 Bowman Chrome Draft Gold Refractors

*GOLD REF 1-165: 10X TO 25X BASIC
*GOLD REF 1-165: 12.5X TO 25X BASIC RC
*GOLD REF 1-165: 12.5X TO 30X BASIC RC YR
1-165 ODDS 1:155 BOWMAN DRAFT HOBBY
1-165 ODDS 1:323 BOWMAN DRAFT HOBBY
*GOLD REF AU 166-180: 4X TO 8X BASIC
166-180 AU ODDS 1:1857 BOW.DRAFT HOB
166-180 AU ODDS 1:1856 BOW.DRAFT RET
STATED PRINT RUN 50 SERIAL #'d SETS
20 Robinson Cano 40.00 80.00
129 Justin Verlander FY 250.00 600.00

2005 Bowman Chrome Draft X-Fractors

*XF 1-165: 2.5X TO 6X BASIC
*XF 1-165: 1X TO 2.5X BASIC RC
1-165 ODDS 1:31 BOWMAN DRAFT HOBBY
1-165 ODDS 1:64 BOWMAN DRAFT RETAIL
*XF AU 166-180: 1X TO 2X BASIC
166-180 AU ODDS 1:372 BOW.DRAFT HOB
166-180 AU ODDS 1:371 BOW.DRAFT RET
STATED PRINT RUN 250 SERIAL #'d SETS
129 Justin Verlander FY 60.00 150.00

2005 Bowman Chrome Draft AFLAC Exchange Cards

BASIC ODDS 1:109 BOW.DRAFT H
REFRACTOR ODDS 1:2184 BOW.DRAFT H
X-FRACTOR ODDS 1:4369 BOW.DRAFT H
BLUE REF ODDS 1:7261 BOW.DRAFT H
GOLD REF ODDS 1:21,937 BOW.DRAFT H
RED REF ODDS 1:1,031,040 BOW.DRAFT H
SUP-FRAC ODDS 1:1,031,040 BOW.DRAFT H
REFRACTOR PRINT RUN 500 CARDS
X-FRACTOR PRINT RUN 250 CARDS
BLUE REF PRINT RUN 150 CARDS
GOLD REF PRINT RUN 50 CARDS
RED REF PRINT RUN 1 CARD
SUPER-FRACTOR PRINT RUN 1 CARD
PLATES PRINT RUN 1 SET PER COLOR
NO RED/SUPER PRICING DUE TO SCARCITY
NO PLATES PRICING DUE TO SCARCITY
EXCHANGE DEADLINE 12/26/06
1 Basic Set 15.00 30.00
3 Refractor Set/500 90.00 150.00
4 Blue Refractor Set/150 250.00 400.00
5 Gold Refractor Set/50 700.00 1000.00
8 X-Fractor Set/250 175.00 300.00

2005 Bowman Chrome Draft AFLAC

COMP.FACT.SET (14) 8.00 20.00
ONE SET VIA MAIL PER AFLAC EXCH.CARD
BASIC ODDS 1:109 '05 BOW.DRAFT HOB.
SETS ACTUALLY SENT OUT JANUARY, 2007
EXCHANGE DEADLINE 12/26/06
REFRACTOR ODDS 1:2184 BOW.DRAFT H
REF PRINT RUN 500 SER.#'d SETS
X-FRACTOR ODDS 1:4369 BOW.DRAFT H
BLUE REF ODDS 1:7261 BOW.DRAFT H
BLUE REF PRINT RUN 150 SER.#'d SETS
GOLD REF ODDS 1:21,937 BOW.DRAFT H
GOLD REF PRINT RUN 50 SER.#'d SETS
RED REF ODDS 1:1,031,040 BOW.DRAFT H
RED REF PRINT RUN 1 SER.#'d SET
NO RED PRICING DUE TO SCARCITY
SUPER ODDS 1:1,031,040 BOW.DRAFT H
SUPER-FRAC PRINT RUN 1 SER.#'d SET
NO SUPER PRICING DUE TO SCARCITY
PLATE PRINT RUN 1 SET PER COLOR
BLACK-CYAN-MAGENTA-YELLOW ISSUED
NO PLATE PRICING DUE TO SCARCITY
1 Billy Rowell 1.50 4.00
2 Kasey Kiker 1.00 2.50
3 Chris Marrero 2.00 5.00
4 Jeremy Jeffress .60 1.50
5 Kyle Drabek 1.00 2.50
6 Chris Parmelee 1.00 2.50
7 Colton Willems .60 1.50
8 Cody Johnson .60 1.50
9 Hank Conger 1.00 2.50
10 Cory Rasmus .60 1.50
11 David Christensen .60 1.50
12 Chris Tillman 1.00 2.50
13 Torre Langley .60 1.50
14 Robby Alcombrack .60 1.50

2005 Bowman Chrome Draft AFLAC Refractors

COMP.FACT.SET (14) 50.00 100.00
*REF: 1.2X TO 3X BASIC
ONE SET VIA MAIL PER EXCH.CARD
STATED ODDS 1:2184 BOW.DRAFT H
STATED PRINT RUN 500 SER.#'d SETS
EXCHANGE DEADLINE 12/26/06
SETS ACTUALLY SENT OUT JANUARY, 2007

2005 Bowman Chrome Draft AFLAC Blue Refractors

COMP.FACT.SET (14) 150.00 300.00
*BLUE REF: 4X TO 10X BASIC
ONE SET VIA MAIL PER EXCH.CARD
STATED ODDS 1:7261 BOW.DRAFT H
STATED PRINT RUN 150 SER.#'d SETS
EXCHANGE DEADLINE 12/26/06
SETS ACTUALLY SENT OUT JANUARY, 2007

2005 Bowman Chrome Draft AFLAC Gold Refractors

*GOLD REF: 12X TO 30X BASIC
ONE SET VIA MAIL PER EXCH.CARD
STATED ODDS 1:21,937 BOW.DRAFT H
STATED PRINT RUN 50 SER.#'d SETS
EXCHANGE DEADLINE 12/26/06
SETS ACTUALLY SENT OUT JANUARY, 2007

2005 Bowman Chrome Draft AFLAC X-Fractors

COMP.FACT.SET (14) 100.00 200.00
*X-FRAC: 2.5X TO 6X BASIC
STATED ODDS 1:4369 BOW.DRAFT H
ONE SET VIA MAIL PER EXCH.CARD
STATED PRINT RUN 250 SER.#'d SETS
EXCHANGE DEADLINE 12/26/06
SETS ACTUALLY SENT OUT JANUARY, 2007

2006 Bowman Chrome

COMP.SET w/o AU's (220) 30.00 60.00
COMMON CARD (1-200) .20 .50
COMMON ROOKIE (201-220) .25 .60
219 AU ODDS 1:2734 HOBBY, 1:6617 RETAIL
221-224 AU ODDS 1:27 HOBBY, 1:65 RETAIL
1-220 PLATE ODDS 1:836 HOBBY
219 AU PLATE ODDS 1:292,536 HOBBY
221-224 AU PLATES ODDS 1:9,000 HOBBY
PLATE PRINT RUN 1 SET PER COLOR
BLACK-CYAN-MAGENTA-YELLOW ISSUED
NO PLATE PRICING DUE TO SCARCITY
1 Nick Swisher .30 .75
2 Ted Lilly .20 .50
3 John Smoltz .50 1.25
4 Lyle Overbay .20 .50
5 Alfonso Soriano .30 .75
6 Javier Vazquez .20 .50
7 Ronnie Belliard .20 .50
8 Jose Reyes .30 .75
9 Brian Roberts .20 .50
10 Curt Schilling .30 .75
11 Adam Dunn .30 .75
12 Zack Greinke .50 1.25
13 Carlos Guillen .20 .50
14 Jon Garland .20 .50
15 Robinson Cano .30 .75
16 Chris Burke .20 .50
17 Barry Zito .30 .75
18 Russ Adams .20 .50
19 Chris Capuano .20 .50
20 Scott Rolen .30 .75
21 Kerry Wood .20 .50
22 Scott Kazmir .30 .75
23 Brandon Webb .30 .75
24 Jeff Kent .20 .50
25 Albert Pujols .60 1.50
26 C.C. Sabathia .30 .75
27 Adrian Beltre .50 1.25
28 Brad Wilkerson .20 .50
29 Randy Wolf .20 .50
30 Jason Bay .20 .50
31 Austin Kearns .20 .50
32 Clint Barmes .20 .50
33 Mike Sweeney .20 .50
34 Kevin Youkilis .20 .50
35 Justin Morneau .30 .75
36 Scott Podsednik .20 .50
37 Jason Giambi .20 .50
38 Steve Finley .20 .50
39 Morgan Ensberg .20 .50
40 Eric Chavez .20 .50
41 Roy Halladay .30 .75
42 Horacio Ramirez .20 .50
43 Ben Sheets .20 .50
44 Chris Carpenter .30 .75
45 Andruw Jones .20 .50
46 Carlos Zambrano .30 .75
47 Jonny Gomes .20 .50
48 Shawn Green .20 .50
49 Moises Alou .20 .50
50 Ichiro Suzuki .60 1.50
51 Juan Pierre .20 .50
52 Grady Sizemore .30 .75
53 Kazuo Matsui .20 .50
54 Jose Vidro .20 .50
55 Jake Peavy .20 .50
56 Dallas McPherson .20 .50
57 Ryan Howard .40 1.00
58 Zach Duke .20 .50
59 Michael Young .20 .50
60 Todd Helton .30 .75
61 David DeJesus .20 .50
62 Ivan Rodriguez .30 .75
63 Johan Santana .30 .75
64 Danny Haren .20 .50
65 Derek Jeter 1.25 3.00
66 Greg Maddux .60 1.50
67 Jorge Cantu .20 .50
68 J.J. Hardy .20 .50
69 Victor Martinez .30 .75
70 David Wright .40 1.00
71 Ryan Church .20 .50

72 Khalil Greene .20 .50
73 Jimmy Rollins .30 .75
74 Hank Blalock .20 .50
75 Pedro Martinez .30 .75
76 Chris Shelton .20 .50
77 Felipe Lopez .20 .50
78 Jeff Francis .20 .50
79 Andy Sisco .20 .50
80 Hideki Matsui .50 1.25
81 Ken Griffey Jr. 1.00 2.50
82 Nomar Garciaparra .30 .75
83 Kevin Millwood .20 .50
84 Paul Konerko .30 .75
85 A.J. Burnett .20 .50
86 Mike Piazza .50 1.25
87 Brian Giles .20 .50
88 Johnny Damon .30 .75
89 Jim Thome .30 .75
90 Roger Clemens .60 1.50
91 Aaron Rowand .20 .50
92 Rafael Furcal .20 .50
93 Gary Sheffield .20 .50
94 Mike Cameron .20 .50
95 Carlos Delgado .20 .50
96 Jorge Posada .30 .75
97 Denny Bautista .20 .50
98 Mike Maroth .20 .50
99 Brad Radke .20 .50
100 Alex Rodriguez .60 1.50
101 Freddy Garcia .20 .50
102 Oliver Perez .20 .50
103 Jon Lieber .20 .50
104 Melvin Mora .20 .50
105 Travis Hafner .20 .50
106 Alex Rios .20 .50
107 Derek Lowe .20 .50
108 Luis Castillo .20 .50
109 Livan Hernandez .20 .50
110 Tadahito Iguchi .20 .50
111 Shawn Chacon .20 .50
112 Frank Thomas .50 1.25
113 Josh Beckett .20 .50
114 Aubrey Huff .20 .50
115 Derrek Lee .20 .50
116 Chien-Ming Wang .30 .75
117 Joe Crede .20 .50
118 Torii Hunter .20 .50
119 J.D. Drew .20 .50
120 Troy Glaus .20 .50
121 Sean Casey .20 .50
122 Edgar Renteria .20 .50
123 Craig Wilson .20 .50
124 Adam Eaton .20 .50
125 Jeff Francoeur .50 1.25
126 Bruce Chen .20 .50
127 Cliff Floyd .20 .50
128 Jeremy Reed .20 .50
129 Jake Westbrook .20 .50
130 Wily Mo Pena .20 .50
131 Toby Hall .20 .50
132 David Ortiz .50 1.25
133 David Eckstein .20 .50
134 Brady Clark .20 .50
135 Marcus Giles .20 .50
136 Aaron Hill .20 .50
137 Mark Kotsay .20 .50
138 Carlos Lee .20 .50
139 Roy Oswalt .30 .75
140 Chone Figgins .20 .50
141 Mike Mussina .30 .75
142 Orlando Hernandez .20 .50
143 Magglio Ordonez .30 .75
144 Jim Edmonds .30 .75
145 Bobby Abreu .20 .50
146 Nick Johnson .20 .50
147 Carlos Beltran .30 .75
148 Jhonny Peralta .20 .50
149 Pedro Feliz .20 .50
150 Miguel Tejada .30 .75
151 Luis Gonzalez .20 .50
152 Carl Crawford .30 .75
153 Yadier Molina .60 1.50
154 Rich Harden .20 .50
155 Tim Wakefield .30 .75
156 Rickie Weeks .20 .50
157 Johnny Estrada .20 .50
158 Gustavo Chacin .20 .50
159 Dan Johnson .20 .50
160 Willy Taveras .20 .50
161 Garret Anderson .20 .50
162 Randy Johnson .50 1.25
163 Jermaine Dye .20 .50
164 Joe Mauer .30 .75
165 Ervin Santana .20 .50
166 Jeremy Bonderman .20 .50
167 Garrett Atkins .20 .50
168 Manny Ramirez .50 1.25
169 Brad Eldred .20 .50
170 Chase Utley .30 .75
171 Mark Loretta .20 .50
172 John Patterson .20 .50
173 Tom Glavine .30 .75
174 Dontrelle Willis .20 .50
175 Mark Teixeira .30 .75
176 Felix Hernandez .30 .75
177 Cliff Lee .30 .75
178 Jason Schmidt .20 .50
179 Chad Tracy .20 .50
180 Rocco Baldelli .20 .50
181 Aramis Ramirez .20 .50
182 Andy Pettitte .30 .75
183 Mark Mulder .20 .50
184 Geoff Jenkins .20 .50
185 Chipper Jones .50 1.25
186 Vernon Wells .20 .50
187 Bobby Crosby .20 .50
188 Lance Berkman .30 .75
189 Vladimir Guerrero .30 .75
190 Coco Crisp .20 .50
191 Brad Penny .20 .50
192 Jose Guillen .20 .50
193 Brett Myers .20 .50
194 Miguel Cabrera .50 1.25
195 Bartolo Colon .20 .50
196 Craig Biggio .30 .75
197 Tim Hudson .30 .75
198 Mark Prior .30 .75
199 Mark Buehrle .30 .75
200 Barry Bonds .75 2.00
201 Anderson Hernandez (RC) .25 .60
202 Jose Capellan (RC) .25 .60
203 Jeremy Accardo RC .25 .60
204 Hanley Ramirez (RC) .40 1.00
205 Matt Capps (RC) .25 .60
206 Jonathan Papelbon (RC) 1.25 3.00
207 Chuck James (RC) .25 .60
208 Matt Cain (RC) 1.50 4.00
209 Cole Hamels (RC) .75 2.00
210 Jason Botts (RC) .25 .60
211 Lastings Milledge (RC) .25 .60
212 Conor Jackson (RC) .40 1.00
213 Yusmeiro Petit (RC) .25 .60
214 Alay Soler RC .25 .60
215 Willy Aybar (RC) .25 .60
216 Adam Loewen (RC) .25 .60
217 Justin Verlander (RC) 2.00 5.00
218 Francisco Liriano (RC) .60 1.50
219 Kenji Johjima RC .60 1.50
219A Kenji Johjima AU 6.00 15.00
220 Craig Hansen RC .60 1.50
221 Prince Fielder AU (RC) 8.00 20.00
222 Josh Barfield AU (RC) 6.00 15.00
223 Fausto Carmona AU (RC) 6.00 15.00
224 James Loney AU (RC) 6.00 15.00

2006 Bowman Chrome Refractors

*REF 1-200: 1.5X TO 4X BASIC
*REF 201-220: 1X TO 2.5X BASIC
1-220 ODDS 1:4 HOB, 1:6 RET
219 AU ODDS 1:5100 HOB, 1:12,432 RET
219 AU PRINT RUN 250 SERIAL #'d CARDS
*REF AU 221-224: .5X TO 1.2X BASIC
221-224 AU ODDS 1:82 HOB, 1:200 RET
221-224 AU PRINT RUN 500 SER.#'d SETS
219A Kenji Johjima AU/250 10.00 25.00

2006 Bowman Chrome Blue Refractors

*BLUE REF 1-200: 4X TO 10X BASIC
*BLUE REF 201-220: 4X TO 10X BASIC
1-220 ODDS 1:25 HOB, 1:73 RET
219 AU ODDS 1:16,877 HOB, 1:61,760 RET
219 AU PRINT RUN 75 SERIAL #'d CARDS
*BLUE REF AU 221-224: .75X TO 2X BASIC
221-224 AU ODDS 1:266 HOB, 1:890 RET
STATED PRINT RUN 150 SERIAL #'d SETS
219A Kenji Johjima AU/75 15.00 40.00

2006 Bowman Chrome Gold Refractors

*GOLD REF 1-200: 6X TO 15X BASIC
*GOLD REF 201-220: 5X TO 12X BASIC
1-220 ODDS 1:74 HOB, 1:247 RET
219 AU ODDS 1:26,000 HOB, 1:52,937 RET
*GOLD REF AU 221-224: 2X TO 5X BASIC
221-224 AU ODDS 1:820 HOB, 1:1910 RET
STATED PRINT RUN 50 SERIAL #'d SETS
219A Kenji Johjima AU 20.00 50.00
224 James Loney AU 50.00 100.00

2006 Bowman Chrome Orange Refractors

*ORANGE REF 1-200: 15X TO 40X BASIC
1-220 ODDS 1:181 HOB, 1:182 RET
219 AU ODDS 1:62,686 HOB, 1:62,607 RET
221-224 AU ODDS 1:1640 HOB, 1:3820 RET
STATED PRINT RUN 25 SERIAL #'d SETS
NO RC/AU PRICING DUE TO SCARCITY

2006 Bowman Chrome X-Fractors

*X-FRACTOR 1-200: 3X TO 8X BASIC
*X-FRACTOR 201-220: 2.5X TO 6X BASIC
1-220 ODDS 1:15 HOB, 1:44 RET
1-220 PRINT RUN 250 SERIAL #'d SETS
219 AU ODDS 1:10,205 HOB 1:28,500 RET
219 AU PRINT RUN 125 SERIAL #'d CARDS
*X-FRAC AU 221-224: .6X TO 1.5X BASIC
221-224 AU ODDS 1:182 HOB, 1:478 RET
221-224 AU PRINT RUN 225 SERIAL #'d SETS
219A Kenji Johjima AU/125 12.50 30.00

2006 Bowman Chrome Prospects

COMP.SET w/o AU's (220) 75.00 150.00
COMP.SERIES 1 SET (110) 30.00 60.00
COMP.SERIES 2 SET (110) 40.00 80.00
1-110 TWO PER HOBBY PACK
1-110 FOUR PER HTA PACK
111-220 TWO PER HOB/RET PACKS
221-247 AU ODDS 1:27 HOB, 1:65 RET
1-110 PLATE ODDS 1:588 HOB,1:575 HTA
111-220 PLATE ODDS 1:836 HOBBY
221-247 AU PLATES 1: 9000 HOBBY
PLATE PRINT RUN 1 PER COLOR
BLACK-CYAN-MAGENTA-YELLOW ISSUED
NO PLATE PRICING DUE TO SCARCITY
1-110 ISSUED IN BOWMAN PACKS
111-247 ISSUED IN BOW.CHROME PACKS
EXCHANGE DEADLINE 8/31/08
BC1 Alex Gordon 1.25 3.00
BC2 Jonathan George .40 1.00
BC3 Scott Walter .40 1.00
BC4 Brian Holliday .40 1.00
BC5 Ben Copeland .40 1.00
BC6 Bobby Wilson .40 1.00
BC7 Mayker Sandoval .40 1.00
BC8 Alejandro de Aza .60 1.50
BC9 David Munoz .40 1.00
BC10 Josh LeBlanc .40 1.00
BC11 Philippe Valiquette .40 1.00
BC12 Edwin Bellorin .40 1.00
BC13 Jason Quarles .40 1.00
BC14 Mark Trumbo 1.00 2.50
BC15 Steve Kelly .40 1.00
BC16 Jamie Hoffman .40 1.00
BC17 Joe Bauserman .40 1.00
BC18 Nick Adenhart .40 1.00
BC19 Mike Butia .40 1.00
BC20 Jon Weber .40 1.00
BC21 Luis Valdez .40 1.00
BC22 Rafael Rodriguez .40 1.00
BC23 Wyatt Toregas .40 1.00
BC24 John Vanden Berg .40 1.00
BC25 Mike Connolly .40 1.00
BC26 Mike O'Connor .40 1.00
BC27 Garrett Mock .40 1.00
BC28 Bill Layman .40 1.00
BC29 Luis Pena .40 1.00
BC30 Billy Killian .40 1.00
BC31 Ross Ohlendorf .40 1.00
BC32 Mark Kaiser .40 1.00
BC33 Ryan Costello .40 1.00
BC34 Dale Thayer .40 1.00
BC35 Steve Garrabrants .40 1.00
BC36 Samuel Deduno .40 1.00
BC37 Juan Portes .40 1.00
BC38 Javier Martinez .40 1.00
BC39 Clint Sammons .40 1.00
BC40 Andrew Kown .40 1.00
BC41 Matt Tolbert .40 1.00
BC42 Michael Ekstrom .40 1.00
BC43 Shawn Norris .40 1.00
BC44 Diory Hernandez .40 1.00
BC45 Chris Maples .40 1.00
BC46 Aaron Hathaway .40 1.00
BC47 Steven Baker .40 1.00
BC48 Greg Creek .40 1.00
BC49 Collin Mahoney .40 1.00
BC50 Corey Ragsdale .40 1.00
BC51 Ariel Nunez .40 1.00
BC52 Max Ramirez .60 1.50
BC53 Eric Rodland .40 1.00
BC54 Dante Brinkley .40 1.00
BC55 Casey Craig .40 1.00
BC56 Ryan Spilborghs .40 1.00
BC57 Fredy Deza .40 1.00
BC58 Jeff Frazier .40 1.00
BC59 Vince Cordova .40 1.00
BC60 Oswaldo Navarro .40 1.00
BC61 Jarod Rine .40 1.00
BC62 Jordan Tata .40 1.00
BC63 Ben Julianel .40 1.00
BC64 Yung-Chi Chen .60 1.50
BC65 Carlos Torres .40 1.00
BC66 Juan Francia .40 1.00
BC67 Brett Smith .40 1.00
BC68 Francisco Leandro .40 1.00
BC69 Chris Turner .40 1.00
BC70 Matt Joyce 2.00 5.00
BC71 Jason Jones .40 1.00
BC72 Jose Diaz .40 1.00
BC73 Kevin Ool .40 1.00
BC74 Nate Bumstead .40 1.00
BC75 Omir Santos .40 1.00
BC76 Shawn Riggans .40 1.00
BC77 Ofilio Castro .40 1.00
BC78 Mike Rozier .40 1.00
BC79 Wilkin Ramirez .60 1.50
BC80 Yobal Duenas .40 1.00
BC81 Adam Bourassa .40 1.00
BC82 Tony Granadillo .40 1.00
BC83 Brad McCann .40 1.00
BC84 Dustin Majewski .40 1.00
BC85 Kelvin Jimenez .40 1.00
BC86 Mark Reed .40 1.00
BC87 Asdrubal Cabrera 2.00 5.00
BC88 James Barthmaier .40 1.00
BC89 Brandon Boggs .40 1.00
BC90 Raul Valdez .40 1.00
BC91 Jose Campusano .40 1.00
BC92 Henry Owens .40 1.00
BC93 Tug Hulett .40 1.00
BC94 Nate Gold .40 1.00
BC95 Lee Mitchell .40 1.00
BC96 John Hardy .40 1.00
BC97 Aaron Wideman .40 1.00
BC98 Brandon Roberts .40 1.00
BC99 Lou Santangelo .40 1.00
BC100 Kyle Kendrick 1.00 2.50
BC101 Michael Collins .40 1.00
BC102 Camilo Vazquez .40 1.00
BC103 Mark McLemore .40 1.00
BC104 Alexander Peralta .40 1.00
BC105 Josh Whitesell .40 1.00
BC106 Carlos Guevara .40 1.00
BC107 Michael Aubrey .60 1.50
BC108 Brandon Chaves .40 1.00
BC109 Leonard Davis .40 1.00
BC110 Kendry Morales 1.00 2.50
BC111 Koby Clemens .60 1.50
BC112 Lance Broadway .40 1.00
BC113 Cameron Maybin 1.25 3.00
BC114 Mike Aviles .60 1.50
BC115 Kyle Blanks 1.50 4.00
BC116 Chris Dickerson .60 1.50
BC117 Sean Gallagher .40 1.00
BC118 Jamar Hill .40 1.00
BC119 Garrett Mock .40 1.00
BC120 Russ Rohlicek .40 1.00
BC121 Clete Thomas .40 1.00
BC122 Elvis Andrus 1.25 3.00
BC123 Brandon Moss .40 1.00
BC124 Mark Holliman .40 1.00
BC125 Jose Tabata .60 1.50
BC126 Corey Wimberly .40 1.00
BC127 Bobby Wilson .40 1.00
BC128 Edward Mujica .40 1.00
BC129 Hunter Pence 1.50 4.00
BC130 Adam Heether .40 1.00
BC131 Andy Wilson .40 1.00
BC132 Radhames Liz .40 1.00
BC133 Garrett Patterson .40 1.00
BC134 Carlos Gomez .75 2.00
BC135 Jared Lansford .40 1.00
BC136 Jose Arredondo .40 1.00
BC137 Renee Cortez .40 1.00
BC138 Francisco Rosario .40 1.00
BC139 Brian Stokes .40 1.00
BC140 Will Thompson .40 1.00
BC141 Ernesto Frieri .40 1.00
BC142 Jose Mijares .40 1.00
BC143 Jeremy Slayden .40 1.00
BC144 Brandon Fahey .40 1.00
BC145 Jason Windsor .40 1.00
BC146 Shawn Nottingham .40 1.00
BC147 Dallas Trahern .40 1.00
BC148 Jon Niese 1.00 2.50
BC149 A.J. Shappi .40 1.00
BC150 Jordan Pals .40 1.00
BC151 Tim Moss .40 1.00
BC152 Stephen Marek .40 1.00
BC153 Mat Gamel 1.00 2.50
BC154 Sean Henn .40 1.00
BC155 Matt Guillory .40 1.00
BC156 Brandon Jones .40 1.00
BC157 Gary Galvez .40 1.00
BC158 Shane Lindsay 1.00 2.50
BC159 Jesus Reina .40 1.00
BC160 Lorenzo Cain 2.00 5.00
BC161 Chris Britton .40 1.00
BC162 Yovani Gallardo 1.25 3.00
BC163 Matt Walker .40 1.00
BC164 Shaun Cumberland .40 1.00
BC165 Ryan Patterson .40 1.00
BC166 Michael Hollimon .40 1.00
BC167 Eude Brito .40 1.00
BC168 John Bowker .40 1.00
BC169 James Avery .40 1.00
BC170 John Bannister .40 1.00
BC171 Juan Ciriaco .40 1.00
BC172 Manuel Corpas .40 1.00
BC173 Leo Rosales .40 1.00
BC174 Tim Kennelly .40 1.00
BC175 Adam Russell .40 1.00
BC176 Jeremy Hellickson 1.25 3.00
BC177 Ryan Klosterman .40 1.00
BC178 Evan Meek .40 1.00
BC179 Steve Murphy .40 1.00
BC180 Scott Feldman .40 1.00
BC181 Pablo Sandoval 1.50 4.00
BC182 Dexter Fowler 1.25 3.00
BC183 Jairo Cuevas .40 1.00
BC184 Andrew Pinckney .40 1.00
BC185 Marino Salas .40 1.00
BC186 Justin Christian .40 1.00
BC187 Ching-Lung Lo .40 1.00
BC188 Randy Roth .40 1.00
BC189 Andy Sonnanstine .40 1.00
BC190 Josh Outman .40 1.00
BC191 Yuber Rodriguez .40 1.00
BC192 Hainley Statia .40 1.00
BC193 Kevin Estrada .40 1.00
BC194 Jeff Karstens .40 1.00
BC195 Corey Coles .40 1.00
BC196 Gustavo Espinoza .40 1.00
BC197 Brian Horwitz .40 1.00
BC198 Landon Jacobsen .40 1.00
BC199 Ben Krosschell .40 1.00
BC200 Jason Jaramillo .40 1.00
BC201 Josh Wilson .40 1.00
BC202 Jason Ray .40 1.00
BC203 Brent Dlugach .40 1.00
BC204 Cesar Jimenez .40 1.00
BC205 Eric Haberer .40 1.00
BC206 Felipe Paulino .40 1.00
BC207 Alcides Escobar 1.50 4.00
BC208 Jose Ascanio .40 1.00
BC209 Yoel Hernandez .40 1.00
BC210 Geoff Vandel .40 1.00
BC211 Travis Denker .40 1.00
BC212 Ramon Alvarado .40 1.00
BC213 Welinson Baez .40 1.00
BC214 Chris Kolkhorst .40 1.00
BC215 Emiliano Fruto .40 1.00
BC216 Luis Cota .40 1.00
BC217 Mark Worrell .40 1.00
BC218 Cla Meredith .40 1.00
BC219 Emmanuel Garcia .40 1.00
BC220 B.J. Szymanski .40 1.00
BC221 Alex Gordon AU 12.00 30.00
BC223 Justin Upton AU 15.00 40.00
BC224 Sean West AU 4.00 10.00
BC225 Tyler Greene AU 4.00 10.00
BC226 Josh Kinney AU 4.00 10.00
BC227 Pedro Lopez AU 4.00 10.00
BC228 Troy Patton AU 4.00 10.00
BC229 Chris Iannetta AU 4.00 10.00
BC230 Jared Wells AU 4.00 10.00
BC231 Brandon Wood AU 4.00 10.00
BC232 Josh Geer AU 4.00 10.00
BC233 Cesar Carrillo AU 4.00 10.00
BC234 Franklin Gutierrez AU 4.00 10.00
BC235 Matt Garza AU 4.00 10.00
BC236 Eli Iorg AU 4.00 10.00
BC237 Trevor Bell AU 4.00 10.00
BC238 Jeff Lyman AU 4.00 10.00
BC239 Jon Lester AU 25.00 60.00
BC240 Kendry Morales AU 5.00 12.00
BC241 J. Brent Cox AU 4.00 10.00
BC242 Jose Bautista AU 10.00 25.00
BC243 Josh Sullivan AU 4.00 10.00
BC244 Brandon Snyder AU 4.00 10.00
BC245 Elvin Puello AU 4.00 10.00
BC247 Jacob Marceaux AU 4.00 10.00

2006 Bowman Chrome Prospects Refractors

*REF 1-110: 1.25X TO 3X BASIC
*REF 111-220: 1.25X TO 3X BASIC
1-110 ODDS 1:36 HOBBY, 1:12 HTA
111-220 ODDS 1:22 HOBBY, 1:61 RETAIL
*REF AU 221-247: .5X TO 1.2X BASIC
221-247 AU ODDS 1:82 HOB, 1:200 RET
STATED PRINT RUN 500 SERIAL #'d SETS
1-110 ISSUED IN BOWMAN PACKS
111-247 ISSUED IN BOW.CHROME PACKS
EXCHANGE DEADLINE 8/31/08

2006 Bowman Chrome Prospects Blue Refractors

*BLUE REF 1-220: 2.5X TO 6X BASIC
1-110 ODDS 1:118 HOBBY, 1:39 HTA
111-220 ODDS 1:205 HOBBY
*BLUE AU 221-247: .75X TO 2X BASIC
221-247 AU ODDS 1:266 HOB, 1:890 RET
STATED PRINT RUN 150 SERIAL #'d SETS
1-110 ISSUED IN BOWMAN PACKS
111-247 ISSUED IN BOW.CHROME PACKS
EXCHANGE DEADLINE 8/31/08

2006 Bowman Chrome Prospects Gold Refractors

*GOLD REF 1-110: 3X TO 8X BASIC
*GOLD REF 111-220: 3X TO 8X BASIC
1-110 ODDS 1:355 HOBBY, 1:116 HTA
111-220 ODDS: 1:74 HOBBY
COMMON AUTO (221-247) 15.00 40.00
221-247 AU ODDS 1:820 HOB, 1:1910 RET
STATED PRINT RUN 50 SERIAL #'d SETS
1-110 ISSUED IN BOWMAN PACKS
111-247 ISSUED IN BOW.CHROME PACKS
EXCHANGE DEADLINE 8/31/08
BC221 Alex Gordon AU 100.00 200.00

2006 Bowman Chrome Prospects Orange Refractors

1-110 ODDS 1:710 HOBBY, 1:233 HTA
111-220 ODDS 1:181 HOBBY
221-247 AU ODDS 1:1640 HOB, 1:3820 RET
STATED PRINT RUN 25 SERIAL #'d SETS
1-110 ISSUED IN BOWMAN PACKS
111-247 ISSUED IN BOW.CHROME PACKS
NO PRICING DUE TO SCARCITY
EXCHANGE DEADLINE 8/31/08

2006 Bowman Chrome Prospects X-Fractors

*X-F 1-220: 1.5X TO 4X BASIC
1-110 ODDS 1:72 HOBBY, 1:23 HTA
111-220 ODDS 1:15 HOBBY
1-220 PRINT RUN 250 SERIAL #'d SETS
*X-F AU 221-247: .6X TO 1.5X BASIC
221-247 AU ODDS 1:182 HOB, 1:478 RET
221-247 AU PRINT RUN 225 SERIAL #'d SETS
1-110 ISSUED IN BOWMAN PACKS
111-247 ISSUED IN BOW.CHROME PACKS
EXCHANGE DEADLINE 8/31/08

2006 Bowman Chrome Draft

COMPLETE SET (55) 15.00 40.00
COMMON RC (1-55) .40 1.00
APPX. ODDS 1:2 HOBBY, 1:2 RETAIL
ODDS INFO PROVIDED BY BECKETT
OVERALL PLATE ODDS 1:990 HOBBY
PLATE PRINT RUN 1 SET PER COLOR
BLACK-CYAN-MAGENTA-YELLOW ISSUED
NO PLATE PRICING DUE TO SCARCITY
1 Matt Kemp (RC) 1.00 2.50
2 Taylor Tankersley (RC) .40 1.00
3 Mike Napoli RC .60 1.50
4 Brian Bannister (RC) .40 1.00
5 Melky Cabrera (RC) .60 1.50
6 Bill Bray (RC) .40 1.00
7 Brian Anderson (RC) .40 1.00
8 Jered Weaver (RC) 1.25 3.00
9 Chris Duncan (RC) .60 1.50
10 Boof Bonser (RC) .60 1.50
11 Mike Rouse (RC) .40 1.00
12 David Pauley (RC) .40 1.00
13 Russ Martin (RC) .60 1.50
14 Jeremy Sowers (RC) .40 1.00
15 Kevin Reese (RC) .40 1.00
16 John Rheinecker (RC) .40 1.00
17 Tommy Murphy (RC) .40 1.00
18 Sean Marshall (RC) .40 1.00
19 Jason Kubel (RC) .40 1.00
20 Chad Billingsley (RC) .60 1.50
21 Kendry Morales (RC) 1.00 2.50
22 Jon Lester RC 1.50 4.00
23 Brandon Fahey RC .40 1.00
24 Josh Johnson (RC) 1.00 2.50
25 Kevin Frandsen (RC) .40 1.00
26 Casey Janssen RC .40 1.00
27 Scott Thorman (RC) .40 1.00
28 Scott Mathieson (RC) .40 1.00
29 Jeremy Hermida (RC) .40 1.00
30 Dustin Nippert (RC) .40 1.00
31 Kevin Thompson (RC) .40 1.00
32 Bobby Livingston (RC) .40 1.00
33 Travis Ishikawa (RC) .60 1.50
34 Jeff Mathis (RC) .40 1.00
35 Charlie Haeger RC .60 1.50
36 Josh Willingham (RC) .60 1.50
37 Taylor Buchholz (RC) .40 1.00
38 Joel Guzman (RC) .40 1.00
39 Zach Jackson (RC) .40 1.00
40 Howie Kendrick (RC) .75 2.00
41 T.J. Beam (RC) .40 1.00
42 Ty Taubenheim RC .60 1.50
43 Erick Aybar (RC) .40 1.00
44 Anibal Sanchez (RC) .40 1.00
45 Michael Pelfrey RC 1.00 2.50
46 Shawn Hill (RC) .40 1.00
47 Chris Roberson (RC) .40 1.00
48 Carlos Villanueva RC .40 1.00
49 Andre Ethier (RC) 1.25 3.00
50 Anthony Reyes (RC) .40 1.00
51 Franklin Gutierrez (RC) .40 1.00
52 Angel Guzman (RC) .40 1.00
53 Michael O'Connor RC .40 1.00
54 James Shields RC 1.25 3.00
55 Nate McLouth (RC) .40 1.00

2006 Bowman Chrome Draft Refractors

*REF: 1.25X TO 3X BASIC
STATED ODDS 1:11 HOBBY, 1:11 RETAIL

2006 Bowman Chrome Draft Blue Refractors

*BLUE REF: 3X TO 8X BASIC
STATED ODDS 1:50 HOBBY, 1:94 RETAIL
STATED PRINT RUN 150 SER.#'d SETS

2006 Bowman Chrome Draft Gold Refractors

*GOLD REF: 5X TO 12X BASIC
STATED ODDS 1:197 H, 1:388 R
STATED PRINT RUN 50 SER.#'d SETS

2006 Bowman Chrome Draft Orange Refractors

STATED ODDS 1:395 HOBBY, 1:770 RETAIL
STATED PRINT RUN 25 SER.#'d SETS
NO PRICING DUE TO SCARCITY

2006 Bowman Chrome Draft X-Fractors

*X-F: 2X TO 5X BASIC
STATED ODDS 1:32 H, 1:74 R
STATED PRINT RUN 299 SER.#'d SETS

2006 Bowman Chrome Draft Draft Picks

APPX. ODDS 1:1 HOBBY, 1:1 RETAIL
ODDS INFO PROVIDED BY BECKETT
66-90 AU ODDS 1:50 HOB, 1:51 RET.
1-65 PLATE ODDS 1:990 HOBBY
66-90 AU PLATE ODDS 1:13,200 HOBBY
PLATE PRINT RUN 1 SET PER COLOR
BLACK-CYAN-MAGENTA-YELLOW ISSUED
NO PLATE PRICING DUE TO SCARCITY
1 Tyler Colvin .60 1.50
2 Chris Marrero .60 1.50
3 Hank Conger .60 1.50
4 Chris Parmelee .60 1.50
5 Jason Place .40 1.00
6 Billy Rowell 1.00 2.50
7 Travis Snider 1.25 3.00
8 Colton Willems .40 1.00
9 Chase Fontaine .40 1.00
10 Jon Jay .60 1.50
11 Wade Leblanc .60 1.50
12 Justin Masterson .60 1.50
13 Gary Daley .40 1.00
14 Justin Edwards .40 1.00
15 Charlie Yarbrough .40 1.00
16 Cyle Hankerd .40 1.00
17 Zach McAllister .40 1.00
18 Tyler Robertson .40 1.00
19 Joe Smith .40 1.00
20 Nate Culp .40 1.00
21 John Holdzkom .40 1.00
22 Patrick Bresnehan .40 1.00
23 Chad Lee .40 1.00
24 Ryan Morris .40 1.00
25 D'Arby Myers .40 1.00
26 Garrett Olson .40 1.00
27 Jon Still .40 1.00
28 Brandon Rice .40 1.00
29 Chris Davis .75 2.00
30 Zack Daeges .40 1.00
31 Bobby Henson .40 1.00
32 George Kontos .40 1.00
33 Jermaine Mitchell .40 1.00
34 Adam Coe .40 1.00
35 Dustin Richardson .40 1.00
36 Allen Craig 1.00 2.50
37 Austin McClune .40 1.00
38 Doug Fister .60 1.50
39 Corey Madden .40 1.00
40 Justin Jacobs .40 1.00
41 Jim Negrych .40 1.00
42 Tyler Norrick .40 1.00
43 Adam Davis .40 1.00
44 Brett Logan .40 1.00
45 Brian Omogrosso .40 1.00
46 Kyle Drabek .60 1.50
47 Jamie Ortiz .40 1.00
48 Alex Presley .60 1.50
49 Terrance Warren .40 1.00
50 David Christensen .40 1.00
51 Helder Velazquez .40 1.00
52 Matt McBride .40 1.00
53 Quintin Berry 1.00 2.50
54 Michael Eisenberg .40 1.00
55 Dan Garcia .40 1.00
56 Scott Cousins .40 1.00
57 Sean Land .40 1.00
58 Kristopher Medlen 2.00 5.00
59 Tyler Reves .40 1.00
60 John Shelby .40 1.00
61 Jordan Newton .40 1.00
62 Ricky Orta .40 1.00
63 Jason Donald .40 1.00
64 David Huff .40 1.00
65 Brett Sinkbeil .40 1.00
66 Evan Longoria AU 20.00 50.00
67 Cody Johnson AU 4.00 10.00
68 Kris Johnson AU 4.00 10.00
69 Kasey Kiker AU 4.00 10.00
70 Ronnie Bourquin AU 4.00 10.00
71 Adrian Cardenas AU 4.00 10.00
72 Matt Antonelli AU 4.00 10.00
73 Brooks Brown AU 4.00 10.00
74 Steven Evarts AU 4.00 10.00
75 Joshua Butler AU 4.00 10.00
76 Chad Huffman AU 4.00 10.00
77 Steven Wright AU 4.00 10.00
78 Cory Rasmus AU 4.00 10.00
79 Brad Furnish AU 4.00 10.00
80 Andrew Carpenter AU 4.00 10.00
81 Dustin Evans AU 4.00 10.00
82 Tommy Hickman AU 4.00 10.00
83 Matt Long AU 4.00 10.00
84 Clayton Kershaw AU 300.00 800.00
85 Kyle McCulloch AU 4.00 10.00
86 Pedro Beato AU 4.00 10.00
87 Kyler Burke AU 4.00 10.00
88 Stephen Englund AU 4.00 10.00
89 Michael Felix AU 4.00 10.00
90 Sean Watson AU 4.00 10.00

2006 Bowman Chrome Draft Draft Picks Refractors

*REF 1-65: 1.25X TO 3X BASIC
1-65 ODDS 1:11 HOBBY, 1:11 RETAIL
*REF AU 66-90: .5X TO 1.2X BASIC AU
AU 66-90 ODDS 1:156 HOB, 1:157 RET
66-90 AU PRINT RUN 500 SER.#'d SETS
84 Clayton Kershaw AU 600.00 1500.00

2006 Bowman Chrome Draft Draft Picks Blue Refractors

*BLUE REF 1-65: 5X TO 12X BASIC
1-65 STATED ODDS 1:50 H, 1:94 R
1-65 PRINT RUN 199 SER.#'d SETS
*BLUE AU 66-90: 1.25X TO 3X BASIC AU
66-90 STATED ODDS 1:535 H, 1:535 R
66-90 PRINT RUN 150 SER.#'d SETS
84 Clayton Kershaw AU 1250.00 3000.00

2006 Bowman Chrome Draft Draft Picks Gold Refractors

*GOLD REF 1-65: 10X TO 25X BASIC
1-65 STATED ODDS 1:197 H, 1:388 R
66-90 AU ODDS 1:1575 H, 1:1600 R
STATED PRINT RUN 50 SER.#'d SETS
66 Evan Longoria AU 200.00 400.00
67 Cody Johnson AU 20.00 50.00
68 Kris Johnson AU 20.00 50.00
70 Ronnie Bourquin AU 20.00 50.00
73 Brooks Brown AU 20.00 50.00
74 Steven Evarts AU 20.00 50.00
75 Joshua Butler AU 20.00 50.00
77 Steven Wright AU 20.00 50.00
78 Cory Rasmus AU 20.00 50.00
79 Brad Furnish AU 20.00 50.00
80 Andrew Carpenter AU 20.00 50.00
81 Dustin Evans AU 20.00 50.00
82 Tommy Hickman AU 20.00 50.00
83 Matt Long AU 20.00 50.00
84 Clayton Kershaw AU 2500.00 6000.00
85 Kyle McCulloch AU 20.00 50.00
86 Pedro Beato AU 20.00 50.00
87 Kyler Burke AU 20.00 50.00
88 Stephen Englund AU 20.00 50.00
89 Michael Felix AU 20.00 50.00
90 Sean Watson AU 20.00 50.00

2006 Bowman Chrome Draft Draft Picks Orange Refractors

1-65 STATD ODDS 1:395 HOB.,1:770 RET.
66-90 AU ODDS 1:3232 HOB.,1:3232 RET.
STATED PRINT RUN 25 SERIAL #'d SETS
NO PRICING DUE TO SCARCITY

2006 Bowman Chrome Draft Draft Picks X-Fractors

*X-F 1-65: 2X TO 5X BASIC
1-65 STATED ODDS 1:32 H, 1:74 R
1-65 PRINT RUN 299 SER.#'d SETS
*X-F AU 66-90: .75X TO 2X BASIC
66-90 AU STATED ODDS 1:351 H, 1:353 R
66-90 AU PRINT RUN 225 SER.#'d SETS
84 Clayton Kershaw AU 750.00 2000.00

2006 Bowman Chrome Draft Future's Game Prospects

COMPLETE SET (45) 10.00 25.00
APPX. ODDS 1:2 HOBBY, 1:2 RETAIL
ODDS INFO PROVIDED BY BECKETT
OVERALL PLATE ODDS 1:990 HOBBY
PLATE PRINT RUN 1 SET PER COLOR
BLACK-CYAN-MAGENTA-YELLOW ISSUED
NO PLATE PRICING DUE TO SCARCITY
1 Nick Adenhart .40 1.00
2 Joel Guzman .40 1.00
3 Ryan Braun 2.00 5.00
4 Carlos Carrasco .60 1.50
5 Neil Walker .60 1.50
6 Pablo Sandoval 1.50 4.00
7 Gio Gonzalez .60 1.50
8 Joey Votto 3.00 8.00
9 Luis Cruz .40 1.00
10 Nolan Reimold .60 1.50
11 Juan Salas .40 1.00
12 Josh Fields .40 1.00
13 Yovani Gallardo 1.25 3.00
14 Radhames Liz .40 1.00
15 Eric Patterson .40 1.00
16 Cameron Maybin 1.25 3.00
17 Edgar Martinez .40 1.00
18 Hunter Pence 1.50 4.00
19 Philip Hughes 1.00 2.50
20 Trent Oeltjen .40 1.00
21 Nick Pereira .40 1.00
22 Wladimir Balentien .40 1.00
23 Stephen Drew .75 2.00
24 Davis Romero .40 1.00
25 Joe Koshansky .40 1.00
26 Chin Lung Hu .40 1.00
27 Jason Hirsh .40 1.00
28 Jose Tabata .60 1.50
29 Eric Hurley .40 1.00
30 Yung Chi Chen .60 1.50
31 Howie Kendrick .75 2.00
32 Humberto Sanchez .40 1.00
33 Alex Gordon 1.25 3.00
34 Yunel Escobar .40 1.00
35 Travis Buck .40 1.00
36 Billy Butler 1.00 2.50
37 Homer Bailey 1.00 2.50
38 George Kottaras .40 1.00
39 Kurt Suzuki .40 1.00
40 Joaquin Arias .40 1.00
41 Matt Lindstrom .40 1.00
42 Sean Smith .40 1.00
43 Carlos Gonzalez 1.00 2.50
44 Jaime Garcia 2.00 5.00
45 Jose Garcia .40 1.00

2006 Bowman Chrome Draft Future's Game Prospects Refractors

*REF: .75X TO 2X BASIC
STATED ODDS 1:11 HOBBY, 1:11 RETAIL

2006 Bowman Chrome Draft Future's Game Prospects Blue Refractors

*BLUE REF: 1.5X TO 4X BASIC
STATED ODDS 1:50 HOBBY, 1:94 RETAIL
STATED PRINT RUN 199 SER.#'d SETS

2006 Bowman Chrome Draft Future's Game Prospects Gold Refractors

*GOLD REF: 4X TO 10X BASIC
STATED ODDS 1:197 H, 1:388 R
STATED PRINT RUN 50 SER.#'d SETS
6 Pablo Sandoval 100.00 200.00

2006 Bowman Chrome Draft Future's Game Prospects Orange Refractors
STATED ODDS 1:395 HOBBY, 1:770 RETAIL
STATED PRINT RUN 25 SERIAL #'d SETS
NO PRICING DUE TO SCARCITY

2006 Bowman Chrome Draft Future's Game Prospects X-Fractors
*X-F: 1.25X TO 3X BASIC
STATED ODDS 1:32 H, 1:74 R
STATED PRINT RUN 299 SER.#'d SETS

2007 Bowman Chrome
COMPLETE SET (220) 30.00 60.00
COMMON CARD (1-190) .20 .50
COMMON ROOKIE (191-220) .30 .75
1-220 PLATE ODDS 1:1054 HOBBY
PLATE PRINT RUN 1 SET PER COLOR
BLACK-CYAN-MAGENTA-YELLOW ISSUED
NO PLATE PRICING DUE TO SCARCITY
1 Hanley Ramirez .30 .75
2 Justin Verlander .50 1.25
3 Ryan Zimmerman .30 .75
4 Jered Weaver .30 .75
5 Stephen Drew .20 .50
6 Jonathan Papelbon .50 1.25
7 Melky Cabrera .20 .50
8 Francisco Liriano .20 .50
9 Prince Fielder .30 .75
10 Dan Uggla .20 .50
11 Jeremy Sowers .20 .50
12 Carlos Quentin .20 .50
13 Chuck James .20 .50
14 Andre Ethier .30 .75
15 Cole Hamels .40 1.00
16 Kenji Johjima .50 1.25
17 Chad Billingsley .30 .75
18 Ian Kinsler .30 .75
19 Jason Hirsh .20 .50
20 Nick Markakis .40 1.00
21 Jeremy Hermida .20 .50
22 Ryan Shealy .20 .50
23 Scott Olsen .20 .50
24 Russell Martin .20 .50
25 Conor Jackson .20 .50
26 Erik Bedard .20 .50
27 Brian McCann .20 .50
28 Michael Barrett .20 .50
29 Brandon Phillips .20 .50
30 Garrett Atkins .20 .50
31 Freddy Garcia .20 .50
32 Mark Loretta .20 .50
33 Craig Biggio .30 .75
34 Jeremy Bonderman .20 .50
35 Johan Santana .30 .75
36 Jorge Posada .30 .75
37 Victor Martinez .30 .75
38 Carlos Delgado .20 .50
39 Gary Matthews Jr. .20 .50
40 Mike Cameron .20 .50
41 Adrian Beltre .50 1.25
42 Freddy Sanchez .20 .50
43 Austin Kearns .20 .50
44 Mark Buehrle .30 .75
45 Miguel Cabrera .50 1.25
46 Josh Beckett .20 .50
47 Chone Figgins .20 .50
48 Edgar Renteria .20 .50
49 Derek Lowe .20 .50
50 Ryan Howard .40 1.00
51 Shawn Green .20 .50
52 Jason Giambi .20 .50
53 Ervin Santana .20 .50
54 Aaron Hill .20 .50
55 Roy Oswalt .30 .75
56 Dan Haren .20 .50
57 Jose Vidro .20 .50
58 Kevin Millwood .20 .50
59 Jim Edmonds .30 .75
60 Carl Crawford .30 .75
61 Randy Wolf .20 .50
62 Paul LoDuca .20 .50
63 Johnny Estrada .20 .50
64 Brian Roberts .20 .50
65 Manny Ramirez .50 1.25
66 Jose Contreras .20 .50
67 Josh Barfield .20 .50
68 Juan Pierre .20 .50
69 David DeJesus .20 .50
70 Gary Sheffield .20 .50
71 Michael Young .20 .50
72 Randy Johnson .50 1.25
73 Rickie Weeks .20 .50
74 Brian Giles .20 .50
75 Ichiro Suzuki .60 1.50
76 Nick Swisher .30 .75
77 Justin Morneau .30 .75
78 Scott Kazmir .30 .75
79 Lyle Overbay .20 .50
80 Alfonso Soriano .30 .75
81 Brandon Webb .30 .75
82 Joe Crede .20 .50
83 Corey Patterson .20 .50
84 Kenny Rogers .20 .50
85 Ken Griffey Jr. 1.00 2.50
86 Cliff Lee .30 .75
87 Mike Lowell .20 .50
88 Marcus Giles .20 .50
89 Orlando Cabrera .20 .50
90 Derek Jeter 1.25 3.00
91 Ramon Hernandez .20 .50
92 Carlos Guillen .20 .50
93 Bill Hall .20 .50
94 Michael Cuddyer .20 .50
95 Miguel Tejada .30 .75
96 Todd Helton .30 .75
97 C.C. Sabathia .30 .75
98 Tadahito Iguchi .20 .50
99 Jose Reyes .30 .75
100 David Wright .40 1.00
101 Barry Zito .30 .75
102 Jake Peavy .20 .50
103 Richie Sexson .20 .50
104 A.J. Burnett .20 .50
105 Eric Chavez .20 .50
106 Vernon Wells .20 .50
107 Grady Sizemore .30 .75
108 Bronson Arroyo .20 .50
109 Mike Mussina .30 .75
110 Magglio Ordonez .30 .75
111 Anibal Sanchez .20 .50
112 Jeff Francoeur .50 1.25
113 Kevin Youkilis .20 .50
114 Aubrey Huff .20 .50
115 Carlos Zambrano .30 .75
116 Mark Teahen .20 .50
117 Mark Mulder .20 .50
118 Pedro Martinez .30 .75
119 Hideki Matsui .50 1.25
120 Mike Piazza .50 1.25
121 Jason Schmidt .20 .50
122 Greg Maddux .60 1.50
123 Joe Blanton .20 .50
124 Chris Carpenter .30 .75
125 David Ortiz .50 1.25
126 Alex Rios .20 .50
127 Nick Johnson .20 .50
128 Carlos Lee .20 .50
129 Pat Burrell .20 .50
130 Ben Sheets .20 .50
131 Derrek Lee .20 .50
132 Adam Dunn .30 .75
133 Jermaine Dye .20 .50
134 Curt Schilling .30 .75
135 Chad Tracy .20 .50
136 Vladimir Guerrero .30 .75
137 Melvin Mora .20 .50
138 John Smoltz .50 1.25
139 Craig Monroe .20 .50
140 Dontrelle Willis .20 .50
141 Jeff Francis .20 .50
142 Chipper Jones .50 1.25
143 Frank Thomas .50 1.25
144 Brett Myers .20 .50
145 Tom Glavine .30 .75
146 Robinson Cano .30 .75
147 Jeff Kent .20 .50
148 Scott Rolen .30 .75
149 Roy Halladay .30 .75
150 Joe Mauer .40 1.00
151 Bobby Abreu .20 .50
152 Matt Cain .30 .75
153 Hank Blalock .20 .50
154 Chris Young .20 .50
155 Jake Westbrook .20 .50
156 Javier Vazquez .20 .50
157 Garret Anderson .20 .50
158 Aramis Ramirez .20 .50
159 Mark Kotsay .20 .50
160 Matt Kemp .40 1.00
161 Adrian Gonzalez .40 1.00
162 Felix Hernandez .30 .75
163 David Eckstein .20 .50
164 Curtis Granderson .40 1.00
165 Paul Konerko .30 .75
166 Alex Rodriguez .60 1.50
167 Tim Hudson .30 .75
168 J.D. Drew .20 .50
169 Chien-Ming Wang .30 .75
170 Jimmy Rollins .30 .75
171 Matt Morris .20 .50
172 Raul Ibanez .30 .75
173 Mark Teixeira .30 .75
174 Ted Lilly .20 .50
175 Albert Pujols .60 1.50
176 Carlos Beltran .30 .75
177 Lance Berkman .30 .75
178 Ivan Rodriguez .30 .75
179 Torii Hunter .20 .50
180 Johnny Damon .30 .75
181 Chase Utley .30 .75
182 Jason Bay .30 .75
183 Jeff Weaver .20 .50
184 Troy Glaus .20 .50
185 Rocco Baldelli .20 .50
186 Rafael Furcal .20 .50
187 Jim Thome .30 .75
188 Travis Hafner .20 .50
189 Matt Holliday .50 1.25
190 Andruw Jones .20 .50
191 Andrew Miller RC 1.25 3.00
192 Ryan Braun RC .30 .75
193 Oswaldo Navarro RC .30 .75
194 Mike Rabelo RC .30 .75
195 Delwyn Young (RC) .30 .75
196 Miguel Montero (RC) .30 .75
197 Matt Lindstrom (RC) .30 .75
198 Josh Hamilton (RC) 1.00 2.50
199 Elijah Dukes RC .50 1.25
200 Sean Henn (RC) .30 .75
201 Delmon Young (RC) .50 1.25
202 Alexi Casilla RC .50 1.25
203 Hunter Pence (RC) 1.00 2.50
204 Jeff Baker (RC) .30 .75
205 Hector Gimenez (RC) .30 .75
206 Ubaldo Jimenez (RC) 1.00 2.50
207 Adam Lind (RC) .30 .75
208 Joaquin Arias (RC) .30 .75
209 David Murphy (RC) .30 .75
210 Daisuke Matsuzaka RC 1.25 3.00
211 Jerry Owens (RC) .30 .75
212 Ryan Sweeney (RC) .30 .75
213 Kei Igawa RC .75 2.00
214 Mitch Maier RC .30 .75
215 Philip Humber (RC) .30 .75
216 Troy Tulowitzki (RC) 1.00 2.50
217 Tim Lincecum RC 1.50 4.00
218 Michael Bourn (RC) .50 1.25
219 Hideki Okajima RC 1.50 4.00
220 Josh Fields (RC) .30 .75

2007 Bowman Chrome Refractors
*REF 1-190: 1.25X TO 3X BASIC
*REF 191-220: .75X TO 2X BASIC
1-220 ODDS 1:4 HOBBY, 1:6 RETAIL

2007 Bowman Chrome Blue Refractors
*BLUE REF 1-190: 3X TO 8X BASIC
*BLUE REF 191-220: 2X TO 5X BASIC
1-220 ODDS 1:30 HOBBY, 1:205 RETAIL
STATED PRINT RUN 150 SERIAL #'d SETS

2007 Bowman Chrome Gold Refractors
*GOLD REF 1-190: 8X TO 20X BASIC
*GOLD REF 191-220: 5X TO 12X BASIC
1-220 ODDS 1:88 HOBBY, 1:615 RETAIL
STATED PRINT RUN 50 SERIAL #'d SETS

2007 Bowman Chrome Orange Refractors
*ORANGE REF 1-190: 8X TO 20X BASIC
1-220 ODDS 1:176 HOBBY, 1:1220 RETAIL
STATED PRINT RUN 25 SERIAL #'d SETS
NO RC 191-220 PRICING DUE TO SCARCITY
75 Ichiro Suzuki 40.00 80.00
85 Ken Griffey Jr. 40.00 100.00
169 Chien-Ming Wang 60.00 120.00

2007 Bowman Chrome X-Fractors
*X-FRACTOR 1-190: 2.5X TO 6X BASIC
*X-FRACTOR 191-220: 1.5X TO 4X BASIC
1-220 ODDS 1:18 HOBBY, 1:123 RETAIL
STATED PRINT RUN 250 SER.#'d SETS

2007 Bowman Chrome Prospects

COMP.SET w/o AU's (220) 40.00 100.00
COMP.SERIES 1 SET (110) 20.00 50.00
COMP.SERIES 2 SET (110) 20.00 50.00
221-256 AU ODDS 1:29 HOB, 1:59 RET
1-110 PLATE ODDS 1:1468 H, 1:212 HTA
111-220 PLATE ODDS 1:1054 HOBBY
221-256 AU PLATE ODDS 1:9668 HOBBY
PLATE PRINT RUN 1 SET PER COLOR
BLACK-CYAN-MAGENTA-YELLOW ISSUED
NO PLATE PRICING DUE TO SCARCITY
1-110 ISSUED IN BOWMAN PACKS
111-256 ISSUED IN BOW.CHROME PACKS
EXCHANGE DEADLINE 8/31/2009
BC1 Cooper Brannon .30 .75
BC2 Jason Taylor .30 .75
BC3 Shawn O'Malley .30 .75
BC4 Robert Alcombrack .30 .75
BC5 Dellin Betances 1.00 2.50
BC6 Jeremy Papelbon .30 .75
BC7 Adam Carr .30 .75
BC8 Matthew Clarkson .30 .75
BC9 Darin McDonald .30 .75
BC10 Brandon Rice .30 .75
BC11 Matthew Sweeney 1.00 2.50
BC12 Scott Deal .30 .75
BC13 Brennan Boesch .50 1.25
BC14 Scott Taylor .30 .75
BC15 Michael Brantley .75 2.00
BC16 Yahmed Yema .30 .75
BC17 Brandon Morrow 1.50 4.00
BC18 Cole Garner .30 .75
BC19 Erik Lis .50 1.25
BC20 Lucas French .30 .75
BC21 Aaron Cunningham .50 1.25
BC22 Ryan Schreppel .30 .75
BC23 Kevin Russo .30 .75
BC24 Yohan Pino .50 1.25
BC25 Michael Sullivan .30 .75
BC26 Trey Shields .30 .75
BC27 Daniel Matienzo .30 .75
BC28 Chuck Lofgren .75 2.00
BC29 Gerrit Simpson .30 .75
BC30 David Haehnel .30 .75
BC31 Marvin Lowrance .30 .75
BC32 Kevin Ardoin .30 .75
BC33 Edwin Maysonet .30 .75
BC34 Derek Griffith .30 .75
BC35 Sam Fuld 1.00 2.50
BC36 Chase Wright .75 2.00
BC37 Brandon Roberts .30 .75
BC38 Kyle Aselton .30 .75
BC39 Steven Sollmann .30 .75
BC40 Mike Devaney .30 .75
BC41 Charlie Fermaint .30 .75
BC42 Jesse Litsch .50 1.25
BC43 Bryan Hansen .30 .75
BC44 Ramon Garcia .30 .75
BC45 John Otness .30 .75
BC46 Trey Hearne .30 .75
BC47 Habelito Hernandez .30 .75
BC48 Edgar Garcia .30 .75
BC49 Seth Fortenberry .30 .75
BC50 Reid Brignac .50 1.25
BC51 Derek Rodriguez .30 .75
BC52 Ervin Alcantara .30 .75
BC53 Thomas Hottovy .30 .75
BC54 Jesus Flores .30 .75
BC55 Matt Palmer .30 .75
BC56 Brian Henderson .30 .75
BC57 John Gragg .30 .75
BC58 Jay Garthwaite .30 .75
BC59 Esmerling Vasquez .30 .75
BC60 Gilberto Mejia .30 .75
BC61 Aaron Jensen .30 .75
BC62 Cedric Brooks .30 .75
BC63 Brandon Mann .30 .75
BC64 Myron Leslie .30 .75
BC65 Ray Aguilar .30 .75
BC66 Jesus Guzman .50 1.25
BC67 Sean Thompson .30 .75
BC68 Jarrett Hoffpauir .30 .75
BC69 Matt Goodson .30 .75
BC70 Neal Musser .30 .75
BC71 Tony Abreu .75 2.00
BC72 Tony Peguero .30 .75
BC73 Michael Bertram .30 .75
BC74 Randy Wells .75 2.00
BC75 Bradley Davis .30 .75
BC76 Jay Sawatski .30 .75
BC77 Vic Buttler .30 .75
BC78 Jose Oyervidez .30 .75
BC79 Doug Deeds .30 .75
BC80 Dan Dement .30 .75
BC81 Spike Lundberg .30 .75
BC82 Ricardo Nanita .30 .75
BC83 Brad Knox .30 .75
BC84 Will Venable .50 1.25
BC85 Greg Smith .50 1.25
BC86 Pedro Powell .30 .75
BC87 Gabriel Medina .30 .75
BC88 Duke Sardinha .30 .75
BC89 Mike Madsen .30 .75
BC90 Rayner Bautista .30 .75
BC91 T.J. Nall .30 .75
BC92 Neil Sellers .30 .75
BC93 Andrew Dobies .30 .75
BC94 Leo Daigle .30 .75
BC95 Brian Duensing .50 1.25
BC96 Vincent Blue .30 .75
BC97 Fernando Rodriguez .30 .75
BC98 Derin McMains .30 .75
BC99 Adam Bass .30 .75
BC100 Justin Ruggiano .50 1.25
BC101 Jared Burton .30 .75
BC102 Mike Parisi .30 .75
BC103 Aaron Peel .30 .75
BC104 Evan Englebrook .30 .75
BC105 Sendy Vasquez .30 .75
BC106 Desmond Jennings 1.25 3.00
BC107 Clay Harris .30 .75
BC108 Cody Strait .30 .75
BC109 Ryan Mullins .30 .75
BC110 Ryan Webb .30 .75
BC111 Mike Carp 1.00 2.50
BC112 Gregory Porter .30 .75
BC113 Joe Ness .30 .75
BC114 Matt Camp .30 .75
BC115 Carlos Fisher .30 .75
BC116 Bryan Bass .30 .75
BC117 Jeff Baisley .50 1.25
BC118 Burke Badenhop .50 1.25
BC119 Grant Psomas .30 .75
BC120 Eric Young Jr. .50 1.25
BC121 Henry Rodriguez .30 .75
BC122 Carlos Fernandez-Oliva .50 1.25
BC123 Chris Errecart .50 1.25
BC124 Brandon Hynick .75 2.00
BC125 Jose Constanza .75 2.00
BC126 Steve Delabar .30 .75
BC127 Raul Barron .30 .75
BC128 Nick DeBarr .30 .75
BC129 Reegie Corona .50 1.25
BC130 Thomas Fairchild .30 .75
BC131 Bryan Byrne .30 .75
BC132 Kurt Mertins .30 .75
BC133 Erik Averill .30 .75
BC134 Matt Young .30 .75
BC135 Ryan Rogowski .30 .75
BC136 Andrew Bailey 1.25 3.00
BC137 Jonathan Van Every .30 .75
BC138 Scott Shoemaker .30 .75
BC139 Steve Singleton .30 .75
BC140 Mitch Atkins .30 .75
BC141 Robert Rohrbaugh .50 1.25
BC142 Ole Sheldon .30 .75
BC143 Adam Ricks .30 .75
BC144 Daniel Mayora .75 2.00
BC145 Johnny Cueto 1.00 2.50
BC146 Jim Fasano .30 .75
BC147 Jared Goedert .75 2.00
BC148 Jonathan Ash .30 .75
BC149 Derek Miller .50 1.25
BC150 Juan Miranda .50 1.25
BC151 J.R. Mathes .30 .75
BC152 Craig Cooper .50 1.25
BC153 Drew Locke .30 .75
BC154 Michael MacDonald .30 .75
BC155 Ryan Norwood .30 .75
BC156 Tony Butler .75 2.00
BC157 Pat Dobson .30 .75
BC158 Cody Ehlers .30 .75
BC159 Dan Fournier .30 .75
BC160 Joe Gaetti .30 .75
BC161 Mark Wagner .50 1.25
BC162 Tommy Hanson 1.00 2.50
BC163 Sharlon Schoop .30 .75
BC164 Woods Fines .30 .75
BC165 Chad Boyd .30 .75
BC166 Kala Kaaihue .50 1.25
BC167 Chris Salamida .30 .75
BC168 Brendan Katin .30 .75
BC169 Terrance Blunt .30 .75
BC170 Tobi Stoner .30 .75
BC171 Phil Coke .50 1.25
BC172 O.D. Gonzalez .30 .75
BC173 Christopher Cody .30 .75
BC174 Cedric Hunter .75 2.00
BC175 Whit Robbins .30 .75
BC176 Chris Begg .30 .75
BC177 Nathan Southard .30 .75
BC178 Dan Brauer .30 .75
BC179 Jared Keel .30 .75
BC180 Chance Douglass .30 .75
BC181 Daniel Murphy 1.50 4.00
BC182 Anthony Hatch .30 .75
BC183 Justin Byler .30 .75
BC184 Scott Lewis .75 2.00
BC185 Andrew Fie .30 .75
BC186 Chorye Spoone .50 1.25
BC187 Cole Bruce .30 .75
BC188 Adam Cowart .75 2.00
BC189 Chris Nowak .30 .75
BC190 Gorkys Hernandez .75 2.00
BC191 Devin Ivany .30 .75
BC192 Jordan Smith .30 .75
BC193 Philip Britton .30 .75
BC194 Cole Gillespie .50 1.25
BC195 Brett Anderson .75 2.00
BC196 Joe Mather .30 .75
BC197 Eddie Degerman .30 .75
BC198 Ronald Prettyman .30 .75
BC199 Patrick Reilly .30 .75
BC200 Tyler Clippard .50 1.25
BC201 Nick Van Stratten .30 .75
BC202 Todd Redmond .30 .75
BC203 Michael Martinez .30 .75
BC204 Alberto Bastardo .30 .75
BC205 Vasili Spanos .30 .75
BC206 Shane Benson .30 .75
BC207 Brent Johnson .30 .75
BC208 Brett Campbell .30 .75
BC209 Dustin Martin .30 .75
BC210 Chris Carter 1.00 2.50
BC211 Alfred Joseph .30 .75
BC212 Carlos Leon .30 .75
BC213 Gabriel Sanchez .50 1.25
BC214 Carlos Corporan .30 .75
BC215 Emerson Frostad .30 .75
BC216 Karl Gelinas .30 .75
BC217 Ryan Finan .30 .75
BC218 Noe Rodriguez .30 .75
BC219 Archie Gilbert .30 .75
BC220 Jeff Locke .75 2.00
BC221 Fernando Martinez AU 6.00 15.00
BC222 Jeremy Papelbon AU 3.00 8.00
BC223 Ryan Adams AU 3.00 8.00
BC224 Chris Perez AU 4.00 10.00
BC225 J.R. Towles AU 3.00 8.00
BC226 Tommy Mendoza AU 3.00 8.00
BC227 Jeff Samardzija AU 5.00 12.00
BC228 Sergio Perez AU 3.00 8.00
BC229 Justin Reed AU 3.00 8.00
BC230 Luke Hochevar AU 3.00 8.00
BC231 Ivan De Jesus Jr. AU 3.00 8.00
BC232 Kevin Mulvey AU 3.00 8.00
BC233 Chris Coghlan AU 4.00 10.00
BC234 Trevor Cahill AU 3.00 8.00
BC235 Peter Bourjos AU 3.00 8.00
BC236 Joba Chamberlain AU 3.00 8.00
BC237 Josh Rodriguez AU 3.00 8.00
BC238 Tim Lincecum AU 20.00 50.00
BC239 Josh Papelbon AU 3.00 8.00
BC240 Greg Reynolds AU 3.00 8.00
BC241 Wes Hodges AU 3.00 8.00
BC242 Chad Reineke AU 3.00 8.00
BC243 Emmanuel Burriss AU 4.00 10.00
BC244 Henry Sosa AU 3.00 8.00
BC245 Cesar Nicolas AU 3.00 8.00
BC246 Young Il Jung AU 3.00 8.00
BC247 Eric Patterson AU 3.00 8.00
BC248 Hunter Pence AU 8.00 20.00
BC249 Dellin Betances AU 10.00 25.00
BC250 Will Venable AU 3.00 8.00
BC251 Zach McAllister AU 3.00 8.00
BC252 Mark Hamilton AU 3.00 8.00
BC253 Paul Estrada AU 3.00 8.00
BC254 Brad Lincoln AU 3.00 8.00
BC255 Cedric Hunter AU 3.00 8.00
BC256 Chad Rodgers AU 3.00 8.00

2007 Bowman Chrome Prospects Refractors
*REF 1-110: 2X TO 5X BASIC CHROME
*REF 111-220: 2X TO 5X BASIC CHROME
1-110 ODDS 1:48 H, 1:8 HTA, 1:142 R
111-220 ODDS 1:27 HOB, 1:186 RET
*REF AU 221-256: .5X TO 1.2X BASIC
221-256 AU ODDS 1:89 HOB, 1:197 RET
STATED PRINT RUN 500 SERIAL #'d SETS
1-110 ISSUED IN BOWMAN PACKS
111-256 ISSUED IN BOW.CHROME PACKS
EXCHANGE DEADLINE 8/31/2009

2007 Bowman Chrome Prospects Blue Refractors
*BLUE 1-110: 4X TO 10X BASIC CHROME
*BLUE 111-220: 4X TO 10X BASIC CHROME
1-110 ODDS 1:481 H, 1:80 HTA, 1:1375 R
111-220 ODDS 1:30 H, 1:205 R
*BLUE AU 221-256: 1X TO 2.5X BASIC
221-256 AU ODDS 1:296 HOB, 1:825 RET
STATED PRINT RUN 150 SER.#'d SETS
1-110 ISSUED IN BOWMAN PACKS
111-256 ISSUED IN BOW.CHROME PACKS
EXCHANGE DEADLINE 8/31/2009

2007 Bowman Chrome Prospects Gold Refractors
*GOLD 1-110: 12X TO 30X BASIC CHROME
*GOLD 111-220: 12X TO 30X BASIC CHROME
1-110 ODDS 1:481 H, 1:80 HTA, 1:1375 R
111-220 ODDS 1:88 HOB, 1:615 RET
221-256 AU ODDS 1:889 HOB, 1:8500 RET
STATED PRINT RUN 50 SER.#'d SETS
1-110 ISSUED IN BOWMAN PACKS
111-256 ISSUED IN BOW.CHROME PACKS
EXCHANGE DEADLINE 8/31/2009
BC221 Fernando Martinez AU 50.00 100.00
BC222 Jeremy Papelbon AU 10.00 25.00
BC223 Ryan Adams AU 10.00 25.00
BC224 Chris Perez AU 40.00 80.00
BC225 J.R. Towles AU 10.00 25.00
BC226 Tommy Mendoza AU 10.00 25.00
BC227 Jeff Samardzija AU 15.00 40.00
BC228 Sergio Perez AU 10.00 25.00
BC229 Justin Reed AU 10.00 25.00
BC230 Luke Hochevar AU 10.00 25.00
BC231 Ivan De Jesus Jr. AU 10.00 25.00
BC232 Kevin Mulvey AU 10.00 25.00
BC233 Chris Coghlan AU 40.00 80.00
BC234 Trevor Cahill AU 10.00 25.00
BC235 Peter Bourjos AU 10.00 25.00
BC236 Joba Chamberlain AU 10.00 25.00
BC237 Josh Rodriguez AU 10.00 25.00
BC238 Tim Lincecum AU 100.00 250.00
BC239 Josh Papelbon AU 10.00 60.00
BC240 Greg Reynolds AU 10.00 60.00
BC241 Wes Hodges AU 10.00 60.00
BC242 Chad Reineke AU 10.00 60.00
BC243 Emmanuel Burriss AU 10.00 60.00
BC244 Henry Sosa AU 10.00 60.00
BC245 Cesar Nicolas AU 10.00 60.00
BC246 Young Il Jung AU 10.00 60.00
BC247 Eric Patterson AU 10.00 25.00
BC249 Dellin Betances AU 50.00 120.00
BC250 Will Venable AU 10.00 25.00
BC251 Zach McAllister AU 10.00 25.00
BC252 Mark Hamilton AU 10.00 25.00
BC253 Paul Estrada AU 10.00 25.00
BC254 Brad Lincoln AU 10.00 25.00
BC255 Cedric Hunter AU 10.00 25.00
BC256 Chad Rodgers AU 10.00 25.00

2007 Bowman Chrome Prospects Orange Refractors
1-110 ODDS 1:961 H, 1:160 HTA, 1:2800 R
111-220 ODDS 1:176 HOB, 1:1220 RET
221-256 AU ODDS 1:1780 HOB, 1:3650 RET
STATED PRINT RUN 25 SER.#'d SETS
1-110 ISSUED IN BOWMAN PACKS
111-220 ISSUED IN BOW.CHROME PACKS
NO PRICING DUE TO SCARCITY
EXCHANGE DEADLINE 8/31/2009

2007 Bowman Chrome Prospects X-Fractors
*X-F 1-110: 2.5X TO 6X BASIC CHROME
*X-F 111-220: 2.5X TO 6X BASIC CHROME
1-110 ODDS 1:87 H, 1:15 HTA, 1:260 R
111-220 ODDS 1:18 H, 1:123 R
1-110 PRINT RUN 275 SER.#'d SETS
111-220 PRINT RUN 250 SER.#'d SETS
*X-F AU 221-256: .6X TO 1.5.X BASIC
221-256 AU ODDS 1:198 HOB, 1:480 RET
211-256 PRINT RUN 225 SERIAL #'d SETS
1-110 ISSUED IN BOWMAN PACKS
111-256 ISSUED IN BOW.CHROME PACKS
EXCHANGE DEADLINE 8/31/2009

2007 Bowman Chrome Draft
COMPLETE SET (55) 15.00 40.00
COMMON RC (1-55) .25 .60
OVERALL PLATE ODDS 1:1294 HOBBY
PLATE PRINT RUN 1 SET PER COLOR
BLACK-CYAN-MAGENTA-YELLOW ISSUED
NO PLATE PRICING DUE TO SCARCITY
BDP1 Travis Buck (RC) .25 .60
BDP2 Matt Chico (RC) .25 .60
BDP3 Justin Upton RC .75 2.00
BDP4 Chase Wright RC .60 1.50
BDP5 Kevin Kouzmanoff (RC) .25 .60
BDP6 John Danks RC .40 1.00
BDP7 Alejandro De Aza RC .40 1.00
BDP8 Jamie Vermilyea RC .25 .60
BDP9 Jesus Flores RC .25 .60
BDP10 Glen Perkins (RC) .25 .60
BDP11 Tim Lincecum RC 1.25 3.00
BDP12 Cameron Maybin RC .40 1.00
BDP13 Brandon Morrow RC 1.25 3.00
BDP14 Mike Rabelo RC .25 .60
BDP15 Alex Gordon RC .75 2.00
BDP16 Zack Segovia (RC) .25 .60
BDP17 Jon Knott (RC) .25 .60
BDP18 Joba Chamberlain RC .40 1.00
BDP19 Danny Putnam (RC) .25 .60
BDP20 Matt DeSalvo (RC) .25 .60
BDP21 Fred Lewis (RC) .40 1.00
BDP22 Sean Gallagher (RC) .25 .60
BDP23 Brandon Wood (RC) .25 .60
BDP24 Dennis Dove (RC) .25 .60
BDP25 Hunter Pence (RC) .75 2.00
BDP26 Jarrod Saltalamacchia (RC) .40 1.00
BDP27 Ben Francisco (RC) .25 .60
BDP28 Doug Slaten RC .25 .60
BDP29 Tony Abreu RC .60 1.50
BDP30 Billy Butler (RC) .40 1.00
BDP31 Jesse Litsch RC .40 1.00
BDP32 Nate Schierholtz (RC) .25 .60
BDP33 Jared Burton RC .25 .60
BDP34 Matt Brown (RC) .25 .60
BDP35 Dallas Braden RC .40 1.00
BDP36 Carlos Gomez RC .50 1.25
BDP37 Brian Stokes (RC) .25 .60
BDP38 Kory Casto (RC) .25 .60
BDP39 Mark McLemore (RC) .25 .60
BDP40 Andy LaRoche (RC) .25 .60
BDP41 Tyler Clippard (RC) .40 1.00
BDP42 Curtis Thigpen (RC) .25 .60
BDP43 Yunel Escobar (RC) .25 .60
BDP44 Andy Sonnanstine RC .25 .60
BDP45 Felix Pie (RC) .25 .60
BDP46 Homer Bailey (RC) .40 1.00
BDP47 Kyle Kendrick RC .60 1.50
BDP48 Angel Sanchez RC .25 .60
BDP49 Phil Hughes (RC) .60 1.50
BDP50 Ryan Braun (RC) 1.25 3.00
BDP51 Kevin Slowey (RC) .60 1.50
BDP52 Brendan Ryan (RC) .25 .60
BDP53 Yovani Gallardo (RC) .60 1.50
BDP54 Mark Reynolds RC .75 2.00
237 Barry Bonds 1.00 2.50

2007 Bowman Chrome Draft Refractors
*REF: 1X TO 2.5X BASIC
STATED ODDS 1:11 HOBBY,1:11 RETAIL

2007 Bowman Chrome Draft Blue Refractors
*BLUE REF: 2X TO 5X BASIC
STATED ODDS 1:58 HOBBY,1:171 RETAIL
STATED PRINT RUN 199 SER.#'d SETS

2007 Bowman Chrome Draft Gold Refractors
*GOLD REF: 5X TO 12X BASIC
STATED ODDS 1:232 H, 1:659 R
STATED PRINT RUN 50 SER.#'d SETS

2007 Bowman Chrome Draft Orange Refractors
STATED ODDS 1:463 H, 1:1349 R
STATED PRINT RUN 25 SER.#'d SETS
NO PRICING DUE TO SCARCITY

2007 Bowman Chrome Draft X-Fractors
*X-F: 1.5X TO 4X BASIC
STATED ODDS 1:39 HOBBY,1:106 RETAIL
STATED PRINT RUN 299 SER.#'d SETS

2007 Bowman Chrome Draft Draft Picks
66-95 AU ODDS 1:38 HOBBY,1:575 RETAIL
1-65 PLATE ODDS 1:1294 HOBBY
66-95 AU PLATE ODDS 1:14,255 HOBBY
PLATE PRINT RUN 1 SET PER COLOR
BLACK-CYAN-MAGENTA-YELLOW ISSUED
NO PLATE PRICING DUE TO SCARCITY
BDPP1 Cody Crowell .30 .75
BDPP2 Karl Bolt .50 1.25
BDPP3 Corey Brown .50 1.25
BDPP4 Tyler Mach .50 1.25
BDPP5 Trevor Pippin .50 1.25
BDPP6 Ed Easley .30 .75
BDPP7 Cory Luebke .30 .75
BDPP8 Darin Mastroianni .30 .75
BDPP9 Ryan Zink .50 1.25
BDPP10 Brandon Hamilton .30 .75
BDPP11 Kyle Lotzkar .50 1.25
BDPP12 Freddie Freeman 5.00 12.00
BDPP13 Nicholas Barnese .50 1.25
BDPP14 Travis d'Arnaud .50 1.25
BDPP15 Eric Eiland .30 .75
BDPP16 John Ely .30 .75
BDPP17 Oliver Marmol .30 .75
BDPP18 Eric Sogard .30 .75
BDPP19 Lars Davis .30 .75
BDPP20 Sam Runion .30 .75
BDPP21 Austin Gallagher .50 1.25
BDPP22 Matt West .50 1.25
BDPP23 Derek Norris .75 2.00
BDPP24 Taylor Holiday .50 1.25
BDPP25 Dustin Biell .30 .75
BDPP26 Julio Borbon .50 1.25
BDPP27 Brant Rustich .50 1.25
BDPP28 Andrew Lambo .50 1.25
BDPP29 Cory Kluber 1.50 4.00
BDPP30 Justin Jackson .50 1.25
BDPP31 Scott Carroll .30 .75
BDPP32 Danny Rams .30 .75
BDPP33 Thomas Eager .30 .75
BDPP34 Matt Dominguez .75 2.00
BDPP35 Steven Souza 1.00 2.50
BDPP36 Craig Heyer .30 .75
BDPP37 Michael Taylor 1.25 3.00
BDPP38 Drew Bowman .30 .75
BDPP39 Frank Gailey .30 .75
BDPP40 Jeremy Hefner .30 .75
BDPP41 Reynaldo Navarro .50 1.25
BDPP42 Daniel Descalso .50 1.25
BDPP43 Leroy Hunt .30 .75
BDPP44 Jason Kiley .30 .75
BDPP45 Ryan Pope .75 2.00
BDPP46 Josh Horton .30 .75
BDPP47 Jason Monti .30 .75
BDPP48 Richard Lucas .30 .75
BDPP49 Jonathan Lucroy .75 2.00
BDPP50 Sean Doolittle .30 .75
BDPP51 Mike McDade .50 1.25
BDPP52 Charlie Culberson .50 1.25
BDPP53 Michael Moustakas .75 2.00
BDPP54 Jason Heyward 2.00 5.00
BDPP55 David Price 1.00 2.50
BDPP56 Brad Mills .30 .75
BDPP57 John Tolisano 1.00 2.50
BDPP58 Jarrod Parker .75 2.00
BDPP59 Wendell Fairley .50 1.25
BDPP60 Gary Gattis .30 .75
BDPP61 Madison Bumgarner 3.00 8.00
BDPP62 Danny Payne .30 .75
BDPP63 Jake Smolinski 1.00 2.50
BDPP64 Matt LaPorta 1.00 2.50
BDPP65 Jackson Williams .30 .75
BDPP111 Daniel Moskos AU 3.00 8.00
BDPP112 Ross Detwiler AU 3.00 8.00
BDPP113 Tim Alderson AU 3.00 8.00
BDPP114 Beau Mills AU 3.00 8.00
BDPP115 Devin Mesoraco AU 6.00 15.00
BDPP116 Kyle Lotzkar AU 3.00 8.00
BDPP117 Blake Beavan AU 3.00 8.00
BDPP118 Peter Kozma AU 3.00 8.00
BDPP119 Chris Withrow AU 3.00 8.00
BDPP120 Cory Luebke AU 3.00 8.00
BDPP121 Nick Schmidt AU 3.00 8.00
BDPP122 Michael Main AU 3.00 8.00
BDPP123 Aaron Poreda AU 3.00 8.00
BDPP124 James Simmons AU 3.00 8.00
BDPP125 Ben Revere AU 3.00 8.00
BDPP126 Joe Savery AU 3.00 8.00
BDPP127 Jonathan Gilmore AU 3.00 8.00
BDPP128 Todd Frazier AU 6.00 15.00
BDPP129 Matt Mangini AU 3.00 8.00
BDPP130 Casey Weathers AU 3.00 8.00
BDPP131 Nick Noonan AU 3.00 8.00
BDPP132 Kellen Kulbacki AU 3.00 8.00
BDPP133 Michael Burgess AU 3.00 8.00
BDPP134 Nick Hagadone AU 3.00 8.00
BDPP135 Clayton Mortensen AU 3.00 8.00
BDPP136 Justin Jackson AU 3.00 8.00
BDPP137 Ed Easley AU 3.00 8.00
BDPP138 Corey Brown AU 3.00 8.00
BDPP139 Danny Payne AU 3.00 8.00
BDPP140 Travis d'Arnaud AU 8.00 20.00

2007 Bowman Chrome Draft Draft Picks Refractors
*REF 1-65: 1.5X TO 4X BASIC
1-65 ODDS 1:11 HOBBY,1:11 RETAIL
*REF AU 66-95: .5X TO 1.2X BASIC AU
AU 66-95 ODDS 1:118 H, 1:1700 R
66-95 AU PRINT RUN 500 SER.#'d SETS

2007 Bowman Chrome Draft Draft Picks Blue Refractors
*BLUE REF 1-65: 4X TO 10X BASIC
1-65 ODDS 1:58 HOBBY, 1:171 HOBBY
1-65 PRINT RUN 199 SER.#'d SETS
*BLUE REF AU 66-95: 1X TO 2.5X BASIC AU
AU 66-95 ODDS 1:400 H, 1:12,000 R
66-95 AU PRINT RUN 150 SER.#'d SETS

2007 Bowman Chrome Draft Draft Picks Gold Refractors
*GOLD REF 1-65: 8X TO 20X BASIC
1-65 ODDS 1:232 H, 1:659 R
1-65 PRINT RUN 50 SER.#'d SETS
COMMON AUTO (66-95) 30.00 60.00
AU 66-95 ODDS 1:1270 H, 1:9440 R
66-95 AU PRINT RUN 50 SER.#'d SETS
BDPP111 Daniel Moskos AU 12.50 30.00
BDPP112 Ross Detwiler AU 12.50 30.00
BDPP113 Tim Alderson AU 12.50 30.00
BDPP114 Beau Mills AU 12.50 30.00
BDPP115 Devin Mesoraco AU 40.00 100.00
BDPP116 Kyle Lotzkar AU 12.50 30.00
BDPP117 Blake Beavan AU 12.50 30.00
BDPP118 Peter Kozma AU 12.50 30.00
BDPP119 Chris Withrow AU 12.50 30.00
BDPP120 Cory Luebke AU 12.50 30.00
BDPP121 Nick Schmidt AU 12.50 30.00

BDPP122 Michael Main AU 12.50 30.00
BDPP123 Aaron Poreda AU 12.50 30.00
BDPP124 James Simmons AU 12.50 30.00
BDPP125 Ben Revere AU 12.50 30.00
BDPP126 Joe Savery AU 12.00 30.00
BDPP127 Jonathan Gilmore AU 12.00 30.00
BDPP129 Matt Mangini AU 12.50 30.00
BDPP130 Casey Weathers AU 12.50 30.00
BDPP131 Nick Noonan AU 12.50 30.00
BDPP132 Kellen Kulbacki AU 12.50 30.00
BDPP133 Michael Burgess AU 12.50 30.00
BDPP134 Nick Hagadone AU 12.50 30.00
BDPP135 Clayton Mortensen AU 12.50 30.00
BDPP136 Justin Jackson AU 12.50 30.00
BDPP137 Ed Easley AU 12.50 30.00
BDPP138 Corey Brown AU 12.50 30.00
BDPP139 Danny Payne AU 12.50 30.00
BDPP140 Travis d'Arnaud AU 75.00 150.00

2007 Bowman Chrome Draft Draft Picks Orange Refractors

1-65 STATED ODDS 1:463 H,1:1349 R
66-95 AU ODDS 1:2345 H, 1:28,320 R
STATED PRINT RUN 25 SERIAL #'d SETS
NO PRICING DUE TO SCARCITY

2007 Bowman Chrome Draft Draft Picks X-Fractors

*X-F 1-65: 2.5X TO 6X BASIC
1-65 STATED ODDS 1:39 H, 1:106 R
1-65 PRINT RUN 299 SER.#'d SETS
*X-F AU 66-95: .6X TO 1.5X BASIC
66-95 AU STATED ODDS 1:262 H,1:14,000 R
66-95 AU PRINT RUN 225 SER.#'d SETS

2007 Bowman Chrome Draft Future's Game Prospects

COMPLETE SET (45) 12.50 30.00
OVERALL PLATE ODDS 1:1294 HOBBY
PLATE PRINT RUN 1 SET PER COLOR
BLACK-CYAN-MAGENTA-YELLOW ISSUED
NO PLATE PRICING DUE TO SCARCITY
BDPP66 Pedro Beato .20 .50
BDPP67 Collin Balester .20 .50
BDPP68 Carlos Carrasco .30 .75
BDPP69 Clay Buchholz .60 1.50
BDPP70 Emiliano Fruto .20 .50
BDPP71 Joba Chamberlain .30 .75
BDPP72 Deolis Guerra .40 1.00
BDPP73 Kevin Mulvey .50 1.25
BDPP74 Franklin Morales .30 .75
BDPP75 Luke Hochevar .60 1.50
BDPP76 Henry Sosa .30 .75
BDPP77 Clayton Kershaw 5.00 12.00
BDPP78 Rich Thompson .20 .50
BDPP79 Chuck Lofgren .50 1.25
BDPP80 Rick VandenHurk .20 .50
BDPP81 Michael Madsen .20 .50
BDPP82 Robinzon Diaz .20 .50
BDPP83 Jeff Niemann .30 .75
BDPP84 Max Ramirez .20 .50
BDPP85 Geovany Soto .75 2.00
BDPP86 Elvis Andrus .50 1.25
BDPP87 Bryan Anderson .20 .50
BDPP88 German Duran .75 2.00
BDPP89 J.R. Towles .60 1.50
BDPP90 Alcides Escobar .50 1.25
BDPP91 Brian Bocock .20 .50
BDPP92 Chin-Lung Hu .20 .50
BDPP93 Adrian Cardenas .20 .50
BDPP94 Freddy Sandoval .20 .50
BDPP95 Chris Coghlan .60 1.50
BDPP96 Craig Stansberry .20 .50
BDPP97 Brent Lillibridge .20 .50
BDPP98 Joey Votto 1.25 3.00
BDPP99 Evan Longoria 2.00 5.00
BDPP100 Wladimir Balentien .20 .50
BDPP101 Johnny Whittleman .20 .50
BDPP102 Gorkys Hernandez .50 1.25
BDPP103 Jay Bruce 1.25 3.00
BDPP104 Matt Tolbert .20 .50
BDPP105 Jacoby Ellsbury 1.25 3.00
BDPP106 Michael Saunders .60 1.50
BDPP107 Cameron Maybin .30 .75
BDPP108 Carlos Gonzalez .50 1.25
BDPP109 Colby Rasmus .50 1.25
BDPP110 Justin Upton .60 1.50

2007 Bowman Chrome Draft Future's Game Prospects Refractors

*REF: 1X TO 2.5X BASIC
STATED ODDS 1:11 HOBBY,1:11 RETAIL

2007 Bowman Chrome Draft Future's Game Prospects Blue Refractors

*BLUE REF: 2X TO 5X BASIC
STATED ODDS 1:58 HOBBY,1:171 RETAIL
STATED PRINT RUN 199 SER.#'d SETS

2007 Bowman Chrome Draft Future's Game Prospects Gold Refractors

*GOLD REF: 5X TO 12X BASIC
STATED ODDS 1:232 H, 1:659 R
STATED PRINT RUN 50 SER.#'d SETS

2007 Bowman Chrome Draft Future's Game Prospects Orange Refractors

STATED ODDS 1:463 H, 1:1349 R
STATED PRINT RUN 25 SER.#'d SETS
NO PRICING DUE TO SCARCITY

2007 Bowman Chrome Draft Future's Game Prospects X-Fractors

*X-F: 1.5X TO 4X BASIC
STATED ODDS 1:39 HOBBY,1:106 RETAIL
STATED PRINT RUN 299 SER.#'d SETS

2007 Bowman Chrome Draft Future's Game Prospects Bases

STATED ODDS 1:633 HOBBY
STATED PRINT RUN 135 SER.#'d SETS
BDPP86 Elvis Andrus 4.00 10.00
BDPP87 Bryan Anderson 3.00 8.00
BDPP88 German Duran 3.00 8.00
BDPP89 J.R. Towles 3.00 8.00
BDPP91 Brian Bocock 3.00 8.00
BDPP92 Chin-Lung Hu 10.00 25.00
BDPP93 Adrian Cardenas 3.00 8.00
BDPP94 Freddy Sandoval 3.00 8.00
BDPP95 Chris Coghlan 3.00 8.00
BDPP97 Brent Lillibridge 4.00 10.00
BDPP98 Joey Votto 5.00 12.00
BDPP99 Evan Longoria 12.50 30.00
BDPP101 Johnny Whittleman 3.00 8.00
BDPP102 Gorkys Hernandez 4.00 10.00
BDPP103 Jay Bruce 6.00 15.00
BDPP105 Jacoby Ellsbury 6.00 15.00
BDPP106 Michael Saunders 4.00 10.00
BDPP108 Carlos Gonzalez 4.00 10.00
BDPP109 Colby Rasmus 6.00 15.00
BDPP110 Justin Upton 10.00 25.00

2008 Bowman Chrome

COMPLETE SET (220) 15.00 40.00
COMMON CARD (1-190) .20 .50
COMMON ROOKIE (1-220) .60 1.50
1-220 PLATE ODDS 1:1382 HOBBY
PLATE PRINT RUN 1 SET PER COLOR
BLACK-CYAN-MAGENTA-YELLOW ISSUED
NO PLATE PRICING DUE TO SCARCITY
1 Ryan Braun .30 .75
2 David DeJesus .20 .50
3 Brandon Phillips .20 .50
4 Mark Teixeira .30 .75
5 Daisuke Matsuzaka .30 .75
6 Justin Upton .30 .75
7 Jered Weaver .30 .75
8 Todd Helton .30 .75
9 Adam Jones .30 .75
10 Erik Bedard .20 .50
11 Jason Bay .30 .75
12 Cole Hamels .40 1.00
13 Bobby Abreu .20 .50
14 Carlos Zambrano .30 .75
15 Vladimir Guerrero .30 .75
16 Joe Blanton .20 .50
17 Paul Maholm .20 .50
18 Adrian Gonzalez .30 .75
19 Brandon Webb .30 .75
20 Carl Crawford .30 .75
21 A.J. Burnett .20 .50
22 Dmitri Young .20 .50
23 Jeremy Hermida .20 .50
24 C.C. Sabathia .30 .75
25 Adam Dunn .30 .75
26 Matt Garza .20 .50
27 Adrian Beltre .50 1.25
28 Kevin Millwood .20 .50
29 Manny Ramirez .50 1.25
30 Javier Vazquez .20 .50
31 Carlos Delgado .20 .50
32 Torii Hunter .20 .50
33 Ivan Rodriguez .30 .75
34 Nick Markakis .40 1.00
35 Gil Meche .20 .50
36 Garrett Atkins .20 .50
37 Fausto Carmona .20 .50
38 Joe Mauer .40 1.00
39 Tom Glavine .30 .75
40 Hideki Matsui .50 1.25
41 Scott Rolen .30 .75
42 Tim Lincecum .30 .75
43 Prince Fielder .30 .75
44 Kazuo Matsui .20 .50
45 Tom Gorzelanny .20 .50
46 Lance Berkman .30 .75
47 David Ortiz .50 1.25
48 Dontrelle Willis .20 .50
49 Travis Hafner .20 .50
50 Aaron Harang .20 .50
51 Chris Young .20 .50
52 Vernon Wells .20 .50
53 Francisco Liriano .20 .50
54 Eric Chavez .20 .50
55 Phil Hughes .20 .50
56 Melvin Mora .20 .50
57 Johan Santana .30 .75
58 Brian McCann .30 .75
59 Pat Burrell .20 .50
60 Chris Carpenter .30 .75
61 Brian Giles .20 .50
62 Jose Reyes .30 .75
63 Hanley Ramirez .30 .75
64 Ubaldo Jimenez .20 .50
65 Felix Pie .20 .50
66 Jeremy Bonderman .20 .50
67 Jimmy Rollins .30 .75
68 Miguel Tejada .30 .75
69 Derek Lowe .20 .50
70 Alex Gordon .30 .75
71 John Maine .20 .50
72 Alfonso Soriano .30 .75
73 Ben Sheets .20 .50
74 Hunter Pence .30 .75
75 Magglio Ordonez .30 .75
76 Josh Beckett .20 .50
77 Victor Martinez .30 .75
78 Mark Buehrle .30 .75
79 Jason Varitek .50 1.25
80 Chien-Ming Wang .30 .75
81 Ken Griffey Jr. 1.00 2.50
82 Billy Butler .20 .50
83 Brad Penny .20 .50
84 Carlos Beltran .30 .75
85 Curt Schilling .30 .75
86 Jorge Posada .30 .75
87 Andruw Jones .20 .50
88 Bobby Crosby .20 .50
89 Freddy Sanchez .20 .50
90 Barry Zito .30 .75
91 Miguel Cabrera .50 1.25
92 B.J. Upton .30 .75
93 Matt Cain .30 .75
94 Lyle Overbay .20 .50
95 Austin Kearns .20 .50
96 Alex Rodriguez .60 1.50
97 Rich Harden .20 .50
98 Justin Morneau .30 .75
99 Oliver Perez .20 .50
100 Gary Matthews .20 .50
101 Matt Holliday .50 1.25
102 Justin Verlander .50 1.25
103 Orlando Cabrera .30 .75
104 Rich Hill .20 .50
105 Tim Hudson .30 .75
106 Ryan Zimmerman .30 .75
107 Roy Oswalt .30 .75
108 Nick Swisher .30 .75
109 Raul Ibanez .30 .75
110 Kelly Johnson .20 .50
111 Alex Rios .20 .50
112 John Lackey .30 .75
113 Robinson Cano .30 .75
114 Michael Young .20 .50
115 Jeff Francis .20 .50
116 Grady Sizemore .30 .75
117 Mike Lowell .20 .50
118 Aramis Ramirez .20 .50
119 Stephen Drew .20 .50
120 Yovani Gallardo .20 .50
121 Chase Utley .30 .75
122 Dan Haren .20 .50
123 Yunel Escobar .20 .50
124 Greg Maddux .60 1.50
125 Garret Anderson .20 .50
126 Aubrey Huff .20 .50
127 Paul Konerko .30 .75
128 Dan Uggla .20 .50
129 Roy Halladay .30 .75
130 Andre Ethier .30 .75
131 Orlando Hernandez .20 .50
132 Troy Tulowitzki .50 1.25
133 Carlos Guillen .20 .50
134 Scott Kazmir .30 .75
135 Aaron Rowand .20 .50
136 Jim Edmonds .30 .75
137 Jermaine Dye .20 .50
138 Orlando Hudson .20 .50
139 Derrek Lee .20 .50
140 Travis Buck .30 .75
141 Zack Greinke .50 1.25
142 Jeff Kent .20 .50
143 John Smoltz .50 1.25
144 David Wright .30 .75
145 Joba Chamberlain .20 .50
146 Adam LaRoche .20 .50
147 Kevin Youkilis .20 .50
148 Troy Glaus .30 .75
149 Nick Johnson .20 .50
150 J.J. Hardy .20 .50
151 Felix Hernandez .30 .75
152 Gary Sheffield .20 .50
153 Albert Pujols .60 1.50
154 Chuck James .20 .50
155 Kosuke Fukudome RC 4.00 10.00
155b Kosuke Fukudome Japan 4.00 10.00
155c Fukudome No Sig/1600 * 10.00 25.00
156 Eric Byrnes .20 .50
157 Brad Hawpe .20 .50
158 Delmon Young .30 .75
159 Brian Roberts .20 .50
160 Russ Martin .20 .50
161 Hank Blalock .20 .50
162 Yadier Molina .60 1.50
163 Jeremy Guthrie .20 .50
164 Chipper Jones .50 1.25
165 Johnny Damon .30 .75
166 Ryan Garko .20 .50
167 Jake Peavy .20 .50
168 Chone Figgins .20 .50
169 Edgar Renteria .20 .50
170 Jim Thome .30 .75
171 Carlos Pena .30 .75
172 Dustin Pedroia .50 1.25
173 Brett Myers .20 .50
174 Josh Hamilton .30 .75
175 Randy Johnson .50 1.25
176 Ichiro Suzuki .60 1.50
177 Aaron Hill .20 .50
178 Corey Hart .20 .50
179 Jarrod Saltalamacchia .20 .50
180 Jeff Francoeur .30 .75
181 Derek Jeter 1.25 3.00
182 Curtis Granderson .30 .75
183 James Loney .20 .50
184 Brian Bannister .20 .50
185 Carlos Lee .20 .50
186 Pedro Martinez .30 .75
187 Asdrubal Cabrera .30 .75
188 Kenji Johjima .20 .50
189 Jacoby Ellsbury .40 1.00
190 Ryan Howard .30 .75
191 Sean Rodriguez (RC) .60 1.50
192 Justin Ruggiano RC 1.00 2.50
193 Jed Lowrie (RC) .60 1.50
194 Joey Votto (RC) 5.00 12.00
195 Denard Span (RC) 1.00 2.50
196 Brad Harman RC 1.00 2.50
197 Jeff Niemann (RC) .60 1.50
198 Chin-Lung Hu (RC) .60 1.50
199 Luke Hochevar RC 1.00 2.50
200 German Duran RC 1.00 2.50
201 Troy Patton (RC) .60 1.50
202 Hiroki Kuroda RC 1.50 4.00
203 David Purcey (RC) .60 1.50
204 Armando Galarraga RC 1.00 2.50
205 John Bowker (RC) .60 1.50
206 Nick Blackburn RC 1.00 2.50
207 Hernan Iribarren (RC) 1.00 2.50
208 Greg Smith RC .60 1.50
209 Alberto Gonzalez RC 1.00 2.50
210 Justin Masterson RC 1.50 4.00
211 Brian Barton RC 1.00 2.50
212 Robinzon Diaz (RC) .60 1.50
213 Clete Thomas RC 1.00 2.50
214 Kazuo Fukumori RC 1.00 2.50
215 Jayson Nix (RC) .60 1.50
216 Evan Longoria RC 3.00 8.00
217 Johnny Cueto RC 1.50 4.00
218 Matt Tolbert RC 1.00 2.50
219 Masahide Kobayashi RC 1.00 2.50
220 Callix Crabbe (RC) .60 1.50

2008 Bowman Chrome Refractors

*REF 1-190: 1X TO 2.5X BASIC
*REF 1-221: .6X TO 1.5X BASIC
1-221 ODDS

2008 Bowman Chrome Blue Refractors

*BLUE REF 1-190: 2.5X TO 6X BASIC
*BLUE REF 1-221: 1.2X TO 3X BASIC
1-221 ODDS 1:66 HOBBY
STATED PRINT RUN 150 SERIAL #'d SETS
198 Chin-Lung Hu 10.00 25.00
204 Armando Galarraga 10.00 25.00

2008 Bowman Chrome Gold Refractors

*GOLD REF 1-190: 4X TO 10X BASIC
*GOLD REF 1-221: 2X TO 5X BASIC
1-221 ODDS 1:197 HOBBY
STATED PRINT RUN 50 SERIAL #'d SETS
42 Tim Lincecum 15.00 40.00
80 Chien-Ming Wang 60.00 120.00
96 Alex Rodriguez 20.00 50.00
176 Ichiro Suzuki 20.00 50.00
181 Derek Jeter 30.00 60.00
189 Jacoby Ellsbury 15.00 40.00
198 Chin-Lung Hu 30.00 60.00
204 Armando Galarraga 30.00 60.00
210 Justin Masterson 20.00 50.00

2008 Bowman Chrome Orange Refractors

STATED ODDS 1:393 HOBBY
STATED PRINT RUN 25 SER.#'d SETS
NO PRICING DUE TO SCARCITY

2008 Bowman Chrome X-Fractors

*X-FRACTOR 1-190: 2X TO 5X BASIC
*X-FRACTOR 1-221: 1X TO 2.5X BASIC
1-221 ODDS 1:40 HOBBY
STATED PRINT RUN 250 SER.#'d SETS
155 Kosuke Fukudome 10.00 25.00
155b Kosuke Fukudome Japan 10.00 25.00
198 Chin-Lung Hu 5.00 12.00
204 Armando Galarraga 8.00 20.00

2008 Bowman Chrome Head of the Class Dual Autograph

STATED ODDS 1:1773 HOBBY
STATED PRINT RUN 350 SER.#'d SETS
CH Joba/P.Hughes 4.00 10.00
FL Prince Fielder/Matt LaPorta 8.00 20.00
LP E.Logoria/D.Price 12.00 30.00

2008 Bowman Chrome Head of the Class Dual Autograph X-Fractors

*X-F: .6X TO 1.5X BASIC
STATED ODDS 1:12,823 HOBBY
STATED PRINT RUN 50 SER.#'d SETS

2008 Bowman Chrome Head of the Class Dual Autograph Refractors

*REF: .5X TO 1.2X BASIC
STATED ODDS 1:6298 HOBBY
STATED PRINT RUN 99 SER.#'d SETS

2008 Bowman Chrome Prospects

COMP.SET w/o AU's (220) 30.00 60.00
COMP.SET w/o AU's (1-110) 12.50 30.00
COMP.SET w/o AU's (131-240) 12.50 30.00
111-130 AU ODDS 1:37 HOBBY
241-285 AU ODDS 1:31 HOBBY
1-110 PLATE ODDS 1:732 HOBBY
111=130 AU PLATE ODDS 1:4700 HOBBY
131-240 PLATE ODDS 1:1132 HOBBY
241-285 AU PLATES 1:10,471 HOBBY
PLATE PRINT RUN 1 SET PER COLOR
BLACK-CYAN-MAGENTA-YELLOW ISSUED
NO PLATE PRICING DUE TO SCARCITY
BCP1 Max Sapp .20 .50
BCP2 Jamie Richmond .20 .50
BCP3 Darren Ford .20 .50
BCP4 Sergio Romo 1.00 2.50
BCP5 Jacob Butler .20 .50
BCP6 Glenn Gibson .20 .50
BCP7 Tom Hagan .20 .50
BCP8 Michael McCormick .20 .50
BCP9 Gregorio Petit .30 .75
BCP10 Bobby Parnell .20 .50
BCP11 Jeff Kindel .30 .75
BCP12 Anthony Claggett .30 .75
BCP13 Christopher Frey .20 .50
BCP14 Jonah Nickerson .30 .75
BCP15 Anthony Martinez .20 .50
BCP16 Rusty Ryal .30 .75
BCP17 Justin Berg .30 .75
BCP18 Gerardo Parra .20 .50
BCP19 Wesley Wright .20 .50
BCP20 Stephen Chapman .20 .50
BCP21 Chance Chapman .20 .50
BCP22 Brett Pill .60 1.50
BCP23 Zachary Phillips .30 .75
BCP24 John Raynor .50 1.25
BCP25 Danny Duffy .50 1.25
BCP26 Brian Finegan .20 .50
BCP27 Jonathan Venters .20 .50
BCP28 Steve Tolleson .20 .50
BCP29 Ben Jukich .30 .75
BCP30 Matthew Weston .20 .50
BCP31 Kyle Mura .20 .50
BCP32 Luke Hetherington .20 .50
BCP33 Michael Daniel .30 .75
BCP34 Jake Renshaw .20 .50
BCP35 Greg Halman .30 .75
BCP36 Ryan Khoury .20 .50
BCP37 Ryan Ouellette .20 .50
BCP38 Mike Brantley .50 1.25
BCP39 Eric Brown .20 .50
BCP40 Jose Duarte .20 .50
BCP41 Eli Tintor .20 .50
BCP42 Kent Sakamoto .20 .50
BCP43 Luke Montz .20 .50
BCP44 Alex Cobb .20 .50
BCP45 Michael McKenry .20 .50
BCP46 Javier Castillo .20 .50
BCP47 Jeffrey Stevens .20 .50
BCP48 Greg Burns .20 .50
BCP49 Blake Johnson .20 .50
BCP50 Austin Jackson 1.00 2.50
BCP51 Anthony Recker .20 .50
BCP52 Luis Durango .20 .50
BCP53 Engel Beltre .60 1.50
BCP54 Seth Bynum .20 .50
BCP55 Ryan Strieby .30 .75
BCP56 Iggy Suarez .20 .50
BCP57 Ryan Morris .30 .75
BCP58 Scott Van Slyke .60 1.50
BCP59 Tyler Kolodny .60 1.50
BCP60 Joseph Martinez .20 .50
BCP61 Aaron Mathews .20 .50
BCP62 Phillip Cuadrado .20 .50
BCP63 Alex Liddi .30 .75
BCP64 Alex Burnett .30 .75
BCP65 Brian Barton .30 .75
BCP66 David Welch .20 .50
BCP67 Kyle Reynolds .20 .50
BCP68 Francisco Hernandez .20 .50
BCP69 Logan Morrison 1.00 2.50
BCP70 Ronald Ramirez .20 .50
BCP71 Brad Miller .20 .50
BCP72 Braedyn Pruitt .30 .75
BCP73 Jason Fernandez .30 .75
BCP74 Joseph Mahoney .20 .50
BCP75 Quentin Davis .30 .75
BCP76 P.J. Walters .20 .50
BCP77 Jordan Czarniecki .20 .50
BCP78 Jonathan Mota .20 .50
BCP79 Michael Hernandez .20 .50
BCP80 James Guerrero .20 .50
BCP81 Chris Johnson .30 .75
BCP82 Daniel Cortes .50 1.25
BCP83 Sal Sanchez .30 .75
BCP84 Sean Henry .20 .50
BCP85 Caleb Gindl .20 .50
BCP86 Tommy Everidge .20 .50
BCP87 Matt Rizzotti .20 .50
BCP88 Luis Munoz .20 .50
BCP89 Matthew Klimas .20 .50
BCP90 Angel Reyes .20 .50
BCP91 Sean Danielson .20 .50
BCP92 Omar Poveda .20 .50
BCP93 Mario Lisson .20 .50
BCP94 Brian Mathews .20 .50
BCP95 Matthew Buschmann .20 .50
BCP96 Greg Thomson .20 .50
BCP97 Matt Inouye .20 .50
BCP98 Aneury Rodriguez .30 .75
BCP99 Brad Harman .30 .75
BCP100 Aaron Bates .50 1.25
BCP101 Graham Taylor .20 .50
BCP102 Ken Holmberg .20 .50
BCP103 Greg Dowling .20 .50
BCP104 Ronnie Ray .20 .50
BCP105 Michael Wlodarczyk .20 .50
BCP106 Jose Martinez .30 .75
BCP107 Jason Stephens .30 .75
BCP108 Will Rhymes .20 .50
BCP109 Joey Side .20 .50
BCP110 Brandon Waring .30 .75
BCP111 David Price AU 12.00 30.00
BCP112 Michael Moustakas AU 5.00 12.00
BCP113 Matt LaPorta AU 3.00 8.00
BCP114 Wendell Fairley AU 3.00 8.00
BCP115 Josh Vitters AU 3.00 8.00
BCP116 Jonathan Bachanov AU 3.00 8.00
BCP117 Edward Kunz AU 3.00 8.00
BCP118 Matt Dominguez AU 3.00 8.00
BCP119 Kyle Lotzkar AU 3.00 8.00
BCP120 M.Bumgarner AU 40.00 100.00
BCP121 Jason Heyward AU 8.00 20.00
BCP122 Julio Borbon AU 3.00 8.00
BCP123 Josh Smoker AU 3.00 8.00
BCP124 Jarrod Parker AU 3.00 8.00
BCP125 Kevin Ahrens AU 3.00 8.00
BCP126 J.P. Arencibia AU 3.00 8.00
BCP127 Josh Bell AU 3.00 8.00
BCP128 Scott Cousins AU 3.00 8.00
BCP129 Brandon Hynick AU 3.00 8.00
BCP130 Alan Johnson AU 3.00 8.00
BCP131 Zhenwang Zhang .30 .75
BCP132 Chris Nash .20 .50
BCP133 Sergio Morales .20 .50
BCP134 Carlos Santana .60 1.50
BCP135 Carlos Monasterios .20 .50
BCP136 Quincy Latimore .20 .50
BCP137 Yamaico Navarro .60 1.50
BCP138 Ryan Mullins .20 .50
BCP139 Collin DeLome .30 .75
BCP140 Hector Correa .20 .50
BCP141 Mitch Canham .20 .50
BCP142 Robert Fish .20 .50
BCP143 Ryan Royster .20 .50
BCP144 Eric Barrett .20 .50
BCP145 Deibinson Romero .30 .75
BCP146 Jeff Gerbe .20 .50
BCP147 Lucas Duda .60 1.50
BCP148 Bryan Morris .30 .75
BCP149 Andrew Romine .20 .50
BCP150 Glenn Gibson .20 .50
BCP151 Danny Brezeale .20 .50
BCP152 Shairon Martis .30 .75
BCP153 Helder Velazquez .20 .50
BCP154 Alan Farina .20 .50
BCP155 Brandon Barnes .20 .50
BCP156 Waldis Joaquin .20 .50
BCP157 Luis De La Cruz .20 .50
BCP158 Yunesky Sanchez .20 .50
BCP159 Mitch Hilligross .20 .50
BCP160 Vin Mazzaro .60 1.50
BCP161 Marcus Davis .20 .50
BCP162 Tony Barnette .20 .50
BCP163 Joe Benson .50 1.25
BCP164 Jake Arrieta .50 1.25
BCP165 Alfredo Silverio .50 1.25
BCP166 Duane Below .20 .50
BCP167 Kai Liu .30 .75
BCP168 Zach Britton .60 1.50
BCP169 Jamie Pedroza .30 .75
BCP170 Frank Herrmann .20 .50
BCP171 Justin Turner 10.00 25.00
BCP172 Jeff Manship .20 .50
BCP173 Paul Winterling .20 .50
BCP174 Nathan Vineyard .30 .75
BCP175 Jason Delaney .20 .50
BCP176 Ivan Nova 1.25 3.00
BCP177 Esmailyn Gonzalez .60 1.50
BCP178 Brett Cecil .30 .75
BCP179 Jose Martinez .20 .50
BCP180 Brad Peacock .60 1.50
BCP181 Justin Snyder .30 .75
BCP182 Steve Garrison .20 .50
BCP183 Joe Mahoney .20 .50
BCP184 Graham Godfrey .20 .50
BCP185 Larry Wiliams .20 .50
BCP186 Jeremy Haynes .20 .50
BCP187 Brent Brewer .50 1.25
BCP188 Jhoulys Chacin .30 .75
BCP189 Nevin Ashley .30 .75
BCP190 Justin Cassel .20 .50
BCP191 Jon Jay .30 .75
BCP192 Chris Huseby .20 .50
BCP193 D.J. Jones .30 .75
BCP194 David Bromberg .30 .75
BCP195 Juan Francisco .50 1.25
BCP196 Zach Jevne .20 .50
BCP197 Darwin Barney 1.00 2.50
BCP198 Jose Ortegano .30 .75
BCP199 Dominic Brown 1.25 3.00
BCP200 Kyle Ginley .20 .50
BCP201 David Wood .20 .50
BCP202 Jhonny Nunez .20 .50
BCP203 Carlos Rivero .50 1.25
BCP204 Anthony Varvaro .20 .50
BCP205 Christian Lopez .20 .50
BCP206 Travis Banwart .20 .50
BCP207 Rhyne Hughes .20 .50
BCP208 Heath Rollins .30 .75
BCP209 Zack Cozart .60 1.50
BCP210 Mike Dunn .20 .50
BCP211 Chris Pettit .20 .50
BCP212 Dan Berlind .20 .50
BCP213 Ernesto Mejia .30 .75
BCP214 Hector Rondon .30 .75
BCP215 Jose Vallejo .30 .75
BCP216 Kyle Schmidt .20 .50
BCP217 Bubba Bell .50 1.25
BCP218 Charlie Furbush .20 .50
BCP219 Pedro Baez .50 1.25
BCP220 Brandon MaGee .20 .50
BCP221 Clint Robinson .20 .50
BCP222 Fabio Castillo .30 .75
BCP223 Brad Emaus .30 .75
BCP224 Mike DeJesus .20 .50
BCP225 Brandon Laird .30 .75
BCP226 R.J. Seidel .20 .50
BCP227 Agustin Murillo .20 .50
BCP228 Trevor Reckling .60 1.50
BCP229 Hector Gomez .50 1.25
BCP230 Jordan Norberto .20 .50
BCP231 Steve Hill .20 .50
BCP232 Hassan Pena .20 .50
BCP233 Justin Henry .30 .75
BCP234 Chase Lirette .20 .50
BCP235 Christian Marrero .30 .75
BCP236 Will Kline .20 .50
BCP237 Johan Limonta .20 .50
BCP238 Duke Welker .20 .50
BCP239 Jeudy Valdez .30 .75
BCP240 Elvin Ramirez .20 .50
BCP241 Josh Kreuzer AU 3.00 8.00
BCP242 Ryan Zink AU 3.00 8.00
BCP243 Matt Harrison AU 3.00 8.00
BCP244 Dustin Richardson AU 3.00 8.00
BCP245 Fautino De Los Santos AU 3.00 8.00
BCP246 Austin Jackson AU 3.00 8.00
BCP247 Jordan Schafer AU 3.00 8.00
BCP248 Daryl Thompson AU 3.00 8.00
BCP249 Lars Anderson AU 3.00 8.00
BCP250 Tim Bascom AU 3.00 8.00
BCP251 Brandon Hicks AU 3.00 8.00
BCP252 David Kopp AU 3.00 8.00
BCP253 Danny Lehmann AU 3.00 8.00
BCP254 Zimmerman AU UER 3.00 8.00
BCP255 Cale Iorg AU 3.00 8.00
BCP256 Austin Romine AU 3.00 8.00
BCP257 Chaz Roe AU 3.00 8.00
BCP258 Danny Rams AU 3.00 8.00
BCP259 Daniel Bard AU 3.00 8.00
BCP260 Engel Beltre AU 3.00 8.00
BCP261 Michael Watt AU 3.00 8.00
BCP262 Brennan Boesch AU 3.00 8.00
BCP263 Matt Latos AU 4.00 10.00
BCP264 John Jaso AU 3.00 8.00
BCP265 Adrian Alaniz AU 3.00 8.00
BCP266 Matt Green AU 3.00 8.00
BCP267 Andrew Lambo AU 3.00 8.00
BCP268 Michael McCardell AU 3.00 8.00
BCP269 Chris Valaika AU 3.00 8.00
BCP270 Cole Rohrbough AU 3.00 8.00
BCP271 Andrew Brackman AU 3.00 8.00
BCP272 Bud Norris AU 3.00 8.00
BCP273 Ryan Kalish AU 3.00 8.00
BCP274 Jake McGee AU 3.00 8.00
BCP275 Aaron Cunningham AU 3.00 8.00
BCP276 Mitch Boggs AU 3.00 8.00
BCP277 Bradley Suttle AU 3.00 8.00
BCP278 Henry Rodriguez AU 3.00 8.00
BCP279 Mario Lisson AU 3.00 8.00
BCP280 Ludovicus Van Mil AU 3.00 8.00
BCP281 Angel Villalona AU 3.00 8.00
BCP282 Mark Melancon AU 3.00 8.00
BCP283 Brian Dinkelman AU 3.00 8.00
BCP284 Daniel McCutchen AU 3.00 8.00
BCP285 Rene Tosoni AU 3.00 8.00

2008 Bowman Chrome Prospects Refractors

*REF 1-110: 2.5X TO 6X BASIC
*REF 131-240: 2.5X TO 6X BASIC
1-110 ODDS 1:34 HOBBY,1:88 RETAIL
131-240 ODDS 1:40 HOBBY
1-110 PRINT RUN 599 SER.#'d SETS
131-240 PRINT RUN 500 SER.#'d SETS
*REF AU 111-130: .5X TO 1.2X BASIC
*REF AU 241-285: .5X TO 1.2X BASIC
111-130 AU ODDS 1:113 HOBBY
241-285 AU ODDS 1:88 HOBBY
111-130 AU PRINT RUN 500 SER.#'d SETS
241-285 AU PRINT RUN 500 SER.#'d SETS

2008 Bowman Chrome Prospects Blue Refractors

*BLUE 1-110: 5X TO 12X BASIC
*BLUE 131-240: 5X TO 12X BASIC
1-110 ODDS 1:126 HOBBY,1:350 RETAIL
131-240 ODDS 1:131 HOBBY
1-110 PRINT RUN 150 SER.#'d SETS
131-240 PRINT RUN 150 SER.#'d SETS
*BLUE AU 111-130: 1.2X TO 3X BASIC
*BLUE AU 241-285: 1.2X TO 3X BASIC
111-130 AU ODDS 1:372 HOBBY
241-285 AU ODDS 1:295 HOBBY
111-130 AU PRINT RUN 150 SER.#'d SETS
241-285 AU PRINT RUN 150 SER.#'d SETS
BCP120 M.Bumgarner AU 150.00 400.00

2008 Bowman Chrome Prospects Gold Refractors

*GOLD 1-110: 12X TO 30X BASIC
*GOLD 131-240: 12X TO 30X BASIC
1-110 ODDS 1:380 HOB, 1:1040 RET
131-240 ODDS 1:393 HOBBY
1-110 PRINT RUN 50 SER.#'d SETS
131-240 PRINT RUN 50 SER.#'d SETS
111-130 AU ODDS 1:1155 HOBBY
241-285 AU ODDS 1:953 HOBBY
111-130 AU PRINT RUN 50 SER.#'d SETS
241-285 AU PRINT RUN 50 SER.#'d SETS
BCP111 David Price AU 75.00 200.00
BCP120 M.Bumgarner AU 500.00 1000.00

2008 Bowman Chrome Prospects Orange Refractors

1-110 ODDS 1:750 HOB, 1:2075 RET
111-130 AU ODDS 1:2495 HOBBY
131-240 ODDS 1:785 HOBBY
241-285 AU ODDS 1:1784 HOBBY
STATED PRINT RUN 25 SER.#'d SETS
NO PRICING DUE TO SCARCITY

2008 Bowman Chrome Prospects X-Fractors

*X-F 1-110: 3X TO 8X BASIC
*X-F 131-240: 3X TO 8X BASIC
1-110 ODDS 1:65 HOBBY,1:188 RETAIL
131-240 ODDS 1:79 HOBBY
1-110 PRINT RUN 275 SER.#'d SETS
131-240 PRINT RUN 250 SER.#'d SETS
*X-F AU 111-130: .6X TO 1.5X BASIC
*X-F AU 241-285: .6X TO 1.5X BASIC
111-130 X-F AU ODDS 1:226 HOBBY
241-285 X-F AU ODDS 1:175 HOBBY
111-130 AU PRINT RUN 275 SER.#'d SETS
241-285 AU PRINT RUN 250 SER.#'d SETS

2008 Bowman Chrome Draft

COMP.SET w/o AU's (55) 12.50 30.00
COMMON CARD (1-60) .25 .60
COMMON AUTO 4.00 10.00
AU ODDS 1:627 HOBBY
OVERALL PLATE ODDS 1:750 HOBBY
AUTO PLATE ODDS 1:49,870 HOBBY
PLATE PRINT RUN 1 SET PER COLOR
BLACK-CYAN-MAGENTA-YELLOW ISSUED
NO PLATE PRICING DUE TO SCARCITY
BDP1 Nick Adenhart (RC) .25 .60
BDP2 Michael Aubrey RC .40 1.00
BDP3 Mike Aviles RC .40 1.00
BDP4 Burke Badenhop RC .40 1.00
BDP5 Wladimir Balentien (RC) .25 .60
BDP6a Collin Balester (RC) .25 .60
BDP6b Collin Balester AU 4.00 10.00
BDP7 Josh Banks (RC) .25 .60
BDP8 Wes Bankston (RC) .25 .60
BDP9 Joey Votto (RC) 2.00 5.00
BDP10 Mitch Boggs (RC) .25 .60
BDP11 Jay Bruce (RC) .75 2.00
BDP12 Chris Carter (RC) .40 1.00
BDP13 Justin Christian RC .40 1.00
BDP14 Chris Davis RC .50 1.25
BDP15a Blake DeWitt (RC) .40 1.00
BDP15b Blake DeWitt AU 8.00 20.00
BDP16 Nick Evans RC .25 .60
BDP17 Jaime Garcia RC 1.00 2.50
BDP18 Brett Gardner (RC) .60 1.50
BDP19 Carlos Gonzalez (RC) .60 1.50
BDP20 Matt Harrison (RC) .40 1.00
BDP21 Micah Hoffpauir RC .75 2.00
BDP22 Nick Hundley (RC) .25 .60
BDP23 Eric Hurley (RC) .25 .60
BDP24 Elliot Johnson (RC) .25 .60
BDP25 Matt Joyce RC .60 1.50
BDP26a Clayton Kershaw RC 25.00 60.00
BDP26b Clayton Kershaw AU 250.00 600.00
BDP27a Evan Longoria RC 1.25 3.00
BDP27b Evan Longoria AU 20.00 50.00
BDP28 Matt Macri (RC) .25 .6
BDP29 Chris Perez RC .40 1.0
BDP30 Max Ramirez RC .25 .6
BDP31 Greg Reynolds RC .40 1.0
BDP32 Brooks Conrad (RC) .25 .6
BDP33 Max Scherzer RC 6.00 15.0
BDP34 Daryl Thompson (RC) .25 .6
BDP35 Taylor Teagarden RC .40 1.0
BDP36 Rich Thompson RC .40 1.0
BDP37 Ryan Tucker (RC) .25 .6
BDP38 Jonathan Van Every RC .25 .6
BDP39a Chris Volstad (RC) .25 .6
BDP39b Chris Volstad AU 4.00 10.0
BDP40 Michael Hollimon RC .25 .6
BDP41 Brad Ziegler RC 1.25 3.
BDP42 Jamie D'Antona (RC) .25 .
BDP43 Clayton Richard (RC) .25 .

BDP44 Edgar Gonzalez (RC) .25 .60
BDP45 Bryan LaHair RC 2.00 5.00
BDP46 Warner Madrigal (RC) .25 .60
BDP47 Reid Brignac (RC) .40 1.00
BDP48 David Robertson RC .60 1.50
BDP49 Nick Stavinoha RC .40 1.00
BDP50 Jai Miller (RC) .25 .60
BDP51 Charlie Morton (RC) .75 2.00
BDP52 Brandon Boggs (RC) .40 1.00
BDP53 Joe Mather RC .40 1.00
BDP54 Gregorio Petit RC .40 1.00
BDP55 Jeff Samardzija RC .75 2.00

2008 Bowman Chrome Draft Refractors

*REF: 1X TO 2.5X BASIC
RANDOM INSERTS IN PACKS
*REF AU: .5X TO 1.2X BASIC AU
REF AUTO ODDS 1:2,000 PACKS
REF AUTO PRINT RUN 99 SER.#'d SETS

2008 Bowman Chrome Draft Blue Refractors

*BLUE REF: 2.5X TO 6X BASIC
STATED ODDS 1:76 HOBBY
STATED PRINT RUN 99 SER.#'d SETS

2008 Bowman Chrome Draft Gold Refractors

*GOLD REF: 5X TO 12X BASIC
STATED ODDS 1:150 HOBBY
STATED PRINT RUN 50 SER.#'d SETS
*GODL REF AU: 1.2X TO 3X BASIC AU
GLD.REF AUTO ODDS 1:3965 PACKS
GLD.REF AU PRINT RUN 50 SER.#'d SETS

2008 Bowman Chrome Draft Orange Refractors

STATED ODDS 1:301 HOBBY
AUTO ODDS 1:7962 HOBBY
STATED PRINT RUN 25 SER.#'d SETS
NO PRICING DUE TO SCARCITY

2008 Bowman Chrome Draft X-Fractors

*X-F: 1.2X TO 3X BASIC
STATED ODDS 1:38 HOBBY
STATED PRINT RUN 199 SER.#'d SETS

2008 Bowman Chrome Draft Prospects

COMP.SET w/o AU's (110) 20.00 50.00
STATED AUTO ODDS 1:38 HOBBY
OVERALL PLATE ODDS 1:750 HOBBY
AUTO PLATE ODDS 1:13,732 HOBBY
PLATE PRINT RUN 1 SET PER COLOR
BLACK-CYAN-MAGENTA-YELLOW ISSUED
NO PLATE PRICING DUE TO SCARCITY
EXCHANGE DEADLINE 11/30/2010
BDPP1 Rick Porcello DP 1.00 2.50
BDPP2 Braeden Schlehuber DP .30 .75
BDPP3 Kenny Wilson DP .30 .75
BDPP4 Jeff Lanning DP .30 .75
BDPP5 Kevin Dubler DP .30 .75
BDPP6 Eric Campbell DP .50 1.25
BDPP7 Tyler Chatwood DP .50 1.25
BDPP8 Tyreace House DP .30 .75
BDPP9 Adrian Nieto DP .30 .75
BDPP10 Robbie Grossman DP .50 1.25
BDPP11 Jordan Danks DP .75 2.00
BDPP12 Jay Austin DP .30 .75
BDPP13 Ryan Perry DP .50 1.25
BDPP14 Ryan Chaffee DP .50 1.25
BDPP15 Niko Vasquez DP .75 2.00
BDPP16 Shane Dyer DP .30 .75
BDPP17 Benji Gonzalez DP .30 .75
BDPP18 Miles Reagan DP .30 .75
BDPP19 Anthony Ferrara DP .30 .75
BDPP20 Markus Brisker DP .30 .75
BDPP21 Justin Bristow DP .30 .75
BDPP22 Richard Bleier DP .50 1.25
BDPP23 Jeremy Beckham DP .50 1.25
BDPP24 Xavier Avery DP .75 2.00
BDPP25 Christian Vazquez DP 1.25 3.00
BDPP26 Nick Romero DP .30 .75
BDPP27 Trey Watten DP .30 .75
BDPP28 Brett Jacobson DP .30 .75
BDPP29 Tyler Sample DP .30 .75
BDPP30 T.J. Steele DP .50 1.25
BDPP31 Christian Friedrich DP .75 2.00
BDPP32 Graham Hicks DP .50 1.25
BDPP33 Shane Peterson DP .50 1.25
BDPP34 Brett Hunter DP .30 .75
BDPP35 Tim Federowicz DP .50 1.25
BDPP36 Isaac Galloway DP .50 1.25
BDPP37 Logan Schafer DP .30 .75
BDPP38 Paul Demny DP .30 .75
BDPP39 Clayton Shunick DP .30 .75
BDPP40 Andrew Liebel DP .30 .75
BDPP41 Brandon Crawford DP .75 2.00
BDPP42 Blake Tekotte DP .50 1.25
BDPP43 Jason Corder DP .30 .75
BDPP44 Bryan Shaw DP .30 .75
BDPP45 Edgar Olmos DP .30 .75
BDPP46 Dusty Coleman DP .30 .75
BDPP47 Johnny Giavotella DP 1.00 2.50
BDPP48 Tyson Ross DP .50 1.25
BDPP49 Brent Morel DP .50 1.25
BDPP50 Dennis Raben DP .50 1.25
BDPP51 Jake Odorizzi DP 1.00 2.50
BDPP52 Ryne White DP .50 1.25
BDPP53 Devaris Strange-Gordon DP 1.00 2.50
BDPP54 Tim Murphy DP .30 .75
BDPP55 Jake Jefferies DP .30 .75
BDPP56 Anthony Capra DP .30 .75
BDPP57 Kyle Weiland DP .75 2.00
BDPP58 Anthony Bass DP .50 1.25
BDPP59 Scott Green DP .30 .75
BDPP60 Zeke Spruill DP .75 2.00
BDPP61 L.J. Hoes DP .30 .75
BDPP62 Tyler Cline DP .30 .75
BDPP63 Matt Cerda DP .30 .75
BDPP64 Bobby Lanigan DP .30 .75
BDPP65 Mike Sheridan DP .30 .75
BDPP66 Carlos Carrasco FG .50 1.25
BDPP67 Nate Schierholtz FG .30 .75
BDPP68 Jesus Delgado FG .30 .75
BDPP70 Shairon Martis FG .50 1.25
BDPP71 Matt LaPorta FG .50 1.25
BDPP72 Eddie Morlan FG .30 .75
BDPP73 Greg Golson FG .30 .75
BDPP74 Julio Pimentel FG .30 .75
BDPP75 Dexter Fowler FG .50 1.25
BDPP76 Henry Rodriguez FG .30 .75
BDPP77 Cliff Pennington FG .30 .75
BDPP78 Hector Rondon FG .50 1.25
BDPP79 Wes Hodges FG .30 .75
BDPP80 Polin Trinidad FG .30 .75
BDPP81 Chris Getz FG .30 .75
BDPP82 Wellington Castillo FG .30 .75
BDPP83 Mat Gamel FG .75 2.00
BDPP84 Pablo Sandoval FG 1.25 3.00
BDPP85 Jason Donald FG .30 .75
BDPP86 Jesus Montero FG .50 1.25
BDPP87 Jamie D'Antona FG .30 .75
BDPP88 Will Inman FG .30 .75
BDPP89 Elvis Andrus FG .75 2.00
BDPP90 Taylor Teagarden FG .50 1.25
BDPP91 Scott Campbell FG .30 .75
BDPP92 Jake Arrieta FG .75 2.00
BDPP93 Juan Francisco FG .75 2.00
BDPP94 Lou Marson FG .30 .75
BDPP95 Luke Hughes FG .30 .75
BDPP96 Bryan Anderson FG .30 .75
BDPP97 Ramiro Pena FG .30 .75
BDPP98 Jesse Todd FG .30 .75
BDPP99 Gorkys Hernandez FG .30 .75
BDPP100 Casey Weathers FG .30 .75
BDPP101 Fernando Martinez FG .50 1.25
BDPP102 Clayton Richard FG .30 .75
BDPP103 Gerardo Parra FG .30 .75
BDPP104 Kevin Pucetas FG .50 1.25
BDPP105 Wilkin Ramirez FG .30 .75
BDPP106 Ryan Mattheus FG .30 .75
BDPP107 Angel Villalona FG .75 2.00
BDPP108 Brett Anderson FG .50 1.25
BDPP109 Chris Valaika FG .30 .75
BDPP110 Trevor Cahill FG .75 2.00
BDPP111 Wilmer Flores AU 4.00 10.00
BDPP112 Lonnie Chisenhall AU 4.00 10.00
BDPP113 Carlos Gutierrez AU 4.00 10.00
BDPP114 Derek Holland AU 5.00 12.00
BDPP115 Michael Stanton AU 150.00 400.00
BDPP116 Ike Davis AU 4.00 10.00
BDPP117 Anthony Hewitt AU 4.00 10.00
BDPP118 Gordon Beckham AU 4.00 10.00
BDPP119 Daniel Schlereth AU 4.00 10.00
BDPP120 Zach Collier AU 4.00 10.00
BDPP121 Evan Frederickson AU 4.00 10.00
BDPP122 Mike Montgomery AU 4.00 10.00
BDPP123 Cody Adams AU 4.00 10.00
BDPP124 Brad Hand AU 4.00 10.00
BDPP125 Josh Reddick AU 4.00 10.00
BDPP127 Jesus Montero AU 4.00 10.00
BDPP128 Buster Posey AU 75.00 200.00
BDPP142 Michael Inoa AU 4.00 10.00

2008 Bowman Chrome Draft Prospects Refractors

*REF: 1.5X TO 4X BASIC
RANDOM INSERTS IN PACKS
*REF AU: .5X TO 1.2X BASIC
REF.AU ODDS 1:118 HOBBY
REF.AU PRINT RUN 500 SER.#'d SETS
EXCHANGE DEADLINE 11/30/2010
BDPP115 Michael Stanton AU 400.00 800.00
BDPP128 Buster Posey AU 150.00 300.00

2008 Bowman Chrome Draft Prospects Blue Refractors

*BLUE REF: 4X TO 10X BASIC
STATED ODDS 1:76 HOBBY
STATED PRINT RUN 99 SER.#'d SETS
*BLUE REF AU: 1X TO 2.5X BASIC
BLUE REF.AU ODDS 1:396 HOBBY
BLUE REF.AU PRINT RUN 150 SER.#'d SETS
EXCHANGE DEADLINE 11/30/2010
BDPP36 Isaac Galloway DP 15.00 40.00
BDPP115 Michael Stanton AU 800.00 1200.00
BDPP128 Buster Posey AU 300.00 600.00

2008 Bowman Chrome Draft Prospects Gold Refractors

*GOLD REF: 12.5X TO 30X BASIC
STATED ODDS 1:150 HOBBY
STATED PRINT RUN 50 SER.#'d SETS
*GOLD REF AU: 1X TO 2.5X BASIC
GOLD REF.AU ODDS 1:1258 HOBBY
GOLD AU PRINT RUN 50 SER.#'d SETS
EXCHANGE DEADLINE 11/30/2010
BDPP9 Adrian Nieto DP 20.00 50.00
BDPP36 Isaac Galloway DP 30.00 60.00
BDPP51 Jake Odorizzi DP 30.00 60.00
BDPP57 Kyle Weiland DP 30.00 60.00
BDPP114 Derek Holland AU 50.00 100.00
BDPP115 Michael Stanton AU 1500.00 2000.00
BDPP128 Buster Posey AU 800.00 1200.00

2008 Bowman Chrome Draft Prospects Orange Refractors

STATED ODDS 1:301 HOBBY
AUTO ODDS 1:2700 HOBBY
STATED PRINT RUN 25 SER.#'d SETS
NO PRICING DUE TO SCARCITY

2008 Bowman Chrome Draft Prospects X-Fractors

*X-F: 2.5X TO 6X BASIC
STATED ODDS 1:38 HOBBY
STATED PRINT RUN 199 SER.#'d SETS
*X-F AU: .6X TO 1.5X BASIC
X-F.AU ODDS 1:270 HOBBY
X-F.AU PRINT RUN 225 SER.#'d SETS
EXCHANGE DEADLINE 11/30/2010
BDPP115 Michael Stanton AU 500.00 800.00
BDPP128 Buster Posey AU 250.00 400.00

2009 Bowman Chrome

COMPLETE SET (220) 75.00 150.00
COMMON CARD (1-190) .20 .50
COMMON ROOKIE .60 1.50
PRINTING PLATE ODDS 1:538 HOBBY
PLATE PRINT RUN 1 SET PER COLOR
BLACK-CYAN-MAGENTA-YELLOW ISSUED
NO PLATE PRICING DUE TO SCARCITY
1 David Wright .40 1.00
2 Albert Pujols .60 1.50
3 Alex Rodriguez .60 1.50
4 Chase Utley .30 .75
5 Chien-Ming Wang .30 .75
6 Jimmy Rollins .30 .75
7 Ken Griffey Jr. 1.00 2.50
8 Manny Ramirez .50 1.25
9 Chipper Jones .50 1.25
10 Ichiro Suzuki .60 1.50
11 Justin Morneau .30 .75
12 Hanley Ramirez .30 .75
13 Cliff Lee .30 .75
14 Ryan Howard .40 1.00
15 Ian Kinsler .30 .75
16 Jose Reyes .30 .75
17 Ted Lilly .20 .50
18 Miguel Cabrera .50 1.25
19 Nate McLouth .20 .50
20 Josh Beckett .20 .50
21 John Lackey .30 .75
22 David Ortiz .50 1.25
23 Carlos Lee .20 .50
24 Adam Dunn .30 .75
25 B.J. Upton .30 .75
26 Curtis Granderson .40 1.00
27 David DeJesus .20 .50
28 CC Sabathia .30 .75
29 Russell Martin .20 .50
30 Torii Hunter .20 .50
31 Rich Harden .20 .50
32 Johnny Damon .30 .75
33 Cristian Guzman .20 .50
34 Grady Sizemore .30 .75
35 Jorge Posada .30 .75
36 Placido Polanco .20 .50
37 Ryan Ludwick .30 .75
38 Dustin Pedroia .50 1.25
39 Matt Garza .20 .50
40 Prince Fielder .30 .75
41 Rick Ankiel .20 .50
42 David Huff RC .60 1.50
43 Erik Bedard .20 .50
44 Ryan Braun .30 .75
45 Ervin Santana .20 .50
46 Brian Roberts .20 .50
47 Mike Jacobs .20 .50
48 Phil Hughes .20 .50
49 Justin Masterson .20 .50
50 Felix Hernandez .30 .75
51 Stephen Drew .20 .50
52 Bobby Abreu .20 .50
53 Jay Bruce .30 .75
54 Josh Hamilton .30 .75
55 Garrett Atkins .20 .50
56 Jacoby Ellsbury .40 1.00
57 Johan Santana .30 .75
58 James Shields .20 .50
59 Sergio Escalona RC 1.00 2.50
60 Carlos Pena .30 .75
61 Matt Kemp .40 1.00
62 Joey Votto .50 1.25
63 Raul Ibanez .30 .75
64 Casey Kotchman .20 .50
65 Hunter Pence .30 .75
66 Daniel Murphy RC 2.50 6.00
67 Carlos Beltran .30 .75
68 Evan Longoria .30 .75
69 Daisuke Matsuzaka .30 .75
70 Cole Hamels .40 1.00
71 Robinson Cano .30 .75
72 Clayton Kershaw .75 2.00
73 Kenji Johjima .30 .75
74 Kazuo Matsui .20 .50
75 Jayson Werth .30 .75
76 Brian McCann .30 .75
77 Barry Zito .30 .75
78 Glen Perkins .20 .50
79 Jeff Francoeur .30 .75
80 Derek Jeter 1.25 3.00
81 Ryan Doumit .20 .50
82 Dan Haren .20 .50
83 Justin Duchscherer .20 .50
84 Marlon Byrd .20 .50
85 Derek Lowe .20 .50
86 Pat Burrell .20 .50
87 Jair Jurrjens .20 .50
88 Zack Greinke .50 1.25
89 Jon Lester .30 .75
90 Justin Verlander .50 1.25
91 Jorge Cantu .20 .50
92 John Maine .20 .50
93 Brad Hawpe .20 .50
94 Mike Aviles .20 .50
95 Victor Martinez .30 .75
96 Ryan Dempster .20 .50
97 Miguel Tejada .30 .75
98 Joe Mauer .40 1.00
99 Scott Olsen .20 .50
100 Tim Lincecum .30 .75
101 Francisco Liriano .20 .50
102 Chris Iannetta .20 .50
103 Greg Burke RC 1.00 2.50
104 Milton Bradley .20 .50
105 John Lannan .20 .50
106 Yovani Gallardo .20 .50
107 Luke French (RC) .60 1.50
108 Jermaine Dye .20 .50
109 Dioner Navarro .20 .50
110 Joba Chamberlain .20 .50
111 Nelson Cruz .50 1.25
112 Johnny Cueto .30 .75
113 Adam LaRoche .20 .50
114 Aaron Rowand .20 .50
115 Jason Bay .30 .75
116 Roy Halladay .30 .75
117 Mark Teixeira .30 .75
118 Gavin Floyd .20 .50
119 Magglio Ordonez .30 .75
120 Rafael Furcal .20 .50
121 Mark Buehrle .30 .75
122 Alexi Casilla .20 .50
123 Scott Kazmir .20 .50
124 Nick Swisher .30 .75
125 Carlos Gomez .20 .50
126 Javier Vazquez .20 .50
127 Paul Konerko .30 .75
128 Nolan Reimold (RC) .60 1.50
129 Gerardo Parra RC 1.00 2.50
130 Josh Johnson .30 .75
131 Carlos Zambrano .30 .75
132 Chris Davis .30 .75
133 Bobby Crosby .20 .50
134 Alex Gordon .30 .75
135 Chris Young .20 .50
136 Carlos Delgado .20 .50
137 Adam Wainwright .30 .75
138 Justin Upton .30 .75
139 Chris Coghlan RC 1.50 4.00
140 J.D. Drew .20 .50
141 Adam Lind .20 .50
142 Mike Lowell .20 .50
143 Lance Berkman .30 .75
144 J.J. Hardy .20 .50
145 A.J. Burnett .20 .50
146 Jake Peavy .20 .50
147 Xavier Paul (RC) .60 1.50
148 Matt Holliday .50 1.25
149 Carl Crawford .30 .75
150 Andre Ethier .30 .75
151 Howie Kendrick .20 .50
152 Ryan Zimmerman .30 .75
153 Troy Tulowitzki .50 1.25
154 Brett Myers .20 .50
155 Chris Young .20 .50
156 Jered Weaver .30 .75
157 Jeff Clement .20 .50
158 Alex Rios .20 .50
159 Shane Victorino .20 .50
160 Jeremy Hermida .20 .50
161 James Loney .20 .50
162 Michael Young .20 .50
163 Aramis Ramirez .20 .50
164 Geovany Soto .30 .75
165 Aubrey Huff .20 .50
166 Rick Porcello RC 2.00 5.00
167 Vernon Wells .20 .50
168 Chone Figgins .20 .50
169 Carlos Quentin .20 .50
170 Chad Billingsley .30 .75
171 Matt Cain .30 .75
172 Derrek Lee .20 .50
173 A.J. Pierzynski .20 .50
174 Daniel Bard RC .60 1.50
175 Bobby Scales RC 1.00 2.50
176 Alfonso Soriano .30 .75
177 Adrian Gonzalez .40 1.00
178 Andrew McCutchen (RC) 3.00 8.00
179 Nick Markakis .40 1.00
180 Brandon Webb .30 .75
181 Vladimir Guerrero .30 .75
182 Roy Oswalt .30 .75
183 Adam Jones .30 .75
184 Edinson Volquez .20 .50
185 Gordon Beckham RC 1.00 2.50
186 Joe Saunders .20 .50
187 Yadier Molina .60 1.50
188 Kevin Youkilis .20 .50
189 Dan Uggla .20 .50
190 Kosuke Fukudome .30 .75
191 Matt LaPorta RC 1.00 2.50
192 Trevor Cahill RC 1.50 4.00
193 Derek Holland RC 1.00 2.50
194 Michael Bowden (RC) .60 1.50
195 Andrew Carpenter RC 1.00 2.50
196 Phil Coke RC 1.00 2.50
197 Graham Taylor RC 1.00 2.50
198 Alcides Escobar RC 1.00 2.50
199 Dexter Fowler (RC) 1.00 2.50
200 Mat Gamel RC 1.50 4.00
201 Jordan Zimmermann RC 1.50 4.00
202 Greg Golson (RC) .60 1.50
203 Andrew Bailey RC 1.50 4.00
204 David Hernandez RC .60 1.50
205 George Kottaras (RC) .60 1.50
206 Lou Marson (RC) .60 1.50
207 Shairon Martis RC 1.00 2.50
208 Juan Miranda RC 1.00 2.50
209 Tyler Greene (RC) .60 1.50
210 Jonathon Niese RC 1.00 2.50
211 Bobby Parnell RC 1.00 2.50
212 Colby Rasmus (RC) 1.00 2.50
213 David Price RC 1.25 3.00
214 Angel Salome (RC) .60 1.50
215 Gaby Sanchez RC 1.00 2.50
216 Freddy Sandoval (RC) .60 1.50
217 Travis Snider RC 1.00 2.50
218 Will Venable RC .60 1.50
219 Brett Anderson RC 1.00 2.50
220 Josh Outman RC 1.00 2.50

2009 Bowman Chrome Refractors

*REF VET: 1X TO 2.5X BASIC
*REF RC: .6X TO 1.5X BASIC RC
STATED ODDS 1:4 HOBBY

2009 Bowman Chrome Blue Refractors

*BLUE VET: 2X TO 6X BASIC
*BLUE RC: 1.2X TO 3X BASIC RC
STATED ODDS 1:17 HOBBY
STATED PRINT RUN 150 SER.#'d SETS

2009 Bowman Chrome Gold Refractors

*GOLD VET: 5X TO 12X BASIC
*GOLD RC: 2X TO 5X BASIC RC
STATED ODDS 1:50 HOBBY
STATED PRINT RUN 50 SER.#'d SETS

2009 Bowman Chrome X-Fractors

*XF VET: 1.5X TO 4X BASIC
*XF RC: 1X TO 2.5X BASIC RC
STATED ODDS 1:10 HOBBY
STATED PRINT RUN 250 SER.#'d SETS

2009 Bowman Chrome Prospects

COMP.SET w/o AU's (160) 30.00 60.00
BOWMAN AU ODDS 1:47 HOBBY
BOW.CHR AU ODDS 1:34 HOBBY
PRINTING PLATE ODDS 1:538 HOBBY
AU PRINT.PLATE ODDS 1:7400 HOBBY
PLATE PRINT RUN 1 SET PER COLOR
BLACK-CYAN-MAGENTA-YELLOW ISSUED
NO PLATE PRICING DUE TO SCARCITY
BCP1 Neftali Feliz .30 .75
BCP2 Oscar Tejada .20 .50
BCP3 Greg Veloz .20 .50
BCP4 Julio Teheran .60 1.50
BCP5 Michael Almanzar .30 .75
BCP6 Stolmy Pimentel .30 .75
BCP7 Matthew Moore 1.50 4.00
BCP8 Jericho Jones .20 .50
BCP9 Kelvin de la Cruz .50 1.25
BCP10 Jose Ceda .20 .50
BCP11 Jesse Darcy .20 .50
BCP12 Kenneth Gilbert .20 .50
BCP13 Will Smith .30 .75
BCP14 Samuel Freeman .20 .50
BCP15 Adam Reifer .20 .50
BCP16 Ehire Adrianza .50 1.25
BCP17 Michael Pineda .50 1.25
BCP18 Jordan Walden .30 .75
BCP19 Angel Morales .30 .75
BCP20 Neil Ramirez .20 .50
BCP21 Kyeong Kang .30 .75
BCP22 Luis Jimenez .20 .50
BCP23 Tyler Flowers .50 1.25
BCP24 Petey Paramore .30 .75
BCP25 Jeremy Hamilton .20 .50
BCP26 Tyler Yockey .30 .75
BCP27 Sawyer Carroll .30 .75
BCP28 Jeremy Farrell .20 .50
BCP29 Tyson Brummett .20 .50
BCP30 Alex Buchholz .30 .75
BCP31 Luis Sumoza .30 .75
BCP32 Jonathan Waltenbury .30 .75
BCP33 Edgar Osuna .20 .50
BCP34 Curt Smith .20 .50
BCP35 Evan Bigley .30 .75
BCP36 Miguel Fermin .20 .50
BCP37 Ben Lasater .20 .50
BCP38 David Freese .60 1.50
BCP39 Jon Kibler .30 .75
BCP40 Cristian Beltre .30 .75
BCP41 Alfredo Figaro .20 .50
BCP42 Marc Rzepczynski .30 .75
BCP43 Joshua Collmenter .30 .75
BCP44 Adam Mills .20 .50
BCP45 Wilson Ramos .60 1.50
BCP46 Esmil Rogers .20 .50
BCP47 Jon Mark Owings .20 .50
BCP48 Chris Johnson .30 .75
BCP49 Abraham Almonte .20 .50
BCP50 Patrick Ryan .20 .50
BCP51 Yefri Carvajal .50 1.25
BCP52 Ruben Tejada .20 .50
BCP53 Edilio Colina .30 .75
BCP54 Wilber Bucardo .30 .75
BCP55 Nelson Perez .30 .75
BCP56 Andrew Rundle .30 .75
BCP57 Anthony Ortega .20 .50
BCP58 Wilin Rosario .30 .75
BCP59 Parker Frazier .20 .50
BCP60 Kyle Farrell .20 .50
BCP61 Erik Komatsu .30 .75
BCP62 Michael Stutes .20 .50
BCP63 David Genao .30 .75
BCP64 Jack Cawley .20 .50
BCP65 Jacob Goldberg .20 .50
BCP66 Jarred Bogany .20 .50
BCP67 Jason McEachern .20 .50
BCP68 Matt Rigoli .20 .50
BCP69 Jose Duran .30 .75
BCP70 Justin Greene .30 .75
BCP71 Nino Leyja .30 .75
BCP72 Michael Swinson .30 .75
BCP73 Miguel Flores .30 .75
BCP74 Nick Buss .20 .50
BCP75 Brett Oberholtzer .30 .75
BCP76 Pat McAnaney .30 .75
BCP77 Sean Conner .20 .50
BCP78 Ryan Verdugo .30 .75
BCP79 Will Atwood .20 .50
BCP80 Tommy Johnson .50 1.25
BCP81 Rene Garcia .30 .75
BCP82 Robert Brooks .30 .75
BCP83 Seth Garrison .20 .50
BCP84 Steven Upchurch .20 .50
BCP85 Zach Moore .20 .50
BCP86 Derrick Phillips .20 .50
BCP87 Dominic De La Osa .50 1.25
BCP88 Jose Barajas .20 .50
BCP89 Bryan Petersen .20 .50
BCP90 Michael Cisco .30 .75
BCP91 Rinku Singh AU 6.00 15.00
BCP92 Dinesh Kumar Patel AU 3.00 8.00
BCP93 Matt Miller AU 3.00 8.00
BCP94 Pat Venditte AU 3.00 8.00
BCP95 Zach Putnam AU 3.00 8.00
BCP96 Robbie Grossman AU 3.00 8.00
BCP97 Tommy Hanson AU 3.00 8.00
BCP98 Graham Hicks AU 3.00 8.00
BCP99 Matt Mitchell AU 3.00 8.00
BCP100 Christopher Marrero AU 3.00 8.00
BCP101 Freddie Freeman AU 125.00 300.00
BCP102 Chris Johnson AU 3.00 8.00
BCP103 Edgar Olmos AU 3.00 8.00
BCP104 Argenis Diaz AU 3.00 8.00
BCP105 Brett Anderson AU 3.00 8.00
BCP106 Juancarlos Sulbaran AU 3.00 8.00
BCP107 Cody Scarpetta AU 3.00 8.00
BCP108 Carlos Santana AU 12.00 30.00
BCP109 Brad Emaus AU 3.00 8.00
BCP110 Dayan Viciedo AU 3.00 8.00
BCP111b Tim Federowicz AU 3.00 8.00
BCP111a Beamer Weems AU 3.00 8.00
BCP112a Logan Morrison AU 6.00 15.00
BCP112b Allen Craig AU 3.00 8.00
BCP113b Kyle Weiland AU 3.00 8.00
BCP113a Greg Halman AU 3.00 8.00
BCP114a Logan Forsythe AU 3.00 8.00
BCP114b Connor Graham AU 3.00 8.00
BCP115 Lance Lynn AU 3.00 8.00
BCP116 Javier Rodriguez AU 3.00 8.00
BCP117 Josh Lindblom AU 3.00 8.00
BCP118 Blake Tekotte AU 3.00 8.00
BCP119 Johnny Giavotella AU 3.00 8.00
BCP120 Jason Knapp AU 3.00 8.00
BCP121 Charlie Blackmon AU 50.00 120.00
BCP122 David Hernandez AU 3.00 8.00
BCP123 Adam Moore AU 3.00 8.00
BCP124 Bobby Lanigan AU 3.00 8.00
BCP125 Jay Austin AU 3.00 8.00
BCP126 Quinton Miller AU 3.00 8.00
BCP127 Eric Sogard AU 3.00 8.00
BCP128 Efrain Nieves .30 .75
BCP129 Kam Mickolio .20 .50
BCP130 Terrell Alliman .20 .50
BCP131 J.R. Higley .30 .75
BCP132 Rashun Dixon .50 1.25
BCP133 Brian Baisley .20 .50
BCP134 Tim Collins .30 .75
BCP135 Kyle Greenwalt .50 1.25
BCP136 C.J. Lee .20 .50
BCP137 Hector Correa .20 .50
BCP138 Wily Peralta .30 .75
BCP139 Bryan Price .20 .50
BCP140 Jarrod Holloway .20 .50
BCP141 Alfredo Silverio .20 .50
BCP142 Brad Dydalewicz .30 .75
BCP143 Alexander Torres .30 .75
BCP144 Chris Hicks .20 .50
BCP145 Andy Parrino .20 .50
BCP146 Christopher Schwinden .20 .50
BCP147 Matt Mitchell .20 .50
BCP148 Mathew Kennelly .20 .50
BCP149 Freddy Galvis .30 .75
BCP150 Mauricio Robles .50 1.25
BCP151 Kevin Eichhorn .20 .50
BCP152 Dan Hudson .30 .75
BCP153 Carlos Martinez .30 .75
BCP154 Danny Carroll .20 .50
BCP155 Maikel Cleto .20 .50
BCP156 Michael Affronti .20 .50
BCP157 Mike Pontius .30 .75
BCP158 Richard Castillo .20 .50
BCP159 Jon Redding .20 .50
BCP160 Aaron King .20 .50
BCP161 Mark Hallberg .20 .50
BCP162 Chris Luck .50 1.25
BCP163 Wilmer Font .20 .50
BCP164 Chad Lundahl .20 .50
BCP165 Isaias Asencio .20 .50
BCP166 Denny Almonte .30 .75
BCP167 Carmen Angelini .20 .50
BCP168 Paul Clemens .20 .50
BCP169 Federico Hernandez .30 .75
BCP170 Mario Martinez .30 .75
BCP171 Bryan Shaw .20 .50
BCP172 Bryan Augenstein .20 .50
BCP173 Santos Rodriguez .30 .75
BCP174 Delvi Cid .30 .75
BCP175 Todd Doolittle .20 .50
BCP176 Rossmel Perez .20 .50
BCP177 Philippe-Alexandre Valiquette .20 .50
BCP178 Julian Sampson .30 .75
BCP179 Eric Farris .20 .50
BCP180 Taylor Harbin .20 .50
BCP181 Clayton Cook .30 .75
BCP182 Jovan Rosa .20 .50
BCP183 Starlin Castro 1.00 2.50
BCP184 Brock Huntzinger .20 .50
BCP185 Jack McGeary .20 .50
BCP186 Moises Sierra .50 1.25
BCP187 Luis Exposito .50 1.25
BCP188 Danny Farquhar .20 .50
BCP189 Layton Hiller .20 .50
BCP190 Michael Harrington .20 .50
BCP191 Nate Tenbrink .20 .50
BCP192 Jason Rook .20 .50
BCP193 Ryan Kulik .20 .50
BCP194 Kennil Gomez .20 .50
BCP195 Brad James .20 .50
BCP196 John Anderson .20 .50
BCP197 Pernell Halliman .20 .50

2009 Bowman Chrome Prospects Refractors

*REF 1-197: 2.5X TO 6X BASIC
1-90 ODDS 1:22 HOBBY
128-197 ODDS 1:15 HOBBY
NON-AU PRINT RUN 599 SER.#'d SETS
*REF AU: .5X TO 1.2X BASIC
BOW.REF.AU ODDS 1:95 HOBBY
BOW.CHR. AU ODDS 1:70 HOBBY
AUTO PRINT RUN 500 SER.#'d SETS

2009 Bowman Chrome Prospects Blue Refractors

*BLUE REF: 5X TO 12X BASIC
BLUE 1-90 ODDS 1:90 HOBBY
BLUE 128-197 ODDS 1:17 HOBBY
BLUE NON-AU PRT RUN 150 SER.#'d SETS
*BLUE REF AU: .75X TO 2X BASIC
BOW.BLU.REF AU ODDS 1:314 HOBBY
BOW.CHR.BLU.REF ODDS 1:246 HOBBY
BLUE REF AU PRINT RUN 150 SER.#'d SETS

2009 Bowman Chrome Prospects Gold Refractors

*GOLD REF: 10X TO 25X BASIC
GOLD 1-90 ODDS 1:271 HOBBY
GOLD 128-197 ODDS 1:50 HOBBY
GOLD PRINT RUN 50 SER.#'d SETS
*GOLD REF AU: 2X TO 5X BASIC
BOW.GLD.REF AU ODDS 1:943 HOBBY
BOW.CHR.GLD.REF AU ODDS 1:715 HOBBY
GOLD REF AU PRINT RUN 50 SER.#'d SETS

2009 Bowman Chrome Prospects Orange Refractors

1-90 STATED ODDS 1:542 HOBBY
91-110 STATED ODDS 1:1500 HOBBY
111-127 STATED ODDS 1:1882 HOBBY
128-197 STATED ODDS 1:100 HOBBY
STATED PRINT RUN 25 SER.#'d SETS
NO PRICING DUE TO SCARCITY

2009 Bowman Chrome Prospects X-Fractors

*X-FRAC: 4X TO 10X BASIC
X-FRAC 1-90 ODDS 1:45 HOBBY
X-FRAC 128-197 ODDS 1:10 HOBBY
1-90 X-F PRINT RUN 299 SER.#'d SETS
128-197 X-F PRINT RUN 250 SER.#'d SETS
*X-F AU: .6X TO 1.5X BASIC
BOW.X-F AU ODDS 1:198 HOBBY
BOW.CHR.X-F AU ODDS 1:144 HOBBY
X-F AU PRINT RUN 250 SER.#'d SETS

2009 Bowman Chrome WBC Prospects

21-60 PRINTING PLATE ODDS 1:538 HOBBY
PLATE PRINT RUN 1 SET PER COLOR
BLACK-CYAN-MAGENTA-YELLOW ISSUED
NO PLATE PRICING DUE TO SCARCITY
BCW1 Yu Darvish 1.50 4.00
BCW2 Phillippe Aumont .60 1.50
BCW3 Concepcion Rodriguez .40 1.00
BCW4 Michel Enriquez .40 1.00
BCW5 Yulieski Gourriel 1.25 3.00
BCW6 Shinnosuke Abe .60 1.50
BCW7 Gift Ngoepe .40 1.00
BCW8 Dylan Lindsay .60 1.50
BCW9 Nick Weglarz .40 1.00
BCW10 Mitch Dening .40 1.00
BCW11 Justin Erasmus .40 1.00
BCW12 Aroldis Chapman 2.00 5.00
BCW13 Alex Liddi .60 1.50
BCW14 Alexander Smit .40 1.00
BCW15 Juan Carlos Sulbaran .40 1.00
BCW16 Cheng-Min Peng .60 1.50
BCW17 Chenhao Li .40 1.00
BCW18 Tao Bu .40 1.00
BCW19 Gregory Halman .60 1.50
BCW20 Fu-Te Ni .60 1.50
BCW21 Norichika Aoki .60 1.50
BCW22 Hisashi Iwakuma 1.25 3.00
BCW23 Tae Kyun Kim .40 1.00
BCW24 Dae Ho Lee .40 1.00
BCW25 Wang Chao .40 1.00
BCW26 Yi-Chuan Lin .60 1.50
BCW27 James Beresford .40 1.00
BCW28 Shuichi Murata .60 1.50
BCW29 Hung-Wen Chen .40 1.00
BCW30 Masahiro Tanaka 2.00 5.00
BCW31 Kao Kuo-Ching .40 1.00
BCW32 Po Yu Lin .40 1.00
BCW33 Yolexis Ulacia .40 1.00
BCW34 Kwang-Hyun Kim 1.25 3.00
BCW35 Kenley Jansen 1.25 3.00
BCW36 Luis Durango .40 1.00
BCW37 Ray Chang .40 1.00
BCW38 Hein Robb .40 1.00
BCW39 Kyuji Fujikawa 1.00 2.50
BCW40 Ruben Tejada .40 1.00
BCW41 Hector Olivera 1.25 3.00
BCW42 Bryan Engelhardt .40 1.00
BCW43 Dennis Neuman .40 1.00
BCW44 Vladimir Garcia .40 1.00
BCW45 Michihiro Ogasawara .60 1.50
BCW46 Yen-Wen Kuo .40 1.00
BCW47 Takahiro Mahara .40 1.00
BCW48 Hiroyuki Nakajima .60 1.50
BCW49 Yoennis Cespedes 1.50 4.00
BCW50 Alfredo Despaigne 1.00 2.50
BCW51 Suk Min-Yoon .40 1.00
BCW52 Chih-Hsien Chiang 1.00 2.50
BCW53 Hyun-Soo Kim .40 1.00
BCW54 Chih-Kang Kao .40 1.00
BCW55 Frederich Cepeda .60 1.50
BCW56 Yi-Feng Kuo .40 1.00
BCW57 Toshiya Sugiuchi .40 1.00
BCW58 Shunsuke Watanabe .60 1.50
BCW59 Max Ramirez .40 1.00
BCW60 Brad Harman .40 1.00

2009 Bowman Chrome WBC Prospects Refractors

*REF: 2X TO 5X BASIC
1-20 ODDS 1:22 HOBBY
21-60 ODDS 1:15 HOBBY
1-20 PRINT RUN 599 SER.#'d SETS
21-60 PRINT RUN 500 SER.#'d SETS

2009 Bowman Chrome WBC Prospects Blue Refractors

*BLUE REF: 3X TO 8X BASIC
1-20 ODDS 1:90 HOBBY
21-60 ODDS 1:17 HOBBY
STATED PRINT RUN 150 SER.#'d SETS

2009 Bowman Chrome WBC Prospects Gold Refractors

*GOLD REF: 6X TO 15X BASIC
1-20 ODDS 1:271 HOBBY
21-60 ODDS 1:50 HOBBY
STATED PRINT RUN 50 SER.#'d SETS

2009 Bowman Chrome WBC Prospects X-Fractors

*X-F: 2.5X TO 6X BASIC
1-20 ODDS 1:45 HOBBY
21-60 ODDS 1:10 HOBBY
1-20 PRINT RUN 299 SER.#'d SETS
21-60 PRINT RUN 250 SER.#'d SETS

2009 Bowman Chrome Draft

COMPLETE SET (55) 10.00 25.00
COMMON CARD (1-55) .30 .75
OVERALL PLATE ODDS 1:1531 HOBBY
PLATE PRINT RUN 1 SET PER COLOR
BLACK-CYAN-MAGENTA-YELLOW ISSUED
NO PLATE PRICING DUE TO SCARCITY
BDP1 Tommy Hanson RC .75 2.00
BDP2 Jeff Manship RC .30 .75
BDP3 Trevor Bell (RC) .30 .75
BDP4 Trevor Cahill RC .75 2.00
BDP5 Trent Oeltjen (RC) .30 .75
BDP6 Wyatt Toregas RC .30 .75
BDP7 Kevin Mulvey RC .30 .75
BDP8 Rusty Ryal RC .30 .75
BDP9 Mike Carp (RC) .50 1.25
BDP10 Jorge Padilla (RC) .30 .75
BDP11 J.D. Martin (RC) .30 .75
BDP12 Dusty Ryan RC .30 .75
BDP13 Alex Avila RC 1.00 2.50
BDP14 Brandon Allen (RC) .30 .75
BDP15 Tommy Everidge (RC) .50 1.25
BDP16 Bud Norris RC .30 .75
BDP17 Neftali Feliz RC .50 1.25
BDP18 Mat Latos RC 1.00 2.50
BDP19 Ryan Perry RC .75 2.00
BDP20 Craig Tatum (RC) .30 .75
BDP21 Chris Tillman RC .50 1.25
BDP22 Jhoulys Chacin RC .50 1.25
BDP23 Michael Saunders RC .75 2.00
BDP24 Jeff Stevens RC .30 .75

BDP25 Luis Valdez RC .30 .75
BDP26 Robert Manuel RC .30 .75
BDP27 Ryan Webb (RC) .30 .75
BDP28 Marc Rzepczynski RC .50 1.25
BDP29 Travis Schlichting (RC) .50 1.25
BDP30 Barbaro Canizares RC .30 .75
BDP31 Brad Mills RC .30 .75
BDP32 Dusty Brown (RC) .30 .75
BDP33 Tim Wood RC .30 .75
BDP34 Drew Sutton RC .50 1.25
BDP35 Jarrett Hoffpauir (RC) .30 .75
BDP36 Jose Lobaton RC .30 .75
BDP37 Aaron Bates RC .30 .75
BDP38 Clayton Mortensen RC .30 .75
BDP39 Ryan Sadowski RC .30 .75
BDP40 Fu-Te Ni RC .50 1.25
BDP41 Casey McGehee (RC) .30 .75
BDP42 Omir Santos RC .30 .75
BDP43 Brent Leach RC .50 1.25
BDP44 Diory Hernandez RC .30 .75
BDP45 Wilkin Castillo RC .30 .75
BDP46 Trevor Crowe RC .30 .75
BDP47 Sean West (RC) .50 1.25
BDP48 Clayton Richard (RC) .30 .75
BDP49 Julio Borbon RC .30 .75
BDP50 Kyle Blanks RC .50 1.25
BDP51 Jeff Gray RC .30 .75
BDP52 Gio Gonzalez (RC) .50 1.25
BDP53 Vin Mazzaro RC .30 .75
BDP54 Josh Reddick RC .50 1.25
BDP55 Fernando Martinez RC .75 2.00

2009 Bowman Chrome Draft Refractors

*REF: 1X TO 2.5X BASIC
STATED ODDS 1:11 HOBBY

2009 Bowman Chrome Draft Blue Refractors

*BLUE REF: 2.5X TO 6X BASIC
STATED ODDS 1:49 HOBBY
STATED PRINT RUN 99 SER.#'d SETS
BDP40 Fu-Te Ni 15.00 40.00

2009 Bowman Chrome Draft Gold Refractors

*GOLD: 4X TO 10X BASIC
STATED ODDS 1:96 HOBBY
STATED PRINT RUN 50 SER.#'d SETS
BDP40 Fu-Te Ni 30.00 80.00

2009 Bowman Chrome Draft Purple Refractors

*PURPLE: 2X TO 5X BASIC
RANDOM INSERTS IN RETAIL PACKS

2009 Bowman Chrome Draft X-Fractors

*X-F: 1.5X TO 4X BASIC
STATED ODDS 1:24 HOBBY
STATED PRINT RUN 199 SER.#'d SETS
BDP40 Fu-Te Ni 6.00 15.00

2009 Bowman Chrome Draft Prospects

COMP.SET w/o AU's (75) 12.50 30.00
STATED AU ODDS 1:24 HOBBY
OVERALL PLATE ODDS 1:1531 HOBBY
OVERALL AUTO PLATE ODDS 1:7973 HOBBY
PLATE PRINT RUN 1 SET PER COLOR
BLACK-CYAN-MAGENTA-YELLOW ISSUED
NO PLATE PRICING DUE TO SCARCITY
BDPP1 Tanner Bushue .50 1.25
BDPP2 Billy Hamilton 1.00 2.50
BDPP3 Enrique Hernandez 4.00 10.00
BDPP4 Virgil Hill .30 .75
BDPP5 Josh Hodges .50 1.25
BDPP6 Christopher Lovett .30 .75
BDPP7 Michael Belfiore .30 .75
BDPP8 Jobduan Morales .30 .75
BDPP9 Anthony Morris .30 .75
BDPP10 Telvin Nash 1.00 2.50
BDPP11 Brooks Pounders .50 1.25
BDPP12 Kyle Rose .30 .75
BDPP13 Seth Schwindenhammer .50 1.25
BDPP14 Patrick Lehman .50 1.25
BDPP15 Mathew Weaver .50 1.25
BDPP16 Brian Dozier 1.50 4.00
BDPP17 Sequoyah Stonecipher .50 1.25
BDPP18 Shannon Wilkerson .30 .75
BDPP19 Jerry Sullivan .30 .75
BDPP20 Jamie Johnson .30 .75
BDPP21 Kent Matthes .30 .75
BDPP22 Ben Paulsen .30 .75
BDPP23 Matthew Davidson 1.00 2.50
BDPP24 Benjamin Carlson .30 .75
BDPP25 Brock Holt .50 1.25
BDPP26 Ben Orloff .30 .75
BDPP27 D.J. LeMahieu 5.00 12.00
BDPP28 Erik Castro .50 1.25
BDPP29 James Jones .30 .75
BDPP30 Cory Burns .30 .75
BDPP31 Chris Wade .30 .75
BDPP32 Jaff Decker .50 1.25
BDPP33 Naoya Washiya .30 .75
BDPP34 Brandt Walker .30 .75
BDPP35 Jordan Henry .50 1.25
BDPP36 Austin Adams .30 .75
BDPP37 Andrew Bellatti .50 1.25
BDPP38 Paul Applebee .50 1.25
BDPP39 Robert Stock .50 1.25
BDPP40 Michael Flacco .30 .75
BDPP41 Jonathan Meyer .30 .75
BDPP42 Cody Rogers .50 1.25
BDPP43 Matt Heidenreich .30 .75
BDPP44 David Holmberg .75 2.00
BDPP45 Mycal Jones .30 .75
BDPP46 David Hale .75 2.00
BDPP47 Dusty Odenbach .30 .75
BDPP48 Robert Hefflinger .30 .75
BDPP49 Buddy Baumann .30 .75
BDPP50 Thomas Berryhill .30 .75
BDPP51 Darrell Ceciliani .30 .75
BDPP52 Derek McCallum .30 .75
BDPP53 Taylor Freeman .30 .75
BDPP54 Tyler Townsend .50 1.25
BDPP55 Tobias Streich .50 1.25
BDPP56 Ryan Jackson .30 .75
BDPP57 Chris Herrmann .50 1.25
BDPP58 Robert Shields .30 .75
BDPP59 Devin Fuller .30 .75
BDPP60 Brad Stillings .30 .75
BDPP61 Ryan Goins .50 1.25
BDPP62 Chase Austin .30 .75
BDPP63 Brett Nommensen .30 .75
BDPP64 Egan Smith .30 .75
BDPP65 Daniel Mahoney .30 .75
BDPP66 Darin Gorski .30 .75
BDPP67 Dustin Dickerson .50 1.25
BDPP68 Victor Black .50 1.25
BDPP69 Dallas Keuchel 2.50 6.00
BDPP70 Nate Baker .30 .75
BDPP71 David Nick .50 1.25
BDPP72 Brian Moran .30 .75
BDPP73 Mark Fleury .30 .75
BDPP74 Brett Wallach .50 1.25
BDPP75 Adam Buschini .30 .75
BDPP76 Tony Sanchez AU 3.00 8.00
BDPP77 Eric Arnett AU 3.00 8.00
BDPP78 Tim Wheeler AU 3.00 8.00
BDPP79 Matt Hobgood AU 3.00 8.00
BDPP80 Matt Bashore AU 3.00 8.00
BDPP81 Randal Grichuk AU 8.00 20.00
BDPP82 A.J. Pollock AU 8.00 20.00
BDPP83 Reymond Fuentes AU 3.00 8.00
BDPP84 Jiovanni Mier AU 3.00 8.00
BDPP85 Steve Matz AU 10.00 25.00
BDPP86 Zack Wheeler AU 8.00 20.00
BDPP87 Mike Minor AU 3.00 8.00
BDPP88 Jared Mitchell AU 5.00 12.00
BDPP89 Mike Trout AU 5000.00 10000.00
BDPP90 Alex White AU 3.00 8.00
BDPP91 Bobby Borchering AU 3.00 8.00
BDPP92 Chad James AU 3.00 8.00
BDPP93 Tyler Matzek AU 3.00 8.00
BDPP94 Max Stassi AU 3.00 8.00
BDPP95 Drew Storen AU 5.00 12.00
BDPP96 Brad Boxberger AU 3.00 8.00
BDPP97 Mike Leake AU 3.00 8.00

2009 Bowman Chrome Draft Prospects Refractors

*REF: 1.5X TO 4X BASIC
STATED ODDS 1:11 HOBBY
*REF AU: .5X TO 1.2X BASIC AU
STATED AUTO ODDS 1:71 HOBBY
AUTO PRINT RUN 500 SER.#'d SETS
BDPP89 Mike Trout AU 8000.00 12000.00

2009 Bowman Chrome Draft Prospects Blue Refractors

*BLUE REF: 4X TO 10X BASIC
STATED ODDS 1:49 HOBBY
STATED PRINT RUN 99 SER.#'d SETS
*BLUE REF AU: 1X TO 2.5X BASIC AU
STATED AUTO ODDS 1:241 HOBBY
AUTO PRINT RUN 150 SER.#'d SETS
BDPP89 Mike Trout AU 15000.00 20000.00

2009 Bowman Chrome Draft Prospects Gold Refractors

*GOLD REF: 8X TO 20X BASIC
STATED ODDS 1:96 HOBBY
STATED PRINT RUN 50 SER.#'d SETS
*GOLD REF AU: 2X TO 5X BASIC AU
STATED AUTO ODDS 1:736 HOBBY
AUTO PRINT RUN 50 SER.#'d SETS
BDPP2 Billy Hamilton 150.00 250.00
BDPP89 Mike Trout AU 25000.00 30000.00

2009 Bowman Chrome Draft Prospects Orange Refractors

STATED ODDS 1:192 HOBBY
STATED AUTO ODDS 1:1545 HOBBY
STATED PRINT RUN 25 SER.#'d SETS
NO PRICING DUE TO SCARCITY

2009 Bowman Chrome Draft Prospects Purple Refractors

*PURPLE: 2X TO 5X BASIC
RANDOM INSERTS IN RETAIL PACKS

2009 Bowman Chrome Draft Prospects X-Fractors

*X-F: 2.5X TO 6X BASIC
STATED ODDS 1:24 HOBBY
STATED PRINT RUN 199 SER.#'d SETS
*X-F AU: .6X TO 1.5X BASIC AU
STATED AUTO ODDS 1:159 HOBBY
AUTO PRINT RUN 225 SER.#'d SETS
BDPP89 Mike Trout AU 10000.00 15000.00

2009 Bowman Chrome Draft WBC Prospects

COMPLETE SET (35) 8.00 20.00
OVERALL PLATE ODDS 1:1531 HOBBY
PLATE PRINT RUN 1 SET PER COLOR
BLACK-CYAN-MAGENTA-YELLOW ISSUED
NO PLATE PRICING DUE TO SCARCITY
BDPW1 Ichiro Suzuki 1.00 2.50
BDPW2 Yu Darvish 1.25 3.00
BDPW3 Phillippe Aumont .50 1.25
BDPW4 Derek Jeter 2.00 5.00
BDPW5 Dustin Pedroia .75 2.00
BDPW6 Earl Agnoly .30 .75
BDPW7 Jose Reyes .50 1.25
BDPW8 Michel Enriquez .30 .75
BDPW9 David Ortiz .75 2.00
BDPW10 Chunhua Dong .50 1.25
BDPW11 Munenori Kawasaki 1.50 4.00
BDPW12 Arquimedes Nieto .30 .75
BDPW13 Bernie Williams .50 1.25
BDPW14 Pedro Lazo .30 .75
BDPW15 Jing-Chao Wang .50 1.25
BDPW16 Chris Barnwell .30 .75
BDPW17 Elmer Dessens .30 .75
BDPW18 Russell Martin .30 .75
BDPW19 Luca Panerati .30 .75
BDPW20 Adam Dunn .50 1.25
BDPW21 Andy Gonzalez .30 .75
BDPW22 Daisuke Matsuzaka .50 1.25
BDPW23 Daniel Berg .30 .75
BDPW24 Aroldis Chapman 1.50 4.00
BDPW25 Justin Morneau .50 1.25
BDPW26 Miguel Cabrera .75 2.00
BDPW27 Magglio Ordonez .50 1.25
BDPW28 Shawn Bowman .30 .75
BDPW29 Robbie Cordemans .30 .75
BDPW30 Paolo Espino .30 .75
BDPW31 Chipper Jones .75 2.00
BDPW32 Frederich Cepeda .50 1.25
BDPW33 Ubaldo Jimenez .30 .75
BDPW34 Seiichi Uchikawa .50 1.25
BDPW35 Norichika Aoki .50 1.25

2009 Bowman Chrome Draft WBC Prospects Refractors

*REF: 1X TO 2.5X BASIC
STATED ODDS 1:11 HOBBY

2009 Bowman Chrome Draft WBC Prospects Blue Refractors

*BLUE REF: 2.5X TO 6X BASIC
STATED ODDS 1:49 HOBBY
STATED PRINT RUN 99 SER.#'d SETS

2009 Bowman Chrome Draft WBC Prospects Gold Refractors

*GOLD: 4X TO 10X BASIC
STATED ODDS 1:96 HOBBY
STATED PRINT RUN 50 SER.#'d SETS

2009 Bowman Chrome Draft WBC Prospects Orange Refractors

STATED ODDS 1:192 HOBBY
STATED PRINT RUN 25 SER.#'d SETS
NO PRICING DUE TO SCARCITY

2009 Bowman Chrome Draft WBC Prospects Purple Refractors

*PURPLE: 1.2X TO 3X BASIC
RANDOM INSERTS IN RETAIL PACKS

2009 Bowman Chrome Draft WBC Prospects X-Fractors

*X-F: 1.5X TO 4X BASIC
STATED ODDS 1:24 HOBBY
STATED PRINT RUN 199 SER.#'d SETS

2010 Bowman Chrome

COMP.SET w/o AU's (220) 40.00 80.00
COMMON CARD (1-180) .20 .50
COMMON RC (181-220) .60 1.50
COMMON AU 3.00 8.00
BOW.STATED AU ODDS 1:113 HOBBY
STRASBURG AU ODDS 1:3810 HOBBY
BOW.CHR.PLATE ODDS 1:1405 HOBBY
STRASBURG AU PLATE ODDS 1:12,000 HOBBY
EXCHANGE DEADLINE 9/30/2013
1 Ryan Braun .30 .75
2 Will Venable .20 .50
3 Zack Greinke .50 1.25
4 Matt Kemp .40 1.00
5 Jair Jurrjens .20 .50
6 Josh Hamilton .30 .75
7 Josh Beckett .20 .50
8 Jake Peavy .20 .50
9 Luke Hochevar .20 .50
10 Ryan Zimmerman .30 .75
11 Robinson Cano .30 .75
12 Magglio Ordonez .30 .75
13 Brian Roberts .20 .50
14 A.J. Burnett .20 .50
15 Chris Carpenter .30 .75
16 Clayton Kershaw .75 2.00
17 Jayson Werth .30 .75
18 Alexei Ramirez .30 .75
19 Ricky Romero .20 .50
20 Andrew McCutchen .50 1.25
21 Chad Billingsley .30 .75
22 David Ortiz .50 1.25
23 Rajai Davis .20 .50
24 Trevor Cahill .20 .50
25 Dan Haren .20 .50
26 Dan Uggla .20 .50
27 Ryan Dempster .20 .50
28 Koji Uehara .20 .50
29 Carlos Gonzalez .30 .75
30 Justin Upton .30 .75
31 Elvis Andrus .30 .75
32 James Loney .20 .50
33 Matt Garza .20 .50
34 Brandon Phillips .20 .50
35 Miguel Cabrera .50 1.25
36 Shane Victorino .30 .75
37 Kyle Blanks .20 .50
38 Troy Tulowitzki .50 1.25
39 Chipper Jones .50 1.25
40 Todd Helton .30 .75
41 Derrek Lee .20 .50
42 Michael Bourn .20 .50
43 Jose Lopez .20 .50
44 Hunter Pence .30 .75
45 Edinson Volquez .20 .50
46 Miguel Montero .20 .50
47 Kevin Youkilis .20 .50
48 Adrian Gonzalez .40 1.00
49 Carl Crawford .30 .75
50 Stephen Drew .20 .50
51 Carlos Pena .30 .75
52 Ubaldo Jimenez .20 .50
53 Martin Prado .20 .50
54 Alcides Escobar .30 .75
55 Jeff Niemann .20 .50
56 Andre Ethier .30 .75
57 Michael Cuddyer .20 .50
58 Howard Kendrick .20 .50
59 Scott Rolen .30 .75
60 Adam Lind .30 .75
61 Prince Fielder .30 .75
62 David Price .40 1.00
63 Johnny Cueto .30 .75
64 John Maine .20 .50
65 Nick Markakis .40 1.00
66 Kosuke Fukudome .30 .75
67 Yadier Molina .60 1.50
68 Aramis Ramirez .20 .50
69 Billy Butler .20 .50
70 Wandy Rodriguez .20 .50
71 Ben Zobrist .30 .75
72 Victor Martinez .30 .75
73 Jorge Posada .30 .75
74 Adam Wainwright .30 .75
75 Vernon Wells .20 .50
76 Gordon Beckham .20 .50
77 Nelson Cruz .50 1.25
78 Kevin Slowey .20 .50
79 Paul Maholm .20 .50
80 Johan Santana .30 .75
81 Kazuo Matsui .20 .50
82 Jon Lester .30 .75
83 Clay Buchholz .20 .50
84 Alex Gordon .30 .75
85 Justin Morneau .30 .75
86 B.J. Upton .30 .75
87 Justin Verlander .50 1.25
88 Carlos Quentin .20 .50
89 Dustin Pedroia .50 1.25
90 Josh Willingham .30 .75
91 Alex Rios .20 .50
92 David Wright .40 1.00
93 Adam Dunn .30 .75
94 Jhoulys Chacin .20 .50
95 Andrew Bailey .20 .50
96 Derek Holland .20 .50
97 Kenshin Kawakami .30 .75
98 Jered Weaver .30 .75
99 Freddy Sanchez .20 .50
100 Matt Holliday .50 1.25
101 Bobby Abreu .20 .50
102 Ryan Doumit .20 .50
103 Kurt Suzuki .20 .50
104 Yovani Gallardo .20 .50
105 Daisuke Matsuzaka .30 .75
106 Francisco Liriano .20 .50
107 Jimmy Rollins .30 .75
108 James Shields .20 .50
109 Chase Utley .30 .75
110 Jeff Francoeur .30 .75
111 Tim Hudson .30 .75
112 Brad Hawpe .20 .50
113 Cole Hamels .40 1.00
114 Alfonso Soriano .30 .75
115 Lance Berkman .30 .75
116 Torii Hunter .20 .50
117 Chris Tillman .20 .50
118 Alex Rodriguez .60 1.50
119 Pablo Sandoval .30 .75
120 Ryan Howard .40 1.00
121 Rick Porcello .30 .75
122 Hanley Ramirez .30 .75
123 Brian McCann .30 .75
124 Kendry Morales .20 .50
125 Josh Johnson .30 .75
126 Joe Mauer .40 1.00
127 Grady Sizemore .30 .75
128 J.A. Happ .30 .75
129 Ichiro .60 1.50
130 Aaron Hill .20 .50
131 Mark Teixeira .30 .75
132 Tim Lincecum .30 .75
133 Denard Span .20 .50
134 Roy Oswalt .30 .75
135 Manny Ramirez .50 1.25
136 Jorge De La Rosa .20 .50
137 Joey Votto .50 1.25
138 Neftali Feliz .20 .50
139 Yunel Escobar .20 .50
140 Carlos Zambrano .30 .75
141 Erick Aybar .20 .50
142 Albert Pujols .60 1.50
143 Felix Hernandez .30 .75
144 Adam Jones .30 .75
145 Jacoby Ellsbury .40 1.00
146 Mark Reynolds .20 .50
147 Derek Jeter 1.25 3.00
148 Scott Baker .20 .50
149 Jose Reyes .30 .75
150 Jason Kubel .20 .50
151 Shin-Soo Choo .30 .75
152 Raul Ibanez .30 .75
153 Matt Cain .30 .75
154 Mark Buehrle .30 .75
155 Ken Griffey Jr. 1.00 2.50
156 Carlos Lee .20 .50
157 Chris Coghlan .20 .50
158 CC Sabathia .30 .75
159 Brett Anderson .20 .50
160 Ian Kinsler .30 .75
161 Mat Latos .30 .75
162 Carlos Beltran .30 .75
163 Dexter Fowler .30 .75
164 Michael Young .20 .50
165 Evan Longoria .30 .75
166 Curtis Granderson .40 1.00
167 Rich Harden .20 .50
168 Hideki Matsui .50 1.25
169 Edwin Jackson .20 .50
170 Miguel Tejada .30 .75
171 John Lackey .30 .75
172 Vladimir Guerrero .30 .75
173 Max Scherzer .50 1.25
174 Jason Bay .30 .75
175 Javier Vazquez .20 .50
176 Johnny Damon .30 .75
177 Cliff Lee .30 .75
178 Chone Figgins .20 .50
179 Kevin Millwood .20 .50
180 Roy Halladay .30 .75
181 Drew Butera (RC) .60 1.50
182 Matt Carson (RC) .60 1.50
183 Ian Desmond (RC) 1.00 2.50
184 Kila Ka'aihue (RC) 1.00 2.50
185 Brian Matusz RC 1.50 4.00
186 Mike Leake RC 2.00 5.00
187 Jenrry Mejia RC 1.00 2.50
188 Austin Jackson RC 1.00 2.50
189 Scott Sizemore RC 1.00 2.50
190 Jason Heyward RC 2.50 6.00
191 Travis Wood (RC) 1.00 2.50
192 Josh Donaldson RC 3.00 8.00
193 John Ely RC .60 1.50
194 Eric Young Jr. (RC) .60 1.50
195 Jason Donald RC .60 1.50
196 Andrew Cashner RC .60 1.50
197 Kevin Russo RC .60 1.50
198A Austin Jackson AU 4.00 10.00
198B Mike Stanton RC 5.00 12.00
199A Scott Sizemore AU 5.00 12.00
199B Drew Storen RC 1.00 2.50
200A Jason Heyward AU 6.00 15.00
200B Jonathan Lucroy RC 1.50 4.00
201 Wade Davis (RC) 1.00 2.50
202 Jon Jay RC 1.00 2.50
203 Ike Davis RC 1.25 3.00
204 Michael Brantley RC 1.00 2.50
205A Stephen Strasburg RC 5.00 12.00
205B Stephen Strasburg AU 25.00 60.00
206 Drew Stubbs RC 1.50 4.00
207 Daniel McCutchen RC 1.00 2.50
208 Brennan Boesch RC 1.50 4.00
209A Henry Rodriguez AU 3.00 8.00
209B Wilson Ramos RC 1.50 4.00
210 Chris Heisey RC 1.00 2.50
211A Michael Dunn AU 3.00 8.00
211B Starlin Castro RC 1.50 4.00
212A Drew Stubbs AU 3.00 8.00
212B Trevor Plouffe (RC) 1.50 4.00
213A Brandon Allen AU 3.00 8.00
213B Luis Atilano RC .60 1.50
214A Daniel McCutchen AU 3.00 8.00
214B Carlos Santana RC 2.00 5.00
215A Juan Francisco AU 3.00 8.00
215B Allen Craig RC 1.50 4.00
216A Eric Hacker AU 3.00 8.00
216B Ruben Tejada RC 1.00 2.50
217A Michael Brantley AU 10.00 25.00
217B Andy Oliver RC .60 1.50
218A Dustin Richardson AU 3.00 8.00
218B Tyler Colvin RC 1.00 2.50
219A Josh Thole AU 4.00 10.00
219B Cesar Valdez RC .60 1.50
220A Daniel Hudson AU 3.00 8.00
220B Lance Zawadzki RC .60 1.50

2010 Bowman Chrome Refractors

*REF VET: 1X TO 2.5X BASIC
*REF RC: .6X TO 1.5X BASIC RC
REF ODDS 1:4 HOBBY
*REF AU: .6X TO 1.5X BASIC
REF AU ODDS 1:277 HOBBY
STRASBURG AU ODDS 1:105 HOBBY
REF AU PRINT RUN 500 SER.#'d SETS
EXCHANGE DEADLINE 9/30/2013

2010 Bowman Chrome Blue Refractors

*BLUE VET: 2.5X TO 6X BASIC
*BLUE RC: 1.2X TO 3X BASIC
BLUE REF ODDS 1:48 HOBBY
STATED PRINT RUN 150 SER.#'d SETS
*BLUE AU: .75X TO 2X BASIC
BLUE AU ODDS 1:545 HOBBY
BLUE STRASBURG AU ODDS 1:352 HOBBY
BLUE AU PRINT RUN 250 SER.#'d SETS
EXCHANGE DEADLINE 9/30/2013

2010 Bowman Chrome Gold Refractors

*GOLD VET: 5X TO 12X BASIC
*GOLD RC: 2X TO 5X BASIC
GOLD REF ODDS 1:142 HOBBY
STATED PRINT RUN 50 SER.#'d SETS
*GOLD AU: 1.2X TO 3X BASIC
GOLD AU ODDS 1:2733 HOBBY
GOLD STRASBURG AU ODDS 1:1073 HOBBY
GOLD AU PRINT RUN 50 SER.#'d SETS
EXCHANGE DEADLINE 9/30/2013
200A Jason Heyward AU 20.00 50.00
205B Stephen Strasburg AU 300.00 500.00
213A Brandon Allen AU 20.00 50.00

2010 Bowman Chrome 18U USA Baseball

COMPLETE SET (20) 15.00 40.00
STATED ODDS 1:4 HOBBY
18BC1 Cody Buckel 1.50 4.00
18BC2 Nick Castellanos 3.00 8.00
18BC3 Garin Cecchini 2.00 5.00
18BC4 Sean Coyle .60 1.50
18BC5 Nicky Delmonico 1.00 2.50
18BC6 Kevin Gausman 3.00 8.00
18BC7 Cory Hahn .60 1.50
18BC8 Bryce Harper 25.00 60.00
18BC9 Kavin Keyes .60 1.50
18BC10 Manny Machado 10.00 25.00
18BC11 Connor Mason .60 1.50
18BC12 Ladson Montgomery .60 1.50
18BC13 Phillip Pfeifer .60 1.50
18BC14 Brian Ragira .60 1.50
18BC15 Robbie Ray .60 1.50
18BC16 Kyle Ryan .60 1.50
18BC17 Jameson Taillon 1.00 2.50
18BC18 A.J. Vanegas 1.00 2.50
18BC19 Karsten Whitson 1.00 2.50
18BC20 Tony Wolters 1.00 2.50

2010 Bowman Chrome 18U USA Baseball Refractors

*REF: .75X TO 2X BASIC
STATED ODDS 1:16 HOBBY
STATED PRINT RUN 777 SER.#'d SETS

2010 Bowman Chrome 18U USA Baseball Blue Refractors

*BLUE REF: 2X TO 5X BASIC
STATED ODDS 1:46 HOBBY
STATED PRINT RUN 250 SER.#'d SETS

2010 Bowman Chrome 18U USA Baseball Gold Refractors

*GOLD REF: 3X TO 8X BASIC
STATED ODDS 1:228 HOBBY
STATED PRINT RUN 50 SER.#'d SETS

2010 Bowman Chrome 18U USA Baseball Orange Refractors

STATED ODDS 1:463 HOBBY
STATED PRINT RUN 25 SER.#'d SETS

2010 Bowman Chrome 18U USA Baseball Autographs

STATED ODDS 1:207 HOBBY
PRINTING PLATE ODDS 1:24,605 HOBBY
AA Albert Almora 5.00 12.00
AV A.J. Vanegas 3.00 8.00
BR Brian Ragira 4.00 10.00
BS Bubba Starling 4.00 10.00
CL Christian Lopes 3.00 8.00
CM Christian Montgomery 3.00 8.00
DC Daniel Camarena 3.00 8.00
DM Dillon Maples 3.00 8.00
ES Elvin Soto 3.00 8.00
FL Francisco Lindor 50.00 120.00
HO Henry Owens 5.00 12.00
JH John Hochstatter 3.00 8.00
JS John Simms 3.00 8.00
LM Lance McCullers 5.00 12.00
ML Marcus Littlewood 3.00 8.00
ND Nicky Delmonico 3.00 8.00
PP Phillip Pfeifer III 3.00 8.00
TW Tony Wolters 3.00 8.00
BSW Blake Swihart 6.00 15.00
MIL Michael Lorenzen 4.00 10.00

2010 Bowman Chrome 18U USA Baseball Autographs Refractors

*REF: .6X TO 1.5X BASIC
STATED ODDS 1:646 HOBBY
STATED PRINT RUN 199 SER.#'d SETS

2010 Bowman Chrome 18U USA Baseball Autographs Blue Refractors

*BLUE REF: 1X TO 2.5X BASIC
STATED ODDS 1:1310 HOBBY
STATED PRINT RUN 99 SER.#'d SETS

2010 Bowman Chrome 18U USA Baseball Autographs Gold Refractors

*GOLD REF: 1.5X TO 4X BASIC
STATED ODDS 1:2630 HOBBY
STATED PRINT RUN 50 SER.#'d SETS

2010 Bowman Chrome 18U USA Baseball Autographs Orange Refractors

STATED ODDS 1:5410 HOBBY
STATED PRINT RUN 25 SER.#'d SETS

2010 Bowman Chrome Prospects

COMP.SET w/o AU's (220) 60.00 120.00
BOW.STATED AU ODDS 1:38 HOBBY
BOW.CHR.STATED AU ODDS 1:24 HOBBY
PLATE ODDS 1:1405 HOBBY
PLATE AU ODDS 1:12,000 HOBBY
BCP1 Stephen Strasburg 2.00 5.00
BCP2 Melky Mesa .50 1.25
BCP3 Cole McCurry .30 .75
BCP4 Tyler Henley .30 .75
BCP5 Andrew Cashner .30 .75
BCP6 Konrad Schmidt .30 .75
BCP7 Jean Segura 1.50 4.00
BCP8 Jon Gaston .50 1.25
BCP9 Nick Santomauro .30 .75
BCP10 Aroldis Chapman 1.25 3.00
BCP11 Logan Watkins .30 .75
BCP12 Bo Bowman .30 .75
BCP13 Jeff Antigua .30 .75
BCP14 Matt Adams 1.00 2.50
BCP15 Joseph Cruz .50 1.25
BCP16 Sebastian Valle .50 1.25
BCP17 Stefan Gartrell .30 .75
BCP18 Pedro Ciriaco 1.00 2.50
BCP19 Tyson Gillies .75 2.00
BCP20 Casey Crosby .30 .75
BCP21 Luis Exposito .30 .75
BCP22 Welington Dotel .30 .75
BCP23 Alexander Torres .30 .75
BCP24 Byron Wiley .30 .75
BCP25 Pedro Florimon .30 .75
BCP26 Cody Satterwhite .50 1.25
BCP27 Craig Clark 1.25 3.00
BCP28 Jason Christian .30 .75
BCP29 Tommy Mendonca .30 .75
BCP30 Ryan Dent .30 .75
BCP31 Jhan Marinez .30 .75
BCP32 Eric Niesen .30 .75
BCP33 Gustavo Nunez .30 .75
BCP34 Scott Shaw .30 .75
BCP35 Welinton Ramirez .30 .75
BCP36 Trevor May 1.25 3.00
BCP37 Mitch Moreland .50 1.25
BCP38 Nick Czyz .30 .75
BCP39 Edinson Rincon .30 .75
BCP40 Domingo Santana 1.00 2.50
BCP41 Carson Blair .30 .75
BCP42 Rashun Dixon .30 .75
BCP43 Alexander Colome .75 2.00
BCP44 Allan Dykstra .30 .75
BCP45 J.J. Hoover .30 .75
BCP46 Abner Abreu .50 1.25
BCP47 Daniel Nava .30 .75
BCP48 Simon Castro .30 .75
BCP49 Brian Baisley .30 .75
BCP50 Tony Delmonico .30 .75
BCP51 Chase D'Arnaud .30 .75
BCP52 Sheng-An Kuo .30 .75
BCP53 Leandro Castro .30 .75
BCP54 Charlie Leesman .30 .75
BCP55 Caleb Joseph .30 .75
BCP56 Rolando Gomez .30 .75
BCP57 John Lamb .75 2.00
BCP58 Adam Wilk .50 1.25
BCP59 Randall Delgado .50 1.25
BCP60 Neil Medchill .50 1.25
BCP61 Josh Donaldson 1.50 4.00
BCP62 Zach Gentile .30 .75
BCP63 Kiel Roling .30 .75
BCP64 Wes Freeman .30 .75
BCP65 Brian Pellegrini .50 1.25
BCP66 Kyle Jensen .30 .75
BCP67 Evan Anundsen .30 .75
BCP68 Hak-Ju Lee .50 1.25
BCP69 C.J. Retherford .30 .75
BCP70 Dillon Gee .75 2.00
BCP71 Bo Greenwell .30 .75
BCP72 Matt Tucker .50 1.25
BCP73 Joe Serafin .30 .75
BCP74 Matt Brown .30 .75
BCP75 Alexis Oliveras .30 .75
BCP76 James Beresford .30 .75
BCP77 Steve Lombardozzi .50 1.25
BCP78 Curtis Petersen .30 .75
BCP79 Eric Farris .30 .75
BCP80 Yen-Wen Kuo .30 .75
BCP81 Caleb Brewer .30 .75
BCP82 Jacob Elmore .50 1.25
BCP83 Jared Clark .50 1.25
BCP84 Yowill Espinal .50 1.25
BCP85 Jae-Hoon Ha .30 .75
BCP86 Michael Wing .30 .75
BCP87 Wilmer Font .30 .75
BCP88 Jake Kahaulelio .30 .75
BCP89A Dustin Ackley .50 1.25
BCP89B Dustin Ackley AU 4.00 10.00
BCP90A Donavan Tate .30 .75
BCP90B Donavan Tate AU 3.00 8.00
BCP91A Nolan Arenado 10.00 25.00
BCP91B Nolan Arenado AU 150.00 400.00
BCP92A Rex Brothers .30 .75
BCP92B Rex Brothers AU 3.00 8.00
BCP93A Brett Jackson 1.00 2.50
BCP93B Brett Jackson AU 3.00 8.00
BCP94A Chad Jenkins .30 .75
BCP94B Chad Jenkins AU 3.00 8.00
BCP95A Slade Heathcott 1.00 2.50
BCP95B Slade Heathcott AU 4.00 10.00
BCP96A J.R. Murphy .50 1.25
BCP96B J.R. Murphy AU 3.00 8.00
BCP97A Patrick Schuster .30 .75
BCP97B Patrick Schuster AU 3.00 8.00
BCP98A Alexia Amarista .30 .75
BCP98B Alexia Amarista AU 3.00 8.00
BCP99A Thomas Neal .50 1.25
BCP99B Thomas Neal AU 3.00 8.00
BCP100A Starlin Castro .75 2.00
BCP100B Starlin Castro AU 8.00 20.00
BCP101A Anthony Rizzo 4.00 10.00
BCP101B Anthony Rizzo AU 75.00 200.00
BCP102A Felix Doubront .30 .75
BCP102B Felix Doubront AU 3.00 8.00
BCP103A Nick Franklin .75 2.00
BCP103B Nick Franklin AU 3.00 8.00
BCP104A Anthony Gose .50 1.25
BCP104B Anthony Gose AU 3.00 8.00
BCP105A Julio Teheran .50 1.25
BCP105B Julio Teheran AU 6.00 15.00
BCP106A Grant Green .30 .75
BCP106B Grant Green AU 3.00 8.00
BCP107A David Lough .30 .75
BCP107B David Lough AU 3.00 8.00
BCP108A Jose Iglesias 1.00 2.50
BCP108B Jose Iglesias AU 5.00 12.00
BCP109A Jaff Decker .75 2.00
BCP109B Jaff Decker AU 3.00 8.00
BCP110A D.J. LeMahieu 3.00 8.00
BCP110B D.J. LeMahieu AU 50.00 120.00
BCP111A Craig Clark 1.25 3.00
BCP111B Craig Clark AU 3.00 8.00
BCP112A Jefry Marte .30 .75
BCP112B Jefry Marte AU 3.00 8.00
BCP113A Josh Donaldson 1.50 4.00
BCP113B Josh Donaldson AU 12.00 30.00
BCP114A Steven Hensley .30 .75
BCP114B Steven Hensley AU 3.00 8.00
BCP115A James Darnell .50 1.25
BCP115B James Darnell AU 3.00 8.00
BCP116A Kirk Nieuwenhuis .30 .75
BCP116B Kirk Nieuwenhuis AU 3.00 8.00
BCP117A Wil Myers .75 2.00
BCP117B Wil Myers AU 12.00 30.00
BCP118A Bryan Mitchell .30 .75
BCP118B Bryan Mitchell AU 3.00 8.00
BCP119A Martin Perez .75 2.00
BCP119B Martin Perez AU 4.00 10.00
BCP120 Taylor Sinclair .30 .75
BCP121 Max Walla .30 .75
BCP122 Darin Ruf 1.25 3.00
BCP123 Nicholas Hernandez .75 2.00
BCP124 Salvador Perez 1.50 4.00
BCP125 Yan Gomes .50 1.25
BCP126 Riaan Spanjer-Furstenburg .30 .75
BCP127 Andrei Lobanov .30 .75
BCP128 Eliezer Mesa .30 .75
BCP129 Scott Barnes .30 .75
BCP130 Jerry Sands .75 2.00
BCP131 Chris Masters .30 .75
BCP132 Brandon Short .30 .75
BCP133 Rafael Dolis .30 .75
BCP134 Kevin Coddington .30 .75
BCP135 Jordan Pacheco .75 2.00
BCP136 Mike Zuanich .30 .75
BCP137 Jose Altuve 5.00 12.00
BCP138 Jimmy Paredes .75 2.00
BCP139 Yohan Flande .30 .75
BCP140 Drew Cumberland .30 .75
BCP141 Jose Yepez .30 .75
BCP142 Joe Gardner .30 .75
BCP143 Michael Kirkman .30 .75
BCP144 Thomas Di Benedetto .30 .75
BCP145 Blake Lalli .30 .75
BCP146 Avery Barnes .30 .75
BCP147 Brayan Villareal .30 .75
BCP148 Zoilo Almonte 2.50 6.00
BCP149 Tommy Pham .50 1.25
BCP150 Vince Belnome .30 .75
BCP151 Carlos Pimentel .30 .75
BCP152 Jeremy Barnes .30 .75
BCP153 Josh Stinson .30 .75
BCP154 Brady Shoemaker .30 .75
BCP155 Rudy Owens .50 1.25
BCP156 Kevin Mahoney .30 .75
BCP157 Luke Putkonen .30 .75
BCP158 Taylor Green .30 .75
BCP159 Anderson Hidalgo .30 .75
BCP160 Jonathan Villar .75 2.00
BCP161 Justin Bour .75 2.00
BCP162 Evan Bronson .30 .75
BCP163 Rossmel Perez .30 .75
BCP164 Jacob Cowan .30 .75
BCP165 J.D. Martinez 4.00 10.00

BCP166 Chris Schwinden .30 .75
BCP167 Rawley Bishop .30 .75
BCP168 Tim Pahuta .30 .75
BCP169 Buck Afenir .30 .75
BCP170 Eduardo Nunez .75 2.00
BCP171 Ethan Hollingsworth .30 .75
BCP172 Brad Correll .30 .75
BCP173 Armando Rodriguez .30 .75
BCP174 Ryan Wiegand .30 .75
BCP175 Terry Doyle .30 .75
BCP176 Grant Hogue .50 1.25
BCP177 Stephen Parker .30 .75
BCP178 Nathan Adcock .50 1.25
BCP179 Will Middlebrooks .50 1.25
BCP180 Chris Archer 1.00 2.50
BCP181A T.J. McFarland .30 .75
BCP181B T.J. McFarland AU 3.00 8.00
BCP182A Alex Liddi .50 1.25
BCP182B Alex Liddi AU 3.00 8.00
BCP183A Liam Hendriks .75 2.00
BCP183B Liam Hendriks AU 3.00 8.00
BCP184A Ozzie Martinez .30 .75
BCP184B Ozzie Martinez AU 3.00 8.00
BCP185A Eury Perez .30 .75
BCP185B Eury Perez AU 3.00 8.00
BCP186A Jhan Marinez .30 .75
BCP186B Jhan Marinez AU 3.00 8.00
BCP187A Carlos Peguero .50 1.25
BCP187B Carlos Peguero AU 3.00 8.00
BCP188A Tyler Chatwood .30 .75
BCP188B Tyler Chatwood AU 3.00 8.00
BCP189A Francisco Peguero .30 .75
BCP189B Francisco Peguero AU 4.00 10.00
BCP190A Pedro Baez .30 .75
BCP190B Pedro Baez AU 3.00 8.00
BCP191A Wilkin Ramirez .30 .75
BCP191B Wilkin Ramirez AU 3.00 8.00
BCP192A Wilin Rosario .30 .75
BCP192B Wilin Rosario AU 3.00 8.00
BCP193A Dan Tuttle .30 .75
BCP193B Dan Tuttle AU 3.00 8.00
BCP194A Trevor Reckling .30 .75
BCP194B Trevor Reckling AU 3.00 8.00
BCP195A Kyle Seager .75 2.00
BCP195B Kyle Seager AU 6.00 15.00
BCP196A Jason Kipnis 1.25 3.00
BCP196B Jason Kipnis AU 5.00 12.00
BCP197A Jeurys Familia .75 2.00
BCP197B Jeurys Familia AU 3.00 8.00
BCP198A Adeinis Hechavarria .30 .75
BCP198B Adeinis Hechavarria AU 3.00 8.00
BCP199A Aroldis Chapman 1.25 3.00
BCP199B Aroldis Chapman AU 12.00 30.00
BCP200A Everett Williams .30 .75
BCP200B Everett Williams AU 3.00 8.00
BCP201A Ehire Adrianza .30 .75
BCP201B Ehire Adrianza AU 5.00 12.00
BCP202A Kyle Gibson 1.25 3.00
BCP202B Kyle Gibson AU 3.00 8.00
BCP203A Max Kepler 1.00 2.50
BCP203B Max Kepler AU 12.00 30.00
BCP204A Shelby Miller 1.50 4.00
BCP204B Shelby Miller AU 4.00 10.00
BCP205A Miguel Sano 2.00 5.00
BCP205B Miguel Sano AU 15.00 40.00
BCP206A Scooter Gennett .60 1.50
BCP206B Scooter Gennett AU 5.00 12.00
BCP207A Gary Sanchez 3.00 8.00
BCP207B Gary Sanchez AU 20.00 50.00
BCP208A Graham Stoneburner .50 1.25
BCP208B Graham Stoneburner AU 3.00 8.00
BCP209 Josh Satin .50 1.25
BCP210A Matt Davidson 1.00 2.50
BCP210B Matt Davidson AU 3.00 8.00
BCP211A Arodys Vizcaino .75 2.00
BCP211B Arodys Vizcaino AU 3.00 8.00
BCP212A Anthony Bass .30 .75
BCP212B Anthony Bass AU 3.00 8.00
BCP213A Robinson Chirinos .30 .75
BCP213B Robinson Chirinos AU 3.00 8.00
BCP214A Trayce Thompson .75 2.00
BCP214B Trayce Thompson AU 3.00 8.00
BCP215A Simon Castro .30 .75
BCP215B Simon Castro AU 3.00 8.00
BCP216A Corban Joseph .30 .75
BCP216B Corban Joseph AU 3.00 8.00
BCP217 Noel Arguelles .50 1.25
BCP218A Daniel Fields .30 .75
BCP218B Daniel Fields AU 3.00 8.00
BCP219A Robbie Erlin .75 2.00
BCP219B Robbie Erlin AU 4.00 10.00
BCP220A Juan Urbina .50 1.25
BCP220B Juan Urbina AU 3.00 8.00
BCP221 Marc Krauss AU 4.00 10.00
BCP222 Ryan Wheeler AU 4.00 10.00

2010 Bowman Chrome Prospects Refractors

1-110 REF: 1.5X TO 4X BASIC
111-220 REF: 1.5X TO 4X BASIC
BOW.ODDS 1:16 HOBBY
BOW.CHR.ODDS 1:39 HOBBY
1-110 PRINT RUN 777 SER.#'d SETS
111-220 PRINT RUN 500 SER.#'d SETS
*REF AU: .5X TO 1.2X BASIC
BOW.REF AU ODDS 1:96 HOBBY
BOW.CHR.REF AU ODDS 1:105 HOBBY
REF AU PRINT RUN 500 SER.#'d SETS
BCP110B D.J. LeMahieu AU 75.00 200.00
BCP137 Jose Altuve 75.00 200.00

2010 Bowman Chrome Prospects Blue Refractors

*BLUE REF: 3X TO 8X BASIC
BOW.ODDS 1:46 HOBBY
BOW.CHR.ODDS 1:48 HOBBY
1-110 PRINT RUN 250 SER.#'d SETS
111-220 PRINT RUN 150 SER.#'d SETS
*BLUE REF AU: 1.2X TO 3X BASIC
BOW.BLUE AU ODDS 1:139 HOBBY
BOW.CHR.BLUE AU ODDS 1:352 HOBBY
BLUE AU PRINT RUN 150 SER.#'d SETS
BCP91B Nolan Arenado AU 500.00 1000.00
BCP110B D.J. LeMahieu AU 125.00 300.00
BCP137 Jose Altuve 300.00 600.00

2010 Bowman Chrome Prospects Gold Refractors

*GOLD REF: 8X TO 20X BASIC
BOW.ODDS 1:228 HOBBY
BOW.CHR.ODDS 1:142 HOBBY
STATED PRINT RUN 50 SER.#'d SETS
*GOLD REF AU: 2.5X TO 6X BASIC
BOW.GOLD AU ODDS 1:957 HOBBY
BOW.CHR.GOLD AU ODDS 1:1073 HOBBY
GOLD AU PRINT RUN 50 SER.#'d SETS
BCP91B Nolan Arenado AU 1200.00 1500.00
BCP93A Brett Jackson 30.00 60.00
BCP100A Starlin Castro 40.00 80.00
BCP110B D.J. LeMahieu AU 400.00 800.00
BCP113B Josh Donaldson AU 125.00 250.00
BCP137 Jose Altuve 800.00 1200.00

2010 Bowman Chrome Prospects Green X-Fractors

*X-F: 1.2X TO 3X BASIC
RANDOM INSERTS IN RETAIL PACKS

2010 Bowman Chrome Prospects Orange Refractors

BOW.STATED ODDS 1:463 HOBBY
BOW.STATED AU ODDS 1:1917 HOBBY
BOW.CHR.ODDS 1:284 HOBBY
BOW.CHR.AU ODDS 1:2200 HOBBY
STATED PRINT RUN 25 SER.#'d SETS

2010 Bowman Chrome Prospects Purple Refractors

*REF: 1X TO 2.5X BASIC
1-110 PRINT RUN 999 SER.#'d SETS
111-220 PRINT RUN 899 SER.#'d SETS
BCP1 Stephen Strasburg 12.00 30.00
BCP137 Jose Altuve 40.00 100.00

2010 Bowman Chrome Topps 100 Prospects

STATED ODDS 1:28 HOBBY
STATED PRINT RUN 999 SER.#'d SETS
*REF: .5X TO 1.2X BASIC
REFRACTOR ODDS 1:55 HOBBY
REFRACTOR PRINT RUN 499 SER.#'d SETS
*GOLD REF: 2X TO 5X BASIC
GOLD REF ODDS 1:610 HOBBY
GOLD REF PRINT RUN 50 SER.#'d SETS
SUPERFRACTOR ODDS 1:19,684 HOBBY
SUPERFRACTOR PRINT RUN 1 SER.#'d SET
TPC1 Stephen Strasburg 4.00 10.00
TPC2 Aroldis Chapman 2.00 5.00
TPC3 Jason Heyward 2.00 5.00
TPC4 Jesus Montero .50 1.25
TPC5 Mike Stanton 4.00 10.00
TPC6 Mike Moustakas 1.25 3.00
TPC7 Kyle Drabek .75 2.00
TPC8 Tyler Matzek 1.25 3.00
TPC9 Austin Jackson .75 2.00
TPC10 Starlin Castro 1.25 3.00
TPC11 Todd Frazier 1.25 3.00
TPC12 Carlos Santana 1.50 4.00
TPC13 Josh Vitters .50 1.25
TPC14 Neftali Feliz .50 1.25
TPC15 Tyler Flowers .75 2.00
TPC16 Alcides Escobar .75 2.00
TPC17 Ike Davis 1.00 2.50
TPC18 Domonic Brown 2.00 5.00
TPC19 Donavan Tate .50 1.25
TPC20 Buster Posey 4.00 10.00
TPC21 Dustin Ackley .75 2.00
TPC22 Desmond Jennings .75 2.00
TPC23 Brandon Allen .50 1.25
TPC24 Freddie Freeman 6.00 15.00
TPC25 Jake Arrieta 1.25 3.00
TPC26 Bobby Borchering .75 2.00
TPC27 Logan Morrison .75 2.00
TPC28 Christian Friederich .75 2.00
TPC29 Wilmer Flores .75 2.00
TPC30 Austin Romine .75 2.00
TPC31 Tony Sanchez 1.25 3.00
TPC32 Madison Bumgarner 5.00 12.00
TPC33 Mike Montgomery .75 2.00
TPC34 Andrew Lambo .50 1.25
TPC35 Derek Norris .75 2.00
TPC36 Chris Withrow .50 1.25
TPC37 Thomas Neal .75 2.00
TPC38 Trevor Reckling .50 1.25
TPC39 Andrew Cashner .50 1.25
TPC40 Daniel Hudson .75 2.00
TPC41 Jiovanni Mier .75 2.00
TPC42 Grant Green .50 1.25
TPC43 Jeremy Hellickson 1.25 3.00
TPC44 Felix Doubront .50 1.25
TPC45 Martin Perez 1.25 3.00
TPC46 Jenrry Mejia .75 2.00
TPC47 Adrian Cardenas .50 1.25
TPC48 Ivan DeJesus Jr. .50 1.25
TPC49 Nolan Arenado 15.00 40.00
TPC50 Slade Heathcott 1.50 4.00
TPC51 Ian Desmond .75 2.00
TPC52 Michael Taylor .75 2.00
TPC53 Jaime Garcia .75 2.00
TPC54 Jose Tabata .75 2.00
TPC55 Josh Bell .50 1.25
TPC56 Jarrod Parker 1.25 3.00
TPC57 Matt Dominguez 1.25 3.00
TPC58 Koby Clemens .75 2.00
TPC59 Angel Morales .50 1.25
TPC60 Juan Francisco .75 2.00
TPC61 John Ely .50 1.25
TPC62 Brett Jackson 1.50 4.00
TPC63 Chad Jenkins .50 1.25
TPC64 Jose Iglesias 1.50 4.00
TPC65 Logan Forsythe .50 1.25
TPC66 Alex Liddi .75 2.00
TPC67 Eric Arnett .50 1.25
TPC68 Wilkin Ramirez .50 1.25
TPC69 Lars Anderson .75 2.00
TPC70 Jared Mitchell .75 2.00
TPC71 Mike Leake 1.50 4.00
TPC72 D.J. LeMahieu 5.00 12.00
TPC73 Chris Marrero .50 1.25
TPC74 Matt Moore 4.00 10.00
TPC75 Jordan Brown .50 1.25
TPC76 Christopher Parmelee .50 1.25
TPC77 Ryan Kalish .75 2.00
TPC78 A.J. Pollock 1.25 3.00
TPC79 Alex White .75 2.00
TPC80 Scott Sizemore .75 2.00
TPC81 Jay Austin .50 1.25
TPC82 Zach McAllister .75 2.00
TPC83 Max Stassi .75 2.00
TPC84 Robert Stock .50 1.25
TPC85 Jake McGee 1.00 2.50
TPC86 Zack Wheeler 1.50 4.00
TPC87 Chase D'Arnaud .50 1.25
TPC88 Danny Duffy .75 2.00
TPC89 Josh Lindblom .50 1.25
TPC90 Anthony Gose .75 2.00
TPC91 Simon Castro .50 1.25
TPC92 Chris Carter .75 2.00
TPC93 Matt Hobgood 1.25 3.00
TPC94 Ben Revere .75 2.00
TPC95 Mat Gamel .50 1.25
TPC96 Anthony Hewitt .50 1.25
TPC97 Julio Teheran .75 2.00
TPC98 Josh Reddick .50 1.25
TPC99 Hank Conger .50 1.25
TPC100 Jordan Walden .50 1.25

2010 Bowman Chrome USA Baseball

COMPLETE SET (22) 10.00 25.00
STATED ODDS 1:4 HOBBY
BC1 Trevor Bauer 6.00 15.00
BC2 Chad Bettis .60 1.50
BC3 Bryce Brentz 1.50 4.00
BC4 Michael Choice 1.00 2.50
BC5 Gerrit Cole 12.00 30.00
BC6 Christian Colon 1.00 2.50
BC7 Blake Forsythe .60 1.50
BC8 Yasmani Grandal 1.00 2.50
BC9 Sonny Gray 1.50 4.00
BC10 Rick Hague .60 1.50
BC11 Tyler Holt .60 1.50
BC12 Casey McGrew .60 1.50
BC13 Brad Miller 1.50 4.00
BC14 Matt Newman .60 1.50
BC15 Nick Pepitone .60 1.50
BC16 Drew Pomeranz 1.50 4.00
BC17 T.J. Walz .60 1.50
BC18 Cody Wheeler .60 1.50
BC19 Andy Wilkins .60 1.50
BC20 Asher Wojciechowski 1.50 4.00
BC21 Kolten Wong 1.00 2.50
BC22 Tony Zych .60 1.50

2010 Bowman Chrome USA Baseball Refractors

*REF: .75X TO 2X BASIC
STATED ODDS 1:16 HOBBY
STATED PRINT RUN 777 SER.#'d SETS

2010 Bowman Chrome USA Baseball Blue Refractors

*BLUE REF: 2X TO 5X BASIC
STATED ODDS 1:46 HOBBY
STATED PRINT RUN 250 SER.#'d SETS

2010 Bowman Chrome USA Baseball Gold Refractors

*GOLD REF: 4X TO 10X BASIC
STATED ODDS 1:228 HOBBY
STATED PRINT RUN 50 SER.#'d SETS

2010 Bowman Chrome USA Baseball Orange Refractors

STATED ODDS 1:463 HOBBY
STATED PRINT RUN 25 SER.#'d SETS

2010 Bowman Chrome USA Baseball Dual Autographs

STATED ODDS 1:1393 HOBBY
STATED PRINT RUN 500 SER.#'d SETS
USAD1 B.Starling/L.McCullers 8.00 20.00
USAD2 Elvin Soto 6.00 15.00
Blake Swihart
USAD3 Nicky Delmonico 6.00 15.00
Tony Wolters
USAD4 Henry Owens 6.00 15.00
Phillip Pfeifer III
USAD5 Christian Montgomery 6.00 15.00
John Simms
USAD6 Albert Almora 10.00 25.00
Brian Ragira
USAD7 Marcus Littlewood 6.00 15.00
Christian Lopes
USAD8 Dillon Maples 6.00 15.00
A.J. Vanegas
USAD9 Daniel Camarena 6.00 15.00
John Hochstatter
USAD10 F.Lindor/M.Lorenzen 20.00 50.00

2010 Bowman Chrome USA Baseball Buyback Autographs

ISSUED VIA WRAPPER REDEMPTION PROGRAM
STATED PRINT RUN 100 SER.#'d SETS
BC3 Bryce Brentz 20.00 50.00
BC4 Michael Choice 20.00 50.00
BC6 Christian Colon 12.50 30.00
BC8 Yasmani Grandal 12.50 30.00
BC16 Drew Pomeranz 10.00 25.00
18BC8 Bryce Harper 1000.00 1500.00
18BC10 Manny Machado 250.00 500.00
18BC17 Jameson Taillon 20.00 50.00

2010 Bowman Chrome USA Baseball Wrapper Redemption Autographs

ISSUED VIA WRAPPER REDEMPTION PROGRAM
STATED PRINT RUN 99 SER.#'d SETS
WR3 Kyle Winkler 6.00 15.00
WR6 AJ Vanegas 6.00 15.00
WR7 Albert Almora 20.00 50.00
WR8 Blake Swihart 30.00 60.00
WR9 Brian Ragira 6.00 15.00
WR10 Bubba Starling 15.00 40.00
WR11 Christian Lopes 6.00 15.00
WR12 Daniel Camarena 6.00 15.00
WR13 Dillon Maples 12.50 30.00
WR14 Elvin Soto 10.00 25.00
WR15 Francisco Lindor 30.00 60.00
WR16 Henry Owens 20.00 50.00
WR17 John Simms 6.00 15.00
WR18 Lance McCullers 6.00 15.00
WR19 Marcus Littlewood 10.00 25.00
WR20 Michael Lorenzen 6.00 15.00
WR21 Phillip Pfeifer 10.00 25.00
WR22 Alex Dickerson 6.00 15.00
WR23 Andrew Maggi 6.00 15.00
WR24 Brad Miller 50.00 100.00
WR25 Brett Mooneyham 10.00 25.00
WR26 Brian Johnson 12.50 30.00
WR27 George Springer 125.00 300.00
WR28 Gerrit Cole 100.00 200.00
WR29 Jackie Bradley Jr. 75.00 200.00
WR30 Jason Esposito 10.00 25.00
WR32 Matt Barnes 20.00 50.00
WR33 Mikie Mahtook 10.00 25.00
WR34 Nick Ramirez 15.00 40.00
WR35 Noe Ramirez 6.00 15.00
WR36 Nolan Fontana 10.00 25.00
WR37 Peter O'Brien 20.00 50.00
WR38 Ryan Wright 6.00 15.00
WR39 Scott McGough 6.00 15.00
WR40 Sean Gilmartin 15.00 40.00
WR41 Steve Rodriguez 6.00 15.00
WR42 Tyler Anderson 6.00 15.00

2010 Bowman Chrome USA Baseball Wrapper Redemption Autographs Black

ISSUED VIA WRAPPER REDMPTION PROGRAM
STATED PRINT RUN 25 SER.#'d SETS

2010 Bowman Chrome USA Stars

COMPLETE SET (20) 6.00 15.00
USA1 Albert Almora 2.00 5.00
USA2 Daniel Camarena .60 1.50
USA3 Nicky Delmonico 1.00 2.50
USA4 John Hochstatter .60 1.50
USA5 Francisco Lindor 8.00 20.00
USA6 Marcus Littlewood 1.00 2.50
USA7 Christian Lopes 1.00 2.50
USA8 Michael Lorenzen .60 1.50
USA9 Dillon Maples .60 1.50
USA10 Lance McCullers 1.00 2.50
USA11 Christian Montgomery .60 1.50
USA12 Henry Owens 1.00 2.50
USA13 Phillip Pfeifer III .60 1.50
USA14 Brian Ragira .60 1.50
USA15 John Simms 1.00 2.50
USA16 Elvin Soto .60 1.50
USA17 Bubba Starling 1.00 2.50
USA18 Blake Swihart 1.50 4.00
USA19 A.J. Vanegas 1.00 2.50
USA20 Tony Wolters 1.00 2.50

2010 Bowman Chrome USA Stars Refractors

*REF: 1X TO 2.5X BASIC
STATED ODDS 1:39 HOBBY
STATED PRINT RUN 500 SER.#'d SETS

2010 Bowman Chrome USA Stars Blue Refractors

*BLUE REF: 2X TO 5X BASIC
STATED ODDS 1:48 HOBBY
STATED PRINT RUN 150 SER.#'d SETS

2010 Bowman Chrome USA Stars Gold Refractors

*GOLD REF: 5X TO 12X BASIC
STATED ODDS 1:142 HOBBY
STATED PRINT RUN 50 SER.#'d SETS

2010 Bowman Chrome USA Stars Orange Refractors

STATED ODDS 1:284 HOBBY
STATED PRINT RUN 25 SER.#'d SETS

2010 Bowman Chrome Wrapper Redemption Autographs

ISSUED VIA WRAPPER REDEMPTION PROGRAM
STATED PRINT RUN 100 SER.#'d SETS
WR1 Buster Posey 125.00 250.00
WR2 Mike Stanton 125.00 250.00
WR3 Mike Moustakas 40.00 80.00
WR4 Miguel Sano 200.00 300.00
WR5 Dustin Ackley 40.00 80.00

2010 Bowman Chrome Draft

COMP.SET w/o AU (110) 15.00 40.00
BDP1A Stephen Strasburg RC 2.50 6.00
BDP1B Stephen Strasburg AU 125.00 250.00
BDP2 Josh Bell (RC) .30 .75
BDP3 Ivan Nova RC 1.50 4.00
BDP4 Starlin Castro RC .75 2.00
BDP5 John Axford RC .30 .75
BDP6 Colin Curtis RC .30 .75
BDP7 Brennan Boesch RC .75 2.00
BDP8 Ike Davis RC .60 1.50
BDP9 Madison Bumgarner RC 3.00 8.00
BDP10 Austin Jackson RC .50 1.25
BDP11 Andrew Cashner RC .30 .75
BDP12 Jose Tabata RC .50 1.25
BDP13 Wade Davis (RC) .50 1.25
BDP14 Ian Desmond (RC) .50 1.25
BDP15 Felix Doubront RC .30 .75
BDP16 Danny Worth RC .30 .75
BDP17 John Ely RC .30 .75
BDP18 Jon Jay RC .50 1.25
BDP19 Mike Leake RC 1.00 2.50
BDP20 Daniel Nava RC .30 .75
BDP21 Brad Lincoln RC .50 1.25
BDP22 Jonathan Lucroy RC .75 2.00
BDP23 Brian Matusz RC .75 2.00
BDP24 Chris Nelson (RC) .50 1.25
BDP25 Andy Oliver RC .30 .75
BDP26 Adam Ottavino RC .30 .75
BDP27 Trevor Plouffe (RC) .75 2.00
BDP28 Vance Worley RC 1.25 3.00
BDP29 Daniel McCutchen RC .50 1.25
BDP30 Mike Stanton RC 2.50 6.00
BDP31 Drew Storen RC .50 1.25
BDP32 Tyler Colvin RC .50 1.25
BDP33 Travis Wood (RC) .50 1.25
BDP34 Eric Young Jr. (RC) .30 .75
BDP35 Sam Demel RC .30 .75
BDP36 Wellington Castillo RC .30 .75
BDP37 Sam LeCure (RC) .30 .75
BDP38 Danny Valencia RC 2.00 5.00
BDP39 Fernando Salas RC .30 .75
BDP40 Jason Heyward RC 1.25 3.00
BDP41 Jake Arrieta RC .75 2.00
BDP42 Kevin Russo RC .30 .75
BDP43 Josh Donaldson RC 1.50 4.00
BDP44 Luis Atilano RC .30 .75
BDP45 Jason Donald RC .30 .75
BDP46 Jonny Venters RC .30 .75
BDP47 Bryan Anderson (RC) .30 .75
BDP48 Jay Sborz (RC) .30 .75
BDP49 Chris Heisey RC .50 1.25
BDP50 Daniel Hudson RC .50 1.25
BDP51 Ruben Tejada RC .50 1.25
BDP52 Jeffrey Marquez RC .50 1.25
BDP53 Brandon Hicks RC .50 1.25
BDP54 Jeanmar Gomez RC .50 1.25
BDP55 Erik Kratz RC .50 1.25
BDP56 Lorenzo Cain RC .75 2.00
BDP57 Jhan Marinez RC .30 .75
BDP58 Omar Beltre (RC) .30 .75
BDP59 Drew Stubbs RC .75 2.00
BDP60 Alex Sanabia RC .30 .75
BDP61 Buster Posey RC 2.50 6.00
BDP62 Anthony Slama RC .30 .75
BDP63 Brad Davis RC .30 .75
BDP64 Logan Morrison RC .50 1.25
BDP65 Luke Hughes (RC) .30 .75
BDP66 Thomas Diamond (RC) .30 .75
BDP67 Tommy Manzella (RC) .30 .75
BDP68 Jordan Smith RC .30 .75
BDP69 Carlos Santana RC 1.00 2.50
BDP70 Domonic Brown RC 1.25 3.00
BDP71 Scott Sizemore RC .50 1.25
BDP72 Jordan Brown RC .30 .75
BDP73 Josh Thole RC .50 1.25
BDP74 Jordan Norberto RC .30 .75
BDP75 Dayan Viciedo RC .50 1.25
BDP76 Josh Tomlin RC .75 2.00
BDP77 Adam Moore RC .30 .75
BDP78 Kenley Jansen RC 1.00 2.50
BDP79 Juan Francisco RC .50 1.25
BDP80 Blake Wood RC .30 .75
BDP81 John Hester RC .30 .75
BDP82 Lucas Harrell (RC) .30 .75
BDP83 Neil Walker (RC) .50 1.25
BDP84 Cesar Valdez RC .30 .75
BDP85 Lance Zawadzki RC .30 .75
BDP86 Rommie Lewis RC .30 .75
BDP87 Steve Tolleson RC .30 .75
BDP88 Jeff Frazier (RC) .30 .75
BDP89 Drew Butera (RC) .30 .75
BDP90 Michael Brantley RC .50 1.25
BDP91 Mitch Moreland RC .50 1.25
BDP92 Alex Burnett RC .30 .75
BDP93 Allen Craig RC .75 2.00
BDP94 Sergio Santos (RC) .30 .75
BDP95 Matt Carson (RC) .30 .75
BDP96 Jenrry Mejia RC .50 1.25
BDP97 Rhyne Hughes RC .30 .75
BDP98 Tyson Ross RC .30 .75
BDP99 Argenis Diaz RC .50 1.25
BDP100 Hisanori Takahashi RC .50 1.25
BDP101 Cole Gillespie RC .30 .75
BDP102 Ryan Kalish RC .50 1.25
BDP103 J.P. Arencibia RC .60 1.50
BDP104 Peter Bourjos RC .50 1.25
BDP105 Justin Turner RC 2.50 6.00
BDP106 Michael Dunn RC .30 .75
BDP107 Mike McCoy RC .30 .75
BDP108 Will Rhymes RC .30 .75
BDP109 Wilson Ramos RC .75 2.00
BDP110 Josh Butler RC .30 .75

2010 Bowman Chrome Draft Refractors

*REF: .75X TO 2X BASIC

2010 Bowman Chrome Draft Blue Refractors

*BLUE REF: 2X TO 5X BASIC
STATED PRINT RUN 199 SER.#'d SETS

2010 Bowman Chrome Draft Gold Refractors

*GOLD REF: 3X TO 8X BASIC
STATED PRINT RUN 50 SER.#'d SETS
BDP1 Stephen Strasburg 30.00 80.00
BDP30 Mike Stanton 20.00 50.00
BDP61 Buster Posey 50.00 100.00

2010 Bowman Chrome Draft Orange Refractors

STATED PRINT RUN 25 SER.#'d SETS

2010 Bowman Chrome Draft Purple Refractors

*PURPLE REF: .75X TO 2X BASIC

2010 Bowman Chrome Draft Prospect Autographs

BDPP61 Michael Choice 3.00 8.00
BDPP62 Zack Cox 3.00 8.00
BDPP63 Bryce Brentz 3.00 8.00
BDPP64 Chance Ruffin 3.00 8.00
BDPP65 Mike Olt 4.00 10.00
BDPP66 Kellin Deglan 3.00 8.00
BDPP67 Yasmani Grandal 4.00 10.00
BDPP68 Kolbrin Vitek 3.00 8.00
BDPP69 Justin O'Conner 3.00 8.00
BDPP70 Gary Brown 4.00 10.00
BDPP71 Mike Foltynewicz 8.00 20.00
BDPP72 Chevez Clarke 3.00 8.00
BDPP73 Cito Culver 3.00 8.00
BDPP74 Aaron Sanchez 6.00 15.00
BDPP75 Noah Syndergaard 40.00 100.00
BDPP76 Taylor Lindsey 3.00 8.00
BDPP77 Josh Sale 3.00 8.00
BDPP78 Christian Yelich 200.00 500.00
BDPP79 Jameson Taillon 6.00 15.00
BDPP80 Manny Machado 100.00 250.00
BDPP81 Christian Colon 3.00 8.00
BDPP82 Drew Pomeranz 6.00 15.00
BDPP83 Delino DeShields 4.00 10.00
BDPP84 Matt Harvey 12.00 30.00
BDPP85 Ryan Bolden 3.00 8.00
BDPP86 Deck McGuire 3.00 8.00
BDPP87 Zach Lee 3.00 8.00
BDPP88 Alex Wimmers 3.00 8.00
BDPP89 Kaleb Cowart 3.00 8.00
BDPP90 Mike Kvasnicka 3.00 8.00
BDPP91 Jake Skole 3.00 8.00
BDPP92 Chris Sale 60.00 150.00

2010 Bowman Chrome Draft Prospect Autographs Refractors

*REF: .5X TO 1.2X BASIC
STATED PRINT RUN 500 SER.#'d SETS
BDPP78 Christian Yelich 300.00 600.00
BDPP80 Manny Machado 200.00 500.00

2010 Bowman Chrome Draft Prospect Autographs Blue Refractors

*BLUE REF: 1.2X TO 3X BASIC
STATED PRINT RUN 150 SER.#'d SETS
BDPP75 Noah Syndergaard 100.00 250.00
BDPP78 Christian Yelich 1000.00 2000.00
BDPP80 Manny Machado 500.00 1000.00

2010 Bowman Chrome Draft Prospect Autographs Gold Refractors

*GOLD REF: 2X TO 5X BASIC
STATED PRINT RUN 50 SER.#'d SETS
BDPP75 Noah Syndergaard 150.00 400.00
BDPP78 Christian Yelich 2000.00 3000.00
BDPP80 Manny Machado 1000.00 1500.00

2010 Bowman Chrome Draft Prospect Autographs Orange Refractors

STATED PRINT RUN 25 SER.#'d SETS

2010 Bowman Chrome Draft Prospects

BDPP1 Sam Tuivailala .30 .75
BDPP2 Alex Burgos .30 .75
BDPP3 Henry Ramos .50 1.25
BDPP4 Pat Dean .20 .50
BDPP5 Ryan Brett .30 .75
BDPP6 Jesse Biddle .30 .75
BDPP7 Leon Landry .50 1.25
BDPP8 Ryan LaMarre .30 .75
BDPP9 Josh Rutledge 1.25 3.00
BDPP10 Tyler Thornburg .50 1.25
BDPP11 Carter Jurica .20 .50
BDPP12 J.R. Bradley .20 .50
BDPP13 Devin Lohman .20 .50
BDPP14 Addison Reed .50 1.25
BDPP15 Micah Gibbs .30 .75
BDPP16 Derek Dietrich .50 1.25
BDPP18 Stephen Pryor .20 .50
BDPP19 Eddie Rosario 1.50 4.00
BDPP20 Blake Forsythe .20 .50
BDPP21 Rangel Ravelo .20 .50
BDPP22 Nick Longmire .30 .75
BDPP23 Andrelton Simmons .75 2.00
BDPP24 Chad Bettis .20 .50
BDPP25 Peter Tago .30 .75
BDPP26 Tyrell Jenkins .60 1.50
BDPP27 Marcus Knecht .20 .50
BDPP28 Seth Blair .30 .75
BDPP29 Brodie Greene .20 .50
BDPP30 Jason Martinson .20 .50
BDPP31 Bryan Morgado .30 .75
BDPP32 Eric Cantrell .20 .50
BDPP33 Niko Goodrum .60 1.50
BDPP34 Bobby Doran .20 .50
BDPP35 Cody Wheeler .20 .50
BDPP36 Cole Leonida .20 .50
BDPP37 Nate Roberts .20 .50
BDPP38 Dave Filak .20 .50
BDPP39 Taijuan Walker .50 1.25
BDPP40 Hayden Simpson .30 .75
BDPP41 Cameron Rupp .30 .75
BDPP42 Ben Heath .20 .50
BDPP43 Tyler Waldron .20 .50
BDPP44 Greg Garcia .20 .50
BDPP45 Vincent Velasquez .75 2.00
BDPP46 Jake Lemmerman .60 1.50
BDPP47 Russell Wilson 10.00 25.00
BDPP48 Cody Stanley .20 .50
BDPP49 Matt Suschak .20 .50
BDPP50 Logan Darnell .20 .50
BDPP51 Kevin Keyes .20 .50
BDPP52 Thomas Royse .20 .50
BDPP53 Scott Alexander .20 .50
BDPP54 Tony Thompson .20 .50
BDPP55 Seth Rosin .30 .75
BDPP56 Mickey Wiswall .20 .50
BDPP57 Albert Almora .60 1.50
BDPP58 Cole Billingsley .30 .75
BDPP58 Cody Hawn .30 .75
BDPP59 Drew Vettleson .30 .75
BDPP60 Matt Lipka .75 2.00
BDPP61 Michael Choice .30 .75
BDPP62 Zack Cox .60 1.50
BDPP63 Bryce Brentz .50 1.25
BDPP64 Chance Ruffin .20 .50
BDPP65 Mike Olt .60 1.50
BDPP66 Kellin Deglan .20 .50
BDPP67 Yasmani Grandal .30 .75
BDPP68 Kolbrin Vitek .50 1.25
BDPP69 Justin O'Conner .20 .50
BDPP70 Gary Brown 1.00 2.50
BDPP71 Mike Foltynewicz .50 1.25
BDPP72 Chevez Clarke .30 .75
BDPP73 Cito Culver .30 .75
BDPP74 Aaron Sanchez .75 2.00
BDPP75 Noah Syndergaard .75 2.00
BDPP76 Taylor Lindsey .30 .75
BDPP77 Josh Sale .60 1.50
BDPP78 Christian Yelich 20.00 50.00
BDPP79 Jameson Taillon .30 .75
BDPP80 Manny Machado 10.00 25.00
BDPP81 Christian Colon .30 .75
BDPP82 Drew Pomeranz .50 1.25
BDPP83 Delino DeShields .30 .75
BDPP84 Matt Harvey 1.25 3.00
BDPP85 Ryan Bolden .20 .50
BDPP86 Deck McGuire .30 .75
BDPP87 Zach Lee .50 1.25
BDPP88 Alex Wimmers .30 .75
BDPP89 Kaleb Cowart .30 .75
BDPP90 Mike Kvansnicka .20 .50
BDPP91 Jake Skole .30 .75
BDPP92 Chris Sale 3.00 8.00
BDPP93 Sean Brady .20 .50
BDPP94 Marc Brakeman .20 .50
BDPP95 Alex Bregman 3.00 8.00
BDPP96 Ryan Burr .50 1.25
BDPP97 Chris Chinea .30 .75
BDPP98 Troy Conyers .20 .50
BDPP99 Zach Green .20 .50
BDPP100 Carson Kelly .60 1.50
BDPP101 Timmy Lopes .20 .50
BDPP102 Adrian Marin .30 .75
BDPP103 Chris Okey .20 .50
BDPP104 Matt Olson 2.50 6.00
BDPP105 Ivan Pelaez .20 .50
BDPP106 Felipe Perez .20 .50
BDPP107 Nelson Rodriguez .30 .75
BDPP108 Corey Seager 15.00 40.00
BDPP109 Lucas Sims .50 1.25
BDPP110 Nick Travieso .30 .75

2010 Bowman Chrome Draft Prospects Refractors

*REF: 2X TO 5X BASIC

2010 Bowman Chrome Draft Prospects Blue Refractors

*BLUE REF: 4X TO 10X BASIC
STATED PRINT RUN 199 SER.#'d SETS
BDPP47 Russell Wilson 125.00 250.00

2010 Bowman Chrome Draft Prospects Gold Refractors

*GOLD REF: 8X TO 20X BASIC
STATED PRINT RUN 50 SER.#'d SETS

2010 Bowman Chrome Draft Prospects Orange Refractors

STATED PRINT RUN 25 SER.#'d SETS

2010 Bowman Chrome Draft Prospects Purple Refractors

*PURPLE REF: 1.2X TO 3X BASIC

2010 Bowman Chrome Draft USA Baseball Autographs

USAA1 Albert Almora 10.00 25.00
USAA2 Cole Billingsley 4.00 10.00
USAA3 Sean Brady 4.00 10.00
USAA4 Marc Brakeman 4.00 10.00
USAA5 Alex Bregman 30.00 80.00
USAA6 Ryan Burr 4.00 10.00
USAA7 Chris Chinea 4.00 10.00
USAA8 Troy Conyers 4.00 10.00
USAA9 Zach Green 4.00 10.00
USAA10 Carson Kelly 6.00 15.00
USAA11 Timmy Lopes 4.00 10.00
USAA12 Adrian Marin 4.00 10.00
USAA13 Chris Okey 8.00 20.00
USAA14 Matt Olson 30.00 80.00
USAA15 Ivan Pelaez 4.00 10.00
USAA16 Felipe Perez 4.00 10.00
USAA17 Nelson Rodriguez 5.00 12.00
USAA18 Corey Seager 100.00 250.00
USAA19 Lucas Sims 10.00 25.00
USAA20 Sheldon Neuse 4.00 10.00

2010 Bowman Chrome Draft USA Baseball Autographs Refractors

*REF: .5X TO 1.2X BASIC
STATED PRINT RUN 199 SER.#'d SETS

2010 Bowman Chrome Draft USA Baseball Autographs Blue Refractors

*BLUE REF: .75X TO 2X BASIC
STATED PRINT RUN 99 SER.#'d SETS

2010 Bowman Chrome Draft USA Baseball Autographs Gold Refractors

*GOLD REF: 1.25X TO 3X BASIC
STATED PRINT RUN 50 SER.#'d SETS

2010 Bowman Chrome Draft USA Baseball Autographs Orange Refractors

STATED PRINT RUN 25 SER.#'d SETS

2011 Bowman Chrome

COMP.SET w/o AU's (220) 20.00 50.00
COMMON RC (171-220) .40 1.00
STATED PLATE ODDS 1:960 HOBBY
PLATE PRINT RUN 1 SET PER COLOR
BLACK-CYAN-MAGENTA-YELLOW ISSUED
NO PLATE PRICING DUE TO SCARCITY
EXCHANGE DEADLINE 9/30/2014
1 Buster Posey .60 1.50
2 Alex Avila .30 .75
3 Edwin Jackson .20 .50
4 Miguel Montero .20 .50
5 Albert Pujols .60 1.50
6 Carlos Santana .50 1.25
7 Marlon Byrd .20 .50
8 Hanley Ramirez .30 .75
9 Josh Hamilton .30 .75
10 Matt Kemp .40 1.00
11 Shane Victorino .30 .75
12 Domonic Brown .40 1.00
13 Chipper Jones .50 1.25
14 Joey Votto .50 1.25
15 Brandon Phillips .20 .50
16 Jason Heyward .40 1.00
17 Curtis Granderson .40 1.00

18 Brian McCann .30 .75
19 Dustin Pedroia .50 1.25
20 Chris Johnson .20 .50
21 Brian Matusz .20 .50
22 Mark Teixeira .30 .75
23 Miguel Tejada .30 .75
24 Ryan Howard .40 1.00
25 Adrian Beltre .50 1.25
26 Joe Mauer .40 1.00
27 Logan Morrison .20 .50
28 Brian Wilson .50 1.25
29 Carlos Lee .20 .50
30 Ian Kinsler .30 .75
31 Shin-Soo Choo .30 .75
32 Adam Wainwright .30 .75
33 Carlos Gonzalez .30 .75
34 Lance Berkman .30 .75
35 Jon Lester .30 .75
36 Miguel Cabrera .50 1.25
37 Justin Verlander .50 1.25
38 Tyler Colvin .20 .50
39 Matt Cain .30 .75
40 Brett Anderson .20 .50
41 Gordon Beckham .20 .50
42 David DeJesus .20 .50
43 Jonathan Sanchez .20 .50
44 Jorge De La Rosa .20 .50
45 Torii Hunter .20 .50
46 Andrew McCutchen .50 1.25
47 Mat Latos .30 .75
48 CC Sabathia .30 .75
49 Brett Myers .20 .50
50 Ryan Zimmerman .30 .75
51 Trevor Cahill .20 .50
52 Clayton Kershaw .75 2.00
53 Andre Ethier .30 .75
54 Justin Upton .30 .75
55 B.J. Upton .30 .75
56 J.P. Arencibia .20 .50
57 Phil Hughes .20 .50
58 Tim Hudson .30 .75
59 Francisco Liriano .20 .50
60 Ike Davis .20 .50
61 Delmon Young .30 .75
62 Paul Konerko .30 .75
63 Carlos Beltran .30 .75
64 Mike Stanton .50 1.25
65 Adam Jones .30 .75
66 Jimmy Rollins .30 .75
67 Alex Rios .20 .50
68 Chad Billingsley .30 .75
69 Tommy Hanson .20 .50
70 Travis Wood .20 .50
71 Magglio Ordonez .30 .75
72 Jake Peavy .20 .50
73 Adrian Gonzalez .40 1.00
74 Aaron Hill .20 .50
75 Kendrys Morales .20 .50
76 Ryan Dempster .20 .50
77 Hunter Pence .30 .75
78 Josh Beckett .20 .50
79 Mark Reynolds .20 .50
80 Drew Stubbs .20 .50
81 Dan Haren .20 .50
82 Chris Carpenter .30 .75
83 Mitch Moreland .20 .50
84 Starlin Castro .30 .75
85 Roy Halladay .30 .75
86 Stephen Drew .20 .50
87 Aramis Ramirez .20 .50
88 Daniel Hudson .20 .50
89 Alexei Ramirez .30 .75
90 Rickie Weeks .20 .50
91 Will Venable .20 .50
92 David Price .40 1.00
93 Dan Uggla .20 .50
94 Austin Jackson .20 .50
95 Evan Longoria .30 .75
96 Ryan Ludwick .20 .50
97 Chase Utley .30 .75
98 Johnny Cueto .30 .75
99 Billy Butler .20 .50
100 David Wright .40 1.00
101 Jose Reyes .30 .75
102 Robinson Cano .30 .75
103 Josh Johnson .30 .75
104 Chris Coghlan .20 .50
105 David Ortiz .50 1.25
106 Jay Bruce .30 .75
107 Jayson Werth .30 .75
108 Matt Holliday .50 1.25
109 John Danks .20 .50
110 Franklin Gutierrez .20 .50
111 Zack Greinke .50 1.25
112 Jacoby Ellsbury .40 1.00
113 Madison Bumgarner .40 1.00
114 Mike Leake .30 .75
115 Carl Crawford .30 .75
116 Clay Buchholz .20 .50
117 Gavin Floyd .20 .50
118 Mike Minor .20 .50
119 Jose Tabata .20 .50
120 Jason Castro .20 .50
121 Chris Young .20 .50
122 Jose Bautista .30 .75
123 Felix Hernandez .30 .75
124 Dexter Fowler .30 .75
125 Tim Lincecum .30 .75
126 Todd Helton .30 .75
127 Ubaldo Jimenez .20 .50
128 Yovani Gallardo .20 .50
129 Derek Jeter 1.25 3.00
130 Wade Davis .20 .50
131 Nelson Cruz .50 1.25
132 Michael Cuddyer .20 .50
133 Mark Buehrle .30 .75
134 Danny Valencia .30 .75
135 Ichiro Suzuki .60 1.50
136 Brett Wallace .20 .50
137 Troy Tulowitzki .50 1.25
138 Pedro Alvarez .40 1.00
139 Brandon Morrow .20 .50
140 Jered Weaver .30 .75
141 Michael Young .20 .50
142 Wandy Rodriguez .20 .50
143 Alfonso Soriano .30 .75
144 Roy Oswalt .30 .75
145 Brian Roberts .20 .50
146 Jaime Garcia .30 .75
147 Edinson Volquez .20 .50
148 Vladimir Guerrero .30 .75
149 Cliff Lee .30 .75
150 Johnny Damon .30 .75
151 Alex Rodriguez .60 1.50
152 Nick Markakis .40 1.00
153 Cole Hamels .40 1.00
154 Prince Fielder .30 .75
155 Kurt Suzuki .20 .50
156 Ryan Braun .30 .75
157 Justin Morneau .30 .75
158 Elvis Andrus .30 .75
159 Stephen Strasburg .50 1.25
160 Adam Lind .30 .75
161 Corey Hart .20 .50
162 Adam Dunn .30 .75
163 Bobby Abreu .20 .50
164 Gaby Sanchez .20 .50
165 Ian Kennedy .20 .50
166 Kevin Youkilis .20 .50
167 Vernon Wells .20 .50
168 Matt Garza .20 .50
169 Victor Martinez .30 .75
170 Casey McGehee .20 .50
171 Jake McGee (RC) .75 2.00
172 Lars Anderson RC .60 1.50
173 Mark Trumbo (RC) 1.00 2.50
174 Konrad Schmidt RC .40 1.00
175 Mike Trout RC 300.00 800.00
176 Brent Morel RC .40 1.00
177 Aroldis Chapman RC 1.25 3.00
178 Greg Halman RC .60 1.50
179 Jeremy Hellickson RC 1.00 2.50
180 Yunesky Maya RC .40 1.00
181 Kyle Drabek RC .60 1.50
182 Ben Revere RC .60 1.50
183 Desmond Jennings RC .60 1.50
184 Brandon Beachy RC 1.00 2.50
185 Freddie Freeman RC 10.00 25.00
186 Randall Delgado RC .60 1.50
187 John Lindsey RC .40 1.00
188 Mark Rogers (RC) .40 1.00
189 Brian Bogusevic (RC) .40 1.00
190 Yonder Alonso RC .60 1.50
191 Gregory Infante RC .40 1.00
192 Dillon Gee RC .60 1.50
193 Ozzie Martinez RC .40 1.00
194 Brandon Snyder (RC) .40 1.00
195 Daniel Descalso RC .40 1.00
196A Eric Hosmer RC 2.50 6.00
196B Eric Hosmer AU EXCH 75.00 150.00
197 Lucas Duda RC 1.00 2.50
198 Cory Luebke RC .40 1.00
199 Hank Conger RC .60 1.50
200 Chris Sale RC 3.00 8.00
201 Julio Teheran RC .60 1.50
202 Danny Duffy RC .60 1.50
203 Brandon Belt RC 1.00 2.50
204 Ivan Nova (RC) .60 1.50
205 Danny Espinosa RC .40 1.00
206 Alexi Ogando RC 1.00 2.50
207 Darwin Barney RC 1.25 3.00
208 Jordan Walden RC .40 1.00
209 Tsuyoshi Nishioka RC 1.25 3.00
210 Zach Britton RC 1.00 2.50
211 Andrew Cashner (RC) .40 1.00
212A Dustin Ackley RC .60 1.50
212B Dustin Ackley AU 8.00 20.00
213 Carlos Peguero RC .60 1.50
214 Hector Noesi RC .60 1.50
215 Eduardo Nunez RC 1.00 2.50
216 Michael Pineda RC 1.00 2.50
217 Alex Cobb RC .40 1.00
218 Ivan DeJesus Jr. RC .40 1.00
219 Scott Cousins RC .40 1.00
220 Aaron Crow RC .60 1.50

2011 Bowman Chrome Refractors

*REF: 1X TO 2.5X BASIC
*REF RC: .5X TO 1.2X BASIC RC
STATED ODDS 1:4 HOBBY

2011 Bowman Chrome Blue Refractors

*BLUE REF: 2X TO 5X BASIC
*BLUE REF RC: 2X TO 5X BASIC RC
STATED ODDS 1:31 HOBBY
STATED PRINT RUN 150 SER.#'d SETS

2011 Bowman Chrome Gold Canary Diamond

STATED ODDS 1:3840 HOBBY
STATED PRINT RUN 1 SER.#'d SET
NO PRICING DUE TO SCARCITY

2011 Bowman Chrome Gold Refractors

*GOLD REF: 6X TO 15X BASIC
*GOLD REF RC: 3X TO 8X BASIC RC
STATED ODDS 1:94 HOBBY
STATED PRINT RUN 50 SER.#'d SETS
EXCHANGE DEADLINE 9/30/2014
196B Eric Hosmer AU EXCH 250.00 400.00
212B Dustin Ackley AU 40.00 80.00

2011 Bowman Chrome Orange Refractors

STATED ODDS 1:198 HOBBY
STATED PRINT RUN 25 SER.#'d SETS
NO PRICING DUE TO SCARCITY
EXCHANGE DEADLINE 9/30/2014

2011 Bowman Chrome Red Refractors

STATED ODDS 1:900 HOBBY
STATED PRINT RUN 5 SER.#'d SETS
NO PRICING DUE TO SCARCITY

2011 Bowman Chrome 18U USA National Team Refractors

STATED ODDS 1:2063 HOBBY
STATED PLATE ODDS 1:365,000 HOBBY
PLATE PRINT RUN 1 SET PER COLOR
BLACK-CYAN-MAGENTA-YELLOW ISSUED
NO PLATE PRICING DUE TO SCARCITY
EXCHANGE DEADLINE 10/26/2012
18U1 Albert Almora 2.50 6.00
18U2 Alex Bregman 12.00 30.00
18U3 Gavin Cecchini 2.50 6.00
18U4 Troy Conyers 1.50 4.00
18U6 Chase DeJong 3.00 8.00
18U8 Carson Fulmer 3.00 8.00
18U13 Cole Irvin 2.50 6.00
18U15 Jeremy Martinez 1.50 4.00
18U17 Chris Okey 1.50 4.00
18U18 Cody Poteet 1.50 4.00
18U19 Nelson Rodriguez 2.50 6.00
18U21 Addison Russell 5.00 12.00
18U22 Clate Schmidt 1.50 4.00
18U24 Hunter Virant 1.50 4.00
18U25 Walker Weickel 1.50 4.00
18U26 Mikey White 1.50 4.00
18U28 Jesse Winker 10.00 25.00

2011 Bowman Chrome 18U USA National Team Blue Refractors

*BLUE: 1.2X TO 3X BASIC
STATED ODDS 1:13,205 HOBBY
STATED PRINT RUN 99 SER.#'d SETS
EXCHANGE DEADLINE 10/26/2012

2011 Bowman Chrome 18U USA National Team Gold Refractors

*GOLD REF: 1.5X TO 4X BASIC
STATED ODDS 1:27,000 HOBBY
STATED PRINT RUN 50 SER.#'d SETS
EXCHANGE DEADLINE 10/26/2012

2011 Bowman Chrome 18U USA National Team Orange Refractors

STATED ODDS 1:50,685 HOBBY
STATED PRINT RUN 25 SER.#'d SETS
NO PRICING DUE TO SCARCITY
EXCHANGE DEADLINE 10/26/2012

2011 Bowman Chrome 18U USA National Team Red Refractors

STATED ODDS 1:253,424 HOBBY
STATED PRINT RUN 5 SER.#'d SETS
NO PRICING DUE TO SCARCITY
EXCHANGE DEADLINE 10/26/2012

2011 Bowman Chrome 18U USA National Team X-Fractors

*XFRACTOR: .6X TO 1.5X BASIC
STATED ODDS 1:4281 HOBBY
STATED PRINT RUN 299 SER.#'d SETS
EXCHANGE DEADLINE 10/26/2012

2011 Bowman Chrome 18U USA National Team Autographs Refractors

STATED ODDS 1:192 HOBBY
STATED PRINT RUN 417 SER.#'d SETS
STATED PLATE ODDS 1:15,839 HOBBY
PLATE PRINT RUN 1 SET PER COLOR
BLACK-CYAN-MAGENTA-YELLOW ISSUED
NO PLATE PRICING DUE TO SCARCITY
18U1 Albert Almora 12.00 30.00
18U2 Alex Bregman 30.00 80.00
18U3 Gavin Cecchini 4.00 10.00
18U4 Troy Conyers 4.00 10.00
18U6 Chase DeJong 4.00 10.00
18U8 Carson Fulmer 8.00 20.00
18U13 Cole Irvin 4.00 10.00
18U15 Jeremy Martinez 4.00 10.00
18U15 Clate Schmidt 4.00 10.00
18U17 Chris Okey 3.00 8.00
18U18 Cody Poteet 4.00 10.00
18U19 Nelson Rodriguez 4.00 10.00
18U21 Addison Russell 12.00 30.00
18U24 Hunter Virant 4.00 10.00
18U25 Walker Weickel 4.00 10.00
18U26 Mikey White 4.00 10.00
18U28 Jesse Winker 25.00 60.00

2011 Bowman Chrome 18U USA National Team Autographs Blue Refractors

*BLUE REF: .75X TO 2X BASIC
STATED ODDS 1:829 HOBBY
STATED PRINT RUN 99 SER.#'d SETS

2011 Bowman Chrome 18U USA National Team Autographs Gold Refractors

*GOLD REF: 1.5X TO 4X BASIC
STATED ODDS 1:1695 HOBBY
STATED PRINT RUN 50 SER.#'d SETS

2011 Bowman Chrome 18U USA National Team Autographs Orange Refractors

STATED ODDS 1:3625 HOBBY
STATED PRINT RUN 25 SER.#'d SETS
NO PRICING DUE TO SCARCITY

2011 Bowman Chrome 18U USA National Team Autographs Red Refractors

STATED ODDS 1:15,919 HOBBY
STATED PRINT RUN 5 SER.#'d SETS
NO PRICING DUE TO SCARCITY

2011 Bowman Chrome 18U USA National Team Autographs Superfractors

STATED ODDS 1:63,356 HOBBY
STATED PRINT RUN 1 SER.#'d SET
NO PRICING DUE TO SCARCITY

2011 Bowman Chrome 18U USA National Team Autographs X-Fractors

*X-FRACTOR: .5X TO 1.2X BASIC
STATED ODDS 1:268 HOBBY
STATED PRINT RUN 299 SER.#'d SETS

2011 Bowman Chrome Bryce Harper Retail Exclusive

INSERTED IN RETAIL VALUE BOXES
BCE1G Bryce Harper Gold 8.00 20.00
BCE1R Bryce Harper Red 4.00 10.00
BCE1S Bryce Harper Silver 4.00 10.00

2011 Bowman Chrome Futures

COMPLETE SET (25) 12.50 30.00
STATED ODDS 1:9 HOBBY
MICRO-FRAC. ODDS 1:2035 HOBBY
MICRO-FRAC. PRINT RUN 25 SER.#'d SETS
NO MICRO-FRAC.PRICING AVAILABLE
1 Bryce Harper 8.00 20.00
2 Manny Machado 4.00 10.00
3 Jameson Taillon .60 1.50
4 Delino DeShields Jr. .40 1.00
5 Grant Green .40 1.00
6 Devin Mesoraco 1.00 2.50
7 Anthony Ranaudo 1.00 2.50
8 Stetson Allie .60 1.50
9 Shelby Miller 2.00 5.00
10 Arodys Vizcaino .60 1.50
11 Manny Banuelos 1.00 2.50
12 Jonathan Singleton .60 1.50
13 Tyler Matzek .60 1.50
14 Gary Sanchez 2.00 5.00
15 Jean Segura 1.50 4.00
16 Peter Tago .40 1.00
17 Matt Dominguez .60 1.50
18 Miguel Sano .75 2.00
19 Jesus Montero .40 1.00
20 Josh Sale .60 1.50
21 Brett Jackson .60 1.50
22 Mike Montgomery .60 1.50
23 Chris Archer .75 2.00
24 Jacob Turner 1.50 4.00
25 Wil Myers 1.00 2.50

2011 Bowman Chrome Futures Refractors

*REF: .5X TO 1.2X BASIC

2011 Bowman Chrome Futures Fusion-Fractors 99

*FUSION: 2X TO 5X BASIC
STATED ODDS 1:512 HOBBY
STATED PRINT RUN 99 SER.#'d SETS
1 Bryce Harper 30.00 60.00

2011 Bowman Chrome Futures Future-Fractors

*FUTURE: .6X TO 1.5X BASIC

2011 Bowman Chrome Prospect Autographs

111-220 PLATE ODDS 1:9051 HOBBY
PLATE PRINT RUN 1 SET PER COLOR
BLACK-CYAN-MAGENTA-YELLOW ISSUED
NO PLATE PRICING DUE TO SCARCITY
EXCHANGE DEADLINE 4/30/2014
BCP80 Dee Gordon 3.00 8.00
BCP81 Blake Forsythe 3.00 8.00
BCP82 Jurickson Profar 6.00 15.00
BCP83 Jedd Gyorko 3.00 8.00
BCP84 Matt Hague 3.00 8.00
BCP85 Mason Williams 3.00 8.00
BCP86 Stetson Allie 3.00 8.00
BCP87 Jarred Cosart 3.00 8.00
BCP88 Wagner Mateo 3.00 8.00
BCP89 Allen Webster 3.00 8.00
BCP90 Adron Chambers 3.00 8.00
BCP91 Blake Smith 3.00 8.00
BCP92 J.D. Martinez 40.00 100.00
BCP93 Brandon Belt 10.00 25.00
BCP94 Drake Britton 3.00 8.00
BCP95 Addison Reed 3.00 8.00
BCP96 Adonis Cardona 3.00 8.00
BCP97 Yordy Cabrera 3.00 8.00
BCP98 Tony Wolters 3.00 8.00
BCP99 Paul Goldschmidt 60.00 150.00
BCP100 Sean Coyle 3.00 8.00
BCP101 Rymer Liriano 3.00 8.00
BCP102 Eric Thames 3.00 8.00
BCP103 Brian Fletcher 3.00 8.00
BCP104 Ben Gamel 3.00 8.00
BCP105 Kyle Russell 3.00 8.00
BCP106 Sammy Solis 3.00 8.00
BCP107 Garin Cecchini 3.00 8.00
BCP108 Carlos Perez 3.00 8.00
BCP110 Jonathan Villar 3.00 8.00
BCP111A Adam Warren 3.00 8.00
BCP111B Bryce Harper 250.00 600.00
BCP112 Rick Hague 3.00 8.00
BCP113 Carlos Perez 3.00 8.00
BCP130 Hunter Morris 3.00 8.00
BCP131 Jean Segura 3.00 8.00
BCP132 Melky Mesa 3.00 8.00
BCP133 Manny Banuelos 3.00 8.00
BCP134 Chris Archer 3.00 8.00
BCP157 Danny Brewer 3.00 8.00
BCP158 David Bromberg 3.00 8.00
BCP160 A.J. Cole 3.00 8.00
BCP161 Alex Colome 3.00 8.00
BCP162 Brody Colvin 3.00 8.00
BCP163 Khris Davis 4.00 10.00
BCP164 Cutter Dykstra 3.00 8.00
BCP165 Nathan Eovaldi 4.00 10.00
BCP167 Garrett Gould 3.00 8.00
BCP168 Brandon Guyer 3.00 8.00
BCP169 Shaeffer Hall 3.00 8.00
BCP170 Reese Havens 3.00 8.00
BCP171 Luis Heredia 3.00 8.00
BCP172 Aaron Hicks 6.00 15.00
BCP173 Bryan Holaday 3.00 8.00
BCP174 Brad Holt 3.00 8.00
BCP175 Brett Lawrie 4.00 10.00
BCP176 Matt Lollis 3.00 8.00
BCP178 Starling Marte 8.00 20.00
BCP179 Ethan Martin 3.00 8.00
BCP180 Trey McNutt 3.00 8.00
BCP182 Keyvius Sampson 3.00 8.00
BCP183 Jordan Swagerty 3.00 8.00
BCP184 Dickie Joe Thon 3.00 8.00
BCP185 Jacob Turner 3.00 8.00
BCP186 Christopher Wallace 3.00 8.00
BCP189 Kendrick Perkins 3.00 8.00
BCP192 Enny Romero 3.00 8.00
BCP212 Brock Holt 3.00 8.00
BCP214 Brandon Laird 3.00 8.00
BCP220 Matt Moore 4.00 10.00

2011 Bowman Chrome Prospect Autographs Refractors

*REF: .6X TO 1.5X BASIC
111-220 STATED ODDS 1:88 HOBBY
STATED PRINT RUN 500 SER.#'d SETS
EXCHANGE DEADLINE 4/30/2014

2011 Bowman Chrome Prospect Autographs Blue Refractors

*BLUE REF: 1.2X TO 3X BASIC
111-220 STATED ODDS 1:295 HOBBY
STATED PRINT RUN 150 SER.#'d SETS
EXCHANGE DEADLINE 4/30/2014

2011 Bowman Chrome Prospect Autographs Gold Refractors

*GOLD REF: 1.5X TO 4X BASIC
111-220 STATED ODDS 1:916 HOBBY
STATED PRINT RUN 50 SER.#'d SETS
EXCHANGE DEADLINE 4/30/2014

2011 Bowman Chrome Prospect Autographs Orange Refractors

111-220 STATED ODDS 1:1936 HOBBY
STATED PRINT RUN 25 SER.#'d SETS
NO PRICING DUE TO SCARCITY
EXCHANGE DEADLINE 4/30/2014

2011 Bowman Chrome Prospect Autographs Red Refractors

111-220 STATED ODDS 1:8675 HOBBY
STATED PRINT RUN 5 SER.#'d SETS
NO PRICING DUE TO SCARCITY
EXCHANGE DEADLINE 4/30/2014

2011 Bowman Chrome Prospects

COMPLETE SET (221) 40.00 80.00
1-110 ISSUED IN BOWMAN
111-220 ISSUED IN BOWMAN CHROME
STATED PLATE ODDS 1:960 HOBBY
PLATE PRINT RUN 1 SET PER COLOR
BLACK-CYAN-MAGENTA-YELLOW ISSUED
NO PLATE PRICING DUE TO SCARCITY
BCP1 Bryce Harper 6.00 15.00
BCP2 Chris Dennis .25 .60
BCP3 Jeremy Barfield .25 .60
BCP4 Nate Freiman .25 .60
BCP5 Tyler Moore .60 1.50
BCP6 Anthony Carter .25 .60
BCP7 Ryan Cavan .25 .60
BCP8 Stephen Vogt .40 1.00
BCP9 Carlo Testa .25 .60
BCP10 Erik Davis .25 .60
BCP11 Jack Shuck .60 1.50
BCP12 Charles Brewer .25 .60
BCP13 Alex Castellanos .40 1.00
BCP14 Anthony Vasquez .25 .60
BCP15 Michael Brenly .25 .60
BCP16 Kody Hinze .40 1.00
BCP17 Hector Noesi .40 1.00
BCP18 Tyler Bortnick .25 .60
BCP19 Thomas Layne .25 .60
BCP20 Everett Teaford .25 .60
BCP21 Jose Pirela .40 1.00
BCP22 Joel Carreno .25 .60
BCP23 Vinnie Catricala .75 2.00
BCP24 Tom Koehler .25 .60
BCP25 Jonathan Schoop .40 1.00
BCP26 Chun-Hsiu Chen .60 1.50
BCP27 Amaury Rivas .25 .60
BCP28 Oswaldo Arcia .25 .60
BCP29 Johermyn Chavez .25 .60
BCP30 Michael Spina .25 .60
BCP31 Kyle McPherson .40 1.00
BCP32 Albert Cartwright .25 .60
BCP33 Joseph Wieland .60 1.50
BCP34 Ben Paulsen .25 .60
BCP35 Jason Hagerty .25 .60
BCP36 Marcell Ozuna 1.00 2.50
BCP37 Dave Sappelt .75 2.00
BCP38 Eduardo Escobar .25 .60
BCP39 Aaron Baker .25 .60
BCP40 Deryk Hooker .25 .60
BCP41 Ty Morrison .25 .60
BCP42 Keon Broxton .25 .60
BCP43 Corey Jones .25 .60
BCP44 Manny Banuelos .60 1.50
BCP45 Brandon Guyer .40 1.00
BCP46 Juan Nicasio .25 .60
BCP47 Sean Ochinko .25 .60
BCP48 Adam Warren .40 1.00
BCP49 Phillip Cerreto .25 .60
BCP50 Mychal Givens .25 .60
BCP51 James Fuller .25 .60
BCP52 Ronnie Welty .25 .60
BCP53 Dan Straily 1.25 3.00
BCP54 Gabriel Jacobo .25 .60
BCP55 David Rubinstein .25 .60
BCP56 Kevin Mailloux .25 .60
BCP57 Angel Castillo .25 .60
BCP58 Adrian Salcedo .40 1.00
BCP59 Ronald Bermudez .25 .60
BCP60 Jarek Cunningham .40 1.00
BCP61 Matt Magill .40 1.00
BCP62 Willie Cabrera .25 .60
BCP63 Austin Hyatt .40 1.00
BCP64 Cody Puckett .40 1.00
BCP65 Jacob Goebbert .40 1.00
BCP66 Matt Carpenter 2.00 5.00
BCP67 Dan Klein .40 1.00
BCP68 Sean Ratliff .25 .60
BCP69 Elih Villanueva .25 .60
BCP70 Wade Gaynor .25 .60
BCP71 Evan Crawford .25 .60
BCP72 Avisail Garcia .40 1.00
BCP73 Kevin Rivers .25 .60
BCP74 Jim Gallagher .25 .60
BCP75 Brian Broderick .25 .60
BCP76 Tyson Auer .25 .60
BCP77 Matt Klinker .25 .60
BCP78 Cole Figueroa .25 .60
BCP79 Rafael Ynoa .25 .60
BCP80 Dee Gordon .40 1.00
BCP81 Blake Forsythe .25 .60
BCP82 Jurickson Profar .60 1.50
BCP83 Jedd Gyorko .60 1.50
BCP84 Matt Hague .40 1.00
BCP85 Mason Williams .60 1.50
BCP86 Stetson Allie .40 1.00
BCP87 Jarred Cosart .40 1.00
BCP88 Wagner Mateo .60 1.50
BCP89 Allen Webster .40 1.00
BCP90 Adron Chambers .25 .60
BCP91 Blake Smith .25 .60
BCP92 J.D. Martinez 2.00 5.00
BCP93 Brandon Belt .60 1.50
BCP94 Drake Britton .25 .60
BCP95 Addison Reed .25 .60
BCP96 Adonis Cardona .40 1.00
BCP97 Yordy Cabrera .25 .60
BCP98 Tony Wolters .25 .60
BCP99 Paul Goldschmidt 3.00 8.00
BCP100 Sean Coyle .40 1.00
BCP101 Rymer Liriano .60 1.50
BCP102 Eric Thames 1.25 3.00
BCP103 Brian Fletcher .25 .60
BCP104 Ben Gamel .40 1.00
BCP105 Kyle Russell .40 1.00
BCP106 Sammy Solis .25 .60
BCP107 Garin Cecchini .60 1.50
BCP108 Carlos Perez .25 .60
BCP109 Darin Mastroianni .25 .60
BCP110 Jonathan Villar .60 1.50
BCP111 Bryce Harper 6.00 15.00
BCP112 Aaron Altherr .25 .60
BCP113 Oswaldo Arcia .25 .60
BCP114 Kyle Blair .25 .60
BCP115 Nick Bucci .25 .60
BCP116 Jose Casilla .25 .60
BCP117 Zach Cates .25 .60
BCP118 Dimaster Delgado .25 .60
BCP119 Jose DePaula .25 .60
BCP120 Zack Dodson .25 .60
BCP121 John Gast .25 .60
BCP122 Cesar Hernandez .25 .60
BCP123 Kyle Higashioka 8.00 20.00
BCP124 Luke Jackson .40 1.00
BCP125 Jiwan James .25 .60
BCP126 Jonathan Joseph .25 .60
BCP127A Gustavo Pierre .25 .60
BCP127B Ryan Tatusko .40 1.00
BCP128 Jeff Kobernus .25 .60
BCP129 Tom Koehler .25 .60
BCP130 Hunter Morris .25 .60
BCP131 Jean Segura 1.00 2.50
BCP132 Melky Mesa .25 .60
BCP133 Manny Banuelos .60 1.50
BCP134 Chris Archer .50 1.25
BCP135 Ian Krol .25 .60
BCP136 Trystan Magnuson .25 .60
BCP137 Roman Mendez .25 .60
BCP138 Tyler Moore .60 1.50
BCP139 Ramon Morla .25 .60
BCP140 Ty Morrison .25 .60
BCP141 Tyler Pastornicky .40 1.00
BCP142 Jon Pettibone .25 .60
BCP143 Zach Quate .25 .60
BCP144 J.C. Ramirez .25 .60
BCP145 Elmer Reyes .25 .60
BCP146 Aderlin Rodriguez .25 .60
BCP147 Conner Crumbliss .40 1.00
BCP148 David Rohm .25 .60
BCP149 Adrian Sanchez .25 .60
BCP150 Tommy Shirley .25 .60
BCP151 Matt Packer .25 .60
BCP152 Jake Thompson .25 .60
BCP153 Miguel Velazquez .25 .60
BCP154 Dakota Watts .25 .60
BCP155 Chase Whitley 1.25 3.00
BCP156 Cameron Bedrosian .25 .60
BCP157 Daniel Brewer .25 .60
BCP158 Dave Bromberg .25 .60
BCP159 Jorge Polanco 1.00 2.50
BCP160 A.J. Cole .40 1.00
BCP161 Alex Colome .25 .60
BCP162 Brody Colvin .25 .60
BCP163 Khris Davis 1.25 3.00
BCP164 Cutter Dykstra .25 .60
BCP165 Nathan Eovaldi .60 1.50
BCP166 Ramon Flores .60 1.50
BCP167 Garrett Gould .25 .60
BCP168 Brandon Guyer .40 1.00
BCP169 Shaeffer Hall .40 1.00
BCP170 Reese Havens .25 .60
BCP171 Luis Heredia .25 .60
BCP172 Aaron Hicks .40 1.00
BCP173 Bryan Holaday .25 .60
BCP174 Brad Holt .25 .60
BCP175 Brett Lawrie 1.00 2.50
BCP176 Matt Lollis .40 1.00
BCP177 Cesar Puello .40 1.00
BCP178 Starling Marte .60 1.50
BCP179 Ethan Martin .25 .60
BCP180 Trey McNutt .25 .60
BCP181 Anthony Ranaudo .60 1.50
BCP182 Keyvius Sampson .25 .60
BCP183 Jordan Swagerty .40 1.00
BCP184 Dickie Joe Thon .40 1.00
BCP185 Jacob Turner 1.00 2.50
BCP186 Rob Brantly .60 1.50
BCP187 Arquimedes Caminero .25 .60
BCP188 Miles Head .40 1.00
BCP189 Erasmo Ramirez .25 .60
BCP190 Ryan Pressly .40 1.00
BCP191 Colton Cain .25 .60
BCP192 Enny Romero .25 .60
BCP193 Zack Von Rosenberg .25 .60
BCP194 Tyler Skaggs .60 1.50
BCP195 Michael Blanke .25 .60
BCP196 Juan Duran .40 1.00
BCP197 Kyle Parker .40 1.00
BCP198 Jake Marisnick .40 1.00
BCP199 Manuel Soliman .25 .60
BCP200 Jordany Valdespin .25 .60
BCP201 Brock Holt .25 .60
BCP202 Chris Owings .25 .60
BCP203 Cameron Garfield .25 .60
BCP204 Rob Scahill .25 .60
BCP205 Ronnie Welty .25 .60
BCP206 Scott Maine .25 .60
BCP207 Kyle Smit .25 .60
BCP208 Spencer Arroyo .25 .60
BCP209 Mariekson Gregorious 6.00 15.00
BCP210 Neftali Soto .40 1.00
BCP211 Wade Gaynor .25 .60
BCP212 Chris Carpenter .25 .60
BCP213 Josh Judy .25 .60
BCP214 Brandon Laird .40 1.00
BCP215 Peter Tago .25 .60
BCP216 Andy Dirks .60 1.50
BCP217 Steve Cishek ERR NNO .25 .60
BCP218 Cory Riordan .25 .60
BCP219 Fernando Abad .25 .60
BCP220 Matt Moore .60 1.50

2011 Bowman Chrome Prospects Refractors

*REF: 2X TO 5X BASIC
111-220 STATED ODDS 1:28 HOBBY
1-110 PRINT RUN 799 SER.#'d SETS
111-220 PRINT RUN 500 SER.#'d SETS
BCP1 Bryce Harper 40.00 100.00
BCP111 Bryce Harper 40.00 100.00

2011 Bowman Chrome Prospects Blue Refractors

*BLUE REF: 4X TO 10X BASIC
111-220 STATED ODDS 1:31 HOBBY
1-110 PRINT RUN 250 SER.#'d SETS
111-220 PRINT RUN 150 SER.#'d SETS
BCP1 Bryce Harper 50.00 120.00
BCP111 Bryce Harper 50.00 120.00

2011 Bowman Chrome Prospects Gold Canary Diamond

STATED ODDS 1:3840 HOBBY
STATED PRINT RUN 1 SER.#'d SET
NO PRICING DUE TO SCARCITY

2011 Bowman Chrome Prospects Gold Refractors

*GOLD REF: 10X TO 25X BASIC
111-220 STATED ODDS 1:94 HOBBY
STATED PRINT RUN 50 SER.#'d SETS
BCP1 Bryce Harper 250.00 500.00
BCP111 Bryce Harper 250.00 500.00

2011 Bowman Chrome Prospects Green X-Fractors

*GREEN XF: 1.5X TO 4X BASIC
RETAIL ONLY PARALLEL
BCP111 Bryce Harper 12.00 30.00
BCP220 Matt Moore 6.00 15.00

2011 Bowman Chrome Prospects Orange Refractors

111-220 STATED ODDS 1:198 HOBBY
STATED PRINT RUN 25 SER.#'d SETS
NO PRICING DUE TO SCARCITY

2011 Bowman Chrome Prospects Purple Refractors

*PURPLE REF: 2.5X TO 6X BASIC
1-110 PRINT RUN 700 SER.#'d SETS
111-220 PRINT RUN 799 SER.#'d SETS
BCP1 Bryce Harper 25.00 60.00
BCP111 Bryce Harper 25.00 60.00

2011 Bowman Chrome Prospects Red Refractors

111-220 STATED ODDS 1:900 HOBBY
STATED PRINT RUN 5 SER.#'d SETS
NO PRICING DUE TO SCARCITY

2011 Bowman Chrome Rookie Autographs

PLATE PRINT RUN 1 SET PER COLOR
BLACK-CYAN-MAGENTA-YELLOW ISSUED
NO PLATE PRICING DUE TO SCARCITY
EXCHANGE DEADLINE 4/30/2014
191 Jake McGee 4.00 10.00
192 Lars Anderson 4.00 10.00
195 Jeremy Jeffress 4.00 10.00
196 Brent Morel 4.00 10.00
197 Aroldis Chapman 10.00 25.00
198 Greg Halman 4.00 10.00
199 Jeremy Hellickson 4.00 10.00
200 Yunesky Maya 4.00 10.00
201 Kyle Drabek 4.00 10.00
203 Desmond Jennings 4.00 10.00
205 Freddie Freeman 75.00 200.00
209 Brian Bogusevic 4.00 10.00
210 Yonder Alonso 3.00 8.00
212 Dillon Gee 4.00 10.00
220 Chris Sale 12.00 30.00

2011 Bowman Chrome Rookie Autographs Refractors

*REF: .5X TO 1.2X BASIC
STATED PRINT RUN 500 SER.#'d SETS
EXCHANGE DEADLINE 4/30/2014

2011 Bowman Chrome Rookie Autographs Blue Refractors

*BLUE REF: .6X TO 1.5X BASIC
STATED PRINT RUN 250 SER.#'d SETS
EXCHANGE DEADLINE 4/30/2014

2011 Bowman Chrome Rookie Autographs Gold Refractors

*GOLD REF: 1X TO 2.5X BASIC
STATED PRINT RUN 50 SER.#'d SETS
EXCHANGE DEADLINE 4/30/2014

2011 Bowman Chrome Throwbacks

COMPLETE SET (25) 10.00 25.0
STATED ODDS 1:8 HOBBY
ATOMIC ODDS 1:25,353 HOBBY
ATOMIC PRINT RUN 1 SER.#'d SET
NO ATOMIC PRICING DUE TO SCARCITY
X-FRACTOR ODDS 1:1013 HOBBY
X-FRACTOR PRINT RUN 25 SER.#'d SETS
NO X-FRACTOR PRICING AVAILABLE
37 Chipper Jones 1.00 2.5
103 Alex Rodriguez 1.25 3.0
340 Albert Pujols 6.00 15.0
351A Ichiro Suzuki English 1.25 3.0
351B Ichiro Suzuki Japanese 1.25 3.0
BCT1 Tony Sanchez .60 1.5
BCT2 Dee Gordon .60 1.5
BCT3 Anthony Rizzo 4.00 10.0
BCT4 Nick Franklin .60 1.5
BCT5 Jameson Taillon .60 1.5
BCT6 Wil Myers 1.00 2.5
BCT7 Grant Green .40 1.
BCT8 Jacob Turner 1.50 4.
BCT9 Tyler Matzek .60 1.5
BCT10 Bryce Harper 4.00 10.
BCT11 Manny Banuelos 1.00 2.5
BCT12 Brett Lawrie 1.50 4.
BCT13 Devin Mesoraco 1.00 2.
BCT14 Shelby Miller 2.00 5.

BCT15 Delino DeShields Jr. .40 1.00
BCT16 Dustin Ackley .60 1.50
BCT17 Manny Machado 4.00 10.00
BCT18 Lonnie Chisenhall .60 1.50
BCT19 Arodys Vizcaino .60 1.50
BCT20 Stetson Allie .60 1.50

2011 Bowman Chrome Throwbacks Refractors

*REF: 2.5X TO 6X BASIC
STATED ODDS 1:256 HOBBY
STATED PRINT RUN 99 SER.#'d SETS

2011 Bowman Chrome Draft

COMPLETE SET (110) 12.50 30.00
COMMON CARD (1-110) .30 .75
STATED PLATE ODDS 1:928 HOBBY
PLATE PRINT RUN 1 SET PER COLOR
BLACK-CYAN-MAGENTA-YELLOW ISSUED
NO PLATE PRICING DUE TO SCARCITY
1 Mike Moustakas RC .75 2.00
2 Ryan Adams RC .30 .75
3 Alexi Amarista RC .30 .75
4 Anthony Bass RC .30 .75
5 Pedro Beato RC .30 .75
6 Bruce Billings RC .30 .75
7 Charlie Blackmon RC 6.00 15.00
8 Brian Broderick RC .30 .75
9 Rex Brothers RC .30 .75
10 Tyler Chatwood RC .30 .75
11 Jose Altuve RC 3.00 8.00
12 Salvador Perez RC 1.25 3.00
13 Mark Hamburger RC .30 .75
14 Matt Carpenter RC 2.50 6.00
15 Ezequiel Carrera RC .30 .75
16 Jose Ceda RC .30 .75
17 Andrew Brown RC .50 1.25
18 Maikel Cleto RC .30 .75
19 Steve Cishek RC .30 .75
20 Lonnie Chisenhall RC .50 1.25
21 Henry Sosa RC .30 .75
22 Tim Collins RC .30 .75
23 Josh Collmenter RC .30 .75
24 David Cooper RC .30 .75
25 Brandon Crawford RC .50 1.25
26 Brandon Laird RC .50 1.25
27 Tony Cruz RC .75 2.00
28 Chase d'Arnaud RC .30 .75
29 Fautino De Los Santos RC .30 .75
30 Rubby De La Rosa RC .75 2.00
31 Andy Dirks RC .75 2.00
32 Jarrod Dyson RC .50 1.25
33 Cody Eppley RC .30 .75
34 Logan Forsythe RC .30 .75
35 Todd Frazier RC .75 2.00
36 Eric Fryer RC .50 1.25
37 Charlie Furbush RC .30 .75
38 Cory Gearrin RC .30 .75
39 Graham Godfrey RC .30 .75
40 Dee Gordon RC .50 1.25
41 Brandon Gomes RC .30 .75
42 Bryan Shaw RC .30 .75
43 Brandon Guyer RC .50 1.25
44 Mark Hamilton RC .50 1.25
45 Brad Hand RC .30 .75
46 Anthony Recker RC .30 .75
47 Jeremy Horst RC .50 1.25
48 Tommy Hottovy (RC) .50 1.25
49 Jose Iglesias RC .50 1.25
50 Craig Kimbrel RC .75 2.00
51 Josh Judy RC .30 .75
52 Cole Kimball RC .30 .75
53 Alan Johnson RC .30 .75
54 Brandon Kintzler RC .30 .75
55 Pete Kozma RC .75 2.00
56 D.J. LeMahieu RC 4.00 10.00
57 Duane Below RC .50 1.25
58 Josh Lindblom RC .50 1.25
59 Zack Cozart RC .75 2.00
60 Al Alburquerque RC .30 .75
61 Trystan Magnuson RC .30 .75
62 Michael Martinez RC .50 1.25
63 Michael McKenry RC .50 1.25
64 Daniel Moskos RC .30 .75
65 Lance Lynn RC .75 2.00
66 Juan Nicasio RC .30 .75
67 Joe Paterson RC .50 1.25
68 Lance Pendleton RC .30 .75
69 Luis Perez RC .30 .75
70 Anthony Rizzo RC 3.00 8.00
71 Joel Carreno RC .30 .75
72 Alex Presley RC .50 1.25
73 Vinnie Pestano RC .30 .75
74 Aneury Rodriguez RC .30 .75
75 Josh Rodriguez RC .30 .75
76 Eduardo Sanchez RC .50 1.25
77 Matt Young RC .30 .75
78 Amauri Sanit RC .30 .75
79 Nathan Eovaldi RC .75 2.00
80 Javy Guerra (RC) .50 1.25
81 Eric Sogard RC .30 .75
82 Henderson Alvarez RC .30 .75
83 Ryan Lavarnway RC 1.25 3.00
84 Michael Stutes RC .50 1.25
85 Everett Teaford RC .30 .75
86 Blake Tekotte RC .30 .75
87 Eric Thames RC 1.50 4.00
88 Arodys Vizcaino RC .50 1.25
89 Rene Tosoni RC .30 .75
90 Alex White RC .30 .75
91 Brayan Villarreal RC .30 .75
92 Tony Watson RC .30 .75
93 Johnny Giavotella RC .30 .75
94 Kevin Whelan (RC) .30 .75
95 Mike Nickeas (RC) .30 .75
96 Elih Villanueva RC .30 .75
97 Tom Wilhelmsen RC .30 .75
98 Adam Wilk RC .50 1.25
99 Mike Wilson (RC) .30 .75
100 Jerry Sands RC .75 2.00
101 Mike Trout RC 250.00 600.00
102 Kyle Weiland RC .30 .75
103 Kyle Seager RC .75 2.00
104 Jason Kipnis RC 1.00 2.50
105 Chance Ruffin RC .30 .75
106 J.B. Shuck RC .75 2.00
107 Jacob Turner RC 1.25 3.00
108 Paul Goldschmidt RC 4.00 10.00
109 Justin Sellers RC .50 1.25
110 Trayvon Robinson (RC) .50 1.25

2011 Bowman Chrome Draft Refractors

*REF: .75X TO 2X BASIC
STATED ODDS 1:4 HOBBY

2011 Bowman Chrome Draft Blue Refractors

*BLUE REF: 2X TO 5X BASIC
STATED ODDS 1:41 HOBBY
STATED PRINT RUN 199 SER.#'d SETS

2011 Bowman Chrome Draft Gold Canary Diamond

STATED ODDS 1:7410 HOBBY
STATED PRINT RUN 1 SER.#'d SET
NO PRICING DUE TO SCARCITY

2011 Bowman Chrome Draft Gold Refractors

*GOLD REF: 3X TO 8X BASIC
STATED ODDS 1:162 HOBBY
STATED PRINT RUN 50 SER.#'d SETS

2011 Bowman Chrome Draft Orange Refractors

STATED ODDS 1:324 HOBBY
STATED PRINT RUN 25 SER.#'d SETS
NO PRICING DUE TO SCARCITY

2011 Bowman Chrome Draft Purple Refractors

*PURPLE REF: .75X TO 2X BASIC

2011 Bowman Chrome Draft Red Refractors

STATED ODDS 1:1620 HOBBY
STATED PRINT RUN 5 SER.#'d SETS
NO PRICING DUE TO SCARCITY

2011 Bowman Chrome Draft 16U USA National Team Autographs

STATED ODDS 1:763 HOBBY
STATED PLATE ODDS 1:20,280 HOBBY
PLATE PRINT RUN 1 SET PER COLOR
BLACK-CYAN-MAGENTA-YELLOW ISSUED
NO PLATE PRICING DUE TO SCARCITY
AM Austin Meadows 30.00 80.00
AP Arden Pabst 4.00 10.00
BB Bryson Brigman 4.00 10.00
CP Christian Pelaez 4.00 10.00
CS Carson Sands 4.00 10.00
DN Dom Nunez 4.00 10.00
DT Dany Toussaint 8.00 20.00
HM Hunter Mercado-Hood 4.00 10.00
JD Joe DeMers 4.00 10.00
JJ Jake Jarvis 4.00 10.00
JS Jordan Sheffield 5.00 12.00
KT Keegan Thompson 4.00 10.00
MV Matt Vogel 4.00 10.00
NC Nick Ciuffo 5.00 12.00
RU Riley Unroe 4.00 10.00
SF Steven Farinaro 4.00 10.00
TA Tyler Alamo 4.00 10.00
TC Trevor Clifton 4.00 10.00
WA William Abreu 5.00 12.00
ZC Zach Collins 4.00 10.00

2011 Bowman Chrome Draft 16U USA National Team Autographs Refractors

*REF: .6X TO 1.5X BASIC
STATED ODDS 1:410 HOBBY
STATED PRINT RUN 199 SER.#'d SETS

2011 Bowman Chrome Draft 16U USA National Team Autographs Blue Refractors

*BLUE REF: .75X TO 2X BASIC
STATED ODDS 1:825 HOBBY
STATED PRINT RUN 99 SER.#'d SETS

2011 Bowman Chrome Draft 16U USA National Team Autographs Gold Refractors

*GOLD REF: 1.2X TO 3X BASIC
STATED ODDS 1:1635 HOBBY
STATED PRINT RUN 50 SER.#'d SETS

2011 Bowman Chrome Draft 16U USA National Team Autographs Orange Refractors

STATED ODDS 1:3273 HOBBY
STATED PRINT RUN 25 SER.#'d SETS
NO PRICING DUE TO SCARCITY

2011 Bowman Chrome Draft 16U USA National Team Autographs Purple Refractors

STATED ODDS 1:8176 HOBBY
STATED PRINT RUN 10 SER.#'d SETS
NO PRICING DUE TO SCARCITY

2011 Bowman Chrome Draft 16U USA National Team Autographs Red Refractors

STATED ODDS 1:16,348 HOBBY
STATED PRINT RUN 5 SER.#'d SETS
NO PRICING DUE TO SCARCITY

2011 Bowman Chrome Draft Prospects

COMPLETE SET (110) 20.00 50.00
STATED PLATE ODDS 1:928 HOBBY
PLATE PRINT RUN 1 SET PER COLOR
BLACK-CYAN-MAGENTA-YELLOW ISSUED
NO PLATE PRICING DUE TO SCARCITY
BDPP1 John Hicks UER .40 1.00
BDPP2 Cody Asche .60 1.50
BDPP3 Tyler Anderson .25 .60
BDPP4 Jack Armstrong .40 1.00
BDPP5 Pratt Maynard .25 .60
BDPP6 Javier Baez 3.00 8.00
BDPP7 Kenneth Peoples-Walls .25 .60
BDPP8 Matt Barnes .40 1.00
BDPP9 Trevor Bauer 2.50 6.00
BDPP10 Daniel Vogelbach .75 2.00
BDPP11 Mike Wright UER .25 .60
BDPP12 Dante Bichette .40 1.00
BDPP13 Hudson Boyd .25 .60
BDPP14 Archie Bradley .75 2.00
BDPP15 Matthew Skole .40 1.00
BDPP16 Jed Bradley .40 1.00
BDPP17 Tyler Pill .25 .60
BDPP18 Dylan Bundy .75 2.00
BDPP19 Harold Martinez .40 1.00
BDPP20 Will Lamb .25 .60
BDPP21 Harold Riggins .25 .60
BDPP22 Zach Cone .40 1.00
BDPP23 Kyle Gaedele .25 .60
BDPP24 Kyle Crick .60 1.50
BDPP25 C.J. Cron .75 2.00
BDPP26 Nicholas Delmonico .25 .60
BDPP27 Alex Dickerson .40 1.00
BDPP28 Tony Cingrani 1.25 3.00
BDPP29 Jose Fernandez 1.00 2.50
BDPP30 Michael Fulmer .60 1.50
BDPP31 Carl Thomore .25 .60
BDPP32 Sean Gilmartin .25 .60
BDPP33 Tyler Goeddel .25 .60
BDPP34 Drew Gagnon .25 .60
BDPP35 Sonny Gray .60 1.50
BDPP36 Larry Greene .40 1.00
BDPP37 Nick Martini .25 .60
BDPP38 Taylor Guerrieri .25 .60
BDPP39 Jake Hager .25 .60
BDPP40 James Harris .25 .60
BDPP41 Travis Harrison .40 1.00
BDPP42 Nick DeSantiago .40 1.00
BDPP43 Chase Larsson .25 .60
BDPP44 Logan Moore .25 .60
BDPP45 Mason Hope .25 .60
BDPP46 Adrian Houser .40 1.00
BDPP47 Sean Buckley .25 .60
BDPP48 Rick Anton .25 .60
BDPP49 Scott Woodward .40 1.00
BDPP50 David Goforth .25 .60
BDPP51 Taylor Jungmann .40 1.00
BDPP52 Blake Snell 1.00 2.50
BDPP53 Francisco Lindor 5.00 12.00
BDPP54 Mikie Mahtook .60 1.50
BDPP55 Brandon Martin .40 1.00
BDPP56 Kevin Quackenbush .40 1.00
BDPP57 Kevin Matthews .25 .60
BDPP58 C.J. McElroy .25 .60
BDPP59 Anthony Meo .25 .60
BDPP60 Justin James .40 1.00
BDPP61 Levi Michael UER .40 1.00
BDPP62 Joseph Musgrove 1.25 3.00
BDPP63 Brandon Nimmo 1.25 3.00
BDPP64 Brandon Culbreth .25 .60
BDPP65 Javaris Reynolds .25 .60
BDPP66 Adam Ehrlich .25 .60
BDPP67 Henry Owens .40 1.00
BDPP68 Joe Panik .60 1.50
BDPP69 Jace Peterson .25 .60
BDPP70 Lance Jeffries .25 .60
BDPP71 Matthew Budgell .25 .60
BDPP72 Dan Gamache .25 .60
BDPP73 Christopher Lee .25 .60
BDPP74 Kyle Kubitza .25 .60
BDPP75 Nick Ahmed .25 .60
BDPP76 Josh Parr .25 .60
BDPP77 Dwight Smith .25 .60
BDPP78 Steven Gruver .25 .60
BDPP79 Jeffrey Soptic .25 .60
BDPP80 Cory Spangenberg .40 1.00
BDPP81 George Springer 1.50 4.00
BDPP82 Bubba Starling .40 1.00
BDPP83 Robert Stephenson .50 1.25
BDPP84 Trevor Story 8.00 20.00
BDPP85 Madison Boer .25 .60
BDPP86 Blake Swihart .40 1.00
BDPP87 Kellen Moen .25 .60
BDPP88 Joe Tuschak .25 .60
BDPP89 Keenyn Walker .25 .60
BDPP90 Kolten Wong .40 1.00
BDPP91 William Abreu .40 1.00
BDPP92 Tyler Alamo .25 .60
BDPP93 Bryson Brigman .25 .60
BDPP94 Nick Ciuffo .25 .60
BDPP95 Trevor Clifton .25 .60
BDPP96 Zach Collins .40 1.00
BDPP97 Joe DeMers .25 .60
BDPP98 Steven Farinaro .25 .60
BDPP99 Jake Jarvis .25 .60
BDPP100 Austin Meadows 6.00 15.00
BDPP101 Hunter Mercado-Hood .25 .60
BDPP102 Dom Nunez .25 .60
BDPP103 Arden Pabst .25 .60
BDPP104 Christian Pelaez .25 .60
BDPP105 Carson Sands .25 .60
BDPP106 Jordan Sheffield .25 .60
BDPP107 Keegan Thompson .25 .60
BDPP108 Dany Toussaint .40 1.00
BDPP109 Riley Unroe .25 .60
BDPP110 Matt Vogel .25 .60

2011 Bowman Chrome Draft Prospects Refractors

*REF: 1.5X TO 4X BASIC
STATED ODDS 1:4 HOBBY

2011 Bowman Chrome Draft Prospects Blue Refractors

*BLUE REF: 4X TO 10X BASIC
STAED ODDS 1:41 HOBBY
STATED PRINT RUN 199 SER.#'d SETS

2011 Bowman Chrome Draft Prospects Gold Canary Diamond

STATED ODDS 1:7410 HOBBY
STATED PRINT RUN 1 SER.#'d SET
NO PRICING DUE TO SCARCITY

2011 Bowman Chrome Draft Prospects Gold Refractors

*GOLD REF: 10X TO 25X BASIC
STAED ODDS 1:162 HOBBY
STATED PRINT RUN 50 SER.#'d SETS

2011 Bowman Chrome Draft Prospects Orange Refractors

STATED ODDS 1:324 HOBBY
STATED PRINT RUN 25 SER.#'d SETS
NO PRICING DUE TO SCARCITY

2011 Bowman Chrome Draft Prospects Purple Refractors

*PURPLE REF: 2X TO 5X BASIC

2011 Bowman Chrome Draft Prospects Red Refractors

STATED ODDS 1:1620 HOBBY
STATED PRINT RUN 5 SER.#'d SETS
NO PRICING DUE TO SCARCITY

2011 Bowman Chrome Draft Prospect Autographs

STATED ODDS 1:37 HOBBY
STATED PLATE ODDS 1:120,000 HOBBY
PLATE PRINT RUN 1 SET PER COLOR
BLACK-CYAN-MAGENTA-YELLOW ISSUED
NO PLATE PRICING DUE TO SCARCITY
EXCHANGE DEADLINE 11/30/2014
AB Archie Bradley 5.00 12.00
BM Brandon Martin 3.00 8.00
BN Brandon Nimmo 10.00 25.00
BS Bubba Starling 6.00 15.00
BSN Blake Snell 25.00 60.00
BSW Blake Swihart 5.00 12.00
CC C.J. Cron 4.00 10.00
CS Cory Spangenberg 3.00 8.00
DB Dylan Bundy 12.00 30.00
DV Daniel Vogelbach 8.00 20.00
FL Francisco Lindor 150.00 400.00
GS George Springer 60.00 150.00
JB Jed Bradley 3.00 8.00
JBA Javier Baez 150.00 400.00
JF Jose Fernandez 10.00 25.00
JH James Harris 3.00 8.00
JHA Jake Hager 3.00 8.00
JP Joe Panik 6.00 15.00
KCR Kyle Crick 3.00 8.00
KM Kevin Matthews 3.00 8.00
KW Kolten Wong 8.00 20.00
KWA Keenyn Walker 3.00 8.00
LG Larry Greene 3.00 8.00
MB Matt Barnes 3.00 8.00
MF Michael Fulmer 6.00 15.00
RS Robert Stephenson 8.00 20.00
SGR Sonny Gray 15.00 40.00
TA Tyler Anderson 3.00 8.00
TB Trevor Bauer 60.00 150.00
TG Tyler Goeddel 3.00 8.00
TGU Taylor Guerrieri 3.00 8.00
TH Travis Harrison 3.00 8.00
TJ Taylor Jungmann 4.00 10.00
TS Trevor Story 75.00 200.00

2011 Bowman Chrome Draft Prospect Autographs Refractors

*REF: .6X TO 1.5X BASIC
STATED ODDS 1:101 HOBBY
STATED PRINT RUN 500 SER.#'d SETS
EXCHANGE DEADLINE 11/30/2014
FL Francisco Lindor 250.00 500.00

2011 Bowman Chrome Draft Prospect Autographs Blue Refractors

*BLUE REF: 1.2X TO 3X BASIC
STATED ODDS 1:337 HOBBY
STATED PRINT RUN 150 SER.#'d SETS
EXCHANGE DEADLINE 11/30/2014
FL Francisco Lindor 400.00 800.00

2011 Bowman Chrome Draft Prospect Autographs Gold Refractors

*GOLD REF: 2.5X TO 6X BASIC
STATED ODDS 1:1004 HOBBY
STATED PRINT RUN 50 SER.#'d SETS
EXCHANGE DEADLINE 11/30/2014
FL Francisco Lindor 800.00 1200.00

2011 Bowman Chrome Draft Prospect Autographs Orange Refractors

STATED ODDS 1:2008 HOBBY
STATED PRINT RUN 25 SER.#'d SETS
NO PRICING DUE TO SCARCITY
EXCHANGE DEADLINE 11/30/2014

2011 Bowman Chrome Draft Prospect Autographs Purple Refractors

STATED ODDS 1:5050 HOBBY
STATED PRINT RUN 10 SER.#'d SETS
NO PRICING DUE TO SCARCITY
EXCHANGE DEADLINE 11/30/2014

2011 Bowman Chrome Draft Prospect Autographs Red Refractors

STATED ODDS 1:10,150 HOBBY
STATED PRINT RUN 5 SER.#'d SETS
NO PRICING DUE TO SCARCITY
EXCHANGE DEADLINE 11/30/2014

2012 Bowman Chrome

COMPLETE SET (220) 20.00 50.00
STATED PLATE ODDS 1:986 HOBBY
PLATE PRINT RUN 1 SET PER COLOR
BLACK-CYAN-MAGENTA-YELLOW ISSUED
NO PLATE PRICING DUE TO SCARCITY
1 Roy Halladay .25 .60
2 Josh Johnson .25 .60
3 Buster Posey .40 1.00
4 Jeremy Hellickson .20 .50
5 Giancarlo Stanton .30 .75
6 Alex Liddi RC .30 .75
7 Mat Latos .25 .60
8 Anibal Sanchez .20 .50
9 Hanley Ramirez .25 .60
10 Derek Jeter .75 2.00
11 Derek Norris RC .30 .75
12 Daniel Hudson .20 .50
13 Brandon Morrow .20 .50
14 Pablo Sandoval .25 .60
15 Josh Beckett .20 .50
16 David Price .25 .60
17 Tim Hudson .25 .60
18 Joe Benson RC .30 .75
19 Doug Fister .20 .50
20 Nick Markakis .25 .60
21 Brad Peacock RC .30 .75
22 Adam Jones .25 .60
23 Billy Butler .20 .50
24 Kirk Nieuwenhuis RC .30 .75
25 Jordan Danks RC .30 .75
26 CC Sabathia .25 .60
27 Zack Greinke .30 .75
28 Mark Reynolds .20 .50
29 Jose Bautista .25 .60
30 Brett Lawrie RC .40 1.00
31 Cole Hamels .25 .60
32 Jayson Werth .25 .60
33 Carl Crawford .25 .60
34 Chipper Jones .30 .75
35 Ervin Santana .20 .50
36 Miguel Cabrera .30 .75
37 Michael Pineda .20 .50
38 Brandon Beachy .20 .50
39 Liam Hendriks RC .30 .75
40 Alex Gordon .25 .60
41 Martin Prado .20 .50
42 Tim Lincecum .25 .60
43 Vance Worley .25 .60
44 Yoenis Cespedes RC .75 2.00
45 Clayton Kershaw .50 1.25
46 Devin Mesoraco RC .30 .75
47 Andrelton Simmons RC .50 1.25
48 B.J. Upton .25 .60
49 Ivan Nova .25 .60
50 Nyjer Morgan .20 .50
51 Carlos Santana .25 .60
52 Norichika Aoki RC .40 1.00
53 David Wright .25 .60
54 Joey Votto .30 .75
55 Felix Hernandez .25 .60
56 Troy Tulowitzki .30 .75
57 Dellin Betances RC .50 1.25
58 Evan Longoria .25 .60
59 Addison Reed RC .30 .75
60 Derek Holland .20 .50
61 Gio Gonzalez .25 .60
62 Shin-Soo Choo .25 .60
63 Jose Reyes .20 .50
64 Ian Kinsler .25 .60
65 Jimmy Rollins .25 .60
66 Alex Rodriguez .40 1.00
67 Cory Luebke .20 .50
68 J.D. Martinez .30 .75
69 Carlos Gonzalez .25 .60
70 Chris Archer RC .30 .75
71 Yovani Gallardo .25 .60
72 Kevin Youkilis .30 .75
73 Neftali Feliz .20 .50
74 Xavier Avery RC .30 .75
75 Jemile Weeks RC .20 .50
76 Matt Hague RC .30 .75
77 Drew Smyly RC .30 .75
78 Yadier Molina .40 1.00
79 Yunel Escobar .20 .50
80 Jason Motte .20 .50
81 Drew Hutchison RC .40 1.00
82 Jordany Valdespin RC .40 1.00
83 Justin Masterson .20 .50
84 Yu Darvish RC .75 2.00
85 Alex Avila .20 .50
86 Nick Swisher .25 .60
87 Mark Teixeira .25 .60
88 Dan Haren .20 .50
89 Jaime Garcia .25 .60
90 Melky Cabrera .20 .50
91 Brian Dozier RC 1.00 2.50
92 Matt Garza .20 .50
93 Hunter Pence .25 .60
94 Brandon Phillips .20 .50
95 Ubaldo Jimenez .20 .50
96 Prince Fielder .25 .60
97 Matt Kemp .25 .60
98 Freddie Freeman .40 1.00
99 Jarrod Parker RC .40 1.00
100 Daniel Bard .20 .50
101 Corey Hart .20 .50
102 Ike Davis .20 .50
103 Curtis Granderson .25 .60
104 Eric Hosmer .25 .60
105 Madison Bumgarner .25 .60
106 Michael Bourn .20 .50
107 Albert Pujols .40 1.00
108 Matt Moore RC .50 1.25
109 Matt Holliday .30 .75
110 Tyler Pastornicky RC .50 1.25
111 Colby Rasmus .25 .60
112 Nelson Cruz .30 .75
113 Craig Kimbrel .25 .60
114 Desmond Jennings .25 .60
115 Irving Falu RC .30 .75
116 Jon Lester .20 .50
117 John Axford .20 .50
118 Wilin Rosario RC .50 1.25
119 Todd Helton .25 .60
120 Ryan Zimmerman .25 .60
121 Josh Hamilton .25 .60
122 Paul Konerko .20 .50
123 Dee Gordon .20 .50
124 J.P. Arencibia .20 .50
125 J.J. Hardy .20 .50
126 David Ortiz .30 .75
127 Shane Victorino .25 .60
128 James Shields .20 .50
129 Mariano Rivera .40 1.00
130 Jon Niese .20 .50
131 Paul Goldschmidt .30 .75
132 Aramis Ramirez .20 .50
133 Emilio Bonifacio .20 .50
134 Salvador Perez .25 .60
135 C.J. Wilson .20 .50
136 Jhonny Peralta .20 .50
137 Chris Parmelee RC .50 1.25
138 Ryan Howard .25 .60
139 Mark Trumbo .20 .50
140 Asdrubal Cabrera .25 .60
141 Lucas Duda .25 .60
142 Dan Uggla .25 .60
143 Rickie Weeks .20 .50
144 Johnny Cueto .25 .60
145 Shaun Marcum .20 .50
146 Elvis Andrus .25 .60
147 Michael Young .20 .50
148 Donovan Solano RC 2.50 6.00
149 Adrian Beltre .30 .75
150 Drew Pomeranz RC .30 .75
151 Lance Berkman .25 .60
152 Heath Bell .20 .50
153 Dustin Ackley .20 .50
154 Stephen Strasburg .30 .75
155 Ichiro Suzuki .40 1.00
156 Michael Cuddyer .20 .50
157 Mike Trout 20.00 50.00
158 Brett Gardner .25 .60
159 Wade Miley RC .40 1.00
160 Chris Young .20 .50
161 Jordan Zimmermann .25 .60
162 Matt Dominguez RC .40 1.00
163 Jay Bruce .25 .60
164 Max Scherzer .30 .75
165 Ricky Romero .20 .50
166 Brandon McCarthy .20 .50
167 Brian McCann .25 .60
168 Jordan Pacheco RC .30 .75
169 Chris Carpenter .25 .60
170 Joe Mauer .25 .60
171 Carlos Ruiz .20 .50
172 Jacoby Ellsbury .25 .60
173 Trevor Bauer RC 1.50 4.00
174 Ryan Braun .20 .50
175 Torii Hunter .25 .60
176 Tommy Hanson .20 .50
177 Elian Herrera RC .50 1.25
178 Quintin Berry RC .50 1.25
179 Adam Lind .25 .60
180 Andrew McCutchen .30 .75
181 Adrian Gonzalez .25 .60
182 Jose Valverde .25 .60
183 Justin Upton .25 .60
184 Hisashi Iwakuma RC .60 1.50
185 Wei-Yin Chen RC .75 2.00
186 Ted Lilly .20 .50
187 Jeremy Hefner RC .30 .75
188 Kole Calhoun RC .40 1.00
189 Will Middlebrooks RC .40 1.00
190 Starlin Castro .25 .60
191 Adam Wainwright .25 .60
192 Ian Kennedy .20 .50
193 Michael Morse .20 .50
194 Mike Moustakas .25 .60
195 Matt Cain .25 .60
196 Tom Milone RC .30 .75
197 Chase Utley .25 .60
198 Ryan Vogelsong .20 .50
199 Wily Peralta RC .30 .75
200 Jered Weaver .25 .60
201 Cliff Lee .25 .60
202 Jason Heyward .25 .60
203 Jesus Montero RC .30 .75
204 Clay Buchholz .20 .50
205 David Freese .20 .50
206 Justin Morneau .25 .60
207 Christian Friedrich RC .30 .75
208 Mike Napoli .20 .50
209 Robinson Cano .25 .60
210 Aroldis Chapman .30 .75
211 Alexi Ogando .20 .50
212 Brennan Boesch .20 .50
213 R.A. Dickey .25 .60
214 Bryce Harper RC 10.00 25.00
215 Matt Adams RC .40 1.00
216 Jamie Moyer .20 .50
217 Dustin Pedroia .30 .75
218 Justin Verlander .30 .75
219 Miguel Montero .20 .50
220 Ben Zobrist .25 .60

2012 Bowman Chrome Refractors

*REF: 1X TO 2.5X BASIC
*REF RC: .6X TO 1.5X BASIC RC
STATED ODDS 1:4 HOBBY
214 Bryce Harper 30.00 80.00

2012 Bowman Chrome Blue Refractors

*BLUE REF: 1.5X TO 4X BASIC
*BLUE REF RC: 1.5X TO 4X BASIC RC
STATED ODDS 1:19 HOBBY
STATED PRINT RUN 250 SER.#'d SETS
157 Mike Trout 125.00 300.00
214 Bryce Harper 75.00 200.00

2012 Bowman Chrome Gold Refractors

*GOLD REF: 6X TO 15X BASIC
*GOLD REF RC: 4X TO 10X BASIC RC
STATED ODDS 1:96 HOBBY
STATED PRINT RUN 50 SER.#'d SETS
44 Yoenis Cespedes 15.00 40.00
70 Chris Archer 8.00 20.00
155 Ichiro Suzuki 20.00 50.00
214 Bryce Harper 125.00 300.00

2012 Bowman Chrome Green Refractors

*GREEN REF: 1.2X TO 3X BASIC
*GREEN REF RC: .75X TO 2X BASIC RC
214 Bryce Harper 40.00 100.00

2012 Bowman Chrome Purple Refractors

*PURPLE REF: 1.5X TO 4X BASIC
*PURPLE REF RC: 1.5X TO 4X BASIC RC
STATED ODDS 1:24 HOBBY
STATED PRINT RUN 199 SER.#'d SETS
214 Bryce Harper 75.00 200.00

2012 Bowman Chrome X-Fractors

*X-FRAC: 1X TO 2.5X BASIC
*X-FRAC RC: .6X TO 1.5X BASIC RC
214 Bryce Harper 30.00 80.00

2012 Bowman Chrome Franchise All-Stars

COMPLETE SET (20) 12.50 30.00
STATED ODDS 1:12 HOBBY
AP J.Profar/E.Andrus .60 1.50
BG Ryan Braun/Scooter Gennett .75 2.00
BGO Anthony Gose/Jose Bautista .60 1.50
BM W.Myers/B.Butler .75 2.00
BT C.Beltran/O.Taveras .75 2.00
CA Robinson Cano/Tyler Austin .75 2.00
CC M.Cabrera/N.Castellanos 1.50 4.00
CL A.Cabrera/F.Lindor 4.00 10.00
GA Arenado/Gonzalez 2.00 5.00
HH Felix Hernandez/Danny Hultzen .75 2.00
HO Mike Olt/Josh Hamilton .60 1.50
JB D.Bundy/A.Jones 1.00 2.50
MC G.Cole/A.McCutchen 3.00 8.00
OB X.Bogaerts/D.Ortiz 2.00 5.00
PJ T.Joseph/B.Posey 1.00 2.50
SF Fernandez/Stanton 1.25 3.00
TS J.Segura/M.Trout 5.00 12.00
VH B.Hamilton/J.Votto .75 2.00
VR B.Rondon/J.Verlander .75 2.00
WW Zack Wheeler/David Wright 1.00 2.50

2012 Bowman Chrome Futures Game

STATED ODDS 1:12 HOBBY
AG Anthony Gose .60 1.50
AM Alfredo Marte .30 .75
AP Ariel Pena .50 1.25
AS Ali Solis 1.25 3.00
BH Billy Hamilton .60 1.50
BR Bruce Rondon .30 .75
CB Christian Bethancourt .50 1.25
CY Christian Yelich 4.00 10.00
DB Dylan Bundy 1.00 2.50
DH Danny Hultzen .75 2.00
ER Enny Romero .30 .75
FL Francisco Lindor 4.00 10.00
FR Felipe Rivero .75 2.00
GC Gerrit Cole 3.00 8.00
JA Jesus Aguilar 3.00 8.00
JF Jose Fernandez 1.25 3.00
JH Jae-Hoon Ha .30 .75
JO Jake Odorizzi .60 1.50
JP Jurickson Profar .60 1.50
JR Julio Rodriguez .50 1.25
JS Jonathan Singleton .60 1.50
JSE Jean Segura .75 2.00
JT Jameson Taillon .60 1.50
KL Kyle Lotzkar .30 .75
KW Kolten Wong .50 1.25
MB Matt Barnes .50 1.25
MC Michael Choice .50 1.25
MM Manny Machado 3.00 8.00
MO Mike Olt .60 1.50
NA Nolan Arenado 2.00 5.00
NC Nick Castellanos 1.50 4.00
OA Oswaldo Arcia .30 .75
OT Oscar Taveras .75 2.00
RB Rob Brantly .75 2.00
RL Rymer Liriano .50 1.25
SG Scooter Gennett .75 2.00
TA Tyler Austin .75 2.00
TJ Tommy Joseph 1.00 2.50
TS Tyler Skaggs .75 2.00
TW Taijuan Walker .60 1.50
WF Wilmer Flores .60 1.50
WM Wil Myers .75 2.00
XB Xander Bogaerts 2.00 5.00
YV Yordano Ventura .50 1.25
ZW Zack Wheeler 1.00 2.50

2012 Bowman Chrome Legends In The Making Die Cuts

STATED ODDS 1:24 HOBBY
AC Aroldis Chapman 1.00 2.50
AP Albert Pujols 1.25 3.00
BH Bryce Harper 5.00 12.00
BL Brett Lawrie .75 2.00
BP Buster Posey 1.25 3.00
CG Carlos Gonzalez .75 2.00
CK Clayton Kershaw 1.50 4.00
DB Dylan Bundy 1.25 3.00
DF David Freese .60 1.50
DP Dustin Pedroia 1.00 2.50
FH Felix Hernandez .75 2.00
JE Jacoby Ellsbury .75 2.00
JV Justin Verlander 1.00 2.50
JW Jered Weaver .75 2.00
MC Miguel Cabrera 1.00 2.50
MK Matt Kemp .75 2.00
MM Matt Moore 1.00 2.50
PF Prince Fielder .75 2.00
RB Ryan Braun .60 1.50
RC Robinson Cano .75 2.00
SS Stephen Strasburg 1.00 2.50
TB Trevor Bauer 3.00 8.00
TT Troy Tulowitzki 1.00 2.50
YC Yoenis Cespedes 1.50 4.00
YD Yu Darvish 1.50 4.00

2012 Bowman Chrome Prospect Autographs

BOWMAN GRP A ODDS 1:42 HOB
BOWMAN GRP B ODDS 1: 1118 HOB
BOWMAN GRP C ODDS 1:1289 HOB
BOWMAN GRP D ODDS 1:1672 HOB
BOW.CHR. ODDS 1:19 HOBBY
BOW.CHR.PLATE ODDS 1:8125 HOB
PLATE PRINT RUN 1 SET PER COLOR
BLACK-CYAN-MAGENTA-YELLOW ISSUED
NO PLATE PRICING DUE TO SCARCITY
EXCHANGE DEADLINE 04/30/2015
AC Adam Conley 3.00 8.00
AG Avisail Garcia 10.00 25.00
BC Bobby Crocker 3.00 8.00
BH Billy Hamilton 4.00 10.00
BM Boss Moanaroa 3.00 8.00
CD Chase Davidson 3.00 8.00
CV Christian Villanueva 3.00 8.00
FH Frazier Hall 3.00 8.00
FR Felipe Rivero 4.00 10.00
FS Felix Sterling 3.00 8.00
JC Jose Campos 3.00 8.00
JG Jonathan Griffin 3.00 8.00

JH John Hellweg 3.00 8.00
JM Jake Marisnick 4.00 10.00
JP James Paxton 10.00 25.00
JR Josh Rutledge 3.00 8.00
JS Jonathan Singleton 3.00 8.00
KS Kevan Smith 3.00 8.00
MH Miles Head 3.00 8.00
MO Marcell Ozuna 25.00 60.00
MS Matt Szczur 5.00 12.00
NC Nick Castellanos 25.00 60.00
NM Nomar Mazara 15.00 40.00
PM Pratt Maynard 3.00 8.00
RG Ronald Guzman 10.00 25.00
RO Rougned Odor 10.00 25.00
RS Ravel Santana 3.00 8.00
SD Shawon Dunston Jr. 3.00 8.00
SG Scooter Gennett 6.00 15.00
SN Sean Nolin 3.00 8.00
TA Tyler Austin 8.00 20.00
TC Tony Cingrani 3.00 8.00
TM Trevor May 3.00 8.00
TS Tyler Skaggs 6.00 15.00
WJ Williams Jerez 3.00 8.00
ZD Zeke DeVoss 3.00 8.00
ACH Andrew Chafin 3.00 8.00
BMI Brad Miller 3.00 8.00
CBU Cody Buckel 3.00 8.00
JRG J.R. Graham 3.00 8.00
JSO Jorge Soler 15.00 40.00
BCP9 Eddie Rosario 10.00 25.00
BCP18 Brandon Drury 15.00 40.00
BCP20 Jeimer Candelario 8.00 20.00
BCP31 Nick Maronde 3.00 8.00
BCP43 Rookie Davis 3.00 8.00
BCP52 Dean Green 3.00 8.00
BCP58 Cheslor Cuthbert 3.00 8.00
BCP62 Kes Carter 3.00 8.00
BCP66 Jackie Bradley Jr. 10.00 25.00
BCP74 Eric Arce 3.00 8.00
BCP75 Dillon Maples 3.00 8.00
BCP77 Clay Holmes 3.00 8.00
BCP79 Josh Bell 40.00 100.00
BCP80 Matt Purke 3.00 8.00
BCP83 Jacob Anderson 3.00 8.00
BCP84 Bryan Brickhouse 3.00 8.00
BCP86 Gerrit Cole 75.00 200.00
BCP87 Danny Hultzen 3.00 8.00
BCP88 Anthony Rendon 50.00 120.00
BCP89 Austin Hedges 4.00 10.00
BCP91 Dillon Howard 3.00 8.00
BCP92 Nick Delmonico 8.00 20.00
BCP93 Brandon Jacobs 3.00 8.00
BCP94 Charlie Tilson 3.00 8.00
BCP97 Andrew Susac 3.00 8.00
BCP98 Greg Bird 6.00 15.00
BCP99 Dante Bichette 3.00 8.00
BCP100 Tommy Joseph 3.00 8.00
BCP101 Julio Rodriguez 3.00 8.00
BCP102 Oscar Taveras 4.00 10.00
BCP103 Drew Hutchison 3.00 8.00
BCP104 Joc Pederson 30.00 80.00
BCP105 Xander Bogaerts 60.00 150.00
BCP106 Tyler Collins 3.00 8.00
BCP107 Joe Ross 4.00 10.00
BCP108 Carlos Martinez 6.00 15.00
BCP109 Andrelton Simmons 10.00 25.00
BCP110 Daniel Norris 3.00 8.00

2012 Bowman Chrome Prospect Autographs Blue Refractors

*BLUE REF: 1.5X TO 4X BASIC
BOWMAN ODDS 1:429 HOBBY
BOW.CHR.ODDS 1:252 HOBBY
STATED PRINT RUN 150 SER.#'d SETS
BOW.EXCH DEADLINE 04/30/2015
BC EXCH DEADLINE 09/30/2015

2012 Bowman Chrome Prospect Autographs Blue Wave Refractors

STATED PRINT RUN 50 SER.#'d SETS
AC Adam Conley 6.00 15.00
AG Avisail Garcia 20.00 50.00
BC Bobby Crocker 6.00 15.00
BH Billy Hamilton 15.00 40.00
BM Boss Moanaroa 6.00 15.00
CD Chase Davidson 6.00 15.00
CV Christian Villanueva 6.00 15.00
FH Frazier Hall 6.00 15.00
FR Felipe Rivero 8.00 20.00
FS Felix Sterling 6.00 15.00
JC Jose Campos 6.00 15.00
JG Jonathan Griffin 6.00 15.00
JH John Hellweg 6.00 15.00
JM Jake Marisnick 8.00 20.00
JP James Paxton 50.00 120.00
JR Josh Rutledge 6.00 15.00
JS Jonathan Singleton 6.00 15.00
KS Kevan Smith 6.00 15.00
MH Miles Head 6.00 15.00
MO Marcell Ozuna 50.00 120.00
MS Matt Szczur 10.00 25.00
NC Nick Castellanos 50.00 120.00
NM Nomar Mazara 30.00 80.00
PM Pratt Maynard 6.00 15.00
RG Ronald Guzman 25.00 60.00
RO Rougned Odor 30.00 80.00
RS Ravel Santana 6.00 15.00
SD Shawon Dunston Jr. 6.00 15.00
SG Scooter Gennett 30.00 80.00
SN Sean Nolin 6.00 15.00
TA Tyler Austin 15.00 40.00
TC Tony Cingrani 6.00 15.00
TM Trevor May 6.00 15.00
TS Tyler Skaggs 12.00 30.00
WJ Williams Jerez 6.00 15.00
ZD Zeke DeVoss 6.00 15.00
ACH Andrew Chafin 6.00 15.00
BMI Brad Miller 6.00 15.00
CBU Cody Buckel 6.00 15.00
JRG J.R. Graham 6.00 15.00
BCP9 Eddie Rosario 20.00 50.00
BCP18 Brandon Drury 30.00 80.00
BCP20 Jeimer Candelario 15.00 40.00
BCP31 Nick Maronde 6.00 15.00
BCP43 Rookie Davis 6.00 15.00
BCP52 Dean Green 6.00 15.00
BCP58 Cheslor Cuthbert 6.00 15.00
BCP62 Kes Carter 6.00 15.00
BCP66 Jackie Bradley Jr. 20.00 50.00
BCP74 Eric Arce 6.00 15.00
BCP75 Dillon Maples 6.00 15.00
BCP77 Clay Holmes 6.00 15.00
BCP79 Josh Bell 500.00 1000.00
BCP80 Matt Purke 6.00 15.00
BCP83 Jacob Anderson 6.00 15.00
BCP84 Bryan Brickhouse 6.00 15.00
BCP86 Gerrit Cole 500.00 1000.00
BCP87 Danny Hultzen 6.00 15.00
BCP88 Anthony Rendon 100.00 250.00
BCP89 Austin Hedges 8.00 20.00
BCP91 Dillon Howard 6.00 15.00
BCP92 Nick Delmonico 15.00 40.00
BCP93 Brandon Jacobs 6.00 15.00
BCP94 Charlie Tilson 6.00 15.00
BCP97 Andrew Susac 6.00 15.00
BCP98 Greg Bird 12.00 30.00
BCP99 Dante Bichette 6.00 15.00
BCP100 Tommy Joseph 6.00 15.00
BCP101 Julio Rodriguez 6.00 15.00
BCP102 Oscar Taveras 8.00 20.00
BCP103 Drew Hutchison 6.00 15.00
BCP104 Joc Pederson 75.00 200.00
BCP105 Xander Bogaerts 125.00 300.00
BCP106 Tyler Collins 6.00 15.00
BCP107 Joe Ross 8.00 20.00
BCP108 Carlos Martinez 12.00 30.00
BCP109 Andrelton Simmons 20.00 50.00
BCP110 Daniel Norris 6.00 15.00

2012 Bowman Chrome Prospect Autographs Gold Refractors

*GOLD REF: 2X TO 5X BASIC
BOWMAN ODDS 1:1300 HOBBY
BOW.CHR.ODDS 1:755 HOBBY
STATED PRINT RUN 50 SER.#'d SETS
BOW.EXCH DEADLINE 04/30/2015
BC EXCH DEADLINE 09/30/2015
BCP79 Josh Bell 500.00 1000.00
BCP86 Gerrit Cole 500.00 1000.00

2012 Bowman Chrome Prospect Autographs Refractors

*REF: .6X TO 1.5X BASIC
BOW.ODDS 1:132 HOBBY
BOW.CHR.ODDS 1:75 HOBBY
STATED PRINT RUN 500 SER.#'d SETS
BOW.EXCH DEADLINE 04/30/2015
BC EXCH DEADLINE 09/30/2015

2012 Bowman Chrome Prospects

COMP.BOW.SET (1-110) 12.50 30.00
COMP.BC SET W/O VAR (111-220) 12.50 30.00
BOW.CHR.ODDS 1:986 HOBBY
PLATE PRINT RUN 1 SET PER COLOR
BLACK-CYAN-MAGENTA-YELLOW ISSUED
NO PLATE PRICING DUE TO SCARCITY
BCP1 Justin Nicolino .30 .75
BCP2 Myrio Richard .25 .60
BCP3 Francisco Lindor 2.00 5.00
BCP4 Nathan Freiman .25 .60
BCP5 A.J. Jimenez .25 .60
BCP6 Noah Perio .25 .60
BCP7 Adonys Cardona .25 .60
BCP8 Nick Kingham .25 .60
BCP9 Eddie Rosario .50 1.25
BCP10 Bryce Harper 6.00 15.00
BCP11 Philip Wunderlich .25 .60
BCP12 Rafael Ortega .25 .60
BCP13 Tyler Gagnon .25 .60
BCP14 Brenny Paulino .25 .60
BCP15 Jose Campos .30 .75
BCP16 Jesus Galindo .25 .60
BCP17 Tyler Austin .40 1.00
BCP18 Brandon Drury .40 1.00
BCP19 Richard Jones .25 .60
BCP20 Jeimer Candelario .30 .75
BCP21 Jose Osuna .25 .60
BCP22 Claudio Custodio .30 .75
BCP23 Jake Marisnick .30 .75
BCP24 J.R. Graham .25 .60
BCP25 Raul Alcantara .25 .60
BCP26 Joseph Staley .25 .60
BCP27 Josh Bowman .25 .60
BCP28 Josh Edgin .25 .60
BCP29 Keith Couch .25 .60
BCP30 Kyrell Hudson .25 .60
BCP31 Nick Maronde .30 .75
BCP32 Mario Yepez .25 .60
BCP33 Matthew West .25 .60
BCP34 Matthew Szczur .30 .75
BCP35 Devon Ethier .25 .60
BCP36 Michael Brady .25 .60
BCP37 Michael Crouse .25 .60
BCP38 Michael Gonzales .25 .60
BCP39 Mike Murray .25 .60
BCP40 Paul Hoilman .25 .60
BCP41 Zach Walters .30 .75
BCP42 Tim Crabbe .25 .60
BCP43 Rookie Davis .25 .60
BCP44 Adam Duvall 2.50 6.00
BCP45 Angelys Nina .25 .60
BCP46 Anthony Fernandez .25 .60
BCP47 Ariel Pena .25 .60
BCP48 Boone Whiting .25 .60
BCP49 Brandon Brown .25 .60
BCP50 Brennan Smith .25 .60
BCP51 Brett Krill .30 .75
BCP52 Dean Green .25 .60
BCP53 Casey Haerther .25 .60
BCP54 Casey Lawrence .25 .60
BCP55 Jose Vinicio .30 .75
BCP56 Kyle Simon .25 .60
BCP57 Chris Rearick .25 .60
BCP58 Cheslor Cuthbert .25 .60
BCP59 Daniel Corcino .30 .75
BCP60 Danny Barnes .25 .60
BCP61 David Medina .25 .60
BCP62 Kes Carter .25 .60
BCP63 Todd McInnis .25 .60
BCP64 Edwar Cabrera .25 .60
BCP65 Emilio King .25 .60
BCP66 Jackie Bradley .60 1.50
BCP67 J.T. Wise .25 .60
BCP68 Jeff Malm .25 .60
BCP69 Jonathan Galvez .25 .60
BCP70 Luis Heredia .25 .60
BCP71 Jonathon Berti .25 .60
BCP72 Jabari Blash .25 .60
BCP73 Will Swanner .25 .60
BCP74 Eric Arce .25 .60
BCP75 Dillon Maples .25 .60
BCP76 Ian Gac .25 .60
BCP77 Clay Holmes .25 .60
BCP78 Nick Castellanos .75 2.00
BCP79 Josh Bell 1.00 2.50
BCP80 Matt Purke .25 .60
BCP81 Taylor Whitenton .25 .60
BCP82 Dayan Diaz .30 .75
BCP83 Jacob Anderson .30 .75
BCP84 Bryan Brickhouse .25 .60
BCP85 Levi Michael .25 .60
BCP86 Gerrit Cole 5.00 12.00
BCP87 Danny Hultzen .40 1.00
BCP88 Anthony Rendon 1.50 4.00
BCP89 Austin Hedges .25 .60
BCP90 Robby Price .25 .60
BCP91 Dillon Howard .30 .75
BCP92 Nick Delmonico .25 .60
BCP93 Brandon Jacobs .30 .75
BCP94 Charlie Tilson .25 .60
BCP95 Luis Angel .25 .60
BCP96 Greg Billo .25 .60
BCP97 Andrew Susac .30 .75
BCP98 Greg Bird .30 .75
BCP99 Dante Bichette .30 .75
BCP100 Tommy Joseph .50 1.25
BCP101 Julio Rodriguez .25 .60
BCP102 Oscar Taveras .40 1.00
BCP103 Drew Hutchison .30 .75
BCP104 Joc Pederson 2.50 6.00
BCP105 Xander Bogaerts 1.00 2.50
BCP106 Tyler Collins .30 .75
BCP107 Joe Ross .25 .60
BCP108 Carlos Martinez .40 1.00
BCP109 Andrelton Simmons .40 1.00
BCP110 Daniel Norris .30 .75
BCP111 Rob Rasmussen .25 .60
BCP112A Maikel Franco .60 1.50
BCP112B M.Franco Fld SP 15.00 40.00
BCP113 Granden Goetzman .25 .60
BCP114A Will Lamb .25 .60
BCP114B W.Lamb Follow thr SP 12.50 30.00
BCP115 Sam Stafford .25 .60
BCP116 Boss Moanaroa .25 .60
BCP117 Shawon Dunston Jr. .30 .75
BCP118A Matt Dean .25 .60
BCP118B M.Dean w/Glove SP 12.50 30.00
BCP119A Kevin Pillar .30 .75
BCP119B K.Pillar Throw SP 10.00 25.00
BCP120 Jorge Soler 1.00 2.50
BCP121 Ravel Santana .25 .60
BCP122 Felipe Rivero .40 1.00
BCP123 Drew Leachman .30 .75
BCP124 Julio Morban .30 .75
BCP125 Donald Lutz .40 1.00
BCP126 Christian Bergman .25 .60
BCP127 Michael Earley .25 .60
BCP128A Jeremy Nowak .25 .60
BCP128B J.Nowak Bat down SP 12.50 30.00
BCP129 Tyler Kelly .25 .60
BCP130A Kyle Hendricks 1.50 4.00
BCP130B Hendricks Red Jsy SP 20.00 50.00
BCP131 Mike O'Neill .30 .75
BCP132 Garrett Wittels .30 .75
BCP133 Jon Talley .30 .75
BCP134 Daniel Santana .30 .75
BCP135 Starlin Rodriguez .25 .60
BCP136 Gregory Hopkins .25 .60
BCP137A Colin Walsh .30 .75
BCP137B C.Walsh Fld SP 10.00 25.00
BCP138A Chris Hawkins .30 .75
BCP138B C.Hawkins Batting SP 12.50 30.00
BCP139 Lane Adams .25 .60
BCP140 Brent Keys .25 .60
BCP141 Hanser Alberto .30 .75
BCP142 Tyler Massey .25 .60
BCP143 Alen Hanson .30 .75
BCP144A Blair Walters .25 .60
BCP144B Walt Hand together SP 12.50 30.00
BCP145A Jordan Scott .25 .60
BCP145B Jordan Scott Running SP 6.00 15.00
BCP146 Jamal Austin .25 .60
BCP147 Joel Caminero .25 .60
BCP148 JaDamion Williams .25 .60
BCP149 Mike Gallic .25 .60
BCP150 Kenny Vargas .50 1.25
BCP151 Camden Maron .25 .60
BCP152 Roberto De La Cruz .25 .60
BCP153 Luis Mateo .25 .60
BCP154 William Beckwith .30 .75
BCP155 Art Charles .25 .60
BCP156 Guillermo Pimentel .25 .60
BCP157 Cameron Seitzer .25 .60
BCP158 Anthony Garcia .25 .60
BCP159 Tyler Rahmatulla .25 .60
BCP160 Gary Apelian .25 .60
BCP161 Derek Christensen .25 .60
BCP162 Tim Shibuya .25 .60
BCP163 Wilsen Palacios .25 .60
BCP164 Brandon Eckerle .25 .60
BCP165 Carlos Valenzuela .30 .75
BCP166 Wander Ramos .25 .60
BCP167 Juaner Aguasvivas .25 .60
BCP168 Willy Garcia .30 .75
BCP169A Brian Pointer .30 .75
BCP169B B.Pointer Swing SP 10.00 25.00
BCP170 Austin Brice .25 .60
BCP171 Matthew Summers .25 .60
BCP172 O'Koyea Dickson .30 .75
BCP173 David Kandilas .25 .60
BCP174 Francisco Arcia .30 .75
BCP175 Taylor Siemens .25 .60
BCP176 Aaron Brooks .25 .60
BCP177 Yeison Hernandez .25 .60
BCP178 Jesus Solorzano .25 .60
BCP179 Narciso Mesa .25 .60
BCP180 Brian Humphries .25 .60
BCP181 Estarlin Martinez .25 .60
BCP182 Gregory Polanco .50 1.25
BCP183 Garrett Buechele .30 .75
BCP184 Austin Barnes .40 1.00
BCP185 Logan Pevny .25 .60
BCP186 Frank Lafreniere .25 .60
BCP187A Joshua Magee .25 .60
BCP187B J.Magee Fld SP 10.00 25.00
BCP188A Michael Antonio .25 .60
BCP188B M.Antonio Throw SP 10.00 25.00
BCP189A Julio Concepcion .25 .60
BCP189B Julio Concepcion Throwing SP 6.00 15.00
BCP190 Daniel Paolini .25 .60
BCP191 Danny Winkler .25 .60
BCP192 Felix Munoz .25 .60
BCP193 Evan Marshall .25 .60
BCP194 Manuel Hernandez .25 .60
BCP195 Ben Alsup .25 .60
BCP196 Montreal Robertson .25 .60
BCP197 Miguel Chalas .25 .60
BCP198A Bobby Bundy .25 .60
BCP198B B.Bundy Glv up SP 12.50 30.00
BCP199 Gabriel Lino .30 .75
BCP200A Eduardo Rodriguez .75 2.00
BCP200B Rodriguez Leg up SP 10.00 25.00
BCP201 Matt Benedict .25 .60
BCP202 Nate Jones .25 .60
BCP203 Marcos Camarena .30 .75
BCP204 Matt Hoffman .25 .60
BCP205A Kenny Faulk .25 .60
BCP205B Kenny Faulk Arm down SP 6.00 15.00
BCP206 Jordan Shipers .25 .60
BCP207 Forrest Snow .40 1.00
BCP208 Theo Bowe .30 .75
BCP209 David Freitas .25 .60
BCP210 Carlos Alonso .30 .75
BCP211A Domingo Tapia .30 .75
BCP211B D.Tapia White jsy SP 8.00 20.00
BCP212 Juan Lagares .50 1.25
BCP213A Junior Lake .25 .60
BCP213B J.Lake Fld SP 6.00 15.00
BCP214 Kevin Chapman .25 .60
BCP215A Jake Buchanan .30 .75
BCP215B Buch Grey jsy SP 12.50 30.00
BCP216 Wilfredo Tovar .30 .75
BCP217 Manny Machado 1.50 4.00
BCP218 John Hellweg .25 .60
BCP219 Matthew Neil .25 .60
BCP220 Ruben Alaniz .25 .60

2012 Bowman Chrome Prospects Blue Refractors

*BLUE REF: 3X TO 8X BASIC
BOWMAN ODDS 1:108 HOBBY
BOW.CHR.ODDS 1:19 HOBBY
STATED PRINT RUN 250 SER.#'d SETS

2012 Bowman Chrome Prospects Blue Wave Refractors

*BLUE WAVE: 2.5X TO 6X BASIC

2012 Bowman Chrome Prospects Gold Refractors

*GOLD REF: 8X TO 20X BASIC
BOWMAN ODDS 1:544 HOBBY
BOW.CHR.ODDS 1:96 HOBBY
STATED PRINT RUN 50 SER.#'d SETS
BCP117 Shawon Dunston Jr. 10.00 25.00

2012 Bowman Chrome Prospects Green Refractors

*GREEN REF: 1.5X TO 4X BASIC

2012 Bowman Chrome Prospects Purple Refractors

*PURPLE REF: 3X TO 8X BASIC
BOW.CHR.ODDS 1:24 HOBBY
STATED PRINT RUN 199 SER.#'d SETS

2012 Bowman Chrome Prospects Refractors

*1-110 REF: 2X TO 5X BASIC
*111-220 REF: 1.2X TO 3X BASIC
BOW.ODDS 1:54 HOBBY
BOW.CHR.ODDS 1:4 HOBBY
1-110 PRINT RUN 500 SER.#'d SETS

2012 Bowman Chrome Prospects X-Fractors

*X-FRAC: 2X TO 5X BASIC

2012 Bowman Chrome Rookie Autographs

GROUP A ODDS 1:2275 HOBBY
GROUP B ODDS 1:556 HOBBY
PLATE PRINT RUN 1 SET PER COLOR
BLACK-CYAN-MAGENTA-YELLOW ISSUED
NO PLATE PRICING DUE TO SCARCITY
EXCHANGE DEADLINE 04/30/2015
BH Bryce Harper 150.00 300.00
TB Trevor Bauer 20.00 50.00
WM Will Middlebrooks 5.00 12.00
YD Yu Darvish 100.00 200.00
204 Jeff Locke 6.00 15.00
209 Yu Darvish 100.00 200.00
210 Jesus Montero 8.00 20.00
211 Matt Moore 10.00 25.00
212 Drew Pomeranz 5.00 12.00
213 Jarrod Parker 5.00 12.00
214 Devin Mesoraco 5.00 12.00
215 Joe Benson 3.00 8.00
216 Brad Peacock 3.00 8.00
217 Dellin Betances 3.00 8.00
218 Wilin Rosario 5.00 12.00
220 Addison Reed 4.00 10.00

2012 Bowman Chrome Rookie Autographs Blue Refractors

*BLUE REF: .75X TO 2X BASIC
BOW.ODDS 1:1940 HOBBY
BOW.CHR.ODDS 1:3810 HOBBY
STATED PRINT RUN 250 SER.#'d SETS
BOW.EXCH DEADLINE 04/30/2015
BC EXCH DEADLINE 09/30/2015
BH Bryce Harper/99 200.00 400.00
YD Yu Darvish/99 200.00 400.00
209 Yu Darvish/250 200.00 400.00

2012 Bowman Chrome Rookie Autographs Gold Refractors

*GOLD REF: 1.5X TO 4X BASIC
BOW.ODDS 1:7050 HOBBY
BOW.CHR.ODDS 1:7515 HOBBY
STATED PRINT RUN 50 SER.#'d SETS
BOW.EXCH DEADLINE 04/30/2015
BC EXCH DEADLINE 09/30/2015
BH Bryce Harper 400.00 600.00
YD Yu Darvish EXCH 500.00 800.00
209 Yu Darvish 400.00 600.00

2012 Bowman Chrome Rookie Autographs Refractors

*REF: .5X TO 1.2X BASIC
STATED ODDS 1:990 HOBBY
STATED PRINT RUN 500 SER.#'d SETS
EXCHANGE DEADLINE 04/30/2015

2012 Bowman Chrome Draft

COMPLETE SET (55) 8.00 20.00
STATED PLATE ODDS 1:1600 HOBBY
PLATE PRINT RUN 1 SET PER COLOR
NO PLATE PRICING DUE TO SCARCITY
1 Trevor Bauer RC 2.50 6.00
2 Tyler Pastornicky RC .50 1.25
3 A.J. Griffin RC .60 1.50
4 Yoenis Cespedes RC 1.25 3.00
5 Drew Smyly RC .50 1.25
6 Jose Quintana RC .50 1.25
7 Yasmani Grandal RC .50 1.25
8 Tyler Thornburg RC .60 1.50
9 A.J. Pollock RC .75 2.00
10 Bryce Harper RC 8.00 20.00
11 Joe Kelly RC .75 2.00
12 Steve Clevenger RC .30 .75
13 Tanner Scheppers RC .30 .75
14 Casey Crosby RC .60 1.50
15 Wade Miley RC .60 1.50
16 Quintin Berry RC .75 2.00
17 Martin Perez RC .75 2.00
18 Addison Reed RC .50 1.25
19 Liam Hendriks RC .50 1.25
20 Matt Moore RC .75 2.00
21 Wilin Rosario RC .50 1.25
22 Jarrod Parker RC .60 1.50
23 Matt Adams RC .60 1.50
24 Devin Mesoraco RC .50 1.25
25 Jordan Pacheco RC .50 1.25
26 Irving Falu RC .50 1.25
27 Edwar Cabrera RC .50 1.25
28 Stephen Pryor RC .30 .75
29 Norichika Aoki RC .60 1.50
30 Jesus Montero RC .50 1.25
31 Drew Pomeranz RC .50 1.25
32 Jordany Valdespin RC .60 1.50
33 Andrelton Simmons RC .75 2.00
34 Xavier Avery RC .50 1.25
35 Chris Archer RC .50 1.25
36 Drew Hutchison RC .60 1.50
37 Dallas Keuchel RC 2.50 6.00
38 Leonys Martin RC .50 1.25
39 Brian Dozier RC 1.50 4.00
40 Will Middlebrooks RC .60 1.50
41 Kirk Nieuwenhuis RC .50 1.25
42 Jeremy Hefner RC .50 1.25
43 Derek Norris RC .50 1.25
44 Tom Milone RC .50 1.25
45 Wei-Yin Chen RC 1.25 3.00
46 Christian Friedrich RC .50 1.25
47 Kole Calhoun RC .60 1.50
48 Wily Peralta RC .50 1.25
49 Hisashi Iwakuma RC 1.00 2.50
50 Yu Darvish RC 1.25 3.00
51 Elian Herrera RC .75 2.00
52 Anthony Gose RC .60 1.50
53 Brett Jackson RC .75 2.00
54 Alex Liddi RC .50 1.25
55 Matt Hague RC .50 1.25

2012 Bowman Chrome Draft Refractors

*REF: 1.2X TO 3X BASIC
STATED PRINT RUN 300 SER.#'d SETS
STATED PRINT RUN 1:4 HOBBY
10 Bryce Harper 20.00 50.00

2012 Bowman Chrome Draft Blue Refractors

*BLUE REF: 1.2X TO 3X BASIC
STATED PRINT RUN 250 SER.#'d SETS
STATED PRINT RUN 1:26 HOBBY
10 Bryce Harper 30.00 80.00

2012 Bowman Chrome Draft Gold Refractors

*GOLD REF: 3X TO 8X BASIC
STATED PRINT RUN 50 SER.#'d SETS
STATED PRINT RUN 1:128 HOBBY
4 Yoenis Cespedes 30.00 60.00
10 Bryce Harper 60.00 120.00
50 Yu Darvish 40.00 80.00

2012 Bowman Chrome Draft Draft Pick Autographs

STATED ODDS 1:41 HOBBY
STATED PLATE ODDS 1:11,250 HOBBY
PLATE PRINT RUN 1 SET PER COLOR
NO PLATE PRICING DUE TO SCARCITY
EXCHANGE DEADLINE 11/30/2015
AA Albert Almora 15.00 40.00
AAU Austin Aune 4.00 10.00
AH Andrew Heaney 5.00 12.00
AR Addison Russell 25.00 60.00
BJ Brian Johnson 8.00 20.00
BM Bruce Maxwell 4.00 10.00
CH Courtney Hawkins 4.00 10.00
CS Corey Seager 100.00 250.00
CST Chris Stratton 4.00 10.00
DD David Dahl 20.00 50.00
DDA D.J. Davis 4.00 10.00
DM Deven Marrero 4.00 10.00
GC Gavin Cecchini 6.00 15.00
JG Joey Gallo 25.00 60.00
JR James Ramsey 4.00 10.00
KB Keon Barnum 4.00 10.00
KG Kevin Gausman 12.00 30.00
KP Kevin Plawecki 4.00 10.00
KZ Kyle Zimmer 3.00 8.00
LB Lewis Brinson 15.00 40.00
LS Lucas Sims 8.00 20.00
MF Max Fried 30.00 80.00
MH Mitch Haniger 15.00 30.00
MN Mitch Nay 4.00 10.00
MS Marcus Stroman 20.00 50.00
MSM Matthew Smoral 4.00 10.00
MW Michael Wacha 10.00 25.00
MZ Mike Zunino 10.00 25.00
NF Nolan Fontana 4.00 10.00
NT Nick Travieso 4.00 10.00
NW Nick Williams 8.00 20.00
PB Paul Blackburn 4.00 10.00
PL Pat Light 4.00 10.00
RS Richie Shaffer 4.00 10.00
SB Steve Bean 4.00 10.00
ST Stryker Trahan 4.00 10.00
SW Shane Watson 4.00 10.00
TH Ty Hensley 4.00 10.00
TN Tyler Naquin 20.00 50.00
TT Tyrone Taylor 5.00 12.00

2012 Bowman Chrome Draft Draft Pick Autographs Refractors

*REF: .5X TO 1.2X BASIC
STATED PRINT RUN 1:90 HOBBY
EXCHANGE DEADLINE 11/30/2015

2012 Bowman Chrome Draft Draft Pick Autographs Blue Refractors

*BLUE REF: 1.2X TO 3X BASIC
STATED PRINT RUN 150 SER.#'d SETS
STATED PRINT RUN 1:299 HOBBY
EXCHANGE DEADLINE 11/30/2015
CS Corey Seager 600.00 1000.00

2012 Bowman Chrome Draft Draft Pick Autographs Blue Wave Refractors

*BLUE WAVE: .6X TO 1.5X BASIC
STATED PRINT RUN 50 SER.#'d SETS

2012 Bowman Chrome Draft Draft Pick Autographs Gold Refractors

*GOLD REF: 2X TO 5X BASIC
STATED PRINT RUN 50 SER.#'d SETS
STATED PRINT RUN 1:893 HOBBY
EXCHANGE DEADLINE 11/30/2015
CS Corey Seager 1000.00 1500.00
DD David Dahl 200.00 400.00
JG Joey Gallo 200.00 500.00

2012 Bowman Chrome Draft Draft Picks

COMPLETE SET (165) 15.00 40.00
STATED PLATE ODDS 1:1600 HOBBY
PLATE PRINT RUN 1 SET PER COLOR
NO PLATE PRICING DUE TO SCARCITY
BDPP1 Lucas Sims .30 .75
BDPP2 Kevin Gausman .75 2.00
BDPP3 Brian Johnson .25 .60
BDPP4 Pierce Johnson .30 .75
BDPP5 Keon Barnum .25 .60
BDPP6 Paul Blackburn .25 .60
BDPP7 Nick Travieso .30 .75
BDPP8 Jesse Winker 4.00 10.00
BDPP9 Tyler Naquin .40 1.00
BDPP10 Kyle Zimmer .30 .75
BDPP11 Jesmuel Valentin .30 .75
BDPP12 Andrew Heaney .30 .75
BDPP13 Victor Roache .50 1.25
BDPP14 Mitch Haniger .60 1.50
BDPP15 Luke Bard .25 .60
BDPP16 Jose Berrios 2.00 5.00
BDPP17 Gavin Cecchini .30 .75
BDPP18 Kevin Plawecki .30 .75
BDPP19 Ty Hensley .30 .75
BDPP20 Matt Olson 3.00 8.00
BDPP21 Mitch Gueller .25 .60
BDPP22 Shane Watson .30 .75
BDPP23 Barrett Barnes .30 .75
BDPP24 Travis Jankowski .30 .75
BDPP25 Mike Zunino .40 1.00
BDPP26 Michael Wacha .50 1.25
BDPP27 James Ramsey .25 .60
BDPP28 Patrick Wisdom .25 .60
BDPP29 Steve Bean .30 .75
BDPP30 Richie Shaffer .30 .75
BDPP31 Lewis Brinson .75 2.00
BDPP32 Joey Gallo .75 2.00
BDPP33 D.J. Davis .30 .75
BDPP34 Tyler Gonzalez .30 .75
BDPP35 Marcus Stroman .40 1.00
BDPP36 Matt Smoral .25 .60
BDPP37 Branden Kline .25 .60
BDPP38 Jacob Thompson .30 .75
BDPP39 Austin Aune .30 .75
BDPP40 Peter O'Brien .40 1.00
BDPP41 Bruce Maxwell .25 .60
BDPP42 Dylan Cozens .40 1.00
BDPP43 Wyatt Mathisen .25 .60
BDPP44 Spencer Edwards .25 .60
BDPP45 Jamie Jarmon .25 .60
BDPP46 R.J. Alvarez .25 .60
BDPP47 Bryan De La Rosa .25 .60
BDPP48 Adrian Marin .25 .60
BDPP49 Austin Maddox .25 .60
BDPP50 Fernando Perez .25 .60
BDPP51 Austin Schotts .25 .60
BDPP52 Avery Romero .25 .60
BDPP53 Kolby Copeland .25 .60
BDPP54 Jonathan Sandfort .25 .60
BDPP55 Alex Yarbrough .25 .60
BDPP56 Justin Black .25 .60
BDPP57 Ty Buttrey .25 .60
BDPP58 Austin Dean .25 .60
BDPP59 Andrew Pullin .30 .75
BDPP60 Bralin Jackson .25 .60
BDPP61 Lex Rutledge .25 .60
BDPP62 Jordan John .25 .60
BDPP63 Andre Martinez .25 .60
BDPP64 Eric Wood .30 .75
BDPP65 Derek Self .25 .60
BDPP66 Jacob Wilson .25 .60
BDPP67 Joe Bircher .25 .60
BDPP68 Matthew Price .25 .60
BDPP69 Hudson Randall .25 .60
BDPP70 Jorge Fernandez .25 .60
BDPP71 Nathan Minnich .25 .60
BDPP72 Yoenny Gonzalez .25 .60
BDPP73 Steven Schils .25 .60
BDPP74 Thomas Coyle .25 .60
BDPP75 Ron Miller .25 .60
BDPP76 Rowan Wick .25 .60
BDPP77 Mike Dodig .25 .60
BDPP78 John Kuchno .25 .60
BDPP79 Caleb Frare .30 .75
BDPP80 William Carmona .25 .60
BDPP81 Clayton Henning .25 .60
BDPP82 Connor Lien .25 .60
BDPP83 Michael Meyers .25 .60
BDPP84 Julio Felix .25 .60
BDPP85 Alexander Muren .25 .60
BDPP86 Jacob Stallings .30 .75
BDPP87 Max Foody .25 .60
BDPP88 Taylor Hawkins .25 .60
BDPP89 Jeffrey Wendelken .25 .60
BDPP90 Steven Golden .25 .60
BDPP91 Brett Wiley .25 .60
BDPP92 John Silviano .25 .60
BDPP93 Tyler Tewell .25 .60
BDPP94 Sean McAdams .30 .75
BDPP95 Michael Vaughn .25 .60
BDPP96 Jake Proctor .25 .60
BDPP97 Richard Bielski .25 .60
BDPP98 Charles Gillies .25 .60
BDPP99 Erick Gonzalez .25 .60
BDPP100 Bennett Pickar .25 .60
BDPP101 Christopher Beck .25 .60
BDPP102 Brandon Brennan .25 .60
BDPP103 Eddie Butler .25 .60
BDPP104 David Dahl .75 2.00
BDPP105 Ryan Gibbard .25 .60
BDPP106 Hunter Scantling .25 .60
BDPP107 Zach Isler .25 .60
BDPP108 Joshua Turley .25 .60
BDPP109 Johendi Jiminian .25 .60
BDPP110 Jake Lamb .40 1.00
BDPP111 Mike Morin .25 .60
BDPP112 Parker Morin .25 .60
BDPP113 Scott Oberg .25 .60
BDPP114 Correlle Prime .25 .60
BDPP115 Mark Sappington .25 .60
BDPP116 Sam Selman .30 .75
BDPP117 Paul Sewald .25 .60
BDPP118 Matt Wessinger .25 .60
BDPP119 Max White .25 .60
BDPP120 Adam Giacalone .30 .75
BDPP121 Jeffrey Popick .25 .60
BDPP122 Alfredo Rodriguez .25 .60
BDPP123 Nick Routt .25 .60
BDPP124 Abe Ruiz .25 .60
BDPP125 Jason Stolz .25 .60
BDPP126 Ben Waldrip .25 .60
BDPP127 Eric Stamets .25 .60
BDPP128 Chris Cowell .25 .60
BDPP129 Fernelys Sanchez .25 .60
BDPP130 Kevin McKague .30 .75
BDPP131 Rashad Brown .25 .60
BDPP132 Jorge Saez .25 .60
BDPP133 Shaun Valeriote .25 .60
BDPP134 Will Hurt .25 .60
BDPP135 Nicholas Grim .30 .75
BDPP136 Patrick Merkling .25 .60
BDPP137 Jonathan Murphy .25 .60
BDPP138 Bryan Lippincott .25 .60
BDPP139 Austin Chubb .25 .60
BDPP140 Joseph Almaraz .25 .60
BDPP141 Robert Ravago .25 .60
BDPP142 Will Hudgins .25 .60
BDPP143 Tommy Richards .25 .60
BDPP144 Chad Carman .40 1.00
BDPP145 Joel Licon .25 .60
BDPP146 Jimmy Rider .25 .60
BDPP147 Jason Wilson .25 .60
BDPP148 Justin Jackson .25 .60
BDPP149 Casey McCarthy .25 .60
BDPP150 Hunter Bailey .25 .60
BDPP151 Jake Pintar .25 .60
BDPP152 David Cruz .25 .60
BDPP153 Mike Mudron .25 .60
BDPP154 Benjamin Kline .25 .60
BDPP155 Bryan Haar .25 .60
BDPP156 Patrick Claussen .25 .60
BDPP157 Derrick Bleeker .25 .60
BDPP158 Edward Sappelt .25 .60
BDPP159 Jeremy Lucas .25 .60
BDPP160 Josh Martin .25 .60
BDPP161 Robert Benincasa .25 .60
BDPP162 Craig Manuel .25 .60
BDPP163 Taylor Ard .25 .60
BDPP164 Dominic Leone .25 .60
BDPP165 Kevin Brady .25 .60

2012 Bowman Chrome Draft Draft Picks Refractors

*REF: 1.2X TO 3X BASIC
STATED PRINT RUN 1:4 HOBBY

2012 Bowman Chrome Draft Draft Picks Blue Refractors

*BLUE REF: 3X TO 8X BASIC
STATED PRINT RUN 250 SER.#'d SETS
STATED PRINT RUN 1:26 HOBBY

2012 Bowman Chrome Draft Draft Picks Blue Wave Refractors

*BLUE WAVE: 2.5X TO 6X BASIC

2012 Bowman Chrome Draft Draft Picks Gold Refractors

*GOLD REF: 10X TO 25X BASIC
STATED PRINT RUN 50 SER.#'d SETS
STATED PRINT RUN 1:128 HOBBY

2012 Bowman Chrome Draft Rookie Autographs

STATED ODDS 1:6700 HOBBY
EXCHANGE DEADLINE 11/30/2015
BH Bryce Harper 150.00 300.00
YD Yu Darvish EXCH 100.00 200.00

2013 Bowman Chrome

COMPLETE SET (220) 30.00 60.00
STATED PLATE ODDS 1:1015 HOBBY
PLATE PRINT RUN 1 SET PER COLOR
BLACK-CYAN-MAGENTA-YELLOW ISSUED
NO PLATE PRICING DUE TO SCARCITY

1 Bryce Harper .50 1.25
2 Wil Myers RC .60 1.50
3 Jose Reyes .25 .60
4 Rob Brantly RC .40 1.00
5 Elvis Andrus .25 .60
6 Matt Moore .25 .60
7 Starling Marte .25 .60
8 Kyuji Fujikawa RC .60 1.50
9 Aaron Hicks RC .60 1.50
10 Brandon Maurer RC .50 1.25
11 Casey Kelly RC .50 1.25
12 Jeurys Familia RC .60 1.50
13 Mike Minor .20 .50
14 Alex Wood RC .50 1.25
15 Joey Votto .30 .75
16 Curtis Granderson .25 .60
17 Ben Revere .20 .50
18 Giancarlo Stanton .30 .75
19 Mariano Rivera .40 1.00
20 Tim Lincecum .25 .60
21 Billy Butler .20 .50
22 Yonder Alonso .20 .50
23 Adeiny Hechavarria RC .50 1.25
24 Nolan Arenado RC 8.00 20.00
25 Felix Hernandez .25 .60
26 C.J. Wilson .20 .50
27 Tommy Milone .20 .50
28 Kyle Gibson RC .60 1.50
29 Carlos Ruiz .20 .50
30 Gerrit Cole RC 2.50 6.00
31 Avisail Garcia RC .50 1.25
32 Ike Davis .20 .50
33 Jordan Zimmermann .25 .60
34 Yoenis Cespedes .30 .75
35 Carlos Beltran .25 .60
36 Troy Tulowitzki .30 .75
37 Wei-Yin Chen .20 .50
38 Adam Wainwright .25 .60
39 Oswaldo Arcia RC .40 1.00
40 Alex Gordon .25 .60
41 Marco Scutaro .25 .60
42 Jon Lester .25 .60
43 Mike Morse .20 .50
44 Jedd Gyorko RC .50 1.25
45 Nelson Cruz .30 .75
46 Yu Darvish .30 .75
47 Josh Beckett .20 .50
48 Kevin Youkilis .20 .50
49 Zack Wheeler RC .75 2.00
50 Mike Trout 2.50 6.00
51 Fernando Rodney .20 .50
52 Jason Kipnis .25 .60
53 Tim Hudson .25 .60
54 Alex Colome RC .40 1.00
55 Alfredo Marte RC .40 1.00
56 Jason Heyward .25 .60
57 Jurickson Profar RC .50 1.25
58 Craig Kimbrel .25 .60
59 Adam Dunn .25 .60
60 Hanley Ramirez .25 .60
61 Jacoby Ellsbury .25 .60
62 Jonathan Pettibone RC .60 1.50
63 Jered Weaver .25 .60
64 Eury Perez RC .50 1.25
65 Jeff Samardzija .20 .50
66 Matt Kemp .25 .60
67 Carlos Santana .25 .60
68 Brett Marshall RC .50 1.25
69 Ryan Vogelsong .20 .50
70 Edwin Encarnacion .30 .75
71 Mike Zunino RC .60 1.50
72 Buster Posey .40 1.00
73 Ben Zobrist .25 .60
74 Madison Bumgarner .25 .60
75 Robinson Cano .25 .60
76 Jake Odorizzi RC .50 1.25
77 Eric Hosmer .25 .60
78 Yasiel Puig RC 1.50 4.00
79 Hisashi Iwakuma .25 .60
80 Ryan Zimmerman .25 .60
81 Adam Warren RC .40 1.00
82 Jake Peavy .20 .50
83 Mike Olt RC .50 1.25
84 Homer Bailey .20 .50
85 Barry Zito .25 .60
86 Wade Miley .20 .50
87 Nick Swisher .25 .60
88 Roy Halladay .25 .60
89 Jackie Bradley Jr. RC 1.00 2.50
90 Jose Bautista .25 .60
91 Will Middlebrooks .20 .50
92 Yasmani Grandal .20 .50
93 Allen Craig .25 .60
94 Brandon Phillips .20 .50
95 Lance Lynn .20 .50
96 Justin Upton .25 .60
97 Anthony Rendon RC 2.50 6.00
98 Ian Desmond .20 .50
99 Matt Harrison .20 .50
100 Justin Verlander .30 .75
101 Adrian Gonzalez .25 .60
102 Chris Davis .25 .60
103 Jose Fernandez RC 1.00 2.50
104 Dexter Fowler .25 .60
105 A.J. Burnett .20 .50
106 Derek Holland .20 .50
107 Cole Hamels .25 .60
108 Marcell Ozuna RC 1.00 2.50
109 James Shields .20 .50
110 Josh Hamilton .25 .60
111 Desmond Jennings .25 .60
112 Jaime Garcia .25 .60
113 Shin-Soo Choo .25 .60
114 Freddie Freeman .40 1.00
115 Nate Karns RC .40 1.00
116 Shelby Miller RC 1.00 2.50
117 Johnny Cueto .25 .60
118 Jay Bruce .25 .60
119 Chris Sale .30 .75
120 Alex Rios .25 .60
121 Michael Wacha RC .50 1.25
122 Mike Moustakas .25 .60
123 Adam Eaton RC .60 1.50
124 Joe Nathan .20 .50
125 Mark Trumbo .20 .50
126 David Freese .20 .50
127 Todd Frazier .20 .50
128 Austin Jackson .20 .50
129 Anthony Rizzo .40 1.00
130 Nick Maronde RC .50 1.25
131 Mat Latos .25 .60
132 Salvador Perez .25 .60
133 Albert Pujols .40 1.00
134 Dylan Bundy RC 1.00 2.50
135 Allen Webster RC .50 1.25
136 Andrew McCutchen .30 .75
137 Jason Motte .20 .50
138 Joe Mauer .25 .60
139 Trevor Rosenthal RC .75 2.00
140 Nick Franklin RC .50 1.25
141 Asdrubal Cabrera .25 .60
142 B.J. Upton .25 .60
143 Aaron Hill .20 .50
144 Jean Segura .25 .60
145 Josh Willingham .25 .60
146 Michael Bourn .20 .50
147 Didi Gregorius RC 1.50 4.00
148 Jon Jay .20 .50
149 Evan Longoria .25 .60
150 Matt Cain .25 .60
151 Yovani Gallardo .20 .50
152 Paul Goldschmidt .30 .75
153 Brett Lawrie .25 .60
154 Hyun-Jin Ryu RC 1.00 2.50
155 Jayson Werth .25 .60
156 R.A. Dickey .25 .60
157 Adrian Beltre .30 .75
158 Hunter Pence .25 .60
159 Adam Jones .25 .60
160 Brandon Morrow .20 .50
161 Coco Crisp .20 .50
162 Dustin Pedroia .30 .75
163 Ian Kennedy .20 .50
164 Stephen Strasburg .30 .75
165 Jon Niese .20 .50
166 Vidal Nuno RC .40 1.00
167 Matt Holliday .30 .75
168 Carter Capps RC .40 1.00
169 Ryan Howard .25 .60
170 David Ortiz .30 .75
171 Alex Rodriguez .40 1.00
172 CC Sabathia .25 .60
173 David Wright .25 .60
174 Wilin Rosario .20 .50
175 Ryan Braun .25 .60
176 Angel Pagan .20 .50
177 Josh Reddick .20 .50
178 Miguel Montero .20 .50
179 Corey Hart .20 .50
180 Cliff Lee .25 .60
181 Kevin Gausman RC 1.25 3.00
182 Melky Cabrera .20 .50
183 Jesus Montero .20 .50
184 Doug Fister .20 .50
185 Jim Johnson .20 .50
186 Carlos Gonzalez .25 .60
187 Starlin Castro .20 .50
188 Tyler Skaggs RC .60 1.50
189 Tony Cingrani RC .75 2.00
190 Matt Magill RC .40 1.00
191 Mark Reynolds .20 .50
192 Bruce Rondon RC .40 1.00
193 Prince Fielder .25 .60
194 Jose Altuve .25 .60
195 Chase Headley .20 .50
196 Andre Ethier .25 .60
197 Hiroki Kuroda .20 .50
198 Gio Gonzalez .25 .60
199 Mark Teixeira .25 .60
200 Miguel Cabrera .30 .75
201 Aroldis Chapman .30 .75
202 Nate Freiman RC .40 1.00
203 Ian Kinsler .25 .60
204 Trevor Bauer .40 1.00
205 Manny Machado RC 2.50 6.00
206 Josh Johnson .25 .60
207 Melky Mesa RC .50 1.25
208 Michael Young .20 .50
209 Evan Gattis RC .75 2.00
210 Yadier Molina .40 1.00
211 Kris Medlen .25 .60
212 Sean Doolittle RC .40 1.00
213 Torii Hunter .20 .50
214 Brian McCann .25 .60
215 Derek Jeter .75 2.00
216 Mike Kickham RC .40 1.00
217 Carlos Martinez RC .60 1.50
218 Paco Rodriguez RC .60 1.50
219 David Price .25 .60
220 Clayton Kershaw .50 1.25

2013 Bowman Chrome Blue Refractors

*BLUE REF: 2.5X TO 6X BASIC
*BLUE REF RC: 1.2X TO 3X BASIC RC
STATED ODDS 1:21 HOBBY
STATED PRINT RUN 250 SER.#'d SETS
2 Wil Myers 8.00 20.00
205 Manny Machado 8.00 20.00
209 Evan Gattis 6.00 15.00

2013 Bowman Chrome Gold Refractors

*GOLD REF: 8X TO 20X BASIC
*GOLD REF RC: 4X TO 10X BASIC RC
STATED ODDS 1:105 HOBBY
STATED PRINT RUN 50 SER.#'d SETS
1 Bryce Harper 20.00 50.00
49 Zack Wheeler 8.00 20.00
50 Mike Trout 25.00 60.00
71 Mike Zunino 15.00 40.00
78 Yasiel Puig 100.00 200.00
200 Miguel Cabrera 20.00 50.00
205 Manny Machado 40.00 80.00
215 Derek Jeter 30.00 60.00

2013 Bowman Chrome Green Refractors

*GREEN REF: 2X TO 5X BASIC
*GREEN REF RC: 1X TO 2.5X BASIC RC
78 Yasiel Puig 15.00 40.00

2013 Bowman Chrome Magenta Refractors

*MAGENTA REF: 12X TO 30X BASIC
*MAGENTA REF RC: 6X TO 15X BASIC RC
STATED ODDS 1:101 HOBBY
STATED PRINT RUN 35 SER.#'d SETS
215 Derek Jeter 40.00 100.00

2013 Bowman Chrome Orange Refractors

*ORANGE REF: 12X TO 30X BASIC
*ORANGE REF RC: 6X TO 15X BASIC RC
STATED ODDS 1:210 HOBBY
STATED PRINT RUN 25 SER.#'d SETS
1 Bryce Harper 30.00 80.00
30 Gerrit Cole 30.00 80.00
49 Zack Wheeler 12.00 30.00
50 Mike Trout 40.00 100.00
72 Buster Posey 30.00 80.00
78 Yasiel Puig 200.00 300.00
100 Justin Verlander 25.00 60.00
103 Jose Fernandez 30.00 80.00
134 Dylan Bundy 25.00 60.00
197 Hiroki Kuroda 15.00 40.00
205 Manny Machado 60.00 120.00
209 Evan Gattis 25.00 60.00
210 Yadier Molina 15.00 40.00
215 Derek Jeter 60.00 150.00

2013 Bowman Chrome Purple Refractors

*PURPLE REF: 2.5X TO 6X BASIC
*PURPLE REF RC: 1.2X TO 3X BASIC RC
STATED ODDS 1:26 HOBBY
STATED PRINT RUN 199 SER.#'d SETS
205 Manny Machado 8.00 20.00
209 Evan Gattis 6.00 15.00

2013 Bowman Chrome Refractors

*REF: 1.5X TO 4X BASIC
*REF RC: .75X TO 2X BASIC RC
STATED ODDS 1:4 HOBBY

2013 Bowman Chrome X-Fractors

*XFRACTOR: 1X TO 2.5X BASIC
*XFRACTOR RC: .6X TO 1.5X BASIC RC
78 Yasiel Puig 10.00 25.00

2013 Bowman Chrome Fit the Bill

STATED ODDS 1:630 HOBBY
STATED PRINT RUN 99 SER.#'d SETS
AC Aroldis Chapman 5.00 12.00
AM Andrew McCutchen 5.00 12.00
AR Anthony Rizzo 6.00 15.00
BH Bryce Harper 10.00 25.00
BP Buster Posey 15.00 40.00
CG Carlos Gonzalez 4.00 10.00
CK Clayton Kershaw 8.00 20.00
CKR Craig Kimbrel 4.00 10.00
CS Chris Sale 5.00 12.00
DP David Price 4.00 10.00
DW David Wright 4.00 10.00
EL Evan Longoria 4.00 10.00
FH Felix Hernandez 4.00 10.00
GS Giancarlo Stanton 5.00 12.00
JH Jason Heyward 4.00 10.00
JU Justin Upton 8.00 20.00
MH Matt Harvey 4.00 10.00
MM Manny Machado 12.00 30.00
MMO Matt Moore 4.00 10.00
MT Mike Trout 12.00 30.00
PG Paul Goldschmidt 10.00 25.00
SS Stephen Strasburg 5.00 12.00
YC Yoenis Cespedes 5.00 12.00
YD Yu Darvish 5.00 12.00
YP Yasiel Puig 15.00 40.00

2013 Bowman Chrome Fit the Bill X-Fractors

*X-FRACTORS: 1X TO 2.5X BASIC
STATED ODDS 1:1943 HOBBY
STATED PRINT RUN 24 SER.#'d SETS

2013 Bowman Chrome Rising Through the Ranks Mini

COMPLETE SET (30) 15.00 40.00
STATED ODDS 1:18 HOBBY
AA Albert Almora 1.00 2.50
AB Archie Bradley .50 1.25
AH Alen Hanson .60 1.50
AM Alex Meyer .50 1.25
AR Addison Russell .75 2.00
CC C.J. Cron .60 1.50
CCO Carlos Correa 6.00 15.00
CS Corey Seager 2.50 6.00
DD David Dahl .60 1.50
DP Dorssys Paulino .60 1.50
DV Dan Vogelbach .75 2.00
FL Francisco Lindor 4.00 10.00
GP Gregory Polanco 1.00 2.50
GS Gary Sanchez 1.50 4.00
JG Joey Gallo 1.50 4.00
JP Joc Pederson 1.25 3.00
JS Jorge Soler 1.00 2.50
KC Kyle Crick .75 2.00
KCO Kaleb Cowart .60 1.50
KZ Kyle Zimmer .60 1.50
MB Matt Barnes .60 1.50
MF Michael Fulmer .75 2.00
MFR Max Fried 2.00 5.00
MW Mason Williams .60 1.50
RQ Roman Quinn .75 2.00
RS Robert Stephenson .50 1.25
TA Tyler Anderson .50 1.25
TAU Tyler Austin .75 2.00
TG Taylor Guerrieri .50 1.25
XB Xander Bogaerts 1.50 4.00

2013 Bowman Chrome Rising Through the Ranks Mini Blue Refractor

*BLUE REF: 1.2X TO 3X BASIC
STATED ODDS 1:231 HOBBY
STATED PRINT RUN 250 SER.#'d SETS

2013 Bowman Chrome Rising Through the Ranks Mini Autographs

STATED ODDS 1:14,860 HOBBY
STATED PRINT RUN 25 SER.#'d SETS
EXCHANGE DEADLINE 9/30/2016
DD David Dahl 4.00 10.00
DV Dan Vogelbach 6.00 15.00
JS Jorge Soler 6.00 15.00
MF Michael Fulmer 10.00 25.00

2013 Bowman Chrome Cream of the Crop Mini Refractors

STATED ODDS 1:6 HOBBY
A1 Kaleb Cowart .30 .75
A2 C.J. Cron .30 .75
A3 Nick Maronde .30 .75
A4 Taylor Lindsey .25 .60
A5 R.J. Alvarez .25 .60
AB1 Julio Teheran .30 .75
AB2 Christian Bethancourt .40 1.00
AB3 Lucas Sims .30 .75
AB4 J.R. Graham .25 .60
AB5 Sean Gilmartin .25 .60
AD1 Tyler Skaggs .40 1.00
AD2 Archie Bradley .25 .60
AD3 Matt Davidson .30 .75
AD4 Adam Eaton .40 1.00
AD5 Stryker Trahan .25 .60
BO1 Dylan Bundy .60 1.50
BO2 Kevin Gausman .75 2.00
BO3 Jonathan Schoop .25 .60
BO4 L.J. Hoes .30 .75
BO5 Nick Delmonico .30 .75
CC1 Javier Baez 1.00 2.50
CC2 Jorge Soler .50 1.25
CC3 Albert Almora .50 1.25
CC4 Dan Vogelbach .40 1.00
CC5 Jeimer Candelario .30 .75
CI1 Trevor Bauer .50 1.25
CI2 Francisco Lindor 2.00 5.00
CI3 Dorssys Paulino .30 .75
CI4 Tyler Naquin .40 1.00
CI5 Ronny Rodriguez .25 .60
CR1 Billy Hamilton .30 .75
CR2 Robert Stephenson .25 .60
CR3 Tony Cingrani .50 1.25
CR4 Daniel Corcino .25 .60
CR5 Nick Travieso .30 .75
DT1 Nick Castellanos .75 2.00
DT2 Bruce Rondon .25 .60
DT3 Avisail Garcia .30 .75
DT4 Jake Thompson .25 .60
DT5 Danry Vasquez .25 .60
HA1 Carlos Correa 3.00 8.00
HA2 Jonathan Singleton .30 .75
HA3 George Springer 1.00 2.50
HA4 Delino DeShields .25 .60
HA5 Jarred Cosart .30 .75
MB1 Wily Peralta .25 .60
MB2 Tyler Thornburg .30 .75
MB3 Hunter Morris .30 .75
MB4 Taylor Jungmann .25 .60
MB5 Johnny Hellweg .25 .60
MM1 Jose Fernandez .60 1.50
MM2 Christian Yelich 2.00 5.00
MM3 Jake Marisnick .30 .75
MM4 Justin Nicolino .25 .60
MM5 Andrew Heaney .30 .75
MT1 Miguel Sano .30 .75
MT2 Byron Buxton 1.25 3.00
MT3 Oswaldo Arcia .25 .60
MT4 Alex Meyer .25 .60
MT5 Eddie Rosario .50 1.25
OA1 Addison Russell .40 1.00
OA2 Michael Choice .25 .60
OA3 Miles Head .30 .75
OA4 Sonny Gray .40 1.00
OA5 Grant Green .40 1.00
PP1 Jesse Biddle .30 .75
PP2 Tommy Joseph .50 1.25
PP3 Ethan Martin .25 .60
PP4 Roman Quinn .40 1.00
PP5 Adam Morgan .25 .60
SM1 Mike Zunino .40 1.00
SM2 Taijuan Walker .30 .75
SM3 Danny Hultzen .30 .75
SM4 Brad Miller .30 .75
SM5 James Paxton .30 .75
TR1 Jurickson Profar .30 .75
TR2 Mike Olt .30 .75
TR3 Cody Buckel .25 .60
TR4 Joey Gallo .75 2.00
TR5 Jairo Beras .40 1.00
WN1 Anthony Rendon 1.50 4.00
WN2 Brian Goodwin .30 .75
WN3 Lucas Giolito .40 1.00
WN4 A.J. Cole .30 .75
WN5 Matt Skole .30 .75
BRS1 Xander Bogaerts .75 2.00
BRS2 Matt Barnes .30 .75
BRS3 Jackie Bradley .60 1.50
BRS4 Allen Webster .30 .75
BRS5 Bryce Brentz .25 .60
CRO1 David Dahl .30 .75
CRO2 Nolan Arenado 6.00 15.00
CRO3 Trevor Story 1.25 3.00
CRO4 Jayson Aquino .25 .60
CRO5 Kyle Parker .25 .60
CWS1 Courtney Hawkins .25 .60
CWS2 Trayce Thompson .40 1.00
CWS3 Keon Barnum .25 .60
CWS4 Carlos Sanchez .25 .60
CWS5 Erik Johnson .25 .60
KCR1 Bubba Starling .30 .75
KCR2 Kyle Zimmer .30 .75
KCR3 Adalberto Mondesi .40 1.00
KCR4 Jorge Bonifacio .30 .75
KCR5 Orlando Calixte .30 .75
LAD1 Corey Seager 1.25 3.00
LAD2 Joc Pederson .60 1.50
LAD3 Yasiel Puig 1.00 2.50
LAD4 Hyun-Jin Ryu .60 1.50
LAD5 Zach Lee .30 .75
NYM1 Travis d'Arnaud .30 .75
NYM2 Zack Wheeler .50 1.25
NYM3 Noah Syndergaard .30 .75
NYM4 Michael Fulmer .40 1.00
NYM5 Wilmer Flores .30 .75
NYY1 Gary Sanchez .75 2.00
NYY2 Mason Williams .30 .75
NYY3 Tyler Austin .40 1.00
NYY4 Mark Montgomery .40 1.00
NYY5 Ty Hensley .30 .75
PPI1 Gerrit Cole 1.50 4.00
PPI2 Jameson Taillon .30 .75
PPI3 Gregory Polanco .50 1.25
PPI4 Alen Hanson .30 .75
PPI5 Luis Heredia .30 .75
SDP1 Jedd Gyorko .30 .75
SDP2 Rymer Liriano .25 .60
SDP3 Max Fried 1.00 2.50
SDP4 Austin Hedges .30 .75
SDP5 Casey Kelly .30 .75
SFG1 Kyle Crick .40 1.00
SFG2 Gary Brown .25 .60
SFG3 Joe Panik .40 1.00
SFG4 Clayton Blackburn .40 1.00
SFG5 Chris Stratton .25 .60
STL1 Oscar Taveras .30 .75
STL2 Shelby Miller .60 1.50
STL3 Carlos Martinez .40 1.00
STL4 Trevor Rosenthal .50 1.25
STL5 Kolten Wong .25 .60
TBJ1 Aaron Sanchez .30 .75
TBJ2 D.J. Davis .30 .75
TBJ3 Sean Nolin .30 .75
TBJ4 Marcus Stroman .40 1.00
TBJ5 Daniel Norris .30 .75
TBR1 Wil Myers .40 1.00
TBR2 Taylor Guerrieri .25 .60
TBR3 Jake Odorizzi .30 .75
TBR4 Hak-Ju Lee .25 .60
TBR5 Blake Snell .30 .75

2013 Bowman Chrome Cream of the Crop Mini Blue Wave Refractors

*REF: 2.5X TO 6X BASIC
STATED ODDS 1:98 HOBBY
STATED PRINT RUN 250 SER.#'d SETS

2013 Bowman Chrome Prospect Autographs

BOW. ODDS 1:38 HOBBY
BOW.CHROME ODDS 1:20 HOBBY
PLATE PRINT RUN 1 SET PER COLOR
BLACK-CYAN-MAGENTA-YELLOW ISSUED
NO PLATE PRICING DUE TO SCARCITY
BOW.EXCH DEADLINE 5/31/2016
BOW.CHR EXCH DEADLINE 9/30/2016
AA Andrew Aplin 3.00 8.00
AAL Arismendy Alcantara 3.00 8.00
AH Alen Hanson 4.00 10.00
AM Alex Meyer 3.00 8.00
AM Adalberto Mejia 3.00 8.00
AMO Adalberto Mondesi 25.00 60.00
AP Adys Portillo 3.00 8.00
AR Andre Rienzo 3.00 8.00
AS Austin Schotts 3.00 8.00
AW Adam Walker 3.00 8.00
BB Byron Buxton 75.00 200.00
BG Brian Goodwin 3.00 8.00
CA Cody Asche 3.00 8.00
CB Christian Bethancourt 3.00 8.00
CBL Clayton Blackburn 3.00 8.00
CC Carlos Correa 60.00 150.00
CE C.J. Edwards 3.00 8.00
CG Cameron Gallagher 3.00 8.00
CT Carlos Tocci 5.00 12.00
DC Dylan Cozens 4.00 10.00
DC Daniel Corcino 3.00 8.00
DG Deivi Grullon 3.00 8.00
DH Dilson Herrera 5.00 12.00
DL Dan Langfield 3.00 8.00
DP Dorssys Paulino 3.00 8.00
DV Danry Vasquez 3.00 8.00
EB Eddie Butler 3.00 8.00
EE Edwin Escobar 3.00 8.00
EJ Erik Johnson 3.00 8.00
ER Eduardo Rodriguez 5.00 12.00
GA Gioskar Amaya 3.00 8.00
GG Gabriel Guerrero 3.00 8.00
GP Gregory Polanco 6.00 15.00
HC Harold Castro 3.00 8.00
HL Hak-Ju Lee 3.00 8.00
HO Henry Owens 3.00 8.00
JA Jorge Alfaro 5.00 12.00
JA Jayson Aquino 3.00 8.00
JB Jorge Bonifacio 5.00 12.00
JB Jose Berrios 12.00 30.00
JBA Jeremy Baltz 3.00 8.00
JBE Jairo Beras 3.00 8.00
JBI Jesse Biddle 3.00 8.00
JC J.T. Chargois 3.00 8.00
JL Jake Lamb 4.00 10.00
JM Julio Morban 3.00 8.00
JN Justin Nicolino 3.00 8.00
JN Jimmy Nelson 3.00 8.00
JP Jose Peraza 4.00 10.00
JPO Jorge Polanco 5.00 12.00
JT Jake Thompson 3.00 8.00
KD Keury de la Cruz 3.00 8.00
KP Kevin Pillar 4.00 10.00
KS Kyle Smith 3.00 8.00
LG Lucas Giolito 20.00 50.00
LM Lance McCullers 10.00 25.00
LMA Luis Mateo 3.00 8.00
LME Luis Merejo 3.00 8.00
LS Luis Sardinas 3.00 8.00
LT Luis Torrens 3.00 8.00
MA Miguel Almonte 3.00 8.00
MAJ Miguel Andujar 40.00 100.00
MC Mauricio Cabrera 4.00 10.00
MK Mike Kickham 3.00 8.00
MM Mark Montgomery 3.00 8.00
MO Matt Olson 25.00 60.00
MR Matt Reynolds 3.00 8.00
MS Matthew Skole 3.00 8.00
MW Mac Williamson 4.00 10.00
MWI Matt Wisler 3.00 8.00
NT Nik Turley 3.00 8.00
NTR Nick Tropeano 3.00 8.00
OA Oswaldo Arcia 4.00 10.00
OG Onelki Garcia 3.00 8.00
PK Patrick Kivlehan 3.00 8.00
PL Patrick Leonard 4.00 10.00
PW Patrick Wisdom 3.00 8.00
RD Rafael De Paula 3.00 8.00
RM Rafael Montero 3.00 8.00
RN Renato Nunez 6.00 15.00
RO Roberto Osuna 4.00 10.00
RQ Roman Quinn 3.00 8.00
RR Rio Ruiz 3.00 8.00
RRO Ronny Rodriguez 3.00 8.00
SP Stephen Piscotty 5.00 12.00
SR Stefen Romero 3.00 8.00
SS Sam Selman 3.00 8.00
TG Tyler Glasnow 40.00 100.00
TH Tyler Heineman 3.00 8.00
TM Tom Murphy 5.00 12.00
TP Tyler Pike 3.00 8.00
TW Taijuan Walker 3.00 8.00
VR Victor Roache 4.00 10.00
VS Victor Sanchez 3.00 8.00
WF Wilfredo Rodriguez 3.00 8.00
WM Wyatt Mathisen 3.00 8.00
YA Yeison Asencio 3.00 8.00
YP Yasiel Puig 60.00 150.00
YV Yordano Ventura 6.00 15.00

2013 Bowman Chrome Prospect Autographs Blue Refractors

*BLUE REF: 1.2X TO 3X BASIC
BOW.ODDS 1:578 HOBBY
BOW.CHROME ODDS 1:227 HOBBY
STATED PRINT RUN 150 SER.#'d SETS
BOW.EXCH DEADLINE 5/31/2016
BOW.CHR EXCH DEADLINE 9/30/2016
CC Carlos Correa 500.00 1000.00
JB Jose Berrios 60.00 150.00
MAJ Miguel Andujar 125.00 300.00

2013 Bowman Chrome Prospect Autographs Blue Wave Refractors

STATED PRINT RUN 50 SER.#'d SETS
AA Andrew Aplin 10.00 25.00
AAL Arismendy Alcantara 10.00 25.00
AH Alen Hanson 12.00 30.00
AM Alex Meyer 10.00 25.00
AM Adalberto Mejia 10.00 25.00
AP Adys Portillo 6.00 15.00
AR Andre Rienzo 10.00 25.00
AS Austin Schotts 10.00 25.00
AW Adam Walker 10.00 25.00
BB Byron Buxton 600.00 1500.00
BG Brian Goodwin 20.00 50.00
CA Cody Asche 8.00 20.00
CB Christian Bethancourt 12.00 30.00
CC Carlos Correa 600.00 1200.00
CE C.J. Edwards 20.00 50.00
CG Cameron Gallagher 6.00 15.00
CT Carlos Tocci 20.00 50.00
DC Dylan Cozens 40.00 100.00
DC Daniel Corcino 12.00 30.00
DG Deivi Grullon 30.00 60.00
DH Dilson Herrera 20.00 50.00
DL Dan Langfield 12.00 30.00
DP Dorssys Paulino 12.00 30.00
DV Danry Vasquez 12.50 30.00
EB Eddie Butler 25.00 60.00
EE Edwin Escobar 20.00 50.00
EJ Erik Johnson 6.00 15.00
ER Eduardo Rodriguez 60.00 150.00
GA Gioskar Amaya 20.00 50.00
GG Gabriel Guerrero 6.00 15.00
HC Harold Castro 8.00 20.00
HL Hak-Ju Lee 10.00 25.00
HO Henry Owens 10.00 25.00
JA Jayson Aquino 8.00 20.00
JB Jorge Bonifacio 20.00 50.00
JB Jose Berrios 100.00 250.00
JBA Jeremy Baltz 10.00 25.00
JBE Jairo Beras 10.00 25.00
JBI Jesse Biddle 6.00 15.00
JC J.T. Chargois 6.00 15.00
JL Jake Lamb 8.00 20.00
JM Julio Morban 6.00 15.00
JN Justin Nicolino 12.50 30.00
JN Jimmy Nelson 12.50 30.00
JP Jose Peraza 40.00 100.00
JPO Jorge Polanco 25.00 60.00
JT Jake Thompson 8.00 20.00
KD Keury de la Cruz 8.00 20.00
KP Kevin Pillar 20.00 50.00
KS Kyle Smith 8.00 20.00
LG Lucas Giolito 100.00 250.00
LM Lance McCullers
LMA Luis Mateo 8.00 20.00
LME Luis Merejo 15.00 40.00
LS Luis Sardinas 6.00 15.00
LT Luis Torrens 30.00 80.00
MA Miguel Almonte 12.00 30.00
MAJ Miguel Andujar 150.00 400.00
MC Mauricio Cabrera 15.00 40.00
MK Mike Kickham 6.00 15.00
MM Mark Montgomery 6.00 15.00
MR Matt Reynolds 15.00 40.00
MS Matthew Skole 15.00 40.00
MW Mac Williamson 20.00 50.00
MWI Matt Wisler 10.00 25.00
NT Nik Turley 10.00 25.00
NTR Nick Tropeano 10.00 25.00
OA Oswaldo Arcia 15.00 40.00
OG Onelki Garcia 12.50 30.00
PK Patrick Kivlehan 15.00 40.00
PL Patrick Leonard
PW Patrick Wisdom 15.00 40.00
RD Rafael De Paula 15.00 40.00
RM Rafael Montero 6.00 15.00
RN Renato Nunez 25.00 60.00
RO Roberto Osuna
RQ Roman Quinn 6.00 15.00
RR Rio Ruiz
RRO Ronny Rodriguez 15.00 40.00
SP Stephen Piscotty 10.00 25.00
SR Stefen Romero 10.00 25.00
SS Sam Selman 15.00 40.00
TG Tyler Glasnow 75.00 200.00
TH Tyler Heineman 10.00 25.00
TM Tom Murphy 12.00 30.00
TP Tyler Pike 10.00 25.00
TW Taijuan Walker 25.00 60.00
VR Victor Roache 12.00 30.00
VS Victor Sanchez 12.00 30.00
WF Wilfredo Rodriguez 6.00 15.00
WM Wyatt Mathisen 6.00 15.00
YA Yeison Asencio 6.00 15.00
YP Yasiel Puig 125.00 300.00
YV Yordano Ventura 25.00 60.00

2013 Bowman Chrome Prospect Autographs Gold Refractors

*GOLD REF: 2.5X TO 6X BASIC
BOW.STATED ODDS 1:1734 HOBBY
BOW.CHROME ODDS 1:682 HOBBY
STATED PRINT RUN 50 SER.#'d SETS
BOW.EXCH DEADLINE 5/31/2016
BOW.CHR EXCH DEADLINE 9/30/2016
BB Byron Buxton 750.00 2000.00
CC Carlos Correa 600.00 1200.00
JB Jose Berrios 100.00 250.00
LS Luis Sardinas 30.00 60.00
MAJ Miguel Andujar 150.00 400.00
YP Yasiel Puig 400.00 800.00

2013 Bowman Chrome Prospect Autographs Refractors

*REF: .5X TO 1.2X BASIC
BOW.STATED ODDS 1:174 HOBBY
BOW.CHROME ODDS 1:68 HOBBY
STATED PRINT RUN 500 SER.#'d SETS
BOW.EXCH DEADLINE 5/31/2016
BOW.CHROME DEADLINE 9/30/2016
JB Jose Berrios 25.00 60.00

2013 Bowman Chrome Prospects

BOWMAN PRINTING PLATE ODDS 1:1881
PLATE PRINT RUN 1 SET PER COLOR
BLACK-CYAN-MAGENTA-YELLOW ISSUED
NO PLATE PRICING DUE TO SCARCITY
BCP1 Byron Buxton 3.00 8.00
BCP2 Jonathan Griffin .25 .60
BCP3 Mark Montgomery .40 1.00
BCP4 Gioskar Amaya .25 .60
BCP5 Lucas Giolito .40 1.00
BCP6 Danny Salazar .50 1.25
BCP7 Jesse Hahn .25 .60
BCP8 Tayler Scott .25 .60
BCP9 Ji-Man Choi .30 .75
BCP10 Tony Renda .25 .60
BCP11 Jamie Callahan .25 .60
BCP12 Collin Wiles .25 .60
BCP13 Tanner Rahier .30 .75
BCP14 Max White .25 .60
BCP15 Jeff Gelalich .25 .60
BCP16 Tyler Gonzales .25 .60
BCP17 Mitch Nay .25 .60
BCP18 Dane Phillips .25 .60
BCP19 Carson Kelly .30 .75
BCP20 Darwin Rivera .25 .60
BCP21 Arismendy Alcantara .40 1.00
BCP22 Brandon Maurer .30 .75
BCP23 Jin-De Jhang .25 .60
BCP24 Bruce Rondon .25 .60
BCP25 Jonathan Schoop .25 .60
BCP26 Cory Hall .25 .60
BCP27 Cory Vaughn .25 .60
BCP28 Danny Muno .25 .60
BCP29 Edwin Diaz .50 1.25
BCP30 Willians Astudillo .25 .60
BCP31 Hansel Robles .25 .60
BCP32 Harold Castro .25 .60
BCP33 Ismael Guillon .25 .60
BCP34 Jeremy Moore .25 .60
BCP35 Jose Cisnero .25 .60
BCP36 Jose Peraza .25 .60
BCP37 Jose Ramirez .30 .75
BCP38 Christian Villanueva .25 .60
BCP39 Brett Gerritse .25 .60
BCP40 Kris Hall .25 .60
BCP41 Matt Stites .25 .60
BCP42 Matt Wisler .25 .60
BCP43 Matthew Koch .25 .60
BCP44 Micah Johnson .30 .75
BCP45 Michael Reed .25 .60
BCP46 Michael Snyder .25 .60
BCP47 Michael Taylor .25 .60
BCP48 Nolan Sanburn .25 .60
BCP49 Patrick Leonard .25 .60
BCP50 Rafael Montero .25 .60
BCP51 Ronnie Freeman .25 .60
BCP52 Stephen Piscotty .50 1.25
BCP53 Steven Moya .40 1.00
BCP54 Chris McFarland .25 .60
BCP55 Todd Kibby .25 .60
BCP56 Tyler Heineman .25 .60
BCP57 Wade Hinkle .25 .60
BCP58 Wilfredo Rodriguez .25 .60
BCP59 William Cuevas .25 .60
BCP60 Yordano Ventura .30 .75
BCP61 Zach Bird .25 .60
BCP62 Socrates Brito .40 1.00
BCP63 Ben Rowen .25 .60
BCP64 Seth Maness .25 .60
BCP65 Corey Dickerson .30 .75
BCP66 Travis Witherspoon .25 .60
BCP67 Travis Shaw .25 .60
BCP68 Lenny Linsky .25 .60
BCP69 Anderson Feliz .25 .60
BCP70 Casey Stevenson .25 .60
BCP71 Pedro Ruiz .25 .60
BCP72 Christian Bethancourt .40 1.00
BCP73 Pedro Guerra .25 .60
BCP74 Ronald Guzman .40 1.00
BCP75 Jake Thompson .25 .60
BCP76 Brian Goodwin .30 .75
BCP77 Jorge Bonifacio .30 .75
BCP78 Dilson Herrera .75 2.00
BCP79 Gregory Polanco .50 1.25
BCP80 Alex Meyer .25 .60
BCP81 Gabriel Encinas .25 .60
BCP82 Yeicok Calderon .25 .60
BCP83 Rio Ruiz .25 .60
BCP84 Luis Sardinas .25 .60
BCP85 Fu-Lin Kuo .30 .75

BCP86 Kelvin De Leon .25 .60
BCP87 Wyatt Mathisen .25 .60
BCP88 Dorssys Paulino .30 .75
BCP89 William Oliver .25 .60
BCP90 Rony Bautista .25 .60
BCP91 Gabriel Guerrero .30 .75
BCP92 Patrick Kivlehan .25 .60
BCP93 Ericson Leonora .25 .60
BCP94 Mikeson Oliberto .25 .60
BCP95 Roman Quinn .40 1.00
BCP96 Shane Broyles .25 .60
BCP97 Cody Buckel .25 .60
BCP98 Clayton Blackburn .40 1.00
BCP99 Evan Rutckyj .25 .60
BCP100 Carlos Correa 3.00 8.00
BCP101 Ronny Rodriguez .25 .60
BCP102 Jayson Aquino .25 .60
BCP103 Adalberto Mondesi .40 1.00
BCP104 Victor Sanchez .30 .75
BCP105 Jairo Beras .40 1.00
BCP106 Stefen Romero .25 .60
BCP107 Alfredo Escalera-Maldonado .30 .75
BCP108 Kevin Medrano .25 .60
BCP109 Carlos Sanchez .25 .60
BCP110 Sam Selman .25 .60
BCP111 Daniel Watts .25 .60
BCP112A Nolan Fontana .30 .75
BCP112B N.Fontana SP VAR 10.00 25.00
BCP113A Addison Russell .40 1.00
BCP113B A.Russell SP VAR 15.00 40.00
BCP114 Mauricio Cabrera .25 .60
BCP115 Marco Hernandez .25 .60
BCP116 Jack Leathersich .25 .60
BCP117 Edwin Escobar .30 .75
BCP118 Onelki Garcia .30 .75
BCP119 Arismendy Alcantara .40 1.00
BCP120A Deven Marrero .25 .60
BCP120B D.Marrero SP VAR 15.00 40.00
BCP121 Adam Walker .30 .75
BCP122 Erik Johnson .25 .60
BCP123A Stryker Trahan .25 .60
BCP123B S.Trahan SP VAR 6.00 15.00
BCP124 Dan Langfield .25 .60
BCP125A Corey Seager 1.25 3.00
BCP125B C.Seager SP VAR 15.00 40.00
BCP126 Harold Castro .25 .60
BCP127A Victor Roache .30 .75
BCP127B V.Roache SP VAR 10.00 25.00
BCP128 Deivi Grullon .25 .60
BCP129 Francellis Montas .25 .60
BCP130 Mike Piazza .25 .60
BCP131 Miguel Almonte .25 .60
BCP132 Renato Nunez .50 1.25
BCP133 Tzu-Wei Lin .30 .75
BCP134 Tyler Glasnow 1.00 2.50
BCP135 Zach Eflin .30 .75
BCP136 Gustavo Cabrera .60 1.50
BCP137 J.T. Chargois .25 .60
BCP138A Max Fried 1.00 2.50
BCP139 Ty Buttrey .25 .60
BCP140 Jimmy Nelson .25 .60
BCP141 Alexis Rivera .25 .60
BCP142 Jeremy Rathjen .25 .60
BCP143 Ismael Guillon .25 .60
BCP144 C.J. Edwards .40 1.00
BCP145 Jorge Martinez .25 .60
BCP146 Nik Turley .25 .60
BCP147 Jeremy Baltz .25 .60
BCP148 Wilfredo Rodriguez .25 .60
BCP149 Matt Wisler .25 .60
BCP150A Henry Owens .30 .75
BCP150B H.Owens SP VAR 10.00 25.00
BCP151 Luis Merejo .25 .60
BCP152A Pat Light .25 .60
BCP152B P.Light SP VAR 6.00 15.00
BCP153 Rainy Lara .25 .60
BCP154A Chris Stratton .25 .60
BCP154B C.Stratton SP VAR 15.00 40.00
BCP155 Taylor Dugas .30 .75
BCP156 Andrew Toles .25 .60
BCP157 Matt Reynolds .30 .75
BCP158A Tyrone Taylor .25 .60
BCP158B T.Taylor SP VAR 10.00 25.00
BCP159 Andry Ubiera .30 .75
BCP160 Miguel Andujar 2.00 5.00
BCP161 Jake Lamb .40 1.00
BCP162 Parker Bridwell .25 .60
BCP163 Matt Curry .25 .60
BCP164 Viosergy Rosa .25 .60
BCP165 Carlos Tocci .25 .60
BCP166 Ryan Court .25 .60
BCP167 Breyvic Valera .30 .75
BCP168 David Holmberg .25 .60
BCP169 Derek Jones .25 .60
BCP170 R.J. Alvarez .25 .60
BCP171 Adalberto Mejia .25 .60
BCP172 Saxon Butler .25 .60
BCP173 Nestor Molina .25 .60
BCP174 Rafael De Paula .25 .60
BCP175 Adys Portillo .25 .60
BCP176 Yohander Mendez .25 .60
BCP177 Cameron Gallagher .25 .60
BCP178A Rock Shoulders .25 .60
BCP178B R.Shoulders SP VAR 10.00 25.00
BCP179 Nick Tropeano .25 .60
BCP180 Tyler Heineman .25 .60
BCP181 Wade Hinkle .25 .60
BCP182 Roberto Osuna .25 .60
BCP183 Drew Steckenrider .25 .60
BCP184 Austin Schotts .30 .75
BCP185 Joan Gregorio .30 .75
BCP186 Dylan Cozens .25 .60
BCP187 Jose Peraza .25 .60
BCP188 Mitch Brown .25 .60
BCP189 Yeison Asencio .25 .60
BCP190A Danry Vasquez .25 .60
BCP191 Jose Berrios .40 1.00
BCP192 Cody Asche .40 1.00
BCP193 Julian Yan .25 .60
BCP194A Tyler Pike .25 .60
BCP194B T.Pike SP VAR 6.00 15.00
BCP195 Gabriel Encinas .25 .60
BCP196 Luis Mateo .25 .60
BCP197 Michael Perez .25 .60
BCP198 Hanser Alberto .25 .60
BCP199 Andrew Aplin .25 .60
BCP200A Lance McCullers .25 .60
BCP200B L.McCullers SP VAR 10.00 25.00
BCP201 Tom Murphy .25 .60
BCP202 Patrick Leonard .25 .60
BCP203 B.J. Boyd .25 .60
BCP204A Rafael Montero .25 .60
BCP204B R.Montero SP VAR 15.00 40.00
BCP205 Kyle Smith .25 .60
BCP206A Albert Almora .50 1.25
BCP206B A.Almora SP VAR 15.00 40.00
BCP207A Eduardo Rodriguez .75 2.00
BCP207B E.Rodriguez SP VAR 12.50 30.00
BCP208 Anthony Alford .25 .60
BCP209 Dustin Geiger .25 .60
BCP210 Andre Rienzo .25 .60
BCP211 Jin-De Jhang .25 .60
BCP212 Jorge Polanco .60 1.50
BCP213A Jorge Alfaro .50 1.25
BCP213B J.Alfaro SP VAR 10.00 25.00
BCP214 Luis Torrens .25 .60
BCP215 Luiz Gohara .30 .75
BCP216 Luigi Rodriguez .25 .60
BCP217A Courtney Hawkins .25 .60
BCP217B C.Hawkins SP VAR 10.00 25.00
BCP218 Tommy Kahnle .25 .60
BCP219 Keury de la Cruz .25 .60
BCP220 Mac Williamson .40 1.00

2013 Bowman Chrome Prospects Refractors

*REF 1-110: 2.5X TO 6X BASIC
*REF 111-220: 2X TO 5X BASIC
BOWMAN ODDS 1:67 HOBBY
1-110 PRINT RUN 500 SER.#'d SETS
111-220 ARE NOT SERIAL NUMBERED

2013 Bowman Chrome Prospects Black Refractors

*BLK 1-110 REF: 6X TO 15X BASIC
BOWMAN ODDS 1:217 HOBBY
1-110 PRINT RUN 99 SER.#'d SETS
111-220 PRINT RUN 15 SER.#'d SETS
NO PRICING ON QTY 15

2013 Bowman Chrome Prospects Blue Refractors

*BLUE REF: 5X TO 12X BASIC
BOWMAN ODDS 1:134 HOBBY
STATED PRINT RUN 250 SER.#'d SETS

2013 Bowman Chrome Prospects Blue Wave Refractors

*BLUE WAVE REF: 4X TO 10X BASIC

2013 Bowman Chrome Prospects Gold Refractors

*GOLD REF: 10X TO 25X BASIC
BOWMAN ODDS 1:670 HOBBY
STATED PRINT RUN 50 SER.#'d SETS

2013 Bowman Chrome Prospects Green Refractors

*GREEN REF: 2.5X TO 6X BASIC

2013 Bowman Chrome Prospects Magenta Refractors

*MAGENTA REF: 12X TO 30X BASIC
STATED PRINT RUN 35 SER.#'d SETS

2013 Bowman Chrome Prospects Purple Refractors

*PURPLE REF: 5X TO 12X BASIC
STATED PRINT RUN 199 SER.#'d SETS

2013 Bowman Chrome Prospects X-Fractors

*X-FRACTORS: 3X TO 8X BASIC

2013 Bowman Chrome Rookie Autographs

BOW.ODDS 1:316 HOBBY
BOW.CHROME ODDS 1:2444 HOBBY
PLATE PRINT RUN 1 SET PER COLOR
BLACK-CYAN-MAGENTA-YELLOW ISSUED
NO PLATE PRICING DUE TO SCARCITY
BOW.EXCH DEADLINE 5/31/2016
BOW.CHR.EXCH DEADLINE 9/30/2016
AE Adam Eaton 3.00 8.00
AG Avisail Garcia 3.00 8.00
BM Brandon Maurer 4.00 10.00
BR Bruce Rondon 10.00 25.00
CK Casey Kelly 3.00 8.00
DB Dylan Bundy 10.00 25.00
DR Darin Ruf 3.00 8.00
EG Evan Gattis 20.00 50.00
HJR Hyun-Jin Ryu 50.00 120.00
JF Jeurys Familia 3.00 8.00
JO Jake Odorizzi 5.00 12.00
JP J.Profar Field 15.00 40.00
JP J.Profar Throw 12.00 30.00
MM Manny Machado 25.00 60.00
MO Mike Olt 6.00 15.00
NM Nick Maronde 3.00 8.00
PR Paco Rodriguez 4.00 10.00
SM Shelby Miller 5.00 12.00
TS Tyler Skaggs 3.00 8.00
WM Wil Myers 20.00 50.00

2013 Bowman Chrome Rookie Autographs Refractors

*REF: .5X TO 1.2X BASIC
STATED ODDS 1:729 HOBBY
STATED PRINT RUN 500 SER.#'d SETS
BOW.EXCH DEADLINE 05/31/2016

2013 Bowman Chrome Rookie Autographs Blue Refractors

*BLUE REF: .75X TO 2X BASIC
*BLUE REF/99: .75X TO 2X BASIC
STATED ODDS 1:1121 HOBBY
BOW.CHROME ODDS 1:6297 HOBBY
STATED PRINT RUN 250 SER.#'d SETS
BOW.CHR. PRINT RUN 99 SER.#'d SETS
EXCHANGE DEADLINE 05/31/2016
BOW.CHR.EXCH DEADLINE 9/30/2016
EG Evan Gattis 40.00 100.00
HJR Hyun-Jin Ryu 100.00 250.00

2013 Bowman Chrome Rookie Autographs Gold Refractors

*GOLD REF: 1.2X TO 3X BASIC
BOWMAN ODDS 1:5602 HOBBY
BOW.CHROME ODDS 1:12,522 HOBBY
STATED PRINT RUN 50 SER.#'d SETS
BOW.EXCH DEADLINE 05/31/2016
BOW.CHR.EXCH DEADLINE 9/30/2016
DB Dylan Bundy 40.00 100.00
HJR Hyun-Jin Ryu 125.00 300.00

2013 Bowman Rookie Reprint Blue Sapphire Refractors

COMPLETE SET (64) 40.00 100.00
BOWMAN ODDS 1:24 HOBBY
BOW.PLATINUM ODDS 1:20 HOBBY
BOW.CHROME ODDS 1:18 HOBBY
68 Jim Thome .40 1.00
71 David Ortiz .60 1.50
78 Yasiel Puig 12.50 30.00
AB Adrian Beltre .60 1.50
AG Adrian Gonzalez .50 1.25
AJ Andruw Jones .40 1.00
AK Al Kaline .60 1.50
AM Andrew McCutchen .60 1.50
AP Andy Pettitte .50 1.25
264 Albert Pujols .75 2.00
AR Alex Rodriguez .75 2.00
350 Alfonso Soriano .50 1.25
BF Bob Feller .50 1.25
BH Bryce Harper 1.00 2.50
BP Buster Posey .75 2.00
CB Carlos Beltran .50 1.25
CG Curtis Granderson .50 1.25
CK Clayton Kershaw 1.00 2.50
CS CC Sabathia .50 1.25
CU Chase Utley .50 1.25
15 Derek Jeter 6.00 15.00
DS Duke Snider .50 1.25
DW David Wright .50 1.25
EL Evan Longoria .50 1.25
EM Eddie Mathews .60 1.50
FH Felix Hernandez .50 1.25
FT Frank Thomas .60 1.50
BCP86 Gerrit Cole 2.50 6.00
HA Hank Aaron 1.25 3.00
JH Josh Hamilton .50 1.25
JR Jose Reyes .50 1.25
JR Jackie Robinson .60 1.50
174 Justin Verlander .60 1.50
JV Joey Votto .60 1.50
MC Matt Cain .50 1.25
MH Matt Holliday .60 1.50
MK Matthew Kemp .50 1.25
MR Mariano Rivera .75 2.00
MS Michael Stanton .60 1.50
MT Mark Teixeira .50 1.25
MT Mike Trout 10.00 25.00
PF Prince Fielder .50 1.25
PK Paul Konerko .50 1.25
PR Phil Rizzuto .50 1.25
RB Ryan Braun .50 1.25
BDP124 Robinson Cano .50 1.25
RH Roy Halladay .50 1.25
SM Stan Musial 1.00 2.50
SS Stephen Strasburg .60 1.50
378 Todd Helton .50 1.25
TH Torii Hunter .40 1.00
TL Tim Lincecum .50 1.25
98 Ted Williams 1.25 3.00
WF Whitey Ford .50 1.25
WM Willie Mays 1.25 3.00
WS Warren Spahn .50 1.25
YD Yu Darvish .60 1.50
181 Jimmy Rollins .50 1.25
220 Ken Griffey Jr. 1.25 3.00
242 Ernie Banks .60 1.50
266 John Smoltz .60 1.50
379 Joe Mauer .50 1.25
421 Jose Bautista .50 1.25
BDP138 Ryan Howard .50 1.25

2013 Bowman Chrome Draft

STATED PLATE ODDS 1:2230 HOBBY
PLATE PRINT RUN 1 SET PER COLOR
BLACK-CYAN-MAGENTA-YELLOW ISSUED
NO PLATE PRICING DUE TO SCARCITY
1 Yasiel Puig RC 1.25 3.00
2 Tyler Skaggs RC .50 1.25
3 Nathan Karns RC .30 .75
4 Manny Machado RC 2.00 5.00
5 Anthony Rendon RC 2.00 5.00
6 Gerrit Cole RC 2.00 5.00
7 Sonny Gray RC .50 1.25
8 Henry Urrutia RC .40 1.00
9 Zoilo Almonte RC .40 1.00
10 Jose Fernandez RC .75 2.00
11 Danny Salazar RC .60 1.50
12 Nick Franklin RC .40 1.00
13 Mike Kickham RC .30 .75
14 Alex Colome RC .30 .75
15 Josh Phegley RC .30 .75
16 Drake Britton RC .40 1.00
17 Marcell Ozuna RC .75 2.00
18 Oswaldo Arcia RC .30 .75
19 Didi Gregorius RC 1.25 3.00
20 Zack Wheeler RC .60 1.50
21 Michael Wacha RC .75 2.00
22 Kyle Gibson RC .30 .75
23 Johnny Hellweg RC .30 .75
24 Dylan Bundy RC .75 2.00
25 Tony Cingrani RC .60 1.50
26 Jurickson Profar RC .40 1.00
27 Scooter Gennett RC .50 1.25
28 Grant Green RC .50 1.25
29 Brad Miller RC .40 1.00
30 Hyun-Jin Ryu RC .75 2.00
31 Jedd Gyorko RC .40 1.00
32 Shelby Miller RC .75 2.00
33 Sean Nolin RC .30 .75
34 Allen Webster RC .40 1.00
35 Corey Dickerson RC .40 1.00
36 Jarred Cosart RC .40 1.00
37 Evan Gattis RC .60 1.50
38 Kevin Gausman RC 1.00 2.50
39 Alex Wood RC .40 1.00
40 Christian Yelich RC 2.50 6.00
41 Nolan Arenado RC 3.00 8.00
42 Matt Magill RC .30 .75
43 Jackie Bradley Jr. RC .75 2.00
44 Mike Zunino RC .50 1.25
45 Wil Myers RC .50 1.25

2013 Bowman Chrome Draft Black Refractors

*BLACK REF: 5X TO 12X BASIC
STATED ODDS 1:224 HOBBY
STATED PRINT RUN 35 SER.#'d SETS
10 Jose Fernandez 10.00 25.00

2013 Bowman Chrome Draft Black Wave Refractors

*BLACK WAVE: 2X TO 5X BASIC

2013 Bowman Chrome Draft Blue Refractors

*BLUE REF: 2X TO 5X BASIC
STATED ODDS 1:93 HOBBY
STATED PRINT RUN 99 SER.#'d SETS

2013 Bowman Chrome Draft Blue Wave Refractors

*BLUE WAVE: 1.5X TO 4X BASIC

2013 Bowman Chrome Draft Gold Refractors

*GOLD REF: 5X TO 12X BASIC
STATED ODDS 1:185 HOBBY
STATED PRINT RUN 50 SER.#'d SETS
4 Manny Machado 30.00 60.00

2013 Bowman Chrome Draft Green Refractors

*GREEN REF: 2.5X TO 6X BASIC
STATED ODDS 1:124 HOBBY
STATED PRINT RUN 75 SER.#'d SETS

2013 Bowman Chrome Draft Orange Refractors

*ORANGE REF: 6X TO 15X BASIC
STATED PRINT RUN 25 SER.#'d SETS
4 Manny Machado 40.00 80.00

2013 Bowman Chrome Draft Red Wave Refractors

*RED WAVE: 6X TO 15X BASIC
STATED PRINT RUN 25 SER.#'d SETS
4 Manny Machado 40.00 80.00
10 Jose Fernandez 30.00 60.00

2013 Bowman Chrome Draft Silver Wave Refractors

*SILVER WAVE: 6X TO 15X BASIC
STATED PRINT RUN 25 SER.#'d SETS
10 Jose Fernandez 30.00 60.00

2013 Bowman Chrome Draft Draft Pick Autographs

STATED ODDS 1:35 HOBBY
K.BRYANT ISSUED IN 14 BOW.INCEPTION
EXCHANGE DEADLINE 11/30/2016
AB Aaron Blair 3.00 8.00
AC Andrew Church 3.00 8.00
AJ Aaron Judge 300.00 800.00
AK Andrew Knapp 3.00 8.00
AM Austin Meadows 30.00 80.00
BS Braden Shipley 3.00 8.00
BT Blake Taylor 3.00 8.00
CA Chris Anderson 3.00 8.00
CF Clint Frazier 40.00 100.00
CM Colin Moran 3.00 8.00
CS Chance Sisco 6.00 15.00
CSA Cord Sandberg 8.00 20.00
DP D.J. Peterson 3.00 8.00
DPE Dustin Peterson 3.00 8.00
DS Dominic Smith 15.00 40.00
EJ Eric Jagielo 3.00 8.00
HD Hunter Dozier 3.00 8.00
HG Hunter Green 3.00 8.00
HH Hunter Harvey 3.00 8.00
HR Hunter Renfroe 3.00 8.00
IC Ian Clarkin 3.00 8.00
JC J.P. Crawford 3.00 8.00
JCR Jonathon Crawford 3.00 8.00
JD Jon Denney 3.00 8.00
JG Jonathan Gray 3.00 8.00
JH Josh Hart 3.00 8.00
JW Justin Williams 6.00 15.00
KB K.Brynt Issued in 2014 150.00 400.00
KF Kevin Franklin 3.00 8.00
KS Kohl Stewart 3.00 8.00
KZ Kevin Ziomek 3.00 8.00
MG Marco Gonzales 8.00 20.00
ML Michael Lorenzen 3.00 8.00
NC Nick Ciuffo 3.00 8.00
OM Oscar Mercado 8.00 20.00
PE Phil Ervin 3.00 8.00
RE Ryan Eades 3.00 8.00
RJ Ryder Jones 3.00 8.00
RK Robert Kaminsky 3.00 8.00
RM Reese McGuire 4.00 10.00
RMC Ryan McMahon 20.00 50.00
RU Riley Unroe 3.00 8.00
TA Tim Anderson 50.00 120.00
TB Trey Ball 3.00 8.00
TD Travis Demeritte 3.00 8.00
TDA Tyler Danish 3.00 8.00
TW Trevor Williams 3.00 8.00
TWI Tom Windle 3.00 8.00

2013 Bowman Chrome Draft Draft Pick Autographs Black Refractors

*BLACK REF: 2.5X TO 6X BASIC
STATED ODDS 1:1097 HOBBY
STATED PRINT RUN 35 SER.#'d SETS
EXCHANGE DEADLINE 11/30/2016

2013 Bowman Chrome Draft Draft Pick Autographs Black Wave Refractors

*BLACK WAVE: 1.5X TO 4X BASIC
STATED PRINT RUN 50 SER.#'d SETS
EXCHANGE DEADLINE 11/30/2016

2013 Bowman Chrome Draft Draft Pick Autographs Blue Refractors

*BLUE REF: 1.5X TO 4X BASIC
STATED ODDS 1:659 HOBBY
STATED PRINT RUN 99 SER.#'d SETS
EXCHANGE DEADLINE 11/30/2016

2013 Bowman Chrome Draft Draft Pick Autographs Blue Wave Refractors

*BLUE WAVE: 1.5X TO 4X BASIC
STATED PRINT RUN 50 SER.#'d SETS
EXCHANGE DEADLINE 11/30/2016

2013 Bowman Chrome Draft Draft Pick Autographs Gold Refractors

*GOLD: 2.5X TO 6X BASIC
STATED ODDS 1:1309 HOBBY
STATED PRINT RUN 50 SER.#'d SETS
EXCHANGE DEADLINE 11/30/2016

2013 Bowman Chrome Draft Draft Pick Autographs Green Refractors

*GREEN REF: 1.5X TO 4X BASIC
STATED ODDS 1:872 HOBBY
STATED PRINT RUN 75 SER.#'d SETS
EXCHANGE DEADLINE 11/30/2016

2013 Bowman Chrome Draft Draft Pick Autographs Refractors

*REFRACTORS: .5X TO 1.2X BASIC
STATED ODDS 1:132 HOBBY
EXCHANGE DEADLINE 11/30/2016

2013 Bowman Chrome Draft Draft Picks

STATED PLATE ODDS 1:2230 HOBBY
PLATE PRINT RUN 1 SET PER COLOR
BLACK-CYAN-MAGENTA-YELLOW ISSUED
NO PLATE PRICING DUE TO SCARCITY
BDPP1 Dominic Smith .40 1.00
BDPP2 Kohl Stewart .30 .75
BDPP3 Josh Hart .25 .60
BDPP4 Nick Ciuffo .25 .60
BDPP5 Austin Meadows .60 1.50
BDPP6 Marco Gonzales .40 1.00
BDPP7 Jonathon Crawford .25 .60
BDPP8 D.J. Peterson .25 .60
BDPP9 Aaron Blair .25 .60
BDPP10 Dustin Peterson .25 .60
BDPP11 Billy Mckinney .30 .75
BDPP12 Braden Shipley .25 .60
BDPP13 Tim Anderson 1.00 2.50
BDPP14 Chris Anderson .30 .75
BDPP15 Clint Frazier 1.25 3.00
BDPP16 Hunter Renfroe .40 1.00
BDPP17 Andrew Knapp .25 .60
BDPP18 Corey Knebel .25 .60
BDPP19 Aaron Judge 12.00 30.00
BDPP20 Colin Moran .30 .75
BDPP21 Ian Clarkin .25 .60
BDPP22 Teddy Stankiewicz .30 .75
BDPP23 Blake Taylor .25 .60
BDPP24 Hunter Green .25 .60
BDPP25 Kevin Franklin .25 .60
BDPP26 Jonathan Gray .30 .75
BDPP27 Reese McGuire .30 .75
BDPP28 Travis Demeritte .30 .75
BDPP29 Kevin Ziomek .25 .60
BDPP30 Tom Windle .25 .60
BDPP31 Ryan McMahon .60 1.50
BDPP32 J.P. Crawford .60 1.50
BDPP33 Hunter Harvey .30 .75
BDPP34 Chance Sisco .50 1.25
BDPP35 Riley Unroe .25 .60
BDPP36 Oscar Mercado .40 1.00
BDPP37 Gosuke Katoh .30 .75
BDPP38 Andrew Church .25 .60
BDPP39 Casey Meisner .25 .60
BDPP40 Ivan Wilson .25 .60
BDPP41 Drew Ward .30 .75
BDPP42 Thomas Milone .25 .60
BDPP43 Jon Denney .30 .75
BDPP44 Jan Hernandez .25 .60
BDPP45 Cord Sandberg .30 .75
BDPP46 Jake Sweaney .25 .60
BDPP47 Patrick Murphy .25 .60
BDPP48 Carlos Salazar .25 .60
BDPP49 Stephen Gonsalves .30 .75
BDPP50 Jonah Heim .25 .60
BDPP51 Kean Wong .25 .60
BDPP52 Tyler Wade .40 1.00
BDPP53 Austin Kubitza .25 .60
BDPP54 Trevor Williams .25 .60
BDPP55 Trae Arbet .25 .60
BDPP56 Ian McKinney .25 .60
BDPP57 Robert Kaminsky .30 .75
BDPP58 Brian Navarreto .25 .60
BDPP59 Alex Murphy .25 .60
BDPP60 Jordon Austin .30 .75
BDPP61 Jacob Nottingham .25 .60
BDPP62 Chris Rivera .25 .60
BDPP63 Trey Williams .40 1.00
BDPP64 Conner Greene .25 .60
BDPP65 Ian Stiffler .25 .60
BDPP66 Phil Ervin .25 .60
BDPP67 Roel Ramirez .25 .60
BDPP68 Michael Lorenzen .30 .75
BDPP69 Jason Martin .25 .60
BDPP70 Aaron Blanton .25 .60
BDPP71 Dylan Manwaring .25 .60
BDPP72 Luis Guillorme .30 .75
BDPP73 Brennan Middleton .25 .60
BDPP74 Austin Nicely .25 .60
BDPP75 Ian Hagenmiller .25 .60
BDPP76 Nelson Molina .25 .60
BDPP77 Denton Keys .30 .75
BDPP78 Kendall Coleman .25 .60
BDPP79 Alec Grosser .25 .60
BDPP80 Ricardo Bautista .25 .60
BDPP81 John Costa .25 .60
BDPP82 Joseph Odom .25 .60
BDPP83 Elier Rodriguez .25 .60
BDPP84 Miles Williams .25 .60
BDPP85 Derrick Penilla .25 .60
BDPP86 Bryan Hudson .25 .60
BDPP87 Jordan Barnes .25 .60
BDPP88 Tyler Kinley .25 .60
BDPP89 Randolph Gassaway .25 .60
BDPP90 Blake Higgins .30 .75
BDPP91 Caleb Kellogg .25 .60
BDPP92 Joseph Monge .25 .60
BDPP93 Steven Negron .25 .60
BDPP94 Justin Williams .30 .75
BDPP95 William White .25 .60
BDPP96 Jared Wilson .25 .60
BDPP97 Niko Spezial .25 .60
BDPP98 Gabe Speier .25 .60
BDPP99 Juan Avila .25 .60
BDPP100 Jason Kanzler .25 .60
BDPP101 Tyler Brosius .25 .60
BDPP102 Tyler Vail .25 .60
BDPP103 Adam Landecker .25 .60
BDPP104 Ethan Carnes .25 .60
BDPP105 Austin Wilson .30 .75
BDPP106 Jon Keller .25 .60
BDPP107 Gaither Bumgardner .25 .60
BDPP108 Garrett Gordon .25 .60
BDPP109 Connor Oliver .25 .60
BDPP110 Cody Harris .25 .60
BDPP111 Brandon Easton .25 .60
BDPP112 Matt Derosier .25 .60
BDPP113 Jeremy Hadley .25 .60
BDPP114 Will Morris .25 .60
BDPP115 Sean Hurley .25 .60
BDPP116 Orrin Sears .25 .60
BDPP117 Sean Townsley .25 .60
BDPP118 Chad Christensen .25 .60
BDPP119 Travis Ott .25 .60
BDPP120 Justin Maffei .25 .60
BDPP121 Reed Harper .25 .60
BDPP122 Adam Westmoreland .25 .60
BDPP123 Adrian Castano .25 .60
BDPP124 Hyrum Formo .25 .60
BDPP125 Jake Stone .30 .75
BDPP126 Joel Effertz .25 .60
BDPP127 Matt Southard .25 .60
BDPP128 Jorge Perez .25 .60
BDPP129 Willie Medina .25 .60
BDPP130 Ty Afenir .25 .60

2013 Bowman Chrome Draft Draft Picks Black Refractors

*BLACK REF: 15X TO 40X BASIC
STATED ODDS 1:224 HOBBY
STATED PRINT RUN 35 SER.#'d SETS
BDPP19 Aaron Judge 250.00 600.00

2013 Bowman Chrome Draft Draft Picks Black Wave Refractors

*BLACK WAVE: 4X TO 10X BASIC
BDPP19 Aaron Judge 125.00 300.00

2013 Bowman Chrome Draft Draft Picks Blue Refractors

*BLUE REF: 6X TO 15X BASIC
STATED ODDS 1:93 HOBBY
STATED PRINT RUN 99 SER.#'d SETS
BDPP19 Aaron Judge 200.00 500.00

2013 Bowman Chrome Draft Draft Picks Blue Wave Refractors

*BLUE WAVE: 3X TO 8X BASIC
BDPP19 Aaron Judge 100.00 250.00

2013 Bowman Chrome Draft Draft Picks Gold Refractors

*GOLD REF: 15X TO 40X BASIC
STATED ODDS 1:185 HOBBY
STATED PRINT RUN 50 SER.#'d SETS
BDPP19 Aaron Judge 250.00 600.00

2013 Bowman Chrome Draft Draft Picks Green Refractors

*GREEN REF: 6X TO 15X BASIC
STATED ODDS 1:124 HOBBY
STATED PRINT RUN 75 SER.#'d SETS
BDPP19 Aaron Judge 200.00 500.00

2013 Bowman Chrome Draft Draft Picks Orange Refractors

*ORANGE REF: 20X TO 50X BASIC
STATED ODDS 1:372 HOBBY
STATED PRINT RUN 25 SER.#'d SETS
BDPP19 Aaron Judge 300.00 800.00

2013 Bowman Chrome Draft Draft Picks Red Wave Refractors

*RED WAVE: 20X TO 50X BASIC
STATED PRINT RUN 25 SER.#'d SETS
BDPP19 Aaron Judge 300.00 800.00

2013 Bowman Chrome Draft Draft Picks Refractors

*REF: 2X TO 5X BASIC
STATED ODDS 1:3 HOBBY
BDPP19 Aaron Judge 40.00 100.00

2013 Bowman Chrome Draft Draft Picks Silver Wave Refractors

*SILVER WAVE: 20X TO 50X BASIC
STATED PRINT RUN 25 SER.#'d SETS
BDPP19 Aaron Judge 300.00 800.00

2013 Bowman Chrome Draft Refractors

*REF: 1.2X TO 3X BASIC CARDS
STATED ODDS 1:3 HOBBY

2013 Bowman Chrome Draft Rookie Autographs

STATED ODDS 1:38,000 HOBBY
EXCHANGE DEADLINE 11/30/2016
YP Yasiel Puig 125.00 250.00

2013 Bowman Chrome Draft Top Prospects

STATED PLATE ODDS 1:2230 HOBBY
PLATE PRINT RUN 1 SET PER COLOR
BLACK-CYAN-MAGENTA-YELLOW ISSUED
NO PLATE PRICING DUE TO SCARCITY
TP1 Byron Buxton 1.00 2.50
TP2 Tyler Austin .30 .75
TP3 Mason Williams .25 .60
TP4 Albert Almora .40 1.00
TP5 Joey Gallo .60 1.50
TP6 Jesse Biddle .25 .60
TP7 David Dahl .25 .60
TP8 Kevin Gausman .60 1.50
TP9 Jorge Soler .40 1.00
TP10 Carlos Correa 2.50 6.00
TP11 Preston Tucker .30 .75
TP12 Jameson Taillon .25 .60
TP13 Joc Pederson .50 1.25
TP14 Max Fried .75 2.00
TP15 Taijuan Walker .25 .60
TP16 Chris Bostick .20 .50
TP17 Francisco Lindor 1.50 4.00
TP18 Daniel Vogelbach .30 .75
TP19 Kaleb Cowart .25 .60
TP20 George Springer .75 2.00
TP21 Yordano Ventura .25 .60
TP22 Noah Syndergaard .25 .60
TP23 Ty Hensley .25 .60
TP24 C.J. Cron .25 .60
TP25 Addison Russell .30 .75
TP26 Kyle Crick .30 .75
TP27 Javier Baez .75 2.00
TP28 Kolten Wong .20 .50
TP29 Taylor Guerrieri .20 .50
TP30 Archie Bradley .20 .50
TP31 Gary Sanchez .60 1.50
TP32 Billy Hamilton .25 .60
TP33 Alen Hanson .25 .60
TP34 Jonathan Singleton .25 .60
TP35 Mark Montgomery .30 .75
TP36 Nick Castellanos .60 1.50
TP37 Courtney Hawkins .20 .50
TP38 Gregory Polanco .40 1.00
TP39 Matt Barnes .25 .60
TP40 Xander Bogaerts .60 1.50
TP41 Dorssys Paulino .25 .60
TP42 Corey Seager 1.00 2.50
TP43 Alex Meyer .20 .50
TP44 Aaron Sanchez .25 .60
TP45 Miguel Sano .25 .60

2013 Bowman Chrome Draft Top Prospects Black Refractors

*BLACK REF:8X TO 20X BASIC
STATED ODDS 1:224 HOBBY
STATED PRINT RUN 35 SER.#'d SETS

2013 Bowman Chrome Draft Top Prospects Black Wave Refractors

*BLACK WAVE: 2X TO 5X BASIC

2013 Bowman Chrome Draft Top Prospects Blue Refractors

*BLUE REF: 3X TO 8X BASIC
STATED ODDS 1:93 HOBBY
STATED PRINT RUN 99 SER.#'d SETS

2013 Bowman Chrome Draft Top Prospects Blue Wave Refractors

*BLUE WAVE REF: 1.5X TO 4X BASIC

2013 Bowman Chrome Draft Top Prospects Gold Refractors

*GOLD REF: 8X TO 20X BASIC
STATED ODDS 1:185 HOBBY
STATED PRINT RUN 50 SER.#'d SETS

2013 Bowman Chrome Draft Top Prospects Green Refractors

*GREEN REF: 4X TO 10X BASIC
STATED ODDS 1:124 HOBBY
STATED PRINT RUN 75 SER.#'d SETS

2013 Bowman Chrome Draft Top Prospects Orange Refractors

*ORANGE REF: 20X TO 50X BASIC
STATED ODDS 1:372 HOBBY
STATED PRINT RUN 25 SER.#'d SETS

2013 Bowman Chrome Draft Top Prospects Red Wave Refractors

*RED WAVE: 12X TO 30X BASIC
STATED PRINT RUN 25 SER.#'d SETS
TP10 Carlos Correa 25.00 60.00

2013 Bowman Chrome Draft Top Prospects Refractors

*REF: 1.2X TO 3X BASIC
STATED ODDS 1:3 HOBBY

2013 Bowman Chrome Draft Top Prospects Silver Wave Refractors

*SILVER WAVE: 10X TO 25X BASIC
STATED PRINT RUN 25 SER.#'d SETS
TP10 Carlos Correa 20.00 50.00

2014 Bowman Chrome

COMP.SET w/o SP's (220) 20.00 50.00
STATED PLATE ODDS 1:1740 HOBBY
PLATE PRINT RUN 1 SET PER COLOR
BLACK-CYAN-MAGENTA-YELLOW ISSUED
NO PLATE PRICING DUE TO SCARCITY
1A Xander Bogaerts RC 1.00 2.50
1B Xander Bogaerts/99 12.00 30.00
2A Nick Castellanos RC 1.00 2.50
2B Nick Castellanos/99 20.00 50.00
3 Erisbel Arruebarrena RC .30 .75
4 Jeff Kobernus RC .30 .75
5A Jose Abreu RC 2.50 6.00
5B Jose Abreu/99 20.00 50.00
6 Yangervis Solarte RC .30 .75
7 Jonathan Schoop RC .30 .75
8 John Ryan Murphy RC .30 .75
9 Travis d'Arnaud RC .40 1.00
10 Marcus Semien RC 1.50 4.00
11 Luis Sardinas RC .30 .75
12 Oscar Taveras RC .40 1.00
13 Josmil Pinto RC .30 .75
14 Gregory Polanco RC .50 1.25
15 Wilmer Flores RC .40 1.00
16A Yordano Ventura RC .40 1.00
16B Yordano Ventura/99 8.00 20.00
17 Matt Davidson RC .40 1.00
18 Michael Choice RC .30 .75
19A Alex Guerrero RC .40 1.00
20 Kolten Wong RC .40 1.00
21A Taijuan Walker RC .30 .75
21B Taijuan Walker/99 8.00 20.00
22 Jon Singleton RC .40 1.00
23 Rougned Odor RC .75 2.00
24 Chris Owings RC .30 .75
25A James Paxton RC .50 1.25
25B James Paxton/99 10.00 25.00
26 Garin Cecchini RC .30 .75
27A Billy Hamilton RC .40 1.00

27B Billy Hamilton/99 8.00 20.00
28 Roenis Elias RC .30 .75
29A George Springer RC 1.25 3.00
30A Masahiro Tanaka RC 1.00 2.50
30B Masahiro Tanaka/99 20.00 50.00
31 Mike Trout 1.50 4.00
32 Salvador Perez .25 .60
33 Carlos Gomez .20 .50
34 Chris Sale .30 .75
35 Stephen Strasburg .30 .75
36 Max Scherzer .30 .75
37 Carlos Gonzalez .25 .60
38 Buster Posey .40 1.00
39 Jayson Werth .25 .60
40 Jose Fernandez .30 .75
41 Madison Bumgarner .25 .60
42 Adam Wainwright .25 .60
43 Freddie Freeman .40 1.00
44 Paul Goldschmidt .30 .75
45 Jose Bautista .25 .60
46 Anthony Rendon .30 .75
47 Pedro Alvarez .20 .50
48 Chris Archer .20 .50
49 Felix Hernandez .25 .60
50 David Price .25 .60
51 Gio Gonzalez .25 .60
52 Michael Wacha .25 .60
53 Evan Longoria .25 .60
54 Troy Tulowitzki .30 .75
55 Hanley Ramirez .25 .60
56 Brandon Belt .25 .60
57 Tony Cingrani .25 .60
58 Yovani Gallardo .20 .50
59 Justin Verlander .30 .75
60 Yadier Molina .40 1.00
61 Starlin Castro .20 .50
62 Giancarlo Stanton .30 .75
63 Shin-Soo Choo .25 .60
64 Hyun-Jin Ryu .25 .60
65 John Lackey .25 .60
66 Andrew Cashner .20 .50
67 Sonny Gray .25 .60
68 Matt Carpenter .30 .75
69 Ryan Braun .25 .60
70 Starling Marte .25 .60
71 Adam Jones .25 .60
72 Jacoby Ellsbury .25 .60
73 Mark Trumbo .20 .50
74 Austin Jackson .20 .50
75 Anthony Rizzo .40 1.00
76 Matt Garza .20 .50
77 Anibal Sanchez .20 .50
78 James Shields .20 .50
79 Ben Zobrist .25 .60
80 Juan Lagares .20 .50
81 David Wright .25 .60
82 Matt Adams .20 .50
83 Albert Pujols .40 1.00
84 Jeff Samardzija .20 .50
85 Johnny Cueto .25 .60
86 Garrett Richards .25 .60
87 Justin Masterson .20 .50
88 Gerrit Cole .30 .75
89 Derek Jeter .75 2.00
90 Adeiny Hechavarria .20 .50
91 Andrew McCutchen .30 .75
92 Ryan Zimmerman .25 .60
93 Nelson Cruz .30 .75
94 Alex Rios .25 .60
95 Chris Tillman .20 .50
96 Francisco Liriano .20 .50
97 Bartolo Colon .20 .50
98 Zack Wheeler .25 .60
99 Brett Gardner .25 .60
100 Curtis Granderson .25 .60
101 Adrian Beltre .30 .75
102 Daniel Murphy .25 .60
103 Ian Kinsler .25 .60
104 Prince Fielder .25 .60
105 Alex Cobb .20 .50
106 Julio Teheran .25 .60
107 Alex Wood .20 .50
108 Dan Straily .20 .50
109 CC Sabathia .25 .60
110 Hiroki Kuroda .20 .50
111 A.J. Burnett .20 .50
112 Cliff Lee .25 .60
113 Carlos Santana .25 .60
114 Todd Frazier .20 .50
115 Jason Kipnis .25 .60
116 Robinson Cano .25 .60
117 Christian Yelich .40 1.00
118 Justin Upton .25 .60
119 Khris Davis .30 .75
120 Jean Segura .25 .60
121 Domonic Brown .25 .60
122 Ryan Howard .25 .60
123 Chase Utley .25 .60
124 Jimmy Rollins .25 .60
125 Jay Bruce .25 .60
126 Joey Votto .30 .75
127 Chris Davis .20 .50
128 Manny Machado .30 .75
129 Ubaldo Jimenez .20 .50
130 Jon Lester .25 .60
131 Clay Buchholz .20 .50
132 Jake Peavy .20 .50
133 Jason Castro .20 .50
134 Joe Mauer .25 .60
135 Josh Hamilton .25 .60
136 Jered Weaver .25 .60
137 Eric Hosmer .25 .60
138 Alex Gordon .25 .60
139 Billy Butler .20 .50
140 David Ortiz .30 .75
141 Brian McCann .25 .60
142 Carlos Beltran .25 .60
143 Yoenis Cespedes .30 .75
144 Hisashi Iwakuma .25 .60
145 Wil Myers .20 .50
146 Yu Darvish .30 .75
147 Edwin Encarnacion .30 .75
148 Jose Reyes .25 .60
149 Andrelton Simmons .20 .50
150 Ervin Santana .20 .50
151 Craig Kimbrel .25 .60
152 Mat Latos .25 .60
153 Wilin Rosario .20 .50
154 Aroldis Chapman .30 .75
155 Kenley Jansen .25 .60
156 Matt Kemp .25 .60
157 Adrian Gonzalez .25 .60
158 Clayton Kershaw .50 1.25
159 Yasiel Puig .30 .75
160 Zack Greinke .30 .75
161 Jonathon Niese .20 .50
162 Marlon Byrd .20 .50
163 Cole Hamels .25 .60
164 Tyson Ross .20 .50
165 Chase Headley .20 .50
166 Everth Cabrera .20 .50
167 Ian Kennedy .20 .50
168 Pablo Sandoval .25 .60
169 Matt Cain .25 .60
170 Tim Hudson .25 .60
171 Hunter Pence .25 .60
172 Jhonny Peralta .20 .50
173 Shelby Miller .25 .60
174 Matt Holliday .30 .75
175 Bryce Harper .50 1.25
176 Jordan Zimmermann .25 .60
177 Angel Pagan .20 .50
178 Doug Fister .20 .50
179 Wilson Ramos .20 .50
180 Edinson Volquez .20 .50
181 Dan Haren .20 .50
182 Homer Bailey .20 .50
183 Jonathan Papelbon .25 .60
184 Huston Street .20 .50
185 Greg Holland .20 .50
186 Joe Nathan .20 .50
187 Trevor Rosenthal .25 .60
188 Addison Reed .20 .50
189 David Robertson .20 .50
190 Fernando Rodney .20 .50
191 Shane Victorino .25 .60
192 Mike Minor .20 .50
193 Ian Desmond .20 .50
194 Dustin Pedroia .30 .75
195 Josh Donaldson .25 .60
196 Jonathan Lucroy .25 .60
197 Mike Napoli .20 .50
198 Jose Altuve .25 .60
199 Jason Heyward .25 .60
200 Alexei Ramirez .25 .60
201 Kyle Seager .20 .50
202 Michael Brantley .25 .60
203 Brian Dozier .25 .60
204 Brandon Moss .20 .50
205 Dee Gordon .20 .50
206 Victor Martinez .25 .60
207 Alcides Escobar .25 .60
208 Phil Hughes .20 .50
209 Corey Kluber .25 .60
210 Jose Quintana .20 .50
211 Dallas Keuchel .25 .60
212 Jason Hammel .25 .60
213 Henderson Alvarez .20 .50
214 Scott Kazmir .20 .50
215 Jesse Chavez .20 .50
216 Drew Pomeranz .25 .60
217 Drew Hutchison .20 .50
218 Aaron Harang .20 .50
219 Jarred Cosart .20 .50
220 Josh Beckett .20 .50

2014 Bowman Chrome Black Static Refractors

*STATIC REF RC: 5X TO 12X BASIC
*STATIC REF VET: 8X TO 20X BASIC
STATED ODDS 1:205 HOBBY
STATED PRINT RUN 35 SER.#'d SETS
31 Mike Trout 40.00 100.00
89 Derek Jeter 50.00 120.00

2014 Bowman Chrome Blue Refractors

*BLUE REF RC: 2X TO 5X BASIC
*BLUE REF VET: 3X TO 8X BASIC
STATED ODDS 1:29 HOBBY
STATED PRINT RUN 250 SER.#'d SETS

2014 Bowman Chrome Bubble Refractors

*BUB REF RC: 3X TO 8X BASIC
*BUB REF VET: 5X TO 12X BASIC
STATED ODDS 1:68 HOBBY
STATED PRINT RUN 99 SER.#'d SETS
89 Derek Jeter 25.00 60.00

2014 Bowman Chrome Gold Refractors

*GOLD REF RC: 3X TO 8X BASIC
*GOLD REF VET: 5X TO 12X BASIC
STATED ODDS 1:138 HOBBY
STATED PRINT RUN 50 SER.#'d SETS
31 Mike Trout 30.00 80.00
89 Derek Jeter 40.00 100.00

2014 Bowman Chrome Green Refractors

*GREEN REF RC: 3X TO 8X BASIC
*GREEN REF VET: 5X TO 12X BASIC
STATED ODDS 1:90 HOBBY
STATED PRINT RUN 75 SER.#'d SETS

2014 Bowman Chrome Orange Refractors

*ORANGE REF RC: 5X TO 12X BASIC
*ORANGE REF VET: 8X TO 20X BASIC
STATED ODDS 1:276 HOBBY
STATED PRINT RUN 25 SER.#'d SETS
31 Mike Trout 50.00 120.00
89 Derek Jeter 60.00 150.00
158 Clayton Kershaw 40.00 80.00

2014 Bowman Chrome Purple Refractors

*PURP REF RC: 2X TO 5X BASIC
*PURP REF VET: 3X TO 8X BASIC
STATED ODDS 1:47 HOBBY
STATED PRINT RUN 150 SER.#'d SETS
31 Mike Trout 10.00 25.00
89 Derek Jeter 12.00 30.00

2014 Bowman Chrome Refractors

*REF RC: 1.2X TO 3X BASIC
*REF VET: 2X TO 5X BASIC
STATED ODDS 1:15 HOBBY
STATED PRINT RUN 500 SER.#'d SETS

2014 Bowman Chrome Bowman Scout Top 5 Mini Refractors

STATED ODDS 1:6 HOBBY
BMA1 C.J. Cron .50 1.25
BMA2 Zach Borenstein .60 1.50
BMA3 Kaleb Cowart .50 1.25
BMA4 Hunter Green .50 1.25
BMA5 Alex Yarbrough .50 1.25
BMAB1 Lucas Sims .50 1.25
BMAB2 Christian Bethancourt .50 1.25
BMAB3 Jason Hursh .50 1.25
BMAB4 J.R. Graham .50 1.25
BMAB5 Jose Peraza .50 1.25
BMAD1 Archie Bradley .50 1.25
BMAD2 Matt Davidson .60 1.50
BMAD3 Chris Owings .50 1.25
BMAD4 Daniel Palka .50 1.25
BMAD5 Brandon Drury .50 1.25
BMBO1 Dylan Bundy .60 1.50
BMBO2 Eduardo Rodriguez .60 1.50
BMBO3 Hunter Harvey .50 1.25
BMBO4 Jonathan Schoop .50 1.25
BMBO5 Michael Ohlman .50 1.25
BMCC1 Javier Baez 2.00 5.00
BMCC2 Kris Bryant 5.00 12.00
BMCC3 C.J. Edwards .60 1.50
BMCC4 Jorge Soler 1.00 2.50
BMCC5 Albert Almora .75 2.00
BMCI1 Francisco Lindor 4.00 10.00
BMCI2 Clint Frazier 2.00 5.00
BMCI3 Tyler Naquin .75 2.00
BMCI4 Dorssys Paulino .50 1.25
BMCI5 Trevor Bauer 1.00 2.50
BMCR1 Billy Hamilton .60 1.50
BMCR2 Robert Stephenson .50 1.25
BMCR3 Phil Ervin .50 1.25
BMCR4 Seth Mejias-Brean .50 1.25
BMCR5 Nick Travieso .50 1.25
BMDT1 Nick Castellanos 1.50 4.00
BMDT2 Devon Travis .50 1.25
BMDT3 Jonathon Crawford .50 1.25
BMDT4 Jake Thompson .50 1.25
BMDT5 Corey Knebel .50 1.25
BMHA1 Carlos Correa 2.50 6.00
BMHA2 Mark Appel .60 1.50
BMHA3 George Springer 2.00 5.00
BMHA4 Lance McCullers .50 1.25
BMHA5 Delino DeShields .50 1.25
BMMB1 Jimmy Nelson .50 1.25
BMMB2 Tyrone Taylor .50 1.25
BMMB3 Devin Williams 1.25 3.00
BMMB4 Victor Roache .50 1.25
BMMB5 Taylor Jungmann .50 1.25
BMMM1 Andrew Heaney .50 1.25
BMMM2 Colin Moran .50 1.25
BMMM3 Justin Nicolino .50 1.25
BMMM4 Jake Marisnick .50 1.25
BMMM5 Trevor Williams .50 1.25
BMMT1 Byron Buxton 2.50 6.00
BMMT2 Miguel Sano .60 1.50
BMMT3 Alex Meyer .50 1.25
BMMT4 Kohl Stewart .50 1.25
BMMT5 Eddie Rosario 1.00 2.50
BMOA1 Addison Russell .75 2.00
BMOA2 Michael Ynoa .50 1.25
BMOA3 Billy McKinney .60 1.50
BMOA4 Renato Nunez 1.00 2.50
BMOA5 B.J. Boyd .50 1.25
BMPP1 Maikel Franco .60 1.50
BMPP2 Jesse Biddle .60 1.50
BMPP3 J.P. Crawford .50 1.25
BMPP4 Miguel Alfredo Gonzalez .50 1.25
BMPP5 Roman Quinn .75 2.00
BMSM1 Taijuan Walker .50 1.25
BMSM2 D.J. Peterson .50 1.25
BMSM3 Danny Hultzen .50 1.25
BMSM4 Victor Sanchez .50 1.25
BMSM5 Chris Taylor 2.50 6.00
BMTR1 Joey Gallo 1.00 2.50
BMTR2 Jorge Alfaro .60 1.50
BMTR3 Rougned Odor 1.25 3.00
BMTR4 Michael Choice .50 1.25
BMTR5 Luis Sardinas .50 1.25
BMWN1 Lucas Giolito .75 2.00
BMWN2 A.J. Cole .50 1.25
BMWN3 Brian Goodwin .50 1.25
BMWN4 Nathan Karns .50 1.25
BMWN5 Jake Johansen .60 1.50
BMBRS1 Xander Bogaerts 1.50 4.00
BMBRS2 Henry Owens .60 1.50
BMBRS3 Garin Cecchini .50 1.25
BMBRS4 Mookie Betts 10.00 25.00
BMBRS5 Anthony Ranaudo .50 1.25
BMCRO1 Jonathan Gray .60 1.50
BMCRO2 Eddie Butler .50 1.25
BMCRO3 David Dahl .60 1.50
BMCRO4 Rosell Herrera .75 2.00
BMCRO5 Raimel Tapia .60 1.50
BMCWS1 Jose Abreu 4.00 10.00
BMCWS2 Erik Johnson .50 1.25
BMCWS3 Micah Johnson .50 1.25
BMCWS4 Tim Anderson 1.00 2.50
BMCWS5 Courtney Hawkins .50 1.25
BMKCR1 Yordano Ventura .60 1.50
BMKCR2 Kyle Zimmer .50 1.25
BMKCR3 Raul Mondesi .75 2.00
BMKCR4 Bubba Starling .60 1.50
BMKCR5 Hunter Dozier .50 1.25
BMLAD1 Joc Pederson 1.25 3.00
BMLAD2 Julio Urias 2.50 6.00
BMLAD3 Corey Seager 2.50 6.00
BMLAD4 Chris Anderson .50 1.25
BMLAD5 Zach Lee .50 1.25
BMNYM1 Noah Syndergaard .60 1.50
BMNYM2 Travis d'Arnaud .60 1.50
BMNYM3 Rafael Montero .50 1.25
BMNYM4 Kevin Plawecki .50 1.25
BMNYM5 Wilmer Flores .60 1.50
BMNYY1 Gary Sanchez 1.50 4.00
BMNYY2 Masahiro Tanaka 1.50 4.00
BMNYY3 Tyler Austin .50 1.25
BMNYY4 Rafael De Paula .50 1.25
BMNYY5 Mason Williams .50 1.25
BMPPI1 Gregory Polanco .75 2.00
BMPPI2 Tyler Glasnow 2.00 5.00
BMPPI3 Alen Hanson .50 1.25
BMPPI4 Jameson Taillon .60 1.50
BMPPI5 Austin Meadows 1.25 3.00
BMSDP1 Austin Hedges .50 1.25
BMSDP2 Max Fried 2.00 5.00
BMSDP3 Rymer Liriano .50 1.25
BMSDP4 Matt Wisler .50 1.25
BMSDP5 Jace Peterson .50 1.25
BMSFG1 Kyle Crick .50 1.25
BMSFG2 Clayton Blackburn .75 2.00
BMSFG3 Edwin Escobar .50 1.25
BMSFG4 Martin Agosta .50 1.25
BMSFG5 Mac Williamson .60 1.50
BMSTL1 Oscar Taveras .60 1.50
BMSTL2 Kolten Wong .60 1.50
BMSTL3 Carlos Martinez .60 1.50
BMSTL4 Stephen Piscotty .60 1.50
BMSTL5 James Ramsey .50 1.25
BMTBJ1 Aaron Sanchez .50 1.25
BMTBJ2 Marcus Stroman .75 2.00
BMTBJ3 Roberto Osuna .50 1.25
BMTBJ4 D.J. Davis .50 1.25
BMTBJ5 Daniel Norris .60 1.50
BMTBR1 Taylor Guerrieri .50 1.25
BMTBR2 Hak-Ju Lee .50 1.25
BMTBR3 Andrew Toles .60 1.50
BMTBR4 Dylan Floro .60 1.50
BMTBR5 Jeff Ames .50 1.25

2014 Bowman Chrome Bowman Scout Top 5 Mini Blue Refractors

*BLUE REF: 1X TO 2.5X BASIC
STATED ODDS 1:65 HOBBY
STATED PRINT RUN 250 SER.#'d SETS

2014 Bowman Chrome Bowman Scout Top 5 Mini Gold Refractors

*GOLD REF: 3X TO 8X BASIC
STATED ODDS 1:540 HOBBY
STATED PRINT RUN 25 SER.#'d SETS
BMCC2 Kris Bryant 60.00 120.00
BMLAD2 Julio Urias 20.00 50.00

2014 Bowman Chrome Bowman Scout Top 5 Mini Orange Refractors

*ORANGE REF: 2.5X TO 6X BASIC
STATED ODDS 1:326 HOBBY
STATED PRINT RUN 50 SER.#'d SETS
BMCC2 Kris Bryant 30.00 80.00

2014 Bowman Chrome Bowman Scout Top 5 Mini Purple Refractors

*PURPLE REF: 1.5X TO 4X BASIC
STATED PRINT RUN 99 SER.#'d SETS
BMCC2 Kris Bryant 25.00 60.00
BMMT1 Byron Buxton 12.00 30.00

2014 Bowman Chrome Dualing Die-Cut Refractors

COMPLETE SET (25) 15.00 40.00
STATED ODDS 1:18 HOBBY
DDCAG J.Gray/M.Appel .60 1.50
DDCAS R.Stephenson/A.Almora .75 2.00
DDCASO J.Abreu/J.Soler 2.50 6.00
DDCAV Velasquez/Alfaro .75 2.00
DDCBC C.Correa/B.Buxton 2.50 6.00
DDCBR J.Baez/A.Russell 2.00 5.00
DDCBS A.Sanchez/M.Betts 10.00 25.00
DDCCC G.Cecchini/G.Cecchini .50 1.25
DDCDB D.Dahl/A.Bradley .60 1.50
DDCGN L.Giolito/B.Nimmo .75 2.00
DDCHS A.Heaney/N.Syndergaard .60 1.50
DDCLM R.Mondesi/F.Lindor 4.00 10.00
DDCMB C.Moran/K.Bryant 2.50 6.00
DDCMC K.Crick/B.McKinney .60 1.50
DDCMF C.Frazier/A.Meadows 2.00 5.00
DDCMFR R.Montero/M.Franco .60 1.50
DDCOS G.Sanchez/H.Owens 1.50 4.00
DDCPE C.Edwards/S.Piscotty .60 1.50
DDCSB E.Butler/C.Seager 2.50 6.00
DDCSW T.Walker/G.Springer 2.00 5.00
DDCTP Polanco/Taveras .75 2.00
DDCUR J.Urias/H.Renfroe 2.50 6.00
DDCVC N.Castellanos/Y.Ventura 1.50 4.00
DDCWP J.Pederson/M.Wisler 1.25 3.00
DDCZM K.Zimmer/A.Meyer .50 1.25

2014 Bowman Chrome Dualing Die-Cut Atomic Refractors

*ATOMIC REF: .75X TO 2X BASIC
STATED ODDS 1:924 HOBBY
STATED PRINT RUN 99 SER.#'d SETS

2014 Bowman Chrome Dualing Die-Cut Shimmer Refractors

*SHIMMER REF: 1.5X TO 4X BASIC
STATED ODDS 1:1835 HOBBY
STATED PRINT RUN 50 SER.#'d SETS

2014 Bowman Chrome Dualing Die-Cut X-Fractors

*X-FRACTOR: 2.5X TO 6X BASIC
STATED ODDS 1:3660 HOBBY
STATED PRINT RUN 25 SER.#'d SETS

2014 Bowman Chrome Fire Die-Cut Refractors

STATED ODDS 1:18 HOBBY
FDCAB Archie Bradley .50 1.25
FDCAH Andrew Heaney .50 1.25
FDCAHE Austin Hedges .50 1.25
FDCAR Addison Russell .75 2.00
FDCBB Byron Buxton 2.50 6.00
FDCBH Bryce Harper 1.25 3.00
FDCBHA Billy Hamilton .60 1.50
FDCCC Carlos Correa 2.50 6.00
FDCCO Chris Owings .50 1.25
FDCFL Francisco Lindor 4.00 10.00
FDCGP Gregory Polanco .75 2.00
FDCGS George Springer 2.00 5.00
FDCJA Jose Abreu 4.00 10.00
FDCJB Javier Baez 2.00 5.00
FDCJG Jonathan Gray .60 1.50
FDCKB Kris Bryant 4.00 10.00
FDCKW Kolten Wong .60 1.50
FDCMA Mark Appel .60 1.50
FDCMD Matt Davidson .60 1.50
FDCMF Maikel Franco .60 1.50
FDCMS Miguel Sano .60 1.50
FDCMT Masahiro Tanaka 1.50 4.00
FDCMTR Mike Trout 4.00 10.00
FDCNC Nick Castellanos 1.50 4.00
FDCNS Noah Syndergaard .60 1.50
FDCOT Oscar Taveras .60 1.50
FDCTD Travis d'Arnaud .60 1.50
FDCTW Taijuan Walker .50 1.25
FDCXB Xander Bogaerts 1.50 4.00
FDCYV Yordano Ventura .60 1.50

2014 Bowman Chrome Fire Die-Cut Atomic Refractors

*DC ATOMIC: 1X TO 2.5X BASIC
STATED ODDS 1:770 HOBBY
STATED PRINT RUN 99 SER.#'d SETS
FDCJA Jose Abreu 10.00 25.00
FDCKB Kris Bryant 12.00 30.00
FDCMTR Mike Trout 12.00 30.00

2014 Bowman Chrome Fire Die-Cut X-Fractors

*X-FRACTORS: 1.5X TO 4X BASIC
STATED ODDS 1:3070 HOBBY
STATED PRINT RUN 25 SER.#'d SETS
FDCJA Jose Abreu 20.00 50.00
FDCKB Kris Bryant 25.00 60.00
FDCMTR Mike Trout 20.00 50.00

2014 Bowman Chrome Fire Die-Cut Refractor Autographs

STATED ODDS 1:9250 HOBBY
STATED PRINT RUN 25 SER.#'d SETS
EXCHANGE DEADLIN 9/30/2017
FDAAB Archie Bradley EXCH 20.00 50.00
FDABH Bryce Harper EXCH 100.00 200.00
FDABHA Billy Hamilton EXCH 25.00 60.00
FDAJB Javier Baez EXCH 30.00 80.00
FDAKB Kris Bryant 300.00 600.00
FDAMS Miguel Sano EXCH 60.00 150.00
FDAMTR Mike Trout 300.00 500.00
FDAOT Oscar Taveras 25.00 60.00
FDATW Taijuan Walker 20.00 50.00

2014 Bowman Chrome Franchise Dual Autograph Refractors

STATED ODDS 1:9800 HOBBY
STATED PRINT RUN 25 SER.#'d SETS
EXCHANGE DEADLINE 4/30/2017
DFAAC Correa/Appel EXCH 60.00 120.00
DFABA Bryant/Alcantara 300.00 400.00
DFABB M.Barnes/M.Betts 40.00 100.00
DFABJ B.Johnson/M.Barnes 10.00 25.00
DFAHS J.Hursh/L.Sims 30.00 80.00
DFAJM D.Maples/P.Johnson 15.00 40.00
DFAMB D.Marrero/M.Betts 40.00 100.00
DFAOB M.Barnes/H.Owens 30.00 80.00
DFAWB T.Wade/G.Bird 40.00 100.00

2014 Bowman Chrome Mini

STATED ODDS 1:18 HOBBY
MCAB Archie Bradley .40 1.00
MCAG Alex Guerrero .50 1.25
MCAH Andrew Heaney .40 1.00
MCAM Austin Meadows 1.00 2.50
MCAMC Andrew McCutchen .60 1.50
MCAP Albert Pujols .75 2.00
MCAR Addison Russell .60 1.50
MCBB Byron Buxton 2.00 5.00
MCBH Bryce Harper 1.00 2.50
MCBHA Billy Hamilton .50 1.25
MCCC Carlos Correa 2.00 5.00
MCCE C.J. Edwards .50 1.25
MCCF Clint Frazier 1.50 4.00
MCCK Clayton Kershaw 1.00 2.50
MCCS Chris Sale .60 1.50
MCCY Christian Yelich .75 2.00
MCFF Freddie Freeman .75 2.00
MCFL Francisco Lindor 3.00 8.00
MCGC Gerrit Cole .60 1.50
MCGP Gregory Polanco .60 1.50
MCGS George Springer 1.50 4.00
MCGST Giancarlo Stanton .60 1.50
MCHR Hyun-Jin Ryu .50 1.25
MCJA Jose Abreu 3.00 8.00
MCJB Javier Baez 1.50 4.00
MCJF Jose Fernandez .60 1.50
MCJG Jonathan Gray .50 1.25
MCJS Jorge Soler .75 2.00
MCJU Julio Urias 2.00 5.00
MCKB Kris Bryant 6.00 15.00
MCKZ Kyle Zimmer .40 1.00
MCMA Mark Appel .50 1.25
MCMB Madison Bumgarner .50 1.25
MCMC Miguel Cabrera .60 1.50
MCMF Maikel Franco .50 1.25
MCMS Miguel Sano .50 1.25
MCMT Mike Trout 3.00 8.00
MCMTA Masahiro Tanaka 1.25 3.00
MCMW Michael Wacha .50 1.25
MCNC Nick Castellanos 1.25 3.00
MCNS Noah Syndergaard .50 1.25
MCOT Oscar Taveras .50 1.25
MCPG Paul Goldschmidt .60 1.50
MCSS Stephen Strasburg .60 1.50
MCWM Wil Myers .40 1.00
MCXB Xander Bogaerts 1.25 3.00
MCYC Yoenis Cespedes .60 1.50
MCYD Yu Darvish .60 1.50
MCYP Yasiel Puig .60 1.50
MCYV Yordano Ventura .50 1.25

2014 Bowman Chrome Mini Die-Cut Black Wave Refractors

*BLACK WAVE: 3X TO 8X BASIC
RANDOM INSERTS IN PACKS
STATED PRINT RUN 25 SER.#'d SETS
MCMT Mike Trout 40.00 100.00

2014 Bowman Chrome Mini Die-Cut Blue Wave Refractors

*DC BLUE WAVE: 1X TO 2.5X BASIC
STATED ODDS 1:465 HOBBY
STATED PRINT RUN 99 SER.#'d SETS
MCMT Mike Trout 12.00 30.00

2014 Bowman Chrome Mini Die-Cut Gold Refractors

*GOLD REF: 2.5X TO 6X BASIC
STATED ODDS 1:915 HOBBY
STATED PRINT RUN 50 SER.#'d SETS
MCMT Mike Trout 30.00 80.00

2014 Bowman Chrome Mini Die-Cut Refractors

*DC REF: .75X TO 2X BASIC
STATED ODDS 1:18 HOBBY
STATED PRINT RUN 150 SER.#'d SETS
MCMT Mike Trout 10.00 25.00

2014 Bowman Chrome Mini Autograph Gold Refractors

*GOLD REF: .75X TO 2X BASIC
STATED ODDS 1:3465 HOBBY
STATED PRINT RUN 25 SER.#'d SETS
EXCHANGE DEADLINE 4/30/2017

2014 Bowman Chrome Mini Autograph Purple Refractors

STATED PRINT RUN 50 SER.#'d SETS
EXCHANGE DEADLINE 4/30/2017
CMACF Clint Frazier 20.00 50.00
CMAGS George Springer 30.00 80.00
CMAJA Jeff Ames EXCH 5.00 12.00
CMAJU Julio Urias 60.00 150.00
CMAMA Mark Appel 25.00 60.00
CMAMD Matt Davidson EXCH 10.00 25.00
CMAMF Maikel Franco 30.00 80.00
CMAMJ Micah Johnson EXCH 20.00 50.00
CMAOT Oscar Taveras 20.00 50.00
CMATD Travis d'Arnaud EXCH 12.00 30.00

2014 Bowman Chrome Prospect Autographs

BOW.STATED ODDS 1:42 HOBBY
BOW.CHR.ODDS 1:13 HOBBY
PLATE PRINT RUN 1 SET PER COLOR
BLACK-CYAN-MAGENTA-YELLOW ISSUED
NO PLATE PRICING DUE TO SCARCITY
BOW.EXCH DEADLINE 4/30/2017
BOW.CHR.EXCH 6/30/2017
BCAPAA Aristides Aquino 12.00 30.00
BCAPAAV Abiatal Avelino 3.00 8.00
BCAPAB Akeem Bostick 3.00 8.00
BCAPABR Aaron Brooks 5.00 12.00
BCAPAM Adam Morgan 3.00 8.00
BCAPAMA Adrian Marin 3.00 8.00
BCAPAN Austin Nola 10.00 25.00
BCAPAR Anthony Ranaudo 3.00 8.00
BCAPARI Armando Rivero 3.00 8.00
BCAPAS Anthony Santander 4.00 10.00
BCAPAT Andrew Toles 4.00 10.00
BCAPATH Andrew Thurman 3.00 8.00
BCAPAW Austin Wilson 3.00 8.00
BCAPAY Alex Yarbrough 3.00 8.00
BCAPBB Billy Burns 3.00 8.00
BCAPBD Brandon Dixon 3.00 8.00
BCAPBL Ben Lively 3.00 8.00
BCAPBT Brandon Trinkwon 4.00 10.00
BCAPBV Breyvic Valera 3.00 8.00
BCAPCA Cody Anderson 3.00 8.00
BCAPCB Christian Binford 3.00 8.00
BCAPCBO Chris Bostick 4.00 10.00
BCAPCC Carlos Contreras 3.00 8.00
BCAPCD Chase DeJong 3.00 8.00
BCAPCF Chris Flexen 4.00 10.00
BCAPCK Chris Kohler 3.00 8.00
BCAPCKN Corey Knebel 3.00 8.00
BCAPCM Casey Meisner 3.00 8.00
BCAPCP Cesar Puello 3.00 8.00
BCAPCR Cody Reed 3.00 8.00
BCAPCT Chris Taylor 6.00 20.00
BCAPDF Dylan Floro 4.00 10.00
BCAPDH David Holmberg 3.00 8.00
BCAPDM Daniel McGrath 4.00 10.00
BCAPDN Dom Nunez 3.00 8.00
BCAPDP Daniel Palka 3.00 8.00
BCAPDR Daniel Robertson 4.00 10.00
BCAPDT Devon Travis 3.00 8.00
BCAPDU Duane Underwood 3.00 8.00
BCAPDUN Dylan Unsworth 3.00 8.00
BCAPDW Daniel Winkler 3.00 8.00
BCAPDWI Devin Williams 20.00 50.00
BCAPED Edwin Diaz 6.00 15.00
BCAPEM Edwin Moreno 3.00 8.00
BCAPFB Franklin Barreto 5.00 12.00
BCAPFC Franchy Cordero 20.00 50.00
BCAPFL Fred Lewis 3.00 8.00
BCAPFR Franmil Reyes 25.00 60.00
BCAPGE Gabriel Encinas 4.00 10.00
BCAPGK Gosuke Katoh 6.00 15.00
BCAPGR Gabriel Rosa 3.00 8.00
BCAPGY Gabriel Ynoa 4.00 10.00
BCAPIK Isiah Kiner-Faleta 5.00 12.00
BCAPJAB Jose Abreu 60.00 150.00
BCAPJB Jake Barrett 4.00 10.00
BCAPJBE Javier Betancourt 4.00 10.00
BCAPJF Johnny Field 3.00 8.00
BCAPJG Joan Gregorio 3.00 8.00
BCAPJH Jose Herrera 3.00 8.00
BCAPJHA Josh Hader 6.00 15.00
BCAPJHU Jason Hursh 3.00 8.00
BCAPJJ JaCoby Jones 5.00 12.00
BCAPJJO Jacob Johansen 4.00 10.00
BCAPJM Jacob May 4.00 10.00
BCAPJMA Jason Martin 5.00 12.00
BCAPJMC Jeff McNeil 40.00 100.00
BCAPJN Jacob Nottingham 4.00 10.00
BCAPJR Jose Ramirez 3.00 8.00
BCAPJRE Jonathan Reynoso 3.00 8.00
BCAPJRO Jose Rondon 3.00 8.00
BCAPJS Jacob Scavuzzo 5.00 12.00
BCAPJSI Juan Silva 3.00 8.00
BCAPJSW Jake Sweaney 3.00 8.00
BCAPJU Julio Urias 30.00 80.00
BCAPJUR Jose Urena 4.00 10.00
BCAPJW Jesse Winker 40.00 100.00
BCAPJWE Jamie Westbrook 3.00 8.00
BCAPKB Kris Bryant 75.00 200.00
BCAPKD Kelly Dugan 3.00 8.00
BCAPKF Kendry Flores 3.00 8.00
BCAPKM Ketel Marte 30.00 80.00
BCAPKP Kyle Parker 4.00 10.00
BCAPKW Kean Wong 3.00 8.00
BCAPLJ Luke Jackson 3.00 8.00
BCAPLM Leonardo Molina 3.00 8.00
BCAPLR Luigi Rodriguez 3.00 8.00
BCAPLT Lewis Thorpe 3.00 8.00
BCAPLW LeVon Washington 3.00 8.00
BCAPMA Mark Appel 4.00 10.00
BCAPMB Mookie Betts 600.00 1500.00
BCAPMF Maikel Franco 4.00 10.00
BCAPMFE Michael Feliz 4.00 10.00
BCAPMJ Micah Johnson 3.00 8.00
BCAPMM Mike Mayers 3.00 8.00
BCAPMMA Manuel Margot 5.00 12.00
BCAPMMC Matt McPhearson 3.00 8.00
BCAPMO Michael O'Neill 3.00 8.00
BCAPMTA Michael Taylor 4.00 10.00
BCAPMW Matt Whitehouse 3.00 8.00
BCAPNK Nick Kingham 4.00 10.00
BCAPNM Nathan Mikolas 3.00 8.00
BCAPPJ Pierce Johnson 4.00 10.00
BCAPPT Preston Tucker 4.00 10.00
BCAPRB Rony Bautista 3.00 8.00
BCAPRC Ryan Casteel 3.00 8.00
BCAPRG Robert Gsellman 4.00 10.00
BCAPRH Rosell Herrera 5.00 12.00
BCAPRHE Ryon Healy 5.00 12.00
BCAPRHA Ryan Hafner 3.00 8.00
BCAPRMC Ryan McNeil 3.00 8.00
BCAPRT Raimel Tapia 4.00 10.00
BCAPRU Richard Urena 4.00 10.00
BCAPSG Severino Gonzalez 3.00 8.00
BCAPSMB Seth Mejias-Brean 3.00 8.00
BCAPTA Trae Arbet 3.00 8.00
BCAPTB Ty Buttrey 3.00 8.00
BCAPTC Tim Cooney 3.00 8.00
BCAPTMA Tyler Mahle 3.00 8.00
BCAPTN Tucker Neuhaus 3.00 8.00
BCAPTS Teddy Stankiewicz 3.00 8.00
BCAPTW Tyler Wade 6.00 15.00
BCAPWG Willy Garcia 3.00 8.00
BCAPWR Wendell Rijo 3.00 8.00
BCAPYA Yency Almonte 3.00 8.00
BCAPYG Yimi Garcia 3.00 8.00
BCAPYM Yohander Mendez 3.00 8.00
BCAPZB Zach Borenstein 4.00 10.00

2014 Bowman Chrome Prospect Autographs Black Refractors

*BLACK REF: .75X TO 2X BASIC
BOW.ODDS 1:775 HOBBY
STATED PRINT RUN 99 SER.#'d SETS
BOW.EXCH DEADLINE 4/30/2017
BOW.CHR.EXCH DEADLINE 9/30/2017
BCAPKB Kris Bryant 200.00 500.00

2014 Bowman Chrome Prospect Autographs Black Wave Refractors

*BLACK WAVE REF: 1.2X TO 3X BASIC
STATED PRINT RUN 50 SER.#'d SETS
BOW.EXCH DEADLINE 4/30/2017
BOW.CHR.EXCH DEADLINE 6/30/2017
BCAPKB Kris Bryant 300.00 800.00

2014 Bowman Chrome Prospect Autographs Blue Refractors

*BLUE REF: 1X TO 2.5X BASIC
BOW.ODDS 1:515 HOBBY
BOW.CHR.ODDS 1:207 HOBBY
STATED PRINT RUN 150 SER.#'d SETS
BOW.EXCH DEADLINE 4/30/2017
BOW.CHR.EXCH DEADLINE 9/30/2017
BCAPKB Kris Bryant 200.00 500.00

2014 Bowman Chrome Prospect Autographs Blue Wave Refractors

*BLUE WAVE REF: 1.2X TO 3X BASIC
STATED PRINT RUN 50 SER.#'d SETS
BOW.EXCH DEADLINE 4/30/2017
BOW.CHR.EXCH DEADLINE 6/30/2017
BCAPKB Kris Bryant 300.00 800.00

2014 Bowman Chrome Prospect Autographs Bubble Refractors

*BUBBLE REF: .75X TO 2X BASIC
STATED ODDS 1:340 HOBBY
STATED PRINT RUN 99 SER.#'d SET
EXCHANGE DEADLINE 9/30/2017

2014 Bowman Chrome Prospect Autographs Gold Refractors

*GOLD REF: 2X TO 5X BASIC
BOW.ODDS 1:1555 HOBBY
BOW.CHR.ODDS 1:614 HOBBY
STATED PRINT RUN 50 SER.#'d SETS
BOW.EXCH DEADLINE 4/30/2017
BOW.CHR.EXCH DEADLINE 6/30/2017
BCAPKB Kris Bryant 400.00 1000.00

2014 Bowman Chrome Prospect Autographs Green Refractors

*GREEN REF: .75X TO 2X BASIC
BOW.ODDS 1:1035 HOBBY
BOW.CHR.ODDS 1:410 HOBBY
STATED PRINT RUN 150 SER.#'d SETS
BOW.EXCH DEADLINE 4/30/2017
BOW.CHR.EXCH DEADLINE 6/30/2017
BCAPKB Kris Bryant 200.00 500.00

2014 Bowman Chrome Prospect Autographs Refractors

*REF: .5X TO 1.2X BASIC
BOW.STATED ODDS 1:155 HOBBY
BOW.CHR ODDS 1:82 HOBBY
STATED PRINT RUN 500 SER.#'d SETS
BOW.EXCH DEADLINE 4/30/2017
BOW.CHR.EXCH 9/30/2017

2014 Bowman Chrome Prospects

COMPLETE SET (110) 15.00 40.00
PLATE PRINT RUN 1 SET PER COLOR
BLACK-CYAN-MAGENTA-YELLOW ISSUED
NO PLATE PRICING DUE TO SCARCITY
BCP1 Jason Hursh .25 .60
BCP2 Trey Ball .25 .60
BCP3 Jacob May .30 .75
BCP4 Rosell Herrera .40 1.00

BCP5 Mark Appel .30 .75
BCP6 Julio Urias 1.25 3.00
BCP7 Devin Williams .60 1.50
BCP8 Ryan Eades .25 .60
BCP9 Eric Jagielo .25 .60
BCP10 Zach Borenstein .30 .75
BCP11 Jake Barrett .30 .75
BCP12 Wendell Rijo .25 .60
BCP13 Armando Rivero .25 .60
BCP14 Chris Taylor 1.25 3.00
BCP15 Edwin Diaz .50 1.25
BCP16 Dylan Floro .30 .75
BCP17 Jose Abreu 3.00 8.00
BCP18 Luke Jackson .25 .60
BCP19 Billy Burns .25 .60
BCP20 Leonardo Molina .25 .60
BCP21 Billy McKinney .30 .75
BCP22 Chris Flexen .30 .75
BCP23 Kyle Parker .30 .75
BCP24 Pierce Johnson .30 .75
BCP25 Kris Bryant 6.00 15.00
BCP26 Micah Johnson .25 .60
BCP27 Raimel Tapia .30 .75
BCP28 Preston Tucker .30 .75
BCP29 Christian Binford .25 .60
BCP30 Ty Buttrey .25 .60
BCP31 Brandon Trinkwon .30 .75
BCP32 Lewis Thorpe .25 .60
BCP33 Devon Travis .25 .60
BCP34 Cesar Puello .25 .60
BCP35 Tyler Wade .40 1.00
BCP36 Daniel Robertson .30 .75
BCP37 Maikel Franco .30 .75
BCP38 Cody Reed .25 .60
BCP39 Sam Moll .25 .60
BCP40 Logan Vick .25 .60
BCP41 Gus Schlosser .25 .60
BCP42 Levon Washington .25 .60
BCP43 Chris Beck .25 .60
BCP44 Tim Cooney .25 .60
BCP45 Michael Feliz .30 .75
BCP46 Jamie Westbrook .25 .60
BCP47 Alex Reyes .40 1.00
BCP48 Trevor Gretzky .25 .60
BCP49 Isiah Kiner-Falefa .40 1.00
BCP50 Shawn Pleffner .25 .60
BCP51 Hunter Dozier .25 .60
BCP52 Hunter Renfroe .30 .75
BCP53 Ryder Jones .25 .60
BCP54 Tyler Danish .25 .60
BCP55 Matt McPhearson .25 .60
BCP56 Gosuke Katoh .40 1.00
BCP57 Andrew Thurman .25 .60
BCP58 Jordan Paroubeck .25 .60
BCP59 Tucker Neuhaus .25 .60
BCP60 Dillon Overton .25 .60
BCP61 Ryon Healy .40 1.00
BCP62 Chase Anderson .25 .60
BCP63 Daniel Palka .25 .60
BCP64 Duane Underwood .25 .60
BCP65 Carlos Contreras .25 .60
BCP66 Ben Lively .25 .60
BCP67 Anthony Santander .30 .75
BCP68 Melvin Mercedes .25 .60
BCP69 Josh Hader .50 1.25
BCP70 Yimi Garcia .25 .60
BCP71 Orlando Arcia .40 1.00
BCP72 Matthew Bowman .25 .60
BCP73 Jacob deGrom 30.00 80.00
BCP74 John Gant .25 .60
BCP75 Robert Gsellman .30 .75
BCP76 Gabriel Ynoa .30 .75
BCP77 Anthony Aliotti .25 .60
BCP78 Chris Bostick .30 .75
BCP79 Drew Granier .25 .60
BCP80 Austin Wright .25 .60
BCP81 Brandon Cumpton .25 .60
BCP82 Kendry Flores .25 .60
BCP83 Jason Rogers .25 .60
BCP84 Ryne Stanek .25 .60
BCP85 Nomar Mazara .60 1.50
BCP86 Victor Payano .25 .60
BCP87 Franklin Barreto .30 .75
BCP88 Santiago Nessy .25 .60
BCP89 Michael Ratterree .25 .60
BCP90 Manuel Margot .40 1.00
BCP91 Gabriel Rosa .25 .60
BCP92 Nelson Rodriguez .30 .75
BCP93 Yency Almonte .25 .60
BCP94 Bobby Coyle .25 .60
BCP95 Pat Stover .25 .60
BCP96 Wuilmer Becerra .25 .60
BCP97 Miller Diaz .25 .60
BCP98 Akeel Morris .25 .60
BCP99 Kenny Giles .30 .75
BCP100 Brian Ragira .25 .60
BCP101 Victor De Leon .30 .75
BCP102 Steven Ramos .25 .60
BCP103 Chris Kohler .25 .60
BCP104 Seth Mejias-Brean .25 .60
BCP105 Miguel Alfredo Gonzalez .25 .60
BCP106 Alexander Guerrero .30 .75
BCP107 Jose Herrera .25 .60
BCP108 Tyler Marlette .25 .60
BCP109 Mookie Betts 30.00 80.00
BCP110 Joe Wendle .50 1.25

2014 Bowman Chrome Prospects Black Refractors

*BLACK REF: 5X TO 12X BASIC
STATED ODDS 1:229 HOBBY
STATED PRINT RUN 99 SER.#'d SETS

2014 Bowman Chrome Prospects Black Wave Refractors

*BLACK WAVE: 3X TO 8X BASIC

2014 Bowman Chrome Prospects Blue Refractors

*BLUE REF: 3X TO 8X BASIC
STATED ODDS 1:91 HOBBY
STATED PRINT RUN 250 SER.#'d SETS

2014 Bowman Chrome Prospects Blue Wave Refractors

*BLUE WAVE: 2X TO 5X BASIC

2014 Bowman Chrome Prospects Gold Refractors

*GOLD REF: 8X TO 20X BASIC
STATED ODDS 1:453 HOBBY
STATED PRINT RUN 50 SER.#'d SETS
BCP6 Julio Urias 25.00 60.00
BCP17 Jose Abreu 60.00 150.00

2014 Bowman Chrome Prospects Green Refractors

*GREEN REF: 6X TO 15X BASIC
STATED ODDS 1:303 HOBBY
STATED PRINT RUN 75 SER.#'d SETS

2014 Bowman Chrome Prospects Green Wave Refractors

*GREEN WAVE: 10X TO 25X BASIC
STATED PRINT RUN 25 SER.#'d SETS
BCP6 Julio Urias 25.00 60.00

2014 Bowman Chrome Prospects Orange Refractors

*ORANGE REF: 10X TO 25X BASIC
STATED ODDS 1:908 HOBBY
STATED PRINT RUN 25 SER.#'d SETS

2014 Bowman Chrome Prospects Orange Wave Refractors

*ORANGE WAVE: 4X TO 10X BASIC

2014 Bowman Chrome Prospects Purple Refractors

*PURPLE REF: 4X TO 10X BASIC
STATED PRINT RUN 199 SER.#'d SETS

2014 Bowman Chrome Prospects Red Wave Refractors

*RED WAVE: 10X TO 25X BASIC
STATED PRINT RUN 25 SER.#'d SETS
BCP6 Julio Urias 25.00 60.00

2014 Bowman Chrome Prospects Refractors

*REF: 2X TO 5X BASIC
STATED ODDS 1:45 HOBBY
STATED PRINT RUN 500 SER.#'d SETS

2014 Bowman Chrome Prospects Silver Wave Refractors

*SILVER WAVE: 10X TO 25X BASIC
STATED PRINT RUN 25 SER.#'d SETS
BCP6 Julio Urias 25.00 60.00

2014 Bowman Chrome Prospects Series 2

PRINTING PLATE ODDS 1:1740 HOBBY
PLATE PRINT RUN 1 SET PER COLOR
BLACK-CYAN-MAGENTA-YELLOW ISSUED
NO PLATE PRICING DUE TO SCARCITY
BCP1 Shae Simmons .25 .60
BCP2 Kean Wong .25 .60
BCP3 Gosuke Katoh .40 1.00
BCP4 Franklin Barreto .40 1.00
BCP5 Ryan Casteel .25 .60
BCP6 Akeem Bostick .25 .60
BCP7 Carlos Contreras .25 .60
BCP8 Alberto Tirado .25 .60
BCP9 Willy Garcia .25 .60
BCP10 Richard Urena .30 .75
BCP11 Isiah Kiner-Falefa .40 1.00
BCP12 Jamie Westbrook .25 .60
BCP13 Franmil Reyes .75 2.00
BCP14 Kelly Dugan .25 .60
BCP15 Jose Rondon .25 .60
BCP16 Ben Lively .25 .60
BCP17 LeVon Washington .25 .60
BCP18 Luigi Rodriguez .25 .60
BCP19 Jordan Patterson .25 .60
BCP20 Cody Anderson .25 .60
BCP21 R.J. Alvarez .25 .60
BCP22 Andy Burns .25 .60
BCP23 Daniel Winkler .25 .60
BCP24 Vincent Velasquez .40 1.00
BCP25 Teddy Stankiewicz .25 .60
BCP26 Dillon Overton .25 .60
BCP27 Nick Kingham .30 .75
BCP28 Austin Wilson .25 .60
BCP29 Manuel Margot .40 1.00
BCP30 Dom Nunez .25 .60
BCP31 Jacob Nottingham .30 .75
BCP32 Michael Feliz .30 .75
BCP33 Adrian Marin .25 .60
BCP34 Trevor Gretzky .25 .60
BCP35 Nick Ramirez .25 .60
BCP36 Juan Silva .25 .60
BCP37 Jonathan Reynoso .25 .60
BCP38 Daniel Palka .25 .60
BCP39 Raul Mondesi .40 1.00
BCP40 Michael Taylor .30 .75
BCP41 Joe Wendle .50 1.25
BCP42 Tim Cooney .25 .60
BCP43 Yimi Garcia .25 .60
BCP44 Cody Reed .25 .60
BCP45 Jose Urena .30 .75
BCP46 Andrew Thurman .25 .60
BCP47 Corey Knebel .25 .60
BCP48 Michael O'Neill .25 .60
BCP49 Devin Williams .60 1.50
BCP50 Tyler Marlette .25 .60
BCP51 Gabriel Ynoa .30 .75
BCP52 Tyler Mahle .25 .60
BCP53 Jason Martin .40 1.00
BCP54 Spencer Patton .25 .60
BCP55 Aaron Brooks .40 1.00
BCP56 Jeff McNeil 1.50 4.00
BCP57 Johnny Field .25 .60
BCP58 Nathan Mikolas .25 .60
BCP59 Ryan McNeil .25 .60
BCP60 Trae Arbet .25 .60
BCP61 Austin Nola .30 .75
BCP62 Brandon Dixon .25 .60
BCP63 Ryan Hafner .25 .60
BCP64 Matt Whitehouse .25 .60
BCP65 Fred Lewis .25 .60
BCP66 Dylan Unsworth .25 .60
BCP67 Ryan Kussmaul .30 .75
BCP68 JaCoby Jones .40 1.00
BCP69 Breyvic Valera .25 .60
BCP70 Jose Ramirez .25 .60
BCP71 Michael Ohlman .25 .60
BCP72 Sebastian Vader .25 .60
BCP73 Robert Whalen .25 .60
BCP74 Tim Berry .25 .60
BCP75 Chris Heston .25 .60
BCP76 Jeff Ames .25 .60
BCP77 Harold Ramirez .40 1.00
BCP78 Luis Severino .40 1.00
BCP79 Bobby Wahl .25 .60
BCP80 Thairo Estrada .75 2.00
BCP81 Logan Bawcom .25 .60
BCP82 Rafael Medina .25 .60
BCP83 Elvis Araujo .25 .60
BCP84 Stuart Turner .25 .60
BCP85 Chad Pinder .25 .60
BCP86 Cam Perkins .25 .60
BCP87 Jose Pujols .25 .60
BCP88 Jake Sanchez .25 .60
BCP89 Dawel Lugo .25 .60
BCP90 Victor Caratini .75 2.00
BCP91 Dalton Pompey .40 1.00
BCP92 L.J. Mazzilli .25 .60
BCP93 Buck Farmer .25 .60
BCP94 Kevin Encarnacion .25 .60
BCP95 Taylor Cole .25 .60
BCP96 Felix Jorge .25 .60
BCP97 Ariel Soriano .25 .60
BCP98 Amaurys Minier .25 .60
BCP99 Wilmer Oberto .25 .60
BCP100 Yonathan Mejia .25 .60

2014 Bowman Chrome Prospects Series 2 Error Card Variations

STATED ODDS 1:928 HOBBY
PECAB Andy Burns 4.00 10.00
PECAB Aaron Books 6.00 15.00
PECAT Andrew Thurboy 4.00 10.00
PECAW Austin Wilson 4.00 10.00
PECBL Ben Lively 4.00 10.00
PECBV Valera Breyvic 4.00 10.00
PECCK Evel Knebel 4.00 10.00
PECCR Cody Write 4.00 10.00
PECDW Daniel Winkler 4.00 10.00
PECGK Gosuke Katoh 6.00 15.00
PECJR Jose Ramirez 4.00 10.00
PECJW Joe Wendle 8.00 20.00
PECKW Kean Wrong 4.00 10.00
PECMM Manuel Margot 5.00 12.00
PECMO Michael Ohlboy 4.00 10.00
PECMR Mario Rodriguez 4.00 10.00
PECMT Taylor Michael 5.00 12.00
PECNK Nick Princeham 5.00 12.00
PECRA P.J. Alvarez 4.00 10.00
PECRM Raul Mondesi III 6.00 15.00
PECSS Shea Simmons 4.00 10.00
PECTM Tyler Earthlette 4.00 10.00
PECTS Teddy Stankiewich 4.00 10.00
PECVV Vincent Velazquez 6.00 15.00
PECYG Yimi Garcia 4.00 10.00

2014 Bowman Chrome Prospects Series 2 Short Prints

STATED ODDS 1:288 HOBBY
PSAT Andrew Thurman 2.50 6.00
PSAW Austin Wilson 2.50 6.00
PSFB Franklin Barreto 4.00 10.00
PSGK Gosuke Katoh 4.00 10.00
PSKW Kean Wong 2.50 6.00
PSMM Manuel Margot 4.00 10.00
PSNK Nick Kingham 3.00 8.00
PSSS Shae Simmons 2.50 6.00
PSVV Vincent Velasquez 4.00 10.00
PSYG Yimi Garcia 2.50 6.00

2014 Bowman Chrome Prospects Series 2 Black Static Refractors

*BLACK STATIC: 8X TO 20X BASIC
STATED ODDS 1:205 HOBBY
STATED PRINT RUN 35 SER.#'d SETS
BCP78 Luis Severino 25.00 60.00
BCP91 Dalton Pompey 25.00 60.00

2014 Bowman Chrome Prospects Series 2 Black Wave Refractors

*BLACK WAVE: 3X TO 8X BASIC
RANDOM INSERTS IN PACKS

2014 Bowman Chrome Prospects Series 2 Blue Refractors

*BLUE REF: 3X TO 8X BASIC
STATED ODDS 1:29 HOBBY
STATED PRINT RUN 250 SER.#'d SETS

2014 Bowman Chrome Prospects Series 2 Blue Wave Refractors

*BLUE WAVE: 2X TO 5X BASIC
RANDOM INSERTS IN PACKS

2014 Bowman Chrome Prospects Series 2 Bubble Refractors

*BUBBLE REF: 5X TO 12X BASIC
STATED ODDS 1:63 HOBBY
STATED PRINT RUN 99 SER.#'d SETS

2014 Bowman Chrome Prospects Series 2 Gold Refractors

*GOLD: 8X TO 20X BASIC
STATED ODDS 1:138 HOBBY
STATED PRINT RUN 50 SER.#'d SETS
BCP78 Luis Severino 25.00 60.00

2014 Bowman Chrome Prospects Series 2 Green Refractors

*GREEN REF: 6X TO 15X BASIC
STATED ODDS 1:90 HOBBY
STATED PRINT RUN 75 SER.#'d SETS

2014 Bowman Chrome Prospects Series 2 Orange Refractors

*ORANGE REF: 10X TO 25X BASIC
STATED ODDS 1:276 HOBBY
STATED PRINT RUN 25 SER.#'d SETS
BCP78 Luis Severino 30.00 80.00
BCP91 Dalton Pompey 30.00 80.00

2014 Bowman Chrome Prospects Series 2 Pink Wave Refractors

*PINK WAVE: 6X TO 15X BASIC
STATED ODDS 1:35,000 HOBBY
STATED PRINT RUN 65 SER.#'d SETS

2014 Bowman Chrome Prospects Series 2 Purple Refractors

*PURPLE REF: 4X TO 10X BASIC
STATED ODDS 1:47 HOBBY
STATED PRINT RUN 150 SER.#'d SETS

2014 Bowman Chrome Prospects Series 2 Red Wave Refractors

*RED WAVE: 8X TO 20X BASIC
RANDOM INSERTS IN PACKS
STATED PRINT RUN 25 SER.#'d SETS
BCP78 Luis Severino 25.00 60.00
BCP91 Dalton Pompey 25.00 60.00

2014 Bowman Chrome Prospects Series 2 Refractors

*REF: 2X TO 5X BASIC
STATED ODDS 1:15 HOBBY
STATED PRINT RUN 500 SER.#'d SETS

2014 Bowman Chrome Prospects Series 2 Silver Wave Refractors

*SILVER WAVE: 8X TO 20X BASIC
RANDOM INSERTS IN PACKS
STATED PRINT RUN 25 SER.#'d SETS

2014 Bowman Chrome Rookie Autographs

BOW.ODDS 1:960 HOBBY
BOW.CHR.ODDS 1:1835 HOBBY
BOW.CHR.PLATE ODDS 1:116,000 HOBBY
PLATE PRINT RUN 1 SET PER COLOR
BLACK-CYAN-MAGENTA-YELLOW ISSUED
NO PLATE PRICING DUE TO SCARCITY
BOW.EXCH DEADLINE 4/30/2017
BOW.CHR.EXCH DEADLINE 9/30/2017
BCARAG Alex Guerrero 8.00 20.00
BCARBH Billy Hamilton 8.00 20.00
BCARCO Chris Owings 3.00 8.00
BCARER Enny Romero 3.00 8.00
BCARJA Jose Abreu 40.00 100.00
BCARJK Jeff Kobernus 3.00 8.00
BCARJM Jake Marisnick 3.00 8.00
BCARJN Jimmy Nelson 3.00 8.00
BCARJR J.R. Murphy 3.00 8.00
BCARJS Jonathan Schoop 12.00 30.00
BCARKW Kolten Wong 4.00 10.00
BCARMC Michael Choice 3.00 8.00
BCARMD Matt Davidson 4.00 10.00
BCARNC Nick Castellanos 12.00 30.00
BCAROT Oscar Taveras 4.00 10.00
BCARTD Travis d'Arnaud 4.00 10.00
BCARTW Taijuan Walker 6.00 15.00
BCARWF Wilmer Flores 4.00 10.00
BCARYS Yangervis Solarte 3.00 8.00
BCARYV Yordano Ventura 8.00 20.00

2014 Bowman Chrome Rookie Autographs Black Refractors

*BLACK REF: 1.5X TO 4X BASIC
STATED ODDS 1:1452 HOBBY
STATED PRINT RUN 35 SER.#'d SETS
EXCHANGE DEADLINE 4/30/2017

2014 Bowman Chrome Rookie Autographs Blue Refractors

*BLUE REF: .6X TO 1.5X BASIC
BOW.ODDS 1:938 HOBBY
BOW.CHR.ODDS 1:3060 HOBBY
BOWMAN PRINT RUN 250 SER.#'d SETS
BOW.CHR. PRINT RUN 150 SER.#'d SETS
BOW.EXCH DEADLINE 4/30/2017
BOW.CHR.EXCH DEADLINE 9/30/2017

2014 Bowman Chrome Rookie Autographs Bubble Refractors

*BUBBLE REF: .75X TO 2X BASIC
STATED ODDS 1:4620 HOBBY
STATED PRINT RUN 99 SER.#'d SETS
EXCHANGE DEADLINE 9/30/2017

2014 Bowman Chrome Rookie Autographs Gold Refractors

*GOLD REF: 1X TO 2.5X BASIC
BOW.ODDS 1:4700 HOBBY
BOW.CHR.ODDS 1:9250 HOBBY
STATED PRINT RUN 50 SER.#'d SETS
BOW.EXCH DEADLINE 4/30/2017
BOW.CHR.EXCH DEADLINE 9/30/2017
BCARBH Billy Hamilton 20.00 50.00
BCARJS Jonathan Schoop 60.00 150.00

2014 Bowman Chrome Rookie Autographs Green Refractors

*GREEN REF/75: .75X TO 2X BASIC
BOWMAN PRINT RUN 20 SER.#'d SETS
BOW.CHR PRINT RUN 75 SER.#'d SETS
NO BOWMAN PRICING DUE TO SCARCITY
BOW.EXCH DEADLINE 4/30/2017
BOW.CHR.EXCH DEADLINE 9/30/2017

2014 Bowman Chrome Rookie Autographs Orange Refractors

*ORANGE: 1.5X TO 4X BASIC
BOW.ODDS 1:9400 HOBBY
BOW.CHR.ODDS 1:13,000 HOBBY
STATED PRINT RUN 25 SER.#'d SETS
BOW.EXCH DEADLINE 4/30/2017
BOW.CHR.EXCH DEADLINE 9/30/2017
BCARAG Alex Guerrero 40.00 100.00
BCARXB Xander Bogaerts 150.00 250.00

2014 Bowman Chrome Rookie Autographs Orange Wave Refractors

*ORANGE WAVE: 1.5X TO 4X BASIC
PRINT RUNS B/WN 25-35 COPIES PER
EXCHANGE DEADLINE 4/30/2017
BCARXB Xander Bogaerts/25 150.00 250.00

2014 Bowman Chrome Rookie Autographs Refractors

*REF: .5X TO 1.2X BASIC
STATED ODDS 1:1005 HOBBY
STATED PRINT RUN 500 SER.#'d SETS
EXCHANGE DEADLINE 4/30/2017

2014 Bowman Chrome Top 100 Prospects

STATED ODDS 1:12 HOBBY
BTP1 Byron Buxton 2.50 6.00
BTP2 Oscar Taveras .60 1.50
BTP3 Miguel Sano .60 1.50
BTP4 Xander Bogaerts 1.50 4.00
BTP5 Carlos Correa 2.50 6.00
BTP6 Javier Baez 2.00 5.00
BTP7 Taijuan Walker .50 1.25
BTP8 Kris Bryant 5.00 12.00
BTP9 Archie Bradley .50 1.25
BTP10 Billy Hamilton .60 1.50
BTP11 Mark Appel .60 1.50
BTP12 Francisco Lindor 4.00 10.00
BTP13 Dylan Bundy .60 1.50
BTP14 Gregory Polanco .75 2.00
BTP15 Travis d'Arnaud .60 1.50
BTP16 Tyler Glasnow 2.00 5.00
BTP17 Jonathan Gray .60 1.50
BTP18 Kyle Crick .50 1.25
BTP19 George Springer 2.00 5.00
BTP20 Robert Stephenson .50 1.25
BTP21 C.J. Edwards .60 1.50
BTP22 Lucas Giolito .75 2.00
BTP23 Lance McCullers .50 1.25
BTP24 Alex Meyer .50 1.25
BTP25 Eddie Butler .50 1.25
BTP26 Andrew Heaney .50 1.25
BTP27 Nick Castellanos 1.50 4.00
BTP28 Clint Frazier 2.00 5.00
BTP29 Maikel Franco .60 1.50
BTP30 Jameson Taillon .60 1.50
BTP31 Noah Syndergaard .60 1.50
BTP32 Masahiro Tanaka 1.50 4.00
BTP33 Addison Russell .75 2.00
BTP34 Jose Abreu 4.00 10.00
BTP35 Austin Meadows 1.25 3.00
BTP36 Alen Hanson .50 1.25
BTP37 D.J. Peterson .50 1.25
BTP38 Kevin Gausman .75 2.00
BTP39 Carlos Martinez .60 1.50
BTP40 Joc Pederson 1.25 3.00
BTP41 Jorge Soler 1.00 2.50
BTP42 Gary Sanchez 1.50 4.00
BTP43 Albert Almora .75 2.00
BTP44 Julio Urias 2.50 6.00
BTP45 Aaron Sanchez .50 1.25
BTP46 Yordano Ventura .60 1.50
BTP47 David Dahl .60 1.50
BTP48 Phil Ervin .50 1.25
BTP49 Kyle Zimmer .50 1.25
BTP50 Erik Johnson .50 1.25
BTP51 Henry Owens .60 1.50
BTP52 Danny Hultzen .50 1.25
BTP53 Colin Moran .50 1.25
BTP54 Kohl Stewart .50 1.25
BTP55 C.J. Cron .50 1.25
BTP56 Austin Hedges .50 1.25
BTP57 Corey Seager 2.50 6.00
BTP58 Lucas Sims .50 1.25
BTP59 Victor Sanchez .50 1.25
BTP60 Garin Cecchini .50 1.25
BTP61 Chris Anderson .50 1.25
BTP62 Raul Mondesi .75 2.00
BTP63 Delino DeShields .50 1.25
BTP64 Tyler Austin .50 1.25
BTP65 Bubba Starling .60 1.50
BTP66 Mookie Betts 10.00 25.00
BTP67 Chris Owings .50 1.25
BTP68 Jesse Biddle .60 1.50
BTP69 Kolten Wong .60 1.50
BTP70 Jonathan Singleton .60 1.50
BTP71 Micah Johnson .50 1.25
BTP72 Taylor Guerrieri .50 1.25
BTP73 Mike Foltynewicz .50 1.25
BTP74 Jorge Alfaro .60 1.50
BTP75 Joey Gallo 1.00 2.50
BTP76 Rafael De Paula .50 1.25
BTP77 Rougned Odor 1.25 3.00
BTP78 Mason Williams .50 1.25
BTP79 Chris Taylor 2.50 6.00
BTP80 Rafael Montero .50 1.25
BTP81 Michael Choice .50 1.25
BTP82 Eddie Rosario 1.00 2.50
BTP83 Max Fried 2.00 5.00
BTP84 Anthony Ranaudo .50 1.25
BTP85 A.J. Cole .50 1.25
BTP86 Matt Davidson .60 1.50
BTP87 Devon Travis .75 2.00
BTP88 Jackie Bradley Jr. .75 2.00
BTP89 Rosell Herrera .75 2.00
BTP90 Lewis Thorpe .50 1.25
BTP91 Luis Heredia .50 1.25
BTP92 Hak-Ju Lee .50 1.25
BTP93 Marcus Stroman .75 2.00
BTP94 Jose Berrios .75 2.00
BTP95 Christian Bethancourt .50 1.25
BTP96 Miguel Andujar 1.50 4.00
BTP97 Edwin Diaz 1.00 2.50
BTP98 Dan Vogelbach .75 2.00
BTP99 Preston Tucker .60 1.50
BTP100 Josh Bell 1.00 2.50

2014 Bowman Chrome Top 100 Prospects Die Cut Refractors

*REF: 2.5X TO 6X BASIC
STATED ODDS 1:247 HOBBY
STATED PRINT RUN 99 SER.#'d SETS

2014 Bowman Chrome Top 100 Prospects Die Cut X-Fractor Autographs

STATED ODDS 1:10,203 HOBBY
STATED PRINT RUN 24 SER.#'d SETS
BTP1 Byron Buxton 250.00 350.00
BTP11 Mark Appel 100.00 200.00
BTP12 Francisco Lindor 30.00 80.00
BTP15 Travis d'Arnaud 15.00 40.00
BTP19 George Springer 60.00 150.00
BTP29 Maikel Franco 60.00 150.00
BTP34 Jose Abreu 300.00 500.00
BTP64 Tyler Austin 12.00 30.00

2014 Bowman Chrome Draft

STATED PLATE ODDS 1:5200 HOBBY
PLATE PRINT RUN 1 SET PER COLOR
BLACK-CYAN-MAGENTA-YELLOW ISSUED
NO PLATE PRICING DUE TO SCARCITY
CDP1 Tyler Kolek .30 .75
CDP2 Kyle Schwarber 1.25 3.00
CDP3 Alex Jackson .40 1.00
CDP4 Aaron Nola 2.00 5.00
CDP5 Kyle Freeland .60 1.50
CDP6 Jeff Hoffman .50 1.25
CDP7 Michael Conforto .60 1.50
CDP8 Max Pentecost .30 .75
CDP9 Kodi Medeiros .30 .75
CDP10 Trea Turner 1.00 2.50
CDP11 Tyler Beede .50 1.25
CDP12 Sean Newcomb .50 1.25
CDP14 Erick Fedde .30 .75
CDP15 Nick Howard .30 .75
CDP16 Casey Gillaspie .50 1.25
CDP17 Bradley Zimmer .50 1.25
CDP18 Grant Holmes .30 .75
CDP19 Derek Hill .30 .75
CDP20 Cole Tucker .30 .75
CDP21 Matt Chapman 4.00 10.00
CDP22 Michael Chavis 1.50 4.00
CDP23 Luke Weaver 1.00 2.50
CDP24 Foster Griffin .30 .75
CDP25 Alex Blandino .30 .75
CDP26 Luis Ortiz .30 .75
CDP27 Justus Sheffield .60 1.50
CDP28 Braxton Davidson .30 .75
CDP29 Michael Kopech 2.00 5.00
CDP30 Jack Flaherty 2.00 5.00
CDP32 Ryan Ripken .40 1.00
CDP33 Forrest Wall .50 1.25
CDP34 Blake Anderson .30 .75
CDP35 Derek Fisher .50 1.25
CDP36 Mike Papi .30 .75
CDP37 Connor Joe .30 .75
CDP38 Chase Vallot .30 .75
CDP39 Jacob Gatewood .30 .75
CDP40 A.J. Reed .60 1.50
CDP41 Justin Twine .30 .75
CDP42 Spencer Adams .40 1.00
CDP43 Jake Stinnett .30 .75
CDP44 Nick Burdi .30 .75
CDP45 Matt Imhof .30 .75
CDP46 Ryan Castellani .30 .75
CDP47 Sean Reid-Foley .30 .75
CDP48 Monte Harrison .60 1.50
CDP49 Michael Gettys .40 1.00
CDP50 Aramis Garcia .30 .75
CDP51 Joe Gatto .30 .75
CDP52 Cody Reed .30 .75
CDP53 Jacob Lindgren .40 1.00
CDP54 Scott Blewett .30 .75
CDP55 Taylor Sparks .30 .75
CDP56 Ti'Quan Forbes .30 .75
CDP57 Cameron Varga .30 .75
CDP58 Grant Hockin .30 .75
CDP59 Alex Verdugo .60 1.50
CDP60 Austin DeCarr .30 .75
CDP61 Sam Travis .40 1.00
CDP62 Trey Supak .30 .75
CDP63 Marcus Wilson .30 .75
CDP64 Zech Lemond .30 .75
CDP65 Jakson Reetz .30 .75
CDP66 Jeff Brigham .30 .75
CDP67 Chris Ellis .30 .75
CDP68 Gareth Morgan .30 .75
CDP69 Mitch Keller .50 1.25
CDP70 Spencer Turnbull .30 .75
CDP71 Daniel Gossett .30 .75
CDP72 Garrett Fulenchek .30 .75
CDP73 Brett Graves .30 .75
CDP74 Ronnie Williams .30 .75
CDP75 Isan Diaz .75 2.00
CDP76 Andrew Morales .30 .75
CDP77 Brent Honeywell .50 1.25
CDP78 Carson Sands .30 .75
CDP79 Dylan Cease .75 2.00
CDP80 Jace Fry .30 .75
CDP81 J.D. Davis .50 1.25
CDP82 Austin Cousino .30 .75
CDP83 Aaron Brown .30 .75
CDP84 Milton Ramos .30 .75
CDP85 Brian Gonzalez .30 .75
CDP86 Bobby Bradley .40 1.00
CDP87 Chad Sobotka .30 .75
CDP88 Jonathan Holder .30 .75
CDP89 Nick Wells .30 .75
CDP90 Josh Morgan .30 .75
CDP91 Brian Anderson .30 .75
CDP92 Mark Zagunis .30 .75
CDP93 Michael Cederoth .40 1.00
CDP94 Dylan Davis .40 1.00
CDP95 Matt Railey .30 .75
CDP96 Eric Skoglund .30 .75
CDP97 Wyatt Strahan .30 .75
CDP98 John Richy .30 .75
CDP99 Grayson Greiner .30 .75
CDP100 Jordan Luplow .30 .75
CDP101 Jake Cosart .40 1.00
CDP102 Michael Mader .30 .75
CDP103 Brian Schales .30 .75
CDP104 Brett Austin .30 .75
CDP105 Ryan Yarbrough .50 1.25
CDP106 Chris Oliver .30 .75
CDP107 Matt Morgan .30 .75
CDP108 Trace Loehr .30 .75
CDP109 Austin Gomber .40 1.00
CDP110 Casey Soltis .30 .75
CDP111 Troy Stokes .30 .75
CDP112 Nick Torres .30 .75
CDP113 Jeremy Rhoades .30 .75
CDP114 Jordan Montgomery .60 1.50
CDP115 Gavin LaValley .30 .75
CDP116 Brett Martin .30 .75
CDP117 Sam Hentges .30 .75
CDP118 Taylor Gushue .30 .75
CDP119 Jordan Schwartz .30 .75
CDP120 Justin Steele .30 .75
CDP121 Jake Reed .30 .75
CDP122 Rhys Hoskins 3.00 8.00
CDP123 Kevin Padlo .30 .75
CDP124 Lane Thomas .50 1.25
CDP125 Dustin DeMuth .30 .75
CDP126 Nick Gordon .40 1.00
CDP127 Auston Bousfield .30 .75
CDP128 Jordan Foley .30 .75
CDP129 Corey Ray .30 .75
CDP130 Jared Walker .30 .75
CDP131 Tejay Antone .30 .75
CDP132 Shane Zeile .30 .75

2014 Bowman Chrome Draft Black Refractors

*BLACK REF: 3X TO 8X BASIC
STATED ODDS 1:116 HOBBY
STATED PRINT RUN 75 SER.#'d SETS

2014 Bowman Chrome Draft Blue Refractors

*BLUE REF: 2X TO 5X BASIC
STATED ODDS 1:37 HOBBY
STATED PRINT RUN 399 SER.#'d SETS

2014 Bowman Chrome Draft Blue Wave Refractors

*BLUE WAVE: 2X TO 5X BASIC
STATED ODDS 1:524 HOBBY

2014 Bowman Chrome Draft Gold Refractors

*GOLD REF: 6X TO 15X BASIC
STATED ODDS 1:418 HOBBY
STATED PRINT RUN 50 SER.#'d SETS
CDP2 Kyle Schwarber 50.00 100.00
CDP7 Michael Conforto 50.00 100.00

2014 Bowman Chrome Draft Green Refractors

*GREEN REF: 2.5X TO 6X BASIC
STATED ODDS 1:133 HOBBY
STATED PRINT RUN 150 SER.#'d SETS

2014 Bowman Chrome Draft Orange Refractors

*ORANGE REF: 8X TO 20X BASIC
STATED ODDS 1:834 HOBBY
STATED PRINT RUN 25 SER.#'d SETS
CDP2 Kyle Schwarber 50.00 120.00
CDP7 Michael Conforto 50.00 120.00

2014 Bowman Chrome Draft Purple Ice Refractors

*PURPLE ICE: X TO X BASIC
RANDOM INSERTS IN PACKS
STATED PRINT RUN 99 SER.#'d SETS

2014 Bowman Chrome Draft Red Ice Refractors

*RED ICE: X TO X BASIC
RANDOM INSERTS IN PACKS
STATED PRINT RUN 150 SER.#'d SETS

2014 Bowman Chrome Draft Red Wave Refractors

*RED WAVE REF: 8X TO 20X BASIC
RANDOM INSERTS IN PACKS
STATED PRINT RUN 25 SER.#'d SETS
CDP2 Kyle Schwarber 50.00 120.00
CDP7 Michael Conforto 50.00 120.00

2014 Bowman Chrome Draft Refractors

*REFRACTOR: .75X TO 2X BASIC
STATED ODDS 1:3 HOBBY
STATED MANZIEL ODDS 1:19,000 HOBBY
CDP31 Johnny Manziel 3.00 8.00

2014 Bowman Chrome Draft Silver Wave Refractors

*SILVER WAVE REF: 8X TO 20X BASIC
RANDOM INSERTS IN PACKS
STATED PRINT RUN 25 SER.#'d SETS
CDP2 Kyle Schwarber 50.00 120.00
CDP7 Michael Conforto 50.00 120.00

2014 Bowman Chrome Draft Draft Pick Autographs

STATED ODDS 1:37 HOBBY
STATED PLATE ODDS 1:16,300 HOBBY
PLATE PRINT RUN 1 SET PER COLOR
BLACK-CYAN-MAGENTA-YELLOW ISSUED
NO PLATE PRICING DUE TO SCARCITY
EXCHANGE DEADLINE 11/30/2017
BCAAB Alex Blandino 3.00 8.00
BCAAD Austin DeCarr 3.00 8.00
BCAAG Aramis Garcia 3.00 8.00
BCAAJ Alex Jackson 4.00 10.00
BCAAN Aaron Nola 20.00 50.00
BCAAR A.J. Reed 3.00 8.00
BCAAV Alex Verdugo 20.00 50.00
BCABAN Blake Anderson 3.00 8.00
BCABD Braxton Davidson 3.00 8.00
BCABGO Brian Gonzalez 3.00 8.00
BCABZ Bradley Zimmer 12.00 30.00
BCACE Chris Ellis 3.00 8.00
BCACJ Connor Joe 3.00 8.00
BCACS Carson Sands 3.00 8.00
BCACSO Chad Sobotka 3.00 8.00
BCACT Cole Tucker 3.00 8.00
BCACV Chase Vallot 3.00 8.00
BCACVA Cameron Varga 3.00 8.00
BCADC Dylan Cease 15.00 40.00
BCADF Derek Fisher 4.00 10.00
BCADH Derek Hill 3.00 8.00
BCAPDO Dillon Overton 3.00 8.00
BCAEF Erick Fedde 3.00 8.00
BCAFG Foster Griffin 3.00 8.00
BCAFW Forrest Wall 5.00 12.00
BCAGF Garrett Fulenchek 3.00 8.00
BCAGH Grant Holmes 3.00 8.00
BCAGHO Grant Hockin 3.00 8.00
BCAGM Gareth Morgan 3.00 8.00
BCAJB Jeff Brigham 3.00 8.00
BCAJF Jack Flaherty 30.00 80.00
BCAJG Jacob Gatewood 3.00 8.00
BCAJGA Joe Gatto 3.00 8.00
BCAJH Jeff Hoffman 5.00 12.00
BCAJL Jacob Lindgren 4.00 10.00
BCAJR Jakson Reetz 3.00 8.00
BCAJS Justus Sheffield 8.00 20.00

BCAJST Jake Stinnett 3.00 8.00
BCAJT Justin Twine 3.00 8.00
BCAKF Kyle Freeland 10.00 25.00
BCAKM Kodi Medeiros 3.00 8.00
BCAKS Kyle Schwarber 20.00 50.00
BCALO Luis Ortiz 3.00 8.00
BCALW Luke Weaver 3.00 8.00
BCAMCH Matt Chapman 30.00 80.00
BCAMG Michael Gettys 4.00 10.00
BCAMH Monte Harrison 6.00 15.00
BCAMI Matt Imhof 3.00 8.00
BCAMIC Michael Chavis 25.00 60.00
BCAMK Michael Kopech 30.00 80.00
BCAMP Max Pentecost 3.00 8.00
BCAMPA Mike Papi 3.00 8.00
BCAMW Marcus Wilson 3.00 8.00
BCANB Nick Burdi 3.00 8.00
BCANG Nick Gordon 4.00 10.00
BCANH Nick Howard 3.00 8.00
BCANW Nick Wells 3.00 8.00
BCAMC Conforto Issued in '15 BC 30.00 80.00
BCARC Ryan Castellani 3.00 8.00
BCARR Ryan Ripken 4.00 10.00
BCARW R.Williams Issued in '15 BC 3.00 8.00
BCASA Spencer Adams 4.00 10.00
BCASB Scott Blewett 3.00 8.00
BCASN Sean Newcomb 5.00 12.00
BCASRF Sean Reid-Foley 3.00 8.00
BCATB Tyler Beede 5.00 12.00
BCATF Ti'Quan Forbes 3.00 8.00
BCATK Tyler Kolek 3.00 8.00
BCATS Taylor Sparks 3.00 8.00
BCATSU Trey Supak 3.00 8.00
BCATT Trea Turner 40.00 100.00
BCAZL Zech Lemond 3.00 8.00

2014 Bowman Chrome Draft Draft Pick Autographs Black Refractors

*BLACK REF: 2X TO 5X BASIC
STATED ODDS 1:781 HOBBY
STATED PRINT RUN 35 SER.#'d SETS
EXCHANGE DEADLINE 11/30/2017
BCABD Braxton Davidson 60.00 150.00

2014 Bowman Chrome Draft Draft Pick Autographs Blue Refractors

*BLUE REF: 1.2X TO 3X BASIC
STATED ODDS 1:436 HOBBY
STATED PRINT RUN 150 SER.#'d SETS
EXCHANGE DEADLINE 11/30/2017

2014 Bowman Chrome Draft Draft Pick Autographs Gold Refractors

*GOLD REF: 1.2X TO 3X BASIC
STATED ODDS 1:1310 HOBBY
STATED PRINT RUN 50 SER.#'d SETS
EXCHANGE DEADLINE 11/30/2017
BCABD Braxton Davidson 60.00 150.00

2014 Bowman Chrome Draft Draft Pick Autographs Green Refractors

*GREEN REF: 1X TO 2.5X BASIC
STATED ODDS 1:664 HOBBY
STATED PRINT RUN 99 SER.#'d SETS
EXCHANGE DEADLINE 11/30/2017

2014 Bowman Chrome Draft Draft Pick Autographs Refractors

*REF: .5X TO 1.2X BASIC
STATED ODDS 1:131 HOBBY
EXCHANGE DEADLINE 11/30/2017
BCAJM Johnny Manziel 15.00 40.00

2014 Bowman Chrome Draft Future of the Franchise Mini

STATED ODDS 1:12 HOBBY
*BLUE/99: 1X TO 2.5X BASIC
FFAJ Alex Jackson .50 1.25
FFBS Braden Shipley .40 1.00
FFBSW Blake Swihart .50 1.25
FFCC Carlos Correa 2.00 5.00
FFCCO Clint Coulter .40 1.00
FFCE C.J. Edwards .50 1.25
FFCF Clint Frazier 1.50 4.00
FFCG Casey Gillaspie .60 1.50
FFDD David Dahl .50 1.25
FFDH Derek Hill .40 1.00
FFDR Daniel Robertson .50 1.25
FFDS Dominic Smith .40 1.00
FFHH Hunter Harvey .40 1.00
FFHR Hunter Renfroe .50 1.25
FFJA Jorge Alfaro .50 1.25
FFJC J.P. Crawford .40 1.00
FFJH Jeff Hoffman .60 1.50
FFJU Julio Urias 2.00 5.00
FFJW Jesse Winker 1.50 4.00
FFKZ Kyle Zimmer .40 1.00
FFLG Lucas Giolito .60 1.50
FFLS Lucas Sims .40 1.00
FFLSE Luis Severino .60 1.50
FFMS Miguel Sano .50 1.25
FFRK Rob Kaminsky .40 1.00
FFSN Sean Newcomb .60 1.50
FFTA Tim Anderson .75 2.00
FFTB Tyler Beede .60 1.50
FFTG Tyler Glasnow 1.50 4.00
FFTK Tyler Kolek .40 1.00

2014 Bowman Chrome Draft Scouts Breakout Die-Cut Refractors

STATED ODDS 1:96 HOBBY
*X-FRACTOR/99: .5X TO 1.2X BASIC
BSBAB Aaron Blair .75 2.00
BSBAJ Aaron Judge 12.00 30.00
BSBAR Alex Reyes 1.25 3.00
BSBBJ Brian Johnson .75 2.00
BSBBL Ben Lively .75 2.00
BSBBP Brett Phillips 1.00 2.50
BSBCP Chad Pinder .75 2.00
BSBCS Chance Sisco 1.50 4.00
BSBCW Chad Wallach 1.25 3.00
BSBDR Daniel Robertson 1.00 2.50
BSBES Edmundo Sosa .75 2.00
BSBFM Francellis Montas .75 2.00
BSBGG Gabriel Guerrero .75 2.00
BSBJB Jake Bauers 1.25 3.00
BSBJD Jose De Leon 1.25 3.00
BSBJH Jabari Henry 1.50 4.00
BSBJJ JaCoby Jones 1.25 3.00
BSBJL Jordy Lara .75 2.00
BSBJP Jose Peraza .75 2.00
BSBJW Justin Williams 1.00 2.50
BSBKW Kyle Waldrop .75 2.00
BSBKZ Kevin Ziomek .75 2.00
BSBLS Luis Severino 1.25 3.00
BSBLW LeVon Washington .75 2.00
BSBMM Marcos Molina 1.00 2.50
BSBMO Matt Olson 4.00 10.00
BSBNL Nick Longhi 1.25 3.00
BSBNM Nomar Mazara 2.00 5.00
BSBRM Ryan McMahon 1.25 3.00
BSBRN Renato Nunez 1.50 4.00
BSBSC Sean Coyle .75 2.00
BSBSM Steven Matz 1.00 2.50
BSBTD Tyler Danish .75 2.00
BSBTG Tayron Guerrero .75 2.00
BSBWL Will Locante .75 2.00

2014 Bowman Chrome Draft Scouts Breakout Die-Cut Autographs

STATED ODDS 1:4640 HOBBY
STATED PRINT RUN 99 SER.#'d SETS
EXCHANGE DEADLINE 11/30/2017
BSAAR Alex Reyes 20.00 50.00
BSAES Edmundo Sosa 12.00 30.00
BSAKW Kyle Waldrop 6.00 15.00
BSALS Luis Severino 40.00 100.00
BSALW LeVon Washington 6.00 15.00
BSAMO Matt Olson 15.00 40.00
BSANL Nick Longhi 10.00 25.00
BSATD Tyler Danish 6.00 15.00
BSATG Tayron Guerrero EXCH 6.00 15.00

2014 Bowman Chrome Draft Top Prospects

STATED PLATE ODDS 1:5200 HOBBY
PLATE PRINT RUN 1 SET PER COLOR
BLACK-CYAN-MAGENTA-YELLOW ISSUED
NO PLATE PRICING DUE TO SCARCITY
CTP1 Kohl Stewart .30 .75
CTP2 Miguel Sano .40 1.00
CTP3 Carlos Correa 1.50 4.00
CTP4 Mark Appel .40 1.00
CTP5 Jameson Taillon .40 1.00
CTP6 Raul Mondesi .50 1.25
CTP7 Jorge Alfaro .40 1.00
CTP8 Max Fried 1.25 3.00
CTP9 Lucas Giolito .50 1.25
CTP10 Austin Meadows .75 2.00
CTP11 Clint Frazier 1.25 3.00
CTP12 Colin Moran .30 .75
CTP13 Lucas Sims .30 .75
CTP14 Julio Urias 1.50 4.00
CTP15 David Dahl .40 1.00
CTP16 Josh Bell .60 1.50
CTP17 Braden Shipley .30 .75
CTP18 D.J. Peterson .30 .75
CTP19 Jose Berrios .50 1.25
CTP20 Trey Ball .30 .75
CTP21 Rosell Herrera .50 1.25
CTP22 J.P. Crawford .30 .75
CTP23 Reese McGuire .30 .75
CTP24 Phil Ervin .30 .75
CTP25 Jesse Winker 1.25 3.00
CTP26 Dominic Smith .30 .75
CTP27 Hunter Harvey .30 .75
CTP28 Vincent Velasquez .50 1.25
CTP29 Gabriel Guerrero .30 .75
CTP30 Brandon Nimmo .50 1.25
CTP31 Jose Peraza .30 .75
CTP32 Hunter Renfroe .40 1.00
CTP33 Eloy Jimenez 4.00 10.00
CTP34 Alen Hanson .30 .75
CTP35 Albert Almora .50 1.25
CTP36 Lance McCullers .30 .75
CTP37 Rafael Devers 3.00 8.00
CTP38 Luis Severino .50 1.25
CTP39 Aaron Judge 5.00 12.00
CTP40 Peter O'Brien .40 1.00
CTP41 Corey Seager 1.50 4.00
CTP42 Aaron Blair .30 .75
CTP43 Ben Lively .30 .75
CTP44 Daniel Robertson .40 1.00
CTP45 Josh Hader .60 1.50
CTP46 Hunter Dozier .30 .75
CTP47 Tim Anderson .60 1.50
CTP48 Tyler Danish .30 .75
CTP49 Alex Gonzalez .50 1.25
CTP50 JaCoby Jones .50 1.25
CTP51 Eric Jagielo .30 .75
CTP52 Rob Kaminsky .30 .75
CTP53 Lewis Brinson .50 1.25
CTP54 Travis Demeritte .40 1.00
CTP55 Luis Torrens .30 .75
CTP56 Ian Clarkin .30 .75
CTP57 Josh Hart .30 .75
CTP58 Michael Lorenzen .30 .75
CTP59 Robert Stephenson .30 .75
CTP60 Ryan McMahon .50 1.25
CTP61 Tyler Glasnow 1.25 3.00
CTP62 Kris Bryant 3.00 8.00
CTP63 Kyle Crick .30 .75
CTP64 Mason Williams .30 .75
CTP65 Christian Binford .30 .75
CTP66 Jake Thompson .30 .75
CTP67 Sean Coyle .30 .75
CTP68 James Ramsey .30 .75
CTP69 Byron Buxton 1.50 4.00
CTP70 Nick Williams .40 1.00
CTP71 Miguel Almonte .30 .75
CTP72 C.J. Edwards .40 1.00
CTP73 Delino DeShields .30 .75
CTP74 Trevor Story 1.50 4.00
CTP75 Raimel Tapia .40 1.00
CTP76 Michael Feliz .40 1.00
CTP77 Brandon Drury .30 .75
CTP78 Franklin Barreto .50 1.25
CTP79 Chris Stratton .30 .75
CTP80 Joey Gallo .60 1.50
CTP81 Christian Arroyo 2.00 5.00
CTP82 Mac Williamson .40 1.00
CTP83 Clayton Blackburn .50 1.25
CTP84 Blake Swihart .40 1.00
CTP85 Gosuke Katoh .50 1.25
CTP86 Roberto Osuna .30 .75
CTP87 Courtney Hawkins .30 .75
CTP88 Tyler Naquin .50 1.25
CTP89 Devon Travis .30 .75
CTP90 Nomar Mazara .75 2.00

2014 Bowman Chrome Draft Top Prospects Black Refractors

*BLACK REF: 2.5X TO 6X BASIC
STATED ODDS 1:116 HOBBY
STATED PRINT RUN 75 SER.#'d SETS
CTP39 Aaron Judge 50.00 120.00

2014 Bowman Chrome Draft Top Prospects Blue Refractors

*BLUE REF: 1.5X TO 4X BASIC
STATED ODDS 1:37 HOBBY
STATED PRINT RUN 399 SER.#'d SETS
CTP39 Aaron Judge 30.00 80.00

2014 Bowman Chrome Draft Top Prospects Blue Wave Refractors

*BLUE WAVE: 1.5X TO 4X BASIC
STATED ODDS 1:524 HOBBY
CTP39 Aaron Judge 30.00 80.00

2014 Bowman Chrome Draft Top Prospects Gold Refractors

*GOLD REF: 5X TO 12X BASIC
STATED ODDS 1:418 HOBBY
STATED PRINT RUN 50 SER.#'d SETS
CTP39 Aaron Judge 100.00 250.00

2014 Bowman Chrome Draft Top Prospects Green Refractors

*GREEN REF: 2X TO 5X BASIC
STATED ODDS 1:133 HOBBY
STATED PRINT RUN 150 SER.#'d SETS
CTP39 Aaron Judge 40.00 100.00

2014 Bowman Chrome Draft Top Prospects Orange Refractors

*ORANGE REF: 6X TO 15X BASIC
STATED ODDS 1:834 HOBBY
STATED PRINT RUN 25 SER.#'d SETS
CTP39 Aaron Judge 125.00 300.00

2014 Bowman Chrome Draft Top Prospects Purple Ice Refractors

*PURPLE ICE: X TO X BASIC
RANDOM INSERTS IN PACKS
STATED PRINT RUN 99 SER.#'d SETS

2014 Bowman Chrome Draft Top Prospects Red Ice Refractors

*RED ICE: X TO X BASIC
RANDOM INSERTS IN PACKS
STATED PRINT RUN 150 SER.#'d SETS

2014 Bowman Chrome Draft Top Prospects Red Wave Refractors

*RED WAVE REF: 6X TO 15X BASIC
RANDOM INSERTS IN PACKS
STATED PRINT RUN 25 SER.#'d SETS
CTP39 Aaron Judge 125.00 300.00

2014 Bowman Chrome Draft Top Prospects Refractors

*REFRACTOR: .6X TO 1.5X BASIC
STATED ODDS 1:3 HOBBY

2014 Bowman Chrome Draft Top Prospects Silver Wave Refractors

*SILVER WAVE REF: 6X TO 15X BASIC
RANDOM INSERTS IN PACKS
STATED PRINT RUN 25 SER.#'d SETS
CTP39 Aaron Judge 125.00 300.00

2015 Bowman Chrome

COMPLETE SET (200) 25.00 60.00
STATED PLATE ODDS 1:5068 HOBBY
PLATE PRINT RUN 1 SET PER COLOR
BLACK-CYAN-MAGENTA-YELLOW ISSUED
NO PLATE PRICING DUE TO SCARCITY
1 Miguel Cabrera .30 .75
2 Michael Brantley .25 .60
3 Yasmani Grandal .20 .50
4 Byron Buxton RC 2.00 5.00
5 Daniel Murphy .25 .60
6 Clay Buchholz .20 .50
7 James Loney .20 .50
8 Dee Gordon .20 .50
9 Khris Davis .30 .75
10 Trevor Rosenthal .25 .60
11 Jered Weaver .25 .60
12 Lucas Duda .25 .60
13 James Shields .20 .50
14 Jacob Lindgren RC .50 1.25
15 Michael Bourn .20 .50
16 Yunel Escobar .20 .50
17 George Springer .25 .60
18 Ryan Howard .25 .60
19 Justin Upton .25 .60
20 Zach Britton .25 .60
21 Santiago Casilla .20 .50
22 Max Scherzer .30 .75
23 Carlos Carrasco .20 .50
24 Angel Pagan .20 .50
25 Wade Miley .20 .50
26 Ryan Braun .25 .60
27 Carlos Gonzalez .25 .60
28 Chase Utley .25 .60
29 Brandon Moss .20 .50
30 Juan Lagares .20 .50
31 David Robertson .25 .60
32 Carlos Santana .25 .60
33 Ender Inciarte RC .40 1.00
34 Jimmy Rollins .25 .60
35 J.D. Martinez .30 .75
36 Yadier Molina .40 1.00
37 Ryan Zimmerman .25 .60
38 Stephen Strasburg .30 .75
39 Torii Hunter .20 .50
40 Anibal Sanchez .20 .50
41 Michael Cuddyer .20 .50
42 Jorge De La Rosa .20 .50
43 Shane Greene .20 .50
44 John Lackey .25 .60
45 Hyun-Jin Ryu .25 .60
46 Lance Lynn .20 .50
47 David Freese .20 .50
48 Russell Martin .20 .50
49 Jose Iglesias .25 .60
50 Pablo Sandoval .25 .60
51 Will Middlebrooks .20 .50
52 Joe Mauer .25 .60
53 Chris Archer .20 .50
54 Starling Marte .25 .60
55 Jason Heyward .25 .60
56 Taijuan Walker .20 .50
57 Pedro Alvarez .20 .50
58 Jose Fernandez .30 .75
59 Marlon Byrd .20 .50
60 Neil Walker .20 .50
61 Mike Moustakas .25 .60
62 Trevor Bauer .40 1.00
63 Steven Souza Jr. .25 .60
64 Michael Saunders .25 .60
65 Andrew Miller .25 .60
66 Melky Cabrera .20 .50
67 Denard Span .20 .50
68 Yovani Gallardo .20 .50
69 Wade Davis .20 .50
70 Nelson Cruz .30 .75
71 Chris Carter .20 .50
72 Alex Avila .25 .60
73 Mark Melancon .20 .50
74 Zack Cozart .20 .50
75 Jeff Samardzija .20 .50
76 Jake Marisnick .20 .50
77 Kolten Wong .25 .60
78 Josh Collmenter .20 .50
79 Alex Rios .25 .60
80 Dustin Ackley .20 .50
81 Felix Hernandez .25 .60
82 Curtis Granderson .25 .60
83 Jean Segura .25 .60
84 Adam LaRoche .20 .50
85 Hunter Pence .25 .60
86 Francisco Liriano .20 .50
87 Josh Donaldson .25 .60
88 Kendrys Morales .20 .50
89 Francisco Lindor RC 10.00 25.00
90 Freddie Freeman .40 1.00
91 Rick Porcello .25 .60
92 Tyson Ross .20 .50
93 Billy Butler .20 .50
94 Scott Kazmir .20 .50
95 Martin Prado .20 .50
96 Pat Neshek .20 .50
97 Travis Wood .20 .50
98 Brandon Phillips .20 .50
99 Jayson Werth .25 .60
100 Buster Posey .40 1.00
101 Norichika Aoki .20 .50
102 Prince Fielder .25 .60
103 Brett Lawrie .25 .60
104 Cole Hamels .25 .60
105 Jon Lester .25 .60
106 Aaron Hill .20 .50
107 Wei-Yin Chen .20 .50
108 Joe Panik .25 .60
109 DJ LeMahieu .30 .75
110 Carlos Correa RC 4.00 10.00
111 Robinson Cano .25 .60
112 Neftali Feliz .20 .50
113 Adam Jones .25 .60
114 Asdrubal Cabrera .25 .60
115 Wil Myers .25 .60
116 Matt Kemp .25 .60
117 Fernando Rodney .20 .50
118 Addison Reed .20 .50
119 Aroldis Chapman .30 .75
120 Brian Dozier .25 .60
121 Edinson Volquez .20 .50
122 Chris Tillman .20 .50
123 Huston Street .20 .50
124 Todd Frazier .20 .50
125 Miguel Montero .20 .50
126 Francisco Rodriguez .25 .60
127 Avisail Garcia .25 .60
128 Yoenis Cespedes .25 .60
129 Nick Swisher .25 .60
130 Jason Grilli .20 .50
131 Giancarlo Stanton .30 .75
132 Yordano Ventura .25 .60
133 Jordan Zimmermann .25 .60
134 Stephen Vogt .25 .60
135 Anthony DeSclafani .20 .50
136 Dustin Pedroia .30 .75
137 Steve Pearce .30 .75
138 Koji Uehara .20 .50
139 Mitch Moreland .20 .50
140 Albert Pujols .40 1.00
141 Jacoby Ellsbury .25 .60
142 Matt Adams .20 .50
143 Alex Wood .20 .50
144 Adrian Beltre .30 .75
145 Julio Teheran .25 .60
146 Nick Markakis .25 .60
147 Alexei Ramirez .25 .60
148 Salvador Perez .25 .60
149 Gerrit Cole .30 .75
150 Matt Harvey .25 .60
151 Gregory Polanco .25 .60
152 Glen Perkins .20 .50
153 Ichiro Suzuki .40 1.00
154 Dallas Keuchel .25 .60
155 Hanley Ramirez .25 .60
156 Alex Rodriguez .40 1.00
157 Brett Gardner .25 .60
158 Howie Kendrick .20 .50
159 Danny Santana .20 .50
160 Nolan Arenado .50 1.25
161 Addison Russell RC 1.25 3.00
162 Delino DeShields Jr. RC .40 1.00
163 Kevin Plawecki RC .40 1.00
164 Michael Lorenzen RC .40 1.00
165 Brandon Finnegan RC .40 1.00
166 A.J. Cole RC .40 1.00
167 Joc Pederson RC 1.50 4.00
168 Jake Lamb RC .60 1.50
169 Chi Chi Gonzalez RC .60 1.50
170 Keone Kela RC .50 1.25
171 Jorge Soler RC .60 1.50
172 Yasmany Tomas RC .50 1.25
173 Roberto Osuna RC .40 1.00
174 Rusney Castillo RC .50 1.25
175 Carlos Rodon RC 1.00 2.50
176 Eddie Rosario RC .75 2.00
177 Tim Cooney RC .40 1.00
178 Javier Baez RC 3.00 8.00
179 Dalton Pompey RC .50 1.25
180 Blake Swihart RC .50 1.25
181 Daniel Norris RC .40 1.00
182 Devon Travis RC .40 1.00
183 Raisel Iglesias RC .50 1.25
184 Preston Tucker RC .60 1.50
185 Joey Gallo RC .75 2.00
186 Miguel Castro RC .40 1.00
187 Michael Taylor RC .40 1.00
188 Austin Hedges RC .40 1.00
189 Jung Ho Kang RC .40 1.00
190 Archie Bradley RC .40 1.00
191 James McCann RC .60 1.50
192 Noah Syndergaard RC .75 2.00
193 Mark Canha RC .60 1.50
194 Paulo Orlando RC .60 1.50
195 Kendall Graveman RC .40 1.00
196 Eduardo Rodriguez RC .40 1.00
197 Anthony Ranaudo RC .40 1.00
198 Maikel Franco RC .50 1.25
199 Odubel Herrera RC .60 1.50
200 Kris Bryant RC 4.00 10.00

2015 Bowman Chrome Blue Refractors

*BLUE REF VET: 4X TO 10X BASIC
*BLUE REF RC: 2X TO 5X BASIC
STATED ODDS 1:68 HOBBY
STATED PRINT RUN 150 SER.#'d SETS
200 Kris Bryant 25.00 60.00

2015 Bowman Chrome Gold Refractors

*GOLD REF VET: 8X TO 20X BASIC
*GOLD REF RC: 4X TO 10X BASIC
STATED ODDS 1:204 HOBBY
STATED PRINT RUN 50 SER.#'d SETS
4 Byron Buxton 10.00 25.00
108 Joe Panik 8.00 20.00
110 Carlos Correa 75.00 200.00
153 Ichiro Suzuki 10.00 25.00
189 Jung Ho Kang 25.00 60.00
200 Kris Bryant 75.00 200.00

2015 Bowman Chrome Green Refractors

*GREEN REF VET: 6X TO 15X BASIC
*GREEN REF RC: 3X TO 8X BASIC
STATED ODDS 1:103 HOBBY
STATED PRINT RUN 99 SER.#'d SETS
4 Byron Buxton 8.00 20.00
110 Carlos Correa 40.00 100.00
200 Kris Bryant 30.00 80.00

2015 Bowman Chrome Orange Refractors

*ORANGE REF VET: 8X TO 20X BASIC
*ORANGE REF RC: 4X TO 10X BASIC
STATED ODDS 1:151 HOBBY
STATED PRINT RUN 25 SER.#'d SETS
4 Byron Buxton 12.00 30.00
108 Joe Panik 10.00 25.00
110 Carlos Correa 100.00 250.00
189 Jung Ho Kang 30.00 80.00
200 Kris Bryant 100.00 250.00

2015 Bowman Chrome Purple Refractors

*PURPLE REF VET: 3X TO 8X BASIC
*PURPLE REF RC: 1.5X TO 4X BASIC
STATED ODDS 1:41 HOBBY
STATED PRINT RUN 250 SER.#'d SETS
200 Kris Bryant 15.00 40.00

2015 Bowman Chrome Refractors

*REF VET: 2X TO 5X BASIC
*REF RC: 1X TO 2.5X BASIC
STATED ODDS 1:21 HOBBY
STATED PRINT RUN 499 SER.#'d SETS
4 Byron Buxton 3.00 8.00
108 Joe Panik 2.50 6.00
110 Carlos Correa 15.00 40.00
200 Kris Bryant 12.00 30.00

2015 Bowman Chrome Bowman Scouts Top 100

COMPLETE SET (100) 75.00 150.00
STATED ODDS 1:8 HOBBY
*DIECUT/99: 2X TO 5X BASIC
BTP1 Byron Buxton 2.00 5.00
BTP2 Kris Bryant 4.00 10.00
BTP3 Carlos Correa 2.00 5.00
BTP4 Addison Russell 1.25 3.00
BTP5 Daniel Norris .40 1.00
BTP6 Jorge Soler .60 1.50
BTP7 Joey Gallo .75 2.00
BTP8 Miguel Sano .50 1.25
BTP9 Noah Syndergaard .75 2.00
BTP10 Lucas Giolito .75 2.00
BTP11 Julio Urias 1.25 3.00
BTP12 Francisco Lindor 3.00 8.00
BTP13 Carlos Rodon 1.00 2.50
BTP14 Tyler Glasnow 1.50 4.00
BTP15 Corey Seager 2.00 5.00
BTP16 J.P. Crawford .40 1.00
BTP17 Archie Bradley .40 1.00
BTP18 Kyle Schwarber 1.50 4.00
BTP19 Jon Gray .40 1.00
BTP20 Tyler Kolek .40 1.00
BTP21 Dylan Bundy .50 1.25
BTP22 Alex Jackson .50 1.25
BTP23 Luis Severino .50 1.25
BTP24 Hunter Harvey .40 1.00
BTP25 Henry Owens .40 1.00
BTP26 Nick Gordon .50 1.25
BTP27 Braden Shipley .40 1.00
BTP28 Jameson Taillon .50 1.25
BTP29 Michael Conforto .50 1.25
BTP30 Robert Stephenson .40 1.00
BTP31 Kyle Zimmer .40 1.00
BTP32 Blake Swihart .50 1.25
BTP33 Joc Pederson 1.50 4.00
BTP34 Andrew Heaney .40 1.00
BTP35 Jose Peraza .40 1.00
BTP36 Josh Bell .75 2.00
BTP37 Aaron Nola .60 1.50
BTP38 Dalton Pompey .50 1.25
BTP39 Raul Mondesi .60 1.50
BTP40 Austin Meadows 1.00 2.50
BTP41 Kevin Plawecki .40 1.00
BTP42 Jeff Hoffman .50 1.25
BTP43 Michael Taylor .40 1.00
BTP44 Mark Appel .40 1.00
BTP45 Rusney Castillo .50 1.25
BTP46 Brandon Finnegan .40 1.00
BTP47 Marco Gonzales .60 1.50
BTP48 Kohl Stewart .40 1.00
BTP49 Eduardo Rodriguez .40 1.00
BTP50 C.J. Edwards .60 1.50
BTP51 Jose Berrios .60 1.50
BTP52 Austin Hedges .40 1.00
BTP53 Aaron Judge 8.00 20.00
BTP54 D.J. Peterson .40 1.00
BTP55 Dilson Herrera .50 1.25
BTP56 Aaron Blair .40 1.00
BTP57 Clint Frazier 1.50 4.00
BTP58 Maikel Franco .50 1.25
BTP59 Trea Turner 1.25 3.00
BTP60 Manuel Margot .40 1.00
BTP61 Alex Reyes .50 1.25
BTP62 David Dahl .50 1.25
BTP63 Reynaldo Lopez .50 1.25
BTP64 Daniel Robertson .40 1.00
BTP65 Nick Kingham .40 1.00
BTP66 Aaron Sanchez .50 1.25
BTP67 Tim Anderson .75 2.00
BTP68 Eddie Butler .40 1.00
BTP69 Rafael Montero .40 1.00
BTP70 Jorge Alfaro .60 1.50
BTP71 Matt Olson 2.00 5.00
BTP72 Gary Sanchez 1.25 3.00
BTP73 Ozhaino Albies 4.00 10.00
BTP74 Garin Cecchini .40 1.00
BTP75 Mike Foltynewicz .40 1.00
BTP76 Grant Holmes .50 1.25
BTP77 Sean Manaea .40 1.00
BTP78 Touki Toussaint .50 1.25
BTP79 Tyrone Taylor .40 1.00
BTP80 Kyle Crick .50 1.25
BTP81 Max Pentecost .40 1.00
BTP82 Alex Meyer .40 1.00
BTP83 Steven Matz .50 1.25
BTP84 Franklin Barreto .50 1.25
BTP85 Casey Gillaspie .60 1.50
BTP86 Albert Almora .50 1.25
BTP87 Lucas Sims .40 1.00
BTP88 Willy Adames .60 1.50
BTP89 Derek Hill .50 1.25
BTP90 Tyler Beede .50 1.25
BTP91 Bradley Zimmer .60 1.50
BTP92 Stephen Piscotty .50 1.25
BTP93 Sean Newcomb .50 1.25
BTP94 Rafael Devers 2.50 6.00
BTP95 Kyle Freeland .50 1.25
BTP96 Robbie Ray .40 1.00
BTP97 Lance McCullers .40 1.00
BTP98 Matt Wisler .40 1.00
BTP99 Luis Ortiz .40 1.00
BTP100 Max Fried 1.50 4.00

2015 Bowman Chrome Bowman Scouts Top 100 Autographs Die Cut Orange

STATED ODDS 1:2424 HOBBY
STATED PRINT RUN 25 SER.#'d SETS
EXCHANGE DEADLINE 4/30/2018
BTP1 Byron Buxton 75.00 150.00
BTP2 Kris Bryant 300.00 500.00
BTP5 Daniel Norris 20.00 50.00
BTP6 Jorge Soler 75.00 150.00
BTP7 Joey Gallo EXCH 125.00 250.00
BTP9 Noah Syndergaard 40.00 100.00
BTP10 Lucas Giolito 40.00 100.00
BTP12 Francisco Lindor 40.00 100.00
BTP13 Carlos Rodon 100.00 200.00
BTP14 Tyler Glasnow 25.00 60.00
BTP16 J.P. Crawford 40.00 100.00
BTP17 Archie Bradley 25.00 60.00
BTP18 Kyle Schwarber 100.00 200.00
BTP21 Dylan Bundy 20.00 50.00
BTP22 Alex Jackson 12.00 30.00
BTP24 Hunter Harvey 25.00 60.00
BTP26 Nick Gordon 20.00 50.00
BTP28 Jameson Taillon 20.00 50.00
BTP32 Blake Swihart 30.00 80.00
BTP33 Joc Pederson 150.00 250.00
BTP36 Josh Bell 30.00 80.00
BTP42 Jeff Hoffman 12.00 30.00
BTP45 Rusney Castillo 12.00 30.00
BTP52 Austin Hedges 20.00 50.00
BTP53 Aaron Judge 75.00 200.00
BTP57 Clint Frazier 25.00 60.00
BTP59 Trea Turner 20.00 50.00
BTP61 Alex Reyes 20.00 50.00
BTP62 David Dahl 12.00 30.00
BTP65 Nick Kingham 10.00 25.00
BTP66 Aaron Sanchez 12.00 30.00
BTP72 Gary Sanchez 60.00 150.00
BTP76 Grant Holmes 25.00 60.00
BTP78 Touki Toussaint 25.00 60.00
BTP80 Kyle Crick 12.00 30.00
BTP81 Max Pentecost 30.00 80.00
BTP89 Derek Hill 30.00 80.00
BTP91 Bradley Zimmer 125.00 250.00
BTP93 Sean Newcomb 20.00 50.00
BTP94 Rafael Devers 125.00 300.00
BTP96 Robbie Ray 10.00 25.00
BTP97 Lance McCullers 20.00 50.00
BTP98 Matt Wisler 20.00 50.00

2015 Bowman Chrome Bowman Scouts Update

COMPLETE SET (25) 10.00 25.00
STATED ODDS 1:6 HOBBY
*DIECUT/99: 2X TO 5X BASIC
BSUAC A.J. Cole .40 1.00
BSUAG Alex Gonzalez .60 1.50
BSUAH Alen Hanson .40 1.00
BSUAR Amed Rosario .60 1.50
BSUBN Brandon Nimmo .60 1.50
BSUCM Colin Moran .40 1.00
BSUDS Dominic Smith .40 1.00
BSUEF Erick Fedde .40 1.00
BSUFW Forrest Wall .40 1.00
BSUGB Greg Bird .50 1.25
BSUHD Hunter Dozier .40 1.00
BSUHR Hunter Renfroe .60 1.50
BSUJW Jesse Winker 1.50 4.00
BSULJ Luke Jackson .40 1.00
BSUMF Michael Feliz .40 1.00
BSUMH Monte Harrison .60 1.50
BSUNM Nomar Mazara .60 1.50
BSUNW Nick Williams .50 1.25
BSUOA Orlando Arcia .50 1.25
BSURK Rob Kaminsky .40 1.00
BSURM Reese McGuire .40 1.00
BSURR Rob Refsnyder .40 1.00
BSURT Raimel Tapia .60 1.50
BSUSA Spencer Adams .40 1.00
BSUYT Yasmany Tomas .50 1.25

2015 Bowman Chrome Bowman Scouts Update Die Cut Autographs

STATED ODDS 1:1276 HOBBY
EXCHANGE DEADLINE 8/31/2017
*ORANGE/25: .6X TO 1.5X BASIC
BSUAC A.J. Cole 4.00 10.00
BSUCM Colin Moran 4.00 10.00
BSUDS Dominic Smith 4.00 10.00
BSUEF Erick Fedde 4.00 10.00
BSUFW Forrest Wall 4.00 10.00
BSUMF Michael Feliz 4.00 10.00
BSURM Reese McGuire 4.00 10.00
BSUSA Spencer Adams 4.00 10.00

2015 Bowman Chrome Dual Autographs

STATED ODDS 1:8466 HOBBY
STATED PRINT RUN 25 SER.#'d SETS
EXCHANGE DEADLINE 8/31/2017
BDAAR Adames/Rondon 40.00 100.00
BDABS J.Baez/J.Soler 25.00 60.00
BDABSA B.Buxton/M.Sano 40.00 100.00
BDADG C.Gonzalez/D.Dahl 20.00 50.00
BDADN A.Sanchez/D.Norris 25.00 60.00
BDADS deGrom/Syndergaard 250.00 600.00
BDAGS Scherzer/Giolito EXCH 30.00 80.00
BDAJC R.Cano/A.Jackson 20.00 50.00
BDAKF T.Kolek/J.Fernandez 20.00 50.00
BDAOP Porcello/Owens EXCH 10.00 25.00
BDARA C.Rodon/J.Abreu 25.00 60.00
BDASJ Judge/Severino 125.00 250.00
BDATG Tomas/Goldschmidt 20.00 50.00

2015 Bowman Chrome Farm's Finest Minis

COMPLETE SET (150) 75.00 150.00
STATED ODDS 1:6 HOBBY
*PURPLE/250: .6X TO 1.5X BASIC
*BLUE/150: .75X TO 2X BASIC
*GREEN/99: 1X TO 2.5X BASIC
*GOLD/50: 1.5X TO 4X BASIC
*ORANGE/25: 3X TO 8X BASIC
FFMAB Archie Bradley .40 1.00
FFMABL Aaron Blair .40 1.00
FFMAC A.J. Cole .40 1.00
FFMADR Adrian Rondon .50 1.25
FFMAG Alex Gonzalez .60 1.50
FFMAH Andrew Heaney .40 1.00
FFMAHE Austin Hedges .40 1.00
FFMAJ Aaron Judge 6.00 15.00
FFMAJA Alex Jackson .50 1.25
FFMAK Austin Kubitza .40 1.00
FFMALB Alex Blandino .40 1.00
FFMAM Austin Meadows 1.00 2.50
FFMAN Aaron Nola .60 1.50
FFMAR Addison Russell 1.25 3.00
FFMARE Alex Reyes .50 1.25
FFMARO Avery Romero .40 1.00
FFMAS Aaron Sanchez .50 1.25
FFMAV Alex Verdugo .60 1.50
FFMAVE Andrew Velazquez .40 1.00
FFMAW Austin Wilson .40 1.00
FFMBB Byron Buxton 2.00 5.00
FFMBD Brandon Drury .40 1.00
FFMBDA Braxton Davidson .40 1.00
FFMBF Buck Farmer .40 1.00
FFMBFI Brandon Finnegan .40 1.00
FFMBL Ben Lively .40 1.00
FFMBN Brandon Nimmo .60 1.50
FFMBS Braden Shipley .40 1.00
FFMBSW Blake Swihart .50 1.25
FFMBZ Bradley Zimmer .60 1.50
FFMCA Christian Arroyo 1.25 3.00
FFMCB Christian Binford .40 1.00
FFMCBL Clayton Blackburn .60 1.50
FFMCC Carlos Correa 2.00 5.00
FFMCE C.J. Edwards .60 1.50
FFMCEL Chris Ellis .40 1.00
FFMCF Clint Frazier 1.50 4.00
FFMCG Casey Gillaspie .60 1.50
FFMCH Courtney Hawkins .40 1.00
FFMCM Colin Moran .40 1.00
FFMCR Carlos Rodon 1.00 2.50
FFMCS Chance Sisco .75 2.00
FFMCSE Corey Seager 2.00 5.00
FFMCW Christian Walker .75 2.00
FFMDA Dariel Alvarez .40 1.00
FFMDB Dylan Bundy .50 1.25
FFMDD David Dahl .50 1.25
FFMDH Derek Hill .50 1.25
FFMDN Daniel Norris .40 1.00
FFMDO Dillon Overton .40 1.00
FFMDP D.J. Peterson .40 1.00
FFMDPO Dalton Pompey .50 1.25
FFMDR Daniel Robertson .40 1.00
FFMEB Eddie Butler .40 1.00
FFMEF Erick Fedde .40 1.00
FFMEJ Eric Jagielo .40 1.00
FFMFB Franklin Barreto .50 1.25
FFMFL Francisco Lindor 3.00 8.00
FFMFM Francellis Montas .50 1.25
FFMGB Greg Bird .50 1.25

FFMGG Gabby Guerrero .40 1.00
FFMGH Grant Holmes .50 1.25
FFMGS Gary Sanchez 1.25 3.00
FFMHH Hunter Harvey .40 1.00
FFMHO Henry Owens .40 1.00
FFMHR Hunter Renfroe .60 1.50
FFMJA Jorge Alfaro .60 1.50
FFMJAG Jacob Gatewood .40 1.00
FFMJB Jose Berrios .60 1.50
FFMJBE Josh Bell .75 2.00
FFMJC J.P. Crawford .40 1.00
FFMJG Jon Gray .40 1.00
FFMJGA Joe Gatto .40 1.00
FFMJH Josh Hader .50 1.25
FFMJHO Jeff Hoffman .50 1.25
FFMJJ JaCoby Jones .50 1.25
FFMJN Justin Nicolino .40 1.00
FFMJOG Joey Gallo .75 2.00
FFMJOU Jose Urena .40 1.00
FFMJP Jose Peraza .40 1.00
FFMJPE Joc Pederson 1.50 4.00
FFMJR James Ramsey .40 1.00
FFMJRO Jose Rondon .40 1.00
FFMJS Jorge Soler .60 1.50
FFMJT Jameson Taillon .50 1.25
FFMJU Julio Urias 1.25 3.00
FFMJW Jesse Winker 1.50 4.00
FFMJWI Justin Williams .40 1.00
FFMKB Kris Bryant 4.00 10.00
FFMKC Kyle Crick .50 1.25
FFMKF Kyle Freeland .50 1.25
FFMKM Kodi Medeiros .40 1.00
FFMKME Keury Mella .40 1.00
FFMKP Kevin Plawecki .40 1.00
FFMKS Kyle Schwarber 1.50 4.00
FFMKST Kohl Stewart .40 1.00
FFMKZ Kevin Ziomek .40 1.00
FFMKZI Kyle Zimmer .40 1.00
FFMLG Lucas Giolito .75 2.00
FFMLO Luis Ortiz .40 1.00
FFMLS Lucas Sims .40 1.00
FFMLSE Luis Severino .50 1.25
FFMMA Mark Appel .40 1.00
FFMMC Michael Conforto .50 1.25
FFMMF Max Fried 1.50 4.00
FFMMFO Mike Foltynewicz .40 1.00
FFMMFR Maikel Franco .50 1.25
FFMMG Marco Gonzales .60 1.50
FFMMH Monte Harrison .60 1.50
FFMMJ Micah Johnson .40 1.00
FFMML Michael Lorenzen .40 1.00
FFMMM Manuel Margot .40 1.00
FFMMO Matt Olson 2.00 5.00
FFMMP Max Pentecost .40 1.00
FFMMS Miguel Sano .50 1.25
FFMMT Michael Taylor .40 1.00
FFMMW Matt Wisler .40 1.00
FFMNG Nick Gordon .50 1.25
FFMNM Nomar Mazara .60 1.50
FFMNS Noah Syndergaard .75 2.00
FFMNT Nick Tropeano .40 1.00
FFMOA Ozhaino Albies 4.00 10.00
FFMOAR Orlando Arcia .50 1.25
FFMPE Phil Ervin .40 1.00
FFMPK Patrick Kivlehan .40 1.00
FFMRC Rusney Castillo .50 1.25
FFMRD Rafael Devers 2.50 6.00
FFMRK Rob Kaminsky .40 1.00
FFMRL Reynaldo Lopez .50 1.25
FFMRM Raul Mondesi .60 1.50
FFMRN Renato Nunez .75 2.00
FFMRQ Roman Quinn .60 1.50
FFMRS Robert Stephenson .40 1.00
FFMRT Raimel Tapia .60 1.50
FFMSM Steven Moya .50 1.25
FFMSMA Sean Manaea .40 1.00
FFMSN Sean Newcomb .50 1.25
FFMSP Stephen Piscotty .50 1.25
FFMSTM Steven Matz .50 1.25
FFMTA Tim Anderson .75 2.00
FFMTB Tyler Beede .50 1.25
FFMTC Tim Cooney .40 1.00
FFMTG Tyler Glasnow 1.50 4.00
FFMTK Tyler Kolek .40 1.00
FFMTN Tyler Naquin .60 1.50
FFMTT Touki Toussaint .50 1.25
FFMTTA Tyrone Taylor .40 1.00
FFMTTU Trea Turner 1.25 3.00
FFMTW Trevor Williams .40 1.00
FFMWA Willy Adames .60 1.50

2015 Bowman Chrome Farm's Finest Minis Autographs

STATED ODDS 1:775 HOBBY
EXCHANGE DEADLINE 4/30/2018
*GOLD/50: .6X TO 1.5X BASIC
*ORANGE/25: .75X TO 2X BASIC
FFMAB Archie Bradley 4.00 10.00
FFMABL Aaron Blair 4.00 10.00
FFMAJ Aaron Judge 60.00 150.00
FFMAJA Alex Jackson 5.00 12.00
FFMAM Austin Meadows 10.00 25.00
FFMARE Alex Reyes 8.00 20.00
FFMARO Avery Romero 4.00 10.00
FFMAS Aaron Sanchez 5.00 12.00
FFMBF Buck Farmer 4.00 10.00
FFMBS Braden Shipley 4.00 10.00
FFMBSW Blake Swihart 5.00 12.00
FFMCE C.J. Edwards 6.00 15.00
FFMCF Clint Frazier 8.00 20.00
FFMCR Carlos Rodon 10.00 25.00
FFMDB Dylan Bundy 5.00 12.00
FFMDD David Dahl 10.00 25.00
FFMDH Derek Hill 5.00 12.00
FFMDP D.J. Peterson 4.00 10.00
FFMFL Francisco Lindor 8.00 20.00
FFMGH Grant Holmes 5.00 12.00
FFMGS Gary Sanchez 30.00 80.00
FFMHH Hunter Harvey 6.00 15.00
FFMHO Henry Owens EXCH 4.00 10.00
FFMJA Jorge Alfaro 6.00 15.00
FFMJC J.P. Crawford EXCH 4.00 10.00
FFMJHO Jeff Hoffman 5.00 12.00
FFMJN Justin Nicolino 4.00 10.00
FFMJP Jose Peraza 6.00 15.00
FFMJS Jorge Soler 15.00 40.00
FFMKB Kris Bryant 60.00 150.00
FFMKF Kyle Freeland 5.00 12.00
FFMKS Kyle Schwarber 15.00 40.00
FFMKST Kohl Stewart 4.00 10.00
FFMLG Lucas Giolito 12.00 30.00
FFMLSE Luis Severino 20.00 50.00
FFMMC Michael Conforto 25.00 60.00
FFMMF Max Fried 6.00 15.00
FFMMJ Micah Johnson 4.00 10.00
FFMMO Matt Olson 12.00 30.00
FFMMS Miguel Sano 8.00 20.00
FFMMT Michael Taylor 4.00 10.00
FFMNG Nick Gordon 12.00 30.00
FFMNS Noah Syndergaard 25.00 60.00
FFMRC Rusney Castillo 5.00 12.00
FFMRD Rafael Devers 50.00 120.00
FFMRS Robert Stephenson 10.00 25.00
FFMSM Steven Moya 5.00 12.00
FFMSN Sean Newcomb 5.00 12.00
FFMTB Tyler Beede 5.00 12.00
FFMTG Tyler Glasnow 10.00 25.00
FFMTK Tyler Kolek 8.00 20.00
FFMTT Touki Toussaint 5.00 12.00
FFMTTU Trea Turner 15.00 40.00

2015 Bowman Chrome Farm's Finest Minis Autographs Gold Refractors

*GOLD REF: .6X TO 1.5X BASIC
RANDOM INSERTS IN PACKS
STATED PRINT RUN 50 SER.#'d SETS
EXCHANGE DEADLINE 4/30/2018

2015 Bowman Chrome Farm's Finest Minis Autographs Orange Refractors

*ORANGE REF: .75X TO 2X BASIC
STATED ODDS 1:727 HOBBY
STATED PRINT RUN 25 SER.#'d SETS
EXCHANGE DEADLINE 4/30/2018

2015 Bowman Chrome Lucky Redemption Autographs

EXCH 1 ODDS 1:38,390 HOBBY
EXCH 2 ODDS 1:38,390 HOBBY
EXCH 3 ODDS 1:38,390 HOBBY
EXCH 4 ODDS 1:38,390 HOBBY
EXCH 5 ODDS 1:38,390 HOBBY
EXCHANGE DEADLINE 4/30/2018
1 Kyle Schwarber EXCH 150.00 250.00
LRKS Kyle Schwarber 150.00 250.00

2015 Bowman Chrome Prime Position Autographs

STATED ODDS 1:581 HOBBY
EXCHANGE DEADLINE 8/31/2017
*GREEN: .75X TO 2X BASIC
*GOLD/50: 1X TO 2.5X BASIC
*ORANGE/25: 1.2X TO 3X BASIC
PPAAJ Alex Jackson 4.00 10.00
PPAAM Austin Meadows 5.00 12.00
PPABB Byron Buxton 8.00 20.00
PPABS Blake Swihart 4.00 10.00
PPACF Clint Frazier 15.00 40.00
PPADP D.J. Peterson 3.00 8.00
PPADS Dominic Smith 3.00 8.00
PPAFL Francisco Lindor 15.00 40.00
PPAKS Kyle Schwarber 20.00 50.00
PPALG Lucas Giolito 6.00 15.00
PPAMO Matt Olson 8.00 20.00
PPARS Robert Stephenson 3.00 8.00
PPATG Tyler Glasnow 8.00 20.00

2015 Bowman Chrome Prospect Autographs

BOW.STATED ODDS 1:86 HOBBY
BOW.CHR.ODDS 1:13 HOBBY
BOW.PLATE ODDS 1:16,064 HOBBY
BOW.CHR.PLATE ODDS 1:12,406 HOBBY
PLATE PRINT RUN 1 SET PER COLOR
NO PLATE PRICING DUE TO SCARCITY
BOW.EXCH.DEADLINE 4/30/2018
BOW.CHR.EXCH. 8/31/2017
BCAPABR Aaron Brown 3.00 8.00
BCAPAC Austin Cousino 3.00 8.00
BCAPAD Austin Dean 3.00 8.00
BCAPAG Arquimedes Gamboa 4.00 10.00
BCAPAGA Amir Garrett 3.00 8.00
BCAPAK Austin Kubitza 3.00 8.00
BCAPAM Amaurys Minier 3.00 8.00
BCAPAMO Akeel Morris 3.00 8.00
BCAPAMR Amed Rosario 12.00 30.00
BCAPAR Alex Reyes 4.00 10.00
BCAPARO Adrian Rondon 4.00 10.00
BCAPAS Antonio Senzatela 4.00 10.00
BCAPASA Adrian Sampson 3.00 8.00
BCAPAV Austin Voth 3.00 8.00
BCAPAVR Avery Romero 3.00 8.00
BCAPBB Bobby Bradley 15.00 40.00
BCAPBG Brett Graves 3.00 8.00
BCAPBH Brent Honeywell 12.00 30.00
BCAPBP Brett Phillips 3.00 8.00
BCAPBW Bobby Wahl 3.00 8.00
BCAPCA Carlos Asuaje 3.00 8.00
BCAPCBE Cody Bellinger 300.00 800.00
BCAPCG Casey Gillaspie 5.00 12.00
BCAPCP Corelle Prime 3.00 8.00
BCAPCP Chad Pinder 4.00 10.00
BCAPCR Cody Reed 4.00 10.00
BCAPCR Carlos Rodon 12.00 30.00
BCAPCS Casey Soltis 3.00 8.00
BCAPCSI Carson Smith 3.00 8.00
BCAPDA Dariel Alvarez 3.00 8.00
BCAPDC Daniel Carbonell 4.00 10.00
BCAPDD Drew Dosch 3.00 8.00
BCAPDG Dermis Garcia 5.00 12.00
BCAPDGE Domingo German 25.00 60.00
BCAPDM Dixon Machado 4.00 10.00
BCAPDS Darnell Sweeney 3.00 8.00
BCAPDW Drew Ward 3.00 8.00
BCAPEB Endrys Briceno 3.00 8.00
BCAPEG Erik Gonzalez 3.00 8.00
BCAPEH Eric Haase 3.00 8.00
BCAPES Edmundo Sosa 4.00 10.00
BCAPFM Francellis Montas 4.00 10.00
BCAPFP Fernando Perez 3.00 8.00
BCAPGG Grayson Greiner 3.00 8.00
BCAPGL Gilbert Lara 4.00 10.00
BCAPGT Gleyber Torres 250.00 600.00
BCAPGU Giovanny Urshela 25.00 60.00
BCAPHO Hector Olivera 4.00 10.00
BCAPHR Harold Ramirez 4.00 10.00
BCAPIS Isael Soto 3.00 8.00
BCAPJB Jake Bauers 5.00 12.00
BCAPJBE Jordan Betts 3.00 8.00
BCAPJC Jake Cave 3.00 8.00
BCAPJD J.D. Davis 5.00 12.00
BCAPJDE Jose De Leon 5.00 12.00
BCAPJG Jarlin Garcia 4.00 10.00
BCAPJH Juan Herrera 3.00 8.00
BCAPJL Jairo Labourt 3.00 8.00
BCAPJL Jorge Lopez 3.00 8.00
BCAPJLU Jordan Luplow 3.00 8.00
BCAPJM Juan Meza 3.00 8.00
BCAPJM Jorge Mateo 10.00 25.00
BCAPJMO Jon Moscot 3.00 8.00
BCAPJOM Josh Morgan 3.00 8.00
BCAPJR Jefry Rodriguez 3.00 8.00
BCAPJS Justin Steele 3.00 8.00
BCAPJU Jhoan Urena 3.00 8.00
BCAPJUL Julian Leon 3.00 8.00
BCAPJW Joe Wendle 8.00 20.00
BCAPKM Keury Mella 3.00 8.00
BCAPLG Luiz Gohara 3.00 8.00
BCAPLM Logan Moon 3.00 8.00
BCAPLS Luis Severino 20.00 50.00
BCAPLY Luis Ysla 3.00 8.00
BCAPMC Miguel Castro 3.00 8.00
BCAPMD Marcos Diplan 3.00 8.00
BCAPMDL Michael De Leon 3.00 8.00
BCAPMM Marcos Molina 3.00 8.00
BCAPMRA Milton Ramos 3.00 8.00
BCAPMS Mallex Smith 5.00 12.00
BCAPMY Mike Yastrzemski 40.00 100.00
BCAPNP Nick Pivetta 3.00 8.00
BCAPNS Nolan Sanburn 3.00 8.00
BCAPOA Orlando Arcia 4.00 10.00
BCAPOAL Ozhaino Albies 75.00 200.00
BCAPPO Peter O'Brien 5.00 12.00
BCAPPS Pedro Severino 3.00 8.00
BCAPRD Rafael Devers 100.00 250.00
BCAPRI Raisel Iglesias 4.00 10.00
BCAPRL Reynaldo Lopez 4.00 10.00
BCAPRM Ryan Merritt 5.00 12.00
BCAPRR Robert Refsnyder 4.00 10.00
BCAPRT Rowdy Tellez 5.00 12.00
BCAPSA Sergio Alcantara 3.00 8.00
BCAPSB Stephen Bruno 3.00 8.00
BCAPSG Stephen Gonsalves 3.00 8.00
BCAPSK Spencer Kieboom 3.00 8.00
BCAPSM Simon Mercedes 3.00 8.00
BCAPSO Steven Okert 3.00 8.00
BCAPSST Seth Streich 3.00 8.00
BCAPSTU Spencer Turnbull 3.00 8.00
BCAPTB Tim Berry 3.00 8.00
BCAPTBL Ty Blach 4.00 10.00
BCAPTGO Trevor Gott 3.00 8.00
BCAPTH Teoscar Hernandez 20.00 50.00
BCAPTL Trace Loehr 3.00 8.00
BCAPTM Trey Michalczewski 3.00 8.00
BCAPTT Touki Toussaint 4.00 10.00
BCAPTW Tyler Wagner 3.00 8.00
BCAPVA Victor Arano 3.00 8.00
BCAPVC Victor Caratini 5.00 12.00
BCAPVR Victor Reyes 3.00 8.00
BCAPWA Willy Adames 10.00 25.00
BCAPWD Wilmer Difo 3.00 8.00
BCAPWG Wilkerman Garcia 4.00 10.00
BCAPWP Wes Parsons 3.00 8.00
BCAPYL Yoan Lopez 3.00 8.00
BCAPYT Yasmany Tomas 4.00 10.00
BCAPZB Zach Bird 3.00 8.00
BCAPZR Zac Reininger 3.00 8.00

2015 Bowman Chrome Prospect Autographs Blue Refractors

*BLUE REF: .75X TO 2X BASIC
BOW.ODDS 1:427 HOBBY
BOW.CHR.ODDS 1:328 HOBBY
STATED PRINT RUN 150 SER.#'d SETS
BOW.EXCH DEADLINE 4/30/2018
BOW.CHR.EXCH 8/31/2017
BCAPCBE Cody Bellinger 1250.00 3000.00
BCAPKS Kyle Schwarber 15.00 40.00
BCAPNG Nick Gordon 8.00 20.00
BCAPTK Tyler Kolek 6.00 15.00

2015 Bowman Chrome Prospect Autographs Gold Refractors

*GOLD REF: 1.2X TO 3X BASIC
BOW.STATED ODDS 1:1278 HOBBY
BOW.CHR.ODDS 1:982 HOBBY
STATED PRINT RUN 50 SER.#'d SETS
BOW.EXCH.DEADLINE 4/30/2018
BOW.CHR.EXCH 5/31/2017
BCAPCBE Cody Bellinger 2000.00 5000.00
BCAPKS Kyle Schwarber 25.00 60.00
BCAPNG Nick Gordon 12.00 30.00
BCAPTK Tyler Kolek 10.00 25.00

2015 Bowman Chrome Prospect Autographs Green Refractors

*GREEN REF: 1X TO 2.5X BASIC
BOW.STATED ODDS 1:191 RETAIL
BOW.CHR.ODDS 1:496 HOBBY
STATED PRINT RUN 99 SER.#'d SETS
BOW.EXCH.DEADLINE 4/30/2018
BOW.CHR.EXCH. 8/31/2017
BCAPCBE Cody Bellinger 1500.00 4000.00
BCAPKS Kyle Schwarber 20.00 50.00
BCAPNG Nick Gordon 10.00 25.00
BCAPTK Tyler Kolek 8.00 20.00

2015 Bowman Chrome Prospect Autographs Orange Refractors

*ORANGE REF: 1.5X TO 4X BASIC
BOW.STATED ODDS 1:606 HOBBY
BOW.CHR.ODDS 1:452 HOBBY
STATED PRINT RUN 25 SER.#'d SETS
BOW.EXCH DEADLINE 4/30/2018
BOW.CHR.EXCH 8/31/2017
BCAPCBE Cody Bellinger 2500.00 6000.00
BCAPKS Kyle Schwarber 30.00 80.00
BCAPNG Nick Gordon 15.00 40.00
BCAPTK Tyler Kolek 12.00 30.00

2015 Bowman Chrome Prospect Autographs Purple Refractors

*PURPLE REF: .6X TO 1.5X BASIC
BOW.STATED ODDS 1:197 HOBBY
BOW.STATED ODDS 1:256 HOBBY
STATED PRINT RUN 250 SER.#'d SETS
BOW.CHR.EXCH 8/31/2017
BOW.EXCH DEADLINE 4/30/2018
BCAPCBE Cody Bellinger 750.00 2000.00
BCAPKS Kyle Schwarber 12.00 30.00
BCAPNG Nick Gordon 6.00 15.00
BCAPTK Tyler Kolek 5.00 12.00

2015 Bowman Chrome Prospect Autographs Refractors

*REF: .5X TO 1.2X BASIC
BOW.ODDS 1:129 HOBBY
BOW.CHR.ODDS 1:99 HOBBY
STATED PRINT RUN 499 SER.#'d SETS
BOW.EXCH DEADLINE 4/30/2018
BOW.CHR.EXCH 8/31/2017
BCAPCBE Cody Bellinger 600.00 1500.00

2015 Bowman Chrome Prospect Profiles Minis

COMPLETE SET (25) 10.00 25.00
STATED ODDS 1:6 HOBBY
*GREEN/99: 1.2X TO 3X BASIC
PP1 Byron Buxton 2.00 5.00
PP2 Carlos Correa 2.00 5.00
PP3 Corey Seager 2.00 5.00
PP4 Joey Gallo .75 2.00
PP5 Lucas Giolito .75 2.00
PP6 Francisco Lindor 3.00 8.00
PP7 Julio Urias 1.25 3.00
PP8 Miguel Sano .50 1.25
PP9 Tyler Glasnow 1.50 4.00
PP10 Kyle Schwarber 1.50 4.00
PP11 Alex Jackson .50 1.25
PP12 Robert Stephenson .40 1.00
PP13 Braden Shipley .40 1.00
PP14 Jameson Taillon .50 1.25
PP15 Mark Appel .40 1.00
PP16 Steven Matz .50 1.25
PP17 Raul Mondesi .60 1.50
PP18 Luis Severino .50 1.25
PP19 Jose Berrios .60 1.50
PP20 Tyler Kolek .40 1.00
PP21 Aaron Judge 6.00 15.00
PP22 Hunter Harvey .40 1.00
PP23 Jose Peraza .40 1.00
PP24 Henry Owens .40 1.00
PP25 Nick Gordon .50 1.25

2015 Bowman Chrome Prospect Profiles Minis Gold Refractors

*GOLD: 2X TO 5X BASIC
STATED ODDS 1:1628 HOBBY
STATED PRINT RUN 50 SER.#'d SETS
PP2 Carlos Correa 20.00 50.00

2015 Bowman Chrome Prospect Profiles Minis Orange Refractors

*ORANGE: 2.5X TO 6X BASIC
STATED ODDS 1:1204 HOBBY
STATED PRINT RUN 25 SER.#'d SETS
PP2 Carlos Correa 25.00 60.00

2015 Bowman Chrome Prospects

COMPLETE SET (250) 25.00 60.00
BOW.PLATE ODDS 1:6523 HOBBY
BOW.CHR.PLATE ODDS 1:5068 HOBBY
PLATE PRINT RUN 1 SET PER COLOR
NO PLATE PRICING DUE TO SCARCITY
BCP1 Tyler Kolek .25 .60
BCP2 Jose Queliz .25 .60
BCP3 Kevin Plawecki .25 .60
BCP4 Jen-Ho Tseng .25 .60
BCP5 Dixon Machado .30 .75
BCP6 Pedro Severino .25 .60
BCP7 Roman Quinn .40 1.00
BCP8 A.J. Cole .25 .60
BCP9 Fernando Perez .25 .60
BCP10 Logan Moon .25 .60
BCP11 Giovanny Urshela 1.50 4.00
BCP12 Emerson Jimenez .25 .60
BCP13 Dermis Garcia .40 1.00
BCP14 Marco Gonzales .40 1.00
BCP15 Jeremy Rhoades .25 .60
BCP16 Joe Ross .25 .60
BCP17 Trevor Gott .25 .60
BCP18 Forrest Wall .25 .60
BCP19 David Dahl .30 .75
BCP20 Adrian Sampson .25 .60
BCP21 Alex Verdugo .40 1.00
BCP22 Williams Perez .30 .75
BCP23 Alex Reyes .30 .75
BCP24 Ty Blach .30 .75
BCP25 Yasmany Tomas .30 .75
BCP26 Hunter Harvey .25 .60
BCP27 Touki Toussaint .30 .75
BCP28 Austin Voth .25 .60
BCP29 Luis Lugo .25 .60
BCP30 Teoscar Hernandez 1.00 2.50
BCP31 Jimmy Reed .25 .60
BCP32 Austin Kubitza .25 .60
BCP33 Miguel Sano .30 .75
BCP34 Rafael Devers 1.50 4.00
BCP35 Harold Ramirez .30 .75
BCP36 Alex Meyer .25 .60
BCP37 Archie Bradley .25 .60
BCP38 Tim Cooney .25 .60
BCP39 Jorge Lopez .25 .60
BCP40 Ryan Merritt .40 1.00
BCP41 Carlos Correa 1.25 3.00
BCP42 Rafael Bautista .25 .60
BCP43 Francisco Mejia .60 1.50
BCP44 Robert Stephenson .25 .60
BCP45 James Dykstra .25 .60
BCP46 Tyler DeLoach .25 .60
BCP47 Kyle Lloyd .25 .60
BCP48 Erik Gonzalez .25 .60
BCP49 Sal Romano .25 .60
BCP50 Julio Urias .75 2.00
BCP51 Juan Herrera .25 .60
BCP52 Jon Gray .25 .60
BCP53 Corey Littrell .25 .60
BCP54 Chris Stratton .25 .60
BCP55 Conrad Gregor .25 .60
BCP56 Hunter Dozier .25 .60
BCP57 Jantzen Witte .40 1.00
BCP58 Kyle Schwarber 1.00 2.50
BCP59 Champ Stuart .25 .60
BCP60 James Needy .25 .60
BCP61 Willy Adames .40 1.00
BCP62 Jose De Leon .40 1.00
BCP63 Buddy Borden .25 .60
BCP64 Jordan Betts .25 .60
BCP65 Gabriel Quintana .25 .60
BCP66 Gareth Morgan .25 .60
BCP67 Matt Andriese .25 .60
BCP68 Raimel Tapia .40 1.00
BCP69 Drew Ward .25 .60
BCP70 Carlos Asuaje .25 .60
BCP71 Ozhaino Albies 6.00 15.00
BCP72 Josh Bell .50 1.25
BCP73 Kyle Zimmer .25 .60
BCP74 Greg Bird .30 .75
BCP75 Nick Gordon .30 .75
BCP76 Aaron Blair .25 .60
BCP77 T.J. Chism .25 .60
BCP78 Marcos Molina .25 .60
BCP79 Avery Romero .25 .60
BCP80 Jose Peraza .25 .60
BCP81 Tim Anderson .50 1.25
BCP82 Nick Travieso .25 .60
BCP83 Matt Wisler .25 .60
BCP84 Nick Petree .25 .60
BCP85 Mark Appel .25 .60
BCP86 Frank Schwindel .30 .75
BCP87 Jorge Mateo .75 2.00
BCP88 Reese McGuire .25 .60
BCP89 Tyler Naquin .40 1.00
BCP90 Nate Smith .25 .60
BCP91 Jose Berrios .40 1.00
BCP92 Henry Owens .25 .60
BCP93 Justin Nicolino .25 .60
BCP94 Jairo Labourt .25 .60
BCP95 Edmundo Sosa .30 .75
BCP96 Seth Streich .25 .60
BCP97 Victor Reyes .25 .60
BCP98 Jhoan Urena .25 .60
BCP99 Adam Engel .25 .60
BCP100 Kris Bryant 2.50 6.00
BCP101 Rio Ruiz .25 .60
BCP102 Wes Parsons .25 .60
BCP103 Raisel Iglesias .30 .75
BCP104 Robert Refsnyder .30 .75
BCP105 Aaron Slegers .25 .60
BCP106 Tim Berry .25 .60
BCP107 Nick Williams .30 .75
BCP108 Jack Reinheimer .30 .75
BCP109 Domingo Santana .30 .75
BCP110 Chad Pinder .30 .75
BCP111 Andre Wheeler .25 .60
BCP112 Chih-Wei Hu .40 1.00
BCP113 Gary Sanchez .75 2.00
BCP114 Ryan McMahon .40 1.00
BCP115 Taylor Williams .25 .60
BCP116 Nelson Gomez .30 .75
BCP117 Addison Russell .75 2.00
BCP118 Domingo German .40 1.00
BCP119 Scott Schebler .40 1.00
BCP120 Joe Jackson .25 .60
BCP121 Gilbert Lara .30 .75
BCP122 Hunter Renfroe .40 1.00
BCP123 Rob Kaminsky .25 .60
BCP124 Steven Matz .30 .75
BCP125 Luis Severino .30 .75
BCP126 Austin Meadows .60 1.50
BCP127 Luis Heredia .25 .60
BCP128 Victor Alcantara .25 .60
BCP129 Trevor Frank .25 .60
BCP130 Jake Johansen .25 .60
BCP131 JaCoby Jones .30 .75
BCP132 Jake Bauers .40 1.00
BCP133 Trey Ball .25 .60
BCP134 Aaron Nola .40 1.00
BCP135 Orlando Arcia .30 .75
BCP136 Keury Mella .25 .60
BCP137 Brett Phillips .25 .60
BCP138 Mike Yastrzemski 6.00 15.00
BCP139 Jose Valdez .25 .60
BCP140 Eric Haase .25 .60
BCP141 Jaycob Brugman .30 .75
BCP142 Albert Almora .30 .75
BCP143 Tyler Wagner .25 .60
BCP144 Francellis Montas .30 .75
BCP145 Dariel Alvarez .25 .60
BCP146 Raul Alcantara .25 .60
BCP147 Ricardo Sanchez .25 .60
BCP148 Jarlin Garcia .30 .75
BCP149 Colin Moran .25 .60
BCP150 Carlos Rodon .60 1.50
BCP151 Kyle Lloyd .25 .60
BCP152 Matt Olson 1.25 3.00
BCP153 J.P. Crawford .25 .60
BCP154 Tony Kemp .25 .60
BCP155 Alen Hanson .25 .60
BCP156 C.J. Edwards .40 1.00
BCP157 Christian Arroyo .75 2.00
BCP158 Amir Garrett .25 .60
BCP159 Justin Steele .25 .60
BCP160 D.J. Peterson .25 .60
BCP161 Edwin Diaz .50 1.25
BCP162 Max Pentecost .25 .60
BCP163 Jon Moscot .25 .60
BCP164 Carson Smith .25 .60
BCP165 Luiz Gohara .25 .60
BCP166 Nick Wells .25 .60
BCP167 Trace Loehr .25 .60
BCP168 Kodi Medeiros .25 .60
BCP169 Stephen Piscotty .30 .75
BCP170 Jorge Alfaro .40 1.00
BCP171 Dan Vogelbach .40 1.00
BCP172 Bobby Wahl .25 .60
BCP173 Parker Bridwell .25 .60
BCP174 Joe Wendle .50 1.25
BCP175 Rowan Wick .25 .60
BCP176 Pierce Johnson .25 .60
BCP177 Nolan Sanburn .25 .60
BCP178 Mitch Keller .30 .75
BCP179 Tyrell Jenkins .30 .75
BCP180 Brandon Nimmo .40 1.00
BCP181 Bobby Bradley .30 .75
BCP182 Sean Newcomb .30 .75
BCP183 Antonio Senzatela .30 .75
BCP184 Dawel Lugo .25 .60
BCP185 Endrys Briceno .25 .60
BCP186 Eloy Jimenez .75 2.00
BCP187 Kyle Freeland .30 .75
BCP188 Max Fried 1.00 2.50
BCP189 Daniel Carbonell .30 .75
BCP190 Chance Sisco .50 1.25
BCP191 Amaurys Minier .25 .60
BCP192 Jake Thompson .25 .60
BCP193 Justin O'Conner .25 .60
BCP194 Andrew Velazquez .25 .60
BCP195 Derek Hill .30 .75
BCP196 Brandon Drury .25 .60
BCP197 Kohl Stewart .25 .60
BCP198 Luis Ysla .25 .60
BCP199 Mallex Smith .40 1.00
BCP200 Lucas Giolito .50 1.25
BCP201 Luke Jackson .25 .60
BCP202 Nick Kingham .25 .60
BCP203 Tyler Glasnow 1.00 2.50
BCP204 Jake Cave .25 .60
BCP205 Jefry Rodriguez .25 .60
BCP206 Monte Harrison .40 1.00
BCP207 Jesse Winker 1.00 2.50
BCP208 Alex Jackson .30 .75
BCP209 Eric Jagielo .25 .60
BCP210 Correlle Prime .25 .60
BCP211 Lucas Sims .25 .60
BCP212 Ian Clarkin .25 .60
BCP213 Austin Brice .25 .60
BCP214 J.D. Davis .40 1.00
BCP215 Simon Mercedes .25 .60
BCP216 Casey Gillaspie .40 1.00
BCP217 Spencer Kieboom .25 .60
BCP218 Michael Conforto .30 .75
BCP219 Stephen Bruno .25 .60
BCP220 Victor Caratini .75 2.00
BCP221 Spencer Turnbull .25 .60
BCP222 Tyler Danish .25 .60
BCP223 Bradley Zimmer .40 1.00
BCP224 Dominic Smith .25 .60
BCP225 Matt Chapman .75 2.00
BCP226 Miguel Almonte .25 .60
BCP227 Franklin Barreto .30 .75
BCP228 Braden Shipley .25 .60
BCP229 Luis Ortiz .25 .60
BCP230 Manuel Margot .25 .60
BCP231 Amed Rosario .40 1.00
BCP232 Felix Jorge .25 .60
BCP233 Cody Reed .30 .75
BCP234 Raul Mondesi .40 1.00
BCP235 Kyle Crick .30 .75
BCP236 Jeff Hoffman .30 .75
BCP237 Grant Holmes .30 .75
BCP238 Billy McKinney .30 .75
BCP239 Jake Gatewood .25 .60
BCP240 Clint Frazier 1.00 2.50
BCP241 Wilmer Difo .25 .60
BCP242 Alex Blandino .25 .60
BCP243 Zac Reininger .25 .60
BCP244 Austin Cousino .25 .60
BCP245 Grayson Greiner .25 .60
BCP246 Reynaldo Lopez .30 .75
BCP247 Jameson Taillon .30 .75
BCP248 Daniel Robertson .25 .60
BCP249 Michael De Leon .25 .60
BCP250 Corey Seager 1.25 3.00

2015 Bowman Chrome Prospects Black Asia Refractors

*BLACK REF: 1.5X TO 4X BASIC
DISTRIBUTED IN ASIA

2015 Bowman Chrome Prospects Black Wave Asia Refractors

*BLACK WAVE REF: 1.5X TO 4X BASIC
DISTRIBUTED IN ASIA

2015 Bowman Chrome Prospects Blue Refractors

*BLUE REF: 2X TO 5X BASIC
BOW.ODDS 1:175 HOBBY
BOW.CHR.ODDS 1:136 HOBBY
STATED PRINT RUN 150 SER.#'d SETS

2015 Bowman Chrome Prospects Blue Wave Refractors

*BLUE WAVE REF: 1.5X TO 4X BASIC
RANDOM INSERTS IN PACKS

2015 Bowman Chrome Prospects Gold Refractors

*GOLD REF: 5X TO 12X BASIC
BOW.ODDS 1:525 HOBBY
BOW.CHR.ODDS 1:407 HOBBY
STATED PRINT RUN 50 SER.#'d SETS

2015 Bowman Chrome Prospects Green Refractors

*GREEN REF: 2.5X TO 6X BASIC
BOW.ODDS 1:44 RETAIL
BOW.CHR.ODDS 1:206 HOBBY
STATED PRINT RUN 99 SER.#'d SETS

2015 Bowman Chrome Prospects Orange Refractors

*ORANGE REF: 6X TO 15X BASIC
BOW.ODDS 1:243 HOBBY
BOW.CHR.ODDS 1:302 HOBBY
STATED PRINT RUN 25 SER.#'d SETS

2015 Bowman Chrome Prospects Orange Wave Refractors

*ORANGE WAVE REF: 4X TO 8X BASIC
RANDOM INSERTS IN PACKS

2015 Bowman Chrome Prospects Purple Refractors

*PURPLE REF: 1.5X TO 4X BASIC
BOW.ODDS 1:105 HOBBY
BOW.CHR.ODDS 1:82 HOBBY
STATED PRINT RUN 250 SER.#'d SETS

2015 Bowman Chrome Prospects Refractors

*REF: 1.5X TO 4X BASIC
BOW.STATED ODDS 1:53 HOBBY
BOW.CHR.STATED ODDS 1:41 HOBBY
STATED PRINT RUN 499 SER.#'d SETS

2015 Bowman Chrome Rookie Autographs

BOW.STATED ODDS 1:295 HOBBY
BOW.CHR. ODDS 1:355 HOBBY
BOW.EXCH DEADLINE 4/30/2018
BOW.CHR.EXCH. 8/31/2017
BCARAB Archie Bradley 3.00 8.00
BCARAR Anthony Ranaudo 3.00 8.00
BCARBB Byron Buxton 50.00 120.00
BCARBBR Bryce Brentz 3.00 8.00
BCARBF Brandon Finnegan 3.00 8.00
BCARBFA Buck Farmer 3.00 8.00
BCARCR Carlos Rodon 10.00 25.00
BCARCS Cory Spangenberg 3.00 8.00
BCARCW Christian Walker 10.00 25.00
BCARDC Daniel Corcino 3.00 8.00
BCARDH Dilson Herrera 4.00 10.00
BCARDN Daniel Norris 3.00 8.00
BCARDP Dalton Pompey 4.00 10.00
BCARDT Devon Travis 3.00 8.00
BCARFL Francisco Lindor 25.00 60.00
BCARJB Javier Baez 30.00 80.00
BCARJHK Jung Ho Kang 3.00 8.00
BCARJL Jake Lamb 5.00 12.00
BCARJM James McCann 5.00 12.00
BCARJP J.Pederson Gray jsy 12.00 30.00
BCARJPE J.Pederson White jsy 12.00 30.00
BCARJR Jason Rogers 3.00 8.00
BCARJS J.Soler Face Rt 10.00 25.00
BCARJSO J.Soler Face Left 10.00 25.00
BCARKB Kris Bryant 60.00 150.00
BCARKG Kendall Graveman 3.00 8.00
BCARMB Matt Barnes 3.00 8.00
BCARMFO Mike Foltynewicz 3.00 8.00
BCARMT Michael Taylor 3.00 8.00
BCARNS Noah Syndergaard 20.00 50.00
BCARRC Rusney Castillo 4.00 10.00
BCARRI Raisel Iglesias 4.00 10.00
BCARRL Rymer Liriano 3.00 8.00
BCARSM Steven Moya 4.00 10.00
BCARTM Trevor May 3.00 8.00
BCARYT Yasmany Tomas 4.00 10.00

2015 Bowman Chrome Rookie Autographs Blue Refractors

*BLUE REF: .6X TO 1.5X BASIC
BOW.STATED ODDS 1:1278 HOBBY
BOW.CHR. ODDS 1:2729 HOBBY
STATED PRINT RUN 150 SER.#'d SETS
BOW.EXCH DEADLINE 4/30/2018
BOW.CHR.EXCH. 8/31/2017
BCARDP Dalton Pompey 10.00 25.00
BCARKB Kris Bryant 250.00 500.00
BCARMF Maikel Franco 6.00 15.00
BCARNS Noah Syndergaard 40.00 100.00

2015 Bowman Chrome Rookie Autographs Gold Refractors

*GOLD REF: 1X TO 2.5X BASIC
BOW.STATED ODDS 1:3839 HOBBY
BOW.CHR. ODDS 1:6368 HOBBY
STATED PRINT RUN 50 SER.#'d SETS
BOW.EXCH DEADLINE 4/30/2018
BOW.CHR.EXCH. 8/31/2017
BCARCW Christian Walker 50.00 120.00
BCARDP Dalton Pompey 30.00 80.00
BCARJP J.Pederson Gray jsy 60.00 150.00
BCARJPE J.Pederson White jsy 60.00 150.00
BCARJS J.Soler Face Rt 50.00 120.00
BCARJSO J.Soler Face Left 50.00 120.00
BCARKB Kris Bryant 400.00 800.00
BCARKG Kendall Graveman 12.00 30.00
BCARMF Maikel Franco 10.00 25.00
BCARNS Noah Syndergaard 175.00 350.00
BCARSM Steven Moya 12.00 30.00
BCARYT Yasmany Tomas 20.00 50.00

2015 Bowman Chrome Rookie Autographs Green Refractors

*GREEN REF: .75X TO 2X BASIC
BOW.STATED ODDS 1:572 RETAIL
BOW.CHR. ODDS 1:3227 HOBBY
STATED PRINT RUN 99 SER.#'d SETS
BOW.EXCH DEADLINE 4/30/2018
BOW.CHR.EXCH. 8/31/2017
BCARCW Christian Walker 30.00 80.00
BCARDP Dalton Pompey 12.00 30.00
BCARKB Kris Bryant 300.00 600.00
BCARMF Maikel Franco 8.00 20.00
BCARNS Noah Syndergaard 50.00 120.00

2015 Bowman Chrome Rookie Autographs Orange Refractors

*ORANGE REF: 2X TO 5X BASIC
BOW.STATED ODDS 1:1819 HOBBY
BOW.CHR. ODDS 1:2949 HOBBY
STATED PRINT RUN 25 SER.#'d SETS
BOW.EXCH DEADLINE 4/30/2018
BOW.CHR.EXCH. 8/31/2017
BCARAB Archie Bradley 12.00 30.00
BCARBBR Bryce Brentz 10.00 25.00
BCARCW Christian Walker 75.00 200.00
BCARDP Dalton Pompey 60.00 150.00
BCARDT Devon Travis 12.00 30.00
BCARJP J.Pederson Gray jsy 75.00 200.00
BCARJPE J.Pederson White jsy 75.00 200.00
BCARJS J.Soler Face Rt 60.00 150.00
BCARJSO J.Soler Face Left 60.00 150.00
BCARKG Kendall Graveman 25.00 60.00
BCARMF Maikel Franco 20.00 50.00
BCARSM Steven Moya 25.00 60.00
BCARYT Yasmany Tomas 40.00 100.00

2015 Bowman Chrome Rookie Autographs Refractors

*REF: .5X TO 1.2X BASIC
BOW.STATED ODDS 1:385 HOBBY
BOW.CHR. ODDS 1:640 HOBBY
STATED PRINT RUN 499 SER.#'d SETS
BOW.EXCH DEADLINE 4/30/2018
BOW.CHR.EXCH. 8/31/2017
BCARMF Maikel Franco 5.00 12.00

2015 Bowman Chrome Rookie Recollections

COMPLETE SET (7) 3.00 8.00
STATED ODDS 1:24 HOBBY
RRIBW Bernie Williams .50 1.25
RRICB Carlos Baerga .40 1.00
RRIFT Frank Thomas .60 1.50
RRIJG Juan Gonzalez .40 1.00
RRIJO John Olerud .40 1.00
RRIMA Moises Alou .40 1.00
RRIMG Marquis Grissom .40 1.00

2015 Bowman Chrome Rookie Recollections Autographs

STATED ODDS 1:2560 HOBBY
EXCHANGE DEADLINE 4/30/2018
*REF/99: .5X TO 1.2X BASIC
*GOLD REF/50: 1X TO 2.5X BASIC
RRBW Bernie Williams 30.00 80.00
RRCB Carlos Baerga 4.00 10.00
RRFT Frank Thomas 50.00 120.00
RRJG Juan Gonzalez 4.00 10.00
RRJO John Olerud 8.00 20.00
RRMA Moises Alou 8.00 20.00
RRMG Marquis Grissom 8.00 20.00

2015 Bowman Chrome Series Next Die Cuts

COMPLETE SET (35) 15.00 40.00
STATED ODDS 1:9 HOBBY
*GREEN/99: 1X TO 2.5X BASIC
*PURPLE/25: 2.5X TO 6X BASIC
SNAB Archie Bradley .40 1.00
SNAR Addison Russell 1.25 3.00
SNBF Brandon Finnegan .40 1.00
SNBH Billy Hamilton .50 1.25
SNBHA Bryce Harper 1.00 2.50
SNBS Blake Swihart .50 1.25
SNCR Carlos Rodon 1.00 2.50
SNCY Christian Yelich .75 2.00
SNDB Dellin Betances .50 1.25
SNDN Daniel Norris .40 1.00
SNDT Devon Travis .40 1.00
SNGC Gerrit Cole .60 1.50
SNGP Gregory Polanco .50 1.25
SNGS George Springer .50 1.25
SNJA Jose Abreu .60 1.50
SNJB Javier Baez 3.00 8.00
SNJD Jacob deGrom 1.25 3.00
SNJF Jose Fernandez .60 1.50
SNJP Joc Pederson 1.50 4.00
SNJPA Joe Panik .50 1.25
SNJS Jorge Soler .60 1.50
SNJT Julio Teheran .50 1.25
SNKB Kris Bryant 4.00 10.00
SNKP Kevin Plawecki .40 1.00
SNKV Kennys Vargas .40 1.00
SNKW Kolten Wong .50 1.25
SNMAT Masahiro Tanaka .50 1.25
SNMBE Mookie Betts 1.25 3.00
SNMF Maikel Franco .50 1.25
SNMT Mike Trout 3.00 8.00
SNRC Rusney Castillo .50 1.25
SNSG Sonny Gray .50 1.25
SNTW Taijuan Walker .40 1.00
SNXB Xander Bogaerts .60 1.50
SNYP Yasiel Puig .60 1.50

2015 Bowman Chrome Series Next Die Cuts Autographs Green Haze Refractors

STATED ODDS 1:3227 HOBBY
PRINT RUNS B/WN 10-99 COPIES PER
NO PRICING ON QTY 10
EXCHANGE DEADLINE 8/31/2017
*PURPLE/25: .75X TO 2X BASIC
SNAB Archie Bradley/99 10.00 25.00
SNAR Addison Russell/99 8.00 20.00
SNBF Brandon Finnegan/99 4.00 10.00
SNBS Blake Swihart/99 10.00 25.00
SNDN Daniel Norris/99 10.00 25.00
SNGP Gregory Polanco/99 8.00 20.00
SNJB Javier Baez/99 10.00 25.00
SNJD Jacob deGrom/99 50.00 120.00
SNJF Jose Fernandez/99 25.00 60.00
SNKP Kevin Plawecki/99 6.00 15.00
SNKV Kennys Vargas/99 10.00 25.00
SNRC Rusney Castillo/99 5.00 12.00
SNSG Sonny Gray/99 5.00 12.00

2015 Bowman Chrome Draft

COMPLETE SET (200) 20.00 50.00
STATED PLATE ODDS 1:500 HOBBY
PLATE PRINT RUN 1 SET PER COLOR
NO PLATE PRICING DUE TO SCARCITY
1 Dansby Swanson 1.50 4.00
2 Yoan Lopez .25 .60
3 Bailey Falter .25 .60
4 Casey Gillaspie .40 1.00
5 Demi Orimoloye .30 .75
6 Steven Duggar .25 .60
7 Tyler Alexander .25 .60
8 Courtney Hawkins .25 .60
9 Casey Hughston .25 .60
10 Kolby Allard .25 .60
11 Austin Meadows .60 1.50
12 Joe McCarthy .25 .60
13 Tyler Stephenson .60 1.50
14 Ashe Russell .25 .60
15 Dylan Moore .25 .60
16 Donnie Dewees .40 1.00
17 Beau Burrows .25 .60
18 Greg Pickett .25 .60
19 Parker French .25 .60
20 Cam Gibson .30 .75
21 Braden Bishop .25 .60
22 Ryan Kellogg .25 .60
23 Monte Harrison .40 1.00
24 Zack Erwin .25 .60
25 J.P. Crawford .25 .60
26 Ryan McMahon .40 1.00
27 Kyle Holder .30 .75
28 Ian Happ 1.00 2.50
29 Anthony Hermelyn .25 .60
30 Jimmy Herget .25 .60
31 Mike Nikorak .25 .60
32 Alex Young .25 .60
33 Tyler Mark .25 .60
34 Trent Clark .25 .60
35 Benton Moss .25 .60
36 Matt Withrow .25 .60
37 Chris Shaw .25 .60
38 Manuel Margot .25 .60
39 Lucas Giolito .50 1.25
40 Chase Ingram .25 .60
41 Lucas Herbert .25 .60
42 Trey Supak .25 .60
43 Blake Trahan .25 .60
44 Jeff Degano .30 .75
45 Desmond Lindsay .40 1.00
46 Walker Buehler 1.50 4.00
47 Cody Ponce .25 .60
48 Adam Brett Walker .25 .60
49 Tyler Danish .25 .60
50 Dillon Tate .30 .75
51 Thomas Szapucki .25 .60
52 Spencer Adams .25 .60
53 Kevin Duchene .25 .60
54 Blake Perkins .25 .60
55 Thomas Eshelman .25 .60
56 Lucas Williams .25 .60
57 David Fletcher 2.50 6.00
58 James Kaprielian .25 .60
59 Preston Morrison .25 .60
60 Ryan Burr .25 .60
61 Brett Lilek .25 .60
62 Trevor Megill .25 .60
63 Jordy Lara .25 .60
64 Kevin Newman .60 1.50
65 Luis Ortiz .25 .60
66 Cornelius Randolph .25 .60
67 Domingo Leyba .25 .60
68 Sean Reid-Foley .30 .75
69 Josh Naylor .30 .75
70 Michael Matuella .30 .75
71 Cole Tucker .25 .60
72 Kyle Wilcox .25 .60
73 Forrest Wall .25 .60
74 Alex Jackson .30 .75
75 Kyle Tucker 2.00 5.00
76 Hunter Harvey .25 .60
77 Brandon Waddell .25 .60
78 Travis Neubeck .25 .60
79 Ronnie Jebavy .25 .60
80 Ryan Mountcastle 6.00 15.00
81 Kyle Zimmer .25 .60
82 A.J. Reed .30 .75
83 Alex Reyes .30 .75
84 Garrett Whitley .40 1.00
85 Derek Hill .30 .75
86 Ryan Clark .25 .60
87 Andrew Sopko .25 .60
88 Breckin Williams .25 .60
89 Tate Matheny .25 .60
90 Kyle Crick .30 .75
91 Andrew Moore .30 .75
92 Hutton Moyer .25 .60
93 Jordan Ramsey .25 .60
94 Javier Medina .25 .60
95 Jack Wynkoop .25 .60
96 Triston McKenzie .75 2.00
97 Jose De Leon .40 1.00
98 Justin Cohen .25 .60
99 Mark Mathias .30 .75
100 Julio Urias .75 2.00
101 Jared Foster .25 .60
102 Roman Quinn .40 1.00
103 Max Wotell .25 .60
104 Jake Gatewood .25 .60
105 Willy Adames .40 1.00
106 Rafael Devers 1.50 4.00
107 Blake Snell .30 .75
108 Cody Poteet .25 .60
109 Bryce Denton .40 1.00
110 Nolan Watson .25 .60
111 Tyler Nevin .40 1.00
112 Antonio Santillan .30 .75
113 Mac Marshall .25 .60
114 Mariano Rivera .40 1.00
115 Grant Hockin .25 .60
116 Raul Mondesi .40 1.00
117 Richie Martin .25 .60
118 Carson Fulmer .25 .60
119 Mikey White .30 .75
120 Lucas Sims .25 .60
121 Peter Lambert .25 .60
122 Roman Collins .25 .60
123 Austin Allen .30 .75
124 David Thompson .30 .75
125 Ka'ai Tom .25 .60
126 Renato Nunez .50 1.25
127 Zech Lemond .25 .60
128 Nick Gordon .30 .75
129 Phil Bickford .25 .60
130 Taylor Ward .40 1.00
131 Corey Taylor .25 .60
132 Chris Ellis .25 .60
133 Michael Chavis .60 1.50
134 Cody Jones .25 .60
135 Tyrone Taylor .25 .60
136 Tyler Jay .25 .60
137 Ke'Bryan Hayes 15.00 40.00
138 Scott Kingery .40 1.00
139 Carl Wise .30 .75
140 Juan Hillman .25 .60
141 Bowdien Derby .25 .60
142 D.J. Peterson .25 .60
143 Jacob Nix .25 .60
144 Josh Staumont .30 .75
145 Nathan Kirby .30 .75
146 D.J. Stewart .25 .60
147 Matt Hall .25 .60
148 Kohl Stewart .25 .60
149 Drew Jackson .30 .75
150 Aaron Judge 4.00 10.00
151 Nick Plummer .30 .75
152 David Dahl .30 .75
153 Brian Mundell .25 .60
154 Bradley Zimmer .40 1.00
155 Tanner Rainey .25 .60
156 JC Cardenas .25 .60
157 Austin Riley 3.00 8.00
158 Kevin Kramer .30 .75
159 Hunter Renfroe .40 1.00
160 Grant Holmes .30 .75
161 Isaiah White .30 .75
162 Justin Jacome .25 .60
163 Amed Rosario .40 1.00
164 Josh Bell .50 1.25
165 Eric Jenkins .25 .60
166 Reese McGuire .25 .60
167 Sean Newcomb .30 .75
168 Reynaldo Lopez .30 .75
169 Conor Biggio .25 .60
170 Andrew Suarez .30 .75
171 Trey Ball .25 .60
172 Austin Rei .30 .75
173 Drew Finley .25 .60
174 Skye Bolt .30 .75
175 Daniel Robertson .25 .60
176 Avery Romero .25 .60
177 Jon Harris .30 .75
178 Christin Stewart .30 .75
179 Nelson Rodriguez .30 .75
180 Austin Smith .25 .60
181 Michael Soroka 1.50 4.00
182 Andrew Benintendi 4.00 10.00
183 Matt Crownover .25 .60
184 Franklin Barreto .30 .75
185 Willie Calhoun .40 1.00
186 Braxton Davidson .25 .60
187 Jake Woodford .25 .60
188 Ryan McKenna .25 .60
189 Ryan Helsley .30 .75
190 Carson Sands .25 .60
191 Tyler Beede .30 .75
192 Jeff Hendrix .30 .75
193 Nick Howard .40 1.00
194 Chris Betts .30 .75
195 Jagger Rusconi .25 .60
196 Matt Olson 1.25 3.00
197 Jake Cronenworth 3.00 8.00
198 Alex Robinson .25 .60
199 Albert Almora .30 .75
200 Brendan Rodgers 1.00 2.50

2015 Bowman Chrome Draft Blue Refractors

*BLUE REF: 2X TO 5X BASIC
STATED ODDS 1:134 HOBBY
STATED PRINT RUN 150 SER.#'d SETS
1 Dansby Swanson 15.00 40.00
182 Andrew Benintendi 30.00 80.00

2015 Bowman Chrome Draft Gold Refractors

*GOLD REF: 6X TO 15X BASIC
STATED ODDS 1:401 HOBBY
STATED PRINT RUN 50 SER.#'d SETS
1 Dansby Swanson 50.00 120.00
182 Andrew Benintendi 100.00 250.00

2015 Bowman Chrome Draft Green Refractors

*GREEN REF: 2.5X TO 6X BASIC
STATED ODDS 1:203 HOBBY
STATED PRINT RUN 99 SER.#'d SETS
1 Dansby Swanson 20.00 50.00
182 Andrew Benintendi 40.00 100.00

2015 Bowman Chrome Draft Orange Refractors

*ORANGE REF: 8X TO 20X BASIC
STATED ODDS 1:283 HOBBY
STATED PRINT RUN 25 SER.#'d SETS
1 Dansby Swanson 30.00 80.00
182 Andrew Benintendi 125.00 300.00

2015 Bowman Chrome Draft Refractors

*REF: .75X TO 2X BASIC
STATED ODDS 1:3 HOBBY
182 Andrew Benintendi 8.00 20.00

2015 Bowman Chrome Draft Sky Blue Refractors

*SKY BLUE: 1X TO 2.5X BASIC
STATED ODDS 1:12 HOBBY

2015 Bowman Chrome Draft Draft Pick Autographs

STATED ODDS 1:39 HOBBY
PLATE ODDS 1:16,666 HOBBY
PLATE PRINT RUN 1 SET PER COLOR
NO PLATE PRICING DUE TO SCARCITY
BCAAB Andrew Benintendi 20.00 50.00
BCAAR Ashe Russell 5.00 12.00
BCAARI Austin Riley 50.00 120.00
BCAASM Austin Smith 3.00 8.00
BCAASU Andrew Suarez 4.00 10.00
BCAAY Alex Young 3.00 8.00
BCABB Beau Burrows 3.00 8.00
BCABL Brett Lilek 3.00 8.00
BCABR Brendan Rodgers 20.00 50.00
BCACB Chris Betts 4.00 10.00
BCACBI Conor Biggio 3.00 8.00
BCACF Carson Fulmer 3.00 8.00
BCACG Cam Gibson 4.00 10.00
BCACP Cody Ponce 3.00 8.00
BCACS Chris Shaw 3.00 8.00
BCACST Christin Stewart 4.00 10.00
BCADD Donnie Dewees 5.00 12.00
BCADF Drew Finley 3.00 8.00
BCADL Desmond Lindsay 5.00 12.00
BCADS Dansby Swanson 20.00 50.00
BCADST D.J. Stewart 3.00 8.00
BCADT Dillon Tate 4.00 10.00
BCAEJ Eric Jenkins 3.00 8.00
BCAGW Garrett Whitley 5.00 12.00
BCAIH Ian Happ 25.00 60.00
BCAJD Jeff Degano 4.00 10.00
BCAJHI Juan Hillman 3.00 8.00
BCAJK James Kaprielian 3.00 8.00
BCAJN Josh Naylor 10.00 25.00
BCAJNI Jacob Nix 3.00 8.00
BCAJW Jake Woodford 3.00 8.00
BCAKA Kolby Allard 5.00 12.00
BCAKH Kyle Holder 4.00 10.00
BCAKHA Ke'Bryan Hayes 200.00 500.00
BCAKN Kevin Newman 8.00 20.00
BCAKT Kyle Tucker 50.00 120.00
BCALH Lucas Herbert 3.00 8.00
BCAMM Michael Matuella 4.00 10.00
BCAMR Mariano Rivera 5.00 12.00
BCAMS Michael Soroka 30.00 80.00
BCAMW Mike Nikorak 3.00 8.00
BCAMWO Max Wotell 3.00 8.00
BCANK Nathan Kirby 4.00 10.00
BCANN Nick Neidert 3.00 8.00
BCANP Nick Plummer 4.00 10.00
BCANW Nolan Watson 3.00 8.00
BCAPB Phil Bickford 3.00 8.00
BCAPL Peter Lambert 3.00 8.00
BCARM Richie Martin 3.00 8.00
BCARMO Ryan Mountcastle 75.00 200.00
BCASK Scott Kingery 8.00 20.00
BCATC Trent Clark 25.00 60.00
BCATE Thomas Eshelman 3.00 8.00
BCATJ Tyler Jay 3.00 8.00
BCATMA Tate Matheny 3.00 8.00
BCATN Tyler Nevin 5.00 12.00
BCATR Tanner Rainey 3.00 8.00
BCATS Tyler Stephenson 15.00 40.00
BCATW Taylor Ward 5.00 12.00
BCAWB Walker Buehler 75.00 200.00

2015 Bowman Chrome Draft Draft Pick Autographs Black Refractors

*BLACK REF: 1.2X TO 3X BASIC
RANDOM INSERTS IN PACKS
STATED PRINT RUN 35 SER.#'d SETS
BCADS Dansby Swanson 200.00 500.00
BCAWB Walker Buehler 300.00 800.00

2015 Bowman Chrome Draft Draft Pick Autographs Gold Refractors

*GOLD REF: 1.2X TO 3X BASIC
STATED ODDS 1:1324 HOBBY
STATED PRINT RUN 50 SER.#'d SETS
BCADS Dansby Swanson 200.00 500.00
BCAWB Walker Buehler/50 300.00 800.00

2015 Bowman Chrome Draft Draft Pick Autographs Green Refractors

*GREEN REF: 1X TO 2.5X BASIC
STATED ODDS 1:669 HOBBY
STATED PRINT RUN 99 SER.#'d SETS

2015 Bowman Chrome Draft Draft Pick Autographs Orange Refractors

*ORANGE REF: 1.5X TO 4X BASIC
STATED ODDS 1:935 HOBBY
STATED PRINT RUN 25 SER.#'d SETS
BCADS Dansby Swanson 250.00 600.00
BCAWB Walker Buehler 400.00 1000.00

2015 Bowman Chrome Draft Draft Pick Autographs Purple Refractors

*PURPLE REF: .6X TO 1.5X BASIC
STATED ODDS 1:265 HOBBY
STATED PRINT RUN 250 SER.#'d SETS

2015 Bowman Chrome Draft Draft Pick Autographs Refractors

*REF: .5X TO 1.2X BASIC
STATED ODDS 1:133 HOBBY

2015 Bowman Chrome Draft Prime Pairings Autographs

STATED ODDS 1:10,384 HOBBY
STATED PRINT RUN 25 SER.#'d SETS
PPAASO M.Soroka/K.Allard 15.00 40.00
PPABB T.Beede/P.Bickford 12.00 30.00
PPAFA S.Adams/C.Fulmer 50.00 120.00
PPAKC I.Clarkin/J.Kaprielian 60.00 150.00
PPASR B.Rodgers/D.Swanson 300.00 500.00
PPAWR G.Whitley/D.Robertson 12.00 30.00

2015 Bowman Chrome Draft Scouts Fantasy Impacts

STATED ODDS 1:12 HOBBY
*GOLD/50: 1.5X TO 4X BASIC
*ORANGE/25: 2X TO 5X BASIC
BSIAB Andrew Benintendi 2.00 5.00
BSICF Carson Fulmer .40 1.00
BSIDS Dansby Swanson 2.50 6.00
BSIDT Dillon Tate .50 1.25
BSIIH Ian Happ 1.50 4.00
BSIJA Jorge Alfaro .60 1.50
BSIJC J.P. Crawford .40 1.00
BSIJK James Kaprielian .40 1.00
BSIKC Kyle Crick .50 1.25
BSIKF Kyle Freeland .50 1.25
BSIKN Kevin Newman 1.00 2.50
BSIKZ Kyle Zimmer .40 1.00
BSILG Lucas Giolito .75 2.00
BSIMO Matt Olson 2.00 5.00
BSITA Tim Anderson .75 2.00
BSITE Thomas Eshelman .40 1.00
BSITG Tyler Glasnow 1.50 4.00
BSITJ Tyler Jay .40 1.00
BSIWB Walker Buehler 2.50 6.00
BSIYL Yoan Lopez .40 1.00

2015 Bowman Chrome Draft Teams of Tomorrow Die Cuts

STATED ODDS 1:24 HOBBY
PRINTING PLATES RANDOMLY INSERTED
PLATE PRINT RUN 1 SET PER COLOR
NO PLATE PRICING DUE TO SCARCITY
*GOLD/50: 1X TO 2.5X BASIC
*ORANGE/25: 1.5X TO 4X BASIC
TDC1 T.Ball/A.Benintendi 2.00 5.00
TDC2 D.Swanson/D.Leyba 2.50 6.00
TDC3 B.Rodgers/K.Freeland 1.50 4.00
TDC4 L.Ortiz/D.Tate .50 1.25
TDC5 K.Tucker/T.Hernandez 3.00 8.00
TDC6 Tyler Jay .50 1.25
Nick Gordon
TDC7 C.Fulmer/T.Danish .40 1.00
TDC8 I.Happ/B.McKinney 1.50 4.00
TDC9 C.Randolph/R.Quinn .60 1.50
TDC10 Tyler Stephenson 1.50 4.00
Jesse Winker
TDC11 Josh Naylor .50 1.25
Avery Romero
TDC12 Garrett Whitley .60 1.50
Casey Gillaspie
TDC13 K.Allard/B.Davidson .40 1.00
TDC14 Trent Clark .60 1.50
Monte Harrison
TDC15 J.Kaprielian/J.Mateo 1.25 3.00
TDC16 Tyler Beede .50 1.25
Phil Bickford
TDC17 K.Newman/A.Meadows 1.00 2.50
TDC18 R.Martin/M.Olson 2.00 5.00
TDC19 Kyle Zimmer .40 1.00
Ashe Russell
TDC20 Derek Hill .50 1.25
Beau Burrows

2015 Bowman Chrome Draft Top of the Class

STATED ODDS 1:118 HOBBY BOXES
*ORANGE/25: 1.5X TO 4X BASIC
TOCAB Andrew Benintendi 8.00 20.00
TOCBR Brendan Rodgers 6.00 15.00
TOCCF Carson Fulmer 1.50 4.00
TOCCR Cornelius Randolph 1.50 4.00
TOCDS Dansby Swanson 10.00 25.00
TOCDT Dillon Tate 2.00 5.00
TOCIH Ian Happ 6.00 15.00
TOCKT Kyle Tucker 12.00 30.00
TOCTJ Tyler Jay 1.50 4.00
TOCTS Tyler Stephenson 4.00 10.00

2015 Bowman Chrome Draft Top of the Class Autographs

STATED ODDS 1:458 HOBBY BOXES
STATED PRINT RUN 25 SER.#'d SETS
TOCAB Andrew Benintendi 300.00 500.00
TOCBR Brendan Rodgers 150.00 300.00
TOCCF Carson Fulmer 125.00 250.00
TOCDS Dansby Swanson 800.00 1000.00
TOCIH Ian Happ 150.00 300.00
TOCKT Kyle Tucker 250.00 500.00

2016 Bowman Chrome

COMPLETE SET (100) 25.00 60.00
STATED PLATE ODDS 1:1239 HOBBY
PLATE PRINT RUN 1 SET PER COLOR
BLACK-CYAN-MAGENTA-YELLOW ISSUED
NO PLATE PRICING DUE TO SCARCITY
1 Mike Trout 1.50 4.00
2 David Ortiz .30 .75
3 Albert Pujols .40 1.00
4 Jacob deGrom .60 1.50
5 Maikel Franco .25 .60
6 Josh Reddick .20 .50
7 Byung-Ho Park RC .50 1.25
8 Manny Machado .30 .75
9 Jose Fernandez .30 .75
10 Nomar Mazara RC .60 1.50
11 Freddie Freeman .40 1.00
12 Hunter Pence .25 .60
13 Wade Davis .20 .50
14 Jameson Taillon RC .50 1.25
15 Seung-Hwan Oh RC 1.00 2.50
16 Tyler White RC .40 1.00
17 Felix Hernandez .25 .60
18 Noah Syndergaard .25 .60
19 Josh Donaldson .25 .60
20 Aledmys Diaz RC .60 1.50
21 Troy Tulowitzki .30 .75
22 Mookie Betts .60 1.50
23 Paul Goldschmidt .30 .75
24 Dustin Pedroia .30 .75
25 Kenta Maeda RC .75 2.00
26 Zack Greinke .30 .75
27 Miguel Sano RC .60 1.50
28 Andrew McCutchen .30 .75
29 Jon Gray RC .40 1.00
30 Aaron Nola RC .75 2.00
31 Kyle Schwarber RC 1.25 3.00
32 Francisco Lindor .30 .75
33 Jose Abreu .30 .75
34 Robinson Cano .25 .60
35 Evan Longoria .25 .60
36 Mallex Smith RC .40 1.00
37 Ichiro Suzuki .40 1.00
38 Dallas Keuchel .25 .60
39 Carlos Correa .30 .75
40 Corey Seager RC 4.00 10.00
41 Michael Fulmer RC .60 1.50
42 Tyson Ross .20 .50
43 Adam Jones .25 .60
44 Jason Heyward .25 .60
45 Anthony Rizzo .40 1.00
46 Carl Edwards Jr. RC .50 1.25
47 Yu Darvish .30 .75
48 Stephen Piscotty RC .60 1.50
49 David Price .25 .60
50 Clayton Kershaw .50 1.25
51 Trea Turner RC 1.25 3.00
52 Nelson Cruz .30 .75
53 Chris Sale .30 .75
54 Buster Posey .40 1.00
55 Jose Berrios RC .60 1.50
56 Salvador Perez .25 .60
57 Trevor Story RC 2.00 5.00
58 Madison Bumgarner .25 .60
59 Evan Gattis .20 .50
60 Julio Urias RC 1.25 3.00
61 Todd Frazier .20 .50
62 Yadier Molina .40 1.00
63 Dellin Betances .25 .60
64 J.D. Martinez .30 .75
65 Chris Archer .20 .50
66 Adam Wainwright .25 .60
67 Luis Severino RC .50 1.25
68 Henry Owens RC .50 1.25
69 Aroldis Chapman .30 .75
70 Kris Bryant .40 1.00
71 Sean Manaea RC .40 1.00
72 Yoenis Cespedes .30 .75
73 Ryan Braun .25 .60
74 Eric Hosmer .25 .60
75 Jacoby Ellsbury .25 .60
76 Adrian Gonzalez .25 .60
77 Edwin Encarnacion .30 .75
78 Adrian Beltre .30 .75
79 Max Scherzer .30 .75
80 Joey Votto .30 .75
81 Masahiro Tanaka .25 .60
82 Michael Conforto RC .50 1.25
83 Albert Almora RC .50 1.25
84 A.J. Pollock .20 .50
85 Sonny Gray .25 .60
86 Miguel Cabrera .30 .75
87 Jose Bautista .25 .60
88 James Shields .20 .50
89 Jake Arrieta .25 .60
90 Gary Sanchez RC 1.25 3.00
91 Giancarlo Stanton .30 .75
92 Hector Olivera RC .50 1.25
93 Aaron Blair RC .40 1.00
94 Byron Buxton .30 .75
95 Justin Upton .25 .60
96 Nolan Arenado .50 1.25
97 Craig Kimbrel .25 .60
98 Blake Snell RC .50 1.25
99 Robert Stephenson RC .40 1.00
100 Bryce Harper .50 1.25

2016 Bowman Chrome Blue Refractors

*BLUE REF VET: 4X TO 10X BASIC
*BLUE REF RC: 2X TO 5X BASIC
STATED ODDS 1:34 HOBBY
STATED PRINT RUN 150 SER.#'d SETS

2016 Bowman Chrome Gold Refractors

*GOLD REF VET: 8X TO 20X BASIC
*GOLD REF RC: 4X TO 10X BASIC
STATED ODDS 1:100 HOBBY
STATED PRINT RUN 50 SER.#'d SETS

2016 Bowman Chrome Green Refractors

*GREEN REF VET: 4X TO 10X BASIC
*GREEN REF RC: 2X TO 5X BASIC
STATED ODDS 1:51 HOBBY
STATED PRINT RUN 99 SER.#'d SETS

2016 Bowman Chrome Orange Refractors

*ORANGE REF VET: 10X TO 25X BASIC
*ORANGE REF RC: 5X TO 12X BASIC
STATED ODDS 1:199 HOBBY
STATED PRINT RUN 25 SER.#'d SETS

2016 Bowman Chrome Purple Refractors

*PURPLE REF VET: 2X TO 5X BASIC
*PURPLE REF RC: 1X TO 2.5X BASIC
c
STATED PRINT RUN 250 SER.#'d SETS

2016 Bowman Chrome Refractors

*REF VET: 1.5X TO 4X BASIC
*REF RC: .75X TO 2X BASIC
STATED ODDS 1:10 HOBBY
STATED PRINT RUN 499 SER.#'d SETS

2016 Bowman Chrome Vending '16 Bowman

COMPLETE SET (100) 12.00 30.00
FOUND IN VENDING BOXES
1 Mike Trout 2.00 5.00
2 Josh Donaldson .30 .75
3 Albert Pujols .50 1.25
5 Paul Goldschmidt .40 1.00
6 Yasmany Tomas .25 .60
7 Freddie Freeman .50 1.25
10 David Ortiz .40 1.00
11 Manny Machado .40 1.00
12 Chris Davis .25 .60
13 Mookie Betts .75 2.00
14 Adam Jones .30 .75
16 Xander Bogaerts .40 1.00
17 Jon Lester .30 .75
18 Jake Arrieta .30 .75
20 Kris Bryant .50 1.25
23 Chris Sale .40 1.00
27 Joey Votto .40 1.00
28 Francisco Lindor .40 1.00
30 Carlos Correa .40 1.00
33 Miguel Cabrera .40 1.00
34 Ian Kinsler .30 .75
38 Dallas Keuchel .30 .75
39 Jose Altuve .30 .75
40 Clayton Kershaw .60 1.50
41 Lorenzo Cain .25 .60
43 Eric Hosmer .30 .75
45 Zack Greinke .40 1.00
47 Yasiel Puig .40 1.00
48 Giancarlo Stanton .40 1.00
49 Jose Fernandez .40 1.00
50 Ichiro Suzuki .50 1.25
51 Ryan Braun .30 .75
52 Byron Buxton .40 1.00
53 Brian Dozier .30 .75
55 Yoenis Cespedes .40 1.00
56 Matt Harvey .30 .75
57 Jacob deGrom .75 2.00
58 Noah Syndergaard .30 .75
59 Dellin Betances .30 .75
60 Masahiro Tanaka .30 .75
61 Alex Rodriguez .50 1.25
62 Sonny Gray .25 .60
64 Stephen Vogt .30 .75
67 Odubel Herrera .30 .75
68 Andrew McCutchen .40 1.00
70 Buster Posey .50 1.25
73 Tyson Ross .25 .60
75 Jung Ho Kang .25 .60
76 Madison Bumgarner .30 .75
78 Brandon Belt .30 .75
80 Felix Hernandez .30 .75
85 Chris Archer .25 .60
86 Kevin Kiermaier .30 .75
87 Prince Fielder .30 .75
91 Jose Bautista .30 .75
92 David Price .30 .75
94 Wei-Yin Chen .25 .60
96 Stephen Strasburg .40 1.00
97 Garrett Richards .30 .75
98 David Peralta .25 .60
99 Julio Teheran .30 .75
100 Bryce Harper .60 1.50
101 Adam Eaton .25 .60
103 Jay Bruce .30 .75
104 Carlos Gonzalez .30 .75
110 Matt Kemp .30 .75
112 Kyle Seager .25 .60
113 Marcus Stroman .30 .75
115 Trevor Rosenthal .30 .75
117 Michael Brantley .30 .75
118 Adam Wainwright .30 .75
119 Wade Davis .25 .60
122 Kyle Schwarber .75 2.00
123 Stephen Piscotty .40 1.00
124 Carl Edwards Jr. .30 .75
125 Aaron Nola .50 1.25
126 Hector Olivera .30 .75
127 Rob Refsnyder .30 .75
128 Jose Peraza .30 .75
129 Henry Owens .30 .75
130 Trea Turner .75 2.00
131 Michael Conforto .30 .75
132 Greg Bird .30 .75
133 Richie Shaffer .25 .60
134 Jon Gray .25 .60
135 Luis Severino .30 .75
136 Miguel Almonte .25 .60
137 Brandon Drury .40 1.00
138 Zach Lee .25 .60
139 Kyle Waldrop .30 .75
140 Miguel Sano .40 1.00
142 Frankie Montas .30 .75
143 Gary Sanchez .75 2.00
144 Ketel Marte .50 1.25
145 Trayce Thompson .40 1.00
146 Jorge Lopez .25 .60
147 Max Kepler .40 1.00
148 Tom Murphy .25 .60
149 Raul Mondesi .50 1.25
150 Corey Seager 2.50 6.00

2016 Bowman Chrome AFL Fall Stars

COMP.SET w/o SP (20) 8.00 20.00
STATED ODDS 1:6 HOBBY
SP ODDS 1:1981 HOBBY
SP PRINT RUN 250 SER.#'d SETS
*BLUE/150: .75X TO 2X BASIC
*GOLD/50: 2X TO 5X BASIC
*ORANGE/25: 2.5X TO 6X BASIC
AFLAB Alex Blandino .40 1.00
AFLABW Adam Brett Walker .40 1.00
AFLAD Austin Dean .40 1.00
AFLAE Adam Engel .40 1.00
AFLAM Austin Meadows 1.00 2.50
AFLCA Christian Arroyo .75 2.00
AFLCF Clint Frazier 1.50 4.00
AFLCP Chad Pinder .40 1.00
AFLDF Derek Fisher .40 1.00
AFLDP D.J. Peterson .40 1.00
AFLJB Jake Bauers .60 1.50
AFLJP Jurickson Profar .50 1.25
AFLKF Kyle Freeland .50 1.25
AFLLS Lucas Sims .40 1.00
AFLNB Renato Nunez .75 2.00
AFLRM Reese McGuire .40 1.00
AFLRT Raimel Tapia .50 1.25
AFLSGS Sanchez MVP SP/250 15.00 40.00
AFLSM Sean Manaea .40 1.00
AFLST Sam Travis .50 1.25
AFLWC Willson Contreras 1.00 2.50

2016 Bowman Chrome AFL Fall Stars Autographs

STATED ODDS 1:416 HOBBY
STATED SP ODDS 1:9659 HOBBY
STATED PRINT RUN 25 SER.#'d SETS
NO PRICING ON QTY 17 OR LESS
BOW.CHR.EXCH.DEADLINE 8/31/2018
*GOLD/50: .6X TO 1.5X BASIC
AFLABW Adam Brett Walker/199 3.00 8.00
AFLAGS Gary Sanchez MVP SP/50 75.00 200.00
AFLCP Chad Pinder/22 3.00 8.00
AFLDP D.J. Peterson
AFLJB Jake Bauers/50 6.00 15.00
AFLJP Jurickson Profar/75 10.00 25.00
AFLLS Lucas Sims/199 4.00 10.00
AFLWC Willson Contreras/199 10.00 25.00

2016 Bowman Chrome AFL Fall Stars Relic Autographs

STATED ODDS 1:2752 HOBBY
STATED PRINT RUN 25 SER.#'d SETS
BOW.CHR.EXCH.DEADLINE 8/31/2018
AFLRAB Alex Blandino 30.00 80.00
AFLRAE Adam Engel 8.00 20.00
AFLRDF Derek Fisher 12.00 30.00
AFLRGS Gary Sanchez 150.00 250.00
AFLRJC Jeimer Candelario 20.00 50.00
AFLRJP Jurickson Profar 10.00 25.00
AFLRRM Reese McGuire 8.00 20.00

2016 Bowman Chrome AFL Fall Stars Relics

STATED ODDS 1:626 HOBBY
STATED PRINT RUN 99 SER.#'d SETS
*ORANGE/25: .75X TO 2X BASIC
AFLRABW Adam Brett Walker 3.00 8.00
AFLRAD Austin Dean 3.00 8.00
AFLRAK Andrew Knapp 3.00 8.00
AFLRAM Austin Meadows 8.00 20.00
AFLRCA Christian Arroyo 8.00 20.00
AFLRCF Clint Frazier 12.00 30.00
AFLRCP Chad Pinder 3.00 8.00
AFLRDP D.J. Peterson 3.00 8.00
AFLRGS Gary Sanchez 25.00 60.00
AFLRJB Jake Bauers 5.00 12.00
AFLRJP Jurickson Profar 8.00 20.00
AFLRKF Kyle Freeland 4.00 10.00
AFLRLS Lucas Sims 3.00 8.00
AFLRRN Renato Nunez 6.00 15.00
AFLRRT Rowdy Tellez 5.00 12.00
AFLRRTA Raimel Tapia 4.00 10.00
AFLRSM Sean Manaea 8.00 20.00
AFLRST Sam Travis 4.00 10.00

2016 Bowman Chrome Bowman Scouts Top 100

STATED ODDS 1:8 HOBBY
*GREEN/99: .75X TO 2X BASIC
*GOLD/50: 2X TO 5X BASIC
*ORANGE/25: 3X TO 8X BASIC
BTP1 Corey Seager 4.00 10.00
BTP2 Byron Buxton .60 1.50
BTP3 Lucas Giolito .60 1.50

BTP4 J.P. Crawford .40 1.00
BTP5 Alex Reyes .50 1.25
BTP6 Orlando Arcia .50 1.25
BTP7 Julio Urias 1.25 3.00
BTP8 Tyler Glasnow 1.50 4.00
BTP9 Anderson Espinoza .50 1.25
BTP10 Brendan Rodgers .60 1.50
BTP11 Blake Snell .50 1.25
BTP12 Jose Berrios .60 1.50
BTP13 Steven Matz .40 1.00
BTP14 Trea Turner 1.25 3.00
BTP15 Gleyber Torres 6.00 15.00
BTP16 Dansby Swanson 1.50 4.00
BTP17 Alex Bregman 2.00 5.00
BTP18 Manuel Margot .40 1.00
BTP19 Ozzie Albies 2.00 5.00
BTP20 Jose De Leon .40 1.00
BTP21 Andrew Benintendi 1.25 3.00
BTP22 Nomar Mazara .60 1.50
BTP23 Victor Robles 1.50 4.00
BTP24 A.J. Reed .40 1.00
BTP25 Joey Gallo .50 1.25
BTP26 Sean Newcomb .50 1.25
BTP27 Jorge Lopez .40 1.00
BTP28 Aaron Blair .40 1.00
BTP29 Max Kepler .60 1.50
BTP30 Rafael Devers 1.25 3.00
BTP31 Aaron Judge 3.00 8.00
BTP32 Archie Bradley .40 1.00
BTP33 Bradley Zimmer .60 1.50
BTP34 Jorge Mateo .50 1.25
BTP35 Carson Fulmer .40 1.00
BTP36 Brett Phillips .40 1.00
BTP37 Kolby Allard .40 1.00
BTP38 Raul Mondesi .75 2.00
BTP39 Lewis Brinson .60 1.50
BTP40 Jeff Hoffman .50 1.25
BTP41 Anthony Alford .40 1.00
BTP42 Brady Aiken 1.00 2.50
BTP43 Jon Gray .40 1.00
BTP44 Robert Stephenson .40 1.00
BTP45 Mark Appel .40 1.00
BTP46 Dillon Tate .50 1.25
BTP47 Austin Meadows 1.00 2.50
BTP48 Willy Adames .60 1.50
BTP49 Ian Happ .75 2.00
BTP50 Clint Frazier 1.50 4.00
BTP51 Francis Martes .40 1.00
BTP52 Jake Thompson .40 1.00
BTP53 David Dahl .50 1.25
BTP54 Dylan Bundy .50 1.25
BTP55 Kyle Tucker 2.00 5.00
BTP56 Franklin Barreto .40 1.00
BTP57 Josh Bell .75 2.00
BTP58 Brent Honeywell .60 1.50
BTP59 Tyler Stephenson 1.00 2.50
BTP60 Jesse Winker 1.50 4.00
BTP61 Jose Peraza .50 1.25
BTP62 Trent Clark .40 1.00
BTP63 Brian Johnson .40 1.00
BTP64 Jameson Taillon .50 1.25
BTP65 Miguel Almonte .40 1.00
BTP66 Sean Manaea .40 1.00
BTP67 Jon Harris .50 1.25
BTP68 Willson Contreras 2.50 6.00
BTP69 Dominic Smith .40 1.00
BTP70 James Kaprielian .40 1.00
BTP71 Marco Gonzales .50 1.25
BTP72 Amir Garrett .40 1.00
BTP73 Gary Sanchez 1.25 3.00
BTP74 Hector Olivera .50 1.25
BTP75 Michael Fulmer .60 1.50
BTP76 Phil Bickford .40 1.00
BTP77 Hunter Renfroe .50 1.25
BTP78 Nick Gordon .40 1.00
BTP79 Nick Williams .50 1.25
BTP80 Cody Reed .40 1.00
BTP81 Grant Holmes .50 1.25
BTP82 Tyler Jay .40 1.00
BTP83 Tyler Kolek .50 1.25
BTP84 Bobby Bradley .50 1.25
BTP85 Alex Jackson .50 1.25
BTP86 Gavin Cecchini .40 1.00
BTP87 Tim Anderson 1.50 4.00
BTP88 Christian Arroyo .75 2.00
BTP89 Hunter Harvey .40 1.00
BTP90 Franklyn Kilome .50 1.25
BTP91 Cornelius Randolph .40 1.00
BTP92 Sean Reid-Foley .50 1.25
BTP93 Rob Kaminsky .40 1.00
BTP94 Jake Bauers .60 1.50
BTP95 Mac Williamson .40 1.00
BTP96 Ke'Bryan Hayes 2.00 5.00
BTP97 Beau Burrows .40 1.00
BTP98 Josh Naylor .50 1.25
BTP99 Edwin Diaz .75 2.00
BTP100 Brandon Nimmo .60 1.50

2016 Bowman Chrome Bowman Scouts Top 100 Autographs Gold

STATED ODDS 1:3386 HOBBY
EXCHANGE DEADLINE 3/31/2018
BTP2 Byron Buxton 15.00 40.00
BTP3 Lucas Giolito 30.00 80.00
BTP5 Alex Reyes 10.00 25.00
BTP10 Brendan Rodgers 20.00 50.00
BTP11 Blake Snell 20.00 50.00
BTP12 Jose Berrios 20.00 50.00
BTP14 Trea Turner 30.00 80.00
BTP16 Dansby Swanson 50.00 120.00
BTP17 Alex Bregman 60.00 150.00
BTP21 Andrew Benintendi 40.00 100.00
BTP31 Aaron Judge 75.00 200.00
BTP35 Carson Fulmer 12.00 30.00
BTP46 Dillon Tate 15.00 40.00
BTP47 Austin Meadows 30.00 80.00
BTP48 Willy Adames 20.00 50.00

2016 Bowman Chrome Bowman Scouts Updates

COMPLETE SET (25) 5.00 12.00
STATED ODDS 1:3 HOBBY
*BLUE/150: .75X TO 2X BASIC
*GOLD/50: 2X TO 5X BASIC
*ORANGE/25: 2.5X TO 6X BASIC
BSUAJ Ariel Jurado .40 1.00
BSUAR Austin Riley 1.25 3.00
BSUAS Antonio Senzatela .40 1.00
BSUAV Alex Verdugo .60 1.50
BSUCB Cody Bellinger 6.00 15.00
BSUCE Chris Ellis .40 1.00
BSUCS Connor Sadzeck .40 1.00
BSUDJ Drew Jackson .40 1.00
BSUDU Duane Underwood .40 1.00
BSUJC Jharel Cotton .40 1.00
BSUJF Jack Flaherty 2.50 6.00
BSUJG Jarlin Garcia .40 1.00
BSUJM Joe Musgrove 1.25 3.00
BSUJN Jacob Nottingham .40 1.00
BSUJO Jhailyn Ortiz .75 2.00
BSUKN Kevin Newman .60 1.50
BSUMC Mike Clevinger .75 2.00
BSUMS Michael Soroka 1.25 3.00
BSUNP Nick Plummer .50 1.25
BSURG Ruddy Giron .40 1.00
BSURL Reynaldo Lopez .40 1.00
BSUTM Trey Mancini 1.25 3.00
BSUTO Tyler O'Neill .50 1.25
BSUTW Taylor Ward .50 1.25
BSUYA Yadier Alvarez .50 1.25

2016 Bowman Chrome Bowman Scouts Updates Autographs

STATED ODDS 1:543 HOBBY
STATED PRINT RUN 199 SER.#'d SETS
BOW.CHR.EXCH.DEADLINE 8/31/2018
*GOLD REF: .75X TO 2X BASIC
BSUAJ Ariel Jurado 3.00 8.00
BSUAR Austin Riley 60.00 150.00
BSUCS Connor Sadzeck 3.00 8.00
BSUDJ Drew Jackson 3.00 8.00
BSUJC Jharel Cotton 3.00 8.00
BSUJO Jhailyn Ortiz 6.00 15.00
BSUKN Kevin Newman 5.00 12.00
BSUMC Mike Clevinger 6.00 15.00
BSUMS Michael Soroka 10.00 25.00
BSUNP Nick Plummer 4.00 10.00
BSUTM Trey Mancini 10.00 25.00
BSUTO Tyler O'Neill 4.00 10.00
BSUTW Taylor Ward 4.00 10.00
BSUYA Yadier Alvarez 10.00 25.00

2016 Bowman Chrome Out of the Gate

COMPLETE SET (10) 8.00 20.00
STATED ODDS 1:12 HOBBY
*BLUE/150: 1.2X TO 3X BASIC
*GOLD/50: 2X TO 5X BASIC
*ORANGE/25: 2.5X TO 6X BASIC
OOG1 Trevor Story 2.00 5.00
OOG2 Tyler White .40 1.00
OOG3 Aledmys Diaz .60 1.50
OOG4 Kenta Maeda .75 2.00
OOG5 Michael Conforto .50 1.25
OOG6 Nomar Mazara .60 1.50
OOG7 Aaron Nola .75 2.00
OOG8 Byung-ho Park .50 1.25
OOG9 Stephen Piscotty .60 1.50
OOG10 Blake Snell .50 1.25

2016 Bowman Chrome Prime Position Autographs

STATED ODDS 1:432 HOBBY
STATED PRINT RUN 250 SER.#'d SETS
BOW.CHR.EXCH.DEADLINE 8/31/2018
*GREEN/99: .6X TO 1.5X BASIC
*GOLD/50: .75X TO 2X BASIC
*ORANGE/25: 1X TO 2.5X BASIC
PPAAB Andrew Benintendi 25.00 60.00
PPAAJ Aaron Judge 60.00 150.00
PPAAR A.J. Reed 4.00 10.00
PPAARE Alex Reyes 10.00 25.00
PPACS Corey Seager 20.00 50.00
PPADS Dansby Swanson 15.00 40.00
PPAJB Jose Berrios 6.00 15.00
PPAKS Kyle Schwarber 12.00 30.00
PPAMS Miguel Sano 8.00 20.00
PPANM Nomar Mazara 8.00 20.00
PPAOA Orlando Arcia 5.00 12.00
PPARD Rafael Devers 20.00 50.00
PPATS Tyler Stephenson 10.00 25.00
PPAYM Yoan Moncada 40.00 100.00

2016 Bowman Chrome Prospect Autographs

BOW.ODDS 1:56 HOBBY
BOW.CHR.ODDS 1:11 HOBBY
BOW.PLATE ODDS 1:17,849 HOBBY
BOW.CHR.PLATE ODDS 1:5568 HOBBY
PLATE PRINT RUN 1 SET PER COLOR
NO PLATE PRICING DUE TO SCARCITY
BOW.EXCH.DEADLINE 3/31/2018
BOW.CHR.EXCH.DEADLINE 8/31/2018
BCAPAG Austin Gomber 3.00 8.00
BCAPASA Antonio Santillan EXCH 3.00 8.00
BCAPCG Conner Greene 3.00 8.00
BCAPCK Chad Kuhl 4.00 10.00
BCAPCR Cornelius Randolph 3.00 8.00
BCAPCS Connor Sadzeck 3.00 8.00
BCAPCZ Corey Zangari 3.00 8.00
BCAPDFO Dustin Fowler 4.00 10.00
BCAPDP David Paulino 4.00 10.00
BCAPEJM Eddy Julio Martinez 4.00 10.00
BCAPFR Franklin Reyes 3.00 8.00
BCAPHJP Hoy-Jun Park 4.00 10.00
BCAPID Isan Diaz 6.00 15.00
BCAPJA Jonah Arenado 4.00 10.00
BCAPJF Junior Fernandez 5.00 12.00
BCAPJFA Jacob Faria 3.00 8.00
BCAPJG Jeison Guzman 3.00 8.00
BCAPJGU Javier Guerra 3.00 8.00
BCAPJJ Jahmai Jones 8.00 20.00
BCAPJOS Jordan Stephens 3.00 8.00
BCAPJP Jermaine Palacios 4.00 10.00
BCAPJS Jaime Schultz 3.00 8.00
BCAPMG Mike Gerber 3.00 8.00
BCAPOC Oneal Cruz 30.00 80.00
BCAPRO Raffy Ozuna 3.00 8.00
BCAPRW Ryan Williams 3.00 8.00
BCAPSH Sam Howard 3.00 8.00
BCAPSTR Sam Travis 4.00 10.00
BCAPTA Tyler Alexander 3.00 8.00
BCAPTJ Tyrell Jenkins 3.00 8.00
BCAPVA Victor Alcantara 3.00 8.00
BCAPWC Willie Calhoun 5.00 12.00
BCAPYG Yeudy Garcia 3.00 8.00
CPAAA Anthony Alford 8.00 20.00
CPAAB Alex Bregman 75.00 200.00
CPAABA Anthony Banda 3.00 8.00
CPAAE Anderson Espinoza 4.00 10.00
CPAAEN Adam Engel 3.00 8.00
CPAAJ Ariel Jurado 3.00 8.00
CPAAS Anfernee Seymour 3.00 8.00
CPABL Brady Lail 3.00 8.00
CPABM Billy McKinney 4.00 10.00
CPABR Brendan Rodgers 15.00 40.00
CPACB Corey Black 3.00 8.00
CPADA Domingo Acevedo 5.00 12.00
CPADAS Dansby Swanson 20.00 50.00
CPADC Daz Cameron 10.00 25.00
CPADD David Denson 3.00 8.00
CPADH David Hess 3.00 8.00
CPADJ Drew Jackson 3.00 8.00
CPADL Domingo Leyba 3.00 8.00
CPADP Daniel Poncedeleon 4.00 10.00
CPAFK Franklyn Kilome 4.00 10.00
CPAFM Francis Martes 3.00 8.00
CPAFT Fernando Tatis Jr. 1500.00 4000.00
CPAHB Harrison Bader 12.00 30.00
CPAIA Iolana Akau 5.00 12.00
CPAJC Jharel Cotton 3.00 8.00
CPAJGU Jordan Guerrero 3.00 8.00
CPAJMU Joe Musgrove 25.00 60.00
CPAJN John Norwood 3.00 8.00
CPAJO Jhailyn Ortiz 6.00 15.00
CPAJP Jordan Patterson 3.00 8.00
CPAJS Juan Soto 2000.00 5000.00
CPAJT Jesus Tinoco 3.00 8.00
CPAJY Juan Yepez 3.00 8.00
CPAKK Kevin Kramer 4.00 10.00
CPAKM Kenta Maeda 30.00 80.00
CPALF Lucius Fox 5.00 12.00
CPAMC Mike Clevinger 12.00 30.00
CPAMD Mauricio Dubon 12.00 30.00
CPAMW Mikey White 3.00 8.00
CPAMZ Mark Zagunis 3.00 8.00
CPANS Nate Smith 3.00 8.00
CPAOD Oscar De La Cruz 4.00 10.00
CPAPD Paul DeJong 20.00 50.00
CPARB Rafael Bautista 3.00 8.00
CPARG Ruddy Giron 3.00 8.00
CPARS Ricardo Sanchez 3.00 8.00
CPASC Samuel Coonrod 3.00 8.00
CPASG Stone Garrett 3.00 8.00
CPASR Sal Romano 3.00 8.00
CPATM Trey Mancini 20.00 50.00
CPATO Tyler O'Neill 20.00 50.00
CPATW Tyler White 3.00 8.00
CPAVG Vladimir Guerrero Jr. 500.00 1200.00
CPAVR Victor Robles 40.00 100.00
CPAWC Willson Contreras 30.00 80.00
CPAWH Wei-Chieh Huang 3.00 8.00
CPAYA Yadier Alvarez 4.00 10.00
CPAYM Yoan Moncada 100.00 250.00
CPAYMU Yairo Munoz 3.00 8.00

2016 Bowman Chrome Prospect Autographs Blue Refractors

*BLUE REF: 1X TO 2.5X BASIC
BOW.ODDS 1:483 HOBBY
BOW.CHR.ODDS 1:139 HOBBY
STATED PRINT RUN 150 SER.#'D SETS
BOW.EXCH.DEADLINE 3/31/2018
BOW.CHR.EXCH.DEADLINE 8/31/2018

2016 Bowman Chrome Prospect Autographs Green Refractors

*GREEN REF: 1.2X TO 3X BASIC
INSERTED IN RETAIL PACKS
BOW.CHR.ODDS 1:208 HOBBY
STATED PRINT RUN 99 SER.#'D SETS
BOW.EXCH.DEADLINE 3/31/2018
BOW.CHR.EXCH.DEADLINE 8/31/2018

2016 Bowman Chrome Prospect Autographs Gold Refractors

*GOLD REF: 1.5X TO 4X BASIC
BOW.STATED ODDS 1:1448 HOBBY
STATED PRINT RUN 50 SER.#'d SETS
BOW.EXCH.DEADLINE 3/31/2018
BOW.CHR.EXCH.DEADLINE 8/31/2018

2016 Bowman Chrome Prospect Autographs Orange Refractors

*ORANGE REF: 3X TO 8X BASIC
BOW.STATED ODDS 1:687 HOBBY
BOW.CHR.ODDS 1:372 HOBBY
STATED PRINT RUN 25 SER.#'d SETS
BOW.EXCH.DEADLINE 3/31/2018
BOW.CHR.EXCH.DEADLINE 8/31/2018

2016 Bowman Chrome Prospect Autographs Purple Refractors

*PURPLE REF: .6X TO 1.5X BASIC
BOW.STATED ODDS 1:290 HOBBY
BOW.CHR.ODDS 1:83 HOBBY
STATED PRINT RUN 250 SER.#'d SETS
BOW.EXCH.DEADLINE 3/31/2018
BOW.CHR.EXCH.DEADLINE 8/31/2018

2016 Bowman Chrome Prospect Autographs Refractors

*REF: .5X TO 1.2X BASIC
BOW.ODDS 1:145 HOBBY
BOW.CHR.ODDS 1:42 HOBBY
STATED PRINT RUN 499 SER.#'D SETS
BOW.EXCH.DEADLINE 3/31/2018
BOW.CHR.EXCH.DEADLINE 8/31/2018

2016 Bowman Chrome Prospects

COMPLETE SET (250) 20.00 50.00
BOW.PLATE ODDS 1:4119 HOBBY
BOW.CHR.PLATE ODDS 1:4116 HOBBY
PLATE PRINT RUN 1 SET PER COLOR
NO PLATE PRICING DUE TO SCARCITY
BCP1 Daz Cameron .25 .60
BCP2 Orlando Arcia .30 .75
BCP3 Domingo Leyba .25 .60
BCP4 Alex Bregman 8.00 20.00
BCP5 Yadier Alvarez .30 .75
BCP6 Touki Toussaint .30 .75
BCP7 Brady Aiken .60 1.50
BCP8 Billy McKinney .30 .75
BCP9 Stone Garrett .25 .60
BCP10 Victor Robles 1.00 2.50
BCP11 Wei-Chieh Huang .25 .60
BCP12 Jomar Reyes .40 1.00
BCP13 Lucius Fox .40 1.00
BCP14 Samuel Coonrod .25 .60
BCP15 Seuly Matias 2.00 5.00
BCP16 Willson Contreras 1.50 4.00
BCP17 Fernando Tatis Jr. 100.00 250.00
BCP18 Starling Heredia .40 1.00
BCP19 Drew Jackson .25 .60
BCP20 Ruddy Giron .25 .60
BCP21 Anfernee Seymour .25 .60
BCP22 Iolana Akau .40 1.00
BCP23 Kevin Padlo .25 .60
BCP24 Brady Lail .25 .60
BCP25 Dillon Tate .30 .75
BCP26 Jharel Cotton .25 .60
BCP27 John Norwood .25 .60
BCP28 Manny Sanchez .30 .75
BCP29 Juan Yepez .25 .60
BCP30 David Denson .25 .60
BCP31 Jhailyn Ortiz .50 1.25
BCP32 Wander Javier .40 1.00
BCP33 Sal Romano .25 .60
BCP34 Francis Martes .25 .60
BCP35 Domingo Acevedo .40 1.00
BCP36 Mark Zagunis .25 .60
BCP37 Franklyn Kilome .30 .75
BCP38 Trey Mancini .75 2.00
BCP39 Corey Black .25 .60
BCP40 Anderson Espinoza .30 .75
BCP41 Jordan Guerrero .25 .60
BCP42 Mauricio Dubon .30 .75
BCP43 Paul DeJong 1.50 4.00
BCP44 Mikey White .25 .60
BCP45 Andrew Suarez .30 .75
BCP46 Kevin Kramer .30 .75
BCP47 Nate Smith .25 .60
BCP48 Ariel Jurado .25 .60
BCP49 Rafael Bautista .25 .60
BCP50 Dansby Swanson 1.00 2.50
BCP51 Anthony Banda .25 .60
BCP52 Mike Clevinger .50 1.25
BCP53 Daniel Poncedeleon .30 .75
BCP54 Ian Kahaloa .25 .60
BCP55 Vladimir Guerrero Jr. 40.00 100.00
BCP56 Logan Allen .25 .60
BCP57 Kyle Survance Jr. .25 .60
BCP58 Omar Carrizales .25 .60
BCP59 Anthony Alford .25 .60
BCP60 Kyle Tucker 1.25 3.00
BCP61 Tyler Jay .25 .60
BCP62 Andrew Benintendi .75 2.00
BCP63 Carson Fulmer .25 .60
BCP64 Ian Happ .50 1.25
BCP65 Sean Newcomb .30 .75
BCP66 Tyler Stephenson .60 1.50
BCP67 Josh Naylor .30 .75
BCP68 Garrett Whitley .30 .75
BCP69 Kolby Allard .25 .60
BCP70 Trent Clark .25 .60
BCP71 James Kaprielian .25 .60
BCP72 Phil Bickford .25 .60
BCP73 Kevin Newman .40 1.00
BCP74 Richie Martin .25 .60
BCP75 Ashe Russell .25 .60
BCP76 Beau Burrows .25 .60
BCP77 Nick Plummer .30 .75
BCP78 Walker Buehler .75 2.00
BCP79 D.J. Stewart .25 .60
BCP80 Taylor Ward .30 .75
BCP81 Mike Nikorak .25 .60
BCP82 Michael Soroka .75 2.00
BCP83 Kyle Holder .30 .75
BCP84 Chris Shaw .25 .60
BCP85 Ke'Bryan Hayes 2.50 6.00
BCP86 Nolan Watson .25 .60
BCP87 Christin Stewart .30 .75
BCP88 Ryan Mountcastle 1.25 3.00
BCP89 Jack Flaherty 1.50 4.00
BCP90 Raimel Tapia .30 .75
BCP91 Michael Fulmer .40 1.00
BCP92 A.J. Reed .25 .60
BCP93 Gavin Cecchini .25 .60
BCP94 Jorge Mateo .30 .75
BCP95 Amed Rosario .40 1.00
BCP96 Daniel Robertson .25 .60
BCP97 Nick Gordon .25 .60
BCP98 Rob Kaminsky .25 .60
BCP99 Amir Garrett .25 .60
BCP100 Brendan Rodgers .40 1.00
BCP101 Duane Underwood .25 .60
BCP102 Alen Hanson .30 .75
BCP103 Jorge Alfaro .40 1.00
BCP104 Grant Holmes .30 .75
BCP105 Nick Williams .30 .75
BCP106 Tyler Wade .40 1.00
BCP107 Jake Thompson .25 .60
BCP108 Alex Reyes .30 .75
BCP109 Rafael Devers .75 2.00
BCP110 Ozzie Albies 1.25 3.00
BCP111 Alex Young .30 .75
BCP112 Tyrell Jenkins .25 .60
BCP113 Max Fried .40 1.00
BCP114 Chance Sisco .50 1.25
BCP115 Michael Kopech .75 2.00
BCP116 Pierce Johnson .25 .60
BCP117 Tyler Danish .25 .60
BCP118 Keury Mella .25 .60
BCP119 Alex Blandino .25 .60
BCP120 Justus Sheffield .50 1.25
BCP121 Jeff Hoffman .30 .75
BCP122 Ryan McMahon .40 1.00
BCP123 JaCoby Jones .30 .75
BCP124 Colin Moran .25 .60
BCP125 Derek Fisher .25 .60
BCP126 Scott Blewett .25 .60
BCP127 Jeimer Candelario .30 .75
BCP128 Fernando Perez .25 .60
BCP129 Andrew Knapp .25 .60
BCP130 Sean Manaea .25 .60
BCP131 Jake Bauers .40 1.00
BCP132 Rowdy Tellez .40 1.00
BCP133 Gabby Guerrero .25 .60
BCP134 Christian Arroyo .50 1.25
BCP135 Adam Brett Walker II .25 .60
BCP136 Brett Phillips .25 .60
BCP137 Lewis Brinson .40 1.00
BCP138 Bubba Starling .30 .75
BCP139 Chad Pinder .25 .60
BCP140 Chris Bostick .25 .60
BCP141 Luke Weaver .40 1.00
BCP142 Kenta Maeda .50 1.25
BCP143 Luiz Gohara .25 .60
BCP144 Yoan Lopez .25 .60
BCP145 Courtney Hawkins .25 .60
BCP146 Austin Dean .25 .60
BCP147 Matt Chapman .75 2.00
BCP148 Yoan Moncada 6.00 15.00
BCP149 Nick Travieso .25 .60
BCP150 Lucas Giolito .40 1.00
BCP151 Jose De Leon .25 .60
BCP152 Willy Adames .40 1.00
BCP153 Dustin Fowler .30 .75
BCP154 Chad Kuhl .30 .75
BCP155 Roman Quinn .40 1.00
BCP156 Yeudy Garcia .25 .60
BCP157 Cody Reed .25 .60
BCP158 Sam Howard .25 .60
BCP159 Josh Staumont .30 .75
BCP160 Franklin Barreto .25 .60
BCP161 Shane Dawson .25 .60
BCP162 Austin Gomber .25 .60
BCP163 Blake Trahan .25 .60
BCP164 Wilkerman Garcia .30 .75
BCP165 Austin Rei .25 .60
BCP166 Todd Hankins .25 .60
BCP167 Ben Lively .25 .60
BCP168 Victor Alcantara .25 .60
BCP169 Willie Calhoun .40 1.00
BCP170 D.J. Wilson .30 .75
BCP171 Dylan Cease .40 1.00
BCP172 Connor Sadzeck .25 .60
BCP173 Donny Sands .30 .75
BCP174 Kyle Freeland .30 .75
BCP175 David Dahl .30 .75
BCP176 Junior Fernandez .40 1.00
BCP177 Antonio Santillan .25 .60
BCP178 Jahmai Jones .30 .75
BCP179 Forrest Wall .25 .60
BCP180 Andrew Stevenson .25 .60
BCP181 Clayton Blackburn .25 .60
BCP182 Cody Bellinger 8.00 20.00
BCP183 Raffy Ozuna .25 .60
BCP184 Anderson Miller .25 .60
BCP185 Travis Blankenhorn 1.25 3.00
BCP186 Jacob Faria .25 .60
BCP187 George Iskenderian .25 .60
BCP188 Alex Verdugo .40 1.00
BCP189 Brent Honeywell .40 1.00
BCP190 Spencer Adams .25 .60
BCP191 Ryan McKenna .25 .60
BCP192 Chance Adams .40 1.00
BCP193 Jaime Schultz .25 .60
BCP194 Michael Soroka .75 2.00
BCP195 Helmis Rodriguez .25 .60
BCP196 Juan Hillman .25 .60
BCP197 Jermaine Palacios .30 .75
BCP198 Reese McGuire .25 .60
BCP199 Yohander Mendez .25 .60
BCP200 Eloy Jimenez 1.00 2.50
BCP201 Hoy-Jun Park .30 .75
BCP202 Austin Riley .75 2.00
BCP203 Isaiah White .25 .60
BCP204 Oneal Cruz 6.00 15.00
BCP205 Mac Marshall .25 .60
BCP206 Jalen Miller .25 .60
BCP207 Mitch Keller .30 .75
BCP208 Franklin Reyes .25 .60
BCP209 Josh Sborz .40 1.00
BCP210 Manuel Margot .25 .60
BCP211 Tyler Beede .30 .75
BCP212 Magneuris Sierra .75 2.00
BCP213 David Paulino .30 .75
BCP214 Bradley Zimmer .40 1.00
BCP215 Ray Black .25 .60
BCP216 Josh Hader .30 .75
BCP217 Zach Eflin .30 .75
BCP218 Ali Sanchez .25 .60
BCP219 Yadir Drake .30 .75
BCP220 Jose Adames .25 .60
BCP221 Ryan Williams .25 .60
BCP222 Conner Greene .25 .60
BCP223 Zack Erwin .25 .60
BCP224 Sean Reid-Foley .30 .75
BCP225 Joe Jimenez .30 .75
BCP226 Nick Burdi .25 .60
BCP227 Jairo Beras .25 .60
BCP228 Blake Perkins .25 .60
BCP229 Sam Travis .30 .75
BCP230 Stephen Gonsalves .25 .60
BCP231 Dakota Chalmers .25 .60
BCP232 Isan Diaz .50 1.25
BCP233 Taylor Guerrieri .25 .60
BCP234 Andrew Moore .30 .75
BCP235 Tyler Alexander .25 .60
BCP236 Gleyber Torres 6.00 15.00
BCP237 Kohl Stewart .25 .60
BCP238 Demi Orimoloye .25 .60
BCP239 Hunter Renfroe .30 .75
BCP240 Jonah Arenado .30 .75
BCP241 Mike Gerber .25 .60
BCP242 Nellie Rodriguez .30 .75
BCP243 Braden Bishop .25 .60
BCP244 Jacob Nottingham .25 .60
BCP245 Bryce Denton .40 1.00
BCP246 Harold Ramirez .30 .75
BCP247 Luis Ortiz .25 .60
BCP248 Ricardo Pinto .30 .75
BCP249 Triston McKenzie .75 2.00
BCP250 Austin Meadows .60 1.50

2016 Bowman Chrome Prospects Black and Gold Refractors

*BLACK/GLD.REF: .6X TO 1.5X BASIC
INSERTED IN VENDING BOXES

2016 Bowman Chrome Prospects Blue Refractors

*BLUE REF: 2X TO 5X BASIC
BOW.ODDS 1:110 HOBBY
BOW.CHR.ODDS 1:111 HOBBY
STATED PRINT RUN 150 SER.#'d SETS

2016 Bowman Chrome Prospects Blue Shimmer Refractors

*BLUE SHIMMER: 2X TO 5X BASIC
RANDOM INSERTS IN PACKS

2016 Bowman Chrome Prospects Gold Refractors

*GOLD REF: 5X TO 12X BASIC
BOW.ODDS 1:329 HOBBY
BOW.CHR.ODDS 1:331 HOBBY
STATED PRINT RUN 50 SER.#'d SETS

2016 Bowman Chrome Prospects Green Refractors

*GREEN REF: 2.5X TO 6X BASIC
BOW.INSERTED IN RETAIL PACKS
BOW.CHR.ODDS 1:51 HOBBY
STATED PRINT RUN 99 SER.#'d SETS

2016 Bowman Chrome Prospects Green Shimmer Refractors

*GRN SHIM REF: 2.5X TO 6X BASIC
STATED ODDS 1:167 HOBBY
STATED PRINT RUN 99 SER.#'d SETS

2016 Bowman Chrome Prospects Orange Refractors

*ORANGE REF: 8X TO 20X BASIC
BOW.ODDS 1:165 HOBBY
BOW.CHR.ODDS 1:199 HOBBY
STATED PRINT RUN 25 SER.#'d SETS

2016 Bowman Chrome Prospects Orange Shimmer Refractors

*ORNG SHIM REF/25: 8X TO 20X BASIC
*ORNG SHIM REF: 2.5X TO 6X BASIC
BOW.ODDS 1:658 HOBBY
BOW.CHR.RANDOMLY INSERTED
1-150 PRINT RUN 25 SER.#'d SETS
151-250 ARE NOT SERIAL NUMBERED

2016 Bowman Chrome Prospects Purple Refractors

*PURPLE REF: 1.5X TO 4X BASIC
BOW.ODDS 1:66 HOBBY
BOW.CHR.ODDS 1:67 HOBBY
STATED PRINT RUN 250 SER.#'d SETS

2016 Bowman Chrome Prospects Refractors

*REF: 1.5X TO 4X BASIC
BOW.ODDS 1:33 HOBBY
BOW.CHR.ODDS 1:34 HOBBY
STATED PRINT RUN 499 SER.#'d SETS

2016 Bowman Chrome Refractors That Never Were

STATED ODDS 1:331 HOBBY
STATED PRINT RUN 499 SER.#'d SETS
*ORANGE/25: 2.5X TO 6X BASIC
RTNWAK Al Kaline 1.25 3.00
RTNWCD Carlos Delgado .75 2.00
RTNWCJ Chipper Jones 1.25 3.00
RTNWJG Juan Gonzalez .75 2.00
RTNWJR Jackie Robinson 1.25 3.00
RTNWJS John Smoltz 1.25 3.00
RTNWMP Mike Piazza 1.25 3.00
RTNWPM Pedro Martinez 1.00 2.50
RTNWVG Vladimir Guerrero 1.00 2.50
RTNWWM Willie Mays 2.50 6.00

2016 Bowman Chrome Refractors That Never Were Autographs

STATED ODDS 1:2181 HOBBY
STATED PRINT RUN 99 SER.#'d SETS
BOW.CHR.EXCH.DEADLINE 8/31/2018
RTNWAK Al Kaline 40.00 100.00
RTNWCD Carlos Delgado 8.00 20.00
RTNWCJ Chipper Jones 40.00 100.00
RTNWJG Juan Gonzalez 8.00 20.00
RTNWJS John Smoltz 20.00 50.00
RTNWMP Mike Piazza 60.00 150.00

2016 Bowman Chrome Rookie Autographs

BOW.ODDS 1:339 HOBBY
BOW.CHR.ODDS 1:174 HOBBY
BOW.PLATE ODDS 1:65,446 HOBBY
BOW.CHR.PLATE ODDS 1:18,202 HOBBY
PLATE PRINT RUN 1 SET PER COLOR
NO PLATE PRICING DUE TO SCARCITY
BOW.EXCH.DEADLINE 3/31/2018
BOW.CHR.EXCH.DEADLINE 8/31/2018
CRAAN Aaron Nola 15.00 40.00
CRACE Carl Edwards Jr. 4.00 10.00
CRAGB Greg Bird 4.00 10.00
CRAHO Hector Olivera 4.00 10.00
CRAHOW Henry Owens 4.00 10.00
CRALS Luis Severino 4.00 10.00
CRAMS Sano Wht jrsy 10.00 25.00
CRARR Rob Refsnyder 4.00 10.00
CRASP Stephen Piscotty 5.00 12.00
CRATT Trea Turner 25.00 60.00
BCARAR A.J. Reed 3.00 8.00
BCARBP Byung-Ho Park 4.00 10.00
BCARBS Blake Snell 10.00 25.00
BCARFM Frankie Montas 4.00 10.00
BCARJBE Jose Berrios 10.00 25.00
BCARJP Jose Peraza 4.00 10.00
BCARLS Luis Severino 4.00 10.00
BCARMR Matt Reynolds 3.00 8.00
BCARTT Trayce Thompson 5.00 12.00

2016 Bowman Chrome Rookie Autographs Blue Refractors

*BLUE REF: 1X TO 2.5X BASIC
BOW.ODDS 1:1693 HOBBY
BOW.CHR.ODDS 1:480 HOBBY
STATED PRINT RUN 150 SER.#'d SETS
BOW.EXCH.DEADLINE 3/31/2018
BOW.CHR.EXCH.DEADLINE 8/31/2018
CRACS C.Seager Bttng 100.00 250.00
CRAJG Jon Gray 8.00 20.00
CRAKS Schwarber Wht jrsy 40.00 100.00
CRAMC Michael Conforto 30.00 80.00
BCARAA Albert Almora 20.00 50.00
BCARCS C.Seager Fldng 100.00 250.00
BCARHO Henry Owens 10.00 25.00
BCARJU Julio Urias 25.00 60.00
BCARKEM Kenta Maeda 10.00 25.00
BCARKS Schwarber Blue jrsy 30.00 80.00
BCARLG Lucas Giolito 12.00 30.00
BCARMS Sano Blue jrsy 15.00 40.00
BCARRM Raul Mondesi 30.00 80.00

2016 Bowman Chrome Rookie Autographs Gold Refractors

*GOLD REF: 1.5X TO 4X BASIC
BOW.ODDS 1:5078 HOBBY
BOW.CHR.ODDS 1:1439 HOBBY
STATED PRINT RUN 50 SER.#'d SETS
BOW.EXCH.DEADLINE 3/31/2018
BOW.CHR.EXCH.DEADLINE 8/31/2018
CRACS C.Seager Bttng 150.00 400.00
CRAJG Jon Gray 12.00 30.00
CRAKS Schwarber Wht jrsy 60.00 150.00
CRAMC Michael Conforto 75.00 200.00
BCARAA Albert Almora 30.00 80.00
BCARBP Byung-Ho Park 40.00 100.00
BCARCS C.Seager Fldng 150.00 400.00
BCARHO Henry Owens 15.00 40.00
BCARJU Julio Urias 40.00 100.00
BCARKEM Kenta Maeda 15.00 40.00
BCARKS Schwarber Blue jrsy 50.00 120.00
BCARLG Lucas Giolito 20.00 50.00
BCARMS Sano Blue jrsy 25.00 60.00
BCARRM Raul Mondesi 50.00 120.00

2016 Bowman Chrome Rookie Autographs Green Refractors

*GREEN REF: 1.2X TO 3X BASIC
INSERTED IN RETAIL PACKS
BOW.CHR.ODDS 1:727 HOBBY
STATED PRINT RUN 99 SER.#'d SETS
BOW.EXCH.DEADLINE 3/31/2018
BOW.CHR.EXCH.DEADLINE 8/31/2018
CRACS C.Seager Bttng 125.00 300.00
CRAJG Jon Gray 10.00 25.00
CRAKS Schwarber Wht jrsy 50.00 120.00
CRAMC Michael Conforto 40.00 100.00
BCARAA Albert Almora 25.00 60.00
BCARCS C.Seager Fldng 125.00 300.00
BCARHO Henry Owens 12.00 30.00
BCARJU Julio Urias 30.00 80.00
BCARKEM Kenta Maeda 12.00 30.00
BCARKS Schwarber Blue jrsy 40.00 100.00
BCARLG Lucas Giolito 15.00 40.00
BCARMS Sano Blue jrsy 20.00 50.00
BCARRM Raul Mondesi 40.00 100.00

2016 Bowman Chrome Rookie Autographs Orange Refractors

*ORANGE REF: 3X TO 8X BASIC
BOW.ODDS 1:2414 HOBBY
BOW.CHR.ODDS 1:1294 HOBBY
STATED PRINT RUN 25 SER.#'d SETS
BOW.EXCH.DEADLINE 3/31/2018
BOW.CHR.EXCH.DEADLINE 8/31/2018
CRACS C.Seager Bttng 300.00 600.00
CRAJG Jon Gray 25.00 60.00
CRAKS Schwarber Wht jrsy 100.00 250.00
CRAMC Michael Conforto 150.00 400.00
BCARAA Albert Almora 60.00 150.00
BCARBP Byung-Ho Park 75.00 200.00
BCARCS C.Seager Fldng 300.00 600.00
BCARHO Henry Owens 30.00 80.00
BCARJU Julio Urias 80.00 200.00
BCARKEM Kenta Maeda 30.00 80.00
BCARKS Schwarber Blue jrsy 100.00 250.00
BCARLG Lucas Giolito 40.00 100.00
BCARMS Sano Blue jrsy 50.00 120.00
BCARRM Raul Mondesi 60.00 150.00

2016 Bowman Chrome Rookie Autographs Refractors

*REF: .5X TO 1.2X BASIC
BOW.ODDS 1:509 HOBBY
BOW.CHR.ODDS 1:155 HOBBY
STATED PRINT RUN 499 SER.#'d SETS
BOW.EXCH.DEADLINE 3/31/2018
BOW.CHR.EXCH.DEADLINE 8/31/2018
CRACS C.Seager Bttng 60.00 150.00
CRAJG Jon Gray 4.00 10.00
CRAKS Schwarber Wht jrsy 30.00 80.00
BCARCS C.Seager Fldng 60.00 150.00
BCARHO Henry Owens 5.00 12.00
BCARJU Julio Urias 12.00 30.00
BCARKEM Kenta Maeda 5.00 12.00
BCARLG Lucas Giolito 6.00 15.00
BCARMS Sano Blue jrsy 8.00 20.00
BCARRM Raul Mondesi 15.00 40.00

2016 Bowman Chrome Rookie Recollections

COMPLETE SET (7) 4.00 10.00
STATED ODDS 1:24 HOBBY
*GOLD/99: 2.5X TO 6X BASIC
*GOLD/50: 4X TO 10X BASIC
*ORANGE/25: 5X TO 12X BASIC
RRBB Bret Boone .40 1.00
RRCJ Chipper Jones .60 1.50
RRIR Ivan Rodriguez .50 1.25
RRJB Jeff Bagwell .50 1.25
RRJC Jeff Conine .40 1.00
RRLG Luis Gonzalez .50 1.25
RRRK Ryan Klesko .40 1.00

2016 Bowman Chrome Rookie Recollections Autographs

STATED ODDS 1:2414 HOBBY
PRINT RUNS B/WN 75-200 COPIES PER
EXCHANGE DEADLINE 3/31/2018
*GOLD/50: .6X TO 1.5X BASIC
RRABB Bret Boone/200 5.00 12.00
RRACE Carl Everett/150 5.00 12.00
RRACJ Chipper Jones/75 50.00 120.00
RRAIR Ivan Rodriguez/150 20.00 50.00
RRAJB Jeff Bagwell/75 25.00 60.00
RRAJC Jeff Conine/150 5.00 12.00
RRALG Luis Gonzalez/200 6.00 15.00
RRAPH Pat Hentgen EXCH 5.00 12.00
RRARK Ryan Klesko/200 5.00 12.00

2016 Bowman Chrome Sophomore Standouts Autographs

STATED ODDS 1:2561 HOBBY
EXCHANGE DEADLINE 3/31/2018

*GOLD/50: .6X TO 1.5X BASIC
SSABS Blake Swihart 5.00 12.00
SSACC Carlos Correa 75.00 200.00
SSAFL Francisco Lindor 15.00 40.00
SSAJP Joc Pederson 6.00 15.00
SSAJS Jorge Soler 6.00 15.00
SSAKB Kris Bryant 75.00 200.00
SSANS Noah Syndergaard 15.00 40.00
SSARC Rusney Castillo 4.00 10.00
SSASM Steven Matz 4.00 10.00

2016 Bowman Chrome Turn Two

STATED ODDS 1:24 HOBBY
*GREEN/99: 1X TO 2.5X BASIC
*GOLD/50: 1.2X TO 3X BASIC
*ORANGE/25: 3X TO 8X BASIC
TTAP A.Alford/M.Pentecost .30 .75
TTBB T.Beede/P.Bickford .40 1.00
TTBC Bregman/Cameron 1.50 4.00
TTBJ T.Jay/J.Berrios .50 1.25
TTBO F.Barreto/M.Olson 1.50 4.00
TTCT J.Crawford/J.Thompson .30 .75
TTDM Devers/Benintendi 1.00 2.50
TTFA T.Anderson/C.Fulmer 1.25 3.00
TTFH D.Hill/M.Fulmer .50 1.25
TTGL R.Lopez/L.Giolito .50 1.25
TTGM T.Glasnow/A.Meadows 1.25 3.00
TTHS H.Harvey/D.Stewart .30 .75
TTJG A.Jackson/L.Gohara .40 1.00
TTJM Judge/Mateo 2.50 6.00
TTKN J.Naylor/T.Kolek .40 1.00
TTMR A.Russell/R.Mondesi .60 1.50
TTNE V.Alcantara/J.Gatto .30 .75
TTNR A.Rosario/B.Nimmo .50 1.25
TTPC T.Clark/B.Phillips .30 .75
TTRD Rodgers/Dahl .50 1.25
TTRF J.Flaherty/A.Reyes 2.00 5.00
TTRR H.Renfroe/M.Margot .40 1.00
TTSL B.Shipley/Y.Lopez .30 .75
TTSN Newcomb/Swanson 1.25 3.00
TTSS T.Stephenson/R.Stephenson .75 2.00
TTTB D.Tate/L.Brinson .50 1.25
TTTM Torres/McKinney 5.00 12.00
TTUD Urias/De Leon 1.00 2.50
TTWA W.Adames/G.Whitley .50 1.25
TTZF B.Zimmer/C.Frazier 1.25 3.00

2016 Bowman Chrome Turn Two Autographs Gold

STATED ODDS 1:3386 HOBBY
EXCHANGE DEADLINE 3/31/2018
TTBC Bregman/Cameron 75.00 200.00
TTBJ Jay/Berrios 20.00 50.00
TTFH Hill/Fulmer 25.00 60.00
TTGM Glasnow/Meadows 40.00 100.00
TTJM Judge/Mateo 75.00 200.00
TTKN Naylor/Kolek 15.00 40.00
TTPC Clark/Phillips 40.00 100.00
TTRD Rodgers/Dahl 50.00 120.00
TTSN Sean Newcomb 75.00 200.00
Dansby Swanson
TTSS Stephenson/Stephenson 30.00 80.00
TTTB Tate/Brinson 30.00 80.00
TTWA Adames/Whitley 20.00 50.00

2016 Bowman Chrome Draft

COMPLETE SET (200) 20.00 50.00
STATED PLATE ODDS 1:947 HOBBY
PLATE PRINT RUN 1 SET PER COLOR
NO PLATE PRICING DUE TO SCARCITY
BDC1 Mickey Moniak 2.50 6.00
BDC2 Thomas Jones .25 .60
BDC3 Dylan Carlson 15.00 40.00
BDC4 Cole Irvin .60 1.50
BDC5 Kevin Gowdy .40 1.00
BDC6 Dakota Hudson .40 1.00
BDC7 Walker Robbins .25 .60
BDC8 Khalil Lee .40 1.00
BDC9 Logan Ice .25 .60
BDC10 Braxton Garrett .30 .75
BDC11 Anfernee Grier .30 .75
BDC12 Kyle Hart .25 .60
BDC13 Taylor Trammell 3.00 8.00
BDC14 Brian Serven .25 .60
BDC15 Buddy Reed .30 .75
BDC16 Carter Kieboom 1.50 4.00
BDC17 Jimmy Lambert .30 .75
BDC18 Nick Solak 2.00 5.00
BDC19 Alexis Torres .30 .75
BDC20 Cal Quantrill .25 .60
BDC21 JaVon Shelby .25 .60
BDC22 Kyle Funkhouser .30 .75
BDC23 Dom Thompson-Williams .40 1.00
BDC24 Jeremy Martinez .60 1.50
BDC25 A.J. Puk .40 1.00
BDC26 Brett Cumberland .40 1.00
BDC27 Mason Thompson .25 .60
BDC28 Easton McGee .25 .60
BDC29 Justin Dunn .25 .60
BDC30 Matt Manning .40 1.00
BDC31 Delvin Perez .75 2.00
BDC32 Nolan Jones .40 1.00
BDC33 Matt Krook .25 .60
BDC34 Stephen Alemais .40 1.00
BDC35 Joey Wentz .40 1.00
BDC36 Ben Bowden .25 .60
BDC37 Drew Harrington .25 .60
BDC38 C.J. Chatham .30 .75
BDC39 Will Craig .25 .60
BDC40 Zack Collins .30 .75
BDC41 Skylar Szynski .25 .60
BDC42 Sheldon Neuse .30 .75
BDC43 Nicholas Lopez .40 1.00
BDC44 Heath Quinn .50 1.25
BDC45 Alex Speas .30 .75
BDC46 Cody Sedlock .25 .60
BDC47 Blake Tiberi .30 .75
BDC48 Mario Feliciano .30 .75
BDC49 Brett Adcock .25 .60
BDC50 Riley Pint .25 .60
BDC51 Jacob Heyward .25 .60
BDC52 Hudson Potts .30 .75
BDC53 Ronnie Dawson .25 .60
BDC54 Nick Hanson .25 .60
BDC55 Forrest Whitley 1.00 2.50
BDC56 Ryan Hendrix .25 .60
BDC57 Eric Lauer .30 .75
BDC58 Tyson Miller .30 .75
BDC59 Jesus Luzardo 1.50 4.00
BDC60 Kyle Lewis 10.00 25.00
BDC61 Connor Justus .25 .60
BDC62 Cole Stobbe .25 .60
BDC63 Garrett Hampson .50 1.25
BDC64 Cole Ragans .30 .75
BDC65 Kyle Muller .30 .75
BDC66 Logan Shore .30 .75
BDC67 Gavin Lux 10.00 25.00
BDC68 Shane Bieber 10.00 25.00
BDC69 T.J. Zeuch .30 .75
BDC70 Joshua Lowe .25 .60
BDC71 Justin Alleman .25 .60
BDC72 Ryan Howard .25 .60
BDC73 Jake Fraley .30 .75
BDC74 Bo Bichette 25.00 60.00
BDC75 DJ Peters 1.25 3.00
BDC76 Jake Rogers 1.25 3.00
BDC77 Bryan Reynolds .75 2.00
BDC78 Colton Welker .40 1.00
BDC79 Nick Banks .25 .60
BDC80 Will Benson .40 1.00
BDC81 Cavan Biggio 6.00 15.00
BDC82 Braden Webb .25 .60
BDC83 Chris Okey .25 .60
BDC84 Will Smith 3.00 8.00
BDC85 A.J. Puckett .30 .75
BDC86 Colby Woodmansee .30 .75
BDC87 Andy Yerzy .25 .60
BDC88 J.B. Woodman .40 1.00
BDC89 Corbin Burnes 6.00 15.00
BDC90 Alex Kirilloff 8.00 20.00
BDC91 Robert Tyler .25 .60
BDC92 Pete Alonso 12.00 30.00
BDC93 Alec Hansen .30 .75
BDC94 Daniel Johnson .25 .60
BDC95 Mike Shawaryn .30 .75
BDC96 Daulton Jefferies .30 .75
BDC97 Jordan Sheffield .25 .60
BDC98 Conner Capel .25 .60
BDC99 Bobby Dalbec 10.00 25.00
BDC100 Corey Ray .30 .75
BDC101 Ben Rortvedt .30 .75
BDC102 Tim Lynch .40 1.00
BDC103 Charles Leblanc .25 .60
BDC104 Dane Dunning .75 2.00
BDC105 Bryson Brigman .25 .60
BDC106 Nolan Martinez .30 .75
BDC107 Connor Jones .30 .75
BDC108 Alex Call .25 .60
BDC109 Reggie Lawson .25 .60
BDC110 Matt Thaiss .25 .60
BDC111 Bryse Wilson .75 2.00
BDC112 Zack Burdi .30 .75
BDC113 Nolan Williams .25 .60
BDC114 Mark Ecker .25 .60
BDC115 Michael Paez .40 1.00
BDC116 Zach Jackson .25 .60
BDC117 Joe Rizzo .25 .60
BDC118 Ryan Boldt .30 .75
BDC119 Mikey York .25 .60
BDC120 Ian Anderson 6.00 15.00
BDC121 Austin Meadows .60 1.50
BDC122 Nick Gordon .25 .60
BDC123 Forrest Wall .25 .60
BDC124 Antonio Senzatela .25 .60
BDC125 Justus Sheffield .50 1.25
BDC126 Christian Arroyo .50 1.25
BDC127 Dylan Cease .40 1.00
BDC128 Scott Kingery .40 1.00
BDC129 Daniel Palka .25 .60
BDC130 Bradley Zimmer .40 1.00
BDC131 Amir Garrett .25 .60
BDC132 Dillon Tate .30 .75
BDC133 Domingo Leyba .25 .60
BDC134 Tyler Jay .25 .60
BDC135 Sean Reid-Foley .30 .75
BDC136 James Kaprielian .25 .60
BDC137 Kyle Tucker 1.25 3.00
BDC138 Derek Fisher .25 .60
BDC139 Tyler O'Neill .30 .75
BDC140 Anderson Espinoza .30 .75
BDC141 Christin Stewart .30 .75
BDC142 Grant Holmes .30 .75
BDC143 Gleyber Torres 6.00 15.00
BDC144 Mitch Keller .30 .75
BDC145 Francis Martes .25 .60
BDC146 Nellie Rodriguez .25 .60
BDC147 Chih-Wei Hu .30 .75
BDC148 Anthony Banda .25 .60
BDC149 Trent Clark .25 .60
BDC150 Brendan Rodgers .40 1.00
BDC151 Ryan Cordell .25 .60
BDC152 Daz Cameron .25 .60
BDC153 Billy McKinney .30 .75
BDC154 Jomar Reyes .40 1.00
BDC155 Jake Bauers .40 1.00
BDC156 Willy Adames .40 1.00
BDC157 Josh Hader .30 .75
BDC158 Luis Ortiz .25 .60
BDC159 Erick Fedde .25 .60
BDC160 Rafael Devers .75 2.00
BDC161 Francisco Mejia .40 1.00
BDC162 Kolby Allard .25 .60
BDC163 Ronnie Williams .25 .60
BDC164 Matt Chapman .75 2.00
BDC165 Austin Riley .75 2.00
BDC166 Austin Dean .25 .60
BDC167 Ryan McMahon .40 1.00
BDC168 Anfernee Seymour .25 .60
BDC169 Marcos Diplan .25 .60
BDC170 Anthony Alford .25 .60
BDC171 Nick Neidert .25 .60
BDC172 Bobby Bradley .30 .75
BDC173 Tyler Wade .40 1.00
BDC174 Chase De Jong .30 .75
BDC175 Brett Phillips .25 .60
BDC176 Dominic Smith .25 .60
BDC177 Touki Toussaint .30 .75
BDC178 Reese McGuire .25 .60
BDC179 Franklin Barreto .25 .60
BDC180 Ian Happ .50 1.25
BDC181 Javier Guerra .25 .60
BDC182 Tyler Beede .30 .75
BDC183 Drew Jackson .25 .60
BDC184 Brent Honeywell .40 1.00
BDC185 Michael Gettys .25 .60
BDC186 Rhys Hoskins 1.00 2.50
BDC187 Dylan Cozens .25 .60
BDC188 Jon Harris .30 .75
BDC189 Phil Bickford .25 .60
BDC190 Amed Rosario .40 1.00
BDC191 Eloy Jimenez 1.00 2.50
BDC192 Jack Flaherty 1.50 4.00
BDC193 Alex Young .30 .75
BDC194 Andrew Sopko .25 .60
BDC195 Rafael Bautista .25 .60
BDC196 Chris Shaw .25 .60
BDC197 Mike Gerber .25 .60
BDC198 Kevin Newman .40 1.00
BDC199 Ryan Mountcastle 1.25 3.00
BDC200 Lucius Fox .40 1.00

2016 Bowman Chrome Draft Blue Refractors

*BLUE REF: 2X TO 5X BASIC
STATED ODDS 1:26 HOBBY
STATED PRINT RUN 150 SER.#'d SETS

2016 Bowman Chrome Draft Gold Refractors

*GOLD REF: 5X TO 12X BASIC
STATED ODDS 1:76 HOBBY
STATED PRINT RUN 50 SER.#'d SETS

2016 Bowman Chrome Draft Green Refractors

*GREEN REF: 2.5X TO 6X BASIC
STATED ODDS 1:39 HOBBY
STATED PRINT RUN 99 SER.#'d SETS

2016 Bowman Chrome Draft Orange Refractors

*ORANGE REF: 8X TO 20X BASIC
STATED ODDS 1:152 HOBBY
STATED PRINT RUN 25 SER.#'d SETS

2016 Bowman Chrome Draft Purple Refractors

*PURPLE REF: 1.5X TO 4X BASIC
STATED ODDS 1:16 HOBBY
STATED PRINT RUN 250 SER.#'d SETS

2016 Bowman Chrome Draft Refractors

*REFRACTORS: .75X TO 2X BASIC
RANDOM INSERTS IN PACKS

2016 Bowman Chrome Draft Sky Blue Refractors

*SKY BLUE: 1X TO 2.5X BASIC
STATED ODDS 1:8 HOBBY

2016 Bowman Chrome Draft Draft Dividends

COMPLETE SET (15) 6.00 15.00
STATED ODDS 1:4 HOBBY
*GOLD/50: 1.2X TO 3X BASIC
DDAP A.J. Puk .60 1.50
DDAY Alex Young .50 1.25
DDBL Brett Lilek .40 1.00
DDCQ Cal Quantrill .40 1.00
DDCR Corey Ray .50 1.25
DDDD Dane Dunning 1.25 3.00
DDDH Dakota Hudson .60 1.50
DDDJ Daulton Jefferies .50 1.25
DDEL Eric Lauer .50 1.25
DDJD Justin Dunn .40 1.00
DDJS Jordan Sheffield .40 1.00
DDMT Matt Thaiss .40 1.00
DDTZ T.J. Zeuch .50 1.25
DDWC Will Craig .40 1.00
DDZC Zack Collins .50 1.25

2016 Bowman Chrome Draft Draft Dividends Autographs

STATED ODDS 1:750 HOBBY
STATED PRINT RUN 50 SER.#'d SETS
EXCHANGE DEADLINE 11/30/2018
*GOLD/50: .5X TO 1.2X BASIC
DDAP A.J. Puk 8.00 20.00
DDCQ Cal Quantrill 5.00 12.00
DDCR Corey Ray 6.00 15.00
DDEL Eric Lauer 6.00 15.00
DDJD Justin Dunn 5.00 12.00
DDMT Matt Thaiss 5.00 12.00
DDTZ T.J. Zeuch 6.00 15.00
DDWC Will Craig 10.00 25.00
DDZC Zack Collins 10.00 25.00

2016 Bowman Chrome Draft Draft Night Autographs

STATED ODDS 1:3733 HOBBY
STATED PRINT RUN 99 SER.#'d SETS
EXCHANGE DEADLINE 11/30/2018
*GOLD/50: .5X TO 1.2X BASIC
DNAIA Ian Anderson 15.00 40.00
DNAWB Will Benson 20.00 50.00

2016 Bowman Chrome Draft Draft Pick Autographs

STATED ODDS 1:7 HOBBY
PRINTING PLATE ODDS 1:3389 HOBBY
PLATE PRINT RUN 1 SET PER COLOR
NO PLATE PRICING DUE TO SCARCITY
EXCHANGE DEADLINE 11/30/2018
CDAAG Anfernee Grier 4.00 10.00
CDAAH Alec Hansen 4.00 10.00
CDAAK Alex Kirilloff 60.00 150.00
CDAAP A.J. Puk 20.00 50.00
CDAAY Andy Yerzy 3.00 8.00
CDABB Ben Bowden 3.00 8.00
CDABD Bobby Dalbec 100.00 250.00
CDABG Braxton Garrett 4.00 10.00
CDABOB Bo Bichette 200.00 500.00
CDABRE Buddy Reed 4.00 10.00
CDABRR Bryan Reynolds 12.00 30.00
CDABW Bryse Wilson 12.00 30.00
CDACB Cavan Biggio 40.00 100.00
CDACC C.J. Chatham 4.00 10.00
CDACJ Connor Jones 4.00 10.00
CDACO Chris Okey 3.00 8.00
CDACQ Cal Quantrill 3.00 8.00
CDACR Corey Ray 4.00 10.00
CDACRA Cole Ragans 4.00 10.00
CDACS Cody Sedlock 3.00 8.00
CDADC Dylan Carlson 125.00 300.00
CDADD Dane Dunning 10.00 25.00
CDADH Dakota Hudson 6.00 15.00
CDADJ Daulton Jefferies 4.00 10.00
CDADP Delvin Perez 10.00 25.00
CDAEL Eric Lauer 4.00 10.00
CDAFW Forrest Whitley 12.00 30.00
CDAGH Garrett Hampson 6.00 15.00
CDAGL Gavin Lux 125.00 300.00
CDAHS Hudson Potts 10.00 25.00
CDAIA Ian Anderson 40.00 100.00
CDAJD Justin Dunn 8.00 20.00
CDAJF Jake Fraley 4.00 10.00
CDAJL Joshua Lowe 10.00 25.00
CDAJLU Jesus Luzardo 25.00 60.00
CDAJR Joe Rizzo 3.00 8.00
CDAJS Jordan Sheffield 3.00 8.00
CDAKL Kyle Lewis 125.00 300.00
CDAKM Kyle Muller 8.00 20.00
CDAMM Matt Manning 15.00 40.00
CDAMM Mickey Moniak 30.00 80.00
CDAMT Matt Thaiss 3.00 8.00
CDANJ Nolan Jones 40.00 100.00
CDANM Nolan Martinez 4.00 10.00
CDAPA Pete Alonso 150.00 400.00
CDARD Ronnie Dawson 3.00 8.00
CDARP Riley Pint 3.00 8.00
CDART Robert Tyler 3.00 8.00
CDATL Tim Lynch 5.00 12.00
CDATT Taylor Trammell 40.00 100.00
CDATZ T.J. Zeuch 4.00 10.00
CDAWB Will Benson 5.00 12.00
CDAWC Will Craig 3.00 8.00
CDAWS Will Smith 30.00 80.00
CDAZB Zack Burdi 4.00 10.00
CDAZC Zack Collins 4.00 10.00

2016 Bowman Chrome Draft Draft Pick Autographs Black Refractors

*BLACK REF: 1.5X TO 4X BASIC
RANDOM INSERTS IN PACKS
STATED PRINT RUN 75 SER.#'d SETS
EXCHANGE DEADLINE 11/30/2018

2016 Bowman Chrome Draft Draft Pick Autographs Blue Refractors

*BLUE REF: 1X TO 2.5X BASIC
STATED ODDS 1:91 HOBBY
STATED PRINT RUN 150 SER.#'d SETS
EXCHANGE DEADLINE 11/30/2018

2016 Bowman Chrome Draft Draft Pick Autographs Blue Wave Refractors

*BLUE WAVE REF: 1X TO 2.5X BASIC
STATED ODDS 1:91 HOBBY
STATED PRINT RUN 150 SER.#'d SETS
EXCHANGE DEADLINE 11/30/2018

2016 Bowman Chrome Draft Draft Pick Autographs Gold Refractors

*GOLD REF: 2.5X TO 6X BASIC
STATED ODDS 1:271 HOBBY
STATED PRINT RUN 50 SER.#'d SETS
EXCHANGE DEADLINE 11/30/2018

2016 Bowman Chrome Draft Draft Pick Autographs Gold Wave Refractors

*GOLD WAVE REF: 2.5X TO 6X BASIC
STATED ODDS 1:271 HOBBY
STATED PRINT RUN 50 SER.#'d SETS
EXCHANGE DEADLINE 11/30/2018

2016 Bowman Chrome Draft Draft Pick Autographs Green Refractors

*GREEN REF: 1.2X TO 3X BASIC
STATED ODDS 1:137 HOBBY
STATED PRINT RUN 99 SER.#'d SETS
EXCHANGE DEADLINE 11/30/2018

2016 Bowman Chrome Draft Draft Pick Autographs Orange Refractors

*ORANGE REF: 3X TO 8X BASIC
STATED ODDS 1:540 HOBBY
STATED PRINT RUN 25 SER.#'d SETS
EXCHANGE DEADLINE 11/30/2018

2016 Bowman Chrome Draft Draft Pick Autographs Purple Refractors

*PURPLE REF: .6X TO 1.5X BASIC
STATED ODDS 1:54 HOBBY
STATED PRINT RUN 250 SER.#'d SETS
EXCHANGE DEADLINE 11/30/2018

2016 Bowman Chrome Draft Draft Pick Autographs Refractors

*REF: .5X TO 1.2X BASIC
STATED ODDS 1:28 HOBBY
STATED PRINT RUN 499 SER.#'d SETS
EXCHANGE DEADLINE 11/30/2018

2016 Bowman Chrome Draft MLB Draft History

COMPLETE SET (15) 6.00 15.00
STATED ODDS 1:6 HOBBY
*GOLD/50: 4X TO 10X BASIC
MLBDBJ Bo Jackson .60 1.50
MLBDCB Craig Biggio .50 1.25
MLBDCJ Chipper Jones .60 1.50
MLBDCR Cal Ripken Jr. 2.00 5.00
MLBDFT Frank Thomas .60 1.50
MLBDGM Greg Maddux .75 2.00
MLBDJB Johnny Bench .60 1.50
MLBDKGJ Ken Griffey Jr. 1.25 3.00
MLBDMP Mike Piazza .60 1.50
MLBDNG Nomar Garciaparra .50 1.25
MLBDNR Nolan Ryan 2.00 5.00
MLBDOS Ozzie Smith .75 2.00
MLBDRC Roger Clemens .75 2.00
MLBDRJ Reggie Jackson .50 1.25
MLBDTG Tom Glavine .50 1.25

2016 Bowman Chrome Draft MLB Draft History Autographs

STATED ODDS 1:750 HOBBY
STATED PRINT RUN 99 SER.#'d SETS
EXCHANGE DEADLINE 11/30/2018
MLBDABJ Bo Jackson 40.00 100.00
MLBDACJ Chipper Jones 40.00 100.00
MLBDACR Cal Ripken Jr. 50.00 120.00
MLBDAFT Frank Thomas 40.00 100.00
MLBDAGM Greg Maddux 40.00 100.00
MLBDAJB Johnny Bench 40.00 100.00
MLBDAKGJ Ken Griffey Jr. 250.00 500.00
MLBDAMP Mike Piazza 50.00 120.00
MLBDANR Nolan Ryan 75.00 200.00
MLBDARC Roger Clemens 30.00 80.00

2016 Bowman Chrome Draft Scouts Fantasy Impacts

COMPLETE SET (20) 6.00 15.00
STATED ODDS 1:3 HOBBY
*GOLD/50: 1.5X TO 4X BASIC
BSIAM Austin Meadows 1.00 2.50
BSIAP A.J. Puk .60 1.50
BSIBM Billy McKinney .50 1.25
BSIBZ Bradley Zimmer .60 1.50
BSICA Christian Arroyo .75 2.00
BSICD Chase De Jong .50 1.25
BSICQ Cal Quantrill .40 1.00
BSICR Corey Ray .50 1.25
BSIDC Dylan Cozens .40 1.00
BSIDS Dominic Smith .40 1.00
BSIFB Franklin Barreto .40 1.00
BSIFM Francis Martes .40 1.00
BSIJD Justin Dunn .40 1.00
BSIKL Kyle Lewis 4.00 10.00
BSIMT Matt Thaiss .40 1.00
BSITB Tyler Beede .50 1.25
BSITZ T.J. Zeuch .50 1.25
BSIWC Will Craig .40 1.00
BSIZB Zack Burdi .50 1.25
BSIZC Zack Collins .50 1.25

2016 Bowman Chrome Draft Scouts Fantasy Impacts Autographs

STATED ODDS 1:1484 HOBBY
STATED PRINT RUN 50 SER.#'d SETS
EXCHANGE DEADLINE 11/30/2018
BSIAP A.J. Puk 12.00 30.00
BSIBM Billy McKinney 8.00 20.00
BSICD Chase De Jong
BSICQ Cal Quantrill 6.00 15.00
BSICR Corey Ray 10.00 25.00
BSIDS Dominic Smith
BSIJD Justin Dunn 12.00 30.00
BSITB Tyler Beede 12.00 30.00
BSIZB Zack Burdi 8.00 20.00
BSIZC Zack Collins 8.00 20.00

2016 Bowman Chrome Draft Top of the Class Box Topper

*GOLD/50: .5X TO 1.2X BASIC
TOCAP A.J. Puk 2.50 6.00
TOCBG Braxton Garrett 2.00 5.00
TOCCQ Cal Quantrill 1.50 4.00
TOCCR Corey Ray 2.00 5.00
TOCFW Forrest Whitley 6.00 15.00
TOCIA Ian Anderson 8.00 20.00
TOCJL Joshua Lowe 1.50 4.00
TOCKL Kyle Lewis 30.00 80.00
TOCMM Matt Manning 2.50 6.00
TOCMM Mickey Moniak 12.00 30.00
TOCNS Nick Senzel 30.00 80.00
TOCRP Riley Pint 1.50 4.00
TOCWB Will Benson 2.50 6.00
TOCZC Zack Collins 2.00 5.00

2016 Bowman Chrome Draft Top of the Class Box Topper Autographs Orange

STATED ODDS 1:140 HOBBY BOXES
STATED PRINT RUN 35 SER.#'d SETS
EXCHANGE DEADLINE 11/30/2018
TOCAP A.J. Puk 30.00 80.00
TOCBG Braxton Garrett 30.00 80.00
TOCCQ Cal Quantrill
TOCCR Corey Ray 100.00 250.00
TOCFW Forrest Whitley 30.00 80.00
TOCIA Ian Anderson 40.00 100.00
TOCMM Mickey Moniak 125.00 300.00
TOCMM Matt Manning 40.00 100.00
TOCRP Riley Pint 10.00 25.00
TOCZC Zack Collins 50.00 120.00

2017 Bowman Chrome

SP ODDS 1:119 HOBBY
PLATE PRINT RUN 1 SET PER COLOR
BLACK-CYAN-MAGENTA-YELLOW ISSUED
NO PLATE PRICING DUE TO SCARCITY
1 Kris Bryant .40 1.00
2 Jesse Winker RC 1.50 4.00
3 Paul Goldschmidt .30 .75
4 Zack Greinke .30 .75
5 Albert Pujols .40 1.00
6A Alex Reyes RC .50 1.25
6B Reyes SP Pntng up 5.00 12.00
7 Byron Buxton .30 .75
8 Ichiro .40 1.00
9 Miguel Cabrera .30 .75
10 Sonny Gray .25 .60
11 Wil Myers .25 .60
12A Alex Bregman RC 2.00 5.00
12B Bregman SP On bench 8.00 20.00
13 David Ortiz .30 .75
14 Robinson Cano .25 .60
15 Chris Sale .30 .75
16 Stephen Piscotty .25 .60
17 Masahiro Tanaka .25 .60
18 Joe Jimenez RC .50 1.25
19 Justin Verlander .30 .75
20 Andrew Miller .25 .60
21 Kyle Schwarber .30 .75
22A Jharel Cotton RC .40 1.00
22B Cotton SP Grn jrsy 4.00 10.00
23 Francisco Lindor .30 .75
24 Cole Hamels .25 .60
25 Corey Seager .30 .75
26 Xander Bogaerts .30 .75
27 Cody Bellinger RC 5.00 12.00
28 Ryan Braun .25 .60
29 Christian Arroyo RC .60 1.50
30 Ryon Healy RC .50 1.25
31A David Dahl RC .50 1.25
31B Dahl SP Prple jrsy 5.00 12.00
32 Jose Quintana .20 .50
33 Jacob deGrom .60 1.50
34 Salvador Perez .25 .60
35 Manny Machado .30 .75
36 Yoenis Cespedes .30 .75
37 Maikel Franco .25 .60
38 Adam Duvall .25 .60
39 Jose Bautista .25 .60
40 Mark Melancon .20 .50
41 Corey Kluber .25 .60
42 Mitch Haniger RC .60 1.50
43 Carson Fulmer RC .40 1.00
44 Jordan Montgomery RC .60 1.50
45 Joe Musgrove RC 1.25 3.00
46 Felix Hernandez .25 .60
47 Zach Britton .25 .60
48 Anthony Rizzo .40 1.00
49 Rougned Odor .25 .60
50A Yoan Moncada RC 1.25 3.00
50B Moncada SP Blck jrsy 8.00 20.00
51 Josh Donaldson .25 .60
52 Trea Turner .25 .60
53 Manny Margot RC .40 1.00
54 Brian Dozier .30 .75
55 Trevor Story .30 .75
56A Aaron Judge RC 5.00 12.00
56B Judge SP In dugout 50.00 125.00
57A Yulieski Gurriel RC .60 1.50
57B Gurriel SP Blue jrsy 6.00 15.00
58 Michael Fulmer .20 .50
59 Braden Shipley RC .40 1.00
60 Odubel Herrera .25 .60
61 Jeff Hoffman RC .40 1.00
62 Joey Votto .30 .75
63 Mookie Betts .60 1.50
64 Gary Sanchez .30 .75
65 Aroldis Chapman .30 .75
66 Giancarlo Stanton .30 .75
67 Noah Syndergaard .25 .60
68A Andrew Benintendi RC 1.25 3.00
68B Benintendi SP Gatorade 12.00 30.00
69 Chris Archer .20 .50
70 Josh Bell RC 1.00 2.50
71 Aledmys Diaz .25 .60
72 Nolan Arenado .50 1.25
73 Evan Longoria .25 .60
74 Ryan Schimpf .20 .50
75A Jose De Leon RC .40 1.00
75B De Leon SP Thrwng rght 4.00 10.00
76 Max Scherzer .30 .75
77A Orlando Arcia RC .60 1.50
77B Arcia SP Sit w/bat 6.00 15.00
78 Jose Abreu .30 .75
79 Jonathan Villar .20 .50
80A Tyler Glasnow RC 1.50 4.00
80B Glasnow SP Whte jrsy 15.00 40.00
81A Robert Gsellman RC .40 1.00
81B Gsellman SP Bckwrds hat 4.00 10.00
82 Carlos Correa .30 .75
83 Khris Davis .30 .75
84A Jorge Alfaro RC .50 1.25
84B Alfaro SP At bat 5.00 12.00
85 Raimel Tapia RC .50 1.25
86A Dansby Swanson RC 1.00 2.50
86B Swanson SP Blue jrsy 10.00 25.00
87 Jose Altuve .25 .60
88A Hunter Renfroe RC .50 1.25
88B Renfroe SP Blue jrsy 5.00 12.00
89 Freddie Freeman .40 1.00
90 Gregory Polanco .25 .60
91 Buster Posey .40 1.00
92 Gerrit Cole .30 .75
93 Clayton Kershaw .50 1.25
94 Danny Duffy .20 .50
95 Amir Garrett RC .40 1.00
96 Bryce Harper .50 1.25
97 Adrian Beltre .30 .75
98 Eric Hosmer .25 .60
99 Matt Kemp .25 .60
100 Mike Trout 1.50 4.00

2017 Bowman Chrome Blue Refractors

*BLUE REF VET: 4X TO 10X BASIC
*BLUE REF RC: 2X TO 5X BASIC
STATED ODDS 1:60 HOBBY
STATED PRINT RUN 150 SER.#'d SETS
56 Aaron Judge 50.00 120.00
100 Mike Trout 12.00 30.00

2017 Bowman Chrome Gold Refractors

*GOLD REF VET: 8X TO 20X BASIC
*GOLD REF RC: 4X TO 10X BASIC
STATED ODDS 1:178 HOBBY
STATED PRINT RUN 50 SER.#'d SETS
1 Kris Bryant 30.00 80.00
13 David Ortiz 10.00 25.00
56 Aaron Judge 125.00 300.00
84 Jorge Alfaro 15.00 40.00
100 Mike Trout 40.00 100.00

2017 Bowman Chrome Green Refractors

*GREEN REF VET: 4X TO 10X BASIC
*GREEN REF RC: 2X TO 5X BASIC
STATED ODDS 1:90 HOBBY
STATED PRINT RUN 99 SER.#'d SETS
56 Aaron Judge 50.00 120.00
100 Mike Trout 12.00 30.00

2017 Bowman Chrome Orange Refractors

*ORANGE REF VET: 10X TO 25X BASIC
*ORANGE REF RC: 5X TO 12X BASIC
STATED ODDS 1:356 HOBBY
STATED PRINT RUN 25 SER.#'d SETS
1 Kris Bryant 40.00 100.00
13 David Ortiz 12.00 30.00
56 Aaron Judge 150.00 400.00
84 Jorge Alfaro 20.00 50.00
100 Mike Trout 50.00 120.00

2017 Bowman Chrome Purple Refractors

*PURPLE REF VET: 2X TO 5X BASIC
*PURPLE REF RC: 1X TO 2.5X BASIC
STATED ODDS 1:36 HOBBY
STATED PRINT RUN 250 SER.#'d SETS
56 Aaron Judge 30.00 80.00
100 Mike Trout 8.00 20.00

2017 Bowman Chrome Refractors

*REF VET: 1.5X TO 4X BASIC
*REF RC: .75X TO 2X BASIC
STATED ODDS 1:18 HOBBY
STATED PRINT RUN 499 SER.#'d SETS
56 Aaron Judge 20.00 50.00

2017 Bowman Chrome '16 AFL Fall Stars

COMP.SET w/o SP (20) 12.00 30.00
STATED ODDS 1:6 HOBBY
SP ODDS 1:3569 HOBBY
SP PRINT RUN 250 SER.#'d SETS
*ORANGE/25: 2X TO 5X BASIC
AFLAA Anthony Alford .40 1.00
AFLAV Alex Verdugo .60 1.50
AFLBA Brian Anderson .50 1.25
AFLBP Brett Phillips .50 1.25
AFLBZ Bradley Zimmer .50 1.25
AFLCB Cody Bellinger 3.00 8.00
AFLCK Carson Kelly .50 1.25
AFLDL Dawel Lugo .40 1.00
AFLDS D.J. Stewart .40 1.00
AFLDT Dillon Tate .40 1.00
AFLEJ Eloy Jimenez 1.50 4.00
AFLFB Franklin Barreto .40 1.00
AFLGB Greg Bird .50 1.25
AFLGT Gleyber Torres 6.00 15.00
AFLIH Ian Happ .75 2.00
AFLNG Nick Gordon .40 1.00
AFLPDJ Paul DeJong 1.25 3.00
AFLTO Tyler O'Neill .50 1.25
AFLWC Willie Calhoun .60 1.50
AFLSWC Calhoun MVP/250 10.00 20.00
AFLYM Yoan Moncada 1.25 3.00

2017 Bowman Chrome '16 AFL Fall Stars Autograph Relics

STATED ODDS 1:1334 HOBBY
STATED PRINT RUN 50 SER.#'d SETS
EXCHANGE DEADLINE 8/31/2019
AFLRBP Brett Phillips 20.00 50.00
AFLRDL Dawel Lugo 25.00 60.00
AFLREJ Eloy Jimenez 75.00 200.00
AFLRFB Franklin Barreto 25.00 60.00
AFLRGT Gleyber Torres 75.00 300.00
AFLRRO Ryan O'Hearn 30.00 80.00
AFLRWC Willie Calhoun EXCH 25.00 60.00

2017 Bowman Chrome '16 AFL Fall Stars Relics

STATED ODDS 1:450 HOBBY
STATED PRINT RUN 99 SER.#'d SETS
*ORANGE/25: .6X TO 1.5X BASIC
AFLRAA Anthony Alford 3.00 8.00
AFLRBA Brian Anderson 4.00 10.00
AFLRBH Brent Honeywell 10.00 25.00
AFLRBP Brett Phillips 4.00 10.00
AFLRBZ Bradley Zimmer 4.00 10.00
AFLRCB Cody Bellinger 20.00 50.00
AFLRDL Dawel Lugo 3.00 8.00
AFLRDP David Paulino 4.00 10.00
AFLRDS D.J. Stewart 3.00 8.00
AFLREJ Eloy Jimenez 8.00 20.00
AFLRFB Franklin Barreto 3.00 8.00
AFLRFM Francis Martes 3.00 8.00
AFLRGT Gleyber Torres 8.00 20.00
AFLRHB Harrison Bader 3.00 8.00
AFLRNG Nick Gordon 3.00 8.00
AFLRPD Paul DeJong 4.00 10.00
AFLRRM Ryan McMahon 5.00 12.00
AFLRRO Ryan O'Hearn 6.00 15.00
AFLRTO Tyler O'Neill 8.00 20.00
AFLRTW Taylor Ward 8.00 20.00
AFLRWC Willie Calhoun 5.00 12.00

2017 Bowman Chrome '48 Bowman Autographs

STATED ODDS 1:38,095 HOBBY
STATED PRINT RUN 25 SER.#'d SETS
EXCHANGE DEADLINE 3/31/2019
48BHA Hank Aaron 250.00 500.00
48BKB Kris Bryant 250.00 500.00
48BSK Sandy Koufax 400.00 800.00

2017 Bowman Chrome '48 Bowman Refractors

COMPLETE SET (10) 6.00 15.00
STATED ODDS 1:24 HOBBY
*GREEN/99: 2.5X TO 6X BASIC
*GOLD/50: 4X TO 10X BASIC
*ORANGE/25: 5X TO 12X BASIC
48BAB Alex Bregman 2.00 5.00
48BGS Giancarlo Stanton .60 1.50
48BHA Hank Aaron 1.25 3.00
48BJC J.P. Crawford .40 1.00
48BKB Kris Bryant .75 2.00
48BMT Mike Trout 3.00 8.00
48BPR Phil Rizzuto .50 1.25
48BSK Sandy Koufax 1.25 3.00
48BWS Warren Spahn .50 1.25
48BYM Yoan Moncada 1.25 3.00

2017 Bowman Chrome '51 Bowman Refractors

COMPLETE SET (19) 20.00 50.00
STATED ODDS 1:24 HOBBY
*GREEN/99: 2.5X TO 6X BASIC
*GOLD/50: 4X TO 10X BASIC
*ORANGE/25: 5X TO 12X BASIC
1 Whitey Ford .50 1.25
2 Ted Williams 1.25 3.00
3 Monte Irvin .50 1.25
4 Phil Rizzuto .50 1.25
5 Duke Snider .50 1.25
6 Bob Feller .50 1.25
7 Alex Bregman 2.00 5.00
8 Kris Bryant .75 2.00
9 Mike Trout 3.00 8.00
10 Bryce Harper 1.00 2.50
11 Carlos Correa .60 1.50
12 Xander Bogaerts .60 1.50
13 Clayton Kershaw 1.00 2.50
15 Corey Seager .60 1.50

16 Yoan Moncada 1.25 3.00
17 J.P. Crawford .40 1.00
18 Dansby Swanson 1.00 2.50
19 Austin Meadows 1.00 2.50
20 Brendan Rodgers .50 1.25

2017 Bowman Chrome '92 Bowman Autographs

STATED ODDS 1:14,772 HOBBY
STATED PRINT RUN 25 SER.#'d SETS
EXCHANGE DEADLINE 3/31/2019
92BAB Alex Bregman 75.00 200.00
92BAR Anthony Rizzo EXCH 60.00 150.00
92BCJ Chipper Jones 100.00 250.00
92BGM Greg Maddux 100.00 250.00
92BJM Jorge Mateo EXCH 60.00 150.00
92BMM Mark McGwire 60.00 150.00
92BMP Mike Piazza 150.00 300.00
92BSN Sean Newcomb 50.00 120.00

2017 Bowman Chrome '92 Bowman Refractors

COMPLETE SET (20) 6.00 15.00
STATED ODDS 1:12 HOBBY
*GREEN/99: 2X TO 5X BASIC
*GOLD/50: 3X TO 8X BASIC
*ORANGE/25: 4X TO 10X BASIC
92BAB Alex Bregman 2.00 5.00
92BAR Anthony Rizzo .75 2.00
92BBH Bryce Harper 1.00 2.50
92BCJ Chipper Jones .60 1.50
92BDS Darryl Strawberry .40 1.00
92BDSW Dansby Swanson 1.00 2.50
92BGM Greg Maddux .75 2.00
92BIR Ivan Rodriguez .50 1.25
92BJM Jorge Mateo .40 1.00
92BKB Kris Bryant .75 2.00
92BKGJ Ken Griffey Jr. 1.25 3.00
92BMM Mark McGwire 1.00 2.50
92BMP Mike Piazza .60 1.50
92BNA Nolan Arenado 1.00 2.50
92BNS Noah Syndergaard .50 1.25
92BOA Orlando Arcia .60 1.50
92BRD Rafael Devers .75 2.00
92BSN Sean Newcomb .50 1.25
92BXB Xander Bogaerts .60 1.50
92BYC Yoenis Cespedes .60 1.50

2017 Bowman Chrome Ascent Autographs

STATED ODDS 1:19671 HOBBY
STATED PRINT RUN 150 SER.#'d SETS
EXCHANGE DEADLINE 3/31/2019
*ORANGE/25: .75X TO 2X BASIC
BAAD Aledmys Diaz 6.00 15.00
BAAR Anthony Rizzo 30.00 80.00
BAARU Addison Russell EXCH 15.00 40.00
BABH Bryce Harper 100.00 250.00
BACC Carlos Correa 30.00 80.00
BACS Corey Seager
Inserted in '18 Transcendent VIP Packs
BAFL Francisco Lindor 30.00 80.00
BAJA Jose Altuve 20.00 50.00
BAKB Kris Bryant EXCH 75.00 200.00
BAMT Mike Trout 200.00 400.00
BANM Nomar Mazara 20.00 50.00
BANS Noah Syndergaard 15.00 40.00
BASM Steven Matz 5.00 12.00
BASP Stephen Piscotty 6.00 15.00
BATS Trevor Story 8.00 20.00
BAWC Willson Contreras 15.00 40.00

2017 Bowman Chrome Autograph Relics

STATED ODDS 1:263 HOBBY
STATED PRINT RUN 150 SER.#'d SETS
EXCHANGE DEADLINE 8/31/2019
CARAR Amed Rosario 15.00 40.00
CARAV Alex Verdugo 25.00 60.00
CARCWH Chih-Wei Hu 15.00 40.00
CARDC Dylan Cozens 6.00 15.00
CARDL Dawel Lugo 6.00 15.00
CAREJ Eloy Jimenez 30.00 80.00
CARFB Franklin Barreto 4.00 10.00
CARFR Francisco Rios 4.00 10.00
CARGB Greg Bird 5.00 12.00
CARGT Gleyber Torres 60.00 150.00
CARJJ Joe Jimenez 5.00 12.00
CARPD Paul DeJong 10.00 25.00
CARSN Sean Newcomb 5.00 12.00
CARTO Tyler O'Neill 5.00 12.00
CARWC Willie Calhoun 8.00 20.00

2017 Bowman Chrome Autograph Relics Gold Refractors

*GOLD REF: .5X TO 1.2X BASIC
STATED ODDS 1:1020 HOBBY
STATED PRINT RUN 50 SER.#'d SETS
EXCHANGE DEADLINE 8/31/2019
CARCWH Chih-Wei Hu 60.00 150.00
CAREJ Eloy Jimenez 60.00 150.00

2017 Bowman Chrome Autograph Relics Orange Refractors

*ORANGE REF: .75X TO 2X BASIC
STATED ODDS 1:1734 HOBBY
STATED PRINT RUN 25 SER.#'d SETS
EXCHANGE DEADLINE 8/31/2019
CARCWH Chih-Wei Hu 100.00 250.00
CARDL Dawel Lugo 40.00 100.00
CAREJ Eloy Jimenez 150.00 400.00

2017 Bowman Chrome Lucky Autograph Redemptions

STATED ODDS 1:28,952 HOBBY
EXCHANGE DEADLINE 3/31/2019
LARIH Ian Happ 10.00 25.00

2017 Bowman Chrome Prime Chrome Inscription Autographs

STATED ODDS 1:1039 HOBBY
STATED PRINT RUN 75 SER.#'d SETS
EXCHANGE DEADLINE 8/31/2019
BIAAE Anderson Espinoza 5.00 12.00
BIAAP A.J. Puk 12.00 30.00
BIABR Blake Rutherford 8.00 20.00
BIACK Carter Kieboom 40.00 100.00
BIACR Corey Ray 8.00 20.00
BIAGT Gleyber Torres 50.00 120.00
BIAIA Ian Anderson 40.00 100.00
BIAJG Jason Groome 10.00 25.00
BIAJM Jorge Mateo 12.00 30.00
BIAKL Kyle Lewis 40.00 100.00
BIAKM Kevin Maitan 8.00 20.00
BIALAB Luis Alexander Basabe 8.00 20.00
BIALG Lourdes Gurriel Jr. 20.00 50.00
BIALT Leody Taveras 25.00 60.00
BIAMK Mitch Keller 10.00 25.00
BIAMM Mickey Moniak 25.00 60.00
BIANS Nick Senzel
BIASN Sean Newcomb 6.00 15.00
BIATC Trevor Clifton EXCH 5.00 12.00
BIATH Torii Hunter Jr. 6.00 15.00
BIAWC Willie Calhoun

2017 Bowman Chrome Prime Chrome Inscription Autographs Orange Refractors

*ORANGE REF: .6X TO 1.5X BASIC
RANDOM INSERTS IN PACKS
STATED PRINT RUN 25 SER.#'d SETS
EXCHANGE DEADLINE 8/31/2019
BIABR Blake Rutherford 125.00 300.00
BIACK Carter Kieboom 100.00 250.00
BIAGT Gleyber Torres 150.00 400.00
BIAKM Kevin Maitan 12.00 30.00
BIALAB Luis Alexander Basabe 15.00 40.00
BIALT Leody Taveras 40.00 100.00
BIAWC Willie Calhoun 50.00 120.00

2017 Bowman Chrome Prospect Autographs

BOW.STATED ODDS 1:68 HOBBY
BOW.CHR.STATED ODDS 1:11 HOBBY
BOW.PLATE ODDS 1:18,095 HOBBY
PLATE PRINT RUN 1 SET PER COLOR
BLACK-CYAN-MAGENTA-YELLOW ISSUED
NO PLATE PRICING DUE TO SCARCITY
BOW.EXCH.DEADLINE 3/31/2019
BOW.CHR.EXCH.DEADLINE 8/31/2019
CPAAA Albert Abreu 4.00 10.00
CPAACA Andrew Calica 3.00 8.00
CPAAE Anderson Espinoza 3.00 8.00
CPAAG Abrahan Gutierrez 5.00 12.00
CPAAH Austin Hays 20.00 50.00
CPAAI Andy Ibanez 3.00 8.00
CPAAK Anthony Kay 4.00 10.00
CPAAM Adrian Morejon 5.00 12.00
CPAAME Adonis Medina 5.00 12.00
CPAAP Angel Perdomo 3.00 8.00
CPAAPU A.J. Puckett 3.00 8.00
CPAAR Alfredo Rodriguez 4.00 10.00
CPAAS Andrew Sopko 3.00 8.00
CPAAST Andrew Stevenson 4.00 10.00
CPAAT Anderson Tejeda 8.00 20.00
CPAATI Alberto Tirado 3.00 8.00
CPABB Bryson Brigman 3.00 8.00
CPABBI Braden Bishop 5.00 12.00
CPABM Brian Mundell 3.00 8.00
CPABR Blake Rutherford 8.00 20.00
CPACAD Chance Adams 4.00 10.00
CPACF Clint Frazier 20.00 50.00
CPACH C.J. Hinojosa 3.00 8.00
CPACHR Christian Arroyo 5.00 12.00
CPACP Chris Paddack 20.00 50.00
CPACS Cole Stobbe 3.00 8.00
CPACWH Chih-Wei Hu 3.00 8.00
CPADF David Fletcher 8.00 20.00
CPADG Daniel Gossett 3.00 8.00
CPADL Dawel Lugo 3.00 8.00
CPADLA Dinelson Lamet 15.00 40.00
CPADT David Thompson 4.00 10.00
CPAEG Elniery Garcia 3.00 8.00
CPAEJ Eloy Jimenez 150.00 400.00
CPAFJ Felix Jorge 3.00 8.00
CPAFM Francisco Mejia 6.00 15.00
CPAFP Freddy Peralta 10.00 25.00
CPAFR Francisco Rios 3.00 8.00
CPAFRO Fernando Romero 3.00 8.00
CPAGH Gage Hinsz 3.00 8.00
CPAGJ Griffin Jax 3.00 8.00
CPAGL Grayson Long 3.00 8.00
CPAGT Gleyber Torres 60.00 150.00
CPAHQ Heath Quinn 4.00 10.00
CPAIW Isaiah White 3.00 8.00
CPAJAZ Jose Azocar 3.00 8.00
CPAJC Jazz Chisholm 75.00 200.00
CPAJD Jon Duplantier 5.00 12.00
CPAJF Jameson Fisher 3.00 8.00
CPAJG Jason Groome 10.00 25.00
CPAJHE Jacob Heyward 3.00 8.00
CPAJJ Joe Jimenez 4.00 10.00
CPAJM Justin Maese 3.00 8.00
CPAJMI Jalen Miller 3.00 8.00
CPAJO Josh Ockimey 4.00 10.00
CPAJO Jorge Ona 4.00 10.00
CPAJP Jose Pujols 4.00 10.00
CPAJS Jesus Sanchez 40.00 100.00
CPAJSB Josh Sborz 3.00 8.00
CPAJT Jose Trevino 3.00 8.00
CPAJT Jose Taveras 4.00 10.00
CPAKA Keegan Akin 4.00 10.00
CPAKF Kyle Funkhouser 4.00 10.00
CPAKL Khalil Lee 10.00 25.00
CPAKM Kevin Maitan 5.00 12.00
CPALA Luis Arraez 25.00 60.00
CPALA Lazarito Armenteros 6.00 15.00
CPALAB Luis Alexander Basabe 5.00 12.00
CPALAL Luis Almanzar 3.00 8.00
CPALB Lewis Brinson 5.00 12.00
CPALCA Luis Carpio 3.00 8.00
CPALE Lucas Erceg 3.00 8.00
CPALGU Lourdes Gurriel Jr. 25.00 60.00
CPALI Logan Ice 3.00 8.00
CPALT Leody Taveras 10.00 25.00
CPAMG Miguel Gomez 3.00 8.00
CPAMK Michael Kopech 12.00 30.00
CPAMK Mitch Keller 10.00 25.00
CPAMM Mickey Moniak 6.00 15.00
CPAMS Magneuris Sierra 3.00 8.00
CPAMSC Max Schrock 5.00 12.00
CPAMV Meibrys Viloria 3.00 8.00
CPAMW Mitchell White 3.00 8.00
CPANB Nick Banks 3.00 8.00
CPANS Nick Senzel 20.00 50.00
CPANSO Nick Solak 12.00 30.00
CPAOP Ofelky Peralta 3.00 8.00
CPAPC P.J. Conlon 3.00 8.00
CPAPW Patrick Weigel 3.00 8.00
CPARA Ronald Acuna 1000.00 2500.00
CPARH Ryan Howard 4.00 10.00
CPAROH Ryan O'Hearn 6.00 15.00
CPARR Roniel Raudes 3.00 8.00
CPASA Sandy Alcantara 15.00 40.00
CPASD Steven Duggar 3.00 8.00
CPASH Starling Heredia 4.00 10.00
CPASS Sixto Sanchez 50.00 120.00
CPATC Trevor Clifton 3.00 8.00
CPATC Taylor Clarke 3.00 8.00
CPATF T.J. Friedl 3.00 8.00
CPATH Torii Hunter Jr. 4.00 10.00
CPATM Triston McKenzie 15.00 40.00
CPATN Tomas Nido 3.00 8.00
CPATS Thomas Szapucki 4.00 10.00
CPAVG Vladimir Gutierrez 3.00 8.00
CPAWB Wuilmer Becerra 3.00 8.00
CPAWJ Wander Javier 5.00 12.00
CPAYCC Yu-Cheng Chang 8.00 20.00
CPAYD Yusniel Diaz 12.00 30.00

2017 Bowman Chrome Prospect Autographs 70th Blue Refractors

*70TH BLUE: 1.2X TO 3X BASIC
BOW.STATED ODDS 1:1463 HOBBY
BOW.EXCH.DEADLINE 3/31/2019
BOW.CHR.EXCH.DEADLINE 8/31/2019
CPAAE Anderson Espinoza 20.00 50.00
CPAAME Adonis Medina 40.00 100.00
CPAEG Elniery Garcia 20.00 50.00
CPAEJ Eloy Jimenez 500.00 1000.00
CPAKM Kevin Maitan 15.00 40.00
CPANS Nick Senzel 300.00 600.00
CPAYCC Yu-Cheng Chang 30.00 80.00

2017 Bowman Chrome Prospect Autographs Blue Refractors

*BLUE REF: 1X TO 2.5X BASIC
BOW.STATED ODDS 1:488 HOBBY
BOW.CHR.STATED ODDS 1:196 HOBBY
STATED PRINT RUN 150 SER.#'D SETS
BOW.EXCH.DEADLINE 3/31/2019
BOW.CHR.EXCH.DEADLINE 8/31/2019

2017 Bowman Chrome Prospect Autographs Blue Mega Refractors

*BLUE REF: 1X TO 2.5X BASIC
STATED PRINT RUN 150 SER.#'D SETS
EXCHANGE DEADLINE 8/31/2019

2017 Bowman Chrome Prospect Autographs Gold Refractors

*GOLD: 1.5X TO 4X BASIC
BOW.ODDS 1:1463 HOBBY
BOW.CHR.ODDS 1:588 HOBBY
STATED PRINT RUN 50 SER.#'d SETS
EXCHANGE DEADLINE 3/31/2019
BOW.CHR.EXCH.DEADLINE 8/31/2019

2017 Bowman Chrome Prospect Autographs Gold Shimmer Refractors

*GOLD SHIMMER: 1.5X TO 4X BASIC
BOW.STATED ODDS 1:1463 HOBBY
STATED PRINT RUN 50 SER.#'d SETS
BOW.EXCH.DEADLINE 3/31/2019
BOW.CHR.EXCH.DEADLINE 8/31/2019

2017 Bowman Chrome Prospect Autographs Green Refractors

*GREEN REF: 1.2X TO 3X BASIC
RANDOM INSERTS IN BOW.RET PACKS
BOW.CHR.STATED ODDS 1:297
STATED PRINT RUN 99 SER.#'D SETS
BOW.EXCH.DEADLINE 3/31/2019
BOW.CHR.EXCH.DEADLINE 8/31/2019

2017 Bowman Chrome Prospect Autographs Green Shimmer Refractors

*GREEN REF: 1.2X TO 3X BASIC
RANDOMLY INSERTED IN RETAIL PACKS
STATED PRINT RUN 99 SER.#'D SETS
BOW.EXCH.DEADLINE 3/31/2019
BOW.CHR.EXCH.DEADLINE 8/31/2019

2017 Bowman Chrome Prospect Autographs Orange Refractors

*ORANGE REF: 3X TO 8X BASIC
STATED ODDS 1:744 HOBBY
BOW,CHR.STATED ODDS 1:655 HOBBY
STATED PRINT RUN 25 SER.#'d SETS
BOW.EXCH.DEADLINE 3/31/2019
BOW.CHR.EXCH.DEADLINE 8/31/2019

2017 Bowman Chrome Prospect Autographs Orange Shimmer Refractors

*ORANGE SHIMMER: 3X TO 8X BASIC
BOW.STATED ODDS 1:744 HOBBY
STATED PRINT RUN 25 SER.#'d SETS
BOW.EXCH.DEADLINE 3/31/2019
BOW.CHR.EXCH.DEADLINE 8/31/2019

2017 Bowman Chrome Prospect Autographs Orange Wave Refractors

*ORANGE WAVE REF: 3X TO 8X BASIC
STATED PRINT RUN 25 SER.#'d SETS
BOW.CHR.EXCH.DEADLINE 8/31/2019

2017 Bowman Chrome Prospect Autographs Purple Refractors

*PURPLE REF: .6X TO 1.5X BASIC
BOW.CHR.STATED ODDS 1:118 HOBBY
BOW.STATED ODDS 1:293 HOBBY
STATED PRINT RUN 250 SER.#'d SETS
BOW.EXCH.DEADLINE 3/31/2019
BOW.CHR.EXCH.DEADLINE 8/31/2019

2017 Bowman Chrome Prospect Autographs Refractors

*REF: .5X TO 1.2X BASIC
BOW.STATED ODDS 1:147 HOBBY
BOW.CHR.ODDS 1:59 HOBBY
STATED PRINT RUN 499 SER.#'D SETS
BOW.EXCH.DEADLINE 3/31/2019
BOW.CHR.EXCH.DEADLINE 8/31/2019

2017 Bowman Chrome Prospects

COMPLETE SET (250) 100.00 250.00
BOW.PLATE ODDS 1:5838 HOBBY
BOW.CHR.PLATE ODDS 1:4116 HOBBY
PLATE PRINT RUN 1 SET PER COLOR
NO PLATE PRICING DUE TO SCARCITY
BCP1 Nick Senzel 1.50 4.00
BCP2 Gavin Lux 1.00 2.50
BCP3 Ronald Guzman .30 .75
BCP4 A.J. Puckett .25 .60
BCP5 Mike Soroka .75 2.00
BCP6 Roniel Raudes .25 .60
BCP7 Lucas Erceg .25 .60
BCP8 Luis Almanzar .25 .60
BCP9 Beau Burrows .25 .60
BCP10 Chase Vallot .25 .60
BCP11 P.J. Conlon .25 .60
BCP12 Erick Fedde .25 .60
BCP13 Rookie Davis .25 .60
BCP14 Chris Shaw .25 .60
BCP15 Nick Burdi .25 .60
BCP16 Clint Frazier .50 1.25
BCP17 Luiz Gohara .25 .60
BCP18 Lourdes Gurriel Jr. .40 1.00
BCP19 Eric Jenkins .25 .60
BCP20 Angel Perdomo .25 .60
BCP21 Dustin May 1.25 3.00
BCP22 Freddy Peralta .40 1.00
BCP23 Jarlin Garcia .25 .60
BCP24 Tyler O'Neill .30 .75
BCP25 Lazarito Armenteros .50 1.25
BCP26 Paul DeJong .75 2.00
BCP27 Antonio Senzatela .25 .60
BCP28 Kyle Tucker .60 1.50
BCP29 Aramis Garcia .25 .60
BCP30 Willie Calhoun .40 1.00
BCP31 Chance Adams .30 .75
BCP32 Vladimir Guerrero Jr. 3.00 8.00
BCP33 Braxton Garrett .25 .60
BCP34 Yeudy Garcia .25 .60
BCP35 Dane Dunning .75 2.00
BCP36 Andy Ibanez .25 .60
BCP37 Francisco Rios .25 .60
BCP38 Joe Jimenez .30 .75
BCP39 Dylan Cozens .25 .60
BCP40 Mauricio Dubon .30 .75
BCP41 Franklyn Kilome .30 .75
BCP42 Chance Sisco .50 1.25
BCP43 Sandy Alcantara .30 .75
BCP44 Stephen Gonsalves .25 .60
BCP45 Grant Holmes .25 .60
BCP46 Dakota Chalmers .25 .60
BCP47 Kolby Allard .25 .60
BCP48 Tyler Alexander .25 .60
BCP49 Phil Bickford .25 .60
BCP50 Eloy Jimenez 1.00 2.50
BCP51 Francisco Mejia .40 1.00
BCP52 Kohl Stewart .25 .60
BCP53 Garrett Whitley .25 .60
BCP54 Anderson Espinoza .25 .60
BCP55 Cal Quantrill .25 .60
BCP56 Tetsuto Yamada .50 1.25
BCP57 Tyler Beede .25 .60
BCP58 Jake Bauers .30 .75
BCP59 Ariel Jurado .25 .60
BCP60 Austin Voth .25 .60
BCP61 Tyler Stephenson .60 1.50
BCP62 Yoshitomo Tsutsugo .60 1.50
BCP63 Dominic Smith .25 .60
BCP64 Matt Thaiss .25 .60
BCP65 Austin Meadows .60 1.50
BCP66 Mitch Keller .30 .75
BCP67 Jahmai Jones .25 .60
BCP68 Alex Speas .25 .60
BCP69 Nolan Jones .40 1.00
BCP70 Kevin Newman .40 1.00
BCP71 T.J. Friedl .25 .60
BCP72 Oscar De La Cruz .25 .60
BCP73 Victor Robles .60 1.50
BCP74 Patrick Weigel .25 .60
BCP75 Ryan Mountcastle 1.25 3.00
BCP76 Amed Rosario .40 1.00
BCP77 Nick Solak 1.00 2.50
BCP78 Abrahan Gutierrez .40 1.00
BCP79 Yu-Cheng Chang .40 1.00
BCP80 Gleyber Torres 4.00 10.00
BCP81 J.D. Davis .30 .75
BCP82 Walker Buehler .60 1.50
BCP83 Andrew Sopko .25 .60
BCP84 Brent Honeywell .30 .75
BCP85 Kyle Funkhouser .30 .75
BCP86 Brian Mundell .25 .60
BCP87 Brian Anderson .30 .75
BCP88 Brendan Rodgers .30 .75
BCP89 Josh Staumont .25 .60
BCP90 Cody Sedlock .25 .60
BCP91 D.J. Stewart .25 .60
BCP92 Wuilmer Becerra .25 .60
BCP93 Nate Smith .25 .60
BCP94 Alfredo Rodriguez .30 .75
BCP95 Daz Cameron .25 .60
BCP96 Taylor Ward .30 .75
BCP97 Takahiro Norimoto .25 .60
BCP98 Tomoyuki Sugano .40 1.00
BCP99 Drew Jackson .25 .60
BCP100 Kevin Maitan .40 1.00
BCP101 Rafael Devers .50 1.25
BCP102 Alex Kirilloff .60 1.50
BCP103 Jack Flaherty 1.50 4.00
BCP104 Adonis Medina .40 1.00
BCP105 Ke'Bryan Hayes 1.25 3.00
BCP106 Josh Hader .30 .75
BCP107 Luis Urias 1.00 2.50
BCP108 Donnie Dewees .25 .60
BCP109 Kyle Freeland .30 .75
BCP110 Matt Chapman .75 2.00
BCP111 Sam Coonrod .25 .60
BCP112 Andrew Suarez .25 .60
BCP113 David Fletcher .75 2.00
BCP114 Tyler Jay .25 .60
BCP115 Franklin Barreto .25 .60
BCP116 Michael Kopech .75 2.00
BCP117 Rhys Hoskins 1.00 2.50
BCP118 Triston McKenzie .75 2.00
BCP119 Luis Garcia 2.00 5.00
BCP120 Harold Ramirez .30 .75
BCP121 Blake Rutherford .40 1.00
BCP122 Matt Manning .40 1.00
BCP123 Josh Morgan .25 .60
BCP124 Dylan Cease .40 1.00
BCP125 Kyle Lewis .50 1.25
BCP126 Nick Neidert .25 .60
BCP127 Ronald Acuna 75.00 200.00
BCP128 Luis Ortiz .25 .60
BCP129 Isael Soto .25 .60
BCP130 Adrian Morejon .40 1.00
BCP131 Mark Zagunis .25 .60
BCP132 Justus Sheffield .40 1.00
BCP133 Jaime Schultz .25 .60
BCP134 Fernando Romero .25 .60
BCP135 Mickey Moniak .50 1.25
BCP136 Jorge Bonifacio .25 .60
BCP137 Jomar Reyes .25 .60
BCP138 Thomas Szapucki .30 .75
BCP139 Sean Reid-Foley .25 .60
BCP140 Willy Adames .30 .75
BCP141 Yang Hyeon-Jong .30 .75
BCP142 Bo Bichette 1.00 2.50
BCP143 Harrison Bader .40 1.00
BCP144 Travis Demeritte .25 .60
BCP145 Juan Hillman .25 .60
BCP146 Francis Martes .25 .60
BCP147 Wilkerman Garcia .30 .75
BCP148 Christin Stewart .30 .75
BCP149 Cody Bellinger 4.00 10.00
BCP150 Jason Groome .50 1.25
BCP151 Amed Rosario .40 1.00
BCP152 Andrew Moore .30 .75
BCP153 Albert Abreu .30 .75
BCP154 Max Schrock .40 1.00
BCP155 Jonathan Arauz .30 .75
BCP156 Max Fried 1.00 2.50
BCP157 Bobby Bradley .30 .75
BCP158 Leody Taveras 3.00 8.00
BCP159 Jacob Nottingham .25 .60
BCP160 Fernando Tatis Jr. 8.00 20.00
BCP161 Austin Riley .75 2.00
BCP162 Trevor Clifton .25 .60
BCP163 Anthony Banda .25 .60
BCP164 Richard Urena .40 1.00
BCP165 Reggie Lawson .25 .60
BCP166 Felix Jorge .25 .60
BCP167 Clint Frazier .50 1.25
BCP168 Jorge Ona .30 .75
BCP169 Brandon Woodruff .75 2.00
BCP170 Sam Travis .30 .75
BCP171 Derek Fisher .30 .75
BCP172 Touki Toussaint .30 .75
BCP173 Forrest Whitley .60 1.50
BCP174 Scott Kingery .40 1.00
BCP175 Jorge Mateo .25 .60
BCP176 Joshua Lowe .25 .60
BCP177 Rowdy Tellez .25 .60
BCP178 Kevin Kramer .25 .60
BCP179 Desmond Lindsay .25 .60
BCP180 Juan Soto 10.00 25.00
BCP181 Isan Diaz .60 1.50
BCP182 Rob Kaminsky .25 .60
BCP183 Domingo Acevedo .25 .60
BCP184 Brian Anderson .30 .75
BCP185 Andy Yerzy .25 .60
BCP186 Brent Honeywell .30 .75
BCP187 Tirso Ornelas .30 .75
BCP188 Rafael Devers .50 1.25
BCP189 Adam Ravenelle .25 .60
BCP190 Mitchell White .25 .60
BCP191 Dawel Lugo .25 .60
BCP192 Vladimir Gutierrez .25 .60
BCP193 Max Povse .25 .60
BCP194 Delvin Perez .40 1.00
BCP195 Jacob Nix .25 .60
BCP196 Josh Sborz .25 .60
BCP197 Torii Hunter Jr. .30 .75
BCP198 Jaime Schultz .25 .60
BCP199 Yasel Antuna 1.25 3.00
BCP200 Jason Groome .50 1.25
BCP201 Nick Gordon .25 .60
BCP202 Brett Phillips .30 .75
BCP203 Yairo Munoz .25 .60
BCP204 Bryan Reynolds .40 1.00
BCP205 Dakota Hudson .40 1.00
BCP206 Miguelangel Sierra .50 1.25
BCP207 Jazz Chisholm 10.00 25.00
BCP208 DJ Peters .60 1.50
BCP209 Jacob Faria .25 .60
BCP210 Sixto Sanchez 8.00 20.00
BCP211 Braden Bishop .40 1.00
BCP212 Ryan O'Hearn .50 1.25
BCP213 Garrett Stubbs .25 .60
BCP214 Paul DeJong .75 2.00
BCP215 Trent Clark .25 .60
BCP216 Jose Albertos .60 1.50
BCP217 Ryan McMahon .40 1.00
BCP218 Khalil Lee .40 1.00
BCP219 Victor Robles .60 1.50
BCP220 Steven Duggar .25 .60
BCP221 Franklin Perez .40 1.00
BCP222 Tomas Nido .25 .60
BCP223 Justin Dunn .25 .60
BCP224 Austin Hays .60 1.50
BCP225 Nick Senzel .75 2.00
BCP226 Starling Heredia .30 .75
BCP227 Bryson Brigman .25 .60
BCP228 Jesus Sanchez 1.25 3.00
BCP229 Yusniel Diaz .75 2.00
BCP230 Eloy Jimenez 1.00 2.50
BCP231 Brendan Rodgers .30 .75
BCP232 Ian Anderson .75 2.00
BCP233 Mark Zagunis .25 .60
BCP234 Jameson Fisher .25 .60
BCP235 Michael Kopech .75 2.00
BCP236 Keegan Akin .30 .75
BCP237 James Kaprielian .25 .60
BCP238 Jeisson Rosario .30 .75
BCP239 Carter Kieboom .40 1.00
BCP240 Nick Williams .30 .75
BCP241 Brandon Marsh 3.00 8.00
BCP242 Wander Javier .40 1.00
BCP243 Chris Paddack .60 1.50
BCP244 Luis Alexander Basabe .40 1.00
BCP245 Zack Burdi .25 .60
BCP246 Anthony Kay .30 .75
BCP247 Anderson Tejeda .40 1.00
BCP248 Daniel Gossett .25 .60
BCP249 Heath Quinn .30 .75
BCP250 Gleyber Torres 4.00 10.00

2017 Bowman Chrome Prospects 70th Blue Refractors

*70TH BLUE REF: 1.5X TO 4X BASIC
BOW.ODDS 1:94 HOBBY
BOW.CHR.ODDS 1:45 HOBBY

2017 Bowman Chrome Prospects Blue Refractors

*BLUE REF: 2X TO 5X BASIC
BOW.ODDS 1:157 HOBBY
BOW.CHR.ODDS 1:60 HOBBY
STATED PRINT RUN 150 SER.#'d SETS

2017 Bowman Chrome Prospects Blue Shimmer Refractors

*BLUE SHIMMER: 2X TO 5X BASIC
BOW.ODDS 1:157 HOBBY
BOW.CHR.ODDS 1:60 HOBBY
BCP151-BCP250 PRINT RUN 150 SER.#'d SETS

2017 Bowman Chrome Prospects Gold Refractors

*GOLD REF: 5X TO 12X BASIC
BOW.ODDS 1:469 HOBBY
BOW.CHR.ODDS 1:178 HOBBY
STATED PRINT RUN 50 SER.#'d SETS

2017 Bowman Chrome Prospects Gold Shimmer Refractors

*GOLD REF: 5X TO 12X BASIC
BOW.ODDS 1:469 HOBBY
BOW.CHR.ODDS 1:178 HOBBY

2017 Bowman Chrome Prospects Green Refractors

*GREEN REF: 2.5X TO 6X BASIC
RANDOMLY INSERTED IN RETAIL PACKS
BOW.CHR.ODDS 1:90 HOBBY
STATED PRINT RUN 99 SER.#'d SETS

2017 Bowman Chrome Prospects Green Shimmer Refractors

*GRN SHIM REF: 2.5X TO 6X BASIC
RANDOMLY INSERTED IN RETAIL PACKS
BOW.CHR.ODDS 1:90 HOBBY
STATED PRINT RUN 99 SER.#'d SETS

2017 Bowman Chrome Prospects Orange Refractors

*ORANGE REF: 8X TO 20X BASIC
BOW.ODDS 1:203 HOBBY
BOW.CHR.ODDS 1:356 HOBBY
STATED PRINT RUN 25 SER.#'d SETS

2017 Bowman Chrome Prospects Orange Shimmer Refractors

*ORNG SHIM REF/25: 8X TO 20X BASIC
BOW.ODDS 1:203 HOBBY
BOW.CHR.ODDS 1:356 HOBBY
STATED PRINT RUN 25 SER.#'d SETS

2017 Bowman Chrome Prospects Purple Refractors

*PURPLE REF: 2X TO 5X BASIC
BOW.ODDS 1:94 HOBBY
BOW.CHR.ODDS 1:36 HOBBY
STATED PRINT RUN 250 SER.#'d SETS

2017 Bowman Chrome Prospects Purple Shimmer Refractors

*PRPLE SHIMMER: 2X TO 5X BASIC
STATED ODDS 1:36 HOBBY

2017 Bowman Chrome Prospects Refractors

*REF: 1.5X TO 4X BASIC
BOW.ODDS 1:47 HOBBY
BOW.CHR.ODDS 1:18 HOBBY
STATED PRINT RUN 499 SER.#'d SETS

2017 Bowman Chrome Refractors That Never Were

STATED ODDS 1:179 HOBBY
STATED PRINT RUN 499 SER.#'d SETS
RTNWAP Andy Pettitte 2.00 5.00
RTNWBW Bernie Williams 2.00 5.00
RTNWCS Curt Schilling 2.00 5.00
RTNWDJ Derek Jeter 6.00 15.00
RTNWIR Ivan Rodriguez 2.00 5.00
RTNWMI Monte Irvin 2.00 5.00
RTNWRK Ralph Kiner 2.00 5.00
RTNWRR Robin Roberts 2.00 5.00
RTNWRS Red Schoendienst 2.00 5.00
RTNWWS Warren Spahn 2.00 5.00

2017 Bowman Chrome Refractors That Never Were Orange Refractors

*ORANGE REF: 1X TO 2.5X BASIC
STATED ODDS 1:3569 HOBBY
STATED PRINT RUN 25 SER.#'d SETS
RTNWDJ Derek Jeter 25.00 60.00

2017 Bowman Chrome Refractors That Never Were Autographs

STATED ODDS 1:3134 HOBBY
PRINT RUNS B/WN 30-99 COPIES PER
EXCHANGE DEADLINE 8/31/2019
RTNWAP Andy Pettitte/99 20.00 50.00
RTNWBW Bernie Williams/99
RTNWDJ Derek Jeter/30 400.00 800.00
RTNWIR Ivan Rodriguez/99 15.00 40.00

2017 Bowman Chrome Rookie Autographs

BOW.STATED ODDS 1:260 HOBBY
2017 Bowman Chrome Prospect Autographs Orange Refractors
BOW.PLATE ODDS 1:48,253 HOBBY
PLATE PRINT RUN 1 SET PER COLOR
BLACK-CYAN-MAGENTA-YELLOW ISSUED
NO PLATE PRICING DUE TO SCARCITY
BOW.EXCH.DEADLINE 3/31/2019
2017 Bowman Chrome Prospect Autographs Orange Refractors
BCARAB A.Bregman Htting 20.00 50.00
BCARAG Amir Garrett 3.00 8.00
BCARBZ Bradley Zimmer 4.00 10.00
BCARCA Christian Arroyo 5.00 12.00
BCARCB Cody Bellinger 125.00 300.00
BCARGC Gavin Cecchini 3.00 8.00
BCARHD Hunter Dozier 6.00 15.00
BCARJDL De Leon TB jrsy 3.00 8.00
BCARJH Jeff Hoffman 3.00 8.00
BCARJHA Josh Hader 8.00 20.00
BCARJT Jake Thompson 3.00 8.00
BCARMM Manny Margot 3.00 8.00
BCARRG Robert Gsellman 3.00 8.00
BCARRL Reynaldo Lopez 3.00 8.00
BCARTM Trey Mancini 8.00 20.00
BCARYG Gurriel Ornge jrsy 12.00 30.00
BCARYM Moncada CHI jrsy 25.00 60.00
CRAAB Bregman Trwng 20.00 50.00
CRAABE Andrew Benintendi 15.00 40.00
CRAAJ Aaron Judge 125.00 300.00
CRAAR Alex Reyes 4.00 10.00
CRACF Carson Fulmer 3.00 8.00
CRADD David Dahl 4.00 10.00
CRADS Dansby Swanson 20.00 50.00
CRAHR Hunter Renfroe 4.00 10.00
CRAJA Jorge Alfaro 4.00 10.00
CRAJCO Jharel Cotton 3.00 8.00
CRAJDL De Leon LAD jrsy 3.00 8.00
CRAJMU Joe Musgrove 15.00 40.00
CRART Raimel Tapia 4.00 10.00
CRATA Tyler Austin 4.00 10.00
CRATG Tyler Glasnow 15.00 40.00
CRAYG Gurriel Blue jrsy 12.00 30.00
CRAYM Moncada CHI jrsy 40.00 100.00

2017 Bowman Chrome Rookie Autographs Blue Refractors

*BLUE REF: .6X TO 1.5X BASIC
BOW.STATED ODDS 1:1300 HOBBY
BOW.CHR.STATED ODDS 1:519 HOBBY
PRINT RUNS B/WN 125-150 COPIES PER1
BOW.EXCH.DEADLINE 3/31/2019
BOW.CHR.EXCH.DEADLINE 8/31/2019
CRAAB Bregman Trwng 30.00 80.00
CRAABE Andrew Benintendi 40.00 100.00
CRAAJ Aaron Judge 300.00 600.00

2017 Bowman Chrome Rookie Autographs Gold Refractors

*GOLD REF: 1.2X TO 3X BASIC
BOW.STATED ODDS 1:3892 HOBBY
BOW.CHR.STATED ODDS 1:1559 HOBBY
STATED PRINT RUN 50 SER.#'d SETS
BOW.EXCH.DEADLINE 3/31/2019
BOW.CHR.EXCH.DEADLINE 8/31/2019
BCARCB Cody Bellinger 400.00 800.00
CRAAB Bregman Trwng 60.00 150.00
CRAABE Andrew Benintendi 75.00 200.00
CRAAJ Aaron Judge 400.00 800.00
CRAYM Moncada CHI jrsy 150.00 400.00

2017 Bowman Chrome Rookie Autographs Green Refractors

*GREEN REF: .6X TO 1.5X BASIC
RANDOM INSERTS IN BOW.RETAIL PACKS
BOW.CHR.STATED ODDS 1:786 HOBBY
STATED PRINT RUN 99 SER.#'d SETS
BOW.EXCH.DEADLINE 3/31/2019
BOW.CHR.EXCH.DEADLINE 8/31/2019
CRAAB Bregman Trwng 30.00 80.00
CRAABE Andrew Benintendi 40.00 100.00
CRAAJ Aaron Judge 300.00 600.00
CRAYM Moncada CHI jrsy 75.00 200.00

2017 Bowman Chrome Rookie Autographs Orange Refractors

*ORANGE REF: 2.5X TO 6X BASIC
BOW.STATED ODDS 1:1983 HOBBY
BOW.CHR.STATED ODDS 1:1734 HOBBY
STATED PRINT RUN 25 SER.#'d SETS
BOW.EXCH.DEADLINE 3/31/2019
BOW.CHR.EXCH.DEADLINE 8/31/2019
BCARCB Cody Bellinger 1000.00 1500.00
CRAAB Bregman Trwng 125.00 300.00
CRAABE Andrew Benintendi 150.00 400.00
CRAAJ Aaron Judge 500.00 1000.00
CRAYM Moncada CHI jrsy 200.00 500.00

2017 Bowman Chrome Rookie Autographs Refractors

*REF: .5X TO 1.2X BASIC
BOW.STATED ODDS 1:391 HOBBY
BOW.CHR.STATED ODDS 1:156 HOBBY
STATED PRINT RUN 499 SER.#'d SETS
BOW.EXCH.DEADLINE 3/31/2019
BOW.CHR.EXCH.DEADLINE 8/31/2019

2017 Bowman Chrome Rookie of the Year Favorites Autographs

STATED ODDS 1:1951 HOBBY
STATED PRINT RUN 150 SER.#'d SETS
EXCHANGE DEADLINE 3/31/2019
*ORANGE/25: .75X TO 2X BASIC
ROYFAB Alex Bregman 20.00 50.00
ROYFABE Andrew Benintendi 50.00 120.00
ROYFAJ Aaron Judge 100.00 250.00
ROYFDD David Dahl 6.00 15.00
ROYFDS Dansby Swanson 15.00 40.00
ROYFHR Hunter Renfroe 8.00 20.00
ROYFJDL Jose De Leon 5.00 12.00
ROYFTG Tyler Glasnow 12.00 30.00
ROYFYG Yulieski Gurriel 8.00 20.00
ROYFYM Yoan Moncada 50.00 120.00

2017 Bowman Chrome Rookie of the Year Favorites Refractors

COMPLETE SET (15) 6.00 15.00
STATED ODDS 1:8 HOBBY
*GREEN/99: 1.5X TO 4X BASIC
*GOLD/50: 3X TO 8X BASIC
*ORANGE/25: 4X TO 10X BASIC
ROYF1 Yoan Moncada 1.25 3.00
ROYF2 Dansby Swanson 1.00 2.50
ROYF3 Alex Bregman 2.00 5.00
ROYF4 Yulieski Gurriel .60 1.50
ROYF5 Andrew Benintendi 1.25 3.00
ROYF6 Jose De Leon .40 1.00

ROYF7 Tyler Glasnow 1.50 4.00
ROYF8 David Dahl .50 1.25
ROYF9 Aaron Judge 3.00 8.00
ROYF10 Orlando Arcia .60 1.50
ROYF11 Hunter Renfroe .50 1.25
ROYF12 Josh Bell 1.00 2.50
ROYF13 Carson Fulmer .40 1.00
ROYF14 Alex Reyes .50 1.25
ROYF15 Jharel Cotton .40 1.00

2017 Bowman Chrome Scouts Top 100 Autographs

STATED ODDS 1:1668 HOBBY
PRINT RUNS B/WN 50-150 COPIES PER
EXCHANGE DEADLINE 3/31/2019
BTP1 Yoan Moncada 50.00 120.00
BTP2 Alex Reyes 10.00 25.00
BTP3 Dansby Swanson 30.00 80.00
BTP4 Andrew Benintendi 75.00 200.00
BTP5 Lucas Giolito 12.00 30.00
BTP12 Brendan Rodgers 15.00 40.00
BTP13 Nick Senzel 60.00 150.00
BTP24 Jason Groome 50.00 120.00
BTP25 Riley Pint 20.00 50.00
BTP26 Corey Ray 6.00 15.00
BTP29 A.J. Puk 8.00 20.00
BTP31 Ian Anderson 30.00 80.00
BTP35 A.J. Reed 5.00 12.00
BTP39 Jorge Mateo 15.00 40.00
BTP40 Francisco Mejia 25.00 60.00
BTP43 Francis Martes 5.00 12.00
BTP44 Brent Honeywell 8.00 20.00
BTP45 Aaron Judge 100.00 250.00
BTP46 Ian Happ 30.00 80.00
BTP50 Luke Weaver 6.00 15.00
BTP54 Forrest Whitley 8.00 20.00
BTP55 Cody Reed 8.00 20.00
BTP56 Sean Newcomb 6.00 15.00
BTP58 Cal Quantrill 5.00 12.00
BTP59 Leody Taveras 30.00 80.00
BTP60 Juan Soto 125.00 300.00
BTP65 Trent Clark 5.00 12.00
BTP70 Cody Sedlock 8.00 20.00
BTP74 Kyle Tucker 25.00 60.00
BTP79 Delvin Perez 30.00 80.00
BTP82 Bradley Zimmer 15.00 40.00
BTP83 Matt Thaiss 10.00 25.00
BTP84 Gavin Lux 8.00 20.00
BTP90 James Kaprielian 12.00 30.00
BTP91 Phil Bickford 5.00 12.00

2017 Bowman Chrome Scouts Top 100 Refractors

STATED ODDS 1:8 HOBBY
*GREEN/99: .1X TO 2.5X BASIC
*GOLD/50: 2X TO 5X BASIC
*ORANGE/25: 3X TO 8X BASIC
BTP1 Yoan Moncada 1.25 3.00
BTP2 Alex Reyes .50 1.25
BTP3 Dansby Swanson 1.00 2.50
BTP4 Andrew Benintendi 1.25 3.00
BTP5 Lucas Giolito .50 1.25
BTP6 Tyler Glasnow 1.50 4.00
BTP7 Amed Rosario .60 1.50
BTP8 Eloy Jimenez 1.50 4.00
BTP9 J.P. Crawford .40 1.00
BTP10 Victor Robles 1.00 2.50
BTP11 Austin Meadows 1.00 2.50
BTP12 Brendan Rodgers .50 1.25
BTP13 Nick Senzel 1.25 3.00
BTP14 Rafael Devers .75 2.00
BTP15 Ozzie Albies 1.50 4.00
BTP16 Clint Frazier .75 2.00
BTP17 Cody Bellinger 6.00 15.00
BTP18 Jose De Leon .40 1.00
BTP19 Gleyber Torres 6.00 15.00
BTP20 Anderson Espinoza .40 1.00
BTP21 Mitch Keller .50 1.25
BTP22 Manny Margot .40 1.00
BTP23 Kolby Allard .40 1.00
BTP24 Jason Groome .75 2.00
BTP25 Riley Pint .40 1.00
BTP26 Corey Ray .50 1.25
BTP27 Mickey Moniak .75 2.00
BTP28 Lewis Brinson .60 1.50
BTP29 A.J. Puk .60 1.50
BTP30 Willy Adames .50 1.25
BTP31 Ian Anderson 1.25 3.00
BTP32 Michael Kopech 1.25 3.00
BTP33 Jeff Hoffman .40 1.00
BTP34 Kyle Lewis .75 2.00
BTP35 A.J. Reed .40 1.00
BTP36 Luis Ortiz .40 1.00
BTP37 Dominic Smith .40 1.00
BTP38 Josh Hader .50 1.25
BTP39 Jorge Mateo .40 1.00
BTP40 Francisco Mejia .60 1.50
BTP41 Josh Bell 1.00 2.50
BTP42 Tyler O'Neill .50 1.25
BTP43 Francis Martes .40 1.00
BTP44 Brent Honeywell .50 1.25
BTP45 Aaron Judge 5.00 12.00
BTP46 Ian Happ .75 2.00
BTP47 Zack Collins .50 1.25
BTP48 Nick Gordon .40 1.00
BTP49 Braxton Garrett .40 1.00
BTP50 Luke Weaver .50 1.25
BTP51 Anthony Alford .40 1.00
BTP52 Reynaldo Lopez .40 1.00
BTP53 Amir Garrett .40 1.00
BTP54 Forrest Whitley 1.00 2.50
BTP55 Cody Reed .40 1.00
BTP56 Sean Newcomb .50 1.25
BTP57 Kevin Newman .60 1.50
BTP58 Cal Quantrill .40 1.00
BTP59 Leody Taveras 1.50 4.00
BTP60 Juan Soto 10.00 25.00
BTP61 Brady Aiken 1.00 2.50
BTP62 Alex Verdugo .60 1.50
BTP63 Dylan Cease .60 1.50
BTP64 Yadier Alvarez .60 1.50
BTP65 Trent Clark .40 1.00
BTP66 Franklin Barreto .40 1.00
BTP67 Hunter Renfroe .50 1.25
BTP68 Jack Flaherty 2.50 6.00
BTP69 Matt Manning .60 1.50
BTP70 Cody Sedlock .40 1.00
BTP71 Carson Fulmer .40 1.00
BTP72 Trevor Clifton .40 1.00
BTP73 Robert Stephenson .40 1.00
BTP74 Kyle Tucker 1.00 2.50
BTP75 Jahmai Jones .40 1.00
BTP76 Franklyn Kilome .50 1.25
BTP77 Isan Diaz 1.00 2.50
BTP78 Justin Dunn .40 1.00
BTP79 Delvin Perez .60 1.50
BTP80 Erick Fedde .40 1.00
BTP81 Justus Sheffield .60 1.50
BTP82 Bradley Zimmer .50 1.25
BTP83 Matt Thaiss .40 1.00
BTP84 Gavin Lux 1.50 4.00
BTP85 Triston McKenzie 1.25 3.00
BTP86 Tyler Beede .40 1.00
BTP87 Sean Reid-Foley .40 1.00
BTP88 Blake Rutherford .60 1.50
BTP89 Chance Sisco .75 2.00
BTP90 James Kaprielian .40 1.00
BTP91 Phil Bickford .40 1.00
BTP92 Kevin Maitan .60 1.50
BTP93 Albert Almora .40 1.00
BTP94 Raimel Tapia .50 1.25
BTP95 Luis Urias 1.50 4.00
BTP96 Yohander Mendez .40 1.00
BTP97 Vladimir Guerrero Jr. 5.00 12.00
BTP98 Alex Kirilloff 1.00 2.50
BTP99 Matt Chapman 1.25 3.00
BTP100 Hunter Dozier .40 1.00

2017 Bowman Chrome Scouts Top 100 Update

STATED ODDS 1:3 HOBBY
*ORANGE/25: 2X TO 5X BASIC
BSUAH Alec Hansen .40 1.00
BSUAM Adonis Medina .60 1.50
BSUAR Adrian Rondon .50 1.25
BSUBB Bo Bichette 1.50 4.00
BSUCA Chance Adams .50 1.25
BSUCK Carson Kelly .50 1.25
BSUDC Dylan Cozens .40 1.00
BSUDD Dane Dunning 1.25 3.00
BSUDF Dustin Fowler .50 1.25
BSUFR Fernando Romero .40 1.00
BSUGH Garrett Hampson .60 1.50
BSUID Isan Diaz 1.00 2.50
BSUJJ Joe Jimenez .50 1.25
BSULC Luis Castillo 1.25 3.00
BSULE Lucas Erceg .40 1.00
BSULG Luiz Gohara .40 1.00
BSUMM Michael Matuella .50 1.25
BSUMS Mike Soroka 1.25 3.00
BSUPDJ Paul DeJong 1.25 3.00
BSURA Ronald Acuna 12.00 30.00
BSURR Roniel Raudes .40 1.00
BSUSG Stephen Gonsalves .40 1.00
BSUTS Thomas Szapucki .50 1.25
BSUTT Taylor Trammell 2.50 6.00
BSUWB Walker Buehler 1.00 2.50

2017 Bowman Chrome Scouts Top 100 Update Autographs

STATED ODDS 1:1039 HOBBY
STATED PRINT RUN 150 SER.#'d SETS
EXCHANGE DEADLINE 8/31/2019
BSUAH Alec Hansen 8.00 20.00
BSUAR Adrian Rondon 5.00 12.00
BSUBB Bo Bichette 25.00 60.00
BSUCK Carson Kelly 5.00 12.00
BSUDC Dylan Cozens 4.00 10.00
BSUDD Dane Dunning 8.00 20.00
BSUDF Dustin Fowler 5.00 12.00
BSUGH Garrett Hampson 6.00 15.00
BSUJJ Joe Jimenez 5.00 12.00
BSULE Lucas Erceg 8.00 20.00
BSUMM Michael Matuella 5.00 12.00
BSUPDJ Paul DeJong 8.00 20.00
BSURA Ronald Acuna 125.00 300.00
BSURR Roniel Raudes 4.00 10.00
BSUTS Thomas Szapucki 8.00 20.00
BSUTT Taylor Trammell 20.00 50.00
BSUWB Walker Buehler 15.00 40.00

2017 Bowman Chrome Sensation Autographs

STATED ODDS 1:786 HOBBY
STATED PRINT RUN 99 SER.#'d SETS
EXCHANGE DEADLINE 8/31/2019
CSAAA Albert Abreu 8.00 20.00
CSAAE Anderson Espinoza 5.00 12.00
CSABR Blake Rutherford 8.00 20.00
CSACR Corey Ray 6.00 15.00
CSAGT Gleyber Torres 40.00 100.00
CSAIA Ian Anderson 6.00 15.00
CSAJG Jason Groome 10.00 25.00
CSAJM Jorge Mateo 6.00 15.00
CSAKL Kyle Lewis 10.00 25.00
CSAKM Kevin Maitan 8.00 20.00
CSALA Lazarito Armenteros 10.00 25.00
CSALG Lourdes Gurriel Jr. 10.00 25.00
CSALT Leody Taveras 30.00 80.00
CSAMK Mitch Keller 6.00 15.00
CSAMM Mickey Moniak 12.00 30.00
CSANS Nick Senzel 30.00 80.00
CSASH Starling Heredia 6.00 15.00
CSASN Sean Newcomb 6.00 15.00
CSATC Trevor Clifton EXCH 5.00 12.00
CSATH Torii Hunter Jr. 6.00 15.00
CSAWC Willie Calhoun 15.00 40.00

2017 Bowman Chrome Sensation Autographs Gold Refractors

*GOLD REF: .6X TO 1.5X BASIC
STATED ODDS 1:1559 HOBBY
STATED PRINT RUN 50 SER.#'d SETS
EXCHANGE DEADLINE 8/31/2019
CSABR Blake Rutherford 10.00 25.00
CSAMM Mickey Moniak 15.00 40.00
CSANS Nick Senzel 40.00 100.00

2017 Bowman Chrome Sensation Autographs Orange Refractors

*ORANGE REF: .6X TO 1.5X BASIC
STATED ODDS 1:1734 HOBBY
STATED PRINT RUN 25 SER.#'d SETS
EXCHANGE DEADLINE 8/31/2019
CSAAA Albert Abreu 25.00 60.00
CSABR Blake Rutherford
CSAMM Mickey Moniak 20.00 50.00
CSANS Nick Senzel 50.00 120.00

2017 Bowman Chrome Talent Pipeline Refractors

COMPLETE SET (30) 20.00 50.00
STATED ODDS 1:12 HOBBY
*GREEN/99: .6X TO 1.5X BASIC
*GOLD/50: 1.2X TO 3X BASIC
*ORANGE/25: 2.5X TO 6X BASIC
TPARI Alex Young .40 1.00
Taylor Clarke
Anthony Banda
TPATL Allard/Albies/Ellis 1.50 4.00
TPBAL Sedlock/Lee/Sisco .75 2.00
TPBOS Devers/Tavarez/Travis .75 2.00
TPCHI Jimenez/Happ/Zagunis 1.50 4.00
TPCHW Zack Collins .50 1.25
Spencer Adams
Zack Burdi
TPCIN Senzel/Mahle/Garrett 1.25 3.00
TPCLE Francisco Mejia .60 1.50
Nellie Rodriguez
Bradley Zimmer
TPCOL Brendan Rodgers .60 1.50
Ryan McMahon
Kyle Freeland
TPDET Manning/Stewart/Jimenez .60 1.50
TPHOU Tuc/Mar/Fis 1.00 2.50
TPKCR Vallot/O'Hearn/Bonifacio .75 2.00
TPLAA Matt Thaiss 1.25 3.00
David Fletcher
Nate Smith
TPLAD Alvarez/Calhoun/Bellinger 6.00 15.00
TPMIA Stone Garrett .40 1.00
Austin Dean
J.T. Riddle
TPMIL Ray/Phillips/Brinson .60 1.50
TPMIN Nick Gordon .40 1.00
Tyler Jay
Jake Reed
TPNYM Dunn/Rosario/Nimmo .60 1.50
TPNYY Trrs/Shffld/Frzr 6.00 15.00
TPOAK Puk/Munoz/Barreto .60 1.50
TPPHI Moniak/Cozens/Crawford .75 2.00
TPPIT Mitch Keller 1.00 2.50
Kevin Newman
Austin Meadows
TPSDP Anderson Espinoza .50 1.25
Austin Allen
Dinelson Lamet
TPSEA Lewis/O'Neill/Peterson .75 2.00
TPSFG Reynolds/Arroyo/Blackburn .60 1.50
TPSTL Flaherty/Bader/Valera 2.50 6.00
TPTBR Joshua Lowe .50 1.25
Willy Adames
Jacob Faria
TPTEX Tvrs/Ibnz/Gzmn 1.50 4.00
TPTOR Sean Reid-Foley .60 1.50
Richard Urena
A.J. Jimenez
TPWAS Robles/Fedde/Voth 1.00 2.50

2017 Bowman Chrome Draft

COMPLETE SET (200) 20.00 50.00
STATED PLATE ODDS 1:1136 HOBBY
PLATE PRINT RUN 1 SET PER COLOR
BLACK-CYAN-MAGENTA-YELLOW ISSUED
NO PLATE PRICING DUE TO SCARCITY
BDC1 Royce Lewis 2.50 6.00
BDC2 Jacob Gonzalez .75 2.00
BDC3 Seth Elledge .25 .60
BDC4 Stuart Fairchild .30 .75
BDC5 Franklin Perez .40 1.00
BDC6 Jeter Downs .50 1.25
BDC7 Yu-Cheng Chang .40 1.00
BDC8 T.J. Friedl .25 .60
BDC9 Alex Scherff .40 1.00
BDC10 Nick Solak 1.00 2.50
BDC11 Lincoln Henzman .25 .60
BDC12 Heliot Ramos 8.00 20.00
BDC13 Riley Adams .30 .75
BDC14 Wyatt Mills .25 .60
BDC15 Alex Faedo .40 1.00
BDC16 Marcos Diplan .25 .60
BDC17 Daulton Varsho .40 1.00
BDC18 Jacob Heatherly .25 .60
BDC19 Lourdes Gurriel Jr. .40 1.00
BDC20 Zach Kirtley .30 .75
BDC21 Cal Quantrill .25 .60
BDC22 Jacob Heyward .25 .60
BDC23 Alec Hansen .25 .60
BDC24 Quinn Brodey .25 .60
BDC25 MacKenzie Gore 10.00 25.00
BDC26 Mitch Keller .30 .75
BDC27 Joey Morgan .30 .75
BDC28 Juan Hillman .25 .60
BDC29 Freddy Peralta .40 1.00
BDC30 Morgan Cooper .30 .75
BDC31 Brett Netzer .30 .75
BDC32 Alex Lange .40 1.00
BDC33 Hans Crouse .60 1.50
BDC34 Michael Kopech .75 2.00
BDC35 Cole Ragans .25 .60
BDC36 Kolby Allard .25 .60
BDC37 Matt Manning .40 1.00
BDC38 Bo Bichette 1.00 2.50
BDC39 Ronald Acuna 15.00 40.00
BDC40 Cristian Pache 1.25 3.00
BDC41 Ryan Vilade .40 1.00
BDC42 Tyler Freeman .25 .60
BDC43 Cory Abbott .25 .60
BDC44 Shane Baz .40 1.00
BDC45 Brian Miller .30 .75
BDC46 Luis Campusano .30 .75
BDC47 A.J. Puk .40 1.00
BDC48 Griffin Canning .40 1.00
BDC49 Justin Dunn .25 .60
BDC50 Jorge Mateo .25 .60
BDC51 Trevor Clifton .25 .60
BDC52 Carter Kieboom .40 1.00
BDC53 Trevor Rogers 3.00 8.00
BDC54 Tommy Doyle .25 .60
BDC55 Adam Hall .40 1.00
BDC56 Will Benson .25 .60
BDC57 Ariel Jurado .25 .60
BDC58 Forrest Whitley .60 1.50
BDC59 Daniel Tillo .40 1.00
BDC60 Austin Beck 1.00 2.50
BDC61 Jahmai Jones .25 .60
BDC62 Adonis Medina .40 1.00
BDC63 Blayne Enlow .30 .75
BDC64 Ryley Widell .40 1.00
BDC65 Tanner Houck 1.25 3.00
BDC66 Caden Lemons .25 .60
BDC67 Buddy Reed .25 .60
BDC68 T.J. Zeuch .25 .60
BDC69 Vladimir Gutierrez .25 .60
BDC70 Anderson Espinoza .25 .60
BDC71 Fernando Tatis Jr. 8.00 20.00
BDC72 Eloy Jimenez 1.00 2.50
BDC73 Jose Taveras .30 .75
BDC74 Christopher Seise .40 1.00
BDC75 Keston Hiura 3.00 8.00
BDC76 Charlie Barnes .25 .60
BDC77 Connor Seabold .25 .60
BDC78 David Peterson .50 1.25
BDC79 Seth Corry .25 .60
BDC80 Blake Rutherford .40 1.00
BDC81 Conner Uselton .40 1.00
BDC82 D.L. Hall .30 .75
BDC83 Peter Alonso 2.50 6.00
BDC84 Glenn Otto .25 .60
BDC85 Gavin Sheets .40 1.00
BDC86 Luis Gonzalez .30 .75
BDC87 Taylor Walls .25 .60
BDC88 Ernie Clement .30 .75
BDC89 Dylan Carlson 1.50 4.00
BDC90 Drew Waters 1.50 4.00
BDC91 Christin Stewart .30 .75
BDC92 Cal Mitchell .50 1.25
BDC93 Troy Bacon .40 1.00
BDC94 Zac Lowther .30 .75
BDC95 Jo Adell 10.00 25.00
BDC96 Francisco Rios .25 .60
BDC97 Mason House .40 1.00
BDC98 Corey Ray .30 .75
BDC99 Anfernee Grier .25 .60
BDC100 Brendan McKay 1.00 2.50
BDC101 Kacy Clemens .30 .75
BDC102 Isan Diaz .60 1.50
BDC103 Drew Strotman .25 .60
BDC104 Will Gaddis .25 .60
BDC105 Jacob Pearson .25 .60
BDC106 Tyler Ivey .25 .60
BDC107 Nick Allen .30 .75
BDC108 Andy Ibanez .25 .60
BDC109 J.J. Matijevic .30 .75
BDC110 KJ Harrison .40 1.00
BDC111 Riley Pint .25 .60
BDC112 Franklyn Kilome .30 .75
BDC113 Peyton Remy .40 1.00
BDC114 Scott Kingery .40 1.00
BDC115 Adam Haseley .50 1.25
BDC116 Will Smith .60 1.50
BDC117 Anderson Tejeda .40 1.00
BDC118 Quentin Holmes .30 .75
BDC119 Nate Pearson 6.00 15.00
BDC120 Kyle Wright .75 2.00
BDC121 Matthew Whatley .25 .60
BDC122 Brent Rooker .60 1.50
BDC123 Daulton Jefferies .30 .75
BDC124 Taylor Ward .30 .75
Missing card number
BDC125 Triston McKenzie .75 2.00
BDC126 Scott Hurst .30 .75
BDC127 Noah Bremer .25 .60
BDC128 Angel Perdomo .25 .60
BDC129 Touki Toussaint .30 .75
BDC130 A.J. Puckett .25 .60
BDC131 Lucas Erceg .25 .60
BDC132 Riley Mahan .25 .60
BDC133 Corbin Martin .25 .60
BDC134 Jordan Sheffield .25 .60
BDC135 Lazarito Armenteros .50 1.25
BDC136 Dylan Cease .40 1.00
BDC137 Kevin Newman .40 1.00
BDC138 Hagen Danner .30 .75
BDC139 Mark Vientos .40 1.00
BDC140 Justus Sheffield .40 1.00
BDC141 Bubba Thompson .40 1.00
BDC142 Desmond Lindsay .25 .60
BDC143 J.B. Bukauskas .40 1.00
BDC144 Freddy Tarnok .30 .75
BDC145 Blake Hunt .25 .60
BDC146 David Thompson .30 .75
BDC147 Delvin Perez .40 1.00
BDC148 Peter Solomon .30 .75
BDC149 Brendan Murphy .25 .60
BDC150 Vladimir Guerrero Jr. 3.00 8.00
BDC151 Yusniel Diaz .75 2.00
BDC152 Dillon Tate .25 .60
BDC153 Nonie Williams .25 .60
BDC154 Kyle Lewis .50 1.25
BDC155 Bobby Dalbec 1.50 4.00
BDC156 Ian Anderson .75 2.00
BDC157 Brendan Rodgers .30 .75
BDC158 Drew Ellis .40 1.00
BDC159 Joseph Dunand .50 1.25
BDC160 Kevin Maitan .40 1.00
BDC161 Kramer Robertson .50 1.25
BDC162 Juan Soto 15.00 40.00
BDC163 Chris Okey .25 .60
BDC164 Tristen Lutz .40 1.00
BDC165 Wil Crowe .40 1.00
BDC166 Taylor Trammell 1.50 4.00
BDC167 Trevor Stephan .40 1.00
BDC168 Matt Tabor .25 .60
BDC169 James Marinan .40 1.00
BDC170 Cody Sedlock .25 .60
BDC171 Gavin Lux 1.00 2.50
BDC172 MJ Melendez .40 1.00
BDC173 Kade McClure .25 .60
BDC174 Dylan Busby .25 .60
BDC175 Kevin Merrell .30 .75
BDC176 Dawel Lugo .25 .60
BDC177 Jake Burger .50 1.25
BDC178 Evan White 2.50 6.00
BDC179 Carl Stajduhar .25 .60
BDC180 Connor Wong .40 1.00
BDC181 Canaan Smith .75 2.00
BDC182 Nick Raquet .25 .60
BDC183 Kyle Tucker .60 1.50
BDC184 Sam Carlson .30 .75
BDC185 Wuilmer Becerra .25 .60
Missing card number
BDC186 Dane Dunning .75 2.00
BDC187 Joe Perez .30 .75
BDC188 Brendon Little .30 .75
BDC189 Will Craig .25 .60
BDC190 Ricardo De La Torre .25 .60
BDC191 Nick Gordon .25 .60
BDC192 Kevin Smith .25 .60
BDC193 Cole Brannen .40 1.00
BDC194 Logan Warmoth .40 1.00
BDC195 Pavin Smith .40 1.00
BDC196 Colton Hock .30 .75
BDC197 Clarke Schmidt .40 1.00
BDC198 Cash Case .40 1.00
BDC199 Luis Ortiz .25 .60
BDC200 Gleyber Torres 4.00 10.00

2017 Bowman Chrome Draft 70th Blue Refractors

*70TH BLUE REF: 2X TO 5X BASIC
STATED ODDS 1:23 HOBBY
STATED PRINT RUN 200 SER.#'d SETS

2017 Bowman Chrome Draft Blue Refractors

*BLUE REF: 2X TO 5X BASIC
STATED ODDS 1:31 HOBBY
STATED PRINT RUN 150 SER.#'d SETS

2017 Bowman Chrome Draft Facsimile Variations

STATED ODDS 1:173 HOBBY
BD1 Royce Lewis 12.00 30.00
BD25 MacKenzie Gore 8.00 20.00
BD60 Austin Beck 4.00 10.00
BD70 Anderson Espinoza 1.00 2.50
BD80 Blake Rutherford 8.00 20.00
BD95 Jo Adell 30.00 80.00
BD100 Brendan McKay 5.00 12.00
BD115 Adam Haseley 2.00 5.00
BD120 Kyle Wright 3.00 8.00
BD135 Lazarito Armenteros 4.00 10.00
BD140 Justus Sheffield 1.50 4.00
BD150 Vladimir Guerrero Jr. 12.00 30.00
BD160 Kevin Maitan 1.50 4.00
BD195 Pavin Smith 8.00 20:00

2017 Bowman Chrome Draft Gold Refractors

*GOLD REF: 5X TO 12X BASIC
STATED ODDS 1:91 HOBBY
STATED PRINT RUN 50 SER.#'d SETS

2017 Bowman Chrome Draft Green Refractors

*GREEN REF: 2.5X TO 6X BASIC
STATED ODDS 1:46 HOBBY
STATED PRINT RUN 99 SER.#'d SETS

2017 Bowman Chrome Draft Image Variation Autographs

STATED ODDS 1:898 HOBBY
STATED PRINT RUN 99 SER.#'d SETS
EXCHANGE DEADLINE 11/30/2019
BD1 Royce Lewis 150.00 300.00
BD25 MacKenzie Gore 75.00 200.00
BD60 Austin Beck 100.00 250.00
BD95 Jo Adell 250.00 500.00
BD100 Brendan McKay 150.00 400.00
BD115 Adam Haseley 60.00 150.00
BD120 Kyle Wright 50.00 120.00
BD160 Kevin Maitan 50.00 120.00

2017 Bowman Chrome Draft Orange Refractors

*ORANGE REF: 8X TO 20X BASIC
STATED ODDS 1:182 HOBBY
STATED PRINT RUN 25 SER.#'d SETS

2017 Bowman Chrome Draft Purple Refractors

*PURPLE REF: 1.5X TO 4X BASIC
STATED ODDS 1:19 HOBBY
STATED PRINT RUN 250 SER.#'d SETS

2017 Bowman Chrome Draft Refractors

*REFRACTORS: .75X TO 2X BASIC
RANDOM INSERTS IN PACKS

2017 Bowman Chrome Draft Sky Blue Refractors

*SKY BLUE REF: 1X TO 2.5X BASIC
STATED ODDS 1:8 HOBBY
STATED PRINT RUN 399 SER.#'d SETS

2017 Bowman Chrome Draft Autographs

STATED ODDS 1:8 HOBBY
PRINTING PLATE ODDS 1:3917 HOBBY
PLATE PRINT RUN 1 SET PER COLOR
BLACK-CYAN-MAGENTA-YELLOW ISSUED
NO PLATE PRICING DUE TO SCARCITY
EXCHANGE DEADLINE 11/30/2019
CDAAB Austin Beck 6.00 15.00
CDAAF Alex Faedo 5.00 12.00
CDAAH Adam Haseley 8.00 20.00
CDABE Blayne Enlow 4.00 10.00
CDABH Blake Hunt 3.00 8.00
CDABM Brendan McKay 15.00 40.00
CDABMI Brian Miller 4.00 10.00
CDABMU Brendan Murphy 3.00 8.00
CDABN Brett Netzer 4.00 10.00
CDABR Brent Rooker 12.00 30.00
CDABT Bubba Thompson 5.00 12.00
CDACA Cory Abbott 3.00 8.00
CDACB Cole Brannen 5.00 12.00
CDACBA Charlie Barnes 3.00 8.00
CDACC Cash Case 5.00 12.00
CDACH Colton Hock 4.00 10.00
CDACL Caden Lemons 3.00 8.00
CDACMA Corbin Martin 3.00 8.00
CDACS Clarke Schmidt 15.00 40.00
CDACSE Christopher Seise 5.00 12.00
CDACW Connor Wong 5.00 12.00
CDADB Dylan Busby 3.00 8.00
CDADE Drew Ellis 5.00 12.00
CDADH D.L. Hall 15.00 40.00
CDADP David Peterson 15.00 40.00
CDADW Drew Waters 40.00 100.00
CDAEC Ernie Clement 4.00 10.00
CDAEW Evan White 25.00 60.00
CDAGC Griffin Canning 5.00 12.00
CDAGS Gavin Sheets 5.00 12.00
CDAHC Hans Crouse 8.00 20.00
CDAHD Hagen Danner 4.00 10.00
CDAHR Heliot Ramos 50.00 120.00
CDAJA Jo Adell 400.00 800.00
CDAJB Jake Burger 6.00 15.00
CDAJD Jeter Downs 40.00 100.00
CDAJJM J.J. Matijevic 6.00 15.00
CDAJM Joey Morgan 4.00 10.00
CDAJP Joe Perez 4.00 10.00
CDAJPE Jacob Pearson 3.00 8.00
CDAKC Kacy Clemens 4.00 10.00
CDAKH Keston Hiura 75.00 200.00
CDAKM Kevin Merrell 4.00 10.00
CDAKMC Kade McClure 3.00 8.00
CDAKS Kevin Smith 3.00 8.00
CDAKW Kyle Wright 8.00 20.00
CDALC Luis Campusano 25.00 60.00
CDALG Luis Gonzalez 4.00 10.00
CDALH Lincoln Henzman 3.00 8.00
CDALW Logan Warmoth 5.00 12.00
CDAMC Morgan Cooper 4.00 10.00
CDAMG MacKenzie Gore 60.00 150.00
CDAMJM MJ Melendez 5.00 12.00
CDAMT Matt Tabor 3.00 8.00
CDAMV Mark Vientos 20.00 50.00
CDANP Nick Pratto 5.00 12.00
CDANPE Nate Pearson 40.00 100.00
CDAPS Pavin Smith 5.00 12.00
CDAPSO Peter Solomon 4.00 10.00
CDAQB Quinn Brodey 3.00 8.00
CDAQH Quentin Holmes 4.00 10.00
CDARL Royce Lewis 60.00 150.00
CDARM Riley Mahan 3.00 8.00
CDARV Ryan Vilade 12.00 30.00
CDASB Shane Baz 12.00 30.00
CDASC Sam Carlson 4.00 10.00
CDASCO Seth Corry 8.00 20.00
CDASF Stuart Fairchild 4.00 10.00
CDATD Tommy Doyle 3.00 8.00
CDATH Tanner Houck 20.00 50.00
CDATL Tristen Lutz 5.00 12.00
CDATR Trevor Rogers 25.00 60.00
CDATW Taylor Walls 3.00 8.00
CDAWG Will Gaddis 3.00 8.00
CDAZK Zach Kirtley 4.00 10.00
CDAZL Zac Lowther 4.00 10.00

2017 Bowman Chrome Draft Autographs 70th Blue Refractors

*70TH BLUE REF: 1.5X TO 4X BASIC
STATED ODDS 1:223 HOBBY
STATED PRINT RUN 70 SER.#'d SETS
EXCHANGE DEADLINE 11/30/2019

2017 Bowman Chrome Draft Autographs Black Refractors

*BLACK REF: 1.5X TO 4X BASIC
STATED ODDS 1:124 HOBBY
STATED PRINT RUN 75 SER.#'d SETS
EXCHANGE DEADLINE 11/30/2019

2017 Bowman Chrome Draft Autographs Blue Refractors

*BLUE REF: 1X TO 2.5X BASIC
STATED ODDS 1:105 HOBBY
STATED PRINT RUN 150 SER.#'d SETS
EXCHANGE DEADLINE 11/30/2019

2017 Bowman Chrome Draft Autographs Blue Wave Refractors

*BLUE WAVE REF: 1X TO 2.5X BASIC
STATED ODDS 1:105 HOBBY
STATED PRINT RUN 150 SER.#'d SETS
EXCHANGE DEADLINE 11/30/2019

2017 Bowman Chrome Draft Autographs Gold Refractors

*GOLD REF: 2.5X TO 6X BASIC
STATED ODDS 1:313 HOBBY
STATED PRINT RUN 50 SER.#'d SETS
EXCHANGE DEADLINE 11/30/2019
CDAJA Jo Adell 1000.00 2000.00

2017 Bowman Chrome Draft Autographs Gold Wave Refractors

*GOLD WAVE REF: 2.5X TO 6X BASIC
STATED ODDS 1:313 HOBBY
STATED PRINT RUN 50 SER.#'d SETS
EXCHANGE DEADLINE 11/30/2019
CDAJA Jo Adell 1000.00 2000.00

2017 Bowman Chrome Draft Autographs Green Refractors

*GREEN REF: 1.2X TO 3X BASIC
STATED ODDS 1:158 HOBBY
STATED PRINT RUN 99 SER.#'d SETS
EXCHANGE DEADLINE 11/30/2019

2017 Bowman Chrome Draft Autographs Orange Refractors

*ORANGE REF: 3X TO 8X BASIC
STATED ODDS 1:435 HOBBY
STATED PRINT RUN 25 SER.#'d SETS
EXCHANGE DEADLINE 11/30/2019
CDAJA Jo Adell 2000.00 3000.00

2017 Bowman Chrome Draft Autographs Purple Refractors

*PURPLE REF: .6X TO 1.5X BASIC
STATED ODDS 1:63 HOBBY
STATED PRINT RUN 250 SER.#'d SETS
EXCHANGE DEADLINE 11/30/2019

2017 Bowman Chrome Draft Autographs Refractors

*REF: .5X TO 1.2X BASIC
STATED ODDS 1:32 HOBBY
STATED PRINT RUN 499 SER.#'d SETS
EXCHANGE DEADLINE 11/30/2019

2017 Bowman Chrome Draft Class of '17 Autographs

STATED ODDS 1:119 HOBBY
STATED PRINT RUN 250 SER.#'d SETS
EXCHANGE DEADLINE 11/30/2019
*GOLD/50: .75X TO 2X BASIC
C17AAB Austin Beck 10.00 25.00
C17AAF Alex Faedo 8.00 20.00
C17AAH Adam Haseley 12.00 30.00
C17ABM Brendan McKay 10.00 25.00
C17ABMC Brendan McKay 10.00 25.00
C17ABMI Brian Miller 6.00 15.00
C17ABR Brent Rooker 12.00 30.00
C17ACS Clarke Schmidt 8.00 20.00
C17ACSE Christopher Seise 8.00 20.00
C17ADP David Peterson 10.00 25.00
C17AEW Evan White 12.00 30.00
C17AJA Jo Adell 30.00 80.00
C17AJB Jake Burger 12.00 30.00
C17AJD Jeter Downs 10.00 25.00
C17AKH Keston Hiura 15.00 40.00
C17AKM Kevin Merrell 6.00 15.00
C17AKW Kyle Wright 10.00 25.00
C17ALW Logan Warmoth 8.00 20.00
C17AMG MacKenzie Gore 20.00 50.00
C17AMV Mark Vientos 12.00 30.00
C17ANPE Nate Pearson 30.00 80.00
C17APS Pavin Smith 8.00 20.00
C17AQH Quentin Holmes 20.00 50.00
C17ARL Royce Lewis 40.00 100.00
C17ARV Ryan Vilade 8.00 20.00
C17ASB Shane Baz 8.00 20.00
C17ATH Tanner Houck 25.00 60.00
C17ATL Tristen Lutz 8.00 20.00
C17ATR Trevor Rogers 12.00 30.00

2017 Bowman Chrome Draft Defining Moments

COMPLETE SET (21) 8.00 20.00
STATED ODDS 1:3 HOBBY
*REF/250: .5X TO 1.2X BASIC
*GOLD REF/50: 1.2X TO 3X BASIC
BDMAB Austin Beck 1.00 2.50
BDMAH Adam Haseley .50 1.25
BDMBM Brendan McKay 1.00 2.50
BDMBMC Brendan McKay 1.00 2.50
BDMCS Clarke Schmidt .40 1.00
BDMEJ Eloy Jimenez 1.00 2.50
BDMFT Fernando Tatis Jr. 2.50 6.00
BDMGT Gleyber Torres 4.00 10.00
BDMJA Jo Adell 3.00 8.00
BDMJB Jake Burger .50 1.25
BDMJM Jorge Mateo .25 .60
BDMKH Keston Hiura 1.25 3.00
BDMKM Kevin Maitan .40 1.00
BDMKW Kyle Wright .75 2.00
BDMMG MacKenzie Gore 2.00 5.00
BDMMM Mickey Moniak .50 1.25
BDMNS Nick Senzel .75 2.00
BDMPS Pavin Smith .40 1.00
BDMRA Ronald Acuna 4.00 10.00
BDMRL Royce Lewis 2.00 5.00

2017 Bowman Chrome Draft Defining Moments Autographs Refractors

STATED ODDS 1:600 HOBBY
STATED PRINT RUN 99 SER.#'d SETS
EXCHANGE DEADLINE 11/30/2019
*GOLD/50: .5X TO 1.2X BASIC
BDMAAB Austin Beck 25.00 60.00
BDMAAH Adam Haseley 15.00 40.00
BDMABM Brendan McKay 25.00 60.00
BDMABMC Brendan McKay 25.00 60.00
BDMACS Clarke Schmidt 6.00 15.00
BDMAGT Gleyber Torres 40.00 100.00
BDMAJA Jo Adell 30.00 80.00
BDMAKH Keston Hiura 25.00 60.00
BDMAKM Kevin Maitan 6.00 15.00
BDMAKW Kyle Wright
BDMAMG MacKenzie Gore 25.00 60.00
BDMAMM Mickey Moniak 15.00 40.00
BDMAPS Pavin Smith 12.00 30.00
BDMARL Royce Lewis

2017 Bowman Chrome Draft Draft Night Autographs

STATED ODDS 1:1796 HOBBY
STATED PRINT RUN 99 SER.#'d SETS
EXCHANGE DEADLINE 11/30/2019
DNAJA Jo Adell 125.00 300.00
DNATR Trevor Rogers 15.00 40.00

2017 Bowman Chrome Draft Draft Night Autographs Gold Refractors

*GOLD: .5X TO 1.2X BASIC
STATED ODDS 1:3570 HOBBY
STATED PRINT RUN 50 SER.#'d SETS
EXCHANGE DEADELINE 11/30/2019
DNAJA Jo Adell 150.00 400.00

2017 Bowman Chrome Draft MLB Draft History

COMPLETE SET (10) 4.00 10.00
STATED ODDS 1:6 HOBBY
*REF/250: 1.2X TO 3X BASIC
*GOLD REF/50: 3X TO 8X BASIC
MLBDAP Andy Pettitte .50 1.25
MLBDBL Barry Larkin .50 1.25
MLBDCF Carlton Fisk .50 1.25
MLBDDJ Derek Jeter 1.50 4.00
MLBDJT Jim Thome .50 1.25
MLBDRH Rickey Henderson .60 1.50
MLBDRHA Roy Halladay .50 1.25
MLBDRJ Randy Johnson .60 1.50
MLBDRS Ryne Sandberg 1.25 3.00
MLBDWB Wade Boggs .50 1.25

2017 Bowman Chrome Draft MLB Draft History Autographs Refractors

STATED ODDS 1:1795 HOBBY
STATED PRINT RUN 99 SER.#'d SETS
EXCHANGE DEADLINE 11/30/2019
MLBDAAP Andy Pettitte 8.00 20.00
MLBDADJ Derek Jeter 200.00 500.00
MLBDARH Rickey Henderson 30.00 80.00
MLBDARJ Randy Johnson 25.00 60.00
MLBDARS Ryne Sandberg 25.00 60.00

2017 Bowman Chrome Draft Recommended Viewing

COMPLETE SET (15) 4.00 10.00
STATED ODDS 1:3 HOBBY

*REF/250: .5X TO 1.2X BASIC
*GOLD REF/50: 1.2X TO 3X BASIC
RVARI Smith/Ellis .40 1.00
RVATL Waters/Wright 1.50 4.00
RVCWS Burger/Sheets .50 1.25
RVHOU Martin/Bukauskas .40 1.00
RVLAA Adell/Canning 3.00 8.00
RVMIL Hiura/Lutz 1.25 3.00
RVMIN Lewis/Rooker 2.00 5.00
RVNYY Sauer/Schmidt .40 1.00
RVOAK Merrell/Beck 1.00 2.50
RVPHI Haseley/Howard .75 2.00
RVPIT Jennings/Baz .40 1.00
RVSDP Campusano/Gore 2.00 5.00
RVSEA White/Carlson .60 1.50
RVSFG Ramos/Gonzalez 2.50 6.00
RVTAM Walls/McKay 1.00 2.50

2017 Bowman Chrome Draft Top of The Class Box Topper

STATED ODDS 1:36 HOBBY BOXES
STATED PRINT RUN 99 SER.#'d SETS
*GOLD/50: .5X TO 1.2X BASIC
TOCAB Austin Beck 8.00 20.00
TOCAH Adam Haseley 3.00 8.00
TOCBM Brendan McKay 8.00 20.00
TOCBMC Brendan McKay 8.00 20.00
TOCCS Clarke Schmidt 2.50 6.00
TOCJA Jo Adell 20.00 50.00
TOCJB Jake Burger 12.00 30.00
TOCJBU J.B. Bukauskas 2.50 6.00
TOCKH Keston Hiura 8.00 20.00
TOCKW Kyle Wright 8.00 20.00
TOCMG MacKenzie Gore 12.00 30.00
TOCPS Pavin Smith 12.00 30.00
TOCRL Royce Lewis 12.00 30.00
TOCSB Shane Baz 2.50 6.00
TOCTR Trevor Rogers 4.00 10.00

2017 Bowman Chrome Draft Top of The Class Box Topper Autographs Refractors

STATED ODDS 1:1769 HOBBY BOXES
STATED PRINT RUN 35 SER.#'d SETS
EXCHANGE DEADLINE 11/30/2019
TOCAB Austin Beck
TOCAH Adam Haseley 12.00 30.00
TOCBM Brendan McKay 75.00 200.00
TOCBMC Brendan McKay 75.00 200.00
TOCCS Clarke Schmidt
TOCJA Jo Adell 60.00 150.00
TOCJB Jake Burger
TOCJBU J.B. Bukauskas
TOCKH Keston Hiura 40.00 100.00
TOCKW Kyle Wright 30.00 80.00
TOCMG MacKenzie Gore 50.00 120.00
TOCPS Pavin Smith 10.00 25.00
TOCRL Royce Lewis 75.00 200.00
TOCSB Shane Baz
TOCTR Trevor Rogers 20.00 50.00

2017 Bowman Chrome Mega Box Autograph Refractors

STATED ODDS 1:18 RETAIL
*GREEN/99: .6X TO 1.5X BASIC
*ORANGE/25: 1.2X TO 3X BASIC
BMAAE Anderson Espinoza 6.00 15.00
BMAAI Andy Ibanez 6.00 15.00
BMABD Bobby Dalbec 10.00 25.00
BMADA Domingo Acevedo 6.00 15.00
BMADC Dylan Cozens 12.00 30.00
BMAFM Francisco Mejia 25.00 60.00
BMAJG Jason Groome 12.00 30.00
BMAJJ Jahmai Jones 6.00 15.00
BMAJM Jorge Mateo 20.00 50.00
BMAJS Justus Sheffield 10.00 25.00
BMAKM Kevin Maitan 10.00 25.00
BMALC Luis Castillo 20.00 50.00
BMALGJ Lourdes Gurriel Jr. 10.00 25.00
BMAMK Mitch Keller 20.00 50.00
BMAMM Mickey Moniak 50.00 120.00
BMANS Nick Senzel 150.00 300.00
BMARR Roniel Raudes 10.00 25.00
BMASN Sean Newcomb 10.00 25.00
BMATS Thomas Szapucki 8.00 20.00
BMAWB Wuilmer Becerra 6.00 15.00
BMAZC Zack Collins 12.00 30.00

2017 Bowman Chrome Mega Box Prospects Refractors

*PURPLE/250: .5X TO 1.2X BASIC
*GREEN/99: .6X TO 1.5X BASIC
BCP1 Nick Senzel 3.00 8.00
BCP3 Ronald Guzman 1.25 3.00
BCP4 A.J. Puckett 1.00 2.50
BCP6 Roniel Raudes 1.00 2.50
BCP7 Lucas Erceg 1.00 2.50
BCP8 Luis Almanzar 1.00 2.50
BCP9 Beau Burrows 1.00 2.50
BCP10 Chase Vallot 1.00 2.50
BCP11 P.J. Conlon 1.00 2.50
BCP12 Erick Fedde 1.00 2.50
BCP13 Rookie Davis 1.00 2.50
BCP14 Chris Shaw 1.00 2.50
BCP16 Clint Frazier 2.00 5.00
BCP18 Lourdes Gurriel Jr. 1.50 4.00
BCP20 Angel Perdomo 1.00 2.50
BCP22 Freddy Peralta 1.50 4.00
BCP23 Jarlin Garcia 1.00 2.50
BCP24 Tyler O'Neill 1.25 3.00
BCP25 Lazarito Armenteros 2.00 5.00
BCP27 Antonio Senzatela 1.00 2.50
BCP28 Kyle Tucker 2.50 6.00
BCP30 Willie Calhoun 1.50 4.00
BCP31 Shohei Otani UER 80.00 200.00
Ohtani
BCP32 Vladimir Guerrero Jr. 5.00 12.00
BCP33 Braxton Garrett 1.00 2.50
BCP36 Andy Ibanez 1.00 2.50
BCP37 Francisco Rios 1.00 2.50
BCP39 Dylan Cozens 1.00 2.50
BCP40 Mauricio Dubon 1.25 3.00
BCP41 Franklyn Kilome 1.25 3.00
BCP42 Chance Sisco 2.00 5.00
BCP43 Sandy Alcantara 1.25 3.00
BCP44 Stephen Gonsalves 1.00 2.50
BCP45 Grant Holmes 1.00 2.50
BCP47 Kolby Allard 1.00 2.50
BCP50 Eloy Jimenez 4.00 10.00
BCP51 Francisco Mejia 1.50 4.00
BCP54 Anderson Espinoza 1.00 2.50
BCP55 Cal Quantrill 1.00 2.50
BCP57 Tyler Beede 1.00 2.50
BCP59 Ariel Jurado 1.00 2.50
BCP61 Tyler Stephenson 2.50 6.00
BCP63 Dominic Smith 1.00 2.50
BCP65 Austin Meadows 2.50 6.00
BCP66 Mitch Keller 1.25 3.00
BCP67 Jahmai Jones 1.00 2.50
BCP68 Alex Speas 1.00 2.50
BCP69 Nolan Jones 1.50 4.00
BCP70 Kevin Newman 1.50 4.00
BCP71 T.J. Friedl 1.00 2.50
BCP72 Oscar De La Cruz 1.00 2.50
BCP73 Victor Robles 2.50 6.00
BCP74 Patrick Weigel 1.00 2.50
BCP76 Amed Rosario 1.50 4.00
BCP77 Nick Solak 4.00 10.00
BCP78 Abrahan Gutierrez 1.50 4.00
BCP79 Yu-Cheng Chang 1.50 4.00
BCP80 Gleyber Torres 15.00 40.00
BCP83 Andrew Sopko 1.00 2.50
BCP84 Brent Honeywell 1.25 3.00
BCP85 Kyle Funkhouser 1.25 3.00
BCP88 Brendan Rodgers 1.25 3.00
BCP89 Josh Staumont 1.00 2.50
BCP92 Wuilmer Becerra 1.00 2.50
BCP94 Alfredo Rodriguez 1.25 3.00
BCP95 Daz Cameron 1.00 2.50
BCP99 Drew Jackson 1.00 2.50
BCP100 Kevin Maitan 1.50 4.00
BCP101 Rafael Devers 2.00 5.00
BCP103 Jack Flaherty 6.00 15.00
BCP104 Adonis Medina 1.50 4.00
BCP106 Josh Hader 1.25 3.00
BCP107 Luis Urias 4.00 10.00
BCP109 Kyle Freeland 1.25 3.00
BCP110 Matt Chapman 3.00 8.00
BCP113 David Fletcher 3.00 8.00
BCP114 Tyler Jay 1.00 2.50
BCP115 Franklin Barreto 1.00 2.50
BCP116 Michael Kopech 3.00 8.00
BCP117 Rhys Hoskins 4.00 10.00
BCP118 Triston McKenzie 3.00 8.00
BCP119 Luis Garcia 8.00 20.00
BCP121 Blake Rutherford 1.50 4.00
BCP124 Dylan Cease 1.50 4.00
BCP127 Ronald Acuna 125.00 300.00
BCP128 Luis Ortiz 1.00 2.50
BCP130 Adrian Morejon 1.50 4.00
BCP132 Justus Sheffield 1.50 4.00
BCP134 Fernando Romero 1.00 2.50
BCP135 Mickey Moniak 2.00 5.00
BCP137 Jomar Reyes 1.00 2.50
BCP138 Thomas Szapucki 1.25 3.00
BCP140 Willy Adames 1.25 3.00
BCP141 Yang Hyeon-Jong 1.25 3.00
BCP142 Bo Bichette 4.00 10.00
BCP143 Harrison Bader 1.50 4.00
BCP145 Juan Hillman 1.00 2.50
BCP148 Christin Stewart 1.25 3.00
BCP149 Cody Bellinger 15.00 40.00
BCP150 Jason Groome 2.00 5.00

2017 Bowman Chrome Mega Box Prospects Orange Refractors

*ORANGE: 1.5X TO 4X BASIC
STATED ODDS 1:56 RETAIL
STATED PRINT RUN 25 SER.#'d SETS
BCP1 Nick Senzel 40.00 100.00
BCP31 Shohei Otani UER 1200.00 2500.00
Ohtani
BCP100 Kevin Maitan 125.00 300.00

2017 Bowman Chrome Mega Box Rookie of the Year Favorites Autographs Refractors

STATED ODDS 1:122 RETAIL
STATED PRINT RUN 75 SER.#'d SETS
*ORANGE/25: .75X TO 2X BASIC
ROYFAAB Alex Bregman 30.00 80.00
ROYFAABE Andrew Benintendi 75.00 200.00
ROYFAAJ Aaron Judge 200.00 400.00
ROYFAAR Alex Reyes 10.00 25.00
ROYFACF Carson Fulmer 5.00 12.00
ROYFADD David Dahl 10.00 25.00
ROYFADS Dansby Swanson 25.00 60.00
ROYFAHR Hunter Renfroe 12.00 30.00
ROYFAJA Jorge Alfaro 20.00 50.00
ROYFAJC Jharel Cotton
ROYFAJDL Jose De Leon 10.00 25.00
ROYFAOA Orlando Arcia 20.00 50.00
ROYFAYG Yulieski Gurriel 10.00 25.00
ROYFAYM Yoan Moncada 75.00 200.00

2017 Bowman Chrome Mega Box Rookie of the Year Favorites Refractors

STATED ODDS 1:4 RETAIL
*PURPLE/250: .6X TO 1.5X BASIC
*GREEN/99: 1.2X TO 3X BASIC
*ORANGE/25: 2X TO 5X BASIC
ROYFIAB Alex Bregman 3.00 8.00
ROYFIABE Andrew Benintendi 2.00 5.00
ROYFIAJ Aaron Judge 50.00 120.00
ROYFIAR Alex Reyes .75 2.00
ROYFICF Carson Fulmer .60 1.50
ROYFIDD David Dahl .75 2.00
ROYFIDS Dansby Swanson 1.50 4.00
ROYFIHR Hunter Renfroe .75 2.00
ROYFIJA Jorge Alfaro .75 2.00
ROYFIJC Jharel Cotton .60 1.50
ROYFIJDL Jose De Leon .60 1.50
ROYFILW Luke Weaver .75 2.00
ROYFIMM Manny Margot .60 1.50
ROYFIOA Orlando Arcia 1.00 2.50
ROYFIRH Ryan Healy .75 2.00
ROYFIRL Reynaldo Lopez .60 1.50
ROYFITA Tyler Austin .75 2.00
ROYFITG Tyler Glasnow 2.50 6.00
ROYFIYG Yulieski Gurriel .60 1.50
ROYFIYM Yoan Moncada 2.00 5.00

2017 Bowman Chrome Mega Box Talent Pipeline Refractors

STATED ODDS 1:2 RETAIL
*PURPLE/250: .5X TO 1.2X BASIC
*GREEN/99: 1X TO 2.5X BASIC
*ORANGE/25: 1.5X TO 4X BASIC
TPARI Alex Young .40 1.00
Taylor Clarke
Anthony Banda
TPATL Allard/Albies/Ellis 1.50 4.00
TPBAL Sdlck/Lee/Ssco .75 2.00
TPBOS Dvrs/Tvrz/Trvs .75 2.00
TPCHI Jmnz/Happ/Zgns 1.50 4.00
TPCHW Zack Collins .50 1.25
Spencer Adams
Zack Burdi
TPCIN Snzl/Mhle/Grrtt 1.25 3.00
TPCLE Francisco Mejia .60 1.50
Nellie Rodriguez
Bradley Zimmer
TPCOL Brendan Rodgers .60 1.50
Ryan McMahon
Kyle Freeland
TPDET Mnnng/Stwrt/Jmnz .60 1.50
TPHOU Tckr/Mrts/Fsher 1.00 2.50
TPKCR Vallot/O'Hearn/Bonifacio .75 2.00
TPLAA Matt Thaiss 1.25 3.00
David Fletcher
Nate Smith
TPLAD Alvrz/Clhn/Bllngr 6.00 15.00
TPMIA Stone Garrett .40 1.00
Austin Dean
J.T. Riddle
TPMIL Ray/Phllps/Brnsn .60 1.50
TPMIN Nick Gordon .40 1.00
Tyler Jay
Jake Reed
TPNYM Dunn/Rsro/Nmmo .60 1.50
TPNYY Trrs/Shffld/Frzr 6.00 15.00
TPOAK Puk/Mnz/Brrto .60 1.50
TPPHI Mnk/Czns/Crwfrd .75 2.00
TPPIT Mitch Keller 1.00 2.50
Kevin Newman
Austin Meadows
TPSDP Anderson Espinoza .50 1.25
Austin Allen
Dinelson Lamet
TPSEA Lewis/O'Neill/Peterson .75 2.00
TPSFG Rynlds/Arryo/Blckbrn .60 1.50
TPSTL Flhrty/Bdr/Vlra 2.50 6.00
TPTBR Joshua Lowe .50 1.25
Willy Adames
Jacob Faria
TPTEX Tvrs/Ibnz/Gzmn 1.50 4.00
TPTOR Sean Reid-Foley .60 1.50
Richard Urena
A.J. Jimenez
TPWAS Rbls/Fdde/Vth 1.00 2.50

2018 Bowman Chrome

COMPLETE SET (100)
1 Shohei Ohtani RC 30.00 80.00
2 Byron Buxton .30 .75
3 Scott Kingery RC .60 1.50
4 Michael Fulmer .20 .50
5 Starlin Castro .20 .50
6 Anthony Rizzo .40 1.00
7 Mookie Betts .60 1.50
8 Rafael Devers RC 1.25 3.00
9 Nelson Cruz .30 .75
10 Gary Sanchez .30 .75
11 Amed Rosario RC .50 1.25
12 Tyler O'Neill RC .60 1.50
13 Christian Yelich .40 1.00
14 Yoan Moncada .30 .75
15 Justin Verlander .30 .75
16 Jordan Hicks RC .75 2.00
17 Joey Lucchesi RC .40 1.00
18 Lucas Giolito .25 .60
19 Sandy Alcantara RC .40 1.00
20 Ender Inciarte .20 .50
21 Clint Frazier RC .75 2.00
22 Aaron Nola .25 .60
23 Alex Gordon .25 .60
24 Salvador Perez .25 .60
25 Rhys Hoskins RC 1.50 4.00
26 Cole Hamels .25 .60
27 Yoenis Cespedes .30 .75
28 Odubel Herrera .25 .60
29 Albert Pujols .40 1.00
30 Yu Darvish .30 .75
31 Francisco Lindor .30 .75
32 Joey Votto .30 .75
33 Francisco Mejia RC .50 1.25
34 Walker Buehler RC 2.00 5.00
35 Nick Williams RC .50 1.25
36 Ryan McMahon RC 1.00 2.50
37 Mike Trout 1.50 4.00
38 Adrian Beltre .30 .75
39 Billy Hamilton .25 .60
40 Ronald Acuna Jr. RC 25.00 60.00
41 Tyler Mahle RC .50 1.25
42 Matt Chapman .30 .75
43 Johnny Cueto .25 .60
44 Dominic Smith RC .50 1.25
45 Carlos Correa .30 .75
46 Josh Harrison .20 .50
47 Alex Verdugo RC .60 1.50
48 Yadier Molina .40 1.00
49 Josh Bell .25 .60
50 Kris Bryant .40 1.00
51 Willie Calhoun RC .60 1.50
52 Victor Robles RC 1.00 2.50
53 Andrew Benintendi .30 .75
54 Garrett Cooper RC .40 1.00
55 Matt Olson .30 .75
56 Andrew Stevenson RC .40 1.00
57 Corey Seager .30 .75
58 J.D. Martinez .30 .75
59 Buster Posey .40 1.00
60 Justin Upton .25 .60
61 Miguel Cabrera .30 .75
62 Roberto Osuna .20 .50
63 Chris Archer .20 .50
64 Mike Soroka RC 1.25 3.00
65 J.P. Crawford RC .40 1.00
66 Paul Goldschmidt .30 .75
67 Ichiro .40 1.00
68 Harrison Bader RC .60 1.50
69 Miguel Andujar RC 1.50 4.00
70 Nolan Arenado .50 1.25
71 Giancarlo Stanton .30 .75
72 Jack Flaherty RC 1.50 4.00
73 Kevin Kiermaier .25 .60
74 Tim Beckham .25 .60
75 Justin Bour .20 .50
76 Tomas Nido RC .40 1.00
77 Chance Sisco RC .50 1.25
78 Todd Frazier .20 .50
79 Charlie Blackmon .30 .75
80 Dustin Fowler RC .40 1.00
81 Zack Granite RC .40 1.00
82 Eric Hosmer .25 .60
83 Gleyber Torres RC 4.00 10.00
84 Bryce Harper .50 1.25
85 Manny Machado .30 .75
86 Hunter Renfroe .20 .50
87 Austin Hays RC .60 1.50
88 Cody Bellinger .60 1.50
89 Lorenzo Cain .20 .50
90 Brian Dozier .25 .60
91 Troy Tulowitzki .30 .75
92 Ozzie Albies RC 1.25 3.00
93 Paul DeJong .30 .75
94 Max Scherzer .30 .75
95 Jose Ramirez .25 .60
96 Freddie Freeman .40 1.00
97 Jake Lamb .25 .60
98 Clayton Kershaw .50 1.25
99 Luiz Gohara RC .40 1.00
100 Aaron Judge .75 2.00

2018 Bowman Chrome Blue Refractors

*BLUE REF VET: 4X TO 10X BASIC
*BLUE REF RC: 2X TO 5X BASIC
STATED ODDS 1:XX HOBBY
STATED PRINT RUN 150 SER.#'d SETS
37 Mike Trout 15.00 40.00

2018 Bowman Chrome Gold Refractors

*GOLD REF VET: 8X TO 20X BASIC
*GOLD REF RC: 4X TO 10X BASIC
STATED ODDS 1:XX HOBBY
STATED PRINT RUN 50 SER.#'d SETS
37 Mike Trout 60.00 150.00
69 Miguel Andujar 30.00 80.00
83 Gleyber Torres 30.00 80.00

2018 Bowman Chrome Green Refractors

*GREEN REF VET: 5X TO 12X BASIC
*GREEN REF RC: 2.5X TO 6X BASIC
STATED ODDS 1:XX HOBBY
STATED PRINT RUN 99 SER.#'d SETS
37 Mike Trout 20.00 50.00

2018 Bowman Chrome Orange Refractors

*ORANGE REF VET: 10X TO 25X BASIC
*ORANGE REF RC: 5X TO 12X BASIC
STATED ODDS 1:421 HOBBY
STATED PRINT RUN 25 SER.#'d SETS
3 Scott Kingery 20.00 50.00
37 Mike Trout 75.00 200.00
69 Miguel Andujar 40.00 100.00
72 Jack Flaherty 20.00 50.00
83 Gleyber Torres 40.00 100.00

2018 Bowman Chrome Purple Refractors

*PURPLE REF VET: 2X TO 5X BASIC
*PURPLE REF RC: 1X TO 2.5X BASIC
STATED ODDS 1:XX HOBBY
STATED PRINT RUN 250 SER.#'d SETS
37 Mike Trout 8.00 20.00

2018 Bowman Chrome Refractors

*REF VET: 1.5X TO 4X BASIC
*REF RC: .75X TO 2X BASIC
STATED ODDS 1:XX HOBBY
STATED PRINT RUN 499 SER.#'d SETS
37 Mike Trout 6.00 15.00

2018 Bowman Chrome Rookie Image Varitations

STATED ODDS 1:XX HOBBY
1 Ohtani Crrng bag 40.00 100.00
8 Devers Swgng bat 8.00 20.00
11 Amed Rosario 3.00 8.00
Blue sleeve
21 Frazier Warm-ups 5.00 12.00
25 Hoskins Pullover 3.00 8.00
33 Francisco Mejia 3.00 8.00
Wearing gear
35 Nick Williams 3.00 8.00
Gray jersey
44 Dominic Smith 3.00 8.00
Wearing pullover
47 Alex Verdugo 4.00 10.00
Front of jersey showing
52 Robles T-Shirt 6.00 15.00
65 J.P. Crawford 2.50 6.00
White jersey
68 Bader Whte jrsy 4.00 10.00
72 Jack Flaherty 10.00 25.00
Batting
87 Austin Hays 4.00 10.00
No helmet
92 Albies Pullover 8.00 20.00

2018 Bowman Chrome Rookie Image Variation Autographs

STATED ODDS 1:XX HOBBY
STATED PRINT RUN 25 SER.#'d SETS
EXCHANGE DEADLINE 8/31/2020
1 Shohei Ohtani 1500.00 2500.00
8 Rafael Devers 150.00 400.00
11 Amed Rosario EXCH 20.00 50.00
21 Clint Frazier 30.00 80.00
25 Rhys Hoskins 250.00 500.00
33 Francisco Mejia
44 Dominic Smith
52 Victor Robles 200.00 400.00
65 J.P. Crawford 15.00 40.00
68 Harrison Bader 25.00 60.00
72 Jack Flaherty 60.00 150.00
87 Austin Hays 60.00 150.00
92 Ozzie Albies 50.00 125.00

2018 Bowman Chrome '17 AFL Fall Stars Refractors

STATED ODDS 1:XX HOBBY
*ATOMIC/150: 1.2X TO 3X BASE
*ORANGE/25: 4X TO 10X BASE
AFLAA Adbert Alzolay .50 1.25
AFLCR Corey Ray .50 1.25
AFLDB David Bote 1.00 2.50
AFLEF Estevan Florial .60 1.50
AFLJS Justus Sheffield .50 1.25
AFLKT Kyle Tucker 1.00 2.50
AFLLU Luis Urias .75 2.00
AFLMB Matt Beaty .50 1.25
AFLMF Matt Festa .40 1.00
AFLMK Mitch Keller .50 1.25
AFLMT Matt Thaiss .40 1.00
AFLRA Ronald Acuna 12.00 30.00
AFLSA Sandy Alcantara .40 1.00
AFLSN Sheldon Neuse .40 1.00
AFLTJ Tyler Jay .40 1.00
AFLTN Tomas Nido .40 1.00
AFLTS Tanner Scott .40 1.00
AFLTT Touki Toussaint .50 1.25
AFLTZ T.J. Zeuch .40 1.00
AFLVR Victor Robles 1.00 2.50
AFLSVR Victor Robles MVP SP 1.25 3.00

2018 Bowman Chrome '17 AFL Fall Stars Autographs

STATED ODDS 1:XXX HOBBY
PRINT RUNS B/WN 40-150 COPIES PER
EXCHANGE DEADLINE 8/31/2020
AFLAA Adbert Alzolay/150 5.00 12.00
AFLCR Corey Ray/45 6.00 15.00
AFLDB David Bote/90 20.00 50.00
AFLEF Estevan Florial/150 20.00 50.00
AFLJS Justus Sheffield
AFLMB Matt Beaty/105 5.00 12.00
AFLMF Matt Festa/150 4.00 10.00
AFLMK Mitch Keller/150 6.00 15.00
AFLMT Matt Thaiss/100 10.00 25.00
AFLRA Ronald Acuna/150 100.00 250.00
AFLSA Sandy Alcantara/150 4.00 10.00
AFLSN Sheldon Neuse/150 4.00 10.00
AFLTJ Tyler Jay/80 4.00 10.00
AFLTN Tomas Nido/150 4.00 10.00
AFLTS Tanner Scott/40 6.00 15.00
AFLTT Touki Toussaint/75 15.00 40.00
AFLTZ T.J. Zeuch/150 4.00 10.00
AFLVR Victor Robles/150 10.00 25.00
AFLSVR Victor Robles MVP/100 10.00 25.00

2018 Bowman Chrome '17 AFL Fall Stars Autograph Relics

STATED ODDS 1:XXX HOBBY
STATED PRINT RUN 50 SER.#'d SETS
EXCHANGE DEADLINE 8/31/2020
AFLRAA Adbert Alzolay 10.00 25.00
AFLRDB David Bote 30.00 80.00
AFLRFM Francisco Mejia EXCH 12.00 30.00
AFLRLU Luis Urias
AFLRMB Matt Beaty 12.00 30.00
AFLRMF Matt Festa 8.00 20.00
AFLRSA Sandy Alcantara 8.00 20.00
AFLRSN Sheldon Neuse 8.00 20.00
AFLRTE Thairo Estrada 60.00 150.00
AFLRTN Tomas Nido 8.00 20.00

2018 Bowman Chrome '17 AFL Fall Stars Relics

STATED ODDS 1:XXX HOBBY
STATED PRINT RUN 99 SER.#'d SETS
AFLRAA Adbert Alzolay 4.00 10.00
AFLRAR Austin Riley 10.00 25.00
AFLRBB Braden Bishop 10.00 25.00
AFLRCR Corey Ray 4.00 10.00
AFLRDB David Bote 12.00 30.00
AFLRFM Francisco Mejia 4.00 10.00
AFLRJH Jordan Hicks 6.00 15.00
AFLRJS Justus Sheffield 4.00 10.00
AFLRKT Kyle Tucker 8.00 20.00
AFLRLU Luis Urias 6.00 15.00
AFLRMB Matt Beaty 4.00 10.00
AFLRMF Matt Festa 3.00 8.00
AFLRMK Mitch Keller 4.00 10.00
AFLRRA Ronald Acuna 25.00 60.00
AFLRRM Ryan Mountcastle 15.00 40.00
AFLRSA Sandy Alcantara 3.00 8.00
AFLRSN Sheldon Neuse 3.00 8.00
AFLRTE Thairo Estrada 5.00 12.00
AFLRTN Tomas Nido 3.00 8.00
AFLRTT Touki Toussaint 5.00 12.00

2018 Bowman Chrome '17 AFL Fall Stars Relics Orange Refractors

*ORANGE: .6X TO 1.5X BASIC
STATED ODDS 1:XXX HOBBY
STATED PRINT RUN 25 SER.#'d SETS
AFLRRA Ronald Acuna 125.00 300.00

2018 Bowman Chrome Autograph Relics

STATED ODDS 1:XXX HOBBY
STATED PRINT RUN 150 SER.#'d SETS
EXCHANGE DEADLINE 8/31/2020
BCARAA Adbert Alzolay/150 8.00 20.00
BCARAR Amed Rosario/150 6.00 15.00
BCARCF Clint Frazier/150 12.00 30.00
BCARCS Chance Sisco/150 5.00 12.00
BCARDS Dominic Smith/125 5.00 12.00
BCARFM Francisco Mejia EXCH 8.00 20.00
BCARGT Gleyber Torres/150 50.00 120.00
BCARJC J.P. Crawford/150 6.00 15.00
BCARJF Jack Flaherty/150 25.00 60.00
BCARKB Kris Bryant/75 50.00 120.00
BCARLE Luis Escobar/150 4.00 10.00
BCARLSE Luis Severino/150 5.00 12.00
BCARLU Luis Urias/150 20.00 50.00
BCARMT Mike Trout/30
BCARNS Noah Syndergaard/75 10.00 25.00
BCARPD Paul DeJong
BCARRD Rafael Devers/150 12.00 30.00
BCARSN Sheldon Neuse/150 5.00 12.00
BCARTE Thairo Estrada/150 8.00 20.00
BCARVR Victor Robles/150 10.00 25.00
BCARWM Whit Merrifield/150 12.00 30.00

2018 Bowman Chrome Autograph Relics Gold Refractors

*GOLD REF: .6X TO 1.5X BASIC
STATED ODDS 1:XXX HOBBY
STATED PRINT RUN 50 SER.#'d SETS
EXCHANGE DEADLINE 8/31/2020

2018 Bowman Chrome Autograph Relics Orange Refractors

*ORANGE REF: 1X TO 2.5X BASIC
STATED ODDS 1:XXX HOBBY
STATED PRINT RUN 25 SER.#'d SETS
EXCHANGE DEADLINE 8/31/2020
BCARCS Chance Sisco 50.00 120.00
BCARFM Francisco Mejia EXCH 40.00 100.00
BCARMT Mike Trout 250.00 500.00
BCARPD Paul DeJong 25.00 60.00

2018 Bowman Chrome Bowman Birthdays Refractors

STATED ODDS 1:8 HOBBY
*ATOMIC REF/150: 1.2X TO 3X BASE
*GREEN REF/99: 1.5X TO 4X BASE
*ORANGE REF/25: 5X TO 12X BASE
BBBB Byron Buxton .40 1.00
BBFL Francisco Lindor .40 1.00
BBJG Joey Gallo .30 .75
BBKS Kyle Schwarber .40 1.00
BBLM Lance McCullers Jr. .25 .60
BBLW Luke Weaver .30 .75
BBMC Michael Conforto .30 .75
BBMCH Matt Chapman .40 1.00
BBMF Michael Fulmer .25 .60
BBMK Max Kepler .30 .75
BBNW Nick Williams .30 .75
BBPD Paul DeJong .40 1.00
BBRH Rhys Hoskins 1.00 2.50
BBTG Tyler Glasnow .40 1.00
BBTT Trea Turner .30 .75

2018 Bowman Chrome Dual Prospect Autographs Refractors

RANDOM INSERTS IN PACKS
STATED PRINT RUN 25 SER.#'d SETS
EXCHANGE DEADLINE 3/31/2020
DBAGM Greene/McKay 250.00 500.00
DBAKI Isabel/Kendall
DBALG Gore/Lewis 60.00 150.00
DBALL Littell/Lewis 60.00 150.00
DBASL Siri/Long 200.00 400.00

2018 Bowman Chrome Hashtag Bowman Trending Refractors

STATED ODDS 1:6 HOBBY
*ATOMIC REF/150: 1X TO 2.5X BASE
*GREEN REF/99: 1.2X TO 3X BASE
*ORANGE REF/25: 3X TO 8X BASE
AP A.J. Puk .40 1.00
BB Bo Bichette 1.00 2.50
CA Chance Adams .40 1.00
CQ Cal Quantrill .25 .60
FP Franklin Perez .30 .75
FR Fernando Romero .25 .60
FT Fernando Tatis Jr. 2.50 6.00
JS Jesus Sanchez .40 1.00
LT Leody Taveras .40 1.00
LU Luis Urias .50 1.25
MC Michael Chavis .40 1.00
NG Nick Gordon .25 .60
RA Ronald Acuna 8.00 20.00
SG Stephen Gonsalves .25 .60
SK Scott Kingery .40 1.00
SS Sixto Sanchez .75 2.00
TM Triston McKenzie .75 2.00
TT Taylor Trammell .40 1.00
VG Vladimir Guerrero Jr. 2.50 6.00
YD Yusniel Diaz .75 2.00

2018 Bowman Chrome Peaks of Potential Refractors

STATED ODDS 1:XX HOBBY
*ATOMIC/150: .75X TO 2X BASE
*ORANGE/25: 2X TO 5X BASE
PPAA Aramis Ademan .50 1.25
PPAAL Adbert Alzolay .50 1.25
PPAG Andres Gimenez 1.00 2.50
PPBB Bo Bichette 1.50 4.00
PPBM Brandon Marsh .60 1.50
PPBMC Brendan McKay .60 1.50
PPCB Corbin Burnes 3.00 8.00
PPCP Cristian Pache 2.00 5.00
PPCW Colton Welker .40 1.00
PPEF Estevan Florial .60 1.50
PPFP Franklin Perez .50 1.25
PPFT Fernando Tatis Jr. 4.00 10.00
PPGT Gleyber Torres 4.00 10.00
PPHG Hunter Greene 1.25 3.00
PPHR Heliot Ramos .60 1.50
PPJA Jo Adell 1.50 4.00
PPJB Jake Burger .40 1.00
PPJG Jorge Guzman .40 1.00
PPJH Jordan Hicks .75 2.00
PPJS Jesus Sanchez .60 1.50
PPKR Keibert Ruiz 2.00 5.00
PPLR Luis Robert 6.00 15.00
PPLU Luis Urias .75 2.00
PPMG MacKenzie Gore .75 2.00
PPMW Mitchell White .40 1.00
PPRL Royce Lewis 1.50 4.00
PPSM Sean Murphy .60 1.50
PPSN Sheldon Neuse .40 1.00
PPSS Sixto Sanchez 1.25 3.00
PPYA Yordan Alvarez 3.00 8.00

2018 Bowman Chrome Peaks of Potential Autographs

STATED ODDS 1:XXX HOBBY
STATED PRINT RUN 99 SER.#'d SETS
EXCHANGE DEADLINE 8/31/2020
*ORNGE REF/25: .6X TO 1.5X BASE
PPAAA Aramis Ademan 4.00 10.00
PPAAAL Adbert Alzolay 6.00 15.00
PPAAG Andres Gimenez 8.00 20.00
PPABM Brandon Marsh 12.00 30.00
PPABMC Brendan McKay 10.00 25.00
PPACB Corbin Burnes 30.00 80.00
PPACP Cristian Pache 12.00 30.00
PPACW Colton Welker 3.00 8.00
PPAEF Estevan Florial 50.00 120.00
PPAFP Franklin Perez 10.00 25.00
PPAGT Gleyber Torres EXCH 40.00 100.00
PPAHG Hunter Greene 20.00 50.00
PPAHR Heliot Ramos 12.00 30.00
PPAJA Jo Adell 40.00 100.00
PPAJB Jake Burger 6.00 15.00
PPAJG Jorge Guzman 6.00 15.00
PPAKR Keibert Ruiz 15.00 40.00
PPALR Luis Robert 50.00 120.00
PPALU Luis Urias EXCH 20.00 50.00
PPAMG MacKenzie Gore 6.00 15.00
PPAMW Mitchell White 6.00 15.00
PPARL Royce Lewis 20.00 50.00
PPASN Sheldon Neuse 3.00 8.00
PPASS Sixto Sanchez 15.00 40.00
PPAZL Zack Littell 6.00 15.00

2018 Bowman Chrome Prospect Autographs

OVERALL AUTO ODDS 1:24 HOBBY
STATED PLATE ODDS 1:18,041 HOBBY
PLATE PRINT RUN 1 SET PER COLOR
BLACK-CYAN-MAGENTA-YELLOW ISSUED
NO PLATE PRICING DUE TO SCARCITY
BOW.EXCH.DEADLINE 3/31/2020
BOW.CHR.EXCH 3/31/2020
BCPAAA Aramis Ademan 4.00 10.00
BCPAAAL Austin Allen 4.00 10.00
BCPAAB Akil Baddoo 25.00 60.00
CPAAA Adbert Alzolay 10.00 25.00
CPAAG Andres Gimenez 25.00 60.00
CPABC Brett Cumberland 3.00 8.00
CPABHE Brayan Hernandez 3.00 8.00
CPABMC Brendan McKay 5.00 12.00
CPABW Jose Adolis Garcia 50.00 120.00
CPACB Corbin Burnes 12.00 30.00
CPACD Chris DeVito 3.00 8.00
CPACM Cedric Mullins 12.00 30.00
CPACP Cristian Pache 50.00 120.00
CPACR Chris Rodriguez 3.00 8.00
CPACRI Carlos Rincon 4.00 10.00
CPACW Colton Welker 12.00 30.00
CPADG Daniel Gonzalez 3.00 8.00
CPADH Darick Hall 3.00 8.00
CPADJ Daniel Johnson 3.00 8.00
CPADP DJ Peters 15.00 40.00
CPADS Dennis Santana 3.00 8.00
CPAEF Estevan Florial 40.00 100.00
CPAEO Edward Olivares 5.00 12.00
CPAEPA Eric Pardinho 4.00 10.00
CPAGD Greg Deichmann 4.00 10.00
CPAGL Gavin LaValley 3.00 8.00
CPAHF Heath Fillmyer 3.00 8.00
CPAHG Hunter Greene 40.00 100.00
CPAII Ibandel Isabel 5.00 12.00
CPAJB Jaime Barria 4.00 10.00
CPAJBU J.B. Bukauskas 3.00 8.00
CPAJG Jose Gomez 3.00 8.00
CPAJH Jordan Humphreys 3.00 8.00
CPAJHI Jordan Hicks 6.00 15.00
CPAJJR JoJo Romero 4.00 10.00
CPAJK Jeren Kendall 4.00 10.00
CPAJN James Nelson 3.00 8.00
CPAJRI Jake Ring 3.00 8.00
CPAJRO Jake Rogers 4.00 10.00
CPAJS Jose Siri 3.00 8.00
CPAJW Joey Wentz 4.00 10.00
CPAKC Kyle Cody 3.00 8.00
CPAKR Keibert Ruiz 20.00 50.00
CPAKY Kyle Young 4.00 10.00
CPALA Logan Allen 3.00 8.00
CPALE Luis Escobar 3.00 8.00
CPALR Luis Robert 400.00 1000.00
CPAMA Micker Adolfo 8.00 20.00
CPAMB Michel Baez 3.00 8.00
CPAMD Matthias Dietz 3.00 8.00
CPAMGO MacKenzie Gore 20.00 50.00
CPAMH Matt Hall 3.00 8.00
CPAMM Michael Mercado 4.00 10.00
CPAMMI McKenzie Mills 3.00 8.00
CPAMS Mike Shawaryn 3.00 8.00
CPAMSA Matt Sauer 3.00 8.00
CPANF Nick Fanti 3.00 8.00
CPAPA Pedro Avila 3.00 8.00
CPARH Ryan Helsley 4.00 10.00
CPARL Royce Lewis 8.00 20.00
CPARS Ranger Suarez 3.00 8.00
CPASCC Shao-Ching Chiang 4.00 10.00
CPASF Sandro Fabian 3.00 8.00
CPASH Spencer Howard 15.00 40.00
CPASHI Sam Hilliard 6.00 15.00
CPASL Shed Long 4.00 10.00
CPASMU Sean Murphy 10.00 25.00
CPASR Seth Romero 3.00 8.00
CPATH Thomas Hatch 4.00 10.00
CPATL Travis Lakins 3.00 8.00
CPAWA Willie Abreu 3.00 8.00
CPAYA Yordan Alvarez 150.00 400.00
CPAZL Zack Littell 3.00 8.00
BCPAAF Antoni Flores 4.00 10.00
BCPAAW Alex Wells 3.00 8.00
BCPABG Brusdar Graterol 8.00 20.00
BCPABL Brendon Little 3.00 8.00
BCPABM Brandon Marsh 20.00 50.00
BCPACB Charcer Burks 3.00 8.00
BCPACC Conner Capel 3.00 8.00
BCPACF Cole Freeman 4.00 10.00
BCPACK Carter Kieboom 20.00 50.00
BCPACP Chase Pinder 4.00 10.00
BCPACS Connor Seabold 3.00 8.00
BCPACT Chris Torres 3.00 8.00
BCPADH Darwinzon Hernandez 4.00 10.00
BCPADM Dustin May 15.00 40.00
BCPADV Daulton Varsho 4.00 10.00
BCPAED Eduardo Diaz 4.00 10.00
BCPAEDL Enyel De Los Santos 4.00 10.00
BCPAER Edwin Rios 12.00 30.00
BCPAES Evan Steele 4.00 10.00
BCPAFP Franklin Perez 4.00 10.00
BCPAGSO Gregory Soto 3.00 8.00
BCPAJAL Jose Albertos 3.00 8.00
BCPAJD Joe Dunand 4.00 10.00
BCPAJG Jorge Guzman 3.00 8.00
BCPAJL Joey Lucchesi 3.00 8.00

BCPAJLO Jonathan Loaisiga 10.00 25.00
BCPAJS Jairo Solis 4.00 10.00
BCPAKM Kevin Maitan 4.00 10.00
BCPAKR Kristian Robinson 75.00 200.00
BCPALG Luis Guillorme 3.00 8.00
BCPALGA Luis Garcia 20.00 50.00
BCPALM Luis Medina 20.00 50.00
BCPALR Leonardo Rivas 3.00 8.00
BCPALS Logan Shore 3.00 8.00
BCPALSA LoLo Sanchez 4.00 10.00
BCPALU Luis Urias 15.00 40.00
BCPALW LaMonte Wade 3.00 8.00
BCPAMB Mike Baumann 3.00 8.00
BCPANA Nick Allen 3.00 8.00
BCPANL Nicky Lopez 5.00 12.00
BCPARAD Riley Adams 4.00 10.00
BCPARAR Rogelio Armenteros 3.00 8.00
BCPARW Russell Wilson 200.00 500.00
BCPASB Shane Bieber 40.00 100.00
BCPASN Sheldon Neuse 3.00 8.00
BCPATF Tyler Freeman 25.00 60.00
BCPATO Trevor Oaks 3.00 8.00
BCPATS Trevor Stephan 3.00 8.00
BCPAWCO William Contreras 20.00 50.00

2018 Bowman Chrome Prospect Autographs Atomic Refractors

*ATMOIC REF: 1.2X TO 3X BASIC
STATED ODDS 1:XX HOBBY
STATED PRINT RUN 100 SER.#'D SETS
EXCHANGE DEADLINE 3/31/2020

2018 Bowman Chrome Prospect Autographs Blue Refractors

*BLUE REF: 1.2X TO 3X BASIC
STATED ODDS 1:XX HOBBY
STATED PRINT RUN 150 SER.#'D SETS
BOW.EXCH.DEADLINE 3/31/2020
BOW.CHR.EXCH 8/31/2020
BCPAYA Yasel Antuna 30.00 80.00

2018 Bowman Chrome Prospect Autographs Gold Refractors

*GOLD REF: 1.5X TO 4X BASIC
STATED ODDS 1:XX HOBBY
STATED PRINT RUN 50 SER.#'D SETS
BOW.EXCH.DEADLINE 3/31/2020
BOW.CHR.EXCH 8/31/2020
BCPAYA Yasel Antuna 40.00 100.00

2018 Bowman Chrome Prospect Autographs Gold Shimmer Refractors

*GOLD SHMR REF: 1.5X TO 4X BASIC
STATED ODDS 1:XX HOBBY
STATED PRINT RUN 50 SER.#'D SETS
BOW.EXCH.DEADLINE 3/31/2020
BOW.CHR.EXCH 8/31/2020
BCPAYA Yasel Antuna 40.00 100.00

2018 Bowman Chrome Prospect Autographs Green Refractors

*GREEN REF: 1.2X TO 3X BASIC
STATED ODDS 1:XX HOBBY
STATED PRINT RUN 99 SER.#'D SETS
BOW.EXCH.DEADLINE 3/31/2020
BOW.CHR.EXCH 8/31/2020
BCPAYA Yasel Antuna 30.00 80.00

2018 Bowman Chrome Prospect Autographs Green Atomic Refractors

*GRN ATOMIC REF: 1.2X TO 3X BASIC
STATED ODDS 1:XX HOBBY
STATED PRINT RUN 99 SER.#'D SETS
BOW.EXCH.DEADLINE 3/31/2020
BOW.CHR.EXCH 8/31/2020
BCPAYA Yasel Antuna 30.00 80.00

2018 Bowman Chrome Prospect Autographs Green Shimmer Refractors

*GRN SHMMR REF: 1.2X TO 3X BASIC
STATED ODDS 1:XX HOBBY
STATED PRINT RUN 99 SER.#'D SETS
BOW.EXCH.DEADLINE 3/31/2020
BOW.CHR.EXCH 8/31/2020

2018 Bowman Chrome Prospect Autographs Orange Refractors

*ORANGE REF: 3X TO 8X BASIC
STATED ODDS 1:XX HOBBY
STATED PRINT RUN 25 SER.#'D SETS
BOW.EXCH.DEADLINE 3/31/2020
BOW.CHR.EXCH 8/31/2020
BCPAYA Yasel Antuna 75.00 200.00

2018 Bowman Chrome Prospect Autographs Orange Shimmer Refractors

*ORNGE SHMMR REF: 3X TO 8X BASIC
STATED ODDS 1:XX HOBBY
STATED PRINT RUN 25 SER.#'D SETS
BOW.EXCH.DEADLINE 3/31/2020
BOW.CHR.EXCH 8/31/2020

2018 Bowman Chrome Prospect Autographs Orange Wave Refractors

*ORNGE WAVE REF: 3X TO 8X BASIC
STATED ODDS 1:XX HOBBY
STATED PRINT RUN 25 SER.#'D SETS
BOW.EXCH.DEADLINE 3/31/2020
BOW.CHR.EXCH 8/31/2020
BCPARW Russell Wilson 300.00 800.00
BCPAYA Yasel Antuna 75.00 200.00

2018 Bowman Chrome Prospect Autographs Purple Refractors

*PURPLE REF: .75X TO 2X BASIC
STATED ODDS 1:53 HOBBY JUMBO
STATED PRINT RUN 250 SER.#'D SETS
BOW.EXCH.DEADLINE 3/31/2020
BOW.CHR.EXCH 8/31/2020

2018 Bowman Chrome Prospect Autographs Refractors

*REF: .5X TO 1.2X BASIC
STATED ODDS 1:27 HOBBY JUMBO
STATED PRINT RUN 499 SER.#'D SETS
BOW.EXCH.DEADLINE 3/31/2020
BOW.CHR.EXCH 8/31/2020

2018 Bowman Chrome Prospects

PRINTING PLATE ODDS 1:7838 HOBBY
PLATE PRINT RUN 1 SET PER COLOR
BLACK-CYAN-MAGENTA-YELLOW ISSUED
NO PLATE PRICING DUE TO SCARCITY
BCP1 Ronald Acuna 8.00 20.00
BCP2 Bryan Mata .25 .60
BCP3 Daniel Johnson .20 .50
BCP4 Hunter Harvey .20 .50
BCP5 Aaron Knapp .20 .50
BCP6 Austin Beck .25 .60
BCP7 Carter Kieboom .30 .75
BCP8 Cole Ragans .20 .50
BCP9 Alex Jackson .20 .50
BCP10 Justin Williams .20 .50
BCP11 Rowdy Tellez .20 .50
BCP12 Thomas Hatch .25 .60
BCP13 Sam Hilliard .40 1.00
BCP14 Kyle Wright .50 1.25
BCP15 Tyler O'Neill .30 .75
BCP16 Michael Mercado .25 .60
BCP17 Kevin Newman .30 .75
BCP18 Eric Lauer .25 .60
BCP19 Johan Mieses .30 .75
BCP20 Will Smith .50 1.25
BCP21 Luis Robert 20.00 50.00
BCP22 Yadier Alvarez .25 .60
BCP23 Jeren Kendall .25 .60
BCP24 Bobby Bradley .25 .60
BCP25 Drew Ellis .25 .60
BCP26 Alfredro Rodriguez .20 .50
BCP27 Jose Trevino .20 .50
BCP28 Kolby Allard .20 .50
BCP29 Taylor Ward .25 .60
BCP30 Cornelius Randolph .20 .50
BCP31 DJ Peters .50 1.25
BCP32 Domingo Acevedo .20 .50
BCP33 James Nelson .20 .50
BCP34 Josh Ockimey .20 .50
BCP35 Marcos Molina .20 .50
BCP36 Dennis Santana .20 .50
BCP37 Jake Burger .20 .50
BCP38 Mitch Keller .25 .60
BCP39 Colton Welker .20 .50
BCP40 Pedro Avila .20 .50
BCP41 Jason Martin .20 .50
BCP42 Braxton Garrett .20 .50
BCP43 Brendan Rodgers .25 .60
BCP44 James Kaprielian .20 .50
BCP45 Greg Deichmann .25 .60
BCP46 Cristian Pache 1.00 2.50
BCP47 Ibandel Isabel .30 .75
BCP48 Hunter Greene 1.25 3.00
BCP49 Nick Gordon .20 .50
BCP50 Eloy Jimenez .75 2.00
BCP51 Adonis Medina .30 .75
BCP52 Juan Soto 6.00 15.00
BCP53 Miguelangel Sierra .20 .50
BCP54 Alex Lange .20 .50
BCP55 Kyle Tucker .50 1.25
BCP56 TJ Zeuch .20 .50
BCP57 Luis Urias .40 1.00
BCP58 Sean Murphy .30 .75
BCP59 Oscar De La Cruz .20 .50
BCP60 Brian Miller .20 .50
BCP61 Matt Thaiss .20 .50
BCP62 Kyle Cody .20 .50
BCP63 Dylan Cozens .20 .50
BCP64 MJ Melendez .20 .50
BCP65 Scott Kingery .30 .75
BCP66 Jordan Humphreys .20 .50
BCP67 Michel Baez .20 .50
BCP68 Brendan McKay .30 .75
BCP69 Justus Sheffield .25 .60
BCP70 Merandy Gonzalez .20 .50
BCP71 Touki Toussaint .25 .60
BCP72 Andres Gimenez .50 1.25
BCP73 Adrian Morejon .20 .50
BCP74 Austin Voth .20 .50
BCP75 Luis Garcia .30 .75
BCP76 Isaac Paredes 1.00 2.50
BCP77 Jake Kalish .20 .50
BCP78 Shed Long .25 .60
BCP79 Keibert Ruiz 1.00 2.50
BCP80 Matt Hall .20 .50
BCP81 Nick Pratto .25 .60
BCP82 Justin Dunn .25 .60
BCP83 Ian Anderson .60 1.50
BCP84 Franklyn Kilome .25 .60
BCP85 Dane Dunning .60 1.50
BCP86 Michael Kopech .75 2.00
BCP87 McKenzie Mills .20 .50
BCP88 Quentin Holmes .20 .50
BCP89 Mike Soroka .60 1.50
BCP90 Stephen Gonsalves .20 .50
BCP91 Spencer Howard 2.00 5.00
BCP92 Ryan Vilade .20 .50
BCP93 Royce Lewis .75 2.00
BCP94 Adam Haseley .30 .75
BCP95 Jorge Mateo .20 .50
BCP96 Junior Fernandez .30 .75
BCP97 Corey Ray .25 .60
BCP98 Evan White .50 1.25
BCP99 Logan Allen .20 .50
BCP100 Gleyber Torres 2.00 5.00
BCP101 Zack Littell .20 .50
BCP102 Matt Sauer .20 .50
BCP103 Mitchell White .20 .50
BCP104 Nick Solak .75 2.00
BCP105 Jorge Ona .20 .50
BCP106 D.J. Stewart .20 .50
BCP107 D.L. Hall .20 .50
BCP108 Chris Rodriguez .20 .50
BCP109 Sam Howard .20 .50
BCP110 Eric Pardinho .25 .60
BCP111 JoJo Romero .25 .60
BCP112 Aramis Garcia .20 .50
BCP113 Taylor Clarke .20 .50
BCP114 Fernando Tatis Jr. 5.00 12.00
BCP115 Cal Quantrill .20 .50
BCP116 Khalil Lee .20 .50
BCP117 C.J. Chatham .25 .60
BCP118 Lazaro Armenteros .40 1.00
BCP119 Gavin LaValley .20 .50
BCP120 Nick Senzel .60 1.50
BCP121 Jose Adolis Garcia 8.00 20.00
BCP122 Ronald Guzman .20 .50
BCP123 Jordan Hicks .40 1.00
BCP124 Alex Faedo .30 .75
BCP125 J.B. Bukauskas .20 .50
BCP126 Jesus Luzardo .30 .75
BCP127 Josh Lowe .20 .50
BCP128 Yu-Cheng Chang .25 .60
BCP129 Kyle Young .25 .60
BCP130 Christin Stewart .25 .60
BCP131 MacKenzie Gore .40 1.00
BCP132 Corbin Burnes 1.50 4.00
BCP133 Tyler Stephenson .50 1.25
BCP134 Wander Javier .30 .75
BCP135 Bryse Wilson .30 .75
BCP136 Jo Adell .75 2.00
BCP137 Pete Alonso 2.00 5.00
BCP138 Delvin Perez .20 .50
BCP139 Travis Lakins .20 .50
BCP140 Blake Rutherford .25 .60
BCP141 Blayne Enlow .20 .50
BCP142 A.J. Puk .30 .75
BCP143 Heliot Ramos .30 .75
BCP144 Jahmai Jones .20 .50
BCP145 Adbert Alzolay .25 .60
BCP146 Will Craig .20 .50
BCP147 Forrest Whitley .30 .75
BCP148 Trevor Rogers .50 1.25
BCP149 Steven Duggar .20 .50
BCP150 Vladimir Guerrero Jr. 2.00 5.00
BCP151 Russell Wilson 1.00 2.50
BCP152 Luis Garcia .75 2.00
BCP153 Enyel De Los Santos .25 .60
BCP154 Cole Brannen .25 .60
BCP155 Austin Riley .60 1.50
BCP156 Taylor Trammell .30 .75
BCP157 Luis Ortiz .20 .50
BCP158 Nick Allen .20 .50
BCP159 LaMonte Wade .20 .50
BCP160 Kyle Tucker .50 1.25
BCP161 Luis Medina .30 .75
BCP162 Brian Mundell .20 .50
BCP163 Tanner Houck .50 1.25
BCP164 Connor Seabold .20 .50
BCP165 Sheldon Neuse .20 .50
BCP166 Brent Rooker .25 .60
BCP167 Ryan Mountcastle 1.00 2.50
BCP168 Trevor Stephan .20 .50
BCP169 Bryse Wilson .30 .75
BCP170 Charcer Burks .20 .50
BCP171 Jeter Downs .30 .75
BCP172 Tyler Freeman .20 .50
BCP173 Yasel Antuna .40 1.00
BCP174 Keston Hiura .50 1.25
BCP175 Dylan Cease .30 .75
BCP176 Dakota Hudson .30 .75
BCP177 Alec Hansen .20 .50
BCP178 Sixto Sanchez .60 1.50
BCP179 Peter Lambert .20 .50
BCP180 Jorge Guzman .20 .50
BCP181 Joe Perez .25 .60
BCP182 Brandon Marsh .30 .75
BCP183 Triston McKenzie .60 1.50
BCP184 Rogelio Armenteros .20 .50
BCP185 Franklin Perez .25 .60
BCP186 Kristian Robinson 10.00 25.00
BCP187 Kyle Funkhouser .25 .60
BCP188 Jon Duplantier .20 .50
BCP189 Nolan Jones .30 .75
BCP190 Patrick Weigel .20 .50
BCP191 Aramis Ademan .25 .60
BCP192 Carter Kieboom .30 .75
BCP193 D.J. Daniels .20 .50
BCP194 Fernando Romero .20 .50
BCP195 Nicky Lopez .30 .75
BCP196 Darwinzon Hernandez .25 .60
BCP197 Jake Bauers .25 .60
BCP198 Daulton Varsho .25 .60
BCP199 Bo Bichette .75 2.00
BCP200 Willy Adames .25 .60
BCP201 Shane Baz .25 .60
BCP202 Logan Shore .20 .50
BCP203 Austin Allen .25 .60
BCP204 Isan Diaz .50 1.25
BCP205 David Peterson .40 1.00
BCP206 Tony Santillan .20 .50
BCP207 Chris Torres .20 .50
BCP208 Chance Adams .30 .75
BCP209 Matt Manning .30 .75
BCP210 Mickey Moniak .50 1.25
BCP211 Cody Sedlock .20 .50
BCP212 Jay Groome .25 .60
BCP213 Shane Bieber 4.00 10.00
BCP214 Pavin Smith .30 .75
BCP215 Luis Urias .40 1.00
BCP216 Beau Burrows .25 .60
BCP217 Mike Baumann .20 .50
BCP218 Brusdar Graterol .40 1.00
BCP219 Riley Pint .20 .50
BCP220 Anderson Espinoza .20 .50
BCP221 Freddy Peralta .20 .50
BCP222 Chase Pinder .25 .60
BCP223 Michael Chavis .30 .75
BCP224 Zack Burdi .20 .50
BCP225 Eduardo Diaz .25 .60
BCP226 Daz Cameron .20 .50
BCP227 Austin Meadows .50 1.25
BCP228 Will Benson .20 .50
BCP229 Jose Albertos .20 .50
BCP230 Zack Collins .25 .60
BCP231 Justin Williams .20 .50
BCP232 Jairo Solis .25 .60
BCP233 Brendon Little .20 .50
BCP234 Albert Abreu .20 .50
BCP235 Dillon Tate .20 .50
BCP236 Garrett Hampson .30 .75
BCP237 Kevin Maitan .25 .60
BCP238 Monte Harrison .30 .75
BCP239 Gregory Soto .20 .50
BCP240 Leody Taveras .30 .75
BCP241 Riley Adams .25 .60
BCP242 Bobby Dalbec 1.25 3.00
BCP243 Gavin Sheets .25 .60
BCP244 Kyle Lewis .40 1.00
BCP245 Evan Steele .25 .60
BCP247 LoLo Sanchez .25 .60
BCP248 Luis Guillorme .20 .50
BCP249 Nate Pearson .60 1.50
BCP250 Nick Senzel .60 1.50

2018 Bowman Chrome Prospects Aqua Refractors

*AQUA REF: 2.5X TO 6X BASIC
STATED ODDS 1:132 HOBBY
STATED PRINT RUN 125 SER.#'d SETS

2018 Bowman Chrome Prospects Aqua Shimmer Refractors

*AQUA SHIM REF: 2.5X TO 6X BASIC
STATED ODDS 1:132 HOBBY
STATED PRINT RUN 125 SER.#'d SETS

2018 Bowman Chrome Prospects Atomic Refractors

*ATOMIC REF: 1.5X TO 4X BASIC
STATED ODDS 1:24 HOBBY

2018 Bowman Chrome Prospects Blue Refractors

*BLUE REF: 2X TO 5X BASIC
STATED ODDS 1:209 HOBBY
STATED PRINT RUN 150 SER.#'d SETS

2018 Bowman Chrome Prospects Blue Shimmer Refractors

*BLUE SHIM REF: 2X TO 5X BASIC
STATED ODDS 1:209 HOBBY
STATED PRINT RUN 150 SER.#'d SETS

2018 Bowman Chrome Prospects Canary Yellow Refractors

*CANARY YELLOW REF: 4X TO 10X BASIC
STATED ODDS 1:417 HOBBY
STATED PRINT RUN 75 SER.#'d SETS

2018 Bowman Chrome Prospects Gold Refractors

*GOLD REF: 6X TO 15X BASIC
STATED ODDS 1:626 HOBBY
STATED PRINT RUN 50 SER.#'d SETS

2018 Bowman Chrome Prospects Gold Shimmer Refractors

*GOLD SHIM REF: 6X TO 15X BASIC
STATED ODDS 1:626 HOBBY
STATED PRINT RUN 50 SER.#'d SETS

2018 Bowman Chrome Prospects Green Refractors

*GREEN REF: 3X TO 8X BASIC
STATED ODDS 1:150 RETAIL
STATED PRINT RUN 99 SER.#'d SETS

2018 Bowman Chrome Prospects Green Shimmer Refractors

*GREEN SHIM REF: 3X TO 8X BASIC
STATED ODDS 1:150 RETAIL
STATED PRINT RUN 99 SER.#'d SETS

2018 Bowman Chrome Prospects Orange Refractors

*ORANGE REF: 10X TO 25X BASIC
STATED ODDS 1:292 HOBBY
STATED PRINT RUN 25 SER.#'d SETS

2018 Bowman Chrome Prospects Orange Shimmer Refractors

*ORANGE SHIM REF: 10X TO 25X BASIC
STATED ODDS 1:292 HOBBY
STATED PRINT RUN 25 SER.#'d SETS

2018 Bowman Chrome Prospects Purple Refractors

*PURPLE REF: 1.5X TO 4X BASIC
STATED ODDS 1:126 HOBBY
STATED PRINT RUN 250 SER.#'d SETS

2018 Bowman Chrome Prospects Purple Shimmer Refractors

*PRPL SHMMR REF: 1X TO 2.5X BASIC
STATED ODDS 1:XX HOBBY
STATED PRINT RUN 665 SER.#'d SETS

2018 Bowman Chrome Prospects Refractors

*REF: 1.2X TO 3X BASIC
STATED ODDS 1:63 HOBBY
STATED PRINT RUN 499 SER.#'d SETS

2018 Bowman Chrome Prime Chrome Signatures

STATED ODDS 1:XXX HOBBY
STATED PRINT RUN 50 SER.#'d SETS
EXCHANGE DEADLINE 8/31/2020
PCSAA Aramis Ademan 12.00 30.00
PCSAAL Adbert Alzolay 12.00 30.00
PCSAB Austin Beck 10.00 25.00
PCSBL Brendon Little
PCSBM Brandon Marsh 30.00 80.00
PCSBMC Brendan McKay 30.00 80.00
PCSCB Corbin Burnes 40.00 100.00
PCSCP Cristian Pache 40.00 100.00
PCSEDL Enyel De Los Santos 20.00 50.00
PCSEF Estevan Florial 100.00 250.00
PCSFP Franklin Perez 6.00 15.00
PCSGS Gregory Soto 6.00 15.00
PCSHG Hunter Greene 40.00 100.00
PCSJA Jo Adell EXCH 40.00 100.00
PCSJB Jake Burger 6.00 15.00
PCSJG Jorge Guzman 6.00 15.00
PCSKH Keston Hiura 15.00 40.00
PCSKM Kevin Maitan 5.00 12.00
PCSKR Keibert Ruiz 20.00 50.00
PCSLR Luis Robert 30.00 80.00
PCSLU Luis Urias 40.00 100.00
PCSMG MacKenzie Gore 12.00 30.00
PCSMW Mitchell White 4.00 10.00
PCSNL Nicky Lopez 15.00 40.00
PCSRL Royce Lewis 25.00 60.00
PCSSB Shane Bieber 20.00 50.00
PCSSN Sheldon Neuse 10.00 25.00

2018 Bowman Chrome Prime Chrome Signatures Orange Refractors

*ORANGE REF: .5X TO 1.2X BASIC
STATED ODDS 1:XXX HOBBY
STATED PRINT RUN 25 SER.#'d SETS
EXCHANGE DEADLINE 8/31/2020
PCSBL Brendon Little 15.00 40.00
PCSBM Brandon Marsh 150.00 400.00
PCSCP Cristian Pache 100.00 250.00
PCSFP Franklin Perez 20.00 50.00
PCSKH Keston Hiura 40.00 100.00

2018 Bowman Chrome Rookie Autographs

STATED ODDS 1:XXX
PRINTING PLATES RANDOMLY INSERTED
PLATE PRINT RUN 1 SET PER COLOR
BLACK-CYAN-MAGENTA-YELLOW ISSUED
NO PLATE PRICING DUE TO SCARCITY
BOW.EXCH.DEADLINE 3/31/2020
BOW.CHR.EXCH. 8/31/2020
CRAAB Anthony Banda 3.00 8.00
CRAAH Austin Hays 5.00 12.00
CRAAR Amed Rosario 5.00 12.00
CRAAV Alex Verdugo 6.00 15.00
CRACF Clint Frazier 25.00 60.00
CRACS Chance Sisco 4.00 10.00
CRADS Dominic Smith 4.00 10.00
CRAHB Harrison Bader 5.00 12.00
CRAJF Jack Flaherty 12.00 30.00
CRAMA Miguel Andujar 15.00 40.00
CRAND Nicky Delmonico 3.00 8.00
CRARD Rafael Devers 40.00 100.00
CRARH Rhys Hoskins 30.00 80.00
CRARM Ryan McMahon 8.00 20.00
CRASO S.Ohtani Ptchng 400.00 1000.00
CRATM Tyler Mahle 4.00 10.00
CRAVR Victor Robles 25.00 60.00
CRAWB Walker Buehler 50.00 120.00
BCRAAR Amed Rosario 5.00 12.00
BCRAAS Andrew Stevenson 3.00 8.00
BCRAAV Alex Verdugo 6.00 15.00
BCRACF Clint Frazier 25.00 60.00
BCRAFM Francisco Mejia 4.00 10.00
BCRAGA Greg Allen 3.00 8.00
BCRAGC Garrett Cooper 3.00 8.00
BCRAGT Gleyber Torres 75.00 200.00
BCRAJD J.D. Davis 4.00 10.00
BCRAJF Jack Flaherty 12.00 30.00
BCRALS Lucas Sims 3.00 8.00
BCRAOA Ozzie Albies 40.00 100.00
BCRARA Ronald Acuna 300.00 800.00
BCRARD Rafael Devers 40.00 100.00
BCRARU Richard Urena 3.00 8.00
BCRASA Sandy Alcantara 3.00 8.00
BCRASO S.Ohtani Bttng 400.00 1000.00
BCRATN Tomas Nido 3.00 8.00
BCRAVR Victor Robles 25.00 60.00
BCRAWA Willy Adames 4.00 10.00

2018 Bowman Chrome Rookie Autographs Atomic Refractors

*ATOMIC REF: .75X TO 2X BASIC
STATED ODDS 1:733 HOBBY
STATED PRINT RUN 100 SER.#'d SETS
EXCHANGE DEADLINE 3/31/2020

2018 Bowman Chrome Rookie Autographs Blue Refractors

*BLUE REF: .75X TO 2X BASIC
STATED ODDS 1:84 JUMBO
STATED PRINT RUN 150 SER.#'d SETS
BOW.EXCH.DEADLINE 3/31/2020
BOW.CHR.EXCH. 8/31/2020

2018 Bowman Chrome Rookie Autographs Gold Refractors

*GOLD REF: 1.2X TO 3X BASIC
STATED ODDS 1:1438 HOBBY
STATED PRINT RUN 50 SER.#'d SETS
BOW.EXCH.DEADLINE 3/31/2020
BOW.CHR.EXCH. 8/31/2020

2018 Bowman Chrome Rookie Autographs Green Refractors

*GREEN REF: .75X TO 2X BASIC
STATED ODDS 1:397 RETAIL
STATED PRINT RUN 99 SER.#'d SETS
BOW.EXCH.DEADLINE 3/31/2020
BOW.CHR.EXCH. 8/31/2020

2018 Bowman Chrome Rookie Autographs Orange Refractors

*ORANGE REF: 2.5X TO 6X BASIC
STATED ODDS 1:858 HOBBY
STATED PRINT RUN 25 SER.#'d SETS
BOW.EXCH.DEADLINE 3/31/2020
BOW.CHR.EXCH. 8/31/2020

2018 Bowman Chrome Rookie Autographs Refractors

*REF: .6X TO 1.2X BASIC
STATED ODDS 1:XXX HOBBY JUMBO
STATED PRINT RUN 499 SER.#'D SETS
BOW.EXCH.DEADLINE 3/31/2020
BOW.CHR.EXCH. 8/31/2020

2018 Bowman Chrome Rookie of the Year Favorites Refractors

STATED ODDS 1:8 HOBBY
*ATOMIC REF: 1X TO 2.5X BASIC
*GREEN REF/99: 2.5X TO 6X BASIC
*ORNGE REF/25: 8X TO 20X BASIC
ROYFAB Anthony Banda .25 .60
ROYFAR Amed Rosario .30 .75
ROYFAV Alex Verdugo .40 1.00
ROYFCF Clint Frazier .50 1.25
ROYFDS Dominic Smith .30 .75
ROYFFM Francisco Mejia .30 .75
ROYFHB Harrison Bader .40 1.00
ROYFJC J.P. Crawford .25 .60
ROYFJF Jack Flaherty 1.00 2.50
ROYFNW Nick Williams .30 .75
ROYFOA Ozzie Albies .75 2.00
ROYFRD Rafael Devers .75 2.00
ROYFRH Rhys Hoskins 1.00 2.50
ROYFVR Victor Robles .60 1.50
ROYFWC Willie Calhoun .40 1.00

2018 Bowman Chrome Rookie of the Year Favorites Autographs Refractors

STATED ODDS 1:2176 HOBBY
STATED PRINT RUN 150 SER. #'d SETS
EXCHANGE DEADLINE 3/31/2020
*GOLD REF/50: .6X TO 1.5X BASE
ROYFAAB Anthony Banda 5.00 12.00
ROYFAAR Amed Rosario 20.00 50.00
ROYFAAV Alex Verdugo 8.00 20.00
ROYFACF Clint Frazier 20.00 50.00
ROYFAHB Harrison Bader 8.00 20.00
ROYFAJF Jack Flaherty 20.00 50.00
ROYFARD Rafael Devers 25.00 60.00
ROYFAVR Victor Robles 25.00 60.00

2018 Bowman Chrome Rookie of the Year Favorites Autographs Orange Refractors

*ORANGE/25: .75X TO 2X BASIC
STATED ODDS 1:3876 HOBBY
STATED PRINT RUN 25 SER. #'d SETS
EXCHANGE DEADLINE 3/31/2020
ROYFAVR Victor Robles 125.00 300.00

2018 Bowman Chrome Scouts Top 100

STATED ODDS 1:4 HOBBY
*ATOMIC REF/150: 1.5X TO 4X BASIC
*GREEN REF/99: 1.5X TO 4X BASIC
*GOLD REF/50: 3X TO 8X BASIC
*ORNGE REF/25: 5X TO 12X BASIC
BTP1 Vladimir Guerrero Jr. 2.50 6.00
BTP2 Ronald Acuna 8.00 20.00
BTP3 Victor Robles .60 1.50
BTP4 Gleyber Torres 2.50 6.00
BTP5 Eloy Jimenez 1.00 2.50
BTP6 Walker Buehler 1.25 3.00
BTP7 Alex Reyes .30 .75
BTP8 Michael Kopech 1.00 2.50
BTP9 Mitch Keller .30 .75
BTP10 Fernando Tatis Jr. 2.50 6.00
BTP11 Hunter Greene .75 2.00
BTP12 Bo Bichette 1.00 2.50
BTP13 MacKenzie Gore .50 1.25
BTP14 Brendan Rodgers .30 .75
BTP15 Francisco Mejia .30 .75
BTP16 Nick Senzel .75 2.00
BTP17 Kyle Tucker .60 1.50
BTP18 Nick Gordon .25 .60
BTP19 A.J. Puk .40 1.00
BTP20 Royce Lewis 1.00 2.50
BTP21 Luiz Gohara .25 .60
BTP22 Brent Honeywell .40 1.00
BTP23 Forrest Whitley .40 1.00
BTP24 Triston McKenzie .75 2.00
BTP25 Mike Soroka .75 2.00
BTP26 Austin Hays .40 1.00
BTP27 Willy Adames .30 .75
BTP28 Alex Verdugo .40 1.00
BTP29 Luis Robert 4.00 10.00
BTP30 Sixto Sanchez .75 2.00
BTP31 Scott Kingery .40 1.00
BTP32 Michael Chavis .40 1.00
BTP33 Franklin Perez .30 .75
BTP34 Alec Hansen .25 .60
BTP35 Ian Anderson .75 2.00
BTP36 Chance Sisco .30 .75
BTP37 J.P. Crawford .25 .60
BTP38 Pavin Smith .40 1.00
BTP39 Jo Adell 1.00 2.50
BTP40 Lewis Brinson .25 .60
BTP41 Brendan McKay .40 1.00
BTP42 Jack Flaherty 1.00 2.50
BTP43 Kyle Lewis .50 1.25
BTP44 Juan Soto 6.00 15.00
BTP45 Estevan Florial .40 1.00
BTP46 Keston Hiura .60 1.50
BTP47 Cal Quantrill .25 .60
BTP48 Shane Baz .30 .75
BTP49 Carson Kelly .25 .60
BTP50 Justus Sheffield .30 .75
BTP51 Leody Taveras .40 1.00
BTP52 Kevin Newman .40 1.00
BTP53 Nate Pearson .75 2.00
BTP54 Heliot Ramos .40 1.00
BTP55 Yordan Alvarez 2.00 5.00
BTP56 Michel Baez .25 .60
BTP57 Jon Duplantier .25 .60
BTP58 Jahmai Jones .25 .60
BTP59 Jay Groome .30 .75
BTP60 Luis Urias .50 1.25
BTP61 Dylan Cease .40 1.00
BTP62 Bobby Bradley .30 .75
BTP63 Ryan McMahon .60 1.50
BTP64 Nick Pratto .30 .75
BTP65 Keibert Ruiz 1.25 3.00
BTP66 Trevor Rogers .60 1.50
BTP67 Chance Adams .40 1.00
BTP68 Jesus Luzardo .40 1.00
BTP69 Chris Shaw .25 .60
BTP70 Adam Haseley .40 1.00
BTP71 Jesus Sanchez .40 1.00
BTP72 Corbin Burnes 2.00 5.00
BTP73 Cole Ragans .25 .60
BTP74 Anthony Alford .25 .60
BTP75 Austin Meadows .60 1.50
BTP76 Kolby Allard .25 .60
BTP77 Carter Kieboom .40 1.00
BTP78 D.L. Hall .25 .60
BTP79 Sam Travis .25 .60
BTP80 David Peterson .50 1.25
BTP81 Tyler Mahle .30 .75
BTP82 Bryse Wilson .40 1.00
BTP83 Victor Caratini .30 .75
BTP84 Taylor Trammell .40 1.00
BTP85 Dane Dunning .75 2.00
BTP86 Adbert Alzolay .30 .75
BTP87 Riley Pint .25 .60
BTP88 J.B. Bukauskas .25 .60
BTP89 Matt Manning .40 1.00
BTP90 Brandon Marsh .40 1.00
BTP91 Andres Gimenez .60 1.50
BTP92 Monte Harrison .40 1.00
BTP93 Jeren Kendall .30 .75
BTP94 Stephen Gonsalves .25 .60
BTP95 Albert Abreu .25 .60
BTP96 Franklin Barreto .25 .60
BTP97 Jorge Mateo .25 .60
BTP98 Christian Arroyo .25 .60
BTP99 Willie Calhoun .40 1.00
BTP100 Austin Riley .75 2.00

2018 Bowman Chrome Scouts Top 100 Autographs Refractors

STATED ODDS 1:1383 HOBBY
STATED PRINT RUN 50 SER. #'d SETS
EXCHANGE DEADLINE 3/31/2020
BTP2 Ronald Acuna 300.00 600.00
BTP3 Victor Robles 30.00 80.00
BTP4 Gleyber Torres 125.00 300.00
BTP6 Walker Buehler 50.00 120.00
BTP7 Alex Reyes
BTP8 Michael Kopech 25.00 60.00
BTP9 Mitch Keller 8.00 20.00
BTP11 Hunter Greene 100.00 250.00
BTP14 Brendan Rodgers 15.00 40.00
BTP19 A.J. Puk 10.00 25.00
BTP20 Royce Lewis 40.00 100.00
BTP26 Austin Hays 10.00 25.00
BTP28 Alex Verdugo 25.00 60.00
BTP32 Michael Chavis 10.00 25.00
BTP35 Ian Anderson 20.00 50.00
BTP36 Chance Sisco 25.00 60.00
BTP37 J.P. Crawford 6.00 15.00
BTP38 Pavin Smith 10.00 25.00
BTP40 Lewis Brinson 6.00 15.00
BTP41 Brendan McKay 40.00 100.00
BTP42 Jack Flaherty 25.00 60.00
BTP46 Keston Hiura 20.00 50.00
BTP47 Cal Quantrill 6.00 15.00
BTP48 Shane Baz 8.00 20.00
BTP50 Justus Sheffield 25.00 60.00
BTP53 Nate Pearson 20.00 50.00
BTP54 Heliot Ramos 25.00 60.00
BTP56 Michel Baez 30.00 80.00
BTP57 Jon Duplantier 6.00 15.00
BTP58 Jahmai Jones 6.00 15.00
BTP59 Jay Groome 8.00 20.00
BTP63 Ryan McMahon 15.00 40.00
BTP64 Nick Pratto 25.00 60.00
BTP65 Keibert Ruiz 30.00 80.00
BTP66 Trevor Rogers
BTP68 Jesus Luzardo
BTP69 Chris Shaw 15.00 40.00
BTP70 Adam Haseley 10.00 25.00
BTP72 Corbin Burnes 40.00 100.00
BTP77 Carter Kieboom 25.00 60.00
BTP79 Sam Travis 6.00 15.00
BTP80 David Peterson 12.00 30.00
BTP81 Tyler Mahle 8.00 20.00
BTP86 Adbert Alzolay
BTP87 Riley Pint 6.00 15.00
BTP88 J.B. Bukauskas 6.00 15.00
BTP91 Andres Gimenez 15.00 40.00
BTP93 Jeren Kendall 25.00 60.00
BTP95 Albert Abreu 12.00 30.00
BTP96 Franklin Barreto 6.00 15.00
BTP97 Jorge Mateo 10.00 25.00
BTP98 Christian Arroyo 6.00 15.00

2018 Bowman Chrome Talent Pipeline Refractors

STATED ODDS 1:12 HOBBY
*ATOMIC REF/150: .75X TO 2X BASIC
*GREEN REF/99: 1X TO 2.5X BASIC
*ORANGE REF/25: 2X TO 5X BASIC
TPARI Jon Duplantier .30 .75
Anthony Banda
Alex Young
TPATL Braves 4.00 10.00
TPBAL Chance Sisco 1.50 4.00
Ryan Mountcastle
Alex Wells
TPBOS Tzu-Wei Lin .50 1.25
Michael Chavis
Jay Groome
TPCHI Cubs .40 1.00
TPCHW White Sox 1.25 3.00
TPCIN Reds 1.00 2.50
TPCLE Nellie Rodriguez 1.00 2.50
Triston McKenzie
Bobby Bradley
TPCOL Brendan Rodgers .40 1.00
Sam Howard
Riley Pint
TPDET Tigers .50 1.25
TPHOU Forrest Whitley .50 1.25
Rogelio Armenteros
Yordan Alvarez
TPKCR Josh Staumont .30 .75
Foster Griffin
Khalil Lee
TPLAA Fetcher/Thaiss/Jones 1.00 2.50
TPLAD Dodgers 1.50 4.00
TPMIA John Norwood .30 .75
Victor Payano
Braxton Garrett
TPMIL Dubon/Ortiz/Hiura .75 2.00
TPMIN Twins 1.25 3.00
TPNYM Mets .75 2.00
TPNYY Yankees 3.00 8.00
TPOAK Paul Blackburn .50 1.25
A.J. Puk
Jesus Luzardo
TPPHI Phillies 1.00 2.50
TPPIT Austin Meadows .75 2.00
Mitch Keller
Will Craig
TPSDP Padres 3.00 8.00
TPSEA Max Povse .60 1.50
Kyle Lewis
Braden Bishop
TPSFG Chris Shaw .30 .75
C.J. Hinojosa
Ryan Howard
TPSTL Cardinals .60 1.50
TPTBR Ryas .50 1.25
TPTEX Rangers .50 1.25
TPTOR Jays 3.00 8.00
TPWAS Nationals 8.00 20.00

2018 Bowman Chrome Draft

COMPLETE SET (200) 20.00 50.00
STATED PLATE ODDS 1:1198 HOBBY
PLATE PRINT RUN 1 SET PER COLOR
BLACK-CYAN-MAGENTA-YELLOW ISSUED
NO PLATE PRICING DUE TO SCARCITY
BDC1 Casey Mize 2.00 5.00
BDC2 Matt Vierling .50 1.25
BDC3 Brusdar Graterol .50 1.25
BDC4 Lawrence Butler .40 1.00
BDC5 Terrin Vavra .50 1.25

BDC6 Jarred Kelenic 20.00 50.00
BDC7 Yusniel Diaz .75 2.00
BDC8 Lenny Torres .30 .75
BDC9 Shane McClanahan .40 1.00
BDC10 Blayne Enlow .25 .60
BDC11 Brice Turang .75 2.00
BDC12 Tim Cate .40 1.00
BDC13 Pedro Avila .25 .60
BDC14 Kyle Isbel .60 1.50
BDC15 Devin Mann .40 1.00
BDC16 Jazz Chisholm 1.00 2.50
BDC17 Luis Medina .40 1.00
BDC18 Adrian Morejon .25 .60
BDC19 Arbert Cipion .25 .60
BDC20 Trevor Stephan .25 .60
BDC21 Drew Ellis .30 .75
BDC22 Taylor Trammell .40 1.00
BDC23 Jayson Schroeder .25 .60
BDC24 Joe Jacques .25 .60
BDC25 Alec Bohm 15.00 40.00
BDC26 Beau Burrows .30 .75
BDC27 Jonathan Stiever .25 .60
BDC28 Parker Meadows .50 1.25
BDC29 Jonathan Ornelas .60 1.50
BDC30 Matthew Liberatore .30 .75
BDC31 Greyson Jenista .40 1.00
BDC32 Bo Bichette 1.00 2.50
BDC33 Durbin Feltman .40 1.00
BDC34 Nick Sandlin .25 .60
BDC35 Jahmai Jones .25 .60
BDC36 Brandon Marsh .40 1.00
BDC37 Lency Delgado .50 1.25
BDC38 Nick Madrigal 5.00 12.00
BDC39 Kris Bubic .40 1.00
BDC40 Oneil Cruz .40 1.00
BDC41 Alex Faedo .40 1.00
BDC42 Thomas Ponticelli .25 .60
BDC43 Bryan Lavastida .25 .60
BDC44 Nick Schnell .25 .60
BDC45 Cal Mitchell .40 1.00
BDC46 Nick Solak 1.00 2.50
BDC47 Brennen Davis 2.00 5.00
BDC48 Ethan Hankins .30 .75
BDC49 Keston Hiura .60 1.50
BDC50 Ke'Bryan Hayes 1.25 3.00
BDC51 Jeremiah Jackson .40 1.00
BDC52 Lolo Sanchez .30 .75
BDC53 Gregory Soto .25 .60
BDC54 Nicky Lopez .40 1.00
BDC55 Jake Wong .25 .60
BDC56 Jordan Groshans 1.25 3.00
BDC57 Josh Breaux .30 .75
BDC58 Hunter Greene .75 2.00
BDC59 Dylan Cease .40 1.00
BDC60 Carlos Cortes .30 .75
BDC61 Korry Howell .25 .60
BDC62 Joey Wentz .30 .75
BDC63 Logan Gilbert .40 1.00
BDC64 Ryan Rolison .50 1.25
BDC65 Anthony Seigler .60 1.50
BDC66 Jorge Guzman .25 .60
BDC67 Mark Vientos .40 1.00
BDC68 Chris Paddack .60 1.50
BDC69 Kole Cottam .30 .75
BDC70 Trevor Larnach 1.50 4.00
BDC71 Monte Harrison .40 1.00
BDC72 Aramis Ademan .30 .75
BDC73 Grayson Rodriguez .50 1.25
BDC74 Nick Gordon .25 .60
BDC75 Sixto Sanchez .75 2.00
BDC76 Joe Gray .40 1.00
BDC77 Drevian Williams-Nelson .25 .60
BDC78 Tanner Dodson .30 .75
BDC79 Ryan Vilade .25 .60
BDC80 Blake Rivera .25 .60
BDC81 Adam Haseley .40 1.00
BDC82 Braydon Fisher 1.00 2.50
BDC83 Kevon Jackson .25 .60
BDC84 Ryder Green .30 .75
BDC85 Jawuan Harris .25 .60
BDC86 Mitch Keller .30 .75
BDC87 Royce Lewis 1.00 2.50
BDC88 Jordyn Adams 4.00 10.00
BDC89 Korey Holland .25 .60
BDC90 Thad Ward .25 .60
BDC91 Sean Murphy .40 1.00
BDC92 Calvin Coker .25 .60
BDC93 Carter Kieboom .40 1.00
BDC94 Jake McCarthy .40 1.00
BDC95 Braxton Ashcraft .30 .75
BDC96 Colton Eastman .60 1.50
BDC97 Mitchell White .25 .60
BDC98 Nick Pratto .30 .75
BDC99 Alex McKenna .30 .75
BDC100 Brendan McKay .40 1.00
BDC101 Mike Shawaryn .25 .60
BDC102 Levi Kelly .25 .60
BDC103 Osiris Johnson .30 .75
BDC104 Justin Jarvis .25 .60
BDC105 Ford Proctor .30 .75
BDC106 Ezequiel Pagan .30 .75
BDC107 Jo Adell 1.00 2.50
BDC108 Jon Duplantier .25 .60
BDC109 Luken Baker .40 1.00
BDC110 Grant Little .25 .60
BDC111 Micah Bello .40 1.00
BDC112 Jonathan India 5.00 12.00
BDC113 Will Banfield .30 .75
BDC114 Keibert Ruiz 1.25 3.00
BDC115 Grant Koch .25 .60
BDC116 Jeren Kendall .30 .75
BDC117 Nolan Gorman 1.50 4.00
BDC118 Nate Pearson .75 2.00
BDC119 Corbin Martin .25 .60
BDC120 Shed Long .30 .75
BDC121 Kody Clemens .40 1.00
BDC122 Josh Naylor .30 .75
BDC123 Sheldon Neuse .25 .60
BDC124 Nick Decker .50 1.25
BDC125 Cole Roederer .75 2.00
BDC126 Albert Abreu .25 .60
BDC127 Dallas Woolfolk .25 .60
BDC128 Adonis Medina .40 1.00
BDC129 Tristan Pompey .25 .60
BDC130 Michel Baez .25 .60
BDC131 Pavin Smith .40 1.00
BDC132 Brian Miller .25 .60
BDC133 Heliot Ramos .40 1.00
BDC134 Cadyn Grenier .30 .75
BDC135 Brady Singer 1.25 3.00
BDC136 Andres Gimenez .60 1.50
BDC137 Griffin Roberts .25 .60
BDC138 Greg Deichmann .30 .75
BDC139 Sean Hjelle .30 .75
BDC140 Kenen Irizarry .40 1.00
BDC141 Alfonso Rivas .25 .60
BDC142 Daniel Lynch .30 .75
BDC143 Matt Mercer .25 .60
BDC144 Sean Guilbe .30 .75
BDC145 Matt Manning .40 1.00
BDC146 Alec Hansen .25 .60
BDC147 Jackson Goddard .25 .60
BDC148 Jesus Luzardo .40 1.00
BDC149 Nick Dunn .75 2.00
BDC150 MacKenzie Gore .50 1.25
BDC151 Jeter Downs .40 1.00
BDC152 Grant Witherspoon .30 .75
BDC153 Griffin Conine .50 1.25
BDC154 Adam Hill .25 .60
BDC155 Alek Thomas 1.00 2.50
BDC156 Tyler Frank .25 .60
BDC157 Sean Wymer .25 .60
BDC158 Connor Scott .30 .75
BDC159 Owen White .40 1.00
BDC160 Jameson Hannah .40 1.00
BDC161 Mike Siani .30 .75
BDC162 Triston McKenzie .75 2.00
BDC163 Bobby Bradley .30 .75
BDC164 Mason Denaburg .30 .75
BDC165 Nico Hoerner 1.25 3.00
BDC166 Matt Thaiss .25 .60
BDC167 Ryan Mountcastle 1.25 3.00
BDC168 Eloy Jimenez 1.00 2.50
BDC169 Logan Allen .25 .60
BDC170 Dane Dunning .75 2.00
BDC171 Triston Casas 6.00 15.00
BDC172 Bryan Mata .30 .75
BDC173 Cole Winn .40 1.00
BDC174 Leury Tejada .25 .60
BDC175 Sam Carlson .30 .75
BDC176 Raynel Delgado .60 1.50
BDC177 Leody Taveras .40 1.00
BDC178 Justin Dunn .30 .75
BDC179 Jeremy Eierman .25 .60
BDC180 Jesus Sanchez .40 1.00
BDC181 Simeon Woods-Richardson .30 .75
BDC182 Ryan Weathers .30 .75
BDC183 Ian Anderson .75 2.00
BDC184 Matt Sauer .25 .60
BDC185 Adam Wolf .30 .75
BDC186 Grant Lavigne 1.25 3.00
BDC187 Estevan Florial .40 1.00
BDC188 Luis Robert 8.00 20.00
BDC189 J.B. Bukauskas .25 .60
BDC190 Josh Stowers .60 1.50
BDC191 Brent Rooker .30 .75
BDC192 Ryan Jeffers .50 1.25
BDC193 Noah Naylor .40 1.00
BDC194 Cody Deason .25 .60
BDC195 Cal Quantrill .25 .60
BDC196 Jackson Kowar 1.50 4.00
BDC197 Griffin Canning .25 .60
BDC198 Travis Swaggerty .75 2.00
BDC199 Alex Kirilloff .40 1.00
BDC200 Lazaro Armenteros .50 1.25

2018 Bowman Chrome Draft Blue Refractors

*BLUE REF: 2X TO 5X BASIC
STATED ODDS 1:32 HOBBY
STATED PRINT RUN 150 SER.#'d SETS
BDC117 Nolan Gorman 50.00 120.00
BDC165 Nico Hoerner 15.00 40.00
BDC188 Luis Robert 60.00 150.00

2018 Bowman Chrome Draft Gold Refractors

*GOLD REF: 5X TO 12X BASIC
STATED ODDS 1:96 HOBBY
STATED PRINT RUN 50 SER.#'d SETS
BDC2 Matt Vierling 15.00 40.00
BDC81 Adam Haseley 15.00 40.00
BDC117 Nolan Gorman 125.00 300.00
BDC165 Nico Hoerner 40.00 100.00
BDC188 Luis Robert 100.00 250.00
BDC193 Noah Naylor 10.00 25.00

2018 Bowman Chrome Draft Green Refractors

*GREEN REF: 2.5X TO 6X BASIC
STATED ODDS 1:49 HOBBY
STATED PRINT RUN 99 SER.#'d SETS
BDC117 Nolan Gorman 60.00 150.00
BDC165 Nico Hoerner 20.00 50.00
BDC188 Luis Robert 75.00 200.00

2018 Bowman Chrome Draft Purple Refractors

*PURPLE REF: 1.5X TO 4X BASIC
STATED ODDS 1:20 HOBBY
STATED PRINT RUN 250 SER.#'d SETS
BDC117 Nolan Gorman 15.00 40.00
BDC165 Nico Hoerner 12.00 30.00
BDC188 Luis Robert 50.00 120.00

2018 Bowman Chrome Draft Refractors

*REF: .75X TO 2X BASIC
RANDOM INSERTS IN PACKS
BDC188 Luis Robert 20.00 50.00

2018 Bowman Chrome Draft Sky Blue Refractors

*SKY BLUE REF: 1X TO 2.5X BASIC
RANDOM INSERTS IN PACKS
STATED PRINT RUN 402 SER.#'d SETS
BDC117 Nolan Gorman 15.00 40.00
BDC165 Nico Hoerner 8.00 20.00
BDC188 Luis Robert 25.00 60.00

2018 Bowman Chrome Draft Sparkle Refractors

*SPARKLE REF: 1.5X TO 4X BASIC
STATED ODDS 1:24 HOBBY
BDC117 Nolan Gorman 15.00 40.00
BDC165 Nico Hoerner 12.00 30.00
BDC188 Luis Robert 50.00 120.00

2018 Bowman Chrome Draft Image Variation Refractors

STATED ODDS 1:196 HOBBY
BDC1 Casey Mize
White Jersey
BDC3 Brusdar Graterol
Gray Pants
BDC6 Jarred Kelenic
Gray Jersey
BDC20 Trevor Stephan
New York visable on jersey
BDC25 Alec Bohm
Red Jersey
BDC32 Bo Bichette
Fielding
BDC38 Nick Madrigal
Fielding
BDC72 Aramis Ademan
Ball visable
BDC87 Royce Lewis
Hand on bat barrel
BDC93 Carter Kieboom
No hat
BDC112 Jonathan India
Running
BDC182 Ryan Weathers
White Jersey
BDC198 Travis Swaggerty
Tipping helmet

2018 Bowman Chrome Draft Image Variation Autographs Refractors

STATED ODDS 1:948 HOBBY
STATED PRINT RUN 99 SER.#'d SETS
EXCHANGE DEADLINE 11/30/2020
BDC1 Casey Mize 100.00 250.00
BDC6 Jarred Kelenic 400.00 1000.00
BDC25 Alec Bohm 250.00 600.00
BDC38 Nick Madrigal 80.00 200.00
BDC93 Carter Kieboom 75.00 200.00
BDC112 Jonathan India 150.00 400.00
BDC182 Ryan Weathers 25.00 60.00

2018 Bowman Chrome Draft Orange Refractors

*ORANGE REF: 8X TO 20X BASIC
STATED ODDS 1:130 HOBBY
STATED PRINT RUN 25 SER.#'d SETS
BDC2 Matt Vierling 25.00 60.00
BDC81 Adam Haseley 25.00 60.00
BDC117 Nolan Gorman 200.00 500.00
BDC165 Nico Hoerner 60.00 150.00
BDC188 Luis Robert 250.00 600.00
BDC193 Noah Naylor 15.00 40.00

2018 Bowman Chrome Draft '98 Bowman

STATED ODDS 1:6 HOBBY
*REF/250: .5X TO 1.2X BASE
*GOLD REF/50: 2.5X TO 6X BASE
98BAB Alec Bohm 1.50 4.00
98BBS Brady Singer 1.25 3.00
98BCM Casey Mize 2.00 5.00
98BGR Grayson Rodriguez .50 1.25
98BJI Jonathan India 1.50 4.00
98BJK Jarred Kelenic 2.50 6.00
98BNM Nick Madrigal 1.00 2.50
98BRW Ryan Weathers .30 .75
98BTC Triston Casas 3.00 8.00
98BTS Travis Swaggerty .75 2.00

2018 Bowman Chrome Draft '98 Bowman Autographs

STATED ODDS 1:948 HOBBY
STATED PRINT RUN 99 SER.#'d SETS
EXCHANGE DEADLINE 11/30/2020
98BAAB Alec Bohm 40.00 100.00
98BACM Casey Mize 50.00 125.00
98BAJI Jonathan India 100.00 250.00
98BAJK Jarred Kelenic 60.00 150.00
98BANM Nick Madrigal 25.00 60.00
98BARW Ryan Weathers 20.00 50.00
98BATS Travis Swaggerty 20.00 50.00

2018 Bowman Chrome Draft Autographs

OVERALL AUTO ODDS 1:8 HOBBY
STATED PLATE ODDS 1:3987 HOBBY
PLATE PRINT RUN 1 SET PER COLOR
BLACK-CYAN-MAGENTA-YELLOW ISSUED
NO PLATE PRICING DUE TO SCARCITY
EXCHANGE DEADLINE 11/30/2020
CDAAB Alec Bohm 150.00 400.00
CDAAS Anthony Seigler 8.00 20.00
CDAAT Alek Thomas 30.00 80.00
CDABA Braxton Ashcraft 4.00 10.00
CDABS Brady Singer 20.00 50.00
CDABT Brice Turang 15.00 40.00
CDACC Carlos Cortes 4.00 10.00
CDACG Cadyn Grenier 4.00 10.00
CDACM Casey Mize 50.00 120.00
CDACR Cole Roederer 10.00 25.00
CDACSC Connor Scott 8.00 20.00
CDACW Cole Winn 5.00 12.00
CDADL Daniel Lynch 12.00 30.00
CDAEH Ethan Hankins 6.00 15.00
CDAGC Griffin Conine 10.00 25.00
CDAGJ Greyson Jenista 5.00 12.00
CDAGL Grant Lavigne 10.00 25.00
CDAGR Grayson Rodriguez 25.00 60.00
CDAGRO Griffin Roberts 3.00 8.00
CDAJA Jordyn Adams 25.00 60.00
CDAJBR Josh Breaux 6.00 15.00
CDAJE Jeremy Eierman 3.00 8.00
CDAJG Jordan Groshans 30.00 80.00
CDAJGR Joe Gray 5.00 12.00
CDAJI Jonathan India 50.00 120.00
CDAJJ Jeremiah Jackson 40.00 100.00
CDAJK Jarred Kelenic 200.00 500.00
CDAJKO Jackson Kowar 10.00 25.00
CDAJM Jake McCarthy 5.00 12.00
CDAJOG Josiah Gray 15.00 40.00
CDAJS Josh Stowers 8.00 20.00
CDAJSC Jayson Schroeder 3.00 8.00
CDAJW Jake Wong 3.00 8.00
CDAKB Kris Bubic 6.00 15.00
CDAKC Kody Clemens 5.00 12.00
CDALB Luken Baker 10.00 25.00
CDALG Logan Gilbert 25.00 60.00
CDALT Lenny Torres 4.00 10.00
CDAMD Mason Denaburg 4.00 10.00
CDAML Matthew Liberatore 15.00 40.00
CDANG Nolan Gorman 60.00 150.00
CDANH Nico Hoerner 25.00 60.00
CDANM Nick Madrigal 40.00 100.00
CDANN Noah Naylor 12.00 30.00
CDANS Nick Schnell 3.00 8.00
CDAOJ Osiris Johnson 4.00 10.00
CDAOW Owen White 5.00 12.00
CDAPM Parker Meadows 6.00 15.00
CDARG Ryder Green 4.00 10.00
CDARJ Ryan Jeffers 10.00 25.00
CDARR Ryan Rolison 6.00 15.00
CDARW Ryan Weathers 4.00 10.00
CDASM Shane McClanahan 12.00 30.00
CDASWR Simeon Woods-Richardson 4.00 10.00
CDATC Triston Casas 60.00 150.00
CDATCA Tim Cate 5.00 12.00
CDATD Tanner Dodson 4.00 10.00
CDATF Tyler Frank 5.00 12.00
CDATL Trevor Larnach 25.00 60.00
CDATP Tristan Pompey 3.00 8.00
CDATS Travis Swaggerty 10.00 25.00
CDAWB Will Banfield 4.00 10.00

2018 Bowman Chrome Draft Autographs Black Refractors

*BLACK REF: 1.5X TO 4X BASIC
STATED ODDS 1:144 HOBBY
STATED PRINT RUN 75 SER.#'d SETS
EXCHANGE DEADLINE 11/30/2020

2018 Bowman Chrome Draft Autographs Blue Refractors

*BLUE REF: 1X TO 2.5X BASIC
STATED ODDS 1:107 HOBBY
STATED PRINT RUN 150 SER.#'d SETS
EXCHANGE DEADLINE 11/30/2020

2018 Bowman Chrome Draft Autographs Blue Wave Refractors

*BLUE WAVE REF: 1X TO 2.5X BASIC
STATED ODDS 1:107 HOBBY
STATED PRINT RUN 150 SER.#'d SETS
EXCHANGE DEADLINE 11/30/2020

2018 Bowman Chrome Draft Autographs Gold Refractors

*GOLD REF: 2.5X TO 6X BASIC
STATED ODDS 1:319 HOBBY
STATED PRINT RUN 50 SER.#'d SETS
EXCHANGE DEADLINE 11/30/2020
CDAAT Alek Thomas/50 300.00 800.00

2018 Bowman Chrome Draft Autographs Gold Wave Refractors

*GOLD WAVE REF: 2.5X TO 6X BASIC
STATED ODDS 1:319 HOBBY
STATED PRINT RUN 50 SER.#'d SETS
EXCHANGE DEADLINE 11/30/2020
CDAAT Alek Thomas 300.00 800.00

2018 Bowman Chrome Draft Autographs Green Refractors

*GREEN REF: 1.2X TO 3X BASIC
STATED ODDS 1:161 HOBBY
STATED PRINT RUN 99 SER.#'d SETS
EXCHANGE DEADLINE 11/30/2020

2018 Bowman Chrome Draft Autographs Orange Refractors

*ORANGE REF: 3X TO 8X BASIC
STATED ODDS 1:430 HOBBY
STATED PRINT RUN 25 SER.#'d SETS
EXCHANGE DEADLINE 11/30/2020
CDAAT Alek Thomas/25 1000.00 2000.00

2018 Bowman Chrome Draft Autographs Purple Refractors

*PURPLE REF: .6X TO 1.5X BASIC
STATED ODDS 1:64 HOBBY
STATED PRINT RUN 250 SER.#'d SETS
EXCHANGE DEADLINE 11/30/2020

2018 Bowman Chrome Draft Autographs Refractors

*REF: .5X TO 1.2X BASIC
STATED ODDS 1:32 HOBBY
PRINT RUNS B/WN 485-499 COPIES PER
EXCHANGE DEADLINE 11/30/2020

2018 Bowman Chrome Draft Autographs Sparkle Refractors

*SPARKEL REF: 1.5X TO 4X BASIC
STATED ODDS 1:225 HOBBY
STATED PRINT RUN 71 SER.#'d SETS
EXCHANGE DEADLINE 11/30/2020

2018 Bowman Chrome Draft Class of '18 Autographs

STATED ODDS 1:114 HOBBY
STATED PRINT RUN 250 SER.#'d SETS
EXCHANGE DEADLINE 11/30/2020
*GOLD/50: 1X TO 2.5X BASIC
C18AAB Alec Bohm 30.00 80.00
C18AAS Anthony Seigler 10.00 25.00
C18ABS Brady Singer 15.00 40.00
C18ABT Brice Turang 6.00 15.00
C18ACG Cadyn Grenier 5.00 12.00
C18ACM Casey Mize 30.00 80.00
C18ACSC Connor Scott 5.00 12.00
C18ACW Cole Winn 6.00 15.00
C18AGR Grayson Rodriguez EXCH 10.00 25.00
C18AJA Jordyn Adams 15.00 40.00
C18AJG Jordan Groshans 12.00 30.00
C18AJI Jonathan India 50.00 120.00
C18AJK Jarred Kelenic 60.00 150.00
C18AJKO Jackson Kowar 12.00 30.00
C18AJM Jake McCarthy 6.00 15.00
C18AKB Kris Bubic 6.00 15.00
C18ALG Logan Gilbert 10.00 25.00
C18AMD Mason Denaburg EXCH 5.00 12.00
C18AML Matthew Liberatore 10.00 25.00
C18ANG Nolan Gorman 50.00 120.00
C18ANH Nico Hoerner 40.00 100.00
C18ANM Nick Madrigal 15.00 40.00
C18ANN Noah Naylor 6.00 15.00
C18ANS Nick Schnell 8.00 20.00
C18ARR Ryan Rolison 8.00 20.00
C18ARW Ryan Weathers 12.00 30.00
C18ASM Shane McClanahan 6.00 15.00
C18ATC Triston Casas 15.00 40.00
C18ATL Trevor Larnach 12.00 30.00
C18ATS Travis Swaggerty 8.00 20.00

2018 Bowman Chrome Draft Draft Night Autographs

STATED ODDS 1:1896 HOBBY
STATED PRINT RUN 99 SER.#'d SETS
EXCHANGE DEADLINE 11/30/2020
*GOLD/50: .5X TO 1.2X BASIC
DNAAB Alec Bohm 40.00 100.00
DNAAS Anthony Seigler 25.00 60.00
DNATC Triston Casas 15.00 40.00
DNATS Travis Swaggerty 20.00 50.00

2018 Bowman Chrome Draft Franchise Futures

STATED ODDS 1:3 HOBBY
*REF/250: .5X TO 1.2X BASE
*GOLD REF/50: 1.2X TO 3X BASE
FFARI McCarthy/Thomas 1.00 2.50
FFBAL Grenier/Rodriguez .50 1.25
FFCIN Siani/India 1.50 4.00
FFCWS Pilkington/Madrigal 1.00 2.50
FFDET Clemens/Mize 2.00 5.00
FFKCR Kowar/Singer 1.25 3.00
FFNYM Cortes/Kelenic 2.50 6.00
FFNYY Seigler/Breaux .60 1.50
FFSDP Xavier Edwards .75 2.00
Ryan Weathers
FFSEA Stowers/Gilbert .60 1.50

2018 Bowman Chrome Draft Recommended Viewing

STATED ODDS 1:3 HOBBY
*REF/250: .5X TO 1.2X BASE
*GOLD REF/50: 1.2X TO 3X BASE
RVBT Kris Bubic .40 1.00
Lenny Torres
RVCS Stowers/Conine .60 1.50
RVGC Casas/Gorman 3.00 8.00
RVGE Xavier Edwards .75 2.00
Cadyn Grenier
RVGT Thomas/Gray 1.00 2.50
RVKH Ethan Hankins .75 2.00
Jackson Kowar
RVLJ Jenista/Lavigne 1.25 3.00
RVMG Groshans/Madrigal 1.00 2.50
RVMI Madrigal/India 1.50 4.00
RVMS Mize/Singer 2.00 5.00
RVSM Jake McCarthy .40 1.00
Nick Schnell
RVSN Naylor/Seigler .60 1.50
RVWC Tim Cate .40 1.00
Owen White
RVWL Liberatore/Winn .40 1.00
RVWRA Simeon Woods-Richardson .30 .75
Braxton Ashcraft

2018 Bowman Chrome Draft Recommended Viewing Dual Autographs

STATED ODDS 1:633 HOBBY
STATED PRINT RUN 99 SER.#'d SETS
EXCHANGE DEADLINE 11/30/2020
*GOLD/50: .5X TO 1.2X BASIC
RVACS Conine/Stowers EXCH 15.00 40.00
RVAGC Gorman/Casas 100.00 250.00
RVAJB Breaux/Jeffers 10.00 25.00
RVAKH Kowar/Hankins EXCH 10.00 25.00
RVALJ Lavigne/Jenista EXCH 25.00 60.00
RVAMG Groshans/Madrigal 40.00 100.00
RVAMI India/Madrigal 60.00 150.00
RVAMS Singer/Mize 40.00 100.00
RVASN Seigler/Naylor EXCH 12.00 30.00
RVAWC Cate/White EXCH 8.00 20.00
RVAWL Winn/Liberatore EXCH 20.00 50.00

2018 Bowman Chrome Draft Top of the Class Box Topper

STATED ODDS 1:46 HOBBY BOXES
STATED PRINT RUN 99 SER.#'d SETS
*GOLD/50: .5X TO 1.2X BASIC
TOCAB Alec Bohm 10.00 25.00
TOCCM Casey Mize 12.00 30.00
TOCGR Grayson Rodriguez 3.00 8.00
TOCJA Jordyn Adams 6.00 15.00
TOCJB Joey Bart 25.00 60.00
TOCJG Jordan Groshans 5.00 12.00
TOCJI Jonathan India 10.00 25.00
TOCJK Jarred Kelenic 15.00 40.00
TOCML Matthew Liberatore 2.00 5.00
TOCNM Nick Madrigal 6.00 15.00
TOCRW Ryan Weathers 2.00 5.00
TOCTS Travis Swaggerty 5.00 12.00

2018 Bowman Chrome Draft Top of the Class Box Topper Autographs

STATED ODDS 1:2184 HOBBY BOXES
STATED PRINT RUN 35 SER.#'d SETS
EXCHANGE DEADLINE 11/30/2020
TOCAB Alec Bohm 30.00 80.00
TOCCM Casey Mize 40.00 100.00
TOCGR Grayson Rodriguez
TOCJA Jordyn Adams
TOCJG Jordan Groshans 15.00 40.00
TOCJI Jonathan India 125.00 300.00
TOCJK Jarred Kelenic
TOCML Matthew Liberatore
TOCNM Nick Madrigal 30.00 80.00
TOCRW Ryan Weathers
TOCTS Travis Swaggerty 15.00 40.00

2019 Bowman Chrome

1 Ronald Acuna Jr. 1.50 4.00
2 Chris Davis .20 .50
3 Jake Bauers RC .60 1.50
4 Yasiel Puig .30 .75
5 Jake Cave RC .50 1.25
6 Corey Kluber .25 .60
7 Christin Stewart RC .50 1.25
8 David Peralta .20 .50
9 DJ Stewart RC .50 1.25
10 Brandon Lowe RC .60 1.50
11 Kolby Allard RC .60 1.50
12 Jonathan Loaisiga RC .50 1.25
13 Francisco Lindor .30 .75
14 Dansby Swanson .30 .75
15 Blake Snell .25 .60
16 Chance Adams RC .40 1.00
17 Brandon Belt .25 .60
18 Eddie Rosario .25 .60
19 Ian Kinsler .25 .60
20 Starling Marte .25 .60
21 Yoan Moncada .30 .75
22 Whit Merrifield .30 .75
23 Miguel Cabrera .30 .75
24 Dakota Hudson RC .50 1.25
25 Kyle Tucker RC 1.00 2.50
26 Fernando Tatis Jr. RC 25.00 60.00
27 Nolan Arenado .50 1.25
28 Rowdy Tellez RC .60 1.50
29 Cedric Mullins RC .75 2.00
30 Lourdes Gurriel Jr. .25 .60
31 Manny Machado .30 .75
32 Corbin Burnes RC 3.00 8.00
33 Josh Hader .25 .60
34 Taylor Ward RC .40 1.00
35 Mark Trumbo .20 .50
36 Enyel De Los Santos RC .40 1.00
37 Ryan Borucki RC .40 1.00
38 Giancarlo Stanton .30 .75
39 Joey Votto .30 .75
40 Willians Astudillo RC .40 1.00
41 Billy Hamilton .25 .60
42 Keston Hiura RC 1.25 3.00
43 Josh James RC .60 1.50
44 Juan Soto 1.00 2.50
45 Griffin Canning RC .60 1.50
46 Khris Davis .30 .75
47 Cal Quantrill RC .40 1.00
48 Pete Alonso RC 4.00 10.00
49 Jacob deGrom .60 1.50
50 Shohei Ohtani .50 1.25
51 Josh Bell .25 .60
52 Charlie Blackmon .30 .75
53 Luis Urias RC .60 1.50
54 Brad Keller .20 .50
55 Bryce Harper .50 1.25
56 Anthony Rizzo .40 1.00
57 Zack Greinke .30 .75
58 Justus Sheffield RC .60 1.50
59 Jon Duplantier RC .40 1.00
60 Alex Bregman .30 .75
61 Rhys Hoskins .40 1.00
62 Bryse Wilson RC .50 1.25
63 Christian Yelich .40 1.00
64 Clayton Kershaw .50 1.25
65 Lewis Brinson .20 .50
66 Robinson Cano .25 .60
67 Ramon Laureano RC .75 2.00
68 Joey Gallo .25 .60
69 Jose Abreu .30 .75
70 Nelson Cruz .30 .75
71 Edwin Encarnacion .30 .75
72 Buster Posey .40 1.00
73 Vladimir Guerrero Jr. RC 8.00 20.00
74 Carter Kieboom RC .60 1.50
75 Mookie Betts .60 1.50
76 Kyle Wright RC .60 1.50
77 Brian Anderson .20 .50
78 Blake Treinen .20 .50
79 Willy Adames .20 .50
80 Nicholas Castellanos .30 .75
81 Eloy Jimenez RC 1.50 4.00
82 Michael Kopech RC 1.25 3.00
83 Jose Altuve .25 .60
84 Austin Riley RC 2.00 5.00
85 Chris Sale .30 .75
86 Kris Bryant .40 1.00
87 Marcus Stroman .25 .60
88 Danny Jansen RC .40 1.00
89 Touki Toussaint RC .50 1.25
90 Aaron Judge .75 2.00
91 Yusei Kikuchi RC .60 1.50
92 Ryan O'Hearn RC .40 1.00
93 Paul DeJong .30 .75
94 Miles Mikolas .30 .75
95 Ronald Guzman .20 .50
96 Mitch Haniger .25 .60
97 Victor Robles .40 1.00
98 Nick Senzel RC 1.25 3.00
99 Justin Turner .30 .75
100 Mike Trout 1.50 4.00

2019 Bowman Chrome Blue Refractors

*BLUE REF VET: 4X TO 10X BASIC
*BLUE REF RC: 2X TO 5X BASIC
STATED ODDS 1:71 HOBBY
STATED PRINT RUN 150 SER.#'d SETS
26 Fernando Tatis Jr. 150.00 400.00
42 Keston Hiura 10.00 25.00
48 Pete Alonso 30.00 80.00
73 Vladimir Guerrero Jr. 40.00 100.00
81 Eloy Jimenez 12.00 30.00
100 Mike Trout 25.00 60.00

2019 Bowman Chrome Gold Refractors

*GOLD REF VET: 8X TO 20X BASIC
*GOLD REF RC: 4X TO 10X BASIC
STATED ODDS 1:211 HOBBY
STATED PRINT RUN 50 SER.#'d SETS
1 Ronald Acuna Jr. 50.00 120.00
26 Fernando Tatis Jr. 300.00 800.00
42 Keston Hiura 20.00 50.00
48 Pete Alonso 60.00 150.00
55 Bryce Harper 30.00 80.00
73 Vladimir Guerrero Jr. 75.00 200.00
81 Eloy Jimenez 25.00 60.00
100 Mike Trout 100.00 250.00

2019 Bowman Chrome Green Refractors

*GREEN REF VET: 5X TO 12X BASIC
*GREEN REF RC: 2.5X TO 6X BASIC
STATED ODDS 1:107 HOBBY
STATED PRINT RUN 99 SER.#'d SETS
26 Fernando Tatis Jr. 200.00 500.00
42 Keston Hiura 12.00 30.00
48 Pete Alonso 40.00 100.00
73 Vladimir Guerrero Jr. 50.00 120.00
81 Eloy Jimenez 15.00 40.00
100 Mike Trout 30.00 80.00

2019 Bowman Chrome Orange Refractors

*ORANGE REF VET: 10X TO 25X BASIC
*ORANGE REF RC: 5X TO 12X BASIC
STATED ODDS 1:XXX HOBBY
STATED PRINT RUN 25 SER.#'d SETS
1 Ronald Acuna Jr. 60.00 150.00
26 Fernando Tatis Jr. 400.00 1000.00
42 Keston Hiura 25.00 60.00
48 Pete Alonso 75.00 200.00
55 Bryce Harper 40.00 100.00
73 Vladimir Guerrero Jr. 100.00 250.00
81 Eloy Jimenez 30.00 80.00
100 Mike Trout 125.00 300.00

2019 Bowman Chrome Purple Refractors

*PURPLE REF VET: 2X TO 5X BASIC
*PURPLE REF RC: 1X TO 2.5X BASIC
STATED ODDS 1:43 HOBBY
STATED PRINT RUN 250 SER.#'d SETS
1 Ronald Acuna Jr. 8.00 20.00
26 Fernando Tatis Jr. 75.00 200.00
42 Keston Hiura 5.00 12.00
48 Pete Alonso 25.00 60.00
73 Vladimir Guerrero Jr. 25.00 60.00
81 Eloy Jimenez 6.00 15.00
100 Mike Trout 12.00 30.00

2019 Bowman Chrome Refractors

*REF VET: 1.5X TO 4X BASIC
*REF RC: .75X TO 2X BASIC
STATED ODDS 1:21 HOBBY
STATED PRINT RUN 499 SER.#'d SETS
1 Ronald Acuna Jr. 6.00 15.00
26 Fernando Tatis Jr. 50.00 120.00
42 Keston Hiura 4.00 10.00
48 Pete Alonso 20.00 50.00
73 Vladimir Guerrero Jr. 20.00 50.00
81 Eloy Jimenez 5.00 12.00
100 Mike Trout 10.00 25.00

2019 Bowman Chrome Rookie Image Variations

STATED ODDS 1:141 HOBBY
3 Jake Bauers 5.00 12.00
7 Christin Stewart 4.00 10.00
11 Kolby Allard 5.00 12.00
16 Chance Adams 3.00 8.00
25 Kyle Tucker 8.00 20.00
29 Cedric Mullins 6.00 15.00
32 Corbin Burnes 25.00 60.00
37 Ryan Borucki 3.00 8.00
42 Chris Shaw 3.00 8.00
53 Luis Urias 5.00 12.00
58 Justus Sheffield 5.00 12.00
76 Kyle Wright 5.00 12.00
82 Michael Kopech 10.00 25.00
88 Danny Jansen 2.50 6.00
92 Ryan O'Hearn 3.00 8.00

2019 Bowman Chrome Rookie Image Variation Autographs

STATED ODDS 1:7728 HOBBY
STATED PRINT RUN 25 SER.#'d SETS
EXCHANGE DEADLINE 8/31/2021
11 Kolby Allard 30.00 80.00
16 Chance Adams 15.00 40.00
58 Justus Sheffield 25.00 60.00
76 Kyle Wright 25.00 60.00

2019 Bowman Chrome '18 AFL Fall Stars

STATED ODDS 1:6 HOBBY
STATED MVP SP ODDS 1:4186 HOBBY
*ATOMIC/150: 1.2X TO 3X BASE
*ORANGE/25: 4X TO 10X BASE
AFLAG Andres Gimenez 1.00 2.50
AFLBD Bobby Dalbec 2.50 6.00
AFLBR Buddy Reed .40 1.00
AFLSBR Buddy Reed MVP/250 8.00 20.00
AFLCB Cavan Biggio 2.00 5.00
AFLCK Carter Kieboom .60 1.50
AFLCP Cristian Pache 1.00 2.50
AFLDC Daz Cameron .40 1.00
AFLDH Darwinzon Hernandez .40 1.00
AFLDJ Daniel Johnson .40 1.00
AFLDV Daulton Varsho .60 1.50
AFLEF Estevan Florial .60 1.50
AFLEW Evan White 1.00 2.50
AFLFW Forrest Whitley .60 1.50
AFLGS Gregory Soto .40 1.00
AFLJD Jon Duplantier .40 1.00
AFLJPM Julio Pablo Martinez .40 1.00
AFLJR Jake Rogers .50 1.25
AFLJY Jordan Yamamoto .40 1.00
AFLKH Keston Hiura 1.25 3.00
AFLKR Keibert Ruiz 2.00 5.00
AFLLJC Li-Jen Chu .50 1.25
AFLLR Luis Robert 3.00 8.00
AFLNH Nico Hoerner 1.25 3.00
AFLNP Nate Pearson 1.25 3.00
AFLPA Pete Alonso 3.00 8.00
AFLRH Ronaldo Hernandez .40 1.00
AFLRM Ryan McKenna .40 1.00
AFLSL Shed Long .60 1.50
AFLVGJ Vladimir Guerrero Jr. 2.50 6.00
AFLZB Zack Burdi .40 1.00

2019 Bowman Chrome '18 AFL Fall Stars Autograph Relics

STATED ODDS 1:4275 HOBBY
STATED PRINT RUN 50 SER.#'d SETS
EXCHANGE DEADLINE 8/31/2021
AFLRBD Bobby Dalbec 15.00 40.00
AFLRDH Darwinzon Hernandez 8.00 20.00
AFLRKH Keston Hiura 25.00 60.00
AFLRKR Keibert Ruiz 40.00 100.00
AFLRNH Nico Hoerner 50.00 120.00
AFLRPA Peter Alonso 125.00 300.00
AFLRRM Ryan McKenna 8.00 20.00

2019 Bowman Chrome '18 AFL Fall Stars Autographs

STATED ODDS 1:727 HOBBY
STATED MVP ODDS 1:18,955 HOBBY
PRINT RUNS B/WN 50-150 COPIES PER
EXCHANGE DEADLINE 8/31/2021

AFLBR Buddy Reed/50 6.00 15.00
AFLSBR Buddy Reed MVP/100 5.00 12.00
AFLCK Carter Kieboom/75 10.00 25.00
AFLDC Daz Cameron/110 4.00 10.00
AFLDJ Daniel Johnson/150 4.00 10.00
AFLDV Daulton Varsho/150 8.00 20.00
AFLEW Evan White/150 12.00 30.00
AFLGS Gregory Soto/150 4.00 10.00
AFLJPM Julio Pablo Martinez/150 4.00 10.00
AFLJR Jake Rogers/150 8.00 20.00
AFLJY Jordan Yamamoto/150 8.00 20.00
AFLKH Keston Hiura/150 20.00 50.00
AFLLJC Li-Jen Chu/150 5.00 12.00
AFLLR Luis Robert/110 60.00 150.00
AFLNH Nico Hoerner/150 8.00 20.00
AFLNP Nate Pearson/50 15.00 40.00
AFLPA Pete Alonso/75 60.00 150.00
AFLRH Ronaldo Hernandez/150 6.00 15.00
AFLRM Ryan McKenna/150 4.00 10.00
AFLSL Shed Long/150 6.00 15.00
AFLZB Zack Burdi/150 4.00 10.00

2019 Bowman Chrome '18 AFL Fall Stars Relics

STATED ODDS 1:483 HOBBY
STATED PRINT RUN 99 SER.#'d SETS
*ORANGE/25: .6X TO 1.5X BASIC
AFLRAG Andres Gimenez 8.00 20.00
AFLRBD Bobby Dalbec 20.00 50.00
AFLRCB Cavan Biggio 10.00 25.00
AFLRCK Carter Kieboom 5.00 12.00
AFLRCP Cristian Pache 8.00 20.00
AFLRCT Cole Tucker 5.00 12.00
AFLRDH Darwinzon Hernandez 3.00 8.00
AFLREF Estevan Florial 8.00 20.00
AFLREW Evan White 8.00 20.00
AFLRFW Forrest Whitley 5.00 12.00
AFLRJD Jon Duplantier 3.00 8.00
AFLRJJ Jahmai Jones 3.00 8.00
AFLRKH Keston Hiura 8.00 20.00
AFLRKL Khalil Lee 3.00 8.00
AFLRKR Keibert Ruiz 15.00 40.00
AFLRLR Luis Robert 12.00 30.00
AFLRNH Nico Hoerner 10.00 25.00
AFLRNP Nate Pearson 10.00 25.00
AFLRPA Peter Alonso 10.00 25.00
AFLRRM Ryan McKenna 3.00 8.00
AFLRSL Shed Long 8.00 20.00
AFLRVGJ Vladimir Guerrero Jr. 20.00 50.00

2019 Bowman Chrome 30th Anniversary

STATED ODDS 1:8 HOBBY
*ATOMIC REF/150: 2.5X TO 6X BASE
*GREEN REF/99: 2.5X TO 6X BASE
*GOLD REF/50: 4X TO 10X BASIC
*ORANGE REF/25: 8X TO 20X BASE
B30AJ Aaron Judge 1.00 2.50
B30AK Alex Kirilloff .40 1.00
B30AN Aaron Nola .30 .75
B30AR Anthony Rizzo .50 1.25
B30BB Bo Bichette .75 2.00
B30BM Brendan McKay .40 1.00
B30BR Brendan Rodgers .40 1.00
B30BS Blake Snell .30 .75
B30CK Carter Kieboom .40 1.00
B30CKE Clayton Kershaw .60 1.50
B30CM Casey Mize .60 1.50
B30CP Cristian Pache .60 1.50
B30DC Dylan Cease .40 1.00
B30EF Estevan Florial .40 1.00
B30EJ Eloy Jimenez 1.00 2.50
B30FL Francisco Lindor .40 1.00
B30FTJ Fernando Tatis Jr. 2.50 6.00
B30FW Forrest Whitley .40 1.00
B30GT Gleyber Torres .75 2.00
B30HG Hunter Greene .40 1.00
B30IA Ian Anderson .75 2.00
B30JA Jo Adell 1.00 2.50
B30JAL Jose Altuve .30 .75
B30JB Joey Bart .75 2.00
B30JD Jacob deGrom .75 2.00
B30JL Jesus Luzardo .40 1.00
B30JPM Julio Pablo Martinez .25 .60
B30JS Justus Sheffield .40 1.00
B30JSO Juan Soto 1.25 3.00
B30KB Kris Bryant .50 1.25
B30KR Keibert Ruiz 1.25 3.00
B30KT Kyle Tucker .60 1.50
B30LU Luis Urias .40 1.00
B30MA Miguel Amaya .40 1.00
B30MB Mookie Betts .75 2.00
B30MG MacKenzie Gore .50 1.25
B30MK Michael Kopech .75 2.00
B30MKE Mitch Keller .30 .75
B30MT Mike Trout 3.00 8.00
B30NG Nolan Gorman .75 2.00
B30NM Nick Madrigal 1.00 2.50
B30NS Nick Senzel .75 2.00
B30RAJ Ronald Acuna Jr. 2.00 5.00
B30RLE Royce Lewis .50 1.25
B30SB Seth Beer .60 1.50
B30SO Shohei Ohtani .60 1.50
B30SS Sixto Sanchez .75 2.00
B30VGJ Vladimir Guerrero Jr. 1.50 4.00
B30WF Wander Franco 5.00 12.00
B30YA Yordan Alvarez 1.25 3.00

2019 Bowman Chrome 30th Anniversary Autographs

STATED ODDS 1:5887 HOBBY
PRINT RUNS B/WN 10-30 COPIES PER
NO PRICING ON QTY 10
EXCHANGE DEADLINE 3/31/2021
B30AR Anthony Rizzo/30 30.00 80.00
B30BS Blake Snell/30 12.00 30.00
B30CM Casey Mize/30 30.00 80.00
B30CP Cristian Pache/30 75.00 200.00
B30FL Francisco Lindor/30 40.00 100.00
B30FTJ Fernando Tatis Jr./30 150.00 400.00
B30HG Hunter Greene/30 15.00 40.00
B30JA Jo Adell/30 40.00 100.00
B30JAL Jose Altuve 12.00 30.00
B30JB Joey Bart/30 100.00 250.00
B30JD Jacob deGrom/30 40.00 100.00
B30JS Justus Sheffield/30 30.00 80.00
B30JSO Juan Soto/30 40.00 100.00
B30KB Kris Bryant/20 50.00 120.00
B30KR Keibert Ruiz/30 20.00 50.00
B30KT Kyle Tucker/30 40.00 100.00
B30LU Luis Urias/30 15.00 40.00
B30MA Miguel Amaya/30 20.00 50.00
B30MG MacKenzie Gore/30 40.00 100.00
B30MK Michael Kopech/30 10.00 25.00
B30MKE Mitch Keller/30 12.00 30.00
B30NM Nick Madrigal/30 40.00 100.00
B30RAJ Ronald Acuna Jr./30 100.00 250.00
B30SB Seth Beer/30 50.00 120.00
B30SS Sixto Sanchez/30 20.00 50.00
B30WF Wander Franco/30 400.00 800.00

2019 Bowman Chrome AFL Alumni

STATED ODDS 1:144 HOBBY
*ORANGE REF/25: 1.2X TO 3X BASE
AFLAAJ Aaron Judge 8.00 20.00
AFLAAP Albert Pujols 4.00 10.00
AFLABB Byron Buxton 3.00 8.00
AFLABH Bryce Harper 5.00 12.00
AFLABP Buster Posey 4.00 10.00
AFLACB Cody Bellinger 6.00 15.00
AFLACK Craig Kimbrel 2.50 6.00
AFLACS Corey Seager 3.00 8.00
AFLADG Didi Gregorius 2.50 6.00
AFLADJ Derek Jeter 10.00 25.00
AFLAFL Francisco Lindor 3.00 8.00
AFLAGB Greg Bird 2.50 6.00
AFLAGS Gary Sanchez 3.00 8.00
AFLAGT Gleyber Torres 6.00 15.00
AFLAHB Harrison Bader 2.50 6.00
AFLAIH Ian Happ 2.50 6.00
AFLAKB Kris Bryant 4.00 10.00
AFLAKD Khris Davis 3.00 8.00
AFLAMB Mookie Betts 6.00 15.00
AFLAMP Mike Piazza 3.00 8.00
AFLAMT Mike Trout 12.00 30.00
AFLANA Nolan Arenado 5.00 12.00
AFLARB Ryan Braun 2.50 6.00
AFLARAJ Ronald Acuna Jr. 15.00 40.00

2019 Bowman Chrome AFL Alumni Autographs

STATED ODDS 1:3806 HOBBY
PRINT RUNS B/WN 14-75 COPIES PER
NO PRICING ON QTY 14 OR LESS
EXCHANGE DEADLINE 8/31/2021
AFLABP Buster Posey/30 25.00 60.00
AFLADG Didi Gregorius/75 12.00 30.00
AFLAFL Francisco Lindor/60 25.00 60.00
AFLAIH Ian Happ/75 8.00 20.00
AFLAKB Kris Bryant/40 30.00 80.00
AFLAMT Mike Trout/25 250.00 500.00
AFLARAJ Ronald Acuna Jr./60 60.00 150.00

2019 Bowman Chrome Autograph Relics

STATED ODDS 1:490 HOBBY
PRINT RUNS B/WN 30-150 COPIES PER
EXCHANGE DEADLINE 8/31/2021
*GOLD/50: .6X TO 1.5X BASIC
BCARAK Andrew Knizner/150 6.00 15.00
BCARAR Anthony Rizzo/75 20.00 50.00
BCARBD Bobby Dalbec/150 25.00 60.00
BCARCR Corey Ray/150 4.00 10.00
BCARDH Darwinzon Hernandez/150 4.00 10.00
BCARDJ Danny Jansen/150 4.00 10.00
BCARFTJ Fernando Tatis Jr. 200.00 500.00
BCARJSO Juan Soto/75 50.00 120.00
BCARKB Kris Bryant/75 50.00 120.00
BCARKH Keston Hiura/150 25.00 60.00
BCARKR Keibert Ruiz/150 10.00 25.00
BCARLU Luis Urias/150 15.00 40.00
BCARMA Miguel Amaya/150 6.00 15.00
BCARMAN Miguel Andujar/75 15.00 40.00
BCARMM Miles Mikolas/150 6.00 15.00
BCARMT Mike Trout/30 300.00 600.00
BCARNH Nico Hoerner/150 15.00 40.00
BCARNL Nate Lowe/150 30.00 80.00
BCARPA Peter Alonso/150 125.00 300.00
BCARPD Paul DeJong/150 8.00 20.00
BCARSM Seuly Matias 8.00 20.00

2019 Bowman Chrome Autograph Relics Orange Refractors

*ORANGE REF: 1X TO 2.5X BASIC
STATED ODDS 1:1523 HOBBY
STATED PRINT RUN 25 SER.#'d SETS
EXCHANGE DEADLINE 8/31/2021
BCARMT Mike Trout 400.00 800.00

2019 Bowman Chrome Bowman Sterling Continuity

STATED ODDS 1:24 HOBBY
*ATOMIC REF/150: 2X TO 5X BASE
*GOLD REF/50: 3X TO 8X BASIC
*ORANGE REF/25: 5X TO 12X BASE
BS1 Shohei Ohtani .75 2.00
BS2 Joey Bart 2.50 6.00
BS3 Brusdar Graterol .40 1.00
BS4 Seuly Matias .40 1.00
BS5 Casey Mize .75 2.00
BS6 Aramis Ademan .30 .75
BS7 Kris Bryant .60 1.50
BS8 Alec Bohm 2.00 5.00
BS9 Estevan Florial .50 1.25
BS10 Wander Franco 6.00 15.00
BS11 Jonathan India 2.00 5.00
BS12 Luis Urias .50 1.25
BS13 Ronaldo Hernandez .30 .75
BS14 Jarred Kelenic 1.50 4.00
BS15 Yordan Alvarez 4.00 10.00
BS16 Kyle Tucker .75 2.00
BS17 Genesis Cabrera .50 1.25
BS18 Nick Madrigal 1.25 3.00
BS19 Julio Pablo Martinez .30 .75
BS20 Mike Trout 3.00 8.00

2019 Bowman Chrome Bowman Sterling Continuity Autographs

STATED ODDS 1:3226 HOBBY
STATED PRINT RUN 99 SER.#'d SETS
EXCHANGE DEADLINE 3/31/2021
BSAAB Alec Bohm 15.00 40.00
BSABG Brusdar Graterol 12.00 30.00
BSACM Casey Mize 30.00 80.00
BSAGC Genesis Cabrera 8.00 20.00
BSAJB Joey Bart 30.00 80.00
BSAJK Jarred Kelenic 40.00 100.00
BSAJPM Julio Pablo Martinez 15.00 40.00
BSAKT Kyle Tucker 15.00 40.00
BSALU Luis Urias 12.00 30.00
BSANM Nick Madrigal 20.00 50.00
BSARH Ronaldo Hernandez 5.00 12.00
BSASM Seuly Matias 6.00 15.00
BSAWF Wander Franco 125.00 300.00

2019 Bowman Chrome Bowman Sterling Continuity Autographs Orange Refractors

*ORANGE REF: .75X TO 2X BASIC
STATED ODDS 1:5226 HOBBY
STATED PRINT RUN 25 SER.#'d SETS
EXCHANGE DEADLINE 3/31/2021
BSAKB Kris Bryant 125.00 300.00
BSAMT Mike Trout 400.00 800.00

2019 Bowman Chrome Dual Prospect Autographs

STATED ODDS 1:20,656 HOBBY
STATED PRINT RUN 25 SER.#'d SETS
EXCHANGE DEADLINE 3/31/2021
DPACW Cruz/Wilson 30.00 80.00
DPAHPM Martinez/Hernandez 10.00 25.00
DPAKM Knizner/Montero 75.00 200.00
DPALH Lowe/Hernandez 25.00 60.00
DPAMB McKenna/Bannon 40.00 100.00
DPAMS Mize/Singer
DPARM Rodriguez/Marte

2019 Bowman Chrome Elite Farmhands

STATED ODDS 1:12 HOBBY
*ATOMIC REF/150: 1X TO 2.5X BASE
*ORANGE REF/25: 3X TO 8X BASE
EFBB Bo Bichette 1.00 2.50
EFCM Casey Mize .75 2.00
EFJA Jordyn Adams .50 1.25
EFJB Joey Bart 1.00 2.50
EFJI Jonathan India 2.00 5.00
EFJK Jarred Kelenic 1.50 4.00
EFJPM Julio Pablo Martinez .30 .75
EFMA Miguel Amaya .50 1.25
EFNG Nolan Gorman 1.00 2.50
EFRL Royce Lewis .60 1.50
EFSM Seuly Matias .40 1.00
EFTS Travis Swaggerty .50 1.25
EFVMJ Victor Mesa Jr. .60 1.50
EFVVM Victor Victor Mesa .60 1.50
EFWF Wander Franco 6.00 15.00

2019 Bowman Chrome Elite Farmhands Autographs

STATED ODDS 1:2133 HOBBY
STATED PRINT RUN 75 SER.#'d SETS
EXCHANGE DEADLINE 8/31/2021
*ORANGE/25: .5X TO 1.5X BASIC
EFACM Casey Mize 12.00 30.00
EFAFTJ Fernando Tatis Jr. 100.00 250.00
EFAJA Jordyn Adams 5.00 12.00
EFAJB Joey Bart 30.00 80.00
EFAJK Jarred Kelenic 50.00 120.00
EFASM Seuly Matias 4.00 10.00
EFAVMJ Victor Mesa Jr. 6.00 15.00
EFAVVM Victor Victor Mesa 6.00 15.00
EFAWF Wander Franco 100.00 250.00

2019 Bowman Chrome Prime Chrome Signatures

STATED ODDS 1:1282 HOBBY
STATED PRINT RUN 50 SER.#'d SETS
EXCHANGE DEADLINE 8/31/2021
*ORANGE/25: .5X TO 1.2X BASIC
PCSAB Alec Bohm 30.00 80.00
PCSAK Andrew Knizner 5.00 12.00
PCSCM Casey Mize 20.00 50.00
PCSDC Diego Cartaya 20.00 50.00
PCSEJ Eloy Jimenez 20.00 50.00
PCSEM Elehuris Montero 20.00 50.00
PCSFTJ Fernando Tatis Jr. EXCH 125.00 300.00
PCSGC Genesis Cabrera 6.00 15.00
PCSJA Jordyn Adams 8.00 20.00
PCSJB Joey Bart 40.00 100.00
PCSJI Jonathan India 20.00 50.00
PCSJK Jarred Kelenic 100.00 250.00
PCSJPM Julio Pablo Martinez 25.00 60.00
PCSJR Julio Rodriguez 60.00 150.00
PCSLG Luis Garcia 25.00 60.00
PCSMA Miguel Amaya 15.00 40.00
PCSNH Nico Hoerner 25.00 60.00
PCSNM Nick Madrigal 25.00 60.00
PCSRH Ronaldo Hernandez 3.00 8.00
PCSRM Ronny Mauricio 20.00 50.00
PCSSB Seth Beer 8.00 20.00
PCSSM Seuly Matias 12.00 30.00
PCSTW Travis Swaggerty 10.00 25.00
PCSVGJ Vladimir Guerrero Jr. 200.00 500.00
PCSVMJ Victor Mesa Jr. 10.00 25.00
PCSVVM Victor Victor Mesa 6.00 15.00
PCSWF Wander Franco 100.00 250.00

2019 Bowman Chrome Prospect Autographs

BOW.STATED ODDS 1:69 HOBBY
BOW.CHR.STATED ODDS 1:9 HOBBY
BOW.PRINTING PLATE ODDS 1:17,064 HOBBY
PLATE PRINT RUN 1 SET PER COLOR
BLACK-CYAN-MAGENTA-YELLOW ISSUED
NO PLATE PRICING DUE TO SCARCITY
BOW.EXCH.DEADLINE 3/31/2021
BOW.CHR.EXCH.DEADLINE 8/31/2021
CPAAB Alec Bohm 60.00 150.00
CPAABE Andrew Bechtold 3.00 8.00
CPAAC Aaron Civale 12.00 30.00
CPAAC Alexander Canario 30.00 80.00
CPAAK Alejandro Kirk 30.00 80.00
CPAAK Andrew Knizner 6.00 15.00
CPAAKL Adam Kloffenstein 5.00 12.00
CPAAT Abraham Toro 6.00 15.00
CPAAW Austin Warner 3.00 8.00
CPABA Bryan Abreu 5.00 12.00
CPABA Blaze Alexander 3.00 8.00
CPABB Brandon Bielak 3.00 8.00
CPABBU Brock Burke 3.00 8.00
CPABD Brock Deatherage 3.00 8.00
CPABH Brewer Hicklen 5.00 12.00
CPABK Blaine Knight 4.00 10.00
CPABM Brailyn Marquez 30.00 80.00
CPABR Brayan Rocchio 12.00 30.00
CPABS Brady Singer 10.00 25.00
CPACC Conner Capel 4.00 10.00
CPACG Casey Golden 8.00 20.00
CPACH Carlos Hernandez 3.00 8.00
CPACI Cole Irvin 3.00 8.00
CPACJ Cristian Javier 12.00 30.00
CPACM Casey Mize 20.00 50.00
CPACMI Cal Mitchell 5.00 12.00
CPACR Cal Raleigh 20.00 50.00
CPACR Cam Roegner 3.00 8.00
CPACS Chad Spanberger 3.00 8.00
CPACSA Cristian Santana 5.00 12.00
CPADC Derian Cruz 3.00 8.00
CPADCA Diego Cartaya 30.00 80.00
CPADD Danny Diaz 5.00 12.00
CPADF Durbin Feltman 3.00 8.00
CPADG Deivi Garcia 30.00 80.00
CPADK Dean Kremer 4.00 10.00
CPADTW Dom Thompson-Williams 4.00 10.00
CPAEC Edward Cabrera 10.00 25.00
CPAEJ Eloy Jimenez 40.00 100.00
CPAEM Elehuris Montero 10.00 25.00
CPAEMO Eli Morgan 3.00 8.00
CPAER Esteury Ruiz 4.00 10.00
CPAEU Edwin Uceta 4.00 10.00
CPAEW Eli White 5.00 12.00
CPAFM Francisco Morales 4.00 10.00
CPAFN Freudis Nova 20.00 50.00
CPAGC Gabriel Cancel 5.00 12.00
CPAGCA Genesis Cabrera 5.00 12.00
CPAGG Gregory Guerrero 5.00 12.00
CPAGP Geraldo Perdomo 25.00 60.00
CPAGW Garrett Whitlock 10.00 25.00
CPAIG Isiah Gilliam 4.00 10.00
CPAIP Israel Pineda 5.00 12.00
CPAIW Isranel Wilson 4.00 10.00
CPAJA Jorge Alcala 3.00 8.00
CPAJB James Bourque 3.00 8.00
CPAJB Joey Bart 100.00 250.00
CPAJD Jose Devers 8.00 20.00
CPAJDU Jhoan Duran 5.00 12.00
CPAJH Jonathan Hernandez 3.00 8.00
CPAJHA Jameson Hannah 4.00 10.00
CPAJM Jonatan Machado 5.00 12.00
CPAJO Jared Oliva 8.00 20.00
CPAJOR Jonathan Ornelas 4.00 10.00
CPAJPM Julio Pablo Martinez 3.00 8.00
CPAJR Julio Rodriguez 125.00 300.00
CPAJS Jose Suarez 3.00 8.00
CPAJY Jordan Yamamoto 3.00 8.00
CPAKP Konnor Pilkington 3.00 8.00
CPAKT Keegan Thompson 3.00 8.00
CPALG Luis Garcia 12.00 30.00
CPALGI Luis Gil 10.00 25.00
CPALJ Leonardo Jimenez 6.00 15.00
CPALR Lyon Richardson 4.00 10.00
CPALS Livan Soto 4.00 10.00
CPALW Logan Webb 5.00 12.00
CPAMA Melvin Adon 5.00 12.00
CPAMAM Miguel Amaya 20.00 50.00
CPAME Mason Englert 3.00 8.00
CPAMG Moises Gomez 5.00 12.00
CPAMG Mateo Gil 4.00 10.00
CPAMH Miguel Hiraldo 10.00 25.00
CPAMK Michael King 5.00 12.00
CPAML Marco Luciano 250.00 600.00
CPAMM Matt Mercer 3.00 8.00
CPAMMA Mason Martin 25.00 60.00
CPAMS Mike Siani 5.00 12.00
CPAMV Matt Vierling 5.00 12.00
CPANG Nick Green 4.00 10.00
CPANL Nate Lowe 40.00 100.00
CPANM Nick Madrigal 20.00 50.00
CPANMA Noelvi Marte 125.00 300.00
CPAOM Orelvis Martinez 60.00 150.00
CPAOM Owen Miller 6.00 15.00
CPAPH Payton Henry 3.00 8.00
CPAPS Patrick Sandoval 3.00 8.00
CPAQTC Quintin Torres-Costa 3.00 8.00
CPARB Rylan Bannon 6.00 15.00
CPARC Ryan Costello 4.00 10.00
CPARF Ryan Feltner 3.00 8.00
CPARG Richard Gallardo 4.00 10.00
CPARH Ronaldo Hernandez 6.00 15.00
CPARL Reggie Lawson 3.00 8.00
CPARM Ronny Mauricio 60.00 150.00
CPARM Ryan McKenna 3.00 8.00
CPARMC Ryan McKenna 3.00 8.00
CPARO Robinson Ortiz 3.00 8.00
CPARR Roberto Ramos 3.00 8.00
CPASB Seth Beer 20.00 50.00
CPASH Sean Hjelle 4.00 10.00
CPASHE Sam Hentges 3.00 8.00
CPASM Seuly Matias 4.00 10.00
CPASN Shervyen Newton 6.00 15.00
CPASW Steele Walker 4.00 10.00
CPATA Telmito Agustin 4.00 10.00
CPATA Telmito Agustin 4.00 10.00
CPATO Tirso Ornelas 3.00 8.00
CPATP Tyler Phillips 3.00 8.00
CPATR Tommy Romero 4.00 10.00
CPATV Terrin Vavra 6.00 15.00
CPAVE Vince Fernandez 3.00 8.00
CPAVF Vince Fernandez 4.00 10.00
CPAVGJ Vladimir Guerrero Jr. 75.00 200.00
CPAVMJ Victor Mesa Jr. 6.00 15.00
CPAVVM Victor Victor Mesa 12.00 30.00
CPAWF Wander Franco 600.00 1500.00
CPAWP Wenceel Perez 5.00 12.00
CPAWS Will Stewart 3.00 8.00
CPAYDR Yefri Del Rosario 3.00 8.00
CPAZB Zack Brown 3.00 8.00

2019 Bowman Chrome Prospect Autographs Atomic Refractors

*ATMOIC REF: .75X TO 2X BASIC
STATED ODDS 1:725 HOBBY
STATED PRINT RUN 100 SER.#'D SETS
EXCHANGE DEADLINE 3/31/2021

2019 Bowman Chrome Prospect Autographs Blue Refractors

*BLUE REF: .75X TO 2X BASIC
BOW.STATED ODDS 1:483 HOBBY
BOW.CHR.STATED ODDS 1:201 HOBBY
STATED PRINT RUN 150 SER.#'D SETS
BOW.EXCH.DEADLINE 3/31/2021
BOW.CHR.EXCH.DEADLINE 8/31/2021

2019 Bowman Chrome Prospect Autographs Gold Refractors

*GOLD REF: 1.5X TO 4X BASIC
BOW.STATED ODDS 1:1399 HOBBY
BOW.CHR.STATED ODDS 1:592 HOBBY
BOW.STATED PRINT RUN 50 SER.#'D SETS
EXCHANGE DEADLINE 3/31/2021
BOW.CHR.EXCH.DEADLINE 8/31/2021
CPAFM Francisco Morales 15.00 40.00
CPAJRO Julio Rodriguez 800.00 1500.00
CPAMG Mateo Gil 25.00 60.00

2019 Bowman Chrome Prospect Autographs Gold Shimmer Refractors

*GOLD SHMR REF: 1.5X TO 4X BASIC
BOW.STATED ODDS 1:1399 HOBBY
STATED PRINT RUN 50 SER.#'D SETS
BOW.EXCH.DEADLINE 3/31/2021
BOW.CHR.EXCH.DEADLINE 8/31/2021
CPAFM Francisco Morales 15.00 40.00
CPAJRO Julio Rodriguez 800.00 1500.00
CPAMG Mateo Gil 25.00 60.00

2019 Bowman Chrome Prospect Autographs Green Refractors

*GREEN REF: .75X TO 2X BASIC
BOW.STATED ODDS 1:366 BLASTER
BOW.CHR.STATED ODDS 1:304 HOBBY
STATED PRINT RUN 99 SER.#'D SETS
BOW.EXCH.DEADLINE 3/31/2021
BOW.CHR.EXCH.DEADLINE 8/31/2021

2019 Bowman Chrome Prospect Autographs Green Atomic Refractors

*GREEN ATMOIC REF: .75X TO 2X BASIC
RANDOM INSERTS IN PACKS
STATED PRINT RUN 99 SER.#'D SETS
BOW.CHR.EXCH.DEADLINE 8/31/2021

2019 Bowman Chrome Prospect Autographs Green Shimmer Refractors

*GRN SHMMR REF: .75X TO 2X BASIC
STATED ODDS 1:366 BLASTER
STATED PRINT RUN 99 SER.#'D SETS
BOW.EXCH.DEADLINE 3/31/2021

2019 Bowman Chrome Prospect Autographs HTA Choice Refractors

2019 Bowman Chrome Prospect Autographs Blue Refractors
2019 Bowman Chrome Prospect Autographs Blue Refractors
2019 Bowman Chrome Prospect Autographs Blue Refractors
2019 Bowman Chrome Prospect Autographs Blue Refractors

2019 Bowman Chrome Prospect Autographs Orange Refractors

*ORNGE REF: 3X TO 8X BASIC
BOW.STATED ODDS 1:793 HOBBY
BOW.CHR.STATED ODDS 1:636 HOBBY
STATED PRINT RUN 25 SER.#'D SETS
BOW.EXCH.DEADLINE 3/31/2021
BOW.CHR.EXCH.DEADLINE 8/31/2021
CPAFM Francisco Morales 30.00 80.00
CPAJRO Julio Rodriguez 1500.00 3000.00
CPAMG Mateo Gil 50.00 120.00

2019 Bowman Chrome Prospect Autographs Orange Shimmer Refractors

*ORNGE SHMMR REF: 3X TO 8X BASIC
STATED ODDS 1:793 HOBBY
STATED PRINT RUN 25 SER.#'D SETS
BOW.EXCH.DEADLINE 3/31/2021
CPAJRO Julio Rodriguez 1500.00 3000.00
CPAMG Mateo Gil 50.00 120.00

2019 Bowman Chrome Prospect Autographs Orange Wave Refractors

*ORNGE WAVE REF: 3X TO 8X BASIC
RANDOM INSERTS IN PACKS
STATED PRINT RUN 25 SER.#'D SETS
BOW.CHR.EXCH.DEADLINE 8/31/2021
CPAFM Francisco Morales 30.00 80.00

2019 Bowman Chrome Prospect Autographs Purple Refractors

*PURPLE REF: .6X TO 1.5X BASIC
BOW.STATED ODDS 1:312 HOBBY
BOW.CHR.STATED ODDS 1:120 HOBBY
STATED PRINT RUN 250 SER.#'D SETS
BOW.EXCH.DEADLINE 3/31/2021
BOW.CHR.EXCH.DEADLINE 8/31/2021

2019 Bowman Chrome Prospect Autographs Refractors

*REF: .5X TO 1.2X BASIC
BOW.STATED ODDS 1:151 HOBBY
BOW.CHR.STATED ODDS 1:61 HOBBY
STATED PRINT RUN 499 SER.#'D SETS
BOW.EXCH.DEADLINE 3/31/2021
BOW.CHR.EXCH.DEADLINE 8/31/2021

2019 Bowman Chrome Prospect Autographs Speckle Refractors

*SPECKLE REF: .6X TO 1.5X BASIC
STATED ODDS 1:261 HOBBY
STATED PRINT RUN 299 SER.#'D SETS
EXCHANGE DADLINE 3/31/2021

2019 Bowman Chrome Prospects

BOW.PLATE ODDS 1:8920 HOBBY
PLATE PRINT RUN 1 SET PER COLOR
BLACK-CYAN-MAGENTA-YELLOW ISSUED
NO PLATE PRICING DUE TO SCARCITY
BCP1 Vladimir Guerrero Jr. 2.50 6.00
BCP2 Alec Bohm 1.25 3.00
BCP3 Justin Dunn .20 .50
BCP4 Jo Adell .75 2.00
BCP5 Victor Victor Mesa .40 1.00
BCP6 Brusdar Graterol .25 .60
BCP7 Tirso Ornelas .20 .50
BCP8 Nick Neidert .20 .50
BCP9 Taylor Widener .20 .50
BCP10 Adrian Morejon .20 .50
BCP11 Derian Cruz .20 .50
BCP12 Corey Ray .20 .50
BCP13 Jarred Kelenic 1.00 2.50
BCP14 Seth Beer .50 1.25
BCP15 Ethan Hankins .25 .60
BCP16 Cole Tucker .30 .75
BCP17 A.J. Puk .30 .75
BCP18 Leody Taveras .30 .75
BCP19 Logan Allen .20 .50
BCP20 Blake Rutherford .20 .50
BCP21 Freudis Nova .30 .75
BCP22 Daniel Johnson .20 .50
BCP23 Rylan Bannon .25 .60
BCP24 Taylor Trammell .30 .75
BCP25 Fernando Tatis Jr. 4.00 10.00
BCP26 Beau Burrows .20 .50
BCP27 Jay Groome .20 .50
BCP28 Adam Haseley .30 .75
BCP29 Adonis Medina .30 .75
BCP30 Julio Pablo Martinez .20 .50
BCP31 Evan White .50 1.25
BCP32 Cristian Javier .25 .60
BCP33 Julio Rodriguez 12.00 30.00
BCP34 Domingo Acevedo .20 .50
BCP35 Miguel Amaya .30 .75
BCP36 Ryan Vilade .20 .50
BCP37 JoJo Romero .20 .50
BCP38 Sandro Fabian .20 .50
BCP39 Franklyn Kilome .20 .50
BCP40 Triston McKenzie .60 1.50
BCP41 Ryan Mountcastle 1.00 2.50
BCP42 Jordyn Adams .30 .75
BCP43 Nick Senzel .60 1.50
BCP44 Luis Robert 3.00 8.00
BCP45 Brent Rooker .25 .60
BCP46 Anthony Seigler .30 .75
BCP47 Ian Anderson .60 1.50
BCP48 Griffin Canning .30 .75
BCP49 Casey Mize .50 1.25
BCP50 Joey Bart 3.00 8.00
BCP51 Hunter Greene .30 .75
BCP52 Forrest Whitley .30 .75
BCP53 Blaze Alexander .20 .50
BCP54 Keston Hiura .60 1.50
BCP55 Chris Paddack .40 1.00
BCP56 Franklin Perez .20 .50
BCP57 Joey Wentz .20 .50
BCP58 Kevin Smith .20 .50
BCP59 Nico Hoerner .60 1.50
BCP60 Nolan Gorman .60 1.50
BCP61 Jazz Chisholm .75 2.00
BCP62 Cristian Pache .50 1.25
BCP63 Nick Madrigal .75 2.00
BCP64 Luis Garcia .75 2.00
BCP65 Colton Welker .20 .50
BCP66 Ryan Weathers .20 .50
BCP67 Jonathan Duplantier .20 .50
BCP68 Reggie Lawson .20 .50
BCP69 Orelvis Martinez 8.00 20.00
BCP70 Sixto Sanchez .60 1.50
BCP71 Ke'Bryan Hayes 1.00 2.50
BCP72 Brewer Hicklen .30 .75
BCP73 MacKenzie Gore .40 1.00
BCP74 Estevan Florial .30 .75
BCP75 Cole Winn .30 .75
BCP76 Zack Collins .25 .60
BCP77 Andres Gimenez .50 1.25
BCP78 Alex Faedo .25 .60
BCP79 Logan Webb .30 .75
BCP80 Dustin May .60 1.50
BCP81 Ryan McKenna .20 .50
BCP82 Marco Luciano 20.00 50.00
BCP83 Heliot Ramos .30 .75
BCP84 Aramis Ademan .20 .50
BCP85 Matt Manning .30 .75
BCP86 Daz Cameron .20 .50
BCP87 Chad Spanberger .20 .50
BCP88 Brent Honeywell .25 .60
BCP89 Esteury Ruiz .25 .60
BCP90 Keegan Thompson .20 .50
BCP91 Will Smith .50 1.25
BCP92 Michael Chavis .30 .75
BCP93 Travis Swaggerty .30 .75
BCP94 Dane Dunning .60 1.50
BCP95 Lyon Richardson .25 .60
BCP96 Jesus Luzardo .30 .75
BCP97 Noelvi Marte 10.00 25.00
BCP98 Carter Kieboom .30 .75
BCP99 Nate Pearson .60 1.50
BCP100 Wander Franco 40.00 100.00
BCP101 Ryan Costello .25 .60
BCP102 Jonathan India 2.00 5.00
BCP103 Royce Lewis .40 1.00
BCP104 Victor Mesa Jr. 2.00 5.00
BCP105 Brendan McKay .30 .75
BCP106 Michel Baez .20 .50
BCP107 Ronny Mauricio .50 1.25
BCP108 Anthony Kay .20 .50
BCP109 Yusniel Diaz .30 .75
BCP110 Brady Singer 1.00 2.50
BCP111 Bo Bichette .60 1.50
BCP112 Matthew Liberatore .20 .50
BCP113 Dylan Cease .30 .75
BCP114 Edward Cabrera .30 .75
BCP115 Jeter Downs .30 .75
BCP116 Luken Baker .25 .60
BCP117 Shane Baz .20 .50
BCP118 Keibert Ruiz 1.00 2.50
BCP119 Jonathan Hernandez .20 .50
BCP120 Matt Mercer .20 .50
BCP121 Ryan Helsley .25 .60
BCP122 Cole Ragans .20 .50
BCP123 Yordan Alvarez 3.00 8.00
BCP124 DJ Peters .30 .75
BCP125 Cal Quantrill .20 .50
BCP126 Drew Waters .60 1.50
BCP127 Peter Alonso 2.00 5.00
BCP128 MJ Melendez .30 .75
BCP129 Austin Riley 1.00 2.50
BCP130 Gavin Lux .75 2.00
BCP131 Brandon Marsh .75 2.00
BCP132 Andrew Knizner .30 .75
BCP133 Mitch Keller .25 .60
BCP134 Cristian Santana .30 .75
BCP135 Jesus Sanchez .30 .75
BCP136 Peter Lambert .30 .75
BCP137 Brock Burke .20 .50
BCP138 Alex Kirilloff .30 .75
BCP139 DL Hall .20 .50
BCP140 Bryan Mata .20 .50
BCP141 Austin Beck .20 .50
BCP142 Genesis Cabrera .30 .75
BCP143 Brendan Rodgers .30 .75
BCP144 Sean Murphy .25 .60
BCP145 Roberto Ramos .25 .60
BCP146 Ronaldo Hernandez .20 .50
BCP147 Albert Abreu .20 .50
BCP148 William Contreras .25 .60
BCP149 Jose de la Cruz .60 1.50
BCP150 Eloy Jimenez .75 2.00
BCP151 Royce Lewis .40 1.00
BCP152 Zack Brown .20 .50
BCP153 Robinson Ortiz .20 .50
BCP154 Bobby Dalbec 1.25 3.00
BCP155 Nolan Jones .30 .75
BCP156 Tim Tebow 1.50 4.00
BCP157 Bryan Abreu .30 .75
BCP158 Taylor Trammell .30 .75
BCP159 Adbert Alzolay .20 .50
BCP160 Roansy Contreras .50 1.25
BCP161 Spencer Howard .60 1.50
BCP162 Michael King .30 .75
BCP163 Alec Bohm 1.25 3.00
BCP164 Micker Adolfo .20 .50
BCP165 Kristian Robinson 1.00 2.50
BCP166 Eric Pardinho .25 .60
BCP167 Jarred Kelenic 1.00 2.50
BCP168 Eli White .30 .75
BCP169 Nick Green .25 .60
BCP170 Owen Miller .25 .60
BCP171 Brice Turang .25 .60
BCP172 Mitchell White .20 .50
BCP173 Nick Madrigal .75 2.00
BCP174 Joey Bart .60 1.50
BCP175 Parker Meadows .25 .60
BCP176 Jose Devers .30 .75
BCP177 Austin Warner .20 .50
BCP178 Jahmai Jones .20 .50
BCP179 Daulton Varsho .20 .50
BCP180 Leonardo Jimenez .30 .75
BCP181 Grayson Rodriguez .40 1.00
BCP182 Estevan Florial .30 .75
BCP183 Sean Hjelle .25 .60
BCP184 Miguel Hiraldo .60 1.50
BCP185 Jesus Sanchez .30 .75
BCP186 Alex Kirilloff .30 .75
BCP187 Genesis Cabrera .30 .75
BCP188 Richard Gallardo .25 .60
BCP189 Kyle Funkhouser .20 .50
BCP190 Nick Pratto .20 .50
BCP191 Geraldo Perdomo 4.00 10.00
BCP192 Logan Gilbert .30 .75
BCP193 Anderson Tejeda .30 .75
BCP194 Bo Naylor .20 .50
BCP195 Kyle Muller .20 .50
BCP196 Ryan Rolison .20 .50
BCP197 Hansel Moreno .20 .50
BCP198 Jameson Hannah .25 .60
BCP199 Tony Santillan .20 .50
BCP200 Victor Victor Mesa .40 1.00
BCP201 Briam Campusano .20 .50
BCP202 Alejandro Kirk .75 2.00
BCP203 Jordan Yamamoto .20 .50
BCP204 Isiah Gilliam .25 .60
BCP205 Sixto Sanchez .60 1.50
BCP206 Wander Javier .30 .75
BCP207 Corey Ray .20 .50
BCP208 Aramis Ademan .20 .50
BCP209 Brayan Rocchio .75 2.00
BCP210 Hans Crouse .20 .50
BCP211 Shaun Anderson .20 .50
BCP212 Lazaro Armenteros .25 .60
BCP213 Triston Casas .75 2.00
BCP214 Deon Stafford .25 .60
BCP215 Khalil Lee .20 .50
BCP216 Wenceel Perez .30 .75
BCP217 Jorge Mateo .20 .50
BCP218 Luis Gil .30 .75
BCP219 Mason Englert .20 .50
BCP220 Konnor Pilkington .20 .50
BCP221 Nolan Gorman .60 1.50
BCP222 Garrett Whitlock .30 .75
BCP223 Mason Denaburg .25 .60
BCP224 Joe Jacques .20 .50
BCP225 Jhoan Duran .30 .75
BCP226 Grant Lavigne .25 .60
BCP227 Corbin Martin .20 .50
BCP228 Mike Siani .30 .75
BCP229 Ryan Feltner .20 .50
BCP230 Hudson Potts .20 .50
BCP231 Ryan McKenna .20 .50
BCP232 Tommy Wilson .20 .50
BCP233 J.B. Bukauskas .20 .50
BCP234 Bo Bichette .60 1.50
BCP235 Keibert Ruiz 1.00 2.50
BCP236 Patrick Sandoval .20 .50
BCP237 Luis Garcia .75 2.00
BCP238 Cam Roegner .20 .50
BCP239 Brendan McKay .30 .75
BCP240 Casey Mize .50 1.25
BCP241 Deivi Garcia 2.00 5.00
BCP242 Quintin Torres-Costa .20 .50
BCP243 Yefri Del Rosario .20 .50
BCP244 Francisco Morales .25 .60
BCP245 MacKenzie Gore .40 1.00
BCP246 Sam Hentges .20 .50
BCP247 Israel Pineda .30 .75
BCP248 Shervyen Newton .30 .75
BCP249 Clarke Schmidt .30 .75
BCP250 Jo Adell .75 2.00

2019 Bowman Chrome Prospects Aqua Refractors

*AQUA REF: 2.5X TO 6X BASIC
STATED ODDS 1:151 HOBBY
STATED PRINT RUN 125 SER.#'d SETS

2019 Bowman Chrome Prospects Aqua Shimmer Refractors
*AQUA SHIM REF: 2.5X TO 6X BASIC
STATED ODDS 1:151 HOBBY
STATED PRINT RUN 125 SER.#'d SETS

2019 Bowman Chrome Prospects Atomic Refractors
*ATOMIC REF: 1.5X TO 4X BASIC
STATED ODDS 1:24 HOBBY

2019 Bowman Chrome Prospects Blue Refractors
*BLUE REF: 2X TO 5X BASIC
BOW.STATED ODDS 1:238 HOBBY
BOW.CHR.ODDS 1:71 HOBBY
STATED PRINT RUN 150 SER.#'d SETS

2019 Bowman Chrome Prospects Blue Shimmer Refractors
*BLUE SHIM REF: 2X TO 5X BASIC
STATED ODDS 1:238 HOBBY
STATED PRINT RUN 150 SER.#'d SETS

2019 Bowman Chrome Prospects Gold Refractors
*GOLD REF: 6X TO 15X BASIC
BOW.STATED ODDS 1:711 HOBBY
BOW.CHR.ODDS 1:211 HOBBY
STATED PRINT RUN 50 SER.#'d SETS

2019 Bowman Chrome Prospects Gold Shimmer Refractors
*GOLD SHIM REF: 6X TO 15X BASIC
BOW.STATED ODDS 1:711 HOBBY
BOW.CHR.ODDS 1:211 HOBBY
STATED PRINT RUN 50 SER.#'d SETS

2019 Bowman Chrome Prospects Green Refractors
*GREEN REF: 3X TO 8X BASIC
BOW.STATED ODDS 1:141 RETAIL
BOW.CHR.ODDS 1:107 HOBBY
STATED PRINT RUN 99 SER.#'d SETS

2019 Bowman Chrome Prospects Green Shimmer Refractors
*GREEN SHIM REF: 3X TO 8X BASIC
BOW.STATED ODDS 1:141 RETAIL
BOW.CHR.ODDS 1:107 HOBBY
STATED PRINT RUN 99 SER.#'d SETS

2019 Bowman Chrome Prospects Orange Refractors
*ORANGE REF: 10X TO 25X BASIC
BOW.STATED ODDS 1:329 HOBBY
BOW.CHR.ODDS 1:421 HOBBY
STATED PRINT RUN 25 SER.#'d SETS

2019 Bowman Chrome Prospects Orange Shimmer Refractors
*ORANGE SHIM REF: 10X TO 25X BASIC
BOW.CHR.ODDS 1:421 HOBBY
BOW.STATED ODDS 1:329 HOBBY
STATED PRINT RUN 25 SER.#'d SETS

2019 Bowman Chrome Prospects Purple Refractors
*PURPLE REF: 1.5X TO 4X BASIC
BOW.STATED ODDS 1:143 HOBBY
BOW.CHR.ODDS 1:43 HOBBY
STATED PRINT RUN 250 SER.#'d SETS

2019 Bowman Chrome Prospects Purple Shimmer Refractors
*PURPLE SHIM REF: 1.2X TO 3X BASIC
BOW.CHR.ODDS 1:15 HOBBY

2019 Bowman Chrome Prospects Refractors
*REF: 1.2X TO 3X BASIC
BOW.STATED ODDS 1:72 HOBBY
BOW.CHR.ODDS 1:21 HOBBY
STATED PRINT RUN 499 SER.#'d SETS

2019 Bowman Chrome Prospects Speckle Refractors
*SPECKLE REF: 1.5X TO 4X BASIC
STATED ODDS 1:119 HOBBY
STATED PRINT RUN 299 SER.#'d SETS

2019 Bowman Chrome Prospects Yellow Refractors
*YELLOW REF: 4X TO 10X BASIC
STATED ODDS 1:474 HOBBY
STATED PRINT RUN 75 SER.#'d SETS

2019 Bowman Chrome Ready for the Show
STATED ODDS 1:6 HOBBY
*ATOMIC REF/150: 2.5X TO 6X BASE
*GREEN REF/99: 2.5X TO 6X BASE
*GOLD REF/50: 4X TO 10X BASIC
*ORANGE REF/25: 8X TO 20X BASE
RFTS1 Vladimir Guerrero Jr. 1.50 4.00
RFTS2 Bo Bichette .75 2.00
RFTS3 Triston McKenzie .75 2.00
RFTS4 Mitch Keller .30 .75
RFTS5 Will Smith .60 1.50
RFTS6 Jon Duplantier .25 .60
RFTS7 Austin Riley 1.25 3.00
RFTS8 Ryan Mountcastle 1.25 3.00
RFTS9 Nick Senzel .75 2.00
RFTS10 Fernando Tatis Jr. 4.00 10.00
RFTS11 Peter Alonso 2.00 5.00
RFTS12 Forrest Whitley .40 1.00
RFTS13 Yusniel Diaz .40 1.00
RFTS14 Brendan McKay .40 1.00
RFTS15 Jesus Luzardo .40 1.00
RFTS16 Brendan Rodgers .40 1.00
RFTS17 Yordan Alvarez 1.25 3.00
RFTS18 Keston Hiura .75 2.00
RFTS19 Brent Honeywell .30 .75
RFTS20 Eloy Jimenez 1.00 2.50

2019 Bowman Chrome Rookie Autographs
BOW.STATED ODDS 1:551 HOBBY
BOW.CHR.STATED ODDS 1:482 HOBBY
BOW.PRINTING PLATE ODDS 1:69,259 HOBBY
PLATE PRINT RUN 1 SET PER COLOR
BLACK-CYAN-MAGENTA-YELLOW ISSUED
NO PLATE PRICING DUE TO SCARCITY
BOW.EXCH.DEADLINE 3/31/2021
BOW.CHR.EXCH.8/31/2021
CRACA C.Adams Blue jrsy 3.00 8.00
CRACA C.Adams Gry jrsy 3.00 8.00
CRACB C.Burns Arm back 30.00 80.00
CRACB C.Burns Leg Up 30.00 80.00
CRACM Cedric Mullins 8.00 20.00
CRACST Chris Shaw 3.00 8.00
CRADJ Danny Jansen Batting 5.00 12.00
CRADJ Danny Jansen Catching 5.00 12.00
CRADS DJ Stewart 4.00 10.00
CRAFTJ Fernando Tatis Jr. 150.00 400.00
CRAJB Jake Bauers 5.00 12.00
CRAJC Jake Cave 4.00 10.00
CRAJS J.Sheffield M's 5.00 12.00
CRAJS J.Sheffield Yanks 5.00 12.00
CRAKA Kolby Allard 5.00 12.00
CRAKT Kyle Tucker 15.00 40.00
CRAKW K.Wright Face forward 4.00 10.00
CRAKW K.Wright Face right 4.00 10.00
CRALU Luis Urias 5.00 12.00
CRAMK Michael Kopech 12.00 30.00
CRARB Ryan Borucki 3.00 8.00
CRARB Ryan Borucki 3.00 8.00
CRAROG Ryan O'Hearn 3.00 8.00
CRAWA Willians Astudillo 3.00 8.00
CRAYK Y.Kikuchi EXCH 10.00 25.00
CRAYK Y.Kikuchi Drk blue jrsy 10.00 25.00

2019 Bowman Chrome Rookie Autographs Atomic Refractors
*ATOMIC REF: .6X TO 1.5X BASIC
STATED ODDS 1:2751 HOBBY
STATED PRINT RUN 100 SER.#'d SETS
EXCHANGE DEADLINE 3/31/2021

2019 Bowman Chrome Rookie Autographs Blue Refractors
*BLUE REF: .6X TO 1.5X BASIC
BOW.STATED ODDS 1:1834 JUMBO
BOW.CHR.STATED ODDS 1:2133
STATED PRINT RUN 150 SER.#'d SETS
BOW.EXCH.DEADLINE 3/31/2021
BOW.CHR.EXCH.DEADLINE 8/31/2021
CRAKH Keston Hiura 50.00 120.00

2019 Bowman Chrome Rookie Autographs Gold Refractors
*GOLD REF: 1.2X TO 3X BASIC
BOW.STATED ODDS 1:5502 HOBBY
BOW.CHR.STATED ODDS 1:2404 HOBBY
STATED PRINT RUN 50 SER.#'d SETS
BOW.EXCH.DEADLINE 3/31/2021
BOW.CHR.EXCH.DEADLINE 8/31/2021
CRAFTJ Fernando Tatis Jr. 600.00 1500.00
CRAKH Keston Hiura 100.00 250.00
CRAPA Pete Alonso 500.00 1000.00
CRAVGJ Vladimir Guerrero Jr. 400.00 800.00

2019 Bowman Chrome Rookie Autographs Green Refractors
*GREEN REF: .6X TO 1.5X BASIC
BOW.STATED ODDS 1:1442 RETAIL
BOW.CHR.STATED ODDS 1:3231 HOBBY
STATED PRINT RUN 99 SER.#'d SETS
BOW.EXCH.DEADLINE 3/31/2021
BOW.CHR.EXCH.DEADLINE 8/31/2021
CRAFTJ Fernando Tatis Jr. 300.00 800.00
CRAKH Keston Hiura 50.00 120.00
CRAPA Pete Alonso 250.00 500.00
CRAVGJ Vladimir Guerrero Jr. 200.00 400.00

2019 Bowman Chrome Rookie Autographs Orange Refractors
*ORANGE REF: 2X TO 5X BASIC
BOW.STATED ODDS 1:3226 HOBBY
BOW.CHR.STATED ODDS 1:2570 HOBBY
STATED PRINT RUN 25 SER.#'d SETS
BOW.EXCH.DEADLINE 3/31/2021
BOW.CHR.EXCH.DEADLINE 8/31/2021
CRAFTJ Fernando Tatis Jr. 1000.00 2500.00
CRAKH Keston Hiura 150.00 400.00
CRAPA Pete Alonso 800.00 1500.00
CRAVGJ Vladimir Guerrero Jr. 600.00 1200.00

2019 Bowman Chrome Rookie Autographs Refractors
*REF: .6X TO 1.2X BASIC
BOW.STATED ODDS 1:552 HOBBY
BOW.CHR.STATED ODDS 1:642 HOBBY
STATED PRINT RUN 499 SER.#'D SETS
BOW.EXCH.DEADLINE 3/31/2021
BOW.CHR.EXCH 8/31/2021
CRAKH Keston Hiura 40.00 100.00

2019 Bowman Chrome Rookie of the Year Favorites
STATED ODDS 1:11 HOBBY
*ATOMIC REF/150: 2.5X TO 6X BASE
*GREEN REF/99: 2.5X TO 6X BASE
*GOLD REF/50: 4X TO 10X BASIC
*ORANGE REF/25: 8X TO 20X BASE
ROYF1 Kyle Tucker .60 1.50
ROYF2 Brandon Lowe .40 1.00
ROYF3 Dawel Lugo .40 1.00
ROYF4 Luis Urias .40 1.00
ROYF5 Chance Adams .25 .60
ROYF6 Danny Jansen .25 .60
ROYF7 Kyle Wright .40 1.00
ROYF8 Chris Shaw .25 .60
ROYF9 Kolby Allard .40 1.00
ROYF10 Christin Stewart .30 .75
ROYF11 Justus Sheffield .40 1.00

2019 Bowman Chrome Rookie of the Year Favorites Autographs
STATED ODDS 1:2500 HOBBY
STATED PRINT RUN 150 SER.#'d SETS
EXCHANGE DEADLINE 3/31/2021
*GOLD REF/50: .6X TO 1.5X BASIC
*ORANGE REF/25: 1X TO 2.5X BASIC
ROYFCM Cedric Mullins 12.00 30.00
ROYFKW Kyle Wright 6.00 15.00
ROYFACB Corbin Burnes 12.00 30.00
ROYFADJ Danny Jansen 4.00 10.00
ROYFAJB Jake Bauers 6.00 15.00
ROYFAJS Justus Sheffield 6.00 15.00
ROYFAKA Kolby Allard 6.00 15.00
ROYFAKT Kyle Tucker 10.00 25.00
ROYFALU Luis Urias 10.00 25.00
ROYFAMK Michael Kopech 10.00 25.00
ROYFROH Ryan O'Hearn 4.00 10.00

2019 Bowman Chrome Scouts Top 100
STATED ODDS 1:4 HOBBY
*ATOMIC REF/150: 2.5X TO 6X BASE
*GREEN REF/99: 2.5X TO 6X BASE
*GOLD REF/50: 4X TO 10X BASIC
*ORANGE REF/25: 6X TO 15X BASE
BTP1 Vladimir Guerrero Jr. 1.50 4.00
BTP2 Eloy Jimenez 1.00 2.50
BTP3 Fernando Tatis Jr. 4.00 10.00
BTP4 Wander Franco 2.50 6.00
BTP5 Forrest Whitley .40 1.00
BTP6 Victor Robles .50 1.25
BTP7 Bo Bichette .75 2.00
BTP8 Michael Kopech .75 2.00
BTP9 Jo Adell 1.00 2.50
BTP10 Royce Lewis .50 1.25
BTP11 Nick Senzel .75 2.00
BTP12 Casey Mize .60 1.50
BTP13 Alex Kirilloff .40 1.00
BTP14 MacKenzie Gore .50 1.25
BTP15 Kyle Tucker .60 1.50
BTP16 Brendan Rodgers .40 1.00
BTP17 Jesus Luzardo .40 1.00
BTP18 Sixto Sanchez .75 2.00
BTP19 Dylan Cease .40 1.00
BTP20 Justus Sheffield .40 1.00
BTP21 Mitch Keller .30 .75
BTP22 Mike Soroka .40 1.00
BTP23 Nick Madrigal 1.00 2.50
BTP24 Keibert Ruiz 1.25 3.00
BTP25 Ian Anderson .75 2.00
BTP26 Taylor Trammell .40 1.00
BTP27 Keston Hiura .75 2.00
BTP28 Touki Toussaint .30 .75
BTP29 Brent Honeywell .30 .75
BTP30 Adrian Morejon .25 .60
BTP31 Cristian Pache .60 1.50
BTP32 Ke'Bryan Hayes 1.25 3.00
BTP33 Joey Bart 2.50 6.00
BTP34 Griffin Canning .40 1.00
BTP35 Francisco Mejia .30 .75
BTP36 Andres Gimenez .60 1.50
BTP37 Brendan McKay .40 1.00
BTP38 Brady Singer 1.25 3.00
BTP39 Jarred Kelenic 1.25 3.00
BTP40 Luis Urias .40 1.00
BTP41 Austin Riley 1.25 3.00
BTP42 Alex Reyes .30 .75
BTP43 A.J. Puk .40 1.00
BTP44 Carter Kieboom .40 1.00
BTP45 Hunter Greene .40 1.00
BTP46 Yordan Alvarez 1.25 3.00
BTP47 Luis Robert 2.00 5.00
BTP48 Kyle Wright .40 1.00
BTP49 Corbin Burnes 2.00 5.00
BTP50 Sean Murphy .30 .75
BTP51 Jon Duplantier .25 .60
BTP52 Peter Alonso 3.00 8.00
BTP53 Alex Verdugo .30 .75
BTP54 Luis Garcia 1.00 2.50
BTP55 Nolan Gorman .75 2.00
BTP56 Jonathan Loaisiga .30 .75
BTP57 Jesus Sanchez .40 1.00
BTP58 Bryse Wilson .30 .75
BTP59 Luiz Gohara .25 .60
BTP60 Dakota Hudson .30 .75
BTP61 Chris Paddack .50 1.25
BTP62 Triston McKenzie .75 2.00
BTP63 Jazz Chisholm 1.00 2.50
BTP64 Jason Groome .25 .60
BTP65 Adonis Medina .40 1.00
BTP66 Dustin May .75 2.00
BTP67 Yusniel Diaz .40 1.00
BTP68 Jonathan India 1.50 4.00
BTP69 D.L. Hall .25 .60
BTP70 Oneil Cruz .40 1.00
BTP71 Estevan Florial .40 1.00
BTP72 Sandy Alcantara .25 .60
BTP73 Travis Swaggerty .40 1.00
BTP74 Nate Pearson .75 2.00
BTP75 Leody Taveras .40 1.00
BTP76 Ronny Mauricio .60 1.50
BTP77 Matthew Liberatore .25 .60
BTP78 Brandon Marsh .40 1.00
BTP79 Khalil Lee .25 .60
BTP80 Alex Scherff .40 1.00
BTP81 Miguel Amaya .40 1.00
BTP82 Brice Turang .30 .75
BTP83 Jackson Kowar .75 2.00
BTP84 Daz Cameron .25 .60
BTP85 Nolan Jones .40 1.00
BTP86 Franklin Perez .25 .60
BTP87 Cole Winn .25 .60
BTP88 Kyle Lewis .50 1.25
BTP89 Brusdar Graterol .30 .75
BTP90 Logan Allen .25 .60
BTP91 Taylor Widener .25 .60
BTP92 Grayson Rodriguez .50 1.25
BTP93 Michel Baez .25 .60
BTP94 Corey Ray .30 .75
BTP95 Evan White .60 1.50
BTP96 Peter Lambert .40 1.00
BTP97 George Valera .50 1.25
BTP98 Matt Manning .40 1.00
BTP99 Luis Patino .40 1.00
BTP100 Julio Pablo Martinez .25 .60

2019 Bowman Chrome Scouts Top 100 Autographs
STATED ODDS 1:1832 HOBBY
PRINT RUNS B/WN 20-50 COPIES PER
EXCHANGE DEADLINE 3/31/2021
BTP3 Fernando Tatis Jr./50 125.00 300.00
BTP4 Wander Franco/50 125.00 300.00
BTP8 Michael Kopech/50 15.00 40.00
BTP9 Jo Adell/50 30.00 80.00
BTP10 Royce Lewis/50 15.00 40.00
BTP12 Casey Mize/50 30.00 80.00
BTP14 MacKenzie Gore/50 10.00 25.00
BTP15 Kyle Tucker/50 20.00 50.00
BTP18 Sixto Sanchez/50 20.00 50.00
BTP20 Justus Sheffield/50 8.00 20.00
BTP21 Mitch Keller/50 6.00 15.00
BTP23 Nick Madrigal/50 30.00 80.00
BTP24 Keibert Ruiz/50 20.00 50.00
BTP27 Keston Hiura/35 20.00 50.00
BTP28 Touki Toussaint/50 6.00 15.00
BTP31 Cristian Pache/50 40.00 100.00
BTP33 Joey Bart/50 60.00 150.00
BTP34 Griffin Canning/50 10.00 25.00
BTP38 Brady Singer/50 15.00 40.00
BTP39 Jarred Kelenic/50 100.00 250.00
BTP43 A.J. Puk/20 40.00 100.00
BTP44 Carter Kieboom/50 8.00 20.00
BTP45 Hunter Greene/50 15.00 40.00
BTP47 Luis Robert/35 50.00 120.00
BTP48 Kyle Wright/50 8.00 20.00
BTP49 Corbin Burnes/50 25.00 60.00
BTP50 Sean Murphy/50 6.00 15.00
BTP51 Jon Duplantier/50 5.00 12.00
BTP55 Nolan Gorman/50 25.00 60.00
BTP56 Jonathan Loaisiga/50 6.00 15.00
BTP57 Jesus Sanchez/50 8.00 20.00
BTP58 Bryse Wilson/50 6.00 15.00
BTP60 Dakota Hudson/50 6.00 15.00
BTP66 Dustin May/50 20.00 50.00
BTP67 Yusniel Diaz/50 8.00 20.00
BTP68 Jonathan India/50 25.00 60.00
BTP72 Sandy Alcantara/50 5.00 12.00
BTP73 Travis Swaggerty/50 8.00 20.00
BTP74 Nate Pearson/50 8.00 20.00
BTP76 Ronny Mauricio/50 12.00 30.00
BTP77 Matthew Liberatore/50 5.00 12.00
BTP78 Brandon Marsh/50 8.00 20.00
BTP81 Miguel Amaya/50 8.00 20.00
BTP82 Brice Turang/50 6.00 15.00
BTP83 Jackson Kowar/50 10.00 25.00
BTP84 Daz Cameron/50 8.00 20.00
BTP86 Franklin Perez/50 5.00 12.00
BTP87 Cole Winn/50 8.00 20.00
BTP91 Taylor Widener/50 5.00 12.00
BTP93 Michel Baez/50 5.00 12.00
BTP94 Corey Ray/50 15.00 40.00
BTP95 Evan White/50 12.00 30.00
BTP96 Peter Lambert/50 8.00 20.00
BTP100 Julio Pablo Martinez/50 30.00 80.00

2019 Bowman Chrome Stat Tracker
STATED ODDS 1:3 HOBBY
*ATOMIC REF/150: 1X TO 2.5X BASE
*ORANGE REF/25: 3X TO 8X BASE
STAB Alec Bohm 1.50 4.00
STAK Andrew Knizner .40 1.00
STAM Adonis Medina .40 1.00
STBD Brock Deatherage .25 .60
STBS Brady Singer 1.25 3.00
STBT Brice Turang .30 .75
STCM Casey Mize .60 1.50
STCS Connor Scott .30 .75
STDW Drew Waters .75 2.00
STEM Elehuris Montero .40 1.00
STGC Genesis Cabrera .40 1.00
STHC Hans Crouse .25 .60
STJA Jordyn Adams .40 1.00
STJB Joey Bart .75 2.00
STJG Jordan Groshans .50 1.25
STJI Jonathan India 1.50 4.00
STJK Jarred Kelenic 1.25 3.00
STJPM Julio Pablo Martinez .25 .60
STMA Miguel Amaya .40 1.00
STNG Nolan Gorman .75 2.00
STNH Nico Hoerner .75 2.00
STNM Nick Madrigal 1.00 2.50
STRH Ronaldo Hernandez .25 .60
STRM Ronny Mauricio .60 1.50
STRW Ryan Weathers .25 .60
STSB Seth Beer .60 1.50
STSM Seuly Matias .30 .75
STTS Travis Swaggerty .40 1.00
STVB Vidal Brujan 2.00 5.00
STWF Wander Franco 5.00 12.00

2019 Bowman Chrome Stat Tracker Autographs
STATED ODDS 1:777 HOBBY
STATED PRINT RUN 75 SER.#'d SETS
EXCHANGE DEADLINE 8/31/2021
*ORANGE/25: .6X TO 1.5X BASIC
STAAK Andrew Knizner 8.00 20.00
STABS Brady Singer 10.00 25.00
STABT Brice Turang 8.00 20.00
STACM Casey Mize 8.00 20.00
STACS Connor Scott 12.00 30.00
STAEM Elehuris Montero 6.00 15.00
STAFTJ Fernando Tatis Jr. EXCH 125.00 300.00
STAGC Genesis Cabrera 5.00 12.00
STAJA Jordyn Adams 5.00 12.00
STAJB Joey Bart 25.00 60.00
STAJG Jordan Groshans 6.00 15.00
STAJI Jonathan India 20.00 50.00
STAMA Miguel Amaya 10.00 25.00
STANH Nico Hoerner 20.00 50.00
STANM Nick Madrigal 10.00 25.00
STARH Ronaldo Hernandez 3.00 8.00
STARM Ronny Mauricio 8.00 20.00
STASB Seth Beer 12.00 30.00
STASM Seuly Matias 8.00 20.00
STAWF Wander Franco 75.00 200.00

2019 Bowman Chrome Talent Pipeline
STATED ODDS 1:12 HOBBY
*ATOMIC REF/150: 2X TO 5X BASE
*GREEN REF/99: 2X TO 5X BASE
*GOLD REF/50: 3X TO 8X BASIC
*ORANGE REF/25: 5X TO 12X BASE
TPARI Jazz Chisholm 1.25 3.00
 Taylor Clarke
 Taylor Widener
TPATL Riley/Anderson/Contreras 1.50 4.00
TPBAL DJ Stewart 1.50 4.00
 Ryan Mountcastle
 DL Hall
TPBOS Josh Ockimey 2.00 5.00
 Bryan Mata
 Bobby Dalbec
TPCHI Alzolay/Hatch/Hoerner 1.00 2.50
TPCIN Long/Greene/Senzel 1.00 2.50
TPCLE Yu Chang 1.00 2.50
 Triston McKenzie
 Nolan Jones
TPCOL Brendan Rodgers .50 1.25
 Colton Welker
 Roberto Ramos
TPCWS Collins/Jimenez/Rutherford 1.25 3.00
TPDET Hall/Mize/Rogers .75 2.00
TPHOU Alvarez/Whitley/Beer 1.50 4.00
TPKCR Lopez/Lee/Matias .50 1.25
TPLAA Thaiss/Adell/Marsh 1.25 3.00
TPLAD Smith/White/Kendall .75 2.00
TPMIA Nick Neidert .40 1.00
 Austin Dean
 Tristan Pompey
TPMIL Burnes/Hiura/Lutz 2.50 6.00
TPMIN Nick Gordon .50 1.25
 Brent Rooker
 Alex Kirilloff
TPNYM Alonso/Gimenez/Kay 2.50 6.00
TPNYY Adams/Stephan/Florial .50 1.25
TPOAK Jesus Luzardo .50 1.25
 Skye Bolt
 Austin Beck
TPPHI Ranger Suarez .50 1.25
 Darick Hall
 Adam Haseley
TPPIT Mitch Keller 1.50 4.00
 Ke'Bryan Hayes
 Luis Escobar
TPSDP Urias/Gore/Naylor .60 1.50
TPSEA Ian Miller .75 2.00
 Evan White
 Braden Bishop
TPSFG Shaw/Anderson/Bart 1.00 2.50
TPSTL Knizner/Montero/Cabrera .50 1.25
TPTBR Honeywell/Hernandez/Solak 1.25 3.00
TPTEX Andy Ibanez .50 1.25
 Jonathan Hernandez
 Leody Taveras
TPTOR Vlad Jr/Pearson/Bichette 2.00 5.00
TPWAS Ward/Garcia/Kieboom 1.25 3.00

2019 Bowman Chrome Draft
COMPLETE SET (200) 30.00 80.00
STATED PLATE ODDS 1:1241 HOBBY
PLATE PRINT RUN 1 SET PER COLOR
BLACK-CYAN-MAGENTA-YELLOW ISSUED
NO PLATE PRICING DUE TO SCARCITY
BDC1 Adley Rutschman 20.00 50.00
BDC2 Jarred Kelenic 1.25 3.00
BDC3 Alek Manoah .50 1.25
BDC4 Grant McCray .40 1.00
BDC5 Brock Deatherage .25 .60
BDC6 Matt Wallner .50 1.25
BDC7 Josh Jung 2.50 6.00
BDC8 Andres Gimenez .60 1.50
BDC9 Jackson Kowar .75 2.00
BDC10 Logan Davidson .25 .60
BDC11 Isaiah Campbell .50 1.25
BDC12 Blake Walston .40 1.00
BDC13 Izzy Wilson .25 .60
BDC14 Yordys Valdes .50 1.25
BDC15 Alec Marsh .30 .75
BDC16 Ryan Zeferjahn .30 .75
BDC17 Brady McConnell .40 1.00
BDC18 Jordan Groshans .50 1.25
BDC19 Sammy Siani .30 .75
BDC20 Kristian Robinson 1.25 3.00
BDC21 Eric Pardinho .30 .75
BDC22 Gunnar Henderson .50 1.25
BDC23 Joseph Ortiz .30 .75
BDC24 Justin Slaten .25 .60
BDC25 Drew Waters .75 2.00
BDC26 Cal Mitchell .40 1.00
BDC27 Daniel Espino .30 .75
BDC28 Ethan Small .30 .75
BDC29 Logan Wyatt .40 1.00
BDC30 Estevan Florial .40 1.00
BDC31 Hunter Bishop 2.50 6.00
BDC32 Thomas Dillard .50 1.25
BDC33 DL Hall .25 .60
BDC34 T.J. Sikkema .40 1.00
BDC35 Dominic Fletcher .25 .60
BDC36 Antoine Kelly .50 1.25
BDC37 Albert Abreu .25 .60
BDC38 Mateo Gil .30 .75
BDC39 Brett Baty 3.00 8.00
BDC40 Brandon Lewis .40 1.00
BDC41 Jamari Baylor .60 1.50
BDC42 Nolan Gorman .75 2.00
BDC43 Jack Little .40 1.00
BDC44 Quinn Priester .30 .75
BDC45 Freudis Nova .40 1.00
BDC46 Royce Lewis .50 1.25
BDC47 Tyler Callihan .30 .75
BDC48 Matthew Allan 2.00 5.00
BDC49 Will Stewart .25 .60
BDC50 Riley Greene 6.00 15.00
BDC51 Ethan Hankins .30 .75
BDC52 Derian Cruz .25 .60
BDC53 Andre Pallante .30 .75
BDC54 Dane Dunning .75 2.00
BDC55 Matt Mercer .25 .60
BDC56 Chris Murphy .25 .60
BDC57 Michael Busch .75 2.00
BDC58 James Beard .75 2.00
BDC59 Braden Shewmake .75 2.00
BDC60 Julio Rodriguez 2.00 5.00
BDC61 JJ Goss .30 .75
BDC62 Ronny Mauricio .60 1.50
BDC63 Dasan Brown .60 1.50
BDC64 Michael Toglia 1.25 3.00
BDC65 Keoni Cavaco 1.25 3.00
BDC66 Greg Jones 1.25 3.00
BDC67 Shea Langeliers 1.50 4.00
BDC68 Evan Fitterer .60 1.50
BDC69 Hudson Head 1.25 3.00
BDC70 Tony Locey .30 .75
BDC71 Julio Pablo Martinez .25 .60
BDC72 Jake Agnos .40 1.00
BDC73 Matt Gorski .40 1.00
BDC74 Peyton Burdick 1.00 2.50
BDC75 Brewer Hicklen .40 1.00
BDC76 Kyle Stowers .40 1.00
BDC77 Erik Rivera .50 1.25
BDC78 Leonardo Jimenez .40 1.00
BDC79 Bryson Stott 5.00 12.00
BDC80 Cristian Santana .40 1.00
BDC81 Davis Wendzel .40 1.00
BDC82 Jake Sanford .50 1.25
BDC83 Casey Golden .40 1.00
BDC84 Tirso Ornelas .25 .60
BDC85 CJ Abrams 5.00 12.00
BDC86 Josh Smith .50 1.25
BDC87 Triston Casas 1.00 2.50
BDC88 Victor Victor Mesa .50 1.25
BDC89 Sixto Sanchez .75 2.00
BDC90 Seth Johnson .25 .60
BDC91 Ryan Jensen .40 1.00
BDC92 Tim Tebow 1.25 3.00
BDC93 Wander Franco 6.00 15.00
BDC94 Matthew Thompson .30 .75
BDC95 Jake Mangum 1.00 2.50
BDC96 Jake Guenther .30 .75
BDC97 Jonathan India 1.50 4.00
BDC98 Jack Kochanowicz .30 .75
BDC99 Noah Song .75 2.00
BDC100 Andrew Vaughn 10.00 25.00
BDC101 Anthony Prato .25 .60
BDC102 Domingo Acevedo .25 .60
BDC103 MacKenzie Gore .50 1.25
BDC104 Zack Thompson .40 1.00
BDC105 Nick Quintana .50 1.25
BDC106 Kyle Isbel .30 .75
BDC107 Ryan Weathers .25 .60
BDC108 Andre Lipcius .30 .75
BDC109 Tyler Baum .30 .75
BDC110 Conner Capel .30 .75
BDC111 Michael Massey .30 .75
BDC112 Diosbel Arias .25 .60
BDC113 Brandon Williamson .40 1.00
BDC114 Jeter Downs .40 1.00
BDC115 George Kirby .40 1.00
BDC116 Graeme Stinson .25 .60
BDC117 Brent Rooker .30 .75
BDC118 Eric Yang .30 .75
BDC119 Josh Wolf .30 .75
BDC120 Andrew Schultz .25 .60
BDC121 Grayson Rodriguez .50 1.25
BDC122 MJ Melendez .40 1.00
BDC123 Bryant Packard .40 1.00
BDC124 Aramis Ademan .25 .60
BDC125 Corbin Carroll 2.00 5.00
BDC126 Kyle McCann .30 .75
BDC127 Matthew Liberatore .25 .60
BDC128 Beau Philip .40 1.00
BDC129 Aaron Schunk .50 1.25
BDC130 Brice Turang .30 .75
BDC131 Rece Hinds 1.50 4.00
BDC132 Jimmy Lewis .25 .60
BDC133 Will Robertson .40 1.00
BDC134 Joey Bart .75 2.00
BDC135 Miguel Amaya .40 1.00
BDC136 Jonathan Ornelas .30 .75
BDC137 Vince Fernandez .30 .75
BDC138 Grant Gambrell .30 .75
BDC139 Matthew Lugo .75 2.00
BDC140 Korey Lee .50 1.25
BDC141 Nasim Nunez .25 .60
BDC142 Denyi Reyes .30 .75
BDC143 Moises Gomez .40 1.00
BDC144 John Rave .25 .60
BDC145 Grae Kessinger .40 1.00
BDC146 Isiah Gilliam .30 .75
BDC147 Ryne Nelson .30 .75
BDC148 Ryan Garcia .25 .60
BDC149 Matt Canterino .30 .75
BDC150 J.J. Bleday 5.00 12.00
BDC151 Ryan Costello .30 .75
BDC152 Tyler Fitzgerald .30 .75
BDC153 Spencer Steer .25 .60
BDC154 Jose Devers .40 1.00
BDC155 Blaze Alexander .25 .60
BDC156 John Doxakis .30 .75
BDC157 Armani Smith .75 2.00
BDC158 Jordyn Adams .40 1.00
BDC159 Sean Hjelle .30 .75
BDC160 Cristian Javier .30 .75
BDC161 Jared Triolo .40 1.00
BDC162 Alec Bohm 1.50 4.00
BDC163 Jahmai Jones .25 .60
BDC164 Deivi Garcia 2.50 6.00
BDC165 Brennan Malone .25 .60
BDC166 Cameron Cannon .50 1.25
BDC167 Glenallen Hill Jr. .40 1.00
BDC168 Evan Edwards .25 .60
BDC169 Shervyen Newton .40 1.00
BDC170 Travis Swaggerty .40 1.00
BDC171 Anthony Seigler .40 1.00
BDC172 Evan White .60 1.50
BDC173 Luken Baker .30 .75
BDC174 Trejyn Fletcher .40 1.00
BDC175 Spencer Brickhouse .60 1.50
BDC176 Daulton Varsho .40 1.00
BDC177 Hayden Wesneski .30 .75
BDC178 Chase Strumpf 1.25 3.00
BDC179 Logan Gilbert .40 1.00
BDC180 Joshua Mears 1.25 3.00
BDC181 Matt Vierling .40 1.00
BDC182 Will Wilson 1.25 3.00
BDC183 Logan Driscoll .40 1.00
BDC184 Tyler Freeman .25 .60
BDC185 Ian Anderson .75 2.00
BDC186 Owen Miller .30 .75
BDC187 Kody Hoese 1.50 4.00
BDC188 Grant Lavigne .30 .75
BDC189 Nick Lodolo .50 1.25
BDC190 Clarke Schmidt .40 1.00
BDC191 Erik Miller .60 1.50
BDC192 Seth Beer .60 1.50
BDC193 Alejandro Kirk 1.00 2.50
BDC194 Drey Jameson .25 .60
BDC195 Christian Cairo .40 1.00
BDC196 Kameron Misner .60 1.50
BDC197 Tommy Henry .30 .75
BDC198 Lazaro Armenteros .30 .75
BDC199 Kendall Williams .40 1.00
BDC200 Cooper Johnson .40 1.00

2019 Bowman Chrome Draft Blue Refractors
*BLUE REF: 2X TO 5X BASIC
STATED ODDS 1:34 HOBBY
STATED PRINT RUN 150 SER.#'d SETS

2019 Bowman Chrome Draft Gold Refractors
*GOLD REF: 5X TO 12X BASIC
STATED ODDS 1:100 HOBBY
STATED PRINT RUN 50 SER.#'d SETS

2019 Bowman Chrome Draft Green Refractors
*GREEN REF: 2.5X TO 6X BASIC
STATED ODDS 1:51 HOBBY
STATED PRINT RUN 99 SER.#'d SETS

2019 Bowman Chrome Draft Orange Refractors
*ORANGE REF: 8X TO 20X BASIC
STATED ODDS 1:134 HOBBY
STATED PRINT RUN 25 SER.#'d SETS

2019 Bowman Chrome Draft Purple Refractors
*PURPLE REF: 1.5X TO 4X BASIC
STATED ODDS 1:20 HOBBY
STATED PRINT RUN 250 SER.#'d SETS

2019 Bowman Chrome Draft Refractors
*REF: .75X TO 2X BASIC
RANDOM INSERTS IN PACKS

2019 Bowman Chrome Draft Sky Blue Refractors
*SKY BLUE REF: 1X TO 2.5X BASIC
STATED ODDS 1:8 HOBBY

2019 Bowman Chrome Draft Sparkle Refractors
*SPARKLE REF: 1.5X TO 4X BASIC
STATED ODDS 1:24 HOBBY

2019 Bowman Chrome Draft Image Variations
STATED ODDS 1:203 HOBBY
BDC1 Adley Rutschman 30.00 80.00
BDC3 Alek Manoah 8.00 20.00
BDC7 Josh Jung 12.00 30.00
BDC31 Hunter Bishop 12.00 30.00
BDC50 Riley Greene 25.00 60.00
BDC67 Shea Langeliers 8.00 20.00
BDC85 CJ Abrams 15.00 40.00
BDC88 Victor Victor Mesa 8.00 20.00
BDC93 Wander Franco 30.00 80.00
BDC100 Andrew Vaughn 12.00 30.00
BDC134 Joey Bart 12.00 30.00
BDC150 J.J. Bleday 20.00 50.00
BDC189 Nick Lodolo 8.00 20.00
BDC192 Seth Beer 10.00 25.00

2019 Bowman Chrome Draft Image Variation Autographs
STATED ODDS 1:691 HOBBY
STATED PRINT RUN 99 SER.#'d SETS
EXCHANGE DEADLINE 11/30/2021
BDC1 Adley Rutschman 400.00 800.00
BDC7 Josh Jung 250.00 500.00
BDC50 Riley Greene 250.00 500.00
BDC67 Shea Langeliers 150.00 300.00
BDC85 CJ Abrams 200.00 400.00
BDC88 Victor Victor Mesa 40.00 100.00
BDC93 Wander Franco 300.00 600.00
BDC100 Andrew Vaughn 250.00 500.00
BDC134 Joey Bart 125.00 300.00
BDC150 J.J. Bleday 200.00 400.00
BDC189 Nick Lodolo 50.00 120.00
BDC192 Seth Beer 50.00 120.00

2019 Bowman Chrome Draft Autographs
STATED ODDS 1:9 HOBBY
PRINTING PLATE ODDS 1:3201 HOBBY
PLATE PRINT RUN 1 SET PER COLOR
BLACK-CYAN-MAGENTA-YELLOW ISSUED
NO PLATE PRICING DUE TO SCARCITY
EXCHANGE DEADLINE 11/30/2021
CDAAK Antoine Kelly 6.00 15.00
CDAAL Andre Lipcius 4.00 10.00
CDAAM Alek Manoah 20.00 50.00
CDAAMA Alec Marsh 4.00 10.00
CDAAR Adley Rutschman 200.00 500.00
CDAAS Aaron Schunk 8.00 20.00
CDAAV Andrew Vaughn 150.00 400.00
CDABB Brett Baty 40.00 100.00
CDABM Brennan Malone 3.00 8.00
CDABMC Brady McConnell 5.00 12.00
CDABP Beau Philip 8.00 20.00
CDABS Bryson Stott 25.00 60.00
CDABSH Braden Shewmake 20.00 50.00
CDABW Blake Walston 5.00 12.00
CDABWI Brandon Williamson 8.00 20.00
CDACA CJ Abrams 200.00 500.00
CDACC Corbin Carroll 60.00 150.00
CDACCA Cameron Cannon 6.00 15.00
CDACS Chase Strumpf 15.00 40.00
CDADB Dasan Brown 8.00 20.00
CDADE Daniel Espino 12.00 30.00
CDADF Dominic Fletcher 8.00 20.00
CDADJ Drey Jameson 3.00 8.00
CDADW Davis Wendzel 8.00 20.00
CDAES Ethan Small 6.00 15.00
CDAGH Gunnar Henderson 30.00 80.00
CDAGJ Greg Jones 15.00 40.00
CDAGK George Kirby 20.00 50.00
CDAGM Grant McCray 5.00 12.00
CDAHB Hunter Bishop 40.00 100.00
CDAIC Isaiah Campbell 6.00 15.00
CDAJB Jamari Baylor 8.00 20.00
CDAJD John Doxakis 4.00 10.00
CDAJJ Josh Jung 60.00 150.00
CDAJJB J.J. Bleday 75.00 200.00
CDAJJG JJ Goss 4.00 10.00
CDAJK Jack Kochanowicz 4.00 10.00
CDAJL Jimmy Lewis 3.00 8.00
CDAJM Joshua Mears 20.00 50.00
CDAJS Josh Smith 6.00 15.00
CDAJSA Jake Sanford 10.00 25.00
CDAJT Jared Triolo 5.00 12.00

CDAJW Josh Wolf 4.00 10.00
CDAKC Keoni Cavaco 20.00 50.00
CDAKH Kody Hoese 20.00 50.00
CDAKM Kameron Misner 25.00 60.00
CDAKP Kyren Paris 15.00 40.00
CDAKS Kyle Stowers 5.00 12.00
CDAKW Kendall Williams 5.00 12.00
CDALD Logan Davidson 3.00 8.00
CDALDR Logan Driscoll 5.00 12.00
CDALW Logan Wyatt 5.00 12.00
CDAMB Michael Busch 25.00 60.00
CDAMC Matt Canterino 4.00 10.00
CDAMG Matt Gorski 5.00 12.00
CDAML Matthew Lugo
CDAMT Michael Toglia 15.00 40.00
CDAMTH Matthew Thompson 10.00 25.00
CDAMW Matt Wallner 10.00 25.00
CDANL Nick Lodolo 15.00 40.00
CDANN Nasim Nunez 8.00 20.00
CDANQ Nick Quintana 6.00 15.00
CDANS Noah Song 10.00 25.00
CDAPB Peyton Burdick 30.00 80.00
CDAQP Quinn Priester 25.00 60.00
CDARG Riley Greene 150.00 400.00
CDARGA Ryan Garcia 3.00 8.00
CDARH Rece Hinds 25.00 60.00
CDARJ Ryan Jensen 5.00 12.00
CDARN Ryne Nelson 4.00 10.00
CDARZ Ryan Zeferjahn 4.00 10.00
CDASJ Seth Johnson 3.00 8.00
CDASL Shea Langeliers 40.00 100.00
CDASS Sammy Siani 4.00 10.00
CDASST Spencer Steer 3.00 8.00
CDATB Tyler Baum 4.00 10.00
CDATC Tyler Callihan 12.00 30.00
CDATH Tommy Henry 4.00 10.00
CDATJS T.J. Sikkema 5.00 12.00
CDAWW Will Wilson 10.00 25.00
CDAZT Zack Thompson 10.00 25.00

2019 Bowman Chrome Draft Autographs Black Refractors

*BLACK REF: 1X TO 2.5X BASIC
STATED ODDS 1:117 HOBBY
STATED PRINT RUN 75 SER.#'D SETS
EXCHANGE DEADLINE 11/30/2021
CDAKM Kameron Misner 50.00 120.00
CDAML Matthew Lugo 40.00 100.00

2019 Bowman Chrome Draft Autographs Blue Refractors

*BLUE REF: .75X TO 2X BASIC
STATED ODDS 1:86 HOBBY
STATED PRINT RUN 150 SER.#'D SETS
EXCHANGE DEADLINE 11/30/2021
CDAKM Kameron Misner 40.00 100.00
CDAML Matthew Lugo 30.00 80.00

2019 Bowman Chrome Draft Autographs Blue Wave Refractors

*BLUE WAVE REF: .75X TO 2X BASIC
STATED ODDS 1:86 HOBBY
STATED PRINT RUN 150 SER.#'D SETS
EXCHANGE DEADLINE 11/30/2021
CDAKM Kameron Misner 40.00 100.00
CDAML Matthew Lugo 30.00 80.00

2019 Bowman Chrome Draft Autographs Gold Refractors

*GOLD REF: 1.5X TO 4X BASIC
STATED ODDS 1:256 HOBBY
STATED PRINT RUN 50 SER.#'D SETS
EXCHANGE DEADLINE 11/30/2021
CDAKM Kameron Misner 75.00 200.00
CDAML Matthew Lugo 60.00 150.00

2019 Bowman Chrome Draft Autographs Gold Wave Refractors

*GOLD WAVE REF: 1.5X TO 4X BASIC
STATED ODDS 1:256 HOBBY
STATED PRINT RUN 50 SER.#'D SETS
EXCHANGE DEADLINE 11/30/2021
CDAKM Kameron Misner 75.00 200.00
CDAML Matthew Lugo 60.00 150.00

2019 Bowman Chrome Draft Autographs Green Refractors

*GREEN REF: .75X TO 2X BASIC
STATED ODDS 1:130 HOBBY
STATED PRINT RUN 99 SER.#'D SETS
EXCHANGE DEADLINE 11/30/2021
CDAKM Kameron Misner 40.00 100.00
CDAML Matthew Lugo 30.00 80.00

2019 Bowman Chrome Draft Autographs Orange Refractors

*ORANGE REF: 3X TO 8X BASIC
STATED ODDS 1:350 HOBBY
STATED PRINT RUN 25 SER.#'D SETS
EXCHANGE DEADLINE 11/30/2021
CDAKM Kameron Misner 150.00 400.00
CDAML Matthew Lugo 125.00 300.00

2019 Bowman Chrome Draft Autographs Purple Refractors

*PURPLE REF: .6X TO 1.5X BASIC
STATED ODDS 1:52 HOBBY
STATED PRINT RUN 250 SER.#'D SETS
EXCHANGE DEADLINE 11/30/2021
CDAKM Kameron Misner 30.00 80.00
CDAML Matthew Lugo 25.00 60.00

2019 Bowman Chrome Draft Autographs Refractors

*REF: .5X TO 1.2X BASIC
STATED ODDS 1:26 HOBBY
STATED PRINT RUN 499 SER.#'D SETS
EXCHANGE DEADLINE 11/30/2021
CDAML Matthew Lugo 20.00 50.00

2019 Bowman Chrome Draft Autographs Sparkle Refractors

*SPARKLE REF: 1X TO 2.5X BASIC
STATED ODDS 1:180 HOBBY
STATED PRINT RUN 71 SER.#'D SETS
EXCHANGE DEADLINE 11/30/2021
CDAKM Kameron Misner 50.00 120.00
CDAML Matthew Lugo 40.00 100.00

2019 Bowman Chrome Draft Bowman 30th Anniversary

STATED ODDS 1:12 HOBBY
*ATOMIC REF/150: 2X TO 5X BASE
*ORANGE REF/25: 6X TO 15X BASE
B30AR Adley Rutschman 2.00 5.00
B30AV Andrew Vaughn 1.00 2.50
B30CJA CJ Abrams 1.50 4.00
B30JB Joey Bart 1.00 2.50
B30JJ Josh Jung 1.00 2.50
B30JJB J.J. Bleday 1.50 4.00
B30RG Riley Greene 2.00 5.00
B30SB Seth Beer .75 2.00
B30VVM Victor Victor Mesa .60 1.50
B30WF Wander Franco 2.00 5.00

2019 Bowman Chrome Draft Bowman 30th Anniversary Autographs

STATED ODDS 1:967 HOBBY
STATED PRINT RUN 99 SER.#'d SETS
EXCHANGE DEADLINE 11/30/2021
*ORANGE/25: .6X TO 1.5X BASIC
B30AAR Adley Rutschman 100.00 250.00
B30AAV Andrew Vaughn 40.00 100.00
B30ACJA CJ Abrams 50.00 120.00
B30AJB Joey Bart 40.00 100.00
B30AJJB J.J. Bleday 50.00 120.00
B30ANL Nick Lodolo 10.00 25.00
B30ARG Riley Greene 40.00 100.00
B30ASB Seth Beer 12.00 30.00
B30AVVM Victor Victor Mesa 12.00 30.00
B30AWF Wander Franco 100.00 250.00

2019 Bowman Chrome Draft Class of '19 Autographs

STATED ODDS 1:116 HOBBY
STATED PRINT RUN 99 SER.#'d SETS
EXCHANGE DEADLINE 11/30/2021
C19AAM Alek Manoah 10.00 25.00
C19AAR Adley Rutschman 50.00 120.00
C19AAV Andrew Vaughn 40.00 100.00
C19ABB Brett Baty 15.00 40.00
C19ABM Brennan Malone 5.00 12.00
C19ABS Bryson Stott 10.00 25.00
C19ABSH Braden Shewmake 10.00 25.00
C19ABW Blake Walston 5.00 12.00
C19ACC Corbin Carroll 12.00 30.00
C19ACJA CJ Abrams 25.00 60.00
C19ADE Daniel Espino 8.00 20.00
C19AES Ethan Small 4.00 10.00
C19AGJ Greg Jones 8.00 20.00
C19AGK George Kirby 5.00 12.00
C19AHB Hunter Bishop 15.00 40.00
C19AJJ Josh Jung 15.00 40.00
C19AJJB J.J. Bleday 20.00 50.00
C19AKC Keoni Cavaco 10.00 25.00
C19AKH Kody Hoese 15.00 40.00
C19AKL Korey Lee 15.00 40.00
C19ALD Logan Davidson 8.00 20.00
C19AMB Michael Busch 10.00 25.00
C19AMT Michael Toglia 12.00 30.00
C19ANL Nick Lodolo 12.00 30.00
C19AQP Quinn Priester 6.00 15.00
C19ARG Riley Greene 30.00 80.00
C19ARJ Ryan Jensen 5.00 12.00
C19ASL Shea Langeliers 15.00 40.00
C19ASS Sammy Siani 8.00 20.00
C19AWW Will Wilson 10.00 25.00
C19AZT Zack Thompson 5.00 12.00

2019 Bowman Chrome Draft Class of '19 Autographs Gold Refractors

*GOLD REF: .6X TO 1.5X BASIC
STATED ODDS 1:670 HOBBY
STATED PRINT RUN 50 SER.#'d SETS
EXCHANGE DEADLINE 11/30/2021

2019 Bowman Chrome Draft Draft Night Autographs

STATED ODDS 1:3233 HOBBY
STATED PRINT RUN 99 SER.#'d SETS
EXCHANGE DEADLINE 11/30/2021
*GOLD/50: .5X TO 1.2X BASIC
*ORANGE/25: .6X TO 1.5X BASIC
DNABB Brett Baty 30.00 80.00
DNABM Brennan Malone 10.00 25.00
DNADE Daniel Espino 12.00 30.00

2019 Bowman Chrome Draft Draft Pick Breakdown

STATED ODDS 1:6 HOBBY
*REF/250: .6X TO 1.5X BASE
*GREEN REF/250: .75X TO 2X BASE
*GOLD REF/50: 1.5X TO 4X BASE
BSBAM Alek Manoah .50 1.25
BSBAR Adley Rutschman 1.50 4.00
BSBAV Andrew Vaughn .75 2.00
BSBCA CJ Abrams 1.25 3.00
BSBHB Hunter Bishop .75 2.00
BSBJJ Josh Jung .75 2.00
BSBJJB J.J. Bleday 1.25 3.00
BSBNL Nick Lodolo .50 1.25
BSBRG Riley Greene 1.50 4.00
BSBSL Shea Langeliers .50 1.25

2019 Bowman Chrome Draft Draft Pick Breakdown Autographs

STATED ODDS 1:967 HOBBY
STATED PRINT RUN 99 SER.#'d SETS
EXCHANGE DEADLINE 11/30/2021
BSBAAM Alek Manoah 10.00 25.00
BSBAAR Adley Rutschman 60.00 150.00
BSBAAV Andrew Vaughn 30.00 80.00
BSBACA CJ Abrams 20.00 50.00
BSBAJJ Josh Jung 25.00 60.00
BSBAJJB J.J. Bleday 25.00 60.00
BSBANL Nick Lodolo 12.00 30.00
BSBARG Riley Greene 25.00 60.00
BSBASL Shea Langeliers 20.00 50.00

2019 Bowman Chrome Draft Draft Progression

STATED ODDS 1:3 HOBBY
*REF/250: .6X TO 1.5X BASE
*GREEN REF/250: .75X TO 2X BASE
*GOLD REF/50: 1.5X TO 4X BASE
DPRARI Smith/Carroll/McCarthy .40 1.00
DPRATL Waters/Jenista/Langeliers .75 2.00
DPRBAL Rutschman/Rodriguez/Hall 1.50 4.00
DPRCIN Lodolo/Greene/India 1.50 4.00
DPRCWS Vaughn/Burger/Madrigal 1.00 2.50
DPRDET Greene/Faedo/Mize 1.50 4.00
DPRMIA Scott/Bleday/Rogers 1.25 3.00
DPRNYM Cortes/Baty/Peterson .50 1.25
DPRPIT Priester/Mitchell/Swaggerty .40 1.00
DPRSDP Abrams/Gore/Weathers 1.25 3.00
DPRSFG Bishop/Bart/Ramos .75 2.00
DPRSTL Thompson/Kirtley/Gorman .75 2.00
DPRTEX Seise/Jung/Winn .75 2.00
DPRTOR Pearson/Groshans/Manoah .75 2.00

2019 Bowman Chrome Draft Franchise Futures

STATED ODDS 1:3 HOBBY
*REF/250: .6X TO 1.5X BASE
*GREEN REF/250: .75X TO 2X BASE
*GOLD REF/50: 1.5X TO 4X BASE
FFAM C.Abrams/J.Mears 1.25 3.00
FFBM J.Bleday/K.Misner 1.25 3.00
FFCW M.Wallner/K.Cavaco .60 1.50
FFGQ N.Quintana/R.Greene 1.50 4.00
FFHB M.Busch/K.Hoese .75 2.00
FFLS S.Langeliers/B.Shewmake .75 2.00
FFPS S.Siani/Q.Priester .30 .75
FFRH A.Rutschman/G.Henderson 1.50 4.00
FFVT A.Vaughn/M.Thompson .75 2.00
FFWMA B.Walston/B.Malone .40 1.00

2019 Bowman Chrome Draft Franchise Futures Autographs

STATED ODDS 1:745 HOBBY
STATED PRINT RUN 99 SER.#'d SETS
EXCHANGE DEADLINE 11/30/2021
*GOLD/50: .5X TO 1.2X BASIC
*ORANGE/25: .6X TO 1.5X BASIC
FFAAM C.Abrams/J.Mears 25.00 60.00
FFABM J.Bleday/K.Misner 30.00 80.00
FFACW M.Wallner/K.Cavaco 20.00 50.00
FFAGQ N.Quintana/R.Greene 30.00 80.00
FFAHB Busch/Hoese EXCH 30.00 80.00
FFAJG J.Goss/G.Jones 10.00 25.00
FFALS S.Langeliers/B.Shewmake 30.00 80.00
FFAMW K.Williams/A.Manoah 10.00 25.00
FFAPS S.Siani/Q.Priester 6.00 15.00
FFARH Rtschmn/Hndrsn EXCH 75.00 200.00
FFAWMA B.Walston/B.Malone 8.00 20.00

2019 Bowman Chrome Draft Top of the Class Box Toppers

RANDOM INSERTS IN HOBBY BOXES
STATED PRINT RUN 99 SER.#'d SETS
*GOLD/50: .5X TO 1.2X BASIC
TOCAM Alek Manoah 4.00 10.00
TOCAR Adley Rutschman 12.00 30.00
TOCAV Andrew Vaughn 6.00 15.00
TOCBB Brett Baty 4.00 10.00
TOCCJA CJ Abrams 10.00 25.00
TOCHB Hunter Bishop 6.00 15.00
TOCJJ Josh Jung 6.00 15.00
TOCJJB J.J. Bleday 10.00 25.00
TOCKC Keoni Cavaco 5.00 12.00
TOCNL Nick Lodolo 4.00 10.00
TOCRG Riley Greene 12.00 30.00
TOCSL Shea Langeliers 4.00 10.00

2019 Bowman Chrome Draft Top of the Class Box Toppers Autographs

STATED ODDS 1:2278 HOBBY BOXES
STATED PRINT RUN 35 SER.#'d SETS
EXCHANGE DEADLINE 11/30/2021
TOCAM Alek Manoah 12.00 30.00
TOCAR Adley Rutschman 100.00 250.00
TOCAV Andrew Vaughn 40.00 100.00
TOCBB Brett Baty 60.00 150.00
TOCCJA CJ Abrams 50.00 120.00
TOCJJ Josh Jung 50.00 120.00
TOCJJB J.J. Bleday 30.00 80.00
TOCKC Keoni Cavaco 40.00 100.00
TOCNL Nick Lodolo 25.00 60.00
TOCRG Riley Greene 60.00 150.00
TOCSL Shea Langeliers 25.00 60.00

2020 Bowman Chrome

1 Mike Trout 1.50 4.00
2 Manny Machado .30 .75
3 Francisco Lindor .30 .75
4 Paul Goldschmidt .30 .75
5 Brusdar Graterol RC .60 1.50
6 Whit Merrifield .30 .75
7 Andres Munoz RC .60 1.50
8 Luis Robert RC 6.00 15.00
9 Zack Collins RC .50 1.25
10 Jose Berrios .25 .60
11 Randy Arozarena RC 6.00 15.00
12 John Means .30 .75
13 Aaron Judge .75 2.00
14 Yadier Molina .40 1.00
15 Logan Allen RC .40 1.00
16 Anthony Kay RC .40 1.00
17 J.D. Martinez .30 .75
18 Kris Bryant .40 1.00
19 Willie Calhoun .20 .50
20 Justin Dunn RC .50 1.25
21 Buster Posey .40 1.00
22 Freddie Freeman .40 1.00
23 Keston Hiura .40 1.00
24 Jordan Yamamoto RC .40 1.00
25 Yordan Alvarez RC 3.00 8.00
26 Rhys Hoskins .40 1.00
27 Jacob deGrom .60 1.50
28 Ronald Acuna Jr. 1.50 4.00
29 Stephen Strasburg .30 .75
30 Sheldon Neuse RC .50 1.25
31 Mookie Betts 1.00 2.50
32 Gleyber Torres .60 1.50
33 Eugenio Suarez .25 .60
34 A.J. Puk RC .60 1.50
35 Bryce Harper .50 1.25
36 Aaron Civale RC .75 2.00
37 Yoshi Tsutsugo RC 1.00 2.50
38 Mauricio Dubon RC .50 1.25
39 Yusei Kikuchi .25 .60
40 Jorge Alfaro .20 .50
41 Blake Snell .25 .60
42 Evan Longoria .25 .60
43 Matt Chapman .30 .75
44 Nico Hoerner RC 1.50 4.00
45 Josh Bell .25 .60
46 Charlie Blackmon .30 .75
47 Bobby Bradley RC .40 1.00
48 Adrian Morejon RC .40 1.00
49 Yu Chang RC .60 1.50
50 Bo Bichette RC 6.00 15.00
51 Michel Baez RC .40 1.00
52 Eddie Rosario .25 .60
53 Matthew Boyd .20 .50
54 Juan Soto 1.00 2.50
55 Gerrit Cole .50 1.25
56 Alex Bregman .30 .75
57 Adbert Alzolay RC .50 1.25
58 Shohei Ohtani .50 1.25
59 Salvador Perez .25 .60
60 Austin Meadows .30 .75
61 Nolan Arenado .50 1.25
62 Jesus Luzardo RC .75 2.00
63 Seth Brown RC .40 1.00
64 Trent Grisham RC 1.50 4.00
65 Pete Alonso .75 2.00
66 Alex Young RC .40 1.00
67 Corey Kluber .25 .60
68 Justin Verlander .30 .75
69 Hyun-jin Ryu .25 .60
70 Mike Clevinger .25 .60
71 Shogo Akiyama RC .60 1.50
72 Dylan Cease RC .60 1.50
73 Ketel Marte .25 .60
74 Tony Gonsolin RC 1.50 4.00
75 Marcus Semien .30 .75
76 Christian Yelich .40 1.00
77 Xander Bogaerts .30 .75
78 Vladimir Guerrero Jr. .50 1.25
79 Aristides Aquino RC 1.00 2.50
80 Brendan McKay RC .60 1.50
81 Zac Gallen RC 1.00 2.50
82 Fernando Tatis Jr. 1.50 4.00
83 Gavin Lux RC 4.00 10.00
84 Bryan Reynolds .25 .60
85 Tim Anderson .30 .75
86 Miguel Cabrera .30 .75
87 Sean Murphy RC .60 1.50
88 Trey Mancini .30 .75
89 Joey Votto .30 .75
90 Kyle Lewis RC 4.00 10.00
91 Abraham Toro RC .50 1.25
92 Anthony Rizzo .40 1.00
93 Anthony Rendon .30 .75
94 Dan Vogelbach .20 .50
95 Eduardo Escobar .20 .50
96 Dustin May RC 1.25 3.00
97 Isan Diaz RC .60 1.50
98 Nick Solak RC 1.50 4.00
99 Jose Abreu .30 .75
100 Cody Bellinger .60 1.50

2020 Bowman Chrome Blue Refractors

*BLUE REF VET: 4X TO 10X BASIC
*BLUE REF RC: 2X TO 5X BASIC
STATED ODDS 1:XX HOBBY
STATED PRINT RUN 150 SER.#'d SETS
1 Mike Trout 40.00 100.00
8 Luis Robert 75.00 200.00
11 Randy Arozarena 60.00 150.00
25 Yordan Alvarez 30.00 80.00
31 Mookie Betts 15.00 40.00
50 Bo Bichette 100.00 250.00
54 Juan Soto 15.00 40.00
82 Fernando Tatis Jr. 50.00 120.00
90 Kyle Lewis 60.00 150.00
100 Cody Bellinger 10.00 25.00

2020 Bowman Chrome Gold Refractors

*GOLD REF VET: 8X TO 20X BASIC
*GOLD REF RC: 4X TO 10X BASIC
STATED ODDS 1:XXX HOBBY
STATED PRINT RUN 50 SER.#'d SETS
1 Mike Trout 125.00 300.00
8 Luis Robert 125.00 300.00
11 Randy Arozarena 125.00 300.00
25 Yordan Alvarez 60.00 150.00
31 Mookie Betts 50.00 120.00
50 Bo Bichette 200.00 500.00
54 Juan Soto 30.00 80.00
82 Fernando Tatis Jr. 100.00 250.00
90 Kyle Lewis 125.00 300.00
100 Cody Bellinger 20.00 50.00

2020 Bowman Chrome Green Refractors

*GREEN REF VET: 5X TO 12X BASIC
*GREEN REF RC: 2.5X TO 6X BASIC
STATED ODDS 1:XXX HOBBY
STATED PRINT RUN 99 SER.#'d SETS
1 Mike Trout 50.00 120.00
8 Luis Robert 100.00 250.00
11 Randy Arozarena 75.00 200.00
25 Yordan Alvarez 40.00 100.00
31 Mookie Betts 25.00 60.00
50 Bo Bichette 125.00 300.00
54 Juan Soto 20.00 50.00
82 Fernando Tatis Jr. 60.00 150.00
90 Kyle Lewis 75.00 200.00
100 Cody Bellinger 12.00 30.00

2020 Bowman Chrome Orange Refractors

*ORANGE REF VET: 10X TO 25X BASIC
*ORANGE REF RC: 5X TO 12X BASIC
STATED ODDS 1:XXX HOBBY
STATED PRINT RUN 25 SER.#'d SETS
1 Mike Trout 150.00 400.00
8 Luis Robert 150.00 400.00
11 Randy Arozarena 150.00 400.00
25 Yordan Alvarez 75.00 200.00
31 Mookie Betts 60.00 150.00
50 Bo Bichette 250.00 600.00
54 Juan Soto 40.00 100.00
82 Fernando Tatis Jr. 125.00 300.00
90 Kyle Lewis 150.00 400.00
100 Cody Bellinger 25.00 60.00

2020 Bowman Chrome Purple Refractors

*PURPLE REF VET: 2X TO 5X BASIC
*PURPLE REF RC: 1X TO 2.5X BASIC
STATED ODDS 1:XX HOBBY
STATED PRINT RUN 250 SER.#'d SETS
1 Mike Trout 20.00 50.00
8 Luis Robert 50.00 120.00
11 Randy Arozarena 30.00 80.00
25 Yordan Alvarez 15.00 40.00
31 Mookie Betts 12.00 30.00
50 Bo Bichette 50.00 120.00
54 Juan Soto 8.00 20.00
82 Fernando Tatis Jr. 25.00 60.00
90 Kyle Lewis 30.00 80.00
100 Cody Bellinger 5.00 12.00

2020 Bowman Chrome Refractors

*REF VET: 1.5X TO 4X BASIC
*REF RC: .75X TO 2X BASIC
STATED ODDS 1:XX HOBBY
STATED PRINT RUN 499 SER.#'d SETS
1 Mike Trout 15.00 40.00
8 Luis Robert 40.00 100.00
11 Randy Arozarena 25.00 60.00
25 Yordan Alvarez 12.00 30.00
31 Mookie Betts 10.00 25.00
50 Bo Bichette 40.00 100.00
54 Juan Soto 6.00 15.00
82 Fernando Tatis Jr. 10.00 25.00
90 Kyle Lewis 25.00 60.00
100 Cody Bellinger 4.00 10.00

2020 Bowman Chrome Rookie Image Variations

STATED ODDS 1:XXX HOBBY
5 Brusdar Graterol sitting 8.00 20.00
25 Yordan Alvarez running 40.00 100.00
30 Sheldon Neuse wearing helmet 3.00 8.00
34 A.J. Puk sitting 4.00 10.00
44 Nico Hoerner no hat 10.00 25.00
50 Bo Bichette running 60.00 150.00
51 Michel Baez looking up 2.50 6.00
62 Jesus Luzardo green jsy 6.00 15.00
72 Dylan Cease grass in background 4.00 10.00
79 Aristides Aquino running out d 6.00 15.00
80 Brendan McKay blue jsy 4.00 10.00
83 Gavin Lux blue shirt 12.00 30.00
87 Sean Murphy sunglasses on hat 4.00 10.00
90 Kyle Lewis catching 20.00 50.00
96 Dustin May batting 8.00 20.00

2020 Bowman Chrome Rookie Image Variation Autographs

STATED ODDS 1:XXX HOBBY
STATED PRINT RUN 25 SER.#'d SETS
EXCHANGE DEADLINE 8/31/2022
44 Nico Hoerner
79 Aristides Aquino 40.00 100.00
80 Brendan McKay
90 Kyle Lewis 200.00 500.00
96 Dustin May 200.00 500.00

2020 Bowman Chrome '19 AFL MVP

STATED ODDS 1:XX HOBBY
STATED PRINT RUN 250 SER.#'d SETS
AFLSRL Royce Lewis 4.00 10.00

2020 Bowman Chrome '19 AFL MVP Autographs

STATED ODDS 1:XXX HOBBY
STATED PRINT RUN 100 SER.#'d SETS
AFLSRL Royce Lewis 25.00 60.00

2020 Bowman Chrome '19 Fall Stars

STATED ODDS 1:XX HOBBY
*ATOMIC/150: 1.2X TO 3X BASE
*ORANGE/25: 2.5X TO 6X BASE
AFLAB Alec Bohm 3.00 8.00
AFLAG Andres Gimenez .75 2.00
AFLBM Brandon Marsh .50 1.25
AFLCJC C.J. Chatham .40 1.00
AFLDK Dean Kremer .40 1.00
AFLDL Daniel Lynch .30 .75
AFLFW Forrest Whitley .50 1.25
AFLGD Greg Deichmann .40 1.00
AFLGP Geraldo Perdomo .30 .75
AFLHR Heliot Ramos .50 1.25
AFLIH Ivan Herrera .50 1.25
AFLJA Jo Adell 1.25 3.00
AFLJB Joey Bart 1.00 2.50
AFLJD Jarren Duran 1.25 3.00
AFLJJM JJ Matijevic .40 1.00
AFLJL Josh Lowe .30 .75
AFLJR Julio Rodriguez 2.00 5.00
AFLKI Kyle Isbel .30 .75
AFLLG Luis Garcia 1.25 3.00
AFLMA Miguel Amaya .30 .75
AFLNJ Nolan Jones .50 1.25
AFLNN Nick Neidert .30 .75
AFLOC Oneil Cruz .40 1.00
AFLSB Seth Beer .60 1.50
AFLSBA Shane Baz .30 .75
AFLSH Spencer Howard 1.00 2.50
AFLTH Trey Harris .40 1.00
AFLTS Tyler Stephenson .75 2.00
AFLVB Vidal Brujan 2.50 6.00
AFLVVM Victor Victor Mesa .50 1.25

2020 Bowman Chrome '19 Fall Stars Autograph Relics

STATED ODDS 1:XXX HOBBY
STATED PRINT RUN 50 SER.#'d SETS
EXCHANGE DEADLINE 8/31/2022
AFLRAB Alec Bohm
AFLRIH Ivan Herrera 40.00 100.00
AFLRJA Jo Adell 40.00 100.00
AFLRJD Jarren Duran 60.00 150.00
AFLRSB Seth Beer
AFLRTH Trey Harris 25.00 60.00
AFLRVVM Victor Victor Mesa

2020 Bowman Chrome '19 Fall Stars Autographs

STATED ODDS 1:XXX HOBBY
EXCHANGE DEADLINE 8/31/2022
AFLAB Alec Bohm 40.00 100.00
AFLBM Brandon Marsh 6.00 15.00
AFLDK Dean Kremer 6.00 15.00
AFLDL Daniel Lynch 4.00 10.00
AFLGP Geraldo Perdomo 6.00 15.00
AFLHR Heliot Ramos 6.00 15.00
AFLJB Joey Bart 20.00 50.00
AFLJD Jarren Duran 15.00 40.00
AFLJJM JJ Matijevic 5.00 12.00
AFLLG Luis Garcia 10.00 25.00
AFLMA Miguel Amaya 10.00 25.00
AFLSB Seth Beer 8.00 20.00
AFLSH Spencer Howard 12.00 30.00
AFLVVM Victor Victor Mesa 6.00 15.00

2020 Bowman Chrome '19 Fall Stars Relics

STATED ODDS 1:XXX HOBBY
STATED PRINT RUN 99 SER.#'d SETS
*ORANGE/25: .6X TO 1.5X BASIC
AFLRTS Tyler Stephenson 8.00 20.00
AFLRAB Alec Bohm 12.00 30.00
AFLRAG Andres Gimenez 8.00 20.00
AFLRBM Brandon Marsh 5.00 12.00
AFLRCJC C.J. Chatham 4.00 10.00
AFLRDK Dean Kremer 8.00 20.00
AFLRDL Daniel Lynch 3.00 8.00
AFLRGD Greg Deichmann 4.00 10.00
AFLRIH Ivan Herrera 10.00 25.00
AFLRJA Jo Adell 8.00 20.00
AFLRJD Jarren Duran 10.00 25.00
AFLRJJM JJ Matijevic 4.00 10.00
AFLRJR Julio Rodriguez 10.00 25.00
AFLRLG Luis Garcia 12.00 30.00
AFLRMA Miguel Amaya 3.00 8.00
AFLRNN Nick Neidert 3.00 8.00
AFLRRL Royce Lewis 6.00 15.00
AFLRSB Seth Beer 6.00 15.00
AFLRTH Trey Harris 4.00 10.00
AFLRVVM Victor Victor Mesa 5.00 12.00

2020 Bowman Chrome '90 Bowman

STATED ODDS 1:8 HOBBY
*ATOMIC REF/150: 2.5X TO 6X BASE
*GREEN REF/99: 2.5X TO 6X BASE
*GOLD REF/50: 4X TO 10X BASIC
*ORANGE REF/25: 8X TO 20X BASE
90BAA Aristides Aquino .60 1.50
90BAB Alec Bohm 1.50 4.00
90BAK Alex Kirilloff .50 1.25
90BAP A.J. Puk .40 1.00
90BAR Adley Rutschman 1.50 4.00
90BAV Andrew Vaughn 1.00 2.50
90BBB Bo Bichette 2.00 5.00
90BBH Bryce Harper .60 1.50
90BBWJ Bobby Witt Jr. 1.50 4.00
90BCA CJ Abrams .75 2.00
90BCK Clayton Kershaw .60 1.50
90BCM Casey Mize .75 2.00
90BCP Cristian Pache .75 2.00
90BCY Christian Yelich .50 1.25
90BDC Dylan Carlson 1.00 2.50
90BDCE Dylan Cease .40 1.00
90BDH DL Hall .25 .60
90BDW Drew Waters .60 1.50
90BFW Forrest Whitley .40 1.00
90BGL Gavin Lux 1.25 3.00
90BGT Gleyber Torres .75 2.00
90BIA Ian Anderson .75 2.00
90BJA Jo Adell 1.00 2.50
90BJB Joey Bart .75 2.00
90BJJB JJ Bleday .75 2.00
90BJK Jarred Kelenic 1.25 3.00
90BJL Jesus Luzardo .50 1.25
90BJR Julio Rodriguez 1.50 4.00
90BJS Juan Soto 1.25 3.00
90BKL Kyle Lewis 2.00 5.00
90BLR Luis Robert 2.00 5.00
90BMG MacKenzie Gore .50 1.25
90BML Matthew Liberatore .30 .75
90BMM Matt Manning .30 .75
90BMS Max Scherzer .40 1.00
90BMT Mike Trout 2.00 5.00
90BNG Nolan Gorman .50 1.25
90BNH Nico Hoerner 1.00 2.50
90BNP Nate Pearson .75 2.00
90BPA Pete Alonso 1.00 2.50
90BRAJ Ronald Acuna Jr. 1.50 4.00
90BRG Riley Greene 1.00 2.50
90BRL Royce Lewis .60 1.50
90BSH Spencer Howard .75 2.00
90BSM Sean Murphy .40 1.00
90BSS Sixto Sanchez .75 2.00
90BTT Taylor Trammell .40 1.00
90BWF Wander Franco 5.00 12.00
90BXB Xander Bogaerts .40 1.00
90BYA Yordan Alvarez 2.50 6.00

2020 Bowman Chrome '90 Bowman Autographs

BOW.STATED ODDS 1:4,400 HOBBY
BOW.CHR.ODDS 1:XXX HOBBY
STATED PRINT RUN 30 SER.#'d SETS
BOW.CHR.EXCH.DEADLINE 8/31/2022
90BAA Aristides Aquino 15.00 40.00
90BAP A.J. Puk 10.00 25.00
90BAR Adley Rutschman 75.00 200.00
90BAV Andrew Vaughn 25.00 60.00
90BBB Bo Bichette 100.00 250.00
90BBWJ Bobby Witt Jr. 75.00 200.00
90BCA C.J. Abrams 50.00 120.00
90BCM Casey Mize 30.00 80.00
90BDC Dylan Carlson 60.00 150.00
90BDCE Dylan Cease 10.00 25.00
90BGL Gavin Lux 75.00 200.00
90BGT Gleyber Torres 50.00 120.00
90BJA Jo Adell 100.00 250.00
90BJB Joey Bart 30.00 80.00
90BJK Jarred Kelenic 60.00 150.00
90BJL Jesus Luzardo 30.00 80.00
90BJR Julio Rodriguez 60.00 150.00
90BKL Kyle Lewis 75.00 200.00
90BMG MacKenzie Gore 30.00 80.00
90BML Matthew Liberatore 50.00 12.00
90BMM Matt Manning 50.00 120.00
90BMS Max Scherzer 50.00 12.00
90BMT Mike Trout 500.00 1000.00
90BNG Nolan Gorman
90BNH Nico Hoerner 50.00 120.00
90BRAJ Ronald Acuna Jr. 150.00 400.00
90BRG Riley Greene 75.00 200.00
90BRL Royce Lewis 30.00 80.00
90BSH Spencer Howard 40.00 100.00
90BSM Sean Murphy 25.00 60.00
90BSS Sixto Sanchez 40.00 100.00
90BWF Wander Franco 125.00 300.00
90BYA Yordan Alvarez 125.00 300.00

2020 Bowman Chrome Autograph Relics

STATED ODDS 1:XXX HOBBY
PRINT RUNS B/WN 30-75 COPIES PER
EXCHANGE DEADLINE 8/31/2022
*GOLD/50: .4X TO 1X BASIC
*GOLD/25: .75X TO 2X BASIC
BCARAA Aristides Aquino/75 15.00 40.00
BCARAR Austin Riley/75 20.00 50.00
BCARBH Bryce Harper/40 125.00 300.00
BCARBR Brendan Rodgers/75 6.00 15.00
BCARGS George Springer/75 15.00 40.00
BCARJA Jose Altuve/50 15.00 40.00
BCARJR Jake Rogers/75 6.00 15.00
BCARJS Jorge Soler/75 8.00 20.00
BCARKN Kevin Newman/75 6.00 15.00
BCARMC Michael Chavis/75 8.00 20.00
BCARMT Mike Trout/30 400.00 1000.00
BCARPA Pete Alonso/75 30.00 80.00
BCARRAJ Ronald Acuna Jr./75 75.00 200.00

2020 Bowman Chrome Dawn of Glory

DG1 Sherten Apostel 1.50 4.00
DG2 Gus Varland .40 1.00
DG3 Jasseel De La Cruz .50 1.25
DG4 Nick Lodolo .50 1.25
DG5 Jarren Duran 1.25 3.00
DG6 Isaac Paredes 1.00 2.50
DG7 Dylan File .40 1.00
DG8 Joe Ryan .40 1.00
DG9 Ruben Cardenas .40 1.00
DG10 Sam Huff .60 1.50
DG11 Lewin Diaz .30 .75
DG12 Andrew Vaughn 1.25 3.00
DG13 Adley Rutschman 2.00 5.00
DG14 Jordan Balazovic .60 1.50
DG15 Kevin Smith .30 .75

2020 Bowman Chrome Dawn of Glory Autographs

STATED ODDS 1:XXX HOBBY
STATED PRINT RUN 99 SER.#'d SETS
EXCHANGE DEADLINE 8/31/2022
*ORANGE/25: .5X TO 1.2X BASIC
DGAAR Adley Rutschman 30.00 80.00
DGAAV Andrew Vaughn 12.00 30.00
DGAJB Jordan Balazovic EXCH 10.00 25.00
DGAJD Jarren Duran 15.00 40.00
DGAJR Joe Ryan 10.00 25.00
DGAKS Kevin Smith 6.00 15.00
DGANL Nick Lodolo 8.00 20.00
DGARC Ruben Cardenas 8.00 20.00
DGASA Sherten Apostel 12.00 30.00
DGASH Sam Huff 12.00 30.00

2020 Bowman Chrome Dual Prospect Autographs

STATED ODDS 1:17,538 HOBBY
STATED PRINT RUN 25 SER.#'d SETS
EXCHANGE DEADLINE 3/31/2022
DPABE Bleday/Encarnacion 200.00 500.00
DPACP Patino/Cantillo 125.00 300.00
DPAHA Arias/Huff 75.00 200.00
DPARH Hall/Rutschman 200.00 500.00
DPAVA Amaya/Vargas 50.00 120.00
DPAVP Pereira/Volpe 125.00 300.00

2020 Bowman Chrome Farm to Fame

STATED ODDS 1:XXX HOBBY
*ORANGE/25: .75X TO 2X BASIC
FTFBL Barry Larkin 3.00 8.00
FTFCF Carlton Fisk 3.00 8.00
FTFCJ Chipper Jones 4.00 10.00
FTFCY Carl Yastrzemski 6.00 15.00
FTFEM Edgar Martinez 3.00 8.00
FTFFT Frank Thomas 4.00 10.00
FTFGB George Brett 10.00 25.00
FTFHA Hank Aaron 8.00 20.00
FTFIR Ivan Rodriguez 3.00 8.00
FTFJB Johnny Bench 4.00 10.00
FTFMR Mariano Rivera 5.00 12.00
FTFNR Nolan Ryan 12.00 30.00
FTFOS Ozzie Smith 5.00 12.00
FTFPM Pedro Martinez 3.00 8.00
FTFRC Rod Carew 3.00 8.00
FTFRF Rollie Fingers 3.00 8.00
FTFRH Rickey Henderson 15.00 4.00
FTFRJ Reggie Jackson 3.00 8.00
FTFRY Robin Yount 4.00 10.00
FTFSC Steve Carlton 3.00 8.00
FTFTP Tony Perez 3.00 8.00
FTFWB Wade Boggs 3.00 8.00
FTFWM Willie Mays 8.00 20.00
FTFCRJ Cal Ripken Jr. 12.00 30.00

2020 Bowman Chrome Farm to Fame Autographs

RANDOM INSERTS IN PACKS
EXCHANGE DEADLINE 8/31/2022
FTFBL Barry Larkin 75.00 200.00
FTFCF Carlton Fisk 20.00 50.00
FTFCJ Chipper Jones 60.00 150.00

FTFCY Carl Yastrzemski 75.00 200.00
FTFFT Frank Thomas 40.00 100.00
FTFHA Hank Aaron 400.00 1000.00
FTFIR Ivan Rodriguez 25.00 60.00
FTFJB Johnny Bench 40.00 100.00
FTFMR Mariano Rivera 100.00 250.00
FTFNR Nolan Ryan 200.00 500.00
FTFOS Ozzie Smith 25.00 60.00
FTFPM Pedro Martinez 50.00 120.00
FTFRF Rollie Fingers 50.00 120.00
FTFSC Steve Carlton 15.00 40.00
FTFTP Tony Perez 15.00 40.00
FTFWB Wade Boggs 30.00 80.00
FTFCRJ Cal Ripken Jr. 75.00 200.00

2020 Bowman Chrome Hidden Finds

STATED ODDS 1:24 HOBBY
*ATOMIC REF/150: 2.5X TO 6X BASE
*GOLD REF/50: 4X TO 10X BASIC
*ORANGE REF/25: 8X TO 20X BASE
HFCM Cedric Mullins .30 .75
HFCP Chris Paddack .40 1.00
HFDJ Danny Jansen .25 .60
HFGV Gus Varland .30 .75
HFIG Isiah Gilliam .30 .75
HFJB Jordan Balazovic .50 1.25
HFJC Joey Cantillo .25 .60
HFJCA Jake Cave .30 .75
HFJD Jarren Duran 1.00 2.50
HFJDM J.D. Martinez .40 1.00
HFJM Jeff McNeil .30 .75
HFJY Jordan Yamamoto .25 .60
HFLA Logan Allen .25 .60
HFMK Mike King .40 1.00
HFMM Max Muncy .30 .75
HFPG Paul Goldschmidt .40 1.00
HFRB Ryan Borucki .25 .60
HFRH Rhys Hoskins .50 1.25
HFRT Rowdy Tellez .30 .75
HFSH Sam Huff .50 1.25

2020 Bowman Chrome Hidden Finds Autographs

BOW.STATED ODDS 1:XXX HOBBY
BOW.CHR.STATED ODDS 1:XXX HOBBY
STATED PRINT RUN 99 SER.#'d SETS
BOW.EXCH.DEADLINE 3/31/2022
BOW.CHR.EXCHANGE DEADLINE 8/31/2022
HFCP Chris Paddack 6.00 15.00
HFGV Gus Varland 5.00 12.00
HFIG Isiah Gilliam 5.00 12.00
HFJC Joey Cantillo 4.00 10.00
HFJDM J.D. Martinez
HFJM Jeff McNeil 12.00 30.00
HFJY Jordan Yamamoto 4.00 10.00
HFLA Logan Allen 4.00 10.00
HFMM Max Muncy 5.00 12.00
HFPG Paul Goldschmidt
HFRH Rhys Hoskins
HFSH Sam Huff 20.00 50.00

2020 Bowman Chrome Hidden Finds Autographs Orange Refractors

*ORANGE REF: .75X TO 2X BASIC
BOW.STATED ODDS 1:3835 HOBBY
BOW.CHR.STATED ODDS 1:XXX HOBBY
STATED PRINT RUN 25 SER.#'d SETS
BOW.EXCH.DEADLINE 3/31/2022
BOW.CHR.EXCHANGE DEADLINE 8/31/2022
HFJDM J.D. Martinez 20.00 50.00
HFPG Paul Goldschmidt 25.00 60.00
HFRH Rhys Hoskins 15.00 40.00

2020 Bowman Chrome Prime Chrome Signatures

STATED ODDS 1:XXX HOBBY
STATED PRINT RUN 50 SER.#'d SETS
EXCHANGE DEADLINE 8/31/2022
*ORANGE/25: .5X TO 1.2X BASIC
PCSAR Adley Rutschman 40.00 100.00
PCSASP Alex Speas 6.00 15.00
PCSAV Andrew Vaughn 20.00 50.00
PCSAVO Anthony Volpe 25.00 60.00
PCSBB Brett Baty 15.00 40.00
PCSBD Brenton Doyle 20.00 50.00
PCSBWJ Bobby Witt Jr. 50.00 120.00
PCSED Ezequiel Duran 10.00 25.00
PCSGJ Gilberto Jimenez 15.00 40.00
PCSGM Gabriel Moreno 5.00 12.00
PCSJA Jacob Amaya 12.00 30.00
PCSJB Jordan Balazovic EXCH 6.00 15.00
PCSJDU Jarren Duran 15.00 40.00
PCSJR Jackson Rutledge 12.00 30.00
PCSKC Keoni Cavaco 6.00 15.00
PCSKS Kevin Smith 3.00 8.00
PCSLD Lewin Diaz 8.00 20.00
PCSML Max Lazar
PCSNH Niko Hulsizer 25.00 60.00
PCSNL Nick Lodolo 6.00 15.00
PCSRC Ruben Cardenas 6.00 15.00
PCSRG Riley Greene 25.00 60.00
PCSSA Sherten Apostel 25.00 60.00
PCSSH Sam Huff 15.00 40.00
PCSWW Will Wilson 8.00 20.00
PCSXE Xavier Edwards 15.00 40.00

2020 Bowman Chrome Prospect Autographs

RANDOM INSERTS IN PACKS
BOW.PLATE ODDS 1:11,389 HOBBY
BOW.CHR.PLATE ODDS 1:XXXX HOBBY
PLATE PRINT RUN 1 SET PER COLOR
BLACK-CYAN-MAGENTA-YELLOW ISSUED
NO PLATE PRICING DUE TO SCARCITY
BOW.EXCH.DEADLINE 3/31/2022
BOW.CHR.EXCH.DEADLINE 8/31/2022
CPAAA Aaron Ashby 6.00 15.00
CPAAC Antonio Cabello 6.00 15.00
CPAAD Andrew Dalquist 3.00 8.00
CPAAG Anthony Garcia 10.00 25.00
CPAAH Austin Hansen 4.00 10.00
CPAAH Adam Hall 4.00 10.00
CPAAHI Adam Hill 3.00 8.00
CPAAP Andy Pages 10.00 25.00
CPAAR Adley Rutschman 60.00 150.00
CPAAS Alvaro Seijas 3.00 8.00
CPAAS Alex Speas 3.00 8.00
CPAASH Austin Shenton 8.00 20.00
CPAASH Aaron Shortridge 4.00 10.00
CPAAV Anthony Volpe 25.00 60.00
CPAAV Alex Vesia 3.00 8.00
CPAAVA Andrew Vaughn 40.00 100.00
CPABB Ben Braymer 5.00 12.00
CPABBA Bryce Ball 40.00 100.00
CPABD Brennen Davis 60.00 150.00
CPABD Brenton Doyle 25.00 60.00
CPABH Brandon Howlett 5.00 12.00
CPABL Brandon Lewis 5.00 12.00
CPABL Bayron Lora 100.00 250.00
CPABP Bryant Packard 4.00 10.00
CPABW Brady Whalen 5.00 12.00
CPABWJ Bobby Witt Jr. 300.00 800.00
CPACB Cody Bolton 4.00 10.00
CPACBA Colin Barber 10.00 25.00
CPACC Connor Cannon 10.00 25.00
CPACG Chris Gittens 12.00 30.00
CPACJ Cooper Johnson 3.00 8.00
CPACK Christian Koss 6.00 15.00
CPACR Chandler Redmond 6.00 15.00
CPACS Canaan Smith 5.00 12.00
CPACT Curtis Terry 8.00 20.00
CPACV Chris Vallimont 3.00 8.00
CPADA Diosbel Arias 4.00 10.00
CPADA Drew Avans 4.00 10.00
CPADF Dylan File 4.00 10.00
CPADJ Damon Jones 4.00 10.00
CPADM Drew Millas 4.00 10.00
CPADMA Devin Mann 5.00 12.00
CPAED Ezequiel Duran 12.00 30.00
CPAEL Ethan Lindow 4.00 10.00
CPAEM Erik Miller 4.00 10.00
CPAEP Everson Pereira 15.00 40.00
CPAEPE Erick Pena 100.00 250.00
CPAERI Erik Rivera 3.00 8.00
CPAFA Francisco Alvarez 60.00 150.00
CPAFP Ford Proctor 3.00 8.00
CPAGHJ Glenallen Hill Jr. 6.00 15.00
CPAGJ Gilberto Jimenez 40.00 100.00
CPAGL Grant Little 4.00 10.00
CPAGM Gabriel Moreno 15.00 40.00
CPAGMA Gunner Mayer 3.00 8.00
CPAGST Graeme Stinson 3.00 8.00
CPAGV Gus Varland 8.00 20.00
CPAHH Hogan Harris 3.00 8.00
CPAHY Hector Yan 4.00 10.00
CPAIH Ivan Herrera 25.00 60.00
CPAIP Isaac Paredes 15.00 40.00
CPAJA Jacob Amaya 12.00 30.00
CPAJBE James Beard 5.00 12.00
CPAJBR Jordan Brewer 10.00 25.00
CPAJC Joey Cantillo 3.00 8.00
CPAJD Jarren Duran 75.00 200.00
CPAJDC Jasseel De La Cruz 5.00 12.00
CPAJDI Jhon Diaz 30.00 80.00
CPAJDO Jasson Dominguez 750.00 2000.00
CPAJE Jerar Encarnacion 15.00 40.00
CPAJG Joe Genord 4.00 10.00
CPAJJB J.J. Bleday 20.00 50.00
CPAJMA Joan Martinez 4.00 10.00
CPAJP Jeremy Pena 20.00 50.00
CPAJR Jackson Rutledge 10.00 25.00
CPAJRY Joe Ryan 6.00 15.00
CPAJS Junior Santos 4.00 10.00
CPAJS Jonathan Stiever 3.00 8.00
CPAJT Jhon Torres 10.00 25.00
CPAKK Karl Kauffmann 3.00 8.00
CPAKS Kevin Smith 3.00 8.00
CPAKSI Kendall Simmons 10.00 25.00
CPALA Luisangel Acuna 100.00 250.00
CPALD Lewin Diaz 6.00 15.00
CPALD Lency Delgado 3.00 8.00
CPALK Levi Kelly 3.00 8.00
CPALM Luis Matos 100.00 250.00
CPALOH Logan O'Hoppe 5.00 12.00
CPALP Luis Patino 30.00 80.00
CPALV Leonel Valera 6.00 15.00
CPAMB Micah Bello 4.00 10.00
CPAMF Mario Feliciano 8.00 20.00
CPAMH Michael Harris 75.00 200.00
CPAML Max Lazar 4.00 10.00
CPAMM Michael Massey 4.00 10.00
CPAMV Miguel Vargas 15.00 40.00
CPANH Niko Hulsizer 10.00 25.00
CPANK Nick Kahle 4.00 10.00
CPAOE Omar Estevez 10.00 25.00
CPAOG Oscar Gonzalez 6.00 15.00
CPAOP Oswald Peraza 30.00 80.00
CPAOR Osiel Rodriguez 8.00 20.00
CPAPC Philip Clarke 3.00 8.00
CPAPN Packy Naughton 3.00 8.00
CPAPP Pedro Pages 6.00 15.00
CPAPR Paul Richan 3.00 8.00
CPAQC Quin Cotton 8.00 20.00
CPARC Ruben Cardenas 4.00 10.00
CPARF Randy Florentino 4.00 10.00
CPARG Riley Greene 12.00 30.00
CPARP Robert Puason 100.00 250.00
CPARPE Ryan Pepiot 12.00 30.00
CPARS Raimfer Salinas 8.00 20.00
CPARV Ricky Vanasco 5.00 12.00
CPASA Sherten Apostel 25.00 60.00
CPASG Seth Gray 5.00 12.00
CPASH Sam Huff 25.00 60.00
CPASP Stephen Paolini 10.00 25.00
CPATD Tony Dibrell 3.00 8.00
CPATDI Thomas Dillard 3.00 8.00
CPATDY Tyler Dyson 3.00 8.00
CPATH Trey Harris 8.00 20.00
CPATI Tyler Ivey 4.00 10.00
CPATJ Taylor Jones 3.00 8.00
CPATM Tucupita Marcano 25.00 60.00
CPATS Tarik Skubal 15.00 40.00
CPATT Tahnaj Thomas 8.00 20.00
CPATW Thad Ward 5.00 12.00
CPAUB Ulrich Bojarski 5.00 12.00
CPAVB Vidal Brujan 50.00 120.00
CPAVG Vaughn Grissom 15.00 40.00
CPAWH Will Holland 5.00 12.00
CPAWP Wilderd Patino 20.00 50.00
CPAXE Xavier Edwards 25.00 60.00
CPAYG Yoendrys Gomez 8.00 20.00
CPAZH Zack Hess 4.00 10.00
CPAZW Zach Watson 4.00 10.00

2020 Bowman Chrome Prospect Autographs Atomic Refractors

*ATOMIC REF: .75X TO 2X BASIC
STATED ODDS 1:742 HOBBY
STATED PRINT RUN 100 SER.#'D SETS
EXCHANGE DEADLINE 3/31/2022
CPABWJ Bobby Witt Jr. 750.00 2000.00

2020 Bowman Chrome Prospect Autographs Blue Refractors

*BLUE REF: .75X TO 2X BASIC
BOW.STATED ODDS 1:495 HOBBY
BOW.CHR.STATED ODDS 1:XXX HOBBY
STATED PRINT RUN 150 SER.#'D SETS
BOW.EXCH.DEADLINE 3/31/2022
BOW.CHR.EXCH.DEADLINE 8/31/2022
CPABWJ Bobby Witt Jr. 750.00 2000.00

2020 Bowman Chrome Prospect Autographs Gold Refractors

*GOLD REF: 1.5X TO 4X BASIC
BOW.STATED ODDS 1:1483 HOBBY
BOW.CHR.STATED ODDS 1:XXX BLASTER
STATED PRINT RUN 50 SER.#'D SETS
BOW.EXCH.DEADLINE 3/31/2022
BOW.CHR.EXCH.DEADLINE 8/31/2022
CPABWJ Bobby Witt Jr. 1500.00 4000.00

2020 Bowman Chrome Prospect Autographs Gold Shimmer Refractors

*GOLD SHIM REF: 1.5X TO 4X BASIC
BOW.STATED ODDS 1:1483 HOBBY
BOW.CHR.STATED ODDS 1:XXX BLASTER
STATED PRINT RUN 50 SER.#'D SETS
BOW.EXCH.DEADLINE 3/31/2022
BOW.CHR.EXCH.DEADLINE 8/31/2022
CPABWJ Bobby Witt Jr. 1500.00 4000.00

2020 Bowman Chrome Prospect Autographs Green Refractors

*GREEN REF: .75X TO 2X BASIC
BOW.STATED ODDS 1:576 BLASTER
BOW.CHR.STATED ODDS 1:XXX BLASTER
STATED PRINT RUN 99 SER.#'D SETS
BOW.EXCH.DEADLINE 3/31/2022
BOW.CHR.EXCH.DEADLINE 8/31/2022
CPABWJ Bobby Witt Jr. 750.00 2000.00

2020 Bowman Chrome Prospect Autographs Green Atomic Refractors

*GREEN ATOMIC REF: .75X TO 2X BASIC
BOW.CHR.STATED ODDS 1:XXX BLASTER
STATED PRINT RUN 99 SER.#'D SETS
BOW.CHR.EXCH.DEADLINE 8/31/2022

2020 Bowman Chrome Prospect Autographs Green Shimmer Refractors

*GREEN SHIM REF: .75X TO 2X BASIC
STATED ODDS 1:576 BLASTER
STATED PRINT RUN 99 SER.#'D SETS
EXCHANGE DEADLINE 3/31/2022
CPABWJ Bobby Witt Jr. 750.00 2000.00

2020 Bowman Chrome Prospect Autographs HTA Choice Refractors

*HTA CHOICE REF: .75X TO 2X BASIC
BOW.CHR.STATED ODDS 1:XXX HOBBY
STATED PRINT RUN 150 SER.#'D SETS
BOW.CHR.EXCH.DEADLINE 8/31/2022

2020 Bowman Chrome Prospect Autographs Orange Refractors

*ORANGE REF: 3X TO 8X BASIC
BOW.STATED ODDS 1:914 HOBBY
BOW.CHR.STATED ODDS 1:XXX HOBBY
STATED PRINT RUN 25 SER.#'D SETS
BOW.EXCH.DEADLINE 3/31/2022
BOW.CHR.EXCH.DEADLINE 8/31/2022
CPABWJ Bobby Witt Jr. 3000.00 8000.00

2020 Bowman Chrome Prospect Autographs Orange Shimmer Refractors

*ORANGE SHIM REF: 3X TO 8X BASIC
STATED ODDS 1:914 HOBBY
STATED PRINT RUN 25 SER.#'D SETS
EXCHANGE DEADLINE 3/31/2022
CPABWJ Bobby Witt Jr. 3000.00 8000.00

2020 Bowman Chrome Prospect Autographs Orange Wave Refractors

*ORANGE WAVE REF: 3X TO 8X BASIC
BOW.CHR.STATED ODDS 1:XXX HOBBY
STATED PRINT RUN 25 SER.#'D SETS
EXCHANGE DEADLINE 8/31/2022

2020 Bowman Chrome Prospect Autographs Purple Refractors

*PURPLE REF: .6X TO 1.5X BASIC
BOW.STATED ODDS 1:319 HOBBY
BOW.CHR.STATED ODDS 1:XXX HOBBY
STATED PRINT RUN 250 SER.#'D SETS
BOW.EXCH.DEADLINE 3/31/2022
BOW.CHR.EXCH.DEADLINE 8/31/2022
CPABWJ Bobby Witt Jr. 600.00 1500.00

2020 Bowman Chrome Prospect Autographs Refractors

*REF: .5X TO 1.2X BASIC
BOW.STATED ODDS 1:160 HOBBY
BOW.CHR.STATED ODDS 1:XXX HOBBY
STATED PRINT RUN 499 SER.#'D SETS
BOW.EXCH.DEADLINE 3/31/2022
BOW.CHR.EXCH.DEADLINE 8/31/2022
CPABWJ Bobby Witt Jr. 600.00 1500.00

2020 Bowman Chrome Prospect Autographs Speckle Refractors

*SPECKLE REF: .6X TO 1.5X BASIC
STATED ODDS 1:267 HOBBY
STATED PRINT RUN 299 SER.#'D SETS
EXCHANGE DEADLINE 3/31/2022
CPABWJ Bobby Witt Jr. 600.00 1500.00

2020 Bowman Chrome Prospect Autographs Yellow Refractors

*YELLOW REF: .75X TO 2X BASIC
STATED ODDS 1:5221 BLASTER
STATED PRINT RUN 75 SER.#'D SETS
EXCHANGE DEADLINE 3/31/2022
CPABWJ Bobby Witt Jr. 750.00 2000.00

2020 Bowman Chrome Prospects

BOW.PLATE ODDS 1:11,389 HOBBY
PLATE PRINT RUN 1 SET PER COLOR
BLACK-CYAN-MAGENTA-YELLOW ISSUED
NO PLATE PRICING DUE TO SCARCITY
BCP1 Wander Franco 2.00 5.00
BCP2 Drew Waters .50 1.25
BCP3 Jacob Amaya .75 2.00
BCP4 Kody Hoese .60 1.50
BCP5 Cristian Pache .60 1.50
BCP6 Zack Thompson .20 .50
BCP7 Briam Campusano .20 .50
BCP8 Jasson Dominguez 20.00 50.00
BCP9 Aaron Shortridge .25 .60
BCP10 Xavier Edwards .75 2.00
BCP11 Jesus Sanchez .30 .75
BCP12 Ronaldo Hernandez .20 .50
BCP13 Blake Rutherford .20 .50
BCP14 Ulrich Bojarski .30 .75
BCP15 Jordyn Adams .25 .60
BCP16 Austin Beck .25 .60
BCP17 Niko Hulsizer .50 1.25
BCP18 Triston Casas .50 1.25
BCP19 Julio Rodriguez 1.25 3.00
BCP20 Shane Baz .20 .50
BCP21 Shea Langeliers .40 1.00
BCP22 Grayson Rodriguez .30 .75
BCP23 Ruben Cardenas .25 .60
BCP24 Mason Denaburg .20 .50
BCP25 Bobby Witt Jr. 5.00 12.00
BCP26 Andrew Vaughn .75 2.00
BCP27 Kristian Robinson .60 1.50
BCP28 Ronny Mauricio .50 1.25
BCP29 Alec Bohm 1.25 3.00
BCP30 Jhon Diaz .60 1.50
BCP31 Estevan Florial .30 .75
BCP32 Elehuris Montero .25 .60
BCP33 Sam Huff .40 1.00
BCP34 Zack Brown .20 .50
BCP35 Brice Turang .20 .50
BCP36 Ryan Mountcastle 1.00 2.50
BCP37 Wilfred Astudillo .25 .60
BCP38 Gus Varland .25 .60
BCP39 Nick Lodolo .30 .75
BCP40 Tyler Freeman .25 .60
BCP41 Rece Hinds .25 .60
BCP42 Brady Singer 1.00 2.50
BCP43 Cal Mitchell .20 .50
BCP44 Ethan Hankins .25 .60
BCP45 Daz Cameron .20 .50
BCP46 Sherten Apostel 1.00 2.50
BCP47 Hunter Greene .30 .75
BCP48 Josiah Gray .30 .75
BCP49 Brailyn Marquez .50 1.25
BCP50 Adley Rutschman 1.25 3.00
BCP51 Everson Pereira .50 1.25
BCP52 Bayron Lora 6.00 15.00
BCP53 Clarke Schmidt .30 .75
BCP54 Brady McConnell .25 .60
BCP55 Spencer Howard .60 1.50
BCP56 Cristian Javier .25 .60
BCP57 Aaron Ashby .20 .50
BCP58 Logan Gilbert .25 .60
BCP59 Glenallen Hill Jr. .30 .75
BCP60 Alvaro Seijas .20 .50
BCP61 Jeremy Pena .50 1.25
BCP62 CJ Abrams .60 1.50
BCP63 Franklin Perez .20 .50
BCP64 Tanner Houck .50 1.25
BCP65 Damon Jones .25 .60
BCP66 Nolan Gorman .40 1.00
BCP67 Ke'Bryan Hayes 1.00 2.50
BCP68 Bryson Stott .50 1.25
BCP69 Canaan Smith .30 .75
BCP70 Forrest Whitley .30 .75
BCP71 Drew Mendoza .50 1.25
BCP72 Jazz Chisholm .75 2.00
BCP73 Jonathan India 1.25 3.00
BCP74 MacKenzie Gore .40 1.00
BCP75 Seth Beer .40 1.00
BCP76 Joey Cantillo .20 .50
BCP77 Evan White .50 1.25
BCP78 Chris Vallimont .20 .50
BCP79 Sixto Sanchez .60 1.50
BCP80 Alex Kirilloff .40 1.00
BCP81 Tristen Lutz .25 .60
BCP82 Freudis Nova .20 .50
BCP83 Tim Cate .20 .50
BCP84 Daniel Lynch .20 .50
BCP85 Antonio Cabello .60 1.50
BCP86 Bobby Dalbec 1.25 3.00
BCP87 Colton Welker .20 .50
BCP88 Logan Davidson .25 .60
BCP89 Matthew Liberatore .25 .60
BCP90 Adam Hall .25 .60
BCP91 Jackson Rutledge .30 .75
BCP92 Dane Dunning .60 1.50
BCP93 Royce Lewis .50 1.25
BCP94 Jarred Kelenic 1.00 2.50
BCP95 Nolan Jones .30 .75
BCP96 Jerar Encarnacion .60 1.50
BCP97 Ian Anderson .60 1.50
BCP98 Alek Thomas .25 .60
BCP99 Matt Manning .25 .60
BCP100 Jo Adell .75 2.00
BCP101 Nick Madrigal .75 2.00
BCP102 Owen Miller .20 .50
BCP103 Marco Luciano .75 2.00
BCP104 Jordan Groshans .40 1.00
BCP105 Nick Allen .20 .50
BCP106 Dylan Carlson .75 2.00
BCP107 Cole Winn .20 .50
BCP108 Tarik Skubal 1.00 2.50
BCP109 Oscar Gonzalez .40 1.00
BCP110 Aramis Ademan .20 .50
BCP111 Oneil Cruz .25 .60
BCP112 Joey Bart .60 1.50
BCP113 Josh Jung .50 1.25
BCP114 Luis Garcia .75 2.00
BCP115 Jasseel De La Cruz .30 .75
BCP116 J.J. Bleday .60 1.50
BCP117 Joe Ryan .25 .60
BCP118 Keoni Cavaco .20 .50
BCP119 Hans Crouse .20 .50
BCP120 Isaac Paredes .60 1.50
BCP121 Grant Lavigne .20 .50
BCP122 Riley Greene .75 2.00
BCP123 Jordan Balazovic .40 1.00
BCP124 Nate Pearson .60 1.50
BCP125 Deivi Garcia 1.00 2.50
BCP126 Luis Garcia .75 2.00
BCP127 Leody Taveras .30 .75
BCP128 Bryan Mata .20 .50
BCP129 Hunter Bishop .40 1.00
BCP130 Taylor Trammell .30 .75
BCP131 Miguel Vargas .50 1.25
BCP132 Luis Gil .25 .60
BCP133 Grant Little .25 .60
BCP134 Gunnar Henderson .25 .60
BCP135 Eric Pardinho .25 .60
BCP136 Miguel Amaya .20 .50
BCP137 Ryan Rolison .25 .60
BCP138 Jorge Mateo .25 .60
BCP139 Anthony Volpe 2.50 6.00
BCP140 Nick Bennett .25 .60
BCP141 Brennen Davis .40 1.00
BCP142 Casey Mize .60 1.50
BCP143 Keibert Ruiz 1.00 2.50
BCP144 Jarren Duran .75 2.00
BCP145 Robert Puason 8.00 20.00
BCP146 Travis Swaggerty .25 .60
BCP147 Will Wilson .25 .60
BCP148 Heliot Ramos .30 .75
BCP149 Alek Manoah .25 .60
BCP150 Luis Robert 5.00 12.00
BCP151 Alex Kirilloff .40 1.00
BCP152 Michael Busch .50 1.25
BCP153 Daulton Jefferies .20 .50
BCP154 Mark Vientos .20 .50
BCP155 Diego Cartaya .40 1.00
BCP156 Monte Harrison .30 .75
BCP157 Nolan Jones .30 .75
BCP158 Alex Faedo .25 .60
BCP159 Bayron Lora 6.00 15.00
BCP160 Bobby Witt Jr. 5.00 12.00
BCP161 Noah Song .25 .60
BCP162 Nolan Gorman .40 1.00
BCP163 Wander Franco 2.00 5.00
BCP164 Tanner Houck .50 1.25
BCP165 Kyle Isbel .20 .50
BCP166 Brandon Marsh .30 .75
BCP167 Mickey Moniak .50 1.25
BCP168 Brice Turang .20 .50
BCP169 Noelvi Marte .75 2.00
BCP170 Yusniel Diaz .30 .75
BCP171 Elehuris Montero .25 .60
BCP172 Sixto Sanchez .60 1.50
BCP173 Robert Puason 2.50 6.00
BCP174 Jackson Kowar .60 1.50
BCP175 Julio Rodriguez 1.25 3.00
BCP176 Steele Walker .30 .75
BCP177 Tony Santillan .20 .50
BCP178 Mike Siani .20 .50
BCP179 Shane McCarthy .20 .50
BCP180 Keoni Cavaco .20 .50
BCP181 Daulton Varsho .30 .75
BCP182 Ryan Castellani .20 .50
BCP183 Adonis Medina .30 .75
BCP184 MacKenzie Gore .40 1.00
BCP185 Jay Groome .20 .50
BCP186 Andres Gimenez .50 1.25
BCP187 Tristen Lutz .25 .60
BCP188 Leody Taveras .30 .75
BCP189 Triston McKenzie .60 1.50
BCP190 Simeon Woods Richardson .30 .75
BCP191 Kyle Muller .20 .50
BCP192 Forrest Whitley .30 .75
BCP193 Korey Lee .25 .60
BCP194 Freudis Nova .20 .50
BCP195 Royce Lewis .50 1.25
BCP196 Keegan Akin .20 .50
BCP197 Quinn Priester .25 .60
BCP198 Francisco Alvarez .60 1.50
BCP199 Luis Garcia .75 2.00
BCP200 Brennan Malone .20 .50
BCP201 Cristian Pache .60 1.50
BCP202 Geraldo Perdomo .20 .50
BCP203 Ethan Hearn .30 .75
BCP204 Jesus Sanchez .30 .75
BCP205 Tim Cate .20 .50
BCP206 Cole Roederer .40 1.00
BCP207 Jorge Mateo .25 .60
BCP208 Triston Casas .50 1.25
BCP209 Matthew Liberatore .25 .60
BCP210 Keibert Ruiz 1.00 2.50
BCP211 Blake Rutherford .20 .50
BCP212 Jarred Kelenic 1.00 2.50
BCP213 Marco Luciano .75 2.00
BCP214 Deivi Garcia 1.00 2.50
BCP215 Sean Hjelle .30 .75
BCP216 Clarke Schmidt .30 .75
BCP217 Mason Denaburg .20 .50
BCP218 Luis Campusano .30 .75
BCP219 Braden Shewmake .30 .75
BCP220 Ke'Bryan Hayes 1.00 2.50
BCP221 Shane Baz .20 .50
BCP222 Corbin Carroll .30 .75
BCP223 Estevan Florial .30 .75
BCP224 Isaac Paredes .60 1.50
BCP225 Michael Toglia .20 .50
BCP226 Alejandro Kirk .50 1.25
BCP227 Jeter Downs .30 .75
BCP228 Tyler Stephenson .50 1.25
BCP229 Matt Manning .25 .60
BCP230 Luis Garcia .75 2.00
BCP231 Ryan Jensen .25 .60
BCP232 Dane Dunning .60 1.50
BCP233 William Contreras .25 .60
BCP234 Bo Naylor .25 .60
BCP235 Luis Patino .30 .75
BCP236 Dylan Carlson .75 2.00
BCP237 Sam Huff .40 1.00
BCP238 D.L. Hall .20 .50
BCP239 Jackson Rutledge .30 .75
BCP240 Ryan Vilade .20 .50
BCP241 Vidal Brujan 1.50 4.00
BCP242 Seth Corry .20 .50
BCP243 Jasson Dominguez 6.00 15.00
BCP244 Jeremiah Jackson .20 .50
BCP245 Orelvis Martinez .50 1.25
BCP246 Kyren Paris .20 .50
BCP247 Brett Baty .60 1.50
BCP248 Corey Ray .20 .50
BCP249 Trevor Larnach .40 1.00
BCP250 Casey Mize .60 1.50

2020 Bowman Chrome Prospects Aqua Refractors

*AQUA REF: 2X TO 5X BASIC
STATED ODDS 1:162 HOBBY
STATED PRINT RUN 125 SER.#'d SETS
BCP1 Wander Franco 12.00 30.00
BCP8 Jasson Dominguez 150.00 400.00
BCP25 Bobby Witt Jr. 30.00 80.00
BCP86 Bobby Dalbec 10.00 25.00
BCP112 Joey Bart 5.00 12.00

2020 Bowman Chrome Prospects Aqua Shimmer Refractors

*AQUA SHIM REF: 2X TO 5X BASIC
STATED ODDS 1:162 HOBBY
STATED PRINT RUN 125 SER.#'d SETS
BCP1 Wander Franco 12.00 30.00
BCP8 Jasson Dominguez 150.00 400.00
BCP25 Bobby Witt Jr. 30.00 80.00
BCP86 Bobby Dalbec 10.00 25.00
BCP112 Joey Bart 5.00 12.00

2020 Bowman Chrome Prospects Atomic Refractors

*ATOMIC REF: 1.5X TO 4X BASIC
STATED ODDS 1:24 HOBBY
BCP1 Wander Franco 10.00 25.00
BCP8 Jasson Dominguez 125.00 300.00
BCP25 Bobby Witt Jr. 25.00 60.00
BCP86 Bobby Dalbec 8.00 20.00

2020 Bowman Chrome Prospects Blue Refractors

*BLUE REF: 2X TO 5X BASIC
BOW.STATED ODDS 1:307 HOBBY
BOW.CHR.STATED ODDS 1:XXX HOBBY
STATED PRINT RUN 150 SER.#'d SETS
BCP1 Wander Franco 12.00 30.00
BCP8 Jasson Dominguez 150.00 400.00
BCP25 Bobby Witt Jr. 30.00 80.00
BCP86 Bobby Dalbec 10.00 25.00
BCP112 Joey Bart 5.00 12.00
BCP163 Wander Franco 20.00 50.00
BCP198 Francisco Alvarez 8.00 20.00
BCP226 Alejandro Kirk 8.00 20.00
BCP247 Brett Baty 6.00 15.00

2020 Bowman Chrome Prospects Blue Shimmer Refractors

*BLUE SHIM REF: 2X TO 5X BASIC
STATED ODDS 1:307 HOBBY
STATED PRINT RUN 150 SER.#'d SETS
BCP1 Wander Franco 12.00 30.00
BCP8 Jasson Dominguez 150.00 400.00
BCP25 Bobby Witt Jr. 30.00 80.00
BCP86 Bobby Dalbec 10.00 25.00
BCP112 Joey Bart 5.00 12.00

2020 Bowman Chrome Prospects Gold Refractors

*GOLD REF: 6X TO 15X BASIC
BOW.STATED ODDS 1:919 HOBBY
BOW.CHR.STATED ODDS 1:XXX HOBBY
STATED PRINT RUN 50 SER.#'d SETS
BCP1 Wander Franco 40.00 100.00
BCP8 Jasson Dominguez 500.00 1200.00
BCP25 Bobby Witt Jr. 100.00 250.00
BCP86 Bobby Dalbec 30.00 80.00
BCP112 Joey Bart 15.00 40.00
BCP163 Wander Franco 60.00 150.00
BCP198 Francisco Alvarez 25.00 60.00
BCP226 Alejandro Kirk 25.00 60.00
BCP247 Brett Baty 20.00 50.00

2020 Bowman Chrome Prospects Gold Shimmer Refractors

*GOLD SHIM REF: 6X TO 15X BASIC
BOW.STATED ODDS 1:919 HOBBY
BOW.CHR.STATED ODDS 1:XX HOBBY
STATED PRINT RUN 50 SER.#'d SETS
BCP1 Wander Franco 40.00 100.00
BCP8 Jasson Dominguez 500.00 1200.00
BCP25 Bobby Witt Jr. 100.00 250.00
BCP86 Bobby Dalbec 30.00 80.00
BCP112 Joey Bart 15.00 40.00
BCP163 Wander Franco 60.00 150.00
BCP198 Francisco Alvarez 25.00 60.00
BCP226 Alejandro Kirk 25.00 60.00
BCP247 Brett Baty 20.00 50.00

2020 Bowman Chrome Prospects Green Refractors

*GREEN REF: 3X TO 8X BASIC
BOW.STATED ODDS 1:218 RETAIL
BOW.CHR.STATED ODDS 1:XXX RETAIL
STATED PRINT RUN 99 SER.#'d SETS
BCP1 Wander Franco 20.00 50.00
BCP8 Jasson Dominguez 250.00 600.00
BCP25 Bobby Witt Jr. 50.00 120.00
BCP86 Bobby Dalbec 15.00 40.00
BCP112 Joey Bart 8.00 20.00
BCP163 Wander Franco 30.00 80.00
BCP198 Francisco Alvarez 12.00 30.00
BCP226 Alejandro Kirk 12.00 30.00
BCP247 Brett Baty 10.00 25.00

2020 Bowman Chrome Prospects Green Shimmer Refractors

*GREEN SHIM REF: 3X TO 8X BASIC
BOW.STATED ODDS 1:218 RETAIL
BOW.CHR.STATED ODDS 1:XXX RETAIL
STATED PRINT RUN 99 SER.#'d SETS
BCP1 Wander Franco 20.00 50.00
BCP8 Jasson Dominguez 250.00 600.00
BCP25 Bobby Witt Jr. 50.00 120.00
BCP86 Bobby Dalbec 15.00 40.00
BCP112 Joey Bart 8.00 20.00
BCP163 Wander Franco 30.00 80.00
BCP198 Francisco Alvarez 12.00 30.00
BCP226 Alejandro Kirk 12.00 30.00
BCP247 Brett Baty 10.00 25.00

2020 Bowman Chrome Prospects Orange Refractors

*ORANGE REF: 10X TO 25X BASIC
BOW.STATED ODDS 1:367 HOBBY
BOW.CHR.STATED ODDS 1:367 HOBBY
STATED PRINT RUN 25 SER.#'d SETS
BCP1 Wander Franco 60.00 150.00
BCP8 Jasson Dominguez 750.00 2000.00
BCP25 Bobby Witt Jr. 150.00 400.00
BCP86 Bobby Dalbec 50.00 120.00
BCP112 Joey Bart 25.00 60.00
BCP163 Wander Franco 100.00 250.00
BCP198 Francisco Alvarez 40.00 100.00
BCP226 Alejandro Kirk 40.00 100.00
BCP247 Brett Baty 30.00 80.00

2020 Bowman Chrome Prospects Orange Shimmer Refractors

*ORANGE SHIM REF: 10X TO 25X BASIC
BOW.STATED ODDS 1:367 HOBBY
BOW.CHR.STATED ODDS 1:XXX HOBBY
STATED PRINT RUN 25 SER.#'d SETS
BCP1 Wander Franco 60.00 150.00
BCP8 Jasson Dominguez 750.00 2000.00
BCP25 Bobby Witt Jr. 150.00 400.00
BCP86 Bobby Dalbec 50.00 120.00
BCP112 Joey Bart 25.00 60.00
BCP163 Wander Franco 100.00 250.00
BCP198 Francisco Alvarez 40.00 100.00
BCP226 Alejandro Kirk 40.00 100.00
BCP247 Brett Baty 30.00 80.00

2020 Bowman Chrome Prospects Purple Refractors

*PURPLE REF: 1.5X TO 4X BASIC
BOW.STATED ODDS 1:185 HOBBY
BOW.CHR.STATED ODDS 1:XXX HOBBY
STATED PRINT RUN 250 SER.#'d SETS
BCP1 Wander Franco 10.00 25.00
BCP8 Jasson Dominguez 125.00 300.00
BCP25 Bobby Witt Jr. 25.00 60.00
BCP86 Bobby Dalbec 8.00 20.00
BCP163 Wander Franco 15.00 40.00
BCP198 Francisco Alvarez 6.00 15.00
BCP226 Alejandro Kirk 6.00 15.00
BCP247 Brett Baty 5.00 12.00

2020 Bowman Chrome Prospects Purple Shimmer Refractors

*PURPLE SHIM REF: 1X TO 2.5X BASIC
STATED ODDS 1:XXX HOBBY
BCP163 Wander Franco 10.00 25.00
BCP198 Francisco Alvarez 4.00 10.00
BCP226 Alejandro Kirk 4.00 10.00

2020 Bowman Chrome Prospects Refractors

*REF: 1.2X TO 3X BASIC
BOW.STATED ODDS 1:93 HOBBY
BOW.CHR.STATED ODDS 1:XX HOBBY
STATED PRINT RUN 499 SER.#'d SETS
BCP8 Jasson Dominguez 100.00 250.00
BCP163 Wander Franco 12.00 30.00
BCP198 Francisco Alvarez 5.00 12.00
BCP226 Alejandro Kirk 5.00 12.00
BCP247 Brett Baty 4.00 10.00

2020 Bowman Chrome Prospects Speckle Refractors

*SPECKLE REF: 1.5X TO 4X BASIC
STATED ODDS 1:155 HOBBY
STATED PRINT RUN 299 SER.#'d SETS
BCP1 Wander Franco 10.00 25.00
BCP8 Jasson Dominguez 125.00 300.00
BCP25 Bobby Witt Jr. 25.00 60.00
BCP86 Bobby Dalbec 8.00 20.00

2020 Bowman Chrome Prospects Yellow Refractors

*YELLOW REF: 4X TO 10X BASIC
STATED ODDS 1:613 HOBBY
STATED PRINT RUN 75 SER.#'d SETS
BCP1 Wander Franco 25.00 60.00
BCP8 Jasson Dominguez 300.00 800.00
BCP25 Bobby Witt Jr. 60.00 150.00
BCP86 Bobby Dalbec 20.00 50.00
BCP112 Joey Bart 10.00 25.00

2020 Bowman Chrome Rookie Autographs

BOW.STATED ODDS 1:667 HOBBY
BOW.CHR.STATED ODDS 1:XXX HOBBY
BOW.PLATE ODDS 1:18,527 HOBBY
PLATE PRINT RUN 1 SET PER COLOR
BLACK-CYAN-MAGENTA-YELLOW ISSUED
NO PLATE PRICING DUE TO SCARCITY
BOW.EXCH.DEADLINE 3/31/2022
BOW.CHR.EXCH.DEADLINE 8/31/2022
CRAAA Aristides Aquino 15.00 40.00
CRAAK Anthony Kay 3.00 8.00
CRAAM Andres Munoz 5.00 12.00
CRAAP A.J. Puk 5.00 12.00
CRABB Bobby Bradley 3.00 8.00
CRABG Brusdar Graterol 8.00 20.00
CRABM McKay Arm Frwrd 5.00 12.00
CRADC Dylan Cease 10.00 25.00
CRADM Dustin May 30.00 80.00
CRAGL Gavin Lux 25.00 60.00
CRAID Isan Diaz 5.00 12.00
CRAJD Justin Dunn 4.00 10.00
CRAJF Jake Fraley 6.00 15.00
CRAJL Jesus Luzardo 12.00 30.00
CRAJY Jordan Yamamoto 3.00 8.00
CRAKL Kyle Lewis 60.00 150.00
CRALA Logan Allen 3.00 8.00
CRALR L.Robert Face Rght 250.00 600.00
CRALR L.Robert Face Lft 250.00 600.00
CRAMD Mauricio Dubon 6.00 15.00
CRANH Nico Hoerner 20.00 50.00
CRANS Nick Solak 15.00 40.00
CRASB Seth Brown 3.00 8.00
CRATG Trent Grisham 25.00 60.00
CRAYA Yordan Alvarez 50.00 120.00
CRAYT Yoshi Tsutsugo 25.00 60.00
CRAZC Zack Collins 8.00 20.00

2020 Bowman Chrome Rookie Autographs Atomic Refractors

*ATOMIC REF: .75X TO 2X BASIC
STATED ODDS 1:2917 HOBBY
STATED PRINT RUN 100 SER.#'d SETS
EXCHANGE DEADLINE 3/31/2022
CRAAAQ Aristides Aquino 25.00 60.00
CRAYC Yu Chang 20.00 50.00

2020 Bowman Chrome Rookie Autographs Blue Refractors

*BLUE REF: .6X TO 1.5X BASIC
BOW.STATED ODDS 1:1946 HOBBY
BOW.CHR.STATED ODDS 1:XXX HOBBY
STATED PRINT RUN 150 SER.#'d SETS
BOW.EXCH.DEADLINE 3/31/2022
BOW.CHR.EXCH.DEADLINE 8/31/2022
CRAAAQ Aristides Aquino 20.00 50.00
CRADL Domingo Leyba 6.00 15.00
CRAYC Yu Chang 15.00 40.00

2020 Bowman Chrome Rookie Autographs Gold Refractors

*GOLD REF: 1.2X TO 3X BASIC
BOW.STATED ODDS 1:5847 HOBBY
BOW.CHR.STATED ODDS 1:XXX HOBBY
STATED PRINT RUN 50 SER.#'d SETS
BOW.EXCH.DEADLINE 3/31/2022
BOW.CHR.EXCH.DEADLINE 8/31/2022
CRAAAQ Aristides Aquino 40.00 100.00
CRABBI Bo Bichette 300.00 800.00
CRABM McKay Arm Back 15.00 40.00
CRADL Domingo Leyba 12.00 30.00
CRAYC Yu Chang 30.00 80.00

2020 Bowman Chrome Rookie Autographs Green Refractors

*GREEN REF: .75X TO 2X BASIC
BOW.STATED ODDS 1:2264 BLASTER
BOW.CHR.STATED ODDS 1:XXX HOBBY
STATED PRINT RUN 99 SER.#'d SETS
BOW.EXCH.DEADLINE 3/31/2022
BOW.CHR.EXCH.DEADLINE 8/31/2022
CRAAAQ Aristides Aquino 25.00 60.00
CRADL Domingo Leyba 8.00 20.00
CRAYC Yu Chang 20.00 50.00

2020 Bowman Chrome Rookie Autographs Orange Refractors

*ORANGE REF: 2X TO 5X BASIC
BOW.STATED ODDS 1:3575 HOBBY
BOW.CHR.STATED ODDS 1:XXX HOBBY
STATED PRINT RUN 25 SER.#'d SETS
BOW.EXCH.DEADLINE 3/31/2022
BOW.CHR.EXCH.DEADLINE 8/31/2022
CRAAAQ Aristides Aquino 60.00 150.00
CRABBI Bo Bichette 500.00 1200.00
CRABM McKay Arm Back 25.00 60.00
CRADL Domingo Leyba 20.00 50.00
CRAYC Yu Chang 50.00 120.00

2020 Bowman Chrome Rookie Autographs Refractors

*REF: .5X TO 1.2X BASIC
BOW.STATED ODDS 1:798 HOBBY
BOW.CHR.STATED ODDS 1:XXX HOBBY
STATED PRINT RUN 499 SER.#'d SETS
BOW.EXCH.DEADLINE 3/31/2022
BOW.CHR.EXCH.DEADLINE 8/31/2022
CRADL Domingo Leyba 5.00 12.00

2020 Bowman Chrome Rookie Autographs Yellow Refractors

*YELLOW REF: .75X TO 2X BASIC
STATED ODDS 1:5139 HOBBY
STATED PRINT RUN 75 SER.#'d SETS
EXCHANGE DEADLINE 3/31/2022
CRAAAQ Aristides Aquino 25.00 60.00
CRABBI Bo Bichette 200.00 500.00
CRABM McKay Arm Back 10.00 25.00
CRAYC Yu Chang 20.00 50.00

2020 Bowman Chrome Rookie of the Year Favorites

STATED ODDS 1:8 HOBBY
*ATOMIC REF/150: 2.5X TO 6X BASE
*GREEN REF/99: 2.5X TO 6X BASE
*GOLD REF/50: 4X TO 10X BASIC
*ORANGE REF/25: 8X TO 20X BASE
ROYFAA Adbert Alzolay .30 .75
ROYFAAQ Aristides Aquino .60 1.50
ROYFAC Aaron Civale .50 1.25
ROYFAP A.J. Puk .40 1.00
ROYFBB Bo Bichette 4.00 10.00
ROYFBM Brendan McKay .40 1.00
ROYFDC Dylan Cease .40 1.00
ROYFDM Dustin May .75 2.00
ROYFGL Gavin Lux 1.25 3.00
ROYFJL Jesus Luzardo .50 1.25
ROYFJY Jordan Yamamoto .25 .60
ROYFKL Kyle Lewis 2.00 5.00
ROYFNH Nico Hoerner 1.00 2.50
ROYFSM Sean Murphy .40 1.00
ROYFYA Yordan Alvarez 2.50 6.00

2020 Bowman Chrome Rookie of the Year Favorites Autographs

STATED ODDS 1:2653 HOBBY
STATED PRINT RUN 150 SER.#'d SETS
EXCHANGE DEADLINE 3/31/2022
*GOLD REF/50: .5X TO 1.2X
*ORANGE REF/25: .6X TO 1.5X
ROYFAAAQ Aristides Aquino 20.00 50.00
ROYFAAJP A.J. Puk 5.00 12.00
ROYFABB Bobby Bradley 3.00 8.00
ROYFABM Brendan McKay 10.00 25.00
ROYFADC Dylan Cease 10.00 25.00
ROYFAGL Gavin Lux 50.00 120.00
ROYFAJL Jesus Luzardo 6.00 15.00
ROYFAJY Jordan Yamamoto 3.00 8.00
ROYFANH Nico Hoerner
ROYFAYA Yordan Alvarez 40.00 100.00
ROYFAZC Zack Collins 4.00 10.00

2020 Bowman Chrome Scouts Top 100

STATED ODDS 1:4 HOBBY
*ATOMIC REF/150: 2.5X TO 6X BASE
*GREEN REF/99: 2.5X TO 6X BASE
*GOLD REF/50: 4X TO 10X BASIC
*GARY VEE/55: 4X TO 10X BASIC
*ORANGE REF/25: 8X TO 20X BASE
BTP1 Wander Franco 3.00 8.00
BTP2 Luis Robert 3.00 8.00
BTP3 Jo Adell 1.00 2.50
BTP4 MacKenzie Gore .50 1.25
BTP5 Gavin Lux 1.25 3.00
BTP6 Jesus Luzardo .50 1.25
BTP7 Adley Rutschman 1.50 4.00
BTP8 Forrest Whitley .40 1.00
BTP9 Joey Bart .75 2.00
BTP10 Nate Pearson .75 2.00
BTP11 Casey Mize .75 2.00
BTP12 Jarred Kelenic 1.25 3.00
BTP13 Cristian Pache .75 2.00
BTP14 Brendan McKay .40 1.00
BTP15 Dylan Carlson 1.00 2.50
BTP16 Julio Rodriguez 1.50 4.00
BTP17 Matt Manning .30 .75
BTP18 Alex Kirilloff .50 1.25
BTP19 Carter Kieboom .30 .75
BTP20 Dustin May .75 2.00
BTP21 Royce Lewis .60 1.50
BTP22 Brendan Rodgers .40 1.00
BTP23 Sixto Sanchez .75 2.00
BTP24 Ian Anderson .75 2.00
BTP25 Bobby Witt Jr. 1.50 4.00
BTP26 Luis Patino .40 1.00
BTP27 A.J. Puk .40 1.00
BTP28 Andrew Vaughn 1.00 2.50
BTP29 Alec Bohm 1.50 4.00
BTP30 Drew Waters .60 1.50
BTP31 Michael Kopech .50 1.25
BTP32 DL Hall .25 .60
BTP33 Nico Hoerner 1.00 2.50
BTP34 Taylor Trammell .40 1.00
BTP35 Riley Greene 1.00 2.50
BTP36 Spencer Howard .75 2.00
BTP37 Matthew Liberatore .30 .75
BTP38 Mitch Keller .40 1.00
BTP39 Tarik Skubal 1.25 3.00
BTP40 CJ Abrams .75 2.00
BTP41 Brusdar Graterol .40 1.00
BTP42 Nick Madrigal 1.00 2.50
BTP43 Nolan Gorman .50 1.25
BTP44 Ke'Bryan Hayes 1.25 3.00
BTP45 Daniel Lynch .25 .60
BTP46 Logan Gilbert .30 .75
BTP47 Jordan Groshans .50 1.25
BTP48 Jesus Sanchez .40 1.00
BTP49 Grayson Rodriguez .40 1.00
BTP50 Nolan Jones .40 1.00
BTP51 Hunter Greene .40 1.00
BTP52 Triston Casas .60 1.50
BTP53 Jasson Dominguez 8.00 20.00
BTP54 Adrian Morejon .25 .60
BTP55 Kyle Wright .40 1.00
BTP56 JJ Bleday .75 2.00
BTP57 Marco Luciano 1.00 2.50
BTP58 Evan White .60 1.50
BTP59 Bobby Dalbec 1.50 4.00
BTP60 Jeter Downs .40 1.00
BTP61 Alek Thomas .30 .75
BTP62 Brady Singer 1.25 3.00
BTP63 Kristian Robinson .75 2.00
BTP64 Justin Dunn .30 .75
BTP65 Keibert Ruiz 1.25 3.00
BTP66 Jonathan India 1.50 4.00
BTP67 Ronny Mauricio .60 1.50
BTP68 Kyle Muller .25 .60
BTP69 Oneil Cruz .30 .75
BTP70 Deivi Garcia 1.25 3.00
BTP71 Bryse Wilson .30 .75
BTP72 Justus Sheffield .40 1.00
BTP73 Andres Gimenez .60 1.50
BTP74 Bryan Mata .25 .60
BTP75 Daulton Varsho .40 1.00
BTP76 Nick Lodolo .40 1.00
BTP77 Francisco Alvarez .75 2.00
BTP78 Josiah Gray .40 1.00
BTP79 Sean Murphy .40 1.00
BTP80 Heliot Ramos .40 1.00
BTP81 Jackson Kowar .75 2.00
BTP82 Vidal Brujan 2.00 5.00
BTP83 Shane Baz .25 .60
BTP84 Yusniel Diaz .40 1.00
BTP85 Triston McKenzie .75 2.00
BTP86 George Valera .50 1.25
BTP87 Hunter Bishop .50 1.25
BTP88 Ryan Mountcastle 1.25 3.00
BTP89 Trevor Larnach .50 1.25
BTP90 Corbin Carroll .40 1.00
BTP91 Tyler Freeman .30 .75
BTP92 Hans Crouse .25 .60
BTP93 Shane McClanahan .30 .75
BTP94 Edward Cabrera .40 1.00
BTP95 Luis Garcia 1.00 2.50
BTP96 Luis Campusano .40 1.00
BTP97 Brailyn Marquez .60 1.50
BTP98 Tony Gonsolin 1.00 2.50
BTP99 Elehuris Montero .30 .75
BTP100 Ronaldo Hernandez .25 .60

2020 Bowman Chrome Scouts Top 100 Autographs

STATED ODDS 1:1300 HOBBY
STATED PRINT RUN 50 SER.#'d SETS
EXCHANGE DEADLINE 3/31/2022
BTP1 Wander Franco 125.00 300.00
BTP3 Jo Adell 60.00 150.00
BTP4 MacKenzie Gore 50.00 120.00
BTP5 Gavin Lux 50.00 120.00
BTP6 Jesus Luzardo 10.00 25.00
BTP7 Adley Rutschman 75.00 200.00
BTP9 Joey Bart 30.00 80.00
BTP11 Casey Mize 30.00 80.00
BTP12 Jarred Kelenic 60.00 150.00
BTP14 Brendan McKay 15.00 40.00
BTP15 Dylan Carlson 40.00 100.00
BTP16 Julio Rodriguez 50.00 120.00
BTP17 Matt Manning 40.00 100.00
BTP19 Carter Kieboom 6.00 15.00
BTP21 Royce Lewis 25.00 60.00
BTP22 Brendan Rodgers 12.00 30.00
BTP23 Sixto Sanchez 20.00 50.00
BTP25 Bobby Witt Jr. 125.00 300.00
BTP27 A.J. Puk 20.00 50.00
BTP28 Andrew Vaughn 20.00 50.00
BTP31 Michael Kopech 10.00 25.00
BTP33 Nico Hoerner 20.00 50.00
BTP35 Riley Greene 40.00 100.00
BTP36 Spencer Howard 40.00 100.00
BTP37 Matthew Liberatore 15.00 40.00
BTP38 Mitch Keller 8.00 20.00
BTP39 Tarik Skubal 25.00 60.00
BTP40 C.J. Abrams 40.00 100.00
BTP41 Brusdar Graterol 8.00 20.00
BTP42 Nick Madrigal 15.00 40.00
BTP43 Nolan Gorman 10.00 25.00
BTP46 Logan Gilbert 6.00 15.00
BTP47 Jordan Groshans 10.00 25.00
BTP49 Grayson Rodriguez 15.00 40.00
BTP51 Hunter Greene 30.00 80.00
BTP52 Triston Casas 30.00 80.00
BTP53 Jasson Dominguez 300.00 800.00
BTP55 Kyle Wright 12.00 30.00
BTP58 Evan White 30.00 80.00
BTP59 Bobby Dalbec 15.00 40.00
BTP60 Jeter Downs 15.00 40.00
BTP61 Alek Thomas 15.00 40.00
BTP62 Brady Singer 15.00 40.00
BTP63 Kristian Robinson 20.00 50.00
BTP65 Keibert Ruiz 25.00 60.00
BTP66 Jonathan India 25.00 60.00
BTP67 Ronny Mauricio 20.00 50.00
BTP68 Kyle Muller 10.00 25.00
BTP70 Deivi Garcia 20.00 50.00
BTP71 Bryse Wilson 6.00 15.00
BTP72 Justus Sheffield 8.00 20.00
BTP75 Daulton Varsho 30.00 80.00
BTP76 Nick Lodolo 10.00 25.00
BTP78 Josiah Gray 10.00 25.00
BTP79 Sean Murphy
BTP80 Heliot Ramos 12.00 30.00
BTP81 Jackson Kowar 15.00 40.00
BTP88 Ryan Mountcastle 25.00 60.00
BTP89 Trevor Larnach 20.00 50.00
BTP90 Corbin Carroll 8.00 20.00
BTP91 Tyler Freeman 10.00 25.00
BTP93 Shane McClanahan 12.00 30.00
BTP95 Luis Garcia 15.00 40.00
BTP97 Brailyn Marquez 20.00 50.00
BTP99 Elehuris Montero 6.00 15.00
BTP100 Ronaldo Hernandez 5.00 12.00

2020 Bowman Chrome Spanning the Globe

STATED ODDS 1:6 HOBBY
*ATOMIC REF/150: 2.5X TO 6X BASE
*GREEN REF/99: 2.5X TO 6X BASE
*GOLD REF/50: 4X TO 10X BASIC
*ORANGE REF/25: 8X TO 20X BASE
STGAA Adbert Alzolay .30 .75
STGAM Andres Munoz .40 1.00
STGCM Casey Mize .75 2.00
STGDB Dasan Brown .60 1.50
STGEP Eric Pardinho .30 .75
STGHR Heliot Ramos .40 1.00
STGIP Isaac Paredes .75 2.00
STGJA Jo Adell 1.00 2.50
STGJB Jordan Balazovic .50 1.25
STGJD Jasson Dominguez 8.00 20.00
STGJL Jesus Luzardo .50 1.25
STGLP Luis Patino .40 1.00
STGLR Luis Robert 2.00 5.00
STGMA Miguel Amaya .25 .60
STGML Matthew Lugo .40 1.00
STGRH Ronaldo Hernandez .25 .60
STGUB Ulrich Bojarski .40 1.00
STGVVM Victor Victor Mesa .40 1.00
STGWF Wander Franco 4.00 10.00
STGYC Yu Chang .40 1.00

2020 Bowman Chrome Stat Track

STATED ODDS 1:XX HOBBY
*ATOMIC/150: 1.2X TO 3X BASE
*ORANGE/25: 2.5X TO 6X BASE
ST1 Jordan Balazovic .60 1.50
ST2 Sam Huff .60 1.50
ST3 Niko Hulsizer .75 2.00
ST4 Riley Greene 1.25 3.00
ST5 Max Lazar .40 1.00
ST6 Cristian Pache 1.00 2.50
ST7 Glenallen Hill Jr. .50 1.25
ST8 Bayron Lora 1.50 4.00
ST9 Jarren Duran 1.25 3.00
ST10 Alek Manoah .40 1.00
ST11 Bobby Witt Jr. 2.00 5.00
ST12 Ulrich Bojarski .50 1.25
ST13 Antonio Cabello 1.00 2.50
ST14 Brenton Doyle 1.50 4.00
ST15 Daniel Espino .40 1.00
ST16 Anthony Volpe 1.25 3.00
ST17 Will Wilson .40 1.00
ST18 Adley Rutschman 2.00 5.00
ST19 Everson Pereira .75 2.00
ST20 Joe Ryan .40 1.00
ST21 Isaac Paredes 1.00 2.50
ST22 Ethan Lindow .40 1.00
ST23 Alvaro Seijas .30 .75
ST24 Lewin Diaz .30 .75
ST25 Andrew Vaughn 1.25 3.00
ST26 Braden Shewmake .50 1.25
ST27 George Kirby .50 1.25
ST28 Ezequiel Duran .60 1.50
ST29 Xavier Edwards 1.25 3.00
ST30 Canaan Smith .50 1.25

2020 Bowman Chrome Stat Track Autographs

STATED ODDS 1:XXX HOBBY
STATED PRINT RUN 99 SER.#'d SETS
EXCHANGE DEADLINE 8/31/2022
*ORANGE/25: .5X TO 1.2X BASIC
STAAM Alek Manoah 4.00 10.00
STAAR Adley Rutschman 25.00 60.00
STAAS Alvaro Seijas 6.00 15.00
STAAV Andrew Vaughn 12.00 30.00
STAAVO Anthony Volpe 12.00 30.00
STABD Brenton Doyle 20.00 50.00
STABWJ Bobby Witt Jr. 100.00 250.00
STACS Canaan Smith 8.00 20.00
STAED Ezequiel Duran 10.00 25.00
STAEL Ethan Lindow 6.00 15.00
STAEP Everson Pereira 12.00 30.00
STAGHJ Glenallen Hill Jr. 5.00 12.00
STAJB Jordan Balazovic EXCH 10.00 25.00
STAJD Jarren Duran 15.00 40.00
STAJR Joe Ryan 6.00 15.00
STALD Lewin Diaz 6.00 15.00
STAML Max Lazar 4.00 10.00
STANH Niko Hulsizer 8.00 20.00
STARG Riley Greene 15.00 40.00
STASH Sam Huff 12.00 30.00
STAXE Xavier Edwards 8.00 20.00

2020 Bowman Chrome Talent Pipeline

STATED ODDS 1:12 HOBBY
*ATOMIC REF/150: 1.2X TO 3X BASE
*GREEN REF/99: 1.2X TO 3X BASE
*GOLD REF/50: 4X TO 10X BASIC
*ORANGE REF/25: 5X TO 12X BASE
TPARI Rbnsn/Wdnr/Beer .75 2.00
TPATL Andrsn/Shwmke/Lnglrs .75 2.00
TPBAL Mntcstle/Diaz/Rtschmn 1.50 4.00
TPBOS Dlbc/Css/Drn 1.50 4.00
TPCHI Clftn/Thmpsn/Rdrr .50 1.25
TPCIN Inda/Grne/Rdrgz 1.50 4.00
TPCLE Daniel Johnson .40 1.00
Nolan Jones
Bo Naylor
TPCOL Roberto Ramos .25 .60
Grant Lavigne
Colton Welker
TPCWS Adlfo/Rbrt/Vghn 2.00 5.00
TPDET Cmrn/Grne/Mize 1.00 2.50
TPHOU Forrest Whitley .40 1.00
J.J. Matijevic
Freudis Nova
TPKCR Foster Griffin .40 1.00
Khalil Lee
Kris Bubic
TPLAA Adll/Jns/Adms 1.00 2.50
TPLAD Ptrs/Dwns/Hse .75 2.00
TPMIA Chshlm/Snchz/Bldy 1.00 2.50
TPMIL Corey Ray .25 .60
Jake Gatewood
Brice Turang
TPMIN Rkr/Lws/Blzvc .60 1.50
TPNYM Ali Sanchez .75 2.00
Andres Gimenez
Brett Baty
TPNYY Grca/Schmdt/Flrl 1.25 3.00
TPOAK Alfonso Rivas .30 .75
Greg Deichmann
Lazaro Armenteros
TPPHI Jns/Bohm/Grca 1.50 4.00
TPPIT Ke'Bryan Hayes 1.25 3.00
Oneil Cruz
Cal Mitchell
TPSDP Gttys/Abrms/Trmmll .75 2.00
TPSEA Klnic/RdrgzKnpp 1.50 4.00
TPSFG Bshp/Bart/Mllr .75 2.00
TPSTL Crlsn/Mntro/Grmn 1.00 2.50
TPTBR Brjn/Frnco/Pdlo 2.50 6.00
TPTEX Huff/Tvrs/Ibnz .50 1.25
TPTOR Smth/Prsn/Prdnho .75 2.00
TPWAS Wil Crowe 1.00 2.50
Luis Garcia
Jackson Rutledge

2020 Bowman Chrome Draft

STATED PLATE ODDS 1:XXX HOBBY
PLATE PRINT RUN 1 SET PER COLOR
BLACK-CYAN-MAGENTA-YELLOW ISSUED
NO PLATE PRICING DUE TO SCARCITY
BD1 Niko Hulsizer .60 1.50
BD2 Jackson Kowar .75 2.00
BD3 Korey Lee .30 .75
BD4 Milan Tolentino .40 1.00
BD5 Jeter Downs .40 1.00
BD6 Hans Crouse .25 .60
BD7 Mike Siani .25 .60
BD8 Dane Acker .40 1.00
BD9 Ryan Jensen .30 .75
BD10 Shane Baz .25 .60
BD11 Trei Cruz 1.00 2.50
BD12 Emerson Hancock 1.00 2.50
BD13 Joey Cantillo .25 .60
BD14 Nick Loftin .40 1.00
BD15 Rece Hinds .30 .75
BD16 Jared Shuster .50 1.25
BD17 Jesse Franklin V 1.00 2.50
BD18 Kaden Polcovich .40 1.00
BD19 Ben Hernandez .40 1.00
BD20 Spencer Strider .40 1.00
BD21 Tyler Brown .40 1.00
BD22 Keoni Cavaco .25 .60
BD23 Case Williams .30 .75
BD24 Cade Cavalli .50 1.25
BD25 Burl Carraway .50 1.25
BD26 Daniel Espino .30 .75
BD27 Oswald Peraza .60 1.50
BD28 Zach DeLoach 1.00 2.50
BD29 Nick Yorke 1.25 3.00
BD30 Clayton Beeter .60 1.50
BD31 Joe Ryan .30 .75
BD32 Jordan Groshans .50 1.25
BD33 Gage Workman 1.00 2.50
BD34 Austin Hendrick 6.00 15.00
BD35 Jimmy Glowenke .50 1.25
BD36 Ryan Rolison .30 .75
BD37 Logan Gilbert .30 .75
BD38 Bobby Miller 1.00 2.50
BD39 Robert Hassell 8.00 20.00
BD40 JJ Goss .25 .60
BD41 Reid Detmers .60 1.50
BD42 Michael Busch .60 1.50
BD43 Chris McMahon .40 1.00
BD44 Xavier Edwards 1.00 2.50
BD45 Alec Burleson .40 1.00
BD46 Freddy Zamora .40 1.00
BD47 Travis Swaggerty .30 .75
BD48 Sammy Infante 1.00 2.50
BD49 Owen Caissie .50 1.25
BD50 Max Meyer 1.00 2.50
BD51 Logan Allen .25 .60
BD52 Landon Knack .60 1.50
BD53 Quinn Priester .30 .75
BD54 Colt Keith 1.25 3.00
BD55 Jarren Duran 1.00 2.50
BD56 Austin Wells 6.00 15.00
BD57 Jordan Walker 8.00 20.00
BD58 Jordan Balazovic .50 1.25
BD59 Masyn Winn 2.00 5.00
BD60 Carson Tucker 2.00 5.00
BD61 Nick Bitsko .75 2.00
BD62 Daniel Cabrera 1.00 2.50
BD63 Marco Raya .50 1.25
BD64 Kyle Nicolas .40 1.00
BD65 Oneil Cruz .30 .75
BD66 Hunter Barnhart .25 .60
BD67 Cole Henry .30 .75
BD68 Tristen Lutz .30 .75
BD69 Petey Halpin .60 1.50
BD70 Jared Jones .40 1.00
BD71 Connor Phillips .40 1.00
BD72 Pete Crow-Armstrong 3.00 8.00
BD73 Casey Martin .75 2.00
BD74 Bryce Bonnin .40 1.00
BD75 Daniel Lynch .25 .60
BD76 Tekoah Roby .25 .60
BD77 Isaiah Greene 1.00 2.50
BD78 Tyler Freeman .30 .75
BD79 Heliot Ramos .40 1.00
BD80 Miguel Amaya .25 .60
BD81 Nick Gonzales 8.00 20.00
BD82 DL Hall .25 .60
BD83 Triston Casas .60 1.50
BD84 Christian Chamberlain .40 1.00
BD85 Slade Cecconi .30 .75
BD86 Tink Hence .40 1.00
BD87 Adisyn Coffey .25 .60
BD88 Asa Lacy 4.00 10.00
BD89 Geraldo Perdomo .25 .60
BD90 Nick Garcia .40 1.00
BD91 Nick Swiney .50 1.25
BD92 Matthew Dyer .40 1.00
BD93 CJ Van Eyk .40 1.00
BD94 Alerick Soularie .30 .75
BD95 Garrett Crochet 8.00 20.00
BD96 Ian Seymour .25 .60
BD97 Zavier Warren .25 .60
BD98 Ed Howard 12.00 30.00
BD99 Justin Lange .25 .60
BD100 Ian Bedell .30 .75
BD101 Aaron Shortridge .30 .75
BD102 Trevor Larnach .50 1.25
BD103 David Calabrese .50 1.25
BD104 Quin Cotton .25 .60
BD105 Luke Little .40 1.00
BD106 Drew Romo .60 1.50
BD107 Zac Veen 15.00 40.00
BD108 Brady McConnell .30 .75
BD109 Sam Weatherly .25 .60
BD110 Jordan Nwogu 1.00 2.50
BD111 Jordan Westburg .60 1.50
BD112 Zach McCambley .25 .60
BD113 Trevor Hauver .40 1.00
BD114 Corbin Carroll .40 1.00
BD115 Tanner Burns .40 1.00
BD116 Jackson Miller .60 1.50
BD117 Carter Baumler .40 1.00
BD118 Garrett Mitchell 12.00 30.00
BD119 Tyler Soderstrom 3.00 8.00
BD120 Holden Powell .30 .75
BD121 Spencer Torkelson 25.00 60.00
BD122 Heston Kjerstad 6.00 15.00
BD123 Alexander Canario .25 .60
BD124 Justin Foscue 1.00 2.50
BD125 Levi Prater .30 .75
BD126 Evan Carter .60 1.50
BD127 Bryce Jarvis .30 .75
BD128 Werner Blakely .30 .75
BD129 Casey Schmitt .60 1.50
BD130 Hudson Haskin 1.00 2.50
BD131 Daxton Fulton .40 1.00
BD132 Luis Gil .30 .75
BD133 Zach Daniels .40 1.00
BD134 Jeff Criswell .30 .75
BD135 Shane McClanahan .30 .75
BD136 Alika Williams .30 .75
BD137 Gilberto Jimenez 1.25 3.00
BD138 Trent Palmer .30 .75
BD139 Alex Santos .75 2.00
BD140 Bryson Stott .60 1.50
BD141 Ethan Hankins .30 .75
BD142 Kody Hoese .75 2.00
BD143 Francisco Alvarez .75 2.00
BD144 Dillon Dingler 1.25 3.00
BD145 Carson Ragsdale .40 1.00
BD146 Patrick Bailey 8.00 20.00
BD147 Liam Norris .25 .60
BD148 RJ Dabovich .25 .60
BD149 Carmen Mlodzinski .30 .75
BD150 AJ Vukovich 2.50 6.00
BD151 Jasson Dominguez 8.00 20.00
BD152 Bobby Witt Jr. 5.00 12.00
BD153 Andrew Vaughn 1.00 2.50
BD154 Adley Rutschman 1.50 4.00
BD155 Robert Puason .75 2.00
BD156 Jay Groome .25 .60
BD157 Will Klein .30 .75
BD158 Zach Britton .30 .75
BD159 Owen Miller .25 .60
BD160 Logan Hofmann .25 .60
BD161 Ronaldo Hernandez .25 .60
BD162 Jack Blomgren .40 1.00
BD163 Adam Seminaris .30 .75
BD164 Bailey Horn .30 .75
BD165 Joe Boyle .40 1.00
BD166 Ryan Murphy .30 .75
BD167 Thomas Saggese .25 .60
BD168 George Kirby .40 1.00
BD169 Jeremiah Jackson .25 .60
BD170 Shane Drohan .30 .75
BD171 Brandon Pfaadt .25 .60
BD172 Blake Rutherford .25 .60
BD173 Hayden Cantrelle .25 .60
BD174 Mark Vientos .25 .60
BD175 Michael Toglia .25 .60
BD176 Mitchell Parker .25 .60
BD177 Jackson Rutledge .40 1.00
BD178 Anthony Volpe 1.00 2.50
BD179 Nick Lodolo .40 1.00
BD180 Riley Greene 1.00 2.50
BD181 JJ Bleday .75 2.00
BD182 Kyle Isbel .25 .60
BD183 Shea Langeliers .50 1.25
BD184 Brett Baty .75 2.00
BD185 Jerar Encarnacion .75 2.00
BD186 Aaron Ashby .25 .60
BD187 Brennen Davis .50 1.25
BD188 Julio Rodriguez 1.50 4.00
BD189 CJ Abrams .75 2.00
BD190 Marco Luciano 1.00 2.50
BD191 Grayson Rodriguez .40 1.00
BD192 Kristian Robinson .75 2.00
BD193 Jordyn Adams .30 .75
BD194 Nolan Gorman .50 1.25
BD195 Alek Thomas .30 .75
BD196 Hunter Greene .40 1.00
BD197 Josh Jung .60 1.50
BD198 Matthew Liberatore .30 .75
BD199 Ronny Mauricio .60 1.50
BD200 Hunter Bishop .50 1.25

2020 Bowman Chrome Draft Blue Refractors

*BLUE REF: 2X TO 5X BASIC
STATED ODDS 1:XXX HOBBY
STATED PRINT RUN 150 SER.#'d SETS
BD12 Emerson Hancock 20.00 50.00
BD16 Jared Shuster 10.00 25.00
BD49 Owen Caissie 12.00 30.00
BD55 Jarren Duran 10.00 25.00
BD57 Jordan Walker 50.00 120.00
BD62 Daniel Cabrera 15.00 40.00
BD72 Pete Crow-Armstrong 40.00 100.00
BD77 Isaiah Greene 12.00 30.00
BD81 Nick Gonzales 60.00 150.00
BD88 Asa Lacy 30.00 80.00
BD121 Spencer Torkelson 125.00 300.00
BD140 Bryson Stott 6.00 15.00
BD151 Jasson Dominguez 100.00 250.00
BD152 Bobby Witt Jr. 60.00 150.00
BD154 Adley Rutschman 12.00 30.00

2020 Bowman Chrome Draft Gold Refractors

*GOLD REF: 5X TO 12X BASIC
STATED ODDS 1:XXX HOBBY
STATED PRINT RUN 50 SER.#'d SETS
BD12 Emerson Hancock 50.00 120.00
BD16 Jared Shuster 30.00 80.00
BD49 Owen Caissie 30.00 80.00
BD55 Jarren Duran 25.00 60.00
BD57 Jordan Walker 125.00 300.00
BD62 Daniel Cabrera 40.00 100.00
BD72 Pete Crow-Armstrong 100.00 250.00
BD77 Isaiah Greene 30.00 80.00
BD81 Nick Gonzales 150.00 400.00
BD88 Asa Lacy 75.00 200.00
BD121 Spencer Torkelson 300.00 800.00
BD140 Bryson Stott 30.00 80.00
BD145 Carson Ragsdale 25.00 60.00
BD151 Jasson Dominguez 400.00 1000.00
BD152 Bobby Witt Jr. 150.00 400.00
BD154 Adley Rutschman 30.00 80.00

2020 Bowman Chrome Draft Green Refractors

*GREEN REF: 2.5X TO 6X BASIC
STATED ODDS 1:XXX HOBBY
STATED PRINT RUN 99 SER.#'d SETS
BD12 Emerson Hancock 25.00 60.00
BD16 Jared Shuster 15.00 40.00
BD49 Owen Caissie 15.00 40.00
BD55 Jarren Duran 12.00 30.00
BD57 Jordan Walker 60.00 150.00
BD62 Daniel Cabrera 20.00 50.00
BD72 Pete Crow-Armstrong 50.00 120.00
BD73 Casey Martin 15.00 40.00
BD77 Isaiah Greene 15.00 40.00
BD81 Nick Gonzales 75.00 200.00
BD88 Asa Lacy 40.00 100.00
BD121 Spencer Torkelson 150.00 400.00
BD140 Bryson Stott 8.00 20.00
BD145 Carson Ragsdale 6.00 15.00
BD151 Jasson Dominguez 125.00 300.00
BD152 Bobby Witt Jr. 75.00 200.00
BD154 Adley Rutschman 15.00 40.00

2020 Bowman Chrome Draft Orange Refractors

*ORANGE REF: 8X TO 20X BASIC
STATED ODDS 1:XXX HOBBY
STATED PRINT RUN 25 SER.#'d SETS
BD12 Emerson Hancock 75.00 200.00
BD16 Jared Shuster 50.00 120.00
BD38 Bobby Miller 40.00 100.00
BD49 Owen Caissie 50.00 120.00
BD55 Jarren Duran 40.00 100.00
BD57 Jordan Walker 200.00 500.00
BD62 Daniel Cabrera 60.00 150.00
BD72 Pete Crow-Armstrong 150.00 400.00
BD77 Isaiah Greene 50.00 120.00
BD81 Nick Gonzales 250.00 600.00
BD88 Asa Lacy 125.00 300.00
BD113 Trevor Hauver 15.00 40.00
BD117 Carter Baumler 15.00 40.00
BD121 Spencer Torkelson 500.00 1200.00
BD137 Gilberto Jimenez 40.00 100.00
BD140 Bryson Stott 50.00 120.00
BD145 Carson Ragsdale 40.00 100.00
BD151 Jasson Dominguez 600.00 1500.00
BD152 Bobby Witt Jr. 250.00 600.00
BD153 Andrew Vaughn 40.00 100.00
BD154 Adley Rutschman 50.00 120.00
BD190 Marco Luciano 40.00 100.00

2020 Bowman Chrome Draft Purple Refractors

*PURPLE REF: 1.5X TO 4X BASIC
STATED ODDS 1:XXX HOBBY
STATED PRINT RUN 250 SER.#'d SETS
BD12 Emerson Hancock 15.00 40.00
BD16 Jared Shuster 4.00 10.00
BD49 Owen Caissie 10.00 25.00
BD62 Daniel Cabrera 12.00 30.00
BD72 Pete Crow-Armstrong 30.00 80.00
BD77 Isaiah Greene 10.00 25.00
BD88 Asa Lacy 25.00 60.00
BD121 Spencer Torkelson 100.00 250.00
BD140 Bryson Stott 5.00 12.00
BD151 Jasson Dominguez 75.00 200.00
BD152 Bobby Witt Jr. 30.00 80.00
BD154 Adley Rutschman 10.00 25.00

2020 Bowman Chrome Draft Refractors

*REF: .75X TO 2X BASIC
RANDOM INSERTS IN PACKS
BD152 Bobby Witt Jr. 15.00 40.00

2020 Bowman Chrome Draft Sky Blue Refractors

*SKY BLUE REF: 1X TO 2.5X BASIC
STATED ODDS 1:XXX HOBBY
BD12 Emerson Hancock 6.00 15.00
BD72 Pete Crow-Armstrong 12.00 30.00
BD77 Isaiah Greene 6.00 15.00
BD88 Asa Lacy 15.00 40.00
BD151 Jasson Dominguez 50.00 120.00
BD152 Bobby Witt Jr. 20.00 50.00
BD154 Adley Rutschman 6.00 15.00

2020 Bowman Chrome Draft Sparkle Refractors

*SPARKLE REF: 1.5X TO 4X BASIC
STATED ODDS 1:XXX HOBBY
BD12 Emerson Hancock 12.00 30.00
BD72 Pete Crow-Armstrong 15.00 40.00
BD77 Isaiah Greene 8.00 20.00
BD88 Asa Lacy 20.00 50.00
BD121 Spencer Torkelson 100.00 250.00
BD151 Jasson Dominguez 60.00 150.00
BD152 Bobby Witt Jr. 25.00 60.00
BD154 Adley Rutschman 8.00 20.00

2020 Bowman Chrome Draft Image Variations

STATED ODDS 1:XXX HOBBY
BD12 Emerson Hancock 8.00 20.00
BD34 Austin Hendrick 40.00 100.00
BD39 Robert Hassell 25.00 60.00
BD41 Reid Detmers 12.00 30.00
BD81 Nick Gonzales 50.00 120.00
BD88 Asa Lacy 20.00 50.00
BD107 Zac Veen 30.00 80.00
BD121 Spencer Torkelson 75.00 200.00
BD122 Heston Kjerstad 30.00 80.00
BD146 Patrick Bailey 20.00 50.00
BD151 Jasson Dominguez 50.00 120.00
BD152 Bobby Witt Jr. 25.00 60.00
BD153 Andrew Vaughn 8.00 20.00
BD154 Adley Rutschman 20.00 50.00
BD155 Robert Puason 12.00 30.00

2020 Bowman Chrome Draft Image Variation Autographs

STATED ODDS 1:XXX HOBBY BOXES
STATED PRINT RUN 99 SER.#'d SETS
EXCHANGE DEADLINE 11/30/2022
BD151 Jasson Dominguez 400.00 1000.00
BD154 Adley Rutschman 100.00 250.00
BD155 Robert Puason 75.00 200.00
BDC12 Emerson Hancock 75.00 200.00
BDC39 Robert Hassell 250.00 600.00
BDC50 Max Meyer 75.00 200.00
BDC81 Nick Gonzales 150.00 400.00
BDC88 Asa Lacy 100.00 250.00
BDC121 Spencer Torkelson 600.00 1500.00
BDC122 Heston Kjerstad 150.00 400.00

2020 Bowman Chrome Draft 1st Edition Autographs

STATED ODDS 1:XXX HOBBY
STATED PRINT RUN 30 SER.#'d SETS
EXCHANGE DEADLINE 11/30/2022
*BLUE/20: .4X TO 1X BASIC
CDAAL Asa Lacy 200.00 500.00
CDABJA Bryce Jarvis 60.00 150.00
CDACCA Cade Cavalli
CDACS Casey Schmitt 60.00 150.00
CDACT Carson Tucker
CDAJC Jeff Criswell 30.00 80.00
CDAJF Justin Foscue
CDAJS Jared Shuster 50.00 125.00
CDAMM Max Meyer 100.00 250.00
CDANB Nick Bitsko 125.00 300.00
CDAPB Patrick Bailey 250.00 600.00
CDARD Reid Detmers
CDARHA Robert Hassell 250.00 600.00
CDAST Spencer Torkelson 1250.00 3000.00
CDAZD Zach DeLoach
CDAZV Zac Veen 750.00 2000.00

2020 Bowman Chrome Draft 20 in '20

STATED ODDS 1:XXX HOBBY
*REF/250: .6X TO 1.5.X BASE
*GREEN REF/99: .75X TO 2X BASE
*GOLD REF/50: 1.5X TO 4X BASE
20IN20AH Austin Hendrick 4.00 10.00
20IN20AL Asa Lacy 1.50 4.00
20IN20BJ Bryce Jarvis .30 .75
20IN20CC Cade Cavalli .50 1.25
20IN20CT Carson Tucker .75 2.00
20IN20EH Ed Howard 2.00 5.00
20IN20EHA Emerson Hancock 1.00 2.50
20IN20GC Garrett Crochet .60 1.50
20IN20HK Heston Kjerstad 2.00 5.00
20IN20JF Justin Foscue 1.00 2.50
20IN20MM Max Meyer 1.00 2.50
20IN20NB Nick Bitsko .75 2.00
20IN20NG Nick Gonzales 1.25 3.00
20IN20NY Nick Yorke 1.25 3.00
20IN20PB Patrick Bailey .75 2.00
20IN20PC Pete Crow-Armstrong .75 2.00
20IN20RD Reid Detmers .60 1.50
20IN20RH Robert Hassell 2.00 5.00
20IN20ST Spencer Torkelson 3.00 8.00
20IN20ZV Zac Veen 1.25 3.00

2020 Bowman Chrome Draft 20 in '20 Autographs

STATED ODDS 1:XXX HOBBY
STATED PRINT RUN 99 SER.#'d SETS
EXCHANGE DEADLINE 11/30/2022
20IN20AAH Austin Hendrick EXCH 60.00 150.00
20IN20AAL Asa Lacy 40.00 100.00
20IN20ACT Carson Tucker 20.00 50.00
20IN20AEHA Emerson Hancock 25.00 60.00
20IN20ANG Nick Gonzales 50.00 120.00

20IN20ARD Reid Detmers 12.00 30.00
20IN20ARHA Robert Hassell 50.00 125.00
20IN20AST Spencer Torkelson 200.00 500.00
20IN20AZV Zac Veen 50.00 120.00

2020 Bowman Chrome Draft Applied Pressure

STATED ODDS 1:XXX HOBBY
*ATOMIC REF/150: 2.5X TO 6X BASIC
*ORANGE REF/25: 8X TO 20X BASIC
APAA Aaron Ashby .25 .60
APAS Aaron Shortridge .30 .75
APBC Burl Carraway .50 1.25
APBD Brennen Davis .50 1.25
APJB Jordan Balazovic .50 1.25
APJC Joey Cantillo .25 .60
APJD Jarren Duran 1.00 2.50
APJR Joe Ryan .30 .75
APKI Kyle Isbel .25 .60
APMS Mike Siani .25 .60

2020 Bowman Chrome Draft Applied Pressure Autographs

STATED ODDS 1:XXX HOBBY
STATED PRINT RUN 99 SER.#'d SETS
EXCHANGE DEADLINE 11/30/2022
*ORANGE/25: .6X TO 1.5X BASIC
APDCAAA Aaron Ashby 8.00 20.00
APDCAAS Aaron Shortridge 5.00 12.00
APDCABB Bryce Ball 40.00 100.00
APDCABC Burl Carraway 8.00 20.00
APDCABD Brennen Davis 30.00 80.00
APDCAJD Jarren Duran 25.00 60.00
APDCAJR Joe Ryan 10.00 25.00
APDCAMS Mike Siani 10.00 25.00
APDCANH Niko Hulsizer EXCH 10.00 25.00
APDCAQC Quin Cotton EXCH 8.00 20.00

2020 Bowman Chrome Draft Autographs

STATED ODDS 1:XXX HOBBY
PRINTING PLATE ODDS 1:XXX HOBBY
PLATE PRINT RUN 1 SET PER COLOR
BLACK-CYAN-MAGENTA-YELLOW ISSUED
NO PLATE PRICING DUE TO SCARCITY
EXCHANGE DEADLINE 11/30/2022
CDAAB Alec Burleson 10.00 25.00
CDAAC Adisyn Coffey 3.00 8.00
CDAAH Austin Hendrick 100.00 250.00
CDAAL Asa Lacy 60.00 150.00
CDAASAN Alex Santos 10.00 25.00
CDAASE Adam Seminaris 4.00 10.00
CDAASO Alerick Soularie 10.00 25.00
CDAAV AJ Vukovich 25.00 60.00
CDAAW Alika Williams 12.00 30.00
CDAAWE Austin Wells 75.00 200.00
CDABB Bryce Bonnin 5.00 12.00
CDABBE Bradlee Beesley 8.00 20.00
CDABC Burl Carraway 6.00 15.00
CDABE Bryce Elder 10.00 25.00
CDABHO Bailey Horn 4.00 10.00
CDABJA Bryce Jarvis 6.00 15.00
CDABM Bobby Miller 25.00 60.00
CDABP Brandon Pfaadt 3.00 8.00
CDACB Carter Baumler 5.00 12.00
CDACBE Clayton Beeter 10.00 25.00
CDACC Christian Chamberlain 5.00 12.00
CDACHE Cole Henry 4.00 10.00
CDACM Casey Martin 25.00 60.00
CDACML Carmen Mlodzinski 4.00 10.00
CDACMM Chris McMahon 5.00 12.00
CDACRA Carson Ragsdale 5.00 12.00
CDACS Casey Schmitt 8.00 20.00
CDACT Carson Tucker 30.00 80.00
CDACV CJ Van Eyk 8.00 20.00
CDACWI Case Williams 4.00 10.00
CDADA Dane Acker 5.00 12.00
CDADC David Calabrese 8.00 20.00
CDADCA Daniel Cabrera 12.00 30.00
CDADCR Trent Palmer 4.00 10.00
CDADD Dillon Dingler 12.00 30.00
CDADF Daxton Fulton 6.00 15.00
CDAEC Evan Carter 40.00 100.00
CDAEH Ed Howard 100.00 250.00
CDAEHA Emerson Hancock 30.00 80.00
CDAEO Eric Orze 3.00 8.00
CDAFZ Freddy Zamora 12.00 30.00
CDAGC Garrett Crochet 50.00 120.00
CDAGM Garrett Mitchell 125.00 300.00
CDAGW Gage Workman 12.00 30.00
CDAHB Hunter Barnhart 3.00 8.00
CDAHCA Hayden Cantrelle 6.00 15.00
CDAHK Heston Kjerstad 100.00 250.00
CDAHP Holden Powell 4.00 10.00
CDAIB Ian Bedell 4.00 10.00
CDAIG Isaiah Greene 20.00 50.00
CDAIS Ian Seymour 3.00 8.00
CDAJB Jack Blomgren 5.00 12.00
CDAJBO Joe Boyle 5.00 12.00
CDAJC Jeff Criswell 4.00 10.00
CDAJF Justin Foscue 25.00 60.00
CDAJFR Jesse Franklin V 15.00 40.00
CDAJGL Jimmy Glowenke 6.00 15.00
CDAJH Jeff Hakanson 3.00 8.00
CDAJL Justin Lange 6.00 15.00
CDAJM Jackson Miller 6.00 15.00
CDAJN Jordan Nwogu 20.00 50.00
CDAJW Jordan Walker 100.00 250.00
CDAKC Keith Colt 12.00 30.00
CDAKNI Kyle Nicolas 5.00 12.00
CDAKR Kala'i Rosario 15.00 40.00
CDALH Logan Hofmann 3.00 8.00
CDALK Landon Knack 8.00 20.00
CDALL Luke Little 8.00 20.00
CDALP Levi Prater 4.00 10.00
CDAMD Matthew Dyer 5.00 12.00
CDAMH Tink Hence 8.00 20.00
CDAMM Max Meyer 30.00 80.00
CDAMR Marco Raya 6.00 15.00
CDAMT Milan Tolentino 10.00 25.00
CDANB Nick Bitsko 10.00 25.00
CDANG Nick Garcia 8.00 20.00
CDANGO Nick Gonzales 75.00 200.00
CDANL Nick Loftin 10.00 25.00
CDANS Nick Swiney 6.00 15.00
CDANY Nick Yorke 40.00 100.00
CDAOC Owen Caissie 15.00 40.00
CDAPB Patrick Bailey 12.00 30.00
CDAPC Pete Crow-Armstrong 75.00 200.00
CDAPH Petey Halpin 15.00 40.00
CDARD Reid Detmers 25.00 60.00
CDARDA RJ Dabovich 3.00 8.00
CDARH Kaden Polcovich 6.00 15.00
CDARHA Robert Hassell 100.00 250.00
CDARM Ryan Murphy 4.00 10.00
CDASD Shane Drohan 4.00 10.00
CDASG Saul Garza 8.00 20.00
CDASI Sammy Infante 12.00 30.00
CDASS Spencer Strider 5.00 12.00
CDAST Spencer Torkelson 400.00 1000.00
CDATB Tanner Burns 8.00 20.00
CDATBR Tyler Brown 5.00 12.00
CDATC Trei Cruz 10.00 25.00
CDATH Trevor Hauver 15.00 40.00
CDATR Tekoah Roby 3.00 8.00
CDATS Tyler Soderstrom 50.00 120.00
CDATSA Thomas Saggese 10.00 25.00
CDAWB Werner Blakely 15.00 40.00
CDAWK Will Klein 4.00 10.00
CDAZB Zach Britton 10.00 25.00
CDAZD Zach DeLoach 20.00 50.00
CDAZDA Zach Daniels 12.00 30.00
CDAZM Zach McCambley 3.00 8.00
CDAZV Zac Veen 125.00 300.00
CDAZW Zavier Warren 8.00 20.00

2020 Bowman Chrome Draft Autographs Black Refractors

*BLACK REF: 1.2X TO 3X BASIC
STATED ODDS 1:XXX HOBBY
STATED PRINT RUN 75 SER.#'D SETS
EXCHANGE DEADLINE 11/30/2022
CDABH Ben Hernandez 15.00 40.00
CDACCA Cade Cavalli 40.00 100.00
CDACP Connor Phillips 20.00 50.00
CDADR Drew Romo 50.00 120.00
CDAFZ Freddy Zamora 50.00 12.00
CDAHH Hudson Haskin 40.00 100.00
CDAJJ Jared Jones 30.00 80.00
CDAJS Jared Shuster 40.00 100.00
CDAJWE Jordan Westburg 60.00 150.00
CDASC Slade Cecconi EXCH 40.00 100.00

2020 Bowman Chrome Draft Autographs Blue Refractors

*BLUE REF: .75X TO 2X BASIC
STATED ODDS 1:XXX HOBBY
STATED PRINT RUN 150 SER.#'D SETS
EXCHANGE DEADLINE 11/30/2022
CDABH Ben Hernandez 10.00 25.00
CDACCA Cade Cavalli 25.00 60.00
CDACP Connor Phillips 12.00 30.00
CDADR Drew Romo 30.00 80.00
CDAHH Hudson Haskin 25.00 60.00
CDAJJ Jared Jones 20.00 50.00
CDAJS Jared Shuster 25.00 60.00
CDAJWE Jordan Westburg 40.00 100.00
CDASC Slade Cecconi EXCH 25.00 60.00

2020 Bowman Chrome Draft Autographs Blue Wave Refractors

*BLUE WAVE REF: .75X TO 2X BASIC
STATED ODDS 1:XXX HOBBY
STATED PRINT RUN 150 SER.#'D SETS
EXCHANGE DEADLINE 11/30/2022
CDABH Ben Hernandez 10.00 25.00
CDACCA Cade Cavalli 25.00 60.00
CDACP Connor Phillips 12.00 30.00
CDADR Drew Romo 30.00 80.00
CDAHH Hudson Haskin 25.00 60.00
CDAJJ Jared Jones 20.00 50.00
CDAJS Jared Shuster 25.00 60.00
CDAJWE Jordan Westburg 40.00 100.00
CDASC Slade Cecconi EXCH 25.00 60.00

2020 Bowman Chrome Draft Autographs Gold Refractors

*GOLD REF: 1.5X TO 4X BASIC
STATED ODDS 1:XXX HOBBY
STATED PRINT RUN 50 SER.#'D SETS
EXCHANGE DEADLINE 11/30/2022
CDABH Ben Hernandez 20.00 50.00
CDACCA Cade Cavalli 50.00 120.00
CDACP Connor Phillips 25.00 60.00
CDADR Drew Romo 60.00 150.00
CDAFZ Freddy Zamora 60.00 150.00
CDAHH Hudson Haskin 50.00 125.00
CDAJJ Jared Jones 40.00 100.00
CDAJS Jared Shuster 50.00 120.00
CDAJWE Jordan Westburg 75.00 200.00
CDASC Slade Cecconi EXCH 50.00 120.00
CDAST Spencer Torkelson 3000.00 8000.00

2020 Bowman Chrome Draft Autographs Gold Wave Refractors

*GRN WAVE REF: 1X TO 2.5X BASIC
STATED ODDS 1:XXX HOBBY
STATED PRINT RUN 99 SER.#'D SETS
EXCHANGE DEADLINE 11/30/2022
CDABH Ben Hernandez 20.00 50.00
CDACCA Cade Cavalli 50.00 120.00
CDACP Connor Phillips 25.00 60.00
CDADR Drew Romo 60.00 150.00
CDAFZ Freddy Zamora 60.00 150.00
CDAHH Hudson Haskin 50.00 125.00
CDAJJ Jared Jones 40.00 100.00
CDAJS Jared Shuster 50.00 120.00
CDAJWE Jordan Westburg 75.00 200.00
CDASC Slade Cecconi EXCH 50.00 120.00
CDAST Spencer Torkelson 3000.00 8000.00

2020 Bowman Chrome Draft Autographs Green Refractors

*GREEN REF: 1X TO 2.5X BASIC
STATED ODDS 1:XXX HOBBY
STATED PRINT RUN 99 SER.#'D SETS
EXCHANGE DEADLINE 11/30/2022
CDABH Ben Hernandez 12.00 30.00
CDACCA Cade Cavalli 30.00 80.00
CDACP Connor Phillips 15.00 40.00
CDADR Drew Romo 40.00 100.00
CDAFZ Freddy Zamora 40.00 100.00
CDAHH Hudson Haskin 30.00 80.00
CDAJJ Jared Jones 25.00 60.00
CDAJS Jared Shuster 30.00 80.00
CDAJWE Jordan Westburg 50.00 120.00
CDASC Slade Cecconi EXCH 30.00 80.00

2020 Bowman Chrome Draft Autographs Orange Refractors

*ORANGE REF: 3X TO 8X BASIC
STATED ODDS 1:XXX HOBBY
STATED PRINT RUN 25 SER.#'D SETS
EXCHANGE DEADLINE 11/30/2022
CDABH Ben Hernandez 40.00 100.00
CDACCA Cade Cavalli 100.00 250.00
CDACP Connor Phillips 50.00 120.00
CDADR Drew Romo 125.00 300.00
CDAFZ Freddy Zamora 125.00 300.00
CDAHH Hudson Haskin 150.00 400.00
CDAJJ Jared Jones 75.00 200.00
CDAJS Jared Shuster 100.00 250.00
CDAJWE Jordan Westburg 150.00 400.00
CDASC Slade Cecconi EXCH 100.00 250.00
CDAST Spencer Torkelson 8000.00 15000.00

2020 Bowman Chrome Draft Autographs Purple Refractors

*PURPLE REF: .6X TO 1.5X BASIC
STATED ODDS 1:XXX HOBBY
STATED PRINT RUN 250 SER.#'D SETS
EXCHANGE DEADLINE 11/30/2022
CDABH Ben Hernandez 8.00 20.00
CDACCA Cade Cavalli 20.00 50.00
CDACP Connor Phillips 10.00 25.00
CDADR Drew Romo 25.00 60.00
CDAHH Hudson Haskin 20.00 50.00
CDAJJ Jared Jones 15.00 40.00
CDAJS Jared Shuster 20.00 50.00
CDAJWE Jordan Westburg 30.00 80.00
CDASC Slade Cecconi EXCH 20.00 50.00

2020 Bowman Chrome Draft Autographs Refractors

*REF: .5X TO 1.2X BASIC
STATED ODDS 1:XXX HOBBY
STATED PRINT RUN 499 SER.#'D SETS
EXCHANGE DEADLINE 11/30/2022
CDABH Ben Hernandez 6.00 15.00
CDACCA Cade Cavalli 15.00 40.00
CDACP Connor Phillips 8.00 20.00
CDADR Drew Romo 20.00 50.00
CDAHH Hudson Haskin 15.00 40.00
CDAJJ Jared Jones 12.00 30.00
CDAJS Jared Shuster 15.00 40.00
CDAJWE Jordan Westburg 25.00 60.00
CDASC Slade Cecconi EXCH 15.00 40.00

2020 Bowman Chrome Draft Autographs Sparkle Refractors

*SPARKLE REF: 1.2X TO 3X BASIC
STATED ODDS 1:XXX HOBBY
STATED PRINT RUN 71 SER.#'D SETS
EXCHANGE DEADLINE 11/30/2022
CDABH Ben Hernandez 12.00 30.00
CDACCA Cade Cavalli 30.00 80.00
CDACP Connor Phillips 15.00 40.00
CDADR Drew Romo 40.00 100.00
CDAFZ Freddy Zamora 40.00 100.00
CDAHH Hudson Haskin 30.00 80.00
CDAJJ Jared Jones 25.00 60.00
CDAJS Jared Shuster 30.00 80.00
CDAJWE Jordan Westburg 50.00 120.00
CDASC Slade Cecconi EXCH 30.00 80.00

2020 Bowman Chrome Draft Class of '20 Autographs

STATED ODDS 1:XXX HOBBY
STATED PRINT RUN 99 SER.#'d SETS
EXCHANGE DEADLINE 11/30/2022
*GOLD/50: .6X TO 1.5X BASIC
C20AAH Austin Hendrick EXCH 60.00 150.00
C20AAL Asa Lacy 25.00 60.00
C20AAW Alika Williams 8.00 20.00
C20ABH Ben Hernandez 5.00 12.00
C20ABJ Bryce Jarvis 4.00 10.00
C20ACC Cade Cavalli 10.00 25.00
C20ACM Carmen Mlodzinski 4.00 10.00
C20ACT Carson Tucker 12.00 30.00
C20ACV CJ Van Eyk EXCH 5.00 12.00
C20ADD Dillon Dingler 10.00 25.00
C20ADDU Daxton Fulton 5.00 12.00
C20ADR Drew Romo 8.00 20.00
C20AEH Ed Howard 50.00 120.00
C20AEHA Emerson Hancock 20.00 50.00
C20AGM Garrett Mitchell 40.00 100.00
C20AHH Hudson Haskin 12.00 30.00
C20AJFO Justin Foscue 12.00 30.00
C20AJWA Jordan Walker 30.00 80.00
C20AMM Max Meyer 15.00 40.00
C20ANB Nick Bitsko 10.00 25.00
C20ANG Nick Gonzales 60.00 150.00
C20ANL Nick Loftin 5.00 12.00
C20ANY Nick Yorke 15.00 40.00
C20APB Patrick Bailey 12.00 30.00
C20APC Pete Crow-Armstrong 50.00 120.00
C20ARD Reid Detmers 12.00 30.00
C20ARH Robert Hassell 30.00 80.00
C20AST Spencer Torkelson 100.00 250.00
C20ATB Tanner Burns 5.00 12.00
C20ATS Tyler Soderstrom 20.00 50.00
C20AZV Zac Veen 30.00 80.00

2020 Bowman Chrome Draft Draft Night Autographs

STATED ODDS 1:XXX HOBBY
STATED PRINT RUN 99 SER.#'d SETS
EXCHANGE DEADLINE 11/30/2022
*GOLD REF/50: .5X TO 1.2X
*ORANGE REF/25: .6X TO 1.5X BASIC
DNAAL Asa Lacy 40.00 100.00
DNAMM Max Meyer 25.00 60.00
DNANG Nick Gonzales 30.00 80.00
DNARD Reid Detmers 12.00 30.00
DNARH Robert Hassell 40.00 100.00
DNAST Spencer Torkelson 200.00 500.00
DNAZV Zac Veen 60.00 150.00

2020 Bowman Chrome Draft Franchise Futures

STATED ODDS 1:XXX HOBBY
*REF/250: 1.2X TO 3X BASE
*GREEN REF/99: 1.5X TO 4X BASE
*GOLD REF/50: 3X TO 8X BASE
FFAN Lacy/Loftin 1.50 4.00
FFCE DeLoach/Hancock 1.00 2.50
FFDR Detmers/Calabrese .60 1.50
FFEB Howard/Carraway 2.00 5.00
FFHJ Kjerstad/Westburg 2.00 5.00
FFJZ Romo/Veen 1.25 3.00
FFMD Meyer/Fulton 1.00 2.50
FFNC Mlodzinski/Gonzales 1.25 3.00
FFRJ Lange/Hassel 2.00 5.00
FFSD Dingler/Torkelson 2.50 6.00

2020 Bowman Chrome Draft Franchise Futures Dual Autographs

STATED ODDS 1:XXX HOBBY
STATED PRINT RUN 99 SER.#'d SETS
EXCHANGE DEADLINE 11/30/2022
*GOLD/50: .5X TO 1.2X BASIC
*ORANGE/25: .6X TO 1.5X BASIC
FFAEZ DeLoach/Hancock 50.00 120.00
FFAHW Westburg/Kjerstad 60.00 150.00
FFAJE Carter/Foscue 40.00 100.00
FFARD Clbrse/Dtmrs EXCH 30.00 80.00

2020 Bowman Chrome Draft Glimpses of Greatness

STATED ODDS 1:XXX HOBBY
*REF/250: .6X TO 1.5X BASE
*GREEN REF/99: .75X TO 2X BASE
*GOLD REF/50: 1.5X TO 4X BASE
GOGAL Asa Lacy 1.50 4.00
GOGAR Adley Rutschman 1.50 4.00
GOGAV Andrew Vaughn 1.00 2.50
GOGBW Bobby Witt Jr. 1.50 4.00
GOGCA CJ Abrams .75 2.00
GOGEH Emerson Hancock 1.00 2.50
GOGHK Heston Kjerstad 2.00 5.00
GOGJB JJ Bleday .75 2.00
GOGJD Jasson Dominguez 3.00 8.00
GOGML Marco Luciano 1.00 2.50
GOGMM Max Meyer 1.00 2.50
GOGNG Nick Gonzales 1.25 3.00
GOGRG Riley Greene 1.00 2.50
GOGST Spencer Torkelson 5.00 12.00
GOGZV Zac Veen 1.25 3.00

2020 Bowman Chrome Draft Top of the Class Box Topper

RANDOM INSERTS IN HOBBY BOXES
STATED PRINT RUN 99 SER.#'d SETS
*GOLD/50: .5X TO 1.2X BASIC
TOCAL Asa Lacy 12.00 30.00
TOCEHA Emerson Hancock 10.00 25.00
TOCGM Reid Detmers 12.00 30.00
TOCHK Heston Kjerstad
TOCJK Robert Hassell 12.00 30.00
TOCMA Austin Hendrick 12.00 30.00
TOCMM Max Meyer 8.00 20.00
TOCNG Nick Gonzales 12.00 30.00
TOCPB Patrick Bailey
TOCRD Garrett Crochet 12.00 30.00
TOCST Spencer Torkelson 25.00 60.00
TOCZV Zac Veen 12.00 30.00

2020 Bowman Chrome Draft Top of the Class Box Topper Autographs

STATED ODDS 1:XXX HOBBY BOXES
STATED PRINT RUN 35 SER.#'d SETS
EXCHANGE DEADLINE 11/30/2022
TOCAL Asa Lacy 30.00 80.00
TOCEHA Emerson Hancock 30.00 80.00
TOCHK Heston Kjerstad
TOCMM Max Meyer 30.00 80.00
TOCNG Nick Gonzales
TOCRD Reid Detmers 40.00 100.00
TOCRH Robert Hassell 50.00 120.00
TOCST Spencer Torkelson 125.00 300.00
TOCZV Zac Veen 100.00 250.00

2021 Bowman Chrome '91 Bowman Refractors

STATED ODDS 1:8 HOBBY
91BAB Alec Bohm 3.00 8.00
91BAJ Aaron Judge 1.25 3.00
91BAL Asa Lacy 1.50 4.00
91BAR Adley Rutschman 2.50 6.00
91BBW Bobby Witt Jr. 3.00 8.00
91BCB Cody Bellinger 1.00 2.50
91BCM Casey Mize 2.50 6.00
91BCP Cristian Pache 3.00 8.00
91BDC Dylan Carlson 4.00 10.00
91BFT Fernando Tatis Jr. 2.50 6.00
91BHK Heston Kjerstad 1.50 4.00
91BJA Jo Adell 2.00 5.00
91BJB Joey Bart 1.00 2.50
91BJK Jarred Kelenic 1.50 4.00
91BJR Julio Rodriguez 2.00 5.00
91BJS Juan Soto 1.50 4.00
91BLR Luis Robert 1.50 4.00
91BMG MacKenzie Gore .60 1.50
91BMT Mike Trout 2.50 6.00
91BNP Nate Pearson 1.50 4.00
91BRA Ronald Acuna Jr. 2.00 5.00
91BRL Royce Lewis .75 2.00
91BSS Sixto Sanchez 1.50 4.00
91BST Spencer Torkelson 3.00 8.00
91BWF Wander Franco 3.00 8.00

2021 Bowman Chrome '91 Bowman Aqua Refractors

*AQUA: 1.5X TO 4X BASIC
STATED ODDS 1:XX HOBBY
STATED PRINT RUN 125 SER.#'d SETS
91BAB Alec Bohm 15.00 40.00
91BBW Bobby Witt Jr. 40.00 100.00
91BJA Jo Adell 12.00 30.00
91BWF Wander Franco 50.00 120.00

2021 Bowman Chrome '91 Bowman Atomic Refractors

*ATOMIC: 1.5X TO 4X BASIC
STATED ODDS 1:XX HOBBY
STATED PRINT RUN 150 SER.#'d SETS
91BAB Alec Bohm 15.00 40.00
91BBW Bobby Witt Jr. 40.00 100.00
91BJA Jo Adell 12.00 30.00
91BWF Wander Franco 50.00 120.00

2021 Bowman Chrome '91 Bowman Gold Refractors

*GOLD: 3X TO 8X BASIC
STATED ODDS 1:XX HOBBY
STATED PRINT RUN 50 SER.#'d SETS
91BAB Alec Bohm 40.00 100.00
91BBW Bobby Witt Jr. 75.00 200.00
91BJA Jo Adell 25.00 60.00
91BWF Wander Franco 100.00 250.00

2021 Bowman Chrome '91 Bowman Green Refractors

*GREEN: 2X TO 5X BASIC
STATED ODDS 1:XX RETAIL
STATED PRINT RUN 99 SER.#'d SETS
91BAB Alec Bohm 25.00 60.00
91BBW Bobby Witt Jr. 50.00 120.00
91BJA Jo Adell 15.00 40.00
91BWF Wander Franco 60.00 150.00

2021 Bowman Chrome '91 Bowman Orange Refractors

*ORANGE: 5X TO 12X BASIC
STATED ODDS 1:XX HOBBY
STATED PRINT RUN 25 SER.#'d SETS
91BAB Alec Bohm 60.00 150.00
91BAJ Aaron Judge 20.00 50.00
91BBW Bobby Witt Jr. 125.00 300.00
91BDC Dylan Carlson 60.00 150.00
91BJA Jo Adell 40.00 100.00
91BJS Juan Soto 30.00 80.00
91BLR Luis Robert 40.00 100.00
91BMT Mike Trout 200.00 500.00
91BWF Wander Franco 150.00 400.00

2021 Bowman Chrome '91 Bowman Autographs Refractors

STATED ODDS 1:XX HOBBY
STATED PRINT RUN 30 SER.#'d SETS
EXCHANGE DEADLINE 3/31/23
91BAB Alec Bohm 75.00 200.00
91BAJ Aaron Judge
91BAL Asa Lacy 30.00 80.00
91BAR Adley Rutschman
91BBW Bobby Witt Jr.
91BCB Cody Bellinger 100.00 250.00
91BCM Casey Mize
91BHK Heston Kjerstad 50.00 120.00
91BJA Jo Adell 100.00 250.00
91BJB Joey Bart 60.00 150.00
91BJS Juan Soto 100.00 250.00
91BMT Mike Trout 400.00 1000.00
91BNP Nate Pearson 30.00 80.00
91BRA Ronald Acuna Jr.
91BST Spencer Torkelson
91BWF Wander Franco 400.00 1000.00

2021 Bowman Chrome 1st Edition Prospect Autographs Refractors

STATED ODDS 1:376 HOBBY
STATED PRINT RUN 50 SER.#'d SETS
*BLUE: .6X TO 1.5X BASIC
BFEAAH Austin Hendrick 100.00 250.00
BFEAAL Asa Lacy 30.00 80.00
BFEAAS Aaron Sabato 300.00 800.00
BFEABJ Blaze Jordan 800.00 2000.00
BFEAEH Emerson Hancock 20.00 50.00
BFEAGM Garrett Mitchell 125.00 300.00
BFEAHK Heston Kjerstad 75.00 200.00
BFEAMA Mick Abel 200.00 500.00
BFEAMM Max Meyer 40.00 100.00
BFEANG Nick Gonzales 100.00 250.00
BFEAPB Patrick Bailey 40.00 100.00
BFEAST Spencer Torkelson 200.00 500.00
BFEAZV Zac Veen 60.00 150.00

2021 Bowman Chrome Dual Prospect Autographs

STATED ODDS 1:XX HOBBY
STATED PRINT RUN 25 SER.#'d SETS
EXCHANGE DEADLINE 3/31/23
DPABJ N.Yorke/B.Jordan EXCH 250.00 600.00
DPAJK K.Alcantara/J.Dominguez EXCH
DPASR R.Greene/S.Torkelson EXCH 300.00 800.00

2021 Bowman Chrome Futurist Refractors

STATED ODDS 1:6 HOBBY
FUTAH Austin Hendrick 1.00 2.50
FUTAL Asa Lacy 1.50 4.00
FUTBJ Blaze Jordan 3.00 8.00
FUTBW Bobby Witt Jr. 2.00 5.00
FUTCA CJ Abrams 1.00 2.50
FUTCC Corbin Carroll .50 1.25
FUTEH Emerson Hancock .75 2.00
FUTFA Francisco Alvarez .75 2.00
FUTGM Garrett Mitchell 2.00 5.00
FUTHK Heston Kjerstad 1.50 4.00
FUTJD Jasson Dominguez 4.00 10.00
FUTMA Mick Abel .50 1.25
FUTML Marco Luciano 1.25 3.00
FUTMM Max Meyer .75 2.00
FUTNG Nick Gonzales 1.00 2.50
FUTRD Reid Detmers .75 2.00
FUTRG Riley Greene 1.25 3.00
FUTRH Robert Hassell 2.00 5.00
FUTST Spencer Torkelson 2.00 5.00
FUTZV Zac Veen 1.00 2.50

2021 Bowman Chrome Futurist Aqua Refractors

*AQUA: 1.5X TO 4X BASIC
STATED ODDS 1:XX HOBBY
STATED PRINT RUN 125 SER.#'d SETS
FUTBJ Blaze Jordan 20.00 50.00

2021 Bowman Chrome Futurist Atomic Refractors

*ATOMIC: 1.5X TO 4X BASIC
STATED ODDS 1:XX HOBBY
STATED PRINT RUN 150 SER.#'d SETS
FUTBJ Blaze Jordan 20.00 50.00

2021 Bowman Chrome Futurist Gold Refractors

*GOLD: 3X TO 8X BASIC
STATED ODDS 1:XX HOBBY
STATED PRINT RUN 50 SER.#'d SETS
FUTBJ Blaze Jordan 40.00 100.00
FUTST Spencer Torkelson 25.00 60.00

2021 Bowman Chrome Futurist Green Refractors

*GREEN: 2X TO 5X BASIC
STATED ODDS 1:XX RETAIL
STATED PRINT RUN 99 SER.#'d SETS
FUTBJ Blaze Jordan 25.00 60.00

2021 Bowman Chrome Futurist Orange Refractors

*ORANGE: 5X TO 12X BASIC
STATED ODDS 1:XX HOBBY
STATED PRINT RUN 25 SER.#'d SETS
FUTBJ Blaze Jordan 60.00 150.00
FUTST Spencer Torkelson 40.00 100.00

2021 Bowman Chrome Positional Promise Refractors

STATED ODDS 1:24 HOBBY
*ATOMIC/150: 1.5X TO 4X BASIC
*AQUA/125: 1.5X TO 4X BASIC
*GREEN/99: 2X TO 5X BASIC
POSAL Asa Lacy 1.50 4.00
POSAR Adley Rutschman 2.00 5.00
POSAV Andrew Vaughn 1.25 3.00
POSBB Brett Baty 1.00 2.50
POSBW Bobby Witt Jr. 2.00 5.00
POSEH Emerson Hancock .75 2.00
POSFA Francisco Alvarez .75 2.00
POSHK Heston Kjerstad 1.50 4.00
POSJB JJ Bleday 1.00 2.50
POSJD Jasson Dominguez 4.00 10.00
POSKR Kristian Robinson 1.00 2.50
POSMM Max Meyer .75 2.00
POSMT Michael Toglia .30 .75
POSNG Nick Gonzales 1.00 2.50
POSNL Nick Lodolo .50 1.25
POSRG Riley Greene 1.25 3.00
POSST Spencer Torkelson 2.00 5.00
POSWF Wander Franco 3.00 8.00
POSXE Xavier Edwards 1.00 2.50
POSZV Zac Veen 1.00 2.50

2021 Bowman Chrome Positional Promise Gold Refractors

*GOLD: 3X TO 8X BASIC
STATED ODDS 1:XX HOBBY
STATED PRINT RUN 50 SER.#'d SETS
POSAR Adley Rutschman 25.00 60.00

2021 Bowman Chrome Positional Promise Orange Refractors

*ORANGE: 5X TO 12X BASIC
STATED ODDS 1:XX HOBBY
STATED PRINT RUN 25 SER.#'d SETS
POSAR Adley Rutschman 40.00 100.00
POSBW Bobby Witt Jr. 40.00 100.00
POSJB JJ Bleday 20.00 50.00

2021 Bowman Chrome Positional Promise Autographs Refractors

STATED ODDS 1:XX HOBBY
STATED PRINT RUN 99 SER.#'d SETS
EXCHANGE DEADLINE 3/31/23
POSPAL Asa Lacy
POSPAV Andrew Vaughn
POSPFA Francisco Alvarez 25.00 60.00
POSPMM Max Meyer 10.00 25.00
POSPNG Nick Gonzales 20.00 50.00
POSPRG Riley Greene 20.00 50.00
POSPZV Zac Veen

2021 Bowman Chrome Positional Promise Autographs Orange Refractors

*ORANGE/25: .6X TO 1.5X BASIC
STATED ODDS 1:XX HOBBY
STATED PRINT RUN 25 SER.#'d SETS
EXCHANGE DEADLINE 3/31/23
POSPFA Francisco Alvarez 60.00 150.00

2021 Bowman Chrome Prospect Autographs

STATED ODDS 1:XX HOBBY
EXCHANGE DEADLINE 3/31/23
CPAAC Austin Cox 5.00 12.00
CPAAH Austin Hendrick 25.00 60.00
CPAAL Asa Lacy 15.00 40.00
CPAAM Austin Martin EXCH 300.00 800.00
CPAAS Aaron Sabato 50.00 120.00
CPAAV Alexander Vargas 25.00 60.00
CPABB Brainer Bonaci 15.00 40.00
CPABE Breidy Encarnacion 4.00 10.00
CPABJ Blaze Jordan 150.00 400.00
CPABW Beck Way 8.00 20.00
CPADC Darryl Collins 12.00 30.00
CPADK D'Shawn Knowles 10.00 25.00
CPADM Daniel Montano 5.00 12.00
CPAED Eddy Diaz 8.00 20.00
CPAER Endy Rodriguez 12.00 30.00
CPAEY Eddy Yean 12.00 30.00
CPAFV Freddy Valdez 20.00 50.00
CPAGA Gabriel Arias 40.00 100.00
CPAHC Hyun-il Choi 10.00 25.00
CPAHH Heriberto Hernandez 40.00 100.00
CPAHK Heston Kjerstad 25.00 60.00
CPAHP Hedbert Perez 100.00 250.00
CPAIJ Ivan Johnson 12.00 30.00
CPAIM Ismael Mena 25.00 60.00
CPAJB Ji-Hwan Bae 15.00 40.00
CPAJE Jeferson Espinal 20.00 50.00
CPAJK Jared Kelley 15.00 40.00
CPAJP Jairo Pomares 30.00 80.00
CPAJR Johan Rojas 25.00 60.00
CPAJS Jose Salas 25.00 60.00
CPAJT Jose Tena 15.00 40.00
CPAJV Jake Vogel 25.00 60.00
CPAJW Jeremy Wu-Yelland 8.00 20.00
CPAKA Kevin Alcantara 75.00 200.00
CPAKF Kohl Franklin 12.00 30.00
CPALF Luis Frias 6.00 15.00
CPALS Luis Santana 12.00 30.00
CPAMA Maximo Acosta 100.00 250.00
CPAMB Mariel Bautista 6.00 15.00
CPAMM Michael McAvene 10.00 25.00
CPAMS Marcus Smith 12.00 30.00
CPAMW Mac Wainwright 12.00 30.00
CPANG Nick Gonzales 25.00 60.00
CPANM Nick Maton 40.00 100.00
CPAPB Patrick Bailey 10.00 25.00
CPARH Robert Hassell 20.00 50.00
CPART Riley Thompson 12.00 30.00
CPASE Stevie Emanuels 4.00 10.00
CPASG Sandy Gaston 5.00 12.00
CPAST Spencer Torkelson EXCH 100.00 250.00
CPAWH William Holmes 4.00 10.00
CPAYC Yoelqui Cespedes 100.00 250.00
CPAYS Yunior Severino 12.00 30.00
CPAZV Zac Veen 25.00 60.00
CPAAAM Adael Amador 20.00 50.00
CPAAGO Antonio Gomez 12.00 30.00
CPAAMA Angel Martinez 20.00 50.00
CPAARA Alexander Ramirez 30.00 80.00
CPAARE Adinso Reyes 20.00 50.00
CPACMA Coby Mayo 20.00 50.00
CPADMA Dylan MacLean 3.00 8.00
CPAEHA Emerson Hancock 12.00 30.00
CPAEHO Ed Howard 25.00 60.00
CPAGMI Garrett Mitchell EXCH 50.00 120.00
CPAJCL Jackson Cluff 6.00 15.00
CPAJDL Jeremy De La Rosa 60.00 150.00
CPAJED Jake Eder 10.00 25.00
CPAJRO Jose Rodriguez 15.00 40.00
CPAMAB Mick Abel 40.00 100.00
CPAMME Max Meyer 10.00 25.00
CPARDC Brayan Buelvas 25.00 60.00
CPAYSA Yolbert Sanchez 20.00 50.00

2021 Bowman Chrome Prospect Autographs Atomic Refractors

*ATOMIC: .8X TO 2X BASIC
STATED ODDS 1:XX HOBBY
STATED PRINT RUN 100 SER.#'d SETS
EXCHANGE DEADLINE 3/31/23
CPAAM Austin Martin EXCH 1500.00 3000.00
CPAAS Aaron Sabato 200.00 500.00
CPAAV Alexander Vargas 125.00 300.00
CPABB Brainer Bonaci 60.00 150.00
CPABJ Blaze Jordan 500.00 1200.00
CPABW Beck Way 25.00 60.00
CPADC Darryl Collins 30.00 80.00
CPADK D'Shawn Knowles 50.00 120.00
CPADM Daniel Montano 12.00 30.00
CPAER Endy Rodriguez 50.00 120.00
CPAFV Freddy Valdez 60.00 150.00
CPAGA Gabriel Arias 125.00 300.00
CPAHC Hyun-il Choi 40.00 100.00
CPAHH Heriberto Hernandez 150.00 400.00
CPAHK Heston Kjerstad 50.00 120.00
CPAHP Hedbert Perez 300.00 800.00
CPAIM Ismael Mena 75.00 200.00
CPAJB Ji-Hwan Bae 50.00 120.00
CPAJE Jeferson Espinal 60.00 150.00
CPAJK Jared Kelley 75.00 200.00
CPAJP Jairo Pomares 150.00 400.00
CPAJR Johan Rojas 100.00 250.00
CPAJS Jose Salas 150.00 400.00
CPAKA Kevin Alcantara 400.00 1000.00
CPALF Luis Frias 15.00 40.00
CPALS Luis Santana 30.00 80.00
CPAMA Maximo Acosta 500.00 1200.00
CPAMM Michael McAvene 25.00 60.00
CPAMS Marcus Smith 40.00 100.00
CPAMW Mac Wainwright 40.00 100.00
CPANG Nick Gonzales 60.00 150.00
CPANM Nick Maton 100.00 250.00
CPAPB Patrick Bailey 40.00 100.00
CPARH Robert Hassell 50.00 120.00
CPAYC Yoelqui Cespedes 300.00 800.00
CPAYS Yunior Severino 30.00 80.00
CPAZV Zac Veen 75.00 200.00
CPAAGO Antonio Gomez 40.00 100.00
CPAAMA Angel Martinez 100.00 250.00
CPAARA Alexander Ramirez 250.00 600.00
CPAARE Adinso Reyes 60.00 150.00
CPACMA Coby Mayo 150.00 400.00
CPAGMI Garrett Mitchell 125.00 300.00
CPAJCL Jackson Cluff 20.00 50.00
CPAJDL Jeremy De La Rosa 150.00 400.00
CPARDC Brayan Buelvas 60.00 150.00
CPAYSA Yolbert Sanchez 50.00 120.00

2021 Bowman Chrome Prospect Autographs Blue Refractors

*BLUE/150: .8X TO 2X BASIC
STATED ODDS 1:XX HOBBY
STATED PRINT RUN 150 SER.#'d SETS
EXCHANGE DEADLINE 3/31/23
CPAAM Austin Martin EXCH 1500.00 3000.00
CPAAS Aaron Sabato 200.00 500.00
CPAAV Alexander Vargas 125.00 300.00
CPABB Brainer Bonaci 60.00 150.00
CPABJ Blaze Jordan 500.00 1200.00
CPABW Beck Way 25.00 60.00
CPADC Darryl Collins 30.00 80.00
CPADK D'Shawn Knowles 50.00 120.00
CPADM Daniel Montano 12.00 30.00
CPAER Endy Rodriguez 50.00 120.00
CPAFV Freddy Valdez 60.00 150.00
CPAGA Gabriel Arias 125.00 300.00
CPAHC Hyun-il Choi 40.00 100.00
CPAHH Heriberto Hernandez 150.00 400.00
CPAHK Heston Kjerstad 40.00 100.00
CPAHP Hedbert Perez 300.00 800.00
CPAIM Ismael Mena 75.00 200.00
CPAJB Ji-Hwan Bae 50.00 120.00
CPAJE Jeferson Espinal 60.00 150.00
CPAJK Jared Kelley 75.00 200.00
CPAJP Jairo Pomares 150.00 400.00
CPAJR Johan Rojas 100.00 250.00
CPAJS Jose Salas 150.00 400.00
CPAKA Kevin Alcantara 400.00 1000.00
CPALF Luis Frias 15.00 40.00
CPALS Luis Santana 30.00 80.00
CPAMA Maximo Acosta 500.00 1200.00
CPAMM Michael McAvene 25.00 60.00
CPAMS Marcus Smith 40.00 100.00
CPAMW Mac Wainwright 40.00 100.00
CPANG Nick Gonzales 60.00 150.00
CPANM Nick Maton 100.00 250.00
CPAPB Patrick Bailey 40.00 100.00
CPARH Robert Hassell 50.00 120.00
CPAYC Yoelqui Cespedes 300.00 800.00
CPAYS Yunior Severino 30.00 80.00
CPAZV Zac Veen 75.00 200.00
CPAAGO Antonio Gomez 40.00 100.00
CPAAMA Angel Martinez 100.00 250.00
CPAARA Alexander Ramirez 250.00 600.00

CPAARE Adinso Reyes 60.00 150.00
CPACMA Coby Mayo 150.00 400.00
CPAGMI Garrett Mitchell 125.00 300.00
CPAJCL Jackson Cluff 20.00 50.00
CPAJDL Jeremy De La Rosa 150.00 400.00
CPARDC Brayan Buelvas 60.00 150.00
CPAYSA Yolbert Sanchez 50.00 120.00

2021 Bowman Chrome Prospect Autographs Gold Refractors

*GOLD/50: 1.5X TO 4X BASIC
STATED ODDS 1:XX HOBBY
STATED PRINT RUN 50 SER.#'d SETS
EXCHANGE DEADLINE 3/31/23
CPAAM Austin Martin EXCH 3000.00 6000.00
CPAAS Aaron Sabato 400.00 1000.00
CPAAV Alexander Vargas 250.00 600.00
CPABB Brainer Bonaci 125.00 300.00
CPABJ Blaze Jordan 1000.00 2500.00
CPADC Darryl Collins 75.00 200.00
CPADK D'Shawn Knowles 100.00 250.00
CPADM Daniel Montano 25.00 60.00
CPAER Endy Rodriguez 100.00 250.00
CPAFV Freddy Valdez 125.00 300.00
CPAGA Gabriel Arias 400.00 1000.00
CPAHC Hyun-il Choi 75.00 200.00
CPAHH Heriberto Hernandez 400.00 1000.00
CPAHK Heston Kjerstad 100.00 250.00
CPAHP Hedbert Perez 600.00 1500.00
CPAIM Ismael Mena 150.00 400.00
CPAJB Ji-Hwan Bae 100.00 250.00
CPAJE Jeferson Espinal 250.00 600.00
CPAJK Jared Kelley 150.00 400.00
CPAJP Jairo Pomares 300.00 800.00
CPAJR Johan Rojas 200.00 500.00
CPAJS Jose Salas 300.00 800.00
CPAJV Jake Vogel 150.00 400.00
CPAKA Kevin Alcantara 800.00 2000.00
CPALF Luis Frias 30.00 80.00
CPALS Luis Santana 60.00 150.00
CPAMA Maximo Acosta 1000.00 2500.00
CPAMM Michael McAvene 50.00 120.00
CPAMS Marcus Smith 75.00 200.00
CPAMW Mac Wainwright 75.00 200.00
CPANG Nick Gonzales 125.00 300.00
CPANM Nick Maton 200.00 500.00
CPAPB Patrick Bailey 75.00 200.00
CPARH Robert Hassell 100.00 250.00
CPAYC Yoelqui Cespedes 600.00 1500.00
CPAYS Yunior Severino 60.00 150.00
CPAZV Zac Veen 150.00 400.00
CPAAGO Antonio Gomez 75.00 200.00
CPAAMA Angel Martinez 200.00 500.00
CPAARA Alexander Ramirez 500.00 1200.00
CPAARE Adinso Reyes 150.00 400.00
CPACMA Coby Mayo 300.00 800.00
CPADMA Dylan MacLean 30.00 80.00
CPAGMI Garrett Mitchell 250.00 600.00
CPAJCL Jackson Cluff 40.00 100.00
CPAJDL Jeremy De La Rosa 300.00 800.00
CPARDC Brayan Buelvas 150.00 400.00
CPAYSA Yolbert Sanchez 100.00 250.00

2021 Bowman Chrome Prospect Autographs Gold Shimmer Refractors

*GOLD SHMR/50: 1.5X TO 4X BASIC
STATED ODDS 1:XX HOBBY
STATED PRINT RUN 50 SER.#'d SETS
EXCHANGE DEADLINE 3/31/23
CPAAM Austin Martin EXCH 3000.00 6000.00
CPAAS Aaron Sabato 400.00 1000.00
CPAAV Alexander Vargas 250.00 600.00
CPABB Brainer Bonaci 125.00 300.00
CPABJ Blaze Jordan 1000.00 2500.00
CPADC Darryl Collins 75.00 200.00
CPADK D'Shawn Knowles 100.00 250.00
CPADM Daniel Montano 25.00 60.00
CPAER Endy Rodriguez 100.00 250.00
CPAFV Freddy Valdez 125.00 300.00
CPAGA Gabriel Arias 400.00 1000.00
CPAHC Hyun-il Choi 75.00 200.00
CPAHH Heriberto Hernandez 400.00 1000.00
CPAHK Heston Kjerstad 100.00 250.00
CPAHP Hedbert Perez 600.00 1500.00
CPAIM Ismael Mena 150.00 400.00
CPAJB Ji-Hwan Bae 100.00 250.00
CPAJE Jeferson Espinal 250.00 600.00
CPAJK Jared Kelley 150.00 400.00
CPAJP Jairo Pomares 300.00 800.00
CPAJR Johan Rojas 200.00 500.00
CPAJS Jose Salas 300.00 800.00
CPAJV Jake Vogel 150.00 400.00
CPAKA Kevin Alcantara 800.00 2000.00
CPALF Luis Frias 30.00 80.00
CPALS Luis Santana 60.00 150.00
CPAMA Maximo Acosta 1000.00 2500.00
CPAMM Michael McAvene 50.00 120.00
CPAMS Marcus Smith 75.00 200.00
CPAMW Mac Wainwright 75.00 200.00
CPANG Nick Gonzales 125.00 300.00
CPANM Nick Maton 200.00 500.00
CPAPB Patrick Bailey 75.00 200.00
CPARH Robert Hassell 100.00 250.00
CPAYC Yoelqui Cespedes 600.00 1500.00
CPAYS Yunior Severino 60.00 150.00
CPAZV Zac Veen 150.00 400.00
CPAAGO Antonio Gomez 75.00 200.00
CPAAMA Angel Martinez 200.00 500.00
CPAARA Alexander Ramirez 500.00 1200.00
CPAARE Adinso Reyes 150.00 400.00
CPACMA Coby Mayo 300.00 800.00
CPADMA Dylan MacLean 30.00 80.00
CPAGMI Garrett Mitchell 250.00 600.00
CPAJCL Jackson Cluff 40.00 100.00
CPAJDL Jeremy De La Rosa 300.00 800.00
CPARDC Brayan Buelvas 150.00 400.00
CPAYSA Yolbert Sanchez 100.00 250.00

2021 Bowman Chrome Prospect Autographs Green Refractors

*GREEN/99: .8X TO 2X BASIC
STATED ODDS 1:XX RETAIL
STATED PRINT RUN 99 SER.#'d SETS
EXCHANGE DEADLINE 3/31/23
CPAAM Austin Martin EXCH 1500.00 3000.00
CPAAS Aaron Sabato 200.00 500.00
CPAAV Alexander Vargas 125.00 300.00
CPABB Brainer Bonaci 60.00 150.00
CPABJ Blaze Jordan 500.00 1200.00
CPABW Beck Way 25.00 60.00
CPADC Darryl Collins 30.00 80.00
CPADK D'Shawn Knowles 50.00 120.00
CPADM Daniel Montano 12.00 30.00
CPAER Endy Rodriguez 50.00 120.00
CPAFV Freddy Valdez 60.00 150.00
CPAGA Gabriel Arias 125.00 300.00
CPAHC Hyun-il Choi 40.00 100.00
CPAHH Heriberto Hernandez 150.00 400.00
CPAHK Heston Kjerstad 50.00 120.00
CPAHP Hedbert Perez 300.00 800.00
CPAIM Ismael Mena 75.00 200.00
CPAJB Ji-Hwan Bae 50.00 120.00
CPAJE Jeferson Espinal 60.00 150.00
CPAJK Jared Kelley 75.00 200.00
CPAJP Jairo Pomares 150.00 400.00
CPAJR Johan Rojas 100.00 250.00
CPAJS Jose Salas 150.00 400.00
CPAKA Kevin Alcantara 400.00 1000.00
CPALF Luis Frias 15.00 40.00
CPALS Luis Santana 30.00 80.00
CPAMA Maximo Acosta 500.00 1200.00
CPAMM Michael McAvene 25.00 60.00
CPAMS Marcus Smith 40.00 100.00
CPAMW Mac Wainwright 40.00 100.00
CPANG Nick Gonzales 60.00 150.00
CPANM Nick Maton 100.00 250.00
CPAPB Patrick Bailey 40.00 100.00
CPARH Robert Hassell 50.00 120.00
CPAYC Yoelqui Cespedes 300.00 800.00
CPAYS Yunior Severino 30.00 80.00
CPAZV Zac Veen 75.00 200.00
CPAAGO Antonio Gomez 40.00 100.00
CPAAMA Angel Martinez 100.00 250.00
CPAARA Alexander Ramirez 250.00 600.00
CPAARE Adinso Reyes 60.00 150.00
CPACMA Coby Mayo 150.00 400.00
CPAGMI Garrett Mitchell 125.00 300.00
CPAJCL Jackson Cluff 20.00 50.00
CPAJDL Jeremy De La Rosa 150.00 400.00
CPARDC Brayan Buelvas 60.00 150.00
CPAYSA Yolbert Sanchez 50.00 120.00

2021 Bowman Chrome Prospect Autographs Green Shimmer Refractors

*GREEN SHMR/99: .8X TO 2X BASIC
STATED ODDS 1:XX RETAIL
STATED PRINT RUN 99 SER.#'d SETS
EXCHANGE DEADLINE 3/31/23
CPAAM Austin Martin EXCH 1500.00 3000.00
CPAAS Aaron Sabato 200.00 500.00
CPAAV Alexander Vargas 125.00 300.00
CPABB Brainer Bonaci 60.00 150.00
CPABJ Blaze Jordan 500.00 1200.00
CPABW Beck Way 25.00 60.00
CPADC Darryl Collins 30.00 80.00
CPADK D'Shawn Knowles 50.00 120.00
CPADM Daniel Montano 12.00 30.00
CPAER Endy Rodriguez 50.00 120.00
CPAFV Freddy Valdez 60.00 150.00
CPAGA Gabriel Arias 125.00 300.00
CPAHC Hyun-il Choi 40.00 100.00
CPAHH Heriberto Hernandez 150.00 400.00
CPAHK Heston Kjerstad 50.00 120.00
CPAHP Hedbert Perez 300.00 800.00
CPAIM Ismael Mena 75.00 200.00
CPAJB Ji-Hwan Bae 50.00 120.00
CPAJE Jeferson Espinal 60.00 150.00
CPAJK Jared Kelley 75.00 200.00
CPAJP Jairo Pomares 150.00 400.00
CPAJR Johan Rojas 100.00 250.00
CPAJS Jose Salas 150.00 400.00
CPAKA Kevin Alcantara 400.00 1000.00
CPALF Luis Frias 15.00 40.00
CPALS Luis Santana 30.00 80.00
CPAMA Maximo Acosta 500.00 1200.00
CPAMM Michael McAvene 25.00 60.00
CPAMS Marcus Smith 40.00 100.00
CPAMW Mac Wainwright 40.00 100.00
CPANG Nick Gonzales 60.00 150.00
CPANM Nick Maton 100.00 250.00
CPAPB Patrick Bailey 40.00 100.00
CPARH Robert Hassell 50.00 120.00
CPAYC Yoelqui Cespedes 300.00 800.00
CPAYS Yunior Severino 30.00 80.00
CPAZV Zac Veen 75.00 200.00
CPAAGO Antonio Gomez 40.00 100.00
CPAAMA Angel Martinez 100.00 250.00
CPAARA Alexander Ramirez 250.00 600.00
CPAARE Adinso Reyes 60.00 150.00
CPACMA Coby Mayo 150.00 400.00
CPAGMI Garrett Mitchell 125.00 300.00
CPAJCL Jackson Cluff 20.00 50.00
CPAJDL Jeremy De La Rosa 150.00 400.00
CPARDC Brayan Buelvas 60.00 150.00
CPAYSA Yolbert Sanchez 50.00 120.00

2021 Bowman Chrome Prospect Autographs Orange Refractors

*ORANGE: 3X TO 8X BASIC
STATED ODDS 1:XX HOBBY
STATED PRINT RUN 25 SER.#'d SETS
EXCHANGE DEADLINE 3/31/23
CPAAM Austin Martin EXCH 6000.00 12000.00
CPAAS Aaron Sabato 800.00 2000.00
CPAAV Alexander Vargas 500.00 1200.00
CPABB Brainer Bonaci 250.00 600.00
CPABJ Blaze Jordan 2000.00 5000.00
CPADC Darryl Collins 150.00 400.00
CPADK D'Shawn Knowles 200.00 500.00
CPADM Daniel Montano 50.00 120.00
CPAER Endy Rodriguez 200.00 500.00
CPAFV Freddy Valdez 250.00 600.00
CPAGA Gabriel Arias 800.00 2000.00
CPAHC Hyun-il Choi 150.00 400.00
CPAHH Heriberto Hernandez 800.00 2000.00
CPAHK Heston Kjerstad 200.00 500.00
CPAHP Hedbert Perez 1250.00 3000.00
CPAIM Ismael Mena 300.00 800.00
CPAJB Ji-Hwan Bae 200.00 500.00
CPAJE Jeferson Espinal 500.00 1200.00
CPAJK Jared Kelley 300.00 800.00
CPAJP Jairo Pomares 600.00 1500.00
CPAJR Johan Rojas 400.00 1000.00
CPAJS Jose Salas 600.00 1500.00
CPAJT Jose Tena 150.00 400.00
CPAJV Jake Vogel 300.00 800.00
CPAKA Kevin Alcantara 1500.00 4000.00
CPALF Luis Frias 60.00 150.00
CPALS Luis Santana 125.00 300.00
CPAMA Maximo Acosta 2000.00 5000.00
CPAMM Michael McAvene 100.00 250.00
CPAMS Marcus Smith 150.00 400.00
CPAMW Mac Wainwright 150.00 400.00
CPANG Nick Gonzales 250.00 600.00
CPANM Nick Maton 400.00 1000.00
CPAPB Patrick Bailey 150.00 400.00
CPARH Robert Hassell 200.00 500.00
CPASG Sandy Gaston 60.00 150.00
CPAYC Yoelqui Cespedes 1250.00 3000.00
CPAYS Yunior Severino 125.00 300.00
CPAZV Zac Veen 300.00 800.00
CPAAGO Antonio Gomez 150.00 400.00
CPAAMA Angel Martinez 400.00 1000.00
CPAARA Alexander Ramirez 1000.00 2500.00
CPAARE Adinso Reyes 300.00 800.00
CPACMA Coby Mayo 600.00 1500.00
CPADMA Dylan MacLean 60.00 150.00
CPAGMI Garrett Mitchell 500.00 1200.00
CPAJCL Jackson Cluff 75.00 200.00
CPAJDL Jeremy De La Rosa 600.00 1500.00
CPARDC Brayan Buelvas 300.00 800.00
CPAYSA Yolbert Sanchez 200.00 500.00

2021 Bowman Chrome Prospect Autographs Orange Shimmer Refractors

*ORANGE SHMR/25: 3X TO 8X BASIC
STATED ODDS 1:XX HOBBY
STATED PRINT RUN 25 SER.#'d SETS
EXCHANGE DEADLINE 3/31/23
CPAAM Austin Martin EXCH 6000.00 12000.00
CPAAS Aaron Sabato 800.00 2000.00
CPAAV Alexander Vargas 500.00 1200.00
CPABB Brainer Bonaci 250.00 600.00
CPABJ Blaze Jordan 2000.00 5000.00
CPADC Darryl Collins 150.00 400.00
CPADK D'Shawn Knowles 200.00 500.00
CPADM Daniel Montano 50.00 120.00
CPAER Endy Rodriguez 200.00 500.00
CPAFV Freddy Valdez 250.00 600.00
CPAGA Gabriel Arias 800.00 2000.00
CPAHC Hyun-il Choi 150.00 400.00
CPAHH Heriberto Hernandez 800.00 2000.00
CPAHK Heston Kjerstad 200.00 500.00
CPAHP Hedbert Perez 1250.00 3000.00
CPAIM Ismael Mena 300.00 800.00
CPAJB Ji-Hwan Bae 200.00 500.00
CPAJE Jeferson Espinal 500.00 1200.00
CPAJK Jared Kelley 300.00 800.00
CPAJP Jairo Pomares 600.00 1500.00
CPAJR Johan Rojas 400.00 1000.00
CPAJS Jose Salas 600.00 1500.00
CPAJT Jose Tena 150.00 400.00
CPAJV Jake Vogel 300.00 800.00
CPAKA Kevin Alcantara 1500.00 4000.00
CPALF Luis Frias 60.00 150.00
CPALS Luis Santana 125.00 300.00
CPAMA Maximo Acosta 2000.00 5000.00
CPAMM Michael McAvene 100.00 250.00
CPAMS Marcus Smith 150.00 400.00
CPAMW Mac Wainwright 150.00 400.00
CPANG Nick Gonzales 250.00 600.00
CPANM Nick Maton 400.00 1000.00
CPAPB Patrick Bailey 150.00 400.00
CPARH Robert Hassell 200.00 500.00
CPASG Sandy Gaston 60.00 150.00
CPAYC Yoelqui Cespedes 1250.00 3000.00
CPAYS Yunior Severino 125.00 300.00
CPAZV Zac Veen 300.00 800.00
CPAAGO Antonio Gomez 150.00 400.00
CPAAMA Angel Martinez 400.00 1000.00
CPAARA Alexander Ramirez 1000.00 2500.00
CPAARE Adinso Reyes 300.00 800.00
CPACMA Coby Mayo 600.00 1500.00
CPADMA Dylan MacLean 60.00 150.00
CPAGMI Garrett Mitchell 500.00 1200.00
CPAJCL Jackson Cluff 75.00 200.00
CPAJDL Jeremy De La Rosa 600.00 1500.00
CPARDC Brayan Buelvas 300.00 800.00
CPAYSA Yolbert Sanchez 200.00 500.00

2021 Bowman Chrome Prospect Autographs Purple Refractors

*PURPLE/250: .6X TO 1.5X BASIC
STATED ODDS 1:XX HOBBY
STATED PRINT RUN 250 SER.#'d SETS
EXCHANGE DEADLINE 3/31/23
CPAAM Austin Martin EXCH 800.00 2000.00
CPAAV Alexander Vargas 75.00 200.00
CPABB Brainer Bonaci 50.00 120.00
CPABJ Blaze Jordan 400.00 1000.00
CPABW Beck Way 15.00 40.00
CPADK D'Shawn Knowles 40.00 100.00
CPADM Daniel Montano 10.00 25.00
CPAER Endy Rodriguez 40.00 100.00
CPAFV Freddy Valdez 50.00 120.00
CPAGA Gabriel Arias 100.00 250.00
CPAHC Hyun-il Choi 30.00 80.00
CPAHH Heriberto Hernandez 125.00 300.00
CPAHP Hedbert Perez 200.00 500.00
CPAJB Ji-Hwan Bae 30.00 80.00
CPAJE Jeferson Espinal 50.00 120.00
CPAJK Jared Kelley 40.00 100.00
CPAJS Jose Salas 125.00 300.00
CPAKA Kevin Alcantara 250.00 600.00
CPALF Luis Frias 12.00 30.00
CPALS Luis Santana 25.00 60.00
CPAMA Maximo Acosta 250.00 600.00
CPAMM Michael McAvene 20.00 50.00
CPAMS Marcus Smith 30.00 80.00
CPANG Nick Gonzales 50.00 120.00
CPAYC Yoelqui Cespedes 250.00 600.00
CPAYS Yunior Severino 25.00 60.00
CPAZV Zac Veen 50.00 120.00
CPAAGO Antonio Gomez 30.00 80.00
CPAARA Alexander Ramirez 100.00 250.00
CPAARE Adinso Reyes 50.00 120.00
CPACMA Coby Mayo 75.00 200.00
CPAJCL Jackson Cluff 15.00 40.00
CPAJDL Jeremy De La Rosa 125.00 300.00
CPAYSA Yolbert Sanchez 40.00 100.00

2021 Bowman Chrome Prospect Autographs Refractors

*REF.: .5X TO 1.2X BASIC
STATED ODDS 1:XX HOBBY
STATED PRINT RUN 499 SER.#'d SETS
EXCHANGE DEADLINE 3/31/23
CPAAM Austin Martin EXCH 600.00 1500.00
CPAAV Alexander Vargas 60.00 150.00
CPABB Brainer Bonaci 25.00 60.00
CPAER Endy Rodriguez 30.00 80.00
CPAFV Freddy Valdez 40.00 100.00
CPAGA Gabriel Arias 60.00 150.00
CPAHC Hyun-il Choi 15.00 40.00
CPAHH Heriberto Hernandez 75.00 200.00
CPAHP Hedbert Perez 150.00 400.00
CPAJE Jeferson Espinal 40.00 100.00
CPAJK Jared Kelley 30.00 80.00
CPAKA Kevin Alcantara 200.00 500.00
CPAMA Maximo Acosta 200.00 500.00
CPANG Nick Gonzales 40.00 100.00
CPAYC Yoelqui Cespedes 200.00 500.00
CPAYS Yunior Severino 20.00 50.00
CPAAGO Antonio Gomez 25.00 60.00
CPAARE Adinso Reyes 30.00 80.00
CPACMA Coby Mayo 60.00 150.00
CPAJDL Jeremy De La Rosa 100.00 250.00

2021 Bowman Chrome Prospect Autographs Speckle Refractors

*SPECKLE/299: .6X TO 1.5X BASIC
STATED ODDS 1:XX HOBBY
STATED PRINT RUN 299 SER.#'d SETS
EXCHANGE DEADLINE 3/31/23
CPAAM Austin Martin EXCH 800.00 2000.00
CPAAV Alexander Vargas 75.00 200.00
CPABB Brainer Bonaci 50.00 120.00
CPABJ Blaze Jordan 400.00 1000.00
CPABW Beck Way 15.00 40.00
CPADM Daniel Montano 10.00 25.00
CPAER Endy Rodriguez 40.00 100.00
CPAFV Freddy Valdez 50.00 120.00
CPAGA Gabriel Arias 100.00 250.00
CPAHC Hyun-il Choi 25.00 60.00
CPAHH Heriberto Hernandez 125.00 400.00
CPAHP Hedbert Perez 200.00 500.00
CPAJB Ji-Hwan Bae 30.00 80.00
CPAJE Jeferson Espinal 50.00 120.00
CPAJK Jared Kelley 40.00 100.00
CPAJS Jose Salas 100.00 250.00
CPAKA Kevin Alcantara 250.00 600.00
CPALF Luis Frias 12.00 30.00
CPALS Luis Santana 25.00 60.00
CPAMA Maximo Acosta 250.00 600.00
CPAMM Michael McAvene 20.00 50.00
CPAMS Marcus Smith 30.00 80.00
CPANG Nick Gonzales 50.00 120.00
CPAYC Yoelqui Cespedes 250.00 600.00
CPAYS Yunior Severino 25.00 60.00
CPAZV Zac Veen 50.00 120.00
CPAAGO Antonio Gomez 30.00 80.00
CPAARA Alexander Ramirez 100.00 250.00
CPAARE Adinso Reyes 50.00 120.00
CPACMA Coby Mayo 75.00 200.00
CPAJCL Jackson Cluff 15.00 40.00
CPAJDL Jeremy De La Rosa 125.00 300.00
CPAYSA Yolbert Sanchez 40.00 100.00

2021 Bowman Chrome Prospect Autographs Yellow Refractors

*YELLOW/75: .8X TO 2X BASIC
STATED ODDS 1:XX HOBBY
STATED PRINT RUN 75 SER.#'d SETS
EXCHANGE DEADLINE 3/31/23
CPAAM Austin Martin EXCH 1500.00 3000.00
CPAAS Aaron Sabato 200.00 500.00
CPAAV Alexander Vargas 125.00 300.00
CPABB Brainer Bonaci 60.00 150.00
CPABJ Blaze Jordan 500.00 1200.00
CPABW Beck Way 25.00 60.00
CPADC Darryl Collins 30.00 80.00
CPADK D'Shawn Knowles 50.00 120.00
CPADM Daniel Montano 12.00 30.00
CPAER Endy Rodriguez 50.00 120.00
CPAFV Freddy Valdez 60.00 150.00
CPAGA Gabriel Arias 200.00 500.00
CPAHC Hyun-il Choi 40.00 100.00
CPAHH Heriberto Hernandez 200.00 500.00
CPAHK Heston Kjerstad 50.00 120.00
CPAHP Hedbert Perez 300.00 800.00
CPAIM Ismael Mena 75.00 200.00
CPAJB Ji-Hwan Bae 50.00 120.00
CPAJE Jeferson Espinal 100.00 250.00
CPAJK Jared Kelley 75.00 200.00
CPAJP Jairo Pomares 150.00 400.00
CPAJR Johan Rojas 100.00 250.00
CPAJS Jose Salas 150.00 400.00
CPAKA Kevin Alcantara 400.00 1000.00
CPALF Luis Frias 15.00 40.00
CPALS Luis Santana 30.00 80.00
CPAMA Maximo Acosta 500.00 1200.00
CPAMM Michael McAvene 25.00 60.00
CPAMS Marcus Smith 40.00 100.00
CPAMW Mac Wainwright 40.00 100.00
CPANG Nick Gonzales 60.00 150.00
CPANM Nick Maton 100.00 250.00
CPAPB Patrick Bailey 40.00 100.00
CPARH Robert Hassell 50.00 120.00
CPAYC Yoelqui Cespedes 300.00 800.00
CPAYS Yunior Severino 30.00 80.00
CPAZV Zac Veen 75.00 200.00
CPAAGO Antonio Gomez 40.00 100.00
CPAAMA Angel Martinez 100.00 250.00
CPAARA Alexander Ramirez 250.00 600.00
CPAARE Adinso Reyes 60.00 150.00
CPACMA Coby Mayo 150.00 400.00
CPAGMI Garrett Mitchell 125.00 300.00
CPAJCL Jackson Cluff 20.00 50.00
CPAJDL Jeremy De La Rosa 150.00 400.00
CPARDC Brayan Buelvas 60.00 150.00
CPAYSA Yolbert Sanchez 50.00 120.00

2021 Bowman Chrome Prospects

STATED ODDS 1:XX HOBBY
BCP1 Bobby Witt Jr. 4.00 10.00
BCP2 Freddy Zamora .40 1.00
BCP3 Zac Veen .75 2.00
BCP4 Riley Greene 1.00 2.50
BCP5 Nick Maton .25 .60
BCP6 James Beard .40 1.00
BCP7 Maximo Acosta 6.00 15.00
BCP8 Marco Luciano 1.00 2.50
BCP9 Forrest Whitley .40 1.00
BCP10 Brice Turang .25 .60
BCP11 Jeremy Pena .60 1.50
BCP12 Ed Howard 2.00 5.00
BCP13 Jasson Dominguez 4.00 10.00
BCP14 CJ Abrams .75 2.00
BCP15 Colton Welker .25 .60
BCP16 Clayton Beeter .60 1.50
BCP17 Bryson Stott .75 2.00
BCP18 Hunter Bishop .50 1.25
BCP19 Vidal Brujan 2.00 5.00
BCP20 Nick Lodolo .40 1.00
BCP21 Adinso Reyes 1.50 4.00
BCP22 Pete Crow-Armstrong .75 2.00
BCP23 Ronny Mauricio .60 1.50
BCP24 Oneil Cruz .30 .75
BCP25 Jeremy De La Rosa 5.00 12.00
BCP26 Reid Detmers .60 1.50
BCP27 Alek Manoah .30 .75
BCP28 Shea Langeliers .50 1.25
BCP29 Matthew Liberatore .30 .75
BCP30 Jordyn Adams .30 .75
BCP31 Alek Thomas .30 .75
BCP32 Dax Fulton .40 1.00
BCP33 Eddy Diaz .25 .60
BCP34 Nick Gonzales .75 2.00
BCP35 Nolan Jones .40 1.00
BCP36 Ismael Mena .40 1.00
BCP37 Jeisson Rosario .40 1.00
BCP38 Josh Jung .60 1.50
BCP39 Kody Hoese .75 2.00
BCP40 Yolbert Sanchez .50 1.25
BCP41 Justin Foscue .60 1.50
BCP42 Mick Abel .60 1.50
BCP43 Jackson Kowar .75 2.00
BCP44 Bryce Jarvis .30 .75
BCP45 Robert Puason .60 1.50
BCP46 Jonathan India 1.50 4.00
BCP47 Austin Wells 1.00 2.50
BCP48 Braden Shewmake .40 1.00
BCP49 Gunnar Henderson .30 .75
BCP50 Oswald Peraza .60 1.50
BCP51 Tyler Soderstrom .60 1.50
BCP52 Liover Peguero .40 1.00
BCP53 Francisco Alvarez .60 1.50
BCP54 Daniel Lynch .25 .60
BCP55 Austin Hendrick 2.00 5.00
BCP56 Freudis Nova .25 .60
BCP57 Wander Franco 3.00 8.00
BCP58 Logan Gilbert .30 .75
BCP59 Jake Vogel .30 .75
BCP60 Seth Beer .50 1.25
BCP61 Jordan Balazovic .25 .60
BCP62 Isaiah Greene .75 2.00
BCP63 Royce Lewis .60 1.50
BCP64 Andrew Dalquist .25 .60
BCP65 Brennen Davis .50 1.25
BCP66 Max Meyer .60 1.50
BCP67 Brett Baty .75 2.00
BCP68 Ryan Vilade .25 .60
BCP69 Heliot Ramos .40 1.00
BCP70 Jordan Groshans .50 1.25
BCP71 Blaze Jordan 15.00 40.00
BCP72 Dillon Dingler .50 1.25
BCP73 Keoni Cavaco .25 .60
BCP74 Matthew Thompson .30 .75
BCP75 Bobby Miller 1.00 2.50
BCP76 Yusniel Diaz .40 1.00
BCP77 Carson Tucker .75 2.00
BCP78 Emerson Hancock .60 1.50
BCP79 Luis Garcia 1.00 2.50
BCP80 Trevor Larnach .50 1.25
BCP81 Drew Waters .60 1.50
BCP82 Antonio Gomez .40 1.00
BCP83 Asa Lacy 1.25 3.00
BCP84 Triston Casas .60 1.50
BCP85 Anthony Volpe 1.00 2.50
BCP86 Julio Rodriguez 1.50 4.00
BCP87 Austin Martin 20.00 50.00
BCP88 Andrew Vaughn 1.50 4.00
BCP89 Gabriel Arias 4.00 10.00
BCP90 Nolan Gorman .50 1.25
BCP91 Tyler Callihan .30 .75
BCP92 Casey Martin .75 2.00
BCP93 JJ Bleday .75 2.00
BCP94 Trent Deveaux .30 .75
BCP95 Simeon Woods Richardson .40 1.00
BCP96 Spencer Torkelson 6.00 15.00
BCP97 Kevin Alcantara 8.00 20.00
BCP98 Jordan Westburg .60 1.50
BCP99 Cade Cavalli .50 1.25
BCP100 Terrin Vavra .50 1.25
BCP101 Xavier Edwards .75 2.00
BCP102 Jarred Kelenic 1.25 3.00
BCP103 Jackson Rutledge .40 1.00
BCP104 Blake Walston .40 1.00
BCP105 MacKenzie Gore .50 1.25
BCP106 Jared Kelley .25 .60
BCP107 Jeter Downs .40 1.00
BCP108 Patrick Bailey .50 1.25
BCP109 Geraldo Perdomo .25 .60
BCP110 Jose Salas .25 .60
BCP111 Matt Manning .30 .75
BCP112 Brandon Marsh .40 1.00
BCP113 C.J. Chatham .30 .75
BCP114 Nick Yorke 1.00 2.50
BCP115 Logan Davidson .30 .75
BCP116 Elehuris Montero .30 .75
BCP117 George Kirby .40 1.00
BCP118 Grayson Rodriguez .40 1.00
BCP119 Tyler Freeman .25 .60
BCP120 Robert Hassell 1.50 4.00
BCP121 Adley Rutschman 1.50 4.00
BCP122 DL Hall .25 .60
BCP123 Daniel Espino .30 .75
BCP124 Bo Naylor .30 .75
BCP125 Aaron Sabato 6.00 15.00
BCP126 Drew Romo .60 1.50
BCP127 Hunter Greene .40 1.00
BCP128 Jose Tena .60 1.50
BCP129 Garrett Mitchell 1.50 4.00
BCP130 Hyun-il Choi .40 1.00
BCP131 Christopher Morel .25 .60
BCP132 Taylor Trammell .40 1.00
BCP133 Mario Feliciano .40 1.00
BCP134 Shane Baz .25 .60
BCP135 Jarren Duran 1.00 2.50
BCP136 Kristian Robinson .75 2.00
BCP137 Michael Toglia .25 .60
BCP138 Heston Kjerstad 1.25 3.00
BCP139 Bayron Lora 1.25 3.00
BCP140 Yunior Severino .30 .75
BCP141 Edward Cabrera .40 1.00
BCP142 Corbin Carroll .40 1.00
BCP143 Nick Bitsko .75 2.00
BCP144 Nick Loftin .40 1.00
BCP145 Alexander Ramirez 4.00 10.00
BCP146 Jordan Walker .75 2.00
BCP147 Nick Allen .25 .60
BCP148 Miguel Amaya .25 .60
BCP149 Ivan Johnson .40 1.00
BCP150 Josiah Gray .40 1.00

2021 Bowman Chrome Prospects Aqua Refractors

*AQUA: 2X TO 5X BASIC
STATED ODDS 1:XX HOBBY
STATED PRINT RUN 125 SER.#'d SETS
BCP1 Bobby Witt Jr. 40.00 100.00
BCP7 Maximo Acosta 100.00 250.00
BCP12 Ed Howard 25.00 60.00
BCP13 Jasson Dominguez 60.00 150.00
BCP21 Adinso Reyes 25.00 60.00
BCP25 Jeremy De La Rosa 30.00 80.00
BCP57 Wander Franco 40.00 100.00
BCP71 Blaze Jordan 125.00 300.00
BCP86 Julio Rodriguez 25.00 60.00
BCP87 Austin Martin 200.00 500.00
BCP89 Gabriel Arias 30.00 80.00
BCP96 Spencer Torkelson 75.00 200.00
BCP97 Kevin Alcantara 100.00 250.00
BCP102 Jarred Kelenic 15.00 40.00
BCP121 Adley Rutschman 30.00 80.00
BCP125 Aaron Sabato 60.00 150.00
BCP145 Alexander Ramirez 40.00 100.00

2021 Bowman Chrome Prospects Aqua Shimmer Refractors

*AQUA SHMR: 2X TO 5X BASIC
STATED ODDS 1:XX HOBBY
STATED PRINT RUN 125 SER.#'d SETS
BCP1 Bobby Witt Jr. 40.00 100.00
BCP7 Maximo Acosta 100.00 250.00
BCP12 Ed Howard 25.00 60.00
BCP13 Jasson Dominguez 60.00 150.00
BCP21 Adinso Reyes 25.00 60.00
BCP25 Jeremy De La Rosa 30.00 80.00
BCP57 Wander Franco 40.00 100.00
BCP71 Blaze Jordan 125.00 300.00
BCP86 Julio Rodriguez 25.00 60.00
BCP87 Austin Martin 200.00 500.00
BCP89 Gabriel Arias 30.00 80.00
BCP96 Spencer Torkelson 75.00 200.00
BCP97 Kevin Alcantara 100.00 250.00
BCP102 Jarred Kelenic 15.00 40.00
BCP121 Adley Rutschman 30.00 80.00
BCP125 Aaron Sabato 60.00 150.00
BCP145 Alexander Ramirez 40.00 100.00

2021 Bowman Chrome Prospects Atomic Refractors

*ATOMIC: 1X TO 2.5X BASIC
STATED ODDS 1:XX HOBBY
BCP1 Bobby Witt Jr. 20.00 50.00
BCP7 Maximo Acosta 50.00 120.00
BCP12 Ed Howard 10.00 25.00
BCP13 Jasson Dominguez 30.00 80.00
BCP21 Adinso Reyes 12.00 30.00
BCP57 Wander Franco 12.00 30.00
BCP71 Blaze Jordan 60.00 150.00
BCP86 Julio Rodriguez 12.00 30.00
BCP87 Austin Martin 100.00 250.00
BCP89 Gabriel Arias 15.00 40.00
BCP96 Spencer Torkelson 20.00 50.00
BCP97 Kevin Alcantara 40.00 100.00
BCP102 Jarred Kelenic 8.00 20.00
BCP121 Adley Rutschman 8.00 20.00
BCP125 Aaron Sabato 30.00 80.00
BCP145 Alexander Ramirez 20.00 50.00

2021 Bowman Chrome Prospects Blue Refractors

*BLUE: 2X TO 5X BASIC
STATED ODDS 1:XX HOBBY
STATED PRINT RUN 150 SER.#'d SETS
BCP1 Bobby Witt Jr. 40.00 100.00
BCP7 Maximo Acosta 100.00 250.00
BCP12 Ed Howard 25.00 60.00
BCP13 Jasson Dominguez 60.00 150.00
BCP21 Adinso Reyes 25.00 60.00
BCP25 Jeremy De La Rosa 30.00 80.00
BCP57 Wander Franco 40.00 100.00
BCP71 Blaze Jordan 125.00 300.00
BCP86 Julio Rodriguez 25.00 60.00
BCP87 Austin Martin 200.00 500.00
BCP89 Gabriel Arias 30.00 80.00
BCP96 Spencer Torkelson 75.00 200.00
BCP97 Kevin Alcantara 100.00 250.00
BCP102 Jarred Kelenic 15.00 40.00
BCP121 Adley Rutschman 30.00 80.00
BCP125 Aaron Sabato 60.00 150.00
BCP145 Alexander Ramirez 40.00 100.00

2021 Bowman Chrome Prospects Blue Shimmer Refractors

*BLUE SHMR: 2X TO 5X BASIC
STATED ODDS 1:XX HOBBY
STATED PRINT RUN 150 SER.#'d SETS
BCP1 Bobby Witt Jr. 40.00 100.00
BCP7 Maximo Acosta 100.00 250.00
BCP12 Ed Howard 25.00 60.00
BCP13 Jasson Dominguez 60.00 150.00
BCP21 Adinso Reyes 25.00 60.00
BCP25 Jeremy De La Rosa 30.00 80.00
BCP57 Wander Franco 40.00 100.00
BCP71 Blaze Jordan 125.00 300.00
BCP86 Julio Rodriguez 25.00 60.00
BCP87 Austin Martin 200.00 500.00
BCP89 Gabriel Arias 30.00 80.00
BCP96 Spencer Torkelson 75.00 200.00
BCP97 Kevin Alcantara 100.00 250.00
BCP102 Jarred Kelenic 15.00 40.00
BCP121 Adley Rutschman 30.00 80.00
BCP125 Aaron Sabato 60.00 150.00
BCP145 Alexander Ramirez 40.00 100.00

2021 Bowman Chrome Prospects Die Cuts

STATED ODDS 1:1419 HOBBY
STATED PRINT RUN 49 SER.#'d SETS
CPDCAH Austin Hendrick 60.00 150.00
CPDCAL Asa Lacy 25.00 60.00
CPDCAM Austin Martin 400.00 1000.00
CPDCAR Adley Rutschman 75.00 200.00
CPDCAS Aaron Sabato
CPDCBJ Blaze Jordan
CPDCEH Ed Howard 50.00 120.00
CPDCGM Garrett Mitchell 60.00 150.00
CPDCHK Heston Kjerstad 30.00 80.00
CPDCJD Jasson Dominguez 200.00 500.00
CPDCMA Mick Abel 100.00 250.00
CPDCML Marco Luciano 60.00 150.00
CPDCMM Max Meyer 25.00 60.00
CPDCNG Nick Gonzales 50.00 120.00
CPDCRH Robert Hassell 100.00 250.00
CPDCST Spencer Torkelson 125.00 300.00
CPDCWF Wander Franco 400.00 1000.00
CPDCZV Zac Veen 75.00 200.00
CPDCBWJ Bobby Witt Jr. 150.00 400.00
CPDCJDO Jeter Downs 30.00 80.00

2021 Bowman Chrome Prospects Fuchsia Refractors

*FUCHSIA: 1.5X TO 4X BASIC
STATED ODDS 1:XX HOBBY
STATED PRINT RUN 199 SER.#'d SETS
BCP1 Bobby Witt Jr. 30.00 80.00
BCP7 Maximo Acosta 75.00 200.00
BCP12 Ed Howard 20.00 50.00
BCP13 Jasson Dominguez 50.00 120.00
BCP21 Adinso Reyes 20.00 50.00
BCP57 Wander Franco 30.00 80.00
BCP71 Blaze Jordan 100.00 250.00
BCP86 Julio Rodriguez 20.00 50.00
BCP87 Austin Martin 150.00 400.00
BCP89 Gabriel Arias 25.00 60.00
BCP96 Spencer Torkelson 60.00 150.00
BCP97 Kevin Alcantara 75.00 200.00
BCP102 Jarred Kelenic 12.00 30.00
BCP121 Adley Rutschman 25.00 60.00
BCP125 Aaron Sabato 50.00 120.00
BCP145 Alexander Ramirez 30.00 80.00

2021 Bowman Chrome Prospects Fuchsia Shimmer Refractors

*FUCHSIA SHMR: 1.5X TO 4X BASIC
STATED ODDS 1:XX HOBBY
STATED PRINT RUN 199 SER.#'d SETS
BCP1 Bobby Witt Jr. 30.00 80.00
BCP7 Maximo Acosta 75.00 200.00
BCP12 Ed Howard 20.00 50.00
BCP13 Jasson Dominguez 50.00 120.00
BCP21 Adinso Reyes 20.00 50.00
BCP57 Wander Franco 30.00 80.00
BCP71 Blaze Jordan 100.00 250.00
BCP86 Julio Rodriguez 20.00 50.00
BCP87 Austin Martin 150.00 400.00
BCP89 Gabriel Arias 25.00 60.00
BCP96 Spencer Torkelson 60.00 150.00
BCP97 Kevin Alcantara 75.00 200.00
BCP102 Jarred Kelenic 12.00 30.00
BCP121 Adley Rutschman 25.00 60.00
BCP125 Aaron Sabato 50.00 120.00
BCP145 Alexander Ramirez 30.00 80.00

2021 Bowman Chrome Prospects Gold Refractors

*GOLD: 5X TO 12X BASIC
STATED ODDS 1:XX HOBBY
STATED PRINT RUN 50 SER.#'d SETS
BCP1 Bobby Witt Jr. 100.00 250.00
BCP4 Riley Greene 40.00 100.00
BCP7 Maximo Acosta 250.00 600.00
BCP12 Ed Howard 60.00 150.00
BCP13 Jasson Dominguez 150.00 400.00
BCP21 Adinso Reyes 60.00 150.00
BCP25 Jeremy De La Rosa 60.00 150.00
BCP57 Wander Franco 100.00 250.00
BCP71 Blaze Jordan 300.00 800.00
BCP86 Julio Rodriguez 60.00 150.00
BCP87 Austin Martin 300.00 800.00
BCP89 Gabriel Arias 75.00 200.00
BCP96 Spencer Torkelson 150.00 400.00
BCP97 Kevin Alcantara 250.00 600.00
BCP102 Jarred Kelenic 40.00 100.00
BCP121 Adley Rutschman 75.00 200.00
BCP125 Aaron Sabato 150.00 400.00
BCP145 Alexander Ramirez 100.00 250.00

2021 Bowman Chrome Prospects Gold Shimmer Refractors

*GOLD SHMR: 5X TO 12X BASIC
STATED ODDS 1:XX HOBBY
STATED PRINT RUN 50 SER.#'d SETS
BCP1 Bobby Witt Jr. 100.00 250.00
BCP4 Riley Greene 40.00 100.00
BCP7 Maximo Acosta 250.00 600.00
BCP12 Ed Howard 60.00 150.00
BCP13 Jasson Dominguez 150.00 400.00
BCP21 Adinso Reyes 60.00 150.00
BCP25 Jeremy De La Rosa 60.00 150.00
BCP57 Wander Franco 100.00 250.00
BCP71 Blaze Jordan 300.00 800.00
BCP86 Julio Rodriguez 60.00 150.00
BCP87 Austin Martin 300.00 800.00
BCP89 Gabriel Arias 75.00 200.00
BCP96 Spencer Torkelson 150.00 400.00
BCP97 Kevin Alcantara 250.00 600.00
BCP102 Jarred Kelenic 40.00 100.00
BCP121 Adley Rutschman 75.00 200.00
BCP125 Aaron Sabato 150.00 400.00
BCP145 Alexander Ramirez 100.00 250.00

2021 Bowman Chrome Prospects Green Mini-Diamond Refractors

*GRN DIAMOND: 2.5X TO 6X BASIC

STATED ODDS 1:XX HOBBY
STATED PRINT RUN 99 SER.#'d SETS
BCP1 Bobby Witt Jr. 50.00 120.00
BCP7 Maximo Acosta 125.00 300.00
BCP12 Ed Howard 30.00 80.00
BCP13 Jasson Dominguez 75.00 200.00
BCP21 Adinso Reyes 30.00 80.00
BCP25 Jeremy De La Rosa 40.00 100.00
BCP57 Wander Franco 50.00 120.00
BCP71 Blaze Jordan 150.00 400.00
BCP86 Julio Rodriguez 30.00 80.00
BCP87 Austin Martin 250.00 600.00
BCP89 Gabriel Arias 40.00 100.00
BCP96 Spencer Torkelson 100.00 250.00
BCP97 Kevin Alcantara 125.00 300.00
BCP102 Jarred Kelenic 20.00 50.00
BCP121 Adley Rutschman 40.00 100.00
BCP125 Aaron Sabato 75.00 200.00
BCP145 Alexander Ramirez 50.00 120.00

2021 Bowman Chrome Prospects Green Refractors

*GREEN: 2.5X TO 6X BASIC
STATED ODDS 1:XX RETAIL
STATED PRINT RUN 99 SER.#'d SETS
BCP1 Bobby Witt Jr. 50.00 120.00
BCP7 Maximo Acosta 125.00 300.00
BCP12 Ed Howard 30.00 80.00
BCP13 Jasson Dominguez 75.00 200.00
BCP21 Adinso Reyes 30.00 80.00
BCP25 Jeremy De La Rosa 40.00 100.00
BCP57 Wander Franco 50.00 120.00
BCP71 Blaze Jordan 150.00 400.00
BCP86 Julio Rodriguez 30.00 80.00
BCP87 Austin Martin 250.00 600.00
BCP89 Gabriel Arias 40.00 100.00
BCP96 Spencer Torkelson 100.00 250.00
BCP97 Kevin Alcantara 125.00 300.00
BCP102 Jarred Kelenic 20.00 50.00
BCP121 Adley Rutschman 40.00 100.00
BCP125 Aaron Sabato 75.00 200.00
BCP145 Alexander Ramirez 50.00 120.00

2021 Bowman Chrome Prospects Green Shimmer Refractors

*GREEN SHMR: 2.5X TO 6X BASIC
STATED ODDS 1:XX RETAIL
STATED PRINT RUN 99 SER.#'d SETS
BCP1 Bobby Witt Jr. 50.00 120.00
BCP7 Maximo Acosta 125.00 300.00
BCP12 Ed Howard 30.00 80.00
BCP13 Jasson Dominguez 75.00 200.00
BCP21 Adinso Reyes 30.00 80.00
BCP25 Jeremy De La Rosa 40.00 100.00
BCP57 Wander Franco 50.00 120.00
BCP71 Blaze Jordan 150.00 400.00
BCP86 Julio Rodriguez 30.00 80.00
BCP87 Austin Martin 250.00 600.00
BCP89 Gabriel Arias 40.00 100.00
BCP96 Spencer Torkelson 100.00 250.00
BCP97 Kevin Alcantara 125.00 300.00
BCP102 Jarred Kelenic 20.00 50.00
BCP121 Adley Rutschman 40.00 100.00
BCP125 Aaron Sabato 75.00 200.00
BCP145 Alexander Ramirez 50.00 120.00

2021 Bowman Chrome Prospects Orange Refractors

*ORANGE: 8X TO 20X BASIC
STATED ODDS 1:XX HOBBY
STATED PRINT RUN 25 SER.#'d SETS
BCP1 Bobby Witt Jr. 150.00 400.00
BCP4 Riley Greene 60.00 150.00
BCP7 Maximo Acosta 400.00 100.00
BCP12 Ed Howard 100.00 250.00
BCP13 Jasson Dominguez 250.00 600.00
BCP21 Adinso Reyes 100.00 250.00
BCP25 Jeremy De La Rosa 100.00 250.00
BCP57 Wander Franco 150.00 400.00
BCP71 Blaze Jordan 500.00 1200.00
BCP86 Julio Rodriguez 100.00 250.00
BCP87 Austin Martin 400.00 1000.00
BCP89 Gabriel Arias 125.00 300.00
BCP96 Spencer Torkelson 250.00 600.00
BCP97 Kevin Alcantara 400.00 1000.00
BCP102 Jarred Kelenic 60.00 150.00
BCP121 Adley Rutschman 125.00 300.00
BCP125 Aaron Sabato 250.00 600.00
BCP145 Alexander Ramirez 150.00 400.00

2021 Bowman Chrome Prospects Orange Shimmer Refractors

*ORANGE SHMR: 8X TO 20X BASIC
STATED ODDS 1:XX HOBBY
STATED PRINT RUN 25 SER.#'d SETS
BCP1 Bobby Witt Jr. 150.00 400.00
BCP4 Riley Greene 60.00 150.00
BCP7 Maximo Acosta 400.00 100.00
BCP12 Ed Howard 100.00 250.00
BCP13 Jasson Dominguez 250.00 600.00
BCP21 Adinso Reyes 100.00 250.00
BCP25 Jeremy De La Rosa 100.00 250.00
BCP57 Wander Franco 150.00 400.00
BCP71 Blaze Jordan 500.00 1200.00
BCP86 Julio Rodriguez 100.00 250.00
BCP87 Austin Martin 400.00 1000.00
BCP89 Gabriel Arias 125.00 300.00
BCP96 Spencer Torkelson 250.00 600.00
BCP97 Kevin Alcantara 400.00 1000.00
BCP102 Jarred Kelenic 60.00 150.00
BCP121 Adley Rutschman 125.00 300.00
BCP125 Aaron Sabato 250.00 600.00
BCP145 Alexander Ramirez 150.00 400.00

2021 Bowman Chrome Prospects Purple Refractors

*PURPLE: 1.2X TO 3X BASIC
STATED ODDS 1:XX HOBBY
STATED PRINT RUN 250 SER.#'d SETS
BCP1 Bobby Witt Jr. 25.00 60.00
BCP7 Maximo Acosta 60.00 150.00
BCP12 Ed Howard 12.00 30.00
BCP13 Jasson Dominguez 40.00 100.00
BCP21 Adinso Reyes 15.00 40.00
BCP57 Wander Franco 15.00 40.00
BCP71 Blaze Jordan 75.00 200.00
BCP86 Julio Rodriguez 15.00 40.00
BCP87 Austin Martin 125.00 300.00
BCP89 Gabriel Arias 20.00 50.00
BCP96 Spencer Torkelson 50.00 120.00
BCP97 Kevin Alcantara 60.00 150.00
BCP102 Jarred Kelenic 10.00 25.00
BCP121 Adley Rutschman 20.00 50.00
BCP125 Aaron Sabato 40.00 100.00
BCP145 Alexander Ramirez 25.00 60.00

2021 Bowman Chrome Prospects Refractors

*REF.: 1X TO 2.5X BASIC
STATED ODDS 1:XX HOBBY
STATED PRINT RUN 499 SER.#'d SETS
BCP1 Bobby Witt Jr. 20.00 50.00
BCP7 Maximo Acosta 50.00 120.00
BCP12 Ed Howard 10.00 25.00
BCP13 Jasson Dominguez 30.00 80.00
BCP21 Adinso Reyes 12.00 30.00
BCP57 Wander Franco 12.00 30.00
BCP71 Blaze Jordan 60.00 150.00
BCP86 Julio Rodriguez 12.00 30.00
BCP87 Austin Martin 125.00 300.00
BCP89 Gabriel Arias 15.00 40.00
BCP96 Spencer Torkelson 20.00 50.00
BCP97 Kevin Alcantara 50.00 120.00
BCP102 Jarred Kelenic 8.00 20.00
BCP121 Adley Rutschman 15.00 40.00
BCP125 Aaron Sabato 30.00 80.00
BCP145 Alexander Ramirez 20.00 50.00

2021 Bowman Chrome Prospects Speckle Refractors

*SPECKLE: 1.2X TO 3X BASIC
STATED ODDS 1:XX HOBBY
STATED PRINT RUN 299 SER.#'d SETS
BCP1 Bobby Witt Jr. 25.00 60.00
BCP7 Maximo Acosta 60.00 150.00
BCP12 Ed Howard 12.00 30.00
BCP13 Jasson Dominguez 40.00 100.00
BCP21 Adinso Reyes 15.00 40.00
BCP57 Wander Franco 15.00 40.00
BCP71 Blaze Jordan 75.00 200.00
BCP86 Julio Rodriguez 15.00 40.00
BCP87 Austin Martin 125.00 300.00
BCP89 Gabriel Arias 20.00 50.00
BCP96 Spencer Torkelson 50.00 120.00
BCP97 Kevin Alcantara 60.00 150.00
BCP102 Jarred Kelenic 10.00 25.00
BCP121 Adley Rutschman 20.00 50.00
BCP125 Aaron Sabato 40.00 100.00
BCP145 Alexander Ramirez 25.00 60.00

2021 Bowman Chrome Prospects Yellow Mini-Diamond Refractors

*YLW DIAMOND: 3X TO 8X BASIC
STATED ODDS 1:XX HOBBY
STATED PRINT RUN 75 SER.#'d SETS
BCP1 Bobby Witt Jr. 60.00 150.00
BCP7 Maximo Acosta 150.00 400.00
BCP12 Ed Howard 40.00 100.00
BCP13 Jasson Dominguez 100.00 250.00
BCP21 Adinso Reyes 40.00 100.00
BCP25 Jeremy De La Rosa 50.00 120.00
BCP57 Wander Franco 60.00 150.00
BCP71 Blaze Jordan 200.00 500.00
BCP86 Julio Rodriguez 40.00 100.00
BCP87 Austin Martin 250.00 600.00
BCP89 Gabriel Arias 50.00 120.00
BCP96 Spencer Torkelson 100.00 250.00
BCP97 Kevin Alcantara 150.00 400.00
BCP102 Jarred Kelenic 25.00 60.00
BCP121 Adley Rutschman 50.00 120.00
BCP125 Aaron Sabato 100.00 250.00
BCP145 Alexander Ramirez 60.00 150.00

2021 Bowman Chrome Prospects Yellow Refractors

*YELLOW: 3X TO 8X BASIC
STATED ODDS 1:XX HOBBY
STATED PRINT RUN 75 SER.#'d SETS
BCP1 Bobby Witt Jr. 60.00 150.00
BCP7 Maximo Acosta 150.00 400.00
BCP12 Ed Howard 40.00 100.00
BCP13 Jasson Dominguez 100.00 250.00
BCP21 Adinso Reyes 40.00 100.00
BCP25 Jeremy De La Rosa 50.00 120.00
BCP57 Wander Franco 60.00 150.00
BCP71 Blaze Jordan 200.00 500.00
BCP86 Julio Rodriguez 40.00 100.00
BCP87 Austin Martin 250.00 600.00
BCP89 Gabriel Arias 50.00 120.00
BCP96 Spencer Torkelson 100.00 250.00
BCP97 Kevin Alcantara 150.00 400.00
BCP102 Jarred Kelenic 25.00 60.00
BCP121 Adley Rutschman 50.00 120.00
BCP125 Aaron Sabato 100.00 250.00
BCP145 Alexander Ramirez 60.00 150.00

2021 Bowman Chrome Rookie Autographs

STATED ODDS 1:XX HOBBY
EXCHANGE DEADLINE 3/31/23
*REF./499: .5X TO 1.2X BASIC
*BLUE/150: .6X TO 1.5X BASIC
CRAAB Alec Bohm 75.00 200.00
CRAAG Andres Gimenez
CRACJ Cristian Javier 30.00 80.00
CRACM Casey Mize 40.00 100.00
CRACP Cristian Pache 60.00 150.00
CRADC Dylan Carlson 100.00 250.00
CRADG Deivi Garcia
CRAJA Jo Adell
CRAJB Joey Bart 40.00 100.00
CRAJS Jesus Sanchez 25.00 60.00
CRAKH Ke'Bryan Hayes 100.00 250.00
CRALG Luis Garcia 25.00 60.00
CRALT Leody Taveras 10.00 25.00
CRANM Nick Madrigal 40.00 100.00
CRANP Nate Pearson 20.00 50.00
CRARM Ryan Mountcastle 40.00 100.00
CRASS Sixto Sanchez 15.00 40.00
CRAJCR Jake Cronenworth 40.00 100.00

2021 Bowman Chrome Rookie Autographs Atomic Refractors

*ATOMIC/100: .8X TO 2X BASIC
STATED ODDS 1:XX HOBBY
STATED PRINT RUN 100 SER.#'d SETS
EXCHANGE DEADLINE 3/31/23
CRAJB Joey Bart 100.00 250.00
CRANP Nate Pearson 60.00 150.00

2021 Bowman Chrome Rookie Autographs Gold Refractors

*GOLD/50: 1.2X TO 3X BASIC
STATED ODDS 1:XX HOBBY
STATED PRINT RUN 50 SER.#'d SETS
EXCHANGE DEADLINE 3/31/23
CRAJB Joey Bart 200.00 500.00
CRALT Leody Taveras 40.00 100.00
CRANP Nate Pearson 100.00 250.00
CRAJCR Jake Cronenworth 250.00 600.00

2021 Bowman Chrome Rookie Autographs Green Refractors

*GREEN/99: .8X TO 2X BASIC
STATED ODDS 1:XX RETAIL
STATED PRINT RUN 99 SER.#'d SETS
EXCHANGE DEADLINE 3/31/23
CRAJB Joey Bart 125.00 300.00
CRANP Nate Pearson 60.00 150.00

2021 Bowman Chrome Rookie Autographs Orange Refractors

*ORANGE/25: 2X TO 5X BASIC
STATED ODDS 1:XX HOBBY
STATED PRINT RUN 25 SER.#'d SETS
EXCHANGE DEADLINE 3/31/23
CRAJB Joey Bart 300.00 800.00
CRALT Leody Taveras 60.00 150.00
CRANP Nate Pearson 150.00 400.00
CRAJCR Jake Cronenworth 400.00 1000.00

2021 Bowman Chrome Rookie Autographs Yellow Refractors

*YELLOW/75: .8X TO 2X BASIC
STATED ODDS 1:XX HOBBY
STATED PRINT RUN 75 SER.#'d SETS
EXCHANGE DEADLINE 3/31/23
CRAJB Joey Bart 125.00 300.00
CRANP Nate Pearson 60.00 150.00

2021 Bowman Chrome Rookie of the Year Favorites Refractors

STATED ODDS 1:8 HOBBY
*ATOMIC/150: 1.5X TO 4X BASIC
*AQUA/125: 1.5X TO 4X BASIC
*GREEN/99: 2X TO 5X BASIC
*GOLD/50: 3X TO 8X BASIC
RRYAB Alec Bohm 3.00 8.00
RRYAG Andres Gimenez .75 2.00
RRYCJ Cristian Javier .75 2.00
RRYCM Casey Mize 2.50 6.00
RRYDC Dylan Carlson 3.00 8.00
RRYEW Evan White 2.00 5.00
RRYJA Jo Adell 2.00 5.00
RRYJB Joey Bart 1.00 2.50
RRYJC Jake Cronenworth 2.00 5.00
RRYKH Ke'Bryan Hayes 3.00 8.00
RRYLG Luis Garcia 1.50 4.00
RRYNM Nick Madrigal 2.50 6.00
RRYNP Nate Pearson 1.00 2.50
RRYRM Ryan Mountcastle 3.00 8.00
RRYSS Sixto Sanchez .75 2.00

2021 Bowman Chrome Rookie of the Year Favorites Orange Refractors

*ORANGE: 5X TO 12X BASIC
STATED ODDS 1:XX HOBBY
STATED PRINT RUN 25 SER.#'d SETS
RRYAB Alec Bohm 50.00 120.00

2021 Bowman Chrome Rookie of the Year Favorites Autographs Refractors

STATED ODDS 1:XX HOBBY
STATED PRINT RUN 150 SER.#'d SETS
EXCHANGE DEADLINE 3/31/23
ROYFAB Alec Bohm EXCH 60.00 150.00
ROYFDC Dylan Carlson 100.00 250.00
ROYFEW Evan White 20.00 50.00
ROYFJA Jo Adell EXCH 40.00 100.00
ROYFJB Joey Bart 40.00 100.00
ROYFJC Jake Cronenworth 25.00 60.00
ROYFNM Nick Madrigal 25.00 60.00
ROYFNP Nate Pearson 25.00 60.00
ROYFSH Spencer Howard 10.00 25.00
ROYFSHU Sam Huff 20.00 50.00

2021 Bowman Chrome Rookie of the Year Favorites Autographs Gold Refractors

*GOLD/50: .5X TO 1.2X BASIC
STATED ODDS 1:XX HOBBY
STATED PRINT RUN 50 SER.#'d SETS
EXCHANGE DEADLINE 3/31/23
ROYFDC Dylan Carlson 200.00 500.00
ROYFJC Jake Cronenworth 50.00 120.00
ROYFNM Nick Madrigal 50.00 120.00

2021 Bowman Chrome Rookie of the Year Favorites Autographs Orange Refractors

*ORANGE/25: .6X TO 1.5X BASIC
STATED ODDS 1:XX HOBBY
STATED PRINT RUN 25 SER.#'d SETS
EXCHANGE DEADLINE 3/31/23
ROYFDC Dylan Carlson 250.00 600.00
ROYFJC Jake Cronenworth 75.00 200.00
ROYFNM Nick Madrigal 60.00 150.00

2021 Bowman Chrome Scouts Top 100 Refractors

STATED ODDS 1:4 HOBBY
BTP1 Wander Franco 3.00 8.00
BTP2 Gavin Lux 1.00 2.50
BTP3 Luis Robert 1.50 4.00
BTP4 Adley Rutschman 2.00 5.00
BTP5 MacKenzie Gore .60 1.50
BTP6 Jo Adell 2.00 5.00
BTP7 Spencer Torkelson 2.00 5.00
BTP8 Casey Mize 2.50 6.00
BTP9 Nate Pearson 1.50 4.00
BTP10 Royce Lewis .75 2.00
BTP11 Bobby Witt Jr. 6.00 15.00
BTP12 Jarred Kelenic 1.50 4.00
BTP13 Jesus Luzardo .50 1.25
BTP14 Cristian Pache 3.00 8.00
BTP15 Joey Bart 1.00 2.50
BTP16 Brendan McKay .40 1.00
BTP17 Andrew Vaughn 1.25 3.00
BTP18 Dylan Carlson 2.50 6.00
BTP19 Julio Rodriguez 2.00 5.00
BTP20 Austin Martin 8.00 20.00
BTP21 Forrest Whitley .50 1.25
BTP22 Sixto Sanchez 1.50 4.00
BTP23 Matt Manning .40 1.00
BTP24 CJ Abrams 1.00 2.50
BTP25 Drew Waters .75 2.00
BTP26 Luis Patino 1.25 3.00
BTP27 JJ Bleday 1.00 2.50
BTP28 Alec Bohm 5.00 12.00
BTP29 Riley Greene 1.25 3.00
BTP30 Asa Lacy 1.50 4.00
BTP31 Alex Kirilloff 1.25 3.00
BTP32 Sean Murphy .30 .75
BTP33 Spencer Howard 1.00 2.50
BTP34 Marco Luciano 1.25 3.00
BTP35 Emerson Hancock .75 2.00
BTP36 Grayson Rodriguez .50 1.25
BTP37 Nick Gonzales 1.00 2.50
BTP38 Max Meyer .75 2.00
BTP39 Ian Anderson 2.00 5.00
BTP40 Logan Gilbert .40 1.00
BTP41 Nick Madrigal 2.50 6.00
BTP42 Ke'Bryan Hayes 3.00 8.00
BTP43 Nolan Jones .50 1.25
BTP44 Kristian Robinson 1.00 2.50
BTP45 Jeter Downs .50 1.25
BTP46 Vidal Brujan 2.50 6.00
BTP47 Tarik Skubal 1.50 4.00
BTP48 Nolan Gorman .60 1.50
BTP49 Nick Lodolo .50 1.25
BTP50 Alek Thomas .40 1.00
BTP51 Luis Campusano .30 .75
BTP52 Hunter Greene .50 1.25
BTP53 Jasson Dominguez 4.00 10.00
BTP54 Zac Veen 1.00 2.50
BTP55 Josh Jung .75 2.00
BTP56 Evan White 2.00 5.00
BTP57 Taylor Trammell .50 1.25
BTP58 Matthew Liberatore .40 1.00
BTP59 Brady Singer 1.50 4.00
BTP60 A.J. Puk .50 1.25
BTP61 Daniel Lynch .30 .75
BTP62 Heston Kjerstad 1.50 4.00
BTP63 Garrett Mitchell 2.00 5.00
BTP64 Ronny Mauricio .75 2.00
BTP65 Francisco Alvarez .75 2.00
BTP66 Oneil Cruz .40 1.00
BTP67 Heliot Ramos .50 1.25
BTP68 Jazz Chisholm 1.25 3.00
BTP69 Josiah Gray .50 1.25
BTP70 Brailyn Marquez 1.50 4.00
BTP71 DL Hall .30 .75
BTP72 Shea Langeliers .60 1.50
BTP73 Hunter Bishop .60 1.50
BTP74 Xavier Edwards 1.00 2.50
BTP75 Keibert Ruiz 1.00 2.50
BTP76 Sam Huff .60 1.50
BTP77 Jordan Groshans .60 1.50
BTP78 Daulton Varsho .75 2.00
BTP79 Triston Casas .75 2.00
BTP80 Brennen Davis .60 1.50
BTP81 Brandon Marsh .50 1.25
BTP82 Robert Hassell 2.00 5.00
BTP83 Reid Detmers .75 2.00
BTP84 Jesus Sanchez 1.00 2.50
BTP85 Trevor Larnach .60 1.50
BTP86 Austin Hendrick 2.50 6.00
BTP87 Geraldo Perdomo .30 .75
BTP88 Brusdar Graterol .40 1.00
BTP89 Andres Gimenez .75 2.00
BTP90 Edward Cabrera .50 1.25
BTP91 Jordan Balazovic .30 .75
BTP92 Bryson Stott 1.00 2.50
BTP93 Clarke Schmidt .50 1.25
BTP94 Mick Abel .50 1.25
BTP95 Corbin Carroll .50 1.25
BTP96 Shane Baz .30 .75
BTP97 Deivi Garcia 2.50 6.00
BTP98 Brett Baty 1.00 2.50
BTP99 Garrett Crochet .50 1.25
BTP100 Ryan Mountcastle 3.00 8.00

2021 Bowman Chrome Scouts Top 100 Aqua Refractors

*AQUA: 1.5X TO 4X BASIC
STATED ODDS 1:XX HOBBY
STATED PRINT RUN 125 SER.#'d SETS
BTP53 Jasson Dominguez 15.00 40.00

2021 Bowman Chrome Scouts Top 100 Atomic Refractors

*ATOMIC: 1.5X TO 4X BASIC
STATED ODDS 1:XX HOBBY
STATED PRINT RUN 150 SER.#'d SETS
BTP53 Jasson Dominguez 30.00 80.00

2021 Bowman Chrome Scouts Top 100 Gold Refractors

*GOLD: 3X TO 8X BASIC
STATED ODDS 1:XX HOBBY
STATED PRINT RUN 50 SER.#'d SETS
BTP53 Jasson Dominguez 30.00 80.00

2021 Bowman Chrome Scouts Top 100 Green Refractors

*GREEN: 2X TO 5X BASIC
STATED ODDS 1:XX RETAIL
STATED PRINT RUN 99 SER.#'d SETS
BTP53 Jasson Dominguez 20.00 50.00

2021 Bowman Chrome Scouts Top 100 Orange Refractors

*ORANGE: 5X TO 12X BASIC
STATED ODDS 1:XX HOBBY
STATED PRINT RUN 25 SER.#'d SETS
BTP53 Jasson Dominguez 50.00 120.00

2021 Bowman Chrome Scouts Top 100 Autographs Refractors

STATED ODDS 1:XX HOBBY
STATED PRINT RUN 50 SER.#'d SETS
EXCHANGE DEADLINE 3/31/23
BTP1 Wander Franco 200.00 500.00
BTP2 Gavin Lux 30.00 80.00
BTP3 Luis Robert
BTP4 Adley Rutschman
BTP5 Mackenzie Gore
BTP6 Jo Adell
BTP7 Spencer Torkelson
BTP8 Casey Mize 30.00 80.00
BTP9 Nate Pearson 15.00 40.00
BTP10 Royce Lewis 25.00 60.00
BTP11 Bobby Witt Jr.
BTP12 Jarred Kelenic 25.00 60.00
BTP13 Jesus Luzardo 15.00 40.00
BTP14 Cristian Pache 40.00 100.00
BTP15 Joey Bart
BTP16 Brendan McKay
BTP17 Andrew Vaughn 40.00 100.00
BTP18 Dylan Carlson
BTP19 Julio Rodriguez 100.00 250.00
BTP20 Austin Martin 150.00 400.00
BTP22 Sixto Sanchez 12.00 30.00
BTP23 Matt Manning 40.00 100.00
BTP24 CJ Abrams
BTP26 Luis Patino
BTP27 JJ Bleday 12.00 30.00
BTP28 Alec Bohm
BTP29 Riley Greene 40.00 100.00
BTP30 Asa Lacy
BTP32 Sean Murphy 8.00 20.00
BTP33 Spencer Howard 12.00 30.00
BTP34 Marco Luciano 40.00 100.00
BTP35 Emerson Hancock 25.00 60.00
BTP36 Grayson Rodriguez
BTP37 Nick Gonzales 50.00 120.00
BTP38 Max Meyer 10.00 25.00
BTP39 Ian Anderson
BTP41 Nick Madrigal 40.00 100.00
BTP42 Ke'Bryan Hayes 100.00 250.00
BTP45 Jeter Downs 40.00 100.00
BTP47 Tarik Skubal 40.00 100.00
BTP48 Nolan Gorman 50.00 120.00
BTP49 Nick Lodolo
BTP50 Alek Thomas 10.00 25.00
BTP51 Luis Campusano
BTP53 Jasson Dominguez
BTP54 Zac Veen 20.00 50.00
BTP56 Evan White 5.00 12.00
BTP62 Heston Kjerstad 40.00 100.00
BTP100 Ryan Mountcastle 60.00 150.00

2021 Bowman Chrome Talent Pipeline Refractors

STATED ODDS 1:12 HOBBY
*ATOMIC/150: 1.5X TO 4X BASIC
*AQUA/125: 1.5X TO 4X BASIC
*GREEN/99: 2X TO 5X BASIC
*GOLD/50: 3X TO 8X BASIC
*ORANGE/25: 5X TO 12X BASIC
TPATL Langeliers/Waters/Shewmake .75 2.00
TPBAL Bannon/Rutschman/Diaz 2.50 6.00
TPBOS Chatham/Duran/Casas 1.25 3.00
TPCHI Rivas/Davis/Abbott .60 1.50
TPCOL Bowden/Rolison/Welker .30 .75
TPDET Short/Greene/Manning 1.25 3.00
TPHOU Ivey/Nova/Whitley .50 1.25
TPLAD Gray/Hoese/Peters 1.00 2.50
TPMIA Cabrera/Bleday/Eveld 1.00 2.50
TPMIL Turang/Ray/Feliciano .50 1.25
TPMIN Gordon/Lewis/Javier .75 2.00
TPNYM Carpio/Mauricio/Gilliam .75 2.00
TPNYY Stephan/Peraza/Alvarez .75 2.00
TPOAK Barrera/Allen/Holmes .30 .75
TPPHI Jones/Maton/Morales .30 .75
TPPIT Cruz/Weiman/Swaggerty .40 1.00
TPSEA Rodriguez/McCaughan/Kelenic 2.00 5.00
TPSFG Corry/Adon/Ramos .50 1.25
TPSTL Gorman/Montero/Capel .60 1.50
TPTBR Franco/Brujan/Honeywell 2.50 6.00

2018 Bowman Chrome Mega Box Prospects Refractors

BCP1 Ronald Acuna 12.00 30.00
BCP2 Bryan Mata .40 1.00
BCP3 Daniel Johnson .30 .75
BCP5 Aaron Knapp .30 .75
BCP6 Austin Beck .40 1.00
BCP7 Carter Kieboom .50 1.25
BCP8 Cole Ragans .30 .75
BCP10 Justin Williams .30 .75
BCP12 Thomas Hatch .40 1.00
BCP13 Sam Hilliard .60 1.50
BCP14 Kyle Wright .75 2.00
BCP16 Michael Mercado .40 1.00
BCP17 Kevin Newman .50 1.25
BCP19 Johan Mieses .50 1.25
BCP21 Luis Robert 30.00 80.00
BCP22 Yadier Alvarez .40 1.00
BCP23 Jeren Kendall .40 1.00
BCP24 Bobby Bradley .40 1.00
BCP25 Drew Ellis .40 1.00
BCP28 Kolby Allard .30 .75
BCP31 DJ Peters .75 2.00
BCP32 Domingo Acevedo .30 .75
BCP36 Dennis Santana .30 .75
BCP37 Jake Burger .30 .75
BCP38 Mitch Keller .40 1.00
BCP39 Colton Welker .30 .75
BCP40 Pedro Avila .30 .75
BCP43 Brendan Rodgers .40 1.00
BCP44 James Kaprielian .30 .75
BCP45 Greg Deichmann .40 1.00
BCP46 Cristian Pache 1.50 4.00
BCP47 Ibandel Isabel .50 1.25
BCP48 Hunter Greene 2.50 6.00
BCP49 Nick Gordon .30 .75
BCP50 Eloy Jimenez 1.25 3.00
BCP52 Juan Soto 10.00 25.00
BCP55 Kyle Tucker .75 2.00
BCP57 Luis Urias .60 1.50
BCP58 Sean Murphy .50 1.25
BCP62 Kyle Cody .30 .75
BCP63 Dylan Cozens .30 .75
BCP65 Scott Kingery .50 1.25
BCP66 Jordan Humphreys .30 .75
BCP67 Michel Baez .30 .75
BCP68 Brendan McKay
BCP69 Justus Sheffield .40 1.00
BCP70 Merandy Gonzalez .30 .75
BCP71 Touki Toussaint .40 1.00
BCP72 Andres Gimenez .75 2.00
BCP77 Jake Kalish .30 .75
BCP78 Shed Long .40 1.00
BCP79 Keibert Ruiz 1.50 4.00
BCP80 Matt Hall .30 .75
BCP83 Ian Anderson 1.00 2.50
BCP85 Dane Dunning 1.00 2.50
BCP86 Michael Kopech 1.25 3.00
BCP87 McKenzie Mills .30 .75
BCP88 Quentin Holmes .30 .75
BCP89 Mike Soroka 1.00 2.50
BCP90 Stephen Gonsalves .30 .75
BCP91 Spencer Howard 3.00 8.00
BCP92 Ryan Vilade .30 .75
BCP93 Royce Lewis 1.25 3.00
BCP94 Adam Haseley .50 1.25
BCP95 Jorge Mateo .30 .75
BCP97 Corey Ray .40 1.00
BCP99 Logan Allen .30 .75
BCP100 Gleyber Torres 3.00 8.00
BCP101 Zack Littell .30 .75
BCP102 Matt Sauer .30 .75
BCP103 Mitchell White .30 .75
BCP104 Nick Solak 1.25 3.00
BCP107 D.L. Hall .30 .75
BCP108 Chris Rodriguez .30 .75
BCP110 Eric Pardinho .40 1.00
BCP111 JoJo Romero .40 1.00
BCP113 Taylor Clarke .30 .75
BCP114 Fernando Tatis Jr. 3.00 8.00
BCP115 Cal Quantrill .30 .75
BCP116 Khalil Lee .30 .75
BCP118 Lazaro Armenteros .60 1.50
BCP120 Nick Senzel 1.00 2.50
BCP121 Jose Adolis Garcia 8.00 20.00
BCP123 Jordan Hicks .60 1.50
BCP125 J.B. Bukauskas .30 .75
BCP126 Jesus Luzardo .50 1.25
BCP131 MacKenzie Gore .60 1.50
BCP132 Corbin Burnes 2.50 6.00
BCP135 Bryse Wilson .50 1.25
BCP136 Jo Adell 1.25 3.00
BCP137 Pete Alonso 3.00 8.00
BCP139 Travis Lakins .30 .75
BCP141 Blayne Enlow .30 .75
BCP142 A.J. Puk .50 1.25
BCP143 Heliot Ramos .50 1.25
BCP144 Jahmai Jones .30 .75
BCP145 Adbert Alzolay .40 1.00
BCP147 Forrest Whitley .50 1.25
BCP148 Trevor Rogers .75 2.00
BCP150 Vladimir Guerrero Jr. 3.00 8.00

2018 Bowman Chrome Mega Box Prospects Gold Refractors

*GOLD REF: 4X TO 10X BASIC
STATED ODDS 1:31 PACKS
STATED PRINT RUN 50 SER.#'d SETS
BCP100 Gleyber Torres 40.00 100.00

2018 Bowman Chrome Mega Box Prospects Green Refractors

*GREEN REF: 2X TO 5X BASIC
STATED ODDS 1:16 PACKS
STATED PRINT RUN 99 SER.#'d SETS
BCP100 Gleyber Torres 20.00 50.00

2018 Bowman Chrome Mega Box Prospects Orange Refractors

*ORANGE REF: 6X TO 15X BASIC
STATED ODDS 1:62 PACKS
STATED PRINT RUN 25 SER.#'d SETS
BCP100 Gleyber Torres 60.00 150.00

2018 Bowman Chrome Mega Box Prospects Purple Refractors

*PURPLE REF: 1X TO 2.5X BASIC
STATED ODDS 1:7 PACKS
STATED PRINT RUN 250 SER.#'d SETS
BCP100 Gleyber Torres 10.00 25.00

2018 Bowman Chrome Mega Box Prospects Image Variaton Refractors

STATED ODDS 1:69 PACKS
BCP1 Ronald Acuna 200.00 500.00
BCP7 Carter Kieboom 20.00 50.00
BCP14 Kyle Wright 12.00 30.00
BCP38 Mitch Keller 10.00 25.00
BCP50 Eloy Jimenez 30.00 80.00
BCP61 Brendan McKay 20.00 50.00
BCP68 Brendan McKay 20.00 50.00
BCP93 Royce Lewis 20.00 50.00
BCP100 Gleyber Torres 50.00 125.00

2018 Bowman Chrome Mega Box Prospects Image Variaton Autograph Refractors

STATED ODDS 1:853 PACKS
STATED PRINT RUN 25 SER.#'d SETS
EXCHANGE DEADLINE 4/30/2020
BCP1 Ronald Acuna 600.00 1200.00
BCP7 Carter Kieboom 100.00 250.00
BCP14 Kyle Wright 60.00 150.00
BCP38 Mitch Keller 30.00 80.00
BCP61 Brendan McKay 75.00 200.00
BCP68 Brendan McKay 75.00 200.00
BCP93 Royce Lewis 100.00 250.00
BCP100 Gleyber Torres 300.00 600.00

2018 Bowman Chrome Mega Box Autograph Refractors

STATED ODDS 1:19 PACKS
EXCHANGE DEADLINE 4/30/2020
*GREEN/99: .75X TO 2X BASIC
BMAAA Adbert Alzolay 8.00 20.00
BMABE Blayne Enlow 4.00 10.00
BMABM Brendan McKay 30.00 80.00
BMAEF Estevan Florial 60.00 150.00
BMAHC Hans Crouse 10.00 25.00
BMAHG Hunter Greene 75.00 200.00
BMAII Ibandel Isabel 12.00 30.00
BMAJH Jordan Hicks 12.00 30.00
BMAJHU Jordan Humphreys 4.00 10.00
BMAJMI Johan Mieses 10.00 25.00
BMAJS Jose Siri 8.00 20.00
BMAKR Keibert Ruiz 40.00 100.00
BMAMB Michel Baez 12.00 30.00
BMAMG Merandy Gonzalez 4.00 10.00
BMAMS Mike Shawaryn 4.00 10.00
BMAQH Quentin Holmes 4.00 10.00
BMARV Ryan Vilade 5.00 12.00
BMASH Spencer Howard 12.00 30.00
BMASL Shed Long 5.00 12.00
BMATH Thomas Hatch 5.00 12.00
BMAWA Willie Abreu 4.00 10.00
BMAZL Zack Littell 4.00 10.00

2018 Bowman Chrome Mega Box Autograph Orange Refractors

*ORANGE REF: 2X TO 5X BASIC
STATED ODDS 1:300 PACKS
STATED PRINT RUN 25 SER.#'d SETS
EXCHANGE DEADLINE 4/30/2020
BMAHG Hunter Greene 300.00 600.00
BMAII Ibandel Isabel 40.00 100.00
BMAJH Jordan Hicks 100.00 250.00

2018 Bowman Chrome Mega Box Hashtag Trending Refractors

STATED ODDS 1:4 PACKS
*PURPLE/250: .6X TO 1.5X BASIC
*GREEN/99: 1X TO 2.5X BASIC
*ORANGE/25: 4X TO 10X BASIC
AP A.J. Puk .50 1.25
BB Bo Bichette 1.25 3.00
CA Chance Adams .50 1.25
CQ Cal Quantrill .30 .75
FP Franklin Perez .40 1.00
FR Fernando Romero .30 .75
FT Fernando Tatis Jr. 3.00 8.00
JS Jesus Sanchez .50 1.25
LT Leody Taveras .50 1.25
LU Luis Urias .60 1.50
MC Michael Chavis .50 1.25
NG Nick Gordon .30 .75
RA Ronald Acuna 10.00 25.00
SG Stephen Gonsalves .30 .75
SK Scott Kingery .50 1.25
SS Sixto Sanchez 1.00 2.50
TM Triston McKenzie 1.00 2.50
TT Taylor Trammell .50 1.25
VG Vladimir Guerrero Jr. 3.00 8.00
YD Yusniel Diaz 1.00 2.50

2018 Bowman Chrome Mega Box Ohtani Bowman Chrome Rookie Autograph Redemption

RANDOM INSERTS IN PACKS
EXCHANGE DEADLINE 4/30/2020
CRASO Shohei Ohtani 1000.00 1500.00

2018 Bowman Chrome Mega Box Rookie of the Year Favorites Refractors

STATED ODDS 1:2 PACKS
ROYFAB Anthony Banda .30 .75
ROYFAH Austin Hays .50 1.25
ROYFAR Amed Rosario .40 1.00
ROYFAV Alex Verdugo .50 1.25
ROYFCF Clint Frazier .60 1.50
ROYFDF Dustin Fowler .30 .75
ROYFDS Dominic Smith .40 1.00
ROYFFM Francisco Mejia .40 1.00
ROYFHB Harrison Bader .50 1.25
ROYFJC J.P. Crawford .30 .75
ROYFJF Jack Flaherty 1.25 3.00
ROYFND Nicky Delmonico .30 .75
ROYFNW Nick Williams .40 1.00
ROYFOA Ozzie Albies 1.00 2.50
ROYFRD Rafael Devers 1.00 2.50
ROYFRH Rhys Hoskins 1.25 3.00
ROYFSO Shohei Ohtani 20.00 50.00
ROYFVR Victor Robles .75 2.00
ROYFWB Walker Buehler 1.50 4.00
ROYFWC Willie Calhoun .50 1.25

2018 Bowman Chrome Mega Box Rookie of the Year Favorites Green Refractors

*GREEN REF: 1X TO 2.5X BASIC
STATED ODDS 1:78 PACKS
STATED PRINT RUN 99 SER.#'d SETS
ROYFOA Ozzie Albies 15.00 40.00
ROYFSO Shohei Ohtani 150.00 400.00

2018 Bowman Chrome Mega Box Rookie of the Year Favorites Orange Refractors

*ORANGE REF: 5X TO 12X BASIC
STATED ODDS 1:307 PACKS
STATED PRINT RUN 25 SER.#'d SETS
ROYFOA Ozzie Albies 30.00 80.00
ROYFSO Shohei Ohtani 300.00 600.00

2018 Bowman Chrome Mega Box Rookie of the Year Favorites Purple Refractors

*PURPLE REF: .6X TO 1.5X BASIC
STATED ODDS 1:31 PACKS
STATED PRINT RUN 250 SER.#'d SETS
ROYFOA Ozzie Albies 10.00 25.00
ROYFSO Shohei Ohtani 75.00 200.00

2018 Bowman Chrome Mega Box Rookie of the Year Favorites Autographs Refractors

STATED ODDS 1:102 PACKS
STATED PRINT RUN 99 SER.#'d SETS
EXCHANGE DEADLINE 4/30/2020
*ORANGE/25: 1.2X TO 3X BASIC
ROYFAAB Anthony Banda 8.00 20.00
ROYFAAR Amed Rosario 10.00 25.00
ROYFAAV Alex Verdugo 12.00 30.00
ROYFACF Clint Frazier 25.00 60.00
ROYFACS Chance Sisco 15.00 40.00
ROYFADS Dominic Smith 10.00 25.00
ROYFAFM Francisco Mejia 20.00 50.00
ROYFAHB Harrison Bader 12.00 30.00
ROYFAJC J.P. Crawford 8.00 20.00
ROYFAJF Jack Flaherty 30.00 80.00
ROYFAMA Miguel Andujar 75.00 200.00
ROYFAOA Ozzie Albies 100.00 250.00
ROYFARD Rafael Devers 25.00 60.00

ROYFATM Tyler Mahle 10.00 25.00
ROYFAVR Victor Robles 25.00 60.00

2019 Bowman Chrome Mega Box Prospects Refractors

BCP1 Vladimir Guerrero Jr. 2.00 5.00
BCP2 Alec Bohm 2.00 5.00
BCP4 Jo Adell 1.25 3.00
BCP5 Victor Victor Mesa .60 1.50
BCP7 Tirso Ornelas .30 .75
BCP10 Adrian Morejon .30 .75
BCP11 Derian Cruz .30 .75
BCP13 Jarred Kelenic 1.50 4.00
BCP14 Seth Beer .75 2.00
BCP17 A.J. Puk .50 1.25
BCP18 Leody Taveras .50 1.25
BCP19 Logan Allen .30 .75
BCP20 Blake Rutherford .30 .75
BCP21 Freudis Nova 1.00 2.50
BCP23 Rylan Bannon .40 1.00
BCP24 Taylor Trammell .50 1.25
BCP25 Fernando Tatis Jr. 5.00 12.00
BCP30 Julio Pablo Martinez .30 .75
BCP32 Cristian Javier .40 1.00
BCP33 Julio Rodriguez 6.00 15.00
BCP35 Miguel Amaya .50 1.25
BCP40 Triston McKenzie 1.00 2.50
BCP41 Ryan Mountcastle 1.50 4.00
BCP43 Nick Senzel 1.00 2.50
BCP44 Luis Robert 15.00 40.00
BCP47 Ian Anderson 1.00 2.50
BCP48 Griffin Canning .50 1.25
BCP49 Casey Mize .75 2.00
BCP50 Joey Bart 4.00 10.00
BCP51 Hunter Greene .50 1.25
BCP52 Forrest Whitley .50 1.25
BCP53 Blaze Alexander .30 .75
BCP54 Keston Hiura 1.00 2.50
BCP55 Chris Paddack .60 1.50
BCP56 Franklin Perez .30 .75
BCP60 Nolan Gorman 1.00 2.50
BCP62 Cristian Pache .75 2.00
BCP63 Nick Madrigal 1.25 3.00
BCP64 Luis Garcia 1.25 3.00
BCP66 Ryan Weathers .30 .75
BCP67 Jon Duplantier .30 .75
BCP68 Reggie Lawson .30 .75
BCP69 Orelvis Martinez 2.50 6.00
BCP70 Sixto Sanchez 1.00 2.50
BCP71 Ke'Bryan Hayes 1.50 4.00
BCP72 Brewer Hicklen .50 1.25
BCP73 MacKenzie Gore .60 1.50
BCP74 Estevan Florial .50 1.25
BCP77 Andres Gimenez .75 2.00
BCP78 Alex Faedo .40 1.00
BCP79 Logan Webb .50 1.25
BCP80 Dustin May 1.00 2.50
BCP81 Ryan McKenna .30 .75
BCP82 Marco Luciano 25.00 60.00
BCP83 Heliot Ramos .50 1.25
BCP85 Matt Manning .50 1.25
BCP87 Chad Spanberger .30 .75
BCP88 Brent Honeywell .40 1.00
BCP89 Esteury Ruiz .40 1.00
BCP90 Keegan Thompson .30 .75
BCP92 Michael Chavis .50 1.25
BCP93 Travis Swaggerty .50 1.25
BCP94 Dane Dunning 1.00 2.50
BCP95 Lyon Richardson .40 1.00
BCP96 Jesus Luzardo .50 1.25
BCP97 Noelvi Marte 3.00 8.00
BCP98 Carter Kieboom .50 1.25
BCP100 Wander Franco 25.00 60.00
BCP101 Ryan Costello .40 1.00
BCP102 Jonathan India 2.50 6.00
BCP103 Royce Lewis .60 1.50
BCP104 Victor Mesa Jr. 2.00 5.00
BCP105 Brendan McKay .50 1.25
BCP107 Ronny Mauricio .75 2.00
BCP109 Yusniel Diaz .50 1.25
BCP110 Brady Singer 1.50 4.00
BCP111 Bo Bichette 1.00 2.50
BCP112 Matthew Liberatore .30 .75
BCP113 Dylan Cease .50 1.25
BCP114 Edward Cabrera .50 1.25
BCP118 Keibert Ruiz 1.50 4.00
BCP119 Jonathan Hernandez .30 .75
BCP120 Matt Mercer .30 .75
BCP123 Yordan Alvarez 5.00 12.00
BCP127 Peter Alonso 4.00 10.00
BCP129 Austin Riley 1.50 4.00
BCP130 Gavin Lux 1.25 3.00
BCP132 Andrew Knizner .50 1.25
BCP133 Mitch Keller .40 1.00
BCP134 Cristian Santana .50 1.25
BCP135 Jesus Sanchez .50 1.25
BCP137 Brock Burke .30 .75
BCP138 Alex Kirilloff .50 1.25
BCP142 Genesis Cabrera .50 1.25
BCP143 Brendan Rodgers .50 1.25
BCP144 Sean Murphy .40 1.00
BCP145 Roberto Ramos .40 1.00
BCP146 Ronaldo Hernandez .30 .75
BCP149 Jose de la Cruz 1.00 2.50
BCP150 Eloy Jimenez 1.25 3.00

2019 Bowman Chrome Mega Box Prospects Gold Refractors

*GOLD REF: 4X TO 10X BASIC
STATED ODDS 1:62 PACKS
STATED PRINT RUN 50 SER.#'d SETS

2019 Bowman Chrome Mega Box Prospects Green Refractors

*GREEN REF: 2X TO 5X BASIC
STATED ODDS 1:32 PACKS
STATED PRINT RUN 99 SER.#'d SETS

2019 Bowman Chrome Mega Box Prospects Orange Refractors

*ORANGE REF: 6X TO 15X BASIC
STATED ODDS 1:126 PACKS
STATED PRINT RUN 25 SER.#'d SETS

2019 Bowman Chrome Mega Box Prospects Purple Refractors

*PURPLE REF: 1X TO 2.5X BASIC
STATED ODDS 1:13 PACKS
STATED PRINT RUN 250 SER.#'d SETS

2019 Bowman Chrome Mega Box Prospects Image Variation Refractors

STATED ODDS 1:140 PACKS
BCP1 Vladimir Guerrero Jr. 50.00 120.00
BCP4 Jo Adell 30.00 80.00
BCP25 Fernando Tatis Jr. 30.00 80.00
BCP43 Nick Senzel 20.00 50.00
BCP49 Casey Mize 40.00 100.00
BCP50 Joey Bart 75.00 200.00
BCP60 Nolan Gorman 30.00 80.00
BCP100 Wander Franco 150.00 400.00
BCP107 Ronny Mauricio 40.00 100.00
BCP150 Eloy Jimenez 20.00 50.00

2019 Bowman Chrome Mega Box Prospects Image Variation Autograph Refractors

STATED ODDS 1:1531 PACKS
STATED PRINT RUN 25 SER.#'d SETS
BCP1 Vladimir Guerrero Jr. 800.00 1200.00
BCP25 Fernando Tatis Jr. 150.00 400.00
BCP49 Casey Mize 200.00 500.00
BCP50 Joey Bart 400.00 800.00
BCP60 Nolan Gorman 200.00 500.00
BCP100 Wander Franco 1500.00 2000.00
BCP107 Ronny Mauricio 200.00 500.00
BCP150 Eloy Jimenez 150.00 400.00

2019 Bowman Chrome Mega Box Autographs Refractors

STATED ODDS 1:16 PACKS
*GREEN REF/99: .75X TO 2X
BMAAB Alec Bohm 15.00 40.00
BMAAK Andrew Knizner 10.00 25.00
BMAAT Alek Thomas 8.00 20.00
BMABA Blaze Alexander 4.00 10.00
BMABB Brock Burke 4.00 10.00
BMABD Bobby Dalbec 8.00 20.00
BMACM Casey Mize 40.00 100.00
BMACS Cristian Santana 6.00 15.00
BMACSP Chad Spanberger 4.00 10.00
BMAEJ Eloy Jimenez 40.00 100.00
BMAFN Freudis Nova 20.00 50.00
BMAGJ Greyson Jenista 5.00 12.00
BMAJA Jordyn Adams 6.00 15.00
BMAJB Joey Bart 60.00 150.00
BMAJG Joe Gray 5.00 12.00
BMAJJ Jeremiah Jackson 6.00 15.00
BMAJPM Julio Pablo Martinez 4.00 10.00
BMAKC Kody Clemens 5.00 12.00
BMAKT Keegan Thompson 4.00 10.00
BMALB Luken Baker 5.00 12.00
BMANH Nico Hoerner 12.00 30.00
BMARB Rylan Bannon 5.00 12.00
BMASB Seth Beer 15.00 40.00
BMAVGJ Vladimir Guerrero Jr. 100.00 250.00
BMAWB Will Banfield 4.00 10.00
BMAWF Wander Franco 250.00 500.00

2019 Bowman Chrome Mega Box Autographs Orange Refractors

*ORANGE REF: 1.5X TO 4X BASIC
STATED ODDS 1:300 PACKS
STATED PRINT RUN 25 SER.#'d SETS
BMAAK Andrew Knizner 75.00 200.00
BMAJA Jordyn Adams 75.00 200.00
BMAJPM Julio Pablo Martinez 15.00 40.00
BMARB Rylan Bannon 60.00 150.00

2019 Bowman Chrome Mega Box Ready for the Show Refractors

STATED ODDS 1:4 PACKS
*PURPLE/250: .6X TO 1.5X BASIC
*GREEN/99: 1X TO 2.5X BASIC
*GOLD/50: 2X TO 5X BASIC
*ORANGE/25: 4X TO 10X BASIC
RFTS1 Vladimir Guerrero Jr. 1.50 4.00
RFTS2 Bo Bichette .75 2.00
RFTS3 Triston McKenzie .75 2.00
RFTS4 Mitch Keller .30 .75
RFTS5 Will Smith .60 1.50
RFTS6 Jon Duplantier .25 .60
RFTS7 Austin Riley 1.25 3.00
RFTS8 Ryan Mountcastle 1.25 3.00
RFTS9 Nick Senzel .75 2.00
RFTS10 Fernando Tatis Jr. 4.00 10.00
RFTS11 Peter Alonso 2.00 5.00
RFTS12 Forrest Whitley .40 1.00
RFTS13 Yusniel Diaz .40 1.00
RFTS14 Brendan McKay .40 1.00
RFTS15 Jesus Luzardo .40 1.00
RFTS16 Brendan Rodgers .40 1.00
RFTS17 Yordan Alvarez 2.00 5.00
RFTS18 Keston Hiura .75 2.00
RFTS19 Brent Honeywell .30 .75
RFTS20 Eloy Jimenez 1.00 2.50

2019 Bowman Chrome Mega Box Rookie of the Year Favorites Autograph Refractors

STATED ODDS 1:207 PACKS
STATED PRINT RUN 99 SER.#'d SETS
*ORANGE/25: .75X TO 2X BASIC
ROYFACA Chance Adams 3.00 8.00
ROYFACB Corbin Burnes 20.00 50.00
ROYFACM Cedric Mullins 10.00 25.00
ROYFACST Chris Shaw 10.00 25.00
ROYFADJ Danny Jansen 8.00 20.00
ROYFADL Dawel Lugo 5.00 12.00
ROYFAJB Jake Bauers 5.00 12.00
ROYFAKA Kolby Allard 5.00 12.00
ROYFAKT Kyle Tucker 12.00 30.00
ROYFAKW Kyle Wright 8.00 20.00
ROYFALU Luis Urias 10.00 25.00
ROYFAMK Michael Kopech 10.00 25.00
ROYFARB Ryan Borucki 3.00 8.00
ROYFAROH Ryan O'Hearn 3.00 8.00
ROYFASD Steven Duggar 15.00 40.00

2019 Bowman Chrome Mega Box Rookie of the Year Favorites Refractors

STATED ODDS 1:2 PACKS
*PURPLE/250: .6X TO 1.5X BASIC
*GREEN/99: 1X TO 2.5X BASIC
*ORANGE/25: 4X TO 10X BASIC
ROYF1 Kyle Tucker .60 1.50
ROYF2 Dakota Hudson .30 .75
ROYF3 Dawel Lugo .40 1.00
ROYF4 Kevin Newman .40 1.00
ROYF5 Chance Adams .25 .60
ROYF6 Danny Jansen .25 .60
ROYF7 Kyle Wright .40 1.00
ROYF8 Chris Shaw .25 .60
ROYF9 Kolby Allard .40 1.00
ROYF10 Christin Stewart .30 .75
ROYF11 Rowdy Tellez .40 1.00
ROYF12 Kohl Stewart .30 .75
ROYF13 Brandon Lowe .40 1.00
ROYF14 Luis Urias .40 1.00
ROYF15 Justus Sheffield .40 1.00
ROYF16 Touki Toussaint .30 .75
ROYF17 Josh James .40 1.00
ROYF18 Jacob Nix .30 .75
ROYF19 Jonathan Loaisiga .30 .75
ROYF20 Willians Astudillo .25 .60

2020 Bowman Chrome Mega Box Prospects Refractors

BCP1 Wander Franco 5.00 12.00
BCP2 Drew Waters .75 2.00
BCP3 Jacob Amaya 1.25 3.00
BCP4 Kody Hoese 1.00 2.50
BCP5 Cristian Pache 2.00 5.00
BCP8 Jasson Dominguez 30.00 80.00
BCP9 Aaron Shortridge .40 1.00
BCP10 Xavier Edwards 1.25 3.00
BCP11 Jesus Sanchez .50 1.25
BCP14 Ulrich Bojarski .50 1.25
BCP15 Jordyn Adams .40 1.00
BCP16 Austin Beck .40 1.00
BCP17 Niko Hulsizer .75 2.00
BCP18 Triston Casas .75 2.00
BCP19 Julio Rodriguez 3.00 8.00
BCP23 Ruben Cardenas .40 1.00
BCP25 Bobby Witt Jr. 12.00 30.00
BCP26 Andrew Vaughn 1.25 3.00
BCP27 Kristian Robinson 1.00 2.50
BCP28 Ronny Mauricio .75 2.00
BCP29 Alec Bohm 2.00 5.00
BCP30 Jhon Diaz 1.00 2.50
BCP31 Estevan Florial .50 1.25
BCP33 Sam Huff .60 1.50
BCP34 Zack Brown .30 .75
BCP35 Brice Turang .30 .75
BCP36 Ryan Mountcastle 1.50 4.00
BCP37 Wilfred Astudillo .40 1.00
BCP38 Gus Varland .40 1.00
BCP39 Nick Lodolo .50 1.25
BCP42 Brady Singer 1.50 4.00
BCP44 Ethan Hankins .40 1.00
BCP46 Sherten Apostel 1.50 4.00
BCP47 Hunter Greene .50 1.25
BCP50 Adley Rutschman 4.00 10.00
BCP51 Everson Pereira .75 2.00
BCP53 Clarke Schmidt .50 1.25
BCP54 Brady McConnell .40 1.00
BCP55 Spencer Howard 1.00 2.50
BCP56 Cristian Javier .40 1.00
BCP57 Aaron Ashby .30 .75
BCP59 Glenallen Hill Jr. .50 1.25
BCP60 Alvaro Seijas .30 .75
BCP61 Jeremy Pena .75 2.00
BCP62 CJ Abrams 1.00 2.50
BCP63 Franklin Perez .30 .75
BCP65 Damon Jones .40 1.00
BCP66 Nolan Gorman .60 1.50
BCP67 Ke'Bryan Hayes 1.50 4.00
BCP70 Forrest Whitley .50 1.25
BCP72 Jazz Chisholm 1.25 3.00
BCP76 Joey Cantillo .30 .75
BCP78 Chris Vallimont .30 .75
BCP80 Alex Kirilloff .60 1.50
BCP82 Freudis Nova .30 .75
BCP83 Tim Cate .30 .75
BCP85 Antonio Cabello 1.00 2.50
BCP87 Colton Welker .30 .75
BCP88 Logan Davidson .40 1.00
BCP89 Matthew Liberatore .40 1.00
BCP91 Jackson Rutledge .50 1.25
BCP92 Dane Dunning 1.00 2.50
BCP93 Royce Lewis .75 2.00
BCP94 Jarred Kelenic 1.50 4.00
BCP95 Nolan Jones .50 1.25
BCP96 Jerar Encarnacion 1.00 2.50
BCP98 Alek Thomas .40 1.00
BCP99 Matt Manning .40 1.00
BCP100 Jo Adell 1.25 3.00
BCP101 Nick Madrigal 1.25 3.00
BCP106 Dylan Carlson 1.25 3.00
BCP108 Tarik Skubal 1.50 4.00
BCP109 Oscar Gonzalez .60 1.50
BCP110 Aramis Ademan .30 .75
BCP111 Oneil Cruz .40 1.00
BCP112 Joey Bart 1.00 2.50
BCP113 Josh Jung .75 2.00
BCP114 Luis Garcia 1.25 3.00
BCP115 Jasseel De La Cruz .50 1.25
BCP116 J.J. Bleday 1.00 2.50
BCP117 Joe Ryan .40 1.00
BCP119 Hans Crouse .30 .75
BCP121 Grant Lavigne .30 .75
BCP122 Riley Greene 1.25 3.00
BCP123 Jordan Balazovic .60 1.50
BCP124 Nate Pearson 1.00 2.50
BCP125 Deivi Garcia 1.50 4.00
BCP128 Bryan Mata .30 .75
BCP130 Taylor Trammell .50 1.25
BCP131 Miguel Vargas .75 2.00
BCP134 Gunnar Henderson .40 1.00
BCP136 Miguel Amaya .30 .75
BCP139 Anthony Volpe 3.00 8.00
BCP140 Nick Bennett .40 1.00
BCP142 Casey Mize 1.00 2.50
BCP143 Keibert Ruiz 1.50 4.00
BCP144 Jarren Duran 3.00 8.00
BCP145 Robert Puason 10.00 25.00
BCP149 Alek Manoah .40 1.00
BCP150 Luis Robert 6.00 15.00
BCP151 Alex Kirilloff .60 1.50
BCP152 Michael Busch .75 2.00
BCP153 Daulton Jefferies .30 .75
BCP154 Mark Vientos .30 .75
BCP155 Diego Cartaya .60 1.50
BCP156 Monte Harrison .50 1.25
BCP157 Nolan Jones .50 1.25
BCP158 Alex Faedo .40 1.00
BCP160 Bobby Witt Jr. 6.00 15.00
BCP161 Noah Song .40 1.00
BCP162 Nolan Gorman .60 1.50
BCP163 Wander Franco 5.00 12.00
BCP164 Tanner Houck .75 2.00
BCP165 Kyle Isbel .30 .75
BCP166 Brandon Marsh .50 1.25
BCP167 Mickey Moniak .75 2.00
BCP168 Brice Turang .30 .75
BCP169 Noelvi Marte 1.25 3.00
BCP170 Yusniel Diaz .50 1.25
BCP171 Elehuris Montero .40 1.00
BCP172 Sixto Sanchez 1.00 2.50
BCP173 Robert Puason 3.00 8.00
BCP174 Jackson Kowar 1.00 2.50
BCP175 Julio Rodriguez 3.00 8.00
BCP176 Steele Walker .50 1.25
BCP177 Tony Santillan .30 .75
BCP178 Mike Siani .30 .75
BCP179 Shane McCarthy .30 .75
BCP180 Keoni Cavaco .30 .75
BCP181 Daulton Varsho .50 1.25
BCP182 Ryan Castellani .30 .75
BCP183 Adonis Medina .50 1.25
BCP184 MacKenzie Gore .60 1.50
BCP185 Jay Groome .30 .75
BCP186 Andres Gimenez .75 2.00
BCP187 Tristen Lutz .40 1.00
BCP188 Leody Taveras .50 1.25
BCP189 Triston McKenzie 1.00 2.50
BCP190 Simeon Woods Richardson .50 1.25
BCP191 Kyle Muller .30 .75
BCP192 Forrest Whitley .50 1.25
BCP193 Korey Lee .40 1.00
BCP194 Freudis Nova .30 .75
BCP195 Royce Lewis .75 2.00
BCP196 Keegan Akin .30 .75
BCP197 Quinn Priester .40 1.00
BCP198 Francisco Alvarez 3.00 8.00
BCP199 Luis Garcia 1.25 3.00
BCP200 Brennan Malone .30 .75
BCP201 Cristian Pache 2.00 5.00
BCP202 Geraldo Perdomo .30 .75
BCP203 Ethan Hearn .50 1.25
BCP204 Jesus Sanchez .50 1.25
BCP205 Tim Cate .30 .75
BCP206 Cole Roederer .60 1.50
BCP207 Jorge Mateo .40 1.00
BCP208 Triston Casas .75 2.00
BCP209 Matthew Liberatore .40 1.00
BCP210 Keibert Ruiz 1.50 4.00
BCP211 Blake Rutherford .30 .75
BCP212 Jarred Kelenic 1.50 4.00
BCP213 Marco Luciano 1.25 3.00
BCP214 Deivi Garcia 1.50 4.00
BCP215 Sean Hjelle .50 1.25
BCP216 Clarke Schmidt .50 1.25
BCP217 Mason Denaburg .30 .75
BCP218 Luis Campusano .50 1.25
BCP219 Braden Shewmake .50 1.25
BCP220 Ke'Bryan Hayes 1.50 4.00
BCP221 Shane Baz .30 .75
BCP222 Corbin Carroll .50 1.25
BCP223 Estevan Florial .50 1.25
BCP224 Isaac Paredes 1.00 2.50
BCP225 Michael Toglia .30 .75
BCP226 Alejandro Kirk .75 2.00
BCP227 Jeter Downs .50 1.25
BCP228 Tyler Stephenson .75 2.00
BCP229 Matt Manning .40 1.00
BCP230 Luis Garcia 1.25 3.00
BCP231 Ryan Jensen .40 1.00
BCP232 Dane Dunning 1.00 2.50
BCP233 William Contreras .40 1.00
BCP234 Bo Naylor .40 1.00
BCP235 Luis Patino .50 1.25
BCP236 Dylan Carlson 1.25 3.00
BCP237 Sam Huff .60 1.50
BCP238 D.L. Hall .30 .75
BCP239 Jackson Rutledge .50 1.25
BCP240 Ryan Vilade .30 .75
BCP241 Vidal Brujan 2.50 6.00
BCP242 Seth Corry .30 .75
BCP243 Jasson Dominguez 15.00 40.00
BCP244 Jeremiah Jackson .30 .75
BCP245 Orelvis Martinez .75 2.00
BCP246 Kyren Paris .30 .75
BCP247 Brett Baty 1.00 2.50
BCP248 Corey Ray .30 .75
BCP249 Trevor Larnach .60 1.50
BCP250 Casey Mize 1.00 2.50

2020 Bowman Chrome Mega Box Prospects Blue Refractors

*BLUE REF: 1.2X TO 3X BASIC
BOW.MEGA ODDS 1:32 HOBBY
BOW.CHR.MEGA ODDS 1:19 HOBBY
STATED PRINT RUN 150 SER.#'d SETS
BCP5 Cristian Pache 8.00 20.00
BCP8 Jasson Dominguez 150.00 400.00
BCP145 Robert Puason 50.00 120.00
BCP173 Robert Puason 12.00 30.00
BCP201 Cristian Pache 8.00 20.00
BCP243 Jasson Dominguez 60.00 150.00

2020 Bowman Chrome Mega Box Prospects Gold Refractors

*GOLD REF: 4X TO 10X BASIC
BOW.MEGA ODDS 1:95 HOBBY
BOW.CHR.MEGA ODDS 1:56 HOBBY
STATED PRINT RUN 50 SER.#'d SETS
BCP5 Cristian Pache 20.00 50.00
BCP8 Jasson Dominguez 500.00 1000.00
BCP29 Alec Bohm 30.00 80.00
BCP46 Sherten Apostel 30.00 80.00
BCP94 Jarred Kelenic 25.00 60.00
BCP112 Joey Bart 40.00 100.00
BCP145 Robert Puason 150.00 400.00
BCP173 Robert Puason 40.00 100.00
BCP198 Francisco Alvarez 25.00 60.00
BCP201 Cristian Pache 20.00 50.00
BCP212 Jarred Kelenic 25.00 60.00
BCP243 Jasson Dominguez 200.00 500.00

2020 Bowman Chrome Mega Box Prospects Green Refractors

*GREEN REF: 1.5X TO 4X BASIC
BOW.MEGA ODDS 1:48 HOBBY
BOW.CHR.MEGA ODDS 1:29 HOBBY
STATED PRINT RUN 99 SER.#'d SETS
BCP5 Cristian Pache 10.00 25.00
BCP8 Jasson Dominguez 200.00 500.00
BCP29 Alec Bohm 12.00 30.00
BCP94 Jarred Kelenic 10.00 25.00
BCP112 Joey Bart 15.00 40.00
BCP145 Robert Puason 60.00 150.00
BCP173 Robert Puason 15.00 40.00
BCP201 Cristian Pache 10.00 25.00
BCP212 Jarred Kelenic 10.00 25.00
BCP243 Jasson Dominguez 75.00 200.00

2020 Bowman Chrome Mega Box Prospects Orange Refractors

*ORANGE REF: 6X TO 15X BASIC
BOW.MEGA ODDS 1:189 HOBBY
BOW.CHR.MEGA ODDS 1:112 HOBBY
STATED PRINT RUN 25 SER.#'d SETS
BCP5 Cristian Pache 30.00 80.00
BCP8 Jasson Dominguez 600.00 1500.00
BCP29 Alec Bohm 50.00 120.00
BCP46 Sherten Apostel 50.00 120.00
BCP94 Jarred Kelenic 40.00 100.00
BCP112 Joey Bart 60.00 150.00
BCP145 Robert Puason 250.00 600.00
BCP173 Robert Puason 60.00 150.00
BCP198 Francisco Alvarez 40.00 100.00
BCP201 Cristian Pache 30.00 80.00
BCP212 Jarred Kelenic 40.00 100.00
BCP243 Jasson Dominguez 300.00 800.00

2020 Bowman Chrome Mega Box Prospects Pink Refractors

*PINK REF: 1.2X TO 3X BASIC
BOW.MEGA ODDS 1:24 HOBBY
BOW.CHR.MEGA ODDS 1:15 HOBBY
STATED PRINT RUN 199 SER.#'d SETS
BCP5 Cristian Pache 8.00 20.00
BCP145 Robert Puason 50.00 120.00
BCP201 Cristian Pache 8.00 20.00
BCP243 Jasson Dominguez 60.00 150.00

2020 Bowman Chrome Mega Box Prospects Purple Refractors

*PURPLE REF: 1X TO 2.5X BASIC
BOW.MEGA ODDS 1:19 HOBBY
BOW.CHR.MEGA ODDS 1:12 HOBBY
STATED PRINT RUN 250 SER.#'d SETS
BCP145 Robert Puason 40.00 100.00

2020 Bowman Chrome Mega Box Prospects Image Variation Refractors

BOW.MEGA ODDS 1:210 HOBBY
BOW.CHR.MEGA ODDS 1:125 HOBBY
BCP25 Bobby Witt Jr. 40.00 100.00
BCP26 Andrew Vaughn 15.00 40.00
BCP50 Adley Rutschman 25.00 60.00
BCP91 Jackson Rutledge 10.00 25.00
BCP94 Jarred Kelenic 20.00 50.00
BCP139 Anthony Volpe 25.00 60.00
BCP142 Casey Mize 12.00 30.00
BCP144 Jarren Duran 15.00 40.00
BCP145 Robert Puason 40.00 100.00
BCP150 Luis Robert 60.00 150.00
BCP151 Alex Kirilloff 8.00 20.00
BCP159 Bayron Lora 40.00 100.00
BCP162 Nolan Gorman 8.00 20.00
BCP192 Forrest Whitley 6.00 15.00
BCP195 Royce Lewis 10.00 25.00
BCP218 Luis Campusano 10.00 25.00
BCP220 Ke'Bryan Hayes 20.00 50.00
BCP241 Vidal Brujan 30.00 80.00
BCP243 Jasson Dominguez 60.00 150.00

2020 Bowman Chrome Mega Box Prospects Image Variation Autograph Refractors

BOW.MEGA ODDS 1:2037 HOBBY
BOW.CHR.MEGA ODDS 1:1570 HOBBY
STATED PRINT RUN 25 SER.#'d SETS
BCP25 Bobby Witt Jr. 500.00 1200.00
BCP26 Andrew Vaughn
BCP50 Adley Rutschman
BCP91 Jackson Rutledge 40.00 100.00
BCP94 Jarred Kelenic
BCP139 Anthony Volpe 125.00 300.00
BCP142 Casey Mize
BCP144 Jarren Duran 100.00 250.00
BCP145 Robert Puason 300.00 800.00
BCP150 Luis Robert 1000.00 2000.00
BCP151 Alex Kirilloff
BCP159 Bayron Lora
BCP162 Nolan Gorman 60.00 150.00
BCP192 Forrest Whitley
BCP195 Royce Lewis 30.00 80.00
BCP218 Luis Campusano
BCP220 Ke'Bryan Hayes 75.00 200.00
BCP241 Vidal Brujan
BCP243 Jasson Dominguez 800.00 1500.00

2020 Bowman Chrome Mega Box Dawn of Glory Autograph Refractors

STATED ODDS 1:186 HOBBY
STATED PRINT RUN 99 SER.#'d SETS
DGAAR Adley Rutschman 30.00 80.00
DGAAV Andrew Vaughn 15.00 40.00
DGAGV Gus Varland 5.00 12.00
DGAJD Jarren Duran 15.00 40.00
DGAJR Joe Ryan 5.00 12.00
DGAKS Kevin Smith 4.00 10.00
DGALD Lewin Diaz 4.00 10.00
DGANL Nick Lodolo 6.00 15.00
DGASA Sherten Apostel 12.00 30.00
DGASH Sam Huff 12.00 30.00
DGAJDL Jasseel De La Cruz 6.00 15.00

2020 Bowman Chrome Mega Box Dawn of Glory Autograph Orange Refractors

*ORANGE/25: .6X TO 1.5X
STATED ODDS 1:733 HOBBY
STATED PRINT RUN 25 SER.#'d SETS
DGAAV Andrew Vaughn 30.00 80.00

2020 Bowman Chrome Mega Box Dawn of Glory Refractors

STATED ODDS 1:2 HOBBY
*BLUE/150: .6X TO 1.5X
*GREEN/99: 1X TO 2.5X
DG1 Sherten Apostel 2.00 5.00
DG2 Gus Varland .50 1.25
DG3 Jasseel De La Cruz .60 1.50
DG4 Nick Lodolo .60 1.50
DG5 Jarren Duran 1.50 4.00
DG6 Isaac Paredes 1.25 3.00
DG7 Dylan File .50 1.25
DG8 Joe Ryan .50 1.25
DG9 Ruben Cardenas .50 1.25
DG10 Sam Huff .75 2.00
DG11 Lewin Diaz .40 1.00
DG12 Andrew Vaughn 1.50 4.00
DG13 Adley Rutschman 2.50 6.00
DG14 Jordan Balazovic .75 2.00
DG15 Kevin Smith .40 1.00
DG16 Jo Adell 1.50 4.00
DG17 Casey Mize 1.25 3.00
DG18 Joey Bart 1.25 3.00
DG19 MacKenzie Gore .75 2.00
DG20 Wander Franco 4.00 10.00

2020 Bowman Chrome Mega Box Dawn of Glory Gold Refractors

*GOLD/50: 1.2X TO 3X
STATED ODDS 1:280 HOBBY
STATED PRINT RUN 50 SER.#'d SETS
DG20 Wander Franco 40.00 100.00

2020 Bowman Chrome Mega Box Dawn of Glory Orange Refractors

*ORANGE/25: 2.5X TO 6X
STATED ODDS 1:560 HOBBY
STATED PRINT RUN 25 SER.#'d SETS
DG20 Wander Franco 75.00 200.00

2020 Bowman Chrome Mega Box Farm to Fame Refractors

STATED ODDS 1:80 HOBBY
FTFBL Barry Larkin 2.00 5.00
FTFCF Carlton Fisk 8.00 20.00
FTFCJ Chipper Jones 10.00 25.00
FTFCY Carl Yastrzemski 8.00 20.00
FTFEM Edgar Martinez 8.00 20.00
FTFFT Frank Thomas 15.00 40.00
FTFGB George Brett 5.00 12.00
FTFHA Hank Aaron 10.00 25.00
FTFIR Ivan Rodriguez 2.00 5.00
FTFJB Johnny Bench 10.00 25.00
FTFMR Mariano Rivera 8.00 20.00
FTFNR Nolan Ryan 15.00 40.00
FTFOS Ozzie Smith 10.00 25.00
FTFPM Pedro Martinez 3.00 8.00
FTFRC Rod Carew 5.00 12.00
FTFRF Rollie Fingers 6.00 15.00
FTFRH Rickey Henderson 20.00 50.00
FTFRJ Reggie Jackson 6.00 15.00
FTFRY Robin Yount 5.00 12.00
FTFSC Steve Carlton 2.00 5.00
FTFTP Tony Perez 2.00 5.00
FTFWB Wade Boggs 6.00 15.00
FTFWM Willie Mays 8.00 20.00
FTFCRJ Cal Ripken Jr. 12.00 30.00

2020 Bowman Chrome Mega Box Farm to Fame Orange Refractors

*ORANGE/25: .6X TO 1.5X
STATED ODDS 1:560 HOBBY
STATED PRINT RUN 25 SER.#'d SETS
FTFEM Edgar Martinez 15.00 40.00
FTFNR Nolan Ryan 40.00 100.00
FTFPM Pedro Martinez 20.00 50.00
FTFCRJ Cal Ripken Jr. 40.00 100.00

2020 Bowman Chrome Mega Box Prospect Autograph Refractors

BOW.MEGA ODDS 1:16 HOBBY
BOW.CHR.MEGA ODDS 1:9 HOBBY
*BLUE REF/150: .6X TO 1.5X
BMAAA Aaron Ashby 8.00 20.00
BMAAR Adley Rutschman 40.00 100.00
BMAAS Aaron Shortridge 5.00 12.00
BMAAV Andrew Vaughn 15.00 40.00
BMAAVO Anthony Volpe 40.00 100.00
BMABM Brady McConnell 5.00 12.00
BMABS Braden Shewmake 6.00 15.00
BMABWJ Bobby Witt Jr. 100.00 250.00
BMACJA CJ Abrams 25.00 60.00
BMAGH Gunnar Henderson 20.00 50.00
BMAGHJ Glenallen Hill Jr. 6.00 15.00
BMAJA Jacob Amaya 8.00 20.00
BMAJC Joey Cantillo 4.00 10.00
BMAJD Jasson Dominguez 300.00 800.00
BMAJDU Jarren Duran 15.00 40.00
BMAJE Jerar Encarnacion 8.00 20.00
BMAJJG JJ Goss 4.00 10.00
BMAJR Joe Ryan 5.00 12.00
BMAJS Jake Sanford 6.00 15.00
BMAKS Kyle Stowers 4.00 10.00
BMANH Niko Hulsizer 10.00 25.00
BMARG Riley Greene 20.00 50.00
BMARH Rece Hinds 5.00 12.00
BMASL Shea Langeliers 8.00 20.00
BMASS Sammy Siani 4.00 10.00
BMATS Tarik Skubal 8.00 20.00
BMATSI T.J. Sikkema 4.00 10.00
BMAUB Ulrich Bojarski 8.00 20.00
BCMAAH Austin Hansen 5.00 12.00
BCMAAP Andy Pages 10.00 25.00
BCMAAR Adley Rutschman 40.00 100.00
BCMAAS Alex Speas 4.00 10.00
BCMAAV Andrew Vaughn 25.00 60.00
BCMACS Canaan Smith 10.00 25.00
BCMADE Daniel Espino 5.00 12.00
BCMAEL Ethan Lindow 5.00 12.00
BCMAGM Gabriel Moreno 15.00 40.00
BCMAHB Hunter Bishop 10.00 25.00
BCMAJD Jasson Dominguez 300.00 600.00
BCMAJE Jerar Encarnacion 8.00 20.00
BCMAKS Kevin Smith 4.00 10.00
BCMALD Lewin Diaz 6.00 15.00
BCMALM Luis Matos 20.00 50.00
BCMAML Max Lazar 5.00 12.00
BCMANL Nick Lodolo 6.00 15.00
BCMARG Riley Greene 20.00 50.00
BCMARP Robert Puason 30.00 80.00
BCMATS Tarik Skubal 8.00 20.00
BCMAJDU Jarren Duran 15.00 40.00
BCMAMLU Matthew Lugo 6.00 15.00

2020 Bowman Chrome Mega Box Prospect Autograph Green Refractors

*GREEN REF: .75X TO 2X BASIC
BOW.MEGA ODDS 1:195 HOBBY
BOW.CHR.MEGA ODDS 1:121 HOBBY
STATED PRINT RUN 99 SER.#'d SETS
BMAJE Jerar Encarnacion 25.00 60.00
BCMAJE Jerar Encarnacion 25.00 60.00
BCMARP Robert Puason 75.00 200.00

2020 Bowman Chrome Mega Box Prospect Autograph Orange Refractors

*ORANGE REF: 1.5X TO 4X BASIC
BOW.MEGA ODDS 1:767 HOBBY
BOW.CHR.MEGA ODDS 1:478 HOBBY
STATED PRINT RUN 25 SER.#'d SETS
BMAJA Jacob Amaya 60.00 150.00
BMAJD Jasson Dominguez 2000.00 4000.00
BMAJE Jerar Encarnacion 50.00 120.00
BMARG Riley Greene 100.00 250.00
BMATS Tarik Skubal 40.00 100.00
BCMAAP Andy Pages 100.00 250.00
BCMAJD Jasson Dominguez 2000.00 4000.00
BCMAJE Jerar Encarnacion 50.00 120.00
BCMARG Riley Greene 100.00 250.00
BCMARP Robert Puason 150.00 400.00
BCMATS Tarik Skubal 40.00 100.00

2020 Bowman Chrome Mega Box Rookie of the Year Favorites Autograph Refractors

STATED ODDS 1:311 HOBBY
STATED PRINT RUN 99 SER.#'d SETS
*ORANGE/25: .6X TO 1.5X BASIC
ROYFAAJP A.J. Puk 12.00 30.00
ROYFABB Bobby Bradley 3.00 8.00
ROYFABM Brendan McKay 12.00 30.00
ROYFADC Dylan Cease 6.00 15.00
ROYFAGL Gavin Lux 60.00 150.00
ROYFAJY Jordan Yamamoto 6.00 15.00
ROYFASB Seth Brown 10.00 25.00
ROYFAYA Yordan Alvarez 60.00 150.00

2020 Bowman Chrome Mega Box Rookie of the Year Favorites Refractors

STATED ODDS 1:2 HOBBY
*PURPLE/250: .6X TO 1.5X BASIC
*PINK/199: .6X TO 1.5X BASIC
*BLUE/150: .75X TO 2X BASIC
*GREEN/99: 1X TO 2.5X BASIC
*ORANGE/25: 2.5X TO 6X BASIC
ROYFAA Adbert Alzolay .50 1.25
ROYFAAQ Aristides Aquino 1.00 2.50
ROYFAC Aaron Civale .75 2.00
ROYFAP A.J. Puk .60 1.50
ROYFAT Abraham Toro .50 1.25
ROYFBB Bo Bichette 3.00 8.00
ROYFBM Brendan McKay .60 1.50
ROYFBR Brusdar Graterol .60 1.50
ROYFDC Dylan Cease .60 1.50
ROYFDM Dustin May 1.25 3.00
ROYFGL Gavin Lux 2.00 5.00
ROYFJD Justin Dunn .50 1.25
ROYFJL Jesus Luzardo .75 2.00
ROYFJY Jordan Yamamoto .40 1.00
ROYFKL Kyle Lewis 3.00 8.00
ROYFNH Nico Hoerner 1.50 4.00
ROYFSB Seth Brown .40 1.00
ROYFSH Sam Hilliard .60 1.50
ROYFSM Sean Murphy .60 1.50
ROYFYA Yordan Alvarez 4.00 10.00

2020 Bowman Chrome Mega Box Spanning the Globe Refractors

STATED ODDS 1:4 HOBBY
STGAA Adbert Alzolay .50 1.25
STGAM Andres Munoz .60 1.50
STGCM Casey Mize 1.25 3.00
STGDB Dasan Brown 1.00 2.50
STGEP Eric Pardinho .50 1.25
STGHR Heliot Ramos .60 1.50
STGIP Isaac Paredes 1.25 3.00
STGJA Jo Adell 1.50 4.00
STGJB Jordan Balazovic .75 2.00
STGJD Jasson Dominguez 10.00 25.00
STGJL Jesus Luzardo .75 2.00
STGLP Luis Patino .60 1.50
STGLR Luis Robert 6.00 15.00
STGMA Miguel Amaya .40 1.00
STGML Matthew Lugo .60 1.50
STGRH Ronaldo Hernandez .40 1.00
STGUB Ulrich Bojarski .60 1.50
STGVVM Victor Victor Mesa .60 1.50
STGWF Wander Franco 4.00 10.00
STGYC Yu Chang .60 1.50

2020 Bowman Chrome Mega Box Spanning the Globe Blue Refractors

*BLUE: .75X TO 2X BASIC
STATED ODDS 1:157 HOBBY
STATED PRINT RUN 150 SER.#'d SETS
STGJD Jasson Dominguez 50.00 120.00

2020 Bowman Chrome Mega Box Spanning the Globe Green Refractors

*GREEN: 1X TO 2.5X BASIC

STATED ODDS 1:238 HOBBY
STATED PRINT RUN 99 SER.#'d SETS
STGJD Jasson Dominguez 60.00 150.00

2020 Bowman Chrome Mega Box Spanning the Globe Orange Refractors

*ORANGE: 2.5X TO 6X BASIC
STATED ODDS 1:940 HOBBY
STATED PRINT RUN 25 SER.#'d SETS
STGJD Jasson Dominguez 150.00 400.00

2020 Bowman Chrome Mega Box Spanning the Globe Pink Refractors

*PINK: .6X TO 1.5X BASIC
STATED ODDS 1:119 HOBBY
STATED PRINT RUN 199 SER.#'d SETS
STGJD Jasson Dominguez 40.00 100.00

2020 Bowman Chrome Mega Box Spanning the Globe Purple Refractors

*PURPLE: .6X TO 1.5X BASIC
STATED ODDS 1:95 HOBBY
STATED PRINT RUN 250 SER.#'d SETS
STGJD Jasson Dominguez 40.00 100.00

2021 Bowman Chrome Mega Box Prospects Refractors

BCP1 Bobby Witt Jr. 4.00 10.00
BCP3 Zac Veen 4.00 10.00
BCP4 Riley Greene 4.00 10.00
BCP5 Nick Maton 8.00 20.00
BCP7 Maximo Acosta 15.00 40.00
BCP8 Marco Luciano 4.00 10.00
BCP9 Forrest Whitley .50 1.25
BCP12 Ed Howard 1.50 4.00
BCP13 Jasson Dominguez 10.00 25.00
BCP14 CJ Abrams 1.00 2.50
BCP17 Bryson Stott 1.00 2.50
BCP18 Hunter Bishop .60 1.50
BCP19 Vidal Brujan 4.00 10.00
BCP20 Nick Lodolo .50 1.25
BCP21 Adinso Reyes 1.25 3.00
BCP23 Ronny Mauricio .75 2.00
BCP25 Jeremy De La Rosa 10.00 25.00
BCP26 Reid Detmers .75 2.00
BCP28 Shea Langeliers .60 1.50
BCP29 Matthew Liberatore .40 1.00
BCP30 Jordyn Adams .40 1.00
BCP31 Alek Thomas .40 1.00
BCP33 Eddy Diaz .30 .75
BCP34 Nick Gonzales 1.00 2.50
BCP35 Nolan Jones .50 1.25
BCP36 Ismael Mena 5.00 12.00
BCP37 Jeisson Rosario .50 1.25
BCP38 Josh Jung .75 2.00
BCP40 Yolbert Sanchez 4.00 10.00
BCP42 Mick Abel 4.00 10.00
BCP45 Robert Puason .75 2.00
BCP46 Jonathan India 2.00 5.00
BCP48 Braden Shewmake .50 1.25
BCP51 Tyler Soderstrom .75 2.00
BCP53 Francisco Alvarez .75 2.00
BCP54 Daniel Lynch .30 .75
BCP55 Austin Hendrick 2.50 6.00
BCP57 Wander Franco 6.00 15.00
BCP58 Logan Gilbert .40 1.00
BCP59 Jake Vogel 5.00 12.00
BCP61 Jordan Balazovic .30 .75
BCP63 Royce Lewis .75 2.00
BCP65 Brennen Davis .60 1.50
BCP66 Max Meyer .75 2.00
BCP67 Brett Baty 1.00 2.50
BCP69 Heliot Ramos .50 1.25
BCP71 Blaze Jordan 15.00 40.00
BCP73 Keoni Cavaco .30 .75
BCP74 Matthew Thompson .40 1.00
BCP78 Emerson Hancock .75 2.00
BCP81 Drew Waters .75 2.00
BCP82 Antonio Gomez .50 1.25
BCP83 Asa Lacy 1.50 4.00
BCP84 Triston Casas .75 2.00
BCP85 Anthony Volpe 1.25 3.00
BCP86 Julio Rodriguez 4.00 10.00
BCP87 Austin Martin 15.00 40.00
BCP88 Andrew Vaughn 6.00 15.00
BCP89 Gabriel Arias 8.00 20.00
BCP90 Nolan Gorman .60 1.50
BCP93 JJ Bleday 1.00 2.50
BCP94 Trent Deveaux .40 1.00
BCP95 Simeon Woods Richardson .50 1.25
BCP96 Spencer Torkelson 8.00 20.00
BCP97 Kevin Alcantara 12.00 30.00
BCP98 Jordan Westburg .75 2.00
BCP99 Cade Cavalli .60 1.50
BCP101 Xavier Edwards 1.00 2.50
BCP102 Jarred Kelenic 5.00 12.00
BCP103 Jackson Rutledge .50 1.25
BCP105 MacKenzie Gore .60 1.50
BCP106 Jared Kelley 4.00 10.00
BCP107 Jeter Downs .50 1.25
BCP108 Patrick Bailey .60 1.50
BCP109 Geraldo Perdomo .30 .75
BCP110 Jose Salas 4.00 10.00
BCP111 Matt Manning .40 1.00
BCP114 Nick Yorke 1.25 3.00
BCP116 Elehuris Montero .40 1.00
BCP117 George Kirby 6.00 15.00
BCP118 Grayson Rodriguez .50 1.25
BCP120 Robert Hassell 2.00 5.00
BCP121 Adley Rutschman 3.00 8.00
BCP125 Aaron Sabato 12.00 30.00
BCP127 Hunter Greene .50 1.25
BCP128 Jose Tena 5.00 12.00
BCP129 Garrett Mitchell 2.00 5.00
BCP130 Hyun-il Choi .50 1.25
BCP131 Christopher Morel 4.00 10.00
BCP132 Taylor Trammell .50 1.25
BCP135 Jarren Duran 4.00 10.00
BCP136 Kristian Robinson 1.00 2.50
BCP138 Heston Kjerstad 1.50 4.00
BCP139 Bayron Lora 1.50 4.00
BCP140 Yunior Severino .40 1.00
BCP142 Corbin Carroll .50 1.25
BCP145 Alexander Ramirez 6.00 15.00
BCP148 Miguel Amaya .30 .75
BCP149 Ivan Johnson 4.00 10.00
BCP150 Josiah Gray .50 1.25

2021 Bowman Chrome Mega Box Prospects Gold Refractors

*GOLD/50: 4X TO 10X BASIC
STATED ODDS 1:140 HOBBY
STATED PRINT RUN 50 SER.#'d SETS
BCP1 Bobby Witt Jr. 50.00 120.00

2021 Bowman Chrome Mega Box Prospects Orange Refractors

*ORANGE/25: 4X TO 10X BASIC
STATED ODDS 1:279 HOBBY
STATED PRINT RUN 25 SER.#'d SETS
BCP1 Bobby Witt Jr. 75.00 200.00

2021 Bowman Chrome Mega Box Prospects Image Variation Refractors

STATED ODDS 1:310 HOBBY
BCP3 Zac Veen
looking left
BCP34 Nick Gonzales
helmet on
BCP55 Austin Hendrick
no helmet
BCP57 Wander Franco
blue jsy
BCP71 Blaze Jordan 60.00 150.00
running
BCP87 Austin Martin 100.00 250.00
white jsy
BCP96 Spencer Torkelson 30.00 80.00
no sunglasses
BCP125 Aaron Sabato
front of jsy visible
BCP129 Garrett Mitchell
holding helmet
BCP138 Heston Kjerstad 20.00 50.00
gray jsy

2021 Bowman Chrome Mega Box Futurist Refractors

STATED ODDS 1:4 HOBBY
*PURPLE/250: .6X TO 1.5X BASIC
*PINK/199: .6X TO 1.5X BASIC
*BLUE/150: .8X TO 2X BASIC
*GREEN/99: 1X TO 2.5X BASIC
*ORANGE/25: 4X TO 10X BASIC
FUTAH Austin Hendrick 3.00 8.00
FUTAL Asa Lacy 2.00 5.00
FUTBJ Blaze Jordan 4.00 10.00
FUTBW Bobby Witt Jr. 2.50 6.00
FUTCA CJ Abrams 1.25 3.00
FUTCC Corbin Carroll .60 1.50
FUTEH Emerson Hancock 1.00 2.50
FUTFA Francisco Alvarez 1.00 2.50
FUTGM Garrett Mitchell 2.50 6.00
FUTHK Heston Kjerstad 2.00 5.00
FUTJD Jasson Dominguez 4.00 10.00
FUTMA Mick Abel .60 1.50
FUTML Marco Luciano 1.50 4.00
FUTMM Max Meyer 1.00 2.50
FUTNG Nick Gonzales 1.25 3.00
FUTRD Reid Detmers 1.00 2.50
FUTRG Riley Greene 1.50 4.00
FUTRH Robert Hassell 2.50 6.00
FUTST Spencer Torkelson 2.50 6.00
FUTZV Zac Veen 1.25 3.00

2021 Bowman Chrome Mega Box Futurist Autograph Refractors

STATED ODDS 1:1380 HOBBY
EXCHANGE DEADLINE 4/30/23
*ORANGE/25: .6X TO 1.5X BASIC
FAHK Heston Kjerstad
FAMM Max Meyer
FANG Nick Gonzales
FARG Riley Greene
FARH Robert Hassell 20.00 50.00

2021 Bowman Chrome Mega Box Prospect Autograph Refractors

STATED ODDS 1:15 HOBBY
EXCHANGE DEADLINE 4/30/23
BMAAH Austin Hendrick 20.00 50.00
BMAAM Austin Martin 200.00 500.00
BMAAW Austin Wells 15.00 40.00
BMABJ Blaze Jordan 125.00 300.00
BMACC Cade Cavalli 20.00 50.00
BMACM Coby Mayo 20.00 50.00
BMACT Carson Tucker 12.00 30.00
BMADD Dillon Dingler 20.00 50.00
BMADR Drew Romo 15.00 40.00
BMAEH Emerson Hancock 15.00 40.00
BMAFV Freddy Valdez 12.00 30.00
BMAGM Garrett Mitchell EXCH
BMAHH Heriberto Hernandez 20.00 50.00
BMAHK Heston Kjerstad 30.00 80.00
BMAIJ Ivan Johnson 10.00 25.00
BMAIM Ismael Mena 20.00 50.00
BMAJD Jeremy De La Rosa 25.00 60.00
BMAJK Jared Kelley 20.00 50.00
BMAJS Jose Salas 20.00 50.00
BMAMM Max Meyer 15.00 40.00
BMANG Nick Gonzales 30.00 80.00
BMANY Nick Yorke 20.00 50.00
BMAPB Patrick Bailey 12.00 30.00
BMAPC Pete Crow-Armstrong 25.00 60.00
BMARD Reid Detmers 15.00 40.00
BMARH Robert Hassell 25.00 60.00
BMAST Spencer Torkelson EXCH 75.00 200.00
BMATS Tyler Soderstrom 20.00 50.00
BMAYS Yolbert Sanchez 12.00 30.00
BMAZV Zac Veen 25.00 60.00
BMAAMA Angel Martinez 20.00 50.00
BMAAVA Alexander Vargas 20.00 50.00
BMAEHO Ed Howard 30.00 80.00

2021 Bowman Chrome Mega Box Prospect Autograph Blue Refractors

*BLUE/150: .6X TO 1.5X BASIC
STATED ODDS 1:139 HOBBY
STATED PRINT RUN 150 SER.#'d SETS
EXCHANGE DEADLINE 4/30/23
BMAAH Austin Hendrick 40.00 100.00
BMAJD Jeremy De La Rosa 60.00 150.00

2021 Bowman Chrome Mega Box Prospect Autograph Green Refractors

*GREEN/99: .8X TO 2X BASIC
STATED ODDS 1:210 HOBBY
STATED PRINT RUN 99 SER.#'d SETS
EXCHANGE DEADLINE 4/30/23
BMAAH Austin Hendrick 50.00 120.00
BMAHH Heriberto Hernandez 50.00 120.00
BMAJD Jeremy De La Rosa 75.00 200.00
BMAJS Jose Salas 50.00 120.00

2021 Bowman Chrome Mega Box Prospect Autograph Orange Refractors

*ORANGE/25: 1.5X TO 4X BASIC
STATED ODDS 1:829 HOBBY
STATED PRINT RUN 25 SER.#'d SETS
EXCHANGE DEADLINE 4/30/23
BMAAH Austin Hendrick 100.00 250.00
BMAHH Heriberto Hernandez 100.00 250.00
BMAIJ Ivan Johnson 50.00 120.00
BMAJD Jeremy De La Rosa 150.00 400.00
BMAJS Jose Salas 100.00 250.00

2021 Bowman Chrome Mega Box Rookie of the Year Favorites Refractors

STATED ODDS 1:2 HOBBY
*PURPLE/250: .6X TO 1.5X BASIC
*PINK/199: .6X TO 1.5X BASIC
*BLUE/150: .8X TO 2X BASIC
*GREEN/99: 1X TO 2.5X BASIC
*ORANGE/25: 4X TO 10X BASIC
RRYAB Alec Bohm 4.00 10.00
RRYAG Andres Gimenez 1.00 2.50
RRYBD Bobby Dalbec 5.00 12.00
RRYCJ Cristian Javier 1.00 2.50
RRYCM Casey Mize 3.00 8.00
RRYCP Cristian Pache 4.00 10.00
RRYDC Dylan Carlson 3.00 8.00
RRYEW Evan White 2.50 6.00
RRYIA Ian Anderson 2.50 6.00
RRYJA Jo Adell 5.00 12.00
RRYJB Joey Bart 1.25 3.00
RRYJC Jake Cronenworth 4.00 10.00
RRYKH Ke'Bryan Hayes 4.00 10.00
RRYLG Luis Garcia 2.00 5.00
RRYNM Nick Madrigal 3.00 8.00
RRYNP Nate Pearson 2.00 5.00
RRYRM Ryan Mountcastle 4.00 10.00
RRYSS Sixto Sanchez 2.00 5.00
RRYTM Triston McKenzie 1.25 3.00
RRYJCH Jazz Chisholm 4.00 10.00

2013 Bowman Chrome Mini

COMPLETE SET (330) 15.00 40.00
PLATE PRINT RUN 1 SET PER COLOR
BLACK-CYAN-MAGENTA-YELLOW ISSUED
NO PLATE PRICING DUE TO SCARCITY
1 Byron Buxton 1.50 4.00
2 Stefen Romero .30 .75
3 Justin Williams .40 1.00
4 Jacob Nottingham .30 .75
5 Justin Maffei .30 .75
6 Jeremy Moore .30 .75
7 Tzu-Wei Lin .40 1.00
8 Jonathon Crawford .30 .75
9 Edwin Escobar .40 1.00
10 Gregory Polanco .60 1.50
11 Riley Unroe .30 .75
12 Carlos Tocci .30 .75
13 Luis Guillorme .40 1.00
14 Tayler Scott .30 .75
15 Victor Roache .40 1.00
16 Francellis Montas .40 1.00
17 Kean Wong .30 .75
18 Andrew Aplin .30 .75
19 Jose Ramirez .40 1.00
20 Courtney Hawkins .30 .75
21 Aaron Blair .30 .75
22 Keury de la Cruz .30 .75
23 Chris Stratton .30 .75
24 R.J. Alvarez .30 .75
25 Jimmy Nelson .30 .75
26 Danry Vasquez .30 .75
27 Steven Moya .50 1.25
28 Nik Turley .30 .75
29 Cody Asche .50 1.25
30 Carlos Correa 4.00 10.00
31 Steven Negron .30 .75
32 Gabe Speier .30 .75
33 Collin Wiles .30 .75
34 Michael Taylor .30 .75
35 Ben Rowen .30 .75
36 Roel Ramirez .30 .75
37 Ivan Wilson .30 .75
38 Ian Hagenmiller .30 .75
39 Mike Piazza .30 .75
40 Austin Meadows .75 2.00
41 Denton Keys .40 1.00
42 Ericson Leonora .30 .75
43 Ian Clarkin .30 .75
44 Danny Muno .30 .75
45 Brennan Middleton .30 .75
46 Jan Hernandez .30 .75
47 Mac Williamson .50 1.25
48 Christian Bethancourt .50 1.25
49 Kevin Medrano .30 .75
50 Braden Shipley .30 .75
51 Michael Perez .30 .75
52 Cory Hall .30 .75
53 Todd Kibby .30 .75
54 Jordon Austin .40 1.00
55 Jeff Gelalich .30 .75
56 Joan Gregorio .40 1.00
57 Brian Navarreto .30 .75
58 Pedro Guerra .30 .75
59 Matthew Koch .30 .75
60 Henry Owens .40 1.00
61 Michael Lorenzen .40 1.00
62 Cord Sandberg .40 1.00
63 Andrew Toles .30 .75
64 Luis Torrens .30 .75
65 Tim Anderson 1.25 3.00
66 Derrick Penilla .30 .75
67 Orrin Sears .30 .75
68 Jayson Aquino .30 .75
69 Drew Ward .40 1.00
70 Hunter Renfroe .50 1.25
71 Rainy Lara .30 .75
72 Jonathan Griffin .30 .75
73 Joseph Monge .30 .75
74 Cory Vaughn .30 .75
75 Tyler Wade .50 1.25
76 Matt Derosier .30 .75
77 Jorge Bonifacio .40 1.00
78 Jesse Hahn .30 .75
79 Ricardo Bautista .30 .75
80 Eduardo Rodriguez 1.00 2.50
81 Casey Stevenson .30 .75
82 Zach Bird .30 .75
83 Ji-Man Choi .40 1.00
84 Anthony Alford .30 .75
85 Evan Rutckyj .30 .75
86 Nolan Fontana .40 1.00
87 Travis Witherspoon .30 .75
88 Breyvic Valera .40 1.00
89 Socrates Brito .50 1.25
90 Billy Mckinney .40 1.00
91 Parker Bridwell .30 .75
92 Tony Renda .30 .75
93 Danny Salazar .60 1.50
94 Randolph Gassaway .30 .75
95 Gioskar Amaya .30 .75
96 Ty Afenir .30 .75
97 Deivi Grullon .30 .75
98 Wyatt Mathisen .30 .75
99 Jamie Callahan .30 .75
100 Adalberto Mondesi .50 1.25
101 Yordano Ventura .40 1.00
102 Jonah Heim .30 .75
103 Tyler Vail .30 .75
104 Ronnie Freeman .30 .75
105 Kevin Ziomek .30 .75
106 Elier Rodriguez .30 .75
107 Stephen Gonsalves .30 .75
108 Jake Sweaney .30 .75
109 Marco Hernandez .30 .75
110 Jose Berrios .50 1.25
111 Victor Sanchez .40 1.00
112 Tyrone Taylor .30 .75
113 Ty Buttrey .30 .75
114 Stryker Trahan .30 .75
115 Travis Shaw .30 .75
116 Jordan Barnes .30 .75
117 Roman Quinn .50 1.25
118 Shane Broyles .30 .75
119 Luis Merejo .30 .75
120 Luis Sardinas .30 .75
121 B.J. Boyd .30 .75
122 Jake Stone .40 1.00
123 Zach Eflin .40 1.00
124 Patrick Kivlehan .30 .75
125 Alex Murphy .30 .75
126 Andre Rienzo .30 .75
127 Adam Landecker .30 .75
128 Tyler Kinley .30 .75
129 Dan Langfield .30 .75
130 D.J. Peterson .30 .75
131 Jeremy Baltz .30 .75
132 Viosergy Rosa .30 .75
133 Tom Windle .30 .75
134 Mikeson Oliberto .30 .75
135 Drew Steckenrider .30 .75
136 Sean Hurley .30 .75
137 Corey Dickerson .40 1.00
138 Andrew Church .30 .75
139 Will Morris .30 .75
140 Lucas Giolito .50 1.25
141 Andry Ubiera .40 1.00
142 Oscar Mercado .50 1.25
143 Blake Higgins .40 1.00
144 Carlos Sanchez .30 .75
145 Tom Murphy .30 .75
146 Brandon Maurer .40 1.00
147 Hanser Alberto .30 .75
148 Gaither Bumgardner .30 .75
149 Jon Keller .30 .75
150 Addison Russell .50 1.25
151 Jason Kanzler .30 .75
152 Casey Meisner .30 .75
153 Mark Montgomery .50 1.25
154 David Holmberg .30 .75
155 Aaron Blanton .30 .75
156 Ryan McMahon .75 2.00
157 Luiz Gohara .40 1.00
158 Hunter Green .30 .75
159 Tommy Kahnle .30 .75
160 Tyler Glasnow 1.25 3.00
161 Yeison Asencio .30 .75
162 Daniel Watts .30 .75
163 Robert Kaminsky .40 1.00
164 Anderson Feliz .30 .75
165 Jake Thompson .30 .75
166 Luigi Rodriguez .30 .75
167 Ronny Rodriguez .30 .75
168 J.T. Chargois .30 .75
169 Matt Stites .30 .75
170 Marco Gonzales .50 1.25
171 Matt Reynolds .40 1.00
172 Adam Westmoreland .30 .75
173 Alexis Rivera .30 .75
174 Andrew Knapp .30 .75
175 Dylan Manwaring .30 .75
176 Tyler Pike .30 .75
177 Darwin Rivera .30 .75
178 Kyle Smith .30 .75
179 Miles Williams .30 .75
180 Max Fried 1.25 3.00
181 Ian McKinney .30 .75
182 Jorge Martinez .30 .75
183 Alec Grosser .30 .75
184 Jason Martin .30 .75
185 Pat Light .30 .75
186 Christian Villanueva .30 .75
187 Chris Rivera .30 .75
188 Micah Johnson .40 1.00
189 Dustin Geiger .30 .75
190 Clayton Blackburn .50 1.25
191 Gosuke Katoh .40 1.00
192 Reed Harper .30 .75
193 William Oliver .30 .75
194 Michael Snyder .30 .75
195 Miguel Andujar 2.50 6.00
196 Ryan Court .30 .75
197 Jorge Perez .30 .75
198 Renato Nunez .60 1.50
199 Jose Cisnero .30 .75
200 Albert Almora .60 1.50
201 Lenny Linsky .30 .75
202 Max White .30 .75
203 Cody Buckel .30 .75
204 Dorssys Paulino .40 1.00
205 Willians Astudillo .30 .75
206 Niko Spezial .30 .75
207 Mauricio Cabrera .30 .75
208 Jon Denney .40 1.00
209 Dylan Cozens .30 .75
210 Dominic Smith .50 1.25
211 Trevor Williams .30 .75
212 Rio Ruiz .30 .75
213 Chris McFarland .30 .75
214 Kris Hall .30 .75
215 Teddy Stankiewicz .40 1.00
216 Julian Yan .30 .75
217 Adys Portillo .30 .75
218 Nick Tropeano .30 .75
219 Austin Wilson .40 1.00
220 Colin Moran .40 1.00
221 Caleb Kellogg .30 .75
222 Nolan Sanburn .30 .75
223 Carson Kelly .40 1.00
224 Mitch Brown .30 .75
225 Hansel Robles .30 .75
226 Matt Curry .30 .75
227 Kendall Coleman .30 .75
228 Alfredo Escalera-Maldonado .40 1.00
229 Luis Mateo .40 1.00
230 Jonathan Schoop .30 .75
231 Corey Knebel .30 .75
232 Tyler Gonzales .30 .75
233 Deven Marrero .30 .75
234 Taylor Dugas .40 1.00
235 Michael Reed .30 .75
236 Cameron Gallagher .30 .75
237 Erik Johnson .30 .75
238 Edwin Diaz .60 1.50
239 Stephen Piscotty .60 1.50
240 Rafael DePaula .30 .75
241 Adam Walker .40 1.00
242 Pedro Ruiz .30 .75
243 Seth Maness .30 .75
244 Alex Meyer .30 .75
245 Phil Ervin .30 .75
246 Ian Stiffler .30 .75
247 Gabriel Guerrero .40 1.00
248 Connor Oliver .30 .75
249 Nestor Molina .30 .75
250 C.J. Edwards .50 1.25
251 Travis Ott .30 .75
252 Kelvin De Leon .30 .75
253 Trey Williams .50 1.25
254 Josh Hart .30 .75
255 Brett Gerritse .30 .75
256 Ronald Guzman .50 1.25
257 Kevin Franklin .30 .75
258 Jairo Beras .50 1.25
259 Joseph Odom .30 .75
260 Lance McCullers .30 .75
261 Matt Southard .30 .75
262 Nick Ciuffo .30 .75
263 Trae Arbet .30 .75
264 Jake Lamb .50 1.25
265 Sam Selman .30 .75
266 Onelki Garcia .40 1.00
267 Austin Kubitza .30 .75
268 Brian Goodwin .40 1.00
269 Austin Schotts .40 1.00
270 J.P. Crawford .50 1.25
271 Derek Jones .30 .75
272 Blake Taylor .30 .75
273 Patrick Murphy .30 .75
274 Roberto Osuna .30 .75
275 Tanner Rahier .40 1.00
276 William White .30 .75
277 William Cuevas .30 .75
278 Rock Shoulders .30 .75
279 Rony Bautista .30 .75
280 Kohl Stewart .40 1.00
281 Nelson Molina .30 .75
282 Chris Anderson .40 1.00
283 Garrett Gordon .30 .75
284 Ethan Carnes .30 .75
285 Willie Medina .30 .75
286 Dustin Peterson .30 .75
287 Travis Demeritte .40 1.00
288 Carlos Salazar .30 .75
289 Dane Phillips .30 .75
290 Corey Seager 1.50 4.00
291 Sean Townsley .30 .75
292 Adalberto Mejia .30 .75
293 Jorge Polanco .75 2.00
294 Tyler Brosius .30 .75
295 Thomas Milone .30 .75
296 Chance Sisco .60 1.50
297 Reese McGuire .40 1.00
298 Yeicok Calderon .30 .75
299 Austin Nicely .30 .75
300 Jorge Alfaro .60 1.50
301 Jack Leathersich .30 .75
302 Miguel Almonte .30 .75
303 Bruce Rondon .30 .75
304 Fu-Lin Kuo .40 1.00
305 Gustavo Cabrera .75 2.00
306 Jeremy Rathjen .30 .75
307 Bryan Hudson .30 .75
308 Yohander Mendez .30 .75
309 Saxon Butler .30 .75
310 Jonathan Gray .40 1.00
311 Aaron Judge 15.00 40.00
312 Dilson Herrera 1.00 2.50
313 Mitch Nay .30 .75
314 Hunter Harvey .40 1.00
315 Clint Frazier 1.50 4.00
316 Gerrit Cole 2.00 5.00
317 Anthony Rendon 2.00 5.00
318 Christian Yelich 2.50 6.00
319 Evan Gattis .60 1.50
320 Henry Urrutia .40 1.00
321 Hyun-Jin Ryu .75 2.00
322 Jose Fernandez .75 2.00
323 Jurickson Profar .40 1.00
324 Manny Machado 2.00 5.00
325 Michael Wacha .40 1.00
326 Shelby Miller .75 2.00
327 Sonny Gray .50 1.25
328 Wil Myers .50 1.25
329 Zack Wheeler .60 1.50
330 Yasiel Puig 1.25 3.00

2013 Bowman Chrome Mini Black Refractors

*BLACK REF: 5X TO 12X BASIC
STATED PRINT RUN 25 SER.#'d SETS
311 Aaron Judge 200.00 500.00

2013 Bowman Chrome Mini Blue Refractors

*BLUE REF: 2X TO 5X BASIC
STATED PRINT RUN 99 SER.#'d SETS
311 Aaron Judge 100.00 250.00

2013 Bowman Chrome Mini Gold Refractors

*GOLD REF: 3X TO 3X BASIC
STATED PRINT RUN 50 SER.#'d SETS
311 Aaron Judge 150.00 400.00

2013 Bowman Chrome Mini Green Refractors

*GREEN REF: 2.5X TO 6X BASIC
STATED PRINT RUN 75 SER.#'d SETS
311 Aaron Judge 125.00 300.00

2013 Bowman Chrome Mini Refractors

*REFRACTORS: 1X TO 2.5X BASIC
STATED PRINT RUN 125 SER.#'d SETS
311 Aaron Judge 40.00 100.00

2013 Bowman Chrome Mini X-fractors

*X-FRACTORS: 2X TO 5X BASIC
STATED PRINT RUN 100 SER.#'d SETS
311 Aaron Judge 100.00 250.00

2014 Bowman Chrome Mini Factory Set

PRINTING PLATE RANDOMLY INSERTED
PLATE PRINT RUN 1 SET PER COLOR
BLACK-CYAN-MAGENTA-YELLOW ISSUED
NO PLATE PRICING DUE TO SCARCITY
1 Kris Bryant 2.00 5.00
2 Julio Urias 1.00 2.50
3 Travis d'Arnaud .25 .60
4 R.J. Alvarez .20 .50
5 Akeem Bostick .20 .50
6 Kelly Dugan .20 .50
7 Ryan Hafner .20 .50
8 Ryan Kussmaul .25 .60
9 Ryan McNeil .20 .50
10 Dom Nunez .20 .50
11 Cam Perkins .20 .50
12 Franmil Reyes .60 1.50
13 Dylan Unsworth .20 .50
14 Robert Whalen .20 .50
15 Spencer Adams .25 .60
16 Bobby Bradley .25 .60
17 Michael Chavis 1.00 2.50
18 Dustin DeMuth .20 .50
19 Ti'Quan Forbes .20 .50
20 Taylor Gushue .20 .50
21 Brent Honeywell .30 .75
22 Michael Kopech 1.25 3.00
23 Brett Martin .20 .50
24 Corey Ray .20 .50
25 Ryan Ripken .25 .60
26 Casey Soltis .20 .50
27 Nick Torres .20 .50
28 Alex Verdugo .40 1.00
29 Mark Zagunis .20 .50
30 Franklin Barreto .30 .75
31 Billy Burns .20 .50
32 Victor De Leon .20 .50
33 Dylan Floro .25 .60
34 Alexander Guerrero .25 .60
35 Isiah Kiner-Falefa .30 .75
36 Seth Mejias-Brean .20 .50
37 Dillon Overton .20 .50
38 Cody Reed .20 .50
39 Gabriel Rosa .20 .50
40 Chris Taylor 1.00 2.50
41 Taijuan Walker .20 .50
42 Jeff Ames .20 .50
43 Aaron Brooks .30 .75
44 Fred Lewis .20 .50
45 Rafael Medina .20 .50
46 Michael O'Neill .20 .50
47 Chad Pinder .20 .50
48 Jonathan Reynoso .20 .50
49 Ariel Soriano .20 .50
50 Jose Urena .25 .60
51 Matt Whitehouse .20 .50
52 Blake Anderson .20 .50
53 Jeff Brigham .20 .50
54 Isan Diaz .50 1.25
55 Austin Gomber .25 .60
56 Monte Harrison .40 1.00
57 Rhys Hoskins 2.00 5.00
58 Gavin LaValley .20 .50
59 Chris Oliver .20 .50
60 A.J. Reed .40 1.00
61 Carson Sands .20 .50
62 Taylor Sparks .20 .50
63 Sam Travis .25 .60
64 Jared Walker .20 .50
65 Jake Barrett .25 .60
66 Jacob deGrom 20.00 50.00
67 Maikel Franco .25 .60
68 Josh Hader .40 1.00
69 Chris Kohler .20 .50
70 Melvin Mercedes .20 .50
71 Daniel Palka .20 .50
72 Alex Reyes .30 .75
73 Anthony Santander .25 .60
74 Lewis Thorpe .20 .50
75 Levon Washington .20 .50
76 Cody Anderson .20 .50
77 Andy Burns .20 .50
78 Kevin Encarnacion .20 .50
79 Chris Heston .20 .50
80 Dawel Lugo .20 .50
81 Yonathan Mejia .20 .50
82 Wilmer Oberto .20 .50
83 Luigi Rodriguez .20 .50
84 Richard Urena .25 .60
85 Austin Wilson .20 .50
86 Brian Anderson .20 .50
87 Aaron Brown .20 .50
88 Jake Cosart .25 .60
89 Chris Ellis .20 .50
90 Jace Fry .20 .50
91 Brian Gonzalez .20 .50
92 Sam Hentges .20 .50
93 Zech Lemond .20 .50
94 Jordan Montgomery .40 1.00
95 Luis Ortiz .20 .50
96 Cody Reed .20 .50
97 Brian Schales .20 .50
98 Miguel Sano .25 .60
99 Forrest Wall .30 .75
100 Anthony Aliotti .20 .50
101 Wuilmer Becerra .20 .50
102 Michael Choice .20 .50
103 Miller Diaz .20 .50
104 John Gant .20 .50
105 Ryon Healy .30 .75
106 Ben Lively .20 .50
107 Leonardo Molina .20 .50
108 Jordan Paroubeck .20 .50
109 D.J. Peterson .20 .50
110 Gus Schlosser .20 .50
111 Andrew Thurman .20 .50
112 Joe Wendle .40 1.00
113 Elvis Araujo .20 .50
114 Victor Caratini .60 1.50
115 Thairo Estrada .60 1.50
116 JaCoby Jones .30 .75
117 Tyler Mahle .20 .50
118 Nathan Mikolas .20 .50
119 Dalton Pompey .30 .75
120 Jose Rondon .20 .50
121 Teddy Stankiewicz .20 .50
122 Sebastian Vader .20 .50
123 Daniel Winkler .20 .50
124 Brett Austin .20 .50
125 Nick Burdi .20 .50
126 Austin Cousino .20 .50
127 Garrett Fulenchek .20 .50
128 Nick Gordon .25 .60
129 Carlos Correa 1.00 2.50
130 Jacob Lindgren .25 .60
131 Andrew Morales .20 .50
132 Kevin Padlo .20 .50
133 Jake Reed .20 .50
134 Jake Stinnett .20 .50
135 Spencer Turnbull .20 .50
136 Luke Weaver .60 1.50
137 Yency Almonte .20 .50
138 Mookie Betts 4.00 10.00
139 Carlos Contreras .20 .50
140 Yimi Garcia .20 .50
141 Jose Herrera .20 .50
142 Manuel Margot .30 .75
143 Sam Moll .20 .50
144 Victor Payano .20 .50
145 Wendell Rijo .20 .50
146 Jonathan Schoop .20 .50
147 Devon Travis .20 .50
148 Devin Williams .50 1.25
149 Trae Arbet .20 .50
150 Ryan Casteel .20 .50
151 Buck Farmer .20 .50
152 Felix Jorge .20 .50
153 Adrian Marin .20 .50
154 Amaurys Minier .20 .50
155 Michael Ohlman .20 .50
156 Jose Pujols .20 .50
157 Jake Sanchez .20 .50
158 Breyvic Valera .20 .50
159 Kean Wong .20 .50
160 Ryan Castellani .20 .50
161 Braxton Davidson .20 .50
162 Raul Mondesi .30 .75
163 Aramis Garcia .20 .50
164 Daniel Gossett .20 .50
165 Grant Hockin .20 .50
166 Trace Loehr .20 .50
167 Gareth Morgan .20 .50
168 Mike Papi .20 .50
169 Jakson Reetz .20 .50
170 Lucas Giolito .30 .75
171 Troy Stokes .20 .50
172 Chase Anderson .20 .50
173 Christian Binford .20 .50
174 Tim Cooney .20 .50
175 Michael Feliz .25 .60
176 Kenny Giles .25 .60
177 Rosell Herrera .30 .75
178 Tyler Marlette .20 .50
179 Akeel Morris .20 .50
180 Shawn Pleffner .20 .50
181 Armando Rivero .20 .50
182 Ryne Stanek .20 .50
183 Brandon Trinkwon .25 .60
184 Austin Wright .20 .50
185 Erisbel Arruebarrena .20 .50
186 Johnny Field .20 .50
187 Clint Frazier .75 2.00
188 Raul Mondesi .30 .75
189 Jordan Patterson .20 .50
190 Harold Ramirez .30 .75
191 Roenis Elias .20 .50
192 Vincent Velasquez .30 .75
193 Kolten Wong .25 .60
194 Alex Blandino .20 .50
195 Dylan Cease .50 1.25
196 Dylan Davis .25 .60
197 Derek Fisher .30 .75
198 Jacob Gatewood .20 .50
199 Brett Graves .20 .50

200 Jeff Hoffman .30 .75
201 Connor Joe .20 .50
202 Jordan Luplow .20 .50
203 Josh Morgan .20 .50
204 Sean Reid-Foley .20 .50
205 Justus Sheffield .40 1.00
206 Wyatt Strahan .20 .50
207 Braden Shipley .20 .50
208 Justin Twine .20 .50
209 Ronnie Williams .20 .50
210 Tim Anderson .40 1.00
211 Miguel Alfredo Gonzalez .20 .50
212 Jason Hursh .20 .50
213 Jacob May .25 .60
214 Jorge Alfaro .25 .60
215 C.J. Edwards .25 .60
216 Daniel Robertson .25 .60
217 Blake Swihart .25 .60
218 Joey Gallo .40 1.00
219 Gabriel Ynoa .25 .60
220 Logan Bawcom .20 .50
221 Taylor Cole .20 .50
222 Willy Garcia .20 .50
223 Nick Kingham .25 .60
224 L.J. Mazzilli .20 .50
225 Austin Nola .25 .60
226 Spencer Patton .20 .50
227 Jose Ramirez .20 .50
228 Juan Silva .20 .50
229 Alberto Tirado .20 .50
230 Bobby Wahl .20 .50
231 Chris Owings .20 .50
232 Scott Blewett .20 .50
233 Michael Cederoth .25 .60
234 J.D. Davis .30 .75
235 Jack Flaherty 1.25 3.00
236 Joe Gatto .20 .50
237 Grayson Greiner .20 .50
238 Jonathan Holder .20 .50
239 Mitch Keller .30 .75
240 Michael Mader .20 .50
241 Michael Taylor .25 .60
242 Matt Railey .20 .50
243 Dominic Smith .25 .60
244 Trey Supak .20 .50
245 Chase Vallot .20 .50
246 Rougned Odor .50 1.25
247 Orlando Arcia .30 .75
248 Zach Borenstein .25 .60
249 Brandon Cumpton .20 .50
250 Kendry Flores .20 .50
251 Drew Granier .20 .50
252 Luke Jackson .20 .50
253 Santiago Nessy .20 .50
254 Steven Ramos .20 .50
255 Nelson Rodriguez .25 .60
256 Tim Berry .20 .50
257 Brandon Dixon .20 .50
258 Trevor Gretzky .20 .50
259 Corey Knebel .20 .50
260 Jeff McNeil 1.25 3.00
261 Kohl Stewart .20 .50
262 James Paxton .30 .75
263 Nick Ramirez .20 .50
264 Shae Simmons .20 .50
265 Stuart Turner .20 .50
266 Jamie Westbrook .20 .50
267 Luis Sardinas .20 .50
268 Albert Almora .30 .75
269 Matt Chapman 1.25 3.00
270 Austin DeCarr .20 .50
271 Jordan Foley .20 .50
272 Michael Gettys .25 .60
273 Foster Griffin .20 .50
274 Grant Holmes .20 .50
275 Johnny Manziel
276 Milton Ramos .20 .50
277 John Richy .20 .50
278 Corey Seager 1.00 2.50
279 Lane Thomas .30 .75
280 Cameron Varga .20 .50
281 Ryan Yarbrough .30 .75
282 Trey Ball .20 .50
283 Matthew Bowman .20 .50
284 Wilmer Flores .25 .60
285 Robert Gsellman .25 .60
286 Eric Jagielo .20 .50
287 Matt McPhearson .20 .50
288 Tucker Neuhaus .20 .50
289 Michael Ratterree .20 .50
290 Jason Rogers .20 .50
291 Raimel Tapia .25 .60
292 Logan Vick .20 .50
293 Casey Gillaspie .30 .75
294 Aaron Nola 1.25 3.00
295 Michael Conforto .40 1.00
296 Kyle Freeland .40 1.00
297 Bradley Zimmer .30 .75
298 Nick Howard .20 .50
299 Erick Fedde .20 .50
300 Trea Turner .60 1.50
301 Kodi Medeiros .20 .50
302 Kyle Schwarber .75 2.00
303 Tyler Beede .30 .75
304 Alex Jackson .25 .60
305 Max Pentecost .20 .50
306 Nomar Mazara .50 1.25
307 Tyler Kolek .20 .50
308 Sean Newcomb .30 .75
309 Luis Severino .30 .75
310 Hunter Harvey .20 .50
311 Hunter Dozier .20 .50
312 Jose Berrios .30 .75
313 Cole Tucker .20 .50
314 Derek Hill .20 .50
315 Austin Meadows .50 1.25
316 Gosuke Katoh .30 .75
317 Mark Appel .25 .60
318 Tyler Glasnow .75 2.00
319 J.P. Crawford .20 .50
320 Masahiro Tanaka .60 1.50
321 Jose Abreu 1.50 4.00
322 Gregory Polanco .30 .75
323 George Springer .75 2.00
324 Oscar Taveras .25 .60
325 Billy Hamilton .25 .60
326 Nick Castellanos .60 1.50
327 Garin Cecchini .20 .50
328 Xander Bogaerts .60 1.50
329 Yordano Ventura .25 .60
330 Jon Singleton .25 .60

2014 Bowman Chrome Mini Factory Set Black Shimmer Refractors

*BLACK SHIMMER: 3X TO 8X BASIC
OVERALL 30 REF.PER FACTORY SET

2014 Bowman Chrome Mini Factory Set Blue Refractors

*BLUE REF: 4X TO 10X BASIC
OVERALL 30 REF.PER FACTORY SET
STATED PRINT RUN 20 SER.#'d SETS
1 Kris Bryant 40.00 100.00

2014 Bowman Chrome Mini Factory Set Refractors

*REF: 1.5X TO 4X BASIC
OVERALL 30 REF.PER FACTORY SET

2014 Bowman Chrome Mini Factory Set Yellow Refractors

*YELLOW REF: 5X TO 12X BASIC
OVERALL 30 REF.PER FACTORY SET
STATED PRINT RUN 25 SER.#'d SETS
1 Kris Bryant 40.00 100.00

2017 Bowman Chrome Mini

OVERALL 30 PARALLELS PER SET
PLATE PRINT RUN 1 SET PER COLOR
BLACK-CYAN-MAGENTA-YELLOW ISSUED
NO PLATE PRICING DUE TO SCARCITY
2 Jesse Winker 1.50 4.00
4 Jeff Hoffman .40 1.00
18 Joe Jimenez .50 1.25
20 Manny Margot .40 1.00
22 Carson Fulmer .40 1.00
23 Andrew Benintendi 1.25 3.00
25 Yoan Moncada 1.25 3.00
26 Teoscar Hernandez 1.50 4.00
27 Reynaldo Lopez .40 1.00
27 Cody Bellinger 6.00 15.00
29 Yulieski Gurriel .60 1.50
29 Christian Arroyo .60 1.50
32 Aaron Judge 5.00 12.00
34 Robert Gsellman .40 1.00
35 Ryon Healy .50 1.25
41 Orlando Arcia .60 1.50
42 Jose De Leon .40 1.00
42 Mitch Haniger .60 1.50
44 Jordan Montgomery .60 1.50
54 David Dahl .50 1.25
55 Rob Segedin .40 1.00
56 Tyler Glasnow 1.50 4.00
57 Dansby Swanson 1.00 2.50
60 Jorge Alfaro .50 1.25
62 Jake Thompson .40 1.00
63 Hunter Dozier .40 1.00
64 Matt Strahm .40 1.00
66 Gavin Cecchini .40 1.00
70 Josh Bell 1.00 2.50
75 Alex Bregman 2.00 5.00
78 Raimel Tapia .50 1.25
83 Braden Shipley .40 1.00
86 Tyler Austin .50 1.25
89 Jharel Cotton .40 1.00
92 Joe Musgrove 1.25 3.00
95 Amir Garrett .40 1.00
98 Alex Reyes .50 1.25
99 Hunter Renfroe .50 1.25

2017 Bowman Chrome Mini 70th Blue Refractors

*70TH BLUE REF: 2X TO 5X BASIC
OVERALL 30 PARALLELS PER SET
STATED PRINT RUN 70 SER.#'d SETS

2017 Bowman Chrome Mini Black Shimmer Refractors

*BLACK SHIMMER REF: 2X TO 5X BASIC
OVERALL 30 PARALLELS PER SET
STATED PRINT RUN 100 SER.#'d SETS

2017 Bowman Chrome Mini Blue Shimmer Refractors

*BLUE SHIMMER REF: 1.5X TO 4X BASIC
OVERALL 30 PARALLELS PER SET
STATED PRINT RUN 150 SER.#'d SETS

2017 Bowman Chrome Mini Gold Refractors

*GOLD REF: 2.5X TO 6X BASIC
OVERALL 30 PARALLELS PER SET
STATED PRINT RUN 50 SER.#'d SETS

2017 Bowman Chrome Mini Green Refractors

*GREEN REF: 2X TO 5X BASIC
OVERALL 30 PARALLELS PER SET
STATED PRINT RUN 99 SER.#'d SETS

2017 Bowman Chrome Mini Orange Refractors

*ORANGE REF: 5X TO 12X BASIC
OVERALL 30 PARALLELS PER SET
STATED PRINT RUN 25 SER.#'d SETS

2017 Bowman Chrome Mini Refractors

*REF: .75X TO 2X BASIC
OVERALL 30 PARALLELS PER SET

2017 Bowman Chrome Mini Prospects

OVERALL 30 PARALLELS PER SET
PLATE PRINT RUN 1 SET PER COLOR
BLACK-CYAN-MAGENTA-YELLOW ISSUED
NO PLATE PRICING DUE TO SCARCITY
BCP1 Nick Senzel .75 2.00
BCP2 Gavin Lux 1.00 2.50
BCP3 Ronald Guzman .30 .75
BCP4 A.J. Puckett .25 .60
BCP5 Mike Soroka .75 2.00
BCP6 Roniel Raudes .25 .60
BCP7 Lucius Erceg .25 .60
BCP8 Luis Almanzar .25 .60
BCP9 Beau Burrows .25 .60
BCP10 Chase Vallot .25 .60
BCP11 P.J. Conlon .25 .60
BCP12 Erick Fedde .25 .60
BCP13 Rookie Davis .25 .60
BCP14 Chris Shaw .25 .60
BCP15 Nick Burdi .25 .60
BCP16 Clint Frazier .50 1.25
BCP17 Luiz Gohara .25 .60
BCP18 Lourdes Gurriel Jr. .40 1.00
BCP19 Eric Jenkins .25 .60
BCP20 Angel Perdomo .25 .60
BCP21 Dustin May 1.25 3.00
BCP22 Freddy Peralta .40 1.00
BCP23 Jarlin Garcia .25 .60
BCP24 Tyler O'Neill .30 .75
BCP25 Lazarito Armenteros .50 1.25
BCP26 Paul De Jong .75 2.00
BCP27 Antonio Senzatela .25 .60
BCP28 Kyle Tucker .60 1.50
BCP29 Aramis Garcia .25 .60
BCP30 Willie Calhoun .40 1.00
BCP31 Chance Adams .30 .75
BCP32 Vladimir Guerrero Jr. 3.00 8.00
BCP33 Braxton Garrett .25 .60
BCP34 Yeudy Garcia .25 .60
BCP35 Dane Dunning .75 2.00
BCP36 Andy Ibanez .25 .60
BCP37 Francisco Rios .25 .60
BCP38 Joe Jimenez .30 .75
BCP39 Dylan Cozens .25 .60
BCP40 Mauricio Dubon .30 .75
BCP41 Franklyn Kilome .25 .60
BCP42 Chance Sisco .50 1.25
BCP43 Sandy Alcantara .30 .75
BCP44 Stephen Gonsalves .25 .60
BCP45 Grant Holmes .25 .60
BCP46 Dakota Chalmers .25 .60
BCP47 Kolby Allard .25 .60
BCP48 Tyler Alexander .25 .60
BCP49 Phil Bickford .25 .60
BCP50 Eloy Jimenez 1.00 2.50
BCP51 Francisco Mejia .40 1.00
BCP52 Kohl Stewart .25 .60
BCP53 Garrett Whitley .25 .60
BCP54 Anderson Espinoza .25 .60
BCP55 Cal Quantrill .25 .60
BCP56 Tetsuto Yamada .50 1.25
BCP57 Tyler Beede .25 .60
BCP58 Jake Bauers .30 .75
BCP59 Ariel Jurado .25 .60
BCP60 Austin Voth .25 .60
BCP61 Tyler Stephenson .60 1.50
BCP62 Yoshitomo Tsutsugo .60 1.50
BCP63 Dominic Smith .25 .60
BCP64 Matt Thaiss .25 .60
BCP65 Austin Meadows .60 1.50
BCP66 Mitch Keller .30 .75
BCP67 Jahmai Jones .25 .60
BCP68 Alex Speas .25 .60
BCP69 Nolan Jones .40 1.00
BCP70 Kevin Newman .40 1.00
BCP71 T.J. Friedl .25 .60
BCP72 Oscar De La Cruz .25 .60
BCP73 Victor Robles .60 1.50
BCP74 Patrick Weigel .25 .60
BCP75 Ryan Mountcastle 1.25 3.00
BCP76 Amed Rosario .40 1.00
BCP77 Nick Solak 1.00 2.50
BCP78 Abrahan Gutierrez .40 1.00
BCP79 Yu-Cheng Chang .40 1.00
BCP80 Gleyber Torres 4.00 10.00
BCP81 J.D. Davis .30 .75
BCP82 Walker Buehler .60 1.50
BCP83 Andrew Sopko .25 .60
BCP84 Brent Honeywell .30 .75
BCP85 Kyle Funkhouser .30 .75
BCP86 Brian Mundell .25 .60
BCP87 Brian Anderson .30 .75
BCP88 Brendan Rodgers .30 .75
BCP89 Josh Staumont .25 .60
BCP90 Cody Sedlock .25 .60
BCP91 D.J. Stewart .25 .60
BCP92 Wuilmer Becerra .25 .60
BCP93 Nate Smith .25 .60
BCP94 Alfredo Rodriguez .30 .75
BCP95 Daz Cameron .25 .60
BCP96 Taylor Ward .30 .75
BCP97 Takahiro Norimoto .25 .60
BCP98 Tomoyuki Sugano .40 1.00
BCP99 Drew Jackson .25 .60
BCP100 Kevin Maitan .40 1.00
BCP101 Rafael Devers .50 1.25
BCP102 Alex Kirilloff .60 1.50
BCP103 Jack Flaherty 1.50 4.00
BCP104 Adonis Medina .40 1.00
BCP105 Ke'Bryan Hayes 1.25 3.00
BCP106 Josh Hader .30 .75
BCP107 Luis Urias 1.00 2.50
BCP108 Donnie Dewees .25 .60
BCP109 Kyle Freeland .30 .75
BCP110 Matt Chapman .75 2.00
BCP111 Sam Coonrod .25 .60
BCP112 Andrew Suarez .25 .60
BCP113 David Fletcher .75 2.00
BCP114 Tyler Jay .25 .60
BCP115 Franklin Barreto .25 .60
BCP116 Michael Kopech .75 2.00
BCP117 Rhys Hoskins 1.00 2.50
BCP118 Triston McKenzie .75 2.00
BCP119 Luis Garcia 2.00 5.00
BCP120 Harold Ramirez .30 .75
BCP121 Blake Rutherford .40 1.00
BCP122 Matt Manning .40 1.00
BCP123 Josh Morgan .25 .60
BCP124 Dylan Cease .40 1.00
BCP125 Kyle Lewis .50 1.25
BCP126 Nick Neidert .25 .60
BCP127 Ronald Acuna 30.00 80.00
BCP128 Luis Ortiz .25 .60
BCP129 Isael Soto .25 .60
BCP130 Adrian Morejon .40 1.00
BCP131 Mark Zagunis .25 .60
BCP132 Justus Sheffield .40 1.00
BCP133 Jaime Schultz .25 .60
BCP134 Fernando Romero .25 .60
BCP135 Mickey Moniak .50 1.25
BCP136 Jorge Bonifacio .25 .60
BCP137 Jomar Reyes .25 .60
BCP138 Thomas Szapucki .30 .75
BCP139 Sean Reid-Foley .25 .60
BCP140 Willy Adames .30 .75
BCP141 Yang Hyeon-Jong .30 .75
BCP142 Bo Bichette 1.00 2.50
BCP143 Harrison Bader .40 1.00
BCP144 Travis Demeritte .25 .60
BCP145 Juan Hillman .25 .60
BCP146 Francis Martes .25 .60
BCP147 Wilkerman Garcia .30 .75
BCP148 Christin Stewart .30 .75
BCP149 Cody Bellinger 4.00 10.00
BCP150 Jason Groome .50 1.25
BCP152 Andrew Moore .30 .75
BCP153 Albert Abreu .30 .75
BCP154 Max Schrock .40 1.00
BCP155 Jonathan Arauz .30 .75
BCP156 Max Fried 1.00 2.50
BCP157 Bobby Bradley .30 .75
BCP158 Leody Taveras 3.00 8.00
BCP159 Jacob Nottingham .25 .60
BCP160 Fernando Tatis Jr. 2.50 6.00
BCP161 Austin Riley .75 2.00
BCP162 Trevor Clifton .25 .60
BCP163 Anthony Banda .25 .60
BCP164 Richard Urena .40 1.00
BCP165 Reggie Lawson .25 .60
BCP166 Felix Jorge .25 .60
BCP168 Jorge Ona .30 .75
BCP169 Brandon Woodruff .75 2.00
BCP170 Sam Travis .30 .75
BCP171 Derek Fisher .30 .75
BCP172 Touki Toussaint .30 .75
BCP173 Forrest Whitley .60 1.50
BCP174 Scott Kingery .40 1.00
BCP175 Jorge Mateo .25 .60
BCP176 Joshua Lowe .25 .60
BCP177 Rowdy Tellez .25 .60
BCP178 Kevin Kramer .25 .60
BCP179 Desmond Lindsay .25 .60
BCP180 Juan Soto 8.00 20.00
BCP181 Isan Diaz .60 1.50
BCP182 Rob Kaminsky .25 .60
BCP183 Domingo Acevedo .25 .60
BCP185 Andy Yerzy .25 .60
BCP187 Tirso Ornelas .30 .75
BCP189 Adam Ravenelle .25 .60
BCP190 Mitchell White .25 .60
BCP191 Dawel Lugo .25 .60
BCP192 Vladimir Gutierrez .25 .60
BCP193 Max Povse .25 .60
BCP194 Delvin Perez .40 1.00
BCP195 Jacob Nix .25 .60
BCP196 Josh Sborz .25 .60
BCP197 Torii Hunter Jr. .30 .75
BCP199 Yasel Antuna 1.25 3.00
BCP201 Nick Gordon .25 .60
BCP202 Brett Phillips .30 .75
BCP203 Yairo Munoz .25 .60
BCP204 Bryan Reynolds .40 1.00
BCP205 Dakota Hudson .40 1.00
BCP206 Miguelangel Sierra .50 1.25
BCP207 Jazz Chisholm 10.00 25.00
BCP208 DJ Peters .60 1.50
BCP209 Jacob Faria .25 .60
BCP210 Sixto Sanchez 4.00 10.00
BCP211 Braden Bishop .40 1.00
BCP212 Ryan O'Hearn .50 1.25
BCP213 Garrett Stubbs .25 .60
BCP215 Trent Clark .25 .60
BCP216 Jose Albertos .60 1.50
BCP217 Ryan McMahon .40 1.00
BCP218 Khalil Lee .40 1.00
BCP220 Steven Duggar .25 .60
BCP221 Franklin Perez .40 1.00
BCP222 Tomas Nido .25 .60
BCP223 Justin Dunn .25 .60
BCP224 Austin Hays .60 1.50
BCP226 Starling Heredia .30 .75
BCP227 Bryson Brigman .25 .60
BCP228 Jesus Sanchez 1.25 3.00
BCP229 Yusniel Diaz .75 2.00
BCP232 Ian Anderson .75 2.00
BCP234 Jameson Fisher .25 .60
BCP236 Keegan Akin .30 .75
BCP237 James Kaprielian .25 .60
BCP238 Jeisson Rosario .30 .75
BCP239 Carter Kieboom .40 1.00
BCP240 Nick Williams .30 .75
BCP241 Brandon Marsh 3.00 8.00
BCP242 Wander Javier .40 1.00
BCP243 Chris Paddack .60 1.50
BCP244 Luis Alexander Basabe .40 1.00
BCP245 Zack Burdi .25 .60
BCP246 Anthony Kay .30 .75
BCP247 Anderson Tejeda .40 1.00
BCP248 Daniel Gossett .25 .60
BCP249 Heath Quinn .30 .75

2017 Bowman Chrome Mini Prospects 70th Blue Refractors

*70TH BLUE REF: 2.5X TO 6X BASIC
OVERALL 30 PARALLELS PER SET
STATED PRINT RUN 70 SER.#'d SETS
BCP127 Ronald Acuna 125.00 300.00

2017 Bowman Chrome Mini Prospects Black Shimmer Refractors

*BLACK SHIMMER: 2X TO 5X BASIC
OVERALL 30 PARALLELS PER SET
STATED PRINT RUN 100 SER.#'d SETS
BCP127 Ronald Acuna 100.00 250.00

2017 Bowman Chrome Mini Prospects Blue Shimmer Refractors

*BLUE SHIMMER REF: 1.5X TO 4X BASIC
OVERALL 30 PARALLELS PER SET
STATED PRINT RUN 150 SER.#'d SETS
BCP127 Ronald Acuna 75.00 200.00

2017 Bowman Chrome Mini Prospects Gold Refractors

*GOLD REF: 3X TO 8X BASIC
OVERALL 50 PARALLELS PER SET
STATED PRINT RUN 50 SER.#'d SETS
BCP127 Ronald Acuna 150.00 400.00

2017 Bowman Chrome Mini Prospects Green Refractors

*GREEN REF: 2X TO 5X BASIC
OVERALL 30 PARALLELS PER SET
STATED PRINT RUN 99 SER.#'d SETS
BCP127 Ronald Acuna 100.00 250.00

2017 Bowman Chrome Mini Prospects Orange Refractors

*ORANGE REF: 4X TO 10X BASIC
OVERALL 30 PARALLELS PER SET
STATED PRINT RUN 25 SER.#'d SETS
BCP127 Ronald Acuna 200.00 500.00

2017 Bowman Chrome Mini Prospects Refractors

*REF: 1.2X TO 3X BASIC
OVERALL 30 PARALLELS PER SET
BCP127 Ronald Acuna 40.00 100.00

2020 Bowman Chrome Sapphire Prospects

BCP1 Wander Franco 15.00 40.00
BCP2 Drew Waters 8.00 20.00
BCP3 Jacob Amaya 5.00 12.00
BCP4 Kody Hoese 4.00 10.00
BCP5 Cristian Pache 12.00 30.00
BCP6 Zack Thompson 1.25 3.00
BCP7 Briam Campusano 1.25 3.00
BCP8 Jasson Dominguez 300.00 600.00
BCP9 Aaron Shortridge 1.50 4.00
BCP10 Xavier Edwards 10.00 25.00
BCP11 Jesus Sanchez 2.00 5.00
BCP12 Ronaldo Hernandez 1.25 3.00
BCP13 Blake Rutherford 1.25 3.00
BCP14 Ulrich Bojarski 2.00 5.00
BCP15 Jordyn Adams 1.50 4.00
BCP16 Austin Beck 1.50 4.00
BCP17 Niko Hulsizer 3.00 8.00
BCP18 Triston Casas 3.00 8.00
BCP19 Julio Rodriguez 12.00 30.00
BCP20 Shane Baz 4.00 10.00
BCP21 Shea Langeliers 2.50 6.00
BCP22 Grayson Rodriguez 2.00 5.00
BCP23 Ruben Cardenas 1.50 4.00
BCP24 Mason Denaburg 1.25 3.00
BCP25 Bobby Witt Jr. 75.00 200.00
BCP26 Andrew Vaughn 5.00 12.00
BCP27 Kristian Robinson 4.00 10.00
BCP28 Ronny Mauricio 3.00 8.00
BCP29 Alec Bohm 8.00 20.00
BCP30 Jhon Diaz 4.00 10.00
BCP31 Estevan Florial 4.00 10.00
BCP32 Elehuris Montero 1.50 4.00
BCP33 Sam Huff 15.00 40.00
BCP34 Zack Brown 1.25 3.00
BCP35 Brice Turang 1.25 3.00
BCP36 Ryan Mountcastle 6.00 15.00
BCP37 Wilfred Astudillo 1.50 4.00
BCP38 Gus Varland 1.50 4.00
BCP39 Nick Lodolo 2.00 5.00
BCP40 Tyler Freeman 1.50 4.00
BCP41 Rece Hinds 1.50 4.00
BCP42 Brady Singer 5.00 12.00
BCP43 Cal Mitchell 1.25 3.00
BCP44 Ethan Hankins 1.50 4.00
BCP45 Daz Cameron 1.25 3.00
BCP46 Sherten Apostel 6.00 15.00
BCP47 Hunter Greene 2.00 5.00
BCP48 Josiah Gray 2.00 5.00
BCP49 Brailyn Marquez 3.00 8.00
BCP50 Adley Rutschman 8.00 20.00
BCP51 Everson Pereira 3.00 8.00
BCP53 Clarke Schmidt 5.00 12.00
BCP54 Brady McConnell 1.50 4.00
BCP55 Spencer Howard 4.00 10.00
BCP56 Cristian Javier 3.00 8.00
BCP57 Aaron Ashby 1.25 3.00
BCP58 Logan Gilbert 1.50 4.00
BCP59 Glenallen Hill Jr. 5.00 12.00
BCP60 Alvaro Seijas 1.25 3.00
BCP61 Jeremy Pena 3.00 8.00
BCP62 CJ Abrams 4.00 10.00
BCP63 Franklin Perez 1.25 3.00
BCP64 Tanner Houck 3.00 8.00
BCP65 Damon Jones 1.50 4.00
BCP66 Nolan Gorman 2.50 6.00
BCP67 Ke'Bryan Hayes 6.00 15.00
BCP68 Bryson Stott 3.00 8.00
BCP69 Canaan Smith 2.00 5.00
BCP70 Forrest Whitley 2.00 5.00
BCP71 Drew Mendoza 3.00 8.00
BCP72 Jazz Chisholm 5.00 12.00
BCP73 Jonathan India 8.00 20.00
BCP74 MacKenzie Gore 2.50 6.00
BCP75 Seth Beer 2.50 6.00
BCP76 Joey Cantillo 1.25 3.00
BCP77 Evan White 4.00 10.00
BCP78 Chris Vallimont 1.25 3.00
BCP79 Sixto Sanchez 6.00 15.00
BCP80 Alex Kirilloff 6.00 15.00
BCP81 Tristen Lutz 1.50 4.00
BCP82 Freudis Nova 1.25 3.00
BCP83 Tim Cate 1.25 3.00
BCP84 Daniel Lynch 1.25 3.00
BCP85 Antonio Cabello 4.00 10.00
BCP86 Bobby Dalbec 8.00 20.00
BCP87 Colton Welker 1.25 3.00
BCP88 Logan Davidson 1.50 4.00
BCP89 Matthew Liberatore 1.50 4.00
BCP90 Adam Hall 1.50 4.00
BCP91 Jackson Rutledge 5.00 12.00
BCP92 Dane Dunning 4.00 10.00
BCP93 Royce Lewis 3.00 8.00
BCP94 Jarred Kelenic 12.00 30.00
BCP95 Nolan Jones 2.00 5.00
BCP96 Jerar Encarnacion 8.00 20.00
BCP97 Ian Anderson 4.00 10.00
BCP98 Alek Thomas 1.50 4.00
BCP99 Matt Manning 1.50 4.00
BCP100 Jo Adell 6.00 15.00
BCP101 Nick Madrigal 5.00 12.00
BCP102 Owen Miller 1.25 3.00
BCP103 Marco Luciano 5.00 12.00
BCP104 Jordan Groshans 2.50 6.00
BCP105 Nick Allen 1.25 3.00
BCP106 Dylan Carlson 5.00 12.00
BCP107 Cole Winn 1.25 3.00
BCP108 Tarik Skubal 20.00 50.00
BCP109 Oscar Gonzalez 2.50 6.00
BCP110 Aramis Ademan 1.25 3.00
BCP111 Oneil Cruz 1.50 4.00
BCP112 Joey Bart 5.00 12.00
BCP113 Josh Jung 3.00 8.00
BCP114 Luis Garcia 5.00 12.00
BCP115 Jasseel De La Cruz 4.00 10.00
BCP116 J.J. Bleday 4.00 10.00
BCP117 Joe Ryan 1.50 4.00
BCP118 Keoni Cavaco 1.25 3.00
BCP119 Hans Crouse 1.25 3.00
BCP120 Isaac Paredes 4.00 10.00
BCP121 Grant Lavigne 1.25 3.00
BCP122 Riley Greene 8.00 20.00
BCP123 Jordan Balazovic 2.50 6.00
BCP124 Nate Pearson 4.00 10.00
BCP125 Deivi Garcia 4.00 10.00
BCP126 Luis Garcia 5.00 12.00
BCP127 Leody Taveras 2.00 5.00
BCP128 Bryan Mata 1.25 3.00
BCP129 Hunter Bishop 2.50 6.00
BCP130 Taylor Trammell 2.00 5.00
BCP131 Miguel Vargas 3.00 8.00
BCP132 Luis Gil 1.50 4.00
BCP133 Grant Little 1.50 4.00
BCP134 Gunnar Henderson 1.50 4.00
BCP135 Eric Pardinho 1.50 4.00
BCP136 Miguel Amaya 1.25 3.00
BCP137 Ryan Rolison 1.50 4.00
BCP138 Jorge Mateo 1.50 4.00
BCP139 Anthony Volpe 10.00 25.00
BCP140 Nick Bennett 1.25 3.00
BCP141 Brennen Davis 6.00 15.00
BCP142 Casey Mize 4.00 10.00
BCP143 Keibert Ruiz 6.00 15.00
BCP144 Jarren Duran 30.00 80.00
BCP145 Robert Puason 40.00 100.00
BCP146 Travis Swaggerty 1.50 4.00
BCP147 Will Wilson 1.50 4.00
BCP148 Heliot Ramos 2.00 5.00
BCP149 Alek Manoah 1.50 4.00
BCP150 Luis Robert 100.00 250.00

2020 Bowman Chrome Sapphire Prospects Orange

*ORANGE: .6X TO 1.5X BASIC
STATED ODDS 1:XX HOBBY
STATED PRINT RUN 75 SER.#'d SETS
BCP1 Wander Franco 50.00 120.00
BCP4 Kody Hoese 12.00 30.00
BCP5 Cristian Pache 40.00 100.00
BCP8 Jasson Dominguez 500.00 1000.00
BCP25 Bobby Witt Jr. 200.00 500.00
BCP26 Andrew Vaughn 25.00 60.00
BCP29 Alec Bohm 15.00 40.00
BCP31 Estevan Florial 8.00 20.00
BCP50 Adley Rutschman 40.00 100.00
BCP62 CJ Abrams 20.00 50.00
BCP94 Jarred Kelenic 30.00 80.00
BCP96 Jerar Encarnacion 30.00 80.00
BCP100 Jo Adell 30.00 80.00
BCP103 Marco Luciano 20.00 50.00
BCP106 Dylan Carlson 30.00 80.00
BCP108 Tarik Skubal 30.00 80.00
BCP112 Joey Bart 12.00 30.00
BCP141 Brennen Davis 20.00 50.00
BCP142 Casey Mize 15.00 40.00
BCP143 Keibert Ruiz 6.00 15.00
BCP144 Jarren Duran 100.00 250.00
BCP145 Robert Puason 150.00 400.00

2020 Bowman Chrome Sapphire Prospects Purple

*PURPLE: 1X TO 2.5X BASIC
STATED ODDS 1:XX HOBBY
STATED PRINT RUN 20 SER.#'d SETS
BCP1 Wander Franco 125.00 400.00
BCP4 Kody Hoese 20.00 50.00
BCP5 Cristian Pache 60.00 150.00
BCP8 Jasson Dominguez 1000.00 2000.00
BCP25 Bobby Witt Jr. 300.00 800.00
BCP26 Andrew Vaughn 40.00 100.00
BCP29 Alec Bohm 25.00 60.00
BCP31 Estevan Florial 25.00 60.00
BCP50 Adley Rutschman 60.00 150.00
BCP62 CJ Abrams 30.00 80.00
BCP66 Nolan Gorman 20.00 50.00
BCP68 Bryson Stott 30.00 80.00
BCP69 Canaan Smith 20.00 50.00
BCP94 Jarred Kelenic 50.00 120.00
BCP96 Jerar Encarnacion 100.00 250.00
BCP100 Jo Adell 60.00 150.00
BCP103 Marco Luciano 30.00 80.00
BCP106 Dylan Carlson 50.00 120.00
BCP108 Tarik Skubal 50.00 120.00
BCP112 Joey Bart 20.00 50.00
BCP141 Brennen Davis 30.00 80.00
BCP142 Casey Mize 25.00 60.00
BCP143 Keibert Ruiz 12.00 30.00
BCP144 Jarren Duran 150.00 400.00
BCP145 Robert Puason 200.00 500.00

2020 Bowman Chrome Draft Sapphire

BD1 Niko Hulsizer 3.00 8.00
BD2 Jackson Kowar 4.00 10.00
BD3 Korey Lee 1.50 4.00
BD4 Milan Tolentino 4.00 10.00
BD5 Jeter Downs 2.00 5.00
BD6 Hans Crouse 1.25 3.00
BD7 Mike Siani 1.25 3.00
BD8 Dane Acker 2.00 5.00
BD9 Ryan Jensen 1.50 4.00
BD10 Shane Baz 1.25 3.00
BD11 Trei Cruz 2.00 5.00
BD12 Emerson Hancock 8.00 20.00
BD13 Joey Cantillo 1.25 3.00
BD14 Nick Loftin 3.00 8.00
BD15 Rece Hinds 1.50 4.00
BD16 Jared Shuster 8.00 20.00
BD17 Jesse Franklin V 3.00 8.00
BD18 Kaden Polcovich 2.00 5.00
BD19 Ben Hernandez 2.00 5.00
BD20 Spencer Strider 2.00 5.00
BD21 Tyler Brown 2.00 5.00
BD22 Keoni Cavaco 1.25 3.00
BD23 Case Williams 1.50 4.00
BD24 Cade Cavalli 2.50 6.00
BD25 Burl Carraway 2.50 6.00
BD26 Daniel Espino 1.50 4.00
BD27 Oswald Peraza 3.00 8.00
BD28 Zach DeLoach 5.00 12.00
BD29 Nick Yorke 8.00 20.00
BD30 Clayton Beeter 3.00 8.00
BD31 Joe Ryan 1.50 4.00
BD32 Jordan Groshans 2.50 6.00
BD33 Gage Workman 5.00 12.00
BD34 Austin Hendrick 25.00 60.00
BD35 Jimmy Glowenke 2.50 6.00
BD36 Ryan Rolison 1.50 4.00
BD37 Logan Gilbert 1.50 4.00
BD38 Bobby Miller 5.00 12.00
BD39 Robert Hassell 30.00 60.00
BD40 JJ Goss 1.25 3.00
BD41 Reid Detmers 6.00 15.00
BD42 Michael Busch 3.00 8.00
BD43 Chris McMahon 2.00 5.00
BD44 Xavier Edwards 5.00 12.00
BD45 Alec Burleson 2.00 5.00
BD46 Freddy Zamora 2.00 5.00
BD47 Travis Swaggerty 1.50 4.00
BD48 Sammy Infante 8.00 20.00
BD49 Owen Caissie 6.00 15.00
BD50 Max Meyer 8.00 20.00
BD51 Logan Allen 1.25 3.00
BD52 Landon Knack 3.00 8.00
BD53 Quinn Priester 1.50 4.00
BD54 Colt Keith 6.00 15.00
BD55 Jarren Duran 12.00 30.00
BD56 Austin Wells 12.00 30.00
BD57 Jordan Walker 30.00 80.00
BD58 Jordan Balazovic 2.50 6.00
BD59 Masyn Winn 6.00 15.00
BD60 Carson Tucker 8.00 20.00
BD61 Nick Bitsko 4.00 10.00
BD62 Daniel Cabrera 6.00 15.00
BD63 Marco Raya 2.50 6.00
BD64 Kyle Nicolas 2.00 5.00
BD65 Oneil Cruz 1.50 4.00
BD66 Hunter Barnhart 1.25 3.00
BD67 Cole Henry 1.50 4.00
BD68 Tristen Lutz 1.50 4.00
BD69 Petey Halpin 3.00 8.00
BD70 Jared Jones 2.00 5.00
BD71 Connor Phillips 3.00 8.00
BD72 Pete Crow-Armstrong 20.00 50.00
BD73 Casey Martin 8.00 20.00
BD74 Bryce Bonnin 2.00 5.00
BD75 Daniel Lynch 1.25 3.00
BD76 Tekoah Roby 1.25 3.00
BD77 Isaiah Greene 8.00 20.00
BD78 Tyler Freeman 1.50 4.00
BD79 Heliot Ramos 2.00 5.00
BD80 Miguel Amaya 1.25 3.00
BD81 Nick Gonzales 20.00 50.00
BD82 DL Hall 1.25 3.00
BD83 Triston Casas 3.00 8.00
BD84 Christian Chamberlain 2.00 5.00
BD85 Slade Cecconi 1.50 4.00
BD86 Tink Hence 2.00 5.00
BD87 Adisyn Coffey 1.25 3.00
BD88 Asa Lacy 12.00 30.00
BD89 Geraldo Perdomo 1.25 3.00
BD90 Nick Garcia 2.00 5.00
BD91 Nick Swiney 2.50 6.00
BD92 Matthew Dyer 2.00 5.00
BD93 CJ Van Eyk 2.00 5.00
BD94 Alerick Soularie 1.50 4.00
BD95 Garrett Crochet 12.00 30.00
BD96 Ian Seymour 1.25 3.00
BD97 Zavier Warren 1.25 3.00
BD98 Ed Howard 30.00 80.00
BD99 Justin Lange 1.25 3.00
BD100 Ian Bedell 1.50 4.00
BD101 Aaron Shortridge 1.50 4.00
BD102 Trevor Larnach 2.50 6.00
BD103 David Calabrese 2.50 6.00
BD104 Quin Cotton 1.25 3.00
BD105 Luke Little 2.00 5.00
BD106 Drew Romo 3.00 8.00
BD107 Zac Veen 20.00 50.00
BD108 Brady McConnell 1.50 4.00
BD109 Sam Weatherly 1.25 3.00
BD110 Jordan Nwogu 6.00 15.00
BD111 Jordan Westburg 3.00 8.00
BD112 Zach McCambley 1.25 3.00
BD113 Trevor Hauver 5.00 12.00
BD114 Corbin Carroll 2.00 5.00
BD115 Tanner Burns 2.00 5.00
BD116 Jackson Miller 3.00 8.00
BD117 Carter Baumler 2.00 5.00
BD118 Garrett Mitchell 15.00 40.00
BD119 Tyler Soderstrom 15.00 40.00
BD120 Holden Powell 1.50 4.00
BD121 Spencer Torkelson 100.00 250.00
BD122 Heston Kjerstad 25.00 60.00
BD123 Alexander Canario 1.25 3.00
BD124 Justin Foscue 8.00 20.00
BD125 Levi Prater 1.50 4.00
BD126 Evan Carter 8.00 8.00
BD127 Bryce Jarvis 1.50 4.00
BD128 Werner Blakely 1.50 4.00
BD129 Casey Schmitt 3.00 8.00
BD130 Hudson Haskin 5.00 12.00
BD131 Daxton Fulton 2.00 5.00
BD132 Luis Gil 1.50 4.00
BD133 Zach Daniels 2.00 5.00
BD134 Jeff Criswell 1.50 4.00
BD135 Shane McClanahan 1.50 4.00
BD136 Alika Williams 1.50 4.00
BD137 Gilberto Jimenez 10.00 25.00
BD138 Trent Palmer 1.50 4.00
BD139 Alex Santos 4.00 10.00
BD140 Bryson Stott 3.00 8.00
BD141 Ethan Hankins 1.50 4.00
BD142 Kody Hoese 1.50 4.00
BD143 Francisco Alvarez 10.00 25.00
BD144 Dillon Dingler 6.00 15.00
BD145 Carson Ragsdale 2.00 5.00
BD146 Patrick Bailey 8.00 20.00
BD147 Liam Norris 1.25 3.00
BD148 RJ Dabovich 1.25 3.00

BD149 Carmen Mlodzinski 1.50 4.00
BD150 AJ Vukovich 4.00 10.00
BD151 Jasson Dominguez 60.00 150.00
BD152 Bobby Witt Jr. 25.00 60.00
BD153 Andrew Vaughn 5.00 12.00
BD154 Adley Rutschman 12.00 30.00
BD155 Robert Puason 6.00 15.00
BD156 Jay Groome 1.25 3.00
BD157 Will Klein 1.50 4.00
BD158 Zach Britton 1.50 4.00
BD159 Owen Miller 1.25 3.00
BD160 Logan Hofmann 1.25 3.00
BD161 Ronaldo Hernandez 1.25 3.00
BD162 Jack Blomgren 2.00 5.00
BD163 Adam Seminaris 1.50 4.00
BD164 Bailey Horn 1.50 4.00
BD165 Joe Boyle 2.00 5.00
BD166 Ryan Murphy 1.50 4.00
BD167 Thomas Saggese 1.25 3.00
BD168 George Kirby 2.00 5.00
BD169 Jeremiah Jackson 1.25 3.00
BD170 Shane Drohan 1.50 4.00
BD171 Brandon Pfaadt 1.25 3.00
BD172 Blake Rutherford 1.25 3.00
BD173 Hayden Cantrelle 1.25 3.00
BD174 Mark Vientos 1.25 3.00
BD175 Michael Toglia 1.25 3.00
BD176 Mitchell Parker 1.25 3.00
BD177 Jackson Rutledge 2.00 5.00
BD178 Anthony Volpe 5.00 12.00
BD179 Nick Lodolo 2.00 5.00
BD180 Riley Greene 5.00 12.00
BD181 JJ Bleday 4.00 10.00
BD182 Kyle Isbel 1.25 3.00
BD183 Shea Langeliers 2.50 6.00
BD184 Brett Baty 4.00 10.00
BD185 Jerar Encarnacion 4.00 10.00
BD186 Aaron Ashby 1.25 3.00
BD187 Brennen Davis 2.50 6.00
BD188 Julio Rodriguez 8.00 20.00
BD189 CJ Abrams 8.00 20.00
BD190 Marco Luciano 10.00 25.00
BD191 Grayson Rodriguez 2.00 5.00
BD192 Kristian Robinson 4.00 10.00
BD193 Jordyn Adams 1.50 4.00
BD194 Nolan Gorman 2.50 6.00
BD195 Alek Thomas 1.50 4.00
BD196 Hunter Greene 2.00 5.00
BD197 Josh Jung 3.00 8.00
BD198 Matthew Liberatore 1.50 4.00
BD199 Ronny Mauricio 3.00 8.00
BD200 Hunter Bishop 2.50 6.00

2020 Bowman Chrome Draft Sapphire Aqua

*AQUA: 1X TO 2.5X BASIC
STATED ODDS 1:6 HOBBY
STATED PRINT RUN 20 SER.#'d SETS
BD12 Emerson Hancock 50.00 120.00
BD17 Jesse Franklin V 50.00 120.00
BD34 Austin Hendrick 75.00 200.00
BD38 Bobby Miller 25.00 60.00
BD39 Robert Hassell 100.00 250.00
BD49 Owen Caissie 60.00 150.00
BD50 Max Meyer 40.00 100.00
BD56 Austin Wells 100.00 250.00
BD57 Jordan Walker 100.00 250.00
BD59 Masyn Winn 25.00 60.00
BD60 Carson Tucker 75.00 200.00
BD62 Daniel Cabrera 50.00 120.00
BD72 Pete Crow-Armstrong 150.00 400.00
BD73 Casey Martin 60.00 150.00
BD81 Nick Gonzales 125.00 300.00
BD88 Asa Lacy 100.00 250.00
BD95 Garrett Crochet 75.00 200.00
BD98 Ed Howard 200.00 500.00
BD110 Jordan Nwogu 50.00 120.00
BD119 Tyler Soderstrom 75.00 200.00
BD121 Spencer Torkelson 600.00 1200.00
BD122 Heston Kjerstad 125.00 300.00
BD124 Justin Foscue 50.00 120.00
BD136 Alika Williams 20.00 50.00
BD137 Gilberto Jimenez 30.00 80.00
BD140 Bryson Stott 30.00 80.00
BD143 Francisco Alvarez 50.00 120.00
BD144 Dillon Dingler 25.00 60.00
BD146 Patrick Bailey 30.00 80.00
BD150 AJ Vukovich 100.00 250.00
BD151 Jasson Dominguez 200.00 500.00
BD152 Bobby Witt Jr. 75.00 200.00
BD153 Andrew Vaughn 25.00 60.00
BD178 Anthony Volpe 40.00 100.00
BD180 Riley Greene 25.00 60.00
BD188 Julio Rodriguez 40.00 100.00
BD190 Marco Luciano 50.00 120.00
BD196 Hunter Greene 8.00 20.00
BD197 Josh Jung 15.00 40.00

2020 Bowman Chrome Draft Sapphire Green

*GREEN: .6X TO 1.5X BASIC
STATED ODDS 1:3 HOBBY
STATED PRINT RUN 50 SER.#'d SETS
BD12 Emerson Hancock 30.00 80.00
BD17 Jesse Franklin V 30.00 80.00
BD34 Austin Hendrick 50.00 120.00
BD38 Bobby Miller 15.00 40.00
BD39 Robert Hassell 60.00 150.00
BD49 Owen Caissie 40.00 100.00
BD50 Max Meyer 25.00 60.00
BD56 Austin Wells 50.00 120.00
BD57 Jordan Walker 60.00 150.00
BD59 Masyn Winn 15.00 40.00
BD60 Carson Tucker 50.00 120.00
BD62 Daniel Cabrera 25.00 60.00
BD72 Pete Crow-Armstrong 100.00 250.00
BD73 Casey Martin 25.00 60.00
BD81 Nick Gonzales 75.00 200.00
BD88 Asa Lacy 50.00 120.00
BD95 Garrett Crochet 50.00 120.00
BD98 Ed Howard 125.00 300.00
BD110 Jordan Nwogu 25.00 60.00
BD119 Tyler Soderstrom 50.00 120.00
BD121 Spencer Torkelson 250.00 600.00
BD122 Heston Kjerstad 75.00 200.00
BD124 Justin Foscue 25.00 60.00
BD137 Gilberto Jimenez 20.00 50.00
BD140 Bryson Stott 20.00 50.00
BD143 Francisco Alvarez 30.00 80.00
BD144 Dillon Dingler 15.00 40.00
BD146 Patrick Bailey 20.00 50.00
BD150 AJ Vukovich 40.00 100.00
BD151 Jasson Dominguez 125.00 300.00
BD152 Bobby Witt Jr. 50.00 120.00
BD153 Andrew Vaughn 15.00 40.00
BD180 Riley Greene 15.00 40.00
BD188 Julio Rodriguez 25.00 60.00
BD190 Marco Luciano 30.00 80.00
BD197 Josh Jung 10.00 25.00

2020 Bowman Chrome Draft Sapphire Orange

*ORANGE: 1X TO 2.5X BASIC
STATED ODDS 1:5 HOBBY
STATED PRINT RUN 25 SER.#'d SETS
BD12 Emerson Hancock 50.00 120.00
BD17 Jesse Franklin V 50.00 120.00
BD34 Austin Hendrick 75.00 200.00
BD38 Bobby Miller 25.00 60.00
BD39 Robert Hassell 100.00 250.00
BD49 Owen Caissie 60.00 150.00
BD50 Max Meyer 40.00 100.00
BD56 Austin Wells 100.00 250.00
BD57 Jordan Walker 100.00 250.00
BD59 Masyn Winn 25.00 60.00
BD60 Carson Tucker 75.00 200.00
BD62 Daniel Cabrera 50.00 120.00
BD72 Pete Crow-Armstrong 150.00 400.00
BD73 Casey Martin 60.00 150.00
BD81 Nick Gonzales 125.00 300.00
BD88 Asa Lacy 100.00 250.00
BD95 Garrett Crochet 75.00 200.00
BD98 Ed Howard 200.00 500.00
BD110 Jordan Nwogu 50.00 120.00
BD119 Tyler Soderstrom 75.00 200.00
BD121 Spencer Torkelson 600.00 1200.00
BD122 Heston Kjerstad 125.00 300.00
BD124 Justin Foscue 50.00 120.00
BD136 Alika Williams 20.00 50.00
BD137 Gilberto Jimenez 30.00 80.00
BD140 Bryson Stott 30.00 80.00
BD143 Francisco Alvarez 50.00 120.00
BD144 Dillon Dingler 25.00 60.00
BD146 Patrick Bailey 30.00 80.00
BD150 AJ Vukovich 100.00 250.00
BD151 Jasson Dominguez 200.00 500.00
BD152 Bobby Witt Jr. 75.00 200.00
BD153 Andrew Vaughn 25.00 60.00
BD178 Anthony Volpe 40.00 100.00
BD180 Riley Greene 25.00 60.00
BD188 Julio Rodriguez 40.00 100.00
BD190 Marco Luciano 50.00 120.00
BD196 Hunter Greene 8.00 20.00
BD197 Josh Jung 15.00 40.00

2020 Bowman Chrome Draft Sapphire Yellow

*YELLOW: .5X TO 1.2X BASIC
STATED ODDS 1:2 HOBBY
STATED PRINT RUN 99 SER.#'d SETS
BD12 Emerson Hancock 25.00 60.00
BD17 Jesse Franklin V 25.00 60.00
BD34 Austin Hendrick 40.00 100.00
BD38 Bobby Miller 12.00 30.00
BD39 Robert Hassell 50.00 120.00
BD49 Owen Caissie 30.00 80.00
BD56 Austin Wells 40.00 100.00
BD57 Jordan Walker 50.00 120.00
BD59 Masyn Winn 12.00 30.00
BD60 Carson Tucker 40.00 100.00
BD62 Daniel Cabrera 20.00 50.00
BD72 Pete Crow-Armstrong 75.00 200.00
BD73 Casey Martin 20.00 50.00
BD81 Nick Gonzales 60.00 150.00
BD88 Asa Lacy 30.00 80.00
BD95 Garrett Crochet 40.00 100.00
BD98 Ed Howard 100.00 250.00
BD110 Jordan Nwogu 20.00 50.00
BD119 Tyler Soderstrom 40.00 100.00
BD121 Spencer Torkelson 200.00 500.00
BD122 Heston Kjerstad 40.00 100.00
BD124 Justin Foscue 20.00 50.00
BD137 Gilberto Jimenez 15.00 40.00
BD143 Francisco Alvarez 25.00 60.00
BD144 Dillon Dingler 12.00 30.00
BD146 Patrick Bailey 15.00 40.00
BD150 AJ Vukovich 30.00 80.00
BD151 Jasson Dominguez 100.00 250.00
BD152 Bobby Witt Jr. 40.00 100.00
BD153 Andrew Vaughn 12.00 30.00
BD180 Riley Greene 12.00 30.00
BD188 Julio Rodriguez 20.00 50.00
BD190 Marco Luciano 25.00 60.00
BD197 Josh Jung 8.00 20.00

2001 Bowman Heritage Promos

COMPLETE SET (5) 90.00 150.00
ONE SET PER ATTENDEE AT CLE NAT'L
STATED PRINT RUN 500 SETS
PRINT RUN INFO PROVIDED BY TOPPS
1 Roberto Alomar 4.00 10.00
2 Albert Pujols 60.00 150.00
3 C.C. Sabathia 4.00 10.00
4 Mark McGwire 10.00 25.00
5 Juan Gonzalez 3.20 8.00

2001 Bowman Heritage

COMPLETE SET (440) 125.00 200.00
COMP.SET w/o SP's (330) 20.00 50.00
COMMON CARD (1-330) .15 .40
COMMON RC (1-330) .15 .40
COMMON CARD (331-440) .75 2.00
SP STATED ODDS 1:2
VINTAGE BUYBACK ODDS 1:24,481
1 Chipper Jones .40 1.00
2 Pete Harnisch .15 .40
3 Brian Giles .15 .40
4 J.T. Snow .15 .40
5 Bartolo Colon .15 .40
6 Jorge Posada .25 .60
7 Shawn Green .15 .40
8 Derek Jeter 1.00 2.50
9 Benito Santiago .15 .40
10 Ramon Hernandez .15 .40
11 Bernie Williams .25 .60
12 Greg Maddux .60 1.50
13 Barry Bonds 1.00 2.50
14 Roger Clemens .75 2.00
15 Miguel Tejada .15 .40
16 Pedro Feliz .15 .40
17 Jim Edmonds .15 .40
18 Tom Glavine .25 .60
19 David Justice .15 .40
20 Rich Aurilia .15 .40
21 Jason Giambi .15 .40
22 Orlando Hernandez .15 .40
23 Shawn Estes .15 .40
24 Nelson Figueroa .15 .40
25 Terrence Long .15 .40
26 Mike Mussina .25 .60
27 Eric Davis .15 .40
28 Jimmy Rollins .15 .40
29 Andy Pettitte .25 .60
30 Shawon Dunston .15 .40
31 Tim Hudson .15 .40
32 Jeff Kent .15 .40
33 Scott Brosius .15 .40
34 Livan Hernandez .15 .40
35 Alfonso Soriano .25 .60
36 Mark McGwire 1.00 2.50
37 Russ Ortiz .15 .40
38 Fernando Vina .15 .40
39 Ken Griffey Jr. .75 2.00
40 Edgar Renteria .15 .40
41 Kevin Brown .15 .40
42 Robb Nen .15 .40
43 Paul LoDuca .15 .40
44 Bobby Abreu .15 .40
45 Adam Dunn .25 .60
46 Osvaldo Fernandez .15 .40
47 Marvin Benard .15 .40
48 Mark Gardner .15 .40
49 Alex Rodriguez .50 1.25
50 Preston Wilson .15 .40
51 Roberto Alomar .25 .60
52 Ben Davis .15 .40
53 Derek Bell .15 .40
54 Ken Caminiti .15 .40
55 Barry Zito .25 .60
56 Scott Rolen .25 .60
57 Geoff Jenkins .15 .40
58 Mike Cameron .15 .40
59 Ben Grieve .15 .40
60 Chuck Knoblauch .15 .40
61 Matt Lawton .15 .40
62 Chan Ho Park .15 .40
63 Lance Berkman .15 .40
64 Carlos Beltran .15 .40
65 Dean Palmer .15 .40
66 Alex Gonzalez .15 .40
67 Larry Walker .15 .40
68 Magglio Ordonez .15 .40
69 Ellis Burks .15 .40
70 Mark Mulder .15 .40
71 Randy Johnson .40 1.00
72 John Smoltz .25 .60
73 Jerry Hairston Jr. .15 .40
74 Pedro Martinez .25 .60
75 Fred McGriff .25 .60
76 Sean Casey .15 .40
77 C.C. Sabathia .15 .40
78 Todd Helton .25 .60
79 Brad Penny .15 .40
80 Mike Sweeney .15 .40
81 Billy Wagner .15 .40
82 Mark Buehrle .25 .60
83 Cristian Guzman .15 .40
84 Jose Vidro .15 .40
85 Pat Burrell .15 .40
86 Jermaine Dye .15 .40
87 Brandon Inge .15 .40
88 David Wells .15 .40
89 Mike Piazza .60 1.50
90 Jose Cabrera .15 .40
91 Cliff Floyd .15 .40
92 Matt Morris .15 .40
93 Raul Mondesi .15 .40
94 Joe Kennedy RC .25 .60
95 Jack Wilson RC .25 .60
96 Andruw Jones .25 .60
97 Mariano Rivera .40 1.00
98 Mike Hampton .15 .40
99 Roger Cedeno .15 .40
100 Jose Cruz .15 .40
101 Mike Lowell .15 .40
102 Pedro Astacio .15 .40
103 Joe Mays .15 .40
104 John Franco .15 .40
105 Tim Redding .15 .40
106 Sandy Alomar Jr. .15 .40
107 Bret Boone .15 .40
108 Josh Towers RC .25 .60
109 Matt Stairs .15 .40
110 Chris Truby .15 .40
111 Jeff Suppan .15 .40
112 J.C. Romero .15 .40
113 Felipe Lopez .15 .40
114 Ben Sheets .25 .60
115 Frank Thomas .40 1.00
116 A.J. Burnett .15 .40
117 Tony Clark .15 .40
118 Mac Suzuki .15 .40
119 Brad Radke .15 .40
120 Jeff Shaw .15 .40
121 Nick Neugebauer .15 .40
122 Kenny Lofton .15 .40
123 Jacque Jones .15 .40
124 Brent Mayne .15 .40
125 Carlos Hernandez .15 .40
126 Shane Spencer .15 .40
127 John Lackey .15 .40
128 Sterling Hitchcock .15 .40
129 Darren Dreifort .15 .40
130 Rusty Greer .15 .40
131 Michael Cuddyer .15 .40
132 Tyler Houston .15 .40
133 Chin-Feng Chen .15 .40
134 Ken Harvey .15 .40
135 Marquis Grissom .15 .40
136 Russell Branyan .15 .40
137 Eric Karros .15 .40
138 Josh Beckett .25 .60
139 Todd Zeile .15 .40
140 Corey Koskie .15 .40
141 Steve Sparks .15 .40
142 Bobby Seay .15 .40
143 Tim Raines Jr. .15 .40
144 Julio Zuleta .15 .40
145 Jose Lima .15 .40
146 Dante Bichette .15 .40
147 Randy Keisler .15 .40
148 Brent Butler .15 .40
149 Antonio Alfonseca .15 .40
150 Bryan Rekar .15 .40
151 Jeffrey Hammonds .15 .40
152 Larry Bigbie .15 .40
153 Blake Stein .15 .40
154 Robin Ventura .15 .40
155 Rondell White .15 .40
156 Juan Silvestre .15 .40
157 Marcus Thames .15 .40
158 Sidney Ponson .15 .40
159 Juan A. Pena RC .15 .40
160 C.J. Nitkowski .15 .40
161 Adam Everett .15 .40
162 Eric Munson .15 .40
163 Jason Isringhausen .15 .40
164 Brad Fullmer .15 .40
165 Miguel Olivo .15 .40
166 Fernando Tatis .15 .40
167 Freddy Garcia .15 .40
168 Tom Goodwin .15 .40
169 Armando Benitez .15 .40
170 Paul Konerko .15 .40
171 Jeff Cirillo .15 .40
172 Shane Reynolds .15 .40
173 Kevin Tapani .15 .40
174 Joe Crede .40 1.00
175 Omar Infante RC 1.25 3.00
176 Jake Peavy RC 1.00 2.50
177 Corey Patterson .15 .40
178 Mike Penney RC .15 .40
179 Jeromy Burnitz .15 .40
180 David Segui .15 .40
181 Marcus Giles .15 .40
182 Paul O'Neill .25 .60
183 John Olerud .15 .40
184 Andy Benes .15 .40
185 Brad Cresse .15 .40
186 Ricky Ledee .15 .40
187 Allen Levrault UER .15 .40
188 Royce Clayton .15 .40
189 Kelly Johnson RC 1.25 3.00
190 Quilvio Veras .15 .40
191 Mike Williams .15 .40
192 Jason Lane RC .25 .60
193 Rick Helling .15 .40
194 Tim Wakefield .15 .40
195 James Baldwin .15 .40
196 Cody Ransom RC .15 .40
197 Bobby Kielty .15 .40
198 Bobby Jones .15 .40
199 Steve Cox .15 .40
200 Jamal Strong RC .15 .40
201 Steve Lomasney .15 .40
202 Brian Cardwell RC .15 .40
203 Mike Matheny .15 .40
204 Jeff Randazzo RC .15 .40
205 Aubrey Huff .15 .40
206 Chuck Finley .15 .40
207 Denny Bautista RC .25 .60
208 Terry Mulholland .15 .40
209 Rey Ordonez .15 .40
210 Keith Surkont RC .15 .40
211 Orlando Cabrera .15 .40
212 Juan Encarnacion .15 .40
213 Dustin Hermanson .15 .40
214 Luis Rivas .15 .40
215 Mark Quinn .15 .40
216 Randy Velarde .15 .40
217 Billy Koch .15 .40
218 Ryan Rupe .15 .40
219 Keith Ginter .15 .40
220 Woody Williams .15 .40
221 Ryan Franklin .15 .40
222 Aaron Myette .15 .40
223 Joe Borchard RC .15 .40
224 Nate Cornejo .15 .40
225 Julian Tavarez .15 .40
226 Kevin Millwood .15 .40
227 Travis Hafner RC 2.00 5.00
228 Charles Nagy .15 .40
229 Mike Lieberthal .15 .40
230 Jeff Nelson .15 .40
231 Ryan Dempster .15 .40
232 Andres Galarraga .15 .40
233 Chad Durbin .15 .40
234 Timo Perez .15 .40
235 Troy O'Leary .15 .40
236 Kevin Young .15 .40
237 Gabe Kapler .15 .40
238 Juan Cruz RC .15 .40
239 Masato Yoshii .15 .40
240 Aramis Ramirez .15 .40
241 Matt Cooper RC .15 .40
242 Randy Flores RC .15 .40
243 Rafael Furcal .15 .40
244 David Eckstein .15 .40
245 Matt Clement .15 .40
246 Craig Biggio .25 .60
247 Rick Reed .15 .40
248 Jose Macias .15 .40
249 Alex Escobar .15 .40
250 Roberto Hernandez .15 .40
251 Andy Ashby .15 .40
252 Tony Armas Jr. .15 .40
253 Jamie Moyer .15 .40
254 Jason Tyner .15 .40
255 Charles Kegley RC .15 .40
256 Jeff Conine .15 .40
257 Francisco Cordova .15 .40
258 Ted Lilly .15 .40
259 Joe Randa .15 .40
260 Jeff D'Amico .15 .40
261 Albie Lopez .15 .40
262 Kevin Appier .15 .40
263 Richard Hidalgo .15 .40
264 Omar Daal .15 .40
265 Ricky Gutierrez .15 .40
266 John Rocker .15 .40
267 Ray Lankford .15 .40
268 Beau Hale RC .15 .40
269 Tony Blanco RC .15 .40
270 Derrek Lee UER .25 .60
271 Jamey Wright .15 .40
272 Alex Gordon .15 .40
273 Jeff Weaver .15 .40
274 Jaret Wright .15 .40
275 Jose Hernandez .15 .40
276 Bruce Chen .15 .40
277 Todd Hollandsworth .15 .40
278 Wade Miller .15 .40
279 Luke Prokopec .15 .40
280 Rafael Soriano RC .15 .40
281 Damion Easley .15 .40
282 Darren Oliver .15 .40
283 Brandon Duckworth RC .15 .40
284 Aaron Herr .15 .40
285 Ray Durham .15 .40
286 Wilmy Caceras RC .15 .40
287 Ugueth Urbina .15 .40
288 Scott Seabol .15 .40
289 Lance Niekro RC .25 .60
290 Trot Nixon .15 .40
291 Adam Kennedy .15 .40
292 Brian Schmitt RC .15 .40
293 Grant Roberts .15 .40
294 Benny Agbayani .15 .40
295 Travis Lee .15 .40
296 Erick Almonte RC .15 .40
297 Jim Thome .25 .60
298 Eric Young .15 .40
299 Dan Denham RC .15 .40
300 Boof Bonser RC .15 .40
301 Denny Neagle .15 .40
302 Kenny Rogers .15 .40
303 J.D. Closser .15 .40
304 Chase Utley RC 6.00 15.00
305 Rey Sanchez .15 .40
306 Sean McGowan .15 .40
307 Justin Pope RC .15 .40
308 Torii Hunter .15 .40
309 B.J. Surhoff .15 .40
310 Aaron Heilman RC .20 .50
311 Gabe Gross RC .25 .60
312 Lee Stevens .15 .40
313 Todd Hundley .15 .40
314 Macay McBride RC .40 1.00
315 Edgar Martinez .25 .60
316 Omar Vizquel .25 .60
317 Reggie Sanders .15 .40
318 John-Ford Griffin RC .15 .40
319 T.Salmon UER Glaus Photo .15 .40
320 Pokey Reese .15 .40
321 Jay Payton .15 .40
322 Doug Glanville .15 .40
323 Greg Vaughn .15 .40
324 Ruben Sierra .15 .40
325 Kip Wells .15 .40
326 Carl Everett .15 .40
327 Garret Anderson .15 .40
328 Jay Bell .15 .40
329 Barry Larkin .25 .60
330 Jeff Mathis RC .25 .60
331 Adrian Gonzalez SP 5.00 12.00
332 Juan Rivera SP .75 2.00
333 Tony Alvarez SP .75 2.00
334 Xavier Nady SP .75 2.00
335 Josh Hamilton 1.50 4.00
336 Will Smith SP RC .75 2.00
337 Israel Alcantara SP .75 2.00
338 Chris George SP .75 2.00
339 Sean Burroughs SP .75 2.00
340 Jack Cust SP .75 2.00
341 Henry Mateo SP RC .75 2.00
342 Carlos Pena SP .75 2.00
343 J.R. House SP .75 2.00
344 Carlos Silva SP .75 2.00
345 Mike Rivera SP RC .75 2.00
346 Adam Johnson SP .75 2.00
347 Scott Heard SP .75 2.00
348 Alex Cintron SP .75 2.00
349 Miguel Cabrera SP 15.00 40.00
350 Nick Johnson SP .75 2.00
351 Albert Pujols SP RC 30.00 80.00
352 Ichiro Suzuki SP RC 8.00 20.00
353 Carlos Delgado SP .75 2.00
354 Troy Glaus SP .75 2.00
355 Sammy Sosa SP 1.25 3.00
356 Ivan Rodriguez SP 1.25 3.00
357 Vladimir Guerrero SP 1.25 3.00
358 Manny Ramirez Sox SP 1.25 3.00
359 Luis Gonzalez SP .75 2.00
360 Roy Oswalt SP 1.25 3.00
361 Moises Alou SP .75 2.00
362 Juan Gonzalez SP .75 2.00
363 Tony Gwynn SP 1.50 4.00
364 Hideo Nomo SP 1.25 3.00
365 Tsuyoshi Shinjo SP RC 1.25 3.00
366 Kazuhiro Sasaki SP .75 2.00
367 Cal Ripken SP 4.00 10.00
368 Rafael Palmeiro SP 1.25 3.00
369 J.D. Drew SP .75 2.00
370 Doug Mientkiewicz SP .75 2.00
371 Jeff Bagwell SP 1.25 3.00
372 Darin Erstad SP .75 2.00
373 Tom Gordon SP .75 2.00
374 Ben Petrick SP .75 2.00
375 Eric Milton SP .75 2.00
376 Nomar Garciaparra SP 2.00 5.00
377 Julio Lugo SP .75 2.00
378 Tino Martinez SP 1.25 3.00
379 Javier Vazquez SP .75 2.00
380 Jeremy Giambi SP .75 2.00
381 Marty Cordova SP .75 2.00
382 Adrian Beltre SP .75 2.00
383 John Burkett SP .75 2.00
384 Aaron Boone SP .75 2.00
385 Eric Chavez SP .75 2.00
386 Curt Schilling SP .75 2.00
387 Cory Lidle UER SP .75 2.00
388 Jason Schmidt SP .75 2.00
389 Johnny Damon SP 1.25 3.00
390 Steve Finley SP .75 2.00
391 Edgardo Alfonzo SP .75 2.00
392 Jose Valentin SP .75 2.00
393 Jose Canseco SP 1.25 3.00
394 Ryan Klesko SP .75 2.00
395 David Cone SP .75 2.00
396 Jason Kendall UER SP .75 2.00
397 Placido Polanco SP .75 2.00
398 Glendon Rusch SP .75 2.00
399 Aaron Sele SP .75 2.00
400 D'Angelo Jimenez SP .75 2.00
401 Mark Grace SP 1.25 3.00
402 Al Leiter SP .75 2.00
403 Brian Jordan SP .75 2.00
404 Phil Nevin SP .75 2.00
405 Brent Abernathy SP .75 2.00
406 Kerry Wood SP .75 2.00
407 Alex Gonzalez SP .75 2.00
408 Robert Fick SP .75 2.00
409 Dmitri Young UER SP .75 2.00
410 Wes Helms SP .75 2.00
411 Trevor Hoffman SP .75 2.00
412 Rickey Henderson SP 1.25 3.00
413 Bobby Higginson SP .75 2.00
414 Gary Sheffield SP .75 2.00
415 Darryl Kile SP .75 2.00
416 Richie Sexson SP .75 2.00
417 Frank Menechino SP RC .75 2.00
418 Javy Lopez SP .75 2.00
419 Carlos Lee SP .75 2.00
420 Jon Lieber SP .75 2.00
421 Hank Blalock SP RC 1.25 3.00
422 Marlon Byrd SP RC 1.25 3.00
423 Jason Kinchen SP RC .75 2.00
424 Morgan Ensberg SP RC 2.00 5.00
425 Greg Nash SP RC .75 2.00
426 Dennis Tankersley SP RC .75 2.00
427 Nate Murphy SP RC .75 2.00
428 Chris Smith SP RC .75 2.00
429 Jake Gautreau SP RC .75 2.00
430 John VanBenschoten SP RC .75 2.00
431 Travis Thompson SP RC .75 2.00
432 Orlando Hudson SP RC 1.25 3.00
433 Jerome Williams SP RC 1.25 3.00
434 Kevin Reese SP RC .75 2.00
435 Ed Rogers SP RC .75 2.00
436 Ryan Jamison SP RC .75 2.00
437 Adam Pettyjohn SP RC .75 2.00
438 Hee Seop Choi SP RC 1.25 3.00
439 Justin Morneau SP RC 5.00 12.00
440 Mitch Jones SP RC .75 2.00

2001 Bowman Heritage Chrome

*CHROME STARS: 4X TO 10X BASIC CARDS
*CHROME RC'S: 2.5X TO 6X BASIC CARDS
STATED ODDS 1:12

2001 Bowman Heritage '48 Reprints

COMPLETE SET (13) 4.00 10.00
STATED ODDS 1:2
1 Ralph Kiner .40 1.00
2 Johnny Mize .40 1.00
3 Bobby Thomson .40 1.00
4 Yogi Berra .60 1.50
5 Phil Rizzuto .50 1.25
6 Bob Feller .40 1.00
7 Enos Slaughter .40 1.00
8 Stan Musial .75 2.00
9 Hank Sauer .40 1.00
10 Ferris Fain .40 1.00
11 Red Schoendienst .40 1.00
12 Allie Reynolds .40 1.00
13 Johnny Sain .40 1.00

2001 Bowman Heritage '48 Reprints Autographs

GROUP 1 ODDS 1:3,018
GROUP 2 ODDS 1:3,074
OVERALL ODDS 1:1,523
1 Warren Spahn 1 30.00 80.00
2 Bob Feller 2 30.00 80.00

2001 Bowman Heritage '48 Reprints Relics

BAT ODDS 1:2,113
JERSEY ODDS 1:2,905
SEAT GROUP A ODDS 1:97
SEAT GROUP B ODDS 1:194
SEAT GROUP C ODDS 1:291
SEAT OVERALL ODDS 1:53
BHMBF Bob Feller Seat A 6.00 15.00
BHMBT Bobby Thomson Seat C 6.00 15.00
BHMES Enos Slaughter Seat C 6.00 15.00
BHMFF Ferris Fain Seat A 6.00 15.00
BHMHS Hank Sauer Seat A 6.00 15.00
BHMJM Johnny Mize Seat C 8.00 20.00
BHMPR Phil Rizzuto Seat B 8.00 20.00
BHMRK Ralph Kiner Seat B 6.00 15.00
BHMRS Red Schoendienst Bat 6.00 15.00
BHMSM1 Stan Musial Seat C 12.50 30.00
BHMYB1 Yogi Berra Seat B 10.00 25.00
BHMYB2 Yogi Berra Jsy 15.00 40.00

2001 Bowman Heritage Autographs

GROUP A ODDS 1:775
GROUP B ODDS 1:664
OVERALL ODDS 1:358
HAAR Alex Rodriguez B 25.00 60.00
HABB Barry Bonds A 40.00 100.00
HARC Roger Clemens A 15.00 40.00

2002 Bowman Heritage

COMP.SET w/o SP's (324) 25.00 50.00
COMMON CARD (1-439) .15 .40
COMMON SP .75 2.00
SP STATED ODDS 1:2
1 Brent Abernathy .15 .40
2 Jermaine Dye .15 .40
3 James Shanks RC .15 .40
4 Chris Flinn RC .15 .40
5 Mike Peeples SP RC .75 2.00
6 Gary Sheffield .15 .40
7 Livan Hernandez SP .75 2.00
8 Jeff Austin RC .15 .40
9 Jeremy Giambi .15 .40
10 Adam Roller RC .15 .40
11 Sandy Alomar Jr. SP .75 2.00
12 Matt Williams SP .75 2.00
13 Hee Seop Choi .15 .40
14 Jose Offerman .15 .40
15 Robin Ventura .15 .40
16 Craig Biggio .25 .60
17 David Wells .15 .40
18 Rob Henkel RC .15 .40
19 Edgar Martinez .25 .60
20 Matt Morris SP .75 2.00
21 Jose Valentin .15 .40
22 Barry Bonds 1.00 2.50
23 Justin Schuda RC .15 .40
24 Josh Phelps .15 .40
25 John Rodriguez RC .20 .50
26 Angel Pagan RC 1.25 3.00
27 Aramis Ramirez .15 .40
28 Jack Wilson .15 .40
29 Roger Clemens .75 2.00
30 Kazuhisa Ishii RC .20 .50
31 Carlos Beltran .15 .40
32 Drew Henson SP .75 2.00
33 Kevin Young SP .75 2.00
34 Juan Cruz SP .75 2.00
35 Curtis Legendre RC .15 .40
36 Jose Morban RC .15 .40
37 Ricardo Cordova SP RC .75 2.00
38 Adam Everett .15 .40
39 Mark Prior .25 .60
40 Jose Bautista RC 3.00 8.00
41 Travis Foley RC .15 .40
42 Kerry Wood .15 .40
43 B.J. Surhoff .15 .40
44 Moises Alou .15 .40
45 Joey Hammond .15 .40
46 Eric Bruntlett RC .15 .40
47 Carlos Guillen .15 .40
48 Joe Crede .15 .40
49 Dan Phillips RC .15 .40
50 Jason LaRue .15 .40
51 Javy Lopez .15 .40
52 Larry Bigbie SP .75 2.00
53 Chris Baker RC .15 .40
54 Marty Cordova .15 .40
55 C.C. Sabathia .15 .40
56 Mike Piazza .60 1.50
57 Brian Giles .15 .40
58 Mike Bordick SP .75 2.00
59 Tyler Houston SP .75 2.00
60 Gabe Kapler .15 .40
61 Ben Broussard .15 .40
62 Steve Finley SP .75 2.00
63 Koyie Hill .15 .40
64 Jeff D'Amico .15 .40
65 Edwin Almonte RC .15 .40
66 Pedro Martinez .25 .60
66B Nomar Garciaparra 66 .60 1.50
67 Travis Fryman SP .75 2.00
68 Brady Clark SP .75 2.00
69 Reed Johnson SP RC 1.50 4.00
70 Mark Grace SP 1.25 3.00
71 Tony Batista SP .75 2.00
72 Roy Oswalt .15 .40
73 Pat Burrell SP .75 2.00
74 Dennis Tankersley .15 .40
75 Ramon Ortiz .15 .40
76 Neal Frendling SP RC .75 2.00
77 Omar Vizquel SP 1.25 3.00
78 Hideo Nomo .40 1.00
79 Orlando Hernandez SP .75 2.00
80 Andy Pettitte .25 .60
81 Cole Barthel RC .15 .40
82 Bret Boone .15 .40
83 Alfonso Soriano .15 .40
84 Brandon Duckworth .15 .40
85 Ben Grieve .15 .40
86 Mike Rosamond SP RC .75 2.00
87 Luke Prokopec .15 .40
88 Chone Figgins RC .60 1.50
89 Rick Ankiel SP .75 2.00
90 David Eckstein .15 .40
91 Corey Koskie .15 .40
92 David Justice .15 .40
93 Jimmy Alvarez RC .15 .40
94 Jason Schmidt .15 .40
95 Reggie Sanders .15 .40
96 Victor Alvarez RC .15 .40
97 Brett Roneberg RC .15 .40
98 D'Angelo Jimenez .15 .40
99 Hank Blalock .25 .60
100 Juan Rivera .15 .40
101 Mark Buehrle SP .75 2.00
102 Juan Uribe .15 .40
103 Royce Clayton SP .75 2.00
104 Brett Kay RC .15 .40
105 John Olerud .15 .40
106 Richie Sexson .15 .40
107 Chipper Jones .40 1.00
108 Adam Dunn .15 .40
109 Tim Salmon SP 1.25 3.00
110 Eric Karros .15 .40
111 Jose Vidro .15 .40
112 Jerry Hairston Jr. .15 .40
113 Anastacio Martinez RC .15 .40
114 Robert Fick SP .75 2.00
115 Randy Johnson .40 1.00
116 Trot Nixon SP .75 2.00
117 Nick Bierbrodt SP .75 2.00
118 Jim Edmonds .15 .40
119 Rafael Palmeiro .25 .60
120 Jose Macias .15 .40
121 Josh Beckett .15 .40
122 Sean Douglass .15 .40
123 Jeff Kent .15 .40
124 Tim Redding .15 .40

125 Xavier Nady	.15	.40
126 Carl Everett	.15	.40
127 Joe Randa	.15	.40
128 Luke Hudson SP	.75	2.00
129 Eric Miller RC	.15	.40
130 Melvin Mora	.15	.40
131 Adrian Gonzalez	.15	.40
132 Larry Walker SP	.75	2.00
133 Nic Jackson SP RC	.75	2.00
134 Mike Lowell SP	.75	2.00
135 Jim Thome	.25	.60
136 Eric Milton	.15	.40
137 Rich Thompson SP RC	.75	2.00
138 Placido Polanco SP	.75	2.00
139 Juan Pierre	.15	.40
140 David Segui	.15	.40
141 Chuck Finley	.15	.40
142 Felipe Lopez	.15	.40
143 Toby Hall	.15	.40
144 Fred Bastardo RC	.15	.40
145 Troy Glaus	.15	.40
146 Todd Helton	.25	.60
147 Ruben Gotay SP RC	1.25	3.00
148 Darin Erstad	.15	.40
149 Ryan Gripp SP RC	.75	2.00
150 Orlando Cabrera	.15	.40
151 Jason Young RC	.15	.40
152 Sterling Hitchcock SP	.75	2.00
153 Miguel Tejada	.15	.40
154 Al Leiter	.15	.40
155 Taylor Buchholz RC	.20	.50
156 Juan M. Gonzalez RC	.15	.40
157 Damion Easley	.15	.40
158 Jimmy Gobble RC	.15	.40
159 Dennis Ulacia SP RC	.75	2.00
160 Shane Reynolds SP	.75	2.00
161 Javier Colina	.15	.40
162 Frank Thomas	.40	1.00
163 Chuck Knoblauch	.15	.40
164 Sean Burroughs	.15	.40
165 Greg Maddux	.60	1.50
166 Jason Ellison RC	.30	.75
167 Tony Womack	.15	.40
168 Randall Shelley SP RC	.75	2.00
169 Jason Marquis	.15	.40
170 Brian Jordan	.15	.40
171 Vicente Padilla	.15	.40
172 Barry Zito	.15	.40
173 Matt Allegra SP RC	.75	2.00
174 Ralph Santana SP RC	.75	2.00
175 Carlos Lee	.15	.40
176 Richard Hidalgo SP	.75	2.00
177 Kevin Deaton RC	.15	.40
178 Juan Encarnacion	.15	.40
179 Mark Quinn	.15	.40
180 Rafael Furcal	.15	.40
181 G.Anderson UER Figgins	.15	.40
182 David Wright RC	4.00	10.00
183 Jose Reyes	.25	.60
184 Mario Ramos SP RC	.75	2.00
185 J.D. Drew	.15	.40
186 Juan Gonzalez	.15	.40
187 Nick Neugebauer	.15	.40
188 Alejandro Giron RC	.15	.40
189 John Burkett	.15	.40
190 Ben Sheets	.15	.40
191 Vinny Castilla SP	.75	2.00
192 Cory Lidle	.15	.40
193 Fernando Vina	.15	.40
194 Russell Branyan SP	.75	2.00
195 Ben Davis	.15	.40
196 Angel Berroa	.15	.40
197 Alex Gonzalez	.15	.40
198 Jared Sandberg	.15	.40
199 Travis Lee SP	.75	2.00
200 Luis DePaula SP RC	.75	2.00
201 Ramon Hernandez SP	.75	2.00
202 Brandon Inge	.15	.40
203 Aubrey Huff	.15	.40
204 Mike Rivera	.15	.40
205 Brad Nelson RC	.15	.40
206 Colt Griffin SP RC	.75	2.00
207 Joel Pineiro	.15	.40
208 Adam Pettyjohn	.15	.40
209 Mark Redman	.15	.40
210 Roberto Alomar SP	1.25	3.00
211 Denny Neagle	.15	.40
212 Adam Kennedy	.15	.40
213 Jason Arnold SP RC	.75	2.00
214 Jamie Moyer	.15	.40
215 Aaron Boone	.15	.40
216 Doug Glanville	.15	.40
217 Nick Johnson SP	.75	2.00
218 Mike Cameron SP	.75	2.00
219 Tim Wakefield SP	.75	2.00
220 Todd Stottlemyre SP	.75	2.00
221 Mo Vaughn SP	.75	2.00
222 Vladimir Guerrero	.40	1.00
223 Bill Ortega	.15	.40
224 Kevin Brown	.15	.40
225 Peter Bergeron SP	.75	2.00
226 Shannon Stewart SP	.75	2.00
227 Eric Chavez	.15	.40
228 Clint Weibl RC	.15	.40
229 Todd Hollandsworth SP	.75	2.00
230 Jeff Bagwell	.25	.60
231 Chad Qualls RC	.20	.50
232 Ben Howard RC	.15	.40
233 Rondell White SP	.75	2.00
234 Fred McGriff	.25	.60
235 Steve Cox SP	.75	2.00
236 Chris Tritle RC	.15	.40
237 Eric Valent	.15	.40
238 Joe Mauer RC	3.00	8.00
239 Shawn Green	.15	.40
240 Jimmy Rollins	.15	.40
241 Edgar Renteria	.15	.40
242 Edwin Yan RC	.15	.40
243 Noochie Varner RC	.15	.40
244 Kris Benson SP	.75	2.00
245 Mike Hampton	.15	.40
246 So Taguchi RC	.20	.50
247 Sammy Sosa	.40	1.00
248 Terrence Long	.15	.40
249 Jason Bay RC	2.00	5.00
250 Kevin Millar SP	.75	2.00
251 Albert Pujols	.75	2.00
252 Chris Latham RC	.15	.40
253 Eric Byrnes	.15	.40
254 Napoleon Calzado SP RC	.75	2.00
255 Bobby Higginson	.15	.40
256 Ben Molina	.15	.40
257 Torii Hunter SP	.75	2.00
258 Jason Giambi	.15	.40
259 Bartolo Colon	.15	.40
260 Benito Baez	.15	.40
261 Ichiro Suzuki	.75	2.00
262 Mike Sweeney	.15	.40
263 Brian West RC	.15	.40
264 Brad Penny	.15	.40
265 Kevin Millwood SP	.75	2.00
266 Orlando Hudson	.15	.40
267 Doug Mientkiewicz	.15	.40
268 Luis Gonzalez SP	.75	2.00
269 Jay Caligiuri RC	.15	.40
270 Nate Cornejo SP	.75	2.00
271 Lee Stevens	.15	.40
272 Eric Hinske	.15	.40
273 Antwon Rollins RC	.15	.40
274 Bobby Jenks RC	.60	1.50
275 Joe Mays	.15	.40
276 Josh Shaffer RC	.15	.40
277 Jonny Gomes RC	1.00	2.50
278 Bernie Williams	.25	.60
279 Ed Rogers	.15	.40
280 Carlos Delgado	.15	.40
281 Raul Mondesi SP	.75	2.00
282 Jose Ortiz	.15	.40
283 Cesar Izturis	.15	.40
284 Ryan Dempster SP	.75	2.00
285 Brian Daubach	.15	.40
286 Hansel Izquierdo RC	.15	.40
287 Mike Lieberthal SP	.75	2.00
288 Marcus Thames	.15	.40
289 Nomar Garciaparra	.60	1.50
290 Brad Fullmer	.15	.40
291 Tino Martinez	.25	.60
292 James Barrett RC	.15	.40
293 Jacque Jones	.15	.40
294 Nick Alvarez SP RC	.75	2.00
295 Jason Grove SP RC	.75	2.00
296 Mike Wilson SP RC	.75	2.00
297 J.T. Snow	.15	.40
298 Cliff Floyd	.15	.40
299 Todd Hundley SP	.75	2.00
300 Tony Clark SP	.75	2.00
301 Demetrius Heath RC	.15	.40
302 Morgan Ensberg	.15	.40
303 Cristian Guzman	.15	.40
304 Frank Catalanotto	.15	.40
305 Jeff Weaver	.15	.40
306 Tim Hudson	.15	.40
307 Scott Wiggins SP RC	.75	2.00
308 Shea Hillenbrand SP	.75	2.00
309 Todd Walker SP	.75	2.00
310 Tsuyoshi Shinjo	.15	.40
311 Adrian Beltre	.15	.40
312 Craig Kuzmic RC	.15	.40
313 Paul Konerko	.15	.40
314 Scott Hairston RC	.20	.50
315 Chan Ho Park	.15	.40
316 Jorge Posada	.25	.60
317 Chris Snelling RC	.30	.75
318 Keith Foulke	.15	.40
319 John Smoltz	.25	.60
320 Ryan Church SP RC	1.50	4.00
321 Mike Mussina	.25	.60
322 Tony Armas Jr. SP	.75	2.00
323 Craig Counsell	.15	.40
324 Marcus Giles	.15	.40
325 Greg Vaughn	.15	.40
326 Curt Schilling	.15	.40
327 Jeromy Burnitz	.15	.40
328 Eric Byrnes	.15	.40
329 Johnny Damon Sox	.25	.60
330 Michael Floyd SP RC	.75	2.00
331 Edgardo Alfonzo	.15	.40
332 Jeremy Hill RC	.15	.40
333 Josh Bonifay RC	.15	.40
334 Byung-Hyun Kim	.15	.40
335 Keith Ginter	.15	.40
336 Ronald Acuna SP RC	.75	2.00
337 Mike Hill SP RC	.75	2.00
338 Sean Casey	.15	.40
339 Matt Anderson SP	.75	2.00
340 Dan Wright	.15	.40
341 Ben Petrick	.15	.40
342 Mike Sirotka SP	.75	2.00
343 Alex Rodriguez	.50	1.50
344 Einar Diaz	.15	.40
345 Derek Jeter	1.00	2.50
346 Jeff Conine	.15	.40
347 Ray Durham SP	.75	2.00
348 Wilson Betemit SP	.75	2.00
349 Jeffrey Hammonds	.15	.40
350 Dan Trumble RC	.15	.40
351 Phil Nevin SP	.75	2.00
352 A.J. Burnett	.15	.40
353 Bill Mueller	.15	.40
354 Charles Nagy	.15	.40
355 Rusty Greer SP	.75	2.00
356 Jason Botts RC	.20	.50
357 Magglio Ordonez	.15	.40
358 Kevin Appier	.15	.40
359 Brad Radke	.15	.40
360 Chris George	.15	.40
361 Chris Piersoll RC	.15	.40
362 Ivan Rodriguez	.25	.60
363 Jim Kavourias RC	.15	.40
364 Rick Helling SP	.75	2.00
365 Dean Palmer	.15	.40
366 Rich Aurilia SP	.75	2.00
367 Ryan Vogelsong	.15	.40
368 Matt Lawton	.15	.40
369 Wade Miller	.15	.40
370 Dustin Hermanson	.15	.40
371 Craig Wilson	.15	.40
372 Todd Zeile SP	.75	2.00
373 Jon Guzman RC	.15	.40
374 Ellis Burks	.15	.40
375 Robert Cosby SP RC	.75	2.00
376 Jason Kendall	.15	.40
377 Scott Rolen SP	1.25	3.00
378 Andruw Jones	.25	.60
379 Greg Sain RC	.15	.40
380 Paul LoDuca	.15	.40
381 Scotty Layfield RC	.15	.40
382 Tomo Ohka	.15	.40
383 Garrett Guzman RC	.15	.40
384 Jack Cust SP	.75	2.00
385 Shayne Wright RC	.15	.40
386 Derrek Lee	.25	.60
387 Jesus Medrano RC	.15	.40
388 Javier Vazquez	.15	.40
389 Preston Wilson SP	.75	2.00
390 Gavin Floyd RC	.40	1.00
391 Sidney Ponson SP	.75	2.00
392 Jose Hernandez	.15	.40
393 Scott Erickson SP	.75	2.00
394 Jose Valverde RC	.15	.40
395 Mark Hamilton SP RC	.75	2.00
396 Brad Cresse	.15	.40
397 Danny Bautista	.15	.40
398 Ray Lankford SP	.75	2.00
399 Miguel Batista SP	.75	2.00
400 Brent Butler	.15	.40
401 Manny Delcarmen SP RC	1.25	3.00
402 Kyle Farnsworth SP	.75	2.00
403 Freddy Garcia	.15	.40
404 Joe Jiannetti RC	.15	.40
405 Josh Barfield RC	1.00	2.50
406 Corey Patterson	.15	.40
407 Josh Towers	.15	.40
408 Carlos Pena	.15	.40
409 Jeff Cirillo	.15	.40
410 Jon Lieber	.15	.40
411 Woody Williams SP	.75	2.00
412 Richard Lane SP RC	.75	2.00
413 Alex Gonzalez	.15	.40
414 Wilkin Ruan	.15	.40
415 Geoff Jenkins	.15	.40
416 Carlos Hernandez	.15	.40
417 Matt Clement SP	.75	2.00
418 Jose Cruz Jr.	.15	.40
419 Jake Mauer RC	.15	.40
420 Matt Childers RC	.15	.40
421 Tom Glavine SP	1.25	3.00
422 Ken Griffey Jr.	.75	2.00
423 Anderson Hernandez RC	.15	.40
424 John Suomi RC	.15	.40
425 Doug Sessions RC	.15	.40
426 Jaret Wright	.15	.40
427 Rolando Viera SP RC	.75	2.00
428 Aaron Sele	.15	.40
429 Dmitri Young	.15	.40
430 Ryan Klesko	.15	.40
431 Kevin Tapani SP	.75	2.00
432 Joe Kennedy	.15	.40
433 Austin Kearns	.15	.40
434 Roger Cedeno SP	.75	2.00
435 Lance Berkman	.15	.40
436 Frank Menechino	.15	.40
437 Brett Myers	.15	.40
438 Bob Abreu	.15	.40
439 Shawn Estes SP	.75	2.00

2002 Bowman Heritage Black Box

STATED ODDS 1:2

13 Hee Seop Choi	.30	.75
22 Barry Bonds	2.00	5.00
23 Justin Schuda	.25	.60
27 Aramis Ramirez	.30	.75
30 Kazuhisa Ishii	.30	.75
39 Mark Prior	.50	1.25
41 Travis Foley	.25	.60
56 Mike Piazza	1.25	3.00
66 Nomar Garciaparra	.50	1.25
72 Roy Oswalt	.30	.75
96 Victor Alvarez	.25	.60
99 Hank Blalock	.50	1.25
107 Chipper Jones	.75	2.00
108 Adam Dunn	.30	.75
120 Jose Macias	.30	.75
121 Josh Beckett	.30	.75
139 Juan Pierre	.30	.75
143 Toby Hall	.30	.75
145 Troy Glaus	.30	.75
146 Todd Helton	.50	1.25
153 Miguel Tejada	.30	.75
167 Tony Womack	.30	.75
180 Rafael Furcal	.30	.75
182 David Wright	4.00	10.00
185 J.D. Drew	.30	.75
222 Vladimir Guerrero	.75	2.00
227 Eric Chavez	.30	.75
238 Joe Mauer	3.00	8.00
240 Jimmy Rollins	.30	.75
246 So Taguchi	.30	.75
247 Sammy Sosa	.75	2.00
251 Albert Pujols	1.50	4.00
258 Jason Giambi	.30	.75
261 Ichiro Suzuki	1.50	4.00
266 Orlando Hudson	.30	.75
269 Jay Caligiuri	.25	.60
274 Bobby Jenks	1.00	2.50
275 Joe Mays	.30	.75
277 Jonny Gomes	1.50	4.00
310 Tsuyoshi Shinjo	.30	.75
314 Scott Hairston	.30	.75
316 Jorge Posada	.50	1.25
317 Chris Snelling	.50	1.25
335 Keith Ginter	.30	.75
343 Alex Rodriguez	1.00	2.50
345 Derek Jeter	2.00	5.00
362 Ivan Rodriguez	.50	1.25
390 Gavin Floyd	.60	1.50
396 Brad Cresse	.30	.75
405 Josh Barfield	1.50	4.00
414 Wilkin Ruan	.30	.75
416 Carlos Hernandez	.30	.75
418 Jose Cruz Jr.	.30	.75
422 Ken Griffey Jr.	1.50	4.00
433 Austin Kearns	.30	.75

2002 Bowman Heritage Chrome Refractors

*CHROME: 4X TO 10X BASIC CARDS
*CHROME SP's: .75X TO 2X BASIC SP'S
*CHROME RC's: 3X TO 8X BASIC RC'S
STATED ODDS 1:16
STATED PRINT RUN 350 SERIAL #'d SETS

2002 Bowman Heritage Gold Chrome Refractors

*GOLD: 6X TO 15X BASIC CARDS
*GOLD SP'S: 1.25X TO 3X BASIC SP'S
*GOLD RC'S: 5X TO 12X BASIC RC'S
STATED ODDS 1:32
STATED PRINT RUN 175 SERIAL #'d SETS

2002 Bowman Heritage '54 Reprints

COMPLETE SET (20)	20.00	50.00
STATED ODDS 1:12		
BHRAR Allie Reynolds	.75	2.00
BHRBF Bob Feller	.75	2.00
BHRCL Clem Labine	.75	2.00
BHRDC Del Crandall	.75	2.00
BHRDL Don Larsen	.75	2.00
BHRDM Don Mueller	.75	2.00
BHRDS Duke Snider	2.00	5.00
BHRDW Dave Williams	.75	2.00
BHRES Enos Slaughter	.75	2.00
BHRGM Gil McDougald	.75	2.00
BHRHW Hoyt Wilhelm	.75	2.00
BHRJL Johnny Logan	.75	2.00
BHRJP Jim Piersall	.75	2.00
BHRNF Nellie Fox	1.25	3.00
BHRPR Phil Rizzuto	1.25	3.00
BHRRA Richie Ashburn	1.25	3.00
BHRWF Whitey Ford	1.25	3.00
BHRWM Willie Mays	4.00	10.00
BHRWW Wes Westrum	.75	2.00
BHRYB Yogi Berra	2.00	5.00

2002 Bowman Heritage '54 Reprints Autographs

STATED ODDS 1:126
*SPEC.ED: .75X TO 2X BASIC AUTOS
SPEC.ED STATED ODDS 1:1910
SPEC.ED. PRINT RUN 54 SERIAL #'d SETS

BHRACL Clem Labine	6.00	15.00
BHRADC Del Crandall	8.00	20.00
BHRADM Don Mueller	6.00	15.00
BHRADW Dave Williams	6.00	15.00
BHRAJL Johnny Logan	6.00	15.00
BHRAYB Yogi Berra	25.00	60.00

2002 Bowman Heritage Autographs

GROUP A STATED ODDS 1:620
GROUP B STATED ODDS 1:89
GROUP C STATED ODDS 1:103
OVERALL STATED ODDS 1:45

BHAAP Albert Pujols A	100.00	250.00
BHACI Cesar Izturis B	4.00	10.00
BHADH Drew Henson B	4.00	10.00
BHAHB Hank Blalock C	6.00	15.00
BHAJM Joe Mauer C	50.00	120.00
BHAJR Juan Rivera C	6.00	15.00
BHAKG Keith Ginter B	4.00	10.00
BHAKI Kazuhisa Ishii A	6.00	15.00
BHALB Lance Berkman B	6.00	15.00
BHAMP Mark Prior B	6.00	15.00
BHAPL Paul LoDuca C	6.00	15.00
BHARO Roy Oswalt B	6.00	15.00
BHATH Toby Hall B	4.00	10.00

2002 Bowman Heritage Relics

GROUP A JSY ODDS 1:1910
GROUP B JSY ODDS 1:1551
GROUP C JSY ODDS 1:138
GROUP D JSY ODDS 1:207
GROUP E JSY ODDS 1:165
GROUP F JSY ODDS 1:2072
GROUP G JSY ODDS 1:653
OVERALL JSY ODDS 1:47
GROUP A UNI ODDS 1:1551
GROUP B UNI ODDS 1:855
GROUP C UNI ODDS 1:124
GROUP D UNI ODDS 1:284
OVERALL UNI ODDS 1:75

BHAP Albert Pujols Uni C	10.00	25.00
BHBB Barry Bonds Uni D	10.00	25.00
BHCD Carlos Delgado Jsy G	4.00	10.00
BHCJ Chipper Jones Jsy C	6.00	15.00
BHDE Darin Erstad Uni C	4.00	10.00
BHEA Edgardo Alfonzo Jsy C	4.00	10.00
BHEC Eric Chavez Jsy C	4.00	10.00
BHEM Edgar Martinez Jsy C	6.00	15.00
BHFT Frank Thomas Jsy F	6.00	15.00
BHGM Greg Maddux Jsy C	6.00	15.00
BHIR Ivan Rodriguez Uni B	6.00	15.00
BHJB Josh Beckett Jsy E	4.00	10.00
BHJE Jim Edmonds Jsy D	4.00	10.00
BHJS John Smoltz Jsy C	6.00	15.00
BHJT Jim Thome Jsy E	6.00	15.00
BHKS Kazuhiro Sasaki Jsy C	4.00	10.00
BHLW Larry Walker Jsy C	4.00	10.00
BHMP Mike Piazza Uni A	6.00	15.00
BHMR Mariano Rivera Uni C	6.00	15.00
BHNG Nomar Garciaparra Jsy A	8.00	20.00
BHPK Paul Konerko Jsy E	4.00	10.00
BHPW Preston Wilson Jsy B	4.00	10.00
BHSR Scott Rolen Jsy C	6.00	15.00
BHTG Tony Gwynn Jsy D	6.00	15.00
BHTH Todd Helton Jsy D	6.00	15.00
BHTS Tim Salmon Uni C	6.00	15.00

2003 Bowman Heritage

COMPLETE SET (300)	20.00	50.00
COMMON CARD (1-160)	.15	.40
COMMON CARD (161-170)	.15	.40
COMMON CARD (171A-180C)	.15	.40
COMMON CARD (181-280)	.15	.40
1 Jorge Posada	.25	.60
2 Todd Helton	.25	.60
3 Marcus Giles	.15	.40
4 Eric Chavez	.15	.40
5 Edgar Martinez	.25	.60
6 Luis Gonzalez	.15	.40
7 Corey Patterson	.15	.40
8 Preston Wilson	.15	.40
9 Ryan Klesko	.15	.40
10 Randy Johnson	.40	1.00
11 Jose Guillen	.15	.40
12 Carlos Lee	.15	.40
13 Steve Finley	.15	.40
14 A.J. Pierzynski	.15	.40
15 Troy Glaus	.15	.40
16 Darin Erstad	.15	.40
17 Moises Alou	.15	.40
18 Torii Hunter	.15	.40
19 Marlon Byrd	.15	.40
20 Mark Prior	.25	.60
21 Shannon Stewart	.15	.40
22 Craig Biggio	.25	.60
23 Johnny Damon	.25	.60
24 Robert Fick	.15	.40
25 Jason Giambi	.15	.40
26 Fernando Vina	.15	.40
27 Aubrey Huff	.15	.40
28 Benito Santiago	.15	.40
29 Jay Gibbons	.15	.40
30 Ken Griffey Jr.	.75	2.00
31 Rocco Baldelli	.15	.40
32 Pat Burrell	.15	.40
33 A.J. Burnett	.15	.40
34 Omar Vizquel	.25	.60
35 Greg Maddux	.50	1.25
36 Cliff Floyd	.15	.40
37 C.C. Sabathia	.25	.60
38 Geoff Jenkins	.15	.40
39 Ty Wigginton	.15	.40
40 Jeff Kent	.15	.40
41 Orlando Hudson	.15	.40
42 Edgardo Alfonzo	.15	.40
43 Greg Myers	.15	.40
44 Melvin Mora	.15	.40
45 Sammy Sosa	.40	1.00
46 Russ Ortiz	.15	.40
47 Josh Beckett	.15	.40
48 David Wells	.15	.40
49 Woody Williams	.15	.40
50 Alex Rodriguez	.50	1.25
51 Randy Wolf	.15	.40
52 Carlos Beltran	.25	.60
53 Austin Kearns	.15	.40
54 Trot Nixon	.15	.40
55 Ivan Rodriguez	.25	.60
56 Shea Hillenbrand	.15	.40
57 Roberto Alomar	.25	.60
58 John Olerud	.15	.40
59 Michael Young	.15	.40
60 Garret Anderson	.15	.40
61 Mike Lieberthal	.15	.40
62 Adam Dunn	.25	.60
63 Raul Ibanez	.25	.60
64 Kenny Lofton	.15	.40
65 Ichiro Suzuki	.50	1.25
66 Jarrod Washburn	.15	.40
67 Shawn Chacon	.15	.40
68 Alex Gonzalez	.15	.40
69 Roy Halladay	.25	.60
70 Vladimir Guerrero	.25	.60
71 Hee Seop Choi	.15	.40
72 Jody Gerut	.15	.40
73 Ray Durham	.15	.40
74 Mark Teixeira	.25	.60
75 Hank Blalock	.15	.40
76 Jerry Hairston Jr.	.15	.40
77 Erubiel Durazo	.15	.40
78 Frank Catalanotto	.15	.40
79 Jacque Jones	.15	.40
80 Bobby Abreu	.15	.40
81 Mike Hampton	.15	.40
82 Zach Day	.15	.40
83 Jimmy Rollins	.25	.60
84 Joel Pineiro	.15	.40
85 Brett Myers	.15	.40
86 Frank Thomas	.40	1.00
87 Aramis Ramirez	.15	.40
88 Paul Lo Duca	.15	.40
89 Dmitri Young	.15	.40
90 Brian Giles	.15	.40
91 Jose Cruz Jr.	.15	.40
92 Derek Lowe	.15	.40
93 Mark Buehrle	.25	.60
94 Wade Miller	.15	.40
95 Derek Jeter	1.00	2.50
96 Bret Boone	.15	.40
97 Tony Batista	.15	.40
98 Sean Casey	.15	.40
99 Eric Hinske	.15	.40
100 Albert Pujols	.50	1.25
101 Runelvys Hernandez	.15	.40
102 Vernon Wells	.15	.40
103 Kerry Wood	.15	.40
104 Lance Berkman	.25	.60
105 Alfonso Soriano	.25	.60
106 Bill Mueller	.15	.40
107 Bartolo Colon	.15	.40
108 Andy Pettitte	.25	.60
109 Rafael Furcal	.15	.40
110 Dontrelle Willis	.15	.40
111 Carl Crawford	.25	.60
112 Scott Rolen	.25	.60
113 Chipper Jones	.40	1.00
114 Magglio Ordonez	.25	.60
115 Bernie Williams	.25	.60
116 Roy Oswalt	.25	.60
117 Kevin Brown	.15	.40
118 Cristian Guzman	.15	.40
119 Kazuhisa Ishii	.15	.40
120 Larry Walker	.25	.60
121 Miguel Tejada	.25	.60
122 Manny Ramirez	.40	1.00
123 Mike Mussina	.25	.60
124 Mike Lowell	.15	.40
125 Scott Podsednik	.15	.40
126 Aaron Boone	.15	.40
127 Carlos Delgado	.15	.40
128 Jose Vidro	.15	.40
129 Brad Radke	.15	.40
130 Rafael Palmeiro	.25	.60
131 Mark Mulder	.15	.40
132 Jason Schmidt	.15	.40
133 Gary Sheffield	.15	.40
134 Richie Sexson	.15	.40
135 Barry Zito	.25	.60
136 Tom Glavine	.25	.60
137 Jim Edmonds	.25	.60
138 Andruw Jones	.15	.40
139 Pedro Martinez	.25	.60
140 Curt Schilling	.25	.60
141 Phil Nevin	.15	.40
142 Nomar Garciaparra	.25	.60
143 Vicente Padilla	.15	.40
144 Kevin Millwood	.15	.40
145 Shawn Green	.15	.40
146 Jeff Bagwell	.25	.60
147 Hideo Nomo	.40	1.00
148 Fred McGriff	.25	.60
149 Matt Morris	.15	.40
150 Roger Clemens	.50	1.25
151 Jerome Williams	.15	.40
152 Orlando Cabrera	.15	.40
153 Tim Hudson	.25	.60
154 Mike Sweeney	.15	.40
155 Jim Thome	.25	.60
156 Rich Aurilia	.15	.40
157 Mike Piazza	.40	1.00
158 Edgar Renteria	.15	.40
159 Javy Lopez	.15	.40
160 Jamie Moyer	.15	.40
161 Miguel Cabrera DI	2.00	5.00
162 Adam Loewen DI RC	.15	.40
163 Jose Reyes DI	.40	1.00
164 Zack Greinke DI	2.00	5.00
165 Gavin Floyd DI	.15	.40
166 Jeremy Guthrie DI	.15	.40
167 Victor Martinez DI	.25	.60
168 Rich Harden DI	.25	.60
169 Joe Mauer DI	.40	1.00
170 Khalil Greene DI	.25	.60
171A Willie Mays	.75	2.00
171B Willie Mays DI	.75	2.00
171C Willie Mays KN	.75	2.00
172A Phil Rizzuto	.25	.60
172B Phil Rizzuto DI	.25	.60
172C Phil Rizzuto KN	.25	.60
173A Al Kaline	.25	.60
173B Al Kaline DI	.25	.60
173C Al Kaline KN	.25	.60
174A Warren Spahn	.25	.60
174B Warren Spahn DI	.25	.60
174C Warren Spahn KN	.25	.60
175A Jimmy Piersall	.15	.40
175B Jimmy Piersall DI	.15	.40
175C Jimmy Piersall KN	.15	.40
176A Luis Aparicio	.25	.60
176B Luis Aparicio DI	.25	.60
176C Luis Aparicio KN	.25	.60
177A Whitey Ford	.25	.60
177B Whitey Ford DI	.25	.60
177C Whitey Ford KN	.25	.60
178A Harmon Killebrew	.40	1.00
178B Harmon Killebrew DI	.40	1.00
178C Harmon Killebrew KN	.40	1.00
179A Duke Snider	.25	.60
179B Duke Snider DI	.25	.60
179C Duke Snider KN	.25	.60
180A Roberto Clemente	1.00	2.50
180B Roberto Clemente DI	1.00	2.50
180C Roberto Clemente KN	1.00	2.50
181 David Martinez KN RC	.15	.40
182 Felix Pie KN RC	.25	.60
183 Kevin Correia KN RC	.15	.40
184 Brandon Webb KN RC	.50	1.25
185 Matt Diaz KN RC	.25	.60
186 Lew Ford KN RC	.15	.40
187 Jeremy Griffiths KN RC	.15	.40
188 Matt Hensley KN RC	.15	.40
189 Danny Garcia KN RC	.15	.40
190 Elizardo Ramirez KN RC	.15	.40
191 Greg Aquino KN RC	.15	.40
192 Felix Sanchez KN RC	.15	.40
193 Kelly Shoppach KN RC	.25	.60
194 Bubba Nelson KN RC	.15	.40
195 Mike O'Keefe KN RC	.15	.40
196 Hanley Ramirez KN RC	1.25	3.00
197 Todd Wellemeyer KN RC	.15	.40
198 Dustin Moseley KN RC	.15	.40
199 Eric Crozier KN RC	.15	.40
200 Ryan Shealy KN RC	.15	.40
201 Jeremy Bonderman KN RC	.60	1.50
202 Bo Hart KN RC	.15	.40
203 Dusty Brown KN RC	.15	.40
204 Rob Hammock KN RC	.15	.40
205 Jorge Piedra KN RC	.15	.40
206 Jason Kubel KN RC	.50	1.25
207 Stephen Randolph KN RC	.15	.40
208 Andy Sisco KN RC	.15	.40
209 Matt Kata KN RC	.15	.40
210 Robinson Cano KN RC	6.00	15.00
211 Ben Francisco KN RC	.15	.40
212 Arnie Munoz KN RC	.15	.40
213 Ozzie Chavez KN RC	.15	.40
214 Beau Kemp KN RC	.15	.40
215 Travis Wong KN RC	.15	.40
216 Brian McCann KN RC	1.25	3.00
217 Aquilino Lopez KN RC	.15	.40
218 Bobby Basham KN RC	.15	.40
219 Tim Olson KN RC	.15	.40
220 Nathan Panther KN RC	.15	.40
221 Wil Ledezma KN RC	.15	.40
222 Josh Willingham KN RC	.50	1.25
223 David Cash KN RC	.15	.40
224 Oscar Villarreal KN RC	.15	.40
225 Jeff Duncan KN RC	.15	.40
226 Dan Haren KN RC	.75	2.00
227 Michel Hernandez KN RC	.15	.40
228 Matt Murton KN RC	.15	.40
229 Clay Hensley KN RC	.15	.40
230 Tyler Johnson KN RC	.15	.40
231 Tyler Martin KN RC	.15	.40
232 J.D. Durbin KN RC	.15	.40
233 Shane Victorino KN RC	.50	1.25
234 Rajai Davis KN RC	.15	.40
235 Chien-Ming Wang KN RC	.60	1.50
236 Travis Ishikawa KN RC	.40	1.00
237 Eric Eckenstahler KN	.15	.40
238 Dustin McGowan KN RC	.15	.40
239 Prentice Redman KN RC	.15	.40
240 Haj Turay KN RC	.15	.40
241 Matt DeMarco KN RC	.15	.40
242 Lou Palmisano KN RC	.15	.40
243 Eric Reed KN RC	.15	.40
244 Willie Eyre KN RC	.15	.40
245 Ferdin Tejeda KN RC	.15	.40
246 Michael Garciaparra KN RC	.15	.40
247 Michael Hinckley KN RC	.15	.40
248 Branden Florence KN RC	.15	.40
249 Trent Oeltjen KN RC	.15	.40
250 Mike Neu KN RC	.15	.40
251 Chris Lubanski KN RC	.15	.40
252 Brandon Wood KN RC	1.00	2.50
253 Delmon Young KN RC	1.00	2.50
254 Matt Harrison KN RC	.60	1.50
255 Chad Billingsley KN RC	.75	2.00
256 Josh Anderson KN RC	.15	.40
257 Brian McFall KN RC	.15	.40
258 Ryan Wagner KN RC	.15	.40
259 Billy Hogan KN RC	.15	.40
260 Nate Spears KN RC	.15	.40
261 Ryan Harvey KN RC	.15	.40
262 Wes Littleton KN RC	.15	.40
263 Xavier Paul KN RC	.15	.40
264 Sean Rodriguez KN RC	.25	.60
265 Brian Finch KN RC	.15	.40
266 Josh Rainwater KN RC	.15	.40
267 Brian Snyder KN RC	.15	.40
268 Eric Duncan KN RC	.15	.40
269 Rickie Weeks KN RC	.50	1.25
270 Tim Battle KN RC	.15	.40
271 Scott Beerer KN RC	.15	.40
272 Aaron Hill KN RC	.50	1.25
273 Casey Abrams KN RC	.15	.40
274 Jonathan Fulton KN RC	.15	.40
275 Todd Jennings KN RC	.15	.40
276 Jordan Pratt KN RC	.15	.40
277 Tom Gorzelanny KN RC	.25	.60
278 Matt Lorenzo KN RC	.15	.40
279 Jarrod Saltalamacchia KN RC	.75	2.00
280 Mike Wagner KN RC	.15	.40

2003 Bowman Heritage Autographs

STATED ODDS 1:1014		
253 Delmon Young KN	3.00	8.00

2003 Bowman Heritage Box Toppers

COMPLETE SET (8)	10.00	25.00
*BOX TOPPER: .4X TO 1X BASIC		
ONE PER SEALED BOX		

2003 Bowman Heritage Facsimile Signature

*FACSIMILE 1-160: 1X TO 2.5X BASIC
*FACSIMILE 161-170: 1X TO 2.5X BASIC
*FACSIMILE 171A-180C: 1X TO 2.5X BASIC
*FACSIMILE 181-280: 1X TO 2.5X BASIC
ONE PER PACK

2003 Bowman Heritage Rainbow

COMPLETE SET (100)	30.00	80.00
*RAINBOW: .5X TO 1.2X BASIC		
ONE PER PACK		

2003 Bowman Heritage Diamond Cuts Relics

BAT ODDS 1:133
JSY GROUP A ODDS 1:28
JSY GROUP B ODDS 1:936
JSY GROUP C ODDS 1:626
UNI ODDS 1:35
GOLD STATED ODDS 1:8193
GOLD PRINT RUN 1 SERIAL #'d SET
NO GOLD PRICING DUE TO SCARCITY
*RED BAT: .6X TO 1.5X BASIC BAT
*RED JSY: 1X TO 2.5X BASIC JSY
*RED UNI: 1X TO 2.5X BASIC UNI
RED STATED ODDS 1:143
RED PRINT RUN 56 SERIAL #'d SETS

AJ Andruw Jones Jsy A	4.00	10.00
AK Austin Kearns Jsy A	3.00	8.00
AP Albert Pujols Bat	10.00	25.00
AR1 Alex Rodriguez Bat	6.00	15.00
AR2 Alex Rodriguez Jsy A	4.00	10.00
AS Alfonso Soriano Bat	4.00	10.00
BB Bret Boone Jsy A	3.00	8.00
BM Brett Myers Jsy A	3.00	8.00
BW Bernie Williams Uni	4.00	10.00
BZ Barry Zito Uni	3.00	8.00
CB Craig Biggio Uni	4.00	10.00
CF Cliff Floyd Uni	3.00	8.00
CG Cristian Guzman Jsy A	3.00	8.00
CJ1 Chipper Jones Bat	6.00	15.00
CJ2 Chipper Jones Jsy A	4.00	10.00
EC Eric Chavez Uni	3.00	8.00
GS Gary Sheffield Uni	3.00	8.00
HB Hank Blalock Bat	4.00	10.00
HN Hideo Nomo Jsy A	4.00	10.00
JA Jeremy Affeldt Uni	3.00	8.00
JB Jeff Bagwell Jsy A	4.00	10.00
JE Jim Edmonds Uni	3.00	8.00
JG Jason Giambi Uni	3.00	8.00
JJ Jason Jennings Jsy A	3.00	8.00
JL Javy Lopez Jsy A	3.00	8.00
JLP Josh Phelps Jsy C	3.00	8.00
JR Jose Reyes Jsy A	3.00	8.00
JV Javier Vazquez Jsy A	3.00	8.00
JW Jarrod Washburn Uni	3.00	8.00
KI Kazuhiro Sasaki Jsy A	3.00	8.00
KM Kevin Millwood Jsy A	3.00	8.00
KW Kerry Wood Uni	3.00	8.00
MA Moises Alou Jsy C	3.00	8.00
MG Mark Grace Jsy B	4.00	10.00
ML Mike Lowell Jsy A	3.00	8.00
MM Mark Mulder Uni	3.00	8.00
MS Mike Sweeney Jsy A	3.00	8.00
MT Miguel Tejada Uni	3.00	8.00
PL Paul Lo Duca Jsy A	3.00	8.00
PM Pedro Martinez Jsy A	4.00	10.00
RC Roberto Clemente Bat	20.00	50.00

RH Rickey Henderson Bat 6.00 15.00
RP1 Rafael Palmeiro Bat 6.00 15.00
RP2 Rafael Palmeiro Uni 4.00 10.00
SR1 Scott Rolen Bat 6.00 15.00
SR2 Scott Rolen Uni 4.00 10.00
SS1 Sammy Sosa Bat 6.00 15.00
SS2 Sammy Sosa Jsy A 4.00 10.00
TA Tony Armas Jr. Jsy A 3.00 8.00
TG Troy Glaus Uni 3.00 8.00
TH Todd Helton Jsy A 4.00 10.00
THA Tim Hudson Uni 3.00 8.00
TW Ty Wigginton Uni 3.00 8.00
VG Vladimir Guerrero Bat 6.00 15.00
VW Vernon Wells Jsy A 3.00 8.00

2003 Bowman Heritage Olbermann Autograph

STATED ODDS 1:1421
KOA Keith Olbermann 25.00 60.00

2003 Bowman Heritage Signs of Greatness

STATED ODDS 1:30
RED INK STATED ODDS 1:32,141
RED INK PRINT RUN 1 SERIAL #'d SET
NO RED INK PRICING DUE TO SCARCITY
BF Brian Finch 3.00 8.00
BS Brian Snyder 3.00 8.00
CB Chad Billingsley 6.00 15.00
DW Dontrelle Willis 3.00 8.00
FP Felix Pie 3.00 8.00
JD Jeff Duncan 3.00 8.00
KY Kevin Youkilis 4.00 10.00
MM Matt Murton 3.00 8.00
RC Robinson Cano 30.00 80.00
RH Rich Harden 3.00 8.00
RW Rickie Weeks 4.00 10.00
TG Tom Gorzelanny 3.00 8.00

2004 Bowman Heritage

COMPLETE SET (351) 175.00 300.00
COMP.SET w/o SP's (300) 25.00 50.00
COMMON ACTIVE .15 .40
COMMON RETIRED .15 .40
COMMON UMPIRE .15 .40
COMMON RC .15 .40
COMMON DP RC .30 .75
COMMON SP 1.25 3.00
COMMON SP RC 1.25 3.00
SP STATED ODDS 1:3 HOBBY, 1:3 RETAIL
SP's: 2/9/13/21/25/40B/46/48B/50/55/61
SP's: 77/80/87/89/95/100/104/109/127/130
SP's: 132/141/183A/189/204/206/208/210
SP's: 213/216/220/224/228/234/240/243
SP's: 246/249/259/268/270-271/282/291
SP's: 304/318/327/334/342/348
PLATES STATED ODDS 1:240 HOBBY
PLATES PRINT RUN 1 #'d SET PER COLOR
PLATES: BLACK, CYAN, MAGENTA & YELLOW
NO PLATES PRICING DUE TO SCARCITY
ROOP BINDER ODDS 1:240 HOBBY
ROOP BINDER EXCH.DEADLINE 12/31/05
1 Tom Glavine .25 .60
2 Mike Piazza SP 3.00 8.00
3 Sidney Ponson .15 .40
4 Jerry Hairston Jr. .15 .40
5 Jermaine Dye .15 .40
6 Bobby Crosby .15 .40
7 Carlos Zambrano .25 .60
8 Moises Alou .15 .40
9 Alex Rodriguez SP 4.00 10.00
10 Derek Jeter 1.00 2.50
11 Rafael Furcal .15 .40
12 J.D. Drew .15 .40
13 Joe Mauer SP 2.50 6.00
14 Brad Radke .15 .40
15 Johnny Damon .25 .60
16 Derek Lowe .15 .40
17 Pat Burrell .15 .40
18 Mike Lieberthal .15 .40
19 Cliff Lee .25 .60
20 Ronnie Belliard .15 .40
21 Eric Gagne SP 1.25 3.00
22 Brad Penny .15 .40
23 Al Kaline RET .40 1.00
24 Mike Maroth .15 .40
25 Magglio Ordonez SP 2.00 5.00
26 Mark Buehrle .25 .60
27 Jack Wilson .15 .40
28 Oliver Perez .15 .40
29 Red Schoendienst RET .25 .60
30 Yadier Molina FY RC 20.00 50.00
31 Ryan Freel .15 .40
32 Adam Dunn .25 .60
33 Paul Konerko .25 .60
34 Esteban Loaiza .15 .40
35 Ivan Rodriguez .25 .60
36 Carlos Guillen .15 .40
37 Adrian Beltre .40 1.00
38 C.C. Sabathia .25 .60
39 Hideo Nomo .40 1.00
40A Victor Martinez .25 .60
40B V.Martinez Pedro Stats SP 2.00 5.00
41 Bobby Abreu .15 .40
42 Randy Wolf .15 .40
43 Johnny Estrada .15 .40
44 Russ Ortiz .15 .40
45 Kenny Rogers .15 .40
46 Hank Blalock SP 1.25 3.00
47 David Ortiz .40 1.00
48A Pedro Martinez .25 .60
48B P.Martinez Victor Stats SP 2.00 5.00
49 Austin Kearns .15 .40
50 Ken Griffey Jr. SP 6.00 15.00
51 Mark Prior .25 .60
52 Kerry Wood .15 .40
53 Eric Chavez .15 .40
54 Tim Hudson .25 .60
55 Rafael Palmeiro SP 2.00 5.00
56 Javy Lopez .15 .40
57 Jason Bay .25 .60
58 Craig Wilson .15 .40
59 Whitey Ford RET .25 .60
60 Jason Giambi .15 .40
61 Scott Rolen SP 2.00 5.00
62 Matt Morris .15 .40
63 Javier Vazquez .15 .40
64 Jim Thome .25 .60
65 Don Zimmer RET .15 .40
66 Shawn Green .15 .40
67 Don Larsen RET .15 .40
68 Gary Sheffield .15 .40
69 Jorge Posada .25 .60
70 Bernie Williams .25 .60
71 Chipper Jones .40 1.00
72 Andruw Jones .15 .40
73 John Thomson .15 .40
74 Jim Edmonds .25 .60
75 Albert Pujols .50 1.25
76 Chris Carpenter .25 .60
77 Aubrey Huff SP 1.25 3.00
78 Carl Crawford .25 .60
79 Victor Zambrano .15 .40
80 Alfonso Soriano SP 2.00 5.00
81 Lance Berkman .25 .60
82 Mike Sweeney .15 .40
83 Ken Harvey .15 .40
84 Angel Berroa .15 .40
85 A.J. Burnett .15 .40
86 Mike Lowell .15 .40
87 Miguel Cabrera SP 3.00 8.00
88 Preston Wilson .15 .40
89 Todd Helton SP 2.00 5.00
90 Larry Walker Cards .25 .60
91 Vladimir Guerrero .25 .60
92 Garret Anderson .15 .40
93 Bartolo Colon .15 .40
94 Scott Hairston .15 .40
95 Richie Sexson SP 1.25 3.00
96 Sean Casey .15 .40
97 John Podres RET .15 .40
98 Andy Pettitte .25 .60
99 Roy Oswalt .25 .60
100 Roger Clemens SP 4.00 10.00
101 Scott Podsednik .15 .40
102 Ben Sheets .15 .40
103 Lyle Overbay .15 .40
104 Nick Johnson SP 1.25 3.00
105 Zach Day .15 .40
106 Jose Reyes .25 .60
107 Khalil Greene .25 .60
108 Sean Burroughs .15 .40
109 David Wells SP 1.25 3.00
110 Jason Schmidt .15 .40
111 Neifi Perez .15 .40
112 Edgar Renteria .15 .40
113 Rich Aurilia .15 .40
114 Edgar Martinez .25 .60
115 Joel Pineiro .15 .40
116 Mark Teixeira .25 .60
117 Michael Young .15 .40
118 Ricardo Rodriguez .15 .40
119 Carlos Delgado .15 .40
120 Roy Halladay .25 .60
121 Jose Guillen .15 .40
122 Troy Glaus .15 .40
123 Shea Hillenbrand .15 .40
124 Luis Gonzalez .15 .40
125 Horacio Ramirez .15 .40
126 Melvin Mora .15 .40
127 Miguel Tejada SP 2.00 5.00
128 Manny Ramirez .40 1.00
129 Tim Wakefield .25 .60
130 Curt Schilling SP 2.00 5.00
131 Aramis Ramirez .15 .40
132 Sammy Sosa SP 3.00 8.00
133 Matt Clement .15 .40
134 Juan Uribe .15 .40
135 Dontrelle Willis .15 .40
136 Paul Lo Duca .15 .40
137 Juan Pierre .15 .40
138 Kevin Brown .15 .40
139 B.Giles .15 .40
M.Giles
140 Brian Giles .15 .40
141 Nomar Garciaparra SP 2.00 5.00
142 Cesar Izturis .15 .40
143 Don Newcombe RET .15 .40
144 Craig Biggio .25 .60
145 Carlos Beltran .25 .60
146 Torii Hunter .15 .40
147 Livan Hernandez .15 .40
148 Cliff Floyd .15 .40
149 Barry Zito .25 .60
150 Mark Mulder .15 .40
151 Rocco Baldelli .15 .40
152 Bret Boone .15 .40
153 Jamie Moyer .15 .40
154 Ichiro Suzuki .50 1.25
155 Brett Myers .15 .40
156 Carl Pavano .15 .40
157 Josh Beckett .15 .40
158 Randy Johnson .40 1.00
159 Trot Nixon .15 .40
160 Dmitri Young .15 .40
161 Jacque Jones .15 .40
162 Lew Ford .15 .40
163 Jose Vidro .15 .40
164 Mark Kotsay .15 .40
165 A.J. Pierzynski .15 .40
166 Dewon Brazelton .15 .40
167 Jeromy Burnitz .15 .40
168 Johan Santana .25 .60
169 Greg Maddux .50 1.25
170 Carl Erskine RET .15 .40
171 Robin Roberts RET .25 .60
172 Freddy Garcia .15 .40
173 Carlos Lee .15 .40
174 Jeff Bagwell .25 .60
175 Jeff Kent .15 .40
176 Kazuhisa Ishii .15 .40
177 Orlando Cabrera .15 .40
178 Shannon Stewart .15 .40
179 Mike Cameron .15 .40
180 Mike Mussina .25 .60
181 Frank Thomas .40 1.00
182 Jaret Wright .15 .40
183A Alex Gonzalez Marlins SP 1.25 3.00
183B Alex Gonzalez Padres .15 .40
184 Matt Lawton .15 .40
185 Derrek Lee .15 .40
186 Omar Vizquel .25 .60
187 Jeremy Bonderman .15 .40
188 Jake Westbrook .15 .40
189 Zack Greinke SP 5.00 12.00
190 Chad Tracy .15 .40
191 Rondell White .15 .40
192 Alex Gonzalez .15 .40
193 Geoff Jenkins .15 .40
194 Ralph Kiner RET .25 .60
195 Al Leiter .15 .40
196 Kevin Millwood .15 .40
197 Jason Kendall .15 .40
198 Kris Benson .15 .40
199 Ryan Klesko .15 .40
200 Mark Loretta .15 .40
201 Richard Hidalgo .15 .40
202 Reed Johnson .15 .40
203 Luis Castillo .15 .40
204 Jon Zeringue DP SP RC 1.25 3.00
205 Matt Bush DP RC .50 1.25
206 Kurt Suzuki DP SP RC 2.00 5.00
207 Mark Rogers DP RC .50 1.25
208 Jason Vargas DP SP RC 2.00 5.00
209 Homer Bailey DP RC .50 1.25
210 Ray Liotta DP SP RC 1.25 3.00
211 Eric Campbell DP RC .30 .75
212 Thomas Diamond DP RC .30 .75
213 Gaby Hernandez DP SP RC 2.00 5.00
214 Neil Walker DP RC .50 1.25
215 Bill Bray DP RC .30 .75
216 Wade Davis DP SP RC 3.00 8.00
217 David Purcey DP RC .50 1.25
218 Scott Elbert DP RC .30 .75
219 Josh Fields DP RC .50 1.25
220 Josh Johnson DP SP RC 1.25 3.00
221 Chris Lambert DP RC .30 .75
222 Trevor Plouffe DP RC .75 2.00
223 Bruce Froemming UMP .15 .40
224 Matt Macri DP SP RC 2.00 5.00
225 Greg Golson DP RC .30 .75
226 Philip Hughes DP RC .75 2.00
227 Kyle Waldrop DP RC .30 .75
228 Matt Tuiasosopo DP SP RC 3.00 8.00
229 Richie Robnett DP RC .30 .75
230 Taylor Tankersley DP RC .30 .75
231 Blake DeWitt DP RC .50 1.25
232 Charlie Reliford UMP .15 .40
233 Eric Hurley DP RC .30 .75
234 Jordan Parraz DP SP RC 2.00 5.00
235 J.P. Howell DP RC .30 .75
236 Dana DeMuth UMP .15 .40
237 Zach Jackson DP RC .30 .75
238 Justin Orenduff DP RC .50 1.25
239 Brad Thompson FY RC .25 .60
240 J.C. Holt DP SP RC 1.25 3.00
241 Matt Fox DP RC .30 .75
242 Danny Putnam DP RC .30 .75
243 Daryl Jones DP SP RC 1.25 3.00
244 Jon Poterson DP RC .30 .75
245 Gio Gonzalez DP RC .50 1.25
246 Lucas Harrell DP SP RC 1.25 3.00
247 Jerry Crawford UMP .15 .40
248 Jay Rainville DP RC .30 .75
249 Donnie Smith DP SP RC 1.25 3.00
250 Huston Street DP RC .50 1.25
251 Jeff Marquez DP RC .30 .75
252 Reid Brignac DP RC .75 2.00
253 Yusmeiro Petit FY RC .40 1.00
254 K.C. Herren DP RC .30 .75
255 Dale Scott UMP .15 .40
256 Erick San Pedro DP RC .30 .75
257 Ed Montague UMP .15 .40
258 Billy Buckner DP RC .30 .75
259 Mitch Einertson DP SP RC 1.25 3.00
260 Aarom Baldiris FY RC .15 .40
261 Conor Jackson FY RC .50 1.25
262 Rick Reed UMP .15 .40
263 Ervin Santana FY RC .40 1.00
264 Gerry Davis UMP .15 .40
265 Merkin Valdez FY RC .15 .40
266 Joey Gathright FY RC .15 .40
267 Alberto Callaspo FY RC .40 1.00
268 Carlos Quentin FY SP RC 5.00 12.00
269 Gary Darling UMP .15 .40
270 Jeff Salazar FY SP RC 1.25 3.00
271 Akinori Otsuka FY SP RC 1.25 3.00
272 Joe Brinkman UMP .15 .40
273 Omar Quintanilla FY RC .15 .40
274 Brian Runge UMP .15 .40
275 Tom Mastny FY RC .15 .40
276 John Hirschbeck UMP .15 .40
277 Warner Madrigal FY RC .15 .40
278 Joe West UMP .15 .40
279 Paul Maholm FY RC .25 .60
280 Larry Young UMP .15 .40
281 Mike Reilly UMP .15 .40
282 Kazuo Matsui FY SP RC 2.00 5.00
283 Randy Marsh UMP .15 .40
284 Frank Francisco FY RC .15 .40
285 Zach Duke FY RC .25 .60
286 Tim McClelland UMP .15 .40
287 Jesse Crain FY RC .25 .60
288 Hector Gimenez FY RC .15 .40
289 Marland Williams FY RC .15 .40
290 Brian Gorman UMP .15 .40
291 Jose Capellan FY SP RC 1.25 3.00
292 Tim Welke UMP .15 .40
293 Javier Guzman FY RC .15 .40
294 Paul McAnulty FY RC .15 .40
295 Hector Made FY RC .15 .40
296 Jon Connolly FY RC .15 .40
297 Don Sutton FY RC .15 .40
298 Fausto Carmona FY RC .25 .60
299 Ramon Ramirez FY RC .15 .40
300 Brad Snyder FY RC .15 .40
301 Chin-Lung Hu FY RC .15 .40
302 Rudy Guillen FY RC .15 .40
303 Matt Moses FY RC .25 .60
304 Brad Halsey FY SP RC 1.25 3.00
305 Erick Aybar FY RC .40 1.00
306 Brad Sullivan FY RC .15 .40
307 Nick Gorneault FY RC .15 .40
308 Craig Ansman FY RC .15 .40
309 Ricky Nolasco FY RC .25 .60
310 Luke Hughes FY RC .40 1.00
311 Danny Gonzalez FY RC .15 .40
312 Josh Labandeira FY RC .15 .40
313 Donald Levinski FY RC .15 .40
314 Vince Perkins FY RC .15 .40
315 Tommy Murphy FY RC .15 .40
316 Chad Bentz FY RC .15 .40
317 Chris Shelton FY RC .15 .40
318 Nyjer Morgan FY SP RC 1.25 3.00
319 Kody Kirkland FY RC .15 .40
320 Blake Hawksworth FY RC .15 .40
321 Alex Romero FY RC .15 .40
322 Mike Gosling FY RC .15 .40
323 Ryan Buddé FY RC .15 .40
324 Kevin Howard FY RC .15 .40
325 Wanell Macia FY RC .15 .40
326 Travis Blackley FY RC .15 .40
327 Kazuhito Tadano FY SP RC 1.25 3.00
328 Shingo Takatsu FY RC .15 .40
329 Joaquin Arias FY RC .40 1.00
330 Juan Cedeno FY RC .15 .40
331 Bobby Brownlie FY RC .15 .40
332 Lastings Milledge FY RC .25 .60
333 Estee Harris FY RC .15 .40
334 Tim Stauffer FY SP RC 2.00 5.00
335 Jon Knott FY RC .15 .40
336 David Aardsma FY RC .15 .40
337 Wardell Starling FY RC .15 .40
338 Dioner Navarro FY RC .25 .60
339 Logan Kensing FY RC .15 .40
340 Jason Hirsh FY RC .15 .40
341 Matt Creighton FY RC .15 .40
342 Felix Hernandez FY SP RC 6.00 15.00
343 Kyle Sleeth FY RC .15 .40
344 Dustin Nippert FY RC .15 .40
345 Anthony Lerew FY RC .15 .40
346 Chris Saenz FY RC .15 .40
347 Steve Palermo SUP .15 .40
348 Barry Bonds SP 5.00 12.00

2004 Bowman Heritage Black and White

COMPLETE SET (351) 225.00 325.00
*B/W: 1X TO 2.5X BASIC
*B/W: .6X TO 1.5X BASIC RC
*B/W: .5X TO 1.2X BASIC DP RC
*B/W: .12X TO .3X BASIC SP
*B/W: .06X TO .15X BASIC SP RC
*B/W: .1X TO .25X BASIC DP SP RC
ONE PER PACK

2004 Bowman Heritage Mahogany

STATED ODDS 1:39 HOBBY
STATED PRINT RUN 25 SERIAL #'d SETS
NO RC YR PRICING DUE TO SCARCITY

2004 Bowman Heritage Commissioner's Cut

STATED ODDS 1:320,720 HOBBY
STATED PRINT RUN 1 SERIAL #'d SET
NO PRICING DUE TO SCARCITY

2004 Bowman Heritage Signs of Authority

STATED ODDS 1:49 HOBBY, 1:107 RETAIL
*RED: .5X TO 1.2X BASIC
RED STATED ODDS 1:499 HOB, 1:1019 RET
RED PRINT RUN 55 SERIAL #'d SETS
BF Bruce Froemming 6.00 15.00
BG Brian Gorman 6.00 15.00
BR Brian Runge 6.00 15.00
CM Charlie Reliford 6.00 15.00
DD Dana DeMuth 6.00 15.00
DS Dale Scott 6.00 15.00
EM Ed Montague 6.00 15.00
ER Rick Reed 6.00 15.00
GD Gerry Davis 6.00 15.00
GDA Gary Darling 6.00 15.00
JB Joe Brinkman 6.00 15.00
JC Jerry Crawford 6.00 15.00
JH John Hirschbeck 6.00 15.00
JW Joe West 6.00 15.00
LY Larry Young 6.00 15.00
MR Mike Reilly 6.00 15.00
RM Randy Marsh 6.00 15.00
SP Steve Palermo 6.00 15.00
TM Tim McClelland 6.00 15.00
TW Tim Welke 6.00 15.00

2004 Bowman Heritage Signs of Glory

STATED ODDS 1:246 HOBBY, 1:503 RETAIL
*RED: 1.25X TO 3X BASIC
RED ODDS 1:2019 HOBBY, 1:3961 RETAIL
RED PRINT RUN 55 SERIAL #'d SETS
BK Bob Kuzava 5.00 12.00
BS Bobby Shantz 5.00 12.00
GK George Kell 10.00 25.00
MS Bill Skowron 10.00 25.00
PR Preacher Roe 6.00 15.00

2004 Bowman Heritage Signs of Greatness

STATED ODDS 1:57 HOBBY, 1:122 RETAIL
*RED: 1.5X TO 4X BASIC
RED ODDS 1:999 HOBBY, 1:2038 RETAIL
RED PRINT RUN 55 SERIAL #'d SETS
CL Chris Lambert 2.50 6.00
GG Greg Golson 2.50 6.00
JM Jeff Marquez 2.50 6.00
JR Jay Rainville 2.50 6.00
MB Matt Bush 4.00 10.00
MR Mark Rogers 4.00 10.00
NW Neil Walker 4.00 10.00
PH Philip Hughes 6.00 15.00
TD Thomas Diamond 2.50 6.00
TP Trevor Plouffe 6.00 15.00

2004 Bowman Heritage Threads of Greatness

GROUP A ODDS 1:339 H, 1:799 R
GROUP B ODDS 1:229 H, 1:534 R
GROUP C ODDS 1:128 H, 1:279 R
GROUP D ODDS 1:48 H, 1:109 R
GROUP E ODDS 1:261 H, 1:621 R
GROUP F ODDS 1:26 H, 1:49 R
*GOLD: 1.2X TO 3X BASIC C-F
*GOLD: 1X TO 2.5X BASIC B
*GOLD: .75X TO 2X BASIC A
RED ODDS 1:115 HOBBY, 1:264 RETAIL
RED PRINT RUN 55 SERIAL #'d SETS
AB Adrian Beltre Bat C 2.00 5.00
AEP Andy Pettitte Uni F 3.00 8.00
AGB Armando Benitez Jsy F 2.00 5.00
AJ Andruw Jones Bat A 6.00 15.00
AMB Angel Berroa Bat B 3.00 8.00
AP Albert Pujols Jsy B 8.00 20.00
AP2 Albert Pujols Bat F 6.00 15.00
AR Alex Rodriguez Bat A 10.00 25.00
AS Alfonso Soriano Bat D 2.00 5.00
BB Bret Boone Bat C 2.00 5.00
BB2 Bret Boone Jsy F 2.00 5.00
BC Bobby Cox Uni F 4.00 10.00
BW Bernie Williams Bat C 3.00 8.00
BZ Barry Zito Uni F 2.00 5.00
CE Carl Everett Uni F 2.00 5.00
CS C.C. Sabathia Jsy F 2.00 5.00
DJ Dave Justice Uni F 3.00 8.00
DW Dontrelle Willis Jsy D 3.00 8.00
EC Eric Chavez Bat D 2.00 5.00
EC2 Eric Chavez Uni D 2.00 5.00
FT Frank Thomas Jsy F 3.00 8.00
GS Gary Sheffield Bat D 3.00 8.00
HB Hank Blalock Bat A 4.00 10.00
HB2 Hank Blalock Jsy F 2.00 5.00
HN Hideo Nomo Jsy E 3.00 8.00
JAG Juan Gonzalez Jsy B 3.00 8.00
JB Jeff Bagwell Bat C 3.00 8.00
JB2 Jeff Bagwell Jsy F 3.00 8.00
JD Johnny Damon Uni D 3.00 8.00
JDS Jason Schmidt Jsy C 2.00 5.00
JG Jason Giambi Uni F 2.00 5.00
JG2 Jason Giambi Jsy D 2.00 5.00
JL Javy Lopez Jsy B 3.00 8.00
JM Joe Mauer Bat B 4.00 10.00
JO John Olerud Bat E 3.00 8.00
JO2 John Olerud Jsy F 3.00 8.00
JPB Josh Beckett Jsy A 4.00 10.00
JPB2 Josh Beckett Bat D 2.00 5.00
JR Jose Reyes Jsy A 4.00 10.00
JS John Smoltz Jsy B 4.00 10.00
JS2 John Smoltz Jsy F 3.00 8.00
JT Jim Thome Jsy D 3.00 8.00
JT2 Jim Thome Bat E 3.00 8.00
JW Jarrod Washburn Uni F 2.00 5.00
KM Kevin Millwood Jsy F 2.00 5.00
KW Kerry Wood Jsy B 3.00 8.00
KW2 Kerry Wood Bat D 2.00 5.00
LB Lance Berkman Bat D 2.00 5.00
LB2 Lance Berkman Jsy D 2.00 5.00
MA Moises Alou Jsy A 8.00 20.00
MC Miguel Cabrera Bat D 6.00 15.00
MCD Mike McDougal Jsy F 2.00 5.00
MCT Mark Teixeira Jsy D 3.00 8.00
ML Mike Lowell Jsy F 2.00 5.00
MM Mark Mulder White Uni F 2.00 5.00
MM2 Mark Mulder White Uni F 2.00 5.00
MP Mike Piazza Bat D 4.00 10.00
MP2 Mike Piazza Jsy A 6.00 15.00
MR Manny Ramirez Uni B 4.00 10.00
MR2 Manny Ramirez Bat D 3.00 8.00
MS Mike Sweeney Bat F 2.00 5.00
MT Miguel Tejada Bat A 4.00 10.00
MT2 Miguel Tejada White Uni F 2.00 5.00
MT3 Miguel Tejada Gray Uni F 2.00 5.00
MY Michael Young Jsy A 4.00 10.00
NG Nomar Garciaparra Bat F 4.00 10.00
OV Omar Vizquel Bat C 3.00 8.00
PB Pat Burrell Bat D 2.00 5.00
PL Paul LoDuca Bat C 2.00 5.00
RB Rocco Baldelli Bat B 3.00 8.00
RC Roger Clemens Uni F 4.00 10.00
RH Roy Halladay Jsy F 2.00 5.00
RS Ruben Sierra Bat C 2.00 5.00
SS Sammy Sosa Blue Jsy A 6.00 15.00
SS2 Sammy Sosa Bat C 3.00 8.00
SS3 Sammy Sosa White Jsy F 3.00 8.00
TB Tony Batista Jsy D 2.00 5.00
TH Todd Helton Jsy D 3.00 8.00
VW Vernon Wells Jsy D 2.00 5.00
WB Wade Boggs Jsy A 6.00 15.00

2005 Bowman Heritage

COMPLETE SET (350) 50.00 120.00
COMP.SET w/o SP's (300) 8.00 20.00
COMMON CARD (1-300) .15 .40
COMMON RC (1-300) .15 .40
COMMON SP (301-350) 1.00 2.50
COM.SP RC (301-350) .30 .75
301-350 SP ODDS 1:3 H, 1:3 R
PLATES STATED ODDS 1:343 HOBBY
PLATES PRINT RUN 1 #'d SET PER COLOR
PLATES: BLACK, CYAN, MAGENTA & YELLOW
NO PLATES PRICING DUE TO SCARCITY
ROOP BINDER EXCH ODDS 1:240 H
ROOP BINDER EXCH.DEADLINE 12/31/07
1 Steven White FY RC .15 .40
2 Jorge Posada .25 .60
3 Brett Myers .15 .40
4 Pat Burrell .15 .40
5 Grady Sizemore .25 .60
6 Jeff Weaver .15 .40
7 Jeff Kent .15 .40
8 Mark Kotsay .15 .40
9 Nick Swisher .25 .60
10 Scott Rolen .25 .60
11 Matt Morris .15 .40
12 Luis Castillo .15 .40
13 Pedro Feliz .15 .40
14 Omar Vizquel .25 .60
15 Edgar Renteria .15 .40
16 David Wells .15 .40
17 Chad Cordero .15 .40
18 Brad Wilkerson .15 .40
19 Kelly Johnson .15 .40
20 Johnny Estrada .15 .40
21 Brian Roberts .15 .40
22 Jeromy Burnitz .15 .40
23 Magglio Ordonez .25 .60
24 Adam Dunn .25 .60
25 Randy Johnson .40 1.00
26 Derek Jeter 1.00 2.50
27 Jon Lieber .15 .40
28 Jim Thome .25 .60
29 Ronnie Belliard .15 .40
30 Jake Westbrook .15 .40
31 Bengie Molina .15 .40
32 J.D. Drew .15 .40
33 Rich Harden .15 .40
34 David Eckstein .15 .40
35 Scott Podsednik .15 .40
36 Mark Buehrle .25 .60
37 Barry Bonds .60 1.50
38 Brian Schneider .15 .40
39 Tim Wakefield .25 .60
40 Craig Wilson .15 .40
41 Jose Vidro .15 .40
42 Jacque Jones .15 .40
43 Felix Hernandez .50 1.25
44 Nomar Garciaparra .25 .60
45 Neifi Perez .15 .40
46 Brandon Inge .15 .40
47 Felipe Lopez .15 .40
48 Ken Griffey Jr. .75 2.00
49 Robinson Cano .50 1.25
50 Jason Giambi .15 .40
51 Mike Lieberthal .15 .40
52 Bobby Abreu .15 .40
53 C.C. Sabathia .25 .60
54 Aaron Boone .15 .40
55 Milton Bradley .15 .40
56 Derek Lowe .15 .40
57 Barry Zito .25 .60
58 Jim Edmonds .25 .60
59 Jon Garland .15 .40
60 Tadahito Iguchi RC .25 .60
61 Jason Schmidt .15 .40
62 David Ortiz .40 1.00
63 Matt Lawton .15 .40
64 Zach Duke .15 .40
65 Gary Sheffield .15 .40
66 Chipper Jones .40 1.00
67 Sammy Sosa .40 1.00
68 Rafael Palmeiro .25 .60
69 Carlos Zambrano .25 .60
70 Aramis Ramirez .15 .40
71 Chris Shelton .15 .40
72 Wily Mo Pena .15 .40
73 Mike Mussina .25 .60
74 Chien-Ming Wang .60 1.50
75 Randy Wolf .15 .40
76 Jimmy Rollins .25 .60
77 Chase Utley .25 .60
78 Kevin Millwood .15 .40
79 Victor Martinez .25 .60
80 Morgan Ensberg .15 .40
81 Bartolo Colon .15 .40
82 Bobby Crosby .15 .40
83 Dan Johnson .15 .40
84 Dan Haren .15 .40
85 Yadier Molina 6.00 15.00
86 Mark Mulder .15 .40
87 Russell Branyan .15 .40
88 Lyle Overbay .15 .40
89 Edgardo Alfonzo .15 .40
90 Mike Matheny .15 .40
91 J.T. Snow .15 .40
92 Curt Schilling .25 .60
93 Oliver Perez .15 .40
94 Mark Redman .15 .40
95 Esteban Loaiza .15 .40
96 Livan Hernandez .15 .40
97 Ryan Church .15 .40
98 Kyle Davies .15 .40
99 Mike Hampton .15 .40
100 Jeff Francoeur .40 1.00
101 Javy Lopez .15 .40
102 Mark Prior .25 .60
103 Kerry Wood .15 .40
104 Carlos Guillen .15 .40
105 Dmitri Young .15 .40
106 David Wright .30 .75
107 Cliff Floyd .15 .40
108 Carlos Beltran .25 .60
109 Melky Cabrera RC .50 1.25
110 Carl Pavano .15 .40
111 Jamie Moyer .15 .40
112 Joel Pineiro .15 .40
113 Adrian Beltre .40 1.00
114 Jhonny Peralta .15 .40
115 Travis Hafner .15 .40
116 Cesar Izturis .15 .40
117 Brad Penny .15 .40
118 Garret Anderson .15 .40
119 Scott Kazmir .40 1.00
120 Aubrey Huff .15 .40
121 Larry Walker .25 .60
122 Albert Pujols .50 1.25
123 Paul Konerko .25 .60
124 Frank Thomas .40 1.00
125 Phil Nevin .15 .40
126 Brian Giles .15 .40
127 Ramon Hernandez .15 .40
128 Johnny Damon .25 .60
129 Trot Nixon .15 .40
130 Rocco Baldelli .15 .40
131 Carl Crawford .25 .60
132 Alfonso Soriano .25 .60
133 Mark Teixeira .25 .60
134 Gustavo Chacin .15 .40
135 Vernon Wells .15 .40
136 Erik Bedard .15 .40
137 Daniel Cabrera .15 .40
138 Michael Barrett .15 .40
139 Greg Maddux .50 1.25
140 Javier Vazquez .15 .40
141 Chad Tracy .15 .40
142 Michael Young .15 .40
143 Kenny Rogers .15 .40
144 Mike Piazza .40 1.00
145 Jose Reyes .25 .60
146 Geoff Jenkins .15 .40
147 Carlos Lee .15 .40
148 Brady Clark .15 .40
149 Torii Hunter .15 .40
150 Johan Santana .25 .60
151 Steve Finley .15 .40
152 Darin Erstad .15 .40
153 Jake Peavy .15 .40
154 Xavier Nady .15 .40
155 Ryan Klesko .15 .40
156 Ichiro Suzuki .50 1.25
157 Richie Sexson .15 .40
158 Raul Ibanez .25 .60
159 Freddy Garcia .15 .40
160 Brad Hawpe .15 .40
161 Jeff Francis .15 .40
162 Todd Helton .25 .60
163 Clint Barmes .15 .40
164 Rodrigo Lopez .15 .40
165 Melvin Mora .15 .40
166 Brandon Webb .25 .60
167 Shawn Green .15 .40
168 Moises Alou .15 .40
169 Matt Clement .15 .40
170 John Smoltz .40 1.00
171 Rafael Furcal .15 .40
172 Jeff Bagwell .25 .60
173 Roger Clemens .50 1.25
174 Dontrelle Willis .15 .40
175 Paul Lo Duca .15 .40
176 Zack Greinke .50 1.25
177 David DeJesus .15 .40
178 Mike Sweeney .15 .40
179 Ben Sheets .15 .40
180 Doug Davis .15 .40
181 Mike Cameron .15 .40
182 Lance Berkman .25 .60
183 Craig Biggio .25 .60
184 Shannon Stewart .15 .40
185 Joe Mauer .30 .75
186 Justin Morneau .25 .60
187 Mike Maroth .15 .40
188 Ivan Rodriguez .25 .60
189 Luis Gonzalez .15 .40
190 Troy Glaus .15 .40
191 Adam Eaton .15 .40
192 Khalil Greene .15 .40
193 Mike Lowell .15 .40
194 Miguel Cabrera .40 1.00
195 Roy Halladay .25 .60
196 Ted Lilly .15 .40
197 Alex Rios .15 .40
198 Josh Beckett .15 .40
199 A.J. Burnett .15 .40
200 Juan Pierre .15 .40
201 Marcus Giles .15 .40
202 Craig Tatum FY RC .15 .40
203 Hayden Penn FY RC .15 .40
204 C.J. Smith FY RC .15 .40
205 Matt Albers FY RC .15 .40
206 Jared Gothreaux FY RC .15 .40
207 Mike Rodriguez FY RC .15 .40
208 Hernan Iribarren FY RC .15 .40
209 Manny Parra FY RC .40 1.00
210 Kevin Collins FY RC .15 .40
211 Buck Coats FY RC .15 .40
212 Jeremy West FY RC .15 .40
213 Ian Bladergroen FY RC .15 .40
214 Chuck Tiffany FY RC .40 1.00
215 Andy LaRoche FY RC .15 .40
216 Frank Diaz FY RC .15 .40
217 Jai Miller FY RC .15 .40
218 Tony Giarratano FY RC .15 .40
219 Danny Zell FY RC .15 .40
220 Justin Verlander FY RC 3.00 8.00
221 Ryan Sweeney FY RC .25 .60
222 Brandon McCarthy FY RC .25 .60
223 Jerry Owens FY RC .15 .40
224 Glen Perkins FY RC .15 .40
225 Kevin West FY RC .15 .40
226 Billy Butler FY RC .75 2.00
227 Shane Costa FY RC .15 .40
228 Erik Schindewolf FY RC .15 .40
229 Miguel Montero FY RC .50 1.25
230 Stephen Drew FY RC .50 1.25
231 Matt DeSalvo FY RC .15 .40
232 Ben Jones FY RC .15 .40
233 Bill McCarthy FY RC .15 .40
234 Chuck James FY RC .40 1.00
235 Brandon Sing FY RC .15 .40
236 Andy Santana FY RC .15 .40
237 Brendan Ryan FY RC .15 .40
238 Wes Swackhamer FY RC .15 .40
239 Jeff Niemann FY RC .40 1.00
240 Ian Kinsler FY RC .75 2.00
241 Micah Furtado FY RC .15 .40
242 Ryan Mount FY RC .15 .40
243 P.J. Phillips FY RC .15 .40
244 Trevor Bell FY RC .15 .40
245 Jered Weaver FY RC .75 2.00
246 Eddy Martinez FY RC .15 .40
247 Brian Bannister FY RC .25 .60
248 Philip Humber FY RC .40 1.00
249 Michael Rogers FY RC .15 .40
250 Landon Powell FY RC .15 .40
251 Kennard Bibbs FY RC .15 .40
252 Nelson Cruz FY RC 2.00 5.00
253 Paul Kelly FY RC .15 .40
254 Kevin Slowey FY RC .75 2.00
255 Brandon Snyder FY RC .40 1.00
256 Nolan Reimold FY RC .60 1.50
257 Brian Stavisky FY RC .15 .40
258 Javier Herrera FY RC .15 .40
259 Russ Martin FY RC .50 1.25
260 Matthew Kemp FY RC .75 2.00
261 Wade Townsend FY RC .15 .40
262 Nick Touchstone FY RC .15 .40
263 Ryan Feierabend FY RC .15 .40
264 Bobby Livingston FY RC .15 .40
265 Wladimir Balentien FY RC .25 .60
266 Keiichi Yabu FY RC .15 .40
267 Craig Italiano FY RC .15 .40
268 Ryan Goleski FY RC .15 .40
269 Ryan Garko FY RC .15 .40
270 Mike Bourn FY RC .40 1.00
271 Scott Mathieson FY RC .15 .40
272 Scott Mitchinson FY RC .15 .40
273 Tyler Greene FY RC .15 .40
274 Mark McCormick FY RC .15 .40

275 Daryl Jones FY RC .15 .40
276 Travis Chick FY RC .15 .40
277 Luis Hernandez FY RC .15 .40
278 Steve Doetsch FY RC .15 .40
279 Chris Vines FY RC .15 .40
280 Mike Costanzo FY RC .15 .40
281 Matt Maloney FY RC .15 .40
282 Matt Goyen FY RC .15 .40
283 Jacob Marceaux FY RC .15 .40
284 David Gassner FY RC .15 .40
285 Ricky Barrett FY RC .15 .40
286 Jon Egan FY RC .15 .40
287 Scott Blue FY RC .15 .40
288 Steven Bondurant FY RC .15 .40
289 Kevin Melillo FY RC .15 .40
290 Brad Corley FY RC .15 .40
291 Brent Lillibridge FY RC .15 .40
292 Mike Morse FY RC .50 1.25
293 Justin Thomas FY RC .15 .40
294 Nick Webber FY RC .15 .40
295 Mitch Boggs FY RC .15 .40
296 Jeff Lyman FY RC .15 .40
297 Jordan Schafer FY RC .75 2.00
298 Ismael Ramirez FY RC .15 .40
299 Chris B.Young FY RC .50 1.25
300 Brian Miller FY RC .15 .40
301 Jason Bay SP 1.00 2.50
302 Tim Hudson SP 1.50 4.00
303 Miguel Tejada SP 1.50 4.00
304 Jeremy Bonderman SP 1.00 2.50
305 Alex Rodriguez SP 3.00 8.00
306 Rickie Weeks SP 1.00 2.50
307 Manny Ramirez SP 2.50 6.00
308 Nick Johnson SP 1.00 2.50
309 Andruw Jones SP 1.00 2.50
310 Hideki Matsui SP 4.00 10.00
311 Jeremy Reed SP 1.00 2.50
312 Dallas McPherson SP 1.00 2.50
313 Vladimir Guerrero SP 1.50 4.00
314 Eric Chavez SP 1.00 2.50
315 Chris Carpenter SP 1.50 4.00
316 Aaron Hill SP 1.50 4.00
317 Derrek Lee SP 1.00 2.50
318 Mark Loretta SP 1.00 2.50
319 Garrett Atkins SP 1.00 2.50
320 Hank Blalock SP 1.00 2.50
321 Chris Young SP 1.50 4.00
322 Roy Oswalt SP 1.50 4.00
323 Carlos Delgado SP 1.00 2.50
324 Pedro Martinez SP 1.50 4.00
325 Jeff Clement FY SP RC .30 .75
326 Jimmy Shull FY SP RC .30 .75
327 Daniel Carte FY SP RC .30 .75
328 Travis Buck FY SP RC .30 .75
329 Chris Volstad FY SP RC .75 2.00
330 A.McCutchen FY SP RC 4.00 10.00
331 Cliff Pennington FY SP RC .30 .75
332 John Mayberry Jr. FY SP RC .75 2.00
333 C.J. Henry FY SP RC .50 1.25
334 Ricky Romero FY SP RC .50 1.25
335 Aaron Thompson FY SP RC .50 1.25
336 Cesar Carrillo FY SP RC .50 1.25
337 Jacoby Ellsbury FY SP RC 2.50 6.00
338 Matt Garza FY SP RC .50 1.25
339 Colby Rasmus FY SP RC .75 2.00
340 Ryan Zimmerman FY SP RC 1.50 4.00
341 Ryan Braun FY SP RC 2.50 6.00
342 Brent Lillibridge FY SP .30 .75
343 Jay Bruce FY SP RC 2.50 6.00
344 Matt Green FY SP RC .30 .75
345 Brent Cox FY SP RC .30 .75
346 Jed Lowrie FY SP RC .30 .75
347 Beau Jones FY SP RC .75 2.00
348 Eli Iorg FY SP RC .30 .75
349 Chaz Roe FY SP RC .30 .75
350 Mickey Mantle 15.00 40.00
NNO Roop Binder Redemption 6.00 15.00

2005 Bowman Heritage Draft Pick Variation

COMPLETE SET (25) 30.00 60.00
*DP VAR: .4X TO 1X BASIC
ONE 5-CARD DPV PACK PER HOBBY BOX

2005 Bowman Heritage Mahogany

COMPLETE SET (350) 75.00 150.00
*MAH 1-300: 1X TO 2.5X BASIC
*MAH 1-300: .6X TO 1.5X BASIC RC
ONE MAHOGANY OR RELIC PER PACK
ON AVG. 22 MAHOG'S PER 24 CT. BOX
150 Johan Santana .60 1.50
185 Joe Mauer .75 2.00
301 Jason Bay .40 1.00
302 Tim Hudson .60 1.50
303 Miguel Tejada .60 1.50
304 Jeremy Bonderman .40 1.00
305 Alex Rodriguez 1.25 3.00
306 Rickie Weeks .40 1.00
307 Manny Ramirez 1.00 2.50
308 Nick Johnson .40 1.00
309 Andruw Jones .40 1.00
310 Hideki Matsui 1.50 4.00
311 Jeremy Reed .40 1.00
312 Dallas McPherson .40 1.00
313 Vladimir Guerrero .60 1.50
314 Eric Chavez .40 1.00
315 Chris Carpenter .60 1.50
316 Aaron Hill .60 1.50
317 Derrek Lee .40 1.00
318 Mark Loretta .40 1.00
319 Garrett Atkins .40 1.00
320 Hank Blalock .40 1.00
321 Chris Young .60 1.50
322 Roy Oswalt .60 1.50
323 Carlos Delgado .40 1.00
324 Pedro Martinez .60 1.50
325 Jeff Clement .40 1.00
326 Jimmy Shull .40 1.00
327 Daniel Carte .40 1.00
328 Travis Buck .40 1.00
329 Chris Volstad 1.00 2.50
330 Andrew McCutchen 5.00 12.00
331 Cliff Pennington .40 1.00
332 John Mayberry Jr. 1.00 2.50
333 C.J. Henry .60 1.50
334 Ricky Romero .60 1.50
335 Aaron Thompson .60 1.50
336 Cesar Carrillo .60 1.50
337 Jacoby Ellsbury 3.00 8.00
338 Matt Garza .60 1.50
339 Colby Rasmus 1.00 2.50
340 Ryan Zimmerman 2.00 5.00
341 Ryan Braun 3.00 8.00
342 Brent Lillibridge .40 1.00
343 Jay Bruce 3.00 8.00
344 Matt Green .40 1.00
345 Brent Cox .40 1.00
346 Jed Lowrie .40 1.00
347 Beau Jones 1.00 2.50
348 Eli Iorg .40 1.00
349 Chaz Roe .40 1.00

2005 Bowman Heritage Mini

COMPLETE SET (350) 75.00 150.00
*MINI 1-300: 1X TO 2.5X BASIC
*MINI 1-300: .6X TO 1.5X BASIC RC
ONE MINI OR BLUE/RED BACK PER PACK
ON AVG. 20 MINI'S PER 24 CT. BOX
150 Johan Santana .60 1.50
185 Joe Mauer .75 2.00
301 Jason Bay .40 1.00
302 Tim Hudson .60 1.50
303 Miguel Tejada .60 1.50
304 Jeremy Bonderman .40 1.00
305 Alex Rodriguez 1.25 3.00
306 Rickie Weeks .40 1.00
307 Manny Ramirez 1.00 2.50
308 Nick Johnson .40 1.00
309 Andruw Jones .40 1.00
310 Hideki Matsui 1.50 4.00
311 Jeremy Reed .40 1.00
312 Dallas McPherson .40 1.00
313 Vladimir Guerrero .60 1.50
314 Eric Chavez .40 1.00
315 Chris Carpenter .60 1.50
316 Aaron Hill .60 1.50
317 Derrek Lee .40 1.00
318 Mark Loretta .40 1.00
319 Garrett Atkins .40 1.00
320 Hank Blalock .40 1.00
321 Chris Young .60 1.50
322 Roy Oswalt .60 1.50
323 Carlos Delgado .40 1.00
324 Pedro Martinez .60 1.50
325 Jeff Clement .40 1.00
326 Jimmy Shull .40 1.00
327 Daniel Carte .40 1.00
328 Travis Buck .40 1.00
329 Chris Volstad 1.00 2.50
330 Andrew McCutchen 5.00 12.00
331 Cliff Pennington .40 1.00
332 John Mayberry Jr. 1.00 2.50
333 C.J. Henry .60 1.50
334 Ricky Romero .60 1.50
335 Aaron Thompson .60 1.50
336 Cesar Carrillo .60 1.50
337 Jacoby Ellsbury 3.00 8.00
338 Matt Garza .60 1.50
339 Colby Rasmus 1.00 2.50
340 Ryan Zimmerman 2.00 5.00
341 Ryan Braun 3.00 8.00
342 Brent Lillibridge .40 1.00
343 Jay Bruce 3.00 8.00
344 Matt Green .40 1.00
345 Brent Cox .40 1.00
346 Jed Lowrie .40 1.00
347 Beau Jones 1.00 2.50
348 Eli Iorg .40 1.00
349 Chaz Roe .40 1.00
350 Mystery Redemption 10.00 25.00

2005 Bowman Heritage Red

STATED ODDS 1:1374 HOBBY
STATED PRINT RUN 1 SERIAL #'d SET
NO PRICING DUE TO SCARCITY

2005 Bowman Heritage '51 Topps Heritage Blue Backs

OVERALL 51 HERITAGE ODDS 1:6 H/R
1 Adam Dunn 1.25 3.00
2 Zach Duke .75 2.00
3 Alex Rodriguez 1.25 3.00
4 Vladimir Guerrero .60 1.50
5 Andruw Jones .75 2.00
6 Travis Chick .75 2.00
7 Alfonso Soriano 1.25 3.00
8 Scott Rolen 1.25 3.00
9 Brian Bannister 1.25 3.00
10 Randy Johnson 1.00 2.50
11 Barry Bonds 1.50 4.00
12 Pat Burrell .75 2.00
13 Barry Zito .60 1.50
14 Nomar Garciaparra .60 1.50
15 C.C. Sabathia 1.25 3.00
16 Miguel Tejada 1.25 3.00
17 Hideki Matsui 3.00 8.00
18 John Smoltz 2.00 5.00
19 Ken Griffey Jr. 2.00 5.00
20 Chris Carpenter .60 1.50
21 Ian Kinsler 2.00 5.00
22 Chuck Tiffany 2.00 5.00
23 Gary Sheffield .75 2.00
24 Mark Mulder .75 2.00
25 Ichiro Suzuki 1.25 3.00
26 Kerry Wood .75 2.00
27 Jose Reyes 1.25 3.00
28 Derrek Lee .40 1.00
29 Justin Verlander 8.00 20.00
30 Johnny Damon 1.25 3.00
31 Chris Volstad 1.00 2.50
32 Jeremy Bonderman .75 2.00
33 David Ortiz 1.00 2.50
34 Morgan Ensberg .75 2.00
35 Mark Buehrle .60 1.50
36 Chuck James 2.00 5.00
37 Miguel Cabrera 1.00 2.50
38 Magglio Ordonez 1.25 3.00
39 Michael Young .40 1.00
40 Carlos Beltran 1.25 3.00
41 Nick Johnson .75 2.00
42 Billy Butler 2.00 5.00
43 Brian Giles .75 2.00
44 Paul Konerko 1.25 3.00
45 Roy Oswalt 1.25 3.00
46 Bobby Abreu .75 2.00
47 Sammy Sosa 1.00 2.50
48 Aramis Ramirez .75 2.00
49 Torii Hunter .75 2.00
50 Aubrey Huff .40 1.00
51 Vernon Wells .75 2.00
52 Joe Mauer .75 2.00

2005 Bowman Heritage '51 Topps Heritage Red Backs

OVERALL 51 HERITAGE ODDS 1:6 H/R
1 Andy LaRoche .40 1.00
2 Mike Piazza 2.00 5.00
3 Pedro Martinez 1.25 3.00
4 Wladimir Balentien .60 1.50
5 Tim Hudson .60 1.50
6 Richie Sexson .75 2.00
7 Carlos Delgado .75 2.00
8 Derek Jeter 5.00 12.00
9 Ryan Zimmerman 2.00 5.00
10 Mark Teixeira .60 1.50
11 David Wright .75 2.00
12 Jake Peavy .40 1.00
13 Jose Vidro .75 2.00
14 Jim Thome 1.25 3.00
15 Carlos Zambrano 1.25 3.00
16 Hank Blalock .75 2.00
17 Johan Santana .60 1.50
18 Cliff Pennington .40 1.00
19 Rafael Palmeiro 1.25 3.00
20 Curt Schilling 1.25 3.00
21 Brandon McCarthy .60 1.50
22 Stephen Drew 1.25 3.00
23 Jeff Niemann 2.00 5.00
24 Eric Chavez .75 2.00
25 Hernan Iribarren .75 2.00
26 Jered Weaver 4.00 10.00
27 Edgar Renteria .75 2.00
28 Travis Hafner .75 2.00
29 Frank Thomas 1.00 2.50
30 Brian Roberts .75 2.00
31 Anthony Reyes .60 1.50
32 Scott Kazmir 2.00 5.00
33 Carlos Lee .75 2.00
34 Jimmy Rollins 1.25 3.00
35 Garret Anderson .75 2.00
36 Jason Schmidt .75 2.00
37 Jon Garland .75 2.00
38 Dontrelle Willis .75 2.00
39 C.J. Henry 1.25 3.00
40 Greg Maddux 2.50 6.00
41 Todd Helton 1.25 3.00
42 Ivan Rodriguez 1.25 3.00
43 Chipper Jones 2.00 5.00
44 Rich Harden .75 2.00
45 Mark Prior 1.25 3.00
46 Roy Halladay .60 1.50
47 Albert Pujols 1.25 3.00
48 Roger Clemens 2.50 6.00
49 Andrew McCutchen 5.00 12.00
50 Scott Podsednik .75 2.00
51 Manny Ramirez 2.00 5.00
52 Carl Crawford 1.25 3.00
53 Jim Edmonds 1.25 3.00
54 Wily Mo Pena .75 2.00

2005 Bowman Heritage Future Greatness Jersey Relics

GROUP A ODDS 1:1004 H, 1:3350 R
GROUP B ODDS 1:270 H, 1:1237 R
GROUP C ODDS 1:205 H, 1:875 R
GROUP D ODDS 1:61 H, 1:210 R
GROUP E ODDS 1:141 H, 1:500 R
*RAINBOW: .75X TO 2X GRP C-E
*RAINBOW: .75X TO 2X GRP B
*RAINBOW: .5X TO 1.2X GRP A
OVERALL RAINBOW ODDS 1:183 H, 1:735 R
RAINBOW PRINT RUN 51 SERIAL #'d SETS
OVERALL RAINBOW RED ODDS 1:7841 H
RAINBOW RED PRINT RUN 1 #'d SET
NO R'BOW RED PRICING DUE TO SCARCITY
AH Aaron Hill D 2.00 5.00
AM Arnie Munoz D 2.00 5.00
AMA Andy Marte D 3.00 8.00
BB Bryan Bullington D 2.00 5.00
BT Brad Thompson A 3.00 8.00
CE Clint Everts B 2.00 5.00
DM Dallas McPherson C 2.00 5.00
DY Delmon Young A 10.00 25.00
EE Edwin Encarnacion C 3.00 8.00
FC Fausto Carmona A 3.00 8.00
FP Felix Pie C 3.00 8.00
GF Gavin Floyd D 2.00 5.00
JB Joe Blanton D 3.00 8.00
JC Jorge Cortes B 2.00 5.00
JCO Jesus Cota D 2.00 5.00
JF Jeff Francis D 3.00 8.00
JG Joel Guzman E 3.00 8.00
JGA Jairo Garcia B 2.00 5.00
JK Jason Kubel A 3.00 8.00
JM Justin Morneau D 3.00 8.00
JMA Jeff Mathis B 3.00 8.00
JP Juan Perez E 2.00 5.00
KH Koyie Hill B 2.00 5.00
MC Matt Cain D 4.00 10.00
RG Ruben Gotay B 2.00 5.00
RW Rickie Weeks D 3.00 8.00
SC Shin Soo Choo C 3.00 8.00
TB Tony Blanco E 2.00 5.00
VM Val Majewski D 2.00 5.00
WL Wil Ledezma E 2.00 5.00
YP Yusmeiro Petit D 3.00 8.00

2005 Bowman Heritage Pieces of Greatness Relics

GROUP A ODDS 1:167 H, 1:555 R
GROUP B ODDS 1:47 H, 1:155 R
GROUP C ODDS 1:55 H, 1:188 R
AD Adam Dunn Bat A 3.00 8.00
AP Albert Pujols Jsy B 6.00 15.00
AR Alex Rodriguez Bat A 6.00 15.00
BB Barry Bonds Uni A 8.00 20.00
BC Bobby Crosby Uni C 3.00 8.00
BM Brett Myers Jsy A 3.00 8.00
BR Brian Roberts Bat B 3.00 8.00
BZ Barry Zito Uni C 3.00 8.00
CB Carlos Beltran Bat B 3.00 8.00
CD Carlos Delgado Bat B 3.00 8.00
DW Dontrelle Willis Jsy C 3.00 8.00
DWR David Wright Bat B 4.00 10.00
EC Eric Chavez Uni C 3.00 8.00
IS Ichiro Suzuki Jsy C 6.00 15.00
JB Josh Beckett Uni B 3.00 8.00
JD Johnny Damon Bat B 3.00 8.00
JG Josh Gibson Seat C 6.00 15.00
JK Jeff Kent Bat A 3.00 8.00
JS John Smoltz Jsy B 3.00 8.00
JT Jim Thome Bat B 3.00 8.00
MC Miguel Cabrera Bat A 3.00 8.00
MM Mark Mulder Uni B 3.00 8.00
MMO Melvin Mora Bat B 3.00 8.00
MR Manny Ramirez Bat B 3.00 8.00
MT Miguel Tejada Bat C 3.00 8.00
PK Paul Konerko Bat B 3.00 8.00
PM Pedro Martinez Bat B 3.00 8.00
RC Roger Clemens Jsy A 6.00 15.00
RH Rich Harden Jsy A 3.00 8.00
TG Troy Glaus Bat B 3.00 8.00
TH Todd Helton Jsy B 3.00 8.00

2005 Bowman Heritage Pieces of Greatness Rainbow Relics

*RAINBOW: .75X TO 2X GRP B-C
*RAINBOW: .75X TO 2X GRP A
OVERALL RAINBOW ODDS 1:183 H, 1:735 R
STATED PRINT RUN 51 SERIAL #'d SETS
RED STATED ODDS 1:7841 HOBBY
RED PRINT RUN 1 SERIAL #'d SET
NO RED PRICING DUE TO SCARCITY
BB Barry Bonds Uni 30.00 60.00
IS Ichiro Suzuki Jsy 30.00 60.00
JG Josh Gibson Seat 30.00 60.00

2005 Bowman Heritage Signs of Greatness

GROUP A ODDS 1:153 H, 1:154 R
GROUP B ODDS 1:40 H, 1:40 R
GROUP C ODDS 1:74 H, 1:75 R
*RED INK: 1.25X TO 3X BASIC
RED INK ODDS 1:634 H, 1:635 R
RED INK PRINT RUN 51 SERIAL #'d SETS
NO RC YR RED INK PRICING AVAILABLE
AG Angel Guzman C 3.00 8.00
AM Andrew McCutchen B 12.00 30.00
BL Brent Lillibridge B 4.00 10.00
CT Curtis Thigpen A 3.00 8.00
DJ Dan Johnson A 4.00 10.00
DL Donny Lucey A 3.00 8.00
DP David Purcey C 5.00 12.00
EM Eddy Martinez B 5.00 12.00
HS Huston Street C 6.00 15.00
JB Jay Bruce B 6.00 15.00
JH J.P. Howell C 3.00 8.00
JJ Jason Jaramillo B 3.00 8.00
JM John Mayberry Jr. B 4.00 10.00
JP Jon Papelbon C 4.00 10.00
JZ Jon Zeringue B 3.00 8.00
MB Matt Bush A 4.00 10.00
MG Matt Green B 3.00 8.00
PB Patrick Bryant A 3.00 8.00
PH Philip Humber B 6.00 15.00
RB Ryan Braun B 5.00 12.00
RR Ricky Romero B 5.00 12.00
RZ Ryan Zimmerman B 6.00 15.00
SE Scott Elbert C 3.00 8.00
TC Travis Chick B 3.00 8.00
TD Thomas Diamond B 3.00 8.00
WW Wesley Whisler B 3.00 8.00
ZJ Zach Jackson A 3.00 8.00

2006 Bowman Heritage

COMPLETE SET (300) 75.00 150.00
COMP.SET w/o SP's (250) 15.00 40.00
COMMON CARD (1-300) .15 .40
COMMON RC (1-300) .15 .40
COMMON SP (202-300) 2.00 5.00
COM.SP RC (202-300) 2.00 5.00
202-300 SP ODDS 1:3 H, 1:3 R
SP CL: EVEN #s B/WN 202-300
OVERALL PLATE ODDS 1:497 HOBBY
PLATE PRINT RUN 1 SET PER COLOR
BLACK-CYAN-MAGENTA-YELLOW ISSUED
NO PLATE PRICING DUE TO SCARCITY
1 David Wright .30 .75
2 Andruw Jones .15 .40
3 Ryan Howard .30 .75
4 Jason Bay .15 .40
5 Paul Konerko .25 .60
6 Jake Peavy .15 .40
7 Todd Jones .15 .40
8 Troy Glaus .15 .40
9 Rocco Baldelli .15 .40
10 Rafael Furcal .15 .40
11 Freddy Sanchez .15 .40
12 Jermaine Dye .15 .40
13 A.J. Burnett .15 .40
14 Michael Cuddyer .15 .40
15 Barry Zito .25 .60
16 Chipper Jones .40 1.00
17 Paul LoDuca .15 .40
18 Mark Mulder .15 .40
19 Raul Ibanez .25 .60
20 Carlos Delgado .15 .40
21 Marcus Giles .15 .40
22 Dan Haren .15 .40
23 Justin Morneau .25 .60
24 Livan Hernandez .15 .40
25 Ken Griffey Jr. .75 2.00
26 Aaron Hill .15 .40
27 Tadahito Iguchi .15 .40
28 Nate Robertson .15 .40
29 Kevin Millwood .15 .40
30 Jim Thome .25 .60
31 Aubrey Huff .15 .40
32 Dontrelle Willis .15 .40
33 Khalil Greene .15 .40
34 Doug Davis .15 .40
35 Ivan Rodriguez .25 .60
36 Rickie Weeks .15 .40
37 Jhonny Peralta .15 .40
38 Yadier Molina .50 1.25
39 Eric Chavez .15 .40
40 Alfonso Soriano .25 .60
41 Pat Burrell .15 .40
42 B.J. Ryan .15 .40
43 Carl Crawford .25 .60
44 Preston Wilson .15 .40
45 Jorge Posada .25 .60
46 Carlos Zambrano .25 .60
47 Mark Teahen .15 .40
48 Nick Johnson .15 .40
49 Mark Kotsay .15 .40
50 Derek Jeter 1.00 2.50
51 Moises Alou .15 .40
52 Ryan Freel .15 .40
53 Shannon Stewart .15 .40
54 Casey Blake .15 .40
55 Edgar Renteria .15 .40
56 Frank Thomas .40 1.00
57 Ty Wigginton .15 .40
58 Jeff Kent .15 .40
59 Chien-Ming Wang .25 .60
60 Josh Beckett .15 .40
61 Chase Utley .25 .60
62 Gary Matthews .15 .40
63 Torii Hunter .15 .40
64 Bobby Jenks .15 .40
65 Wilson Betemit .15 .40
66 Jeremy Bonderman .15 .40
67 Scott Rolen .25 .60
68 Brad Penny .15 .40
69 Jacque Jones .15 .40
70 Jose Reyes .25 .60
71 Brian Roberts .15 .40
72 John Smoltz .40 1.00
73 Johnny Estrada .15 .40
74 Ronnie Belliard .15 .40
75 Vladimir Guerrero .25 .60
76 A.J. Pierzynski .15 .40
77 Garrett Atkins .15 .40
78 Adam LaRoche .15 .40
79 Mark Loretta .15 .40
80 Todd Helton .25 .60
81 Jose Vidro .15 .40
82 Carlos Guillen .15 .40
83 Michael Barrett .15 .40
84 Lyle Overbay .15 .40
85 Travis Hafner .15 .40
86 Shea Hillenbrand .15 .40
87 Julio Lugo .15 .40
88 Tim Hudson .25 .60
89 Scott Podsednik .15 .40
90 Roy Halladay .25 .60
91 Bartolo Colon .15 .40
92 Ryan Langerhans .15 .40
93 Tom Glavine .25 .60
94 Kenny Rogers .15 .40
95 Robinson Cano .25 .60
96 Mark Prior .25 .60
97 Jason Schmidt .15 .40
98 Bengie Molina .15 .40
99 Jon Lieber .15 .40
100 Alex Rodriguez .50 1.25
101 Scott Kazmir .25 .60
102 Jeff Francoeur .40 1.00
103 Chris Carpenter .25 .60
104 Juan Uribe .15 .40
105 Mariano Rivera .50 1.25
106 Rich Harden .15 .40
107 Jack Wilson .15 .40
108 Austin Kearns .15 .40
109 Marcus Thames .15 .40
110 Miguel Tejada .25 .60
111 Chone Figgins .15 .40
112 Bronson Arroyo .15 .40
113 Chad Cordero .15 .40
114 Bill Hall .15 .40
115 Curt Schilling .25 .60
116 David Eckstein .15 .40
117 Ramon Hernandez .15 .40
118 Eric Byrnes .15 .40
119 Clint Barmes .15 .40
120 Bobby Abreu .15 .40
121 Joe Crede .15 .40
122 Derek Lowe .15 .40
123 Jason Marquis .15 .40
124 Erik Bedard .15 .40
125 Derrek Lee .15 .40
126 Brian McCann .15 .40
127 Magglio Ordonez .25 .60
128 Ben Sheets .15 .40
129 Brandon Inge .15 .40
130 Miguel Cabrera .40 1.00
131 Jim Edmonds .25 .60
132 John Lackey .25 .60
133 Kevin Mench .15 .40
134 Adrian Beltre .40 1.00
135 Curtis Granderson .30 .75
136 Shawn Green .15 .40
137 Jose Contreras .15 .40
138 Joe Nathan .15 .40
139 Bobby Crosby .15 .40
140 Johnny Damon .25 .60
141 Brad Hawpe .15 .40
142 Brandon Phillips .15 .40
143 Victor Martinez .25 .60
144 Jimmy Rollins .25 .60
145 Corey Patterson .15 .40
146 Grady Sizemore .25 .60
147 Placido Polanco .15 .40
148 Mike Lowell .15 .40
149 Francisco Rodriguez .25 .60
150 Ichiro Suzuki .50 1.25
151 Kris Benson .15 .40
152 Scott Hatteberg .15 .40
153 Akinori Otsuka .15 .40
154 Cesar Izturis .15 .40
155 Roger Clemens .50 1.25
156 Kerry Wood .15 .40
157 Tom Gordon .15 .40
158 Sean Casey .15 .40
159 Jose Lopez .15 .40
160 Orlando Hernandez .15 .40
161 Aramis Ramirez .15 .40
162 J.D. Drew .15 .40
163 David DeJesus .15 .40
164 Craig Biggio .25 .60
165 Brett Myers .15 .40
166 C.C. Sabathia .25 .60
167 Zach Duke .15 .40
168 Luis Castillo .15 .40
169 Hideki Matsui .40 1.00
170 Brian Giles .15 .40
171 Coco Crisp .15 .40
172 Richie Sexson .15 .40
173 Nomar Garciaparra .25 .60
174 Roy Oswalt .25 .60
175 David Ortiz .40 1.00
176 Matt Morris .15 .40
177 Felipe Lopez .15 .40
178 Garret Anderson .15 .40
179 Kevin Youkilis .15 .40
180 Alex Rios .15 .40
181 Jon Garland .15 .40
182 Luis Gonzalez .15 .40
183 Cliff Floyd .15 .40
184 Juan Encarnacion .15 .40
185 Nick Swisher .25 .60
186 Mike Cameron .15 .40
187 Jose Castillo .15 .40
188 Ray Durham .15 .40
189 Jorge Cantu .15 .40
190 Andy Pettitte .25 .60
191 Chad Tracy .15 .40
192 Adrian Gonzalez .30 .75
193 Jose Valentin .15 .40
194 Mark Buehrle .25 .60
195 Huston Street .15 .40
196 Chris Capuano .15 .40
197 Aaron Rowand .15 .40
198 Billy Wagner .15 .40
199 Orlando Cabrera .15 .40
200 Albert Pujols .50 1.25
201 Dan Uggla (RC) .25 .60
202 Alay Soler SP RC 2.00 5.00
203 Matt Kemp (RC) .40 1.00
204 Mike Napoli SP RC 1.25 3.00
205 Joel Zumaya (RC) .40 1.00
206 Mike Pelfrey SP RC 2.00 5.00
207 Ian Kinsler (RC) .50 1.25
208 Josh Willingham SP (RC) 3.00 8.00
209 Erick Aybar (RC) .15 .40
210 Willie Eyre SP (RC) 2.00 5.00
211 Kendry Morales (RC) .40 1.00
212 Scott Thorman SP (RC) 2.00 5.00
213 Hanley Ramirez (RC) .25 .60
214 Boof Bonser SP (RC) 2.00 5.00
215 Anthony Reyes (RC) .15 .40
216 Justin Huber SP (RC) 2.00 5.00
217 Yusmeiro Petit (RC) .15 .40
218 Jason Bartlett SP (RC) 2.00 5.00
219 Shin-Soo Choo (RC) .25 .60
220 Francisco Liriano SP (RC) 2.00 5.00
221 Craig Hansen RC .40 1.00
222 Ricky Nolasco SP (RC) 2.00 5.00
223 Adam Loewen (RC) .15 .40
224 Scott Olsen SP (RC) 2.00 5.00
225 Cole Hamels (RC) .50 1.25
226 Martin Prado SP (RC) 3.00 8.00
227 James Loney (RC) .25 .60
228 Kevin Thompson SP (RC) 2.00 5.00
229 Adam Jones RC 1.50 4.00
230 Josh Johnson SP (RC) 3.00 8.00
231 Anderson Hernandez (RC) .15 .40
232 Tony Gwynn Jr. SP (RC) 2.00 5.00
233 Casey Janssen RC .15 .40
234 Taylor Tankersley SP (RC) 2.00 5.00
235 Mike Thompson RC .15 .40
236 Jeremy Sowers SP (RC) 2.00 5.00
237 Anibal Sanchez (RC) .15 .40
238 Adam Wainwright SP (RC) 2.00 5.00
239 Rich Hill (RC) .40 1.00
240 Russ Martin SP (RC) 2.00 5.00
241 Joe Inglett RC .15 .40
242 Tony Pena SP (RC) 2.00 5.00
243 Josh Sharpless RC .15 .40
244 Darrell Rasner SP (RC) 2.00 5.00
245 Joe Saunders (RC) .15 .40
246 Jon Lester SP RC 2.00 5.00
247 Jeremy Hermida (RC) .15 .40
248 Chad Billingsley SP (RC) 2.00 5.00
249 Bobby Livingston (RC) .15 .40
250 Justin Verlander SP (RC) 6.00 15.00
251 Mickey Mantle 1.25 3.00
252 Hank Blalock SP 2.00 5.00
253 Manny Ramirez .40 1.00
254 Mike Mussina SP 2.00 5.00
255 Greg Maddux .50 1.25
256 Jason Giambi SP 2.00 5.00
257 Mark Teixeira .25 .60
258 Carlos Beltran SP 3.00 8.00
259 Matt Holliday .40 1.00
260 Pedro Martinez SP 2.00 5.00
261 Joe Mauer .25 .60
262 Melvin Mora SP 2.00 5.00
263 Mike Piazza .40 1.00
264 B.J. Upton SP 2.00 5.00
265 Vernon Wells .15 .40
266 Gary Sheffield SP 2.00 5.00
267 Randy Johnson .40 1.00
268 Ryan Zimmerman SP 1.25 3.00
269 Lance Berkman .25 .60
270 Johan Santana SP 2.00 5.00
271 Carlos Lee .15 .40
272 Brandon Webb SP 3.00 8.00
273 Adam Dunn .25 .60
274 Michael Young SP 2.00 5.00
275 Barry Bonds .60 1.50
276 Jonathan Papelbon SP (RC) 2.00 5.00
277 Howie Kendrick (RC) .30 .75
278 Melky Cabrera SP (RC) 2.00 5.00
279 Jered Weaver (RC) .50 1.25
280 Josh Barfield SP (RC) 2.00 5.00
281 Chuck James (RC) .15 .40
282 Lastings Milledge SP (RC) 1.25 3.00
283 Nick Markakis (RC) .30 .75
284 Jose Capellan SP (RC) 2.00 5.00
285 Prince Fielder (RC) .75 2.00
286 Jason Botts SP (RC) 2.00 5.00
287 Eliezer Alfonzo RC .15 .40
288 Sean Marshall SP (RC) 2.00 5.00
289 Ryan Garko (RC) .15 .40
290 Stephen Drew SP (RC) 1.50 4.00
291 Joel Guzman (RC) .15 .40
292 Hong-Chih Kuo SP (RC) 2.00 5.00
293 Zach Miner (RC) .15 .40
294 Angel Guzman SP (RC) 2.00 5.00
295 Andre Ethier (RC) .50 1.25
296 Fausto Carmona SP (RC) 2.00 5.00
297 Ronny Paulino (RC) .15 .40
298 Matt Cain SP (RC) 8.00 20.00
299 Carlos Quentin (RC) .25 .60
300 Kenji Johjima SP RC 1.00 2.50

2006 Bowman Heritage Black

STATED ODDS 1:1990 HOBBY
STATED PRINT RUN 1 SERIAL #'d SET
NO PRICING DUE TO SCARCITY

2006 Bowman Heritage Mini

COMPLETE SET (300) 100.00 200.00
*MINI 1-300: 1X TO 2.5X BASIC
*MINI 1-300: 1X TO 2.5X BASIC RC
COMMON BASIC SP (202-300) .40 1.00
BASIC SP SEMIS 202-300 .60 1.50
BASIC SP UNLISTED 202-300 1.00 2.50
OVERALL ODDS ONE PER PACK
NO SHORT PRINTS IN MINI SET

2006 Bowman Heritage Chrome

COMPLETE SET (300) 75.00 150.00
*CHROME 1-300: 1X TO 2.5X BASIC
*CHROME 1-300: 1X TO 2.5X BASIC RC
COMMON BASIC SP (202-300) .40 1.00
BASIC SP SEMIS 202-300 .60 1.50
BASIC SP UNLISTED 202-300 1.00 2.50
APPX. ODDS ONE PER PACK
ON AVG. 22 CHROME PER 24 CT.BOX
NO SHORT PRINTS IN CHROME SET

2006 Bowman Heritage White

*WHITE 1-300: .4X TO 1X BASIC
*WHITE 1-300: .4X TO 1X BASIC RC
COMMON BASIC SP (202-300) .40 1.00
BASIC SP SEMIS 202-300 .60 1.50
BASIC SP UNLISTED 202-300 1.00 2.50
STATED ODDS 1:6 HOBBY, 1:6 RETAIL
NO SHORT PRINTS IN WHITE SET

2006 Bowman Heritage Mini Draft Pick Variations

*DP VAR: 1X TO 2.5X BASIC
ONE 5-CARD DPV PACK PER HOBBY BOX
76 Evan Longoria 5.00 12.00
77 Adrian Cardenas 1.25 3.00
82 Matthew Sulentic .75 2.00
85 Clayton Kershaw 6.00 15.00
87 Chris Parmelee 1.25 3.00
88 Billy Rowell 1.50 4.00
90 Chris Marrero .75 2.00
95 Chad Huffman .75 2.00

2006 Bowman Heritage Pieces of Greatness

GROUP A ODDS 1:98 H, 1:99 R
GROUP B ODDS 1:82 H, 1:82 R
GROUP C ODDS 1:28 H, 1:28 R
GROUP D ODDS 1:43 H, 1:43 R
AD Adam Dunn Bat A 2.00 5.00
AJ Andruw Jones Jsy D 1.25 3.00
AJ2 Andruw Jones Bat C 1.25 3.00
AJP A.J. Pierzynski Bat A 1.25 3.00
AL Adam LaRoche Jsy B 1.25 3.00
AP Albert Pujols Bat C 4.00 10.00
AP2 Albert Pujols Jsy D 4.00 10.00
AR Alex Rodriguez Bat A 4.00 10.00
ARA Aramis Ramirez Bat A 1.25 3.00
BB Barry Bonds Jsy A 5.00 12.00
BR Brian Roberts Bat B 1.25 3.00
BW Brad Wilkerson Bat A 1.25 3.00
BZ Barry Zito Jsy C 2.00 5.00
CB Craig Biggio Jsy C 2.00 5.00
CF Cliff Floyd Bat B 1.25 3.00
CJ Chipper Jones Bat C 3.00 8.00
CJ2 Chipper Jones Jsy D 3.00 8.00
CS Curt Schilling Jsy C 2.00 5.00
CU Chase Utley Bat A 2.00 5.00
DE David Eckstein Bat A 1.25 3.00
DL Derrek Lee Bat B 1.25 3.00
DO David Ortiz Bat C 3.00 8.00
DW Dontrelle Willis Jsy D 1.25 3.00
EE Edwin Encarnacion Jsy C 3.00 8.00
GM Greg Maddux Bat B 4.00 10.00
GS Gary Sheffield Bat D 1.25 3.00
HB Hank Blalock Bat A 1.25 3.00
JD Jermaine Dye Bat C 1.25 3.00
JF Jeff Francoeur Bat A 3.00 8.00
JK Jeff Kent Jsy C 1.25 3.00
JL Javy Lopez Jsy C 1.25 3.00
JT Jim Thome Bat G 2.00 5.00
LB Lance Berkman Jsy C 2.00 5.00
MB Milton Bradley Bat A 1.25 3.00
ME Morgan Ensberg Jsy C 1.25 3.00
ML Mike Lowell Bat A 1.25 3.00
MO Magglio Ordonez Bat C 2.00 5.00
MR Manny Ramirez Bat D 3.00 8.00
MY Michael Young Jsy C 1.25 3.00
NJ Nick Johnson Bat B 1.25 3.00
NS Nick Swisher Bat C 2.00 5.00
RC Robinson Cano Bat C 2.00 5.00
RF Rafael Furcal Bat C 1.25 3.00
RH Ryan Howard Jsy C 2.50 6.00
SP Scott Podsednik Bat B 1.25 3.00
TH Torii Hunter Bat B 1.25 3.00
THE Todd Helton Jsy D 2.00 5.00
VG Vladimir Guerrero Bat B 2.00 5.00
VM Victor Martinez Bat B 2.00 5.00
XN Xavier Nady Bat C 1.25 3.00

2006 Bowman Heritage Pieces of Greatness White

*WHITE: .5X TO 1.2X BASIC
OVERALL WHITE ODDS 1:387 H,1:387 R
STATED PRINT RUN 49 SERIAL #'d SETS
BLACK STATED ODDS 1:12,016 HOBBY
BLACK PRINT RUN 1 SERIAL #'d SET
NO BLACK PRICING DUE TO SCARCITY

2006 Bowman Heritage Prospects

COMPLETE SET (100) 15.00 40.00
COMMON CARD (1-100) .15 .40
OVERALL PLATE ODDS 1:1494 HOBBY
PLATE PRINT RUN 1 SET PER COLOR
BLACK-CYAN-MAGENTA-YELLOW ISSUED
NO PLATE PRICING DUE TO SCARCITY
1 Justin Upton 1.25 3.00
2 Koby Clemens .25 .60
3 Lance Broadway .15 .40
4 Cameron Maybin .50 1.25
5 Garrett Mock .15 .40
6 Alex Gordon .50 1.25
7 Ben Copeland .15 .40
8 Nick Adenhart .15 .40
9 Yung-Chi Chen .25 .60
10 Tim Moss .15 .40
11 Francisco Leandro .15 .40
12 Brad McCann .15 .40
13 Dallas Trahern .15 .40
14 Dustin Majewski .15 .40
15 James Barthmaier .15 .40
16 Nate Gold .15 .40
17 John Hardy .15 .40
18 Mark McLemore .15 .40
19 Michael Aubrey .25 .60
20A Mark Holliman .15 .40
20B Mark Holliman UER .15 .40
Michael Holliman,Tigers,pictured
21 Bobby Wilson .15 .40
22 Radhames Liz .15 .40
23 Jose Tabata .25 .60
24 Jared Lansford .15 .40
25 Brent Dlugach .15 .40
26 Steve Garrabrants .15 .40
27 Eric Haberer .15 .40
28 Chris Dickerson .25 .60
29 Wellinson Baez .15 .40
30 Chris Kolkhorst .15 .40
31 Brandon Moss .15 .40
32 Corey Wimberly .15 .40
33 Ryan Patterson .15 .40
35 John Bannister .15 .40
36 Pablo Sandoval .60 1.50
37 Dexter Fowler .50 1.25
38 Elvis Andrus .50 1.25
39 Jason Windsor .15 .40
40 B.J. Szymanski .15 .40
41 Yovani Gallardo .50 1.25
42 John Bowker .15 .40
43 Justin Christian .15 .40
44 Andy Sonnanstine .15 .40
45 Jeremy Slayden .15 .40
46 Brandon Jones .15 .40
47 Travis Denker .15 .40
48 Emmanuel Garcia .15 .40
49 Landon Jacobsen .15 .40
50 Kevin Estrada .15 .40
51 Ross Ohlendorf .15 .40
52 Wyatt Toregas .15 .40
53 Andrew Kown .15 .40
54 Steve Kelly .15 .40
55 Mike Butia .15 .40
56 Mike Connolly .15 .40
57 Brian Horwitz .15 .40
58 Dale Thayer .15 .40
59 Diory Hernandez .15 .40
60 Samuel Deduno .15 .40
61 Jamie Hoffman .15 .40
62 Matt Tolbert .15 .40
63 Michael Ekstrom .15 .40
64 Chris Maples .15 .40
65 Adam Coe .15 .40
66 Max Ramirez .25 .60
67 Evan MacLane .15 .40
68 Jose Campusano .15 .40
69 Lou Santangelo .15 .40
70 Shawn Riggans .15 .40
71 Kyle Kendrick .40 1.00
72 Oswaldo Navarro .15 .40
73 Eric Rodland .15 .40
74 Omir Santos .15 .40
75 Kyle McCulloch .15 .40
76 Evan Longoria 4.00 10.00
77 Adrian Cardenas .15 .40
78 Steven Wright .15 .40
79 Andrew Carpenter .15 .40
80 Dustin Evans .15 .40
81 Chad Tracy .15 .40
82 Matthew Sulentic .40 1.00
83 Adam Ottavino .15 .40
84 Matt Long .15 .40
85 Clayton Kershaw 10.00 25.00
86 Matt Antonelli .15 .40
87 Chris Parmelee .25 .60
88 Billy Rowell .40 1.00
89 Chase Fontaine .15 .40
90 Chris Marrero .25 .60
91 Jamie Ortiz .15 .40
92 Sean Watson .15 .40
93 Brooks Brown .15 .40
94 Brad Furnish .15 .40
95 Chad Huffman .40 1.00
96 Pedro Beato .15 .40
97 Kyler Burke .15 .40
98 Stephen Englund .15 .40
99 Tyler Norrick .15 .40
100 Brett Sinkbeil .15 .40

2006 Bowman Heritage Prospects Black

STATED ODDS 1:6008 HOBBY
STATED PRINT RUN 1 SERIAL #'d SET
NO PRICING DUE TO SCARCITY

2006 Bowman Heritage Prospects White

*WHITE: .4X TO 1X BASIC
STATED ODDS 1:6 HOBBY, 1:6 RETAIL

2006 Bowman Heritage Signs of Greatness

GROUP A ODDS 1:719 H, 1:719 R
GROUP B ODDS 1:42 H, 1:42 R
GROUP C ODDS 1:61 H, 1:63 R
GROUP D ODDS 1:2172 H, 1:2175 R
RED INK ODDS 1:9737 HOBBY
RED INK PRINT RUN 5 SERIAL #'d SETS
NO RED INK PRICING DUE TO SCARCITY
SILVER INK ODDS 28,238 H,1:9500 R
SILVER INK PRINT RUN 1 SER.#'d SET
NO SILVER PRICING DUE TO SCARCITY
EXCHANGE DEADLINE 12/31/08
AG Alex Gordon B 10.00 25.00
BB Brian Bogusevic B 3.00 8.00
BS Brandon Snyder B 3.00 8.00
BW Brandon Wood A 6.00 15.00
CI Craig Italiano B 3.00 8.00
CM Cameron Maybin B 3.00 8.00
JC Jesus Cota B 3.00 8.00
JCL Jeff Clement B 3.00 8.00
JS Jarrod Saltalamacchia C 6.00 15.00
JU Justin Upton D 10.00 25.00
KW Kevin Whelan B 3.00 8.00
LB Lance Broadway B 4.00 10.00
MM Matt Maloney B 6.00 15.00
RT Ryan Tucker C 3.00 8.00
SG Sean Gallagher B 5.00 12.00
SL Sam LeCure C 3.00 8.00
ST Steve Tolleson B 3.00 8.00
WT Wade Townsend C 3.00 8.00

2007 Bowman Heritage

COMP.SET w/o SPs (251) 15.00 40.00
COMMON CARD (1-200) .15 .40
COMMON ROOKIE (201-251) .20 .50
COMMON SP (181-200) 1.25 3.00
COMMON SP RC (226-250) 1.50 4.00
SP ODDS 1:3 HOBBY
NO SIG CARDS ARE SHORT PRINTS
COMP.SET INCLUDES ALL MANTLE VAR.
OVERALL PLATE ODDS 1:463 HOBBY
PLATE PRINT RUN 1 SET PER COLOR
BLACK-CYAN-MAGENTA-YELLOW ISSUED
NO PLATE PRICING DUE TO SCARCITY
1 Jeff Francoeur .40 1.00
2 Jered Weaver .25 .60
3 Derrek Lee .15 .40
4 Todd Helton .25 .60
5 Shawn Hill .15 .40
6 Ivan Rodriguez .25 .60
7 Mickey Mantle 1.25 3.00
8 Ramon Hernandez .15 .40
9 Randy Johnson .40 1.00
10 Jermaine Dye .15 .40
11 Brian Roberts .15 .40
12 Hank Blalock .15 .40
13 Chien-Ming Wang .25 .60
14 Mike Lowell .15 .40
15 Brandon Webb .25 .60
16 Kelly Johnson .15 .40
17 Nick Johnson .15 .40
18 Zach Duke .15 .40
19 Aaron Hill .15 .40
20 Miguel Tejada .25 .60
21 Mark Buehrle .25 .60
22 Michael Young .15 .40
23 Carlos Delgado .15 .40
24 Anibal Sanchez .15 .40
25 Vladimir Guerrero .25 .60
26 Russell Martin .15 .40
27 Lance Berkman .25 .60
28 Bobby Crosby .15 .40
29 Javier Vazquez .15 .40
30 Manny Ramirez .40 1.00
31 Rich Hill .15 .40
32 Mike Sweeney .15 .40
33 Jeff Kent .15 .40
34 Noah Lowry .15 .40
35 Alfonso Soriano .25 .60
36 Paul Lo Duca .15 .40
37 J.D. Drew .15 .40
38 C.C Sabathia .25 .60
39 Craig Biggio .25 .60
40 Adam Dunn .25 .60
41 Josh Beckett .25 .60
42 Carlos Guillen .15 .40
43 Jeff Francis .15 .40
44 Orlando Hudson .15 .40
45 Grady Sizmore .25 .60
46 Jason Jennings .15 .40
47 Mark Teixeira .25 .60
48 Freddy Garcia .15 .40
49 Adrian Gonzalez .30 .75
50 Albert Pujols .50 1.25
51 Tom Glavine .25 .60
52 J.J. Hardy .15 .40
53 Bobby Abreu .15 .40
54 Bartolo Colon .15 .40
55 Garrett Atkins .15 .40
56 Moises Alou .15 .40
57 Cliff Lee .25 .60
58 Michael Cuddyer .15 .40
59 Brandon Phillips .15 .40
60 Jeremy Bonderman .15 .40
61 Rickie Weeks .15 .40
62 Chris Carpenter .25 .60
63 Frank Thomas .40 1.00
64 Victor Martinez .25 .60
65 Dontrelle Willis .15 .40
66 Jim Thome .25 .60
67 Aaron Rowand .15 .40
68 Andy Pettitte .25 .60
69 Brian McCann .15 .40
70 Roger Clemens .50 1.25
71 Gary Matthews .15 .40
72 Bronson Arroyo .15 .40
73 Jeremy Hermida .15 .40
74 Eric Chavez .15 .40
75 David Ortiz .40 1.00
76 Stephen Drew .15 .40
77 Ronnie Belliard .15 .40
78 James Shields .15 .40
79 Richie Sexson .15 .40
80 Johan Santana .25 .60
81 Orlando Cabrera .15 .40
82 Aramis Ramirez .15 .40
83 Greg Maddux .50 1.25
84 Reggie Sanders .15 .40
85 Carlos Zambrano .25 .60
86 Bengie Molina .15 .40
87 David DeJesus .15 .40
88 Adam Wainwright .25 .60
89 Conor Jackson .15 .40
90 David Wright .30 .75
91 Ryan Garko .15 .40
92 Bill Hall .15 .40
93 Marcus Giles .15 .40
94 Kenny Rogers .15 .40
95 Joe Mauer .30 .75
96 Hanley Ramirez .25 .60
97 Brian Giles .15 .40
98 Dan Haren .15 .40
99 Robinson Cano .25 .60
100 Ryan Howard .30 .75
101 Andruw Jones .15 .40
102 Aaron Harang .15 .40
103 Hideki Matsui .40 1.00
104 Nick Swisher .25 .60
105 Pedro Martinez .25 .60
106 Felipe Lopez .15 .40
107 Erik Bedard .15 .40
108 Rafael Furcal .15 .40
109 Curt Schilling .25 .60
110 Jose Reyes .25 .60
111 Adam LaRoche .15 .40
112 Mike Mussina .25 .60
113 Melvin Mora .15 .40
114 Zack Greinke .40 1.00
115 Justin Morneau .25 .60
116 Ervin Santana .15 .40
117 Ken Griffey Jr. .75 2.00
118 David Eckstein .15 .40
119 Jamie Moyer .15 .40
120 Jorge Posada .25 .60
121 Justin Verlander .40 1.00
122 Sammy Sosa .40 1.00
123 Jason Schmidt .15 .40
124 Josh Willingham .25 .60
125 Roy Oswalt .25 .60
126 Travis Hafner .15 .40
127 John Maine .15 .40
128 Willy Taveras .15 .40
129 Magglio Ordonez .25 .60
130 Barry Zito .25 .60
131 Prince Fielder .25 .60
132 Michael Barrett .15 .40
133 Livan Hernandez .15 .40
134 Troy Glaus .15 .40
135 Rocco Baldelli .15 .40
136 Jason Giambi .15 .40
137 Austin Kearns .15 .40
138 Dan Uggla .15 .40
139 Pat Burrell .15 .40
140 Carlos Beltran .25 .60
141 Carlos Quentin .15 .40
142 Johnny Estrada .15 .40
143 Torii Hunter .15 .40
144 Carlos Lee .15 .40
145 Mike Piazza .40 1.00
146 Mark Teahen .15 .40
147 Juan Pierre .15 .40
148 Paul Konerko .25 .60
149 Freddy Sanchez .15 .40
150 Derek Jeter 1.00 2.50
151 Orlando Hernandez .15 .40
152 Raul Ibanez .25 .60
153 John Smoltz .40 1.00
154 Scott Rolen .25 .60
155 Jimmy Rollins .25 .60
156 A.J. Burnett .15 .40
157 Jason Varitek .40 1.00
158 Ben Sheets .15 .40
159 Matt Cain .25 .60
160 Carl Crawford .25 .60
161 Jeff Suppan .15 .40
162 Tadahito Iguchi .15 .40
163 Kevin Millwood .15 .40
164 Chris Duncan .15 .40
165 Rich Harden .15 .40
166 Joe Crede .15 .40
167 Chipper Jones .40 1.00
168 Gary Sheffield .15 .40
169 Cole Hamels .30 .75
170 Jason Bay .25 .60
171 Jhonny Peralta .15 .40
172 Aubrey Huff .15 .40
173 Xavier Nady .15 .40
174 Kazuo Matsui .15 .40
175 Vernon Wells .15 .40
176 Johnny Damon .25 .60
177 Jim Edmonds .25 .60
178 Jose Vidro .15 .40
179 Garret Anderson .15 .40
180 Alex Rios .15 .40
181a Ichiro Suzuki .50 1.25
181b Ichiro Suzuki SP 3.00 8.00
182a Jake Peavy .15 .40
182b Jake Peavy SP 1.25 4.00
No Signature
183a Ian Kinsler .25 .60
183b Ian Kinsler SP 1.25 4.00
No Signature
184a Tom Gorzelanny .15 .40
184b Tom Gorzelanny SP 1.25 4.00
No Signature
185a Miguel Cabrera .40 1.00
185b Miguel Cabrera SP 2.00 5.00
186a Scott Kazmir .25 .60
186b Scott Kazmir SP 2.00 5.00
No Signature
187a Matt Holliday .40 1.00
187b Matt Holliday SP 2.00 5.00
No Signature
188a Roy Halladay .25 .60
188b Roy Halladay SP 1.25 4.00
No Signature
189a Ryan Zimmerman .25 .60
189b Ryan Zimmerman SP 2.00 5.00
No Signature
190a Alex Rodriguez .50 1.25
190b Alex Rodriguez SP 3.00 8.00
191a Kenji Johjima .40 1.00
191b Kenji Johjima SP 2.00 5.00
No Signature
192a Gil Meche .15 .40
192b Gil Meche SP 1.25 4.00
No Signature
193a Chase Utley .25 .60
193b Chase Utley SP 2.00 5.00
No Signature
194a Jeremy Sowers .15 .40
194b Jeremy Sowers SP 1.25 3.00
No Signature
195a John Lackey .25 .60
195b John Lackey SP 1.25 3.00
No Signature
196a Nick Markakis .30 .75
196b Nick Markakis SP 2.00 5.00
No Signature
197a Tim Hudson .25 .60
197b Tim Hudson SP 1.25 3.00
No Signature
198a B.J. Upton .15 .40
198b B.J. Upton SP 1.25 3.00
No Signature
199a Felix Hernandez .25 .60
199b Felix Hernandez SP 2.00 5.00
No Signature
200a Barry Bonds .60 1.50
200b Barry Bonds SP 4.00 10.00
201 Jarrod Saltalamacchia (RC) .30 .75
202 Tim Lincecum RC 1.00 2.50
203 Kory Casto (RC) .20 .50
204 Sean Henn (RC) .20 .50
205 Hector Gimenez (RC) .20 .50
206 Homer Bailey (RC) .30 .75
207 Yunel Escobar (RC) .20 .50
208 Matt Lindstrom (RC) .20 .50
209 Tyler Clippard (RC) .30 .75
210 Joe Smith RC .20 .50
211 Tony Abreu RC .50 1.25
212 Billy Butler (RC) .30 .75
213 Gustavo Molina RC .20 .50
214 Brian Stokes (RC) .20 .50
215 Kevin Slowey (RC) .50 1.25
216 Curtis Thigpen (RC) .20 .50
217 Carlos Gomez RC .40 1.00
218 Rick Vanden Hurk RC .20 .50
219 Michael Bourn (RC) .30 .75
220 Jeff Baker (RC) .20 .50
221 Andy LaRoche (RC) .20 .50
222 Andy Sonnanstine RC .20 .50
223 Chase Wright RC .50 1.25
224 Mark Reynolds RC .60 1.50
225 Matt Chico (RC) .20 .50
226a Hunter Pence (RC) .60 1.50
226b Hunter Pence SP 3.00 8.00
227a John Danks RC .30 .75
227b John Danks SP 1.50 4.00
No Signature
228a Elijah Dukes RC .30 .75
228b Elijah Dukes SP 2.50 6.00
No Signature
229a Kei Igawa RC .50 1.25
229b Kei Igawa SP 2.50 6.00
No Signature
230a Felix Pie (RC) .20 .50
230b Felix Pie SP 1.50 4.00
No Signature
231a Jesus Flores RC .20 .50
231b Jesus Flores SP 1.50 4.00
No Signature
232a Dallas Braden RC .30 .75
232b Dallas Braden SP 2.50 6.00
No Signature
233a Akinori Iwamura RC .50 1.25
233b Akinori Iwamura SP 2.50 6.00
No Signature
234a Ryan Braun (RC) 1.00 2.50
234b Ryan Braun SP 3.00 8.00
235a Alex Gordon RC .60 1.50
235b Alex Gordon SP 3.00 8.00
236a Micah Owings (RC) .20 .50
236b Micah Owings SP 1.50 4.00
No Signature
237a Kevin Kouzmanoff (RC) .20 .50
237b Kevin Kouzmanoff SP 1.50 4.00
No Signature
238a Glen Perkins (RC) .20 .50
238b Glen Perkins SP 1.50 4.00
No Signature
239a Danny Putnam (RC) .20 .50
239b Danny Putnam SP 1.50 4.00
No Signature
240a Philip Hughes (RC) .50 1.25
240b Philip Hughes SP 3.00 8.00
241a Ryan Sweeney (RC) .20 .50
241b Ryan Sweeney SP 1.50 4.00
No Signature
242a Josh Hamilton (RC) .60 1.50
242b Josh Hamilton SP 5.00 12.00
243a Hideki Okajima RC 1.00 2.50
243b Hideki Okajima SP 3.00 8.00
244a Adam Lind (RC) .20 .50
244b Adam Lind SP 1.50 4.00
No Signature
245a Travis Buck (RC) .20 .50
245b Travis Buck SP 1.50 4.00
No Signature
246a Miguel Montero (RC) .20 .50
246b Miguel Montero SP 1.50 4.00
No Signature
247a Brandon Morrow RC .75 2.00
247b Brandon Morrow SP 2.50 6.00
248a Troy Tulowitzki (RC) .60 1.50
248b Troy Tulowitzki SP 2.50 6.00
249a Delmon Young (RC) .30 .75
249b Delmon Young SP 2.50 6.00
No Signature
250a Daisuke Matsuzaka RC .75 2.00
250b Daisuke Matsuzaka SP 4.00 10.00
251 Joba Chamberlain RC .30 .75

2007 Bowman Heritage Black

*BLACK 1-200: 8X TO 20X BASIC
*BLACK 201-251: 6X TO 15X BASIC RC
COMMON BASIC SP (180-250) 3.00 8.00
BASIC SP SEMIS 5.00 12.00
BASIC SP UNLISTED 8.00 20.00
STATED ODDS 1:52 HOBBY, 1:97 RETAIL
NO SHORT PRINTS IN BLACK SET
181b I.Suzuki No Sig 10.00 25.00
190b A.Rodriguez No Sig 10.00 25.00
200b B.Bonds No Sig 12.00 30.00
226b H.Pence No Sig 10.00 25.00
234b R.Braun No Sig 15.00 40.00
240b P.Hughes No Sig 8.00 20.00
243b H.Okajima No Sig 15.00 40.00
250b D.atsuzaka No Sig 12.00 30.00

2007 Bowman Heritage Rainbow Foil

COMPLETE SET (299) 75.00 150.00
*CHROME 1-200: 1X TO 2.5X BASIC
*CHROME 201-250: .75X TO 2X BASIC RC
COMMON BASIC SP (180-250) .40 1.00
BASIC SP SEMIS .60 1.50
BASIC SP UNLISTED 1.00 2.50
APPX.ODDS 1:1 HOBBY
NO SHORT PRINTS IN CHROME SET
COMP.SET INCLUDES ALL MANTLE VAR.
181b I.Suzuki No Sig 1.25 3.00
190b A.Rodriguez No Sig 1.25 3.00
200b B.Bonds No Sig 1.50 4.00
226b H.Pence No Sig 1.25 3.00
234b R.Braun No Sig 2.00 5.00
235b A.Gordon No Sig 1.25 3.00
240b P.Hughes No Sig 1.00 2.50
243b H.Okajima No Sig 2.00 5.00
250b D.Matsuzaka No Sig 1.50 4.00

2007 Bowman Heritage Red

STATED ODDS 1:1569 HOBBY
STATED PRINT RUN 1 SER.#'d SET
NO PRICING DUE TO SCARCITY

2007 Bowman Heritage Checklists

COMMON CHECKLIST (1-3) .10 .25

2007 Bowman Heritage Mantle Short Prints

COMPLETE SET (5) 12.50 30.00
COMMON CARD 2.50 6.00
OVERALL SP ODDS 1:3 HOBBY
OVERALL PLATE ODDS 1:463 HOBBY
PLATE PRINT RUN 1 SET PER COLOR
BLACK-CYAN-MAGENTA-YELLOW ISSUED
NO PLATE PRICING DUE TO SCARCITY

2007 Bowman Heritage Mantle Short Prints Black

COMMON CARD 10.00 25.00
OVERALL BLACK ODDS 1:52 HOB,1:97 RET
STATED PRINT RUN 52 SER.#'d SETS

2007 Bowman Heritage Mantle Short Prints Rainbow Foil

COMPLETE SET (5) 15.00 40.00
COMMON CARD 3.00 8.00
OVERALL FOIL ODDS ONE PER PACK

2007 Bowman Heritage Mantle Short Prints Red

OVERALL RED ODDS 1:1569 HOBBY
STATED PRINT RUN 1 SER.#'d SET
NO PRICING DUE TO SCARCITY

2007 Bowman Heritage Pieces of Greatness

GROUP A ODDS 1:83 HOBBY,1:166 RETAIL
GROUP B ODDS 1:22 HOBBY,1:46 RETAIL
GROUP C ODDS 1:119 HOBBY,1:238 RETAIL
GROUP D ODDS 1:325 HOBBY,1:660 RETAIL
GROUP E ODDS 1:104 HOBBY,1:211 RETAIL
GROUP F ODDS 1:687 HOBBY,1:687 RETAIL
GROUP G ODDS 1:452 HOBBY,1:953 RETAIL
AD Adam Dunn Jsy C 3.00 8.00
AE Andre Ethier Jsy B 3.00 8.00
AG Alex Gonzalez Bat B 3.00 8.00
AJ Andruw Jones Bat C 3.00 8.00
AL Adam LaRoche Jsy B 3.00 8.00
AR Aramis Ramirez Bat A 3.00 8.00
ARO Alex Rodriguez Bat C 6.00 15.00
BB Barry Bonds Jsy A 6.00 15.00
BC Bobby Crosby Bat B 3.00 8.00
BG Brian Giles Bat A 3.00 8.00
BL Brad Lidge Jsy E 3.00 8.00
BZ Barry Zito Pants C 3.00 8.00
CB Craig Biggio Jsy B 3.00 8.00
CBE Carlos Beltran Bat B 3.00 8.00
CH Cole Hamels Jsy A 4.00 10.00
CK Cory Koskie Bat B 3.00 8.00
CP Corey Patterson Bat B 3.00 8.00
CS Curt Schilling Jsy C 3.00 8.00
CT Chad Tracy Bat B 3.00 8.00
CU Chase Utley Bat A 4.00 10.00
DE Darin Erstad Bat B 3.00 8.00
DO David Ortiz Bat B 3.00 8.00
DO2 David Ortiz Jsy A 3.00 8.00
DW Dontrelle Willis Jsy E 3.00 8.00
DWR David Wright Pants A 5.00 12.00
EC Eric Chavez Pants B 3.00 8.00
FT Frank Thomas Bat A 4.00 10.00
GM Greg Maddux Bat A 4.00 10.00
GS Gary Sheffield Bat B 3.00 8.00
GSI Grady Sizmore Jsy B 3.00 8.00
HM Hideki Matsui Bat A 4.00 10.00
IR Ivan Rodriguez Jsy E 3.00 8.00
JB Jeremy Bonderman Jsy B 3.00 8.00
JD Johnny Damon Bat A 3.00 8.00
JDD J.D. Drew Jsy B 3.00 8.00
JE Juan Encarnacion Bat B 3.00 8.00
JF Jeff Franceour Bat B 3.00 8.00
JFR Jeff Francis Jsy B 3.00 8.00
JK Jeff Kent Jsy A 3.00 8.00
JM Joe Mauer Bat B 3.00 8.00
JR Jose Reyes Jsy B 4.00 10.00
LB Lance Berkman Jsy A 3.00 8.00
LG Luis Gonzalez Bat B 3.00 8.00
MC Miguel Cabrera Jsy B 3.00 8.00
ML Mike Lowell Pants A 3.00 8.00
MM Mark Mulder Pants E 3.00 8.00
MO Magglio Ordonez Bat D 3.00 8.00
MP Mike Piazza Bat E 4.00 10.00
MR Manny Ramirez Jsy C 3.00 8.00
MR2 Manny Ramirez Bat G 3.00 8.00
MT Mark Teixeira Bat A 3.00 8.00
MTE Miguel Tejada Pants B 3.00 8.00
NS Nick Swisher Bat A 3.00 8.00
PK Paul Konerko Pants B 3.00 8.00
PK2 Paul Konerko Jsy B 3.00 8.00
RB Rocco Baldelli Jsy F 3.00 8.00
RC Robinson Cano Bat B 4.00 10.00
RC2 Robinson Cano Jsy B 4.00 10.00
RF Rafael Furcal Bat B 3.00 8.00
RH Rich Harden Jsy B 3.00 8.00
SG Shawn Green Bat B 3.00 8.00
TH Todd Helton Jsy B 3.00 8.00
TH2 Todd Helton Bat B 3.00 8.00
THU Tim Hudson Pants A 3.00 8.00
TI Tadahito Iguchi Bat A 3.00 8.00
TN Trot Nixon Bat A 3.00 8.00
TW Tim Wakefield Pants B 3.00 8.00
VG Vladimir Guerrero Bat B 3.00 8.00
YM Yadier Molina Jsy D 3.00 8.00

2007 Bowman Heritage Pieces of Greatness Black

*BLACK: .75X TO 2X BASIC
STATED ODDS 1:221 HOBBY,1:429 RETAIL
STATED PRINT RUN 52 SER.#'d SETS

2007 Bowman Heritage Pieces of Greatness Red

STATED ODDS 1:6854 HOBBY
STATED PRINT RUN 1 SER.#'d SET
NO PRICING DUE TO SCARCITY

2007 Bowman Heritage Prospects

COMPLETE SET (100) 15.00 40.00
STATED ODDS TWO PER PACK
OVERALL PLATE ODDS 1:1175 HOBBY
PLATE PRINT RUN 1 SET PER COLOR
BLACK-CYAN-MAGENTA-YELLOW ISSUED
NO PLATE PRICING DUE TO SCARCITY
BHP1 Thomas Fairchild .20 .50
BHP2 Peter Bourjos .30 .75
BHP3 Brett Campbell .20 .50
BHP4 Cesar Nicolas .20 .50
BHP5 Kala Kaaihue .30 .75
BHP6 Zach McAllister .30 .75
BHP7 Chad Reineke .20 .50
BHP8 Anthony Hatch .20 .50
BHP9 Cedric Hunter .50 1.25
BHP10 Chris Carter .60 1.50
BHP11 Tommy Hanson .60 1.50
BHP12 Dellin Betances .60 1.50
BHP13 John Otness .20 .50
BHP14 Derin McMains .20 .50
BHP15 Greg Reynolds .50 1.25
BHP16 Jonathan Van Every .20 .50
BHP17 Eddie Degerman .20 .50
BHP18 Cody Strait .20 .50
BHP19 Noe Rodriguez .20 .50
BHP20 Young-Il Jung .50 1.25
BHP21 Reegie Corona .30 .75
BHP22 Carlos Corporan .20 .50
BHP23 Chance Douglass .20 .50
BHP24 Leo Daigle .20 .50
BHP25 Jeff Samardzija .75 2.00
BHP26 Mark Wagner .30 .75
BHP27 Chuck Lofgren .50 1.25
BHP28 Bryan Byrne .20 .50
BHP29 Daniel Mayora .50 1.25
BHP30 Gorkys Hernandez .50 1.25
BHP31 Joshua Rodriguez .20 .50
BHP32 Brad Knox .20 .50
BHP33 Scott Lewis .50 1.25
BHP34 Joe Gaetti .20 .50
BHP35 Michael Saunders .60 1.50
BHP36 Brendan Katin .20 .50
BHP37 Brennan Boesch 3.00 8.00
BHP38 Jay Garthwaite .20 .50
BHP39 Mike Devaney .20 .50
BHP40 J.R. Towles .60 1.50
BHP41 Joe Ness .20 .50
BHP42 Michael Martinez .20 .50
BHP43 Justin Byler .20 .50
BHP44 Chris Coghlan .60 1.50
BHP45 Eric Young Jr. .30 .75
BHP46 J.R. Mathes .20 .50
BHP47 Ivan De Jesus Jr. .30 .75
BHP48 Woods Fines .20 .50
BHP49 Andrew Fie .20 .50
BHP50 Luke Hochevar .60 1.50
BHP51 Will Venable .30 .75
BHP52 Todd Redmond .20 .50
BHP53 Matthew Sweeney .60 1.50
BHP54 Trevor Cahill .50 1.25
BHP55 Mike Carp .60 1.50
BHP56 Henry Sosa .30 .75
BHP57 Emerson Frostad .20 .50
BHP58 Jeremy Jeffress .20 .50
BHP59 Whit Robbins .20 .50
BHP60 Joba Chamberlain .30 .75
BHP61 Raul Barron .20 .50
BHP62 Aaron Cunningham .30 .75
BHP63 Greg Smith .30 .75
BHP64 Jeff Baisley .30 .75
BHP65 Vic Buttler .20 .50
BHP66 Steve Singleton .20 .50
BHP67 Josh Papelbon .20 .50
BHP68 Ryan Finan .20 .50
BHP69 Deolis Guerra .40 1.00
BHP70 Vasili Spanos .20 .50
BHP71 Patrick Reilly .20 .50
BHP72 Thomas Hottovy .20 .50
BHP73 Daniel Murphy 1.00 2.50
BHP74 Matt Young .20 .50
BHP75 Brian Bocock .20 .50
BHP76 Chris Salamida .20 .50
BHP77 Nathan Southard .20 .50
BHP78 Brandon Hynick .50 1.25
BHP79 Chris Nowak .20 .50
BHP80 Reid Brignac .30 .75
BHP81 Cole Garner .20 .50
BHP82 Nick Van Stratten .20 .50
BHP83 Jeremy Papelbon .20 .50
BHP84 Jarrett Hoffpauir .20 .50
BHP85 Kevin Mulvey .50 1.25
BHP86 Matt Miller .20 .50
BHP87 Devin Ivany .20 .50
BHP88 Marcus Sanders .20 .50
BHP89 Michael MacDonald .20 .50
BHP90 Gabriel Sanchez .30 .75
BHP91 Ryan Norwood .20 .50
BHP92 Jim Fasano .20 .50
BHP93 Ryan Adams .30 .75
BHP94 Evan Englebrook .20 .50
BHP95 Juan Miranda .30 .75
BHP96 Gregory Porter .20 .50
BHP97 Shane Benson .20 .50
BHP98 Sam Fuld .60 1.50
BHP99 Cooper Brannan .20 .50
BHP100 Fernando Martinez .75 2.00

2007 Bowman Heritage Prospects Black

*BLACK: 4X TO 10X BASIC
STATED ODDS 1:153 HOBBY,1:295 RETAIL
STATED PRINT RUN 52 SER.#'d SETS
BHP37 Brennan Boesch 3.00 8.00

2007 Bowman Heritage Prospects Red

STATED ODDS 1:4740 HOBBY
STATED PRINT RUN 1 SER.#'d SET
NO PRICING DUE TO SCARCITY

2007 Bowman Heritage Red Man Box Topper

ONE PER HOBBY BOX TOPPER
AG Alex Gordon 2.50 6.00
AK Akinori Iwamura 2.00 5.00
AP Albert Pujols 2.50 6.00
AR Alex Rodriguez 2.50 6.00
AS Alfonso Soriano 1.25 3.00
BB Barry Bonds 3.00 8.00
DM Daisuke Matsuzaka 3.00 8.00
DO David Ortiz 2.00 5.00
DW David Wright 1.50 4.00
DY Delmon Young 1.25 3.00
FH Matt Holliday 2.00 5.00
FP Felix Pie .75 2.00
HM Hideki Matsui 2.00 5.00
HP Hunter Pence 2.50 6.00
IS Ichiro Suzuki 2.50 6.00
JH Josh Hamilton 2.50 6.00
JR Jose Reyes 1.25 3.00
KI Kei Igawa 2.00 5.00
MC Miguel Cabrera 2.00 5.00
MM Mickey Mantle 6.00 15.00
MR Manny Ramirez 2.00 5.00
PH Phil Hughes 2.00 5.00
RH Ryank Howard 1.50 4.00
TT Troy Tulowitzki 2.50 6.00
VG Vladimir Guerrero 1.25 3.00

2007 Bowman Heritage Signs of Greatness

GROUP A ODDS 1:339 HOBBY,1:405 RETAIL
GROUP B ODDS 1:47 HOBBY, 1:53 RETAIL
GROUP C ODDS 1:58 HOBBY, 1:68 RETAIL
GROUP D ODDS 1:350 HOBBY,1:410 RETAIL
GROUP E ODDS 1:238 HOBBY,1:232 RETAIL
GROUP F ODDS 1:389 HOBBY,1:445 RETAIL
GROUP G ODDS 1:4450 HOBBY,1:4800 RETAIL
GROUP H ODDS 1:8100 HOBBY,1:7850 RETAIL
EXCH DEADLINE 10/31/2009
AF Andrew Fie G 3.00 8.00
AO Adam Ottavino D 3.00 8.00
BJ Blake Johnson C 3.00 8.00
BL Brad Lincoln E 3.00 8.00
CA Carlos Arroyo D 3.00 8.00
CC Carl Crawford C 6.00 15.00
CH Cole Hamels C 8.00 20.00
CJ Chipper Jones B 30.00 60.00
CS Chorye Spoone G 3.00 8.00
DW David Wright A 40.00 80.00
EJ Elliot Johnson F 3.00 8.00
GG Glenn Gibson F 3.00 8.00
GM Garrett Mock D 3.00 8.00
JB John Buck D 3.00 8.00
JC Jorge Cantu D 3.00 8.00
JCB Jordan Brown F 6.00 15.00
JH J.P. Howell C 3.00 8.00
JL Jeff Locke G 6.00 15.00
JM Jeff Manship F 6.00 15.00
JP Jorge Posada C 30.00 60.00
JT J.R. Towles G 6.00 15.00
JW Johnny Whittleman H 3.00 8.00
MM Matt Maloney E 3.00 8.00
MT Mike Thompson F 3.00 8.00
NR Nolan Reimold C 8.00 20.00
RD Rajai Davis E 3.00 8.00
SE Stephen Englund G 3.00 8.00
SJ Seth Johnston G 3.00 8.00
SK Sean Kazmar G 3.00 8.00
SP Steve Pearce G 10.00 25.00
SS Scott Sizemore F 4.00 10.00
TG Tony Giarratano F 3.00 8.00
WCS Cody Strait G 3.00 8.00
WJB Joe Benson F 3.00 8.00

2007 Bowman Heritage Signs of Greatness Black

*BLACK: .75X TO 2X BASIC
STATED ODDS 1:590 HOBBY,1:695 RETAIL
STATED PRINT RUN 52 SER.#'d SETS
EXCH DEADLINE 10/31/2009
CJ Chipper Jones 75.00 150.00
DW David Wright 60.00 120.00
JL Jeff Locke 40.00 80.00
SP Steve Pearce 60.00 120.00

2007 Bowman Heritage Signs of Greatness Red
STATED ODDS 1:14,500 HOBBY
STATED PRINT RUN 1 SER.#'d SET
NO PRICING DUE TO SCARCITY

2019 Bowman Heritage
COMPLETE SET (118) 25.00 60.00
53VR1 Mike Trout 1.50 4.00
53VR2 Justin Verlander .30 .75
53VR3 Chris Archer .20 .50
53VR4 Carter Kieboom RC .60 1.50
53VR5 Whit Merrifield .30 .75
53VR6 Josh Hader .25 .60
53VR7 Chance Adams RC .40 1.00
53VR8 Yoan Moncada .30 .75
53VR9 Zack Greinke .30 .75
53VR10 Juan Soto 1.00 2.50
53VR11 Willy Adames .20 .50
53VR12 Ronald Acuna Jr. 1.50 4.00
53VR13 David Fletcher RC 1.25 3.00
53VR14 Josh James RC .60 1.50
53VR15 Evan Longoria .25 .60
53VR16 Joey Wendle .25 .60
53VR17 Michael Chavis RC .60 1.50
53VR18 Ryan Helsley RC .50 1.25
53VR19 Jake Cave RC .50 1.25
53VR20 Kyle Freeland .25 .60
53VR21 Jacob deGrom .60 1.50
53VR22 Scooter Gennett .25 .60
53VR23 Aaron Judge .75 2.00
53VR24 Rowdy Tellez RC .60 1.50
53VR25 Kolby Allard RC .60 1.50
53VR26 Vladimir Guerrero Jr. RC 2.50 6.00
53VR27 DJ Stewart RC .50 1.25
53VR28 Ryan O'Hearn RC .40 1.00
53VR29 Taylor Ward RC .40 1.00
53VR30 Fernando Tatis Jr. RC 6.00 15.00
53VR31 Mookie Betts .60 1.50
53VR32 Keston Hiura RC 1.25 3.00
53VR33 Jon Duplantier RC .40 1.00
53VR34 Brandon Crawford .25 .60
53VR35 Aramis Garcia RC .40 1.00
53VR36 Danny Jansen RC .40 1.00
53VR37 Michael Kopech RC 1.25 3.00
53VR38 Eddie Rosario .25 .60
53VR39 Maikel Franco .25 .60
53VR40 Cedric Mullins RC .75 2.00
53VR41 Willians Astudillo RC .40 1.00
53VR42 Brian Anderson .20 .50
53VR43 Kevin Newman RC .60 1.50
53VR44 Jose Altuve .25 .60
53VR45 Ramon Laureano RC .75 2.00
53VR46 Chris Shaw RC .40 1.00
53VR47 Nick Senzel RC 1.25 3.00
53VR48 Kyle Tucker RC 1.00 2.50
53VR49 Trey Mancini .25 .60
53VR50 Bryce Harper .50 1.25
53VR51 Steven Duggar RC .50 1.25
53VR52 Nicholas Castellanos .30 .75
53VR53 Dakota Hudson RC .50 1.25
53VR54 Salvador Perez .25 .60
53VR55 Mitch Keller RC .50 1.25
53VR56 Jose Abreu .30 .75
53VR57 Paul Goldschmidt .30 .75
53VR58 Edwin Diaz .25 .60
53VR59 Cal Quantrill RC .40 1.00
53VR60 Clayton Kershaw .50 1.25
53VR61 Kevin Pillar .20 .50
53VR62 Ronald Guzman .20 .50
53VR63 Amed Rosario .25 .60
53VR64 Mychal Givens .20 .50
53VR65 Marcus Stroman .25 .60
53VR66 Ryan Borucki RC .40 1.00
53VR67 J.T. Realmuto .30 .75
53VR68 Rougned Odor .25 .60
53VR69 Francisco Arcia RC .60 1.50
53VR70 Eric Hosmer .25 .60
53VR71 J.D. Martinez .30 .75
53VR72 Dawel Lugo RC .60 1.50
53VR73 Christin Stewart RC .50 1.25
53VR74 Starling Marte .25 .60
53VR75 Max Scherzer .30 .75
53VR76 Peter Lambert RC .60 1.50
53VR77 Griffin Canning RC .60 1.50
53VR78 Luis Urias RC .60 1.50
53VR79 Brad Keller RC .40 1.00
53VR80 Ozzie Albies .30 .75
53VR81 Sean Reid-Foley RC .40 1.00
53VR82 Justus Sheffield RC .60 1.50
53VR83 Bryse Wilson RC .50 1.25
53VR84 Luis Guillorme RC .40 1.00
53VR85 Matt Chapman .30 .75
53VR86 Enyel De Los Santos RC .40 1.00
53VR87 Matt Carpenter .30 .75
53VR88 Touki Toussaint RC .50 1.25
53VR89 Jose Ramirez .25 .60
53VR90 Jeff McNeil RC 1.00 2.50
53VR91 Andrew Knizner RC .60 1.50
53VR92 Shohei Ohtani .50 1.25
53VR93 Anthony Rizzo .40 1.00
53VR94 Eloy Jimenez RC 1.50 4.00
53VR95 Mitch Haniger .25 .60
53VR96 Adolis Garcia RC 2.50 6.00
53VR97 Giancarlo Stanton .30 .75
53VR98 Khris Davis .30 .75
53VR99 Miguel Cabrera .30 .75
53VR100 Christian Yelich .40 1.00
53VR101 Cody Bellinger .60 1.50
53VR102 Brandon Lowe RC .60 1.50
53VR103 Kevin Kramer RC .50 1.25
53VR104 Jose Berrios .25 .60
53VR105 Jake Bauers RC .60 1.50
53VR106 Francisco Lindor .30 .75
53VR107 Will Smith RC 1.00 2.50
53VR108 Corbin Burnes RC 3.00 8.00
53VR109 Kyle Wright RC .60 1.50
53VR110 Chris Paddack RC .75 2.00
53VR111 Wil Myers .25 .60
53VR112 Nolan Arenado .50 1.25
53VR113 Jonathan Loaisiga RC .50 1.25
53VR114 Eugenio Suarez .25 .60
53VR115 Yadier Molina .40 1.00
53VR116 Kris Bryant .40 1.00
53VR117 Aaron Nola .25 .60
53VR118 Pete Alonso RC 3.00 8.00

2019 Bowman Heritage Black and White
*BW: 1.2X TO 3X BASIC
*BW RC: .6X TO 1.5X BASIC RC
RANDOM INSERTS IN PACKS
53VR26 Vladimir Guerrero Jr. 15.00 40.00
53VR30 Fernando Tatis Jr. 20.00 50.00
53VR118 Pete Alonso 10.00 25.00

2019 Bowman Heritage Chrome Prospect Autographs
RANDOM INSERTS IN PACKS
PRINTING PLATES RANDOMLY INSERTED
PLATE PRINT RUN 1 SET PER COLOR
BLACK-CYAN-MAGENTA-YELLOW ISSUED
NO PLATE PRICING DUE TO SCARCITY
53PAAB Alec Bohm 15.00 40.00
53PABD Brock Deatherage 3.00 8.00
53PACC Conner Capel 4.00 10.00
53PACM Casey Mize 20.00 50.00
53PACMI Cal Mitchell 5.00 12.00
53PACS Cristian Santana 5.00 12.00
53PACSP Chad Spanberger 3.00 8.00
53PADK Dean Kremer 4.00 10.00
53PAGC Gabriel Cancel 5.00 12.00
53PAJB Joey Bart 30.00 80.00
53PAJPM Julio Pablo Martinez 3.00 8.00
53PAJR Julio Rodriguez 50.00 120.00
53PAMG Mateo Gil 4.00 10.00
53PAML Marco Luciano 40.00 100.00
53PAMM Mason Martin 10.00 25.00
53PANM Nick Madrigal 12.00 30.00
53PARB Rylan Bannon 4.00 10.00
53PARC Ryan Costello 4.00 10.00
53PARR Roberto Ramos 4.00 10.00
53PASW Steele Walker
53PAVF Vince Fernandez 4.00 10.00
53PAVMJ Victor Mesa Jr. 6.00 15.00
53PAVVM Victor Victor Mesa 6.00 15.00
53PAWF Wander Franco 100.00 250.00

2019 Bowman Heritage Chrome Prospect Autographs Gold Refractors
*GOLD REF: 1X TO 2.5X BASIC
RANDOM INSERTS IN PACKS
STATED PRINT RUN 50 SER.#'d SETS
53PASW Steele Walker 10.00 25.00
53PAWF Wander Franco 400.00 1000.00

2019 Bowman Heritage Chrome Prospect Autographs Orange Refractors
*ORANGE REF: 1.2X TO 3X BASIC
RANDOM INSERTS IN PACKS
STATED PRINT RUN 25 SER.#'d SETS
53PASW Steele Walker 12.00 30.00
53PAWF Wander Franco 500.00 1200.00

2019 Bowman Heritage Chrome Prospects
RANDOM INSERTS IN PACKS
*REF/199: 2X TO 5X BASIC
*BLUE REF/99: 4X TO 10X BASIC
*YLLW REF/75: 5X TO 12X BASIC
*GOLD REF/50: 6X TO 15X BASIC
*ORNGE REF/25: 10X TO 25X BASIC
53CP1 Wander Franco 4.00 10.00
53CP2 Blake Rutherford .20 .50
53CP3 Heliot Ramos .30 .75
53CP4 Beau Burrows .20 .50
53CP5 Ronny Mauricio .50 1.25
53CP6 Drew Waters .60 1.50
53CP7 Matt Mercer .20 .50
53CP8 Brewer Hicklen .30 .75
53CP9 Ryan Vilade .20 .50
53CP10 Chad Spanberger .20 .50
53CP11 Dylan Cease .30 .75
53CP12 Edward Cabrera .30 .75
53CP13 Jordyn Adams .30 .75
53CP14 Austin Beck .20 .50
53CP15 Alex Faedo .25 .60
53CP16 Domingo Acevedo .20 .50
53CP17 Matt Manning .30 .75
53CP18 Julio Rodriguez 1.50 4.00
53CP19 Reggie Lawson .20 .50
53CP20 Anthony Seigler .30 .75
53CP21 Jose de la Cruz .60 1.50
53CP22 MJ Melendez .30 .75
53CP23 Alex Kirilloff .30 .75
53CP24 Adonis Medina .30 .75
53CP25 Victor Mesa Jr. .40 1.00
53CP26 Sixto Sanchez .60 1.50
53CP27 William Contreras .25 .60
53CP28 Hunter Greene .30 .75
53CP29 Noelvi Marte .75 2.00
53CP30 Orelvis Martinez .50 1.25
53CP31 Adam Haseley .30 .75
53CP32 Travis Swaggerty .30 .75
53CP33 Seth Beer .50 1.25
53CP34 Brendan Rodgers .30 .75
53CP35 Jarred Kelenic 1.00 2.50
53CP36 Nick Madrigal .75 2.00
53CP37 Julio Pablo Martinez .20 .50
53CP38 Kevin Smith .20 .50
53CP39 Taylor Trammell .30 .75
53CP40 Taylor Widener .20 .50
53CP41 Ryan McKenna .20 .50
53CP42 Brandon Marsh .30 .75
53CP43 Franklyn Kilome .20 .50
53CP44 Lyon Richardson .25 .60
53CP45 DJ Peters .30 .75
53CP46 Royce Lewis .40 1.00
53CP47 Gavin Lux .75 2.00
53CP48 Colton Welker .20 .50
53CP49 Alec Bohm 1.25 3.00
53CP50 Luis Robert 1.50 4.00
53CP51 Ryan Mountcastle 1.00 2.50
53CP52 Brent Rooker .25 .60
53CP53 Brent Honeywell .25 .60
53CP54 Nick Neidert .20 .50
53CP55 Daniel Johnson .20 .50
53CP56 Derian Cruz .20 .50
53CP57 Aramis Ademan .20 .50
53CP58 Joey Wentz .20 .50
53CP59 Anthony Kay .20 .50
53CP60 Nate Pearson .60 1.50
53CP61 Ian Anderson .60 1.50
53CP62 Forrest Whitley .30 .75
53CP63 Cole Ragans .20 .50
53CP64 Ronaldo Hernandez .20 .50
53CP65 Jeter Downs .30 .75
53CP66 Sandro Fabian .20 .50
53CP67 Cristian Santana .30 .75
53CP68 Keibert Ruiz 1.00 2.50
53CP69 Ke'Bryan Hayes 1.00 2.50
53CP70 Cristian Pache .50 1.25
53CP71 Joey Bart .60 1.50
53CP72 Cole Winn .20 .50
53CP73 Jonathan India 1.25 3.00
53CP74 Ryan Weathers .20 .50
53CP75 Luken Baker .25 .60
53CP76 Justin Dunn .20 .50
53CP77 Nolan Gorman .60 1.50
53CP78 Bo Bichette .60 1.50
53CP79 Esteury Ruiz .25 .60
53CP80 Genesis Cabrera .30 .75
53CP81 Sean Murphy .25 .60
53CP82 Ryan Costello .25 .60
53CP83 Freudis Nova .30 .75
53CP84 Albert Abreu .20 .50
53CP85 Jazz Chisholm .75 2.00
53CP86 Logan Webb .30 .75
53CP87 Shane Baz .20 .50
53CP88 Marco Luciano 1.25 3.00
53CP89 Nico Hoerner .60 1.50
53CP90 A.J. Puk .30 .75
53CP91 Jesus Sanchez .30 .75
53CP92 Cole Tucker .30 .75
53CP93 Blaze Alexander .20 .50
53CP94 Triston McKenzie .60 1.50
53CP95 Franklin Perez .20 .50
53CP96 Jonathan Hernandez .20 .50
53CP97 Rylan Bannon .25 .60
53CP98 Andres Gimenez .50 1.25
53CP99 Keegan Thompson .20 .50
53CP100 Jo Adell .75 2.00
53CP101 Evan White .50 1.25
53CP102 Dustin May .60 1.50
53CP103 Daz Cameron .20 .50
53CP104 Brady Singer 1.00 2.50
53CP105 Victor Victor Mesa .40 1.00
53CP106 Ethan Hankins .25 .60
53CP107 Yusniel Diaz .30 .75
53CP108 Brock Burke .20 .50
53CP109 Bryan Mata .20 .50
53CP110 Luis Garcia .75 2.00
53CP111 Matthew Liberatore .20 .50
53CP112 Adrian Morejon .20 .50
53CP113 DL Hall .20 .50
53CP114 Cristian Javier .25 .60
53CP115 Michel Baez .20 .50
53CP116 Roberto Ramos .25 .60
53CP117 Dane Dunning .60 1.50
53CP118 Jesus Luzardo .30 .75
53CP119 MacKenzie Gore .40 1.00
53CP120 Brendan McKay .30 .75
53CP121 Leody Taveras .30 .75
53CP122 JoJo Romero .20 .50
53CP123 Tirso Ornelas .20 .50
53CP124 Jay Groome .20 .50
53CP125 Estevan Florial .30 .75
53CP126 Brusdar Graterol .25 .60
53CP127 Miguel Amaya .30 .75
53CP128 Corey Ray .20 .50
53CP129 Casey Mize .50 1.25

2019 Bowman Heritage Chrome Rookie Autographs
RANDOM INSERTS IN PACKS
PRINTING PLATES RANDOMLY INSERTED
PLATE PRINT RUN 1 SET PER COLOR
BLACK-CYAN-MAGENTA-YELLOW ISSUED
NO PLATE PRICING DUE TO SCARCITY
53RACB Corbin Burnes
53RAEJ Eloy Jimenez 40.00 100.00
53RAKW Kyle Wright 5.00 12.00
53RAVGJ Vladimir Guerrero Jr. 75.00 200.00

2019 Bowman Heritage Chrome Rookie Autographs Gold Refractors
53RACB Corbin Burnes 15.00 40.00

2019 Bowman Heritage Chrome Rookie Autographs Orange Refractors
53RACB Corbin Burnes 25.00 60.00

2019 Bowman Heritage Prospects
53P1 Wander Franco 4.00 10.00
53P2 Blake Rutherford .20 .50
53P3 Heliot Ramos .30 .75
53P4 Beau Burrows .20 .50
53P5 Ronny Mauricio .50 1.25
53P6 Drew Waters .60 1.50
53P7 Matt Mercer .20 .50
53P8 Brewer Hicklen .30 .75
53P9 Ryan Vilade .20 .50
53P10 Chad Spanberger .20 .50
53P11 Dylan Cease .30 .75
53P12 Edward Cabrera .30 .75
53P13 Jordyn Adams .30 .75
53P14 Austin Beck .20 .50
53P15 Alex Faedo .25 .60
53P16 Domingo Acevedo .20 .50
53P17 Matt Manning .30 .75
53P18 Julio Rodriguez 1.50 4.00
53P19 Reggie Lawson .20 .50
53P20 Anthony Seigler .30 .75
53P21 Jose de la Cruz .60 1.50
53P22 MJ Melendez .30 .75
53P23 Alex Kirilloff .30 .75
53P24 Adonis Medina .30 .75
53P25 Victor Mesa Jr. .40 1.00
53P26 Sixto Sanchez .60 1.50
53P27 William Contreras .25 .60
53P28 Hunter Greene .30 .75
53P29 Noelvi Marte .75 2.00
53P30 Orelvis Martinez .50 1.25
53P31 Adam Haseley .30 .75
53P32 Travis Swaggerty .30 .75
53P33 Seth Beer .50 1.25
53P34 Brendan Rodgers .30 .75
53P35 Jarred Kelenic 1.00 2.50
53P36 Nick Madrigal .75 2.00
53P37 Julio Pablo Martinez .20 .50
53P38 Kevin Smith .20 .50
53P39 Taylor Trammell .30 .75
53P40 Taylor Widener .20 .50
53P41 Ryan McKenna .20 .50
53P42 Brandon Marsh .30 .75
53P43 Franklyn Kilome .20 .50
53P44 Lyon Richardson .25 .60
53P45 DJ Peters .30 .75
53P46 Royce Lewis .40 1.00
53P47 Gavin Lux .75 2.00
53P48 Colton Welker .20 .50
53P49 Alec Bohm 1.25 3.00
53P50 Luis Robert 1.50 4.00
53P51 Ryan Mountcastle 1.00 2.50
53P52 Brent Rooker .25 .60
53P53 Brent Honeywell .25 .60
53P54 Nick Neidert .20 .50
53P55 Daniel Johnson .20 .50
53P56 Derian Cruz .20 .50
53P57 Aramis Ademan .20 .50
53P58 Joey Wentz .20 .50
53P59 Anthony Kay .20 .50
53P60 Nate Pearson .60 1.50
53P61 Ian Anderson .60 1.50
53P62 Forrest Whitley .30 .75
53P63 Cole Ragans .20 .50
53P64 Ronaldo Hernandez .20 .50
53P65 Jeter Downs .30 .75
53P66 Sandro Fabian .20 .50
53P67 Cristian Santana .30 .75
53P68 Keibert Ruiz 1.00 2.50
53P69 Ke'Bryan Hayes 1.00 2.50
53P70 Cristian Pache .50 1.25
53P71 Joey Bart .60 1.50
53P72 Cole Winn .20 .50
53P73 Jonathan India 1.25 3.00
53P74 Ryan Weathers .20 .50
53P75 Luken Baker .25 .60
53P76 Justin Dunn .20 .50
53P77 Nolan Gorman .60 1.50
53P78 Bo Bichette .60 1.50
53P79 Esteury Ruiz .25 .60
53P80 Genesis Cabrera .30 .75
53P81 Sean Murphy .25 .60
53P82 Ryan Costello .25 .60
53P83 Freudis Nova .30 .75
53P84 Albert Abreu .20 .50
53P85 Jazz Chisholm .75 2.00
53P86 Logan Webb .30 .75
53P87 Shane Baz .20 .50
53P88 Marco Luciano 1.25 3.00
53P89 Nico Hoerner .60 1.50
53P90 A.J. Puk .30 .75
53P91 Jesus Sanchez .30 .75
53P92 Cole Tucker .30 .75
53P93 Blaze Alexander .20 .50
53P94 Triston McKenzie .60 1.50
53P95 Franklin Perez .20 .50
53P96 Jonathan Hernandez .20 .50
53P97 Rylan Bannon .25 .60
53P98 Andres Gimenez .50 1.25
53P99 Keegan Thompson .20 .50
53P100 Jo Adell .75 2.00
53P101 Evan White .50 1.25
53P102 Dustin May .60 1.50
53P103 Daz Cameron .20 .50
53P104 Brady Singer 1.00 2.50
53P105 Victor Victor Mesa .40 1.00
53P106 Ethan Hankins .25 .60
53P107 Yusniel Diaz .30 .75
53P108 Brock Burke .20 .50
53P109 Bryan Mata .20 .50
53P110 Luis Garcia .75 2.00
53P111 Matthew Liberatore .20 .50
53P112 Adrian Morejon .20 .50
53P113 DL Hall .20 .50
53P114 Cristian Javier .25 .60
53P115 Michel Baez .20 .50
53P116 Roberto Ramos .25 .60
53P117 Dane Dunning .60 1.50
53P118 Jesus Luzardo .30 .75
53P119 MacKenzie Gore .40 1.00
53P120 Brendan McKay .30 .75
53P121 Leody Taveras .30 .75
53P122 JoJo Romero .20 .50
53P123 Tirso Ornelas .20 .50
53P124 Jay Groome .20 .50
53P125 Estevan Florial .30 .75
53P126 Brusdar Graterol .25 .60
53P127 Miguel Amaya .30 .75
53P128 Corey Ray .20 .50
53P129 Casey Mize .50 1.25
53P130 Yordan Alvarez 1.00 2.50
53P131 Logan Allen .20 .50
53P132 Zack Collins .25 .60

2019 Bowman Heritage Prospects Black and White
*BW: 1.2X TO 3X BASIC
RANDOM INSERTS IN PACKS
53P18 Julio Rodriguez 10.00 25.00

2020 Bowman Heritage
1 Mike Trout 3.00 8.00
2 Aaron Judge 1.00 2.50
3 Ketel Marte .30 .75
4 Francisco Lindor .40 1.00
5 Isan Diaz RC .75 2.00
6 Jordan Yamamoto RC .50 1.25
7 Mike Soroka .40 1.00
8 Cavan Biggio .50 1.25
9 Max Muncy .30 .75
10 Juan Soto 2.00 8.00
11 Sean Murphy RC .75 2.00
12 Rhys Hoskins .50 1.25
13 Shane Bieber .40 1.00
14 Willie Calhoun .25 .60
15 Justin Dunn RC .60 1.50
16 Travis Demeritte RC .75 2.00
17 Anthony Kay RC .50 1.25
18 Luis Robert RC 6.00 15.00
19 Adbert Alzolay RC .60 1.50
20 Bobby Bradley RC .50 1.25
21 Ramon Laureano .30 .75
22 Kris Bryant .50 1.25
23 Abraham Toro RC .60 1.50
24 Randy Arozarena RC 3.00 8.00
25 Yordan Alvarez RC 3.00 8.00
26 Shohei Ohtani .60 1.50
27 Ronald Acuna Jr. 1.50 4.00
28 Lorenzo Cain .25 .60
29 Eduardo Escobar .25 .60
30 Matthew Boyd .25 .60
31 Bryan Reynolds .30 .75
32 Jose Berrios .30 .75
33 Nolan Arenado .60 1.50
34 John Means .40 1.00
35 Logan Allen RC .50 1.25
36 Robel Garcia RC .50 1.25
37 Whit Merrifield .40 1.00
38 Dustin May RC 1.50 4.00
39 Junior Fernandez RC .50 1.25
40 Aaron Civale RC 1.00 2.50
41 George Springer .30 .75
42 Michel Baez RC .50 1.25
43 Joey Votto .40 1.00
44 Seth Brown RC .50 1.25
45 Mookie Betts .75 2.00
46 Austin Nola RC .75 2.00
47 Fernando Tatis Jr. 2.50 6.00
48 Zack Collins RC .60 1.50
49 Eddie Rosario .30 .75
50 Vladimir Guerrero Jr. .60 1.50
51 Dan Vogelbach .25 .60
52 Bo Bichette RC 4.00 10.00
53 Max Scherzer .40 1.00
54 Bryce Harper .60 1.50
55 Paul DeJong .40 1.00
56 Luis Castillo .30 .75
57 Francisco Mejia .30 .75
58 Dylan Cease RC .75 2.00
59 Lucas Giolito .30 .75
60 Jose Urena .25 .60
61 Jesus Luzardo RC 1.00 2.50
62 Kevin Newman .40 1.00
63 Tony Gonsolin RC 2.00 5.00
64 A.J. Puk RC .75 2.00
65 Adrian Morejon RC .50 1.25
66 Yu Chang RC .75 2.00
67 Sheldon Neuse RC .60 1.50
68 Blake Snell .30 .75
69 Alex Young RC .50 1.25
70 Nomar Mazara .25 .60
71 Gavin Lux RC 2.50 6.00
72 Nico Hoerner RC 2.00 5.00
73 Matt Chapman .40 1.00
74 Gleyber Torres .75 2.00
75 Zac Gallen RC 1.25 3.00
76 Mauricio Dubon RC .60 1.50
77 Jeff McNeil .30 .75
78 Kyle Lewis RC 2.50 6.00
79 Aristides Aquino RC 1.25 3.00
80 Yusei Kikuchi .30 .75
81 Willy Adames .25 .60
82 Trevor Story .40 1.00
83 Trent Grisham RC 2.00 5.00
84 Starlin Castro .25 .60
85 Cody Bellinger .75 2.00
86 Buster Posey .50 1.25
87 Hanser Alberto .25 .60
88 Jose Altuve .30 .75
89 Brusdar Graterol RC .75 2.00
90 Andres Munoz RC .75 2.00
91 Hunter Dozier .25 .60
92 Mike Yastrzemski .60 1.50
93 Miguel Cabrera .40 1.00
94 Jack Flaherty .40 1.00
95 Xander Bogaerts .40 1.00
96 Nick Solak 1.00 2.50
97 Tim Anderson .40 1.00
98 Pete Alonso 1.00 2.50
99 Javier Baez .50 1.25
100 Christian Yelich .50 1.25

2020 Bowman Heritage Black and White
*BW: 1.4X TO 4X BASIC
*BW RC: .8X TO 2X BASIC RC
STATED ODDS 1:3 HOBBY
18 Luis Robert 15.00 40.00
25 Yordan Alvarez 10.00 25.00
79 Aristides Aquino 3.00 8.00

2020 Bowman Heritage Chrome Prospect Autographs
STATED ODDS 1:XX HOBBY
EXCHANGE DEADLINE XX/XX/XX
92PAAA Aaron Ashby 2.50 6.00
92PAAH Adam Hall 5.00 12.00
92PAAV Anthony Volpe 15.00 40.00
92PABB Ben Braymer 4.00 10.00
92PABD Brennen Davis 12.00 30.00
92PABH Brandon Howlett 4.00 10.00
92PACC Connor Cannon 6.00 15.00
92PADJ Damon Jones 3.00 8.00
92PAGV Gus Varland 3.00 8.00
92PAJC Joey Cantillo 5.00 12.00
92PAJD Jarren Duran 15.00 40.00
92PAPC Philip Clarke 2.50 6.00
92PARP Robert Puason 20.00 50.00
92PASA Sherten Apostel 10.00 25.00
92PAAHI Adam Hill 2.50 6.00
92PAASH Aaron Shortridge 3.00 8.00
92PAAVA Andrew Vaughn 20.00 50.00
92PABBA Bryce Ball 10.00 25.00
92PAJDO Jasson Dominguez 250.00 600.00
92PAJJB JJ Bleday
92PAJRY Joe Ryan 5.00 12.00

2020 Bowman Heritage Chrome Prospect Autographs Gold Refractors
*GOLD: .6X TO 1.5X BASIC
STATED ODDS 1:XX HOBBY
STATED PRINT RUN 50 SER.#'d SETS
EXCHANGE DEADLINE XX/XX/XX
92PAAV Anthony Volpe 75.00 200.00
92PAGV Gus Varland 8.00 20.00
92PAJD Jarren Duran 50.00 120.00
92PAPC Philip Clarke 6.00 15.00
92PARP Robert Puason 40.00 100.00
92PAASH Aaron Shortridge 10.00 25.00
92PAAVA Andrew Vaughn 60.00 150.00
92PABBA Bryce Ball 40.00 100.00
92PAJDO Jasson Dominguez 800.00 1500.00
92PAJJB JJ Bleday 25.00 60.00
92PAJRY Joe Ryan 12.00 30.00

2020 Bowman Heritage Chrome Prospect Autographs Orange Refractors
*ORANGE: .8X TO 2X BASIC
STATED ODDS 1:XX HOBBY
STATED PRINT RUN 25 SER.#'d SETS
EXCHANGE DEADLINE XX/XX/XX
92PAAV Anthony Volpe 125.00 300.00
92PACC Connor Cannon 15.00 40.00
92PAGV Gus Varland 10.00 25.00
92PAJD Jarren Duran 60.00 150.00
92PAPC Philip Clarke 8.00 20.00
92PARP Robert Puason 50.00 120.00
92PAASH Aaron Shortridge 12.00 30.00
92PAAVA Andrew Vaughn 100.00 250.00
92PABBA Bryce Ball 50.00 120.00
92PAJDO Jasson Dominguez 1000.00 2000.00
92PAJJB JJ Bleday 50.00 120.00
92PAJRY Joe Ryan 15.00 40.00

2020 Bowman Heritage Chrome Prospect Autographs Refractors
*REF: .5X TO 1.2X BASIC
STATED ODDS 1:XX HOBBY
STATED PRINT RUN 99 SER.#'d SETS
EXCHANGE DEADLINE XX/XX/XX
92PAAV Anthony Volpe 30.00 80.00
92PAJD Jarren Duran 40.00 100.00
92PAPC Philip Clarke 5.00 12.00
92PAJDO Jasson Dominguez 400.00 1000.00
92PAJJB JJ Bleday 20.00 50.00
92PAJRY Joe Ryan 8.00 20.00

2020 Bowman Heritage Chrome Prospects
STATED ODDS 1:XX HOBBY
92CPAA Aaron Ashby .60 1.50
92CPAB Alec Bohm 4.00 10.00
92CPAC Antonio Cabello 2.00 5.00
92CPAH Adam Hall .75 2.00
92CPAK Alex Kirilloff 1.25 3.00
92CPAM Alek Manoah .75 2.00
92CPAR Adley Rutschman 4.00 10.00
92CPAS Alvaro Seijas .60 1.50
92CPAT Alek Thomas .75 2.00
92CPAV Andrew Vaughn 2.50 6.00
92CPBB Brett Baty 1.25 3.00
92CPBC Briam Campusano .60 1.50
92CPBD Bobby Dalbec 4.00 10.00
92CPBL Bayron Lora 3.00 8.00
92CPBM Brady McConnell .75 2.00
92CPBR Blake Rutherford .60 1.50
92CPBS Bryson Stott 1.50 4.00
92CPBT Brice Turang .60 1.50
92CPBW Bobby Witt Jr. 5.00 12.00
92CPCA CJ Abrams 2.00 5.00
92CPCJ Cristian Javier .75 2.00
92CPCM Casey Mize 2.00 5.00
92CPCP Cristian Pache 2.00 5.00
92CPCS Clarke Schmidt 1.00 2.50
92CPCV Chris Vallimont .60 1.50
92CPCW Cole Winn .60 1.50
92CPDC Dylan Carlson 2.50 6.00
92CPDD Dane Dunning 2.00 5.00
92CPDG Deivi Garcia 3.00 8.00
92CPDJ Damon Jones .75 2.00
92CPDL Daniel Lynch .60 1.50
92CPDM Drew Mendoza 1.50 4.00
92CPDW Drew Waters 1.50 4.00
92CPEF Estevan Florial 1.00 2.50
92CPEH Ethan Hankins .75 2.00
92CPEM Elehuris Montero .75 2.00
92CPEP Eric Pardinho .75 2.00
92CPEW Evan White 1.50 4.00
92CPFN Freudis Nova .60 1.50
92CPFP Franklin Perez .60 1.50
92CPFW Forrest Whitley 1.00 2.50
92CPGH Gunnar Henderson .75 2.00
92CPGL Grant Lavigne .60 1.50
92CPGR Grayson Rodriguez 1.00 2.50
92CPGV Gus Varland .75 2.00
92CPHB Hunter Bishop 1.25 3.00
92CPHC Hans Crouse .60 1.50
92CPHF Sam Huff 1.25 3.00
92CPHG Hunter Greene 1.00 2.50
92CPHR Heliot Ramos 1.00 2.50
92CPIA Ian Anderson 2.00 5.00
92CPIP Isaac Paredes 2.00 5.00
92CPJA Jordyn Adams .75 2.00
92CPJB Joey Bart 1.25 3.00
92CPJC Jazz Chisholm 2.50 6.00
92CPJD Jhon Diaz 2.00 5.00
92CPJE Jerar Encarnacion 2.00 5.00
92CPJG Jordan Groshans 1.25 3.00
92CPJI Jonathan India 4.00 10.00
92CPJJ JJ Bleday 2.00 5.00
92CPJK Jarred Kelenic 3.00 8.00
92CPJM Jorge Mateo .75 2.00
92CPJO Jo Adell 2.50 6.00
92CPJP Jeremy Pena 1.50 4.00
92CPJR Jackson Rutledge 1.00 2.50
92CPJS Jesus Sanchez 1.00 2.50
92CPKC Keoni Cavaco .60 1.50
92CPKH Ke'Bryan Hayes 3.00 8.00
92CPKR Keibert Ruiz 3.00 8.00
92CPLD Logan Davidson .75 2.00
92CPLG Luis Garcia 2.50 6.00
92CPLT Leody Taveras 1.00 2.50
92CPMA Miguel Amaya .60 1.50
92CPMD Mason Denaburg .60 1.50
92CPMG MacKenzie Gore 1.25 3.00
92CPML Matthew Liberatore .75 2.00
92CPMM Matt Manning .75 2.00
92CPMV Miguel Vargas 1.50 4.00
92CPNA Nick Allen .60 1.50
92CPNB Nick Bennett .75 2.00
92CPNG Nolan Gorman 1.25 3.00
92CPNH Niko Hulsizer 1.50 4.00
92CPNJ Nolan Jones 1.00 2.50
92CPNL Nick Lodolo 1.00 2.50
92CPNM Nick Madrigal 2.50 6.00
92CPNP Nate Pearson 2.00 5.00
92CPOC Oneil Cruz .75 2.00
92CPOG Oscar Gonzalez 1.25 3.00
92CPOM Owen Miller .60 1.50
92CPRC Ruben Cardenas .75 2.00
92CPRG Riley Greene 2.50 6.00
92CPRH Ronaldo Hernandez .60 1.50
92CPRL Royce Lewis 1.50 4.00
92CPRM Ronny Mauricio 1.50 4.00
92CPRP Robert Puason 2.00 5.00
92CPRR Ryan Rolison .75 2.00
92CPSA Sherten Apostel 3.00 8.00
92CPSB Shane Baz .60 1.50
92CPSH Spencer Howard 2.00 5.00
92CPSL Shea Langeliers 1.25 3.00
92CPSS Sixto Sanchez 2.00 5.00
92CPTC Tim Cate .60 1.50
92CPTF Tyler Freeman .75 2.00
92CPTH Tanner Houck 1.50 4.00
92CPTL Tristen Lutz .75 2.00
92CPTS Travis Swaggerty .75 2.00
92CPTT Taylor Trammell 1.00 2.50
92CPUB Ulrich Bojarski 1.00 2.50
92CPWA Wilfred Astudillo .75 2.00
92CPWF Wander Franco 6.00 15.00
92CPWW Will Wilson .75 2.00
92CPXE Xavier Edwards 2.50 6.00
92CPZB Zack Brown .60 1.50
92CPZT Zack Thompson .60 1.50
92CPADE Aramis Ademan .60 1.50
92CPAMA Jacob Amaya 2.50 6.00
92CPBCK Austin Beck .75 2.00
92CPBER Seth Beer 1.25 3.00
92CPBLZ Jordan Balazovic 1.25 3.00
92CPCAN Joey Cantillo .60 1.50
92CPCAS Triston Casas 1.50 4.00
92CPDAL Bryan Mata .60 1.50
92CPDAZ Daz Cameron .60 1.50
92CPDLC Jasseel De La Cruz 1.00 2.50
92CPDUR Jarren Duran 2.50 6.00
92CPDVS Brennen Davis 1.25 3.00
92CPGCA Luis Garcia 2.50 6.00
92CPGHJ Glenallen Hill Jr. 1.00 2.50
92CPGIL Luis Gil .75 2.00
92CPGRY Josiah Gray 1.00 2.50
92CPHSE Kody Hoese 2.00 5.00
92CPJAS Jasson Dominguez 20.00 50.00
92CPJNG Josh Jung 1.50 4.00
92CPLTL Grant Little .75 2.00
92CPLUC Marco Luciano 2.50 6.00
92CPMAR Brailyn Marquez 1.50 4.00
92CPMNT Ryan Mountcastle 3.00 8.00
92CPPRR Everson Pereira 1.50 4.00
92CPREC Rece Hinds .75 2.00
92CPROB Kristian Robinson 2.00 5.00
92CPROD Julio Rodriguez 4.00 10.00
92CPRYN Joe Ryan .75 2.00
92CPSHR Aaron Shortridge .75 2.00
92CPSMT Canaan Smith 1.00 2.50
92CPSNG Brady Singer 3.00 8.00
92CPSWG Cal Mitchell .60 1.50
92CPTRK Tarik Skubal 1.50 4.00
92CPVOL Anthony Volpe 2.50 6.00
92CPWHT Logan Gilbert .75 2.00
92CPWLK Colton Welker .60 1.50

2020 Bowman Heritage Chrome Prospects Blue Refractors
*BLUE: 1X TO 2.5X BASIC
STATED ODDS 1:XX HOBBY
STATED PRINT RUN 99 SER.#'d SETS
92CPAR Adley Rutschman 15.00 40.00
92CPBL Bayron Lora 8.00 20.00
92CPBW Bobby Witt Jr. 15.00 40.00
92CPCP Cristian Pache 10.00 25.00
92CPDG Deivi Garcia 10.00 25.00
92CPJK Jarred Kelenic 15.00 40.00
92CPRG Riley Greene 8.00 20.00
92CPRP Robert Puason 10.00 25.00
92CPWF Wander Franco 40.00 100.00
92CPJAS Jasson Dominguez 75.00 200.00
92CPVOL Anthony Volpe 8.00 20.00

2020 Bowman Heritage Chrome Prospects Gold Refractors
*GOLD: 2X TO 5X BASIC
STATED ODDS 1:XX HOBBY
STATED PRINT RUN 50 SER.#'d SETS
92CPAR Adley Rutschman 40.00 100.00
92CPBL Bayron Lora 15.00 40.00
92CPBW Bobby Witt Jr. 30.00 80.00
92CPCP Cristian Pache 20.00 50.00
92CPDG Deivi Garcia 20.00 50.00
92CPJK Jarred Kelenic 30.00 80.00
92CPRG Riley Greene 15.00 40.00
92CPRP Robert Puason 20.00 50.00
92CPWF Wander Franco 75.00 200.00
92CPJAS Jasson Dominguez 150.00 400.00
92CPVOL Anthony Volpe 15.00 40.00

2020 Bowman Heritage Chrome Prospects Orange Refractors
*ORANGE: 2.5X TO 6X BASIC
STATED ODDS 1:XX HOBBY
STATED PRINT RUN 25 SER.#'d SETS
92CPAR Adley Rutschman 50.00 120.00
92CPBL Bayron Lora 20.00 50.00
92CPBW Bobby Witt Jr. 40.00 100.00
92CPCP Cristian Pache 25.00 60.00
92CPDG Deivi Garcia 25.00 60.00
92CPJK Jarred Kelenic 40.00 100.00
92CPRG Riley Greene 20.00 50.00
92CPRP Robert Puason 25.00 60.00
92CPWF Wander Franco 40.00 100.00
92CPJAS Jasson Dominguez 400.00 800.00
92CPVOL Anthony Volpe 20.00 50.00

2020 Bowman Heritage Chrome Prospects Refractors
*REF: .6X TO 1.5X BASIC
STATED ODDS 1:XX HOBBY
STATED PRINT RUN 199 SER.#'d SETS
92CPBW Bobby Witt Jr. 10.00 25.00
92CPCP Cristian Pache 6.00 15.00
92CPDG Deivi Garcia 6.00 15.00
92CPJK Jarred Kelenic 10.00 25.00
92CPRP Robert Puason 4.00 10.00
92CPJAS Jasson Dominguez 60.00 150.00
92CPVOL Anthony Volpe 5.00 12.00

2020 Bowman Heritage Chrome Prospects Yellow Refractors
*YELLOW: 1.2X TO 3X BASIC
STATED ODDS 1:XX HOBBY
STATED PRINT RUN 75 SER.#'d SETS
92CPAR Adley Rutschman 25.00 60.00
92CPBL Bayron Lora 10.00 25.00
92CPBW Bobby Witt Jr. 20.00 50.00
92CPCP Cristian Pache 12.00 30.00
92CPDG Deivi Garcia 12.00 301.00
92CPJK Jarred Kelenic 20.00 50.00
92CPRG Riley Greene 10.00 25.00
92CPRP Robert Puason 12.00 30.00
92CPWF Wander Franco 50.00 120.00
92CPJAS Jasson Dominguez 100.00 250.00
92CPVOL Anthony Volpe 10.00 25.00

2020 Bowman Heritage Prospects Image Variations
STATED ODDS 1:XX HOBBY
BHP1 Wander Franco 12.00 30.00
BHP5 Cristian Pache 4.00 10.00
BHP8 Jasson Dominguez 40.00 100.00
BHP19 Julio Rodriguez 8.00 20.00
BHP25 Bobby Witt Jr. 8.00 20.00
BHP26 Andrew Vaughn 5.00 12.00
BHP29 Alec Bohm 8.00 20.00
BHP50 Casey Mize 4.00 10.00
BHP62 CJ Abrams 4.00 10.00
BHP74 MacKenzie Gore 2.50 6.00
BHP79 Sixto Sanchez 4.00 10.00
BHP93 Royce Lewis 3.00 8.00
BHP94 Jarred Kelenic 6.00 15.00
BHP100 Jo Adell 5.00 12.00
BHP106 Dylan Carlson 5.00 12.00
BHP112 Joey Bart 4.00 10.00
BHP116 JJ Bleday 4.00 10.00
BHP122 Riley Greene 5.00 12.00
BHP145 Robert Puason 4.00 10.00
BHP150 Adley Rutschman 8.00 20.00

2020 Bowman Heritage Chrome Rookie Autographs
STATED ODDS 1:XX HOBBY
EXCHANGE DEADLINE XX/XX/XX
92RABM Brendan McKay 6.00 15.00
92RAJL Jesus Luzardo 8.00 20.00
92RALR Luis Robert
92RAYA Yordan Alvarez 30.00 80.00
92RAAAQ Aristides Aquino 6.00 15.00

2020 Bowman Heritage Chrome Rookie Autographs Gold Refractors
*GOLD: .6X TO 1.5X BASIC
STATED ODDS 1:XX HOBBY
STATED PRINT RUN 50 SER.#'d SETS
EXCHANGE DEADLINE XX/XX/XX
92RALR Luis Robert 400.00 1000.00
92RAYA Yordan Alvarez 75.00 200.00

2020 Bowman Heritage Chrome Rookie Autographs Orange Refractors
*ORANGE: .8X TO 2X BASIC
STATED ODDS 1:XX HOBBY
STATED PRINT RUN 25 SER.#'d SETS
EXCHANGE DEADLINE XX/XX/XX
92RALR Luis Robert 800.00 1500.00
92RAYA Yordan Alvarez 200.00 500.00

2020 Bowman Heritage Chrome Rookie Autographs Refractors
*REF: .5X TO 1.2X BASIC
STATED ODDS 1:XX HOBBY
STATED PRINT RUN 99 SER.#'d SETS
EXCHANGE DEADLINE XX/XX/XX
92RAYA Yordan Alvarez 50.00 120.00

2020 Bowman Heritage Prospects
STATED ODDS 1:XX HOBBY
BHP1 Wander Franco 3.00 8.00
BHP2 Drew Waters .75 2.00
BHP3 Jacob Amaya 1.25 3.00
BHP4 Kody Hoese 1.00 2.50
BHP5 Cristian Pache 1.00 2.50
BHP6 Zack Thompson .30 .75
BHP7 Briam Campusano .30 .75
BHP8 Jasson Dominguez 8.00 20.00
BHP9 Aaron Shortridge .40 1.00
BHP10 Xavier Edwards 1.25 3.00
BHP11 Jesus Sanchez .50 1.25
BHP12 Ronaldo Hernandez .30 .75
BHP13 Blake Rutherford .30 .75
BHP14 Ulrich Bojarski .50 1.25
BHP15 Jordyn Adams .40 1.00
BHP16 Austin Beck .40 1.00
BHP17 Niko Hulsizer .75 2.00
BHP18 Triston Casas .75 2.00
BHP19 Julio Rodriguez 1.25 3.00
BHP20 Shane Baz .30 .75
BHP21 Shea Langeliers .60 1.50
BHP22 Grayson Rodriguez .50 1.25
BHP23 Ruben Cardenas .40 1.00
BHP24 Mason Denaburg .30 .75
BHP25 Bobby Witt Jr. 4.00 10.00
BHP26 Andrew Vaughn 1.25 3.00
BHP27 Kristian Robinson 1.00 2.50
BHP28 Ronny Mauricio .75 2.00
BHP29 Alec Bohm 2.00 5.00
BHP30 Jhon Diaz 1.00 2.50
BHP31 Estevan Florial .50 1.25
BHP32 Elehuris Montero .40 1.00
BHP33 Sam Huff .60 1.50
BHP34 Zack Brown .30 .75
BHP35 Brice Turang .30 .75
BHP36 Ryan Mountcastle 1.50 4.00
BHP37 Wilfred Astudillo .40 1.00
BHP38 Gus Varland .40 1.00
BHP39 Nick Lodolo .50 1.25
BHP40 Tyler Freeman .40 1.00
BHP41 Rece Hinds .40 1.00
BHP42 Brady Singer 1.50 4.00
BHP43 Cal Mitchell .30 .75
BHP44 Ethan Hankins .40 1.00
BHP45 Daz Cameron .30 .75
BHP46 Sherten Apostel 1.50 4.00
BHP47 Hunter Greene .50 1.25
BHP48 Josiah Gray .50 1.25
BHP49 Brailyn Marquez .75 2.00
BHP50 Casey Mize 1.00 2.50
BHP51 Everson Pereira .75 2.00
BHP52 Bayron Lora 1.50 4.00
BHP53 Clarke Schmidt .50 1.25
BHP54 Brady McConnell .40 1.00
BHP55 Spencer Howard 1.00 2.50
BHP56 Cristian Javier .40 1.00
BHP57 Aaron Ashby .30 .75
BHP58 Logan Gilbert .40 1.00
BHP59 Glenallen Hill Jr. .50 1.25
BHP60 Alvaro Seijas .30 .75
BHP61 Jeremy Pena .75 2.00
BHP62 CJ Abrams 1.00 2.50
BHP63 Franklin Perez .30 .75
BHP64 Tanner Houck .75 2.00
BHP65 Damon Jones .40 1.00
BHP66 Nolan Gorman .60 1.50
BHP67 Ke'Bryan Hayes 1.50 4.00
BHP68 Bryson Stott .75 2.00
BHP69 Canaan Smith .50 1.25
BHP70 Forrest Whitley .50 1.25
BHP71 Drew Mendoza .75 2.00
BHP72 Jazz Chisholm 1.25 3.00
BHP73 Jonathan India 2.00 5.00
BHP74 MacKenzie Gore .60 1.50
BHP75 Seth Beer .60 1.50
BHP76 Joey Cantillo .30 .75
BHP77 Evan White .75 2.00
BHP78 Chris Vallimont .30 .75
BHP79 Sixto Sanchez 1.00 2.50
BHP80 Alex Kirilloff .60 1.50
BHP81 Tristen Lutz .40 1.00
BHP82 Freudis Nova .30 .75
BHP83 Tim Cate .30 .75
BHP84 Daniel Lynch .30 .75
BHP85 Antonio Cabello 1.00 2.50
BHP86 Bobby Dalbec 2.00 5.00
BHP87 Colton Welker .30 .75
BHP88 Logan Davidson .40 1.00
BHP89 Matthew Liberatore .40 1.00
BHP90 Adam Hall .40 1.00
BHP91 Jackson Rutledge .50 1.25
BHP92 Dane Dunning 1.00 2.50
BHP93 Royce Lewis .75 2.00
BHP94 Jarred Kelenic 1.50 4.00
BHP95 Nolan Jones .50 1.25
BHP96 Jerar Encarnacion 1.00 2.50
BHP97 Ian Anderson 1.00 2.50
BHP98 Alek Thomas .40 1.00
BHP99 Matt Manning .40 1.00
BHP100 Jo Adell 1.25 3.00
BHP101 Nick Madrigal 1.25 3.00
BHP102 Owen Miller .30 .75
BHP103 Marco Luciano 1.25 3.00
BHP104 Jordan Groshans .60 1.50
BHP105 Nick Allen .30 .75
BHP106 Dylan Carlson 1.25 3.00
BHP107 Cole Winn .30 .75
BHP108 Tarik Skubal 1.50 4.00
BHP109 Oscar Gonzalez .60 1.50
BHP110 Aramis Ademan .30 .75
BHP111 Oneil Cruz .40 1.00
BHP112 Joey Bart 1.00 2.50
BHP113 Josh Jung .75 2.00
BHP114 Luis Garcia 1.25 3.00
BHP115 Jasseel De La Cruz .50 1.25
BHP116 JJ Bleday 1.00 2.50
BHP117 Joe Ryan .40 1.00
BHP118 Keoni Cavaco .30 .75
BHP119 Hans Crouse .30 .75
BHP120 Isaac Paredes 1.00 2.50
BHP121 Grant Lavigne .30 .75
BHP122 Riley Greene 1.25 3.00
BHP123 Jordan Balazovic .60 1.50
BHP124 Nate Pearson 1.00 2.50
BHP125 Deivi Garcia 1.50 4.00
BHP126 Luis Garcia 1.25 3.00
BHP127 Leody Taveras .50 1.25
BHP128 Bryan Mata .30 .75
BHP129 Hunter Bishop .60 1.50
BHP130 Taylor Trammell .50 1.25
BHP131 Miguel Vargas .75 2.00
BHP132 Luis Gil .40 1.00
BHP133 Grant Little .40 1.00
BHP134 Gunnar Henderson .40 1.00
BHP135 Eric Pardinho .40 1.00
BHP136 Miguel Amaya .30 .75
BHP137 Ryan Rolison .40 1.00
BHP138 Jorge Mateo .40 1.00
BHP139 Anthony Volpe 1.25 3.00
BHP140 Nick Bennett .40 1.00
BHP141 Brennen Davis .60 1.50
BHP142 Brett Baty 1.00 2.50
BHP143 Keibert Ruiz 1.50 4.00
BHP144 Jarren Duran 1.25 3.00
BHP145 Robert Puason 1.00 2.50
BHP146 Travis Swaggerty .40 1.00
BHP147 Will Wilson .40 1.00
BHP148 Heliot Ramos .50 1.25
BHP149 Alek Manoah .40 1.00
BHP150 Adley Rutschman 2.00 5.00

2020 Bowman Heritage Prospects Black and White
*BW: 1X TO 2.5X BASIC
STATED ODDS 1:XX HOBBY
BHP8 Jasson Dominguez 25.00 60.00
BHP29 Alec Bohm 6.00 15.00
BHP150 Adley Rutschman 6.00 15.00

2017 Bowman High Tek
BHTAE Anderson Espinoza .40 1.00
BHTAI Andy Ibanez .40 1.00
BHTAK Alex Kiriloff 1.00 2.50
BHTAM Adrian Morejon .60 1.50
BHTAME Austin Meadows 1.00 2.50
BHTAP A.J. Puk .60 1.50
BHTAR Amed Rosario .60 1.50
BHTARO Alfredo Rodriguez .50 1.25
BHTBB Bo Bichette 1.50 4.00
BHTBG Braxton Garrett .40 1.00
BHTBR Brendan Rodgers .50 1.25
BHTCB Cody Bellinger 4.00 10.00
BHTCF Clint Frazier .75 2.00
BHTCR Corey Ray .50 1.25
BHTCS Cody Sedlock .40 1.00
BHTDC Dylan Cozens .40 1.00
BHTEJ Eloy Jimenez 1.50 4.00
BHTFM Francisco Mejia .60 1.50
BHTFR Fernando Romero .40 1.00
BHTFW Forrest Whitley 1.00 2.50
BHTGT Gleyber Torres 6.00 15.00
BHTIA Ian Anderson 1.25 3.00
BHTID Isan Diaz 1.00 2.50
BHTIH Ian Happ .75 2.00
BHTJC J.P. Crawford .40 1.00
BHTJD Justin Dunn .40 1.00
BHTJF Junior Fernandez .60 1.50
BHTJG Jason Groome .75 2.00
BHTJM Jorge Mateo .40 1.00
BHTJO Jhailyn Ortiz .75 2.00
BHTJS Justus Sheffield .60 1.50
BHTKL Kyle Lewis .75 2.00
BHTKM Kevin Maitan .60 1.50
BHTLA Lazarito Armenteros .75 2.00
BHTLB Lewis Brinson .60 1.50
BHTLC Luis Castillo 1.25 3.00
BHTLF Lucius Fox .40 1.00
BHTLGJ Lourdes Gurriel Jr. .60 1.50
BHTMK Mitch Keller .50 1.25
BHTMM Mickey Moniak .75 2.00
BHTMMA Matt Manning .60 1.50
BHTNS Nick Senzel 1.25 3.00
BHTOA Ozzie Albies 1.50 4.00
BHTPC P.J. Conlon .40 1.00
BHTPW Patrick Weigel .40 1.00
BHTRD Rafael Devers .75 2.00
BHTRH Rhys Hoskins 1.50 4.00
BHTRR Roniel Raudes .40 1.00
BHTSN Sean Newcomb .50 1.25
BHTTO Tyler O'Neill .50 1.25
BHTTS Thomas Szapucki .50 1.25
BHTVR Victor Robles 1.00 2.50
BHTWB Wuilmer Becerra .40 1.00
BHTWC Willie Calhoun .60 1.50
BHTYA Yadier Alvarez .60 1.50
BHTZC Zack Collins .50 1.25

2017 Bowman High Tek Circuit Board
*CIRCUIT: .6X TO 1.5X BASIC
STATED ODDS 1:3 HOBBY

2017 Bowman High Tek Diamond Dots
*DIAMOND DOTS: 1.5X TO 4X BASIC
STATED ODDS 1:18 HOBBY

2017 Bowman High Tek Gold Rainbow
*GOLD RAINBOW: 1.5X TO 4X BASIC
RANDOM INSERTS IN PACKS
STATED PRINT RUN 50 SER.#'d SETS
BHTCB Cody Bellinger 25.00 60.00

2017 Bowman High Tek Green Rainbow
*GREEN RAINBOW: 1X TO 2.5X BASIC
RANDOM INSERTS IN PACKS
STATED PRINT RUN 99 SER.#'d SETS
BHTCB Cody Bellinger 15.00 40.00

2017 Bowman High Tek Hexagon
*HEXAGON: .75X TO 2X BASIC
STATED ODDS 1:6 HOBBY

2017 Bowman High Tek Orange Magma Diffractors
*ORANGE MAGMA: 2.5X TO 6X BASIC
RANDOM INSERTS IN PACKS
STATED PRINT RUN 25 SER.#'d SETS
BHTCB Cody Bellinger 40.00 100.00

2017 Bowman High Tek Pinwheel
*PINWHEEL: .5X TO 1.2X BASIC
RANDOM INSERTS IN PACKS

2017 Bowman High Tek Shatter
*SHATTER: .75X TO 2X BASIC
STATED ODDS 1:4 HOBBY

2017 Bowman High Tek Squiggles and Dots
*SQUIG DOTS: 1.2X TO 3X BASIC
STATED ODDS 1:12 HOBBY

2017 Bowman High Tek Stripes and Arrows
*STRIPE ARROW: .5X TO 1.2X BASIC
RANDOM INSERTS IN PACKS

2017 Bowman High Tek Tidal Diffractors
*TIDAL DIFF: .75X TO 2X BASIC
RANDOM INSERTS IN PACKS
STATED PRINT RUN 199 SER.#'d SETS
BHTCB Cody Bellinger 12.00 30.00

2017 Bowman High Tek '17 Bowman Rookie Autographs
RANDOM INSERTS IN PACKS
STATED PRINT RUN 50 SER.#;d SETS
EXCHANGE DEADLINE 9/30/2019
17BTAB Alex Bregman 40.00 100.00
17BTAJ Aaron Judge 250.00 500.00
17BTDD David Dahl 20.00 50.00
17BTYG Yulieski Gurriel 12.00 30.00
17BTABE Andrew Benintendi 40.00 100.00

2017 Bowman High Tek '17 Bowman Rookies
RANDOM INSERTS IN PACKS
STATED PRINT RUN 75 SER.#;d SETS
17BTAB Alex Bregman 12.00 30.00
17BTABE Andrew Benintendi 8.00 20.00
17BTAJ Aaron Judge 60.00 150.00
17BTAR Alex Reyes 3.00 8.00
17BTDD David Dahl 3.00 8.00
17BTDS Dansby Swanson 6.00 15.00
17BTJDL Jose De Leon 2.50 6.00
17BTTG Tyler Glasnow 10.00 25.00
17BTYG Yulieski Gurriel 4.00 10.00
17BTYM Yoan Moncada 8.00 20.00

2017 Bowman High Tek '92 Bowman
RANDOM INSERTS IN PACKS
STATED PRINT RUN 75 SER.#;d SETS
92BAR Amed Rosario 8.00 20.00
92BBR Brendan Rodgers 2.50 6.00
92BCR Corey Ray 2.50 6.00
92BEJ Eloy Jimenez 5.00 12.00
92BIA Ian Anderson 6.00 15.00
92BJC J.P. Crawford 6.00 15.00
92BJG Jason Groome 4.00 10.00
92BJM Jorge Mateo 2.00 5.00
92BKM Kevin Maitan 6.00 15.00
92BLA Lazarito Armenteros 5.00 12.00
92BLGJ Lourdes Gurriel Jr. 3.00 8.00
92BMM Mickey Moniak 4.00 10.00
92BNS Nick Senzel 6.00 15.00
92BVR Victor Robles 5.00 12.00
92BYA Yadier Alvarez 3.00 8.00

2017 Bowman High Tek '92 Bowman Autographs
RANDOM INSERTS IN PACKS
STATED PRINT RUN 35 SER.#;d SETS
EXCHANGE DEADLINE 9/30/2019
92BAR Amed Rosario 10.00 25.00
92BBR Brendan Rodgers 15.00 40.00
92BCR Corey Ray 8.00 20.00
92BEJ Eloy Jimenez 100.00 250.00
92BIA Ian Anderson 20.00 50.00
92BJG Jason Groome 12.00 30.00
92BJM Jorge Mateo 6.00 15.00
92BKM Kevin Maitan 10.00 25.00
92BLA Lazarito Armenteros 12.00 30.00
92BLGJ Lourdes Gurriel Jr. 25.00 60.00
92BMM Mickey Moniak 12.00 30.00
92BNS Nick Senzel 40.00 100.00
92BYA Yadier Alvarez 10.00 25.00

2017 Bowman High Tek Autographs
RANDOM INSERTS IN PACKS
EXCHANGE DEADLINE 9/30/2019
BHTAE Anderson Espinoza 2.50 6.00
BHTAK Alex Kiriloff 10.00 25.00
BHTAM Adrian Morejon 3.00 8.00
BHTAP A.J. Puk 5.00 12.00
BHTAR Amed Rosario 4.00 10.00
BHTARO Alfredo Rodriguez 3.00 8.00
BHTBB Bo Bichette 40.00 100.00
BHTBG Braxton Garrett 2.50 6.00
BHTBR Brendan Rodgers 6.00 15.00
BHTCR Corey Ray 3.00 8.00
BHTCS Cody Sedlock 2.50 6.00
BHTDC Dylan Cozens 2.50 6.00
BHTEJ Eloy Jimenez
BHTFM Francisco Mejia 5.00 12.00
BHTFW Forrest Whitley 10.00 25.00
BHTGT Gleyber Torres 25.00 60.00
BHTIA Ian Anderson 12.00 30.00
BHTID Isan Diaz 6.00 15.00
BHTJD Justin Dunn 2.50 6.00
BHTJF Junior Fernandez 4.00 10.00
BHTJG Jason Groome 5.00 12.00
BHTJM Jorge Mateo
BHTJS Justus Sheffield 4.00 10.00
BHTKL Kyle Lewis 30.00 80.00
BHTKM Kevin Maitan 4.00 10.00
BHTLA Lazarito Armenteros 5.00 12.00
BHTLC Luis Castillo 8.00 20.00
BHTLF Lucius Fox 2.50 6.00
BHTLGJ Lourdes Gurriel Jr. 6.00 15.00
BHTMK Mitch Keller 4.00 10.00
BHTMM Mickey Moniak 5.00 12.00
BHTMMA Matt Manning 4.00 10.00
BHTNS Nick Senzel 8.00 20.00
BHTPC P.J. Conlon 2.50 6.00
BHTPW Patrick Weigel 2.50 6.00
BHTRH Rhys Hoskins 10.00 25.00
BHTRR Roniel Raudes 2.50 6.00
BHTSN Sean Newcomb 3.00 8.00
BHTTS Thomas Szapucki 3.00 8.00
BHTWB Wuilmer Becerra 2.50 6.00
BHTWC Willie Calhoun 6.00 15.00
BHTYA Yadier Alvarez 4.00 10.00
BHTZC Zack Collins 3.00 8.00

2017 Bowman High Tek Autographs Gold Rainbow
*GOLD RAINBOW: .75X TO 2X BASIC
RANDOM INSERTS IN PACKS
STATED PRINT RUN 50 SER.#'d SETS
EXCHANGE DEADLINE 9/30/2019
BHTFM Francisco Mejia 10.00 25.00
BHTJM Jorge Mateo 5.00 12.00
BHTMK Mitch Keller 20.00 50.00

2017 Bowman High Tek Autographs Green Rainbow
*GREEN RAINBOW: .5X TO 1.2X BASIC
RANDOM INSERTS IN PACKS
STATED PRINT RUN 99 SER.#'d SETS
EXCHANGE DEADLINE 9/30/2019
BHTJM Jorge Mateo 3.00 8.00

2017 Bowman High Tek Autographs Orange Magma Diffractors
*ORANGE MAGMA: 1X TO 2.5X BASIC
RANDOM INSERTS IN PACKS
STATED PRINT RUN 25 SER.#'d SETS
EXCHANGE DEADLINE 9/30/2019
BHTAK Alex Kiriloff 30.00 80.00
BHTBR Brendan Rodgers 12.00 30.00
BHTEJ Eloy Jimenez 75.00 200.00
BHTFM Francisco Mejia 12.00 30.00
BHTMK Mitch Keller 25.00 60.00
BHTNS Nick Senzel 20.00 50.00

2017 Bowman High Tek Autographs Rush Diffractors
*RUSH DIF: .5X TO 1.2X BASIC
RANDOM INSERTS IN PACKS
EXCHANGE DEADLINE 9/30/2019
BHTJM Jorge Mateo 3.00 8.00

2017 Bowman High Tek Autographs Tidal Diffractors
*TIDAL DIF: .5X TO 1.2X BASIC
RANDOM INSERTS IN PACKS
STATED PRINT RUN 199 SER.#'d SETS
EXCHANGE DEADLINE 9/30/2019
BHTJM Jorge Mateo 3.00 8.00

2017 Bowman High Tek Bashers
RANDOM INSERTS IN PACKS
STATED PRINT RUN 75 SER.#;d SETS
BBH Bryce Harper 5.00 12.00
BCB Cody Bellinger 30.00 80.00
BDC Dylan Cozens 2.00 5.00
BJO Jhailyn Ortiz 4.00 10.00
BKB Kris Bryant 4.00 10.00
BKL Kyle Lewis 4.00 10.00
BMC Miguel Cabrera 8.00 20.00
BMT Mike Trout 30.00 80.00
BNA Nolan Arenado 5.00 12.00
BNS Nick Senzel 6.00 15.00
BRC Robinson Cano 2.50 6.00
BRH Rhys Hoskins 8.00 20.00
BTO Tyler O'Neill 2.50 6.00
BWC Willie Calhoun 3.00 8.00
BZC Zack Collins 2.50 6.00

2017 Bowman High Tek Bashers Autographs
RANDOM INSERTS IN PACKS
STATED PRINT RUN 50 SER.#;d SETS
EXCHANGE DEADLINE 9/30/2019
BBH Bryce Harper 50.00 120.00
BDC Dylan Cozens 12.00 30.00
BKB Kris Bryant 100.00 250.00
BKL Kyle Lewis 8.00 20.00
BMT Mike Trout 200.00 400.00
BNS Nick Senzel 30.00 80.00
BRH Rhys Hoskins 75.00 200.00
BZC Zack Collins

2017 Bowman High Tek Foundations of the Franchise
RANDOM INSERTS IN PACKS
STATED PRINT RUN 50 SER.#;d SETS
FFAR Nolan Arenado 5.00 12.00
Brendan Rodgers
FFARA Orlando Arcia 3.00 8.00
Corey Ray
FFBD Devers/Betts 12.00 30.00
FFBJ Bryant/Jimenez 12.00 30.00
FFCL Cano/Lewis 4.00 10.00
FFCT Castro/Torres 30.00 80.00
FFDG Nick Gordon 3.00 8.00
Brian Dozier
FFDP Diaz/Perez 3.00 8.00
FFFC Maikel Franco 2.50 6.00
J.P. Crawford
FFHR Harper/Robles 12.00 30.00
FFKB Kershaw/Bellinger 15.00 40.00
FFLM Mejia/Lindor 3.00 8.00
FFMM Austin Meadows 5.00 12.00
Starling Marte
FFSA Swanson/Albies 8.00 20.00
FFSD Justin Dunn 2.50 6.00
Noah Syndergaard

2018 Bowman High Tek
RHTAR Amed Rosario .50 1.25
RHTAV Alex Verdugo .60 1.50
RHTCF Clint Frazier .75 2.00
RHTFM Francisco Mejia .50 1.25
RHTJC J.P. Crawford .40 1.00
RHTNW Nick Williams .50 1.25
RHTOA Ozzie Albies 1.25 3.00
RHTRD Rafael Devers 1.25 3.00
RHTRH Rhys Hoskins 1.50 4.00
RHTSO Shohei Ohtani 10.00 25.00
RHTVR Victor Robles 1.00 2.50

2018 Bowman High Tek Circle Gear
*CIRCLE GEAR: 1.5X TO 4X BASIC
STATED ODDS 1:XXX

2018 Bowman High Tek Circuit Board
*CIRCUIT BOARD: 1.2X TO 3X BASIC
STATED ODDS 1:XXX

2018 Bowman High Tek Dots Bow Tie
*DOTS BOW TIE: .6X TO 1.5X BASIC
STATED ODDS 1:XXX

2018 Bowman High Tek Gold Rainbow
*GOLD RAINBOW: 2X TO 5X BASIC
STATED ODDS 1:XXX
STATED PRINT RUN 50 SER.#'d SETS
RHTSO Shohei Ohtani 30.00 80.00

2018 Bowman High Tek Green Rainbow
*GREEN RAINBOW: 1X TO 2.5X BASIC
STATED ODDS 1:XXX
STATED PRINT RUN 99 SER.#'d SETS
RHTSO Shohei Ohtani 15.00 40.00

2018 Bowman High Tek Lightning Tree
*LIGHTNING TREE: 1.2X TO 3X BASIC
STATED ODDS 1:XXX

2018 Bowman High Tek Ocean Blue Tidal
*OCEAN BLUE: 1.5X TO 4X BASIC
STATED ODDS 1:XXX
STATED PRINT RUN 75 SER.#'d SETS
RHTSO Shohei Ohtani 25.00 60.00

2018 Bowman High Tek Orange Magma Diffractors
*ORANGE MAGMA: 3X TO 8X BASIC
STATED ODDS 1:XXX
STATED PRINT RUN 25 SER.#'d SETS
RHTSO Shohei Ohtani 50.00 120.00

2018 Bowman High Tek Purple Rainbow
*PURPLE RAINBOW: .75X TO 2X BASIC
STATED ODDS 1:XXX
STATED PRINT RUN 191 SER.#'d SETS
RHTSO Shohei Ohtani 12.00 30.00

2018 Bowman High Tek Shatter
*SHATTER: 1.5X TO 4X BASIC
STATED ODDS 1:XXX

2018 Bowman High Tek Stripes
*STRIPES: .5X TO 1.2X BASIC
STATED ODDS 1:XXX

2018 Bowman High Tek Zig Zag
*ZIG ZAG: .6X TO 1.5X BASIC
STATED ODDS 1:XXX

2018 Bowman High Tek First Bowman TEK
STATED ODDS 1:XX HOBBY
STATED PRINT RUN 99 SER.#'d SETS
*BLUE/25: .6X TO 1.5X BASIC
FBTAA Adbert Alzolay 1.25 3.00
FBTAG Andres Gimenez 2.50 6.00
FBTBM Bryan Mata 1.25 3.00
FBTHG Hunter Greene 3.00 8.00
FBTJH Jordan Hicks 2.00 5.00
FBTJK Jeren Kendall 1.25 3.00
FBTKR Keibert Ruiz 5.00 12.00
FBTLR Luis Robert 15.00 40.00
FBTMB Michel Baez 1.00 2.50
FBTRM Ronny Mauricio 2.50 6.00
FBTZL Zack Littell 1.00 2.50

2018 Bowman High Tek First Bowman TEK Autographs
STATED ODDS 1:XX HOBBY
STATED PRINT RUN 99 SER.#'d SETS
EXCHANGE DEADLINE 8/31/2020
*BLUE/25: .6X TO 1.5X BASIC
FBTAA Adbert Alzolay 5.00 12.00
FBTAG Andres Gimenez 10.00 25.00
FBTBM Bryan Mata 8.00 20.00
FBTHG Hunter Greene 12.00 30.00
FBTJH Jordan Hicks 10.00 25.00
FBTJK Jeren Kendall 5.00 12.00
FBTKR Keibert Ruiz 20.00 50.00
FBTLR Luis Robert 40.00 100.00
FBTMB Michel Baez 4.00 10.00
FBTZL Zack Littell 4.00 10.00

2018 Bowman High Tek Prospect Autographs
STATED ODDS 1:XX HOBBY
EXCHANGE DEADLINE 8/31/2020
*PURPLE/150: .5X TO 1.2X
*GREEN/99: .6X TO 1.5X
*BLUE/75: .75X TO 2X
*GOLD/50: 1X TO 2.5X
*ORANGE/25: 1.2X TO 3X
PHTAA Adbert Alzolay 3.00 8.00
PHTAB Austin Beck 3.00 8.00
PHTAF Alex Faedo 4.00 10.00
PHTAG Andres Gimenez 8.00 20.00
PHTAH Adam Haseley 3.00 8.00
PHTBM Brendan McKay 4.00 10.00
PHTBR Brent Rooker 3.00 8.00
PHTCB Corbin Burnes 10.00 25.00
PHTCP Cristian Pache 30.00 80.00
PHTCW Colton Welker 2.50 6.00
PHTDH D.L. Hall 2.50 6.00
PHTDJ Daniel Johnson 2.50 6.00
PHTEW Evan White 6.00 15.00
PHTFP Franklin Perez 3.00 8.00
PHTGT Gleyber Torres 30.00 80.00
PHTHG Hunter Greene 8.00 20.00
PHTHR Heliot Ramos 10.00 25.00
PHTII Ibandel Isabel 6.00 15.00
PHTJA Jo Adell 25.00 60.00
PHTJB Jake Burger 2.50 6.00
PHTJD Jeter Downs 8.00 20.00
PHTJG Jorge Guzman 2.50 6.00
PHTJK Jeren Kendall 3.00 8.00
PHTJS Jesus Sanchez 4.00 10.00
PHTKH Keston Hiura 8.00 20.00
PHTKR Keibert Ruiz 6.00 15.00
PHTKW Kyle Wright 8.00 20.00
PHTLR Luis Robert 60.00 150.00
PHTMB Michel Baez 2.50 6.00
PHTMG MacKenzie Gore 12.00 30.00
PHTMW Mitchell White 2.50 6.00
PHTNP Nick Pratto 3.00 8.00
PHTPS Pavin Smith 4.00 10.00
PHTRA Ronald Acuna 75.00 200.00
PHTRL Royce Lewis 12.00 30.00
PHTRV Ryan Vilade 2.50 6.00
PHTSB Shane Baz 3.00 8.00
PHTSL Shed Long 3.00 8.00
PHTSS Sixto Sanchez 8.00 20.00
PHTTL Tristen Lutz 3.00 8.00

2018 Bowman High Tek Prospects
PHTAA Adbert Alzolay .40 1.00
PHTAB Austin Beck .40 1.00
PHTAF Alex Faedo .50 1.25
PHTAG Andres Gimenez .75 2.00
PHTAH Adam Haseley .50 1.25
PHTBM Brendan McKay .50 1.25
PHTBR Brent Rooker .40 1.00
PHTBRO Brendan Rodgers .40 1.00
PHTCB Corbin Burnes 2.50 6.00
PHTCP Cristian Pache 1.50 4.00
PHTCW Colton Welker .30 .75
PHTDH D.L. Hall .30 .75
PHTDJ Daniel Johnson .30 .75
PHTEW Evan White .75 2.00
PHTFP Franklin Perez .40 1.00
PHTGT Gleyber Torres 3.00 8.00
PHTHG Hunter Greene 1.00 2.50
PHTHR Heliot Ramos .50 1.25
PHTII Ibandel Isabel .50 1.25
PHTJA Jo Adell 1.25 3.00
PHTJB Jake Burger .30 .75
PHTJD Jeter Downs .50 1.25
PHTJG Jorge Guzman .30 .75
PHTJH Jordan Hicks .60 1.50
PHTJK Jeren Kendall .40 1.00
PHTJM Jorge Mateo .30 .75
PHTJS Jesus Sanchez .50 1.25
PHTKH Keston Hiura .75 2.00
PHTKR Keibert Ruiz 1.50 4.00
PHTKW Kyle Wright .75 2.00
PHTLR Luis Robert 5.00 12.00
PHTMB Michel Baez .30 .75
PHTMG MacKenzie Gore .60 1.50
PHTMW Mitchell White .30 .75
PHTNP Nick Pratto .40 1.00
PHTPS Pavin Smith .50 1.25
PHTRA Ronald Acuna 10.00 25.00
PHTRL Royce Lewis 1.25 3.00
PHTRM Ronny Mauricio .75 2.00
PHTRV Ryan Vilade .30 .75
PHTSB Shane Baz .40 1.00
PHTSL Shed Long .40 1.00
PHTSM Sean Murphy .50 1.25
PHTSS Sixto Sanchez 1.00 2.50
PHTTL Tristen Lutz .40 1.00

2018 Bowman High Tek Prospects Circle Gear
*CIRCLE GEAR: 1.5X TO 4X BASIC
STATED ODDS 1:XXX

2018 Bowman High Tek Prospects Circuit Board
*CIRCUIT BOARD: 1.2X TO 3X BASIC
STATED ODDS 1:XXX

2018 Bowman High Tek Prospects Dots Bow Tie
*DOTS BOW TIE: .6X TO 1.5X BASIC
STATED ODDS 1:XXX

2018 Bowman High Tek Prospects Gold Rainbow
*GOLD RAINBOW: 2X TO 5X BASIC
STATED ODDS 1:XXX
STATED PRINT RUN 50 SER.#'d SETS

2018 Bowman High Tek Prospects Green Rainbow
*GREEN RAINBOW: 1X TO 2.5X BASIC
STATED ODDS 1:XXX
STATED PRINT RUN 99 SER.#'d SETS

2018 Bowman High Tek Prospects Lightning Tree
*LIGHTNING TREE: 1.2X TO 3X BASIC
STATED ODDS 1:XXX

2018 Bowman High Tek Prospects Ocean Blue Tidal
*OCEAN BLUE: 1.5X TO 4X BASIC
STATED ODDS 1:XXX
STATED PRINT RUN 75 SER.#'d SETS

2018 Bowman High Tek Prospects Orange Magma Diffractors
*ORANGE MAGMA: 2.5X TO 6X BASIC
STATED ODDS 1:XXX
STATED PRINT RUN 25 SER.#'d SETS

2018 Bowman High Tek Prospects Purple Rainbow
*PURPLE RAINBOW: .75X TO 2X BASIC
STATED ODDS 1:XXX
STATED PRINT RUN 191 SER.#'d SETS

2018 Bowman High Tek Prospects Shatter
*SHATTER: 1.5X TO 4X BASIC
STATED ODDS 1:XXX

2018 Bowman High Tek Prospects Stripes
*STRIPES: .5X TO 1.2X BASIC
STATED ODDS 1:XXX

2018 Bowman High Tek Prospects Zig Zag
*ZIG ZAG: .6X TO 1.5X BASIC
STATED ODDS 1:XXX

2018 Bowman High Tek PyroTEKnics
STATED ODDS 1:XXX HOBBY
STATED PRINT RUN 99 SER.#'d SETS
*BLUE/25: .6X TO 1.5X BASIC
PYAR Amed Rosario 1.25 3.00
PYBM Brendan McKay 1.50 4.00
PYBR Brendan Rodgers 1.25 3.00
PYCF Clint Frazier 2.00 5.00
PYGT Gleyber Torres 10.00 25.00
PYHG Hunter Greene 3.00 8.00
PYJB Jake Burger 1.00 2.50
PYLR Luis Robert 15.00 40.00
PYRA Ronald Acuna 30.00 80.00
PYRD Rafael Devers 3.00 8.00
PYRH Rhys Hoskins 4.00 10.00
PYRL Royce Lewis 4.00 10.00
PYSO Shohei Ohtani 20.00 50.00
PYVR Victor Robles 2.50 6.00
PYVGJ Vladimir Guerrero Jr. 15.00 40.00

2018 Bowman High Tek PyroTEKnics Autographs
STATED ODDS 1:XX HOBBY
PRINT RUNS B/WN 50-75 COPIES PER
EXCHANGE DEADLINE 8/31/2020
*BLUE/25: .6X TO 1.5X BASIC
PYAR Amed Rosario/50 5.00 12.00
PYBM Brendan McKay/75 10.00 25.00
PYGT Gleyber Torres/75 30.00 80.00
PYHG Hunter Greene EXCH 12.00 30.00
PYJB Jake Burger/75 4.00 10.00
PYLR Luis Robert/75 60.00 150.00
PYRA Ronald Acuna/75 100.00 250.00
PYRD Rafael Devers/50 15.00 40.00
PYRH Rhys Hoskins/50 20.00 50.00
PYRL Royce Lewis/50 20.00 50.00
PYVR Victor Robles/50 10.00 25.00

2018 Bowman High Tek Rookie Autographs
STATED ODDS 1:XX HOBBY
EXCHANGE DEADLINE 8/31/2020
*PURPLE/150: .5X TO 1.2X
*GREEN/99: .6X TO 1.5X
*BLUE/75: .75X TO 2X
*GOLD/50: 1X TO 2.5X
*ORANGE/25: 1.2X TO 3X
RHTAR Amed Rosario 3.00 8.00
RHTOA Ozzie Albies 12.00 30.00
RHTRD Rafael Devers 20.00 50.00
RHTRH Rhys Hoskins 12.00 30.00
RHTSO Shohei Ohtani EXCH 150.00 300.00
RHTVR Victor Robles 10.00 25.00

2018 Bowman High Tek Tides of Youth
STATED ODDS 1:XXX HOBBY
STATED PRINT RUN 99 SER.#'d SETS
*BLUE/25: .6X TO 1.5X BASIC
TYAB Austin Beck 1.25 3.00

TYAF Alex Faedo 1.50 4.00
TYAH Adam Haseley 1.50 4.00
TYAR Amed Rosario 1.25 3.00
TYAV Alex Verdugo 1.50 4.00
TYBM Brendan McKay 1.50 4.00
TYCF Clint Frazier 2.00 5.00
TYCP Cristian Pache 5.00 12.00
TYFM Francisco Mejia 1.25 3.00
TYGT Gleyber Torres 10.00 25.00
TYHG Hunter Greene 3.00 8.00
TYHR Heliot Ramos 1.50 4.00
TYJA Jo Adell 4.00 10.00
TYJB Jake Burger 1.00 2.50
TYJC J.P. Crawford 1.00 2.50
TYJK Jeren Kendall 1.25 3.00
TYJM Jorge Mateo 1.00 2.50
TYJS Jesus Sanchez 1.50 4.00
TYKR Keibert Ruiz 5.00 12.00
TYLR Luis Robert 15.00 40.00
TYMG MacKenzie Gore 2.00 5.00
TYNW Nick Williams 1.25 3.00
TYOA Ozzie Albies 3.00 8.00
TYRA Ronald Acuna 12.00 30.00
TYRD Rafael Devers 3.00 8.00
TYRH Rhys Hoskins 4.00 10.00
TYRL Royce Lewis 4.00 10.00
TYSO Shohei Ohtani 20.00 50.00
TYVR Victor Robles 2.50 6.00
TYWB Walker Buehler 5.00 12.00

2018 Bowman High Tek Tides of Youth Autographs

STATED ODDS 1:XX HOBBY
STATED PRINT RUN 75 COPIES PER
EXCHANGE DEADLINE 8/31/2020
TYAB Austin Beck/75 5.00 12.00
TYAF Alex Faedo/75 6.00 15.00
TYAH Adam Haseley/75 4.00 10.00
TYAV Alex Verdugo/75 8.00 20.00
TYBM Brendan McKay/75 10.00 25.00
TYFM Francisco Mejia/75 8.00 20.00
TYGT Gleyber Torres/75 30.00 80.00
TYHG Hunter Greene/75 12.00 30.00
TYHR Heliot Ramos/75 6.00 15.00
TYJA Jo Adell/75 25.00 60.00
TYJB Jake Burger/75 4.00 10.00
TYKR Keibert Ruiz/75 20.00 50.00
TYLR Luis Robert/75 60.00 150.00
TYMG MacKenzie Gore/75 8.00 20.00
TYOA Ozzie Albies/75 20.00 50.00
TYRA Ronald Acuna/75 75.00 200.00
TYRD Rafael Devers/75 15.00 40.00
TYRH Rhys Hoskins/75 20.00 50.00
TYRL Royce Lewis/75 20.00 50.00
TYVR Victor Robles/75 10.00 25.00

2018 Bowman High Tek Tides of Youth Autographs Blue

*BLUE: .6X TO 1.5X BASIC
STATED ODDS 1:XX HOBBY
STATED PRINT RUN 25 SER.#'d SETS
EXCHANGE DEADLINE 8/31/2020
TYAR Amed Rosario 8.00 20.00

2013 Bowman Inception Rookie Autographs

PRINTING PLATE ODDS 1:390 HOBBY
PLATE PRINT RUN 1 SET PER COLOR
BLACK-CYAN-MAGENTA-YELLOW ISSUED
NO PLATE PRICING DUE TO SCARCITY
EXCHANGE DEADLINE 06/30/2016
AE Adam Eaton 3.00 8.00
AG Avisail Garcia 4.00 10.00
CK Casey Kelly 3.00 8.00
DB Dylan Bundy 8.00 20.00
DG Didi Gregorius 10.00 25.00
DR Darin Ruf 3.00 8.00
JF Jeurys Familia 3.00 8.00
JO Jake Odorizzi 3.00 8.00
JP Jurickson Profar 4.00 10.00
MM Manny Machado 30.00 80.00
MO Mike Olt EXCH 4.00 10.00
RH Ryu Hyun-Jin 12.00 30.00
SM Shelby Miller 6.00 15.00
TC Tony Cingrani 3.00 8.00
TS Tyler Skaggs 4.00 10.00

2013 Bowman Inception Rookie Autographs Blue

*BLUE: .5X TO 1.2X BASIC
STATED ODDS 1:21 HOBBY
STATED PRINT RUN 75 SER.#'d SETS
EXCHANGE DEADLINE 06/30/2016

2013 Bowman Inception Rookie Autographs Gold

*GOLD: .5X TO 1.2X BASIC
STATED ODDS 1:16 HOBBY
STATED PRINT RUN 99 SER.#'d SETS
EXCHANGE DEADLINE 06/30/2016

2013 Bowman Inception Rookie Autographs Green

*GREEN: 1.2X TO 3X BASIC
STATED ODDS 1:63 HOBBY
STATED PRINT RUN 25 SER.#'d SETS
EXCHANGE DEADLINE 06/30/2016

2013 Bowman Inception Rookie Autographs Orange

*ORANGE: .6X TO 1.5X BASIC
STATED ODDS 1:32 HOBBY
STATED PRINT RUN 50 SER.#'d SETS
EXCHANGE DEADLINE 06/30/2016

2013 Bowman Inception Dual Rise Autographs

STATED ODDS 1:94 HOBBY
STATED PRINT RUN 25 SER.#'d SETS
EXCHANGE DEADLINE 06/30/2016
AM T.Austin/M.Montgomery 15.00 40.00
AS A.Almora/J.Soler 100.00 200.00
BG D.Bundy/K.Gausman
BM Bundy/Machado EXCH 100.00 200.00
CB Correa/Buxton EXHC 150.00 300.00
HP A.Hanson/G.Polanco 90.00 150.00
MT Myers/Taveras EXCH 125.00 250.00
PC Profar/Correa EXCH 60.00 120.00
SB Sano/Buxton EXCH 75.00 200.00
SP Seager/Puig 150.00 300.00

2013 Bowman Inception Jumbo Relic Autographs

STATED ODDS 1:64 HOBBY
PRINT RUNS B/WN 11-25 COPIES PER
NO PANIC PRICING AVAILABLE
EXCHANGE DEADLINE 06/30/2016
AR Anthony Rendon 15.00 40.00
BH Billy Hamilton 20.00 50.00
BR Bruce Rondon 12.50 30.00
CM Carlos Martinez 20.00 50.00
FR Felipe Rivero 6.00 15.00
GC Gerrit Cole 20.00 50.00
GS George Springer 12.50 30.00
JG Jedd Gyorko EXCH 15.00 40.00
JP Jurickson Profar 40.00 80.00
JS Jonathan Schoop 30.00 60.00
MC Michael Choice 10.00 25.00
MM Manny Machado 20.00 50.00
MZ Mike Zunino 30.00 60.00
RS Richie Shaffer 6.00 15.00

2013 Bowman Inception Patch Autographs

STATED ODDS 1:46 HOBBY
PRINT RUNS B/WN 4-35 COPIES PER
NO MACHADO PRICING AVAILABLE
EXCHANGE DEADLINE 06/30/2016
AR Anthony Rendon EXCH 20.00 50.00
BH Billy Hamilton 30.00 60.00
DB Dylan Bundy/25 50.00 100.00
FR Felipe Rivero 6.00 15.00
GC Gerrit Cole 15.00 40.00
GS George Springer 20.00 50.00
JO Jake Odorizzi 12.50 30.00
JP Jurickson Profar 15.00 40.00
JS Jonathan Singleton 15.00 40.00
JSC Jonathan Schoop 20.00 50.00
MC Michael Choice 20.00 50.00
NC Nick Castellanos 20.00 50.00
RL Rymer Liriano 6.00 15.00
RS Richie Shaffer 6.00 15.00
WM Wil Myers 50.00 100.00

2013 Bowman Inception Prospect Autographs

PRINTING PLATE ODDS 1:130 HOBBY
PLATE PRINT RUN 1 SET PER COLOR
BLACK-CYAN-MAGENTA-YELLOW ISSUED
NO PLATE PRICING DUE TO SCARCITY
EXCHANGE DEADLINE 06/30/2016
AA Albert Almora 5.00 12.00
AH Alen Hanson 3.00 8.00
AR Addison Russell 6.00 15.00
BB Byron Buxton 6.00 15.00
BBA Barrett Barnes 3.00 8.00
BH Billy Hamilton 5.00 12.00
BM Brad Miller 3.00 8.00
BS Bubba Starling 4.00 10.00
CBL Clayton Blackburn 3.00 8.00
CC Carlos Correa 25.00 60.00
CH Courtney Hawkins 3.00 8.00
CS Corey Seager 30.00 80.00
DC Daniel Corcino 3.00 8.00
DD David Dahl 3.00 8.00
EB Eddie Butler 3.00 8.00
GA Gioskar Amaya 3.00 8.00
GP Gregory Polanco 4.00 10.00
JB J.O. Berrios 8.00 20.00
JBI Jesse Biddle 3.00 8.00
JBO Jorge Bonifacio 3.00 8.00
JF Jose Fernandez 15.00 40.00
JM Jake Marisnick 3.00 8.00
JN Justin Nicolino 3.00 8.00
JS Jonathan Singleton 3.00 8.00
JSO Jorge Soler 5.00 12.00
KG Kevin Gausman 3.00 8.00
KP Kevin Pillar 3.00 8.00
KZ Kyle Zimmer 6.00 15.00
LG Lucas Giolito 4.00 10.00
LM Lance McCullers 3.00 8.00
MF Max Fried 3.00 8.00
MH Miles Head 3.00 8.00
MM Mark Montgomery 3.00 8.00
MO Matt Olson 6.00 15.00
MS Miguel Sano 10.00 25.00
MZ Mike Zunino 8.00 20.00
NC Nick Castellanos 5.00 12.00
OT Oscar Taveras 3.00 8.00
PW Patrick Wisdom 3.00 8.00
RG Ronald Guzman 3.00 8.00
SP Stephen Piscotty 4.00 10.00
SR Stefen Romero 3.00 8.00
ST Stryker Trahan 3.00 8.00
TA Tyler Austin 8.00 20.00
TD Travis d'Arnaud 5.00 12.00
TW Taijuan Walker 4.00 10.00
YP Yasiel Puig 30.00 80.00

2013 Bowman Inception Prospect Autographs Blue

*BLUE: .5X TO 1.2X BASIC
STATED ODDS 1:7 HOBBY
STATED PRINT RUN 75 SER.#'d SETS
EXCHANGE DEADLINE 06/30/2016

2013 Bowman Inception Prospect Autographs Gold

*GOLD: .5X TO 1.2X BASIC
STATED ODDS 1:6 HOBBY
STATED PRINT RUN 99 SER.#'d SETS
EXCHANGE DEADLINE 06/30/2016

2013 Bowman Inception Prospect Autographs Green

*GREEN: 1.2X TO 3X BASIC
STATED ODDS 1:21 HOBBY
STATED PRINT RUN 25 SER.#'d SETS
EXCHANGE DEADLINE 06/30/2016
BS Bubba Starling 12.00 30.00

2013 Bowman Inception Prospect Autographs Orange

*ORANGE: .6X TO 1.5X BASIC
STATED ODDS 1:11 HOBBY
STATED PRINT RUN 50 SER.#'d SETS
EXCHANGE DEADLINE 06/30/2016

2013 Bowman Inception Relic Autographs

EXCHANGE DEADLINE 06/30/2016
AR Anthony Rendon 6.00 15.00
BB Bryce Brentz 4.00 8.00
BM Brad Miller 4.00 10.00
CS Carlos Sanchez 4.00 8.00
FR Felipe Rivero 4.00 10.00
GB Gary Brown 3.00 8.00
GS George Springer 12.00 30.00
HL Hak-Ju Lee 3.00 8.00
JM Jake Marisnick 4.00 8.00
JO Jake Odorizzi 4.00 8.00
JP James Paxton 6.00 15.00
JPE Joc Pederson 8.00 20.00
JS Jonathan Singleton 3.00 8.00
MC Michael Choice 5.00 12.00
MH Miles Head 4.00 10.00
MZ Mike Zunino 5.00 12.00
NC Nick Castellanos 4.00 10.00
NF Nick Franklin 4.00 10.00
RL Rymer Liriano 4.00 10.00
RS Richie Shaffer 4.00 10.00
SH Slade Heathcott 4.00 10.00
TJ Tommy Joseph 4.00 10.00
WM Wil Myers 4.00 10.00
XB Xander Bogaerts 25.00 60.00
YV Yordano Ventura 10.00 25.00

2013 Bowman Inception Relic Autographs Blue

*BLUE: 1X TO 2.5X BASIC
STATED ODDS 1:38 HOBBY
STATED PRINT RUN 25 SER.#'d SETS
EXCHANGE DEADLINE 06/30/2016

2013 Bowman Inception Relic Autographs Red

*RED: .6X TO 1.5X BASIC
STATED ODDS 1:19 HOBBY
STATED PRINT RUN 50 SER.#'d SETS
EXCHANGE DEADLINE 06/30/2016

2013 Bowman Inception Silver Signings

STATED ODDS 1:38 HOBBY
STATED PRINT RUN 25 SER.#'d SETS
EXCHANGE DEADLINE 06/30/2016
AE Adam Eaton 20.00 50.00
AG Avisail Garcia 20.00 50.00
AH Alen Hanson 20.00 50.00
AR Addison Russell 40.00 80.00
BB Byron Buxton 200.00 400.00
BH Billy Hamilton EXCH 50.00 100.00
CC Carlos Correa 150.00 250.00
CS Corey Seager 75.00 200.00
DB Dylan Bundy 20.00 50.00
DD David Dahl 30.00 60.00
JF Jose Fernandez 50.00 100.00
JP Jurickson Profar EXCH 40.00 80.00
JS Jonathan Singleton 20.00 50.00
JSO Jorge Soler 60.00 120.00
MM Manny Machado EXCH 90.00 150.00
MO Mike Olt 20.00 50.00
MS Miguel Sano 40.00 80.00
MZ Mike Zunino 20.00 50.00
NC Nick Castellanos 40.00 80.00
OT Oscar Taveras 20.00 50.00
RH Ryu Hyun-Jin EXCH 50.00 100.00
TA Tyler Austin 20.00 50.00
TD Travis d'Arnaud 20.00 50.00
WM Wil Myers 60.00 120.00
YP Yasiel Puig 250.00 500.00

2014 Bowman Inception Rookie Autographs

EXCHANGE DEADLINE 6/30/2017
RABH Billy Hamilton 4.00 10.00
RAEJ Erik Johnson 3.00 8.00
RAJS Jonathan Schoop 3.00 8.00
RAKW Kolten Wong 4.00 10.00
RAMC Michael Choice 3.00 8.00
RAMS Marcus Semien 15.00 40.00
RANC Nick Castellanos 10.00 25.00
RATW Taijuan Walker 3.00 8.00
RAYV Yordano Ventura 6.00 15.00

2014 Bowman Inception Rookie Autographs Blue

*BLUE: .5X TO 1.2X BASIC
STATED PRINT RUN 75 SER.#'d SETS
EXCHANGE DEADLINE 6/30/2017

2014 Bowman Inception Rookie Autographs Gold

*GOLD: .5X TO 1.2X BASIC
STATED PRINT RUN 99 SER.#'d SETS
EXCHANGE DEADLINE 6/30/2017

2014 Bowman Inception Rookie Autographs Green

*GREEN: .75X TO 2X BASIC
STATED PRINT RUN 25 SER.#'d SETS
EXCHANGE DEADLINE 6/30/2017

2014 Bowman Inception Rookie Autographs Pink

*PINK: .6X TO 1.5X BASIC
STATED PRINT RUN 50 SER.#'d SETS
EXCHANGE DEADLINE 6/30/2017

2014 Bowman Inception Inceptioned Autographs

STATED PRINT RUN 35 SER.#'d SETS
EXCHANGE DEADLINE 6/30/2017
IBAAB Archie Bradley 20.00 50.00
IBAAM Austin Meadows 30.00 60.00
IBABB Byron Buxton 150.00 250.00
IBABH Billy Hamilton 20.00 50.00
IBACF Clint Frazier 25.00 60.00
IBADP D.J. Peterson 15.00 40.00
IBADS Dominic Smith 15.00 40.00
IBAFL Francisco Lindor 125.00 300.00
IBAGS Gary Sanchez 75.00 200.00
IBAJA Jose Abreu 150.00 300.00
IBAJB Jorge Bonifacio 20.00 50.00
IBAJG Jonathan Gray 25.00 60.00
IBAJS Jorge Soler 40.00 100.00
IBAJU Julio Urias EXCH 80.00 200.00
IBAKB Kris Bryant 300.00 600.00
IBAMA Mark Appel EXCH 20.00 50.00
IBAMF Maikel Franco 30.00 80.00
IBAMJ Micah Johnson 15.00 40.00
IBANC Nick Castellanos 20.00 50.00
IBANS Noah Syndergaard 40.00 100.00
IBARM Rafael Montero 15.00 40.00
IBATW Taijuan Walker 15.00 40.00

2014 Bowman Inception Patch Autographs

STATED PRINT RUN 25 SER.#'d SETS
EXCHANGE DEADLINE 6/30/2017
APAA Arismendy Alcantara 10.00 25.00
APAB Archie Bradley 20.00 50.00
APAR Anthony Ranaudo 10.00 25.00
APBB Byron Buxton 50.00 100.00
APCC Carlos Correa 60.00 120.00
APCK Corey Knebel 15.00 40.00
APDT Devon Travis 30.00 60.00
APEB Eddie Butler 20.00 50.00
APER Eduardo Rodriguez 12.00 30.00
APERO Eddie Rosario 20.00 50.00
APGP Gregory Polanco 15.00 40.00
APJAL Jorge Alfaro 20.00 50.00
APJB Jake Barrett 12.00 30.00
APJB Jorge Bonifacio 10.00 25.00
APJS Jorge Soler 20.00 50.00
APMA Miguel Almonte 10.00 25.00
APNS Noah Syndergaard 50.00 120.00
APPOB Peter O'Brien 12.00 30.00
APRM Rafael Montero 10.00 25.00
APSP Stephen Piscotty 25.00 60.00
APSS Shae Simmons 10.00 25.00
APTW Taijuan Walker 10.00 25.00

2014 Bowman Inception Relic Autographs

EXCHANGE DEADLINE 6/30/2017
ARAA Arismendy Alcantara 4.00 10.00
ARAB Archie Bradley 4.00 10.00
ARAH Alen Hanson 4.00 10.00
ARAR Anthony Ranaudo 4.00 10.00
ARBB Byron Buxton 12.00 30.00
ARCC Carlos Correa 15.00 40.00
ARCK Corey Knebel 4.00 10.00
ARCM Colin Moran 4.00 10.00
ARDD Delino DeShields 4.00 10.00
ARDT Devon Travis 4.00 10.00
ARER Eduardo Rodriguez 5.00 12.00
ARGP Gregory Polanco 6.00 15.00
ARGS George Springer 10.00 25.00
ARJAL Jorge Alfaro 5.00 12.00
ARJB Jorge Bonifacio 4.00 10.00
ARJBA Jake Barrett 5.00 12.00
ARJBI Jesse Biddle 5.00 12.00
ARJR James Ramsey 4.00 10.00
ARJS Jorge Soler 8.00 20.00
ARKP Kyle Parker EXCH 5.00 12.00
ARMA Miguel Almonte 4.00 10.00
ARMF Maikel Franco 5.00 12.00
ARMS Marcus Semien 20.00 50.00
ARMSA Miguel Sano 5.00 12.00
ARNS Noah Syndergaard 12.00 30.00
ARPOB Peter O'Brien 5.00 12.00
ARRD Rafael De Paula 4.00 10.00
ARRM Rafael Montero 4.00 10.00
ARSP Stephen Piscotty 5.00 12.00
ARSR Stefen Romero 4.00 10.00
ARSS Shae Simmons 4.00 10.00
ARTA Tyler Austin 4.00 10.00
ARTW Taijuan Walker 4.00 10.00
ARXB Xander Bogaerts 15.00 40.00

2014 Bowman Inception Relic Autographs Green

*GREEN: .75X TO 2X BASIC
STATED PRINT RUN 25 SER.#'d SETS
EXCHANGE DEADLINE 6/30/2017
ARERO Eddie Rosario 15.00 40.00
ARKB Kris Bryant EXCH 250.00 500.00

2014 Bowman Inception Relic Autographs Pink

*PINK: .6X TO 1.5X BASIC
STATED PRINT RUN 50 SER.#'d SETS
EXCHANGE DEADLINE 6/30/2017
ARERO Eddie Rosario 12.00 30.00

2014 Bowman Inception Silver Signings

STATED PRINT RUN 25 SER.#'d SETS
EXCHANGE DEADLINE 6/30/2017
SSAB Archie Bradley 12.00 30.00
SSAM Austin Meadows 30.00 80.00
SSBB Byron Buxton 60.00 150.00
SSBH Billy Hamilton 15.00 40.00
SSCF Clint Frazier 50.00 125.00
SSDP D.J. Peterson 12.00 30.00
SSDS Dominic Smith 20.00 50.00
SSFL Francisco Lindor 75.00 200.00
SSGS Gary Sanchez 100.00 200.00
SSJA Jose Abreu 100.00 200.00
SSJB Jorge Bonifacio 12.00 30.00
SSJG Jonathan Gray 20.00 50.00
SSJS Jorge Soler 30.00 60.00
SSJU Julio Urias 60.00 150.00
SSKB Kris Bryant 250.00 500.00
SSMA Mark Appel EXCH 15.00 40.00
SSMF Maikel Franco 15.00 40.00
SSMJ Micah Johnson 12.00 30.00
SSMS Miguel Sano 15.00 40.00
SSNC Nick Castellanos 12.00 30.00
SSRM Rafael Montero 12.00 30.00
SSTW Taijuan Walker 15.00 40.00

2014 Bowman Inception Prospect Autographs

PAAA Arismendy Alcantara 3.00 8.00
PAAB Archie Bradley 3.00 8.00
PAAG Alexander Guerrero 4.00 10.00
PAAH Alen Hanson 3.00 8.00
PAAJ Aaron Judge 60.00 150.00
PAAM Adalberto Mejia 3.00 8.00
PAAME Austin Meadows 6.00 15.00
PAAR Anthony Ranaudo 3.00 8.00
PAAW Adam Walker 3.00 8.00
PABB Byron Buxton 15.00 40.00
PABM Billy McKinney 4.00 10.00
PACA Chris Anderson 3.00 8.00
PACC Carlos Correa 15.00 40.00
PACF Clint Frazier 4.00 10.00
PACT Carlos Tocci 3.00 8.00
PADF Dylan Floro 4.00 10.00
PADP Daniel Palka 3.00 8.00
PADPE D.J. Peterson 3.00 8.00
PADR Daniel Robertson 4.00 10.00
PADS Dominic Smith 3.00 8.00
PAEB Eddie Butler 3.00 8.00
PAEE Edwin Escobar 3.00 8.00
PAEJ Eric Jagielo 3.00 8.00
PAFL Francisco Lindor 25.00 60.00
PAGS Gary Sanchez 40.00 100.00
PAJA Jose Abreu 15.00 40.00
PAJB Javier Baez 15.00 40.00
PAJBO Jorge Bonifacio 3.00 8.00
PAJD Jon Denney 3.00 8.00
PAJG Jonathan Gray 4.00 10.00
PAJH Jason Hursh 3.00 8.00
PAJL Jake Lamb 5.00 12.00
PAJP Jose Peraza 3.00 8.00
PAJPO Jorge Polanco 8.00 20.00
PAJS Jorge Soler 3.00 8.00
PAJU Julio Urias 8.00 20.00
PAKP Kevin Plawecki 3.00 8.00
PALJ Luke Jackson 3.00 8.00
PALM Leonardo Molina 3.00 8.00
PAMA Mark Appel 4.00 10.00
PAMF Maikel Franco 4.00 10.00
PAMJ Micah Johnson 3.00 8.00
PAMS Miguel Sano 8.00 20.00
PANS Noah Syndergaard 8.00 20.00
PAOM Oscar Mercado 5.00 12.00
PAOT Oscar Taveras 4.00 10.00
PAPE Phil Ervin 5.00 12.00
PARK Robert Kaminsky 3.00 8.00
PARM Rafael Montero 3.00 8.00
PARMC Reese McGuire 3.00 8.00
PARN Renato Nunez 6.00 15.00
PARO Roberto Osuna 3.00 8.00
PARYM Ryan McMahon 5.00 12.00
PATA Tim Anderson 15.00 40.00
PATD Travis Demeritte 4.00 10.00
PATM Tom Murphy 3.00 8.00
PATP Tyler Pike 3.00 8.00

2014 Bowman Inception Prospect Autographs Blue

*BLUE: .5X TO 1.2X BASIC
STATED PRINT RUN 75 SER.#'d SETS
EXCHANGE DEADLINE 6/30/2017
PAKB Kris Bryant 200.00 400.00

2014 Bowman Inception Prospect Autographs Gold

*GOLD: .5X TO 1.2X BASIC
STATED PRINT RUN 99 SER.#'d SETS
EXCHANGE DEADLINE 6/30/2017

2014 Bowman Inception Prospect Autographs Green

*GREEN: .75X TO 2X BASIC
STATED PRINT RUN 25 SER.#'d SETS
EXCHANGE DEADLINE 6/30/2017
PAKB Kris Bryant 300.00 600.00

2014 Bowman Inception Prospect Autographs Pink

*PINK: .6X TO 1.5X BASIC
STATED PRINT RUN 50 SER.#'d SETS
EXCHANGE DEADLINE 6/30/2017
PAKB Kris Bryant 250.00 500.00

2015 Bowman Inception Rookie Autographs

RANDOM INSERTS IN PACKS
EXCHANGE DEADLINE 6/30/2018
*BLUE/150: .5X TO 1.2X BASIC
*GREEN/99: .5X TO 1.2X BASIC
*GOLD/50: .6X TO 1.5X BASIC
*ORANGE/25: .75X TO 2X BASIC
RABB Bryce Brentz 3.00 8.00
RABF Brandon Finnegan 5.00 12.00
RACW Christian Walker 5.00 12.00
RADH Dilson Herrera 4.00 10.00
RADN Daniel Norris 3.00 8.00
RAEE Edwin Escobar 3.00 8.00
RAJB Javier Baez 15.00 40.00
RAJL Jake Lamb 5.00 12.00
RAJP Joc Pederson 10.00 25.00
RAMF Maikel Franco 10.00 25.00
RAMT Michael Taylor 3.00 8.00
RARC Rusney Castillo 4.00 10.00
RARL Rymer Liriano 3.00 8.00
RASM Steven Moya 4.00 10.00

2015 Bowman Inception Autographs

STATED ODDS 1:11 HOBBY
EXCHANGE DEADLINE 6/30/2018
*ORANGE/25:.6X TO 1.5X BASIC
BIAAB Archie Bradley 15.00 40.00
BIAAJ Alex Jackson 50.00 120.00
BIAAJU Aaron Judge 75.00 200.00
BIAAME Austin Meadows 6.00 15.00
BIAAN Aaron Nola 8.00 20.00
BIAAR Addison Russell 12.00 30.00
BIABB Byron Buxton EXCH 40.00 100.00
BIABS Blake Swihart 20.00 50.00
BIACE C.J. Edwards 15.00 40.00
BIACR Carlos Rodon 10.00 25.00
BIAHH Hunter Harvey 6.00 15.00
BIAHO Henry Owens 15.00 40.00
BIAJA Jorge Alfaro 10.00 25.00
BIAJB Jose Berrios 6.00 15.00
BIAJGA Joey Gallo EXCH 12.00 30.00
BIAJHK Jung-Ho Kang 40.00 100.00
BIAKB Kris Bryant 150.00 300.00
BIALG Lucas Giolito 20.00 50.00
BIALS Luis Severino 8.00 20.00
BIAMA Miguel Almonte 6.00 15.00
BIAMC Michael Conforto 75.00 200.00
BIAMS Miguel Sano 20.00 50.00
BIATG Tyler Glasnow 15.00 40.00
BIATK Tyler Kolek EXCH 6.00 15.00
BIAYT Yasmany Tomas 8.00 20.00

2015 Bowman Inception Jumbo Patch Autographs

STATED ODDS 1:19 HOBBY
PRINT RUNS B/WN 40-50 COPIES PER
EXCHANGE DEADLINE 6/30/2018
IAPAB Archie Bradley/40 8.00 20.00
IAPBB Byron Buxton/50 EXCH 20.00 50.00
IAPBS Braden Shipley/50 8.00 20.00
IAPCB Christian Binford/50 8.00 20.00
IAPDP D.J. Peterson/50 8.00 20.00
IAPFL Francisco Lindor/50 60.00 150.00
IAPGG Gabby Guerrero/50 8.00 20.00
IAPHD Hunter Dozier/50 15.00 40.00
IAPHH Hunter Harvey/50 8.00 20.00
IAPHO Henry Owens/44 8.00 20.00
IAPHR Hunter Renfroe/50 12.00 30.00
IAPJB Jose Berrios/44 12.00 30.00
IAPJBA Javier Baez/50 30.00 80.00
IAPJC J.P. Crawford/50 8.00 20.00
IAPJG Joey Gallo/50 15.00 40.00
IAPJP Jose Peraza/50 15.00 40.00
IAPJT Jake Thompson/50 8.00 20.00
IAPJU Julio Urias/50 30.00 80.00
IAPJW Jesse Winker/50 15.00 40.00
IAPKC Kyle Crick/50 25.00 60.00
IAPLG Lucas Giolito/44 25.00 60.00
IAPLS Luis Severino/50 30.00 80.00
IAPMF Michael Feliz/50 8.00 20.00
IAPMJ Micah Johnson/50 8.00 20.00
IAPMO Matt Olson/50 20.00 50.00
IAPMS Miguel Sano/50 20.00 50.00
IAPRN Renato Nunez/50 15.00 40.00
IAPRS Robert Stephenson/44 8.00 20.00
IAPSC Sean Coyle/50 8.00 20.00

2015 Bowman Inception Origins Autographs

STATED ODDS 1:45 HOBBY
STATED PRINT RUN 25 SER.#'d SETS
EXCHANGE DEADLINE 6/30/2018
OAAJ Aaron Judge 75.00 200.00
OABH Bryce Harper 200.00 400.00
OABL Ben Lively 6.00 15.00
OACB Christian Binford 6.00 15.00
OACE C.J. Edwards 20.00 50.00
OAEJ Eric Jagielo 6.00 15.00
OAGH Grant Holmes 20.00 50.00
OAHH Hunter Harvey 20.00 50.00
OAJB Jose Berrios 20.00 50.00
OAJD Jacob deGrom 125.00 300.00
OAJG Joey Gallo EXCH 75.00 200.00
OAJH Josh Hader 15.00 40.00
OALO Luis Ortiz 6.00 15.00
OAMO Matt Olson 15.00 40.00
OAMS Mike Stanton EXCH 75.00 200.00
OAMT Mike Trout 150.00 300.00
OARM Ryan McMahon 20.00 50.00
OATA Tim Anderson 12.00 30.00
OATB Tyler Beede 8.00 20.00

2015 Bowman Inception Prospect Autographs

RANDOM INSERTS IN PACKS
EXCHANGE DEADLINE 6/30/2018
*BLUE/150: .5X TO 1.2X BASIC
*GREEN/99: .5X TO 1.2X BASIC
*GOLD/50: .6X TO 1.5X BASIC
*ORANGE/25: .75X TO 2X BASIC
PAAB Aaron Blair 3.00 8.00
PAABL Alex Blandino 3.00 8.00
PAAJ Aaron Judge 60.00 150.00
PAAM Austin Meadows 8.00 20.00
PAAN Aaron Nola 5.00 12.00
PABL Ben Lively 3.00 8.00
PABP Brett Phillips 3.00 8.00
PABS Braden Shipley 3.00 8.00
PABSW Blake Swihart 4.00 10.00
PABZ Bradley Zimmer 5.00 12.00
PACB Christian Binford 3.00 8.00
PACE C.J. Edwards 5.00 12.00
PACM Colin Moran 3.00 8.00
PACR Carlos Rodon 8.00 20.00
PADP D.J. Peterson 3.00 8.00
PAEJ Eric Jagielo 3.00 8.00
PAFB Franklin Barreto 4.00 10.00
PAFM Francellis Montas 4.00 10.00
PAGG Gabby Guerrero 3.00 8.00
PAGH Grant Holmes 4.00 10.00
PAHH Hunter Harvey 3.00 8.00
PAHO Henry Owens 3.00 8.00
PAHR Hunter Renfroe 5.00 12.00
PAJA Jorge Alfaro 5.00 12.00
PAJB Jose Berrios 5.00 12.00
PAJH Jeff Hoffman 4.00 10.00
PAJHA Josh Hader 6.00 15.00
PAJHK Jung-Ho Kang 25.00 60.00
PAJT Jake Thompson 3.00 8.00
PAJW Jesse Winker 6.00 15.00
PAKB Kris Bryant 75.00 200.00
PAKF Kyle Freeland 4.00 10.00
PAKP Kevin Plawecki 3.00 8.00
PAKS Kyle Schwarber 12.00 30.00
PAKST Kohl Stewart 3.00 8.00
PAKZ Kevin Ziomek 3.00 8.00
PALG Lucas Giolito 10.00 25.00
PALO Luis Ortiz 3.00 8.00
PALS Luis Severino 10.00 25.00
PAMA Miguel Almonte 3.00 8.00
PAMC Michael Conforto 15.00 40.00
PAMH Monte Harrison 5.00 12.00
PAMM Manuel Margot 3.00 8.00
PAMO Matt Olson 8.00 20.00
PAMP Max Pentecost 3.00 8.00
PAMS Miguel Sano 4.00 10.00
PANG Nick Gordon 4.00 10.00
PANS Noah Syndergaard 12.00 30.00
PARM Ryan McMahon 5.00 12.00
PASC Sean Coyle 3.00 8.00
PASN Sean Newcomb 4.00 10.00
PATA Tim Anderson 12.00 30.00
PATB Tyler Beede 4.00 10.00
PATG Tyler Glasnow 8.00 20.00
PATT Trea Turner 10.00 25.00
PAYT Yasmany Tomas 4.00 10.00

2015 Bowman Inception Relic Autographs

RANDOM INSERTS IN PACKS
EXCHANGE DEADLINE 6/30/2018
*GREEN/99: .5X TO 1.2X BASIC
*GOLD/50: .6X TO 1.5X BASIC
*ORANGE/25: .75X TO 2X BASIC
IARAB Archie Bradley 3.00 8.00
IARBB Byron Buxton 8.00 20.00
IARBS Braden Shipley 3.00 8.00
IARCB Christian Binford 3.00 8.00
IARCE C.J. Edwards 5.00 12.00
IARDP D.J. Peterson 3.00 8.00
IARFL Francisco Lindor 30.00 80.00
IARGG Gabby Guerrero 3.00 8.00
IARHH Hunter Harvey 4.00 10.00
IARHO Henry Owens 3.00 8.00
IARHR Hunter Renfroe 5.00 12.00
IARJA Jorge Alfaro 5.00 12.00
IARJB Jose Berrios 6.00 15.00
IARJBA Javier Baez 20.00 50.00
IARJC J.P. Crawford 3.00 8.00
IARJG Joey Gallo 12.00 30.00
IARJRA James Ramsey 3.00 8.00
IARJT Jake Thompson 3.00 8.00
IARJW Jesse Winker 6.00 15.00
IARKB Kris Bryant 75.00 200.00
IARKC Kyle Crick 4.00 10.00
IARLG Lucas Giolito 6.00 15.00
IARLS Luis Severino 6.00 15.00
IARMF Michael Feliz 3.00 8.00
IARMJ Micah Johnson 3.00 8.00
IARMO Matt Olson 8.00 20.00
IARMS Miguel Sano 4.00 10.00
IARRH Rosell Herrera 3.00 8.00
IARRN Renato Nunez 6.00 15.00
IARRS Robert Stephenson 3.00 8.00
IARSC Sean Coyle 3.00 8.00

2016 Bowman Inception Rookie Autographs

RANDOM INSERTS IN PACKS
EXCHANGE DEADLINE 6/30/2018
*PURPLE/150: .5X TO 1.2X BASIC
*BLUE/99: .5X TO 1.2X BASIC
*GREEN/50: .6X TO 1.5X BASIC
*GOLD/25: .75X TO 2X BASIC
RAAN Aaron Nola 6.00 15.00
RABP Byung-Ho Park 4.00 10.00
RACS Corey Seager 25.00 60.00
RAGB Greg Bird 4.00 10.00
RAHOL Hector Olivera 4.00 10.00
RAHOW Henry Owens 4.00 10.00
RAJG Jon Gray 3.00 8.00
RAKMAE Kenta Maeda 6.00 15.00
RAKS Kyle Schwarber 20.00 50.00
RALS Luis Severino 4.00 10.00
RAMC Michael Conforto 6.00 15.00
RAMS Miguel Sano 8.00 20.00
RARM Raul Mondesi 6.00 15.00
RASP Stephen Piscotty 6.00 15.00
RATT Trea Turner 15.00 40.00

2016 Bowman Inception Inceptionized Prospect Autographs

PRINT RUNS B/WN 30-300 COPIES PER
EXCHANGE DEADLINE 6/30/2018
*GOLD/25: .5X TO 1.2X BASIC
IBPAAA Anthony Alford/60 6.00 15.00
IBPAAB Alex Bregman EXCH 150.00 300.00
IBPAAE Anderson Espinoza/300 10.00 25.00
IBPAAJ Ariel Jurado/200 6.00 15.00
IBPABR Brendan Rodgers/30 12.00 30.00
IBPADC Daz Cameron EXCH 6.00 15.00
IBPADJ Drew Jackson EXCH 6.00 15.00
IBPADS Dansby Swanson/30 75.00 150.00
IBPAFK Franklyn Kilome/212 8.00 20.00
IBPAFM Francis Martes/60 12.00 30.00
IBPAJC Jharel Cotton/30 10.00 25.00
IBPAJGU Jordan Guerrero/60
IBPAJO Jhailyn Ortiz/200 12.00 30.00
IBPATM Trey Mancini/60 20.00 50.00
IBPATO Tyler O'Neill/30
IBPAVR Victor Robles/110 20.00 50.00
IBPAWC Willson Contreras/30 40.00 100.00
IBPAYA Yadier Alvarez/300 10.00 25.00
IBPAYM Yoan Moncada/50 175.00 350.00

2016 Bowman Inception Inceptionized Veteran Autographs

PRINT RUNS B/WN 30-100 COPIES PER
EXCHANGE DEADLINE 6/30/2018
IBVABH Bryce Harper/30 150.00 300.00
IBVACC Carlos Correa/30 25.00 60.00
IBVACS Chris Sale/30 30.00 80.00
IBVAFL Francisco Lindor EXCH 40.00 100.00
IBVAJD Jacob deGrom EXCH 60.00 150.00
IBVAKW Kolten Wong/100 12.00 30.00
IBVAMM Manny Machado/30 75.00 200.00
IBVANS Noah Syndergaard EXCH
IBVASG Sonny Gray/63 12.00 30.00

2016 Bowman Inception Jumbo Patch Autographs

PRINT RUNS B/WN 44-50 COPIES PER
EXCHANGE DEADLINE 6/30/2018
*GOLD/25: .5X TO 1.2X BASIC
IAJPABL Alex Blandino
IAJPAG Amir Garrett
IAJPAJ Aaron Judge/50 100.00 250.00
IAJPAM Austin Meadows
IAJPAREY Alex Reyes/50 20.00 50.00
IAJPBS Blake Snell
IAJPBZ Bradley Zimmer
IAJPCE Carl Edwards Jr.
IAJPCS Corey Seager
IAJPDS Dominic Smith/50 15.00 40.00
IAJPED Edwin Diaz
IAJPJBE Jose Berrios/50 15.00 40.00
IAJPKME Keury Mella
IAJPLG Lucas Giolito
IAJPLSE Luis Severino/50
IAJPLSI Lucas Sims/50 10.00 25.00
IAJPMCO Michael Conforto
IAJPMO Matt Olson
IAJPOAL Ozzie Albies
IAJPOAR Orlando Arcia
IAJPPO Peter O'Brien
IAJPRD Rafael Devers
IAJPRM Reese McGuire/50
IAJPRN Renato Nunez
IAJPRT Raimel Tapia/44
IAJPTB Tyler Beede

IAJPTT Trea Turner
IAJPWC Willson Contreras/50
IAJPWH Wei-Chieh Huang

2016 Bowman Inception Origins Autographs

STATED PRINT RUN 25 SER.#'d SETS
EXCHANGE DEADLINE 6/30/2018
OAAB Alex Bregman
OAAJ Aaron Judge 75.00 200.00
OABR Brendan Rodgers 25.00 60.00
OABS Blake Snell
OACS Corey Seager 60.00 150.00
OADC Daz Cameron EXCH 15.00 40.00
OADS Dansby Swanson 175.00 350.00
OAJD Jose De Leon
OAJP Joc Pederson 20.00 50.00
OAKS Kyle Schwarber 50.00 125.00
OALG Lucas Giolito 25.00 60.00
OASP Stephen Piscotty 30.00 80.00
OATT Trea Turner 20.00 50.00
OAMCO Michael Conforto EXCH 30.00 80.00

2016 Bowman Inception Prospect Autographs

RANDOM INSERTS IN PACKS
EXCHANGE DEADLINE 6/30/2018
PAAA Anthony Alford 3.00 8.00
PAABE Andrew Benintendi 10.00 25.00
PAABR Alex Bregman 15.00 40.00
PAAE Anderson Espinoza 5.00 12.00
PAAJUD Aaron Judge 60.00 150.00
PAAJUR Ariel Jurado 3.00 8.00
PAAREE A.J. Reed 5.00 12.00
PAAREY Alex Reyes 4.00 10.00
PAARU Ashe Russell 3.00 8.00
PABBR Bobby Bradley 4.00 10.00
PABBU Beau Burrows 3.00 8.00
PABP Brett Phillips 3.00 8.00
PABR Brendan Rodgers
PABS Blake Snell 6.00 15.00
PACF Carson Fulmer 3.00 8.00
PACR Cornelius Randolph 3.00 8.00
PACSA Connor Sadzeck 3.00 8.00
PADC Daz Cameron 3.00 8.00
PADJ Drew Jackson 3.00 8.00
PADS Dansby Swanson
PADT Dillon Tate
PAFK Franklyn Kilome 4.00 10.00
PAFM Francis Martes 3.00 8.00
PAGT Gleyber Torres 50.00 120.00
PAHC Hunter Cole 3.00 8.00
PAIH Ian Happ 6.00 15.00
PAJBE Jose Berrios 5.00 12.00
PAJC Jharel Cotton 3.00 8.00
PAJDE Jose De Leon 6.00 15.00
PAJGO Jordan Guerrero 3.00 8.00
PAJK James Kaprielian 3.00 8.00
PAJM Jorge Mateo 5.00 12.00
PAJO Jhailyn Ortiz 4.00 10.00
PAJSH Justus Sheffield 6.00 15.00
PAKA Kolby Allard 3.00 8.00
PAKH Ke'Bryan Hayes 20.00 50.00
PALF Lucius Fox 5.00 12.00
PALS Lucas Sims 3.00 8.00
PAMCL Mike Clevinger 6.00 15.00
PAMF Michael Fulmer 4.00 10.00
PAMM Manuel Margot 5.00 12.00
PAMSM Mallex Smith 3.00 8.00
PANG Nick Gordon 3.00 8.00
PAOAL Ozzie Albies 15.00 40.00
PAOAR Orlando Arcia 4.00 10.00
PARD Rafael Devers 20.00 50.00
PARM Richie Martin 3.00 8.00
PATC Trent Clark 3.00 8.00
PATM Trey Mancini 6.00 15.00
PATO Tyler O'Neill 4.00 10.00
PATS Tyler Stephenson 8.00 20.00
PATT Touki Toussaint 4.00 10.00
PATW Taylor Ward 4.00 10.00
PAVR Victor Robles 10.00 25.00
PAYA Yadier Alvarez 6.00 15.00
PAYM Yoan Moncada 30.00 80.00

2016 Bowman Inception Prospect Autographs Blue

*BLUE: .5X TO 1.2X BASIC
STATED PRINT RUN 99 SER.#'d SETS
EXCHANGE DEADLINE 6/30/2018
PABR Brendan Rodgers 12.00 30.00
PADS Dansby Swanson 30.00 80.00
PADT Dillon Tate 5.00 12.00

2016 Bowman Inception Prospect Autographs Gold

*GOLD: .75X TO 2X BASIC
STATED PRINT RUN 25 SER.#'d SETS
EXCHANGE DEADLINE 6/30/2018
PABR Brendan Rodgers 20.00 50.00
PADS Dansby Swanson 50.00 120.00
PADT Dillon Tate 8.00 20.00

2016 Bowman Inception Prospect Autographs Green

*GREEN: .6X TO 1.5X BASIC
STATED PRINT RUN 50 SER.#'d SETS
EXCHANGE DEADLINE 6/30/2018
PABR Brendan Rodgers 15.00 40.00
PADS Dansby Swanson 40.00 100.00
PADT Dillon Tate 6.00 15.00

2016 Bowman Inception Prospect Autographs Purple

*PURPLE: .5X TO 1.2X BASIC
STATED PRINT RUN 150 SER.#'d SETS
EXCHANGE DEADLINE 6/30/2018
PABR Brendan Rodgers 12.00 30.00
PADS Dansby Swanson 30.00 80.00
PADT Dillon Tate 5.00 12.00

2016 Bowman Inception Relic Autographs

RANDOM INSERTS IN PACKS
EXCHANGE DEADLINE 6/30/2018
*BLUE/99: .5X TO 1.2X BASIC
*GREEN/50: .6X TO 1.5X BASIC
*GOLD/25: .75X TO 2X BASIC
IARAG Amir Garrett 5.00 12.00
IARAJ Aaron Judge 75.00 200.00
IARAN Aaron Nola 6.00 15.00
IARAREE A.J. Reed 6.00 15.00
IARAREY Alex Reyes 8.00 20.00
IARAW Adam Brett Walker II 3.00 8.00
IARBS Blake Snell 5.00 12.00
IARCP Chad Pinder 3.00 8.00
IARCS Corey Seager 25.00 60.00
IARDS Dominic Smith 3.00 8.00
IARHOL Hector Olivera 4.00 10.00
IARJBA Jake Bauers 5.00 12.00
IARJBE Jose Berrios 5.00 12.00
IARJD J.D. Davis 4.00 10.00
IARJP Jose Peraza 4.00 10.00
IARKME Keury Mella 3.00 8.00
IARLG Lucas Giolito 8.00 20.00
IARLS Lucas Sims 3.00 8.00
IARMO Matt Olson 8.00 20.00
IAROAL Ozzie Albies 20.00 50.00
IAROAR Orlando Arcia 5.00 12.00
IARRD Rafael Devers 25.00 60.00
IARRM Reese McGuire 3.00 8.00
IARTB Tyler Beede 4.00 10.00
IARTT Trea Turner 15.00 40.00
IARWH Wei-Chieh Huang 3.00 8.00

2016 Bowman Inception Veteran Relic Autographs

STATED PRINT RUN 35 SER.#'d SETS
EXCHANGE DEADLINE 6/30/2018
IVARCKE Clayton Kershaw 100.00 250.00
IVARCKL Corey Kluber 20.00 50.00
IVARCS Chris Sale 25.00 60.00
IVARFF Freddie Freeman 30.00 80.00
IVARJD Jacob deGrom 100.00 250.00
IVARJP Joc Pederson 20.00 50.00
IVARMA Matt Adams
IVARMC Matt Carpenter
IVARMM Manny Machado 20.00 50.00
IVARNS Noah Syndergaard 20.00 50.00
IVARSG Sonny Gray 20.00 50.00

2006 Bowman Originals

COMMON CARD (1-35) .40 1.00
COMMON ROOKIE (36-55) .50 1.25
OVERALL PRINTING PLATE ODDS 1:86
PLATE PRINT RUN 1 SET PER COLOR
BLACK-CYAN-MAGENTA-YELLOW ISSUED
NO PLATE PRICING DUE TO SCARCITY
1 David Wright .75 2.00
2 Derek Jeter 2.50 6.00
3 Eric Chavez .40 1.00
4 Ken Griffey Jr. 2.00 5.00
5 Albert Pujols 1.25 3.00
6 Ryan Howard .75 2.00
7 Joe Mauer .60 1.50
8 Andruw Jones .40 1.00
9 Nomar Garciaparra .60 1.50
10 Michael Young .40 1.00
11 Miguel Tejada .60 1.50
12 Alfonso Soriano .60 1.50
13 Alex Rodriguez 1.25 3.00
14 Paul Konerko .60 1.50
15 Carl Crawford .60 1.50
16 Nick Johnson .40 1.00
17 Jim Thome .60 1.50
18 Ivan Rodriguez .60 1.50
19 Chipper Jones 1.00 2.50
20 Pedro Martinez .60 1.50
21 Carlos Delgado .40 1.00
22 Roger Clemens 1.25 3.00
23 Mark Teixeira .60 1.50
24 Manny Ramirez 1.00 2.50
25 Barry Bonds 1.50 4.00
26 Vernon Wells .40 1.00
27 Vladimir Guerrero .60 1.50
28 Miguel Cabrera 1.00 2.50
29 Victor Martinez .60 1.50
30 Derrek Lee .40 1.00
31 Carlos Lee .40 1.00
32 Ichiro Suzuki 1.25 3.00
33 Johan Santana .60 1.50
34 David Ortiz 1.00 2.50
35 Jason Bay .40 1.00
36 Kendry Morales (RC) 1.25 3.00
37 Nick Markakis (RC) 1.00 2.50
38 Conor Jackson (RC) .75 2.00
39 Justin Verlander (RC) 4.00 10.00
40 Ryan Zimmerman (RC) 1.50 4.00
41 Jeremy Hermida (RC) .50 1.25
42 Dan Uggla (RC) .75 2.00
43 Matt Kemp (RC) 1.25 3.00
44 Lastings Milledge (RC) .50 1.25
45 Kenji Johjima RC 1.25 3.00
46 Ian Kinsler (RC) 1.50 4.00
47 Hanley Ramirez (RC) .75 2.00
48 Melky Cabrera (RC) .75 2.00
49 Willy Aybar (RC) .50 1.25
50 Jonathan Papelbon (RC) 2.50 6.00
51 Prince Fielder (RC) 2.50 6.00
52 Cole Hamels (RC) 1.50 4.00
53 Josh Barfield (RC) .50 1.25
54 Alay Soler RC .50 1.25
55 Russ Martin (RC) .75 2.00

2006 Bowman Originals Black

*BLACK: 1X TO 2.5X BASIC
*BLACK RC: .75X TO 2X BASIC RC
STATED ODDS 1:4
STATED PRINT RUN 99 SERIAL #'d SETS

2006 Bowman Originals Blue

*BLUE: .6X TO 1.5X BASIC
*BLUE RC: .5X TO 1.2X BASIC RC
STATED ODDS 1:2
STATED PRINT RUN 249 SERIAL #'d SETS

2006 Bowman Originals Red

STATED ODDS 1:347
STATED PRINT RUN 1 SERIAL #'d SET
NO PRICING DUE TO SCARCITY

2006 Bowman Originals Buyback Autographs

GROUP A ODDS 1:3600
GROUP B ODDS 1:768
GROUP C ODDS 1:38
GROUP D ODDS 1:3
GROUP E ODDS 1:26
GROUP F ODDS 1:1
GROUP G ODDS 1:31
GROUP A PRINT RUN B/WN 10-20 PER
GROUP B PRINT RUN 50 CARDS
GROUP C PRINT RUN B/WN 1-61 PER
GROUP D PRINT RUN B/WN 1-466 PER
GROUP E PRINT RUN B/WN 1-472 PER
GROUP F PRINT RUN B/WN 1-1000 PER
GROUP G PRINT RUN B/WN 1-544 PER
NO PRICING ON QTY OF 25 OR LESS
2 A.Loewen 05 BCDP/198 F 5.00 12.00
11 A.Loewen 05 BDP/719 F 4.00 10.00
12 A.Loewen 05 BDPGLD/68 F 5.00 12.00
15 A.Gonzalez 00 B/976 F 6.00 15.00
18 A.Pujols 02 B/50 C 40.00 80.00
24 A.Pujols 05 B/44 C 60.00 120.00
25 A.Gordon 06 BCPROS/32 C 10.00 25.00
26 A.Gordon 06 BPROS/49 C 12.00 30.00
47 A.McCutchen 04 BAFLAC/391 F 40.00 100.00
50 A.McCutchen 05 BDP/561 F 20.00 50.00
51 A.McCutchen 06 BDPGLD/33 F 60.00 150.00
55 A.Jones 04 B/48 C 4.00 10.00
56 A.Jones 04 BH/28 C 8.00 20.00
57 A.Jones 04 BH/34 C 6.00 15.00
58 A.LaRoche 05 B/66 F 10.00 25.00
63 A.LaRoche 05 BDP/734 F 4.00 10.00
64 A.LaRoche 05 BDPGLD/60 F 8.00 20.00
75 B.Upton 04 BDP/120 F 12.50 30.00
77 B.Upton 05 BCDP/136 F 12.50 30.00
85 B.Upton 05 BDP/667 F 8.00 20.00
89 B.Jones 05 BAFLAC/329 F 4.00 10.00
90 B.Jones 05 BAFLAC/33 F 8.00 20.00
92 B.Jones 05 BCDP/63 F 5.00 12.00
95 B.Jones 05 BDP/576 F 4.00 10.00
98 B.Buckner 04 BC/182 E 6.00 15.00
100 B.Buckner 04 BDP/432 E 4.00 10.00
101 B.Buckner 04 BDPGLD/33 E 8.00 20.00
102 B.Buckner 04 BH/99 E 6.00 15.00
104 B.Wagner 01 BH/99 D 8.00 20.00
108 B.Wagner 94 BB/37 D 10.00 25.00
109 B.Wagner 95 B/56 D 8.00 20.00
110 B.Wagner 96 B/47 D 10.00 25.00
111 B.Wagner 96 BB/64 D 8.00 20.00
116 B.Wagner 97 B/90 D 8.00 20.00
117 B.Wagner 97 BC/38 D 10.00 25.00
123 B.Phillips 01 B/26 F 6.00 15.00
124 B.Phillips 01 BC/46 F 6.00 15.00
126 B.Phillips 02 B/335 F 6.00 15.00
127 B.Phillips 02 BC/67 F 5.00 12.00
128 B.Phillips 02 BCDP/28 F 6.00 15.00
131 B.Phillips 02 BDP/140 F 10.00 25.00
133 B.Phillips 02 BDPGLD/32 F 6.00 15.00
135 B.Phillips 03 B/257 F 4.00 10.00
136 B.Phillips 03 BC/35 F 10.00 25.00
141 B.Snyder 05 BDP/461 D 4.00 10.00
145 B.Wood 05 BCDP/239 F 6.00 15.00
150 B.Wood 05 BDP/627 F 6.00 15.00
153 B.Wood 05 BDPGLD/100 F 6.00 15.00
155 B.Cox 05 BCDP/240 F 5.00 12.00
159 B.Cox 05 BDP/688 F 4.00 10.00
161 B.Cox 05 BDPGLD/66 F 5.00 12.00
165 C.Crawford 00 B/40 F 10.00 25.00
167 C.Crawford 00 BC/37 F 10.00 25.00
171 C.Crawford 02 B/279 F 4.00 10.00
178 C.Crawford 04 B/30 F 8.00 20.00
181 C.Crawford 05 B/71 F 6.00 15.00
184 C.Crawford 05 BH/71 F 6.00 15.00
186 C.Crawford 06 B/334 F 4.00 10.00
188 C.Silva 00 B/996 F 4.00 10.00
190 C.Ramos 05 BCDP/161 F 5.00 12.00
196 C.Ramos 05 BDP/732 F 4.00 10.00
197 C.Ramos 05 BDPGLD/76 F 5.00 12.00
200 C.Utley 02 B/303 D 15.00 40.00
203 C.Utley 06 B/150 D 12.50 30.00
204 C.Roe 05 BCDP/132 F 5.00 12.00
210 C.Roe 05 BDP/774 F 4.00 10.00
212 C.Roe 05 BDPGLD/73 F 5.00 12.00
224 C.Young OF 05 B/81 F 15.00 40.00
228 C.Young OF 05 BDP/558 F 8.00 20.00
229 C.Young OF 05 BDPGLD/88 F 20.00 50.00
232 C.Young OF 05 BH/44 F 20.00 50.00
235 C.Young P 05 BCDP/146 F 12.50 30.00
242 C.Young P 05 BDP/772 F 10.00 25.00
243 C.Young P 05 BDPGLD/70 F 12.50 30.00
245 C.Barmes 03 B/61 F 5.00 12.00
246 C.Barmes 05 BCDP/113 F 5.00 12.00
249 C.Barmes 05 BDP/430 F 4.00 10.00
251 C.Barmes 06 B/375 F 4.00 10.00
252 C.Jackson 04 B/78 F 8.00 20.00
258 C.Jackson 05 BDP/457 F 5.00 12.00
261 C.Jackson 06 B/360 F 5.00 12.00
265 C. Italiano 05 BCDP/163 F 5.00 12.00
268 C. Italiano 05 BDP/658 F 4.00 10.00
269 C. Italiano 05 BDPGLD/160 F 5.00 12.00
276 D. Johnson 05 BCDP/101 F 5.00 12.00
281 D. Johnson 05 BDP/575 F 4.00 10.00
283 D. Johnson 05 BH/29 F 6.00 15.00
284 D. Johnson 06 B/276 F 4.00 10.00
287 D. Wright 02 B/264 F 12.00 30.00
290 D. Wright 04 BDP/45 F 15.00 40.00
292 D. Wright 05 B/64 F 15.00 40.00
294 D. Wright 05 BH/62 F 15.00 40.00
295 D. Wright 06 B/543 F 12.00 30.00
297 D. Lee 04 B/61 C 5.00 12.00
307 D. Willis 04 B/78 F 8.00 20.00
310 D. Willis 04 BH/79 F 8.00 20.00
311 D. Willis 05 B/147 F 8.00 20.00
313 D. Willis 05 BC/36 F 10.00 25.00
315 D. Willis 05 BH/55 F 8.00 20.00
319 D. Willis 06 B/525 F 5.00 12.00
327 E. Iorg 05 BDP/672 F 4.00 10.00
328 E. Iorg 05 BDPGLD/151 F 5.00 12.00
332 E. Chavez 02 B/301 D 4.00 10.00
335 E. Chavez 05 B/70 D 5.00 12.00
336 E. Chavez 05 BH/62 D 5.00 12.00
338 E. Chavez 06 B/34 D 6.00 15.00
339 E. Santana 04 B/76 F 6.00 15.00
340 E. Santana 04 BH/62 F 15.00 40.00
341 E. Santana 05 B/67 F 5.00 12.00
343 E. Santana 05 BCDP/109 F 5.00 12.00
348 E. Santana 05 BDP/51 F 5.00 12.00
349 E. Santana 05 BDP/544 F 4.00 10.00
351 E. Santana 06 B/369 F 4.00 10.00
354 F. Carmona 04 BDP/56 D 6.00 15.00
357 F. Carmona 05 BDP/263 D 4.00 10.00
359 F. Cordero 00 B/140 D 5.00 12.00
360 F. Cordero 00 BC/64 D 5.00 12.00
364 F. Cordero 98 B/138 D 8.00 20.00
365 F. Cordero 98 BB/87 D 5.00 12.00
367 F. Cordero 98 BC/49 D 6.00 15.00
370 F. Liriano 02 B/212 F 6.00 15.00
371 F. Liriano 02 BDP/63 F 6.00 15.00
373 F. Liriano 05 BCDP/142 F 6.00 15.00
375 F. Liriano 05 BDP/350 F 6.00 15.00
378 F. Liriano 06 B/222 F 6.00 15.00
383 G. Atkins 05 BDP/581 F 4.00 10.00
385 G. Atkins 05 BDPGLD/27 F 6.00 15.00
386 G. Atkins 06 B/209 F 5.00 12.00
390 G. Atkins 06 BGLD/38 F 6.00 15.00
391 G. Chacin 05 BH/30 D 6.00 15.00
393 G. Chacin 06 B/468 D 4.00 10.00
396 H. Ramirez 05 BCDP/98 F 10.00 25.00
399 H. Ramirez 05 BDP/435 F 4.00 10.00
400 H. Ramirez 06 B/466 F 4.00 10.00
402 H. Street 05 BDP/54 5.00 12.00
404 J. Bay 02 B/298 D 4.00 10.00
406 J. Bay 04 BH/58 D 5.00 12.00
407 J. Bay 05 B/70 D 5.00 12.00
408 J. Bay 06 B/50 D 5.00 12.00
409 J. Botts 02 B/269 F 4.00 10.00
412 J. Botts 02 BH/46 F 6.00 15.00
413 J. Botts 06 B/29 F 6.00 15.00
414 J. Botts 06 B/577 F 4.00 10.00
418 J. Botts 06 BGLD/31 F 6.00 15.00
419 J. Kubel 03 B/77 D 5.00 12.00
424 J. Kubel 04 BCDP/127 D 5.00 12.00
428 J. Kubel 04 BDP/232 D 5.00 12.00
433 J. Marquis 00 B/944 F 4.00 10.00
436 J. Marquis 98 B/26 F 6.00 15.00
438 J. Bruce 05 BDP/434 D 4.00 10.00
439 J. Bruce 05 BDPGLD/66 D 20.00 50.00
442 J. Lowrie 05 BDP/716 F 6.00 15.00
443 J. Lowrie 05 BDPGLD/141 F 6.00 15.00
447 J. Mathis 01 BDP/71 D 5.00 12.00
451 J. Mathis 03 BDP/127 D 5.00 12.00
453 J. Mathis 04 BCDP/97 D 5.00 12.00
454 J. Mathis 04 BDP/185 D 5.00 12.00
457 J. Williams 02 B/292 D 4.00 10.00
459 J. Williams 03 BCDP/45 D 6.00 15.00
460 J. Williams 03 BDP/48 D 6.00 15.00
461 J. Williams 04 B/97 D 5.00 12.00
462 J. Guzman 02 B/274 D 4.00 10.00
465 J. Guzman 02 BDP/90 D 10.00 25.00
466 J. Guzman 04 BC/54 D 5.00 12.00
467 J. Guzman 04 BDP/53 D 5.00 12.00
469 J. Zumaya 04 B/96 F 10.00 25.00
472 J. Zumaya 05 BCDP/233 F 4.00 10.00
478 J. Zumaya 05 BDP/582 F 4.00 10.00
479 J. Zumaya 05 BDPGLD/57 F 6.00 15.00
483 J. Drennen 05 BAFLAC/78 D 8.00 20.00
486 J. Drennen 06 BDP/387 D 4.00 10.00
489 J.Van Benschoten 01 BDP/51 D 5.00 12.00
490 J. Van Benschoten 02 B/272 D 4.00 10.00
492 J. Van Benschoten 03 BCDP/26 D 6.00 15.00
493 J. Van Benschoten 03 BDP/130 D 5.00 12.00
495 J. Gomes 02 B/341 F 5.00 12.00
496 J. Gomes 02 BC/27 F 10.00 25.00
499 J. Gomes 04 B/175 F 8.00 20.00
506 J. Gomes 06 B/363 F 4.00 10.00
511 J. Barfield 02 B/178 F 8.00 20.00
524 J. Barfield 05 BDP/557 F 4.00 10.00
526 J. Barfield 05 BDPGLD/31 F 6.00 15.00
529 J. Geer 05 BCDP/138 D 5.00 12.00
531 J. Geer 05 BDP/343 D 4.00 10.00
534 J. Huber 02 BDP/26 F 12.00 30.00
536 J. Huber 03 BCDP/37 F 12.00 30.00
539 J. Huber 03 BDP/99 F 5.00 12.00
545 J. Huber 05 BDP/572 F 4.00 10.00
547 J. Huber 05 BDPGLD/32 F 6.00 15.00
550 J. Upton 04 BAFLAC/1000 F 8.00 20.00
551 K. Gregg 00 B/988 F 4.00 10.00
554 L. Milledge 04 B/158 F 12.00 30.00
558 L. Milledge 05 BCDP/166 F 12.00 30.00
560 L. Milledge 05 BDP/632 F 10.00 25.00
561 L. Milledge 05 BDPGLD/27 F 15.00 40.00
563 M. Loretta 05 B/110 D 5.00 12.00
565 M. Loretta 05 BH/73 D 5.00 12.00
566 M. Loretta 06 B/289 D 4.00 10.00
582 M. Cain 04 BDP/36 D 10.00 25.00
586 M. Cain 06 B/389 D 6.00 15.00
590 M. Maloney 05 B/350 D 6.00 15.00
595 M. Maloney 05 BH/50 D 30.00 60.00
601 M. Torra 06 BDP/456 D 6.00 15.00
603 M. Cabrera 05 B/95 F 10.00 25.00
606 M. Cabrera 05 BCDP/191 F 10.00 25.00
612 M. Cabrera 05 BDP/606 F 6.00 15.00
613 M. Cabrera 05 BDPGLD/60 F 20.00 50.00
616 M. Valdez 04 B/70 D 5.00 12.00
619 M. Valdez 04 BH/66 D 5.00 12.00
621 M. Valdez 05 BDP/325 D 4.00 10.00
622 M. Valdez 05 BDP/41 D 6.00 15.00
627 M. Owings 06 BDP/648 F 6.00 15.00
628 M. Owings 06 BDPGLD/138 F 12.00 30.00
631 M. Bowden 05 BDP/449 D 8.00 20.00
632 M. Bowden 05 BDPGLD/27 D 15.00 40.00
633 M. Cabrera 02 B/130 D 20.00 50.00
634 M. Cabrera 03 B/70 D 20.00 50.00
635 M. Cabrera 04 B/70 D 20.00 50.00
637 M. Cabrera 05 B/69 D 20.00 50.00
639 M. Cabrera 05 BH/63 D 20.00 50.00
641 M. Cabrera 06 B/98 D 20.00 50.00
645 M. Costanzo 06 BDP/466 D 5.00 12.00
648 M. Lamb 00 B/993 F 4.00 10.00
649 M. Ensberg 01 BDP/74 D 5.00 12.00
650 M. Ensberg 02 B/334 D 4.00 10.00
655 M. Ensberg 06 B/64 D 5.00 12.00
661 N. Swisher 05 BH/73 D 5.00 12.00
663 N. Swisher 06 B/342 D 4.00 10.00
668 N. Swisher 06 BGLD/31 D 6.00 15.00
670 N. Reimold 05 BCDP/30 D 12.00 30.00
671 N. Reimold 05 BDP/419 D 8.00 20.00
674 N. Reimold 05 BH/41 D 12.00 30.00
677 R. Harden 02 B/263 D 5.00 12.00
678 R. Harden 03 B/70 D 5.00 12.00
679 R.Harden 03 BDP/68 D 5.00 12.00
681 R. Harden 04 B/87 D 5.00 12.00
682 R. Harden 05 B/82 D 5.00 12.00
686 R. Nolasco 04 B/256 D 4.00 10.00
687 R. Nolasco 04 BC/148 D 5.00 12.00
693 R. Nolasco 04 BH/52 D 5.00 12.00
698 R. Cano 04 BDP/72 D 30.00 60.00
701 R. Cano 05 BCDP/90 D 20.00 50.00
702 R. Cano 05 BDP/222 D 10.00 25.00
705 R. Cano 06 B/101 D 8.00 20.00
706 R. Oswalt 02 B/199 D 4.00 10.00
709 R. Oswalt 04 B/61 D 6.00 15.00
710 R. Oswalt 04 BH/63 D 6.00 15.00
711 R. Oswalt 05 B/96 D 6.00 15.00
712 R. Oswalt 06 B/42 D 6.00 15.00
713 R. Martin 05 B/96 F 6.00 15.00
715 R. Martin 05 BCDP/252 F 6.00 15.00
718 R. Martin 05 BDP/577 F 6.00 15.00
719 R. Martin 05 BDPGLD/33 F 12.00 30.00
724 R. Garko 05 BDP/394 F 4.00 10.00
726 R. Garko 06 B/580 F 4.00 10.00
728 R. Howard 03 BDP/50 B 10.00 25.00
729 S. Elbert 04 BCDP/60 D 10.00 25.00
731 S. Elbert 04 BDP/330 D 8.00 20.00
733 S. Elbert 04 BH/79 D 15.00 40.00
734 S. Kazmir 05 B/155 F 8.00 20.00
736 S. Kazmir 05 BH/99 F 10.00 25.00
738 S. Kazmir 06 B/661 F 4.00 10.00
742 S. Kazmir 06 BGLD/26 F 6.00 15.00
744 S. Mathieson 05 B/72 E 5.00 12.00
754 S. Mathieson 05 BDP/472 E 4.00 10.00
759 S. Thorman 00 B/980 F 4.00 10.00
761 S. West 05 BCDP/70 D 12.00 30.00
764 S. West 05 BDP/394 D 4.00 10.00
765 S. West 05 BDPGLD/35 D 10.00 25.00
766 S. Marcum 03 BCDP/153 D 5.00 12.00
767 S. Marcum 03 BDP/138 D 5.00 12.00
768 S. Marcum 03 BDPGLD/33 D 6.00 15.00
769 S. Marcum 05 B/133 D 5.00 12.00
770 S. Marcum 05 BC/26 D 6.00 15.00
775 T. Buck 05 BCDP/134 F 8.00 20.00
777 T. Buck 05 BDP/747 F 5.00 12.00
778 T. Buck 05 BDPGLD/60 F 20.00 50.00
782 T. Buck 05 BS/44 F 20.00 50.00
784 T. Hafner 02 B/280 F 5.00 12.00
787 T. Hafner 03 BCDP/45 F 10.00 25.00
790 T. Hafner 03 BDP/114 F 6.00 15.00
792 T. Hafner 05 B/96 F 6.00 15.00
794 T. Hafner 06 B/386 F 4.00 10.00
804 T. Bell 05 BDP/689 F 4.00 10.00
806 T. Bell 05 BDPGLD/134 F 5.00 12.00
807 T. Bell 05 BH/28 F 6.00 15.00
809 T. Patton 05 BCDP/211 F 8.00 20.00
813 T. Patton 05 BDP/736 F 4.00 10.00
814 T. Patton 05 BDPGLD/50 F 5.00 12.00
817 V. Wells 00 B/56 F 4.00 10.00
820 V. Wells 01 B/29 F 4.00 10.00
823 V. Wells 04 B/96 F 4.00 10.00
826 V. Wells 05 B/100 F 4.00 10.00
828 V. Wells 05 BH/52 F 4.00 10.00
831 V. Wells 06 B/426 F 4.00 10.00
838 V. Wells 98 B/40 F 4.00 10.00
842 V. Wells 99 B/68 F 4.00 10.00
849 V. Guerrero 05 B/45 C 20.00 50.00
851 W. Townsend 05 BCDP/53 D 5.00 12.00
853 W. Townsend 05 BDP/423 D 4.00 10.00
856 W. Mo Pena 00 B/79 D 5.00 12.00
857 W. Mo Pena 00 BB/27 D 6.00 15.00
860 W. Mo Pena 02 B/134 D 5.00 12.00
863 W. Mo Pena 02 BDP/70 D 5.00 12.00
865 W. Mo Pena 03 B/62 D 5.00 12.00
866 W. Mo Pena 05 B/69 D 5.00 12.00
868 X. Nady 01 BDP/192 F 5.00 12.00
869 X. Nady 02 B/294 F 4.00 10.00
870 X. Nady 02 BC/41 F 6.00 15.00
875 X. Nady 03 BCDP/72 F 5.00 12.00
877 X. Nady 03 BDP/213 F 5.00 12.00
878 X. Nady 03 BDPGLD/33 F 6.00 15.00
879 X. Nady 05 BH/105 F 5.00 12.00
884 Y. Escobar 06 BCDP/28 D 15.00 40.00
885 Y. Escobar 06 BDP/395 D 4.00 10.00
886 Y. Escobar 06 BDPGLD/69 D 30.00 60.00
888 Y. Petit 04 BDP/102 F 5.00 12.00
891 Y. Petit 04 BH/68 F 5.00 12.00
893 Y. Petit 05 BCDP/160 F 5.00 12.00
897 Y. Petit 05 BDP/630 F 4.00 10.00

2006 Bowman Originals Prospects

COMMON CARD (1-55) .40 1.00
OVERALL PRINTING PLATE ODDS 1:86
PLATE PRINT RUN 1 SET PER COLOR
BLACK-CYAN-MAGENTA-YELLOW ISSUED
NO PLATE PRICING DUE TO SCARCITY
1 Cameron Maybin 1.25 3.00
2 Koby Clemens .60 1.50
3 Lance Broadway .40 1.00
4 Chris Dickerson .60 1.50
5 Garrett Mock .40 1.00
6 Ben Copeland .40 1.00
7 Nick Adenhart .40 1.00
8 Brad McCann .40 1.00
9 Dustin Majewski .40 1.00
10 Jimmy Barthmaier .40 1.00
11 Michael Aubrey .60 1.50
12 Evan Longoria 5.00 12.00
13 Clayton Kershaw 30.00 80.00
14 Juan Francia .40 1.00
15 Elvis Andrus 1.25 3.00
16 Mark Trumbo 1.00 2.50
17 Shawn Riggans .40 1.00
18 Asdrubal Cabrera 2.00 5.00
19 Mark McLemore .40 1.00
20 Radhames Liz .40 1.00
21 Mat Gamel 1.00 2.50
22 Wilkin Ramirez .60 1.50
23 Jared Lansford .40 1.00
24 Hunter Pence 1.50 4.00
25 Justin Upton 3.00 8.00
26 Brent Dlugach .40 1.00
27 B.J. Szymanski .40 1.00
28 Stephen Marek .40 1.00
29 Shaun Cumberland .40 1.00
30 Yovani Gallardo 1.25 3.00
31 Will Venable .40 1.00
32 A.J. Shappi .40 1.00
33 Dallas Trahern .40 1.00
34 Jason Jaramillo .40 1.00
35 Jose Tabata .60 1.50
36 Jose Campusano .40 1.00
37 Ryan Patterson .40 1.00
38 Andrew Pinckney .40 1.00
39 Dexter Fowler 1.25 3.00
40 Cody Johnson .40 1.00
41 Steve Murphy .40 1.00
42 Mark Reed .40 1.00
43 Chris Iannetta .40 1.00
44 Michael Hollimon .40 1.00
45 Omir Santos .40 1.00
46 Diory Hernandez .40 1.00
47 Matt Tolbert .40 1.00
48 Jeff Frazier .40 1.00
49 Max Ramirez .60 1.50
50 Alex Gordon 1.25 3.00
51 Steve Garrabrants .40 1.00
52 Steven Baker .40 1.00
53 Ryan Klosterman .40 1.00
54 Michael Collins .40 1.00
55 Corey Wimberly .40 1.00

2006 Bowman Originals Prospects Black

*BLACK: .75X TO 2X BASIC
STATED ODDS 1:4
STATED PRINT RUN 99 SERIAL #'d SETS

2006 Bowman Originals Prospects Blue

*BLUE: .6X TO 1.5X BASIC
STATED ODDS 1:2
STATED PRINT RUN 249 SERIAL #'d SETS

2006 Bowman Originals Prospects Red

STATED ODDS 1:347
STATED PRINT RUN 1 SERIAL #'d SET
NO PRICING DUE TO SCARCITY

2011 Bowman Perfect Game All-American Classic

AA Albert Almora 8.00 20.00
AB Alex Bregman 5.00 12.00
AF Austin Fairchild
AP Andrew Pullin 5.00 12.00
AR Addison Russell 8.00 20.00
CC Carlos Correa 30.00 80.00
CF Carson Fulmer 3.00 8.00
CH Chris Harvey 5.00 12.00
CHA Courtney Hawkins 6.00 15.00
CJH C.J. Hinojosa 4.00 10.00
CJS C.J. Saylor 4.00 10.00
CO Corey Oswalt
CP Cody Poteet
CS Clate Schmidt 5.00 12.00
CSE Corey Seager 25.00 60.00
DD David Dahl 10.00 25.00
DR Daniel Robertson 5.00 12.00
DU Duane Underwood 4.00 10.00
HV Hunter Virant 4.00 10.00
JG Joey Gallo 15.00 40.00
JGO Jason Goldstein 4.00 10.00
JH Josh Henderson 4.00 10.00
JW Jesse Winker 6.00 15.00
JWI Jameis Winston 30.00 80.00
KB Keon Barnum 5.00 12.00
KP Kayden Porter 6.00 15.00
LG Lucas Giolito 10.00 25.00
LM Lance McCullers 6.00 15.00
LS Lucas Sims 6.00 15.00
MC Matthew Crownover
MF Max Fried 8.00 20.00
MS Matthew Smoral 4.00 10.00
MT Mitchell Traver 4.00 10.00
NR Nelson Rodriguez
NW Nick Williams 4.00 10.00
RB Ryan Burr
RM Ryan McNeil 3.00 8.00
RR Rio Ruiz 5.00 12.00
RW Rhett Wiseman
SB Skye Bolt
SG Steven Golden 5.00 12.00
TC Taylore Cherry 4.00 10.00
TR Tanner Rahier 5.00 12.00
TS Tucker Simpson
TW Trey Williams 5.00 12.00
WW Walker Weickel 4.00 10.00

2011 Bowman Perfect Game All-American Classic Autographs

13 BOW.ODDS 1:2059 HOBBY
14 BOW.ODDS 1:1150 HOBBY
14 BOW.CHR.ODDS 1:1020 HOBBY
15 BOW.CHR.ODDS 1:1440 HOBBY
16 BOW.CHR.ODDS 1:1083 HOBBY
PRINT RUNS B/WN 199-235 COPIES PER
AB Alex Bregman/199 30.00 80.00
AR Addison Russell/229 50.00 120.00
CC Carlos Correa/235 200.00 400.00
CF Carson Fulmer/199 6.00 15.00
CH Courtney Hawkins/233 10.00 25.00
CS Corey Seager/225 60.00 150.00
DD David Dahl/235 40.00 100.00
DR Daniel Robertson/225 10.00 25.00
DU Duane Underwood/199 5.00 12.00
JG Joey Gallo/235 30.00 80.00
JW Jesse Winker/225 30.00 80.00
JWI Jameis Winston/199 40.00 100.00
KB Keon Barnum/235 8.00 20.00
LG Lucas Giolito/235 30.00 80.00
LM Lance McCullers/225 12.00 30.00
LS Lucas Sims/225 10.00 25.00
MF Max Fried/235 30.00 80.00
NR Nelson Rodriguez/199 4.00 10.00
NW Nick Williams/199 20.00 50.00
RR Rio Ruiz/199 8.00 20.00
TR Tanner Rahier/225 10.00 25.00

2012 Bowman Perfect Game All-American Classic

COMPLETE SET (48) 100.00 175.00
AM Austin Meadows 8.00 20.00
AP A.J. Puk 2.50 6.00
BC Brady Corless 2.00 5.00
BM Billy McKinney 2.00 5.00
BMO Brett Morales 2.00 5.00
BN Brian Navarreto 4.00 10.00
CB Cavan Biggio 6.00 15.00
CF Clint Frazier 10.00 25.00
CH Clinton Hollon 6.00 15.00
CO Chris Oakley 3.00 8.00
COK Chris Okey 2.50 6.00
CR Christopher Rivera 3.00 8.00
CS Corder Sandberg 5.00 12.00
CSH Casey Shane 2.00 5.00
DB Derik Beauprez 2.00 5.00
DD Dustin Driver 2.50 6.00
DM Dane McFarland 2.50 6.00
DS Dominic Smith 6.00 15.00
GK Gosuke Katoh 2.00 5.00
IC Ian Clarkin 6.00 15.00
JB Jared Brasher 2.00 5.00
JC John Paul Crawford 3.00 8.00
JH Josh Hart 2.50 6.00
JHE Jan Hernandez 4.00 10.00
JM Jeremy Martinez 5.00 12.00
JMA Joey Martarano 2.50 6.00
JS John Sternagel 2.00 5.00
JSH Jordan Sheffield 4.00 10.00
JW Jonah Wesely 2.00 5.00
JWI Justin Williams 10.00 25.00
KC Kacy Clemens 5.00 12.00
KD Kevin Davis 3.00 8.00
KF Kevin Franklin 2.50 6.00
KS Kohl Stewart 6.00 15.00
MP Mayky Perez 4.00 10.00
NB Nicholas Banks 2.50 6.00
NC Nick Ciuffo 4.00 10.00
OM Oscar Mercado 10.00 25.00
RB Ronald Trey Ball III 6.00 15.00
RBO Ryan Boldt 4.00 10.00
RK Robert Kaminsky 5.00 12.00
RM Reese McGuire 4.00 10.00
RT Rowdy Tellez 4.00 10.00
RTY Robert Tyler 2.00 5.00
SG Stephen Gonsalves 5.00 12.00
SN Sheldon Neuse 3.00 8.00
TD Travis Demeritte 3.00 8.00
ZC Zack Collins 4.00 10.00

2012 Bowman Perfect Game All-American Classic Autographs

13 BOW.DFT.ODDS 1:619 HOBBY
14 BOW.ODDS 1:1150 HOBBY
14 BOW.CHR.ODDS 1:1020 HOBBY
15 BOW.ODDS 1:1278 HOBBY
PRINT RUNS B/WN 210-235 COPIES PER
AJ Alex Jackson/200 30.00 80.00
AM Austin Meadows/235 20.00 50.00
AP A.J. Puk/199 6.00 15.00
BM Billy McKinney/235 12.00 30.00
CB Cavan Biggio/199 20.00 50.00
CF Clint Frazier/235 20.00 50.00
CS Cord Sandberg/235 12.00 30.00
DS Dominic Smith/235 15.00 40.00
GK Gosuke Katoh/210 10.00 25.00
IC Ian Clarkin/210 12.00 30.00
JC John Paul Crawford/235 15.00 40.00
JG Joe Gatto/200 4.00 10.00
JW Justin Williams/235 8.00 20.00
KS Kohl Stewart/225 10.00 25.00
LW Levon Washington/225 4.00 10.00
MH Monte Harrison/200 4.00 10.00
MK Michael Kopech/200 15.00 40.00
NC Nick Ciuffo/235 10.00 25.00
RK Rob Kaminsky/210 12.00 30.00
RM Reese McGuire/210 12.00 30.00
RT Rowdy Tellez/225 12.00 30.00
SN Sheldon Neuse/199 6.00 15.00
TB Trey Ball/235 12.00 30.00
TD Travis Demeritte/210 12.00 30.00

2013 Bowman Perfect Game All-American Classic Autographs

'17 BOW.CHR.ODDS 1:1562 HOBBY
PRINT RUNS B/WN 199-200 COPIES PER
'17 BOW.CHR.EXCH 8/31/2019
PGAP A.J. Puk/199 10.00 25.00
PGDH Derek Hill/199 12.00 30.00
PGGD Greg Deichmann/199 8.00 20.00
PGJGA Jacob Gatewood/199 12.00 30.00
PGJH Jack Flaherty/199 25.00 60.00
PGKME Kodi Medeiros/199 12.00 30.00
PGMK Michael Kopech/200 15.00 40.00
PGTKO Tyler Kolek/199 25.00 60.00
PGZC Zack Collins/199 5.00 12.00

2010 Bowman Platinum

COMMON CARD (1-100) .15 .40
COMMON RC (1-100) .40 1.00
1 Stephen Strasburg RC 3.00 8.00
2 Derek Jeter 1.00 2.50
3 Felix Doubront RC .40 1.00
4 Miguel Cabrera .40 1.00
5 Albert Pujols .50 1.25
6 Domonic Brown RC 1.50 4.00
7 Ryan Braun .25 .60
8 Justin Upton .25 .60
9 Dustin Pedroia .40 1.00
10 Shin-Soo Choo .25 .60
11 Jake Arrieta RC 1.00 2.50
12 Hanley Ramirez .25 .60
13 Matt Kemp .30 .75
14 Joe Mauer .30 .75
15 Joey Votto .40 1.00
16 Andrew Cashner RC .40 1.00
17 Josh Hamilton .25 .60
18 Buster Posey RC 3.00 8.00
19 Ubaldo Jimenez .15 .40
20 Peter Bourjos RC .60 1.50
21 CC Sabathia .25 .60
22 Alfonso Soriano .25 .60
23 Carlos Santana RC 1.25 3.00
24 Kevin Youkilis .15 .40
25 Brian McCann .25 .60
26 Troy Tulowitzki .40 1.00
27 Hunter Pence .25 .60
28 Jay Sborz (RC) .40 1.00
29 Andre Ethier .25 .60
30 Kendry Morales .15 .40

31 Brian Matusz RC 1.00 2.50
32 Vladimir Guerrero .25 .60
33 Prince Fielder .25 .60
34 J.P. Arencibia RC .75 2.00
35 Roy Halladay .25 .60
36 Mark Teixeira .25 .60
37 Ryan Kalish RC .60 1.50
38 Tim Lincecum .25 .60
39 Andrew McCutchen .40 1.00
40 Johan Santana .25 .60
41 Josh Bell (RC) .40 1.00
42 Daniel Nava RC .40 1.00
43 Manny Ramirez .40 1.00
44 Ichiro Suzuki .50 1.25
45 Pablo Sandoval .25 .60
46 Chris Coghlan .15 .40
47 Mike Leake RC 1.25 3.00
48 Adrian Gonzalez .30 .75
49 Torii Hunter .15 .40
50 Brennan Boesch RC 1.00 2.50
51 Justin Verlander .40 1.00
52 Matt Holliday .40 1.00
53 Evan Longoria .25 .60
54 Adam Jones .25 .60
55 Wade Davis (RC) .60 1.50
56 Jose Reyes .60 1.50
57 Martin Prado .15 .40
58 Brad Lincoln RC .60 1.50
59 Billy Butler .15 .40
60 Mat Latos .25 .60
61 Logan Morrison RC .60 1.50
62 Ryan Howard .30 .75
63 Cliff Lee .25 .60
64 Adam Dunn .25 .60
65 David Ortiz .40 1.00
66 Ike Davis RC .75 2.00
67 Victor Martinez .25 .60
68 Josh Johnson .25 .60
69 Dayan Viciedo RC .60 1.50
70 Jimmy Rollins .25 .60
71 Jered Weaver .25 .60
72 Robinson Cano .25 .60
73 Madison Bumgarner RC 4.00 10.00
74 Clayton Kershaw .60 1.50
75 Tommy Hanson .15 .40
76 Carl Crawford .25 .60
77 Trevor Plouffe (RC) 1.00 2.50
78 Roy Oswalt .25 .60
79 Austin Jackson RC .60 1.50
80 Dan Haren .15 .40
81 Gordon Beckham .15 .40
82 Zack Greinke .40 1.00
83 Neil Walker (RC) .60 1.50
84 Vernon Wells .15 .40
85 Lance Berkman .25 .60
86 Mike Stanton RC 3.00 8.00
87 Ryan Zimmerman .25 .60
88 Nick Markakis .30 .75
89 Jose Tabata RC .60 1.50
90 Chipper Jones .40 1.00
91 Jason Heyward RC 1.50 4.00
92 Alex Rodriguez .50 1.25
93 Matt Cain .25 .60
94 Justin Morneau .25 .60
95 Jon Lester .25 .60
96 Starlin Castro RC 1.00 2.50
97 Chase Utley .25 .60
98 Felix Hernandez .25 .60
99 Wilson Ramos RC 1.00 2.50
100 David Wright .30 .75

2010 Bowman Platinum Refractors
*REF VET: 2X TO 5X BASIC
*REF RC: .6X TO 1.5X BASIC
STATED PRINT RUN 999 SER.#'d SETS

2010 Bowman Platinum Gold Refractors
*GOLD VET: 2.5X TO 6X BASIC
*GOLD RC: 1X TO 2.5X RC
STATED PRINT RUN 539 SER.#'d SETS

2010 Bowman Platinum Dual Relic Autographs Refractors
STATED PRINT RUN 99 SER.#'d SETS
AJ T.Anderson/B.Johnson 6.00 15.00
BM M.Barnes/S.McGough 8.00 20.00
BS J.Bradley Jr./G.Springer 30.00 80.00
DM A.Dickerson/A.Maggi 6.00 15.00
ER J.Esposito/S.Rodriguez 6.00 15.00
FM N.Fontana/M.Mahtook 6.00 15.00
GC S.Gray/G.Cole 20.00 50.00
MW B.Miller/R.Wright 6.00 15.00
RW N.Ramirez/K.Winkler 6.00 15.00
SH S.Strasburg/J.Heyward 125.00 250.00

2010 Bowman Platinum Hexagraph Autographs
STATED PRINT RUN 6 SER.#'d SETS

2010 Bowman Platinum Prospect Autographs Refractors
AC Alexander Colome 5.00 12.00
ACH Aroldis Chapman 10.00 25.00
AH Adeiny Hechavarria 2.00 5.00
AW Alex Wilson 2.00 5.00
AWE Allen Webster 3.00 8.00
CA Chris Archer 6.00 15.00
CD Chase D'Arnaud 2.00 5.00
CO Chris Owings 2.00 5.00
DM Dan Merklinger 2.00 5.00
ET Eric Thames 5.00 12.00
FF Freddie Freeman 30.00 80.00
FM Fabio Martinez 2.00 5.00
GH Gorkys Hernandez 2.00 5.00
IK Ian Krol 2.00 5.00
JDM J.D. Martinez 25.00 60.00
JH Jordan Henry 2.00 5.00
JJ Jake Jefferies 2.00 5.00
JK Joe Kelly 2.00 5.00
JL Josh Lindblom 2.00 5.00
JM Jesus Montero 2.00 5.00
JMA Justin Marks 2.00 5.00
JMC Jake McGee 4.00 10.00
JMI Jiovanni Mier 3.00 8.00
JP Jarrod Parker 5.00 12.00
JR Javier Rodriguez 2.00 5.00
JS Jerry Sands 5.00 12.00
JS Jonathan Singleton 5.00 12.00
KSA Keyvius Sampson 5.00 12.00
LC Lonnie Chisenhall 3.00 8.00
LS Logan Schafer 2.00 5.00
MR Matt Rizzotti 2.00 5.00
MRO Mauricio Robles 2.00 5.00
MS Miguel Sano 5.00 12.00
MT Mike Trout 400.00 800.00
NB Nick Barnese 2.00 5.00
NN Nick Noonan 2.00 5.00
NT Nate Tenbrink 2.00 5.00
PC Pat Corbin 6.00 15.00
PG Paul Goldschmidt 20.00 50.00
RC Ryan Chaffee 2.00 5.00
RP Rich Poythress 2.00 5.00
RU Rudy Owens 3.00 8.00
SG Steve Garrison 2.00 5.00
SH Steven Hensley 2.00 5.00
TS Tony Sanchez 5.00 12.00

2010 Bowman Platinum Prospect Autographs Blue Refractors
*BLUE: .75X TO 2X BASIC
STATED PRINT RUN 99 SER.#'d SETS
MT Mike Trout 1500.00 2000.00

2010 Bowman Platinum Prospect Autographs Green Refractors
*GREEN: .6X TO 1.5X BASIC
STATED PRINT RUN 199 SER.#'d SETS
MT Mike Trout 600.00 1200.00

2010 Bowman Platinum Prospect Autographs Red Refractors
STATED PRINT RUN 10 SER.#'d SETS

2010 Bowman Platinum Prospect Dual Autographs Refractors
STATED PRINT RUN 99 SER.#'d SETS
BD J.Bradley Jr./A.Dickerson 15.00 40.00
CB G.Cole/M.Barnes 12.50 30.00
GE S.Gray/J.Esposito 8.00 20.00
GW S.Gilmartin/K.Winkler 8.00 20.00
JM B.Jackson/J.Mitchell 8.00 20.00
JM B.Johnson/B.Mooneyham 8.00 20.00
MF M.Mahtook/N.Fontana 8.00 20.00
MS B.Miller/G.Springer 15.00 40.00
OR P.O'Brien/S.Rodriguez 8.00 20.00
RR N.Ramirez/N.Ramirez 8.00 20.00
WM R.Wright/A.Maggi 8.00 20.00

2010 Bowman Platinum Prospects
PP1 Jerry Sands 1.00 2.50
PP2 Desmond Jennings .60 1.50
PP3 Jeremy Hellickson 1.00 2.50
PP4 Jesus Montero .40 1.00
PP5 Mike Trout 75.00 200.00
PP6 Dustin Ackley .60 1.50
PP7 Zach Britton 1.25 3.00
PP8 Adeiny Hechavarria .40 1.00
PP9 Mike Moustakas 1.00 2.50
PP10 Aroldis Chapman 1.50 4.00
PP11 Lonnie Chisenhall .60 1.50
PP12 Mike Montgomery .60 1.50
PP13 Freddie Freeman 5.00 12.00
PP14 Kyle Drabek .60 1.50
PP15 Grant Green .40 1.00
PP16 Brett Jackson 1.25 3.00
PP17 Slade Heathcott 1.25 3.00
PP18 Mike Minor .60 1.50
PP19 Austin Romine .60 1.50
PP20 Kyle Gibson 1.50 4.00
PP21 Chris Withrow .40 1.00
PP22 John Lamb 1.00 2.50
PP23 J.D. Martinez 5.00 12.00
PP24 Donavan Tate .40 1.00
PP25 Shelby Miller 2.00 5.00
PP26 Jose Iglesias 1.25 3.00
PP27 Hak-Ju Lee .60 1.50
PP28 Miguel Sano 2.50 6.00
PP29 Tyler Anderson .60 1.50
PP30 Matt Barnes 1.00 2.50
PP31 Jackie Bradley Jr. 1.50 4.00
PP32 Gerrit Cole 4.00 10.00
PP33 Alex Dickerson .40 1.00
PP34 Jason Esposito 1.00 2.50
PP35 Nolan Fontana .60 1.50
PP36 Sean Gilmartin .60 1.50
PP37 Sonny Gray 1.00 2.50
PP38 Brian Johnson .40 1.00
PP39 Andrew Maggi .40 1.00
PP40 Mikie Mahtook 1.00 2.50
PP41 Scott McGough 1.00 2.50
PP42 Brad Miller 1.00 2.50
PP43 Brett Mooneyham 1.00 2.50
PP44 Peter O'Brien 1.00 2.50
PP45 Nick Ramirez .60 1.50
PP46 Noe Ramirez .60 1.50
PP47 Steve Rodriguez .60 1.50
PP48 George Springer 2.50 6.00
PP49 Kyle Winkler .60 1.50
PP50 Ryan Wright .40 1.00

2010 Bowman Platinum Prospects Refractors Thick Stock
*REF: .75X TO 2X BASIC
STATED PRINT RUN 999 SER.#'d SETS

2010 Bowman Platinum Prospects Refractors Thin Stock
*REF: .75X TO 2X BASIC
STATED PRINT RUN 999 SER.#'d SETS

2010 Bowman Platinum Prospects Blue Refractors
*BLUE REF: 1.5X TO 4X BASIC
STATED PRINT RUN 99 SER.#'d SETS

2010 Bowman Platinum Prospects Gold Refractors Thick Stock
*GOLD REF: 1X TO 2.5X BASIC
STATED PRINT RUN 539 SER.#'d SETS

2010 Bowman Platinum Prospects Gold Refractors Thin Stock
*GOLD REF: 1X TO 2.5X BASIC
STATED PRINT RUN 539 SER.#'d SETS

2010 Bowman Platinum Prospects Green Refractors
*GREEN REF: 1X TO 2.5X BASIC
STATED PRINT RUN 499 SER.#'d SETS

2010 Bowman Platinum Prospects Purple Refractors
*PURPLE REF: .6X TO 1.5X BASIC

2010 Bowman Platinum Prospects Red Refractors
STATED PRINT RUN 25 SER.#'d SETS

2010 Bowman Platinum Relic Autographs Refractors
STATED PRINT RUN 740 SER.#'d SETS
STRASBURG PRINT RUN 240 SER.#'d SETS
AC Andrew Cashner 5.00 12.00
AD Alex Dickerson 5.00 12.00
AM Andrew Maggi 6.00 15.00
AMC Andrew McCutchen 15.00 40.00
BC Brett Cecil 5.00 12.00
BJ Brian Johnson 5.00 12.00
BL Brad Lincoln 5.00 12.00
BM Brad Miller 6.00 15.00
BMO Brett Mooneyham 5.00 12.00
CJ Chris Johnson 5.00 12.00
CP Carlos Pena 5.00 12.00
GC Gerrit Cole 25.00 60.00
GS George Springer 15.00 40.00
JB Jackie Bradley Jr. 10.00 25.00
JBA Jose Bautista 6.00 15.00
JE Jason Esposito 5.00 12.00
JH Jason Heyward 5.00 12.00
JJ Josh Johnson 5.00 12.00
JT Jose Tabata 5.00 12.00
KW Kyle Winkler 5.00 12.00
MB Matt Barnes 8.00 20.00
MM Mikie Mahtook 5.00 12.00
NC Nelson Cruz 5.00 12.00
NF Nolan Fontana 5.00 12.00
NR Nick Ramirez 5.00 12.00
NRA Noe Ramirez 5.00 12.00
PF Prince Fielder 6.00 15.00
PO Peter O'Brien 5.00 12.00
PS Pablo Sandoval 6.00 15.00
RC Robinson Cano 8.00 20.00
RH Ryan Howard 12.00 30.00
RW Ryan Wright 5.00 12.00
SC Starlin Castro 5.00 12.00
SG Sean Gilmartin 5.00 12.00
SGR Sonny Gray 5.00 12.00
SM Scott McGough 10.00 25.00
SR Steve Rodriguez 5.00 12.00
SS Stephen Strasburg/240 40.00 100.00
TA Tyler Anderson 5.00 12.00

2010 Bowman Platinum Relic Autographs Blue Refractors
*BLUE: .75X TO 2X BASIC
STATED PRINT RUN 50 SER.#'d SETS

2010 Bowman Platinum Relic Autographs Green Refractors
*GREEN: .6X TO 1.5X BASIC
STATED PRINT RUN 199 SER.#'d SETS

2010 Bowman Platinum Relic Autographs Red Refractors
STATED PRINT RUN 10 SER.#'d SETS

2010 Bowman Platinum Triple Autographs
STATED PRINT RUN 89 SER.#'d SETS
AJM And/Johnson/Moon 10.00 25.00
CBG Cole/Barnes/Gray 25.00 60.00
CVM Wright/Vitters/Moustakas 15.00 40.00
MMF Maggi/Mahtook/Fontana 10.00 25.00
MOW Miller/O'Brien/Wright 12.00 30.00
REG Ramirez/Esposito/Gilmartin 10.00 25.00
RWM Ramirez/Winkler/McGough 12.00 30.00
SBD Springer/Bradley/Dickerson 12.00 40.00
SPM Santana/Posey/Montero 40.00 80.00
TRU Tillman/Reimold/Uehara 10.00 25.00

2011 Bowman Platinum
COMPLETE SET (100) 10.00 25.00
COMMON CARD (1-100) .12 .30
COMMON RC (1-100) .30 .75
1 Ryan Howard .25 .60
2 Josh Rodriguez RC .30 .75
3 Adam Jones .25 .60
4 Jon Lester .25 .60
5 Brad Emaus RC .30 .75
6 Miguel Cabrera .30 .75
7 Hank Conger RC .50 1.25
8 Hanley Ramirez .25 .60
9 Derek Jeter .75 2.00
10 Austin Jackson .12 .30
11 Justin Upton .20 .50
12 Jimmy Rollins .20 .50
13 Carlos Santana .30 .75
14 Jeremy Hellickson RC .75 2.00
15 Roy Oswalt .20 .50
16 Carl Crawford .20 .50
17 Ryan Braun .20 .50
18 Adam Dunn .20 .50
19 Carlos Gonzalez .20 .50
20 Pedro Alvarez RC .60 1.50
21 Mark Trumbo (RC) .75 2.00
22 Daniel Descalso RC .30 .75
23 Mike Stanton .30 .75
24 Andre Ethier .20 .50
25 Brandon Beachy RC .75 2.00
26 Robinson Cano .20 .50
27 Jake McGee (RC) .60 1.50
28 Buster Posey .40 1.00
29 Brent Morel RC .30 .75
30 Felix Hernandez .20 .50
31 Adrian Gonzalez .25 .60
32 Jason Heyward .25 .60
33 Madison Bumgarner .25 .60
34 Nick Markakis .25 .60
35 Chris Sale RC 2.50 6.00
36 Johan Santana .20 .50
37 Josh Johnson .20 .50
38 Manny Ramirez .30 .75
39 Brian McCann .20 .50
40 Clay Buchholz .12 .30
41 Gordon Beckham .12 .30
42 Ubaldo Jimenez .12 .30
43 Joey Votto .30 .75
44 Jeremy Jeffress RC .30 .75
45 Torii Hunter .12 .30
46 Kendry Morales .12 .30
47 Cory Luebke RC .30 .75
48 Mark Teixeira .20 .50
49 Joe Mauer .25 .60
50 Mat Latos .20 .50
51 Jose Bautista .20 .50
52 Brandon Belt RC .75 2.00
53 David Ortiz .30 .75
54 Matt Cain .20 .50
55 Michael Pineda RC .75 2.00
56 Jered Weaver .20 .50
57 Freddie Freeman RC 5.00 12.00
58 Clayton Kershaw .50 1.25
59 Justin Morneau .20 .50
60 CC Sabathia .20 .50
61 Jayson Werth .20 .50
62 David Wright .25 .60
63 Prince Fielder .20 .50
64 Hunter Pence .20 .50
65 Albert Pujols .40 1.00
66 Dustin Pedroia .30 .75
67 Victor Martinez .20 .50
68 Stephen Strasburg .30 .75
69 Jose Reyes .20 .50
70 Zack Greinke .30 .75
71 Dan Haren .12 .30
72 Tim Lincecum .20 .50
73 Ryan Zimmerman .20 .50
74 Starlin Castro .20 .50
75 Josh Hamilton .20 .50
76 Yonder Alonso RC .50 1.25
77 Dan Uggla .12 .30
78 Jonathan Sanchez .12 .30
79 Andrew McCutchen .30 .75
80 Billy Butler .12 .30
81 Carlos Pena .12 .30
82 Justin Verlander .30 .75
83 Cole Hamels .25 .60
84 Ike Davis .12 .30
85 Jacoby Ellsbury .25 .60
86 Chipper Jones .30 .75
87 Cliff Lee .20 .50
88 Vernon Wells .12 .30
89 Shin-Soo Choo .20 .50
90 Alex Rodriguez .40 1.00
91 Troy Tulowitzki .30 .75
92 Kevin Youkilis .12 .30
93 Aroldis Chapman RC 1.00 2.50
94 Chase Utley .20 .50
95 Kyle Drabek RC .50 1.25
96 Matt Kemp .25 .60
97 Evan Longoria .20 .50
98 Matt Holliday .30 .75
99 Roy Halladay .20 .50
100 Ichiro Suzuki .40 1.00

2011 Bowman Platinum Emerald
*EMERALD: 2X TO 5X BASIC
*EMERALD RC: .75X TO 2X BASIC RC

2011 Bowman Platinum Gold
*GOLD: 1.5X TO 4X BASIC
*GOLD RC: .6X TO 1.5X BASIC RC

2011 Bowman Platinum Ruby
*RUBY: 3X TO 8X BASIC
*RUBY RC: 1.2X TO 3X BASIC RC

2011 Bowman Platinum Dual Autographs
STATED PRINT RUN 89 SER.#'d SETS
RED PRINT RUN 10 SER.#'d SETS
NO RED PRICING DUE TO SCARCITY
SUPERFRACTOR PRINT RUN 1 SER.#'d SET
NO SUPERFRACTOR PRICING AVAILABLE
EXCHANGE DEADLINE 7/31/2014
CM L.Chisenhall/M.Moustakas 8.00 20.00
DT Jaff Decker/Donavan Tate 5.00 12.00
GC G.Green/M.Choice 5.00 12.00
GL D.Gordon/L.Landry 5.00 12.00
HT B.Harper/J.Taillon 100.00 250.00
MC M.Machado/C.Colon 20.00 50.00
MM M.Montgomery/M.Moustakas 8.00 20.00
NW Hector Noesi/Adam Warren 5.00 12.00
SD Jake Skole/Kellin Deglan EXCH 3.00 8.00
SM G.Sanchez/J.Montero 30.00 80.00

2011 Bowman Platinum Dual Autographs Red Refractors
STATED PRINT RUN 10 SER.#'d SETS
NO PRICING DUE TO SCARCITY
EXCHANGE DEADLINE 7/31/2014

2011 Bowman Platinum Dual Relic Autographs
STATED PRINT RUN 89 SER.#'d SETS
RED PRINT RUN 10 SER.#'d SETS
NO RED PRICING DUE TO SCARCITY
SUPERFRACTOR PRINT RUN 1 SER.#'d SET
NO SUPERFRACTOR PRICING AVAILABLE
EXCHANGE DEADLINE 7/31/2014
CB S.Castro/M.Byrd 10.00 25.00
CP J.Chamberlain/R.Perry 10.00 25.00
DP I.Davis/A.Pagan 12.50 30.00
GC A.Gonzalez/C.Crawford 20.00 50.00
HK D.Haren/S.Kazmir 10.00 25.00
IV R.Ibanez/S.Victorino 10.00 25.00
JS J.Johnson/M.Stanton 30.00 60.00
JU A.Jones/J.Upton 15.00 40.00
JW C.Johnson/B.Wallace EXCH 10.00 25.00
KB I.Kinsler/G.Beckham 10.00 25.00
SB D.Span/B.Boesch 10.00 25.00
SM P.Sandoval/C.McGehee 10.00 25.00

2011 Bowman Platinum Dual Relic Autographs Red Refractors
STATED PRINT RUN 10 SER.#'d SETS
NO PRICING DUE TO SCARCITY
EXCHANGE DEADLINE 7/31/2014

2011 Bowman Platinum Hexagraph Patches
STATED PRINT RUN 10 SER.#'d SETS
NO PRICING DUE TO SCARCITY

2011 Bowman Platinum Hexagraphs
STATED PRINT RUN 10 SER.#'d SETS
NO PRICING DUE TO SCARCITY

2011 Bowman Platinum Prospect Autograph Refractors
PLATE PRINT RUN 1 SET PER COLOR
BLACK-CYAN-MAGENTA-YELLOW ISSUED
NO PLATE PRICING DUE TO SCARCITY
EXCHANGE DEADLINE 7/31/2014
AF Anderson Feliz 3.00 8.00
AW Alex Wimmers 3.00 8.00
AWA Adam Warren 3.00 8.00
BE Brett Eibner 4.00 10.00
BG Brandon Guyer 3.00 8.00
BH Bryce Harper 100.00 250.00
BHO Brad Holt 3.00 8.00
CD Cutter Dykstra 3.00 8.00
CR Clint Robinson 3.00 8.00
CS Cody Scarpetta 3.00 8.00
DD Delino DeShields 3.00 8.00
DJ Dickie Joe Thon 3.00 8.00
DM Deck McGuire 3.00 8.00
DS Domingo Santana 6.00 15.00
GR Garrett Richards 4.00 10.00
HN Hector Noesi 3.00 8.00
HS Hayden Simpson 3.00 8.00
JB Joe Benson 3.00 8.00
JJ Jiwan James 3.00 8.00
JP Jimmy Paredes 4.00 10.00
JPA Jordan Pacheco 4.00 10.00
JSE Jean Segura 3.00 8.00
JSW Jordan Swagerty 3.00 8.00
JT Jameson Taillon 4.00 10.00
KP Kyle Parker 6.00 15.00
KS Kyle Seager 6.00 15.00
LL Leon Landry 3.00 8.00
MC Michael Choice 4.00 10.00
MD Miguel De Los Santos 3.00 8.00
MF Mike Foltynewicz 3.00 8.00
MH Matt Harvey 6.00 15.00
MM Manny Machado EXCH 15.00 40.00
RD Rashun Dixon 3.00 8.00
RDE Randall Delgado 3.00 8.00
SH Shaeffer Hall 3.00 8.00
SM Shelby Miller 3.00 8.00
TS Tyler Skaggs 4.00 10.00
NNO Mystery EXCH 10.00 25.00

2011 Bowman Platinum Prospect Autograph Blue Refractors
*BLUE: .75X TO 2X BASIC
STATED PRINT RUN 99 SER.#'d SETS
EXCHANGE DEADLINE 7/31/2014
BH Bryce Harper 150.00 400.00

2011 Bowman Platinum Prospect Autograph Gold Refractors
*GOLD : 1.2X TO 3X BASIC
STATED PRINT RUN 50 SER.#'d SETS
EXCHANGE DEADLINE 7/31/2014
BH Bryce Harper 300.00 600.00
DM Deck McGuire 15.00 40.00

2011 Bowman Platinum Prospect Autograph Green Refractors
*GREEN : .5X TO 1.2X BASIC
STATED PRINT RUN 399 SER.#'d SETS
EXCHANGE DEADLINE 7/31/2014
BH Bryce Harper 125.00 300.00

2011 Bowman Platinum Prospect Autograph Red Refractors
STATED PRINT RUN 10 SER.#'d SETS
NO PRICING DUE TO SCARCITY
EXCHANGE DEADLINE 7/31/2014

2011 Bowman Platinum Prospects
COMPLETE SET (100) 40.00 80.00
PLATE PRINT RUN 1 SET PER COLOR
BLACK-CYAN-MAGENTA-YELLOW ISSUED
NO PLATE PRICING DUE TO SCARCITY
BPP1 Bryce Harper 8.00 20.00
BPP2 Dee Gordon .60 1.50
BPP3 Jesus Montero .60 1.50
BPP4 Daniel Fields .40 1.00
BPP5 Deck McGuire .40 1.00
BPP6 Zach Lee .60 1.50
BPP7 Travis D'Arnaud .60 1.50
BPP8 Anderson Feliz .40 1.00
BPP9 Blake Smith .40 1.00
BPP10 Jonathan Singleton .60 1.50
BPP11 Kyle Seager 1.00 2.50
BPP12 Avisail Garcia .60 1.50
BPP13 Miguel De Los Santos .40 1.00
BPP14 Ronnie Welty .40 1.00
BPP15 Ryan Lavarnway 1.50 4.00
BPP16 Yasmani Grandal .60 1.50
BPP17 Kolbrin Vitek .60 1.50
BPP18 Zack Cox .60 1.50
BPP19 Jimmy Paredes 1.00 2.50
BPP20 Joe Benson .40 1.00
BPP21 Austin Hyatt .60 1.50
BPP22 Corban Joseph .40 1.00
BPP23 Josh Zeid .40 1.00
BPP24 Oswaldo Arcia .40 1.00
BPP25 Jacob Turner 1.50 4.00
BPP26 Jose Iglesias .60 1.50
BPP27 Jarred Cosart .60 1.50
BPP28 Shaeffer Hall .60 1.50
BPP29 Manny Banuelos 1.00 2.50
BPP30 Tyler Skaggs 1.00 2.50
BPP31 Domingo Santana 1.00 2.50
BPP32 Dustin Ackley .60 1.50
BPP33 Dickie Joe Thon .60 1.50
BPP34 Jurickson Profar 1.00 2.50
BPP35 Tony Wolters .40 1.00
BPP36 Aderlin Rodriguez .40 1.00
BPP37 Cito Culver 1.50 4.00
BPP38 Billy Hamilton .75 2.00
BPP39 Yorman Rodriguez .60 1.50
BPP40 Matt Dominguez .60 1.50
BPP41 Delino DeShields .40 1.00
BPP42 Brandon Short .60 1.50
BPP43 Michael Choice .60 1.50
BPP44 Wilmer Flores .60 1.50
BPP45 Jake Marisnick .60 1.50
BPP46 Leon Landry .60 1.50
BPP47 Derek Norris .40 1.00
BPP48 Mike Foltynewicz .40 1.00
BPP49 Rashun Dixon .40 1.00
BPP50 Drew Pomeranz .60 1.50
BPP51 Alex Wimmers .40 1.00
BPP52 Cody Scarpetta .40 1.00
BPP53 Eduardo Escobar .40 1.00
BPP54 Jake Skole .40 1.00
BPP55 David Cooper .40 1.00
BPP56 Jarrod Parker 1.00 2.50
BPP57 Jacob Goebbert .60 1.50
BPP58 Carlos Perez .40 1.00
BPP59 Kevin Mailloux .40 1.00
BPP60 Drew Vettleson .40 1.00
BPP61 Hayden Simpson .40 1.00
BPP62 Hector Noesi .60 1.50
BPP63 Jonathan Schoop .60 1.50
BPP64 Nick Franklin .60 1.50
BPP65 Jameson Taillon .60 1.50
BPP66 Matt Harvey 2.50 6.00
BPP67 Keon Broxton .40 1.00
BPP68 Allen Webster .60 1.50
BPP69 Kyle Parker .60 1.50
BPP70 Brad Brach .40 1.00
BPP71 Johermyn Chavez .40 1.00
BPP72 Shelby Miller 2.00 5.00
BPP73 Julio Teheran .60 1.50
BPP74 Jordan Swagerty .60 1.50
BPP75 Sean Coyle .60 1.50
BPP76 Kyle Russell .60 1.50
BPP77 Cutter Dykstra .40 1.00
BPP78 Brad Holt .40 1.00
BPP79 Chun-Hsiu Chen 1.00 2.50
BPP80 Brandon Guyer .60 1.50
BPP81 Cesar Puello .60 1.50
BPP82 Garrett Richards 1.00 2.50
BPP83 Manny Machado 4.00 10.00
BPP84 Jared Mitchell .60 1.50
BPP85 Brody Colvin .40 1.00
BPP86 Tim Beckham 1.00 2.50
BPP87 Adron Chambers .40 1.00
BPP88 Marcell Ozuna 1.50 4.00
BPP89 Sammy Solis .40 1.00
BPP90 Gary Brown 1.00 2.50
BPP91 Kaleb Cowart .60 1.50
BPP92 Trey McNutt .40 1.00
BPP93 Jordan Pacheco .40 1.00
BPP94 Adam Warren .60 1.50
BPP95 Matt Lipka .60 1.50
BPP96 Christian Colon .40 1.00
BPP97 Carlos Perez .40 1.00
BPP98 Matt Moore 1.00 2.50
BPP99 Chris Archer .75 2.00
BPP100 Jaff Decker .40 1.00

2011 Bowman Platinum Prospects Refractors
*REF: .5X TO 1.2X BASIC
BPP1 Bryce Harper 10.00 25.00

2011 Bowman Platinum Prospects Blue Refractors
*BLUE: 1.2X TO 3X BASIC
STATED PRINT RUN 199 SER.#'d SETS
BPP1 Bryce Harper 30.00 80.00

2011 Bowman Platinum Prospects Gold Canary Diamond Refractors
STATED PRINT RUN 1 SER.#'d SET
NO PRICING DUE TO SCARCITY

2011 Bowman Platinum Prospects Gold Refractors
*GOLD: 3X TO 8X BASIC
STATED PRINT RUN 50 SER.#'d SETS
BPP1 Bryce Harper 125.00 250.00

2011 Bowman Platinum Prospects Green Refractors
*GREEN: .75X TO 2X BASIC
STATED PRINT RUN 599 SER.#'d SETS
BPP1 Bryce Harper 15.00 40.00

2011 Bowman Platinum Prospects Purple Refractors
*PURPLE: .6X TO 1.5X BASIC
BPP1 Bryce Harper 8.00 20.00

2011 Bowman Platinum Prospects Red Refractors
STATED PRINT RUN 25 SER.#'d SETS
NO PRICING DUE TO SCARCITY

2011 Bowman Platinum Prospects X-Fractors
*X-FRACTOR: .5X TO 1.2X BASIC

2011 Bowman Platinum Relic Autograph Refractors
PRINT RUN B/WN 115-1166 COPIES PER
2011 Bowman Platinum Relic Autograph Blue Refractors
AJ Austin Jackson/115 6.00 15.00
AR Adam Rosales/1166 4.00 10.00
BC Brett Cecil EXCH 4.00 10.00
CM Cristhian Martinez/1166 4.00 10.00
EB Emilio Bonifacio/1166 4.00 10.00
EE Edwin Encarnacion/1166 4.00 10.00
EM Evan Meek/1166 4.00 10.00
FF Freddie Freeman/115 20.00 50.00
FM Franklin Morales/1166 4.00 10.00
JA J.P. Arencibia/666 5.00 12.00
JC Jesse Crain/1166 4.00 10.00
JF Juan Francisco/1166 4.00 10.00
JM Jake McGee/1166 4.00 10.00
JM Jhan Marinez/1166 4.00 10.00
JM John McDonald/1166 4.00 10.00
JM Juan Miranda/1166 4.00 10.00
LN Leo Nunez/1166 4.00 10.00
MR Max Ramirez/1166 4.00 10.00
OM Ozzie Martinez/1166 4.00 10.00
RT Robinson Tejeda/1166 4.00 10.00
SC Starlin Castro/666 8.00 20.00
TB Trevor Bell EXCH 4.00 10.00
YN Yamaico Navarro/1166 4.00 10.00
JHL Jeremy Hellickson/115 6.00 15.00

2011 Bowman Platinum Relic Autograph Blue Refractors
*BLUE: .6X TO 1.5X BASIC pr/666-1166
*BLUE: .4X TO 1X BASIC pr/115
STATED PRINT RUN 99 SER.#'d SETS
EXCHANGE DEADLINE 7/31/2014

2011 Bowman Platinum Relic Autograph Gold Refractors
STATED PRINT RUN 25 SER.#'d SETS
NO PRICING DUE TO SCARCITY
EXCHANGE DEADLINE 7/31/2014

2011 Bowman Platinum Relic Autograph Green Refractors
*GREEN: .5X TO 1.2X BASIC
STATED PRINT RUN 199 SER.#'d SETS
EXCHANGE DEADLINE 7/31/2014

2011 Bowman Platinum Relic Autograph Red Refractors
STATED PRINT RUN 10 SER.#'d SETS
NO PRICING DUE TO SCARCITY
EXCHANGE DEADLINE 7/31/2014

2011 Bowman Platinum Team USA National Team Autographs
EXCHANGE DEADLINE 12/31/2012
BR Brady Rodgers 3.00 8.00
CE Chris Elder 4.00 10.00
DF Dominic Ficociello 5.00 12.00
DL David Lyon 3.00 8.00
DM Deven Marrero 3.00 8.00
EW Erich Weiss 4.00 10.00
HM Hoby Milner 4.00 10.00
KG Kevin Gausman 8.00 20.00
MA Mark Appel 6.00 15.00
ML Michael Lorenzen 3.00 8.00
MR Matt Reynolds 4.00 10.00
MS Marcus Stroman 6.00 15.00
NNO Mystery EXCH 10.00 25.00

2011 Bowman Platinum Triple Autographs Red Refractors
STATED PRINT RUN 10 SER.#'d SETS
NO PRICING DUE TO SCARCITY
EXCHANGE DEADLINE 7/31/2014

2011 Bowman Platinum Triple Autographs
STATED PRINT RUN 89 SER.#'d SETS
RED PRINT RUN 10 SER.#'d SETS
NO RED PRICING DUE TO SCARCITY
SUPERFRACTOR PRINT RUN 1 SER.#'d SET
NO SUPERFRACTOR PRICING AVAILABLE
EXCHANGE DEADLINE 7/31/2014
CWJ Castro/Wall/John 15.00 40.00
FHD Free/How/Davis 40.00 100.00
HKW Har/Kaz/Wald 8.00 20.00
HSB Hey/Stan/D.Brow 75.00 150.00
MAC Mon/Ack/Chis EXCH 15.00 40.00
PMM Pos/Mauer/Mon EXCH 30.00 80.00
SPG Soto/Pena/Garza 10.00 25.00

2012 Bowman Platinum
COMPLETE SET (100) 15.00 40.00
STATED PLATE ODDS 1:1118 HOBBY
PLATE PRINT RUN 1 SET PER COLOR
BLACK-CYAN-MAGENTA-YELLOW ISSUED
NO PLATE PRICING DUE TO SCARCITY
1 Michael Pineda .20 .50
2 Joe Mauer .25 .60
3 Liam Hendriks RC .50 1.25
4 Adrian Beltre .30 .75
5 Josh Johnson .25 .60
6 Miguel Cabrera .30 .75
7 Matt Kemp .25 .60
8 Ichiro Suzuki .40 1.00
9 Yu Darvish RC 1.25 3.00
10 Carlos Gonzalez .25 .60
11 Jose Reyes .20 .50
12 Eric Hosmer .25 .60
13 Jay Bruce .25 .60
14 Derek Jeter .75 2.00
15 Lance Berkman .25 .60
16 Mike Trout 10.00 25.00
17 Tyler Pastornicky RC .50 1.25
18 Tommy Hanson .20 .50
19 Dustin Pedroia .30 .75
20 Prince Fielder .25 .60
21 Yoenis Cespedes RC 1.25 3.00
22 Jose Bautista .25 .60
23 Ian Kennedy .20 .50
24 Chipper Jones .30 .75
25 Jeremy Hellickson .20 .50
26 James Shields .20 .50
27 Brian McCann .25 .60
28 David Price .25 .60
29 Mike Napoli .25 .60
30 Adrian Gonzalez .25 .60
31 Andre Ethier .25 .60
32 Giancarlo Stanton .30 .75
33 Adam Jones .25 .60
34 Ryan Braun .25 .60
35 Joey Votto .30 .75
36 Alex Rodriguez .40 1.00
37 Justin Verlander .30 .75
38 Ian Kinsler .25 .60
39 Justin Upton .25 .60
40 Ubaldo Jimenez .20 .50
41 Carlos Santana .25 .60

42 Rickie Weeks .20 .50
43 Mark Teixeira .25 .60
44 Leonys Martin RC .50 1.25
45 Mariano Rivera .40 1.00
46 Andrew McCutchen .30 .75
47 Ryan Howard .25 .60
48 Kirk Nieuwenhuis RC .50 1.25
49 Robinson Cano .25 .60
50 Josh Beckett .20 .50
51 Troy Tulowitzki .30 .75
52 Addison Reed RC .50 1.25
53 Desmond Jennings .25 .60
54 Evan Longoria .25 .60
55 Clayton Kershaw .50 1.25
56 Bryce Harper RC 8.00 20.00
57 Buster Posey .40 1.00
58 Paul Konerko .20 .50
59 Josh Hamilton .25 .60
60 Brad Peacock RC .50 1.25
61 C.J. Wilson .20 .50
62 Alex Gordon .25 .60
63 Dan Uggla .25 .60
64 David Ortiz .30 .75
65 Jesus Montero .20 .50
66 Michael Morse .20 .50
67 Cole Hamels .25 .60
68 Albert Pujols .40 1.00
69 Drew Pomeranz RC .50 1.25
70 Jon Lester .20 .50
71 Tim Hudson .25 .60
72 Curtis Granderson .25 .60
73 Madison Bumgarner .25 .60
74 Nelson Cruz .30 .75
75 Kevin Youkilis .30 .75
76 Tim Lincecum .25 .60
77 Pablo Sandoval .25 .60
78 Jered Weaver .25 .60
79 Starlin Castro .25 .60
80 Stephen Strasburg .30 .75
81 Hisashi Iwakuma RC 1.00 2.50
82 David Freese .20 .50
83 Devin Mesoraco RC .50 1.25
84 Justin Morneau .25 .60
85 Felix Hernandez .25 .60
86 Ryan Zimmerman .25 .60
87 Zack Greinke .30 .75
88 CC Sabathia .25 .60
89 Hanley Ramirez .25 .60
90 David Wright .25 .60
91 Cliff Lee .25 .60
92 Wilin Rosario RC .50 1.25
93 Roy Halladay .25 .60
94 Mat Latos .25 .60
95 Asdrubal Cabrera .25 .60
96 Jarrod Parker RC .60 1.50
97 Matt Holliday .30 .75
98 Freddie Freeman .40 1.00
99 Matt Moore RC .75 2.00
100 Jacoby Ellsbury .25 .60

2012 Bowman Platinum Emerald
*EMERALD: 2X TO 5X BASIC
*EMERALD RC: .75X TO 2X BASIC RC
STATED ODDS 1:10 HOBBY

2012 Bowman Platinum Gold
*GOLD: 1.5X TO 4X BASIC
*GOLD RC: .6X TO 1.5X BASIC RC
STATED ODDS 1:5 HOBBY

2012 Bowman Platinum Ruby
*RUBY: 3X TO 8X BASIC
*RUBY RC: 1.2X TO 3X BASIC RC
STATED ODDS 1:20 HOBBY

2012 Bowman Platinum Blue National Promo
ISSUED AT 2012 NATIONAL CONVENTION
STATED PRINT RUN 499 SER.#'d SETS
9 Yu Darvish 4.00 10.00
21 Yoenis Cespedes 4.00 10.00
44 Leonys Martin 1.50 4.00
52 Addison Reed 1.50 4.00
56 Bryce Harper 25.00 60.00
60 Brad Peacock 1.50 4.00
65 Jesus Montero 1.50 4.00
69 Drew Pomeranz 1.50 4.00
81 Norichika Aoki 2.00 5.00
83 Devin Mesoraco 1.50 4.00
92 Wilin Rosario 1.50 4.00
96 Jarrod Parker 2.00 5.00
99 Matt Moore 2.50 6.00

2012 Bowman Platinum Cutting Edge Stars
STATED ODDS 1:10 HOBBY
I Ichiro Suzuki 1.25 3.00
AC Allen Craig .75 2.00
AG Adrian Gonzalez .75 2.00
AM Andrew McCutchen 1.00 2.50
AP Albert Pujols 1.25 3.00
BH Bryce Harper 6.00 15.00
BL Brett Lawrie .75 2.00
BM Brian McCann .75 2.00
BP Buster Posey 1.25 3.00
CG Carlos Gonzalez .75 2.00
CJ Chipper Jones 1.00 2.50
DA Dustin Ackley .60 1.50
DF David Freese .60 1.50
DH Daniel Hudson .60 1.50
DJ Derek Jeter 2.50 6.00
DO David Ortiz 1.00 2.50
DU Dan Uggla .75 2.00
DW David Wright .75 2.00
EH Eric Hosmer .75 2.00
EL Evan Longoria .75 2.00
FF Freddie Freeman 1.25 3.00
HB Heath Bell .60 1.50
HR Hanley Ramirez .75 2.00
IK Ian Kinsler .75 2.00
IN Ivan Nova .75 2.00
JB Jose Bautista .75 2.00
JM Jason Motte .60 1.50
JS James Shields .60 1.50
JU Justin Upton .75 2.00
JV Justin Verlander 1.00 2.50
MC Miguel Cabrera 1.00 2.50
MM Matt Moore 1.00 2.50
MP Michael Pineda .60 1.50
MT Mark Trumbo .60 1.50
NC Nelson Cruz 1.00 2.50
PF Prince Fielder .75 2.00
PG Paul Goldschmidt 1.00 2.50
RB Ryan Braun .60 1.50
RC Robinson Cano .75 2.00
RR Ricky Romero .60 1.50
SC Starlin Castro .75 2.00
TT Troy Tulowitzki 1.00 2.50
YA Yonder Alonso .60 1.50
YD Yu Darvish 1.50 4.00
YG Yovani Gallardo .75 2.00
ZG Zack Greinke 1.00 2.50
IKE Ian Kennedy .60 1.50
JDM J.D. Martinez 1.00 2.50
JMO Jesus Montero .60 1.50
MMS Michael Morse .60 1.50

2012 Bowman Platinum Cutting Edge Stars Relics
STATED ODDS 1:490 HOBBY
STATED PRINT RUN 50 SER.#'d SETS
AG Adrian Gonzalez 8.00 20.00
AM Andrew McCutchen 12.50 30.00
AP Albert Pujols 8.00 20.00
BM Brian McCann 8.00 20.00
BP Buster Posey 12.50 30.00
CJ Chipper Jones 12.50 30.00
DJ Derek Jeter 12.50 30.00
DO David Ortiz 8.00 20.00
DU Dan Uggla 4.00 10.00
DW David Wright 8.00 20.00
EH Eric Hosmer 6.00 15.00
EL Evan Longoria 8.00 20.00
FF Freddie Freeman 8.00 20.00
HR Hanley Ramirez 6.00 15.00
IK Ian Kinsler 4.00 10.00
JS James Shields 5.00 12.00
JU Justin Upton 6.00 15.00
JV Justin Verlander 12.50 30.00
NC Nelson Cruz 4.00 10.00
RB Ryan Braun 8.00 20.00
RR Ricky Romero 4.00 10.00
TT Troy Tulowitzki 6.00 15.00
YG Yovani Gallardo 4.00 10.00
ZG Zack Greinke 4.00 10.00
JBA Jose Bautista 5.00 12.00

2012 Bowman Platinum Dual Autographs
STATED ODDS 1:1066 HOBBY
STATED PRINT RUN 50 SER.#'d SETS
EXCHANGE DEADLINE 06/30/2015
BJ T.Jungmann/J.Bradley 15.00 40.00
BS Blake Swihart/Matt Barnes 15.00 40.00
CT J.Taillon/G.Cole 50.00 100.00
HM Brandon Martin/Jake Hager 15.00 40.00
HP Paxton/Hultzen EXCH 20.00 50.00
JP J.Panik/T.Joseph 15.00 40.00
LB J.Baez/F.Lindor 40.00 80.00
SB J.Bell/B.Starling EXCH 40.00 80.00
ST Terdoslavich/Simmons EXCH 40.00 80.00
TT O.Taveras/C.Tilson 60.00 120.00

2012 Bowman Platinum Jumbo Relic Autograph Refractors
STATED ODDS 1:180 HOBBY
PRINTING PLATE ODDS 1:11,186 HOBBY
PLATE PRINT RUN 1 SET PER COLOR
BLACK-CYAN-MAGENTA-YELLOW ISSUED
NO PLATE PRICING DUE TO SCARCITY
EXCHANGE DEADLINE 06/30/2015
AG Anthony Gose EXCH 5.00 12.00
BH Bryce Harper 100.00 200.00
DH Danny Hultzen 6.00 15.00
GC Gerrit Cole 15.00 40.00
JP Joe Panik 12.50 30.00
JS Jean Segura 5.00 12.00
MA Matt Adams 8.00 20.00
MC Michael Choice 5.00 12.00
NA Nolan Arenado 60.00 150.00

2012 Bowman Platinum Jumbo Relic Autograph Blue Refractors
*BLUE: .6X TO 1.5X BASIC
STATED ODDS 1:258 HOBBY
STATED PRINT RUN 199 SER.#'d SETS
EXCHANGE DEADLINE 06/30/2015

2012 Bowman Platinum Jumbo Relic Autograph Gold Refractors
*GOLD: 1.2X TO 3X BASIC
STATED ODDS 1:1025 HOBBY
STATED PRINT RUN 50 SER.#'d SETS
EXCHANGE DEADLINE 06/30/2015
BH Bryce Harper 150.00 300.00

2012 Bowman Platinum Prospect Autographs
STATED ODDS 1:14 HOBBY
PRINTING PLATE ODDS 1:2728 HOBBY
PLATE PRINT RUN 1 SET PER COLOR
BLACK-CYAN-MAGENTA-YELLOW ISSUED
NO PLATE PRICING DUE TO SCARCITY
EXCHANGE DEADLINE 06/30/2015
AR Anthony Rendon 25.00 60.00
ASU Andrew Susac 3.00 8.00
BB Bryan Brickhouse 3.00 8.00
BJ Brandon Jacobs 4.00 10.00
BS Bubba Starling EXCH 4.00 10.00
CC Carter Capps 3.00 8.00
CH Clay Holmes 3.00 8.00
CT Charlie Tilson 3.00 8.00
DB Dylan Bundy 10.00 25.00
DBU David Buchanan 3.00 8.00
DC Daniel Corcino 3.00 8.00
DH Danny Hultzen 3.00 8.00
DM Dillon Maples 3.00 8.00
DN Daniel Norris 4.00 10.00
DNO Derek Norris EXCH 3.00 8.00
EA Eric Arce 3.00 8.00
GB Greg Bird 15.00 40.00
GC Gerrit Cole 10.00 25.00
GP Guillermo Pimentel EXCH 3.00 8.00
JB Josh Bell 8.00 20.00
JG Jonathan Galvez 3.00 8.00
JM Jermaine Mitchell 3.00 8.00
JR Joe Ross 3.00 8.00
JT Joe Terdoslavich 3.00 8.00
KC Kole Calhoun 3.00 8.00
LM Levi Michael 3.00 8.00
MM Mikie Mahtook 3.00 8.00
MP Matt Purke 6.00 15.00
MW Mike Wright 3.00 8.00
OA Oswaldo Arcia 3.00 8.00
RR Robbie Ray 6.00 15.00
TB Trevor Bauer 10.00 25.00
TBK Tyler Bortnick 3.00 8.00
TC Tyler Collins 3.00 8.00
TJ Tyrell Jenkins EXCH 3.00 8.00
TN Telvin Nash 4.00 10.00
TW Taijuan Walker 3.00 8.00
VC Vinnie Catricala 4.00 10.00
YA Yazy Arbelo 3.00 8.00
YC Yoenis Cespedes 12.50 30.00
YD Yu Darvish 30.00 80.00

2012 Bowman Platinum Prospect Autographs Blue Refractors
*BLUE: .6X TO 1.5X BASIC
STATED ODDS 1:145 HOBBY
STATED PRINT RUN 199 SER.#'d SETS
EXCHANGE DEADLINE 06/30/2015

2012 Bowman Platinum Prospect Autographs Gold Refractors
*GOLD: 1X TO 2.5X BASIC
STATED ODDS 1:450 HOBBY
STATED PRINT RUN 50 SER.#'d SETS
EXCHANGE DEADLINE 06/30/2015
DB Dylan Bundy 15.00 40.00
TB Trevor Bauer 20.00 50.00

2012 Bowman Platinum Prospect Autographs Green Refractors
*GREEN: .5X TO 1.2X BASIC
STATED ODDS 1:74 HOBBY
STATED PRINT RUN 399 SER.#'d SETS
EXCHANGE DEADLINE 06/30/2015

2012 Bowman Platinum Prospects
COMPLETE SET (100) 50.00 100.00
PRINTING PLATE ODDS 1:1118 HOBBY
PLATE PRINT RUN 1 SET PER COLOR
BLACK-CYAN-MAGENTA-YELLOW ISSUED
NO PLATE PRICING DUE TO SCARCITY
BPP1 Matt Adams .75 2.00
BPP2 Nolan Arenado 2.50 6.00
BPP3 Manny Banuelos .75 2.00
BPP4 Trevor Bauer 3.00 8.00
BPP5 Chad Bettis .60 1.50
BPP6 Gary Brown .60 1.50
BPP7 Garin Cecchini .75 2.00
BPP8 Michael Choice .60 1.50
BPP9 Travis d'Arnaud .75 2.00
BPP10 Brandon Drury 1.00 2.50
BPP11 Robbie Erlin .75 2.00
BPP12 Wilmer Flores .75 2.00
BPP13 Anthony Gose .75 2.00
BPP14 Robbie Grossman .60 1.50
BPP15 Jedd Gyorko .75 2.00
BPP16 Billy Hamilton .75 2.00
BPP17 Joe Terdoslavich .75 2.00
BPP18 Matt Harvey 4.00 10.00
BPP19 Brett Jackson 1.00 2.50
BPP20 Hak-Ju Lee .60 1.50
BPP21 Taylor Lindsey .60 1.50
BPP22 Rymer Liriano .60 1.50
BPP23 Manny Machado 4.00 10.00
BPP24 Starling Marte .75 2.00
BPP25 Trevor May .60 1.50
BPP26 Will Middlebrooks .75 2.00
BPP27 Shelby Miller 1.25 3.00
BPP28 Mike Montgomery .60 1.50
BPP29 Jake Odorizzi .75 2.00
BPP30 Mike Olt .75 2.00
BPP31 Marcell Ozuna 1.50 4.00
BPP32 Joe Panik 1.00 2.50
BPP33 Wily Peralta .60 1.50
BPP34 Martin Perez 1.00 2.50
BPP35 Jurickson Profar .75 2.00
BPP36 Eddie Rosario 1.25 3.00
BPP37 Keenyn Walker .60 1.50
BPP38 Gary Sanchez 2.00 5.00
BPP39 Miguel Sano .75 2.00
BPP40 Jonathan Schoop .60 1.50
BPP41 Jonathan Singleton .75 2.00
BPP42 Tyler Skaggs 1.00 2.50
BPP43 Alexi Amarista .60 1.50
BPP44 Noah Syndergaard .75 2.00
BPP45 Jameson Taillon .75 2.00
BPP46 Taijuan Walker .75 2.00
BPP47 Allen Webster .75 2.00
BPP48 Zack Wheeler 1.25 3.00
BPP49 Christian Yelich 5.00 12.00
BPP50 Drew Hutchison .75 2.00
BPP51 Oscar Taveras 1.00 2.50
BPP52 A.J. Cole .75 2.00
BPP53 Jake Marisnick .75 2.00
BPP54 Nick Franklin .75 2.00
BPP55 Nestor Molina .60 1.50
BPP56 Jeurys Familia 1.00 2.50
BPP57 Tim Wheeler .75 2.00
BPP58 Jonathan Galvez .60 1.50
BPP59 Vincent Catricala .60 1.50
BPP60 Keyvius Sampson .60 1.50
BPP61 Archie Bradley .40 1.00
BPP62 Brian Dozier 2.00 5.00
BPP63 John Lamb .60 1.50
BPP64 Dylan Bundy 1.25 3.00
BPP65 Jean Segura 1.00 2.50
BPP66 Daniel Corcino .75 2.00
BPP67 Tyler Thornburg .75 2.00
BPP68 Yorman Rodriguez .40 1.00
BPP69 Gerrit Cole 4.00 10.00
BPP70 Tyler Pastornicky .75 2.00
BPP71 Zach Cone .75 2.00
BPP72 Brandon Jacobs .75 2.00
BPP73 Kevin Matthews .60 1.50
BPP74 Jake Hager .60 1.50
BPP75 Sean Buckley .60 1.50
BPP76 Andrelton Simmons 1.00 2.50
BPP77 Julio Rodriguez .60 1.50
BPP78 Sonny Gray 1.00 2.50
BPP79 Jabari Blash .60 1.50
BPP80 Wil Myers 1.00 2.50
BPP81 Jarred Cosart .60 1.50
BPP82 Chris Archer .60 1.50
BPP83 Guillermo Pimentel .60 1.50
BPP84 Tyler Matzek .40 1.00
BPP85 Javier Baez 2.50 6.00
BPP86 Cory Spangenberg .60 1.50
BPP87 John Hellweg .60 1.50
BPP88 Chad James .60 1.50
BPP89 Telvin Nash .60 1.50
BPP90 Mason Williams 1.00 2.50
BPP91 Heath Hembree .75 2.00
BPP92 Bryce Brentz .60 1.50
BPP93 Anthony Ranaudo .75 2.00
BPP94 Tommy Joseph 1.25 3.00
BPP95 Trey McNutt .60 1.50
BPP96 Matt Davidson .75 2.00
BPP97 Nick Castellanos 2.00 5.00
BPP98 Jordan Swagerty .60 1.50
BPP99 Sebastian Valle .60 1.50
BPP100 Bubba Starling .75 2.00

2012 Bowman Platinum Prospects Refractors
*REF: .5X TO 1.2X BASIC
STATED ODDS 1:4 HOBBY

2012 Bowman Platinum Prospects Blue Refractors
*BLUE: 1.2X TO 3X BASIC
STATED ODDS 1:31 HOBBY
STATED PRINT RUN 199 SER.#'d SETS

2012 Bowman Platinum Prospects Gold Refractors
*GOLD: 2.5X TO 6X BASIC
STATED ODDS 1:123 HOBBY
STATED PRINT RUN 50 SER.#'d SETS
BPP51 Oscar Taveras 30.00 60.00

2012 Bowman Platinum Prospects Green Refractors
*GREEN: .6X TO 1.5X BASIC
STATED ODDS 1:16 HOBBY
STATED PRINT RUN 399 SER.#'d SETS

2012 Bowman Platinum Prospects Purple Refractors
*REF: .5X TO 1.2X BASIC

2012 Bowman Platinum Prospects X-Fractors
*X-FRACTORS: .6X TO 1.5X BASIC
STATED ODDS 1:20 HOBBY

2012 Bowman Platinum Prospects Blue National Promo
ISSUED AT 2012 NATIONAL CONVENTION
STATED PRINT RUN 499 SER.#'d SETS
BPP4 Trevor Bauer 8.00 20.00
BPP23 Manny Machado 10.00 25.00
BPP27 Shelby Miller 3.00 8.00
BPP35 Jurickson Profar 2.00 5.00
BPP39 Miguel Sano 2.00 5.00
BPP42 Tyler Skaggs 2.50 6.00
BPP45 Jameson Taillon 2.00 5.00
BPP52 A.J. Cole 2.00 5.00
BPP64 Dylan Bundy 3.00 8.00
BPP69 Gerrit Cole 10.00 25.00
BPP70 Tyler Pastornicky 1.50 4.00
BPP100 Bubba Starling 2.00 5.00

2012 Bowman Platinum Relic Autographs
STATE ODDS 1:43 HOBBY
PRINTING PLATE ODDS 1:3608 HOBBY
PLATE PRINT RUN 1 SET PER COLOR
BLACK-CYAN-MAGENTA-YELLOW ISSUED
NO PLATE PRICING DUE TO SCARCITY
EXCHANGE DEADLINE 06/30/2015
AE Andre Ethier EXCH 6.00 15.00
AG Adrian Gonzalez 8.00 20.00
AR Anthony Rizzo 20.00 50.00
BL Brett Lawrie 4.00 10.00
CG Carlos Gonzalez 8.00 20.00
CM Carlos Martinez 6.00 15.00
DH Daniel Hudson 4.00 10.00
DM Devin Mesoraco 4.00 10.00
DP Dustin Pedroia 20.00 50.00
DU Dan Uggla 5.00 12.00
EH Eric Hosmer 15.00 40.00
FH Felix Hernandez 12.50 30.00
FM Francisco Martinez 6.00 15.00
JB Jay Bruce 8.00 20.00
JD Jaff Decker 4.00 10.00
JJ Jon Jay 4.00 10.00
JM J.D. Martinez 12.00 30.00
JMO Jesus Montero 8.00 20.00
JPX James Paxton 12.00 30.00
JW Jered Weaver EXCH 12.50 30.00
MD Matt Dominguez 4.00 10.00
MM Matt Moore 5.00 12.00
MMS Mike Morse 5.00 12.00
MO Mike Olt 8.00 20.00
MS Matt Szczur 4.00 10.00
MT Mike Trout 200.00 500.00
NC Nelson Cruz 8.00 20.00
PG Paul Goldschmidt 25.00 60.00
RZ Ryan Zimmerman 10.00 25.00
SM Starling Marte 5.00 12.00
TT Tyler Thornburg 5.00 12.00
YD Yu Darvish 125.00 250.00

2012 Bowman Platinum Relic Autographs Blue Refractors
*BLUE: .5X TO 1.2X BASIC
STATED ODDS 1:101 HOBBY
STATED PRINT RUN 199 SER.#'d SETS
EXCHANGE DEADLINE 06/30/2015
MT Mike Trout 250.00 600.00
YD Yu Darvish 150.00 300.00

2012 Bowman Platinum Relic Autographs Gold Refractors
*GOLD: .75X TO 2X BASIC
STATED ODDS 1:297 HOBBY
STATED PRINT RUN 50 SER.#'d SETS
EXCHANGE DEADLINE 06/30/2015
AG Adrian Gonzalez 10.00 25.00
DP Dustin Pedroia 30.00 60.00
MT Mike Trout 400.00 1000.00
SC Starlin Castro 20.00 50.00
YD Yu Darvish 250.00 350.00

2012 Bowman Platinum Top Prospects
STATED ODDS 1:5 HOBBY
AG Anthony Gose .75 2.00
BB Bryce Brentz .60 1.50
BD Brian Dozier 2.00 5.00
BH Billy Hamilton .75 2.00
BJ Brett Jackson 1.00 2.50
BS Bubba Starling .75 2.00
CS Cory Spangenberg .60 1.50
CY Christian Yelich 5.00 12.00
ER Eddie Rosario 1.25 3.00
GB Gary Brown .60 1.50
GC Gerrit Cole 4.00 10.00
JG Jedd Gyorko .75 2.00
JL John Lamb .60 1.50
JM Jake Marisnick .75 2.00
JP Jurickson Profar .75 2.00
JR Julio Rodriguez .60 1.50
JS Jean Segura 1.00 2.50
JT Jameson Taillon .75 2.00
KS Keyvius Sampson .60 1.50
MA Matt Adams .75 2.00
MB Manny Banuelos .75 2.00
MC Michael Choice .60 1.50
MH Matt Harvey 4.00 10.00
MM Manny Machado 4.00 10.00
MS Miguel Sano .75 2.00
MW Mason Williams 1.00 2.50
NA Nolan Arenado 2.50 6.00
NC Nick Castellanos 2.00 5.00
NS Noah Syndergaard .75 2.00
OT Oscar Taveras 1.00 2.50
RE Robbie Erlin .75 2.00
RL Rymer Liriano .60 1.50
SM Shelby Miller 1.25 3.00
TB Trevor Bauer 3.00 8.00
Td Travis d'Arnaud .75 2.00
TL Taylor Lindsey .60 1.50
TM Trevor May .60 1.50
TS Tyler Skaggs 1.00 2.50
TT Tyler Thornburg .75 2.00
TW Tim Wheeler .75 2.00
VC Vincent Catricala .60 1.50
WM Wil Myers 1.00 2.50
ZW Zack Wheeler 1.25 3.00
JGZ Jonathan Galvez .60 1.50
JPK Joe Panik 1.00 2.50
JSN Jonathan Singleton .75 2.00
JSW Jordan Swagerty .60 1.50
SME Starling Marte .75 2.00
TJW Taijuan Walker .75 2.00
WMK Will Middlebrooks .75 2.00

2013 Bowman Platinum
COMPLETE SET (100) 15.00 40.00
STATED PLATE ODDS 1:1490 HOBBY
PLATE PRINT RUN 1 SET PER COLOR
BLACK-CYAN-MAGENTA-YELLOW ISSUED
NO PLATE PRICING DUE TO SCARCITY
1 Albert Pujols .30 .75
2 Mike Trout 2.00 5.00
3 Jered Weaver .20 .50
4 Norichika Aoki .15 .40
5 Jacoby Ellsbury .20 .50
6 Jose Bautista .20 .50
7 Adam Wainwright .30 .75
8 David Freese .15 .40
9 Ryan Braun .20 .50
10 Yoenis Cespedes .25 .60
11 Paul Goldschmidt .40 1.00
12 Evan Gattis RC .60 1.50
13 Mark Trumbo .25 .60
14 Yadier Molina .30 .75
15 Carl Crawford .20 .50
16 Starlin Castro .15 .40
17 Ryan Howard .30 .75
18 Anthony Rizzo .30 .75
19 Justin Upton .30 .75
20 Matt Kemp .20 .50
21 Aaron Hicks RC .50 1.25
22 Adrian Gonzalez .30 .75
23 Clayton Kershaw .40 1.00
24 Alfredo Marte RC .30 .75
25 Chase Utley .30 .75
26 Edwin Encarnacion .40 1.00
27 Matt Cain .20 .50
28 Buster Posey .50 1.25
29 Mariano Rivera .50 1.25
30 Brandon Maurer RC .40 1.00
31 Felix Hernandez .20 .50
32 Oswaldo Arcia RC .30 .75
33 Josh Reddick .15 .40
34 Jose Reyes .20 .50
35 Giancarlo Stanton .25 .60
36 David Wright .20 .50
37 R.A. Dickey .20 .50
38 Michael Young .15 .40
39 Bryce Harper .40 1.00
40 Stephen Strasburg .25 .60
41 Gio Gonzalez .20 .50
42 Manny Machado RC 2.00 5.00
43 Adam Jones .20 .50
44 Jarrod Parker .15 .40
45 Cliff Lee .20 .50
46 Chase Headley .15 .40
47 Carlos Ruiz .15 .40
48 Cole Hamels .20 .50
49 Mike Olt RC .60 1.50
50 Rob Brantly RC .30 .75
51 Andrew McCutchen .25 .60
52 Kris Medlen .20 .50
53 Freddie Freeman .30 .75
54 Josh Hamilton .20 .50
55 Adrian Beltre .25 .60
56 Yu Darvish .25 .60
57 Adam Eaton RC .50 1.25
58 David Price .20 .50
59 Evan Longoria .20 .50
60 Will Middlebrooks .15 .40
61 Dustin Pedroia .25 .60
62 Tony Cingrani RC .60 1.50
63 Jason Heyward .20 .50
64 Joey Votto .25 .60
65 Shelby Miller RC 1.25 3.00
66 Salvador Perez .20 .50
67 Aroldis Chapman .25 .60
68 Johnny Cueto .20 .50
69 Troy Tulowitzki .25 .60
70 Carlos Gonzalez .20 .50
71 Tim Lincecum .20 .50
72 Billy Butler .15 .40
73 Justin Verlander .25 .60
74 Jake Odorizzi RC .60 1.50
75 Prince Fielder .20 .50
76 Miguel Cabrera .25 .60
77 Joe Mauer .20 .50
78 Robinson Cano .20 .50
79 Tyler Skaggs RC .50 1.25
80 Adeiny Hechavarria RC .60 1.50
81 Derek Jeter .60 1.50
82 Alex Rodriguez .30 .75
83 CC Sabathia .20 .50
84 Jackie Bradley Jr. RC .75 2.00
85 Jose Fernandez RC 1.25 3.00
86 Jeurys Familia RC .50 1.25
87 Trevor Rosenthal RC 1.00 2.50
88 Didi Gregorius RC 1.25 3.00
89 Kevin Youkilis .15 .40
90 Jedd Gyorko RC .60 1.50
91 Darin Ruf RC 1.00 2.50
92 Paul Konerko .20 .50
93 Pablo Sandoval .20 .50
94 Paco Rodriguez RC .50 1.25
95 Carlos Beltran .20 .50
96 Hyun-Jin Ryu RC 1.25 3.00
97 Chris Sale .25 .60
98 Avisail Garcia RC .60 1.50
99 Dylan Bundy RC .75 2.00
100 Jurickson Profar RC .60 1.50

2013 Bowman Platinum Gold
*GOLD: 1.5X TO 4X BASIC
*GOLD RC: .75X TO 2X BASIC RC
STATED ODDS 1:5 HOBBY

2013 Bowman Platinum Ruby
*RUBY: 2.5X TO 6X BASIC
*RUBY RC: 1.2X TO 3X BASIC RC
STATED ODDS 1:20 HOBBY

2013 Bowman Platinum Sapphire
*SAPPHIRE: 2X TO 5X BASIC
*SAPPHIRE RC: 1X TO 2.5X BASIC RC
STATED ODDS 1:10 HOBBY

2013 Bowman Platinum Cutting Edge Stars
STATED ODDS 1:10 HOBBY
AD Raul Mondesi .60 1.50
AJ Adam Jones .50 1.25
AM Andrew McCutchen .60 1.50
AP Albert Pujols .75 2.00
AR Anthony Rendon 2.50 6.00
BH Bryce Harper 1.00 2.50
BP Buster Posey .75 2.00
CC C.J. Cron .50 1.25
CG Carlos Gonzalez .50 1.25
CK Clayton Kershaw 1.00 2.50
CSA Chris Sale .60 1.50
DB Dylan Bundy 1.00 2.50
DD David Dahl .50 1.25
DJ Derek Jeter 1.50 4.00
DW David Wright .50 1.25
EL Evan Longoria .50 1.25
FH Felix Hernandez .50 1.25
FL Francisco Lindor 3.00 8.00
GG Gio Gonzalez .50 1.25
GS George Springer 1.50 4.00
GST Giancarlo Stanton .60 1.50
HR Hanley Ramirez .50 1.25
JB Jose Bautista .50 1.25
JH Jeremy Hellickson .40 1.00
JK Jason Kipnis .50 1.25
JM Joe Mauer .50 1.25
JP Jurickson Profar .50 1.25
JS James Shields .40 1.00
JT Julio Teheran .50 1.25
JV Joey Votto .60 1.50
JVE Justin Verlander .60 1.50
JW Jered Weaver .50 1.25
KZ Kyle Zimmer .50 1.25
MB Matt Barnes .50 1.25
MC Miguel Cabrera .60 1.50
MK Matt Kemp .50 1.25
MM Manny Machado 2.50 6.00
MR Mariano Rivera .75 2.00
MT Mark Trumbo .40 1.00
MTR Mike Trout 5.00 12.00
MZ Mike Zunino .60 1.50
NC Nick Castellanos 1.25 3.00
PF Prince Fielder .50 1.25
RB Ryan Braun .50 1.25
RC Robinson Cano .50 1.25
SS Stephen Strasburg .60 1.50
YC Yoenis Cespedes .60 1.50
YD Yu Darvish .60 1.50
YG Yovani Gallardo .40 1.00
YP Yasiel Puig 1.50 4.00

2013 Bowman Platinum Cutting Edge Stars Relics
STATED ODDS 1:626 HOBBY
STATED PRINT RUN 50 SER.#'d SETS
AJ Adam Jones 8.00 20.00
AM Andrew McCutchen 8.00 20.00
AR Anthony Rendon 10.00 25.00
BH Bryce Harper 15.00 40.00
BP Buster Posey 12.50 30.00
CS Chris Sale 6.00 15.00
DB Dylan Bundy 6.00 15.00
DJ Derek Jeter 15.00 40.00
FH Felix Hernandez 4.00 10.00
GG Gio Gonzalez 4.00 10.00
GS Giancarlo Stanton 8.00 20.00
JB Jose Bautista 10.00 25.00
JV Justin Verlander 8.00 20.00
JVO Joey Votto 6.00 15.00
JW Jered Weaver 4.00 10.00
MC Miguel Cabrera 12.50 30.00
MK Matt Kemp 6.00 15.00
MR Mariano Rivera 8.00 20.00
MT Mike Trout 20.00 50.00
PF Prince Fielder 10.00 25.00
RB Ryan Braun 4.00 10.00
RC Robinson Cano 10.00 25.00
SS Stephen Strasburg 10.00 25.00
YC Yoenis Cespedes 6.00 15.00
YD Yu Darvish 6.00 15.00

2013 Bowman Platinum Diamonds in the Rough
STATED ODDS 1:20 HOBBY
AA Arismendy Alcantara .60 1.50
BV Breyvic Valera .50 1.25
CE C.J. Edwards .60 1.50
CT Carlos Tocci .40 1.00
DH Dilson Herrera 1.25 3.00
HA Hanser Alberto .40 1.00
HR Hansel Robles .40 1.00
IG Ismael Guillon .40 1.00
JJ Jin-De Jhang .40 1.00
JP Jorge Polanco 1.00 2.50
LM Luis Merejo .40 1.00
MH Marco Hernandez .40 1.00
MS Michael Snyder .40 1.00
WH Wade Hinkle .40 1.00
WR Wilfredo Rodriguez .40 1.00

2013 Bowman Platinum Diamonds in the Rough Autographs
STATED ODDS 1:2095 HOBBY
STATED PRINT RUN 50 SER.#'d SETS
EXCHANGE DEADLINE 07/31/2016
CE C.J. Edwards 20.00 50.00
CT Carlos Tocci EXCH 30.00 60.00
DH Dilson Herrera 20.00 50.00
IG Ismael Guillon EXCH 30.00 60.00
JJ Jin-De Jhang EXCH 40.00 80.00
JP Jorge Polanco 30.00 60.00
LM Luis Merejo EXCH 15.00 40.00

2013 Bowman Platinum Jumbo Relic Autographs Blue Refractors
*BLUE REF: .5X TO 1.2X BASIC
STATED ODDS 1:388 HOBBY
STATED PRINT RUN 199 SER.#'d SETS
EXCHANGE DEADLINE 07/31/2016

2013 Bowman Platinum Jumbo Relic Autographs Gold Refractors
*GOLD REF: 1.2X TO 3X BASIC
STATED ODDS 1:1775 HOBBY
STATED PRINT RUN 50 SER.#'d SETS
PRICING FOR BASIC PATCHES
PREMIUM PATCHES MAY SELL FOR MORE
EXCHANGE DEADLINE 07/31/2016

2013 Bowman Platinum Jumbo Relic Autographs Refractors
STATED ODDS 1:243 HOBBY
STATED PLATE ODDS 1:21,282 HOBBY
PLATE PRINT RUN 1 SET PER COLOR
BLACK-CYAN-MAGENTA-YELLOW ISSUED
NO PLATE PRICING DUE TO SCARCITY
EXCHANGE DEADLINE 07/31/2016
AG Avisail Garcia 6.00 15.00
AR Anthony Rendon 12.00 30.00
GS George Springer 12.00 30.00
HL Hak-Ju Lee 4.00 10.00
JS Jonathan Singleton 5.00 12.00
MD Matt Davidson 5.00 12.00
PL Patrick Leonard 4.00 10.00
TC Tyler Collins 4.00 10.00

2013 Bowman Platinum Prospect Autographs
STATED ODDS 1:14 HOBBY
STATED PLATE ODDS 1:4026 HOBBY
PLATE PRINT RUN 1 SET PER COLOR
BLACK-CYAN-MAGENTA-YELLOW ISSUED
NO PLATE PRICING DUE TO SCARCITY
EXCHANGE DEADLINE 07/31/2016
AC Adam Conley 3.00 8.00
AM Anthony Meo 3.00 8.00
AR Addison Russell 10.00 25.00
BB Byron Buxton 12.00 30.00
BL Barret Loux 3.00 8.00
BT Beau Taylor 3.00 8.00
CC Carlos Correa 25.00 60.00
CM Carlos Martinez 6.00 15.00
DD David Dahl 5.00 12.00
DP Dorssys Paulino 3.00 8.00
DS Danny Salazar 3.00 8.00
JA Jorge Alfaro 4.00 10.00
JAM Jeff Ames 3.00 8.00
JB Jose Berrios 6.00 15.00
JBI Jesse Biddle 3.00 8.00
JG J.R. Graham 3.00 8.00
JH John Hellweg 3.00 8.00
KD Keury de la Cruz 3.00 8.00
LM Luis Mateo 3.00 8.00
LMC Lance McCullers 3.00 8.00
MF Maikel Franco 5.00 10.00
MK Max Kepler 4.00 10.00
MKI Michael Kickham 3.00 8.00
MM Matt Magill 3.00 8.00
MO Marcell Ozuna 3.00 8.00
MON Mike O'Neill 3.00 8.00
MS Miguel Sano 3.00 8.00
MZ Mike Zunino 3.00 8.00
NA Nick Ahmed 3.00 8.00
NR Nate Roberts 3.00 8.00
OC Orlando Calixte 3.00 8.00
PO Peter O'Brien 5.00 12.00
RO Rougned Odor 6.00 15.00
SD Shawon Dunston Jr. 3.00 8.00
TM Trevor May 3.00 8.00
TS Tayler Scott 3.00 8.00
WS Will Swanner 3.00 8.00

2013 Bowman Platinum Prospect Autographs Blue Refractors
*BLUE REF: .6X TO 1.5X BASIC
STATED ODDS 1:142 HOBBY
STATED PRINT RUN 199 SER.#'d SETS
EXCHANGE DEADLINE 07/31/2016

2013 Bowman Platinum Prospect Autographs Gold Refractors
*GOLD REF: .75X TO 2X BASIC
STATED ODDS 1:565 HOBBY
STATED PRINT RUN 50 SER.#'d SETS
EXCHANGE DEADLINE 07/31/2016
JA Jorge Alfaro 8.00 20.00
JBI Jesse Biddle 15.00 40.00

2013 Bowman Platinum Prospect Autographs Green Refractors
*GREEN REF: .5X TO 1.2X BASIC
STATED ODDS 1:69 HOBBY
STATED PRINT RUN 399 SER.#'d SETS
EXCHANGE DEADLINE 07/31/2016

2013 Bowman Platinum Prospects
STATED PLATE ODDS 1:1490 HOBBY
PLATE PRINT RUN 1 SET PER COLOR
BLACK-CYAN-MAGENTA-YELLOW ISSUED
NO PLATE PRICING DUE TO SCARCITY
EXCHANGE DEADLINE 07/31/2016
BPP1 Oscar Taveras .30 .75
BPP2 Travis d'Arnaud .30 .75
BPP3 Lewis Brinson .30 .75
BPP4 Gerrit Cole 1.50 4.00
BPP5 Zack Wheeler .50 1.25
BPP6 Wil Myers .40 1.00
BPP7 Miguel Sano .30 .75
BPP8 Xander Bogaerts .75 2.00
BPP9 Billy Hamilton .30 .75
BPP10 Javier Baez 1.00 2.50
BPP11 Mike Zunino .40 1.00
BPP12 Christian Yelich 2.00 5.00
BPP13 Taijuan Walker .30 .75
BPP14 Jameson Taillon .30 .75
BPP15 Nick Castellanos .75 2.00
BPP16 Archie Bradley .25 .60
BPP17 Danny Hultzen .30 .75
BPP18 Taylor Guerrieri .25 .60
BPP19 Byron Buxton 1.25 3.00
BPP20 David Dahl .30 .75
BPP21 Francisco Lindor 2.00 5.00
BPP22 Bubba Starling .30 .75
BPP23 Carlos Correa 3.00 8.00
BPP24 Jonathan Singleton .30 .75
BPP25 Anthony Rendon 1.50 4.00
BPP26 Gregory Polanco .50 1.25
BPP27 Carlos Martinez .40 1.00
BPP28 Jorge Soler .50 1.25
BPP29 Matt Barnes .30 .75
BPP30 Kevin Gausman .75 2.00
BPP31 Albert Almora .50 1.25
BPP32 Alen Hanson .30 .75
BPP33 Addison Russell .40 1.00
BPP34 Gary Sanchez .75 2.00
BPP35 Noah Syndergaard .30 .75
BPP36 Victor Roache .30 .75
BPP37 Mason Williams .30 .75
BPP38 George Springer 1.00 2.50
BPP39 Aaron Sanchez .30 .75
BPP40 Nolan Arenado 2.50 6.00
BPP41 Corey Seager 1.25 3.00
BPP42 Kyle Zimmer .30 .75
BPP43 Tyler Austin .40 1.00
BPP44 Kyle Crick .40 1.00
BPP45 Robert Stephenson .25 .60
BPP46 Joc Pederson .60 1.50
BPP47 Brian Goodwin .30 .75
BPP48 Kaleb Cowart .30 .75
BPP49A Yasiel Puig 1.00 2.50
NCA49 Yasiel Puig AU 250.00 500.00
BPP50 Mike Piazza .25 .60
BPP51 Alex Meyer .25 .60
BPP52 Jake Marisnick .30 .75
BPP53 Lucas Sims .30 .75
BPP54 Brad Miller .30 .75
BPP55 Max Fried 1.00 2.50
BPP56 Eddie Rosario .50 1.25
BPP57 Justin Nicolino .25 .60
BPP58 Cody Buckel .25 .60
BPP59 Jesse Biddle .30 .75
BPP60 James Paxton .30 .75
BPP61 Allen Webster .30 .75
BPP62 Kyle Gibson .40 1.00
BPP63 Nick Franklin .30 .75
BPP64 Dorssys Paulino .30 .75
BPP65 Courtney Hawkins .25 .60
BPP66 Delino DeShields .25 .60
BPP67 Joey Gallo .75 2.00
BPP68 Hak-Ju Lee .25 .60
BPP69 Kolten Wong .25 .60
BPP70 Renato Nunez .50 1.25
BPP71 Michael Choice .25 .60
BPP72 Luis Heredia .30 .75
BPP73 C.J. Cron .30 .75
BPP74 Lucas Giolito .40 1.00
BPP75 Daniel Vogelbach .40 1.00
BPP76 Austin Hedges .30 .75
BPP77 Matt Davidson .30 .75
BPP78 Gary Brown .25 .60
BPP79 Daniel Corcino .25 .60
BPP80 D.J. Davis .30 .75
BPP81 Victor Sanchez .30 .75
BPP82 Joe Ross .25 .60
BPP83 Joe Panik .40 1.00
BPP84 Jose Berrios .40 1.00
BPP85 Trevor Story 1.25 3.00
BPP86 Stefen Romero .25 .60
BPP87 Andrew Heaney .30 .75
BPP88 Mark Montgomery .40 1.00
BPP89 Deven Marrero .25 .60
BPP90 Marcell Ozuna .60 1.50
BPP91 Michael Wacha .30 .75
BPP92 Gavin Cecchini .30 .75
BPP93 Richie Shaffer .25 .60
BPP94 Ty Hensley .30 .75
BPP95 Nick Williams .30 .75
BPP96 Tyrone Taylor .25 .60
BPP97 Christian Bethancourt .40 1.00
BPP98 Roman Quinn .40 1.00
BPP99 Luis Sardinas .25 .60
BPP100 Jonathan Schoop .25 .60

2013 Bowman Platinum Chrome Prospects Refractors
*REFRACTORS: .75X TO 2X BASIC
STATED ODDS 1:4 HOBBY

2013 Bowman Platinum Chrome Prospects Blue Refractors
*BLUE REF: 2.5X TO 6X BASIC
STATED ODDS 1:39 HOBBY
STATED PRINT RUN 199 SER.#'d SETS

2013 Bowman Platinum Chrome Prospects Gold Refractors
*GOLD REF: 8X TO 20X BASIC
STATED ODDS 1:157 HOBBY
STATED PRINT RUN 50 SER.#'d SETS
BPCP19 Byron Buxton 40.00 80.00

2013 Bowman Platinum Chrome Prospects Green Refractors
*GREEN REF: 2X TO 5X BASIC
STATED ODDS 1:20 HOBBY
STATED PRINT RUN 399 SER.#'d SETS

2013 Bowman Platinum Chrome Prospects Purple Refractors
*PURPLE REF: 1X TO 2.5X BASIC

2013 Bowman Platinum Chrome Prospects X-Fractors
*X-FRACTOR: 1.2X TO 3X BASIC
STATED ODDS 1:20 HOBBY

2013 Bowman Platinum Relic Autographs
STATED ODDS 1:43 HOBBY
STATED PLATE ODDS 1:3464 HOBBY
PLATE PRINT RUN 1 SET PER COLOR
BLACK-CYAN-MAGENTA-YELLOW ISSUED
NO PLATE PRICING DUE TO SCARCITY
EXCHANGE DEADLINE 07/31/2016
AG Anthony Gose 4.00 10.00
BH Billy Hamilton 4.00 10.00
BHA Bryce Harper 200.00 300.00
BM Brad Miller 5.00 12.00
CB Christian Bethancourt 6.00 15.00
CO Chris Owings 4.00 10.00
CS Cory Spangenberg 4.00 10.00
CY Christian Yelich 6.00 150.00
DB Dylan Bundy 10.00 25.00
DHU Danny Hultzen 4.00 10.00
GB Gary Brown 4.00 10.00
GC Gerrit Cole 20.00 50.00
HR Hyun-Jin Ryu EXCH 20.00 50.00
JC Jarred Cosart 4.00 10.00
JF Jeurys Familia 4.00 10.00
JM Jake Marisnick 4.00 10.00
JMO Julio Morban 4.00 10.00
JP Joe Panik 12.00 30.00
JPA James Paxton 4.00 10.00
JPR Jurickson Profar 6.00 15.00
KW Kolten Wong 4.00 10.00
MB Matt Barnes 4.00 10.00
MC Michael Choice 4.00 10.00
MD Matt Davidson 4.00 10.00
MM Manny Machado EXCH 15.00 40.00
MO Mike Olt 4.00 10.00
MS Matt Skole 4.00 10.00
MZ Mike Zunino 4.00 10.00
NA Nolan Arenado 60.00 150.00
NC Nick Castellanos 10.00 25.00
NF Nick Franklin EXCH 5.00 12.00
OA Oswaldo Arcia 4.00 10.00
OT Oscar Taveras 5.00 12.00
RS Richie Shaffer 4.00 10.00
SH Slade Heathcott 6.00 15.00
TB Trevor Bauer 4.00 10.00
TC Tony Cingrani 8.00 20.00
WM Will Middlebrooks 6.00 15.00
WMY Wil Myers 20.00 50.00
YD Yu Darvish 60.00 120.00
YV Yordano Ventura 6.00 15.00
ZW Zack Wheeler 4.00 10.00

2013 Bowman Platinum Relic Autographs Blue Refractors
*BLUE REF: .5X TO 1.2X BASIC
STATED ODDS 1:77 HOBBY
STATED PRINT RUN 199 SER.#'d SETS
EXCHANGE DEADLINE 07/31/2016

2013 Bowman Platinum Relic Autographs Gold Refractors
*GOLD REF: 1X TO 2.5X BASIC
STATED ODDS 1:306 HOBBY
STATED PRINT RUN 50 SER.#'d SETS
EXCHANGE DEADLINE 07/31/2016
BM Brad Miller 25.00 60.00
CB Christian Bethancourt 25.00 60.00
MD Matt Davidson 20.00 50.00
MM Manny Machado EXCH 30.00 80.00
NC Nick Castellanos 20.00 50.00
NF Nick Franklin EXCH 20.00 50.00
WMY Wil Myers 40.00 80.00

2013 Bowman Platinum Top Prospects
STATED ODDS 1:5 HOBBY
AA Albert Almora .60 1.50
AB Archie Bradley .30 .75
AH Alen Hanson .40 1.00
AM Alex Meyer .30 .75
AR Anthony Rendon 2.00 5.00
ARU Addison Russell .50 1.25
BB Byron Buxton 1.50 4.00
BG Brian Goodwin .40 1.00
BH Billy Hamilton .40 1.00
BS Bubba Starling .40 1.00
CB Cody Buckel .30 .75
CC Carlos Correa 4.00 10.00
CH Courtney Hawkins .30 .75
CS Corey Seager 1.50 4.00
CY Christian Yelich 2.50 6.00
DD David Dahl .40 1.00
DP Dorssys Paulino .40 1.00
DV Daniel Vogelbach .50 1.25
FL Francisco Lindor 2.50 6.00
GC Gerrit Cole 2.00 5.00
GP Gregory Polanco .60 1.50
GS Gary Sanchez 1.00 2.50
GSP George Springer 1.25 3.00
JB Javier Baez 1.25 3.00
JF Jose Fernandez .75 2.00
JG Joey Gallo 1.00 2.50
JP Joc Pederson .75 2.00
JS Jonathan Singleton .40 1.00
JSO Jorge Soler .60 1.50
JT Jameson Taillon .40 1.00
KC Kaleb Cowart .40 1.00
KG Kevin Gausman 1.00 2.50
KW Kolten Wong .30 .75
MB Matt Barnes .40 1.00
MS Miguel Sano .40 1.00
MW Mason Williams .40 1.00
MZ Mike Zunino .50 1.25
NA Nolan Arenado 3.00 8.00
NC Nick Castellanos 1.00 2.50
NS Noah Syndergaard .40 1.00
OA Oswaldo Arcia .30 .75
OT Oscar Taveras .40 1.00
TA Tyler Austin .50 1.25
TD Travis d'Arnaud .40 1.00
TG Taylor Guerrieri .30 .75
TW Taijuan Walker .40 1.00
WM Wil Myers .50 1.25
XB Xander Bogaerts 1.00 2.50
YP Yasiel Puig 1.25 3.00
ZW Zack Wheeler .60 1.50

2013 Bowman Platinum Orange National Convention
COMPLETE SET (100) 150.00 400.00
ISSUED AT THE 2013 NSCC IN CHICAGO
STATED PRINT RUN 125 SER.#'d SETS
NC1 Oscar Taveras 1.25 3.00
NC2 Travis d'Arnaud 1.25 3.00
NC3 Lewis Brinson 1.25 3.00
NC4 Gerrit Cole 6.00 15.00
NC5 Zack Wheeler 2.00 5.00
NC6 Wil Myers 1.50 4.00
NC7 Miguel Sano 1.25 3.00
NC8 Xander Bogaerts 3.00 8.00
NC9 Billy Hamilton 1.25 3.00
NC10 Javier Baez 4.00 10.00
NC11 Mike Zunino 1.50 4.00
NC12 Christian Yelich 8.00 20.00
NC13 Taijuan Walker 1.25 3.00
NC14 Jameson Taillon 1.25 3.00
NC15 Nick Castellanos 3.00 8.00
NC16 Archie Bradley 1.00 2.50
NC17 Danny Hultzen 1.25 3.00
NC18 Taylor Guerrieri 1.00 2.50
NC19 Byron Buxton 12.50 30.00
NC20 David Dahl 1.25 3.00
NC21 Francisco Lindor 8.00 20.00
NC22 Bubba Starling 1.25 3.00
NC23 Carlos Correa 12.50 30.00
NC24 Jonathan Singleton 1.25 3.00
NC25 Anthony Rendon 6.00 15.00
NC26 Gregory Polanco 2.00 5.00
NC27 Carlos Martinez 1.50 4.00
NC28 Jorge Soler 2.00 5.00
NC29 Matt Barnes 1.25 3.00
NC30 Kevin Gausman 3.00 8.00
NC31 Albert Almora 2.00 5.00
NC32 Alen Hanson 1.25 3.00
NC33 Addison Russell 1.50 4.00
NC34 Gary Sanchez 3.00 8.00
NC35 Noah Syndergaard 1.25 3.00
NC36 Victor Roache 1.25 3.00
NC37 Mason Williams 1.25 3.00
NC38 George Springer 4.00 10.00
NC39 Aaron Sanchez 1.25 3.00
NC40 Nolan Arenado 10.00 25.00
NC41 Corey Seager 5.00 12.00
NC42 Kyle Zimmer 1.25 3.00
NC43 Tyler Austin 1.50 4.00
NC44 Kyle Crick 1.50 4.00
NC45 Robert Stephenson 1.00 2.50
NC46 Joc Pederson 2.50 6.00
NC47 Brian Goodwin 1.25 3.00
NC48 Kaleb Cowart 1.25 3.00
NC49 Yasiel Puig 60.00 120.00
NC50 Mike Piazza 1.00 2.50
NC51 Alex Meyer 1.00 2.50
NC52 Jake Marisnick 1.25 3.00
NC53 Lucas Sims 1.25 3.00
NC54 Brad Miller 1.25 3.00
NC55 Max Fried 4.00 10.00
NC56 Eddie Rosario 2.00 5.00
NC57 Justin Nicolino 1.00 2.50
NC58 Cody Buckel 1.00 2.50
NC59 Jesse Biddle 1.25 3.00
NC60 James Paxton 1.25 3.00
NC61 Allen Webster 1.25 3.00
NC62 Kyle Gibson 1.50 4.00
NC63 Nick Franklin 1.25 3.00
NC64 Dorssys Paulino 1.25 3.00
NC65 Courtney Hawkins 1.00 2.50
NC66 Delino DeShields 1.00 2.50
NC67 Joey Gallo 3.00 8.00
NC68 Hak-Ju Lee 1.00 2.50
NC69 Kolten Wong 1.00 2.50
NC70 Renato Nunez 2.00 5.00
NC71 Michael Choice 1.00 2.50
NC72 Luis Heredia 1.25 3.00
NC73 C.J. Cron 1.25 3.00
NC74 Lucas Giolito 1.50 4.00
NC75 Daniel Vogelbach 1.50 4.00
NC76 Austin Hedges 1.25 3.00
NC77 Matt Davidson 1.25 3.00
NC78 Gary Brown 1.00 2.50
NC79 Daniel Corcino 1.00 2.50
NC80 D.J. Davis 1.25 3.00
NC81 Victor Sanchez 1.25 3.00
NC82 Joe Ross 1.00 2.50
NC83 Joe Panik 1.50 4.00
NC84 Jose Berrios 1.50 4.00
NC85 Trevor Story 5.00 12.00
NC86 Stefen Romero 1.00 2.50
NC87 Andrew Heaney 1.25 3.00
NC88 Mark Montgomery 1.50 4.00
NC89 Deven Marrero 1.00 2.50
NC90 Marcell Ozuna 2.50 6.00
NC91 Michael Wacha 1.25 3.00
NC92 Gavin Cecchini 1.25 3.00
NC93 Richie Shaffer 1.00 2.50
NC94 Ty Hensley 1.25 3.00
NC95 Nick Williams 1.25 3.00
NC96 Tyrone Taylor 1.00 2.50
NC97 Christian Bethancourt 1.50 4.00
NC98 Roman Quinn 1.50 4.00
NC99 Luis Sardinas 1.00 2.50
NC100 Jonathan Schoop 1.00 2.50

2014 Bowman Platinum
COMPLETE SET (100) 15.00 40.00
PLATE PRINT RUN 1 SET PER COLOR
BLACK-CYAN-MAGENTA-YELLOW ISSUED
NO PLATE PRICING DUE TO SCARCITY
1 Taijuan Walker .15 .40
2 Mike Trout 1.25 3.00
3 Andrew McCutchen .25 .60
4 Josh Donaldson .20 .50
5 Carlos Gomez .15 .40
6 Miguel Cabrera .25 .60
7 Matt Carpenter .25 .60
8 Evan Longoria .20 .50
9 Chris Davis .15 .40
10 Paul Goldschmidt .25 .60
11 Manny Machado .25 .60
12 Clayton Kershaw .40 1.00
13 Max Scherzer .25 .60
14 Anibal Sanchez .15 .40
15 Adam Wainwright .20 .50
16 Matt Harvey .20 .50
17 Felix Hernandez .20 .50
18 Cliff Lee .20 .50
19 Chris Sale .25 .60
20 Yu Darvish .25 .60
21 Joey Votto .25 .60
22 Robinson Cano .20 .50
23 David Wright .20 .50
24 Troy Tulowitzki .25 .60
25 David Price .20 .50
26 Stephen Strasburg .25 .60
27 James Shields .15 .40
28 Buster Posey .30 .75
29 Carlos Santana .20 .50
30 Jason Heyward .20 .50
31 Giancarlo Stanton .25 .60
32 Pablo Sandoval .20 .50
33 Jose Bautista .20 .50
34 CC Sabathia .20 .50
35 Hisashi Iwakuma .20 .50
36 Jose Fernandez .25 .60
37 Yasiel Puig .25 .60
38 Adrian Beltre .25 .60
39 Carlos Gonzalez .20 .50
40 Bryce Harper .40 1.00
41 Madison Bumgarner .20 .50
42 Cole Hamels .20 .50
43 Jon Lester .20 .50
44 Matt Moore .20 .50
45 Hanley Ramirez .20 .50
46 Dustin Pedroia .25 .60
47 Ryan Braun .20 .50
48 Yadier Molina .30 .75
49 Freddie Freeman .30 .75
50 Danny Salazar .20 .50
51 Tony Cingrani .20 .50
52 Gio Gonzalez .20 .50
53 Jacoby Ellsbury .20 .50
54 Salvador Perez .20 .50
55 Jason Kipnis .20 .50
56 Jean Segura .20 .50
57 Zack Greinke .25 .60
58 Francisco Liriano .15 .40
59 Zack Wheeler .20 .50
60 Matt Cain .20 .50
61 Mat Latos .20 .50
62 Craig Kimbrel .20 .50
63 Aroldis Chapman .25 .60
64 Jose Reyes .20 .50
65 Edwin Encarnacion .25 .60
66 Anthony Rizzo .30 .75
67 Pedro Alvarez .15 .40
68 Jay Bruce .20 .50
69 Prince Fielder .20 .50
70 Justin Upton .20 .50
71 David Ortiz .25 .60
72 Matt Holliday .25 .60
73 Shelby Miller .20 .50
74 Jered Weaver .20 .50
75 Xander Bogaerts RC 1.00 2.50
76 Jose Abreu RC 2.50 6.00
77 Masahiro Tanaka RC 1.00 2.50
78 Billy Hamilton RC .40 1.00
79 Travis d'Arnaud RC .40 1.00
80 James Paxton RC .50 1.25
81 Nick Castellanos RC 1.00 2.50
82 Wilmer Flores RC .40 1.00
83 Jake Marisnick RC .30 .75
84 Yordano Ventura RC .40 1.00
85 Matt Davidson RC .40 1.00
86 Kevin Gausman RC .50 1.25
87 Kolten Wong RC .40 1.00
88 Jimmy Nelson RC .30 .75
89 Marcus Semien RC 1.50 4.00
90 Chris Owings RC .30 .75
91 Michael Choice RC .30 .75
92 Jonathan Schoop RC .30 .75
93 Erik Johnson RC .30 .75
94 Christian Bethancourt RC .30 .75
95 Tony Sanchez RC .30 .75
96 Oscar Taveras RC .40 1.00
97 Jon Singleton RC .40 1.00
98 J.R. Murphy RC .30 .75
99 Enny Romero RC .30 .75
100 Alex Guerrero RC .40 1.00

2014 Bowman Platinum Gold
*GOLD: 1X TO 2.5X BASIC
*GOLD RC: .5X TO 1.2X BASIC RC

2014 Bowman Platinum Ruby
*RUBY: 1.5X TO 4X BASIC
*RUBY RC: .75X TO 2X BASIC RC

2014 Bowman Platinum Sapphire
*SAPPHIRE: 1.2X TO 3X BASIC
*SAPPHIRE RC: .6X TO 1.5X BASIC RC

2014 Bowman Platinum Chrome Prospects Refractors
*REFRACTORS: .5X TO 1.2X BASIC

2014 Bowman Platinum Chrome Prospects Blue Refractors
*BLUE REF: 1.5X TO 4X BASIC
STATED PRINT RUN 199 SER.#'d SETS

2014 Bowman Platinum Chrome Prospects Gold Refractors
*GOLD REF: 5X TO 12X BASIC
STATED PRINT RUN 50 SER.#'d SETS

2014 Bowman Platinum Chrome Prospects Green Refractors
*GREEN REF: 1.2X TO 3X BASIC
STATED PRINT RUN 399 SER.#'d SETS

2014 Bowman Platinum Chrome Prospects Japan Fractors
*JAPAN REF: 5X TO 12X BASIC
STATED PRINT RUN 35 SER.#'d SETS

2014 Bowman Platinum Chrome Prospects Red Refractors
*RED REF: 6X TO 15X BASIC
STATED PRINT RUN 25 SER.#'d SETS

2014 Bowman Platinum Chrome Prospects X-Fractors
*X-FRACTOR: .75X TO 2X BASIC

2014 Bowman Platinum Cutting Edge Stars
CESAM Andrew McCutchen .75 2.00
CESBB Byron Buxton 2.50 6.00
CESBH Bryce Harper 1.25 3.00
CESBHA Billy Hamilton .60 1.50
CESBP Buster Posey 1.00 2.50
CESCC Carlos Correa 2.50 6.00
CESDJ Derek Jeter 2.00 5.00
CESDO David Ortiz .75 2.00
CESHI Hisashi Iwakuma .60 1.50
CESJA Jose Abreu 4.00 10.00
CESJB Javier Baez 2.00 5.00
CESJF Jose Fernandez .75 2.00
CESMC Miguel Cabrera .75 2.00
CESMT Masahiro Tanaka 1.50 4.00
CESMTR Mike Trout 4.00 10.00
CESTW Taijuan Walker .50 1.25
CESWM Wil Myers .50 1.25
CESXB Xander Bogaerts 1.50 4.00
CESYD Yu Darvish .75 2.00
CESYP Yasiel Puig .75 2.00

2014 Bowman Platinum Cutting Edge Stars Blue Refractors
*BLUE REF: 1.5X T O 4X BASIC
STATED PRINT RUN 49 SER.#'d SETS
CESDJ Derek Jeter 12.00 30.00
CESMTR Mike Trout 20.00 50.00

2014 Bowman Platinum Cutting Edge Stars Autographs
STATED PRINT RUN 25 SER.#'d SETS
EXCHANGE DEADLINE 7/31/2017
CEBP Buster Posey EXCH 40.00 100.00
CECC Carlos Correa 40.00 100.00
CEJA Jose Abreu 250.00 400.00
CEJB Javier Baez 50.00 120.00
CEMC Miguel Cabrera 60.00 150.00
CEMTR Mike Trout 250.00 400.00
CETW Taijuan Walker 8.00 20.00

2014 Bowman Platinum Cutting Edge Stars Relics
STATED PRINT RUN 49 SER.#'d SETS
CESDAM Andrew McCutchen 5.00 12.00
CESDBB Byron Buxton 15.00 40.00
CESDBH Bryce Harper 8.00 20.00
CESDBP Buster Posey 6.00 15.00
CESDCC Carlos Correa 30.00 80.00
CESDDJ Derek Jeter 20.00 50.00
CESDDO David Ortiz 5.00 12.00
CESDHI Hisashi Iwakuma 4.00 10.00
CESDMC Miguel Cabrera 5.00 12.00
CESDMT Mike Trout 20.00 50.00
CESDWM Wil Myers 3.00 8.00
CESDXB Xander Bogaerts 10.00 25.00
CESDYD Yu Darvish 5.00 12.00
CESDYP Yasiel Puig 5.00 12.00
CESDMTA Masahiro Tanaka 10.00 25.00

2014 Bowman Platinum Dual Autographs
STATED PRINT RUN 25 SER.#'d SETS
EXCHANGE DEADLINE 7/31/2017
DAAM L.McCullers/M.Appel 100.00 200.00
DAAT A.Almora/O.Taveras 20.00 50.00
DAAV A.Almora/D.Vogelbach 20.00 50.00
DABA A.Almora/J.Baez 60.00 150.00
DABJ B.Johnson/M.Barnes 12.00 30.00
DABS B.Buxton/M.Sano 100.00 200.00
DACC G.Cecchini/G.Cecchini 12.00 30.00
DAGH A.Heaney/L.Giolito 40.00 80.00
DANH A.Heaney/J.Nicolino 20.00 50.00
DASO R.Odor/L.Sardinas 30.00 80.00

2014 Bowman Platinum Five Tool Die Cuts
5TDCAA Albert Almora 3.00 8.00
5TDCAJ Adam Jones 2.50 6.00
5TDCAM Andrew McCutchen 3.00 8.00
5TDCAME Austin Meadows 5.00 12.00
5TDCBB Byron Buxton 10.00 25.00
5TDCBH Bryce Harper 5.00 12.00
5TDCBS Bubba Starling 2.50 6.00
5TDCCF Clint Frazier 8.00 20.00
5TDCCG Carlos Gonzalez 2.50 6.00
5TDCDW David Wright 2.50 6.00
5TDCGP Gregory Polanco 3.00 8.00
5TDCGS George Springer 8.00 20.00
5TDCJE Jacoby Ellsbury 2.50 6.00
5TDCMT Mike Trout 15.00 40.00
5TDCYP Yasiel Puig 3.00 8.00

2014 Bowman Platinum Jumbo Relic Autographs Refractors
EXCHANGE DEADLINE 7/31/2017
AJRAA Albert Almora 8.00 20.00
AJRBB Byron Buxton 20.00 50.00
AJRCM Colin Moran 4.00 10.00
AJRDD Delino DeShields 4.00 10.00
AJRGC Garin Cecchini 4.00 10.00

2014 Bowman Platinum Jumbo Relic Autographs Blue Refractors
*BLUE REF: .4X TO 1X BASIC
STATED PRINT RUN 199 SER.#'d SETS
EXCHANGE DEADLINE 7/31/2017

2014 Bowman Platinum Jumbo Relic Autographs Gold Refractors
*GOLD REF: .75X TO 2X BASIC
STATED PRINT RUN 50 SER.#'d SETS
EXCHANGE DEADLINE 7/31/2017

2014 Bowman Platinum Jumbo Relic Autographs Red Refractors
*RED REF: 1X TO 2.5X BASIC
STATED PRINT RUN 25 SER.#'d SETS
EXCHANGE DEADLINE 7/31/2017

2014 Bowman Platinum Platinum Cut Relic Autographs
STATED PRINT RUN 49 SER.#'d SETS
EXCHANGE DEADLINE 7/31/2017
APCAA Albert Almora 15.00 40.00
APCAB Archie Bradley 8.00 20.00
APCBB Byron Buxton 40.00 100.00
APCBH Bryce Harper EXCH 125.00 250.00
APCCC Carlos Correa 50.00 100.00
APCCM Colin Moran 8.00 20.00
APCCO Chris Owings 8.00 20.00
APCDD Delino DeShields 8.00 20.00
APCFL Francisco Lindor 60.00 150.00
APCGC Garin Cecchini 8.00 20.00
APCGS George Springer 30.00 80.00
APCMC Miguel Cabrera 60.00 150.00
APCMS Miguel Sano 10.00 25.00
APCMT Mike Trout 150.00 250.00
APCNC Nick Castellanos 25.00 60.00
APCTW Taijuan Walker 8.00 20.00
APCYV Yordano Ventura 10.00 25.00
APCZW Zack Wheeler 10.00 25.00

2014 Bowman Platinum Prospect Autographs
PLATE PRINT RUN 1 SET PER COLOR
BLACK-CYAN-MAGENTA-YELLOW ISSUED
NO PLATE PRICING DUE TO SCARCITY
EXCHANGE DEADLINE 07/31/2017
APAG Alexander Guerrero 8.00 20.00
APAK Akeem Bostick 3.00 8.00
APAT Andrew Thurman 3.00 8.00
APBB Bryce Bandilla 3.00 8.00
APBBU Byron Buxton 5.00 12.00
APBS Braden Shipley 3.00 8.00
APCB Christian Binford 3.00 8.00
APCC Curt Casali 3.00 8.00
APCCO Carlos Correa 15.00 40.00
APCF Chris Flexen 4.00 10.00
APCFR Clint Frazier 12.00 30.00
APCS Cord Sandberg 3.00 8.00
APCT Chris Taylor 6.00 15.00
APCV Cory Vaughn 3.00 8.00
APDR Daniel Robertson 4.00 10.00
APDT Devon Travis 3.00 8.00
APER Eduardo Rodriguez 6.00 15.00
APGY Gabriel Ynoa 4.00 10.00
APHR Hunter Renfroe 6.00 15.00
APJA Jose Abreu 15.00 40.00
APJB Jake Barrett 4.00 10.00
APJBA Javier Baez 25.00 60.00
APJC Jose Campos 3.00 8.00
APJG Joan Gregorio 3.00 8.00
APJS Jake Sweaney 3.00 8.00
APKB Kris Bryant 175.00 350.00
APLT Lewis Thorpe 3.00 8.00
APMA Miguel Almonte 3.00 8.00
APMAP Mark Appel 4.00 10.00
APMR Michael Ratterree 3.00 8.00
APMS Miguel Sano 3.00 8.00
APOT Oscar Taveras 4.00 10.00
APRH Rosell Herrera 5.00 12.00
APRHE Ryon Healy 5.00 12.00
APRT Raimel Tapia 4.00 10.00
APSG Sean Gilmartin 3.00 8.00
APSS Shae Simmons 3.00 8.00
APSSC Scott Schebler 8.00 20.00
APTD Tyler Danish 3.00 8.00
APWR Wendell Rijo 3.00 8.00
APYG Yimi Garcia 3.00 8.00
APZB Zach Borenstein 4.00 10.00

2014 Bowman Platinum Prospect Autographs Blue Refractors
*BLUE REF: .6X TO 1.5X BASIC
STATED PRINT RUN 199 SER.#'d SETS
EXCHANGE DEADLINE 07/31/2017

2014 Bowman Platinum Prospect Autographs Camo Refractors
*CAMO REF: 1X TO 2.5X BASIC
STATED PRINT RUN 35 SER.#'d SETS
EXCHANGE DEADLINE 07/31/2017
APAG Alexander Guerrero 30.00 80.00
APCCO Carlos Correa 60.00 150.00
APKB Kris Bryant 300.00 600.00

2014 Bowman Platinum Prospect Autographs Gold Refractors
*GOLD REF: .75X TO 2X BASIC
STATED PRINT RUN 50 SER.#'d SETS
EXCHANGE DEADLINE 07/31/2017
APCCO Carlos Correa 50.00 120.00

2014 Bowman Platinum Prospect Autographs Green Refractors
*GREEN REF: .5X TO 1.2X BASIC
STATED PRINT RUN 399 SER.#'d SETS
EXCHANGE DEADLINE 07/31/2017

2014 Bowman Platinum Prospect Autographs Red Refractors
*RED REF: 1X TO 2.5X BASIC
STATED PRINT RUN 25 SER.#'d SETS
EXCHANGE DEADLINE 07/31/2017
APCCO Carlos Correa 60.00 150.00
APKB Kris Bryant 300.00 600.00

2014 Bowman Platinum Prospects
PLATE PRINT RUN 1 SET PER COLOR
BLACK-CYAN-MAGENTA-YELLOW ISSUED
NO PLATE PRICING DUE TO SCARCITY
EXCHANGE DEADLINE 07/31/2017
BPP1 Francisco Lindor 2.00 5.00
BPP2 Jorge Soler .50 1.25
BPP3 Andrew Susac .30 .75
BPP4 Braden Shipley .25 .60
BPP5 Jose Berrios .40 1.00
BPP6 Gary Sanchez .75 2.00
BPP7 Kyle Zimmer .25 .60
BPP8 Taylor Guerrieri .25 .60
BPP9 Max Fried 1.00 2.50
BPP10 Byron Buxton 1.25 3.00
BPP11 Alex Meyer .25 .60
BPP12 Jonathan Gray .30 .75
BPP13 Austin Hedges .25 .60
BPP14 Mason Williams .25 .60
BPP15 Alen Hanson .25 .60
BPP16 Bubba Starling .30 .75
BPP17 Jesse Biddle .30 .75
BPP18 Kyle Crick .25 .60
BPP19 Joc Pederson .60 1.50
BPP20 Carlos Correa 1.25 3.00
BPP21 Raul Mondesi .40 1.00
BPP22 Corey Seager 1.25 3.00
BPP23 Andrew Heaney .25 .60
BPP24 Clint Frazier 1.00 2.50
BPP25 Henry Owens .30 .75
BPP26 Roberto Osuna .25 .60
BPP27 Arismendy Alcantara .25 .60
BPP28 Matt Barnes .25 .60
BPP29 David Dahl .30 .75
BPP30 Addison Russell .40 1.00
BPP31 Zach Lee .25 .60
BPP32 Justin Nicolino .25 .60
BPP33 Lance McCullers .25 .60
BPP34 Kohl Stewart .25 .60
BPP35 Mike Foltynewicz .25 .60
BPP36 Eddie Rosario .50 1.25
BPP37 Tyler Austin .25 .60
BPP38 Lucas Giolito .40 1.00
BPP39 Austin Meadows .60 1.50
BPP40 Kris Bryant 3.00 8.00
BPP41 Daniel Robertson .30 .75
BPP42 Colin Moran .25 .60
BPP43 A.J. Cole .25 .60
BPP44 Garin Cecchini .25 .60
BPP45 Eddie Butler .25 .60
BPP46 Julio Urias 1.25 3.00
BPP47 Marcus Stroman .40 1.00
BPP48 Lucas Sims .25 .60
BPP49 Clayton Blackburn .40 1.00
BPP50 Javier Baez 1.00 2.50
BPP51 Rougned Odor .60 1.50
BPP52 Tyler Glasnow 1.00 2.50
BPP53 Rosell Herrera .40 1.00
BPP54 Eduardo Rodriguez .30 .75
BPP55 Devon Travis .25 .60
BPP56 Hunter Dozier .25 .60
BPP57 Delino DeShields .25 .60
BPP58 Domingo Santana .40 1.00
BPP59 Michael Ynoa .25 .60
BPP60 Aaron Sanchez .25 .60
BPP61 Billy McKinney .30 .75
BPP62 D.J. Peterson .25 .60
BPP63 Chris Taylor 1.25 3.00
BPP64 Joey Gallo .50 1.25
BPP65 Dominic Smith .25 .60
BPP66 Brandon Nimmo .40 1.00
BPP67 J.P. Crawford .25 .60
BPP68 Maikel Franco .30 .75
BPP69 Brian Goodwin .25 .60
BPP70 Mark Appel .30 .75
BPP71 Dan Vogelbach .40 1.00
BPP72 C.J. Edwards .30 .75
BPP73 Luis Heredia .25 .60
BPP74 Josh Bell .50 1.25
BPP75 Reese McGuire .25 .60
BPP76 Nick Kingham .30 .75
BPP77 Marco Gonzales .40 1.00
BPP78 Stephen Piscotty .30 .75
BPP79 Rob Kaminsky .25 .60
BPP80 Jorge Alfaro .30 .75
BPP81 Jake Barrett .30 .75
BPP82 Stryker Trahan .25 .60
BPP83 Trevor Story 1.25 3.00
BPP84 Chris Anderson .25 .60
BPP85 Rymer Liriano .25 .60
BPP86 Hunter Renfroe .30 .75
BPP87 Chris Stratton .25 .60
BPP88 Joe Panik .40 1.00
BPP89 Christian Arroyo 1.50 4.00
BPP90 Albert Almora .40 1.00
BPP91 Luis Sardinas .25 .60
BPP92 Jairo Beras .25 .60
BPP93 Hak-Ju Lee .25 .60
BPP94 Arodys Vizcaino .25 .60
BPP95 Dorssys Paulino .25 .60
BPP96 Slade Heathcott .30 .75
BPP97 Courtney Hawkins .25 .60
BPP98 Tim Anderson .50 1.25
BPP99 Nick Travieso .25 .60
BPP100 Robert Stephenson .25 .60

2014 Bowman Platinum Relic Autographs
PLATE PRINT RUN 1 SET PER COLOR
BLACK-CYAN-MAGENTA-YELLOW ISSUED
NO PLATE PRICING DUE TO SCARCITY
EXCHANGE DEADLINE 07/31/2017
ARAC A.J. Cole 3.00 8.00
ARARI Andre Rienzo 3.00 8.00
ARAS Andrew Susac 4.00 10.00
ARASA Aaron Sanchez 4.00 10.00
ARCCO Carlos Contreras 3.00 8.00
ARCK Corey Knebel 3.00 8.00
ARCY Christian Yelich 30.00 80.00
ARDG David Goforth 3.00 8.00
ARDH Dilson Herrera 15.00 40.00
ARDT Devon Travis 3.00 8.00

AREB Eddie Butler 3.00 8.00
AREG Evan Gattis 3.00 8.00
ARER Eduardo Rodriguez 4.00 10.00
ARGP Gregory Polanco 5.00 12.00
ARJB Jake Barrett 4.00 10.00
ARJBI Jesse Biddle 4.00 10.00
ARJM James McCann 8.00 20.00
ARJP Joc Pederson 8.00 20.00
ARJS Jorge Soler 10.00 25.00
ARKC Kyle Crick 3.00 8.00
ARKP Kyle Parker 4.00 10.00
ARKS Keyvius Sampson 3.00 8.00
ARMB Mookie Betts 100.00 250.00
ARMM Mike Montgomery 3.00 8.00
ARMST Marcus Stroman 5.00 12.00
ARMSTI Matt Stites 3.00 8.00
ARMW Mason Williams 3.00 8.00
ARMY Michael Ynoa 3.00 8.00
ARNS Noah Syndergaard 15.00 40.00
ARPO Peter O'Brien EXCH 4.00 10.00
ARSP Stephen Piscotty 8.00 20.00
ARSR Stefen Romero 3.00 8.00
ARTA Tyler Austin 3.00 8.00
ARTL Taylor Lindsey 3.00 8.00
ARTN Tyler Naquin 5.00 12.00
ARYA Yeison Asencio 3.00 8.00

2014 Bowman Platinum Relic Autographs Blue Refractors

*BLUE REF: .5X TO 1.2X BASIC
STATED PRINT RUN 199 SER.#'d SETS
EXCHANGE DEADLINE 07/31/2017
ARAB Archie Bradley 8.00 20.00
ARMS Miguel Sano 10.00 25.00
ARWM Wil Myers 4.00 10.00
ARZW Zack Wheeler 5.00 12.00
AJRBM B.Nimmo Retail Excl 6.00 15.00
AJRCB Bethancourt Retail Excl 8.00 20.00
AJRCCR C.Cron Retail Excl 8.00 20.00

2014 Bowman Platinum Relic Autographs Gold Refractors

*GOLD REF: .75X TO 2X BASIC
STATED PRINT RUN 50 SER.#'d SETS
EXCHANGE DEADLINE 07/31/2017
ARAB Archie Bradley 10.00 25.00
ARCC Carlos Correa 25.00 60.00
ARMS Miguel Sano 12.00 30.00
ARWM Wil Myers 6.00 15.00
ARZW Zack Wheeler 8.00 20.00

2014 Bowman Platinum Relic Autographs Red Refractors

*RED REF: 1X TO 2.5X BASIC
STATED PRINT RUN 25 SER.#'d SETS
EXCHANGE DEADLINE 07/31/2017
ARAB Archie Bradley 12.00 30.00
ARBH Billy Hamilton EXCH 40.00 100.00
ARCC Carlos Correa 30.00 80.00
ARGS George Springer 30.00 80.00
ARMS Miguel Sano 15.00 40.00
ARMTR Mike Trout 200.00 400.00
ARWM Wil Myers 8.00 20.00
ARZW Zack Wheeler 10.00 25.00

2014 Bowman Platinum Toolsy Die Cuts

TDCAA Albert Almora .60 1.50
TDCAH Austin Hedges .40 1.00
TDCAHA Alen Hanson .40 1.00
TDCAHE Austin Hedges .40 1.00
TDCAM Austin Meadows 1.00 2.50
TDCAR Addison Russell .60 1.50
TDCBB Byron Buxton 2.00 5.00
TDCBG Brian Goodwin .40 1.00
TDCBH Billy Hamilton .50 1.25
TDCCB Christian Bethancourt .40 1.00
TDCCC C.J. Cron .40 1.00
TDCCCO Carlos Correa 2.00 5.00
TDCCH Courtney Hawkins .40 1.00
TDCCM Colin Moran .40 1.00
TDCCS Corey Seager 2.00 5.00
TDCDD Delino DeShields .40 1.00
TDCDDA David Dahl .50 1.25
TDCDP D.J. Peterson .40 1.00
TDCDS Dominic Smith .40 1.00
TDCDV Dan Vogelbach .60 1.50
TDCFL Francisco Lindor 3.00 8.00
TDCGC Garin Cecchini .40 1.00
TDCGP Gregory Polanco .60 1.50
TDCGS George Springer 1.50 4.00
TDCGSA Gary Sanchez 1.25 3.00
TDCHL Hak-Ju Lee .40 1.00
TDCJA Jose Abreu 3.00 8.00
TDCJAL Jorge Alfaro .50 1.25
TDCJB Javier Baez 1.50 4.00
TDCJC J.P. Crawford .40 1.00
TDCJCR J.P. Crawford .40 1.00
TDCJG Joey Gallo .75 2.00
TDCJP Joc Pederson 1.00 2.50
TDCJS Jorge Soler .75 2.00
TDCJSI Jonathan Singleton .50 1.25
TDCKB Kris Bryant 4.00 10.00
TDCKW Kolten Wong .50 1.25
TDCLS Luis Sardinas .40 1.00
TDCMB Mookie Betts 8.00 20.00
TDCMF Maikel Franco .50 1.25
TDCMJ Micah Johnson .40 1.00
TDCMS Miguel Sano .50 1.25
TDCMW Mason Williams .40 1.00
TDCNC Nick Castellanos 1.25 3.00
TDCOT Oscar Taveras .50 1.25
TDCRM Raul Mondesi .60 1.50
TDCRMC Reese McGuire .40 1.00
TDCRW Russell Wilson 5.00 12.00
TDCTA Tyler Austin .40 1.00
TDCXB Xander Bogaerts 1.25 3.00

2014 Bowman Platinum Top Prospects Die Cuts

TPAA Albert Almora .50 1.25
TPAB Archie Bradley .30 .75
TPAH Alen Hanson .30 .75
TPAHE Andrew Heaney .30 .75
TPAM Austin Meadows .75 2.00
TPAR Addison Russell .50 1.25
TPAS Aaron Sanchez .30 .75
TPBB Byron Buxton 1.50 4.00
TPCC C.J. Cron .30 .75
TPCE C.J. Edwards .40 1.00
TPCF Clint Frazier 1.25 3.00
TPDD David Dahl .40 1.00
TPEB Eddie Butler .30 .75
TPFL Francisco Lindor 2.50 6.00
TPGP Gregory Polanco .50 1.25
TPGS Gary Sanchez 1.00 2.50
TPGSP George Springer 1.25 3.00
TPJA Jose Abreu 2.50 6.00
TPJB Javier Baez 1.25 3.00
TPJS Jorge Soler .60 1.50
TPKB Kris Bryant 3.00 8.00
TPLG Lucas Giolito .50 1.25
TPLM Lance McCullers .30 .75
TPMA Mark Appel .40 1.00
TPMF Maikel Franco .40 1.00
TPMS Miguel Sano .40 1.00
TPMT Masahiro Tanaka 1.00 2.50
TPOT Oscar Taveras .40 1.00
TPPE Phil Ervin .30 .75
TPTG Tyler Glasnow 1.25 3.00

2014 Bowman Platinum Top Prospects Die Cuts Refractors

*REF: 2X TO 5X BASIC
STATED PRINT RUN 25 SER.#'d SETS

2014 Bowman Platinum Top Prospects Die Cuts Blue Refractors

*BLUE REF: 1.5X TO 4X BASIC
STATED PRINT RUN 49 SER.#'d SETS

2016 Bowman Platinum

COMPLETE SET (100) 20.00 50.00
PRINTING PLATE ODDS 1:742 RETAIL
PLATE PRINT RUN 1 SET PER COLOR
BLACK-CYAN-MAGENTA-YELLOW ISSUED
NO PLATE PRICING DUE TO SCARCITY
1 Mike Trout 2.50 6.00
2 Gary Sanchez RC 1.50 4.00
3 Miguel Cabrera .50 1.25
4 Carl Edwards Jr. RC .60 1.50
5 Kris Bryant .60 1.50
6 Gerrit Cole .50 1.25
7 Dustin Pedroia .50 1.25
8 Paul Goldschmidt .50 1.25
9 Jose Abreu .50 1.25
10 Carlos Rodon .50 1.25
11 Michael Fulmer RC .75 2.00
12 Brian McCann .40 1.00
13 Francisco Lindor .50 1.25
14 Evan Longoria .40 1.00
15 Stephen Piscotty RC .75 2.00
16 Chris Sale .50 1.25
17 Jeurys Familia .40 1.00
18 Ryan Braun .40 1.00
19 Aaron Blair RC .50 1.25
20 Troy Tulowitzki .50 1.25
21 Nolan Arenado .75 2.00
22 Byung-Ho Park RC .60 1.50
23 Yoenis Cespedes .50 1.25
24 Hector Olivera RC .60 1.50
25 Kyle Seager .30 .75
26 Julio Urias RC 1.50 4.00
27 Aroldis Chapman .50 1.25
28 Henry Owens RC .60 1.50
29 Jose Fernandez .50 1.25
30 Jose Peraza RC .60 1.50
31 Cole Hamels .40 1.00
32 Kyle Schwarber RC 1.50 4.00
33 Giancarlo Stanton .50 1.25
34 Anthony Rizzo .60 1.50
35 Albert Almora RC .60 1.50
36 Buster Posey .60 1.50
37 Jose Berrios RC .75 2.00
38 Jon Lester .40 1.00
39 Mookie Betts 1.00 2.50
40 Corey Seager RC 5.00 12.00
41 Matt Harvey .40 1.00
42 Seung-hwan Oh RC 1.25 3.00
43 Zack Greinke .50 1.25
44 Wade Davis .30 .75
45 Yu Darvish .50 1.25
46 Tyler Naquin RC .75 2.00
47 Jorge Soler .50 1.25
48 Matt Carpenter .50 1.25
49 Jake Arrieta .40 1.00
50 Bryce Harper .75 2.00
51 Raul Mondesi RC 1.00 2.50
52 David Wright .40 1.00
53 Felix Hernandez .40 1.00
54 Wil Myers .40 1.00
55 Andrew McCutchen .50 1.25
56 Jameson Taillon RC .60 1.50
57 Prince Fielder .40 1.00
58 Joey Votto .50 1.25
59 Blake Snell RC .60 1.50
60 Joey Gallo .40 1.00
61 Freddie Freeman .60 1.50
62 Eric Hosmer .40 1.00
63 Kenta Maeda RC 1.00 2.50
64 Luis Severino RC .60 1.50
65 Nomar Mazara RC .75 2.00
66 Max Scherzer .50 1.25
67 Dee Gordon .30 .75
68 Craig Kimbrel .40 1.00
69 Michael Conforto RC .60 1.50
70 Sonny Gray .40 1.00
71 Brian Dozier .40 1.00
72 Noah Syndergaard .40 1.00
73 Edwin Encarnacion .50 1.25
74 Rob Refsnyder RC .60 1.50
75 Dallas Keuchel .40 1.00
76 Ichiro Suzuki .60 1.50
77 David Ortiz .50 1.25
78 Trea Turner RC 1.50 4.00
79 Josh Donaldson .40 1.00
80 Jose Altuve .40 1.00
81 Eddie Rosario .40 1.00
82 A.J. Pollock .30 .75
83 Salvador Perez .40 1.00
84 Miguel Sano RC .75 2.00
85 Adam Jones .40 1.00
86 Joc Pederson .40 1.00
87 Tyson Ross .30 .75
88 Robert Stephenson RC .50 1.25
89 J.D. Martinez .50 1.25
90 Tyler White RC .50 1.25
91 Sean Manaea RC .50 1.25
92 Madison Bumgarner .40 1.00
93 Byron Buxton .50 1.25
94 Jacob deGrom 1.00 2.50
95 Jon Gray RC .50 1.25
96 David Price .40 1.00
97 Carlos Correa .50 1.25
98 Trevor Story RC 2.50 6.00
99 Aaron Nola RC 1.00 2.50
100 Clayton Kershaw .75 2.00

2016 Bowman Platinum Green

*GREEN: 2.5X TO 6X BASIC
*GREEN RC: 1.5X TO 4X BASIC RC
STATED ODDS 1:31 RETAIL
STATED PRINT RUN 99 SER.#'d SETS
5 Kris Bryant 10.00 25.00

2016 Bowman Platinum Ice

*ICE: 1.2X TO 3X BASIC
*ICE RC: .75X TO 2X BASIC RC
RANDOM INSERTS IN PACKS
5 Kris Bryant 5.00 12.00

2016 Bowman Platinum Orange

*ORANGE: 3X TO 8X BASIC
*ORANGE RC: 2X TO 5X BASIC RC
STATED ODDS 1:119 RETAIL
STATED PRINT RUN 25 SER.#'d SETS
50 Bryce Harper 12.00 30.00

2016 Bowman Platinum Purple

*PURPLE: 1.5X TO 4X BASIC
*PURPLE RC: 1X TO 2.5X BASIC RC
STATED ODDS 1:12 RETAIL
STATED PRINT RUN 250 SER.#'d SETS
5 Kris Bryant 6.00 15.00

2016 Bowman Platinum Autographs

STATED ODDS 1:635 RETAIL
PAAN Aaron Nola 6.00 15.00
PAAP A.J. Pollock 3.00 8.00
PABB Byron Buxton 8.00 20.00
PABHP Byung-Ho Park 4.00 10.00
PABS Blake Snell 4.00 10.00
PACC Carlos Correa 25.00 60.00
PACR Carlos Rodon
PACS Corey Seager
PAER Eddie Rosario 4.00 10.00
PAFM Frankie Montas 4.00 10.00
PAJB Jose Berrios 5.00 12.00
PAJF Jeurys Familia 4.00 10.00
PAJG Joey Gallo
PAJU Julio Urias 15.00 40.00
PAKB Kris Bryant 75.00 200.00
PAKM Kenta Maeda
PAKS Kyle Schwarber
PALS Luis Severino 6.00 15.00
PAMF Michael Fulmer 12.00 30.00
PAMS Max Scherzer 15.00 40.00
PAMSA Miguel Sano 5.00 12.00
PAMT Mike Trout 125.00 250.00
PARS Robert Stephenson 3.00 8.00
PATS Trevor Story 12.00 30.00

2016 Bowman Platinum Autographs Green

*GREEN: .6X TO 1.5X BASIC
STATED ODDS 1:1091 RETAIL
STATED PRINT RUN 75 SER.#'d SETS
PACR Carlos Rodon 6.00 15.00
PACS Corey Seager 100.00 250.00
PAJG Joey Gallo
PAKB Kris Bryant
PAKM Kenta Maeda 40.00 100.00
PAKS Kyle Schwarber 30.00 80.00
PAMT Mike Trout

2016 Bowman Platinum Autographs Orange

*ORANGE: .75X TO 2X BASIC
STATED ODDS 1:2775 RETAIL
STATED PRINT RUN 25 SER.#'d SETS
PACR Carlos Rodon 10.00 25.00
PACS Corey Seager 150.00 400.00
PAJG Joey Gallo 8.00 20.00
PAKB Kris Bryant
PAKM Kenta Maeda 60.00 150.00
PAKS Kyle Schwarber 50.00 120.00
PAMT Mike Trout

2016 Bowman Platinum Next Generation

STATED ODDS 1:2 RETAIL
*PURPLE/250: 1.5X TO 4X BASIC
*GREEN/99: 2X TO 6X BASIC
*ORANGE/25: 3X TO 8X BASIC
NG1 Kaleb Cowart .40 1.00
NG2 Brandon Drury .60 1.50
NG3 Hector Olivera .50 1.25
NG4 Dylan Bundy .50 1.25
NG5 Henry Owens .50 1.25
NG6 Kris Bryant .75 2.00
NG7 Carlos Rodon .60 1.50
NG8 Jose Peraza .50 1.25
NG9 Francisco Lindor .60 1.50
NG10 Trevor Story 2.00 5.00
NG11 Daniel Norris .40 1.00
NG12 Carlos Correa .60 1.50
NG13 Raul Mondesi .75 2.00
NG14 Kenta Maeda .75 2.00
NG15 Justin Bour .50 1.25
NG16 Jorge Lopez .40 1.00
NG17 Miguel Sano .60 1.50
NG18 Jacob deGrom 1.25 3.00
NG19 Luis Severino .50 1.25
NG20 Sean Manaea .40 1.00
NG21 Odubel Herrera .50 1.25
NG22 Gregory Polanco .50 1.25
NG23 Colin Rea .40 1.00
NG24 Chris Heston .40 1.00
NG25 Ketel Marte .75 2.00
NG26 Randal Grichuk .40 1.00
NG27 Blake Snell .50 1.25
NG28 Nomar Mazara .60 1.50
NG29 Roberto Osuna .40 1.00
NG30 Trea Turner 1.25 3.00

2016 Bowman Platinum Next Generation Prospects

STATED ODDS 1:2 RETAIL
*PURPLE/250: 1X TO 2.5X BASIC
*GREEN/99: 1.2X TO 3X BASIC
*ORANGE/25: 2X TO 5X BASIC
NGP1 Taylor Ward .50 1.25
NGP2 Braden Shipley .40 1.00
NGP3 Dansby Swanson 1.50 4.00
NGP4 Hunter Harvey .40 1.00
NGP5 Yoan Moncada 1.00 2.50
NGP6 Gleyber Torres 6.00 15.00
NGP7 Carson Fulmer .40 1.00
NGP8 Jesse Winker 1.50 4.00
NGP9 Bradley Zimmer .60 1.50
NGP10 Brendan Rodgers .60 1.50
NGP11 Beau Burrows .40 1.00
NGP12 Alex Bregman 2.50 6.00
NGP13 Kyle Zimmer .40 1.00
NGP14 Jose De Leon .40 1.00
NGP15 Tyler Kolek .50 1.25
NGP16 Orlando Arcia .50 1.25
NGP17 Tyler Jay .40 1.00
NGP18 Dominic Smith .40 1.00
NGP19 Jorge Mateo .50 1.25
NGP20 Franklin Barreto .40 1.00
NGP21 J.P. Crawford .40 1.00
NGP22 Tyler Glasnow 1.50 4.00
NGP23 Manuel Margot .40 1.00
NGP24 Christian Arroyo .75 2.00
NGP25 Alex Jackson .50 1.25
NGP26 Alex Reyes .50 1.25
NGP27 Brent Honeywell .60 1.50
NGP28 Lewis Brinson .60 1.50
NGP29 Anthony Alford .40 1.00
NGP30 Lucas Giolito .60 1.50

2016 Bowman Platinum Platinum Cut Autographs

STATED ODDS 1:2258 RETAIL
STATED PRINT RUN 25 SER.#'d SETS
PCAAA Anthony Alford
PCAAB Alex Bregman 75.00 200.00
PCAABE Andrew Benintendi 60.00 150.00
PCAAE Anderson Espinoza
PCAAJ Aaron Judge 125.00 300.00
PCAAR A.J. Reed 8.00 20.00
PCAARE Alex Reyes 40.00 100.00
PCABR Brendan Rodgers
PCABZ Bradley Zimmer
PCACF Carson Fulmer 8.00 20.00
PCADD David Dahl 50.00 120.00
PCADS Dansby Swanson 75.00 200.00
PCADT Dillon Tate
PCAIH Ian Happ
PCAJB Josh Bell 25.00 60.00
PCAJG Javier Guerra 12.00 30.00
PCAJM Jorge Mateo 10.00 25.00
PCAKA Kolby Allard 20.00 50.00
PCAKT Kyle Tucker
PCALF Lucius Fox
PCALG Lucas Giolito
PCALS Lucas Sims 8.00 20.00
PCAOA Orlando Arcia
PCARD Rafael Devers 75.00 200.00
PCASN Sean Newcomb 10.00 25.00
PCAVG Vladimir Guerrero Jr. 300.00 600.00
PCAVR Victor Robles
PCAWC Willson Contreras
PCAYM Yoan Moncada

2016 Bowman Platinum Platinum Presence

STATED ODDS 1:4 RETAIL
*GREEN/99: 1X TO 2.5X BASIC
*ORANGE/25: X TO X BASIC
PP1 Yoan Moncada 1.00 2.50
PP2 Dansby Swanson 1.50 4.00
PP3 Vladimir Guerrero Jr. 8.00 20.00
PP4 Alex Bregman 2.00 5.00
PP5 Brendan Rodgers .60 1.50
PP6 Daz Cameron .40 1.00
PP7 Lucius Fox .60 1.50
PP8 Andrew Benintendi 1.25 3.00
PP9 Ian Happ .75 2.00
PP10 Lucas Giolito .60 1.50
PP11 David Dahl .50 1.25
PP12 Jose De Leon .40 1.00
PP13 Alex Reyes .50 1.25
PP14 Kolby Allard .40 1.00
PP15 Orlando Arcia .50 1.25
PP16 Francis Martes .40 1.00
PP17 Anderson Espinoza .50 1.25
PP18 Domingo Acevedo .60 1.50
PP19 Javier Guerra .40 1.00
PP20 Rafael Devers 1.25 3.00
PP21 Josh Bell .75 2.00
PP22 Austin Meadows 1.00 2.50
PP23 J.P. Crawford .40 1.00
PP24 Anthony Alford .40 1.00
PP25 Aaron Judge 10.00 25.00
PP26 Sean Newcomb .50 1.25
PP27 Tyler Glasnow 1.50 4.00
PP28 Franklin Barreto .40 1.00
PP29 Jorge Mateo .50 1.25
PP30 Victor Robles 1.50 4.00

2016 Bowman Platinum Platinum Presence Autographs

STATED ODDS 1:1518 RETAIL
STATED PRINT RUN 99 SER.#'d SETS
PPAAB Alex Bregman
PPAABE Andrew Benintendi
PPAAE Anderson Espinoza 6.00 15.00
PPAAR Alex Reyes 10.00 25.00
PPABR Brendan Rodgers
PPADA Domingo Acevedo 10.00 25.00
PPADC Daz Cameron
PPADD David Dahl 4.00 10.00
PPADS Dansby Swanson
PPAFM Francis Martes 3.00 8.00
PPAIH Ian Happ 6.00 15.00
PPAJG Javier Guerra 3.00 8.00
PPAKA Kolby Allard 6.00 15.00
PPALF Lucius Fox
PPALG Lucas Giolito 5.00 12.00
PPAOA Orlando Arcia 6.00 15.00
PPARD Rafael Devers 20.00 50.00
PPAVGJ Vladimir Guerrero Jr.
PPAWC Willson Contreras
PPAYM Yoan Moncada

2016 Bowman Platinum Platinum Presence Autographs Green

*GREEN: .5X TO 1.2X BASIC
STATED ODDS 1:1091 RETAIL
STATED PRINT RUN 75 SER.#'d SETS
PPAAB Alex Bregman 40.00 100.00
PPAABE Andrew Benintendi 40.00 100.00
PPABR Brendan Rodgers 6.00 15.00
PPADC Daz Cameron 4.00 10.00
PPADS Dansby Swanson 40.00 100.00
PPALF Lucius Fox 8.00 20.00
PPAVGJ Vladimir Guerrero Jr. 125.00 300.00
PPAWC Willson Contreras 25.00 60.00
PPAYM Yoan Moncada 40.00 100.00

2016 Bowman Platinum Platinum Presence Autographs Orange

*ORANGE: .6X TO 1.5X BASIC
STATED ODDS 1:3237 RETAIL
STATED PRINT RUN 25 SER.#'d SETS
PPAAB Alex Bregman 60.00 150.00
PPAABE Andrew Benintendi 60.00 150.00
PPABR Brendan Rodgers 10.00 25.00
PPADC Daz Cameron 6.00 15.00
PPADS Dansby Swanson 60.00 150.00
PPALF Lucius Fox 12.00 30.00
PPAVGJ Vladimir Guerrero Jr. 200.00 500.00
PPAWC Willson Contreras 40.00 100.00
PPAYM Yoan Moncada 60.00 150.00

2016 Bowman Platinum Top Prospects

SP ODDS 1:100 RETAIL
PRINTING PLATE ODDS 1:742 RETAIL
PLATE PRINT RUN 1 SET PER COLOR
BLACK-CYAN-MAGENTA-YELLOW ISSUED
NO PLATE PRICING DUE TO SCARCITY
*ICE: .6X TO 1.5X BASIC
*PURPLE/250: .75X TO 2X BASIC
*GREEN/99: 1X TO 2.5X BASIC
TPAA Anthony Alford .30 .75
TPAB Alex Bregman 1.50 4.00
TPABE Andrew Benintendi 1.00 2.50
TPABW Adam Brett Walker II .30 .75
TPAE Anderson Espinoza .40 1.00
TPAEN Adam Engel .30 .75
TPAG Amir Garrett .30 .75
TPAJ Judge SP Rnnng 40.00 100.00
TPAJU Ariel Jurado .30 .75
TPAR A.J. Reed .30 .75
TPARE Alex Reyes .40 1.00
TPARO Amed Rosario .50 1.25
TPAS Antonio Santillan .30 .75
TPASE Antonio Senzatela .30 .75
TPAV Alex Verdugo .50 1.25
TPBA Brady Aiken .75 2.00
TPBD Braxton Davidson .30 .75
TPBH Brent Honeywell .50 1.25
TPBM Billy McKinney .40 1.00
TPBP Brett Phillips .30 .75
TPBR Brendan Rodgers .50 1.25
TPBZ Zimmer SP Bttng 40.00 100.00
TPCA Arroyo SP Fldng 20.00 50.00
TPCB Cody Bellinger 5.00 12.00
TPCF Clint Frazier SP 40.00 100.00
TPCFU Carson Fulmer SP 20.00 50.00
TPCG Conner Greene .30 .75
TPCR Cornelius Randolph .30 .75
TPCRE Cody Reed .30 .75
TPDA Domingo Acevedo .50 1.25
TPDC Daz Cameron .30 .75
TPDD David Dahl .40 1.00
TPDDE David Denson .30 .75
TPDSM Dominic Smith .30 .75
TPDJ Drew Jackson .30 .75
TPDP David Paulino .40 1.00
TPDS Dansby Swanson 1.25 3.00
TPDT Dillon Tate .40 1.00
TPFB Franklin Barreto .30 .75
TPFM Francis Martes .30 .75
TPFT Fernando Tatis Jr. 15.00 40.00
TPGH Grant Holmes .40 1.00
TPGT Gleyber Torres 5.00 12.00
TPGW Garrett Whitley .40 1.00
TPHR Harold Ramirez .40 1.00
TPHR Hunter Renfroe SP
TPIH Ian Happ .60 1.50
TPJC Jharel Cotton .30 .75
TPJC Crwfrd SP Rnnng 10.00 25.00
TPJDL Jose De Leon SP 20.00 50.00
TPJF Jacob Faria .30 .75
TPJG Javier Guerra .30 .75
TPJGU Jordan Guerrero .30 .75
TPJH Jeff Hoffman .40 1.00
TPJM Jorge Mateo .40 1.00
TPJMU Joe Musgrove 1.00 2.50
TPJN Josh Naylor .40 1.00
TPJO Jhailyn Ortiz .60 1.50
TPJR Jomar Reyes .50 1.25
TPJS Justus Sheffield .60 1.50
TPJT Jake Thompson .30 .75
TPJUF Junior Fernandez .50 1.25
TPJW Jesse Winker 1.25 3.00
TPKA Kolby Allard .30 .75
TPKK Kevin Kramer .40 1.00
TPKP Kevin Padlo .30 .75
TPKT Kyle Tucker 1.50 4.00
TPKZ Kyle Zimmer .30 .75
TPLB Lewis Brinson SP 12.00 30.00
TPLF Lucius Fox .50 1.25
TPLG Lucas Giolito .50 1.25
TPLO Luis Ortiz .30 .75
TPLW Luke Weaver .50 1.25
TPMD Mauricio Dubon .40 1.00
TPMM Manuel Margot .30 .75
TPNG Nick Gordon .30 .75
TPNS Nate Smith .30 .75
TPNW Nick Williams .40 1.00
TPOA Orlando Arcia .40 1.00
TPOAL Ozzie Albies 1.50 4.00
TPRB Rafael Bautista .30 .75
TPRD Rafael Devers 1.00 2.50
TPRG Ruddy Giron .30 .75
TPRM Reese McGuire .30 .75
TPRMC Ryan McMahon .50 1.25
TPRR Rio Ruiz .30 .75
TPRRA Roniel Raudes .50 1.25
TPSG Stone Garrett .30 .75
TPSK Scott Kingery .50 1.25
TPSN Sean Newcomb .40 1.00
TPTA Tim Anderson 1.25 3.00
TPTC Trent Clark .30 .75
TPTG Tyler Glasnow 1.25 3.00
TPTJ Tyler Jay .30 .75
TPTM Trey Mancini 1.00 2.50
TPTO Tyler O'Neill .40 1.00
TPTS Tyler Stephenson .75 2.00
TPTT Touki Toussaint .40 1.00
TPTW Taylor Ward .40 1.00
TPVG Vladimir Guerrero Jr. 5.00 12.00
TPVR Victor Robles 1.25 3.00
TPWA Willy Adames .50 1.25
TPWC1 Willson Contreras 2.00 5.00
TPWC2 Cntrrs SP Bttng 25.00 60.00
TPWCH Wei-Chieh Huang .30 .75
TPWG Wilkerman Garcia .40 1.00
TPWJ Wander Javier .50 1.25
TPYG Yeudy Garcia .30 .75
TPYL Yoan Lopez .30 .75
TPYM Yoan Moncada .75 2.00

2016 Bowman Platinum Top Prospects Orange

*ORANGE: 2X TO 5X BASIC
STATED ODDS 1:119 RETAIL
STATED PRINT RUN 25 SER.#'d SETS
TPABE Andrew Benintendi 20.00 50.00

2016 Bowman Platinum Top Prospects Autographs

STATED ODDS 1:105 RETAIL
TPAAA Anthony Alford 2.50 6.00
TPAAB Alex Bregman
TPAABE Andrew Benintendi 25.00 60.00
TPAABW Adam Brett Walker II 2.50 6.00
TPAAE Anderson Espinoza 4.00 10.00
TPAAJU Ariel Jurado 2.50 6.00
TPAAR A.J. Reed 2.50 6.00
TPAARE Alex Reyes 5.00 12.00
TPABD Braxton Davidson 2.50 6.00
TPABM Billy McKinney
TPABR Brendan Rodgers
TPACR Cornelius Randolph 2.50 6.00
TPADA Domingo Acevedo 4.00 10.00
TPADC Daz Cameron
TPADD David Dahl 3.00 8.00
TPADJ Drew Jackson 2.50 6.00
TPADS Dansby Swanson
TPADT Dillon Tate 3.00 8.00
TPAFM Francis Martes 2.50 6.00
TPAGH Grant Holmes 3.00 8.00
TPAGW Garrett Whitley 3.00 8.00
TPAIH Ian Happ 15.00 40.00
TPAJG Javier Guerra 2.50 6.00
TPAJM Jorge Mateo 3.00 8.00
TPAKA Kolby Allard 2.50 6.00
TPAKP Kevin Padlo 2.50 6.00
TPALF Lucius Fox
TPALG Lucas Giolito 4.00 10.00
TPALW Luke Weaver 4.00 10.00
TPAMM Manuel Margot 2.50 6.00
TPANG Nick Gordon 2.50 6.00
TPAOA Orlando Arcia 3.00 8.00
TPARD Rafael Devers 8.00 20.00
TPARM Reese McGuire 2.50 6.00
TPARR Rio Ruiz 2.50 6.00
TPASN Sean Newcomb 3.00 8.00
TPATT Touki Toussaint 3.00 8.00
TPAVGJ Vladimir Guerrero Jr.
TPAVR Victor Robles 12.00 30.00
TPAWA Willy Adames 4.00 10.00
TPAWC Willson Contreras 10.00 25.00
TPAYM Yoan Moncada 50.00 120.00

2016 Bowman Platinum Top Prospects Autographs Green

*GREEN: .6X TO 1.5X BASIC
STATED ODDS 1:562 RETAIL
STATED PRINT RUN 75 SER.#'d SETS
TPAAB Alex Bregman 50.00 120.00
TPABM Billy McKinney 5.00 12.00
TPABR Brendan Rodgers 6.00 15.00
TPADC Daz Cameron 4.00 10.00
TPADS Dansby Swanson 40.00 100.00
TPALF Lucius Fox 10.00 25.00
TPAVGJ Vladimir Guerrero Jr. 125.00 300.00
TPAYM Yoan Moncada

2016 Bowman Platinum Top Prospects Autographs Orange

*ORANGE: 1X TO 2.5X BASIC
STATED ODDS 1:1646 RETAIL
STATED PRINT RUN 25 SER.#'d SETS
TPAAB Alex Bregman 75.00 200.00
TPABM Billy McKinney 8.00 20.00
TPABR Brendan Rodgers 10.00 25.00
TPADC Daz Cameron 6.00 15.00
TPADS Dansby Swanson 60.00 150.00
TPALF Lucius Fox 15.00 40.00
TPAVGJ Vladimir Guerrero Jr. 200.00 500.00
TPAYM Yoan Moncada 100.00 250.00

2016 Bowman Platinum Top Prospects Autographs Purple

*PURPLE: .5X TO 1.2X BASIC
STATED ODDS 1:289 RETAIL
STATED PRINT RUN 150 SER.#'d SETS
TPAAB Alex Bregman 40.00 100.00
TPABM Billy McKinney 4.00 10.00
TPABR Brendan Rodgers 5.00 12.00
TPADC Daz Cameron 3.00 8.00
TPADS Dansby Swanson 30.00 80.00
TPALF Lucius Fox 8.00 20.00
TPAVGJ Vladimir Guerrero Jr. 100.00 250.00
TPAYM Yoan Moncada

2017 Bowman Platinum

COMP.SET w/o SP's (100) 25.00 60.00
STATED SP ODDS 1:165 RETAIL
1A Kris Bryant .50 1.25
1B Bryant SP w/Bat 5.00 12.00
2 Bryce Harper .60 1.50
3 Daniel Murphy .30 .75
4 Dellin Betances .30 .75
5 Nomar Mazara .25 .60
6 Cole Hamels .30 .75
7 Matt Carpenter .40 1.00
8 Joey Votto .40 1.00
9 Stephen Strasburg .40 1.00
10 Aledmys Diaz .30 .75
11 Jake Thompson RC .40 1.00
12 Carson Fulmer RC .40 1.00
13A Andrew Benintendi RC 1.25 3.00
13B Bnntndi SP Dugout 12.00 30.00
14 David Ortiz .40 1.00
15 Gregory Polanco .30 .75
16 Starling Marte .30 .75
17 Jharel Cotton RC .40 1.00
18 Gavin Cecchini RC .40 1.00
19 Jackie Bradley Jr. .40 1.00
20 Anthony Rizzo .50 1.25
21 Francisco Lindor .40 1.00
22 Robert Gsellman RC .40 1.00
23 Max Scherzer .40 1.00
24 Trevor Story .40 1.00
25A Yoan Moncada RC 1.25 3.00
25B Mncda SP Glasses 8.00 20.00
26 Paul Goldschmidt .40 1.00
27 Amir Garrett RC .40 1.00
28 Tyler Glasnow RC 1.50 4.00
29 Nelson Cruz .40 1.00
30 Brandon Belt .30 .75
31 Tim Anderson .40 1.00
32 A.J. Pollock .25 .60
33 Evan Longoria .30 .75
34 Manny Machado .40 1.00
35 David Dahl RC .50 1.25
36 Jameson Taillon .30 .75
37 Danny Salazar .30 .75
38 Yoenis Cespedes .40 1.00
39 Braden Shipley RC .40 1.00
40 Jon Lester .30 .75
41 Andrew McCutchen .40 1.00
42 Robinson Cano .30 .75
43 Ryon Healy RC .50 1.25
44 Mark Trumbo .25 .60
45 Carlos Correa .40 1.00
46 Antonio Senzatela RC .40 1.00
47 Raimel Tapia RC .50 1.25
48 Freddie Freeman .50 1.25
49 Giancarlo Stanton .40 1.00
50 Corey Seager .40 1.00
51 Matt Strahm RC .40 1.00
52 Julio Urias .40 1.00
53 Nolan Arenado .60 1.50
54 Stephen Piscotty .30 .75
55 Joe Musgrove RC 1.25 3.00
56 Josh Donaldson .30 .75
57 Jose Altuve .30 .75
58 Yulieski Gurriel RC .60 1.50
59 Odubel Herrera .30 .75
60 Kenta Maeda .30 .75
61 Jorge Alfaro RC .50 1.25
62 Reynaldo Lopez RC .40 1.00
63A Mookie Betts .75 2.00
63B Betts SP Red jrsy 6.00 15.00
64 Ryan Braun .30 .75
65 Gary Sanchez .40 1.00
66 Craig Kimbrel .30 .75
67 Yu Darvish .40 1.00
68 Michael Fulmer .25 .60
69 Jose De Leon RC .40 1.00
70 Jose Bautista .30 .75
71 Chris Sale .40 1.00
72 Alex Reyes RC .50 1.25
73 Troy Tulowitzki .40 1.00
74 Andrew Miller .30 .75
75A Alex Bregman RC 2.00 5.00
75B Bregman SP Thrwng 12.00 30.00
76 Cody Bellinger RC 6.00 15.00
77 George Springer .30 .75
78A Dansby Swanson RC 1.00 2.50
78B Swanson SP w/Bat 6.00 15.00
79 Tyler Austin RC .50 1.25
80 Felix Hernandez .30 .75
81 Jacob deGrom .75 2.00
82 Clayton Kershaw .60 1.50
83 Ben Zobrist .30 .75
84 Ichiro .50 1.25
85 Noah Syndergaard .30 .75
86 Willson Contreras .40 1.00
87 Kyle Schwarber .40 1.00
88 Hunter Renfroe RC .50 1.25
89 Manny Margot RC .40 1.00
90 Jake Lamb .30 .75
91 Aaron Judge RC 5.00 12.00
92 Orlando Arcia RC .60 1.50
93 Jeff Hoffman RC .40 1.00
94 Wil Myers .30 .75
95 Jake Arrieta .30 .75
96 Buster Posey .50 1.25
97 Xander Bogaerts .40 1.00
98 Miguel Cabrera .40 1.00
99 Trea Turner .30 .75
100A Mike Trout 2.00 5.00
100B Trout SP No hat 20.00 50.00

2017 Bowman Platinum Green

*GREEN: 1.5X TO 4X BASIC
*GREEN RC: 1X TO 2.5X BASIC RC
STATED ODDS 1:84 RETAIL
STATED PRINT RUN 99 SER.#'d SETS

2017 Bowman Platinum Ice

*ICE: .6X TO 1.5X BASIC
*ICE RC: .6X TO 1.5X BASIC RC
RANDOM INSERTS IN PACKS

2017 Bowman Platinum Orange

*ORANGE: 5X TO 12X BASIC
*ORANGE RC: 3X TO 8X BASIC RC
STATED ODDS 1:329 RETAIL
STATED PRINT RUN 25 SER.#'d SETS

2017 Bowman Platinum Purple

*PURPLE: 1.2X TO 3X BASIC
*PURPLE RC: .75X TO 2X BASIC RC

STATED ODDS 1:33 RETAIL
STATED PRINT RUN 250 SER.#'d SETS

2017 Bowman Platinum MLB Autographs

STATED ODDS 1:390 RETAIL
PRINT RUNS B/WN 60-250 COPIES PER
EXCHANGE DEADLINE 6/30/2019
*GREEN/75: .5X TO 1.2X BASIC
MLBAAB Alex Bregman/60 20.00 50.00
MLBAABE Andrew Benintendi/100 30.00 80.00
MLBAAR Alex Reyes/80 8.00 20.00
MLBADB Dellin Betances/80 4.00 10.00
MLBADS Dansby Swanson
MLBAJD Jacob deGrom
MLBAJU Julio Urias
MLBAKB Kris Bryant
MLBALG Lucas Giolito/70 20.00 50.00
MLBARH Ryon Healy/250 5.00 12.00
MLBAYG Yulieski Gurriel/70 10.00 25.00

2017 Bowman Platinum MLB Autographs Orange

*ORANGE: .75X TO 2X BASIC
STATED ODDS 1:1186 RETAIL
STATED PRINT RUN 25 SER.#'d SETS
EXCHANGE DEADLINE 6/30/2019
MLBADS Dansby Swanson 40.00 100.00
MLBAJD Jacob deGrom 30.00 80.00

2017 Bowman Platinum Next Generation

STATED ODDS 1:5 RETAIL
*PURPLE/250: 1X TO 2.5X BASIC
*GREEN/99: 1.5X TO 4X BASIC
*ORANGE/25: 2X TO 5X BASIC
BNGAA Anthony Alford .25 .60
BNGAB Anthony Banda .25 .60
BNGAE Anderson Espinoza .25 .60
BNGAM Austin Meadows .60 1.50
BNGAR Amed Rosario .40 1.00
BNGBG Braxton Garrett .25 .60
BNGBR Brendan Rodgers .30 .75
BNGCA Christian Arroyo .40 1.00
BNGCB Cody Bellinger 4.00 10.00
BNGCS Cody Sedlock .25 .60
BNGEJ Eloy Jimenez 1.00 2.50
BNGFB Franklin Barreto .25 .60
BNGFM Francisco Mejia .40 1.00
BNGFMA Francis Martes .25 .60
BNGGT Gleyber Torres 4.00 10.00
BNGHB Harrison Bader .60 1.50
BNGJC J.P. Crawford .25 .60
BNGJJ Jahmai Jones .25 .60
BNGJS Josh Staumont .25 .60
BNGKL Kyle Lewis .50 1.25
BNGLB Lewis Brinson .40 1.00
BNGLT Leody Taveras 1.00 2.50
BNGMM Matt Manning .40 1.00
BNGNG Nick Gordon .25 .60
BNGNS Nick Senzel .75 2.00
BNGOA Ozzie Albies 1.00 2.50
BNGRD Rafael Devers .50 1.25
BNGVR Victor Robles .60 1.50
BNGWA Willy Adames .30 .75
BNGZC Zack Collins .30 .75

2017 Bowman Platinum Platinum Cut Autographs

STATED ODDS 1:553 RETAIL
STATED PRINT RUN 25 SER.#'d SETS
EXCHANGE DEADLINE 6/30/2019
PCAAA Anthony Alford
PCAAE Anderson Espinoza
PCAAK Alex Kirilloff
PCAAR Amed Rosario 60.00 150.00
PCAAV Alex Verdugo 40.00 100.00
PCABD Bobby Dalbec 15.00 40.00
PCABR Blake Rutherford EXCH 40.00 100.00
PCACB Cody Bellinger EXCH 150.00 400.00
PCACR Corey Ray 6.00 15.00
PCADC Dylan Cozens 5.00 12.00
PCAEJ Eloy Jimenez 60.00 150.00
PCAFB Franklin Barreto
PCAFM Francisco Mejia 40.00 100.00
PCAGL Gavin Lux 60.00 150.00
PCAGT Gleyber Torres 60.00 150.00
PCAIA Ian Anderson 20.00 50.00
PCAJG Jason Groome 30.00 80.00
PCAJM Jorge Mateo 25.00 60.00
PCAKL Kyle Lewis 20.00 50.00
PCAKM Kevin Maitan 8.00 20.00
PCAMK Mitch Keller 10.00 25.00
PCAMM Mickey Moniak 20.00 50.00
PCANS Nick Senzel 50.00 120.00
PCASN Sean Newcomb
PCATC Trevor Clifton
PCAWC Willie Calhoun 20.00 50.00
PCAZC Zack Collins

2017 Bowman Platinum Platinum Presence

STATED ODDS 1:10 RETAIL
*ORANGE/25: 2X TO 5X BASIC
PPAB Alex Bregman 1.50 4.00
PPABE Andrew Benintendi 1.00 2.50
PPAE Anderson Espinoza .30 .75
PPAJ Aaron Judge 8.00 20.00
PPAR Anthony Rizzo .60 1.50
PPARE Alex Reyes .40 1.00
PPARO Amed Rosario .50 1.25
PPBH Bryce Harper .75 2.00
PPCC Carlos Correa .50 1.25
PPCF Clint Frazier .60 1.50
PPCR Corey Ray .40 1.00
PPCS Corey Seager .50 1.25
PPDP Dustin Pedroia .50 1.25
PPDS Dansby Swanson .75 2.00
PPGT Gleyber Torres 5.00 12.00
PPJC J.P. Crawford .30 .75
PPJD Josh Donaldson .40 1.00
PPJG Jason Groome .60 1.50
PPKB Kris Bryant .60 1.50
PPKL Kyle Lewis .60 1.50
PPMM Mickey Moniak .60 1.50
PPMMA Manny Machado .50 1.25
PPMT Mike Trout 2.50 6.00
PPNS Nick Senzel 1.00 2.50
PPOA Orlando Arcia .50 1.25
PPPG Paul Goldschmidt .50 1.25
PPTG Tyler Glasnow 1.25 3.00
PPTS Trevor Story .50 1.25
PPVR Victor Robles .75 2.00
PPYM Yoan Moncada 1.00 2.50

2017 Bowman Platinum Platinum Presence Green

*GREEN: 1.2X TO 3X BASIC
STATED ODDS 1:277 RETAIL
STATED PRINT RUN 99 SER.#'d SETS
PPAJ Aaron Judge 40.00 100.00

2017 Bowman Platinum Platinum Presence Orange

*ORANGE: 2.5X TO 6X BASIC
STATED ODDS 1:1100 RETAIL
STATED PRINT RUN 25 SER.#'d SETS
PPAJ Aaron Judge 125.00 300.00
PPKB Kris Bryant 20.00 50.00
PPMT Mike Trout 20.00 50.00

2017 Bowman Platinum Platinum Presence Autographs

STATED ODDS 1:415 RETAIL
STATED PRINT RUN 50 SER.#'d SETS
EXCHANGE DEADLINE 6/30/2019
PPAB Alex Bregman 15.00 40.00
PPABE Andrew Benintendi 40.00 100.00
PPAJ Aaron Judge 200.00 400.00
PPAR Anthony Rizzo 20.00 50.00
PPARE Alex Reyes 8.00 20.00
PPARO Amed Rosario 25.00 60.00
PPCC Carlos Correa 15.00 40.00
PPCR Corey Ray 6.00 15.00
PPGT Gleyber Torres 40.00 100.00
PPJG Jason Groome 8.00 20.00
PPKB Kris Bryant 30.00 80.00
PPKL Kyle Lewis 15.00 40.00
PPMM Mickey Moniak 25.00 60.00
PPNS Nick Senzel 12.00 30.00
PPYM Yoan Moncada 30.00 80.00

2017 Bowman Platinum Rookie Radar

STATED ODDS 1:5 RETAIL
RRAB Alex Bregman 1.50 4.00
RRABE Andrew Benintendi 1.00 2.50
RRAJ Aaron Judge 6.00 15.00
RRAR Alex Reyes .40 1.00
RRCA Christian Arroyo .50 1.25
RRCB Cody Bellinger 5.00 12.00
RRDD David Dahl .40 1.00
RRDS Dansby Swanson .75 2.00
RRHR Hunter Renfroe .40 1.00
RRJA Jorge Alfaro .40 1.00
RRJC Jharel Cotton .30 .75
RRJDL Jose De Leon .30 .75
RRLW Luke Weaver .40 1.00
RRMM Manny Margot .30 .75
RROA Orlando Arcia .50 1.25
RRRT Raimel Tapia .40 1.00
RRTA Tyler Austin .40 1.00
RRTG Tyler Glasnow 1.25 3.00
RRYG Yulieski Gurriel .50 1.25
RRYM Yoan Moncada 1.00 2.50

2017 Bowman Platinum Rookie Radar Green

*GREEN: 1.2X TO 3X BASIC
STATED ODDS 1:416 RETAIL
STATED PRINT RUN 99 SER.#'d SETS
RRAJ Aaron Judge 40.00 100.00
RRCB Cody Bellinger 30.00 80.00

2017 Bowman Platinum Rookie Radar Orange

*ORANGE: 2.5X TO 6X BASIC
STATED ODDS 1:1643 RETAIL
STATED PRINT RUN 25 SER.#'d SETS
RRAJ Aaron Judge 75.00 200.00
RRCB Cody Bellinger 60.00 150.00

2017 Bowman Platinum Rookie Radar Purple

*PURPLE: .75X TO 2X BASIC
STATED ODDS 1:165 RETAIL
STATED PRINT RUN 250 SER.#'d SETS
RRAJ Aaron Judge 25.00 60.00
RRCB Cody Bellinger 20.00 50.00

2017 Bowman Platinum Rookie Radar Autographs

STATED ODDS 1:553 RETAIL
STATED PRINT RUN 50 SER.#'d SETS
EXCHANGE DEADLINE 6/30/2019
RRAB Alex Bregman 15.00 40.00
RRABE Andrew Benintendi 40.00 100.00
RRAJ Aaron Judge 200.00 400.00
RRAR Alex Reyes 8.00 20.00
RRDD David Dahl 8.00 20.00
RRDS Dansby Swanson 40.00 100.00
RRHR Hunter Renfroe 10.00 25.00
RRJA Jorge Alfaro 15.00 40.00
RRJDL Jose De Leon 10.00 25.00
RRLW Luke Weaver 8.00 20.00
RRMM Manny Margot 6.00 15.00
RRTA Tyler Austin 8.00 20.00
RRYG Yulieski Gurriel 12.00 30.00
RRYM Yoan Moncada 30.00 80.00

2017 Bowman Platinum Tools of the Craft Autographs Hitting

HITTING ODDS 1:587 RETAIL
PRINT RUNS B/WN 7-35 COPIES PER
NO PRICING ON QTY 10 OR LESS
EXCHANGE DEADLINE 6/30/2019
*SPEED: .4X TO 1X HITTING
*ARM: .4X TO 1X HITTING
*POWER: .4X TO 1X HITTING
*GLOVE: .4X TO 1X HITTING
TOCAAA Anthony Alford/35 4.00 10.00
TOCAAB Alex Bregman/35 20.00 50.00
TOCAABE Andrew Benintendi/35 30.00 80.00
TOCAAI Andy Ibanez/35 10.00 25.00
TOCAAV Alex Verdugo/35 20.00 50.00
TOCABP Brett Phillips/35 10.00 25.00
TOCABR Blake Rutherford/35 50.00 120.00
TOCACB Cody Bellinger/35 75.00 200.00
TOCACS Corey Seager/35 25.00 60.00
TOCAFB Franklin Barreto/35 10.00 25.00
TOCAGT Gleyber Torres/35 40.00 100.00
TOCAJA Jose Altuve/35 25.00 60.00
TOCAJM Jorge Mateo/35 20.00 50.00
TOCAKL Kyle Lewis/35 10.00 25.00
TOCAMM Mickey Moniak/35 25.00 60.00
TOCANS Nick Senzel/35 30.00 80.00
TOCAWC Willie Calhoun/35 10.00 25.00

2017 Bowman Platinum Top Prospects

COMP.SET w/o SP's (100) 25.00 60.00
STATED SP ODDS 1:146 RETAIL
TPAA Anthony Alford .25 .60
TPAE Anderson Espinoza .25 .60
TPAI Andy Ibanez .25 .60
TPAK Alex Kirilloff .60 1.50
TPAM Austin Meadows SP 12.00 30.00
TPAMO Adrian Morejon SP 10.00 25.00
TPAP A.J. Puk .50 1.25
TPAR Amed Rosario .40 1.00
TPARO Alfredo Rodriguez .30 .75
TPAS Andrew Sopko .25 .60
TPAV Alex Verdugo .40 1.00
TPBA Brady Aiken .60 1.50
TPBB Bo Bichette SP 20.00 50.00
TPBD Bobby Dalbec 1.50 4.00
TPBH Brent Honeywell .30 .75
TPBM Brandon Marsh .60 1.50
TPBP Brett Phillips .30 .75
TPBR Blake Rutherford .40 1.00
TPBRO Brendan Rodgers .30 .75
TPBW Brandon Woodruff .75 2.00
TPBX Braxton Garrett .25 .60
TPBZ Bradley Zimmer SP 6.00 15.00
TPCA Chance Adams .30 .75
TPCF Clint Frazier .50 1.25
TPCK Carter Kieboom .40 1.00
TPCQ Cal Quantrill .25 .60
TPCR Corey Ray .30 .75
TPCR Ray SP Running 10.00 25.00
TPCS Cody Sedlock SP 5.00 12.00
TPDC Dylan Cozens .25 .60
TPDCE Dylan Cease .40 1.00
TPDL Dawel Lugo .25 .60
TPDLA Dinelson Lamet .25 .60
TPDS Dominic Smith SP 10.00 25.00
TPEJ Eloy Jimenez 1.00 2.50
TPFB Franklin Barreto .25 .60
TPFM Francisco Mejia .40 1.00
TPFR Fernando Romero .25 .60
TPFRI Francisco Rios .25 .60
TPFW Forrest Whitley .60 1.50
TPGL Gavin Lux 1.00 2.50
TPGT Gleyber Torres 4.00 10.00
TPIA Ian Anderson .75 2.00
TPID Isan Diaz SP 12.00 30.00
TPIH Ian Happ .50 1.25
TPJC J.P. Crawford .25 .60
TPJD Justin Dunn .25 .60
TPJF Junior Fernandez .40 1.00
TPJG Jason Groome .50 1.25
TPJG Jason Groome SP 6.00 15.00
Hand at knee
TPJH Josh Hader .30 .75
TPJJ Joe Jimenez .30 .75
TPJJO Jahmai Jones .25 .60
TPJK James Kaprielian .25 .60
TPJM Jorge Mateo .25 .60
TPJO Jhailyn Ortiz .50 1.25
TPJS Juan Soto 6.00 15.00
TPJSH Justus Sheffield SP 12.00 30.00
TPKA Kolby Allard .25 .60
TPKF Kyle Funkhouser .25 .60
TPKL Kyle Lewis .50 1.25
TPKM Kevin Maitan .40 1.00
TPKN Kevin Newman .40 1.00
TPKT Kyle Tucker .60 1.50
TPLA Lazarito Armenteros .50 1.25
TPLAB Luis Alexander Basabe .40 1.00
TPLB Lewis Brinson .40 1.00
TPLC Luis Castillo .75 2.00
TPLF Lucius Fox .25 .60
TPLGJ Lourdes Gurriel Jr. .40 1.00
TPLO Luis Ortiz .25 .60
TPLT Leody Taveras 1.00 2.50
TPLU Luis Urias 1.00 2.50
TPMC Matt Chapman .75 2.00
TPMF Max Fried 1.00 2.50
TPMK Mitch Keller .30 .75
TPMKO Michael Kopech .75 2.00
TPMM Mickey Moniak .50 1.25
TPMM Mickey Moniak SP 8.00 20.00
Throwing
TPMMA Matt Manning SP 8.00 20.00
TPNG Nick Gordon .25 .60
TPNJ Nolan Jones .40 1.00
TPNS Nick Senzel .75 2.00
TPNW Nick Williams .30 .75
TPOA Ozzie Albies SP 20.00 50.00
TPOD Oscar de la Cruz .25 .60
TPPC P.J. Conlon .25 .60
TPPW Patrick Weigel .25 .60
TPRD Rafael Devers .50 1.25
TPRH Rhys Hoskins 1.00 2.50
TPRP Riley Pint .25 .60
TPRR Raudy Read .30 .75
TPRRA Roniel Raudes .25 .60
TPSN Sean Newcomb .30 .75
TPSS Sixto Sanchez 4.00 10.00
TPTAC Taylor Clarke .25 .60
TPTC Trevor Clifton .25 .60
TPTCL Trent Clark .25 .60
TPTF T.J. Friedl .25 .60
TPTJ Thomas Jones .25 .60
TPTM Triston McKenzie .75 2.00
TPTO Tyler O'Neill .30 .75
TPTS Thomas Szapucki .30 .75
TPTT Taylor Trammell 1.50 4.00
TPVR Victor Robles .60 1.50
TPWA Willy Adames .30 .75
TPWB Will Benson .30 .75
TPWBE Wuilmer Becerra .25 .60
TPWC Willie Calhoun .40 1.00
TPWCR Will Craig .25 .60
TPYA Yadier Alvarez .40 1.00
TPYCC Yu-Cheng Chang .40 1.00
TPZC Zack Collins .30 .75

2017 Bowman Platinum Top Prospects Blue Ice

*BLUE ICE: .75X TO 2X BASIC
RANDOM INSERTS IN PACKS

2017 Bowman Platinum Top Prospects Green

*GREEN: 1.2X TO 3X BASIC
STATED ODDS 1:84 RETAIL
STATED PRINT RUN 99 SER.#'d SETS
TPSS Sixto Sanchez 15.00 40.00

2017 Bowman Platinum Top Prospects Orange

*ORANGE: 3X TO 8X BASIC
STATED ODDS 1:287 RETAIL
STATED PRINT RUN 25 SER.#'d SETS

2017 Bowman Platinum Top Prospects Purple

*PURPLE: 1X TO 2.5X BASIC
STATED ODDS 1:121 RETAIL
STATED PRINT RUN 250 SER.#'d SETS

2017 Bowman Platinum Top Prospects White Ice

*WHITE ICE: .75X TO 2X BASIC
RANDOM INSERTS IN PACKS

2017 Bowman Platinum Top Prospects Autographs

STATED ODDS 1:19 RETAIL
EXCHANGE DEADLINE 6/30/2019
TPAA Anthony Alford 3.00 8.00
TPAE Anderson Espinoza 3.00 8.00
TPAI Andy Ibanez 3.00 8.00
TPAK Alex Kirilloff 15.00 40.00
TPAR Amed Rosario 15.00 40.00
TPAS Andrew Sopko 3.00 8.00
TPAV Alex Verdugo 5.00 12.00
TPBD Bobby Dalbec 20.00 50.00
TPBP Brett Phillips 4.00 10.00
TPBR Blake Rutherford 5.00 12.00
TPCK Carter Kieboom 8.00 20.00
TPCR Corey Ray 6.00 15.00
TPDC Dylan Cozens 6.00 15.00
TPDLA Dinelson Lamet 3.00 8.00
TPEJ Eloy Jimenez 30.00 80.00
TPFB Franklin Barreto 3.00 8.00
TPFM Francisco Mejia 6.00 15.00
TPFRI Francisco Rios 3.00 8.00
TPFW Forrest Whitley 6.00 15.00
TPGT Gleyber Torres 30.00 80.00
TPIA Ian Anderson 25.00 60.00
TPIH Ian Happ 8.00 20.00
TPJG Jason Groome 10.00 25.00
TPJJ Joe Jimenez 4.00 10.00
TPJJO Jahmai Jones 3.00 8.00
TPJM Jorge Mateo 3.00 8.00
TPJS Juan Soto 125.00 300.00
TPKL Kyle Lewis 6.00 15.00
TPKM Kevin Maitan 5.00 12.00
TPLA Lazarito Armenteros 8.00 20.00
TPLAB Luis Alexander Basabe 5.00 12.00
TPLGJ Lourdes Gurriel Jr. 5.00 12.00
TPMK Mitch Keller 4.00 10.00
TPMM Mickey Moniak 10.00 25.00
TPNS Nick Senzel 25.00 60.00
TPPC P.J. Conlon 3.00 8.00
TPRR Raudy Read 4.00 10.00
TPRRA Roniel Raudes 3.00 8.00
TPSN Sean Newcomb 4.00 10.00
TPTC Trevor Clifton 3.00 8.00
TPTM Triston McKenzie 8.00 20.00
TPWB Will Benson 3.00 8.00
TPWC Willie Calhoun 8.00 20.00
TPWCR Will Craig 3.00 8.00
TPZC Zack Collins 4.00 10.00

2017 Bowman Platinum Top Prospects Autographs Blue

*BLUE: .75X TO 2X BASIC
RANDOM INSERTS IN PACKS
STATED PRINT RUN 20 SER.#'d SETS
EXCHANGE DEADLINE 6/30/2019
TPLA Lazarito Armenteros 30.00 80.00

2017 Bowman Platinum Top Prospects Autographs Green

*GREEN: .6X TO 1.5X BASIC
STATED ODDS 1:158 RETAIL
STATED PRINT RUN 75 SER.#'d SETS
EXCHANGE DEADLINE 6/30/2019

2017 Bowman Platinum Top Prospects Autographs Orange

*ORANGE: .75X TO 2X BASIC
STATED ODDS 1:320 RETAIL
STATED PRINT RUN 25 SER.#'d SETS
EXCHANGE DEADLINE 6/30/2019
TPLA Lazarito Armenteros 30.00 80.00

2017 Bowman Platinum Top Prospects Autographs Purple

*PURPLE: .5X TO 1.2X BASIC
STATED ODDS 1:79 RETAIL
STATED PRINT RUN 150 SER.#'d SETS
EXCHANGE DEADLINE 6/30/2019

2018 Bowman Platinum

1 Kris Bryant .40 1.00
2 Rafael Devers RC 1.00 2.50
3 Jon Lester .25 .60
4 Paul DeJong .30 .75
5 Lorenzo Cain .20 .50
6 Freddie Freeman .40 1.00
7 Max Scherzer .30 .75
8 Nick Williams RC .40 1.00
9 Corey Kluber .25 .60
10 Jake Lamb .25 .60
11 Carlos Correa .30 .75
12 Daniel Murphy .25 .60
13 Victor Robles RC .75 2.00
14 Francisco Mejia RC .40 1.00
15 Joey Votto .30 .75
16 Robinson Cano .25 .60
17 Andrew McCutchen .30 .75
18 Joe Mauer .25 .60
19 Jonathan Schoop .20 .50
20 Justin Smoak .20 .50
21 Josh Bell .25 .60
22 Yoan Moncada .30 .75
23 Clayton Kershaw .50 1.25
24 Matt Carpenter .30 .75
25 Christian Yelich .40 1.00
26 Luiz Gohara RC .30 .75
27 Javier Baez .40 1.00
28 Manny Machado .30 .75
29 Austin Hays RC .50 1.25
30 George Springer .25 .60
31 Marcell Ozuna .30 .75
32 Cody Bellinger .60 1.50
33 Byron Buxton .30 .75
34 Shohei Ohtani RC 8.00 20.00
35 Dominic Smith RC .40 1.00
36 Carlos Santana .25 .60
37 Alex Bregman .30 .75
38 Ender Inciarte .20 .50
39 Miguel Cabrera .30 .75
40 Andrew Benintendi .30 .75
41 Ozzie Albies RC 1.00 2.50
42 Corey Seager .30 .75
43 Willie Calhoun RC .50 1.25
44 Tyler Mahle RC .40 1.00
45 Hunter Renfroe .20 .50
46 Kevin Kiermaier .25 .60
47 Alcides Escobar .25 .60
48 Josh Donaldson .25 .60
49 Mike Trout 1.50 4.00
50 Joey Gallo .25 .60
51 Wil Myers .25 .60
52 Eric Thames .25 .60
53 Rhys Hoskins RC 1.25 3.00
54 Jose Altuve .25 .60
55 Khris Davis .30 .75
56 Gregory Polanco .25 .60
57 Yoenis Cespedes .30 .75
58 Michael Fulmer .20 .50
59 Chance Sisco RC .40 1.00
60 Jose Abreu .30 .75
61 Josh Harrison .20 .50
62 Chris Sale .30 .75
63 Anthony Rizzo .40 1.00
64 Alex Verdugo RC .50 1.25
65 Charlie Blackmon .30 .75
66 Albert Pujols .40 1.00
67 Harrison Bader RC .50 1.25
68 Buster Posey .40 1.00
69 Adrian Beltre .30 .75
70 Paul Goldschmidt .30 .75
71 Felix Hernandez .25 .60
72 Giancarlo Stanton .30 .75
73 Luis Severino .25 .60
74 Ryan McMahon RC .75 2.00
75 Noah Syndergaard .25 .60
76 Nolan Arenado .50 1.25
77 Mookie Betts .60 1.50
78 Starlin Castro .20 .50
79 Clint Frazier RC .60 1.50
80 Francisco Lindor .30 .75
81 Stephen Piscotty .20 .50
82 Amed Rosario RC .40 1.00
83 Gary Sanchez .30 .75
84 Dee Gordon .20 .50
85 Cole Hamels .25 .60
86 Aaron Judge .75 2.00
87 Adam Jones .25 .60
88 Chris Archer .20 .50
89 Marcus Stroman .25 .60
90 Dansby Swanson .30 .75
91 Evan Longoria .25 .60
92 Zack Greinke .30 .75
93 Billy Hamilton .25 .60
94 Jack Flaherty RC 1.25 3.00
95 Justin Verlander .30 .75
96 Gerrit Cole .30 .75
97 Walker Buehler RC 1.50 4.00
98 Salvador Perez .25 .60
99 Justin Bour .20 .50
100 Bryce Harper .50 1.25

2018 Bowman Platinum Blue

*BLUE: 1.2X TO 3X BASIC
*BLUE RC: .75X TO 2X BASIC
STATED ODDS 1:78 RETAIL
STATED PRINT RUN 150 SER.#'d SETS
34 Shohei Ohtani 12.00 30.00
49 Mike Trout 6.00 15.00

2018 Bowman Platinum Green

*GREEN: 1.5X TO 4X BASIC
*GREEN RC: 1X TO 2.5X BASIC
STATED ODDS 1:119 RETAIL
STATED PRINT RUN 99 SER.#'d SETS
34 Shohei Ohtani 15.00 40.00
49 Mike Trout 8.00 20.00

2018 Bowman Platinum Ice

*ICE: .75X TO 2X BASIC
*ICE RC: .5X TO 1.2X BASIC
FOUR PER VALUE BOX
49 Mike Trout 4.00 10.00

2018 Bowman Platinum Orange

*ORANGE: 5X TO 12X BASIC
*ORANGE RC: 3X TO 8X BASIC
STATED ODDS 1:191 RETAIL
STATED PRINT RUN 25 SER.#'d SETS
34 Shohei Ohtani 50.00 120.00
49 Mike Trout 25.00 60.00

2018 Bowman Platinum Purple

*PURPLE: 1X TO 2.5X BASIC
*PURPLE RC: .6X TO 1.5X BASIC
STATED ODDS 1:47 RETAIL
STATED PRINT RUN 250 SER.#'d SETS
49 Mike Trout 5.00 12.00

2018 Bowman Platinum Sky Blue

*SKY BLUE: 1X TO 2.5X BASIC
*SKY BLUE RC: .6X TO 1.5X BASIC
INSERTED IN FAT PACKS
49 Mike Trout 5.00 12.00

2018 Bowman Platinum Base Set Photo Variations

STATED ODDS 1:391 RETAIL
1 Bryant Gray jrsy 3.00 8.00
2 Devers Snglsss 5.00 12.00
23 Krshw Blue shirt 8.00 20.00
32 Bllngr Ctchng 4.00 10.00
34 Ohtani w/Bag 12.00 30.00
49 Trout Snglsss 20.00 50.00
54 Altuve w/Glove 6.00 15.00
80 Lindor T-shirt 6.00 15.00
86 Judge Bat on shldr 10.00 25.00
100 Harper Knee up 4.00 10.00

2018 Bowman Platinum 80 Grade Prospect Autographs

STATED ODDS 1:556 RETAIL
STATED PRINT RUN 80 SER.#'d SETS
EXCHANGE DEADLINE 6/30/2020
80GAAA Albert Abreu 5.00 12.00
80GAAP A.J. Puk
80GABM Brendan McKay 8.00 20.00
80GAGT Gleyber Torres 50.00 125.00
80GAHG Hunter Greene 15.00 40.00
80GAHR Heliot Ramos 8.00 20.00
80GAIA Ian Anderson
80GAJA Jo Adell 40.00 100.00
80GAJB Jake Burger 10.00 25.00
80GAJG Jay Groome 6.00 15.00
80GAKH Keston Hiura 15.00 40.00
80GAKM Kevin Maitan 6.00 15.00
80GAKR Keibert Ruiz 8.00 20.00
80GALR Luis Robert 75.00 200.00
80GAMB Michel Baez 5.00 12.00
80GAMK Michael Kopech 20.00 50.00
80GARL Royce Lewis 10.00 25.00

2018 Bowman Platinum Die Cut Autographs

STATED ODDS 1:617 RETAIL
PRINT RUNS B/WN 25-50 COPIES PER
EXCHANGE DEADLINE 6/30/2020
PCAABR Alex Bregman/25 20.00 50.00
PCAAG Andres Gimenez/50 15.00 40.00
PCAAH Austin Hays/50 25.00 60.00
PCAAJ Aaron Judge
PCAAR Amed Rosario 10.00 25.00
PCAAV Alex Verdugo/25 12.00 30.00
PCACK Carter Kieboom/50 12.00 30.00
PCACP Christian Pache/25 25.00 60.00
PCACS Chris Shaw/50 12.00 30.00
PCAFM Francisco Mejia/50 6.00 15.00
PCAGT Gleyber Torres
PCAHC Hans Crouse/50 8.00 20.00
PCAHR Heliot Ramos/50 25.00 60.00
PCAJH Jordan Hicks/50 10.00 25.00
PCAJK James Kaprielian/50 10.00 25.00
PCAKM Kevin Maitan/25 6.00 15.00
PCAKR Keibert Ruiz/25 20.00 50.00
PCAMB Michel Baez/50 10.00 25.00
PCAMK Mitch Keller/25 12.00 30.00
PCAMKO Michael Kopech/25 20.00 50.00
PCAMT Mike Trout
PCANS Nick Senzel/25 25.00 60.00
PCAOA Ozzie Albies EXCH 30.00 80.00
PCAPD Paul DeJong/25 8.00 20.00
PCARA Ronald Acuna Jr./50 75.00 200.00
PCARL Royce Lewis 15.00 40.00
PCARM Ryan Mountcastle/50 25.00 60.00
PCASA Sandy Alcantara
PCASB Shane Baz
PCATL Tristen Lutz/50 8.00 20.00
PCATR Trevor Rogers
PCAVR Victor Robles/25 30.00 80.00

2018 Bowman Platinum Hunter Greene Short Print Autographs

STATED ODDS 1:6615 RETAIL
STATED PRINT RUN 10 SER.#'d SETS
EXCHANGE DEADLINE 6/30/2020
HG1 Hunter Greene 75.00 200.00
HG2 Hunter Greene 75.00 200.00
HG3 Hunter Greene 75.00 200.00
HG4 Hunter Greene 75.00 200.00
HG5 Hunter Greene 75.00 200.00
HG6 Hunter Greene 75.00 200.00
HG7 Hunter Greene 75.00 200.00
HG8 Hunter Greene 75.00 200.00
HG9 Hunter Greene 75.00 200.00
HG10 Hunter Greene 75.00 200.00

2018 Bowman Platinum Hunter Greene Short Prints

STATED ODDS 1:234 RETAIL
HG1 Hunter Greene 2.50 6.00
HG2 Hunter Greene 2.50 6.00
HG3 Hunter Greene 2.50 6.00
HG4 Hunter Greene 2.50 6.00
HG5 Hunter Greene 2.50 6.00
HG6 Hunter Greene 2.50 6.00
HG7 Hunter Greene 2.50 6.00
HG8 Hunter Greene 2.50 6.00
HG9 Hunter Greene 2.50 6.00
HG10 Hunter Greene 2.50 6.00

2018 Bowman Platinum Platinum Presence

STATED ODDS 1:10 RETAIL
*PURPLE/250: 1.2X TO 3X BASIC
*GREEN/99: 1.5X TO 4X BASIC
*ORANGE/25: 6X TO 15X BASIC
PP1 Nick Senzel .75 2.00
PP2 Jo Adell 1.00 2.50
PP3 Keston Hiura .60 1.50
PP4 Michel Baez .25 .60
PP5 Austin Hays .40 1.00
PP6 Heliot Ramos .40 1.00
PP7 Alex Verdugo .40 1.00
PP8 Albert Abreu .25 .60
PP9 Michael Kopech 1.00 2.50
PP10 Kris Bryant .50 1.25
PP11 Luis Robert .60 1.50
PP12 Amed Rosario .30 .75
PP13 Brendan McKay .40 1.00
PP14 Colton Welker .25 .60
PP15 Mitch Keller .30 .75
PP16 Mike Trout 2.00 5.00
PP17 Clayton Kershaw .60 1.50
PP18 Francisco Lindor .40 1.00
PP19 Jose Altuve .30 .75
PP20 Nolan Arenado .60 1.50

2018 Bowman Platinum Platinum Presence Autographs

STATED ODDS 1:892 RETAIL
STATED PRINT RUN 50 SER.#'d SETS
EXCHANGE DEADLINE 6/30/2020
PPAAA Albert Abreu 8.00 20.00
PPAAH Austin Hays 8.00 20.00
PPAAR Amed Rosario 10.00 25.00
PPAAV Alex Verdugo 8.00 20.00
PPABM Brendan McKay 8.00 20.00
PPACW Colton Welker 6.00 15.00
PPAHR Heliot Ramos 15.00 40.00
PPAJA Jo Adell 40.00 100.00
PPAKB Kris Bryant
PPAKH Keston Hiura 10.00 25.00
PPALR Luis Robert 50.00 120.00
PPAMB Michel Baez 5.00 12.00
PPAMK Mitch Keller 6.00 15.00
PPAMKO Michael Kopech 20.00 50.00
PPANS Nick Senzel 15.00 40.00

2018 Bowman Platinum Prismatic Prodigies

STATED ODDS 1:5 RETAIL
*PURPLE/250: 1.5X TO 4X BASIC
*GREEN/99: 2X TO 5X BASIC
*ORANGE/25: 6X TO 15X BASIC
PPP1 Eloy Jimenez 1.00 2.50
PPP2 D.L. Hall .25 .60
PPP3 Tanner Houck .60 1.50
PPP4 Jake Burger .25 .60
PPP5 Colton Welker .25 .60
PPP6 Franklin Perez .30 .75
PPP7 Forrest Whitley .40 1.00
PPP8 Nick Pratto .30 .75
PPP9 Jay Groome .30 .75
PPP10 Royce Lewis 1.00 2.50
PPP11 Gleyber Torres 2.00 5.00
PPP12 Lazarito Armenteros .50 1.25
PPP13 Evan White .60 1.50
PPP14 Brendan McKay .40 1.00
PPP15 Bubba Thompson .40 1.00
PPP17 Jon Duplantier .25 .60
PPP18 Cristian Pache 1.25 3.00
PPP19 Adbert Alzolay .30 .75
PPP20 Tony Santillan .25 .60
PPP21 Brendan Rodgers .30 .75
PPP22 Jeren Kendall .30 .75
PPP23 Trevor Rogers .60 1.50
PPP24 Corbin Burnes 2.00 5.00
PPP25 Peter Alonso 2.50 6.00
PPP26 Adam Haseley .40 1.00
PPP27 Mitch Keller .30 .75
PPP28 MacKenzie Gore .50 1.25
PPP29 Heliot Ramos .40 1.00
PPP30 Jordan Hicks .50 1.25
PPP31 Seth Romero .25 .60
PPP32 Ryan Mountcastle 1.25 3.00
PPP33 Steven Duggar .25 .60
PPP34 Fernando Tatis Jr. 2.50 6.00
PPP35 Andres Gimenez .60 1.50
PPP36 Alex Faedo .40 1.00
PPP37 Kyle Wright .60 1.50
PPP38 Keston Hiura .60 1.50
PPP39 Brandon Marsh .40 1.00
PPP40 Carter Kieboom .40 1.00

2018 Bowman Platinum Prismatic Prodigies Autographs

STATED ODDS 1:498 RETAIL
STATED PRINT RUN 50 SER.#'d SETS
EXCHANGE DEADLINE 6/30/2020
PPPAAA Adbert Alzolay 6.00 15.00
PPPAAF Alex Faedo 8.00 20.00
PPPABMC Brendan McKay 8.00 20.00
PPPABR Brendan Rodgers 10.00 25.00
PPPABT Bubba Thompson 8.00 20.00
PPPACB Corbin Burnes 20.00 50.00
PPPACP Cristian Pache 12.00 30.00
PPPACW Colton Welker 6.00 15.00
PPPAEW Evan White
PPPAGT Gleyber Torres 60.00 150.00
PPPAHR Heliot Ramos 15.00 40.00
PPPAJB Jake Burger
PPPAJD Jon Duplantier 5.00 12.00
PPPAJG Jay Groome
PPPAJH Jordan Hicks 10.00 25.00
PPPAJK Jeren Kendall 6.00 15.00
PPPAKW Kyle Wright
PPPALA Lazarito Armenteros
PPPAMK Mitch Keller 6.00 15.00
PPPANP Nick Pratto 6.00 15.00
PPPAPA Peter Alonso 40.00 100.00
PPPARL Royce Lewis EXCH 20.00 50.00
PPPATH Tanner Houck 12.00 30.00
PPPATR Trevor Rogers 12.00 30.00

2018 Bowman Platinum Rookie Autograph Pieces

STATED ODDS 1:374 RETAIL
STATED PRINT RUN 99 SER.#'d SETS
EXCHANGE DEADLINE 6/30/2020
*ORANGE/25: .6X TO 1.5X BASIC
PRAPAH Austin Hays 5.00 12.00
PRAPAR Amed Rosario 8.00 20.00
PRAPAS Andrew Stevenson 3.00 8.00
PRAPAV Alex Verdugo 5.00 12.00
PRAPBW Brandon Woodruff 10.00 25.00
PRAPCF Clint Frazier
PRAPDS Dominic Smith 4.00 10.00
PRAPFM Francisco Mejia 8.00 20.00
PRAPHB Harrison Bader 5.00 12.00
PRAPJF Jack Flaherty 12.00 30.00
PRAPLS Lucas Sims 3.00 8.00
PRAPMG Miguel Gomez 3.00 8.00
PRAPND Nicky Delmonico 3.00 8.00
PRAPRD Rafael Devers EXCH 15.00 40.00
PRAPRM Ryan McMahon 6.00 15.00
PRAPSO Shohei Ohtani
PRAPTM Tyler Mahle 4.00 10.00
PRAPTN Tomas Nido 4.00 10.00
PRAPVR Victor Robles 10.00 25.00
PRAPZG Zack Granite

2018 Bowman Platinum Rookie Revelations

STATED ODDS 1:5 RETAIL
*PURPLE/250: 1.5X TO 4X BASIC

*GREEN/99: 2X TO 5X BASIC
*ORANGE/25: 6X TO 15X BASIC
RR1 Rhys Hoskins 1.00 2.50
RR2 Victor Robles .60 1.50
RR3 Francisco Mejia .30 .75
RR4 Miguel Andujar 1.00 2.50
RR5 Brandon Woodruff .75 2.00
RR6 Max Fried 1.00 2.50
RR7 Ozzie Albies .75 2.00
RR8 J.P. Crawford .25 .60
RR9 Shohei Ohtani 6.00 15.00
RR10 Tyler Mahle .30 .75
RR11 Andrew Stevenson .25 .60
RR12 Nicky Delmonico .25 .60
RR13 Rafael Devers .75 2.00
RR14 Amed Rosario .30 .75
RR15 Clint Frazier .50 1.25
RR16 Alex Verdugo .40 1.00
RR17 Nick Williams .30 .75
RR18 Willie Calhoun .40 1.00
RR19 Walker Buehler 1.25 3.00
RR20 Harrison Bader .40 1.00

2018 Bowman Platinum Rookie Revelations Autographs

STATED ODDS 1:707 RETAIL
STATED PRINT RUN 50 SER.#'d SETS
EXCHANGE DEADLINE 6/30/2020
RRAAR Amed Rosario/50 10.00 25.00
RRAAS Andrew Stevenson/99
RRAAV Alex Verdugo/50 8.00 20.00
RRAFM Francisco Mejia/50 6.00 15.00
RRAMA Miguel Andujar/99
RRAMF Max Fried/99
RRAND Nicky Delmonico/99
RRAOA Ozzie Albies/50
RRARD Rafael Devers/50
RRARH Rhys Hoskins/50 40.00 100.00
RRASO Shohei Ohtani/50 300.00 600.00
RRATM Tyler Mahle/99
RRAVR Victor Robles/99 8.00 20.00

2018 Bowman Platinum Top Prospect Autographs

STATED ODDS 1:15 RETAIL
EXCHANGE DEADLINE 6/30/2020
*BLUE/150: .5X TO 1.2X BASE
*GREEN/99: .5X TO 1.2X BASE
*ORANGE/25: 1X TO 2.5X BASE
TOP1 Brendan McKay 4.00 10.00
TOP2 Ronald Acuna 75.00 200.00
TOP3 Gleyber Torres 40.00 100.00
TOP4 Hunter Greene 15.00 40.00
TOP5 Royce Lewis 20.00 50.00
TOP6 MacKenzie Gore 8.00 20.00
TOP8 Luis Robert 60.00 150.00
TOP10 Kevin Maitan 3.00 8.00
TOP11 Jo Adell 30.00 80.00
TOP12 Mitch Keller 3.00 8.00
TOP13 Keston Hiura 15.00 40.00
TOP14 Michael Kopech 6.00 15.00
TOP15 Peter Alonso 40.00 100.00
TOP17 Jay Groome 3.00 8.00
TOP18 Keibert Ruiz 4.00 10.00
TOP19 Adbert Alzolay 3.00 8.00
TOP20 Joey Wentz 3.00 8.00
TOP21 Cristian Pache 15.00 40.00
TOP22 Gavin Lux 25.00 60.00
TOP23 McKenzie Mills 2.50 6.00
TOP24 Michel Baez 2.50 6.00
TOP25 Albert Abreu 4.00 10.00
TOP26 P.J. Conlon 2.50 6.00
TOP27 Dennis Santana 2.50 6.00
TOP29 Heliot Ramos 4.00 10.00
TOP31 Dawel Lugo 2.50 6.00
TOP32 Andres Gimenez 4.00 10.00
TOP33 Sean Murphy 4.00 10.00
TOP34 Tyler Freeman 2.50 6.00
TOP35 Kelvin Gutierrez 2.50 6.00
TOP36 Hans Crouse 4.00 10.00
TOP37 Matt Festa 2.50 6.00
TOP38 MJ Melendez 2.50 6.00
TOP40 Drew Ellis 3.00 8.00
TOP41 Corbin Martin 2.50 6.00
TOP42 Kacy Clemens 3.00 8.00
TOP43 CJ Chatham 3.00 8.00
TOP44 Kevin Kramer 2.50 6.00
TOP45 Jose Adolis Garcia 15.00 40.00
TOP46 Enyel De Los Santos 3.00 8.00
TOP47 Carter Kieboom 8.00 20.00
TOP48 Brian Mundell 2.50 6.00
TOP53 Quentin Holmes 2.50 6.00
TOP54 Johan Mieses 4.00 10.00
TOP55 Keegan Akin 3.00 8.00
TOP71 Daniel Johnson 2.50 6.00
TOP73 Brayan Hernandez 2.50 6.00
TOP80 Shane Bieber 20.00 50.00
TOP81 Trevor Stephan 2.50 6.00
TOP82 Nick Allen 2.50 6.00
TOP93 Evan White 6.00 15.00
TOP97 Jordan Hicks 4.00 10.00
TOP99 Jeren Kendall 4.00 10.00

2018 Bowman Platinum Top Prospect Autographs Ice

*ICE: .6X TO 1.5X BASIC
STATED ODDS 1:247 RETAIL
STATED PRINT RUN 50 SER.#'d SETS
EXCHANGE DEADLINE 6/30/2020
TOP2 Ronald Acuna 125.00 300.00

2018 Bowman Platinum Top Prospects

TOP1 Brendan McKay .40 1.00
TOP2 Ronald Acuna Jr. 8.00 20.00
TOP3 Gleyber Torres 2.50 6.00
TOP4 Hunter Greene .75 2.00
TOP5 Royce Lewis 1.00 2.50
TOP6 MacKenzie Gore .50 1.25
TOP7 A.J. Puk .40 1.00
TOP8 Luis Robert 4.00 10.00
TOP9 Jake Burger .25 .60
TOP10 Kevin Maitan .30 .75
TOP11 Jo Adell 1.00 2.50
TOP12 Mitch Keller .30 .75
TOP13 Keston Hiura .60 1.50
TOP14 Michael Kopech 1.00 2.50
TOP15 Peter Alonso 2.50 6.00
TOP16 Kyle Tucker .60 1.50
TOP17 Jay Groome .30 .75
TOP18 Keibert Ruiz 1.25 3.00
TOP19 Adbert Alzolay .30 .75
TOP20 Joey Wentz .30 .75
TOP21 Cristian Pache 1.25 3.00
TOP22 Gavin Lux 1.00 2.50
TOP23 McKenzie Mills .25 .60
TOP24 Michel Baez .25 .60
TOP25 Albert Abreu .25 .60
TOP26 P.J. Conlon .25 .60
TOP27 Dennis Santana .25 .60
TOP28 Zack Littell .25 .60
TOP29 Heliot Ramos .40 1.00
TOP30 Hudson Potts .30 .75
TOP31 Dawel Lugo .25 .60
TOP32 Andres Gimenez .60 1.50
TOP33 Sean Murphy .40 1.00
TOP34 Tyler Freeman .25 .60
TOP35 Kelvin Gutierrez .25 .60
TOP36 Hans Crouse .40 1.00
TOP37 Matt Festa .25 .60
TOP38 MJ Melendez .25 .60
TOP39 Jacob Gonzalez .50 1.25
TOP40 Drew Ellis .30 .75
TOP41 Corbin Martin .25 .60
TOP42 Kacy Clemens .30 .75
TOP43 C.J. Chatham .30 .75
TOP44 Kevin Kramer .25 .60
TOP45 Jose Adonis Garcia 2.50 6.00
TOP46 Enyel De Los Santos .30 .75
TOP47 Carter Kieboom .40 1.00
TOP48 Brian Mundell .25 .60
TOP49 Jorge Guzman .25 .60
TOP50 Merandy Gonzalez .25 .60
TOP51 Jordan Humphreys .25 .60
TOP52 Matt Beaty .30 .75
TOP53 Quentin Holmes .25 .60
TOP54 Johan Mieses .40 1.00
TOP55 Keegan Akin .30 .75
TOP56 Vladimir Guerrero Jr. 2.50 6.00
TOP57 Estevan Florial .40 1.00
TOP58 Alex Faedo .40 1.00
TOP59 Zack Burdi .25 .60
TOP60 Eloy Jimenez 1.00 2.50
TOP61 Mickey Moniak .60 1.50
TOP62 Bo Bichette 1.00 2.50
TOP63 Riley Pint .25 .60
TOP64 Cole Brannen .30 .75
TOP65 J.B. Bukauskas .25 .60
TOP66 Seth Romero .25 .60
TOP67 Shed Long .30 .75
TOP68 Pedro Avila .25 .60
TOP69 Thomas Hatch .30 .75
TOP70 Isaac Paredes 1.25 3.00
TOP71 Daniel Johnson .25 .60
TOP72 Greg Deichmann .30 .75
TOP73 Brayan Hernandez .25 .60
TOP74 Gregory Soto .25 .60
TOP75 Franklin Perez .30 .75
TOP76 Nicky Lopez .40 1.00
TOP77 LoLo Sanchez .30 .75
TOP78 Nick Senzel .75 2.00
TOP79 Sheldon Neuse .25 .60
TOP80 Shane Bieber 5.00 12.00
TOP81 Trevor Stephan .25 .60
TOP82 Nick Allen .25 .60
TOP83 Ryan Mountcastle 1.25 3.00
TOP84 Colton Welker .25 .60
TOP85 Shane Baz .30 .75
TOP86 Tristen Lutz .30 .75
TOP87 Chris Shaw .25 .60
TOP88 Corbin Burnes 2.00 5.00
TOP89 D.L. Hall .25 .60
TOP90 Tanner Houck .60 1.50
TOP91 Nick Pratto .30 .75
TOP92 Lazarito Armenteros .50 1.25
TOP93 Evan White .60 1.50
TOP94 Bubba Thompson .40 1.00
TOP96 Jon Duplantier .25 .60
TOP97 Jordan Hicks .50 1.25
TOP98 Brendan Rodgers .30 .75
TOP99 Jeren Kendall .30 .75
TOP100 Trevor Rogers .60 1.50

2018 Bowman Platinum Top Prospects Blue

*BLUE: 1X TO 2.5X BASIC
STATED ODDS 1:78 RETAIL
STATED PRINT RUN 150 SER.#'d SETS

2018 Bowman Platinum Top Prospects Green

*GREEN: 1.2X TO 3X BASIC
STATED ODDS 1:119 RETAIL
STATED PRINT RUN 99 SER.#'d SETS

2018 Bowman Platinum Top Prospects Ice

*ICE: .6X TO 1.5X BASIC
FOUR PER VALUE BOX

2018 Bowman Platinum Top Prospects Orange

*ORANGE: 4X TO 10X BASIC
STATED ODDS 1:191 RETAIL
STATED PRINT RUN 25 SER.#'d SETS

2018 Bowman Platinum Top Prospects Purple

*PURPLE: .75X TO 2X BASIC
STATED ODDS 1:47 RETAIL
STATED PRINT RUN 250 SER.#'d SETS

2018 Bowman Platinum Top Prospects Sky Blue

*SKY BLUE: .75X TO 2X BASIC
INSERTED IN FAT PACKS

2019 Bowman Platinum

COMPLETE SET (100) 12.00 30.00
1 Mike Trout 1.50 4.00
2 Shohei Ohtani .50 1.25
3 Taylor Ward RC .30 .75
4 Albert Pujols .40 1.00
5 Jose Altuve .25 .60
6 Kyle Tucker RC .75 2.00
7 Josh James RC .50 1.25
8 Carlos Correa .30 .75
9 Alex Bregman .30 .75
10 Justin Verlander .30 .75
11 Khris Davis .30 .75
12 Ramon Laureano .40 1.00
13 Matt Chapman .30 .75
14 Danny Jansen RC .30 .75
15 Lourdes Gurriel Jr. .25 .60
16 Rowdy Tellez RC .50 1.25
17 Ryan Borucki RC .30 .75
18 Ronald Acuna Jr. 1.50 4.00
19 Touki Toussaint RC .40 1.00
20 Kolby Allard RC .50 1.25
21 Ozzie Albies .30 .75
22 Christian Yelich .40 1.00
23 Josh Hader .25 .60
24 Corbin Burnes RC 2.50 6.00
25 Paul Goldschmidt .30 .75
26 Harrison Bader .25 .60
27 Dakota Hudson RC .40 1.00
28 Yadier Molina .40 1.00
29 Kris Bryant .40 1.00
30 Anthony Rizzo .40 1.00
31 Javier Baez .40 1.00
32 Zack Greinke .30 .75
33 Jake Lamb .25 .60
34 Clayton Kershaw .50 1.25
35 Walker Buehler .40 1.00
36 A.J. Pollock .20 .50
37 Cody Bellinger .60 1.50
38 Corey Seager .30 .75
39 Max Muncy .25 .60
40 Buster Posey .40 1.00
41 Brandon Crawford .25 .60
42 Steven Duggar RC .40 1.00
43 Dereck Rodriguez .20 .50
44 Francisco Lindor .30 .75
45 Jose Ramirez .25 .60
46 Corey Kluber .25 .60
47 Justus Sheffield RC .50 1.25
48 Yusei Kikuchi RC .50 1.25
49 Mitch Haniger .25 .60
50 Austin Dean RC .30 .75
51 Brian Anderson .20 .50
52 Jacob deGrom .60 1.50
53 Noah Syndergaard .25 .60
54 Edwin Diaz .25 .60
55 Robinson Cano .25 .60
56 Juan Soto 1.00 2.50
57 Max Scherzer .30 .75
58 Victor Robles .40 1.00
59 Cedric Mullins RC .60 1.50
60 Trey Mancini .25 .60
61 Luis Urias RC .50 1.25
62 Eric Hosmer .25 .60
63 Rhys Hoskins .40 1.00
64 Andrew McCutchen .30 .75
65 Aaron Nola .25 .60
66 Chris Archer .20 .50
67 Kevin Newman RC .50 1.25
68 Starling Marte .25 .60
69 Joey Gallo .25 .60
70 Nomar Mazara .20 .50
71 Blake Snell .25 .60
72 Willy Adames .20 .50
73 Austin Meadows .30 .75
74 Mookie Betts .60 1.50
75 Andrew Benintendi .30 .75
76 Rafael Devers .40 1.00
77 J.D. Martinez .30 .75
78 Chris Sale .30 .75
79 David Price .25 .60
80 Joey Votto .30 .75
81 Yasiel Puig .30 .75
82 Scooter Gennett .25 .60
83 Nolan Arenado .50 1.25
84 Trevor Story .30 .75
85 Charlie Blackmon .30 .75
86 Whit Merrifield .30 .75
87 Ryan O'Hearn RC .30 .75
88 Salvador Perez .25 .60
89 Miguel Cabrera .30 .75
90 Christin Stewart RC .40 1.00
91 Willians Astudillo RC .30 .75
92 Eddie Rosario .25 .60
93 Jose Berrios .25 .60
94 Jose Abreu .30 .75
95 Michael Kopech RC 1.00 2.50
96 Chance Adams RC .30 .75
97 Gleyber Torres .60 1.50
98 Aaron Judge .75 2.00
99 Miguel Andujar .30 .75
100 Giancarlo Stanton .30 .75

2019 Bowman Platinum Blue

*BLUE: 1.2X TO 3X BASIC
*BLUE RC: .75X TO 2X BASIC
STATED ODDS 1:132 MEGA
STATED PRINT RUN 150 SER.#'d SETS
1 Mike Trout 6.00 15.00

2019 Bowman Platinum Gold

*GOLD: 4X TO 10X BASIC
*GOLD RC: 2.5X TO 6X BASIC
STATED ODDS 1:396 MEGA
STATED PRINT RUN 50 SER.#'d SETS
1 Mike Trout 20.00 50.00

2019 Bowman Platinum Green

*GREEN: 1.5X TO 4X BASIC
*GREEN RC: 1X TO 2.5X BASIC
STATED ODDS 1:200 MEGA
STATED PRINT RUN 99 SER.#'d SETS
1 Mike Trout 8.00 20.00

2019 Bowman Platinum Ice

*ICE: .75X TO 2X BASIC
*ICE RC: .5X TO 1.2X BASIC
STATED ODDS 1:2 BLASTER
1 Mike Trout 4.00 10.00

2019 Bowman Platinum Orange

*ORANGE: 5X TO 12X BASIC
*ORANGE RC: 3X TO 8X BASIC
STATED ODDS 1:287 MEGA
STATED PRINT RUN 25 SER.#'d SETS
1 Mike Trout 25.00 60.00

2019 Bowman Platinum Purple

*PURPLE: 1X TO 2.5X BASIC
*PURPLE RC: .6X TO 1.5X BASIC
STATED ODDS 1:80 MEGA
STATED PRINT RUN 250 SER.#'d SETS
1 Mike Trout 5.00 12.00

2019 Bowman Platinum Sky Blue

*SKY BLUE: 1X TO 2.5X BASIC
*SKY BLUE RC: .6X TO 1.5X BASIC
RANDOM INSERTS IN PACKS
1 Mike Trout 5.00 12.00

2019 Bowman Platinum Base Set Variations

STATED ODDS 1:275 JUMBO
*ICE: .5X TO 1.2X BASIC
*PURPLE/250: 1.2X TO 3X BASIC
*BLUE/150: 1.2X TO 3X BASIC
*GREEN/99: 1.5X TO 4X BASIC
*GOLD/50: 2.5X TO 6X BASIC
*ORANGE/25: 3X TO 8X BASIC
1 Mike Trout 25.00 60.00
2 Shohei Ohtani 15.00 40.00
9 Alex Bregman 6.00 15.00
18 Ronald Acuna Jr. 15.00 40.00
20 Pete Alonso 5.00 12.00
22 Christian Yelich 8.00 20.00
23 Fernando Tatis Jr. 12.00 30.00
27 Vladimir Guerrero Jr. 4.00 10.00
48 Yusei Kikuchi 6.00 15.00
56 Juan Soto 10.00 25.00
63 Rhys Hoskins 8.00 20.00
74 Mookie Betts 8.00 20.00
74 Eloy Jimenez 2.50 6.00
97 Gleyber Torres 8.00 20.00

2019 Bowman Platinum Die Cut Autographs

STATED ODDS 1:1582 JUMBO
PRINT RUNS B/WN 25-50 COPIES PER
EXCHANGE DEADLINE 5/31/2021
PCABB Brock Burke/50 8.00 20.00
PCABD Bobby Dalbec/50 25.00 60.00
PCACMI Casey Mize/25 20.00 50.00
PCACS Chad Spanberger/50 4.00 10.00
PCADH Dakota Hudson
PCADR Dereck Rodriguez/50 15.00 40.00
PCAEJ Eloy Jimenez/25 40.00 100.00
PCAEW Evan White/50
PCAJA Jordyn Adams
PCAJI Jonathan India/25 12.00 30.00
PCAJL Jesus Luzardo/50 15.00 40.00
PCAJS Justus Sheffield/25
PCAJSO Juan Soto/25 40.00 100.00
PCAKA Kolby Allard EXCH 12.00 30.00
PCAKB Kris Bryant/25
PCAKH Keston Hiura/50 20.00 50.00
PCAKT Kyle Tucker/25
PCALU Luis Urias/25 15.00 40.00
PCAMM Max Muncy/50 15.00 40.00
PCANM Nick Madrigal/25
PCAPA Pete Alonso/50 75.00 200.00
PCARA Ronald Acuna Jr./25 50.00 120.00
PCASB Seth Beer/50 50.00 120.00
PCASO Shohei Ohtani
PCAVG Vladimir Guerrero Jr./25 100.00 250.00
PCAWA Willy Adames/50 10.00 25.00
PCAWF Wander Franco/50 125.00 300.00

2019 Bowman Platinum Platinum Pieces Autograph Relics

STATED ODDS 1:1049 JUMBO
PRINT RUNS B/WN 30-99 COPIES PER
EXCHANGE DEADLINE 5/31/2021
PPARAG Adolis Garcia/99 25.00 60.00
PPARBN Brandon Nimmo/99 5.00 12.00
PPARDC Dylan Cozens/99 4.00 10.00
PPARDJ Danny Jansen/99 6.00 15.00
PPARJF Jack Flaherty/99 6.00 15.00
PPARJH Josh Hader/99 6.00 15.00
PPARJM Jeff McNeil/99 15.00 40.00
PPARJN Jacob Nix/99 5.00 12.00
PPARKA Kolby Allard/99 6.00 15.00
PPARKB Kris Bryant/30 30.00 80.00
PPARKN Kevin Newman/99 10.00 25.00
PPARKS Kohl Stewart 5.00 12.00
PPARKT Kyle Tucker 10.00 25.00
PPARKW Kyle Wright 6.00 15.00
PPARRA Ronald Acuna Jr./50 40.00 100.00
PPARRB Ryan Borucki 4.00 10.00
PPARRD Rafael Devers/50 20.00 50.00
PPARRO Ryan O'Hearn 4.00 10.00
PPARSK Scott Kingery 5.00 12.00
PPARVR Victor RoCbles 8.00 20.00

2019 Bowman Platinum Platinum Pieces Autograph Relics Orange

*ORANGE: .6X TO 1.5X p/r 99
*ORANGE: .5X TO 1.2X p/r 30-50
STATED ODDS 1:1400 MEGA
STATED PRINT RUN 25 SER.#'d SETS
EXCHANGE DEADLINE 5/31/2021
PPARSK Scott Kingery 20.00 50.00

2019 Bowman Platinum Platinum Presence

STATED ODDS 1:4 JUMBO
*PURPLE/250: .75X TO 2X BASIC
*GREEN/99: 1X TO 2.5X BASIC
*ORANGE/25: 4X TO 10X BASIC
PP1 Yusei Kikuchi .40 1.00
PP2 Vladimir Guerrero Jr. 1.50 4.00
PP3 Eloy Jimenez 1.00 2.50
PP4 Matt Chapman .40 1.00
PP5 Seth Beer .60 1.50
PP6 Joey Bart .75 2.00
PP7 Wander Franco 5.00 12.00
PP8 Gleyber Torres .75 2.00
PP9 Juan Soto 1.25 3.00
PP10 Victor Victor Mesa .50 1.25
PP11 Jacob deGrom .75 2.00
PP12 Miguel Andujar .40 1.00
PP13 Keibert Ruiz 1.25 3.00
PP14 Rafael Devers .50 1.25
PP15 Victor Robles .50 1.25
PP16 Rhys Hoskins .50 1.25
PP17 Christian Yelich .50 1.25
PP18 Jose Ramirez .30 .75
PP19 Aaron Judge 1.00 2.50
PP20 Ronald Acuna Jr. 2.00 5.00

2019 Bowman Platinum Platinum Presence Autographs

STATED ODDS 1:12540 JUMBO
STATED PRINT RUN 50 SER.#'d SETS
EXCHANGE DEADLINE 5/31/2021
PPAEJ Eloy Jimenez 15.00 40.00
PPAJB Joey Bart 25.00 60.00
PPAJD Jacob deGrom 30.00 80.00
PPAJR Jose Ramirez 8.00 20.00
PPAJS Juan Soto 40.00 100.00
PPAKR Keibert Ruiz 12.00 30.00
PPAMA Miguel Andujar 10.00 25.00
PPARD Rafael Devers 15.00 40.00
PPARH Rhys Hoskins 20.00 50.00
PPASB Seth Beer 20.00 50.00
PPAVG Vladimir Guerrero Jr. 125.00 300.00
PPAVM Victor Victor Mesa 12.00 30.00
PPAVR Victor Robles 8.00 20.00
PPAWF Wander Franco 125.00 300.00
PPAYK Yusei Kikuchi 12.00 30.00

2019 Bowman Platinum Prismatic Prodigies

STATED ODDS 1:2 JUMBO
*PURPLE/250: .75X TO 2X BASIC
*GREEN/99: 1X TO 2.5X BASIC
*ORANGE/25: 4X TO 10X BASIC
PPP1 Jo Adell 1.00 2.50
PPP2 Victor Victor Mesa .50 1.25
PPP3 Jonathan India 1.50 4.00
PPP4 Jordan Groshans .50 1.25
PPP5 Jarred Kelenic 1.25 3.00
PPP6 Triston Casas 1.00 2.50
PPP7 Brady Singer 1.25 3.00
PPP8 Nolan Gorman .75 2.00
PPP9 Jesus Luzardo .40 1.00
PPP10 Estevan Florial .40 1.00
PPP11 William Contreras .30 .75
PPP12 Mark Vientos .40 1.00
PPP13 Alec Bohm 1.50 4.00
PPP14 Carter Kieboom .40 1.00
PPP15 Miguel Amaya .40 1.00
PPP16 Corey Ray .25 .60
PPP17 Travis Swaggerty .40 1.00
PPP18 Taylor Widener .25 .60
PPP19 Grant Lavigne .30 .75
PPP20 Keibert Ruiz 1.25 3.00
PPP21 Bobby Dalbec 1.50 4.00
PPP22 Joey Bart .75 2.00
PPP23 Yusniel Diaz .40 1.00
PPP24 Wander Franco 5.00 12.00
PPP25 Luis Robert 2.00 5.00
PPP26 Ethan Hankins .30 .75
PPP27 Casey Mize .60 1.50
PPP28 Brusdar Graterol .30 .75
PPP29 Seth Beer .60 1.50
PPP30 Cole Winn .25 .60
PPP31 Anthony Seigler .40 1.00
PPP32 Vladimir Guerrero Jr. 1.50 4.00
PPP33 Nick Solak 1.00 2.50
PPP34 Alex Kirilloff .40 1.00
PPP35 Bo Bichette .75 2.00
PPP36 Hunter Greene .40 1.00
PPP37 Nico Hoerner .75 2.00
PPP38 Garrett Whitlock .40 1.00
PPP39 Nick Madrigal 1.00 2.50
PPP40 Matthew Liberatore .25 .60

2019 Bowman Platinum Prismatic Prodigies Autographs

STATED ODDS 1:1270 JUMBO
STATED PRINT RUN 50 SER.#'d SETS
EXCHANGE DEADLINE 5/31/2021
PPPAAB Alec Bohm 10.00 25.00
PPPAAS Anthony Seigler 6.00 15.00
PPPABG Brusdar Graterol
PPPABS Brady Singer 12.00 30.00
PPPACK Carter Kieboom 6.00 15.00
PPPACM Casey Mize 25.00 60.00
PPPACR Corey Ray 4.00 10.00
PPPACW Cole Winn 4.00 10.00
PPPAEF Estevan Florial 15.00 40.00
PPPAEH Ethan Hankins 5.00 12.00
PPPAGL Grant Lavigne 5.00 12.00
PPPAJA Jo Adell 20.00 50.00
PPPAJB Joey Bart 40.00 100.00
PPPAJG Jordan Groshans
PPPAJI Jonathan India 20.00 50.00
PPPAJK Jarred Kelenic 60.00 150.00
PPPAJL Jesus Luzardo
PPPAKR Keibert Ruiz 12.00 30.00
PPPALR Luis Robert 50.00 120.00
PPPAMA Miguel Amaya 6.00 15.00
PPPANG Nolan Gorman 20.00 50.00
PPPANM Nick Madrigal 15.00 40.00
PPPASB Seth Beer 20.00 50.00
PPPATC Triston Casas 15.00 40.00
PPPATS Travis Swaggerty 6.00 15.00
PPPATW Taylor Widener 4.00 10.00
PPPAVM Victor Victor Mesa 12.00 30.00
PPPAWC William Contreras
PPPAWF Wander Franco 125.00 300.00
PPPAYD Yusniel Diaz 6.00 15.00

2019 Bowman Platinum Prolific Power

STATED ODDS 1:165 JUMBO
POW1 Jo Adell 4.00 10.00
POW2 Ronaldo Hernandez 1.00 2.50
POW3 Keibert Ruiz 5.00 12.00
POW4 Carter Kieboom 1.50 4.00
POW5 Nolan Gorman 3.00 8.00
POW6 Wander Franco 20.00 50.00
POW7 Joey Bart 3.00 8.00
POW8 Vladimir Guerrero Jr. 6.00 15.00
POW9 Ibandel Isabel 1.50 4.00
POW10 Corey Ray 1.00 2.50

2019 Bowman Platinum Refined Autographs

STATED ODDS 1:960 JUMBO
PRINT RUNS B/WN 15-99 COPIES PER
NO PRICING ON QTY 15
EXCHANGE DEADLINE 5/31/2021
RAAK Andrew Knizner/99 8.00 20.00
RABB Brock Burke/99 3.00 8.00
RACK Carter Kieboom/99 12.00 30.00
RACR Corey Ray/99 3.00 8.00
RADH Darwinzon Hernandez/99 3.00 8.00
RADM Dustin May/99 10.00 25.00
RAEJ Eloy Jimenez/20 40.00 100.00
RAJL Jesus Luzardo/99 5.00 12.00
RAKR Keibert Ruiz/99 15.00 40.00
RAMS Brandon Marsh/99 6.00 15.00
RANL Nicky Lopez/99 6.00 15.00
RANS Nick Solak/99 6.00 15.00
RARL Royce Lewis/30
RARM Ryan McKenna/99 3.00 8.00
RARMO Ryan Mountcastle/99 10.00 25.00
RARR Roberto Ramos/99 4.00 10.00
RASL Fernando Tatis Jr./40 125.00 300.00
RASN Sheldon Neuse/99 3.00 8.00
RATW Taylor Widener/99 3.00 8.00
RAWF Wander Franco/99 100.00 250.00

2019 Bowman Platinum Renowned Rookies

STATED ODDS 1:2 JUMBO
*PURPLE/250: .75X TO 2X BASIC
*GREEN/99: 1X TO 2.5X BASIC
*ORANGE/25: 4X TO 10X BASIC
RR1 Yusei Kikuchi .40 1.00
RR2 Willians Astudillo .25 .60
RR3 Ramon Laureano .50 1.25
RR4 Jeff McNeil .60 1.50
RR5 Justus Sheffield .40 1.00
RR6 Dakota Hudson .30 .75
RR7 Josh James .40 1.00
RR8 Chance Adams .25 .60
RR9 Luis Urias .40 1.00
RR10 Rowdy Tellez .40 1.00
RR11 Danny Jansen .25 .60
RR12 Ryan O'Hearn .25 .60
RR13 Michael Kopech .75 2.00
RR14 Corbin Burnes 2.00 5.00
RR15 Kolby Allard .40 1.00
RR16 Cionel Perez .25 .60
RR17 Touki Toussaint .30 .75
RR18 Brad Keller .25 .60
RR19 Christin Stewart .30 .75
RR20 Kevin Newman .40 1.00

2019 Bowman Platinum Renowned Rookies Autographs

STATED ODDS 1:2540 JUMBO
STATED PRINT RUN 50 SER.#'d SETS
EXCHANGE DEADLINE 5/31/2021
RRACA Chance Adams 4.00 10.00
RRACB Corbin Burnes 12.00 30.00
RRADH Dakota Hudson 12.00 30.00
RRADJ Danny Jansen
RRAJJ Josh James
RRAJM Jeff McNeil 25.00 60.00
RRAJS Justus Sheffield
RRAKA Kolby Allard
RRALU Luis Urias 12.00 30.00
RRAMK Michael Kopech 12.00 30.00
RRARL Ramon Laureano 20.00 50.00
RRARO Ryan O'Hearn 4.00 10.00
RRART Rowdy Tellez 6.00 15.00
RRAWA Willians Astudillo 4.00 10.00
RRAYK Yusei Kikuchi 12.00 30.00

2019 Bowman Platinum Top Prospect Autographs

STATED ODDS 1:24 JUMBO
EXCHANGE DEADLINE 5/31/2021
*BLUE/150: .5X TO 1.2X BASE
*GREEN/99: .5X TO 1.2X BASE
*ICE/50: .6X TO 1.5X BASIC
*ORANGE/25: .75X TO 2X BASE
TOP1 Vladimir Guerrero Jr. 60.00 150.00
TOP2 Shervyen Newton 4.00 10.00
TOP3 Casey Mize 6.00 15.00
TOP4 Joey Bart 20.00 50.00
TOP5 Nick Madrigal 8.00 20.00
TOP6 Alec Bohm 25.00 60.00
TOP7 Jonathan India 6.00 15.00
TOP8 Jarred Kelenic 25.00 60.00
TOP9 Wander Franco 75.00 200.00
TOP10 Estevan Florial 10.00 25.00
TOP11 Victor Victor Mesa 8.00 20.00
TOP12 Seuly Matias 3.00 8.00
TOP13 Jordan Groshans 8.00 20.00
TOP14 Victor Mesa Jr. 6.00 15.00
TOP15 Jordyn Adams 4.00 10.00
TOP16 Nick Solak 5.00 12.00
TOP18 Logan Gilbert 4.00 10.00
TOP19 Brady Singer 8.00 20.00
TOP20 Nolan Gorman 12.00 30.00
TOP21 Luis Garcia 10.00 25.00
TOP22 Elehuris Montero 4.00 10.00
TOP23 Yusniel Diaz 4.00 10.00
TOP24 Keegan Thompson 2.50 6.00
TOP25 Anthony Seigler 4.00 10.00
TOP26 Luis Arraez 8.00 20.00
TOP27 Nico Hoerner 12.00 30.00
TOP28 Seth Beer 6.00 15.00
TOP29 Jose Azocar 2.50 6.00
TOP30 Logan Webb 4.00 10.00
TOP31 Bobby Dalbec 15.00 40.00
TOP32 Nicky Lopez 4.00 10.00
TOP33 Miguel Amaya 4.00 10.00
TOP34 Ethan Hankins 3.00 8.00
TOP35 Shane McClanahan 3.00 8.00
TOP36 Taylor Widener 2.50 6.00
TOP37 Dauris Valdez 2.50 6.00
TOP38 Pablo Olivares 4.00 10.00
TOP39 Chad Spanberger 2.50 6.00
TOP40 Tristan Pompey 3.00 8.00
TOP41 Alex Royalty 2.50 6.00
TOP42 Griffin Conine 4.00 10.00
TOP43 Owen White 2.50 6.00
TOP44 Josiah Gray 8.00 20.00
TOP45 Luken Baker 3.00 8.00
TOP46 Brewer Hicklen 4.00 10.00
TOP47 Cash Case 3.00 8.00
TOP48 Connor Wong 3.00 8.00
TOP49 Griffin Canning 4.00 10.00
TOP50 Liam Jenkins 2.50 6.00
TOP51 Adam Wolf 4.00 10.00
TOP52 Ronaldo Hernandez 2.50 6.00
TOP53 Tommy Romero 3.00 8.00
TOP54 Blaze Alexander 2.50 6.00
TOP55 Owen Miller 3.00 8.00
TOP56 Matt Mercer 2.50 6.00
TOP57 Ronny Mauricio 10.00 25.00
TOP59 Andrew Knizner 4.00 10.00
TOP60 Freudis Nova 6.00 15.00
TOP62 Tirso Ornelas 5.00 12.00

2019 Bowman Platinum Top Prospects

TOP1 Vladimir Guerrero Jr. 1.50 4.00
TOP2 Shervyen Newton .40 1.00
TOP3 Casey Mize .60 1.50
TOP4 Joey Bart .75 2.00
TOP5 Nick Madrigal 1.00 2.50
TOP6 Alec Bohm 1.50 4.00
TOP7 Jonathan India 1.50 4.00
TOP8 Jarred Kelenic 1.25 3.00
TOP9 Wander Franco 5.00 12.00
TOP10 Estevan Florial .40 1.00
TOP11 Victor Victor Mesa .50 1.25
TOP12 Seuly Matias .30 .75
TOP13 Jordan Groshans .50 1.25
TOP14 Victor Mesa Jr. .50 1.25
TOP15 Jordyn Adams .40 1.00
TOP16 Nick Solak 1.00 2.50
TOP17 Matthew Liberatore .25 .60
TOP18 Logan Gilbert .40 1.00
TOP19 Brady Singer 1.25 3.00
TOP20 Nolan Gorman .75 2.00
TOP21 Luis Garcia 1.00 2.50
TOP22 Elehuris Montero .40 1.00
TOP23 Yusniel Diaz .40 1.00
TOP24 Keegan Thompson .25 .60
TOP25 Anthony Seigler .40 1.00
TOP26 Luis Arraez 1.00 2.50
TOP27 Nico Hoerner .75 2.00
TOP28 Seth Beer .60 1.50
TOP29 Jose Azocar .25 .60
TOP30 Logan Webb .40 1.00
TOP31 Bobby Dalbec 1.50 4.00
TOP32 Nicky Lopez .40 1.00
TOP33 Miguel Amaya .40 1.00
TOP34 Ethan Hankins .30 .75
TOP35 Shane McClanahan .30 .75
TOP36 Taylor Widener .25 .60
TOP37 Dauris Valdez .25 .60
TOP38 Pablo Olivares .40 1.00
TOP39 Chad Spanberger .25 .60
TOP40 Tristan Pompey .30 .75
TOP41 Alex Royalty .25 .60
TOP42 Griffin Conine .40 1.00
TOP43 Owen White .25 .60
TOP44 Josiah Gray .40 1.00
TOP45 Luken Baker .30 .75
TOP46 Brewer Hicklen .40 1.00
TOP47 Cash Case .30 .75
TOP48 Connor Wong .30 .75
TOP49 Griffin Canning .40 1.00
TOP50 Liam Jenkins .25 .60
TOP51 Adam Wolf .40 1.00
TOP52 Ronaldo Hernandez .25 .60
TOP53 Tommy Romero .30 .75
TOP54 Blaze Alexander .25 .60
TOP55 Owen Miller .30 .75
TOP56 Matt Mercer .25 .60
TOP57 Ronny Mauricio .60 1.50
TOP58 Diego Cartaya .50 1.25
TOP59 Andrew Knizner .40 1.00
TOP60 Freudis Nova .40 1.00
TOP61 Brice Turang .30 .75
TOP62 Tirso Ornelas .25 .60
TOP63 Julio Rodriguez 2.00 5.00
TOP64 Sheldon Neuse .25 .60
TOP65 Will Smith .60 1.50
TOP66 Cristian Javier .30 .75
TOP67 Noelvi Marte 1.00 2.50
TOP68 Rylan Bannon .30 .75
TOP69 Josh Breaux .30 .75
TOP70 Deivi Garcia 10.00 25.00
TOP71 Alex Kirilloff .40 1.00
TOP72 Jo Adell 1.00 2.50
TOP73 Brendan Rodgers .40 1.00
TOP74 Carter Kieboom .40 1.00
TOP75 Brock Deatherage .25 .60
TOP76 James Marvel .40 1.00
TOP77 Jose de la Cruz .75 2.00
TOP78 Carlos Cortes .25 .60
TOP79 Eli Morgan .25 .60
TOP80 Matt Vierling .40 1.00
TOP81 Royce Lewis .50 1.25
TOP82 Bo Bichette .75 2.00
TOP83 Mackenzie Gore .50 1.25
TOP84 Hunter Greene .40 1.00
TOP85 Brendan McKay .40 1.00
TOP86 Keston Hiura .75 2.00
TOP87 Pedro Castellanos .25 .60
TOP88 Luis Robert 4.00 10.00
TOP89 Andres Munoz .40 1.00
TOP90 Sean Murphy .30 .75
TOP91 Cristian Pache .60 1.50
TOP92 Heliot Ramos .40 1.00
TOP93 Jon Duplantier .25 .60
TOP94 Nate Pearson .75 2.00
TOP95 Ryan Weathers .25 .60
TOP96 Alek Thomas .40 1.00
TOP97 Triston Casas 1.00 2.50
TOP98 Cole Roederer .75 2.00
TOP99 Triston McKenzie .75 2.00
TOP100 Yordan Alvarez 4.00 10.00

2019 Bowman Platinum Top Prospects Blue

*BLUE: 1X TO 2.5X BASIC
STATED ODDS 1:55 JUMBO
STATED PRINT RUN 150 SER.#'d SETS

2019 Bowman Platinum Top Prospects Gold

*GOLD: 3X TO 8X BASIC
STATED ODDS 1:165 JUMBO
STATED PRINT RUN 50 SER.#'d SETS

2019 Bowman Platinum Top Prospects Green

*GREEN: 1.2X TO 3X BASIC
STATED ODDS 1:84 JUMBO
STATED PRINT RUN 99 SER.#'d SETS

2019 Bowman Platinum Top Prospects Ice

*ICE: .6X TO 1.5X BASIC
STATED ODDS 1:4 BLASTER

2019 Bowman Platinum Top Prospects Orange
*ORANGE: 4X TO 10X BASIC
STATED ODDS 1:287 MEGA
STATED PRINT RUN 25 SER.#'d SETS

2019 Bowman Platinum Top Prospects Purple
*PURPLE: .75X TO 2X BASIC
STATED ODDS 1:33 JUMBO
STATED PRINT RUN 250 SER.#'d SETS

2019 Bowman Platinum Top Prospects Sky Blue
*SKY BLUE: .75X TO 2X BASIC
STATED ODDS 1:2 JUMBO

2020 Bowman Platinum
1 Mookie Betts .60 1.50
2 Max Scherzer .30 .75
3 DJ LeMahieu .30 .75
4 John Means .30 .75
5 Shohei Ohtani .50 1.25
6 Gleyber Torres .60 1.50
7 J.D. Martinez .30 .75
8 Nick Solak RC 1.25 3.00
9 Isan Diaz RC .50 1.25
10 Paul DeJong .30 .75
11 Ozzie Albies .30 .75
12 Gavin Lux RC 1.50 4.00
13 Bryce Harper .50 1.25
14 Justin Dunn RC .40 1.00
15 Manny Machado .30 .75
16 Freddie Freeman .40 1.00
17 Chris Paddack .30 .75
18 Nico Hoerner RC 1.25 3.00
19 Brendan McKay RC .50 1.25
20 Trey Mancini .30 .75
21 Corey Kluber .25 .60
22 J.T. Realmuto .30 .75
23 Anthony Rizzo .40 1.00
24 Vladimir Guerrero Jr. .50 1.25
25 Clayton Kershaw .50 1.25
26 Francisco Lindor .30 .75
27 Whit Merrifield .30 .75
28 Giancarlo Stanton .30 .75
29 Luis Robert RC 4.00 10.00
30 Josh Bell .25 .60
31 Nolan Arenado .50 1.25
32 Ketel Marte .25 .60
33 Didi Gregorius .25 .60
34 Elvis Andrus .25 .60
35 Andrew Benintendi .30 .75
36 Kris Bryant .40 1.00
37 Keston Hiura .40 1.00
38 Nick Senzel .30 .75
39 Miguel Cabrera .30 .75
40 Alex Bregman .30 .75
41 Starling Marte .25 .60
42 Stephen Strasburg .30 .75
43 Matt Chapman .30 .75
44 Rafael Devers .40 1.00
45 A.J. Puk RC .50 1.25
46 Jose Altuve .25 .60
47 Zack Greinke .30 .75
48 Eloy Jimenez .60 1.50
49 Pete Alonso .75 2.00
50 Kyle Lewis RC 2.50 6.00
51 Jesus Luzardo RC .60 1.50
52 Eugenio Suarez .25 .60
53 Jeff McNeil .25 .60
54 Nick Castellanos .30 .75
55 Trevor Story .30 .75
56 Chris Sale .30 .75
57 Cavan Biggio .40 1.00
58 Jorge Soler .30 .75
59 Aristides Aquino RC .75 2.00
60 Justin Verlander .30 .75
61 Blake Snell .25 .60
62 Ronald Acuna Jr. 1.25 3.00
63 Buster Posey .40 1.00
64 Anthony Rendon .30 .75
65 Mike Trout 1.50 4.00
66 Austin Meadows .30 .75
67 Shane Bieber .30 .75
68 Aaron Judge .75 2.00
69 George Springer .25 .60
70 Aaron Nola .25 .60
71 Jack Flaherty .30 .75
72 Javier Baez .40 1.00
73 Rhys Hoskins .40 1.00
74 Christian Yelich .40 1.00
75 Jordan Yamamoto RC .30 .75
76 Paul Goldschmidt .30 .75
77 Walker Buehler .40 1.00
78 Bo Bichette RC 2.50 6.00
79 Jacob deGrom .60 1.50
80 Mike Soroka .30 .75
81 Fernando Tatis Jr. 1.50 4.00
82 Cody Bellinger .60 1.50
83 Juan Soto 1.00 2.50
84 Noah Syndergaard .25 .60
85 Yadier Molina .40 1.00
86 Bryan Reynolds .25 .60
87 Josh Hader .25 .60
88 Zac Gallen RC .75 2.00
89 Josh Donaldson .25 .60
90 Joey Votto .30 .75
91 Carlos Correa .30 .75
92 Mike Yastrzemski .50 1.25
93 Jose Ramirez .25 .60
94 Nelson Cruz .30 .75
95 Tim Anderson .30 .75
96 Albert Pujols .40 1.00
97 Xander Bogaerts .30 .75
98 Hyun-Jin Ryu .25 .60
99 Gerrit Cole .50 1.25
100 Yordan Alvarez RC 3.00 8.00

2020 Bowman Platinum Blue
BLUE: 1.2X TO 3X BASIC
BLUE RC: .8X TO 2X BASIC RC
RANDOM INSERTS IN PACKS
STATED PRINT RUN 150 SER.#'d SETS

2020 Bowman Platinum Gold
GOLD: 3X TO 8X BASIC
GOLD RC: 2X TO 5X BASIC RC
RANDOM INSERTS IN PACKS
STATED PRINT RUN 50 SER.#'d SETS
29 Luis Robert 40.00 100.00
50 Kyle Lewis 20.00 50.00
78 Bo Bichette 20.00 50.00

2020 Bowman Platinum Green
*GREEN: 1.5X TO 4X BASIC
*GREEN RC: 1X TO 2.5X BASIC RC
RANDOM INSERTS IN PACKS
STATED PRINT RUN 99 SER.#'d SETS
50 Kyle Lewis 10.00 25.00
78 Bo Bichette 10.00 25.00

2020 Bowman Platinum Orange
*ORANGE: 5X TO 12X BASIC
*ORANGE RC: 3X TO 8X BASIC RC
RANDOM INSERTS IN PACKS
STATED PRINT RUN 25 SER.#'d SETS
29 Luis Robert 60.00 150.00
50 Kyle Lewis 30.00 80.00
65 Mike Trout 30.00 80.00
78 Bo Bichette 30.00 80.00

2020 Bowman Platinum Pink
*PINK: 1.2X TO 3X BASIC
*PINK RC: .8X TO 2X BASIC RC
RANDOM INSERTS IN PACKS
STATED PRINT RUN 199 SER.#'d SETS

2020 Bowman Platinum Purple
*PURPLE: 1X TO 2.5X BASIC
*PURPLE RC: .6X TO 1.5X BASIC RC
RANDOM INSERTS IN PACKS
STATED PRINT RUN 250 SER.#'d SETS

2020 Bowman Platinum Teal
*TEAL: 1X TO 2.5X BASIC
*TEAL RC: .6X TO 1.5X BASIC RC
RANDOM INSERTS IN PACKS
STATED PRINT RUN 299 SER.#'d SETS

2020 Bowman Platinum Cut Autographs
RANDOM INSERTS IN PACKS
PRINT RUNS B/WN 25-50 COPIES PER
EXCHANGE DEADLINE XX/XX/XX
PCAAA Aristides Aquino/50 10.00 25.00
PCAAB Alec Bohm/25 50.00 120.00
PCAAM Andres Munoz/50 6.00 15.00
PCAAR Adley Rutschman/25 40.00 100.00
PCAAT Alek Thomas/50 5.00 12.00
PCABH Bryce Harper
PCABM Brendan McKay/25 8.00 20.00
PCABW Bobby Witt Jr./25 60.00 150.00
PCACA CJ Abrams/50 12.00 30.00
PCACB Cavan Biggio/50 25.00 60.00
PCAGC Gerrit Cole/25 30.00 80.00
PCAGR Grayson Rodriguez/50 6.00 15.00
PCAJB Joey Bart/25 20.00 50.00
PCAJK Jarred Kelenic/50 40.00 100.00
PCAJR Julio Rodriguez
PCAKH Keston Hiura
PCAKL Kyle Lewis/50 50.00 120.00
PCALA Luis Arraez/50 8.00 20.00
PCAMY Mike Yastrzemski/50 25.00 60.00
PCANH Nico Hoerner
PCAPA Pete Alonso/25 30.00 80.00
PCARA Ronald Acuna Jr./25 60.00 150.00
PCARG Riley Greene/25 20.00 50.00
PCASB Seth Beer
PCATA Tim Anderson/50 8.00 20.00
PCATL Trevor Larnach/50 8.00 20.00
PCAVG Vladimir Guerrero Jr./25 30.00 80.00
PCAWB Walker Buehler/25 30.00 80.00
PCAYA Yordan Alvarez/25 50.00 120.00

2020 Bowman Platinum Platinum Pieces Autograph Relics
RANDOM INSERTS IN PACKS
PRINT RUNS B/WN 35-99 COPIES PER
EXCHANGE DEADLINE XX/XX/XX
PPARAA Adbert Alzolay/99 4.00 10.00
PPARAC Aaron Civale/99 6.00 15.00
PPARAM Andres Munoz/99 5.00 12.00
PPARAT Abraham Toro/99 4.00 10.00
PPARBB Bobby Bradley/99 3.00 8.00
PPARBH Bryce Harper
PPARGL Gavin Lux/75 15.00 40.00
PPARID Isan Diaz/99 5.00 12.00
PPARJC Johan Camargo/99 3.00 8.00
PPARJM Jeff McNeil/99 8.00 20.00
PPARJY Jordan Yamamoto/99 3.00 8.00
PPARMK Mike King/99 5.00 12.00
PPARMT Matt Thaiss/99 4.00 10.00
PPARNS Noah Syndergaard/35 10.00 25.00
PPARRM Ryan McMahon/99 5.00 12.00
PPARRY Ryan Yarbrough/99 3.00 8.00
PPARSB Seth Brown/99 3.00 8.00
PPARSM Sean Murphy/99 5.00 12.00
PPARTZ T.J. Zeuch/99 3.00 8.00
PPARYA Yordan Alvarez/45 40.00 100.00
PPARAAQ Aristides Aquino/99 8.00 20.00
PPARJLU Jesus Luzardo/99 6.00 15.00

2020 Bowman Platinum Platinum Pieces Autograph Relics Orange
*ORANGE: .5X TO 1.2X p/r 75-99
*ORANGE: .6X TO 1.5X p/r 35-45
RANDOM INSERTS IN PACKS
STATED PRINT RUN 25 SER.#'d SETS
EXCHANGE DEADLINE XX/XX/XX
PPARBH Bryce Harper 100.00 250.00
PPARNS Noah Syndergaard 20.00 50.00

2020 Bowman Platinum Polished Gems
RANDOM INSERTS IN PACKS
PG1 Mike Trout 2.00 5.00
PG2 Ketel Marte .30 .75
PG3 Ronald Acuna Jr. 1.50 4.00
PG4 Dansby Swanson .40 1.00
PG5 Eloy Jimenez .75 2.00
PG6 Lucas Giolito .30 .75
PG7 Mike Clevinger .30 .75
PG8 Jorge Soler .40 1.00
PG9 Walker Buehler .50 1.25
PG10 Will Smith .40 1.00
PG11 Josh Hader .30 .75
PG12 Keston Hiura .50 1.25
PG13 Pete Alonso 1.00 2.50
PG14 Gio Urshela .40 1.00
PG15 Gleyber Torres .75 2.00
PG16 DJ LeMahieu .40 1.00
PG17 Chris Paddack .40 1.00
PG18 Jack Flaherty .40 1.00
PG19 Austin Meadows .40 1.00
PG20 Victor Robles .50 1.25

2020 Bowman Platinum Polished Gems Green
*GREEN: 1.2X TO 3X BASIC
RANDOM INSERTS IN PACKS
STATED PRINT RUN 99 SER.#'d SETS
PG1 Mike Trout 10.00 25.00

2020 Bowman Platinum Polished Gems Orange
*ORANGE: 4X TO 10X BASIC
RANDOM INSERTS IN PACKS
STATED PRINT RUN 25 SER.#'d SETS
PG1 Mike Trout 30.00 80.00
PG3 Ronald Acuna Jr. 40.00 100.00

2020 Bowman Platinum Polished Gems Purple
*PURPLE: .8X TO 2X BASIC
RANDOM INSERTS IN PACKS
STATED PRINT RUN 250 SER.#'d SETS
PG1 Mike Trout 6.00 15.00

2020 Bowman Platinum Polished Gems Autographs
RANDOM INSERTS IN PACKS
PRINT RUNS B/WN 25-50 COPIES PER
EXCHANGE DEADLINE XX/XX/XX
PGAAM Austin Meadows/50 6.00 15.00
PGACP Chris Paddack/50 6.00 15.00
PGADS Dansby Swanson/50 8.00 20.00
PGAEJ Eloy Jimenez/50 12.00 30.00
PGAGT Gleyber Torres/25 25.00 60.00
PGAJF Jack Flaherty/50 15.00 40.00
PGAJH Josh Hader/50 5.00 12.00
PGAJS Jorge Soler/50 6.00 15.00
PGAKH Keston Hiura/50 8.00 20.00
PGAKM Ketel Marte
PGAMT Mike Trout
PGAPA Pete Alonso/50 25.00 60.00
PGARA Ronald Acuna Jr./25 60.00 150.00
PGAVR Victor Robles/50 8.00 20.00
PGAWB Walker Buehler/50 12.00 30.00
PGAWS Will Smith/41 10.00 25.00

2020 Bowman Platinum Precious Elements
RANDOM INSERTS IN PACKS
PE1 Jo Adell 1.00 2.50
PE2 Alek Thomas .30 .75
PE3 Cristian Pache .75 2.00
PE4 Adley Rutschman 1.50 4.00
PE5 Bobby Dalbec 1.50 4.00
PE6 Miguel Amaya .25 .60
PE7 Andrew Vaughn 1.00 2.50
PE8 Nick Lodolo .40 1.00
PE9 Nolan Jones .40 1.00
PE10 Colton Welker .25 .60
PE11 Casey Mize .75 2.00
PE12 J.J. Matijevic .30 .75
PE13 Bobby Witt Jr. 1.50 4.00
PE14 Keibert Ruiz 1.25 3.00
PE15 Jesus Sanchez .40 1.00
PE16 Antoine Kelly .50 1.25
PE17 Royce Lewis .60 1.50
PE18 Brett Baty .75 2.00
PE19 Jasson Dominguez 4.00 10.00
PE20 Jorge Mateo .30 .75
PE21 Alec Bohm 1.50 4.00
PE22 Travis Swaggerty .30 .75
PE23 MacKenzie Gore .50 1.25
PE24 Joey Bart .75 2.00
PE25 Jarred Kelenic 1.25 3.00
PE26 Nolan Gorman .50 1.25
PE27 Wander Franco 2.50 6.00
PE28 Josh Jung .60 1.50
PE29 Jordan Groshans .50 1.25
PE30 Tim Cate .25 .60

2020 Bowman Platinum Precious Elements Green
*GREEN: 1.2X TO 3X BASIC
RANDOM INSERTS IN PACKS
STATED PRINT RUN 99 SER.#'d SETS
PE19 Jasson Dominguez 40.00 100.00

2020 Bowman Platinum Precious Elements Orange
*ORANGE: 4X TO 10X BASIC
RANDOM INSERTS IN PACKS
STATED PRINT RUN 25 SER.#'d SETS
PE19 Jasson Dominguez 75.00 200.00

2020 Bowman Platinum Precious Elements Purple
*PURPLE: .8X TO 2X BASIC
RANDOM INSERTS IN PACKS
STATED PRINT RUN 250 SER.#'d SETS
PE19 Jasson Dominguez 25.00 60.00

2020 Bowman Platinum Precious Elements Autographs
RANDOM INSERTS IN PACKS
STATED PRINT RUN 25 SER.#'d SETS
EXCHANGE DEADLINE XX/XX/XX
PEAB Alec Bohm 30.00 80.00
PEAAK Antoine Kelly 8.00 20.00
PEAAR Adley Rutschman 30.00 80.00
PEAAT Alek Thomas 5.00 12.00
PEAAV Andrew Vaughn 15.00 40.00
PEABB Brett Baty 12.00 30.00
PEABD Bobby Dalbec 10.00 25.00
PEABW Bobby Witt Jr. 50.00 120.00
PEACM Casey Mize 20.00 50.00
PEACW Colton Welker 4.00 10.00
PEAJA Jo Adell 25.00 60.00
PEAJB Joey Bart 15.00 40.00
PEAJD Jasson Dominguez 100.00 250.00
PEAJG Jordan Groshans 8.00 20.00
PEAJJ Josh Jung 10.00 25.00
PEAJK Jarred Kelenic 40.00 100.00
PEAKR Keibert Ruiz 20.00 50.00
PEAMA Miguel Amaya 4.00 10.00
PEAMG MacKenzie Gore 8.00 20.00
PEANG Nolan Gorman 10.00 25.00
PEANL Nick Lodolo 6.00 15.00
PEARL Royce Lewis 10.00 25.00
PEATC Tim Cate 4.00 10.00
PEATS Travis Swaggerty 10.00 25.00
PEAWF Wander Franco 50.00 120.00

2020 Bowman Platinum Precision Autographs
RANDOM INSERTS IN PACKS
STATED PRINT RUN 25 SER.#'d SETS
EXCHANGE DEADLINE XX/XX/XX
PP1 Mike Soroka 8.00 20.00
PP2 Casey Mize 25.00 60.00
PP3 Matt Manning 6.00 15.00
PP6 Brady Singer 10.00 25.00
PP7 Clayton Kershaw 40.00 100.00
PP10 Gerrit Cole 30.00 80.00
PP11 Jesus Luzardo 10.00 25.00
PP12 A.J. Puk 8.00 20.00
PP13 Chris Paddack 8.00 20.00
PP14 Max Scherzer 25.00 60.00

2020 Bowman Platinum Refined Autographs
RANDOM INSERTS IN PACKS
PRINT RUNS B/WN 25-99 COPIES PER
EXCHANGE DEADLINE XX/XX/XX
RABD Bobby Dalbec/99 20.00 50.00
RACJ Cristian Javier/99 4.00 10.00
RACM Casey Mize/25 25.00 60.00
RACP Cristian Pache/45 20.00 50.00
RADG Deivi Garcia/99 20.00 50.00
RAJA Jo Adell/99 12.00 30.00
RAJB Joey Bart/25 20.00 50.00
RAJD Jarren Duran/99 10.00 25.00
RAJG Josiah Gray/99 5.00 12.00
RAJI Jonathan India/50 10.00 25.00
RAJK Jarred Kelenic/50 40.00 100.00
RAMM Matt Manning/99 4.00 10.00
RANM Nick Madrigal/40 15.00 40.00
RASB Seth Beer/99 6.00 15.00
RAWC William Contreras/99 4.00 10.00
RAWF Wander Franco/99 50.00 120.00

2020 Bowman Platinum Renowned Rookies
RANDOM INSERTS IN PACKS
RR1 Brendan McKay .40 1.00
RR2 Yordan Alvarez 2.50 6.00
RR3 Luis Robert 2.00 5.00
RR4 Bo Bichette 2.00 5.00
RR5 Gavin Lux 1.25 3.00
RR6 Nico Hoerner 1.00 2.50
RR7 Aristides Aquino .60 1.50
RR8 A.J. Puk .40 1.00
RR9 Jesus Luzardo .50 1.25
RR10 Kyle Lewis 2.00 5.00
RR11 Adbert Alzolay .30 .75
RR12 Justin Dunn .30 .75
RR13 Nick Solak 1.00 2.50
RR14 Anthony Kay .25 .60
RR15 Seth Brown .25 .60
RR16 Jose Urquidy .30 .75
RR17 Sean Murphy .40 1.00
RR18 Shun Yamaguchi .30 .75
RR19 Shogo Akiyama .40 1.00
RR20 Jordan Yamamoto .25 .60

2020 Bowman Platinum Renowned Rookies Green
*GREEN: 1.2X TO 3X BASIC
RANDOM INSERTS IN PACKS
STATED PRINT RUN 99 SER.#'d SETS
RR3 Luis Robert 12.00 30.00

2020 Bowman Platinum Renowned Rookies Orange
*ORANGE: 4X TO 10X BASIC
RANDOM INSERTS IN PACKS
STATED PRINT RUN 25 SER.#'d SETS
RR3 Luis Robert 40.00 100.00

2020 Bowman Platinum Renowned Rookies Purple
*PURPLE: .8X TO 2X BASIC
RANDOM INSERTS IN PACKS
STATED PRINT RUN 250 SER.#'d SETS
RR3 Luis Robert 8.00 20.00

2020 Bowman Platinum Renowned Rookies Autographs
RANDOM INSERTS IN PACKS
STATED PRINT RUN 25 SER.#'d SETS
EXCHANGE DEADLINE XX/XX/XX
RRAAA Adbert Alzolay 5.00 12.00
RRAAK Anthony Kay 4.00 10.00
RRAAP A.J. Puk 6.00 15.00
RRABM Brendan McKay 6.00 15.00
RRAGL Gavin Lux 20.00 50.00
RRAJD Justin Dunn 5.00 12.00
RRAJL Jesus Luzardo 8.00 20.00
RRAKL Kyle Lewis 30.00 80.00
RRALR Luis Robert 75.00 200.00
RRANH Nico Hoerner 15.00 40.00
RRANS Nick Solak 8.00 20.00
RRASB Seth Brown 4.00 10.00
RRAYA Yordan Alvarez 40.00 100.00
RRAAAQ Aristides Aquino 10.00 25.00

2020 Bowman Platinum Top Prospect Autographs
RANDOM INSERTS IN PACKS
EXCHANGE DEADLINE XX/XX/XX
*PURPLE/199: .5X TO 1.2X BASIC
*BLUE/150: .5X TO 1.2X BASIC
*GREEN/99: .5X TO 1.2X BASIC
*ICE/50: .6X TO 1.5X BASIC
*ORANGE/25: .8X TO 2X BASIC
TOP1 Casey Golden 4.00 10.00
TOP5 Jacob Amaya 3.00 8.00
TOP6 Quinn Priester 5.00 12.00
TOP7 Peyton Burdick 3.00 8.00
TOP10 CJ Abrams 25.00 60.00
TOP11 Grayson Rodriguez 4.00 10.00
TOP13 Rece Hinds 5.00 12.00
TOP15 Adley Rutschman 30.00 80.00
TOP18 Josh Smith 3.00 8.00
TOP20 Xavier Edwards 6.00 15.00
TOP22 Alek Manoah 6.00 15.00
TOP23 Jackson Rutledge 4.00 10.00
TOP24 Davis Wendzel 4.00 10.00
TOP25 Bobby Witt Jr. 30.00 80.00
TOP26 JJ Bleday 8.00 20.00
TOP30 Edwin Uceta 3.00 8.00
TOP31 Bo Naylor 3.00 8.00
TOP33 Blake Walston 4.00 10.00
TOP34 Kody Hoese 5.00 12.00
TOP35 Adam Kloffenstein 4.00 10.00
TOP37 Logan Davidson 3.00 8.00
TOP41 Logan Wyatt 4.00 10.00
TOP43 Kris Bubic 4.00 10.00
TOP44 Canaan Smith 4.00 10.00
TOP45 Antoine Kelly 3.00 8.00
TOP46 Brett Baty 8.00 20.00
TOP47 Hogan Harris 2.50 6.00
TOP48 Ryne Nelson 3.00 8.00
TOP49 Kendall Williams 4.00 10.00
TOP50 Joe Ryan 3.00 8.00
TOP51 Tim Cate 2.50 6.00
TOP52 Jeremy Pena 6.00 15.00
TOP53 Greg Jones 3.00 8.00
TOP54 Korey Lee 3.00 8.00
TOP55 Andrew Vaughn 15.00 40.00
TOP56 Ryan Jeffers 3.00 8.00
TOP59 Joey Cantillo 2.50 6.00
TOP60 Ryan Jensen 3.00 8.00
TOP62 Ryan Zeferjahn 3.00 8.00
TOP64 Riley Greene 10.00 25.00
TOP66 Aaron Schunk 5.00 12.00
TOP68 Terrin Vavra 5.00 12.00
TOP69 Zack Thompson 5.00 12.00
TOP70 Gunnar Henderson 5.00 12.00
TOP71 Dominic Fletcher 5.00 12.00
TOP75 Logan Driscoll 4.00 10.00
TOP78 Jake Latz 2.50 6.00
TOP79 Corbin Carroll 8.00 20.00
TOP81 Devin Mann 5.00 12.00
TOP82 Bryce Ball 8.00 20.00
TOP83 Michael Toglia 2.50 6.00
TOP84 Joey Bart 10.00 25.00
TOP86 Kameron Misner 4.00 10.00
TOP89 Sam Huff 5.00 12.00
TOP91 Ethan Small 3.00 8.00
TOP92 Nick Lodolo 4.00 10.00
TOP95 Andy Pages 3.00 8.00
TOP96 Marshall Kasowski 4.00 10.00
TOP97 Josh Jung 10.00 25.00
TOP98 Jarren Duran 20.00 50.00
TOP100 Matt Wallner 5.00 12.00

2020 Bowman Platinum Top Prospects
RANDOM INSERTS IN PACKS
*CHARTREUSE: .6X TO 1.5X BASIC
*ICE: .6X TO 1.5X BASIC
TOP1 Casey Golden .40 1.00
TOP2 William Contreras .30 .75
TOP3 Evan White .60 1.50
TOP4 Jordan Balazovic .50 1.25
TOP5 Jacob Amaya 1.00 2.50
TOP6 Quinn Priester .30 .75
TOP7 Peyton Burdick 1.00 2.50
TOP8 Jo Adell 1.00 2.50
TOP9 Will Wilson .30 .75
TOP10 CJ Abrams .75 2.00
TOP11 Grayson Rodriguez .40 1.00
TOP12 Ryan Garcia .25 .60
TOP13 Rece Hinds .30 .75
TOP14 Hunter Bishop .50 1.25
TOP15 Adley Rutschman 1.50 4.00
TOP16 Gilberto Jimenez 1.25 3.00
TOP17 Jonathan India 1.50 4.00
TOP18 Josh Smith .50 1.25
TOP19 Keoni Cavaco .25 .60
TOP20 Xavier Edwards 1.00 2.50
TOP21 Braden Shewmake .40 1.00
TOP22 Alek Manoah .30 .75
TOP23 Jackson Rutledge .40 1.00
TOP24 Davis Wendzel .40 1.00
TOP25 Bobby Witt Jr. 1.50 4.00
TOP26 JJ Bleday .75 2.00
TOP27 Alex Faedo .30 .75
TOP28 Casey Mize .75 2.00
TOP29 Anthony Volpe 1.00 2.50
TOP30 Edwin Uceta .30 .75
TOP31 Bo Naylor .30 .75
TOP32 Alec Bohm 1.50 4.00
TOP33 Blake Walston .40 1.00
TOP34 Kody Hoese .75 2.00
TOP35 Adam Kloffenstein .40 1.00
TOP36 Seth Beer .50 1.25
TOP37 Logan Davidson .30 .75
TOP38 JJ Goss .25 .60
TOP39 Matt Canterino .30 .75
TOP40 Noelvi Marte 1.00 2.50
TOP41 Logan Wyatt .40 1.00
TOP42 Trevor Larnach .50 1.25
TOP43 Kris Bubic .40 1.00
TOP44 Canaan Smith .40 1.00
TOP45 Antoine Kelly .50 1.25
TOP46 Brett Baty .75 2.00
TOP47 Hogan Harris .25 .60
TOP48 Ryne Nelson .30 .75
TOP49 Kendall Williams .40 1.00
TOP50 Joe Ryan .30 .75
TOP51 Tim Cate .25 .60
TOP52 Jeremy Pena .60 1.50
TOP53 Greg Jones .30 .75
TOP54 Korey Lee .30 .75
TOP55 Andrew Vaughn 1.00 2.50
TOP56 Ryan Jeffers .30 .75
TOP57 Deivi Garcia 1.25 3.00
TOP58 Tyler Nevin .40 1.00
TOP59 Joey Cantillo .25 .60
TOP60 Ryan Jensen .30 .75
TOP61 T.J. Sikkema .25 .60
TOP62 Ryan Zeferjahn .30 .75
TOP63 Brandon Bielak .25 .60
TOP64 Riley Greene 1.00 2.50
TOP65 Daniel Lynch .25 .60
TOP66 Aaron Schunk .50 1.25
TOP67 Luis Gil .30 .75
TOP68 Terrin Vavra .50 1.25
TOP69 Zack Thompson .25 .60
TOP70 Gunnar Henderson .30 .75
TOP71 Dominic Fletcher .25 .60
TOP72 Shea Langeliers .50 1.25
TOP73 Joshua Mears .50 1.25
TOP74 Mason Martin .50 1.25
TOP75 Logan Driscoll .40 1.00
TOP76 Ezequiel Duran .40 1.00
TOP77 Keibert Ruiz 1.25 3.00
TOP78 Jake Latz .25 .60
TOP79 Corbin Carroll .40 1.00
TOP80 Ford Proctor .25 .60
TOP81 Devin Mann .40 1.00
TOP82 Bryce Ball 1.25 3.00
TOP83 Michael Toglia .25 .60
TOP84 Joey Bart .75 2.00
TOP85 Kyle Stowers .25 .60
TOP86 Kameron Misner .40 1.00
TOP87 Seth Corry .25 .60
TOP88 Alexander Canario .25 .60
TOP89 Sam Huff .50 1.25
TOP90 Jarred Kelenic 1.25 3.00
TOP91 Ethan Small .30 .75
TOP92 Nick Lodolo .40 1.00
TOP93 Josiah Gray .40 1.00
TOP94 Julio Rodriguez 1.50 4.00
TOP95 Andy Pages .30 .75
TOP96 Marshall Kasowski .40 1.00
TOP97 Josh Jung .60 1.50
TOP98 Jarren Duran 1.00 2.50
TOP99 Matt Manning .30 .75
TOP100 Matt Wallner .50 1.25
TOP101 Jasson Dominguez 4.00 10.00
TOP102 Robert Puason .75 2.00

2020 Bowman Platinum Top Prospects Blue
*BLUE: 1X TO 2.5X BASIC
RANDOM INSERTS IN PACKS
STATED PRINT RUN 150 SER.#'d SETS
TOP101 Jasson Dominguez 30.00 80.00

2020 Bowman Platinum Top Prospects Gold
*GOLD: 2.5X TO 6X BASIC
RANDOM INSERTS IN PACKS
STATED PRINT RUN 50 SER.#'d SETS
TOP32 Alec Bohm 12.00 30.00
TOP101 Jasson Dominguez 75.00 200.00

2020 Bowman Platinum Top Prospects Green
*GREEN: 1.2X TO 3X BASIC
RANDOM INSERTS IN PACKS
STATED PRINT RUN 99 SER.#'d SETS
TOP101 Jasson Dominguez 40.00 100.00

2020 Bowman Platinum Top Prospects Orange
*ORANGE: 4X TO 10X BASIC
RANDOM INSERTS IN PACKS
STATED PRINT RUN 25 SER.#'d SETS
TOP32 Alec Bohm 20.00 50.00
TOP101 Jasson Dominguez 125.00 300.00

2020 Bowman Platinum Top Prospects Pink
*PINK: 1X TO 2.5X BASIC
RANDOM INSERTS IN PACKS
STATED PRINT RUN 199 SER.#'d SETS
TOP101 Jasson Dominguez 30.00 80.00

2020 Bowman Platinum Top Prospects Purple
*PURPLE: .8X TO 2X BASIC
RANDOM INSERTS IN PACKS
STATED PRINT RUN 250 SER.#'d SETS
TOP101 Jasson Dominguez 25.00 60.00

2020 Bowman Platinum Top Prospects Teal
*TEAL: .8X TO 2X BASIC
RANDOM INSERTS IN PACKS
STATED PRINT RUN 299 SER.#'d SETS
TOP101 Jasson Dominguez 25.00 60.00

2004 Bowman Sterling
COMMON FY .75 2.00
FY ODDS APPX.TWO PER HOBBY PACK
COMMON FY AU 3.00 8.00
FY AU ODDS APPX.ONE PER HOBBY PACK
COMMON AU-GU 4.00 10.00
AU-GU ODDS APPX.ONE PER HOBBY PACK
AU-GU 1:2 WRAPPER ODDS IS AN ERROR
COMMON AU-GU RC 4.00 10.00
COMMON GU 2.00 5.00
GU ODDS APPX. 1.5 PER HOBBY PACK
GU 1:2 WRAPPER ODDS IS AN ERROR
AB Angel Berroa Bat 2.00 5.00
ABA Aarom Baldiris FY RC .40 1.00
AC Alberto Callaspo FY AU RC 4.00 10.00
AD Adam Dunn Bat 2.00 5.00
AER Alex Rodriguez Bat 6.00 15.00
AJ Andruw Jones Jsy 3.00 8.00
AK Austin Kearns Jsy 2.00 5.00
ANR Aramis Ramirez Bat 2.00 5.00
AP Albert Pujols Jsy 8.00 20.00
AR Alex Romero FY AU RC 3.00 8.00
AW Adam Wainwright AU Jsy 6.00 15.00
AWH A.Whittington FY RC .40 1.00
AZ Alec Zumwalt FY AU RC 3.00 8.00
BB Brian Bixler AU Jsy RC 4.00 10.00
BBR Bill Bray FY RC .40 1.00
BBU Billy Buckner FY RC .40 1.00
BC2 Bobby Crosby Jsy 2.00 5.00
BD Blake DeWitt AU Jsy RC 6.00 15.00
BE Brad Eldred FY RC .40 1.00
BH B.Hawksworth FY AU RC 4.00 10.00
BT Brad Thompson FY RC .60 1.50
BU B.J. Upton AU Bat 4.00 10.00
BW Bernie Williams Jsy 3.00 8.00
CA Chris Aguila FY AU RC 3.00 8.00
CB Craig Biggio Jsy 3.00 8.00
CC Chad Cordero AU Jsy 6.00 15.00
CG Christian Garcia AU Jsy RC 6.00 15.00
CH Chin-Lung Hu FY RC .40 1.00
CIB Carlos Beltran Bat 2.00 5.00
CJ Conor Jackson FY RC 1.25 3.00
CL Chris Lubanski AU Bat 4.00 10.00
CLA Chris Lambert FY RC .40 1.00
CN Chris Nelson FY RC .40 1.00
CQ Carlos Quentin FY AU RC 4.00 10.00
CT Curtis Thigpen FY RC .40 1.00
DD David DeJesus AU Jsy 6.00 15.00
DP Danny Putnam AU Jsy RC 4.00 10.00
DPU David Purcey FY RC .60 1.50
DW David Wright AU Jsy 10.00 25.00
DWW Dontrelle Willis Jsy 3.00 8.00
DY Delmon Young AU Bat 5.00 12.00
EG Eric Gagne Jsy 2.00 5.00
EH Eric Hurley FY RC .40 1.00
ESP Erick San Pedro FY RC .40 1.00
FC Fausto Carmona FY RC .60 1.50
FG Freddy Guzman FY RC .40 1.00
FH Felix Hernandez FY RC 6.00 15.00
FP Felix Pie AU Jsy 10.00 25.00
FT Frank Thomas Bat 3.00 8.00
GG Greg Golson FY RC .40 1.00
GH Gaby Hernandez FY RC .60 1.50
GIG Gio Gonzalez FY RC .60 1.50
GS Gary Sheffield Bat 2.00 5.00
HB Homer Bailey AU Jsy RC 3.00 8.00
HC Hee Seop Choi Bat 2.00 5.00
HG Hector Gimenez FY AU RC 3.00 8.00
HJB Hank Blalock Bat 2.00 5.00
HM Hector Made FY RC .40 1.00
HS Huston Street AU Jsy RC 5.00 12.00
IR Ivan Rodriguez Bat 3.00 8.00
JB Jeff Bagwell Jsy 3.00 8.00
JC Jose Capellan FY RC .40 1.00
JCR Jesse Crain FY RC .60 1.50
JD Johnny Damon Bat 3.00 8.00
JE Johnny Estrada Bat 2.00 5.00
JFI Josh Fields FY RC .60 1.50
JG Joey Gathright FY RC .40 1.00
JH Jesse Hoover FY RC .40 1.00
JK Jason Kendall Bat 2.00 5.00
JM Jeff Marquez AU Jsy RC 4.00 10.00
JO Justin Orenduff FY RC .60 1.50
JP Juan Pierre Bat 2.00 5.00
JPH J.P. Howell FY RC .40 1.00
JR Jay Rainville FY AU RC 5.00 12.00
JS Jeremy Sowers FY AU RC 3.00 8.00
JZ Jon Zeringue FY RC .40 1.00
KCH K.C. Herren FY RC .40 1.00
KS Kurt Suzuki FY RC .60 1.50
KT Kazuhito Tadano FY RC .40 1.00
KW Kerry Wood Jsy 2.00 5.00
KWA Kyle Waldrop AU Jsy RC 4.00 10.00
LB Lance Berkman Jsy 2.00 5.00
LC Luis Castillo Jsy 2.00 5.00
LH Linc Holdzkom FY AU RC 3.00 8.00
LN Laynce Nix Bat 2.00 5.00
MA Moises Alou Bat 2.00 5.00
MAM Mark Mulder Jsy 2.00 5.00
MAR Manny Ramirez Bat 3.00 8.00
MB Matt Bush AU Jsy RC 3.00 8.00
MC Miguel Cabrera Bat 3.00 8.00
MCT Mark Teixeira Bat 3.00 8.00
ME Mitch Einertson FY RC .40 1.00
MF Mike Ferris FY RC .40 1.00
MFO Matt Fox FY RC .40 1.00
MJP Mike Piazza Bat 3.00 8.00
MM Matt Moses FY AU RC 6.00 15.00
MMC Matt Macri FY RC .60 1.50
MP Mark Prior Jsy 3.00 8.00
MR Mike Rouse FY AU RC 3.00 8.00
MRO Mark Rogers FY RC .60 1.50
MT M.Tuiasosopo AU Bat RC 6.00 15.00
MT1 Miguel Tejada Bat 2.00 5.00
MT2 Miguel Tejada Jsy 2.00 5.00
MW Marland Williams FY RC .40 1.00
MY Michael Young Bat 2.00 5.00
NJ Nick Johnson Bat 2.00 5.00
NM Nyjer Morgan FY RC .40 1.00
NS Nate Schierholtz FY RC .40 1.00
NW Neil Walker FY RC .60 1.50
OQ Omar Quintanilla FY RC .40 1.00
PGM Paul Maholm FY RC .60 1.50
PH Philip Hughes FY RC 1.00 2.50
PL Paul LoDuca Bat 2.00 5.00
PR Pokey Reese Bat 2.00 5.00
RB Rocco Baldelli Bat 2.00 5.00
RBR Reid Brignac FY RC 1.00 2.50
RC Robinson Cano AU Jsy 10.00 25.00
RH Ryan Harvey AU Bat 6.00 15.00
RJH Richard Hidalgo Bat 2.00 5.00
RM Ryan Meaux FY AU RC 3.00 8.00
RO Russ Ortiz Jsy 2.00 5.00
RP Rafael Palmeiro Bat 3.00 8.00
SK Scott Kazmir AU Jsy RC 3.00 8.00
SO Scott Olsen AU Jsy RC 4.00 10.00
SS Sammy Sosa Jsy 3.00 8.00
SSM Seth Smith FY RC .60 1.50
TD Thomas Diamond FY RC .40 1.00
TG Troy Glaus Bat 2.00 5.00
TLH Todd Helton Bat 3.00 8.00
TM Tino Martinez Bat 3.00 8.00
TMG Tom Glavine Jsy 3.00 8.00
TP Trevor Plouffe AU Jsy RC 4.00 10.00
TT T.Tankersley AU Jsy RC 4.00 10.00
VG Vladimir Guerrero Bat 3.00 8.00
VP Vince Perkins FY AU RC 4.00 10.00
YP Yusmeiro Petit FY RC 1.00 2.50
ZD Zach Duke FY RC .60 1.50
ZJ Zach Jackson FY RC .40 1.00

2004 Bowman Sterling Refractors
*REF.FY: 1.25X TO 3X BASIC
FY ODDS 1:4 HOBBY
*REF.FY AU: 1X TO 2.5X BASIC FY AU
FY AU ODDS 1:8 HOBBY
*REF.AU-GU: .6X TO 1.5X BASIC AU-GU
AU-GU ODDS 1:9 HOBBY
*REF.GU: .6X TO 1.5X BASIC GU
GU ODDS 1:5 HOBBY
STATED PRINT RUN 199 SERIAL #'d SETS
BD Blake DeWitt AU Jsy 8.00 20.00
FP Felix Pie AU Jsy 12.50 30.00

2004 Bowman Sterling Original Autographs
GROUP A ODDS 1:221 HOBBY
GROUP B ODDS 1:25 HOBBY
GROUP A = A.ROD/BONDS
GROUP B = CHAVEZ/REYES/SORIANO

PRINT RUNS B/WN 1-106 COPIES PER
NO PRICING ON QTY OF 25 OR LESS
ISSUED IN HOBBY BOX LOADER PACKS
AR11 Alex Rodriguez 03BC/28 60.00 120.00
AS7 Alfonso Soriano 02B/54 4.00 10.00
AS8 Alfonso Soriano 02BC/33 10.00 25.00
AS9 Alfonso Soriano 03B/102 8.00 20.00
AS10 Alfonso Soriano 03BC/49 8.00 20.00
AS11 Alfonso Soriano 04B/26 10.00 25.00
EC10 Eric Chavez 02B/68 10.00 25.00
EC11 Eric Chavez 02BC/21 12.50 30.00
EC12 Eric Chavez 03B/106 10.00 25.00
EC13 Eric Chavez 03BC/22 12.50 30.00
JR1 Jose Reyes 02B/52 10.00 25.00
JR2 Jose Reyes 02BD/22 20.00 50.00
JR3 Jose Reyes 02BD/34 20.00 50.00
JR4 Jose Reyes 02BC/31 20.00 50.00
JR5 Jose Reyes 02BCD/41 10.00 25.00
JR6 Jose Reyes 03BD/92 10.00 25.00

2005 Bowman Sterling

COMMON CARD .60 1.50
BASIC CARDS APPX.TWO PER HOBBY PACK
BASIC CARDS APPX.TWO PER RETAIL PACK
AU GROUP A ODDS 1:2 HOBBY
AU GROUP B ODDS 1:3 HOBBY
AU-GU GROUP A ODDS 1:2 H, 1:2 R
AU-GU GROUP B ODDS 1:37 H, 1:37 R
AU-GU GROUP C ODDS 1:11 H, 1:11 R
AU-GU GROUP D ODDS 1:10 H, 1:10 R
AU-GU GROUP E ODDS 1:27 H, 1:27 R
AU-GU GROUP F ODDS 1:13 H, 1:13 R
GU GROUP A ODDS 1:3 H, 1:3 R
GU GROUP B ODDS 1:5 H, 1:5 R
GU GROUP C ODDS 1:6 H, 1:6 R
ACL Andy LaRoche RC .60 1.50
AL Adam Lind AU Bat B 4.00 10.00
AM A.McCutchen AU Jsy D RC 15.00 40.00
AP Albert Pujols Jsy B 6.00 15.00
AR Alex Rodriguez Jsy B UER 6.00 15.00
ARA Aramis Ramirez Bat A 2.00 5.00
AS Alfonso Soriano Bat A 2.00 5.00
AT Aaron Thompson AU A RC 4.00 10.00
BA Brian Anderson RC 1.00 2.50
BB Billy Buckner AU Jsy A 4.00 10.00
BBU Billy Butler RC 3.00 8.00
BC Brent Cox AU Jsy D RC 6.00 15.00
BCR Brad Corley RC .60 1.50
BE Brad Eldred AU Jsy C 4.00 10.00
BH Brett Hayes RC .60 1.50
BJ Beau Jones AU Jsy A RC 8.00 20.00
BL B.Livingston AU Jsy A RC 4.00 10.00
BLB Barry Bonds Jsy C 6.00 15.00
BM B.McCarthy AU Jsy A RC 4.00 10.00
BMU Bill Mueller Jsy C 2.00 5.00
BRB Brian Bogusevic RC .60 1.50
BS Brandon Sing AU A RC 4.00 8.00
BSN Brandon Snyder RC 1.50 4.00
BZ Barry Zito Uni A 2.00 5.00
CB Carlos Beltran Bat A 2.00 5.00
CBU Clay Buchholz RC 3.00 8.00
CC Cesar Carrillo RC 1.00 2.50
CD Carlos Delgado Jsy A 2.00 5.00
CH C.J. Henry AU B RC 3.00 8.00
CHE Chase Headley RC 1.00 2.50
CI Craig Italiano RC .60 1.50
CJ Chuck James RC 1.50 4.00
CLT Chuck Tiffany RC 1.50 4.00
CN Chris Nelson AU Jsy A 4.00 10.00
CP Cliff Pennington AU B RC 4.00 10.00
CPP C.Pignatiello AU Jsy A RC 4.00 10.00
CR Colby Rasmus AU Jsy A RC 4.00 10.00
CRA Cesar Ramos RC .60 1.50
CRO Chaz Roe AU Jsy A RC 4.00 10.00
CS C.J. Smith AU Jsy A RC 4.00 10.00
CSU Curt Schilling Jsy C 3.00 8.00
CT Curtis Thigpen AU Jsy A 4.00 10.00
CV Chris Volstad AU B RC 3.00 8.00
DC Dan Carte RC .60 1.50
DL Derrek Lee Bat A 3.00 8.00
DO David Ortiz Bat A 3.00 8.00
DP Dustin Pedroia AU Jsy A 30.00 80.00
DT Drew Thompson RC .60 1.50
DW Dontrelle Willis Jsy C 2.00 5.00
EC Eric Chavez Uni B 2.00 5.00
EI Eli Iorg AU Jsy C RC 3.00 8.00
EM Eddy Martinez AU A RC 4.00 10.00
GK George Kottaras AU A RC 3.00 8.00
GM Greg Maddux Jsy C 4.00 10.00
GO Garrett Olson AU A RC 3.00 8.00
GS Gary Sheffield Bat A 2.00 5.00
HAS Henry Sanchez RC 1.00 2.50
HB Hank Blalock Bat A 2.00 5.00
HI Hernan Iribarren RC .60 1.50
HM Hideki Matsui AS Jsy C 6.00 15.00
HS Hum Sanchez AU A RC 8.00 20.00
IR Ivan Rodriguez Bat A 3.00 8.00
JB Jay Bruce AU Jsy D RC 6.00 15.00
JBE Josh Beckett Uni A 2.00 5.00
JC Jeff Clement RC .60 1.50
JCN John Nelson AU Uni A RC 4.00 10.00
JD Johnny Damon Bat A 3.00 8.00
JDR John Drennen RC .60 1.50
JE J.Ellsbury AU Jsy E RC 5.00 12.00
JEG Jon Egan RC .60 1.50
JF Josh Fields AU Jsy A 4.00 10.00
JG Josh Geer AU Jsy A RC 4.00 10.00
JGI Josh Gibson Seat C 8.00 20.00
JL Jed Lowrie AU Jsy F RC 4.00 10.00
JLY Jeff Lyman RC .60 1.50
JM John Mayberry Jr. AU A RC 8.00 20.00
JMA Jacob Marceaux RC .60 1.50
JN Jeff Niemann AU Jsy A RC 4.00 10.00
JO Justin Olson AU Jsy A RC 4.00 10.00
JP Jorge Posada Bat A 3.00 8.00
JPE Jim Edmonds Jsy B 2.00 5.00
JS John Smoltz Jsy A 3.00 8.00
JV J.Verlander AU Jsy A RC 60.00 150.00
JW Josh Wall RC 1.00 2.50
JWE Jered Weaver RC 3.00 8.00
KG Khalil Greene Jsy B 3.00 8.00
KM Kevin Millar Bat A 2.00 5.00
KS Kevin Slowey RC 3.00 8.00
KW Kevin Whelan RC .60 1.50
LWJ Chipper Jones Bat A 3.00 8.00
MA Matt Albers AU A RC 4.00 10.00
MAM Matt Maloney RC .60 1.50
MB M.Bowden AU Jsy A RC 4.00 10.00
MC Mike Conroy AU Jsy A RC 4.00 10.00
MCA Miguel Cabrera Jsy A 3.00 8.00
MCO Mike Costanzo RC .60 1.50
MG Matt Green AU A RC 3.00 8.00
MGA Matt Garza RC 1.00 2.50
MGI Marcus Giles AS Jsy B 2.00 5.00
MM Mark Mulder Uni B 2.00 5.00
MMC Mark McCormick RC .60 1.50
MP Mike Piazza Bat A 3.00 8.00
MPR Mark Prior Jsy B 3.00 8.00
MR Manny Ramirez Bat A 3.00 8.00
MT Miguel Tejada Uni A 2.00 5.00
MTE Mark Teixeira Bat A 3.00 8.00
MTO Matt Torra RC .60 1.50
MY Michael Young Bat A 2.00 5.00
NH Nick Hundley RC .60 1.50
NR Nolan Reimold RC 2.50 6.00
NW Nick Webber RC .60 1.50
PH Philip Humber AU Jsy A RC 4.00 10.00
PK Paul Kelly RC .60 1.50
PL Paul Lo Duca Bat A 2.00 5.00
PM Pedro Martinez Jsy A 3.00 8.00
PP P.J. Phillips RC .60 1.50
RB Ryan Braun AU A RC 10.00 25.00
RBE Ronnie Belliard Bat A 2.00 5.00
RF Rafael Furcal Jsy A 2.00 5.00
RM Russ Martin AU Jsy F RC 5.00 12.00
RMO Ryan Mount RC .60 1.50
RR Ricky Romero RC 1.00 2.50
RT Raul Tablado AU Jsy A RC 4.00 10.00
RZ Ryan Zimmerman RC 3.00 8.00
SD Stephen Drew RC 2.00 5.00
SE Scott Elbert AU Jsy A 4.00 10.00
SM Steve Marek AU Jsy A RC 4.00 10.00
SR Scott Rolen Jsy B 3.00 8.00
SS Sammy Sosa Bat A 3.00 8.00
SW Steven White AU B RC 3.00 8.00
TB Trevor Bell AU Jsy C RC 4.00 10.00
TBU Travis Buck RC .60 1.50
TC Travis Chick AU A RC 3.00 8.00
TG Tyler Greene RC .60 1.50
TH Torii Hunter Bat A 2.00 5.00
THE Tyler Herron RC .60 1.50
THU Tim Hudson Uni A 2.00 5.00
TI Tadahito Iguchi RC 1.00 2.50
TLH Todd Helton Jsy B 3.00 8.00
TM Tyler Minges AU Jsy A RC 4.00 10.00
TM Tino Martinez Bat A 3.00 8.00
TN Trot Nixon Bat A 2.00 5.00
TT Troy Tulowitzki RC 6.00 15.00
TW Travis Wood RC 1.50 4.00
VG Vladimir Guerrero Bat A 3.00 8.00
VM Victor Martinez Bat A 2.00 5.00
WT Wade Townsend RC .60 1.50
YE Yunel Escobar RC 2.50 6.00
ZS Zach Simons RC .60 1.50

2005 Bowman Sterling Refractors

*REF: 1.25X TO 3X BASIC
BASIC ODDS 1:6 H, 1:6 R
*REF AU: 1X TO 2.5X BASIC AU
AU ODDS 1:13 HOBBY
*REF AU-GU: .6X TO 1.5X BASIC AU-GU
AU-GU ODDS 1:9 H, 1:9 R
*REF GU: .6X TO 1.5X BASIC GU
GU ODDS 1:6 H, 1: R
STATED PRINT RUN 199 SERIAL #'d SETS
BE Brad Eldred AU Jsy 12.50 30.00

2005 Bowman Sterling Black Refractors

BASIC ODDS 1:5 BOX-LOADER
NO BASIC PRICING DUE TO SCARCITY
AU ODDS 1:17 BOX-LOADER
NO AU PRICING DUE TO SCARCITY
AU-GU ODDS 1:8 BOX-LOADER
NO AU-GU PRICING DUE TO SCARCITY
*BLACK GU: 2X TO 5X BASIC GU
GU ODDS 1:5 BOX-LOADER
ONE BOX-LOADER PACK PER HOBBY BOX
STATED PRINT RUN 25 SERIAL #'d SETS
BLB Barry Bonds Jsy 60.00 120.00

2005 Bowman Sterling MLB Logo Patch Autograph

STATED ODDS 1:665 BOX-LOADER
ONE BOX-LOADER PACK PER HOBBY BOX
STATED PRINT RUN 1 SERIAL #'d SET
NO PRICING DUE TO SCARCITY

2005 Bowman Sterling Original Autographs

GROUP A ODDS 1:665 BOX-LOADER
GROUP B ODDS 1:250 BOX-LOADER
GROUP C ODDS 1:63 BOX-LOADER
GROUP D ODDS 1:50 BOX-LOADER
GROUP E ODDS 1:42 BOX-LOADER
GROUP F ODDS 1:28 BOX-LOADER
GROUP G ODDS 1:25 BOX-LOADER
GROUP H ODDS 1:21 BOX-LOADER
GROUP I ODDS 1:6 BOX-LOADER
ONE BOX-LOADER PACK PER HOBBY BOX
PRINT RUNS B/WN 1-160 COPIES PER
NO PRICING ON QTY OF 13 OR LESS
AJ1 Andruw Jones 98 B/18 20.00 50.00
AJ2 Andruw Jones 99 B/18 20.00 50.00
AJ6 Andruw Jones 02 B/122 6.00 15.00
AJ8 Andruw Jones 03 B/112 6.00 15.00
AJ9 Andruw Jones 03 BC/18 20.00 50.00
AJ10 Andruw Jones 04 B/71 6.00 15.00
DL1 Derrek Lee 95 B/27 10.00 25.00
DL2 Derrek Lee 96 B/29 10.00 25.00
DL3 Derrek Lee 96 BB/15 12.50 30.00
DL4 Derrek Lee 97 BC/16 12.50 30.00
DL5 Derrek Lee 98 B/22 10.00 25.00
DL6 Derrek Lee 04 B/92 6.00 15.00
DW1 David Wright 04 BD/98 6.00 15.00
DW3 David Wright 05 B/139 6.00 15.00
GA3 Garret Anderson 03 B/33 6.00 15.00
GA4 Garret Anderson 04 B/33 6.00 15.00
GA5 Garret Anderson 04 BC/36 6.00 15.00
GA6 Garret Anderson 05 B/48 5.00 12.00
JR1 Jeremy Reed 04 BD/82 4.00 10.00
JR2 Jeremy Reed 04 BCD/48 5.00 12.00
MC2 M.Cabrera 02 BD/26 100.00 200.00
MC4 M.Cabrera 03 BD/27 100.00 200.00
MC5 M.Cabrera 03 BCD/25 100.00 200.00
MC6 M.Cabrera 04 B/127 20.00 50.00
MC7 M.Cabrera 04 BC/25 100.00 200.00
MC8 M.Cabrera 05 B/154 20.00 50.00
MC9 M.Cabrera 05 BC/25 100.00 200.00
MK1 Mark Kotsay 97 B/18 20.00 50.00
MK3 Mark Kotsay 98 B/56 8.00 20.00
MK4 Mark Kotsay 98 BC/23 10.00 25.00
MK5 Mark Kotsay 99 B/75 6.00 15.00
MK6 Mark Kotsay 99 BC/23 10.00 25.00
MK7 Mark Kotsay 05 B/160 6.00 15.00
MK8 Mark Kotsay 05 BC/46 8.00 20.00
MY1 Michael Young 04 B/148 6.00 15.00
MY2 Michael Young 04 BC/64 8.00 20.00
MY3 Michael Young 05 B/92 6.00 15.00

2006 Bowman Sterling

COMMON ROOKIE .75 2.00
COMMON AUTO RC 3.00 8.00
AU RC AUTO ODDS 1:4 HOBBY
COMMON AU-GU RC 4.00 10.00
AU-GU RC ODDS 1:4 HOBBY
COMMON GU VET 2.50 6.00
GU VET ODDS 1:4 HOBBY
OVERALL PLATE ODDS 1:23 BOXES
PLATE PRINT RUN 1 SET PER COLOR
BLACK-CYAN-MAGENTA-YELLOW ISSUED
NO PLATE PRICING DUE TO SCARCITY
EXCHANGE DEADLINE 12/31/08
AD Adam Dunn Jsy 2.50 6.00
AE Andre Ethier AU (RC) 3.00 8.00
AER Alex Rodriguez Bat 10.00 25.00
AJ Andruw Jones Jsy 3.00 8.00
ALR A.Reyes Jsy AU (RC) EXCH 4.00 10.00
ALS Alay Soler RC .75 2.00
AP Albert Pujols Jsy 8.00 20.00
AP2 Albert Pujols Bat 8.00 20.00
APS Alfonso Soriano Bat 4.00 10.00
AR Aramis Ramirez Bat UER 3.00 8.00
AS Anibal Sanchez (RC) .75 2.00
BA Brian Anderson (RC) .75 2.00
BB Brian Bannister (RC) .75 2.00
BL B.Livingston Jsy AU (RC) 4.00 10.00
BLB Barry Bonds Bat 6.00 15.00
BON Boof Bonser (RC) 1.25 3.00
BR Brian Roberts Jsy 2.50 6.00
BZ Ben Zobrist (RC) 4.00 10.00
CB Carlos Beltran Jsy 2.50 6.00
CB2 Carlos Beltran Bat 2.50 6.00
CC Chris Carpenter Jsy 4.00 10.00
CH Cole Hamels Jsy AU (RC) 10.00 25.00
CHJ Chuck James (RC) .75 2.00
CI Chris Iannetta Jsy AU RC 4.00 10.00
CJ Conor Jackson (RC) 1.25 3.00
CJJ Casey Janssen RC .75 2.00
CQ Carlos Quentin (RC) 1.25 3.00
CRB Chad Billingsley (RC) 1.25 3.00
CRH Craig Hansen RC 2.00 5.00
CS Curt Schilling Jsy 3.00 8.00
DG David Gassner (RC) .75 2.00
DO David Ortiz Bat 4.00 10.00
DP David Pauley (RC) .75 2.00
DU Dan Uggla (RC) 1.25 3.00
DW David Wright Jsy 6.00 15.00
DWW Dontrelle Willis Jsy 2.50 6.00
EC Eric Chavez Pants 2.50 6.00
EG Enrique Gonzalez (RC) .75 2.00
FG Franklin Gutierrez (RC) .75 2.00
FL Francisco Liriano (RC) 2.00 5.00
GS Grady Sizemore Jsy 4.00 10.00
HB Hank Blalock Jsy 2.50 6.00
HK1 Howie Kendrick (RC) 1.50 4.00
HK2 Howie Kendrick Jsy AU 6.00 15.00
HM Hideki Matsui Bat 6.00 15.00
HP Hayden Penn (RC) .75 2.00
HR Hanley Ramirez (RC) 1.25 3.00
IK Ian Kinsler AU (RC) 4.00 10.00
IR Ivan Rodriguez Jsy 3.00 8.00
IS Ichiro Suzuki Jsy 10.00 25.00
JAS Johan Santana Jsy 4.00 10.00
JB J.Bulger Jsy AU (RC) EXCH 3.00 8.00
JBS Jeremy Sowers (RC) .75 2.00
JCB Jason Botts AU (RC) 3.00 8.00
JD Joey Devine RC .75 2.00
JDD Johnny Damon Bat 4.00 10.00
JHT Jim Thome Bat 4.00 10.00
JI Joe Inglett AU RC 5.00 12.00
JJ Josh Johnson (RC) 2.00 5.00
JK Jeff Karstens RC .75 2.00
JL James Loney (RC) 1.25 3.00
JLB Josh Barfield AU (RC) 3.00 8.00
JM Jeff Mathis (RC) .75 2.00
JP Jonathan Papelbon (RC) 4.00 10.00
JRH Rich Harden Jsy 2.50 6.00
JS James Shields RC 2.50 6.00
JT Jack Taschner Jsy AU (RC) 4.00 10.00
JTA Jordan Tata RC .75 2.00
JTL Jon Lester Jsy AU RC 15.00 40.00
JV Justin Verlander (RC) 6.00 15.00
JW Jered Weaver (RC) 2.50 6.00
JZ Joel Zumaya (RC) 2.00 5.00
KF Kevin Frandsen (RC) .75 2.00
KJ Kenji Johjima RC 2.00 5.00
KM Kendry Morales (RC) 2.00 5.00
LB Lance Berkman Jsy 3.00 8.00
LM Lastings Milledge AU (RC) 8.00 20.00
LWJ Chipper Jones Jsy 4.00 10.00
MC Miguel Cabrera Jsy 3.00 8.00
MC2 Miguel Cabrera Bat 3.00 8.00
MCC Melky Cabrera (RC) 1.25 3.00
MCM Mickey Mantle Bat 30.00 60.00
MCT Mark Teixeira Bat 3.00 8.00
ME Morgan Ensberg Jsy 2.50 6.00
MJP Mike Piazza Bat 4.00 10.00
MK Matt Kemp (RC) 2.00 5.00
MM Mark Mulder Pants 2.50 6.00
MN Mike Napoli Jsy AU RC 4.00 10.00
MP Martin Prado Jsy AU (RC) 5.00 12.00
MPP Mike Pelfrey RC 2.00 5.00
MR Manny Ramirez Jsy 4.00 10.00
MR2 Manny Ramirez Bat 4.00 10.00
MS Matt Smith (RC) 1.25 3.00
MT Miguel Tejada Pants 2.50 6.00
NM Nick Markakis (RC) 1.50 4.00
PF Prince Fielder Jsy AU (RC) 6.00 15.00
PK Paul Konerko Bat 3.00 8.00
PM Pedro Martinez Pants 3.00 8.00
RC Robinson Cano Bat 5.00 12.00
RH Ryan Howard Jsy 8.00 20.00
RK Ryan Garko (RC) .75 2.00
RM Russ Martin (RC) 1.25 3.00
RN Ricky Nolasco AU (RC) 3.00 8.00
RP Ronny Paulino Jsy AU (RC) 6.00 15.00
RZ Ryan Zimmerman (RC) 2.50 6.00
SD Stephen Drew (RC) 1.50 4.00
SM Scott Mathieson (RC) .75 2.00
SO Scott Olsen (RC) .75 2.00
SR Scott Rolen Pants 3.00 8.00
TGJ Tony Gwynn Jr (RC) .75 2.00
TH Todd Helton Jsy 3.00 8.00
TT Taylor Tankersley (RC) .75 2.00
VG Vladimir Guerrero Jsy 3.00 8.00
WA Willy Aybar (RC) .75 2.00
YP Yusmeiro Petit Jsy AU (RC) 4.00 10.00
ZM Zach Miner AU (RC) 3.00 8.00

2006 Bowman Sterling Refractors

*REF RC: .6X TO 1.5X BASIC
RC ODDS 1:6 HOBBY
*REF AU RC: .6X TO 1.5X BASIC AU
AU RC ODDS 1:5 HOBBY
*REF AU-GU RC: .5X TO 1.2X BASIC AU-GU
AU-GU RC ODDS 1:20 HOBBY
*REF GU VET: .5X TO 1.2X BASIC GU
GU VET ODDS 1:7 HOBBY
STATED PRINT RUN 199 SERIAL #'d SETS
EXCHANGE DEADLINE 12/31/08
BLB Barry Bonds Bat 12.50 30.00
HK2 Howie Kendrick Jsy AU 10.00 25.00
HM Hideki Matsui Bat 12.50 30.00
MCM Mickey Mantle Bat 40.00 80.00

2006 Bowman Sterling Gold Refractors

STATED GOLD RC ODDS 1:18 BOXES
STATED PRINT RUN 10 SERIAL #'d SETS
NO PRICING DUE TO SCARCITY

2006 Bowman Sterling Original Autographs

GROUP A ODDS 1:356 BOXES
GROUP B ODDS 1:90 BOXES
GROUP C ODDS 1:45 BOXES
GROUP D ODDS 1:8 BOXES
PRINT RUNS B/WN 1-233 COPIES PER
NO PRICING ON QTY OF 25 OR LESS
EXCHANGE DEADLINE 12/31/08
JD5 J.Damon 02 B/47 C 6.00 15.00
JM1 J.Morneau 02 B/199 D 10.00 25.00
JM2 J.Morneau 06 B/48 D 12.50 30.00
JP1 J.Papelbon 03 BD/71 D 30.00 60.00
JP2 J.Papelbon 06 B/225 D 15.00 40.00
JV1 J.Verlander 05 BD/233 D 30.00 60.00
JV3 J.Verlander 06 B/59 D 40.00 80.00

2006 Bowman Sterling Prospects

COMMON CARD .60 1.50
GROUP A AUTO ODDS 1:2 HOBBY
GROUP B AUTO ODDS 1:2 HOBBY
OVERALL PLATE ODDS 1:23 BOXES
PLATE PRINT RUN 1 SET PER COLOR
BLACK-CYAN-MAGENTA-YELLOW ISSUED
NO PLATE PRICING DUE TO SCARCITY
EXCHANGE DEADLINE 12/31/08
AC Adrian Cardenas AU A 4.00 10.00
ADC Adam Coe .60 1.50
AG Alex Gordon AU B 8.00 20.00
AJC Asdrubal Cabrera 3.00 8.00
AO Adam Ottovino AU A 5.00 12.00
AP Andrew Pinckney .50 1.25
AS A.J. Shappi .60 1.50
BA Brandon Allen AU B 4.00 10.00
BB Brooks Brown AU A 3.00 8.00
BC Ben Copeland .60 1.50
BD Brent Dlugach .60 1.50
BF Brad Furnish AU A 3.00 8.00
BH Brett Hayes AU B 3.00 8.00
BJ Brandon Jones .60 1.50
BJS B.J. Szymanski .60 1.50
BM Brandon Moss AU A 3.00 8.00
BS Brandon Snyder AU B 3.00 8.00
BSI Brett Sinkbeil AU B 6.00 15.00
BW Brandon Wood AU B 6.00 15.00
BWM Brad McCann .60 1.50
CD Chris Dickerson AU A 4.00 10.00
CD Chris Dickerson 1.00 2.50
CH Chase Headley AU B 8.00 20.00
CHH Chad Huffman AU B 3.00 8.00
CJ Cody Johnson AU B 3.00 8.00
CK Clayton Kershaw AU A 125.00 300.00
CM Cameron Maybin AU A 8.00 20.00
CMT Matt Tolbert .60 1.50
CP Chris Parmelee AU B 3.00 8.00
CR Cory Rasmus AU A 5.00 12.00
CT Chad Tracy AU A 3.00 8.00
CW Colton Willems AU B 3.00 8.00
CW Corey Wimberly .60 1.50
DE Dustin Evans AU A 3.00 8.00
DF Dexter Fowler 2.00 5.00
DH Daniel Haigwood AU B 3.00 8.00
DHU David Huff AU B 3.00 8.00
DIH Diory Hernandez .60 1.50
DM Dustin Majewski .60 1.50
DT Dallas Trahern .60 1.50
EA Elvis Andrus 2.00 5.00
EL Evan Longoria AU B 10.00 25.00
EM Evan MacLane .60 1.50
EP Elvin Puello AU A 3.00 8.00
GLM Garrett Mock .60 1.50
GM Garrett Mock AU B 3.00 8.00
HC Hank Conger AU B 5.00 12.00
HP Hunter Pence 2.50 6.00
JAC Jose Campusano .60 1.50
JBU Joshua Butler AU A 3.00 8.00
JC Jeff Clement AU B 3.00 8.00
JF Juan Francia .60 1.50
JJ Jeremy Jeffress AU B 4.00 10.00
JJ Jason Jaramillo .60 1.50
JKF Jeff Frazier .60 1.50
JN Jason Neighborgall AU B 3.00 8.00
JR Joshua Rodriguez AU A 3.00 8.00
JRB Jimmy Barthmaier .60 1.50
JS Jarrod Saltalamacchia AU A 3.00 8.00
JT Jose Tabata 1.00 2.50
JTL Jared Lansford .60 1.50
JU Justin Upton AU B 6.00 15.00
JW Johnny Whittleman AU B 8.00 20.00
KB Kyler Burke AU A 3.00 8.00
KC Koby Clemens AU A 4.00 10.00
KD Kyle Drabek AU B 3.00 8.00
KJ Kris Johnson AU A 3.00 8.00
KK Kasey Kiker AU B 3.00 8.00
KM Kyle McCulloch AU B 3.00 8.00
LH Luke Hochevar AU A 3.00 8.00
MA Mike Aviles AU B 4.00 10.00
MAA Matt Antonelli AU B 4.00 10.00
MC Michael Collins .60 1.50
MF Michael Felix AU A 3.00 8.00
MG Mat Gamel 1.50 4.00
MH Michael Hollimon .60 1.50
MM Mark McCormick AU B 3.00 8.00
MO Micah Owings AU B 6.00 15.00
MR Mark Reed .60 1.50
MRA Michael Aubrey 1.00 2.50
MRR Max Ramirez 1.00 2.50
MSM Mark McLemore .60 1.50
MT Mark Trumbo 1.50 4.00
NA Nick Adenhart .60 1.50
ON Oswaldo Navarro .60 1.50
OS Omir Santos .60 1.50
PB Pedro Beato AU A 3.00 8.00
PL Pedro Lopez AU A 3.00 8.00
RB Ronny Bourquin AU B 3.00 8.00
RK Ryan Klosterman .60 1.50
RL Radhames Liz .60 1.50
RP Ryan Patterson .60 1.50
SC Shaun Cumberland .60 1.50
SE Steven Evarts AU A 3.00 8.00
SGG Steve Garrabrants .60 1.50
SM Stephen Marek .60 1.50
SMM Steve Murphy .60 1.50
SR Shawn Riggans .60 1.50
SW Steven Wright AU A 3.00 8.00
SWA Sean Watson AU B 3.00 8.00
TB Travis Buck AU B 6.00 15.00
TC Trevor Crowe AU A 3.00 8.00
TC Tyler Colvin AU B 4.00 10.00
TP Troy Patton AU A 3.00 8.00
WR Wilkin Ramirez 1.00 2.50
WT Wade Townsend AU B 3.00 8.00
WV Will Venable .60 1.50
YC Yung-Chi Chen 1.00 2.50
YG Yovani Gallardo 2.00 5.00

2006 Bowman Sterling Prospects Refractors

*REF: .75X TO 2X BASIC
REF ODDS 1:6 HOBBY
*REF AU: .75X TO 2X BASIC AU
AU ODDS 1:5 HOBBY
STATED PRINT RUN 199 SERIAL #'d SETS
EXCHANGE DEADLINE 12/31/08
HC Hank Conger AU 10.00 25.00
JW Johnny Whittleman AU 15.00 40.00
KB Kyler Burke AU 10.00 25.00
MO Micah Owings AU 12.50 30.00
TB Travis Buck AU 10.00 25.00

2006 Bowman Sterling Prospects Gold Refractors

STATED GOLD ODDS 1:18 BOXES
STATED PRINT RUN 10 SERIAL #'d SETS
NO PRICING DUE TO SCARCITY

2007 Bowman Sterling

COMMON ROOKIE .40 1.00
COMMON AUTO RC 3.00 8.00
AU RC SEMIS 4.00 10.00
AU RC UNLISTED 5.00 12.00
AU RC AUTO ODDS 1:2 PACKS
COMMON GU VET 2.50 6.00
GU VET GROUP A ODDS 1:5 PACKS
GU VET GROUP B ODDS 1:3 PACKS
GU VET GROUP C ODDS 1:253 PACKS
PRINTING PLATE ODDS 1:29 BOXES
PRINTING PLATE AU ODDS 1:41 BOXES
PLATE PRINT RUN 1 SET PER COLOR
BLACK-CYAN-MAGENTA-YELLOW ISSUED
NO PLATE PRICING DUE TO SCARCITY
AAL Adam Lind (RC) .40 1.00
AER Alex Rodriguez Bat A 6.00 15.00
AG Alex Gordon RC 1.25 3.00
AI Akinori Iwamura RC 1.00 2.50
AJ Andruw Jones Bat B 2.50 6.00
AL Andy LaRoche (RC) .40 1.00
AM Andrew Miller RC 1.50 4.00
AP Albert Pujols Jsy A 5.00 12.00
AR Alex Rios Jsy B 2.50 6.00
AS Alfonso Soriano Bat B 2.50 6.00
AS Andy Sonnanstine RC .40 1.00
BB Billy Butler (RC) .60 1.50
BF Ben Francisco (RC) .40 1.00
BLB Barry Bonds Pants A 4.00 10.00
BP Brad Penny Jsy B 2.50 6.00
BR Brian Roberts Jsy A 2.50 6.00
BS Brian Stokes (RC) .40 1.00
BU B.J. Upton Bat B 2.50 6.00
BW Brandon Webb Jsy B 2.50 6.00
BW Brandon Wood (RC) .40 1.00
CAB Craig Biggio Jsy B 3.00 8.00
CAG Carlos Guillen Jsy B 2.50 6.00
CG Carlos Gomez RC .75 2.00
CH Cole Hamels Jsy A 3.00 8.00
CH Chase Headley AU (RC) 3.00 8.00
CL Carlos Lee Jsy B 2.50 6.00
CM Cameron Maybin AU RC 4.00 10.00
CMS Curt Schilling Jsy B 2.50 6.00
CT Curtis Thigpen (RC) .40 1.00
DDY Dmitri Young Jsy B 2.50 6.00
DM Daisuke Matsuzaka RC 1.50 4.00
DMM David Murphy (RC) .40 1.00
DO David Ortiz Bat B 3.00 8.00
DP Danny Putnam (RC) .40 1.00
DW David Wright Bat B 4.00 10.00
DWW Dontrelle Willis Jsy B 2.50 6.00
DY Delmon Young (RC) .60 1.50
EC Eric Chavez Pants B 2.50 6.00
FL Fred Lewis (RC) .60 1.50
FP Felix Pie AU (RC) 3.00 8.00
GO Garrett Olson (RC) .40 1.00
GP Glen Perkins AU (RC) 4.00 10.00
HB Homer Bailey AU (RC) 3.00 8.00
HG Hector Gimenez (RC) .40 1.00
HO Hideki Okajima RC 2.00 5.00
HP Hunter Pence (RC) 1.25 3.00
IS Ichiro Suzuki Bat B 5.00 12.00
JAV Jason Varitek Jsy B 3.00 8.00
JB Jeff Baker (RC) .40 1.00
JBR Jose Reyes Jsy A 3.00 8.00
JC1 Joba Chamberlain RC .60 1.50
JC2 Joba Chamberlain AU 5.00 12.00
JD John Danks AU RC 3.00 8.00
JDF Josh Fields (RC) .40 1.00
JE Jim Edmonds Jsy B 3.00 8.00
JE Jacoby Ellsbury (RC) 2.50 6.00
JF Jesus Flores RC .40 1.00
JH Josh Hamilton AU (RC) 6.00 15.00
JL Jesse Litsch AU RC 3.00 8.00
JQF Jake Fox RC .40 1.00
JR Jo-Jo Reyes (RC) .40 1.00
JS Johan Santana Jsy A 3.00 8.00
JS J.Salty AU (RC) 3.00 8.00
JU Justin Upton RC 1.25 3.00
JV Justin Verlander Jsy B 5.00 12.00
KI Kei Igawa RC 1.00 2.50
KK Kevin Kouzmanoff (RC) .40 1.00
KKS Kurt Suzuki AU (RC) 3.00 8.00
KRK Kyle Kendrick AU RC 3.00 8.00
KS Kevin Slowey AU (RC) 6.00 15.00
LB Lance Berkman Jsy B 2.50 6.00
MAR Manny Ramirez Bat B 2.50 6.00
MB Michael Bourn (RC) .60 1.50
MC Melky Cabrera Bat B 2.50 6.00
MC Matt Chico AU (RC) 3.00 8.00
MCT Mark Teixeira Bat A 2.50 6.00
MF Mike Fontenot (RC) .40 1.00
MH Matt Holliday Jsy B 3.00 8.00
MJO Magglio Ordonez Bat B 2.50 6.00
MK Masumi Kuwata RC .40 1.00
MM Mickey Mantle Jsy C 30.00 60.00
MM Miguel Montero (RC) .40 1.00
MO Micah Owings (RC) .40 1.00
MP Manny Parra (RC) .40 1.00
MR Mark Reynolds RC 1.25 3.00
MSM Mark McLemore (RC) .40 1.00
MT Miguel Tejada Pants B 2.50 6.00
MY Michael Young Jsy B 2.50 6.00
NG Nick Gorneault AU (RC) 3.00 8.00
NS Nate Schierholtz AU (RC) 3.00 8.00
OC Orlando Cabrera Jsy 2.50 6.00
PF Prince Fielder Jsy A 3.00 8.00
PH Phil Hughes (RC) 1.00 2.50
PH Phil Hughes AU (RC) 3.00 8.00
RB Rocco Baldelli Jsy B 2.50 6.00
RB Ryan Braun AU (RC) 5.00 12.00
RC Roger Clemens Jsy B 4.00 10.00
RJC Robinson Cano Bat B 3.00 8.00
RJH Ryan Howard Bat A 4.00 10.00
RS Ryan Sweeney (RC) .40 1.00
RV Rick Vanden Hurk RC .40 1.00
RZ Ryan Zimmerman Bat B 3.00 8.00
SD Shelley Duncan (RC) 1.00 2.50
SG Sean Gallagher (RC) .40 1.00
SK Scott Kazmir Jsy B 2.50 6.00
TA Tony Abreu RC 1.00 2.50
TB Travis Buck (RC) .40 1.00
TC Tyler Clippard (RC) .60 1.50
TH Tim Hudson Jsy B 2.50 6.00
TL Tim Lincecum AU RC 12.00 30.00
TLH Todd Helton Bat A 2.50 6.00
TM Travis Metcalf RC .60 1.50
TW Tim Wakefield Jsy B 2.50 6.00
UJ Ubaldo Jimenez (RC) 1.25 3.00
VG Vladimir Guerrero Jsy A 2.50 6.00
YE Yunel Escobar (RC) .40 1.00
YG Yovani Gallardo AU (RC) 3.00 8.00

2007 Bowman Sterling Refractors

*REF RC: 1X TO 2.5X BASIC
RC ODDS 1:7 PACKS
*REF AU RC: .5X TO 1.2X BASIC AU
AU RC ODDS 1:5 PACKS
*REF GU VET: .5X TO 1.2X BASIC GU
GU VET ODDS 1:8 PACKS
STATED PRINT RUN 199 SERIAL #'d SETS
JH Josh Hamilton AU 8.00 20.00
JU Justin Upton 20.00 50.00
KS Kevin Slowey AU 10.00 25.00

2007 Bowman Sterling Dual Autographs

STATED ODDS 1:5 BOXES
STATED PRINT RUN 275 SER.#'d SETS
BV J.Bruce/J.Votto 15.00 40.00
CH S.Choo/C.Hu 6.00 15.00
GM D.Guerra/F.Martinez 5.00 12.00
HC P.Hughes/J.Chamberlain 10.00 25.00
HP L.Hochevar/D.Price 8.00 20.00
LC E.Longoria/C.Crawford 6.00 15.00
MM J.Maine/L.Milledge 4.00 10.00
PB H.Pence/R.Braun 12.50 30.00
PP J.Papelbon/J.Papelbon 4.00 10.00
PS F.Pie/J.Samardzija 10.00 25.00

2007 Bowman Sterling Dual Autographs Refractors

*REF: .4X TO 1X BASIC
STATED ODDS 1:6 BOXES
STATED PRINT RUN 199 SER.#'d SETS

2007 Bowman Sterling Prospects

COMMON CARD .50 1.25
COMMON AUTO 3.00 8.00
STATED AU ODDS 1:1 PACKS
COMMON AU-GU 3.00 8.00
AU-GU ODDS 1:5 PACKS
PRINTING PLATE ODDS 1:29 BOXES
PRINTING PLATE AU ODDS 1:41 BOXES
PLATE PRINT RUN 1 SET PER COLOR
BLACK-CYAN-MAGENTA-YELLOW ISSUED
NO PLATE PRICING DUE TO SCARCITY
AC Adrian Cardenas Jsy AU 4.00 10.00
AF Andrew Fie .50 1.25
ALC Aaron Cunningham .75 2.00
AP Aaron Poreda AU 3.00 8.00
BB Brian Bocock Jsy AU 3.00 8.00
BB Blake Beavan AU 3.00 8.00
BEL Brad Lincoln .50 1.25
BH Brandon Hamilton .50 1.25
BHB Burke Badenhop .75 2.00
BL Bryan LaHair AU 3.00 8.00
BM Brandon MaGee AU 3.00 8.00
BMI Beau Mills AU 3.00 8.00
BR Ben Revere AU 6.00 15.00
BWH Brandon Hynick 1.25 3.00
CB Collin Balester Jsy AU 3.00 8.00
CC Chris Carter 1.50 4.00
CD Chance Douglass .50 1.25
CG Cole Gillespie AU 3.00 8.00
CH Chin-Lung Hu Jsy AU 4.00 10.00
CH Cedric Hunter 1.25 3.00
CK Clayton Kershaw Jsy AU 75.00 200.00
CL Chuck Lofgren Jsy AU 4.00 10.00
CM Clayton Mortensen AU 3.00 8.00
CN Chris Nowak .50 1.25
CR Colby Rasmus Jsy AU 3.00 8.00
CS Cody Strait .50 1.25
CW Chris Withrow AU 4.00 10.00
CWW Casey Weathers AU 3.00 8.00
DB Daniel Bard AU 3.00 8.00
DBE Dellin Betances 1.50 4.00
DG Deolis Guerra Jsy AU 4.00 10.00
DI Devin Ivany .50 1.25
DJ Desmond Jennings 2.00 5.00
DL Drew Locke .50 1.25
DM Daniel Moskos AU 3.00 8.00
DME Devin Mesoraco AU 4.00 10.00
DMM Derek Miller .75 2.00
DPP David Price AU 12.00 30.00
DS James Simmons AU 3.00 8.00
EE Ed Easley .50 1.25
EL Evan Longoria Jsy AU 6.00 15.00
EL Erik Lis AU 3.00 8.00
EM Emerson Frostad .50 1.25
EY Eric Young Jr. .75 2.00
FF Freddie Freeman 8.00 20.00
GD German Duran Jsy AU 3.00 8.00
GH Gorkys Hernandez 1.25 3.00
GP Gregory Porter .50 1.25
GR Greg Reynolds 1.25 3.00
GS Greg Smith .75 2.00
HS Henry Sosa Jsy AU 4.00 10.00
ID Ivan De Jesus Jr. .75 2.00
IS Ian Stewart Jsy AU 5.00 12.00
JA J.P. Arencibia AU 3.00 8.00
JAA James Avery AU 3.00 8.00
JB Jay Bruce Jsy AU 6.00 15.00
JB Joe Benson AU 5.00 12.00
JBO Julio Borbon AU 6.00 15.00
JG Jonathan Gilmore AU 3.00 8.00
JGA Joe Gaetti .50 1.25
JGO Jared Goedert 1.25 3.00
JH Jason Heyward AU 4.00 10.00
JJ Justin Jackson .75 2.00
JL Jeff Locke 1.25 3.00
JM Joe Mather .50 1.25
JO Josh Outman AU 3.00 8.00
JP Jason Place .75 2.00
JPA Jeremy Papelbon .50 1.25
JPP Josh Papelbon .50 1.25
JS Joe Savery AU 3.00 8.00
JS Jeff Samardzija 2.00 5.00
JSM Jake Smolinski 1.50 4.00
JT J.R. Towles 1.50 4.00
JV Joey Votto Jsy AU 40.00 100.00
JV Josh Vitters AU 3.00 8.00
JVE Jonathan Van Every .50 1.25
JW Johnny Whittleman Jsy AU 3.00 8.00
KA Kevin Ahrens AU 3.00 8.00
KK Kellen Kulbacki AU 3.00 8.00
KK Kala Kaaihue .75 2.00
MB Michael Burgess AU 3.00 8.00
MBB Madison Bumgarner AU 30.00 80.00
MC Mike Carp 1.50 4.00
MCA Mitch Canham AU 3.00 8.00
MD Mike Daniel AU 3.00 8.00
MDE Mike Devaney .50 1.25
MDO Matt Dominguez AU 4.00 10.00
MH Mark Hamilton .50 1.25
MIM Michael Main AU 3.00 8.00
MLP Matt LaPorta AU 3.00 8.00
MM Michael Madsen Jsy AU 3.00 8.00
MM Matt McBride AU 3.00 8.00
MMG Matt Mangini AU 3.00 8.00
MP Mike Parisi AU 3.00 8.00
MS Michael Saunders 1.50 4.00
MY Matt Young .50 1.25
NH Nick Hagadone AU 4.00 10.00
NN Nick Noonan AU 5.00 12.00
NS Nick Schmidt AU 3.00 8.00
OS Ole Sheldon .50 1.25
PB Pedro Beato Jsy AU 3.00 8.00
PK Peter Kozma AU 3.00 8.00
RD Ross Detwiler AU 3.00 8.00
RM Ryan Mount AU 3.00 8.00
RT Rich Thompson .50 1.25
SF Sam Fuld 1.50 4.00
SP Steve Pearce Jsy AU 6.00 15.00
TA Tim Alderson AU 3.00 8.00
TF Todd Frazier AU 6.00 15.00
TF Thomas Fairchild .50 1.25
TM Thomas Manzella AU 3.00 8.00
TS Travis Snider AU 4.00 10.00
TW Ty Weeden AU 3.00 8.00
VB Vic Buttler .50 1.25
VS Vasili Spanos .50 1.25
WF Wendell Fairley AU 3.00 8.00
WT Wade Townsend AU 3.00 8.00
ZM Zach McAllister .75 2.00

2007 Bowman Sterling Prospects Refractors

*REF: 1.2X TO 3X BASIC
REF ODDS 1:7 PACKS
*REF AU: .75X TO 2X BASIC AU
REF AU ODDS 1:5 PACKS
*REF AU-GU RC: .5X TO 1.2X BASIC AU-GU
REF AU-GU ODDS 1:20 PACKS
STATED PRINT RUN 199 SERIAL #'d SETS

2008 Bowman Sterling

COMMON GU VET 2.50 6.00
EXCHANGE DEADLINE 11/30/2010
COMMON RC 1.00 2.50
COMMON RC VAR 1.25 3.00
RC VAR ODDS 1:2 BOXES
RC VAR PRINT RUN 399 SER.#'d SETS
COMMON AU RC 3.00 8.00
AU RC ODDS 1:3 PACKS
PRINTING PLATE ODDS 1:93 PACKS
PRINTING PLATE AU ODDS 1:238 PACKS
PLATE PRINT RUN 1 SET PER COLOR
BLACK-CYAN-MAGENTA-YELLOW ISSUED
NO PLATE PRICING DUE TO SCARCITY
AAG Armando Galarraga AU RC 3.00 8.00
AP Albert Pujols Jsy 5.00 12.00
AR Alex Rodriguez Jsy 5.00 12.00
ARA Aramis Ramirez Mem 2.50 6.00
ARU Adam Russell AU (RC) 3.00 8.00
BG Brett Gardner (RC) 2.50 6.00
BH Brian Horwitz RC 1.00 2.50
BJ Brandon Jones RC 2.50 6.00
BJB Brian Bixler AU (RC) 3.00 8.00
BM Brian McCann Bat 2.50 6.00
BZ Brad Ziegler RC 5.00 12.00
CC Carl Crawford Jsy 2.50 6.00
CD Chris Davis RC 2.00 5.00
CDB Clay Buchholz (RC) 1.50 4.00
CEGa Carlos Gonzalez (RC) 2.50 6.00
CEGb Carlos Gonzalez VAR SP 3.00 8.00
CG Chris Getz AU RC 3.00 8.00
CG Curtis Granderson Mem 3.00 8.00
CH Cole Hamels Jsy 3.00 8.00
CJ Chipper Jones Jsy 3.00 8.00
CKa Clayton Kershaw RC 30.00 80.00
CKb Clayton Kershaw VAR SP 25.00 60.00
CLH Chin-Lung Hu (RC) 1.00 2.50
CM Charlie Morton (RC) 3.00 8.00
CMT Matt Tolbert RC 1.50 4.00
CP Chris Perez AU RC 3.00 8.00
CR Clayton Richard (RC) 1.00 2.50
CRPa Cliff Pennington (RC) 1.00 2.50
CRPb Cliff Pennington VAR SP 1.25 3.00
CU Chase Utley Jsy 4.00 10.00
CW Chien-Ming Wang Jsy 4.00 10.00
DB Daric Barton (RC) 1.00 2.50
DM Daisuke Matsuzaka Jsy 4.00 10.00
DO David Ortiz Jsy 3.00 8.00
DP David Purcey (RC) 1.00 2.50
DW David Wright Bat 4.00 10.00
DY Delmon Young Jsy 2.50 6.00
EH Eric Hurley (RC) 1.00 2.50
EL Evan Longoria AU RC 10.00 25.00
EV Edinson Volquez Jsy 2.50 6.00
FC Fausto Carmona Mem 3.00 8.00
GB Gregor Blanco (RC) 1.00 2.50
GD German Duran RC 1.50 4.00
GR Greg Reynolds RC 1.50 4.00
GS Geovany Soto Jsy 3.00 8.00
GTS Greg Smith AU RC 3.00 8.00
HI Hernan Iribarren (RC) 1.50 4.00
HKa Hiroki Kuroda RC 2.50 6.00
HKb Hiroki Kuroda VAR SP 3.00 8.00
HP Hunter Pence Jsy 3.00 8.00
HR Hanley Ramirez Jsy 2.50 6.00
IS Ichiro Suzuki Jsy 6.00 15.00
JABa Jay Bruce (RC) 3.00 8.00
JABb Jay Bruce VAR SP 4.00 10.00
JB Josh Banks (RC) 1.00 2.50
JBC Jeff Clement (RC) 1.50 4.00
JBR Jose Reyes Jsy 3.00 8.00
JC Joba Chamberlain Jsy 5.00 12.00
JCH Justin Christian RC 1.50 4.00
JCO Johnny Cueto RC 2.50 6.00
JE Jacoby Ellsbury Jsy 4.00 10.00
JH Josh Hamilton Jsy 5.00 12.00
JLa Jed Lowrie (RC) 1.00 2.50
JLb Jed Lowrie VAR SP 1.25 3.00
JMR Justin Ruggiano AU RC 3.00 8.00
JN Jeff Niemann (RC) 1.00 2.50
JR Jimmy Rollins Jsy 3.00 8.00
JSa Jeff Samardzija RC 3.00 8.00
JSb Jeff Samardzija VAR SP 4.00 10.00
JT J.R. Towles RC 1.50 4.00
JU Justin Upton Bat 2.50 6.00
Va Joey Votto (RC) 8.00 20.00
Vb Joey Votto VAR SP 10.00 25.00
Fa Kosuke Fukudome RC 3.00 8.00
Fb Kosuke Fukudome VAR SP 4.00 10.00
Hb Luke Hochevar RC 1.50 4.00
A Michael Aubrey RC 1.50 4.00
C Miguel Cabrera Bat 3.00 8.00
H Matt Holliday Bat 2.50 6.00
J Matt Joyce RC 2.50 6.00
K Masahide Kobayashi RC 1.50 4.00
M Mickey Mantle Jsy 30.00 60.00
R Manny Ramirez Jsy 4.00 10.00
RRa Max Ramirez RC 1.00 2.50
RRb Max Ramirez VAR SP 1.25 3.00
T Mark Teixeira Bat 3.00 8.00
TA Miguel Tejada Mem 2.50 6.00
TH Michael Holliman RC 1.00 2.50
A Nick Adenhart (RC) 1.00 2.50
B Nick Blackburn RC 1.50 4.00
Nick Evans RC 1.00 2.50
Nick Hundley (RC) 1.00 2.50
S Nick Stavinoha RC 1.50 4.00
M Nick Markakis Jsy 4.00 10.00
Prince Fielder Jsy 3.00 8.00
Ryan Braun Jsy 4.00 10.00
Reid Brignac (RC) 1.50 4.00
Ryan Howard Jsy 4.00 10.00
M Jai Miller (RC) 1.00 2.50
Radhames Liz RC 1.50 4.00
Russ Martin Bat 3.00 8.00
Ryan Tucker (RC) 1.00 2.50
SR Sean Rodriguez (RC) 1.00 2.50
SS Seth Smith AU (RC) 3.00 8.00
TL Tim Lincecum Jsy 6.00 15.00
TT Taylor Teagarden AU RC 5.00 12.00
VG Vladimir Guerrero Jsy 2.50 6.00
VM Victor Martinez Jsy 2.50 6.00
WB Wladimir Balentien (RC) 1.00 2.50
WCC Chris Carter (RC) 1.50 4.00

2008 Bowman Sterling Refractors

*GU VET REF: .5X TO 1.2X BASIC
GU VET REF ODDS 1:5 PACKS
GU VET REF PRINT RUN 199 SER.#'d SETS
*RC REF: .5X TO 1.2X BASIC
RC REF ODDS 1:4 PACKS
RC REF PRINT RUN 199 SER.#'d SETS
*RC VAR REF: .4X TO 1X BASIC
RC VAR REF ODDS 1:5 BOXES
RC VAR REF PRINT RUN 149 SER.#'d SETS
*RC AU REF: .5X TO 1.2X BASIC
RC AU REF ODDS 1:5 PACKS
RC AU REF PRINT RUN 199 SER.#'d SETS

2008 Bowman Sterling Gold Refractors

*GU VET GLD: .75X TO 2X BASIC
GU VET GLD ODDS 1:19 PACKS
GU VET GLD PRINT RUN 50 SER.#'d SETS
*RC GLD: 1X TO 2.5X BASIC
RC GLD ODDS 1:15 PACKS
RC GLD PRINT RUN 50 SER.#'d SETS
*RC VAR GLD: .75X TO 2X BASIC
RC VAR GLD ODDS 1:13 BOXES
RC VAR GLD PRINT RUN 50 SER.#'d SETS
*RC AU GLD: .75X TO 2X BASIC
RC AU GLD ODDS 1:21 PACKS
RC AU GLD PRINT RUN 50 SER.#'d SETS
AP Albert Pujols Jsy 12.50 30.00
AR Alex Rodriguez Jsy 12.50 30.00
BZ Brad Ziegler 25.00 60.00
CLH Chin-Lung Hu 4.00 10.00
CW Chien-Ming Wang Jsy 20.00 50.00
DM Daisuke Matsuzaka Jsy 10.00 25.00
HKa Hiroki Kuroda 12.00 30.00
HKb Hiroki Kuroda VAR 12.00 30.00
IS Ichiro Suzuki Jsy 15.00 40.00
JE Jacoby Ellsbury Jsy 15.00 40.00
TT Taylor Teagarden AU 20.00 50.00

2008 Bowman Sterling Dual Autographs

STATED ODDS 1:29 PACKS
STATED PRINT RUN 325 SER.#'d SETS
LS E.Longoria/G.Soto 6.00 15.00
MM J.Montero/M.Melancon 8.00 20.00
PB B.Posey/G.Beckham 20.00 50.00
RS A.Rios/T.Snider 6.00 15.00

2008 Bowman Sterling Dual Autographs Refractors

*REF: .5X TO 1.2X BASIC
STATED ODDS 1:93 PACKS
STATED PRINT RUN 99 SER.#'d SETS

2008 Bowman Sterling Dual Autographs Gold Refractors

*GLD REF: .6X TO 1.5X BASIC
STATED ODDS 1:185 PACKS
STATED PRINT RUN 50 SER.#'d SETS

2008 Bowman Sterling Prospects

COMMON CARD .40 1.00
COMMON AU 3.00 8.00
STATED AUTO ODDS 1:3 PACKS
COMMON JSY AU 5.00 12.00
STATED JSY AU ODDS 1:4 PACKS
PRINTING PLATE ODDS 1:93 PACKS
PRINTING PLATE AU ODDS 1:238 PACKS
PLATE PRINT RUN 1 SET PER COLOR
BLACK-CYAN-MAGENTA-YELLOW ISSUED
NO PLATE PRICING DUE TO SCARCITY
AA Adrian Alaniz .40 1.00
AB Andrew Brackman .60 1.50
AC Alex Cobb .40 1.00
AC Andrew Cashner AU 3.00 8.00
AH Anthony Hewitt AU 4.00 10.00
AJ Austin Jackson 2.00 5.00
AM Aaron Mathews .40 1.00
AMO Adam Moore AU 3.00 8.00
AR Aneury Rodriguez .60 1.50
BB Bubba Bell 1.00 2.50
BC Brett Cecil .60 1.50
BH Brandon Hicks .40 1.00
BHA Brad Hand AU 3.00 8.00
BP Buster Posey AU 40.00 100.00
BS Braeden Schlehuber .40 1.00
BW Brandon Waring .60 1.50
CB Charlie Blackmon AU 25.00 60.00
CC Carlos Carrasco Jsy AU 3.00 8.00
CGU Carlos Gutierrez AU 3.00 8.00
CI Cale Iorg .40 1.00
CJ Chris Johnson .60 1.50
CSA Carlos Santana AU 4.00 10.00
CT Chris Tillman AU 3.00 8.00
CV Chris Valaika .40 1.00
DC Daniel Cortes 1.00 2.50
DD Danny Duffy 1.00 2.50
DH David Hernandez AU 3.00 8.00
DS Daniel Schlereth AU 3.00 8.00
EA Elvis Andrus Jsy AU 4.00 10.00
EB Engel Beltre 1.25 3.00
EH Eric Hacker AU 3.00 8.00
EK Edward Kunz .60 1.50
FM Fernando Martinez Jsy AU 6.00 15.00
FS Fautino de los Santos .40 1.00
GB Gordon Beckham AU 4.00 10.00
GGH Gorkys Hernandez Jsy AU 5.00 12.00
GH Greg Halman AU 6.00 15.00
GP Gerardo Parra .40 1.00
GT Graham Taylor .40 1.00
IDA Ike Davis AU 5.00 12.00
JA Jake Arrieta Jsy AU 12.00 30.00
JB Jonathan Bachanov .40 1.00
JC Jhoulys Chacin .60 1.50
JD Jason Donald Jsy AU 5.00 12.00
JJ Jon Jay .60 1.50
JK Jason Knapp AU 3.00 8.00
JL Jeff Locke AU 3.00 8.00
JLC Jordan Czarniecki .40 1.00
JLI Josh Lindblom AU 3.00 8.00
JM Jake McGee .60 1.50
JM Jesus Montero Jsy AU 5.00 12.00
JR Javier Rodriguez AU 3.00 8.00
JS Justin Snyder .60 1.50
JSM Josh Smoker .40 1.00
JZ Jordan Zimmermann 1.00 2.50
KK Kala Kaaihue AU 3.00 8.00
KW Kenny Wilson .40 1.00
LA Lars Anderson AU 4.00 10.00
LC Lonnie Chisenhall AU 4.00 10.00
LL Lance Lynn AU 5.00 12.00
LM Logan Morrison 2.00 5.00
MB Mike Brantley 1.00 2.50
MC Mitch Canham .40 1.00
MD Michael Daniel .60 1.50
MI Matt Inouye .40 1.00
MM Mark Melancon AU 3.00 8.00
MR Matt Rizzotti .40 1.00
MW Michael Watt .40 1.00
NR Nick Romero .40 1.00
NV Niko Vasquez 1.00 2.50
PT Polin Trinidad AU 3.00 8.00
QM Quinton Miller AU 3.00 8.00
RK Ryan Kalish 1.00 2.50
RM Ryan Morris .60 1.50
RP Rick Porcello 1.25 3.00
RR Rusty Ryal .60 1.50
RT Rene Tosoni .40 1.00
SM Shairon Martis .60 1.50
ST Steve Tolleson .40 1.00
TF Tim Fedroff AU 3.00 8.00
TH Tom Hagan .40 1.00
VM Vin Mazzaro AU 3.00 8.00
XA Xavier Avery 1.00 2.50
YS Yunesky Sanchez .40 1.00
ZB Zach Britton 1.25 3.00

2008 Bowman Sterling Prospects Refractors

*PROS REF: 1X TO 2.5X BASIC
PROS REF ODDS 1:4 PACKS
*PROS AU REF: .75X TO 2X BASIC
PROS AU REF ODDS 1:5 PACKS
*PROS JSY AU REF: .75X TO 2X BASIC
PROS JSY AU REF ODDS 1:28 PACKS
REFRACTOR PRINT RUN 199 SER.#'d SETS
BP Buster Posey AU 75.00 150.00
RP Rick Porcello 15.00 40.00

2008 Bowman Sterling Prospects Gold Refractors

*PROS GLD: 3X TO 8X BASIC
RC GLD ODDS 1:15 PACKS
*PROS AU GLD: 2X TO 5X BASIC
PROS AU GLD ODDS 1:21 PACKS
*PROS JSY AU GLD: 1.5X TO 4X BASIC
PROS JSY AU GLD ODDS 1:113 PACKS
GOLD REF PRINT RUN 50 SER.#'d SETS
BP Buster Posey AU 175.00 350.00

2008 Bowman Sterling WBC Patch

STATED ODDS 1:24 PACKS
EXCHANGE DEADLIN 12/31/2009
1 Yu Darvish 125.00 250.00
2 Ichiro Suzuki 60.00 120.00
8 Chenhao Li 6.00 15.00
9 Xiaotian Zhang 10.00 25.00
10 Po Hsuan Keng 6.00 15.00
12 Yoennis Cespedes 150.00 300.00
16 Masahiro Tanaka 300.00 500.00
17 Gift Ngoepe• 6.00 15.00
18 Juan Carlos Sulbaran 6.00 15.00
22 Alexander Mayeta 6.00 15.00
NNO EXCH Card 50.00 100.00

2009 Bowman Sterling

COMMON CARD 1.00 2.50
COMMON AU 4.00 10.00
OVERALL AUTO ODDS TWO PER PACK
PRINTING PLATE ODDS 1:91 HOBBY
AU PRINTING PLATE ODDS 1:245 HOBBY
PLATE PRINT RUN 1 SET PER COLOR
BLACK-CYAN-MAGENTA-YELLOW ISSUED
NO PLATE PRICING DUE TO SCARCITY
AA Alex Avila RC 3.00 8.00
AB Antonio Bastardo AU RC 4.00 10.00
AB Andrew Bailey RC 2.50 6.00
AC Andrew Carpenter RC 1.50 4.00
AM Andrew McCutchen (RC) 5.00 12.00
BD Brian Duensing RC 1.50 4.00
BN Brad Nelson (RC) 1.00 2.50
BS Bobby Scales RC 1.50 4.00
CC Chris Coghlan RC 2.50 6.00
CM C.McGehee AU (RC) 1.00 2.50
CR Colby Rasmus (RC) 1.50 4.00
CT Chris Tillman AU RC 3.00 8.00
DB Daniel Bard RC 1.00 2.50
DF Dexter Fowler (RC) 1.50 4.00
DH David Hernandez RC 1.00 2.50
DP David Price RC 2.00 5.00
DS Daniel Schlereth AU RC 4.00 10.00
EC Everth Cabrera RC 1.50 4.00
EY Eric Young Jr. RC 1.00 2.50
FC Francisco Cervelli RC 2.50 6.00
FM Fernando Martinez RC 2.50 6.00
FN Fu-Te Ni RC 1.50 4.00
GB Gordon Beckham AU RC 4.00 10.00
GG Greg Golson (RC) 1.00 2.50
GK George Kottaras (RC) 1.00 2.50
GP Gerardo Parra RC 1.50 4.00
JB Julio Borbon RC 1.00 2.50
JC Jhoulys Chacin RC 1.50 4.00
JH Jarrett Hoffpauir (RC) 1.00 2.50
JM Justin Masterson AU (RC) 3.00 8.00
JM Juan Miranda RC 1.50 4.00
JS Jordan Schafer (RC) 1.50 4.00
JZ Jordan Zimmermann RC 2.50 6.00
KB Kyle Blanks RC 1.50 4.00
KK Kenshin Kawakimi RC 1.50 4.00
KU Koji Uehara RC 2.50 6.00
MG Mat Gamel RC 2.50 6.00
ML Mat Latos RC 3.00 8.00
MM Mark Melancon RC 1.00 2.50
MS Michael Saunders RC 2.50 6.00
MT Matt Tuiasosopo (RC) 1.00 2.50
NR Nolan Reimold AU 6.00 15.00
NR Nolan Reimold (RC) 1.00 2.50
RP Ryan Perry AU RC 4.00 10.00
RP Rick Porcello RC 3.00 8.00
SR Shane Robinson RC 1.00 2.50
TC Trevor Crowe RC 1.00 2.50
TG Tyler Greene (RC) 1.00 2.50
TH Tommy Hanson AU RC 6.00 15.00
TS Travis Snider RC 1.50 4.00
WR Wilkin Ramirez RC 1.00 2.50
WV Will Venable RC 1.00 2.50
ABB Aaron Bates RC 1.00 2.50
CTT Carlos Torres RC 1.00 2.50
DFR David Freese RC 3.00 8.00
DHE Diory Hernandez RC 1.00 2.50
DHO Derek Holland RC 1.50 4.00
JHO Jamie Hoffmann RC 1.00 2.50
JMA John Mayberry Jr. (RC) 1.50 4.00

2009 Bowman Sterling Refractors

*REF: .5X TO 1.2X BASIC
REF ODDS 1:4 HOBBY
*REF AUTO: .5X TO 1.2X BASIC AUTO
REF AUTO ODDS 1:5 HOBBY
STATED PRINT RUN 199 SER.#'d SETS
CM Casey McGehee AU 4.00 10.00

2009 Bowman Sterling Gold Refractors

*GOLD REF: 1X TO 2.5X BASIC
GOLD REF ODDS 1:15 HOBBY
*GOLD REF AU: .75X TO 2X BASIC AU
GOLD REF AU ODDS 1:21 HOBBY
STATED PRINT RUN 50 SER.#'d SETS
CM Casey McGehee AU 5.00 12.00

2009 Bowman Sterling Dual Autographs

STATED ODDS 1:8 HOBBY
*REF: .5X TO 1.2 BASIC
REF.ODDS 1:27 HOBBY
REF. PRINT RUN 199 SER.#'d SETS
BLK REF ODDS 1:238 HOBBY
BLK REF PRINT RUN 25 SER.#'d SETS
NO BLACK PRICING DUE TO SCARCITY
*GLD REF: .75X TO 2X BASIC
GLD REF ODDS 1:111 HOBBY
GLD REF PRINT RUN 50 SER.#'d SETS
RED REF ODDS 1:4968 HOBBY
RED REF PRINT RUN 1 SER.#'d SETS
NO RED PRICING DUE TO SCARCITY
BPFC B.Posey/F.Cervelli 20.00 50.00
BPGB B.Posey/G.Beckham 20.00 50.00
CTDH C.Tillman/D.Hernandez 5.00 12.00
JKZC Jason Knapp/Zach Collier 5.00 12.00
JMFD J.Mejia/F.Doubront 5.00 12.00
NRJR N.Reimold/J.Reddick 6.00 15.00
RPCI Ryan Perry/Cale Iorg 5.00 12.00

2009 Bowman Sterling Prospects

OVERALL AUTO ODDS TWO PER PACK
PRINTING PLATE ODDS 1:91 HOBBY
AU PRINTING PLATE ODDS 1:245 HOBBY
PLATE PRINT RUN 1 SET PER COLOR
BLACK-CYAN-MAGENTA-YELLOW ISSUED
NO PLATE PRICING DUE TO SCARCITY
AA Abraham Almonte .75 2.00
AB Alex Buchholz 1.25 3.00
AF Alfredo Figaro .75 2.00
AM Adam Mills .75 2.00
AO Anthony Ortega .75 2.00
AP A.J. Pollock AU 6.00 15.00
AR Andrew Rundle 1.25 3.00
AS Alfredo Silverio .75 2.00
AW Alex White AU 3.00 8.00
BB Bobby Borchering AU 5.00 12.00
BB Brian Baisley .75 2.00
BO Brett Oberholtzer 1.25 3.00
BP Bryan Petersen .75 2.00
CA Carmen Angelini .75 2.00
CH Chris Heisey AU 6.00 15.00
CJ Chad Jenkins AU 3.00 8.00
CL C.J. Lee .75 2.00
CM Carlos Martinez 1.25 3.00
DA Denny Almonte 1.25 3.00
DH Daniel Hudson AU 4.00 10.00
DP Dinesh Patel AU 6.00 15.00
DS Drew Storen AU 3.00 8.00
DV Dayan Viciedo AU 3.00 8.00
EA Eric Arnett AU 3.00 8.00
EA Ehire Adrianza 2.00 5.00
EC Edilio Colina 1.25 3.00
EK Erik Komatsu 1.25 3.00
FG Freddy Galvis 1.25 3.00
GV Greg Veloz .75 2.00
JC Jose Ceda .75 2.00
JG Justin Greene 1.25 3.00
JM Jared Mitchell AU 4.00 10.00
JR Jovan Rosa .75 2.00
JT Julio Teheran 2.50 6.00
JW Jordan Walden 1.25 3.00
KK Kyeong Kang 1.25 3.00
LE Luis Exposito 2.00 5.00
LJ Luis Jimenez .75 2.00
LS Luis Sumoza 1.25 3.00
MA Michael Almanzar 1.25 3.00
MC Michael Cisco 1.25 3.00
MH Matt Hobgood AU 8.00 20.00
ML Mike Leake AU 6.00 15.00
MM Matthew Moore 6.00 15.00
MM Mike Minor AU 3.00 8.00
MP Michael Pineda 2.00 5.00
MS Michael Swinson 1.25 3.00
MT Mike Trout AU 2000.00 4000.00
NB Nick Buss .75 2.00
NP Nelson Perez 1.25 3.00
NR Neil Ramirez .75 2.00
OT Oscar Tejeda 2.50 6.00
PP Petey Paramore 1.25 3.00
PV Pat Venditte AU 3.00 8.00
RD Rashun Dixon 2.00 5.00
RF Reymond Fuentes AU 3.00 8.00
RG Robbie Grossman AU 3.00 8.00
RS Rinku Singh AU 6.00 15.00
RT Ruben Tejada .75 2.00
SC Scott Campbell AU 3.00 8.00
SP Stolmy Pimentel 1.25 3.00
SW Christopher Schwinden .75 2.00
TF Tyler Flowers 2.00 5.00
TM Tyler Matzek AU 3.00 8.00
TS Tony Sanchez AU 5.00 12.00
TW Tim Wheeler AU 3.00 8.00
TY Tyler Yockey 1.25 3.00
WF Wilmer Font .75 2.00
WR Wilin Rosario 1.25 3.00
WS Will Smith 1.25 3.00
ZW Zack Wheeler AU 4.00 10.00
CJA Chad James AU 4.00 10.00
CLU Chad Lundahl .75 2.00
JMM Jiovanni Mier AU 5.00 12.00
JMO Jon Mark Owings .75 2.00
MAF Michael Affronti .75 2.00
RGR Randal Grichuk AU 6.00 15.00
TME Tommy Mendonca AU 5.00 12.00

2009 Bowman Sterling Prospects Refractors

*REF: .5X TO 1.2X BASIC
REF ODDS 1:4 HOBBY
*REF AUTO: .5X TO 1.2X BASIC AUTO
REF AUTO ODDS 1:5 HOBBY
STATED PRINT RUN 199 SER.#'d SETS
MT Mike Trout AU 2000.00 3000.00

2009 Bowman Sterling Prospects Gold Refractors

*GOLD REF: 1.5X TO 4X BASIC
GOLD REF ODDS 1:15 HOBBY
*GOLD REF AU: .6X TO 1.5X BASIC AU
GOLD REF AU ODDS 1:21 HOBBY
STATED PRINT RUN 50 SER.#'d SETS
MT Mike Trout AU 6000.00 8000.00

2009 Bowman Sterling WBC Relics

STATED ODDS ONE PER PACK
AC Aroldis Chapman 10.00 25.00
AM Alexander Mayeta 3.00 8.00
AO Adam Ottavino 3.00 8.00
AS Alexander Smit 3.00 8.00
BW Bernie Williams 3.00 8.00
CL Chenhao Li 3.00 8.00
CR Concepcion Rodriguez 3.00 8.00
DL Dae Ho Lee 4.00 10.00
DN Drew Naylor 3.00 8.00
EG Edgar Gonzalez 3.00 8.00
FC Frederich Cepeda 3.00 8.00
FF Fei Feng 3.00 8.00
FN Fu-Te Ni 5.00 12.00
GH Greg Halman 3.00 8.00
HC Hung-Wen Chen 3.00 8.00
HO Hein Robb 3.00 8.00
HR Hanley Ramirez 3.00 8.00
IS Ichiro Suzuki 10.00 25.00
JC Johnny Cueto 3.00 8.00
JE Justin Erasmus 3.00 8.00
JL Jae Woo Lee 3.00 8.00
JS Juancarlos Sulbaran 3.00 8.00
KF Kosuke Fukudome 5.00 12.00
KK Kwang-Hyun Kim 4.00 10.00
KL Kai Liu 3.00 8.00
LH Luke Hughes 3.00 8.00
LR Luis Rodriguez 3.00 8.00
MC Miguel Cabrera 3.00 8.00
MD Mitchell Dening 3.00 8.00
ME Michel Enriquez 3.00 8.00
MT Miguel Tejada 3.00 8.00
NA Norichika Aoki 6.00 15.00
NP Nick Punto 3.00 8.00
NW Nick Weglarz 3.00 8.00
PA Phillippe Aumont 5.00 12.00
PK Po-Hsuan Keng 3.00 8.00
PM Pedro Martinez 3.00 8.00
RM Russell Martin 3.00 8.00
SA Shinnosuke Abe 5.00 12.00
SC Shin-Soo Choo 5.00 12.00
TK Tae Kyun Kim 4.00 10.00
XZ Xiaotian Zhang 3.00 8.00
YC Yoennis Cespedes 10.00 25.00
YD Yu Darvish 10.00 25.00
YG Yulieski Gourriel 3.00 8.00
HRR Hyun-Jin Ryu 8.00 20.00
JCC Jorge Cantu 3.00 8.00
JLL Jin Young Lee 4.00 10.00
LHH Liam Hendriks 3.00 8.00

2009 Bowman Sterling WBC Relics Refractors

*REF: .5X TO 1.2X BASIC
REF ODDS 1:5 HOBBY
REF PRINT RUN 199 SER.#'d SETS

2009 Bowman Sterling WBC Relics Blue Refractors

*BLUE REF: .5X TO 1.2X BASIC
BLUE REF ODDS ONE PER BOX LOADER
BLUE PRINT RUN 125 SER.#'d SETS
FN Fu-Te Ni 12.50 30.00

2009 Bowman Sterling WBC Relics Gold Refractors

*GOLD REF: .75X TO 2X BASIC
GOLD REF ODDS 1:21 HOBBY
GOLD REF PRINT RUN 50 SER.#'d SETS
FN Fu-Te Ni 30.00 60.00

2010 Bowman Sterling

COMMON CARD .60 1.50
PRINTING PLATE ODDS 1:105 HOBBY
1 Stephen Strasburg RC 5.00 12.00
2 Josh Bell (RC) .60 1.50
3 Starlin Castro RC 1.50 4.00
4 J.P. Arencibia RC 1.25 3.00
5 Brennan Boesch RC 1.50 4.00
6 Ike Davis RC 1.25 3.00
7 Madison Bumgarner RC 6.00 15.00
8 Austin Jackson RC 1.00 2.50
9 Andrew Cashner RC .60 1.50
10 Jose Tabata RC 1.00 2.50
11 Wade Davis (RC) 1.00 2.50
12 Felix Doubront RC .60 1.50
13 Mike Leake RC 2.00 5.00
14 Logan Morrison RC 1.00 2.50
15 Brian Matusz RC 1.50 4.00
16 Trevor Plouffe (RC) 1.50 4.00
17 Mike Stanton RC 5.00 12.00
18 Drew Storen RC 1.00 2.50
19 Tyler Colvin RC 1.00 2.50
20 Jason Heyward RC 2.50 6.00
21 Jake Arrieta RC 1.50 4.00
22 Daniel Hudson RC 1.00 2.50
23 Buster Posey RC 5.00 12.00
24 Neil Walker (RC) 1.00 2.50
25 Carlos Santana RC 2.00 5.00
26 Josh Thole RC 1.00 2.50
27 Dayan Viciedo RC 1.00 2.50
28 Wilson Ramos RC 1.50 4.00
29 Ian Desmond (RC) 1.00 2.50
30 John Ely RC .60 1.50
31 Daniel Nava RC .60 1.50
32 Chris Nelson (RC) 1.00 2.50
33 Andy Oliver RC .60 1.50
34 Danny Valencia RC 4.00 10.00
35 Brad Lincoln RC 1.00 2.50
36 Domonic Brown RC 2.50 6.00
37 Jay Sborz (RC) .60 1.50
38 Daniel McCutchen RC 1.00 2.50
39 Eric Young Jr. (RC) .60 1.50
40 Peter Bourjos RC 1.00 2.50
41 Drew Stubbs RC 1.50 4.00
42 Chris Heisey RC 1.00 2.50
43 Jason Castro RC 1.50 4.00
44 Jason Donald RC .60 1.50
45 Ruben Tejada RC 1.00 2.50
46 Jon Jay RC 1.00 2.50
47 Travis Wood (RC) 1.00 2.50
48 Ryan Kalish RC 1.00 2.50
49 Mike Minor RC 1.00 2.50
50 Brett Wallace RC 1.50 4.00

2010 Bowman Sterling Refractors

*REF: 1.2X TO 3X BASIC
STATED ODDS 1:5 HOBBY
STATED PRINT RUN 199 SER.#'d SETS

2010 Bowman Sterling Gold Refractors

*GOLD REF: 2X TO 5X BASIC
STATED ODDS 1:17 HOBBY
STATED PRINT RUN 50 SER.#'d SETS

2010 Bowman Sterling Dual Relics

STATED PRINT RUN 199 SER.#'d SETS
BL1 A.Pujols/M.Cabrera 6.00 15.00
BL2 D.Jeter/H.Ramirez 8.00 20.00
BL3 Joe Mauer/Brian McCann 4.00 10.00
BL4 A.Rodriguez/E.Longoria 8.00 20.00
BL5 R.Braun/J.Upton 5.00 12.00
BL6 Prince Fielder/Pablo Sandoval 4.00 10.00
BL7 R.Halladay/C.Lee 8.00 20.00
BL8 Josh Hamilton/Nelson Cruz 4.00 10.00
BL9 J.Heyward/M.Stanton 6.00 15.00
BL10 I.Suzuki/A.Pujols 10.00 25.00
BL11 Adrian Gonzalez/Justin Morneau 4.00 10.00
BL12 D.Pedroia/K.Youkilis 5.00 12.00
BL13 Mark Teixeira/Chipper Jones 4.00 10.00
BL14 C.Utley/R.Cano 5.00 12.00
BL15 D.Wright/R.Zimmerman 5.00 12.00
BL16 Jimmy Rollins/Ryan Howard 4.00 10.00
BL17 S.Strasburg/J.Heyward 4.00 10.00
BL18 T.Tulowitzki/C.Gonzalez 5.00 12.00
BL19 D.Jeter/A.Rodriguez 10.00 25.00

2010 Bowman Sterling Dual Relics Refractors

*REF: .5X TO 1.2X BASIC
STATED ODDS 1:4 BOXES
STATED PRINT RUN 99 SER.#'d SETS

2010 Bowman Sterling Dual Relics Gold Refractors

*GOLD REF: .6X TO 1.5X BASIC
STATED ODDS 1:8 BOXES
STATED PRINT RUN 50 SER.#'d SETS

2010 Bowman Sterling Prospect Autographs

RANDOM INSERTS IN PACKS
PRINTING PLATE ODDS 1:250 HOBBY
AC Aroldis Chapman 8.00 20.00
AM Aaron Miller 4.00 10.00
AW Alex Wimmers 3.00 8.00
CB Chad Bettis 3.00 8.00
CR Chance Ruffin 3.00 8.00
CS Chris Sale 10.00 25.00
CY Christian Yelich 60.00 150.00
DD Delino DeShields 4.00 10.00
DM Deck McGuire 3.00 8.00
DP Drew Pomeranz 3.00 8.00
GB Gary Brown 5.00 12.00
HS Hayden Simpson 4.00 10.00
JB Jesse Biddle 6.00 15.00
JS John Singleton 4.00 10.00
JS Jake Skole 4.00 10.00
JT Jameson Taillon 6.00 15.00
JW Justin Wilson 3.00 8.00
KD Kellin Deglan 3.00 8.00
MF Mike Foltynewicz 3.00 8.00
ML Matt Lipka 6.00 15.00
MO Mike Olt 3.00 8.00
PT Peter Tago 3.00 8.00
RL Ryan Lavarnway 3.00 8.00
SB Seth Blair 3.00 8.00
TB Tim Beckham 6.00 15.00
TJ Tyrell Jenkins 3.00 8.00
TL Taylor Lindsey 3.00 8.00
YG Yasmani Grandal 4.00 10.00
ZL Zach Lee 5.00 12.00
CCO Christian Colon 3.00 8.00
CPU Cesar Puello 3.00 8.00
RBO Ryan Bolden 3.00 8.00
TWA Taijuan Walker 3.00 8.00

2010 Bowman Sterling Prospect Autographs Refractors

*REF: .75X TO 2X BASIC
STATED ODDS 1:6 HOBBY
STATED PRINT RUN 199 SER.#'d SETS

2010 Bowman Sterling Prospect Autographs Gold Refractors

*GOLD REF: 1.2X TO 3X BASIC
STATED ODDS 1:21 HOBBY
STATED PRINT RUN 50 SER.#'d SETS

2010 Bowman Sterling Prospects

PRINTING PLATE ODDS 1:105 HOBBY
AA Alexia Amarista .50 1.25
AC Aroldis Chapman 2.00 5.00
AD Allan Dykstra .50 1.25
AH Adeinis Hechavarria .50 1.25
AR Anthony Rizzo 6.00 15.00
AV Arodys Vizcaino 1.25 3.00
BJ Brett Jackson 1.50 4.00
BM Bryan Mitchell .50 1.25
BO Brett Oberholtzer .50 1.25
BS Brandon Short .50 1.25
CA Chris Archer 1.50 4.00
CJ Corban Joseph .50 1.25
CM Chris Masters .50 1.25
CP Carlos Peguero .75 2.00
DA Dustin Ackley .75 2.00
DC Drew Cumberland .50 1.25
DF Daniel Fields .50 1.25
DT Donavan Tate .50 1.25
GG Grant Green .50 1.25
GS Gary Sanchez 15.00 40.00
HL Hak-Ju Lee .75 2.00
JH J.J. Hoover .50 1.25
JI Jose Iglesias 1.50 4.00
JL John Lamb 1.25 3.00
JM J.D. Martinez 6.00 15.00
JS John Singleton 1.25 3.00
KG Kyle Gibson 2.00 5.00
KS Konrad Schmidt .50 1.25
MD Matt Davidson 1.50 4.00
MP Martin Perez 1.25 3.00
MS Miguel Sano 3.00 8.00
NA Nolan Arenado 20.00 50.00
RB Rex Brothers .50 1.25
RE Robbie Erlin 1.25 3.00
SH Steven Hensley .50 1.25
SM Shelby Miller 2.50 6.00
SV Sebastian Valle .75 2.00
TB Tim Beckham 2.00 5.00
TC Tyler Chatwood .50 1.25
TN Thomas Neal .75 2.00
WM Wil Myers 1.25 3.00
YA Yonder Alonso 1.25 3.00
CPU Cesar Puello .50 1.25
FPE Francisco Peguero .50 1.25
JOS Josh Satin .75 2.00
JRM J.R. Murphy .75 2.00
JSA Jerry Sands 1.25 3.00
JSE Jean Segura 2.50 6.00
MKE Max Kepler 1.50 4.00
WMI Will Middlebrooks .75 2.00

2010 Bowman Sterling Prospects Refractors

*REF: 1X TO 2.5X BASIC
STATED ODDS 1:5 HOBBY
STATED PRINT RUN 199 SER.#'d SETS

2010 Bowman Sterling Prospects Gold Refractors

*GOLD REF: 1.5X TO 4X BASIC
STATED ODDS 1:17 HOBBY
STATED PRINT RUN 50 SER.#'d SETS
SM Shelby Miller 15.00 40.00

2010 Bowman Sterling Rookie Autographs

STATED ODDS 1:
STRASBURG ODDS 1:25 HOBBY
EXCHANGE DEADLINE 12/31/2013
PRINTING PLATE ODDS 1:250 HOBBY
STRASBURG PLATE ODDS 1:10,014 HOBBY
1 Stephen Strasburg 30.00 80.00
10 Jose Tabata 4.00 10.00
20 Jason Heyward 6.00 15.00
22 Daniel Hudson 4.00 10.00
25 Carlos Santana 4.00 10.00
34 Danny Valencia 4.00 10.00
36 Domonic Brown 4.00 10.00
43 Josh Tomlin 4.00 10.00
46 Jon Jay 4.00 10.00
47 Travis Wood 4.00 10.00

2010 Bowman Sterling Rookie Autographs Refractors

*REF: .5X TO 1.2X BASIC
STATED ODDS 1:6 HOBBY
STRASBURG ODDS 1:212 HOBBY
STATED PRINT RUN 199 SER.#'d SETS
EXCHANGE DEADLINE 12/31/2013

2010 Bowman Sterling Rookie Autographs Gold Refractors

*GOLD: 1.2X TO 3X BASIC
STATED ODDS 1:21 HOBBY
STRASBURG ODDS 1:852 HOBBY
STATED PRINT RUN 50 SER.#'d SETS
EXCHANGE DEADLINE 12/31/2013

2010 Bowman Sterling USA Baseball Autograph Relics Red

STATED ODDS 1:976 HOBBY
STATED PRINT RUN 1 SER.#'d SET

2010 Bowman Sterling USA Baseball Dual Autographs

NATIONAL TEAM ODDS 1:27 HOBBY
18U TEAM ODDS 1:18 HOBBY
PRINTING PLATE ODDS 1:494 HOBBY
BSDA1 Tony Wolters/Nicky Delmonico 4.00 10.00
BSDA2 P.Pfeifer/H.Owens 8.00 20.00
BSDA3 C.Lopes/F.Lindor 6.00 15.00
BSDA4 B.Starling/L.McCullers 4.00 10.00
BSDA5 B.Swihart/D.Camarena 10.00 25.00
BSDA6 Dillon Maples/A.J. Vanegas 4.00 10.00
BSDA7 M.Lorenzen/C.Montgomery 4.00 10.00
BSDA8 A.Almora/M.Littlewood 4.00 10.00
BSDA9 John Hochstatter/Brian Ragira 4.00 10.00
BSDA10 John Simms/Elvin Soto 4.00 10.00
BSDA11 M.Barnes/B.Miller 6.00 15.00
BSDA12 G.Cole/J.Bradley Jr. 12.00 30.00
BSDA13 S.Gray/G.Springer 12.00 30.00
BSDA14 Ryan Wright/Nolan Fontana 4.00 10.00
BSDA15 Andrew Maggi/Kyle Winkler 4.00 10.00
BSDA16 P.O'Brien/A.Dickerson 10.00 25.00
BSDA17 Jason Esposito/Sean Gilmartin 4.00 10.00
BSDA18 Nick Ramirez/Steve Rodriguez 4.00 10.00
BSDA19 T.Anderson/S.McGough 4.00 10.00
BSDA20 Noe Ramirez/Brett Mooneyham 4.00 10.00
BSDA21 M.Mahtook/B.Johnson 6.00 15.00

2010 Bowman Sterling USA Baseball Dual Autographs Refractors

*REF: .5X TO 1.2X BASIC
STATED ODDS 1:21 HOBBY
STATED PRINT RUN 99 SER.#'d SETS

2010 Bowman Sterling USA Baseball Dual Autographs Gold Refractors

*GOLD REF: .75X TO 2X BASIC
STATED ODDS 1:42 HOBBY
STATED PRINT RUN 50 SER.#'d SETS

2010 Bowman Sterling USA Baseball Relics

RANDOM INSERTS IN PACKS
USAR1 Albert Almora 2.50 6.00
USAR2 Daniel Camarena 2.50 6.00
USAR3 Nicky Delmonico 2.50 6.00
USAR4 John Hochstatter 2.50 6.00
USAR5 Francisco Lindor 4.00 10.00
USAR6 Marcus Littlewood 2.50 6.00
USAR7 Christian Lopes 2.50 6.00
USAR8 Michael Lorenzen 2.50 6.00
USAR9 Dillon Maples 2.50 6.00
USAR10 Lance McCullers 2.50 6.00
USAR11 Ricardo Jacquez 2.50 6.00
USAR12 Henry Owens 2.50 6.00
USAR13 Phillip Pfeifer 2.50 6.00
USAR14 Brian Ragira 2.50 6.00
USAR15 John Simms 2.50 6.00
USAR16 Elvin Soto 2.50 6.00
USAR17 Bubba Starling 3.00 8.00
USAR18 Blake Swihart 2.50 6.00
USAR19 A.J. Vanegas 2.50 6.00
USAR20 Tony Wolters 2.50 6.00
USAR21 Tyler Anderson 2.50 6.00
USAR22 Matt Barnes 3.00 8.00
USAR23 Jackie Bradley Jr. 3.00 8.00
USAR24 Gerrit Cole 4.00 10.00
USAR25 Alex Dickerson 2.50 6.00
USAR26 Jason Esposito 2.50 6.00
USAR27 Nolan Fontana 2.50 6.00
USAR28 Sean Gilmartin 2.50 6.00
USAR29 Sonny Gray 2.50 6.00
USAR30 Brian Johnson 2.50 6.00
USAR31 Andrew Maggi 2.50 6.00
USAR32 Mikie Mahtook 2.50 6.00
USAR33 Scott McGough 2.50 6.00
USAR34 Brad Miller 2.50 6.00
USAR35 Brett Mooneyham 2.50 6.00
USAR36 Peter O'Brien 2.50 6.00
USAR37 Nick Ramirez 2.50 6.00
USAR38 Noe Ramirez 2.50 6.00
USAR39 Steve Rodriguez 2.50 6.00
USAR40 George Springer 6.00 15.00
USAR41 Kyle Winkler 2.50 6.00
USAR42 Ryan Wright 2.50 6.00

2010 Bowman Sterling USA Baseball Relics Refractors

*REF: .5X TO 1.2X BASIC
STATED ODDS 1:6 HOBBY
STATED PRINT RUN 99 SER.#'d SETS

2010 Bowman Sterling USA Baseball Relics Gold Refractors

*GOLD REF: .6X TO 1.5X BASIC
STATED ODDS 1:22 HOBBY
STATED PRINT RUN 50 SER.#'d SETS

2011 Bowman Sterling

COMMON CARD .60 1.50
PRINTING PLATES RANDOMLY INSERTED
PLATE PRINT RUN 1 SET PER COLOR
BLACK-CYAN-MAGENTA-YELLOW ISSUED
NO PLATE PRICING DUE TO SCARCITY
1 Freddie Freeman RC 10.00 25.00
2 Al Alburquerque RC .60 1.50
3 Salvador Perez RC 2.50 6.00
4 Ryan Lavarnway RC 2.50 6.00
5 Jason Kipnis RC 2.00 5.00
6 Arodys Vizcaino RC 1.00 2.50
7 Chance Ruffin RC .60 1.50
8 Dee Gordon RC 1.00 2.50
9 Mike Moustakas RC 1.50 4.00
10 Johnny Giavotella RC .60 1.50
11 Dustin Ackley RC 1.00 2.50
12 Chase d'Arnaud RC .60 1.50
13 Jimmy Paredes RC 1.50 4.00
14 Fautino De Los Santos RC .60 1.50
15 Jose Altuve RC 20.00 50.00
16 Brandon Beachy RC 1.50 4.00
17 Trayvon Robinson (RC) 1.00 2.50
18 Mark Trumbo (RC) 1.50 4.00
19 Jacob Turner RC 2.50 6.00
20 Anthony Rizzo RC 6.00 15.00
21 Kyle Weiland RC .60 1.50
22 Mike Trout RC 400.00 800.00
23 Ben Revere RC 1.00 2.50
24 Hector Noesi RC 1.00 2.50
25 Danny Duffy RC 1.00 2.50
26 Juan Nicasio RC .60 1.50
27 Paul Goldschmidt RC 20.00 50.00
28 Tyler Chatwood RC .60 1.50
29 Eric Thames RC 3.00 8.00
30 Yonder Alonso RC 1.00 2.50
31 Todd Frazier RC 1.50 4.00
32 Andy Dirks RC 1.50 4.00
33 Javy Guerra (RC) 1.00 2.50
34 Michael Stutes RC 1.00 2.50
35 Michael Pineda RC 1.50 4.00
36 Aaron Crow RC 1.00 2.50
37 Alexi Ogando RC 1.50 4.00
38 Alex Cobb RC .60 1.50
39 Brandon Belt RC 1.50 4.00
40 Lonnie Chisenhall RC 1.00 2.50
41 Zach Britton RC 1.50 4.00
42 Jordan Walden RC .60 1.50
43 Jose Iglesias RC 1.00 2.50
44 Julio Teheran RC 1.00 2.50
45 Desmond Jennings RC 1.00 2.50
46 Blake Beavan RC 1.00 2.50
47 Craig Kimbrel RC 1.50 4.00
48 Eric Hosmer RC 4.00 10.00
49 Jerry Sands RC 1.50 4.00
50 Kyle Seager RC 1.50 4.00

2011 Bowman Sterling Refractors

*REF: .75X TO 2X BASIC
STATED ODDS 1:8
STATED PRINT RUN 199 SER.#'d SETS
22 Mike Trout 500.00 1000.00

2011 Bowman Sterling Gold Refractors

*GOLD REF: 2.5X TO 6X BASIC
STATED ODDS 1:31
STATED PRINT RUN 50 SER.#'d SETS
22 Mike Trout 600.00 1200.00

2011 Bowman Sterling Dual Autographs

STATED ODDS 1:10
PRINT RUNS B/WN 225-299 COPIES PER
PRINTING PLATE ODDS 1:703
PLATE PRINT RUN 1 SET PER COLOR
BLACK-CYAN-MAGENTA-YELLOW ISSUED
NO PLATE PRICING DUE TO SCARCITY
EXCHANGE DEADLINE 12/31/2014
AB M.Appel/D.Baxendale 6.00 15.00
AW A.Almora/M.White 8.00 20.00
BC A.Bregman/G.Cecchini 15.00 40.00
DC D.Duffy/A.Crow 4.00 10.00
DW D.Dahl/J.Winker 10.00 25.00
EL Chris Elder 4.00 10.00
Michael Lorenzen
EN J.Elander/T.Naquin 6.00 15.00
FF Dominic Ficociello 4.00 10.00
Nolan Fontana
GJ K.Gausman/B.Johnson 6.00 15.00
ID Cole Irvin 4.00 10.00
Chase DeJong
KG C.Kelly/J.Gallo 6.00 15.00
KK Branden Kline 4.00 10.00
Corey Knebel
LM David Lyon 4.00 10.00
Tom Murphy
MM Hoby Milner 4.00 10.00
Andrew Mitchell
MR D.Marrero/M.Reynolds 4.00 10.00
OC Chris Okey 4.00 10.00
Troy Conyers
OH A.Ogando/M.Hamburger 4.00 10.00
RH B.Revere/L.Hendriks 5.00 12.00
RM N.Rodriguez/J.Martinez 6.00 15.00
RW B.Rodgers/M.Wacha 4.00 10.00
SD J.Sands/R.De La Rosa 6.00 15.00
SP Clate Schmidt 4.00 10.00
Cody Poteet
SW M.Stroman/E.Weiss 4.00 10.00
TB M.Trumbo/B.Belt 6.00 15.00
TBE J.Teheran/B.Beachy 10.00 25.00
TR E.Thames/B.Revere 20.00 50.00
VW H.Virant/W.Weickel 4.00 10.00

2011 Bowman Sterling Dual Autographs Refractors

*REF: .5X TO 1.2X BASIC
STATED ODDS 1:29
STATED PRINT RUN 99 SER.#'d SETS
EXCHANGE DEADLINE 12/31/2014

2011 Bowman Sterling Dual Autographs Black Refractors

STATED ODDS 1:112
STATED PRINT RUN 25 SER.#'d SETS
NO PRICING DUE TO SCARCITY
EXCHANGE DEADLINE 12/31/2014

2011 Bowman Sterling Dual Autographs Gold Refractors

*GOLD REF: .6X TO 1.5X BASIC
STATED ODDS 1:57
STATED PRINT RUN 50 SER.#'d SETS
EXCHANGE DEADLINE 12/31/2014

2011 Bowman Sterling Dual Relics

STATED ODDS 1:1 BOXES
PRINT RUNS B/WN 54-246 PER
AE Dustin Ackley/Danny Espinosa 4.00 10.00
BD Zach Britton/Danny Duffy 4.00 10.00
BF Ryan Braun/Prince Fielder 5.00 12.00
BH Brandon Beachy/Tommy Hanson 6.00 15.00
BJ Zach Britton/Adam Jones 5.00 12.00
CB Starlin Castro/Darwin Barney 6.00 15.00
CD Aaron Crow/Danny Duffy 4.00 10.00
FH F.Freeman/J.Heyward 6.00 15.00
GC C.Granderson/R.Cano 5.00 12.00
GG Curtis Granderson/Carlos Gonzalez/246 4.00
10.00
GJ Curtis Granderson/Adam Jones 4.00 10.00
GK D.Gordon/M.Kemp 6.00 15.00
GS Carlos Gonzalez/Mike Stanton 5.00 12.00
HM E.Hosmer/M.Mustakas 8.00 20.00
HP F.Hernandez/M.Pineda 5.00 12.00
JN D.Jeter/E.Nunez/54 10.00 25.00
MC Mike Moustakas/Lonnie Chisenhall 4.00 10.00
OF Alexi Ogando/Neftali Feliz 4.00 10.00
PB B.Posey/B.Belt 6.00 15.00
PBR Michael Pineda/Zach Britton 4.00 10.00
PH David Price/Jeremy Hellickson 5.00 12.00
PH David Price/Felix Hernandez 4.00 10.00
PHO A.Pujols/M.Holliday 5.00 12.00
PJ David Price/Desmond Jennings 4.00 10.00
SC Carlos Santana/Lonnie Chisenhall 4.00 10.00
SR Mike Stanton/Hanley Ramirez 4.00 10.00
SS Chris Sale/Sergio Santos 4.00 10.00
TC Mark Trumbo/Hank Conger 6.00 15.00
TG Troy Tulowitzki/Carlos Gonzalez 6.00 15.00
VH J.Verlander/R.Halladay 5.00 12.00
WC Jered Weaver/Tyler Chatwood 4.00 10.00
WK Jordan Walden/Craig Kimbrel 4.00 10.00
WW Rickie Weeks/Jemile Weeks 4.00 10.00
ZE Ryan Zimmerman/Danny Espinosa 4.00 10.00

2011 Bowman Sterling Dual Relics Refractors

*REF: .5X TO 1.2X BASIC
STATED PRINT RUNS B/WN 25-99
STATED ODDS 1:4 BOXES
NO PRICING ON QTY 25

2011 Bowman Sterling Dual Relics Gold Refractors

*GOLD REF: .6X TO 1.5X BASIC
STATED PRINT RUN 50 SER.#'d SETS
STATED ODDS 1:8 BOXES
JN Derek Jeter 10.00 25.00
Eduardo Nunez

2011 Bowman Sterling Prospect Autographs

STATED ODDS 1:20
PRINTING PLATE ODDS 1:260
PLATE PRINT RUN 1 SET PER COLOR
BLACK-CYAN-MAGENTA-YELLOW ISSUED
NO PLATE PRICING DUE TO SCARCITY
EXCHANGE DEADLINE 12/31/2014
AB Archie Bradley 3.00 8.00
AH Aaron Hicks 5.00 12.00
BB Bryce Brentz 3.00 8.00
BHO Bryan Holaday 3.00 8.00
BM Brandon Martin 3.00 8.00
BN Brandon Nimmo 4.00 10.00
BS Blake Snell 10.00 25.00
BST Bubba Starling 5.00 12.00
BSW Blake Swihart 4.00 10.00
CB Charles Brewer 3.00 8.00
CC Collin Cowgill 3.00 8.00
CCR C.J. Cron 3.00 8.00
CS Cory Spangenberg 3.00 8.00
CW Christopher Wallace 3.00 8.00
DBU Dylan Bundy 4.00 10.00
DV Dan Vogelbach 5.00 12.00
FL Francisco Lindor 25.00 60.00
GG Garrett Gould 3.00 8.00
GS George Springer 15.00 40.00
JB Javier Baez 30.00 80.00
JB Jed Bradley 3.00 8.00
JF Jose Fernandez 6.00 15.00
JH Jake Hager 3.00 8.00
JHA James Harris 3.00 8.00
JK Jake Skole 3.00 8.00
JP Joe Panik 5.00 12.00
KC Kyle Crick 3.00 8.00
KM Kevin Matthews 3.00 8.00
KW Kolten Wong 4.00 10.00
KWA Keenyn Walker 3.00 8.00
LG Larry Greene 3.00 8.00
MB Manny Banuelos 4.00 10.00
MBA Matt Barnes 3.00 8.00
MF Michael Fulmer 5.00 12.00
MG Mychal Givens 3.00 8.00
MMO Matt Moore 4.00 10.00
RS Robert Stephenson 3.00 8.00
SG Sonny Gray 4.00 10.00
SGI Sean Gilmartin 4.00 10.00
SM Starling Marte 4.00 10.00
TA Tyler Anderson 3.00 8.00
TB Trevor Bauer 20.00 50.00
TG Tyler Goeddel 3.00 8.00
TGU Taylor Guerrieri 3.00 8.00
TH Travis Harrison 3.00 8.00
TJ Taylor Jungmann 4.00 10.00
TS Trevor Story 40.00 100.00
ZC Zach Cone 3.00 8.00
ZL Zach Lee 3.00 8.00

2011 Bowman Sterling Prospect Autographs Refractors

*REF: .5X TO 1.5X BASIC
STATED ODDS 1:6
STATED PRINT RUN 199 SER.#'d SETS
HARPER PRINT RUN 109 SER.#'d SETS
EXCHANGE DEADLINE 12/31/2014
BH Bryce Harper/109 300.00 500.00

2011 Bowman Sterling Prospect Autographs Gold Refractors

*GOLD REF: 1.5X TO 4X BASIC
STATED ODDS 1:21
STATED PRINT RUN 50 SER.#'d SETS
EXCHANGE DEADLINE 12/31/2014
BH Bryce Harper 500.00 700.00

2011 Bowman Sterling Prospects

PRINTING PLATES RANDOMLY INSERTED
PLATE PRINT RUN 1 SET PER COLOR
BLACK-CYAN-MAGENTA-YELLOW ISSUED
NO PLATE PRICING DUE TO SCARCITY
1 Bryce Harper 25.00 60.00
2 Shelby Miller 3.00 8.00
3 Jesus Montero .60 1.50
4 Manny Banuelos 1.50 4.00
5 Wil Myers 1.50 4.00
6 Aaron Hicks 1.00 2.50
7 Matt Moore 1.50 4.00
8 Jameson Taillon 1.00 2.50
9 Manny Machado 6.00 15.00
10 Jonathan Singleton 1.00 2.50
11 Devin Mesoraco 1.50 4.00
12 John Lamb .60 1.50
13 Blake Snell 2.50 6.00
14 Gary Sanchez 3.00 8.00
15 Brett Jackson 1.00 2.50
16 Zack Wheeler 2.00 5.00
17 Jean Segura 2.50 6.00
18 Wilmer Flores 1.00 2.50
19 Miguel Sano 1.25 3.00
20 Larry Greene 1.00 2.50
21 Chris Archer 1.25 3.00
22 Travis d'Arnaud 1.00 2.50
23 George Springer 4.00 10.00
24 Trevor Story 10.00 25.00
25 Jarrod Parker 1.50 4.00
26 Christian Colon .60 1.50
27 Dellin Betances 1.50 4.00
28 Tony Sanchez 1.00 2.50
29 Billy Hamilton 1.25 3.00
30 Tyler Goeddel .60 1.50
31 Dante Bichette 1.00 2.50
32 Trevor Bauer 6.00 15.00
33 Cory Spangenberg 1.00 2.50
34 Javier Baez 8.00 20.00
35 C.J. Cron 2.00 5.00
36 Sonny Gray 1.50 4.00
37 Jake Hager .60 1.50
38 James Harris .60 1.50
39 Brandon Martin 1.00 2.50
40 Joe Panik 1.50 4.00
41 Robert Stephenson 1.25 3.00
42 Jose Fernandez 2.50 6.00
43 Kolten Wong 1.00 2.50
44 Taylor Jungmann 1.00 2.50
45 Francisco Lindor 8.00 20.00
46 Matt Barnes 1.00 2.50
47 Brandon Nimmo 3.00 8.00
48 Bubba Starling 1.00 2.50
49 Dan Vogelbach 2.00 5.00
50 Kevin Matthews .60 1.50

2011 Bowman Sterling Prospects Refractors

*REF: .75X TO 2X BASIC
STATED ODDS 1:8
STATED PRINT RUN 199 SER.#'d SETS

2011 Bowman Sterling Prospects Gold Refractors

*GOLD REF: 2X TO 5X BASIC
STATED ODDS 1:31
STATED PRINT RUN 50 SER.#'d SETS

2011 Bowman Sterling Rookie Autographs

GROUP A STATED ODDS 1:18
GROUP B STATED ODDS 1:10
GROUP C STATED ODDS 1:4
PRINTING PLATE ODDS 1:260
PLATE PRINT RUN 1 SET PER COLOR
BLACK-CYAN-MAGENTA-YELLOW ISSUED
NO PLATE PRICING DUE TO SCARCITY
EXCHANGE DEADLINE 12/31/2014
1 Michael Pineda 3.00 8.00
2 Hector Noesi 3.00 8.00
3 Jerry Sands 3.00 8.00
4 Anthony Rizzo 20.00 50.00
5 Julio Teheran 4.00 10.00
6 Eric Hosmer 20.00 50.00
7 Freddie Freeman 25.00 60.00
8 Dustin Ackley 3.00 8.00
9 Kyle Seager 5.00 12.00
10 Danny Duffy 3.00 8.00
11 Aaron Crow 3.00 8.00
12 Nathan Eovaldi 3.00 8.00
13 Mike Moustakas 12.00 30.00
14 Alex Cobb 3.00 8.00
15 Dee Gordon 4.00 10.00
16 Rubby De La Rosa 3.00 8.00
17 Ben Revere 3.00 8.00
18 Alex White 3.00 8.00
20 Maikel Cleto 3.00 8.00
21 Jemile Weeks 3.00 8.00
22 Brandon Beachy 3.00 8.00
23 Eric Thames 4.00 10.00

2011 Bowman Sterling Rookie Autographs Refractors

*REF: .6X TO 1.5X BASIC
STATED ODDS 1:6
STRASBURG ODDS 1:3018
STATED PRINT RUN 199 SER.#'d SETS
TROUT PRINT RUN 109 SER.#'d SETS
STRASBURG PRINT RUN 25 SER.#'d SETS
NO STRASBURG PRICING AVAILABLE
EXCHANGE DEADLINE 12/31/2014
19 Mike Trout/109 350.00 500.00

2011 Bowman Sterling Rookie Autographs Gold Refractors

*GOLD REF: 1.5X TO 4X BASIC
STATED ODDS 1:21
STATED PRINT RUN 50 SER.#'d SETS
EXCHANGE DEADLINE 12/31/2014
19 Mike Trout 350.00 500.00

2011 Bowman Sterling Rookie Dual Relic X-Fractors

STATED ODDS 1:126
PRINT RUNS B/WN 25-199 COPIES PER
NO PRICING ON QTY 25
AC Aaron Crow 3.00 8.00
AO Alexi Ogando 5.00 12.00
AR Anthony Rizzo 20.00 50.00
BB Brandon Belt 5.00 12.00
BB Brandon Beachy 5.00 12.00
BR Ben Revere 3.00 8.00
CK Craig Kimbrel 5.00 12.00
DA Dustin Ackley 3.00 8.00
DE Danny Espinosa 2.00 5.00
EH Eric Hosmer/25 12.00 30.00
FF Freddie Freeman 30.00 80.00
JW Jordan Walden 2.00 5.00
LC Lonnie Chisenhall 3.00 8.00
MM Mike Moustakas/25 5.00 12.00
MP Michael Pineda 5.00 12.00
MT Mark Trumbo 5.00 12.00
ZB Zach Britton 5.00 12.00

2011 Bowman Sterling Rookie Relics

STATED ODDS 1:18
AC Aaron Crow 3.00 8.00
AO Alexi Ogando 3.00 8.00
AR Anthony Rizzo 6.00 15.00
AW Alex White 3.00 8.00
BB Brandon Belt 4.00 10.00
BB Brandon Beachy 3.00 8.00
BR Ben Revere 3.00 8.00
CK Craig Kimbrel 4.00 10.00
CL Cory Luebke 3.00 8.00
CS Chris Sale 6.00 15.00
DA Dustin Ackley 3.00 8.00
DB Darwin Barney 3.00 8.00
DD Danny Duffy 3.00 8.00
DE Danny Espinosa 3.00 8.00
DJ Desmond Jennings 3.00 8.00
EH Eric Hosmer 4.00 10.00
FF Freddie Freeman 4.00 10.00
JH Jeremy Hellickson 4.00 10.00
JT Justin Turner 3.00 8.00
JW Jordan Walden 3.00 8.00
LC Lonnie Chisenhall 3.00 8.00
MM Mike Moustakas 4.00 10.00
MP Michael Pineda 4.00 10.00
MT Mark Trumbo 5.00 12.00
TC Tyler Chatwood 3.00 8.00
ZB Zach Britton 3.00 8.00
ACO Alex Cobb 3.00 8.00
JWE Jemile Weeks 4.00 10.00
MMI Mike Minor 3.00 8.00

2011 Bowman Sterling Rookie Triple Relic Gold Refractors

STATED ODDS 1:126
PRINT RUNS B/WN 10-50 COPIES PER
NO PRICING ON QTY 10
AC Aaron Crow 4.00 10.00
AO Alexi Ogando 5.00 12.00
AR Anthony Rizzo 10.00 25.00
BB Brandon Belt 10.00 25.00
CK Craig Kimbrel 8.00 20.00
CS Chris Sale 8.00 20.00
DA Dustin Ackley 20.00 50.00
DD Danny Duffy 5.00 12.00
FF Freddie Freeman 15.00 40.00
JW Jordan Walden 4.00 10.00
LC Lonnie Chisenhall 8.00 20.00
MP Michael Pineda/30 8.00 20.00
MT Mark Trumbo 12.50 30.00
ZB Zach Britton 4.00 10.00

2011 Bowman Sterling USA Baseball Dual Relic X-Fractors

COMMON CARD 3.00 8.00
STATED ODDS 1:18 3.00 8.00
STATED PRINT RUN 199 SER.#'d SETS
AM Andrew Mitchell 3.00 8.00
BJ Brian Johnson 3.00 8.00
BK Branden Kline 3.00 8.00
BR Brady Rodgers 3.00 8.00
CE Chris Elder 3.00 8.00
CK Corey Knebel 3.00 8.00
DB DJ Baxendale 4.00 10.00
DF Dominic Ficociello 3.00 8.00
DL David Lyon 3.00 8.00
DM Deven Marrero 4.00 10.00
EW Erich Weiss 3.00 8.00
HM Hoby Milner 3.00 8.00
JE Josh Elander 3.00 8.00
KG Kevin Gausman 3.00 8.00
MA Mark Appel 5.00 12.00
ML Michael Lorenzen 3.00 8.00
MR Matt Reynolds 3.00 8.00
MS Marcus Stroman 4.00 10.00
MW Michael Wacha 5.00 12.00
NF Nolan Fontana 3.00 8.00
TM Tom Murphy 3.00 8.00
TN Tyler Naquin 3.00 8.00

2011 Bowman Sterling USA Baseball Relics

RANDOM INSERTS IN PACKS
AM Andrew Mitchell 3.00 8.00
BJ Brian Johnson 3.00 8.00
BK Branden Kline 3.00 8.00
BR Brady Rodgers 3.00 8.00
CE Chris Elder 3.00 8.00
CK Corey Knebel 3.00 8.00
DB DJ Baxendale 4.00 10.00
DF Dominic Ficociello 3.00 8.00
DL David Lyon 3.00 8.00
DM Deven Marrero 3.00 8.00
EW Erich Weiss 3.00 8.00
HM Hoby Milner 3.00 8.00
JE Josh Elander 3.00 8.00
KG Kevin Gausman 3.00 8.00
MA Mark Appel 4.00 10.00
ML Michael Lorenzen 3.00 8.00
MR Matt Reynolds 3.00 8.00
MS Marcus Stroman 3.00 8.00
MW Michael Wacha 3.00 8.00
NF Nolan Fontana 3.00 8.00
TM Tom Murphy 3.00 8.00
TN Tyler Naquin 3.00 8.00

2011 Bowman Sterling USA Baseball Triple Relic Gold Refractors

STATED ODDS 1:69
STATED PRINT RUN 50 SER.#'d SETS
AM Andrew Mitchell 5.00 12.00
BJ Brian Johnson 5.00 12.00
BK Branden Kline 5.00 12.00
BR Brady Rodgers 5.00 12.00
CE Chris Elder 5.00 12.00
CK Corey Knebel 5.00 12.00
DB DJ Baxendale 6.00 15.00
DF Dominic Ficociello 5.00 12.00
DL David Lyon 5.00 12.00
DM Deven Marrero 6.00 15.00
EW Erich Weiss 5.00 12.00
HM Hoby Milner 5.00 12.00
JE Josh Elander 5.00 12.00
KG Kevin Gausman 5.00 12.00
MA Mark Appel 6.00 15.00
ML Michael Lorenzen 5.00 12.00
MR Matt Reynolds 5.00 12.00
MS Marcus Stroman 5.00 12.00
MW Michael Wacha 8.00 20.00
NF Nolan Fontana 5.00 12.00
TM Tom Murphy 5.00 12.00
TN Tyler Naquin 5.00 12.00

2012 Bowman Sterling

PRINTING PLATE ODDS 1:150 HOBBY
PLATE PRINT RUN 1 SET PER COLOR
NO PLATE PRICING DUE TO SCARCITY
1 Bryce Harper RC 40.00 100.00
2 Wade Miley RC 1.25 3.00
3 Brian Dozier RC 3.00 8.00
4 Brett Jackson RC 1.50 4.00
5 Edwar Cabrera RC 1.00 2.50
6 A.J. Griffin RC 1.25 3.00
7 Leonys Martin RC 1.00 2.50
8 Casey Crosby RC 1.25 3.00
9 Anthony Gose RC 1.25 3.00
10 Yu Darvish RC 2.50 6.00
11 Jarrod Parker RC 1.25 3.00
12 Yasmani Grandal RC 1.00 2.50
13 Addison Reed RC 1.00 2.50
14 Matt Moore RC 1.50 4.00
15 Tyler Thornburg RC 1.25 3.00
16 Jordany Valdespin RC 1.25 3.00
17 Jordan Danks RC 1.00 2.50
18 Martin Perez RC 1.50 4.00
19 Steve Clevenger RC .60 1.50
20 Trevor Bauer RC 5.00 12.00
21 Derek Norris RC 1.00 2.50
22 Tommy Milone RC 1.00 2.50
23 Quintin Berry RC 1.50 4.00
24 Wilin Rosario RC 1.00 2.50
25 Kole Calhoun RC 1.25 3.00
26 Wily Peralta RC 1.00 2.50
27 A.J. Pollock RC 1.50 4.00
28 Wei-Yin Chen RC 2.50 6.00
29 Jeremy Hefner RC 1.00 2.50
30 Yoenis Cespedes RC 2.50 6.00
31 Drew Smyly RC 1.00 2.50
32 Drew Pomeranz RC 1.00 2.50
33 Kirk Nieuwenhuis RC 1.00 2.50
34 Jose Quintana RC 1.00 2.50
35 Stephen Pryor RC .60 1.50
36 Drew Hutchison RC 1.25 3.00
37 Joe Kelly RC 1.50 4.00
38 Andrelton Simmons RC 1.50 4.00
39 Norichika Aoki RC 1.25 3.00
40 Jesus Montero RC 1.00 2.50
41 Matt Adams RC 1.25 3.00
42 Xavier Avery RC 1.00 2.50
43 Chris Archer RC 1.00 2.50
44 Jean Segura RC 2.50 6.00
45 Devin Mesoraco RC 1.00 2.50
46 Liam Hendriks RC 1.00 2.50
47 Jordan Pacheco RC 1.00 2.50
48 Starling Marte RC 1.25 3.00
49 Matt Harvey RC 6.00 15.00
50 Will Middlebrooks RC 1.25 3.00

2012 Bowman Sterling Refractors

*REF: .75X TO 2X BASIC
STATED ODDS 1:6 HOBBY
STATED PRINT RUN 199 SER.#'d SETS
1 Bryce Harper 60.00 150.00
44 Jean Segura 5.00 12.00

2012 Bowman Sterling Gold Refractors

*GOLD REF: 2.5X TO 6X BASIC
STATED ODDS 1:24 HOBBY
STATED PRINT RUN 50 SER.#'d SETS
1 Bryce Harper 100.00 200.00

2012 Bowman Sterling Box Topper Triple Autographs

RANDOM INSERT IN BOXES
EXCHANGE DEADLINE 12/31/2015
ADH Hawkins/Almora/Dahl 100.00 200.00
BHC Bundy/Cole/Hultzen 100.00 175.00
DBA Moore/Yu/Bauer 150.00 250.00
THM Harper/Middle/Trout 500.00 1000.00

2012 Bowman Sterling Dual Autographs Refractors

STATED ODDS 1:69 HOBBY
PRINT RUNS B/WN 38-99 COPIES PER
PRINTING PLATE ODDS 1:1284 HOBBY
PLATE PRINT RUN 1 SET PER COLOR
NO PLATE PRICING DUE TO SCARCITY
EXCHANGE DEADLINE 12/31/2015
AB J.Baez/A.Almora 40.00 80.00
AD A.Almora/D.Dahl 20.00 50.00
BB J.Bradley/X.Bogaerts 75.00 200.00
CT G.Cole/J.Taillon/38 40.00 80.00
GB D.Bundy/K.Gausman 30.00 80.00
HB K.Barnum/C.Hawkins 12.00 30.00
HF Andrew Heaney/Jose Fernandez 30.00 60.00
JL J.Gallo/L.Brinson EXCH 15.00 40.00
OA Austin Aune/Peter O'Brien 12.00 30.00
PC Gavin Cecchini/Kevin Plawecki 12.00 30.00
SV J.Valentin/C.Seager 20.00 50.00

2012 Bowman Sterling Dual Autographs Gold Refractors

*GOLD REF: .75X TO 2X BASIC
STATED ODDS 1:146 HOBBY
STATED PRINT RUN 50 SER.#'d SETS
EXCHANGE DEADLINE 12/31/2015

2012 Bowman Sterling Ichiro Yankees Commemorative Logo Patch

RANDOM INSERTS IN PACKS
STATED PRINT RUN 100 SER.#'d SETS
MPR1 Ichiro Suzuki 40.00 80.00

2012 Bowman Sterling Japanese Player Autographs

EXCHANGE DEADLINE 12/31/2015
HI Hisashi Iwakuma 40.00 80.00
TW Tsuyoshi Wada EXCH 30.00 60.00
YD Yu Darvish/75 125.00 250.00

2012 Bowman Sterling Next In Line

COMPLETE SET (10) 12.50 30.00
STATED ODDS 1:6 HOBBY
NIL1 Tyler Skaggs/Trevor Bauer 3.00 8.00
NIL2 M.Zunino/J.Montero 1.00 2.50
NIL3 A.Rendon/B.Harper 10.00 25.00
NIL4 Bradley/Middlebrooks 1.50 4.00
NIL5 J.Segura/M.Trout 30.00 80.00
NIL6 O.Taveras/M.Adams 1.00 2.50
NIL7 C.Buckel/Y.Darvish 1.50 4.00
NIL8 J.Baez/A.Rizzo 2.50 6.00
NIL9 B.Lawrie/T.d'Arnaud .75 2.00
NIL10 Rymer Liriano/Yasmani Grandal .60 1.50

2012 Bowman Sterling Prospect Autographs

PRINTING PLATE ODDS 1:246 HOBBY
PLATE PRINT RUN 1 SET PER COLOR
NO PLATE PRICING DUE TO SCARCITY
EXCHANGE DEADLINE 12/31/2015
AA Albert Almora 5.00 12.00
AAU Austin Aune 3.00 8.00
AH Andrew Heaney 5.00 12.00
AR Addison Russell 6.00 15.00
BB Barrett Barnes 3.00 8.00
BH Billy Hamilton 5.00 12.00
BJ Brian Johnson 3.00 8.00
BM Bruce Maxwell 3.00 8.00
BS Bubba Starling 3.00 8.00
CH Courtney Hawkins 3.00 8.00
CHE Chris Heston 3.00 8.00
CK Carson Kelly 3.00 8.00
CO Chris Owings 3.00 8.00
CS Corey Seager 25.00 60.00
DB Dylan Bundy 5.00 12.00
DD David Dahl 5.00 12.00
DDA D.J. Davis 3.00 8.00
DM Deven Marrero 3.00 8.00
DS Daniel Straily 5.00 12.00
DV David Vidal 3.00 8.00
EB Eddie Butler 3.00 8.00
FL Francisco Lindor 25.00 60.00
GC Gavin Cecchini 3.00 8.00
GCO Gerrit Cole 20.00 50.00
JC Jamie Callahan 3.00 8.00
JGA Joey Gallo 6.00 15.00
JJ Jamie Jarmon 3.00 8.00
JR James Ramsey 3.00 8.00
JS Jonathan Singleton 3.00 8.00
JSC Jonathan Schoop 4.00 10.00
JV Jesmuel Valentin 4.00 10.00
JWI Jesse Winker 15.00 40.00
KB Keon Barnum 3.00 8.00
KG Kevin Gausman 3.00 8.00
KP Kevin Plawecki 3.00 8.00
KZ Kyle Zimmer 3.00 8.00
LB Lewis Brinson 4.00 10.00
LBA Luke Bard 3.00 8.00
LS Lucas Sims 3.00 8.00
MF Max Fried 12.00 30.00
MH Mitch Haniger 3.00 8.00
MN Mitch Nay 3.00 8.00
MO Matthew Olson 6.00 15.00
MS Marcus Stroman 3.00 8.00
MSM Matthew Smoral 3.00 8.00
MZ Mike Zunino 4.00 10.00
NC Nick Castellanos 6.00 15.00
NF Nolan Fontana 3.00 8.00
NT Nicholas Travieso 3.00 8.00
PB Paul Blackburn 3.00 8.00
PJ Pierce Johnson 3.00 8.00
PL Pat Light 3.00 8.00
PO Peter O'Brien 3.00 8.00
PW Patrick Wisdom 3.00 8.00
RL Rymer Liriano 3.00 8.00
RS Richard Shaffer 3.00 8.00
SB Steve Bean 3.00 8.00
SN Sean Nolin 3.00 8.00
SP Stephen Piscotty 5.00 12.00
ST Stryker Trahan 3.00 8.00
TH Ty Hensley 3.00 8.00
TJ Travis Jankowski 3.00 8.00
TN Tyler Naquin 3.00 8.00
TRE Tony Renda 3.00 8.00
TS Tyler Skaggs 3.00 8.00
TT Tyrone Taylor 4.00 10.00
TW Taijuan Walker 3.00 8.00
VR Victor Roache 3.00 8.00

2012 Bowman Sterling Prospect Autographs Refractors

*REF: .6X TO 1.5X BASIC
STATED ODDS 1:5 HOBBY
STATED PRINT RUN 199 SER.#'d SETS
EXCHANGE DEADLINE 12/31/2015

2012 Bowman Sterling Prospect Autographs Gold Refractors

*GOLD REF: 1.5X TO 4X BASIC
STATED ODDS 1:20 HOBBY
STATED PRINT RUN 50 SER.#'d SETS
EXCHANGE DEADLINE 12/31/2015

2012 Bowman Sterling Prospects

PRINTING PLATE ODDS 1:150 HOBBY
PLATE PRINT RUN 1 SET PER COLOR
NO PLATE PRICING DUE TO SCARCITY
BSP1 Nolan Arenado 5.00 12.00
BSP2 Tyler Austin 2.00 5.00
BSP3 Matt Barnes 1.25 3.00
BSP4 Dante Bichette Jr. 1.50 4.00
BSP5 Xander Bogaerts 5.00 12.00
BSP6 Archie Bradley .75 2.00
BSP7 Jackie Bradley Jr. 3.00 8.00
BSP8 Gary Brown 1.25 3.00
BSP9 Cody Buckel 1.25 3.00
BSP10 Dylan Bundy 2.50 6.00
BSP11 Jose Campos 1.50 4.00
BSP12 Nick Castellanos 4.00 10.00
BSP13 Tony Cingrani 2.50 6.00
BSP14 Gerrit Cole 8.00 20.00
BSP15 Travis d'Arnaud 1.50 4.00
BSP16 Matt Davidson 1.50 4.00
BSP17 Corey Dickerson 1.25 3.00
BSP18 Jose Fernandez 3.00 8.00
BSP19 Nick Franklin 1.50 4.00
BSP20 Billy Hamilton 1.50 4.00
BSP21 Miles Head 1.25 3.00
BSP22 Danny Hultzen 2.00 5.00
BSP23 Francisco Lindor 10.00 25.00

BSP24 Rymer Liriano 1.25 3.00
BSP25 Austin Barnes 2.00 5.00
BSP26 Shelby Miller 2.50 6.00
BSP27 Brad Miller 1.25 3.00
BSP28 Sean Nolin 1.25 3.00
BSP29 Jonathan Galvez 1.25 3.00
BSP30 Chris Owings .75 2.00
BSP31 Marcell Ozuna 3.00 8.00
BSP32 James Paxton 2.00 5.00
BSP33 Alen Hanson 1.50 4.00
BSP34 Jurickson Profar 1.50 4.00
BSP35 Eddie Rosario 2.50 6.00
BSP36 Miguel Sano 1.50 4.00
BSP37 Daniel Vogelbach 2.00 5.00
BSP38 Travis Shaw 1.50 4.00
BSP39 Jonathan Singleton 1.50 4.00
BSP40 Tyler Skaggs 2.00 5.00
BSP41 George Springer 5.00 12.00
BSP42 Bubba Starling 1.50 4.00
BSP43 Jameson Taillon 1.50 4.00
BSP44 Oscar Taveras 2.00 5.00
BSP45 Keury de la Cruz 1.25 3.00
BSP46 Taijuan Walker 1.50 4.00
BSP47 Zack Wheeler 2.50 6.00
BSP48 Mason Williams 2.00 5.00
BSP49 Kolten Wong 1.25 3.00
BSP50 Christian Yelich 10.00 25.00

2012 Bowman Sterling Prospects Refractors

*REF: .6X TO 1.5X BASIC
STATED ODDS 1:6 HOBBY
STATED PRINT RUN 199 SER.#'d SETS

2012 Bowman Sterling Prospects Gold Refractors

*GOLD REF: 2X TO 5X BASIC
STATED ODDS 1:24 HOBBY
STATED PRINT RUN 50 SER.#'d SETS

2012 Bowman Sterling Rookie Autographs

STATED ODDS 1:6 HOBBY
PRINTING PLATE ODDS 1:777 HOBBY
PLATE PRINT RUN 1 SET PER COLOR
NO PLATE PRICING DUE TO SCARCITY
EXCHANGE DEADLINE 12/31/2015
AG Anthony Gose 4.00 10.00
BH Bryce Harper 75.00 150.00
BJ Brett Jackson 3.00 8.00
CA Chris Archer 6.00 15.00
DN Derek Norris 4.00 10.00
JM Jesus Montero 5.00 12.00
JP Jarrod Parker 5.00 12.00
JS Jean Segura 3.00 8.00
KN Kirk Nieuwenhuis 3.00 8.00
MA Matt Adams 5.00 12.00
MM Matt Moore 4.00 10.00
MT Mike Trout 400.00 1000.00
SC Steve Clevenger 3.00 8.00
SM Starling Marte 6.00 15.00
TB Trevor Bauer 10.00 25.00
WM Will Middlebrooks 3.00 8.00
WMI Wade Miley 3.00 8.00
WR Wilin Rosario 3.00 8.00
YC Yoenis Cespedes 15.00 40.00
YD Yu Darvish 90.00 150.00

2012 Bowman Sterling Rookie Autographs Refractors

*REF: .5X TO 1.2X BASIC
STATED ODDS 1:18 HOBBY
STATED PRINT RUN 199 SER.#'d SETS
EXCHANGE DEADLINE 12/31/2015

2012 Bowman Sterling Rookie Autographs Gold Refractors

*GOLD REF: 1.2X TO 3X BASIC
STATED ODDS 1:63 HOBBY
STATED PRINT RUN 50 SER.#'d SETS
EXCHANGE DEADLINE 12/31/2015
BH Bryce Harper 125.00 300.00
YD Yu Darvish 150.00 300.00

2013 Bowman Sterling

PLATE PRINT RUN 1 SET PER COLOR
BLACK-CYAN-MAGENTA-YELLOW ISSUED
NO PLATE PRICING DUE TO SCARCITY
1 Tyler Skaggs RC 1.00 2.50
2 Tony Cingrani RC 1.25 3.00
3 Shelby Miller RC 1.50 4.00
4 Oswaldo Arcia RC .60 1.50
5 Nolan Arenado RC 15.00 40.00
6 Nate Freiman RC .60 1.50
7 Mike Olt RC .75 2.00
8 Matt Magill RC .60 1.50
9 Marcell Ozuna RC 1.50 4.00
10 Manny Machado RC 8.00 20.00
11 Kyuji Fujikawa RC 1.00 2.50
12 Jurickson Profar RC .75 2.00
13 Jose Fernandez RC 1.50 4.00
14 Jedd Gyorko RC .75 2.00
15 Jake Odorizzi RC .75 2.00
16 Jackie Bradley Jr. RC 1.50 4.00
17 Hyun-Jin Ryu RC 1.50 4.00
18 Evan Gattis RC 1.25 3.00
19 Dylan Bundy RC 1.50 4.00
20 Didi Gregorius RC 2.50 6.00
21 Carlos Martinez RC 1.00 2.50
22 Bruce Rondon RC .60 1.50
23 Anthony Rendon RC 4.00 10.00
24 Allen Webster RC .75 2.00
25 Adeiny Hechavarria RC .75 2.00
26 Adam Eaton RC 1.00 2.50
27 Aaron Hicks RC 1.00 2.50
28 Michael Wacha RC .75 2.00
29 Michael Kickham RC .60 1.50
30 Jonathan Pettibone RC 1.00 2.50
31 Nick Franklin RC .75 2.00
32 Yasiel Puig RC 2.50 6.00
33 Gerrit Cole RC 4.00 10.00
34 Zack Wheeler RC 1.25 3.00
35 Wil Myers RC 1.00 2.50
36 Mike Zunino RC 1.00 2.50
37 Alex Wood RC .75 2.00
38 Christian Yelich RC 10.00 25.00
39 Jarred Cosart RC .75 2.00
40 Henry Urrutia RC .75 2.00
41 Sonny Gray RC 1.00 2.50
42 Grant Green RC 1.00 2.50
43 Cody Asche RC 1.00 2.50
44 Kyle Gibson RC 1.00 2.50
45 Josh Phegley RC .60 1.50
46 Brad Miller RC .75 2.00
47 Zoilo Almonte RC .75 2.00
48 Johnny Hellweg RC .60 1.50
49 Drake Britton RC .75 2.00
50 Jonathan Villar RC 1.00 2.50

2013 Bowman Sterling Blue Refractors

*BLUE REF: 2.5X TO 6X BASIC
STATED PRINT RUN 25 SER.#'d SETS

2013 Bowman Sterling Gold Refractors

*GOLD REF: 2X TO 5X BASIC
STATED PRINT RUN 50 SER.#'d SETS

2013 Bowman Sterling Refractors

*REF: 1X TO 2.5X BASIC
STATED PRINT RUN 199 SER.#'d SETS

2013 Bowman Sterling Blue Sapphire Signings

STATED PRINT RUN 25 SER.#'d SETS
EXCHANGE DEADLINE 12/31/2016
BB Byron Buxton 75.00 150.00
HR Hyun-Jin Ryu 25.00 60.00
JP Jurickson Profar 20.00 50.00
MM Manny Machado 50.00 100.00
MS Miguel Sano 12.00 30.00
MT Mike Trout 100.00 200.00
OT Oscar Taveras 20.00 50.00
SM Shelby Miller 40.00 80.00
TD Travis d'Arnaud 5.00 12.00
WM Wil Myers 12.00 30.00

2013 Bowman Sterling Blue Sapphire Signings Ruby

*RUBY: .5X TO 1.2X BASIC
STATED PRINT RUN 25 SER.#'d SETS
EXCHANGE DEADLINE 12/31/2016

2013 Bowman Sterling Dual Autographs Refractors

STATED PRINT RUN 35 SER.#'d SETS
EXCHANGE DEADLINE 12/31/2016
BL F.Lindor/J.Baez 50.00 100.00
CN G.Cecchini/B.Nimmo 12.50 30.00
CS G.Springer/C.Correa 100.00 200.00
DS T.d'Arnaud/N.Syndergaard 60.00 120.00
HM T.Hensley/M.Montgomery 12.50 30.00
LC F.Lindor/C.Correa 90.00 150.00
RD H.Jin Ryu/Y.Darvish 90.00 150.00
RT T.Taylor/V.Roache
RV D.Vogelbach/A.Rizzo 12.50 30.00
ZW M.Zunino/T.Walker 30.00 60.00

2013 Bowman Sterling Asia Exclusive Autographs

HI Hisashi Iwakuma
JT Junichi Tazawa 50.00 100.00
KF Kyuji Fujikawa EXCH
TW Tsuyoshi Wada EXCH
YD Yu Darvish
HR Hyun-Jin Ryu 60.00 120.00

2013 Bowman Sterling Prospect Autographs

PLATE PRINT RUN 1 SET PER COLOR
BLACK-CYAN-MAGENTA-YELLOW ISSUED
NO PLATE PRICING DUE TO SCARCITY
EXCHANGE DEADLINE 12/31/2016
AB Archie Bradley 3.00 8.00
ABL Aaron Blair 3.00 8.00
AC Andrew Church 3.00 8.00
AH Alen Hanson 3.00 8.00
AJ Aaron Judge 75.00 200.00
AK Andrew Knapp 4.00 10.00
AM Austin Meadows 6.00 15.00
AT Andrew Thurman 3.00 8.00
AW Austin Wilson 3.00 8.00
BB Byron Buxton 4.00 10.00
BM Billy McKinney 4.00 10.00
BMI Brad Miller 3.00 8.00
BS Braden Shipley 3.00 8.00
BT Blake Taylor 3.00 8.00
CA Chris Anderson 3.00 8.00
CC Carlos Correa 15.00 40.00
CE C.J. Edwards 3.00 8.00
CF Clint Frazier 6.00 15.00
CH Courtney Hawkins 3.00 8.00
CK Corey Knebel 3.00 8.00
CM Colin Moran 3.00 8.00
CS Chance Sisco 3.00 8.00
CSA Cord Sandberg 3.00 8.00
DO Dillon Overton 3.00 8.00
DP D.J. Peterson 6.00 15.00
DPL Daniel Palka 3.00 8.00
DS Dominic Smith 6.00 15.00
DW Devin Williams 8.00 20.00
EJ Eric Jagielo 3.00 8.00
ER Eduardo Rodriguez 3.00 8.00
GK Gosuke Katoh 3.00 8.00
GP Gregory Polanco 4.00 10.00
HD Hunter Dozier 3.00 8.00
HG Hunter Green 3.00 8.00
HH Hunter Harvey 3.00 8.00
HR Hunter Renfroe 5.00 12.00
IC Ian Clarkin 3.00 8.00
JC J.P. Crawford 6.00 15.00
JCA Jamie Callahan 3.00 8.00
JCR Jonathon Crawford 3.00 8.00
JD Jon Denney 3.00 8.00
JG Jonathan Gray 3.00 8.00
JH Josh Hart 3.00 8.00
JMA Jacob May 3.00 8.00
JMO Julio Morban 3.00 8.00
JP Joc Pederson 10.00 25.00
JS Jorge Soler 5.00 12.00
JSW Jake Sweaney 3.00 8.00
JU Julio Urias 15.00 40.00
JW Justin Williams 3.00 8.00
KF Kevin Franklin 3.00 8.00
KS Kohl Stewart 3.00 8.00
KZ Kevin Ziomek 3.00 8.00
LM L.J. Mazzilli 3.00 8.00
ML Michael Lorenzen 3.00 8.00
MM Matt McPhearson 3.00 8.00
MMO Mark Montgomery 3.00 8.00
MO Michael O'Neill 3.00 8.00
MS Miguel Sano 5.00 12.00
NC Nick Ciuffo 4.00 10.00
NK Nick Kingham 3.00 8.00
NS Noah Syndergaard 10.00 25.00
NTU Nik Turley 3.00 8.00
OM Oscar Mercado 4.00 10.00
OT Oscar Taveras 3.00 8.00
PE Phil Ervin 3.00 8.00
PK Patrick Kivlehan 3.00 8.00
RD Rafael DePaula 3.00 8.00
RE Ryan Eades 3.00 8.00
RH Ryon Healy 5.00 12.00
RJ Ryder Jones 3.00 8.00
RK Robert Kaminsky 3.00 8.00
RM Raul Mondesi 6.00 15.00
RMC Reese McGuire 5.00 12.00
RMM Ryan McMahon 12.00 30.00
RQ Roman Quinn 3.00 8.00
RU Riley Unroe 3.00 8.00
TA Tim Anderson 15.00 40.00
TAU Tyler Austin 3.00 8.00
TB Trey Ball 3.00 8.00
TDA Tyler Danish 3.00 8.00
TN Tucker Neuhaus 3.00 8.00
TW Taijuan Walker 3.00 8.00
TWI Trevor Williams 3.00 8.00
TWN Tom Windle 3.00 8.00
VS Victor Sanchez 3.00 8.00
XB Xander Bogaerts
YV Yordano Ventura 5.00 12.00

2013 Bowman Sterling Prospect Autographs Blue Refractors

*BLUE REF: 1.2X TO 3X BASIC
STATED PRINT RUN 25 SER.#'d SETS
EXCHANGE DEADLINE 12/31/2016

2013 Bowman Sterling Prospect Autographs Gold Refractors

*ORANGE REF: .75X TO 2X BASIC
STATED PRINT RUN 50 SER.#'d SETS
EXCHANGE DEADLINE 12/31/2016

2013 Bowman Sterling Prospect Autographs Green Refractors

*GREEN REF: .5X TO 1.2X BASIC
STATED PRINT RUN 125 SER.#'d SETS
EXCHANGE DEADLINE 12/31/2016

2013 Bowman Sterling Prospect Autographs Orange Refractors

*ORANGE REF: .6X TO 1.5X BASIC
STATED PRINT RUN 75 SER.#'d SETS
EXCHANGE DEADLINE 12/31/2016

2013 Bowman Sterling Prospect Autographs Refractors

*REF: .5X TO 1.2X BASIC
STATED PRINT RUN 150 SER.#'d SETS
EXCHANGE DEADLINE 12/31/2016

2013 Bowman Sterling Prospect Autographs Ruby Refractors

*RUBY REF: .5X TO 1.2X BASIC
STATED PRINT RUN 99 SER.#'d SETS
EXCHANGE DEADLINE 12/31/2016

2013 Bowman Sterling Prospects

PLATE PRINT RUN 1 SET PER COLOR
BLACK-CYAN-MAGENTA-YELLOW ISSUED
NO PLATE PRICING DUE TO SCARCITY
1 Mark Appel 1.00 2.50
2 Xander Bogaerts 2.00 5.00
3 Tyler Austin 1.00 2.50
4 Clint Frazier 3.00 8.00
5 Taylor Guerrieri .60 1.50
6 Taijuan Walker .75 2.00
7 Rafael De Paula .60 1.50
8 Noah Syndergaard .75 2.00
9 Nick Castellanos 2.00 5.00
10 Miguel Sano .75 2.00
11 Kris Bryant 20.00 50.00
12 Pierce Johnson .75 2.00
13 Max Fried 2.50 6.00
14 Matt Barnes .75 2.00
15 Mason Williams .75 2.00
16 Mark Montgomery 1.00 2.50
17 Kolten Wong .60 1.50
18 Dominic Smith 1.00 2.50
19 Austin Meadows 1.50 4.00
20 Jorge Soler 1.25 3.00
21 Jonathan Singleton .75 2.00
22 Joey Gallo 2.00 5.00
23 Joc Pederson 1.50 4.00
24 Jesse Biddle .75 2.00
25 Javier Baez 2.50 6.00
26 Jameson Taillon .75 2.00
27 Gregory Polanco 1.25 3.00
28 George Springer 2.50 6.00
29 Gary Sanchez 2.00 5.00
30 Francisco Lindor 5.00 12.00
31 Dorssys Paulino .75 2.00
32 David Dahl .75 2.00
33 Colin Moran .75 2.00
34 Raul Mondesi 1.00 2.50
35 Courtney Hawkins .60 1.50
36 Kohl Stewart .75 2.00
37 Carlos Correa 20.00 50.00
38 C.J. Cron .75 2.00
39 Byron Buxton 3.00 8.00
40 Bubba Starling .75 2.00
41 Billy Hamilton .75 2.00
42 Archie Bradley .60 1.50
43 Alex Meyer .60 1.50
44 Alen Hanson .75 2.00
45 Addison Russell 1.00 2.50
46 Adam Walker .75 2.00
47 Oscar Taveras .75 2.00
48 Dan Vogelbach 1.00 2.50
49 Trey Ball 1.00 2.50
50 Jonathan Gray .75 2.00

2013 Bowman Sterling Prospects Blue Refractors

*BLUE REF: 2.5X TO 6X BASIC
STATED PRINT RUN 25 SER.#'d SETS
4 Clint Frazier 20.00 50.00
19 Austin Meadows 20.00 50.00

2013 Bowman Sterling Prospects Gold Refractors

*GOLD REF: 2X TO 5X BASIC
STATED PRINT RUN 50 SER.#'d SETS
4 Clint Frazier 15.00 40.00

2013 Bowman Sterling Prospects Refractors

*REF: .75X TO 2X BASIC
STATED PRINT RUN 199 SER.#'d SETS

2013 Bowman Sterling Rookie Autographs

PLATE PRINT RUN 1 SET PER COLOR
BLACK-CYAN-MAGENTA-YELLOW ISSUED
NO PLATE PRICING DUE TO SCARCITY
EXCHANGE DEADLINE 12/31/2016
AE Adam Eaton 3.00 8.00
AW Allen Webster 3.00 8.00
AWO Alex Wood 3.00 8.00
CM Carlos Martinez 6.00 15.00
DB Dylan Bundy 5.00 12.00
DG Didi Gregorius 5.00 12.00
EG Evan Gattis 4.00 10.00
JF Jose Fernandez 20.00 50.00
JG Jedd Gyorko 3.00 8.00
JP Jonathan Pettibone 3.00 8.00
MW Michael Wacha 5.00 12.00
NA Nolan Arenado 60.00 150.00
SM Shelby Miller 3.00 8.00
TC Tony Cingrani 3.00 8.00
TS Tyler Skaggs 3.00 8.00
WM Wil Myers 6.00 15.00
YP Yasiel Puig 60.00 150.00
ZW Zack Wheeler 5.00 12.00

2013 Bowman Sterling Rookie Autographs Gold Refractors

*GOLD REF: .75X TO 2X BASIC
STATED PRINT RUN 50 SER.#'d SETS
EXCHANGE DEADLINE 12/31/2016
AE Adam Eaton 8.00 20.00

2013 Bowman Sterling Rookie Autographs Green Refractors

*GREEN REF: .5X TO 1.2X BASIC
STATED PRINT RUN 125 SER.#'d SETS
EXCHANGE DEADLINE 12/31/2016

2013 Bowman Sterling Rookie Autographs Orange Refractors

*ORANGE REF: .6X TO 1.5X BASIC
STATED PRINT RUN 75 SER.#'d SETS
EXCHANGE DEADLINE 12/31/2016

2013 Bowman Sterling Rookie Autographs Refractors

*REF: .5X TO 1.2X BASIC
STATED PRINT RUN 150 SER.#'d SETS
EXCHANGE DEADLINE 12/31/2016

2013 Bowman Sterling Rookie Autographs Ruby Refractors

*RUBY REF: .5X TO 1.2X BASIC
STATED PRINT RUN 99 SER.#'d SETS
EXCHANGE DEADLINE 12/31/2016

2013 Bowman Sterling Showcase Autographs

STATED PRINT RUN 25 SER.#'d SETS
EXCHANGE DEADLINE 12/31/2016
BB Byron Buxton 150.00 250.00
BH Bryce Harper 150.00 300.00
JP Jurickson Profar 12.00 30.00
MC Miguel Cabrera EXCH 100.00 200.00
MM Manny Machado 75.00 150.00
MT Mike Trout 200.00 350.00
OT Oscar Taveras 10.00 25.00
SM Shelby Miller 50.00 100.00
YD Yu Darvish
YP Yasiel Puig 50.00 120.00

2013 Bowman Sterling The Duel

BA T.Austin/M.Barnes .50 1.25
BJ A.Judge/T.Ball 5.00 12.00
BP J.Pederson/C.Blackburn .75 2.00
CS D.Smith/I.Clarkin .50 1.25
DT M.Trout/Y.Darvish 4.00 10.00
GB T.Guerrieri/X.Bogaerts 1.00 2.50
HH B.Harper/M.Harvey .75 2.00
HM D.Marrero/T.Hensley .40 1.00
JH C.Hawkins/P.Johnson .40 1.00
MB J.Baez/S.Miller 1.25 3.00

2014 Bowman Sterling

PRINTING PLATE ODDS 1:424 HOBBY
PLATE PRINT RUN 1 SET PER COLOR
BLACK-CYAN-MAGENTA-YELLOW ISSUED
NO PLATE PRICING DUE TO SCARCITY
1 Jose Abreu RC 6.00 15.00
2 Alex Guerrero RC 1.00 2.50
3 Andrew Heaney RC .75 2.00
4 Eddie Butler RC .75 2.00
5 Joe Panik RC 1.25 3.00
6 Luis Sardinas RC .75 2.00
7 Taijuan Walker RC .75 2.00
8 Yordano Ventura RC 1.00 2.50
9 Andrew Susac RC 1.00 2.50
10 Billy Hamilton RC 1.00 2.50
11 Chase Anderson RC .75 2.00
12 Jesse Hahn RC 1.00 2.50
13 Arismendy Alcantara RC .75 2.00
14 Cam Bedrosian RC .75 2.00
15 Erisbel Arruebarrena RC .75 2.00
16 Rougned Odor RC 2.00 5.00
17 Mookie Betts RC 20.00 50.00
18 Xander Bogaerts RC 2.50 6.00
19 Michael Choice RC .75 2.00
20 George Springer RC 3.00 8.00
21 Jonathan Schoop RC .75 2.00
22 Rafael Montero RC .75 2.00
23 Tommy La Stella RC .75 2.00
24 Jacob deGrom RC 75.00 200.00
25 Masahiro Tanaka RC 2.50 6.00
26 Nick Castellanos RC 2.50 6.00
27 James Paxton RC 1.25 3.00
28 Kennys Vargas RC .75 2.00
29 Travis d'Arnaud 1.00 2.50
30 Oscar Taveras RC 1.00 2.50
31 Danny Santana RC 1.00 2.50
32 Kolten Wong RC 1.00 2.50
33 Aaron Sanchez RC .75 2.00
34 Matt Davidson RC 1.00 2.50
35 Jimmy Nelson RC .75 2.00
36 Chris Owings RC .75 2.00
37 Kyle Parker RC 1.00 2.50
38 Josmil Pinto RC .75 2.00
39 Stefen Romero RC .75 2.00
40 Jon Singleton RC 1.00 2.50
41 C.J. Cron RC .75 2.00
42 Marcus Stroman RC 1.25 3.00
43 Yangervis Solarte RC .75 2.00
44 Zach Walters RC .75 2.00
45 Jake Marisnick RC .75 2.00
46 Ken Giles RC 1.00 2.50
47 Christian Bethancourt RC .75 2.00
48 Roenis Elias RC .75 2.00
49 Garin Cecchini RC .75 2.00
50 Gregory Polanco RC 1.25 3.00

2014 Bowman Sterling Blue Refractors

*BLUE REF: 1.2X TO 3X BASIC
STATED ODDS 1:68 HOBBY
STATED PRINT RUN 25 SER.#'d SETS

2014 Bowman Sterling Japan Fractors

*JAPAN REF: 1.2X TO 3X BASIC
RELEASED EXCLUSIVELY IN ASIA
STATED PRINT RUN 25 SER.#'d SETS

2014 Bowman Sterling Purple Refractors

*PURPLE REF: 1X TO 2.5X BASIC
STATED ODDS 1:34 HOBBY
STATED PRINT RUN 50 SER.#'d SETS

2014 Bowman Sterling Refractors

*REF: .6X TO 1.5X BASIC
STATED ODDS 1:9 HOBBY
STATED PRINT RUN 199 SER.#'d SETS

2014 Bowman Sterling Box Topper Purple Wave Refractors

STATED ODDS 1:15 HOBBY BOXES
STATED PRINT RUN 50 SER.#'d SETS
*BLACK/35: .5X TO 1.2X BASIC
BBTAB Archie Bradley 2.00 5.00
BBTAJ Alex Jackson 2.50 6.00
BBTAR Addison Russell 3.00 8.00
BBTBB Byron Buxton 10.00 25.00
BBTCC Carlos Correa 10.00 25.00
BBTFL Francisco Lindor 15.00 40.00
BBTGP Gregory Polanco 10.00 25.00
BBTGS George Springer 8.00 20.00
BBTHH Hunter Harvey 2.00 5.00
BBTJA Jose Abreu 15.00 40.00
BBTJB Javier Baez 8.00 20.00
BBTJG Jon Gray 2.50 6.00
BBTJS Jorge Soler 4.00 10.00
BBTKB Kris Bryant 20.00 50.00
BBTKS Kyle Schwarber 8.00 20.00
BBTLG Lucas Giolito 3.00 8.00
BBTMT Masahiro Tanaka 6.00 15.00
BBTNG Nick Gordon 2.50 6.00
BBTOT Oscar Taveras 2.50 6.00
BBTTK Tyler Kolek 2.00 5.00

2014 Bowman Sterling Die Cut Autographs Refractors

STATED ODDS 1:85 HOBBY
STATED PRINT RUN 50 SER.#'d SETS
EXCHANGE DEADLINE 12/31/2017
*BLUE/30: .5X TO 1.2X BASIC
SAAB Archie Bradley EXCH 6.00 15.00
SAAJ Alex Jackson 8.00 20.00
SAAN Aaron Nola 40.00 100.00
SABB Byron Buxton 30.00 80.00
SACC Carlos Correa 75.00 200.00
SACF Clint Frazier 15.00 40.00
SAFL Francisco Lindor 50.00 125.00
SAGP Gregory Polanco 15.00 40.00
SAGS George Springer 25.00 60.00
SAJA Jose Abreu 25.00 60.00
SAJB Javier Baez 25.00 60.00
SAJSO Jorge Soler EXCH 12.00 30.00
SAKS Kyle Schwarber EXCH 75.00 200.00
SALG Lucas Giolito 20.00 50.00
SAMB Mookie Betts 40.00 100.00
SAMS Miguel Sano 20.00 50.00
SANG Nick Gordon 25.00 60.00
SANS Noah Syndergaard 15.00 40.00
SATK Tyler Kolek 25.00 60.00

2014 Bowman Sterling Die Cut Autographs Blue Refractors

*BLUE REF: .5X TO 1.2X BASIC
STATED ODDS 1:142 HOBBY
STATED PRINT RUN 30 SER.#'d SETS
EXCHANGE DEADLINE 12/31/2017

2014 Bowman Sterling Dual Autographs Refractors

STATED ODDS 1:242 HOBBY
STATED PRINT RUN 35 SER.#'d SETS
*BLUE/25: .5X TO 1.2X BASIC
PRINTING PLATE ODDS 1:2118 HOBBY
PLATE PRINT RUN 1 SET PER COLOR
BLACK-CYAN-MAGENTA-YELLOW ISSUED
NO PLATE PRICING DUE TO SCARCITY
EXCHANGE DEADLINE 12/31/2017
BDAAC Abreu/Cabrera 60.00 150.00
BDABT Buxton/Taveras EXCH 25.00 60.00
BDAGS M.Sano/N.Gordon 30.00 80.00
BDAKH Heaney/Kolek EXCH 6.00 15.00
BDASC G.Springer/C.Correa 60.00 150.00
BDASP Puig/Soler EXCH 30.00 80.00

2014 Bowman Sterling Japan Darvish Die Cut Refractors

INSERTED IN BOW.STERLING ASIAN PACKS
STATED PRINT RUN 25 SER.#'d SETS
YD1 Yu Darvish 5.00 12.00
YD2 Yu Darvish 5.00 12.00
YD3 Yu Darvish 5.00 12.00
YD4 Yu Darvish 5.00 12.00
YD5 Yu Darvish 5.00 12.00

2014 Bowman Sterling Japan Darvish Jersey Die Cut

INSERTED IN BOW.STERLING ASIAN PACKS
STATED PRINT RUN 10 SER.#'d SETS
YD1 Yu Darvish 10.00 25.00
YD2 Yu Darvish 10.00 25.00
YD3 Yu Darvish 10.00 25.00
YD4 Yu Darvish 10.00 25.00
YD5 Yu Darvish 10.00 25.00

2014 Bowman Sterling Japan Tanaka Die Cut Refractors

INSERTED IN BOW.STERLING ASIAN PACKS
STATED PRINT RUN 25 SER.#'d SETS
MT1 Masahiro Tanaka 3.00 8.00
MT2 Masahiro Tanaka 3.00 8.00
MT3 Masahiro Tanaka 3.00 8.00
MT4 Masahiro Tanaka 3.00 8.00
MT5 Masahiro Tanaka 3.00 8.00

2014 Bowman Sterling Japan Tanaka Jersey Die Cut

INSERTED IN BOW.STERLING ASIAN PACKS
STATED PRINT RUN 10 SER.#'d SETS
MT1 Masahiro Tanaka 8.00 20.00
MT2 Masahiro Tanaka 8.00 20.00
MT3 Masahiro Tanaka 8.00 20.00
MT4 Masahiro Tanaka 8.00 20.00
MT5 Masahiro Tanaka 8.00 20.00

2014 Bowman Sterling Prospect Autographs

PRINTING PLATE ODDS 1:326 HOBBY
PLATE PRINT RUN 1 SET PER COLOR
BLACK-CYAN-MAGENTA-YELLOW ISSUED
NO PLATE PRICING DUE TO SCARCITY
EXCHANGE DEADLINE 12/31/2017
BSPAAA Albert Almora 5.00 12.00
BSPAABL Alex Blandino 3.00 8.00
BSPAAC A.J. Cole 3.00 8.00
BSPAAH Alen Hanson 3.00 8.00
BSPAAJ Alex Jackson 4.00 10.00
BSPAAME Austin Meadows 8.00 20.00
BSPAAN Aaron Northcraft 3.00 8.00
BSPAANO Aaron Nola 8.00 20.00
BSPABD Braxton Davidson 3.00 8.00
BSPABF Brandon Finnegan 3.00 8.00
BSPABS Blake Swihart 4.00 10.00
BSPABZ Bradley Zimmer 5.00 12.00
BSPACC Carlos Correa 15.00 40.00
BSPACE C.J. Edwards 4.00 10.00
BSPACF Clint Frazier 8.00 20.00
BSPACM Colin Moran 3.00 8.00
BSPACT Cole Tucker 3.00 8.00
BSPACV Chase Vallot 3.00 8.00
BSPADDE Delino DeShields Jr. 3.00 8.00
BSPADF Derek Fisher 5.00 12.00
BSPADH Derek Hill 3.00 8.00
BSPADS Dominic Smith 3.00 8.00
BSPAEF Erick Fedde 3.00 8.00
BSPAER Eduardo Rodriguez 4.00 10.00
BSPAERO Eddie Rosario 6.00 15.00
BSPAFG Foster Griffin 3.00 8.00
BSPAFL Francisco Lindor 20.00 50.00
BSPAGC Gavin Cecchini 3.00 8.00
BSPAGH Grant Holmes 3.00 8.00
BSPAGM Gareth Morgan 3.00 8.00
BSPAGS Gary Sanchez 15.00 40.00
BSPAHH Hunter Harvey 3.00 8.00
BSPAHO Henry Owens 4.00 10.00
BSPAJA Jorge Alfaro 4.00 10.00
BSPAJAG Jacob Gatewood 3.00 8.00
BSPAJB Jorge Bonifacio 3.00 8.00
BSPAJBA Javier Baez 20.00 50.00
BSPAJC J.P. Crawford 3.00 8.00
BSPAJF Jack Flaherty 12.00 30.00
BSPAJGA Joey Gallo 6.00 15.00
BSPAJH Jason Hursh 3.00 8.00
BSPAJHO Jeff Hoffman 5.00 12.00
BSPAJN Justin Nicolino 3.00 8.00
BSPAJPE Jose Peraza 3.00 8.00
BSPAJS Justus Sheffield 4.00 10.00
BSPAKC Kyle Crick 3.00 8.00
BSPAKF Kyle Freeland 3.00 8.00
BSPAKSC Kyle Schwarber 6.00 15.00
BSPAKV Kennys Vargas 3.00 8.00
BSPALG Lucas Giolito 5.00 12.00
BSPALO Luis Ortiz 3.00 8.00
BSPALS Luis Severino 10.00 25.00
BSPALSI Lucas Sims 3.00 8.00
BSPALW Luke Weaver 5.00 12.00
BSPAMBA Matt Barnes 3.00 8.00
BSPAMC Michael Conforto 12.00 30.00
BSPAMF Michael Foltynewicz 3.00 8.00
BSPAMG Mitch Gueller 3.00 8.00
BSPAMIC Michael Chavis 6.00 15.00
BSPAMJ Micah Johnson 3.00 8.00
BSPAMK Michael Kopech 8.00 20.00
BSPAMP Max Pentecost 3.00 8.00
BSPAMPA Mike Papi 3.00 8.00
BSPAMS Miguel Sano 4.00 10.00
BSPANG Nick Gordon 4.00 10.00
BSPANH Nick Howard 3.00 8.00
BSPANS Noah Syndergaard 8.00 20.00
BSPARA Raul Alcantara 3.00 8.00
BSPARS Robert Stephenson 3.00 8.00
BSPASC Sean Coyle 3.00 8.00
BSPASN Sean Newcomb 5.00 12.00
BSPASP Stephen Piscotty 4.00 10.00
BSPATB Tyler Beede 5.00 12.00
BSPATG Tyler Glasnow 8.00 20.00
BSPATK Tyler Kolek 3.00 8.00
BSPATM Tom Murphy 3.00 8.00

2014 Bowman Sterling Prospect Autographs Blue Refractors

*BLUE REF: 1X TO 2.5X BASIC
STATED ODDS 1:53 HOBBY
STATED PRINT RUN 25 SER.#'d SETS
EXCHANGE DEADLINE 12/31/2017
BSPAAB Archie Bradley 8.00 20.00
BSPABB Byron Buxton 15.00 40.00

2014 Bowman Sterling Prospect Autographs Green Refractors

*GREEN REF: .5X TO 1.2X BASIC
STATED ODDS 1:11 HOBBY
STATED PRINT RUN 125 SER.#'d SETS
EXCHANGE DEADLINE 12/31/2017
BSPAAB Archie Bradley 4.00 10.00
BSPABB Byron Buxton 8.00 20.00

2014 Bowman Sterling Prospect Autographs Magenta Refractors

*MAGENTA REF: .6X TO 1.5X BASIC
STATED ODDS 1:14 HOBBY
STATED PRINT RUN 99 SER.#'d SETS
EXCHANGE DEADLINE 12/31/2017
BSPAAB Archie Bradley 5.00 12.00
BSPABB Byron Buxton 10.00 25.00

2014 Bowman Sterling Prospect Autographs Orange Refractors

*ORANGE REF: .6X TO 1.5X BASIC
STATED ODDS 1:18 HOBBY
STATED PRINT RUN 75 SER.#'d SETS
EXCHANGE DEADLINE 12/31/2017
BSPAAB Archie Bradley 5.00 12.00
BSPABB Byron Buxton 10.00 25.00

2014 Bowman Sterling Prospect Autographs Purple Refractors

*PURPLE REF: .75X TO 2X BASIC
STATED ODDS 1:27 HOBBY
STATED PRINT RUN 50 SER.#'d SETS
EXCHANGE DEADLINE 12/31/2017
BSPAAB Archie Bradley 6.00 15.00
BSPABB Byron Buxton 12.00 30.00

2014 Bowman Sterling Prospect Autographs Refractors

*REF: .5X TO 1.2X BASIC
STATED ODDS 1:9 HOBBY
STATED PRINT RUN 150 SER.#'d SETS
EXCHANGE DEADLINE 12/31/2017
BSPAAB Archie Bradley 4.00 10.00
BSPABB Byron Buxton 8.00 20.00

2014 Bowman Sterling Prospects

PRINTING PLATE ODDS 1:424 HOBBY
PLATE PRINT RUN 1 SET PER COLOR
BLACK-CYAN-MAGENTA-YELLOW ISSUED
NO PLATE PRICING DUE TO SCARCITY
BSP1 Kris Bryant 25.00 60.00
BSP2 Francisco Lindor 5.00 12.00
BSP3 Aaron Nola 4.00 10.00
BSP4 J.P. Crawford .60 1.50
BSP5 Miguel Sano .75 2.00
BSP6 Alex Meyer .60 1.50
BSP7 Nick Howard .60 1.50
BSP8 Kodi Medeiros .60 1.50
BSP9 Jon Gray .75 2.00
BSP10 Joey Gallo 1.25 3.00
BSP11 Braden Shipley .60 1.50
BSP12 Robert Stephenson .60 1.50
BSP13 Luis Severino 1.00 2.50
BSP14 Alex Jackson .75 2.00
BSP15 Hunter Harvey .60 1.50
BSP16 Sean Newcomb 1.00 2.50
BSP17 Nick Gordon .75 2.00
BSP18 Colin Moran .60 1.50
BSP19 Mark Appel .75 2.00
BSP20 Carlos Correa 3.00 8.00
BSP21 Jorge Soler 1.25 3.00
BSP22 Michael Conforto 1.25 3.00
BSP23 Tyler Glasnow 2.50 6.00
BSP24 Jorge Alfaro .75 2.00
BSP25 Jeff Hoffman 1.00 2.50
BSP26 Joc Pederson 1.50 4.00
BSP27 Clint Frazier 2.50 6.00
BSP28 David Dahl .75 2.00
BSP29 Tyler Kolek .60 1.50
BSP30 Addison Russell 1.00 2.50
BSP31 Henry Owens .75 2.00
BSP32 Julio Urias 3.00 8.00
BSP33 Maikel Franco .75 2.00
BSP34 Blake Swihart .75 2.00
BSP35 Tyler Beede 1.00 2.50
BSP36 Trea Turner 2.00 5.00
BSP37 Erick Fedde .60 1.50
BSP38 Kohl Stewart .60 1.50
BSP39 Austin Meadows 1.50 4.00
BSP40 Kyle Schwarber 6.00 15.00
BSP41 Kyle Zimmer .60 1.50
BSP42 Max Pentecost .60 1.50
BSP43 Brandon Finnegan .60 1.50
BSP44 Javier Baez 2.50 6.00
BSP45 Noah Syndergaard .75 2.00
BSP46 Archie Bradley .60 1.50
BSP47 Dominic Smith .60 1.50
BSP48 Lucas Giolito 1.00 2.50
BSP49 Kyle Freeland 1.25 3.00
BSP50 Byron Buxton 3.00 8.00

2014 Bowman Sterling Prospects Blue Refractors

*BLUE REF: 1.2X TO 3X BASIC
STATED ODDS 1:68 HOBBY
STATED PRINT RUN 25 SER.#'d SETS

2014 Bowman Sterling Prospects Japan Fractors

*JAPAN REF: 1.2X TO 3X BASIC
RELEASED EXCLUSIVELY IN ASIA
STATED PRINT RUN 25 SER.#'d SETS

2014 Bowman Sterling Prospects Purple Refractors

*PURPLE REF: 1X TO 2.5X BASIC
STATED ODDS 1:34 HOBBY
STATED PRINT RUN 50 SER.#'d SETS

2014 Bowman Sterling Prospects Refractors

*REF: .6X TO 1.5X BASIC
STATED ODDS 1:9 HOBBY
STATED PRINT RUN 199 SER.#'d SETS

2014 Bowman Sterling Rookie Autographs

STATED ODDS 1:5 HOBBY
PRINTING PLATE ODDS 1:1065 HOBBY
PLATE PRINT RUN 1 SET PER COLOR
BLACK-CYAN-MAGENTA-YELLOW ISSUED
NO PLATE PRICING DUE TO SCARCITY
EXCHANGE DEADLINE 12/31/2017
BSRAAA Arismendy Alcantara 3.00 8.00
BSRAAH Andrew Heaney 3.00 8.00

BSRAASU Andrew Susac 4.00 10.00
BSRABH Billy Hamilton 4.00 10.00
BSRACB Cam Bedrosian 3.00 8.00
BSRACC C.J. Cron 3.00 8.00
BSRACO Chris Owings 3.00 8.00
BSRAGC Garin Cecchini 3.00 8.00
BSRAGP Gregory Polanco 5.00 12.00
BSRAGS George Springer 12.00 30.00
BSRAJAG Jesus Aguilar 8.00 20.00
BSRAJN Jimmy Nelson 3.00 8.00
BSRAMB Mookie Betts 100.00 250.00
BSRANC Nick Castellanos 10.00 25.00
BSRAOT Oscar Taveras 4.00 10.00
BSRARE Roenis Elias 3.00 8.00
BSRARO Rougned Odor 6.00 15.00
BSRATL Tommy La Stella 3.00 8.00
BSRAYS Yangervis Solarte 3.00 8.00
BSRAYV Yordano Ventura 4.00 10.00

2014 Bowman Sterling Rookie Autographs Blue Refractors

*BLUE REF: 1X TO 2.5X BASIC
STATED ODDS 1:170 HOBBY
STATED PRINT RUN 25 SER.#'d SETS
EXCHANGE DEADLINE 12/31/2017
BSRAJA Jose Abreu 100.00 250.00
BSRAJPA Joe Panik 20.00 50.00

2014 Bowman Sterling Rookie Autographs Green Refractors

*GREEN REF: .5X TO 1.2X BASIC
STATED ODDS 1:34 HOBBY
STATED PRINT RUN 125 SER.#'d SETS
EXCHANGE DEADLINE 12/31/2017
BSRAJPA Joe Panik 10.00 25.00

2014 Bowman Sterling Rookie Autographs Magenta Refractors

*MAGENTA REF: .6X TO 1.5X BASIC
STATED ODDS 1:43 HOBBY
STATED PRINT RUN 99 SER.#'d SETS
EXCHANGE DEADLINE 12/31/2017
BSRAJPA Joe Panik 12.00 30.00

2014 Bowman Sterling Rookie Autographs Orange Refractors

*ORANGE REF: .6X TO 1.5X BASIC
STATED ODDS 1:57 HOBBY
STATED PRINT RUN 75 SER.#'d SETS
EXCHANGE DEADLINE 12/31/2017
BSRAJA Jose Abreu 60.00 150.00
BSRAJPA Joe Panik 12.00 30.00

2014 Bowman Sterling Rookie Autographs Purple Refractors

*PURPLE REF: .75X TO 2X BASIC
STATED ODDS 1:65 HOBBY
STATED PRINT RUN 50 SER.#'d SETS
EXCHANGE DEADLINE 12/31/2017
BSRAJA Jose Abreu 75.00 200.00
BSRAJPA Joe Panik 15.00 40.00

2014 Bowman Sterling Rookie Autographs Refractors

*REF: .5X TO 1.2X BASIC
STATED ODDS 1:29 HOBBY
STATED PRINT RUN 150 SER.#'d SETS
EXCHANGE DEADLINE 12/31/2017
BSRAJPA Joe Panik 10.00 25.00

2014 Bowman Sterling Showcase Autographs

STATED ODDS 1:340 HOBBY
STATED PRINT RUN 25 SER.#'d SETS
EXCHANGE DEADLINE 12/31/2017
SASBB Byron Buxton 15.00 40.00
SASCC Carlos Correa 100.00 200.00
SASGP Gregory Polanco EXCH 25.00 60.00
SASJA Jose Abreu 40.00 100.00
SASJB Javier Baez 30.00 80.00
SASNG Nick Gordon 10.00 25.00
SASTK Tyler Kolek 10.00 25.00
SASYP Yasiel Puig 60.00 150.00

2018 Bowman Sterling Refractors

BOW.STATED ODDS 1:24 HOBBY
BOW.DFT.ODDS 1:12 HOBBY
BSAB Alec Bohm BD 2.00 5.00
BSAG Andres Gimenez .75 2.00
BSAH Adam Haseley .50 1.25
BSAJ Aaron Judge 1.25 3.00
BSAR Amed Rosario .40 1.00
BSBH Bryce Harper .75 2.00
BSBM Brendan McKay .50 1.25
BSBS Brady Singer BD 1.50 4.00
BSCC Carlos Correa .50 1.25
BSCF Clint Frazier .60 1.50
BSCM Casey Mize BD 2.50 6.00
BSEF Estevan Florial .50 1.25
BSEJ Eloy Jimenez 1.25 3.00
BSFM Francisco Mejia .40 1.00
BSFP Franklin Perez .40 1.00
BSGR Grayson Rodriguez BD .60 1.50
BSGT Gleyber Torres 3.00 8.00
BSHG Hunter Greene 1.00 2.50
BSHR Heliot Ramos .50 1.25
BSJI Jonathan India BD 2.00 5.00
BSJK Jarred Kelenic BD 15.00 40.00
BSJK Jeren Kendall .40 1.00
BSJM Jorge Mateo .30 .75
BSKB Kris Bryant .60 1.50
BSKH Keston Hiura .75 2.00
BSLR Luis Robert 10.00 25.00
BSMB Michel Baez .30 .75
BSMG MacKenzie Gore .60 1.50
BSMK Michael Kopech 1.25 3.00
BSMM Mickey Moniak .75 2.00
BSMT Mike Trout 2.50 6.00
BSNM Nick Madrigal BD 1.25 3.00
BSNP Nick Pratto .40 1.00
BSNW Nick Williams .40 1.00
BSOA Ozzie Albies 1.00 2.50
BSRA Ronald Acuna 10.00 25.00
BSRD Rafael Devers 1.00 2.50
BSRH Rhys Hoskins 1.25 3.00
BSRL Royce Lewis 1.25 3.00
BSRW Ryan Weathers BD .40 1.00
BSSO Shohei Ohtani 8.00 20.00
BSTC Triston Casas BD 4.00 10.00
BSTS Travis Swaggerty BD 1.00 2.50
BSVR Victor Robles .75 2.00
BSVGJ Vladimir Guerrero Jr. 3.00 8.00

2018 Bowman Sterling Atomic Refractors

*ATOMIC: 1.2X TO 3X BASIC
BOW.ODDS 1:823 HOBBY
BOW.DFT.ODDS 1:640 HOBBY
STATED PRINT RUN 150 SER.#'d SETS

2018 Bowman Sterling Orange Refractors

*ORANGE: 4X TO 10X BASIC
BOW.ODDS 1:2185 HOBBY
BOW.DFT.ODDS 1:2575 HOBBY
STATED PRINT RUN 25 SER.#'d SETS

2018 Bowman Sterling Autographs Refractors

BOW.ODDS 1:2791 HOBBY
BOW.DFT.ODDS 1:791 HOBBY
PRINT RUNS B/WN 15-99 COPIES PER
NO PRICING ON QTY 15
BOW.EXCH.DEADLINE 3/31/2020
BOW.CHR.EXCH. 8/31/2020
BOW.DFT.EXCH. 11/30/2020
BSAAB Alec Bohm/99 40.00 100.00
BSAAG Andres Gimenez/99 20.00 50.00
BSAAH Adam Haseley/99 8.00 20.00
BSAAR Amed Rosario/99 6.00 15.00
BSABM Brendan McKay/99 8.00 20.00
BSABS Brady Singer/99 15.00 40.00
BSACF Clint Frazier/99 10.00 25.00
BSACM Casey Mize/99 20.00 50.00
BSAEF Estevan Florial/99 15.00 40.00
BSAFP Franklin Perez/99 6.00 15.00
BSAGT Gleyber Torres/99 50.00 125.00
BSAHG Hunter Greene/99 20.00 50.00
BSAJI Jonathan India/99 25.00 60.00
BSAJK Jarred Kelenic/99
BSAJK Jeren Kendall/99 6.00 15.00
BSAKH Keston Hiura/99 15.00 40.00
BSALR Luis Robert/99 75.00 200.00
BSANM Nick Madrigal/99 20.00 50.00
BSANP Nick Pratto/99 6.00 15.00
BSARD Rafael Devers/99 15.00 40.00
BSARL Royce Lewis/99 20.00 50.00
BSARW Ryan Weathers/99 6.00 15.00
BSASO Shohei Ohtani/30 400.00 800.00
BSATC Triston Casas/99 60.00 150.00
BSATS Travis Swaggerty/99 20.00 50.00
BSAVR Victor Robles/99 20.00 50.00

2018 Bowman Sterling Autographs Orange Refractors

*ORANGE: .75X TO 2X BASIC
BOW.ODDS 1:2677 HOBBY
BOW.DFT.ODDS 1:2102 HOBBY
STATED PRINT RUN 25 SER.#'d SETS
BOW.EXCH.DEADLINE 3/31/2020
BOW.CHR.EXCH. 8/31/2020
BOW.DFT.EXCH. 11/30/2020
BSACM Casey Mize 100.00 250.00
BSAKB Kris Bryant 75.00 200.00
BSASO Shohei Ohtani EXCH 600.00 1000.00

2019 Bowman Sterling Die Cut Autographs

STATED ODDS 1:67 HOBBY
PRINT RUNS B/WN 15-50 COPIES PER
NO PRICING ON QTY 15
EXCHANGE DEADLINE 7/31/2021
*BLUE/25: 4X TO 1X p/r 30
*BLUE/25: .5X TO 1.2X p/r 40-99
SDCAAB Alec Bohm/40 40.00 100.00
SDCACK Carter Kieboom/75 8.00 20.00
SDCACM Casey Mize/30 30.00 80.00
SDCAEM Elehuris Montero/99 8.00 20.00
SDCAJA Jordyn Adams/99 8.00 20.00
SDCAJB Joey Bart/40 50.00 120.00
SDCAJI Jonathan India/50 20.00 50.00
SDCAJK Jarred Kelenic/55 20.00 50.00
SDCAJR Julio Rodriguez/75 60.00 150.00
SDCAJS Justus Sheffield/50 8.00 20.00
SDCALU Luis Urias/55 8.00 20.00
SDCAMA Miguel Amaya/99 8.00 20.00
SDCANM Nick Madrigal/40 20.00 50.00
SDCARH Ronaldo Hernandez/75 8.00 20.00
SDCARM Ronny Mauricio/99 20.00 50.00
SDCASM Seuly Matias/75 6.00 15.00
SDCAWF Wander Franco/65 75.00 200.00
SDCAJPM Julio Pablo Martinez/65 5.00 12.00
SDCAVGJ Vladimir Guerrero Jr./30 150.00 400.00
SDCAVMJ Victor Mesa Jr./75 12.00 30.00
SDCAVVM Victor Victor Mesa/65 15.00 40.00

2019 Bowman Sterling Dual Autographs Refractors

STATED ODDS 1:407 HOBBY
STATED PRINT RUN 25 SER.#'d SETS
EXCHANGE DEADLINE 7/31/2021
DRAFH Hernandez/Franco 200.00 500.00
DRAGJ Guerrero Jr./Jimenez 150.00 400.00
DRAGT Guerrero Jr./Tatis Jr. 400.00 1000.00
DRAKS Kikuchi/Sheffield 20.00 50.00
DRAMM Mesa Jr./Mesa 50.00 120.00
DRAMMA Maitan/Marsh 15.00 40.00
DRAMN Newton/Mauricio 100.00 250.00
DRAMP Mize/Perez 30.00 80.00
DRARF Florial/Robert 100.00 250.00
DRATG Tatis Jr./Gore 200.00 500.00

2019 Bowman Sterling Prospect Autographs

OVERALL AUTO ODDS 1:1 HOBBY
EXCHANGE DEADLINE 7/31/2021
BSPAAB Akil Baddoo 25.00 60.00
BSPAABO Alec Bohm 40.00 100.00
BSPAAK Andrew Knizner 4.00 10.00
BSPAAS Anthony Seigler 6.00 15.00
BSPABA Blaze Alexander 5.00 12.00
BSPABB Brock Burke 2.50 6.00
BSPABD Brock Deatherage 2.50 6.00
BSPABM Brandon Marsh 4.00 10.00
BSPABN Bo Naylor 2.50 6.00
BSPABS Brady Singer 8.00 20.00
BSPABSI Luken Baker 3.00 8.00
BSPABT Brice Turang 3.00 8.00
BSPACK Carter Kieboom 6.00 15.00
BSPACM Casey Mize 30.00 80.00
BSPACS Connor Scott 3.00 8.00
BSPACSA Cristian Santana 4.00 10.00
BSPACSP Chad Spanberger 2.50 6.00
BSPACW Cole Winn 2.50 6.00
BSPADK Dean Kremer 5.00 12.00
BSPADM Dustin May 10.00 25.00
BSPAEM Elehuris Montero 4.00 10.00
BSPAFN Freudis Nova 4.00 10.00
BSPAFP Franklin Perez 2.50 6.00
BSPAGR Grayson Rodriguez 5.00 12.00
BSPAIW Israel Wilson 3.00 8.00
BSPAJA Jordyn Adams 4.00 10.00
BSPAJB Joey Bart 15.00 40.00
BSPAJG Jordan Groshans 5.00 12.00
BSPAJH Jonathan Hernandez 2.50 6.00
BSPAJI Jonathan India 25.00 60.00
BSPAJPM Julio Pablo Martinez 2.50 6.00
BSPAJR Julio Rodriguez 50.00 120.00
BSPAJW Jackson Kowar 5.00 12.00
BSPAKC Kody Clemens 3.00 8.00
BSPAKM Kevin Maitan 3.00 8.00
BSPAKR Keibert Ruiz 12.00 30.00
BSPAMA Miguel Amaya 4.00 10.00
BSPAML Matthew Liberatore 8.00 20.00
BSPAMLU Marco Luciano 40.00 100.00
BSPAMM Matt Mercer 2.50 6.00
BSPANH Nico Hoerner 10.00 25.00
BSPANM Nick Madrigal 10.00 25.00
BSPANMA Noelvi Marte 20.00 50.00
BSPANS Nick Schnell 2.50 6.00
BSPAOM Orelvis Martinez 8.00 20.00
BSPARB Rylan Bannon 5.00 12.00
BSPARH Ronaldo Hernandez 2.50 6.00
BSPARM Ronny Mauricio 15.00 40.00
BSPARR Roberto Ramos 3.00 8.00
BSPASM Seuly Matias 3.00 8.00
BSPASN Sheldon Neuse 2.50 6.00
BSPATL Trevor Larnach 6.00 15.00
BSPATO Tirso Ornelas 2.50 6.00
BSPATS Travis Swaggerty 4.00 10.00
BSPAVF Vince Fernandez 3.00 8.00
BSPAVMJ Victor Mesa Jr. 5.00 12.00
BSPAVVM Victor Victor Mesa 5.00 12.00
BSPAWF Wander Franco EXCH 75.00 200.00

2019 Bowman Sterling Prospect Autographs Blue Refractors

*BLUE REF: 1.5X TO 4X BASIC
STATED ODDS 1:76 HOBBY
STATED PRINT RUN 25 SER.#'d SETS
EXCHANGE DEADLINE 7/31/2021
BSPAEM Elehuris Montero 25.00 60.00
BSPAJK Jarred Kelenic 50.00 120.00
BSPALG Logan Gilbert 20.00 50.00
BSPANM Nick Madrigal 50.00 120.00

2019 Bowman Sterling Prospect Autographs Gold Refractors

*GOLD REF: 1.2X TO 3X BASIC
STATED ODDS 1:38 HOBBY
STATED PRINT RUN 50 SER.#'d SETS
EXCHANGE DEADLINE 7/31/2021
BSPAEM Elehuris Montero 20.00 50.00
BSPAJK Jarred Kelenic 40.00 100.00
BSPALG Logan Gilbert 15.00 40.00
BSPANM Nick Madrigal 40.00 100.00

2019 Bowman Sterling Prospect Autographs Orange Refractors

*ORANGE REF: .75X TO 2X BASIC
STATED ODDS 1:26 HOBBY
STATED PRINT RUN 75 SER.#'d SETS
EXCHANGE DEADLINE 7/31/2021
BSPAJK Jarred Kelenic 25.00 60.00
BSPALG Logan Gilbert 10.00 25.00
BSPANM Nick Madrigal 25.00 60.00

2019 Bowman Sterling Prospect Autographs Refractors

*REF: .5X TO 1.2X BASIC
STATED ODDS 1:13 HOBBY
STATED PRINT RUN 150 SER.#'d SETS
EXCHANGE DEADLINE 7/31/2021
BSPALG Logan Gilbert 6.00 15.00
BSPANM Nick Madrigal 15.00 40.00

2019 Bowman Sterling Prospect Autographs Speckle Refractors

*SPECKLE REF: .6X TO 1.5X BASIC
STATED ODDS 1:20 HOBBY
STATED PRINT RUN 99 SER.#'d SETS
EXCHANGE DEADLINE 7/31/2021
BSPAJK Jarred Kelenic 20.00 50.00
BSPALG Logan Gilbert 8.00 20.00
BSPANM Nick Madrigal 20.00 50.00

2019 Bowman Sterling Prospect Autographs Wave Refractors

*WAVE REF: .5X TO 1.2X BASIC
STATED ODDS 1:16 HOBBY
STATED PRINT RUN 125 SER.#'d SETS
EXCHANGE DEADLINE 7/31/2021
BSPALG Logan Gilbert 6.00 15.00
BSPANM Nick Madrigal 15.00 40.00

2019 Bowman Sterling Prospects

PRINTING PLATE ODDS 1:260 HOBBY
PLATE PRINT RUN 1 SET PER COLOR
BLACK-CYAN-MAGENTA-YELLOW ISSUED
NO PLATE PRICING DUE TO SCARCITY
BPR1 Royce Lewis 1.25 3.00
BPR2 Nolan Jones 1.00 2.50
BPR3 Seth Beer 1.50 4.00
BPR4 Jarred Kelenic 3.00 8.00
BPR5 Triston McKenzie 2.00 5.00
BPR6 Jazz Chisholm 2.50 6.00
BPR7 MacKenzie Gore 1.25 3.00
BPR8 Jesus Luzardo 1.00 2.50
BPR9 Jesus Sanchez 1.00 2.50
BPR10 Ryan Mountcastle 3.00 8.00
BPR11 Luis Robert 5.00 12.00
BPR12 Alex Kirilloff 1.00 2.50
BPR13 Nick Madrigal 2.50 6.00
BPR14 Travis Swaggerty 1.00 2.50
BPR15 Adonis Medina 1.00 2.50
BPR16 Cristian Pache 1.50 4.00
BPR17 Ronaldo Hernandez .60 1.50
BPR18 Victor Mesa Jr. 1.25 3.00
BPR19 Hunter Greene 1.00 2.50
BPR20 Adrian Morejon .60 1.50
BPR21 Joey Bart 2.00 5.00
BPR22 Yordan Alvarez 3.00 8.00
BPR23 Yusniel Diaz 1.00 2.50
BPR24 Jonathan India 4.00 10.00
BPR25 Bo Bichette 3.00 8.00
BPR26 Mitch Keller .75 2.00
BPR27 Ian Anderson 2.00 5.00
BPR28 Brock Deatherage .60 1.50
BPR29 Dylan Cease 1.00 2.50
BPR30 Taylor Trammell 1.00 2.50
BPR31 Wander Franco 8.00 20.00
BPR32 Gavin Lux 2.50 6.00
BPR33 Nolan Gorman 2.00 5.00
BPR34 Casey Mize 1.50 4.00
BPR35 Seuly Matias .75 2.00
BPR36 Ke'Bryan Hayes 3.00 8.00
BPR37 Alec Bohm 4.00 10.00
BPR38 Estevan Florial 1.00 2.50
BPR39 Julio Pablo Martinez .60 1.50
BPR40 Sixto Sanchez 2.00 5.00
BPR41 Jo Adell 2.50 6.00
BPR42 Andres Gimenez 1.50 4.00
BPR43 Matthew Liberatore .60 1.50
BPR44 Dustin May 2.00 5.00
BPR45 Brendan McKay 1.00 2.50
BPR46 Keibert Ruiz 3.00 8.00
BPR47 Drew Waters 3.00 8.00
BPR48 Brady Singer 3.00 8.00
BPR49 Forrest Whitley 1.00 2.50
BPR50 Victor Victor Mesa 1.25 3.00

2019 Bowman Sterling Prospects Blue Refractors

*BLUE REF: 2X TO 5X BASIC
STATED ODDS 1:42 HOBBY
STATED PRINT RUN 25 SER.#'d SETS
BPR22 Yordan Alvarez 50.00 120.00
BPR25 Bo Bichette 25.00 60.00

2019 Bowman Sterling Prospects Gold Refractors

*GOLD REF: 1.2X TO 3X BASIC
STATED ODDS 1:21 HOBBY
STATED PRINT RUN 50 SER.#'d SETS
BPR22 Yordan Alvarez 30.00 80.00
BPR25 Bo Bichette 15.00 40.00

2019 Bowman Sterling Prospects Refractors

*REF: .6X TO 1.5X BASIC
STATED ODDS 1:6 HOBBY
STATED PRINT RUN 199 SER.#'d SETS
BPR22 Yordan Alvarez 12.00 30.00
BPR23 Yusniel Diaz 1.50 4.00
BPR25 Bo Bichette 8.00 20.00

2019 Bowman Sterling Prospects Speckle Refractors

*SPEC REF: .75X TO 2X BASIC
STATED ODDS 1:11 HOBBY
STATED PRINT RUN 99 SER.#'d SETS
BPR22 Yordan Alvarez 15.00 40.00
BPR25 Bo Bichette 10.00 25.00

2019 Bowman Sterling Retrospect

STATED ODDS 1:43 HOBBY
STATED PRINT RUN 99 SER.#'d SETS
*GOLD/50: .6X TO 1.5X BASIC
*BLUE/25: .75X TO 2X BASIC
SRAJ Aaron Judge 6.00 15.00
SRAN Aaron Nola 2.00 5.00
SRAR Anthony Rizzo 3.00 8.00
SRBH Bryce Harper 4.00 10.00
SRCY Christian Yelich 3.00 8.00
SRFF Freddie Freeman 3.00 8.00
SRFL Francisco Lindor 2.50 6.00
SRGS George Springer 2.00 5.00
SRJA Jose Altuve 2.00 5.00
SRJD Jacob deGrom 5.00 12.00
SRJR Jose Ramirez 2.00 5.00
SRJS Juan Soto 8.00 20.00
SRJV Joey Votto 2.50 6.00
SRKB Kris Bryant 3.00 8.00
SRLS Luis Severino 2.00 5.00
SRMA Miguel Andujar 2.50 6.00
SRMC Matt Chapman 2.50 6.00
SRMT Mike Trout 20.00 50.00
SRNS Noah Syndergaard 2.00 5.00
SROA Ozzie Albies 2.50 6.00
SRRAJ Ronald Acuna Jr. 12.00 30.00
SRRH Rhys Hoskins 3.00 8.00
SRSO Shohei Ohtani 4.00 10.00
SRSP Salvador Perez 2.00 5.00
SRYM Yadier Molina 3.00 8.00

2019 Bowman Sterling Retrospect Autographs

STATED ODDS 1:108 HOBBY
PRINT RUNS B/WN 15-50 COPIES PER
NO PRICING ON QTY 15
EXCHANGE DEADLINE 7/31/2021
*BLUE/25: .4X TO 1X p/r 25-35
*BLUE/25: .5X TO 1.2X p/r 45-50
SRAAJ Aaron Judge/25 75.00 200.00
SRAAN Aaron Nola/50 10.00 25.00
SRAAR Anthony Rizzo/45 20.00 50.00
SRACK Corey Kluber/50 8.00 20.00
SRACS Chris Sale/50 10.00 25.00
SRAFF Freddie Freeman/30 30.00 80.00
SRAGS George Springer/30 6.00 15.00
SRAJA Jose Altuve/30 20.00 50.00
SRAJR Jose Ramirez/50 10.00 25.00
SRAJS Juan Soto/35 50.00 120.00
SRAJV Joey Votto/45 15.00 40.00
SRAKB Kris Bryant/45 60.00 150.00
SRALS Luis Severino/35 12.00 30.00
SRAMA Miguel Andujar/30 12.00 30.00
SRANS Noah Syndergaard/30 12.00 30.00
SRARAJ Ronald Acuna Jr./25 125.00 300.00
SRARH Rhys Hoskins/35 15.00 40.00
SRASP Salvador Perez/35 12.00 30.00
SRAWM Whit Merrifield/50 10.00 25.00

2019 Bowman Sterling Rookie Autographs

STATED ODDS 1:36 HOBBY
EXCHANGE DEADLINE 7/31/2021
BSRABL Brandon Lowe 10.00 25.00
BSRABW Bryse Wilson 4.00 10.00
BSRACA Chance Adams 2.50 6.00
BSRACB Corbin Burnes 8.00 20.00
BSRACM Cedric Mullins 8.00 20.00
BSRADL Dawel Lugo 4.00 10.00
BSRAJS Justus Sheffield 4.00 10.00
BSRAKA Kolby Allard 4.00 10.00
BSRAKW Kyle Wright 4.00 10.00
BSRALU Luis Urias 4.00 10.00
BSRARB Ryan Borucki 2.50 6.00

2019 Bowman Sterling Rookie Autographs Blue Refractors

*BLUE REF: 1X TO 2.5X BASIC
STATED ODDS 1:215 HOBBY
STATED PRINT RUN 25 SER.#'d SETS
EXCHANGE DEADLINE 7/31/2021
BSRAMK Michael Kopech 20.00 50.00
BSRAPA Peter Alonso 200.00 500.00
BSRAVGJ Vladimir Guerrero Jr. 200.00 500.00

2019 Bowman Sterling Rookie Autographs Gold Refractors

*GOLD REF: .75X TO 2X BASIC
STATED ODDS 1:108 HOBBY
STATED PRINT RUN 50 SER.#'d SETS
EXCHANGE DEADLINE 7/31/2021
BSRAMK Michael Kopech 15.00 40.00
BSRAPA Peter Alonso 150.00 400.00
BSRAVGJ Vladimir Guerrero Jr. 75.00 200.00

2019 Bowman Sterling Rookie Autographs Orange Refractors

*ORANGE REF: .6X TO 1.5X BASIC
STATED ODDS 1:72 HOBBY
STATED PRINT RUN 75 SER.#'d SETS
EXCHANGE DEADLINE 7/31/2021
BSRAMK Michael Kopech 12.00 30.00
BSRAPA Peter Alonso 125.00 300.00
BSRAVGJ Vladimir Guerrero Jr. 60.00 150.00

2019 Bowman Sterling Rookie Autographs Refractors

*REF: .5X TO 1.2X BASIC
STATED ODDS 1:36 HOBBY
STATED PRINT RUN 150 SER.#'d SETS
EXCHANGE DEADLINE 7/31/2021
BSRAMK Michael Kopech 10.00 25.00

2019 Bowman Sterling Rookie Autographs Speckle Refractors

*SPECKLE REF: .5X TO 1.2X BASIC
STATED ODDS 1:55 HOBBY
STATED PRINT RUN 99 SER.#'d SETS
EXCHANGE DEADLINE 7/31/2021
BSRAMK Michael Kopech 10.00 25.00

2019 Bowman Sterling Rookie Autographs Wave Refractors

*WAVE REF: .5X TO 1.2X BASIC
STATED ODDS 1:43 HOBBY
STATED PRINT RUN 125 SER.#'d SETS
EXCHANGE DEADLINE 7/31/2021
BSRAMK Michael Kopech 10.00 25.00

2019 Bowman Sterling Rookies

PRINTING PLATE ODDS 1:260 HOBBY
PLATE PRINT RUN 1 SET PER COLOR
BLACK-CYAN-MAGENTA-YELLOW ISSUED
NO PLATE PRICING DUE TO SCARCITY
BSR51 Kyle Tucker 1.50 4.00
BSR52 Keston Hiura 2.00 5.00
BSR53 Enyel De Los Santos .60 1.50
BSR54 Jake Bauers 1.00 2.50
BSR55 Brandon Lowe 1.00 2.50
BSR56 Christin Stewart .75 2.00
BSR57 Willians Astudillo .60 1.50
BSR58 Brad Keller .60 1.50
BSR59 Ryan Borucki .60 1.50
BSR60 Kyle Wright 1.00 2.50
BSR61 Pete Alonso 6.00 15.00
BSR62 Rowdy Tellez 1.00 2.50
BSR63 Josh James .75 2.00
BSR64 Jonathan Loaisiga .75 2.00
BSR65 Jake Cave .75 2.00
BSR66 Chance Adams .60 1.50
BSR67 Cedric Mullins 1.25 3.00
BSR68 Ryan O'Hearn .60 1.50
BSR69 Austin Riley 3.00 8.00
BSR70 Eloy Jimenez 2.50 6.00
BSR71 Dawel Lugo 1.00 2.50
BSR72 Bryse Wilson .75 2.00
BSR73 Fernando Tatis Jr. 10.00 25.00
BSR74 Reese McGuire 1.00 2.50
BSR75 Justus Sheffield 1.00 2.50
BSR76 Kevin Newman 1.00 2.50
BSR77 Taylor Ward .60 1.50
BSR78 Brendan Rodgers 1.00 2.50
BSR79 Chris Shaw .60 1.50
BSR80 Heath Fillmyer .60 1.50
BSR81 Touki Toussaint .75 2.00
BSR82 Garrett Hampson 1.00 2.50
BSR83 Kolby Allard 1.00 2.50
BSR84 Corbin Burnes 5.00 12.00
BSR85 Luis Urias 1.00 2.50
BSR86 Ramon Laureano 1.25 3.00
BSR87 Steven Duggar .75 2.00
BSR88 Michael Kopech 2.00 5.00
BSR89 Vladimir Guerrero Jr. 4.00 10.00
BSR90 Cionel Perez .60 1.50
BSR91 Jeff McNeil 1.50 4.00
BSR92 Dean Deetz .60 1.50
BSR93 Dakota Hudson .75 2.00
BSR94 Nick Senzel 2.00 5.00
BSR95 Danny Jansen .60 1.50
BSR96 Sean Reid-Foley .60 1.50
BSR97 David Fletcher 2.00 5.00
BSR98 Kevin Kramer .75 2.00
BSR99 Carter Kieboom 1.00 2.50
BSR100 Yusei Kikuchi 1.00 2.50

2019 Bowman Sterling Rookies Blue Refractors

*BLUE REF: 2X TO 5X BASIC
STATED ODDS 1:42 HOBBY
STATED PRINT RUN 25 SER.#'d SETS
BSR61 Pete Alonso 50.00 120.00
BSR89 Vladimir Guerrero Jr. 50.00 210.00

2019 Bowman Sterling Rookies Gold Refractors

*GOLD REF: 1.2X TO 3X BASIC
STATED ODDS 1:21 HOBBY
STATED PRINT RUN 50 SER.#'d SETS
BSR61 Pete Alonso 30.00 80.00
BSR89 Vladimir Guerrero Jr. 30.00 80.00

2019 Bowman Sterling Rookies Refractors

*REF: .6X TO 1.5X BASIC
STATED ODDS 1:6 HOBBY
STATED PRINT RUN 199 SER.#'d SETS
BSR61 Pete Alonso 15.00 40.00
BSR89 Vladimir Guerrero Jr. 15.00 40.00

2019 Bowman Sterling Rookies Speckle Refractors

*SPEC REF: .75X TO 25X BASIC
STATED ODDS 1:11 HOBBY
STATED PRINT RUN 99 SER.#'d SETS
BSR61 Pete Alonso 20.00 50.00
BSR89 Vladimir Guerrero Jr. 20.00 50.00

2019 Bowman Sterling Triple Autographs Refractors

STATED ODDS 1:809 HOBBY
STATED PRINT RUN 25 SER.#'d SETS
EXCHANGE DEADLINE 7/31/2021
TRAGTJ Jimenez/Tatis Jr/Vladdy Jr 400.00 1000.00
TRAKKS Kikuchi/Sheffield/Kopech 40.00 100.00
TRAMBB Bart/Mize/Bohm 100.00 250.00
TRAMMP Perez/Manning/Mize 75.00 200.00
TRAMNA Alonso/Mauricio/Newton

2020 Bowman Sterling Rookies

BSR51 Bobby Bradley .60 1.50
BSR52 Jaylin Davis 1.00 2.50
BSR53 Abraham Toro .75 2.00
BSR54 Nick Solak 2.50 6.00
BSR55 Brusdar Graterol 1.00 2.50
BSR56 Bo Bichette 5.00 12.00
BSR57 Nico Hoerner 2.50 6.00
BSR58 A.J. Puk 1.00 2.50
BSR59 Jesus Luzardo 1.25 3.00
BSR60 Jordan Yamamoto .60 1.50
BSR61 James Karinchak 6.00 15.00
BSR62 Brendan McKay 1.00 2.50
BSR63 Tony Gonsolin 2.50 6.00
BSR64 Hunter Harvey 1.00 2.50
BSR65 Sean Murphy 1.00 2.50
BSR66 Sam Hilliard 1.00 2.50
BSR67 Isan Diaz 1.00 2.50
BSR68 Kwang-Hyun Kim 1.25 3.00
BSR69 Junior Fernandez .60 1.50
BSR70 Brock Burke .60 1.50
BSR71 Randy Arozarena 5.00 12.00
BSR72 Seth Brown .60 1.50
BSR73 Yu Chang 1.00 2.50
BSR74 Aaron Civale 1.25 3.00
BSR75 Shun Yamaguchi .75 2.00
BSR76 Sheldon Neuse .75 2.00
BSR77 Justin Dunn .75 2.00
BSR78 Travis Demeritte 1.00 2.50
BSR79 Trent Grisham 2.50 6.00
BSR80 Luis Robert 8.00 20.00
BSR81 Kyle Lewis 6.00 15.00
BSR82 Adbert Alzolay .75 2.00
BSR83 Gavin Lux 3.00 8.00
BSR84 Mauricio Dubon .75 2.00
BSR85 Shogo Akiyama 3.00 8.00
BSR86 Andres Munoz 1.00 2.50
BSR87 Dustin May 3.00 8.00
BSR88 Zack Collins .75 2.00
BSR89 Alex Young .60 1.50
BSR90 Adrian Morejon .60 1.50
BSR91 Zac Gallen 1.50 4.00
BSR92 Logan Allen .60 1.50
BSR93 Aristides Aquino 4.00 10.00
BSR94 Jake Rogers .60 1.50
BSR95 Yordan Alvarez 5.00 12.00
BSR96 Anthony Kay .60 1.50
BSR97 Michel Baez .60 1.50
BSR98 Dylan Cease 1.00 2.50
BSR99 Robel Garcia .60 1.50
BSR100 Jose Urquidy .75 2.00

2020 Bowman Sterling Rookies Blue Refractors

*BLUE REF: 2X TO 5X BASIC
STATED ODDS 1:XX HOBBY
STATED PRINT RUN 25 SER.#'d SETS
BSR56 Bo Bichette 50.00 120.00
BSR61 James Karinchak 60.00 150.00
BSR80 Luis Robert 75.00 200.00
BSR81 Kyle Lewis 40.00 100.00

2020 Bowman Sterling Rookies Gold Refractors

*GOLD REF: 1.2X TO 3X BASIC
STATED ODDS 1:XX HOBBY
STATED PRINT RUN 50 SER.#'d SETS
BSR56 Bo Bichette 30.00 80.00
BSR61 James Karinchak 40.00 100.00
BSR80 Luis Robert 50.00 120.00
BSR81 Kyle Lewis 25.00 60.00

2020 Bowman Sterling Rookies Magenta Refractors

*MAGENTA REF: 1X TO 2.5X BASIC
STATED ODDS 1:XX HOBBY
STATED PRINT RUN 75 SER.#'d SETS
BSR56 Bo Bichette 25.00 60.00
BSR61 James Karinchak 30.00 80.00
BSR80 Luis Robert 40.00 100.00
BSR81 Kyle Lewis 20.00 50.00

2020 Bowman Sterling Rookies Refractors

*REF: .6X TO 1.5X BASIC
STATED ODDS 1:XX HOBBY
STATED PRINT RUN 199 SER.#'d SETS
BSR56 Bo Bichette 15.00 40.00
BSR61 James Karinchak 20.00 50.00
BSR80 Luis Robert 25.00 60.00
BSR81 Kyle Lewis 10.00 25.00

2020 Bowman Sterling Rookies Speckle Refractors

*SPEC REF: .75X TO 2X BASIC
STATED ODDS 1:XX HOBBY
STATED PRINT RUN 99 SER.#'d SETS
BSR56 Bo Bichette 20.00 50.00
BSR61 James Karinchak 25.00 60.00
BSR80 Luis Robert 30.00 80.00
BSR81 Kyle Lewis 15.00 40.00

2020 Bowman Sterling Bowman Die Cut Autographs

STATED ODDS 1:XX HOBBY
PRINT RUNS B/WN 75-99 COPIES PER
EXCHANGE DEADLINE 7/31/22
BDCAAA Aristides Aquino/99 15.00 40.00
BDCAAR Adley Rutschman/75 30.00 80.00
BDCAAV Andrew Vaughn/99 50.00 120.00
BDCABM Brendan McKay 20.00
BDCAJJ Josh Jung/99 20.00 50.00
BDCAJL Jesus Luzardo/99 15.00 40.00
BDCAJR Jackson Rutledge/99 6.00 15.00
BDCALP Luis Patino/99 12.00 30.00
BDCANH Nico Hoerner/99 10.00 25.00
BDCANL Nick Lodolo/99 6.00 15.00
BDCARP Robert Puason/99 20.00 50.00
BDCASH Sam Huff/99 12.00 30.00
BDCASL Shea Langeliers/99 12.00 30.00
BDCATS Tarik Skubal/99 20.00 50.00
BDCAXE Xavier Edwards/99 15.00 40.00
BDCAYA Yordan Alvarez/75 60.00 150.00
BDCAAVO Anthony Volpe/99 20.00 50.00
BDCABBA Brett Baty/99 15.00 40.00
BDCABWJ Bobby Witt Jr./99 150.00 400.00
BDCAJJB JJ Bleday/75 15.00 40.00

2020 Bowman Sterling Bowman Die Cut Autographs Blue Refractors

*BLUE REF: .6X TO 1.5X BASIC
STATED ODDS 1:XX HOBBY
STATED PRINT RUN 25 SER.#'d SETS
EXCHANGE DEADLINE 7/31/22
BDCABM Brendan McKay 10.00 25.00
BDCAAVO Anthony Volpe 40.00 100.00
BDCABWJ Bobby Witt Jr. 400.00 1000.00

2020 Bowman Sterling Dual Autographs Refractors

STATED ODDS 1:XX HOBBY
STATED PRINT RUN 25 SER.#'d SETS
BDAAB B.Bichette/Y.Alvarez 125.00 300.00
BDABR H.Ramos/J.Bart 50.00 120.00
BDACD B.Dalbec/T.Casas 50.00 120.00
BDACG D.Carlson/N.Gorman 125.00 300.00
BDAGD D.Garcia/J.Dominguez 400.00 800.00
BDAFH W.Franco/R.Hernandez 75.00 200.00
BDAGA M.Gore/C.Abrams 100.00 250.00
BDALL T.Larnach/R.Lewis 50.00 120.00
BDALP A.Puk/J.Luzardo 25.00 60.00
BDAMG C.Mize/R.Greene 100.00 250.00
BDARM R.Mountcastle/A.Rutschman 100.00 250.00
BDARW E.White/J.Rodriguez
BDATR K.Robinson/A.Thomas 50.00 120.00
BDAVM N.Madrigal/A.Vaughn 75.00 200.00
BDAWS B.Singer/B.Witt Jr. 100.00 250.00

2020 Bowman Sterling Prospects

BPR1 Wander Franco 6.00 15.00
BPR2 Brandon Marsh 1.00 2.50
BPR3 Taylor Trammell 1.00 2.50
BPR4 Alex Kirilloff 1.25 3.00
BPR5 Ronny Mauricio 1.50 4.00
BPR6 Nolan Jones 1.00 2.50
BPR7 Luis Patino 1.00 2.50
BPR8 Royce Lewis 1.50 4.00
BPR9 Oneil Cruz .75 2.00
BPR10 Nick Lodolo 1.00 2.50
BPR11 Jazz Chisholm 2.50 6.00
BPR12 Jarred Kelenic 3.00 8.00
BPR13 Sixto Sanchez 2.00 5.00
BPR14 Josh Jung 1.50 4.00
BPR15 Jasson Dominguez 10.00 25.00
BPR16 Ke'Bryan Hayes 3.00 8.00
BPR17 Alek Thomas .75 2.00
BPR18 Julio Rodriguez 4.00 10.00
BPR19 Vidal Brujan 5.00 12.00
BPR20 Drew Waters 1.50 4.00
BPR21 MacKenzie Gore 1.25 3.00
BPR22 Andrew Vaughn 3.00 8.00
BPR23 Jeter Downs 2.50 6.00
BPR24 Alec Bohm 4.00 10.00
BPR25 Matt Manning .75 2.00
BPR26 CJ Abrams 2.00 5.00
BPR27 Kristian Robinson 2.00 5.00
BPR28 Matthew Liberatore .75 2.00
BPR29 Bobby Witt Jr. 5.00 12.00
BPR30 Cristian Pache 4.00 10.00
BPR31 Forrest Whitley 1.00 2.50
BPR32 Nolan Gorman 1.25 3.00
BPR33 Adley Rutschman 4.00 10.00
BPR34 Jo Adell 4.00 10.00
BPR35 Luis Campusano 3.00 8.00
BPR36 Dylan Carlson 2.50 6.00
BPR37 Nick Madrigal 2.50 6.00
BPR38 Ian Anderson 2.00 5.00
BPR39 Hunter Greene 1.00 2.50
BPR40 Marco Luciano 2.50 6.00
BPR41 Casey Mize 5.00 12.00
BPR42 Logan Gilbert .75 2.00
BPR43 JJ Bleday 2.00 5.00
BPR44 Tarik Skubal 3.00 8.00
BPR45 Spencer Howard 2.00 5.00
BPR46 Grayson Rodriguez 1.00 2.50
BPR47 Evan White 1.50 4.00
BPR48 Riley Greene 2.50 6.00
BPR49 Joey Bart 3.00 8.00
BPR50 Nate Pearson 4.00 10.00

2020 Bowman Sterling Prospects Blue Refractors

*BLUE REF: 2X TO 5X BASIC
STATED ODDS 1:XX HOBBY
STATED PRINT RUN 25 SER.#'d SETS
BPR1 Wander Franco 60.00 150.00
BPR5 Ronny Mauricio 12.00 30.00
BPR15 Jasson Dominguez 125.00 300.00
BPR18 Julio Rodriguez 30.00 80.00
BPR29 Bobby Witt Jr. 60.00 150.00
BPR30 Cristian Pache 30.00 80.00

2020 Bowman Sterling Prospects Gold Refractors

*GOLD REF: 1.2X TO 3X BASIC
STATED ODDS 1:XX HOBBY
STATED PRINT RUN 50 SER.#'d SETS
BPR1 Wander Franco 40.00 100.00
BPR5 Ronny Mauricio 8.00 20.00
BPR15 Jasson Dominguez 75.00 200.00
BPR18 Julio Rodriguez 20.00 50.00
BPR29 Bobby Witt Jr. 40.00 100.00
BPR30 Cristian Pache 20.00 50.00

2020 Bowman Sterling Prospects Magenta Refractors

*MAGENTA REF: 1X TO 2.5X BASIC
STATED ODDS 1:XX HOBBY
STATED PRINT RUN 75 SER.#'d SETS
BPR1 Wander Franco 25.00 60.00
BPR5 Ronny Mauricio 6.00 15.00
BPR15 Jasson Dominguez 40.00 100.00
BPR29 Bobby Witt Jr. 20.00 50.00
BPR30 Cristian Pache 15.00 40.00

2020 Bowman Sterling Prospects Refractors

*REF: .6X TO 1.5X BASIC
STATED ODDS 1:XX HOBBY
STATED PRINT RUN 199 SER.#'d SETS
BPR5 Ronny Mauricio 4.00 10.00
BPR15 Jasson Dominguez 40.00 100.00
BPR29 Bobby Witt Jr. 12.00 30.00
BPR30 Cristian Pache 10.00 25.00

2020 Bowman Sterling Prospects Speckle Refractors

*SPEC REF: .75X TO 2X BASIC
STATED ODDS 1:XX HOBBY
STATED PRINT RUN 99 SER.#'d SETS
BPR1 Wander Franco 20.00 50.00
BPR5 Ronny Mauricio 5.00 12.00
BPR15 Jasson Dominguez 50.00 120.00
BPR29 Bobby Witt Jr. 15.00 40.00
BPR30 Cristian Pache 12.00 30.00

2020 Bowman Sterling Prospect Autographs

STATED ODDS 1:XX HOBBY
EXCHANGE DEADLINE 7/31/22
BSPAAA Aaron Ashby 5.00 12.00
BSPAAM Alek Manoah 12.00 30.00
BSPAAP Andy Pages 6.00 15.00
BSPAAR Adley Rutschman 30.00 80.00
BSPAAV Anthony Volpe 10.00 25.00
BSPAAVA Andrew Vaughn 15.00 40.00
BSPABB Brett Baty 10.00 25.00
BSPABD Brennen Davis 25.00 60.00
BSPABM Brady McConnell 3.00 8.00
BSPABMA Brennan Malone 4.00 10.00
BSPABS Bryson Stott 6.00 15.00
BSPABSH Braden Shewmake 6.00 15.00
BSPABWJ Bobby Witt Jr. 100.00 250.00
BSPACC Corbin Carroll 10.00 25.00
BSPACS Canaan Smith 5.00 12.00
BSPADE Daniel Espino 3.00 8.00
BSPADJ Drey Jameson 2.50 6.00
BSPAGG Grant Gambrell 3.00 8.00
BSPAGHJ Glenallen Hill Jr. 4.00 10.00
BSPAGJ Greg Jones 3.00 8.00
BSPAGV Gus Varland 3.00 8.00
BSPAHB Hunter Bishop 8.00 20.00
BSPAJA Jacob Amaya 5.00 12.00
BSPAJC Joey Cantillo 2.50 6.00
BSPAJD Jasson Dominguez 150.00 400.00
BSPAJDU Jarren Duran 20.00 50.00
BSPAJJB JJ Bleday 12.00 30.00
BSPAJJG JJ Goss 2.50 6.00
BSPAJJU Josh Jung 12.00 30.00
BSPAJP Jeremy Pena 8.00 20.00
BSPAJR Jackson Rutledge 8.00 20.00
BSPAJRY Joe Ryan 3.00 8.00
BSPAJS Jake Sanford 4.00 10.00
BSPAKC Keoni Cavaco 5.00 12.00
BSPAKP Kyren Paris 8.00 20.00
BSPALD Logan Davidson 3.00 8.00
BSPALP Luis Patino 10.00 25.00
BSPAMB Michael Busch 6.00 15.00
BSPAML Matthew Lugo 4.00 10.00
BSPAMT Matthew Thompson 3.00 8.00
BSPAMTO Michael Toglia 2.50 6.00
BSPAMV Miguel Vargas 6.00 15.00
BSPAMW Matt Wallner 5.00 12.00
BSPANL Nick Lodolo 6.00 15.00
BSPAQP Quinn Priester 8.00 20.00
BSPARC Ruben Cardenas 3.00 8.00
BSPARG Riley Greene 12.00 30.00
BSPARH Rece Hinds 3.00 8.00
BSPARP Robert Puason 12.00 30.00
BSPASA Sherten Apostel 5.00 12.00
BSPASH Sam Huff 8.00 20.00
BSPASL Shea Langeliers 8.00 20.00
BSPASS Sammy Siani 5.00 12.00
BSPATS Tarik Skubal 5.00 12.00
BSPAWW Will Wilson 3.00 8.00
BSPAXE Xavier Edwards 6.00 15.00

2020 Bowman Sterling Prospect Autographs Blue Refractors

*BLUE REF: 1X TO 2.5X BASIC
STATED ODDS 1:XX HOBBY
STATED PRINT RUN 25 SER.#'d SETS
EXCHANGE DEADLINE 7/31/22
BSPAAVA Andrew Vaughn 75.00 200.00
BSPABWJ Bobby Witt Jr. 400.00 1000.00
BSPAMV Miguel Vargas 25.00 60.00
BSPARP Robert Puason 50.00 120.00
BSPASH Sam Huff 30.00 80.00

2020 Bowman Sterling Prospect Autographs Gold Refractors

*GOLD REF: .75X TO 2X BASIC
STATED ODDS 1:XX HOBBY
STATED PRINT RUN 50 SER.#'d SETS
EXCHANGE DEADLINE 7/31/22
BSPAAVA Andrew Vaughn 60.00 150.00
BSPABWJ Bobby Witt Jr. 300.00 800.00
BSPAMV Miguel Vargas 20.00 50.00
BSPARP Robert Puason 40.00 100.00
BSPASH Sam Huff 25.00 60.00

2020 Bowman Sterling Prospect Autographs Orange Refractors

*ORANGE REF: .6X TO 1.5X BASIC
STATED ODDS 1:XX HOBBY
STATED PRINT RUN 75 SER.#'d SETS
EXCHANGE DEADLINE 7/31/22
BSPAAVA Andrew Vaughn 50.00 120.00
BSPABWJ Bobby Witt Jr. 250.00 600.00
BSPAMV Miguel Vargas 15.00 40.00
BSPARP Robert Puason 30.00 80.00

2020 Bowman Sterling Prospect Autographs Refractors

*REF: .5X TO 1.2X BASIC
STATED ODDS 1:XX HOBBY
STATED PRINT RUN 150 SER.#'d SETS
EXCHANGE DEADLINE 7/31/22
BSPAAVA Andrew Vaughn 30.00 80.00
BSPABWJ Bobby Witt Jr. 150.00 400.00
BSPAMV Miguel Vargas 12.00 30.00

2020 Bowman Sterling Prospect Autographs Speckle Refractors

*SPEC REF: .5X TO 1.2X BASIC
STATED ODDS 1:XX HOBBY
STATED PRINT RUN 99 SER.#'d SETS
EXCHANGE DEADLINE 7/31/22
BSPAAVA Andrew Vaughn 40.00 100.00
BSPABWJ Bobby Witt Jr. 200.00 500.00
BSPAMV Miguel Vargas 12.00 30.00
BSPARP Robert Puason 25.00 60.00

2020 Bowman Sterling Prospect Autographs Wave Refractors

*WAVE REF: .5X TO 1.2X BASIC
STATED ODDS 1:XX HOBBY
STATED PRINT RUN 125 SER.#'d SETS
EXCHANGE DEADLINE 7/31/22
BSPAAVA Andrew Vaughn 30.00 80.00
BSPABWJ Bobby Witt Jr. 200.00 500.00
BSPAMV Miguel Vargas 12.00 30.00

2020 Bowman Sterling Rookie Autographs Blue Refractors

*BLUE REF: 1X TO 2.5X BASIC
STATED ODDS 1:XX HOBBY
STATED PRINT RUN 25 SER.#'d SETS
EXCHANGE DEADLINE 7/31/22
BSRADM Dustin May 60.00 150.00
BSRAYA Yordan Alvarez 75.00 200.00

2020 Bowman Sterling Rookie Autographs Gold Refractors

*GOLD REF: .75X TO 2X BASIC
STATED ODDS 1:XX HOBBY
STATED PRINT RUN 50 SER.#'d SETS
EXCHANGE DEADLINE 7/31/22
BSRADM Dustin May 50.00 120.00
BSRAYA Yordan Alvarez 60.00 150.00

2020 Bowman Sterling Rookie Autographs Orange Refractors

*ORANGE REF: .6X TO 1.5X BASIC
STATED ODDS 1:XX HOBBY
STATED PRINT RUN 75 SER.#'d SETS
EXCHANGE DEADLINE 7/31/22
BSRADM Dustin May 40.00 100.00

2020 Bowman Sterling Rookie Autographs Refractors

*REF: .5X TO 1.2X BASIC
STATED ODDS 1:XX HOBBY
STATED PRINT RUN 150 SER.#'d SETS
EXCHANGE DEADLINE 7/31/22

2020 Bowman Sterling Rookie Autographs Speckle Refractors

*SPEC REF: .5X TO 1.2X BASIC
STATED ODDS 1:XX HOBBY
STATED PRINT RUN 99 SER.#'d SETS
EXCHANGE DEADLINE 7/31/22
BSRADM Dustin May 25.00 60.00

2020 Bowman Sterling Rookie Autographs Wave Refractors

*WAVE REF: .5X TO 1.2X BASIC
STATED ODDS 1:XX HOBBY
STATED PRINT RUN 125 SER.#'d SETS
EXCHANGE DEADLINE 7/31/22
BSRADM Dustin May 25.00 60.00

2020 Bowman Sterling Sterling First Signs

STATED ODDS 1:XX HOBBY
STATED PRINT RUN 99 SER.#'d SETS
SFSAJ Aaron Judge 6.00 15.00
SFSAR Austin Riley 3.00 8.00
SFSBB Bo Bichette 15.00 40.00
SFSBH Bryce Harper 4.00 10.00
SFSCB Cavan Biggio 3.00 8.00
SFSCK Clayton Kershaw 4.00 10.00
SFSCY Christian Yelich 3.00 8.00
SFSEJ Eloy Jimenez 5.00 12.00
SFSFL Francisco Lindor 2.50 6.00
SFSGS George Springer 2.00 5.00
SFSGT Gleyber Torres 5.00 12.00
SFSJA Jose Altuve 2.00 5.00
SFSKB Kris Bryant 3.00 8.00
SFSKH Keston Hiura 3.00 8.00
SFSMT Mike Trout 25.00 60.00
SFSNA Nolan Arenado 4.00 10.00
SFSOA Ozzie Albies 2.50 6.00
SFSPA Pete Alonso 6.00 15.00
SFSPD Paul DeJong 2.50 6.00
SFSRH Rhys Hoskins 3.00 8.00
SFSXB Xander Bogaerts 2.50 6.00
SFSARI Anthony Rizzo 3.00 8.00
SFSFTJ Fernando Tatis Jr. 20.00 50.00
SFSRAJ Ronald Acuna Jr. 10.00 25.00
SFSVGJ Vladimir Guerrero Jr. 4.00 10.00

2020 Bowman Sterling Sterling First Signs Blue Refractors

*BLUE REF: .8X TO 2X BASIC
STATED ODDS 1:XX HOBBY
STATED PRINT RUN 25 SER.#'d SETS
SFSBB Bo Bichette 50.00 120.00
SFSMT Mike Trout 75.00 200.00

2020 Bowman Sterling Sterling First Signs Gold Refractors

*GOLD REF: .6X TO 1.5X BASIC
STATED ODDS 1:XX HOBBY
STATED PRINT RUN 50 SER.#'d SETS
SFSBB Bo Bichette 40.00 100.00
SFSMT Mike Trout 50.00 120.00

2020 Bowman Sterling Sterling First Signs Autographs

STATED ODDS 1:XX HOBBY
PRINT RUNS B/WN 30-50 COPIES PER
EXCHANGE DEADLINE 7/31/22
SFSABH Bryce Harper
SFSAEJ Eloy Jimenez 30.00 80.00
SFSAGT Gleyber Torres 40.00 100.00
SFSAJA Jose Altuve 12.00 30.00
SFSAMT Mike Trout
SFSARH Rhys Hoskins 20.00 50.00
SFSAXB Xander Bogaerts 20.00 50.00
SFSARAJ Ronald Acuna Jr. 125.00 300.00

2020 Bowman Sterling Sterling First Signs Autographs Blue Refractors

*BLUE REF: .5X TO 1.2X BASIC
STATED ODDS 1:XX HOBBY
STATED PRINT RUN 25 SER.#'d SETS
EXCHANGE DEADLINE 7/31/22
SFSABH Bryce Harper 125.00 300.00
SFSAMT Mike Trout 500.00 1000.00

2020 Bowman Sterling Triple Autographs Refractors

STATED ODDS 1:XX HOBBY
STATED PRINT RUN 25 SER.#'d SETS
BTACGM Gorman/Carlson/Montero 150.00 400.00
BTADRG Downs/Ruiz/Gray 80.00 200.00
BTAFMH Franco/Hernandez/McKay 150.00 400.00
BTAGIL India/Lodolo/Greene 60.00 150.00
BTAKRW Kelenic/Rodriguez/White 100.00 250.00
BTALPM Murphy/Puk/Luzardo 30.00 80.00
BTAMMG Manning/Greene/Mize 150.00 400.00
BTARRM Rutschman/Rodriguez
Mountcastle 100.00 250.00
BTATRV Robinson/Thomas/Varsho 100.00 250.00
BTAWSK Kowar/Witt Jr./Singer 125.00 300.00

2017 Bowman Topps Holiday

THAB Andrew Benintendi .75 2.00
THABR Alex Bregman 1.25 3.00
THAJ Aaron Judge 3.00 8.00
THAM Austin Meadows .60 1.50
THAR Amed Rosario .40 1.00
THARE Alex Reyes .30 .75
THARI Anthony Rizzo .50 1.25
THAS Andrew Sopko .25 .60
THAV Alex Verdugo .40 1.00
THAY Andy Yerzy .25 .60
THBB Bo Bichette 1.00 2.50
THBD Bobby Dalbec 1.50 4.00
THBH Brent Honeywell .30 .75
THBHA Bryce Harper .60 1.50
THBR Bryan Reynolds .40 1.00
THBRO Brendan Rodgers .30 .75
THBRU Blake Rutherford .40 1.00
THBZ Bradley Zimmer .30 .75
THCA Christian Arroyo .40 1.00
THCB Cody Bellinger 4.00 10.00
THCBL Charlie Blackmon .40 1.00
THCC Carlos Correa .40 1.00
THCF Clint Frazier .50 1.25
THCK Clayton Kershaw .60 1.50
THCS Christin Stewart .30 .75
THCSA Chris Sale .40 1.00
THCSE Corey Seager .40 1.00
THCW Colton Welker .25 .60
THDC Dylan Cease .40 1.00
THDD David Dahl .30 .75
THDS Dansby Swanson .60 1.50
THEJ Eloy Jimenez 1.00 2.50
THFB Franklin Barreto .25 .60
THFL Francisco Lindor .40 1.00
THFM Francisco Mejia .40 1.00
THFR Francisco Rios .25 .60
THFW Forrest Whitley .60 1.50
THGL Gavin Lux 1.00 2.50
THGS Giancarlo Stanton .40 1.00
THGT Gleyber Torres 4.00 10.00
THHR Hunter Renfroe .30 .75
THIH Ian Happ .50 1.25
THJA Jorge Alfaro .30 .75
THJAB Jose Abreu .40 1.00
THJAL Jose Altuve .30 .75
THJC Jake Cave .25 .60
THJG Jay Groome .50 1.25
THJL Jesus Luzardo .40 1.00
THJS Justus Sheffield .40 1.00
THJSO Juan Soto 6.00 15.00
THKB Kris Bryant .50 1.25
THKH Kyle Holder .30 .75
THKM Kevin Maitan .40 1.00
THKT Kyle Tucker .60 1.50
THLA Lazarito Armenteros .50 1.25
THLB Lewis Brinson .40 1.00
THLE Lucas Erceg .25 .60
THLT Leody Taveras 1.00 2.50
THMB Mookie Betts .75 2.00
THMC Michael Conforto .30 .75
THMCA Miguel Cabrera .40 1.00
THMF Michael Fulmer .25 .60
THMG Mike Gerber .25 .60
THMK Mitch Keller .30 .75
THMKO Michael Kopech .75 2.00
THMM Mickey Moniak .50 1.25
THMM Manny Machado .40 1.00
THMS Max Scherzer .40 1.00
THMT Mike Trout 2.00 5.00
THNA Nolan Arenado .60 1.50
THNS Nick Senzel .75 2.00
THNSY Noah Syndergaard .30 .75
THOA Ozzie Albies 1.00 2.50
THPC P.J. Conlon .25 .60
THPG Paul Goldschmidt .40 1.00
THPW Patrick Weigel .25 .60
THRA Ronald Acuna 12.00 30.00
THRD Rafael Devers .50 1.25
THRH Rhys Hoskins 1.00 2.50
THRHE Ryon Healy .30 .75
THRM Ryan Mountcastle 1.25 3.00
THRT Raimel Tapia .30 .75
THR Rudolph .20 .50
THSC Santa Claus .20 .50
THSK Scott Kingery .40 1.00
THSN Sean Newcomb .30 .75
THS Snowman .20 .50
THTE Thairo Estrada .40 1.00
THTL Tim Lynch .30 .75
THTM Triston McKenzie .75 2.00
THTMA Trey Mancini .50 1.25
THTS Tyler Stephenson .60 1.50
THTT Taylor Trammell 1.50 4.00
THVGJ Vladimir Guerrero Jr. 3.00 8.00
THVR Victor Robles .60 1.50
THWB Wuilmer Becerra .25 .60
THWBU Walker Buehler .60 .1.50
THWC Willie Calhoun .40 1.00
THYG Yulieski Gurriel .40 1.00
THYM Yoan Moncada .75 2.00

2017 Bowman Topps Holiday Ugly Sweater Green

*UGLY GREEN: 2.5X TO 6X
STATED PRINT RUN 99 SER.#'d SETS

2017 Bowman Topps Holiday Autographs

THAR Amed Rosario/85 6.00 15.00
THARI Anthony Rizzo
THAS Andrew Sopko/35 4.00 10.00
THAY Andy Yerzy/99 4.00 10.00
THBD Bobby Dalbec/99 25.00 60.00
THBH Brent Honeywell/5
THBR Bryan Reynolds/99 6.00 15.00
THCBL Charlie Blackmon/85 6.00 15.00
THCS Christin Stewart/99 5.00 12.00
THDD David Dahl/99 5.00 12.00
THFR Francisco Rios/35 4.00 10.00
THGL Gavin Lux/99 15.00 40.00
THGT Gleyber Torres/65 60.00 150.00
THIH Ian Happ/50 8.00 20.00
THJA Jorge Alfaro/99 5.00 12.00
THJC Jake Cave/99 4.00 10.00
THJG Jay Groome/99 8.00 20.00
THJL Jesus Luzardo/99 6.00 15.00
THJS Justus Sheffield/99 6.00 15.00
THKH Kyle Holder/99 5.00 12.00
THKM Kevin Maitan/99 6.00 15.00
THLE Lucas Erceg/99 4.00 10.00
THMC Michael Conforto/5
THMF Michael Fulmer/50 4.00 10.00
THMG Mike Gerber/99 4.00 10.00
THMK Mitch Keller/99 5.00 12.00
THMM Manny Machado/10
THPW Patrick Weigel/99 4.00 10.00
THRA Ronald Acuna
THRD Rafael Devers/99 8.00 20.00
THRM Ryan Mountcastle/99 20.00 50.00
THRT Raimel Tapia/65 5.00 12.00
THSK Scott Kingery/40 6.00 15.00
THTE Thairo Estrada/99 30.00 80.00
THTL Tim Lynch/99 5.00 12.00
THTM Triston McKenzie/99 12.00 30.00
THTMA Trey Mancini/50 8.00 20.00
THTS Tyler Stephenson/80 10.00 25.00
THTT Taylor Trammell/82 12.00 30.00
THWB Wuilmer Becerra/99 4.00 10.00
THWBU Walker Buehler/10
THYG Yulieski Gurriel

2020 Bowman Transcendent

ONE COMPLETE SET PER BOX
STATED PRINT RUN 100 SER.#'d SETS
1 Wander Franco 30.00 80.00
2 Luis Robert 150.00 400.00
3 Justin Dunn 5.00 12.00
4 Cristian Pache 15.00 40.00
5 Matt Manning 5.00 12.00
6 Bobby Bradley 6.00 15.00
7 Casey Mize 12.00 30.00
8 Yoshi Tsutsugo 8.00 20.00
9 Dylan Carlson 8.00 20.00
10 Sixto Sanchez 8.00 20.00
11 JJ Bleday 30.00 80.00
12 Aaron Civale 8.00 20.00
13 Alec Bohm 25.00 60.00
14 Jasson Dominguez 150.00 400.00
15 Trent Grisham 15.00 40.00
16 Dustin May 10.00 25.00
17 Nick Madrigal 12.00 30.00
18 Royce Lewis 6.00 15.00
19 Jo Adell 15.00 40.00
20 A.J. Puk 6.00 15.00
21 Nico Hoerner 15.00 40.00
22 MacKenzie Gore 10.00 25.00
23 Sean Murphy 12.00 30.00
24 Yordan Alvarez 60.00 150.00
25 Jordan Yamamoto 4.00 10.00
26 Julio Rodriguez 50.00 120.00
27 Adley Rutschman 15.00 40.00
28 Nate Pearson 12.00 30.00
29 Michel Baez 4.00 10.00
30 CJ Abrams 12.00 30.00
31 Shun Yamaguchi 5.00 12.00
32 Nolan Gorman 8.00 20.00
33 Anthony Kay 4.00 10.00
34 Jarred Kelenic 20.00 50.00
35 Brusdar Graterol 6.00 15.00
36 Bo Bichette 75.00 200.00
37 Forrest Whitley 8.00 20.00
38 Marco Luciano 20.00 50.00
39 Bobby Witt Jr. 60.00 150.00
40 Dylan Cease 6.00 15.00
41 Jesus Luzardo 8.00 20.00
42 Shogo Akiyama 6.00 15.00
43 Brendan McKay 12.00 30.00
44 Andrew Vaughn 30.00 80.00
45 Aristides Aquino 10.00 25.00
46 Joey Bart 12.00 30.00
47 Adbert Alzolay 5.00 12.00
48 Kyle Lewis 75.00 200.00
49 Gavin Lux 20.00 50.00
50 Riley Greene 20.00 50.00

2020 Bowman Transcendent Autographs

OVERALL TWENTY EIGHT AUTOS PER BOX
STATED PRINT RUN 25 SER.#'d SETS
*VARIATION/25: .4X TO 1X BASIC
*BLUE/10: .5X TO 1.2X BASIC
*VAR BLUE/10: .5X TO 1.2X BASIC
BTAAR Adley Rutschman 80.00 200.00
BTAAT Alek Thomas 25.00 60.00
BTAAV Andrew Vaughn 50.00 125.00
BTABB Brett Baty 40.00 100.00
BTABBI Bo Bichette 150.00 400.00
BTABL Bayron Lora 100.00 250.00
BTABWJ Bobby Witt Jr. 150.00 400.00
BTACA CJ Abrams 40.00 100.00
BTACM Casey Mize 40.00 100.00
BTACP Cristian Pache 60.00 150.00
BTADG Deivi Garcia 100.00 250.00
BTADL Daniel Lynch 12.00 30.00
BTAEW Evan White 30.00 80.00
BTAGL Gavin Lux 60.00 150.00
BTAHB Hunter Bishop 50.00 120.00
BTAJA Jo Adell 75.00 200.00
BTAJB Joey Bart 40.00 100.00
BTAJD Jasson Dominguez 600.00 1500.00
BTAJG Jordan Groshans 25.00 60.00
BTAJJ Josh Jung 30.00 80.00
BTAJJB JJ Bleday 40.00 100.00
BTAJK Jarred Kelenic 75.00 200.00
BTAJR Julio Rodriguez 80.00 200.00
BTAKH Ke'Bryan Hayes 100.00 250.00
BTAKL Aristides Aquino 30.00 80.00
BTALR Luis Robert 200.00 500.00
BTANG Nolan Gorman 25.00 60.00
BTANH Nico Hoerner 50.00 125.00
BTANL Nick Lodolo 20.00 50.00
BTANP Nate Pearson 25.00 60.00
BTARG Riley Greene 50.00 125.00
BTASH Sam Huff 30.00 80.00
BTATS Tarik Skubal 25.00 60.00
BTATT Taylor Trammell 30.00 80.00
BTAWF Wander Franco 125.00 300.00
BTAYA Yordan Alvarez 75.00 200.00

2011 Bowman Under Armour All-American Autographs

13 BOW.ODDS 1:2059 HOBBY
14 BOW.ODDS 1:1150 HOBBY
15 BOW.ODDS 1:1278 HOBBY
PRINT RUNS B/WN 225-235 COPIES PER
BB Byron Buxton/233 100.00 250.00
CK Carson Kelly/225 6.00 15.00
GC Gavin Cecchini/235 6.00 15.00
JB Jose Berrios/225 20.00 50.00
JC Jamie Callahan/225 6.00 15.00
JV Jesmuel Valentin/225 10.00 25.00
LB Lewis Brinson/235 15.00 40.00
MO Matt Olsen/225 6.00 15.00
NT Nick Travieso/225 10.00 25.00
RR Ryan Ripken/200 15.00 40.00
ST Stryker Trahan/235 10.00 25.00
TG Tyler Gonzales/225 8.00 20.00
TH Ty Hensley/235 10.00 25.00

2012 Bowman Under Armour All-American Autographs

13 BOW.DFT.ODDS 1:619 HOBBY
14 BOW.ODDS 1:1150 HOBBY
14 BOW.CHR.ODDS 1:1020 HOBBY
PRINT RUNS B/WN 199-235 COPIES PER
AJ Alex Jackson/199 10.00 25.00
AM Austin Meadows/220 25.00 60.00
BM Billy McKinney/220 5.00 12.00
CF Clint Frazier/220 30.00 80.00
DS Dominic Smith/220 20.00 50.00
GG Hunter Harvey/235 10.00 25.00
JD Jon Denney/225 4.00 10.00
JP John Paul Crawford/220 15.00 40.00
JW Justin Williams/220 8.00 10.00
MM Matt McPhearson/235 6.00 15.00
NC Nick Ciuffo #220 10.00 25.00
OM Oscar Mercado/220 12.00 30.00
TB Trey Ball/220 4.00 10.00

2013 Bowman Under Armour All-American Autographs

14 BOW.CHR.ODDS 1:1020 HOBBY
15 BOW.ODDS 1:1278 HOBBY
'17 BOW.CHR.ODDS 1:1562 HOBBY
PRINT RUNS B/WN 199-225 COPIES PER
'17 BOW.CHR.EXCH 8/31/2019
1 Dylan Cease/199 6.00 15.00
5 Michael Gettys/200 4.00 10.00
6 Nick Gordon/199 20.00 50.00
7 Foster Griffin/199 4.00 10.00
8 Grant Holmes/225 4.00 10.00
15 Carson Sands/200 4.00 10.00
16 Touki Toussaint/200 8.00 20.00
17 Chase Vallot/200 4.00 10.00
18 Alex Verdugo/200 20.00 50.00

2014 Bowman Under Armour All-American Autographs

15 BOW.CHR.ODDS 1:1440 HOBBY
15 BOW.ODDS 1:2931 HOBBY
18 BOW.DFT,ODDS 1:942 HOBBY
19 BOW.CHR.ODDS 1:1929 HOBBY
PRINT RUNS BW/N 99-225 COPIES PER
17 BOW.EXCH 3/31/2019
18 BOW.DFT EXCH 11/30/2020
19 BOW.CHR EXCH 8/31/2021
UAA2 Chris Betts/225 6.00 15.00
UAA4 Dazmon Cameron/225 10.00 25.00
UAA9 Ke'Bryan Hayes/225 50.00 120.00
UAN2 Kody Clemens/199 12.00 30.00
UAA10 Juan Hillman/199 6.00 15.00
UAA13 Brendan Rodgers/99 25.00 60.00
UAA13 Brendan Rodgers/199 20.00 50.00
UAA16 Kyle Tucker/225 12.00 30.00
UAA17 Seth Beer/199 25.00 60.00
UAA21 Demi Orimoloye/225 12.00 30.00
UAN1 Beau Burrows/199 8.00 20.00
UAN1 Beau Burrows/99 8.00 20.00
UAN13 Austin Riley/225 60.00 150.00
UAN18 Starling Heredia/225 10.00 25.00
UAN20 Nick Plumer/225 15.00 40.00

2015 Bowman Under Armour All-American Autographs

'16 BOW.DRAFT ODDS 1:472 HOBBY
'17 BOW.ODDS 1:2931 HOBBY
'17 BOW.CHR.ODDS 1:1562 HOBBY
'17 BOW.DRAFT ODDS 1:894 HOBBY
PRINT RUNS B/WN 199-225 COPIES PER
'16 BOW.DRAFT EXCH 11/30/2018
'17 BOW.EXCH 3/31/2019
'17 BOW.CHR.EXCH 8/31/2019
'17 BOW.DRAFT EXCH 11/30/2019
UAA4 Will Benson/225 20.00 50.00
UAA11 Thomas Jones/199 6.00 15.00
UAA13 Carter Kieboom/225 25.00 60.00
UAA13 Carter Kieboom/199 25.00 60.00
UAA17 Alex Speas/225 8.00 20.00
UAA18 Colton Welker/199 15.00 40.00
UAN3 Bo Bichette/199 40.00 100.00
UAN10 Jesus Luzardo/225 8.00 20.00
UAN13 Delvin Perez/225 25.00 60.00
UAN14 Riley Pint/225 20.00 50.00
UAN18 Forrest Whitley/199 20.00 50.00
UAN19 Andy Yerzy/225 8.00 20.00
UAN20 Taylor Trammell/199 15.00 40.00

2016 Bowman Under Armour All-American Autographs

'17 BOW.DRAFT ODDS 1:894 HOBBY
'18 BOW.DRAFT ODDS 1:942 HOBBY
'19 BOW.ODDS 1:4146 HOBBY
STATED PRINT RUN 199 SER.#'d SETS
'17 BOW.DRAFT EXCH 11/30/2019
'18 BOW.DRAFT EXCH 11/30/2020
'19 BOW.EXCH 3/31/20201
UAA2 Nick Allen/199 6.00 15.00
UAA3 Triston Casas/199 15.00 40.00
UAA4 Hunter Greene/199 25.00 60.00
UAA7 Quentin Holmes/199 10.00 25.00
UAA9 Royce Lewis/199 40.00 100.00
UAN1 Jordon Adell/199 40.00 100.00
UAN11 Joe Gray/199 10.00 25.00
UAN14 Nick Pratto/199 10.00 25.00
UAN16 Heliot Ramos/199 30.00 80.00

2017 Bowman Under Armour All-American Autographs

'18 BOW.DRAFT ODDS 1:942 HOBBY
'19 BOW.ODDS 1:4146 HOBBY
19 BOW.CHR.ODDS 1:1929 HOBBY
STATED PRINT RUN 199 SER.#'d SETS
'18 BOW.DRAFT EXCH 11/30/2020
'19 BOW.EXCH 3/31/20201
19 BOW.CHR EXCH 8/31/2021
UAA1 Jordyn Adams/199 15.00 40.00
UAA2 Blaze Alexander/199 10.00 25.00
UAA8 Nolan Gorman/199 60.00 150.00
UAA9 Ethan Hankins/199 8.00 20.00
UAN8 Ryan Weathers/199 3.00 8.00
UAN9 Jordan Groshans/199 10.00 25.00
UAA12 Jarred Kelenic/199 75.00 200.00
UAA13 Matthew Liberatore/199 8.00 20.00
UAA18 Alek Thomas/199 6.00 15.00
UAN12 Bo Naylor/199 10.00 25.00
UAN16 Mike Siani/199 4.00 10.00

2018 Bowman Under Armour All-American Autographs

'18 BOW.DRAFT ODDS 1:963 HOBBY
'20 BOW. ODDS 1:4327 HOBBY
STATED PRINT RUN 199 SER.#'d SETS
'19 BOW.DFT EXCH 11/30/20201
'20 BOW.EXCH 3/31/2022
UAA4 Tyler Callihan/199 10.00 25.00
UAA5 Corbin Carroll/199 15.00 40.00
UAN1 CJ Abrams/199 40.00 100.00
UAN5 Daniel Espino 12.00 30.00
Issued in 20 Bowman
UAN8 Riley Greene/199 20.00 50.00
UAA10 Gunnar Henderson 12.00 30.00
Issued in 20 Bowman
UAA20 Bobby Witt Jr 100.00 250.00
Issued in 20 Bowman
UAN10 Rece Hinds/199 8.00 20.00
UAN14 Quinn Priester 8.00 20.00
Issued in 20 Bowman
UAN16 Erik Rivera 12.00 30.00
Issued in 20 Bowman

1994 Bowman's Best

This 200-card standard-size set (produced by Topps) consists of 90 veteran stars, 90 rookies and prospects and 20 Mirror Image cards. The veteran cards have red fronts and are designated 1R-90R. The rookies and prospects cards have blue fronts and are designated 1B-90B. The Mirror Image cards feature a veteran star and a prospect matched by position in a horizontal design. These cards are numbered 91-110. Subsets featured are Super Vet (1R-6R), Super Rookie (82R-90R), and Blue Chip (1B-11B). Rookie Cards include Edgardo Alfonzo, Tony Clark, Brad Fullmer, Chan Ho Park, Jorge Posada and Edgar Renteria.

COMPLETE SET (200) 15.00 40.00
B1 Chipper Jones .50 1.25
B2 Derek Jeter 2.00 5.00
B3 Bill Pulsipher .20 .50
B4 James Baldwin .08 .25
B5 Brooks Kieschnick RC .20 .50
B6 Justin Thompson .08 .25
B7 Midre Cummings .08 .25
B8 Joey Hamilton .08 .25
B9 Pokey Reese .08 .25
B10 Brian Barber .08 .25
B11 John Burke .08 .25
B12 DeShawn Warren .08 .25
B13 Edgardo Alfonzo RC .40 1.00
B14 Eddie Pearson RC .20 .50
B15 Jimmy Haynes .08 .25
B16 Danny Bautista .08 .25
B17 Roger Cedeno .08 .25
B18 Jon Lieber .20 .50
B19 Billy Wagner RC 2.00 5.00
B20 Tate Seefried RC .20 .50
B21 Chad Mottola .08 .25
B22 Jose Malave .08 .25
B23 Terrell Wade RC .20 .50
B24 Shane Andrews .08 .25
B25 Chan Ho Park RC .60 1.50
B26 Kirk Presley RC .20 .50
B27 Robbie Beckett .08 .25
B28 Orlando Miller .08 .25
B29 Jorge Posada RC 4.00 10.00
B30 Frankie Rodriguez .08 .25
B31 Brian L. Hunter .08 .25
B32 Billy Ashley .08 .25
B33 Rondell White .20 .50
B34 John Roper .08 .25
B35 Marc Valdes .08 .25
B36 Scott Ruffcorn .08 .25
B37 Rod Henderson .08 .25
B38 Curtis Goodwin RC .20 .50
B39 Russ Davis .08 .25
B40 Rick Gorecki .08 .25
B41 Johnny Damon .50 1.25
B42 Roberto Petagine .08 .25
B43 Chris Snopek .08 .25
B44 Mark Acre RC .20 .50
B45 Todd Hollandsworth .08 .25
B46 Shawn Green .50 1.25
B47 John Carter RC .20 .50
B48 Jim Pittsley RC .20 .50
B49 John Wasdin RC .20 .50
B50 D.J. Boston RC .20 .50
B51 Tim Clark .08 .25
B52 Alex Ochoa .08 .25
B53 Chad Roper .08 .25
B54 Mike Kelly .08 .25
B55 Brad Fullmer RC .40 1.00
B56 Carl Everett .20 .50
B57 Tim Belk RC .20 .50
B58 Jimmy Hurst RC .20 .50
B59 Mac Suzuki RC .40 1.00
B60 Mike Moore .08 .25
B61 Alan Benes RC .20 .50
B62 Tony Clark RC .60 1.50
B63 Edgar Renteria RC 2.50 6.00
B64 Trey Beamon .08 .25
B65 LaTroy Hawkins RC .40 1.00
B66 Wayne Gomes RC .40 1.00
B67 Ray McDavid .08 .25
B68 John Dettmer .08 .25
B69 Willie Greene .08 .25
B70 Dave Stevens .08 .25
B71 Kevin Orie RC .08 .25
B72 Chad Ogea .08 .25
B73 Ben Van Ryn RC .20 .50
B74 Kym Ashworth RC .20 .50
B75 Dmitri Young .20 .50
B76 Herbert Perry RC .20 .50
B77 Joey Eischen .08 .25
B78 Arquimedez Pozo RC .20 .50
B79 Ugueth Urbina .08 .25
B80 Keith Williams RC .20 .50
B81 John Frascatore RC .20 .50
B82 Garey Ingram RC .20 .50
B83 Aaron Small .20 .50
B84 Olmedo Saenz RC .20 .50
B85 Jesus Tavarez RC .20 .50
B86 Jose Silva RC .40 1.00
B87 Jay Witasick RC .20 .50
B88 Jay Maldonado RC .20 .50
B89 Keith Heberling RC .20 .50
B90 Rusty Greer RC .60 1.50
R1 Paul Molitor .20 .50
R2 Eddie Murray .50 1.25
R3 Ozzie Smith .75 2.00
R4 Rickey Henderson .50 1.25
R5 Lee Smith .20 .50
R6 Dave Winfield .20 .50
R7 Roberto Alomar .30 .75
R8 Matt Williams .20 .50
R9 Mark Grace .30 .75
R10 Lance Johnson .08 .25
R11 Darren Daulton .20 .50
R12 Tom Glavine .30 .75
R13 Gary Sheffield .20 .50
R14 Rod Beck .08 .25
R15 Fred McGriff .30 .75
R16 Joe Carter .20 .50
R17 Dante Bichette .20 .50
R18 Danny Tartabull .08 .25
R19 Juan Gonzalez .20 .50
R20 Steve Avery .08 .25
R21 John Wetteland .20 .50
R22 Ben McDonald .08 .25
R23 Jack McDowell .08 .25
R24 Jose Canseco .30 .75
R25 Tim Salmon .30 .75
R26 Wilson Alvarez .08 .25
R27 Gregg Jefferies .08 .25
R28 John Burkett .08 .25
R29 Greg Vaughn .08 .25
R30 Robin Ventura .20 .50
R31 Paul O'Neill .30 .75
R32 Cecil Fielder .20 .50
R33 Kevin Mitchell .08 .25
R34 Jeff Conine .20 .50
R35 Carlos Baerga .08 .25
R36 Greg Maddux .75 2.00
R37 Roger Clemens 1.00 2.50
R38 Deion Sanders .30 .75
R39 Delino DeShields .08 .25
R40 Ken Griffey Jr. 1.00 2.50
R41 Albert Belle .20 .50
R42 Wade Boggs .30 .75
R43 Andres Galarraga .20 .50
R44 Aaron Sele .08 .25
R45 Don Mattingly 1.25 3.00
R46 David Cone .20 .50
R47 Len Dykstra .20 .50
R48 Brett Butler .20 .50
R49 Bill Swift .08 .25
R50 Bobby Bonilla .20 .50
R51 Rafael Palmeiro .30 .75
R52 Moises Alou .20 .50
R53 Jeff Bagwell .30 .75
R54 Mike Mussina .30 .75
R55 Frank Thomas .50 1.25
R56 Jose Rijo .08 .25
R57 Ruben Sierra .20 .50
R58 Randy Myers .08 .25
R59 Barry Bonds 1.25 3.00
R60 Jimmy Key .20 .50
R61 Travis Fryman .20 .50
R62 John Olerud .20 .50
R63 David Justice .20 .50
R64 Ray Lankford .20 .50
R65 Bob Tewksbury .08 .25
R66 Chuck Carr .08 .25
R67 Jay Buhner .20 .50
R68 Kenny Lofton .20 .50
R69 Marquis Grissom .20 .50

R70 Sammy Sosa .50 1.25
R71 Cal Ripken 1.50 4.00
R72 Ellis Burks .20 .50
R73 Jeff Montgomery .08 .25
R74 Julio Franco .20 .50
R75 Kirby Puckett .50 1.25
R76 Larry Walker .20 .50
R77 Andy Van Slyke .30 .75
R78 Tony Gwynn .60 1.50
R79 Will Clark .30 .75
R80 Mo Vaughn .20 .50
R81 Mike Piazza 1.00 2.50
R82 James Mouton .08 .25
R83 Carlos Delgado .30 .75
R84 Ryan Klesko .20 .50
R85 Javier Lopez .20 .50
R86 Raul Mondesi .20 .50
R87 Cliff Floyd .20 .50
R88 Manny Ramirez .50 1.25
R89 Hector Carrasco .08 .25
R90 Jeff Granger .08 .25
X91 F.Thomas .30 .75
D.Young
X92 F.McGriff .20 .50
B.Kieschnick
X93 M.Williams .08 .25
S.Andrews
X94 C.Ripken .75 2.00
K.Orie
X95 D.Jeter .75 2.00
B.Larkin
X96 K.Griffey Jr. .50 1.25
J.Damon
X97 B.Bonds .60 1.50
R.White
X98 A.Belle .20 .50
J.Hurst
X99 R.Rivera RC .20 .50
R.Mondesi
X100 R.Clemens .50 1.25
S.Ruffcorn
X101 G.Maddux .50 1.25
J.Wasdin
X102 T.Salmon .30 .75
C.Mottola
X103 C.Baerga .08 .25
A.Pozo
X104 M.Piazza .50 1.25
B.Hughes
X105 C.Delgado .30 .75
M.Nieves
X106 J.Posada 1.00 2.50
J.Lopez
X107 M.Ramirez .50 1.25
J.Malave
X108 C.Jones .30 .75
T.Fryman
X109 S.Avery .08 .25
B.Pulsipher
X110 J.Olerud .50 1.25
S.Green

1994 Bowman's Best Refractors

COMPLETE SET (200) 500.00 1000.00
*RED STARS: 4X TO 10X BASIC CARDS
*BLUE STARS: 4X TO 10X BASIC CARDS
*BLUE ROOKIES: 1.5X TO 4X BASIC
*MIRROR IMAGE: 2X TO 5X BASIC
STATED ODDS 1:9
B2 Derek Jeter 75.00 200.00
B63 Edgar Renteria 10.00 25.00

1995 Bowman's Best

This 195 card standard-size set (produced by Topps) consists of 90 veteran stars, 90 rookies and prospects and 15 dual player Mirror Image cards. The packs contain seven cards and the suggested retail price was $5. The veteran cards have red fronts and are designated R1-R90. Cards of rookies and prospects have blue fronts and are designated B1-B90. The Mirror Image cards feature a veteran star and a prospect matched by position in a horizontal design. These cards are numbered X1-X15. Rookie Cards include Bob Abreu, Bartolo Colon, Scott Elarton, Juan Encarnacion, Vladimir Guerrero, Andruw Jones, Hideo Nomo, Rey Ordonez, Scott Rolen and Richie Sexson.

COMPLETE SET (195) 50.00 100.00
COMMON CARD (B1-R90) .20 .50
COMMON CARD (X1-X15) .20 .50
B1 Derek Jeter 1.00 2.50
B2 Vladimir Guerrero RC 20.00 50.00
B3 Bob Abreu RC 3.00 8.00
B4 Chan Ho Park .20 .50
B5 Paul Wilson .20 .50
B6 Chad Ogea .20 .50
B7 Andruw Jones RC 6.00 15.00
B8 Brian Barber .20 .50
B9 Andy Larkin .20 .50
B10 Richie Sexson RC 4.00 10.00
B11 Everett Stull .20 .50
B12 Brooks Kieschnick .20 .50
B13 Matt Murray .20 .50
B14 John Wasdin .20 .50
B15 Shannon Stewart .20 .50
B16 Luis Ortiz .20 .50
B17 Marc Kroon .20 .50
B18 Todd Greene .20 .50
B19 Juan Acevedo RC .40 1.00
B20 Tony Clark .20 .50
B21 Jermaine Dye .20 .50
B22 Derrek Lee .50 1.25
B23 Pat Watkins .20 .50
B24 Pokey Reese .20 .50
B25 Ben Grieve .20 .50
B26 Julio Santana RC .20 .50
B27 Felix Rodriguez RC .40 1.00
B28 Paul Konerko 3.00 8.00
B29 Nomar Garciaparra 2.00 5.00
B30 Pat Ahearne RC .20 .50
B31 Jason Schmidt .50 1.25
B32 Billy Wagner .30 .75
B33 Rey Ordonez RC 1.25 3.00
B34 Curtis Goodwin .20 .50
B35 Sergio Nunez RC .40 1.00
B36 Tim Belk .20 .50
B37 Scott Elarton RC .75 2.00
B38 Jason Isringhausen .20 .50
B39 Trot Nixon .20 .50
B40 Sid Roberson RC .40 1.00
B41 Ron Villone .20 .50
B42 Ruben Rivera .20 .50
B43 Rick Huisman .20 .50
B44 Todd Hollandsworth .20 .50
B45 Johnny Damon .30 .75
B46 Garret Anderson .20 .50
B47 Jeff D'Amico .20 .50
B48 Dustin Hermanson .20 .50
B49 Juan Encarnacion RC 1.25 3.00
B50 Andy Pettitte .30 .75
B51 Chris Stynes .20 .50
B52 Troy Percival .20 .50
B53 LaTroy Hawkins .20 .50
B54 Roger Cedeno .20 .50
B55 Alan Benes .20 .50
B56 Karim Garcia RC .40 1.00
B57 Andrew Lorraine .20 .50
B58 Gary Rath RC .40 1.00
B59 Bret Wagner .20 .50
B60 Jeff Suppan .20 .50
B61 Bill Pulsipher .20 .50
B62 Jay Payton RC 1.25 3.00
B63 Alex Ochoa .20 .50
B64 Ugueth Urbina .20 .50
B65 Armando Benitez .20 .50
B66 George Arias .20 .50
B67 Raul Casanova RC .40 1.00
B68 Matt Drews .20 .50
B69 Jimmy Haynes .20 .50
B70 Jimmy Hurst .20 .50
B71 C.J. Nitkowski .20 .50
B72 Tommy Davis RC .40 1.00
B73 Bartolo Colon RC 2.50 6.00
B74 Chris Carpenter RC 3.00 8.00
B75 Trey Beamon .20 .50
B76 Bryan Rekar .20 .50
B77 James Baldwin .20 .50
B78 Marc Valdes .20 .50
B79 Tom Fordham RC .40 1.00
B80 Marc Newfield .20 .50
B81 Angel Martinez .20 .50
B82 Brian L. Hunter .20 .50
B83 Jose Herrera .20 .50
B84 Glenn Dishman RC .40 1.00
B85 Jacob Cruz RC .75 2.00
B86 Paul Shuey .20 .50
B87 Scott Rolen RC 4.00 10.00
B88 Doug Million .20 .50
B89 Desi Relaford .20 .50
B90 Michael Tucker .20 .50
R1 Randy Johnson .50 1.25
R2 Joe Carter .20 .50
R3 Chili Davis .20 .50
R4 Moises Alou .20 .50
R5 Gary Sheffield .20 .50
R6 Kevin Appier .20 .50
R7 Denny Neagle .20 .50
R8 Ruben Sierra .20 .50
R9 Darren Daulton .20 .50
R10 Cal Ripken 1.50 4.00
R11 Bobby Bonilla .20 .50
R12 Manny Ramirez .30 .75
R13 Barry Bonds 1.25 3.00
R14 Eric Karros .20 .50
R15 Greg Maddux .75 2.00
R16 Jeff Bagwell .30 .75
R17 Paul Molitor .20 .50
R18 Ray Lankford .20 .50
R19 Mark Grace .30 .75
R20 Kenny Lofton .20 .50
R21 Tony Gwynn .60 1.50
R22 Will Clark .30 .75
R23 Roger Clemens 1.00 2.50
R24 Dante Bichette .20 .50
R25 Barry Larkin .30 .75
R26 Wade Boggs .30 .75
R27 Kirby Puckett .50 1.25
R28 Cecil Fielder .20 .50
R29 Jose Canseco .30 .75
R30 Juan Gonzalez .20 .50
R31 David Cone .20 .50
R32 Craig Biggio .30 .75
R33 Tim Salmon .30 .75
R34 David Justice .20 .50
R35 Sammy Sosa .50 1.25
R36 Mike Piazza .75 2.00
R37 Carlos Baerga .20 .50
R38 Jeff Conine .20 .50
R39 Rafael Palmeiro .30 .75
R40 Bret Saberhagen .20 .50
R41 Len Dykstra .20 .50
R42 Mo Vaughn .20 .50
R43 Wally Joyner .20 .50
R44 Chuck Knoblauch .20 .50
R45 Robin Ventura .20 .50
R46 Don Mattingly 1.25 3.00
R47 Dave Hollins .20 .50
R48 Andy Benes .20 .50
R49 Ken Griffey Jr. 1.00 2.50
R50 Albert Belle .20 .50
R51 Matt Williams .20 .50
R52 Rondell White .20 .50
R53 Raul Mondesi .20 .50
R54 Brian Jordan .20 .50
R55 Greg Vaughn .20 .50
R56 Fred McGriff .30 .75
R57 Roberto Alomar .30 .75
R58 Dennis Eckersley .20 .50
R59 Lee Smith .20 .50
R60 Eddie Murray .50 1.25
R61 Kenny Rogers .20 .50
R62 Ron Gant .20 .50
R63 Larry Walker .20 .50
R64 Chad Curtis .20 .50
R65 Frank Thomas .50 1.25
R66 Paul O'Neill .30 .75
R67 Kevin Seitzer .20 .50
R68 Marquis Grissom .20 .50
R69 Mark McGwire 1.50 4.00
R70 Travis Fryman .20 .50
R71 Andres Galarraga .20 .50
R72 Carlos Perez RC .75 2.00
R73 Tyler Green .20 .50
R74 Marty Cordova .20 .50
R75 Shawn Green .20 .50
R76 Vaughn Eshelman .20 .50
R77 John Mabry .20 .50
R78 Jason Bates .20 .50
R79 Jon Nunnally .20 .50
R80 Ray Durham .20 .50
R81 Edgardo Alfonzo .20 .50
R82 Esteban Loaiza .20 .50
R83 Hideo Nomo RC 3.00 8.00
R84 Orlando Miller .20 .50
R85 Alex Gonzalez .20 .50
R86 Mark Grudzielanek RC 1.25 3.00
R87 Julian Tavarez .20 .50
R88 Benji Gil .20 .50
R89 Quilvio Veras .20 .50
R90 Ricky Bottalico .20 .50
X1 B.Davis RC .60 1.50
I.Rodriguez
X2 M.Redman RC .60 1.50
M.Ramirez
X3 R.Taylor RC .60 1.50
D.Sanders
X4 R.Jaroncyk RC .20 .50
S.Green
X5 C.Beltran UER 1.50 4.00
J.Gonz
X6 T.McKnight RC .20 .50
C.Biggio
X7 M.Barrett RC .60 1.50
T.Fryman
X8 C.Jenkins RC .20 .50
M.Vaughn
X9 R.Rivera .50 1.25
F.Thomas
X10 C.Goodwin .20 .50
K.Lofton
X11 B.Hunter .30 .75
T.Gwynn
X12 T.Greene .60 1.50
K.Griffey Jr.
X13 K.Garcia .20 .50
M.Williams
X14 B.Wagner .30 .75
R.Johnson
X15 P.Watkins .30 .75
J.Bagwell

1995 Bowman's Best Refractors

*STARS: 4X TO 10X BASIC CARDS
*ROOKIES: 1.5X TO 4X BASIC CARDS
*MIRROR IMAGE: 1.25X TO 3X BASIC
RED/BLUE REF.STATED ODDS 1:6
MIRROR IMAGE REF.STATED ODDS 1:12
B1 Derek Jeter 60.00 120.00
B2 Vladimir Guerrero 150.00 400.00
B3 Bob Abreu 20.00 50.00
B10 Richie Sexson 8.00 20.00
B73 Bartolo Colon 12.00 30.00

1995 Bowman's Best Jumbo Refractors

COMPLETE SET (10) 50.00 120.00
COMMON CARD (1-10) 2.00 5.00
COMMON DP 1.50 4.00
1 Albert Belle DP 1.50 4.00
2 Ken Griffey Jr 8.00 20.00
3 Tony Gwynn 6.00 15.00
4 Greg Maddux 3.00 8.00
5 Hideo Nomo 6.00 15.00
6 Mike Piazza 6.00 15.00
7 Cal Ripken 12.50 30.00
8 Sammy Sosa 5.00 12.00
9 Frank Thomas 4.00 10.00
10 Cal Ripken 12.50 30.00

1996 Bowman's Best Previews

COMPLETE SET (30) 25.00 60.00
STATED ODDS 1:12
*REFRACTORS: .5X TO 1.2X BASIC PREVIEWS
REFRACTOR STATED ODDS 1:24
*ATOMIC: 1X TO 2.5X BASIC PREVIEWS
ATOMIC STATED ODDS 1:48
BBP1 Chipper Jones 1.00 2.50
BBP2 Alan Benes .40 1.00
BBP3 Brooks Kieschnick .40 1.00
BBP4 Barry Bonds 2.50 6.00
BBP5 Rey Ordonez .40 1.00
BBP6 Tim Salmon .60 1.50
BBP7 Mike Piazza 1.50 4.00
BBP8 Billy Wagner .40 1.00
BBP9 Andruw Jones 1.50 4.00
BBP10 Tony Gwynn 1.25 3.00
BBP11 Paul Wilson .40 1.00
BBP12 Pokey Reese .40 1.00
BBP13 Frank Thomas 1.00 2.50
BBP14 Greg Maddux 1.50 4.00
BBP15 Derek Jeter 5.00 12.00
BBP16 Jeff Bagwell .60 1.50
BBP17 Barry Larkin .60 1.50
BBP18 Todd Greene .40 1.00
BBP19 Ruben Rivera .40 1.00
BBP20 Richard Hidalgo .40 1.00
BBP21 Larry Walker .40 1.00
BBP22 Carlos Baerga .40 1.00
BBP23 Derrick Gibson .40 1.00
BBP24 Richie Sexson .60 1.50
BBP25 Mo Vaughn .40 1.00
BBP26 Hideo Nomo 1.00 2.50
BBP27 Nomar Garciaparra 2.00 5.00
BBP28 Cal Ripken 3.00 8.00
BBP29 Karim Garcia .40 1.00
BBP30 Ken Griffey Jr. 2.00 5.00

1996 Bowman's Best

This 180-card set was (produced by Topps) issued in packs of six cards at the cost of $4.99 per pack. The fronts feature a color action player cutout of 90 outstanding veteran players on a chromium gold background design and 90 up and coming prospects and rookies on a silver design. The backs carry a color player portrait, player information and statistics. Card number 33 was never actually issued. Instead, both Roger Clemens and Rafael Palmeiro are erroneously numbered 32. A chrome reprint of the 1952 Bowman Mickey Mantle was inserted at the rate of one in 24 packs. A Refractor version of the Mantle was seeded at 1:96 packs and an Atomic Refractor version was seeded at 1:192. Notable Rookie Cards include Geoff Jenkins and Mike Sweeney.

COMPLETE SET (180) 15.00 40.00
NUMBER 33 NEVER ISSUED
CLEMENS AND PALMEIRO NUMBERED 32
MANTLE CHROME ODDS 1:24 HOB, 1:20 RET
MANTLE REF.ODDS 1:96 HOB, 1:160 RET
MANTLE ATOMIC ODDS 1:192 HOB,1:320 RET
1 Hideo Nomo .40 1.00
2 Edgar Martinez .25 .60
3 Cal Ripken 1.25 3.00
4 Wade Boggs .25 .60
5 Cecil Fielder .15 .40
6 Albert Belle .15 .40
7 Chipper Jones .40 1.00
8 Ryne Sandberg .60 1.50
9 Tim Salmon .25 .60
10 Barry Bonds 1.00 2.50
11 Ken Caminiti .15 .40
12 Ron Gant .15 .40
13 Frank Thomas .40 1.00
14 Dante Bichette .15 .40
15 Jason Kendall .15 .40
16 Mo Vaughn .15 .40
17 Rey Ordonez .15 .40
18 Henry Rodriguez .15 .40
19 Ryan Klesko .15 .40
20 Jeff Bagwell .25 .60
21 Randy Johnson .40 1.00
22 Jim Edmonds .15 .40
23 Kenny Lofton .15 .40
24 Andy Pettitte .25 .60
25 Brady Anderson .15 .40
26 Mike Piazza .60 1.50
27 Greg Vaughn .15 .40
28 Joe Carter .15 .40
29 Jason Giambi .15 .40
30 Ivan Rodriguez .25 .60
31 Jeff Conine .15 .40
32 Rafael Palmeiro .25 .60
33 Roger Clemens UER .75 2.00
34 Chuck Knoblauch .15 .40
35 Reggie Sanders .15 .40
36 Andres Galarraga .15 .40
37 Paul O'Neill .25 .60
38 Tony Gwynn .50 1.25
39 Paul Wilson .15 .40
40 Garret Anderson .15 .40
41 David Justice .15 .40
42 Eddie Murray .40 1.00
43 Mike Grace RC .20 .50
44 Marty Cordova .15 .40
45 Kevin Appier .15 .40
46 Raul Mondesi .15 .40
47 Jim Thome .25 .60
48 Sammy Sosa .40 1.00
49 Craig Biggio .25 .60
50 Marquis Grissom .15 .40
51 Alan Benes .15 .40
52 Manny Ramirez .25 .60
53 Gary Sheffield .15 .40
54 Mike Mussina .25 .60
55 Robin Ventura .15 .40
56 Johnny Damon .25 .60
57 Jose Canseco .25 .60
58 Juan Gonzalez .15 .40
59 Tino Martinez .25 .60
60 Brian Hunter .15 .40
61 Fred McGriff .25 .60
62 Jay Buhner .15 .40
63 Carlos Delgado .15 .40
64 Moises Alou .15 .40
65 Roberto Alomar .25 .60
66 Barry Larkin .25 .60
67 Vinny Castilla .15 .40
68 Ray Durham .15 .40
69 Travis Fryman .15 .40
70 Jason Isringhausen .15 .40
71 Ken Griffey Jr. .75 2.00
72 John Smoltz .25 .60
73 Matt Williams .15 .40
74 Chan Ho Park .15 .40
75 Mark McGwire 1.25 3.00
76 Jeffrey Hammonds .15 .40
77 Will Clark .25 .60
78 Kirby Puckett .40 1.00
79 Derek Jeter 1.25 3.00
80 Derek Bell .15 .40
81 Eric Karros .15 .40
82 Len Dykstra .15 .40
83 Larry Walker .15 .40
84 Mark Grudzielanek .15 .40
85 Greg Maddux .60 1.50
86 Carlos Baerga .15 .40
87 Paul Molitor .15 .40
88 John Valentin .15 .40
89 Mark Grace .25 .60
90 Ray Lankford .15 .40
91 Andruw Jones .60 1.50
92 Nomar Garciaparra .75 2.00
93 Alex Ochoa .15 .40
94 Derrick Gibson .15 .40
95 Jeff D'Amico .15 .40
96 Ruben Rivera .15 .40
97 Vladimir Guerrero .75 2.00
98 Pokey Reese .15 .40
99 Richard Hidalgo .15 .40
100 Bartolo Colon .40 1.00
101 Karim Garcia .15 .40
102 Ben Davis .15 .40
103 Jay Powell .15 .40
104 Chris Snopek .15 .40
105 Glendon Rusch RC .40 1.00
106 Enrique Wilson .15 .40
107 Antonio Alfonseca RC .40 1.00
108 Wilton Guerrero RC .20 .50
109 Jose Guillen RC 1.50 4.00
110 Miguel Mejia RC .20 .50
111 Jay Payton .15 .40
112 Scott Elarton .15 .40
113 Brooks Kieschnick .15 .40
114 Dustin Hermanson .15 .40
115 Roger Cedeno .15 .40
116 Matt Wagner .15 .40
117 Lee Daniels .15 .40
118 Ben Grieve .15 .40
119 Ugueth Urbina .15 .40
120 Danny Graves .15 .40
121 Dan Donato RC .20 .50
122 Matt Ruebel RC .20 .50
123 Mark Sievert RC .20 .50
124 Chris Stynes .15 .40
125 Jeff Abbott .15 .40
126 Rocky Coppinger RC .20 .50
127 Jermaine Dye .15 .40
128 Todd Greene .15 .40
129 Chris Carpenter .25 .60
130 Edgar Renteria .15 .40
131 Matt Drews .15 .40
132 Edgard Velazquez RC .20 .50
133 Casey Whitten .15 .40
134 Ryan Jones RC .20 .50
135 Todd Walker .15 .40
136 Geoff Jenkins RC .75 2.00
137 Matt Morris RC 1.50 4.00
138 Richie Sexson .25 .60
139 Todd Dunwoody RC .20 .50
140 Gabe Alvarez RC .20 .50
141 J.J. Johnson .15 .40
142 Shannon Stewart .15 .40
143 Brad Fullmer .15 .40
144 Julio Santana .15 .40
145 Scott Rolen .40 1.00
146 Amaury Telemaco .15 .40
147 Trey Beamon .15 .40
148 Billy Wagner .15 .40
149 Todd Hollandsworth .15 .40
150 Doug Million .15 .40
151 Javier Valentin RC .20 .50
152 Wes Helms RC .40 1.00
153 Jeff Suppan .15 .40
154 Luis Castillo RC .60 1.50
155 Bob Abreu .40 1.00
156 Paul Konerko .40 1.00
157 Jamey Wright .15 .40
158 Eddie Pearson .15 .40
159 Jimmy Haynes. .15 .40
160 Derrek Lee .25 .60
161 Damian Moss .15 .40
162 Carlos Guillen RC 1.00 2.50
163 Chris Fussell RC .20 .50
164 Mike Sweeney RC 1.00 2.50
165 Donnie Sadler .15 .40
166 Desi Relaford .15 .40
167 Steve Gibralter .15 .40
168 Neifi Perez .15 .40
169 Antone Williamson .15 .40
170 Marty Janzen RC .20 .50
171 Todd Helton .75 2.00
172 Raul Ibanez RC 1.50 4.00
173 Bill Selby .15 .40
174 Shane Monahan RC .20 .50
175 Robin Jennings .15 .40
176 Bobby Chouinard .15 .40
177 Einar Diaz .15 .40
178 Jason Thompson RC .15 .40
179 Rafael Medina RC .20 .50
180 Kevin Orie .15 .40
NNO 1952 Mantle Atomic Ref. 4.00 10.00
NNO 1952 Mantle Refractor 2.00 5.00
NNO 1952 Mantle Chrome 1.00 2.50

1996 Bowman's Best Atomic Refractors

*GOLD STARS: 6X TO 15X BASIC CARDS
*SILVER STARS: 6X TO 15X BASIC CARDS
*ROOKIES: 4X TO 10X BASIC CARDS
STATED ODDS 1:48 HOB, 1:80 RET

1996 Bowman's Best Refractors

*GOLD STARS: 3X TO 8X BASIC CARDS
*SILVER STARS: 3X TO 8X BASIC CARDS
*ROOKIES: 2X TO 5X BASIC CARDS
STATED ODDS 1:12 HOB, 1:20 RET

1996 Bowman's Best Cuts

COMPLETE SET (15) 30.00 80.00
STATED ODDS 1:24 HOB, 1:40 RET
*REFRACTORS: .6X TO 1.5X BASIC CUTS
REF.STATED ODDS 1:48 HOB, 1:80 RET
*ATOMIC: 1X TO 2.5X BASIC CUTS
ATOMIC STATED ODDS 1:96 HOB, 1:160 RET
1 Ken Griffey Jr. 3.00 8.00
2 Jason Isringhausen .60 1.50
3 Derek Jeter 4.00 10.00
4 Andruw Jones 2.50 6.00
5 Chipper Jones 1.50 4.00
6 Ryan Klesko .60 1.50
7 Raul Mondesi .60 1.50
8 Hideo Nomo 1.50 4.00
9 Mike Piazza 2.50 6.00
10 Manny Ramirez 1.00 2.50
11 Cal Ripken 5.00 12.00
12 Ruben Rivera .60 1.50
13 Tim Salmon 1.00 2.50
14 Frank Thomas 1.50 4.00
15 Jim Thome 1.00 2.50

1996 Bowman's Best Mirror Image

COMPLETE SET (10) 15.00 40.00
STATED ODDS 1:48 HOB, 1:80 RET
*REFRACTORS: .6X TO 1.5X BASIC MI
REFRACTOR ODDS 1:96 HOB, 1:160 RET
*ATOMIC REF: .75X TO 2X BASIC MI
ATOMIC ODDS 1:192 HOB, 1:320 RET
1 F.Thom 2.50 6.00
Helton
Bagw
Sexson
2 R.Alom 1.00 2.50
Biggio
L.Cast
Rela
3 C.Jones 1.50 4.00
Rolen
Boggs
4 Ripken 5.00 12.00
Larkin
Bellhorn
5 A.Belle 1.00 2.50
L.Walker
K.Garcia
6 A.Jones 2.50 6.00
Bonds
Lofton
7 K.Griff 3.00 8.00
Gwynn
Grieve
Vlad
8 M.Piazza 1.50 4.00
I.Rod
B.Davis
9 G.Maddux 2.50 6.00
Mussina
B.Colon
10 J.Washburn 1.50 4.00
R.John
Glav

1997 Bowman's Best Preview

COMPLETE SET (20) 30.00 80.00
STATED ODDS 1:12
*REF: .75X TO 2X BASIC PREVIEWS
REFRACTOR STATED ODDS 1:48
*ATOMIC REF: 1.5X TO 4X BASIC PREVIEWS
ATOMIC STATED ODDS 1:96
DISTRIBUTED IN 1997 BOWMAN SER.1 PACKS
1 Frank Thomas 1.50 4.00
2 Ken Griffey Jr. 3.00 8.00
3 Barry Bonds 4.00 10.00
4 Derek Jeter 4.00 10.00
5 Chipper Jones 1.50 4.00
6 Mark McGwire 5.00 12.00
7 Cal Ripken 5.00 12.00
8 Kenny Lofton .60 1.50
9 Gary Sheffield .60 1.50
10 Jeff Bagwell 1.00 2.50
11 Wilton Guerrero .60 1.50
12 Scott Rolen 1.00 2.50
13 Todd Walker .60 1.50
14 Ruben Rivera .60 1.50
15 Andruw Jones 1.00 2.50
16 Nomar Garciaparra 2.50 6.00
17 Vladimir Guerrero 1.50 4.00
18 Miguel Tejada 1.50 4.00
19 Bartolo Colon .60 1.50
20 Katsuhiro Maeda .60 1.50

1997 Bowman's Best

The 1997 Bowman's Best set (produced by Topps) was issued in one series totalling 200 cards and was distributed in six-card packs (SRP $4.99). The fronts feature borderless color player photos printed on chromium card stock. The cards of the 100 current veteran stars display a classic gold design while the cards of the 100 top prospects carry a sleek silver design. Rookie Cards include Adrian Beltre, Kris Benson, Jose Cruz Jr., Travis Lee, Fernando Tatis, Miguel Tejada and Kerry Wood.

COMPLETE SET (200) 15.00 40.00
1 Ken Griffey Jr. .75 2.00
2 Cecil Fielder .15 .40
3 Albert Belle .15 .40
4 Todd Hundley .15 .40
5 Mike Piazza .60 1.50
6 Matt Williams .15 .40
7 Mo Vaughn .15 .40
8 Ryne Sandberg .60 1.50
9 Chipper Jones .40 1.00
10 Edgar Martinez .25 .60
11 Kenny Lofton .15 .40
12 Ron Gant .15 .40
13 Moises Alou .15 .40
14 Pat Hentgen .15 .40
15 Steve Finley .15 .40
16 Mark Grace .25 .60
17 Jay Buhner .15 .40
18 Jeff Conine .15 .40
19 Jim Edmonds .15 .40
20 Todd Hollandsworth .15 .40
21 Andy Pettitte .25 .60
22 Jim Thome .25 .60
23 Eric Young .15 .40
24 Ray Lankford .15 .40
25 Marquis Grissom .15 .40
26 Tony Clark .15 .40
27 Jermaine Allensworth .15 .40
28 Ellis Burks .15 .40
29 Tony Gwynn .50 1.25
30 Barry Larkin .25 .60
31 John Olerud .15 .40
32 Mariano Rivera .40 1.00
33 Paul Molitor .15 .40
34 Ken Caminiti .15 .40
35 Gary Sheffield .15 .40
36 Al Martin .15 .40
37 John Valentin .15 .40
38 Frank Thomas .40 1.00
39 John Jaha .15 .40
40 Greg Maddux .60 1.50
41 Alex Fernandez .15 .40
42 Dean Palmer .15 .40
43 Bernie Williams .25 .60
44 Deion Sanders .25 .60
45 Mark McGwire 1.25 3.00
46 Brian Jordan .15 .40
47 Bernard Gilkey .15 .40
48 Will Clark .25 .60
49 Kevin Appier .15 .40
50 Tom Glavine .25 .60
51 Chuck Knoblauch .15 .40
52 Rondell White .15 .40
53 Greg Vaughn .15 .40
54 Mike Mussina .25 .60
55 Brian McRae .15 .40
56 Chili Davis .15 .40
57 Wade Boggs .25 .60
58 Jeff Bagwell .25 .60
59 Roberto Alomar .25 .60
60 Dennis Eckersley .15 .40
61 Ryan Klesko .15 .40
62 Manny Ramirez .25 .60
63 John Wetteland .15 .40
64 Cal Ripken 1.25 3.00
65 Edgar Renteria .15 .40
66 Tino Martinez .25 .60
67 Larry Walker .15 .40
68 Gregg Jefferies .15 .40
69 Lance Johnson .15 .40
70 Carlos Delgado .15 .40
71 Craig Biggio .25 .60
72 Jose Canseco .25 .60
73 Barry Bonds 1.00 2.50
74 Juan Gonzalez .15 .40
75 Eric Karros .15 .40
76 Reggie Sanders .15 .40
77 Robin Ventura .15 .40
78 Hideo Nomo .40 1.00
79 David Justice .15 .40
80 Vinny Castilla .15 .40
81 Travis Fryman .15 .40
82 Derek Jeter 1.00 2.50
83 Sammy Sosa .40 1.00
84 Ivan Rodriguez .25 .60
85 Rafael Palmeiro .25 .60
86 Roger Clemens .75 2.00
87 Jason Giambi .15 .40
88 Andres Galarraga .15 .40
89 Jermaine Dye .15 .40
90 Joe Carter .15 .40
91 Brady Anderson .15 .40
92 Derek Bell .15 .40
93 Randy Johnson .40 1.00
94 Fred McGriff .25 .60
95 John Smoltz .25 .60
96 Harold Baines .15 .40
97 Raul Mondesi .15 .40
98 Tim Salmon .25 .60
99 Carlos Baerga .15 .40
100 Dante Bichette .15 .40
101 Vladimir Guerrero .40 1.00
102 Richard Hidalgo .15 .40
103 Paul Konerko .25 .60
104 Alex Gonzalez RC .40 1.00
105 Jason Dickson .15 .40
106 Jose Rosado .15 .40
107 Todd Walker .15 .40
108 Seth Greisinger RC .15 .40
109 Todd Helton .40 1.00
110 Ben Davis .15 .40
111 Bartolo Colon .15 .40
112 Elieser Marrero .15 .40
113 Jeff D'Amico .15 .40
114 Miguel Tejada RC 1.50 4.00
115 Darin Erstad .15 .40
116 Kris Benson RC .40 1.00
117 Adrian Beltre RC 8.00 20.00
118 Neifi Perez .15 .40
119 Pokey Reese .15 .40
120 Carl Pavano .15 .40
121 Juan Melo .15 .40
122 Kevin McGlinchy RC .15 .40
123 Pat Cline .15 .40
124 Felix Heredia RC .15 .40
125 Aaron Boone .15 .40
126 Glendon Rusch .15 .40
127 Mike Cameron .15 .40
128 Justin Thompson .15 .40
129 Chad Hermansen RC .15 .40
130 Sidney Ponson RC .40 1.00
131 Willie Martinez RC .15 .40
132 Paul Wilder RC .15 .40
133 Geoff Jenkins .15 .40
134 Roy Halladay RC 6.00 15.00
135 Carlos Guillen .15 .40
136 Tony Batista .15 .40
137 Todd Greene .15 .40
138 Luis Castillo .15 .40
139 Jimmy Anderson RC .15 .40
140 Edgard Velazquez .15 .40
141 Chris Snopek .15 .40
142 Ruben Rivera .15 .40
143 Javier Valentin .15 .40
144 Brian Rose .15 .40
145 Fernando Tatis RC .15 .40
146 Dean Crow RC .15 .40
147 Karim Garcia .15 .40
148 Dante Powell .15 .40
149 Hideki Irabu RC .25 .60
150 Matt Morris .15 .40
151 Wes Helms .15 .40
152 Russ Johnson .15 .40
153 Jarrod Washburn .15 .40
154 Kerry Wood RC 1.50 4.00
155 Joe Fontenot RC .15 .40
156 Eugene Kingsale .15 .40
157 Terrence Long .15 .40
158 Calvin Maduro .15 .40
159 Jeff Suppan .15 .40
160 DaRond Stovall .15 .40
161 Mark Redman .15 .40
162 Ken Cloude RC .15 .40
163 Bobby Estalella .15 .40
164 Abraham Nunez RC .15 .40
165 Derrick Gibson .15 .40
166 Mike Drumright RC .15 .40
167 Katsuhiro Maeda .15 .40
168 Jeff Liefer .15 .40
169 Ben Grieve .15 .40
170 Bob Abreu .25 .60
171 Shannon Stewart .15 .40
172 Braden Looper RC .30 .75
173 Brant Brown .15 .40
174 Marlon Anderson .15 .40
175 Brad Fullmer .15 .40
176 Carlos Beltran .75 2.00
177 Nomar Garciaparra .60 1.50
178 Derrek Lee .25 .60
179 Valerio De Los Santos RC .15 .40
180 Dmitri Young .15 .40
181 Jamey Wright .15 .40
182 Hiram Bocachica RC .15 .40
183 Wilton Guerrero .15 .40
184 Chris Carpenter .15 .40
185 Scott Spiezio .15 .40

186 Andruw Jones .25 .60
187 Travis Lee RC .25 .60
188 Jose Cruz Jr. RC .25 .60
189 Jose Guillen .15 .40
190 Jeff Abbott .15 .40
191 Ricky Ledee RC .25 .60
192 Mike Sweeney .15 .40
193 Donnie Sadler .15 .40
194 Scott Rolen .25 .60
195 Kevin Orie .15 .40
196 Jason Conti RC .15 .40
197 Mark Kotsay RC .60 1.50
198 Eric Milton RC .25 .60
199 Russell Branyan .15 .40
200 Alex Sanchez RC .25 .60

1997 Bowman's Best Atomic Refractors

*STARS: 5X TO 12X BASIC CARDS
*ROOKIES: 3X TO 8X BASIC CARDS
STATED ODDS 1:24
117 Adrian Beltre 150.00 400.00

1997 Bowman's Best Refractors

*STARS: 2.5X TO 6X BASIC CARDS
*ROOKIES: 1.5X TO 4X BASIC CARDS
STATED ODDS 1:12
117 Adrian Beltre 60.00 150.00

1997 Bowman's Best Autographs

COMPLETE SET (10) 125.00 250.00
STATED ODDS 1:170
*REFRACTOR: .75X TO 2X BASIC AUTO
REFRACTOR STATED ODDS 1:2036
*ATOMIC: 1.5X TO 4X BASIC AUTO
ATOMIC STATED ODDS 1:6107
SKIP-NUMBERED 10-CARD SET
29 Tony Gwynn 15.00 40.00
33 Paul Molitor 10.00 25.00
82 Derek Jeter 125.00 300.00
91 Brady Anderson 6.00 15.00
98 Tim Salmon 6.00 15.00
107 Todd Walker 6.00 15.00
183 Wilton Guerrero 2.00 5.00
185 Scott Spiezio 2.00 5.00
188 Jose Cruz Jr. 6.00 15.00
194 Scott Rolen 6.00 15.00

1997 Bowman's Best Best Cuts

COMPLETE SET (20) 75.00 150.00
STATED ODDS 1:24
*REFRACTOR: .6X TO 1.5X BASIC CUTS
REFRACTOR STATED ODDS 1:48
*ATOMIC: 1X TO 2.5X BASIC CUTS
ATOMIC STATED ODDS 1:96
BC1 Derek Jeter 6.00 15.00
BC2 Chipper Jones 2.50 6.00
BC3 Frank Thomas 2.50 6.00
BC4 Cal Ripken 8.00 20.00
BC5 Mark McGwire 8.00 20.00
BC6 Ken Griffey Jr. 5.00 12.00
BC7 Jeff Bagwell 1.50 4.00
BC8 Mike Piazza 4.00 10.00
BC9 Ken Caminiti 1.00 2.50
BC10 Albert Belle 1.00 2.50
BC11 Jose Cruz Jr. 1.00 2.50
BC12 Wilton Guerrero 1.00 2.50
BC13 Darin Erstad 1.00 2.50
BC14 Andruw Jones 1.50 4.00
BC15 Scott Rolen 1.50 4.00
BC16 Jose Guillen 1.00 2.50
BC17 Bob Abreu 1.50 4.00
BC18 Vladimir Guerrero 2.50 6.00
BC19 Todd Walker 1.00 2.50
BC20 Nomar Garciaparra 4.00 10.00

1997 Bowman's Best Mirror Image

COMPLETE SET (10) 30.00 80.00
STATED ODDS 1:48
*REFRACTORS: .6X TO 1.5X BASIC MI
REFRACTOR STATED ODDS 1:96
*ATOMIC REF: 1.25X TO 3X BASIC MI
ATOMIC STATED ODDS 1:192
*INVERTED: 2X VALUE OF NON-INVERTED
INVERTED: RANDOM INSERTS IN PACKS
INVERTED HAVE LARGER ROOKIE PHOTOS
MI1 Nomar 5.00 12.00
Jeter
Boca
Larkin
MI2 T.Lee 2.00 5.00
Thomas
D.Lee
Bag
MI3 K.Wood 2.00 5.00
Maddux
Benson
MI4 M.Piazza 3.00 8.00
I.Rod
E.Marrero
MI5 J.Cruz 6.00 15.00
Grif
Jones
Bonds
MI6 J.Gonz 1.25 3.00
Guillen
Hidalgo
Shef
MI7 Koner 5.00 12.00
McGwire
Helt
Palm
MI8 W.Guer 1.25 3.00
Biggio
Sadl
Knob
MI9 A.Beltre 2.50 6.00
C.Jones
Branyan
MI10 V.Guer 2.00 5.00
Abreu
Loft
Belle

1997 Bowman's Best Jumbo

*REFRACTORS: 4X BASIC CARDS
*ATOMIC REFRACTORS: 8X BASIC CARDS
1 Ken Griffey Jr. 4.00 10.00
5 Mike Piazza 3.00 8.00
9 Chipper Jones 3.00 8.00
11 Kenny Lofton .75 2.00
29 Tony Gwynn 3.00 8.00
33 Paul Molitor 1.50 4.00
38 Frank Thomas 1.25 3.00
45 Mark McGwire 3.00 8.00
64 Cal Ripken Jr. 6.00 15.00
73 Barry Bonds 3.00 8.00
74 Juan Gonzalez .75 2.00
82 Derek Jeter 6.00 15.00
101 Vladimir Guerrero 1.50 4.00
177 Nomar Garciaparra 2.50 6.00
186 Andruw Jones 2.00 5.00
188 Jose Cruz Jr. .75 2.00

1998 Bowman's Best

The 1998 Bowman's Best set (produced by Topps) consists of 200 standard size cards and was released in August, 1998. The six-card packs retailed for a suggested price of $5 each. The card fronts feature 100 action photos with a gold background showcasing today's veteran players and 100 photos (combining posed shots with action shots) with a silver background showcasing rookies. The Bowman's Best logo sits in the upper right corner and the featured player's name sits in the lower left corner. Rookie Cards include Ryan Anderson, Troy Glaus, Orlando Hernandez, Carlos Lee, Ruben Mateo and Magglio Ordonez.

COMPLETE SET (200) 15.00 40.00
1 Mark McGwire 1.00 2.50
2 Jeromy Burnitz .15 .40
3 Barry Bonds 1.00 2.50
4 Dante Bichette .15 .40
5 Chipper Jones .40 1.00
6 Frank Thomas .40 1.00
7 Kevin Brown .25 .60
8 Juan Gonzalez .15 .40
9 Jay Buhner .15 .40
10 Chuck Knoblauch .15 .40
11 Cal Ripken 1.25 3.00
12 Matt Williams .15 .40
13 Jim Edmonds .15 .40
14 Manny Ramirez .25 .60
15 Tony Clark .15 .40
16 Mo Vaughn .15 .40
17 Bernie Williams .25 .60
18 Scott Rolen .25 .60
19 Gary Sheffield .15 .40
20 Albert Belle .15 .40
21 Mike Piazza .60 1.50
22 John Olerud .15 .40
23 Tony Gwynn .50 1.25
24 Jay Bell .15 .40
25 Jose Cruz Jr. .15 .40
26 Justin Thompson .15 .40
27 Ken Griffey Jr. .75 2.00
28 Sandy Alomar Jr. .15 .40
29 Mark Grudzielanek .15 .40
30 Mark Grace .25 .60
31 Ron Gant .15 .40
32 Javy Lopez .15 .40
33 Jeff Bagwell .25 .60
34 Fred McGriff .25 .60
35 Rafael Palmeiro .25 .60
36 Vinny Castilla .15 .40
37 Andy Benes .15 .40
38 Pedro Martinez .25 .60
39 Andy Pettitte .25 .60
40 Marty Cordova .15 .40
41 Rusty Greer .15 .40
42 Kevin Orie .15 .40
43 Chan Ho Park .15 .40
44 Ryan Klesko .15 .40
45 Alex Rodriguez .60 1.50
46 Travis Fryman .15 .40
47 Jeff King .15 .40
48 Roger Clemens .75 2.00
49 Darin Erstad .15 .40
50 Brady Anderson .15 .40
51 Jason Kendall .15 .40
52 John Valentin .15 .40
53 Ellis Burks .15 .40
54 Brian Hunter .15 .40
55 Paul O'Neill .25 .60
56 Ken Caminiti .15 .40
57 David Justice .15 .40
58 Eric Karros .15 .40
59 Pat Hentgen .15 .40
60 Greg Maddux .60 1.50
61 Craig Biggio .25 .60
62 Edgar Martinez .25 .60
63 Mike Mussina .25 .60
64 Larry Walker .15 .40
65 Tino Martinez .25 .60
66 Jim Thome .25 .60
67 Tom Glavine .25 .60
68 Raul Mondesi .15 .40
69 Marquis Grissom .15 .40
70 Randy Johnson .40 1.00
71 Steve Finley .15 .40
72 Jose Guillen .15 .40
73 Nomar Garciaparra .60 1.50
74 Wade Boggs .25 .60
75 Bobby Higginson .15 .40
76 Robin Ventura .15 .40
77 Derek Jeter 1.00 2.50
78 Andruw Jones .25 .60
79 Ray Lankford .15 .40
80 Vladimir Guerrero .40 1.00
81 Kenny Lofton .15 .40
82 Ivan Rodriguez .25 .60
83 Neifi Perez .15 .40
84 John Smoltz .25 .60
85 Tim Salmon .25 .60
86 Carlos Delgado .15 .40
87 Sammy Sosa .40 1.00
88 Jaret Wright .15 .40
89 Roberto Alomar .25 .60
90 Paul Molitor .15 .40
91 Dean Palmer .15 .40
92 Barry Larkin .25 .60
93 Jason Giambi .15 .40
94 Curt Schilling .15 .40
95 Eric Young .15 .40
96 Denny Neagle .15 .40
97 Moises Alou .15 .40
98 Livan Hernandez .15 .40
99 Todd Hundley .15 .40
100 Andres Galarraga .15 .40
101 Travis Lee .15 .40
102 Lance Berkman .15 .40
103 Orlando Cabrera .15 .40
104 Mike Lowell RC 1.25 3.00
105 Ben Grieve .15 .40
106 Jae Weong Seo RC .25 .60
107 Richie Sexson .15 .40
108 Eli Marrero .15 .40
109 Aramis Ramirez .15 .40
110 Paul Konerko .15 .40
111 Carl Pavano .15 .40
112 Brad Fullmer .15 .40
113 Matt Clement .15 .40
114 Donzell McDonald .15 .40
115 Todd Helton .25 .60
116 Mike Caruso .15 .40
117 Donnie Sadler .15 .40
118 Bruce Chen .15 .40
119 Jarrod Washburn .15 .40
120 Adrian Beltre .15 .40
121 Ryan Jackson RC .15 .40
122 Kevin Millar RC .60 1.50
123 Corey Koskie RC .40 1.00
124 Dermal Brown .15 .40
125 Kerry Wood .15 .40
126 Juan Melo .15 .40
127 Ramon Hernandez .15 .40
128 Roy Halladay .75 2.00
129 Ron Wright .15 .40
130 Darnell McDonald RC .25 .60
131 Odalis Perez RC .60 1.50
132 Alex Cora RC 1.00 2.50
133 Justin Towle .15 .40
134 Juan Encarnacion .15 .40
135 Brian Rose .15 .40
136 Russell Branyan .15 .40
137 Cesar King RC .15 .40
138 Ruben Rivera .15 .40
139 Ricky Ledee .15 .40
140 Vernon Wells .15 .40
141 Luis Rivas RC .40 1.00
142 Brent Butler .15 .40
143 Karim Garcia .15 .40
144 George Lombard .15 .40
145 Masato Yoshii RC .25 .60
146 Braden Looper .15 .40
147 Alex Sanchez .15 .40
148 Kris Benson .15 .40
149 Mark Kotsay .15 .40
150 Richard Hidalgo .15 .40
151 Scott Elarton .15 .40
152 Ryan Minor RC .15 .40
153 Troy Glaus RC 1.50 4.00
154 Carlos Lee RC 1.25 3.00
155 Michael Coleman .15 .40
156 Jason Grilli RC .15 .40
157 Julio Ramirez RC .15 .40
158 Randy Wolf RC .25 .60
159 Ryan Brannan .15 .40
160 Edgard Clemente .15 .40
161 Miguel Tejada .40 1.00
162 Chad Hermansen .15 .40
163 Ryan Anderson RC .15 .40
164 Ben Petrick .15 .40
165 Alex Gonzalez .15 .40
166 Ben Davis .15 .40
167 John Patterson .15 .40
168 Cliff Politte .15 .40
169 Randall Simon .15 .40
170 Javier Vazquez .15 .40
171 Kevin Witt .15 .40
172 Geoff Jenkins .15 .40
173 David Ortiz 1.50 4.00
174 Derrick Gibson .15 .40
175 Abraham Nunez .15 .40
176 A.J. Hinch .15 .40
177 Ruben Mateo RC .15 .40
178 Magglio Ordonez RC 2.00 5.00
179 Todd Dunwoody .15 .40
180 Daryle Ward .15 .40
181 Mike Kinkade RC .15 .40
182 Willie Martinez .15 .40
183 Orlando Hernandez RC .75 2.00
184 Eric Milton .15 .40
185 Eric Chavez .15 .40
186 Damian Jackson .15 .40
187 Jim Parque RC .25 .60
188 Dan Reichert RC .25 .60
189 Mike Drumright .15 .40
190 Todd Walker .15 .40
191 Shane Monahan .15 .40
192 Derrek Lee .25 .60
193 Jeremy Giambi RC .25 .60
194 Dan McKinley RC .15 .40
195 Tony Armas Jr. RC .25 .60
196 Matt Anderson RC .15 .40
197 Jim Chamblee RC .15 .40
198 Francisco Cordero RC .40 1.00
199 Calvin Pickering .15 .40
200 Reggie Taylor .15 .40

1998 Bowman's Best Atomic Refractors

*STARS: 10X TO 25X BASIC CARDS
*YNG.STARS: 10X TO 25X BASIC CARDS
*PROSPECTS: 10X TO 25X BASIC CARDS
*ROOKIES: 6X TO 15X BASIC CARDS
STATED ODDS 1:82
STATED PRINT RUN 100 SERIAL #'d SETS
27 Ken Griffey Jr. 125.00 300.00
43 Chan Ho Park 100.00 200.00
45 Alex Rodriguez 75.00 150.00

1998 Bowman's Best Refractors

COMPLETE SET (200) 1500.00 3000.00
*STARS: 5X TO 12X BASIC CARDS
*ROOKIES: 2.5X TO 6X BASIC CARDS
STATED ODDS 1:20
STATED PRINT RUN 400 SERIAL #'d SETS
122 Kevin Millar 4.00 10.00

1998 Bowman's Best Autographs

COMPLETE SET (10) 200.00 400.00
STATED ODDS 1:180
*REFRACTORS: .75X TO 2X BASIC AU'S
REFRACTOR STATED ODDS 1:2158
*ATOMICS: 2X TO 4X BASIC AU'S
ATOMIC STATED ODDS 1:6437
SKIP-NUMBERED 10-CARD SET
5 Chipper Jones 25.00 60.00
10 Chuck Knoblauch 6.00 15.00
15 Tony Clark 4.00 10.00
20 Albert Belle 6.00 15.00
25 Jose Cruz Jr. 4.00 10.00
105 Ben Grieve 4.00 10.00
110 Paul Konerko 10.00 25.00
115 Todd Helton 6.00 15.00
120 Adrian Beltre 60.00 150.00
125 Kerry Wood 6.00 15.00

1998 Bowman's Best Mirror Image Fusion

COMPLETE SET (20) 15.00 40.00
STATED ODDS 1:12
*REFRACTORS: 1.25X TO 3X BASIC MIRROR
REFRACTOR STATED ODDS 1:809
REF.PRINT RUN 100 SERIAL #'d SETS
ATOMIC STATED ODDS 1:3237
ATOMIC PRINT RUN 25 SERIAL #'d SETS
NO ATOMIC PRICING DUE TO SCARCITY
MI1 F.Thomas 1.50 4.00
D.Ortiz
MI2 C.Knoblauch .50 1.25
E.Wilson
MI3 N.Garciaparra 1.25 3.00
M.Tejada
MI4 A.Rodriguez 1.50 4.00
M.Caruso
MI5 C.Ripken 4.00 10.00
R.Minor
MI6 K.Griffey Jr. 2.50 6.00
B.Grieve
MI7 J.Gonzalez .50 1.25
J.Encarnacion
MI8 J.Cruz Jr. .50 1.25
R.Mateo
MI9 R.Johnson 1.25 3.00
R.Anderson
MI10 I.Rodriguez .75 2.00
A.Hinch
MI11 J.Bagwell .75 2.00
P.Konerko
MI12 M.McGwire 2.00 5.00
T.Lee
MI13 C.Biggio .75 2.00
C.Hermansen
MI14 M.Grudzielanek .40 1.00
A.Gonzalez
MI15 C.Jones 1.25 3.00
A.Beltre
MI16 L.Walker .75 2.00
M.Kotsay
MI17 T.Gwynn 1.25 3.00
G.Lombard
MI18 B.Bonds 2.00 5.00
R.Hidalgo
MI19 G.Maddux 1.50 4.00
K.Wood
MI20 M.Piazza 1.25 3.00
B.Petrick

1998 Bowman's Best Performers

COMPLETE SET (10) 6.00 15.00
STATED ODDS 1:6
*REFRACTORS: 5X TO 12X BASIC PERF.
REFRACTOR STATED ODDS 1:809
REF.PRINT RUN 200 SERIAL #'d SETS
*ATOMIC: 12.5X TO 30X BASIC PERF.
ATOMIC STATED ODDS 1:3237
ATOMIC PRINT RUN 50 SERIAL #'d SETS
BP1 Ben Grieve .60 1.50
BP2 Travis Lee .60 1.50
BP3 Ryan Minor .60 1.50
BP4 Todd Helton 1.00 2.50
BP5 Brad Fullmer .60 1.50
BP6 Paul Konerko .60 1.50
BP7 Adrian Beltre .60 1.50
BP8 Richie Sexson .60 1.50
BP9 Aramis Ramirez .60 1.50
BP10 Russell Branyan .60 1.50

1999 Bowman's Best Pre-Production

COMPLETE SET (3) .75 2.00
PP1 Javy Lopez .40 1.00
PP2 Marlon Anderson .40 1.00
PP3 J.M. Gold .40 1.00

1999 Bowman's Best

The 1999 Bowman's Best set (produced by Topps) consists of 200 standard size cards. The six-card packs, released in August, 1999, retailed for a suggested price of $5 each. The cards are printed on 27-pt. Serillusion stock and feature 85 veteran stars in a striking gold series, 15 Best Performers bonus subset captured in a bronze series, 50 rookies highlighted in a brilliant blue series and 50 prospects shown in a captivating silver series. The fifty rookies and prospects (cards 151-200) were seeded at a rate of one per pack. Notable Rookie Cards included Pat Burrell, Sean Burroughs, Nick Johnson, Austin Kearns, Corey Patterson and Alfonso Soriano.

COMPLETE SET (200) 15.00 40.00
COMP.SET w/o SP's (150) 10.00 25.00
COMMON CARD (1-150) .15 .40
COMMON ROOKIE (151-200) .20 .50
ONE ROOKIE CARD PER PACK
1 Chipper Jones .40 1.00
2 Brian Jordan .15 .40
3 David Justice .15 .40
4 Jason Kendall .15 .40
5 Mo Vaughn .15 .40
6 Jim Edmonds .25 .60
7 Wade Boggs .25 .60
8 Jeromy Burnitz .15 .40
9 Todd Hundley .15 .40
10 Rondell White .15 .40
11 Cliff Floyd .15 .40
12 Sean Casey .15 .40
13 Bernie Williams .25 .60
14 Dante Bichette .15 .40
15 Greg Vaughn .15 .40
16 Andres Galarraga .25 .60
17 Ray Durham .15 .40
18 Jim Thome .25 .60
19 Gary Sheffield .15 .40
20 Frank Thomas .40 1.00
21 Orlando Hernandez .15 .40
22 Ivan Rodriguez .25 .60
23 Jose Cruz Jr. .15 .40
24 Jason Giambi .15 .40
25 Craig Biggio .25 .60
26 Kerry Wood .15 .40
27 Manny Ramirez .40 1.00
28 Curt Schilling .15 .40
29 Mike Mussina .25 .60
30 Tim Salmon .15 .40
31 Mike Piazza .40 1.00
32 Roberto Alomar .25 .60
33 Larry Walker .25 .60
34 Barry Larkin .25 .60
35 Nomar Garciaparra .25 .60
36 Paul O'Neill .25 .60
37 Todd Walker .15 .40
38 Eric Karros .15 .40
39 Brad Fullmer .15 .40
40 John Olerud .15 .40
41 Todd Helton .25 .60
42 Raul Mondesi .15 .40
43 Jose Canseco .25 .60
44 Matt Williams .15 .40
45 Ray Lankford .15 .40
46 Carlos Delgado .15 .40
47 Darin Erstad .15 .40
48 Vladimir Guerrero .25 .60
49 Robin Ventura .15 .40
50 Alex Rodriguez .50 1.25
51 Vinny Castilla .15 .40
52 Tony Clark .15 .40
53 Pedro Martinez .25 .60
54 Rafael Palmeiro .25 .60
55 Scott Rolen .25 .60
56 Tino Martinez .25 .60
57 Tony Gwynn .40 1.00
58 Barry Bonds .60 1.50
59 Kenny Lofton .15 .40
60 Javy Lopez .15 .40
61 Mark Grace .25 .60
62 Travis Lee .15 .40
63 Kevin Brown .25 .60
64 Al Leiter .15 .40
65 Albert Belle .15 .40
66 Sammy Sosa .40 1.00
67 Greg Maddux .50 1.25
68 Mark Kotsay .15 .40
69 Dmitri Young .15 .40
70 Mark McGwire .60 1.50
71 Juan Gonzalez .15 .40
72 Andruw Jones .15 .40
73 Derek Jeter 1.00 2.50
74 Randy Johnson .40 1.00
75 Cal Ripken 1.25 3.00
76 Shawn Green .15 .40
77 Moises Alou .15 .40
78 Tom Glavine .25 .60
79 Sandy Alomar Jr. .15 .40
80 Ken Griffey Jr. .75 2.00
81 Ryan Klesko .15 .40
82 Jeff Bagwell .25 .60
83 Ben Grieve .15 .40
84 John Smoltz .25 .60
85 Roger Clemens .50 1.25
86 Ken Griffey Jr. BP .75 2.00
87 Roger Clemens BP .50 1.25
88 Derek Jeter BP 1.00 2.50
89 Nomar Garciaparra BP .25 .60
90 Mark McGwire BP .60 1.50
91 Sammy Sosa BP .40 1.00
92 Alex Rodriguez BP .50 1.25
93 Greg Maddux BP .50 1.25
94 Vladimir Guerrero BP .25 .60
95 Chipper Jones BP .40 1.00
96 Kerry Wood BP .15 .40
97 Ben Grieve BP .15 .40
98 Tony Gwynn BP .40 1.00
99 Juan Gonzalez BP .15 .40
100 Mike Piazza BP .40 1.00
101 Eric Chavez .15 .40
102 Billy Koch .15 .40
103 Dernell Stenson .15 .40
104 Marlon Anderson .15 .40
105 Ron Belliard .15 .40
106 Bruce Chen .15 .40
107 Carlos Beltran .25 .60
108 Chad Hermansen .15 .40
109 Ryan Anderson .15 .40
110 Michael Barrett .15 .40
111 Matt Clement .15 .40
112 Ben Davis .15 .40
113 Calvin Pickering .15 .40
114 Brad Penny .15 .40
115 Paul Konerko .15 .40
116 Alex Gonzalez .15 .40
117 George Lombard .15 .40
118 John Patterson .15 .40
119 Rob Bell .15 .40
120 Ruben Mateo .15 .40
121 Troy Glaus .15 .40
122 Ryan Bradley .15 .40
123 Carlos Lee .15 .40
124 Gabe Kapler .15 .40
125 Ramon Hernandez .15 .40
126 Carlos Febles .15 .40
127 Mitch Meluskey .15 .40
128 Michael Cuddyer .15 .40
129 Pablo Ozuna .15 .40
130 Jayson Werth .25 .60
131 Ricky Ledee .15 .40
132 Jeremy Giambi .15 .40
133 Danny Klassen .25 .60
134 Mark DeRosa .15 .40
135 Randy Wolf .15 .40
136 Roy Halladay .25 .60
137 Derrick Gibson .15 .40
138 Ben Petrick .15 .40
139 Warren Morris .15 .40
140 Lance Berkman .25 .60
141 Russell Branyan .15 .40
142 Adrian Beltre .40 1.00
143 Juan Encarnacion .15 .40
144 Fernando Seguignol .15 .40
145 Corey Koskie .15 .40
146 Preston Wilson .15 .40
147 Homer Bush .15 .40
148 Daryle Ward .15 .40
149 Joe McEwing RC .20 .50
150 Peter Bergeron RC .20 .50
151 Pat Burrell RC .75 2.00
152 Choo Freeman RC .20 .50
153 Matt Belisle RC .20 .50
154 Carlos Pena RC .60 1.50
155 A.J. Burnett RC .30 .75
156 Doug Mientkiewicz RC .30 .75
157 Sean Burroughs RC .20 .50
158 Mike Zywica RC .20 .50
159 Corey Patterson RC .50 1.25
160 Austin Kearns RC .75 2.00
161 Chip Ambres RC .20 .50
162 Kelly Dransfeldt RC .20 .50
163 Mike Nannini RC .20 .50
164 Mark Mulder RC .60 1.50
165 Jason Tyner RC .20 .50
166 Bobby Seay RC .20 .50
167 Alex Escobar RC .20 .50
168 Nick Johnson RC .50 1.25
169 Alfonso Soriano RC 2.00 5.00
170 Clayton Andrews RC .20 .50
171 C.C. Sabathia RC 1.50 4.00
172 Matt Holliday RC 1.00 2.50
173 Brad Lidge RC .60 1.50
174 Kit Pellow RC .20 .50
175 J.M. Gold RC .20 .50
176 Roosevelt Brown RC .20 .50
177 Eric Valent RC .20 .50
178 Adam Everett RC .30 .75
179 Jorge Toca RC .20 .50
180 Matt Roney RC .20 .50
181 Andy Brown RC .20 .50
182 Phil Norton RC .20 .50
183 Mickey Lopez RC .20 .50
184 Chris George RC .20 .50
185 Arturo McDowell RC .20 .50
186 Jose Fernandez RC .20 .50
187 Seth Etherton RC .20 .50
188 Josh McKinley RC .20 .50
189 Nate Cornejo RC .20 .50
190 Giuseppe Chiaramonte RC .20 .50
191 Mamon Tucker RC .20 .50
192 Ryan Mills RC .20 .50
193 Chad Moeller RC .20 .50
194 Tony Torcato RC .20 .50
195 Jeff Winchester RC .20 .50
196 Rick Elder RC .20 .50
197 Matt Burch RC .20 .50
198 Jeff Urban RC .20 .50
199 Chris Jones RC .20 .50
200 Masao Kida RC .20 .50

1999 Bowman's Best Atomic Refractors

*ATOMIC: 10X TO 25X BASIC CARDS
*ROOKIES: 8X TO 20X BASIC CARDS
STATED ODDS 1:62
STATED PRINT RUN 100 SERIAL #'d SETS
73 Derek Jeter 75.00 150.00

1999 Bowman's Best Refractors

*STARS: 5X TO 12X BASIC CARDS
*ROOKIES: 4X TO 10X BASIC CARDS
STATED ODDS 1:15
STATED PRINT RUN 400 SERIAL #'d SETS
80 Ken Griffey Jr. 25.00 60.00

1999 Bowman's Best Franchise Best Mach I

COMPLETE SET (10) 10.00 25.00
STATED ODDS 1:41
STATED PRINT RUN 3000 SERIAL #'d SETS
*MACH II: .75X TO 2X MACH I
MACH II STATED ODDS 1:124
MACH II PRINT RUN 1000 SERIAL #'d SETS
*MACH III: 1.25X TO 3X MACH I
MACH III STATED ODDS 1:248
MACH III PRINT RUN 500 SERIAL #'d SETS
FB1 Mark McGwire 2.00 5.00
FB2 Ken Griffey Jr. 2.50 6.00
FB3 Sammy Sosa 1.25 3.00
FB4 Nomar Garciaparra .75 2.00
FB5 Alex Rodriguez 1.50 4.00
FB6 Derek Jeter 3.00 8.00
FB7 Mike Piazza 1.25 3.00
FB8 Frank Thomas 1.25 3.00
FB9 Chipper Jones 1.25 3.00
FB10 Juan Gonzalez .50 1.25

1999 Bowman's Best Franchise Favorites

COMPLETE SET (6) 12.50 30.00
STATED ODDS 1:40
FR1A Derek Jeter 4.00 10.00
FR1B Don Mattingly 3.00 8.00
FR1C D.Jeter 4.00 10.00
D.Mattingly
FR2A Scott Rolen 1.00 2.50
FR2B Mike Schmidt 2.50 6.00
FR2C S.Rolen 2.50 6.00
M.Schmidt

1999 Bowman's Best Franchise Favorites Autographs

FR1A/FR2A STATED ODDS 1:1550
FR1B/FR2B STATED ODDS 1:1550
FR1C/FR2C STATED ODDS 1:6174
FR1A Derek Jeter 100.00 200.00
FR1B Don Mattingly 30.00 60.00
FR1C D.Jeter/D.Mattingly 200.00 400.00
FR2A Scott Rolen 6.00 51.00
FR2B Mike Schmidt 15.00 40.00
FR2C S.Rolen/M.Schmidt 30.00 60.00

1999 Bowman's Best Future Foundations Mach I

COMPLETE SET (10) 6.00 15.00
STATED ODDS 1:41
STATED PRINT RUN 3000 SERIAL #'d SETS
*MACH II: .75X TO 2X MACH I
MACH II STATED ODDS 1:124
MACH II PRINT RUN 1000 SERIAL #'d SETS
*MACH III: 1.25X TO 3X MACH I
MACH III STATED ODDS 1:248
MACH III PRINT RUN 500 SERIAL #'d SETS
FF1 Ruben Mateo .40 1.00
FF2 Troy Glaus .40 1.00
FF3 Eric Chavez .40 1.00
FF4 Pat Burrell 1.50 4.00
FF5 Adrian Beltre 1.00 2.50
FF6 Ryan Anderson .40 1.00
FF7 Alfonso Soriano 4.00 10.00
FF8 Brad Penny .40 1.00
FF9 Derrick Gibson .40 1.00
FF10 Bruce Chen .40 1.00

1999 Bowman's Best Mirror Image

COMPLETE SET (10) 10.00 25.00
*REFRACTORS: .75X TO 2X BASIC MIR.IMAGE
REFRACTOR STATED ODDS 1:96
*ATOMIC: 1.25X TO 3X BASIC MIR.IMAGE
ATOMIC STATED ODDS 1:192
M1 A.Rodriguez 1.25 3.00
A.Gonzalez
M2 K.Griffey Jr. 2.00 5.00
R.Mateo
M3 D.Jeter 4.00 10.00
A.Soriano
M4 S.Sosa 1.00 2.50
C.Patterson
M5 G.Maddux 1.25 3.00
B.Chen
M6 C.Jones 1.00 2.50
E.Chavez
M7 V.Guerrero .60 1.50
C.Beltran
M8 F.Thomas 1.00 2.50
N.Johnson
M9 N.Garciaparra .60 1.50
P.Ozuna
M10 M.McGwire 1.50 4.00
P.Burrell

1999 Bowman's Best Rookie Locker Room Autographs

STATED ODDS 1:248
RA1 Pat Burrell 8.00 20.00
RA2 Michael Barrett 4.00 10.00
RA3 Troy Glaus 6.00 15.00
RA4 Gabe Kapler 4.00 10.00
RA5 Eric Chavez 4.00 10.00

1999 Bowman's Best Rookie Locker Room Game Used Bats

STATED ODDS 1:517
RB1 Pat Burrell 6.00 15.00
RB2 Michael Barrett 3.00 8.00
RB3 Troy Glaus 4.00 10.00
RB4 Gabe Kapler 3.00 8.00
RB5 Eric Chavez 3.00 8.00
RB6 Richie Sexson 3.00 8.00

1999 Bowman's Best Rookie Locker Room Game Worn Jerseys

STATED ODDS 1:538
RJ1 Richie Sexson 4.00 10.00
RJ2 Michael Barrett 4.00 10.00
RJ3 Troy Glaus 6.00 15.00
RJ4 Eric Chavez 4.00 10.00

1999 Bowman's Best Rookie of the Year

STATED ODDS 1:95
GRIEVE AU STATED ODDS 1:1239
ROY1 Ben Grieve .75 2.00
ROY2 Kerry Wood .75 2.00
ROY1A Ben Grieve AU 6.00 15.00

2000 Bowman's Best Pre-Production

COMPLETE SET (3) 1.50 4.00
PP1 Larry Walker .60 1.50
PP2 Adam Dunn .60 1.50
PP3 Brett Myers 1.25 3.00

2000 Bowman's Best Previews

COMPLETE SET (10) 8.00 20.00
STATED ODDS 1:18 HOB/RET, 1:8 HTC
BB1 Derek Jeter 2.50 6.00
BB2 Ken Griffey Jr. 2.00 5.00
BB3 Nomar Garciaparra .60 1.50
BB4 Mike Piazza 1.00 2.50
BB5 Alex Rodriguez 1.25 3.00
BB6 Sammy Sosa 1.00 2.50
BB7 Mark McGwire 1.50 4.00
BB8 Pat Burrell .40 1.00
BB9 Josh Hamilton 1.25 3.00
BB10 Adam Platt .40 1.00

2000 Bowman's Best

COMP.SET w/o RC's (150) 10.00 25.00
COMMON CARD (1-150) .15 .40
COMMON ROOKIE (151-200) .50 1.25
RC 151-200 STATED ODDS 1:7
RC 151-200 PRINT RUN 2999 SERIAL #'d SETS
1 Nomar Garciaparra .25 .60
2 Chipper Jones .40 1.00
3 Tony Clark .15 .40
4 Bernie Williams .25 .60
5 Barry Bonds .60 1.50
6 Jermaine Dye .15 .40
7 John Olerud .15 .40
8 Mike Hampton .15 .40
9 Cal Ripken 1.25 3.00

10 Jeff Bagwell .25 .60
11 Troy Glaus .15 .40
12 J.D. Drew .15 .40
13 Jeromy Burnitz .15 .40
14 Carlos Delgado .15 .40
15 Shawn Green .15 .40
16 Kevin Millwood .15 .40
17 Rondell White .15 .40
18 Scott Rolen .25 .60
19 Jeff Cirillo .15 .40
20 Barry Larkin .25 .60
21 Brian Giles .15 .40
22 Roger Clemens .50 1.25
23 Manny Ramirez .40 1.00
24 Alex Gonzalez .15 .40
25 Mark Grace .25 .60
26 Fernando Tatis .15 .40
27 Randy Johnson .40 1.00
28 Roger Cedeno .15 .40
29 Brian Jordan .15 .40
30 Kevin Brown .15 .40
31 Greg Vaughn .15 .40
32 Roberto Alomar .25 .60
33 Larry Walker .25 .60
34 Rafael Palmeiro .25 .60
35 Curt Schilling .25 .60
36 Orlando Hernandez .15 .40
37 Todd Walker .15 .40
38 Juan Gonzalez .15 .40
39 Sean Casey .15 .40
40 Tony Gwynn .40 1.00
41 Albert Belle .15 .40
42 Gary Sheffield .15 .40
43 Michael Barrett .15 .40
44 Preston Wilson .15 .40
45 Jim Thome .25 .60
46 Shannon Stewart .15 .40
47 Mo Vaughn .15 .40
48 Ben Grieve .15 .40
49 Adrian Beltre .40 1.00
50 Sammy Sosa .40 1.00
51 Bob Abreu .15 .40
52 Edgardo Alfonzo .15 .40
53 Carlos Febles .15 .40
54 Frank Thomas .40 1.00
55 Alex Rodriguez .50 1.25
56 Cliff Floyd .15 .40
57 Jose Canseco .25 .60
58 Erubiel Durazo .15 .40
59 Tim Hudson .25 .60
60 Craig Biggio .25 .60
61 Eric Karros .15 .40
62 Mike Mussina .25 .60
63 Robin Ventura .15 .40
64 Carlos Beltran .25 .60
65 Pedro Martinez .25 .60
66 Gabe Kapler .15 .40
67 Jason Kendall .15 .40
68 Derek Jeter 1.00 2.50
69 Magglio Ordonez .25 .60
70 Mike Piazza .40 1.00
71 Mike Lieberthal .15 .40
72 Andres Galarraga .25 .60
73 Raul Mondesi .15 .40
74 Eric Chavez .15 .40
75 Greg Maddux .50 1.25
76 Matt Williams .15 .40
77 Kris Benson .15 .40
78 Ivan Rodriguez .25 .60
79 Pokey Reese .15 .40
80 Vladimir Guerrero .25 .60
81 Mark McGwire .60 1.50
82 Vinny Castilla .15 .40
83 Todd Helton .25 .60
84 Andruw Jones .15 .40
85 Ken Griffey Jr. .75 2.00
86 Mark McGwire BP .60 1.50
87 Derek Jeter BP 1.00 2.50
88 Chipper Jones BP .40 1.00
89 Nomar Garciaparra BP .25 .60
90 Sammy Sosa BP .40 1.00
91 Cal Ripken BP 1.25 3.00
92 Juan Gonzalez BP .15 .40
93 Alex Rodriguez BP .50 1.25
94 Barry Bonds BP .60 1.50
95 Sean Casey BP .15 .40
96 Vladimir Guerrero BP .25 .60
97 Mike Piazza BP .40 1.00
98 Shawn Green BP .15 .40
99 Jeff Bagwell BP .25 .60
100 Ken Griffey Jr. BP .75 2.00
101 Rick Ankiel .25 .60
102 John Patterson .15 .40
103 David Walling .15 .40
104 Michael Restovich .15 .40
105 A.J. Burnett .15 .40
106 Pablo Ozuna .15 .40
107 Chad Hermansen .15 .40
108 Choo Freeman .15 .40
109 Mark Quinn .15 .40
110 Corey Patterson .15 .40
111 Ramon Ortiz .15 .40
112 Vernon Wells .15 .40
113 Milton Bradley .15 .40
114 Gookie Dawkins .15 .40
115 Sean Burroughs .15 .40
116 Wily Mo Pena .15 .40
117 Dee Brown .15 .40
118 C.C. Sabathia .25 .60
119 Adam Kennedy .15 .40
120 Octavio Dotel .15 .40
121 Kip Wells .15 .40
122 Ben Petrick .15 .40
123 Mark Mulder .15 .40
124 Jason Standridge .15 .40
125 Adam Piatt .15 .40
126 Steve Lomasney .15 .40
127 Jayson Werth .25 .60
128 Alex Escobar .15 .40
129 Ryan Anderson .15 .40
130 Adam Dunn .25 .60
131 Ted Lilly .15 .40
132 Brad Penny .15 .40
133 Daryle Ward .15 .40
134 Eric Munson .15 .40
135 Nick Johnson .15 .40
136 Jason Jennings .15 .40
137 Tim Raines Jr. .15 .40
138 Ruben Mateo .15 .40
139 Jack Cust .15 .40
140 Rafael Furcal .25 .60
141 Eric Gagne .15 .40
142 Tony Armas Jr. .15 .40
143 Mike Paradis .15 .40
144 Peter Bergeron .15 .40
145 Alfonso Soriano .40 1.00
146 Josh Hamilton .50 1.25
147 Michael Cuddyer .15 .40
148 Jay Gehrke .15 .40
149 Josh Girdley .15 .40
150 Pat Burrell .15 .40
151 Brett Myers RC 1.50 4.00
152 Scott Seabol RC .50 1.25
153 Keith Reed RC .50 1.25
154 Francisco Rodriguez RC 3.00 8.00
155 Barry Zito RC 4.00 10.00
156 Pat Manning RC .50 1.25
157 Ben Christensen RC .50 1.25
158 Corey Myers RC .50 1.25
159 Wascar Serrano RC .50 1.25
160 Wes Anderson RC .50 1.25
161 Andy Tracy RC .50 1.25
162 Cesar Saba RC .50 1.25
163 Mike Lamb RC .50 1.25
164 Bobby Bradley RC .50 1.25
165 Vince Faison RC .50 1.25
166 Ty Howington RC .50 1.25
167 Ken Harvey RC .50 1.25
168 Josh Kalinowski RC .50 1.25
169 Ruben Salazar RC .50 1.25
170 Aaron Rowand RC 2.50 6.00
171 Ramon Santiago RC .50 1.25
172 Scott Sobkowiak RC .50 1.25
173 Lyle Overbay RC .75 2.00
174 Rico Washington RC .50 1.25
175 Rick Asadoorian RC .50 1.25
176 Matt Ginter RC .50 1.25
177 Jason Stumm RC .50 1.25
178 B.J. Garbe RC .50 1.25
179 Mike MacDougal RC .75 2.00
180 Ryan Christianson RC .50 1.25
181 Kurt Ainsworth RC .50 1.25
182 Brad Baisley RC .50 1.25
183 Ben Broussard RC .75 2.00
184 Aaron McNeal RC .50 1.25
185 John Sneed RC .50 1.25
186 Junior Brignac RC .50 1.25
187 Chance Caple RC .50 1.25
188 Scott Downs RC .50 1.25
189 Matt Cepicky RC .50 1.25
190 Chin-Feng Chen RC 1.50 4.00
191 Johan Santana RC 8.00 20.00
192 Brad Baker RC .50 1.25
193 Jason Repko RC .50 1.25
194 Craig Dingman RC .50 1.25
195 Chris Wakeland RC .50 1.25
196 Rogelio Arias RC .50 1.25
197 Luis Matos RC .50 1.25
198 Rob Ramsay .50 1.25
199 Willie Bloomquist RC 5.00 12.00
200 Tony Pena Jr. RC .50 1.25

2000 Bowman's Best Autographed Baseball Redemptions

STATED ODDS 1:688
EXCHANGE DEADLINE 06/30/01
PRICES REFER TO SIGNED BASEBALLS
1 Josh Hamilton 10.00 25.00
2 Rick Ankiel 15.00 40.00
3 Alfonso Soriano 12.00 30.00
4 Nick Johnson 15.00 40.00
5 Corey Patterson 15.00 40.00

2000 Bowman's Best Bets

COMPLETE SET (10) 3.00 8.00
STATED ODDS 1:15
BBB1 Pat Burrell .40 1.00
BBB2 Alfonso Soriano 1.00 2.50
BBB3 Corey Patterson .40 1.00
BBB4 Eric Munson .40 1.00
BBB5 Sean Burroughs .40 1.00
BBB6 Rafael Furcal .60 1.50
BBB7 Rick Ankiel .60 1.50
BBB8 Nick Johnson .40 1.00
BBB9 Ruben Mateo .40 1.00
BBB10 Josh Hamilton 1.25 3.00

2000 Bowman's Best Franchise 2000

COMPLETE SET (25) 20.00 50.00
STATED ODDS 1:18
F1 Cal Ripken 3.00 8.00
F2 Nomar Garciaparra .60 1.50
F3 Frank Thomas 1.00 2.50
F4 Manny Ramirez 1.00 2.50
F5 Juan Gonzalez .40 1.00
F6 Carlos Beltran .60 1.50
F7 Derek Jeter 2.50 6.00
F8 Alex Rodriguez 1.25 3.00
F9 Ben Grieve .40 1.00
F10 Jose Canseco .60 1.50
F11 Ivan Rodriguez .60 1.50
F12 Mo Vaughn .40 1.00
F13 Randy Johnson 1.00 2.50
F14 Chipper Jones 1.00 2.50
F15 Sammy Sosa 1.00 2.50
F16 Ken Griffey Jr. 2.00 5.00
F17 Larry Walker .60 1.50
F18 Preston Wilson .40 1.00
F19 Jeff Bagwell .60 1.50
F20 Shawn Green .40 1.00
F21 Vladimir Guerrero .60 1.50
F22 Mike Piazza 1.00 2.50
F23 Scott Rolen .60 1.50
F24 Tony Gwynn 1.00 2.50
F25 Barry Bonds 1.50 4.00

2000 Bowman's Best Franchise Favorites

COMPLETE SET (6) 6.00 15.00
STATED ODDS 1:17
FR1A Sean Casey .40 1.00
FR1B Johnny Bench 1.00 2.50
FR1C S.Casey 1.00 2.50
J.Bench
FR2A Cal Ripken 3.00 8.00
FR2B Brooks Robinson .60 1.50
FR2C C.Ripken 3.00 8.00
B.Robinson

2000 Bowman's Best Franchise Favorites Autographs

GROUP A STATED ODDS 1:1291
GROUP B STATED ODDS 1:1291
GROUP C STATED ODDS 1:5153
OVERALL STATED ODDS 1:574
FR1A Sean Casey A 10.00 25.00
FR1B Johnny Bench B 30.00 60.00
FR1C S.Casey/J.Bench C 30.00 60.00
FR2A Cal Ripken A 40.00 80.00
FR2B Brooks Robinson B 15.00 40.00
FR2C C.Ripken/B.Robinson C 150.00 250.00

2000 Bowman's Best Locker Room Collection Autographs

GROUP A STATED ODDS 1:1033
GROUP B STATED ODDS 1:61
OVERALL STATED ODDS 1:57
LRCA1 Carlos Beltran B 8.00 20.00
LRCA2 Rick Ankiel A 6.00 15.00
LRCA3 Vernon Wells A 6.00 15.00
LRCA4 Ruben Mateo A 4.00 10.00
LRCA5 Ben Petrick A 4.00 10.00
LRCA6 Adam Piatt A 4.00 10.00
LRCA7 Eric Munson A 4.00 10.00
LRCA8 Alfonso Soriano A 4.00 10.00
LRCA9 Kerry Wood B 6.00 15.00
LRCA10 Jack Cust A 4.00 10.00
LRCA11 Rafael Furcal A 4.00 10.00
LRCA12 Josh Hamilton 12.50 30.00
LRCA13 Brad Penny A 4.00 10.00
LRCA14 Dee Brown A 4.00 10.00
LRCA15 Milton Bradley A 6.00 15.00
LRCA16 Ryan Anderson A 6.00 15.00
LRCA17 John Patterson A 6.00 15.00
LRCA18 Nick Johnson A 6.00 15.00
LRCA19 Peter Bergeron A 4.00 10.00

2000 Bowman's Best Locker Room Collection Bats

STATED ODDS 1:376
LRCLAP Adam Piatt 3.00 8.00
LRCLBP Ben Petrick 3.00 8.00
LRCLBP Brad Penny 4.00 10.00
LRCLCB Carlos Beltran 4.00 10.00
LRCLDB Dee Brown 3.00 8.00
LRCLEM Eric Munson 3.00 8.00
LRCLJD J.D. Drew 4.00 10.00
LRCLPB Pat Burrell 4.00 10.00
LRCLRA Rick Ankiel 6.00 15.00
LRCLRF Rafael Furcal 4.00 10.00
LRCLVW Vernon Wells 4.00 10.00

2000 Bowman's Best Locker Room Collection Jerseys

STATED ODDS 1:206
LRCJ1 Carlos Beltran 4.00 10.00
LRCJ2 Rick Ankiel 6.00 15.00
LRCJ3 Mark Quinn 3.00 8.00
LRCJ4 Ben Petrick 3.00 8.00
LRCJ5 Adam Piatt 3.00 8.00

2000 Bowman's Best Selections

COMPLETE SET (15) 20.00 50.00
STATED ODDS 1:30
BBS1 Alex Rodriguez 2.00 5.00
BBS2 Ken Griffey Jr. 3.00 8.00
BBS3 Pat Burrell .60 1.50
BBS4 Mark McGwire 2.50 6.00
BBS5 Derek Jeter 4.00 10.00
BBS6 Nomar Garciaparra 1.00 2.50
BBS7 Mike Piazza 1.50 4.00
BBS8 Josh Hamilton 2.00 5.00
BBS9 Cal Ripken 5.00 12.00
BBS10 Jeff Bagwell 1.00 2.50
BBS11 Chipper Jones 1.50 4.00
BBS12 Jose Canseco 1.00 2.50
BBS13 Carlos Beltran 1.00 2.50
BBS14 Kerry Wood .60 1.50
BBS15 Ben Grieve .60 1.50

2000 Bowman's Best Year by Year

COMPLETE SET (10) 8.00 20.00
STATED ODDS 1:23
YY1 S.Sosa 2.00 5.00
K.Griffey Jr.
YY2 N.Garciaparra .60 1.50
V.Guerrero
YY3 A.Rodriguez 1.25 3.00
J.Cirillo
YY4 M.Piazza 1.00 2.50
P.Martinez
YY5 D.Jeter 2.50 6.00
E.Alfonzo
YY6 A.Soriano 1.00 2.50
R.Ankiel
YY7 M.McGwire 1.50 4.00
B.Bonds
YY8 J.Gonzalez .60 1.50
L.Walker
YY9 I.Rodriguez .60 1.50
J.Bagwell
YY10 S.Green 1.00 2.50
M.Ramirez

2001 Bowman's Best Promos

COMPLETE SET (3) 2.00 5.00
PP1 Todd Helton .80 2.00
PP2 Tim Hudson .80 2.00
PP3 Vernon Wells .40 1.00

2001 Bowman's Best

COMP.SET w/o SP's (150) 20.00 50.00
COMMON CARD (1-150) .15 .40
COMMON CARD (151-200) 2.00 5.00
151-185 STATED ODDS 1:7
186-200 EXCLUSIVE RC ODDS 1:15
151-200 PRINT RUN 2999 SERIAL #'d SETS
1 Vladimir Guerrero .40 1.00
2 Miguel Tejada .15 .40
3 Geoff Jenkins .15 .40
4 Jeff Bagwell .25 .60
5 Todd Helton .25 .60
6 Ken Griffey Jr. .75 2.00
7 Nomar Garciaparra .60 1.50
8 Chipper Jones .40 1.00
9 Darin Erstad .15 .40
10 Frank Thomas .40 1.00
11 Jim Thome .25 .60
12 Preston Wilson .15 .40
13 Kevin Brown .15 .40
14 Derek Jeter 1.00 2.50
15 Scott Rolen .25 .60
16 Ryan Klesko .15 .40
17 Jeff Kent .15 .40
18 Raul Mondesi .15 .40
19 Greg Vaughn .15 .40
20 Bernie Williams .25 .60
21 Mike Piazza .60 1.50
22 Richard Hidalgo .15 .40
23 Dean Palmer .15 .40
24 Roberto Alomar .25 .60
25 Sammy Sosa .40 1.00
26 Randy Johnson .40 1.00
27 Manny Ramirez Sox .25 .60
28 Roger Clemens .75 2.00
29 Terrence Long .15 .40
30 Jason Kendall .15 .40
31 Richie Sexson .15 .40
32 David Wells .15 .40
33 Andruw Jones .25 .60
34 Pokey Reese .15 .40
35 Juan Gonzalez .15 .40
36 Carlos Beltran .25 .60
37 Shawn Green .15 .40
38 Mariano Rivera .40 1.00
39 John Olerud .15 .40
40 Jim Edmonds .15 .40
41 Andres Galarraga .15 .40
42 Carlos Delgado .15 .40
43 Kris Benson .15 .40
44 Andy Pettitte .25 .60
45 Jeff Cirillo .15 .40
46 Magglio Ordonez .15 .40
47 Tom Glavine .25 .60
48 Garret Anderson .15 .40
49 Cal Ripken 1.25 3.00
50 Pedro Martinez .25 .60
51 Barry Bonds 1.00 2.50
52 Alex Rodriguez .50 1.25
53 Ben Grieve .15 .40
54 Edgar Martinez .25 .60
55 Jason Giambi .15 .40
56 Jeromy Burnitz .15 .40
57 Mike Mussina .25 .60
58 Moises Alou .15 .40
59 Sean Casey .15 .40
60 Greg Maddux .60 1.50
61 Tim Hudson .15 .40
62 Mark McGwire 1.00 2.50
63 Rafael Palmeiro .25 .60
64 Tony Batista .15 .40
65 Kazuhiro Sasaki .15 .40
66 Jorge Posada .25 .60
67 Johnny Damon .25 .60
68 Brian Giles .15 .40
69 Jose Vidro .15 .40
70 Jermaine Dye .15 .40
71 Craig Biggio .25 .60
72 Larry Walker .25 .60
73 Eric Chavez .15 .40
74 David Segui .15 .40
75 Tim Salmon .25 .60
76 Javy Lopez .15 .40
77 Paul Konerko .15 .40
78 Barry Larkin .25 .60
79 Mike Hampton .15 .40
80 Bobby Higginson .15 .40
81 Mark Mulder .15 .40
82 Pat Burrell .15 .40
83 Kerry Wood .15 .40
84 J.T. Snow .15 .40
85 Ivan Rodriguez .25 .60
86 Edgardo Alfonzo .15 .40
87 Orlando Hernandez .15 .40
88 Gary Sheffield .15 .40
89 Mike Sweeney .15 .40
90 Carlos Lee .15 .40
91 Rafael Furcal .15 .40
92 Troy Glaus .15 .40
93 Bartolo Colon .15 .40
94 Cliff Floyd .15 .40
95 Barry Zito .25 .60
96 J.D. Drew .15 .40
97 Eric Karros .15 .40
98 Jose Valentin .15 .40
99 Ellis Burks .15 .40
100 David Justice .15 .40
101 Larry Barnes .15 .40
102 Rod Barajas .15 .40
103 Tony Pena Jr. .15 .40
104 Jerry Hairston Jr. .15 .40
105 Keith Ginter .15 .40
106 Corey Patterson .15 .40
107 Aaron Rowand .15 .40
108 Miguel Olivo .15 .40
109 Gookie Dawkins .15 .40
110 C.C. Sabathia .15 .40
111 Ben Petrick .15 .40
112 Eric Munson .15 .40
113 Ramon Castro .15 .40
114 Alex Escobar .15 .40
115 Josh Hamilton/2 .30 .75
116 Jason Marquis .15 .40
117 Ben Davis .15 .40
118 Alex Cintron .15 .40
119 Julio Zuleta .15 .40
120 Ben Broussard .15 .40
121 Adam Everett .15 .40
122 Ramon Carvajal RC .15 .40
123 Felipe Lopez .15 .40
124 Alfonso Soriano .25 .60
125 Jayson Werth .15 .40
126 Donzell McDonald .15 .40
127 Jason Hart .15 .40
128 Joe Crede .40 1.00
129 Sean Burroughs .15 .40
130 Jack Cust .15 .40
131 Corey Smith .15 .40
132 Adrian Gonzalez 1.00 2.50
133 J.R. House .15 .40
134 Steve Lomasney .15 .40
135 Tim Raines Jr. .15 .40
136 Tony Alvarez .15 .40
137 Doug Mientkiewicz .15 .40
138 Rocco Baldelli .15 .40
139 Jason Romano .15 .40
140 Vernon Wells .15 .40
141 Mike Bynum .15 .40
142 Xavier Nady .15 .40
143 Brad Wilkerson .15 .40
144 Ben Diggins .15 .40
145 Aubrey Huff .15 .40
146 Eric Byrnes .15 .40
147 Alex Gordon .15 .40
148 Roy Oswalt .40 1.00
149 Brian Esposito .15 .40
150 Scott Seabol .15 .40
151 Erick Almonte RC 2.00 5.00
152 Gary Johnson RC 2.00 5.00
153 Pedro Liriano RC 2.00 5.00
154 Matt White RC 2.00 5.00
155 Luis Montanez RC 2.50 6.00
156 Brad Cresse 2.00 5.00
157 Wilson Betemit RC 3.00 8.00
158 Octavio Martinez RC 2.00 5.00
159 Adam Pettyjohn RC 2.00 5.00
160 Corey Spencer RC 2.00 5.00
161 Mark Burnett RC 2.00 5.00
162 Ichiro Suzuki RC 40.00 100.00
163 Alexis Gomez RC 2.00 5.00
164 Greg Nash RC 2.00 5.00
165 Roberto Miniel RC 2.00 5.00
166 Justin Morneau RC 4.00 10.00
167 Ben Washburn RC 2.00 5.00
168 Bob Keppel RC 2.00 5.00
169 Deivi Mendez RC 2.00 5.00
170 Tsuyoshi Shinjo RC 3.00 8.00
171 Jared Abruzzo RC 2.00 5.00
172 Derrick Van Dusen RC 2.00 5.00
173 Hee Seop Choi RC 3.00 8.00
174 Albert Pujols RC 75.00 200.00
175 Travis Hafner RC 6.00 15.00
176 Ron Davenport RC 2.00 5.00
177 Luis Torres RC 2.00 5.00
178 Jake Peavy RC 5.00 12.00
179 Elvis Corporan RC 2.00 5.00
180 Dave Krynzel 2.00 5.00
181 Tony Blanco RC 2.00 5.00
182 Elpidio Guzman RC 2.00 5.00
183 Matt Butler RC 2.00 5.00
184 Joe Thurston RC 2.00 5.00
185 Andy Beal RC 2.00 5.00
186 Kevin Nulton RC 2.00 5.00
187 Sneideer Santos RC 2.00 5.00
188 Joe Dillon RC 2.00 5.00
189 Jeremy Blevins RC 2.00 5.00
190 Chris Amador RC 2.00 5.00
191 Mark Hendrickson RC 2.00 5.00
192 Willy Aybar RC 2.00 5.00
193 Antoine Cameron RC 2.00 5.00
194 J.J. Johnson RC 2.00 5.00
195 Ryan Ketchner RC 2.00 5.00
196 Bjorn Ivy RC 2.00 5.00
197 Josh Kroeger RC 2.00 5.00
198 Ty Wigginton RC 3.00 8.00
199 Stubby Clapp RC 2.00 5.00
200 Jerrod Riggan RC 2.00 5.00

2001 Bowman's Best Autographs

STATED ODDS 1:95
BBAAG Adrian Gonzalez 10.00 25.00
BBABC Brad Cresse 4.00 10.00
BBAJH Josh Hamilton 10.00 25.00
BBAJR Jon Rauch 4.00 10.00
BBAJRH J.R. House 4.00 10.00
BBASB Sean Burroughs 4.00 10.00
BBATL Terrence Long 4.00 10.00

2001 Bowman's Best Exclusive Autographs

STATED ODDS 1:50
BBEABI Bjorn Ivy 3.00 8.00
BBEAJB Jeremy Blevins 3.00 8.00
BBEAJJ J.J. Johnson 3.00 8.00
BBEAJR Jerrod Riggan 3.00 8.00
BBEAMH Mark Hendrickson 3.00 8.00
BBEASC Stubby Clapp 3.00 8.00
BBEASS Sneideer Santos 3.00 8.00
BBEATW Ty Wigginton 4.00 10.00
BBEAWA Willy Aybar 3.00 8.00

2001 Bowman's Best Franchise Favorites

COMPLETE SET (9) 20.00 50.00
STATED ODDS 1:16
FFAR Alex Rodriguez 2.50 6.00
FFDE Darin Erstad 1.50 4.00
FFDM Don Mattingly 5.00 12.00
FFDW Dave Winfield 1.50 4.00
FFEJ D.Erstad 1.50 4.00
R.Jackson
FFMW D.Mattingly 5.00 12.00
D.Winfield
FFNR Nolan Ryan 5.00 12.00
FFRJ Reggie Jackson 1.50 4.00
FFRR N.Ryan 4.00 10.00
A.Rodriguez

2001 Bowman's Best Franchise Favorites Autographs

SINGLE STATED ODDS 1:556
DOUBLE STATED ODDS 1:4436
FFAAR Alex Rodriguez 30.00 60.00
FFADE Darin Erstad 6.00 15.00
FFADM Don Mattingly 30.00 60.00
FFADW Dave Winfield 15.00 40.00
FFAEJ D.Erstad/R.Jackson 40.00 80.00
FFAMW Mattingly/Winfield 125.00 200.00
FFANR Nolan Ryan 50.00 100.00
FFARJ Reggie Jackson 15.00 40.00
FFARR N.Ryan/A.Rodriguez 175.00 350.00

2001 Bowman's Best Franchise Favorites Relics

STATED JSY ODDS 1:139
STATED JSY/JSY ODDS 1:1114
STATED UNIFORM ODDS 1:307
STATED UNIFORM/UNIFORM ODDS 1:2456
FFAR Alex Rodriguez Jsy 12.50 30.00
FFRBB Biggio U/Bagwell U 15.00 40.00
FFRCB Craig Biggio Uni 6.00 15.00
FFRDE Darin Erstad Jsy 4.00 10.00
FFRDM Don Mattingly Jsy 15.00 40.00
FFRDW Dave Winfield Jsy 4.00 10.00
FFREJ D.Erstad J/R.Jackson J 15.00 40.00
FFRJB Jeff Bagwell Uni 6.00 15.00
FFRMW Mattingly J/Winfield J 15.00 40.00
FFRNR Nolan Ryan Jsy 10.00 25.00
FFRRJ Reggie Jackson Jsy 6.00 15.00
FFRRR N.Ryan J/A.Rod J 20.00 50.00

2001 Bowman's Best Franchise Futures

COMPLETE SET (12) 12.50 30.00
STATED ODDS 1:24
FF1 Josh Hamilton 1.50 4.00
FF2 Wes Helms .75 2.00
FF3 Alfonso Soriano .75 2.00
FF4 Nick Johnson .75 2.00
FF5 Jose Ortiz .75 2.00
FF6 Ben Sheets .75 2.00
FF7 Sean Burroughs .75 2.00
FF8 Ben Petrick .75 2.00
FF9 Corey Patterson .75 2.00
FF10 J.R. House .75 2.00
FF11 Alex Escobar .75 2.00
FF12 Travis Hafner 2.50 6.00

2001 Bowman's Best Impact Players

COMPLETE SET (20) 12.50 30.00
STATED ODDS 1:7
IP1 Mark McGwire 2.00 5.00
IP2 Sammy Sosa .75 2.00
IP3 Manny Ramirez .50 1.25
IP4 Troy Glaus .40 1.00
IP5 Ken Griffey Jr. 1.50 4.00
IP6 Gary Sheffield .40 1.00
IP7 Vladimir Guerrero .75 2.00
IP8 Carlos Delgado .40 1.00
IP9 Jason Giambi .40 1.00
IP10 Frank Thomas .75 2.00
IP11 Vernon Wells .40 1.00
IP12 Carlos Pena .40 1.00
IP13 Joe Crede .75 2.00
IP14 Keith Ginter .40 1.00
IP15 Aubrey Huff .40 1.00
IP16 Brad Cresse .40 1.00
IP17 Austin Kearns .40 1.00
IP18 Nick Johnson .40 1.00
IP19 Josh Hamilton .75 2.00
IP20 Corey Patterson .40 1.00

2001 Bowman's Best Locker Room Collection Jerseys

STATED ODDS 1:133
LRCJEC Eric Chavez 4.00 10.00
LRCJJP Jay Payton 3.00 8.00
LRCJMM Mark Mulder 4.00 10.00
LRCJPR Pokey Reese 3.00 8.00
LRCJPW Preston Wilson 4.00 10.00

2001 Bowman's Best Locker Room Collection Lumber

STATED ODDS 1:267
LRCLAG Adrian Gonzalez 3.00 8.00
LRCLCP Corey Patterson 3.00 8.00
LRCLEM Eric Munson 3.00 8.00
LRCLPB Pat Burrell 4.00 10.00
LRCLSB Sean Burroughs 3.00 8.00

2001 Bowman's Best Rookie Fever

COMPLETE SET (10) 6.00 15.00
STATED ODDS 1:10
RF1 Chipper Jones .60 1.50
RF2 Preston Wilson .40 1.00
RF3 Todd Helton .40 1.00
RF4 Jay Payton .40 1.00
RF5 Ivan Rodriguez .40 1.00
RF6 Manny Ramirez .40 1.00
RF7 Derek Jeter 1.50 4.00
RF8 Orlando Hernandez .40 1.00
RF9 Mark Quinn .40 1.00
RF10 Terrence Long .40 1.00

2002 Bowman's Best

COMP.SET w/o SP's (90) 40.00 100.00
COMMON CARD (1-90) .30 .75
COMMON AUTO A (91-180) 3.00 8.00
AUTO GROUP A ODDS 1:3
COMMON AUTO B (91-180) 4.00 10.00
AUTO GROUP B ODDS 1:19
COMMON BAT (91-180) 2.00 5.00
91-180 BAT STATED ODDS 1:5
181 ISHII BAT EXCHANGE ODDS 1:131
ISHII EXCHANGE DEADLINE 12/31/02
1 Josh Beckett .30 .75
2 Derek Jeter 2.00 5.00
3 Alex Rodriguez 1.00 2.50
4 Miguel Tejada .30 .75
5 Nomar Garciaparra 1.25 3.00
6 Aramis Ramirez .30 .75
7 Jeremy Giambi .30 .75
8 Bernie Williams .50 1.25
9 Juan Pierre .30 .75
10 Chipper Jones .75 2.00
11 Jimmy Rollins .30 .75
12 Alfonso Soriano .30 .75
13 Mark Prior .50 1.25
14 Paul Konerko .30 .75
15 Tim Hudson .30 .75
16 Doug Mientkiewicz .30 .75
17 Todd Helton .50 1.25
18 Moises Alou .30 .75
19 Juan Gonzalez .30 .75
20 Jorge Posada .50 1.25
21 Jeff Kent .30 .75
22 Roger Clemens 1.50 4.00
23 Phil Nevin .30 .75
24 Brian Giles .30 .75
25 Carlos Delgado .30 .75
26 Jason Giambi .30 .75
27 Vladimir Guerrero .75 2.00
28 Cliff Floyd .30 .75
29 Shea Hillenbrand .30 .75
30 Ken Griffey Jr. 1.50 4.00
31 Mike Piazza 1.25 3.00
32 Carlos Pena .30 .75
33 Larry Walker .30 .75
34 Magglio Ordonez .30 .75
35 Mike Mussina .50 1.25
36 Andruw Jones .50 1.25
37 Nick Johnson .30 .75
38 Curt Schilling .30 .75
39 Eric Chavez .30 .75
40 Bartolo Colon .30 .75
41 Eric Hinske .30 .75
42 Sean Burroughs .30 .75
43 Randy Johnson .75 2.00
44 Adam Dunn .30 .75
45 Pedro Martinez .50 1.25
46 Garret Anderson .30 .75
47 Jim Thome .50 1.25
48 Gary Sheffield .30 .75
49 Tsuyoshi Shinjo .30 .75
50 Albert Pujols 1.50 4.00
51 Ichiro Suzuki 1.50 4.00
52 C.C. Sabathia .30 .75
53 Bobby Abreu .30 .75
54 Ivan Rodriguez .50 1.25
55 J.D. Drew .30 .75
56 Jacque Jones .30 .75
57 Jason Kendall .30 .75
58 Javier Vazquez .30 .75
59 Jeff Bagwell .50 1.25
60 Greg Maddux 1.25 3.00
61 Jim Edmonds .30 .75
62 Hank Blalock .50 1.25
63 Jose Vidro .30 .75
64 Kevin Brown .30 .75
65 Mark Teixeira .75 2.00
66 Sammy Sosa .75 2.00
67 Lance Berkman .30 .75
68 Mark Mulder .30 .75
69 Marty Cordova .30 .75
70 Frank Thomas .75 2.00
71 Mike Cameron .30 .75
72 Mike Sweeney .30 .75
73 Barry Bonds 2.00 5.00
74 Troy Glaus .30 .75
75 Barry Zito .30 .75
76 Pat Burrell .30 .75
77 Paul LoDuca .30 .75
78 Rafael Palmeiro .50 1.25
79 Austin Kearns .30 .75
80 Darin Erstad .30 .75
81 Richie Sexson .30 .75
82 Roberto Alomar .50 1.25
83 Roy Oswalt .30 .75
84 Ryan Klesko .30 .75
85 Luis Gonzalez .30 .75
86 Scott Rolen .50 1.25
87 Shannon Stewart .30 .75
88 Shawn Green .30 .75
89 Toby Hall .30 .75
90 Bret Boone .30 .75
91 Casey Kotchman Bat RC 3.00 8.00
92 Jose Valverde AU A RC 3.00 8.00
93 Cole Barthel Bat RC 2.00 5.00
94 Brad Nelson AU A RC 3.00 8.00
95 Mauricio Lara AU A RC 3.00 8.00
96 Ryan Gripp Bat RC 2.00 5.00
97 Brian West AU A RC 3.00 8.00
98 Chris Piersoll AU B RC 4.00 10.00
99 Ryan Church AU B RC 6.00 15.00
100 Javier Colina AU A 3.00 8.00
101 Juan M. Gonzalez AU A RC 3.00 8.00
102 Benito Baez AU A 3.00 8.00
103 Mike Hill Bat RC 2.00 5.00
104 Jason Grove AU B RC 4.00 10.00
105 Koyie Hill AU B 4.00 10.00
106 Mark Outlaw AU A RC 3.00 8.00
107 Jason Bay Bat RC 6.00 15.00
108 Jorge Padilla AU A RC 3.00 8.00
109 Pete Zamora AU A RC 3.00 8.00
110 Joe Mauer AU A RC 20.00 50.00
111 Franklyn German AU A RC 3.00 8.00
112 Chris Flinn AU A RC 3.00 8.00
113 David Wright Bat RC 6.00 15.00
114 Anastacio Martinez AU A RC 3.00 8.00
115 Nic Jackson Bat RC 2.00 5.00
116 Rene Reyes AU A RC 3.00 8.00
117 Colin Young AU A RC 3.00 8.00
118 Joe Orloski AU A RC 3.00 8.00
119 Mike Wilson AU A RC 3.00 8.00
120 Rich Thompson AU A RC 3.00 8.00
121 Jake Mauer AU B RC 4.00 10.00
122 Mario Ramos AU A RC 3.00 8.00
123 Doug Sessions AU B RC 4.00 10.00
124 Doug Devore Bat RC 2.00 5.00
125 Travis Foley AU A RC 3.00 8.00
126 Chris Baker AU A RC 3.00 8.00
127 Michael Floyd AU A RC 3.00 8.00
128 Josh Barfield Bat RC 4.00 10.00
129 Jose Bautista Bat RC 5.00 12.00
130 Gavin Floyd AU A RC 3.00 8.00
131 Jason Botts Bat RC 2.00 5.00
132 Clint Nageotte AU B RC 4.00 10.00
133 Jesus Cota AU B RC 4.00 10.00
134 Ron Calloway Bat RC 2.00 5.00
135 Kevin Cash Bat RC 2.00 5.00
136 Jonny Gomes AU B RC 8.00 20.00
137 Dennis Ulacia AU A RC 3.00 8.00
138 Ryan Snare AU A RC 3.00 8.00
139 Kevin Deaton AU A RC 3.00 8.00
140 Bobby Jenks AU B RC 3.00 8.00
141 Casey Kotchman AU A RC 6.00 15.00
142 Adam Walker AU A RC 3.00 8.00
143 Mike Gonzalez AU A RC 3.00 8.00
144 Ruben Gotay Bat RC 3.00 8.00

145 Jason Grove Bat RC 2.00 5.00
146 Freddy Sanchez AU B RC 5.00 12.00
147 Jason Arnold AU B RC 4.00 10.00
148 Scott Hairston AU A RC 4.00 10.00
149 Jason St. Clair AU B RC 4.00 10.00
150 Chris Tritle Bat RC 2.00 5.00
151 Edwin Yan Bat RC 2.00 5.00
152 Freddy Sanchez Bat RC 5.00 12.00
153 Greg Sain Bat RC 2.00 5.00
154 Yurendell De Caster Bat RC 2.00 5.00
155 Noochie Varner Bat RC 2.00 5.00
156 Nelson Castro AU B RC 4.00 10.00
157 Randall Shelley Bat RC 2.00 5.00
158 Reed Johnson Bat RC 3.00 8.00
159 Ryan Raburn AU A RC 3.00 8.00
160 Jose Morban Bat RC 2.00 5.00
161 Justin Schuda AU A RC 3.00 8.00
162 Henry Pichardo AU A RC 3.00 8.00
163 Josh Bard AU A RC 3.00 8.00
164 Josh Bonifay AU A RC 3.00 8.00
165 Brandon League AU B RC 4.00 10.00
166 Jorge-Julio DePaula AU A RC 3.00 8.00
167 Todd Linden AU B RC 6.00 15.00
168 Francisco Liriano AU A RC 6.00 15.00
169 Chris Snelling AU A RC 5.00 12.00
170 Blake McGinley AU A RC 3.00 8.00
171 Cody McKay AU A RC 3.00 8.00
172 Jason Stanford AU A RC 3.00 8.00
173 Lenny Dinardo AU A RC 3.00 8.00
174 Greg Montalbano AU A RC 3.00 8.00
175 Earl Snyder AU A RC 3.00 8.00
176 Justin Huber AU A RC 3.00 8.00
177 Chris Narveson AU A RC 3.00 8.00
178 Jon Switzer AU A RC 3.00 8.00
179 Ronald Acuna AU A RC 3.00 8.00
180 Chris Duffy Bat RC 3.00 8.00
181 Kazuhisa Ishii Bat RC 3.00 8.00

2002 Bowman's Best Blue

*BLUE 1-90: 1X TO 2.5X BASIC
1-90 STATED ODDS 1:6
1-90 PRINT RUN 300 SERIAL #'d SETS
*BLUE AUTO: .4X TO 1X BASIC AU A
*BLUE AUTO: .3X TO .8X BASIC AU B
AUTO STATED ODDS 1:6
*BLUE BAT: .4X TO 1X BASIC BAT
BAT STATED ODDS 1:14
ISHII BAT EXCHANGE ODDS 1:335
ISHII BAT EXCHANGE DEADLINE 12/31/02
BLUE BATS FEATURE TEAM LOGOS!
140 Bobby Jenks AU 6.00 15.00
181 Kazuhisa Ishii Bat 3.00 8.00

2002 Bowman's Best Gold

*GOLD 1-90: 3X TO 8X BASIC
1-90 STATED ODDS 1:31
1-90 PRINT RUN 50 SERIAL #'d SETS
*GOLD AUTO: 1X TO 2.5X BASIC AU A
*GOLD AUTO: .75X TO 2X BASIC AU B
GOLD AUTO STATED ODDS 1:51
*GOLD BAT: 1X TO 2.5X BASIC BAT
GOLD BAT STATED ODDS 1:115
ISHII BAT EXCHANGE ODDS 1:3444
ISHII BAT EXCHANGE DEADLINE 12/31/02
GOLD BATS FEATURE FACSIMILE AUTOS!
181 Kazuhisa Ishii Bat 8.00 20.00

2002 Bowman's Best Red

*RED 1-90: 1.25X TO 3X BASIC
1-90 STATED ODDS 1:8
1-90 PRINT RUN 200 SERIAL #'d SETS
*RED AUTO: .6X TO 1.5X BASIC AU A
*RED AUTO: .5X TO 1.2X BASIC AU B
AUTO STATED ODDS 1:17
*RED BATS: .6X TO 1.5X BASIC BATS
BAT STATED ODDS 1:39
ISHII BAT EXCHANGE ODDS 1:1117
ISHII BAT EXCHANGE DEADLINE 12/31/02
RED BATS FEATURE STATISTICS!
181 Kazuhisa Ishii Bat 5.00 12.00

2002 Bowman's Best Uncirculated

COMMON EXCH
AU STATED ODDS 1:129
BAT STATED ODDS 1:322
OVERALL STATED ODDS 1:92

2003 Bowman's Best

COMP.SET w/o SP's (50) 15.00 40.00
COMMON CARD .40 1.00
COMMON RC .40 1.00
COMMON AUTO 3.00 8.00
AUTO ODDS ONE PER PACK
COMMON BAT 1.50 4.00
BAT ODDS ONE PER BOX-LOADER PACK
BULLINGTON BOX AU ODDS 1:106 BOXES
AB Andrew Brown FY AU RC 4.00 10.00
AK Austin Kearns .40 1.00
AM Aneudis Mateo FY AU RC 3.00 8.00
AP Albert Pujols 1.25 3.00
AR Alex Rodriguez 1.25 3.00
AS Alfonso Soriano .60 1.50
AW Aron Weston FY AU RC 3.00 8.00
BB Bryan Bullington FY AU RC 3.00 8.00
BC Bernie Castro FY RC .40 1.00
BFL Branden Florence FY AU RC 3.00 8.00
BFR Ben Francisco FY AU RC 3.00 8.00
BH Brendan Harris FY AU RC 4.00 10.00
BJH Bo Hart FY RC .40 1.00
BK Beau Kemp FY AU RC 3.00 8.00
BLB Barry Bonds 1.50 4.00
BM Brian McCann FY AU RC 4.00 10.00
BSG Brian Giles .40 1.00
BWB Bobby Basham FY AU RC 3.00 8.00
BZ Barry Zito .60 1.50
CAD Carlos Duran FY AU RC 3.00 8.00
CDC Chris De La Cruz FY AU RC 3.00 8.00
CJ Chipper Jones 1.00 2.50
CJW C.J. Wilson FY AU 3.00 8.00
CM Charlie Manning FY AU RC 3.00 8.00
CMS Curt Schilling .60 1.50
CS Cory Stewart FY AU RC 3.00 8.00
CSS Corey Shafer FY AU RC 3.00 8.00
CW Chien-Ming Wang FY RC 1.50 4.00
CWA Chien-Ming Wang FY AU 20.00 50.00
DAM Dustin Moseley FY AU RC 3.00 8.00
DC David Cash FY AU RC 3.00 8.00
DH Dan Haren FY AU RC 3.00 8.00
DJ Derek Jeter 2.50 6.00
DM David Martinez FY AU RC 3.00 8.00
DMM Dust. McGowan FY AU RC 4.00 10.00
DR Darrell Rasner FY AU RC 3.00 8.00
DW Doug Waechter FY AU RC 4.00 10.00
DY Dustin Yount FY RC .40 1.00
ERA Elizardo Ramirez FY AU RC 4.00 10.00
ERI Eric Riggs FY AU RC 4.00 10.00
ET Eider Torres FY AU RC 3.00 8.00
FP Felix Pie FY AU RC 3.00 8.00
FS Felix Sanchez FY AU RC 3.00 8.00
FT Ferdin Tejeda FY AU RC 3.00 8.00
GA Greg Aquino FY AU RC 3.00 8.00
GB Gregor Blanco FY AU RC 3.00 8.00
GJA Garret Anderson .40 1.00
GM Greg Maddux 1.25 3.00
GS Gary Schneidmiller FY AU RC 3.00 8.00
HR Hanley Ramirez FY AU RC 12.00 30.00
HRB Hanley Ramirez FY Bat 10.00 25.00
HT Haj Turay FY RC .40 1.00
IS Ichiro Suzuki 1.25 3.00
JB Jeremy Bonderman FY RC 1.50 4.00
JC Jose Contreras FY RC 1.00 2.50
JDD J.D. Durbin FY AU RC 3.00 8.00
JFK Jeff Kent .40 1.00
JG Joey Gomes FY AU RC 3.00 8.00
JGB Joey Gomes FY Bat 1.50 4.00
JGG Jason Giambi .40 1.00
JK Jason Kubel FY AU RC 4.00 10.00
JKB Jason Kubel FY Bat 2.50 6.00
JLB Jaime Bubela FY AU RC 3.00 8.00
JM Jose Morales FY AU RC 3.00 8.00
JMS Jon-Mark Sprowl FY RC .40 1.00
JRG Jeremy Griffiths FY AU RC 3.00 8.00
JT Jim Thome .60 1.50
JV Joe Valentine FY AU RC 3.00 8.00
JW Josh Willingham FY AU RC 6.00 15.00
KBS Kelly Shoppach FY Bat 2.00 5.00
KG Ken Griffey Jr. 2.00 5.00
KJ Kade Johnson FY AU RC 3.00 8.00
KS Kelly Shoppach FY AU RC 4.00 10.00
KY Kevin Youkilis FY AU RC 6.00 15.00
KYE Kevin Youkilis FY Bat 5.00 12.00
LB Lance Berkman .60 1.50
LF Lew Ford FY AU RC 4.00 10.00
LFJ Lew Ford FY Bat 2.00 5.00
LW Larry Walker .60 1.50
MB Matt Bruback FY RC .40 1.00
MD Matt Diaz FY RC .60 1.50
MDA Matt Diaz FY AU 3.00 8.00
MDH Matt Hensley FY AU RC 3.00 8.00
MDM Mark Malaska FY AU RC 3.00 8.00
MH Michel Hernandez FY AU RC 3.00 8.00
MHI Michael Hinckley FY AU RC 4.00 10.00
MJP Mike Piazza 1.00 2.50
MK Matt Kata FY AU RC 3.00 8.00
MNH Matt Hagen FY AU RC 3.00 8.00
MO Mike O'Keefe FY RC .40 1.00
MOR Magglio Ordonez .60 1.50
MP Mark Prior .60 1.50
MR Manny Ramirez 1.00 2.50
MS Mike Sweeney .40 1.00
MT Miguel Tejada .60 1.50
NG Nomar Garciaparra .60 1.50
NL Nook Logan FY AU RC 4.00 10.00
OC Ozzie Chavez FY AU RC 3.00 8.00
PB Pat Burrell .40 1.00
PL Pete LaForest FY AU RC 3.00 8.00
PM Pedro Martinez .60 1.50
PR Prentice Redman FY AU RC 3.00 8.00
RC Ryan Cameron FY AU RC 3.00 8.00
RD Rajai Davis FY AU RC 3.00 8.00
RH Ryan Howard FY AU RC 10.00 25.00
RHJ Ryan Howard FY Bat 4.00 10.00
RJ Randy Johnson 1.00 2.50
RLD Rajai Davis FY Bat 1.50 4.00
RM Ramon Nivar-Martinez FY RC .40 1.00
RS Ryan Shealy FY AU RC 3.00 8.00
RSB Ryan Shealy FY Bat 5.00 12.00
RWH Robbie Hammock FY AU RC 3.00 8.00
SS Sammy Sosa 1.00 2.50
ST Scott Tyler FY AU RC 4.00 10.00
SV Shane Victorino FY RC 1.25 3.00
TA Tyler Adamczyk FY AU RC 3.00 8.00
TH Todd Helton .60 1.50
TI Travis Ishikawa FY AU RC 10.00 25.00
TJ Tyler Johnson FY AU RC 3.00 8.00
TJB T.J. Bohn FY RC .40 1.00
TKH Torii Hunter .40 1.00
TO Tim Olson FY AU RC 3.00 8.00
TS T.Story-Harden FY AU RC 3.00 8.00
TSB T.Story-Harden FY Bat 1.50 4.00
TT Terry Tiffee FY RC .40 1.00
VG Vladimir Guerrero .60 1.50
WE Willie Eyre FY AU RC 3.00 8.00
WL Wil Ledezma FY AU RC 3.00 8.00
WRC Roger Clemens 1.25 3.00
NNO B.Bullington Opened Box AU 10.00 25.00

2003 Bowman's Best Blue

*BLUE: 1.5X TO 4X BASIC
*BLUE FY: 3X TO 8X BASIC FY
BLUE STATED ODDS 1:28
BLUE PRINT RUN 100 SERIAL #'d SETS
*BLUE AUTO: 1X TO 2.5X BASIC AUTO
BLUE AUTO ODDS 1:32
BLUE AUTO PRINT RUN 50 SETS
BLUE AUTO'S NOT SERIAL-NUMBERED
BLUE AU PRINT RUNS PROVIDED BY TOPPS
*BLUE BAT: 1X TO 2.5X BASIC FY BAT
BLUE BAT ODDS 1:22 BOXLOADER PACKS
BLUE BAT PRINT RUN 50 SETS
BLUE BATS NOT SERIAL-NUMBERED
BLUE BAT PRINTS PROVIDED BY TOPPS

2003 Bowman's Best Red

*RED: 3X TO 8X BASIC RED
*RED FY: 3X TO 8X BASIC FY
RED STATED ODDS 1:55
RED STATED PRINT RUN 50 SERIAL #'d SETS
RED AUTO ODDS 1:63
RED AUTO PRINT RUN 25 SETS
RED AU PRINT RUNS PROVIDED BY TOPPS
RED AUTOS NOT SERIAL-NUMBERED
NO RED AUTO PRICING DUE TO SCARCITY
RED BAT ODDS 1:44 BOXLOADER PACKS
RED BAT PRINT RUN 25 SETS
RED BAT PRINT RUNS PROVIDED BY TOPPS
RED BATS NOT SERIAL-NUMBERED
NO RED BAT PRICING DUE TO SCARCITY

2003 Bowman's Best Double Play Autographs

STATED ODDS 1:55
EB Elizardo Ramirez 6.00 15.00
Bryan Bullington
GK Joey Gomes 6.00 15.00
Jason Kubel
HV Dan Haren 6.00 15.00
Joe Valentine
LL Nook Logan 6.00 15.00
Wil Ledezma
RS Prentice Redman 6.00 15.00
Gary Schneidmiller
SB Corey Shafer 6.00 15.00
Gregor Blanco
SR Felix Sanchez 6.00 15.00
Darrell Rasner
YS Kevin Youkilis 6.00 15.00
Kelly Shoppach

2003 Bowman's Best Triple Play Autographs

STATED ODDS 1:219
BCS Brown/Cash/Stewart 10.00 25.00
DRS Rajai/Hanley/Shealy 8.00 20.00

2004 Bowman's Best

COMP.SET w/o SP'S (50) 10.00 25.00
COMMON CARD .30 .75
COMMON RC .40 1.00
COMMON AUTO 3.00 8.00
ONE AUTO PER HOBBY PACK
COMMON RELIC 2.00 5.00
RELIC MINORS 2.00 5.00
RELIC SEMIS 3.00 8.00
RELIC UNLISTED 3.00 8.00
ONE RELIC PER BOX-LOADER PACK
ONE BOX-LOADER PACK PER HOBBY BOX
COMMON AU BOX 6.00 15.00
STAUFFER BOX RANDOM IN HOBBY CASES
OVERALL AU PLATE ODDS 1:391 HOBBY
AU PLATE PRINT RUN 1 SET PER COLOR
BLACK-CYAN-MAGENTA-YELLOW ISSUED
NO AU PLATE PRICING DUE TO SCARCITY
AER Alex Rodriguez 1.00 2.50
AG Adam Greenberg FY AU RC 4.00 10.00
AL Anthony Lerew FY RC .40 1.00
AO Akinori Otsuka FY RC .40 1.00
AP Albert Pujols 1.00 2.50
AS Alfonso Soriano .50 1.25
BB Bobby Brownlie FY AU RC 4.00 10.00
BEM Brandon Medders FY AU RC 3.00 8.00
BG Brian Giles .30 .75
BMS Brad Snyder FY AU RC 4.00 10.00
BP Brayan Pena FY AU RC 3.00 8.00
BS Brad Sullivan FY AU RC 4.00 10.00
CB Carlos Beltran .50 1.25
CD Carlos Delgado .30 .75
CJ Conor Jackson FY AU RC 4.00 10.00
CLH Chin-Lung Hu FY RC .40 1.00
CMA Craig Ansman FY AU RC 3.00 8.00
CMS Curt Schilling .50 1.25
CZ Charlie Zink FY AU RC 3.00 8.00
DA David Aardsma FY AU RC 3.00 8.00
DC Dave Crouthers FY AU RC 3.00 8.00
DDN Dustin Nippert FY AU RC 4.00 10.00
DG Danny Gonzalez FY RC .40 1.00
DK Donald Kelly FY AU RC 3.00 8.00
DL Donald Levinski FY AU RC 3.00 8.00
DM David Murphy FY AU RC 6.00 15.00
DN Dioner Navarro FY AU RC 4.00 10.00
DS Don Sutton FY RC .40 1.00
EA Erick Aybar FY AU RC 3.00 8.00
EC Eric Chavez .30 .75
EH Estee Harris FY AU RC 4.00 10.00
ES Ervin Santana FY AU RC 5.00 12.00
FH Felix Hernandez FY AU RC 20.00 50.00
GA Garret Anderson .30 .75
HB Hank Blalock .30 .75
HM Hector Made FY RC .40 1.00
IR Ivan Rodriguez .50 1.25
IS Ichiro Suzuki 1.00 2.50
JA Joaquin Arias FY AU RC 6.00 10.00
JAV Jose Vidro .30 .75
JC Juan Cedeno FY AU RC 3.00 8.00
JDS Jason Schmidt .30 .75
JE Jesse English FY AU RC 3.00 8.00
JGG Jason Giambi .30 .75
JH Jason Hirsh FY AU RC 10.00 25.00
JJC Jon Connolly FY RC .40 1.00
JK Jon Knott FY AU RC 3.00 8.00
JL Josh Labandeira FY AU RC 3.00 8.00
JLO Javy Lopez .30 .75
JP Jorge Posada .50 1.25
JRG Joey Gathright FY RC .40 1.00
JS Jeff Salazar FY AU RC 4.00 10.00
JSZ Jason Szuminski FY AU RC 3.00 8.00
JT Jim Thome .50 1.25
KC Kory Casto FY AU RC 3.00 8.00
KK Kevin Kouzmanoff FY AU RC 8.00 20.00
KM Kazuo Matsui FY Uni RC 2.00 5.00
KRK Kody Kirkland FY Bat RC 2.00 5.00
KS Kyle Sleeth FY RC .40 1.00
KT Kazuhito Tadano FY Jsy RC 3.00 8.00
LK Logan Kensing FY AU RC 3.00 8.00
LM Lastings Milledge FY AU RC 3.00 8.00
LO Lyle Overbay .30 .75
LTH Luke Hughes FY AU RC 4.00 10.00
LWJ Chipper Jones .75 2.00
MAR Manny Ramirez .75 2.00
MDC Matt Creighton FY AU RC 3.00 8.00
MG Mike Gosling FY RC .40 1.00
MJP Mike Piazza .75 2.00
MO Magglio Ordonez .50 1.25
MT Miguel Tejada .50 1.25
MTC Miguel Cabrera .75 2.00
MV Merkin Valdez FY AU RC 3.00 8.00
MWP Mark Prior .50 1.25
MY Michael Young .30 .75
NAG Nomar Garciaparra .50 1.25
NG Nick Gorneault FY RC .40 1.00
NU Nic Ungs FY AU RC 3.00 8.00
OQ Omar Quintanilla FY AU RC 4.00 10.00
PM Paul Maholm FY AU RC 4.00 10.00
PMM Paul McAnulty FY RC .40 1.00
RB Ryan Budde FY AU RC 3.00 8.00
RC Roger Clemens 1.00 2.50
RG Rudy Guillen FY AU RC 4.00 10.00
RJ Randy Johnson .75 2.00
RN Ricky Nolasco FY AU RC 4.00 10.00
RR Ramon Ramirez FY AU RC 3.00 8.00
RS Richie Sexson .30 .75
RT Rob Tejeda FY AU RC 6.00 15.00
SH Shawn Hill FY AU RC 3.00 8.00
SR Scott Rolen .50 1.25
SS Sammy Sosa .75 2.00
ST Shingo Takatsu FY Jsy RC 3.00 8.00
TB Travis Blackley FY Jsy RC 2.00 5.00
TD Tyler Davidson FY AU RC 4.00 10.00
TJ Terry Jones FY RC .40 1.00
TJS Tim Stauffer FY AU RC 4.00 10.00
TLH Todd Helton .50 1.25
TOH Travis Hanson FY AU RC 4.00 10.00
TRM Tom Mastny FY AU RC 3.00 8.00
TS Todd Self FY RC .40 1.00
VC Vito Chiaravalloti FY AU RC 3.00 8.00
VG Vladimir Guerrero .50 1.25
WM Warner Madrigal FY RC .60 1.50
WS Wardell Starling FY AU RC 3.00 8.00
YM Yadier Molina FY AU RC 200.00 500.00
ZD Zach Duke FY AU RC 5.00 12.00
NNO Tim Stauffer AU Box/100 10.00 25.00

2004 Bowman's Best Green

*GREEN: 1.5X TO 4X BASIC
*GREEN RC'S: 3X TO 8X BASIC RC'S
GREEN ODDS 1:18
GREEN PRINT RUN 100 SERIAL #'d SETS
*GREEN AU'S: 1X TO 2.5X BASIC AU'S
GREEN AU ODDS 1:32 HOBBY
GREEN AU PRINT RUN 50 SETS
GREEN AUTOS NOT SERIAL-NUMBERED
AUTO PRINT RUNS PROVIDED BY TOPPS
RELIC MINORS
RELIC SEMIS
RELIC UNLISTED
*GREEN RELICS: .75X TO 2X BASIC RELICS
GREEN RELIC ODDS 1:31 HOBBY BOXES
GREEN RELIC PRINT RUN 50 SETS
GREEN RELICS NOT SERIAL-NUMBERED
RELIC PRINT RUNS PROVIDED BY TOPPS

2004 Bowman's Best Red

*RED: 5X TO 12X BASIC
RED ODDS 1:90 HOBBY
RED PRINT RUN 20 SERIAL #'d SETS
NO RED RC PRICING DUE TO SCARCITY
RED AUTO ODDS 1:156 HOBBY
RED AU PRINT RUN 10 SETS
RED AU'S ARE NOT SERIAL-NUMBERED
PRINT RUN INFO PROVIDED BY TOPPS
NO RED AU PRICING DUE TO SCARCITY
RED RELIC ODDS 1:154 HOBBY BOXES
RED RELIC PRINT RUN 10 SETS
RED RELICS ARE NOT SERIAL-NUMBERED
PRINT RUN INFO PROVIDED BY TOPPS
NO RED RELIC PRICING DUE TO SCARCITY

2004 Bowman's Best Double Play Autographs

STATED ODDS 1:33 HOBBY
STATED PRINT RUN 236 SETS
CARDS ARE NOT SERIAL NUMBERED
PRINT RUN INFO PROVIDED BY TOPPS
CC M.Creighton/D.Crouthers 8.00 20.00
EN J.English/R.Nolasco 10.00 25.00
HJ T.Hanson/C.Jackson 10.00 25.00
MH L.Milledge/E.Harris 10.00 25.00
MN B.Medders/D.Nippert 6.00 15.00
QS O.Quintanilla/B.Snyder 6.00 15.00
SC T.Stauffer/V.Chiaravalloti 6.00 15.00
SK J.Salazar/J.Knott 6.00 15.00
SV E.Santana/M.Valdez 6.00 15.00
UK N.Ungs/K.Kouzmanoff 12.50 30.00

2004 Bowman's Best Triple Play Autographs

STATED ODDS 1:109 HOBBY
STATED PRINT RUN 236 SETS
CARDS ARE NOT SERIAL NUMBERED
PRINT RUN INFO PROVIDED BY TOPPS
ALS Aardsma/Levinski/Sullivan 6.00 15.00
CBA Cedeno/Brownlie/Arias 6.00 15.00
SSV Stauffer/Santana/Valdez 6.00 15.00

2005 Bowman's Best

COMP.SET w/o SP's (100) 25.00 50.00
COMMON CARD (1-30) .20 .50
COMMON CARD (31-100) .40 1.00
COMMON AU (101-143) 3.00 8.00
101-143 ODDS 1:5 HOBBY
101-143 PRINT RUN 974 SERIAL #'d SETS
OVERALL 1-100 PLATE ODDS 1:345 H
OVERALL 101-143 AU PLATE ODDS 1:805 H
PLATE PRINT RUN 1 SET PER COLOR
BLACK-CYAN-MAGENTA-YELLOW ISSUED
NO PLATE PRICING DUE TO SCARCITY
1 Jose Vidro .20 .50
2 Adam Dunn .30 .75
3 Manny Ramirez .50 1.25
4 Miguel Tejada .30 .75
5 Ken Griffey Jr. 1.00 2.50
6 Pedro Martinez .30 .75
7 Alex Rodriguez .60 1.50
8 Ichiro Suzuki .60 1.50
9 Alfonso Soriano .30 .75
10 Brian Giles .20 .50
11 Roger Clemens .60 1.50
12 Todd Helton .30 .75
13 Ivan Rodriguez .30 .75
14 David Ortiz .50 1.25
15 Sammy Sosa .50 1.25
16 Chipper Jones .50 1.25
17 Mark Buehrle .30 .75
18 Miguel Cabrera .50 1.25
19 Johan Santana .30 .75
20 Randy Johnson .50 1.25
21 Jim Thome .30 .75
22 Vladimir Guerrero .30 .75
23 Dontrelle Willis .20 .50
24 Nomar Garciaparra .30 .75
25 Barry Bonds .75 2.00
26 Curt Schilling .30 .75
27 Carlos Beltran .30 .75
28 Albert Pujols .60 1.50
29 Mark Prior .30 .75
30 Derek Jeter 1.25 3.00
31 Ryan Garko FY RC .40 1.00
32 Eulogio De La Cruz FY RC .40 1.00
33 Luke Scott FY RC 1.00 2.50
34 Shane Costa FY RC .40 1.00
35 Casey McGehee FY RC .60 1.50
36 Jered Weaver FY RC 2.00 5.00
37 Kevin Melillo FY RC .40 1.00
38 D.J. Houlton FY RC .40 1.00
39 Brandon Moorhead FY RC .40 1.00
40 Jerry Owens FY RC .40 1.00
41 Elliot Johnson FY RC .40 1.00
42 Kevin West FY RC .40 1.00
43 Hernan Iribarren FY RC .40 1.00
44 Miguel Montero FY RC 1.25 3.00
45 Craig Tatum FY RC .40 1.00
46 Ryan Sweeney FY RC .60 1.50
47 Micah Furtado FY RC .40 1.00
48 Cody Haerther FY RC .40 1.00
49 Erick Abreu FY RC .40 1.00
50 Chuck Tiffany FY RC 1.00 2.50
51 Tadahito Iguchi FY RC .60 1.50
52 Frank Diaz FY RC .40 1.00
53 Errol Simonitsch FY RC .40 1.00
54 Wade Robinson FY RC .40 1.00
55 Adam Boeve FY RC .40 1.00
56 Steven Bondurant FY RC .40 1.00
57 Jason Motte FY RC .60 1.50
58 Juan Senreiso FY RC .40 1.00
59 Vinny Rottino FY RC .40 1.00
60 Jai Miller FY RC .40 1.00
61 Thomas Pauly FY RC .40 1.00
62 Tony Giarratano FY RC .40 1.00
63 Alexander Smit FY RC .40 1.00
64 Keiichi Yabu FY RC .40 1.00
65 Brian Bannister FY RC .60 1.50
66 Kennard Bibbs FY RC .40 1.00
67 Anthony Reyes FY RC .60 1.50
68 Thomas Oldham FY RC .40 1.00
69 Ben Harrison FY .40 1.00
70 Daryl Thompson FY RC .40 1.00
71 Kevin Collins FY RC .40 1.00
72 Wes Swackhamer FY RC .40 1.00
73 Landon Powell FY RC .40 1.00
74 Matt Brown FY RC .40 1.00
75 Russ Martin FY RC 1.25 3.00
76 Nick Touchstone FY RC .40 1.00
77 Steven White FY RC .40 1.00
78 Ian Bladergroen FY RC .40 1.00
79 Sean Marshall FY RC 1.00 2.50
80 Nick Masset FY RC .40 1.00
81 Ryan Goleski FY RC .40 1.00
82 Matt Campbell FY RC .40 1.00
83 Manny Parra FY RC 1.00 2.50
84 Melky Cabrera FY RC 1.25 3.00
85 Ryan Feierabend FY RC .40 1.00
86 Nate McLouth FY RC .60 1.50
87 Glen Perkins FY RC .60 1.50
88 Kila Kaaihue FY RC 1.00 2.50
89 Dana Eveland FY RC .40 1.00
90 Tyler Pelland FY RC .40 1.00
91 Matt Van Der Bosch FY RC .40 1.00
92 Andy Santana FY RC .40 1.00
93 Eric Nielsen FY RC .40 1.00
94 Brendan Ryan FY RC .40 1.00
95 Ian Kinsler FY RC 2.00 5.00
96 Matthew Kemp FY RC 2.00 5.00
97 Stephen Drew FY RC 1.25 3.00
98 Peeter Ramos FY RC .40 1.00
99 Chris Seddon FY RC .40 1.00
100 Chuck James FY RC 1.00 2.50
101 Travis Chick FY AU RC 3.00 8.00
102 Justin Verlander FY AU RC 50.00 120.00
103 Billy Butler FY AU RC 8.00 20.00
104 Chris B.Young FY AU RC 3.00 8.00
105 Jake Postlewait FY AU RC 3.00 8.00
106 C.J. Smith FY AU RC 3.00 8.00
107 Mike Rodriguez FY AU RC 3.00 8.00
108 Philip Humber FY AU RC 10.00 25.00
109 Jeff Niemann FY AU RC 3.00 8.00
110 Brian Miller FY AU RC 3.00 8.00
111 Chris Vines FY AU RC 3.00 8.00
112 Andy LaRoche FY AU RC 3.00 8.00
113 Mike Bourn FY AU RC 3.00 8.00
114 Wlad Balentein FY AU RC 3.00 8.00
115 Ismael Ramirez FY AU RC 3.00 8.00
116 Hayden Penn FY AU RC 3.00 8.00
117 Pedro Lopez FY AU RC 3.00 8.00
118 Shawn Bowman FY AU RC 3.00 8.00
119 Chad Orvella FY AU RC 3.00 8.00
120 Sean Tracey FY AU RC 3.00 8.00
121 Bobby Livingston FY AU RC 3.00 8.00
122 Michael Rogers FY AU RC 3.00 8.00
123 Willy Mota FY AU RC 3.00 8.00
124 Bran McCarthy FY AU RC 5.00 12.00
125 Mike Morse FY AU RC 8.00 20.00
126 Matt Lindstrom FY AU RC 3.00 8.00
127 Brian Stavisky FY AU RC 3.00 8.00
128 Richie Gardner FY AU RC 3.00 8.00
129 Scott Mitchinson FY AU RC 3.00 8.00
130 Billy McCarthy FY AU RC 3.00 8.00
131 Brandon Sing FY AU RC 3.00 8.00
132 Matt Albers FY AU RC 3.00 8.00
133 George Kottaras FY AU RC 3.00 8.00
134 Luis Hernandez FY AU RC 3.00 8.00
135 Hum Sanchez FY AU RC 3.00 8.00
136 Buck Coats FY AU RC 3.00 8.00
137 Jon Barratt FY AU RC 3.00 8.00
138 Raul Tablado FY AU RC 3.00 8.00
139 Jake Mullinax FY AU RC 3.00 8.00
140 Edgar Varela FY AU RC 3.00 8.00
141 Ryan Garko FY AU 3.00 8.00
142 Nate McLouth FY AU 6.00 15.00
143 Shane Costa FY AU 3.00 8.00

2005 Bowman's Best Black

STATED ODDS 1:1386 HOBBY
STATED PRINT RUN 1 SERIAL #'d SET
NO PRICING DUE TO SCARCITY

2005 Bowman's Best Blue

*BLUE 1-30: 1.25X TO 3X BASIC
*BLUE 31-100: .6X TO 1.5X BASIC
1-100 ODDS 1:4 HOBBY
1-100 PRINT RUN 499 #'d SETS
*BLUE AU 101-143: .5X TO 1.2X BASIC
AU 101-143 PRINT RUN 299 #'d SETS
AU 101-143 ODDS 1:14 HOBBY

2005 Bowman's Best Gold

*GOLD 1-30: 6X TO 15X BASIC
1-100 ODDS 1:69 HOBBY
1-100 PRINT RUN 25 #'d SETS
31-100 NO PRICING DUE TO SCARCITY
AU 101-143 ODDS 1:159 HOBBY
AU 101-143 PRINT RUN 25 #'d SETS
AU 101-143 NO PRICING DUE TO SCARCITY

2005 Bowman's Best Green

*GREEN 1-30: 1X TO 2.5X BASIC
*GREEN 31-100: .5X TO 1.2X BASIC
1-100 ODDS 1:2 HOBBY
1-100 PRINT RUN 899 #'d SETS
*GREEN AU 101-143: .5X TO 1.2X BASIC
AU 101-143 ODDS 1:10 HOBBY
AU 101-143 PRINT RUN 399 #'d SETS

2005 Bowman's Best Red

*RED 1-30: 1.5X TO 4X BASIC
*RED 31-100: 1X TO 2.5X BASIC
1-100 ODDS 1:9 HOBBY
1-100 PRINT RUN 199 #'d SETS
*RED AU 101-143: .6X TO 1.5X BASIC
AU 101-143 ODDS 1:20 HOBBY
AU 101-143 PRINT RUN 199 #'d SETS

2005 Bowman's Best Silver

*SILVER 1-30: 2.5X TO 6X BASIC
*SILVER 31-100: 1.25X TO 3X BASIC
1-100 ODDS 1:18 HOBBY
1-100 PRINT RUN 99 #'d SETS
*SILVER AU 101-143: .75X TO 2X BASIC
AU 101-143 ODDS 1:41 HOBBY
AU 101-143 PRINT RUN 99 #'d SETS

2005 Bowman's Best A-Rod Throwback Autograph

STATED ODDS 1:1402 HOBBY
STATED PRINT RUN 100 SERIAL #'d CARDS
AR Alex Rodriguez 1994 50.00 120.00

2005 Bowman's Best Mirror Image Spokesmen Dual Autograph

STATED ODDS 1:16,300 HOBBY
STATED PRINT RUN 10 SERIAL #'d CARDS
NO PRICING DUE TO SCARCITY

2005 Bowman's Best Mirror Image Throwback Dual Autograph

STATED ODDS 1:2835 HOBBY
STATED PRINT RUN 50 SERIAL #'d CARDS
RR A.Rodriguez/C.Ripken 175.00 350.00

2005 Bowman's Best Shortstops Triple Autograph

STATED ODDS 1:5927 HOBBY
STATED PRINT RUN 25 SERIAL #'d CARDS
NO PRICING DUE TO SCARCITY

2007 Bowman's Best

COMP.SET w/o AU (33) 6.00 15.00
COMMON CARD (1-33) .20 .50
COMMON AU VET VAR (23-33) 3.00 8.00
AU VET VAR GROUP A 1:15 PACKS
AU VET VAR GROUP B 1:122 PACKS
AU VET VAR GROUP C 1:381 PACKS
AU VET VAR GROUP D 1:113 PACKS
COMMON AU VET (34-51) 3.00 8.00
AU VET ODDS 1:2 PACKS
COMMON RC (52-81) .40 1.00
RC ODDS 1:2 PACKS
RC PRINT RUN 799 SER.#'D SETS
GU-RC ODDS 1:35 PACKS
COMMON AU VAR RC (71-81) 3.00 8.00
AU VAR RC ODDS 1:11 PACKS
COMMON AU RC (82-99) 3.00 8.00
AU RC ODDS 1:2 PACKS
PRINTING PLATE ODDS 1:88 PACKS
PRINTING PLATE AU ODDS 1:173 PACKS
PRINTING PLATE GU ODDS 1:8945 PACKS
PLATE PRINT RUN 1 SET PER COLOR
BLACK-CYAN-MAGENTA-YELLOW ISSUED
NO PLATE PRICING DUE TO SCARCITY
1 Jose Reyes .30 .75
2 Derek Jeter 1.25 3.00
3 Vladimir Guerrero .30 .75
4 Ichiro Suzuki .60 1.50
5 Jason Bay .30 .75
6 Joe Mauer .40 1.00
7 Alfonso Soriano .30 .75
8 David Ortiz .50 1.25
9 Andruw Jones .20 .50
10 Roger Clemens .60 1.50
11 Grady Sizemore .30 .75
12 Magglio Ordonez .30 .75
13 Carl Crawford .30 .75
14 Chase Utley .30 .75
15 Mark Teixeira .30 .75
16 Ryan Zimmerman .30 .75
17 Ken Griffey Jr. 1.00 2.50
18 Derrek Lee .20 .50
19 Barry Bonds .75 2.00
20 Chipper Jones .50 1.25
21 Vernon Wells .20 .50
22 Manny Ramirez .50 1.25
23a Alex Rodriguez .60 1.50
23b Alex Rodriguez AU A 25.00 80.00
24a Ryan Howard .40 1.00
24b Ryan Howard AU B 4.00 10.00
25a Tom Glavine .30 .75
25b Tom Glavine AU D 5.00 12.00
26a Gary Sheffield .20 .50
26b Gary Sheffield AU A 8.00 20.00
27a Miguel Cabrera .50 1.25
27b Miguel Cabrera AU A 12.00 30.00
28a Robinson Cano .30 .75
28b Robinson Cano AU A 10.00 25.00
29a David Wright .40 1.00
29b David Wright AU A 6.00 15.00
30a Jim Thome .30 .75
30b Jim Thome AU A 20.00 50.00
31a Albert Pujols .60 1.50
31b Albert Pujols AU C 50.00 120.00
32 Jorge Posada .30 .75
33a Brian McCann .20 .50
33b Brian McCann AU A 6.00 15.00
34 Josh Barfield AU 3.00 8.00
35 Melky Cabrera AU 4.00 10.00
36 Bill Hall AU 3.00 8.00
37 Cole Hamels AU 10.00 25.00
38 Adam LaRoche AU 3.00 8.00
39 Matt Holliday AU 4.00 10.00
40 Jeremy Hermida AU 3.00 8.00
41 Jonathan Papelbon AU 4.00 10.00
42 Hanley Ramirez AU 3.00 8.00
43 Justin Verlander AU 25.00 60.00
44 Andre Ethier AU 3.00 8.00
46 Erik Bedard AU 3.00 8.00
47 Freddy Sanchez AU 3.00 8.00
48 Adrian Gonzalez AU 4.00 10.00
49 Russell Martin AU 5.00 12.00
50 B.J. Upton AU 3.00 8.00
51 Prince Fielder AU 5.00 12.00
52 Tony Abreu RC 1.00 2.50
53 Ben Francisco (RC) .40 1.00
54 Billy Butler (RC) .60 1.50
55 Philip Hughes (RC) 1.00 2.50
56 Josh Fields (RC) .40 1.00
57 Carlos Gomez RC .75 2.00
58 Akinori Iwamura RC 1.00 2.50
59 Matt Brown (RC) .40 1.00
60 Jesus Flores RC .40 1.00
61 Mike Fontenot (RC) .40 1.00
62 Ryan Feierabend (RC) .40 1.00
63 Miguel Montero (RC) .40 1.00
64a Daisuke Matsuzaka RC 1.50 4.00
64b Daisuke Matsuzaka Jsy 5.00 12.00
65 Kei Igawa RC 1.00 2.50
66 Shawn Riggans (RC) .40 1.00
67 Masumi Kuwata RC .40 1.00
68 Kevin Slowey (RC) 1.00 2.50
69 Josh Hamilton (RC) 1.25 3.00
70 Curtis Thigpen (RC) .40 1.00
71a Justin Upton RC 1.25 3.00
71b Justin Upton AU 5.00 12.00
72a Delmon Young (RC) .60 1.50
72b Delmon Young AU 3.00 8.00
73a Brandon Wood (RC) .40 1.00
73b Brandon Wood AU 6.00 15.00
74a Felix Pie (RC) .50 1.25
74b Felix Pie AU 4.00 10.00
75a Alex Gordon RC .50 1.25
75b Alex Gordon AU 6.00 15.00
76a Mark Reynolds RC 1.25 3.00
76b Mark Reynolds AU 3.00 8.00
77a Tyler Clippard (RC) .60 1.50
77b Tyler Clippard AU 4.00 10.00
78a Adam Lind (RC) .40 1.00
78b Adam Lind AU 3.00 8.00
79a Hunter Pence (RC) 1.25 3.00
79b Hunter Pence AU 5.00 12.00
80 Micah Owings (RC) .40 1.00
81a Jarrod Saltalamacchia (RC) .60 1.50
81b Jarrod Saltalamacchia AU 6.00 15.00
82 Kevin Kouzmanoff AU (RC) 3.00 8.00
83 Glen Perkins AU (RC) 3.00 8.00
84 Michael Bourn AU (RC) 3.00 8.00
85 Andrew Miller AU RC 4.00 10.00
86 Fred Lewis AU (RC) 3.00 8.00
88 Joba Chamberlain AU RC 5.00 12.00
89 Hideki Okajima AU RC 3.00 8.00
90 Troy Tulowitzki AU (RC) 6.00 15.00
91 Ryan Sweeney AU (RC) 3.00 8.00
92 Matt Lindstrom AU (RC) 3.00 8.00
93 T.Lincecum AU RC UER 10.00 25.00
94 Homer Bailey AU (RC) 4.00 10.00
95 Matt DeSalvo AU (RC) 3.00 8.00
96 Alejandro De Aza AU RC 3.00 8.00
97 Ryan Braun AU (RC) 5.00 12.00
99 Andy LaRoche AU (RC) 3.00 8.00

2007 Bowman's Best Blue

*VET BLUE: 3X TO 8X BASIC VET
VET ODDS 1:11 PACKS
*AU VET BLUE: .5X TO 1.2X BASIC AU VET
AU VET ODDS 1:14 PACKS
*RC BLUE: 1X TO 2.5X BASIC RC
RC ODDS 1:12 PACKS
*AU RC BLUE: .5X TO 1.2X BASIC AU RC
AU RC ODDS 1:15 PACKS
*GU-RC BLUE: .75X TO 2X BASIC GU-RC
GU-RC ODDS 1:361 PACKS
STATED PRINT RUN 99 SER.#'d SETS

2007 Bowman's Best Gold

*VET GOLD: 4X TO 10X BASIC VET
VET ODDS 1:22 PACKS
*AU VET GOLD: .6X TO 1.5X BASIC AU VET
AU VET ODDS 1:28 PACKS
*RC GOLD: 1.5X TO 4X BASIC RC
RC ODDS 1:24 PACKS
*AU RC GOLD: .6X TO 1.5X BASIC AU RC
AU RC ODDS 1:29 PACKS
*GU-RC GOLD: 1X TO 2.5X BASIC GU-RC
GU-RC ODDS 1:715 PACKS
STATED PRINT RUN 50 SER.#'d SETS

2007 Bowman's Best Green

*VET GREEN: 1.5X TO 4X BASIC VET
VET ODDS 1:5 PACKS
*RC GREEN: .75X TO 2X BASIC RC
RC ODDS 1:5 PACKS
STATED PRINT RUN 249 SER.#'d SETS

2007 Bowman's Best Red

VET ODDS 1:1073 PACKS
AU VET ODDS 1:1325 PACKS
RC ODDS 1:1221 PACKS

AU RC ODDS 1:1376 PACKS
GU-RC ODDS 1:27,456 PACKS
STATED PRINT RUN 1 SER.#'d SETS
NO PRICING DUE TO SCARCITY

2007 Bowman's Best Alex Rodriguez 500

COMPLETE SET (1) 1.50 4.00
COMMON CARD 1.50 4.00
STATED ODDS 1:
COMMON BLUE 8.00 20.00
BLUE ODDS 1:1107 PACKS
BLUE PRINT RUN 33 SER.#'d SETS
GOLD ODDS 1:2532 PACKS
GOLD PRINT RUN 15 SER.#'d SETS
NO GOLD PRICING DUE TO SCARCITY
COMMON GREEN 5.00 12.00
GREEN ODDS 1:361 PACKS
GREEN PRINT RUN 99 SER.#'d SETS
AR Alex Rodriguez 1.25 3.00

2007 Bowman's Best Barry Bonds 756

COMPLETE SET (1) 1.25 3.00
STATED ODDS 1:20 PACKS
PRINTING PLATE ODDS 1:8945 PACKS
PLATE PRINT RUN 1 SET PER COLOR
BLACK-CYAN-MAGENTA-YELLOW ISSUED
NO PLATE PRICING DUE TO SCARCITY
BB Barry Bonds 1.00 2.50

2007 Bowman's Best Prospects

COMMON PROSPECT (1-40) .25 .60
PROSPECT STATED ODDS 1:2 PACKS
PROSPECT PRINT RUN 499 SER.#'d SETS
COMMON PROS.AU VAR (37-40) 3.00 8.00
PROS AU VAR ODDS 1:26 PACKS
COMMON PROS.AUTO (41-60) 3.00 8.00
PROS.AUTO ODDS 1:26 PACKS
PRINTING PLATE ODDS 1:88 PACKS
PRINTING PLATE AU ODDS 1:173 PACKS
PLATE PRINT RUN 1 SET PER COLOR
BLACK-CYAN-MAGENTA-YELLOW ISSUED
NO PLATE PRICING DUE TO SCARCITY
BBP1 Greg Smith .40 1.00
BBP2 J.R. Towles .75 2.00
BBP3 Jeff Locke .60 1.50
BBP4 Henry Sosa .40 1.00
BBP5 Ivan De Jesus Jr. .40 1.00
BBP6 Brad Lincoln .25 .60
BBP7 Josh Papelbon .25 .60
BBP8 Mark Hamilton .25 .60
BBP9 Sam Fuld .75 2.00
BBP10 Thomas Fairchild .25 .60
BBP11 Chris Carter .75 2.00
BBP12 Chuck Lofgren .60 1.50
BBP13 Joe Gaetti .25 .60
BBP14 Zach McAllister .40 1.00
BBP15 Cole Gillespie .40 1.00
BBP16 Jeremy Papelbon .25 .60
BBP17 Mike Carp .75 2.00
BBP18 Cody Strait .25 .60
BBP19 Gorkys Hernandez .60 1.50
BBP20 Andrew Fie .25 .60
BBP21 Erik Lis .40 1.00
BBP22 Chance Douglass .25 .60
BBP23 Vasili Spanos .25 .60
BBP24 Desmond Jennings 1.00 2.50
BBP25 Vic Buttler .25 .60
BBP26 Cedric Hunter .60 1.50
BBP27 Emerson Frostad .25 .60
BBP28 Mike Devaney .25 .60
BBP29 Eric Young Jr. .40 1.00
BBP30 Evan Englebrook .25 .60
BBP31 Aaron Cunningham .40 1.00
BBP32 Dellin Betances .75 2.00
BBP33 Michael Saunders .75 2.00
BBP34 Deolis Guerra .50 1.25
BBP35 Brian Bocock .25 .60
BBP36 Rich Thompson .25 .60
BBP37a Greg Reynolds .60 1.50
BBP37b Greg Reynolds AU 5.00 12.00
BBP38a Jeff Samardzija 1.00 2.50
BBP38b Jeff Samardzija AU 5.00 12.00
BBP39a Evan Longoria 3.00 8.00
BBP39b Evan Longoria AU 10.00 25.00
BBP40a Luke Hochevar .75 2.00
BBP40b Luke Hochevar AU 6.00 15.00
BBP41 James Avery AU 3.00 8.00
BBP42 Joe Mather AU 3.00 8.00
BBP43 Hank Conger AU 4.00 10.00
BBP44 Adam Miller AU 3.00 8.00
BBP45 Clayton Kershaw AU 60.00 150.00
BBP46 Adam Ottavino AU 3.00 8.00
BBP47 Jason Place AU 5.00 12.00
BBP48 Billy Rowell AU 3.00 8.00
BBP49 Brett Sinkbeil AU 3.00 8.00
BBP50 Colton Willems AU 3.00 8.00
BBP51 Cameron Maybin AU 3.00 8.00
BBP52 Jeremy Jeffress AU 3.00 8.00
BBP53 Fernando Martinez AU 3.00 8.00
BBP54 Chris Marrero AU 3.00 8.00
BBP55 Kyle McCulloch AU 3.00 8.00
BBP56 Chris Parmelee AU 3.00 8.00
BBP57 Emmanuel Burris AU 3.00 8.00
BBP58 Chris Coghlan AU 3.00 8.00
BBP59 Chris Perez AU 4.00 10.00
BBP60 David Huff AU 3.00 8.00

2007 Bowman's Best Prospects Blue

*PROS BLUE : .6X TO 1.5X BASIC PROS
PROS ODDS 1:9 PACKS
*PROS AU BLUE: .6X TO 1.5X BASIC PROS AU
PROS AU ODDS 1:16 PACKS
STATED PRINT RUN 99 SER.#'d SETS

2007 Bowman's Best Prospects Gold

*PROS GOLD: .75X TO 2X BASIC PROS
PROS ODDS 1:18 PACKS
*PROS AU GOLD: .75X TO 2X BASIC PROS AU
PROS AU ODDS 1:31 PACKS
STATED PRINT RUN 50 SER.#'d SETS

2007 Bowman's Best Prospects Green

PROS GREEN: .5X TO 1.2X BASIC PROS
STATED ODDS 1:4 PACKS
STATED PRINT RUN 249 SER.#'d SETS

2007 Bowman's Best Prospects Red

PROS. ODDS 1:908 PACKS
PROS. AU ODDS 1:1453 PACKS
STATED PRINT RUN 1 SER.#'d SET
NO PRICING DUE TO SCARCITY

2015 Bowman's Best

COMPLETE SET (100) 30.00 80.00
STATED PLATE ODDS 1:133 MINI BOX
PLATE PRINT RUN 1 SET PER COLOR
BLACK-CYAN-MAGENTA-YELLOW ISSUED
NO PLATE PRICING DUE TO SCARCITY
1 Mike Trout 2.00 5.00
2 James Shields .25 .60
3 Francisco Lindor RC 4.00 10.00
4 Chi Chi Gonzalez RC .75 2.00
5 Felix Hernandez .30 .75
6 Addison Russell RC 1.50 4.00
7 Joey Votto .40 1.00
8 Michael Brantley .30 .75
9 Robinson Cano .30 .75
10 Yasiel Puig .40 1.00
11 Edwin Encarnacion .40 1.00
12 Joey Gallo RC 1.00 2.50
13 Troy Tulowitzki .40 1.00
14 Nelson Cruz .40 1.00
15 Maikel Franco RC .60 1.50
16 Jake Arrieta .30 .75
17 Chris Archer .25 .60
18 Jacob deGrom .75 2.00
19 Adam Jones .30 .75
20 Daniel Norris RC .50 1.25
21 Jose Abreu .40 1.00
22 Masahiro Tanaka .30 .75
23 Yoenis Cespedes .30 .75
24 Anthony Rizzo .50 1.25
25 Bryce Harper .60 1.50
26 Starling Marte .30 .75
27 Byron Buxton RC 2.50 6.00
28 Joc Pederson RC 2.00 5.00
29 Adrian Gonzalez .30 .75
30 Buster Posey .50 1.25
31 Dee Gordon .25 .60
32 Noah Syndergaard RC 1.00 2.50
33 Michael Pineda .25 .60
34 Giancarlo Stanton .40 1.00
35 Freddie Freeman .50 1.25
36 George Springer .30 .75
37 Jose Bautista .30 .75
38 Brian Dozier .30 .75
39 Paul Goldschmidt .40 1.00
40 Eddie Rosario .50 1.25
41 Matt Wisler RC .50 1.25
42 Johnny Cueto .30 .75
43 Dustin Pedroia .40 1.00
44 Alex Meyer RC .50 1.25
45 Chris Sale .40 1.00
46 Yasmany Tomas RC .60 1.50
47 Mookie Betts .75 2.00
48 Zack Greinke .40 1.00
49 Jung Ho Kang RC .50 1.25
50 Kris Bryant RC 5.00 12.00
51 Kyle Seager .25 .60
52 Sonny Gray .30 .75
53 Eric Hosmer .30 .75
54 Devon Travis RC .50 1.25
55 Rusney Castillo RC .60 1.50
56 Jose Altuve .30 .75
57 Matt Harvey .30 .75
58 Carlos Correa RC 2.50 6.00
59 Anthony Rendon .40 1.00
60 Michael Wacha .30 .75
61 Miguel Cabrera .40 1.00
62 Ryan Braun .30 .75
63 Garrett Richards .30 .75
64 Justin Upton .30 .75
65 Brett Gardner .30 .75
66 Todd Frazier .25 .60
67 Archie Bradley RC .50 1.25
68 Dallas Keuchel .30 .75
69 Jacoby Ellsbury .30 .75
70 Adam Wainwright .30 .75
71 Eduardo Rodriguez RC .50 1.25
72 Carlos Beltran .30 .75
73 Cole Hamels .30 .75
74 Charlie Blackmon .40 1.00
75 Josh Donaldson .30 .75
76 Jose Reyes .30 .75
77 Corey Kluber .30 .75
78 Prince Fielder .30 .75
79 Carlos Rodon RC 1.25 3.00
80 A.J. Cole RC .50 1.25
81 Jason Kipnis .30 .75
82 Albert Pujols .50 1.25
83 Max Scherzer .40 1.00
84 Blake Swihart RC .60 1.50
85 Aroldis Chapman .40 1.00
86 Adrian Beltre .40 1.00
87 Trevor Rosenthal .30 .75
88 Madison Bumgarner .30 .75
89 Carlos Gomez .25 .60
90 Andrew McCutchen .40 1.00
91 Hanley Ramirez .30 .75
92 Steven Matz RC .60 1.50
93 Jorge Soler RC .75 2.00
94 David Price .30 .75
95 Billy Hamilton .30 .75
96 Nolan Arenado .60 1.50
97 Gerrit Cole .40 1.00
98 Craig Kimbrel .30 .75
99 Manny Machado .40 1.00
100 Clayton Kershaw .60 1.50

2015 Bowman's Best Atomic Refractors

*ATOMIC REF: 3X TO 8X BASIC
*ATOMIC REF RC: 1.5X TO 4X BASIC
STATED ODDS 1:2 MINI BOXES

2015 Bowman's Best Blue Refractors

*BLUE REF: 2.5X TO 6X BASIC
*BLUE REF RC: 1.2X TO 3X BASIC
STATED ODDS 1:4 MINI BOXES
STATED PRINT RUN 150 SER.#'D SETS
50 Kris Bryant 15.00 40.00
58 Carlos Correa 20.00 50.00

2015 Bowman's Best Gold Refractors

*GOLD REF: 4X TO 10X BASIC
*GOLD REF RC: 2X TO 5X BASIC
STATED ODDS 1:11 MINI BOX
STATED PRINT RUN 50 SER.#'d SETS
30 Buster Posey 12.00 30.00
49 Jung Ho Kang 10.00 25.00
50 Kris Bryant 25.00 60.00
58 Carlos Correa 40.00 100.00
100 Clayton Kershaw 15.00 40.00

2015 Bowman's Best Green Refractors

*GREEN REF: 2.5X TO 6X BASIC
*GREEN REF RC: 1.2X TO 3X BASIC
STATED ODDS 1:6 MINI BOXES
STATED PRINT RUN 99 SER.#'D SETS
50 Kris Bryant 15.00 40.00
58 Carlos Correa 20.00 50.00

2015 Bowman's Best Orange Refractors

*ORANGE REF: 5X TO 12X BASIC
*ORANGE REF RC: 2.5X TO 6X BASIC
STATED ODDS 1:22 MINI BOX
STATED PRINT RUN 25 SER.#'d SETS
30 Buster Posey 15.00 40.00
49 Jung Ho Kang 12.00 30.00
50 Kris Bryant 50.00 120.00
58 Carlos Correa 50.00 120.00
100 Clayton Kershaw 20.00 50.00

2015 Bowman's Best Refractors

*REFRACTOR: 1.2X TO 3X BASIC
*REFRACTOR RC: .6X TO 1.5X BASIC
RANDOM INSERTS IN MINI BOXES
50 Kris Bryant 8.00 20.00

2015 Bowman's Best '95 Bowman's Best Autographs Refractors

STATED ODDS 1:66 MINI BOX
PRINT RUNS B/WN 30-50 COPIES PER
EXCHANGE DEADLINE 12/31/2017
*ORANGE/25: .5X TO 1.2X BASIC
95BBAG Adrian Gonzalez/50 15.00 40.00
95BBAJ Adam Jones/50 8.00 20.00
95BBAR Anthony Rizzo/50 25.00 60.00
95BBCH Cole Hamels/50 40.00 100.00
95BBDO David Ortiz/30 30.00 80.00
95BBEE Edwin Encarnacion/50 10.00 25.00
95BBFF Freddie Freeman/50 20.00 50.00
95BBGS George Springer/50 15.00 40.00
95BBJA Jose Abreu/50 20.00 50.00
95BBJD Jacob deGrom/50 50.00 120.00
95BBJV Joey Votto/50 25.00 60.00
95BBPS Pablo Sandoval/50 8.00 20.00
95BBRB Ryan Braun/50 12.00 30.00
95BBSM Shelby Miller/50 15.00 40.00

2015 Bowman's Best Best of '15 Autographs

OVERALL AUTO ODDS TWO PER MINI BOX
STATED PLATE ODDS 1:233 MINI BOX
PLATE PRINT RUN 1 SET PER COLOR
BLACK-CYAN-MAGENTA-YELLOW ISSUED
NO PLATE PRICING DUE TO SCARCITY
EXCHANGE DEADLINE 12/31/2017
B15AB Alex Blandino 3.00 8.00
B15AG Adrian Gonzalez 6.00 15.00
B15AJ Alex Jackson 4.00 10.00
B15ANB Andrew Benintendi 10.00 25.00
B15ANO Aaron Nola 8.00 20.00
B15AR Alex Reyes 4.00 10.00
B15ARI Anthony Rizzo 20.00 50.00
B15ASR Ashe Russell 3.00 8.00
B15BB Byron Buxton 8.00 20.00
B15BD Braxton Davidson 3.00 8.00
B15BEB Beau Burrows 3.00 8.00
B15BR Brendan Rodgers 6.00 15.00
B15BSN Blake Snell 10.00 25.00
B15BZ Bradley Zimmer 5.00 12.00
B15CD Chase De Jong 4.00 10.00
B15CF Carson Fulmer 3.00 8.00
B15CH Chris Heston 3.00 8.00
B15CR Carlos Rodon 8.00 20.00
B15CRA Cornelius Randolph 3.00 8.00
B15CT Cole Tucker 3.00 8.00
B15DF Derek Fisher 4.00 10.00
B15DM Dixon Machado 4.00 10.00
B15DS Dansby Swanson 10.00 25.00
B15DST D.J. Stewart 3.00 8.00
B15DTA Dillon Tate 4.00 10.00
B15ER Eduardo Rodriguez 3.00 8.00
B15FL Francisco Lindor 40.00 100.00
B15FM Frankie Montas 4.00 10.00
B15GH Grant Holmes 4.00 10.00
B15GW Garrett Whitley 5.00 12.00
B15HR Hanley Ramirez 4.00 10.00
B15IH Ian Happ 8.00 20.00
B15JAL Jose Altuve 15.00 40.00
B15JHK Jung Ho Kang EXCH 15.00 40.00
B15JK James Kaprielian 3.00 8.00
B15JM Jorge Mateo 5.00 12.00
B15JNA Josh Naylor 4.00 10.00
B15JP Joc Pederson 6.00 15.00
B15JW Jacob Wilson 3.00 8.00
B15KA Kolby Allard 3.00 8.00
B15KB Kris Bryant 50.00 120.00
B15KM Kevonte Mitchell 3.00 8.00
B15KME Kodi Medeiros 3.00 8.00
B15KN Kevin Newman 4.00 10.00
B15KT Kyle Tucker 15.00 40.00
B15LG Lucas Giolito 6.00 15.00
B15LW Luke Weaver 5.00 12.00
B15MC Michael Chavis 10.00 25.00
B15MCH Matt Chapman 10.00 25.00
B15MMA Manuel Margot 3.00 8.00
B15MN Mike Nikorak 3.00 8.00
B15MO Matt Olson 8.00 20.00
B15MP Max Pentecost 3.00 8.00
B15MR Mariano Rivera 6.00 15.00
B15MS Miguel Sano 6.00 15.00
B15MSC Max Scherzer 40.00 100.00
B15MWI Matt Wisler 3.00 8.00
B15NG Nick Gordon 4.00 10.00
B15NP Nick Plummer 4.00 10.00
B15NS Noah Syndergaard 20.00 50.00
B15OA Orlando Arcia 4.00 10.00
B15PB Phil Bickford 3.00 8.00
B15PV Pat Venditte 3.00 8.00
B15RD Rafael Devers 20.00 50.00
B15RM Richie Martin 3.00 8.00
B15SG Stephen Gonsalves 3.00 8.00
B15SMA Steven Matz 5.00 12.00
B15SN Sean Newcomb 4.00 10.00
B15TC Trent Clark 3.00 8.00
B15TJ Tyler Jay 3.00 8.00
B15TS Tyler Stephenson 8.00 20.00
B15TT Trea Turner 10.00 25.00
B15TTO Touki Toussaint 4.00 10.00
B15TWA Taylor Ward 5.00 12.00
B15WB Walker Buehler 25.00 60.00
B15WD Wilmer Difo 3.00 8.00
B15YL Yoan Lopez 3.00 8.00

2015 Bowman's Best Best of '15 Autographs Atomic Refractors

*ATOMIC REF: .75X TO 2X BASIC
STATED ODDS 1:20 MINI BOX
STATED PRINT RUN 50 SER.#'d SETS
EXCHANGE DEADLINE 12/31/2017
B15AG Adrian Gonzalez 12.00 30.00
B15CC Carlos Correa 150.00 300.00
B15JG Joey Gallo 12.00 30.00
B15KS Kyle Schwarber 60.00 150.00
B15MT Mike Trout 200.00 400.00
B15SGR Sonny Gray EXCH 8.00 20.00

2015 Bowman's Best Best of '15 Autographs Green Refractors

*GREEN REF: .6X TO 1.5X BASIC
STATED ODDS 1:11 MINI BOX
STATED PRINT RUN 99 SER.#'d SETS
EXCHANGE DEADLINE 12/31/2017
B15CC Carlos Correa 125.00 250.00
B15JG Joey Gallo 10.00 25.00
B15KS Kyle Schwarber 50.00 120.00
B15MT Mike Trout 175.00 350.00
B15SGR Sonny Gray EXCH 6.00 15.00

2015 Bowman's Best Best of '15 Autographs Orange Refractors

*ORANGE REF: 1X TO 2.5X BASIC
STATED ODDS 1:38 MINI BOX
STATED PRINT RUN 25 SER.#'d SETS
EXCHANGE DEADLINE 12/31/2017
B15AG Adrian Gonzalez 15.00 40.00
B15CC Carlos Correa 175.00 350.00
B15JG Joey Gallo 15.00 40.00
B15KS Kyle Schwarber 75.00 200.00
B15MT Mike Trout 250.00 500.00
B15SGR Sonny Gray EXCH 10.00 25.00

2015 Bowman's Best Best of '15 Autographs Refractors

*REFRACTORS: .5X TO 1.2X BASIC
RANDOM INSERTS IN PACKS
EXCHANGE DEADLINE 12/31/2017
B15SGR Sonny Gray EXCH 5.00 12.00

2015 Bowman's Best First Impressions Refractors

STATED ODDS 1:2 MINI BOX
*ATOMIC/50: 1.5X TO 4X BASIC
*ORANGE/25: 2.5X TO 6X BASIC
FIAB Andrew Benintendi 2.50 6.00
FIBR Brendan Rodgers 2.00 5.00
FICF Carson Fulmer .50 1.25
FICR Cornelius Randolph .50 1.25
FIDS Dansby Swanson 3.00 8.00
FIDT Dillon Tate .60 1.50
FIGW Garrett Whitley .75 2.00
FIIH Ian Happ 2.00 5.00
FIJK James Kaprielian .50 1.25
FIJN Josh Naylor .60 1.50
FIKA Kolby Allard .50 1.25
FIKT Kyle Tucker 4.00 10.00
FIPB Phil Bickford .50 1.25
FITJ Tyler Jay .50 1.25
FITS Tyler Stephenson 1.25 3.00

2015 Bowman's Best First Impressions Autographs

STATED ODDS 1:53 MINI BOX
STATED PRINT RUN 99 SER.#'d SETS
EXCHANGE DEADLINE 12/31/2017
*ORANGE/25: .6X TO 1.5X BASIC
FIAB Andrew Benintendi 50.00 120.00
FIBR Brendan Rodgers 20.00 50.00
FICF Carson Fulmer 6.00 15.00
FICR Cornelius Randolph 6.00 15.00
FIDS Dansby Swanson 50.00 120.00
FIDT Dillon Tate 8.00 20.00
FIGW Garrett Whitley 10.00 25.00
FIIH Ian Happ 20.00 50.00
FIJK James Kaprielian 6.00 15.00
FIJN Josh Naylor 8.00 20.00
FIKA Kolby Allard 6.00 15.00
FIKT Kyle Tucker 50.00 125.00
FIPB Phil Bickford 6.00 15.00
FITJ Tyler Jay 6.00 15.00
FITS Tyler Stephenson 15.00 40.00

2015 Bowman's Best Hi Def Heritage Refractors

RANDOM INSERTS IN PACKS
*ATOMIC: 1X TO 2.5X BASIC
*ORANGE/25: 1.5X TO 4X BASIC
HDHAB Archie Bradley .50 1.25
HDHAG Adrian Gonzalez .60 1.50
HDHAJ Alex Jackson .60 1.50
HDHAJO Adam Jones .60 1.50
HDHAP Albert Pujols 1.00 2.50
HDHAR Addison Russell 1.50 4.00
HDHARI Anthony Rizzo 1.00 2.50
HDHBB Byron Buxton 2.50 6.00
HDHBH Bryce Harper 1.25 3.00
HDHBP Buster Posey 1.00 2.50
HDHBS Blake Swihart .60 1.50
HDHCC Carlos Correa 2.50 6.00
HDHCK Corey Kluber .60 1.50
HDHCKE Clayton Kershaw 1.25 3.00
HDHCR Carlos Rodon 1.25 3.00
HDHCS Corey Seager 2.50 6.00
HDHCSA Chris Sale .75 2.00
HDHDO David Ortiz .75 2.00
HDHFL Francisco Lindor 4.00 10.00
HDHGS Giancarlo Stanton .75 2.00
HDHHH Hunter Harvey .50 1.25
HDHHO Henry Owens .50 1.25
HDHJA Jose Abreu .75 2.00
HDHJB Jose Bautista .60 1.50
HDHJC J.P. Crawford .50 1.25
HDHJD Jacob deGrom 1.50 4.00
HDHJG Joey Gallo 1.00 2.50
HDHJL Jon Lester .60 1.50
HDHJP Joc Pederson 2.00 5.00
HDHJS Jorge Soler .75 2.00
HDHJU Julio Urias 1.50 4.00
HDHJV Joey Votto .75 2.00
HDHKB Kris Bryant 5.00 12.00
HDHKP Kevin Plawecki .50 1.25
HDHKS Kyle Schwarber 2.00 5.00
HDHLG Lucas Giolito 1.00 2.50
HDHLS Luis Severino .60 1.50
HDHMC Miguel Cabrera .75 2.00
HDHMS Miguel Sano .60 1.50
HDHMSC Max Scherzer .75 2.00
HDHMT Mike Trout 4.00 10.00
HDHNC Nelson Cruz .75 2.00
HDHNG Nick Gordon .60 1.50
HDHNS Noah Syndergaard 1.00 2.50
HDHPG Paul Goldschmidt .75 2.00
HDHRC Robinson Cano .60 1.50
HDHRD Rafael Devers 3.00 8.00
HDHTG Tyler Glasnow 2.00 5.00
HDHTT Touki Toussaint .60 1.50
HDHYT Yasmany Tomas .60 1.50

2015 Bowman's Best Hi Def Heritage Autographs

STATED ODDS 1:55 MINI BOX
STATED PRINT RUN 50 SER.#'d SETS
EXCHANGE DEADLINE 12/31/2017
HDHAB Archie Bradley 15.00 40.00
HDHAG Adrian Gonzalez 8.00 20.00
HDHAJO Adam Jones 25.00 60.00
HDHAP Albert Pujols 200.00 300.00
HDHARI Anthony Rizzo 20.00 50.00
HDHBB Byron Buxton 25.00 60.00
HDHBS Blake Swihart 6.00 15.00
HDHCC Carlos Correa 150.00 250.00
HDHCK Corey Kluber 8.00 20.00
HDHCR Carlos Rodon 12.00 30.00
HDHHO Henry Owens EXCH 8.00 20.00
HDHJG Joey Gallo 12.00 30.00
HDHJL Jon Lester 15.00 40.00
HDHJP Joc Pederson 25.00 60.00
HDHJS Jorge Soler 15.00 40.00
HDHKB Kris Bryant 150.00 250.00
HDHLG Lucas Giolito 12.00 30.00
HDHLS Luis Severino 25.00 60.00
HDHMS Miguel Sano 20.00 50.00
HDHMSC Max Scherzer EXCH 20.00 50.00
HDHNS Noah Syndergaard 25.00 60.00

2015 Bowman's Best Hi Def Heritage Autographs Orange Refractors

*ORANGE REF: .5X TO 1.2X BASIC
STATED ODDS 1:116 MINI BOX
STATED PRINT RUN 25 SER.#'d SETS
EXCHANGE DEADLINE 12/31/2017

2015 Bowman's Best Mirror Image

COMP.SET w/o UER (20) 10.00 25.00
RANDOM INSERTS IN MINI BOX
BELTRAN UER ODDS 1:399 MINI BOX
MI1 G.Stanton/A.Judge 6.00 15.00
MI2 C.Seager/T.Tulowitzki 1.25 3.00
MI3 K.Schwarber/B.Posey 1.00 2.50
MI4 S.Strasburg/L.Giolito .50 1.25
MI5 J.Bell/E.Hosmer .50 1.25
MI6 J.Urias/C.Kershaw .75 2.00
MI7 K.Bryant/N.Arenado 2.50 6.00
MI8 B.Buxton/C.Blackmon 1.25 3.00
MI9 C.Correa/A.Rodriguez 1.25 3.00
MI10 J.Gallo/J.Donaldson .50 1.25
MI11 J.Pederson/R.Braun 1.00 2.50
MI12 M.Sano/T.Frazier .30 .75
MI13 C.Rodon/D.Price .60 1.50
MI14 A.Nola/J.Shields .40 1.00
MI15 D.Swanson/B.Crawford 1.50 4.00
MI16 B.Rodgers/X.Bogaerts 1.00 2.50
MI17 D.Tate/F.Hernandez .30 .75
MI18 P.Tucker/K.Tucker 2.00 5.00
MI19 M.Trout/A.Benintendi 2.00 5.00
MI20 B.McCann/T.Stephenson .60 1.50
MILG Beltran/Gonzalez UER 2.00 5.00

2015 Bowman's Best Top Prospects

COMPLETE SET (50) 15.00 40.00
STATED PLATE ODDS 1:133 MINI BOX
PLATE PRINT RUN 1 SET PER COLOR
BLACK-CYAN-MAGENTA-YELLOW ISSUED
NO PLATE PRICING DUE TO SCARCITY
TP1 Corey Seager 1.25 3.00
TP2 Miguel Sano .30 .75
TP3 Robert Stephenson .25 .60
TP4 Raul Mondesi .40 1.00
TP5 Luis Severino .30 .75
TP6 Henry Owens .25 .60
TP7 Alex Reyes .30 .75
TP8 Hunter Harvey .25 .60
TP9 Dillon Tate .30 .75
TP10 Carson Fulmer .25 .60
TP11 Tyler Stephenson .60 1.50
TP12 Kolby Allard .25 .60
TP13 Kevin Newman .60 1.50
TP14 Beau Burrows .25 .60
TP15 Frankie Montas .30 .75
TP16 Kyle Schwarber 1.00 2.50
TP17 Braden Shipley .25 .60
TP18 Mark Appel .25 .60
TP19 Austin Meadows .60 1.50
TP20 Jesse Winker 1.00 2.50
TP21 Aaron Judge 4.00 10.00
TP22 Nick Gordon .30 .75
TP23 Ian Happ 1.00 2.50
TP24 Josh Naylor .30 .75
TP25 Lucas Giolito .50 1.25
TP26 James Kaprielian .25 .60
TP27 Ashe Russell .25 .60
TP28 Michael Conforto .30 .75
TP29 Rafael Devers 1.50 4.00
TP30 Tyler Glasnow 1.00 2.50
TP31 Jon Gray .25 .60
TP32 Jameson Taillon .30 .75
TP33 Aaron Nola .40 1.00
TP34 Tyler Kolek .25 .60
TP35 Dansby Swanson 1.50 4.00
TP36 Tyler Jay .25 .60
TP37 Andrew Benintendi 1.25 3.00
TP38 Garrett Whitley .40 1.00
TP39 Phil Bickford .25 .60
TP40 Richie Martin .25 .60
TP41 Bradley Zimmer .40 1.00
TP42 J.P. Crawford .25 .60
TP43 Aaron Blair .25 .60
TP44 Brandon Nimmo .40 1.00
TP45 Brendan Rodgers 1.00 2.50
TP46 Kyle Tucker 2.00 5.00
TP47 Cornelius Randolph .25 .60
TP48 Trent Clark .25 .60
TP49 Josh Bell .50 1.25
TP50 Julio Urias .75 2.00

2015 Bowman's Best Top Prospects Atomic Refractors

*ATOMIC REF: 1.5X TO 4X BASIC
RANDOM INSERST IN MINI BOXES
TP37 Andrew Benintendi 12.00 30.00

2015 Bowman's Best Top Prospects Blue Refractors

*BLUE REF: 1.5X TO 4X BASIC
RANDOM INSERTS IN MINI BOXES
STATED PRINT RUN 150 SER.#'d SETS
TP37 Andrew Benintendi 15.00 40.00

2015 Bowman's Best Top Prospects Gold Refractors

*GOLD REF: 5X TO 12X BASIC
RANDOM INSERTS IN MINI BOXES
STATED PRINT RUN 50 SER.#'d SETS

2015 Bowman's Best Top Prospects Green Refractors

*GREEN REF: 1.5X TO 4X BASIC
RANDOM INSERTS IN MINI BOXES
STATED PRINT RUN 99 SER.#'d SETS
TP37 Andrew Benintendi 20.00 50.00

2015 Bowman's Best Top Prospects Orange Refractors

*ORANGE REF: 6X TO 15X BASIC
RANDOM INSERTS IN MINI BOXES
STATED PRINT RUN 25 SER.#'d SETS

2015 Bowman's Best Top Prospects Refractors

*REFRACTORS: .5X TO 1.2X BASIC
RANDOM INSERST IN MINI BOXES

2016 Bowman's Best

COMPLETE SET (65) 10.00 25.00
1 Mike Trout 2.00 5.00
2 Albert Almora RC .50 1.25
3 Gary Sanchez RC 1.25 3.00
4 Michael Conforto RC .50 1.25
5 Evan Longoria .30 .75
6 Luis Severino RC .50 1.25
7 Dellin Betances .30 .75
8 Carlos Correa .40 1.00
9 Aaron Nola RC .75 2.00
10 Jose Altuve .30 .75
11 Paul Goldschmidt .40 1.00
12 Trevor Story RC 2.00 5.00
13 Dae-Ho Lee RC .60 1.50
14 Blake Snell RC .50 1.25
15 Miguel Sano RC .60 1.50
16 Wil Myers .30 .75
17 Josh Donaldson .30 .75
18 Freddie Freeman .50 1.25
19 Xander Bogaerts .40 1.00
20 Lucas Giolito RC .60 1.50
21 Nomar Mazara RC .60 1.50
22 Andrew McCutchen .40 1.00
23 Ryan Braun .30 .75
24 Julio Urias RC 1.25 3.00
25 Corey Seager RC 4.00 10.00
26 Manny Machado .40 1.00
27 Madison Bumgarner .30 .75
28 Ben Zobrist .30 .75
29 Aledmys Diaz RC .60 1.50
30 Clayton Kershaw .60 1.50
31 Max Scherzer .40 1.00
32 Mookie Betts .75 2.00
33 Nolan Arenado .60 1.50
34 Bryce Harper .60 1.50
35 Chris Sale .40 1.00
36 Jose Berrios RC .60 1.50
37 Jameson Taillon RC .50 1.25
38 Noah Syndergaard .30 .75
39 Kenta Maeda RC .75 2.00
40 Francisco Lindor .40 1.00
41 Jake Arrieta .30 .75
42 Tim Anderson RC 1.50 4.00
43 Rob Refsnyder RC .50 1.25
44 Anthony Rizzo .50 1.25
45 Jon Gray RC .40 1.00
46 Michael Fulmer RC .60 1.50
47 Yoenis Cespedes .40 1.00
48 Yu Darvish .40 1.00
49 Giancarlo Stanton .40 1.00
50 David Ortiz .40 1.00
51 Willson Contreras RC 2.50 6.00
52 Stephen Strasburg .40 1.00
53 Starling Marte .30 .75
54 Buster Posey .50 1.25
55 Tyler Naquin RC .60 1.50
56 Miguel Cabrera .40 1.00
57 Ichiro Suzuki .50 1.25
58 Trea Turner RC 1.25 3.00
59 Stephen Piscotty RC .60 1.50
60 Jose Bautista .30 .75
61 Daniel Murphy .30 .75
62 Felix Hernandez .30 .75
63 Robinson Cano .30 .75
64 Kyle Schwarber RC 1.25 3.00
65 Kris Bryant .50 1.25

2016 Bowman's Best Atomic Refractors

*ATOMIC REF: 3X TO 8X BASIC
*ATOMIC REF RC: 2X TO 5X BASIC RC
STATED ODDS 1:12 HOBBY

2016 Bowman's Best Blue Refractors

*BLUE REF: 2.5X TO 6X BASIC
*BLUE REF RC: 1.5X TO 4X BASIC RC
STATED ODDS 1:16 HOBBY
STATED PRINT RUN 250 SER.#'d SETS

2016 Bowman's Best Gold Refractors

*GOLD REF: 5X TO 12X BASIC
*GOLD REF RC: 3X TO 8X BASIC RC
STATED ODDS 1:79 HOBBY
STATED PRINT RUN 50 SER.#'d SETS

2016 Bowman's Best Green Refractors

*GRN REF: 3X TO 8X BASIC
*GRN REF RC: 2X TO 5X BASIC RC
STATED ODDS 1:49 HOBBY
STATED PRINT RUN 99 SER.#'d SETS

2016 Bowman's Best Orange Refractors

*ORANGE REF: 6X TO 15X BASIC
*ORANGE REF RC: 4X TO 10X BASIC RC
STATED ODDS 1:113 HOBBY
STATED PRINT RUN 25 SER.#'d SETS

2016 Bowman's Best Refractors

*REF: 1X TO 2.5X BASIC
*REF RC: .6X TO 1.5X BASIC RC

2016 Bowman's Best '96 Bowman's Best

STATED ODDS 1:6 HOBBY
96BBI Ichiro Suzuki 1.25 3.00
96BBAA Anthony Alford .60 1.50
96BBAB Andrew Benintendi 2.00 5.00
96BBAE Anderson Espinoza .75 2.00
96BBAG Andres Galarraga .75 2.00
96BBAP Andy Pettitte .75 2.00
96BBAR Alex Reyes .75 2.00
96BBBH Bryce Harper 1.50 4.00
96BBBS Blake Snell .75 2.00
96BBCC Carlos Correa 1.00 2.50
96BBDS Dansby Swanson 2.50 6.00
96BBDW David Wright .75 2.00
96BBHA Hank Aaron 2.00 5.00
96BBJB Jose Berrios 1.00 2.50
96BBJC Jose Canseco .75 2.00
96BBJD Johnny Damon .75 2.00
96BBJM Jorge Mateo .75 2.00
96BBJS John Smoltz 1.00 2.50
96BBKB Kris Bryant 1.25 3.00
96BBKM Kenta Maeda 1.25 3.00
96BBKS Kyle Schwarber 2.00 5.00
96BBLG Lucas Giolito 1.00 2.50
96BBMM Mark McGwire 1.50 4.00
96BBMT Mike Trout 5.00 12.00
96BBNA Nolan Arenado 1.50 4.00
96BBOA Orlando Arcia .75 2.00
96BBOV Omar Vizquel .75 2.00
96BBRD Rafael Devers 2.00 5.00
96BBSN Sean Newcomb .75 2.00
96BBYM Yoan Moncada 1.50 4.00

2016 Bowman's Best '96 Bowman's Best Atomic Refractors

*ATOMIC REF: 1X TO 2.5X BASIC
STATED ODDS 1:96 HOBBY
96BBKB Kris Bryant 20.00 50.00
96BBKS Kyle Schwarber 10.00 25.00
96BBMT Mike Trout 20.00 50.00

2016 Bowman's Best '96 Bowman's Best Orange Refractors

*ORANGE REF: 2X TO 5X BASIC
STATED ODDS 1:375 HOBBY
STATED PRINT RUN 35 SER.#'d SETS
96BBKB Kris Bryant 40.00 100.00
96BBKS Kyle Schwarber 20.00 50.00
96BBMT Mike Trout 40.00 100.00

2016 Bowman's Best '96 Bowman's Best Autographs

STATED ODDS 1:385 HOBBY
PRINT RUNS B/WN 30-99 COPIES PER
EXCHANGE DEADLINE 11/30/2018
96BBAAA Anthony Alford/99 4.00 10.00
96BBAAE Anderson Espinoza/99 5.00 12.00
96BBAAG Andres Galarraga/50 6.00 15.00
96BBAAR Alex Reyes/75 20.00 50.00
96BBADS Dansby Swanson/50 50.00 120.00
96BBAJC Jose Canseco/75 15.00 40.00
96BBAJD Johnny Damon/30 30.00 80.00
96BBAJM Jorge Mateo/99 5.00 12.00
96BBAKS Kyle Schwarber/50 15.00 40.00
96BBALG Lucas Giolito/75 6.00 15.00
96BBAOA Orlando Arcia/99 5.00 12.00
96BBAOV Omar Vizquel/75 5.00 12.00
96BBARD Rafael Devers/75 20.00 50.00
96BBASN Sean Newcomb/99 5.00 12.00

2016 Bowman's Best '96 Bowman's Best Autographs Atomic Refractors

*ATOMIC REF: .6X TO 1.5X BASIC
STATED ODDS 1:768 HOBBY
STATED PRINT RUN 25 SER.#'d SETS
EXCHANGE DEADLINE 11/30/2018

96BBAAP Andy Pettitte 20.00 50.00
96BBABH Bryce Harper 200.00 400.00
96BBACC Carlos Correa 75.00 200.00
96BBADW David Wright 25.00 60.00
96BBAHA Hank Aaron 250.00 400.00
96BBAI Ichiro Suzuki 300.00 600.00
96BBAJD Johnny Damon 30.00 80.00
96BBAJS John Smoltz 25.00 60.00
96BBAKB Kris Bryant 400.00 600.00
96BBAMM Mark McGwire 100.00 250.00
96BBAMT Mike Trout 175.00 350.00

2016 Bowman's Best Baseball America Prospect Forecast

STATED ODDS 1:262 HOBBY
STATED PRINT RUN 150 SER.#'d SETS
*ORANGE/35: .5X TO 1.2X BASIC
BAPFAE Anderson Espinoza 2.00 5.00
BAPFBR Brendan Rodgers 2.50 6.00
BAPFDS Dansby Swanson 6.00 15.00
BAPFGT Gleyber Torres 8.00 20.00
BAPFJM Jorge Mateo 2.00 5.00
BAPFLF Lucius Fox 2.50 6.00
BAPFRD Rafael Devers 4.00 10.00
BAPFSN Sean Newcomb 2.00 5.00
BAPFVR Victor Robles 6.00 15.00
BAPFYM Yoan Moncada 4.00 10.00

2016 Bowman's Best Baseball America Prospect Forecast Autographs

STATED ODDS 1:1,284 HOBBY
STATED PRINT RUN 50 SER.#'d SETS
EXCHANGE DEADLINE 11/30/2018
BAPFAE Anderson Espinoza
BAPFDS Dansby Swanson 20.00 50.00
BAPFGT Gleyber Torres 60.00 150.00
BAPFJM Jorge Mateo 6.00 15.00
BAPFSN Sean Newcomb 4.00 10.00
BAPFYM Yoan Moncada 30.00 80.00

2016 Bowman's Best Best of '16 Autographs

STATED ODDS 1:XX HOBBY
STATED PLATE ODDS 1:1,696 HOBBY
PLATE PRINT RUN 1 SET PER COLOR
BLACK-CYAN-MAGENTA-YELLOW ISSUED
NO PLATE PRICING DUE TO SCARCITY
EXCHANGE DEADLINE 11/30/2018
B16AA Anthony Alford 3.00 8.00
B16AB Anthony Banda 3.00 8.00
B16ABR Alex Bregman 20.00 50.00
B16ABE Andrew Benintendi 10.00 25.00
B16ABL Aaron Blair 3.00 8.00
B16AD Aledmys Diaz 5.00 12.00
B16AE Anderson Espinoza 4.00 10.00
B16AJ Aaron Judge 75.00 200.00
B16AK Alex Kirilloff 15.00 40.00
B16AP A.J. Puk 5.00 12.00
B16AR Alex Reyes 4.00 10.00
B16AR A.J. Reed 3.00 8.00
B16ARO Amed Rosario 5.00 12.00
B16BG Braxton Garrett 4.00 10.00
B16BH Bryce Harper 60.00 150.00
B16BP Buster Posey 20.00 50.00
B16BR Brendan Rodgers 5.00 12.00
B16BS Blake Snell 3.00 8.00
B16CC Carlos Correa 25.00 60.00
B16COR Corey Ray 4.00 10.00
B16CQ Cal Quantrill 3.00 8.00
B16CR Carlos Rodon 5.00 12.00
B16CS Corey Seager 60.00 150.00
B16DD David Dahl 4.00 10.00
B16DJ Drew Jackson 3.00 8.00
B16DS Dansby Swanson 10.00 25.00
B16ED Elias Diaz 3.00 8.00
B16FB Franklin Barreto 3.00 8.00
B16FL Francisco Lindor 20.00 50.00
B16FW Forrest Whitley 6.00 15.00
B16GD Garrett Davila 3.00 8.00
B16GL Gavin Lux 25.00 60.00
B16HOW Henry Owens 4.00 10.00
B16IA Ian Anderson 15.00 40.00
B16JDU Justin Dunn 3.00 8.00
B16JH Josh Hader 4.00 10.00
B16JL Joshua Lowe 3.00 8.00
B16JM Jorge Mateo 4.00 10.00
B16JT Jameson Taillon 4.00 10.00
B16JU Julio Urias
B16KA Kolby Allard 3.00 8.00
B16KB Kris Bryant 60.00 150.00
B16KL Kyle Lewis 30.00 80.00
B16KM Kenta Maeda
B16KN Kevin Newman 5.00 12.00
B16KS Kyle Schwarber 12.00 30.00
B16LG Lucas Giolito 12.00 30.00
B16LS Luis Severino 10.00 25.00
B16MAS Mallex Smith
B16MC Michael Conforto
B16MCL Mike Clevinger 8.00 20.00
B16MM Mickey Moniak 8.00 20.00
B16MMA Matt Manning 10.00 25.00
B16MS Miguel Sano 5.00 12.00
B16MT Mike Trout
B16MTH Matt Thaiss 3.00 8.00
B16NA Nolan Arenado 25.00 60.00
B16NM Nomar Mazara
B16OA Ozzie Albies 15.00 40.00
B16OAR Orlando Arcia 4.00 10.00
B16RD Rafael Devers 15.00 40.00
B16RP Riley Pint 3.00 8.00
B16RS Robert Stephenson 3.00 8.00
B16SM Steven Matz 3.00 8.00
B16SN Sean Newcomb 4.00 10.00
B16ST Sam Travis 4.00 10.00
B16TA Tim Anderson 25.00 60.00
B16TO Tyler O'Neill 4.00 10.00
B16TS Trevor Story 25.00 60.00
B16TT Touki Toussaint EXCH 4.00 10.00
B16VG Vladimir Guerrero Jr. 100.00 250.00
B16WB Will Benson 5.00 12.00
B16WC Will Craig 3.00 8.00
B16WCO Willson Contreras 15.00 40.00
B16YG Yulieski Gurriel 3.00 8.00
B16YM Yoan Moncada 12.00 30.00
B16ZC Zack Collins 4.00 10.00

2016 Bowman's Best Best of '16 Autographs Atomic Refractors

*ATOMIC REF: 1X TO 2.5X BASIC
STATED ODDS 1:271 HOBBY
STATED PRINT RUN 25 SER.#'d SETS
EXCHANGE DEADLINE 11/30/2018
B16JU Julio Urias 50.00 120.00
B16KM Kenta Maeda 40.00 100.00
B16MAS Mallex Smith 10.00 25.00
B16MC Michael Conforto 20.00 50.00
B16MT Mike Trout 250.00 600.00
B16NM Nomar Mazara 12.00 30.00

2016 Bowman's Best Best of '16 Autographs Green Refractors

*GREEN REF: .6X TO 1.5X BASIC
STATED ODDS 1:69 HOBBY
STATED PRINT RUN 99 SER.#'d SETS
EXCHANGE DEADLINE 11/30/2018
B16JU Julio Urias 30.00 80.00
B16KM Kenta Maeda 25.00 60.00
B16MAS Mallex Smith 6.00 15.00
B16MC Michael Conforto 12.00 30.00
B16NM Nomar Mazara 8.00 20.00

2016 Bowman's Best Best of '16 Autographs Orange Refractors

*ORANGE REF: .75X TO 2X BASIC
STATED ODDS 1:135 HOBBY
STATED PRINT RUN 50 SER.#'d SETS
EXCHANGE DEADLINE 11/30/2018
B16JU Julio Urias 40.00 100.00
B16KM Kenta Maeda 30.00 80.00
B16MAS Mallex Smith 8.00 20.00
B16MC Michael Conforto 15.00 40.00
B16MT Mike Trout 200.00 500.00
B16NM Nomar Mazara 10.00 25.00

2016 Bowman's Best Best of '16 Autographs Refractors

*REFRACTORS: .5X TO 1.2X BASIC
STATED ODDS 1:14 HOBBY
EXCHANGE DEADLINE 11/30/2018

2016 Bowman's Best Bowman Choice Autographs

STATED ODDS 1:768 HOBBY
STATED PRINT RUN 50 SER.#'d SETS
EXCHANGE DEADLINE 11/30/2018
BCAAB Alex Bregman 30.00 80.00
BCAAE Anderson Espinoza 8.00 20.00
BCACC Carlos Correa 30.00 80.00
BCACK Clayton Kershaw 50.00 120.00
BCACS Corey Seager 40.00 100.00
BCACSA Chris Sale
BCADO David Ortiz 40.00 100.00
BCAKB Kris Bryant 150.00 300.00
BCALG Lucas Giolito 8.00 20.00
BCANM Nomar Mazara 30.00 80.00
BCAOA Ozzie Albies 12.00 30.00
BCASM Steven Matz 10.00 25.00
BCATO Tyler O'Neill 6.00 15.00
BCAYM Yoan Moncada

2016 Bowman's Best Dual Autographs

STATED ODDS 1:3,072 HOBBY
STATED PRINT RUN 25 SER.#'d SETS
EXCHANGE DEADLINE 11/30/2018
BDAAB O.Arcia/R.Braun
BDABC A.Bregman/C.Correa 125.00 250.00
BDABH K.Bryant/M.Trout 1000.00 1500.00
BDAGH L.Giolito/B.Harper 30.00 80.00
BDAMS K.Maeda/C.Seager EXCH 125.00 250.00
BDAPM D.Pedroia/Y.Moncada 125.00 250.00
BDARF C.Rodon/C.Fulmer 20.00 50.00
BDASF D.Swanson/F.Freeman

2016 Bowman's Best First Impressions Autographs

STATED ODDS 1:385 HOBBY
STATED PRINT RUN 50 SER.#'d SETS
EXCHANGE DEADLINE 11/30/2018
*ATOMIC/25: .6X TO 1.5X BASIC
FIAAK Alex Kirilloff 40.00 100.00
FIAAP A.J. Puk 6.00 15.00
FIABG Braxton Garrett 12.00 30.00
FIACQ Cal Quantrill 4.00 10.00
FIACR Corey Ray 5.00 12.00
FIAFW Forrest Whitley 15.00 40.00
FIAGL Gavin Lux 40.00 100.00
FIAIA Ian Anderson 8.00 20.00
FIAJD Justin Dunn 4.00 10.00
FIAJL Joshua Lowe
FIAKL Kyle Lewis 40.00 100.00
FIAMM Mickey Moniak 25.00 60.00
FIAMMA Matt Manning 6.00 15.00
FIAMT Matt Thaiss 15.00 40.00
FIARP Riley Pint 4.00 10.00
FIAWB Will Benson 6.00 15.00
FIAZC Zack Collins 10.00 25.00

2016 Bowman's Best Mirror Image

COMPLETE SET (20) 8.00 20.00
STATED ODDS 1:4 HOBBY
*ATOMIC: .75X TO 2X BASIC
*ORANGE/25: 2.5X TO 6X BASIC
MI1 M.Moniak/J.Ellsbury 1.50 4.00
MI2 I.Anderson/J.deGrom 1.25 3.00
MI3 R.Pint/J.Verlander .40 1.00
MI4 C.Ray/J.Heyward .30 .75
MI5 A.Puk/A.Miller .40 1.00
MI6 G.Stanton/J.Bour .40 1.00
MI7 M.Manning/N.Syndergaard .40 1.00
MI8 B.Posey/Z.Collins .50 1.25
MI9 A.Jones/K.Lewis 5.00 12.00
MI10 C.Yelich/A.Kirilloff 2.50 6.00
MI11 C.Seager/T.Tulowitzki 2.50 6.00
MI12 B.McCann/W.Contreras 1.50 4.00
MI13 L.Giolito/M.Scherzer .40 1.00
MI14 C.Kershaw/J.Urias .75 2.00
MI15 J.Lester/S.Matz .30 .75
MI16 J.Altuve/Y.Moncada .60 1.50
MI17 F.Lindor/O.Arcia .40 1.00
MI18 X.Bogaerts/D.Swanson 1.00 2.50
MI19 A.Reyes/J.Arrieta .30 .75
MI20 Carpenter/Devers .75 2.00

2016 Bowman's Best Stat Lines

COMPLETE SET (35) 10.00 25.00
STATED ODDS 1:3 HOBBY
*ATOMIC: 1X TO 2.5X BASIC
*ORANGE/25: 2.5X TO 6X BASIC
SLAB Anthony Banda .25 .60
SLABR Alex Bregman 1.25 3.00
SLAE Anderson Espinoza .30 .75
SLAJ Aaron Judge 2.00 5.00
SLAR Alex Reyes .30 .75
SLBH Bryce Harper .60 1.50
SLBP Buster Posey .50 1.25
SLBR Brendan Rodgers .40 1.00
SLBS Blake Snell .30 .75
SLCC Carlos Correa .40 1.00
SLCK Clayton Kershaw .60 1.50
SLCS Corey Seager 2.50 6.00
SLDO David Ortiz .40 1.00
SLDS Dansby Swanson 1.00 2.50
SLFL Francisco Lindor .40 1.00
SLGS Gary Sanchez .75 2.00
SLJA Jake Arrieta .30 .75
SLJAL Jose Altuve .30 .75
SLJH Josh Hader .30 .75
SLJT Jameson Taillon .30 .75
SLJU Julio Urias .75 2.00
SLKB Kris Bryant .50 1.25
SLKM Kenta Maeda .50 1.25
SLLG Lucas Giolito .40 1.00
SLMB Madison Bumgarner .30 .75
SLMC Michael Conforto .30 .75
SLMF Michael Fulmer .40 1.00
SLNA Nolan Arenado .60 1.50
SLNM Nomar Mazara .40 1.00
SLOA Orlando Arcia .30 .75
SLSN Sean Newcomb .30 .75
SLTA Tim Anderson 1.00 2.50
SLTO Tyler O'Neill .30 .75
SLTS Trevor Story 1.25 3.00
SLYM Yoan Moncada .60 1.50

2016 Bowman's Best Stat Lines Autographs

STATED ODDS 1:308 HOBBY
STATED PRINT RUN 50 SER.#'d SETS
EXCHANGE DEADLINE 11/30/2018
SLABR Alex Bregman 15.00 40.00
SLAJ Aaron Judge 40.00 100.00
SLBH Bryce Harper 75.00 200.00
SLBP Buster Posey 30.00 80.00
SLBS Blake Snell 6.00 15.00
SLCC Carlos Correa 30.00 80.00
SLCK Clayton Kershaw 30.00 80.00
SLDO David Ortiz 40.00 100.00
SLDS Dansby Swanson
SLFL Francisco Lindor 20.00 50.00
SLJH Josh Hader
SLJT Jameson Taillon 6.00 15.00
SLKM Kenta Maeda 15.00 40.00
SLMF Michael Fulmer 15.00 40.00
SLNA Nolan Arenado 25.00 60.00
SLNM Nomar Mazara 15.00 40.00
SLOA Orlando Arcia 6.00 15.00
SLSN Sean Newcomb 6.00 15.00
SLTA Tim Anderson 20.00 50.00
SLTO Tyler O'Neill 12.00 30.00
SLTS Trevor Story 15.00 40.00
SLYM Yoan Moncada 60.00 150.00

2016 Bowman's Best Top Prospects

COMPLETE SET (35) 6.00 15.00
*REF: .5X TO 1.2X BASIC
*BLUE/250: 1X TO 2.5X BASIC
*ATOMIC: 1X TO 2.5X BASIC
*GREEN/99: 1.2X TO 3X BASIC
*GOLD/50: 2X TO 5X BASIC
*ORANGE/35: 2.5X TO 6X BASIC
TP1 Yoan Moncada .60 1.50
TP2 Brendan Rodgers .40 1.00
TP3 Jorge Mateo .30 .75
TP4 Anderson Espinoza .30 .75
TP5 Orlando Arcia .30 .75
TP6 Cal Quantrill .25 .60
TP7 Joshua Lowe .25 .60
TP8 Bradley Zimmer .40 1.00
TP9 A.J. Puk .40 1.00
TP10 Will Craig .25 .60
TP11 Rafael Devers .75 2.00
TP12 J.P. Crawford .25 .60
TP13 Gleyber Torres 4.00 10.00
TP14 Riley Pint .25 .60
TP15 Will Benson .25 .60
TP16 Dansby Swanson 1.00 2.50
TP17 Manny Margot .25 .60
TP18 Zack Collins .30 .75
TP19 Ian Anderson 1.25 3.00
TP20 Clint Frazier 1.00 2.50
TP21 Corey Ray .30 .75
TP22 Kyle Lewis 5.00 12.00
TP23 Tyler Glasnow 1.00 2.50
TP24 Francis Martes .25 .60
TP25 Alex Bregman 1.25 3.00
TP26 Braxton Garrett .30 .75
TP27 Alex Kirilloff 2.50 6.00
TP28 Aaron Judge 6.00 15.00
TP29 Andrew Benintendi .75 2.00
TP30 Alex Reyes .30 .75
TP31 Matt Manning .40 1.00
TP32 David Dahl .40 1.00
TP33 Jose De Leon .25 .60
TP34 Austin Meadows .60 1.50
TP35 Mickey Moniak 1.50 4.00

2017 Bowman's Best

COMPLETE SET (65) 10.00 25.00
1 Aaron Judge RC 5.00 12.00
2 Max Scherzer .40 1.00
3 Tyler Glasnow RC 1.50 4.00
4 Daniel Murphy .30 .75
5 Freddie Freeman .50 1.25
6 Alex Reyes RC .50 1.25
7 Clayton Kershaw .60 1.50
8 Manny Machado .40 1.00
9 Jose Altuve .30 .75
10 Corey Seager .40 1.00
11 David Dahl RC .50 1.25
12 Jose De Leon RC .40 1.00
13 Franklin Barreto RC .40 1.00
14 Andrew Benintendi RC 1.25 3.00
15 Paul Goldschmidt .40 1.00
16 Jose Berrios .30 .75
17 Robinson Cano .30 .75
18 Miguel Sano .30 .75
19 Chris Sale .40 1.00
20 Giancarlo Stanton .40 1.00
21 Yoan Moncada RC 1.25 3.00
22 Brett Phillips RC .50 1.25
23 Miguel Cabrera .40 1.00
24 Jose Ramirez .30 .75
25 Mike Trout 2.00 5.00
26 Buster Posey .50 1.25
27 Craig Kimbrel .30 .75
28 Nolan Arenado .60 1.50
29 Yu Darvish .40 1.00
30 Jorge Alfaro RC .50 1.25
31 Bryce Harper .60 1.50
32 Luke Weaver RC .50 1.25
33 Noah Syndergaard .30 .75
34 Christian Arroyo RC .60 1.50
35 Anthony Rizzo .50 1.25
36 Joey Votto .40 1.00
37 Hunter Renfroe RC .40 1.00
38 Ian Happ RC .75 2.00
39 Charlie Blackmon .40 1.00
40 Kenley Jansen .30 .75
41 Yulieski Gurriel RC .60 1.50
42 Lewis Brinson RC .60 1.50
43 Sean Newcomb RC .50 1.25
44 Francisco Lindor .40 1.00
45 Aroldis Chapman .40 1.00
46 Mookie Betts .75 2.00
47 Trey Mancini RC .75 2.00
48 Carlos Correa .40 1.00
49 Josh Donaldson .30 .75
50 Kris Bryant .50 1.25
51 Andrew McCutchen .40 1.00
52 Ichiro .50 1.25
53 Khris Davis .40 1.00
54 Alex Bregman RC 2.00 5.00
55 Raimel Tapia RC .50 1.25
56 George Springer .30 .75
57 Corey Kluber .30 .75
58 Ryon Healy RC .50 1.25
59 Josh Bell RC 1.00 2.50
60 Jake Lamb .30 .75
61 Dansby Swanson RC 1.00 2.50
62 Yoenis Cespedes .40 1.00
63 Wil Myers .30 .75
64 Bradley Zimmer RC .50 1.25
65 Cody Bellinger RC 6.00 15.00

2017 Bowman's Best Atomic Refractors

*ATOMIC REF: 2X TO 5X BASIC
*ATOMIC REF RC: 1.2X TO 3X BASIC RC

2017 Bowman's Best Blue Refractors

*BLUE REF: 2.5X TO 6X BASIC
*BLUE REF RC: 1.5X TO 4X BASIC RC
STATED PRINT RUN 150 SER.#'d SETS

2017 Bowman's Best Gold Refractors

*GOLD REF: 5X TO 12X BASIC
*GOLD REF RC: 3X TO 8X BASIC RC
STATED PRINT RUN 50 SER.#'d SETS

2017 Bowman's Best Green Refractors

*GRN REF: 3X TO 8X BASIC
*GRN REF RC: 2X TO 5X BASIC RC
STATED PRINT RUN 99 SER.#'d SETS

2017 Bowman's Best Orange Refractors

*ORANGE REF: 6X TO 15X BASIC
*ORANGE REF RC: 4X TO 10X BASIC RC
STATED PRINT RUN 25 SER.#'d SETS

2017 Bowman's Best Purple Refractors

*PURPLE REF: 2.5X TO 6X BASIC
*PURPLE REF RC: 1.5X TO 4X BASIC RC
STATED PRINT RUN 250 SER.#'d SETS

2017 Bowman's Best Refractors

*REF: 1X TO 2.5X BASIC
*REF RC: .6X TO 1.5X BASIC RC

2017 Bowman's Best '97 Best Cuts

COMPLETE SET (30) 12.00 30.00
97BCAB Alex Bregman 2.50 6.00
97BCABE Andrew Benintendi 1.50 4.00
97BCAG Andres Galarraga .60 1.50
97BCAJ Aaron Judge 6.00 15.00
97BCBH Bryce Harper 1.25 3.00
97BCCB Cody Bellinger 8.00 20.00
97BCCC Carlos Correa .75 2.00
97BCCS Corey Seager .75 2.00
97BCDC Dylan Cozens .50 1.25
97BCDJ Derek Jeter 2.00 5.00
97BCDS Dominic Smith .50 1.25
97BCEJ Eloy Jimenez 2.00 5.00
97BCGT Gleyber Torres 8.00 20.00
97BCHA Hank Aaron 1.50 4.00
97BCJB Jeff Bagwell .60 1.50
97BCJT Jim Thome .60 1.50
97BCKB Kris Bryant 1.00 2.50
97BCKGJ Ken Griffey Jr. 1.50 4.00
97BCLA Lazarito Armenteros 1.00 2.50
97BCLB Lewis Brinson .75 2.00
97BCMM Mark McGwire 1.25 3.00
97BCMP Mike Piazza .75 2.00
97BCMT Mike Trout 4.00 10.00
97BCNG Nomar Garciaparra .60 1.50
97BCNS Nick Senzel 1.50 4.00
97BCPG Paul Goldschmidt .75 2.00
97BCRH Rhys Hoskins 2.00 5.00
97BCTO Tyler O'Neill .60 1.50
97BCWC Willie Calhoun .75 2.00
97BCYM Yoan Moncada 1.50 4.00

2017 Bowman's Best '97 Best Cuts Atomic Refractors

*ATOMIC REF: 1.2X TO 3X BASIC
97BCKGJ Ken Griffey Jr. 10.00 25.00

2017 Bowman's Best '97 Best Cuts Gold Refractors

*GOLD REF: 2X TO 5X BASIC
STATED PRINT RUN 50 SER.#'d SETS
97BCKB Kris Bryant 15.00 40.00
97BCKGJ Ken Griffey Jr. 30.00 80.00
97BCMP Mike Piazza 15.00 40.00
97BCMT Mike Trout 20.00 50.00

2017 Bowman's Best '97 Best Cuts Autographs

PRINT RUNS B/WN 9-150 COPIES PER
NO PRICING ON QTY 9
EXCHANGE DEADLINE 9/30/2019
97BCAAB Alex Bregman/150 20.00 50.00
97BCAABE Andrew Benintendi EXCH 25.00 60.00
97BCACB Cody Bellinger/150 75.00 200.00
97BCACC Carlos Correa/40 40.00 100.00
97BCADO David Ortiz/30 40.00 100.00
97BCAGT Gleyber Torres/150 60.00 150.00
97BCAHA Hank Aaron/20 200.00 400.00
97BCAJB Jeff Bagwell/50 20.00 50.00
97BCAJT Jim Thome/50 40.00 100.00
97BCAKB Kris Bryant/30 75.00 200.00
97BCALA Lazarito Armenteros/150 12.00 30.00
97BCAMM Mark McGwire/30 40.00 100.00
97BCAMT Mike Trout/20 300.00 500.00
97BCANG Nomar Garciaparra/50 15.00 40.00
97BCANS Nick Senzel/150 25.00 60.00
97BCAPG Paul Goldschmidt/50 25.00 60.00
97BCAYM Yoan Moncada/40 30.00 80.00

2017 Bowman's Best '97 Best Cuts Autographs Atomic Refractors

*ATOMIC REF: .6X TO 1.5X p/r 150
*ATOMIC REF: .5X TO 1.2X p/r 40-50
*ATOMIC REF: .4X TO 1X p/r 20-30
STATED PRINT RUN 50 SER.#'d SETS
EXCHANGE DEADLINE 11/30/2019
97BCAGT Gleyber Torres 125.00 300.00

2017 Bowman's Best '97 Best Cuts Autographs Gold Refractors

*GOLD REF: .5X TO 1.2X p/r 150
*GOLD REF: .4X TO 1X p/r 40-50
STATED PRINT RUN 50 SER.#'d SETS
EXCHANGE DEADLINE 11/30/2019

2017 Bowman's Best Baseball America's Dean's List

COMPLETE SET (40) 12.00 30.00
*ATOMIC REF: 1.5X TO 4X BASIC
*GOLD REF/50: 2.5X TO 6X BASIC
BADLAR Amed Rosario .50 1.25
BADLAS Tony Santillan .30 .75
BADLAV Alex Verdugo .50 1.25
BADLBD Bobby Dalbec 2.00 5.00
BADLBH Bryce Harper .75 2.00
BADLBHO Brent Honeywell .40 1.00
BADLBR Blake Rutherford .50 1.25
BADLCF Clint Frazier .60 1.50
BADLCS Corey Seager .50 1.25
BADLCST Christin Stewart .40 1.00
BADLDC Dylan Cozens .30 .75
BADLDS Dominic Smith .30 .75
BADLEJ Eloy Jimenez 1.25 3.00
BADLFM Francisco Mejia .50 1.25
BADLGT Gleyber Torres 5.00 12.00
BADLJD Jon Duplantier .50 1.25
BADLJG Jason Groome .60 1.50
BADLJM Jorge Mateo .30 .75
BADLJN Josh Naylor .40 1.00
BADLJS Justus Sheffield .50 1.25
BADLJSA Jesus Sanchez 1.50 4.00
BADLKB Kris Bryant .60 1.50
BADLKM Kevin Maitan .50 1.25
BADLLA Lazarito Armenteros .60 1.50
BADLLE Lucas Erceg .30 .75
BADLMK Mitch Keller .40 1.00
BADLMM Mickey Moniak .60 1.50
BADLMT Mike Trout 2.50 6.00
BADLNS Nick Senzel 1.00 2.50
BADLPW Patrick Weigel .30 .75
BADLRA Ronald Acuna 10.00 25.00
BADLRD Rafael Devers .60 1.50
BADLRH Rhys Hoskins 1.25 3.00
BADLRM Ryan Mountcastle 1.50 4.00
BADLSK Scott Kingery .50 1.25
BADLSS Sixto Sanchez 5.00 12.00
BADLTM Triston McKenzie 1.00 2.50
BADLTO Tyler O'Neill .40 1.00
BADLTT Taylor Trammell 2.00 5.00
BADLWC Willie Calhoun .50 1.25

2017 Bowman's Best Baseball America's Dean's List Autographs

STATED PRINT RUN 75 SER.#'d SETS
EXCHANGE DEADLINE 11/30/2019
BADLAS Tony Santillan 4.00 10.00
BADLAV Alex Verdugo 10.00 25.00
BADLBD Bobby Dalbec 25.00 60.00
BADLCF Clint Frazier 8.00 20.00
BADLDC Dylan Cozens 4.00 10.00
BADLDS Dominic Smith 4.00 10.00
BADLEJ Eloy Jimenez 20.00 50.00
BADLFM Francisco Mejia 10.00 25.00
BADLGT Gleyber Torres 30.00 80.00
BADLJG Jason Groome 8.00 20.00
BADLJM Jorge Mateo 8.00 20.00
BADLJN Josh Naylor 8.00 20.00
BADLJS Justus Sheffield 8.00 20.00
BADLKM Kevin Maitan 6.00 15.00
BADLLA Lazarito Armenteros 15.00 40.00
BADLLE Lucas Erceg 5.00 12.00
BADLMK Mitch Keller 6.00 15.00
BADLMM Mickey Moniak 15.00 40.00
BADLNS Nick Senzel 20.00 50.00
BADLPW Patrick Weigel 4.00 10.00
BADLRA Ronald Acuna 150.00 400.00
BADLRD Rafael Devers 10.00 25.00
BADLSK Scott Kingery 20.00 50.00
BADLTM Triston McKenzie 12.00 30.00
BADLTT Taylor Trammell 10.00 25.00
BADLWC Willie Calhoun 6.00 15.00

2017 Bowman's Best Best of '17 Autographs

PLATE PRINT RUN 1 SET PER COLOR
BLACK-CYAN-MAGENTA-YELLOW ISSUED
NO PLATE PRICING DUE TO SCARCITY
EXCHANGE DEADLINE 11/30/2019
B17AB Alex Bregman
B17ABE Andrew Benintendi 20.00 50.00
B17AE Anderson Espinoza 3.00 8.00
B17AF Alex Faedo 4.00 10.00
B17AH Adam Haseley 6.00 15.00
B17AJ Aaron Judge 100.00 250.00
B17AR Anthony Rizzo 20.00 50.00
B17ARO Amed Rosario 5.00 12.00
B17AUB Austin Beck 5.00 12.00
B17AV Alex Verdugo 6.00 15.00
B17BH Bryce Harper 75.00 200.00
B17BM Brendan McKay 10.00 25.00
B17BMC Brendan McKay 10.00 25.00
B17BP Brett Phillips 4.00 10.00
B17BR Blake Rutherford 5.00 12.00
B17CA Christian Arroyo 5.00 12.00
B17CAD Chance Adams 4.00 10.00
B17CB Cody Bellinger
B17CC Carlos Correa 20.00 50.00
B17CF Clint Frazier 8.00 20.00
B17CR Cole Ragans 3.00 8.00
B17CSA Chris Sale 8.00 20.00
B17CSC Clarke Schmidt 12.00 30.00
B17CSE Christopher Seise 4.00 10.00
B17DC Dylan Cozens 3.00 8.00
B17DD Dane Dunning 6.00 15.00
B17DE Drew Ellis 4.00 10.00
B17DF Dustin Fowler 4.00 10.00
B17DF Derek Fisher 5.00 12.00
B17DH D.L. Hall 4.00 10.00
B17DM Daniel Murphy 4.00 10.00
B17DPE David Peterson 4.00 10.00
B17DS Dansby Swanson 15.00 40.00
B17EW Evan White 6.00 15.00
B17FM Francisco Mejia 5.00 12.00
B17GT Gleyber Torres 40.00 100.00
B17HR Heliot Ramos 15.00 40.00
B17IH Ian Happ 8.00 20.00
B17JA Jo Adell 40.00 100.00
B17JB Jorge Bonifacio 3.00 8.00
B17JBU Jake Burger 5.00 12.00
B17JC J.P. Crawford 6.00 12.00
B17JD Jeter Downs 4.00 10.00
B17JDU Jon Duplantier 4.00 10.00
B17JG Jason Groome 5.00 12.00
B17JMO Jordan Montgomery 5.00 12.00
B17JS Justus Sheffield 5.00 12.00
B17KB Kris Bryant 60.00 150.00
B17KH Keston Hiura 8.00 20.00
B17KM Kevin Maitan 5.00 12.00
B17KME Kevin Merrell 4.00 10.00
B17KW Kyle Wright 6.00 15.00
B17LA Lazarito Armenteros 5.00 12.00
B17LB Lewis Brinson 5.00 12.00
B17LE Lucas Erceg 3.00 8.00
B17LGJ Lourdes Gurriel Jr. 4.00 10.00
B17LW Logan Warmoth 4.00 10.00
B17MG MacKenzie Gore 15.00 40.00
B17MK Mitch Keller 5.00 12.00
B17MKO Michael Kopech 5.00 12.00
B17MM Mickey Moniak 8.00 20.00
B17MMA Manny Machado
B17MS Matt Sauer 4.00 10.00
B17MT Mike Trout 250.00 600.00
B17MW Mitchell White 3.00 8.00
B17NPE Nate Pearson 20.00 50.00
B17NS Noah Syndergaard 10.00 25.00
B17NSE Nick Senzel 10.00 25.00
B17PC P.J. Conlon 3.00 8.00
B17PS Pavin Smith 4.00 10.00
B17QH Quentin Holmes 3.00 8.00
B17RA Ronald Acuna 125.00 300.00
B17RL Royce Lewis 15.00 40.00
B17RM Ryan Mountcastle 15.00 40.00
B17RR Roniel Raudes 3.00 8.00
B17SB Shane Baz 3.00 8.00
B17TC Trevor Clifton 3.00 8.00
B17TH Tanner Houck 12.00 30.00
B17TL Tristen Lutz 4.00 10.00
B17TM Triston McKenzie 12.00 30.00
B17TTR Taylor Trammell 15.00 40.00
B17YG Yulieski Gurriel 6.00 15.00
B17YM Yoan Moncada

2017 Bowman's Best Best of '17 Autographs Atomic Refractors

*ATOMIC REF: 1X TO 2.5X BASIC
STATED PRINT RUN 25 SER.#'d SETS
EXCHANGE DEADLINE 11/30/2019
B17AB Alex Bregman 50.00 120.00
B17ABE Andrew Benintendi 60.00 150.00
B17AF Alex Faedo 15.00 40.00
B17AJ Aaron Judge 200.00 500.00
B17AR Anthony Rizzo 40.00 100.00
B17BH Bryce Harper 125.00 300.00
B17BM Brendan McKay 50.00 120.00
B17BMC Brendan McKay 50.00 120.00
B17BR Blake Rutherford 20.00 50.00
B17CB Cody Bellinger 125.00 300.00
B17CC Carlos Correa 50.00 120.00
B17CSA Chris Sale 20.00 50.00
B17GT Gleyber Torres 100.00 250.00
B17JBU Jake Burger 25.00 60.00
B17JD Jeter Downs 30.00 80.00
B17KB Kris Bryant 125.00 300.00
B17LA Lazarito Armenteros 25.00 60.00
B17MK Mitch Keller 25.00 60.00
B17MMA Manny Machado 25.00 60.00
B17MT Mike Trout 250.00 600.00
B17RL Royce Lewis 50.00 120.00
B17TL Tristen Lutz 30.00 80.00
B17YG Yulieski Gurriel 12.00 30.00
B17YM Yoan Moncada 40.00 100.00

2017 Bowman's Best Best of '17 Autographs Gold Refractors

*GOLD REF: .75X TO 2X BASIC
STATED PRINT RUN 50 SER.#'d SETS
EXCHANGE DEADLINE 11/30/2019
B17AB Alex Bregman 40.00 100.00
B17ABE Andrew Benintendi 40.00 100.00
B17AF Alex Faedo 12.00 30.00
B17AJ Aaron Judge 150.00 400.00
B17AR Anthony Rizzo 30.00 80.00
B17BH Bryce Harper 100.00 250.00
B17BM Brendan McKay 40.00 100.00
B17BMC Brendan McKay 40.00 100.00
B17BR Blake Rutherford 15.00 40.00
B17CB Cody Bellinger 100.00 250.00
B17CC Carlos Correa 40.00 100.00
B17CSA Chris Sale 15.00 40.00
B17GT Gleyber Torres 75.00 200.00
B17JBU Jake Burger 20.00 50.00
B17JD Jeter Downs 25.00 60.00
B17KB Kris Bryant 100.00 250.00
B17LA Lazarito Armenteros 20.00 50.00
B17MK Mitch Keller 20.00 50.00
B17MMA Manny Machado 30.00 80.00
B17MT Mike Trout 200.00 500.00
B17RL Royce Lewis 40.00 100.00
B17TL Tristen Lutz 25.00 60.00
B17YG Yulieski Gurriel 10.00 25.00
B17YM Yoan Moncada 30.00 80.00

2017 Bowman's Best Best of '17 Autographs Green Refractors

*GREEN REF: .6X TO 1.5X BASIC
STATED PRINT RUN 99 SER.#'d SETS
EXCHANGE DEADLINE 11/30/2019
B17AB Alex Bregman 30.00 80.00
B17ABE Andrew Benintendi 30.00 80.00
B17AJ Aaron Judge 125.00 300.00
B17AR Anthony Rizzo 25.00 60.00
B17BM Brendan McKay 30.00 80.00
B17BMC Brendan McKay 30.00 80.00
B17BR Blake Rutherford 12.00 30.00
B17CB Cody Bellinger 75.00 200.00
B17CC Carlos Correa 30.00 80.00
B17GT Gleyber Torres 60.00 150.00
B17JBU Jake Burger 12.00 30.00
B17JD Jeter Downs 20.00 50.00
B17KB Kris Bryant 75.00 200.00
B17LA Lazarito Armenteros 12.00 30.00
B17MMA Manny Machado 25.00 60.00
B17YG Yulieski Gurriel 8.00 20.00
B17YM Yoan Moncada 25.00 60.00

2017 Bowman's Best Best of '17 Autographs Refractors

*REFRACTORS: .5X TO 1.2X BASIC
EXCHANGE DEADLINE 11/30/2019

2017 Bowman's Best Dual Autographs

STATED PRINT RUN 25 SER.#'d SETS
EXCHANGE DEADLINE 11/30/2019
BDACB Correa/Bregman 75.00 200.00
BDAGG Bellinger/Gurriel 75.00 200.00
BDAJF Judge/Frazier 300.00 500.00
BDASG Sale/Groome 30.00 80.00
BDASM Swanson/Maitan 25.00 60.00
BDATB Trout/Bryant 600.00 800.00

2017 Bowman's Best Mirror Image

COMPLETE SET (20) 12.00 30.00
MI1 Stanton/Judge 4.00 10.00
MI2 Bellinger/Votto 5.00 12.00
MI3 Benintendi/Yelich 1.00 2.50
MI4 Odor/Moncada 1.00 2.50
MI5 Faria/Fulmer .30 .75
MI6 Pollock/Robles .75 2.00
MI7 Devers/Moustakas .60 1.50
MI8 Scherzer/Kopech 1.00 2.50
MI9 Sano/Maitan .50 1.25
MI10 Rosario/Lindor .50 1.25
MI11 McKay/Rizzo 1.25 3.00
MI12 McKay/Kershaw 1.25 3.00
MI13 Gore/Sale 2.50 6.00
MI14 Wright/Kluber 1.00 2.50
MI15 Beck/Trout 2.50 6.00
MI16 Hosmer/Smith .50 1.25
MI17 Brantley/Haseley .60 1.50
MI18 Hiura/Pedroia 1.50 4.00
MI19 Adell/Betts 4.00 10.00
MI20 Correa/Lewis 2.50 6.00

2017 Bowman's Best Mirror Image Atomic Refractors

*ATOMIC REF: .75X TO 2X BASIC
MI1 Stanton/Judge 12.00 30.00

2017 Bowman's Best Mirror Image Gold Refractors

*GOLD REF: 1.2X TO 3X BASIC
STATED PRINT RUN 50 SER.#'d SETS
MI1 Stanton/Judge 30.00 80.00

2017 Bowman's Best Monochrome Autographs

PRINT RUNS B/WN 30-150 COPIES PER
EXCHANGE DEADLINE 11/30/2019
MAAB Austin Beck/125 10.00 25.00
MAABE Andrew Benintendi EXCH 20.00 50.00
MAABR Alex Bregman/100 15.00 40.00
MAAH Adam Haseley/125 8.00 20.00
MAAJ Aaron Judge/125 60.00 150.00
MAAV Alex Verdugo/125 6.00 15.00
MABM Brendan McKay/125 20.00 50.00
MABMC Brendan McKay/125 20.00 50.00
MABR Blake Rutherford/125 12.00 30.00
MACB Cody Bellinger/100 40.00 100.00
MACF Clint Frazier/125 20.00 50.00
MACS Clarke Schmidt/125 6.00 15.00
MADF Dustin Fowler/125 6.00 15.00
MADH D.L. Hall/150 8.00 20.00
MAEW Evan White/125 10.00 25.00
MAGT Gleyber Torres/125 40.00 100.00
MAJA Jo Adell/125 40.00 100.00
MAJB Jake Burger/125 8.00 20.00
MAJG Jason Groome/125 10.00 25.00
MAKB Kris Bryant/50 75.00 200.00
MAKH Keston Hiura/125 20.00 50.00
MAKM Kevin Maitan/125 6.00 15.00
MAKW Kyle Wright/125 10.00 25.00
MALB Lewis Brinson/125 10.00 25.00
MALG Lourdes Gurriel Jr./125 6.00 15.00
MAMG MacKenzie Gore/125 15.00 40.00
MAMK Michael Kopech/125 12.00 30.00
MAMM Mickey Moniak/150 12.00 30.00
MAMT Mike Trout/30 150.00 400.00

MANS Nick Senzel/100 12.00 30.00
MAPS Pavin Smith/125 5.00 12.00
MARL Royce Lewis/100 25.00 60.00
MASB Shane Baz/125 10.00 25.00
MATR Trevor Rogers/125 10.00 25.00

2017 Bowman's Best Monochrome Autographs Atomic Refractors

*ATOMIC REF: .6X TO 1.5X BASE
STATED PRINT RUN 25 SER.#'d SETS
EXCHANGE DEADLINE 11/30/2019
MAAB Austin Beck 30.00 80.00
MAAH Adam Haseley 25.00 60.00
MAAJ Aaron Judge 125.00 300.00
MAKM Kevin Maitan 10.00 25.00
MAMT Mike Trout 150.00 400.00

2017 Bowman's Best Monochrome Autographs Gold Refractors

*GOLD REF: .5X TO 1.2X BASE
STATED PRINT RUN 50 SER.#'d SETS
EXCHANGE DEADLINE 11/30/2019
MAAB Austin Beck 20.00 50.00
MAAH Adam Haseley 20.00 50.00
MAAJ Aaron Judge 100.00 250.00
MAKM Kevin Maitan 8.00 20.00

2017 Bowman's Best Raking Rookies

COMPLETE SET (10) 12.00 30.00
*ATOMIC REF: .75X TO 2X BASIC
*GOLD REF/50: 1.5X TO 4X BASIC
RRAB Alex Bregman 2.50 6.00
RRABE Andrew Benintendi 1.50 4.00
RRAJ Aaron Judge 6.00 15.00
RRBZ Bradley Zimmer .60 1.50
RRCB Cody Bellinger 8.00 20.00
RRFB Franklin Barreto .50 1.25
RRHR Hunter Renfroe .60 1.50
RRIH Ian Happ 1.00 2.50
RRRH Ryon Healy .60 1.50
RRYG Yulieski Gurriel .75 2.00

2017 Bowman's Best Raking Rookies Autographs

STATED PRINT RUN 99 SER.#'d SETS
EXCHANGE DEADLINE 11/30/2019
RRABE Andrew Benintendi EXCH 50.00 120.00
RRAJ Aaron Judge 100.00 250.00
RRBZ Bradley Zimmer 10.00 25.00
RRCB Cody Bellinger EXCH 40.00 100.00
RRHR Hunter Renfroe 8.00 20.00
RRIH Ian Happ 10.00 25.00
RRRH Ryon Healy 5.00 12.00
RRYG Yulieski Gurriel 6.00 15.00

2017 Bowman's Best Top Prospects

COMPLETE SET (35) 10.00 25.00
*REF: .5X TO 1.2X BASIC
*ATOMIC: 1X TO 2.5X BASIC
*PURPLE/250: 1X TO 2.5X BASIC
*BLUE/150: 1X TO 2.5X BASIC
*GREEN/99: 1.2X TO 3X BASIC
TP1 Amed Rosario .40 1.00
TP2 Austin Meadows .60 1.50
TP3 Mickey Moniak .50 1.25
TP4 Jo Adell 3.00 8.00
TP5 Alex Faedo .40 1.00
TP6 Austin Beck 1.00 2.50
TP7 Clint Frazier .50 1.25
TP8 Victor Robles .60 1.50
TP9 Michael Kopech .75 2.00
TP10 Ronald Acuna 12.00 30.00
TP11 Kyle Wright .75 2.00
TP12 Rafael Devers .50 1.25
TP13 Kevin Maitan .40 1.00
TP14 Jay Groome .50 1.25
TP15 Adam Haseley .50 1.25
TP16 Gleyber Torres 4.00 10.00
TP17 Shane Baz .40 1.00
TP18 Brendan Rodgers .30 .75
TP19 MacKenzie Gore 2.00 5.00
TP20 Brendan McKay 1.00 2.50
TP21 Brendan McKay 1.00 2.50
TP22 Eloy Jimenez 1.00 2.50
TP23 Kyle Tucker .60 1.50
TP24 Clarke Schmidt .40 1.00
TP25 Keston Hiura 1.25 3.00
TP26 Brent Honeywell .30 .75
TP27 Nick Senzel .75 2.00
TP28 Pavin Smith .40 1.00
TP29 Blake Rutherford .40 1.00
TP30 Jake Burger .50 1.25
TP31 Triston McKenzie .75 2.00
TP32 Willy Adames .30 .75
TP33 Vladimir Guerrero Jr. 3.00 8.00
TP34 Evan White .60 1.50
TP35 Royce Lewis 2.00 5.00

2017 Bowman's Best Top Prospects Gold Refractors

*GOLD REF: 2X TO 5X BASIC
STATED PRINT RUN 50 SER.#'d SETS

2017 Bowman's Best Top Prospects Orange Refractors

*ORANGE REF: 2.5X TO 6X BASIC
STATED PRINT RUN 25 SER.#'d SETS

2018 Bowman's Best

1 Shohei Ohtani RC 10.00 25.00
2 Walker Buehler RC 2.00 5.00
3 George Springer .30 .75
4 Rafael Devers RC 1.25 3.00
5 Bryce Harper .60 1.50
6 Andrew McCutchen .40 1.00
7 Chris Sale .40 1.00
8 Cody Bellinger .75 2.00
9 Austin Meadows RC 1.00 2.50
10 Manny Machado .40 1.00
11 Carlos Correa .40 1.00
12 Fernando Romero RC .40 1.00
13 Carlos Carrasco .25 .60
14 Craig Kimbrel .30 .75
15 Justin Verlander .40 1.00
16 Khris Davis .40 1.00
17 Mookie Betts .75 2.00
18 Francisco Lindor .40 1.00
19 Jose Ramirez .30 .75
20 Brian Dozier .30 .75
21 Harrison Bader RC .60 1.50
22 Andrew Benintendi .40 1.00
23 Dustin Fowler RC .40 1.00
24 Joey Votto .40 1.00
25 Aaron Judge 1.00 2.50
26 Nick Williams RC .50 1.25
27 Jose Altuve .30 .75
28 Josh Donaldson .30 .75
29 Juan Soto RC 20.00 50.00
30 Amed Rosario RC .50 1.25
31 Luis Severino .30 .75
32 Didi Gregorius .30 .75
33 Alex Verdugo RC .60 1.50
34 Jose Abreu .40 1.00
35 Trea Turner .30 .75
36 Rhys Hoskins RC 1.50 4.00
37 Victor Robles RC 1.00 2.50
38 J.P. Crawford RC .40 1.00
39 Justin Upton .30 .75
40 Mike Soroka RC 1.25 3.00
41 Jack Flaherty RC 1.50 4.00
42 Jacob deGrom .75 2.00
43 Eddie Rosario .40 1.00
44 Jean Segura .25 .60
45 Aroldis Chapman .40 1.00
46 Clint Frazier RC .75 2.00
47 Charlie Blackmon .40 1.00
48 J.D. Martinez .40 1.00
49 Miguel Andujar RC 1.50 4.00
50 Gleyber Torres RC 5.00 12.00
51 Ronald Acuna Jr. RC 15.00 40.00
52 Anthony Rizzo .50 1.25
53 Freddie Freeman .50 1.25
54 Ozzie Albies RC 1.25 3.00
55 Willy Adames RC .50 1.25
56 Francisco Mejia RC .50 1.25
57 Nolan Arenado .60 1.50
58 Giancarlo Stanton .40 1.00
59 Clayton Kershaw .60 1.50
60 Scott Kingery RC .60 1.50
61 Corey Kluber .30 .75
62 Brian Anderson RC .50 1.25
63 Max Scherzer .40 1.00
64 Paul Goldschmidt .40 1.00
65 Mike Trout 2.00 5.00
66 Javier Baez .50 1.25
67 Christian Yelich .50 1.25
68 Whit Merrifield .40 1.00
69 Blake Snell .30 .75
70 Noah Syndergaard .30 .75

2018 Bowman's Best Atomic Refractors

*ATOMIC REF: 1X TO 2.5X BASIC
*ATOMIC REF RC: .6X TO 1.5X BASIC RC
STATED ODDS 1:12 HOBBY

2018 Bowman's Best Blue Refractors

*BLUE REF: 2.5X TO 6X BASIC
*BLUE REF RC: 1.5X TO 4X BASIC RC
STATED ODDS 1:33 HOBBY
STATED PRINT RUN 150 SER.#'d SETS

2018 Bowman's Best Gold Refractors

*GOLD REF: 5X TO 12X BASIC
*GOLD REF RC: 3X TO 8X BASIC RC
STATED ODDS 1:99 HOBBY
STATED PRINT RUN 50 SER.#'d SETS

2018 Bowman's Best Green Refractors

*GRN REF: 2.5X TO 6X BASIC
*GRN REF RC: 1.5X TO 4X BASIC RC
STATED ODDS 1:50 HOBBY
STATED PRINT RUN 99 SER.#'d SETS

2018 Bowman's Best Orange Refractors

*ORANGE REF: 6X TO 15X BASIC
*ORANGE REF RC: 4X TO 10X BASIC RC
STATED ODDS 1:197 HOBBY
STATED PRINT RUN 25 SER.#'d SETS

2018 Bowman's Best Purple Refractors

*PURPLE REF: 1.2X TO 3X BASIC
*PURPLE REF RC: .75X TO 2X BASIC RC
STATED ODDS 1:20 HOBBY
STATED PRINT RUN 250 SER.#'d SETS

2018 Bowman's Best Refractors

*REF: .75X TO 2X BASIC
*REF RC: .5X TO 1.2X BASIC RC
RANDOM INSERTS IN PACKS

2018 Bowman's Best '98 Best Performers Refractors

STATED ODDS 1:3 HOBBY
*ATOMIC: X TO X BASIC
*GOLD REF/50: X TO X BASIC
98BPAB Alec Bohm 1.50 4.00
98BPAM Austin Meadows .60 1.50
98BPAR Anthony Rizzo .50 1.25
98BPARO Alex Rodriguez .50 1.25
98BPBM Brendan McKay .40 1.00
98BPBS Brady Singer 1.25 3.00
98BPBT Brice Turang .75 2.00
98BPCM Casey Mize 2.00 5.00
98BPCSC Connor Scott .30 .75
98BPDG Didi Gregorius .30 .75
98BPEF Estevan Florial .40 1.00
98BPFL Francisco Lindor .40 1.00
98BPGM Greg Maddux .50 1.25
98BPGR Grayson Rodriguez .50 1.25
98BPGT Gleyber Torres 2.50 6.00
98BPHG Hunter Greene .75 2.00
98BPJA Jordyn Adams 1.00 2.50
98BPJAD Jo Adell 1.00 2.50
98BPJC Jose Canseco .30 .75
98BPJG Jordan Groshans .75 2.00
98BPJI Jonathan India 1.50 4.00
98BPJK Jarred Kelenic 2.50 6.00
98BPJS Juan Soto 6.00 15.00
98BPKB Kris Bryant .50 1.25
98BPML Matthew Liberatore .30 .75
98BPMM Mark McGwire .60 1.50
98BPMT Mike Trout 2.00 5.00
98BPNM Nick Madrigal 1.00 2.50
98BPNN Noah Naylor .40 1.00
98BPOA Ozzie Albies .75 2.00
98BPPM Pedro Martinez .30 .75
98BPRAJ Ronald Acuna Jr. 8.00 20.00
98BPRC Roger Clemens .50 1.25
98BPRH Rhys Hoskins 1.00 2.50
98BPRJ Randy Johnson .40 1.00
98BPRL Royce Lewis 1.00 2.50
98BPRW Ryan Weathers .30 .75
98BPSO Shohei Ohtani 6.00 15.00
98BPTS Travis Swaggerty .75 2.00
98BPWA Willy Adames .30 .75

2018 Bowman's Best '98 Best Performers Autographs

STATED ODDS 1:121 HOBBY
PRINT RUNS B/WN 10-150 COPIES PER
NO PRICING ON QTY 10
EXCHANGE DEADLINE 11/30/2020
*GOLD/50: .5X TO 1.2X BASIC
*ATOMIC/25: .6X TO 1.5X BASIC
98BPAAB Alec Bohm/100 10.00 25.00
98BPAAM Austin Meadows/100 8.00 20.00
98BPAAT Alek Thomas/150 8.00 20.00
98BPABM Brendan McKay/100 6.00 15.00
98BPABS Brady Singer/150 8.00 20.00
98BPACM Casey Mize/75 15.00 40.00
98BPACP Cristian Pache/150 12.00 30.00
98BPACSC Connor Scott/150 4.00 10.00
98BPACW Cole Winn/150 6.00 15.00
98BPACWE Colton Welker/150 4.00 10.00
98BPAEF Estevan Florial/150 15.00 40.00
98BPAGR Grayson Rodriguez/150 8.00 20.00
98BPAHG Hunter Greene/100 20.00 50.00
98BPAJA Jordyn Adams/150 15.00 40.00
98BPAJG Jordan Groshans/150 12.00 30.00
98BPAJI Jonathan India/100 20.00 50.00
98BPAJK Jarred Kelenic/100 40.00 100.00
98BPAJS Juan Soto/100 200.00 500.00
98BPAKB Kris Bryant/50 50.00 120.00
98BPAKR Keibert Ruiz/100 10.00 25.00
98BPALG Logan Gilbert/150 6.00 15.00
98BPALR Luis Robert/150 60.00 150.00
98BPAML Matthew Liberatore/150 5.00 12.00
98BPAMT Mike Trout/30 300.00 500.00
98BPANG Nolan Gorman/150 25.00 60.00
98BPANM Nick Madrigal/100 15.00 40.00
98BPANN Noah Naylor/150 8.00 20.00
98BPAOA Ozzie Albies/100 15.00 40.00
98BPARA Ronald Acuna Jr./50 100.00 250.00
98BPARL Royce Lewis/75 15.00 40.00
98BPARW Ryan Weathers/150 5.00 12.00
98BPASK Scott Kingery/100 6.00 15.00
98BPATC Triston Casas/150 10.00 25.00
98BPATS Travis Swaggerty/150 10.00 25.00

2018 Bowman's Best Best of '18 Autographs

PRINTING PLATE ODDS 1:1442 HOBBY
PLATE PRINT RUN 1 SET PER COLOR
BLACK-CYAN-MAGENTA-YELLOW ISSUED
NO PLATE PRICING DUE TO SCARCITY
EXCHANGE DEADLINE 11/30/2020
B18AA Adbert Alzolay 3.00 8.00
B18AAL Aramis Ademan 3.00 8.00
B18ABO Alec Bohm 25.00 60.00
B18AG Andres Gimenez 6.00 15.00
B18AJ Aaron Judge 60.00 150.00
B18AM Austin Meadows 12.00 30.00
B18AR Anthony Rizzo 20.00 50.00
B18ARO Amed Rosario 3.00 8.00
B18AS Anthony Seigler 4.00 10.00
B18AT Alek Thomas 6.00 15.00
B18AV Alex Verdugo 6.00 15.00
B18BG Brusdar Graterol 3.00 8.00
B18BM Brendan McKay 5.00 12.00
B18BMA Brandon Marsh 4.00 10.00
B18BS Brady Singer 8.00 20.00
B18BSN Blake Snell 3.00 8.00
B18BT Brice Turang 5.00 12.00
B18CK Carter Kieboom 8.00 20.00
B18CM Casey Mize 20.00 50.00
B18CP Cristian Pache 15.00 40.00
B18CSC Connor Scott 3.00 8.00
B18CV Christian Villanueva 2.50 6.00
B18CW Colton Welker 2.50 6.00
B18CWI Cole Winn 4.00 10.00
B18DL Daniel Lynch 3.00 8.00
B18EF Estevan Florial 12.00 30.00
B18EH Ethan Hankins 5.00 12.00
B18EW Evan White 6.00 15.00
B18FP Franklin Perez 3.00 8.00
B18FR Fernando Romero 2.50 6.00
B18FT Fernando Tatis Jr. 100.00 250.00
B18GR Grayson Rodriguez 10.00 25.00
B18HG Hunter Greene 12.00 30.00
B18HR Heliot Ramos 5.00 12.00
B18JA Jose Altuve 12.00 30.00
B18JAD Jo Adell 25.00 60.00
B18JAD Jordyn Adams 6.00 15.00
B18JALEI Jose Albertos 2.50 6.00
B18JD Jeter Downs 4.00 10.00
B18JG Jordan Groshans 8.00 20.00
B18JH Jordan Hicks 6.00 15.00
B18JI Jonathan India 15.00 40.00
B18JK Jeren Kendall 3.00 8.00
B18JKE Jarred Kelenic 60.00 150.00
B18JL Jesus Luzardo 4.00 10.00
B18JS Jose Siri 2.50 6.00
B18JSO Juan Soto 75.00 200.00
B18JST Josh Stowers 3.00 8.00
B18JW Justin Williams 2.50 6.00
B18KB Kris Bryant 50.00 120.00
B18KD Khris Davis 4.00 10.00
B18KH Keston Hiura 6.00 15.00
B18KK Kevin Kramer 2.50 6.00
B18KR Keibert Ruiz 15.00 40.00
B18KRO Josh Breaux 3.00 8.00
B18LE Luis Escobar 2.50 6.00
B18LG Logan Gilbert 4.00 10.00
B18LR Luis Robert 75.00 200.00
B18LU Luis Urias 15.00
B18MD Mason Denaburg 3.00 8.00
B18MG MacKenzie Gore 6.00 15.00
B18ML Matthew Liberatore 6.00 15.00
B18MO Matt Olson 4.00 10.00
B18MT Mike Trout 150.00 400.00
B18NG Nolan Gorman 15.00 40.00
B18NH Nico Hoerner 8.00 20.00
B18NM Nick Madrigal 15.00 40.00
B18NN Noah Naylor 4.00 10.00
B18NSC Nick Schnell 2.50 6.00
B18OA Ozzie Albies 12.00 30.00
B18PD Paul DeJong 4.00 10.00
B18PS Pavin Smith 4.00 10.00
B18RA Ronald Acuna Jr. 75.00 200.00
B18RAD Riley Adams 3.00 8.00
B18RL Royce Lewis 12.00 30.00
B18RR Ryan Rolison 3.00 8.00
B18RW Ryan Weathers 3.00 8.00
B18SA Sandy Alcantara 2.50 6.00
B18SK Scott Kingery 4.00 10.00
B18SM Shane McClanahan 4.00 10.00
B18SO Shohei Ohtani 150.00 400.00
B18TC Triston Casas 12.00 30.00
B18TL Trevor Larnach 8.00 20.00
B18TST Trevor Stephan 2.50 6.00
B18VR Victor Robles 12.00 30.00
B18YA Yordan Alvarez 50.00 120.00

2018 Bowman's Best Best of '18 Autographs Atomic Refractors

*ATOMIC REF: 1X TO 2.5X BASIC
STATED ODDS 1:227 HOBBY
STATED PRINT RUN 25 SER.#'d SETS
EXCHANGE DEADLINE 11/30/2019
B18ABO Alec Bohm 60.00 150.00
B18CF Clint Frazier 20.00 50.00
B18MT Mike Trout 250.00 500.00
B18NG Nolan Gorman 125.00 300.00
B18SO Shohei Ohtani 400.00 800.00

2018 Bowman's Best Best of '18 Autographs Gold Refractors

*GOLD REF: .75X TO 2X BASIC
STATED ODDS 1:115 HOBBY
STATED PRINT RUN 50 SER.#'d SETS
EXCHANGE DEADLINE 11/30/2020
B18CF Clint Frazier 15.00 40.00
B18MT Mike Trout 200.00 500.00
B18NG Nolan Gorman 60.00 150.00
B18SO Shohei Ohtani 300.00 600.00

2018 Bowman's Best Best of '18 Autographs Green Refractors

*GREEN REF: .6X TO 1.5X BASIC
STATED ODDS 1:61 HOBBY
STATED PRINT RUN 99 SER.#'d SETS
EXCHANGE DEADLINE 11/30/2020
B18CF Clint Frazier 12.00 30.00
B18NG Nolan Gorman 50.00 120.00
B18SO Shohei Ohtani 200.00 500.00

2018 Bowman's Best Best of '18 Autographs Refractors

*REFRACTORS: .5X TO 1.2X BASIC
STATED ODDS 1:20 HOBBY
EXCHANGE DEADLINE 11/30/2020
B18CF Clint Frazier 10.00 25.00

2018 Bowman's Best Dual Autographs

STATED ODDS 1:2398 HOBBY
STATED PRINT RUN 25 SER.#'d SETS
EXCHANGE DEADLINE 11/30/2020
DAAA Albertos/Alzolay 40.00 100.00
DAAAL Acuna/Albies 200.00 400.00
DAAM Marsh/Adell 60.00 150.00
DABR Rizzo/Bryant EXCH 125.00 300.00
DAGM McKay/Greene 60.00 150.00
DAVR Ruiz/Verdugo EXCH 30.00 80.00

2018 Bowman's Best Early Indications Refractors

STATED ODDS 1:4 HOBBY
*ATOMIC: .75X TO 2X BASIC
*GOLD REF/50: 1.5X TO 4X BASIC
EI1 Fernando Tatis Jr. 2.50 6.00
EI2 Keston Hiura .60 1.50
EI3 Luis Robert 4.00 10.00
EI4 Brandon Marsh .40 1.00
EI5 Cristian Pache 1.25 3.00
EI6 Jose Siri .25 .60
EI7 Brendan McKay .40 1.00
EI8 Hunter Greene .75 2.00
EI9 Franklin Perez .30 .75
EI10 Brent Rooker .30 .75
EI11 Jeter Downs .40 1.00
EI12 Kevin Kramer .25 .60
EI13 Estevan Florial .40 1.00
EI14 MacKenzie Gore .50 1.25
EI15 Jeren Kendall .30 .75
EI16 Pavin Smith .40 1.00
EI17 Corbin Burnes 2.00 5.00
EI18 Jesus Luzardo .40 1.00
EI19 Carter Kieboom .40 1.00
EI20 Keibert Ruiz 1.25 3.00
EI21 Jo Adell 1.00 2.50
EI22 Jose Albertos .25 .60
EI23 Justin Williams .25 .60
EI24 Heliot Ramos .40 1.00
EI25 Yordan Alvarez 2.00 5.00
EI26 Colton Welker .25 .60
EI27 Luis Urias .50 1.25
EI28 Adbert Alzolay .30 .75
EI29 Michel Baez .25 .60
EI30 Royce Lewis 1.00 2.50

2018 Bowman's Best Early Indications Autographs

STATED ODDS 1:193 HOBBY
STATED PRINT RUN 100 SER.#'d SETS
EXCHANGE DEADLINE 11/30/2020
*GOLD/50: .5X TO 1.2X BASIC
*ATOMIC/25: .6X TO 1.5X BASIC
EIAAA Adbert Alzolay 5.00 12.00
EIABM Brendan McKay 6.00 15.00
EIACK Carter Kieboom 12.00 30.00
EIACP Cristian Pache 12.00 30.00
EIACW Colton Welker 4.00 10.00
EIAEF Estevan Florial 12.00 30.00
EIAFP Franklin Perez 5.00 12.00
EIAHG Hunter Greene 20.00 50.00
EIAHR Heliot Ramos 6.00 15.00
EIAJA Jo Adell 25.00 60.00
EIAJAL Jose Albertos 4.00 10.00
EIAJK Jeren Kendall 5.00 12.00
EIAJL Jesus Luzardo 10.00 25.00
EIAJS Jose Siri 4.00 10.00
EIAJW Justin Williams 4.00 10.00
EIAKH Keston Hiura 10.00 25.00
EIAKR Keibert Ruiz 10.00 25.00
EIALR Luis Robert 25.00 60.00
EIALU Luis Urias 10.00 25.00
EIAMB Michel Baez 4.00 10.00
EIAMG MacKenzie Gore 8.00 20.00
EIAPS Pavin Smith 6.00 15.00
EIARL Royce Lewis 15.00 40.00
EIAYA Yordan Alvarez 25.00 60.00

2018 Bowman's Best Neophyte Sensations Refractors

STATED ODDS 1:18 HOBBY
*ATOMIC: .75X TO 2X BASIC
*GOLD REF/50: 2X TO 5X BASIC
NSAR Amed Rosario .50 1.25
NSGT Gleyber Torres 4.00 10.00
NSJS Juan Soto 10.00 25.00
NSMA Miguel Andujar 1.50 4.00
NSOA Ozzie Albies 1.25 3.00
NSRAJ Ronald Acuna Jr. 12.00 30.00
NSRD Rafael Devers 1.25 3.00
NSRH Rhys Hoskins 1.50 4.00
NSSO Shohei Ohtani 10.00 25.00
NSWB Walker Buehler 2.00 5.00

2018 Bowman's Best Neophyte Sensations Autographs

STATED ODDS 1:512 HOBBY
PRINT RUNS B/WN 50-99 COPIES PER
EXCHANGE DEADLINE 11/30/2020
NSAR Amed Rosario/99 4.00 10.00
NSJS Juan Soto/99 125.00 300.00
NSMA Miguel Andujar/99 12.00 30.00
NSOA Ozzie Albies/99 12.00 30.00
NSRAJ Ronald Acuna Jr./99 75.00 200.00
NSRH Rhys Hoskins/99 20.00 50.00
NSSO Shohei Ohtani/50 200.00 400.00
NSWB Walker Buehler/99 25.00 60.00

2018 Bowman's Best Power Producers Refractors

STATED ODDS 1:6 HOBBY
*ATOMIC: .75X TO 2X BASIC
*GOLD REF/50: 2X TO 5X BASIC
PPAB Alec Bohm 2.50 6.00
PPAJ Aaron Judge 1.50 4.00
PPAR Anthony Rizzo .75 2.00
PPBH Bryce Harper 1.00 2.50
PPBM Brendan McKay .60 1.50
PPEJ Eloy Jimenez 1.50 4.00
PPGT Gleyber Torres 4.00 10.00
PPJA Jo Adell 1.50 4.00
PPJAL Jose Altuve .50 1.25
PPJK Jarred Kelenic 4.00 10.00
PPJS Juan Soto 10.00 25.00
PPKL Kyle Lewis .75 2.00
PPMT Mike Trout 3.00 8.00
PPNG Nolan Gorman 2.50 6.00
PPRAJ Ronald Acuna Jr. 12.00 30.00
PPRH Rhys Hoskins 1.50 4.00
PPSO Shohei Ohtani 10.00 25.00
PPTC Triston Casas 5.00 12.00
PPTL Trevor Larnach 2.50 6.00
PPVGJ Vladimir Guerrero Jr. 4.00 10.00

2018 Bowman's Best Power Producers Autographs

STATED ODDS 1:487 HOBBY
PRINT RUNS B/WN 15-99 COPIES PER
NO PRICING ON QTY 15
EXCHANGE DEADLINE 11/30/2020
PPAB Alec Bohm/99 12.00 30.00
PPAR Anthony Rizzo/35 40.00 100.00
PPBM Brendan McKay/50 10.00 25.00
PPJA Jo Adell/99 25.00 60.00
PPJAL Jose Altuve/40 20.00 50.00
PPJK Jarred Kelenic/99 40.00 100.00
PPJS Juan Soto/99 125.00 300.00
PPNG Nolan Gorman/99 25.00 60.00
PPRAJ Ronald Acuna Jr./40 100.00 250.00
PPRH Rhys Hoskins/75 20.00 50.00
PPTC Triston Casas/99 12.00 30.00
PPTL Trevor Larnach/99 12.00 30.00

2018 Bowman's Best Top Prospects

*REF: .5X TO 1.2X BASIC
*ATOMIC: 1X TO 2.5X BASIC
*PURPLE/250: 1X TO 2.5X BASIC
*BLUE/150: 1X TO 2.5X BASIC
*GREEN/99: 1.2X TO 3X BASIC
TP1 Vladimir Guerrero Jr. 2.50 6.00
TP2 Mitch Keller .30 .75
TP3 Kyle Tucker .60 1.50
TP4 Michael Kopech 1.00 2.50
TP5 Austin Riley .75 2.00
TP6 Jo Adell 1.00 2.50
TP7 Eloy Jimenez 1.00 2.50
TP8 Alec Bohm 1.50 4.00
TP9 Logan Gilbert .40 1.00
TP10 Justus Sheffield .30 .75
TP11 Sixto Sanchez .75 2.00
TP12 Connor Scott .30 .75
TP13 Brendan Rodgers .30 .75
TP14 Jonathan India 1.50 4.00
TP15 Jarred Kelenic 2.50 6.00
TP16 Nick Madrigal 1.00 2.50
TP17 Matthew Liberatore .30 .75
TP18 Royce Lewis 1.00 2.50
TP19 Taylor Trammell .40 1.00
TP20 Travis Swaggerty .75 2.00
TP21 Grayson Rodriguez .50 1.25
TP22 Alek Thomas 1.00 2.50
TP23 Ryan Weathers .30 .75
TP24 Fernando Tatis Jr. 2.50 6.00
TP25 Brendan McKay .40 1.00
TP26 Jordyn Adams 1.00 2.50
TP27 Jordan Groshans .75 2.00
TP29 Triston Casas 3.00 8.00
TP30 Casey Mize 2.00 5.00

2018 Bowman's Best Top Prospects Gold Refractors

*GOLD REF: 2X TO 5X BASIC
STATED ODDS 1:99 HOBBY
STATED PRINT RUN 50 SER.#'d SETS
TP1 Vladimir Guerrero Jr. 40.00 100.00
TP8 Alec Bohm 25.00 60.00

2018 Bowman's Best Top Prospects Orange Refractors

*ORANGE REF: 2.5X TO 6X BASIC
STATED ODDS 1:197
STATED PRINT RUN 25 SER.#'d SETS
TP1 Vladimir Guerrero Jr. 50.00 120.00
TP8 Alec Bohm 30.00 80.00

2019 Bowman's Best

1 Mike Trout 2.00 5.00
2 Chris Paddack RC .75 2.00
3 Michael Kopech RC 1.25 3.00
4 Austin Riley RC 2.00 5.00
5 Nolan Arenado .60 1.50
6 Khris Davis .40 1.00
7 Gary Sanchez .40 1.00
8 Mookie Betts .75 2.00
9 Jacob deGrom .75 2.00
10 Yusei Kikuchi RC .60 1.50
11 Hyun-Jin Ryu .30 .75
12 Nick Senzel RC 1.25 3.00
13 Freddie Freeman .50 1.25
14 Clayton Kershaw .60 1.50
15 Charlie Blackmon .40 1.00
16 Gerrit Cole .40 1.00
17 Josh Bell .30 .75
18 Eloy Jimenez RC 1.50 4.00
19 Paul Goldschmidt .40 1.00
20 Chris Sale .40 1.00
21 Carter Kieboom RC .60 1.50
22 Michael Chavis RC .60 1.50
23 Yasiel Puig .40 1.00
24 Brendan Rodgers RC .60 1.50
25 Aaron Judge 1.00 2.50
26 Vladimir Guerrero Jr. RC 4.00 10.00
27 Kyle Wright RC .60 1.50
28 Jon Duplantier RC .40 1.00
29 Jose Abreu .40 1.00
30 Kris Bryant .50 1.25
31 Joey Gallo .30 .75
32 Pete Alonso RC 5.00 12.00
33 Shohei Ohtani .60 1.50
34 Justus Sheffield RC .60 1.50
35 Francisco Lindor .40 1.00
36 Jeff McNeil RC 1.00 2.50
37 Brandon Lowe RC .60 1.50
38 Alex Bregman .40 1.00
39 Xander Bogaerts .40 1.00
40 Max Scherzer .40 1.00
41 Will Smith RC 1.00 2.50
42 Rhys Hoskins .50 1.25
43 Kyle Tucker RC 1.00 2.50
44 Mitch Keller RC .50 1.25
45 Manny Machado .40 1.00
46 Anthony Rizzo .50 1.25
47 Walker Buehler .50 1.25
48 Trea Turner .30 .75
49 Whit Merrifield .40 1.00
50 Cody Bellinger .75 2.00
51 Justin Verlander .40 1.00
52 Javier Baez .50 1.25
53 Keston Hiura RC 1.25 3.00
54 Ozzie Albies .40 1.00
55 John Means RC 5.00 12.00
56 Bryce Harper .60 1.50
57 Paul DeJong .40 1.00
58 Fernando Tatis Jr. RC 10.00 25.00
59 Juan Soto 1.25 3.00
60 DJ LeMahieu .40 1.00
61 Ronald Acuna Jr. 2.00 5.00
62 Eugenio Suarez .30 .75
63 Griffin Canning RC .60 1.50
64 Gleyber Torres .75 2.00
65 Yoan Moncada .40 1.00
66 Ramon Laureano RC .75 2.00
67 J.D. Martinez .40 1.00
68 Rowdy Tellez RC .60 1.50
69 Jose Altuve .30 .75
70 Christian Yelich .50 1.25

2019 Bowman's Best Atomic Refractors

*ATOMIC REF: 1X TO 2.5X BASIC
*ATOMIC REF RC: .6X TO 1.5X BASIC RC
STATED ODDS 1:12 HOBBY
26 Vladimir Guerrero Jr. 8.00 20.00
32 Pete Alonso 10.00 25.00

2019 Bowman's Best Blue Refractors

*BLUE REF: 2X TO 5X BASIC
*BLUE REF RC: 1.2X TO 3X BASIC RC
STATED ODDS 1:34 HOBBY
STATED PRINT RUN 150 SER.#'d SETS
26 Vladimir Guerrero Jr. 15.00 40.00
32 Pete Alonso 15.00 40.00

2019 Bowman's Best Gold Refractors

*GOLD REF: 4X TO 10X BASIC
*GOLD REF RC: 2.5X TO 6X BASIC RC
STATED ODDS 1:101 HOBBY
STATED PRINT RUN 50 SER.#'d SETS
26 Vladimir Guerrero Jr. 25.00 60.00
32 Pete Alonso 30.00 80.00

2019 Bowman's Best Green Refractors

*GRN REF: 2.5X TO 6X BASIC
*GRN REF RC: 1.5X TO 4X BASIC RC
STATED ODDS 1:51 HOBBY
STATED PRINT RUN 99 SER.#'d SETS
26 Vladimir Guerrero Jr. 20.00 50.00
32 Pete Alonso 20.00 50.00

2019 Bowman's Best Orange Refractors

*ORNG REF: 6X TO 15X BASIC
*ORNG REF RC: 4X TO 10X BASIC RC
STATED ODDS 1:202 HOBBY
STATED PRINT RUN 25 SER.#'d SETS
18 Eloy Jimenez 25.00 60.00
26 Vladimir Guerrero Jr. 50.00 120.00
32 Pete Alonso 40.00 100.00
53 Keston Hiura 20.00 50.00

2019 Bowman's Best Purple Refractors

*PRPL REF: 1.2X TO 3X BASIC
*PRPL REF RC: .8X TO 2X BASIC RC
STATED ODDS 1:21 HOBBY
STATED PRINT RUN 250 SER.#'d SETS
26 Vladimir Guerrero Jr. 10.00 25.00
32 Pete Alonso 12.00 30.00

2019 Bowman's Best '99 Franchise Favorites Refractors

STATED ODDS 1:3 HOBBY
*ATOMIC REF: 1.2X TO 3X BASIC
*GOLD REF/50: 3X TO 8X BASIC
99FFAM Alek Manoah .50 1.25
99FFAR Adley Rutschman 1.50 4.00
99FFAV Andrew Vaughn .75 2.00
99FFBB Brett Baty .50 1.25
99FFBR Brendan Rodgers .40 1.00
99FFCB Cavan Biggio 1.25 3.00
99FFCC Corbin Carroll .40 1.00
99FFCJ Chipper Jones .40 1.00
99FFCM Casey Mize .60 1.50
99FFEJ Eloy Jimenez 1.00 2.50
99FFHB Hunter Bishop .75 2.00
99FFJB Joey Bart .75 2.00
99FFJI Jonathan India 1.50 4.00
99FFJJ Josh Jung .75 2.00
99FFJS Juan Soto 1.25 3.00
99FFKC Keoni Cavaco .60 1.50
99FFKH Keston Hiura .75 2.00
99FFMC Michael Chavis .40 1.00
99FFMM Mark McGwire .60 1.50
99FFMT Mike Trout 4.00 10.00
99FFNG Nolan Gorman .75 2.00
99FFNL Nick Lodolo .50 1.25
99FFNS Nick Senzel .75 2.00
99FFPM Pedro Martinez .30 .75
99FFRG Riley Greene 1.50 4.00
99FFSL Shea Langeliers .50 1.25
99FFSO Shohei Ohtani .60 1.50
99FFWF Wander Franco 5.00 12.00
99FFARI Austin Riley 1.25 3.00
99FFAVO Anthony Volpe 1.00 2.50
99FFBWJ Bobby Witt Jr. 1.50 4.00
99FFCJA CJ Abrams 1.25 3.00
99FFFTJ Fernando Tatis Jr. 8.00 20.00
99FFJJB J.J. Bleday 1.25 3.00
99FFJPM Julio Pablo Martinez .25 .60
99FFKGJ Ken Griffey Jr. .75 2.00
99FFRAJ Ronald Acuna Jr. 2.00 5.00
99FFVGJ Vladimir Guerrero Jr. 1.50 4.00
99FFVMJ Victor Mesa Jr. .50 1.25
99FFVVM Victor Victor Mesa .50 1.25

2019 Bowman's Best '99 Franchise Favorites Atomic Refractors

*ATOMIC REF: 1.2X TO 3X BASIC
STATED ODDS 1:48 HOBBY
99FFAR Adley Rutschman 8.00 20.00
99FFMT Mike Trout 15.00 40.00
99FFBWJ Bobby Witt Jr. 12.00 30.00
99FFFTJ Fernando Tatis Jr. 40.00 100.00
99FFKGJ Ken Griffey Jr. 12.00 30.00
99FFRAJ Ronald Acuna Jr. 8.00 20.00

2019 Bowman's Best '99 Franchise Favorites Gold Refractors

*GOLD REF/50: 3X TO 8X BASIC
STATED ODDS 1:253 HOBBY
STATED PRINT RUN 50 SER.#'d SETS
99FFAR Adley Rutschman 15.00 40.00
99FFMT Mike Trout 40.00 100.00
99FFBWJ Bobby Witt Jr. 30.00 80.00
99FFFTJ Fernando Tatis Jr. 100.00 250.00
99FFKGJ Ken Griffey Jr. 15.00 40.00
99FFRAJ Ronald Acuna Jr. 20.00 50.00

2019 Bowman's Best '99 Franchise Favorites Autographs

STATED ODDS 1:155 HOBBY
PRINT RUNS B/WN 30-150 COPIES PER
EXCHANGE DEADLINE 11/30/2021
99FFAAM Alek Manoah/150 8.00 20.00
99FFAAR Adley Rutschman/60 75.00 200.00
99FFAAV Andrew Vaughn/50 40.00 100.00
99FFABB Brett Baty/150 15.00 40.00
99FFABR Brendan Rodgers/50 8.00 20.00
99FFABS Braden Shewmake/150 10.00 25.00
99FFACB Cavan Biggio/150 15.00 40.00
99FFACC Corbin Carroll/150 12.00 30.00
99FFACJ Chipper Jones/40 75.00 200.00
99FFACM Casey Mize/60 20.00 50.00
99FFAEJ Eloy Jimenez/60 25.00 60.00
99FFAHB Hunter Bishop 15.00 40.00
99FFAJB Joey Bart/50 40.00 100.00
99FFAJJ Josh Jung/120 12.00 30.00
99FFAKC Keoni Cavaco/150 12.00 30.00
99FFAKH Keston Hiura/75 40.00 100.00
99FFAMC Michael Chavis/75 12.00 30.00
99FFANG Nolan Gorman/150 12.00 30.00
99FFANL Nick Lodolo/120 15.00 40.00
99FFANS Nick Senzel/60 15.00 40.00
99FFAPM Pedro Martinez/30 30.00 80.00
99FFAQP Quinn Priester/150 4.00 10.00
99FFARG Riley Greene/50 30.00 80.00
99FFASL Shea Langeliers/100 15.00 40.00
99FFASO Shohei Ohtani/30 75.00 200.00
99FFATS Travis Swaggerty/150 5.00 12.00
99FFAWF Wander Franco/120 80.00 200.00
99FFAZT Zack Thompson/150 5.00 12.00
99FFAARI Austin Riley/60 25.00 60.00
99FFACJA CJ Abrams/100 25.00 60.00
99FFAFTJ Fernando Tatis Jr./60 125.00 300.00
99FFAJJB J.J. Bleday/50 25.00 60.00
99FFAKGJ Ken Griffey Jr. EXCH
99FFAKHO Kody Hoese/150 10.00 25.00
99FFARAJ Ronald Acuna Jr./50 75.00 200.00
99FFAVGJ Vladimir Guerrero Jr./60 50.00 120.00
99FFAVMJ Victor Mesa Jr./150 6.00 15.00
99FFAVVM Victor Victor Mesa/150 6.00 15.00

2019 Bowman's Best '99 Franchise Favorites Autographs Atomic Refractors
*ATOMIC REF: .8X TO 2X p/r 150
*ATOMIC REF: .6X TO 1.5X p/r 100-120
*ATOMIC REF: .5X TO 1.2X p/r 50-75
*ATOMIC REF: .4X TO 1X p/r 30-40
STATED ODDS 1:565 HOBBY
STATED PRINT RUN 25 SER.#'d SETS
EXCHANGE DEADLINE 11/30/2021
99FFACC Corbin Carroll 40.00 100.00
99FFAEJ Eloy Jimenez 75.00 200.00
99FFAHB Hunter Bishop 40.00 100.00
99FFAJJ Josh Jung 30.00 80.00
99FFANS Nick Senzel 25.00 60.00
99FFAWF Wander Franco 200.00 400.00
99FFAFTJ Fernando Tatis Jr. 250.00 600.00

2019 Bowman's Best '99 Franchise Favorites Autographs Gold Refractors
*GOLD REF: .6X TO 1.5X p/r 150
*GOLD REF: .5X TO 1.2X p/r 100-120
*GOLD REF: .4X TO 1X p/r 50-75
STATED ODDS 1:449 HOBBY
STATED PRINT RUN 50 SER.#'d SETS
EXCHANGE DEADLINE 11/30/2021
99FFAJJ Josh Jung 25.00 60.00
99FFAWF Wander Franco 125.00 300.00

2019 Bowman's Best Best of '19 Autographs
STATED ODDS 1:1 HOBBY
EXCHANGE DEADLINE 11/30/2021
B19AB Alec Bohm 25.00 60.00
B19AK Andrew Knizner 4.00 10.00
B19AM Alek Manoah 8.00 20.00
B19AR Adley Rutschman 60.00 150.00
B19ARI Austin Riley 12.00 30.00
B19AV Andrew Vaughn 20.00 50.00
B19BA Blaze Alexander 2.50 6.00
B19BB Brett Baty 10.00 25.00
B19BD Brock Deatherage 2.50 6.00
B19BH Bryce Harper 75.00 200.00
B19BM Brennan Malone 2.50 6.00
B19BR Brendan Rodgers 5.00 12.00
B19BS Bryson Stott 8.00 20.00
B19BSH Braden Shewmake 5.00 12.00
B19CB Cavan Biggio 15.00 40.00
B19CC Corbin Carroll 10.00 25.00
B19CJA CJ Abrams 25.00 60.00
B19CK Carter Kieboom 10.00 25.00
B19CM Casey Mize 12.00 30.00
B19CMI Cal Mitchell 4.00 10.00
B19DC Diego Cartaya 12.00 30.00
B19DE Daniel Espino 3.00 8.00
B19DG Deivi Garcia 20.00 50.00
B19DK Dean Kremer 6.00 15.00
B19DM Dustin May 15.00 40.00
B19EJ Eloy Jimenez 25.00 60.00
B19FTJ Fernando Tatis Jr. 100.00 250.00
B19GC Genesis Cabrera 4.00 10.00
B19GJ Greg Jones 3.00 8.00
B19GK George Kirby 6.00 15.00
B19GL Grant Lavigne 3.00 8.00
B19HB Hunter Bishop 15.00 40.00
B19HG Hunter Greene 10.00 25.00
B19JA Jose Altuve 15.00 40.00
B19JAD Jordyn Adams 4.00 10.00
B19JB Joey Bart 20.00 50.00
B19JBA Jake Bauers 4.00 10.00
B19JD Jon Duplantier 2.50 6.00
B19JI Jonathan India 20.00 50.00
B19JJ Josh James 4.00 10.00
B19JJB J.J. Bleday 10.00 25.00
B19JJU Josh Jung 12.00 30.00
B19JK Jarred Kelenic 40.00 100.00
B19JR Julio Rodriguez 30.00 80.00
B19JS Justus Sheffield 4.00 10.00
B19KB Kris Bryant 30.00 80.00
B19KC Keoni Cavaco 6.00 15.00
B19KH Kody Hoese 10.00 25.00
B19KHI Keston Hiura 15.00 40.00
B19KS Kyle Schwarber 4.00 10.00
B19LG Luis Gil 4.00 10.00
B19MB Michael Busch 4.00 10.00
B19MCH Michael Chavis 12.00 30.00
B19MKE Mitch Keller 5.00 12.00
B19MT Mike Trout 200.00 500.00
B19MTO Michael Toglia 4.00 10.00
B19MW Matt Wallner 5.00 12.00
B19NG Nolan Gorman 12.00 30.00
B19NH Nico Hoerner 12.00 30.00
B19NL Nate Lowe 8.00 20.00
B19NLO Nick Lodolo 6.00 15.00
B19OM Owen Miller 3.00 8.00
B19PA Pete Alonso 50.00 120.00
B19QP Quinn Priester 3.00 8.00
B19RB Rylan Bannon 3.00 8.00
B19RG Riley Greene 40.00 100.00
B19RH Rhys Hoskins 8.00 20.00
B19RHE Ronaldo Hernandez 2.50 6.00
B19RHI Rece Hinds 8.00 20.00
B19ROH Ryan O'Hearn 2.50 6.00
B19RT Rowdy Tellez 4.00 10.00
B19SB Seth Beer 6.00 15.00
B19SL Shea Langeliers 5.00 12.00
B19SN Shervyen Newton 4.00 10.00
B19SO Shohei Ohtani 100.00 250.00
B19TJS TJ Sikkema 4.00 10.00
B19TON Tyler O'Neill 3.00 8.00
B19TS Travis Swaggerty 4.00 10.00
B19VGJ Vladimir Guerrero Jr. 75.00 200.00
B19VMJ Victor Mesa Jr. 6.00 15.00
B19VVM Victor Victor Mesa 5.00 12.00
B19WA Willians Astudillo 2.50 6.00
B19WF Wander Franco 75.00 200.00
B19WS Will Smith 12.00 30.00
B19WW Will Wilson 4.00 10.00
B19YK Yusei Kikuchi 4.00 10.00
B19ZT Zack Thompson 4.00 10.00

2019 Bowman's Best Best of '19 Autographs Atomic Refractors
*ATOMIC REF: 1X TO 2.5X BASIC
STATED ODDS 1:233 HOBBY
STATED PRINT RUN 25 SER.#'d SETS
EXCHANGE DEADLINE 11/30/2021
B19AV Andrew Vaughn 75.00 200.00
B19BH Bryce Harper 200.00 500.00
B19CB Cavan Biggio 60.00 150.00
B19JJB J.J. Bleday 50.00 120.00
B19JJU Josh Jung 60.00 150.00
B19JR Julio Rodriguez 150.00 400.00
B19MT Mike Trout 400.00 800.00
B19PA Pete Alonso 200.00 500.00

2019 Bowman's Best Best of '19 Autographs Blue Refractors
*BLUE REF: .5X TO 1.2X BASIC
STATED ODDS 1:43 HOBBY
STATED PRINT RUN 150 SER.#'d SETS
EXCHANGE DEADLINE 11/30/2021
B19AV Andrew Vaughn 40.00 100.00
B19CB Cavan Biggio 30.00 80.00
B19JJB J.J. Bleday 20.00 50.00

2019 Bowman's Best Best of '19 Autographs Gold Refractors
*GOLD REF: .75X TO 2X BASIC
STATED ODDS 1:117 HOBBY
STATED PRINT RUN 50 SER.#'d SETS
EXCHANGE DEADLINE 11/30/2021
B19AV Andrew Vaughn 60.00 150.00
B19BH Bryce Harper 150.00 400.00
B19CB Cavan Biggio 50.00 120.00
B19JJB J.J. Bleday 30.00 80.00
B19JJU Josh Jung 50.00 120.00
B19MT Mike Trout 250.00 600.00
B19PA Pete Alonso 125.00 300.00

2019 Bowman's Best Best of '19 Autographs Green Refractors
*GRN REF: .6X TO 1.5X BASIC
STATED ODDS 1:64 HOBBY
STATED PRINT RUN 99 SER.#'d SETS
EXCHANGE DEADLINE 11/30/2021
B19AV Andrew Vaughn 50.00 120.00
B19CB Cavan Biggio 40.00 100.00
B19JJB J.J. Bleday 25.00 60.00

2019 Bowman's Best Best of '19 Autographs Refractors
*REF: .5X TO 1.2X BASIC
STATED ODDS 1:21 HOBBY
EXCHANGE DEADLINE 11/30/2021
B19AV Andrew Vaughn 40.00 100.00
B19CB Cavan Biggio 30.00 80.00
B19JJB J.J. Bleday 20.00 50.00

2019 Bowman's Best Dual Autographs
STATED ODDS 1:3278 HOBBY
STATED PRINT RUN 25 SER.#'d SETS
EXCHANGE DEADLINE 11/30/2021
DAGJ V.Guerrero Jr./E.Jimenez 125.00 300.00
DAHH R.Hoskins/B.Harper 150.00 400.00
DAMM V.Mesa Jr./V.Mesa 75.00 200.00
DATO M.Trout/S.Ohtani 500.00 1000.00

2019 Bowman's Best Future Foundations Refractors
STATED ODDS 1:4 HOBBY
*ATOMIC REF: 1.2X TO 3X BASIC
*GOLD REF/50: 3X TO 8X BASIC
FFAB Alec Bohm 1.50 4.00
FFAK Andrew Knizner .40 1.00
FFBA Blaze Alexander .25 .60
FFBB Bo Bichette .75 2.00
FFBD Brock Deatherage .25 .60
FFCK Carter Kieboom .40 1.00
FFCM Casey Mize .60 1.50
FFDK Dean Kremer .30 .75
FFEJ Eloy Jimenez 1.00 2.50
FFEM Elehuris Montero .40 1.00
FFGL Grant Lavigne .30 .75
FFHG Hunter Greene .40 1.00
FFJA Jordyn Adams .40 1.00
FFJB Joey Bart .75 2.00
FFJI Jonathan India 1.50 4.00
FFJR Julio Rodriguez 2.00 5.00
FFNG Nolan Gorman .75 2.00
FFNH Nico Hoerner .75 2.00
FFNL Nate Lowe 1.25 3.00
FFRB Rylan Bannon .30 .75
FFRH Ronaldo Hernandez .25 .60
FFSB Seth Beer .60 1.50
FFSN Shervyen Newton .40 1.00
FFTS Travis Swaggerty .40 1.00
FFWF Wander Franco 2.00 5.00
FFFTJ Fernando Tatis Jr. 4.00 10.00
FFJPM Julio Pablo Martinez .25 .60
FFVGJ Vladimir Guerrero Jr. 1.50 4.00
FFVMJ Victor Mesa Jr. .50 1.25
FFVVM Victor Victor Mesa .50 1.25

2019 Bowman's Best Future Foundations Atomic Refractors
*ATOMIC REF: 1.2X TO 3X BASIC
STATED ODDS 1:48 HOBBY
FFWF Wander Franco 6.00 15.00
FFFTJ Fernando Tatis Jr. 12.00 30.00

2019 Bowman's Best Future Foundations Gold Refractors
*GOLD REF/50: 3X TO 8X BASIC
STATED ODDS 1:336 HOBBY
STATED PRINT RUN 50 SER.#'d SETS
FFAB Alec Bohm 10.00 25.00
FFWF Wander Franco 15.00 40.00

2019 Bowman's Best Future Foundations Autographs
STATED ODDS 1:174 HOBBY
PRINT RUNS B/WN 50-150 COPIES PER
EXCHANGE DEADLINE 11/30/2021
FFAAB Alec Bohm/80 25.00 60.00
FFAAK Andrew Knizner/150 6.00 15.00
FFABA Blaze Alexander/150 8.00 20.00
FFABD Brock Deatherage/150 4.00 10.00
FFACK Carter Kieboom/100 12.00 30.00
FFACM Casey Mize/50 12.00 30.00
FFADK Dean Kremer/150 5.00 12.00
FFAEJ Eloy Jimenez/50 30.00 80.00
FFAHG Hunter Greene/50 15.00 40.00
FFAJA Jordyn Adams/150 6.00 15.00
FFAJB Joey Bart/80 30.00 80.00
FFAJI Jonathan India
FFAJR Julio Rodriguez/150 30.00 80.00
FFANG Nolan Gorman/100 15.00 40.00
FFANH Nico Hoerner/150 12.00 30.00
FFANL Nate Lowe/150 25.00 60.00
FFARH Ronaldo Hernandez/150 4.00 10.00
FFASB Seth Beer/150 10.00 25.00
FFASN Shervyen Newton/150 6.00 15.00
FFATS Travis Swaggerty/100 6.00 15.00
FFAWF Wander Franco/100 60.00 150.00
FFAFTJ Fernando Tatis Jr./150 100.00 250.00
FFAJPM Julio Pablo Martinez/100 4.00 10.00
FFAVGJ Vladimir Guerrero Jr./50 60.00 150.00
FFAVMJ Victor Mesa Jr./150 8.00 20.00
FFAVVM Victor Victor Mesa/100 8.00 20.00

2019 Bowman's Best Future Foundations Autographs Atomic Refractors
STATED ODDS 1:789 HOBBY
STATED PRINT RUN 25 SER.#'d SETS
EXCHANGE DEADLINE 11/30/2021
FFACK Carter Kieboom 25.00 60.00
FFAJI Jonathan India 30.00 80.00
FFAJR Julio Rodriguez 75.00 200.00
FFAWF Wander Franco 125.00 300.00
FFAVGJ Vladimir Guerrero Jr. 100.00 250.00

2019 Bowman's Best Future Foundations Autographs Gold Refractors
STATED ODDS 1:395 HOBBY
STATED PRINT RUN 50 SER.#'d SETS
EXCHANGE DEADLINE 11/30/2021
FFAJI Jonathan India 25.00 60.00
FFAWF Wander Franco 100.00 250.00

2019 Bowman's Best Neophyte Sensations Refractors
STATED ODDS 1:18 HOBBY
*ATOMIC REF: 1.2X TO 3X BASIC
*GOLD REF/50: 3X TO 8X BASIC
NS1 Vladimir Guerrero Jr. 1.50 4.00
NS2 Will Smith .60 1.50
NS3 Austin Riley .75 2.00
NS4 Brandon Lowe .40 1.00
NS5 Pete Alonso 2.00 5.00
NS6 Keston Hiura .75 2.00
NS7 Chris Paddack .50 1.25
NS8 Nick Senzel .75 2.00
NS9 Eloy Jimenez 1.00 2.50
NS10 Fernando Tatis Jr. 4.00 10.00

2019 Bowman's Best Neophyte Sensations Autographs
STATED ODDS 1:499 HOBBY
STATED PRINT RUN 99 SER.#'d SETS
EXCHANGE DEADLINE 11/30/2021
NS1 Vladimir Guerrero Jr. 50.00 120.00
NS2 Will Smith 10.00 25.00
NS3 Austin Riley 20.00 50.00
NS4 Brandon Lowe 10.00 25.00
NS5 Pete Alonso 50.00 120.00
NS6 Keston Hiura 15.00 40.00
NS7 Chris Paddack 15.00 40.00
NS8 Nick Senzel 12.00 30.00
NS9 Eloy Jimenez 20.00 50.00
NS10 Fernando Tatis Jr. 60.00 150.00

2019 Bowman's Best Power Producers Refractors
STATED ODDS 1:6 HOBBY
*ATOMIC REF: 1.2X TO 3X BASIC
*GOLD REF/50: 3X TO 8X BASIC
PPAR Adley Rutschman 1.50 4.00
PPAV Andrew Vaughn .75 2.00
PPBH Bryce Harper .60 1.50
PPCY Christian Yelich .50 1.25
PPEJ Eloy Jimenez 1.00 2.50
PPJB Josh Bell .30 .75
PPJJ Josh Jung .75 2.00
PPMM Manny Machado .40 1.00
PPMT Mike Trout 2.00 5.00
PPNA Nolan Arenado .60 1.50
PPPA Pete Alonso 2.00 5.00
PPRG Riley Greene 1.50 4.00
PPSO Shohei Ohtani .60 1.50
PPANR Anthony Rizzo .50 1.25
PPARI Austin Riley 1.25 3.00
PPFTJ Fernando Tatis Jr. 4.00 10.00
PPJDM J.D. Martinez .40 1.00
PPJJB J.J. Bleday 1.25 3.00
PPRAJ Ronald Acuna Jr. 2.00 5.00
PPVGJ Vladimir Guerrero Jr. 1.50 4.00

2019 Bowman's Best Power Producers Autographs
STATED ODDS 1:399 HOBBY
PRINT RUNS B/WN 25-99 COPIES PER
EXCHANGE DEADLINE 11/30/2021
PPAR Adley Rutschman/99 50.00 120.00
PPAV Andrew Vaughn/99 20.00 50.00
PPCY Christian Yelich/99 30.00 80.00
PPJJ Josh Jung/99 12.00 30.00
PPMM Manny Machado/99 20.00 50.00
PPMT Mike Trout/25 250.00 500.00
PPNA Nolan Arenado/50 25.00 60.00
PPPA Pete Alonso/99 60.00 150.00
PPRG Riley Greene/99 25.00 60.00
PPSO Shohei Ohtani/25 75.00 200.00
PPANR Anthony Rizzo/50 10.00 25.00
PPARI Austin Riley/99 20.00 50.00
PPFTJ Fernando Tatis Jr./99 100.00 250.00
PPRAJ Ronald Acuna Jr./99 50.00 120.00

2019 Bowman's Best Top Prospects
*REF: .6X TO 1.5X BASIC
TP1 Wander Franco 5.00 12.00
TP2 CJ Abrams 1.25 3.00
TP3 Alek Manoah .50 1.25
TP4 Luis Robert 2.00 5.00
TP5 Cristian Pache .60 1.50
TP6 Bryson Stott .75 2.00
TP7 Riley Greene 1.50 4.00
TP8 Josh Jung .75 2.00
TP9 Taylor Trammell .40 1.00
TP10 Bo Bichette .75 2.00
TP11 Corbin Carroll .40 1.00
TP12 Shea Langeliers .50 1.25
TP13 Casey Mize .60 1.50
TP14 Jarred Kelenic 1.25 3.00
TP15 Nolan Gorman .75 2.00
TP16 Keoni Cavaco .60 1.50
TP17 Nick Lodolo .50 1.25
TP18 J.J. Bleday 1.25 3.00
TP19 Sixto Sanchez .75 2.00
TP20 Forrest Whitley .40 1.00
TP21 Joey Bart .75 2.00
TP22 Royce Lewis .50 1.25
TP23 Will Wilson .40 1.00
TP24 MacKenzie Gore .50 1.25
TP25 Andrew Vaughn .75 2.00
TP26 Deivi Garcia 2.50 6.00
TP27 Jo Adell 1.00 2.50
TP28 Hunter Bishop .75 2.00
TP29 Brett Baty .50 1.25
TP30 Adley Rutschman 1.50 4.00

2019 Bowman's Best Top Prospects Atomic Refractors
*ATOMIC REF: 1X TO 2.5X BASIC
STATED ODDS 1:12 HOBBY
TP30 Adley Rutschman 8.00 20.00

2019 Bowman's Best Top Prospects Blue Refractors
*BLUE REF/150: 1.2X TO 3X BASIC
STATED ODDS 1:34 HOBBY
STATED PRINT RUN 150 SER.#'d SETS
TP30 Adley Rutschman 10.00 25.00

2019 Bowman's Best Top Prospects Gold Refractors
*GOLD REF/50: 2X TO 5X BASIC
STATED ODDS 1:101 HOBBY
STATED PRINT RUN 50 SER.#'d SETS
TP30 Adley Rutschman 15.00 40.00

2019 Bowman's Best Top Prospects Green Refractors
*GRN REF/99: 1.5X TO 4X BASIC
STATED ODDS 1:51 HOBBY
STATED PRINT RUN 99 SER.#'d SETS
TP30 Adley Rutschman 12.00 30.00

2019 Bowman's Best Top Prospects Orange Refractors
*ORNG REF/25: 2.5X TO 6X BASIC
STATED ODDS 1:202 HOBBY
STATED PRINT RUN 25 SER.#'d SETS
TP30 Adley Rutschman 20.00 50.00

2019 Bowman's Best Top Prospects Purple Refractors
*PRPL REF/250: 1X TO 2.5X BASIC
STATED ODDS 1:21 HOBBY
STATED PRINT RUN 250 SER.#'d SETS
TP30 Adley Rutschman 8.00 20.00

2020 Bowman's Best
1 Shun Yamaguchi RC .50 1.25
2 Mike Trout 2.00 5.00
3 Fernando Tatis Jr. 2.00 5.00
4 Buster Posey .50 1.25
5 Bo Bichette RC 5.00 12.00
6 Justin Verlander .40 1.00
7 Xander Bogaerts .40 1.00
8 Anthony Rizzo .50 1.25
9 Christian Yelich .50 1.25
10 Luis Robert RC 6.00 15.00
11 Justin Dunn RC .50 1.25
12 Yoshi Tsutsugo RC 1.00 2.50
13 Bobby Bradley RC .40 1.00
14 Kris Bryant .50 1.25
15 Manny Machado .40 1.00
16 Jordan Yamamoto RC .40 1.00
17 Corey Kluber .30 .75
18 Nolan Arenado .60 1.50
19 Dustin May RC 1.25 3.00
20 Mookie Betts .75 2.00
21 Sean Murphy RC .60 1.50
22 Shohei Ohtani .60 1.50
23 Pete Alonso 1.00 2.50
24 Jorge Alfaro .25 .60
25 Gerrit Cole .60 1.50
26 Vladimir Guerrero Jr. .60 1.50
27 Rhys Hoskins .50 1.25
28 Blake Snell .30 .75
29 Jacob deGrom .75 2.00
30 A.J. Puk RC .60 1.50
31 Kyle Lewis RC 3.00 8.00
32 Aristides Aquino RC 1.00 2.50
33 Josh Bell .30 .75
34 Yadier Molina .50 1.25
35 Zac Gallen RC 1.00 2.50
36 Nick Solak RC 1.50 4.00
37 Juan Soto 1.25 3.00
38 J.D. Martinez .40 1.00
39 Max Scherzer .40 1.00
40 Brendan McKay RC .60 1.50
41 Gavin Lux RC 2.00 5.00
42 Starling Marte .30 .75
43 Tim Anderson .40 1.00
44 Francisco Lindor .40 1.00
45 Yordan Alvarez RC 4.00 10.00
46 Nico Hoerner RC 1.50 4.00
47 Trent Grisham RC 1.50 4.00
48 Jesus Luzardo RC .75 2.00
49 Brusdar Graterol RC .60 1.50
50 Adbert Alzolay RC .50 1.25
51 Bryce Harper .60 1.50
52 Dylan Cease RC .60 1.50
53 Ronald Acuna Jr. 1.50 4.00
54 Freddie Freeman .50 1.25
55 Joey Votto .40 1.00
56 Anthony Rendon .40 1.00
57 Dan Vogelbach .25 .60
58 Trey Mancini .40 1.00
59 Albert Pujols .50 1.25
60 Paul Goldschmidt .40 1.00
61 Aaron Judge 1.00 2.50
62 Eddie Rosario .30 .75
63 Cody Bellinger .75 2.00
64 Austin Meadows .40 1.00
65 Jose Altuve .30 .75
66 Mauricio Dubon RC .50 1.25
67 Miguel Cabrera .40 1.00
68 Jorge Soler .40 1.00
69 Matt Chapman .40 1.00
70 Shogo Akiyama RC .60 1.50

2020 Bowman's Best Atomic Refractors
*ATOMIC: 1X TO 2.5X BASIC
*ATOMIC RC: .6X TO 1.5X BASIC
STATED ODDS 1:XX HOBBY
2 Mike Trout 10.00 25.00
5 Bo Bichette 15.00 40.00
10 Luis Robert 20.00 50.00
31 Kyle Lewis 12.00 30.00

2020 Bowman's Best Blue Refractors
*BLUE: 2X TO 5X BASIC
*BLUE RC: 1.2X TO 3X BASIC
STATED ODDS 1:XX HOBBY
STATED PRINT RUN 150 SER.#'d SETS
2 Mike Trout 20.00 50.00
5 Bo Bichette 30.00 80.00
10 Luis Robert 50.00 120.00
31 Kyle Lewis 25.00 60.00

2020 Bowman's Best Gold Refractors
*GOLD: 4X TO 1X BASIC
*GOLD RC: 2.5X TO 6X BASIC
STATED ODDS 1:XX HOBBY
STATED PRINT RUN 50 SER.#'d SETS
2 Mike Trout 40.00 100.00
5 Bo Bichette 60.00 150.00
10 Luis Robert 100.00 250.00
31 Kyle Lewis 50.00 120.00

2020 Bowman's Best Green Refractors
*GREEN: 2.5X TO 6X BASIC
*GREEN RC: 1.5X TO 4X BASIC
STATED ODDS 1:XX HOBBY
STATED PRINT RUN 99 SER.#'d SETS
2 Mike Trout 25.00 60.00
5 Bo Bichette 40.00 100.00
10 Luis Robert 60.00 150.00
31 Kyle Lewis 30.00 80.00

2020 Bowman's Best Orange Refractors
*ORANGE: 6X TO 15X BASIC
*ORANGE RC: 4X TO 10X BASIC
STATED ODDS 1:XX HOBBY
STATED PRINT RUN 25 SER.#'d SETS
2 Mike Trout 60.00 150.00
5 Bo Bichette 100.00 250.00
10 Luis Robert 150.00 400.00
31 Kyle Lewis 75.00 200.00

2020 Bowman's Best Purple Refractors
*PURPLE: 1.2X TO 3X BASIC
*PURPLE RC: .8X TO 2X BASIC
STATED ODDS 1:XX HOBBY
STATED PRINT RUN 250 SER.#'d SETS
2 Mike Trout 12.00 30.00
5 Bo Bichette 20.00 50.00
10 Luis Robert 30.00 80.00
31 Kyle Lewis 15.00 40.00

2020 Bowman's Best Refractors
*REF.: .8X TO 2X BASIC
*REF. RC: .5X TO 1.2X BASIC
STATED ODDS 1:XX HOBBY
10 Luis Robert 10.00 25.00
31 Kyle Lewis 6.00 15.00

2020 Bowman's Best Best of '20 Autographs
STATED ODDS 1:XX HOBBY
EXCHANGE DEADLINE 11/30/22
B20AA Adbert Alzolay 3.00 8.00
B20AB Andrew Benintendi 8.00 20.00
B20AC Antonio Cabello 5.00 12.00
B20AH Austin Hendrick 30.00 80.00
B20AJ Aaron Judge 75.00 200.00
B20AK Anthony Kay 2.50 6.00
B20AV Andrew Vaughn 30.00 80.00
B20AW Austin Wells 20.00 50.00
B20BG Brusdar Graterol 6.00 15.00
B20BJ Bryce Jarvis 3.00 8.00
B20BM Brendan McKay 6.00 15.00
B20BR Bryan Reynolds 6.00 15.00
B20BW Bobby Witt Jr. 100.00 250.00
B20CC Cade Cavalli 5.00 12.00
B20CK Carter Kieboom 8.00 20.00
B20CS Casey Schmitt 3.00 8.00
B20CY Christian Yelich 25.00 60.00
B20DC Dylan Cease 4.00 10.00
B20DD Dillon Dingler 8.00 20.00
B20DF Daxton Fulton 4.00 10.00
B20DM Dustin May 8.00 20.00
B20EH Emerson Hancock 8.00 20.00
B20EP Everson Pereira 10.00 25.00
B20FT Fernando Tatis Jr.
B20GC Garrett Crochet 30.00 80.00
B20GM Garrett Mitchell 25.00 60.00
B20HK Heston Kjerstad 25.00 60.00
B20IH Ivan Herrera 10.00 25.00
B20JD Jasson Dominguez 150.00 400.00
B20JF Justin Foscue 5.00 12.00
B20JL Jesus Luzardo 6.00 15.00
B20JM Jeff McNeil 12.00 30.00
B20JR Jake Rogers 4.00 10.00
B20JS Juan Soto 100.00 250.00
B20JT J.T. Realmuto 12.00 30.00
B20JW Jordan Walker 15.00 40.00
B20JY Jordan Yamamoto 2.50 6.00
B20LA Logan Allen 2.50 6.00
B20LC Luis Castillo 3.00 8.00
B20LR Luis Robert 100.00 250.00
B20LW Logan Webb 10.00 25.00
B20MC Michael Chavis 5.00 12.00
B20MD Mauricio Dubon 5.00 12.00
B20MK Mitch Keller 4.00 10.00
B20MM Max Muncy 8.00 20.00
B20MT Mike Trout 300.00 800.00
B20NB Nick Bitsko 5.00 12.00
B20NG Nick Gonzales 15.00 40.00
B20NH Nico Hoerner 12.00 30.00
B20NS Nick Solak 8.00 20.00
B20NY Nick Yorke 8.00 20.00
B20OC Owen Caissie 10.00 25.00
B20PA Pete Alonso 25.00 60.00
B20PB Patrick Bailey 5.00 12.00
B20PC Pete Crow-Armstrong 15.00 40.00
B20RA Ronald Acuna Jr. 100.00 250.00
B20RD Rafael Devers
B20RH Robert Hassell 20.00 50.00
B20RL Ramon Laureano 6.00 15.00
B20RP Robert Puason 15.00 40.00
B20SA Shogo Akiyama 8.00 20.00
B20SM Sean Murphy 5.00 12.00
B20ST Spencer Torkelson 100.00 250.00
B20SY Shun Yamaguchi EXCH 6.00 15.00
B20TA Tim Anderson 10.00 25.00
B20TG Trent Grisham 15.00 40.00
B20TS Tarik Skubal 10.00 25.00
B20WM Whit Merrifield 6.00 15.00
B20WS Will Smith 6.00 15.00
B20YA Yordan Alvarez 40.00 100.00
B20ZD Zach DeLoach 8.00 20.00
B20ZV Zac Veen 30.00 80.00
B20AAQ Aristides Aquino 10.00 25.00
B20ADR Adley Rutschman 25.00 60.00
B20AMU Andres Munoz 4.00 10.00
B20BBB Bobby Bradley 5.00 12.00
B20BHE Ben Hernandez 4.00 10.00
B20BTY Brett Baty 8.00 20.00
B20CML Carmen Mlodzinski 3.00 8.00
B20EHO Ed Howard 20.00 50.00
B20JDA Jaylin Davis 4.00 10.00
B20JDU Jarren Duran 20.00 50.00
B20JLA Justin Lange 2.50 6.00
B20JSH Jared Shuster 6.00 15.00
B20JST Josh Staumont 5.00 12.00
B20MME Max Meyer 8.00 20.00
B20NGO Nolan Gorman 12.00 30.00
B20NLO Nick Loftin 5.00 12.00
B20RDE Reid Detmers 8.00 20.00
B20TSO Tyler Soderstrom 12.00 30.00

2020 Bowman's Best Best of '20 Autographs Atomic Refractors
*ATOMIC: 1X TO 2.5X BASIC
STATED ODDS 1:XX HOBBY
STATED PRINT RUN 25 SER.#'d SETS
EXCHANGE DEADLINE 11/30/22
B20BM Brendan McKay 25.00 60.00
B20BW Bobby Witt Jr. 250.00 600.00
B20EH Emerson Hancock 30.00 80.00
B20FT Fernando Tatis Jr. 150.00 400.00
B20HK Heston Kjerstad 100.00 250.00
B20IH Ivan Herrera 50.00 120.00
B20JD Jasson Dominguez 500.00 1200.00
B20JL Jesus Luzardo 25.00 60.00
B20JT J.T. Realmuto 40.00 100.00
B20MC Michael Chavis 15.00 40.00
B20MT Mike Trout 600.00 1200.00
B20NG Nick Gonzales 75.00 200.00
B20NY Nick Yorke 40.00 100.00
B20PC Pete Crow-Armstrong 75.00 200.00
B20RA Ronald Acuna Jr. 150.00 400.00
B20RH Robert Hassell 75.00 200.00
B20RP Robert Puason 60.00 150.00
B20SM Sean Murphy 25.00 60.00
B20ST Spencer Torkelson 300.00 800.00
B20TG Trent Grisham 50.00 120.00
B20WS Will Smith 20.00 50.00
B20ADR Adley Rutschman 75.00 200.00
B20EHO Ed Howard 100.00 250.00
B20JST Josh Staumont 15.00 40.00
B20MME Max Meyer 40.00 100.00
B20NGO Nolan Gorman 40.00 100.00
B20TSO Tyler Soderstrom 75.00 200.00

2020 Bowman's Best Best of '20 Autographs Blue Refractors
*BLUE: .5X TO 1.2X BASIC
STATED ODDS 1:XX HOBBY
STATED PRINT RUN 150 SER.#'d SETS
EXCHANGE DEADLINE 11/30/22
B20HK Heston Kjerstad 40.00 100.00
B20IH Ivan Herrera 20.00 50.00
B20NG Nick Gonzales 40.00 100.00
B20NY Nick Yorke 15.00 40.00
B20PC Pete Crow-Armstrong 30.00 80.00
B20RH Robert Hassell 40.00 100.00
B20ST Spencer Torkelson 150.00 400.00
B20NGO Nolan Gorman 20.00 50.00
B20TSO Tyler Soderstrom 20.00 50.00

2020 Bowman's Best Best of '20 Autographs Gold Refractors
*GOLD: .8X TO 2X BASIC
STATED ODDS 1:XX HOBBY
STATED PRINT RUN 50 SER.#'d SETS
EXCHANGE DEADLINE 11/30/22
B20BW Bobby Witt Jr. 200.00 500.00
B20EH Emerson Hancock 25.00 60.00
B20FT Fernando Tatis Jr. 125.00 300.00
B20HK Heston Kjerstad 60.00 150.00
B20IH Ivan Herrera 40.00 100.00
B20JD Jasson Dominguez 400.00 1000.00
B20JL Jesus Luzardo 15.00 40.00
B20LR Luis Robert 250.00 600.00
B20NG Nick Gonzales 60.00 150.00
B20NY Nick Yorke 30.00 80.00
B20PC Pete Crow-Armstrong 60.00 150.00
B20RH Robert Hassell 60.00 150.00
B20RP Robert Puason 50.00 120.00
B20SM Sean Murphy 15.00 40.00
B20ST Spencer Torkelson 250.00 600.00
B20TG Trent Grisham 40.00 100.00
B20WS Will Smith 15.00 40.00
B20ADR Adley Rutschman 60.00 150.00
B20EHO Ed Howard 75.00 200.00
B20JST Josh Staumont 12.00 30.00
B20NGO Nolan Gorman 30.00 80.00
B20TSO Tyler Soderstrom 30.00 80.00

2020 Bowman's Best Best of '20 Autographs Green Refractors
*GREEN: .6X TO 1.5X BASIC
STATED ODDS 1:XX HOBBY
STATED PRINT RUN 99 SER.#'d SETS
EXCHANGE DEADLINE 11/30/22
B20EH Emerson Hancock 20.00 50.00
B20HK Heston Kjerstad 50.00 120.00
B20IH Ivan Herrera 30.00 80.00
B20JL Jesus Luzardo 12.00 30.00
B20NG Nick Gonzales 50.00 120.00
B20NY Nick Yorke 20.00 50.00
B20PC Pete Crow-Armstrong 40.00 100.00
B20RH Robert Hassell 50.00 120.00
B20ST Spencer Torkelson 200.00 500.00
B20WS Will Smith 12.00 30.00
B20NGO Nolan Gorman 25.00 60.00
B20TSO Tyler Soderstrom 25.00 60.00

2020 Bowman's Best Decade's Best
STATED ODDS 1:XX HOBBY
DB1 Yoshi Tsutsugo .60 1.50
DB2 Gavin Lux 1.25 3.00
DB3 Dustin May .75 2.00
DB4 Shogo Akiyama .40 1.00
DB5 Yordan Alvarez 2.50 6.00
DB6 Luis Robert 8.00 20.00
DB7 Jesus Luzardo .50 1.25
DB8 Nico Hoerner 1.00 2.50
DB9 Brendan McKay .40 1.00
DB10 Aristides Aquino .60 1.50

2020 Bowman's Best Decade's Best Atomic Refractors
*ATOMIC: 1.2X TO 3X BASIC
STATED ODDS 1:XX HOBBY
DB6 Luis Robert 50.00 120.00

2020 Bowman's Best Decade's Best Gold Refractors
*GOLD: 3X TO 8X BASIC
STATED ODDS 1:XX HOBBY
STATED PRINT RUN 50 SER.#'d SETS
DB6 Luis Robert 125.00 300.00

2020 Bowman's Best Decade's Best Autographs
STATED ODDS 1:XX HOBBY
STATED PRINT RUN 99 SER.#'d SETS
EXCHANGE DEADLINE 11/30/22
DB1 Yoshi Tsutsugo 10.00 25.00
DB2 Gavin Lux EXCH 40.00 100.00
DB3 Dustin May 40.00 100.00
DB4 Shogo Akiyama 12.00 30.00
DB5 Yordan Alvarez 40.00 100.00
DB6 Luis Robert 125.00 300.00
DB7 Jesus Luzardo 12.00 30.00
DB8 Nico Hoerner 20.00 50.00
DB9 Brendan McKay 12.00 30.00
DB10 Aristides Aquino 12.00 301.00

2020 Bowman's Best Franchise '20 Die Cuts
STATED ODDS 1:XX HOBBY
FFDCAA Aristides Aquino .60 1.50
FFDCAB Alec Bohm 1.50 4.00
FFDCAR Adley Rutschman 1.50 4.00
FFDCBB Bo Bichette 5.00 12.00
FFDCBR Brendan Rodgers .40 1.00
FFDCBW Bobby Witt Jr. 4.00 10.00
FFDCCK Carter Kieboom .30 .75
FFDCCM Casey Mize .75 2.00
FFDCCP Cristian Pache .75 2.00
FFDCFT Fernando Tatis Jr. 2.00 5.00
FFDCGL Gavin Lux 1.25 3.00
FFDCJA Jo Adell 1.00 2.50
FFDCJB Joey Bart .75 2.00
FFDCJD Jeter Downs .40 1.00
FFDCJK Jarred Kelenic 1.25 3.00
FFDCKH Ke'Bryan Hayes 1.25 3.00
FFDCLR Luis Robert 5.00 12.00
FFDCNG Nolan Gorman .50 1.25
FFDCNH Nico Hoerner 1.00 2.50
FFDCNJ Nolan Jones .40 1.00
FFDCNS Nick Solak 1.00 2.50
FFDCPA Pete Alonso 1.00 2.50
FFDCRP Robert Puason .75 2.00
FFDCYA Yordan Alvarez 2.50 6.00
FFDCZG Zac Gallen .60 1.50
FFDCJBL JJ Bleday .75 2.00
FFDCJDO Jasson Dominguez 10.00 25.00
FFDCKHI Keston Hiura .50 1.25
FFDCRLA Ramon Laureano .30 .75
FFDCRLE Royce Lewis .60 1.50

2020 Bowman's Best Franchise '20 Die Cuts Gold Refractors
*GOLD: 3X TO 8X BASIC
STATED ODDS 1:XX HOBBY
STATED PRINT RUN 50 SER.#'d SETS
FFDCFT Fernando Tatis Jr. 50.00 120.00

2020 Bowman's Best Franchise '20 Die Cuts Inverse Color Refractors
*INVRSE CLR: 1.2X TO 3X BASIC
STATED ODDS 1:XX HOBBY
FFDCFT Fernando Tatis Jr. 20.00 50.00

2020 Bowman's Best Franchise '20 Die Cuts Autographs
STATED ODDS 1:XX HOBBY
PRINT RUNS B/WN 100-150 COPIES PER
EXCHANGE DEADLINE 11/30/22
F20AA Aristides Aquino/150 10.00 25.00
F20AB Alec Bohm/150 50.00 120.00
F20AR Adley Rutschman/100 100.00 250.00
F20BR Brendan Rodgers/100 6.00 15.00
F20CK Carter Kieboom/150 10.00 25.00
F20DC Nolan Gorman/150 10.00 25.00
F20GL Gavin Lux/150 30.00 80.00
F20JA Jo Adell/100 25.00 60.00
F20JJ JJ Bleday/100 20.00 50.00
F20KH Keston Hiura/100 12.00 30.00
F20LR Luis Robert/100 150.00 400.00
F20NH Nico Hoerner/150 25.00 60.00
F20NS Nick Solak/150 8.00 20.00
F20PA Pete Alonso/100 40.00 100.00
F20RP Robert Puason/100 30.00 80.00
F20YA Yordan Alvarez/100

2020 Bowman's Best Franchise '20 Die Cuts Autographs Atomic Refractors
*ATOMIC: .6X TO 1.5X BASIC
RANDOM INSERTS IN PACKS
STATED PRINT RUN 25 SER.#'d SETS
F20DC Nolan Gorman 40.00 100.00
F20GL Gavin Lux 60.00 150.00
F20KH Keston Hiura 25.00 60.00

2020 Bowman's Best Franchise '20 Die Cuts Autographs Gold Refractors

*GOLD: .5X TO 1.2X BASIC
RANDOM INSERTS IN PACKS
STATED PRINT RUN 50 SER.#'d SETS
F20DC Nolan Gorman 30.00 80.00
F20KH Keston Hiura 20.00 50.00

2020 Bowman's Best Franchise Favorites

STATED ODDS 1:XX HOBBY
FFAAA Aristides Aquino .60 1.50
FFAAH Austin Hendrick 2.50 6.00
FFAAL Asa Lacy 1.50 4.00
FFAAV Andrew Vaughn 1.00 2.50
FFABJ Bryce Jarvis .30 .75
FFABM Brendan McKay .40 1.00
FFABW Bobby Witt Jr. 4.00 10.00
FFACJ Chipper Jones .40 1.00
FFACR Cal Ripken Jr. 1.25 3.00
FFAEH Emerson Hancock 1.00 2.50
FFAFT Fernando Tatis Jr. 4.00 10.00
FFAGL Gavin Lux 1.25 3.00
FFAGM Garrett Mitchell 2.00 5.00
FFAHK Heston Kjerstad 2.00 5.00
FFAJF Justin Foscue 1.00 2.50
FFAJJ Josh Jung .60 1.50
FFAJL Jesus Luzardo .50 1.25
FFAJS Juan Soto 1.25 3.00
FFAKG Ken Griffey Jr. .75 2.00
FFALR Luis Robert 6.00 15.00
FFAMM Max Meyer 1.00 2.50
FFAMT Mike Trout 4.00 10.00
FFANG Nick Gonzales 1.25 3.00
FFANH Nico Hoerner 1.00 2.50
FFANY Nick Yorke 1.25 3.00
FFAPB Patrick Bailey .75 2.00
FFAPM Pedro Martinez .30 .75
FFARA Ronald Acuna Jr. 1.50 4.00
FFARD Reid Detmers .60 1.50
FFARG Riley Greene 1.00 2.50
FFARH Robert Hassell 3.00 8.00
FFASA Shogo Akiyama .40 1.00
FFASO Shohei Ohtani .60 1.50
FFAST Spencer Torkelson 3.00 8.00
FFAWF Wander Franco 3.00 8.00
FFAYA Yordan Alvarez 2.50 6.00
FFAZV Zac Veen 1.25 3.00
FFAEHO Ed Howard 2.00 5.00
FFANGO Nolan Gorman .50 1.25

2020 Bowman's Best Franchise Favorites Atomic Refractors

*ATOMIC: 1.2X TO 3X BASIC
STATED ODDS 1:XX HOBBY
FFAFT Fernando Tatis Jr. 20.00 50.00
FFAKG Ken Griffey Jr. 15.00 40.00
FFAMT Mike Trout 15.00 40.00

2020 Bowman's Best Franchise Favorites Gold Refractors

*GOLD: 3X TO 8X BASIC
STATED ODDS 1:XX HOBBY
STATED PRINT RUN 50 SER.#'d SETS
FFAFT Fernando Tatis Jr. 50.00 120.00
FFAKG Ken Griffey Jr. 25.00 60.00
FFAMT Mike Trout 40.00 100.00
FFARA Ronald Acuna Jr. 15.00 40.00

2020 Bowman's Best Franchise Favorites Autographs

STATED ODDS 1:XX HOBBY
PRINT RUNS B/WN 40-250 COPIES PER
EXCHANGE DEADLINE 11/30/22
FFABJ Bryce Jarvis/250 8.00 20.00
FFACJ Chipper Jones/40 60.00 150.00
FFACR Cal Ripken Jr./40 100.00 250.00
FFAEH Emerson Hancock/250 12.00 30.00
FFAGL Gavin Lux/60 60.00 150.00
FFAHK Heston Kjerstad/250 40.00 100.00
FFAJF Justin Foscue/250 12.00 30.00
FFAJJ Josh Jung/250 15.00 40.00
FFAJL Jesus Luzardo/250 15.00 40.00
FFAJS Juan Soto/50 100.00 250.00
FFALR Luis Robert/60 400.00 1000.00
FFAMM Max Meyer/108 12.00 30.00
FFANG Nick Gonzales/250 30.00 80.00
FFANH Nico Hoerner/160 25.00 60.00
FFANY Nick Yorke/250 15.00 40.00
FFAPB Patrick Bailey/250 20.00 50.00
FFARA Ronald Acuna Jr./60 75.00 200.00
FFARD Reid Detmers/250 8.00 20.00
FFARG Riley Greene/200 30.00 80.00
FFARH Robert Hassell/250 25.00 60.00
FFASA Shogo Akiyama/250 10.00 25.00
FFAST Spencer Torkelson/60
FFAVB Vidal Brujan/250 20.00 50.00
FFAJJB JJ Bleday/60 20.00 50.00
FFANGO Nolan Gorman/250 12.00 30.00

2020 Bowman's Best Franchise Favorites Autographs Atomic Refractors

*ATOMIC: .8X TO 2X p/r 108-250
*ATOMIC: .5X TO 1.2X p/r 40-60
RANDOM INSERTS IN PACKS
STATED PRINT RUN 25 SER.#'d SETS
FFANY Nick Yorke 30.00 80.00
FFARA Ronald Acuna Jr. 150.00 400.00

2020 Bowman's Best Franchise Favorites Autographs Gold Refractors

*GOLD: .6X TO 1.5X p/r 108-250
*GOLD: .4X TO 1X p/r 40-60
RANDOM INSERTS IN PACKS
STATED PRINT RUN 50 SER.#'d SETS
FFANY Nick Yorke 25.00 60.00

2020 Bowman's Best Power Producers

STATED ODDS 1:XX HOBBY
PPAA Aristides Aquino .60 1.50
PPAJ Aaron Judge 1.00 2.50
PPBH Bryce Harper .60 1.50
PPCB Cody Bellinger .75 2.00
PPCY Christian Yelich .50 1.25
PPES Eugenio Suarez .30 .75
PPJD Jasson Dominguez 6.00 15.00
PPJS Juan Soto 1.25 3.00
PPLR Luis Robert 5.00 12.00
PPMT Mike Trout 3.00 8.00
PPNA Nolan Arenado .60 1.50
PPNG Nick Gonzales 1.25 3.00
PPPA Pete Alonso 1.00 2.50
PPRA Ronald Acuna Jr. 1.50 4.00
PPRH Robert Hassell 2.00 5.00
PPSO Shohei Ohtani .60 1.50
PPST Spencer Torkelson 4.00 10.00
PPVG Vladimir Guerrero Jr. .60 1.50
PPYA Yordan Alvarez 2.50 6.00
PPZV Zac Veen 1.25 3.00

2020 Bowman's Best Power Producers Atomic Refractors

*ATOMIC: 1.2X TO 3X BASIC
STATED ODDS 1:XX HOBBY
PPAJ Aaron Judge 5.00 12.00
PPBH Bryce Harper 6.00 15.00
PPMT Mike Trout 12.00 30.00

2020 Bowman's Best Power Producers Gold Refractors

*GOLD: 3X TO 8X BASIC
STATED ODDS 1:XX HOBBY
STATED PRINT RUN 50 SER.#'d SETS
PPAJ Aaron Judge 12.00 30.00
PPBH Bryce Harper 15.00 40.00
PPMT Mike Trout 30.00 80.00
PPRA Ronald Acuna Jr. 15.00 40.00

2020 Bowman's Best Power Producers Autographs

STATED ODDS 1:XX HOBBY
STATED PRINT RUN 99 SER.#'d SETS
EXCHANGE DEADLINE 11/30/22
PPCB Cody Bellinger 60.00 150.00
PPJD Jasson Dominguez 125.00 300.00
PPJS Juan Soto 75.00 200.00
PPLR Luis Robert 100.00 250.00
PPMT Mike Trout 400.00 800.00
PPNA Nolan Arenado 20.00 50.00
PPNG Nick Gonzales 50.00 120.00
PPPA Pete Alonso 30.00 80.00
PPRA Ronald Acuna Jr. 60.00 150.00
PPRH Robert Hassell 30.00 80.00
PPSO Shohei Ohtani 60.00 150.00
PPST Spencer Torkelson
PPVG Vladimir Guerrero Jr. 40.00 100.00
PPYA Yordan Alvarez 25.00 60.00
PPZV Zac Veen 25.00 60.00

2020 Bowman's Best Top Prospects

STATED ODDS 1:XX HOBBY
TP1 Wander Franco 2.50 6.00
TP2 Emerson Hancock 1.00 2.50
TP3 Garrett Crochet .60 1.50
TP4 Casey Mize .75 2.00
TP5 Jarred Kelenic 1.25 3.00
TP6 Justin Foscue 1.00 2.50
TP7 Heston Kjerstad 2.00 5.00
TP8 Robert Hassell 2.00 5.00
TP9 Dylan Carlson 1.00 2.50
TP10 Royce Lewis .60 1.50
TP11 Nick Yorke 1.25 3.00
TP12 Zac Veen 1.25 3.00
TP13 Adley Rutschman 1.50 4.00
TP14 Joey Bart .75 2.00
TP15 Julio Rodriguez 1.50 4.00
TP16 Patrick Bailey .75 2.00
TP17 Nick Gonzales 1.25 3.00
TP18 Asa Lacy 1.50 4.00
TP19 Andrew Vaughn 1.00 2.50
TP20 Bobby Witt Jr. 1.50 4.00
TP21 Cristian Pache .75 2.00
TP22 Nate Pearson .75 2.00
TP23 Ed Howard 2.00 5.00
TP24 MacKenzie Gore .50 1.25
TP25 Max Meyer 1.00 2.50
TP26 Forrest Whitley .40 1.00
TP27 Jo Adell 1.00 2.50
TP28 Reid Detmers .60 1.50
TP29 Austin Hendrick 2.50 6.00
TP30 Spencer Torkelson 5.00 12.00

2020 Bowman's Best Top Prospects Atomic Refractors

*ATOMIC: 1X TO 2.5X BASIC
STATED ODDS 1:XX HOBBY
TP9 Dylan Carlson 4.00 10.00
TP13 Adley Rutschman 6.00 15.00
TP14 Joey Bart 3.00 8.00
TP30 Spencer Torkelson 15.00 40.00

2020 Bowman's Best Top Prospects Blue Refractors

*BLUE: 1.2X TO 3X BASIC
STATED ODDS 1:XX HOBBY
STATED PRINT RUN 150 SER.#'d SETS
TP3 Garrett Crochet 5.00 12.00
TP9 Dylan Carlson 5.00 12.00
TP13 Adley Rutschman 8.00 20.00
TP14 Joey Bart 4.00 10.00
TP20 Bobby Witt Jr. 6.00 15.00
TP30 Spencer Torkelson 20.00 50.00

2020 Bowman's Best Top Prospects Gold Refractors

*GOLD: 2X TO 5X BASIC
STATED ODDS 1:XX HOBBY
STATED PRINT RUN 50 SER.#'d SETS
TP3 Garrett Crochet 15.00 40.00
TP9 Dylan Carlson 8.00 20.00
TP13 Adley Rutschman 12.00 30.00
TP14 Joey Bart 6.00 15.00
TP16 Patrick Bailey 5.00 12.00
TP19 Andrew Vaughn 6.00 15.00
TP20 Bobby Witt Jr. 15.00 40.00
TP30 Spencer Torkelson 40.00 100.00

2020 Bowman's Best Top Prospects Green Refractors

*GREEN: 1.5X TO 4X BASIC
STATED ODDS 1:XX HOBBY
STATED PRINT RUN 99 SER.#'d SETS
TP3 Garrett Crochet 8.00 20.00
TP9 Dylan Carlson 6.00 15.00
TP13 Adley Rutschman 10.00 25.00
TP14 Joey Bart 5.00 12.00
TP19 Andrew Vaughn 5.00 12.00
TP20 Bobby Witt Jr. 8.00 20.00
TP30 Spencer Torkelson 25.00 60.00

2020 Bowman's Best Top Prospects Orange Refractors

*ORANGE: 2.5X TO 6X BASIC
STATED ODDS 1:XX HOBBY
STATED PRINT RUN 25 SER.#'d SETS
TP3 Garrett Crochet 20.00 50.00
TP9 Dylan Carlson 10.00 25.00
TP13 Adley Rutschman 15.00 40.00
TP14 Joey Bart 8.00 20.00
TP16 Patrick Bailey 6.00 15.00
TP19 Andrew Vaughn 8.00 20.00
TP20 Bobby Witt Jr. 20.00 50.00
TP30 Spencer Torkelson 50.00 120.00

2020 Bowman's Best Top Prospects Purple Refractors

*PURPLE: 1X TO 2.5X BASIC
STATED ODDS 1:XX HOBBY
STATED PRINT RUN 250 SER.#'d SETS
TP9 Dylan Carlson 4.00 10.00
TP13 Adley Rutschman 6.00 15.00
TP14 Joey Bart 3.00 8.00
TP20 Bobby Witt Jr. 5.00 12.00
TP30 Spencer Torkelson 15.00 40.00

2020 Bowman's Best Top Prospects Refractors

*REF.: .6X TO 1.5X BASIC
STATED ODDS 1:XX HOBBY
TP30 Spencer Torkelson 10.00 25.00

1974 Bramac 1933 National League All-Stars

This 18-card set features black-and-white photos of the 1933 All-Stars of the National League. The set measures approximately 2 1/2" by 3 1/4" and was originally available from the producers for $3.

COMPLETE SET (18) 12.50 30.00
1 Paul Waner 1.00 2.50
2 Woody English .40 1.00
3 Dick Bartell .40 1.00
4 Chuck Klein 1.00 2.50
5 Tony Cuccinello .40 1.00
6 Lefty O'Doul .60 1.50
7 Gabby Hartnett 1.00 2.50
8 Lon Warneke .40 1.00
9 Walter Berger .60 1.50
10 Chick Hafey .75 2.00
11 Frank Frisch 1.00 2.50
12 Carl Hubbell 1.50 4.00
13 Bill Hallahan .40 1.00
14 Hal Schumacher .60 1.50
15 Pie Traynor 1.00 2.50
16 Bill Terry 1.00 2.50
17 Pepper Martin .75 2.00
18 Jimmy Wilson .60 1.50

1889 Braves Cabinets Smith

These three cabinets feature members of the 1889 Boston Beaneaters and were produced by the G. Walden Smith studio in Boston. Each of these cabinets measure approximately 4 1/4" by 6 1/2" and feature the player a posed shot in their uniforms. Since the cards are unnumbered, we have sequenced them in alphabetical order.vThere should be more to this set so any additions are greatly appreciated.

COMPLETE SET 2000.00 4000.00
1 Tom Brown 750.00 1500.00
2 Charlie Ganzel 750.00 1500.00
3 Charles Smith 750.00 1500.00

1891 Braves Conly Cabinets

These Cabinets feature members of the 1891 Boston NL team. The players are all pictured in suit and tie. The back features an ad for Conly studios. This set is not numbered so we have sequenced them in alphabetical order.

1 Hugh Duffy 2000.00 3000.00
2 George Haddock 1000.00 1500.00
3 John Irwin 1000.00 1500.00

1899 Braves Chickering Cabinets

These cabinets, which measure approximately 8" by 9 1/2", feature members of the 1899 Boston team which was known as the Beaneaters at that time. The photographs were taken by the Elmer Chickering studio at that time, which was one of the leading photo studios of the time. Since these cabinets are unnumbered, we have sequenced them in alphabetical order. It is very possible that there are other cabinets so any further information is greatly appreciated.

COMPLETE SET 2000.00 40000.00
1 Harvey Bailey 1000.00 2000.00
2 Marty Bergen 1000.00 2000.00
3 William Clarke 1000.00 2000.00
4 Jimmy Collins 2000.00 4000.00
5 Hugh Duffy 2000.00 4000.00
6 Billy Hamilton 2000.00 4000.00
7 Charlie Hickman 1000.00 2000.00
8 Frank Killen 1000.00 2000.00
9 Edward Lewis 1000.00 2000.00
10 Herman Long 1250.00 2500.00
11 Robert Lowe 1250.00 2500.00
12 Jouett Meekin 1000.00 2000.00
13 Kid Nichols 2000.00 4000.00
14 Fred Tenney 1250.00 2500.00
15 Vic Willis 2000.00 4000.00

1932 Braves Team Issue

These blank-backed photos which measure 9" by 12" are a sepia color against cream borders. All photos are copyright 1932 by "Gowell Studios." Since they are unnumbered we have sequenced them in alphabetical order.

COMPLETE SET 75.00 150.00
1 Wally Berger 10.00 20.00
2 Huck Betts 5.00 10.00
3 Ed Brandt 5.00 10.00
4 Bobby Brown 5.00 10.00
5 Ben Cantwell 5.00 10.00
6 Pinky Hargrave 7.50 15.00
7 Fritz Knothe 5.00 10.00
8 Freddie Leach 5.00 10.00
9 Rabbit Maranville 12.50 25.00
10 Bill McKechnie MG 12.50 25.00
11 Randy Moore 5.00 10.00
12 Art Shires 7.50 15.00
13 Al Spohrer 5.00 10.00
14 Bill Urbanski 5.00 10.00
15 Red Worthington 5.00 10.00

1948 Braves Gentles Bread Label

These bread labels were issued one per loaf of Gentles bread. They feature a player photo with a fascimile signature on either the top or bottom with the "Gentles Bread" logo on the other end. These cards are unnumbered so we have sequenced them in alphabetical order. We suspect there might be more additions so any help is appreciated.

COMPLETE SET 600.00 1200.00
1 Tommy Holmes 125.00 250.00
2 Phil Masi 100.00 200.00
3 John Sain 200.00 400.00
4 Warren Spahn 250.00 500.00

1953 Braves Johnston Cookies

The cards in this 25-card set measure approximately 2 9/16" by 3 5/8". The 1953 Johnston's Cookies set of numbered cards features Milwaukee Braves players only. This set is the most plentiful of the three Johnston's Cookies sets and no known scarcities exist. The catalog designation for this set is D356-1.

COMPLETE SET (25) 250.00 500.00
1 Charlie Grimm MG 7.50 15.00
2 John Antonelli 7.50 15.00
3 Vern Bickford 6.00 12.00
4 Bob Buhl 10.00 20.00
5 Lew Burdette 12.50 25.00
6 Dave Cole 7.50 15.00
7 Ernie Johnson 10.00 20.00
8 Dave Jolly 7.50 15.00
9 Don Liddle 7.50 15.00
10 Warren Spahn 50.00 100.00
11 Max Surkont 7.50 15.00
12 Jim Wilson 7.50 15.00
13 Sibbi Sisti 7.50 15.00
14 Walker Cooper 7.50 15.00
15 Del Crandall 10.00 20.00
16 Ebba St.Claire 7.50 15.00
17 Joe Adcock 12.50 25.00
18 George Crowe 7.50 15.00
19 Jack Dittmer 7.50 15.00
20 Johnny Logan 10.00 20.00
21 Ed Mathews 50.00 100.00
22 Bill Bruton 10.00 20.00
23 Sid Gordon 7.50 15.00
24 Andy Pafko 10.00 20.00
25 Jim Pendleton 7.50 15.00

1953 Braves Merrell

This 17-card set features black-and-white art work of the Milwaukee Braves drawn by Marshall Merrell. The set measures 8" by 10" and was printed on heavy card stock. The prints originally were sold for 25 cents each. The cards are unnumbered and checklisted below in alphabetical order.

COMPLETE SET (17) 300.00 600.00
1 Joe Adcock 30.00 60.00
2 Johnny Antonelli 20.00 50.00
3 Billy Bruton 15.00 40.00
4 Bob Buhl 15.00 40.00
5 Lou Burdette 30.00 60.00
6 Del Crandall 20.00 50.00
7 Jack Dittmer 15.00 40.00
8 Sid Gordon 15.00 40.00
9 Charlie Grimm 20.00 50.00
10 Don Liddle 15.00 40.00
11 Johnny Logan 15.00 40.00
12 Ed Mathews 50.00 100.00
13 Andy Pafko 20.00 50.00
14 Jim Pendleton 15.00 40.00
15 Warren Spahn 75.00 150.00
16 Max Surkont 15.00 40.00
17 Jim Wilson 15.00 40.00

1953-54 Braves Spic and Span 3x5

This 27-card set features only members of the Milwaukee Braves. The cards are black and white and approximately 3 1/4" by 5 1/2". Some of the photos in the set are posed against blank backgrounds, but most are posed against seats and a chain link fence, hence the set is sometimes referred to as the "chain link fence" set. There is a facsimile autograph at the bottom of the card. The set was probably issued in 1953 and 1954 since Hank Aaron is not included in the set and Don Liddle, Ebba St.Claire, and Johnny Antonelli were traded from the Braves on February 1, 1954 for Bobby Thomson (who is also in the set). Cards can be found either blank back or with player's name, comment, and logo in blue on the back

COMPLETE SET (28) 600.00 1200.00
1 Joe Adcock 17.50 35.00
2 Johnny Antonelli 15.00 30.00
3 Vern Bickford 12.50 25.00
4 Bill Bruton 15.00 30.00
5 Bob Buhl 15.00 30.00
6 Lew Burdette 17.50 35.00
7 Dick Cole 12.50 25.00
8 Walker Cooper 12.50 25.00
9 Del Crandall 15.00 30.00
10 George Crowe 12.50 25.00
11 Jack Dittmer 12.50 25.00
12 Sid Gordon 12.50 25.00
13 Ernie Johnson 15.00 30.00
14 Dave Jolly 12.50 25.00
15 Don Liddle 12.50 25.00
16 Johnny Logan 15.00 30.00
17 Ed Mathews 75.00 150.00
18 Danny O'Connell 12.50 25.00
19 Andy Pafko 15.00 30.00
20 Jim Pendleton 12.50 25.00
21 Ebba St.Claire 12.50 25.00
22 Warren Spahn 75.00 150.00
23 Max Surkont 12.50 25.00
24 Bobby Thomson 17.50 35.00
25 Bob Thorpe 12.50 25.00
26 Roberto Vargas 12.50 25.00
27 Jim Wilson 12.50 25.00
28 Hank Aaron 150.00 300.00

1953-56 Braves Spic and Span 7x10

This 13-card set features only members of the Milwaukee Braves. The set was issued beginning in 1953 but may have been issued for several years as they seem to be the most common of all the Spic and Span issues. In addition, Danny O'Connell and Bobby Thomson were not on the '53 Braves team. The front of each card shows the logo, "Spic and Span Dry Cleaners ... the Choice of Your Favorite Braves." There is a thick white border around the cards with facsimile autograph in black in the bottom border. The cards have blank backs and are approximately 7" by 10".

COMPLETE SET (13) 100.00 200.00
1 Joe Adcock 6.00 12.00
2 Billy Bruton 5.00 10.00
3 Bob Buhl 5.00 10.00
4 Lew Burdette 6.00 12.00
5 Del Crandall 5.00 10.00
6 Jack Dittmer 4.00 8.00
7 Johnny Logan 5.00 10.00
8 Eddie Mathews 25.00 50.00
9 Chet Nichols 4.00 8.00
10 Danny O'Connell 4.00 8.00
11 Andy Pafko 5.00 10.00
12 Warren Spahn 25.00 50.00
13 Bobby Thomson 6.00 12.00
14 Milwaukee County Stadium 3.00 8.00

1954 Braves Douglas Felts

These circular oversize felts feature members of the 1954 Milwaukee Braves. Against a white baseball background, the player's photo and fascimile signature is set. The backs are blank and since these are unnumbered, we have sequenced them in alphabetical order.

COMPLETE SET 250.00 500.00
1 Joe Adcock 40.00 80.00
2 Bill Bruton 30.00 60.00
3 Bob Buhl 20.00 50.00
4 Lew Burdette 30.00 60.00
5 Del Crandall 30.00 60.00
6 Johnny Logan 20.00 50.00
7 Eddie Mathews 50.00 100.00
8 Danny O'Connell 20.00 50.00
9 Andy Pafko 30.00 60.00
10 Jim Pendleton 20.00 50.00
11 Warren Spahn 60.00 120.00
12 Bobby Thomson 50.00 100.00

1954 Braves Douglas Portraits

These 8" by 10" portraits feature members of the 1954 Milwaukee Braves. The checklist is identical to the Douglas Felt checklist of the same year. The drawings are oin Sepia-toned paper and the backs are blank

COMPLETE SET 500.00 1000.00
1 Joe Adcock 50.00 100.00
2 Bill Bruton 40.00 80.00
3 Bob Buhl 40.00 80.00
4 Lew Burdette 60.00 120.00
5 Del Crandall 40.00 80.00
6 Johnny Logan 40.00 80.00
7 Eddie Mathews 75.00 150.00
8 Danny O'Connell 30.00 60.00
9 Andy Pafko 50.00 100.00
10 Jim Pendleton 30.00 60.00
11 Warren Spahn 100.00 200.00
12 Bobby Thomson 50.00 100.00

1954 Braves Johnston Cookies

The cards in this 35-card set measure approximately 2" by 3 7/8". The 1954 Johnston's Cookies set of color cards of Milwaukee Braves are numbered according to the player's uniform number, except for the non-players, Lacks and Taylor, who are found at the end of the set. The Bobby Thomson card was withdrawn early in the year after his injury and is scarce. The catalog number for this set is D356-2. The Hank Aaron card shows him with uniform number 5, rather than the more familiar 44, that he switched to shortly thereafter.

COMPLETE SET (35) 600.00 1200.00
COMMON SP 100.00 200.00
1 Del Crandall 10.00 20.00
3 Jim Pendleton 6.00 12.00
4 Danny O'Connell 6.00 12.00
5 Hank Aaron 600.00 1200.00
6 Jack Dittmer 6.00 12.00
9 Joe Adcock 10.00 20.00
10 Bob Buhl 7.50 15.00
11 Phil Paine 6.00 12.00
12 Ben Johnson 6.00 12.00
13 Sibbi Sisti 6.00 12.00
15 Charles Gorin 6.00 12.00
16 Chet Nichols 6.00 12.00
17 Dave Jolly 6.00 12.00
19 Jim Wilson 6.00 12.00
20 Ray Crone 6.00 12.00
21 Warren Spahn 40.00 80.00
22 Gene Conley 7.50 15.00
23 Johnny Logan 10.00 20.00
24 Charlie White 6.00 12.00
27 George Metkovich 6.00 12.00
28 Johnny Cooney CO 6.00 12.00
29 Paul Burris 6.00 12.00
31 Bucky Walters CO 7.50 15.00
32 Ernie Johnson 7.50 15.00
33 Lou Burdette 10.00 20.00
34 Bobby Thomson SP 100.00 200.00
35 Bob Keely 6.00 12.00
38 Bill Bruton 7.50 15.00
40 Charlie Grimm MG 10.00 20.00
41 Eddie Mathews 40.00 80.00
42 Sam Calderone 6.00 12.00
47 Joey Jay 7.50 15.00
48 Andy Pafko 7.50 15.00
49 Dr. Charles Lacks/(Unnumbered) 6.00 12.00
50 Joseph F. Taylor/(Unnumbered) 6.00 12.00

1954 Braves Merrell

This set of the Milwaukee Braves measures approximately 8" by 10" and features black-and-white drawings of players by artist, Marshall Merrell. The cards are unnumbered and checklisted below in alphabetical order. This checklist may be incomplete and additions are welcome.

COMPLETE SET 450.00 900.00
1 Hank Aaron 125.00 250.00
2 Joe Adcock 40.00 80.00
3 Bob Buhl 20.00 50.00
4 Charlie Grimm MG 30.00 60.00
5 Johnny Logan 20.00 50.00
6 Ed Mathews 75.00 150.00
7 Danny O'Connell 20.00 50.00
8 Andy Pafko 30.00 60.00
9 Warren Spahn 75.00 150.00
10 Jim Wilson 20.00 50.00

1954 Braves Spic and Span Postcards

This black and white set features only members of the Milwaukee Braves. The cards have postcard backs and measure approximately 3 11/16" by 6". The postcards were issued beginning in 1954. There is a facsimile autograph on the front in black or white ink. The set apparently was also issued with white borders in a 5" by 7" size. The catalog designation for this set is PC756. The front of each card shows the logo, "Spic and Span Dry Cleaners ... the Choice of Your Favorite Braves."

COMPLETE SET (18) 300.00 600.00
1 Henry Aaron 125.00 250.00
2 Joe Adcock 12.50 25.00
3 Billy Bruton 10.00 20.00
4 Bob Buhl 10.00 20.00
5 Lew Burdette 12.50 25.00
6 Gene Conley 10.00 20.00
7 Del Crandall 12.50 25.00
8 Ray Crone 7.50 15.00
9 Jack Dittmer 7.50 15.00
10 Ernie Johnson 10.00 20.00
11 Dave Jolly 7.50 15.00
12 Johnny Logan 10.00 20.00
13 Eddie Mathews 40.00 80.00
14 Chet Nichols 7.50 15.00
15 Danny O'Connell 7.50 15.00
16 Andy Pafko 10.00 20.00
17 Warren Spahn 40.00 80.00
18 Bobby Thomson 12.50 25.00

1955 Braves Golden Stamps

This 32-stamp set features color photos of the Milwaukee Braves and measures approximately 1 15/16" by 2 5/8". The stamps are designed to be placed in a 32-page album which measures approximately 8 3/8" by 10 15/16". The album contains black-and-white drawings of players with their batting averages and life stories. The team's history and other information is also printed in the album. The stamps are unnumbered and listed below according to where they fall in the album.

COMPLETE SET (32) 75.00 150.00
1 1954 Team Photo 5.00 10.00
2 Charlie Grimm MG 5.00 10.00
3 Warren Spahn 7.50 15.00
4 Lew Burdette 4.00 8.00
5 Chet Nichols 1.00 2.00
6 Gene Conley 1.00 2.00
7 Bob Buhl 1.00 2.00
8 Jim Wilson 1.00 2.00
9 Dave Jolly 1.00 2.00
10 Ernie Johnson 1.50 3.00
11 Joey Jay 1.50 3.00
12 Dave Koslo 1.00 2.00
13 Charlie Gorin 1.00 2.00
14 Ray Crone 1.00 2.00
15 Del Crandall 1.50 3.00
16 Joe Adcock 2.00 4.00
17 Jack Dittmer 1.00 2.00
18 Eddie Mathews 10.00 20.00
19 Johnny Logan 1.50 3.00
20 Andy Pafko 1.50 3.00
21 Bill Bruton 1.00 2.00
22 Bobby Thomson 2.00 4.00
23 Charlie White 1.00 2.00
24 Danny O'Connell 1.00 2.00
25 Henry Aaron 12.50 25.00
26 Jim Pendleton 1.00 2.00
27 George Metkovich 1.00 2.00
28 Mel Roach 1.00 2.00
29 John Cooney CO 1.00 2.00
30 Bucky Walters CO 1.50 3.00
31 Charles Lacks TR 1.00 2.00
32 Milwaukee County Stadium 5.00 10.00
XX Album 2.50 5.00

1955 Braves Johnston Cookies

The cards in this 35-card set measure approximately 2 3/4" by 4". This set of Milwaukee Braves issued in 1955 by Johnston Cookies are numbered by the uniform number of the player depicted, except for non-players Lacks, Lewis and Taylor. The cards were issued in strips of six which accounts for the rouletted edges found on single cards. They are larger in size than the two previous sets but are printed on thinner cardboard. Each player in the checklist has been marked to show on which panel or strip he appeared (Pafko appears twice). A complete panel of six cards is worth 25 percent more than the sum of the individual players. The catalog designation for this set is D356-3.

COMPLETE SET (35) 500.00 1000.00
1 Del Crandall P1 12.50 25.00
3 Jim Pendleton P3 7.50 15.00
4 Danny O'Connell P1 7.50 15.00
6 Jack Dittmer P6 7.50 15.00
9 Joe Adcock P2 12.50 25.00
10 Bob Buhl P6 10.00 20.00
11 Phil Paine P5 7.50 15.00
12 Ray Crone P5 7.50 15.00
15 Charlie Gorin P1 7.50 15.00
16 Dave Jolly P4 7.50 15.00
17 Chet Nichols P2 7.50 15.00
18 Chuck Tanner P5 15.00 30.00
19 Jim Wilson P6 7.50 15.00
20 Dave Koslo P4 7.50 15.00
21 Warren Spahn P3 40.00 80.00
22 Gene Conley P3 10.00 20.00
23 Johnny Logan P4 12.50 25.00
24 Charlie White P2 7.50 15.00
28 Johnny Cooney CO P4 7.50 15.00
30 Roy Smalley P3 7.50 15.00
31 Bucky Walters CO P6 10.00 20.00
32 Ernie Johnson P5 10.00 20.00
33 Lew Burdette P1 12.50 25.00
34 Bobby Thomson P6 12.50 25.00
35 Bob Keely P1 7.50 15.00
38 Bill Bruton P4 10.00 20.00
39 George Crowe P3 7.50 15.00
40 Charlie Grimm MG P6 10.00 20.00
41 Eddie Mathews P5 40.00 80.00
44 Hank Aaron P1 200.00 400.00
47 Joey Jay P2 10.00 20.00
48 Andy Pafko P2 P4 10.00 20.00
49 Dr. Charles Leaks P2/(Unnumbered) 7.50 15.00
50 Duffy Lewis P5 10.00 20.00
Trav.Sec./(Unnumbered)
51 Joe Taylor P3/(Unnumbered) 7.50 15.00

1955 Braves Spic and Span Die-Cut

This 18-card, die-cut, set features only members of the Milwaukee Braves. Each player measures differently according to the pose but they are, on average, approximately 8" by 8". The cards could be folded together to stand up. Each card contains a logo in the middle at the bottom and a copyright notice, "1955 Spic and Span Cleaners" in the lower right corner.

COMPLETE SET (18) 2000.00 4000.00
1 Hank Aaron 500.00 1000.00
2 Joe Adcock 100.00 200.00
3 Billy Bruton 60.00 120.00
4 Bob Buhl 60.00 120.00
5 Lew Burdette 100.00 200.00
6 Gene Conley 60.00 120.00
7 Del Crandall 100.00 200.00
8 Jack Dittmer 60.00 120.00
9 Ernie Johnson 75.00 150.00
10 Dave Jolly 60.00 120.00
11 Johnny Logan 75.00 150.00
12 Eddie Mathews 200.00 400.00
13 Chet Nichols 60.00 120.00
14 Danny O'Connell 60.00 120.00
15 Andy Pafko 75.00 150.00
16 Warren Spahn 200.00 400.00
17 Bob Thomson 100.00 200.00
18 Jim Wilson 60.00 120.00

1956-60 Braves Bill and Bob Postcards PPC-741

The Bill and Bob postcards issued during the 1956-60 time period features only Milwaukee Braves. The cards are unnumbered, other than the K card number at the middle base on the reverse, and present some of the most attractive color postcards issued in the postwar period. Three poses of Adcock and two poses each of Bruton and Crandall exist. The Torre card has been seen with a Pepsi advertisment on the reverse. The complete set price includes only one of each player.

COMPLETE SET (15) 600.00 1200.00
1 Hank Aaron 200.00 400.00
2 Joe Adcock (3) 25.00 50.00
3 Bill Bruton (2) 30.00 60.00
4 Bob Buhl 12.50 25.00
5 Lew Burdette 25.00 50.00
6 Gene Conley 20.00 40.00
7 Wes Covington 20.00 40.00
8 Del Crandall (2) 12.50 25.00
9 Chuck Dressen MG 20.00 40.00
10 Charlie Grimm MG 30.00 60.00
11 Fred Haney MG 25.00 50.00
12 Bobby Keely CO 12.50 25.00
13 Ed Mathews 75.00 150.00
14 Warren Spahn 75.00 150.00
15 Frank Torre 30.00 60.00

1957 Braves 8x10

This 12-card set features reddish sepia portraits of the Milwaukee Braves in a combination of photos and drawings printed on a yellowish card. The backs are blank. The cards are unnumbered and checklisted below in alphabetical order.

COMPLETE SET (12) 75.00 150.00
1 Joe Adcock 7.50 15.00
2 Bill Bruton 6.00 12.00
3 Bob Buhl 6.00 12.00
4 Lew Burdette 7.50 15.00
5 Del Crandall 6.00 12.00
6 Johnny Logan 6.00 12.00
7 Ed Mathews 12.50 25.00
8 Danny O'Connell 5.00 10.00
9 Andy Pafko 6.00 12.00
10 Jim Pendleton 5.00 10.00
11 Warren Spahn 15.00 30.00
12 Bob Thomson 7.50 15.00

1957 Braves Spic and Span 4x5

This set contains 20 black and white photos each with a blue-printed message such as "Stay in There and Pitch" and blue facsimile autograph The set features only members of the Milwaukee Braves. Red Schoendienst was traded to the Braves on June 15, 1957 in exchange for Danny O'Connell, Ray Crone, and Bobby Thomson. Wes Covington, Felix Mantilla, and Bob Trowbridge are also listed as shorter-printed (SP) cards as they were apparently mid-season call-ups. The cards are approximately 4 5/16" by 5" with a thick white border and are blank backed. Spic and Span appears in blue in the white border in the lower right corner of the card. Since the cards are unnumbered, they are numbered in alphabetical order in the checklist below.

COMPLETE SET (20) 250.00 500.00
COMMON CARD (1-20) 5.00 10.00
COMMON CARD SP 12.50 25.00
1 Henry Aaron 75.00 150.00
2 Joe Adcock 7.50 15.00
3 Billy Bruton 6.00 12.00
4 Bob Buhl 6.00 12.00
5 Lew Burdette 7.50 15.00
6 Gene Conley 6.00 12.00
7 Wes Covington SP 15.00 30.00
8 Del Crandall 7.50 15.00

9 Ray Crone 5.00 10.00
10 Fred Haney MG 5.00 10.00
11 Ernie Johnson 6.00 12.00
12 Johnny Logan 6.00 12.00
13 Felix Mantilla SP 12.50 25.00
14 Ed Mathews 25.00 50.00
15 Danny O'Connell 5.00 10.00
16 Andy Pafko 6.00 12.00
17 Red Schoendienst SP 30.00 60.00
18 Warren Spahn 25.00 50.00
19 Bobby Thomson 7.50 15.00
20 Bob Trowbridge SP 12.50 25.00

1958 Braves Jay Publishing

This 12-card set of the Milwaukee Braves measures approximately 5" by 7" and features black-and-white player photos in a white border. These cards were packaged 12 to a packet. The backs are blank. The cards are unnumbered and checklisted below in alphabetical order.

COMPLETE SET (12) 30.00 60.00
1 Hank Aaron 7.50 15.00
2 Joe Adcock 2.50 5.00
3 Lew Burdette 2.50 5.00
4 Wes Covington 2.00 4.00
5 Del Crandall 1.50 3.00
6 Robert Hazle 1.50 3.00
7 John Logan 1.50 3.00
8 Eddie Mathews 5.00 10.00
9 Donald McMahon 1.50 3.00
10 Andy Pafko 1.50 3.00
11 Red Schoendienst 4.00 8.00
12 Warren Spahn 5.00 10.00

1959 Braves Jay Publishing

This 12-card set of the Milwaukee Braves measures approximately 5" by 7" and features black-and-white player photos in a white border. These cards were packaged 12 to a packet. The backs are blank. The cards are unnumbered and checklisted below in alphabetical order.

COMPLETE SET 40.00
1 Joe Adcock 2.00 5.00
2 Billy Bruton 1.25 3.00
3 Wes Covington 1.25 3.00
4 Johnny Logan 1.50 4.00
5 Stan Lopata 1.25 3.00
6 Eddie Mathews 3.00 8.00
7 Don McMahon 1.25 3.00
8 Del Rice 1.25 3.00
9 Mel Roach 1.25 3.00
10 Bob Rush 1.25 3.00
11 Bob Trowbridge 1.25 3.00
12 Casey Wise 1.25 3.00

1960 Braves Davison's

These cards measure approximately 3" by 3 5/8" and features black-and-white player photos. The cards are unnumbered and checklisted below in alphabetical order. The checklist may be incomplete and additions are welcome.

COMPLETE SET 20.00 50.00
1 Hank Aaron 12.50 30.00
2 Eddie Mathews 8.00 20.00

1960 Braves Jay Publishing

This 12-card set of the Milwaukee Braves measures approximately 5" by 7" and features black-and-white player photos in a white border. These cards were packaged 12 to a packet. The backs are blank. The cards are unnumbered and checklisted below in alphabetical order.

COMPLETE SET (12) 15.00 40.00
1 Hank Aaron 4.00 10.00
2 Billy Bruton 1.25 3.00
3 Wes Covington 1.25 3.00
4 Charlie Dressen MG 1.25 3.00
5 Bob Giggie .75 2.00
6 Joey Jay 1.25 3.00
7 Stan Lopata .75 2.00
8 Felix Mantilla .75 2.00
9 Bob Rush .75 2.00
10 Red Schoendienst 1.50 4.00
11 Warren Spahn 3.00 8.00
12 Frank Torre 1.25 3.00

1960 Braves Lake to Lake

The cards in this 28-card set measure 2 1/2" by 3 1/4". The 1960 Lake to Lake set of unnumbered, blue tinted cards features Milwaukee Braves players only. For some reason, this set of Braves does not include Eddie Mathews. The cards were issued on milk cartons by Lake to Lake Dairy. Most cards have staple holes in the upper right corner. The backs are in red and give details and prizes associated with the card promotion. Cards with staple holes can be considered very good to excellent at best. The catalog designation for this set is F102-1.

COMPLETE SET (28) 600.00 1200.00
1 Hank Aaron 200.00 400.00
2 Joe Adcock 10.00 25.00
3 Ray Boone 60.00 120.00
4 Bill Bruton 150.00 300.00
5 Bob Buhl 8.00 20.00
6 Lew Burdette 10.00 25.00
7 Chuck Cottier 6.00 15.00
8 Wes Covington 8.00 20.00
9 Del Crandall 10.00 25.00
10 Chuck Dressen MG 8.00 20.00
11 Bob Giggie 6.00 15.00
12 Joey Jay 8.00 20.00
13 Johnny Logan 8.00 20.00
14 Felix Mantilla 6.00 15.00
15 Lee Maye 6.00 15.00
16 Don McMahon 6.00 15.00
17 George Myatt CO 6.00 15.00
18 Andy Pafko CO 8.00 20.00
19 Juan Pizarro 6.00 15.00
20 Mel Roach 6.00 15.00
21 Bob Rush 6.00 15.00
22 Bob Scheffing CO 6.00 15.00
23 Red Schoendienst 15.00 40.00
24 Warren Spahn 40.00 80.00
25 Al Spangler 6.00 15.00
26 Frank Torre 8.00 20.00
27 Carlton Willey 6.00 15.00
28 Whit Wyatt CO 8.00 20.00

1960 Braves Spic and Span

This set features only members of the Milwaukee Braves. These small cards each measure approximately 2 13/16" by 3 1/16". The cards have a thin white border around a black and white photo with no other writing or words on the front. The card backs have the Spic and Span logo at the bottom along with "Photographed and Autographed Exclusively for Spic and Span". A message and facsimile autograph from the player is presented inside a square box all in blue on the card back.

COMPLETE SET (27) 250.00 500.00
1 Henry Aaron 75.00 150.00
2 Joe Adcock 6.00 15.00
3 Billy Bruton 5.00 12.00
4 Bob Buhl 5.00 12.00
5 Lew Burdette 6.00 15.00
6 Chuck Cottier 4.00 10.00
7A Del Crandall ERR/(Reversed negative) 20.00 50.00
7B Del Crandall COR 6.00 15.00
8 Charlie Dressen MG 5.00 12.00
9 Joey Jay 5.00 12.00
10 Johnny Logan 5.00 12.00
11 Felix Mantilla 4.00 10.00
12 Ed Mathews 20.00 50.00
13 Lee Maye 4.00 10.00
14 Don McMahon 4.00 10.00
15 George Myatt CO 4.00 10.00
16 Andy Pafko CO 5.00 12.00
17 Juan Pizarro 4.00 10.00
18 Mel Roach 4.00 10.00
19 Bob Rush 4.00 10.00
20 Bob Scheffing CO 4.00 10.00
21 Red Schoendienst 8.00 20.00
22 Warren Spahn 20.00 50.00
23 Al Spangler 4.00 10.00
24 Frank Torre 5.00 12.00
25 Carl Willey 4.00 10.00
26 Whit Wyatt CO 5.00 12.00

1962 Braves Jay Publishing

This 12-card set of the Milwaukee Braves measures approximately 5" by 7". The fronts feature black-and-white posed player photos with the player's and team name printed below in the white border. These cards were packaged 12 to a packet. The backs are blank. The cards are unnumbered and checklisted below in alphabetical order.

COMPLETE SET (12) 20.00 50.00
1 Hank Aaron 6.00 15.00
2 Joe Adcock 1.50 4.00
3 Frank Bolling .75 2.00
4 Lou Burdette 1.50 4.00
5 Del Crandall 1.50 4.00
6 Eddie Mathews 3.00 8.00
7 Lee Maye .75 2.00
8 Roy McMillan 1.25 3.00
9 Warren Spahn 3.00 8.00
10 George (Birdie) Tebbetts MG .75 2.00
11 Joe Torre 2.00 5.00
12 Carl Willey .75 2.00

1963 Braves Jay Publishing

This set of the Milwaukee Braves measures approximately 5" by 7". The fronts feature black-and-white posed player photos with the player's and team name printed below in the white border. These cards were packaged 12 to a packet. The backs are blank. The cards are unnumbered and checklisted below in alphabetical order. More than the standard 12 cards are listed as the Braves updated this set throughout the 1963 season.

COMPLETE SET 30.00 60.00
1 Hank Aaron 6.00 15.00
2 Tommie Aaron 1.25 3.00
3 Gus Bell 1.25 3.00
4 Frank Bolling .75 2.00
5 Lew Burdette 1.50 4.00
6 Cecil Butler .75 2.00
7 Tony Cloninger 1.25 3.00
8 Jim Constable .75 2.00
9 Del Crandall 1.25 3.00
10 Frank Funk .75 2.00
11 Bob Hendley .75 2.00
12 Norm Larker .75 2.00
13 Eddie Mathews 4.00 10.00
14 Roy McMillan .75 2.00
15 Denis Menke .75 2.00
16 Ron Piche .75 2.00
17 Claude Raymond .75 2.00
18 Amado Samuel .75 2.00
19 Bob Shaw .75 2.00
20 Warren Spahn 4.00 10.00
21 Joe Torre 2.50 6.00
22 Bob Uecker 2.00 5.00

1964 Braves Jay Publishing

This 12-card set of the Milwaukee Braves measures approximately 5" by 7". The fronts feature black-and-white posed player photos with the player's and team name printed below in the white border. These cards were packaged 12 to a packet. The backs are blank. The cards are unnumbered and checklisted below in alphabetical order.

COMPLETE SET (12) 20.00 50.00
1 Hank Aaron 6.00 15.00
2 Frank Bolling .75 2.00
3 Bobby Bragan MG .75 2.00
4 Tony Cloninger .75 2.00
5 Denny Lemaster .75 2.00
6 Eddie Mathews 4.00 10.00
7 Lee Maye .75 2.00
8 Roy McMillan 1.25 3.00
9 Denis Menke .75 2.00
10 Bob Sadowski .75 2.00
11 Warren Spahn 4.00 10.00
12 Joe Torre 2.00 5.00

1965 Braves Jay Publishing

This 12-card set of the Milwaukee Braves measures approximately 5" by 7". The fronts feature black-and-white posed player photos with the player's and team name printed below in the white border. These cards were packaged 12 to a packet. The backs are blank. The cards are unnumbered and checklisted below in alphabetical order. 1965 would prove to be the Braves final season in Milwaukee.

COMPLETE SET (12) 20.00 50.00
1 Hank Aaron 6.00 15.00
2 Wade Blasingame .75 2.00
3 Frank Bolling .75 2.00
4 Bobby Bragan MG .75 2.00
5 Hank Fischer .75 2.00
6 Mack Jones .75 2.00
7 Denny LeMaster .75 2.00
8 Eddie Mathews 3.00 8.00
9 Phil Niekro 4.00 10.00
10 Billy O'Dell .75 2.00
11 Dan Osinski .75 2.00
12 Joe Torre 2.50 6.00

1965 Braves Team Issue

This 12-card set of the 1965 Milwaukee Braves measures approximately 4 7/8" by 7 1/8" and features black-and-white player photos with white borders. The backs are blank. The cards are unnumbered and checklisted below in alphabetical order.

COMPLETE SET (12) 8.00 20.00
1 Sandy Alomar .75 2.00
2 Frank Bolling .75 2.00
3 Ty Cline .75 2.00
4 Mike De La Hoz .75 2.00
5 Hank Fischer .75 2.00
6 Mack Jones .75 2.00
7 Gary Kolb .75 2.00
8 Billy O'Dell .75 2.00
9 Chi Chi Olivo .75 2.00
10 Dan Osinski .75 2.00
11 Bob Sadowski .75 2.00
12 Bob Tiefenauer .75 2.00

1966 Braves Postcards

This 27-card set of the Atlanta Braves features black-and-white player portraits in white borders and measures approximately 4" by 5". The backs are blank. The cards are unnumbered and checklisted below in alphabetical order.

COMPLETE SET (27) 100.00 200.00
1 Hank Aaron 12.50 30.00
2 Ted Abernathy 3.00 8.00
3 Felipe Alou 5.00 12.00
4 Wade Blasingame 3.00 8.00
5 Frank Bolling 3.00 8.00
6 Bobby Bragan MG 4.00 10.00
7 Clay Carroll 3.00 8.00
8 Rico Carty 4.00 10.00
9 Tony Cloninger 3.00 8.00
10 Mike de la Hoz 3.00 8.00
11 Gary Geiger 3.00 8.00
12 John Herrnstein 3.00 8.00
13 Billy Hitchcock CO 3.00 8.00
14 Ken Johnson 3.00 8.00
15 Mack Jones 3.00 8.00
16 Denver Lemaster 3.00 8.00
17 Eddie Mathews 10.00 25.00
18 Denis Menke 3.00 8.00
19 Felix Millan 4.00 10.00
20 Gene Oliver 3.00 8.00
21 Grover Resinger CO 3.00 8.00
22 Dan Schneider 3.00 8.00
23 Ken Silvestri 3.00 8.00
24 Joe Torre 8.00 20.00
25 Arnold Umbach 3.00 8.00
26 Jo Jo White CO 3.00 8.00
27 Whitlow Wyatt CO 4.00 10.00

1966 Braves Volpe

These 12 cards, which measure 8 1/2" by 11" feature members of the 1966 Atlanta Braves in their first year in Atlanta. These cards are unnumbered, so we have sequenced them in alphabetical order. The fronts feature drawings of the players while the back has biographical information, information blurbs and career statistics.

COMPLETE SET 60.00 120.00
1 Hank Aaron 12.50 30.00
2 Felipe Alou 5.00 12.00
3 Frank Bolling 3.00 8.00
4 Bobby Bragan MG 3.00 8.00
5 Rico Carty 4.00 10.00
6 Tony Cloninger 3.00 8.00
7 Mack Jones 3.00 8.00
8 Denny Lemaster 3.00 8.00
9 Eddie Mathews 8.00 20.00
10 Denis Menke 3.00 8.00
11 Lee Thomas 3.00 8.00
12 Joe Torre 5.00 12.00

1967 Braves Irvingdale Dairy

Four Atlanta Braves were featured on the back of one milk carton. If each player photo were cut, it would measure 1 3/4" by 2 5/8". The fronts feature a brown-tinted head-and-shoulders shot, with the player's name below. The backs are blank. The cards are unnumbered and checklisted below in alphabetical order.

COMPLETE SET (4) 150.00 300.00
1 Clete Boyer 50.00 100.00
2 Mack Jones 30.00 60.00
3 Denis Menke 30.00 60.00
4 Joe Torre 60.00 120.00

1967 Braves Photos

These photos were issued by the Atlanta Braves and features members of the 1967 Braves. The tops are black and white portrait photos with the players name on the bottom. The backs are blank so we have sequenced these cards in alphabetical order.

COMPLETE SET (29) 100.00 200.00
1 Hank Aaron 8.00 20.00
2 Felipe Alou 4.00 10.00
3 Wade Blasingame 2.00 5.00
4 Clete Boyer 3.00 8.00
5 Bob Bruce 2.00 5.00
6 Clay Carroll 2.00 5.00
7 Rico Carty 3.00 8.00
8 Ty Cline 2.00 5.00
9 Tony Cloninger 2.00 5.00
10 Mike de la Hoz 2.00 5.00
11 Gary Geiger 2.00 5.00
12 Ramon Hernandez 2.00 5.00
13 Billy Hitchcock MG 2.00 5.00
14 Pat Jarvis 2.00 5.00
15 Ken Johnson 2.00 5.00
16 Mack Jones 2.00 5.00
17 Dick Kelley 2.00 5.00
18 Bob Kennedy CO 2.00 5.00
19 Denver Lemaster 2.00 5.00
20 Orlando Martinez 2.00 5.00
21 Denis Menke 2.00 5.00
22 Felix Millan 2.00 5.00
23 Phil Niekro 8.00 20.00
24 Gene Oliver 2.00 5.00
25 Jay Ritchie 2.00 5.00
26 Joe Torre 8.00 20.00
27 Ken Silvestri CO 2.00 5.00
28 Woody Woodward 2.00 5.00
29 Whitlow Wyatt CO 3.00 8.00

1968 Braves Postcards

This 33-card set of the Atlanta Braves features black-and-white player portraits with white borders. The backs are blank. The cards are unnumbered and checklisted below in alphabetical order.

COMPLETE SET (33) 100.00 200.00
1 Hank Aaron 8.00 20.00
2 Tommie Aaron 2.50 6.00
3 Felipe Alou 3.00 8.00
4 Clete Boyer 2.50 6.00
5 Jim Britton 2.00 5.00
6 Jim Busby CO 2.00 5.00
7 Clay Carroll 2.00 5.00
8 Rico Carty 2.50 6.00
9 Tony Cloninger 2.00 5.00
10 Harry Dorish CO 2.00 5.00
11 Tito Francona 2.00 5.00
12 Billy Goodman CO 2.00 5.00
13 Luman Harris MG 2.00 5.00
14 Sonny Jackson 2.00 5.00
15 Pat Jarvis 2.00 5.00
16 Bob Johnson 2.00 5.00
17 Deron Johnson 2.00 5.00
18 Ken Johnson 2.00 5.00
19 Dick Kelley 2.00 5.00
20 Mike Lum 2.00 5.00
21 Marty Martinez 2.00 5.00
22 Felix Millan 2.50 6.00
23 Phil Niekro 6.00 15.00
24 Mike Page 2.00 5.00
25 Milt Pappas 2.50 6.00
26 Claude Raymond 2.00 5.00
27 Ron Reed 2.00 5.00
28 Ken Silvestri CO 2.00 5.00
29 George Stone 2.00 5.00
30 Bob Tillman 2.00 5.00
31 Joe Torre 5.00 12.00
32 Bob Uecker 3.00 8.00
33 Cecil Upshaw 2.00 5.00

1969 Braves Birthday Party Photo Stamps

This 25-stamp set was distributed as one sheet of postage-size stamps and features black-and-white portraits of the Atlanta Braves. The stamps are unnumbered and checklisted below in alphabetical order.

COMPLETE SET (25) 50.00 100.00
1 Hank Aaron/(dark photo) 8.00 20.00
2 Hank Aaron/(light photo) 8.00 20.00
3 Tommie Aaron 1.50 4.00
4 Clete Boyer 1.50 4.00
5 Rico Carty 1.50 4.00
6 Orlando Cepeda 3.00 8.00
7 Bob Didier 1.25 3.00
8 Ralph Garr 2.00 5.00
9 Gil Garrido 1.25 3.00
10 Tony Gonzalez 1.25 3.00
11 Luman Harris MG 1.25 3.00
12 Sonny Jackson 1.25 3.00
13 Pat Jarvis 1.25 3.00
14 Larry Jaster 1.25 3.00
15 Mike Lum 1.25 3.00
16 Felix Millan 1.50 4.00
17 Jim Nash 1.25 3.00
18 Phil Niekro 3.00 8.00
19 Milt Pappas 1.50 4.00
20 Ron Reed 1.25 3.00
21 George Stone 1.25 3.00
22 Bob Tillman 1.25 3.00
23 Cecil Upshaw 1.25 3.00
24 Hoyt Wilhelm 2.50 6.00
25 Title Stamp 1.25 3.00

1970 Braves Stamps

This eight-stamp set of the Atlanta Braves features black-and-white player portraits measuring approximately 1 1/4" by 1 3/4" with rounded corners. The stamps are unnumbered and checklisted below in alphabetical order.

COMPLETE SET (8) 10.00 25.00
1 Hank Aaron 4.00 10.00
2 Rico Carty 1.25 3.00
3 Orlando Cepeda 2.50 6.00
4 Luman Harris MG .75 2.00
5 Pat Jarvis .75 2.00
6 Felix Millan 1.25 3.00
7 Cecil Upshaw .75 2.00
8 Hoyt Wilhelm 2.00 5.00

1974 Braves Photo Cards

This set of six photo cards was produced by the Atlanta Braves Sales Department. The photos were included in a special brochure promoting the 1974 season. The photo cards measure approximately 7" by 7 1/2" and feature full-bleed color portraits of the Braves' star players. A player autograph facsimile is superimposed on the photo in the upper left corner in white lettering. The backs have a ghosted baseball icon with the words "take 'em out to..." in bold black lettering in the upper left corner. Each card has promotional information regarding season tickets or player highlights from previous seasons. The cards are unnumbered and checklisted below alphabetically.

COMPLETE SET (6) 8.00 20.00
1 Hank Aaron 3.00 8.00
2 Dusty Baker 1.50 4.00
3 Darrell Evans 1.25 3.00
4 Eddie Mathews MG 2.00 5.00
5 Phil Niekro 2.50 6.00
6 Johnny Oates .75 2.00

1974 Braves Team Issue

These 7" by 9" blank-backed full color photos feature members of the Atlanta Braves. The fronts have a full color photo with the players name and team on the bottom. There may be more players in this set so all additions are appreciated. Since these are unnumbered, we have sequenced these photos in alphabetical order.

COMPLETE SET 6.00 15.00
1 Dusty Baker 1.25 3.00
2 Darrell Evans 1.25 3.00
3 Ralph Garr .75 2.00
4 Dave Johnson 1.25 3.00
5 Phil Niekro 2.00 5.00

1975 Braves Postcards

This 38-card set of the Atlanta Bravesw features player photos on postcard-size cards. The cards are unnumbered and checklisted below in alphabetical order.

COMPLETE SET (38) 8.00 20.00
1 Dusty Baker .40 1.00
2 Larvell Blanks .20 .50
3 Bob Beale .20 .50
4 Mike Beard .20 .50
5 Jim Busby CO .20 .50
6 Buzz Capra .20 .50
7 Vic Correll .20 .50
8 Bruce Dal Canton .20 .50
9 Jamie Easterly .20 .50
10 Darrell Evans .60 1.50
11 Ralph Garr .30 .75
12 Clarence Gaston .20 .50
13 Gary Gentry .20 .50
14 Rod Gilbreath .20 .50
15 Ed Goodson .20 .50
16 Eddie Haas CO .20 .50
17 Roric Harrison .20 .50
18 Tom House .20 .50
19 Clyde King .20 .50
20 Dave Johnson .60 1.50
21 Mike Lum .20 .50
22 Dave May .20 .50
23 Carl Morton .20 .50
24 Phil Niekro 1.50 4.00
25 Johnny Oates .20 .50
26 John Odom .20 .50
27 Rowland Office .20 .50
28 Marty Perez .20 .50
29 Biff Pocoroba .20 .50
30 Ron Reed .20 .50
31 Craig Robinson .20 .50
32 Ray Sadecki .20 .50
33 Ken Silvestri CO .20 .50
34 Elias Sosa .20 .50
35 Herm Starrette CO .20 .50
36 Frank Tepedino .30 .75
37 Mike Thompson .20 .50
38 Earl Williams .20 .50

1976 Braves Postcards

This 34-card set of the Atlanta Braves features player photos on postcard-size cards. The cards are unnumbered and checklisted below in alphabetical order.

COMPLETE SET (34) 8.00 20.00
1 Mike Beard .20 .50
2 Vern Benson CO .20 .50
3 Dave Bristol CO .20 .50
4 Chris Cannizzaro .20 .50
5 Buzz Capra .20 .50
6 Darrel Chaney .20 .50
7 Vic Correll .20 .50
8 Terry Crowley .20 .50
9 Bruce Dal Canton .20 .50
10 Adrian Devine .20 .50
11 Darrell Evans .60 1.50
12 Cito Gaston .20 .50
13 Rod Gilbreath .20 .50
14 Eddie Haas CO .20 .50
15 Ken Henderson .20 .50
16 Lee Lacy .20 .50
17 Max Leon .20 .50
18 Dave May .20 .50
19 Andy Messersmith .20 .50
20 Roger Moret .20 .50
21 Carl Morton .20 .50
22 Phil Niekro 1.50 4.00
23 Rowland Office .20 .50
24 Marty Perez .20 .50
25 Biff Pocoroba .20 .50
26 Luis Quintana .20 .50
27 Craig Robinson .20 .50
28 Jerry Royster .20 .50
29 Dick Ruthven .20 .50
30 Elias Sosa .20 .50
31 Herm Starrette CO .20 .50
32 Pablo Torrealba .20 .50
33 Earl Williams .20 .50
34 Jim Wynn .30 .75

1978 Braves Coke

This 14-card set of the Atlanta Braves measures approximately 3" by 4 1/4" and was sponsored by Coca-Cola and Atlanta Radio Station WPLO. The white fronts feature black-and-white drawings of player heads with the player's name and sponsor logos below. The backs carry the player's name, position, biography, and career information with the team and sponsor logos on a white background. The cards are unnumbered and checklisted below in alphabetical order. A poster was also made for this promotion, it has a value of $15.

COMPLETE SET (14) 8.00 20.00
1 Barry Bonnell .40 1.00
2 Jeff Burroughs .60 1.50
3 Rick Camp .40 1.00
4 Gene Garber .60 1.50
5 Rod Gilbreath .40 1.00
6 Bob Horner .75 2.00
7 Glenn Hubbard .40 1.00
8 Gary Matthews .75 2.00
9 Larry McWilliams .40 1.00
10 Dale Murphy 2.00 5.00
11 Phil Niekro 1.50 4.00
12 Rowland Office .40 1.00
13 Biff Pocoroba .40 1.00
14 Jerry Royster .40 1.00

1978 Braves TCC

These 16 standard-size cards feature past members of the Milwaukee Braves. Although the checklist mentions that uniform and card number are the same we have sequenced this set in alphabetical order.

COMPLETE SET (16) 3.00 8.00
1 Hank Aaron .75 2.00
2 Joe Adcock .30 .75
3 Billy Bruton .10 .25
4 Bob Buhl .10 .25
5 Lou Burdette .20 .50
6 Wes Covington .10 .25
7 Del Crandall .20 .50
8 Johnny Logan .10 .25
9 Eddie Mathews .40 1.00
10 Andy Pafko .10 .25
11 Red Schoendienst .30 .75
12 Warren Spahn .40 1.00
13 Joe Torre .50 1.25
14 Bob Uecker .40 1.00
15 Carl Willey .10 .25
16 Checklist .10 .25

1979 Braves Team Issue

These cards, issued on a light stock black and white, actually measure slightly smaller than a postcard. While many of the cards did have the players name printed on them, some did not. These cards are unnumbered so we have sequenced them in alphabetical order.

COMPLETE SET 10.00 25.00
1 Tommy Aaron CO .20 .50
2 Barry Bonnell .20 .50
3 Jeff Burroughs .30 .75
4 Bobby Cox MG Dark Background .30 .75
5 Bobby Cox MG White Background .30 .75
6 Bobby Dews CO .20 .50
7 Pepe Frias .20 .50
8 Gene Garber Portrait .20 .50
9 Gene Garber Kneeling .20 .50
10 Cito Gaston .20 .50
11 Alex Grammas CO .20 .50
12 Bob Horner .40 1.00
13 Glenn Hubbard .20 .50
14 Mike Lum Portrait .20 .50
15 Mike Lum Ready to hit .20 .50
16 Gary Matthews .30 .75
17 Gary Matthews Close up .30 .75
18 Rick Matula .20 .50
19 Joe McLaughlin .20 .50
20 Larry McWilliams .20 .50
21 Ed Miller .20 .50
22 Dale Murphy Name on Card 2.00 5.00
23 Dale Murphy No Name on Card 2.00 5.00
24 Phil Niekro Name on Card 1.25 3.00
25 Phil Niekro No Name on Card 1.25 3.00
26 Rowland Office .20 .50
27 Biff Pocoroba .20 .50
28 Jerry Royster .20 .50
29 Hank Small .20 .50
30 Charlie Spikes .20 .50

1980 Braves 1914 TCMA

This 33-card set features sepia tinted photos of the 1914 World Champion "Miracle Braves" with black-and-white designed borders. The backs carry player information and career statistics. We are missing cards number 31, we would appreciate any identification.

COMPLETE SET (32) 4.00 10.00
1 Joe Connolly .08 .25
2 Lefty Tyler .08 .25
3 Tom Hughes .08 .25
4 Hank Gowdy .20 .50
5 Gene Cocreham .08 .25
6 Larry Gilbert .08 .25
7 George Davis .08 .25
8 Hub Perdue .08 .25
9 Otto Hess
10 Clarence Kraft .08 .25
11 Tommy Griffith .08 .25
12 Johnny Evers .40 1.00
Ira Thomas
Bill Klem
Umpires
13 Oscar Dugey .08 .25
14 Josh Devore .08 .25
15 George Stallings MG .20 .50
16 Rabbit Maranville .40 1.00
17 Paul Strand .08 .25
18 Charlie Deal .08 .25
19 Dick Rudolph .20 .50
20 Butch Schmidt .08 .25
21 Johnny Evers .60 1.50
22 Dick Crutcher .08 .25
23 Possum Whitted .08 .25
24 Fred Mitchell CO .08 .25
25 Herbie Moran .08 .25
26 Bill James .08 .25
27 Ted Cather .08 .25
28 Red Smith .08 .25
29 Less Mann .08 .25
30 Herbie Moran .08 .25
Wally Schang
32 Johnny Evers MVP .20 .50
Receives Gift of Car
33 Jim Gainey .08 .25
Owner

1980 Braves 1957 TCMA

This 42-card set features photos of the 1957 Milwaukee Braves team with blue lettering. The backs carry player information.

COMPLETE SET (42) 10.00 25.00
1 Don McMahon .08 .25
2 Joey Jay .08 .25
3 Phil Paine .08 .25
4 Bob Trowbridge .08 .25
5 Bob Buhl .08 .25
6 Lew Burdette .30 .75
7 Ernie Johnson .08 .25
8 Ray Crone .08 .25
9 Taylor Phillips .08 .25
10 Johnny Logan .20 .50
11 Frank Torre .20 .50
12 John DeMerit .08 .25
13 Red Murff .08 .25
14 Nippy Jones .08 .25
15 Bobby Thomson .30 .75
16 Chuck Tanner .08 .25
17 Charlie Root .20 .50
18 Juan Pizarro .08 .25
19 Hawk Taylor .08 .25
20 Mel Roach .08 .25
21 Bob Hazle .08 .25
22 Del Rice .08 .25
23 Felix Mantilla .08 .25
24 Andy Pafko .20 .50
25 Del Crandall .20 .50
26 Wes Covington .08 .25
27 Eddie Mathews .75 2.00
28 Joe Adcock .40 1.00
29 Dick Cole .08 .25
30 Carl Sawatski .08 .25
31 Warren Spahn .75 2.00
32 Hank Aaron 2.00 5.00
33 Bob Keely .08 .25
34 Johnny Riddle CO .08 .25
35 Connie Ryan .08 .25
36 Harry Hanebrink .08 .25
37 Danny O'Connell .08 .25
38 Fred Haney MG .08 .25
39 Dave Jolly .08 .25
40 Red Schoendienst .60 1.50
41 Gene Conley .08 .25
42 Bill Bruton .20 .50

1981 Braves Police

The cards in this 27-card set measure approximately 2 5/8" by 4 1/8". This first Atlanta Police set features full color cards sponsored by the Braves, the Atlanta Police Department, Coca-Cola and Hostess. The cards are numbered by uniform number, which is contained on the front along with an Atlanta Police Athletic League logo, a black and white Braves logo, and a green bow in the upper right corner of the frameline. The backs feature brief player biographies, logos of Coke and Hostess, and Tips from the Braves. It is reported that 33,000 of these sets were printed. The Terry Harper card is supposed to be slightly more difficult to obtain than other cards in the set.

COMPLETE SET (27) 6.00 15.00
COMMON SP .40 1.00
1 Jerry Royster .08 .25
3 Dale Murphy 1.50 4.00
4 Biff Pocoroba .08 .25
5 Bob Horner .20 .50
6 Bobby Cox MG .40 1.00
9 Luis Gomez .08 .25
10 Chris Chambliss .20 .50
15 Bill Nahorodny .08 .25
16 Rafael Ramirez .08 .25
17 Glenn Hubbard .08 .25
18 Claudell Washington .20 .50
19 Terry Harper SP .40 1.00
20 Bruce Benedict .08 .25
24 John Montefusco .08 .25
25 Rufino Linares .08 .25
26 Gene Garber .20 .50
30 Brian Asselstine .08 .25
34 Larry Bradford .08 .25
35 Phil Niekro 1.00 2.50
37 Rick Camp .08 .25
39 Al Hrabosky .20 .50
40 Tommy Boggs .08 .25
42 Rick Mahler .08 .25
44 Hank Aaron CO 1.50 4.00
45 Ed Miller .08 .25
46 Gaylord Perry 1.00 2.50
49 Preston Hanna .08 .25

1982 Braves Burger King Lids

The cards in this 27-card set measure 3 11/16" diameter. During the summer of 1982, the Atlanta-area chain of Burger King restaurants issued a series of 27 "Collector Lids" in honor of the Atlanta Braves baseball team. A special cup listing the scores of the Braves 13-game season-opening win streak and crowned by a baseball player lid was given with the purchase of a large Coca-Cola. The black and white player photos are printed on a sturdy, glazed cardboard disc, the edges of which are attached to a red plastic rim. These lids are blank backed. The individual's name, height, weight and 1981 record are listed, but the lids are not numbered. The MLB and Burger King logos, as well as the Coca-Cola TM line also appear on the disc.

COMPLETE SET (27) 15.00 40.00
1 Bruce Benedict .40 1.00
2 Steve Bedrosian .75 2.00
3 Tommy Boggs .40 1.00
4 Brett Butler 1.50 4.00
5 Rick Camp .40 1.00
6 Chris Chambliss .75 2.00
7 Ken Dayley .40 1.00
8 Gene Garber .60 1.50
9 Preston Hanna .40 1.00
10 Terry Harper .40 1.00
11 Bob Horner .60 1.50
12 Al Hrabosky .60 1.50
13 Glenn Hubbard .40 1.00
14 Randy Johnson .40 1.00
15 Rufino Linares .40 1.00
16 Rick Mahler .40 1.00
17 Larry McWilliams .40 1.00
18 Dale Murphy 6.00 15.00
19 Phil Niekro 3.00 8.00
20 Biff Pocoroba .40 1.00
21 Rafael Ramirez .40 1.00
22 Jerry Royster .40 1.00
23 Ken Smith .40 1.00
24 Bob Walk .40 1.00
25 Claudell Washington .60 1.50
26 Bob Watson .75 2.00
27 Larry Whisenton .40 1.00

1982 Braves Police

The cards in this 30-card set measure approximately 2 5/8" by 4 1/8". The Atlanta Police Department followed up on their successful 1981 safety set by publishing a new Braves set for 1982. Featured in excellent color photos are manager Joe Torre, 24 players, and 5 coaches. The cards are numbered, by uniform number, on the front only, while the backs contain a short biography of the individual and a Tips from the Braves section. The logos for the Atlanta PAL and the Braves appear on the front; those of Coca-Cola and Hostess are found on the back. A line commemorating Atlanta's record-shattering, season-beginning win streak is located in the upper right corner on every card obverse. The player list on the reverse of the Torre card is a roster list and not a checklist for the set. There were 8,000 sets reportedly printed. The Bob Watson card is supposedly more difficult to obtain than others in this set.

COMPLETE SET (30) 8.00 20.00
COMMON CARD .20 .50
COMMON SP 1.25 3.00
1 Jerry Royster .20 .50
3 Dale Murphy 2.00 5.00
4 Biff Pocoroba .20 .50
5 Bob Horner .30 .75
6 Randy Johnson .20 .50
8 Bob Watson SP 1.25 3.00
9 Joe Torre MG .60 1.50
10 Chris Chambliss .40 1.00
15 Claudell Washington .30 .75
16 Rafael Ramirez .20 .50
17 Glenn Hubbard .20 .50
20 Bruce Benedict .20 .50
22 Brett Butler 1.25 3.00
23 Tommy Aaron CO .30 .75
25 Rufino Linares .20 .50
26 Gene Garber .30 .75
27 Larry McWilliams .20 .50
28 Larry Whisenton .20 .50
32 Steve Bedrosian .60 1.50
35 Phil Niekro 1.25 3.00
37 Rick Camp .20 .50
38 Joe Cowley .20 .50
39 Al Hrabosky .30 .75
42 Rick Mahler .20 .50
43 Bob Walk .20 .50
45 Bob Gibson CO .60 1.50
49 Preston Hanna .20 .50
52 Joe Pignatano CO .20 .50
53 Dal Maxvill CO .20 .50
54 Rube Walker CO .20 .50

1982 Braves Team Issue

This set, which measures approximately 3" by 5" features members of the division winning Atlanta Braves team. The fronts have black and white photos on a glossy stock.Since these cards are unnumbered, we have sequenced them in alphabetical order.

COMPLETE SET (20) 5.00 12.00
1 Jose Alvarez .20 .50
2 Steve Bedrosian .60 1.50
3 Bruce Benedict .20 .50
4 Brett Butler .75 2.00
5 Rick Camp .20 .50
6 Joe Cowley .20 .50
7 Carlos Diaz .20 .50
8 Ken Dayley .20 .50
9 Terry Harper .20 .50
10 Randy Johnson .20 .50
11 Rufino Linares .20 .50
12 Rick Mahler .20 .50
13 Larry McWilliams .20 .50
14 Dale Murphy 1.00 2.50
15 Bob Porter .20 .50
16 Joe Torre MG .60 1.50
17 Bob Walk .20 .50
18 Bob Watson .30 .75
19 Larry Whisenton .20 .50
20 Chief Noc-a-homa MASCOT .20 .50

1983 Braves 53 Fritsch

This 32 card set measures approximately 2 5/8" by 3 3/4". These cards commemorated the 30th anniversary of the Braves move to Milwaukee. The player photos are surrounded by blue borders all the way around. They are identified in the bottom right corner. The backs have vital statistics and bulletpoint career highlights. The cards are numbered by uniform number.

COMPLETE SET (32) 4.00 10.00
1 Del Crandall .20 .50
2 Billy Klaus .08 .25
4 Sid Gordon .20 .50
6 Jack Dittmer .08 .25
9 Joe Adcock .30 .75
10 Bob Buhl .20 .50
11 Murray Wall .08 .25
13 Sibby Sisti .08 .25
14 Paul Burris .08 .25
16 Dave Jolly .08 .25
18 Bob Thorpe .08 .25
19 Jim Wilson .08 .25
20 Dick Donovan .08 .25
21 Warren Spahn 1.00 2.50
22 Virgil Jester .08 .25
23 Johnny Logan .20 .50
28 Johnny Cooney CO .08 .25
29 Luis Marquez .08 .25
30 Dave Cole .08 .25
31 Bucky Walters CO .20 .50
32 Ernie Johnson .08 .25
33 Lew Burdette .40 1.00
34 John Antonelli .20 .50
36 Max Surkont .08 .25
37 George Crowe .08 .25
38 Billy Bruton .20 .50
39 Walker Cooper .08 .25
41 Eddie Mathews 1.00 2.50
42 Ebba St. Claire .08 .25
43 Don Liddle .08 .25
48 Andy Pafko .20 .50
53 Jim Pendleton .08 .25

1983 Braves Police

The cards in this 30-card set measure approximately 2 5/8" by 4 1/8". For the third year in a row, the Atlanta Braves, in cooperation with the Atlanta Police Department, Coca-Cola, and Hostess, issued a full color safety set. The set features Joe Torre, five coaches, and 24 of the Atlanta Braves. Numbered only by uniform number, the statement that the Braves were the 1982 National League Western Division Champions is included on the fronts along with the Braves and Police Athletic biographies, a short narrative on the player, Tips from the Braves, and the Coke and Hostess logos.

COMPLETE SET (30) 6.00 15.00
1 Jerry Royster .08 .25
3 Dale Murphy 1.50 4.00
4 Biff Pocoroba .08 .25
5 Bob Horner .20 .50
6 Randy Johnson .08 .25
8 Bob Watson .30 .75
9 Joe Torre MG .40 1.00
10 Chris Chambliss .30 .75
11 Ken Smith .08 .25
15 Claudell Washington .20 .50
16 Rafael Ramirez .08 .25
17 Glenn Hubbard .08 .25
19 Terry Harper .08 .25
20 Bruce Benedict .08 .25
22 Brett Butler .60 1.50
24 Larry Owen .08 .25
26 Gene Garber .20 .50
27 Pascual Perez .08 .25
29 Craig McMurtry .08 .25
32 Steve Bedrosian .20 .50
33 Pete Falcone .08 .25
35 Phil Niekro .75 2.00
36 Sonny Jackson CO .08 .25
37 Rick Camp .08 .25
45 Bob Gibson CO .75 2.00
49 Rick Behenna .08 .25
51 Terry Forster .08 .25
52 Joe Pignatano CO .08 .25
53 Dal Maxvill CO .08 .25
54 Rube Walker CO .10 .25

1984 Braves Photos

These 31 photos were issued by the Braves and feature members of the 1984 Atlanta Braves. They are unnumbered so we have sequenced them in alphabetical order.

COMPLETE SET 8.00 20.00
1 Luke Appling CO .60 1.50
2 Len Barker .20 .50
3 Steve Bedrosian .30 .75
4 Bruce Benedict .20 .50
5 Rick Camp .20 .50
6 Chris Chambliss .30 .75
7 Jeff Dedmon .20 .50
8 Pete Falcone .20 .50
9 Terry Forster .20 .50
10 Gene Garber .30 .75
11 Bob Gibson CO .75 2.00
12 Terry Harper .20 .50
13 Bob Horner .20 .50
14 Glenn Hubbard .30 .75
15 Randy Johnson .20 .50
16 Brad Komminsk .20 .50
17 Rufino Linares .20 .50
18 Rick Mahler .20 .50
19 Dal Maxvill CO .20 .50
20 Craig McMurtry .20 .50
21 Dale Murphy 1.25 3.00
22 Ken Oberkfell .20 .50
23 Pascual Perez .20 .50
24 Gerald Perry .20 .50
25 Joe Pignatano CO .20 .50
26 Rafael Ramirez .20 .50
27 Jerry Royster .20 .50
28 Paul Runge .20 .50
29 Alex Trevino .20 .50
30 Claudell Washington .20 .50
31 Bob Watson .30 .75

1984 Braves Police

The cards in this 30-card set measure approximately 2 5/8" by 4 1/8". For the fourth straight year, the Atlanta Police Department issued a full color set of Atlanta Braves. The cards were given out two per week by Atlanta police officers. In addition to the police department, the set was sponsored by Coke and Hostess. The backs of the cards of Perez and Ramirez are in Spanish. The Joe Torre card contains the checklist.

COMPLETE SET (30) 4.00 10.00
1 Jerry Royster .08 .25
3 Dale Murphy 1.25 3.00
5 Bob Horner .20 .50
6 Randy Johnson .08 .25
8 Bob Watson .30 .75
9 Joe Torre MG/(Checklist back) .40 1.00
10 Chris Chambliss .20 .50
11 Mike Jorgensen .08 .25
15 Claudell Washington .20 .50
16 Rafael Ramirez .08 .25
17 Glenn Hubbard .08 .25
19 Terry Harper .08 .25
20 Bruce Benedict .08 .25
25 Alex Trevino .08 .25
26 Gene Garber .20 .50
27 Pascual Perez .08 .25
28 Gerald Perry .08 .25
29 Craig McMurtry .08 .25
31 Donnie Moore .08 .25
32 Steve Bedrosian .20 .50
33 Pete Falcone .08 .25
37 Rick Camp .08 .25
39 Len Barker .08 .25
42 Rick Mahler .08 .25
45 Bob Gibson CO .75 2.00
51 Terry Forster .08 .25
52 Joe Pignatano CO .08 .25
53 Dal Maxvill CO .08 .25
54 Rube Walker CO .08 .25
55 Luke Appling CO .60 1.50

1985 Braves Hostess

The cards in this 22 standard-size set features players of the Atlanta Braves. Cards were produced by Topps for Hostess (Continental Baking Co.) and are quite attractive. The card backs are similar in design to the 1985 Topps regular issue; however all photos are different from those that Topps used as these were apparently taken during Spring Training. Cards were available in boxes of Hostess products in packs of four (three players and a contest card). Other than the manager card, the rest of the set is ordered and numbered alphabetically.

COMPLETE SET (22) 3.00 8.00
1 Eddie Haas MG .08 .25
2 Len Barker .08 .25
3 Steve Bedrosian .20 .50
4 Bruce Benedict .08 .25
5 Rick Camp .08 .25
6 Rick Cerone .08 .25
7 Chris Chambliss .20 .50
8 Terry Forster .08 .25
9 Gene Garber .20 .50
10 Albert Hall .08 .25
11 Bob Horner .20 .50
12 Glenn Hubbard .08 .25
13 Brad Komminsk .08 .25
14 Rick Mahler .08 .25
15 Craig McMurtry .08 .25
16 Dale Murphy .40 1.00
17 Ken Oberkfell .08 .25
18 Pascual Perez .08 .25
19 Gerald Perry .08 .25
20 Rafael Ramirez .08 .25
21 Bruce Sutter .60 1.50
22 Claudell Washington .20 .50

1985 Braves Police

The cards in this 30-card set measure 2 5/8" by 4 1/8". For the fifth straight year, the Atlanta Police Department issued a full color set of Atlanta Braves. The set was also sponsored by Coca Cola and Hostess. In the upper right of the obverse is a logo commemorating the 20th anniversary of the Braves in Atlanta. Cards are numbered by uniform number. Cards feature a safety tip on the back. Each card except for Manager Haas has an interesting "Did You Know" fact about the player.

COMPLETE SET (30) 4.00 10.00
2 Albert Hall .08 .25
3 Dale Murphy 1.25 3.00
5 Rick Cerone .08 .25
7 Bobby Wine CO .08 .25
10 Chris Chambliss .20 .50
11 Bob Horner .20 .50
12 Paul Runge .08 .25
15 Claudell Washington .20 .50
16 Rafael Ramirez .08 .25
17 Glenn Hubbard .08 .25
18 Paul Zuvella .08 .25
19 Terry Harper .08 .25
20 Bruce Benedict .08 .25
22 Eddie Haas MG .08 .25
24 Ken Oberkfell .08 .25
26 Gene Garber .20 .50
27 Pascual Perez .08 .25
28 Gerald Perry .08 .25
29 Craig McMurtry .08 .25
32 Steve Bedrosian .20 .50
33 Johnny Sain CO .30 .75
34 Zane Smith .20 .50
36 Brad Komminsk .08 .25
37 Rick Camp .08 .25
39 Len Barker .08 .25
40 Bruce Sutter .60 1.50
42 Rick Mahler .08 .25
51 Terry Forster .08 .25
52 Leo Mazzone CO .08 .25
53 Bobby Dews CO .08 .25

1985 Braves TBS America's Team

This set features four close-up headshots on painted backgrounds. The photos measure 8 1/4" X 10 3/4". In a star-studded rectangular box, the words "America's Team" are emblazoned across the bottom of each picture. The horizontally oriented backs have biography and statistics for the last three seasons (1982-84). The photos are unnumbered and checklisted below alphabetically.

COMPLETE SET (4) 2.50 6.00
1 Brad Komminsk .40 1.00
2 Dale Murphy 1.50 4.00
3 Bruce Sutter 1.25 3.00
4 Claudell Washington .60 1.50

1986 Braves Greats TCMA

This 12-card standard-size set features leading Braves players from all three cities (Boston, Atlanta and Milwaukee). The fronts have player photos, while the backs have a biography, and career statistics.

COMPLETE SET (12) 2.50 6.00
1 Joe Adcock .20 .50
2 Felix Millan .08 .25
3 Rabbit Maranville .40 1.00
4 Eddie Mathews .60 1.50
5 Hank Aaron 1.25 3.00
6 Wally Berger .20 .50
7 Tommy Holmes .20 .50
8 Del Crandall .20 .50
9 Warren Spahn .60 1.50
10 Charles Kid Nichols .30 .75
11 Cecil Upshaw .08 .25
12 Fred Haney MG .08 .25

1986 Braves Police

This 30-card safety set was also sponsored by Coca-Cola. The backs contain the usual biographical info and safety tip. The front features a full-color photo of the player, his name, and uniform number. The cards measure 2 5/8" by 4 1/8". Cards were freely distributed throughout the summer by the Police Departments in the Atlanta area. Cards are numbered below by uniform number.

COMPLETE SET (30) 8.00 20.00
2 Russ Nixon CO .08 .25
3 Dale Murphy 1.25 3.00
4 Bob Skinner CO .08 .25
5 Billy Sample .08 .25
7 Chuck Tanner MG .20 .50
8 Willie Stargell CO .60 1.50
9 Ozzie Virgil .08 .25
10 Chris Chambliss .20 .50
11 Bob Horner .20 .50
14 Andres Thomas .08 .25
15 Claudell Washington .20 .50
16 Rafael Ramirez .08 .25
17 Glenn Hubbard .08 .25
18 Omar Moreno .08 .25
19 Terry Harper .08 .25
20 Bruce Benedict .08 .25
23 Ted Simmons .40 1.00
24 Ken Oberkfell .08 .25
26 Gene Garber .20 .50
29 Craig McMurtry .08 .25
30 Paul Assenmacher .20 .50
33 Johnny Sain CO .30 .75
34 Zane Smith .08 .25
38 Joe Johnson .08 .25
40 Bruce Sutter .60 1.50
42 Rick Mahler .08 .25
46 David Palmer .08 .25
48 Duane Ward .20 .50
49 Jeff Dedmon .08 .25
52 Al Monchak CO .08 .25

1987 Braves 1957 TCMA

This nine-card standard-size set commemorates the 30th anniversary and members of the 1957 World Champion Milwaukee Braves. The player's name and position are displayed on the front. The backs carry highlights and stats from the 1957 season.

COMPLETE SET (9) 2.50 6.00
1 Hank Aaron 1.25 3.00
2 Eddie Mathews .60 1.50
3 Bob Hazle .08 .25
4 Johnny Logan .30 .75
5 Red Schoendienst .50 1.25
6 Wes Covington .20 .50
7 Lew Burdette .40 1.00
8 Warren Spahn .60 1.50
9 Bob Buhl .30 .75

1987 Braves Smokey

The U.S. Forestry Service (in conjunction with the Atlanta Braves) produced this large, attractive 27-card set to commemorate the 43rd birthday of Smokey. The cards feature Smokey the Bear pictured in the top right corner of every card. The card backs give a cartoon fire safety tip. The cards measure approximately 4" by 6" and are subtitled "Wildfire Prevention" on the front. Distribution of the cards was gradual at the stadium throughout the summer.

COMPLETE SET (27) 12.50 30.00
1 Zane Smith .40 1.00
2 Charlie Puleo .40 1.00
3 Randy O'Neal .40 1.00
4 David Palmer .40 1.00
5 Rick Mahler .40 1.00
6 Ed Olwine .40 1.00
7 Jeff Dedmon .40 1.00
8 Paul Assenmacher .50 1.25
9 Gene Garber .50 1.25
10 Jim Acker .40 1.00
11 Bruce Benedict .40 1.00
12 Ozzie Virgil .40 1.00
13 Ted Simmons .75 2.00
14 Dale Murphy 4.00 10.00
15 Graig Nettles .60 1.50
16 Ken Oberkfell .40 1.00
17 Gerald Perry .40 1.00
18 Rafael Ramirez .40 1.00
19 Ken Griffey .60 1.50
20 Andres Thomas .40 1.00
21 Glenn Hubbard .40 1.00
22 Damaso Garcia .40 1.00
23 Gary Roenicke .40 1.00
24 Dion James .40 1.00
25 Albert Hall .40 1.00
26 Chuck Tanner MG .50 1.25
NNO Smokey .40 1.00
Checklist

1989 Braves Dubuque

This 32-card set was sponsored by Dubuque, the meat company that makes the hot dogs sold at Atlanta-Fulton County Stadium. The cards were given away at the ballpark on Sundays and at autograph appearances at card stores. Due to the latter, several of these exist in much larger quantities. The cards measure approximately 2 1/4" by 3 1/2". Almost all the photos were taken during spring training, with the exception of Oddibe McDowell, mid-season additions Mark Eichhorn and John Russell, and coach Brian Snitker. The cards are unnumbered and checklisted below in alphabetical order.

COMPLETE SET (32) 12.00 30.00
COMMON CARD (1-32) .40 1.00
1 Jim Acker .40 1.00
2 Jose Alvarez .40 1.00
3 Paul Assenmacher .40 1.00
4 Bruce Benedict .40 1.00
5 Geronimo Berroa .40 1.00
6 Jeff Blauser .50 1.25
7 Joe Boever .40 1.00
8 Marty Clary .40 1.00
9 Bruce Dal Canton CO .40 1.00
10 Jody Davis .40 1.00
11 Mark Eichhorn .75 2.00
12 Ron Gant 1.25 3.00
13 Tom Glavine 2.50 6.00
14 Tommy Gregg .40 1.00
15 Dion James .40 1.00
16 Clarence Jones CO .40 1.00
17 Derek Lilliquist .40 1.00
18 Roy Majtyka TR .40 1.00
19 Oddibe McDowell .75 2.00
20 Dale Murphy 1.50 4.00
21 Russ Nixon MG .40 1.00
22 Gerald Perry .40 1.00
23 John Russell .75 2.00
24 Lonnie Smith .50 1.25
25 Pete Smith .40 1.00
26 John Smoltz 3.00 8.00
27 Brian Snitker CO .75 2.00
28 Andres Thomas .40 1.00
29 Jeff Treadway .40 1.00
30 Jeff Wetherby .40 1.00
30 Bobby Wine CO .40 1.00
31 Ed Whited .40 1.00

1990 Braves Dubuque Perforated

Given out early in the season, this set's 30 cards are slightly smaller than the other Dubuque Singles set, and was part of a perforated sheet that included a team photo. The backs are similar, but the fronts are all different with portrait shots. The cards are unnumbered and checklisted below in alphabetical order.

COMPLETE SET (30) 12.50 30.00
1 Jeff Blauser .40 1.00
2 Joe Boever .20 .50
3 Francisco Cabrera .20 .50
4 Tony Castillo .20 .50
5 Marty Clary .20 .50
6 Nick Esasky .20 .50
7 Ron Gant .75 2.00
8 Tom Glavine 1.50 4.00
9 Tommy Gregg .20 .50
10 Dwayne Henry .20 .50
11 Joe Hesketh .20 .50
12 Alexis Infante .20 .50
13 David Justice 1.50 4.00
14 Charlie Kerfeld .20 .50
15 Charlie Leibrandt .20 .50
16 Mark Lemke .20 .50
17 Derek Lilliquist .20 .50
18 Rick Luecken .20 .50
19 Oddibe McDowell .20 .50
20 Dale Murphy 1.50 4.00
21 Russ Nixon MG .20 .50
22 Greg Olson .20 .50
23 Jim Presley .20 .50
24 Lonnie Smith .20 .50
25 Pete Smith .20 .50
26 John Smoltz 1.25 3.00
27 Mike Stanton .60 1.50
28 Andres Thomas .20 .50
29 Jeff Treadway .20 .50
30 Ernie Whitt .20 .50

1990 Braves Dubuque Singles

These 35 cards measure approximately 2 1/4" by 3 1/2" and were given out, usually four at a time, on Sundays with subjects available for autographs that day. Several were offered more than once, but Murphy's card was given out once before his trade to the Phillies. The cards issued early in the season featured spring training action shots on their fronts. Those issued later in the season had action photos taken at Atlanta-Fulton County Stadium. The Mark Grant card was given out only on the last Sunday of the season, the only new card to be issued so late. The cards are unnumbered and checklisted below in alphabetical order.

COMPLETE SET (35) 20.00 50.00
COMMON CARD (1-35) .40 1.00
COMMON SP 2.00 5.00
1 Steve Avery .50 1.25
2 Jeff Blauser .50 1.25
3 Joe Boever .40 1.00
4 Francisco Cabrera .40 1.00
5 Pat Corrales CO .40 1.00
6 Bobby Cox MG .60 1.50
7 Nick Esasky .40 1.00
8 Ron Gant .75 2.00
9 Tom Glavine 2.00 5.00
10 Mark Grant SP 2.00 5.00
11 Tommy Gregg .40 1.00
12 Dwayne Henry .40 1.00
13 Homer the Brave/(Mascot) .40 1.00
14 Alexis Infante .40 1.00
15 Clarence Jones CO .40 1.00
16 David Justice 2.00 5.00
17 Jimmy Kremers .40 1.00
18 Charlie Leibrandt .40 1.00
19 Mark Lemke .40 1.00
20 Roy Majtyka TR .40 1.00
21 Leo Mazzone CO .40 1.00
22 Oddibe McDowell .40 1.00
23 Dale Murphy SP 10.00 25.00
24 Phil Niekro 1.25 3.00
25 Greg Olson .40 1.00
26 Jim Presley .40 1.00
27 Rally (Mascot) .40 1.00
28 Lonnie Smith .50 1.25
29 Pete Smith .40 1.00
30 John Smoltz 1.50 4.00
31 Brian Snitker CO .40 1.00
32 Andres Thomas .40 1.00
33 Jeff Treadway .40 1.00
34 Ernie Whitt .40 1.00
35 Jimy Williams CO .40 1.00

1991 Braves Dubuque Perforated

The 1991 Atlanta Braves team set was sponsored by Dubuque. The set was issued in three 10 5/8" by 9 3/8" panels that were attached to form a continuous sheet. The first panel features a team photo. The second and third panels have 15 player cards each; after perforation, the cards measure approximately 2 3/16" by 3 3/16". The front design has a posed head and shoulders color photo, with red borders and diamond designs on the corners of the picture. The cards are unnumbered and checklisted below in alphabetical order.

COMPLETE SET (30) 8.00 20.00
1 Steve Avery .08 .25
2 Rafael Belliard .08 .25
3 Juan Berenguer .08 .25
4 Jeff Blauser .20 .50
5 Sid Bream .08 .25
6 Francisco Cabrera .08 .25
7 Bobby Cox MG .20 .50
8 Nick Esasky .08 .25
9 Marvin Freeman .08 .25
10 Ron Gant .40 1.00
11 Tom Glavine 1.00 2.50
12 Mark Grant .08 .25
13 Tommy Gregg .08 .25
14 Mike Heath .08 .25
15 Danny Heep .08 .25
16 David Justice .75 2.00
17 Charlie Leibrandt .08 .25
18 Mark Lemke .08 .25
19 Kent Mercker .08 .25
20 Otis Nixon .08 .25
21 Greg Olson .08 .25
22 Jeff Parrett .08 .25
23 Terry Pendleton .40 1.00
24 Deion Sanders 1.00 2.50
25 Doug Sisk .08 .25
26 Lonnie Smith .08 .25
27 Pete Smith .08 .25
28 John Smoltz .75 2.00
29 Mike Stanton .20 .50
30 Jeff Treadway .08 .25

1991 Braves Dubuque Standard

These 39 cards were sponsored by Dubuque Meats and measure approximately 2 1/4" by 3 1/2". They were given out, usually three or six at a time, on Sundays with subjects available for autographs that day. Aside from players' uniform numbers on the back, the cards are unnumbered and checklisted below in alphabetical order. Sunday Aug. 25 had six new cards given out for the first time (Hunter, Mitchell, Clancy, Beauchamp, Esasky, Grant). Sunday Sept. 22 had three new cards issued (Pete Smith, Bell, Reynoso) with three previously released. Two Sundays previous to these had featured three previously issued cards each day. The final day of the season (Oct. 6) featured a Deion Sanders card, along with Glavine, Avery, Cox, Gant, Justice, Pendleton and Treadway. A special "apology" card was issued with the cards this day due to no autographs. Black- and blue-lettered varieties exist on at least 30 cards (different printings).

COMPLETE SET (39) 20.00 50.00
1 Steve Avery .40 1.00
2 Jim Beauchamp CO .40 1.00
3 Mike Bell .40 1.00
4 Rafael Belliard .40 1.00
5 Juan Berenguer .40 1.00
6 Jeff Blauser .50 1.25
7 Sid Bream .40 1.00
8 Francisco Cabrera .40 1.00
9 Jim Clancy .40 1.00
10 Pat Corrales CO .40 1.00
11 Bobby Cox MG .50 1.25
12 Nick Esasky .40 1.00
13 Marvin Freeman .40 1.00
14 Ron Gant .75 2.00
15 Tom Glavine 2.00 5.00
16 Mark Grant .40 1.00
17 Tommy Gregg .40 1.00
18 Mike Heath .40 1.00
19 Brian Hunter .40 1.00
20 Clarence Jones CO .40 1.00
21 David Justice 1.25 3.00
22 Charlie Leibrandt .40 1.00
23 Mark Lemke .40 1.00
24 Leo Mazzone CO .40 1.00
25 Kent Mercker .40 1.00
26 Keith Mitchell .40 1.00
27 Otis Nixon .40 1.00
28 Greg Olson .40 1.00
29 Jeff Parrett .40 1.00
30 Terry Pendleton .75 2.00
31 Armando Reynoso .40 1.00
32 Deion Sanders 2.00 5.00
33 Lonnie Smith .40 1.00
34 Pete Smith .40 1.00
35 John Smoltz 1.50 4.00
36 Mike Stanton .50 1.25
37 Jeff Treadway .40 1.00
38 Jimy Williams CO .40 1.00
39 Ned Yost CO .40 1.00

1992 Braves Krystal Postcard Sanders

This postcards features two sport athlete Deion Sanders. This postcard was issued by the Krystal food chain.

1 Deion Sanders 1.25 3.00

1992 Braves Lykes Perforated

The 1992 Atlanta Braves Team Picture Card set was sponsored by Lykes and distributed as an uncut, perforated sheet before a Braves' home game. It consists of three large sheets (each measuring approximately 10 5/8" by 9 3/8") joined together to form one continuous sheet. The first panel features a team photo, while the second and third panels feature 15 player cards each. After perforation, the cards measure approximately 2 1/8" by 3 1/8". The cards are unnumbered and checklisted below in alphabetical order.

COMPLETE SET (30) 5.00 12.00
1 Steve Avery .08 .25
2 Rafael Belliard .08 .25
3 Juan Berenguer .08 .25
4 Damon Berryhill .08 .25
5 Mike Bielecki .08 .25
6 Jeff Blauser .20 .50
7 Sid Bream .08 .25
8 Francisco Cabrera .08 .25
9 Bobby Cox MG .20 .50
10 Nick Esasky .08 .25
11 Marvin Freeman .08 .25
12 Ron Gant .40 1.00
13 Tom Glavine .75 2.00
14 Tommy Gregg .08 .25
15 Brian Hunter .08 .25
16 David Justice .50 1.25
17 Charlie Leibrandt .08 .25
18 Mark Lemke .08 .25
19 Kent Mercker .08 .25
20 Otis Nixon .08 .25
21 Greg Olson .08 .25
22 Alejandro Pena .08 .25
23 Terry Pendleton .40 1.00
24 Deion Sanders .75 2.00
25 Lonnie Smith .20 .50
26 John Smoltz .60 1.50
27 Mike Stanton .20 .50
28 Jeff Treadway .08 .25
29 Jerry Willard .08 .25
30 Mark Wohlers .08 .25

1992 Braves Lykes Standard

These 37 standard-size cards were given out (some more than once) to fans 12 years old and under on Tuesdays. Two different uncut sheets have surfaced, but no complete sets were sold or given away by the Braves. The mascot cards were available on a daily basis. The cards are unnumbered and checklisted below in alphabetical order.

COMPLETE SET (36) 12.50 30.00
COMMON CARD (1-37) .20 .50
COMMON DP .10 .25
1 Steve Avery .20 .50
2 Jim Beauchamp CO .20 .50
3 Rafael Belliard .20 .50
4 Juan Berenguer .20 .50
5 Damon Berryhill .20 .50
6 Mike Bielecki .20 .50
7 Jeff Blauser .40 1.00
8 Sid Bream .20 .50
9 Francisco Cabrera .20 .50
10 Pat Corrales CO .20 .50
11 Bobby Cox MG .40 1.00
12 Marvin Freeman .20 .50
13 Ron Gant .75 2.00
14 Tom Glavine 1.50 4.00
15 Tommy Gregg .20 .50
16 Homer the Brave DP/(Mascot) .08 .25
17 Brian Hunter .20 .50
18 Clarence Jones CO .20 .50
19 David Justice 1.00 2.50
20 Charlie Leibrandt .20 .50
21 Mark Lemke .20 .50
22 Leo Mazzone CO .20 .50
23 Kent Mercker .20 .50
24 Otis Nixon .20 .50
25 Greg Olson .20 .50
26 Alejandro Pena .20 .50
27 Terry Pendleton .75 2.00
28 Rally (Mascot) DP .08 .25
29 Deion Sanders 1.50 4.00
30 Lonnie Smith .40 1.00
31 John Smoltz 1.25 3.00
32 Mike Stanton .20 .50
33 Jeff Treadway .20 .50
34 Jerry Willard .20 .50
35 Jimy Williams CO .20 .50
36 Mark Wohlers .20 .50
37 Ned Yost CO .20 .50

1993 Braves Florida Agriculture

These were given out in eight-card perforated sheets at the Sunshine State Games in Tallahassee in July 1993. The sheets measure approximately 7" by 10" and the cards, when cut from the sheets, are the standard size. Within a baseball icon between the two panels is the result of an "at bat" in a game that used an 11" by 8 1/2" game card, which was also distributed at the Games. The cards are numbered on the back with the numbering essentially following alphabetical order.

COMPLETE SET (8) 4.00 10.00
1 Title Card .40 1.00
2 Steve Avery .40 1.00
3 Jeff Blauser .50 1.25
4 Sid Bream .40 1.00
5 Tom Glavine 1.00 2.50
6 Mark Lemke .40 1.00
7 Greg Olson .40 1.00
8 Terry Pendleton .75 2.00

1993 Braves Lykes Perforated

These 30 cards measure approximately 2 1/8" by 3 1/8" and feature color player photos that are the same as the Dubuque Meats Tuesday giveaway cards, except that Ryan Klesko was only in this set. The cards were issued late in the season and as a result include an early card of Fred McGriff as a Brave. The cards are unnumbered and checklisted below in alphabetical order.

COMPLETE SET (30) 8.00 20.00
1 Steve Avery .08 .25
2 Steve Bedrosian .20 .50
3 Rafael Belliard .08 .25
4 Damon Berryhill .08 .25
5 Jeff Blauser .20 .50
6 Sid Bream .08 .25
7 Francisco Cabrera .08 .25
8 Bobby Cox MG .20 .50
9 Marvin Freeman .08 .25
10 Ron Gant .40 1.00
11 Tom Glavine 1.25 3.00
12 Jay Howell .08 .25
13 Brian Hunter .08 .25
14 David Justice .60 1.50
15 Ryan Klesko .75 2.00
16 Mark Lemke .08 .25
17 Greg Maddux 3.00 8.00
18 Fred McGriff .75 2.00
19 Greg McMichael .08 .25
20 Kent Mercker .08 .25
21 Otis Nixon .08 .25
22 Greg Olson .08 .25
23 Bill Pecota .08 .25
24 Terry Pendleton .30 .75
25 Deion Sanders 1.25 3.00
26 Pete Smith .08 .25
27 John Smoltz .75 2.00
28 Mike Stanton .20 .50
29 Tony Tarasco .08 .25
30 Mark Wohlers .08 .25

1993 Braves Lykes Standard

These 38 standard-size cards feature the same portraits as the perforated Dubuque Meats 1993 set, but with a different design. Each Tuesday, the Braves gave out three different cards, and for the first time, did not repeat any player's card during the season. Mascot cards were offered to youngsters on a daily basis. The cards are unnumbered and checklisted below in alphabetical order. Some near-complete sets surfaced following the season, along with some uncut sheets, but neither the near-complete sets nor the sheets included the cards of Javy Lopez, Fred McGriff, and Tony Tarasco, which were the final Tuesday's handout. The uncut sheet had six rows with six slots per row; thirty-five players are featured, and one slot is blank. The printing on the back of these three cards is slightly different from the other 35 cards, indicating a separate printing.

COMPLETE SET (38) 15.00 40.00
COMMON CARD (1-38) .20 .50
COMMON DP .10 .25
SP COMMONS 1.50 4.00
1 Steve Avery .20 .50
2 Jim Beauchamp CO .20 .50
3 Steve Bedrosian .40 1.00
4 Rafael Belliard .20 .50
5 Damon Berryhill .20 .50
6 Jeff Blauser .40 1.00
7 Sid Bream .20 .50
8 Francisco Cabrera .20 .50
9 Pat Corrales CO .20 .50
10 Bobby Cox MG .40 1.00
11 Marvin Freeman .20 .50
12 Ron Gant .75 2.00
13 Tom Glavine 1.50 4.00
14 Homer the Brave DP/(Mascot) .08 .25
15 Jay Howell .20 .50
16 Brian Hunter .20 .50
17 Clarence Jones CO .20 .50
18 David Justice 1.00 2.50
19 Mark Lemke .20 .50
20 Javy Lopez SP 4.00 10.00
21 Greg Maddux 4.00 10.00
22 Leo Mazzone CO .20 .50
23 Fred McGriff SP 3.00 8.00
24 Greg McMichael .20 .50
25 Kent Mercker .20 .50
26 Otis Nixon .40 1.00
27 Greg Olson .20 .50
28 Bill Pecota .20 .50
29 Terry Pendleton .75 2.00
30 Rally (Mascot) DP .08 .25
31 Deion Sanders 1.50 4.00
32 Pete Smith .20 .50
33 John Smoltz 1.25 3.00
34 Mike Stanton .20 .50
35 Tony Tarasco SP 1.50 4.00
36 Jimy Williams CO .20 .50
37 Mark Wohlers .20 .50
38 Ned Yost CO .20 .50

1993 Braves Postcards

These seven postcards featuring members of the Atlanta Braves, were taken by veteran sports photographer Barry Colla. The full-bleed fronts have the player's photo with their name on the bottom in white letters. The backs are standard postcard backs. Since these cards are unnumbered, we have sequenced them in alphabetical order.

COMPLETE SET (7) 3.00 8.00
1 Steve Avery .20 .50
2 Tom Glavine .75 2.00
3 David Justice .60 1.50
4 Otis Nixon .20 .50
5 Terry Pendleton .30 .75
6 Deion Sanders .60 1.50
7 John Smoltz .60 1.50

1993 Braves Stadium Club

This 30-card standard-size set features the 1993 Atlanta Braves. The set was issued in hobby (plastic box) and retail (blister) form.

COMPLETE SET (30) 4.00 10.00
1 Tom Glavine .40 1.00
2 Bill Pecota .02 .10
3 David Justice .30 .75
4 Mark Lemke .02 .10
5 Jeff Blauser .02 .10
6 Ron Gant .08 .25
7 Greg Olson .02 .10
8 Francisco Cabrera .02 .10
9 Chipper Jones 1.25 3.00
10 Steve Avery .02 .10
11 Kent Mercker .02 .10
12 John Smoltz .30 .75
13 Pete Smith .02 .10
14 Damon Berryhill .02 .10
15 Sid Bream .02 .10
16 Otis Nixon .02 .10
17 Mike Stanton .02 .10
18 Greg Maddux 1.25 3.00
19 Jay Howell .02 .10
20 Rafael Belliard .02 .10
21 Terry Pendleton .20 .50
22 Deion Sanders .30 .75
23 Brian R. Hunter .02 .10
24 Marvin Freeman .02 .10
25 Mark Wohlers .02 .10
26 Ryan Klesko .30 .75
27 Javier Lopez .30 .75
28 Melvin Nieves .02 .10
29 Tony Tarasco .02 .10
30 Ramon Caraballo .02 .10

1994 Braves Lykes Perforated

The 1994 Atlanta Braves Team Picture Card set was sponsored by Lykes, the stadium's hot dog maker. It consists of three 10 5/8" by 9 3/8" sheets and one 10 5/8" by 3 1/8" 5-card strip, all joined together to form one continuous sheet. The first panel features a team photo, with each player identified by row. The second and third panels display 15 player cards each, with the 5-card strip for a total of 35 cards. In contrast to the 1994 Braves Standard set, these cards measure approximately 2 1/8" by 3 1/8" and are perforated. The design of these cards is identical to the standard cards, except that the bio and statistics on the card backs are in team color-coded red and blue print rather than black. The difference in player selection between the perforated and standard sets is instructive. The perforated set omits Sanders (traded) but adds Roberto Kelly (acquired), Mike Mordecai (called up), and Jose Oliva (called up). Also Pat Corrales was omitted from the perforated set. The cards are unnumbered but are arranged alphabetically by column beginning in the upper left corner.

COMPLETE SET (35) 8.00 20.00
1 Steve Avery .08 .25
2 Jim Beauchamp CO .08 .25
3 Steve Bedrosian .20 .50
4 Rafael Belliard .08 .25
5 Mike Bielecki .08 .25
6 Jeff Blauser .20 .50
7 Bobby Cox MG .20 .50
8 Dave Gallagher .08 .25
9 Tom Glavine .75 2.00
10 Milt Hill .08 .25
11 Chipper Jones 2.50 6.00
12 Clarence Jones CO .08 .25
13 David Justice .40 1.00
14 Mike Kelly .08 .25
15 Roberto Kelly .08 .25
16 Ryan Klesko .75 2.00
17 Mark Lemke .20 .50
18 Javier Lopez .75 2.00
19 Greg Maddux 2.50 6.00
20 Leo Mazzone CO .08 .25
21 Fred McGriff .60 1.50
22 Greg McMichael .08 .25
23 Kent Mercker .08 .25
24 Mike Mordecai .08 .25
25 Charlie O'Brien .08 .25
26 Jose Oliva .08 .25
27 Gregg Olson .08 .25
28 Bill Pecota .08 .25
29 Terry Pendleton .40 1.00
30 John Smoltz .60 1.50
31 Mike Stanton .08 .25
32 Tony Tarasco .08 .25
33 Jimy Williams CO .08 .25
34 Mark Wohlers .08 .25
35 Ned Yost CO .08 .25

1994 Braves Lykes Standard

This 34-card standard-size set was sponsored by Lykes, the stadium's hot dog maker. Three cards each were to be given out on nine Tuesdays, but three giveaway dates were lost to the strike. The other seven cards were either of players who were traded (Sanders and Hill) or were not given out at games (Cox, Jones, Kelly, Klesko, and McGriff). These seven cards may be scarcer than the others. The cards are unnumbered and checklisted below in alphabetical order.

COMPLETE SET (34) 15.00 40.00
1 Steve Avery .20 .50
2 Jim Beauchamp CO .20 .50
3 Steve Bedrosian .40 1.00
4 Rafael Belliard .20 .50
5 Mike Bielecki .20 .50
6 Jeff Blauser .40 1.00
7 Pat Corrales CO .20 .50
8 Bobby Cox MG .40 1.00
9 Dave Gallagher .20 .50
10 Tom Glavine 1.25 3.00
11 Milt Hill .20 .50
12 Chipper Jones 2.50 6.00
13 Clarence Jones CO .20 .50
14 David Justice .75 2.00
15 Mike Kelly .20 .50
16 Ryan Klesko .75 2.00
17 Mark Lemke .20 .50
18 Javy Lopez .75 2.00
19 Greg Maddux 2.50 6.00
20 Leo Mazzone CO .20 .50
21 Fred McGriff .75 2.00
22 Greg McMichael .20 .50
23 Kent Mercker .20 .50
24 Charlie O'Brien .20 .50
25 Gregg Olson .20 .50
26 Bill Pecota .20 .50
27 Terry Pendleton .75 2.00
28 Deion Sanders .75 2.00
29 John Smoltz .75 2.00
30 Mike Stanton .20 .50
31 Tony Tarasco .20 .50
32 Jimy Williams CO .20 .50
33 Mark Wohlers .20 .50
34 Ned Yost CO .20 .50

1994 Braves U.S. Playing Cards

These 56 playing standard-size cards have rounded corners, and feature color posed and action player photos on their white-bordered fronts. The set is checklisted below in playing card order by suits and assigned numbers to aces (1), jacks (11), queens (12), and kings (13).

COMPLETE SET (56) 2.50 6.00
1C Ron Gant .08 .25
1D Greg Maddux .40 1.00
1H Dave Justice .08 .25
1S Jeff Blauser .01 .05
2C Chipper Jones .40 1.00
2D Ron Gant .08 .25
2H Mark Lemke .01 .05
2S Mike Stanton .01 .05
3C Terry Pendleton .02 .10
3D Kent Mercker .01 .05
3H Javier Lopez .15 .40
3S Ryan Klesko .20 .50
4C Mark Wohlers .01 .05
4D Greg McMichael .01 .05
4H Rafael Belliard .01 .05
4S Michael Potts .01 .05
5C Pedro Borbon .01 .05
5D Tony Tarasco .01 .05
5H Bill Pecota .01 .05
5S Charlie O'Brien .01 .05
6C Steve Avery .01 .05
6D John Smoltz .08 .25
6H Tom Glavine .20 .50
6S Steve Bedrosian .01 .05
7C Deion Sanders .08 .25
7D Fred McGriff .08 .25
7H Milt Hill .01 .05
7S Javier Lopez .15 .40
8C Dave Justice .08 .25
8D Ron Gant .08 .25
8H Jeff Blauser .02 .10
8S Greg Maddux .40 1.00
9C Dave Gallagher .01 .05
9D Mike Kelly .01 .05
9H Ryan Klesko .02 .10
9S Deion Sanders .08 .25
10C Rafael Belliard .01 .05
10D Steve Bedrosian .01 .05
10H Terry Pendleton .02 .10
10S Ramon Caraballo .01 .05
11C Greg McMichael .01 .05
11D Bill Pecota .01 .05
11H Mike Stanton .01 .05
11S Kent Mercker .01 .05
12C John Smoltz .08 .25
12D Mark Lemke .01 .05
12H Steve Avery .01 .05
12S Mark Wohlers .01 .05
13C Fred McGriff .08 .25
13D Terry Pendleton .02 .10
13H Deion Sanders .08 .25
13S Tom Glavine .20 .50
NNO Featured Players .01 .05

1995 Braves Atlanta Constitution

This eight-card set of the Atlanta Braves measuring approximately 8 1/2" by 11" features color action player photos with a red, blue and yellow inner border and a white outer margin. The backs carry player information and career statistics. Only 5,000 of each card were produced and are sequentially numbered. The profits from this set was donated to the Atlanta Braves Foundation. The cards are unnumbered and checklisted below in alphabetical order.

COMPLETE SET (8) 5.00 12.00
1 Steve Avery .40 1.00
2 Tom Glavine 1.25 3.00
3 Marquis Grissom .40 1.00
4 David Justice 1.00 2.50
5 Ryan Klesko 1.00 2.50
6 Mark Lemke .40 1.00
7 John Smoltz .75 2.00
8 Mark Wohlers .40 1.00

1996 Braves Fleer

These 20 standard-size cards feature the same design as the regular Fleer issue, except they are UV coated, use silver foil and are numbered "x of 20". The team set packs were available at retail locations and hobby shops in 10-card packs for a suggested retail price of $1.99.

COMPLETE SET (20) 2.50 6.00
1 Steve Avery .02 .10
2 Jeff Blauser .02 .10
3 Brad Clontz .02 .10
4 Tom Glavine .20 .50
5 Marquis Grissom .02 .10
6 Chipper Jones .60 1.50
7 David Justice .15 .40
8 Ryan Klesko .07 .20
9 Mark Lemke .02 .10
10 Javier Lopez .07 .20
11 Greg Maddux .75 2.00
12 Fred McGriff .10 .30
13 Greg McMichael .02 .10
14 Eddie Perez .02 .10
15 Jason Schmidt .60 1.50
16 John Smoltz .15 .40
17 Terrell Wade .02 .10
18 Mark Wohlers .02 .10
19 Logo card .02 .10
20 Checklist .02 .10

1997 Braves Score

This 15-card set of the Atlanta Braves was issued in five-card packs with a suggested retail of $1.30 each. The fronts feature color player photos with special team specific color foil stamping. The backs carry player information. Only 100 cases were made for each team. Platinum parallel cards were inserted at a rate of 1:6, Premier parallel cards at a rate of 1:31.

COMPLETE SET (15) 4.00 10.00
*PLATINUM: 4X BASIC CARDS
*PREMIER: 20X BASIC CARDS
1 Ryan Klesko .40 1.00
2 Dave Justice .30 .75
3 Terry Pendleton .08 .25
4 Tom Glavine .50 1.25
5 Javier Lopez .30 .75
6 John Smoltz .40 1.00
7 Jermaine Dye .08 .25
8 Mark Lemke .08 .25
9 Fred McGriff .30 .75
10 Chipper Jones 1.25 3.00
11 Terrell Wade .08 .25
12 Greg Maddux 1.25 3.00
13 Mark Wohlers .08 .25
14 Marquis Grissom .08 .25
15 Andruw Jones .75 2.00

1998 Braves Score

This 15-card set was issued in special retail packs and features color photos of the Atlanta Braves team. The backs carry player information. A special platinum parallel set was also issued and randomly inserted in packs.

COMPLETE SET (15) 3.00 8.00
*PLATINUM: 5X BASIC CARDS
1 Andruw Jones .50 1.25
2 Greg Maddux 1.00 2.50
3 Michael Tucker .08 .25
4 Denny Neagle .08 .25
5 Javier Lopez .40 1.00
6 Ryan Klesko .40 1.00
7 Chipper Jones 1.00 2.50
8 Kenny Lofton .20 .50
9 John Smoltz .40 1.00
10 Jeff Blauser .08 .25
11 Tom Glavine .50 1.25
12 Tony Graffanino .08 .25
13 Terrell Wade .08 .25
14 Fred McGriff .30 .75
15 Mark Wohlers .08 .25

1999 Braves Atlanta Journal-Constitution Jumbos

This 16-card jumbo set was released in conjunction with the Atlanta Journal-Constitution in 1999, and features 16 jumbo photos of the 1999 Atlanta Braves. The photos measure approximately 8"x10". Please note that only 15,000 of each photo were produced. The photos have been put in alphabetical order below for convenience.

COMPLETE SET (16) 20.00 50.00
1 Tom Glavine 2.50 6.00
2 Ozzie Guillen 1.25 3.00
3 Brian Hunter .75 2.00
4 Andruw Jones 2.50 6.00
5 Chipper Jones 3.00 8.00
6 Brian Jordan .75 2.00
7 Ryan Klesko 2.00 5.00
8 Keith Lockhart .75 2.00
9 Javy Lopez 1.50 4.00
10 Greg Maddux 3.00 8.00
11 Otis Nixon .75 2.00
12 Eddie Perez .75 2.00
13 John Rocker 1.25 3.00
14 John Smoltz 2.00 5.00
15 Walt Weiss .75 2.00
16 Gerald Williams .75 2.00

2004 Braves DAV

COMPLETE SET (6) 5.00 10.00
1 J.D. Drew .60 1.50
2 Johnny Estrada .60 1.50
3 Rafael Furcal .60 1.50
4 Marcus Giles .60 1.50
5 Horacio Ramirez .60 1.50
6 John Smoltz 1.00 2.50

2006 Braves Topps

COMPLETE SET (14) 3.00 8.00
ATL1 Chipper Jones .30 .75
ATL2 Andruw Jones .12 .30
ATL3 John Smoltz .30 .75
ATL4 Jeff Francoeur .30 .75
ATL5 Marcus Giles .12 .30
ATL6 Ryan Langerhans .12 .30
ATL7 Edgar Renteria .12 .30
ATL8 Lance Cormier .12 .30
ATL9 Brian McCann .12 .30
ATL10 Tim Hudson .20 .50
ATL11 Mike Hampton .12 .30
ATL12 Wilson Betemit .12 .30
ATL13 Jorge Sosa .12 .30
ATL14 Adam LaRoche .12 .30

2007 Braves Topps

COMPLETE SET (14) 3.00 8.00
ATL1 Chipper Jones .30 .75
ATL2 Bob Wickman .12 .30
ATL3 Chuck James .12 .30
ATL4 John Smoltz .30 .75
ATL5 Andruw Jones .12 .30
ATL6 Edgar Renteria .12 .30
ATL7 Mike Gonzalez .12 .30
ATL8 Rafael Soriano .12 .30
ATL9 Brian McCann .12 .30
ATL10 Tim Hudson .20 .50
ATL11 Matt Diaz .12 .30
ATL12 Jeff Francoeur .30 .75
ATL13 Pete Orr .12 .30
ATL14 Ryan Langerhans .12 .30

2008 Braves Topps

COMPLETE SET (14) 3.00 8.00
ATL1 Tom Glavine .20 .50
ATL2 Jo-Jo Reyes .12 .30
ATL3 Chuck James .12 .30
ATL4 John Smoltz .30 .75
ATL5 Chipper Jones .30 .75
ATL6 Mark Kotsay .12 .30
ATL7 Mark Teixeira .20 .50
ATL8 Rafael Soriano .12 .30
ATL9 Brian McCann .20 .50
ATL10 Tim Hudson .20 .50
ATL11 Matt Diaz .12 .30
ATL12 Jeff Francoeur .20 .50
ATL13 Yunel Escobar .12 .30
ATL14 Kelly Johnson .12 .30

2009 Braves Topps

ATL1 Chipper Jones .40 1.00
ATL2 Tim Hudson .25 .60
ATL3 Casey Kotchman .15 .40
ATL4 Derek Lowe .15 .40
ATL5 Brian McCann .25 .60
ATL6 Jo Jo Reyes .15 .40
ATL7 Yunel Escobar .15 .40
ATL8 Jair Jurrjens .15 .40
ATL9 Josh Anderson .15 .40
ATL10 Jorge Campillo .15 .40
ATL11 Javier Vazquez .15 .40
ATL12 Jeff Francoeur .25 .60
ATL13 Gregor Blanco .15 .40
ATL14 Kelly Johnson .15 .40
ATL15 Bobby Cox MG .15 .40

2010 Braves Topps

ATL1 Chipper Jones .40 1.00
ATL2 Troy Glaus .15 .40
ATL3 Takashi Saito .15 .40
ATL4 Nate McLouth .15 .40
ATL5 Kenshin Kawakami .25 .60
ATL6 Jair Jurrjens .15 .40
ATL7 Brian McCann .25 .60
ATL8 Yunel Escobar .15 .40
ATL9 Jordan Schafer .15 .40
ATL10 Melky Cabrera .15 .40
ATL11 Tommy Hanson .15 .40
ATL12 Kris Medlen .25 .60
ATL13 Matt Diaz .15 .40
ATL14 Martin Prado .15 .40
ATL15 Tim Hudson .25 .60
ATL16 Jason Heyward .60 1.50
ATL17 Billy Wagner .15 .40

2011 Braves Topps

ATL1 Jason Heyward .30 .75
ATL2 Chipper Jones .40 1.00
ATL3 Jair Jurrjens .15 .40
ATL4 Brian McCann .25 .60
ATL5 Mike Minor .15 .40
ATL6 Martin Prado .15 .40
ATL7 Kris Medlen .25 .60
ATL8 Nate McLouth .15 .40
ATL9 Eric Hinske .15 .40
ATL10 Derek Lowe .15 .40
ATL11 Freddie Freeman 2.50 6.00
ATL12 Jonny Venters .15 .40
ATL13 Alex Gonzalez .15 .40
ATL14 Tommy Hanson .15 .40
ATL15 Tim Hudson .25 .60
ATL16 Dan Uggla .15 .40
ATL17 Turner Field .15 .40

2012 Braves Topps

ATL1 Jason Heyward .30 .75
ATL2 Jonny Venters .25 .60
ATL3 Martin Prado .25 .60
ATL4 Tim Hudson .25 .60
ATL5 Freddie Freeman .50 1.25
ATL6 Mike Minor .25 .60
ATL7 Michael Bourn .25 .60
ATL8 Dan Uggla .30 .75
ATL9 Tommy Hanson .25 .60
ATL10 Brandon Beachy .25 .60
ATL11 Jair Jurrjens .25 .60
ATL12 Chipper Jones .40 1.00
ATL13 Craig Kimbrel .30 .75
ATL14 Eric Hinske .25 .60
ATL15 Brian McCann .30 .75
ATL16 Julio Teheran .30 .75
ATL17 Turner Field .15 .40

2013 Braves Topps

COMPLETE SET (17) 3.00 8.00
ATL1 Craig Kimbrel .30 .75
ATL2 Justin Upton .30 .75
ATL3 Jason Heyward .30 .75
ATL4 B.J. Upton .30 .75
ATL5 Tim Hudson .30 .75
ATL6 Brian McCann .30 .75
ATL7 Kris Medlen .20 .50
ATL8 Dan Uggla .30 .75
ATL9 Freddie Freeman .50 1.25
ATL10 Brandon Beachy .15 .40
ATL11 Jordan Walden .15 .40
ATL12 Andrelton Simmons .15 .40
ATL13 Mike Minor .25 .60
ATL14 Julio Teheran .25 .60
ATL15 Juan Francisco .25 .60
ATL16 Paul Maholm .15 .40
ATL17 Turner Field .15 .40

2014 Braves Topps

COMPLETE SET (17) 3.00 8.00
ATL1 Craig Kimbrel .20 .50
ATL2 Justin Upton .20 .50
ATL3 Jason Heyward .20 .50
ATL4 B.J. Upton .15 .40
ATL5 Alex Wood .15 .40
ATL6 Ryan Doumit .15 .40
ATL7 Kris Medlen .20 .50
ATL8 Dan Uggla .15 .40
ATL9 Freddie Freeman .30 .75
ATL10 Brandon Beachy .15 .40
ATL11 Evan Gattis .15 .40
ATL12 Andrelton Simmons .15 .40
ATL13 Mike Minor .20 .50
ATL14 Julio Teheran .20 .50
ATL15 Chris Johnson .15 .40
ATL16 Joey Terdoslavich .15 .40
ATL17 Turner Field .15 .40

2015 Braves Topps

COMPLETE SET (17) 3.00 8.00
AB1 Freddie Freeman .30 .75
AB2 Shelby Miller .20 .50
AB3 Chris Johnson .15 .40
AB4 Alberto Callaspo .15 .40
AB5 Mike Minor .15 .40
AB6 James Russell .15 .40
AB7 Julio Teheran .20 .50
AB8 B.J. Upton .15 .40
AB9 Arodys Vizcaino .15 .40
AB10 Christian Bethancourt .15 .40
AB11 Zoilo Almonte .15 .40
AB12 Andrelton Simmons .15 .40
AB13 Nick Markakis .20 .50
AB14 Alex Wood .15 .40
AB15 Craig Kimbrel .20 .50
AB16 A.J. Pierzynski .15 .40
AB17 Jason Grilli .15 .40

2016 Braves Topps

COMPLETE SET (17) 3.00 8.00
ATL1 Freddie Freeman .30 .75
ATL2 A.J. Pierzynski .15 .40
ATL3 Jace Peterson .15 .40
ATL4 Erick Aybar .15 .40
ATL5 Hector Olivera .20 .50
ATL6 Nick Swisher .20 .50
ATL7 Julio Teheran .20 .50
ATL8 Ender Inciarte .15 .40
ATL9 Nick Markakis .20 .50
ATL10 Bud Norris .15 .40
ATL11 Manny Banuelos .25 .60
ATL12 Matt Wisler .15 .40
ATL13 Arodys Vizcaino .15 .40
ATL14 Adonis Garcia .15 .40
ATL15 Jason Grilli .15 .40
ATL16 Tyler Flowers .15 .40
ATL17 Gordon Beckham .15 .40

2017 Braves Topps

COMPLETE SET (17) 3.00 8.00
ATL1 Dansby Swanson .40 1.00
ATL2 Kurt Suzuki .15 .40
ATL3 Mike Foltynewicz .15 .40
ATL4 Ender Inciarte .15 .40
ATL5 Bartolo Colon .15 .40
ATL6 Adonis Garcia .15 .40
ATL7 Matt Kemp .20 .50
ATL8 Jace Peterson .15 .40
ATL9 Julio Teheran .20 .50
ATL10 Jim Johnson .15 .40
ATL11 R.A. Dickey .20 .50
ATL12 Freddie Freeman .30 .75
ATL13 Nick Markakis .20 .50
ATL14 Tyler Flowers .15 .40
ATL15 Sean Rodriguez .15 .40
ATL16 Matt Wisler .15 .40
ATL17 Arodys Vizcaino .15 .40

2018 Braves Topps

COMPLETE SET (17) 2.50 6.00
AB1 Freddie Freeman .30 .75
AB2 Tyler Flowers .15 .40
AB3 Dansby Swanson .25 .60
AB4 Lucas Sims .15 .40
AB5 Nick Markakis .20 .50
AB6 Ozzie Albies .50 1.25
AB7 A.J. Minter .20 .50
AB8 Mike Foltynewicz .15 .40
AB9 Ender Inciarte .15 .40
AB10 Johan Camargo .15 .40
AB11 Brandon McCarthy .15 .40
AB12 Julio Teheran .20 .50
AB13 Max Fried .60 1.50
AB14 Charlie Culberson .15 .40
AB15 Kurt Suzuki .15 .40
AB16 Sean Newcomb .20 .50
AB17 Arodys Vizcaino .15 .40

2019 Braves Topps

COMPLETE SET (17) 3.00 8.00
AB1 Ronald Acuna Jr. 1.25 3.00
AB2 Freddie Freeman .30 .75
AB3 Ozzie Albies .25 .60
AB4 Dansby Swanson .25 .60
AB5 Ender Inciarte .15 .40
AB6 Mike Foltynewicz .25 .60
AB7 Sean Newcomb .15 .40
AB8 Kevin Gausman .25 .60
AB9 Julio Teheran .20 .50
AB10 Adam Duvall .25 .60
AB11 Tyler Flowers .15 .40
AB12 Arodys Vizcaino .15 .40
AB13 A.J. Minter .20 .50
AB14 Johan Camargo .15 .40
AB15 Brian McCann .20 .50
AB16 Touki Toussaint .20 .50
AB17 Josh Donaldson .20 .50

2020 Braves Topps

ATL1 Ronald Acuna Jr. 1.00 2.50
ATL2 Ozzie Albies .25 .60
ATL3 Freddie Freeman .30 .75
ATL4 Nick Markakis .20 .50
ATL5 Mark Melancon .15 .40
ATL6 Mike Soroka .25 .60
ATL7 Ender Inciarte .15 .40
ATL8 Austin Riley .30 .75
ATL9 Travis d'Arnaud .20 .50
ATL10 Johan Camargo .15 .40
ATL11 Max Fried .25 .60
ATL12 Tyler Flowers .15 .40
ATL13 Dansby Swanson .25 .60
ATL14 Shane Greene .15 .40
ATL15 Adam Duvall .20 .50
ATL16 Chris Martin .15 .40
ATL17 Will Smith .15 .40

2017 Braves Topps National Baseball Card Day

COMPLETE SET (10) 6.00 15.00
ATL1 Dansby Swanson 1.50 4.00
ATL2 Freddie Freeman 1.25 3.00
ATL3 Ender Inciarte .60 1.50
ATL4 Julio Teheran .75 2.00
ATL5 Nick Markakis .75 2.00
ATL6 Mike Foltynewicz .60 1.50
ATL7 Bartolo Colon .60 1.50
ATL8 Matt Kemp .75 2.00
ATL9 Hank Aaron 2.00 5.00
ATL10 Chipper Jones 1.00 2.50

2008 Braves Upper Deck SGA

COMPLETE SET (25) 4.00 10.00
AB1 Kelly Johnson .20 .50
AB2 Clint Sammons .20 .50
AB3 Bobby Cox MG .20 .50
AB4 Jeff Francoeur .30 .75
AB5 Chipper Jones .50 1.25
AB6 Brandon Jones .50 1.25
AB7 Tim Hudson .30 .75
AB8 Brian McCann .30 .75
AB9 Yunel Escobar .20 .50
AB10 Matt Diaz .20 .50
AB11 Mark Teixeira .30 .75
AB12 John Smoltz .50 1.25
AB13 Jeff Bennett .20 .50
AB14 Mike Hampton .20 .50
AB15 Tyler Yates .20 .50
AB16 Royce Ring .20 .50
AB17 Chuck James .20 .50
AB18 Jo Jo Reyes .20 .50
AB19 Buddy Carlyle .20 .50
AB20 Rafael Soriano .20 .50
AB21 Manny Acosta .20 .50
AB22 Tom Glavine .30 .75
AB23 Mike Gonzalez .20 .50
AB24 Blaine Boyer .20 .50
AB25 Peter Moylan .20 .50

1909 H.H. Bregstone PC743

The H.H. Bregstone postcards were issued during the 1909-11 time period. They feature St. Louis Browns and St. Louis Cardinals only. The cards are sepia and black in appearance and are of consistent quality in the printing. Each cards features the line "by H.H. Bregstone, St. Louis" at the bottom of the obverse. The player's last name, his position, and his team are enumerated. The reverses features the letters AZO in the stamp area. B. Gregory of the Trolley League is probably Howie Gregory who played for the Browns that year.

COMPLETE SET (53) 5250.00 10500.00
1 Bill Bailey 125.00 250.00
2 Jap Barbeau 125.00 250.00
3 Shad Barry 125.00 250.00
4 Fred Beebe 125.00 250.00
5 Frank Betcher 125.00 250.00
6 Jack Bliss 125.00 250.00
7 Roger Bresnahan 250.00 500.00
8 Bobby Byrne 125.00 250.00
9 Chappy Charles 125.00 250.00
10 Frank Corridon 125.00 250.00
11 Dade Criss 125.00 250.00
12 Lou Criger 125.00 250.00
13 Joe Delahanty 125.00 250.00
14 Bill Dineen 125.00 250.00
15 Rube Ellis 125.00 250.00
16 Steve Evans 125.00 250.00
17 Art Fromme 125.00 250.00
18 Rube Geyer 125.00 250.00
19 Billy Gilbert 125.00 250.00
20 Bert Graham 125.00 250.00
21 B. Gregory 125.00 250.00
Probably Howie Gregory
22 Art Griggs 125.00 250.00
23 Bob Harmon 125.00 250.00
24 Roy Hartzell 125.00 250.00
25 Irv Higginbotham 125.00 250.00
26 Thomas Higgins 125.00 250.00
27 Danny Hoffman 125.00 250.00
28 Harry Howell 125.00 250.00
29 Miller Huggins 250.00 500.00
30 Rudy Hulswitt 125.00 250.00
31 Johnson 125.00 250.00
32 Tom Jones 125.00 250.00
33 Ed Konetchy 125.00 250.00
34 Johnny Lush 125.00 250.00
35 Lee Magee 125.00 250.00
36 Jimmy McAleer MG 125.00 250.00
37 Stoney McGlynn 125.00 250.00
38 Rebel Oakes 125.00 250.00
39 Tom O'Hara 125.00 250.00
40 Ham Patterson 125.00 250.00
41 Barney Pelty 125.00 250.00
42 Ed Phelps 125.00 250.00
43 Elmer Rieger 125.00 250.00
44 Charlie Rhodes 125.00 250.00
45 Slim Sallee 125.00 250.00
46 Schweitzer 125.00 250.00
47 Wib Smith 125.00 250.00
48 Jim Stephens 125.00 250.00
49 George Stone 125.00 250.00
50 Rube Waddell 250.00 500.00
51 Bobby Wallace 250.00 500.00
52 Jim Williams 125.00 250.00
53 Vic Willis 250.00 500.00

1903-04 Breisch-Williams E107

The cards in this 159-card set measure 1 1/4" by 2 1/2". The black and white cards of this series of "prominent baseball players" were marketed by the Breisch-Williams Company. Judging from the team changes for individual players, the set appears to have been issued in 1903-04. Cards have been found with smaller printing front and back and also with the company name hand stamped on back. There are several names misspelled. The cards have been alphabetized and numbered in the checklist below. A second type (sic Type II) of these cards is also known. These cards have thicker paper stock and more narrow borders. There is no definitive answer, however, as to how many players are available in Type II format. Any further information is greatly appreciated. A Deacon McGuire NY card was recently discovered, but due to market scarcity, no pricing is provided for this card. Due to the fact that most E107's are found in off-grade condition, our pricing references the technical grade of Good.

1 John Anderson/NY AL 900.00 1500.00
2 John Anderson/St. Louis AL 900.00 1500.00
3 Jimmy Barrett: Detroit/(sic, Barret) 900.00 1500.00
4 Ginger Beaumont 1200.00 2000.00
5 Erve Beck 900.00 1500.00
6 Jake Beckley 5000.00 8000.00
7 Harry Bemis: Cleve. 900.00 1500.00
8 Chief Bender/Phila. AL 6000.00 10000.00
9 Bill Bernhard 900.00 1500.00
10 Harry Bay/sic, Bey) 900.00 1500.00
11 Bill Bradley 900.00 1500.00
12 Fritz Buelow 900.00 1500.00
13 Nixey Callahan 900.00 1500.00
14 Scoops Carey 900.00 1500.00
15 Charlie Carr 900.00 1500.00
16 Bill Carrick 900.00 1500.00
17 Doc Casey 900.00 1500.00
18 Frank Chance 9000.00 15000.00
19 Jack Chesbro 6000.00 10000.00
20 Boileryard Clarke/sic, Clark 900.00 1500.00
21 Fred Clarke 7000.00 12000.00
22 Jimmy Collins 5000.00 8000.00
23 Duff Cooley 900.00 1500.00
24 Tommy Corcoran 900.00 1500.00
25 Bill Coughlin/sic, Coughlan) 900.00 1500.00
26 Lou Criger 900.00 1500.00
27 Lave Cross 900.00 1500.00
28 Monte Cross 900.00 1500.00
29 Bill Dahlen/Brooklyn 1200.00 2000.00
30 Bill Dahlen/New York National 3000.00 5000.00
31 Tom Daly 900.00 1500.00
32 George Davis 3000.00 5000.00
33 Harry Davis 900.00 1500.00
34 Ed Delahanty 15000.00 25000.00
35 DeMont: Wash. 900.00 1500.00
36 Pop Dillon/Brooklyn 900.00 1500.00
37 Pop Dillon/Detroit 900.00 1500.00
38 Bill Dinneen/(sic, Dineen) 900.00 1500.00
39 Jiggs Donahue 900.00 1500.00
40 Mike Donlin 1200.00 2000.00
41 Patsy Donovan 900.00 1500.00
42 Patsy Dougherty 900.00 1500.00
43 Klondike Douglass/sic, Douglas) 900.00 1500.00
44 Jack Doyle/Brooklyn 900.00 1500.00
45 Jack Doyle/Phila. NL 900.00 1500.00
46 Lew Drill 900.00 1500.00
47 Jack Dunn 900.00 1500.00
48 Kid Elberfeld/sic, Elberfield 900.00 1500.00
49 Kid Elberfeld/sic, Elberfield 900.00 1500.00
50 Duke Farrell 900.00 1500.00
51 Hobe Ferris 900.00 1500.00
52 Elmer Flick 5000.00 8000.00
53 Buck Freeman 900.00 1500.00
54 Bill Friel/sic, Freil 900.00 1500.00

55 Dave Fultz 900.00 1500.00
56 Ned Garvin 900.00 1500.00
57 Billy Gilbert 900.00 1500.00
58 Harry Gleason 900.00 1500.00
59 Kid Gleason/NY NL 5000.00 8000.00
60 Kid Gleason/Phila. NL 3500.00 6000.00
61 John Gochnaur/Cleve.
sic, Gochnauer 900.00 1500.00
62 Danny Green 900.00 1500.00
63 Noodles Hahn 1200.00 2000.00
64 Bill Hallman 900.00 1500.00
65 Ned Hanlon MG 3000.00 5000.00
66 Dick Harley 900.00 1500.00
67 Jack Harper 900.00 1500.00
68 Topsy Hartsel/sic, Hartsell 900.00 1500.00
69 Emmett Heidrick 900.00 1500.00
70 Charlie Hemphill 900.00 1500.00
71 Weldon Henley 900.00 1500.00
72 Charlie Hickman 900.00 1500.00
73 Harry Howell 900.00 1500.00
74 Frank Isbell/sic, Isabel 900.00 1500.00
75 Fred Jacklitsch/sic, Jacklitzch 900.00 1500.00
76 Charlie Jones 900.00 1500.00
77 Fielder Jones 900.00 1500.00
78 Addie Joss 6000.00 10000.00
79 Mike Kahoe 900.00 1500.00
80 Willie Keeler 9000.00 15000.00
81 Joe Kelley 5000.00 8000.00
82 Brickyard Kennedy 900.00 1500.00
83 Frank Kitson 900.00 1500.00
84 Malachi Kittredge/Boston NL 900.00 1500.00
85 Malachi Kittredge/Wash. 900.00 1500.00
86 Candy LaChance 900.00 1500.00
87 Nap Lajoie 9000.00 15000.00
88 Thomas Leach 900.00 1500.00
89 Watty Lee/Pittsburgh 900.00 1500.00
90 Watty Lee/Washington 900.00 1500.00
91 Sam Leever 900.00 1500.00
92 Herman Long 1200.00 2000.00
93 Billy Lush/Cleveland 900.00 1500.00
94 Billy Lush/Detroit 900.00 1500.00
95 Christy Mathewson 30000.00 50000.00
96 Sport McAllister 900.00 1500.00
97 Jack McCarthy 900.00 1500.00
98 Barry McCormick 900.00 1500.00
99 Ed McFarland 900.00 1500.00
100 Herm McFarland 900.00 1500.00
101 Joe McGinnity 5000.00 8000.00
102 John McGraw 7000.00 12000.00
103 Deacon McGuire/Brooklyn 3000.00 5000.00
104 Deacon McGuire/New York
105 Jock Menefee 900.00 1500.00
106 Sam Mertes 900.00 1500.00
107 Roscoe Miller 900.00 1500.00
108 Fred Mitchell 900.00 1500.00
109 Earl Moore 900.00 1500.00
110 Danny Murphy 900.00 1500.00
111 Jack O'Connor 900.00 1500.00
112 Al Orth 900.00 1500.00
113 Dick Padden 900.00 1500.00
114 Freddy Parent 900.00 1500.00
115 Roy Patterson 900.00 1500.00
116 Heinie Peitz 900.00 1500.00
117 Deacon Phillipe/sic, Phillipi 1200.00 2000.00
118 Wiley Piatt 900.00 1500.00
119 Ollie Pickering 900.00 1500.00
120 Eddie Plank 9000.00 15000.00
121 Ed Poole/Brooklyn 900.00 1500.00
122 Ed Poole/Cinc. 900.00 1500.00
123 Jack Powell/New York AL 900.00 1500.00
124 Jack Powell/StL AL 900.00 1500.00
125 Doc Powers 900.00 1500.00
126 Claude Ritchey/sic, Ritchie 900.00 1500.00
127 Jimmy Ryan 1200.00 2000.00
128 Ossie Schreckengost 900.00 1500.00
129 Kip Selbach 900.00 1500.00
130 Socks Seybold 900.00 1500.00
131 Jimmy Sheckard 900.00 1500.00
132 Ed Siever 900.00 1500.00
133 Harry Smith 900.00 1500.00
134 Tully Sparks 900.00 1500.00
135 Jake Stahl 1200.00 2000.00
136 Harry Steinfeldt 1200.00 2000.00
137 Sammy Strang 900.00 1500.00
138 Willie Sudhoff 900.00 1500.00
139 Joe Sugden 900.00 1500.00
140 Billy Sullivan 1200.00 2000.00
141 Jack Taylor 900.00 1500.00
142 Fred Tenney 900.00 1500.00
143 Roy Thomas 1250.00 1500.00
144 Jack Thoney/Cleve. 900.00 1500.00
145 Jack Thoney/NY AL 900.00 1500.00
146 Happy Townsend 900.00 1500.00
147 George Van Haltren 900.00 1500.00
148 Rube Waddell 7000.00 12000.00
149 Honus Wagner 60000.00 80000.00
150 Bobby Wallace 5000.00 8000.00
151 John Warner 900.00 1500.00
152 Jimmy Wiggs 900.00 1500.00
153 Jimmy Williams 900.00 1500.00
154 Vic Willis 5000.00 8000.00
155 Snake Wiltse 900.00 1500.00
156 George Winter/sic, Winters 900.00 1500.00
157 Bob Wood 900.00 1500.00
158 Joe Yeager 900.00 1500.00
159 Cy Young 15000.00 30000.00
160 Chief Zimmer 900.00 1500.00

1981 George Brett Promo

This promo card was distributed at the St. Louis Card Show in 1981. It commemorates his .390 season. It features an artist's rendition with a Sporting News quote on back. Just 5,000 were issued.

1 George Brett 4.00 10.00

1982 Brett Spotbilt

This one card standard-size set features Kansas City Royals star George Brett. This card features Brett's picture on the card. The letters GB5 (his uniform number) are on the top with the Spot-Bilt words and logo on the bottom. The horizontal back has vital statistics, career stats as well as some career highlights.

5 George Brett .40 1.00

1993 George Brett 3,000 Hit

This one-card set is actually a 16-page booklet honoring George Brett for his 3,000 hits. The front features a strip depicting Brett at bat with a facsimile autograph below. The back displays a color photo of Brett rejoicing after the hit. The inside carries facts about the player with an autographed picture enclosed.

1 George Brett 2.00 5.00

1970 Brewers McDonald's

This 31-card set features cards measuring approximately 2 15/16" by 4 3/8" and was issued during the Brewers' first year in Milwaukee after moving from Seattle. The cards are drawings of the members of the 1970 Milwaukee Brewers and underneath the drawings there is information about the players. These cards are still often found in uncut sheet form and hence have no extra value in that form. The backs are blank. The set is checklisted alphabetically with the number of the sheet being listed next to the players name. There were six different sheets of six cards each although only one sheet contained six players; the other sheets depicted five players and a Brewers' logo.

COMPLETE SET (31) 3.00 8.00
1 Max Alvis 6 .10 .25
2 Bob Bolin 1 .10 .25
3 Gene Brabender 3 .10 .25
4 Dave Bristol 5 MG .20 .50
5 Wayne Comer 2 .10 .25
6 Cal Ermer 3 CO .10 .25
7 John Gelnar 4 .10 .25
8 Greg Goossen 5 .10 .25
9 Tommy Harper 5 .30 .75
10 Mike Hegan 3 .20 .50
11 Mike Hershberger 3 .10 .25
12 Steve Hovley 2 .10 .25
13 John Kennedy 2 .10 .25
14 Lew Krausse 4 .10 .25
15 Ted Kubiak 1 .10 .25
16 George Lauzerique 6 .10 .25
17 Bob Locker 5 .10 .25
18 Roy McMillan 4 CO .20 .50
19 Jerry McNertney 4 .10 .25
20 Bob Meyer 2 .10 .25
21 Jackie Moore 6 CO .20 .50
22 John Morris 1 .10 .25
23 John O'Donoghue 1 .10 .25
24 Marty Pattin 6 .10 .25
25 Rich Rollins 4 .20 .50
26 Phil Roof 5 .10 .25
27 Ted Savage 1 .10 .25
28 Russ Snyder 6 .10 .25
29 Wes Stock 2 CO .20 .50
30 Sandy Valdespino 2 .10 .25
31 Danny Walton 3 .10 .25

1970 Brewers Milk

This 24-card set of the Milwaukee Brewers measures approximately 2 5/8" by 4 1/4" and features blue-and-white player photos. The players name is printed in blue in the white wide bottom border. The cards are unnumbered and checklisted below in alphabetical order.

COMPLETE SET (24) 4.00 10.00
1 Gene Brabender .20 .50
2 Dave Bristol MG .30 .75
3 Wayne Comer .20 .50
4 Cal Ermer CO .20 .50
5 Greg Goossen .20 .50
6 Tom Harper .40 1.00
7 Mike Hegan .30 .75
8 Mike Hershberger .20 .50
9 Steve Hovley .20 .50
10 John Kennedy .20 .50
11 Lew Krausse .20 .50
12 Ted Kubiak .20 .50
13 Bob Locker .20 .50
14 Roy McMillan CO .30 .75
15 Jerry McNertney .20 .50
16 Bob Meyer .20 .50
17 John Morris .20 .50
18 John O'Donoghue .20 .50
19 Marty Pattin .20 .50
20 Rich Rollins .30 .75
21 Phil Roof .20 .50
22 Ted Savage .20 .50
23 Russ Snyder .20 .50
24 Dan Walton .20 .50

1970 Brewers Team Issue

This 12-card set of the Milwaukee Brewers measures approximately 4 1/4" by 7". The fronts display black-and-white player portraits bordered in white. The player's name and team are printed in the top margin. The backs are blank. The cards are unnumbered and checklisted below in alphabetical order.

COMPLETE SET (12) 8.00 20.00
1 Max Alvis .75 2.00
2 Dave Bristol .75 2.00
3 Tommy Harper 1.00 2.50
4 Mike Hegan .75 2.00
5 Mike Hershberger .60 1.50
6 Lew Krausse .60 1.50
7 Ted Kubiak .60 1.50
8 Dave May .60 1.50
9 Jerry McNertney .60 1.50
10 Phil Roof .60 1.50
11 Ted Savage .60 1.50
12 Danny Walton .60 1.50

1971 Brewers Team Issue

This 18-photo set features members of the Milwaukee Brewers. The photos are not dated, but can be identified as a 1971 issue since Bill Voss' card is included in the set and this was his first year with the team. Additionally, Tommy Harper's card is included and 1971 was his final year with the Brewers. The photos are printed on thin paper stock that has a pebbled texture. They measure approximately 4 1/4" by 7" and display black-and-white portraits edged in white. The player's name and team are printed in the top margin. The cards have blank backs and are numbered and checklisted alphabetically below.

COMMON PLAYER (1-18) 8.00 20.00
1 Max Alvis .60 1.50
2 Dave Bristol MG .60 1.50
3 Tommy Harper .75 2.00
4 Mike Hegan .75 2.00
5 Mike Hershberger .60 1.50
6 Lew Krausse .60 1.50
7 Ted Kubiak .60 1.50
8 Dave May .60 1.50
9 Jerry McNertney .60 1.50
10 Bill Parsons .60 1.50
11 Marty Pattin .60 1.50
12 Roberto Pena .60 1.50
13 Ellie Rodriguez .60 1.50
14 Phil Roof .60 1.50
15 Ken Sanders .60 1.50
16 Ted Savage .60 1.50
17 Bill Voss .60 1.50
18 Danny Walton .60 1.50

1975 Brewers Broadcasters

This seven-card standard-size set features four announcer cards and three schedule cards. The cards were issued as a seven-card pack with a piece of Topps gum included. All the cards have on the fronts black and white photos, with orange picture frame borders on a white card face. The backs are gray and present either comments on the announcers or broadcast schedules. The first four cards are numbered on the back.

COMMON PLAYER (1-4) 10.00 25.00
1 Jim Irwin ANN 1.25 3.00
2 Gary Bender ANN 1.50 4.00
3 Bob Uecker ANN 4.00 10.00
4 Merle Harmon ANN 2.00 5.00
x Television Schedule/(unnumbered) 1.25 3.00
x Radio Schedule Part 1/(unnumbered) 1.25 3.00
x Radio Schedule Part 2/(unnumbered) 1.25 3.00

1976 Brewers A and P

This 16-card set of the Milwaukee Brewers measures approximately 5 7/8" by 9". The white-bordered fronts feature color player head photos with a facsimile autograph below. The backs are blank. The cards are unnumbered and checklisted below in alphabetical order. They were issued four at a time over a four week period at participating A and P stores. These cards were made available to customers who bought specially marked items.

COMPLETE SET (16) 8.00 20.00
1 Hank Aaron 4.00 10.00
2 Pete Broberg .20 .50
3 Jim Colborn .20 .50
4 Mike Hegan .20 .50
5 Von Joshua .20 .50
6 Tim Johnson .20 .50
7 Sixto Lezcano .20 .50
8 Charlie Moore .20 .50
9 Don Money .20 .50
10 Darrell Porter .60 1.50
11 George Scott .60 1.50
12 Bill Sharp .20 .50
13 Jim Slaton .20 .50
14 Bill Travers .20 .50
15 Robin Yount 3.00 8.00
16 County Stadium .20 .50

1979 Brewers Team Issue

These cards, which measure 4" by 5 1/2" were issued either on light paper or on card stock. Some of these cards were issued both ways. All values are the same no matter what stock was used. These cards were not numbered so we have sequenced them alphabetically.

COMPLETE SET (29) 6.00 15.00
1 Jerry Augustine .20 .50
2 George Bamberger MG .20 .50
3 Sal Bando .30 .75
4 Mike Caldwell .20 .50
5 Bill Castro .20 .50
6 Cecil Cooper .40 1.00
7 Reggie Cleveland .20 .50
8 Dick Davis .20 .50
9 Ray Fosse .20 .50
10 Bob Galasso .20 .50
11 Jim Gantner .20 .50
12 Moose Haas .20 .50
13 Larry Haney CO .20 .50
14 Larry Hisle .20 .50
15 Frank Howard CO .30 .75
16 Harvey Kuenn CO .30 .75
17 Sixto Lezcano .20 .50
18 Buck Martinez .30 .75
19 Cal McLish CO .20 .50
20 Bob McClure .20 .50
21 Don Money .20 .50
22 Ben Oglivie .20 .50
23 Buck Rodgers CO .20 .50
24 Jim Slaton .20 .50
25 Lary Sorensen .20 .50
26 Gorman Thomas .30 .75
27 Bill Travers .20 .50
28 Jim Wohlford .20 .50
29 Robin Yount 2.00 5.00

1980 Brewers Team Issue

These 24 photos were issued by the team and feature members of the 1980 Milwaukee Brewers. The photos are unnumbered and sequenced in alphabetical order.

COMPLETE SET 6.00 15.00
1 Jerry Augustine .20 .50
2 George Bamberger MG .20 .50
3 Sal Bando .30 .75
4 Mark Brouhard .20 .50
5 Mike Caldwell .20 .50
6 Bill Castro .20 .50
7 Reggie Cleveland .20 .50
8 Dick Davis .20 .50
9 Jim Gantner .30 .75
10 Moose Haas .20 .50
11 Larry Haney CO .20 .50
12 Ron Hansen CO .20 .50
13 Larry Hisle .20 .50
14 Frank Howard CO .30 .75
15 Harvey Kuenn CO .30 .75
16 Sixto Lezcano .20 .50
17 Buck Martinez .30 .75
18 Cal McLish CO .20 .50
19 Don Money .30 .75
20 Ben Oglivie .30 .75
21 Buck Rodgers CO .20 .50
22 Lary Sorenson .20 .50
23 Gorman Thomas .30 .75
24 Robin Yount 2.00 5.00

1982 Brewers Police

The cards in this 30-card set measure approximately 2 13/16" by 4 1/8". This set of Milwaukee Brewers baseball cards is noted for its excellent color photographs set upon a simple white background. The set was initially distributed at the stadium on May 5th, but was also handed out by several local police departments, and credit lines for the Wisconsin State Fair Park Police (no shield design on reverse), Milwaukee, Brookfield, and Wauwatosa PD's have already been found. The reverses feature advice concerning safety measures, social situations, and crime prevention (Romero card in both Spanish and English). The team card carries a checklist which lists the Brewer's coaches separately although they all appear on a single card; VP/GM Harry Dalton is not mentioned on this list but is included in the set.The prices below are for the basic set without regard to the Police Department listed on the backs. Cards from the more obscure corners and small towns of Wisconsin (where fewer cards were produced) will be valued higher.

COMPLETE SET (30) 8.00 20.00
4 Paul Molitor 3.00 8.00
5 Ned Yost .30 .75
7 Don Money .30 .75
9 Larry Hisle .20 .50
10 Bob McClure .20 .50
11 Ed Romero .20 .50
13 Roy Howell .20 .50
15 Cecil Cooper .60 1.50
17 Jim Gantner .40 1.00
19 Robin Yount 2.50 6.00
20 Gorman Thomas .40 1.00
22 Charlie Moore .30 .75
23 Ted Simmons .60 1.50
24 Ben Oglivie .40 1.00
26 Kevin Bass .20 .50
28 Jamie Easterly .20 .50
29 Mark Brouhard .20 .50
30 Moose Haas .20 .50
34 Rollie Fingers 1.00 2.50
35 Randy Lerch .20 .50
41 Jim Slaton .20 .50
45 Doug Jones .60 1.50
46 Jerry Augustine .20 .50
47 Dwight Bernard .20 .50
48 Mike Caldwell .30 .75
50 Pete Vuckovich .40 1.00
NNO Team Card .40 1.00
NNO Harry Dalton GM .20 .50
NNO Buck Rodgers MG .20 .50
NNO Brewer Coaches .20 .50
Ron Hansen
Bob Rodgers MG
Harry

1983 Brewers Gardner's

The cards in this 22-card set measure 2 1/2" by 3 1/2". The 1983 Gardner's Brewers set features Milwaukee Brewer players and manager Harvey Kuenn. Topps printed the set for the Madison (Wisconsin) bakery, hence, the backs are identical to the 1983 Topps backs except for the card number. The fronts of the cards, however, feature all new photos and include the Gardner's logo and the Brewers' logo. Many of the cards are grease laden, as they were issued with packages of bread and hamburger and hot-dog buns. The card numbering for this set is essentially in alphabetical order by player's name (after the manager is listed first).

COMPLETE SET (22) 10.00 25.00
1 Harvey Kuenn MG .60 1.50
2 Dwight Bernard .30 .75
3 Mark Brouhard .30 .75
4 Mike Caldwell .40 1.00
5 Cecil Cooper .60 1.50
6 Marshall Edwards .30 .75
7 Rollie Fingers 1.25 3.00
8 Jim Gantner .50 1.25
9 Moose Haas .30 .75
10 Bob McClure .30 .75
11 Paul Molitor 4.00 10.00
12 Don Money .40 1.00
13 Charlie Moore .40 1.00
14 Ben Oglivie .50 1.25
15 Ed Romero .30 .75
16 Ted Simmons .60 1.50
17 Jim Slaton .30 .75
18 Don Sutton 1.25 3.00
19 Gorman Thomas .60 1.50
20 Pete Vuckovich .50 1.25
21 Ned Yost .40 1.00
22 Robin Yount 3.00 8.00

1983 Brewers Police

The cards in this 30-card set measure approximately 2 13/16" by 4 1/8". The 1983 Police Milwaukee Brewers set contains full color cards issued by the Milwaukee Police Department in conjunction with the Brewers. The cards are numbered on the fronts by the player uniform number and contain the line, "The Milwaukee Police Department Presents the 1983 Milwaukee Braves." The backs contain a brief narrative attributable to the player on the front, the Milwaukee Police logo, and a Milwaukee Brewers logo stating that they were the 1982 American League Champions. In all, 28 variations of these Police sets have been found to date. Prices below are for the basic set without regard to the Police Department listed on the backs of the cards; cards from the more obscure corners and small towns of Wisconsin (whose cards were produced in lesser quantities) will be valued higher.

COMPLETE SET (30) 5.00 12.00
4 Paul Molitor 1.50 4.00
5 Ned Yost .20 .50
7 Don Money .20 .50
8 Rob Picciolo .08 .25
10 Bob McClure .08 .25
11 Ed Romero .08 .25
13 Roy Howell .08 .25
15 Cecil Cooper .30 .75
16 Marshall Edwards .08 .25
17 Jim Gantner .30 .75
19 Robin Yount 1.25 3.00
20 Gorman Thomas .40 1.00
21 Don Sutton .60 1.50
22 Charlie Moore .08 .25
23 Ted Simmons .40 1.00
24 Ben Oglivie .20 .50
26 Bob Skube .08 .25
27 Pete Ladd .08 .25
28 Jamie Easterly .08 .25
30 Moose Haas .08 .25
32 Harvey Kuenn MG .20 .50
34 Rollie Fingers .60 1.50
40 Bob L. Gibson .08 .25
41 Jim Slaton .08 .25
42 Tom Tellmann .08 .25
46 Jerry Augustine .08 .25
48 Mike Caldwell .20 .50
50 Pete Vuckovich .20 .50
NNO Coaches Card .20 .50
Pat Dobson
Ron Hansen
Larry Haney#
NNO Team Photo/(Checklist back) .20 .50

1984 Brewers Gardner's

The cards in this 22-card set measure 2 1/2" by 3 1/2". For the second year in a row, the Gardner Bakery Company issued a set of cards available in packages of Gardner Bakery products. The set was manufactured by Topps, and the backs of the cards are identical to the Topps cards of this year except for the numbers. The Gardner logo appears on the fronts of the cards with the player's name, position abbreviation, the name Brewers, and the words 1984 Series II. The card numbering for this set is essentially in alphabetical order by player's name (after the manager is listed first).

COMPLETE SET (22) 5.00 12.00
1 Rene Lachemann MG .08 .25
2 Mark Brouhard .08 .25
3 Mike Caldwell .20 .50
4 Bobby Clark .08 .25
5 Cecil Cooper .40 1.00
6 Rollie Fingers .75 2.00
7 Jim Gantner .30 .75
8 Moose Haas .08 .25
9 Roy Howell .08 .25
10 Pete Ladd .08 .25
11 Rick Manning .08 .25
12 Bob McClure .08 .25
13 Paul Molitor 1.50 4.00
14 Charlie Moore .20 .50
15 Ben Oglivie .30 .75
16 Ed Romero .08 .25
17 Ted Simmons .40 1.00
18 Jim Sundberg .20 .50
19 Don Sutton .75 2.00
20 Tom Tellmann .08 .25
21 Pete Vuckovich .30 .75
22 Robin Yount 1.25 3.00

1984 Brewers Mr Z's Pizza

These cards were issued as part of a set of Milwaukee Brewers issued as pizza inserts during the 1984 season. These cards feature full color photos of the featured Brewers. There may be additions to this checklist so any help is appreciated. Since these cards are unnumbered, we have sequenced them in alphabetical order.

COMPLETE SET 3.00 8.00
1 Cecil Cooper .75 2.00
2 Jim Gantner .50 1.25
3 Paul Molitor 1.50 4.00
4 Robin Yount 1.25 3.00

1984 Brewers Police

The cards in this 30-card set measure approximately 2 13/16" by 4 1/8". Again this year, the police departments in and around Milwaukee issued sets of the Milwaukee Brewers. Although each set contained the same players and numbers, the individual police departments placed their own name on the fronts of cards to show that they were the particular jurisdiction issuing the set. The backs contain the Brewers logo, a safety tip, and in some cases, a badge of the jurisdiction. To date, 59 variations of this set have been found. Prices below are for the basic set without regard to the Police Department issuing the cards; cards from the more obscure corners and small towns of Wisconsin will be valued higher. Cards are numbered by uniform number.

COMPLETE SET (30) 4.00 10.00
2 Randy Ready .08 .25
4 Paul Molitor 1.25 3.00
8 Jim Sundberg .20 .50
9 Rene Lachemann MG .08 .25
10 Bob McClure .08 .25
11 Ed Romero .08 .25
13 Roy Howell .08 .25
14 Dion James .08 .25
15 Cecil Cooper .30 .75
17 Jim Gantner .30 .75
19 Robin Yount 1.00 2.50
20 Don Sutton .60 1.50
21 Bill Schroeder .08 .25
22 Charlie Moore .08 .25
23 Ted Simmons .40 1.00
24 Ben Oglivie .30 .75
25 Bob Clark .08 .25
27 Pete Ladd .08 .25
28 Rick Manning .08 .25
29 Mark Brouhard .08 .25
30 Moose Haas .08 .25
34 Rollie Fingers .60 1.50
42 Tom Tellmann .08 .25
43 Chuck Porter .08 .25
46 Jerry Augustine .08 .25
47 Jaime Cocanower .08 .25
48 Mike Caldwell .20 .50
50 Pete Vuckovich .20 .50
NNO Coaches Card .08 .25
Dave Garcia
Pat Dobson
Andy Etcheb
NNO Team Photo/(Checklist back) .20 .50

1985 Brewers Gardner's

The cards in this 22-card set measure 2 1/2" by 3 1/2". For the third year in a row, the Gardner Bakery Company issued a set of cards available in packages of Gardner Bakery products. The set was manufactured by Topps, and the backs of the cards are identical to the Topps cards of this year except for the card numbers and copyright information. The Gardner logo appears on the fronts of the cards with the player's name, position abbreviation, and the name Brewers. The card numbering for this set is essentially in alphabetical order.

COMPLETE SET (22) 4.00 10.00
1 George Bamberger MG .20 .50
2 Mark Brouhard .08 .25
3 Bobby Clark .08 .25
4 Jaime Cocanower .08 .25
5 Cecil Cooper .40 1.00
6 Rollie Fingers .60 1.50
7 Jim Gantner .30 .75
8 Moose Haas .08 .25
9 Dion James .08 .25
10 Pete Ladd .08 .25
11 Rick Manning .08 .25
12 Bob McClure .08 .25
13 Paul Molitor 1.50 4.00
14 Charlie Moore .20 .50
15 Ben Oglivie .30 .75
16 Chuck Porter .08 .25
17 Ed Romero .08 .25
18 Bill Schroeder .08 .25
19 Ted Simmons .40 1.00
20 Tom Tellmann .08 .25
21 Pete Vuckovich .30 .75
22 Robin Yount 1.25 3.00

1985 Brewers Police

The cards in this 30-card set measure 2 3/4" by 4 1/8". Again this year, the police departments in and around Milwaukee issued sets of the Milwaukee Brewers. The backs contain the Brewers logo, a safety tip, and in some cases, a badge of the jurisdiction. Prices below are for the basic set without regard to the Police Department issuing the cards; cards from the more obscure corners and small towns of Wisconsin (smaller production) will be valued higher. Cards are numbered by uniform number.

COMPLETE SET (30) 3.00 8.00
2 Randy Ready .08 .25
4 Paul Molitor 1.25 3.00
5 Doug Loman .08 .25
7 Paul Householder .08 .25
10 Bob McClure .08 .25
11 Ed Romero .08 .25
14 Dion James .08 .25
15 Cecil Cooper .40 1.00
17 Jim Gantner .30 .75
18 Danny Darwin .08 .25
19 Robin Yount .75 2.00
21 Bill Schroeder .08 .25
22 Charlie Moore .08 .25
23 Ted Simmons .40 1.00
24 Ben Oglivie .20 .50
26 Brian Giles .08 .25
27 Pete Ladd .08 .25
28 Rick Manning .08 .25
29 Mark Brouhard .08 .25
30 Moose Haas .08 .25
31 George Bamberger MG .20 .50
34 Rollie Fingers .60 1.50
40 Bob L. Gibson .08 .25
41 Ray Searage .08 .25
47 Jaime Cocanower .08 .25
48 Ray Burris .08 .25
49 Ted Higuera .20 .50
50 Pete Vuckovich .20 .50
NNO Team Roster .08 .25
NNO Coaches Card .08 .25
Herm Sterrette
Tony Muser
Frank Ho
NNO Newspaper Carrier .08 .25

1986 Brewers Greats TCMA

This 12-card standard-size set honors the best retired Brewers of the first two decades. The fronts have a player photo and position while the backs have vital statistics, career information and lifetime statistics.

COMPLETE SET (12) 1.25 3.00
1 George Scott .20 .50
2 Pedro Garcia .08 .25
3 Tim Johnson .08 .25
4 Don Money .08 .25
5 Sixto Lezcano .08 .25
6 John Briggs .08 .25
7 Dave May .08 .25
8 Darrell Porter .20 .50
9 Jim Colborn .08 .25
10 Mike Caldwell .20 .50
11 Rollie Fingers .40 1.00
12 Harvey Kuenn MG .20 .50

1986 Brewers Police

This 32-card safety set was also sponsored by WTMJ Radio and Kinney Shoes. The backs contain the usual biographical info and safety tip. The front features a full-color photo of the player, his name, position, and uniform number. The cards measure approximately 2 5/8" by 4 1/8". Cards were freely distributed throughout the summer by the Police Departments in the Milwaukee area. Cards are numbered in alphabetical order.

COMPLETE SET (32) 3.00 8.00
1 George Bamberger MG .08 .25
2 Juan Castillo .08 .25
3 Rick Cerone .08 .25
4 Mark Clear .08 .25
5 Jaime Cocanower .08 .25
6 Cecil Cooper .30 .75
7 Danny Darwin .08 .25
8 Rob Deer .08 .25
9 Mike Felder .08 .25
10 Jim Gantner .08 .25
11 Ted Higuera .20 .50
12 Paul Householder .08 .25
13 Tim Leary .08 .25
14 Rick Manning .08 .25
15 Bob McClure .08 .25
16 Paul Molitor 1.25 3.00
17 Charlie Moore .08 .25
18 Juan Nieves .08 .25
19 Ben Oglivie .20 .50
20 Dan Plesac .20 .50
21 Chuck Porter .08 .25
22 Randy Ready .08 .25
23 Ernest Riles .08 .25
24 Billy Jo Robidoux .08 .25
25 Bill Schroeder .08 .25
26 Ray Searage .08 .25
27 Bill Wegman .08 .25
28 Robin Yount .75 2.00
29 Andy Etchebarren CO .08 .25
Larry Haney CO
Frank Howard
30 Milwaukee Brewers .08 .25

1987 Brewers Police

This 30-card safety set was also sponsored by WTMJ Radio and Kinney Shoes. The backs contain the usual biographical info and safety tip. The front features a full-color photo of the player, his name, position, and uniform number. The cards measure approximately 2 5/8" by 4 1/8". Cards were freely distributed throughout the summer by the Police Departments in the Milwaukee area and throughout other parts of Wisconsin. Cards are numbered below by uniform number. Bosio comes as card number #26 or card#29, there is no difference in the values of the Bosio cards.

COMPLETE SET (30) 3.00 8.00
1 Ernest Riles .08 .25
2 Edgar Diaz .08 .25
3 Juan Castillo .08 .25
4 Paul Molitor 1.00 2.50
5 B.J. Surhoff .75 2.00
7 Dale Sveum .08 .25
9 Greg Brock .08 .25
13 Billy Joe Robidoux .08 .25
14 Jim Paciorek .08 .25
15 Cecil Cooper .30 .75
16 Mike Felder .08 .25
17 Jim Gantner .30 .75
19 Robin Yount .75 2.00
20 Juan Nieves .08 .25
21 Bill Schroeder .08 .25
25 Mark Clear .08 .25
26 Glenn Braggs .08 .25
26 Chris Bosio .08 .25
28 Rick Manning .08 .25
29 Chris Bosio .20 .50
32 Chuck Crim .08 .25
34 Mark Ciardi .08 .25
37 Dan Plesac .20 .50
38 John Henry Johnson .08 .25
40 Mike Birkbeck .08 .25
42 Tom Trebelhorn MG .08 .25
45 Rob Deer .20 .50
46 Bill Wegman .08 .25
49 Teddy Higuera .08 .25
NNO Coaching Staff .08 .25
Andy Etchebarren
Larry Haney
Chu
NNO Brewers Team/(Checklist on back).20 .50

1987 Brewers Team Issue

These cards feature members of the 1987 Milwaukee Brewers. These cards are unnumbered and we have checklisted them below in alphabetical order.

COMPLETE SET (16) 2.50 6.00
1 Glenn Braggs .08 .25
2 Greg Brock .08 .25
3 Mark Clear .08 .25
4 Cecil Cooper .30 .75
5 Rob Deer .08 .25
6 Jim Gantner .30 .75
7 Teddy Higuera .08 .25
8 Paul Molitor 1.00 2.50
9 Juan Nieves .08 .25
10 Dan Plesac .20 .50
11 Billy Jo Robidoux .08 .25
12 Bill Schroeder .08 .25
13 B.J. Surhoff .60 1.50
14 Dale Sveum .08 .25
15 Bill Wegman .08 .25
16 Robin Yount .60 1.50

1988 Brewers Police

This 30-card safety set was also sponsored by WTMJ Radio and Stadia Athletic Shoes. The backs contain the usual biographical info and safety tip. The front features a full-color photo of the player, his name, position, and uniform number. The cards measure approximately 2 7/8" by 4 1/8". Cards were freely distributed throughout the summer by the Police Departments in the Milwaukee area and throughout other parts of Wisconsin. Cards are numbered below by uniform number.

COMPLETE SET (30) 2.50 6.00
1 Ernest Riles .08 .25
3 Juan Castillo .08 .25
4 Paul Molitor 1.00 2.50
5 B.J. Surhoff .60 1.50
7 Dale Sveum .08 .25
9 Greg Brock .08 .25
11 Charlie O'Brien .08 .25
14 Jim Adduci .08 .25
16 Mike Felder .08 .25
17 Jim Gantner .30 .75
19 Robin Yount .60 1.50
20 Juan Nieves .08 .25
21 Bill Schroeder .08 .25
23 Joey Meyer .08 .25
25 Mark Clear .08 .25
26 Glenn Braggs .08 .25
28 Odell Jones .08 .25
29 Chris Bosio .08 .25
30 Steve Kiefer .08 .25
32 Chuck Crim .08 .25
33 Jay Aldrich .08 .25
37 Dan Plesac .20 .50
40 Mike Birkbeck .08 .25
42 Tom Trebelhorn MG .08 .25

43 Dave Stapleton .08 .25
45 Rob Deer .20 .50
46 Bill Wegman .08 .25
49 Ted Higuera .08 .25
NNO Team Photo HOR .20 .50
NNO Manager .08 .25
Coaches HOR
Andy Etchebarren
Larry Haney

1988 Brewers Team Issue

This 37-card set of the 1988 Milwaukee Brewers features black-and-white player portraits with white borders and measures approximately 4" by 5 1/2". The backs are blank. The cards are unnumbered and checklisted below in alphabetical order.

COMPLETE SET (37) 4.00 10.00
1 Jim Adduci .08 .25
2 Don August .08 .25
3 Mike Birkbeck .08 .25
4 Chris Bosio .08 .25
5 Glenn Braggs .08 .25
6 Greg Brock .08 .25
7 Juan Castillo .08 .25
8 Mark Clear .08 .25
9 Chuck Crim .08 .25
10 Rob Deer .08 .25
11 Andy Etchebarren CO .08 .25
12 Mike Felder .08 .25
13 Tom Filer .08 .25
14 Jim Gantner .30 .75
15 Darryl Hamilton .08 .25
16 Larry Haney CO .08 .25
17 Chuck Hartenstein CO .08 .25
18 Ted Higuera .08 .25
19 Dave Hilton CO .08 .25
20 Odell Jones .08 .25
21 Steve Kiefer .08 .25
22 Jeffrey Leonard .08 .25
23 Joey Meyer .08 .25
24 Paul Mirabella .08 .25
25 Paul Molitor .60 1.50
26 Tony Muser CO .08 .25
27 Juan Nieves .08 .25
28 Charlie O'Brien .08 .25
29 Dan Plesac .08 .25
30 Billy Jo Robidoux .08 .25
31 Bill Schroeder .08 .25
32 Dave Stapleton .08 .25
33 B.J. Surhoff .40 1.00
34 Dale Sveum .08 .25
35 Tom Trebelhorn MG .08 .25
36 Bill Wegman .08 .25
37 Robin Yount .50 1.25

1989 Brewers Gardner's

The 1989 Gardner's Brewers set contains 15 standard-size cards. The fronts feature airbrushed mugshots with sky blue backgrounds and white borders. The backs are white and feature career stats. One card was distributed in each specially marked Gardner's bakery product. Cards were issued during the middle of the season. For some reason Riles is included in the set even though he had been traded by the Brewers during the 1988 season.

COMPLETE SET (15) 5.00 12.00
1 Paul Molitor 2.50 6.00
2 Robin Yount 1.50 4.00
3 Jim Gantner .40 1.00
4 Rob Deer .20 .50
5 B.J. Surhoff .60 1.50
6 Dale Sveum .20 .50
7 Ted Higuera .20 .50
8 Dan Plesac .30 .75
9 Bill Wegman .20 .50
10 Juan Nieves .20 .50
11 Greg Brock .20 .50
12 Glenn Braggs .20 .50
13 Joey Meyer .20 .50
14 Earnest Riles .20 .50
15 Don August .20 .50

1989 Brewers Police

The 1989 Police Milwaukee Brewers set contains 30 cards measuring approximately 2 3/4" by 4 1/4". The fronts have color photos with white borders; the backs feature safety tips. The unnumbered cards were given away by various local Wisconsin police departments. The cards are numbered below by uniform number.

COMPLETE SET (30) 3.00 8.00
1 Gary Sheffield 1.50 4.00
4 Paul Molitor 1.00 2.50
5 B.J. Surhoff .40 1.00
6 Bill Spiers .08 .25
7 Dale Sveum .08 .25
9 Greg Brock .08 .25
14 Gus Polidor .08 .25
16 Mike Felder .08 .25
17 Jim Gantner .30 .75
19 Robin Yount .75 2.00
20 Juan Nieves .08 .25
22 Charlie O'Brien .08 .25
23 Joey Meyer .08 .25
25 Dave Engle .08 .25
26 Glenn Braggs .08 .25
27 Paul Mirabella .08 .25
29 Chris Bosio .08 .25
30 Terry Francona .30 .75
32 Chuck Crim .08 .25
37 Dan Plesac .08 .25
38 Don August .08 .25
40 Mike Birkbeck .08 .25
41 Mark Knudson .08 .25
42 Tom Trebelhorn MG .08 .25
45 Rob Deer .08 .25
46 Bill Wegman .08 .25
48 Bryan Clutterbuck .08 .25
49 Teddy Higuera .08 .25
NNO Team Card/(Checklist on back) .20 .50
NNO Coaches Card .08 .25
Duffy Dyer
Andy Etchebarren
Larry

1989 Brewers Yearbook

This 18-card standard size set was issued as an insert in the 1989 Milwaukee Brewer Yearbooks. The yearbook itself had a suggested retail price of 4.95. The card set features 17 of the Brewers and their manager. The cards are dominated by a full-color photo of the player on the top two-thirds of the cards along with the uniform number name and position underneath the player. There is also a large logo on the bottom right of the card commemorating the twentieth anniversary of the Brewers in Milwaukee. The backs only contain the player's name and their career statistics. The set is checklisted below by uniform numbers.

COMPLETE SET (18) 4.00 10.00
1 Gary Sheffield 1.50 4.00
4 Paul Molitor 1.25 3.00
5 B.J. Surhoff .40 1.00
7 Dale Sveum .08 .25
9 Greg Brock .08 .25
17 Jim Gantner .30 .75
19 Robin Yount .75 2.00
20 Juan Nieves .08 .25
26 Glenn Braggs .08 .25
29 Chris Bosio .08 .25
32 Chuck Crim .08 .25
37 Dan Plesac .20 .50
38 Don August .08 .25
40 Mike Birkbeck .08 .25
42 Tom Trebelhorn MG .08 .25
45 Rob Deer .08 .25
46 Bill Wegman .08 .25
49 Ted Higuera .08 .25

1990 Brewers Miller Brewing

This 32-card standard-size set and a plastic binder were sponsored by Miller Brewing Co. and given away to the first 25,000 adults (21 years and older) attending the Brewers' home game against the White Sox on August 4th. The fronts have either action or posed color player photos, with the player's name and position given in white lettering on a black stripe at the bottom of the card face. The backs have biographical information and player statistics. The cards are unnumbered and checklisted below in alphabetical order. The complete set price below does not include the binder.

COMPLETE SET (32) 8.00 20.00
1 Chris Bosio .08 .25
2 Greg Brock .08 .25
3 Chuck Crim .08 .25
4 Rob Deer .08 .25
5 Edgar Diaz .08 .25
6 Tom Edens .08 .25
7 Mike Felder .08 .25
8 Tom Filer .08 .25
9 Jim Gantner .30 .75
10 Darryl Hamilton .08 .25
11 Teddy Higuera .08 .25
12 Mark Knudson .08 .25
13 Bill Krueger .08 .25
14 Paul Mirabella .08 .25
15 Paul Molitor 3.00 8.00
16 Jaime Navarro .08 .25
17 Charlie O'Brien .08 .25
18 Dave Parker .40 1.00
19 Dan Plesac .08 .25
20 Dennis Powell .08 .25
21 Ron Robinson .08 .25
22 Bob Sebra .08 .25
23 Gary Sheffield 1.25 3.00
24 Bill Spiers .08 .25
25 B.J. Surhoff .40 1.00
26 Dale Sveum .08 .25
27 Tom Trebelhorn MG .08 .25
28 Greg Vaughn .60 1.50
29 Randy Veres .08 .25
30 Bill Wegman .08 .25
31 Robin Yount 2.50 6.00
32 Coaches Card .20 .50
Don Baylor
Ray Burris
Duffy Dyer/
XX Album .40 1.00

1990 Brewers Police

This 30-card police set was issued in conjunction with the Fan Appreciation store of Waukesha, Wisconsin and the Waukesha Police department. This set measures approximately 2 13/16" by 4 1/8" and is checklisted in alphabetical order. The front of the card is a full-color photo surrounded by a blue border while the back has anti-crime tips.

COMPLETE SET (30) 3.00 8.00
1 Don August .08 .25
2 Billy Bates .08 .25
3 Chris Bosio .08 .25
4 Glenn Braggs .08 .25
5 Greg Brock .08 .25
6 Chuck Crim .08 .25
7 Rob Deer .08 .25
8 Eddie Diaz .08 .25
9 Mike Felder .08 .25
10 Tom Filer .08 .25
11 Tony Fossas .08 .25
12 Jim Gantner .20 .50
13 Ted Higuera .08 .25
14 Mark Knudson .08 .25
15 Paul Mirabella .08 .25
16 Paul Molitor .75 2.00
17 Jaime Navarro .08 .25
18 Charlie O'Brien .08 .25
19 Dave Parker .40 1.00
20 Dan Plesac .08 .25
21 Gus Polidor .08 .25
22 Gary Sheffield .60 1.50
23 B.J. Surhoff .20 .50
24 Dale Sveum .08 .25
25 Tom Trebelhorn MG .08 .25
26 Greg Vaughn .40 1.00
27 Robin Yount .60 1.50
28 Don Baylor CO .20 .50
Ray Burris CO
Duffy Dyer CO
Andy
29 Milwaukee Brewers .20 .50

1991 Brewers Miller Brewing

This 32-card set was sponsored by the Miller Brewing Company, and the company logo appears in red lettering at the lower right corner of the front. The cards were given away at the Brewers' home game against the Baltimore Orioles on August 17. The standard-size cards feature on the fronts color action player photos inside a pentagonal-shaped design that resembles home plate. A black border on the right side of the pentagon creates the impression of a shadow. The words "91 Brewers" appears in bluish-purple lettering above the photo, with player information given in black lettering in the lower left corner of the card face. The backs are printed in black and present complete Major League statistics. The cards are unnumbered and checklisted below in alphabetical order, with the coaches' card listed at the end.

COMPLETE SET (32) 5.00 12.00
1 Don August .08 .25
2 Jim Austin .08 .25
3 Dante Bichette .40 1.00
4 Chris Bosio .08 .25
5 Kevin D. Brown .08 .25
6 Chuck Crim .08 .25
7 Rick Dempsey .20 .50
8 Jim Gantner .30 .75
9 Darryl Hamilton .08 .25
10 Teddy Higuera .08 .25
11 Darren Holmes .08 .25
12 Jim Hunter .08 .25
13 Mark Knudson .08 .25
14 Mark Lee .08 .25
15 Julio Machado .08 .25
16 Candy Maldonado .08 .25
17 Paul Molitor 2.00 5.00
18 Jaime Navarro .08 .25
19 Edwin Nunez .08 .25
20 Dan Plesac .20 .50
21 Willie Randolph .30 .75
22 Ron Robinson .08 .25
23 Gary Sheffield 1.25 3.00
24 Bill Spiers .08 .25
25 Franklin Stubbs .08 .25
26 B.J. Surhoff .40 1.00
27 Dale Sveum .08 .25
28 Tom Trebelhorn MG .08 .25
29 Greg Vaughn .20 .50
30 Bill Wegman .08 .25
31 Robin Yount 1.50 4.00
32 Coaches Card .20 .50
Don Baylor
Fred Stanley
Duffy Dyer
XX Album .40 1.00

1991 Brewers Police

This 30-card standard-size set was again issued regionally. Among the sponsors were the Waukesha Police Department, Waukesha Sportscards, and Delicious Brand Cookies and Crackers (who are only credited on the back). Many municipalities sponsored these cards.

COMPLETE SET (30) 3.00 8.00
1 Don August .08 .25
2 Dante Bichette .40 1.00
3 Chris Bosio .08 .25
4 Greg Brock .08 .25
5 Kevin D. Brown .08 .25
6 Chuck Crim .08 .25
7 Rick Dempsey .20 .50
8 Jim Gantner .30 .75
9 Darryl Hamilton .20 .50
10 Teddy Higuera .08 .25
11 Mark Lee .08 .25
12 Mark Knudson .08 .25
13 Julio Machado .08 .25
14 Candy Maldonado .08 .25
15 Paul Molitor 1.00 2.50
16 Jaime Navarro .08 .25
17 Edwin Nunez .08 .25
18 Dan Plesac .08 .25
19 Willie Randolph .30 .75
20 Ron Robinson .08 .25
20 Gary Sheffield .75 2.00
21 Bill Spiers .08 .25
22 Franklin Stubbs .08 .25
23 B.J. Surhoff .40 1.00
24 Dale Sveum .08 .25
25 Tom Trebelhorn MG .08 .25
26 Greg Vaughn .40 1.00
27 Bill Wegman .08 .25
28 Robin Yount .75 2.00
NNO0 Coaches Card .20 .50
Don Baylor
Ray Burris
Duffy Dyer/

1992 Brewers Carlson Travel

This 31-card standard-size set was sponsored by Carlson Travel in conjunction with United Airlines and TV Channel 6 (WITI in Milwaukee). It was issued to commemorate the 1982 Milwaukee Brewers team who played in the World Series. The set included a travel coupon entitling the holder to 50.00 off per couple on the next cruise vacation. The cards are unnumbered and checklisted below in alphabetical order.

COMPLETE SET (31) 5.00 12.00
1 Jerry Augustine .08 .25
2 Dwight Bernard .08 .25
3 Mark Brouhard .08 .25
4 Mike Caldwell .20 .50
5 Cecil Cooper .30 .75
6 Marshall Edwards .08 .25
7 Rollie Fingers .75 2.00
8 Jim Gantner .30 .75
9 Moose Haas .08 .25
10 Roy Howell .08 .25
11 Harvey Kuenn MG .20 .50
12 Pete Ladd .08 .25
13 Bob McClure .08 .25
14 Doc Medich .08 .25
15 Paul Molitor 1.50 4.00
16 Don Money .20 .50
17 Charlie Moore .08 .25
18 Ben Oglivie .30 .75
19 Ed Romero .08 .25
20 Ted Simmons .40 1.00
21 Jim Slaton .08 .25
22 Don Sutton .75 2.00
23 Gorman Thomas .30 .75
24 Pete Vuckovich .20 .50
25 Ned Yost .08 .25
26 Robin Yount 1.25 3.00
xx Bernie Brewer/(Team Mascot) .08 .25
XX Coaches .08 .25
Larry Haney
Ron Hansen
Harry Warner
Ca
XX Cecil Cooper .20 .50
Post Season Rally
xx Team Photo .20 .50
xx Carlson Travel Coupon .08 .25

1992 Brewers Police

For the second consecutive year, this 30-card standard-size set was sponsored by the Waukesha Police Department, Waukesha Sports Cards, and Delicious Brand Cookies and Crackers. The cards are unnumbered and checklisted below in alphabetical order. Variations also exist as to the Police Department sponsorship on the cardbacks, such as Franklin PD.

COMPLETE SET (30) 3.00 8.00
1 Andy Allanson .08 .25
2 Jim Austin .08 .25
3 Dante Bichette .40 1.00
4 Ricky Bones .08 .25
5 Chris Bosio .08 .25
6 Mike Fetters .08 .25
7 Scott Fletcher .08 .25
8 Jim Gantner .30 .75
9 Phil Garner MG .20 .50
10 Darryl Hamilton .08 .25
11 Doug Henry .08 .25
12 Teddy Higuera .08 .25
13 Pat Listach .08 .25
14 Tim McIntosh .08 .25
15 Paul Molitor 1.00 2.50
16 Jaime Navarro .08 .25
17 Edwin Nunez .08 .25
18 Jesse Orosco .20 .50
19 Dan Plesac .08 .25
20 Ron Robinson .08 .25
21 Bruce Ruffin .08 .25
22 Kevin Seitzer .20 .50
23 Bill Spiers .08 .25
24 Franklin Stubbs .08 .25
25 William Suero .08 .25
26 B.J. Surhoff .40 1.00
27 Greg Vaughn .20 .50
28 Bill Wegman .08 .25
29 Robin Yount .75 2.00
30 Coaches Card .08 .25
Mike Easler
Bill Castro
Don Rowe/

1992 Brewers Sentry Yount

Sponsored by Sentry Foods, this four-card standard-size card captures four moments in the career of Robin Yount, who reached 3,000 career hits during the 1992 season. The cards are unnumbered and checklisted below in chronological order.

COMPLETE SET (4) 6.00 15.00
COMMON CARD (1-4) 1.60 4.00

1992 Brewers U.S. Oil

Sponsored by U.S. Oil Co. Inc., this four-card set consists of 2 3/4" by 4 1/4" cards and commemorative pins. The pins are attached to an extension of the card that is perforated for removal. With this section attached, the cards measure 2 3/4" by 5 5/8" inches. The cards feature color action shots with bright yellow borders. The player's name appears in a bright blue stripe across the top. The event being commemorated is printed on a bright blue stripe across the bottom. The pins show a baseball player against a yellow home plate design. Blue banners across the top contain the event, and a blue bar at the bottom contains the player's name. The pin attached to the Milwaukee County Stadium card shows a bat, ball, and glove design, and has the words "American League Champions" at the top. The cards are unnumbered and checklisted below in alphabetical order.

COMPLETE SET (4) 2.50 6.00
1 Milwaukee County .40 1.00
Stadium - 1982
2 Paul Molitor 1.25 3.00
3 Juan Nieves .60 1.50
4 Robin Yount 1.25 3.00

1993 Brewers Police

This 31-card standard-size set was sponsored by the Waukesha Police Department, Waukesha Sportscards, and Cher-Make. The fronts display a color action photo on a blue background and are edged in blue. The player's name and position appear in white lettering at the top with "93 Brewers" and the team logo printed in yellow along the left edge. The sponsors are listed at the bottom of the card. The backs have black print on a white background and feature public service tips from the players. The Cher-Make logo is carried on the bottom. The cards are unnumbered and checklisted below in alphabetical order.

COMPLETE SET (30) 3.00 8.00
NNO Jim Austin .08 .25
NNO Ricky Bones .08 .25
NNO Tom Brunansky .20 .50
NNO Alex Diaz .08 .25
NNO Bill Doran .08 .25
NNO Cal Eldred .08 .25
NNO Mike Fetters .08 .25
NNO Phil Garner MG .20 .50
NNO Darryl Hamilton .08 .25
NNO Doug Henry .08 .25
NNO Ted Higuera .08 .25
NNO John Jaha .08 .25
NNO Mark Kiefer .08 .25
NNO Joe Kmak .08 .25
NNO Pat Listach .08 .25
NNO Graeme Lloyd .20 .50
NNO Tim McIntosh .08 .25
NNO Jaime Navarro .08 .25
NNO Dave Nilsson .20 .50
NNO Jesse Orosco .08 .25
NNO Kevin Reimer .08 .25
NNO Bill Spiers .08 .25
NNO William Suero .08 .25
NNO B.J. Surhoff .40 1.00
NNO Dickie Thon .08 .25
NNO Greg Vaughn .40 1.00
NNO Bill Wegman .08 .25
NNO Robin Yount .75 2.00
NNO Robin Yount .40 1.00
Memorable Moment
NNO Title Card .08 .25
NNO Bernie Brewer

1993 Brewers Sentry

Subtitled "Memorable Moments, this four-card standard-size set was sponsored by Sentry Foods and features color player photos on its fronts. The pictures are edged with dark blue lines and so are the cards. In the light blue area at the top between these darker lines appear the set subtitle and the Brewers logo. Near the bottom of the photo the player's exploit and its date are printed in gold foil. The year of issue appears at the bottom in a gold-foil diamond set off by a gold-foil stripe on either side. The white back carries the player's name, position, uniform number, exploit, and date at the top. The player's career highlights and a quote appear beneath within a red-lined rectangle. The Sentry logo at the bottom rounds out the back. The cards are unnumbered and checklisted below in alphabetical order.

COMPLETE SET (4) 3.00 8.00
1 Paul Molitor 1.50 4.00
2 Juan Nieves .40 1.00
3 Dale Sveum .40 1.00
4 Robin Yount 1.25 3.00

1994 Brewers Miller Brewing

Produced in perforated booklets, these Brewers cards were supposed to be issued in four sets to fans attending four different Brewers games at Milwaukee County Stadium. Set 1 (1-94) was issued at the April 24 game vs. Kansas City; set 2 (95-188) was issued at the June 26 game vs. Boston. Sets 3 (189-282) and 4 (283-376) were to be issued at later games (August 21 vs. Oakland; September 18 vs. Detroit), but the intervention of the baseball strike postponed their release. All four sets combined would include every player in the Brewers' 25-year history. The perforated booklets measure approximately 13" by 7" and each contains 94 cards; the individual cards measure the standard size. The gold-bordered cards feature on their fronts black-and-white player head shots. The player's name appears in black lettering within a white bar at the bottom. The white back carries the player's name, biography, years with the Brewers, and statistics therefrom. The cards are unnumbered and checklisted below in alphabetical order within each set. The final two series were released early in 1995.

COMPLETE SET (376) 15.00 40.00
1 Hank Aaron 2.00 5.00
2 Jim Adduci .20 .50
3 Jay Aldrich .20 .50
4 Andy Allanson .20 .50
5 Dave Baldwin .20 .50
6 Sal Bando .20 .50
7 Len Barker .20 .50
8 Kevin Bass .20 .50
9 Ken Berry .20 .50
10 George Canale .20 .50
11 Tom Candiotti .20 .50
12 Mike Capel .20 .50
13 Bobby Darwin .20 .50
14 Danny Darwin .20 .50
15 Brock Davis .20 .50
16 Dick Davis .20 .50
17 Jamie Easterly .20 .50
18 Tom Edens .20 .50
Logo just touching cap
19 Marshall Edwards .20 .50
20 Cal Eldred .20 .50
21 Rob Ellis .20 .50
22 Ed Farmer .20 .50
23 Mike Felder .20 .50
24 John Felske .20 .50
25 Mike Ferraro .20 .50
26 Mike Fetters .20 .50
27 Danny Frisella .20 .50
28 Bob Galasso .20 .50
29 Jim Gantner .20 .50
Head shot
30 Pedro Garcia .20 .50
31 Rob Gardner .20 .50
32 John Gelnar .20 .50
33 Moose Haas .20 .50
34 Darryl Hamilton .20 .50
35 Larry Haney .20 .50
36 Jim Hannan .20 .50
37 Bob Hansen .20 .50
38 Michael Ignasiak .20 .50
39 John Jaha .20 .50
40 Dion James .20 .50
41 Deron Johnson .20 .50
42 John Henry Johnson .20 .50
43 Tim Johnson .20 .50
44 Rickey Keeton .20 .50
45 John Kennedy .20 .50
46 Jim Kern .20 .50
47 Pete Ladd .20 .50
48 Joe Lahoud .20 .50
49 Tom Lampkin .20 .50
50 Dave LaPoint .20 .50
51 George Lauzerique .20 .50
52 Julio Machado .20 .50
53 Alex Madrid .20 .50
54 Candy Maldonado .20 .50
55 Carlos Maldonado .20 .50
56 Rick Manning .20 .50
57 Jaime Navarro .20 .50
58 Ray Newman .20 .50
59 Juan Nieves .20 .50
60 Dave Nilsson .20 .50
61 Charlie O'Brien .20 .50
62 Syd O'Brien .20 .50
63 John O'Donoghue .20 .50
64 Jim Paciorek .20 .50
65 Dave Parker .30 .75
66 Bill Parsons .20 .50
67 Marty Pattin .20 .50
68 Jamie Quirk .20 .50
69 Willie Randolph .30 .75
70 Paul Ratliff .20 .50
71 Lance Rautzhan .20 .50
72 Randy Ready .20 .50
73 Ray Sadecki .20 .50
74 Lenn Sakata .20 .50
75 Ken Sanders .20 .50
76 Ted Savage .20 .50
77 Dick Schofield .20 .50
78 Jim Tatum .20 .50
79 Chuck Taylor .20 .50
80 Tom Tellmann .20 .50
81 Frank Tepedino .20 .50
82 Sandy Valdespino .20 .50
83 Jose Valentin .20 .50
84 Greg Vaughn .20 .50
Head shot
85 Carlos Velazquez .20 .50
86 Rick Waits .20 .50
87 Danny Walton .20 .50
Large space between cap and border
88 Floyd Weaver .20 .50
89 Bill Wegman .20 .50
90 Floyd Wicker .20 .50
91 Al Yates .20 .50
92 Ned Yost .20 .50
93 Mike Young .20 .50
94 Robin Yount 1.25 3.00
Action shot
95 Hank Allen .20 .50
96 Felipe Alou .30 .75
97 Max Alvis .20 .50
98 Larry Anderson .20 .50
99 Rick Auerbach .20 .50
100 Don August .20 .50
101 Billy Bates .20 .50
102 Gary Beare .20 .50
103 Larry Bearnarth .20 .50
104 Andy Beene .20 .50
105 Jerry Bell .20 .50
106 Juan Bell .20 .50
107 Dwight Bernard .20 .50
108 Bernie Carbo .20 .50
109 Jose Cardenal .20 .50
110 Matias Carrillo .20 .50
111 Juan Castillo .20 .50
112 Bill Castro .20 .50
113 Rick Cerone .20 .50
114 Rob Deer .25 .60
115 Rick Dempsey .20 .50
116 Alex Diaz .20 .50
117 Dick Ellsworth .20 .50
118 Narciso Elvira .20 .50
119 Tom Filer .20 .50
120 Rollie Fingers .60 1.50
Head shot
121 Scott Fletcher .20 .50
122 John Flinn .20 .50
123 Rich Folkers .20 .50
124 Tony Fossas .20 .50
125 Chris George .20 .50
126 Bob L. Gibson .20 .50
127 Gus Gil .20 .50
128 Tommy Harper .20 .50
129 Vic Harris .20 .50
130 Paul Hartzell .20 .50
131 Tom Hausman .20 .50
132 Neal Heaton .20 .50
133 Mike Hegan .20 .50
134 Jack Heidemann .20 .50
135 Doug Jones .20 .50
136 Mark Kiefer .20 .50
137 Steve Kiefer .20 .50
138 Ed Kirkpatrick .20 .50
139 Joe Kmak .20 .50
140 Mark Knudson .20 .50
141 Kevin Kobel .20 .50
142 Pete Koegel .20 .50
143 Jack Lazorko .20 .50
144 Tim Leary .20 .50
145 Mark Lee .20 .50
146 Jeffrey Leonard .20 .50
147 Randy Lerch .20 .50
148 Brad Lesley .20 .50
149 Sixto Lezcano .20 .50
150 Josias Manzanillo .20 .50
151 Buck Martinez .20 .50
152 Tom Matchick .20 .50
153 Dave May .20 .50
154 Matt Maysey .20 .50
155 Bob McClure .20 .50
156 Tim McIntosh .20 .50
157 Tim Nordbrook .20 .50
158 Ben Oglivie .20 .50
Action shot
159 Troy O'Leary .20 .50
160 Jim Olander .20 .50
161 Roberto Pena .20 .50
162 Jeff Peterek .20 .50
163 Ray Peters .20 .50
164 Rob Picciolo .20 .50
165 Dan Plesac .20 .50
166 John Poff .20 .50
167 Gus Polidor .20 .50
168 Kevin Reimer .20 .50
169 Andy Replogle .20 .50
170 Jerry Reuss .20 .50
171 Archie Reynolds .20 .50
172 Bob Reynolds .20 .50
173 Ken Reynolds .20 .50
174 Tommie Reynolds .20 .50
175 Ernest Riles .20 .50
176 Bill Schroeder .20 .50
177 George Scott .20 .50
178 Ray Searage .20 .50
179 Bob Sebra .20 .50
180 Kevin Seitzer .20 .50
181 Dick Selma .20 .50
182 Bill Sharp .20 .50
183 Ron Theobald .20 .50
184 Dan Thomas .20 .50
185 Gorman Thomas .30 .75
Holding bat
186 Randy Veres .20 .50
187 Bill Voss .20 .50
188 Jim Wohlford .20 .50
189 Jerry Augustine .20 .50
190 Jim Austin .20 .50
191 Rick Austin .20 .50
192 Kurt Bevacqua .20 .50
193 Tommy Bianco .20 .50
194 Dante Bichette .60 1.50
195 Mike Birkbeck .20 .50
196 Dan Boitano .20 .50
197 Bobby Bolin .20 .50
198 Mark Bomback .20 .50
199 Ricky Bones .20 .50
200 Chris Bosio .20 .50
201 Thad Bosley .20 .50
202 Steve Bowling .20 .50
203 Gene Brabender .20 .50
204 Glenn Braggs .20 .50
205 Mike Caldwell .20 .50
206 Bill Champion .20 .50
207 Mark Ciardi .20 .50
208 Bobby Clark .20 .50
Player's hat doesn't touch border
209 Ron Clark .20 .50
210 Mark Clear .20 .50
211 Reggie Cleveland .20 .50
212 Bryan Clutterbuck .20 .50
213 Jaime Cocanower .20 .50
214 Jim Colborn .20 .50
215 Cecil Cooper .20 .50
Head shot
216 Edgar Diaz .20 .50
217 Frank Dipino .20 .50
218 Dave Engle .20 .50
219 Ray Fosse .20 .50
220 Terry Francona .25 .60
221 Tito Francona .20 .50
222 La Vel Freeman .20 .50
223 Brian Giles .20 .50
224 Bob Heise .20 .50
225 Doug Henry .20 .50
226 Mike Hershberger .20 .50
227 Teddy Higuera .20 .50
228 Sam Hinds .20 .50
229 Fred Holdsworth .20 .50
230 Darren Holmes .20 .50
231 Paul Householder .20 .50
232 Odell Jones .20 .50
233 Brad Komminsk .20 .50
234 Andy Kosco .20 .50
235 Lew Krausse .20 .50
236 Ray Krawczyk .20 .50
237 Bill Krueger .20 .50
238 Ted Kubiak .20 .50
239 Jack Lind .20 .50
240 Frank Linzy .20 .50
241 Pat Listach .20 .50
242 Graeme Lloyd .20 .50
243 Bob Locker .20 .50
244 Skip Lockwood .20 .50
245 Ken McMullen .20 .50
Player's cap doesn't touch border
246 Jerry McNertney .20 .50
247 Doc Medich .20 .50
248 Bob Meyer .20 .50
249 Joey Meyer .20 .50
250 Matt Mieske .20 .50
251 Roger Miller .20 .50
252 Paul Mirabella .20 .50
253 Angel Miranda .20 .50
254 Bobby Mitchell .20 .50
255 Paul Mitchell .20 .50
256 Paul Molitor 1.50 4.00
Action shot
257 Rafael Novoa .20 .50
258 Jesse Orosco .20 .50
259 Carlos Ponce .20 .50
260 Chuck Porter .20 .50
261 Darrell Porter .20 .50
262 Billy Jo Robidoux .20 .50
263 Ron Robinson .20 .50
264 Eduardo Rodriguez .20 .50
265 Ellie Rodriguez .20 .50
266 Rich Rollins .20 .50
267 Ed Romero .20 .50
268 Gary Sheffield 1.00 2.50
269 Bob Sheldon .20 .50
270 Chris Short .20 .50
271 Bob Skube .20 .50
272 Jim Slaton .20 .50
273 Bernie Smith .20 .50
274 Russ Snyder .20 .50
275 Lary Sorensen .20 .50
276 Bill Spiers .20 .50
277 Ed Sprague .20 .50
278 Dickie Thon .20 .50
279 Bill Travers .20 .50
280 Pete Vuckovich .20 .50
281 Clyde Wright .20 .50
282 Jeff Yurak .20 .50
283 Joe Azcue .20 .50
284 Mike Boddicker .20 .50
285 Ken Brett .20 .50
286 John Briggs .20 .50
287 Pete Broberg .20 .50
288 Greg Brock .20 .50
289 Jeff Bronkey .20 .50
290 Mark Brouhard .20 .50
291 Kevin Brown .20 .50
292 Ollie Brown .20 .50
293 Bruce Brubaker .20 .50
294 Tom Brunansky .20 .50
295 Steve Brye .20 .50
296 Bob Burda .20 .50
297 Ray Burris .20 .50
298 Jeff Cirillo .20 .50
299 Bobby Clark .20 .50
Player's hat touches border
300 Bob Coluccio .20 .50
301 Wayne Comer .20 .50
302 Billy Conigliaro .20 .50
303 Cecil Cooper .20 .50
Action shot
304 Barry Cort .20 .50
305 Chuck Crim .20 .50
306 LaFayette Currence .20 .50
307 Kiki Diaz .20 .50
308 Bill Doran .20 .50
309 Al Downing .20 .50
310 Tom Edens .20 .50
Logo partially covering cap

311 Andy Etchebarren .20 .50
312 Rollie Fingers .60 1.50
Action shot
313 Jim Gantner .20 .50
Action shot
314 Greg Goosen .20 .50
315 Brian Harper .20 .50
316 Larry Hisle .20 .50
317 Steve Hovley .20 .50
318 Wilbur Howard .20 .50
319 Roy Howell .20 .50
320 Bob Humphreys .20 .50
321 Jim Hunter .20 .50
322 Dave Huppert .20 .50
323 Von Joshua .20 .50
324 Art Kusnyer .20 .50
325 Doug Loman .20 .50
326 Jim Lonborg .20 .50
327 Marcelino Lopez .20 .50
328 Willie Lozado .20 .50
329 Mike Matheny .20 .50
330 Ken McMullen .20 .50
Player's cap touches blue border
331 Jose Mercedes .20 .50
332 Paul Molitor 1.50 4.00
Head shot
333 Don Money .20 .50
Head Shot
334 Don Money .20 .50
Action Shot
335 Charlie Moore .20 .50
336 Donnie Moore .20 .50
337 John Morris .20 .50
338 Curt Motton .20 .50
339 Willie Mueller .20 .50
340 Tom Murphy .20 .50
341 Tony Muser .20 .50
342 Edwin Nunez .20 .50
343 Ben Oglivie .20 .50
Head shot
344 Pat Osborn .20 .50
345 Dennis Powell .20 .50
346 Jody Reed .20 .50
347 Phil Roof .20 .50
348 Jimmy Rosario .20 .50
349 Bruce Ruffin .20 .50
350 Gary Ryerson .20 .50
351 Bob Scanlan .20 .50
352 Ted Simmons/(Head Shot) .30 .75
353 Ted Simmons/(Action Shot) .30 .75
354 Duane Singleton .20 .50
355 Steve Stanicek .20 .50
356 Fred Stanley .20 .50
357 Dave Stapleton .20 .50
358 Randy Stein .20 .50
359 Earl Stephenson .20 .50
360 Franklin Stubbs .20 .50
361 William Suero .20 .50
362 Jim Sundberg .20 .50
363 B.J. Surhoff .30 .75
364 Gary Sutherland .20 .50
365 Don Sutton .60 1.50
366 Dale Sveum .20 .50
367 Gorman Thomas .20 .50
Head shot
368 Wayne Twitchell .20 .50
369 Dave Valle .20 .50
370 Greg Vaughn .20 .50
Action shot
371 John Vukovich .20 .50
372 Danny Walton .20 .50
Small space between cap and border
373 Turner Ward .20 .50
374 Rick Wrona .20 .50
375 Jim Wynn .20 .50
376 Robin Yount 1.25 3.00
Head shot

1994 Brewers Police

Sponsored by Pick 'n Save and Snickers Ice Cream Bars to celebrate the 25th Anniversary of the Brewers, this 30-card set features, on its fronts, posed color player photos with two-toned green borders. Other than the players' uniform numbers, the cards are unnumbered and checklisted below in alphabetical order.

COMPLETE SET (30) 3.00 8.00
1 Bernie Brewer Mascot .08 .25
2 Ricky Bones .08 .25
3 Jeff Bronkey .08 .25
4 Tom Brunansky .08 .25
5 Jeff D'Amico DP .60 1.50
Kelly Wunsch DP
6 Cal Eldred .08 .25
7 Mike Fetters .08 .25
8 Phil Garner MG .20 .50
9 Darryl Hamilton .08 .25
10 Brian Harper .08 .25
11 Doug Henry .08 .25
12 Teddy Higuera .08 .25
13 Mike Ignasiak .08 .25
14 John Jaha .08 .25
15 Mark Kiefer .08 .25
16 Pat Listach .08 .25
17 Graeme Lloyd .20 .50
18 Matt Mieske .08 .25
19 Jaime Navarro .08 .25
20 Dave Nilsson .20 .50
21 Jesse Orosco .20 .50
22 Jody Reed .08 .25
23 Bob Scanlan .08 .25
24 Kevin Seitzer .20 .50
25 Bill Spiers .08 .25
26 B.J. Surhoff .40 1.00
27 Jose Valentin .30 .75
28 Greg Vaughn .20 .50
29 Turner Ward .08 .25
30 Bill Wegman .08 .25

1994 Brewers Sentry

This eight-card set was issued to honor outstanding achievements by Milwaukee Brewer players. Though the set is sponsored by Sentry Foods, its logo does not appear on the cards. One card was given out each Tuesday night home game through August 30. The fronts feature color player photos inside a blue border with gold and green. A special Brewers' 25th Anniversary logo appears in the top left, while the player's name is printed on a navy bar beneath the picture. On a white background, the back presents the player's outstanding achievement. The cards are unnumbered and checklisted below in alphabetical order.

COMPLETE SET (8) 5.00 12.00
1 Hank Aaron 2.00 5.00
2 Rollie Fingers .75 2.00
3 Pat Listach .40 1.00
4 Paul Molitor 1.50 4.00
5 Paul Molitor 1.50 4.00
Robin Yount
Jim Gantner
6 Juan Nieves .40 1.00
7 Don Sutton .75 2.00
8 Robin Yount 1.25 3.00

1994 Brewers Team Issue

This 29-card set of the 1994 Milwaukee Brewers features black-and-white player portraits with white borders and measures approximately 4" by 5 7/16". The backs are blank. The cards are unnumbered and checklisted below in alphabetical order.

COMPLETE SET (29) 4.00 10.00
1 Ricky Bones .08 .25
2 Jeff Bronkey .08 .25
3 Tom Brunansky .20 .50
4 Alex Diaz .08 .25
5 Cal Eldred .08 .25
6 Mike Fetters .08 .25
7 Phil Garner MG .08 .25
8 Darryl Hamilton .08 .25
9 Brian Harper .08 .25
10 Doug Henry .08 .25
11 Ted Higuera .08 .25
12 John Jaha .20 .50
13 Mark Kiefer .08 .25
14 Pat Listach .08 .25
15 Graeme Lloyd .08 .25
16 Matt Mieske .08 .25
17 Angel Miranda .08 .25
18 Jaime Navarro .08 .25
19 Dave Nilsson .20 .50
20 Jesse Orosco .20 .50
21 Jody Reed .08 .25
22 Bob Scanlan .08 .25
23 Kevin Seitzer .20 .50
24 Bill Spiers .08 .25
25 B.J. Surhoff .40 1.00
26 Jose Valentin .30 .75
27 Greg Vaughn .20 .50
28 Turner Ward .08 .25
29 Bill Wegman .08 .25

1995 Brewers Police

This green bordered standard-size set was issued by Milwaukee area police forces to promote safety among their residents. Since these cards are unnumbered except by uniform number, we have sequenced them in alphabetical order.

COMPLETE SET (33) 4.00 10.00
1 Ricky Bones .08 .25
2 Jeff Bronkey .08 .25
3 Jeff Cirillo .40 1.00
Mike Matheny
4 Cal Eldred .08 .25
5 Mike Fetters .08 .25
6 Phil Garner MG .20 .50
7 Darryl Hamilton .08 .25
8 David Hulse .08 .25
9 Mike Ignasiak .08 .25
10 John Jaha .20 .50
11 Scott Karl .20 .50
Steve Sparks
Alberto Reyes
12 Mark Kiefer .08 .25
Jose Mercedes
13 Pat Listach .08 .25
14 Graeme Lloyd .08 .25
15 Derrick May .08 .25
16 Matt Mieske .08 .25
17 Angel Miranda .08 .25
18 Dave Nilsson .20 .50
19 Joe Oliver .08 .25
20 Bob Scanlan .08 .25
21 Kevin Seitzer .20 .50
22 B.J Surhoff .30 .75
23 Bob Uecker ANN .40 1.00
24 Jose Valentin .20 .50
25 Greg Vaughn .40 1.00
26 Fernando Vina .08 .25
27 Turner Ward .08 .25
28 Bill Wegman .08 .25
29 Bill Castro CO .08 .25
Duffy Dyer CO
Tim Foli CO
Lamar
30 Charlie the Mouse Ad Card .08 .25
31 SqueezeCheese Free Offer .08 .25
32 Iris the Cow Ad Card .08 .25
33 Squeezasaurus Ad Card .08 .25

1996 Brewers Police

This 30-card set features color action photos of the 1996 Milwaukee Brewers. The backs carry a safety message from the player pictured on the front. The cards are unnumbered and checklisted below in alphabetical order.

COMPLETE SET (30) 4.00 10.00
1 Ricky Bones .08 .25
2 Marshall Boze .08 .25
3 Chuck Carr .08 .25
4 Jeff Cirillo .30 .75
5 Cal Eldred .08 .25
6 Mike Fetters .08 .25
7 Ramon Garcia .08 .25
8 Phil Garner MG .20 .50
9 David Hulse .08 .25
10 John Jaha .20 .50
11 Scott Karl .08 .25
12 Jesse Levis .08 .25
13 Pat Listach .08 .25
14 Graeme Lloyd .20 .50
15 Mark Loretta .40 1.00
16 Mike Matheny .08 .25
17 Ben McDonald .08 .25
18 Matt Mieske .08 .25
19 Angel Miranda .08 .25
20 David Nilsson .20 .50
21 Mike Potts .08 .25
22 Kevin Seitzer .20 .50
23 Steve Sparks .08 .25
24 Jose Valentin .30 .75
25 Greg Vaughn .20 .50
26 Fernando Vina .08 .25
27 Turner Ward .08 .25
28 Kevin Wickander .08 .25
29 Coaches Card .08 .25
30 Miller Park .08 .25

1997 Brewers Police

This 29-card set of the Milwaukee Brewers was presented by the Waukesha Police Department, Waukesha Sports Cards, and Delzer Lithograph Company. The cards are unnumbered and checklisted below in alphabetical order.

COMPLETE SET (29) 5.00 12.00
1 Chris Bando CO .08 .25
Bill Castro CO
Jim Gantner CO
La
2 Jeromy Burnitz .30 .75
3 Chuck Carr .08 .25
4 Jeff Cirillo .30 .75
5 Jeff D'Amico .08 .25
6 Eddy Diaz .08 .25
7 Mike Fetters .08 .25
8 Bryce Florie .08 .25
9 Phil Garner MG .08 .25
10 Jeff Huson .08 .25
11 John Jaha .20 .50
12 Doug Jones .20 .50
13 Scott Karl .08 .25
14 Jesse Levis .08 .25
15 Mark Loretta .40 1.00
16 Mike Matheny .08 .25
17 Ben McDonald .08 .25
18 Jose Mercedes .08 .25
19 Matt Mieske .08 .25
20 Angel Miranda .08 .25
21 Marc Newfield .08 .25
22 David Nilsson .20 .50
23 Jackie Robinson 1.25 3.00
24 Tim Unroe .08 .25
25 Jose Valentin .30 .75
26 Ron Villone .08 .25
27 Fernando Vina .08 .25
28 Bob Wickman .30 .75
29 Gerald Williams .08 .25

1998 Brewers Police

This 30 card standard-size set features members of the 1998 Milwaukee Brewers. The cards care sponsored by the Milwaukee Sports Connection as well as the Waukesha Police Department; Waukesha Sports Cards and Delzer Lithograph Co. Since the cards are unnumbered, we have sequenced them in alphabetical order.

COMPLETE SET (30) 3.00 8.00
1 Jeromy Burnitz .30 .75
2 Jeff Cirillo .30 .75
3 Jeff D'Amico .08 .25
4 Cal Eldred .08 .25
5 Chad Fox .08 .25
6 Phil Garner MG .20 .50
7 Marquis Grissom .20 .50
8 Bob Hamelin .08 .25
9 Darrin Jackson .08 .25
10 John Jaha .20 .50
11 Geoff Jenkins .40 1.00
12 Doug Jones .20 .50
13 Jeff Juden .08 .25
14 Scott Karl .08 .25
15 Jesse Levis .08 .25
16 Mark Loretta .40 1.00
17 Mike Matheny .08 .25
18 Jose Mercedes .08 .25
19 Mike Myers .08 .25
20 Marc Newfield .08 .25
21 David Nilsson .20 .50
22 Al Reyes .08 .25
23 Jose Valentin .30 .75
24 Fernando Vina .08 .25
25 Paul Wagner .08 .25
26 Bob Wickman .30 .75
27 Steve Woodard .08 .25
28 Bobby Hughes .08 .25
Eric Owens
29 Bronswell Patrick .08 .25
Brad Woodall
30 Chris Bando CO .08 .25
Bill Castro CO
Lamar Johnson CO/

1999 Brewers Postcards

These 5" by 7" blank backed postcards featured members of the 1999 Milwaukee Brewers. The postcards have a large photo of the player with the Ohio Casualty Group log and Milwaukee County Stadium logo on the bottom. As these cards are unnumbered we have sequenced them in alphabetical order.

COMPLETE SET 3.00 8.00
1 Ron Belliard .30 .75
2 Sean Berry .08 .25
2 Bill Campbell CO .08 .25
4 Lou Collier .08 .25
5 Cal Eldred .08 .25
6 Phil Garner MG .20 .50
7 Marquis Grissom .20 .50
8 Bobby Hughes .08 .25
9 Ron Jackson CO .08 .25
10 Geoff Jenkins .40 1.00
11 Scott Karl .08 .25
12 Jim Lefebvre CO .08 .25
13 Mark Loretta .40 1.00
14 Bob Melvin CO .08 .25
15 Mike Myers .08 .25
16 Alex Ochoa .08 .25
17 Eric Plunk .08 .25
18 Bill Pulsipher .08 .25
19 Rafael Roque .08 .25
20 Jose Valentin .20 .50
21 Fernando Vina .08 .25
22 David Weathers .08 .25
23 Bob Wickman .30 .75
24 Bernie Brewer .08 .25
Mascot

1999 Brewers Safety

This 30-card standard-size set was issued to commemorate the 1999 Milwaukee Brewers. The fronts have a player portrait against a ghosted background of the new stadium. The players name and uniform number is printed next to the photo and the cards say on the bottom "Presented by Midwest Sports Channel and the Milwaukee Brewers". The backs have some biographical information as well as a safety tip. The cards are unnumbered so we have sequenced them in alphabetical order.

COMPLETE SET (30) 4.00 10.00
1 Jim Abbott .20 .50
2 Brian Banks .08 .25
3 Sean Berry .08 .25
4 Jeromy Burnitz .40 1.00
5 Jeff Cirillo .40 1.00
6 Lou Collier .08 .25
7 Cal Eldred .08 .25
8 Valerio De Los Santos .08 .25
9 Chad Fox .08 .25
10 Phil Garner MG .20 .50
11 Marquis Grissom .20 .50
12 Bobby Hughes .08 .25
13 Geoff Jenkins .40 1.00
14 Scott Karl .08 .25
15 Mark Loretta .40 1.00
16 Mike Myers .08 .25
17 David Nilsson .20 .50
18 Alex Ochoa .08 .25
19 Eric Plunk .08 .25
20 Bill Pulsipher .08 .25
21 Al Reyes .08 .25
22 Rafael Roque .08 .25
23 Jose Valentin .20 .50
24 Fernando Vina .08 .25
25 David Weathers .08 .25
26 Bob Wickman .30 .75
27 Steve Woodard .08 .25
28 Steve Faltisek .08 .25
Rich Becker
29 Bob Melvin CO .08 .25
Jim Lefevre CO
Ron Jackson CO
Bil
30 Milwaukee County Stadium .08 .25

2000 Brewers All-Decade 70's

COMPLETE SET (13) 3.20 8.00
1 Hank Aaron 2.00 5.00
2 George Bamberger MG .10 .25
3 Mike Caldwell .10 .25
4 Cecil Cooper .40 1.00
5 Tommy Harper .10 .25
6 Larry Hisle .10 .25
7 Charlie Moore .10 .25
8 Sixto Lezcano .10 .25
9 Don Money .20 .50
10 Ken Sanders .10 .25
11 Jim Slaton .10 .25
12 Gorman Thomas .30 .75
13 Robin Yount 1.60 4.00

2000 Brewers All-Decade 80's

COMPLETE SET (13) 3.20 8.00
1 Mike Caldwell .10 .25
2 Cecil Cooper .30 .75
3 Rollie Fingers .50 1.25
4 Jim Gantner .10 .25
5 Harvey Kuenn MG .10 .25
6 Paul Molitor 1.00 2.50
Batting
7 Paul Molitor 1.00 2.50
Fielding
8 Ben Oglivie .20 .50
9 Ted Simmons .30 .75
10 Gorman Thomas .20 .50
11 Pete Vuckovich .10 .25
12 Robin Yount .80 2.00
Close-Up
13 Robin Yount .80 2.00
Batting

2000 Brewers All-Decade 90's

COMPLETE SET 2.50 6.00
1 Chris Bosio .10 .25
2 Jeromy Burnitz .30 .75
3 Jeff Cirillo .10 .25
4 Phil Garner MG .10 .25
5 John Jaha .20 .50
6 Geoff Jenkins .40 1.00
7 David Nilsson .20 .50
8 B.J. Surboff .30 .75
9 Fernando Vina .10 .25
10 Jose Valentin .10 .25
11 Bill Wegman .10 .25
12 Bob Wickman .20 .50
13 Robin Yount .80 2.00

2000 Brewers Police

COMPLETE SET (30) 3.20 8.00
1 Juan Acevedo .10 .25
2 Kevin Barker .10 .25
3 Ron Belliard .30 .75
4 Jason Bere .10 .25
5 Sean Berry .10 .25
6 Henry Blanco .10 .25
7 Jim Bruske .10 .25
8 Jeromy Burnitz .30 .75
9 Valerio De Los Santos .10 .25
10 Marquis Grissom .20 .50
11 Charlie Hayes .10 .25
12 Jimmy Haynes .10 .25
13 Jose Hernandez .10 .25
14 Tyler Houston .10 .25
15 Geoff Jenkins .40 1.00
16 Curtis Leskanic .10 .25
17 Davey Lopes MG .20 .50
18 Luis Lopez .10 .25
19 Mark Loretta .40 1.00
20 James Mouton .10 .25
21 Lyle Mouton .10 .25
22 Jaime Navarro .10 .25
23 John Snyder .10 .25
24 Everett Stull .10 .25
25 David Weathers .10 .25
26 Bob Wickman .20 .50
27 Matt Williams .10 .25
28 Steve Woodard .10 .25
29 B.Schroeder .10 .25
M.Vasgersian
30 Brewers Coaches .30 .75

2000 Brewers Postcards

COMPLETE SET 6.00 15.00
1 Gary Allenson CO .20 .50
2 Bob Apodaca CO .20 .50
3 Juan Acevado .20 .50
4 Kevin Barker .20 .50
5 Ron Belliard .40 1.00
6 Sean Berry .20 .50
7 Henry Blanco .20 .50
8 Jeromy Burnitz .40 1.00
9 Rod Carew CO .80 2.00
10 Bill Castro CO .20 .50
11 Valerio de los Santos .20 .50
12 Marquis Grissom .30 .75
13 Charlie Hayes .20 .50
14 Jose Hernandez .20 .50
15 Tyler Houston .20 .50
16 Geoff Jenkins .60 1.50
17 Curtis Leskanic .20 .50
18 Luis Lopez .20 .50
19 Mark Loretta .60 1.50
20 James Mouton .20 .50
21 Lyle Mouton .20 .50
22 Jerry Royster CO .20 .50
23 Chris Speier CO .20 .50
24 David Weathers .20 .50
25 Bob Wickman .30 .75
26 Steve Woodard .20 .50

2001 Brewers Police

COMPLETE SET (30) 4.00 10.00
1 Ronnie Belliard .30 .75
2 Henry Blanco .10 .25
3 Raul Casanova .10 .25
4 Will Cunnane .10 .25
5 Jeromy Burnitz .30 .75
6 Jeff D'Amico .10 .25
7 Mike DeJean .10 .25
8 Angel Echevarria .10 .25
9 Tony Fernandez .20 .50
10 Chad Fox .10 .25
11 Jeffrey Hammonds .10 .25
12 Jimmy Haynes .10 .25
13 Jose Hernandez .20 .50
14 Tyler Houston .10 .25
15 Geoff Jenkins .40 1.00
16 Ray King .10 .25
17 Mark Leiter .10 .25
18 Curtis Leskanic .10 .25
19 Dave Lopes MG .20 .50
20 Luis Lopez .10 .25
21 Mark Loretta .40 1.00
22 James Mouton .10 .25
23 Paul Rigdon .10 .25
24 Richie Sexson .40 1.00
25 Ben Sheets .50 1.25
26 David Weathers .10 .25
27 Devon White .10 .25
28 Jamey Wright .10 .25
29 Jerry Royster CO .30 .75
Rod Carew CO
Bill Castro CO
Bo
30 Bill Schroeder ANN .10 .25
Matt Vasgersian ANN

2001 Brewers Walk of Fame

COMPLETE SET 40.00 10.00
1 Hank Aaron 2.00 5.00
2 Rollie Fingers .40 1.00
3 Paul Molitor 1.50 4.00
4 Robin Yount 1.00 2.50

2002 Brewers Police

COMPLETE SET 3.00 8.00
1 Paul Bako .08 .25
2 Ron Belliard .30 .75
3 Mike Buddie .08 .25
4 Jose Cabrera .08 .25
5 Raul Casanova .08 .25
6 Mike DeJean .08 .25
7 Nelson Figueroa .08 .25
8 Chad Fox .08 .25
9 Jeffrey Hammonds .08 .25
10 Lenny Harris .08 .25
11 Jose Hernandez .20 .50
12 Tyler Houston .08 .25
13 Geoff Jenkins .40 1.00
14 Ray King .08 .25
15 Curtis Leskanic .08 .25
16 Luis Lopez .08 .25
17 Mark Loretta .08 .25
18 Nick Neugebauer .08 .25
19 Takahito Nomura .20 .50
20 Alex Ochoa .08 .25
21 Ruben Quevedo .08 .25
22 Paul Rigdon .08 .25
23 Glendon Rusch .08 .25
24 Alex Sanchez .08 .25
25 Richie Sexson .40 1.00
26 Ben Sheets .40 1.00
27 Matt Stairs .08 .25
28 Luis Vizcaino .08 .25
29 Jamey Wright .08 .25
30 Eric Young .20 .50

2002 Brewers Topps

COMPLETE SET 15.00 40.00
1 Don Money 4/19/1978 Topps 2.00 5.00
2 Paul Molitor 5/24/1992 Topps 6.00 15.00
3 Cecil Cooper 6/21 8.00
4 Robin Yount 7/12/1982 Topps 5.00 12.00
5 Gorman Thomas 8/9/1981 Topps 2.50 6.00
6 Ben Oglivie 9/6/1980 Topps 2.00 5.00

2003 Brewers Police

COMPLETE SET 4.00 8.00
1 Brady Clark .30 .75
2 Royce Clayton .10 .25
3 Jason Conti .10 .25
4 Enrique Cruz .10 .25
5 Mike DeJean .10 .25
6 Jayson Durocher .10 .25
7 Valerio de los Santos .10 .25
8 Matt Ford .10 .25
9 John Foster .10 .25
10 Wayne Franklin .10 .25
11 Keith Ginter .10 .25
12 Jeffrey Hammonds .10 .25
13 Wes Helms .20 .50
14 Geoff Jenkins .40 1.00
15 Matt Kinney .10 .25
16 Curtis Leskanic .10 .25
17 Shane Nance .10 .25
18 Keith Osik .10 .25
19 Eddie Perez .10 .25
20 Scott Podsednik .75 2.00
21 Todd Ritchie .10 .25
22 Glendon Rusch .10 .25
23 Alex Sanchez .10 .25
24 Richie Sexson .40 1.00
25 Ben Sheets .30 .75
26 John Vander Wal .10 .25
27 Luis Vizcaino .10 .25
28 Ned Yöst MG .10 .25
29 Eric Young .20 .50
30 The Coaches .10 .25

2003 Brewers Team Issue

COMPLETE SET 7.50 15.00
1 Dave Burba .20 .50
2 Bill Castro CO .20 .50
3 Brady Clark .40 1.00
4 Royce Clayton .20 .50
5 Enrique Cruz .20 .50
6 Rich Donnelly CO .20 .50
7 Leo Estrella .20 .50
8 Wayne Franklin .20 .50
9 Keith Ginter .20 .50
10 Bill Hall .20 .50
11 Brooks Kieschnick .20 .50
11 Geoff Jenkins .60 1.50
13 Matt Kinney .20 .50
14 Mike Maddux .20 .50
15 Shane Nance .20 .50
16 Dave Nelson CO .20 .50
17 Wes Obermueller .20 .50
18 Keith Osik .20 .50
19 Ulice Payne PRES .20 .50
20 Eddie Perez .20 .50
21 Scott Podsednik 1.00 2.50
22 Richie Sexson .60 1.50
23 Ben Sheets 1.00 2.50
24 John Vander Wal .20 .50
25 Luis Vizcaino .20 .50
26 Butch Wynegar CO .20 .50
27 Ned Yost MG .20 .50

2004 Brewers Police

COMPLETE SET 4.00 10.00
1 Gary Bennett .10 .25
2 Jeff Bennett .10 .25
3 Dave Burba .10 .25
4 Chris Capuano .10 .25
5 Brady Clark .30 .75
6 Craig Counsell .10 .25
7 Doug Davis .10 .25
8 Trent Durrington .10 .25
9 Ben Ford .10 .25
10 Keith Ginter .10 .25
11 Ben Grieve .10 .25
12 Bill Hall .20 .50
13 Wes Helms .10 .25
14 Adrian Hernandez .10 .25
15 Geoff Jenkins .40 1.00
16 Brooks Kieschnick .10 .25
17 Matt Kinney .10 .25
18 Dan Kolb .10 .25
19 Chad Moeller .10 .25
20 Paul Molitor .60 1.50
21 Wes Obermueller .10 .25
22 Lyle Overbay .40 1.00
23 Scott Podsednik .40 1.00
24 Ben Sheets .60 1.50
25 Junior Spivey .10 .25
26 Luis Vizcaino .10 .25
27 Ned Yost MG .10 .25
28 Rich Dauer CO .10 .25
Dave Nelson CO
Rich Donnelly CO
M
29 Bernie Brewer .10 .25
Mascot
30 Klement's Brewers Sausages .10 .25

2004 Brewers Team Issue

COMPLETE SET
1 Mike Adams .20 .50
2 Gary Bennett .20 .50
3 Jeff Bennett .20 .50
4 Russell Branyan .20 .50
5 Dave Burba .20 .50
6 Chris Capuano .20 .50
7 Bill Castro CO .20 .50
8 Brady Clark .40 1.00
9 Craig Counsell .20 .50
10 Rich Dauer CO .20 .50
11 Doug Davis .20 .50
12 Rich Donnelly CO .20 .50
13 Trent Durrington .20 .50
14 Ben Ford .20 .50
15 Keith Ginter .20 .50
16 Ben Grieve .20 .50
17 Bill Hall .30 .75
18 Wes Helms .20 .50
19 Adrian Hernandez .20 .50
20 Geoff Jenkins .60 1.50
21 Brooks Kieschnick .20 .50
22 Matt Kinney .20 .50
23 Dan Kolb .20 .50
24 Mike Maddux CO .20 .50
25 Chad Moeller .20 .50
26 Dave Nelson CO .20 .50
27 Wes Obermueller .20 .50
28 Lyle Overbay .60 1.50
29 Scott Podsednik .60 1.50
30 Victor Santos .20 .50
31 Ben Sheets .75 2.00
32 Junior Spivey .20 .50
33 Luis Vizcaino .20 .50
34 Matt Wise .20 .50
35 Butch Wynegar CO .20 .50
36 Ned Yost MG .20 .50
37 Bernie Brewer .20 .50
Mascot

2005 Brewers Police

COMPLETE SET 3.00 8.00
1 Mike Adams .10 .25
2 Jeff Bennett .10 .25
3 Ricky Bottalico .10 .25
4 Russell Branyan .10 .25
5 Chris Capuano .10 .25
6 Jeff Cirillo .10 .25
7 Brady Clark .30 .75
8 Doug Davis .20 .50
9 Jorge De la Rosa .10 .25
10 Gary Glover .10 .25
11 Bill Hall .20 .50
12 J.J. Hardy .30 .75
13 Ben Hendrickson .10 .25
14 Wes Helms .10 .25
15 Geoff Jenkins .40 1.00
16 Dave Krynzel .20 .50
17 Carlos Lee .40 1.00
18 Chris Magruder .10 .25
19 Damian Miller .10 .25
20 Chad Moeller .10 .25
21 Wes Obermueller .10 .25
22 Lyle Overbay .40 1.00
23 Tommy Phelps .10 .25
24 Victor Santos .10 .25
25 Ben Sheets .50 1.25
26 Junior Spivey .10 .25
27 Derrick Turnbow .40 1.00
28 Matt Wise .10 .25
29 Ned Yost MG .10 .25
30 Ned Yost MG .10 .25
Butch Wynegar CO
Bill Castro CO
Mar

2006 Brewers Topps

COMPLETE SET (14) 3.00 8.00
MIL1 Ben Sheets .12 .30
MIL2 Chris Capuano .12 .30
MIL3 Brady Clark .12 .30
MIL4 Jose Capellan .12 .30
MIL5 Geoff Jenkins .12 .30
MIL6 Damian Miller .12 .30
MIL7 Carlos Lee .12 .30
MIL8 Rickie Weeks .12 .30
MIL9 J.J. Hardy .12 .30
MIL10 Russell Branyan .12 .30
MIL11 Tomo Ohka .12 .30
MIL12 Derrick Turnbow .12 .30
MIL13 Bill Hall .12 .30
MIL14 Doug Davis .12 .30

2007 Brewers Police

COMPLETE SET (30) 2.00 5.00
1 Greg Aquino .10 .25
2 Dave Bush .10 .25
3 Chris Capuano .10 .25
4 Francisco Cordero .10 .25
5 Craig Counsell .10 .25
6 Elmer Dessens .10 .25
7 Johnny Estrada .10 .25
8 Prince Fielder .15 .40
9 Tony Graffanino .10 .25
10 Gabe Gross .10 .25
11 Tony Gwynn .10 .25
12 Bill Hall .10 .25
13 Corey Hart .10 .25
14 J.J. Hardy .10 .25
15 Geoff Jenkins .10 .25
16 Corey Koskie .10 .25
17 Kevin Mench .10 .25
18 Damian Miller .10 .25
19 Laynce Nix .10 .25
20 Vinny Rottino .10 .25
21 Dennis Sarfate .10 .25
22 Ben Sheets .10 .25
23 Brian Shouse .10 .25
24 Jeff Suppan .10 .25
25 Derrick Turnbow .10 .25
26 Claudio Vargas .10 .25
27 Carlos Villanueva .10 .25
28 Rickie Weeks .10 .25
29 Matt Wise .10 .25
30 Ned Yost MG .10 .25

2007 Brewers Topps

COMPLETE SET (14) 3.00 8.00
MIL1 Prince Fielder .20 .50
MIL2 Chris Capuano .12 .30
MIL3 J.J. Hardy .12 .30
MIL4 Dave Bush .12 .30
MIL5 Bill Hall .12 .30
MIL6 Ben Sheets .12 .30
MIL7 Johnny Estrada .12 .30

MIL8 Francisco Cordero .12 .30
MIL9 Corey Hart .12 .30
MIL10 Tony Gwynn Jr. .12 .30
MIL11 Geoff Jenkins .12 .30
MIL12 Rickie Weeks .12 .30
MIL13 Jeff Suppan .12 .30
MIL14 Kevin Mench .12 .30

2008 Brewers Topps

COMPLETE SET (14) 3.00 8.00
MIL1 Prince Fielder .20 .50
MIL2 Yovani Gallardo .25 .60
MIL3 J.J. Hardy .12 .30
MIL4 Eric Gagne .12 .30
MIL5 Bill Hall .12 .30
MIL6 Ben Sheets .12 .30
MIL7 Jason Kendall .12 .30
MIL8 Mike Cameron .12 .30
MIL9 Corey Hart .12 .30
MIL10 Ryan Braun .20 .50
MIL11 Carlos Villanueva .12 .30
MIL12 Rickie Weeks .12 .30
MIL13 Jeff Suppan .12 .30
MIL14 Dave Bush .12 .30

2009 Brewers Police

COMPLETE SET (28) 2.00 5.00
1 Ryan Braun .15 .40
2 Dave Bush .10 .25
3 Mike Cameron .10 .25
4 Todd Coffey .10 .25
5 Craig Counsell .10 .25
6 Mark DiFelice .10 .25
7 Tim Dillard .10 .25
8 Chris Duffy .10 .25
9 Prince Fielder .15 .40
10 Yovani Gallardo .10 .25
11 Bill Hall .10 .25
12 J.J. Hardy .10 .25
13 Corey Hart .10 .25
14 Trevor Hoffman .15 .40
15 Jorge Julio .10 .25
16 Jason Kendall .10 .25
17 Braden Looper .10 .25
18 Ken Macha MG .10 .25
19 Seth Mclung .10 .25
20 Brad Nelson .10 .25
21 Manny Parra .10 .25
22 David Riske .10 .25
23 Mike Rivera .10 .25
24 Mitch Stetter .10 .25
25 Jeff Suppan .10 .25
26 R.J. Swindle .10 .25
27 Carlos Villanueva .10 .25
28 Rickie Weeks .10 .25

2009 Brewers Topps

MIL1 Ryan Braun .25 .60
MIL2 Mat Gamel .40 1.00
MIL3 Prince Fielder .25 .60
MIL4 Mike Cameron .15 .40
MIL5 Corey Hart .15 .40
MIL6 Dave Bush .15 .40
MIL7 Trevor Hoffman .25 .60
MIL8 Manny Parra .15 .40
MIL9 Rickie Weeks .15 .40
MIL10 Jason Kendall .15 .40
MIL11 J.J. Hardy .15 .40
MIL12 Jeff Suppan .15 .40
MIL13 Bill Hall .15 .40
MIL14 Yovani Gallardo .15 .40
MIL15 Bernie Brewer .15 .40

2010 Brewers Topps

MIL1 Ryan Braun .25 .60
MIL2 Jody Gerut .15 .40
MIL3 Greg Zaun .15 .40
MIL4 Craig Counsell .15 .40
MIL5 Rickie Weeks .15 .40
MIL6 Mat Gamel .15 .40
MIL7 Prince Fielder .25 .60
MIL8 Felipe Lopez .15 .40
MIL9 Jeff Suppan .15 .40
MIL10 Yovani Gallardo .15 .40
MIL11 Casey McGehee .15 .40
MIL12 Corey Hart .15 .40
MIL13 Trevor Hoffman .25 .60
MIL14 Carlos Gomez .15 .40
MIL15 Alcides Escobar .25 .60
MIL16 Randy Wolf .15 .40
MIL17 Manny Parra .15 .40

2011 Brewers Topps

MIL1 Zack Greinke .40 1.00
MIL2 Ryan Braun .25 .60
MIL3 Yuniesky Betancourt .15 .40
MIL4 Prince Fielder .25 .60
MIL5 Yovani Gallardo .15 .40
MIL6 Carlos Gomez .15 .40
MIL7 Corey Hart .15 .40
MIL8 Mark Rogers .15 .40
MIL9 Jonathan Lucroy .25 .60
MIL10 Casey McGehee .15 .40
MIL11 Chris Narveson .15 .40
MIL12 John Axford .15 .40
MIL13 Rickie Weeks .15 .40
MIL14 Randy Wolf .15 .40
MIL15 Craig Counsell .15 .40
MIL16 Shaun Marcum .15 .40
MIL17 Miller Park .15 .40

2012 Brewers Topps

MIL1 Ryan Braun .25 .60
MIL2 Carlos Gomez .25 .60
MIL3 Zack Greinke .40 1.00
MIL4 Aramis Ramirez .25 .60
MIL5 Mat Gamel .25 .60
MIL6 Shaun Marcum .25 .60
MIL7 Nyjer Morgan .25 .60
MIL8 Rickie Weeks .25 .60
MIL9 Alex Gonzalez .25 .60
MIL10 Yovani Gallardo .30 .75
MIL11 Randy Wolf .25 .60
MIL12 Corey Hart .25 .60
MIL13 Jonathan Lucroy .30 .75
MIL14 John Axford .25 .60
MIL15 Francisco Rodriguez .30 .75
MIL16 Chris Narveson .25 .60
MIL17 Miller Park .25 .60

2013 Brewers Topps

COMPLETE SET (17) 3.00 8.00
MIL1 Ryan Braun .20 .50
MIL2 Carlos Gomez .25 .60
MIL3 Norichika Aoki .15 .40
MIL4 Jean Segura .20 .50
MIL5 Rickie Weeks .25 .60
MIL6 Aramis Ramirez .25 .60
MIL7 Corey Hart .15 .40
MIL8 Yovani Gallardo .25 .60
MIL9 Marco Estrada .15 .40
MIL10 Wily Peralta .15 .40
MIL11 Mike Fiers .25 .60
MIL12 Jonathan Lucroy .20 .50
MIL13 John Axford .15 .40
MIL14 Chris Narveson .15 .40
MIL15 Mat Gamel .15 .40
MIL16 Martin Maldonado .15 .40
MIL17 Miller Park .15 .40

2014 Brewers Topps

COMPLETE SET (17) 3.00 8.00
MIL1 Ryan Braun .20 .50
MIL2 Carlos Gomez .15 .40
MIL3 Sean Halton .15 .40
MIL4 Jean Segura .20 .50
MIL5 Rickie Weeks .20 .50
MIL6 Aramis Ramirez .15 .40
MIL7 Scooter Gennett .20 .50
MIL8 Yovani Gallardo .15 .40
MIL9 Marco Estrada .15 .40
MIL10 Wily Peralta .15 .40
MIL11 Matt Garza .15 .40
MIL12 Jonathan Lucroy .20 .50
MIL13 Kyle Lohse .15 .40
MIL14 Jim Henderson .15 .40
MIL15 Juan Francisco .15 .40
MIL16 Khris Davis .25 .60
MIL17 Miller Park .15 .40

2015 Brewers Topps

COMPLETE SET (17) 3.00 8.00
MB1 Ryan Braun .20 .50
MB2 Carlos Gomez .15 .40
MB3 Matt Garza .15 .40
MB4 Jean Segura .20 .50
MB5 Khris Davis .25 .60
MB6 Gerardo Parra .15 .40
MB7 Adam Lind .20 .50
MB8 Kyle Lohse .15 .40
MB9 Scooter Gennett .20 .50
MB10 Jonathan Lucroy .20 .50
MB11 Aramis Ramirez .15 .40
MB12 Jimmy Nelson .15 .40
MB13 Jonathan Broxton .15 .40
MB14 Wily Peralta .15 .40
MB15 Martin Maldonado .15 .40
MB16 Will Smith .15 .40
MB17 Mike Fiers .15 .40

2016 Brewers Topps

COMPLETE SET (17) 3.00 8.00
MIL1 Jonathan Lucroy .20 .50
MIL2 Ryan Braun .20 .50
MIL3 Corey Knebel .15 .40
MIL4 Scooter Gennett .15 .40
MIL5 Jean Segura .20 .50
MIL6 Khris Davis .25 .60
MIL7 Domingo Santana .20 .50
MIL8 Matt Garza .15 .40
MIL9 Wily Peralta .15 .40
MIL10 Jimmy Nelson .15 .40
MIL11 Taylor Jungmann .15 .40
MIL12 Jonathan Villar .15 .40
MIL13 Jeremy Jeffress .15 .40
MIL14 Will Smith .15 .40
MIL15 Michael Blazek .15 .40
MIL16 Shane Peterson .15 .40
MIL17 Zach Davies .20 .50

2017 Brewers Topps

COMPLETE SET (17) 3.00 8.00
MIL1 Jonathan Villar .15 .40
MIL2 Domingo Santana .20 .50
MIL3 Travis Shaw .15 .40
MIL4 Jimmy Nelson .15 .40
MIL5 Wily Peralta .15 .40
MIL6 Chase Anderson .15 .40
MIL7 Corey Knebel .15 .40
MIL8 Orlando Arcia .25 .60
MIL9 Scooter Gennett .20 .50
MIL10 Kirk Nieuwenhuis .15 .40
MIL11 Hernan Perez .15 .40
MIL12 Ryan Braun .20 .50
MIL13 Zach Davies .15 .40
MIL14 Junior Guerra .15 .40
MIL15 Eric Thames .20 .50
MIL16 Matt Garza .15 .40
MIL17 Keon Broxton .15 .40

2018 Brewers Topps

COMPLETE SET (17) 2.00 5.00
MB1 Ryan Braun .20 .50
MB2 Chase Anderson .15 .40
MB3 Manny Pina .15 .40
MB4 Orlando Arcia .15 .40
MB5 Lewis Brinson .15 .40
MB6 Jonathan Villar .15 .40
MB7 Keon Broxton .15 .40
MB8 Brett Phillips .15 .40
MB9 Zach Davies .15 .40
MB10 Josh Hader .20 .50
MB11 Domingo Santana .20 .50
MB12 Eric Sogard .15 .40
MB13 Travis Shaw .15 .40
MB14 Corey Knebel .15 .40
MB15 Jimmy Nelson .15 .40
MB16 Eric Thames .20 .50
MB17 Hernan Perez .15 .40

2019 Brewers Topps

COMPLETE SET (17) 2.00 5.00
MB1 Christian Yelich .30 .75
MB2 Lorenzo Cain .15 .40
MB3 Jesus Aguilar .20 .50
MB4 Orlando Arcia .15 .40
MB5 Chase Anderson .15 .40
MB6 Jhoulys Chacin .15 .40
MB7 Jimmy Nelson .15 .40
MB8 Travis Shaw .15 .40
MB9 Ben Gamel .20 .50
MB10 Ryan Braun .20 .50
MB11 Corbin Burnes 1.25 3.00
MB12 Josh Hader .20 .50
MB13 Jeremy Jeffress .15 .40
MB14 Brandon Woodruff .25 .60
MB15 Freddy Peralta .25 .60
MB16 Corey Knebel .15 .40
MB17 Zach Davies .15 .40

2020 Brewers Topps

MIL1 Lorenzo Cain .15 .40
MIL2 Christian Yelich .30 .75
MIL3 Ryan Braun .20 .50
MIL4 Brandon Woodruff .25 .60
MIL5 Josh Hader .20 .50
MIL6 Tyrone Taylor .15 .40
MIL7 Orlando Arcia .15 .40
MIL8 Keston Hiura .30 .75
MIL9 Eric Sogard .15 .40
MIL10 Eric Lauer .15 .40
MIL11 Manny Pina .15 .40
MIL12 Ben Gamel .20 .50
MIL13 Ronny Rodriguez .15 .40
MIL14 Bernie Brewer .15 .40
MIL15 Miller Park .15 .40
MIL16 Luis Urias .20 .50
MIL17 Freddy Peralta .15 .40

2017 Brewers Topps National Baseball Card Day

COMPLETE SET (10) 5.00 12.00
MIL1 Keon Broxton .60 1.50
MIL2 Ryan Braun .75 2.00
MIL3 Jonathan Villar .60 1.50
MIL4 Junior Guerra .60 1.50
MIL5 Domingo Santana .75 2.00
MIL6 Travis Shaw .60 1.50
MIL7 Eric Thames .75 2.00
MIL8 Orlando Arcia 1.00 2.50
MIL9 Zach Davies .60 1.50
MIL10 Robin Yount 1.00 2.50

1909 Briggs E97

The cards in this 32-card set measure 1 1/2" by 2 3/4". The C.A. Briggs Company distributed this set in 1909, and it is one of the most highly prized of caramel issues. The cards come in two distinct varieties: one group in color with a brown print checklist on back; the other with identical player poses in black and white with blank backs. A comparison of team and name variations suggests that the black and white set pre-dates the color issue. The list below has been correctly alphabetized and hence does not exactly follow the checklist back order.

COMPLETE SET (32) 25000.00 50000.00
1 Jimmy Austin 500.00 1000.00
2 Joe Birmingham 500.00 1000.00
3 William J. Bradley 500.00 1000.00
4 Kitty Bransfield 500.00 1000.00
5 Howie Camnitz 500.00 1000.00
6 Bill Carrigan 500.00 1000.00
7 Harry Davis 500.00 1000.00
8 Josh Devore 500.00 1000.00
9 Mickey Doolan 500.00 1000.00
10 Bill Durham 500.00 1000.00
11 Jimmy Dygert 500.00 1000.00
12A Topsy Hartsel 600.00 1200.00
12B Topsy Hartsell (Hartsel) 500.00 1000.00
13 Charlie Hemphill 500.00 1000.00
14 Bill Heinchman (Hinchman) 500.00 1000.00
15 Willie Keeler 2500.00 5000.00
16 Joseph J. Kelly (Kelley) 1250.00 2500.00
17 Red Kleinow 500.00 1000.00
18 Rube Kroh 500.00 1000.00
19 Amby McConnell 500.00 1000.00
20 Matty McIntyre 500.00 1000.00
21 Chief Meyers 600.00 1200.00
22 Earl Moore 500.00 1000.00
23 George Mullin 500.00 1000.00
24 Red Murray 500.00 1000.00
25 Simon Nichols (Nicholls) 500.00 1000.00
26 Claude Rossman 500.00 1000.00
27 Admiral Schlei 500.00 1000.00
28A Harry Steinfeldt 600.00 1200.00
28B Harry Steinfeldt/No T in Steinfeldt 1500.00
3000.00
29A Dennis Sullivan:/Boston 5000.00 10000.00
29B Dennis Sullivan:/Chicago 600.00 1200.00
30A Cy Young/Boston Nat'l 2000.00 4000.00
30B Cy Young: Cleveland 1500.00 3000.00

1932 Briggs Chocolate

This set was issued by C.A. Brigss Chocolate company in 1932. The cards feature 31-different sports with each card including an artist's rendering of a sporting event. Although players are not named, it is thought that most were modeled after famous athletes of the time. The cardbacks include a written portion about the sport and an offer from Briggs for free baseball equipment for building a compete set of cards.

24 Baseball 800.00 1500.00

1953-54 Briggs

The cards in this 37-card set measure 2 1/4" by 3 1/2". The 1953-54 Briggs Hot Dog set of color cards contains 25 Senators and 12 known players from the Dodgers, Yankees and Giants. They were issued in two card panels in the Washington, D.C. area as part of the hot dog package itself. The cards are unnumbered and are printed on waxed cardboard, and the style of the Senator cards differs from that of the New York players. The latter appear in poses which also exist in the Dan Dee and Stahl Meyer card sets. The catalog designation is F154. In the checklist below the Washington players are numbered 1-25 alphabetically by name and the New York players are numbered 26-40 similarly.

COMPLETE SET (40) 8000.00 16000.00
COMMON CARD 100.00 200.00
COMMON PLAYER (29-40) 150.00 300.00
1 Jim Busby 100.00 200.00
2 Tommy Byrne 100.00 200.00
3 Gilbert Coan 100.00 200.00
4 Sonny Dixon 100.00 200.00
5 Ed Fitzgerald 100.00 200.00
6 Mickey Grasso 100.00 200.00
7 Mel Hoderlein 100.00 200.00
8 Jackie Jensen 200.00 400.00
9 Connie Marrero 100.00 200.00
10 Carmen Mauro 100.00 200.00
11 Walt Masterson 100.00 200.00
12 Mickey McDermott 100.00 200.00
13 Julio Moreno 100.00 200.00
14 Bob Oldis 100.00 200.00
15 Erwin Porterfield 100.00 200.00
16 Pete Runnels 100.00 200.00
17 Johnny Schmitz 100.00 200.00
18 Angel Scull 100.00 200.00
19 Spec Shea 100.00 200.00
20 Albert Sima 100.00 200.00
21 Chuck Stobbs 100.00 200.00
22 Wayne Terwilliger 100.00 200.00
23 Joe Tipton 100.00 200.00
24 Tom Umphlett 100.00 200.00
25 Mickey Vernon 300.00 600.00
26 Clyde Vollmer 100.00 200.00
27 Gene Verble 100.00 200.00
28 Eddie Yost 100.00 200.00
29 Hank Bauer 300.00 600.00
30 Carl Erskine 300.00 600.00
31 Gil Hodges 500.00 1000.00
32 Monte Irvin 500.00 1000.00
33 Whitey Lockman 300.00 600.00
34 Mickey Mantle 4000.00 8000.00
35 Willie Mays 2000.00 4000.00
36 Gil McDougald 300.00 600.00
37 Don Mueller 300.00 600.00
38 Don Newcombe 300.00 600.00
39 Phil Rizzuto 500.00 1000.00
40 Duke Snider 1000.00 2000.00

1941 Browns W753

The cards in this 29-card set measure approximately 2 1/8" by 2 5/8". The 1941 W753 set features unnumbered cards of the St. Louis Browns. The cards are numbered below alphabetically by player's name. Similar to the W711-2 set, it was issued in a box with a reverse side resembling a mailing label. These sets were also available via mail-order. This set is valued at an extra $100 when still in its original mailing box.

COMPLETE SET (30) 250.00 500.00
1 Johnny Allen 12.50 30.00
2 Elden Auker 12.50 30.00
3 Donald L. Barnes OWN 10.00 25.00
4 Johnny Berardino 20.00 50.00
5 George Caster 10.00 25.00
6 Harland Clift 12.50 30.00
7 Roy J. Cullenbine 10.00 25.00
8 William O. DeWitt GM 10.00 25.00
9 Robert Estalella 10.00 25.00
10 Rick Ferrell 50.00 100.00
11 Dennis W. Galehouse 12.50 30.00
12 Joseph L. Grace 10.00 25.00
13 Frank Grube 10.00 25.00
14 Robert A. Harris 10.00 25.00
15 Donald Heffner 10.00 25.00
16 Fred Hofmann 10.00 25.00
17 Walter F. Judnich 10.00 25.00
18 Jack Kramer 10.00 25.00
19 Chester(Chet) Laabs 10.00 25.00
20 John Lucadello 10.00 25.00
21 George H. McQuinn 10.00 25.00
22 Robert Muncrief Jr. 10.00 25.00
23 John Niggeling 10.00 25.00
24 Fritz Ostermueller 10.00 25.00
25 James(Luke) Sewell MG 12.50 30.00
26 Alan C. Strange 10.00 25.00
27 Bob Swift 10.00 25.00
28 James(Zack) Taylor CO 10.00 25.00
29 Bill Trotter 10.00 25.00
30 Title Card/(Order Coupon on back) 10.00 25.00

1952 Browns Postcards

The 12-card set has glossy black and white with PC backs. It appears that backs determine the year. The 1952 cards have "Post Card" in script block lettering over the top if you lay the card down horizontally. There is a line dividing the back on one side"Correspondence" and the other "Address". There is no postage box. The cards are unnumbered and listed alphabetically.

COMPLETE SET (12) 60.00 120.00
1 Tommy Byrne 8.00 20.00
2 Bob Cain 6.00 15.00
3 Clint Courtney 6.00 15.00
4 Jim Delsing 6.00 15.00
5 Jim Dyck 6.00 15.00
6 Marty Marion 12.50 30.00
7 Cass Michaels 6.00 15.00
8 Bob Nieman 6.00 15.00
9 Satchel Paige 20.00 50.00
10 Duane Pillette 6.00 15.00
11 Jim Rivera 6.00 15.00
12 Bobby Young 6.00 15.00

1953 Browns Postcards

All the 1953 cards have divided backs, but "Photo Post Card" in double block lettering and then "Address" under that in smaller lettering. The only variation known is one of Ned Garver where the "Photo Post Card" is in a different type of lettering. Everything else is the same. The set is unnumbered and listed below in alphabetical order. The Don Larsen card predates his Bowman Rookie Card.

COMPLETE SET (31) 200.00 400.00
1 Neil Berry 6.00 15.00
2 Mike Blyzka 6.00 15.00
3 Harry Breechen 8.00 20.00
4 Bob Cain 6.00 15.00
5 Clint Courtney 6.00 15.00
6 Jim Dyck 6.00 15.00
7 Hank Edwards 6.00 15.00
8 Ned Garver 8.00 20.00
9 Johnny Groth 6.00 15.00
10 Bobo Holloman 8.00 20.00
11 Bill Hunter 6.00 15.00
12 Dick Kokos 6.00 15.00
13 Dick Kryhoski 6.00 15.00
14 Max Lanier 6.00 15.00
15 Don Larsen 10.00 25.00
16 Don Lenhardt 6.00 15.00
17 Dick Littlefield 6.00 15.00
18 Marty Marion 12.50 30.00
19 Babe Martin 6.00 15.00
20 Willy Miranda 6.00 15.00
21 Les Moss 6.00 15.00
22 Bill Norman 6.00 15.00
23 Satchel Paige 30.00 60.00
24 Satchel Paige 30.00 60.00
25 Duane Pillette 6.00 15.00
26 Bob Sheffing 6.00 15.00
27 Roy Sievers 10.00 25.00
28 Marlin Stuart 6.00 15.00
29 Virgil Trucks 6.00 15.00
30 Bill Veeck 12.50 30.00
31 Vic Wertz 8.00 20.00

1996 Browns '44 Fritsch

This 36-card set of the 1944 American League Champion St. Louis Browns Baseball team with a suggested retail price of $10 features an artist's rendition of the player on the front. The backs carry player information, career statistics, and a small cartoon depicting one aspect of the player's career.

COMPLETE SET (36) 4.00 10.00
1 Team Card .08 .25
2 Don Gutteridge .08 .25
3 Milt Byrnes .08 .25
4 Al Hollingsworth .08 .25
5 Willis Hudlin .08 .25
6 Sid Jakucki .08 .25
7 Nelson Potter .20 .50
8 Len Schulte .08 .25
9 Vern Stephens .30 .75
10 Frank Demaree .08 .25
11 Al Zarilla .08 .25
12 Bob Muncrief .08 .25
13 Steve Sundra .08 .25
14 Jack Kramer .08 .25
15 Lefty West .08 .25
16 Denny Galehouse .08 .25
17 Luke Sewell MG .20 .50
18 Joe Schultz .20 .50
19 George McQuinn .30 .75
20 Ellis Clary .08 .25
21 Babe Martin .08 .25
22 Red Hayworth .08 .25
23 Frank Mancuso .08 .25
24 Tex Shirley .08 .25
25 Mike Chartak .08 .25
26 Mark Christman .08 .25
27 Tom Hatley .08 .25
28 Tom Turner .08 .25
29 Floyd Baker .08 .25
30 Mike Kreevich .08 .25
31 George Caster .08 .25
32 Gene Moore .08 .25
33 Chet Laabs .08 .25
34 Sam Zoldak .08 .25
35 Hal Epps .08 .25
36 Checklist .08 .25

1998 Browns Heads Up

These 20 cards, issued in the style of the 1938 Goudey Heads Up set, was issued by the St. Louis Browns historical society and featured living alumnni of the Browns. These cards measure 2 1/2" by 2" and are unnumbered so we have sequenced them in alphabetical order.

COMPLETE SET (20) 3.00 8.00
1 Hank Arft .08 .25
2 Ellis Clary .08 .25
3 Jim Delsing .08 .25
4 Ned Garver .08 .25
5 Don Gutteridge .08 .25
6 Red Hayworth .08 .25
7 Bill Jennings .08 .25
8 Dick Kryhoski .08 .25
9 Don Lenhardt .08 .25
10 Bob Mahoney .08 .25
11 Frank Mancuso .08 .25
12 Babe Martin .08 .25
13 Ed Mickelson .08 .25
14 Stan Musial 2.00 5.00
15 J.W. Porter .08 .25
16 Arthur Richman .08 .25
17 Roy Sievers .20 .50
18 Virgil Trucks .08 .25
19 Jerry Witte .08 .25
20 Al Widmar .08 .25

2003 Browns 1953 50th Anniversary

COMPLETE SET 5.00 10.00
1 Satchel Paige .60 1.50
2 Les Moss .10 .25
3 Roy Sievers .20 .50
4 Bobby Young .10 .25
5 Marlin Stuart .10 .25
6 Billy Hunter .10 .25
7 Don Lenhardt .10 .25
8 Johnny Groth .10 .25
9 Vic Wertz .10 .25
10 Don Larsen .30 .75
11 Clint Courtney .10 .25
12 Dick Kryhoski .10 .25
13 Neil Berry .10 .25
14 Bob Cain .10 .25
15 Willie Miranda .10 .25
16 Hank Edwards .10 .25
17 Dick Kokos .10 .25
18 Jim Pisoni .10 .25
19 Harry Brecheen .20 .50
20 St Louis Browns .20 .50
21 St Louis Browns CL .20 .50
22 Lou Kretlow .10 .25
23 Babe Martin .10 .25
24 Ed Mickelson .10 .25
25 Frank Kellert .10 .25
26 Virgil Trucks .10 .25
27 Dick Littlefield .10 .25
28 Jim Dyck .10 .25
29 Mike Blyzka .10 .25
30 Bob Habenicht .10 .25
31 Max Lanier .10 .25
32 Bob Elliott .10 .25
33 Duane Pillette .10 .25
34 Johnny Lipon .10 .25
35 Bob Turley .40 1.00
36 Vern Stephens .20 .50
37 Hal White .10 .25
38 Dixie Upright .10 .25
39 Bobo Holloman .10 .25
40 Marty Marion MG .20 .50

1887 Buchner Gold Coin N284

The baseball players found in this Buchner set are a part of a larger group of cards portraying policemen, jockeys and actors, all of which were issued with the tobacco brand "Gold Coin." The set is comprised of three major groupings or types. In the first type, nine players from eight teams, plus three Brooklyn players, are all portrayed in identical poses according to position. In the second type, St. Louis has 14 players depicted in poses which are not repeated. The last group contains 53 additional cards which vary according to pose, team change, spelling, etc. These third type cards are indicated in the checklist below by an asterisk. In all, there are 116 individuals portrayed on 142 cards. The existence of an additional player in the set, McClellan of Brooklyn, has never been verified and the card probably doesn't exist. The set was issued circa 1887. The cards are numbered below in alphabetical order within team with teams themselves listed in alphabetical order: Baltimore (1-4), Boston (5-13), Brooklyn (14-17), Chicago (18-26), Detroit (27-35), Indianapolis (36-47), LaCrosse (48-51), Milwaukee (52-55), New York Mets (56-63), New York (64-73), Philadelphia (74-83), Pittsburg (84-92), St. Louis (93-106), and Washington (107-117).

COMPLETE SET (152) 25000.00 50000.00
COMMON ST. LOUIS 200.00 400.00
COMMON CARD * 125.00 250.00
1 Tommy(Oyster) Burns * 250.00 500.00
2 Chris Fulmer * 250.00 500.00
3 Matt Kilroy 250.00 500.00
4 Blondie Purcell * 250.00 500.00
5 John Burdock 300.00 600.00
6 Bill Daley 300.00 600.00
7 Joe Hornung 300.00 600.00
8 Dick Johnston 300.00 600.00
9A King Kelly: Boston 750.00 1500.00
Right field
9B King Kelly: Boston 1250.00 2500.00
Catcher *
10A John Morrell: Boston/(Both hands out- 300.00
600.00
stretched
10B John Morrell: 250.00 500.00
Boston */(Hands clasped
near chin
11A Hoss Radbourn: 600.00 1200.00
Boston
Sic, Radbourne
11B Hoss Radbourn: 750.00 1500.00
Boston */(Sic& Radbourne;
hands
12 Ezra Sutton 300.00 600.00
13 Sam Wise 300.00 600.00
14 Bill McClellan:
Brooklyn
Never confirmed
15 Jimmy Peoples 300.00 600.00
16 Bill Phillips 300.00 600.00
17 Henry Porter 300.00 600.00
18A Cap Anson 1500.00 3000.00
Both hands out-
stretche
18B Cap Anson 3000.00 6000.00
Left hand on hip
righ
19 Tom Burns 300.00 600.00
20A John Clarkson 750.00 1500.00
Chicago
20B John Clarkson: 1000.00 2000.00
Chicago */(Right arm extended&
l
21 Silver Flint 300.00 600.00
22 Fred Pfeffer 300.00 600.00
23 Jimmy Ryan 400.00 800.00
24 Billy Sullivan 400.00 800.00
25 Billy Sunday 750.00 1500.00
26A Ned Williamson: 300.00 600.00
Chicago
Shortstop
26B Ned Williamson: 250.00 500.00
Chicago
Second base *
27 Charlie Bennett 400.00 800.00
28A Dan Brouthers: 750.00 1500.00
Detroit
Fielding
28B Dan Brouthers: 1000.00 2000.00
Detroit *
Batting
29 Fred Dunlap 300.00 600.00
30 Charlie Getzien 300.00 600.00
31 Ned Hanlon 600.00 1200.00
32 Jim Manning 300.00 600.00
33A Hardy Richardson: 300.00 600.00
Detroit/(Hands together in
fr
33B Hardy Richardson: 250.00 500.00
Detroit */(Right hand holding#
34A Sam Thompson: 750.00 1500.00
Detroit
Looking up with
hands at
34B Sam Thompson: 1000.00 2000.00
Detroit *
Hands chest high
35 Deacon White 500.00 1000.00
36 Tug Arundels 300.00 600.00
37 Charley Bassett 300.00 600.00
38 Henry Boyle * 250.00 500.00
39 John Cahill * 250.00 500.00
40A Jerry Denny: 300.00 600.00
Indianapolis/(Hands on knees&
legs
40B Jerry Denny: 250.00 500.00
Indianapolis */(Hands on knees&
le
41A Jack Glasscock: 400.00 800.00
Indianapolis/(Crouching& catch-#
41B Jack Glasscock: 300.00 600.00
Indianapolis *
Hands on knees
42 John Healy 300.00 600.00
43 George Meyers * 250.00 500.00
44 Jack McGeachy 300.00 600.00
45 Mark Polhemus 300.00 600.00
46A Emmett Seery: 300.00 600.00
Indianapolis/(Hands together in
f
46B Emmett Seery: 400.00 800.00
Indianapolis */(Hands outstretched
47 Shomberg 300.00 600.00
48 John Corbett * 250.00 500.00
49 Crowley * 250.00 500.00
50 Kennedy * 250.00 500.00
51 Rooks * 250.00 500.00
52 Forster * 250.00 500.00
53 Hart * 250.00 500.00
54 Morrissy * 250.00 500.00
55 Strauss * 250.00 500.00
56 Ed Cushmann * 250.00 500.00
57 Jim Donohue * 250.00 500.00
58 Dude Esterbrooke * 250.00 500.00
59 Joe Gerhardt * 250.00 500.00
60 Frank Hankinson * 250.00 500.00
61 Jack Nelson * 250.00 500.00
62 Dave Orr * 250.00 500.00
63 James Rosemann * 250.00 500.00
64A Roger Connor: 750.00 1500.00
New York/(Both hands out-
stretch
64B Roger Connor: 1000.00 2000.00
New York */(Hands outstretched&
p
65 Pat Deasley * 250.00 500.00
66A Mike Dorgan 300.00 600.00
Fielding
66B Mike Dorgan 250.00 500.00
Batting *
67A Buck Ewing: 750.00 1500.00
New York (Ball in
left hand& right a
67B Buck Ewing 1000.00 2000.00
New York *
Appears ready to clap
68A Pete Gillespie: 300.00 600.00
New York
Fielding
68B Pete Gillespie: 250.00 500.00
New York
Batting *
69 George Gore 300.00 600.00
70A Tim Keefe: 750.00 1500.00
New York
70B Tim Keefe: 1000.00 2000.00
New York *
Ball just released
from
71A Jim O'Rourke: 750.00 1500.00
New York
Hands cupped in
front
71B Jim O'Rourke: 1000.00 2000.00
New York */(Hands on knees&
looki
72A Danny Richardson: 300.00 600.00
New York
Third base
72B Danny Richardson: 250.00 500.00
New York
Second base*
73A John M. Ward: 750.00 1500.00
New York/(Crouching& catching a
73B John M. Ward: 1000.00 2000.00
New York *
Hands by left knee
73C John M. Ward: 750.00 1500.00
New York *
Hands on knees
74A Ed Andrews: 300.00 600.00
Philadelphia/(Hands together in
fro
74B Ed Andrews: 250.00 500.00
Philadelphia */(Catching& hands
wai
75 Charlie Bastian 300.00 600.00
76 Dan Casey * 250.00 500.00
77 Jack Clements 300.00 600.00
78 Sid Farrar 400.00 800.00
79 Charlie Ferguson 300.00 600.00
80 Jim Fogarty 300.00 600.00
81 Arthur Irwin 300.00 600.00
82A Joel Mulvey: 300.00 600.00
Philadelphia
Hands on knees
82B Joel Mulvey: 250.00 500.00
Philadelphia */(Hands together
abo
83A Pete Wood 300.00 600.00
Philadelphia
Fielding
83B Pete Wood: Phila- 400.00 800.00
delphia HOR (Stealing
a Base)
84 Sam Barkley 300.00 600.00
85 Ed Beecher: 300.00 600.00
86 Tom Brown 300.00 600.00
87 Fred Carroll 300.00 600.00
88 John Coleman 300.00 600.00
89 Jim McCormick 300.00 600.00
90 Doggie Miller 300.00 600.00
91 Pop Smith 300.00 600.00
92 Art Whitney 300.00 600.00
93 Sam Barkley 400.00 800.00
94 Doc Bushong 400.00 800.00
95 Bob Carruthers 500.00 1000.00
96 Charles Comiskey 1250.00 2500.00

97 Dave Foutz	400.00	800.00
98 William Gleason	500.00	1000.00
99 Arlie Latham	600.00	1200.00
100 Jumbo McGinnis	400.00	800.00
101 Hugh Nicol	400.00	800.00
102 James O'Neil	400.00	800.00
103 Yank Robinson	400.00	800.00
104 Sullivan	400.00	800.00
105 Chris Von Der Ahe OWN	1500.00	3000.00
St. Louis/(Photo		
106 Curt Welch	500.00	1000.00
107 Cliff Carroll	300.00	600.00
108 Craig *	250.00	500.00
109 Sam Crane *	250.00	500.00
110 Ed Dailey	300.00	600.00
111 Jim Donnelly	300.00	600.00
112A Jack Farrell:	300.00	600.00
Washington		
Ball in left hand, rig		
112B Jack Farrell:	250.00	500.00
Washington */(Ball in hands		
near		
113 Barney Gilligan	300.00	600.00
114A Paul Hines:	300.00	600.00
Washington		
Fielding		
114B Paul Hines:	250.00	500.00
Washington *		
Batting		
115 Al Myers	300.00	600.00
116 Billy O'Brien	300.00	600.00
117 Jim Whitney	300.00	600.00

1932 Bulgaria Zigaretten Sport Photos

256 Babe Ruth	40.00	80.00
Max Schmeling		

1977 Burger Chef Discs

The individual discs measure approximately 2 1/2" in diameter and contain a burger-related caricature on the reverse. There were nine discs on each tray; five on the front and four on the back. Each tray contained one team and there were 24 different trays, obviously one for each team. On the tray the copyright notice indicates 1977. The player photos are shown without team logos on their caps. We have sequenced this set in the following order: Houston (1-9), St. Louis (10-18), Texas (19-27), Boston (28-36), Baltimore (37-45), Minnesota (46-54), Cleveland (55-63), Kansas City (64-72), Chicago White Sox (73-81), Milwaukee (82-90), Detroit (91-99), San Francisco (100-108), Oakland (109-117), California (118-126), San Diego (127-135), New York Mets (136-144), Los Angeles (145-153), Montreal (154-162), Philadelphia (163-171), New York Yankees (172-180), Pirates (181-189), Chicago Cubs (190-198), Cincinnati (199-207), Atlanta (208-216). No 1977 expansion teams were featured in this set. Complete Panels are worth twice the amount of the values for each team.

COMPLETE SET (216)	75.00	150.00
1 J.R. Richard	.20	.50
2 Enos Cabell	.10	.25
3 Leon Roberts	.10	.25
4 Ken Forsch	.10	.25
5 Roger Metzger	.10	.25
6 Bob Watson	.20	.50
7 Cesar Cedeno	.20	.50
8 Joe Ferguson	.10	.25
9 Jose Cruz	.20	.50
10 Al Hrabosky	.10	.25
11 Keith Hernandez	.60	1.50
12 Pete Falcone	.10	.25
13 Ken Reitz	.10	.25
14 John Denny	.10	.25
15 Lou Brock	1.50	4.00
16 Ted Simmons	.40	1.00
17 Bake McBride	.10	.25
18 Mike Tyson	.10	.25
19 Campy Campaneris	.20	.50
20 Gaylord Perry	1.25	3.00
21 Lenny Randle	.10	.25
22 Bert Blyleven	.40	1.00
23 Jim Sundberg	.20	.50
24 Mike Hargrove	.20	.50
25 Tom Grieve	.20	.50
26 Toby Harrah	.10	.25
27 Juan Beniquez	.10	.25
28 Rick Burleson	.10	.25
29 Jim Rice	.60	1.50
30 Dwight Evans	.40	1.00
31 Fergie Jenkins	1.25	3.00
32 Bill Lee	.10	.25
33 Carlton Fisk	2.50	6.00
34 Luis Tiant	.40	1.00
35 Fred Lynn	.20	.50
36 Carl Yastrzemski	1.50	4.00
37 Al Bumbry	.10	.25
38 Mark Belanger	.20	.50
39 Paul Blair	.10	.25
40 Ross Grimsley	.10	.25
41 Ken Singleton	.20	.50
42 Jim Palmer	1.50	4.00
43 Brooks Robinson	1.50	4.00
44 Doug DeCinces	.20	.50
45 Lee May	.20	.50
46 Tom Johnson	.10	.25
47 Dave Goltz	.10	.25
48 Dan Ford	.10	.25
49 Larry Hisle	.10	.25
50 Mike Cubbage	.10	.25
51 Rod Carew	1.50	4.00
52 Bobby Randall	.10	.25
53 Butch Wynegar	.10	.25
54 Lyman Bostock	.20	.50
55 Duane Kuiper	.10	.25
56 Rick Manning	.10	.25
57 Buddy Bell	.40	1.00
58 Dennis Eckersley	2.00	5.00
59 Wayne Garland	.10	.25
60 Dave LaRoche	.10	.25
61 Rick Waits	.10	.25
62 Ray Fosse	.10	.25
63 Frank Duffy	.10	.25
64 Paul Splittorff	.10	.25
65 Amos Otis	.20	.50
66 Tom Poquette	.10	.25
67 Fred Patek	.10	.25
68 Doug Bird	.10	.25
69 John Mayberry	.10	.25
70 Dennis Leonard	.10	.25
71 George Brett	10.00	25.00
72 Hal McRae	.40	1.00
73 Chet Lemon	.20	.50
74 Jorge Orta	.10	.25
75 Richie Zisk	.10	.25
76 Lamar Johnson	.10	.25
77 Bart Johnson	.10	.25
78 Jack Brohamer	.10	.25
79 Jim Spencer	.10	.25
80 Ralph Garr	.10	.25
81 Bucky Dent	.20	.50
82 Jerry Augustine	.10	.25
83 Jim Slaton	.10	.25
84 Charlie Moore	.10	.25
85 Von Joshua	.10	.25
86 Eduardo Rodriquez	.10	.25
87 Sal Bando	.20	.50
88 Robin Yount	2.50	6.00
89 Sixto Lezcano	.10	.25
90 Bill Travers	.10	.25
91 Ben Oglivie	.10	.25
92 Mark Fidrych	2.00	5.00
93 Aurelio Rodriquez	.10	.25
94 Bill Freehan	.40	1.00
95 John Hiller	.10	.25
96 Rusty Staub	.40	1.00
97 Willie Horton	.20	.50
98 Ron LeFlore	.20	.50
99 Jason Thompson	.20	.50
100 Marty Perez	.10	.25
101 Randy Moffitt	.10	.25
102 Gary Thomasson	.10	.25
103 Jim Barr	.10	.25
104 Larry Herndon	.10	.25
105 Bobby Murcer	.40	1.00
106 John Montefusco	.10	.25
107 Willie Crawford	.10	.25
108 Chris Speier	.10	.25
109 Phil Garner	.40	1.00
110 Mike Torrez	.10	.25
111 Manny Sanguillen	.10	.25
112 Stan Bahnsen	.10	.25
113 Mike Norris	.10	.25
114 Vida Blue	.40	1.00
115 Claudell Washington	.20	.50
116 Bill North	.10	.25
117 Paul Lindblad	.10	.25
118 Paul Hartzell	.10	.25
119 Dave Chalk	.10	.25
120 Ron Jackson	.10	.25
121 Jerry Remy	.10	.25
122 Frank Tanana	.40	1.00
123 Nolan Ryan	10.00	25.00
124 Bobby Bonds	.20	.50
125 Joe Rudi	.20	.50
126 Bobby Grich	.40	1.00
127 Butch Metzger	.10	.25
128 Doug Rader	.10	.25
129 George Hendrick	.20	.50
130 David Winfield	3.00	8.00
131 Gene Tenace	.40	1.00
132 Randy Jones	.10	.25
133 Rollie Fingers	1.25	3.00
134 Mike Ivie	.10	.25
135 Enzo Hernandez	.10	.25
136 Ed Kranepool	.10	.25
137 John Matlack	.10	.25
138 Felix Millan	.10	.25
139 Skip Lockwood	.10	.25
140 John Stearns	.10	.25
141 Dave Kingman	.60	1.50
142 Tom Seaver	2.50	6.00
143 Jerry Koosman	.40	1.00
144 Bud Harrelson	.10	.25
145 Davey Lopes	.20	.50
146 Rick Monday	.10	.25
147 Don Sutton	1.25	3.00
148 Rick Rhoden	.10	.25
149 Doug Rau	.10	.25
150 Steve Garvey	.75	2.00
151 Steve Yeager	.10	.25
152 Reggie Smith	.20	.50
153 Ron Cey	.40	1.00
154 Gary Carter	2.00	5.00
155 Del Unser	.10	.25
156 Tim Foli	.10	.25
157 Barry Foote	.10	.25
158 Ellis Valentine	.10	.25
159 Steve Rogers	.10	.25
160 Tony Perez	1.00	2.50
161 Larry Parrish	.20	.50
162 Dave Cash	.10	.25
163 Greg Luzinski	.40	1.00
164 Bob Boone	.40	1.00
165 Tug McGraw	.40	1.00
166 Jay Johnstone	.20	.50
167 Garry Maddox	.10	.25
168 Mike Schmidt	6.00	15.00
169 Jim Kaat	.60	1.50
170 Larry Bowa	.40	1.00
171 Steve Carlton	2.50	6.00
172 Don Gullett	.10	.25
173 Chris Chambliss	.10	.25
174 Graig Nettles	.40	1.00
175 Willie Randolph	.60	1.50
176 Reggie Jackson	2.50	6.00
177 Thurman Munson	1.00	2.50
178 Catfish Hunter	1.50	4.00
179 Roy White	.20	.50
180 Mickey Rivers	.10	.25
181 Jerry Reuss	.20	.50
182 Rennie Stennett	.10	.25
183 Bill Robinson	.10	.25
184 Frank Taveras	.10	.25
185 Duffy Dyer	.10	.25
186 Willie Stargell	1.50	4.00
187 Dave Parker	1.00	2.50
188 John Candelaria	.20	.50
189 Al Oliver	.40	1.00
190 Joe Wallis	.10	.25
191 Manny Trillo	.10	.25
192 Bill Bonham	.10	.25
193 Rich Reuschel	.20	.50
194 Ray Burris	.10	.25
195 Bill Buckner	.20	.50
196 Jerry Morales	.10	.25
197 Jose Cardenal	.10	.25
198 Bill Madlock	.40	1.00
199 Dan Driessen	.10	.25
200 Dave Concepcion	.40	1.00
201 George Foster	.40	1.00
202 Cesar Geronimo	.10	.25
203 Gary Nolan	.10	.25
204 Pete Rose	4.00	10.00
205 Johnny Bench	2.50	6.00
206 Ken Griffey	.40	1.00
207 Joe Morgan	1.50	4.00
208 Dick Ruthven	.10	.25
209 Phil Niekro	1.25	3.00
210 Gary Matthews	.20	.50
211 Willie Montanez	.10	.25
212 Jerry Royster	.10	.25
213 Andy Messersmith	.10	.25
214 Jeff Burroughs	.20	.50
215 Tom Paciorek	.20	.50
216 Darrel Chaney	.10	.25

1980 Burger King Pitch/Hit/Run

The cards in this 34-card set measure 2 1/2" by 3 1/2". The "Pitch, Hit, and Run" set was a promotion introduced by Burger King in 1980. The cards carry a Burger King logo on the front and those marked by an asterisk in the checklist contain a different photo from that found in the regularly issued Topps series. For example, Nolan Ryan was shown as a California Angel and Joe Morgan was a Cincinnati Red in the 1980 Topps regular set. Cards 1-11 are pitchers, 12-22 are hitters, and 23-33 are speedsters. Within each subgroup, the players are numbered corresponding to the alphabetical order of their names.

COMPLETE SET (34)	10.00	25.00
1 Vida Blue *	.20	.50
2 Steve Carlton	.75	2.00
3 Rollie Fingers	.40	1.00
4 Ron Guidry *	.20	.50
5 Jerry Koosman *	.08	.25
6 Phil Niekro	.50	1.25
7 Jim Palmer *	.75	2.00
8 J.R. Richard	.08	.25
9 Nolan Ryan *	7.50	15.00
Houston Astros		
10 Tom Seaver *	1.00	2.50
11 Bruce Sutter	.40	1.00
12 Don Baylor	.20	.50
13 George Brett	2.50	6.00
14 Rod Carew	.60	1.50
15 George Foster	.08	.25
16 Keith Hernandez *	.20	.50
17 Reggie Jackson *	1.50	4.00
18 Fred Lynn *	.20	.50
19 Dave Parker	.08	.25
20 Jim Rice	.08	.25
21 Pete Rose	1.50	4.00
22 Dave Winfield *	1.25	3.00
23 Bobby Bonds *	.20	.50
24 Enos Cabell	.02	.10
25 Cesar Cedeno	.08	.25
26 Julio Cruz	.02	.10
27 Ron LeFlore *	.08	.25
28 Dave Lopes *	.08	.25
29 Omar Moreno *	.08	.25
30 Joe Morgan *	1.00	2.50
Houston Astros		
31 Bill North	.02	.10
32 Frank Taveras	.02	.10
33 Willie Wilson	.08	.25
NNO Checklist Card TP	.01	.05

1986 Burger King All-Pro

This 20-card standard-size set was distributed in Burger King restaurants across the country. They were produced as panels of three where the middle card was actually a special discount coupon card. The folded panel was given with the purchase of a Whopper. Each individual card measures 2 1/2" by 3 1/2". The team logos have been airbrushed from the pictures. The cards are numbered on the front at the top. Uncut panels are worth 1x to 2x the combined values of the players on said panel.

COMPLETE SET (20)	4.00	10.00
1 Tony Pena	.02	.10
2 Dave Winfield	.50	1.25
3 Fernando Valenzuela	.08	.25
4 Pete Rose	.40	1.25
5 Mike Schmidt	.40	1.25
6 Steve Carlton	.50	1.25
7 Glenn Wilson	.02	.10
8 Jim Rice	.08	.25
9 Wade Boggs	.40	1.25
10 Juan Samuel	.02	.10
11 Dale Murphy	.20	.50
12 Reggie Jackson	.50	1.25
13 Kirk Gibson	.08	.25
14 Eddie Murray	.40	1.25
15 Cal Ripken	2.00	5.00
16 Willie McGee	.08	.25
17 Dwight Gooden	.08	.25
18 Steve Garvey	.20	.50
19 Don Mattingly	1.00	2.50
20 George Brett	1.00	2.50

1987 Burger King All-Pro

This 20-card set consists of ten panels of two cards each joined together along with a promotional coupon. Individual cards measure 2 1/2" by 3 1/2" whereas the panels measure approximately 3 1/2" by 7 5/8". MSA (Mike Schechter Associates produced the cards for Burger King; there are no Major League logos on the cards. The cards are numbered on the front. The set card numbering is almost (but not quite) in alphabetical order by player's name. Uncut panels are worth 1x to 2x the combined value of the players on said panel.

COMPLETE SET (20)	2.50	6.00
1 Wade Boggs	.30	.75
2 Gary Carter	.10	.30
3 Will Clark	.30	.75
4 Roger Clemens	.60	1.50
5 Steve Garvey	.10	.30
6 Ron Darling	.02	.10
7 Pedro Guerrero	.02	.10
8 Von Hayes	.02	.10
9 Rickey Henderson	.40	1.00
10 Keith Hernandez	.07	.20
11 Wally Joyner	.20	.50
12 Mike Krukow	.02	.10
13 Don Mattingly	.60	1.50
14 Ozzie Smith	.30	.75
15 Tony Pena	.02	.10
16 Jim Rice	.07	.20
17 Mike Schmidt	.30	.75
18 Ryne Sandberg	.60	1.50
19 Darryl Strawberry	.07	.20
20 Fernando Valenzuela	.07	.20

1994 Burger King Ripken

Co-sponsored by Coca-Cola and Burger King, this nine-card standard-size set was produced by Pinnacle to honor Baltimore Orioles star shortstop, Cal Ripken Jr. Three-card packs were available for 25 cents with the purchase of a large soft drink at Baltimore and Washington, D.C. Burger Kings, beginning May 22. The cards were available until June 19, or while supplies lasted. Each card was issued in two versions: standard and gold-foil, with the three-card packs containing two standard and one gold foil card. Ripken autographed several hundred cards, which were awarded in a drawing held after the promotion to collectors who had mailed in entry forms. The cards are numbered on the back as "X of 9."

COMPLETE SET (9)	2.50	6.00
COMMON CARD (1-9)	.40	1.00
*GOLD CARDS: 2X BASIC CARDS		

1997 Burger King Ripken

This eight-card set features borderless color action photos of Cal Ripken Jr. and was sponsored by Burger King. The backs carry another photo and a paragraph about an event in the life of Cal Ripken Jr. The set was available in three-card packs beginning August 4, and running through September 13, 1997 at participating Burger Kings for 99 cents a pack with the purchase of a Value Meal. The cards were also available in limited quantities to be purchased separately for $1.15 per pack. Each pack contained a game piece which gave the collector a chance to win a Ripken watch or autographed Ripken balls or jerseys. All proceeds from this promotion benefited the Ripken Charities.

COMPLETE SET (8)	2.50	6.00
COMMON CARD (1-8)	.40	1.00
*GOLD/10000: 1.2X TO 3X BASIC		
AU Cal Ripken Jr. AU	40.00	100.00

1938-59 George Burke PC744

The Burke postcards were issued by Chicago photographer George Burke during the period from 1938 through the 1950's. Because there are hundreds known and new ones are discovered frequently, a checklist has not been provided. The reverses feature the stamped name of "Geo. Burke, his address and the city "Chicago"

COMMON CARD (1938-48)	5.00	10.00
COMMON CARD (1948-on)	2.50	5.00

1978 Burlington Free Press

These newspaper inserts feature members of the Boston Red Sox and the Montreal Expos. Since each team was reasonably near Burlington, Vermont -- that is why the set consists of players from those teams. These cards are unnumbered, so we have sequenced them in alphabetical order. There are probably many additions to this set so any additional information is greatly appreciated.

COMPLETE SET	6.00	15.00
1 Bernie Carbo	.40	1.00
2 Dave Cash	.40	1.00
3 Dick Drago	.40	1.00
4 Pepe Frias	.40	1.00
5 Wayne Garrett	.40	1.00
6 Ross Grimsley	.40	1.00
7 Butch Hobson	.40	1.00
8 Bill Lee	.50	1.25
9 Rudy May	.40	1.00
10 Bob Montgomery	.40	1.00
11 Larry Parrish	.40	1.00
12 Jerry Remy	.40	1.00
13 Rodney Scott	.40	1.00
14 Chris Speier	.40	1.00
15 Wayne Twitchell	.40	1.00
16 Del Unser	.40	1.00
17 Ellis Valentine	.40	1.00
18 Dick Williams MG	.40	1.00

1933 Butter Cream R306

The small, elongated (measuring 1 1/4" by 3 1/2") cards of this 30 card set are unnumbered and contain many cut-down, blurry black and white photos. The producer's name is sometimes printed on the reverse. Despite their limitations, Butter Cream cards are highly prized by collectors. The cards have been alphabetized and numbered for reference in the checklist below. There are two varieties of the back for each card: One says "Your estimate of this year to Sept 1st; and "Your estimate of this year to Oct. 1st. The Babe Ruth card within this set is one of the more legendary rarities of the hobby. How rare is this Ruth card? Rare enough that through 1989 it was generally believed that the R306 set was complete at 29 cards. Two copies of the Ruth card, however, surfaced at the 1989 National Convention in Chicago, pushing the checklist up to 30 cards and establishing the R306 issue as perhaps Ruth's rarest card. Though a third (lower grade) copy was known to exist, according to the information provided in REA's 2008 catalog, it was lost in transit in 1990 in a deal involving hobby legends Lew Lipset and Barry Halper. To this date, the number of known copies remains at a mere two, one of which the whereabouts is unknown and the other – graded VgEx 4 by PSA – was offered for sale in REA's May, 2008 auction ultimately commanding $111,625. The Ruth is, understandably, unpriced due to scarcity and the set price references the collection of the 29 standard R306's. It's been theorized that the Ruth was intentionally short-printed perhaps as a stumbling block to send in all 30 cards for a special prize.

COMPLETE SET (29)	4000.00	8000.00
1 Earl Averill	300.00	600.00
2 Ed Brandt	200.00	400.00
3 Guy T. Bush	200.00	400.00
4 Mickey Cochrane	400.00	800.00
5 Joe Cronin	400.00	800.00
6 George Earnshaw	200.00	400.00
7 Wesley Ferrell	250.00	500.00
8 Jimmy Foxx	500.00	1000.00
(Jimmie)		
9 Frank Frisch	400.00	800.00
10 Charles M. Gelbert	200.00	400.00
11 Lefty Grove	400.00	800.00
12 Gabby Hartnett	300.00	600.00
13 Babe Herman	300.00	600.00
14 Chuck Klein	300.00	600.00
15 Ray Kremer	200.00	400.00
16 Fred Lindstrom	300.00	600.00
17 Ted Lyons	300.00	600.00
18 Pepper Martin	250.00	500.00
19 Robert O'Farrell	200.00	400.00
20 Ed A. Rommell	200.00	400.00
21 Charles Root	200.00	400.00
22 Harold Ruel	200.00	400.00
23 Babe Ruth SP		
24 Al Simmons	400.00	800.00
25 Bill Terry	400.00	800.00
26 George Uhle	200.00	400.00
27 Lloyd Waner	300.00	600.00
28 Paul Waner	400.00	800.00
29 Hack Wilson	300.00	600.00
30 Glenn Wright	200.00	400.00

1933 Butterfinger Canadian V94

These large photos measure approximately 6 1/2" by 8 1/2" and are printed on thin paper stock. The fronts feature black-and-white posed action shots within white borders. A facsimile autograph is inscribed across the picture. The backs are blank.

COMPLETE SET	2000.00	4000.00
1 Earl Averill	40.00	80.00
2 Larry Benton	20.00	40.00
3 Jim Bottomley	40.00	80.00
4 Tom Bridges	25.00	50.00
5 Bob Brown	20.00	40.00
6 Owen T. Carroll	20.00	40.00
7 Mickey Cochrane	62.50	125.00
8 Roger Cramer	25.00	50.00
9 Joe Cronin	62.50	125.00
10 Alvin Crowder	25.00	50.00
11 Dizzy Dean	75.00	150.00
12 Edward Delker	20.00	40.00
13 Bill Dickey	62.50	125.00
14 Rick Ferrell	40.00	80.00
15 Lew Fonseca	25.00	50.00
16A Jimmy Foxx	75.00	150.00
Name spelled Fox		
(Jimmie)		
16B Jimmie Foxx	20.00	40.00
Name spelled correctly		
17 Chuck Fullis	20.00	40.00
18 Lou Gehrig	150.00	300.00
19 Charles Gehringer	62.50	125.00
20 Lefty Gomez	62.50	125.00
21 Lefty Grove	75.00	150.00
22 Mule Haas	20.00	40.00
23 Chick Hafey	40.00	80.00
24 Bucky Harris	40.00	80.00
25 Frank Higgins	20.00	40.00
26 J. Francis Hogan	20.00	40.00
27 Ed Holley	20.00	40.00
28 Waite Hoyt	40.00	80.00
29 Jim Jordan	20.00	40.00
30 Hal Lee	20.00	40.00
31 Gus Mancuso	25.00	50.00
32 Oscar Melillo	20.00	40.00
33 Austin Moore	20.00	40.00
34 Randy Moore	20.00	40.00
35 Joe Morrissey	20.00	40.00
36 Joe Mowry	20.00	40.00
37 Bobo Newsom	25.00	50.00
38 Ernest Orsatti	20.00	40.00
39 Carl Reynolds	20.00	40.00
40 Walter Roettger	20.00	40.00
41 Babe Ruth	200.00	400.00
42 Blondy Ryan	20.00	40.00
43 John Salveson	20.00	40.00
44 Al Simmons	62.50	125.00
45 Al Smith	20.00	40.00
46 Harold Smith	20.00	40.00
47 Allyn Stout	20.00	40.00
48 Fresco Thompson	25.00	50.00
49 Art Veltman	20.00	40.00
50 Johnny Vergez	20.00	40.00
51 Gerald Walker	20.00	40.00
52 Paul Waner	40.00	80.00
53 Burgess Whitehead	20.00	40.00
54 Earl Whitehill	20.00	40.00
55 Robert Weiland	20.00	40.00
56 Jimmy Wilson	25.00	50.00
57 Bob Worthington	20.00	40.00
58 Tom Zachary	25.00	50.00

1934 Butterfinger Premiums R310

This large-size premium set comes either in paper or on heavy cardboard stock with advertising for Butterfinger or other candy at the top. The heavy cardboard Butterfinger display advertising cards are valued at triple the prices in the list below. The cards are unnumbered and Foxx exists as Fox or Foxx. The cards measure approximately 7 3/4" by 9 3/4" and have a thick off-white border around the player photo.

COMPLETE SET (65)	2500.00	5000.00
1 Earl Averill	40.00	80.00
2 Dick Bartell	20.00	40.00
3 Lawrence Benton	20.00	40.00
4 Wally Berger	25.00	50.00
5 Jim Bottomley	40.00	80.00
6 Ralph Boyle	20.00	40.00
7 Tex Carleton	20.00	40.00
8 Owen T. Carroll	20.00	40.00
9 Ben Chapman	20.00	40.00
10 Mickey Cochrane	50.00	100.00
11 Jimmy Collins	20.00	40.00
12 Joe Cronin	50.00	100.00
13 Al Crowder	20.00	40.00
14 Dizzy Dean	100.00	200.00
15 Paul Derringer	25.00	50.00
16 Bill Dickey	50.00	100.00
17 Leo Durocher	50.00	100.00
18 George Earnshaw	20.00	40.00
19 Dick Ferrell	40.00	80.00
20 Lew Fonseca	25.00	50.00
21A Jimmie Fox/(sic& Foxx)	100.00	200.00
21B Jimmie Foxx	100.00	200.00
22 Benny Frey	20.00	40.00
23 Frankie Frisch	50.00	100.00
24 Lou Gehrig	250.00	500.00
25 Charley Gehringer	50.00	100.00
26 Lefty Gomez	50.00	100.00
27 Ray Grabowski	20.00	40.00
28 Lefty Grove	60.00	120.00
29 Mule Haas	20.00	40.00
30 Chick Hafey	40.00	80.00
31 Bucky Harris	40.00	80.00
32 J. Francis Hogan	20.00	40.00
33 Ed Holley	20.00	40.00
34 Rogers Hornsby	75.00	150.00
35 Waite Hoyt	40.00	80.00
36 Walter Johnson	150.00	300.00
37 Jim Jordan	20.00	40.00
38 Joe Kuhel	20.00	40.00
39 Hal Lee	20.00	40.00
40 Gus Mancuso	20.00	40.00
41 Heinie Manush	40.00	80.00
42 Fred Marberry	20.00	40.00
43 Pepper Martin	25.00	50.00
44 Oscar Melillo	20.00	40.00
45 Johnny Moore	20.00	40.00
46 Joe Morrisey	20.00	40.00
47 Joe Mowry	20.00	40.00
48 Bob O'Farrell	20.00	40.00
49 Mel Ott	60.00	120.00
50 Monte Pearson	25.00	50.00
51 Carl Reynolds	20.00	40.00
52 Red Ruffing	40.00	80.00
53 Babe Ruth	300.00	600.00
54 John Ryan	20.00	40.00
55 Al Simmons	40.00	80.00
56 Alfred Smith	40.00	80.00
57 Al Spohrer	20.00	40.00
58 Gus Suhr	20.00	40.00
59 Steve Swetonic	25.00	50.00
60 Dazzy Vance	40.00	80.00
61 Joe Vosmik	20.00	40.00
62 Lloyd Waner	40.00	80.00
63 Paul Waner	40.00	80.00
64 Sam West	20.00	40.00
65 Earl Whitehill	20.00	40.00
66 Jimmy Wilson	20.00	40.00

1989 Cadaco Ellis Disc

The 1989 Cadaco Ellis discs were designed to be used in a game. These are large-sized discs, measuring approximately 3 1/2" in diameter, the standard size which has been used for many decades by the Cadaco Company for the game which was called at one point the Ethan Allen Cadaco game. This set marks the first time that full color photos were used on the front, but with no team logo. The backs contain complete major league statistics on the back. The set is checklisted in alphabetical order.

COMPLETE SET (63)	25.00	60.00
1 Harold Baines	.40	1.00
2 Wade Boggs	.75	2.00
3 Bobby Bonilla	.20	.50
4 George Brett	2.00	5.00
5 Jose Canseco	.75	2.00
6 Gary Carter	.75	2.00
7 Joe Carter	.20	.50
8 Will Clark	.60	1.50
9 Roger Clemens	2.00	5.00
10 Vince Coleman	.08	.25
11 David Cone	.20	.50
12 Eric Davis	.20	.50
13 Glenn Davis	.08	.25
14 Andre Dawson	.60	1.50
15 Shawon Dunston	.08	.25
16 Dennis Eckersley	.75	2.00
17 Carlton Fisk	.75	2.00
18 Scott Fletcher	.08	.25
19 John Franco	.20	.50
20 Julio Franco	.20	.50
21 Gary Gaetti	.20	.50
22 Andres Galarraga	.60	1.50
23 Kirk Gibson	.20	.50
24 Mike Greenwell	.08	.25
25 Mark Gubicza	.08	.25
26 Pedro Guerrero	.08	.25
27 Tony Gwynn	2.00	5.00
28 Rickey Henderson	1.25	3.00
29 Orel Hershiser	.20	.50
30 Kent Hrbek	.08	.25
31 Danny Jackson	.08	.25
32 Barry Larkin	.60	1.50
33 Greg Maddux	2.00	5.00
34 Don Mattingly	2.00	5.00
35 Fred McGriff	.60	1.50
36 Mark McGwire	2.00	5.00
37 Paul Molitor	.75	2.00
38 Tony Pena	.08	.25
39 Gerald Perry	.08	.25
40 Dan Plesac	.08	.25
41 Kirby Puckett	1.00	2.50
42 Johnny Ray	.08	.25
43 Jeff Reardon	.08	.25
44 Cal Ripken	4.00	10.00
45 Babe Ruth	4.00	10.00
46 Nolan Ryan	4.00	10.00
47 Juan Samuel	.08	.25
48 Ryne Sandberg	1.25	3.00
49 Benito Santiago	.08	.25
50 Steve Sax	.08	.25
51 Mike Schmidt	1.25	3.00
52 Kevin Seitzer	.08	.25
53 Ozzie Smith	1.50	4.00
54 Terry Steinbach	.08	.25
55 Dave Stewart	.08	.25
56 Darryl Strawberry	.20	.50
57 Andres Thomas	.08	.25
58 Alan Trammell	.60	1.50
59 Andy Van Slyke	.20	.50
60 Frank Viola	.08	.25
61 Dave Winfield	1.00	2.50
62 Todd Worrell	.20	.50
63 Strategy Disc	.08	.25

1991 Cadaco Ellis Discs

These discs were designed to be used in conjuction with the Cadaco BB game. These discs feature player photos and feature leading stars in the game. Retired superstars Roberto Clemente, Ty Cobb, Lou Gehrig, Babe Ruth and Honus Wagner are also included in this set.

COMPLETE SET (62)	30.00	80.00
1 Roberto Alomar	.60	1.50
2 Harold Baines	.20	.50
3 Craig Biggio	.40	1.00
4 Wade Boggs	1.00	2.50
5 Barry Bonds	2.00	5.00
6 Bobby Bonilla	.08	.25
7 Jose Canseco	.75	2.00
8 Will Clark	.60	1.50
9 Roger Clemens	2.00	5.00
10 Roberto Clemente	3.00	8.00
11 Ty Cobb	2.50	6.00
12 Vince Coleman	.08	.25
13 Eric Davis	.20	.50
14 Glenn Davis	.08	.25
15 Andre Dawson	.60	1.50
16 Delino DeShields	.08	.25
17 Shawon Dunston	.08	.25
18 Cecil Fielder	.20	.50
19 Tony Fernandez	.20	.50
20 Carlton Fisk	.75	2.00
21 Julio Franco	.20	.50
22 Gary Gaetti	.20	.50
23 Lou Gehrig	3.00	8.00-
24 Kirk Gibson	.20	.50
25 Mark Grace	.60	1.50
26 Ken Griffey Jr.	4.00	10.00
27 Kelly Gruber	.08	.25
28 Tony Gwynn	2.00	5.00
29 Rickey Henderson	1.25	3.00
30 Orel Hershiser	.20	.50
31 David Justice	.60	1.50
32 Bo Jackson	.60	1.50
33 Howard Johnson	.08	.25
34 Barry Larkin	.60	1.50
35 Ramon Martinez	.08	.25
36 Don Mattingly	2.00	5.00
37 Fred McGriff	.40	1.00
38 Mark McGwire	1.50	4.00
39 Kevin Mitchell	.08	.25
40 Lance Parrish	.20	.50
41 Tony Pena	.08	.25
42 Kirby Puckett	1.00	2.50
43 Cal Ripken Jr.	4.00	10.00
44 Babe Ruth	4.00	10.00
45 Nolan Ryan	4.00	10.00
46 Bret Saberhagen	.08	.25
47 Chris Sabo	.08	.25
48 Ryne Sandberg	1.50	4.00
49 Benito Santiago	.20	.50
50 Steve Sax	.08	.25
51 Gary Sheffield	1.00	2.50
52 Ruben Sierra	.20	.50
53 Ozzie Smith	1.50	4.00
54 Terry Steinbach	.08	.25
55 Dave Stewart	.08	.25
56 Mickey Tettleton	.08	.25
57 Alan Trammell	.40	1.00
58 Jose Uribe	.08	.25
59 Honus Wagner	1.25	3.00
60 Lou Whitaker	.20	.50
61 Matt Williams	.40	1.00
62 Robin Yount	.75	2.00

1993 Cadaco Discs

These cards were issued as part of the Cadaco games. These discs feature a mix of active players and a few retired players.

COMPLETE SET (62)	30.00	80.00
1 Kevin Appier	.08	.25
2 Carlos Baerga	.08	.25
3 Harold Baines	.20	.50
4 Derek Bell	.08	.25
5 George Bell	.08	.25
6 Jay Bell	.08	.25
7 Mike Boddicker	.08	.25
8 Wade Boggs	.75	2.00
9 Hubie Brooks	.08	.25
10 Jose Canseco	.75	2.00
11 Roger Clemens	1.50	4.00
12 Roberto Clemente	2.50	6.00
13 Ty Cobb	2.00	5.00
14 Alex Cole	.08	.25
15 Jeff Conine	.08	.25
16 Andre Dawson	.60	1.50
17 Shawon Dunston	.08	.25
18 Len Dykstra	.20	.50
19 Carlton Fisk	.75	2.00
20 Darrin Fletcher	.08	.25
21 Gary Gaetti	.20	.50
22 Greg Gagne	.08	.25
23 Mike Gallego	.08	.25
24 Lou Gehrig	2.50	6.00
25 Kirk Gibson	.20	.50
26 Tom Glavine	.60	1.50
27 Mark Grace	.60	1.50
28 Ken Griffey Jr.	2.50	6.00
29 Tony Gwynn	1.50	4.00
30 Charles Hayes	.08	.25
31 Rickey Henderson	1.00	2.50
32 Orel Hershiser	.20	.50
33 Bo Jackson	.60	1.50
34 Howard Johnson	.08	.25
35 Randy Johnson	1.00	2.50
36 Ricky Jordan	.08	.25
37 David Justice	.60	1.50
38 Ray Lankford	.08	.25
39 Ramon Martinez	.08	.25

40 Don Mattingly 1.50 4.00
41 Mark McGwire 1.50 4.00
42 Brian McRae .08 .25
43 Joe Oliver .08 .25
44 Tony Pena .08 .25
45 Kirby Puckett .75 2.00
46 Cal Ripken 3.00 8.00
47 Babe Ruth 3.00 8.00
48 Nolan Ryan 3.00 8.00
49 Bret Saberhagen .08 .25
50 Chris Sabo .08 .25
51 Ryne Sandberg 1.25 3.00
52 Benito Santiago .20 .50
53 Steve Sax .08 .25
54 Gary Sheffield .75 2.00
55 Ozzie Smith 1.50 4.00
56 Dave Stewart .08 .25
57 Darryl Strawberry .20 .50
58 Frank Thomas .75
59 Robin Ventura .20 .50
60 Hector Villanueva .08 .25
61 Honus Wagner 1.50 4.00
62 Lou Whitaker .20 .50

1997 California Lottery

This five-card set features small color head photos of California Baseball Legends. The set measures approximately 4" by 2" and was actually real California scratch-off lottery ticket stubs that could be obtained for $1 a piece. The backs carry the lottery rules and prize information. The cards are unnumbered and checklisted below in alphabetical order.

COMPLETE SET (5) 2.50 6.00
1 Rod Carew .75 2.00
2 Don Drysdale .75 2.00
3 Rollie Fingers .40 1.00
4 Willie McCovey .60 1.50
5 Gaylord Perry .40 1.00

1950-56 Callahan HOF W576

The cards in this 82-card set measure approximately 1 3/4" by 2 1/2". The 1950-56 Callahan Hall of Fame set was issued over a number of years at the Baseball Hall of Fame museum in Cooperstown, New York. New cards were added to the set each year when new members were inducted into the Hall of Fame. The cards with (2) in the checklist exist with two different biographies. The year of each card's first inclusion in the set is also given in parentheses; those not listed parenthetically below were issued in 1950 as well as in all the succeeding years and are hence the most common. Naturally the supply of cards is directly related to how many years a player was included in the set; cards that were not issued until 1955 are much scarcer than those printed all the years between 1950 and 1956. The catalog designation is W576. One frequently finds "complete" sets in the original box; take care to investigate the year of issue, the set may be complete in the sense of all the cards issued up to a certain year, but not all 82 cards below. The box is priced below. For example, a "complete" 1950 set would obviously not include any of the cards marked below with ('52), ('54), or ('55) as none of those cards existed in 1950 since those respective players had not yet been inducted. The complete set price below refers to a set including all 83 cards below. Since the cards are unnumbered, they are numbered below for reference alphabetically by player's name.

COMPLETE SET (83) 400.00 800.00
COMMON CARD '50 2.00 5.00
COMMON CARD '52 3.00 8.00
COMMON CARD '54 4.00 10.00
COMMON CARD '55 5.00 12.00
1 Grover Alexander 3.00 8.00
2 Cap Anson 2.50 6.00
3 Frank Baker '55 5.00 12.00
4 Edward Barrow '54 4.00 10.00
5 Chief Bender (2) '54 4.00 10.00
6 Roger Bresnahan 2.00 5.00
7 Dan Brouthers 2.00 5.00
8 Mordecai Brown 2.00 5.00
9 Morgan Bulkeley 2.00 5.00
10 Jesse Burkett 2.00 5.00
11 Alexander Cartwright 2.00 5.00
12 Henry Chadwick 2.00 5.00
13 Frank Chance 2.00 5.00
14 Happy Chandler '52 50.00 100.00
15 Jack Chesbro 2.00 5.00
16 Fred Clarke 2.00 5.00
17 Ty Cobb 37.50 75.00
18A Mickey Cochrane ERR 4.00 10.00
Name spelled Cochran
18B Mickey Cochrane COR 15.00 30.00
19 Eddie Collins (2) 2.00 5.00
20 Jimmie Collins 2.00 5.00
21 Charles Comiskey 2.00 5.00
22 Tom Connolly '54 4.00 10.00
23 Candy Cummings 2.00 5.00
24 Dizzy Dean '54 12.50 25.00
25 Ed Delahanty 2.00 5.00
26 Bill Dickey '54 (2) 8.00 20.00
27 Joe DiMaggio '55 125.00 250.00
28 Hugh Duffy 2.00 5.00
29 Johnny Evers 2.00 5.00
30 Buck Ewing 2.00 5.00
31 Jimmie Foxx 4.00 10.00
32 Frank Frisch 2.00 5.00
33 Lou Gehrig 40.00 80.00
34 Charles Gehringer 3.00 8.00
35 Clark Griffith 2.00 5.00
36 Lefty Grove 4.00 10.00
37 Gabby Hartnett '55 5.00 12.00
38 Harry Heilmann '52 3.00 8.00
39 Rogers Hornsby 4.00 10.00
40 Carl Hubbell 2.50 6.00
41 Hughie Jennings 2.00 5.00
42 Ban Johnson 2.00 5.00
43 Walter Johnson 8.00 20.00
44 Willie Keeler 2.00 5.00
45 Mike Kelly 2.00 5.00
46 Bill Klem '54 4.00 10.00
47 Napoleon Lajoie 3.00 8.00
48 Kenesaw Landis 2.00 5.00
49 Ted Lyons '55 5.00 12.00
50 Connie Mack 2.00 5.00
51 Rabbit Maranville '54 4.00 10.00
52 Christy Mathewson 8.00 20.00
53 Tommy McCarthy 2.00 5.00
54 Joe McGinnity 2.00 5.00
55 John McGraw 2.50 6.00
56 Kid Nichols 2.00 5.00
57 Jim O'Rourke 2.00 5.00
58 Mel Ott 3.00 8.00
59 Herb Pennock 2.00 5.00
60 Eddie Plank 2.00 5.00
61 Charles Radbourne 2.00 5.00
62 Wilbert Robinson 2.00 5.00
63 Babe Ruth 30.00 80.00
64 Ray Schalk '55 5.00 12.00
65 Al Simmons '54 4.00 10.00
66 George Sisler (2) 2.00 5.00
67 Albert G. Spalding 2.00 5.00
68 Tris Speaker 3.00 8.00
69 Bill Terry '54 5.00 12.00
70 Joe Tinker 2.00 5.00
71 Pie Traynor 2.00 5.00
72 Dazzy Vance '55 5.00 12.00
73 Rube Waddell 2.00 5.00
74 Hans Wagner 10.00 25.00
75 Bobby Wallace '54 4.00 10.00
76 Ed Walsh 2.00 5.00
77 Paul Waner '52 5.00 12.00
78 George Wright 2.00 5.00
79 Harry Wright '54 4.00 10.00
80 Cy Young 5.00 12.00
81 Museum Interior/'54 (2) 4.00 10.00
82 Museum Exterior/'54 (2) 4.00 10.00
XX Presentation Box 2.00 5.00

1996 Canadian Club Autographs

These six cards were issued as premiums by Canadian Club Whiskey. All the cards were signed by the Hall of Fame players. The cards are also accompanied by a certificate of authenticity.

COMPLETE SET (6) 25.00 60.00
1 Ernie Banks 10.00 25.00
2 Rollie Fingers 5.00 12.00
3 Willie Stargell 8.00 20.00
4 Billy Williams 6.00 15.00
5 Brooks Robinson 6.00 15.00
6 Frank Robinson 6.00 15.00

2000 Capcure

COMPLETE SET 20.00 50.00
1 Jason Giambi .60 1.50
2 Ken Griffey Jr 3.00 8.00
3 Tony Gwynn 3.20 8.00
4 Derek Jeter 6.00 15.00
5 Mark McGwire 2.50 6.00
6 Alex Rodriguez 3.00 8.00
7 Sammy Sosa 1.50 4.00
8 Robin Ventura .40 1.00

2001 Capcure

COMPLETE SET (8) 20.00 50.00
1 Jeff Bagwell 1.20 3.00
Carlos Delgado
2 Jay Bell 2.00 5.00
Alex Rodriguez
3 Nomar Garciaparra 3.20 8.00
Sammy Sosa
4 Jason Giambi 2.00 5.00
Mark McGwire
5 Tony Gwynn 2.40 6.00
Ivan Rodriguez
6 Ken Griffey Jr. 4.00 10.00
Robin Ventura
7 Derek Jeter 4.00 10.00
Mike Sweeney
8 Chipper Jones 1.20 3.00
Jim Thome

1974 Capital Publishing

This 110-card set was issued by Capital Publishing Company and features 4 1/8" by 5 1/4" black-and-white photos of great players. The fronts consist of nothing more than the picture of the player while the back has biographical information and statistics. It is believed that cards 106 through 110 are significantly tougher than the rest of the set.

COMPLETE SET (110) 50.00 100.00
COMMON CARD (106-110) .40 1.00
1 Babe Ruth 2.00 5.00
2 Lou Gehrig 1.50 4.00
3 Ty Cobb 1.50 4.00
4 Jackie Robinson 1.50 4.00
5 Roger Connor .40 1.00
6 Harry Heilmann .40 1.00
7 Clark Griffith .40 1.00
8 Ed Walsh .40 1.00
9 Hugh Duffy .40 1.00
10 Russ Christopher .20 .50
11 Snuffy Stirnweiss .20 .50
12 Willie Keeler .60 1.50
13 Buck Ewing .40 1.00
14 Tony Lazzeri .40 1.00
15 King Kelly .60 1.50
16 Jimmy McAleer .20 .50
17 Frank Chance .75 2.00
18 Sam Zoldak .20 .50
19 Christy Mathewson .75 2.00
20 Eddie Collins .75 2.00
21 Cap Anson .75 2.00
22 Steve Evans .20 .50
23 Mordecai Brown .60 1.50
24 Don Black .20 .50
25 Home Run Baker .40 1.00
26 Jack Chesbro .20 .50
27 Gil Hodges .40 1.00
28 Dan Brouthers .40 1.00
29 Don Hoak .20 .50
30 Herb Pennock .40 1.00
31 Vern Stephens .20 .50
32 Cy Young .75 2.00
33 Eddie Cicotte .75 2.00
34 Sam Jones .20 .50
35 Ed Waitkus .20 .50
36 Roger Bresnahan .40 1.00
37 Fred Merkle .20 .50
38 Ed Delehanty .75 2.00
39 Tris Speaker .60 1.50
40 Fred Clarke .40 1.00
41 Johnny Evers .75 2.00
42 Mickey Cochrane .60 1.50
43 Nap Lajoie .75 2.00
44 Charles Comiskey .40 1.00
45 Sam Crawford .40 1.00
46 Ban Johnson .40 1.00
47 Ray Schalk .40 1.00
48 Pat Moran .20 .50
49 Walt Judnich .20 .50
50 Bill Killefer .20 .50
51 Jimmie Foxx .75 2.00
52 Red Rolfe .20 .50
53 Howie Pollett .20 .50
54 Wally Pipp .20 .50
55 Chief Bender .40 1.00
56 Connie Mack .75 2.00
57 Bump Hadley .20 .50
58 Al Simmons .60 1.50
59 Hughie Jennings .40 1.00
60 Johnny Allen .20 .50
61 Fred Snodgrass .20 .50
62 Heinie Manush .40 1.00
63 Dazzy Vance .40 1.00
64 George Sisler .60 1.50
65 Jim Bottomley .40 1.00
66 Roy Chapman .20 .50
67 Hal Chase .20 .50
68 Jack Barry .20 .50
69 George Burns .20 .50
70 Jim Barrett .20 .50
71 Grover Alexander .75 2.00
72 Elmer Flick .20 .50
73 Jake Flowers .20 .50
74 Al Orth .20 .50
75 Cliff Aberson .20 .50
76 Moe Berg .75 2.00
77 Bill Bradley .20 .50
78 Max Bishop .20 .50
79 Jimmy Austin .20 .50
80 Beals Becker .20 .50
81 Jack Clements .20 .50
82 Cy Blanton .20 .50
83 Garland Braxton .20 .50
84 Red Ames .20 .50
85 Hippo Vaughn .20 .50
86 Ray Caldwell .20 .50
87 Clint Brown .20 .50
88 Joe Jackson 1.25 3.00
89 Pete Appleton .20 .50
90 Ed Brandt .20 .50
91 Walter Johnson .75 2.00
92 Dizzy Dean .75 2.00
93 Nick Altrock .20 .50
94 Buck Weaver .75 2.00
95 George Blaeholder .20 .50
96 Jim Bagby Sr. .20 .50
97 Ted Blankenship .20 .50
98 Babe Adams .20 .50
99 Lefty Williams .60 1.50
100 Tommy Bridges .20 .50
101 Rube Benton .20 .50
102 Jim Poole .20 .50
103 Max Butcher .20 .50
104 Larry Benton .20 .50
105 Chick Gandil .60 1.50
106 Lefty Grove 2.00 5.00
107 Roberto Clemente 4.00 10.00
108 Albert Spalding 2.00 5.00
109 Bill Barrett .40 1.00
110 Bob O'Farrell .40 1.00

1986 Card Collectors Company Canseco

These 10 full-bleed standard-size cards features then rookie Jose Canseco. The fronts show the different photos which are available while the backs have information on how to obtain these photos autographed.

COMPLETE SET (10) 4.00 10.00
COMMON CARD .40 1.00

1986 Card Collectors Mantle

This 10-card standard-size set features various photos of Mickey Mantle. The fronts have a mix of photos used by the card companies and more modern photos on front while the back says that these photos are available in an 8" by 10" signed form from Card Collectors for just $15 each or for $139.95 for the group of 10.

COMPLETE SET (10) 8.00 20.00
COMMON CARD (1-10) .80 2.00

1987 Card Collectors McGwire

This 10-card standard-size set features various photos of Mickey Mantle. The fronts have a mix of photos used by the card companies and more modern photos on front while the back says that these photos are available in an 8" by 10" signed form from Card Collectors for just $10 each or for $89.95 for the group of 10. Other than the art-work, all the photos used for this promotion were taken by Barry Colla.

COMPLETE SET (10) 8.00 20.00
COMMON CARD (1-10) .80 2.00

1989 Card Collectors Company Jefferies Boyhood

This 16-card set features borderless color photos of Gregg Jefferies from childhood to adulthood. The backs carry information about the photos.

COMPLETE SET (16) 1.50 4.00
COMMON CARD (1-16) .10 .25

1990 Card Collectors Company Justice Boyhood

This 16-card set depicts different stages of the boyhood of David Justice. The fronts feature various pictures from his life on a red background. The backs carry information about the picture.

COMPLETE SET (16) 1.50 4.00
COMMON CARD (1-16) .10 .25

1991 Card Collectors Company Gooden Boyhood

This 16-card set depicts different stages of the boyhood of Dwight Gooden. The fronts feature various pictures from his early life. The backs carry information about the picture.

COMPLETE SET (16)
COMMON CARD

1908 Cardinals Republic

Issued as a supplement in the St Louis Republic, these photos feature members of the 1908 St Louis Cardinals. There might be more of these so any additions to this checklist is appreciated. Since these are unnumbered, we have sequenced them in alphabetical order.

COMPLETE SET 400.00
1 Fred Beebe 50.00 100.00
2 Robert Byrne 50.00 100.00
3 Ed Konetchy 50.00 100.00
4 John Lush 50.00 100.00

1931 Cardinals Metropolitan

This 30-card set features white-bordered, sepia colored blank-backed photos of the 1931 St. Louis Cardinals and measures approximately 6 1/8" by 9 1/2". The cards are unnumbered and checklisted below in alphabetical order. The words "Metropolitan Studios St. Louis" are in the bottom right hand corner. These photos were sent to fans in an manila envelope. One could order another set from the team for 41 cents.

COMPLETE SET (30) 600.00 1200.00
1 Earl Sparky Adams 15.00 30.00
2 Ray Blades 15.00 30.00
3 James Bottomly 30.00 60.00
4 Sam Breadon PRES 15.00 30.00
5 James Rip Collins 25.00 50.00
6 Dizzy Dean 75.00 150.00
7 Paul Derringer 15.00 30.00
8 Jake Flowers 15.00 30.00
9 Frank Frisch 60.00 120.00
10 Charles Gelbert 15.00 30.00
11 Miguel Gonzales 15.00 30.00
12 Burleigh Grimes 30.00 60.00
13 Charles Chick Hafey 30.00 60.00
14 Jesse Haines 30.00 60.00
15 William Hallahan 15.00 30.00
16 Andrew High 15.00 30.00
17 Sylvester Johnson 15.00 30.00
18 Tony Kaufmann 15.00 30.00
19 James Lindsey 15.00 30.00
20 Gus Mancuso 15.00 30.00
21 Pepper Martin 30.00 60.00
22 Ernest Orsatti 15.00 30.00
23 Charles Rhem 15.00 30.00
24 Branch Rickey VP 30.00 60.00
25 Walter Roettger 15.00 30.00
26 Allyn Stout 15.00 30.00
27 Gabby Street 15.00 30.00
28 Clyde Wares CO 15.00 30.00
29 George Watkins 15.00 30.00
30 James Wilson 15.00 30.00

1935 Cardinals Rice Stix

This two card set features the Dean brothers who won 49 games for the Cardinals in 1934. These cards measure approximately 2 1/4" by 3" and were issued as premiums when shirts were purchased from that St Louis firm.

COMPLETE SET 600.00 1200.00
1 Paul Dafly Dean 250.00 500.00
2 Jay Dizzy Dean 400.00 800.00

1941 Cardinals W754

The cards in this 30-card set measure approximately 2 1/8" by 2 5/8". The 1941 W754 set of unnumbered cards features St. Louis Cardinals. The cards are numbered below alphabetically by player's name. This is another set issued in its own box with the other side being a mailing label. This set is worth about $100 more when still in the original box.

COMPLETE SET (30) 400.00 800.00
1 Sam Breadon OWN 12.50 30.00
2 Jimmy Brown 12.50 30.00
3 Mort Cooper 20.00 50.00
4 Walker Cooper 15.00 40.00
5 Estel Crabtree 12.50 30.00
6 Frank Crespi 12.50 30.00
7 Bill Crouch 12.50 30.00
8 Mike Gonzalez CO 15.00 40.00
9 Harry Gumpert 12.50 30.00
10 John Hopp 15.00 30.00
11 Ira Hutchinson 12.50 30.00
12 Howie Krist 12.50 30.00
13 Eddie Lake 12.50 30.00
14 Max Lanier 20.00 50.00
15 Gus Mancuso 12.50 30.00
16 Marty Marion 40.00 80.00
17 Steve Mesner 12.50 30.00
18 John Mize 75.00 150.00
19 Terry Moore 30.00 60.00
20 Sam Nahem 12.50 30.00
21 Don Padgett 12.50 30.00
22 Branch Rickey GM 60.00 120.00
23 Clyde Shoun 12.50 30.00
24 Enos Slaughter 75.00 150.00
25 Billy Southworth MG 15.00 40.00
26 Coaker Triplett 12.50 30.00
27 Buzzy Wares 12.50 30.00
28 Lon Warneke 15.00 40.00
29 Ernie White 12.50 30.00
30 Title Card/(Order Coupon on back) 12.50 30.00

1953 Cardinals Hunter's Wieners

The cards in this 26 card set measure 2 1/4" by 3 1/2". The 1953 Hunter's Wieners set of full color, blank backed unnumbered cards feature St. Louis Cardinal players only. The cards have red borders and were issued in panels of two on hot dog packages. The catalog designation is F 153-1. We have sequenced this set in alphabetical order.

COMPLETE SET 3000.00 6000.00
1 Steve Bilko 125.00 250.00
2 Alpha Brazle 125.00 250.00
3 Cloyd Boyer 150.00 300.00
4 Cliff Chambers 125.00 250.00
5 Mike Clark 125.00 250.00
6 Jack Crimian 125.00 250.00
7 Les Fusselman 125.00 250.00
8 Harvey Haddix 200.00 400.00
9 Solly Hemus 125.00 250.00
10 Ray Jablonski 125.00 250.00
11 Will Johnson 125.00 250.00
12 Harry Lowrey 125.00 250.00
13 Larry Miggins 125.00 250.00
14 Stuart Miller 125.00 250.00
15 Wilmer Mizell 125.00 250.00
16 Stan Musial 1000.00 2000.00
17 Joe Presko 125.00 250.00
18 Del Rice 125.00 250.00
19 Hal Rice 125.00 250.00
20 Willard Schmidt 125.00 250.00
21 Red Schoendienst 300.00 600.00
22 Dick Sisler 125.00 250.00
23 Enos Slaughter 300.00 600.00
24 Gerry Staley 125.00 250.00
25 Ed Stanky 200.00 400.00
26 Ed Yuhas 125.00 250.00

1954 Cardinals Hunter's Wieners

The cards in this 30 card set measure 2 1/4" by 3 1/2". The 1954 Hunter's Wieners set of full color, blank backed unnumbered cards feature St. Louis Cardinals. They were issued in pairs on the backs of hot dog packages as in 1953; however one of the cards is a statistical record of the player's career. The poses are very similar to those used in the 1953 set; however, there are captions which read "What's My Name" and "What's My Record". The catalog designation is F153-2.

COMPLETE SET 3000.00 6000.00
1 Tom Alston 125.00 250.00
2 Steve Bilko 125.00 250.00
3 Alpha Brazle 125.00 250.00
4 Tom Burgess 125.00 250.00
5 Cot Deal 125.00 250.00
6 Alex Grammas 125.00 250.00
7 Harvey Haddix 150.00 300.00
8 Solly Hemus 125.00 250.00
9 Ray Jablonski 125.00 250.00
10 Royce Lint 125.00 250.00
11 Harry Lowrey 125.00 250.00
12 Memo Luna 125.00 250.00
13 Stu Miller 150.00 300.00
14 Stan Musial 750.00 1500.00
15 Tom Poholsky 125.00 250.00
16 Bill Posedel CO 125.00 250.00
17 Joe Presko 125.00 250.00
18 Vic Raschi 200.00 400.00
19 Dick Rand 125.00 250.00
20 Rip Repulski 125.00 250.00
21 Del Rice 125.00 250.00
22 John Riddle CO 125.00 250.00
23 Mike Ryba CO 125.00 250.00
24 Red Schoendienst 200.00 500.00
25 Dick Schofield 150.00 300.00
26 Enos Slaughter 200.00 500.00
27 Gerry Staley 125.00 250.00
28 Ed Stanky MG 150.00 300.00
29 Ed Yuhas 125.00 250.00
30 Sal Yvars 125.00 250.00

1954-55 Cardinals Postcards

These postcards were issued over a two year period. The top of the card has a picture of the player on top and a message beginning "Dear Cardinal Fan". The backs are blank. Since these cards are unnumbered, we have sequenced them in alphabetical order.

COMPLETE SET 225.00 450.00
1 Luis Arroyo 10.00 25.00
2 Bill Baker 6.00 15.00
3 Ralph Beard 6.00 15.00
4 Ken Boyer 15.00 40.00
5 Al Brazle 6.00 15.00
6 Nelson Burbrink 6.00 15.00
7 Joe Cunningham 8.00 20.00
8 Cot Deal 6.00 15.00
9 Eddie Dyer 6.00 15.00
10 Joe Frazier 6.00 15.00
11 Ben Flowers 6.00 15.00
12 Al Gettel 6.00 15.00
13 Alex Grammas 6.00 15.00
14 Harvey Haddix 8.00 20.00
15 Solly Hemus 6.00 15.00
16 Ray Jablonski 6.00 15.00
17 Larry Jackson 8.00 20.00
18 Gordon Jones 6.00 15.00
19 Paul LaPalme 6.00 15.00
20 Brooks Lawrence 6.00 15.00
21 Royce Lint 6.00 15.00
22 Harry Lowrey 6.00 15.00
23 Wally Moon 8.00 20.00
24 Stan Musial 30.00 60.00
25 Bill Posedel 6.00 15.00
26 Tom Poholsky 6.00 15.00
27 Joe Presko 6.00 15.00
28 Vic Raschi 8.00 20.00
29 Del Rice 6.00 15.00
30 John Riddle 6.00 15.00
31 Rip Repulski 6.00 15.00
32 Mike Ryba 6.00 15.00
33 Bill Sarni 6.00 15.00
34 Will Schmidt 6.00 15.00
35 Red Schoendienst 15.00 40.00
36 Dick Schofield 6.00 15.00
37 Gerry Staley 6.00 15.00
38 Eddie Stanky 8.00 20.00
39 Bill Virdon 10.00 25.00
40 Ben Wade 6.00 15.00
41 Pete Whisenant 6.00 15.00
42 Sal Yvars 6.00 15.00

1955 Cardinals Hunter's Wieners

The cards in this 30 card set measure 2" by 4 3/4". The 1955 Hunter's Wieners set of full color, blank backed, unnumbered cards feature St. Louis Cardinals only. This year presented a different format from the previous two years in that there are two pictures on the front of each card, one full figure shot and a close up bust shot. The card was actually the side panel of the hot dog package rather than the back as in the previous two years. The catalog designation of this scarce regional issue is F153-3. Ken Boyer appears in his rookie season.

COMPLETE SET 3000.00 6000.00
1 Tom Alston 150.00 300.00
2 Ken Boyer 250.00 500.00
3 Harry Elliott 125.00 250.00
4 Jack Faszholz 125.00 250.00
5 Joe Frazier 125.00 250.00
6 Alex Grammas 125.00 250.00
7 Harvey Haddix 150.00 300.00
8 Solly Hemus 125.00 250.00
9 Larry Jackson 150.00 300.00
10 Tony Jacobs 125.00 250.00
11 Gordon Jones 125.00 250.00
12 Paul LaPalme 125.00 250.00
13 Brooks Lawrence 125.00 250.00
14 Wally Moon 150.00 300.00
15 Stan Musial 1000.00 2000.00
16 Tom Poholsky 125.00 250.00
17 Bill Posedel CO 125.00 250.00
18 Vic Raschi 200.00 400.00
19 Rip Repulski 125.00 250.00
20 Del Rice 125.00 250.00
21 John Riddle CO 125.00 250.00
22 Bill Sarni 125.00 250.00
23 Red Schoendienst 250.00 500.00
24 Dick Schofield 150.00 300.00
25 Frank Smith 125.00 250.00
26 Ed Stanky MG 150.00 300.00
27 Bob Tiefenauer 125.00 250.00
28 Bill Virdon 200.00 400.00
29 Fred Walker CO 125.00 250.00
30 Floyd Woolridge 125.00 250.00

1956 Cardinals Postcards

These cards were the first issued in the style the Cardinals would use for many years. The fronts have photos of players in the "Old" Cardinals uniform with Cardinals on it with a thick heavy line right under that word. The backs have postcard backs with a Busch Stadium address. Each card has a 1" border on the bottom which usually contained an facsimile autograph. Since these cards are unnumbered, we have sequenced them in alphabetical order.

COMPLETE SET 125.00 250.00
1 Tom Alston 6.00 15.00
2 Don Blasingame 5.00 12.00
3 Ken Boyer 8.00 20.00
4 Jack Brandt 5.00 12.00
5 Jackie Collum 5.00 12.00
6 Walker Cooper 5.00 12.00
7 Al Dark 6.00 15.00
8 Bob Del Greco 5.00 12.00
9 Murry Dickson 5.00 12.00
10 Chuck Harmon 5.00 12.00
11 Grady Hatton 5.00 12.00
12 Johnny Hopp CO 5.00 12.00
13 Fred Hutchinson MG 5.00 12.00
14 Ray Katt 5.00 12.00
15 Ellis Kinder 5.00 12.00
16 Jim Konstanty 6.00 15.00
17 Larry Jackson 5.00 12.00
18 Dick Littlefield 5.00 12.00
19 Lindy McDaniel 6.00 15.00
20 Vinegar Bend Mizell 5.00 12.00
21 Wally Moon 5.00 12.00
22 Terry Moore CO 6.00 15.00
23 Bobby Morgan 5.00 12.00
24 Stan Musial 15.00 40.00
25 Tom Poholsky 5.00 12.00
26 Bill Posedel CO 5.00 12.00
27 Rip Repulski 5.00 12.00
28 Hank Sauer 6.00 15.00
29 Hal Smith 5.00 12.00
30 Herm Wehmeier 5.00 12.00

1957-58 Cardinals Postcards

These postcards were issued by the St Louis Cardinals over a two year period and the players in the set are wearing the uniform that the Cards wore from 1957 through 1971. The only way a collector can tell the difference between the postcards is that the 1957 cards have a notation for a 2 cent stamp while the 1958 cards have a notation for a 3 cent stamp. Since these cards are unnumbered, we have sequenced them in alphabetical order.

COMPLETE SET 200.00 400.00
1 Ruben Amaro 5.00 12.00
2 Frank Barnes 5.00 12.00
3 Don Blasingame 5.00 12.00
4 Ken Boyer 10.00 25.00
5 Jim Brosnan 6.00 15.00
6 Tom Cheney 5.00 12.00
7 Nelson Chittum 5.00 12.00
8 Walker Cooper 5.00 12.00
9 Joe Cunningham 6.00 15.00
10 Al Dark 6.00 15.00
11 Jim Davis 5.00 12.00
12 Bing Devine GM 5.00 12.00
13 Murry Dickson 5.00 12.00
14 Del Ennis 6.00 15.00
15 Curt Flood 12.50 30.00
16 Gene Freese 5.00 12.00
17 Gene Green 5.00 12.00
18 Stan Hack CO 5.00 12.00
19 Al Hollingsworth 5.00 12.00
20 Fred Hutchinson MG 5.00 12.00
21 Larry Jackson 5.00 12.00
22 Sam Jones 5.00 12.00
23 Eddie Kasko 5.00 12.00
24 Ray Katt 5.00 12.00
25 Hobie Landrith 5.00 12.00
26 Bob Mabe 5.00 12.00
27 Sal Maglie 8.00 20.00
28 Morrie Martin 5.00 12.00
29 Lindy McDaniel 6.00 15.00
30 Von McDaniel 5.00 12.00
31 Lloyd Merritt 5.00 12.00
32 Eddie Miksis 5.00 12.00
33 Bob Miller 5.00 12.00
34 Vinegar Bend Mizell 5.00 12.00
35 Wally Moon 5.00 12.00
36 Terry Moore CO 5.00 12.00
37 Billy Muffett 5.00 12.00
38 Stan Musial 15.00 40.00
39 Irv Noren 5.00 12.00
40 Phil Paine 5.00 12.00
41 Will Schmidt 5.00 12.00
42 Dick Schofield 5.00 12.00
43 Bobby Gene Smith 5.00 12.00
44 Hal Smith 5.00 12.00
45 Chuck Stobbs 5.00 12.00
46 Joe Taylor 5.00 12.00
47 Herman Wehmeier 5.00 12.00
48 Bill Wight 5.00 12.00
49 Hoyt Wilhelm 12.50 30.00

1958 Cardinals Jay Publishing

This 14-card set of the St. Louis Cardinals measures approximately 5" by 7" and features black-and-white player photos in a white border. These cards were packaged 12 to a packet. The backs are blank. The cards are unnumbered and checklisted below in alphabetical order. Changes to the Cardinals roster during the season accounts for more than 12 cards in this set.

COMPLETE SET (14) 30.00 60.00
1 Don Blasingame 1.50 3.00
2 Ken Boyer 4.00 8.00
3 Joe Cunningham 2.00 4.00
4 Alvin Dark 3.00 6.00
5 Del Ennis 1.50 3.00
6 Larry Jackson 1.50 3.00
7 Sam Jones 1.50 3.00
8 Eddie Kasko 1.50 3.00
9 Lindy McDaniel 1.50 3.00
10 Von McDaniel 1.50 3.00
11 Wilmer Mizell 1.50 3.00
12 Wally Moon 1.50 3.00
13 Stan Musial 7.50 15.00
14 Hal Smith 1.50 3.00

1959 Cardinals Jay Publishing

This 12-card set of the St. Louis Cardinals measures approximately 5" by 7" and features black-and-white player photos in a white border. These cards were packaged 12 to a packet. The backs are blank. The cards are unnumbered and checklisted below in alphabetical order.

COMPLETE SET 20.00 50.00
1 Don Blasingame 1.25 3.00
2 Ken Boyer 2.50 6.00
3 Jim Brosnan 1.25 3.00
4 Gino Cimoli 1.25 3.00
5 Joe Cunningham 1.50 4.00
6 Curt Flood 2.50 6.00
7 Alex Grammas 1.25 3.00
8 Gene Green 1.25 3.00
9 Larry Jackson 1.25 3.00
10 Wilmer Mizell 1.25 3.00
11 Stan Musial 6.00 15.00
12 Hal R. Smith 1.25 3.00

1960 Cardinals Jay Publishing

This 12-card set of the St. Louis Cardinals measures approximately 5" by 7". The fronts feature black-and-white posed player photos with the player's and team name printed below in the white border. These cards were packaged 12 in a packet. The backs are blank. The cards are unnumbered and checklisted below in alphabetical order.

COMPLETE SET (12) 15.00 40.00
1 Ken Boyer 2.00 5.00
2 Joe Cunningham 1.25 3.00
3 Curt Flood 1.50 4.00
4 Larry Jackson .75 2.00
5 Ronnie Kline .75 2.00
6 Lindy McDaniel .75 2.00
7 Wilmer Mizell .75 2.00
8 Stan Musial 6.00 15.00
9 Bob Nieman .75 2.00
10 Hal Smith .75 2.00
11 Daryl Spencer .75 2.00
12 Bill White 1.50 4.00

1961 Cardinals Jay Publishing

This 13-card set of the St. Louis Cardinals measures approximately 5" by 7". The fronts feature black-and-white posed player photos with the player's and team name printed below in the white border. These cards were packaged 12 in a packet. The backs are blank. The cards are unnumbered and checklisted below in alphabetical order. Thirteen cards are listed for this set as Walt Moryn is included this year. Since these sets were issued throughout the years, sometimes more than the 12 players listed are included. Additions to this or any other team issue set in the book is appreciated.

COMPLETE SET (13) 6.00 15.00
1 Ken Boyer 1.25 3.00
2 Ernie Broglio .50 1.25
3 Joe Cunningham .75 2.00
4 Curt Flood 1.25 3.00
5 Solly Hemus MG .50 1.25
6 Larry Jackson .50 1.25
7 Julian Javier .75 2.00
8 Lindy McDaniel .50 1.25
9 Walt Moryn .50 1.25
10 Stan Musial 4.00 10.00
11 Hal Smith .50 1.25
12 Daryl Spencer .50 1.25
13 Bill White 1.25 3.00

1962 Cardinals Jay Publishing

The 1962 Jay Cardinals set consists of 14 cards produced by Jay Publishing. The Minoso card establishes the year of the set, since 1962 was Minoso's only year with the Cardinals. The cards measure approximately 4 3/4" by 7" and are printed on thin photographic paper stock. The white fronts feature a black-and-white player portrait with the player's name and the team name below. The backs are blank. The cards are packaged 12 to a packet and originally sold for 25 cents. The cards are unnumbered and checklisted below in alphabetical order. Updates during the season account for the additional cards.

COMPLETE SET (14) 30.00 60.00
1 Ken Boyer 2.00 5.00
2 Ernie Broglio .75 2.00
3 Curt Flood 1.50 4.00
4 Bob Gibson 6.00 15.00
5 Julio Gotay .75 2.00
6 Larry Jackson .75 2.00
7 Julian Javier 1.25 3.00
8 Johnny Keane MG .75 2.00
9 Lindy McDaniel .75 2.00
10 Minnie Minoso 2.00 5.00
11 Stan Musial 6.00 15.00

12 Gene Oliver	.75	2.00
13 Curt Simmons	1.25	3.00
14 Bill White	1.50	4.00

1963-64 Cardinals Jay Publishing

This set of the St. Louis Cardinals measures approximately 5" by 7". The fronts feature black-and-white posed player photos with the player's and team name printed below in the white border. These cards were packaged 12 in a packet. The backs are blank. The cards are unnumbered and checklisted below in alphabetical order. These cards were issued over a two year period and where possible we have identified which year each card was issued.

COMPLETE SET (20)	40.00	80.00
1 Ken Boyer/(With glove)	2.00	5.00
2 Ken Boyer /(With bat)	2.00	5.00
3 Ernie Broglio/(Above waist pose)	.75	2.00
4 Ernie Broglio/(Action photo with glove)	.75	2.00
5 Curt Flood/(Smiling)	1.50	4.00
6 Curt Flood	1.50	4.00
7 Bob Gibson/(Head pose)	5.00	12.00
8 Bob Gibson/(Action pose)	5.00	12.00
9 Dick Groat 64	1.50	4.00
10 Julian Javier	1.25	3.00
11 John Keane MG/(Above waist pose)	.75	2.00
12 John Keane MG/(Full shot)	.75	2.00
13 Dal Maxvill 64	.75	2.00
14 Tim McCarver 64	2.00	5.00
15 Stan Musial 63	6.00	15.00
16 Ray Sadecki/(Without glasses)	.75	2.00
17 Ray Sadecki/(With glasses)	.75	2.00
18 Curt Simmons/(Close up head shot)	1.25	3.00
19 Curt Simmons/(With glove)	1.25	3.00
20 Bill White	1.50	4.00

1965 Cardinals Jay Publishing

This 12-card set of the St. Louis Cardinals measures approximately 5" by 7". The fronts feature black-and-white posed player photos with the player's and team name printed below in the white border. These cards were packaged 12 in a packet. The backs are blank. The cards are unnumbered and checklisted below in alphabetical order.

COMPLETE SET (12)	15.00	40.00
1 Ken Boyer	2.00	5.00
2 Curt Flood	1.50	4.00
3 Bob Gibson	3.00	8.00
4 Dick Groat	1.25	3.00
5 Julian Javier	.75	2.00
6 Tim McCarver	2.00	5.00
7 Bob Purkey	.75	2.00
8 Red Schoendienst MG	2.00	5.00
9 Mike Shannon	1.50	4.00
10 Tracy Stallard	.75	2.00
11 Carl Warwick	.75	2.00
12 Bill White	1.50	4.00

1964 Cardinals Team Issue

This eight-card set measures approximately 4" by 5" and features black-and-white player portraits in a white border with the player's name and position in the bottom margin. The backs are blank. The cards are unnumbered and checklisted below in alphabetical order.

COMPLETE SET (8)	8.00	20.00
1 Ken Boyer	2.00	5.00
2 Curt Flood	1.50	4.00
3 Dick Groat	1.25	3.00
4 Charley James	.75	2.00
5 Julian Javier	1.25	3.00
6 Tim McCarver	2.00	5.00
7 Ray Sadecki	.75	2.00
8 Bill White	1.50	4.00

1965 Cardinals Team Issue

The 28-card set of the St. Louis Cardinals measures approximately 3 1/4" by 5 1/2" and features black-and-white player photos in a white border with a facsimile autograph in the wide bottom margin. The backs are blank. The cards are unnumbered and checklisted below in alphabetical order. Steve Carlton has a card in his Rookie Card year.

COMPLETE SET (28)	40.00	80.00
1 Dennis Aust	.75	2.00
2 Joe Becker CO	.75	2.00
3 Nellie Briles	.75	2.00
4 Lou Brock	3.00	8.00
5 Jerry Buchek	.75	2.00
6 Steve Carlton	6.00	15.00
7 Don Dennis	.75	2.00
8 Curt Flood	1.50	4.00
9 Bob Gibson	3.00	8.00
10 Tito Francona	.75	2.00
11 Phil Gagliano	.75	2.00
12 Larry Jaster	.75	2.00
13 Julian Javier	1.25	3.00
14 George Kernek	.75	2.00
15 Dal Maxvill	1.25	3.00
16 Tim McCarver	2.00	5.00
17 Bob Milliken	.75	2.00
18 Bob Purkey	.75	2.00
19 Ray Sadecki	.75	2.00
20 Red Schoendienst MG	2.00	5.00
21 Joe Schultz	.75	2.00
22 Mike Shannon	1.50	4.00
23 Curt Simmons	1.25	3.00
24 Bob Skinner	.75	2.00
25 Tracy Stallard	.75	2.00
26 Bob Tolan	.75	2.00
27 Ray Washburn	.75	2.00
28 Hal Woodeschick	.75	2.00

1966 Cardinals Team Issue

These 12 black and white photos were available directly from Busch Stadium for twenty-five cents. The cards measure approximately 4 3/4" by 7 and have blank backs. We have dated this set as 1966 was Charlie Smith's last season and Alex Johnson's first season with the Cardinals.

COMPLETE SET (12)	15.00	40.00
1 Lou Brock	3.00	8.00
2 Jerry Buchek	.75	2.00
3 Curt Flood	1.50	4.00
4 Phil Gagliano	.75	2.00
5 Bob Gibson	3.00	8.00
6 Julian Javier	1.25	3.00
7 Alex Johnson	.75	2.00
8 Tim McCarver	2.00	5.00
9 Red Schoendienst MG	2.00	5.00
10 Curt Simmons	1.25	3.00
11 Charlie Smith	.75	2.00
12 Tracy Stallard	.75	2.00

1969 Cardinals Team Issue

These photos, were issued by the St Louis Cardinals and featured members of the two-time defending NL Champions. These photos were designed to be sent out in response to fan requests. Since these photos are unnumbered, we have sequenced them in alphabetical order.

COMPLETE SET (12)	10.00	25.00
1 Nelson Briles	.40	1.00
2 Lou Brock	2.50	6.00
3 Curt Flood	1.00	2.50
4 Bob Gibson	2.50	6.00
5 Julian Javier	.40	1.00
6 Dal Maxvill	.40	1.00
7 Tim McCarver	1.00	2.50
8 Vada Pinson	.75	2.00
9 Red Schoendienst MGR	1.00	2.50
10 Mike Shannon	.60	1.50
11 Joe Torre	1.00	2.50
12 Ray Washburn	.40	1.00

1970 Cardinals Team Issue

This 33-card set of the St. Louis Cardinals measures approximately 4 1/4" by 7" and features black-and-white player photos in a white border. These cards were packaged 12 to a packet and some display facsimile autographs. The backs are blank. The cards are unnumbered and checklisted below in alphabetical order. Updates and changes during the year account for the odd number of cards. This set can be dated to 1970 as that was Richie (Dick) Allen's only season with the Cards.

COMPLETE SET (33)	40.00	80.00
1 Richie Allen Glasses	2.00	5.00
2 Richie Allen Uniform # showing	2.00	5.00
3 Jim Beauchamp	.75	2.00
4 Lou Brock	3.00	8.00
5 Vern Benson CO	.75	2.00
6 Sal Campisi	.75	2.00
7 Jose Cardenal	1.25	3.00
8 Bob Chlupsa	.75	2.00
9 Ed Crosby	.75	2.00
10 George Culver	.75	2.00
11 Vic Davalillo	1.25	3.00
12 Bob Gibson	3.00	8.00
13 Santiago Guzman	.75	2.00
14 Joe Hague	.75	2.00
15 Julian Javier	1.25	3.00
16 Al Hrabosky	1.25	3.00
17 Leron Lee Head and Shoulders	.75	2.00
18 Leron Lee Uniform # Showing	.75	2.00
19 Frank Linzy	.75	2.00
20 Dal Maxvill	.75	2.00
21 Milt Ramirez	.75	2.00
22 Jerry Reuss	1.50	4.00
23 Cookie Rojas	.75	2.00
24 Red Schoendienst	2.00	5.00
25 Mike Shannon	1.50	4.00
26 Ted Simmons	2.50	6.00
27 Dick Sisler CO	.75	2.00
28 Carl Taylor Portrait	.75	2.00
29 Carl Taylor Kneeling	.75	2.00
30 Chuck Taylor	.75	2.00
31 Joe Torre	2.00	5.00
32 Bart Zeller Portrait	.75	2.00
33 Bart Zeller Batting	.75	2.00

1971 Cardinals Team Issue

This 30-card set measures 3 1/4" by 5 1/2" and features black-and-white player portraits with white borders. A facsimile autograph appears in the wider white border area at the bottom. The backs are blank. The cards are unnumbered and checklisted below in alphabetical order.

COMPLETE SET (30)	40.00	80.00
1 Matty Alou	1.25	3.00
2 Jim Beauchamp	.60	1.50
3 Vern Benson CO	.60	1.50
4 Ken Boyer CO	1.50	4.00
5 Lou Brock	4.00	10.00
6 Bob Burda	.60	1.50
7 Jose Cardenal	.75	2.00
8 Steve Carlton	4.00	10.00
9 Reggie Cleveland	.60	1.50
10 Moe Drabowsky	.60	1.50
11 Bob Gibson	4.00	10.00
12 Joe Hague	.60	1.50
13 Julian Javier	.75	2.00
14 George Kissell CO	.60	1.50
15 Frank Linzy	.60	1.50
16 Dal Maxvill	.75	2.00
17 Jerry McNertney	.60	1.50
18 Luis Melendez	.60	1.50
19 Jerry Reuss	1.25	3.00
20 Al Santorini	.60	1.50
21 Red Schoendienst MG	1.50	4.00
22 Barney Schultz CO	.60	1.50
23 Don Shaw	.60	1.50
24 Ted Simmons	1.50	4.00
25 Ted Sizemore	.60	1.50
26 Chuck Taylor	.60	1.50
27 Lee Thomas CO	.60	1.50
28 Joe Torre/(Profile)	1.50	4.00
29 Joe Torre/(Front View)	1.50	4.00
30 Chris Zachary	.60	1.50

1972 Cardinals Team Issue

This 18-card set of the St. Louis Cardinals measures approximately 3 1/4" by 5 1/2" and features black-and-white player portraits with white borders. A facsimile autograph appears in the wide bottom margin. The backs are blank. The cards are unnumbered and checklisted below in alphabetical order.

COMPLETE SET (18)	30.00	60.00
1 Nelson Briles	1.25	3.00
2 Lou Brock	3.00	8.00
3 Steve Carlton	3.00	8.00
4 Donn Clendenon	1.25	3.00
5 Tony Cloninger	1.25	3.00
6 Ed Crosby	1.25	3.00
7 Jose Cruz	1.50	4.00
8 Moe Drabowsky	1.25	3.00
9 Bob Gibson	4.00	10.00
10 Joe Grzenda	1.25	3.00
11 George Kissell CO	1.25	3.00
12 Dal Maxvill	1.25	3.00
13 Billy Muffett CO	1.25	3.00
14 Ted Simmons	2.00	5.00
15 Ted Sizemore	1.25	3.00
16 Scipio Spinks	1.25	3.00
17 Mike Torrez	1.50	4.00
18 Rick Wise	1.50	4.00

1974 Cardinals 1931 Bra-Mac

This 20 card set, which measures 3 1/2" by 5" features members of the 1931 World Champion St Louis Cardinals.

COMPLETE SET	6.00	15.00
1 Burleigh Grimes	.60	1.50
2 Sparky Adams	.20	.50
3 Jesse Haines	.60	1.50
4 Jimmie Wilson	.30	.75
5 Ernie Orsatti	.20	.50
6 Gus Mancuso	.20	.50
7 Ray Blades	.20	.50
8 Frank Frisch	.75	2.00
9 Bill Hallahan	.20	.50
10 George Watkins	.20	.50
11 Pepper Martin	.40	1.00
12 Charlie Gelbert	.20	.50
13 Jake Flowers	.20	.50
14 Jim Lindsey	.20	.50
15 Rip Collins	.20	.50
16 Flint Rhem	.20	.50
17 Paul Derringer	.20	.50
18 Syl Johnson	.20	.50
19 Chick Hafey	.40	1.00
20 Jim Bottomley	.60	1.50

1974 Cardinals 1934 TCMA

This 31-card set of the 1934 World Champion St. Louis Cardinals measures approximately 2 1/4" by 3 5/8" and features black-and-white player photos. Each set includes four jumbo cards measuring approximately 3 5/8" by 4 1/2" and displaying action photos from the 1934 World Series Games with various information on the backs. The cards are unnumbered and checklisted below with the jumbo cards being the last four cards, numbers 28-31.

COMPLETE SET (31)	10.00	25.00
1 Tex Carleton	.20	.50
2 Rip Collins	.40	1.00
3 Cliff Crawford	.20	.50
4 Spud Davis	.20	.50
5 Daffy Dean Dizzy Dean	.75	2.00
6 Paul Dean	.40	1.00
7 Dizzy Dean	1.25	3.00
8 Bill DeLancey	.20	.50
9 Leo Durocher	1.25	3.00
10 Frank Frisch P MG	1.00	2.50
11 Chick Fullis	.20	.50
12 Mike Gonzalez CO	.20	.50
13 Jesse Haines	.75	2.00
14 Bill Hallahan	.40	1.00
15 Francis Healy	.20	.50
16 Jim Lindsey	.20	.50
17 Pepper Martin	.60	1.50
18 Joe Medwick	1.00	2.50
19 Jim Mooney	.20	.50
20 Ernie Orsatti	.20	.50
21 Flint Rhem	.20	.50
22 John Rothrock	.20	.50
23 Dazzy Vance	.75	2.00
24 Bill Walker	.20	.50
25 Buzzy Wares CO	.20	.50
26 Whitey Whitehead	.20	.50
27 Jim Winford	.20	.50
28 Dizzy & Leo Celebrate	.75	2.00
29 Durocher Scores	1.00	2.50
30 Medwick Out Cochrane Catcher	.75	2.00
31 1934 St. Louis Cardinals World Champions	.60	1.50

1974 Cardinals Postcards

These postcards, which were available directly from the Cardinals, feature members of the 1974 St Louis Cardinals. Some of the photos used in 1974 were used in previous years. Since these photos are not numbered, we have sequenced them alphabetically.

COMPLETE SET	8.00	20.00
1 Vern Benson CO	.20	.50
2 Lou Brock	1.00	2.50
3 Jose Cruz	.40	1.00
4 Joe Cunningham FO	.20	.50
5 John Curtis	.20	.50
6 Rich Folkers	.20	.50
7 Bob Forsch	.20	.50
8 Alan Foster	.20	.50
9 Mike Garman	.20	.50
10 Bob Gibson	1.25	3.00
11 Jim Hickman	.20	.50
12 Marc Hill	.20	.50
13 Al Hrabosky	.20	.50
14 George Kissell CO	.20	.50
15 Johnny Lewis CO	.20	.50
16 Bake McBride	.30	.75
17 Tim McCarver	.60	1.50
18 Lynn McGlothen	.20	.50
19 Luis Melendez	.20	.50
20 Orlando Pena	.20	.50
21 Ken Reitz	.20	.50
22 Pete Richert	.20	.50
23 Dave Ricketts	.20	.50
24 Red Schoendienst MG	.40	1.00
25 Barney Schultz	.20	.50
26 Sonny Siebert	.20	.50
27 Ted Simmons	.40	1.00
28 Ted Sizemore	.20	.50
29 Reggie Smith	.30	.75
30 Joe Torre	.60	1.50
31 Mike Tyson	.20	.50

1975 Cardinals Postcards

This 30-card set of the St Louis Cardinals features player photos on postcard-size cards. The cards are unnumbered and checklisted below in alphabetical order.

COMPLETE SET (30)	8.00	20.00
1 Ed Brinkman	.20	.50
2 Lou Brock	1.25	3.00
3 Ron Bryant	.20	.50
4 Danny Cater	.20	.50
5 John Curtis	.20	.50
6 Willie Davis	.30	.75
7 John Denny	.20	.50
8 Jim Dwyer	.20	.50
9 Ron Fairly	.30	.75
10 Bob Forsch	.20	.50
11 Mike Garman	.20	.50
12 Bob Gibson	1.50	4.00
13 Mario Guerrero	.20	.50
14 Keith Hernandez	2.00	5.00
15 Al Hrabosky	.20	.50
16 Teddy Martinez	.20	.50
17 Bake McBride	.20	.50
18 Lynn McGlothen	.20	.50
19 Luis Melendez	.20	.50
20 Tommy Moore	.20	.50
21 Ron Reed	.20	.50
22 Ken Reitz	.20	.50
23 Ken Rudolph	.20	.50
24 Ray Sadecki	.20	.50
25 Ted L. Simmons	.60	1.50
26 Ted Sizemore	.20	.50
27 Reggie Smith	.30	.75
28 Elias Sosa	.20	.50
29 Greg Terlecky	.20	.50
30 Mike Tyson	.20	.50

1975 Cardinals TCMA 1942-46

This 66-card set features the 1942-46 St. Louis Cardinals Team. The fronts display black-and-white player photos while the backs carry player statistics. The cards are unnumbered and checklisted below in alphabetical order with the jumbo cards listed last. The set concludes with several multi-player cards.

1 Buster Adams	.20	.50
2 Red Barrett	.20	.50
3 Johnny Beazley	.20	.50
4 Augie Bergamo	.20	.50
5 Buddy Blattner	.20	.50
6 Al Brazle	.20	.50
7 Harry Brecheen	.40	1.00
8 Jimmy Brown	.20	.50
9 Ken Burkhart	.20	.50
10 Bud Byerly	.20	.50
11 Mort Cooper	.40	1.00
12 Walker Cooper	.40	1.00
13 Estel Crabtree	.20	.50
14 Frank Crespi	.20	.50
15 Jeff Cross	.20	.50
16 Frank Demaree	.20	.50
17 Murry Dickson	.30	.75
18 Blix Donnelly	.20	.50
19 Erv Dusak	.20	.50
20 Eddie Dyer MGR	.20	.50
21 Bill Endicott	.20	.50
22 George Fallon	.20	.50
23 Joe Garagiola	1.00	2.50
24 Debs Garms	.20	.50
25 Mike Gonzalez CO	.20	.50
26 Johnny Grodzicki	.20	.50
27 Harry Gumbert	.20	.50
28 Johnny Hopp	.20	.50
29 Nippy Jones	.20	.50
30 Al Jurisich	.20	.50
31 Lou Klein	.20	.50
32 Clyde Kluttz	.20	.50
33 Howie Krist	.20	.50
34 Whitey Kurowski	.20	.50
35 Max Lanier	.20	.50
36 Danny Litwhiler	.20	.50
37 Bill Lohrman	.20	.50
38 Marty Marion	.75	2.00
39 Freddie Martin	.20	.50
40 Pepper Martin	.75	2.00
41 Terry Moore	.40	1.00
42 George Munger	.20	.50
43 Stan Musial	2.00	5.00
44 Sam Narron	.20	.50
45 Ken O'Dea	.20	.50
46 Howie Pollet	.20	.50
47 Del Rice	.20	.50
48 Ray Sanders	.20	.50
49 Fred Schmidt	.20	.50
50 Red Schoendienst	1.00	2.50
51 Walt Sessi	.20	.50
52 Clyde Shoun	.20	.50
53 Dick Sisler	.20	.50
54 Enos Slaughter	1.00	2.50
55 Billy Southworth MGR	.20	.50
56 Coaker Triplett	.20	.50
57 Emil Verban	.20	.50
58 Harry Walker	.40	1.00
59 Buzzy Ware	.20	.50
60 Lon Warneke	.40	1.00
61 Ernie White	.20	.50
62 Del Wilber	.20	.50
63 Ted Wilks	.20	.50
64 L.Durocher MGR/E.Dyer MGR	.75	2.00
65 Musial/Southworth MGR/Hopp	.75	2.00
66 Musial/Southworth MGR/Sanders	.75	2.00
67 R.Ruffing/J.Beazley	.40	1.00
68 1942 St. Louis Cardinals Team	.40	1.00
69 Sportsman's Park	.40	1.00

1976 Cardinals Postcards

This 35-card set of the St. Louis Cardinals features player photos on postcard-size cards. The cards are unnumbered and checklisted below in alphabetical order.

COMPLETE SET (35)	8.00	20.00
1 Mike Anderson	.20	.50
2 Lou Brock	1.50	4.00
3 Willie Crawford	.20	.50
4 John Curtis	.20	.50
5 Hector Cruz	.20	.50
6 John Denny	.30	.75
7 Ron Fairly	.30	.75
8 Pete Falcone	.20	.50
9 Joe Ferguson	.20	.50
10 Bob Forsch	.20	.50
11 Danny Frisella	.20	.50
12 Preston Gomez CO	.20	.50
13 Bill Greif	.20	.50
14 Vic Harris	.20	.50
15 Keith Hernandez	1.25	3.00
16 Al Hrabosky	.30	.75
17 Don Kessinger	.20	.50
18 Fred Koenig CO	.20	.50
19 Johnny Lewis	.20	.50
20 Bake McBride	.20	.50
21 Lynn McGlothen	.20	.50
22 Luis Melendez	.20	.50
23 Bob Milliken CO	.20	.50
24 Jerry Mumphrey	.20	.50
25 Mike Proly	.20	.50
26 Harry Rasmussen	.20	.50
27 Lee Richard	.20	.50
28 Ken Rudolph	.20	.50
29 Red Schoendienst MG	.60	1.50
30 Ted Simmons	.40	1.00
31 Reggie Smith	.40	1.00
32 Eddie Solomon	.20	.50
33 Mike Tyson	.20	.50
34 Mike Wallace	.20	.50
35 Tom Zimmer	.20	.50

1977 Cardinals 5x7

This 30-card set features black-and-white player portraits in a white border with the player's name and position printed in the bottom margin. The backs are blank. The cards are unnumbered and checklisted below in alphabetical order.

COMPLETE SET (30)	6.00	15.00
1 Mike Anderson	.20	.50
2 Lou Brock	.75	2.00
3 Clay Carroll	.20	.50
4 Heity Cruz	.20	.50
5 John Denny	.20	.50
6 Larry Dierker	.20	.50
7 Rawly Eastwick	.20	.50
8 Pete Falcone	.20	.50
9 Bob Forsch	.20	.50
10 Roger Freed	.20	.50
11 Keith Hernandez	.60	1.50
12 Al Hrabosky	.30	.75
13 Jack Krol CO	.20	.50
14 Butch Metzger	.20	.50
15 Mo Mozzali CO	.20	.50
16 Jerry Mumphrey	.20	.50
17 Claude Osteen CO	.20	.50
18 Mike Phillips	.20	.50
19 Dave Rader	.20	.50
20 Vern Rapp	.20	.50
21 Eric Rasmussen	.20	.50
22 Ken Reitz	.20	.50
23 Sonny Ruberto CO	.20	.50
24 Bobby Schultz	.20	.50
25 Tony Scott	.20	.50
26 Ted Simmons	.60	1.50
27 Garry Templeton	.40	1.00
28 Mike Tyson	.20	.50
29 Tom Underwood	.20	.50
30 John Urrea	.20	.50

1977 Cardinals Team Issue

This 28-card set measures approximately 3 1/4" by 5 1/2" and features black-and-white player portraits in a white border. A facsimile autograph is printed in the wide bottom margin. The backs are blank. The cards are unnumbered and checklisted below in alphabetical order.

COMPLETE SET (28)	4.00	10.00
1 Mike Anderson	.10	.25
2 Lou Brock	1.00	2.50
3 Clay Carroll	.10	.25
4 Heity Cruz	.10	.25
5 John Denny	.20	.50
6 Larry Dierker	.10	.25
7 Pete Falcone	.10	.25
8 Bob Forsch	.10	.25
9 Roger Freed	.10	.25
10 Keith Hernandez	.40	1.00
11 Al Hrabosky	.20	.50
12 Don Kessinger	.10	.25
13 Jack Krol	.10	.25
14 Butch Metzger	.10	.25
15 Maurice Mo Mozzali	.10	.25
16 Jerry Mumphrey	.10	.25
17 Claude Osteen	.10	.25
18 Dave Rader	.10	.25
19 Vern Rapp MG	.10	.25
20 Eric Rasmussen	.10	.25
21 Ken Reitz	.10	.25
22 Sonny Ruberto	.10	.25
23 Buddy Schutz	.10	.25
24 Tony Scott	.10	.25
25 Ted Simmons	.40	1.00
26 Garry Templeton	.30	.75
27 Mike Tyson	.10	.25
28 John Urrea	.10	.25

1978 Cardinals Team Issue

This 37-card set measures approximately 3 1/4" by 5 1/2" and features black-and-white player portraits in a white border. A facsimile autograph is printed in the wide bottom margin. The backs are blank. The cards are unnumbered and checklisted below in alphabetical order.

COMPLETE SET (37)	6.00	15.00
1 Ken Boyer	.40	1.00
2 Lou Brock	1.00	2.50
3 Tom Bruno	.10	.25
4 John Denny	.10	.25
5 Jim Dwyer	.10	.25
6 Pete Falcone	.10	.25
7 Bob Forsch	.10	.25
8 Roger Freed	.10	.25
9 Dave Hamilton	1.00	2.50
10 George Hendrick	.10	.25
11 Keith Hernandez	.40	1.00
12 Dane Iorg	.10	.25
13 Jack Krol	.10	.25
14 Mark Littell	.10	.25
15 Aurelio Lopez	.10	.25
16 Silvio Martinez	.10	.25
17 Dal Maxvill	.10	.25
18 Jerry Morales	.10	.25
19 Maurice Mo Mozzali	.10	.25
20 Jerry Mumphrey	.10	.25
21 Ken Oberkfell	.10	.25
22 Claude Osteen	.10	.25
23 Mike Phillips	.10	.25
24 Eric Rasmussen	.10	.25
25 Ken Reitz	.10	.25
26 Dave Ricketts	.10	.25
27 Sonny Ruberto	.10	.25
28 Red Schoendienst MG	.40	1.00
29 Buddy Schultz	.10	.25
30 Tony Scott	.10	.25
31 Ted Simmons	.40	1.00
32 Gary Sutherland	1.00	2.50
33 Steve Swisher	.10	.25
34 Garry Templeton	.20	.50
35 Mike Tyson	.10	.25
36 Pete Vuckovich	.20	.50
37 John Urrea	.10	.25

1979 Cardinals 5x7

This set features black-and-white player portraits in a white border with the player's name and position printed in the bottom margin. The backs are blank. The cards are unnumbered and checklisted below in alphabetical order. According to published reports at the time, the Tom Grieve card was pulled very early in the season.

COMPLETE SET	8.00	20.00
COMMON CARD	.20	.50
COMMON SP		
1 Ken Boyer MG	.40	1.00
2 Lou Brock	1.00	2.50
3 Tom Bruno	.20	.50
4 Bernie Carbo	.20	.50
5 John Denny	.20	.50
6 Bob Forsch	.20	.50
7 George Frazier	.20	.50
8 Roger Freed	.20	.50
9 John Fulgham	.20	.50
10 Tom Grieve SP	.40	1.00
11 George Hendrick	.20	.50
12 Keith Hernandez	.60	1.50
13 Dane Iorg	.20	.50
14 Terry Kennedy	.30	.75
15 Darold Knowles	.20	.50
16 Jack Krol CO	.20	.50
17 Mark Littell	.20	.50
18 Silvio Martinez	.20	.50
19 Dal Maxvill CO	.20	.50
20 Will McEnaney	.20	.50
21 Jerry Mumphrey	.20	.50
22 Ken Oberkfell	.20	.50
23 Claude Osteen CO	.20	.50
24 Mike Phillips	.20	.50
25 Ken Reitz		
26 Dave Ricketts CO	.20	.50
27 Tony Scott	.20	.50
28 Ted Schoendienst CO	.60	1.50
29 Buddy Schultz	.20	.50
30 Ted Simmons	.40	1.00
31 Steve Swisher number 9 on uniform	.20	.50
32 Steve Swisher No number on uniform	.20	.50
33 Bob Sykes	.20	.50
34 Garry Templeton	.30	.75
35 Roy Thomas	.20	.50
36 Mike Tyson	.20	.50
37 Pete Vuckovich	.30	.75

1981 Cardinals 5x7

This 26-card set features black-and-white player portraits in a white border with the player's name and position printed in the bottom margin. The backs are blank. The cards are unnumbered and checklisted below in alphabetical order.

COMPLETE SET (26)	6.00	15.00
1 Steve Braun	.20	.50
2 Glenn Brummer	.20	.50
3 Larry Dierker	.20	.50
4 Bob Forsch	.20	.50
5 Julio Gonzalez	.20	.50
6 George Hendrick	.40	1.00
7 Keith Hernandez	.75	2.00
8 Tom Herr Uniform number visible	.40	1.00
9 Tom Herr No number visible	.40	1.00
10 Whitey Herzog MG	.60	1.50
11 Chuck Hiller CO	.20	.50
12 Dane Iorg	.20	.50
13 Jim Kaat	.60	1.50
14 Hub Kittle CO	.20	.50
15 Hal Lanier CO	.20	.50
16 Dave LaPoint	.20	.50
17 John Martin	.20	.50
18 Ken Oberkfell Uniform number 10	.20	.50
19 Ken Oberkfell Uniform number 20	.20	.50
20 Jim Otten	.20	.50
21 Darrell Porter	.40	1.00
22 Dave Ricketts CO	.20	.50
23 Orlando Sanchez	.20	.50
24 Red Schoendienst CO	.75	2.00
25 Bob Shirley	.20	.50
26 Gene Tenace	.40	1.00

1982 Cardinals Post-Dispatch

Issued after the 1982 World Series as a supplement in the St Louis Post-Dispatch, these inserts feature the members of the 1982 World Champions St Louis Cardinals. These "cards" have a player photo, information about the player's season and 1982 Regular Season and World Series statistics. Since these are unnumbered, we have sequenced them in alphabetical order.

COMPLETE SET	12.50	30.00
1 Joaquin Andujar	.40	1.00
2 Doug Bair	.40	1.00
3 Steve Braun	.40	1.00
4 Glenn Brummer	.40	1.00
5 Bob Forsch	.40	1.00
6 Julio Gonzalez	.40	1.00
7 David Green	.40	1.00
8 George Hendrick	.50	1.25
9 Keith Hernandez	.60	1.50
10 Tom Herr	.40	1.00
11 Dane Iorg	.40	1.00
12 Jim Kaat	.60	1.50
13 Dave LaPoint	.40	1.00
14 Jeff Lahti	.40	1.00
15 John Martin	.40	1.00
16 Willie McGee	1.25	3.00
17 Steve Mura	.40	1.00
18 Ken Oberkfell	.40	1.00
19 Darrell Porter	.40	1.00
20 Mike Ramsey	.40	1.00
21 Lonnie Smith	.50	1.25
22 Ozzie Smith	1.50	4.00
23 John Stuper	.40	1.00
24 Bruce Sutter	1.00	2.50
25 Gene Tenace	.50	1.25

1983 Cardinals

These cards feature members of the 1983 St. Louis Cardinals. These cards are unnumbered and we have sequenced them in alphabetical order.

COMPLETE SET (31)	4.00	10.00
1 Joaquin Andujar	.20	.50
2 Doug Bair	.08	.25
3 Steve Braun	.08	.25
4 Glenn Brummer	.08	.25
5 Bob Forsch	.08	.25
6 David Green	.08	.25
7 George Hendrick	.20	.50
8 Keith Hernandez	.40	1.00
9 Tom Herr	.08	.25
10 Whitey Herzog MG	.30	.75
11 Chuck Hiller CO	.08	.25
12 Jim Kaat	.30	.75
13 Hub Kittle CO	.08	.25
14 Jeff Lahti	.08	.25
15 Hal Lanier CO	.08	.25
16 David LaPoint	.08	.25
17 Dane Iorg	.08	.25
18 John Martin	.08	.25
19 Willie McGee	1.00	2.50
20 Ken Oberkfell	.08	.25
21 Darrell Porter	.20	.50
22 Jamie Quirk	.08	.25
23 Mike Ramsey	.08	.25
24 Eric Rasmussen	.08	.25
25 Dave Ricketts CO	.08	.25
26 Rafael Santana	.08	.25
27 Red Schoendienst CO	.40	1.00
28 Lonnie Smith	.20	.50
29 Ozzie Smith	1.50	4.00
30 John Stuper	.08	.25
31 Bruce Sutter	.60	1.50

1983 Cardinals Colonial Bread Porter

This one-card set features a blue-and-white photo of the 1982 World Series MVP, Darrell Porter of the World Champion St. Louis Cardinals, holding a loaf of Colonial Bread. The back displays sweepstakes rules for a contest sponsored by Colonial Bread.

1 Darrell Porter	1.25	3.00

1983 Cardinals Greats TCMA

This 12-card standard-size set honors some leading all-time St. Louis Cardinals. These players are noted with their name and position on the front. The backs have vital statistics, a biography as well as career totals.

COMPLETE SET (12)	2.50	6.00
1 Jim Bottomley	.20	.50
2 Rogers Hornsby	.50	1.25
3 Ken Boyer	.30	.75
4 Marty Marion	.30	.75
5 Ducky Medwick	.20	.50
6 Chick Hafey	.20	.50
7 Stan Musial	1.00	2.50
8 Robert Bob Gibson	.50	1.25
9 Harry Brecheen	.08	.25
10 Tim McCarver	.30	.75
11 Alpha Brazle	.08	.25
12 Red Schoendienst MG	.30	.75

1983 Cardinals 1942-1946 TCMA

This 68-card set was printed in 1983 by TCMA and features photos of the 1942-46 St. Louis Cardinals teams. The backs carry player information. Cards numbered 66 and 67 are double-sized cards.

COMPLETE SET (68)	5.00	12.00
1 Jimmy Brown	.02	.10
2 Jeff Cross	.02	.10
3 Lou Klein	.02	.10
4 Danny Litwhiler	.02	.10
5 Sam Narron	.02	.10
6 Estel Crabtree	.02	.10
7 Buzzy Wares	.02	.10
8 Ken O'Dea	.02	.10
9 Buddy Blattner	.02	.10
10 Erv Dusak	.02	.10
11 Ray Sanders	.02	.10
12 Harry Walker	.08	.25
13 Coaker Triplett	.02	.10
14 Stan Musial	2.00	5.00
15 Walker Cooper	.02	.10
16 Whitey Kurowski	.08	.25
17 Enos Slaughter	.40	1.00
18 Terry Moore	.20	.50
19 Johnny Hopp	.02	.10
20 Creepy Grespi	.02	.10
21 Marty Marion	.30	.75
22 Debs Garms	.02	.10

23 Frank Demaree .02 .10
24 George Fallon .02 .10
25 Buster Adams .02 .10
26 Emil Verban .02 .10
27 Augie Bergamo .02 .10
28 Pepper Martin .30 .75
29 Mike Gonzalez CO .02 .10
30 Leo Durocher MG .20 .50
Eddie Dyer MG
31 Red Schoendienst .60 1.50
32 Del Rice .02 .10
33 Joe Garagiola .30 .75
34 Dick Sisler .02 .10
35 Clyde Kluttz .02 .10
36 Bill Endicott .02 .10
37 Nippy Jones .02 .10
38 Walter Sessi .02 .10
39 Del Wilber .02 .10
40 Mort Cooper .02 .10
41 John Beazley .02 .10
42 Howie Krist .02 .10
43 Max Lanier .02 .10
44 Harry Gumbert .02 .10
45 Howie Pollet .02 .10
46 Ernie White .02 .10
47 Murry Dickson .02 .10
48 Lon Warneke .08 .25
49 Bill Lohrmann .02 .10
50 Clyde Shoun .02 .10
51 George Munger .02 .10
52 Harry Brecheen .08 .25
53 Alpha Brazle .02 .10
54 Bud Byerly .02 .10
55 Ted Wilks .02 .10
56 Fred Schmidt .02 .10
57 Al Jurisch .02 .10
58 Red Barrett .02 .10
59 Ken Burkhardt .02 .10
60 Blix Donnelly .02 .10
61 Johnny Grodzicki .02 .10
62 Billy Southworth .02 .10
63 Eddie Dyer MG .02 .10
64 Red Ruffing .20 .50
Bud Beasley
65 Stan Musial .30 .75
Bill Southworth MG
Johnny Hopp
66 Sportsman Park .40 1.00
67 1942 Cardinals Team Picture .40 1.00
68 Stan Musial .30 .75
Bill Southworth MG
Ray Sanders

1984 Cardinals

This 32-card set of the St. Louis Cardinals measures approximately 3 1/4" by 5 1/2" and features white-bordered, black-and-white player portraits. A facsimile autograph appears in the wide bottom margin. The backs are blank. Some personnel changes during the season account for more than 30 cards although they were issued in 30 card sets. The cards are unnumbered and checklisted below in alphabetical order.

COMPLETE SET (32) 3.00 8.00
1 Neil Allen .08 .25
2 Joaquin Andujar .20 .50
3 Steve Braun .08 .25
4 Glenn Brummer .08 .25
5 Ralph Citarella .08 .25
6 Danny Cox .08 .25
7 Bob Forsch .08 .25
8 David Green .08 .25
9 George Hendrick .20 .50
10 Tom Herr .08 .25
11 Whitey Herzog MG .30 .75
12 Rick Horton .08 .25
13 Art Howe .08 .25
14 Mike Jorgensen .08 .25
15 Jeff Lahti .08 .25
16 Tito Landrum .08 .25
17 Hal Lanier CO .08 .25
18 Dave LaPoint .08 .25
19 Nick Leyva CO .08 .25
20 Bill Lyons .08 .25
21 Willie McGee .60 1.50
22 Darrell Porter .20 .50
23 Dave Ricketts CO .08 .25
24 Mike Roarke CO .08 .25
25 Dave Rucker .08 .25
26 Mark Salas .08 .25
27 Red Schoendienst CO .40 1.00
28 Lonnie Smith .08 .25
29 Ozzie Smith 1.25 3.00
30 Bruce Sutter .60 1.50
31 Andy Van Slyke .60 1.50
32 Dave Von Ohlen .08 .25

1984 Cardinals 5x7

This 30-card set features black-and-white player portraits either borderless or in a white border with the player's name and position printed in the bottom margin. The backs are blank. The cards are unnumbered and checklisted below in alphabetical order.

COMPLETE SET (30) 8.00 20.00
1 Neil Allen .20 .50
2 Joaquin Andujar .20 .50
3 Steve Braun .20 .50
4 Glenn Brummer .20 .50
5 Danny Cox .20 .50
6 Bob Forsch .20 .50
7 Jose Gonzalez .20 .50
8 David Green .20 .50
9 George Hendrick .30 .75
10 Tom Herr .20 .50
11 Whitey Herzog MG .40 1.00
12 Ricky Horton .20 .50
13 Art Howe .20 .50
14 Hal Lanier CO .20 .50
15 Dave LaPoint .20 .50
16 Nick Leyva CO .20 .50
17 Bill Lyons .20 .50
18 Willie McGee .75 2.00
19 Tom Nieto .20 .50
20 Terry Pendleton .75 2.00
21 Darrell Porter .30 .75
22 Dave Ricketts CO .20 .50
23 Mike Roarke CO .20 .50
24 Dave Rucker .20 .50
25 Red Schoendienst CO .60 1.50
26 Lonnie Smith .30 .75
27 Ozzie Smith 1.00 2.50
28 John Stuper .20 .50
29 Bruce Sutter .75 2.00
30 Andy Van Slyke .75 2.00

1985 Cardinals Team Issue

These 32 cards represent members of the 1985 St. Louis Cardinals. The fronts have black and white photographs and facsimile autographs. The backs are blank. We have checklisted this set in alphabetical order.

COMPLETE SET (33) 4.00 10.00
1 Neil Allen .08 .25
2 Joaquin Andujar .20 .50
3 Steve Braun .08 .25
4 Bill Campbell .08 .25
5 Jack Clark .30 .75
6 Vince Coleman .40 1.00
7 Danny Cox .08 .25
8 Ken Dayley .08 .25
9 Ivan DeJesus .08 .25
10 Bob Forsch .08 .25
11 Brian Harper .08 .25
12 Andy Hassler .08 .25
13 Tom Herr .08 .25
14 Whitey Herzog MG .30 .75
15 Ricky Horton .08 .25
16 Mike Jorgensen .08 .25
17 Kurt Kepshire .08 .25
18 Hal Lanier CO .08 .25
19 Jeff Lahti .08 .25
20 Tito Landrum .08 .25
21 Tom Lawless .08 .25
22 Johnny Lewis CO .08 .25
23 Nick Leyva CO .08 .25
24 Willie McGee .40 1.00
25 Tom Nieto .08 .25
26 Terry Pendleton .40 1.00
27 Darrell Porter .20 .50
28 Dave Ricketts CO .08 .25
29 Mike Roarke CO .08 .25
30 Red Schoendienst CO .40 1.00
31 Ozzie Smith 1.00 2.50
32 John Tudor .20 .50
33 Andy Van Slyke .40 1.00

1986 Cardinals Team Issue

This 45-card set of the St. Louis Cardinals measures approximately 3 1/4" by 5 1/2" and features white-bordered, black-and-white player portraits. A facsimile autograph appears in the wide bottom margin. The backs are blank. The cards are unnumbered and checklisted below in alphabetical order. This set was updated during the season and that explains the large size of this set.

COMPLETE SET (45) 4.00 10.00
1 Neil Allen .08 .25
2 Joaquin Andujar .20 .50
3 Greg Bargar .08 .25
4 Steve Braun .08 .25
5 Ray Burris .08 .25
6 Bill Campbell .08 .25
7 Jack Clark .30 .75
8 Vince Coleman .40 1.00
9 Tim Conroy .08 .25
10 Dan Cox .08 .25
11 Ken Dayley .08 .25
12 Ivan DeJesus .08 .25
13 Bob Forsch .08 .25
14 Rich Hacker CO .08 .25
15 Brian Harper .08 .25
16 Mike Heath .08 .25
17 Tom Herr .08 .25
18 Whitey Herzog MG .30 .75
19 Rick Horton .08 .25
20 Clint Hurdle .20 .50
21 Mike Jorgensen .08 .25
22 Kurt Kepshire .08 .25
23 Jeff Lahti .08 .25
24 Tito Landrum .08 .25
25 Hal Lanier CO .08 .25
26 Tom Lawless .08 .25
27 Johnny Lewis CO .08 .25
28 Nick Leyva CO .08 .25
29 Greg Mathews .08 .25
30 Willie McGee .40 1.00
31 Tom Nieto .08 .25
32 Jose Oquendo .08 .25
33 Rick Ownbey .08 .25
34 Terry Pendleton .30 .75
35 Pat Perry .08 .25
36 Darrell Porter .08 .25
37 Dave Ricketts CO .08 .25
38 Mike Roarke CO .08 .25
39 Red Schoendienst CO .40 1.00
40 Ozzie Smith 1.00 2.50
41 John Tudor .08 .25
42 Andy Van Slyke .30 .75
43 Andy Van Slyke .30 .75
44 Jerry White .08 .25
45 Todd Worrell .40 1.00

1986 Cardinals IGA Stores

This 14-card set of the St. Louis Cardinals measures approximately 6" by 9". The fronts feature white-framed color player portraits with a facsimile autographed in the lower left. The backs are blank. The cards are unnumbered and checklisted below in alphabetical order.

COMPLETE SET (14) 8.00 20.00
1 Jack Clark .75 2.00
2 Vince Coleman 1.00 2.50
3 Dan Cox .40 1.00
4 Bob Forsch .40 1.00
5 Mike Heath .40 1.00
6 Tom Herr .40 1.00
7 Tito Landrum .40 1.00
8 Jeff Lahti .40 1.00
9 Willie McGee 1.00 2.50
10 Terry Pendleton .75 2.00
11 Ozzie Smith 2.00 5.00
12 John Tudor .40 1.00
13 Andy Van Slyke .75 2.00
14 Todd Worrell 1.00 2.50

1986 Cardinals KAS Discs

This set of discs was distributed by KAS in 1986 to commemorate the Cardinal's "almost" World Championship in 1985. Each disc measures 2 3/4" in diameter. Each disc has a white border on the front. Inside this white border is a full-color photo of the player with his hat airbrushed to erase the team logo on their hat. The statistics on back of the disc give the player's 1985 pitching or hitting record as well as his vital statistics. The discs are numbered on the back.

COMPLETE SET (20) 5.00 12.00
1 Vince Coleman .20 .50
2 Ken Dayley .08 .25
3 Tito Landrum .08 .25
4 Steve Braun .08 .25
5 Danny Cox .08 .25
6 Bob Forsch .08 .25
7 Ozzie Smith 2.50 6.00
8 Brian Harper .08 .25
9 Jack Clark .30 .75
10 Todd Worrell .30 .75
11 Joaquin Andujar .20 .50
12 Tom Nieto .08 .25
13 Kurt Kepshire .08 .25
14 Terry Pendleton .40 1.00
15 Tom Herr .08 .25
16 Darrell Porter .20 .50
17 John Tudor .20 .50
18 Jeff Lahti .08 .25
19 Andy Van Slyke .40 1.00
20 Willie McGee .75 2.00

1986 Cardinals Schnucks Milk

The cards in this set were printed on the sides of Schnucks milk cartons. The set features only members of the St. Louis Cardinals. The cards measure approximately 3 3/4" by 7 1/2" and have black and white photos. The cards are unnumbered and blank backed. The cards are ordered below according to alphabetical order except for the mascot and schedule cards which are listed last.

COMPLETE SET 20.00 50.00
1 Jack Clark 1.25 3.00
2 Vince Coleman 1.50 4.00
3 Tim Conroy .60 1.50
4 Danny Cox .60 1.50
5 Ken Dayley .60 1.50
6 Bob Forsch .60 1.50
7 Mike Heath .60 1.50
8 Tom Herr .60 1.50
9 Rick Horton .60 1.50
10 Clint Hurdle .75 2.00
11 Kurt Kepshire .60 1.50
12 Jeff Lahti .60 1.50
13 Tito Landrum .60 1.50
14 Mike LaValliere .60 1.50
15 Tom Lawless .60 1.50
16 Willie McGee 1.50 4.00
17 Jose Oquendo .60 1.50
18 Rick Ownbey .60 1.50
19 Terry Pendleton 1.50 4.00
20 Pat Perry .60 1.50
21 Ozzie Smith 4.00 10.00
22 John Tudor .75 2.00
23 Andy Van Slyke 1.25 3.00
24 Todd Worrell 1.50 4.00
25 Fred Bird/(Mascot) .60 1.50
26 Cardinals Schedule .60 1.50

1987 Cardinals 1934 TCMA

This nine-card standard-size set honors members of the "Gashouse Gang". This team won the world series and was led by the Dean Brothers who combined for 49 wins, 30 by Dizzy. The fronts have a player portrait as well as name and position. The back describes their 1934 season and has stats for that season as well.

COMPLETE SET (9) 2.00 5.00
1 Dizzy Dean .75 2.00
2 Daffy Dean .20 .50
3 Pepper Martin .30 .75
4 Ripper Collins .08 .25
5 Frankie Frisch P MG .40 1.00
6 Leo Durocher .40 1.00
7 Ducky Medwick .40 1.00
8 Tex Carleton .08 .25
9 Spud Davis .08 .25

1987 Cardinals Smokey

The U.S. Forestry Service (in conjunction with the St. Louis Cardinals) produced this large, attractive 25-card set to commemorate the 43rd birthday of Smokey. The cards feature Smokey the Bear pictured in the top right corner of every card. The card backs give a cartoon fire safety tip. The cards measure approximately 4" by 6" and are subtitled "Wildfire Prevention" on the front. Sets were supposedly available from the Cardinals team for 3.50 postpaid. Also a limited number of 8 1/2" by 12" full-color team photos were available from the team to those who sent in a large SASE. The large team photo is not considered part of the complete set.

COMPLETE SET (25) 5.00 12.00
1 Ray Soff .20 .50
2 Todd Worrell .40 1.00
3 John Tudor .20 .50
4 Pat Perry .20 .50
5 Rick Horton .20 .50
6 Danny Cox .20 .50
7 Bob Forsch .30 .75
8 Greg Mathews .20 .50
9 Bill Dawley .20 .50
10 Steve Lake .20 .50
11 Tony Pena .20 .50
12 Tom Pagnozzi .30 .75
13 Jack Clark .40 1.00
14 Jim Lindeman .20 .50
15 Mike Laga .20 .50
16 Terry Pendleton .40 1.00
17 Ozzie Smith 1.50 4.00
18 Jose Oquendo .20 .50
19 Tom Lawless .20 .50
20 Tom Herr .30 .75
21 Curt Ford .20 .50
22 Willie McGee .60 1.50
23 Tito Landrum .20 .50
24 Vince Coleman .30 .75
25 Whitey Herzog MG .40 1.00
NNO Team Photo (large) 1.25 3.00

1987 Cardinals Team Issue

This 33-card set of the St. Louis Cardinals features black-and-white player photos measuring approximately 3 1/4" by 5 1/2". The cards are unnumbered and checklisted below in alphabetical order.

COMPLETE SET (33) 5.00 12.00
1 Rod Booker .08 .25
2 Jack Clark .30 .75
3 Vince Coleman .08 .25
4 Tim Conroy .08 .25
5 Dan Cox .08 .25
6 Bill Dawley .08 .25
7 Ken Dayley .08 .25
8 Curt Ford .08 .25
9 Bob Forsch .08 .25
10 Richard Hacker CO .08 .25
11 Tom Herr .20 .50
12 Whitey Herzog MG .30 .75
13 Rich Horton .08 .25
14 Steve Lake .08 .25
15 Tito Landrum .08 .25
16 Tom Lawless .08 .25
17 Johnny Lewis CO .08* .25
18 Nick Leyva CO .08 .25
19 Jim Lindeman .08 .25
20 Joe Magrane .08 .25
21 Willie McGee .60 1.50
22 John Morris .08 .25
23 Jose Oquendo .08 .25
24 Tony Pena .20 .50
25 Terry Pendleton .30 .75
26 Pat Perry .08 .25
27 Dave Ricketts CO .08 .25
28 Mike Roarke CO .08 .25
29 Red Schoendienst CO .40 1.00
30 Ozzie Smith 1.25 3.00
31 John Tudor .20 .50
32 Lee Tunnell .08 .25
33 Todd Worrell .30 .75

1988 Cardinals Smokey

The U.S. Forestry Service (in conjunction with the St. Louis Cardinals) produced this attractive 25-card set. The cards feature Smokey the Bear pictured in the lower right corner of every card. The card backs give a cartoon fire safety tip. The cards measure approximately 3" by 5" and are in full color. The cards are numbered on the backs. The sets were distributed on July 19th during the Cardinals' game against the Los Angeles Dodgers to fans 15 years of age and under.

COMPLETE SET (25) 4.00 10.00
1 Whitey Herzog MG .30 .75
2 Danny Cox .08 .25
3 Ken Dayley .08 .25
4 Jose DeLeon .08 .25
5 Bob Forsch .08 .25
6 Joe Magrane .08 .25
7 Greg Mathews .08 .25
8 Scott Terry .08 .25
9 John Tudor .20 .50
10 Todd Worrell .30 .75
11 Steve Lake .08 .25
12 Tom Pagnozzi .20 .50
13 Tony Pena .20 .50
14 Bob Horner .08 .25
15 Tom Lawless .08 .25
16 Jose Oquendo/(Ryne Sandberg also shown on card) .40 1.00
17 Terry Pendleton .30 .75
18 Ozzie Smith 1.50 4.00
19 Vince Coleman .20 .50
20 Curt Ford .08 .25
21 Willie McGee .50 1.25
22 Larry McWilliams .08 .25
23 Steve Peters .08 .25
24 Luis Alicea .08 .25
25 Tom Brunansky .08 .25

1988 Cardinals Team Issue

This 36-card set of the St. Louis Cardinals features black-and-white player photos measuring approximately 3 1/4" by 5 1/2". The cards are unnumbered and checklisted below in alphabetical order.

COMPLETE SET (36) 5.00 12.00
1 Luis Alicea .08 .25
2 Tom Brunansky .20 .50
3 Vince Coleman .20 .50
4 Dan Cox .08 .25
5 Ken Dayley .08 .25
6 Jose DeLeon .08 .25
7 Curt Ford .08 .25
8 Bob Forsch .08 .25
9 Richard Hacker CO .08 .25
10 Whitey Herzog MG .30 .75
11 Bob Horner .08 .25
12 Michael Joyce .08 .25
13 Steve Lake .08 .25
14 Tom Lawless .08 .25
15 Johnny Lewis CO .08 .25
16 Nick Leyva CO .08 .25
17 Jim Lindeman .08 .25
18 Joe Magrane .08 .25
19 Greg Mathews .08 .25
20 Willie McGee .40 1.00
21 Larry McWilliams .08 .25
22 John Morris .08 .25
23 Randy O'Neal .08 .25
24 Jose Oquendo .08 .25
25 Tom Pagnozzi .08 .25
26 Tony Pena .08 .25
27 Terry Pendleton .30 .75
28 Steve Peters .08 .25
29 Dave Ricketts CO .08 .25
30 Mike Roarke CO .08 .25
31 Red Schoendienst CO .40 1.00
32 Ozzie Smith 1.00 2.50
33 Scott Terry .08 .25
34 John Tudor .08 .25
35 Duane Walker .08 .25
36 Todd Worrell .30 .75

1989 Cardinals Smokey

The 1989 Smokey Cardinals set contains 24 cards measuring approximately 4" by 6". The fronts have color photos with white and red borders. The backs feature biographical information. The cards are unnumbered so they are listed below in alphabetical order for reference.

COMPLETE SET (24) 4.00 10.00
1 Tom Brunansky .08 .25
2 Vince Coleman .30 .75
3 John Costello .10 .25
4 Ken Dayley .08 .25
5 Jose DeLeon .08 .25
6 Frank DiPino .08 .25
7 Pedro Guerrero .30 .75
8 Whitey Herzog MG .30 .75
9 Ken Hill .20 .50
10 Tim Jones .08 .25
11 Jim Lindeman .08 .25
12 Joe Magrane .08 .25
13 Willie McGee .40 1.00
14 John Morris .08 .25
15 Jose Oquendo .08 .25
16 Tom Pagnozzi .08 .25
17 Tony Pena .08 .25
18 Terry Pendleton .30 .75
19 Dan Quisenberry .30 .75
20 Ozzie Smith 1.25 3.00
21 Scott Terry .08 .25
22 Milt Thompson .08 .25
23 Denny Walling .08 .25
24 Todd Worrell .30 .75

1989 Cardinals Team Issue

This 34-card set of the St. Louis Cardinals features black-and-white player photos measuring approximately 3 1/4" by 5 1/2". The cards are unnumbered and checklisted below in alphabetical order.

COMPLETE SET (34) 5.00 12.00
1 Tom Brunansky .20 .50
2 Cris Carpenter .08 .25
3 Vince Coleman .20 .50
4 John Costello .08 .25
5 Dan Cox .08 .25
6 Ken Dayley .08 .25
7 Jose DeLeon .08 .25
8 Frank DiPino .08 .25
9 Pedro Guerrero .30 .75
10 Rick Hacker CO .08 .25
11 Whitey Herzog MG .30 .75
12 Ken Hill .20 .50
13 Tim Jones .08 .25
14 Johnny Lewis CO .08 .25
15 Jim Lindeman .08 .25
16 Joe Magrane .08 .25
17 Greg Mathews .08 .25
18 Willie McGee .40 1.00
19 John Morris .08 .25
20 Jose Oquendo .08 .25
21 Tom Pagnozzi .08 .25
22 Tony Pena .08 .25
23 Terry Pendleton .30 .75
24 Ted Power .08 .25
25 Dan Quisenberry .30 .75
26 Dave Ricketts CO .08 .25
27 Jim Riggleman CO .08 .25
28 Mike Roarke CO .08 .25
29 Red Schoendienst CO .40 1.00
30 Ozzie Smith 1.25 3.00
31 Scott Terry .08 .25
32 Milt Thompson .08 .25
33 Denny Walling .08 .25
34 Todd Worrell .30 .75

1990 Cardinals Smokey

This 27-card, approximately 3" by 5", set was issued about the 1990 St. Louis Cardinals in conjunction with the US Forest Service which was using the popular character Smokey the Bear. The set has full color action photos of the Cardinals on the front of the card while the back of the card has fire safety tips on the bottom of the card. The set has been checklisted alphabetically for reference. The cards are unnumbered; not even uniform numbers are displayed prominently.

COMPLETE SET (27) 6.00 15.00
1 Vince Coleman .40 1.00
2 Dave Collins .20 .50
3 Danny Cox .20 .50
4 Ken Dayley .20 .50
5 Frank DiPino .20 .50
6 Jose DeLeon .20 .50
7 Pedro Guerrero .40 1.00
8 Whitey Herzog MG .40 1.00
9 Rick Horton .20 .50
10 Rex Hudler .20 .50
11 Tim Jones .20 .50
12 Joe Magrane .20 .50
13 Greg Mathews .20 .50
14 Willie McGee .75 2.00
15 John Morris .20 .50
16 Tom Niedenfuer .20 .50
17 Jose Oquendo .20 .50
18 Tom Pagnozzi .20 .50
19 Terry Pendleton .40 1.00
20 Bryn Smith .20 .50
21 Lee Smith .40 1.00
22 Ozzie Smith 1.25 3.00
23 Scott Terry .20 .50
24 Milt Thompson .20 .50
25 John Tudor .20 .50
26 Denny Walling .20 .50
27 Todd Zeile .60 1.50

1990 Cardinals Topps TV

This Cardinals team set contains 66 cards measuring the standard size. Cards numbered 1-36 were with the parent club, while cards 37-66 were in the farm system.

COMPLETE FACT. SET (66) 20.00 50.00
1 Whitey Herzog MG .20 .50
2 Steve Braun CO .08 .25
3 Rich Hacker CO .08 .25
4 Dave Ricketts CO .08 .25
5 Jim Riggleman CO .08 .25
6 Mike Roarke CO .08 .25
7 Cris Carpenter .08 .25
8 John Costello .08 .25
9 Danny Cox .08 .25
10 Ken Dayley .08 .25
11 Jose DeLeon .08 .25
12 Frank DiPino .08 .25
13 Ken Hill .08 .25
14 Howard Hilton .08 .25
15 Ricky Horton .08 .25
16 Joe Magrane .08 .25
17 Greg Mathews .08 .25
18 Bryn Smith .08 .25
19 Scott Terry .08 .25
20 Bob Tewksbury .08 .25
21 John Tudor .08 .25
22 Todd Worrell .20 .50
23 Tom Pagnozzi .08 .25
24 Todd Zeile .60 1.50
25 Pedro Guerrero .20 .50
26 Tim Jones .08 .25
27 Jose Oquendo .08 .25
28 Terry Pendleton .60 1.50
29 Ozzie Smith 15.00 40.00
30 Denny Walling .08 .25
31 Tom Brunansky .20 .50
32 Vince Coleman .20 .50
33 Dave Collins .08 .25
34 Willie McGee .60 1.50
35 John Morris .08 .25
36 Milt Thompson .08 .25
37 Gibson Alba .08 .25
38 Scott Arnold .08 .25
39 Rod Brewer .08 .25
40 Greg Carmona .08 .25
41 Mark Clark .20 .50
42 Stan Clarke .08 .25
43 Paul Coleman .08 .25
44 Todd Crosby .08 .25
45 Brad DuVall .08 .25
46 John Ericks .08 .25
47 Ben Figueroa .08 .25
48 Terry Francona .20 .50
49 Ed Fulton .20 .50
50 Bernard Gilkey .60 1.50
51 Ernie Camacho .08 .25
52 Mike Hinkle .08 .25
53 Ray Lankford 3.00 8.00
54 Julian Martinez .08 .25
55 Jesus Mendez .08 .25
56 Mike Milchin .08 .25
57 Mauricio Nunez .08 .25
58 Omar Olivares .60 1.50
59 Geronimo Pena .08 .25
60 Mike Perez .08 .25
61 Gaylen Pitts MG .08 .25
62 Mark Riggins CO .08 .25
63 Tim Sherrill .08 .25
64 Roy Silver .08 .25
65 Ray Stephens .08 .25
66 Craig Wilson .08 .25

1991 Cardinals Police

This 24-card police set was sponsored by the Kansas City Life Insurance Company and distributed by Greater St. Louis Law Enforcement Agencies. The cards measure approximately 2 5/8" by 4 1/8" and feature on the fronts a mix of posed and action color player photos with white borders. The cards are checklisted below by uniform number.

COMPLETE SET (24) 5.00 12.00
1 Ozzie Smith 1.25 3.00
7 Geronimo Pena .20 .50
9 Joe Torre MG .60 1.50
10 Rex Hudler .30 .75
11 Jose Oquendo .20 .50
12 Craig Wilson .20 .50
16 Ray Lankford .75 2.00
19 Tom Pagnozzi .20 .50
21 Gerald Perry .20 .50
23 Bernard Gilkey .30 .75
25 Milt Thompson .20 .50
27 Todd Zeile .60 1.50
28 Pedro Guerrero .40 1.00
29 Rich Gedman .20 .50
34 Felix Jose .20 .50
35 Frank DiPino .20 .50
36 Bryn Smith .20 .50
37 Scott Terry .20 .50
38 Todd Worrell .40 1.00
39 Bob Tewksbury .20 .50
43 Ken Hill .20 .50
47 Lee Smith .40 1.00
48 Jose DeLeon .20 .50
49 Juan Agosto .20 .50

1992 Cardinals McDonald's/Pacific

Produced by Pacific, this 55-card standard-size set commemorates the 100th anniversary of the St. Louis Cardinals. The collection was available at McDonald's restaurants in the greater St. Louis area for 1.49 with a purchase, and was distributed to raise money for Ronald McDonald Children's Charities. The set features black-and-white and color action player photos of players throughout Cardinals' history. The pictures are bordered in gold and include the player's name, the Cardinals 100th anniversary logo, and the McDonald's logo. The back design consists of a posed player photo, biographical and statistical information, and a career summary. There was also an album issued to go with this set. The album is not widely available at this time.

COMPLETE SET (55) 15.00 40.00
1 Jim Bottomley .40 1.00
2 Rip Collins .08 .25
3 Johnny Mize .40 1.00
4 Rogers Hornsby .60 1.50
5 Miller Huggins .40 1.00
6 Marty Marion .30 .75
7 Frank Frisch .40 1.00
8 Whitey Kurowski .08 .25
9 Joe Medwick .40 1.00
10 Terry Moore .30 .75
11 Chick Hafey .40 1.00
12 Pepper Martin .30 .75
13 Bob O'Farrell .08 .25
14 Walker Cooper .08 .25
15 Dizzy Dean .75 2.00
16 Grover C. Alexander .60 1.50
17 Jesse Haines .40 1.00
18 Bill Hallahan .08 .25
19 Mort Cooper .08 .25
20 Burleigh Grimes .40 1.00
21 Red Schoendienst .60 1.50
22 Stan Musial 3.00 8.00
23 Enos Slaughter .60 1.50
24 Keith Hernandez .30 .75
25 Bill White .30 .75
26 Orlando Cepeda .40 1.00
27 Julian Javier .20 .50
28 Dick Groat .20 .50
29 Ken Boyer .40 1.00
30 Lou Brock .60 1.50
31 Mike Shannon .20 .50
32 Curt Flood .30 .75
33 Joe Cunningham .20 .50
34 Reggie Smith .20 .50
35 Ted Simmons .30 .75
36 Tim McCarver .30 .75
37 Tom Herr .08 .25
38 Ozzie Smith 3.00 8.00
39 Joe Torre .40 1.00
40 Terry Pendleton .30 .75
41 Ken Reitz .08 .25
42 Vince Coleman .08 .25
43 Willie McGee .40 1.00
44 Bake McBride .08 .25
45 George Hendrick .08 .25
46 Bob Gibson .60 1.50
47 Whitey Herzog MG .30 .75
48 Harry Brecheen .20 .50
49 Howard Pollet .08 .25
50 John Tudor .08 .25
51 Bob Forsch .08 .25
52 Bruce Sutter .60 1.50
53 Lee Smith .30 .75
54 Todd Worrell .20 .50
55 Al Hrabosky .08 .25
XX Album 2.00 5.00
NNO Checklist .08 .25

1992 Cardinals Police

This 26-card set commemorates the 100th anniversary of the Cardinals. The set was sponsored by the Kansas City Life Insurance Company and distributed by the Greater St. Louis Law Enforcement Agencies. The cards measure 2 5/8" by 4 1/8" and feature color action player photos with white borders. The cards are unnumbered and checklisted below in alphabetical order.

COMPLETE SET (27) 4.00 10.00
1 Juan Agosto .08 .25
2 Cris Carpenter .08 .25
3 Jose DeLeon .08 .25
4 Andres Galarraga .60 1.50
5 Rich Gedman .08 .25
6 Bernard Gilkey .08 .25
7 Pedro Guerrero .20 .50
8 Rex Hudler .20 .50
9 Felix Jose .08 .25
10 Ray Lankford .40 1.00
11 Joe Magrane .08 .25
12 Omar Olivares .08 .25
13 Jose Oquendo .08 .25
14 Tom Pagnozzi .08 .25
15 Geronimo Pena .08 .25
16 Gerald Perry .08 .25
17 Bryn Smith .08 .25
18 Lee Smith .30 .75
19 Ozzie Smith 1.25 3.00
20 Scott Terry .08 .25
21 Bob Tewksbury .08 .25
22 Milt Thompson .08 .25
23 Joe Torre MG .40 1.00
24 Craig Wilson .08 .25
25 Todd Worrell .20 .50
26 Todd Zeile .40 1.00
27 Checklist .08 .25

1993 Cardinals Police

Sponsored by the Kansas City Life Insurance Company, the 26 cards comprising this set measure 2 5/8" by 4" and feature on their fronts blue-bordered color player action photos. The cards are unnumbered and checklisted below in alphabetical order.

COMPLETE SET (26) 3.00 8.00
1 Luis Alicea .08 .25
2 Rene Arocha .08 .25
3 Rod Brewer .08 .25
4 Ozzie Canseco .08 .25
5 Rheal Cormier .08 .25
6 Bernard Gilkey .08 .25
7 Gregg Jefferies .08 .25
8 Brian Jordan .40 1.00
9 Ray Lankford .40 1.00
10 Rob Murphy .08 .25
11 Omar Olivares .08 .25
12 Jose Oquendo .08 .25
13 Donovan Osborne .08 .25
14 Tom Pagnozzi .08 .25
15 Geronimo Pena .08 .25
16 Mike Perez .08 .25
17 Gerald Perry .08 .25
18 Stan Royer .08 .25
19 Lee Smith .30 .75
20 Ozzie Smith 1.25 3.00
21 Bob Tewksbury .08 .25
22 Joe Torre MG .40 1.00
23 Hector Villanueva .08 .25
24 Tracy Woodson .08 .25
25 Todd Zeile .40 1.00
26 Checklist .08 .25

1993 Cardinals Stadium Club

This 30-card standard-size set features the 1993 St. Louis Cardinals. The set was issued in hobby (plastic box) and retail (blister) form.

COMP. FACT SET (30) 1.50 4.00
1 Ozzie Smith .75 2.00
2 Rene Arocha .02 .10
3 Bernard Gilkey .02 .10
4 Jose Oquendo .02 .10
5 Mike Perez .02 .10
6 Tom Pagnozzi .02 .10
7 Rod Brewer .02 .10
8 Joe Magrane .02 .10
9 Todd Zeile .08 .25
10 Bob Tewksbury .02 .10
11 Darrel Deak .02 .10
12 Gregg Jefferies .02 .10
13 Lee Smith .08 .25
14 Ozzie Canseco .02 .10
15 Tom Urbani .02 .10
16 Donovan Osborne .02 .10
17 Ray Lankford .20 .50
18 Rheal Cormier .02 .10
19 Allen Watson .02 .10
20 Geronimo Pena .02 .10
21 Rob Murphy .02 .10
22 Tracy Woodson .02 .10
23 Basil Shabazz .02 .10
24 Omar Olivares .02 .10
25 Brian Jordan .30 .75
26 Les Lancaster .02 .10
27 Sean Lowe .02 .10
28 Hector Villanueva .02 .10
29 Brian Barber .02 .10
30 Aaron Holbert .02 .10

1994 Cardinals Magnets GM

This six-card set featues color action player photos in white borders. The cards are actually magnets that measure approximately 2" by 3". The last two cards of the set were released sparingly because of the Baseball strike of 1994.

COMPLETE SET (6) 8.00 20.00
COMMON CARD (1-4) .80 2.00
COMMON CARD (5-6) 2.00 5.00
1 Ozzie Smith 3.00 8.00
2 Gregg Jefferies .75 2.00
3 Bob Tewksbury .75 2.00
4 Ray Lankford 1.50 4.00
5 Rene Arocha 2.00 5.00
6 Tom Pagnozzi 2.00 5.00

1994 Cardinals Police

Measuring approximately 2 5/8" by 4", this 26-card set was sponsored by Kansas City Life Insurance Company and distributed by Greater St. Louis Law Enforcement Agencies. The cards are unnumbered and checklisted below in alphabetical order.

COMPLETE SET (26) 2.50 6.00
1 Luis Alicea .08 .25
2 Rene Arocha .08 .25
3 Rich Batchelor .08 .25
4 Rheal Cormier .08 .25
5 Bernard Gilkey .08 .25
6 Gregg Jefferies .08 .25
7 Brian Jordan .40 1.00
8 Paul Kilgus .08 .25
9 Ray Lankford .30 .75
10 Rob Murphy .08 .25
11 Omar Olivares .08 .25
12 Jose Oquendo .08 .25
13 Tom Pagnozzi .08 .25
14 Erik Pappas .08 .25
15 Geronimo Pena .08 .25
16 Mike Perez .08 .25
17 Gerald Perry .08 .25
18 Stan Royer .08 .25
19 Ozzie Smith 1.00 2.50
20 Rick Sutcliffe .20 .50
21 Bob Tewksbury .08 .25
22 Joe Torre MG .40 1.00
23 Tom Urbani .08 .25
24 Allen Watson .08 .25
25 Mark Whiten .08 .25
26 Todd Zeile .30 .75

1996 Cardinals Police

This 26-card set measures approximately 2 1/2" by 4". The player's photo, name and uniform number are notated on the front. The back has vital statistics, career stats and a safety tip. The cards are unnumbered so we have sequenced them in alphabetical order.

COMPLETE SET (26) 3.00 8.00
1 Alan Benes .08 .25
2 Andy Benes .08 .25
3 Pat Borders .08 .25
4 Royce Clayton .08 .25
5 Dennis Eckersley .50 1.25
6 Tony Fossas .08 .25
7 Fredbird CL .08 .25
Mascot
8 Ron Gant .20 .50
9 Gary Gaetti .20 .50
10 Mike Gallego .08 .25
11 Rick Honeycutt .08 .25
12 Danny Jackson .08 .25
13 Brian Jordan .20 .50
14 Ray Lankford .30 .75
15 Tony LaRussa MG .40 1.00
16 John Mabry .08 .25
17 T.J. Mathews .08 .25
18 Willie McGee .40 1.00
19 Mike Morgan .08 .25
20 Donovan Osborne .08 .25
21 Tom Pagnozzi .08 .25
22 Mark Petkovsek .08 .25
23 Ozzie Smith 1.00 2.50
24 Todd Stottlemyre .08 .25
25 Mark Sweeney .08 .25
26 Tom Urbani .08 .25

1997 Cardinals Police

Measuring approximately 2 5/8" by 4", this 27-card set was sponsored by Kansas City Life Insurance Company and distributed by Greater St. Louis Law Enforcement Agencies. The fronts feature color action player photos in white borders. The backs carry biographical information, statistics, and a picture illustrating a public service announcement. The cards are unnumbered and checklisted below in alphabetical order.

COMPLETE SET (27) 4.00 10.00
1 Alan Benes .08 .25
2 Andy Benes .08 .25
3 Royce Clayton .08 .25
4 Delino DeShields .20 .50
5 Dennis Eckersley .50 1.25
6 Tony Fossas .08 .25
7 Fredbird(Mascot) CL .08 .25
8 Gary Gaetti .20 .50
9 Ron Gant .20 .50
10 Rick Honeycutt .08 .25
11 Danny Jackson .08 .25
12 Brian Jordan .30 .75
13 Tom Lampkin .08 .25
14 Ray Lankford .20 .50
15 Tony La Russa MG .40 1.00
16 Eric Ludwick .08 .25
17 John Mabry .08 .25
18 T.J. Mathews .08 .25
19 Willie McGee .40 1.00
20 Donovan Osborne .08 .25
21 Tom Pagnozzi .08 .25
22 Mark Petkovsek .08 .25
23 Steve Scarsone .08 .25
24 Danny Sheaffer .08 .25
25 Todd Stottlemyre .08 .25
26 Mark Sweeney .08 .25
27 Dmitri Young .30 .75

1998-09 Cardinals Fox Sports

Issued over a series of years, these standard size cards were designed to do promotions for the Fox Sports Network regional coverage of the St. Louis Cardinals. Apparently issued at a rate of one card per year, the front features a Cardinal star while the back features information about that player. This checklist is incomplete and any additional information is appreciated.

2 Mark McGwire 1.25 3.00
5 Albert Pujols 2.50 6.00
10 Fredbird Mascot .40 1.00
13 Tony LaRussa MG .60 1.50
15 Albert Pujols 2.50 6.00

1998 Cardinals Hunter

This three item card and pin set features three of the most famous personages in St Louis Cardinal history. The blank-backed card featured a photo, and a brief biography of the person featured. There is also an ad for "Hunter Meats". Since these items are unnumbered, we have sequenced them in alphabetical order.

COMPLETE SET (3) 4.00 10.00
1 Jack Buck ANN .75 2.00
2 Bob Gibson 1.50 4.00
3 Stan Musial 2.00 5.00

1998 Cardinals Score

This 15-card set was issued in special retail packs and features color photos of the St. Louis Cardinals team. The backs carry player information. A special platinum parallel set was also issued and randomly inserted in packs.

COMPLETE SET (15) 3.00 8.00
*PLATINUM: 5X BASIC CARDS
1 Andy Benes .08 .25
2 Todd Stottlemyre .08 .25
3 Dennis Eckersley .50 1.25
4 Mark McGwire .75 2.00
5 Dmitri Young .30 .75
6 Ron Gant .20 .50
7 Mike Difelice .08 .25
8 Ray Lankford .20 .50
9 John Mabry .08 .25
10 Royce Clayton .08 .25
11 Alan Benes .08 .25
12 Delino DeShields .08 .25
13 Brian Jordan .20 .50
14 Gary Gaetti .20 .50
15 Matt Morris .40 1.00

1999 Cardinals Safety

This 26 card set features members of the St Louis Cardinals and was sponsored by the Kansas City Life Insurance Company. The fronts of most of these cards feature blurry photos with the words "Cardinals 99" on top and the player name and uniform number on the bottom. The backs give some biographical information and a life aphorism. Since these cards are unnumbered we have sequenced them in alphabetical order.

COMPLETE SET (26) 4.00 10.00
1 Juan Acevedo .08 .25
2 Manny Aybar .08 .25
3 Alan Benes .08 .25
4 Ricky Bottalico .08 .25
5 Kent Bottenfield .08 .25
6 Darren Bragg .08 .25
7 Alberto Castillo .08 .25
8 Eric Davis .20 .50
9 J.D.Drew .40 1.00
10 Shawon Dunston .08 .25
11 John Frascatore .08 .25
12 David Howard .08 .25
13 Ray Lankford .20 .50
14 Tony LaRussa MG .40 1.00
15 Eli Marrero .08 .25
16 Joe McEwing .08 .25
17 Willie McGee .40 1.00
18 Mark McGwire .75 2.00
19 Kent Mercker .08 .25
20 Matt Morris .30 .75
21 Darren Oliver .08 .25
22 Donovan Osborne .08 .25
23 Lance Painter .08 .25
24 Scott Radinsky .08 .25
25 Edgar Renteria .40 1.00
26 Fernando Tatis .08 .25

1999 Cardinals Upper Deck McDonald's

These 15 standard-size cards were available through St. Louis are McDonald restaurants. The cards are similar in design to the 1999 Upper Deck MVP sets.

COMPLETE SET (15) 3.00 8.00
1 J.D. Drew .40 1.00
2 Jose Jiminez .08 .25
3 Mark McGwire .40 1.00
4 Fernando Tatis .08 .25
5 Edgar Renteria .40 1.00
6 Ray Lankford .20 .50
7 Willie McGee .40 1.00
8 Ricky Bottalico .08 .25
9 Eli Marrero .08 .25
10 Kent Bottenfield .08 .25
11 Eric Davis .20 .50
12 Darren Bragg .08 .25
13 Joe McEwing .08 .25
14 Shawon Dunston .08 .25
15 Darren Oliver .08 .25

1999 Cardinals Upper Deck McDonald's McGwire Milestones

This nine-card set honoring Mark McGwire was an insert into the 1999 Cardinal Upper Deck packs available in the St. Louis area. The horizontal cards feature a photo of McGwire against a silvery background. The words "McGwire Milestones" are printed in red and the word milestone is printed in a continous line along the bottom of the card. The back has a black box describing a key homer of 1998 and at the bottom there is a description of three various homer highlights of his career.

COMPLETE SET (M1-M9) 10.00 25.00
COMMON CARD (M1-M9) 1.20 3.00

2000 Cardinals McDonald's

COMPLETE SET (4) 16.00 40.00
1 Jim Edmonds 4.00 10.00
2 Willie McGee 4.00 10.00
3 Mark McGwire 5.00 12.00
4 Fernando Vina 2.00 5.00

2001 Cardinals McDonald's

1 Darryl Kile 3.00 8.00
June 18th, 2001
2 Mike Matheny 3.00 8.00
April 28th, 2001
3 Albert Pujols 8.00 20.00
August 18th, 2001

2001 Cardinals Safety

COMPLETE SET 4.00 10.00
1 Rick Ankiel .10 .25
2 Alan Benes .10 .25
3 Andy Benes .10 .25
4 Bobby Bonilla .20 .50
5 Jack Buck ANN .40 1.00
6 Jason Christiansen .10 .25
7 J.D. Drew .30 .75
8 Jim Edmonds .40 1.00
9 Dustin Hermanson .10 .25
10 Carlos Hernandez .10 .25
11 Mike James .10 .25
12 Darryl Kile .10 .25
13 Steve Kline .10 .25
14 Ray Lankford .30 .75
15 Tony LaRussa MG .20 .50
16 Mike Matheny .10 .25
17 Eli Marrero .10 .25
18 Mark McGwire .60 1.50
19 Matt Morris .20 .50
20 Craig Paquette .10 .25
21 Placido Polanco .10 .25
22 Edgar Renteria .20 .50
23 Larry Sutton .10 .25
24 Mike Timlin .10 .25
25 Dave Veres .10 .25
26 Fernando Vina .10 .25
27 Fredbird .10 .25
Mascot

2002 Cardinals Christian Family Day

NNO Albert Pujols 1.25 3.00

2002 Cardinals Safety

COMPLETE SET 4.00 8.00
1 Rick Ankiel .20 .50
2 Andy Benes .08 .25
3 Mike Difelice .08 .25
4 J.D. Drew .40 1.00
5 Jim Edmonds .40 1.00
6 Luther Hackman .08 .25
7 Jason Isringhausen .08 .25
8 Darryl Kile .20 .50
9 Steve Kline .08 .25
10 Tony LaRussa MG .40 1.00
11 Eli Marrero .08 .25
12 Tino Martinez .30 .75
13 Mike Matheny .08 .25
14 Mike Matthews .08 .25
15 Matt Morris .30 .75
16 Placido Polanco .20 .50
17 Albert Pujols 1.00 2.50
18 Edgar Renteria .40 1.00
19 Kerry Robinson .08 .25
20 Bud Smith .08 .25
21 Gene Stechschulte .08 .25
22 Garrett Stephenson .08 .25
23 Mike Timlin .08 .25
24 Dave Veres .08 .25
25 Fernando Vina .08 .25
26 Woody Williams .08 .25
27 Fredbird (Mascot) .08 .25

2003 Cardinals Safety

COMPLETE SET 4.00 10.00
1 Miguel Cairo .10 .25
2 J.D. Drew .30 .75
3 Jim Edmonds .40 1.00
4 Jeff Fassero .10 .25
5 Joe Girardi .20 .50
6 Dustin Hermanson .10 .25
7 Jason Isringhausen .30 .75
8 Steve Kline .10 .25
9 Tony LaRussa MG .40 1.00
10 Eli Marrero .10 .25
11 Tino Martinez .30 .75
12 Mike Matheny .10 .25
13 Matt Morris .30 .75
14 Orlando Palmeiro .10 .25
15 Eduardo Perez .10 .25
16A Albert Pujols .75 2.00
Batting Stance
16B Albert Pujols .75 2.00
Follow-Through
17 Edgar Renteria .40 1.00
18 Kerry Robinson .10 .25
19 Scott Rolen .60 1.50
20 Jason Simontacchi .10 .25
21 Russ Springer .10 .25
22 Garrett Stephenson .10 .25
23 Brett Tomko .10 .25
24 Fernando Vina .10 .25
25 Woody Williams .10 .25
26 Fredbird .10 .25
Mascot

2004 Cardinals Police

COMPLETE SET 4.00 10.00
1 Marlon Anderson .10 .25
2 Kiko Calero .10 .25
3 Chris Carpenter .15 .40
4 Jim Edmonds .15 .40
5 Cal Eldred .10 .25
6 Dan Haren .10 .25
7 Bo Hart .10 .25
8 Jason Isringhausen .10 .25
9 Ray King .10 .25
10 Steve Kline .10 .25
11 Tony LaRussa MG .15 .40
12 Mike Lincoln .10 .25
13 Jason Marquis .10 .25
14 Mike Matheny .10 .25
15 Matt Morris .10 .25
16 Albert Pujols .30 .75
17 Edgar Renteria .10 .25
18 Scott Rolen .15 .40
19 Reggie Sanders .10 .25
20 Jason Simontacchi .10 .25
21 Jeff Suppan .10 .25
22 So Taguchi .10 .25
23 Julian Tavarez .10 .25
24 Woody Williams .10 .25
25 Busch Stadium .10 .25
26 Fredbird Mascot .10 .25

2005 Cardinals Police

COMP[LETE SET 2.00 5.00
1 Fredbird .10 .25
Mascot
2 Abraham Nunez .10 .25
3 Albert Pujols .30 .75
4 Hector Luna .10 .25
5 Mark Grudzielanek .10 .25
6 Tony LaRussa MG .15 .40
7 Jim Edmonds .15 .40
8 Reggie Sanders .10 .25
9 Jason Marquis .10 .25
10 David Eckstein .10 .25
11 Cal Eldred .10 .25
12 Scott Rolen .15 .40
13 Chris Carpenter .15 .40
14 Mark Mulder .10 .25
15 Roger Cedeno .10 .25
16 Larry Walker .15 .40
17 Matt Morris .10 .25
18 Mike Lincoln .10 .25
19 Jeff Suppan .10 .25
20 Bill Pulsipher .10 .25
21 Jason Isringhausen .10 .25
22 Yadier Molina 1.00 2.50
23 John Mabry .10 .25
24 Julian Tavarez .10 .25
25 Ray King .10 .25
26 Carmen Cali .10 .25
27 So Taguchi .10 .25

2006 Cardinals Police

COMPLETE SET (27) 2.00 5.00
1 Gary Bennett .10 .25
2 Larry Bigbie .10 .25
3 Chris Carpenter .15 .40
4 Deivi Cruz .10 .25
5 David Eckstein .10 .25
6 Jim Edmonds .15 .40
7 Juan Encarnacion .10 .25
8 Randy Flores .10 .25
9 Fredbird• .10 .25
10 Jason Isringhausen .10 .25
11 Tony LaRussa MG .15 .40
12 Braden Looper .10 .25
13 Hector Luna .10 .25
14 Jason Marquis .10 .25
15 Yadier Molina .30 .75
16 Mark Mulder .10 .25
17 Sidney Ponson .10 .25
18 Albert Pujols .30 .75
19 Anthony Reyes .10 .25
20 Ricardo Rincon .10 .25
21 John Rodriguez .10 .25
22 Scott Rolen .15 .40
23 Junior Spivey .10 .25
24 Jeff Suppan .10 .25
25 So Taguchi .10 .25
26 Brad Thompson .10 .25
27 Adam Wainwright .15 .40

2006 Cardinals Topps

COMPLETE SET (14) 3.00 8.00
STL1 Albert Pujols .40 1.00
STL2 Chris Carpenter .20 .50
STL3 Scott Rolen .20 .50
STL4 Jim Edmonds .20 .50
STL5 David Eckstein .12 .30
STL6 So Taguchi .12 .30
STL7 Mark Mulder .12 .30
STL8 Yadier Molina .40 1.00
STL9 Jason Isringhausen .12 .30
STL10 Jason Marquis .12 .30
STL11 Jeff Suppan .12 .30
STL12 John Rodriguez .12 .30
STL13 Sidney Ponson .12 .30
STL14 Edwin Encarnacion .30 .75

2006 Cardinals Upper Deck World Series Champions

1 Ronnie Belliard .20 .50
2 Gary Bennett .20 .50
3 Chris Carpenter .30 .75
4 Chris Duncan .30 .75
5 David Eckstein .20 .50
6 Jim Edmonds .30 .75
7 Juan Encarnacion .20 .50
8 Randy Flores .20 .50
9 Josh Hancock .20 .50
10 Tyler Johnson .20 .50
11 Josh Kinney .20 .50
12 Braden Looper .20 .50
13 Aaron Miles .20 .50
14 Yadier Molina .60 1.50
15 Albert Pujols .60 1.50
16 Anthony Reyes .20 .50
17 John Rodriguez .20 .50
18 Scott Rolen .30 .75
19 Jeff Suppan .20 .50
20 Scott Spiezio .20 .50
21 So Taguchi .20 .50
22 Brad Thompson .20 .50
23 Adam Wainwright .30 .75
24 Jeff Weaver .20 .50
25 Preston Wilson .20 .50

2006 Cardinals Upper Deck World Series Champions Jumbo

WSCC Cardinals Team Photo .40 1.00

2006 Cardinals Upper Deck World Series Champions Memorable Moments

MM1 Albert Pujols .60 1.50
MM2 Juan Encarnacion .20 .50
MM3 So Taguchi .20 .50
MM4 Jeff Suppan .20 .50
MM5 Albert Pujols .60 1.50
MM6 Yadier Molina .60 1.50
MM7 Anthony Reyes .20 .50
MM8 David Eckstein .20 .50
MM9 Jeff Weaver .20 .50

2006 Cardinals Upper Deck World Series Champions MVP

MVP1 David Eckstein .20 .50

2006 Cardinals Upper Deck World Series Champions Season Highlights

SH1 Scott Rolen .30 .75
SH2 Mark Mulder .20 .50
SH3 Albert Pujols .60 1.50
SH4 Albert Pujols .60 1.50
SH5 Chris Carpenter .30 .75
SH6 Juan Encarnacion .20 .50
SH7 Adam Wainwright .30 .75
SH8 Yadier Molina .60 1.50
SH9 So Taguchi .20 .50
SH10 Jeff Suppan .20 .50
SH11 Jim Edmonds .30 .75
SH12 Chris Duncan .30 .75
SH13 Scott Spiezio .20 .50
SH14 Scott Rolen .30 .75
SH15 Ronnie Belliard .20 .50

2007 Cardinals Police

COMPLETE SET (27) 2.00 5.00
1 Gary Bennett .10 .25
2 Chris Carpenter .15 .40
3 Chris Duncan .10 .25
4 David Eckstein .10 .25
5 Jim Edmonds .15 .40
6 Juan Encarnacion .10 .25
7 Randy Flores .10 .25
8 Fredbird .10 .25
9 Josh Hancock .10 .25
10 Jason Isringhausen .10 .25
11 Tyler Johnson .10 .25
12 Adam Kennedy .10 .25
13 Tony LaRussa MG .15 .40
14 Braden Looper .10 .25
15 Aaron Miles .10 .25
16 Yadier Molina .30 .75
17 Mark Mulder .10 .25
18 Albert Pujols .30 .75
19 Anthony Reyes .10 .25
20 Scott Rolen .15 .40
21 Skip Schumaker .10 .25
22 Scott Spiezio .10 .25
23 So Taguchi .10 .25
24 Brad Thompson .10 .25
25 Adam Wainwright .15 .40
26 Kip Wells .10 .25
27 Preston Wilson .10 .25

2007 Cardinals Topps

COMPLETE SET (14) 3.00 8.00
STL1 Albert Pujols .40 1.00
STL2 Scott Rolen .20 .50
STL3 Jason Isringhausen .12 .30
STL4 So Taguchi .12 .30
STL5 Jim Edmonds .20 .50
STL6 Chris Duncan .12 .30
STL7 Yadier Molina .40 1.00
STL8 Anthony Reyes .12 .30
STL9 Adam Wainwright .20 .50
STL10 Chris Carpenter .20 .50
STL11 Juan Encarnacion .12 .30
STL12 Kip Wells .12 .30
STL13 Adam Kennedy .12 .30
STL14 Scott Rolen .20 .50

2008 Cardinals Police

COMPLETE SET (27) 2.00 5.00
1 Rick Ankiel .10 .25
2 Chris Carpenter .15 .40
3 Matt Clement .10 .25
4 Chris Duncan .10 .25
5 Randy Flores .10 .25
6 Ryan Franklin .10 .25
7 Fredbird .10 .25
8 Troy Glaus .15 .40
9 Jason Isringhausen .10 .25
10 Cesar Isturis .10 .25
11 Tyler Johnson .10 .25
12 Adam Kennedy .10 .25
13 Jason Larue .10 .25
14 Tony LaRussa MG .15 .40
15 Braden Looper .10 .25
16 Ryan Ludwick .10 .25
17 Aaron Miles .10 .25
18 Yadier Molina .30 .75
19 Mark Mulder .10 .25
20 Joel Pineiro .10 .25
21 Albert Pujols .30 .75
22 Brendan Ryan .10 .25
23 Skip Schumaker .10 .25
24 Russ Springer .10 .25
25 Brad Thompson .10 .25
26 Adam Wainwright .15 .40
27 Todd Wellemeyer .10 .25

2008 Cardinals Topps

COMPLETE SET (14) 3.00 8.00
STL1 Albert Pujols .40 1.00
STL2 Troy Glaus .20 .50
STL3 Jason Isringhausen .12 .30
STL4 Ryan Ludwick .12 .30
STL5 Anthony Reyes .12 .30
STL6 Chris Duncan .12 .30
STL7 Yadier Molina .40 1.00
STL8 Braden Looper .12 .30
STL9 Adam Wainwright .20 .50
STL10 Chris Carpenter .20 .50
STL11 Rick Ankiel .12 .30
STL12 Scott Spiezio .12 .30
STL13 Adam Kennedy .12 .30
STL14 Brendan Ryan .12 .30

2009 Cardinals All-Star Topps

COMPLETE SET (15) 3.00 8.00
STL1 Albert Pujols .60 1.50
STL2 Chris Carpenter .30 .75
STL3 Ryan Ludwick .30 .75
STL4 Adam Wainwright .30 .75
STL5 Yadier Molina .60 1.50
STL6 Chris Duncan .20 .50
STL7 Rick Ankiel .20 .50
STL8 Joel Pineiro .20 .50
STL9 Troy Glaus .20 .50
STL10 Chris Perez .20 .50
STL11 Brendan Ryan .20 .50
STL12 Todd Wellemeyer .20 .50
STL13 Skip Schumaker .20 .50
STL14 Khalil Greene .20 .50
STL15 Fredbird .20 .50

2009 Cardinals Topps

STL1 Albert Pujols .50 1.25
STL2 Chris Carpenter .25 .60
STL3 Ryan Ludwick .25 .60
STL4 Adam Wainwright .25 .60
STL5 Yadier Molina .50 1.25
STL6 Chris Duncan .15 .40
STL7 Rick Ankiel .15 .40
STL8 Joel Pineiro .15 .40
STL9 Troy Glaus .15 .40
STL10 Chris Perez .15 .40
STL11 Brendan Ryan .15 .40
STL12 Todd Wellemeyer .15 .40
STL13 Skip Schumaker .15 .40
STL14 Khalil Greene .15 .40
STL15 Fredbird .15 .40

2010 Cardinals Topps

STL1 Albert Pujols .50 1.25
STL2 Ryan Franklin .15 .40
STL3 Skip Schumaker .15 .40
STL4 Kyle Lohse .15 .40
STL5 Tyler Greene .15 .40
STL6 Colby Rasmus .25 .60
STL7 Jason LaRue .15 .40
STL8 Adam Wainwright .25 .60
STL9 Matt Holliday .40 1.00
STL10 Julio Lugo .15 .40
STL11 Chris Carpenter .25 .60
STL12 Ryan Ludwick .15 .40
STL13 Jason Motte .15 .40
STL14 Yadier Molina .50 1.25
STL15 Brendan Ryan .15 .40
STL16 Todd Wellemeyer .15 .40
STL17 David Freese .25 .60

2011 Cardinals Topps

STL1 Albert Pujols .50 1.25
STL2 Chris Carpenter .25 .60
STL3 Allen Craig .30 .75
STL4 Ryan Franklin .15 .40
STL5 David Freese .15 .40
STL6 Jaime Garcia .25 .60
STL7 Matt Holliday .40 1.00
STL8 Jon Jay .15 .40
STL9 Yadier Molina .50 1.25
STL10 Colby Rasmus .25 .60
STL11 Skip Schumaker .15 .40
STL12 Adam Wainwright .25 .60
STL13 Jake Westbrook .15 .40
STL14 Pedro Feliz .15 .40
STL15 Lance Berkman .25 .60
STL16 Ryan Theriot .15 .40
STL17 Busch Stadium .15 .40

2012 Cardinals Topps

STL1 David Freese .25 .60
STL2 Jon Jay .40 1.00
STL3 Matt Holliday .40 1.00
STL4 Carlos Beltran .30 .75
STL5 Yadier Molina .50 1.25
STL6 Chris Carpenter .30 .75
STL7 Allen Craig .30 .75
STL8 Skip Schumaker .25 .60
STL9 Rafael Furcal .25 .60
STL10 Adam Wainwright .30 .75
STL11 Kyle Lohse .25 .60
STL12 Lance Berkman .30 .75
STL13 Daniel Descalso .25 .60
STL14 Jaime Garcia .30 .75
STL15 Jason Motte .25 .60
STL16 Fredbird .15 .40
STL17 Busch Stadium .15 .40

2013 Cardinals Topps

COMPLETE SET (17) 3.00 8.00
STL1 Matt Holliday .40 1.00
STL2 Adam Wainwright .30 .75
STL3 Carlos Beltran .20 .50
STL4 Chris Carpenter .20 .50
STL5 Shelby Miller .60 1.50
STL6 David Freese .25 .60
STL7 Yadier Molina .30 .75
STL8 Rafael Furcal .25 .60
STL9 Jaime Garcia .20 .50
STL10 Jason Motte .25 .60
STL11 Daniel Descalso .15 .40
STL12 Jake Westbrook .15 .40
STL13 Lance Lynn .15 .40
STL14 Jon Jay .25 .60
STL15 Allen Craig .20 .50
STL16 Trevor Rosenthal .50 1.25
STL17 Matt Carpenter .25 .60

2014 Cardinals Topps

COMPLETE SET (17) 3.00 8.00
STL1 Matt Holliday .25 .60
STL2 Adam Wainwright .20 .50
STL3 Kolten Wong .20 .50
STL4 Joe Kelly .15 .40
STL5 Shelby Miller .20 .50
STL6 Jhonny Peralta .15 .40
STL7 Yadier Molina .30 .75
STL8 Peter Bourjos .15 .40
STL9 Matt Carpenter .25 .60
STL10 Carlos Martinez .20 .50
STL11 Matt Adams .15 .40
STL12 Michael Wacha .20 .50
STL13 Lance Lynn .15 .40
STL14 Jon Jay .15 .40
STL15 Allen Craig .20 .50
STL16 Trevor Rosenthal .20 .50
STL17 Busch Stadium .15 .40

2015 Cardinals Topps

COMPLETE SET (17) 3.00 8.00
SLC1 Adam Wainwright .20 .50
SLC2 Jon Jay .15 .40
SLC3 Lance Lynn .15 .40
SLC4 Jason Heyward .20 .50
SLC5 Jhonny Peralta .15 .40
SLC6 Trevor Rosenthal .20 .50
SLC7 Michael Wacha .20 .50
SLC8 Matt Carpenter .25 .60
SLC9 Carlos Martinez .20 .50
SLC10 Matt Holliday .25 .60
SLC11 Yadier Molina .30 .75
SLC12 Matt Adams .15 .40
SLC13 Peter Bourjos .15 .40
SLC14 John Lackey .20 .50
SLC15 Kolten Wong .20 .50
SLC16 Jaime Garcia .15 .40
SLC17 Sam Freeman .15 .40

2016 Cardinals Topps

COMPLETE SET (17) 3.00 8.00
STL1 Yadier Molina .30 .75
STL2 Matt Adams .15 .40
STL3 Kolten Wong .20 .50
STL4 Jhonny Peralta .15 .40
STL5 Matt Carpenter .25 .60
STL6 Matt Holliday .25 .60
STL7 Randal Grichuk .15 .40
STL8 Stephen Piscotty .25 .60
STL9 Jedd Gyorko .15 .40
STL10 Mike Leake .15 .40
STL11 Michael Wacha .20 .50
STL12 Carlos Martinez .20 .50
STL13 Adam Wainwright .20 .50
STL14 Trevor Rosenthal .20 .50
STL15 Tommy Pham .15 .40
STL16 Kevin Siegrist .15 .40
STL17 Jaime Garcia .15 .40

2017 Cardinals Topps

COMPLETE SET (17) 3.00 8.00
STL1 Yadier Molina .30 .75
STL2 Jhonny Peralta .15 .40
STL3 Matt Carpenter .25 .60
STL4 Stephen Piscotty .20 .50
STL5 Carlos Martinez .20 .50
STL6 Jedd Gyorko .15 .40
STL7 Kolten Wong .20 .50
STL8 Randal Grichuk .15 .40
STL9 Alex Reyes .20 .50
STL10 Seung-Hwan Oh .30 .75
STL11 Michael Wacha .20 .50
STL12 Trevor Rosenthal .20 .50
STL13 Aledmys Diaz .20 .50
STL14 Adam Wainwright .20 .50
STL15 Jonathan Broxton .15 .40
STL16 Matt Adams .15 .40
STL17 Brandon Moss .15 .40

2018 Cardinals Topps

COMPLETE SET (17) 2.50 6.00
SC1 Yadier Molina .30 .75
SC2 Harrison Bader .25 .60
SC3 Alex Reyes .20 .50
SC4 Kolten Wong .20 .50
SC5 Randal Grichuk .15 .40
SC6 Dexter Fowler .20 .50
SC7 Marcell Ozuna .25 .60
SC8 Jedd Gyorko .15 .40
SC9 Greg Garcia .15 .40
SC10 Jack Flaherty .60 1.50
SC11 Tommy Pham .15 .40
SC12 Matt Carpenter .25 .60
SC13 Adam Wainwright .20 .50
SC14 Michael Wacha .20 .50
SC15 Carlos Martinez .20 .50
SC16 Paul DeJong .25 .60
SC17 Seung-hwan Oh .20 .50

2019 Cardinals Topps

COMPLETE SET (17) 2.50 6.00
SC1 Yadier Molina .30 .75
SC2 Matt Carpenter .25 .60
SC3 Marcell Ozuna .25 .60
SC4 Paul DeJong .25 .60
SC5 Kolten Wong .20 .50
SC6 Harrison Bader .20 .50
SC7 Dexter Fowler .20 .50
SC8 Carlos Martinez .20 .50
SC9 Miles Mikolas .25 .60
SC10 Jack Flaherty .25 .60
SC11 Michael Wacha .20 .50
SC12 Jedd Gyorko .15 .40
SC13 Jose Martinez .20 .50
SC14 Jordan Hicks .20 .50
SC15 John Gant .15 .40

SC16 Adam Wainwright .20 .50
SC17 Paul Goldschmidt .25 .60

2020 Cardinals Topps

STL1 Paul Goldschmidt .25 .60
STL2 Yadier Molina .30 .75
STL3 Paul DeJong .25 .60
STL4 Kolten Wong .20 .50
STL5 Carlos Martinez .20 .50
STL6 Miles Mikolas .15 .40
STL7 Jack Flaherty .25 .60
STL8 Harrison Bader .20 .50
STL9 Dexter Fowler .20 .50
STL10 Marcell Ozuna .25 .60
STL11 Matt Carpenter .25 .60
STL12 Tommy Edman .25 .60
STL13 Adam Wainwright .20 .50
STL14 Andrew Miller .20 .50
STL15 Jose Martinez .15 .40
STL16 Dakota Hudson .20 .50
STL17 Tyler O'Neill .20 .50

2017 Cardinals Topps National® Baseball Card Day

COMPLETE SET (10) 6.00 15.00
STL1 Matt Carpenter 1.00 2.50
STL2 Aledmys Diaz .75 2.00
STL3 Randal Grichuk .60 1.50
STL4 Carlos Martinez .75 2.00
STL5 Yadier Molina 1.25 3.00
STL6 Seung-Hwan Oh 1.25 3.00
STL7 Dexter Fowler .75 2.00
STL8 Stephen Piscotty .75 2.00
STL9 Adam Wainwright .75 2.00
STL10 Ozzie Smith 1.25 3.00

2011 Cardinals Topps World Series Champions

COMPLETE SET (27) 6.00 15.00
COMMON CARD .20 .50
WS1 Albert Pujols .60 1.50
WS2 Nick Punto .20 .50
WS3 David Freese .20 .50
WS4 Rafael Furcal .20 .50
WS5 Lance Berkman .30 .75
WS6 Jon Jay .20 .50
WS7 Matt Holliday .50 1.25
WS8 Yadier Molina .60 1.50
WS9 Ryan Theriot .20 .50
WS10 Allen Craig .40 1.00
WS11 Adron Chambers .20 .50
WS12 Kyle Lohse .20 .50
WS13 Jaime Garcia .30 .75
WS14 Chris Carpenter .30 .75
WS15 Edwin Jackson .20 .50
WS16 Fernando Salas .30 .75
WS17 Skip Schumaker .20 .50
WS18 Jason Motte .20 .50
WS19 Daniel Descalso .20 .50
WS20 Octavio Dotel .20 .50
WS21 NLDS Highlight .20 .50
WS22 NLDS Highlight .20 .50
WS23 NLCS Highlight .20 .50
WS24 NLCS Highlight .20 .50
WS25 WS Highlight .20 .50
WS26 WS Highlight .20 .50
WS27 Tony LaRussa MG .30 .75

1993 Cardtoons

This 115-card unlicensed standard-size set was distributed in eight-card packs with a suggested retail of $1.29. The set uses fanciful cartoon caricatures on its fronts to parody major league baseball players. The borderless cartoons are framed by a thin gold-colored line that terminates in gold-colored baseball icons, which set off the "player's" name at the bottom. The backs carry comical "career highlights" within silver-colored panels on the left sides and team logo caricatures on the right sides. Cards numbered 1-95 were drawn by sports artist Dayne Dudley. The checklist below contains the base set and two subsets called Politics in Baseball (S1-S11) and Field of Greed (FOG1-FOG9). Cards S1-S11 features cartoons by cartoonist Dave Simpson and carries his views of baseball in 1993. Cards FOG1-FOG9 belong to the subset Field of Greed which fitted together to form a nine-piece puzzle. Even though this set does not have a license, it is listed since the company won a suit that allows it to be released as a parody under first admendment rules. The complete set price includes the two subsets.

COMPLETE SET (115) 10.00 25.00
COMMON CARD (1-95) .04 .10
COMMON CARD (S1-S11) .40 1.00
COMMON CARD (FOG1-FOG9) .10 .25
1 Hey Abbott .08 .25
2 Robin Adventura .08 .25
3 Roberto Alamode .30 .75
4 Don Battingly .30 .75
5 Cow Belle .30 .75
6 Jay Bellhop .02 .10
7 Fowl Boggs .30 .75
8 Treasury Bonds .30 .75
9 True Brett .30 .75
10 Wild Pitch Mitch .02 .10
11 Balou's Brothers .02 .10
12 Charlie Bustle .08 .25
13 Brett Butter .02 .10
14 Rambo Canseco .20 .50
15 Roberto Cementie .60 1.50
16 Roger Clemency .30 .75
17 Will Clock .02 .10
18 David Clone .08 .25
19 Tom Clowning .02 .10
20 Mr. Club .20 .50
21 Joe Crater .08 .25
22 Doolin' Daulton .08 .25
23 Chili Dog Davis .08 .25
24 Doug Drawback .02 .10
25 Dennis Excellency .08 .25
26 Silly Fanatic .02 .10
27 Wand Gonzales .30 .75
28 Amazing Grace .20 .50
29 Tom Grapevine .08 .25
30 Marquis Gruesome .08 .25
31 Homerin' Hank .30 .75
32 Kevin Happier .02 .10
33 Pete Harness .02 .10
34 Charlie Haze .02 .10
35 Egotisticky Henderson .20 .50
36 Sayanora Infielder .02 .10
37 Snoozin' Ted & Tarzan Jane .02 .10
38 Cloud Johnson .02 .10
39 Sandy K-Fax .30 .75
40 The Say What Kid .30 .75
41 Tommy Lasagna .08 .25
42 Greg Maddogs .50 1.25
43 Stamp the Man .20 .50
44 Mark McBash .60 1.50
45 Fred McGruff .08 .25
46 Mount Mick .75 2.00
47 Pat Moustache .02 .10
48 Ozzie Myth .30 .75
49 Bob Nukesbury .02 .10
50 Reggie October .30 .75
51 Doctor OK .08 .25
52 Rafael Palmist .20 .50
53 Lose Pinella .02 .10
54 Vince Poleman .02 .10
55 Charlie Puff .02 .10
56 Rob Quibble .02 .10
57 Darryl Razzberry .02 .10
58 Cal Ripkenwinkle .60 1.50
59 Budge Rodriguez .30 .75
60 Ryne Sandbox .30 .75
61 Steve Saxophone .02 .10
62 Harry Scaray .02 .10
63 Scary Shefield .20 .50
64 Ruben Siesta .02 .10
65 Dennis Smartinez .02 .10
66 Lee Smite .08 .25
67 Ken Spiffy Jr. .75 2.00
68 Nails Spikestra .02 .10
69 The Splendid Spinner .60 1.50
70 Toad Stottlemyre .02 .10
71 Raging Tartabull .02 .10
72 Robbery Thompson .02 .10
73 Alan Trampoline .08 .25
74 Monster Truk .02 .10
75 Shawon Tungsten .02 .10
76 Tony Twynn .30 .75
77 Andy Van Tyke .02 .10
78 Derrick Ventriloquist .02 .10
79 Frankie Violin .02 .10
80 Rap Winfielder .30 .75
81 Robinhood Yount .30 .75
82 Swift Justice .02 .10
83 Brat Saberhagen .02 .10
84 Mike Pizzazz .50 1.25
85 Andres Colorado .08 .25
86 Money Bagswell .50 1.25
87 Video Nomo .60 1.50
88 Out of the Park .02 .10
89 Tim Wallet .02 .10
90 Checklist .02 .10
91 Greenback Jack .02 .10
92 Mighty Matt Power Hitter .02 .10
93 Frankenthomas .75 2.00
94 Neon Peon Slanders .30 .75
95 Just Air Jordan 1.00 2.50
FOG1 Strike 1/(Top left of puzzle) .08 .25
FOG2 Strike 2/(Top middle of puzzle) .08 .25
FOG3 Strike 3/(Top right of puzzle) .08 .25
FOG4 Strike 4/(Middle left of puzzle) .08 .25
FOG5 Strike 5/(Middle of puzzle) .08 .25
FOG6 Strike 6/(Middle right of puzzle) .08 .25
FOG7 Strike 7/(Bottom left of puzzle .08 .25
FOG8 Strike 8/(Bottom middle of puzzle).08 .25
FOG9 Strike 9/(Bottom right of puzzle) .08 .25
S1 Pledge of Allegiance .40 1.00
S2 The Wave .40 1.00
S3 Slick Willie .40 1.00
S4 Umpires Convention .40 1.00
S5 The Slide .40 1.00
S6 SH-H-H-H-H-H-H .40 1.00
S7 Throwing Out the First Contract .40 1.00
S8 Babe Rush 1.25 3.00
S10 Let's Play Ball .40 1.00
S11 Role Model .40 1.00
S9 Hot Prospect .40 1.00

1985 CBS Radio Sports

This standard-size set was issued in a six-card pack (complete set) to promote both the telecasts of the CBS Baseball Network and those people announcing the games. Since these cards are unnumbered, we have sequenced them in alphabetical order

COMPLETE SET 12.50 30.00
1 Johnny Bench 10.00 25.00
2 Brent Musberger .75 2.00
3 Lindsey Nelson .75 2.00
4 John Rooney .75 2.00
5 Dick Stockton .75 2.00
6 Bill White 2.00 5.00

1990 CBS/Fox Video

This one card set which measures 3" by 5" features information about three movies which CBS/Fox had released in video form. There is some basic information about each movie along with a photo of the featured star. The other side features a different photo of the star in an old style baseball card format

1 Pride of the Yankees 1.25 3.00
Gary Cooper
Babe Ruth Story

2008 Americana Celebrity Cuts

COMPLETE SET (100) 125.00 200.00
STATED PRINT RUN 499 SERIAL #'d SETS
*CENTURY SILVER/50: .6X TO 1.5X BASE
*CENTURY GOLD/25: .75X TO 2X BASE
UNPRICED CENTURY PLATINUM #'d TO 1
37 Jackie Robinson 2.00 5.00
53 Lou Gehrig 2.00 5.00
81 Stan Musial 2.00 5.00
86 Ted Williams 3.00 8.00
96 Willie Mays 2.00 5.00

2008 Americana Celebrity Cuts Century Material

RANDOM INSERTS IN PACKS
PRINT RUNS B/WN 5-100 COPIES
NO PRICING ON QTY OF 5
37 Jackie Robinson/100 10.00 25.00
53 Lou Gehrig/50 40.00 80.00
81 Stan Musial/100 8.00 20.00
96 Willie Mays/100 10.00 25.00

2008 Americana Celebrity Cuts Century Material Prime

RANDOM INSERTS IN PACKS
PRINT RUNS B/WN 1-50 COPIES PER
NO PRICING ON QTY OF 12 OR LESS
37 Jackie Robinson/50 30.00 60.00
53 Lou Gehrig/5
81 Stan Musial/12
96 Willie Mays/50 12.50 30.00

2008 Americana Celebrity Cuts Century Material Combo

RANDOM INSERTS IN PACKS
PRINT RUNS B/WN 5-50 COPIES PER
NO PRICING ON QTY OF 10 OR LESS
37 Jackie Robinson/50 15.00 40.00
53 Lou Gehrig/50 50.00 100.00
81 Stan Musial/50 10.00 25.00
86 Ted Williams/10
96 Willie Mays/50 12.50 30.00

2008 Americana Celebrity Cuts Century Signature Gold

RANDOM INSERTS IN PACKS
PRINT RUNS B/WN 1-200 COPIES PER
NO PRICING ON QTY OF 14 OR LESS
81 Stan Musial/100 30.00 60.00
96 Willie Mays/50 60.00 120.00

2008 Americana Celebrity Cuts Century Signature Material

RANDOM INSERTS IN PACKS
PRINT RUNS B/WN 1-50 COPIES PER
NO PRICING ON QTY OF 14 OR LESS
81 Stan Musial/50 30.00 60.00
96 Willie Mays/50 75.00 150.00

2008 Americana Celebrity Cuts Century Signature Material Prime

96 Willie Mays/50 75.00 150.00

1989 Cereal Superstars

This 12-card, standard-size set was issued by MSA (Michael Schechter Associates) and celebrates some of the baseball's best players as of 1989. The sets have an attractive design of stars in each of the front corners with the word Superstars on the top of the card and players name, team, and position underneath the full color photo of the player. Like most of the MSA sets there are no team logos used. The vertically oriented backs show career statistics. Reportedly two cards were included in each specially marked Ralston Purina cereal box.

COMPLETE SET (12) 5.00 12.00
1 Ozzie Smith 1.25 3.00
2 Andre Dawson .60 1.50
3 Darryl Strawberry .20 .50
4 Mike Schmidt .75 2.00
5 Orel Hershiser .08 .25
6 Tim Raines .20 .50
7 Roger Clemens 1.50 4.00
8 Kirby Puckett .75 2.00
9 George Brett 1.25 3.00
10 Alan Trammell .60 1.50
11 Don Mattingly 1.50 4.00
12 Jose Canseco .60 1.50

2019 Certified

RANDOM INSERTS IN PACKS
*GREEN: 1X TO 2.5X
*BLUE/99: 1.2X TO 3X
*RED/25: 2.5X TO 6X
*MIRROR GOLD/25: 2.5X TO 6X
1 Mike Trout 1.25 3.00
2 Bryce Harper .40 1.00
3 Aaron Judge .60 1.50
4 Kris Bryant .30 .75
5 Shohei Ohtani .40 1.00
6 Yadier Molina .30 .75
7 Anthony Rizzo .30 .75
8 Mookie Betts .50 1.25
9 Ichiro .30 .75
10 Giancarlo Stanton .25 .60
11 Jose Altuve .20 .50
12 Christian Yelich .30 .75
13 Francisco Lindor .25 .60
14 Albert Pujols .30 .75
15 Joey Votto .25 .60
16 Cody Bellinger .50 1.25
17 Ronald Acuna Jr. 1.25 3.00
18 Khris Davis .25 .60
19 Brendan Rodgers .25 .60
20 Chris Paddack RC .30 .75
21 Eloy Jimenez RC .60 1.50
22 Fernando Tatis Jr. 2.00 5.00
23 Kyle Tucker RC .40 1.00
24 Michael Kopech RC .50 1.25
25 Pete Alonso RC 3.00 8.00
26 Yusei Kikuchi RC .25 .60
27 Christin Stewart RC .20 .50
28 Jeff McNeil RC .40 1.00
29 Mitch Keller RC .20 .50
30 Brandon Lowe RC .25 .60
31 Cole Tucker RC .25 .60
32 Michael Chavis RC .25 .60
33 Bryan Reynolds RC .50 1.25
34 Darwinzon Hernandez RC .15 .40
35 Vladimir Guerrero Jr. RC 3.00 8.00

2020 Certified

RANDOM INSERTS IN PACKS
1 Pete Alonso .60 1.50
2 Shun Yamaguchi RC .30 .75
3 Luis Robert RC 4.00 10.00
4 Giancarlo Stanton .25 .60
5 Kwang-Hyun Kim RC .50 1.25
6 Yadier Molina .30 .75
7 Yordan Alvarez RC 2.50 6.00
8 Bryce Harper .40 1.00
9 Brendan McKay RC .40 1.00
10 Bo Bichette RC 3.00 8.00
11 Aristides Aquino RC .60 1.50
12 Sean Murphy RC .40 1.00
13 Ronald Acuna Jr. 1.50 4.00
14 Mike Trout 2.00 5.00
15 Kris Bryant .30 .75
16 Juan Soto .75 2.00
17 Yoshitomo Tsutsugo RC .60 1.50
18 Robinson Cano .20 .50
19 Shogo Akiyama RC .40 1.00
20 Vladimir Guerrero Jr. .40 1.00
21 Cody Bellinger .50 1.25
22 Nolan Arenado .40 1.00
23 Aaron Judge .60 1.50
24 Christian Yelich .30 .75
25 Gavin Lux RC 1.25 3.00
26 Austin Riley .30 .75
27 Bobby Bradley RC .25 .60
28 Dillon Tate .15 .40
29 Brian Anderson .15 .40
30 Danny Mendick RC .30 .75

1964 Challenge The Yankees

These cards were distributed as part of a baseball game produced in 1964. The cards each measure 4" by 5 3/8" and have square corners. The card fronts show a small black and white inset photo of the player, his name, position, vital statistics and the game outcomes associated with that particular player's card. The colors used on the front of the card are a blue border at the top and a yellow background for the game outcomes at the bottom. The game was played by rolling two dice. The outcomes (two through twelve) on the player's card related to the sum of the two dice. The game was noted for slightly inflated offensive production compared to real life. The cards are blank backed. Since the cards are unnumbered, they are listed below in alphabetical order within group. The first 25 cards are Yankees and the next 25 are All-Stars. Sets were put out in two different years, WG9 1964 and WG10 1965, which are difficult to distinguish. An empty box of either set, with the game pieces intact, is valued at approximately $75.

COMPLETE SET (50) 350.00 700.00
1 Yogi Berra 15.00 40.00
2 Johnny Blanchard 2.00 5.00
3 Jim Bouton 3.00 8.00
4 Clete Boyer 2.50 6.00
5 Marshall Bridges 2.00 5.00
6 Harry Bright 2.00 5.00
7 Al Downing 2.00 5.00
8 Whitey Ford 12.50 30.00
9 Jake Gibbs 2.00 5.00
10 Pedro Gonzalez 2.00 5.00
11 Steve Hamilton 2.00 5.00
12 Elston Howard 4.00 10.00
13 Tony Kubek 4.00 10.00
14 Phil Linz 2.00 5.00
15 Hector Lopez 2.00 5.00
16 Mickey Mantle 150.00 300.00
17 Roger Maris 30.00 60.00
18 Tom Metcalf 2.00 5.00
19 Joe Pepitone 2.50 6.00
20 Hal Reniff 2.00 5.00
21 Bobby Richardson 4.00 10.00
22 Bill Stafford 2.00 5.00
23 Ralph Terry 2.50 6.00
24 Tom Tresh 2.50 6.00
25 Stan Williams 2.00 5.00
26 Hank Aaron 20.00 50.00
27 Tom Cheney 2.50 6.00
28 Del Crandall 2.50 6.00
29 Tito Francona 2.50 6.00
30 Dick Groat 2.50 6.00
31 Al Kaline 12.50 30.00
32 Art Mahaffey 2.50 6.00
33 Frank Malzone 2.50 6.00
34 Juan Marichal 8.00 20.00
35 Eddie Mathews 8.00 20.00
36 Bill Mazeroski 8.00 20.00
37 Ken McBride 2.50 6.00
38 Willie McCovey 8.00 20.00
39 Jim O'Toole 2.50 6.00
40 Milt Pappas 3.00 8.00
41 Ron Perranoski 2.50 6.00
42 Johnny Podres 3.00 8.00
43 Dick Radatz 2.50 6.00
44 Rich Rollins 2.50 6.00
45 Ron Santo 5.00 12.00
46 Moose Skowron 3.00 8.00
47 Duke Snider 15.00 40.00
48 Pete Ward 2.50 6.00
49 Carl Warwick 2.50 6.00
50 Carl Yastrzemski 15.00 40.00

1965 Challenge The Yankees

These cards were distributed as part of a baseball game produced in 1965. The cards each measure 4" by 5 3/8" and have square corners. The card fronts show a small black and white inset photo of the player, his name, position, vital statistics, and the game outcomes associated with that particular player's card. The colors used on the front of the card are a blue border at the top and a yellow background for the game outcomes at the bottom. The game was played by rolling two dice. The outcomes (two through twelve) on the player's card related to the sum of the two dice. The game was noted for slightly inflated offensive production compared to real life. The cards are blank backed. Since the cards are unnumbered, they are listed below in alphabetical order within group. The first 23 cards are Yankees and the next 25 are All-Stars. There were also 18 blank cards included in the set for extra players of your choice. These "Challenge The Yankees" sets were put out in two different years, WG9 1964 and WG10 1965, which are difficult to distinguish.

COMPLETE SET (48) 500.00 1000.00
1 Johnny Blanchard 4.00 10.00
2 Jim Bouton 6.00 15.00
3 Clete Boyer 5.00 12.00
4 Leon Carmel 4.00 10.00
5 Al Downing 4.00 10.00
6 Whitey Ford 15.00 40.00
7 Jake Gibbs 4.00 10.00
8 Pedro Gonzalez 4.00 10.00
9 Steve Hamilton 4.00 10.00
10 Elston Howard 8.00 20.00
11 Tony Kubek 8.00 20.00
12 Phil Linz 4.00 10.00
13 Mickey Mantle 200.00 400.00
14 Roger Maris 50.00 100.00
15 Tom Metcalf 4.00 10.00
16 Pete Mikkelsen 4.00 10.00
17 Joe Pepitone 5.00 12.00
18 Pedro Ramos 4.00 10.00
19 Hal Reniff 4.00 10.00
20 Bobby Richardson 8.00 20.00
21 Bill Stafford 4.00 10.00
22 Mel Stottlemyre 5.00 12.00
23 Tom Tresh 5.00 12.00
24 Henry Aaron 40.00 80.00
25 Joe Christopher 4.00 10.00
26 Vic Davalillo 4.00 10.00
27 Bill Freehan 5.00 12.00
28 Jim Gentile 4.00 10.00
29 Dick Groat 5.00 12.00
30 Al Kaline 20.00 50.00
31 Don Lock 4.00 10.00
32 Art Mahaffey 4.00 10.00
33 Frank Malzone 4.00 10.00
34 Juan Marichal 12.50 30.00
35 Eddie Mathews 12.50 30.00
36 Bill Mazeroski 12.50 30.00
37 Ken McBride 4.00 10.00
38 Tim McCarver 8.00 20.00
39 Willie McCovey 12.50 30.00
40 Jim O'Toole 4.00 10.00
41 Milt Pappas 5.00 12.00
42 Ron Perranoski 4.00 10.00
43 Johnny Podres 5.00 12.00
44 Dick Radatz 4.00 10.00
45 Rich Rollins 4.00 10.00
46 Ron Santo 8.00 20.00
47 Pete Ward 4.00 10.00
48 Carl Yastrzemski 30.00 60.00

1994 Dean Chance Snapple

This pin and card honor the 1964 Cy Young Award-Winning pitching ace Dean Chance. The diamond-shaped pin measures about one inch from corner to corner and features a posed color photo of Chance. The card is 2 1/2" by 5 1/8" and features on its white-bordered front a photo of Chance in his windup. His lifetime pitching record appears below the photo in an area set off by a perforated line. The Snapple and California Angels logo rest at the bottom. The plain white back carries career highlights and the Snapple and Angels logos.

1 Dean Chance .75 2.00

1982 Charboneau Super Joe's

This two-card set features a black-and-white portrait of Cleveland Indians player, Joe Charboneau, on two different size cards. The smaller card is standard size, and the larger one measures approximately 3 1/2" by 5 1/2". The cards are checklisted below with the smaller one listed first.

COMPLETE SET (2) 2.00 5.00
1 Joe Charboneau/(Standard size card) .75 2.00
2 Joe Charboneau/(3 1/2 by 5 1/2 size card) 1.25 3.00

1988 Chef Boyardee

This 24-card set was distributed as a perforated sheet of four rows and six columns of cards in return for ten proofs of purchase of Chef Boyardee products and 1.50 for postage and handling. The card photos on the fronts are in full color with a light blue border but are not shown with team logos. The card backs are numbered and printed in red and blue on gray card stock. Individual cards measure approximately 2 1/2" by 3 1/2" and show the Chef Boyardee logo in the upper right corner of the obverse. Card backs feature year-by-year season statistics since 1984. There is no additional premium for having the sheet intact as opposed to having individual cards neatly cut.

COMPLETE SET (24) 4.00 10.00
1 Mark McGwire .75 2.00
2 Eric Davis .20 .50
3 Jack Morris .20 .50
4 George Bell .08 .25
5 Ozzie Smith .60 1.50
6-Tony Gwynn .60 1.50
7 Cal Ripken 1.25 3.00
8 Todd Worrell .20 .50
9 Larry Parrish .08 .25
10 Gary Carter .40 1.00
11 Ryne Sandberg .40 1.00
12 Keith Hernandez .20 .50
13 Kirby Puckett .40 1.00
14 Mike Schmidt .40 1.00
15 Frank Viola .08 .25
16 Don Mattingly .60 1.50
17 Dale Murphy .30 .75
18A Andre Dawson .30 .75
18B Andre Dawson COR 4.00 10.00
19 Mike Scott .08 .25
20 Rickey Henderson .50 1.25
21 Jim Rice .20 .50
22 Wade Boggs .50 1.25
23 Roger Clemens .60 1.50
24 Fernando Valenzuela .20 .50

1961 Chemstrand Patches

This nine-card set features color star player portraits on 2 1/2" diameter cloth patches which were included with the purchase of a boy's sport shirt for a short period in 1961. The patches were issued one to a cello package with instructions for ironing the patch onto the shirt. The package also offered the opportunity to trade the player patch for a different star. The patches are unnumbered and checklisted below in alphabetical order. Values for unopened cello packs are slightly higher.

COMPLETE SET (9) 175.00 350.00
1 Ernie Banks 15.00 40.00
2 Yogi Berra 15.00 40.00
3 Nellie Fox 15.00 40.00
4 Dick Groat 8.00 20.00
5 Al Kaline 15.00 40.00
6 Harmon Killebrew 15.00 40.00
7 Frank Malzone 8.00 20.00
8 Willie Mays 40.00 80.00
9 Warren Spahn 15.00 40.00

1976 Chevy Prints

These four prints were drawn by Robert Thon, a noted historical illustrator and were commissioned by Chevrolet in honor of the 100th anniversary of the National League (and what is considered organized ball). The fronts feature four highligts from various times in baseball history and the backs have a description of these events.

COMPLETE SET (4) 4.00 10.00
1 The First Game .40 1.00
2 Pepper Martin .75 2.00
Bill Werber
The Gashouse Gang
3 Babe Ruth 2.00 5.00
The Mighty Babe
4 Hank Aaron 2.00 5.00
The Record Breaker

1976 Chicago Greats

This standard-size set features black-and-white action player photos with a red baseball and bat border design. A small, square close-up photo is superimposed on one of the upper corners of the picture. "Chicago's Greats" is printed in red at the bottom. The horizontal backs are white and carry the player's name, biographical information, statistics and career highlights. The cards are unnumbered and checklisted below in alphabetical order. The set was originally available for $2.50 from the producers.

COMPLETE SET (24) 5.00 12.00
1 Luke Appling .30 .75
2 Ernie Banks .60 1.50
3 Zeke Bonura .10 .25
4 Phil Cavarretta .20 .50
5 Jimmie Dykes .20 .50
6 Nellie Fox .40 1.00
7 Larry French .10 .25
8 Charlie Grimm .20 .50
9 Gabby Hartnett .40 1.00
10 Billy Herman .30 .75
11 Mike Kreevich .10 .25
12 Sherm Lollar .10 .25
13 Al Lopez .30 .75
14 Ted Lyons .20 .50
Red Faber
15 Minnie Minoso .30 .75
16 Wally Moses .10 .25
17 Bill Nicholson .10 .25
18 Claude Passeau .10 .25
19 Billy Pierce .20 .50
20 Ron Santo .30 .75
21 Hank Sauer .10 .25
22 Riggs Stephenson .20 .50
23 Bill Veeck OWN .30 .75
24 Philip K. Wrigley OWN .20 .50
25 Checklist .10 .25

1915 Chicago Tribune Supplements

These four newspaper supplements were issued by the Chicago Tribune. Based on the known date of the Eddie Collins card it is presumed that these supplements were supposed to increase interest in the upcoming baseball season. Since these are unnumbered, we have sequenced these in alphabetical order.

1 Roger Bresnahan
2 Eddie Collins (April 18)
3 Vic Saier
4 Joe Tinker

1994 Church's Hometown Stars

A pack containing four standard-size cards from the 28-card Hometown Stars set produced by Pinnacle was offered to consumers who bought a nine-piece family meal at Church's Chicken during April and May. Packs were also sold separately for 69 cents each. Each pack contained three regular cards and one gold foil-stamped card from the set. The gold foil cards are valued at two times the regular cards. A portion of the proceeds from card sales went to Habitat for Humanity, a national volunteer organization that helps families build their own homes. The cards are numbered on the back as "X of 28."

COMPLETE SET (28) 6.00 15.00
*GOLD CARDS: 2X BASIC CARDS
1 Brian McRae .08 .25
2 Dwight Gooden .20 .50
3 Ruben Sierra .20 .50
4 Greg Maddux 1.00 2.50
5 Kirby Puckett .50 1.25
6 Jeff Bagwell .60 1.50
7 Cal Ripken 1.50 4.00
8 Lenny Dykstra .08 .25
9 Tim Salmon .20 .50
10 Matt Williams .20 .50
11 Roberto Alomar .40 1.00
12 Barry Larkin .40 1.00
13 Roger Clemens .75 2.00
14 Mike Piazza 1.00 2.50
15 Travis Fryman .20 .50
16 Ryne Sandberg .60 1.50
17 Robin Ventura .20 .50
18 Gary Sheffield .50 1.25
19 Carlos Baerga .08 .25
20 Jay Bell .08 .25
21 Edgar Martinez .30 .75
22 Phil Plantier .08 .25
23 Danny Tartabull .08 .25
24 Marquis Grissom .08 .25
25 Robin Yount .50 1.25
26 Ozzie Smith .75 2.00
27 Ivan Rodriguez .50 1.25
28 Dante Bichette .20 .50

1994 Church's Show Stoppers

One of ten Show Stoppers cards was inserted in every fourth pack of 1994 Church's Chicken Stars of the Diamond four-card packs. The standard-size inserts were produced by Pinnacle using the "Dufex" printing process and highlight the major leagues' top home run hitters. The colorful metallic fronts feature color player action shots that appear to project from within home plate icons. Team logos are airbrushed away. The player's name appears at the lower right. The light blue back carries a color player head shot on the right, with the player's name, team, and career highlights shown alongside. Statistics for home runs, slugging percentage, and at bat/home run ratio appear near the bottom. The cards are numbered on the back as "X of 10."

COMPLETE SET (10) 8.00 20.00
1 Juan Gonzalez .40 1.00
2 Barry Bonds 2.00 5.00
3 Ken Griffey Jr. 2.50 6.00
4 David Justice .60 1.50
5 Frank Thomas 1.00 2.50
6 Fred McGriff .60 1.50
7 Albert Belle .20 .50
8 Joe Carter .40 1.00
9 Cecil Fielder .40 1.00
10 Mickey Tettleton .20 .50

1996 Circa

The 1996 Circa set (produced by Fleer/SkyBox) was issued in one series totalling 200 cards. The eight-card packs retailed for $1.99 each. The cards feature color action player photos on one of 28 different background designs and colors indicating the player's major league team. The checklist is grouped alphabetically by team with American League teams preceeding National League teams. The backs carry player information and statistics. Notable Rookie Cards include Darin Erstad and Chris Singleton.

COMPLETE SET (200) 10.00 25.00
1 Roberto Alomar .10 .30
2 Brady Anderson .07 .20
3 Rocky Coppinger RC .07 .20
4 Eddie Murray .20 .50
5 Mike Mussina .10 .30
6 Randy Myers .07 .20
7 Rafael Palmeiro .10 .30
8 Cal Ripken .60 1.50
9 Jose Canseco .10 .30
10 Roger Clemens .40 1.00
11 Mike Greenwell .07 .20
12 Tim Naehring .07 .20
13 John Valentin .07 .20
14 Mo Vaughn .07 .20
15 Tim Wakefield .07 .20
16 Jim Abbott .10 .30
17 Garret Anderson .07 .20
18 Jim Edmonds .07 .20
19 Darin Erstad RC .60 1.50
20 Chuck Finley .07 .20
21 Troy Percival .07 .20
22 Tim Salmon .10 .30
23 J.T. Snow .07 .20
24 Wilson Alvarez .07 .20
25 Harold Baines .07 .20
26 Ray Durham .07 .20
27 Alex Fernandez .07 .20
28 Tony Phillips .07 .20
29 Frank Thomas .20 .50
30 Robin Ventura .07 .20
31 Sandy Alomar Jr. .07 .20
32 Albert Belle .07 .20
33 Kenny Lofton .07 .20
34 Dennis Martinez .07 .20
35 Jose Mesa .07 .20
36 Charles Nagy .07 .20
37 Manny Ramirez .10 .30
38 Jim Thome .10 .30
39 Travis Fryman .07 .20
40 Bob Higginson .07 .20
41 Melvin Nieves .07 .20
42 Alan Trammell .07 .20
43 Kevin Appier .07 .20
44 Johnny Damon .10 .30
45 Keith Lockhart .07 .20
46 Jeff Montgomery .07 .20
47 Joe Randa .07 .20
48 Bip Roberts .07 .20
49 Ricky Bones .07 .20
50 Jeff Cirillo .07 .20
51 Marc Newfield .07 .20
52 Dave Nilsson .07 .20
53 Kevin Seitzer .07 .20
54 Ron Coomer .07 .20
55 Marty Cordova .07 .20
56 Roberto Kelly .07 .20
57 Chuck Knoblauch .07 .20
58 Paul Molitor .07 .20
59 Kirby Puckett .20 .50
60 Scott Stahoviak .07 .20
61 Wade Boggs .10 .30
62 David Cone .07 .20
63 Cecil Fielder .07 .20
64 Dwight Gooden .07 .20
65 Derek Jeter .50 1.25
66 Tino Martinez .10 .30
67 Paul O'Neill .10 .30
68 Andy Pettitte .10 .30
69 Ruben Rivera .07 .20
70 Bernie Williams .10 .30
71 Geronimo Berroa .07 .20
72 Jason Giambi .07 .20
73 Mark McGwire .50 1.25
74 Terry Steinbach .07 .20
75 Todd Van Poppel .07 .20
76 Jay Buhner .07 .20
77 Norm Charlton .07 .20
78 Ken Griffey Jr. .40 1.00
79 Randy Johnson .20 .50
80 Edgar Martinez .10 .30
81 Alex Rodriguez .40 1.00
82 Paul Sorrento .07 .20
83 Dan Wilson .07 .20
84 Will Clark .10 .30
85 Kevin Elster .07 .20
86 Juan Gonzalez .07 .20
87 Rusty Greer .07 .20
88 Ken Hill .07 .20
89 Mark McLemore .07 .20
90 Dean Palmer .07 .20
91 Roger Pavlik .07 .20
92 Ivan Rodriguez .10 .30
93 Joe Carter .07 .20
94 Carlos Delgado .07 .20
95 Juan Guzman .07 .20
96 John Olerud .07 .20
97 Ed Sprague .07 .20

98 Jermaine Dye .07 .20
99 Tom Glavine .10 .30
100 Marquis Grissom .07 .20
101 Andruw Jones .30 .75
102 Chipper Jones .20 .50
103 David Justice .07 .20
104 Ryan Klesko .07 .20
105 Greg Maddux .30 .75
106 Fred McGriff .10 .30
107 John Smoltz .10 .30
108 Brant Brown .07 .20
109 Mark Grace .10 .30
110 Brian McRae .07 .20
111 Ryne Sandberg .30 .75
112 Sammy Sosa .20 .50
113 Steve Trachsel .07 .20
114 Bret Boone .07 .20
115 Eric Davis .07 .20
116 Steve Gibralter .07 .20
117 Barry Larkin .10 .30
118 Reggie Sanders .07 .20
119 John Smiley .07 .20
120 Dante Bichette .07 .20
121 Ellis Burks .07 .20
122 Vinny Castilla .07 .20
123 Andres Galarraga .07 .20
124 Larry Walker .07 .20
125 Eric Young .07 .20
126 Kevin Brown .07 .20
127 Greg Colbrunn .07 .20
128 Jeff Conine .07 .20
129 Charles Johnson .07 .20
130 Al Leiter .07 .20
131 Gary Sheffield .07 .20
132 Devon White .07 .20
133 Jeff Bagwell .10 .30
134 Derek Bell .07 .20
135 Craig Biggio .10 .30
136 Doug Drabek .07 .20
137 Brian L.Hunter .07 .20
138 Darryl Kile .07 .20
139 Shane Reynolds .07 .20
140 Brett Butler .07 .20
141 Eric Karros .07 .20
142 Ramon Martinez .07 .20
143 Raul Mondesi .07 .20
144 Hideo Nomo .20 .50
145 Chan Ho Park .07 .20
146 Mike Piazza .30 .75
147 Moises Alou .07 .20
148 Yamil Benitez .07 .20
149 Mark Grudzielanek .07 .20
150 Pedro Martinez .10 .30
151 Henry Rodriguez .07 .20
152 David Segui .07 .20
153 Rondell White .07 .20
154 Carlos Baerga .07 .20
155 John Franco .07 .20
156 Bernard Gilkey .07 .20
157 Todd Hundley .07 .20
158 Jason Isringhausen .07 .20
159 Lance Johnson .07 .20
160 Alex Ochoa .07 .20
161 Rey Ordonez .07 .20
162 Paul Wilson .07 .20
163 Ron Blazier .07 .20
164 Ricky Bottalico .07 .20
165 Jim Eisenreich .07 .20
166 Pete Incaviglia .07 .20
167 Mickey Morandini .07 .20
168 Ricky Otero .07 .20
169 Curt Schilling .07 .20
170 Jay Bell .07 .20
171 Charlie Hayes .07 .20
172 Jason Kendall .07 .20
173 Jeff King .07 .20
174 Al Martin .07 .20
175 Alan Benes .07 .20
176 Royce Clayton .07 .20
177 Brian Jordan .07 .20
178 Ray Lankford .07 .20
179 John Mabry .07 .20
180 Willie McGee .07 .20
181 Ozzie Smith .30 .75
182 Todd Stottlemyre .07 .20
183 Andy Ashby .07 .20
184 Ken Caminiti .07 .20
185 Steve Finley .07 .20
186 Tony Gwynn .25 .60
187 Rickey Henderson .20 .50
188 Wally Joyner .07 .20
189 Fernando Valenzuela .07 .20
190 Greg Vaughn .07 .20
191 Rod Beck .07 .20
192 Barry Bonds .60 1.50
193 Shawon Dunston .07 .20
194 Chris Singleton RC .10 .30
195 Robby Thompson .07 .20
196 Matt Williams .07 .20
197 Barry Bonds CL .30 .75
198 Ken Griffey Jr. CL .25 .60
199 Cal Ripken CL .30 .75
200 Frank Thomas CL .10 .30

1996 Circa Rave

STATED ODDS 1:60
STATED PRINT RUN 150 SERIAL #'d SETS
78 Ken Griffey Jr. 50.00 120.00
198 Ken Griffey Jr. CL 50.00 120.00

1996 Circa Access

COMPLETE SET (30) 60.00 120.00
STATED ODDS 1:12
1 Cal Ripken 6.00 15.00
2 Mo Vaughn .75 2.00
3 Tim Salmon 1.25 3.00
4 Frank Thomas 2.00 5.00
5 Albert Belle .75 2.00
6 Kenny Lofton .75 2.00
7 Manny Ramirez 1.25 3.00
8 Paul Molitor .75 2.00
9 Kirby Puckett 2.00 5.00
10 Paul O'Neill 1.25 3.00
11 Mark McGwire 5.00 12.00
12 Ken Griffey Jr. 4.00 10.00
13 Randy Johnson 2.00 5.00
14 Greg Maddux 3.00 8.00
15 John Smoltz 1.25 3.00
16 Sammy Sosa 2.00 5.00
17 Barry Larkin 1.25 3.00
18 Gary Sheffield .75 2.00
19 Jeff Bagwell 1.25 3.00
20 Hideo Nomo 2.00 5.00
21 Mike Piazza 3.00 8.00
22 Moises Alou .75 2.00
23 Henry Rodriguez .75 2.00
24 Rey Ordonez .75 2.00
25 Jay Bell .75 2.00
26 Ozzie Smith 3.00 8.00
27 Tony Gwynn 2.50 6.00
28 Rickey Henderson 2.00 5.00
29 Barry Bonds 6.00 15.00
30 Matt Williams .75 2.00
P30 Matt Williams Promo .40 1.00

1996 Circa Boss

COMPLETE SET (50) 40.00 100.00
STATED ODDS 1:6
1 Roberto Alomar .60 1.50
2 Cal Ripken 3.00 8.00
3 Jose Canseco .60 1.50
4 Mo Vaughn .40 1.00
5 Tim Salmon .60 1.50
6 Frank Thomas 1.00 2.50
7 Robin Ventura .40 1.00
8 Albert Belle .40 1.00
9 Kenny Lofton .40 1.00
10 Manny Ramirez .60 1.50
11 Dave Nilsson .40 1.00
12 Chuck Knoblauch .40 1.00
13 Paul Molitor .40 1.00
14 Kirby Puckett 1.00 2.50
15 Wade Boggs .60 1.50
16 Dwight Gooden .40 1.00
17 Paul O'Neill .60 1.50
18 Mark McGwire 2.50 6.00
19 Jay Buhner .40 1.00
20 Ken Griffey Jr. 2.00 5.00
21 Randy Johnson 1.00 2.50
22 Will Clark .60 1.50
23 Juan Gonzalez .40 1.00
24 Joe Carter .40 1.00
25 Tom Glavine .60 1.50
26 Ryan Klesko .40 1.00
27 Greg Maddux 1.50 4.00
28 John Smoltz .60 1.50
29 Ryne Sandberg 1.50 4.00
30 Sammy Sosa 1.00 2.50
31 Barry Larkin .60 1.50
32 Reggie Sanders .40 1.00
33 Dante Bichette .40 1.00
34 Andres Galarraga .40 1.00
35 Charles Johnson .40 1.00
36 Gary Sheffield .40 1.00
37 Jeff Bagwell .60 1.50
38 Hideo Nomo 1.00 2.50
39 Mike Piazza 1.50 4.00
40 Moises Alou .40 1.00
41 Henry Rodriguez .40 1.00
42 Rey Ordonez .40 1.00
43 Ricky Otero .40 1.00
44 Jay Bell .40 1.00
45 Royce Clayton .40 1.00
46 Ozzie Smith 1.50 4.00
47 Tony Gwynn 1.25 3.00
48 Rickey Henderson 1.00 2.50
49 Barry Bonds 3.00 8.00
50 Matt Williams .40 1.00
P2 Cal Ripken Promo 1.25 3.00

1997 Circa

The 1997 Circa set (produced by Fleer/SkyBox) was issued in one series totalling 400 cards and was distributed in eight-card foil packs with a suggested retail price of $1.49. The set contains 393 player cards and seven checklist cards. The fronts feature color player photos with new in-your-face graphics that lift the player off the card. The backs carry in-depth player statistics and "Did you know" information. An Alex Rodriguez promo card (P100) was distributed to dealers. Rookie Cards include Brian Giles.

COMPLETE SET (400) 10.00 25.00
1 Kenny Lofton .07 .20
2 Ray Durham .07 .20
3 Mariano Rivera .20 .50
4 Jon Lieber .07 .20
5 Tim Salmon .10 .30
6 Mark Grudzielanek .07 .20
7 Neifi Perez .07 .20
8 Cal Ripken .60 1.50
9 John Olerud .07 .20
10 Edgar Renteria .07 .20
11 Jose Rosado .07 .20
12 Mickey Morandini .07 .20
13 Orlando Miller .07 .20
14 Ben McDonald .07 .20
15 Hideo Nomo .20 .50
16 Fred McGriff .10 .30
17 Sean Berry .07 .20
18 Roger Pavlik .07 .20
19 Aaron Sele .07 .20
20 Joey Hamilton .07 .20
21 Roger Clemens .40 1.00
22 Jose Herrera .07 .20
23 Ryne Sandberg .30 .75
24 Ken Griffey Jr. .40 1.00
25 Barry Bonds .60 1.50
26 Dan Naulty .07 .20
27 Wade Boggs .10 .30
28 Ray Lankford .07 .20
29 Rico Brogna .07 .20
30 Wally Joyner .07 .20
31 F.P. Santangelo .07 .20
32 Vinny Castilla .07 .20
33 Eddie Murray .20 .50
34 Kevin Elster .07 .20
35 Mike Macfarlane .07 .20
36 Jeff Kent .07 .20
37 Orlando Merced .07 .20
38 Jason Isringhausen .07 .20
39 Chad Ogea .07 .20
40 Greg Gagne .07 .20
41 Curt Lyons .07 .20
42 Mo Vaughn .07 .20
43 Rusty Greer .07 .20
44 Shane Reynolds .07 .20
45 Frank Thomas .20 .50
46 Chris Hoiles .07 .20
47 Scott Sanders .07 .20
48 Mark Lemke .07 .20
49 Fernando Vina .07 .20
50 Mark McGwire .50 1.25
51 Bernie Williams .10 .30
52 Bobby Higginson .07 .20
53 Kevin Tapani .07 .20
54 Rich Becker .07 .20
55 Felix Heredia RC .07 .20
56 Delino DeShields .07 .20
57 Rick Wilkins .07 .20
58 Edgardo Alfonzo .07 .20
59 Brett Butler .07 .20
60 Ed Sprague .07 .20
61 Joe Randa .07 .20
62 Ugueth Urbina .07 .20
63 Todd Greene .07 .20
64 Devon White .07 .20
65 Bruce Ruffin .07 .20
66 Mark Gardner .07 .20
67 Omar Vizquel .10 .30
68 Luis Gonzalez .07 .20
69 Tom Glavine .10 .30
70 Cal Eldred .07 .20
71 Wm. VanLandingham .07 .20
72 Jay Buhner .07 .20
73 James Baldwin .07 .20
74 Robin Jennings .07 .20
75 Terry Steinbach .07 .20
76 Billy Taylor .07 .20
77 Armando Benitez .07 .20
78 Joe Girardi .07 .20
79 Jay Bell .07 .20
80 Damon Buford .07 .20
81 Deion Sanders .10 .30
82 Bill Haselman .07 .20
83 John Flaherty .07 .20
84 Todd Stottlemyre .07 .20
85 J.T. Snow .07 .20
86 Felipe Lira .07 .20
87 Steve Avery .07 .20
88 Trey Beamon .07 .20
89 Alex Gonzalez .07 .20
90 Mark Clark .07 .20
91 Shane Andrews .07 .20
92 Randy Myers .07 .20
93 Gary Gaetti .07 .20
94 Jeff Blauser .07 .20
95 Tony Batista .07 .20
96 Todd Worrell .07 .20
97 Jim Edmonds .07 .20
98 Eric Young .07 .20
99 Roberto Kelly .07 .20
100 Alex Rodriguez .30 .75
101 Julio Franco .07 .20
102 Jeff Bagwell .10 .30
103 Bobby Witt .07 .20
104 Tino Martinez .10 .30
105 Shannon Stewart .07 .20
106 Brian Banks .07 .20
107 Eddie Taubensee .07 .20
108 Terry Mulholland .07 .20
109 Lyle Mouton .07 .20
110 Jeff Conine .07 .20
111 Johnny Damon .10 .30
112 Quilvio Veras .07 .20
113 Wilton Guerrero .07 .20
114 Dmitri Young .07 .20
115 Garret Anderson .07 .20
116 Bill Pulsipher .07 .20
117 Jacob Brumfield .07 .20
118 Mike Lansing .07 .20
119 Jose Canseco .10 .30
120 Mike Bordick .07 .20
121 Kevin Stocker .07 .20
122 Frankie Rodriguez .07 .20
123 Mike Cameron .07 .20
124 Tony Womack RC .10 .30
125 Bret Boone .07 .20
126 Moises Alou .07 .20
127 Tim Naehring .07 .20
128 Brant Brown .07 .20
129 Todd Zeile .07 .20
130 Dave Nilsson .07 .20
131 Donne Wall .07 .20
132 Jose Mesa .07 .20
133 Mark McLemore .07 .20
134 Mike Stanton .07 .20
135 Dan Wilson .07 .20
136 Jose Offerman .07 .20
137 David Justice .07 .20
138 Kirt Manwaring .07 .20
139 Raul Casanova .07 .20
140 Ron Coomer .07 .20
141 Dave Hollins .07 .20
142 Shawn Estes .07 .20
143 Darren Daulton .07 .20
144 Turk Wendell .07 .20
145 Darrin Fletcher .07 .20
146 Marquis Grissom .07 .20
147 Andy Benes .07 .20
148 Nomar Garciaparra .30 .75
149 Andy Pettitte .10 .30
150 Tony Gwynn .25 .60
151 Robb Nen .07 .20
152 Kevin Seitzer .07 .20
153 Ariel Prieto .07 .20
154 Scott Karl .07 .20
155 Carlos Baerga .07 .20
156 Wilson Alvarez .07 .20
157 Thomas Howard .07 .20
158 Kevin Appier .07 .20
159 Russ Davis .07 .20
160 Justin Thompson .07 .20
161 Pete Schourek .07 .20
162 John Burkett .07 .20
163 Roberto Alomar .10 .30
164 Darren Holmes .07 .20
165 Travis Miller .07 .20
166 Mark Langston .07 .20
167 Juan Guzman .07 .20
168 Pedro Astacio .07 .20
169 Mark Johnson .07 .20
170 Mark Leiter .07 .20
171 Heathcliff Slocumb .07 .20
172 Dante Bichette .07 .20
173 Brian Giles RC .40 1.00
174 Paul Wilson .07 .20
175 Eric Davis .07 .20
176 Charles Johnson .07 .20
177 Willie Greene .07 .20
178 Geronimo Berroa .07 .20
179 Mariano Duncan .07 .20
180 Robert Person .07 .20
181 David Segui .07 .20
182 Ozzie Guillen .07 .20
183 Osvaldo Fernandez .07 .20
184 Dean Palmer .07 .20
185 Bob Wickman .07 .20
186 Eric Karros .07 .20
187 Travis Fryman .07 .20
188 Andy Ashby .07 .20
189 Scott Stahoviak .07 .20
190 Norm Charlton .07 .20
191 Craig Paquette .07 .20
192 John Smoltz UER .10 .30
193 Orel Hershiser .07 .20
194 Glenallen Hill .07 .20
195 George Arias .07 .20
196 Brian Jordan .07 .20
197 Greg Vaughn .07 .20
198 Rafael Palmeiro .10 .30
199 Darryl Kile .07 .20
200 Derek Jeter .50 1.25
201 Jose Vizcaino .07 .20
202 Rick Aguilera .07 .20
203 Jason Schmidt .07 .20
204 Trot Nixon .07 .20
205 Tom Pagnozzi .07 .20
206 Mark Wohlers .07 .20
207 Lance Johnson .07 .20
208 Carlos Delgado .07 .20
209 Cliff Floyd .07 .20
210 Kent Mercker .07 .20
211 Matt Mieske .07 .20
212 Ismael Valdes .07 .20
213 Shawon Dunston .07 .20
214 Melvin Nieves .07 .20
215 Tony Phillips .07 .20
216 Scott Spiezio .07 .20
217 Michael Tucker .07 .20
218 Matt Williams .07 .20
219 Ricky Otero .07 .20
220 Kevin Ritz .07 .20
221 Darryl Strawberry .07 .20
222 Troy Percival .07 .20
223 Eugene Kingsale .07 .20
224 Julian Tavarez .07 .20
225 Jermaine Dye .07 .20
226 Jason Kendall .07 .20
227 Sterling Hitchcock .07 .20
228 Jeff Cirillo .07 .20
229 Roberto Hernandez .07 .20
230 Ricky Bottalico .07 .20
231 Bobby Bonilla .07 .20
232 Edgar Martinez .10 .30
233 John Valentin .07 .20
234 Ellis Burks .07 .20
235 Benito Santiago .07 .20
236 Terrell Wade .07 .20
237 Armando Reynoso .07 .20
238 Danny Graves .07 .20
239 Ken Hill .07 .20
240 Dennis Eckersley .07 .20
241 Darin Erstad .07 .20
242 Lee Smith UER .07 .20
243 Cecil Fielder .07 .20
244 Tony Clark .07 .20
245 Scott Erickson .07 .20
246 Bob Abreu .10 .30
247 Ruben Sierra .07 .20
248 Chili Davis .07 .20
249 Darryl Hamilton .07 .20
250 Albert Belle .07 .20
251 Todd Hollandsworth .07 .20
252 Terry Adams .07 .20
253 Rey Ordonez .07 .20
254 Steve Finley .07 .20
255 Jose Valentin .07 .20
256 Royce Clayton .07 .20
257 Sandy Alomar Jr. .07 .20
258 Mike Lieberthal .07 .20
259 Ivan Rodriguez .10 .30
260 Rod Beck .07 .20
261 Ron Karkovice .07 .20
262 Mark Gubicza .07 .20
263 Chris Holt .07 .20
264 Jaime Bluma UER .07 .20
265 Francisco Cordova .07 .20
266 Javy Lopez .07 .20
267 Reggie Jefferson .07 .20
268 Kevin Brown .07 .20
269 Scott Brosius .07 .20
270 Dwight Gooden .07 .20
271 Marty Cordova .07 .20
272 Jeff Brantley .07 .20
273 Joe Carter .07 .20
274 Todd Jones .07 .20
275 Sammy Sosa .20 .50
276 Randy Johnson .20 .50
277 B.J. Surhoff .07 .20
278 Chan Ho Park .07 .20
279 Jamey Wright .07 .20
280 Manny Ramirez .10 .30
281 John Franco .07 .20
282 Tim Worrell .07 .20
283 Scott Rolen .10 .30
284 Reggie Sanders .07 .20
285 Mike Fetters .07 .20
286 Tim Wakefield .07 .20
287 Trevor Hoffman .07 .20
288 Donovan Osborne .07 .20
289 Phil Nevin .07 .20
290 Jermaine Allensworth .07 .20
291 Rocky Coppinger .07 .20
292 Tim Raines .07 .20
293 Henry Rodriguez .07 .20
294 Paul Sorrento .07 .20
295 Tom Goodwin .07 .20
296 Raul Mondesi .07 .20
297 Allen Watson .07 .20
298 Derek Bell .07 .20
299 Gary Sheffield .07 .20
300 Paul Molitor .07 .20
301 Shawn Green .07 .20
302 Darren Oliver .07 .20
303 Jack McDowell .07 .20
304 Denny Neagle .07 .20
305 Doug Drabek .07 .20
306 Mel Rojas .07 .20
307 Andres Galarraga .07 .20
308 Alex Ochoa .07 .20
309 Gary DiSarcina .07 .20
310 Ron Gant .07 .20
311 Gregg Jefferies .07 .20
312 Ruben Rivera .07 .20
313 Vladimir Guerrero .20 .50
314 Willie Adams .07 .20
315 Bip Roberts .07 .20
316 Mark Grace .10 .30
317 Bernard Gilkey .07 .20
318 Marc Newfield .07 .20
319 Al Leiter .07 .20
320 Otis Nixon .07 .20
321 Tom Candiotti .07 .20
322 Mike Stanley .07 .20
323 Jeff Fassero .07 .20
324 Billy Wagner .07 .20
325 Todd Walker .07 .20
326 Chad Curtis .07 .20
327 Quinton McCracken .07 .20
328 Will Clark .10 .30
329 Andruw Jones .10 .30
330 Robin Ventura .07 .20
331 Curtis Pride .07 .20
332 Barry Larkin .10 .30
333 Jimmy Key .07 .20
334 David Wells .07 .20
335 Mike Holtz .07 .20
336 Paul Wagner .07 .20
337 Greg Maddux .30 .75
338 Curt Schilling .07 .20
339 Steve Trachsel .07 .20
340 John Wetteland .07 .20
341 Rickey Henderson .20 .50
342 Ernie Young .07 .20
343 Harold Baines .07 .20
344 Bobby Jones .07 .20
345 Jeff D'Amico .07 .20
346 John Mabry .07 .20
347 Pedro Martinez .10 .30
348 Mark Lewis .07 .20
349 Dan Miceli .07 .20
350 Chuck Knoblauch .07 .20
351 John Smiley .07 .20
352 Brady Anderson .07 .20
353 Jim Leyritz .07 .20
354 Al Martin .07 .20
355 Pat Hentgen .07 .20
356 Mike Piazza .30 .75
357 Charles Nagy .07 .20
358 Luis Castillo .07 .20
359 Paul O'Neill .10 .30
360 Steve Reed .07 .20
361 Tom Gordon .07 .20
362 Craig Biggio .10 .30
363 Jeff Montgomery .07 .20
364 Jamie Moyer .07 .20
365 Ryan Klesko .07 .20
366 Todd Hundley .07 .20
367 Bobby Estalella .07 .20
368 Jason Giambi .07 .20
369 Brian Hunter .07 .20
370 Ramon Martinez .07 .20
371 Carlos Garcia .07 .20
372 Hal Morris .07 .20
373 Juan Gonzalez .07 .20
374 Brian McRae .07 .20
375 Mike Mussina .10 .30
376 John Ericks .07 .20
377 Larry Walker .07 .20
378 Chris Gomez .07 .20
379 John Jaha .07 .20
380 Rondell White .07 .20
381 Chipper Jones .20 .50
382 David Cone .07 .20
383 Alan Benes .07 .20
384 Troy O'Leary .07 .20
385 Ken Caminiti .07 .20
386 Jeff King .07 .20
387 Mike Hampton .07 .20
388 Jaime Navarro .07 .20
389 Brad Radke .07 .20
390 Joey Cora .07 .20
391 Jim Thome .10 .30
392 Alex Fernandez .07 .20
393 Chuck Finley .07 .20
394 Andruw Jones CL .07 .20
395 Ken Griffey Jr. CL .25 .60
396 Frank Thomas CL .10 .30
397 Alex Rodriguez CL .20 .50
398 Cal Ripken CL .30 .75
399 Mike Piazza CL .20 .50
400 Greg Maddux CL .20 .50
P100 Alex Rodriguez Promo .75 2.00

1997 Circa Rave

*STARS: 25X TO 60X BASIC CARDS
*ROOKIES: 10X TO 25X BASIC CARDS
STATED ODDS 1:30 HOBBY

1997 Circa Boss

COMPLETE SET (20) 15.00 40.00
STATED ODDS 1:6
*SUPER BOSS: 1.5X TO 4X BASIC BOSS
SUPER BOSS STATED ODDS 1:36
1 Jeff Bagwell .40 1.00
2 Albert Belle .25 .60
3 Barry Bonds 2.00 5.00
4 Ken Caminiti .25 .60
5 Juan Gonzalez .25 .60
6 Ken Griffey Jr. 1.25 3.00
7 Tony Gwynn .75 2.00
8 Derek Jeter 1.50 4.00
9 Andruw Jones .40 1.00
10 Chipper Jones .60 1.50
11 Greg Maddux 1.00 2.50
12 Mark McGwire 1.50 4.00
13 Mike Piazza 1.00 2.50
14 Manny Ramirez .40 1.00
15 Cal Ripken 2.00 5.00
16 Alex Rodriguez 1.00 2.50
17 John Smoltz .40 1.00
18 Frank Thomas .60 1.50
19 Mo Vaughn .25 .60
20 Bernie Williams .40 1.00

1997 Circa Emerald Autographs

COMPLETE SET (6) 125.00 250.00
*EXCH CARDS: .1X TO .25X BASIC AUTO
EXCH CARDS STATED ODDS 1:1000 PACKS
100 Alex Rodriguez 40.00 100.00
241 Darin Erstad 6.00 15.00
251 Todd Hollandsworth 6.00 15.00
283 Scott Rolen 10.00 25.00
308 Alex Ochoa 6.00 15.00
325 Todd Walker 6.00 15.00

1997 Circa Fast Track

COMPLETE SET (10) 6.00 15.00
STATED ODDS 1:24
1 Vladimir Guerrero .60 1.50
2 Todd Hollandsworth .40 1.00
3 Derek Jeter 2.50 6.00
4 Andruw Jones .40 1.00
5 Chipper Jones 1.00 2.50
6 Andy Pettitte .60 1.50
7 Mariano Rivera 1.25 3.00
8 Alex Rodriguez 1.25 3.00
9 Scott Rolen .60 1.50
10 Todd Walker .40 1.00

1997 Circa Icons

COMPLETE SET (12) 40.00 100.00
STATED ODDS 1:36
1 Juan Gonzalez .75 2.00
2 Ken Griffey Jr. 6.00 15.00
3 Tony Gwynn 2.50 6.00
4 Derek Jeter 5.00 12.00
5 Chipper Jones 2.00 5.00
6 Greg Maddux 3.00 8.00
7 Mark McGwire 5.00 12.00
8 Mike Piazza 3.00 8.00
9 Cal Ripken 6.00 15.00
10 Alex Rodriguez 3.00 8.00
11 Frank Thomas 2.00 5.00
12 Matt Williams .75 2.00

1997 Circa Limited Access

COMPLETE SET (15) 12.00 30.00
STATED ODDS 1:18 RETAIL
1 Jeff Bagwell .60 1.50
2 Albert Belle .40 1.00
3 Barry Bonds 1.50 4.00
4 Juan Gonzalez .40 1.00
5 Ken Griffey Jr. 2.00 5.00
6 Tony Gwynn 1.00 2.50
7 Derek Jeter 2.50 6.00
8 Chipper Jones 1.00 2.50
9 Greg Maddux 1.50 4.00
10 Mark McGwire 1.50 4.00
11 Mike Piazza 1.00 2.50
12 Cal Ripken 3.00 8.00
13 Alex Rodriguez 1.25 3.00
14 Frank Thomas 1.00 2.50
15 Mo Vaughn .40 1.00

1997 Circa Rave Reviews

STATED ODDS 1:288
1 Albert Belle 2.50 6.00
2 Barry Bonds 20.00 50.00
3 Juan Gonzalez 2.50 6.00
4 Ken Griffey Jr. 20.00 50.00
5 Tony Gwynn 8.00 20.00
6 Greg Maddux 10.00 25.00
7 Mark McGwire 15.00 40.00
8 Eddie Murray 6.00 15.00
9 Mike Piazza 10.00 25.00
10 Cal Ripken 20.00 50.00
11 Alex Rodriguez 10.00 25.00
12 Frank Thomas 6.00 15.00

1998 Circa Thunder

The 1998 Circa Thunder set, produced by Fleer/SkyBox, was issued in one series totalling 300 cards. The eight-card packs retailed for $1.59 each. Collector's should take note that Marquis Grissom's card was erroneously numbered as 8 instead 280. Both Cal Ripken Jr. and Grissom are numbered as 8. In addition, a Cal Ripken promo card was issued prior to the product's public release. The card was distributed in dealer order forms and hobby media releases. It's identical in design to the standard Circa Thunder Ripken except for the text "PROMOTIONAL SAMPLE" written diagonally across the front and back of the card.

COMPLETE SET (300) 10.00 25.00
1 Ben Grieve .07 .20
2 Derek Jeter .50 1.25
3 Alex Rodriguez .30 .75
4 Paul Molitor .07 .20
5 Nomar Garciaparra .30 .75
6 Fred McGriff .10 .30
7 Kenny Lofton .07 .20
8 Cal Ripken .60 1.50
9 Matt Williams .07 .20
10 Chipper Jones .20 .50
11 Barry Larkin .10 .30
12 Steve Finley .07 .20
13 Billy Wagner .07 .20
14 Rico Brogna .07 .20
15 Tim Salmon .10 .30
16 Hideo Nomo .20 .50
17 Tony Clark .07 .20
18 Jason Kendall .07 .20
19 Juan Gonzalez .07 .20
20 Jeromy Burnitz .07 .20
21 Roger Clemens .40 1.00
22 Mark Grace .10 .30
23 Robin Ventura .07 .20
24 Manny Ramirez .10 .30
25 Mark McGwire .50 1.25
26 Gary Sheffield .07 .20
27 Vladimir Guerrero .20 .50
28 Butch Huskey .07 .20
29 Cecil Fielder .07 .20
30 Rod Myers .07 .20
31 Greg Maddux .30 .75
32 Bill Mueller .07 .20
33 Larry Walker .07 .20
34 Henry Rodriguez .07 .20
35 Mike Mussina .10 .30
36 Ricky Ledee .07 .20
37 Bobby Bonilla .07 .20
38 Curt Schilling .07 .20
39 Luis Gonzalez .07 .20
40 Troy Percival .07 .20
41 Eric Milton .07 .20
42 Mo Vaughn .07 .20
43 Raul Mondesi .07 .20
44 Kenny Rogers .07 .20
45 Frank Thomas .20 .50
46 Jose Canseco .10 .30
47 Tom Glavine .10 .30
48 Rich Butler RC .07 .20
49 Jay Buhner .07 .20
50 Jose Cruz Jr. .07 .20
51 Bernie Williams .10 .30
52 Doug Glanville .07 .20
53 Travis Fryman .07 .20
54 Rey Ordonez .07 .20
55 Jeff Conine .07 .20
56 Trevor Hoffman .07 .20
57 Kirk Rueter .07 .20
58 Ron Gant .07 .20
59 Carl Everett .07 .20
60 Joe Carter .07 .20
61 Livan Hernandez .07 .20
62 John Jaha .07 .20
63 Ivan Rodriguez .10 .30
64 Willie Blair .07 .20
65 Todd Helton .10 .30
66 Kevin Young .07 .20
67 Mike Caruso .07 .20
68 Steve Trachsel .07 .20
69 Marty Cordova .07 .20
70 Alex Fernandez .07 .20
71 Eric Karros .07 .20
72 Reggie Sanders .07 .20
73 Russ Davis .07 .20
74 Roberto Hernandez .07 .20
75 Barry Bonds .60 1.50
76 Alex Gonzalez .07 .20
77 Roberto Alomar .10 .30
78 Troy O'Leary .07 .20
79 Bernard Gilkey .07 .20
80 Ismael Valdes .07 .20
81 Travis Lee .07 .20
82 Brant Brown .07 .20
83 Gary DiSarcina .07 .20
84 Joe Randa .07 .20
85 Jaret Wright .07 .20
86 Quilvio Veras .07 .20
87 Rickey Henderson .20 .50
88 Randall Simon .07 .20
89 Mariano Rivera .20 .50
90 Ugueth Urbina .07 .20
91 Fernando Vina .07 .20
92 Alan Benes .07 .20
93 Dante Bichette .07 .20
94 Karim Garcia .07 .20
95 A.J. Hinch .07 .20
96 Shane Reynolds .07 .20
97 Kevin Stocker .07 .20
98 John Wetteland .07 .20
99 Terry Steinbach .07 .20
100 Ken Griffey Jr. .40 1.00
101 Mike Cameron .07 .20
102 Damion Easley .07 .20
103 Randy Myers .07 .20
104 Jason Schmidt .07 .20
105 Jeff King .07 .20
106 Gregg Jefferies .07 .20
107 Sean Casey .07 .20
108 Mark Kotsay .07 .20
109 Brad Fullmer .07 .20
110 Wilson Alvarez .07 .20
111 Sandy Alomar Jr. .07 .20
112 Walt Weiss .07 .20
113 Doug Jones .07 .20
114 Andy Benes .07 .20
115 Paul O'Neill .10 .30
116 Dennis Eckersley .07 .20
117 Todd Greene .07 .20
118 Bobby Jones .07 .20
119 Darrin Fletcher .07 .20
120 Eric Young .07 .20
121 Jeffrey Hammonds .07 .20
122 Mickey Morandini .07 .20
123 Chuck Knoblauch .07 .20
124 Moises Alou .07 .20
125 Miguel Tejada .20 .50
126 Brian Anderson .07 .20
127 Edgar Renteria .07 .20
128 Mike Lansing .07 .20
129 Quinton McCracken .07 .20
130 Ray Lankford .07 .20
131 Andy Ashby .07 .20
132 Kelvim Escobar .07 .20
133 Mike Lowell RC .50 1.25
134 Randy Johnson .20 .50
135 Andres Galarraga .07 .20
136 Armando Benitez .07 .20
137 Rusty Greer .07 .20
138 Jose Guillen .07 .20
139 Paul Konerko .07 .20
140 Edgardo Alfonzo .07 .20
141 Jim Leyritz .07 .20
142 Mark Clark .07 .20

143 Brian Johnson .07 .20
144 Scott Rolen .10 .30
145 David Cone .07 .20
146 Jeff Shaw .07 .20
147 Shannon Stewart .07 .20
148 Brian Hunter .07 .20
149 Garret Anderson .07 .20
150 Jeff Bagwell .10 .30
151 James Baldwin .07 .20
152 Devon White .07 .20
153 Jim Thome .10 .30
154 Wally Joyner .07 .20
155 Mark Wohlers .07 .20
156 Jeff Cirillo .07 .20
157 Jason Giambi .07 .20
158 Royce Clayton .07 .20
159 Dennis Reyes .07 .20
160 Raul Casanova .07 .20
161 Pedro Astacio .07 .20
162 Todd Dunwoody .07 .20
163 Sammy Sosa .20 .50
164 Todd Hundley .07 .20
165 Wade Boggs .10 .30
166 Robb Nen .07 .20
167 Dan Wilson .07 .20
168 Hideki Irabu .07 .20
169 B.J. Surhoff .07 .20
170 Carlos Delgado .07 .20
171 Fernando Tatis .07 .20
172 Bob Abreu .07 .20
173 David Ortiz .25 .60
174 Tony Womack .07 .20
175 Magglio Ordonez RC .60 1.50
176 Aaron Boone .07 .20
177 Brian Giles .07 .20
178 Kevin Appier .07 .20
179 Chuck Finley .07 .20
180 Brian Rose .07 .20
181 Ryan Klesko .07 .20
182 Mike Stanley .07 .20
183 Dave Nilsson .07 .20
184 Carlos Perez .07 .20
185 Jeff Blauser .07 .20
186 Richard Hidalgo .07 .20
187 Charles Johnson .07 .20
188 Vinny Castilla .07 .20
189 Joey Hamilton .07 .20
190 Bubba Trammell .07 .20
191 Eli Marrero .07 .20
192 Scott Erickson .07 .20
193 Pat Hentgen .07 .20
194 Jorge Fabregas .07 .20
195 Tino Martinez .10 .30
196 Bobby Higginson .07 .20
197 Dave Hollins .07 .20
198 Rolando Arrojo RC .10 .30
199 Joey Cora .07 .20
200 Mike Piazza .30 .75
201 Reggie Jefferson .07 .20
202 John Smoltz .10 .30
203 Bobby Smith .07 .20
204 Tom Goodwin .07 .20
205 Omar Vizquel .10 .30
206 John Olerud .07 .20
207 Matt Stairs .07 .20
208 Bobby Estalella .07 .20
209 Miguel Cairo .07 .20
210 Shawn Green .07 .20
211 Jon Nunnally .07 .20
212 Al Leiter .07 .20
213 Matt Lawton .07 .20
214 Brady Anderson .07 .20
215 Jeff Kent .07 .20
216 Ray Durham .07 .20
217 Al Martin .07 .20
218 Jeff D'Amico .07 .20
219 Kevin Tapani .07 .20
220 Jim Edmonds .07 .20
221 Jose Vizcaino .07 .20
222 Jay Bell .07 .20
223 Ken Caminiti .07 .20
224 Craig Biggio .10 .30
225 Bartolo Colon .07 .20
226 Neifi Perez .07 .20
227 Delino DeShields .07 .20
228 Javier Lopez .07 .20
229 David Wells .07 .20
230 Brad Rigby .07 .20
231 John Franco .07 .20
232 Michael Coleman .07 .20
233 Edgar Martinez .10 .30
234 Francisco Cordova .07 .20
235 Johnny Damon .10 .30
236 Deivi Cruz .07 .20
237 J.T. Snow .07 .20
238 Enrique Wilson .07 .20
239 Rondell White .07 .20
240 Aaron Sele .07 .20
241 Tony Saunders .07 .20
242 Ricky Bottalico .07 .20
243 Cliff Floyd .07 .20
244 Chili Davis .07 .20
245 Brian McRae .07 .20
246 Brad Radke .07 .20
247 Chan Ho Park .07 .20
248 Lance Johnson .07 .20
249 Rafael Palmeiro .10 .30
250 Tony Gwynn .25 .60
251 Denny Neagle .07 .20
252 Dean Palmer .07 .20
253 Jose Valentin .07 .20
254 Matt Morris .07 .20
255 Ellis Burks .07 .20
256 Jeff Suppan .07 .20
257 Jimmy Key .07 .20
258 Justin Thompson .07 .20
259 Brett Tomko .07 .20
260 Mark Grudzielanek .07 .20
261 Mike Hampton .07 .20
262 Jeff Fassero .07 .20
263 Charles Nagy .07 .20
264 Pedro Martinez .10 .30
265 Todd Zeile .07 .20
266 Will Clark .10 .30
267 Abraham Nunez .07 .20
268 Dave Martinez .07 .20
269 Jason Dickson .07 .20
270 Eric Davis .07 .20
271 Kevin Orie .07 .20
272 Derrek Lee .10 .30
273 Andruw Jones .10 .30
274 Juan Encarnacion .07 .20
275 Carlos Baerga .07 .20
276 Andy Pettitte .10 .30
277 Brent Brede .07 .20
278 Paul Sorrento .07 .20
279 Mike Lieberthal .07 .20
280 Marquis Grissom UER 8 .07 .20
281 Darin Erstad .07 .20
282 Willie Greene .07 .20
283 Derek Bell .07 .20
284 Scott Spiezio .07 .20
285 David Segui .07 .20
286 Albert Belle .07 .20
287 Ramon Martinez .07 .20
288 Jeremi Gonzalez .07 .20
289 Shawn Estes .07 .20
290 Ron Coomer .07 .20
291 John Valentin .07 .20
292 Kevin Brown .10 .30
293 Michael Tucker .07 .20
294 Brian Jordan .07 .20
295 Darryl Kile .07 .20
296 David Justice .07 .20
297 Frank Thomas CL .10 .30
298 Alex Rodriguez CL .20 .50
299 Ken Griffey Jr. CL .25 .60
300 Jose Cruz Jr. CL .07 .20
P8 Cal Ripken Promo .75 2.00

1998 Circa Thunder Rave

*STARS: 20X TO 50X BASIC CARDS
*ROOKIES: 12.5X TO 30X BASIC CARDS
100 Ken Griffey Jr. 60.00 150.00

1998 Circa Thunder Boss

COMPLETE SET (20) 15.00 40.00
STATED ODDS 1:6
1 Jeff Bagwell .40 1.00
2 Barry Bonds 2.00 5.00
3 Roger Clemens 1.25 3.00
4 Jose Cruz Jr. .25 .60
5 Nomar Garciaparra 1.00 2.50
6 Juan Gonzalez .25 .60
7 Ken Griffey Jr. 1.25 3.00
8 Tony Gwynn .75 2.00
9 Derek Jeter 1.50 4.00
10 Chipper Jones .60 1.50
11 Travis Lee .25 .60
12 Greg Maddux 1.00 2.50
13 Pedro Martinez .40 1.00
14 Mark McGwire 1.50 4.00
15 Mike Piazza 1.00 2.50
16 Cal Ripken 2.00 5.00
17 Alex Rodriguez 1.00 2.50
18 Scott Rolen .40 1.00
19 Frank Thomas .60 1.50
20 Larry Walker .25 .60

1998 Circa Thunder Fast Track

COMPLETE SET (10) 6.00 15.00
STATED ODDS 1:24
1 Jose Cruz Jr. .50 1.25
2 Juan Encarnacion .50 1.25
3 Brad Fullmer .50 1.25
4 Nomar Garciaparra 2.00 5.00
5 Todd Helton .75 2.00
6 Livan Hernandez .50 1.25
7 Travis Lee .50 1.25
8 Neifi Perez .50 1.25
9 Scott Rolen .75 2.00
10 Jaret Wright .50 1.25

1998 Circa Thunder Limited Access

COMPLETE SET (15) 75.00 150.00
STATED ODDS 1:18 RETAIL
1 Jeff Bagwell 1.50 4.00
2 Roger Clemens 5.00 12.00
3 Jose Cruz Jr. 1.00 2.50
4 Nomar Garciaparra 4.00 10.00
5 Juan Gonzalez 1.00 2.50
6 Ken Griffey Jr. 5.00 12.00
7 Tony Gwynn 3.00 8.00
8 Derek Jeter 6.00 15.00
9 Greg Maddux 4.00 10.00
10 Pedro Martinez 1.50 4.00
11 Mark McGwire 6.00 15.00
12 Mike Piazza 4.00 10.00
13 Alex Rodriguez 4.00 10.00
14 Frank Thomas 2.50 6.00
15 Larry Walker 1.00 2.50

1998 Circa Thunder Quick Strike

COMPLETE SET (12) 30.00 80.00
STATED ODDS 1:36
1 Jeff Bagwell 1.25 3.00
2 Roger Clemens 4.00 10.00
3 Jose Cruz Jr. .75 2.00
4 Nomar Garciaparra 3.00 8.00
5 Ken Griffey Jr. 4.00 10.00
6 Greg Maddux 3.00 8.00
7 Pedro Martinez 1.25 3.00
8 Mark McGwire 5.00 12.00
9 Mike Piazza 3.00 8.00
10 Alex Rodriguez 3.00 8.00
11 Frank Thomas 2.00 5.00
12 Larry Walker .75 2.00

1998 Circa Thunder Rave Review

COMPLETE SET (15) 40.00 100.00
STATED ODDS 1:288
1 Jeff Bagwell 3.00 8.00
2 Barry Bonds 8.00 20.00
3 Roger Clemens 6.00 15.00
4 Jose Cruz Jr. 2.00 5.00
5 Nomar Garciaparra 3.00 8.00
6 Juan Gonzalez 2.00 5.00
7 Ken Griffey Jr. 10.00 25.00
8 Tony Gwynn 5.00 12.00
9 Derek Jeter 12.00 30.00
10 Greg Maddux 6.00 15.00
11 Mark McGwire 8.00 20.00
12 Mike Piazza 5.00 12.00
13 Alex Rodriguez 6.00 15.00
14 Frank Thomas 5.00 12.00
15 Larry Walker 3.00 8.00

1998 Circa Thunder Thunder Boomers

COMPLETE SET (12) 60.00 120.00
STATED ODDS 1:96
1 Jeff Bagwell 2.50 6.00
2 Barry Bonds 12.50 30.00
3 Jay Buhner 1.50 4.00
4 Andres Galarraga 1.50 4.00
5 Juan Gonzalez 1.50 4.00
6 Ken Griffey Jr. 8.00 20.00
7 Tino Martinez 2.50 6.00
8 Mark McGwire 10.00 25.00
9 Mike Piazza 6.00 15.00
10 Frank Thomas 4.00 10.00
11 Jim Thome 2.50 6.00
12 Larry Walker 1.50 4.00

1998 Circa Thunder Rolen Sportsfest

This one card standard-size set was issued by Fleer/SkyBox and distributed at the inaugural SportsFest show in May 1998. The card features the SportsFest 98 logo on the front and is numbered SF1 on the back. While not serial numbered, the back does state that the production on this card is limited to 5,000 cards.

1 Scott Rolen 2.00 5.00

1985 Circle K

The cards in this 33-card set measure 2 1/2" by 3 1/2" and were issued with an accompanying custom box. In 1985, Topps produced this set for Circle K; cards were printed in Ireland. Cards are numbered on the back according to each player's rank on the all-time career Home Run list. The backs are printed in blue and red on white card stock. The card fronts are glossy and each player is named in the lower left corner. Most of the obverses are in color, although the older vintage players are pictured in black and white. Joe DiMaggio was not included in the set; card number 31 does not exist. It was intended to be DiMaggio but he apparently would not consent to be included in the set.

COMP. FACT. SET (33) 2.00 5.00
1 Hank Aaron .30 .75
2 Babe Ruth .60 1.50
3 Willie Mays .30 .75
4 Frank Robinson .08 .25
5 Harmon Killebrew .08 .25
6 Mickey Mantle .60 1.50
7 Jimmie Foxx .08 .25
8 Willie McCovey .08 .25
9 Ted Williams .30 .75
10 Ernie Banks .08 .25
11 Eddie Mathews .08 .25
12 Mel Ott .08 .25
13 Reggie Jackson .20 .50
14 Lou Gehrig .30 .75
15 Stan Musial .20 .50
16 Willie Stargell .08 .25
17 Carl Yastrzemski .08 .25
18 Billy Williams .08 .25
19 Mike Schmidt .20 .50
20 Duke Snider .08 .25
21 Al Kaline .08 .25
22 Johnny Bench .08 .25
23 Frank Howard .02 .10
24 Orlando Cepeda .07 .20
25 Norm Cash .02 .10
26 Dave Kingman .02 .10
27 Rocky Colavito .07 .20
28 Tony Perez .07 .20
29 Gil Hodges .07 .20
30 Ralph Kiner .08 .25
32 Johnny Mize .08 .25
33 Yogi Berra .08 .25
34 Lee May .02 .10

1994 Will Clark Kelly Russell Studios

This is a double matted artist's rendering which measures 14" by 11". It is accompanied by a '93 season highlights panel and baseball card panel. This issued is subtitled "The Texas Thrill." This is part of a big set: need complete set information before we price this.

1 Will Clark 2.00 5.00

1972 Classic Cards

This 120-card set was issued in four series and features sepia player photos printed on beige card stock. The backs carry a checklist of the series in which the player photo displayed on the front is found. The cards are checklisted below according to those checklists. Series 1 consists of cards numbered from 1-30; Series 2, cards numbered from 31-60; Series 3, cards numbered from 61-90; and Series 4, cards numbered from 91-120.

COMPLETE SET (120) 40.00 80.00
1 Clark Griffith .75 2.00
2 Walter Johnson 1.25 3.00
3 Bob Ganley .20 .50
4 Joe Tinker .75 2.00
5 Frank Chance .75 2.00
6 Wid Conroy .20 .50
7 Roger Bresnahan .40 1.00
8 Jack Powell .20 .50
9 Jack Pfeister .20 .50
10 Tom McCarthy .40 1.00
11 Amby McConnell .20 .50
12 Hugh Jennings .40 1.00
13 Ed Lennox .20 .50
14 Moose McCormick .20 .50
15 Fred Merkle .20 .50
16 Dick Hoblitzell .20 .50
17 Bill Dahlen .20 .50
18 Frank Chance .75 2.00
19 George Ferguson .20 .50
20 Howie Camnitz .20 .50
21 Neal Ball .20 .50
22 Charlie Hemphill .20 .50
23 Frank Baker .60 1.50
24 Christy Mathewson .75 2.00
25 Al Burch .20 .50
26 Eddie Grant .40 1.00
27 Red Ames .20 .50
28 Doc Newton .20 .50
29 Pat Moran .20 .50
30 Nap Lajoie .75 2.00
31 Mordecai Brown .60 1.50
32 Bill Abstein .20 .50
33 Ty Cobb 2.00 5.00
34 Billy Campbell .20 .50
35 Claude Rossman .20 .50
36 Topsy Hartsel .20 .50
37 Sam Crawford .60 1.50
38 Red Dooin .20 .50
39 Jack Dunn .20 .50
40 Tom Downey .20 .50
41 Bill Hinchman .20 .50
42 John Titus .20 .50
43 Patsy Dougherty .20 .50
44 Art Devlin .20 .50
45 Nap Lajoie .75 2.00
46 Larry Doyle .20 .50
47 Honus Wagner 1.25 3.00
48 Bull Durham .40 1.00
49 Irv Higginbotham .20 .50
50 George Gibson .20 .50
51 Mike Mowrey .20 .50
52 George Stone .20 .50
53 George Perring .20 .50
54 Orvie Overall .20 .50
55 Hooks Wiltse .20 .50
56 Jack Warhop .20 .50
57 Harry Steinfeldt .40 1.00
58 Bill O'Hara .20 .50
59 Boss Schmidt .20 .50
60 George Mullin .20 .50
61 Buck Herzog .20 .50
62 John Hummell .20 .50
63 Art Fromme .20 .50
64 Kid Elberfeld .20 .50
65 Frank Bowerman .20 .50
66 Roger Bresnahan .40 1.00
67 Andy Coakley .20 .50
68 Jim Pastorius .20 .50
69 Tubby Spencer .20 .50
70 Frank Schulte .20 .50
71 Willie Keeler .40 1.00
72 Joe McGinnity .40 1.00
73 Harry McIntyre .20 .50
74 Harry Lumley .20 .50
75 Nick Maddox .20 .50
76 Cy Barger .20 .50
77 Bill Donovan .20 .50
78 Tim Jordan .20 .50
79 Johnnie Evers .75 2.00
80 Zack Wheat .40 1.00
81 Hippo Vaughn .20 .50
82 Jimmy Sebring .20 .50
83 Tom Tuckey .20 .50
84 Tris Speaker 1.25 3.00
85 John McGraw .75 2.00
86 Billy Purtell .20 .50
87 George Moriarity .20 .50
88 Charlie Smith .20 .50
89 Bill Bergen .20 .50
90 Kitty Bransfield .20 .50
91 Joe Doyle .20 .50
92 Amos Strunk .20 .50
93 Bob Ewing .20 .50
94 Tom Daley .20 .50
95 Joe Delahanty .20 .50
96 Ed Summers .20 .50
97 Joe Lake .20 .50
98 Dave Altizer .20 .50
99 Roger Bresnahan .40 1.00
100 Chief Bender .60 1.50
101 Buck Herzog .20 .50
102 Ira Thomas .20 .50
103 Hal Chase .75 2.00
104 Tom Needham .20 .50
105 Ducky Pearce .20 .50
106 Rube Ellis .20 .50
107 Ed Konetchy .20 .50
108 Harry Lord .20 .50
109 Ossie Schreck .20 .50
110 Heinie Wagner .20 .50
111 Luther Taylor .20 .50
112 Alan Storke .20 .50
113 Bill Powell .20 .50
114 Ham Hyatt .20 .50
115 George Davis .40 1.00
116 Bill Grahame .20 .50
117 Larry McLean .20 .50
118 Jiggs Donohue .20 .50
119 Bill Chappelle .20 .50
120 Billy Purtell .20 .50

1987 Classic Game

This 100-card standard-size set was actually distributed as part of a trivia board game. The card backs contain several trivia questions (and answers) which are used to play the game. A dark green border frames the full-color photo. The games were produced by Game Time, Ltd. and were available in toy stores as well as from card dealers. According to the producers of this game, only 75,000 sets were distributed. The set features Bo Jackson, Wally Joyner, and Barry Larkin in their Rookie Card year.

COMP.FACT SET (100) 25.00 60.00
1 Pete Rose 1.00 2.50
2 Len Dykstra .08 .25
3 Darryl Strawberry .08 .25
4 Keith Hernandez .08 .25
5 Gary Carter .60 1.50
6 Wally Joyner .20 .50
7 Andres Thomas .02 .10
8 Pat Dodson .02 .10
9 Kirk Gibson .08 .25
10 Don Mattingly 2.00 5.00
11 Dave Winfield .60 1.50
12 Rickey Henderson 1.50 4.00
13 Dan Pasqua .02 .10
14 Don Baylor .08 .25
15 Bo Jackson/(Swinging bat in Auburn FB uniform) 20.00 50.00
16 Pete Incaviglia .08 .25
17 Kevin Bass .02 .10
18 Barry Larkin 2.00 5.00
19 Dave Magadan .08 .25
20 Steve Sax .02 .10
21 Eric Davis .08 .25
22 Mike Pagliarulo .02 .10
23 Fred Lynn .08 .25
24 Reggie Jackson .75 2.00
25 Larry Parrish .02 .10
26 Tony Gwynn 2.00 5.00
27 Steve Garvey .08 .25
28 Glenn Davis .02 .10
29 Tim Raines .08 .25
30 Vince Coleman .02 .10
31 Willie McGee .08 .25
32 Ozzie Smith 1.50 4.00
33 Dave Parker .08 .25
34 Tony Pena .02 .10
35 Ryne Sandberg 1.50 4.00
36 Brett Butler .08 .25
37 Dale Murphy .30 .75
38 Bob Horner .02 .10
39 Pedro Guerrero .02 .10
40 Brook Jacoby .02 .10
41 Carlton Fisk .60 1.50
42 Harold Baines .20 .50
43 Rob Deer .02 .10
44 Robin Yount 1.00 2.50
45 Paul Molitor 1.00 2.50
46 Jose Canseco 2.00 5.00
47 George Brett 2.00 5.00
48 Jim Presley .02 .10
49 Rich Gedman .02 .10
50 Lance Parrish .08 .25
51 Eddie Murray 1.00 2.50
52 Cal Ripken 4.00 10.00
53 Kent Hrbek .02 .10
54 Gary Gaetti .08 .25
55 Kirby Puckett 1.25 3.00
56 George Bell .02 .10
57 Tony Fernandez .02 .10
58 Jesse Barfield .02 .10
59 Jim Rice .08 .25
60 Wade Boggs 1.00 2.50
61 Marty Barrett .02 .10
62 Mike Schmidt 1.00 2.50
63 Von Hayes .02 .10
64 Jeff Leonard .02 .10
65 Chris Brown .02 .10
66 Dave Smith .02 .10
67 Mike Krukow .02 .10
68 Ron Guidry .08 .25
69 Rob Woodward .02 .10
70 Rob Murphy .02 .10
71 Andres Galarraga 1.50 4.00
72 Dwight Gooden .08 .25
73 Bob Ojeda .02 .10
74 Sid Fernandez .02 .10
75 Jesse Orosco .02 .10
76 Roger McDowell .02 .10
77 John Tudor UER/(Misspelled Tutor) .02 .10
78 Tom Browning .02 .10
79 Rick Aguilera .02 .10
80 Lance McCullers .02 .10
81 Mike Scott .02 .10
82 Nolan Ryan 4.00 10.00
83 Bruce Hurst .02 .10
84 Roger Clemens 2.00 5.00
85 Dennis Boyd .02 .10
86 Dave Righetti .02 .10
87 Dennis Rasmussen .02 .10
88 Bret Saberhagen .08 .25
89 Mark Langston .02 .10
90 Jack Morris .08 .25
91 Fernando Valenzuela .08 .25
92 Orel Hershiser .08 .25
93 Rick Honeycutt .02 .10
94 Jeff Reardon .02 .10
95 John Habyan .02 .10
96 Goose Gossage .08 .25
97 Todd Worrell .02 .10
98 Floyd Youmans .02 .10
99 Don Aase .02 .10
100 John Franco .08 .25

1987 Classic Update Yellow

This 50-card standard-size set was actually distributed as part of an update to a trivia board game, but (unlike the original Classic game) was sold without the game. The set is sometimes referred to as the "Travel Edition" of the game. The card backs contain several trivia questions (and answers) which are used to play the game. A yellow border frames the full-color photo. The games were produced by Game Time, Ltd. and were available in toy stores as well as from card dealers. Cards are numbered beginning with 101, as they are an extension of the original set. According to the set's producers, reportedly about 1/3 of the 150,000 sets printed were error sets in that they had green backs instead of yellow backs. This "green back" variation/error set is valued at approximately double the prices listed below. Early cards of Barry Bonds and Mark McGwire highlight this set. Most cards issued of Barry Bonds tend to be off center. It is believed that the average centering on this card is approximately 80/20.

COMP.FACT.SET (50) 10.00 25.00
101 Mike Schmidt .40 1.00
102 Eric Davis .08 .25
103 Pete Rose .50 1.25
104 Don Mattingly .50 1.25
105 Wade Boggs .08 .25
106 Dale Murphy .08 .25
107 Glenn Davis .02 .10
108 Wally Joyner .08 .25
109 Bo Jackson 2.50 6.00
110 Cory Snyder .02 .10
111 Jim Lindeman .05 .15
112 Kirby Puckett .30 .75
113 Barry Bonds 10.00 25.00
114 Roger Clemens .60 1.50
115 Oddibe McDowell .02 .10
116 Bret Saberhagen .05 .15
117 Joe Magrane .02 .10
118 Scott Fletcher .02 .10
119 Mark McLemore .05 .15
120 Who Me (Joe Niekro) .05 .15
121 Mark McGwire 5.00 12.00
122 Darryl Strawberry .05 .15
123 Mike Scott .05 .15
124 Andre Dawson .05 .15
125 Jose Canseco .30 .75
126 Kevin McReynolds .02 .10
127 Joe Carter .05 .15
128 Casey Candaele .02 .10
129 Matt Nokes .15 .40
130 Kal Daniels .02 .10
131 Pete Incaviglia .15 .40
132 Benito Santiago .15 .40
133 Barry Larkin .60 1.50
134 Gary Pettis .02 .10
135 B.J. Surhoff .25 .60
136 Juan Nieves .02 .10
137 Jim Deshaies .02 .10
138 Pete O'Brien .02 .10
139 Kevin Seitzer .05 .15
140 Devon White .25 .60
141 Rob Deer .02 .10
142 Kurt Stillwell .02 .10
143 Edwin Correa .02 .10
144 Dion James .02 .10
145 Danny Tartabull .02 .10
146 Jerry Browne .05 .15
147 Ted Higuera .02 .10
148 Jack Clark .05 .15
149 Ruben Sierra .40 1.00
150 M.McGwire .50 1.25
E.Davis

1987 Classic Update Yellow/Green Backs

COMP.FACT.SET (50) 15.00 40.00
*GREENBACK: .4X TO 1X YELLOW
ONE-THIRD OF PRINT RUN ARE GREEN BACKS

1988 Classic Blue

This 50-card blue-bordered standard-size set was actually distributed as part of an update to a trivia board game, but (unlike the original Classic game) was sold without the game. The card backs contain several trivia questions (and answers) which are used to play the game. A blue border frames the full color photo. The games were produced by Game Time, Ltd. and were available in toy stores as well as from card dealers. Cards are numbered beginning with 201 as they are an extension of the original sets.

COMP.FACT. SET (50) 4.00 10.00
201 Eric Davis .05 .15
Dale Murphy
202 B.J. Surhoff .07 .20
203 John Kruk .08 .25
204 Sam Horn .02 .10
205 Jack Clark .05 .15
206 Wally Joyner .05 .15
207 Matt Nokes .02 .10
208 Bo Jackson .08 .25
209 Darryl Strawberry .05 .15
210 Ozzie Smith .60 1.50
211 Don Mattingly .75 2.00
212 Mark McGwire 1.00 2.50
213 Eric Davis .05 .15
214 Wade Boggs .30 .75
215 Dale Murphy .08 .25
216 Andre Dawson .08 .25
217 Roger Clemens .75 2.00
218 Kevin Seitzer .02 .10
219 Benito Santiago .05 .15
220 Tony Gwynn .75 2.00
221 Mike Scott .02 .10
222 Steve Bedrosian .02 .10
223 Vince Coleman .02 .10
224 Rick Sutcliffe .02 .10
225 Will Clark .30 .75
226 Pete Rose .30 1.00
227 Mike Greenwell .02 .10
228 Ken Caminiti .08 .25
229 Ellis Burks .30 1.00
230 Dave Magadan .02 .10
231 Alan Trammell .08 .25
232 Paul Molitor .30 .75
233 Gary Gaetti .05 .15
234 Rickey Henderson .30 1.00
235 Danny Tartabull UER .02 .10
(Photo actually Hal McRae)
236 Bobby Bonilla .05 .15
237 Mike Dunne .02 .10
238 Al Leiter .08 .25
239 John Farrell .02 .10
240 Joe Magrane .02 .10
241 Mike Henneman .05 .15
242 George Bell .02 .10
243 Gregg Jefferies .05 .15
244 Jay Buhner .30 .75
245 Todd Benzinger .02 .10
246 Matt Williams .30 .75
247 Mark McGwire .60 1.50
Don Mattingly
(Unnumbered; game instrucions on back
248 George Brett .50 1.25
249 Jimmy Key .05 .15
250 Mark Langston .02 .10

1988 Classic Red

This 50-card red-bordered standard-size set was actually distributed as part of an update to a trivia board game, but (unlike the original Classic game) was sold without the game. The card backs contain several trivia questions (and answers) which are used to play the game. A red border frames the full color photo. The games were produced by Game Time, Ltd. and were available in toy stores as well as from card dealers. Cards are numbered beginning with 151 as they are an extension of the original sets.

COMP. FACT. SET (50) 5.00 12.00
151 Mark McGwire and .40 1.00
Don Mattingly
152 Don Mattingly .60 1.50
153 Mark McGwire .60 1.50
154 Eric Davis .05 .15
155 Wade Boggs .30 .75
156 Dale Murphy .08 .25
157 Andre Dawson .08 .25
158 Roger Clemens .60 1.50
159 Kevin Seitzer .05 .15
160 Benito Santiago .05 .15
161 Kal Daniels .02 .10
162 John Kruk .08 .25
163 Bill Ripken .02 .10
164 Kirby Puckett .30 .75
165 Jose Canseco .20 .50
166 Matt Nokes .02 .10
167 Mike Schmidt .30 .75
168 Tim Raines .05 .15
169 Ryne Sandberg .50 1.25
170 Dave Winfield .20 .50
171 Dwight Gooden .05 .15
172 Bret Saberhagen .05 .15
173 Willie McGee .05 .15
174 Jack Morris .05 .15
175 Jeff Leonard .02 .10
176 Cal Ripken 1.25 3.00
177 Pete Incaviglia .02 .10
178 Devon White .02 .10
179 Nolan Ryan 1.25 3.00
180 Ruben Sierra .05 .15
181 Todd Worrell .05 .15
182 Glenn Davis .02 .10
183 Frank Viola .02 .10
184 Cory Snyder .02 .10
185 Tracy Jones .02 .10
186 Terry Steinbach .02 .10
187 Julio Franco .05 .15
188 Larry Sheets .02 .10
189 John Marzano .02 .10
190 Kevin Elster .02 .10
191 Vicente Palacios .02 .10
192 Kent Hrbek .02 .10
193 Eric Bell .02 .10
194 Kelly Downs .02 .10
195 Jose Lind .02 .10
196 Dave Stewart .05 .15
197 Mark McGwire and .40 1.00
Jose Canseco
198 Phil Niekro .20 .50
Cleveland Indians
199 Phil Niekro .20 .50
Toronto Blue Jays
200 Phil Niekro .20 .50
Atlanta Braves

1989 Classic Light Blue

The 1989 Classic set contains 100 standard-size cards. The fronts of these cards have light blue borders. The backs feature 1988 and lifetime stats. The cards were distributed with a baseball boardgame. Reportedly there were 150,000 sets produced.

COMP.FACT.SET (100) 8.00 20.00
1 Orel Hershiser .05 .15
2 Wade Boggs .30 .75
3 Jose Canseco .60 1.00
4 Mark McGwire .60 1.50
5 Don Mattingly .75 2.00
6 Gregg Jefferies .05 .15
7 Dwight Gooden .05 .15
8 Darryl Strawberry .05 .15
9 Eric Davis .07 .20
10 Joey Meyer .02 .10
11 Joe Carter .08 .20
12 Paul Molitor .30 .75
13 Mark Grace .30 .75
14 Kurt Stillwell .02 .10
15 Kirby Puckett .30 .75
16 Keith Miller .02 .10
17 Glenn Davis .02 .10
18 Will Clark .20 .50
19 Cory Snyder .02 .10
20 Jose Lind .02 .10
21 Andres Thomas .02 .10
22 Dave Smith .02 .10
23 Mike Scott .02 .10
24 Kevin McReynolds .02 .10
25 B.J. Surhoff .05 .15
26 Mackey Sasser .02 .10
27 Chad Kreuter .02 .10
28 Hal Morris .02 .10
29 Wally Joyner .02 .10
30 Tony Gwynn .75 2.00
31 Kevin Mitchell .05 .15
32 Dave Winfield .30 .75
33 Billy Bean .07 .20
34 Steve Bedrosian .02 .10
35 Ron Gant .05 .15
36 Len Dykstra .05 .15
37 Andre Dawson .08 .25
38 Brett Butler .05 .15
39 Rob Deer .02 .10
40 Tommy John .05 .15
41 Gary Gaetti .05 .15
42 Tim Raines .05 .15
43 George Bell .02 .10
44 Dwight Evans .05 .15
45 Dennis Martinez .05 .15
46 Andres Galarraga .20 .50
47 George Brett .75 2.00
48 Mike Schmidt .40 1.00
49 Dave Stieb .02 .10
50 Rickey Henderson .50 1.25
51 Craig Biggio .75 2.00
52 Mark Lemke .02 .10
53 Chris Sabo .02 .10
54 Jeff Treadway .02 .10
55 Kent Hrbek .05 .15
56 Cal Ripken 1.50 4.00
57 Tim Belcher .02 .10
58 Ozzie Smith .60 1.50
59 Keith Hernandez .05 .15
60 Pedro Guerrero .02 .10
61 Greg Swindell .02 .10
62 Bret Saberhagen .05 .15
63 John Tudor .02 .10
64 Gary Carter .30 .75
65 Kevin Seitzer .02 .10
66 Jesse Barfield .02 .10
67 Luis Medina .02 .10
68 Walt Weiss .02 .10

69 Terry Steinbach .02 .10
70 Barry Larkin .20 .50
71 Pete Rose .30 1.00
72 Luis Salazar .02 .10
73 Benito Santiago .05 .15
74 Kal Daniels .02 .10
75 Kevin Elster .02 .10
76 Rob Dibble .05 .15
77 Bobby Witt .02 .10
78 Steve Searcy .02 .10
79 Sandy Alomar Jr. .08 .25
80 Chili Davis .05 .15
81 Alvin Davis .02 .10
82 Charlie Leibrandt .02 .10
83 Robin Yount .30 .75
84 Mark Carreon .02 .10
85 Pascual Perez .02 .10
86 Dennis Rasmussen .02 .10
87 Ernie Riles .02 .10
88 Melido Perez .02 .10
89 Doug Jones .02 .10
90 Dennis Eckersley .30 .75
91 Bob Welch .05 .15
92 Bob Milacki .02 .10
93 Jeff Robinson .02 .10
94 Mike Henneman .02 .10
95 Randy Johnson 2.00 5.00
96 Ron Jones .02 .10
97 Jack Armstrong .02 .10
98 Willie McGee .05 .15
99 Ryne Sandberg .40 1.00
100 David Cone and .02 .10
Danny Jackson

1989 Classic Travel Orange

The 1989 Classic Travel Orange set contains 50 standard-size cards. The fronts of the cards have orange borders. The backs feature 1988 and lifetime stats. This subset of cards were distributed as a set in blister packs as "Travel Update I" subsets. Reportedly there were 150,000 sets produced. A first year card of Ken Griffey Jr. highlights this set.

COMP.FACT.SET (50) 6.00 15.00
101 Gary Sheffield .60 1.50
102 Wade Boggs .05 .15
103 Jose Canseco .08 .25
104 Mark McGwire .40 1.00
105 Orel Hershiser .02 .10
106 Don Mattingly .25 .60
107 Dwight Gooden .02 .10
108 Darryl Strawberry .02 .10
109 Eric Davis .02 .10
110 Hensley Meulens UER .01 .05
111 Andy Van Slyke .05 .15
112 Al Leiter .08 .25
113 Matt Nokes .01 .05
114 Mike Krukow .01 .05
115 Tony Fernandez .01 .05
116 Fred McGriff .05 .15
117 Barry Bonds .60 1.50
118 Gerald Perry .01 .05
119 Roger Clemens .40 1.00
120 Kirk Gibson .02 .10
121 Greg Maddux .20 .50
122 Bo Jackson .08 .25
123 Danny Jackson .01 .05
124 Dale Murphy .05 .15
125 David Cone .02 .10
126 Tom Browning .01 .05
127 Roberto Alomar .08 .25
128 Alan Trammell .02 .10
129 Ricky Jordan UER .02 .10
Misspelled Jordon
130 Ramon Martinez .02 .10
131 Ken Griffey Jr. 2.50 6.00
132 Gregg Olson .02 .10
133 Carlos Quintana .01 .05
134 Dave West .01 .05
135 Cameron Drew .01 .05
136 Teddy Higuera .01 .05
137 Sil Campusano .01 .05
138 Mark Gubicza .01 .05
139 Mike Boddicker .01 .05
140 Paul Gibson .01 .05
141 Jose Rijo .02 .10
142 John Costello .01 .05
143 Cecil Espy .01 .05
144 Frank Viola .02 .10
145 Erik Hanson .02 .10
146 Juan Samuel .01 .05
147 Harold Reynolds .02 .10
148 Joe Magrane .01 .05
149 Mike Greenwell .01 .05
150 D.Strawberry .02 .10
W.Clark

1989 Classic Travel Purple

The 1989 Classic "Travel Update II" set contains 50 standard-size cards. The fronts have purple (and gray) borders. The set features "two sport" cards of Bo Jackson and Deion Sanders. In addition, a first year card of Ken Griffey Jr highlights this set. The cards were distributed as a set in blister packs.

COMP.FACT.SET (50) 5.00 12.00
151 Jim Abbott .30 .75
152 Ellis Burks .02 .10
153 Mike Schmidt .20 .50
154 Gregg Jefferies .01 .05
155 Mark Grace .08 .25
156 Jerome Walton .05 .15
157 Bo Jackson .08 .25
158 Jack Clark .02 .10
159 Tom Glavine .08 .25
160 Eddie Murray .08 .25
161 John Dopson .01 .05
162 Ruben Sierra .02 .10
163 Rafael Palmeiro .08 .25
164 Nolan Ryan .40 1.00
165 Barry Larkin .05 .15
166 Tommy Herr .01 .05
167 Roberto Kelly .01 .05
168 Glenn Davis .01 .05
169 Glenn Braggs .01 .05
170 Juan Bell .01 .05
171 Todd Burns .01 .05
172 Derek Lilliquist .01 .05
173 Orel Hershiser .02 .10
174 John Smoltz .30 .75
175 O.Guillen .02 .10
E.Burks
176 Kirby Puckett .08 .25
177 Robin Ventura .30 .75
178 Allan Anderson .01 .05
179 Steve Sax .01 .05
180 Will Clark .05 .15
181 Mike Devereaux .01 .05
182 Tom Gordon .08 .25
183 Rob Murphy .01 .05
184 Pete O'Brien .01 .05
185 Cris Carpenter .01 .05
186 Tom Brunansky .01 .05
187 Bob Boone .02 .10
188 Lou Whitaker .02 .10
189 Dwight Gooden .02 .10
190 Mark McGwire .40 1.00
191 John Smiley .01 .05
192 Tommy Gregg .01 .05
193 Ken Griffey Jr. 2.50 6.00
194 Bruce Hurst .01 .05
195 Greg Swindell .01 .05
196 Nelson Liriano .01 .05
197 Randy Myers .02 .10
198 Kevin Mitchell .02 .10
199 Dante Bichette .08 .25
200 Deion Sanders .40 1.00

1990 Classic Blue

The 1990 Classic Blue (Game) set contains 150 standard-size cards, the largest Classic set to date in terms of player selection. The front borders are blue with magenta splotches. The backs feature 1989 and career total stats. The cards were distributed as a set in blister packs. According to distributors of the set, reportedly there were 200,000 sets produced. Reportedly the Sanders "correction" was made at Sanders own request; less than 10 percent of the sets contain the first version and hence it has the higher value in the checklist below. The complete set price below does not include any of the more difficult variation cards. Early cards of Sammy Sosa and Bernie Williams highlight the set.

COMP. FACT SET (150) 4.00 10.00
1 Nolan Ryan .40 1.00
2 Bo Jackson .08 .25
3 Gregg Olson .01 .05
4 Tom Gordon .02 .10
5 Robin Ventura .08 .25
6 Will Clark .05 .15
7 Ruben Sierra .02 .10
8 Mark Grace .05 .15
9 Luis DeLosSantos .01 .05
10 Bernie Williams .40 1.00
11 Eric Davis .02 .10
12 Carney Lansford .02 .10
13 John Smoltz .08 .25
14 Gary Sheffield .08 .25
15 Kent Mercker .02 .10
16 Don Mattingly .25 .60
17 Tony Gwynn .10 .30
18 Ozzie Smith .15 .40
19 Fred McGriff .05 .15
20 Ken Griffey Jr. .40 1.00
21A Deion Sanders Prime Time 1.25 3.00
21B Deion Sanders Prime Time .08 .25
22 Jose Canseco .05 .15
23 Mitch Williams .01 .05
24 Cal Ripken UER .30 .75
25 Bob Geren .01 .05
26 Wade Boggs .05 .15
27 Ryne Sandberg .20 .50
28 Kirby Puckett .08 .25
29 Mike Scott .02 .10
30 Dwight Smith .01 .05
31 Craig Worthington .01 .05
32A Ricky Jordan ERR .01 .05
32B Ricky Jordan COR .01 .05
33 Darryl Strawberry .02 .10
34 Jerome Walton .01 .05
35 John Olerud .20 .50
36 Tom Glavine .05 .15
37 Rickey Henderson .08 .25
38 Rolando Roomes .01 .05
39 Mickey Tettleton .02 .10
40 Jim Abbott .05 .15
41 Dave Righetti .02 .10
42 Mike LaValliere .01 .05
43 Rob Dibble .02 .10
44 Pete Harnisch .01 .05
45 Jose Offerman .02 .10
46 Walt Weiss .01 .05
47 Mike Greenwell .01 .05
48 Barry Larkin .05 .15
49 Dave Gallagher .01 .05
50 Junior Felix .01 .05
51 Roger Clemens .40 1.00
52 Lonnie Smith .02 .10
53 Jerry Browne .01 .05
54 Greg Briley .01 .05
55 Delino DeShields .02 .10
56 Carmelo Martinez .01 .05
57 Craig Biggio .08 .25
58 Dwight Gooden .02 .10
59 McGwire .40 1.00
Bo
Sierra
59B Bo 2.00 5.00
Rubin
McGwire
60 Greg Vaughn .01 .05
61 Roberto Alomar .05 .15
62 Steve Bedrosian .01 .05
63 Devon White .02 .10
64 Kevin Mitchell .01 .05
65 Marquis Grissom .08 .25
66 Brian Holman .01 .05
67 Julio Franco .02 .10
68 Dave West .01 .05
69 Harold Baines .02 .10
70 Eric Anthony .01 .05
71 Glenn Davis .01 .05
72 Mark Langston .01 .05
73 Matt Williams .02 .10
74 Rafael Palmeiro .08 .25
75 Pete Rose Jr. .02 .10
76 Ramon Martinez .01 .05
77 Dwight Evans .05 .15
78 Mackey Sasser .01 .05
79 Mike Schooler .01 .05
80 Dennis Cook .01 .05
81 Orel Hershiser .02 .10
82 Barry Bonds .40 1.00
83 Geronimo Berroa .01 .05
84 George Bell .02 .10
85 Andre Dawson .02 .10
86 John Franco .02 .10
87A Clark 1.25 3.00
Gwynn
87B N.L. Hit Kings .05 .15
88 Glenallen Hill .01 .05
89 Jeff Ballard .01 .05
90 Todd Zeile .02 .10
91 Frank Viola .02 .10
92 Ozzie Guillen .02 .10
93 Jeffrey Leonard .01 .05
94 Dave Smith .01 .05
95 Dave Parker .02 .10
96 Jose Gonzalez .01 .05
97 Dave Stieb .02 .10
98 Charlie Hayes .01 .05
99 Jesse Barfield .02 .10
100 Joey Belle .08 .25
101 Jeff Reardon .02 .10
102 Bruce Hurst .02 .10
103 Luis Medina .01 .05
104 Mike Moore .01 .05
105 Vince Coleman .01 .05
106 Alan Trammell .02 .10
107 Randy Myers .01 .05
108 Frank Tanana .02 .10
109 Craig Lefferts .01 .05
110 John Wetteland .02 .10
111 Chris Gwynn .01 .05
112 Mark Carreon .01 .05
113 Von Hayes .02 .10
114 Doug Jones .01 .05
115 Andres Galarraga .02 .10
116 Carlton Fisk UER .05 .15
117 Paul O'Neill .05 .15
118 Tim Raines .02 .10
119 Tom Brunansky .01 .05
120 Andy Benes .02 .10
121 Mark Portugal .01 .05
122 Willie Randolph .02 .10
123 Jeff Blauser .01 .05
124 Don August .01 .05
125 Chuck Cary .01 .05
126 John Smiley .01 .05
127 Terry Mulholland .01 .05
128 Harold Reynolds .02 .10
129 Hubie Brooks .02 .10
130 Ben McDonald .02 .10
131 Kevin Ritz .01 .05
132 Luis Quinones .01 .05
133A Hensley Meulens ERR .01 .05
133B Hensley Meulens COR .01 .05
134 Bill Spiers UER .01 .05
135 Andy Hawkins .01 .05
136 Alvin Davis .02 .10
137 Lee Smith .02 .10
138 Joe Carter .02 .10
139 Bret Saberhagen .02 .10
140 Sammy Sosa 1.00 2.50
141 Matt Nokes .01 .05
142 Bert Blyleven .02 .10
143 Bobby Bonilla .02 .10
144 Howard Johnson .02 .10
145 Joe Magrane .01 .05
146 Pedro Guerrero .02 .10
147 Robin Yount .15 .40
148 Dan Gladden .01 .05
149 Steve Sax .02 .10
150A Clark .75 2.00
•Mitchell
150B Bay Bombers .05 .15

1990 Classic Update

The 1990 Classic Update set was the second set issued by the Classic Game company in 1990. Sometimes referenced as Classic Pink or Red, this set includes a Juan Gonzalez card. This 50-card, standard-size set was issued in late June of 1990. With a few exceptions, the set numbering is in alphabetical order by player's name. Early cards of Juan Gonzalez and Larry Walker highlight this set.

COMP. FACT. SET (50) 2.50 6.00
T1 Gregg Jefferies .01 .05
T2 Steve Adkins .01 .05
T3 Sandy Alomar Jr. .02 .10
T4 Steve Avery .01 .05
T5 Mike Blowers .01 .05
T6 George Brett .30 .75
T7 Tom Browning .01 .05
T8 Ellis Burks .02 .10
T9 Joe Carter .02 .10
T10 Jerald Clark .01 .05
T11 Hot Corners HOR .30 .75
Matt Williams
Will Clark
T12 Pat Combs .01 .05
T13 Scott Cooper .01 .05
T14 Mark Davis .01 .05
T15 Storm Davis .01 .05
T16 Larry Walker .50 1.25
T17 Brian DuBois .01 .05
T18 Len Dykstra .02 .10
T19 John Franco .02 .10
T20 Kirk Gibson .02 .10
T21 Juan Gonzalez .50 1.25
T22 Tommy Greene .01 .05
T23 Kent Hrbek .02 .10
T24 Mike Huff .01 .05
T25 Bo Jackson .08 .25
T26 Nolan Ryan .75 2.00
Nolan Knows Bo
T27 Roberto Kelly .01 .05
T28 Mark Langston .01 .05
T29 Ray Lankford .20 .50
T30 Kevin Maas .01 .05
T31 Julio Machado .01 .05
T32 Greg Maddux .50 1.25
T33 Mark McGwire .40 1.00
T34 Paul Molitor .10 .30
T35 Hal Morris .01 .05
T36 Dale Murphy .07 .20
T37 Eddie Murray .15 .40
T38 Jaime Navarro .01 .05
T39 Dean Palmer .15 .40
T40 Derek Parks .01 .05
T41 Bobby Rose .01 .05
T42 Wally Joyner .01 .05
T43 Chris Sabo .01 .05
T44 Benito Santiago .02 .10
T45 Mike Stanton .01 .05
T46 Terry Steinbach UER .01 .05
Career BA .725
T47 Dave Stewart .02 .10
T48 Greg Swindell .01 .05
T49 Jose Vizcaino .02 .10
NNO Royal Flush .01 .05
Mark Davis
Bret Saberhagen/(Instruc

1990 Classic Yellow

The 1990 Classic III set is also referenced as Classic Yellow. This set also featured number one draft picks of the current year mixed with the other Classic cards. This 100-card standard-size set also contained a special Nolan Ryan commemorative card, Texas Heat. A very early card of Chipper Jones is included in this set. Card T51 was never issued.

COMP.FACT.SET (100) 4.00 10.00
T1 Ken Griffey Jr. .40 1.00
T2 John Tudor .01 .05
T3 John Kruk .02 .10
T4 Mark Gardner .01 .05
T5 Scott Radinsky .01 .05
T6 John Burkett .01 .05
T7 Will Clark .05 .15
T8 Gary Carter .25 .60
T9 Ted Higuera .01 .05
T10 Dave Parker .02 .10
T11 Dante Bichette .02 .10
T12 Don Mattingly .25 .60
T13 Greg Harris .01 .05
T14 Dave Hollins .02 .10
T15 Matt Nokes .01 .05
T16 Kevin Tapani .08 .25
T17 Shane Mack .01 .05
T18 Randy Myers .02 .10
T19 Greg Olson .01 .05
T20 Shawn Abner .01 .05
T21 Jim Presley .01 .05
T22 Randy Johnson .20 .50
T23 Edgar Martinez .05 .15
T24 Scott Coolbaugh .01 .05
T25 Jeff Treadway .01 .05
T26 Joe Klink .01 .05
T27 Rickey Henderson .08 .25
T28 Sam Horn .01 .05
T29 Kurt Stillwell .01 .05
T30 Andy Van Slyke .05 .15
T31 Willie Banks .01 .05
T32 Jose Canseco .05 .15
T33 Felix Jose .01 .05
T34 Candy Maldonado .01 .05
T35 Carlos Baerga .02 .10
T36 Keith Hernandez .02 .10
T37 Frank Viola .01 .05
T38 Pete O'Brien .01 .05
T39 Pat Borders .01 .05
T40 Mike Heath .01 .05
T41 Kevin Brown .02 .10
T42 Chris Bosio .01 .05
T43 Shawn Boskie .01 .05
T44 Carlos Quintana .01 .05
T45 Juan Samuel .01 .05
T46 Tim Layana .01 .05
T47 Mike Harkey .01 .05
T48 Gerald Perry .01 .05
T49 Mike Witt .01 .05
T50 Joe Orsulak .01 .05
T51 Not Issued
T52 Willie Blair .01 .05
T53 Gene Larkin .01 .05
T54 Jody Reed .01 .05
T55 Jeff Reardon .02 .10
T56 Kevin McReynolds .01 .05
T57 Mike Marshall/(Unnumbered; game.01 .05
instructions on
T58 Eric Yelding .01 .05
T59 Fred Lynn .01 .05
T60 Jim Leyritz .08 .25
T61 John Orton .01 .05
T62 Mike Lieberthal .15 .40
T63 Mike Hartley .01 .05
T64 Kal Daniels .01 .05
T65 Terry Shumpert .01 .05
T66 Sil Campusano .01 .05
T67 Tony Pena .01 .05
T68 Barry Bonds .40 1.00
T69 Roger McDowell .01 .05
T70 Kelly Gruber .01 .05
T71 Willie Randolph .02 .10
T72 Rick Parker .01 .05
T73 Bobby Bonilla .02 .10
T74 Jack Armstrong .01 .05
T75 Hubie Brooks .01 .05
T76 Sandy Alomar Jr. .02 .10
T77 Ruben Sierra .02 .10
T78 Erik Hanson .01 .05
T79 Tony Phillips .01 .05
T80 Rondell White .15 .40
T81 Bobby Thigpen .01 .05
T82 Ron Walden .02 .10
T83 Don Peters .02 .10
T84 Nolan Ryan 6TH .40 1.00
T85 Lance Dickson .02 .10
T86 Ryne Sandberg .15 .40
T87 Eric Christopherson .02 .10
T88 Shane Andrews .02 .10
T89 Marc Newfield .02 .10
T90 Adam Hyzdu .02 .10
T91 N.Ryan .20 .50
R.Ryan
T92 Chipper Jones 1.25 3.00
T93 Frank Thomas .75 2.00
T94 Cecil Fielder .02 .10
T95 Delino DeShields .08 .25
T96 John Olerud .20 .50
T97 David Justice .20 .50
T98 Joe Oliver .01 .05
T99 Alex Fernandez .08 .25
T100 Todd Hundley .08 .25
NNO C.Jones .40 1.00
Matt
Ryan
Viola

1991 Classic Game

The 1991 Classic Baseball Collector's Edition board game is Classic's first Big Game issue since the 1989 Big Game. 100,000 games were produced, and each one included a board game, action spinner, eight stand-up baseball player pieces, action scoreboard, eight-page picture book with tips from five great baseball players (Carew, Spahn, Schmidt, Brock, and Aaron), 200 player cards, and a certificate of limited edition. The standard-size cards have on the fronts glossy color action photos bordered in purple. The backs are purple and white and have biography, statistics, five trivia questions, and an autograph slot.

COMP. FACT SET (200) 8.00 20.00
1 Frank Viola .01 .05
2 Tim Wallach .01 .05
3 Lou Whitaker .02 .10
4 Brett Butler .02 .10
5 Jim Abbott .02 .10
6 Jack Armstrong .01 .05
7 Craig Biggio .08 .25
8 Brian Barnes .01 .05
9 Dennis(Oil Can) Boyd .01 .05
10 Tom Browning .01 .05
11 Tom Brunansky .01 .05
12 Ellis Burks .02 .10
13 Harold Baines .05 .15
14 Kal Daniels .01 .05
15 Mark Davis .01 .05
16 Storm Davis .01 .05
17 Tom Glavine .20 .50
18 Mike Greenwell .01 .05
19 Kelly Gruber .01 .05
20 Mark Gubicza .01 .05
21 Pedro Guerrero .01 .05
22 Mike Harkey .01 .05
23 Orel Hershiser .02 .10
24 Ted Higuera .01 .05
25 Von Hayes .01 .05
26 Andre Dawson .08 .25
27 Shawon Dunston .01 .05
28 Roberto Kelly .01 .05
29 Joe Magrane .01 .05
30 Dennis Martinez .02 .10
31 Kevin McReynolds .01 .05
32 Matt Nokes .01 .05
33 Dan Plesac .01 .05
34 Dave Parker .02 .10
35 Randy Johnson .40 1.00
36 Bret Saberhagen .02 .10
37 Mackey Sasser .01 .05
38 Mike Scott .01 .05
39 Ozzie Smith .40 1.00
40 Kevin Seitzer .01 .05
41 Ruben Sierra .02 .10
42 Kevin Tapani .01 .05
43 Danny Tartabull .01 .05
44 Robby Thompson .01 .05
45 Andy Van Slyke .01 .05
46 Greg Vaughn .02 .10
47 Harold Reynolds .05 .15
48 Will Clark .08 .25
49 Gary Gaetti .02 .10
50 Joe Grahe .01 .05
51 Carlton Fisk .20 .50
52 Robin Ventura .08 .25
53 Ozzie Guillen .02 .10
54 Tom Candiotti .01 .05
55 Doug Jones .01 .05
56 Eric King .01 .05
57 Kirk Gibson .02 .10
58 Tim Costo .01 .05
59 Robin Yount .20 .50
60 Sammy Sosa .60 1.50
61 Jesse Barfield .01 .05
62 Marc Newfield .01 .05
63 Jimmy Key .02 .10
64 Felix Jose .01 .05
65 Mark Whiten .01 .05
66 Tommy Greene .01 .05
67 Kent Mercker .01 .05
68 Greg Maddux .50 1.25
69 Danny Jackson .01 .05
70 Reggie Sanders .02 .10
71 Eric Yelding .01 .05
72 Karl Rhodes .01 .05
73 Fernando Valenzuela .02 .10
74 Chris Nabholz .01 .05
75 Andres Galarraga .08 .25
76 Howard Johnson .01 .05
77 Hubie Brooks .01 .05
78 Terry Mulholland .01 .05
79 Paul Molitor .20 .50
80 Roger McDowell .01 .05
81 Darren Daulton .02 .10
82 Zane Smith .01 .05
83 Ray Lankford .02 .10
84 Bruce Hurst .01 .05
85 Andy Benes .01 .05
86 John Burkett .01 .05
87 Dave Righetti .01 .05
88 Steve Karsay .08 .25
89 D.J. Dozier .01 .05
90 Jeff Bagwell .75 2.00
91 Joe Carter .02 .10
92 Wes Chamberlain .01 .05
93 Vince Coleman .01 .05
94 Pat Combs .01 .05
95 Jerome Walton .01 .05
96 Jeff Conine .01 .05
97 Alan Trammell .05 .15
98 Don Mattingly .40 1.00
99 Ramon Martinez .01 .05
100 Dave Magadan .01 .05
101 Greg Swindell UER/(Misnumbered as T10) .01
.05
102 Dave Stewart .02 .10
103 Gary Sheffield .20 .50
104 George Bell .01 .05
105 Mark Grace .20 .50
106 Steve Sax .01 .05
107 Ryne Sandberg .30 .75
108 Chris Sabo .01 .05
109 Jose Rijo .01 .05
110 Cal Ripken 1.00 2.50
111 Kirby Puckett .20 .50
112 Eddie Murray .20 .50
113 Roberto Alomar .08 .25
114 Randy Myers .01 .05
115 Rafael Palmeiro .08 .25
116 John Olerud .05 .15
117 Gregg Jefferies .01 .05
118 Kent Hrbek .02 .10
119 Marquis Grissom .02 .10
120 Ken Griffey Jr. .75 2.00
121 Dwight Gooden .02 .10
122 Juan Gonzalez .20 .50
123 Ron Gant .02 .10
124 Travis Fryman .08 .25
125 John Franco .02 .10
126 Dennis Eckersley .15 .40
127 Cecil Fielder .02 .10
128 Phil Plantier .01 .05
129 Kevin Mitchell .01 .05
130 Kevin Maas .01 .05
131 Mark McGwire .40 1.00
132 Ben McDonald .01 .05
133 Len Dykstra .02 .10
134 Delino DeShields .02 .10
135 Jose Canseco .20 .50
136 Eric Davis .02 .10
137 George Brett .50 1.25
138 Steve Avery .01 .05
139 Eric Anthony .01 .05
140 Bobby Thigpen .01 .05
141 Ken Griffey Sr. .02 .10
142 Barry Larkin .08 .25
143 Jeff Brantley .01 .05
144 Bobby Bonilla .01 .05
145 Jose Offerman .01 .05
146 Mike Mussina .50 1.25
147 Erik Hanson .01 .05
148 Dale Murphy .15 .40
149 Roger Clemens .50 1.25
150 Tino Martinez .08 .25
151 Todd Van Poppel .08 .25
152 Mo Vaughn .20 .50
153 Derrick May .01 .05
154 Jack Clark .02 .10
155 Dave Hansen .01 .05
156 Tony Gwynn .50 1.25
157 Brian McRae .02 .10
158 Matt Williams .05 .15
159 Kirk Dressendorfer .01 .05
160 Scott Erickson .02 .10
161 Tony Fernandez .01 .05
162 Willie McGee .02 .10
163 Fred McGriff .08 .25
164 Leo Gomez .01 .05
165 Bernard Gilkey .01 .05
166 Bobby Witt .01 .05
167 Doug Drabek .01 .05
168 Rob Dibble .01 .05
169 Glenn Davis .01 .05
170 Danny Darwin .01 .05
171 Eric Karros .20 .50
172 Eddie Zosky .01 .05
173 Todd Zeile .02 .10
174 Tim Raines .02 .10
175 Benito Santiago .02 .10
176 Dan Peltier .01 .05
177 Darryl Strawberry .02 .10
178 Hal Morris .01 .05
179 Hensley Meulens .01 .05
180 John Smoltz .08 .25
181 Frank Thomas .40 1.00
182 Dave Staton .01 .05
183 Scott Chiamparino .01 .05
184 Alex Fernandez .01 .05
185 Mark Lewis .01 .05
186 Bo Jackson .08 .25
187 Mickey Morandini UER
(Photo is actually .01 .05
Darren D
188 Cory Snyder .01 .05
189 Rickey Henderson .20 .50
190 Junior Felix .01 .05
191 Milt Cuyler .01 .05
192 Wade Boggs .15 .40
193 Dave Justice/(Justice Prevails) .20 .50
194 Sandy Alomar Jr. .02 .10
195 Barry Bonds .60 1.50
196 Nolan Ryan 1.00 2.50
197 Rico Brogna .01 .05
198 Steve Decker .01 .05
199 Bob Welch .02 .10
200 Andujar Cedeno .01 .05

1991 Classic I

This 100-card standard-size set features many of the most popular players in the game of baseball as well as some of the more exciting prospects. The set includes trivia questions on the backs of the cards. For the most part the set is arranged alphabetically by team and then alphabetically by players within that team.

COMP.FACT SET (100) 3.00 8.00
T1 John Olerud .05 .15
T2 Tino Martinez .08 .25
T3 Ken Griffey Jr. .75 2.00
T4 Jeromy Burnitz .20 .50
T5 Ron Gant .02 .10
T6 Mike Benjamin .01 .05
T7 Steve Decker .01 .05
T8 Matt Williams .05 .15
T9 Rafael Novoa .01 .05
T10 Kevin Mitchell .01 .05
T11 Dave Justice .08 .25
T12 Leo Gomez .01 .05
T13 Chris Hoiles .01 .05
T14 Ben McDonald .01 .05
T15 David Segui .02 .10
T16 Anthony Telford .01 .05
T17 Mike Mussina .60 1.50
T18 Roger Clemens .50 1.25
T19 Wade Boggs .20 .50
T20 Tim Naehring .01 .05
T21 Joe Carter .02 .10
T22 Phil Plantier .01 .05
T23 Rob Dibble .01 .05
T24 Mo Vaughn .15 .40
T25 Lee Stevens .01 .05
T26 Chris Sabo .01 .05
T27 Mark Grace .08 .25
T28 Derrick May .01 .05
T29 Ryne Sandberg .20 .50
T30 Matt Stark .01 .05
T31 Bobby Thigpen .01 .05
T32 Frank Thomas .30 .75
T33 Don Mattingly .50 1.25
T34 Eric Davis .02 .10
T35 Reggie Jefferson .01 .05
T36 Alex Cole .01 .05
T37 Mark Lewis .01 .05
T38 Tim Costo .01 .05
T39 Sandy Alomar Jr. .02 .10
T40 Travis Fryman .08 .25
T41 Cecil Fielder .02 .10
T42 Milt Cuyler .01 .05
T43 Andujar Cedeno .01 .05
T44 Danny Darwin .01 .05
T45 Randy Hennis .01 .05
T46 George Brett .50 1.25
T47 Jeff Conine .05 .15
T48 Bo Jackson .08 .25
T49 Brian McRae .02 .10
T50 Brent Mayne .01 .05
T51 Eddie Murray .20 .50
T52 Ramon Martinez .01 .05
T53 Jim Neidlinger .01 .05
T54 Jim Poole .01 .05
T55 Tim McIntosh .01 .05
T56 Randy Veres .01 .05
T57 Kirby Puckett .15 .40
T58 Todd Ritchie .02 .10
T59 Rich Garces .01 .05
T60 Moises Alou .08 .25
T61 Delino DeShields .02 .10
T62 Oscar Azocar .01 .05
T63 Kevin Maas .01 .05
T64 Alan Mills .01 .05
T65 John Franco .02 .10
T66 Chris Jelic .01 .05
T67 Dave Magadan .01 .05
T68 Darryl Strawberry .02 .10
T69 Hensley Meulens .01 .05
T70 Juan Gonzalez .25 .60
T71 Reggie Harris .01 .05
T72 Rickey Henderson .20 .50
T73 Mark McGwire .50 1.25
T74 Willie McGee .02 .10
T75 Todd Van Poppel .01 .05
T76 Bob Welch .01 .05
T77 Future Aces .01 .05
Todd Van Poppel
Don Peters
David Za
T78 Len Dykstra .02 .10
T79 Mickey Morandini .01 .05
T80 Wes Chamberlain .01 .05
T81 Barry Bonds .50 1.25
T82 Doug Drabek .01 .05
T83 Randy Tomlin .01 .05
T84 Scott Chiamparino .01 .05
T85 Rafael Palmeiro .08 .25
T86 Nolan Ryan 1.00 2.50
T87 Bobby Witt .01 .05
T88 Fred McGriff .08 .25
T89 Dave Stieb .02 .10
T90 Ed Sprague .02 .10
T91 Vince Coleman .01 .05
T92 Rod Brewer .01 .05
T93 Bernard Gilkey .01 .05
T94 Roberto Alomar .08 .25
T95 Chuck Finley .02 .10
T96 Dale Murphy .08 .25
T97 Jose Rijo .01 .05
T98 Hal Morris .01 .05
T99 Friendly Foes .02 .10
Darryl Strawberry
Dwight Gooden/(
NNO Todd Van Poppel .02 .10
Dave Justice
Ryne Sandberg
Kevi

1991 Classic II

This second issue of the 1991 Classic baseball trivia game contains a small gameboard, accessories, 99 standard-size player cards with trivia questions on the backs, and one "4-in-1" micro player card. The fronts have glossy color action photos with cranberry red borders. The backs have biography, statistics, five trivia questions, and an autograph slot. A first year card of Ivan Rodriguez is featured within this set.

COMP. FACT. SET (100) 3.00 8.00
T1 Ken Griffey Jr. 1.00 2.50
T2 Wil Cordero .01 .05
T3 Cal Ripken 1.25 3.00
T4 D.J. Dozier .01 .05
T5 Darrin Fletcher .01 .05
T6 Glenn Davis .01 .05
T7 Alex Fernandez .01 .05
T8 Cory Snyder .01 .05
T9 Tim Raines .02 .10
T10 Greg Swindell .01 .05
T11 Mark Lewis .01 .05
T12 Rico Brogna .01 .05
T13 Gary Sheffield .20 .50
T14 Paul Molitor .20 .50
T15 Kent Hrbek .02 .10
T16 Scott Erickson .01 .05
T17 Steve Sax .01 .05
T18 Dennis Eckersley .20 .50
T19 Jose Canseco .15 .40
T20 Kirk Dressendorfer .01 .05
T21 Ken Griffey Sr. .02 .10
T22 Erik Hanson .01 .05
T23 Dan Peltier .01 .05
T24 John Olerud .05 .15
T25 Eddie Zosky .01 .05
T26 Steve Avery .02 .05

T27 John Smoltz .15 .40
T28 Frank Thomas .25 .60
T29 Jerome Walton .01 .05
T30 George Bell .01 .05
T31 Jose Rijo .01 .05
T32 Randy Myers .02 .10
T33 Barry Larkin .08 .25
T34 Eric Anthony .01 .05
T35 Dave Hansen .01 .05
T36 Eric Karros .15 .40
T37 Jose Offerman .01 .05
T38 Marquis Grissom .02 .10
T39 Dwight Gooden .02 .10
T40 Gregg Jefferies .01 .05
T41 Pat Combs .01 .05
T42 Todd Zeile .02 .10
T43 Benito Santiago .02 .10
T44 Dave Staton .01 .05
T45 Tony Fernandez .02 .10
T46 Fred McGriff .05 .15
T47 Jeff Brantley .01 .05
T48 Junior Felix .01 .05
T49 Jack Morris .02 .10
T50 Chris George .01 .05
T51 Henry Rodriguez .02 .10
T52 Paul Marak .01 .05
T53 Ryan Klesko .30 .75
T54 Darren Lewis .01 .05
T55 Lance Dickson .01 .05
T56 Anthony Young .01 .05
T57 Willie Banks .01 .05
T58 Mike Bordick .05 .15
T59 Roger Salkeld .01 .05
T60 Steve Karsay .02 .10
T61 Bernie Williams .08 .25
T62 Mickey Tettleton .02 .10
T63 Dave Justice .08 .25
T64 Steve Decker .01 .05
T65 Roger Clemens .60 1.50
T66 Phil Plantier .01 .05
T67 Ryne Sandberg .20 .50
T68 Sandy Alomar Jr. .02 .10
T69 Cecil Fielder .02 .10
T70 George Brett .60 1.50
T71 Delino DeShields .02 .10
T72 Dave Magadan .01 .05
T73 Darryl Strawberry .02 .10
T74 Juan Gonzalez .20 .50
T75 Rickey Henderson .30 .75
T76 Willie McGee .02 .10
T77 Todd Van Poppel .01 .05
T78 Barry Bonds .60 1.50
T79 Doug Drabek .01 .05
T80 Nolan Ryan 300 GW .50 1.25
T81 Roberto Alomar .08 .25
T82 Ivan Rodriguez 1.00 2.50
T83 Dan Opperman .01 .05
T84 Jeff Bagwell .75 2.00
T85 Braulio Castillo .01 .05
T86 Doug Simons .01 .05
T87 Wade Taylor .01 .05
T88 Gary Scott .01 .05
T89 Dave Stewart .02 .10
T90 Mike Simms .01 .05
T91 Luis Gonzalez .40 1.00
T92 Bobby Bonilla .02 .10
T93 Tony Gwynn .40 1.00
T94 Will Clark .15 .40
T95 Rich Rowland .01 .05
T96 Alan Trammell .05 .15
T97 Strikeout Kings .30 .75
Nolan Ryan
Roger Clemens
T98 Joe Carter .02 .10
T99 Jack Clark .02 .10
T100 Steve Decker .01 .05
NNO John Olerud .20 .50
Dwight Gooden
Jose Canseco
Darryl S

1991 Classic III

The third issue of the 1991 Classic baseball trivia game contains a small gameboard, accessories, 99 standard-size player cards with trivia questions on the backs, and one "4-in-1" micro player card. The card fronts are glossy color action photos with grayish-green borders. The horizontal backs feature biography, statistics, and five trivia questions. With few exceptions, the cards are arranged in alphabetical order. First year cards of Pedro Martinez and Ivan Rodriguez are featured within this set.

COMP.FACT.SET (100) 2.00 5.00
T1 Jim Abbott .05 .15
T2 Craig Biggio .05 .15
T3 Wade Boggs .05 .15
T4 Bobby Bonilla .02 .10
T5 Ivan Calderon .01 .05
T6 Jose Canseco .05 .15
T7 Andy Benes .01 .05
T8 Wes Chamberlain .01 .05
T9 Will Clark .05 .15
T10 Royce Clayton .01 .05
T11 Gerald Alexander .01 .05
T12 Chili Davis .02 .10
T13 Eric Davis .02 .10
T14 Andre Dawson .02 .10
T15 Rob Dibble .02 .10
T16 Chris Donnels .01 .05
T17 Scott Erickson .01 .05
T18 Monty Fariss .01 .05
T19 Ruben Amaro Jr. .01 .05
T20 Chuck Finley .02 .10
T21 Carlton Fisk .05 .15
T22 Carlos Baerga .01 .05
T23 Ron Gant .02 .10
T24 D.Justice/R.Gant .02 .10
T25 Mike Gardiner .01 .05
T26 Tom Glavine .05 .15
T27 Joe Grahe .01 .05
T28 Derek Bell .02 .10
T29 Mike Greenwell .01 .05
T30 Ken Griffey Jr. .25 .60
T31 Leo Gomez .01 .05
T32 Tom Goodwin .01 .05
T33 Tony Gwynn .10 .30
T34 Mel Hall .01 .05
T35 Brian Harper .01 .05
T36 Dave Henderson .01 .05
T37 Albert Belle .02 .10
T38 Orel Hershiser .02 .10
T39 Brian Hunter .02 .10
T40 Howard Johnson .01 .05
T41 Felix Jose .01 .05
T42 Wally Joyner .02 .10
T43 Jeff Juden .01 .05
T44 Pat Kelly .01 .05
T45 Jimmy Key .02 .10
T46 Chuck Knoblauch .02 .10
T47 John Kruk .02 .10
T48 Ray Lankford .02 .10
T49 Ced Landrum .01 .05
T50 Scott Livingstone .01 .05
T51 Kevin Maas .01 .05
T52 Greg Maddux .15 .40
T53 Dennis Martinez .02 .10
T54 Edgar Martinez .05 .15
T55 Pedro Martinez 1.25 3.00
T56 Don Mattingly .25 .60
T57 Orlando Merced .01 .05
T58 Keith Mitchell .01 .05
T59 Kevin Mitchell .01 .05
T60 Paul Molitor .02 .10
T61 Jack Morris .02 .10
T62 Hal Morris .01 .05
T63 Kevin Morton .01 .05
T64 Pedro Munoz .01 .05
T65 Eddie Murray .08 .25
T66 Jack McDowell .01 .05
T67 Jeff McNeely .01 .05
T68 Brian McRae .02 .10
T69 Kevin McReynolds .01 .05
T70 Gregg Olson .01 .05
T71 Rafael Palmeiro .05 .15
T72 Dean Palmer .02 .10
T73 Tony Phillips .01 .05
T74 Kirby Puckett .08 .25
T75 Carlos Quintana .01 .05
T76 Pat Rice .01 .05
T77 Cal Ripken .30 .75
T78 Ivan Rodriguez .75 2.00
T79 Nolan Ryan .40 1.00
T80 Bret Saberhagen .02 .10
T81 Tim Salmon .40 1.00
T82 Juan Samuel .01 .05
T83 Ruben Sierra .02 .10
T84 Heathcliff Slocumb .02 .10
T85 Joe Slusarski .01 .05
T86 John Smiley .01 .05
T87 Dave Smith .01 .05
T88 Ed Sprague .01 .05
T89 Todd Stottlemyre .01 .05
T90 Mike Timlin .02 .10
T91 Greg Vaughn .01 .05
T92 Frank Viola .02 .10
T93 Chico Walker .01 .05
T94 Devon White .02 .10
T95 Matt Williams .02 .10
T96 Rick Wilkins .01 .05
T97 Bernie Williams .08 .25
T98 N.Ryan .20 .50
G.Gossage
T99 Gerald Williams .02 .10
NNO 4-in-1 Card .05 .15

1991 Classic Nolan Ryan 10

Produced by Classic Games, Inc. and made exclusively for American Collectibles for Shop at Home TV campaign., this ten card limited edition career celebration standard size set highlights Nolan Ryan's achievements. The fronts display posed and action shots with a split design border. The left half of the card has a mottled green and yellow border and the right half displays a teal green one. A black bar overlaid on the photo lists the team he is portrayed playing for, and the years Nolan was a member of that team. The light green horizontal backs carry biography, statistics, and career summary.

COMP. FACT. SET (10) 8.00 20.00
COMMON PLAYER (1-10) .80 2.00

1992 Classic Game

The 1992 Classic Baseball Collector's Edition game contains 200 standard-size cards. The cards were issued in two boxes labeled "Trivia Cards A" and "Trivia Cards B." The game also included an official Major League Action Spinner, eight stand-up baseball hero player pieces, an action scoreboard, a hand-illustrated game board, and a collectible book featuring tips from a new group of baseball legends. According to Classic, production has been limited to 125,000 games. The fronts display glossy color action photos bordered in dark purple. The Classic logo and the year "1992" appear in the top border, while the player's name is given in white lettering in the bottom border. The horizontally oriented backs present biography, statistics (1991 and career), and five baseball trivia questions.

COMP. FACT. SET (200) 10.00 25.00
1 Chuck Finley .07 .20
2 Craig Biggio .15 .40
3 Luis Gonzalez .20 .50
4 Pete Harnisch .02 .10
5 Jeff Juden .02 .10
6 Harold Baines .07 .20
7 Kirk Dressendorfer .02 .10
8 Dennis Eckersley .20 .50
9 Dave Henderson .02 .10
10 Dave Stewart .07 .20
11 Joe Carter .07 .20
12 Juan Guzman .02 .10
13 Dave Stieb .02 .10
14 Todd Stottlemyre .02 .10
15 Ron Gant .07 .20
16 Brian Hunter .02 .10
17 Dave Justice .15 .40
18 John Smoltz .07 .20
19 Mike Stanton .07 .20
20 Chris George .02 .10
21 Paul Molitor .20 .50
22 Omar Olivares .02 .10
23 Lee Smith .07 .20
24 Ozzie Smith .50 1.25
25 Todd Zeile .07 .20
26 George Bell .02 .10
27 Andre Dawson .15 .40
28 Shawon Dunston .02 .10
29 Mark Grace .15 .40
30 Greg Maddux .75 2.00
31 Dave Smith .02 .10
32 Brett Butler .07 .20
33 Orel Hershiser .07 .20
34 Eric Karros .10 .30
35 Ramon Martinez .02 .10
36 Jose Offerman .02 .10
37 Juan Samuel .02 .10
38 Delino DeShields .07 .20
39 Marquis Grissom .07 .20
40 Tim Wallach .02 .10
41 Eric Gunderson .02 .10
42 Willie McGee .07 .20
43 Dave Righetti .02 .10
44 Robby Thompson .02 .10
45 Matt Williams .10 .30
46 Sandy Alomar Jr. .07 .20
47 Reggie Jefferson .02 .10
48 Mark Lewis .02 .10
49 Robin Ventura .15 .40
50 Tino Martinez .15 .40
51 Roberto Kelly .02 .10
52 Vince Coleman .02 .10
53 Dwight Gooden .07 .20
54 Todd Hundley .07 .20
55 Kevin Maas .02 .10
56 Wade Taylor .02 .10
57 Bryan Harvey .02 .10
58 Leo Gomez .02 .10
59 Ben McDonald .02 .10
60 Ricky Bones .02 .10
61 Tony Gwynn .60 1.50
62 Benito Santiago .07 .20
63 Wes Chamberlain .02 .10
64 Tommy Greene .02 .10
65 Dale Murphy .15 .40
66 Steve Buechele .02 .10
67 Doug Drabek .02 .10
68 Joe Grahe .02 .10
69 Rafael Palmeiro .15 .40
70 Wade Boggs .30 .75
71 Ellis Burks .07 .20
72 Mike Greenwell .02 .10
73 Mo Vaughn .10 .30
74 Derek Bell .02 .10
75 Rob Dibble .02 .10
76 Barry Larkin .15 .40
77 Jose Rijo .02 .10
78 Doug Henry .02 .10
79 Chris Sabo .02 .10
80 Pedro Guerrero .02 .10
81 George Brett .60 1.50
82 Tom Gordon .02 .10
83 Mark Gubicza .02 .10
84 Mark Whiten .02 .10
85 Brian McRae .02 .10
86 Danny Jackson .02 .10
87 Milt Cuyler .02 .10
88 Travis Fryman .07 .20
89 Mickey Tettleton .02 .10
90 Alan Trammell .15 .40
91 Lou Whitaker .07 .20
92 Chili Davis .07 .20
93 Scott Erickson .02 .10
94 Kent Hrbek .07 .20
95 Alex Fernandez .02 .10
96 Carlton Fisk .30 .75
97 Ramon Garcia .02 .10
98 Ozzie Guillen .07 .20
99 Tim Raines .07 .20
100 Bobby Thigpen .02 .10
101 Kirby Puckett .25 .60
102 Bernie Williams .30 .75
103 Dave Hansen .02 .10
104 Kevin Tapani .02 .10
105 Don Mattingly .60 1.50
106 Frank Thomas .25 .60
107 Monty Fariss .02 .10
108 Bo Jackson .15 .40
109 Jim Abbott .07 .20
110 Jose Canseco .20 .50
111 Phil Plantier .02 .10
112 Brian Williams .02 .10
113 Mark Langston .02 .10
114 Wilson Alvarez .02 .10
115 Roberto Hernandez .15 .40
116 Darryl Kile .07 .20
117 Ryan Bowen .02 .10
118 Rickey Henderson .40 1.00
119 Mark McGwire .60 1.50
120 Devon White .02 .10
121 Roberto Alomar .15 .40
122 Kelly Gruber .02 .10
123 Eddie Zosky .02 .10
124 Tom Glavine .10 .30
125 Kal Daniels .02 .10
126 Cal Eldred .02 .10
127 Deion Sanders .20 .50
128 Robin Yount .20 .50
129 Cecil Fielder .07 .20
130 Ray Lankford .07 .20
131 Ryne Sandberg .30 .75
132 Darryl Strawberry .07 .20
133 Chris Haney .02 .10
134 Dennis Martinez .07 .20
135 Bryan Hickerson .02 .10
136 Will Clark .30 .75
137 Hal Morris .02 .10
138 Charles Nagy .02 .10
139 Jim Thome .40 1.00
140 Albert Belle .10 .30
141 Reggie Sanders .02 .10
142 Scott Cooper .02 .10
143 David Cone .15 .40
144 Anthony Young .02 .10
145 Howard Johnson .02 .10
146 Arthur Rhodes .02 .10
147 Scott Aldred .02 .10
148 Mike Mussina .40 1.00
149 Fred McGriff .10 .30
150 Andy Benes .02 .10
151 Ruben Sierra .07 .20
152 Len Dykstra .07 .20
153 Andy Van Slyke .07 .20
154 Orlando Merced .02 .10
155 Barry Bonds .60 1.50
156 John Smiley .02 .10
157 Julio Franco .07 .20
158 Juan Gonzalez .15 .40
159 Ivan Rodriguez .50 1.25
160 Willie Banks .02 .10
161 Eric Davis .10 .30
162 Eddie Murray .20 .50
163 Dave Fleming .02 .10
164 Wally Joyner .02 .10
165 Kevin Mitchell .07 .20
166 Eddie Taubensee .02 .10
167 Danny Tartabull .02 .10
168 Ken Hill .02 .10
169 Willie Randolph .07 .20
170 Kevin McReynolds .02 .10
171 Gregg Jefferies .02 .10
172 Patrick Lennon .02 .10
173 Luis Mercedes .02 .10
174 Glenn Davis .02 .10
175 Bret Saberhagen .07 .20
176 Bobby Bonilla .02 .10
177 Kenny Lofton .15 .40
178 Jose Lind .02 .10
179 Royce Clayton .02 .10
180 Scott Scudder .02 .10
181 Chuck Knoblauch .15 .40
182 Terry Pendleton .02 .10
183 Nolan Ryan 1.25 3.00
184 Rob Maurer .02 .10
185 Brian Bohanon .02 .10
186 Ken Griffey Jr. 1.00 2.50
187 Jeff Bagwell .60 1.50
188 Steve Avery .02 .10
189 Roger Clemens .60 1.50
190 Cal Ripken 1.25 3.00
191 Kim Batiste .02 .10
192 Bip Roberts .02 .10
193 Greg Swindell .02 .10
194 Dave Winfield .20 .50
195 Steve Sax .02 .10
196 Frank Viola .02 .10
197 Mo Sanford .02 .10
198 Kyle Abbott .02 .10
199 Jack Morris .07 .20
200 Andy Ashby .02 .10

1992 Classic I

The first issue of the 1992 Classic baseball trivia game contains a small gameboard, accessories, 99 standard-size player cards with trivia questions on the backs, one "4-in-1" micro player card, and four micro player pieces. The cards have on the fronts glossy color action photos bordered in white. A red, gray, and purple stripe with the year "1992" traverses the top of the card. In a horizontal format, the backs feature biography, statistics, and five trivia questions, printed on a ghosted image of the 26 major league city skylines. The cards are numbered on the back and basically arranged in alphabetical order.

COMP. FACT. SET (100) 3.00 8.00
T1 Jim Abbott .02 .10
T2 Kyle Abbott .01 .05
T3 Scott Aldred .01 .05
T4 Roberto Alomar .10 .30
T5 Wilson Alvarez .01 .05
T6 Andy Ashby .01 .05
T7 Steve Avery .01 .05
T8 Jeff Bagwell .40 1.00
T9 Bret Barberie .01 .05
T10 Kim Batiste .01 .05
T11 Derek Bell .01 .05
T12 Jay Bell .01 .05
T13 Albert Belle .02 .10
T14 Andy Benes .01 .05
T15 Sean Berry .01 .05
T16 Barry Bonds .40 1.00
T17 Ryan Bowen .01 .05
T18 Pena/Wohlers/Mercker .01 .05
T19 Scott Brosius .10 .30
T20 Jay Buhner .02 .10
T21 David Burba .01 .05
T22 Jose Canseco .15 .40
T23 Andujar Cedeno .01 .05
T24 Will Clark .20 .50
T25 Royce Clayton .01 .05
T26 Roger Clemens .40 1.00
T27 David Cone .10 .30
T28 Scott Cooper .01 .05
T29 Chris Cron .01 .05
T30 Len Dykstra .02 .10
T31 Cal Eldred .01 .05
T32 Hector Fajardo .01 .05
T33 Cecil Fielder .02 .10
T34 Dave Fleming .01 .05
T35 Steve Foster .01 .05
T36 Julio Franco .02 .10
T37 Carlos Garcia .01 .05
T38 Tom Glavine .10 .30
T39 Tom Goodwin .01 .05
T40 Ken Griffey Jr. .60 1.50
T41 Chris Haney .01 .05
T42 Bryan Harvey .01 .05
T43 Rickey Henderson 939 .30 .75
T44 Carlos Hernandez .01 .05
T45 Roberto Hernandez .10 .30
T46 Brook Jacoby .01 .05
T47 Howard Johnson .01 .05
T48 Pat Kelly .01 .05
T49 Darryl Kile .02 .10
T50 Chuck Knoblauch .10 .30
T51 R.Lankford/O.Smith .10 .30
T52 Mark Leiter .01 .05
T53 Darren Lewis .01 .05
T54 Scott Livingstone .01 .05
T55 Shane Mack .01 .05
T56 Chito Martinez .01 .05
T57 Dennis Martinez/(The Perfect Game).02 .10
T58 Don Mattingly .40 1.00
T59 Paul McClellan .01 .05
T60 Chuck McElroy .01 .05
T61 Fred McGriff .07 .20
T62 Orlando Merced .01 .05
T63 Luis Mercedes .01 .05
T64 Kevin Mitchell .02 .10
T65 Hal Morris .01 .05
T66 Jack Morris .02 .10
T67 Mike Mussina .30 .75
T68 Denny Neagle .02 .10
T69 Tom Pagnozzi .01 .05
T70 Terry Pendleton .01 .05
T71 Phil Plantier .01 .05
T72 Kirby Puckett .15 .40
T73 Carlos Quintana .01 .05
T74 Willie Randolph .02 .10
T75 Arthur Rhodes .01 .05
T76 Cal Ripken .75 2.00
T77 Ivan Rodriguez .40 1.00
T78 Nolan Ryan .75 2.00
T79 Ryne Sandberg .25 .60
T80 Deion Sanders/(Deion Drops In) .20 .50
T81 Reggie Sanders .02 .10
T82 Mo Sanford .01 .05
T83 Terry Shumpert .01 .05
T84 Tim Spehr .01 .05
T85 Lee Stevens .01 .05
T86 Darryl Strawberry .02 .10
T87 Kevin Tapani .01 .05
T88 Danny Tartabull .01 .05
T89 Frank Thomas .20 .50
T90 Jim Thome .30 .75
T91 Todd Van Poppel .01 .05
T92 Andy Van Slyke .01 .05
T93 John Wehner .01 .05
T94 John Wetteland .02 .10
T95 Devon White .01 .05
T96 Brian Williams .01 .05
T97 Mark Wohlers .01 .05
T98 Robin Yount .20 .50
T99 Eddie Zosky .01 .05
NNO Bonds/Clem/Avery/Ryan .40 1.00

1992 Classic II

The 1992 Series II baseball trivia board game features 99 standard-size new player trivia standard-size cards, one "4-in-1" micro player card, a gameboard, and a spinner. The cards display color action player photos on the fronts. The horizontal backs have a biography, statistics (1991 and career), five trivia questions, and a color drawing of the team's uniform. According to Classic, the production run was 175,000 games.

COMP. FACT. SET (100) 4.00 10.00
T1 Jim Abbott .02 .10
T2 Jeff Bagwell .40 1.00
T3 Jose Canseco .15 .40
T4 Julio Valera .01 .05
T5 Scott Brosius .10 .30
T6 Mark Langston .01 .05
T7 Andy Stankiewicz .01 .05
T8 Gary DiSarcina .01 .05
T9 Pete Harnisch .01 .05
T10 Mark McGwire .40 1.00
T11 Ricky Bones .01 .05
T12 Steve Avery .01 .05
T13 Deion Sanders .15 .40
T14 Mike Mussina .20 .50
T15 Dave Justice .07 .20
T16 Pat Hentgen .10 .30
T17 Tom Glavine .10 .30
T18 Juan Guzman .01 .05
T19 Ron Gant .02 .10
T20 Kelly Gruber .01 .05
T21 Eric Karros .07 .20
T22 Derrick May .01 .05
T23 Dave Hansen .01 .05
T24 Andre Dawson .07 .20
T25 Eric Davis .02 .10
T26 Ozzie Smith .30 .75
T27 Sammy Sosa .30 .75
T28 Lee Smith .02 .10
T29 Ryne Sandberg .20 .50
T30 Robin Yount .15 .40
T31 Matt Williams .07 .20
T32 John Vander Wal .01 .05
T33 Bill Swift .01 .05
T34 Delino DeShields .01 .05
T35 Royce Clayton .01 .05
T36 Moises Alou .02 .10
T37 Will Clark .20 .50
T38 Darryl Strawberry .02 .10
T39 Larry Walker .10 .30
T40 Ramon Martinez .01 .05
T41 Howard Johnson .01 .05
T42 Tino Martinez .10 .30
T43 Dwight Gooden .02 .10
T44 Ken Griffey Jr. .60 1.50
T45 David Cone .10 .30
T46 Kenny Lofton .10 .30
T47 Bobby Bonilla .02 .10
T48 Carlos Baerga .01 .05
T49 Don Mattingly .40 1.00
T50 Sandy Alomar Jr. .02 .10
T51 Lenny Dykstra .02 .10
T52 Tony Gwynn .40 1.00
T53 Felix Jose .01 .05
T54 Rick Sutcliffe .01 .05
T55 Wes Chamberlain .01 .05
T56 Cal Ripken .75 2.00
T57 Kyle Abbott .01 .05
T58 Leo Gomez .01 .05
T59 Gary Sheffield .15 .40
T60 Anthony Young .01 .05
T61 Roger Clemens .40 1.00
T62 Rafael Palmeiro .15 .40
T63 Wade Boggs .20 .50
T64 Andy Van Slyke .02 .10
T65 Ruben Sierra .01 .05
T66 Denny Neagle .02 .10
T67 Nolan Ryan .75 2.00
T68 Doug Drabek .01 .05
T69 Ivan Rodriguez .50 1.25
T70 Barry Bonds .40 1.00
T71 Chuck Knoblauch .10 .30
T72 Reggie Sanders .02 .10
T73 Cecil Fielder .02 .10
T74 Barry Larkin .10 .30
T75 Scott Aldred .01 .05
T76 Rob Dibble .01 .05
T77 Brian McRae .01 .05
T78 Tim Belcher .01 .05
T79 George Brett .40 1.00
T80 Frank Viola .01 .05
T81 Roberto Kelly .01 .05
T82 Jack McDowell .01 .05
T83 Mel Hall .01 .05
T84 Esteban Beltre .01 .05
T85 Robin Ventura .10 .30
T86 George Bell .01 .05
T87 Frank Thomas .25 .60
T88 John Smiley .01 .05
T89 Bobby Thigpen .01 .05
T90 Kirby Puckett .15 .40
T91 Kevin Mitchell .02 .10
T92 Peter Hoy .01 .05
T93 Russ Springer .01 .05
T94 Donovan Osborne .01 .05
T95 Dave Silvestri .01 .05
T96 Chad Curtis .02 .10
T97 Pat Mahomes .01 .05
T98 Danny Tartabull .01 .05
T99 John Doherty .01 .05
NNO Sand/Muss/Sand/Cans .20 .50

1993 Classic Game

The 1993 Classic Game contains 99 trivia standard-size cards, a micro player card, four micro piece stands, a color game board, and a reusable plastic carrying case. As a special bonus, Classic included highlight trivia cards of George Brett and Robin Yount commemorating their 3,000 hits in the 1992 season. The cards feature color action player photos with navy blue borders.

COMP. FACT. SET (100) 5.00 12.00
1 Jim Abbott .02 .10
2 Roberto Alomar .20 .50
3 Moises Alou .02 .10
4 Brady Anderson .02 .10
5 Eric Anthony .01 .05
6 Alex Arias .01 .05
7 Pedro Astacio .01 .05
8 Steve Avery .01 .05
9 Carlos Baerga .01 .05
10 Jeff Bagwell .30 .75
11 George Bell .01 .05
12 Albert Belle .02 .10
13 Craig Biggio .10 .30
14 Barry Bonds .50 1.25
15 Bobby Bonilla .02 .10
16 Mike Bordick .01 .05
17 George Brett/3,000th Hit .50 1.25
18 Jose Canseco .20 .50
19 Joe Carter .02 .10
20 Royce Clayton .01 .05
21 Roger Clemens .50 1.25
22 Greg Colbrunn .01 .05
23 David Cone .10 .30
24 Darren Daulton .02 .10
25 Delino DeShields .01 .05
26 Rob Dibble .01 .05
27 Dennis Eckersley .15 .40
28 Cal Eldred .01 .05
29 Scott Erickson .01 .05
30 Junior Felix .01 .05
31 Tony Fernandez .01 .05
32 Cecil Fielder .02 .10
33 Steve Finley .02 .10
34 Dave Fleming .01 .05
35 Travis Fryman .01 .05
36 Tom Glavine .10 .30
37 Juan Gonzalez .20 .50
38 Ken Griffey Jr. .60 1.50
39 Marquis Grissom .02 .10
40 Juan Guzman .01 .05
41 Tony Gwynn .50 1.25
42 Rickey Henderson .40 1.00
43 Felix Jose .01 .05
44 Wally Joyner .01 .05
45 David Justice .10 .30
46 Eric Karros .02 .10
47 Roberto Kelly .01 .05
48 Ryan Klesko .02 .10
49 Chuck Knoblauch .02 .10
50 John Kruk .02 .10
51 Ray Lankford .02 .10
52 Barry Larkin .10 .30
53 Pat Listach .01 .05
54 Kenny Lofton .10 .30
55 Shane Mack .01 .05
56 Greg Maddux .60 1.50
57 Dave Magadan .01 .05
58 Edgar Martinez .07 .20
59 Don Mattingly .50 1.25
60 Ben McDonald .01 .05
61 Jack McDowell .01 .05
62 Fred McGriff .07 .20
63 Mark McGwire .50 1.25
64 Kevin McReynolds .01 .05
65 Sam Militello .01 .05
66 Paul Molitor .20 .50
67 Jeff Montgomery .02 .10
68 Jack Morris .02 .10
69 Eddie Murray .20 .50
70 Mike Mussina .30 .75
71 Otis Nixon .01 .05
72 Donovan Osborne .01 .05
73 Terry Pendleton .01 .05
74 Mike Piazza 1.00 2.50
75 Kirby Puckett .15 .40
76 Cal Ripken Jr. 1.00 2.50
77 Bip Roberts .01 .05
78 Ivan Rodriguez .30 .75
79 Nolan Ryan 1.00 2.50
80 Ryne Sandberg .40 1.00
81 Deion Sanders .15 .40
82 Reggie Sanders .02 .10
83 Frank Seminara .01 .05
84 Gary Sheffield .15 .40
85 Ruben Sierra .02 .10
86 John Smiley .01 .05
87 Lee Smith .02 .10
88 Ozzie Smith .40 1.00
89 John Smoltz .07 .20
90 Danny Tartabull .01 .05
91 Bob Tewksbury .01 .05
92 Frank Thomas .30 .75
93 Andy Van Slyke .01 .05
94 Mo Vaughn .02 .10
95 Robin Ventura .02 .10
96 Tim Wakefield .10 .30
97 Larry Walker .10 .30
98 Dave Winfield .20 .50
99 Robin Yount/3,000th Hit .20 .50
NNO 4-in-1 Card .50 1.25
Mark McGwire
Sam Militello
Ryan Kle

1995 Classic $10 Phone Cards Promos

These rounded-corner phone cards meaure 2" by 3 1/4". They were handed out at 1995 FanFest as a redemption when a ticket stub was brought to the Classic booth. Packs handed out to dealers also included an usable $10 phone card. The cards are unnumbered and checklisted below in alphabetical order.

COMPLETE SET (8) 12.50 30.00
1 Barry Bonds 2.00 5.00
2 Will Clark .60 1.50
3 Juan Gonzalez .50 1.25
4 Ken Griffey Jr. 2.50 6.00
5 Mike Piazza 2.50 6.00
6 Cal Ripken 4.00 10.00
7 Ozzie Smith 1.50 4.00
8 Frank Thomas .75 2.00

1995 Classic $10 Phone Cards

This 57-phone card set measures approximately 2 1/8" by 3 3/8" and features color action player photos with a $10 calling value. The backs carry the instructions on how to use the cards which expired on 12/31/96. The cards are unnumbered and checklisted below alphabetically according to the team's city or state. We have priced the cards as being unused. Cards which has had its PIN used are priced half the value of the unused cards. A Cal Ripken Jr. autographed phone card along with a certificate of authenticity were randomly distributed. As this card is rarely traded on the secondary market, we have no pricing information on this card.

COMPLETE SET (57) 200.00 400.00
1 Chipper Jones 4.00 10.00
2 David Justice 2.50 6.00
3 Greg Maddux 5.00 12.00
4 Fred McGriff 2.00 5.00
5A Cal Ripken 8.00 20.00
Fielding
5B Cal Ripken 8.00 "20.00
Follow-through
5C Cal Ripken 8.00 20.00
Catching a pop-up
5D Cal Ripken 8.00 20.00
Swinging
6 Mike Mussina 2.50 6.00
7 Jose Canseco 2.50 6.00
8 Mo Vaughn 1.50 4.00
9 Roger Clemens 4.00 10.00
10 Tim Salmon 1.50 4.00
11 Mark Grace 2.50 6.00
12 Sammy Sosa 3.00 8.00
13A Frank Thomas 3.00 8.00
White Letters
13B Frank Thomas 3.00 8.00
Brown Letters
14 Robin Ventura 1.50 4.00
15 Barry Larkin 2.50 6.00
16 Reggie Sanders 1.25 3.00
17 Ron Gant 1.25 3.00
18 Manny Ramirez 3.00 8.00
19 Albert Belle 1.25 3.00
20 Carlos Baerga 1.25 3.00
21 Eddie Murray 2.50 6.00
22 Kenny Lofton 1.50 4.00
23 Andres Galarraga 2.50 6.00
24 Dante Bichette 1.50 4.00
25 Larry Walker 1.50 4.00
26 Cecil Fielder 1.50 4.00
27 Travis Fryman 1.25 3.00
28 Jeff Conine 1.25 3.00
29 Craig Biggio 2.00 5.00
30 Jeff Bagwell 3.00 8.00
31 Kevin Appier 1.25 3.00
32 Hideo Nomo 6.00 15.00
33 Mike Piazza 6.00 15.00
34 Raul Mondesi 2.00 5.00
35 Kirby Puckett 3.00 8.00
36 Carlos Perez 1.25 3.00
37 Jeff Kent 2.00 5.00
38 Don Mattingly 4.00 10.00
39 Paul O'Neill 1.50 4.00
40 Wade Boggs 2.50 6.00
41 Mark McGwire 4.00 10.00
42 Rickey Henderson 4.00 10.00
43 Darren Daulton 1.50 4.00
44 Lenny Dykstra 1.50 4.00
45 Denny Neagle 1.25 3.00
46 Tony Gwynn 4.00 10.00
47A Barry Bonds 4.00 10.00
White Letter

47B Barry Bonds 4.00 10.00
Brown Letters
48 Matt Williams 1.50 4.00
49 Deion Sanders 1.50 4.00
50 Ken Griffey Jr. 5.00 12.00
51 Randy Johnson 4.00 10.00
52 Ozzie Smith 5.00 12.00
53 Juan Gonzalez 1.50 4.00
54 Will Clark 2.50 6.00
55 Ivan Rodriguez 3.00 8.00
56 Joe Carter 1.50 4.00
57 Roberto Alomar 2.50 6.00
AU5 Cal Ripken Jr AU 100.00 200.00

1995 Classic National

This 20-card multi-sport set was issued by Classic to commemorate the 16th National Sports Collectors Convention in St. Louis. The set included a certificate of limited edition, with the serial number out of 9,995 sets produced. One thousand Sprint 20-minute phone cards featuring Ki-Jana Carter and Nolan Ryan were also distributed.

COMPLETE SET (20) 8.00 20.00
NC5 Nolan Ryan 1.50 4.00
NC13 Barry Bonds 1.25 3.00
NNO Nolan Ryan 1.50 4.00
Phone Card

1996 Classic Phone Cards

NNO Cal Ripken/$100
NNO Cal Ripken/2131

1996 Classic Ripken

COMPLETE SET (8) 4.00 10.00
1 Cal Ripken .60 1.50
2 Cal Ripken .60 1.50
3 Cal Ripken .60 1.50
4 Cal Ripken .60 1.50
5 Cal Ripken .60 1.50
6 Cal Ripken .60 1.50
7 Cal Ripken .60 1.50
8 Cal Ripken .60 1.50

1996 Classic 7/11 Phone Cards

These phone cards feature leading major league players. They were available at all participating 7/11 stores for a cost of $5.99 and are good for 15 minutes of phone time. The cards expired on December 31, 1997. Cards which have been used have half the value of unused cards.

COMPLETE SET 40.00 100.00
1A Cal Ripken 8.00 20.00
1B Cal Ripken PROMO 8.00 20.00
2 Frank Thomas 2.50 6.00
3 Hideo Nomo 4.00 10.00
4 Jeff Conine 1.25 3.00
5 Ken Griffey Jr. 5.00 12.00
6 Greg Maddux 5.00 12.00
7 Wade Boggs 3.00 8.00
8 Ivan Rodriguez 3.00 8.00
9 Barry Bonds 4.00 10.00
10 Kirby Puckett 2.50 6.00
11 Mo Vaughn 1.25 3.00
12 Tony Gwynn 4.00 10.00

1998 Classic Collectible Ryan Tickets

These oversize commemorative tickets, which measure approximately 4" by 8" feature Nolan Ryan record setting seven no-hitters. The fronts have photos of Ryan along with a photo of an ticket stub from that game. The back has another photo as well as information about that no-hitter. Since these cards are unnumbered, we have sequenced them in order of no-hitter

COMPLETE SET (7) 15.00 40.00
COMMON CARD (1-7) 2.00 5.00

1997 Classic Sports Brooks Robinson

This one card set was issued by Comcast to introduce the new Clasic Sports Network (as well as other all-sports Cable Channels). The horizontal front has an action photo of Brooks Robinson while the back has descriptions of the new cable networks available.

1 Brooks Robinson 2.00 5.00

2004 Classic Clippings

COMP.SET w/o SP's (75) 6.00 15.00
COMMON CARD (1-75) .12 .30
COMMON CARD (76-110) .75 2.00
COMMON RC (76-110) .75 2.00
76-100 ODDS 1:18 HOBBY, 1:108 RETAIL
101-110 RANDOM INSERTS IN PACKS
76-110 PRINT RUN 500 SERIAL #'d SETS
PROOFS RANDOM INSERTS IN PACKS
OVERALL PARALLEL ODDS 1:18 H, 1:120 R
PROOFS PRINT RUN 1 SET PER COLOR
BLACK-CYAN-MAGENTA-YELLOW ISSUED
NO PROOFS PRICING DUE TO SCARCITY
1 Juan Pierre .12 .30
2 Derek Jeter .75 2.00
3 Jose Reyes .20 .50
4 Eric Chavez .12 .30
5 Alex Rodriguez Yanks .40 1.00
6 Mark Prior .20 .50
7 Carlos Beltran .20 .50
8 Ichiro Suzuki .40 1.00
9 Shawn Green .12 .30
10 Richie Sexson .12 .30
11 Andruw Jones .12 .30
12 Geoff Jenkins .12 .30
13 Luis Gonzalez .12 .30
14 Garret Anderson .12 .30
15 Adam Dunn .20 .50
16 Nomar Garciaparra .20 .50
17 Albert Pujols .40 1.00
18 Jeff Bagwell .20 .50
19 Rocco Baldelli .12 .30
20 Preston Wilson .12 .30
21 Gary Sheffield .12 .30
22 Magglio Ordonez .20 .50
23 Kerry Wood .12 .30
24 Manny Ramirez .30 .75
25 Randy Johnson .30 .75
26 Ken Griffey Jr. .60 1.50
27 Rafael Palmeiro .20 .50
28 Vernon Wells .12 .30
29 Mike Piazza .30 .75
30 Hank Blalock .12 .30
31 Miguel Cabrera .30 .75
32 Jason Giambi .12 .30
33 Troy Glaus .12 .30
34 Angel Berroa .12 .30
35 Greg Maddux .40 1.00
36 Lance Berkman .20 .50
37 Austin Kearns .12 .30
38 Hideo Nomo .30 .75
39 Sammy Sosa .30 .75
40 Jose Vidro .12 .30
41 Curt Schilling .20 .50
42 Melvin Mora .12 .30
43 Scott Podsednik .12 .30
44 Dontrelle Willis .12 .30
45 Roy Halladay .20 .50
46 Hideki Matsui .50 1.25
47 Tom Glavine .20 .50
48 Torii Hunter .12 .30
49 Chipper Jones .30 .75
50 Barry Zito .20 .50
51 Vladimir Guerrero .20 .50
52 Jim Thome .20 .50
53 Shannon Stewart .12 .30
54 Miguel Tejada .20 .50
55 Roy Oswalt .20 .50
56 Jason Kendall .12 .30
57 Brian Giles .12 .30
58 Jason Schmidt .12 .30
59 Pedro Martinez .20 .50
60 Bret Boone .12 .30
61 Josh Beckett .12 .30
62 Scott Rolen .20 .50
63 Aubrey Huff .12 .30
64 Pat Burrell .12 .30
65 Mark Teixeira .20 .50
66 Alfonso Soriano .20 .50
67 Carlos Delgado .12 .30
68 Ivan Rodriguez .20 .50
69 Brandon Webb .12 .30
70 Eric Gagne .12 .30
71 Frank Thomas .30 .75
72 Jody Gerut .12 .30
73 Todd Helton .20 .50
74 Andy Pettitte .20 .50
75 Roger Clemens .40 1.00
76 Rickie Weeks ROO .75 2.00
77 Chien-Ming Wang ROO 3.00 8.00
78 Edwin Jackson ROO .75 2.00
79 Dallas McPherson ROO .75 2.00
80 John Gall ROO RC .75 2.00
81 Ryan Wagner ROO .75 2.00
82 Clint Barmes ROO 1.25 3.00
83 Khalil Greene ROO 1.25 3.00
84 Chin-Hui Tsao ROO .75 2.00
85 Alexis Rios ROO .75 2.00
86 Merkin Valdez ROO RC .75 2.00
87 Aarom Baldiris ROO RC .75 2.00
88 Onil Joseph ROO RC .75 2.00
89 Ruddy Yan ROO .75 2.00
90 Chad Bentz ROO RC .75 2.00
91 Shawn Hill ROO RC .75 2.00
92 Delmon Young ROO 1.25 3.00
93 Hector Gimenez ROO RC .75 2.00
94 William Bergolla ROO RC .75 2.00
95 Ronny Cedeno ROO RC .75 2.00
96 Angel Chavez ROO RC .75 2.00
97 Justin Leone ROO RC .75 2.00
98 Ivan Ochoa ROO RC .75 2.00
99 Ian Snell ROO RC .75 2.00
100 Rich Harden ROO .75 2.00
101 Joe Mauer DEB 1.50 4.00
102 Akinori Otsuka DEB RC .75 2.00
103 Bobby Crosby DEB .75 2.00
104 Garrett Atkins DEB .75 2.00
105 Dan Haren DEB .75 2.00
106 Koyie Hill DEB .75 2.00
107 Kaz Matsui DEB RC 1.25 3.00
108 Adam LaRoche DEB .75 2.00
109 Terrmel Sledge DEB .75 2.00
110 Shingo Takatsu DEB RC .75 2.00

2004 Classic Clippings First Edition

*1ST ED 1-75: 3X TO 8X BASIC
*1ST ED 76-110: .4X TO 1X BASIC
*1ST ED 76-110: .4X TO 1X BASIC RC
OVERALL PARALLEL ODDS 1:18 H, 1:120 R
STATED PRINT RUN 150 SERIAL #'d SETS

2004 Classic Clippings All-Star Lineup Swatch

STATED ODDS 1:28 RETAIL
AJ A.Jones w 3.00 8.00
Sheffield-Javy
AP A.Pujols w 4.00 10.00
Sheffield-Wilson
AR A.Rod w 4.00 10.00
Nomar-Giambi
AS A.Soriano w 2.00 5.00
Delgado-Glaus
BZ B.Zito w 2.00 5.00
Clemens-Halladay
CD C.Delgado w 2.00 5.00
Wells-Halladay
DW D.Willis w 3.00 8.00
Castillo-Lowell
HB H.Blalock w 2.00 5.00
Maggilo-Glaus
HM H.Matsui Base w 4.00 10.00
Ichiro-And
MP M.Prior w 3.00 8.00
Wood-Willis
NG Nomar w 4.00 10.00
A.Rod-Manny
RC R.Clemens w 4.00 10.00
Soriano-Giam
RS R.Sexson w 2.00 5.00
Helton-Pujols
SR S.Rolen w 3.00 8.00
Renteria-Pujols
TH T.Helton w 3.00 8.00
Castillo-Rolen

2004 Classic Clippings All-Star Lineup Triple Swatch

STATED PRINT RUN 75 SERIAL #'d SETS
AST PATCH PRINT RUN 25 SERIAL #'d SETS
AST PATCH NO PRICES DUE TO SCARCITY
OVERALL GU ODDS 1:18 H, AU-GU 1:24 R
CARD SMA FEATURES GU BASE SWATCHES
ALL OTHERS ARE JERSEY SWATCHES
CHR Castillo/Helton/Rolen 6.00 15.00
CWL Castillo/Willis/Lowell 6.00 15.00
CZH Clemens/Zito/Halladay 8.00 20.00
DSG Delgado/Soriano/Glaus 4.00 10.00
GRG Nomar/A.Rod/Giambi 12.50 30.00
HSP Helton/Sexson/Pujols 8.00 20.00
OBG Maggilo/Blalock/Glaus 4.00 10.00
RGR A.Rod/Nomar/Manny 10.00 25.00
RRP Renteria/Rolen/Pujols 15.00 40.00
SCG Soriano/Clemens/Giambi 12.50 30.00
SJL Sheffield/Andruw/Javy 6.00 15.00
SMA Ichiro/Hideki/G.Anderson 15.00 40.00
SPW Sheffield/Pujols/P.Wilson 8.00 20.00
WDH V.Wells/Delgado/Halladay 4.00 10.00
WPW Wood/Prior/Willis 6.00 15.00

2004 Classic Clippings Bat Rack Autograph Bronze

OVERALL AU ODDS 1:18 H, AU-GU 1:24 R
STATED PRINT RUN 75 SERIAL #'d SETS
AH Aubrey Huff 6.00 15.00
EM Edgar Martinez 10.00 25.00
GS Gary Sheffield 10.00 25.00
HB Hank Blalock 6.00 15.00
JB Josh Beckett 6.00 15.00
JE Jim Edmonds 10.00 25.00
JR Jose Reyes 6.00 15.00
MC Miguel Cabrera 20.00 50.00
MT Mark Teixeira 6.00 15.00
RA Roberto Alomar 10.00 25.00

2004 Classic Clippings Bat Rack Quad Green

STATED PRINT RUN 75 SERIAL #'d SETS
GOLD PRINT RUN 10 SERIAL #'d SETS
NO GOLD PRICING DUE TO SCARCITY
*RED: .5X TO 1.2X BASIC
RED PRINT RUN 25 SERIAL #'d SETS
OVERALL GU ODDS 1:18 H, AU-GU 1:24 R
BJPR Bald/Chip/Pierre/Manny 8.00 20.00
BLHD Bagwell/D.Lee/Huff/Delg 8.00 20.00
GTGP Vlad/Tejada/Giambi/Piaz 12.50 30.00
HRMR Helton/Reyes/Kaz/Rolen 15.00 40.00
JRMG Jeter/A.Rod/Kaz/Nomar 10.00 25.00
JRSG Jeter/A.Rod/Shef/Giamb 20.00 50.00
PPRS Pujols/Prior/A.Rod/Schill 15.00 40.00
PRPR Piaz/Reyes/Pujols/Rolen 15.00 40.00
PSCB Pierre/Shef/Cabrera/Bald 8.00 20.00
SABG Sori/Alom/Blalock/Glaus 8.00 20.00
SGEJ Sosa/Vlad/Edmonds/Chip 8.00 20.00
SGWS Schill/Nomar/Webb/Sexs 10.00 25.00
SPCB Sosa/Prior/Cabrera/Beck 8.00 20.00
TBHL Thome/Bag/Helton/D.Lee 8.00 20.00
TBTD Thome/Bag/Teix/Delgado 8.00 20.00

2004 Classic Clippings Bat Rack Triple Green

STATED PRINT RUN 175 SERIAL #'d SETS
*GOLD: .6X TO 1.5X BASIC
GOLD PRINT RUN 25 SERIAL #'d SETS
*RED: .5X TO 1.2X BASIC
RED PRINT RUN 50 SERIAL #'d SETS
OVERALL GU ODDS 1:18 H, AU-GU 1:24 R
ARS Alomar/Reyes/Soriano 6.00 15.00
BHD Baldelli/Huff/Delgado 4.00 10.00
BTH Bagwell/Thome/Helton 6.00 15.00
CPB Cabrera/Pierre/Beckett 6.00 15.00
DHG Delgado/Huff/Giambi 4.00 10.00
GPJ Guerrero/Pierre/Chipper 6.00 15.00
GPS Guerrero/Pujols/Sosa 10.00 25.00
GRB Glaus/Rolen/Blalock 6.00 15.00
GRS Nomar/Manny/Schilling 8.00 20.00
GTH Giambi/Thome/Helton 6.00 15.00
JMG Jeter/K.Matsui/Nomar 15.00 40.00
JRS Jeter/A.Rod/Sheffield 15.00 40.00
PBS Prior/Beckett/Schilling 6.00 15.00
PRE Pujols/Rolen/Edmonds 12.50 30.00
PRM Piazza/Reyes/K.Matsui 10.00 25.00
RTC A.Rod/Tejada/Cabrera 6.00 15.00
SBT Soriano/Blalock/Teixeira 6.00 15.00
SLP Sosa/D.Lee/Prior 6.00 15.00
SRB Sheffield/Manny/Baldelli 6.00 15.00
SWA Sexson/Webb/Alomar 6.00 15.00

2004 Classic Clippings Inserts

1-20 PRINT RUN 750 SERIAL #'d SETS
21-25 PRINT RUN 100 SERIAL #'d SETS
STATED ODDS 1:18 HOBBY, 1:150 RETAIL
1 Nolan Ryan 4.00 10.00
2 Mike Schmidt 2.00 5.00
3 Cal Ripken 4.00 10.00
4 Don Mattingly 2.50 6.00
5 Roger Clemens 1.50 4.00
6 Randy Johnson 1.25 3.00
7 Mark Prior .75 2.00
8 Jim Thome .75 2.00
9 Sammy Sosa 1.25 3.00
10 Pedro Martinez .75 2.00
11 Chipper Jones 1.25 3.00
12 Vladimir Guerrero .75 2.00
13 Albert Pujols 1.50 4.00
14 Ichiro Suzuki 1.50 4.00
15 Derek Jeter 3.00 8.00
16 Alex Rodriguez 1.50 4.00
17 Greg Maddux 1.50 4.00
18 Nomar Garciaparra .75 2.00
19 Mike Piazza 1.25 3.00
20 Ken Griffey Jr. 2.50 6.00
21 Pie Traynor 2.00 5.00
22 Bill Dickey 1.25 3.00
23 George Sisler 2.00 5.00
24 Ted Williams 6.00 15.00
25 Enos Slaughter 2.00 5.00

2004 Classic Clippings Jersey Rack Autograph Bronze

OVERALL AU ODDS 1:18 H, AU-GU 1:24 R
STATED PRINT RUN 149 SERIAL #'d SETS
AB Angel Berroa 4.00 10.00
AP1 Andy Pettitte 15.00 40.00
AP2 Albert Pujols 60.00 150.00
BL Barry Larkin 15.00 40.00
BW Brandon Webb 4.00 10.00
CD Carlos Delgado 10.00 25.00
DH Dan Haren 4.00 10.00
DW Dontrelle Willis 4.00 10.00
EJ Edwin Jackson 4.00 10.00
GA1 Garret Anderson 10.00 25.00
GA2 Garrett Atkins 4.00 10.00
IR Ivan Rodriguez 25.00 60.00
JG Jody Gerut 4.00 10.00
KW Kerry Wood 10.00 25.00
MB Marlon Byrd 4.00 10.00
MC Miguel Cabrera 15.00 40.00
MM1 Mark Mulder 6.00 15.00
MM2 Mike Mussina 10.00 25.00
RB Rocco Baldelli 6.00 15.00
RH Roy Halladay 8.00 20.00
RW Ryan Wagner 4.00 10.00
SR Scott Rolen 10.00 25.00
TH Torii Hunter 6.00 15.00

2004 Classic Clippings Jersey Rack Autograph Gold Patch

*GOLD PATCH p/r 36-55: 1X TO 2.5X BRZ
*GOLD PATCH p/r 21-35: 1X TO 2.5X BRZ
*GOLD PATCH p/r 16-20: 1.25X TO 3X BRZ
OVERALL AU ODDS 1:18 H, AU-GU 1:24 R
PRINT RUNS B/WN 4-55 COPIES PER
NO PRICING ON QTY OF 11 OR LESS
JB Josh Beckett/21 15.00 40.00

2004 Classic Clippings Jersey Rack Autograph Silver

*SILVER: .5X TO 1.2X BRONZE
OVERALL AU ODDS 1:18 H, AU-GU 1:24 R
STATED PRINT RUN 50 SERIAL #'d SETS
JB Josh Beckett 12.50 30.00

2004 Classic Clippings Jersey Rack Triple Blue

STATED PRINT RUN 225 SERIAL #'d SETS
*BRONZE: .4X TO 1X BASIC
BRONZE PRINT RUN 99 SERIAL #'d SETS
GOLD PATCH PRINT RUN 25 SER.#'d SETS
GOLD PATCH NO PRICE DUE TO SCARCITY
*SILVER p/r 64-117: .4X TO 1X BASIC
*SILVER p/r 40-56: .5X TO 1.2X BASIC
*SILVER p/r 20-34: .6X TO 1.5X BASIC
SILVER PRINT B/WN 20-117 COPIES PER
OVERALL GU ODDS 1:18 H, AU-GU 1:24 R
BCP Baldelli/Cabrera/Pujols 8.00 20.00
CPB Clemens/Prior/Beckett 10.00 25.00
CPO Clemens/Pettitte/Oswalt 8.00 20.00
CWB Cabrera/Willis/Beckett 12.50 30.00
DTS Delgado/Tejada/Soriano 4.00 10.00
GMS Nomar/Pedro/Schilling 8.00 20.00
JRG Jeter/A.Rod/Giambi 10.00 25.00
JSW Randy/Sexson/Webb 6.00 15.00
PRL Piazza/I.Rod/Javy 6.00 15.00
PSR Pujols/Sosa/Manny 10.00 25.00
RJG A.Rod/Jeter/Nomar 12.50 30.00
SWP Sosa/Wood/Prior 6.00 15.00
WWB Willis/Webb/Berroa 6.00 15.00
WWS Willis/Wood/Schilling 6.00 15.00
ZHM Zito/Hudson/Mulder 4.00 10.00

2004 Classic Clippings Phenom Lineup Autograph Red

STATED PRINT RUN 150 SERIAL #'d SETS
*GOLD: .6X TO 1.5X BASIC
GOLD PRINT RUN 50 SERIAL #'d SETS
*SILVER: .5X TO 1.2X BASIC
SILVER PRINT RUN 99 SERIAL #'d SETS
OVERALL AU ODDS 1:18 H, AU-GU 1:24 R
AB A.Berroa w/Nomar-A.Rod 4.00 10:00
AL A.LaRoche w/Pujols-Thome 4.00 10.00
AR A.Rios w/Delgado-Wells 6.00 15.00
BC B.Crosby w/Nomar-A.Rod 6.00 15.00
CW C.Wang w/Hideki-Giambi 50.00 120.00
DM D.McPh w/Glaus-And 6.00 15.00
DW D.Willis w/Prior-Wood 6.00 15.00
DY D.Young w/Ichiro-Hideki 10.00 25.00
EJ E.Jackson w/Prior-Wood 4.00 10.00
GS G.Sizemore w/Manny-And 10.00 25.00
HB H.Blalock w/Glaus-A.Rod 6.00 15.00
JG J.Gall w/Pujols-Rolen 4.00 10.00
JR J.Reyes w/Kaz-Weeks 6.00 15.00
KG K.Greene w/Rent-Lowell 10.00 25.00
LN L.Nix w/A.Rod-Garret 4.00 10.00
MC M.Cabrera w/Cast-Lowell 20.00 50.00
MV M.Valdez w/Edwin-Willis 4.00 10.00
RH2 R.Howard w/Thome-Helton 6.00 15.00
RW1 R.Wagner w/Willis-Prior 4.00 10.00
RW2 R.Weeks w/Cast-Reyes 6.00 15.00
SP S.Podsed w 6.00 15.00
Pujols-Andruw

2004 Classic Clippings Press Clippings

STATED ODDS 1:6 HOBBY/RETAIL
1 Josh Beckett .40 1.00
2 Albert Pujols 1.25 3.00
3 Derek Jeter 2.50 6.00
4 Alex Rodriguez 1.25 3.00
5 Jim Thome .60 1.50
6 Angel Berroa .40 1.00
7 Dontrelle Willis .40 1.00
8 Roy Halladay .60 1.50
9 Kerry Wood .40 1.00
10 Mark Prior .60 1.50
11 Roger Clemens 1.25 3.00
12 Hideki Matsui 1.50 4.00
13 Ichiro Suzuki 1.25 3.00
14 Eric Gagne .40 1.00
15 Miguel Cabrera 1.00 2.50
16 Nomar Garciaparra .60 1.50
17 Hank Blalock .40 1.00
18 Chipper Jones 1.00 2.50
19 Sammy Sosa 1.00 2.50
20 Alfonso Soriano .60 1.50

2004 Classic Clippings Signature Edition

STATED PRINT RUN 50 SERIAL #'d SETS
PURPLE PRINT RUN 1 SERIAL #'d SET
NO PURPLE PRICING DUE TO SCARCITY
OVERALL AU ODDS 1:18 H, AU-GU 1:24 R
AP Albert Pujols 150.00 250.00
CR Cal Ripken 100.00 200.00
DM Don Mattingly 40.00 80.00
EJ Edwin Jackson 5.00 12.00
KG Khalil Greene 12.50 30.00
MP Mark Prior 12.50 30.00
MS Mike Schmidt 15.00 40.00
NR Nolan Ryan 60.00 120.00
RJ Randy Johnson 40.00 80.00
RW Rickie Weeks 8.00 20.00
VG Vladimir Guerrero 20.00 50.00

2005 Classic Clippings

COMP.SET w/o SP's (75) 6.00 15.00
COMMON CARD (1-75) .10 .30
COMMON CARD (76-105) .60 1.50
76-105 ODDS 1:9 H, 1:500 R
76-105 PRINT RUN 999 SERIAL #'d SETS
COMMON CARD (106-125) .30 .75
106-125 ODDS 1:6 H, 1:12 R
1 Frank Thomas .30 .75
2 Vladimir Guerrero .20 .50
3 Ken Griffey Jr. .60 1.50
4 Derek Jeter .75 2.00
5 Rafael Palmeiro .20 .50
6 Adrian Beltre .30 .75
7 Khalil Greene .12 .30
8 Richie Sexson .12 .30
9 Roger Clemens .40 1.00
10 Mike Piazza .30 .75
11 Chipper Jones .30 .75
12 Juan Pierre .12 .30
13 Todd Helton .20 .50
14 Ben Sheets .12 .30
15 John Smoltz .30 .75
16 Steve Finley .12 .30
17 Jim Thome .20 .50
18 Vernon Wells .12 .30
19 Melvin Mora .12 .30
20 Dontrelle Willis .12 .30
21 Eric Gagne .12 .30
22 Craig Wilson .12 .30
23 Curt Schilling .20 .50
24 Justin Morneau .20 .50
25 Jason Schmidt .12 .30
26 Kerry Wood .12 .30
27 Ivan Rodriguez .20 .50
28 Rocco Baldelli .12 .30
29 Mark Prior .20 .50
30 Josh Beckett .12 .30
31 Scott Rolen .20 .50
32 Nomar Garciaparra .20 .50
33 Carl Crawford .20 .50
34 Paul Konerko .20 .50
35 Miguel Cabrera .30 .75
36 Hank Blalock .12 .30
37 Sammy Sosa .30 .75
38 Jim Edmonds .20 .50
39 David Ortiz .30 .75
40 Lance Berkman .20 .50
41 Ichiro Suzuki .40 1.00
42 Adam Dunn .20 .50
43 Carlos Guillen .12 .30
44 Alfonso Soriano .20 .50
45 Victor Martinez .20 .50
46 Torii Hunter .12 .30
47 Kaz Matsui .12 .30
48 Andruw Jones .12 .30
49 Matt Holliday .30 .75
50 Eric Chavez .12 .30
51 Randy Johnson .30 .75
52 Lew Ford .12 .30
53 Hideki Matsui .50 1.25
54 Manny Ramirez .30 .75
55 Mark Teixeira .20 .50
56 Jose Vidro .12 .30
57 Mike Sweeney .12 .30
58 Jack Wilson .12 .30
59 Greg Maddux .40 1.00
60 Tony Batista .12 .30
61 Albert Pujols .40 1.00
62 Miguel Tejada .20 .50
63 Carlos Beltran .20 .50
64 Bobby Abreu .12 .30
65 Carlos Delgado .12 .30
66 Travis Hafner .12 .30
67 Scott Podsednik .12 .30
68 Gary Sheffield .12 .30
69 Johan Santana .20 .50
70 Barry Zito .20 .50
71 Pedro Martinez .20 .50
72 Brian Giles .12 .30
73,Garret Anderson .12 .30
74 Jeff Bagwell .20 .50
75 Alex Rodriguez .40 1.00
76 Johnny Bench LGD 1.50 4.00
77 Yogi Berra LGD 1.50 4.00
78 Lou Brock LGD 1.00 2.50
79 Rod Carew LGD 1.00 2.50
80 Orlando Cepeda LGD 1.00 2.50
81 Carlton Fisk LGD 1.00 2.50
82 Bob Gibson LGD 1.00 2.50
83 Reggie Jackson LGD 1.00 2.50
84 Al Kaline LGD 1.50 4.00
85 Harmon Killebrew LGD 1.50 4.00
86 Ralph Kiner LGD 1.00 2.50
87 Willie McCovey LGD 1.00 2.50
88 Eddie Murray LGD 1.00 2.50
89 Phil Rizzuto LGD 1.00 2.50
90 Brooks Robinson LGD 1.00 2.50
91 Nolan Ryan LGD 5.00 12.00
92 Mike Schmidt LGD 2.50 6.00
93 Tom Seaver LGD 1.00 2.50
94 Willie Stargell LGD 1.00 2.50
95 Rollie Fingers LGD 1.00 2.50
96 Dennis Eckersley LGD 1.00 2.50
97 Enos Slaughter LGD 1.00 2.50
98 Jim Palmer LGD 1.00 2.50
99 Warren Spahn LGD 1.00 2.50
100 Joe Morgan LGD 1.00 2.50
101 Richie Ashburn LGD 1.00 2.50
102 Robin Yount LGD 1.50 4.00
103 Bob Feller LGD 1.00 2.50
104 Pee Wee Reese LGD 1.00 2.50
105 Eddie Mathews LGD 1.50 4.00
106 David Wright ROO .60 1.50
107 David Aardsma ROO .30 .75
108 B.J. Upton ROO .50 1.25
109 Scott Kazmir ROO .75 2.00
110 Gavin Floyd ROO .30 .75
111 Jeff Francis ROO .30 .75
112 Dioner Navarro ROO .30 .75
113 Zack Greinke ROO 1.00 2.50
114 Nick Swisher ROO .50 1.25
115 Josh Kroeger ROO .30 .75
116 Ryan Raburn ROO .30 .75
117 Victor Diaz ROO .30 .75
118 Casey Kotchman ROO .30 .75
119 Joey Gathright ROO .30 .75
120 Jon Knott ROO .30 .75
121 J.D. Durbin ROO .30 .75
122 Andres Blanco ROO .30 .75
123 Charlton Jimerson ROO .30 .75
124 Russ Adams ROO .30 .75
125 Justin Verlander ROO RC 6.00 15.00

2005 Classic Clippings Final Edition

OVERALL PARALLEL ODDS 1:18 H, 1:100 R
STATED PRINT RUN 1 SERIAL #'d SET
NO PRICING DUE TO SCARCITY

2005 Classic Clippings First Edition

*1ST ED 1-75: 3X TO 8X BASIC
*1ST ED 76-105: .6X TO 1.5X BASIC
*1ST ED 106-125: 1X TO 2.5X BASIC
OVERALL PARALLEL ODDS 1:18 H, 1:100 R
STATED PRINT RUN 150 SERIAL #'d SETS

2005 Classic Clippings Bat Rack Quad Blue

STATED ODDS 1:118 HOBBY
STATED PRINT RUN 115 SETS
SP PRINT RUNS PROVIDED BY FLEER
CARDS ARE NOT SERIAL-NUMBERED
NO SP PRICING DUE TO SCARCITY
PURPLE PRINT RUN 1 SERIAL #'d SET
NO PURPLE PRICING DUE TO SCARCITY
SILVER PRINT RUN 10 SERIAL #'d SETS
NO SILVER PRICING DUE TO SCARCITY
OVERALL ODDS GU 1:9 H, AU-GU 1:24 R
ADBM Abreu/Dunn/Rocco/Hideki 15.00 40.00
BRDY Boggs/Manny/Doerr/Yaz 15.00 40.00
CMMS Clem/Madl/Maz/Starg 60.00 120.00
CRMP G.Cart/Reyes/Kaz/Piazza 10.00 25.00
GHCK Gwynn/How/Colav/Kaline 30.00 60.00
GPTD Giambi/Raffy/Teix/Delgado 10.00 25.00
GRSS Vlad/Manny/Sosa/Sheffield 10.00 25.00
HJKP Torii/Jacque/Kill/Puckett 15.00 40.00
RTGB I.Rod/Teja/Glaus/Blalock 10.00 25.00
THBP Thome/Helton/Bag/Pujols 15.00 40.00
WJSC Webb/Randy/Schil/Clem 15.00 40.00

2005 Classic Clippings Cut of History Single Autograph Blue

STATED ODDS 1:161 HOBBY
SP PRINT RUNS PROVIDED BY FLEER
SP'S ARE NOT SERIAL-NUMBERED
PURPLE PRINT RUN 1 SERIAL #'d SET
NO PURPLE PRICING DUE TO SCARCITY
SILVER PRINT RUN 25 SERIAL #'d SETS
NO SILVER PRICING AVAILABLE
OVERALL ODDS AU 1:18 H, AU-GU 1:24 R
BB Bill Buckner SP/48 12.00 30.00
BF Bob Feller SP/34 10.00 25.00
BR Brooks Robinson SP/49 15.00 40.00
DG Dwight Gooden SP/50 10.00 25.00
DL Don Larsen SP/49 10.00 25.00
DM Don Mattingly SP/39 30.00 60.00
DS Darryl Strawberry SP/51 10.00 25.00
JB Johnny Bench SP/38 30.00 60.00
JP Jim Palmer SP/50 10.00 25.00
KG Kirk Gibson 4.00 10.00
MW Mookie Wilson SP/49 10.00 25.00

2005 Classic Clippings Cut of History Single Jersey Blue

STATED ODDS 1:21 HOBBY, 1:28 RETAIL
SP PRINT RUNS PROVIDED BY FLEER
SP's ARE NOT SERIAL-NUMBERED
PURPLE PATCH PRINT RUN 1 #'d SET
NO PURPLE PATCH PRICING AVAILABLE
SILVER PATCH PRINT RUN 25 #'d SETS
NO SILVER PATCH PRICING AVAILABLE
OVERALL ODDS GU 1:9 H, AU-GU 1:24 R
BG Bob Gibson 6.00 15.00
BR Brooks Robinson 6.00 15.00
CF Carlton Fisk 6.00 15.00
CR Cal Ripken 12.50 30.00
CY Carl Yastrzemski 8.00 20.00
DG Dwight Gooden 4.00 10.00
DM Don Mattingly 8.00 20.00
DS Darryl Strawberry 4.00 10.00
EM Eddie Murray 6.00 15.00
JB Johnny Bench 6.00 15.00
JM Joe Morgan SP/82 6.00 15.00
MS Mike Schmidt 8.00 20.00
NR Nolan Ryan 10.00 25.00
OC Orlando Cepeda 4.00 10.00
OS Ozzie Smith 6.00 15.00
RJ Reggie Jackson 6.00 15.00
SA Sparky Anderson 4.00 10.00
TS Tom Seaver 6.00 15.00
WM Willie McCovey 6.00 15.00
WS Willie Stargell 6.00 15.00

2005 Classic Clippings Cut of History Dual Autograph Blue

STATED PRINT RUN 49 SETS
PRINT RUN INFO PROVIDED BY FLEER
CARDS ARE NOT SERIAL-NUMBERED
PURPLE PRINT RUN 1 SERIAL #'d SET
NO PURPLE PRICING DUE TO SCARCITY
SILVER PRINT RUN 22 SERIAL #'d SETS
NO SILVER PRICING AVAILABLE
OVERALL ODDS AU 1:18 H, AU-GU 1:24 R
GE K.Gibson/D.Eckersley 15.00 40.00
GS D.Gooden/D.Strawberry 15.00 40.00
WB M.Wilson/B.Buckner 20.00 50.00

2005 Classic Clippings Cut of History Dual Jersey Blue

STATED ODDS 1:112 HOBBY
PURPLE PATCH PRINT RUN 1 #'d SET
NO PURPLE PATCH PRICING AVAILABLE
SILVER PATCH PRINT RUN 15 #'d SETS
NO SILVER PATCH PRICING AVAILABLE
OVERALL ODDS GU 1:9 H, AU-GU 1:24 R
BF J.Bench/C.Fisk 6.00 15.00
BS L.Brock/M.Schmidt 10.00 25.00
CM O.Cepeda/W.McCovey 4.00 10.00
GS D.Gooden/D.Strawberry 4.00 10.00
JY R.Jackson/C.Yastrzemski 8.00 20.00
RS C.Ripken/O.Smith 12.00 30.00
RS N.Ryan/T.Seaver 10.00 25.00
SJ W.Stargell/R.Jackson 6.00 15.00

2005 Classic Clippings Cut of History Triple Autograph Blue

STATED PRINT RUN 15 SETS
PRINT RUN INFO PROVIDED BY FLEER
CARDS ARE NOT SERIAL-NUMBERED
PURPLE PRINT RUN 1 SERIAL #'d SET
SILVER PRINT RUN 5 SERIAL #'d SETS
OVERALL ODDS AU 1:18 H, AU-GU 1:24 R
NO PRICING DUE TO SCARCITY

2005 Classic Clippings Cut of History Triple Jersey Blue

STATED ODDS 1:67 HOBBY
PURPLE PATCH PRINT RUN 1 #'d SET
NO PURPLE PATCH PRICING AVAILABLE
SILVER PATCH PRINT RUN 25 #'d SETS
NO SILVER PATCH PRICING AVAILABLE
OVERALL ODDS GU 1:9 H, AU-GU 1:24 R
ACW Aaron/Clemente/Williams 100.00 175.00
BSG Brock/Ozzie/Gibson 20.00 50.00
JKM Reggie/Killebrew/McCov 15.00 40.00
MMC Murray/McCov/Cepeda 15.00 40.00
MRS Mattingly/Ripken/Schmidt 40.00 80.00
OJM O'Neill/Reggie/Mattingly 20.00 50.00
RCJ Ryan/Clemens/Randy 20.00 50.00

2005 Classic Clippings Diamond Signings Single Blue

STATED ODDS 1:29 HOBBY
SP PRINT RUNS PROVIDED BY FLEER
SP's ARE NOT SERIAL-NUMBERED
NO PRICING ON SP/18-19 AVAILABLE
PURPLE PRINT RUN 1 SERIAL #'d SET
NO PURPLE PRICING DUE TO SCARCITY
SILVER PRINT RUN 25 SERIAL #'d SETS
NO SILVER PRICING AVAILABLE
OVERALL ODDS AU 1:18 H, AU-GU 1:24 R
AB Andres Blanco SP/98 6.00 15.00
BL Brad Lidge SP/97 15.00 40.00
BU B.J. Upton 6.00 15.00
CF Chone Figgins SP/150 6.00 15.00
CJ Charlton Jimerson SP/150 6.00 15.00
CK Casey Kotchman 4.00 10.00
DN Dioner Navarro 4.00 10.00
DW David Wright SP/97 10.00 25.00
GF Gavin Floyd SP/150 6.00 15.00
JB Jason Bay SP/96 6.00 15.00
JM Justin Morneau SP/98 6.00 15.00
JP Jake Peavy 6.00 15.00
JV Justin Verlander SP/150 40.00 100.00
KG Khalil Greene SP/150 4.00 10.00
NS Nick Swisher 6.00 15.00
SK Scott Kazmir SP/200 8.00 20.00
TH Travis Hafner 4.00 10.00
ZG Zack Greinke SP/96 10.00 25.00

2005 Classic Clippings Diamond Signings Dual Blue

STATED PRINT RUN 49 SERIAL #'d SETS
PURPLE PRINT RUN 1 SERIAL #'d SET
NO PURPLE PRICING DUE TO SCARCITY
SILVER PRINT RUN 22 SERIAL #'d SETS
NO SILVER PRICING DUE AVAILABLE
OVERALL ODDS AU 1:18 H, AU-GU 1:24 R
EXCHANGE DEADLINE 03/16/08
FU G.Floyd/C.Utley 20.00 50.00
KM C.Kotchman/J.Morneau 15.00 40.00

2005 Classic Clippings Diamond Signings Triple Blue

PRINT RUNS BETWEEN 8-99 COPIES PER
NO PRICING ON QTY OF 8
PURPLE PRINT RUN 1 SERIAL #'d SET
NO PURPLE PRICING DUE TO SCARCITY
SILVER PRINT RUN 5 SERIAL #'d SETS
NO SILVER PRICING DUE TO SCARCITY
OVERALL ODDS AU 1:18 H, AU-GU 1:24 R
EXCHANGE DEADLINE 03/16/08
FKV Floyd/Kazm/Verlander/99 20.00 50.00
FSJ Figgins/Swish/Jimer/99 12.50 30.00
KMB Kotch/Morneau/Bay/86 12.50 30.00

2005 Classic Clippings Jersey Rack Dual Blue

STATED ODDS 1:100 HOBBY
STATED PRINT RUN 75 SETS
PRINT RUN INFO PROVIDED BY FLEER
CARDS ARE NOT SERIAL NUMBERED
PURPLE PRINT RUN 1 SERIAL #'d SET
NO PURPLE PRICING DUE TO SCARCITY
SILVER PRINT RUN 25 SERIAL #'d SETS
NO SILVER PRICING DUE TO SCARCITY
OVERALL ODDS GU 1:9 H, AU-GU 1:24 R
BW J.Beckett/K.Wood 4.00 10.00
CJ M.Cabrera/A.Jones 6.00 15.00
DB A.Dunn/L.Berkman 4.00 10.00
GS V.Guerrero/S.Sosa 6.00 15.00
GT K.Greene/M.Tejada 6.00 15.00
HB T.Helton/J.Bagwell 6.00 15.00
HE T.Hunter/J.Edmonds 4.00 10.00
JC R.Johnson/R.Clemens 10.00 25.00
JW C.Jones/D.Wright 6.00 15.00
MM H.Matsui/K./Matsui 15.00 40.00
OG D.Ortiz/J.Giambi 6.00 15.00
RB S.Rolen/A.Beltre 6.00 15.00
RS M.Ramirez/G.Sheffield 6.00 15.00
SG J.Smoltz/E.Gagne 6.00 15.00
SM J.Schmidt/P.Martinez 6.00 15.00
SM1 A.Soriano/K.Matsui 4.00 10.00
SP C.Schilling/M.Prior 6.00 15.00

TP J.Thome/M.Piazza 6.00 15.00
WS D.Willis/J.Santana 6.00 15.00

2005 Classic Clippings Jersey Rack Triple Blue

STATED ODDS 1:54 HOBBY
PURPLE PRINT RUN 1 SERIAL #'d SET
NO PURPLE PRICING DUE TO SCARCITY
SILVER PRINT RUN 25 SERIAL #'d SETS
NO SILVER PRICING AVAILABLE
OVERALL ODDS GU 1:9 H, AU-GU 1:24 R
CJS Clemens/Randy/J.Schmidt 10.00 25.00
CSJ Clemens/Schilling/Randy 10.00 25.00
EHJ Edmonds/Torii/Andruw 6.00 15.00
GRS Vlad/Manny/Sheffield 6.00 15.00
GSR Gagne/Smoltz/Rivera 6.00 15.00
HSB Helton/Soriano/Beltre 4.00 10.00
MGT Kaz/Greene/Tejada 6.00 15.00
MRG Hideki/Rivera/Giambi 12.50 30.00
ORM Ortiz/Manny/Pedro 8.00 20.00
PRE Pujols/Rolen/Edmonds 12.50 30.00
PTB Pujols/Thome/Bagwell 10.00 25.00
RBJ Rolen/Beltre/Chipper 6.00 15.00
SDC Sosa/Dunn/Cabrera 6.00 15.00
SJJ Smoltz/Chipper/Andruw 10.00 25.00
SPB J.Schmidt/Prior/Beckett 6.00 15.00
STB Sosa/Tejada/Beltre 6.00 15.00
WPM Wright/Piazza/Kaz 10.00 25.00
WSW Willis/Johan/Wood 6.00 15.00

2005 Classic Clippings MLB Game Worn Jersey Collection

*1 COLOR PATCH: ADD 20%
*2-COLOR+ PATCH: ADD 50%
*3-COLOR+ PATCH: ADD 100%
STATED ODDS 1:8 EXCEL RETAIL
19 David Ortiz 3.00 8.00
20 Mike Piazza 3.00 8.00
21 Adrian Beltre 2.00 5.00
22 Garret Anderson 2.00 5.00
23 Michael Young 2.00 5.00
24 Frank Thomas 3.00 8.00
25 Brian Giles 2.00 5.00
26 Luis Gonzalez 2.00 5.00
27 Eric Chavez 2.00 5.00
28 Jeremy Bonderman 2.00 5.00
29 Bret Boone 2.00 5.00
30 Vernon Wells 2.00 5.00
31 Omar Vizquel 3.00 8.00
32 Mike Lowell 2.00 5.00
33 Marcus Giles 2.00 5.00
34 Junior Spivey 2.00 5.00
35 A.J. Pierzynski 2.00 5.00
36 Jason Kendall 2.00 5.00

2005 Classic Clippings Official Box Score

PRINT RUNS B/WN 1951-1995 COPIES PER
*GOLD: 1.5X TO 4X BASIC
GOLD PRINT RUN B/WN 51-95 COPIES PER
OVERALL INSERT ODDS 1:5 HOB, 1:17 RET
1 Nolan Ryan/1991 4.00 10.00
2 Cal Ripken/1995 4.00 10.00
3 Joe Carter/1993 .50 1.25
4 Bucky Dent/1978 .50 1.25
5 Kirk Gibson/1988 .50 1.25
6 Reggie Jackson/1977 .75 2.00
7 Carlton Fisk/1975 .75 2.00
8 Bobby Thomson/1951 .75 2.00
9 Bill Mazeroski/1960 .75 2.00
10 Don Larsen/1956 .50 1.25

2005 Classic Clippings Press Clippings

STATED ODDS 1:6 HOBBY, 1:24 RETAIL
GOLD PRINT RUN 4 SERIAL #'d SETS
NO GOLD PRICING DUE TO SCARCITY
1 Ichiro Suzuki 1.25 3.00
2 Manny Ramirez 1.00 2.50
3 Albert Pujols 1.25 3.00
4 David Ortiz 1.00 2.50
5 Greg Maddux 1.25 3.00
6 Ken Griffey Jr. 2.00 5.00
7 Vladimir Guerrero .60 1.50
8 Randy Johnson 1.00 2.50
9 Johan Santana .60 1.50
10 Roger Clemens 1.25 3.00
11 Bobby Crosby .40 1.00
12 Jason Bay .40 1.00

2014 Classics

COMPLETE SET (200) 15.00 40.00
1 Adam Jones .20 .50
2 Adam Wainwright .20 .50
3 Adrian Beltre .25 .60
4 Adrian Gonzalez .20 .50
5 Al Kaline .25 .60
6 Herb Pennock .20 .50
7 Albert Pujols .30 .75
8 Andrew McCutchen .25 .60
9 Arky Vaughan .15 .40
10 Bill Dickey .15 .40
11 Bill Terry .15 .40
12 Billy Herman .15 .40
13 Bob Feller .20 .50
14 Bob Gibson .20 .50
15 Brandon Belt .20 .50
16 Brooks Robinson .20 .50
17 Bryce Harper .40 1.00
18 Burleigh Grimes .20 .50
19 Buster Posey .30 .75
20 Cal Ripken .75 2.00
21 Carl Yastrzemski .40 1.00
22 Carlos Gomez .15 .40
23 Carlton Fisk .20 .50
24 Lefty Gomez .15 .40
25 Chipper Jones .25 .60
26 Chris Davis .15 .40
27 Chris Sale .25 .60
28 Chuck Klein .15 .40
29 Clayton Kershaw .40 1.00
30 Dave Bancroft .15 .40
31 David Ortiz .25 .60
32 David Wright .20 .50
33 Derek Jeter .60 1.50
34 Dizzy Dean .20 .50
35 Duke Snider .20 .50
36 Dustin Pedroia .25 .60
37 Earl Averill .15 .40
38 Eddie Collins .20 .50
39 Eddie Murray .20 .50
40 Edwin Encarnacion .25 .60
41 Elston Howard .15 .40
42 Eric Hosmer .20 .50
43 Ernie Banks .25 .60
44 Evan Longoria .20 .50
45 Felix Hernandez .20 .50
46 Frank Chance .20 .50
47 Frank Robinson .20 .50
48 Frank Thomas .25 .60
49 Lefty O'Doul .15 .40
50 Freddie Freeman .30 .75
51 Gabby Hartnett .15 .40
52 George Brett .50 1.25
53 George Kelly .15 .40
54 George Sisler .20 .50
55 Giancarlo Stanton .25 .60
56 Goose Goslin .20 .50
57 Greg Maddux .30 .75
58 Hack Wilson .20 .50
59 Hank Greenberg .25 .60
60 Hanley Ramirez .20 .50
61 Harmon Killebrew .25 .60
62 Harry Heilmann .20 .50
63 Honus Wagner .25 .60
64 Ichiro Suzuki .40 1.00
65 Jackie Robinson .25 .60
66 Jim Bottomley .15 .40
67 Jim Palmer .20 .50
68 Jim Thorpe .40 1.00
69 Jimmie Foxx .25 .60
70 Joe DiMaggio .50 1.25
71 Joe Jackson .30 .75
72 Joe Mauer .20 .50
73 Joe Medwick .15 .40
74 Joe Morgan .20 .50
75 Joey Votto .25 .60
76 Johnny Bench .25 .60
77 Jose Bautista .20 .50
78 Jose Fernandez .25 .60
79 Josh Donaldson .20 .50
80 Josh Gibson .25 .60
81 Juan Marichal .20 .50
82 Justin Upton .20 .50
83 Justin Verlander .25 .60
84 Ken Griffey Jr. .50 1.25
85 Lefty Grove .20 .50
86 Leo Durocher .15 .40
87 Lloyd Waner .20 .50
88 Carl Furillo .15 .40
89 Luke Appling .20 .50
90 Manny Machado .25 .60
91 Mariano Rivera .30 .75
92 Mark McGwire .50 1.25
93 Max Scherzer .25 .60
94 Mel Ott .25 .60
95 Miguel Cabrera .25 .60
96 Mike Piazza .25 .60
97 Mike Trout 1.25 3.00
98 Miller Huggins .15 .40
99 Nap Lajoie .25 .60
100 Nellie Fox .20 .50
101 Nolan Ryan .75 2.00
102 Orlando Cepeda .20 .50
103 Paul Goldschmidt .25 .60
104 Paul Molitor .25 .60
105 Paul Waner .20 .50
106 Pee Wee Reese .20 .50
107 Pete Rose .50 1.25
108 Phil Rizzuto .20 .50
109 Reggie Jackson .20 .50
110 Rick Ferrell .15 .40
111 Rickey Henderson .25 .60
112 Robinson Cano .20 .50
113 Robin Yount .25 .60
114 Rod Carew .20 .50
115 Roger Bresnahan .20 .50
116 Roger Clemens .30 .75
117 Roger Maris .25 .60
118 Barry Bonds .40 1.00
119 Roy Campanella .25 .60
120 Ryan Braun .20 .50
121 Ryne Sandberg .50 1.25
122 Sam Crawford .20 .50
123 Satchel Paige .25 .60
124 Stan Musial .40 1.00
125 Stephen Strasburg .25 .60
126 Steve Carlton .20 .50
127 Ted Kluszewski .20 .50
128 Sonny Gray .20 .50
129 Thurman Munson .25 .60
130 Todd Helton .20 .50
131 Tom Glavine .20 .50
132 Tom Seaver .20 .50
133 Tommy Henrich .15 .40
134 Tony Gwynn .25 .60
135 Tony Lazzeri .20 .50
136 Tony Perez .20 .50
137 Tris Speaker .20 .50
138 Troy Tulowitzki .25 .60
139 Ty Cobb .40 1.00
140 Wade Boggs .20 .50
141 Warren Spahn .20 .50
142 Whitey Ford .20 .50
143 Wil Myers .15 .40
144 Willie Keeler .15 .40
145 Willie McCovey .20 .50
146 Willie Stargell .20 .50
147 Yasiel Puig .25 .60
148 Yoenis Cespedes .25 .60
149 Yogi Berra .25 .60
150 Yu Darvish .25 .60
151 Arismendy Alcantara RC .25 .60
152 Alex Guerrero RC .30 .75
153 Andrew Heaney RC .25 .60
154 Anthony DeSclafani RC .25 .60
155 Billy Hamilton RC .30 .75
156 C.J. Cron RC .25 .60
157 Chris Owings RC .25 .60
158 Christian Bethancourt RC .25 .60
159 Danny Santana RC .30 .75
160 David Hale RC .25 .60
161 Kevin Kiermaier RC .40 1.00
162 Eddie Butler RC .25 .60
163 Aaron Sanchez RC .25 .60
164 Erisbel Arruebarrena RC .25 .60
165 Eugenio Suarez RC 1.00 2.50
166 Garin Cecchini RC .25 .60
167 George Springer RC 1.00 2.50
168 Gregory Polanco RC .40 1.00
169 Mookie Betts RC 12.00 30.00
170 J.R. Murphy RC .25 .60
171 Jace Peterson RC .25 .60
172 Jake Marisnick RC .25 .60
173 James Paxton RC .40 1.00
174 Jimmy Nelson RC .25 .60
175 Jon Singleton RC .30 .75
176 Jonathan Schoop RC .25 .60
177 Jose Abreu RC 2.00 5.00
178 Jose Ramirez RC 2.00 5.00
179 Kolten Wong RC .30 .75
180 Luis Sardinas RC .25 .60
181 Andrew Susac RC .30 .75
182 Marcus Stroman RC .40 1.00
183 Masahiro Tanaka RC .75 2.00
184 Matt Davidson RC .30 .75
185 Robbie Ray RC .25 .60
186 Nick Castellanos RC .75 2.00
187 Oscar Taveras RC .30 .75
188 Rafael Montero RC .25 .60
189 Randal Grichuk RC .40 1.00
190 Rougned Odor RC .60 1.50
191 Christian Vazquez RC .60 1.50
192 Taijuan Walker RC .25 .60
193 Odrisamer Despaigne RC .25 .60
194 Tommy La Stella RC .25 .60
195 Travis d'Arnaud RC .30 .75
196 Chris Taylor RC 1.25 3.00
197 Domingo Santana RC .40 1.00
198 Xander Bogaerts RC .75 2.00
199 Kyle Parker RC .30 .75
200 Yordano Ventura RC .30 .75

2014 Classics Timeless Tributes Gold

*GOLD VET: 8X TO 20X BASIC
*GOLD RC: 5X TO 12X BASIC RC
RANDOM INSERTS IN PACKS
STATED PRINT RUN 25 SER.#'d SETS

2014 Classics Timeless Tributes Silver

*SILVER VET: 4X TO 10X BASIC
*SILVER RC: 2.5X TO 6X BASIC RC
RANDOM INSERTS IN PACKS
STATED PRINT RUN 149 SER.#'d SETS
177 Jose Abreu 6.00 15.00

2014 Classics Champion Materials

RANDOM INSERTS IN PACKS
STATED PRINT RUN 99 SER.#'d SETS
1 Bill Dickey 6.00 15.00
3 Carl Furillo 6.00 15.00
7 Lefty Gomez 10.00 25.00
15 Herb Pennock 8.00 20.00
18 Lefty O'Doul 20.00 50.00

2014 Classics Champion Materials Bats

RANDOM INSERTS IN PACKS
PRINT RUNS B/WN 10-99 SER.#'d SETS
NO PRICING ON QTY 10
2 Bob Meusel/25 6.00 15.00
3 Carl Furillo/99 6.00 15.00
4 Dave Bancroft/99 6.00 15.00
5 Eddie Collins/25 40.00 80.00
6 Frank Chance/25 25.00 60.00
8 George Kelly/99 6.00 15.00
9 Goose Goslin/99 20.00 50.00
10 Heinie Groh/99 6.00 15.00
11 Honus Wagner/25 40.00 100.00
12 Jake Daubert/99 6.00 15.00
13 Jim Bottomley/99 6.00 15.00
14 Joe Jackson/25 150.00 250.00
16 Miller Huggins/25 6.00 15.00
17 Roger Bresnahan/99 75.00 150.00
19 Tony Lazzeri/99 8.00 20.00
20 Tris Speaker/99 8.00 20.00

2014 Classics Classic Combos Bats

RANDOM INSERTS IN PACKS
PRINT RUNS B/WN 5-99 SER.#'d SETS
NO PRICING ON QTY 10 OR LESS
6 H.Groh/J.Daubert/25 10.00 25.00
12 G.Goslin/J.Cronin/25 30.00 80.00
13 E.Averill/W.Kamm/25 15.00 40.00
14 F.Frisch/J.Bottomley/25 40.00 80.00
21 Joe DiMaggio
Bill Dickey/25 25.00 60.00
22 J.Mize/M.Ott/99 12.00 30.00
23 F.Robinson/T.Kluszewski/99 6.00 15.00
27 A.Pujols/M.Trout/99 15.00 40.00
29 D.Jeter/I.Suzuki/99 10.00 25.00

2014 Classics Classic Combos Jerseys

RANDOM INSERTS IN PACKS
PRINT RUNS B/WN 5-99 SER.#'d SETS
NO PRICING ON QTY 5
23 F.Robinson/T.Kluszewski/99 15.00 40.00
25 B.Campaneris/R.Jackson/99 15.00 40.00
26 G.Springer/J.Singleton/99 5.00 12.00
27 A.Pujols/M.Trout/99 15.00 40.00
28 Stanton/Fernandez/99 5.00 12.00
29 D.Jeter/I.Suzuki/99 20.00 50.00
30 M.Tanaka/Y.Darvish/99 20.00 50.00

2014 Classics Classic Cuts

RANDOM INSERTS IN PACKS
PRINT RUNS B/WN 1-99 SER.#'d SETS
NO PRICING ON QTY 10 OR LESS
EXCHANGE DEADLINE 5/19/2016
7 Bobby Thomson/99 10.00 25.00
25 Johnny Pesky/99 15.00 40.00
34 Stan Musial/99 20.00 50.00
36 Lou Boudreau/25 15.00 40.00
39 Warren Spahn/25 40.00 100.00

2014 Classics Classic Lineups

RANDOM INSERTS IN PACKS
PRINT RUNS B/WN 25-99 COPIES PER
1 Ghrngr/Hlmnn/Cbb/99 30.00 80.00
2 Sthwrth/Bttmly/Hrnsby/25 100.00 200.00
3 Msl/Hlmnn/Drchr/99 12.00 30.00
4 Hrtntt/Wlsn/Hrnsby/99 20.00 50.00
5 Frsch/Mdwck/Drchr/25 75.00 150.00
6 Hrmn/Kln/Hrtntt/99 50.00 100.00
7 Ghrngr/Gsln/Grnbrg/99 50.00 100.00
8 Smmns/Ghrngr/Gsln/99 25.00 60.00
9 Hrmn/Grbrg/Knr/99 30.00 80.00
10 Frllo/Sndr/Rbnsn/25 75.00 150.00
11 Mzrski/Hk/Clmnt/99 20.00 50.00
12 Hwrd/Mrs/Brra/99 12.00 30.00
13 Mzrski/Clmnt/Strgll/99 30.00 80.00
14 Kllbrw/Crw/Olva/99 50.00 100.00
15 Pwll/Rbnsn/Rbnsn/99 12.00 30.00
16 Bncrft/Frsch/Klly/99 20.00 50.00
17 Musl/Ghrig/Lzzri/27 60.00 150.00
18 Smmns/Cllns/Fxx/99 30.00 80.00
19 DMggo/Fxx/Wllms/99 25.00 60.00
20 Hdgs/Gllam/Cmpnlla/99 15.00 40.00

2014 Classics Classic Quads Bats

RANDOM INSERTS IN PACKS
PRINT RUNS B/WN 5-99 COPIES PER
NO PRICING ON QTY 10 OR LESS
2 Frsch/Klly/Wlsn/Grh/25 75.00 150.00
8 DMggo/Fxx/Crnn/Wllms/25 60.00 120.00
12 Frllo/Stnky/Rbnsn/Rsr/25 40.00 100.00
16 Pwll/Rbnsn/Rbnsn/Aprco/99 12.00 30.00
19 Gnzlz/Krshw/Rmrz/Pg/75 15.00 40.00

2014 Classics Classic Quads Jerseys

RANDOM INSERTS IN PACKS
PRINT RUNS B/WN 5-99 COPIES PER
NO PRICING ON QTY 5
12 Frllo/Stnky/Rbnsn/Rsr/47 50.00 100.00
15 Pttte/Wllms/Jtr/Psda/98 30.00 60.00
17 Mrgn/Bnch/Rse/Prz/25 50.00 120.00
18 Whtly/Mrphy/Tnka/Slrte/99 12.00 30.00
19 Gnzlz/Krshw/Rmrz/Puig/99 10.00 25.00

2014 Classics Classic Triples Bats

RANDOM INSERTS IN PACKS
PRINT RUNS B/WN 15-99 COPIES PER
NO PRICING ON QTY 15
10 Herman/Greenberg/Kiner/25 60.00 120.00
14 Mazeroski/Clemente/Stargell/99 50.00 100.00
16 Powell/Robinson/Robinson/99 15.00 40.00
21 Jones/Davis/Machado/99 12.00 30.00
22 Ortiz/Pedroia/Bogaerts/99 12.00 30.00
25 Terry/Klein/Frisch/25 15.00 40.00

2014 Classics Classic Triples Jerseys

RANDOM INSERTS IN PACKS
PRINT RUNS B/WN 5-99 COPIES PER
NO PRICING ON QTY 10 OR LESS
9 Sthwrth/Slghtr/Msl/25 150.00 250.00
11 Frllo/Sndr/Rbnsn/25 75.00 150.00
13 Hwrd/Mrs/Brra/25 12.00 30.00
14 Maz/Clmnte/Strgll/25 50.00 100.00
15 Kllbrw/Crw/Olva/25 20.00 50.00
16 Pwll/Rbnsn/Rbnsn/99 10.00 25.00
17 Strwbrry/Crtr/Hrnndz/99 20.00 50.00
18 Abru/Pg/Cspds/99 12.00 30.00
19 McCtchn/Plnco/Mrte/99 25.00 60.00
20 Sprngr/Plnco/Tvrs/99 12.00 30.00
21 Jns/Dvs/Mchdo/99 12.00 30.00
22 Ortz/Pdra/Bgrts/99 20.00 50.00
23 Smmns/Dcky/Ghrngr/25 40.00 80.00

2014 Classics Home Run Heroes

COMPLETE SET (25) 12.00 30.00
RANDOM INSERTS IN PACKS
1 Adrian Beltre .50 1.25
2 Miguel Cabrera .50 1.25
3 Albert Pujols .60 1.50
4 Bill Terry .30 .75
5 Jose Abreu 2.50 6.00
6 Chris Davis .30 .75
7 Chuck Klein .30 .75
8 David Ortiz .50 1.25
9 Eddie Murray .40 1.00
10 Frank Howard .30 .75
11 Frank Thomas .50 1.25
12 Giancarlo Stanton .50 1.25
13 Hack Wilson .40 1.00
14 Hank Greenberg .50 1.25
15 Mike Trout 2.50 6.00
16 Joe DiMaggio 1.00 2.50
17 Johnny Mize .40 1.00
18 Justin Upton .40 1.00
19 Ken Griffey Jr. 1.00 2.50
20 Mel Ott .50 1.25
21 Roger Maris .50 1.25
22 Barry Bonds .75 2.00
23 Sam Crawford .40 1.00
24 Mark McGwire 1.00 2.50
25 Tony Lazzeri .40 1.00

2014 Classics Home Run Heroes Bats

RANDOM INSERTS IN PACKS
PRINT RUNS B/WN 10-99 COPIES PER
NO PRICING ON QTY 10 OR LESS
2 Al Simmons/99 10.00 25.00
3 Albert Pujols/99 5.00 12.00
4 Bill Terry/25 20.00 50.00
5 Bob Meusel/25 10.00 25.00
7 Chuck Klein/25 15.00 40.00
9 Eddie Murray/99 4.00 10.00
10 Frank Howard/99 3.00 8.00
11 Frank Thomas/99 5.00 12.00
12 Giancarlo Stanton/99 5.00 12.00
13 Hack Wilson/25 40.00 80.00
14 Hank Greenberg/25 50.00 100.00
16 Joe DiMaggio/25 20.00 50.00
17 Johnny Mize/25 10.00 25.00
18 Justin Upton/99 4.00 10.00
23 Sam Crawford/25 12.00 30.00
24 Ted Williams/25 20.00 50.00

2014 Classics Home Run Heroes Jerseys

RANDOM INSERTS IN PACKS
PRINT RUNS B/WN 4-99 COPIES PER
NO PRICING ON QTY 10 OR LESS
1 Adrian Beltre/99 5.00 12.00
3 Albert Pujols/99 5.00 12.00
6 Chris Davis/99 3.00 8.00
9 Eddie Murray/99 6.00 15.00
10 Frank Howard/99 6.00 15.00
11 Frank Thomas/99 5.00 12.00
12 Giancarlo Stanton/99 5.00 12.00
16 Joe DiMaggio/25 30.00 60.00
17 Johnny Mize/25 8.00 20.00
18 Justin Upton/99 4.00 10.00
24 Ted Williams/99 20.00 50.00

2014 Classics Home Run Heroes Jerseys HR

RANDOM INSERTS IN PACKS
PRINT RUNS B/WN 4-99 COPIES PER
NO PRICING ON QTY 10 OR LESS
1 Adrian Beltre/99 5.00 12.00
3 Albert Pujols/99 6.00 15.00
8 David Ortiz/99 5.00 12.00
9 Eddie Murray/99 6.00 15.00
10 Frank Howard/25 15.00 40.00
11 Frank Thomas/99 8.00 20.00
12 Giancarlo Stanton/99 5.00 12.00
17 Johnny Mize/25 15.00 40.00
24 Ted Williams/99 20.00 50.00

2014 Classics Home Run Heroes Materials Combos

RANDOM INSERTS IN PACKS
PRINT RUNS B/WN 4-99 COPIES PER
NO PRICING ON QTY 10 OR LESS
1 Adrian Beltre/99 5.00 12.00
2 Al Simmons/25 40.00 80.00
3 Albert Pujols/99 6.00 15.00
6 Chris Davis/99 3.00 8.00
8 David Ortiz/99 5.00 12.00
9 Eddie Murray/99 4.00 10.00
11 Frank Thomas/99 5.00 12.00
12 Giancarlo Stanton/99 5.00 12.00
18 Justin Upton/99 4.00 10.00
24 Ted Williams/25 30.00 60.00

2014 Classics Legendary Lumberjacks

COMPLETE SET (25) 12.00 30.00
RANDOM INSERTS IN PACKS
1 Albert Pujols .60 1.50
2 Ernie Banks .50 1.25
3 Cal Ripken 1.50 4.00
4 Tony Gwynn .50 1.25
5 Derek Jeter 1.25 3.00
6 Dustin Pedroia .50 1.25
7 Earl Averill .30 .75
8 Lefty O'Doul .30 .75
9 Eddie Murray .40 1.00
10 Frank Robinson .40 1.00
11 George Brett 1.00 2.50
12 George Sisler .40 1.00
13 Jose Abreu 2.50 6.00
14 Harry Heilmann .40 1.00
15 Honus Wagner .50 1.25
16 Ichiro Suzuki .75 2.00
17 Giancarlo Stanton .50 1.25
18 Lloyd Waner .40 1.00
19 Miguel Cabrera .50 1.25
20 Nap Lajoie .50 1.25
21 Paul Waner .40 1.00
22 Mike Trout 2.50 6.00
23 Tris Speaker .40 1.00
24 Ty Cobb .75 2.00
25 Willie Keeler .30 .75

2014 Classics Legendary Lumberjacks Bats

RANDOM INSERTS IN PACKS
PRINT RUNS B/WN 10-99 COPIES PER
NO PRICING ON QTY 10
1 Albert Pujols/99 6.00 15.00
2 Bill Dickey/25 8.00 20.00
3 Cal Ripken/99 6.00 15.00
5 Derek Jeter/99 12.00 30.00
6 Dustin Pedroia/99 5.00 12.00
7 Earl Averill/99 3.00 8.00
9 Eddie Murray/99 4.00 10.00
10 Frank Robinson/99 4.00 10.00
11 George Brett/99 6.00 15.00
12 George Sisler/99 8.00 20.00
15 Honus Wagner/25 50.00 100.00
16 Ichiro Suzuki/99 6.00 15.00
17 Joe Jackson/25 50.00 120.00
18 Lloyd Waner/99 4.00 10.00
19 Miguel Cabrera/99 6.00 15.00
20 Nap Lajoie/25 30.00 80.00
21 Paul Waner/25 20.00 50.00
22 Roberto Clemente/25 20.00 50.00

2014 Classics Legendary Lumberjacks Bats Combos

RANDOM INSERTS IN PACKS
PRINT RUNS B/WN 10-99 COPIES PER
NO PRICING ON QTY 10
3 Cal Ripken/99 10.00 25.00
5 Derek Jeter/99 20.00 50.00
6 Dustin Pedroia/99 5.00 12.00
7 Earl Averill/25 15.00 40.00
9 Eddie Murray/99 4.00 10.00
10 Frank Robinson/99 4.00 10.00
16 Ichiro Suzuki/99 8.00 20.00
18 Lloyd Waner/25 10.00 25.00
19 Miguel Cabrera/99 5.00 12.00

2014 Classics Legendary Lumberjacks Bats Signatures

RANDOM INSERTS IN PACKS
PRINT RUNS B/WN 5-25 COPIES PER
NO PRICING ON QTY 10 OR LESS
EXCHANGE DEADLINE 5/19/2016

2014 Classics Legendary Lumberjacks Jerseys

RANDOM INSERTS IN PACKS
PRINT RUNS B/WN 10-99 COPIES PER
NO PRICING ON QTY 10
1 Albert Pujols/99 6.00 15.00
3 Cal Ripken/99 10.00 25.00
4 Charlie Gehringer/25 15.00 40.00
5 Derek Jeter/99 15.00 40.00
6 Dustin Pedroia/99 5.00 12.00
9 Eddie Murray/99 5.00 12.00
10 Frank Robinson/99 4.00 10.00
11 George Brett/25 6.00 15.00
16 Ichiro Suzuki/99 8.00 20.00
19 Miguel Cabrera/99 5.00 12.00
22 Roberto Clemente/25 30.00 60.00

2014 Classics Legendary Players Bats

RANDOM INSERTS IN PACKS
PRINT RUNS B/WN 10-99 COPIES PER
NO PRICING ON QTY 10
8 George Kelly 20.00 50.00
9 Gil Hodges 12.00 30.00
11 Joe DiMaggio 25.00 60.00
15 Miller Huggins 15.00 40.00
16 Paul Waner 5.00 12.00
17 Pee Wee Reese 4.00 10.00
19 Roberto Clemente 12.00 30.00
20 Roger Maris 12.00 30.00
23 Thurman Munson 8.00 20.00
24 Tommy Henrich 3.00 8.00

2014 Classics Legendary Players Materials

RANDOM INSERTS IN PACKS
PRINT RUNS B/WN 25-99 COPIES PER
2 Bob Feller/25 50.00 100.00
3 Lefty O'Doul/99 20.00 50.00
5 Elston Howard/99 25.00 60.00
6 Enos Slaughter/99 6.00 15.00
7 Gabby Hartnett/99 50.00 100.00
9 Gil Hodges/99 10.00 25.00
13 Leo Durocher/99 6.00 15.00
14 Luke Appling/99 4.00 10.00
18 Rick Ferrell/99 10.00 25.00
19 Roberto Clemente/25 20.00 50.00
20 Roger Maris/25 20.00 50.00
21 Herb Pennock/99 12.00 30.00
22 Lefty Gomez/99 50.00 100.00
23 Thurman Munson/99 20.00 50.00
24 Tommy Henrich/99 3.00 8.00
25 Walter Alston/99 6.00 15.00

2014 Classics Membership Materials HOF

RANDOM INSERTS IN PACKS
PRINT RUNS B/WN 1-25 COPIES PER
NO PRICING ON QTY 10 OR LESS
5 George Sisler/25 60.00 120.00
8 Paul Waner/25 15.00 40.00
9 Jim Bottomley/25 30.00 80.00
10 Herb Pennock/25 50.00 100.00
12 Chuck Klein/25 10.00 25.00
15 Gabby Hartnett/25 75.00 150.00
16 Charlie Gehringer/25 20.00 50.00
18 Joe DiMaggio/25 75.00 150.00
19 Ted Williams/25 60.00 150.00
22 Roberto Clemente/25 100.00 200.00
24 Warren Spahn/25 75.00 150.00
25 Early Wynn/25 30.00 60.00

2014 Classics Membership Materials MVP

RANDOM INSERTS IN PACKS
PRINT RUNS B/WN 1-25 COPIES PER
NO PRICING ON QTY 10 OR LESS
3 Jake Daubert/25 40.00 80.00
23 Thurman Munson/25 40.00 80.00

2014 Classics October Heroes

COMPLETE SET (25) 12.00 30.00
RANDOM INSERTS IN PACKS
1 Don Larsen .30 .75
2 Albert Pujols .60 1.50
3 Bill Mazeroski .40 1.00
4 Bob Gibson .40 1.00
5 Herb Pennock .40 1.00
6 Carlos Ruiz .30 .75
7 Carlton Fisk .40 1.00
8 Catfish Hunter .40 1.00
9 David Ortiz .50 1.25
10 Derek Jeter 1.25 3.00
11 Eddie Collins .40 1.00
12 Frank Chance .40 1.00
13 Heinie Groh .30 .75
14 Joe Jackson .60 1.50
15 Johnny Bench .50 1.25
16 Luis Gonzalez .30 .75
17 Pablo Sandoval .40 1.00
18 Lefty Gomez .30 .75
19 Ted Kluszewski .40 1.00
20 Thurman Munson .50 1.25
21 Frank Robinson .40 1.00
22 Mariano Rivera .60 1.50
23 Mike Schmidt .75 2.00
24 Pete Rose 1.00 2.50
25 Reggie Jackson .40 1.00

2014 Classics October Heroes Bats

RANDOM INSERTS IN PACKS
PRINT RUNS B/WN 10-99 COPIES PER
NO PRICING ON QTY 10
2 Albert Pujols/99 5.00 12.00
3 Bill Mazeroski/25 12.00 30.00
5 Bob Meusel/25 6.00 15.00
7 Carlton Fisk/99 4.00 10.00
9 David Ortiz/99 5.00 12.00
10 Derek Jeter/99 8.00 20.00
13 Heinie Groh/99 6.00 15.00
14 Joe Jackson/25 125.00 250.00
17 Pablo Sandoval/99 4.00 10.00
18 Roberto Clemente/25 30.00 80.00
19 Ted Kluszewski/99 4.00 10.00
20 Thurman Munson/99 10.00 25.00

2014 Classics October Heroes Bats Signatures

RANDOM INSERTS IN PACKS
PRINT RUNS B/WN 5-25 COPIES PER
NO PRICING ON QTY 10 OR LESS
EXCHANGE DEADLINE 5/19/2016
4 Bill Mazeroski/25 20.00 50.00
10 David Freese/25 5.00 12.00
15 Joe Carter/25 15.00 40.00

2014 Classics October Heroes Jerseys

RANDOM INSERTS IN PACKS
PRINT RUNS B/WN 4-99 COPIES PER
NO PRICING ON QTY 4
1 Herb Pennock/99 6.00 15.00
4 Bob Gibson/99 10.00 25.00
7 Carlton Fisk/99 4.00 10.00
9 David Ortiz/99 5.00 12.00
10 Derek Jeter/99 12.00 30.00
18 Roberto Clemente/25 40.00 100.00
20 Thurman Munson/99 15.00 40.00

2014 Classics October Heroes Jerseys Signatures

RANDOM INSERTS IN PACKS
PRINT RUNS B/WN 5-25 COPIES PER
NO PRICING ON QTY 10 OR LESS
EXCHANGE DEADLINE 5/19/2016
1 Alan Trammell/25 12.00 30.00
3 Andy Pettitte/25 20.00 50.00
7 Carlos Ruiz/99 5.00 12.00

2014 Classics October Heroes Materials Combos

RANDOM INSERTS IN PACKS
PRINT RUNS B/WN 5-99 COPIES PER
NO PRICING ON QTY 10 OR LESS
1 Herb Pennock/25 50.00 100.00
2 Albert Pujols/99 5.00 12.00
3 Bill Mazeroski/25 20.00 50.00
4 Bob Gibson/99 15.00 40.00
6 Carlos Ruiz/99 3.00 8.00
7 Carlton Fisk/99 4.00 10.00
9 David Ortiz/99 5.00 12.00
10 Derek Jeter/99 12.00 30.00
12 Frank Chance/25 30.00 60.00
13 Heinie Groh/99 10.00 25.00
14 Joe Jackson/25 150.00 250.00
17 Pablo Sandoval/99 10.00 25.00
18 Roberto Clemente/25 50.00 100.00
19 Ted Kluszewski/99 15.00 40.00
20 Thurman Munson/25 50.00 100.00

2014 Classics October Heroes Materials Combos Signatures

RANDOM INSERTS IN PACKS
PRINT RUNS B/WN 5-25 COPIES PER
NO PRICING ON QTY 10 OR LESS
EXCHANGE DEADLINE 5/19/2016
3 Andy Pettitte/25 6.00 15.00
4 Bill Mazeroski/20 12.00 30.00
7 Carlos Ruiz/25 5.00 12.00
10 David Freese/25 5.00 12.00

2014 Classics Players Collection

RANDOM INSERTS IN PACKS
PRINT RUNS B/WN 5-99 COPIES PER
NO PRICING ON QTY 5
2 Derek Jeter/99 15.00 40.00
10 Jose Abreu/25 30.00 80.00
14 Nolan Ryan/25 20.00 50.00
15 Pete Rose/25 15.00 40.00
18 Tony Gwynn/99 6.00 15.00

2014 Classics Significant Signatures Bats Gold

RANDOM INSERTS IN PACKS
PRINT RUNS B/WN 1-25 COPIES PER
NO PRICING ON QTY 10 OR LESS
EXCHANGE DEADLINE 5/19/2016
36 Carlos Sanchez/25 5.00 12.00
73 Jose Abreu/25 40.00 100.00
77 Rougned Odor/25 12.00 30.00

2014 Classics Significant Signatures Bats Silver

RANDOM INSERTS IN PACKS
PRINT RUNS B/WN 5-99 COPIES PER
NO PRICING ON QTY 10 OR LESS
EXCHANGE DEADLINE 5/19/2016
8 Buster Posey 25.00 60.00
36 Carlos Sanchez 4.00 10.00
73 Jose Abreu 15.00 40.00
75 C.J. Cron 4.00 10.00
77 Rougned Odor 10.00 25.00
80 George Springer 10.00 25.00
90 Michael Choice 4.00 10.00

2014 Classics Significant Signatures Silver

*GOLD/25: .5X TO 1.2X SILVER
RANDOM INSERTS IN PACKS
PRINT RUNS B/WN 10-299 COPIES PER
NO PRICING ON QTY 10
EXCHANGE DEADLINE 5/19/2016
1 Aaron Sanchez/299 3.00 8.00
3 Alan Trammell/99 6.00 15.00
5 Austin Hedges/299 3.00 8.00
8 Boog Powell/299 3.00 8.00
10 Carlos Correa/299 20.00 50.00
14 Dave Parker/149 5.00 12.00
19 Doug Harvey/99 5.00 12.00
21 Dylan Bundy/99 4.00 10.00
22 Edgar Martinez/99 12.00 30.00
25 Francisco Lindor/299 20.00 50.00
35 Joe Charboneau/299 6.00 15.00
37 Joey Gallo/299 6.00 15.00
41 Jose Canseco/299 4.00 10.00
45 Kris Bryant/299 50.00 120.00
46 Lance Lynn/299 3.00 8.00
50 Maikel Franco/299 4.00 10.00
51 Matt Adams/299 3.00 8.00
52 Maury Wills/299 3.00 8.00
53 Michael Wacha/299 4.00 10.00
54 Miguel Sano/299 4.00 10.00
56 Mookie Betts/299 60.00 150.00
62 Robert Stephenson/299 3.00 8.00
64 Ron Guidry/25 10.00 25.00
67 Shelby Miller/149 4.00 10.00
70 Steve Garvey/199 3.00 8.00
74 Tony La Russa/25 5.00 12.00
75 Whitey Herzog/25 4.00 10.00
76 Willie Horton/89 3.00 8.00
79 Danny Santana/299 20.00 50.00
80 Robbie Ray/299 3.00 8.00
81 Anthony DeSclafani/299 3.00 8.00
82 Christian Bethancourt/299 3.00 8.00
83 Eddie Butler/299 3.00 8.00
84 Nick Ahmed/299 3.00 8.00
85 Erisbel Arruebarrena/299 6.00 15.00
86 Eugenio Suarez/299 8.00 20.00
87 Garin Cecchini/299 3.00 8.00
88 Alex Guerrero/299 4.00 10.00
89 Jace Peterson/299 3.00 8.00
90 Jacob deGrom/299 200.00 500.00
91 Jake Marisnick/299 3.00 8.00

92 James Paxton/299 5.00 12.00
93 Jon Singleton/299 4.00 10.00
94 Luis Sardinas/299 3.00 8.00
95 Marcus Stroman/299 5.00 12.00
96 Rafael Montero/299 3.00 8.00
97 Randal Grichuk/299 10.00 25.00
98 Arismendy Alcantara/299 3.00 8.00
99 Tanner Roark/299 3.00 8.00
100 Tommy La Stella/299 3.00 8.00

2014 Classics Significant Signatures Jerseys Silver

RANDOM INSERTS IN PACKS
PRINT RUNS B/WN 3-299 COPIES PER
NO PRICING ON QTY 10 OR LESS
EXCHANGE DEADLINE 5/19/2016
3 Andrew McCutchen/149 25.00 60.00
5 Anthony Rizzo/299 20.00 50.00
9 Byron Buxton/299 8.00 20.00
12 Carlos Gomez/199 3.00 8.00
20 Enny Romero/299 3.00 8.00
26 Joe Panik/299 4.00 10.00
29 Freddie Freeman/25 10.00 25.00
30 Gaylord Perry/25 5.00 12.00
35 Harold Baines/299 4.00 10.00
36 Carlos Sanchez/299 3.00 8.00
37 Jameson Taillon/299 4.00 10.00
38 Javier Baez/299 12.00 30.00
42 Jonathan Gray/299 4.00 10.00
45 Josh Donaldson/299 10.00 25.00
47 Kyle Zimmer/299 3.00 8.00
53 Mark Trumbo/25 4.00 10.00
63 Starling Marte/199 6.00 15.00
66 Tony Perez/25 20.00 50.00
71 Tyler Collins/299 3.00 8.00
73 Jose Abreu/299 12.00 30.00
74 Billy Hamilton/299 4.00 10.00
75 C.J. Cron/299 3.00 8.00
76 Chris Owings/299 3.00 8.00
77 Rougned Odor/299 4.00 10.00
78 David Hale/299 3.00 8.00
79 David Holmberg/299 3.00 8.00
80 George Springer/299 12.00 30.00
81 Gregory Polanco/299 5.00 12.00
82 J.R. Murphy/299 3.00 8.00
83 Jimmy Nelson/299 3.00 8.00
84 Jonathan Schoop/299 3.00 8.00
85 Andrew Heaney/299 3.00 8.00
86 Jose Ramirez/299 25.00 60.00
87 Kolten Wong/299 4.00 10.00
88 Marcus Semien/299 15.00 40.00
89 Matt Davidson/299 4.00 10.00
90 Michael Choice/299 3.00 8.00
91 Nick Castellanos/299 10.00 25.00
93 Roenis Elias/299 3.00 8.00
94 Taijuan Walker/299 3.00 8.00
95 Travis d'Arnaud/299 6.00 15.00
96 Wei-Chung Wang/299 15.00 40.00
97 Wilmer Flores/299 4.00 10.00
98 Xander Bogaerts/299 20.00 50.00
99 Yangervis Solarte/299 3.00 8.00
100 Yordano Ventura/299 8.00 20.00

2014 Classics Significant Signatures Jerseys Gold Prime

*GOLD: .5X TO 1.2X SILVER
RANDOM INSERTS IN PACKS
PRINT RUNS B/WN 5-25 COPIES PER
NO PRICING ON QTY 10 OR LESS
EXCHANGE DEADLINE 5/19/2016

2014 Classics Stars of Summer

COMPLETE SET (25) 12.00 30.00
RANDOM INSERTS IN PACKS
1 Adam Jones .40 1.00
2 Adrian Beltre .50 1.25
3 Albert Pujols .60 1.50
4 Andrew McCutchen .50 1.25
5 Anthony Rizzo .60 1.50
6 Aroldis Chapman .50 1.25
7 Bryce Harper .75 2.00
8 Buster Posey .60 1.50
9 Chris Davis .30 .75
10 David Ortiz .50 1.25
11 David Wright .40 1.00
12 Derek Jeter 1.25 3.00
13 Dustin Pedroia .50 1.25
14 Edwin Encarnacion .50 1.25
15 Evan Longoria .40 1.00
16 Felix Hernandez .40 1.00
17 Joey Votto .50 1.25
18 Jose Bautista .40 1.00
19 Justin Upton .40 1.00
20 Masahiro Tanaka 1.00 2.50
21 Miguel Cabrera .50 1.25
22 Paul Goldschmidt .50 1.25
23 Starlin Castro .30 .75
24 Yasiel Puig .50 1.25
25 Yu Darvish .50 1.25

2014 Classics Stars of Summer Bats

RANDOM INSERTS IN PACKS
STATED PRINT RUN 99 SER.#'d SETS
1 Adam Jones 2.50 6.00
2 Adrian Beltre 3.00 8.00
5 Anthony Rizzo 4.00 10.00
7 Bryce Harper 8.00 20.00
8 Buster Posey 4.00 10.00
9 Chris Davis 2.00 5.00
10 David Ortiz 3.00 8.00
11 David Wright 2.50 6.00
12 Derek Jeter 8.00 20.00
13 Dustin Pedroia 3.00 8.00
14 Edwin Encarnacion 3.00 8.00
15 Evan Longoria 2.50 6.00
17 Joey Votto 3.00 8.00
21 Miguel Cabrera 3.00 8.00
23 Starlin Castro 2.00 5.00
24 Yasiel Puig 3.00 8.00

2014 Classics Stars of Summer Bats Signatures

RANDOM INSERTS IN PACKS
PRINT RUNS B/WN 5-25 COPIES PER
NO PRICING ON QTY 10 OR LESS
EXCHANGE DEADLINE 5/19/2016
3 Anthony Rizzo/25 20.00 50.00
4 Buster Posey/25 40.00 80.00
18 Jose Abreu/25 40.00 100.00

2014 Classics Stars of Summer Jerseys

RANDOM INSERTS IN PACKS
STATED PRINT RUN 99 SER.#'d SETS
3 Albert Pujols 5.00 12.00
4 Andrew McCutchen 6.00 15.00
5 Anthony Rizzo 6.00 15.00
7 Bryce Harper 8.00 20.00
8 Buster Posey 6.00 15.00
10 David Ortiz 5.00 12.00
11 David Wright 4.00 10.00
12 Derek Jeter 12.00 30.00
15 Evan Longoria 4.00 10.00
16 Felix Hernandez 4.00 10.00
17 Joey Votto 5.00 12.00
19 Justin Upton 4.00 10.00
20 Masahiro Tanaka 12.00 30.00
21 Miguel Cabrera 5.00 12.00
22 Paul Goldschmidt 5.00 12.00
23 Starlin Castro 3.00 8.00
24 Yasiel Puig 5.00 12.00
25 Yu Darvish 5.00 12.00

2014 Classics Stars of Summer Jerseys Signatures

RANDOM INSERTS IN PACKS
PRINT RUNS B/WN 10-99 COPIES PER
NO PRICING ON QTY 10 OR LESS
EXCHANGE DEADLINE 5/19/2016
3 Anthony Rizzo/25 20.00 50.00
4 Buster Posey/25 40.00 80.00
12 Evan Gattis/99 5.00 12.00
15 George Springer/99 20.00 50.00
17 Gregory Polanco/99 8.00 20.00
18 Jose Abreu/99 40.00 100.00

2014 Classics Stars of Summer Materials Combos

RANDOM INSERTS IN PACKS
STATED PRINT RUN 99 SER.#'d SETS
2 Adrian Beltre 5.00 12.00
3 Albert Pujols 5.00 12.00
5 Anthony Rizzo 6.00 15.00
7 Bryce Harper 8.00 20.00
8 Buster Posey 6.00 15.00
11 David Wright 4.00 10.00
12 Derek Jeter 20.00 50.00
13 Dustin Pedroia 5.00 12.00
14 Edwin Encarnacion 5.00 12.00
15 Evan Longoria 4.00 10.00
16 Felix Hernandez 4.00 10.00
17 Joey Votto 5.00 12.00
19 Justin Upton 4.00 10.00
20 Masahiro Tanaka 20.00 50.00
21 Miguel Cabrera 6.00 15.00
22 Paul Goldschmidt 5.00 12.00
23 Starlin Castro 3.00 8.00
24 Yasiel Puig 6.00 15.00
25 Yu Darvish 8.00 20.00

2014 Classics Stars of Summer Materials Combos Signatures

RANDOM INSERTS IN PACKS
PRINT RUNS B/WN 5-25 COPIES PER
NO PRICING ON QTY 10 OR LESS
EXCHANGE DEADLINE 5/19/2016
3 Anthony Rizzo/25 20.00 50.00
4 Buster Posey/25 40.00 80.00
5 Carlos Gomez/25 8.00 20.00
15 George Springer/25 20.00 50.00
18 Jose Abreu/25 40.00 100.00

2014 Classics Timeless Treasures Bats

RANDOM INSERTS IN PACKS
PRINT RUNS B/WN 25-99 COPIES PER
1 Albert Pujols/99 5.00 12.00
2 Bill Dickey/25 20.00 50.00
4 Bob Meusel/25 2.50 6.00
5 Cal Ripken/99 10.00 25.00
13 Joe Jackson/25 100.00 200.00
15 Mark McGwire/99 5.00 16.00
16 Mike Schmidt/99 5.00 12.00
18 Nolan Ryan/25 8.00 20.00
20 Roger Bresnahan/99 12.00 30.00
22 Ryne Sandberg/99 5.00 12.00
23 Tony Gwynn/99 4.00 10.00
24 Tony Lazzeri/99 3.00 8.00

2014 Classics Timeless Treasures Jerseys

RANDOM INSERTS IN PACKS
PRINT RUNS B/WN 5-99 COPIES PER
NO PRICING ON QTY 5
*PRIME/25: .5X TO 1.2X BASIC
1 Albert Pujols/99 5.00 12.00
3 Bob Gibson/99 8.00 20.00
5 Cal Ripken/99 15.00 40.00
6 Herb Pennock/99 8.00 20.00
8 Elston Howard/99 10.00 25.00
10 Gabby Hartnett/99 40.00 80.00
11 Jackie Robinson/42 20.00 50.00
14 Leo Durocher/99 8.00 20.00
15 Mark McGwire/99 15.00 40.00
16 Mike Schmidt/99 8.00 20.00
18 Nolan Ryan/99 10.00 25.00
19 Rick Ferrell/99 10.00 25.00
21 Rogers Hornsby/25 25.00 60.00
22 Ryne Sandberg/99 10.00 25.00
23 Tony Gwynn/99 5.00 12.00
25 Warren Spahn/25 60.00 120.00

2018 Classics

INSERTED IN '18 CHRONICLES PACKS
*TRIB/199: 1X TO 2.5X BASE
*TRIB RC/199: .6X TO 1.5X BASE RC
*GOLD/99: 1.2X TO 3X BASE
*GOLD RC/99: .75X TO 2X BASE RC
*RED/25: 2X TO 5X BASE
*RED RC/25: 1.2X TO 3X BASE RC
1 Cole Hamels .20 .50
2 Victor Robles RC .60 1.50
3 Andrew McCutchen .25 .60
4 Ryan McMahon RC .60 1.50
5 Nick Williams RC .30 .75
6 Alex Verdugo RC .40 1.00
7 Shohei Ohtani RC 6.00 15.00
8 Madison Bumgarner .20 .50
9 Dominic Smith RC .30 .75
10 Kris Bryant .30 .75
11 Aaron Judge .60 1.50
12 Rafael Devers RC .75 2.00
13 Shohei Ohtani RC 6.00 15.00
14 Josh Donaldson .20 .50
15 Francisco Lindor .25 .60
16 Clint Frazier RC .50 1.25
17 Jose Altuve .20 .50
18 Amed Rosario RC .30 .75
19 Charlie Blackmon .25 .60
20 Yoenis Cespedes .25 .60
21 Bryce Harper .40 1.00
22 Gleyber Torres RC 2.50 6.00
23 Ronald Acuna Jr. RC 8.00 20.00
24 Miguel Andujar RC 1.00 2.50
25 J.P. Crawford RC .25 .60
26 Rhys Hoskins RC 1.00 2.50
27 Anthony Rizzo .30 .75
28 Austin Hays RC .40 1.00
29 Mookie Betts .50 1.25
30 Ozzie Albies RC .75 2.00

2018 Classics Classic Singles

INSERTED IN '18 CHRONICLES PACKS
*HOLO GLD/49: .6X TO 1.5X
*HOLO GLD/25: .75X TO 2X
*RED/25: .75X TO 2X BASIC
1 Mickey Mantle
2 Al Kaline 6.00 15.00
3 Mike Piazza 2.50 6.00
4 Mike Trout 12.00 30.00
5 Yoenis Cespedes 2.50 6.00
6 David Ortiz 2.50 6.00
7 Madison Bumgarner 2.00 5.00
8 Max Scherzer 2.50 6.00
9 Frank Thomas
10 Cal Ripken 8.00 20.00
11 Eddie Mathews
12 Harmon Killebrew
13 Aaron Judge 4.00 10.00
14 Jose Altuve 2.00 5.00
15 Gary Sheffield 1.50 4.00
16 Greg Maddux 3.00 8.00
17 Ryne Sandberg 5.00 12.00
18 Reggie Jackson 4.00 10.00
19 Bob Feller 2.00 5.00
20 Tony Gwynn

2018 Classics Classic Singles Blue

*BLUE/99: .5X TO 1.2X BASIC
*BLUE/49: .6X TO 1.5X BASIC
*BLUE/25: .75X TO 2X BASIC
INSERTED IN '18 CHRONICLES PACKS
PRINT RUNS B/WN 10-99 COPIES PER
NO PRICING ON QTY 15 OR LESS
11 Eddie Mathews/25 6.00 15.00

2018 Classics Classic Singles Gold

*GOLD/99-149: .5X TO 1.2X BASIC
*GOLD/49: .6X TO 1.5X BASIC
*GOLD/25: .75X TO 2X BASIC
INSERTED IN '18 CHRONICLES PACKS
PRINT RUNS B/WN 15-149 COPIES PER
NO PRICING ON QTY 15
1 Mickey Mantle/25 20.00 50.00
20 Tony Gwynn/49 4.00 10.00

2019 Classics

RANDOM INSERTS IN PACKS
*RED/99: 1.5X TO 4X
*BLUE/50: 2X TO 5X
*PINK/25: 3X TO 8X
1 Mike Trout 1.25 3.00
2 Fernando Tatis Jr. RC 2.00 5.00
3 Carlos Correa .25 .60
4 Ryan O'Hearn RC .15 .40
5 Pete Alonso RC 2.00 5.00
6 Kyle Tucker RC .40 1.00
7 Chris Paddack RC .30 .75
8 Bryce Harper .40 1.00
9 Shohei Ohtani .40 1.00
10 Javier Baez .30 .75
11 Aaron Judge .60 1.50
12 Yusei Kikuchi RC .25 .60
13 Eloy Jimenez RC .60 1.50
14 Michael Kopech RC .50 1.25
15 Kris Bryant .30 .75
16 Austin Riley RC .75 2.00
17 Keston Hiura RC .50 1.25
18 Corbin Martin RC .25 .60
19 Nick Senzel RC .50 1.25
20 Carter Kieboom RC .25 .60

2020 Classics

RANDOM INSERTS IN PACKS
1 Yordan Alvarez RC 2.50 6.00
2 Bo Bichette RC 3.00 8.00
3 Aristides Aquino RC .60 1.50
4 Gavin Lux RC 1.25 3.00
5 Luis Robert RC 3.00 8.00
6 Brendan McKay RC .40 1.00
7 Shogo Akiyama RC .40 1.00
8 Yoshitomo Tsutsugo RC .60 1.50
9 Joe Palumbo RC .25 .60
10 Yonathan Daza RC .30 .75
11 Jaylin Davis RC .40 1.00
12 Abraham Toro RC .30 .75
13 Donnie Walton RC .60 1.50
14 Jonathan Hernandez RC .25 .60
15 Rico Garcia RC .40 1.00
16 Cody Bellinger .50 1.25
17 J.D. Martinez .25 .60
18 Adalberto Mondesi .20 .50
19 Aaron Nola .20 .50
20 Mike Clevinger .20 .50
21 Ken Griffey Jr. .50 1.25
22 Jacob deGrom .50 1.25
23 Christian Yelich .30 .75
24 Juan Soto .75 2.00
25 Ronald Acuna Jr. 1.50 4.00

2020 Classics Autographs

RANDOM INSERTS IN PACKS
EXCHANGE DEADLINE 3/18/2022
*RED/50: .6X TO 1.5X BASIC
*RED/25: .8X TO 2X BASIC
*BLUE/25: .8X TO 2X BASIC
1 Victor Caratini 2.50 6.00
2 Rosell Herrera 2.50 6.00
5 Dakota Hudson 3.00 8.00
7 Brad Keller 2.50 6.00
8 Evan White 6.00 15.00
9 Jharel Cotton 2.50 6.00
10 Nick Ciuffo 2.50 6.00
11 Mallex Smith 2.50 6.00
12 Michael Perez 2.50 6.00
13 Randy Dobnak 5.00 12.00
15 Jacob Nix 3.00 8.00
16 A.J. Minter 3.00 8.00
17 David Fletcher 4.00 10.00
18 Kevin Newman 4.00 10.00
20 Nomar Mazara 2.50 6.00
21 Jordan Hicks 3.00 8.00
22 Terrance Gore 2.50 6.00
23 Christin Stewart 2.50 6.00
24 Greg Allen 3.00 8.00
25 Raimel Tapia 2.50 6.00

2020 Classics Autographs Gold

*GOLD/99: .5X TO 1.2X BASIC
*GOLD/50: .6X TO 1.5X BASIC
*GOLD/25: .8X TO 2X BASIC
RANDOM INSERTS IN PACKS
PRINT RUNS B/WN 5-99 COPIES PER
NO PRICING QTY 15 OR LESS
EXCHANGE DEADLINE 3/18/2022
3 Mike Schmidt/25 25.00 60.00
6 Alex Bregman/25 10.00 25.00

1997 Clemens A and P

This one-card set measuring approximately 3 1/2" by 5" features a color action photo of Roger Clemens with a blue Toronoto Blue Jays logo as the background in thin inner white and blue borders and a wider red outer border. The back displays a small player portrait and player information along with sponsor logos.
1 Roger Clemens 2.00 5.00

1997 Clemens The Fan

This one-card set was sponsored by THE FAN 590 Radio Station and distributed to fans who attended the first regular season game played by Roger Clemens as a Toronto Blue Jay on April 2, 1997. The front features a small color action painting of the player. The back displays information on how fans could win one of ten baseballs thrown by Roger Clemens during his first regular season game as a Blue Jay.
1 Roger Clemens 2.00 5.00

2005 Clemens HEB

COMPLETE SET (12)
COMMON CLEMENS

2003 Clemens 300 Upper Deck

COMPLETE SET 5.00 10.00
COMMON CARD 1.00 2.00

1910 Clement Brothers D380

This set, which measures approximately 1 1/2" by 2 3/4" was issued solely in the Rochester NY area. The set features a mix of established major leaguers and some local minor league players.
COMPLETE SET 100000.00 200000.00
1 Whitey Alperman 4000.00 8000.00
2 Bailey 4000.00 8000.00
3 Walter Blair 4000.00 8000.00
4 Ty Cobb 25000.00 50000.00
5 Eddie Collins 2000.00 40000.00
6 Roy Hartzell 4000.00 8000.00
7 Harry Howell 4000.00 8000.00
8 Addie Joss 12500.00 25000.00
9 George McConnell 4000.00 8000.00
10 Fred Osborn 4000.00 8000.00
11 Harry Pattee 4000.00 8000.00
12 Don Carlos Ragan 4000.00 8000.00
13 Oscar Stanage 4000.00 8000.00
14 George Stone 4000.00 8000.00
15 Ed Summers 4000.00 8000.00
16 Joe Tinker 12500.00 25000.00
17 Bert Tooley 4000.00 8000.00
18 Heinie Zimmerman 5000.00 10000.00

1991 Clemente Big League Collectibles

This 19-card set features color photos of Roberto Clemente as he appeared on Topps cards through the years and are printed as stickers. The set was distributed in strips with each strip containing three stickers. The backs are blank. The cards are listed below according to the year of the Topps set in which they originally appeared.
COMPLETE SET (19) 8.00 20.00
COMMON CARD (1-19) .60 1.50

1993 Clemente City Pride

One of these standard-size cards was inserted in a protective sleeve attached to City Pride Bakery plastic bread bags. The bread bag itself contained a "Help Build The Statue" feature, which stated that proceeds from the sale of this bread would go toward constructing a memorial statue to be unveiled before the 1994 All-Star Game at Three Rivers Stadium. Inside team color-coded border stripes (black and mustard), the fronts display full-bleed color or sepia-toned photos. The backs summarize Clemente's life and career with biography, statistics, and career highlights. The cards are unnumbered.
COMPLETE SET (6) 6.00 15.00
COMMON PLAYER (1-6) 1.00 2.50

1972 Clemente Daily Juice

This slightly oversized card featured Pirate great Roberto Clemente. The borderless front has a full color photo of Clemente along with a fascimile signature. The horizontal back has information on how to join the Clemente fan club. These cards are still commonly found as part of uncut sheets.
1 Roberto Clemente 2.00 5.00

1973 Clemente Pictureform

The Roberto Clemente Pictureform set consists of 12 photos and originally sold for $2.00. The black-and-white action photos are in a circle format and measure approximately 8 3/16" in diameter. The photos are bordered by an orange or light blue 1 3/8" border and printed on medium weight paper stock. There are five scored lines surrounding the photo that indicate where to fold the picture to form the pictureform. Once assembled, the pictures form a twelve-sided sphere. No lettering is printed on the front and the backs are blank. The photos were packaged with a large folder which displayed a color posed photo of Clemente on the front. On the inside left side were Clemente's career highlights and quotes from his peers. The inside right contained instructions for assembling the pictureform with line drawn illustrations above and below.
COMPLETE SET (12) 50.00 100.00
COMMON PLAYER (1-12) 4.00 10.00
XX Album 4.00 10.00

1994 Clemente Wendy's

Sponsored by Wendy's restaurants, this standard-size hologram card commemorates Hall of Famer Roberto Clemente. Reportedly only 90,000 of these hologram cards were produced. Framed by black borders, the horizontal front pictures Clemente in batting posture awaiting the pitch. When the holograph is rotated slightly, he is pictured hitting the ball. His name, the team name, and "3000" are printed in the holograph. The horizontal backs presents two color photos of Clemente and career summary. The card is unnumbered.
1 Roberto Clemente 2.00 5.00

1993 Clemente Z-Silk

This ten-card set of silk cachets features artist's paintings of Roberto Clemente. The cards measure the standard-size and have white borders. Roberto Clemente's name is printed along the bottom edge. The cards may be most easily distinguished by the differing overlaid action pictures described below.
COMPLETE SET (10) 2.50 6.00
COMMON PLAYER (1-10) .30 .75

1938 Clopay Foto-Fun R329

This set features sun-developed blue-tinted photos which are self-developed by the sun. They measure approximately 2 3/16" by 2 3/4". The backs are blank. The cards are unnumbered and checklisted below in alphabetical order. Holders in excellent condition are fairly rare and add a value of at least $25 to any individual clopay. It is believed that 100 subjects were issued for this set so any additions to this checklist are appreciated.
COMPLETE SET 2000.00 4000.00
1 Luke Appling 60.00 120.00
2 Morris Arnovich 30.00 60.00
3 Eldon Auker 30.00 60.00
4 Jim Bagby 30.00 60.00
5 Red Barrett 30.00 60.00
6 Roy Bell 30.00 60.00
7 Wally Berger 40.00 80.00
8 Oswald Bluege 30.00 60.00
9 Frenchy Bordagaray 30.00 60.00
10 Tom Bridges 40.00 80.00
11 Dolf Camilli 50.00 100.00
12 Ben Chapman 30.00 60.00
13 Harland Clift 40.00 80.00
14 Harry Craft 30.00 60.00
15 Roger Cramer 40.00 80.00
16 Joe Cronin MG 60.00 120.00
17 Kiki Cuyler 60.00 120.00
18 Babe Dahlgren 30.00 60.00
19 Harry Danning 40.00 80.00
20 Frank Demaree 30.00 60.00
21 Gene Desautels 30.00 60.00
22 Jim Deshong 30.00 60.00
23 Bill Dickey 60.00 120.00
24 Jim Dykes MG 40.00 80.00
25 Lou Fette 30.00 60.00
26 Louis Finney 30.00 60.00
27 Larry French 30.00 60.00
28 Linus Frey 30.00 60.00
29 Deb Garms 30.00 60.00
30 Charles Gehringer 60.00 120.00
31 Lefty Gomez 60.00 120.00
32 Ival Goodman 30.00 60.00
33 Lee Grissom 30.00 60.00
34 Stanley Hack 40.00 80.00
35 Irving Hadley 30.00 60.00
36 Mel Harder 40.00 80.00
37 Rollie Hemsley 30.00 60.00
38 Tommy Henrich 50.00 100.00
39 Billy Herman 40.00 80.00
40 Willard Hershberger 40.00 80.00
41 Michael Higgins 30.00 60.00
42 Oral Hildebrand 30.00 60.00
43 Carl Hubbell 60.00 120.00
44 Willis Hudlin 30.00 60.00
45 Mike Kreevich 30.00 60.00
46 Ralph Kress 30.00 60.00
47 John Lanning 30.00 60.00
48 Lyn Lary 30.00 60.00
49 Cookie Lavagetto 30.00 60.00
50 Thornton Lee 30.00 60.00
51 Ernie Lombardi 60.00 120.00
52 Al Lopez 60.00 120.00
53 Ted Lyons 60.00 120.00
54 Danny MacFayden 30.00 60.00
55 Max Macon 30.00 60.00
56 Pepper Martin 50.00 100.00
57 Joe Marty 30.00 60.00
58 Frank McCormick 30.00 60.00
59 Bill McKechnie MG 50.00 100.00
60 Joe Medwick 60.00 120.00
61 Cliff Melton 30.00 60.00
62 Charles Meyer 30.00 60.00
63 John Mize 60.00 120.00
64 Terry Moore 30.00 60.00
65 Whitey Moore 30.00 60.00
66 Emmett Mueller 30.00 60.00
67 Hugh Mulcahy 30.00 60.00
68 Van Mungo 40.00 80.00
69 John Murphy 40.00 80.00
70 Lynn Nelson 30.00 60.00
71 Mel Ott 60.00 120.00
72 Monte Pearson 30.00 60.00
73 Bill Rogell 30.00 60.00
74 George Selkirk 30.00 60.00
75 Milt Shoffner 30.00 60.00
76 Clyde Shoun 30.00 60.00
77 Al Simmons 60.00 120.00
78 Gus Suhr 30.00 60.00
79 Bill Sullivan 30.00 60.00
80 Cecil Travis 30.00 60.00
81 Pie Traynor MG 60.00 120.00
82 Harold Trosky 30.00 60.00
83 Jim Turner 30.00 60.00
84 Johnny VanderMeer 50.00 100.00
85 Oscar Vitt MG 30.00 60.00
86 Gerald Walker 30.00 60.00
87 Paul Waner 60.00 120.00
88 Lon Warneke 30.00 60.00
89 Rabbit Warstler 30.00 60.00
90 Bob Weiland 30.00 60.00
91 Burgess Whitehead 30.00 60.00
92 Earl Whitehill 30.00 60.00
93 Rudy York 40.00 80.00
94 Del Young 30.00 60.00

1988 CMC Mattingly

This 20-card set featuring Don Mattingly was distributed as part of a Collecting Kit produced by Collector's Marketing Corp. The cards themselves measure approximately 2 1/2" by 3 1/2" and have a light blue border. The card backs describe some aspect of Mattingly's career. Also in the kit were plastic sheets, a small album, a record, a booklet and information on how to join Don's Fan Club. The set price below is for the whole kit as well as the cards. The set was re-issued with a Line Drive logo in 1993 with a different border.
COMPLETE SET (20) 2.50 6.00
COMMON PLAYER (1-20) .20 .50
P1 Don Mattingly .20 .50
Promo

1989 CMC Baseball's Greatest

Issued in a cello packs, this four-card, standard-size set was issued by CMC. On a white card face, the fronts feature either color (number 1) or sepia-tone (numbers 2-4) player photos inside a red and white border whose shape resembles the home plate. The set's title appears in the red border above the picture while the player's name appears in a turquoise diamond at the bottom. The backs have the same design, only with a career summary presented on a gray panel instead of the front photo. The cards are unnumbered and checklisted below alphabetically.
COMPLETE SET 1.25 3.00
1 Roberto Clemente .30 .75
2 Ty Cobb .30 .75
3 Lou Gehrig .30 .75
4 Babe Ruth .40 1.00

1989 CMC Canseco

The 1989 CMC Jose Canseco Collector's Kit set contains 20 numbered standard-size cards. The front borders are Oakland A's green and yellow. The backs are green and white, and feature narratives and facsimile signatures. The cards were distributed as a set in a box along with an album and a booklet as well as other elements by CMC, Collectors Marketing Corporation. Since all the cards in the set feature the same player, cards in the checklist below are differentiated by some other characteristic of the particular card.
COMPLETE SET (20) 2.50 6.00
COMMON PLAYER (1-20) .20 .50
12 Jose Canseco 1.00
Mark McGwire
Bashing after homer
P1 Jose Canseco .40 1.00
Promo

1989 CMC Mantle

The 1989 CMC Mickey Mantle Collector's Kit set contains 20 numbered standard-size cards. The fronts and backs are white, red and navy. The backs feature narratives and facsimile signatures. The cards were distributed as a set in a box along with an album and a booklet as well as other elements by CMC, Collectors Marketing Corporation. Since all the cards in the set feature the same player, cards in the checklist below are differentiated by some other characteristic of the particular card. Some of the cards in this set are sepia-tone photos as the action predates the widespread use of color film. The set was re-issued with a Line Drive logo in 1993 with a different border.
COMPLETE SET (20) 10.00 25.00
COMMON CARD (1-20) .75 2.00

1989 CMC Ruth

The 1989 CMC Babe Ruth Collector's Kit set contains 20 numbered standard-size cards. The front borders are white, red and navy. The backs are blue and white, and feature narratives and facsimile signatures. The cards were distributed as a set in a box along with an album and a booklet as well as other elements by CMC, Collectors Marketing Corporation. Since all the cards in the set feature the same player, cards in the checklist below are differentiated by some other characteristic of the particular card. All of the cards in this set are sepia-tone photos as the action predates the widespread use of color film.
COMPLETE SET (20) 4.00 10.00
COMMON PLAYER (1-20) .20 .50
15 Babe Ruth .30 .75
Jacob Ruppert OWN
17 Babe Ruth .30 .75
Miller Huggins MG
P1 Babe Ruth .40 1.00
Promo for Set

1975 Cobb McCallum

This 20-card set was produced to promote John McCallum's biography on Ty Cobb. The cards measure approximately 2 1/2" X 3 1/2" and feature on the fronts vintage black and white photos, with a hand-drawn artificial wood grain picture frame border. The title to each picture appears in a plaque below the picture. The back has a facsimile autograph and extended caption. The cards are numbered on the back in a baseball icon in the upper right corner. This set was issued at a price of $2.95 upon its release.
COMPLETE SET (20) 12.50 30.00
COMMON PLAYER (1-20) .30 .75
6 Ty Cobb 1.25 3.00
Walter Johnson
11 Ty Cobb .40 1.00
Paul Cobb
12 Ty Cobb 1.00 2.50
Thomas Edison
13 Ty Cobb 1.00 2.50
Tangles with John McGraw
14 Author McCallum with .60 1.50
Cy Young
15 Tris Speaker 2.50 6.00
Joe DiMaggio
and Ty Cobb
16 Ty Cobb 1.25 3.00
Ted Williams

2002-05 Ty Cobb Museum

COMPLETE SET
1 Ty Cobb 2002 2.00 5.00
Drawing, Numbered to 1000
2 Ty Cobb 2003 4.00 10.00
50th Anniversary of Educational Foun
3 Ty Cobb 2004 4.00 10.00
100th Anniversary of Augusta Tourist
4 Ty Cobb 2005 4.00 10.00
100th Anniversary of Tigers debut
PC Ty Cobb 2.00 5.00
Postcard

1952 Coke Tips

This 10-card set features artwork of various Yankees, Giants and Dodgers and was inserted into regional Coca-Cola bottle cartons. The fronts display the artwork depicting the players and team schedules. The backs carry tips on how to play the pictured player's position and other Big-League tips. The cards are unnumbered and checklisted below in alphabetical order. A Willie Mays card, considered a test for this series, is appended at the end of the checklist. It is possible that the Mays card was actually pulled from this series when he entered military service early during the 1952 season.
COMPLETE SET (10) 1250.00 2500.00
1 Hank Bauer 150.00 300.00
2 Carl Furillo 200.00 400.00
3 Gil Hodges 200.00 400.00
4 Ed Lopat 125.00 250.00
5 Gil McDougald 125.00 250.00
6 Don Mueller 100.00 200.00
7 Pee Wee Reese 200.00 400.00
8 Bobby Thomson/(Playing 3rd base) 150.00 300.00
9 Bobby Thomson/(Hitting) 150.00 300.00
10 Wes Westrum 100.00 200.00
T1 Willie Mays 750.00 1500.00
Test
T2 Phil Rizzuto 150.00 400.00
Test

1980 Coke/7-11 NL MVPs

This one-card blank-backed set, sponosred by Coca-Cola and 7-11, features a color posed photo of the co-most valuable players of the 1979 National League.
1 Willie Stargell 2.00 5.00
Keith Hernandez

1981 Coke Team Sets

The cards in this 132-card set measure 2 1/2" by 3 1/2". In 1981, Topps produced 11 sets of 12 cards each for the Coca-Cola Company. Each set features 11 star players for a particular team plus an advertising card with the team name on the front. Although the cards are numbered in the upper right corner of the back from 1 to 11, they are re-numbered below within team, i.e., Boston Red Sox (1-12), Chicago Cubs (13-24), Chicago White Sox (25-36), Cincinnati Reds (37-48), Detroit Tigers (49-60), Houston Astros (61-72), Kansas City Royals (73-84), New York Mets (85-96), Philadelphia Phillies (97-108), Pittsburgh Pirates (109-120), and St. Louis Cardinals (121-132). Within each team the player actually numbered number 1 (on the card back) is the first player below and the player numbered number 11 is the last in that team's list. These player cards are quite similar to the 1981 Topps issue but feature a Coca-Cola logo on both the front and the back. The advertising card for each team features, on its back, an offer for obtaining an uncut sheet of 1981 Topps cards. These promotional cards were actually issued by Coke in only a few of the cities, and most of these cards have reached collectors hands through dealers who have purchased the cards through suppliers. Cards of the following New York Yankees have been discovered: Rick Cerone, Rich Gossage and Reggie Jackson. In addition, a Boston Red Sox of Carlton Fisk has also recently been discovered. Since these cards are so infrequently found, we have not yet placed a value on them.
COMPLETE SET (132) 10.00 25.00
COMMON CARD (1-132) .04 .10
COMMON AD CARDS .02 .05
1 Tom Burgmeier .02 .10
2 Dennis Eckersley .75 2.00
3 Dwight Evans .30 .75
4 Bob Stanley .02 .10
5 Glenn Hoffman .02 .10
6 Carney Lansford .10 .30
7 Frank Tanana .07 .20
8 Tony Perez .60 1.50
9 Jim Rice .15 .40
10 Dave Stapleton .02 .10
11 Carl Yastrzemski 1.25 3.00
12 Red Sox Ad Card/(Unnumbered) .01 .05
13 Tim Blackwell .02 .10
14 Bill Buckner .07 .20
15 Ivan DeJesus .02 .10
16 Leon Durham .02 .10
17 Steve Henderson .02 .10
18 Mike Krukow .02 .10
19 Ken Reitz .02 .10
20 Rick Reuschel .07 .20
21 Scot Thompson .02 .10
22 Dick Tidrow .02 .10
23 Mike Tyson .02 .10
24 Cubs Ad Card/(Unnumbered) .01 .05
25 Britt Burns .02 .10

26 Todd Cruz .02 .10
27 Rich Dotson .02 .10
28 Jim Essian .02 .10
29 Ed Farmer .02 .10
30 Lamar Johnson .02 .10
31 Ron LeFlore .02 .10
32 Chet Lemon .02 .10
33 Bob Molinaro .02 .10
34 Jim Morrison .02 .10
35 Wayne Nordhagen .02 .10
36 White Sox Ad Card/(Unnumbered) .01 .05
37 Johnny Bench 1.50 4.00
38 Dave Collins .02 .10
39 Dave Concepcion .10 .30
40 Dan Driessen .02 .10
41 George Foster .15 .40
42 Ken Griffey .10 .30
43 Tom Hume .02 .10
44 Ray Knight .02 .10
45 Ron Oester .02 .10
46 Tom Seaver 1.50 4.00
47 Mario Soto .02 .10
48 Reds Ad Card/(Unnumbered) .01 .05
49 Champ Summers .02 .10
50 Al Cowens .02 .10
51 Rich Hebner .02 .10
52 Steve Kemp .02 .10
53 Aurelio Lopez .02 .10
54 Jack Morris .60 1.50
55 Lance Parrish .30 .75
56 Johnny Wockenfuss .02 .10
57 Alan Trammell 1.50 4.00
58 Lou Whitaker .75 2.00
59 Kirk Gibson 1.25 3.00
60 Tigers Ad Card/(Unnumbered) .01 .05
61 Alan Ashby .02 .10
62 Cesar Cedeno .07 .20
63 Jose Cruz .10 .30
64 Art Howe .02 .10
65 Rafael Landestoy .02 .10
66 Joe Niekro .07 .20
67 Terry Puhl .02 .10
68 J.R. Richard .07 .20
69 Nolan Ryan 3.00 8.00
70 Joe Sambito .02 .10
71 Don Sutton .75 2.00
72 Astros Ad Card/(Unnumbered) .01 .05
73 Willie Aikens .02 .10
74 George Brett 3.00 8.00
75 Larry Gura .02 .10
76 Dennis Leonard .02 .10
77 Hal McRae .07 .20
78 Amos Otis .07 .20
79 Dan Quisenberry .07 .20
80 U.L. Washington .02 .10
81 John Wathan .02 .10
82 Frank White .07 .20
83 Willie Wilson .07 .20
84 Royals Ad Card/(Unnumbered) .01 .05
85 Neil Allen .02 .10
86 Doug Flynn .02 .10
87 Dave Kingman .15 .40
88 Randy Jones .02 .10
89 Pat Zachry .02 .10
90 Lee Mazzilli .02 .10
91 Rusty Staub .10 .30
92 Craig Swan .02 .10
93 Frank Taveras .02 .10
94 Alex Trevino .02 .10
95 Joel Youngblood .02 .10
96 Mets Ad Card/(Unnumbered) .01 .05
97 Bob Boone .15 .40
98 Larry Bowa .07 .20
99 Steve Carlton .75 2.00
100 Greg Luzinski .15 .40
101 Garry Maddox .02 .10
102 Bake McBride .02 .10
103 Tug McGraw .07 .20
104 Pete Rose 1.25 3.00
105 Mike Schmidt 1.25 3.00
106 Lonnie Smith .02 .10
107 Manny Trillo .02 .10
108 Phillies Ad Card/(Unnumbered) .01 .05
109 Jim Bibby .02 .10
110 John Candelaria .02 .10
111 Mike Easler .02 .10
112 Tim Foli .02 .10
113 Phil Garner .07 .20
114 Bill Madlock .10 .30
115 Omar Moreno .02 .10
116 Ed Ott .02 .10
117 Dave Parker .30 .75
118 Willie Stargell .60 1.50
119 Kent Tekulve .07 .20
120 Pirates Ad Card/(Unnumbered) .01 .05
121 Bob Forsch .02 .10
122 George Hendrick .07 .20
123 Keith Hernandez .15 .40
124 Tom Herr .02 .10
125 Sixto Lezcano .02 .10
126 Ken Oberkfell .02 .10
127 Darrell Porter .07 .20
128 Tony Scott .02 .10
129 Lary Sorensen .02 .10
130 Bruce Sutter .30 .75
131 Garry Templeton .02 .10
132 Cardinals Ad Card/(Unnumbered) .01 .05
BRS1 Carlton Fisk
NYY1 Rick Cerone
NYY2 Rich Gossage
NYY3 Reggie Jackson

1991 Coke Mattingly

This 15-card standard-size set was sponsored by Coca-Cola. The front design features mostly color action player photos on a white and blue pinstripe card face. Each card has a year number on the top edge of the picture, and the Coke logo is superimposed at the lower left corner. In a horizontal format the backs are printed in blue and red, and present career highlights and statistics.

COMPLETE SET (15) 2.50 6.00
COMMON PLAYER (1-15) .20 .50

1993 Coke Case Inserts

These standard-size cards are one per case inserts in the 1993 Coca-Cola set marketed by Collect-A-Card. The Ty Cobb image on the card is from the 1947 Coca-Cola hanging cardboard signs, "All Time Sports Favorite," which featured various sports celebrities. The variegated gray front has a pair of thin red foil lines surrounding an artist's illustration of the player. Below the picture are the player's name in red foil lettering and the words "All-Time Baseball Favorite." A Coke bottle appears in the lower left corner next to the Coca-Cola logo. The horizontal backs also have a variegated gray background and a thin red line surrounding player profile and a historical trivia question. The card is numbered on the back with a "TC" prefix.

COMPLETE SET (2) 8.00 20.00
TC1 Ty Cobb 4.00 10.00
TC2 Ty Cobb 4.00 10.00

1994 Coke Case Inserts

These standard-size cards are one per case inserts in the 1994 Coca-Cola set marketed by Collect-A-Card. The cards features Christy Mathewson in a reprinted ad from 1916. The back describes the ad and gives some more information about Mathewson.

COMPLETE SET (2) 5.00 12.00
CM1 Christy Mathewson 2.50 6.00
CM2 Christy Mathewson 2.50 6.00

1989 Colla Postcards Dawson

These postcards measure 3 1/2" by 5 1/2" and showcase Andre Dawson. The fronts feature color action or posed player shots in a postcard format. The typical postcard backs carry the player's name, position and the team name, along with the team logo.

COMPLETE SET (8) 2.00 5.00
COMMON CARD (1-8) .30 .75

1989 Colla Postcards Greenwell

These postcards measure 3 1/2" by 5 1/2" and showcase Mike Greenwell. The fronts feature color action or posed player shots in a postcard format. The typical postcard backs carry the player's name, position and the team name, along with the team logo.

COMPLETE SET (8) 1.50 4.00
COMMON CARD (1-8) .20 .50

1989 Colla Postcards McGwire

These postcards measure 3 1/2" by 5 1/2" and showcase Mark McGwire. The fronts feature color action or posed player shots in a postcard format. The typical postcard backs carry the player's name, position and the team name, along with the team logo.

COMPLETE SET (8) 6.00 15.00
COMMON CARD (1-8) .80 2.00

1989 Colla Postcards Mitchell

These postcards measure 3 1/2" by 5 1/2" and showcase Kevin Mitchell. The fronts feature color action or posed player shots in a postcard format. The typical postcard backs carry the player's name, position and the team name, along with the team logo.

COMPLETE SET (8) 1.50 4.00
COMMON CARD (1-8) .20 .50

1989 Colla Postcards Ozzie Smith

These postcards measure 3 1/2" by 5 1/2" and showcase Ozzie Smith. The fronts feature color action or posed player shots in a postcard format. The typical postcard backs carry the player's name, position and the team name, along with the team logo.

COMPLETE SET (8) 4.00 10.00
COMMON CARD (1-8) .50 1.25

1990 Colla Canseco

This 12-card standard-size set, issued by noted photographer Barry Colla, features Jose Canseco in various poses. The fronts are beautiful full-color photos while the backs contain notes about Canseco. According to the back of the first card in the set, 20,000 numbered sets were issued.

COMPLETE SET (12) 4.00 10.00
COMMON PLAYER (1-12) .40 1.00

1990 Colla Will Clark

This 12-card standard-size set again features the beautiful photography of Barry Colla; this time Will Clark is the featured player. Again the fronts are borderless photos while the back contains notes about Will Clark. According to card number one, 15,000 numbered sets were produced.

COMPLETE SET (12) 5.00 12.00
COMMON PLAYER (1-12) .50 1.25

1990 Colla Maas

This attractive 12-card standard-size card set was produced by photographer Barry Colla. The set was limited to 7,500 made and each card has some facts relevant to Maas' career on the back of the card. The set was produced to be sold in its own special box and the boxes were issued 24 sets to each bigger box. All of the boxes were produced in the team's colors.

COMPLETE SET (12) 2.50 6.00
COMMON PLAYER (1-12) .20 .50

1990 Colla Mattingly

This 12-card standard-size set honoring Yankee great Don Mattingly features the photography of Barry Colla. The set was limited to 15,000 numbered sets and feature full-color photographs on the borderless fronts along with notes about Mattingly on the back.

COMPLETE SET (12) 4.00 10.00
COMMON PLAYER (1-12) .40 1.00

1990 Colla Postcards Will Clark

These postcards measure 3 1/2" by 5 1/2" and showcase Will Clark. The fronts feature color action or posed player shots in a postcard format. The typical postcard backs carry the player's name, position and the team name, along with the team logo.

COMPLETE SET (8) 4.00 10.00
COMMON CARD (1-8) .50 1.25

1990 Colla Postcards Grace

These postcards measure 3 1/2" by 5 1/2" and showcase Mark Grace. The fronts feature color action or posed player shots in a postcard format. The typical postcard backs carry the player's name, position and the team name, along with the team logo.

COMPLETE SET (8) 3.00 8.00
COMMON CARD (1-8) .40 1.00

1991 Colla Roberto Alomar

This 13-card standard size set features colorful photos of Roberto Alomar by noted photographer Barry Colla. The high gloss borderless color photos were packed in a full color collector's box. Only 7,500 sets were produced, with 24 sets per display carton. The first card of each set bears the registration number.

COMPLETE SET (13) 4.00 10.00
COMMON PLAYER (1-12) .40 1.00

1991 Colla Bonds

This 13-card standard size set features colorful photos of Barry Bonds by noted photographer Barry Colla. The high gloss borderless color photos were packed in a full color collector's box. Only 7,500 sets were produced, with 24 sets per display carton. The first card of each set bears the registration number. This set was issued so late in 1991 that it was actually January 1992 before the set was in general distribution.

COMPLETE SET (13) 5.00 12.00
COMMON PLAYER (1-12) .40 1.00

1991 Colla Joe Carter

This 13-card standard size set features colorful photos of Joe Carter by noted photographer Barry Colla. The high gloss borderless color photos were packed in a full color collector's box. Only 7,500 sets were produced, with 24 sets per display carton. The first card of each set bears the registration number.

COMPLETE SET (13) 4.00 10.00
COMMON PLAYER (1-12) .40 1.00

1991 Colla Gooden

This 13-card standard size set features colorful photos of Dwight Gooden by noted photographer Barry Colla. The high gloss borderless color photos were packed in a full color collector's box. Only 15,000 sets were produced, with 24 sets per display carton. The first card of each set bears the registration number.

COMPLETE SET (13) 4.00 10.00
COMMON CARD (1-13) .40 1.00

1991 Colla Griffey Jr.

This 12-card standard size set features colorful photos of Ken Griffey Jr. by noted photographer Barry Colla. The high gloss borderless color photos were packed in a full color collector's box. Only 15,000 sets were produced, with 24 sets per display carton. The first card of each set bears the registration number.

COMPLETE SET (12) 6.00 15.00
COMMON PLAYER (1-12) .60 1.50

1991 Colla Justice

This 13-card standard size set features colorful photos of Dave Justice by noted photographer Barry Colla. The high gloss borderless color photos were packed in a full color collector's box. Only 15,000 sets were produced, with 24 sets per display carton. The first card of each set bears the registration number.

COMPLETE SET (13) 4.00 10.00
COMMON PLAYER (1-12) .40 1.00

1991 Colla Sandberg

This 13-card standard size set features colorful photos of Ryne Sandberg by noted photographer Barry Colla. The high gloss borderless color photos were packed in a full color collector's box. Only 15,000 sets were produced, with 24 sets per display carton. The first card of each set bears the registration number.

COMPLETE SET (13) 4.00 10.00
COMMON PLAYER (1-12) .40 1.00

1991 Colla Strawberry

This 13-card standard size set features colorful photos of Darryl Strawberry by noted photographer Barry Colla. The high gloss borderless color photos were packed in a full color collector's box. Only 15,000 sets were produced, with 24 sets per display carton. The first card of each set bears the registration number.

COMPLETE SET (13) 3.00 8.00
COMMON PLAYER (1-12) .30 .75

1991 Colla Postcards Sandberg

These postcards measure 3 1/2" by 5 1/2" and showcase Ryne Sandberg. The fronts feature color action or posed player shots in a postcard format. The typical postcard backs carry the player's name, position and the team name, along with the team logo.

COMPLETE SET (8) 2.50 6.00
COMMON CARD (1-8) .40 1.00

1992 Colla All-Stars Promos

The 1992 Colla All-Stars promo set consists of 25 standard-size cards. The fronts feature full-bleed glossy color photos. The backs carry an advertisement for the cards and logos. Though the cards are unnumbered, they are listed below according to the numbering assigned to them on the checklist card. According to the checklist card, the set was issued July 14, 1992 and limited to 25,000 sets.

COMPLETE SET (24) 6.00 15.00
1 Mark McGwire .60 1.50
2 Will Clark .40 1.00
3 Roberto Alomar .40 1.00
4 Ryne Sandberg .50 1.25
5 Cal Ripken 1.50 4.00
6 Ozzie Smith .60 1.50
7 Wade Boggs .50 1.25
8 Terry Pendleton .08 .25
9 Kirby Puckett .50 1.25
10 Chuck Knoblauch .20 .50
11 Ken Griffey Jr. 1.00 2.50
12 Joe Carter .20 .50
13 Sandy Alomar Jr. .08 .25
14 Benito Santiago .20 .50
15 Mike Mussina .30 .75
16 Fred McGriff .30 .75
17 Dennis Eckersley .50 1.25
18 Tony Gwynn .75 2.00
19 Roger Clemens .75 2.00
20 Gary Sheffield .50 1.25
21 Jose Canseco .50 1.25
22 Barry Bonds .75 2.00
23 Ivan Rodriguez .50 1.25
24 Tony Fernandez .08 .25
NNO Juan Guzman/(Checklist) .08 .25

1992 Colla All-Star Game

This 24-card standard-size set was made available at the 1992 All-Star game in San Diego. The cards feature All-Stars from the National and American League. Randomly inserted throughout the sets were 200 numbered and autographed Roberto Alomar cards. The production run was limited to 25,000 sets, and the first card (McGwire) of each set bears the set serial number ("X of 25,000"). The fronts display full-bleed glossy color player photos. The All-Star Game logo and the player's name are superimposed across the bottom of the picture. The backs carry a close-up color photo and All-Star statistics. The cards are numbered in a diamond in the upper left corner.

COMPLETE SET (24) 5.00 12.00
1 Mark McGwire .60 1.50
2 Will Clark .40 1.00
3 Roberto Alomar .40 1.00
4 Ryne Sandberg .50 1.25
5 Cal Ripken 1.25 3.00
6 Ozzie Smith .50 1.25
7 Wade Boggs .50 1.25
8 Terry Pendleton .08 .25
9 Kirby Puckett .50 1.25
10 Chuck Knoblauch .40 1.00
11 Ken Griffey Jr. .75 2.00
12 Joe Carter .20 .50
13 Sandy Alomar Jr. .08 .25
14 Benito Santiago .20 .50
15 Mike Mussina .30 .75
16 Fred McGriff .30 .75
17 Dennis Eckersley .50 1.25
18 Tony Gwynn .60 1.50
19 Roger Clemens .60 1.50
20 Gary Sheffield .50 1.25
21 Jose Canseco .40 1.00
22 Barry Bonds .60 1.50
23 Ivan Rodriguez .40 1.00
24 Tony Fernandez .08 .25

1992 Colla Promos

This 17-card standard-size set consists of promo cards to the various Barry Colla limited edition player sets. The cards feature full-bleed glossy color photos on their fronts. Except for the Thomas card, the backs are horizontally oriented. Some of the backs are gray while others are white. Each back gives the player's name, issue date, production quantity and a toll free phone number for ordering the set. The cards are unnumbered and checklisted below in alphabetical order.

COMPLETE SET (17) 15.00 40.00
1A Roberto Alomar/(English back) 1.25 3.00
1B Roberto Alomar/(French back) 2.00 5.00
2 Jeff Bagwell/(Bat on right shoulder& dark blue j 1.00 2.50
3 Barry Bonds 1.25 3.00
4 Jose Canseco .75 2.00
5A Joe Carter/(English back) .60 1.50
5B Joe Carter/(French back) 1.25 3.00
6 Will Clark .75 2.00
7 Dwight Gooden .60 1.50
8 Ken Griffey Jr. 2.00 5.00
9 Dave Justice 1.00 2.50
10 Kevin Maas .40 1.00
11 Don Mattingly 1.25 3.00
12 Nolan Ryan/(Pitching with arm extended behind bo 2.00 5.00
13 Ryne Sandberg 1.00 2.50
14 Darryl Strawberry .60 1.50
15 Frank Thomas/(Leaning forward& right shoulder n .75 2.00

1992 Colla Bagwell

This 12-card standard-size set features colorful photos of Jeff Bagwell by noted sports photographer Barry Colla. Only 25,000 sets were produced, with 24 sets per display carton. Also the set included an Allocation Rights card, which entitled the holder to purchase the Colla Rookie set. The high gloss borderless color photos were packed in a full color collector's box.

COMPLETE SET (12) 4.00 10.00
COMMON PLAYER (1-12) .40 1.00
AU Jeff Bagwell AU/200 20.00 50.00

1992 Colla Gwynn

This 12-card standard size set features colorful photos of Tony Gwynn by noted photographer Barry Colla. The high gloss borderless color photos were packed in a full color collector's box. Only 7,500 sets were produced, with the first card of each set carrying the set number. The "92 The Colla Collection" icon appears in an upper corner and the player's name is printed toward the bottom of the picture. In light black lettering on white, the horizontal backs present biography (1), notes on Gwynn (2-11), or major league statistics (12) on the left portion and baseball cartoons on the right portion.

COMPLETE SET (12) 4.00 10.00
COMMON PLAYER (1-12) .40 1.00

1992 Colla McGwire

This 12-card standard-size set features colorful photos of Mark McGwire by noted sports photographer Barry Colla. Only 15,000 sets were produced, with 24 sets per display carton. The high gloss borderless color photos were packed in a full color collector's box. The first card of each set bears the set serial number.

COMPLETE SET (12) 4.00 10.00
COMMON PLAYER (1-12) .40 1.00
AU Mark McGwire AU/200 200.00 750.00

1992 Colla Ryan

This 12-card standard-size set features colorful photos of Nolan Ryan by noted sports photographer Barry Colla. Only 25,000 sets were produced, with 24 sets per display carton. The high-gloss borderless color photos were packed in a full color collector's box. The first card of each set bears the set serial number.

COMPLETE SET (12) 4.00 10.00
COMMON PLAYER (1-12) .40 1.00
AU Nolan Ryan AU/200 100.00 250.00

1992 Colla Thomas

This 12-card standard-size set features colorful photos of Frank Thomas by noted sports photographer Barry Colla. Only 25,000 sets were produced, with 24 sets per display carton. Also the set included an Allocation Rights card, which entitled the holder to purchase tbe Colla Rookie set. The high gloss borderless color photos were packed in a full color collector's box. The first card of each set bears the set serial number.

COMPLETE SET (12) 4.00 10.00
COMMON PLAYER (1-12) .40 1.00
AU Frank Thomas AU/200 25.00 60.00

1993 Colla All-Star Game

Issued by noted photographer Barry Colla, this 24-card boxed set was made available at the 1993 All-Star game in Baltimore. The standard-size cards feature 24 All-Stars from the National and American Leagues.

COMPLETE SET (25) 8.00 20.00
1 Roberto Alomar .40 1.00
2 Barry Bonds 1.00 2.50
3 Ken Griffey Jr. 1.25 3.00
4 John Kruk .20 .50
5 Kirby Puckett .60 1.50
6 Darren Daulton .20 .50
7 Wade Boggs .50 1.25
8 Matt Williams .30 .75
9 Cal Ripken 2.00 5.00
10 Ryne Sandberg .75 2.00
11 Ivan Rodriguez .50 1.25
12 Andy Van Slyke .08 .25
13 John Olerud .20 .50
14 Tom Glavine .40 1.00
15 Juan Gonzalez .20 .50
16 David Justice .40 1.00
17 Mike Mussina .40 1.00
18 Tony Gwynn 1.00 2.50
19 Joe Carter .20 .50
20 Barry Larkin .40 1.00
21 Brian Harper .08 .25
22 Ozzie Smith .75 2.00
23 Mark McGwire 1.00 2.50
24 Mike Piazza 2.00 5.00
NNO Checklist Card .08 .25

1993 Colla Postcards Piazza

These postcards measure 3 1/2" by 5 1/2" and showcase Mike Piazza. The fronts feature color action or posed player shots in a postcard format. The typical postcard backs carry the player's name, position and the team name, along with the team logo.

COMPLETE SET (8) 2.50 6.00
COMMON CARD (1-8) .40 1.00

1993 Colla Postcards Ripken Jr.

These postcards measure 3 1/2" by 5 1/2" and showcase Cal Ripken Jr. The fronts feature color action or posed player shots in a postcard format. The typical postcard backs carry the player's name, position and the team name, along with the team logo.

COMPLETE SET (7) 3.00 8.00
COMMON CARD (1-7) .50 1.25

1990 Collect-A-Books

The 1990 Collect-A-Books set was issued by CMC (Collectors Marketing Corp.) in three different sets (boxes) of 12 players apiece. The sets (boxes) were distinguishable by color, red, yellow, or green. The Collect-A-Books were in the style of the 1970 Topps Comic Book inserts but were much more profesionally made. The cards all fit into a nine-pocket sheet (since they are standard size) even though they can be expanded. The set contains an interesting mixture of retired and current players. The concept for this set was created by former major leaguer Jim Bouton.

COMPLETE SET (36) 3.00 8.00
1 Bo Jackson .07 .20
2 Dwight Gooden .07 .20
3 Ken Griffey Jr. .60 1.50
4 Will Clark .20 .50
5 Ozzie Smith .30 .75
6 Orel Hershiser .07 .20
7 Ruben Sierra .07 .20
8 Rickey Henderson .20 .50
9 Robin Yount .15 .40
10 Babe Ruth .60 1.50
11 Ernie Banks .15 .40
12 Carl Yastrzemski .15 .40
13 Don Mattingly .30 .75
14 Nolan Ryan .60 1.50
15 Jerome Walton .02 .10
16 Kevin Mitchell .02 .10
17 Tony Gwynn .40 1.00
18 Dave Stewart .07 .20
19 Roger Clemens .30 .75
20 Darryl Strawberry .07 .20
21 George Brett .30 .75
22 Hank Aaron .40 1.00
23 Ted Williams .40 1.00
24 Warren Spahn .15 .40
25 Jose Canseco .15 .40
26 Wade Boggs .20 .50
27 Jim Abbott .07 .20
28 Eric Davis .07 .20
29 Ryne Sandberg .30 .75
30 Bret Saberhagen .07 .20
31 Mark Grace .15 .40
32 Gregg Olson .02 .10
33 Kirby Puckett .20 .50
34 Lou Gehrig .50 1.25
35 Roberto Clemente .40 1.00
36 Bob Feller .15 .40

1991 Collect-A-Books

This 36-card set, which measures the standard size, was issued by Impel for the second consecutive year. Collectors Marketing Corp., the 1990 Collect-a-Book producer, was a division within the Impel Corporation. This 1991 set was issued under Impel's Line Drive brand. Each book consists of eight pages and fits into a standard size plastic sheet. The set features 27 active stars and nine famous retired stars. An action shot of the player is pictured on the first two pages. The next four pages has textual information broken down into biographical information& two pages of more detailed personal information and a page of statistics. The inside back cover has a quote from the player pictured while the back cover has an attractive drawing of the player. Unlike the 1990 issue, the Collect-A-Books were issued in random packs.

COMPLETE SET (36) 4.00 10.00
1 Roger Clemens .40 1.00
2 Cal Ripken .75 2.00
3 Nolan Ryan .75 2.00
4 Ken Griffey Jr. .60 1.50
5 Bob Welch .02 .10
6 Kevin Mitchell .02 .10
7 Kirby Puckett .25 .60
8 Len Dykstra .07 .20
9 Ben McDonald .02 .10
10 Don Drysdale .15 .40
11 Lou Brock .15 .40
12 Ralph Kiner .15 .40
13 Jose Canseco .20 .50
14 Cecil Fielder .07 .20
15 Ryne Sandberg .30 .75
16 Wade Boggs .20 .50
17 Dwight Gooden .07 .20
18 Ramon Martinez .02 .10
19 Tony Gwynn .30 .75
20 Mark Grace .15 .40
21 Kevin Maas .02 .10
22 Thurman Munson .15 .40
23 Bob Gibson .15 .40
24 Bill Mazeroski .10 .30
25 Rickey Henderson .25 .60
26 Barry Bonds .40 1.00
27 Jose Rijo .02 .10
28 George Brett .30 .75
29 Doug Drabek .02 .10
30 Matt Williams .10 .30
31 Barry Larkin .15 .40
32 Dave Stewart .07 .20
33 Dave Justice .15 .40
34 Harmon Killebrew .15 .40
35 Yogi Berra .15 .40
36 Billy Williams .15 .40

1994 Collector's Choice

Produced by Upper Deck, this 670 standard-size card set was distributed in two series of 320 and 350. Cards were issued in foil-wrapped 12-card packs and factory sets (of which contained five Gold Signature cards for a total of 675 cards). Basic card fronts feature color player action photos with white borders that are highlighted by vertical gray pinstripes. Subsets include Rookie Class (1-20), First Draft Picks (21-30), Top Performers (306-315), Up Close (631-640) and Future Foundation (641-650). Rookie Cards include Michael Jordan and Alex Rodriguez. A legitimate variation on the Alex Rodriguez card (#647) was verified several years after release. The standard card features the "A" from Alex on the card back text in grey/silver whereas the variation features his name in white. It's believed that the A-Rod "White A" variation is a significantly tougher card but exact estimates of it's scarcity are not known. In subsequent years other cards (such as Johnny Damon) were also verified to have this White Letter variation - thus it's generally believed that the entire Future Foundations subset was produced with white (and standard grey) letter variations.

COMPLETE SET (670) 15.00 40.00
COMP.FACT.SET (675) 15.00 40.00
COMPLETE SERIES 1 (320) 6.00 15.00
COMPLETE SERIES 2 (350) 6.00 15.00
SUBSET CARDS HALF VALUE OF BASE CARDS
1 Rich Becker .02 .10
2 Greg Blosser .02 .10
3 Midre Cummings .02 .10
4 Carlos Delgado .10 .30
5 Steve Dreyer RC .02 .10
6 Carl Everett .07 .20
7 Cliff Floyd .07 .20
8 Alex Gonzalez .02 .10
9 Shawn Green .20 .50
10 Butch Huskey .02 .10
11 Mark Hutton .02 .10
12 Miguel Jimenez .02 .10
13 Steve Karsay .02 .10
14 Marc Newfield .02 .10
15 Luis Ortiz .02 .10
16 Manny Ramirez .20 .50
17 Johnny Ruffin .02 .10
18 Scott Stahoviak .02 .10
19 Salomon Torres .02 .10
20 Gabe White .02 .10
21 Brian Anderson RC .08 .25
22 Wayne Gomes RC .02 .10
23 Jeff Granger FDP .02 .10
24 Steve Soderstrom RC .02 .10
25 Trot Nixon RC .60 1.50
26 Kirk Presley RC .02 .10
27 Matt Brunson RC .02 .10
28 Brooks Kieschnick RC .02 .10
29 Billy Wagner RC .50 1.25
30 Matt Drews RC .02 .10
31 Kurt Abbott RC .02 .10
32 Luis Alicea .02 .10
33 Roberto Alomar .10 .30
34 Sandy Alomar Jr. .02 .10
35 Moises Alou .07 .20
36 Wilson Alvarez .02 .10
37 Rich Amaral .02 .10
38 Eric Anthony .02 .10
39 Luis Aquino .02 .10
40 Jack Armstrong .02 .10
41 Rene Arocha .02 .10
42 Rich Aude RC .02 .10
43 Brad Ausmus .10 .30
44 Steve Avery .02 .10
45 Bob Ayrault .02 .10
46 Willie Banks .02 .10
47 Bret Barberie .02 .10
48 Kim Batiste .02 .10
49 Rod Beck .02 .10
50 Jason Bere .02 .10
51 Sean Berry .02 .10
52 Dante Bichette .07 .20
53 Jeff Blauser .02 .10
54 Mike Blowers .02 .10
55 Tim Bogar .02 .10
56 Tom Bolton .02 .10
57 Ricky Bones .02 .10
58 Bobby Bonilla .07 .20
59 Bret Boone .07 .20
60 Pat Borders .02 .10
61 Mike Bordick .02 .10
62 Daryl Boston .02 .10
63 Ryan Bowen .02 .10
64 Jeff Branson .02 .10
65 George Brett .50 1.25
66 Steve Buechele .02 .10
67 Dave Burba .02 .10
68 John Burkett .02 .10
69 Jeromy Burnitz .07 .20
70 Brett Butler .07 .20
71 Rob Butler .02 .10
72 Ken Caminiti .07 .20
73 Cris Carpenter .02 .10
74 Vinny Castilla .07 .20
75 Andujar Cedeno .02 .10
76 Wes Chamberlain .02 .10
77 Archi Cianfrocco .02 .10
78 Dave Clark .02 .10
79 Jerald Clark .02 .10
80 Royce Clayton .02 .10
81 David Cone .07 .20
82 Jeff Conine .07 .20
83 Steve Cooke .02 .10
84 Scott Cooper .02 .10
85 Joey Cora .02 .10
86 Tim Costo .02 .10
87 Chad Curtis .02 .10
88 Ron Darling .02 .10
89 Danny Darwin .02 .10
90 Rob Deer .02 .10
91 Jim Deshaies .02 .10
92 Delino DeShields .02 .10
93 Rob Dibble .07 .20
94 Gary DiSarcina .02 .10
95 Doug Drabek .02 .10
96 Scott Erickson .02 .10
97 Rikkert Faneyte RC .02 .10
98 Jeff Fassero .02 .10
99 Alex Fernandez .02 .10
100 Cecil Fielder .07 .20
101 Dave Fleming .02 .10
102 Darrin Fletcher .02 .10
103 Scott Fletcher .02 .10
104 Mike Gallego .02 .10
105 Carlos Garcia .02 .10
106 Jeff Gardner .02 .10
107 Brent Gates .02 .10
108 Benji Gil .02 .10
109 Bernard Gilkey .02 .10
110 Chris Gomez .02 .10
111 Luis Gonzalez .07 .20
112 Tom Gordon .02 .10
113 Jim Gott .02 .10
114 Mark Grace .10 .30
115 Tommy Greene .02 .10
116 Willie Greene .02 .10
117 Ken Griffey Jr. .40 1.00
118 Bill Gullickson .02 .10
119 Ricky Gutierrez .02 .10
120 Juan Guzman .02 .10
121 Chris Gwynn .02 .10
122 Tony Gwynn .25 .60
123 Jeffrey Hammonds .02 .10
124 Erik Hanson .02 .10
125 Gene Harris .02 .10
126 Greg W. Harris .02 .10
127 Bryan Harvey .02 .10
128 Billy Hatcher .02 .10
129 Hilly Hathaway .02 .10
130 Charlie Hayes .02 .10
131 Rickey Henderson .20 .50
132 Mike Henneman .02 .10
133 Pat Hentgen .02 .10
134 Roberto Hernandez .02 .10
135 Orel Hershiser .07 .20
136 Phil Hiatt .02 .10
137 Glenallen Hill .02 .10
138 Ken Hill .02 .10
139 Eric Hillman .02 .10
140 Chris Hoiles .02 .10
141 Dave Hollins .02 .10
142 David Hulse .02 .10
143 Todd Hundley .02 .10
144 Pete Incaviglia .02 .10
145 Danny Jackson .02 .10
146 John Jaha .02 .10
147 Domingo Jean .02 .10
148 Gregg Jefferies .02 .10
149 Reggie Jefferson .02 .10
150 Lance Johnson .02 .10
151 Bobby Jones .02 .10
152 Chipper Jones .20 .50
153 Todd Jones .02 .10
154 Brian Jordan .07 .20
155 Wally Joyner .07 .20
156 David Justice .07 .20
157 Ron Karkovice .02 .10
158 Eric Karros .07 .20
159 Jeff Kent .10 .30
160 Jimmy Key .07 .20
161 Mark Kiefer .02 .10
162 Darryl Kile .07 .20
163 Jeff King .02 .10
164 Wayne Kirby .02 .10
165 Ryan Klesko .07 .20
166 Chuck Knoblauch .07 .20
167 Chad Kreuter .02 .10
168 John Kruk .07 .20
169 Mark Langston .02 .10
170 Mike Lansing .02 .10
171 Barry Larkin .10 .30
172 Manuel Lee .02 .10
173 Phil Leftwich RC .02 .10
174 Darren Lewis .02 .10
175 Derek Lilliquist .02 .10
176 Jose Lind .02 .10
177 Albie Lopez .02 .10
178 Javier Lopez .07 .20
179 Torey Lovullo .02 .10
180 Scott Lydy .02 .10
181 Mike Macfarlane .02 .10
182 Shane Mack .02 .10
183 Greg Maddux .30 .75
184 Dave Magadan .02 .10
185 Joe Magrane .02 .10
186 Kirk Manwaring .02 .10

187 Al Martin .02 .10
188 Pedro A.Martinez RC .02 .10
189 Pedro Martinez .20 .50
190 Ramon Martinez .02 .10
191 Tino Martinez .10 .30
192 Don Mattingly .50 1.25
193 Derrick May .02 .10
194 David McCarty .02 .10
195 Ben McDonald .02 .10
196 Roger McDowell .02 .10
197 Fred McGriff .10 .30
198 Mark McLemore .02 .10
199 Greg McMichael .02 .10
200 Jeff McNeely .02 .10
201 Brian McRae .02 .10
202 Pat Meares .02 .10
203 Roberto Mejia .02 .10
204 Orlando Merced .02 .10
205 Jose Mesa .02 .10
206 Blas Minor .02 .10
207 Angel Miranda .02 .10
208 Paul Molitor .07 .20
209 Raul Mondesi .07 .20
210 Jeff Montgomery .02 .10
211 Mickey Morandini .02 .10
212 Mike Morgan .02 .10
213 Jamie Moyer .07 .20
214 Bobby Munoz .02 .10
215 Troy Neel .02 .10
216 Dave Nilsson .02 .10
217 John O'Donoghue .02 .10
218 Paul O'Neill .10 .30
219 Jose Offerman .02 .10
220 Joe Oliver .02 .10
221 Greg Olson .02 .10
222 Donovan Osborne .02 .10
223 Jayhawk Owens .02 .10
224 Mike Pagliarulo .02 .10
225 Craig Paquette .02 .10
226 Roger Pavlik .02 .10
227 Brad Pennington .02 .10
228 Eduardo Perez .02 .10
229 Mike Perez .02 .10
230 Tony Phillips .02 .10
231 Hipolito Pichardo .02 .10
232 Phil Plantier .02 .10
233 Curtis Pride RC .08 .25
234 Tim Pugh .02 .10
235 Scott Radinsky .02 .10
236 Pat Rapp .02 .10
237 Kevin Reimer .02 .10
238 Armando Reynoso .02 .10
239 Jose Rijo .02 .10
240 Cal Ripken .60 1.50
241 Kevin Roberson .02 .10
242 Kenny Rogers .07 .20
243 Kevin Rogers .02 .10
244 Mel Rojas .02 .10
245 John Roper .02 .10
246 Kirk Rueter .02 .10
247 Scott Ruffcorn .02 .10
248 Ken Ryan .02 .10
249 Nolan Ryan .75 2.00
250 Bret Saberhagen .07 .20
251 Tim Salmon .10 .30
252 Reggie Sanders .07 .20
253 Curt Schilling .07 .20
254 David Segui .02 .10
255 Aaron Sele .02 .10
256 Scott Servais .02 .10
257 Gary Sheffield .07 .20
258 Ruben Sierra .07 .20
259 Don Slaught .02 .10
260 Lee Smith .07 .20
261 Cory Snyder .02 .10
262 Paul Sorrento .02 .10
263 Sammy Sosa .20 .50
264 Bill Spiers .02 .10
265 Mike Stanley .02 .10
266 Dave Staton .02 .10
267 Terry Steinbach .02 .10
268 Kevin Stocker .02 .10
269 Todd Stottlemyre .02 .10
270 Doug Strange .02 .10
271 Bill Swift .02 .10
272 Kevin Tapani .02 .10
273 Tony Tarasco .02 .10
274 Julian Tavarez RC .07 .20
275 Mickey Tettleton .02 .10
276 Ryan Thompson .02 .10
277 Chris Turner .02 .10
278 John Valentin .02 .10
279 Todd Van Poppel .02 .10
280 Andy Van Slyke .10 .30
281 Mo Vaughn .07 .20
282 Robin Ventura .07 .20
283 Frank Viola .07 .20
284 Jose Vizcaino .02 .10
285 Omar Vizquel .10 .30
286 Larry Walker .07 .20
287 Duane Ward .02 .10
288 Allen Watson .02 .10
289 Bill Wegman .02 .10
290 Turk Wendell .02 .10
291 Lou Whitaker .07 .20
292 Devon White .07 .20
293 Rondell White .07 .20
294 Mark Whiten .02 .10
295 Darrell Whitmore .02 .10
296 Bob Wickman .02 .10
297 Rick Wilkins .02 .10
298 Bernie Williams .10 .30
299 Matt Williams .07 .20
300 Woody Williams .07 .20
301 Nigel Wilson .02 .10
302 Dave Winfield .07 .20
303 Anthony Young .02 .10
304 Eric Young .02 .10
305 Todd Zeile .02 .10
306 McDow .07 .20
Burkett
Glavine TP
307 Randy Johnson TP .10 .30
308 Randy Myers TP .02 .10
309 Jack McDowell TP .02 .10
310 Mike Piazza TP .20 .50
311 Barry Bonds TP .30 .75
312 Andres Galarraga TP .02 .10
313 J.Gonzalez .30 .75
B.Bonds TP
314 Albert Belle TP .07 .20
315 Kenny Lofton TP .02 .10
316 Barry Bonds CL .30 .75
317 Ken Griffey Jr. CL .25 .60
318 Mike Piazza CL .20 .50
319 Kirby Puckett CL .10 .30
320 Nolan Ryan CL .20 .50
321 Roberto Alomar CL .07 .20
322 Roger Clemens CL .20 .50
323 Juan Gonzalez CL .02 .10
324 Ken Griffey Jr. CL .25 .60
325 David Justice CL .02 .10
326 John Kruk CL .02 .10
327 Frank Thomas CL .07 .20
328 Tim Salmon TC .07 .20
329 Jeff Bagwell TC .07 .20
330 Mark McGwire TC .25 .60
331 Roberto Alomar TC .07 .20
332 David Justice TC .02 .10
333 Pat Listach TC .02 .10
334 Ozzie Smith TC .20 .50
335 Ryne Sandberg TC .20 .50
336 Mike Piazza TC .20 .50
337 Cliff Floyd TC .02 .10
338 Barry Bonds TC .30 .75
339 Albert Belle TC .07 .20
340 Ken Griffey Jr. TC .25 .60
341 Gary Sheffield TC .02 .10
342 Dwight Gooden TC .02 .10
343 Cal Ripken TC .30 .75
344 Tony Gwynn TC .10 .30
345 Lenny Dykstra TC .02 .10
346 Andy Van Slyke TC .07 .20
347 Juan Gonzalez TC .02 .10
348 Roger Clemens TC .20 .50
349 Barry Larkin TC .07 .20
350 Andres Galarraga TC .02 .10
351 Kevin Appier TC .02 .10
352 Cecil Fielder TC .02 .10
353 Kirby Puckett TC .10 .30
354 Frank Thomas TC .10 .30
355 Don Mattingly TC .25 .60
356 Bo Jackson .20 .50
357 Randy Johnson .20 .50
358 Darren Daulton .07 .20
359 Charlie Hough .07 .20
360 Andres Galarraga .07 .20
361 Mike Felder .02 .10
362 Chris Hammond .02 .10
363 Shawon Dunston .02 .10
364 Junior Felix .02 .10
365 Ray Lankford .07 .20
366 Darryl Strawberry .07 .20
367 Dave Magadan .02 .10
368 Gregg Olson .02 .10
369 Lenny Dykstra .07 .20
370 Darrin Jackson .02 .10
371 Dave Stewart .07 .20
372 Terry Pendleton .07 .20
373 Arthur Rhodes .02 .10
374 Benito Santiago .07 .20
375 Travis Fryman .07 .20
376 Scott Brosius .07 .20
377 Stan Belinda .02 .10
378 Derek Parks .02 .10
379 Kevin Seitzer .02 .10
380 Wade Boggs .10 .30
381 Wally Whitehurst .02 .10
382 Scott Leius .02 .10
383 Danny Tartabull .02 .10
384 Harold Reynolds .07 .20
385 Tim Raines .07 .20
386 Darryl Hamilton .02 .10
387 Felix Fermin .02 .10
388 Jim Eisenreich .02 .10
389 Kurt Abbott .07 .20
390 Kevin Appier .07 .20
391 Chris Bosio .02 .10
392 Randy Tomlin .02 .10
393 Bob Hamelin .02 .10
394 Kevin Gross .02 .10
395 Wil Cordero .02 .10
396 Joe Girardi .02 .10
397 Orestes Destrade .02 .10
398 Chris Haney .02 .10
399 Xavier Hernandez .02 .10
400 Mike Piazza .40 1.00
401 Alex Arias .02 .10
402 Tom Candiotti .02 .10
403 Kirk Gibson .07 .20
404 Chuck Carr .02 .10
405 Brady Anderson .07 .20
406 Greg Gagne .02 .10
407 Bruce Ruffin .02 .10
408 Scott Hemond .02 .10
409 Keith Miller .02 .10
410 John Wetteland .07 .20
411 Eric Anthony .02 .10
412 Andre Dawson .07 .20
413 Doug Henry .02 .10
414 John Franco .07 .20
415 Julio Franco .07 .20
416 Dave Hansen .02 .10
417 Mike Harkey .02 .10
418 Jack Armstrong .02 .10
419 Joe Orsulak .02 .10
420 John Smoltz .10 .30
421 Scott Livingstone .02 .10
422 Darren Holmes .02 .10
423 Ed Sprague .02 .10
424 Jay Buhner .07 .20
425 Kirby Puckett .20 .50
426 Phil Clark .02 .10
427 Anthony Young .02 .10
428 Reggie Jefferson .02 .10
429 Mariano Duncan .02 .10
430 Tom Glavine .10 .30
431 Dave Henderson .02 .10
432 Melido Perez .02 .10
433 Paul Wagner .02 .10
434 Tim Worrell .02 .10
435 Ozzie Guillen .07 .20
436 Mike Butcher .02 .10
437 Jim Deshaies .02 .10
438 Kevin Young .02 .10
439 Tom Browning .02 .10
440 Mike Greenwell .02 .10
441 Mike Stanton .02 .10
442 John Doherty .02 .10
443 John Dopson .02 .10
444 Carlos Baerga .02 .10
445 Jack McDowell .02 .10
446 Kent Mercker .02 .10
447 Ricky Jordan .02 .10
448 Jerry Browne .02 .10
449 Fernando Vina .02 .10
450 Jim Abbott .10 .30
451 Teddy Higuera .02 .10
452 Tim Naehring .02 .10
453 Jim Leyritz .02 .10
454 Frank Castillo .02 .10
455 Joe Carter .07 .20
456 Craig Biggio .10 .30
457 Geronimo Pena .02 .10
458 Alejandro Pena .02 .10
459 Mike Moore .02 .10
460 Randy Myers .02 .10
461 Greg Myers .02 .10
462 Greg Hibbard .02 .10
463 Jose Guzman .02 .10
464 Tom Pagnozzi .02 .10
465 Marquis Grissom .07 .20
466 Tim Wallach .02 .10
467 Joe Grahe .02 .10
468 Bob Tewksbury .02 .10
469 B.J. Surhoff .07 .20
470 Kevin Mitchell .02 .10
471 Bobby Witt .02 .10
472 Milt Thompson .02 .10
473 John Smiley .02 .10
474 Alan Trammell .07 .20
475 Mike Mussina .10 .30
476 Rick Aguilera .02 .10
477 Jose Valentin .02 .10
478 Harold Baines .07 .20
479 Bip Roberts .02 .10
480 Edgar Martinez .10 .30
481 Rheal Cormier .02 .10
482 Hal Morris .02 .10
483 Pat Kelly .02 .10
484 Roberto Kelly .02 .10
485 Chris Sabo .02 .10
486 Kent Hrbek .07 .20
487 Scott Kamieniecki .02 .10
488 Walt Weiss .02 .10
489 Karl Rhodes .02 .10
490 Derek Bell .02 .10
491 Chili Davis .07 .20
492 Brian Harper .02 .10
493 Felix Jose .02 .10
494 Trevor Hoffman .10 .30
495 Dennis Eckersley .07 .20
496 Pedro Astacio .02 .10
497 Jay Bell .07 .20
498 Randy Velarde .02 .10
499 David Wells .07 .20
500 Frank Thomas .20 .50
501 Mark Lemke .02 .10
502 Mike Devereaux .02 .10
503 Chuck McElroy .02 .10
504 Luis Polonia .02 .10
505 Damion Easley .02 .10
506 Greg A. Harris .02 .10
507 Chris James .02 .10
508 Terry Mulholland .02 .10
509 Pete Smith .02 .10
510 Rickey Henderson .20 .50
511 Sid Fernandez .02 .10
512 Al Leiter .07 .20
513 Doug Jones .02 .10
514 Steve Farr .02 .10
515 Chuck Finley .07 .20
516 Bobby Thigpen .02 .10
517 Jim Edmonds .20 .50
518 Graeme Lloyd .02 .10
519 Dwight Gooden .07 .20
520 Pat Listach .02 .10
521 Kevin Bass .02 .10
522 Willie Banks .02 .10
523 Steve Finley .07 .20
524 Delino DeShields .02 .10
525 Mark McGwire .50 1.25
526 Greg Swindell .02 .10
527 Chris Nabholz .02 .10
528 Scott Sanders .02 .10
529 David Segui .02 .10
530 Howard Johnson .02 .10
531 Jaime Navarro .02 .10
532 Jose Vizcaino .02 .10
533 Mark Lewis .02 .10
534 Pete Harnisch .02 .10
535 Robby Thompson .02 .10
536 Marcus Moore .02 .10
537 Kevin Brown .07 .20
538 Mark Clark .02 .10
539 Sterling Hitchcock .02 .10
540 Will Clark .10 .30
541 Denis Boucher .02 .10
542 Jack Morris .07 .20
543 Pedro Munoz .02 .10
544 Bret Boone .07 .20
545 Ozzie Smith .30 .75
546 Dennis Martinez .07 .20
547 Dan Wilson .02 .10
548 Rick Sutcliffe .07 .20
549 Kevin McReynolds .02 .10
550 Roger Clemens .40 1.00
551 Todd Benzinger .02 .10
552 Bill Haselman .02 .10
553 Bobby Munoz .02 .10
554 Ellis Burks .07 .20
555 Ryne Sandberg .30 .75
556 Lee Smith .07 .20
557 Danny Bautista .02 .10
558 Rey Sanchez .02 .10
559 Norm Charlton .02 .10
560 Jose Canseco .10 .30
561 Tim Belcher .02 .10
562 Denny Neagle .07 .20
563 Eric Davis .07 .20
564 Jody Reed .02 .10
565 Kenny Lofton .07 .20
566 Gary Gaetti .07 .20
567 Todd Worrell .02 .10
568 Mark Portugal .02 .10
569 Dick Schofield .02 .10
570 Andy Benes .02 .10
571 Zane Smith .02 .10
572 Bobby Ayala .02 .10
573 Chip Hale .02 .10
574 Bob Welch .02 .10
575 Deion Sanders .10 .30
576 Dave Nied .02 .10
577 Pat Mahomes .02 .10
578 Charles Nagy .02 .10
579 Otis Nixon .02 .10
580 Dean Palmer .07 .20
581 Roberto Petagine .02 .10
582 Dwight Smith .02 .10
583 Jeff Russell .02 .10
584 Mark Dewey .02 .10
585 Greg Vaughn .02 .10
586 Brian Hunter .02 .10
587 Willie McGee .07 .20
588 Pedro Martinez .20 .50
589 Roger Salkeld .02 .10
590 Jeff Bagwell .10 .30
591 Spike Owen .02 .10
592 Jeff Reardon .07 .20
593 Erik Pappas .02 .10
594 Brian Williams .02 .10
595 Eddie Murray .20 .50
596 Henry Rodriguez .02 .10
597 Erik Hanson .02 .10
598 Stan Javier .02 .10
599 Mitch Williams .02 .10
600 John Olerud .07 .20
601 Vince Coleman .02 .10
602 Damon Berryhill .02 .10
603 Tom Brunansky .02 .10
604 Robb Nen .07 .20
605 Rafael Palmeiro .10 .30
606 Cal Eldred .02 .10
607 Jeff Brantley .02 .10
608 Alan Mills .02 .10
609 Jeff Nelson .02 .10
610 Barry Bonds .60 1.50
611 Carlos Pulido RC .02 .10
612 Tim Hyers RC .02 .10
613 Steve Howe .02 .10
614 Brian Turang RC .02 .10
615 Leo Gomez .02 .10
616 Jesse Orosco .02 .10
617 Dan Pasqua .02 .10
618 Marvin Freeman .02 .10
619 Tony Fernandez .02 .10
620 Albert Belle .07 .20
621 Eddie Taubensee .02 .10
622 Mike Jackson .02 .10
623 Jose Bautista .02 .10
624 Jim Thome .10 .30
625 Ivan Rodriguez .10 .30
626 Ben Rivera .02 .10
627 Dave Valle .02 .10
628 Tom Henke .02 .10
629 Omar Vizquel .10 .30
630 Juan Gonzalez .07 .20
631 Roberto Alomar UP .07 .20
632 Barry Bonds UP .30 .75
633 Juan Gonzalez UP .02 .10
634 Ken Griffey Jr. UP .25 .60
635 Michael Jordan UP 1.00 2.50
636 David Justice UP .02 .10
637 Mike Piazza UP .20 .50
638 Kirby Puckett UP .10 .30
639 Tim Salmon UP .07 .20
640 Frank Thomas UP .10 .30
641 Alan Benes RC .07 .20
642 Johnny Damon .20 .50
643 Brad Fullmer RC .08 .25
644 Derek Jeter .60 1.50
645 Derrek Lee RC .60 1.50
646 Alex Ochoa .02 .10
647 Alex Rodriguez RC 5.00 12.00
648 Jose Silva RC .02 .10
649 Terrell Wade RC .02 .10
650 Preston Wilson .07 .20
651 Shane Andrews .02 .10
652 James Baldwin .02 .10
653 Ricky Bottalico RC .07 .20
654 Tavo Alvarez .02 .10
655 Donnie Elliott .02 .10
656 Joey Eischen .02 .10
657 Jason Giambi .20 .50
658 Todd Hollandsworth .02 .10
659 Brian L.Hunter .02 .10
660 Charles Johnson .07 .20
661 Michael Jordan RC 2.00 5.00
662 Jeff Juden .02 .10
663 Mike Kelly .02 .10
664 James Mouton .02 .10
665 Ray Holbert .02 .10
666 Pokey Reese .02 .10
667 Ruben Santana RC .02 .10
668 Paul Spoljaric .02 .10
669 Luis Lopez .02 .10
670 Matt Walbeck .02 .10
P50 Ken Griffey Jr. Promo .50 1.25

1994 Collector's Choice White Letter Variation

RANDOM PRINTING ERRORS IN PACKS
PRICING AVAIL ONLY ON A-ROD FOR NOW
647 Alex Rodriguez 15.00 40.00

1994 Collector's Choice Gold Signature

*STARS: 6X TO 15X BASIC CARDS
*ROOKIES: 6X TO 15X BASIC CARDS
RANDOM PRINTING ERRORS IN PACKS
FIVE PER FACTORY SET
117 Ken Griffey Jr. 15.00 40.00
635 Michael Jordan UP 8.00 20.00
644 Derek Jeter 150.00 250.00
647 Alex Rodriguez 60.00 150.00

1994 Collector's Choice Gold Signature White Letter Variation

RANDOM PRINTING ERRORS IN PACKS
NO PRICING DUE TO SCARCITY

1994 Collector's Choice Silver Signature

COMPLETE SET (670) 75.00 150.00
COMPLETE SERIES 1 (320) 20.00 50.00
COMPLETE SERIES 2 (350) 40.00 100.00
*STARS: 1.5X TO 4X BASIC CARDS
*ROOKIES: 1X TO 2.5X BASIC CARDS
ONE SILVER SIGNATURE PER PACK
647 Alex Rodriguez 8.00 20.00

1994 Collector's Choice Silver Signature White Letter Variation

RANDOM VARIATIONS IN PACKS
NO PRICING DUE TO SCARCITY

1994 Collector's Choice Home Run All-Stars

COMPLETE SET (8) 1.50 4.00
ONE SET VIA MAIL PER 8TH PRIZE CARD
HA1 Juan Gonzalez .10 .30
HA2 Ken Griffey Jr. .60 1.50
HA3 Barry Bonds 1.00 2.50
HA4 Bobby Bonilla .10 .30
HA5 Cecil Fielder UER HA4 .10 .30
HA6 Albert Belle .10 .30
HA7 David Justice .10 .30
HA8 Mike Piazza .60 1.50

1994 Collector's Choice Team vs. Team

COMPLETE SET (15) 2.00 5.00
ONE UNNUMBERED CARD PER SER.2 PACK
1 R.Alomar .08 .25
F.Thomas
2 B.Bonds .20 .50
K.Griffey
3 R.Clemens .25 .60
D.Mattingly
4 L.Dykstra .02 .10
D.Justice
5 A.Galarraga .10 .30
T.Gwynn
6 D.Gooden .02 .10
G.Sheffield
7 K.Griffey .20 .50
J.Gonzalez
8 B.Larkin .05 .15
J.Bagwell
9 P.Listach .02 .10
A.Belle
10 M.McGwire .25 .60
T.Salmon
11 M.Piazza .20 .50
B.Bonds
12 K.Puckett .08 .25
B.McRae
13 C.Ripken .30 .75
C.Fielder
14 R.Sandberg .15 .40
O.Smith
15 A.Van Slyke .02 .10
C.Floyd

1995 Collector's Choice

Produced by Upper Deck, this set contains 530 standard-size cards issued in 12-card foil hobby and retail packs of which carried a suggested price of 99 cents. The fronts have a color photo with a white border and the player's last name at the bottom in his team's color. The backs have an action photo at the top with statistics and information at the bottom with a silver Upper Deck hologram below that. Subsets featured are Rookie Class (1-27), Future Foundation (28-45), Best of the '90s (51-65) and What's the Call? (86-90). The key Rookie Card in this set is Hideo Nomo. The 55-card Trade set represents the cards a collector received when the five randomly inserted trade cards were redeemed. They are numbered in continuation of the regular Collector's Choice cards but have a "T" suffix. The cards numbered 542-552 were also issued as a bonus to dealers who ordered collector's choice factory sets. The trade cards offer expired on February 1, 1996.

COMPLETE SET (530) 8.00 20.00
COMP.FACT.SET (545) 15.00 30.00
COMMON CARD (1-530) .02 .10
COMP.TRADE SET (55) 4.00 10.00
COMMON TRADE (531-585) .08 .25
TEN TRADE VIA MAIL PER TRD.EXCH.CARD
ONE 542-552 RUN PER DLR.FACT.SET ORDER
SUBSET CARDS HALF VALUE OF BASE CARDS
1 Charles Johnson .07 .20
2 Scott Ruffcorn .02 .10
3 Ray Durham .07 .20
4 Armando Benitez .02 .10
5 Alex Rodriguez .50 1.25
6 Julian Tavarez .02 .10
7 Chad Ogea .02 .10
8 Quilvio Veras .02 .10
9 Phil Nevin .07 .20
10 Michael Tucker .02 .10
11 Mark Thompson .02 .10
12 Rod Henderson .02 .10
13 Andrew Lorraine .02 .10
14 Joe Randa .07 .20
15 Derek Jeter .50 1.25
16 Tony Clark .02 .10
17 Juan Castillo .02 .10
18 Mark Acre .02 .10
19 Orlando Miller .02 .10
20 Paul Wilson .02 .10
21 John Mabry .02 .10
22 Garey Ingram .02 .10
23 Garret Anderson .07 .20
24 Dave Stevens .02 .10
25 Dustin Hermanson .02 .10
26 Paul Shuey .02 .10
27 J.R. Phillips .02 .10
28 Ruben Rivera .02 .10
29 Nomar Garciaparra .50 1.25
30 John Wasdin .02 .10
31 Jim Pittsley .02 .10
32 Scott Elarton RC .08 .25
33 Raul Casanova RC .02 .10
34 Todd Greene .02 .10
35 Bill Pulsipher .02 .10
36 Trey Beamon .02 .10
37 Curtis Goodwin .02 .10
38 Doug Million .02 .10
39 Karim Garcia RC .02 .10
40 Ben Grieve .02 .10
41 Mark Farris .02 .10
42 Juan Acevedo RC .02 .10
43 C.J. Nitkowski .02 .10
44 Travis Miller RC .02 .10
45 Reid Ryan .07 .20
46 Nolan Ryan .75 2.00
47 Robin Yount .30 .75
48 Ryne Sandberg .30 .75
49 George Brett .50 1.25
50 Mike Schmidt .30 .75
51 Cecil Fielder B90 .02 .10
52 Nolan Ryan B90 .40 1.00
53 Rickey Henderson B90 .10 .30
54 Brett .20 .50
Yount
Winfield B90
55 Sid Bream B90 .02 .10
56 Carlos Baerga B90 .02 .10
57 Lee Smith B90 .02 .10
58 Mark Whiten B90 .02 .10
59 Joe Carter B90 .02 .10
60 Barry Bonds B90 .30 .75
61 Tony Gwynn B90 .10 .30
62 Ken Griffey Jr. B90 .25 .60
63 Greg Maddux B90 .20 .50
64 Frank Thomas B90 .20 .50
65 D.Martinez .02 .10
K.Rogers B90
66 David Cone .07 .20
67 Greg Maddux .30 .75
68 Jimmy Key .07 .20
69 Fred McGriff .10 .30
70 Ken Griffey Jr. .40 1.00
71 Matt Williams .07 .20
72 Paul O'Neill .10 .30
73 Tony Gwynn .25 .60
74 Randy Johnson .20 .50
75 Frank Thomas .20 .50
76 Jeff Bagwell .10 .30
77 Kirby Puckett .20 .50
78 Bob Hamelin .02 .10
79 Raul Mondesi .07 .20
80 Mike Piazza .30 .75
81 Kenny Lofton .07 .20
82 Barry Bonds .60 1.50
83 Albert Belle .07 .20
84 Juan Gonzalez .07 .20
85 Cal Ripken .60 1.50
86 Barry Bonds WC .30 .75
87 Mike Piazza WC .20 .50
88 Ken Griffey Jr. WC .25 .60
89 Frank Thomas WC .10 .30
90 Juan Gonzalez WC .02 .10
91 Jorge Fabregas .02 .10
92 J.T. Snow .07 .20
93 Spike Owen .02 .10
94 Eduardo Perez .02 .10
95 Bo Jackson .20 .50
96 Damion Easley .02 .10
97 Gary DiSarcina .02 .10
98 Jim Edmonds .10 .30
99 Chad Curtis .02 .10
100 Tim Salmon .10 .30
101 Chili Davis .07 .20
102 Chuck Finley .07 .20
103 Mark Langston .02 .10
104 Brian Anderson .02 .10
105 Lee Smith .07 .20
106 Phil Leftwich .02 .10
107 Chris Donnels .02 .10
108 John Hudek .02 .10
109 Craig Biggio .10 .30
110 Luis Gonzalez .07 .20
111 Brian L.Hunter .02 .10
112 James Mouton .02 .10
113 Scott Servais .02 .10
114 Tony Eusebio .02 .10
115 Derek Bell .02 .10
116 Doug Drabek .02 .10
117 Shane Reynolds .02 .10
118 Darryl Kile .07 .20
119 Greg Swindell .02 .10
120 Phil Plantier .02 .10
121 Todd Jones .02 .10
122 Steve Ontiveros .02 .10
123 Bobby Witt .02 .10
124 Brent Gates .02 .10
125 Rickey Henderson .20 .50
126 Scott Brosius .07 .20
127 Mike Bordick .02 .10
128 Fausto Cruz .02 .10
129 Stan Javier .02 .10
130 Mark McGwire .50 1.25
131 Geronimo Berroa .02 .10
132 Terry Steinbach .02 .10
133 Steve Karsay .02 .10
134 Dennis Eckersley .07 .20
135 Ruben Sierra .07 .20
136 Ron Darling .02 .10
137 Todd Van Poppel .02 .10
138 Alex Gonzalez .02 .10
139 John Olerud .07 .20
140 Roberto Alomar .10 .30
141 Darren Hall .02 .10
142 Ed Sprague .02 .10
143 Devon White .07 .20
144 Shawn Green .07 .20
145 Paul Molitor .07 .20
146 Pat Borders .02 .10
147 Carlos Delgado .07 .20
148 Juan Guzman .02 .10
149 Pat Hentgen .02 .10
150 Joe Carter .07 .20
151 Dave Stewart .07 .20
152 Todd Stottlemyre .02 .10
153 Dick Schofield .02 .10
154 Chipper Jones .20 .50
155 Ryan Klesko .07 .20
156 David Justice .07 .20
157 Mike Kelly .02 .10
158 Roberto Kelly .02 .10
159 Tony Tarasco .02 .10
160 Javier Lopez .07 .20
161 Steve Avery .02 .10
162 Greg McMichael .02 .10
163 Kent Mercker .02 .10
164 Mark Lemke .02 .10
165 Tom Glavine .10 .30
166 Jose Oliva .02 .10
167 John Smoltz .10 .30
168 Jeff Blauser .02 .10
169 Troy O'Leary .02 .10
170 Greg Vaughn .02 .10
171 Jody Reed .02 .10
172 Kevin Seitzer .02 .10
173 Jeff Cirillo .02 .10
174 B.J. Surhoff .07 .20
175 Cal Eldred .02 .10
176 Jose Valentin .02 .10
177 Turner Ward .02 .10
178 Darryl Hamilton .02 .10
179 Pat Listach .02 .10
180 Matt Mieske .02 .10
181 Brian Harper .02 .10
182 Dave Nilsson .02 .10
183 Mike Fetters .02 .10
184 John Jaha .02 .10
185 Ricky Bones .02 .10
186 Geronimo Pena .02 .10
187 Bob Tewksbury .02 .10
188 Todd Zeile .02 .10
189 Danny Jackson .02 .10
190 Ray Lankford .07 .20
191 Bernard Gilkey .02 .10
192 Brian Jordan .07 .20
193 Tom Pagnozzi .02 .10
194 Rick Sutcliffe .07 .20
195 Mark Whiten .02 .10
196 Tom Henke .02 .10
197 Rene Arocha .02 .10
198 Allen Watson .02 .10
199 Mike Perez .02 .10
200 Ozzie Smith .30 .75
201 Anthony Young .02 .10
202 Rey Sanchez .02 .10
203 Steve Buechele .02 .10
204 Shawon Dunston .02 .10
205 Mark Grace .10 .30
206 Glenallen Hill .02 .10
207 Eddie Zambrano .02 .10
208 Rick Wilkins .02 .10
209 Derrick May .02 .10
210 Sammy Sosa .20 .50
211 Kevin Roberson .02 .10
212 Steve Trachsel .02 .10
213 Willie Banks .02 .10
214 Kevin Foster .02 .10
215 Randy Myers .02 .10
216 Mike Morgan .02 .10
217 Rafael Bournigal .02 .10
218 Delino DeShields .02 .10
219 Tim Wallach .02 .10
220 Eric Karros .07 .20
221 Jose Offerman .02 .10
222 Tom Candiotti .02 .10
223 Ismael Valdes .02 .10
224 Henry Rodriguez .02 .10
225 Billy Ashley .02 .10
226 Darren Dreifort .02 .10
227 Ramon Martinez .02 .10
228 Pedro Astacio .02 .10
229 Orel Hershiser .07 .20
230 Brett Butler .07 .20
231 Todd Hollandsworth .02 .10
232 Chan Ho Park .07 .20
233 Mike Lansing .02 .10
234 Sean Berry .02 .10
235 Rondell White .07 .20
236 Ken Hill .02 .10
237 Marquis Grissom .07 .20
238 Larry Walker .07 .20
239 John Wetteland .07 .20
240 Cliff Floyd .07 .20
241 Joey Eischen .02 .10
242 Lou Frazier .02 .10
243 Darrin Fletcher .02 .10
244 Pedro Martinez .10 .30
245 Wil Cordero .02 .10
246 Jeff Fassero .02 .10
247 Butch Henry .02 .10
248 Mel Rojas .02 .10
249 Kirk Rueter .02 .10
250 Moises Alou .07 .20
251 Rod Beck .02 .10
252 John Patterson .02 .10
253 Robby Thompson .02 .10
254 Royce Clayton .02 .10
255 Wm. VanLandingham .02 .10
256 Darren Lewis .02 .10
257 Kirt Manwaring .02 .10
258 Mark Portugal .02 .10
259 Bill Swift .02 .10
260 Rikkert Faneyte .02 .10
261 Mike Jackson .02 .10
262 Todd Benzinger .02 .10
263 Bud Black .02 .10
264 Salomon Torres .02 .10
265 Eddie Murray .20 .50
266 Mark Clark .02 .10
267 Paul Sorrento .02 .10
268 Jim Thome .10 .30
269 Omar Vizquel .10 .30
270 Carlos Baerga .02 .10
271 Jeff Russell .02 .10
272 Herbert Perry .02 .10
273 Sandy Alomar Jr. .02 .10
274 Dennis Martinez .07 .20
275 Manny Ramirez .10 .30
276 Wayne Kirby .02 .10
277 Charles Nagy .02 .10
278 Albie Lopez .02 .10
279 Jeromy Burnitz .07 .20

280 Dave Winfield .07 .20
281 Tim Davis .02 .10
282 Marc Newfield .02 .10
283 Tino Martinez .10 .30
284 Mike Blowers .02 .10
285 Goose Gossage .07 .20
286 Luis Sojo .02 .10
287 Edgar Martinez .10 .30
288 Rich Amaral .02 .10
289 Felix Fermin .02 .10
290 Jay Buhner .07 .20
291 Dan Wilson .02 .10
292 Bobby Ayala .02 .10
293 Dave Fleming .02 .10
294 Greg Pirkl .02 .10
295 Reggie Jefferson .02 .10
296 Greg Hibbard .02 .10
297 Yorkis Perez .02 .10
298 Kurt Miller .02 .10
299 Chuck Carr .02 .10
300 Gary Sheffield .07 .20
301 Jerry Browne .02 .10
302 Dave Magadan .02 .10
303 Kurt Abbott .02 .10
304 Pat Rapp .02 .10
305 Jeff Conine .07 .20
306 Benito Santiago .07 .20
307 Dave Weathers .02 .10
308 Robb Nen .07 .20
309 Chris Hammond .02 .10
310 Bryan Harvey .02 .10
311 Charlie Hough .07 .20
312 Greg Colbrunn .02 .10
313 David Segui .02 .10
314 Rico Brogna .02 .10
315 Jeff Kent .07 .20
316 Jose Vizcaino .02 .10
317 Jim Lindeman .02 .10
318 Carl Everett .07 .20
319 Ryan Thompson .02 .10
320 Bobby Bonilla .07 .20
321 Joe Orsulak .02 .10
322 Pete Harnisch .02 .10
323 Doug Linton .02 .10
324 Todd Hundley .02 .10
325 Bret Saberhagen .07 .20
326 Kelly Stinnett .02 .10
327 Jason Jacome .02 .10
328 Bobby Jones .02 .10
329 John Franco .07 .20
330 Rafael Palmeiro .10 .30
331 Chris Hoiles .02 .10
332 Leo Gomez .02 .10
333 Chris Sabo .02 .10
334 Brady Anderson .07 .20
335 Jeffrey Hammonds .02 .10
336 Dwight Smith .02 .10
337 Jack Voigt .02 .10
338 Harold Baines .07 .20
339 Ben McDonald .02 .10
340 Mike Mussina .10 .30
341 Bret Barberie .02 .10
342 Jamie Moyer .07 .20
343 Mike Oquist .02 .10
344 Sid Fernandez .02 .10
345 Eddie Williams .02 .10
346 Joey Hamilton .02 .10
347 Brian Williams .02 .10
348 Luis Lopez .02 .10
349 Steve Finley .07 .20
350 Andy Benes .02 .10
351 Andujar Cedeno .02 .10
352 Bip Roberts .02 .10
353 Ray McDavid .02 .10
354 Ken Caminiti .07 .20
355 Trevor Hoffman .07 .20
356 Mel Nieves .02 .10
357 Brad Ausmus .07 .20
358 Andy Ashby .02 .10
359 Scott Sanders .02 .10
360 Gregg Jefferies .02 .10
361 Mariano Duncan .02 .10
362 Dave Hollins .02 .10
363 Kevin Stocker .02 .10
364 Fernando Valenzuela .07 .20
365 Lenny Dykstra .07 .20
366 Jim Eisenreich .02 .10
367 Ricky Bottalico .02 .10
368 Doug Jones .02 .10
369 Ricky Jordan .02 .10
370 Darren Daulton .07 .20
371 Mike Lieberthal .07 .20
372 Bobby Munoz .02 .10
373 John Kruk .07 .20
374 Curt Schilling .07 .20
375 Orlando Merced .02 .10
376 Carlos Garcia .02 .10
377 Lance Parrish .07 .20
378 Steve Cooke .02 .10
379 Jeff King .02 .10
380 Jay Bell .07 .20
381 Al Martin .02 .10
382 Paul Wagner .02 .10
383 Rick White .02 .10
384 Midre Cummings .02 .10
385 Jon Lieber .02 .10
386 Dave Clark .02 .10
387 Don Slaught .02 .10
388 Denny Neagle .07 .20
389 Zane Smith .02 .10
390 Andy Van Slyke .10 .30
391 Ivan Rodriguez .10 .30
392 David Hulse .02 .10
393 John Burkett .02 .10
394 Kevin Brown .07 .20
395 Dean Palmer .07 .20
396 Otis Nixon .02 .10
397 Rick Helling .02 .10
398 Kenny Rogers .07 .20
399 Darren Oliver .02 .10
400 Will Clark .10 .30
401 Jeff Frye .02 .10
402 Kevin Gross .02 .10
403 John Dettmer .02 .10
404 Manny Lee .02 .10
405 Rusty Greer .07 .20
406 Aaron Sele .02 .10
407 Carlos Rodriguez .02 .10
408 Scott Cooper .02 .10
409 John Valentin .02 .10
410 Roger Clemens .40 1.00
411 Mike Greenwell .02 .10
412 Tim Vanegmond .02 .10
413 Tom Brunansky .02 .10
414 Steve Farr .02 .10
415 Jose Canseco .10 .30
416 Joe Hesketh .02 .10
417 Ken Ryan .02 .10
418 Tim Naehring .02 .10
419 Frank Viola .07 .20
420 Andre Dawson .07 .20
421 Mo Vaughn .07 .20
422 Jeff Brantley .02 .10
423 Pete Schourek .02 .10
424 Hal Morris UER
(signature actually Jack Morris) .02 .10
425 Deion Sanders .10 .30
426 Brian R. Hunter .02 .10
427 Bret Boone .07 .20
428 Willie Greene .02 .10
429 Ron Gant .07 .20
430 Barry Larkin .10 .30
431 Reggie Sanders .07 .20
432 Eddie Taubensee .02 .10
433 Jack Morris .07 .20
434 Jose Rijo .02 .10
435 Johnny Ruffin .02 .10
436 John Smiley .02 .10
437 John Roper .02 .10
438 Dave Nied .02 .10
439 Roberto Mejia .02 .10
440 Andres Galarraga .07 .20
441 Mike Kingery .02 .10
442 Curt Leskanic .02 .10
443 Walt Weiss .02 .10
444 Marvin Freeman .02 .10
445 Charlie Hayes .02 .10
446 Eric Young .02 .10
447 Ellis Burks .07 .20
448 Joe Girardi .02 .10
449 Lance Painter .02 .10
450 Dante Bichette .07 .20
451 Bruce Ruffin .02 .10
452 Jeff Granger .02 .10
453 Wally Joyner .07 .20
454 Jose Lind .02 .10
455 Jeff Montgomery .02 .10
456 Gary Gaetti .07 .20
457 Greg Gagne .02 .10
458 Vince Coleman .02 .10
459 Mike Macfarlane .02 .10
460 Brian McRae .02 .10
461 Tom Gordon .02 .10
462 Kevin Appier .07 .20
463 Billy Brewer .02 .10
464 Mark Gubicza .02 .10
465 Travis Fryman .07 .20
466 Danny Bautista .02 .10
467 Sean Bergman .02 .10
468 Mike Henneman .02 .10
469 Mike Moore .02 .10
470 Cecil Fielder .07 .20
471 Alan Trammell .07 .20
472 Kirk Gibson .07 .20
473 Tony Phillips .02 .10
474 Mickey Tettleton .02 .10
475 Lou Whitaker .07 .20
476 Chris Gomez .02 .10
477 John Doherty .02 .10
478 Greg Gohr .02 .10
479 Bill Gullickson .02 .10
480 Rick Aguilera .02 .10
481 Matt Walbeck .02 .10
482 Kevin Tapani .02 .10
483 Scott Erickson .02 .10
484 Steve Dunn .02 .10
485 David McCarty .02 .10
486 Scott Leius .02 .10
487 Pat Meares .02 .10
488 Jeff Reboulet .02 .10
489 Pedro Munoz .02 .10
490 Chuck Knoblauch .07 .20
491 Rich Becker .02 .10
492 Alex Cole .02 .10
493 Pat Mahomes .02 .10
494 Ozzie Guillen .07 .20
495 Tim Raines .07 .20
496 Kirk McCaskill .02 .10
497 Olmedo Saenz .02 .10
498 Scott Sanderson .02 .10
499 Lance Johnson .02 .10
500 Michael Jordan .60 1.50
501 Warren Newson .02 .10
502 Ron Karkovice .02 .10
503 Wilson Alvarez .02 .10
504 Jason Bere .02 .10
505 Robin Ventura .07 .20
506 Alex Fernandez .02 .10
507 Roberto Hernandez .02 .10
508 Norberto Martin .02 .10
509 Bob Wickman .02 .10
510 Don Mattingly .50 1.25
511 Melido Perez .02 .10
512 Pat Kelly .02 .10
513 Randy Velarde .02 .10
514 Tony Fernandez .02 .10
515 Jack McDowell .02 .10
516 Luis Polonia .02 .10
517 Bernie Williams .10 .30
518 Danny Tartabull .02 .10
519 Mike Stanley .02 .10
520 Wade Boggs .10 .30
521 Jim Leyritz .02 .10
522 Steve Howe .02 .10
523 Scott Kamieniecki .02 .10
524 Russ Davis .02 .10
525 Jim Abbott .10 .30
526 Eddie Murray CL .10 .30
527 Alex Rodriguez CL .20 .50
528 Jeff Bagwell CL .07 .20
529 Joe Carter CL .02 .10
530 Fred McGriff CL .07 .20
531T Tony Phillips TRADE .08 .25
532T Dave Magadan TRADE .08 .25
533T Mike Gallego TRADE .08 .25
534T Dave Stewart TRADE .20 .50
535T Todd Stottlemyre TRADE .08 .25
536T David Cone TRADE .20 .50
537T Marquis Grissom TRADE .20 .50
538T Derrick May TRADE .08 .25
539T Joe Oliver TRADE .08 .25
540T Scott Cooper TRADE .08 .25
541T Ken Hill TRADE .08 .25
542T Howard Johnson TRADE DP .08 .25
543T Brian McRae TRADE DP .08 .25
544T Jaime Navarro TRADE DP .08 .25
545T Ozzie Timmons TRADE DP .08 .25
546T Roberto Kelly TRADE DP .08 .25
547T Hideo Nomo TRADE DP 1.50 4.00
548T Shane Andrews TRADE DP .08 .25
549T M.Grudzielanek TRADE DP .40 1.00
550T Carlos Perez TRADE DP .20 .50
551T Henry Rodriguez TRADE DP .08 .25
552T Tony Tarasco TRADE DP .08 .25
553T Glenallen Hill TRADE .08 .25
554T Terry Mulholland TRADE .08 .25
555T Orel Hershiser TRADE .20 .50
556T Darren Bragg TRADE .08 .25
557T John Burkett TRADE .08 .25
558T Bobby Witt TRADE .08 .25
559T Terry Pendleton TRADE .20 .50
560T Andre Dawson TRADE .20 .50
561T Brett Butler TRADE .20 .50
562T Kevin Brown TRADE .20 .50
563T Doug Jones TRADE .08 .25
564T Andy Van Slyke TRADE .40 1.00
565T Jody Reed TRADE .08 .25
566T Fernando Valenzuela TRADE .20 .50
567T Charlie Hayes TRADE .08 .25
568T Benji Gil TRADE .08 .25
569T Mark McLemore TRADE .08 .25
570T Mickey Tettleton TRADE .08 .25
571T Bob Tewksbury TRADE .08 .25
572T Rheal Cormier TRADE .08 .25
573T Vaughn Eshelman TRADE .08 .25
574T Mike Macfarlane TRADE .08 .25
575T Mark Whiten TRADE .08 .25
576T Benito Santiago TRADE .20 .50
577T Jason Bates TRADE .08 .25
578T Bill Swift TRADE .08 .25
579T Larry Walker TRADE .20 .50
580T Chad Curtis TRADE .08 .25
581T Bob Higginson TRADE .40 1.00
582T Marty Cordova TRADE .08 .25
583T Mike Devereaux TRADE .08 .25
584T John Kruk TRADE .20 .50
585T John Wetteland TRADE .20 .50
P172 Ken Griffey Jr. Promo .50 1.25

1995 Collector's Choice Gold Signature

*STARS: 6X TO 15X BASIC CARDS
*ROOKIES: 5X TO 12X BASIC
STATED ODDS 1:35
12 PER GOLD SUPER PACK/15 PER FACT.SET
15 Derek Jeter 20.00 50.00

1995 Collector's Choice Silver Signature

COMPLETE SET (530) 25.00 60.00
*STARS: 1.5X TO 4X BASIC CARDS
*ROOKIES: 1.25X TO 3X BASIC
ONE PER PACK/TWO PER MINI JUMBO
TWELVE PER SUPER PACK

1995 Collector's Choice Crash the All-Star Game

COMPLETE SET (8) 6.00 15.00
*REDEMPTION WINNERS: 3X VALUE
1 Albert Belle .30 .75
2 Barry Bonds 1.50 4.00
3 Fred McGriff .40 1.00
4 Mark McGwire 1.50 4.00
5 Raul Mondesi .20 .50
6 Mike Piazza 1.50 4.00
7 Manny Ramirez .75 2.00
8 Frank Thomas .60 1.50

1995 Collector's Choice Crash the Game

COMPLETE SET (60) 12.50 30.00
STATED ODDS 1:15
*GOLD: 2X TO 5X SILVER CRASH
GOLD: RANDOM INSERTS IN PACKS
THREE DATES PER PLAYER
*EXCHANGE: .2X TO .5X SILVER CRASH
ONE EXCH.SET VIA MAIL PER WINNER
*GOLD EXCH: 1.5X TO 4X SILVER CRASH
ONE EXCH.SET VIA MAIL PER WINNER
CG1 Jeff Bagwell .10 .30
CG1B Jeff Bagwell 8/13 .10 .30
CG1C Jeff Bagwell 9/28 .10 .30
CG2 Albert Belle .07 .20
CG2B Albert Belle 8/26 .07 .20
CG2C Albert Belle 9/20 .07 .20
CG3 Barry Bonds .60 1.50
CG3B Barry Bonds 7/9 .60 1.50
CG3C Barry Bonds 9/6 .60 1.50
CG4 Jose Canseco .10 .30
CG4B Jose Canseco 7/30 W .10 .30
CG4C Jose Canseco 9/3 .10 .30
CG5 Joe Carter .07 .20
CG5B Joe Carter 8/9 .07 .20
CG5C Joe Carter 9/23 .07 .20
CG6 Cecil Fielder .07 .20
CG6B Cecil Fielder 8/2 .07 .20
CG6C Cecil Fielder 10/1 .07 .20
CG7 Juan Gonzalez .07 .20
CG7B Juan Gonzalez 8/13 .07 .20
CG7C Juan Gonzalez 9/3 W .07 .20
CG8 Ken Griffey Jr. .40 1.00
CG8B K.Griffey Jr. 8/24 W .40 1.00
CG8C K.Griffey Jr. 9/15 .40 1.00
CG9 Bob Hamelin .02 .10
CG9B Bob Hamelin 8/1 .02 .10
CG9C Bob Hamelin 9/29 .02 .10
CG10 David Justice .07 .20
CG10B David Justice 7/25 .07 .20
CG10C David Justice 9/17 .07 .20
CG11 Ryan Klesko .07 .20
CG11B Ryan Klesko 8/20 .07 .20
CG11C Ryan Klesko 9/10 .07 .20
CG12 Fred McGriff .10 .30
CG12B Fred McGriff 9/8 .10 .30
CG12C Fred McGriff 9/24 .10 .30
CG13 Mark McGwire .50 1.25
CG13B Mark McGwire 8/3 W .50 1.25
CG13C Mark McGwire 9/27 .50 1.25
CG14 Raul Mondesi .07 .20
CG14B Raul Mondesi 8/13 .07 .20
CG14C Raul Mondesi 9/15 W .07 .20
CG15 Mike Piazza .30 .75
CG15B Mike Piazza 8/27 W .30 .75
CG15C Mike Piazza 9/19 .30 .75
CG16 Manny Ramirez .10 .30
CG16B Manny Ramirez 8/13 .10 .30
CG16C Manny Ramirez 9/26 .10 .30
CG17 Alex Rodriguez 9/10 .50 1.25
CG17B Alex Rodriguez 9/18 .50 1.25
CG17C Alex Rodriguez 9/24 .50 1.25
CG18 Gary Sheffield .07 .20
CG18B Gary Sheffield 8/13 .07 .20
CG18C Gary Sheffield 9/4 W .07 .20
CG19 Frank Thomas .20 .50
CG19B Frank Thomas 8/17 .20 .50
CG19C Frank Thomas 9/23 .20 .50
CG20 Matt Williams .07 .20
CG20B Matt Williams 8/12 .07 .20
CG20C Matt Williams 9/19 .07 .20

1995 Collector's Choice Trade Cards

COMPLETE SET (5) 1.50 4.00
RANDOM INSERTS IN PACKS
TC1 Larry Walker .50 1.25
TC2 David Cone .50 1.25
TC3 Marquis Grissom .50 1.25
TC4 Terry Pendleton .50 1.25
TC5 F.Valenzuela .50 1.25

1996 Collector's Choice

This 790-card standard-size set (produced by Upper Deck) was issued in 12-card packs with 36 packs per box and 20 boxes per case. Suggested retail price on these packs was 99 cents. The fronts of the regular set feature a player photo, his name and team logo. The backs feature another photo, vital stats and a baseball quiz. The set includes the following subsets: 1995 Stat Leaders (2-9), Rookie Class (10-39), Traditional Threads (100-108), Fantasy Team (268-279), International Flavor (325-342), Series 1 Checklists (358-365), Team Checklists (396-423), First HOF Class (500-504), Arizona Fall League (650-666), Award Winners (704-711) and Series 2 Checklists (753-760). Postseason Trade cards were inserted one every 11 packs. These cards had an ordering deadline of May 13 and were each redeemable for 10 cards depicting highlights from the playoffs and World Series, resulting in a 30-card redemption set. Finally, a 30-card Update set was included in each factory set and was also available through a Series 2 wrapper offer. The Cal Ripken Collection cards inserted into these packs, are priced in the Upper Deck area as Upper Deck Ripken Collection. Please check that section for pricing on this set. Notable Rookie Cards include Mike Sweeney.

COMPLETE SET (730) 10.00 25.00
COMP.FACT.SET (790) 12.50 30.00
COMPLETE SERIES 1 (365) 5.00 12.00
COMPLETE SERIES 2 (365) 5.00 12.00
COMMON (1-365/396-760) .07 .20
SUBSET CARDS HALF VALUE OF BASE CARDS
COMP.TRADE SET (30) 6.00 15.00
COMMON TRADE (366T-395T) .15 .40
TEN TRADE CARDS PER TRADE EXCH.CARD
SER.1 TRADE EXCH.STATED ODDS 1:11
COMP.UPDATE SET (30) 2.00 4.00
COMMON UPDATE (761-790) .15 .40
ONE UPDATE SET VIA SER.2 WRAP.OFFER
ONE UPDATE SET PER FACTORY SET
1 Cal Ripken .60 1.50
2 E.Martinez .07 .20
T.Gwynn SL
3 A.Belle .07 .20
D.Bichette SL
4 Belle .07 .20
Vaughn
Bichette SL
5 K.Lofton .07 .20
Q.Veras SL
6 M.Mussina .20 .50
G.Maddux SL
7 R.Johnson .20 .50
H.Nomo SL
8 R.Johnson .20 .50
G.Maddux SL
9 J.Mesa .07 .20
R.Myers SL
10 Johnny Damon .10 .30
11 Rick Krivda .07 .20
12 Roger Cedeno .07 .20
13 Angel Martinez .07 .20
14 Ariel Prieto .07 .20
15 John Wasdin .07 .20
16 Edwin Hurtado .07 .20
17 Lyle Mouton .07 .20
18 Chris Snopek .07 .20
19 Mariano Rivera .40 1.00
20 Ruben Rivera .07 .20
21 Juan Castro RC .07 .20
22 Jimmy Haynes .07 .20
23 Bob Wolcott .07 .20
24 Brian Barber .07 .20
25 Frank Rodriguez .07 .20
26 Jesus Tavarez .07 .20
27 Glenn Dishman .07 .20
28 Jose Herrera .07 .20
29 Chan Ho Park .07 .20
30 Jason Isringhausen .07 .20
31 Doug Johns .07 .20
32 Gene Schall .07 .20
33 Kevin Jordan .07 .20
34 Matt Lawton RC .08 .25
35 Karim Garcia .07 .20
36 George Williams .07 .20
37 Orlando Palmeiro .07 .20
38 Jamie Brewington RC .07 .20
39 Robert Person .07 .20
40 Greg Maddux .30 .75
41 Marquis Grissom .07 .20
42 Chipper Jones .20 .50
43 David Justice .07 .20
44 Mark Lemke .07 .20
45 Fred McGriff .10 .30
46 Javier Lopez .07 .20
47 Mark Wohlers .07 .20
48 Jason Schmidt .10 .30
49 John Smoltz .10 .30
50 Curtis Goodwin .07 .20
51 Greg Zaun .07 .20
52 Armando Benitez .07 .20
53 Manny Alexander .07 .20
54 Chris Hoiles .07 .20
55 Harold Baines .07 .20
56 Ben McDonald .07 .20
57 Scott Erickson .07 .20
58 Jeff Manto .07 .20
59 Luis Alicea .07 .20
60 Roger Clemens .40 1.00
61 Rheal Cormier .07 .20
62 Vaughn Eshelman .07 .20
63 Zane Smith .07 .20
64 Mike Macfarlane .07 .20
65 Erik Hanson .07 .20
66 Tim Naehring .07 .20
67 Lee Tinsley .07 .20
68 Troy O'Leary .07 .20
69 Garret Anderson .07 .20
70 Chili Davis .07 .20
71 Jim Edmonds .07 .20
72 Troy Percival .07 .20
73 Mark Langston .07 .20
74 Spike Owen .07 .20
75 Tim Salmon .10 .30
76 Brian Anderson .07 .20
77 Lee Smith .07 .20
78 Jim Abbott .10 .30
79 Jim Bullinger .07 .20
80 Mark Grace .10 .30
81 Todd Zeile .07 .20
82 Kevin Foster .07 .20
83 Howard Johnson .07 .20
84 Brian McRae .07 .20
85 Randy Myers .07 .20
86 Jaime Navarro .07 .20
87 Luis Gonzalez .07 .20
88 Ozzie Timmons .07 .20
89 Wilson Alvarez .07 .20
90 Frank Thomas .20 .50
91 James Baldwin .07 .20
92 Ray Durham .07 .20
93 Alex Fernandez .07 .20
94 Ozzie Guillen .07 .20
95 Tim Raines .07 .20
96 Roberto Hernandez .07 .20
97 Lance Johnson .07 .20
98 John Kruk .07 .20
99 Mark Portugal .07 .20
100 Don Mattingly TT .25 .60
101 Roger Clemens TT .20 .50
102 Raul Mondesi TT .07 .20
103 Cecil Fielder TT .07 .20
104 Ozzie Smith TT .20 .50
105 Frank Thomas TT .10 .30
106 Sammy Sosa TT .10 .30
107 Fred McGriff TT .07 .20
108 Barry Bonds TT .30 .75
109 Thomas Howard .07 .20
110 Ron Gant .07 .20
111 Eddie Taubensee .07 .20
112 Hal Morris .07 .20
113 Jose Rijo .07 .20
114 Pete Schourek .07 .20
115 Reggie Sanders .07 .20
116 Benito Santiago .07 .20
117 Jeff Brantley .07 .20
118 Julian Tavarez .07 .20
119 Carlos Baerga .07 .20
120 Jim Thome .10 .30
121 Jose Mesa .07 .20
122 Dennis Martinez .07 .20
123 Dave Winfield .07 .20
124 Eddie Murray .20 .50
125 Manny Ramirez .10 .30
126 Paul Sorrento .07 .20
127 Kenny Lofton .07 .20
128 Eric Young .07 .20
129 Jason Bates .07 .20
130 Bret Saberhagen .07 .20
131 Andres Galarraga .07 .20
132 Joe Girardi .07 .20
133 John Vander Wal .07 .20
134 David Nied .07 .20
135 Dante Bichette .07 .20
136 Vinny Castilla .07 .20
137 Kevin Ritz .07 .20
138 Felipe Lira .07 .20
139 Joe Boever .07 .20
140 Cecil Fielder .07 .20
141 John Flaherty .07 .20
142 Kirk Gibson .07 .20
143 Brian Maxcy .07 .20
144 Lou Whitaker .07 .20
145 Alan Trammell .07 .20
146 Bobby Higginson .07 .20
147 Chad Curtis .07 .20
148 Quilvio Veras .07 .20
149 Jerry Browne .07 .20
150 Andre Dawson .07 .20
151 Robb Nen .07 .20
152 Greg Colbrunn .07 .20
153 Chris Hammond .07 .20
154 Kurt Abbott .07 .20
155 Charles Johnson .07 .20
156 Terry Pendleton .07 .20
157 Dave Weathers .07 .20
158 Mike Hampton .07 .20
159 Craig Biggio .10 .30
160 Jeff Bagwell .10 .30
161 Brian L.Hunter .07 .20
162 Mike Henneman .07 .20
163 Dave Magadan .07 .20
164 Shane Reynolds .07 .20
165 Derek Bell .07 .20
166 Orlando Miller .07 .20
167 James Mouton .07 .20
168 Melvin Bunch .07 .20
169 Tom Gordon .07 .20
170 Kevin Appier .07 .20
171 Tom Goodwin .07 .20
172 Greg Gagne .07 .20
173 Gary Gaetti .07 .20
174 Jeff Montgomery .07 .20
175 Jon Nunnally .07 .20
176 Michael Tucker .07 .20
177 Joe Vitiello .07 .20
178 Billy Ashley .07 .20
179 Tom Candiotti .07 .20
180 Hideo Nomo .20 .50
181 Chad Fonville .07 .20
182 Todd Hollandsworth .07 .20
183 Eric Karros .07 .20
184 Roberto Kelly .07 .20
185 Mike Piazza .30 .75
186 Ramon Martinez .07 .20
187 Tim Wallach .07 .20
188 Jeff Cirillo .07 .20
189 Sid Roberson .07 .20
190 Kevin Seitzer .07 .20
191 Mike Fetters .07 .20
192 Steve Sparks .07 .20
193 Matt Mieske .07 .20
194 Joe Oliver .07 .20
195 B.J. Surhoff .07 .20
196 Alberto Reyes .07 .20
197 Fernando Vina .07 .20
198 LaTroy Hawkins .07 .20
199 Marty Cordova .07 .20
200 Kirby Puckett .20 .50
201 Brad Radke .07 .20
202 Pedro Munoz .07 .20
203 Scott Klingenbeck .07 .20
204 Pat Meares .07 .20
205 Chuck Knoblauch .07 .20
206 Scott Stahoviak .07 .20
207 Dave Stevens .07 .20
208 Shane Andrews .07 .20
209 Moises Alou .07 .20
210 David Segui .07 .20
211 Cliff Floyd .07 .20
212 Carlos Perez .07 .20
213 Mark Grudzielanek .07 .20
214 Butch Henry .07 .20
215 Rondell White .07 .20
216 Mel Rojas .07 .20
217 Ugueth Urbina .07 .20
218 Edgardo Alfonzo .07 .20
219 Carl Everett .07 .20
220 John Franco .07 .20
221 Todd Hundley .07 .20
222 Bobby Jones .07 .20
223 Bill Pulsipher .07 .20
224 Rico Brogna .07 .20
225 Jeff Kent .07 .20
226 Chris Jones .07 .20
227 Butch Huskey .07 .20
228 Robert Eenhoorn .07 .20
229 Sterling Hitchcock .07 .20
230 Wade Boggs .10 .30
231 Derek Jeter .50 1.25
232 Tony Fernandez .07 .20
233 Jack McDowell .07 .20
234 Andy Pettitte .10 .30
235 David Cone .07 .20
236 Mike Stanley .07 .20
237 Don Mattingly .50 1.25
238 Geronimo Berroa .07 .20
239 Scott Brosius .07 .20
240 Rickey Henderson .20 .50
241 Terry Steinbach .07 .20
242 Mike Gallego .07 .20
243 Jason Giambi .07 .20
244 Steve Ontiveros .07 .20
245 Dennis Eckersley .07 .20
246 Dave Stewart .07 .20
247 Don Wengert .07 .20
248 Paul Quantrill .07 .20
249 Ricky Bottalico .07 .20
250 Kevin Stocker .07 .20
251 Lenny Dykstra .07 .20
252 Tony Longmire .07 .20
253 Tyler Green .07 .20
254 Mike Williams .07 .20
255 Charlie Hayes .07 .20
256 Mickey Morandini .07 .20
257 Heathcliff Slocumb .07 .20
258 Jeff King .07 .20
259 Midre Cummings .07 .20
260 Mark Johnson .07 .20
261 Freddy Adrian Garcia .07 .20
262 Jon Lieber .07 .20
263 Esteban Loaiza .07 .20
264 Dan Miceli .07 .20
265 Orlando Merced .07 .20
266 Denny Neagle .07 .20
267 Steve Parris .07 .20
268 Greg Maddux FT .20 .50
269 Randy Johnson FT .10 .30
270 Hideo Nomo FT .10 .30
271 Jose Mesa FT .07 .20
272 Mike Piazza FT .20 .50
273 Mo Vaughn FT .07 .20
274 Craig Biggio FT .07 .20
275 Edgar Martinez FT .07 .20
276 Barry Larkin FT .07 .20
277 Sammy Sosa FT .10 .30
278 Dante Bichette FT .07 .20
279 Albert Belle FT .07 .20
280 Ozzie Smith .30 .75
281 Mark Sweeney .07 .20
282 Terry Bradshaw .07 .20
283 Allen Battle .07 .20
284 Danny Jackson .07 .20
285 Tom Henke .07 .20
286 Scott Cooper .07 .20
287 Tripp Cromer .07 .20
288 Bernard Gilkey .07 .20
289 Brian Jordan .07 .20
290 Tony Gwynn .25 .60
291 Brad Ausmus .07 .20
292 Bryce Florie .07 .20
293 Andres Berumen .07 .20
294 Ken Caminiti .07 .20
295 Bip Roberts .07 .20
296 Trevor Hoffman .07 .20
297 Roberto Petagine .07 .20
298 Jody Reed .07 .20
299 Fernando Valenzuela .07 .20
300 Barry Bonds .60 1.50
301 Mark Leiter .07 .20
302 Mark Carreon .07 .20
303 Royce Clayton .07 .20
304 Kirt Manwaring .07 .20
305 Glenallen Hill .07 .20
306 Deion Sanders .10 .30
307 Joe Rosselli .07 .20
308 Robby Thompson .07 .20
309 W. VanLandingham .07 .20
310 Ken Griffey Jr. .40 1.00
311 Bobby Ayala .07 .20
312 Joey Cora .07 .20
313 Mike Blowers .07 .20
314 Darren Bragg .07 .20
315 Randy Johnson .20 .50
316 Alex Rodriguez .40 1.00
317 Andy Benes .15 .40
318 Tino Martinez .10 .30
319 Dan Wilson .07 .20
320 Will Clark .10 .30
321 Jeff Frye .07 .20
322 Benji Gil .07 .20
323 Rick Helling .07 .20
324 Mark McLemore .07 .20
325 Dave Nilsson IF .07 .20
326 Larry Walker IF .07 .20
327 Jose Canseco IF .07 .20
328 Raul Mondesi IF .07 .20
329 Manny Ramirez IF .07 .20
330 Robert Eenhoorn IF .07 .20
331 Chili Davis IF .07 .20
332 Hideo Nomo IF .10 .30
333 Benji Gil IF .07 .20
334 Fernando Valenzuela IF .07 .20
335 Dennis Martinez IF .07 .20
336 Roberto Kelly IF .07 .20
337 Carlos Baerga IF .07 .20
338 Juan Gonzalez IF .07 .20
339 Roberto Alomar IF .07 .20
340 Chan Ho Park IF .07 .20
341 Andres Galarraga IF .07 .20
342 Midre Cummings IF .07 .20
343 Otis Nixon .07 .20
344 Jeff Russell .07 .20
345 Ivan Rodriguez .10 .30
346 Mickey Tettleton .07 .20
347 Bob Tewksbury .07 .20
348 Domingo Cedeno .07 .20
349 Lance Parrish .07 .20
350 Joe Carter .07 .20
351 Devon White .07 .20
352 Carlos Delgado .07 .20
353 Alex Gonzalez .07 .20
354 Darren Hall .07 .20
355 Paul Molitor .07 .20
356 Al Leiter .07 .20
357 Randy Knorr .07 .20
358 Cam .07 .20
Fin
Wil
Pet
Ced
Pla
Bel
Mar
Bro
Shi
Gut CL
359 Hideo Nomo CL .10 .30
360 R.Martinez .07 .20
R.Martinez CL
361 Robin Ventura CL .07 .20
362 Cal Ripken CL .30 .75
363 Ken Caminiti CL .07 .20
364 A.Belle .10 .30
E.Murray CL
365 Randy Johnson CL .10 .30
366T Tony Pena TRADE .15 .40
367T Jim Thome TRADE .25 .60
368T Don Mattingly TRADE 1.00 2.50
369T Jim Leyritz TRADE .15 .40
370T Ken Griffey Jr. TRADE .75 2.00
371T Edgar Martinez TRADE .25 .60
372T Pete Schourek TRADE .15 .40
373T Mark Lewis TRADE .15 .40
374T Chipper Jones TRADE .40 1.00
375T Fred McGriff TRADE .25 .60
376T Javy Lopez TRADE .15 .40
377T Fred McGriff TRADE .25 .60
378T Charlie O'Brien TRADE .15 .40
379T Mike Devereaux TRADE .15 .40
380T Mark Wohlers TRADE .15 .40
381T Bob Wolcott TRADE .15 .40
382T Manny Ramirez TRADE .25 .60
383T Jay Buhner TRADE .15 .40
384T Orel Hershiser TRADE .15 .40
385T Kenny Lofton TRADE .15 .40
386T Greg Maddux TRADE .60 1.50
387T Javier Lopez TRADE .15 .40
388T Kenny Lofton TRADE .15 .40
389T Eddie Murray TRADE .40 1.00
390T Luis Polonia TRADE .15 .40
391T Pedro Borbon TRADE .15 .40
392T Jim Thome TRADE .25 .60

393T Orel Hershiser TRADE .15 .40
394T David Justice TRADE .15 .40
395T Tom Glavine TRADE .25 .60
396 Greg Maddux TC .20 .50
397 Rico Brogna TC .07 .20
398 Darren Daulton TC .07 .20
399 Gary Sheffield TC .07 .20
400 Moises Alou TC .07 .20
401 Barry Larkin TC .07 .20
402 Jeff Bagwell TC .07 .20
403 Sammy Sosa TC .10 .30
404 Ozzie Smith TC .20 .50
405 Jay Bell TC .07 .20
406 Mike Piazza TC .20 .50
407 Dante Bichette TC .07 .20
408 Tony Gwynn TC .10 .30
409 Barry Bonds TC .30 .75
410 Kenny Lofton TC .07 .20
411 Johnny Damon TC .07 .20
412 Frank Thomas TC .10 .30
413 Greg Vaughn TC .07 .20
414 Paul Molitor TC .07 .20
415 Ken Griffey Jr. TC .25 .60
416 Tim Salmon TC .07 .20
417 Juan Gonzalez TC .07 .20
418 Mark McGwire TC .25 .60
419 Roger Clemens TC .20 .50
420 Wade Boggs TC .07 .20
421 Cal Ripken TC .30 .75
422 Cecil Fielder TC .07 .20
423 Joe Carter TC .07 .20
424 Osvaldo Fernandez RC .07 .20
425 Billy Wagner .07 .20
426 George Arias .07 .20
427 Mendy Lopez .07 .20
428 Jeff Suppan .07 .20
429 Rey Ordonez .07 .20
430 Brooks Kieschnick .07 .20
431 Raul Ibanez RC .75 2.00
432 Livan Hernandez RC .30 .75
433 Shannon Stewart .07 .20
434 Steve Cox .07 .20
435 Trey Beamon .07 .20
436 Sergio Nunez .07 .20
437 Jermaine Dye .07 .20
438 Mike Sweeney RC .30 .75
439 Richard Hidalgo .07 .20
440 Todd Greene .07 .20
441 Robert Smith RC .07 .20
442 Rafael Orellano .07 .20
443 Wilton Guerrero RC .07 .20
444 David Doster .07 .20
445 Jason Kendall .07 .20
446 Edgar Renteria .07 .20
447 Scott Spiezio .07 .20
448 Jay Canizaro .07 .20
449 Enrique Wilson .07 .20
450 Bob Abreu .20 .50
451 Dwight Smith .07 .20
452 Jeff Blauser .07 .20
453 Steve Avery .07 .20
454 Brad Clontz .07 .20
455 Tom Glavine .10 .30
456 Mike Mordecai .07 .20
457 Rafael Belliard .07 .20
458 Greg McMichael .07 .20
459 Pedro Borbon .07 .20
460 Ryan Klesko .07 .20
461 Terrell Wade .07 .20
462 Brady Anderson .07 .20
463 Roberto Alomar .10 .30
464 Bobby Bonilla .07 .20
465 Mike Mussina .10 .30
466 Cesar Devarez .07 .20
467 Jeffrey Hammonds .07 .20
468 Mike Devereaux .07 .20
469 B.J. Surhoff .07 .20
470 Rafael Palmeiro .10 .30
471 John Valentin .07 .20
472 Mike Greenwell .07 .20
473 Dwayne Hosey .07 .20
474 Tim Wakefield .07 .20
475 Jose Canseco .10 .30
476 Aaron Sele .07 .20
477 Stan Belinda .07 .20
478 Mike Stanley .07 .20
479 Jamie Moyer .07 .20
480 Mo Vaughn .07 .20
481 Randy Velarde .07 .20
482 Gary DiSarcina .07 .20
483 Jorge Fabregas .07 .20
484 Rex Hudler .07 .20
485 Chuck Finley .07 .20
486 Tim Wallach .07 .20
487 Eduardo Perez .07 .20
488 Scott Sanderson .07 .20
489 J.T. Snow .07 .20
490 Sammy Sosa .20 .50
491 Terry Adams .07 .20
492 Matt Franco RC .07 .20
493 Scott Servais .07 .20
494 Frank Castillo .07 .20
495 Ryne Sandberg .30 .75
496 Rey Sanchez .07 .20
497 Steve Trachsel .07 .20
498 Jose Hernandez .07 .20
499 Dave Martinez .07 .20
500 Babe Ruth FC .40 1.00
501 Ty Cobb FC .20 .50
502 Walter Johnson FC .20 .50
503 Christy Mathewson FC .20 .50
504 Honus Wagner FC .20 .50
505 Robin Ventura .07 .20
506 Jason Bere .07 .20
507 Mike Cameron RC .20 .50
508 Ron Karkovice .07 .20
509 Matt Karchner .07 .20
510 Harold Baines .07 .20
511 Kirk McCaskill .07 .20
512 Larry Thomas .07 .20
513 Danny Tartabull .07 .20
514 Steve Gibralter .07 .20
515 Bret Boone .07 .20
516 Jeff Branson .07 .20
517 Kevin Jarvis .07 .20
518 Xavier Hernandez .07 .20
519 Eric Owens .07 .20
520 Barry Larkin .10 .30
521 Dave Burba .07 .20
522 John Smiley .07 .20
523 Paul Assenmacher .07 .20
524 Chad Ogea .07 .20
525 Orel Hershiser .07 .20
526 Alan Embree .07 .20
527 Tony Pena .07 .20
528 Omar Vizquel .10 .30
529 Mark Clark .07 .20
530 Albert Belle .07 .20
531 Charles Nagy .07 .20
532 Herbert Perry .07 .20
533 Darren Holmes .07 .20
534 Ellis Burks .07 .20
535 Billy Swift .07 .20
536 Armando Reynoso .07 .20
537 Curtis Leskanic .07 .20
538 Quinton McCracken .07 .20
539 Steve Reed .07 .20
540 Larry Walker .07 .20
541 Walt Weiss .07 .20
542 Bryan Rekar .07 .20
543 Tony Clark .07 .20
544 Steve Rodriguez .07 .20
545 C.J. Nitkowski .07 .20
546 Todd Steverson .07 .20
547 Jose Lima .07 .20
548 Phil Nevin .07 .20
549 Chris Gomez .07 .20
550 Travis Fryman .07 .20
551 Mark Lewis .07 .20
552 Alex Arias .07 .20
553 Marc Valdes .07 .20
554 Kevin Brown .07 .20
555 Jeff Conine .07 .20
556 John Burkett .07 .20
557 Devon White .07 .20
558 Pat Rapp .07 .20
559 Jay Powell .07 .20
560 Gary Sheffield .07 .20
561 Jim Dougherty .07 .20
562 Todd Jones .07 .20
563 Tony Eusebio .07 .20
564 Darryl Kile .07 .20
565 Doug Drabek .07 .20
566 Mike Simms .07 .20
567 Derrick May .07 .20
568 Donne Wall .07 .20
569 Greg Swindell .07 .20
570 Jim Pittsley .07 .20
571 Bob Hamelin .07 .20
572 Mark Gubicza .07 .20
573 Chris Haney .07 .20
574 Keith Lockhart .07 .20
575 Mike Macfarlane .07 .20
576 Les Norman .07 .20
577 Joe Randa .07 .20
578 Chris Stynes .07 .20
579 Greg Gagne .07 .20
580 Raul Mondesi .07 .20
581 Delino DeShields .07 .20
582 Pedro Astacio .07 .20
583 Antonio Osuna .07 .20
584 Brett Butler .07 .20
585 Todd Worrell .07 .20
586 Mike Blowers .07 .20
587 Felix Rodriguez .07 .20
588 Ismael Valdes .07 .20
589 Ricky Bones .07 .20
590 Greg Vaughn .07 .20
591 Mark Loretta .07 .20
592 Cal Eldred .07 .20
593 Chuck Carr .07 .20
594 Dave Nilsson .07 .20
595 John Jaha .07 .20
596 Scott Karl .07 .20
597 Pat Listach .07 .20
598 Jose Valentin .07 .20
599 Mike Trombley .07 .20
600 Paul Molitor .07 .20
601 Dave Hollins .07 .20
602 Ron Coomer .07 .20
603 Matt Walbeck .07 .20
604 Roberto Kelly .07 .20
605 Rick Aguilera .07 .20
606 Pat Mahomes .07 .20
607 Jeff Reboulet .07 .20
608 Rich Becker .07 .20
609 Tim Scott .07 .20
610 Pedro Martinez .10 .30
611 Kirk Rueter .07 .20
612 Tavo Alvarez .07 .20
613 Yamil Benitez .07 .20
614 Darrin Fletcher .07 .20
615 Mike Lansing .07 .20
616 Henry Rodriguez .07 .20
617 Tony Tarasco .07 .20
618 Alex Ochoa .07 .20
619 Tim Bogar .07 .20
620 Bernard Gilkey .07 .20
621 Dave Mlicki .07 .20
622 Brent Mayne .07 .20
623 Ryan Thompson .07 .20
624 Pete Harnisch .07 .20
625 Lance Johnson .07 .20
626 Jose Vizcaino .07 .20
627 Doug Henry .07 .20
628 Scott Kamieniecki .07 .20
629 Jim Leyritz .07 .20
630 Ruben Sierra .07 .20
631 Pat Kelly .07 .20
632 Joe Girardi .07 .20
633 John Wetteland .07 .20
634 Melido Perez .07 .20
635 Paul O'Neill .10 .30
636 Jorge Posada .10 .30
637 Bernie Williams .10 .30
638 Mark Acre .07 .20
639 Mike Bordick .07 .20
640 Mark McGwire .50 1.25
641 Fausto Cruz .07 .20
642 Ernie Young .07 .20
643 Todd Van Poppel .07 .20
644 Craig Paquette .07 .20
645 Brent Gates .07 .20
646 Pedro Munoz .07 .20
647 Andrew Lorraine .07 .20
648 Sid Fernandez .07 .20
649 Jim Eisenreich .07 .20
650 Johnny Damon AFL .07 .20
651 Dustin Hermanson AFL .07 .20
652 Joe Randa AFL .07 .20
653 Michael Tucker AFL .07 .20
654 Alan Benes AFL .07 .20
655 Chad Fonville AFL .07 .20
656 David Bell AFL .07 .20
657 Jon Nunnally AFL .07 .20
658 Chan Ho Park AFL .07 .20
659 LaTroy Hawkins AFL .07 .20
660 Jamie Brewington AFL .07 .20
661 Quinton McCracken AFL .07 .20
662 Tim Unroe AFL .07 .20
663 Jeff Ware AFL .07 .20
664 Todd Greene AFL .07 .20
665 Andrew Lorraine AFL .07 .20
666 Ernie Young AFL .07 .20
667 Toby Borland .07 .20
668 Lenny Webster .07 .20
669 Benito Santiago .07 .20
670 Gregg Jefferies .07 .20
671 Darren Daulton .07 .20
672 Curt Schilling .07 .20
673 Mark Whiten .07 .20
674 Todd Zeile .07 .20
675 Jay Bell .07 .20
676 Paul Wagner .07 .20
677 Dave Clark .07 .20
678 Nelson Liriano .07 .20
679 Ramon Morel .07 .20
680 Charlie Hayes .07 .20
681 Angelo Encarnacion .07 .20
682 Al Martin .07 .20
683 Jacob Brumfield .07 .20
684 Mike Kingery .07 .20
685 Carlos Garcia .07 .20
686 Tom Pagnozzi .07 .20
687 David Bell .07 .20
688 Todd Stottlemyre .07 .20
689 Jose Oliva .07 .20
690 Ray Lankford .07 .20
691 Mike Morgan .07 .20
692 John Frascatore .07 .20
693 John Mabry .07 .20
694 Mark Petkovsek .07 .20
695 Alan Benes .07 .20
696 Steve Finley .07 .20
697 Marc Newfield .07 .20
698 Andy Ashby .07 .20
699 Marc Kroon .07 .20
700 Wally Joyner .07 .20
701 Joey Hamilton .07 .20
702 Dustin Hermanson .07 .20
703 Scott Sanders .07 .20
704 Marty Cordova ROY .07 .20
705 Hideo Nomo ROY .10 .30
706 Mo Vaughn MVP .07 .20
707 Barry Larkin MVP .07 .20
708 Randy Johnson CY .10 .30
709 Greg Maddux CY .20 .50
710 Mark McGwire CB .25 .60
711 Ron Gant CB .07 .20
712 Andujar Cedeno .07 .20
713 Brian Johnson .07 .20
714 J.R. Phillips .07 .20
715 Rod Beck .07 .20
716 Sergio Valdez .07 .20
717 Marvin Benard RC .08 .25
718 Steve Scarsone .07 .20
719 Rich Aurilia RC .08 .25
720 Matt Williams .07 .20
721 John Patterson .07 .20
722 Shawn Estes .07 .20
723 Russ Davis .07 .20
724 Rich Amaral .07 .20
725 Edgar Martinez .10 .30
726 Norm Charlton .07 .20
727 Paul Sorrento .07 .20
728 Luis Sojo .07 .20
729 Arquimedez Pozo .07 .20
730 Jay Buhner .07 .20
731 Chris Bosio .07 .20
732 Chris Widger .07 .20
733 Kevin Gross .07 .20
734 Darren Oliver .07 .20
735 Dean Palmer .07 .20
736 Matt Whiteside .07 .20
737 Luis Ortiz .07 .20
738 Roger Pavlik .07 .20
739 Damon Buford .07 .20
740 Juan Gonzalez .07 .20
741 Rusty Greer .07 .20
742 Lou Frazier .07 .20
743 Pat Hentgen .07 .20
744 Tomas Perez .07 .20
745 Juan Guzman .07 .20
746 Otis Nixon .07 .20
747 Robert Perez .07 .20
748 Ed Sprague .07 .20
749 Tony Castillo .07 .20
750 John Olerud .07 .20
751 Shawn Green .07 .20
752 Jeff Ware .07 .20
753 Bich .07 .20
Cast
Gala
Walk CL
754 Greg Maddux CL .20 .50
755 Marty Cordova CL .07 .20
756 Ozzie Smith CL .20 .50
757 John Vander Wal CL .07 .20
758 Andres Galarraga CL .07 .20
759 Frank Thomas CL .10 .30
760 Tony Gwynn CL .10 .30
761 Randy Myers UPD .15 .40
762 Kent Mercker UPD .15 .40
763 David Wells UPD .15 .40
764 Tom Gordon UPD .15 .40
765 Wil Cordero UPD .15 .40
766 Dave Magadan UPD .15 .40
767 Doug Jones UPD .15 .40
768 Kevin Tapani UPD .15 .40
769 Curtis Goodwin UPD .15 .40
770 Julio Franco UPD .15 .40
771 Jack McDowell UPD .15 .40
772 Al Leiter UPD .15 .40
773 Sean Berry UPD .15 .40
774 Bip Roberts UPD .15 .40
775 Jose Offerman UPD .15 .40
776 Ben McDonald UPD .15 .40
777 Dan Serafini UPD .15 .40
778 Ryan McGuire UPD .15 .40
779 Tim Raines UPD .15 .40
780 Tino Martinez UPD .25 .60
781 Kenny Rogers UPD .15 .40
782 Bob Tewksbury UPD .15 .40
783 Rickey Henderson UPD .40 1.00
784 Ron Gant UPD .15 .40
785 Gary Gaetti UPD .15 .40
786 Andy Benes UPD .15 .40
787 Royce Clayton UPD .15 .40
788 Darryl Hamilton UPD .15 .40
789 Ken Hill UPD .15 .40
790 Erik Hanson UPD .15 .40
P100 Ken Griffey Jr. Promo .50 1.25

1996 Collector's Choice Gold Signature

*STARS: 12X TO 30X BASIC CARDS
*ROOKIES: 8X TO 20X BASIC CARDS
STATED ODDS 1:35

1996 Collector's Choice Silver Signature

COMPLETE SET (730) 60.00 120.00
COMPLETE SERIES 1 (365) 30.00 80.00
COMPLETE SERIES 2 (365) 25.00 60.00
*STARS: 1X TO 2.5X BASIC CARDS
*ROOKIES: .75X TO 2X BASIC CARDS
ONE PER PACK

1996 Collector's Choice Crash the Game

COMPLETE SET (90) 20.00 50.00
SER.2 STATED ODDS 1:5
*GOLD: 2X TO 5X BASIC CRASH
GOLD SER.2 STATED ODDS 1:48
THREE DATES PER PLAYER
*EXCH: 2X TO 5X BASIC CRASH
ONE EXCH.CARD VIA MAIL PER WINNER
*GOLD EXCH: 6X TO 15X BASIC CRASH
ONE EXCH.VIA MAIL PER GOLD WINNER
CG1 Chipper Jones .30 .75
CG1B Chipper Jones .30 .75
CG1C Chipper Jones .30 .75
CG2 Fred McGriff .20 .50
CG2B Fred McGriff .20 .50
CG2C Fred McGriff .20 .50
CG3 Rafael Palmeiro .20 .50
CG3B Rafael Palmeiro .20 .50
CG3C Rafael Palmeiro .20 .50
CG4 Cal Ripken 1.00 2.50
CG4B Cal Ripken 1.00 2.50
CG4C Cal Ripken 1.00 2.50
CG5 Jose Canseco .20 .50
CG5B Jose Canseco .20 .50
CG5C Jose Canseco .20 .50
CG6 Mo Vaughn .10 .30
CG6B Mo Vaughn .10 .30
CG6C Mo Vaughn .10 .30
CG7 Jim Edmonds .10 .30
CG7B Jim Edmonds .10 .30
CG7C Jim Edmonds .10 .30
CG8 Tim Salmon .20 .50
CG8B Tim Salmon .20 .50
CG8C Tim Salmon .20 .50
CG9 Sammy Sosa .30 .75
CG9B Sammy Sosa .30 .75
CG9C Sammy Sosa .30 .75
CG10 Frank Thomas .30 .75
CG10B Frank Thomas .30 .75
CG10C Frank Thomas .30 .75
CG11 Albert Belle .10 .30
CG11B Albert Belle .10 .30
CG11C Albert Belle .10 .30
CG12 Manny Ramirez .20 .50
CG12B Manny Ramirez .20 .50
CG12C Manny Ramirez .20 .50
CG13 Jim Thome .20 .50
CG13B Jim Thome .20 .50
CG13C Jim Thome .20 .50
CG14 Dante Bichette .10 .30
CG14B Dante Bichette .10 .30
CG14C Dante Bichette .10 .30
CG15 Vinny Castilla .10 .30
CG15B Vinny Castilla .10 .30
CG15C Vinny Castilla .10 .30
CG16 Larry Walker .10 .30
CG16B Larry Walker .10 .30
CG16C Larry Walker .10 .30
CG17 Cecil Fielder .10 .30
CG17B Cecil Fielder .10 .30
CG17C Cecil Fielder .10 .30
CG18 Gary Sheffield .10 .30
CG18B Gary Sheffield .10 .30
CG18C Gary Sheffield .10 .30
CG19 Jeff Bagwell .20 .50
CG19B Jeff Bagwell .20 .50
CG19C Jeff Bagwell .20 .50
CG20 Eric Karros .10 .30
CG20B Eric Karros .10 .30
CG20C Eric Karros .10 .30
CG21 Mike Piazza .50 1.25
CG21B Mike Piazza .50 1.25
CG21C Mike Piazza .50 1.25
CG22 Ken Caminiti .10 .30
CG22B Ken Caminiti .10 .30
CG22C Ken Caminiti .10 .30
CG23 Barry Bonds 1.00 2.50
CG23B Barry Bonds 1.00 2.50
CG23C Barry Bonds 1.00 2.50
CG24 Matt Williams .10 .30
CG24B Matt Williams .10 .30
CG24C Matt Williams .10 .30
CG25 Jay Buhner .10 .30
CG25B Jay Buhner .10 .30
CG25C Jay Buhner .10 .30
CG26 Ken Griffey Jr. .60 1.50
CG26B Ken Griffey Jr. .60 1.50
CG26C Ken Griffey Jr. .60 1.50
CG27 Ron Gant .10 .30
CG27B Ron Gant .10 .30
CG27C Ron Gant .10 .30
CG28 Juan Gonzalez .10 .30
CG28B Juan Gonzalez .10 .30
CG28C Juan Gonzalez .10 .30
CG29 Mickey Tettleton .10 .30
CG29B Mickey Tettleton .10 .30
CG29C Mickey Tettleton .10 .30
CG30 Joe Carter .10 .30
CG30B Joe Carter .10 .30
CG30C Joe Carter .10 .30

1996 Collector's Choice Griffey A Cut Above

COMPLETE SET (10) 2.50 6.00
COMMON CARD (CA1-CA10) .30 .75
ONE PER SPECIAL RETAIL PACK

1996 Collector's Choice Nomo Scrapbook

COMPLETE SET (5) 1.25 3.00
COMMON CARD (1-5) .40 1.00
SER.2 STATED ODDS 1:12

1996 Collector's Choice You Make the Play

COMPLETE SET (90) 5.00 12.00
ONE BASIC CARD PER SER.1 PACK
*GOLD: 6X TO 15X BASIC PLAY
GOLD SER.1 STATED ODDS 1:35
TWO MAKE THE PLAY CARDS PER PLAYER
EITHER OUTCOME SAME VALUE
1 Kevin Appier .07 .20
2 Carlos Baerga .07 .20
3 Jeff Bagwell .10 .30
4 Jay Bell .07 .20
5 Albert Belle .07 .20
6 Craig Biggio .10 .30
7 Wade Boggs .10 .30
8 Barry Bonds .60 1.50
9 Bobby Bonilla .07 .20
10 Jose Canseco .10 .30
11 Joe Carter .07 .20
12 Darren Daulton .07 .20
13 Cecil Fielder .07 .20
14 Ron Gant .07 .20
15 Juan Gonzalez .07 .20
16 Ken Griffey Jr. .40 1.00
17 Tony Gwynn .25 .60
18 Randy Johnson .20 .50
19 Chipper Jones .20 .50
20 Barry Larkin .10 .30
21 Kenny Lofton .07 .20
22 Greg Maddux .30 .75
23 Don Mattingly .50 1.25
24 Fred McGriff .10 .30
25 Mark McGwire .50 1.25
26 Paul Molitor .07 .20
27 Raul Mondesi .07 .20
28 Eddie Murray .20 .50
29 Hideo Nomo .20 .50
30 Jon Nunnally .07 .20
31 Mike Piazza .30 .75
32 Kirby Puckett .20 .50
33 Cal Ripken .60 1.50
34 Alex Rodriguez .40 1.00
35 Tim Salmon .10 .30
36 Gary Sheffield .07 .20
37 Lee Smith .07 .20
38 Ozzie Smith .30 .75
39 Sammy Sosa .20 .50
40 Frank Thomas .20 .50
41 Greg Vaughn .07 .20
42 Mo Vaughn .07 .20
43 Larry Walker .07 .20
44 Rondell White .07 .20
45 Matt Williams .07 .20

1997 Collector's Choice

This 506-card set (produced by Upper Deck) was distributed in 12-card first series packs with a suggested retail price of $.99 and 14-card second series with a suggested retail price of $1.29. The fronts feature color action player photos while the backs carry player statistics. The first series set contains the following subsets: Rookie Class (1-27), League Leaders (56-63), Postseason (218-224) which recaps action from the 1996 playoffs and World Series Games and Ken Griffey Jr. Checklist (244-249) which also carry collecting tips. The second-series set contains the following: 199 regular player cards, 10 Ken Griffey Jr.'s Hot List (325-334), 18 Rookie Class, 3 Collecting 101 Set checklists, and 30 full-bleed All-Star cards. Notable Rookie Cards include Brian Giles.

COMPLETE SET (506) 10.00 25.00
COMP.FACT.SET (516) 10.00 25.00
COMPLETE SERIES 1 (246) 6.00 15.00
COMPLETE SERIES 2 (260) 6.00 15.00
SUBSET CARDS HALF VALUE OF BASE CARDS
B.WILLIAMS AND D.GOODEN NUMBERED 175
D.GOODEN 176 AVAIL.ONLY IN FACT.SETS
1 Andruw Jones .10 .30
2 Rocky Coppinger .07 .20
3 Jeff D'Amico .07 .20
4 Dmitri Young .07 .20
5 Darin Erstad .07 .20
6 Jermaine Allensworth .07 .20
7 Damian Jackson .07 .20
8 Bill Mueller RC .30 .75
9 Jacob Cruz .07 .20
10 Vladimir Guerrero .20 .50
11 Marty Janzen .07 .20
12 Kevin L. Brown .07 .20
13 Willie Adams .07 .20
14 Wendell Magee .07 .20
15 Scott Rolen .10 .30
16 Matt Beech .07 .20
17 Neifi Perez .07 .20
18 Jamey Wright .07 .20
19 Jose Paniagua .07 .20
20 Todd Walker .07 .20
21 Justin Thompson .07 .20
22 Robin Jennings .07 .20
23 Dario Veras RC .07 .20
24 Brian Lesher RC .07 .20
25 Nomar Garciaparra .30 .75
26 Luis Castillo .07 .20
27 Brian Giles RC .40 1.00
28 Jermaine Dye .07 .20
29 Terrell Wade .07 .20
30 Fred McGriff .10 .30
31 Marquis Grissom .07 .20
32 Ryan Klesko .07 .20
33 Javier Lopez .07 .20
34 Mark Wohlers .07 .20
35 Tom Glavine .10 .30
36 Denny Neagle .07 .20
37 Scott Erickson .07 .20
38 Chris Hoiles .07 .20
39 Roberto Alomar .10 .30
40 Eddie Murray .20 .50
41 Cal Ripken .60 1.50
42 Randy Myers .07 .20
43 B.J. Surhoff .07 .20
44 Rick Krivda .07 .20
45 Jose Canseco .10 .30
46 Heathcliff Slocumb .07 .20
47 Jeff Suppan .07 .20
48 Tom Gordon .07 .20
49 Aaron Sele .07 .20
50 Mo Vaughn .07 .20
51 Darren Bragg .07 .20
52 Wil Cordero .07 .20
53 Scott Bullett .07 .20
54 Terry Adams .07 .20
55 Jackie Robinson .20 .50
56 T.Gwynn .20 .50
A.Rodriguez LL
57 A.Galarraga .25 .60
M.McGwire LL
58 A.Galarraga .07 .20
A.Belle LL
59 E.Young .07 .20
K.Lofton LL
60 J.Smoltz .07 .20
A.Pettitte LL
61 J.Smoltz .20 .50
R.Clemens LL
62 K.Brown .07 .20
J.Guzman LL
63 J.Wetteland .07 .20
T.Worrell
J.Brantley LL
64 Scott Servais .07 .20
65 Sammy Sosa .20 .50
66 Ryne Sandberg .30 .75
67 Frank Castillo .07 .20
68 Rey Sanchez .07 .20
69 Steve Trachsel .07 .20
70 Robin Ventura .07 .20
71 Wilson Alvarez .07 .20
72 Tony Phillips .07 .20
73 Lyle Mouton .07 .20
74 Mike Cameron .07 .20
75 Harold Baines .07 .20
76 Albert Belle .07 .20
77 Chris Snopek .07 .20
78 Reggie Sanders .07 .20
79 Jeff Brantley .07 .20
80 Barry Larkin .10 .30
81 Kevin Jarvis .07 .20
82 John Smiley .07 .20
83 Pete Schourek .07 .20
84 Thomas Howard .07 .20
85 Lee Smith .07 .20
86 Omar Vizquel .10 .30
87 Julio Franco .07 .20
88 Orel Hershiser .07 .20
89 Charles Nagy .07 .20
90 Matt Williams .07 .20
91 Dennis Martinez .07 .20
92 Jose Mesa .07 .20
93 Sandy Alomar Jr. .07 .20
94 Jim Thome .10 .30
95 Vinny Castilla .07 .20
96 Armando Reynoso .07 .20
97 Kevin Ritz .07 .20
98 Larry Walker .07 .20
99 Eric Young .07 .20
100 Dante Bichette .07 .20
101 Quinton McCracken .07 .20
102 John Vander Wal .07 .20
103 Phil Nevin .07 .20
104 Tony Clark .07 .20
105 Alan Trammell .07 .20
106 Felipe Lira .07 .20
107 Curtis Pride .07 .20
108 Bobby Higginson .07 .20
109 Mark Lewis .07 .20
110 Travis Fryman .07 .20
111 Al Leiter .07 .20
112 Devon White .07 .20
113 Jeff Conine .07 .20
114 Charles Johnson .07 .20
115 Andre Dawson .07 .20
116 Edgar Renteria .07 .20
117 Robb Nen .07 .20
118 Kevin Brown .07 .20
119 Derek Bell .07 .20
120 Bob Abreu .10 .30
121 Mike Hampton .07 .20
122 Todd Jones .07 .20
123 Billy Wagner .07 .20
124 Shane Reynolds .07 .20
125 Jeff Bagwell .10 .30
126 Brian L. Hunter .07 .20
127 Jeff Montgomery .07 .20
128 Rod Myers RC .07 .20
129 Tim Belcher .07 .20
130 Kevin Appier .07 .20
131 Mike Sweeney .07 .20
132 Craig Paquette .07 .20
133 Joe Randa .07 .20
134 Michael Tucker .07 .20
135 Raul Mondesi .07 .20
136 Tim Wallach .07 .20
137 Brett Butler .07 .20
138 Karim Garcia .07 .20
139 Todd Hollandsworth .07 .20
140 Eric Karros .07 .20
141 Hideo Nomo .20 .50
142 Ismael Valdes .07 .20
143 Cal Eldred .07 .20
144 Scott Karl .07 .20
145 Matt Mieske .07 .20
146 Mike Fetters .07 .20
147 Mark Loretta .07 .20
148 Fernando Vina .07 .20
149 Jeff Cirillo .07 .20
150 Dave Nilsson .07 .20
151 Kirby Puckett .20 .50
152 Rich Becker .07 .20
153 Chuck Knoblauch .07 .20
154 Marty Cordova .07 .20
155 Paul Molitor .07 .20
156 Rick Aguilera .07 .20
157 Pat Meares .07 .20
158 Frank Rodriguez .07 .20
159 David Segui .07 .20
160 Henry Rodriguez .07 .20
161 Shane Andrews .07 .20
162 Pedro Martinez .10 .30
163 Mark Grudzielanek .07 .20
164 Mike Lansing .07 .20
165 Rondell White .07 .20
166 Ugueth Urbina .07 .20
167 Rey Ordonez .07 .20
168 Robert Person .07 .20
169 Carlos Baerga .07 .20
170 Bernard Gilkey .07 .20
171 John Franco .07 .20
172 Pete Harnisch .07 .20
173 Butch Huskey .07 .20
174 Paul Wilson .07 .20
175 Dwight Gooden ERR .07 .20
176 Bernie Williams .10 .30
177 Wade Boggs .10 .30
178 Ruben Rivera .07 .20
179 Jim Leyritz .07 .20
180 Derek Jeter .50 1.25
181 Tino Martinez .10 .30
182 Tim Raines .07 .20
183 Scott Brosius .07 .20
184 Jason Giambi .07 .20
185 Geronimo Berroa .07 .20
186 Ariel Prieto .07 .20
187 Scott Spiezio .07 .20
188 John Wasdin .07 .20
189 Ernie Young .07 .20
190 Mark McGwire .50 1.25
191 Jim Eisenreich .07 .20
192 Ricky Bottalico .07 .20
193 Darren Daulton .07 .20
194 David Doster .07 .20
195 Gregg Jefferies .07 .20
196 Lenny Dykstra .07 .20
197 Curt Schilling .07 .20
198 Todd Stottlemyre .07 .20
199 Willie McGee .07 .20
200 Ozzie Smith .30 .75
201 Dennis Eckersley .07 .20
202 Ray Lankford .07 .20
203 John Mabry .07 .20
204 Alan Benes .07 .20
205 Ron Gant .07 .20
206 Archi Cianfrocco .07 .20
207 Fernando Valenzuela .07 .20
208 Greg Vaughn .07 .20
209 Steve Finley .07 .20
210 Tony Gwynn .25 .60
211 Rickey Henderson .20 .50
212 Trevor Hoffman .07 .20
213 Jason Thompson .07 .20
214 Osvaldo Fernandez .07 .20
215 Glenallen Hill .07 .20
216 William VanLandingham .07 .20
217 Marvin Benard .07 .20
218 Juan Gonzalez POST .07 .20
219 Roberto Alomar POST .07 .20
220 Brian Jordan POST .07 .20
221 John Smoltz POST .07 .20
222 Javy Lopez POST .07 .20
223 Bernie Williams POST .10 .30
224 J.Leyritz .07 .20
J.Wetteland POST
225 Barry Bonds .60 1.50
226 Rich Aurilia .07 .20
227 Jay Canizaro .07 .20
228 Dan Wilson .07 .20
229 Bob Wolcott .07 .20
230 Ken Griffey Jr. .40 1.00
231 Sterling Hitchcock .07 .20
232 Edgar Martinez .10 .30
233 Joey Cora .07 .20
234 Norm Charlton .07 .20
235 Alex Rodriguez .30 .75
236 Bobby Witt .07 .20
237 Darren Oliver .07 .20
238 Kevin Elster .07 .20
239 Rusty Greer .07 .20
240 Juan Gonzalez .07 .20
241 Will Clark .10 .30
242 Dean Palmer .07 .20
243 Ivan Rodriguez .10 .30
244 Ken Griffey Jr. CL .10 .30
245 Ken Griffey Jr. CL .10 .30
246 Ken Griffey Jr. CL .10 .30
247 Ken Griffey Jr. CL .10 .30
248 Ken Griffey Jr. CL .10 .30
249 Ken Griffey Jr. CL .10 .30
250 Eddie Murray .20 .50
251 Troy Percival .07 .20
252 Garret Anderson .07 .20
253 Allen Watson .07 .20
254 Jason Dickson .07 .20
255 Jim Edmonds .07 .20

256 Chuck Finley .07 .20
257 Randy Velarde .07 .20
258 Shigetoshi Hasegawa RC .15 .40
259 Todd Greene .07 .20
260 Tim Salmon .10 .30
261 Mark Langston .07 .20
262 Dave Hollins .07 .20
263 Gary DiSarcina .07 .20
264 Kenny Lofton .07 .20
265 John Smoltz .10 .30
266 Greg Maddux .30 .75
267 Jeff Blauser .07 .20
268 Alan Embree .07 .20
269 Mark Lemke .07 .20
270 Chipper Jones .20 .50
271 Mike Mussina .10 .30
272 Rafael Palmeiro .10 .30
273 Jimmy Key .07 .20
274 Mike Bordick .07 .20
275 Brady Anderson .07 .20
276 Eric Davis .07 .20
277 Jeffrey Hammonds .07 .20
278 Reggie Jefferson .07 .20
279 Tim Naehring .07 .20
280 John Valentin .07 .20
281 Troy O'Leary .07 .20
282 Shane Mack .07 .20
283 Mike Stanley .07 .20
284 Tim Wakefield .07 .20
285 Brian McRae .07 .20
286 Brooks Kieschnick .07 .20
287 Shawon Dunston .07 .20
288 Kevin Foster .07 .20
289 Mel Rojas .07 .20
290 Mark Grace .10 .30
291 Brant Brown .07 .20
292 Amaury Telemaco .07 .20
293 Dave Martinez .07 .20
294 Jaime Navarro .07 .20
295 Ray Durham .07 .20
296 Ozzie Guillen .07 .20
297 Roberto Hernandez .07 .20
298 Ron Karkovice .07 .20
299 James Baldwin .07 .20
300 Frank Thomas .20 .50
301 Eddie Taubensee .07 .20
302 Bret Boone .07 .20
303 Willie Greene .07 .20
304 Dave Burba .07 .20
305 Deion Sanders .10 .30
306 Reggie Sanders .07 .20
307 Hal Morris .07 .20
308 Pokey Reese .07 .20
309 Tony Fernandez .07 .20
310 Manny Ramirez .10 .30
311 Chad Ogea .07 .20
312 Jack McDowell .07 .20
313 Kevin Mitchell .07 .20
314 Chad Curtis .07 .20
315 Steve Kline .07 .20
316 Kevin Seitzer .07 .20
317 Kirt Manwaring .07 .20
318 Billy Swift .07 .20
319 Ellis Burks .07 .20
320 Andres Galarraga .07 .20
321 Bruce Ruffin .07 .20
322 Mark Thompson .07 .20
323 Walt Weiss .07 .20
324 Todd Jones .07 .20
325 Andruw Jones GHL .07 .20
326 Chipper Jones GHL .10 .30
327 Mo Vaughn GHL .07 .20
328 Frank Thomas GHL .10 .30
329 Albert Belle GHL .07 .20
330 Mark McGwire GHL .25 .60
331 Derek Jeter GHL .25 .60
332 Alex Rodriguez GHL .20 .50
333 Jay Buhner GHL .10 .30
334 Ken Griffey Jr. GHL .25 .60
335 Brian L. Hunter .07 .20
336 Brian Johnson .07 .20
337 Omar Olivares .07 .20
338 Deivi Cruz RC .10 .30
339 Damion Easley .07 .20
340 Melvin Nieves .07 .20
341 Moises Alou .07 .20
342 Jim Eisenreich .07 .20
343 Mark Hutton .07 .20
344 Alex Fernandez .07 .20
345 Gary Sheffield .07 .20
346 Pat Rapp .07 .20
347 Brad Ausmus .07 .20
348 Sean Berry .07 .20
349 Darryl Kile .07 .20
350 Craig Biggio .10 .30
351 Chris Holt .07 .20
352 Luis Gonzalez .07 .20
353 Pat Listach .07 .20
354 Jose Rosado .07 .20
355 Mike Macfarlane .07 .20
356 Tom Goodwin .07 .20
357 Chris Haney .07 .20
358 Chili Davis .07 .20
359 Jose Offerman .07 .20
360 Johnny Damon .10 .30
361 Bip Roberts .07 .20
362 Ramon Martinez .07 .20
363 Pedro Astacio .07 .20
364 Todd Zeile .07 .20
365 Mike Piazza .30 .75
366 Greg Gagne .07 .20
367 Chan Ho Park .07 .20
368 Wilton Guerrero .07 .20
369 Todd Worrell .07 .20
370 John Jaha .07 .20
371 Steve Sparks .07 .20
372 Mike Matheny .07 .20
373 Marc Newfield .07 .20
374 Jeromy Burnitz .07 .20
375 Jose Valentin .07 .20
376 Ben McDonald .07 .20
377 Roberto Kelly .07 .20
378 Bob Tewksbury .07 .20
379 Ron Coomer .07 .20
380 Brad Radke .07 .20
381 Matt Lawton .07 .20
382 Dan Naulty .07 .20
383 Scott Stahoviak .07 .20
384 Matt Wagner .07 .20
385 Jim Bullinger .07 .20
386 Carlos Perez .07 .20
387 Darrin Fletcher .07 .20
388 Chris Widger .07 .20
389 F.P. Santangelo .07 .20
390 Lee Smith .07 .20
391 Bobby Jones .07 .20
392 John Olerud .07 .20
393 Mark Clark .07 .20
394 Jason Isringhausen .07 .20
395 Todd Hundley .07 .20
396 Lance Johnson .07 .20
397 Edgardo Alfonzo .07 .20
398 Alex Ochoa .07 .20
399 Darryl Strawberry .07 .20
400 David Cone .07 .20
401 Paul O'Neill .10 .30
402 Joe Girardi .07 .20
403 Charlie Hayes .07 .20
404 Andy Pettitte .10 .30
405 Mariano Rivera .20 .50
406 Mariano Duncan .07 .20
407 Kenny Rogers .07 .20
408 Cecil Fielder .07 .20
409 George Williams .07 .20
410 Jose Canseco .10 .30
411 Tony Batista .07 .20
412 Steve Karsay .07 .20
413 Dave Telgheder .07 .20
414 Billy Taylor .07 .20
415 Mickey Morandini .07 .20
416 Calvin Maduro .07 .20
417 Mark Leiter .07 .20
418 Kevin Stocker .07 .20
419 Mike Lieberthal .07 .20
420 Rico Brogna .07 .20
421 Mark Portugal .07 .20
422 Rex Hudler .07 .20
423 Mark Johnson .07 .20
424 Esteban Loaiza .07 .20
425 Lou Collier .07 .20
426 Kevin Elster .07 .20
427 Francisco Cordova .07 .20
428 Marc Wilkins .07 .20
429 Joe Randa .07 .20
430 Jason Kendall .07 .20
431 Jon Lieber .07 .20
432 Steve Cooke .07 .20
433 Emil Brown RC .07 .20
434 Tony Womack RC .10 .30
435 Al Martin .07 .20
436 Jason Schmidt .07 .20
437 Andy Benes .07 .20
438 Delino DeShields .07 .20
439 Royce Clayton .07 .20
440 Brian Jordan .07 .20
441 Donovan Osborne .07 .20
442 Gary Gaetti .07 .20
443 Tom Pagnozzi .07 .20
444 Joey Hamilton .07 .20
445 Wally Joyner .07 .20
446 John Flaherty .07 .20
447 Chris Gomez .07 .20
448 Sterling Hitchcock .07 .20
449 Andy Ashby .07 .20
450 Ken Caminiti .07 .20
451 Tim Worrell .07 .20
452 Jose Vizcaino .07 .20
453 Rod Beck .07 .20
454 Wilson Delgado .07 .20
455 Darryl Hamilton .07 .20
456 Mark Lewis .07 .20
457 Mark Gardner .07 .20
458 Rick Wilkins .07 .20
459 Scott Sanders .07 .20
460 Kevin Orie .07 .20
461 Glendon Rusch .07 .20
462 Juan Melo .07 .20
463 Richie Sexson .07 .20
464 Bartolo Colon .07 .20
465 Jose Guillen .07 .20
466 Heath Murray .07 .20
467 Aaron Boone .07 .20
468 Bubba Trammell RC .10 .30
469 Jeff Abbott .07 .20
470 Derrick Gibson .07 .20
471 Matt Morris .07 .20
472 Ryan Jones .07 .20
473 Pat Cline .07 .20
474 Adam Riggs .07 .20
475 Jay Payton .07 .20
476 Derrek Lee .10 .30
477 Eli Marrero .07 .20
478 Lee Tinsley .07 .20
479 Jamie Moyer .07 .20
480 Jay Buhner .07 .20
481 Bob Wells .07 .20
482 Jeff Fassero .07 .20
483 Paul Sorrento .07 .20
484 Russ Davis .07 .20
485 Randy Johnson .20 .50
486 Roger Pavlik .07 .20
487 Damon Buford .07 .20
488 Julio Santana .07 .20
489 Mark McLemore .07 .20
490 Mickey Tettleton .07 .20
491 Ken Hill .07 .20
492 Benji Gil .07 .20
493 Ed Sprague .07 .20
494 Mike Timlin .07 .20
495 Pat Hentgen .07 .20
496 Orlando Merced .07 .20
497 Carlos Garcia .07 .20
498 Carlos Delgado .07 .20
499 Juan Guzman .07 .20
500 Roger Clemens .40 1.00
501 Erik Hanson .07 .20
502 Otis Nixon .07 .20
503 Shawn Green .07 .20
504 Charlie O'Brien .07 .20
505 Joe Carter .07 .20
506 Alex Gonzalez .07 .20

1997 Collector's Choice All-Star Connection

COMPLETE SET (45) 5.00 12.00
SER.2 ODDS 1:1 HOBBY, 2:1 RETAIL
1 Mark McGwire .50 1.25
2 Chuck Knoblauch .07 .20
3 Jim Thome .10 .30
4 Alex Rodriguez .30 .75
5 Ken Griffey Jr. .40 1.00
6 Brady Anderson .07 .20
7 Albert Belle .07 .20
8 Ivan Rodriguez .10 .30
9 Pat Hentgen .07 .20
10 Frank Thomas .20 .50
11 Roberto Alomar .10 .30
12 Robin Ventura .07 .20
13 Cal Ripken .60 1.50
14 Juan Gonzalez .07 .20
15 Manny Ramirez .10 .30
16 Bernie Williams .10 .30
17 Terry Steinbach .07 .20
18 Andy Pettitte .10 .30
19 Jeff Bagwell .10 .30
20 Craig Biggio .10 .30
21 Ken Caminiti .07 .20
22 Barry Larkin .10 .30
23 Tony Gwynn .25 .60
24 Barry Bonds .60 1.50
25 Kenny Lofton .07 .20
26 Mike Piazza .30 .75
27 John Smoltz .10 .30
28 Andres Galarraga .07 .20
29 Ryne Sandberg .30 .75
30 Chipper Jones .20 .50
31 Mark Grudzielanek .07 .20
32 Sammy Sosa .20 .50
33 Steve Finley .07 .20
34 Gary Sheffield .07 .20
35 Todd Hundley .07 .20
36 Greg Maddux .30 .75
37 Mo Vaughn .07 .20
38 Eric Young .07 .20
39 Vinny Castilla .07 .20
40 Derek Jeter .50 1.25
41 Lance Johnson .07 .20
42 Ellis Burks .07 .20
43 Dante Bichette .07 .20
44 Javy Lopez .07 .20
45 Hideo Nomo .20 .50

1997 Collector's Choice Big Shots

COMPLETE SET (19) 25.00 60.00
SER.2 STATED ODDS 1:12
*GOLD: 1.5X TO 4X BASIC BIG SHOT
SER.2 STATED ODDS 1:144
1 Ken Griffey Jr. 2.00 5.00
2 Nomar Garciaparra 1.50 4.00
3 Brian Jordan .40 1.00
4 Scott Rolen .60 1.50
5 Alex Rodriguez 1.50 4.00
6 Larry Walker .40 1.00
7 Mariano Rivera 1.00 2.50
8 Cal Ripken 3.00 8.00
9 Deion Sanders .60 1.50
10 Frank Thomas 1.00 2.50
11 Dean Palmer .40 1.00
12 Ken Caminiti .40 1.00
13 Derek Jeter 2.50 6.00
14 Barry Bonds 3.00 8.00
15 Chipper Jones 1.00 2.50
16 Mo Vaughn .40 1.00
17 Jay Buhner .40 1.00
18 Mike Piazza 1.50 4.00
19 Tony Gwynn 1.25 3.00

1997 Collector's Choice The Big Show

COMPLETE SET (45) 4.00 10.00
SER.1 STATED ODDS 1:1
*WHQ: 8X TO 20X BASIC BIG SHOW
WHQ SER.1 STATED ODDS 1:35
1 Greg Maddux .30 .75
2 Chipper Jones .20 .50
3 Andruw Jones .10 .30
4 John Smoltz .10 .30
5 Cal Ripken .60 1.50
6 Roberto Alomar .10 .30
7 Rafael Palmeiro .10 .30
8 Eddie Murray .20 .50
9 Jose Canseco .10 .30
10 Roger Clemens .40 1.00
11 Mo Vaughn .07 .20
12 Jim Edmonds .07 .20
13 Tim Salmon .10 .30
14 Sammy Sosa .20 .50
15 Albert Belle .07 .20
16 Frank Thomas .20 .50
17 Barry Larkin .10 .30
18 Kenny Lofton .07 .20
19 Manny Ramirez .10 .30
20 Matt Williams .07 .20
21 Dante Bichette .07 .20
22 Gary Sheffield .07 .20
23 Craig Biggio .10 .30
24 Jeff Bagwell .10 .30
25 Todd Hollandsworth .07 .20
26 Raul Mondesi .07 .20
27 Hideo Nomo .20 .50
28 Mike Piazza .30 .75
29 Paul Molitor .07 .20
30 Kirby Puckett .20 .50
31 Rondell White .07 .20
32 Rey Ordonez .07 .20
33 Paul Wilson .07 .20
34 Derek Jeter .50 1.25
35 Andy Pettitte .10 .30
36 Mark McGwire .50 1.25
37 Jason Kendall .07 .20
38 Ozzie Smith .30 .75
39 Tony Gwynn .25 .60
40 Barry Bonds .60 1.50
41 Alex Rodriguez .30 .75
42 Jay Buhner .07 .20
43 Ken Griffey Jr. .40 1.00
44 Randy Johnson .20 .50
45 Juan Gonzalez .07 .20

1997 Collector's Choice Crash the Game

COMPLETE SET (90) 25.00 60.00
SER.2 STATED ODDS 1:5
*INSTANT WIN: 10X TO 20X BASIC CRASH
INSTANT WIN SER.2 STATED ODDS 1:721
1A R.Klesko July 28-30 L .15 .40
1B R.Klesko Aug 8-11 L .15 .40
1C R.Klesko Sept 19-21 L .15 .40
2A C.Jones Aug 15-17 L .40 1.00
2B C.Jones Aug 29-31 L .40 1.00
2C C.Jones Sept 12-14 L .40 1.00
3A A.Jones Aug 22-24 W .25 .60
3B A.Jones Sept 1-3 L .25 .60
3C A.Jones Sept 19-22 L .25 .60
4A B.Anderson July 31-Aug 3 W .15 .40
4B B.Anderson Sept 4-7 L .15 .40
4C B.Anderson Sept 19-22 L .15 .40
5A R.Palmeiro July 29-30 L .25 .60
5B R.Palmeiro Aug 29-31 L .25 .60
5C R.Palmeiro Sept 26-28 L .25 .60
6A C.Ripken Aug 8-10 W 1.25 3.00
6B C.Ripken Sept 1-3 W 1.25 3.00
6C C.Ripken Sept 11-14 L 1.25 3.00
7A M.Vaughn Aug 14-17 L .15 .40
7B M.Vaughn Aug 29-31 W .15 .40
7C M.Vaughn Sept 23-25 W .15 .40
8A S.Sosa Aug 1-3 W .40 1.00
8B S.Sosa Aug 29-31 L .40 1.00
8C S.Sosa Sept 19-21 W .40 1.00
9A A.Belle Aug 7-10 L .15 .40
9B A.Belle Sept 11-14 L .15 .40
9C A.Belle Sept 19-21 W .15 .40
10A F.Thomas Aug 29-31 L .40 1.00
10B F.Thomas Sept 1-3 L .40 1.00
10C F.Thomas Sept 23-25 W .40 1.00
11A M.Ramirez Aug 12-14 W .25 .60
11B M.Ramirez Aug 29-31 L .25 .60
11C M.Ramirez Sept 11-14 W .25 .60
12A J.Thome July 28-30 L .25 .60
12B J.Thome Aug 15-18 W .25 .60
12C J.Thome Sept 19-22 L .25 .60
13A M.Williams Aug 4-5 L .15 .40
13B M.Williams Sept 1-3 W .15 .40
13C M.Williams Sept 23-25 L .15 .40
14A D.Bichette July 24-27 W .15 .40
14B D.Bichette Aug 28-29 L .15 .40
14C D.Bichette Sept 26-28 W .15 .40
15A V.Castilla Aug 12-13 L .15 .40
15B V.Castilla Sept 4-7 W .15 .40
15C V.Castilla Sept 19-21 L .15 .40
16A A.Galarraga Aug 8-10 W .15 .40
16B A.Galarraga Aug 30-31 L .15 .40
16C A.Galarraga Sept 12-14 L .15 .40
17A G.Sheffield Aug 1-3 W .15 .40
17B G.Sheffield Sept 1-3 W .15 .40
17C G.Sheffield Sept 12-14 W .15 .40
18A J.Bagwell Sept 9-10 L .25 .60
18B J.Bagwell Sept 19-22 W .25 .60
18C J.Bagwell Sept 23-25 W .25 .60
19A E.Karros Aug 1-3 L .15 .40
19B E.Karros Aug 15-17 L .15 .40
19C E.Karros Sept 25-28 W .15 .40
20A M.Piazza Aug 11-12 L .60 1.50
20B M.Piazza Sept 5-8 W .60 1.50
20C M.Piazza Sept 19-21 W .60 1.50
21A V.Guerrero Aug 22-24 L .40 1.00
21B V.Guerrero Aug 29-31 L .40 1.00
21C V.Guerrero Sept 19-22 L .40 1.00
22A C.Fielder Aug 29-31 L .15 .40
22B C.Fielder Sept 4-7 L .15 .40
22C C.Fielder Sept 26-28 L .15 .40
23A J.Canseco Sept 12-14 L .25 .60
23B J.Canseco Sept 22-24 L .25 .60
23C J.Canseco Sept 26-28 L .25 .60
24A M.McGwire July 31-Aug 3 L 1.00 2.50
24B M.McGwire Aug 30-31 L 1.00 2.50
24C M.McGwire Sept 19-22 W 1.00 2.50
25A K.Caminiti Aug 8-10 L .15 .40
25B K.Caminiti Sept 4-7 W .15 .40
25C K.Caminiti Sept 17-18 W .15 .40
26A B.Bonds Aug 5-7 L 1.25 3.00
26B B.Bonds Sept 4-7 L 1.25 3.00
26C B.Bonds Sept 23-24 W 1.25 3.00
27A J.Buhner Aug 7-10 L .15 .40
27B J.Buhner Aug 28-29 L .15 .40
27C J.Buhner Sept 1-3 L .15 .40
28A K.Griffey Jr. Aug 22-24 W .75 2.00
28B K.Griffey Jr. Aug 28-29 L .75 2.00
28C K.Griffey Jr. Sept 19-22 W .75 2.00
29A A.Rodriguez July 29-31 L .60 1.50
29B A.Rodriguez Aug 30-31 L .60 1.50
29C A.Rodriguez Sept 12-15 L .60 1.50
30A J.Gonzalez Aug 11-13 W .15 .40
30B J.Gonzalez Aug 30-31 L .15 .40
30C J.Gonzalez Sept 19-21 W .15 .40

1997 Collector's Choice Griffey Clearly Dominant

COMPLETE SET (5) 2.50 6.00
COMMON GRIFFEY (CD1-CD5) .75 2.00
SER.1 STATED ODDS 1:144

1997 Collector's Choice Griffey Clearly Dominant Jumbo

COMMON GRIFFEY (CD1-CD5) 2.00 5.00
STATED PRINT RUN 5000 SER.#'d SETS

1997 Collector's Choice New Frontier

SER.2 STATED ODDS 1:69
NF1 Alex Rodriguez 4.00 10.00
NF2 Tony Gwynn 3.00 8.00
NF3 Jose Canseco 2.00 5.00
NF4 Hideo Nomo 2.00 5.00
NF5 Mark McGwire 5.00 12.00
NF6 Barry Bonds 5.00 12.00
NF7 Juan Gonzalez 1.25 3.00
NF8 Ken Caminiti 1.25 3.00
NF9 Tim Salmon 1.25 3.00
NF10 Mike Piazza 3.00 8.00
NF11 Ken Griffey Jr. 12.50 30.00
NF12 Andres Galarraga 2.00 5.00
NF13 Jay Buhner 1.25 3.00
NF14 Dante Bichette 1.25 3.00
NF15 Frank Thomas 3.00 8.00
NF16 Ryne Sandberg 5.00 12.00
NF17 Roger Clemens 4.00 10.00
NF18 Andruw Jones 1.25 3.00
NF19 Jim Thome 2.00 5.00
NF20 Sammy Sosa 2.00 5.00
NF21 Dave Justice 1.25 3.00
NF22 Deion Sanders 2.00 5.00
NF23 Todd Walker 1.25 3.00
NF24 Kevin Orie 1.25 3.00
NF25 Albert Belle 1.25 3.00
NF26 Jeff Bagwell 2.00 5.00
NF27 Manny Ramirez 2.00 5.00
NF28 Brian Jordan 1.25 3.00
NF29 Derek Jeter 8.00 20.00
NF30 Chipper Jones 3.00 8.00
NF31 Mo Vaughn 1.25 3.00
NF32 Gary Sheffield 1.25 3.00
NF33 Carlos Delgado 1.25 3.00
NF34 Vladimir Guerrero 2.00 5.00
NF35 Cal Ripken 10.00 25.00
NF36 Greg Maddux 5.00 12.00
NF37 Cecil Fielder 1.25 3.00
NF38 Todd Hundley 1.25 3.00
NF39 Mike Mussina 2.00 5.00
NF40 Scott Rolen 2.00 5.00

1997 Collector's Choice Premier Power

COMPLETE SET (20) 15.00 40.00
SER.1 STATED ODDS 1:15
*GOLD: 1.25X TO 3X BASIC PREM.POWER
GOLD SER.1 STATED ODDS 1:69
*JUMBOS: .25X BASIC PREMIER POWER
TEN JUMBO POWERS PER FACTORY SET
PP1 Mark McGwire 2.50 6.00
PP2 Brady Anderson .40 1.00
PP3 Ken Griffey Jr. 2.00 5.00
PP4 Albert Belle .40 1.00
PP5 Juan Gonzalez .40 1.00
PP6 Andres Galarraga .40 1.00
PP7 Jay Buhner .40 1.00
PP8 Mo Vaughn .40 1.00
PP9 Barry Bonds 3.00 8.00
PP10 Gary Sheffield .40 1.00
PP11 Todd Hundley .40 1.00
PP12 Frank Thomas 1.00 2.50
PP13 Sammy Sosa 1.00 2.50
PP14 Ken Caminiti .40 1.00
PP15 Vinny Castilla .40 1.00
PP16 Ellis Burks .40 1.00
PP17 Rafael Palmeiro .60 1.50
PP18 Alex Rodriguez 1.50 4.00
PP19 Mike Piazza 1.50 4.00
PP20 Eddie Murray 1.00 2.50

1997 Collector's Choice Stick'Ums

COMPLETE SET (30) 6.00 15.00
SER.1 STATED ODDS 1:3
1 Ozzie Smith .50 1.25
2 Andruw Jones .20 .50
3 Alex Rodriguez .50 1.25
4 Paul Molitor .10 .30
5 Jeff Bagwell .20 .50
6 Manny Ramirez .20 .50
7 Kenny Lofton .10 .30
8 Albert Belle .10 .30
9 Jay Buhner .10 .30
10 Chipper Jones .30 .75
11 Barry Larkin .20 .50
12 Dante Bichette .10 .30
13 Mike Piazza .50 1.25
14 Andres Galarraga .10 .30
15 Barry Bonds 1.00 2.50
16 Brady Anderson .10 .30
17 Gary Sheffield .10 .30
18 Jim Thome .20 .50
19 Tony Gwynn .40 1.00
20 Cal Ripken 1.00 2.50
21 Sammy Sosa .30 .75
22 Juan Gonzalez .10 .30
23 Greg Maddux .50 1.25
24 Ken Griffey Jr. .60 1.50
25 Mark McGwire .75 2.00
26 Kirby Puckett .30 .75
27 Mo Vaughn .10 .30
28 Vladimir Guerrero .30 .75
29 Ken Caminiti .10 .30
30 Frank Thomas .30 .75

1997 Collector's Choice Stick'Ums Retail

COMPLETE SET (28) 4.00 10.00
1 Brady Anderson .08 .25
2 Jeff Bagwell .30 .75
3 Albert Belle .07 .20
4 Dante Bichette .08 .25
5 Barry Bonds .60 1.50
6 Jay Buhner .08 .25
7 Ken Caminiti .08 .25
8 Andres Galarraga .07 .20
9 Juan Gonzalez .30 .75
10 Ken Griffey Jr. .75 2.00
11 Vladimir Guerrero .40 1.00
12 Tony Gwynn .60 1.50
13 Andruw Jones .50 1.25
14 Chipper Jones .60 1.50
15 Barry Larkin .30 .75
16 Kenny Lofton .08 .25
17 Greg Maddux .75 2.00
18 Mark McGwire .60 1.50
19 Paul Molitor .30 .75
20 Mike Piazza .75 2.00
21 Manny Ramirez .40 1.00
22 Cal Ripken Jr. 1.25 3.00
23 Alex Rodriguez .60 1.50
24 Gary Sheffield .40 1.00
25 Sammy Sosa .50 1.25
26 Frank Thomas .08 .25
27 Jim Thome .30 .75
28 Mo Vaughn .02 .10

1997 Collector's Choice Toast of the Town

COMPLETE SET (30) 100.00 200.00
SER.2 STATED ODDS 1:35
T1 Andruw Jones 1.50 4.00
T2 Chipper Jones 2.50 6.00
T3 Greg Maddux 4.00 10.00
T4 John Smoltz 1.50 4.00
T5 Kenny Lofton 1.00 2.50
T6 Brady Anderson 1.00 2.50
T7 Cal Ripken 8.00 20.00
T8 Mo Vaughn 1.00 2.50
T9 Sammy Sosa 2.50 6.00
T10 Albert Belle 1.00 2.50
T11 Frank Thomas 2.50 6.00
T12 Barry Larkin 1.50 4.00
T13 Manny Ramirez 1.50 4.00
T14 Jeff Bagwell 1.50 4.00
T15 Mike Piazza 4.00 10.00
T16 Paul Molitor 1.00 2.50
T17 Vladimir Guerrero 2.50 6.00
T18 Todd Hundley 1.00 2.50
T19 Derek Jeter 6.00 15.00
T20 Andy Pettitte 1.50 4.00
T21 Bernie Williams 1.50 4.00
T22 Mark McGwire 6.00 15.00
T23 Scott Rolen 1.50 4.00
T24 Ken Caminiti 1.00 2.50
T25 Tony Gwynn 3.00 8.00
T26 Barry Bonds 8.00 20.00
T27 Ken Griffey Jr. 5.00 12.00
T28 Alex Rodriguez 4.00 10.00
T29 Juan Gonzalez 1.00 2.50
T30 Roger Clemens 5.00 12.00

1997 Collector's Choice Update

COMPLETE SET (30) 2.00 5.00
ONE SET VIA MAIL PER 10 SER.2 WRAPPERS
EXCH.DEADLINE: 12/01/97
U1 Jim Leyritz .07 .20
U2 Matt Perisho .07 .20
U3 Michael Tucker .07 .20
U4 Mike Johnson .07 .20
U5 Jaime Navarro .07 .20
U6 Doug Drabek .07 .20
U7 Terry Mulholland .07 .20
U8 Brett Tomko .07 .20
U9 Marquis Grissom .07 .20
U10 David Justice .07 .20
U11 Brian Moehler RC .10 .30
U12 Bobby Bonilla .07 .20
U13 Todd Dunwoody .07 .20
U14 Tony Saunders .07 .20
U15 Jay Bell .07 .20
U16 Jeff King .07 .20
U17 Terry Steinbach .07 .20
U18 Steve Bieser .07 .20
U19 Takashi Kashiwada .07 .20
U20 Hideki Irabu .10 .30
U21 Damon Mashore .07 .20
U22 Quilvio Veras .07 .20
U23 Will Cunnane .07 .20
U24 Jeff Kent .07 .20
U25 J.T. Snow .07 .20
U26 Dante Powell .07 .20
U27 Jose Cruz Jr. .10 .30
U28 John Burkett .07 .20
U29 John Wetteland .07 .20
U30 Benito Santiago .07 .20

1997 Collector's Choice Teams

This set features color action and posed player photos either borderless or in white borders of 13 players each of selected major league baseball teams. The backs carry player information and career statistics. Each set was distributed in a special package along with a foil enhanced die cut 3 1/2" by 5" Home Team Heroes card displaying two star players of that team. The cards are checklisted below by teams with the Home Team Heroes cards, which was also issued seperately, priced as a Upper Deck set.

COMPLETE SET 30.00 80.00
AB Atlanta Braves Logo CL .08 .25
AB1 Andruw Jones .75 2.00
AB2 Kenny Lofton .20 .50
AB3 Fred McGriff .30 .75
AB4 Michael Tucker .08 .25
AB5 Ryan Klesko .20 .50
AB6 Javier Lopez .30 .75
AB7 Mark Wohlers .08 .25
AB8 Tom Glavine .40 1.00
AB9 Denny Neagle .08 .25
AB10 Chipper Jones 1.00 2.50
AB11 Jeff Blauser .08 .25
AB12 Greg Maddux 1.25 3.00
AB13 John Smoltz .30 .75
BO Baltimore Orioles Logo CL .08 .25
BO1 Rocky Coppinger .08 .25
BO2 Scott Erickson .08 .25
BO3 Chris Hoiles .08 .25
BO4 Roberto Alomar .40 1.00
BO5 Cal Ripken Jr. 2.00 5.00
BO6 Randy Myers .20 .50
BO7 B.J. Surhoff .20 .50
BO8 Mike Mussina .40 1.00
BO9 Rafael Palmeiro .40 1.00
BO10 Jimmy Key .20 .50
BO11 Mike Bordick .08 .25
BO12 Brady Anderson .20 .50
BO13 Eric Davis .20 .50
CI Cleveland Indians Logo CL .08 .25
CI1 Brian Giles 1.50 4.00
CI2 Omar Vizquel .30 .75
CI3 Julio Franco .20 .50
CI4 Orel Hershiser .20 .50
CI5 Charles Nagy .08 .25
CI6 Matt Williams .30 .75
CI7 Jose Mesa .20 .50
CI8 Sandy Alomar Jr. .20 .50
CI9 Jim Thome .50 1.25
CI10 David Justice .40 1.00
CI11 Marquis Grissom .20 .50
CI12 Chad Ogea .08 .25
CI13 Manny Ramirez .50 1.25
CR Colorado Rockies Logo CL .08 .25
CR1 Dante Bichette .20 .50
CR2 Vinny Castilla .20 .50
CR3 Kevin Ritz .08 .25
CR4 Larry Walker .40 1.00
CR5 Eric Young .20 .50
CR6 Quinton McCracken .08 .25
CR7 John Vander Wal .08 .25
CR8 Jamey Wright .08 .25
CR9 Mark Thompson .08 .25
CR10 Andres Galarraga .40 1.00
CR11 Ellis Burks .20 .50
CR12 Kirt Manwaring .08 .25
CR13 Walt Weiss .08 .25
CW Chicago White Sox Logo CL .08 .25
CW1 Robin Ventura .40 1.00
CW2 Wilson Alvarez .08 .25
CW3 Tony Phillips .08 .25
CW4 Lyle Mouton .08 .25
CW5 James Baldwin .08 .25
CW6 Harold Baines .08 .25
CW7 Albert Belle .20 .50
CW8 Chris Snopek .08 .25
CW9 Ray Durham .20 .50
CW10 Frank Thomas .50 1.25
CW11 Ozzie Guillen .20 .50
CW12 Roberto Hernandez .20 .50
CW13 Jaime Navarro .08 .25
FM Florida Marlins Logo CL .08 .25
FM1 Luis Castillo .30 .75
FM2 Al Leiter .20 .50
FM3 Devon White .08 .25
FM4 Jeff Conine .08 .25
FM5 Charles Johnson .08 .25
FM6 Edgar Renteria .40 1.00
FM7 Robb Nen .08 .25
FM8 Kevin Brown .20 .50
FM9 Gary Sheffield .50 1.25
FM10 Alex Fernandez .08 .25
FM11 Pat Rapp .08 .25
FM12 Moises Alou .20 .50
FM13 Bobby Bonilla .20 .50
LA Los Angles Dodgers Logo CL .08 .25
LA1 Raul Mondesi .20 .50
LA2 Brett Butler .20 .50
LA3 Todd Hollandsworth .08 .25
LA4 Eric Karros .20 .50
LA5 Hideo Nomo .60 1.50
LA6 Ismael Valdes .08 .25
LA7 Wilton Guerrero .08 .25
LA8 Ramon Martinez .08 .25
LA9 Greg Gagne .08 .25
LA10 Mike Piazza 1.25 3.00
LA11 Chan Ho Park .20 .50
LA12 Todd Worrell .08 .25
LA13 Todd Zeile .20 .50
NY New York Yankees Logo CL .08 .25
NY1 Bernie Williams .40 1.00
NY2 Dwight Gooden .20 .50
NY3 Wade Boggs .50 1.25
NY4 Ruben Rivera .08 .25
NY5 Derek Jeter 2.00 5.00
NY6 Tino Martinez .30 .75
NY7 Tim Raines .20 .50
NY8 Joe Girardi .08 .25
NY9 Charlie Hayes .08 .25
NY10 Andy Pettitte .30 .75
NY11 Cecil Fielder .20 .50
NY12 Paul O'Neill .20 .50
NY13 David Cone .30 .75
SM Seattle Mariners Logo CL .08 .25
SM1 Dan Wilson .08 .25
SM2 Ken Griffey Jr. 1.25 3.00
SM3 Edgar Martinez .30 .75
SM4 Joey Cora .08 .25
SM5 Norm Charlton .08 .25
SM6 Alex Rodriguez 1.50 4.00
SM7 Randy Johnson .75 2.00
SM8 Paul Sorrento .08 .25
SM9 Jamie Moyer .20 .50
SM10 Jay Buhner .20 .50
SM11 Russ Davis .08 .25
SM12 Jeff Fassero .08 .25
SM13 Bob Wells .08 .25
TR Texas Rangers Logo CL .08 .25
TR1 Bobby Witt .08 .25
TR2 Darren Oliver .08 .25
TR3 Rusty Greer .20 .50
TR4 Juan Gonzalez .20 .50
TR5 Will Clark .40 1.00
TR6 Dean Palmer .20 .50
TR7 Ivan Rodriguez .50 1.25
TR8 John Wetteland .20 .50
TR9 Mark McLemore .08 .25
TR10 John Burkett .08 .25
TR11 Benji Gil .08 .25
TR12 Ken Hill .08 .25
TR13 Mickey Tettleton .20 .50

1998 Collector's Choice

The 1998 Collector's Choice set (produced by Upper Deck) was issued in two separate series, each containing 265 cards. Packs for both first and second series contained 14 cards and carried a suggested retail price of $1.29. First series packs went live around March, 1998 and second series packs followed suit in June, 1998. Card fronts feature color glossy action player photos framed by a clean white or gray border. The backs carry statistical information and another color image. The set contains the topical subsets: Checklists (266-270), Cover Glory (1-18), Golden Jubilee (271-279), Rookie Class (100-126/415-432), Masked Marauders (181-189), and Top of the Charts (253-261). Key Rookie Cards in this set include Kevin Millwood and Maggio Ordonez. Card number 202A featuring Kerry Wood was issued in factory sets to replace Tony Barron

COMPLETE SET (530) 15.00 40.00
COMPLETE SERIES 1 (265) 8.00 20.00
COMPLETE SERIES 2 (265) 8.00 20.00
COMP.FACT.SET (530) 20.00 50.00
1 Nomar Garciaparra CG .20 .50
2 Roger Clemens CG .20 .50
3 Larry Walker CG .07 .20
4 Mike Piazza CG .20 .50

5 Mark McGwire CG .25 .60
6 Tony Gwynn CG .10 .30
7 Jose Cruz Jr. CG .07 .20
8 Frank Thomas CG .10 .30
9 Tino Martinez CG .07 .20
10 Ken Griffey Jr. CG .25 .60
11 Barry Bonds CG .30 .75
12 Scott Rolen CG .07 .20
13 Randy Johnson CG .10 .30
14 Ryne Sandberg CG .20 .50
15 Eddie Murray CG .10 .30
16 Kevin Brown CG .07 .20
17 Mike Mussina CG .07 .20
18 Sandy Alomar Jr. CG .07 .20
19 CL1 Griffey .15 .40
Riggs
20 CL2 Garciaparra .10 .30
O'Brien
21 CL 3 Grieve .07 .20
Thomas
Gwynn
22 CL4 McGwire .10 .30
Ripken
23 CL5 Tino Martinez .07 .20
24 Jason Dickson .07 .20
25 Darin Erstad .07 .20
26 Todd Greene .07 .20
27 Chuck Finley .07 .20
28 Garret Anderson .07 .20
29 Dave Hollins .07 .20
30 Rickey Henderson .20 .50
31 John Smoltz .10 .30
32 Michael Tucker .07 .20
33 Jeff Blauser .07 .20
34 Javier Lopez .07 .20
35 Andruw Jones .10 .30
36 Denny Neagle .07 .20
37 Randall Simon .07 .20
38 Mark Wohlers .07 .20
39 Harold Baines .07 .20
40 Cal Ripken .60 1.50
41 Mike Bordick .07 .20
42 Jimmy Key .07 .20
43 Armando Benitez .07 .20
44 Scott Erickson .07 .20
45 Eric Davis .07 .20
46 Bret Saberhagen .07 .20
47 Darren Bragg .07 .20
48 Steve Avery .07 .20
49 Jeff Frye .07 .20
50 Aaron Sele .07 .20
51 Scott Hatteberg .07 .20
52 Tom Gordon .07 .20
53 Kevin Orie .07 .20
54 Kevin Foster .07 .20
55 Ryne Sandberg .30 .75
56 Doug Glanville .07 .20
57 Tyler Houston .07 .20
58 Steve Trachsel .07 .20
59 Mark Grace .10 .30
60 Frank Thomas .20 .50
61 Scott Eyre .07 .20
62 Jeff Abbott .07 .20
63 Chris Clemons .07 .20
64 Jorge Fabregas .07 .20
65 Robin Ventura .07 .20
66 Matt Karchner .07 .20
67 Jon Nunnally .07 .20
68 Aaron Boone .07 .20
69 Pokey Reese .07 .20
70 Deion Sanders .10 .30
71 Jeff Shaw .07 .20
72 Eduardo Perez .07 .20
73 Brett Tomko .07 .20
74 Bartolo Colon .07 .20
75 Manny Ramirez .10 .30
76 Jose Mesa .07 .20
77 Brian Giles .07 .20
78 Richie Sexson .07 .20
79 Orel Hershiser .07 .20
80 Matt Williams .07 .20
81 Walt Weiss .07 .20
82 Jerry DiPoto .07 .20
83 Quinton McCracken .07 .20
84 Neifi Perez .07 .20
85 Vinny Castilla .07 .20
86 Ellis Burks .07 .20
87 John Thomson .07 .20
88 Willie Blair .07 .20
89 Bob Hamelin .07 .20
90 Tony Clark .07 .20
91 Todd Jones .07 .20
92 Deivi Cruz .07 .20
93 Frank Catalanotto RC .15 .40
94 Justin Thompson .07 .20
95 Gary Sheffield .07 .20
96 Kevin Brown .10 .30
97 Charles Johnson .07 .20
98 Bobby Bonilla .07 .20
99 Livan Hernandez .07 .20
100 Paul Konerko .07 .20
101 Craig Counsell .07 .20
102 Magglio Ordonez RC .60 1.50
103 Garrett Stephenson .07 .20
104 Ken Cloude .07 .20
105 Miguel Tejada .20 .50
106 Juan Encarnacion .07 .20
107 Dennis Reyes .07 .20
108 Orlando Cabrera .07 .20
109 Kelvim Escobar .07 .20
110 Ben Grieve .07 .20
111 Brian Rose .07 .20
112 Fernando Tatis .07 .20
113 Tom Evans .07 .20
114 Tom Fordham .07 .20
115 Mark Kotsay .07 .20
116 Mario Valdez .07 .20
117 Jeremi Gonzalez .07 .20
118 Todd Dunwoody .07 .20
119 Javier Valentin .07 .20
120 Todd Helton .10 .30
121 Jason Varitek .20 .50
122 Chris Carpenter .07 .20
123 Kevin Millwood RC .25 .60
124 Brad Fullmer .07 .20
125 Jaret Wright .07 .20
126 Brad Rigby .07 .20
127 Edgar Renteria .07 .20
128 Robb Nen .07 .20
129 Tony Pena .07 .20
130 Craig Biggio .10 .30
131 Brad Ausmus .07 .20
132 Shane Reynolds .07 .20
133 Mike Hampton .07 .20
134 Billy Wagner .07 .20
135 Richard Hidalgo .07 .20
136 Jose Rosado .07 .20
137 Yamil Benitez .07 .20
138 Felix Martinez .07 .20
139 Jeff King .07 .20
140 Jose Offerman .07 .20
141 Joe Vitiello .07 .20
142 Tim Belcher .07 .20
143 Brett Butler .07 .20
144 Greg Gagne .07 .20
145 Mike Piazza .30 .75
146 Ramon Martinez .07 .20
147 Raul Mondesi .07 .20
148 Adam Riggs .07 .20
149 Eddie Murray .20 .50
150 Jeff Cirillo .07 .20
151 Scott Karl .07 .20
152 Mike Fetters .07 .20
153 Dave Nilsson .07 .20
154 Antone Williamson .07 .20
155 Jeff D'Amico .07 .20
156 Jose Valentin .07 .20
157 Brad Radke .07 .20
158 Torii Hunter .07 .20
159 Chuck Knoblauch .07 .20
160 Paul Molitor .07 .20
161 Travis Miller .07 .20
162 Rich Robertson .07 .20
163 Ron Coomer .07 .20
164 Mark Grudzielanek .07 .20
165 Lee Smith .07 .20
166 Vladimir Guerrero .20 .50
167 Dustin Hermanson .07 .20
168 Ugueth Urbina .07 .20
169 F.P. Santangelo .07 .20
170 Rondell White .07 .20
171 Bobby Jones .07 .20
172 Edgardo Alfonzo .07 .20
173 John Franco .07 .20
174 Carlos Baerga .07 .20
175 Butch Huskey .07 .20
176 Rey Ordonez .07 .20
177 Matt Franco .07 .20
178 Dwight Gooden .07 .20
179 Chad Curtis .07 .20
180 Tino Martinez .10 .30
181 Charlie O'Brien MM .07 .20
182 Sandy Alomar Jr. MM .07 .20
183 Raul Casanova MM .07 .20
184 Javier Lopez MM .07 .20
185 Mike Piazza MM .20 .50
186 Ivan Rodriguez MM .07 .20
187 Charles Johnson MM .07 .20
188 Brad Ausmus MM .07 .20
189 Brian Johnson MM .07 .20
190 Wade Boggs .10 .30
191 David Wells .07 .20
192 Tim Raines .07 .20
193 Ramiro Mendoza .07 .20
194 Willie Adams .07 .20
195 Matt Stairs .07 .20
196 Jason McDonald .07 .20
197 Dave Magadan .07 .20
198 Mark Bellhorn .07 .20
199 Ariel Prieto .07 .20
200 Jose Canseco .10 .30
201 Bobby Estalella .07 .20
202 Tony Barron RC .07 .20
202A Kerry Wood
203 Midre Cummings .07 .20
204 Ricky Bottalico .07 .20
205 Mike Grace .07 .20
206 Rico Brogna .07 .20
207 Mickey Morandini .07 .20
208 Lou Collier .07 .20
209 Kevin Polcovich .07 .20
210 Kevin Young .07 .20
211 Jose Guillen .07 .20
212 Esteban Loaiza .07 .20
213 Marc Wilkins .07 .20
214 Jason Schmidt .07 .20
215 Gary Gaetti .07 .20
216 Fernando Valenzuela .07 .20
217 Willie McGee .07 .20
218 Alan Benes .07 .20
219 Eli Marrero .07 .20
220 Mark McGwire .50 1.25
221 Matt Morris .07 .20
222 Trevor Hoffman .07 .20
223 Will Cunnane .07 .20
224 Joey Hamilton .07 .20
225 Ken Caminiti .07 .20
226 Derrek Lee .10 .30
227 Mark Sweeney .07 .20
228 Carlos Hernandez .07 .20
229 Brian Johnson .07 .20
230 Jeff Kent .07 .20
231 Kirk Rueter .07 .20
232 Bill Mueller .07 .20
233 Dante Powell .07 .20
234 J.T. Snow .07 .20
235 Shawn Estes .07 .20
236 Dennis Martinez .07 .20
237 Jamie Moyer .07 .20
238 Dan Wilson .07 .20
239 Joey Cora .07 .20
240 Ken Griffey Jr. .40 1.00
241 Paul Sorrento .07 .20
242 Jay Buhner .07 .20
243 Hanley Frias RC .07 .20
244 John Burkett .07 .20
245 Juan Gonzalez .07 .20
246 Rick Helling .07 .20
247 Darren Oliver .07 .20
248 Mickey Tettleton .07 .20
249 Ivan Rodriguez .10 .30
250 Joe Carter .07 .20
251 Pat Hentgen .07 .20
252 Marty Janzen .07 .20
253 F.Thomas .07 .20
T.Gwynn TOP
254 McGwire .25 .60
Griffey
Walker TOP
255 K.Griffey .15 .40
A.Galarraga TOP
256 B.Hunter .07 .20
T.Womack TOP
257 R.Clemens .10 .30
D.Neagle TOP
258 R.Clemens .20 .50
C.Schilling TOP
259 R.Clemens .20 .50
P.Martinez TOP
260 R.Myers .07 .20
J.Shaw TOP
261 N.Garciaparra .10 .30
S.Rolen TOP
262 Charlie O'Brien .07 .20
263 Shannon Stewart .07 .20
264 Robert Person .07 .20
265 Carlos Delgado .07 .20
266 M.Williams .07 .20
T.Lee CL
267 N.Garciaparra .10 .30
C.Ripken CL
268 M.McGwire .20 .50
M.Piazza CL
269 T.Gwynn .15 .40
K.Griffey Jr. CL
270 F.McGriff .07 .20
J.Cruz Jr. CL
271 Andruw Jones GJ .07 .20
272 Alex Rodriguez GJ .20 .50
273 Juan Gonzalez GJ .07 .20
274 Nomar Garciaparra GJ .20 .50
275 Ken Griffey Jr. GJ .25 .60
276 Tino Martinez GJ .07 .20
277 Roger Clemens GJ .20 .50
278 Barry Bonds GJ .30 .75
279 Mike Piazza GJ .20 .50
280 Tim Salmon .10 .30
281 Gary DiSarcina .07 .20
282 Cecil Fielder .07 .20
283 Ken Hill .07 .20
284 Troy Percival .07 .20
285 Jim Edmonds .07 .20
286 Allen Watson .07 .20
287 Brian Anderson .07 .20
288 Jay Bell .07 .20
289 Jorge Fabregas .07 .20
290 Devon White .07 .20
291 Yamil Benitez .07 .20
292 Jeff Suppan .07 .20
293 Tony Batista .07 .20
294 Brent Brede .07 .20
295 Andy Benes .07 .20
296 Felix Rodriguez .07 .20
297 Karim Garcia .07 .20
298 Omar Daal .07 .20
299 Andy Stankiewicz .07 .20
300 Matt Williams .07 .20
301 Willie Blair .07 .20
302 Ryan Klesko .07 .20
303 Tom Glavine .10 .30
304 Walt Weiss .07 .20
305 Greg Maddux .30 .75
306 Chipper Jones .20 .50
307 Keith Lockhart .07 .20
308 Andres Galarraga .07 .20
309 Chris Hoiles .07 .20
310 Roberto Alomar .10 .30
311 Joe Carter .07 .20
312 Doug Drabek .07 .20
313 Jeffrey Hammonds .07 .20
314 Rafael Palmeiro .10 .30
315 Mike Mussina .10 .30
316 Brady Anderson .07 .20
317 B.J. Surhoff .07 .20
318 Dennis Eckersley .07 .20
319 Jim Leyritz .07 .20
320 Mo Vaughn .07 .20
321 Nomar Garciaparra .30 .75
322 Reggie Jefferson .07 .20
323 Tim Naehring .07 .20
324 Troy O'Leary .07 .20
325 Pedro Martinez .10 .30
326 John Valentin .07 .20
327 Mark Clark .07 .20
328 Rod Beck .07 .20
329 Mickey Morandini .07 .20
330 Sammy Sosa .20 .50
331 Jeff Blauser .07 .20
332 Lance Johnson .07 .20
333 Scott Servais .07 .20
334 Kevin Tapani .07 .20
335 Henry Rodriguez .07 .20
336 Jaime Navarro .07 .20
337 Benji Gil .07 .20
338 James Baldwin .07 .20
339 Mike Cameron .07 .20
340 Ray Durham .07 .20
341 Chris Snopek .07 .20
342 Eddie Taubensee .07 .20
343 Bret Boone .07 .20
344 Willie Greene .07 .20
345 Barry Larkin .10 .30
346 Chris Stynes .07 .20
347 Pete Harnisch .07 .20
348 Dave Burba .07 .20
349 Sandy Alomar Jr. .07 .20
350 Kenny Lofton .07 .20
351 Geronimo Berroa .07 .20
352 Omar Vizquel .10 .30
353 Travis Fryman .07 .20
354 Dwight Gooden .07 .20
355 Jim Thome .10 .30
356 David Justice .07 .20
357 Charles Nagy .07 .20
358 Chad Ogea .07 .20
359 Pedro Astacio .07 .20
360 Larry Walker .07 .20
361 Mike Lansing .07 .20
362 Kirt Manwaring .07 .20
363 Dante Bichette .07 .20
364 Jamey Wright .07 .20
365 Darryl Kile .07 .20
366 Luis Gonzalez .07 .20
367 Joe Randa .07 .20
368 Raul Casanova .07 .20
369 Damion Easley .07 .20
370 Brian Hunter .07 .20
371 Bobby Higginson .07 .20
372 Brian Moehler .07 .20
373 Scott Sanders .07 .20
374 Jim Eisenreich .07 .20
375 Derrek Lee .10 .30
376 Jay Powell .07 .20
377 Cliff Floyd .07 .20
378 Alex Fernandez .07 .20
379 Felix Heredia .07 .20
380 Jeff Bagwell .10 .30
381 Bill Spiers .07 .20
382 Chris Holt .07 .20
383 Carl Everett .07 .20
384 Derek Bell .07 .20
385 Moises Alou .07 .20
386 Ramon Garcia .07 .20
387 Mike Sweeney .07 .20
388 Glendon Rusch .07 .20
389 Kevin Appier .07 .20
390 Dean Palmer .07 .20
391 Jeff Conine .07 .20
392 Johnny Damon .10 .30
393 Jose Vizcaino .07 .20
394 Todd Hollandsworth .07 .20
395 Eric Karros .07 .20
396 Todd Zeile .07 .20
397 Chan Ho Park .07 .20
398 Ismael Valdes .07 .20
399 Eric Young .07 .20
400 Hideo Nomo .20 .50
401 Mark Loretta .07 .20
402 Doug Jones .07 .20
403 Jeromy Burnitz .07 .20
404 John Jaha .07 .20
405 Marquis Grissom .07 .20
406 Mike Matheny .07 .20
407 Todd Walker .07 .20
408 Marty Cordova .07 .20
409 Matt Lawton .07 .20
410 Terry Steinbach .07 .20
411 Pat Meares .07 .20
412 Rick Aguilera .07 .20
413 Otis Nixon .07 .20
414 Derrick May .07 .20
415 Carl Pavano .07 .20
416 A.J. Hinch .07 .20
417 Dave Dellucci RC .15 .40
418 Bruce Chen .07 .20
419 Darron Ingram RC .07 .20
420 Sean Casey .07 .20
421 Mark L. Johnson .07 .20
422 Gabe Alvarez .07 .20
423 Alex Gonzalez .07 .20
424 Daryle Ward .07 .20
425 Russell Branyan .07 .20
426 Mike Caruso .07 .20
427 Mike Kinkade RC .07 .20
428 Ramon Hernandez .07 .20
429 Matt Clement .07 .20
430 Travis Lee .07 .20
431 Shane Monahan .07 .20
432 Rich Butler RC .07 .20
433 Chris Widger .07 .20
434 Jose Vidro .07 .20
435 Carlos Perez .07 .20
436 Ryan McGuire .07 .20
437 Brian McRae .07 .20
438 Al Leiter .07 .20
439 Rich Becker .07 .20
440 Todd Hundley .07 .20
441 Dave Mlicki .07 .20
442 Bernard Gilkey .07 .20
443 John Olerud .07 .20
444 Paul O'Neill .10 .30
445 Andy Pettitte .10 .30
446 David Cone .07 .20
447 Chili Davis .07 .20
448 Bernie Williams .10 .30
449 Joe Girardi .07 .20
450 Derek Jeter .50 1.25
451 Mariano Rivera .20 .50
452 George Williams .07 .20
453 Kenny Rogers .07 .20
454 Tom Candiotti .07 .20
455 Rickey Henderson .20 .50
456 Jason Giambi .07 .20
457 Scott Spiezio .07 .20
458 Doug Glanville .07 .20
459 Desi Relaford .07 .20
460 Curt Schilling .07 .20
461 Bob Abreu .07 .20
462 Gregg Jefferies .07 .20
463 Scott Rolen .10 .30
464 Mike Lieberthal .07 .20
465 Tony Womack .07 .20
466 Jermaine Allensworth .07 .20
467 Francisco Cordova .07 .20
468 Jon Lieber .07 .20
469 Al Martin .07 .20
470 Jason Kendall .07 .20
471 Todd Stottlemyre .07 .20
472 Royce Clayton .07 .20
473 Brian Jordan .07 .20
474 John Mabry .07 .20
475 Ray Lankford .07 .20
476 Delino DeShields .07 .20
477 Ron Gant .07 .20
478 Mark Langston .07 .20
479 Steve Finley .07 .20
480 Tony Gwynn .25 .60
481 Andy Ashby .07 .20
482 Wally Joyner .07 .20
483 Greg Vaughn .07 .20
484 Sterling Hitchcock .07 .20
485 Kevin Brown .10 .30
486 Orel Hershiser .07 .20
487 Charlie Hayes .07 .20
488 Darryl Hamilton .07 .20
489 Mark Gardner .07 .20
490 Barry Bonds .60 1.50
491 Robb Nen .07 .20
492 Kirk Rueter .07 .20
493 Randy Johnson .20 .50
494 Jeff Fassero .07 .20
495 Alex Rodriguez .30 .75
496 David Segui .07 .20
497 Rich Amaral .07 .20
498 Russ Davis .07 .20
499 Bubba Trammell .07 .20
500 Wade Boggs .10 .30
501 Roberto Hernandez .07 .20
502 Dave Martinez .07 .20
503 Dennis Springer .07 .20
504 Paul Sorrento .07 .20
505 Wilson Alvarez .07 .20
506 Mike Kelly .07 .20
507 Albie Lopez .07 .20
508 Tony Saunders .07 .20
509 John Flaherty .07 .20
510 Fred McGriff .10 .30
511 Quinton McCracken .07 .20
512 Terrell Wade .07 .20
513 Kevin Stocker .07 .20
514 Kevin Elster .07 .20
515 Will Clark .10 .30
516 Bobby Witt .07 .20
517 Tom Goodwin .07 .20
518 Aaron Sele .07 .20
519 Lee Stevens .07 .20
520 Rusty Greer .07 .20
521 John Wetteland .07 .20
522 Darrin Fletcher .07 .20
523 Jose Canseco .10 .30
524 Randy Myers .07 .20
525 Jose Cruz Jr. .07 .20
526 Shawn Green .07 .20
527 Tony Fernandez .07 .20
528 Alex Gonzalez .07 .20
529 Ed Sprague .07 .20
530 Roger Clemens .40 1.00

1998 Collector's Choice Prime Choice Reserve

COMPLETE SET (18) 30.00 80.00
*STARS: 15X TO 40X BASIC CARDS
*ROOKIES: 8X TO 20X BASIC CARDS
STATED PRINT RUN 500 SERIAL #'d SETS

1998 Collector's Choice Crash the Game

COMPLETE SET (90) 30.00 80.00
SER.2 STATED ODDS 1:5
*INSTANT WIN: .75X TO 2X BASIC CRASH
INSTANT WIN SER.2 STATED ODDS 1:721
EXPIRATION DATE: 12/1/98
CG1A K.Griffey June 26-28 W .75 2.00
CG1B K.Griffey Jr. July 7 L .75 2.00
CG1C K.Griffey Jr. Sept 21-24 W .75 2.00
CG2A T.Lee July 27-30 L .15 .40
CG2B T.Lee Aug 27-30 L .15 .40
CG2C T.Lee Sept 17-20 L .15 .40
CG3A L.Walker July 17-19 L .15 .40
CG3B L.Walker Aug 27-30 W .15 .40
CG3C L.Walker Sept 25-27 W .15 .40
CG4A T.Clark July 9-12 W .15 .40
CG4B T.Clark June 30-July 2 L .15 .40
CG4C T.Clark Sept 4-6 L .15 .40
CG5A C.Ripken June 22-25 W 1.25 3.00
CG5B C.Ripken July 7 L 1.25 3.00
CG5C C.Ripken Sept 4-6 W 1.25 3.00
CG6A T.Salmon June 22-25 L .25 .60
CG6B T.Salmon Aug 28-30 L .25 .60
CG6C T.Salmon Sept 14-15 L .25 .60
CG7A V.Castilla June30-July2 W .15 .40
CG7B V.Castilla Aug 27-30 W .15 .40
CG7C V.Castilla Sept 7-10 W .15 .40
CG8A F.McGriff June 22-25 L .25 .60
CG8B F.McGriff July 3-5 L .25 .60
CG8C F.McGriff Sept 18-20 W .25 .60
CG9A M.Williams July 17-19 L .15 .40
CG9B M.Williams Sept 14-16 W .15 .40
CG9C M.Williams Sept 18-20 L .15 .40
CG10A M.McGwire July 7 L 1.00 2.50
CG10B M.McGwire July 24-26W 1.00 2.50
CG10C M.McGwire Aug 18-19W 1.00 2.50
CG11A A.Belle July 3-5 L .25 .60
CG11B A.Belle Aug 21-23 W .25 .60
CG11C A.Belle Sept 11-13 L .25 .60
CG12A J.Buhner July 9-12 W .15 .40
CG12B J.Buhner Aug 6-9 L .15 .40
CG12C J.Buhner Sept 24-27 L .15 .40
CG13A V.Guerrero June 22-25 L .40 1.00
CG13B V.Guerrero Aug 10-12 W .40 1.00
CG13C V.Guerrero Sept 14-16 W .40 1.00
CG14A A.Jones July 16-19 W .25 .60
CG14B A.Jones Aug 27-30 W .25 .60
CG14C A.Jones Sept 17-20 L .25 .60
CG15A Nomar July 9-12 L .60 1.50
CG15B Nomar Aug 13-16 W .60 1.50
CG15C Nomar Sept 24-27 W .60 1.50
CG16A K.Caminiti June 26-28 W .15 .40
CG16B K.Caminiti July 13-15 W .15 .40
CG16C K.Caminiti Sept 10-13 L .15 .40
CG17A S.Sosa July 9-12 W .40 1.00
CG17B S.Sosa Aug 27-30 W .40 1.00
CG17C S.Sosa Sept 18-20 L .40 1.00
CG18A B.Grieve June 30-July 2 W .15 .40
CG18B B.Grieve Aug 14-16 L .15 .40
CG18C B.Grieve Sept 24-27 L .15 .40
CG19A M.Vaughn July 7 L .15 .40
CG19B M.Vaughn Sept 7-9 L .15 .40
CG19C M.Vaughn Sept 24-27 W .15 .40
CG20A F.Thomas July 7 L .40 1.00
CG20B F.Thomas July 17-19 W .40 1.00
CG20C F.Thomas Sept 4-6 L .40 1.00
CG21A M.Ramirez July 9-12 L .25 .60
CG21B M.Ramirez Aug 13-16 W .25 .60
CG21C M.Ramirez Sept 18-20 W .25 .60
CG22A J.Bagwell July 7 L .25 .60
CG22B J.Bagwell Aug 28-30 W .25 .60
CG22C J.Bagwell Sept 4-6 W .25 .60
CG23A J.Cruz Jr. July 9-12 L .15 .40
CG23B J.Cruz Jr. Aug 13-16 L .15 .40
CG23C J.Cruz Jr. Sept 18-20 L .15 .40
CG24A A.Rod July 7 W .60 1.50
CG24B A.Rod Aug 6-9 W .60 1.50
CG24C A.Rod Sept 21-23 W .60 1.50
CG25A M.Piazza June 22-25 W .60 1.50
CG25B M.Piazza July 7 L .60 1.50
CG25C M.Piazza Sept 10-13 W .60 1.50
CG26A T.Martinez June 26-28 W .25 .60
CG26B T.Martinez July 9-12 L .25 .60
CG26C T.Martinez Aug 13-16 L .25 .60
CG27A C.Jones July 3-5 L .40 1.00
CG27B C.Jones Aug 23-30 L .40 1.00
CG27C C.Jones Sept 17-20 L .40 1.00
CG28A J.Gonzalez July 7 L .15 .40
CG28B J.Gonzalez Aug 6-9 W .15 .40
CG28C J.Gonzalez Sept 11-13 W .15 .40
CG29A J.Thome June 22-23 L .25 .60
CG29B J.Thome July 23-26 W .25 .60
CG29C J.Thome Sept 24-27 L .25 .60
CG30A B.Bonds July 7 W 1.25 3.00
CG30B B.Bonds Sept 4-6 L 1.25 3.00
CG30C B.Bonds Sept 18-20 W 1.25 3.00

1998 Collector's Choice Evolution Revolution

COMPLETE SET (28) 25.00 60.00
SER.1 STATED ODDS 1:13
ER1 Tim Salmon .60 1.50
ER2 Greg Maddux 1.50 4.00
ER3 Cal Ripken 3.00 8.00
ER4 Mo Vaughn .40 1.00
ER5 Sammy Sosa 1.00 2.50
ER6 Frank Thomas 1.00 2.50
ER7 Barry Larkin .60 1.50
ER8 Jim Thome .60 1.50
ER9 Larry Walker .40 1.00
ER10 Travis Fryman .40 1.00
ER11 Gary Sheffield .40 1.00
ER12 Jeff Bagwell .60 1.50
ER13 Johnny Damon .60 1.50
ER14 Mike Piazza 1.50 4.00
ER15 Jeff Cirillo .40 1.00
ER16 Paul Molitor .40 1.00
ER17 Vladimir Guerrero 1.00 2.50
ER18 Todd Hundley .40 1.00
ER19 Tino Martinez .60 1.50
ER20 Jose Canseco .60 1.50
ER21 Scott Rolen .60 1.50
ER22 Al Martin .40 1.00
ER23 Mark McGwire 2.50 6.00
ER24 Tony Gwynn 1.25 3.00
ER25 Barry Bonds 3.00 8.00
ER26 Ken Griffey Jr. 2.00 5.00
ER27 Juan Gonzalez .40 1.00
ER28 Roger Clemens 2.00 5.00

1998 Collector's Choice Mini Bobbing Heads

COMPLETE SET (30) 8.00 20.00
SER.2 STATED ODDS 1:3
1 Tim Salmon .20 .50
2 Travis Lee .10 .30
3 Matt Williams .10 .30
4 Chipper Jones .30 .75
6A Greg Maddux .50 1.25
6B Cal Ripken 1.00 2.50
7 Nomar Garciaparra .50 1.25
8 Mo Vaughn .10 .30
9 Sammy Sosa .30 .75
10 Frank Thomas .30 .75
11 Kenny Lofton .10 .30
12 Jaret Wright .10 .30
13 Larry Walker .10 .30
14 Tony Clark .10 .30
15 Edgar Renteria .10 .30
16 Jeff Bagwell .20 .50
17 Mike Piazza .50 1.25
18 Vladimir Guerrero .30 .75
19 Derek Jeter .75 2.00
20 Ben Grieve .10 .30
21 Scott Rolen .20 .50
22 Mark McGwire .75 2.00
23 Tony Gwynn .40 1.00
24 Barry Bonds 1.00 2.50
25 Ken Griffey Jr. .60 1.50
26 Alex Rodriguez .50 1.25
27 Fred McGriff .20 .50
28 Juan Gonzalez .10 .30
29 Roger Clemens .60 1.50
30 Jose Cruz Jr. .10 .30

1998 Collector's Choice StarQuest

COMP.DELIV.SET (45) 8.00 20.00
COMMON DELIV (1-45) 2.50 6.00
ONE DELIVERY PER SER.1 PACK
COMP.STUDENT SET (20) 6.00 15.00
COMM.STUDENTS (46-65) 6.00 15.00
STUDENTS SER.1 STATED ODDS 1:21
COMP.POWERS SET (15) 6.00 15.00
COMMON POWERS (66-80) 6.00 15.00
POWERS SER.1 STATED ODDS 1:71
COMP.SUPERSTAR SET (10) 6.00 15.00
COM.SUPERSTAR (81-90) 6.00 15.00
SUPERSTAR SER.1 STATED ODDS 1:145
SQ1 Nomar Garciaparra SD .40 1.00
SQ2 Scott Rolen SD .15 .40
SQ3 Jason Dickson SD .08 .25
SQ4 Jaret Wright SD .08 .25
SQ5 Kevin Orie SD .08 .25
SQ6 Jose Guillen SD .08 .25
SQ7 Matt Morris SD .08 .25
SQ8 Mike Cameron SD .08 .25
SQ9 Kevin Polcovich SD .08 .25
SQ10 Jose Cruz Jr. SD .08 .25
SQ11 Miguel Tejada SD .25 .60
SQ12 Fernando Tatis SD .08 .25
SQ13 Todd Helton SD .15 .40
SQ14 Ken Cloude SD .08 .25
SQ15 Ben Grieve SD .08 .25
SQ16 Dante Powell SD .08 .25
SQ17 Bubba Trammell SD .08 .25
SQ18 Juan Encarnacion SD .08 .25
SQ19 Derrek Lee SD .15 .40
SQ20 Paul Konerko SD .08 .25
SQ21 Richard Hidalgo SD .08 .25
SQ22 Denny Neagle SD .08 .25
SQ23 David Justice SD .08 .25
SQ24 Pedro Martinez SD .15 .40
SQ25 Greg Maddux SD .40 1.00
SQ26 Edgar Martinez SD .08 .25
SQ27 Cal Ripken SD .75 2.00
SQ28 Tim Salmon SD .15 .40
SQ29 Shawn Estes SD .08 .25
SQ30 Ken Griffey Jr. SD .50 1.25
SQ31 Brad Radke SD .08 .25
SQ32 Andy Pettitte SD .15 .40
SQ33 Curt Schilling SD .08 .25
SQ34 Raul Mondesi SD .08 .25
SQ35 Alex Rodriguez SD .40 1.00
SQ36 Jeff Kent SD .08 .25
SQ37 Jeff Bagwell SD .15 .40
SQ38 Juan Gonzalez SD .08 .25
SQ39 Barry Bonds SD .75 2.00
SQ40 Mark McGwire SD .60 1.50
SQ41 Frank Thomas SD .25 .60
SQ42 Ray Lankford SD .08 .25
SQ43 Tony Gwynn SD .30 .75
SQ44 Mike Piazza SD .40 1.00
SQ45 Tino Martinez SD .15 .40
SQ46 Nomar Garciaparra SG 2.50 6.00
SQ47 Paul Molitor SG .60 1.50
SQ48 Chuck Knoblauch SG .60 1.50
SQ49 Rusty Greer SG .60 1.50
SQ50 Cal Ripken SG 5.00 12.00
SQ51 Roberto Alomar SG 1.00 2.50
SQ52 Scott Rolen SG 1.00 2.50
SQ53 Derek Jeter SG 4.00 10.00
SQ54 Mark Grace SG 1.00 2.50
SQ55 Randy Johnson SG 1.50 4.00
SQ56 Craig Biggio SG 1.00 2.50
SQ57 Kenny Lofton SG .60 1.50
SQ58 Eddie Murray SG 1.50 4.00
SQ59 Ryne Sandberg SG 2.50 6.00
SQ60 Rickey Henderson SG 1.50 4.00
SQ61 Darin Erstad SG .60 1.50
SQ62 Jim Edmonds SG .60 1.50
SQ63 Ken Caminiti SG .60 1.50
SQ64 Ivan Rodriguez SG 1.00 2.50
SQ65 Tony Gwynn SG 2.00 5.00
SQ66 Tony Clark SP 1.50 4.00
SQ67 Andres Galarraga SP 1.50 4.00
SQ68 Rafael Palmeiro SP 2.50 6.00
SQ69 Manny Ramirez SP 2.50 6.00
SQ70 Albert Belle SP 2.50 6.00
SQ71 Jay Buhner SP 1.50 4.00
SQ72 Mo Vaughn SP 1.50 4.00
SQ73 Barry Bonds SP 12.50 30.00
SQ74 Chipper Jones SP 4.00 10.00
SQ75 Jeff Bagwell SP 2.50 6.00
SQ76 Jim Thome SP 2.50 6.00
SQ77 Sammy Sosa SP 4.00 10.00
SQ78 Todd Hundley SP 1.50 4.00
SQ79 Matt Williams SP 1.50 4.00
SQ80 Vinny Castilla SP 1.50 4.00
SQ81 Jose Cruz Jr. SS 2.50 6.00
SQ82 Frank Thomas SS 6.00 15.00
SQ83 Juan Gonzalez SS 2.50 6.00
SQ84 Mike Piazza SS 10.00 25.00
SQ85 Alex Rodriguez SS 10.00 25.00
SQ86 Larry Walker SS 2.50 6.00
SQ87 Tino Martinez SS 4.00 10.00
SQ88 Greg Maddux SS 10.00 25.00
SQ89 Mark McGwire SS 15.00 40.00
SQ90 Ken Griffey Jr. SS 12.50 30.00

1998 Collector's Choice StarQuest Single

COMPLETE SET (30) 4.00 10.00
ONE PER SERIES 2 PACK
*DOUBLES: 4X TO 10X SQ SINGLE
DOUBLES SER.2 STATED ODDS 1:21
*TRIPLES: 12.5X TO 30X SQ SINGLE
TRIPLES SER.2 STATED ODDS 1:71
*HR'S: 30X TO 80X SQ SINGLE
HOME RUN: RANDOM INS.IN SER.2 PACKS
HOME RUN PRINT RUN 100 SERIAL #'d SETS
1 Ken Griffey Jr. .40 1.00
2 Jose Cruz Jr. .07 .20
3 Cal Ripken .60 1.50
4 Roger Clemens .40 1.00
5 Frank Thomas .20 .50
6 Derek Jeter .50 1.25
7 Alex Rodriguez .30 .75
8 Andruw Jones .10 .30
9 Vladimir Guerrero .20 .50
10 Mark McGwire .50 1.25
11 Kenny Lofton .07 .20
12 Pedro Martinez .10 .30
13 Greg Maddux .30 .75
14 Larry Walker .07 .20
15 Barry Bonds .60 1.50
16 Chipper Jones .20 .50
17 Jeff Bagwell .10 .30
18 Juan Gonzalez .07 .20
19 Tony Gwynn .25 .60
20 Mike Piazza .30 .75
21 Tino Martinez .10 .30
22 Mo Vaughn .07 .20
23 Ben Grieve .07 .20
24 Scott Rolen .10 .30
25 Nomar Garciaparra .30 .75
26 Paul Konerko .07 .20
27 Jaret Wright .07 .20
28 Gary Sheffield .07 .20
29 Todd Helton .10 .30
30 Travis Lee .07 .20

1998 Collector's Choice Stick 'Ums

COMPLETE SET (30) 8.00 20.00
SER.1 STATED ODDS 1:3
1 Andruw Jones .20 .50
2 Chipper Jones .30 .75
3 Cal Ripken 1.00 2.50
4 Nomar Garciaparra .50 1.25
5 Mo Vaughn .10 .30
6 Ryne Sandberg .50 1.25
7 Sammy Sosa .30 .75
8 Frank Thomas .30 .75
9 Albert Belle .20 .50
10 Jim Thome .20 .50
11 Manny Ramirez .20 .50
12 Larry Walker .10 .30
13 Gary Sheffield .10 .30
14 Jeff Bagwell .20 .50

15 Mike Piazza .50 1.25
16 Paul Molitor .10 .30
17 Pedro Martinez .20 .50
18 Todd Hundley .10 .30
19 Derek Jeter .75 2.00
20 Tino Martinez .20 .50
21 Curt Schilling .10 .30
22 Mark McGwire .75 2.00
23 Tony Gwynn .40 1.00
24 Barry Bonds 1.00 2.50
25 Ken Griffey Jr. .60 1.50
26 Alex Rodriguez .50 1.25
27 Juan Gonzalez .10 .30
28 Ivan Rodriguez .20 .50
29 Roger Clemens .60 1.50
30 Jose Cruz Jr. .10 .30

1998 Collector's Choice Blowups 5x7

These 10 cards measure approximately 5" by 7". These cards were inserted one per second series retail box and feature oversize parallels of a selection of stars from the basic 1998 Collectors Choice set.

COMPLETE SET (10) 5.00 12.00
306 Chipper Jones .60 1.50
321 Nomar Garciaparra .50 1.25
360 Larry Walker .30 .75
450 Derek Jeter 1.25 3.00
463 Scott Rolen .30 .75
480 Tony Gwynn .60 1.50
490 Barry Bonds .60 1.50
495 Alex Rodriguez .75 2.00
525 Jose Cruz Jr. .20 .50
530 Roger Clemens .60 1.50

1998 Collector's Choice Cover Glory 5x7

This 10-card set measures approximately 5" by 7" and features action color player images on a red-and-black background. The backs carry player information with a "headline" and paragraph about the player.

COMPLETE SET (10) 5.00 12.00
1 Nomar Garciaparra .50 1.25
2 Roger Clemens .60 1.50
3 Larry Walker .20 .50
4 Mike Piazza .75 2.00
5 Mark McGwire 1.00 2.50
6 Tony Gwynn .60 1.50
7 Jose Cruz Jr. .20 .50
8 Frank Thomas .30 .75
9 Tino Martinez .20 .50
10 Ken Griffey Jr. 1.25 3.00

1998 Collector's Choice Golden Jubilee 5x7

These nine oversize cards measure approximately 5" by 7" and feature parallel cards of the golden jubilee subset in second series Collector's Choice.

COMPLETE SET (9) 5.00 12.00
271 Andruw Jones .40 1.00
272 Alex Rodriguez .60 1.50
273 Juan Gonzalez .20 .50
274 Nomar Garciaparra .60 1.50
275 Ken Griffey Jr. 1.00 2.50
276 Tino Martinez .20 .50
277 Roger Clemens .60 1.50
278 Barry Bonds .60 1.50
279 Mike Piazza .75 2.00

1998 Collector's Choice Retail Jumbos

These cards were available as a mail-away from Upper Deck. If a collector mailed in 10 wrappers and an amount for postage and handling they received this skip-numbered set from Upper Deck's redemption center.

COMPLETE SET (33) 12.50 30.00
1 Nomar Garciaparra .50 1.25
2 Roger Clemens .60 1.50
3 Larry Walker .25 .60
4 Mike Piazza .75 2.00
5 Mark McGwire .60 1.50
6 Tony Gwynn .60 1.50
7 Jose Cruz Jr. .08 .25
8 Frank Thomas .25 .60
35 Andruw Jones .30 .75
40 Cal Ripken 1.25 3.00
55 Ryne Sandberg .30 .75
60 Frank Thomas .25 .60
95 Gary Sheffield .30 .75
97 Charles Johnson .08 .25
145 Mike Piazza .75 2.00
160 Paul Molitor .30 .75
180 Tino Martinez .08 .25
220 Mark McGwire .60 1.50
225 Ken Caminiti .15 .40
240 Ken Griffey Jr. .75 2.00
242 Jay Buhner .08 .25
245 Juan Gonzalez .25 .60
249 Ivan Rodriguez .30 .75
SQ67 Andres Galarraga .15 .40
SQ68 Rafael Palmeiro .15 .40
SQ69 Manny Ramirez .30 .75
SQ70 Albert Belle .08 .25
SQ71 Jay Buhner .08 .25
SQ72 Mo Vaughn .08 .25
SQ73 Barry Bonds .60 1.50
SQ74 Chipper Jones .60 1.50
SQ75 Jeff Bagwell .30 .75
SQ76 Jim Thome .30 .75

1995 Collector's Choice SE

The 1995 Collector's Choice SE set (produced by Upper Deck) consists of 265 standard-size cards issued in foil packs. The fronts feature color action player photos with blue borders. The player's name, position and the team name are printed on the bottom of the photo. The SE logo in blue-foil appears in a top corner. On a white background, the backs carry another color player photo with a short player biography, career stats and 1994 highlights. Subsets featured include Rookie Class (1-25), Record Pace (26-30), Stat Leaders (137-144), Fantasy Team (249-260). There are no Rookie Cards in this set.

COMPLETE SET (265) 8.00 20.00
1 Alex Rodriguez .75 2.00
2 Derek Jeter .75 2.00
3 Dustin Hermanson .05 .15
4 Bill Pulsipher .05 .15
5 Terrell Wade .05 .15
6 Darren Dreifort .05 .15
7 LaTroy Hawkins .05 .15
8 Alex Ochoa .05 .15
9 Paul Wilson .05 .15
10 Ernie Young .05 .15
11 Alan Benes .05 .15
12 Garret Anderson .10 .30
13 Armando Benitez .05 .15
14 Robert Perez .05 .15
15 Herbert Perry .05 .15
16 Jose Silva .05 .15
17 Orlando Miller .05 .15
18 Russ Davis .05 .15
19 Jason Isringhausen .10 .30
20 Ray McDavid .05 .15
21 Duane Singleton .05 .15
22 Paul Shuey .05 .15
23 Steve Dunn .05 .15
24 Mike Lieberthal .10 .30
25 Chan Ho Park .10 .30
26 Ken Griffey Jr. RP .40 1.00
27 Tony Gwynn RP .20 .50
28 Chuck Knoblauch RP .05 .15
29 Frank Thomas RP .20 .50
30 Matt Williams RP .05 .15
31 Chili Davis .10 .30
32 Chad Curtis .05 .15
33 Brian Anderson .05 .15
34 Chuck Finley .10 .30
35 Tim Salmon .20 .50
36 Bo Jackson .30 .75
37 Doug Drabek .05 .15
38 Craig Biggio .20 .50
39 Ken Caminiti .10 .30
40 Jeff Bagwell .20 .50
41 Darryl Kile .10 .30
42 John Hudek .05 .15
43 Brian L.Hunter .05 .15
44 Dennis Eckersley .10 .30
45 Mark McGwire .75 2.00
46 Brent Gates .05 .15
47 Steve Karsay .05 .15
48 Rickey Henderson .30 .75
49 Terry Steinbach .05 .15
50 Ruben Sierra .10 .30
51 Roberto Alomar .20 .50
52 Carlos Delgado .10 .30
53 Alex Gonzalez .05 .15
54 Joe Carter .10 .30
55 Paul Molitor .10 .30
56 Juan Guzman .05 .15
57 John Olerud .10 .30
58 Shawn Green .10 .30
59 Tom Glavine .20 .50
60 Greg Maddux .50 1.25
61 Roberto Kelly .05 .15
62 Ryan Klesko .10 .30
63 Javier Lopez .10 .30
64 Jose Oliva .05 .15
65 Fred McGriff .20 .50
66 Steve Avery .05 .15
67 David Justice .10 .30
68 Ricky Bones .05 .15
69 Cal Eldred .05 .15
70 Greg Vaughn .05 .15
71 Dave Nilsson .05 .15
72 Jose Valentin .05 .15
73 Matt Mieske .05 .15
74 Todd Zeile .05 .15
75 Ozzie Smith .50 1.25
76 Bernard Gilkey .05 .15
77 Ray Lankford .10 .30
78 Bob Tewksbury .05 .15
79 Mark Whiten .05 .15
80 Gregg Jefferies .05 .15
81 Randy Myers .05 .15
82 Shawon Dunston .05 .15
83 Mark Grace .20 .50
84 Derrick May .05 .15
85 Sammy Sosa .30 .75
86 Steve Trachsel .05 .15
87 Brett Butler .10 .30
88 Delino DeShields .05 .15
89 Orel Hershiser .10 .30
90 Mike Piazza .50 1.25
91 Todd Hollandsworth .05 .15
92 Eric Karros .10 .30
93 Ramon Martinez .05 .15
94 Tim Wallach .05 .15
95 Raul Mondesi .10 .30
96 Larry Walker .10 .30
97 Wil Cordero .05 .15
98 Marquis Grissom .10 .30
99 Ken Hill .05 .15
100 Cliff Floyd .10 .30
101 Pedro Martinez .20 .50
102 John Wetteland .10 .30
103 Rondell White .10 .30
104 Moises Alou .10 .30
105 Barry Bonds .75 2.00
106 Darren Lewis .05 .15
107 Mark Portugal .05 .15
108 Matt Williams .10 .30
109 William VanLandingham .05 .15
110 Bill Swift .05 .15
111 Robby Thompson .05 .15
112 Rod Beck .05 .15
113 Darryl Strawberry .10 .30
114 Jim Thome .20 .50
115 Dave Winfield .10 .30
116 Eddie Murray .30 .75
117 Manny Ramirez .20 .50
118 Carlos Baerga .05 .15
119 Kenny Lofton .10 .30
120 Albert Belle .10 .30
121 Mark Clark .05 .15
122 Dennis Martinez .10 .30
123 Randy Johnson .30 .75
124 Jay Buhner .10 .30
125 Ken Griffey Jr. .60 1.50
126 Goose Gossage .10 .30
127 Tino Martinez .20 .50
128 Reggie Jefferson .05 .15
129 Edgar Martinez .20 .50
130 Gary Sheffield .10 .30
131 Pat Rapp .05 .15
132 Bret Barberie .05 .15
133 Chuck Carr .05 .15
134 Jeff Conine .10 .30
135 Charles Johnson .10 .30
136 Benito Santiago .10 .30
137 Matt Williams STL .05 .15
138 Jeff Bagwell STL .10 .30
139 Kenny Lofton STL .05 .15
140 Tony Gwynn STL .20 .50
141 Jimmy Key STL .05 .15
142 Greg Maddux STL .30 .75
143 Randy Johnson STL .20 .50
144 Lee Smith STL .05 .15
145 Bobby Bonilla .10 .30
146 Jason Jacome .05 .15
147 Jeff Kent .10 .30
148 Ryan Thompson .05 .15
149 Bobby Jones .05 .15
150 Bret Saberhagen .10 .30
151 John Franco .10 .30
152 Lee Smith .10 .30
153 Rafael Palmeiro .20 .50
154 Brady Anderson .10 .30
155 Cal Ripken 1.00 2.50
156 Jeffrey Hammonds .05 .15
157 Mike Mussina .20 .50
158 Chris Hoiles .05 .15
159 Ben McDonald .05 .15
160 Tony Gwynn .40 1.00
161 Joey Hamilton .05 .15
162 Andy Benes .05 .15
163 Trevor Hoffman .10 .30
164 Phil Plantier .05 .15
165 Derek Bell .05 .15
166 Bip Roberts .05 .15
167 Eddie Williams .05 .15
168 Fernando Valenzuela .10 .30
169 Mariano Duncan .05 .15
170 Lenny Dykstra .10 .30
171 Darren Daulton .10 .30
172 Danny Jackson .05 .15
173 Bobby Munoz .05 .15
174 Doug Jones .05 .15
175 Jay Bell .10 .30
176 Zane Smith .05 .15
177 Jon Lieber .05 .15
178 Carlos Garcia .05 .15
179 Orlando Merced .05 .15
180 Andy Van Slyke .20 .50
181 Rick Helling .05 .15
182 Rusty Greer .10 .30
183 Kenny Rogers .10 .30
184 Will Clark .20 .50
185 Jose Canseco .20 .50
186 Juan Gonzalez .10 .30
187 Dean Palmer .10 .30
188 Ivan Rodriguez .20 .50
189 John Valentin .05 .15
190 Roger Clemens .60 1.50
191 Aaron Sele .05 .15
192 Scott Cooper .05 .15
193 Mike Greenwell .05 .15
194 Mo Vaughn .10 .30
195 Andre Dawson .10 .30
196 Ron Gant .10 .30
197 Jose Rijo .10 .30
198 Bret Boone .10 .30
199 Deion Sanders .20 .50
200 Barry Larkin .20 .50
201 Hal Morris .05 .15
202 Reggie Sanders .10 .30
203 Kevin Mitchell .05 .15
204 Marvin Freeman .05 .15
205 Andres Galarraga .10 .30
206 Walt Weiss .05 .15
207 Charlie Hayes .05 .15
208 Dave Nied .05 .15
209 Dante Bichette .10 .30
210 David Cone .10 .30
211 Jeff Montgomery .05 .15
212 Felix Jose .05 .15
213 Mike Macfarlane .05 .15
214 Wally Joyner .10 .30
215 Bob Hamelin .05 .15
216 Brian McRae .05 .15
217 Kirk Gibson .10 .30
218 Lou Whitaker .10 .30
219 Chris Gomez .05 .15
220 Cecil Fielder .10 .30
221 Mickey Tettleton .05 .15
222 Travis Fryman .10 .30
223 Tony Phillips .05 .15
224 Rick Aguilera .05 .15
225 Scott Erickson .05 .15
226 Chuck Knoblauch .10 .30
227 Kent Hrbek .10 .30
228 Shane Mack .05 .15
229 Kevin Tapani .05 .15
230 Kirby Puckett .30 .75
231 Julio Franco .10 .30
232 Jack McDowell .05 .15
233 Jason Bere .05 .15
234 Alex Fernandez .05 .15
235 Frank Thomas .30 .75
236 Ozzie Guillen .10 .30
237 Robin Ventura .10 .30
238 Michael Jordan 1.00 2.50
239 Wilson Alvarez .05 .15
240 Don Mattingly .75 2.00
241 Jim Abbott .20 .50
242 Jim Leyritz .05 .15
243 Paul O'Neill .20 .50
244 Melido Perez .05 .15
245 Wade Boggs .20 .50
246 Mike Stanley .05 .15
247 Danny Tartabull .05 .15
248 Jimmy Key .10 .30
249 Greg Maddux FT .30 .75
250 Randy Johnson FT .20 .50
251 Bret Saberhagen FT .05 .15
252 John Wetteland FT .05 .15
253 Mike Piazza FT .30 .75
254 Jeff Bagwell FT .10 .30
255 Craig Biggio FT .10 .30
256 Matt Williams FT .05 .15
257 Wil Cordero FT .05 .15
258 Kenny Lofton FT .05 .15
259 Barry Bonds FT .40 1.00
260 Dante Bichette FT .05 .15
261 Ken Griffey Jr. CL .40 1.00
262 Goose Gossage CL .05 .15
263 Cal Ripken CL .50 1.25
264 Kenny Rogers CL .05 .15
265 John Valentin CL .05 .15
P125 Ken Griffey Jr. Promo .50 1.25

1995 Collector's Choice SE Gold Signature

*STARS: 10X TO 25X BASIC CARDS
*ROOKIES: 8X TO 20X BASIC
STATED ODDS 1:35
TWELVE GOLD PER GOLD SUPER PACK
261 Ken Griffey Jr. CL 20.00 50.00

1995 Collector's Choice SE Silver Signature

COMPLETE SET (265) 25.00 60.00
*STARS: 1.25X TO 3X BASIC CARDS
*ROOKIES: 1X TO 2.5X BASIC
ONE PER PACK/TWO PER MINI JUMBO
12 PER SILVER SUPER PACK

1994 Collector's Edge Dial Justice

This card measures the standard size. The fronts feature an action player photo on a clear, blue and green background. The Dial logo and team logo appear at the top. The player's name, position and card name are printed in a blue bar at the bottom. The backs are the reverse of the front with career highlights printed in white.

1 David Justice 1.25 3.00

1917 Collins-McCarthy E135

The cards in this 200-card set measure 2" by 3 1/4". Collins-McCarthy, the West Coast manufacturer of Zee Nuts (E137), issued the Baseball's Hall of Fame set of players in 1917. These black and white photos of current players were not only numbered but also listed alphabetically. The set is similar to D328, except that E135 is printed on thinner stock. The complete set price includes all variation cards listed in the checklist below. Recent research indicates that this set was issued in 1917, a good example of that is the Ping Bodie card. Bodie played the full 1916 season for San Francisco and his card indicates he is a member of the White Sox. At least four different back varieties are known: A card with a blank back, Collins-McCarthy, Boston Store and Standard Biscuit.

COMPLETE SET (200) 20000.00 40000.00
1 Sam Agnew 75.00 150.00
2 Grover C. Alexander 150.00 300.00
3 W.E. Alexander 75.00 150.00
4 Leon Ames 75.00 150.00
5 Fred Anderson 75.00 150.00
6 Ed Appleton 75.00 150.00
7 Jimmy Archer 75.00 150.00
8 Jimmy Austin 75.00 150.00
9 Jim Bagby 75.00 150.00
10 H.D. Baird 75.00 150.00
11 Frank Baker 150.00 300.00
12 Dave Bancroft 125.00 250.00
13 Jack Barry 75.00 150.00
14 Joe Benz 75.00 150.00
15 Al Betzel 75.00 150.00
16 Ping Bodie 75.00 150.00
17 Joe Boehling 75.00 150.00
18 Eddie Burns 75.00 150.00
19 George Burns Detroit 75.00 150.00
20 Geo. J. Burns NY 75.00 150.00
21 Joe Bush 100.00 200.00
22 Owen Bush 75.00 150.00
23 Bobbie Byrne 75.00 150.00
24 Forrest Cady 75.00 150.00
25 Max Carey 125.00 250.00
26 Ray Chapman 125.00 250.00
27 Larry Cheney 75.00 150.00
28 Eddie Cicotte 150.00 300.00
29 Tom Clarke 75.00 150.00
30 Ty Cobb 1200.00 2400.00
31 Eddie Collins 150.00 300.00
32 Shauno Collins 75.00 150.00
33 Fred Coumbe 75.00 150.00
34 Harry Coveleski 100.00 200.00
35 Gavvy Cravath 100.00 200.00
36 Sam Crawford 150.00 300.00
37 George Cutshaw 100.00 200.00
38 Jack Daubert 100.00 200.00
39 George Dauss 75.00 150.00
40 Charles Deal 75.00 150.00
41 Wheezer Dell 75.00 150.00
42 William Doak 75.00 150.00
43 Bill Donovan 75.00 150.00
44 Larry Doyle 100.00 200.00
45 Johnny Evers 150.00 300.00
46 Urban Faber 125.00 250.00
47 Happy Felsch 150.00 300.00
48 Bill Fischer 75.00 150.00
49 Ray Fisher 75.00 150.00
50 Art Fletcher 75.00 150.00
51 Eddie Foster 75.00 150.00
52 Jacques Fournier 75.00 150.00
53 Del Gainer 75.00 150.00
54 Bert Gallia 75.00 150.00
55 Chick Gandil 150.00 300.00
56 Larry Gardner 75.00 150.00
57 Joe Gedeon 75.00 150.00
58 Gus Getz 75.00 150.00
59 Frank Gilhooley 75.00 150.00
60 Kid Gleason MG 100.00 200.00
61 Mike Gonzales 75.00 150.00
62 Hank Gowdy 100.00 200.00
63 John Graney 75.00 150.00
64 Tom Griffith 75.00 150.00
65 Heinie Groh 100.00 200.00
66 Bob Groom 75.00 150.00
67 Louis Guisto 75.00 150.00
68 Earl Hamilton 75.00 150.00
69 Harry Harper 75.00 150.00
70 Grover Hartley 75.00 150.00
71 Harry Heilmann 125.00 250.00
72 Claude Hendrix 75.00 150.00
73 Olaf Henriksen 75.00 150.00
74 John Henry 75.00 150.00
75 Buck Herzog 75.00 150.00
76A Hugh High ERR photo actually Claude Williams white stockings 150.00 300.00
76B Hugh High COR black stockings 100.00 200.00
77 Dick Hoblitzell 75.00 150.00
78 Walter Holke 75.00 150.00
79 Harry Hooper 125.00 250.00
80 Rogers Hornsby 300.00 600.00
81 Ivan Howard 75.00 150.00
82 Joe Jackson 1200.00 2400.00
83 Harold Janvrin 75.00 150.00
84 William James 75.00 150.00
85 Charlie Jamieson 75.00 150.00
86 Hugh Jennings MG 125.00 250.00
87 Walter Johnson 350.00 700.00
88 James Johnston 75.00 150.00
89 Fielder Jones 75.00 150.00
90A Joe Judge ERR photo actually Ray Morgan bat right shoulder 150.00 300.00
90B Joe Judge COR(bat left shoulder) 100.00 200.00
91 Hans Lobert 75.00 150.00
92 Benny Kauff 75.00 150.00
93 Wm. Killefer Jr. 75.00 150.00
94 Ed Konetchy 75.00 150.00
95 John Lavan 75.00 150.00
96 Jimmy Lavender 75.00 150.00
97 Nemo Leibold 75.00 150.00
98 Dutch Leonard 100.00 200.00
99 Duffy Lewis 75.00 150.00
100 Tom Long 75.00 150.00
101 Bill Louden 75.00 150.00
102 Fred Luderus 75.00 150.00
103 Lee Magee 75.00 150.00
104 Sherwood Magee 100.00 200.00
105 Al Mamaux 75.00 150.00
106 Leslie Mann 75.00 150.00
107 Rabbit Maranville 125.00 250.00
108 Rube Marquard 150.00 300.00
109 Armando Marsans 75.00 150.00
110 J. Erskine Mayer 75.00 150.00
111 George McBride 75.00 150.00
112 Lew McCarty 75.00 150.00
113 John J. McGraw MG 150.00 300.00
114 Jack McInnis 100.00 200.00
115 Lee Meadows 75.00 150.00
116 Fred Merkle 100.00 200.00
117 Chief Meyers 100.00 200.00
118 Clyde Milan 75.00 150.00
119 Otto Miller 75.00 150.00
120 Clarence Mitchell 75.00 150.00
121A Ray Morgan ERR photo actually Joe Judge bat left shoulder 150.00 300.00
121B Ray Morgan COR (bat right shoulder) 100.00 200.00
122 Guy Morton 75.00 150.00
123 Mike Mowrey 75.00 150.00
124 Elmer Myers 75.00 150.00
125 Hy Myers 75.00 150.00
126 Greasy Neale 100.00 200.00
127 Art Nehf 75.00 150.00
128 J.A. Niehoff 75.00 150.00
129 Steve O'Neill 100.00 200.00
130 Dode Paskert 75.00 150.00
131 Roger Peckinpaugh 100.00 200.00
132 Pol Perritt 75.00 150.00
133 Jeff Pfeffer 75.00 150.00
134 Walter Pipp 125.00 250.00
135 Derril Pratt 75.00 150.00
136 Bill Rariden 75.00 150.00
137 Sam Rice 125.00 250.00
138 Hank Ritter 75.00 150.00
139 Eppa Rixey 125.00 250.00
140 Davey Robertson 75.00 150.00
141 Bob Roth 75.00 150.00
142 Ed Roush 125.00 250.00
143 Clarence Rowland MG 75.00 150.00
144 Dick Rudolph 75.00 150.00
145 William Rumler 75.00 150.00
146A Reb Russell ERR photo actually Mel Wolfgang pitching follow through 150.00 300.00
146B Reb Russell COR standing, hands at side 100.00 200.00
147 Babe Ruth 1800.00 3600.00
148 Vic Saier 75.00 150.00
149 Slim Sallee 75.00 150.00
150 Ray Schalk 125.00 250.00
151 Walter Schang 75.00 150.00
152 Frank Schulte 75.00 150.00
153 Ferd Schupp 75.00 150.00
154 Everett Scott 100.00 200.00
155 Hank Severeid 75.00 150.00
156 Howard Shanks 75.00 150.00
157 Bob Shawkey 100.00 200.00
158 Jimmy Sheckard CO 75.00 150.00
159 Ernie Shore 100.00 200.00
160 Chick Shorten 75.00 150.00
161 Burt Shotton 100.00 200.00
162 George Sisler 150.00 300.00
163 Elmer Smith 75.00 150.00
164 J. Carlisle Smith 75.00 150.00
165 Fred Snodgrass 100.00 200.00
166 Tris Speaker 150.00 300.00
167 Oscar Stanage 75.00 150.00
168 Casey Stengel 500.00 1000.00
169 Milton Stock 75.00 150.00
170 Amos Strunk 75.00 150.00
171 Zeb Terry 75.00 150.00
172 Jeff Tesreau 75.00 150.00
173 Chester Thomas 75.00 150.00
174 Fred Toney 100.00 200.00
175 Terry Turner 75.00 150.00
176 George Tyler 75.00 150.00
177 Jim Vaughn 75.00 150.00
178 Bob Veach 75.00 150.00
179 Oscar Vitt 100.00 200.00
180 Honus Wagner 750.00 1500.00
181 Clarence Walker 75.00 150.00
182 Jim Walsh 75.00 150.00
183 Al Walters 75.00 150.00
184 Bill Wambsganss 75.00 150.00
185 Buck Weaver 150.00 300.00
186 Carl Weilman 75.00 150.00
187 Zack Wheat 150.00 300.00
188 Geo. Whitted 75.00 150.00
189 Joe Wilhoit 75.00 150.00
190A Claude Williams ERR photo actually Hugh High black stockings 150.00 300.00
190B Claude Williams COR (photo correct) 125.00 250.00
191 Fred Williams 100.00 200.00
192 Art Wilson 75.00 150.00
193 Lawton Witt 75.00 150.00
194 Joe Wood 125.00 250.00
195 William Wortman 75.00 150.00
196 Steve Yerkes 75.00 150.00
197 Earl Yingling 75.00 150.00
198 Pep Young(2ndB. Detroit) 75.00 150.00
199 Rollie Zeider 75.00 150.00
200 Heine Zimmerman 75.00 150.00

1962 Colt .45's Booklets

These booklets feature members of the inagural Houston Colt 45's. They were issued and released at various retail outlets. Each booklet is 16 pages and has personal and career information on the players in the set. The following booklets are believed to be in shorter supply: Jim Campbell; J.C. Hartman, Roman Mejias, Jim Pendleton, Paul Richards, Bobby Shantz, Jim Umbricht, Hal Woodeshick, Coaches, Announcers. Umbricht is believed to be by far the hardest booklet to acquire. Three different versions of each booklet exist: they were sponsored by American Tobacco, Pearl Beer and Phillips 66 respectively. All sponsors are valued the same.

COMPLETE SET 125.00 250.00
COMMON PLAYER 2.50 6.00
COMMON SP'S 6.00 15.00
1 Joe Amalfitano 2.50 6.00
2 Bob Aspromonte 3.00 8.00
3 Bob Bruce 2.50 6.00
4 Jim Campbell SP 6.00 15.00
5 Harry Craft MG 2.50 6.00
6 Dick Farrell 2.50 6.00
7 Dave Giusti 2.50 6.00
8 Jim Golden 2.50 6.00
9 J.C. Hartman SP 6.00 15.00
10 Ken Johnson 2.50 6.00
11 Norm Larker 2.50 6.00
12 Bob Lillis 3.00 8.00
13 Don McMahon 2.50 6.00
14 Roman Mejias SP 6.00 15.00
15 Jim Pendleton SP 6.00 15.00
16 Paul Richards GM SP 8.00 20.00
17 Bobby Shantz SP 8.00 20.00
18 Hal Smith 2.50 6.00
19 Al Spangler 2.50 6.00
20 Jim Umbricht SP 20.00 50.00
21 Carl Warwick 2.50 6.00
22 Hal Woodeshick SP 8.00 20.00
23 The Coaches SP 8.00 20.00
24 The Announcers SP 6.00 15.00

1962 Colt .45's Houston Chronicle

This 20-card set features sketches of the Houston Colt .45's team as drawn by Tony Couch and appeared in the Houston Chronicle newspaper. The cards are unnumbered and checklisted below in alphabetical order.

COMPLETE SET (20) 12.50 30.00
1 Joe Amalfitano .60 1.50
2 Bob Aspromonte .75 2.00
3 Don Buddin .60 1.50
4 Al Cicotte .60 1.50
5 Dick Ferrell(Sic) .60 1.50
6 Dick Gernert .60 1.50
7 Jim Golden .60 1.50
8 Al Heist .60 1.50
9 Ken Johnson .60 1.50
10 Norm Larker .60 1.50
11 Roman Mejias .60 1.50
12 Ed Olivares .60 1.50
13 Jim Pendleton .60 1.50
14 Bobby Shantz .75 2.00
15 Hal W. Smith .60 1.50
16 Al Spangler .60 1.50
17 Don Taussig .60 1.50
18 Bobby Tiefenauer .60 1.50
19 Jim Umbricht .60 1.50
20 Hal Woodeshick .60 1.50

1962 Colt .45's Jay Publishing

This 12-card set of the Houston Colt .45's measures approximately 5" by 7". The fronts feature black-and-white posed player photos with the player's and team name printed below in the white border. These cards were packaged 12 in a packet. The backs are blank. The cards are unnumbered and checklisted below in alphabetical order. A complete set in the original envelope is valued at fifty percent higher.

COMPLETE SET (12) 50.00 100.00
1 Joe Amalfitano 4.00 10.00
2 Bob Aspromonte 5.00 12.00
3 Bob Bruce 3.00 8.00
4 Don Buddin 3.00 8.00
5 Harry Craft MG 3.00 8.00
6 Dick Farrell 3.00 8.00
7 Ken Johnson 3.00 8.00
8 Norm Larker 3.00 8.00
9 Roman Mejias 4.00 10.00
10 Paul Richards GM 5.00 12.00
11 Hal Smith 4.00 10.00
12 Al Spangler 3.00 8.00

1963 Colt .45's Jay Publishing

This 12-card set of the Houston Colt .45's measures approximately 5" by 7". The fronts feature black-and-white posed player photos with the player's and team name printed below in the white border. These cards were packaged 12 in a packet. The backs are blank. The cards are unnumbered and checklisted below in alphabetical order.

COMPLETE SET (12) 40.00 80.00
1 Bob Aspromonte 4.00 10.00
2 Bob Bruce 2.50 6.00
3 Harry Craft MG 3.00 8.00
4 Dick Farrell 2.50 6.00
5 Bob Lillis 3.00 8.00
6 Don McMahon 2.50 6.00
7 Jim Pendleton 2.50 6.00
8 Merritt Ranew 2.50 6.00
9 Pete Runnels 2.50 6.00
10 Hal Smith 2.50 6.00
11 Al Spangler 2.50 6.00
12 Carl Warwick 2.50 6.00

1963 Colt .45's Pepsi-Cola

The 1963 Pepsi carton insert set consists of 16 black and white cards portraying Houston Colt 45 players. Cards are often found with the tabs, which contain a schedule and ads. Lillis and Temple are the scarcest commons while Bateman and Warwick were never publicly distributed. The set has a catalog description of F230-3. Rusty Staub appears in his Rookie Card year.

COMPLETE SET 1500.00 3000.00
COMMON CARD .75 2.00
COMMON SP'S 10.00 25.00
COMMON 4 BY 6 4.00 10.00
1 Bob Aspromonte 1.25 3.00
2 John Bateman SP 1250.00 2500.00
3 Bob Bruce 6.00 15.00
4 Jim Campbell .75 2.00
5 Dick Farrell .75 2.00
6 Ernie Fazio .75 2.00
7 Carroll Hardy .75 2.00
8 J.C. Hartman .75 2.00
9 Ken Johnson .75 2.00
10 Bob Lillis SP 10.00 25.00
11 Don McMahon .75 2.00
12 Pete Runnels .75 2.00
13 Al Spangler .75 2.00
14 Rusty Staub 6.00 15.00
15 Johnny Temple SP 10.00 25.00
16 Carl Warwick SP 300.00 600.00
17 Ernie Fazio (4-in x 6-in) 4.00 10.00
18 Pete Runnels (4-in x 6-in) 6.00 15.00
19 Al Spangler (4-in x 6-in) 4.00 10.00
20 Rusty Staub (4-in x 6-in) 10.00 25.00

1964 Colt .45's Jay Publishing

This 12-card set of the Houston Colt .45's measures approximately 5" by 7". The fronts feature black-and-white posed player photos with the player's and team name printed below in the white border. These cards were packaged 12 in a packet. The backs are blank. The cards are unnumbered and checklisted below in alphabetical order.

COMPLETE SET (12) 40.00 80.00
1 Bob Aspromonte 3.00 8.00
2 Bob Bruce 2.50 6.00
3 Harry Craft MG 2.50 6.00
4 Dick Farrell 2.50 6.00
5 Ken Johnson 2.50 6.00
6 Pete Runnels 2.50 6.00
7 Al Spangler 2.50 6.00
8 Rusty Staub 6.00 15.00
9 Johnny Temple 3.00 8.00
10 Carl Warwick 2.50 6.00
11 Hal Woodeshick 2.50 6.00
12 Jim Wynn 5.00 12.00

1995 Comic Images Promo

This standard-size promo card was issued to promote the 90-card "Phil Rizzuto's Baseball - The National Pastime" set. Sporting a chromium finish, the front features a full-bleed color shot of Phil Rizzuto. The back presents an advertisement for the card set. The card is unnumbered.

1 Phil Rizzuto 1.25 3.00

1995 Comic Images

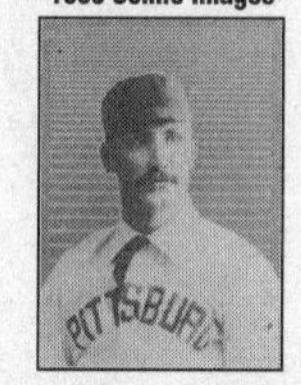

This 90-card standard-size set was produced by Comic Images, who enlisted the help of Hall of Famer Phil Rizzuto. Rizzuto himself autographed 1,000 cards for random insertion. Titled "Phil Rizzuto's Baseball - The National Pastime," set features nostalgic images of players, teams, stadiums, and memorabilia from the turn of the century until the present day.

COMPLETE SET (90) 10.00 25.00
1 Sportsman's Park .08 .25
2 Briggs Stadium .08 .25
3 Shibe Park .08 .25
4 Polo Grounds Print .08 .25
5 Forbes Field .08 .25
6 Cleveland Stadium .08 .25
7 League Park .08 .25
8 Highlander Park .08 .25
9 South Side Park .08 .25
10 Catchers' Mitt .08 .25
11 Baseball Trophy .08 .25
12 Baseball Plate .08 .25
13 Bisque Figure .08 .25
14 Beanbag Toss Game .08 .25
15 Tobacco Carved Figure .08 .25
16 Sunday Magazine .08 .25
17 Street and Smith Sport .08 .25
18 Collier's .08 .25
19 Bluebook .08 .25
20 Chadwick's .08 .25

21 Harper's Weekly .08 .25
22 American Magazine .08 .25
23 Crazy Baseball Stories .08 .25
24 New York Giants .08 .25
25 Cincinnati American .08 .25
26 Chicago White Stockings .08 .25
27 Baltimore Blues .08 .25
28 Chicago White Stockings .08 .25
All-American Team
29 Phillipines Baseball .08 .25
30 Champions .08 .25
31 John McGraw .60 1.50
32 Home Run .08 .25
33 Lorillard Chicago BBC .08 .25
34 Boston BBC .08 .25
35 Out at First .08 .25
36 Coffee Cards .08 .25
37 Uncut Sheet .08 .25
38 Tobin Lithographers .08 .25
39 Uncut Sheet .08 .25
Die Cut
40 Patsy Dougherty .20 .50
41 A Regular Corker .08 .25
42 Barker's Advertising Books .08 .25
43 Toledo BBC Tobacco .08 .25
44 Shredded Wheat .08 .25
45 BVS Advertisment .08 .25
46 Police Gazette Poster .08 .25
47 Japenese Poster .08 .25
48 Safe Hit Vegetable Crate .08 .25
49 Slide, Kelly, Slide Poster .08 .25
50 Peck and Snyder Hat .08 .25
51 Reach Gloves Catalog .08 .25
52 New York Giants Score Card .08 .25
53 Game Card .08 .25
54 Wright and Ditson Guide .08 .25
55 All-Star Game Program .08 .25
56 Stadium Scene .08 .25
57 Currier and Ives Print .08 .25
58 Scorecard Artwork .08 .25
59 Folk Art .08 .25
60 Batter .08 .25
61 Cartoon .08 .25
62 Teddy Roosevelt Cartoon .08 .25
63 Uncle Sam Cartoon .08 .25
64 Casey at the Bat .08 .25
65 Seymour Church Print .08 .25
66 Valentine Card .08 .25
67 Pinup Book .08 .25
68 Uncle Sam WWI Sheet .08 .25
69 Baseball Sheet Music .08 .25
70 Saturday Glove .08 .25
71 Ft Wayne Woman .08 .25
72 Spalding Baseball Guide .08 .25
73 Rally Day Postcard .08 .25
74 Spalding Advertisment Die Cut .08 .25
75 Out Baseball Club Cover .08 .25
76 Jake Beckley .40 1.00
77 Cap Anson .60 1.50
78 St Louis Player .08 .25
79 Sam Thompson .40 1.00
80 Bobby Wallace .40 1.00
81 Fogarty and McGuire .20 .50
82 Yank Robinson .20 .50
83 Charlie Comiskey .40 1.00
84 Picked Off .08 .25
85 Error .08 .25
86 Third Base .08 .25
87 Safe at Home .08 .25
88 Baseball Action .08 .25
89 Great Fielding .08 .25
90 Checklist .08 .25
AU Phil Rizzuto AU 20.00 40.00
NNO Limited Edition
Medallion Card

2000 Cone ALS

1 David Cone 1.25 3.00

1981 Conlon TSN

Issued by The Sporting News, this 100-card set measures approximately 4" by 5" and features the photography of Charles Martin Conlon. The set consists of baseball portraits from 1915-1935. The set was packaged in a brown leatherette case embossed in silver and cost $50 upon issue directly from the Sporting News. The fronts display glossy sepia-tone pictures with white borders on heavy card stock. The words "The Sporting News" are printed at the top and the player's name, position, the year of the photo and the card number are listed at the bottom. The backs are blank. A limited edition set numbered to 1000 and certified was issued in 1993. Those cards are valued the same as the cards issued in 1981

COMPLETE SET (100) 40.00 100.00
1 Ty Cobb 3.00 8.00
2 Hugh Jennings .60 1.50
3 Miller Huggins .60 1.50
4 Babe Ruth 4.00 10.00
5 Lou Gehrig 3.00 8.00
6 John McGraw 1.50 4.00
7 Bill Terry 1.00 2.50
8 Stan Baumgartner .20 .50
9 Christy Mathewson 1.50 4.00
10 Grover Alexander 1.25 3.00
11 Tony Lazzeri .60 1.50
12 Frank Chance 1.00 2.50
Joe Tinker
13 Johnny Evers 1.00 2.50
14 Tris Speaker 1.00 2.50
15 Harry Hooper .60 1.50
16 Duffy Lewis .20 .50
17 Smokey Joe Wood .40 1.00
18 Hugh Duffy .60 1.50
19 Rogers Hornsby 1.50 4.00
20 Earl Averill .60 1.50
21 Dizzy Dean 1.50 4.00
22 Paul Dean .20 .50
23 Frank Frisch .60 1.50
24 Pepper Martin .40 1.00
25 Blondy Ryan .20 .50
26 Hank Gowdy .20 .50
27 Fred Merkle .40 1.00
28 Ernie Lombardi .60 1.50
29 Greasy Neale .40 1.00
30 Morris Badgro .20 .50
31 Jim Thorpe 2.50 6.00
32 Roy Johnson .20 .50
33 Bob Johnson .20 .50
34 Moose Solters .20 .50
35 Specs Toporcer .20 .50
36 Jackie Hayes .20 .50
37 Walter Johnson 2.00 5.00
38 Lefty Grove 1.25 3.00
39 Eddie Collins 1.25 3.00
40 Buck Weaver .60 1.50
41 Cozy Dolan .20 .50
42 Emil Meusel .20 .50
43 Bob Meusel .40 1.00
44 Lefty Gomez .60 1.50
45 Rube Marquard .60 1.50
46 Jeff Tesreau .20 .50
47 Joe Heving .20 .50
48 Johnny Heving .20 .50
49 Rick Ferrell .60 1.50
50 Wes Ferrell .40 1.00
51 Bill Wambsganss .20 .50
52 Ray Chapman .40 1.00
53 Joe Sewell .60 1.50
54 Luke Sewell .20 .50
55 Odell Hale .20 .50
56 Sammy Hale .20 .50
57 Earle Mack .20 .50
58 Connie Mack 1.50 4.00
59 Rube Walberg .20 .50
60 Mule Haas .20 .50
61 Paul Waner 1.00 2.50
62 Lloyd Waner .60 1.50
63 Pie Traynor 1.00 2.50
64 Honus Wagner 2.00 5.00
65 Joe Cronin 1.25 3.00
66 Moon Harris .20 .50
67 Sheriff Harris .20 .50
68 Bucky Harris .60 1.50
69 Alec Gaston .20 .50
70 Milt Gaston .20 .50
71 Casey Stengel 2.00 5.00
72 Amos Rusie .60 1.50
73 Mickey Welch .60 1.50
74 Roger Bresnahan .60 1.50
75 Jesse Burkett .60 1.50
76 Harry Heilmann .60 1.50
77 Heinie Manush .60 1.50
78 Charlie Gehringer 1.00 2.50
79 Hank Greenberg 1.25 3.00
80 Jimmie Foxx 1.50 4.00
81 Al Simmons 1.00 2.50
82 Ed Plank 1.00 2.50
83 George Sisler 1.00 2.50
84 Joe Medwick .60 1.50
85 Mel Ott 1.25 3.00
86 Hack Wilson .60 1.50
87 Jimmy Wilson .20 .50
88 Chuck Klein .60 1.50
89 Gabby Hartnett .60 1.50
90 Heinie Groh .20 .50
91 Ping Bodie .20 .50
92 Ted Lyons .60 1.50
93 Jack(Picus) Quinn .20 .50
94 Oscar Roettger .20 .50
95 Wally Roettger .20 .50
96 Bubbles Hargrave .20 .50
97 Pinky Hargrave .20 .50
98 Sam Crawford .60 1.50
99 Gee Walker .20 .50
100 Homer Summa .20 .50

1983 Conlon Marketcom

This set of 60 Charles Martin Conlon photo cards was produced by Marketcom in conjunction with The Sporting News. The cards are large size, approximately 4 1/2" X 6 1/8" and are in a sepia tone. The players selected for the set are members of the 1933 American and National League All-Star teams as well as Negro League All-Stars. These cards are numbered at the bottom of each reverse. The set numbering is American League (1-24), National League (25-48) and Negro League (49-60). In the upper right corner of each card's obverse is printed "1933 American (National or Negro League as appropriate) All Stars." Each obverse also features a facsimile autograph of the player pictured.

COMPLETE SET (60) 10.00 25.00
1 Jimmy Foxx .30 .75
(Jimmie)
2 Heinie Manush .25 .60
3 Lou Gehrig .75 2.00
4 Al Simmons .25 .60
5 Charlie Gehringer .25 .60
6 Luke Appling .25 .60
7 Mickey Cochrane .25 .60
8 Joe Kuhel .08 .25
9 Bill Dickey .30 .75
10 Pinky Higgins .08 .25
11 Roy Johnson .08 .25
12 Ben Chapman .08 .25
13 Urban Hodapp .08 .25
14 Joe Cronin .25 .60
15 Evar Swanson .08 .25
16 Earl Averill .25 .60
17 Babe Ruth 1.25 3.00
18 Tony Lazzeri .25 .60
19 Alvin Crowder .08 .25
20 Lefty Grove .30 .75
21 Earl Whitehill .08 .25
22 Lefty Gomez .30 .75
23 Mel Harder .08 .25
24 Tommy Bridges .08 .25
25 Chuck Klein .25 .60
26 Spud Davis .08 .25
27 Riggs Stephenson .15 .40
28 Tony Piet .08 .25
29 Bill Terry .25 .60
30 Wes Schulmerich .08 .25
31 Pepper Martin .15 .40
32 Arky Vaughan .25 .60
33 Wally Berger .15 .40
34 Ripper Collins .08 .25
35 Fred Lindstrom .25 .60
36 Chick Fullis .08 .25
37 Paul Waner .30 .75
38 Johnny Frederick .08 .25
39 Joe Medwick .25 .60
40 Pie Traynor .25 .60
41 Frankie Frisch .25 .60
42 Chick Hafey .25 .60
43 Carl Hubbell .30 .75
44 Guy Bush .08 .25
45 Dizzy Dean .40 1.00
46 Hal Schumacher .08 .25
47 Larry French .08 .25
48 Lon Warneke .08 .25
49 Cool Papa Bell .30 .75
50 Oscar Charleston .25 .60
51 Josh Gibson .50 1.25
52 Satchel Paige .50 1.25
53 Dave Malarcher .15 .40
54 John Henry Lloyd .25 .60
55 Rube Foster .30 .75
56 Buck Leonard .30 .75
57 Smoky Joe Williams .30 .75
58 Willie Wells .25 .60
59 Judy Johnson .30 .75
60 Martin DiHigo .25 .60

1986 Conlon Series 1

This 60-card set was produced from the black and white photos in the Charles Martin Conlon collection. Each set comes with a special card which contains the number of that set out of the 12,000 sets which were produced. The cards measure 2 1/2" X 3 1/2" and are printed in sepia tones.

COMPLETE SET (60) 10.00 25.00
1 Lou Gehrig .60 1.50
2 Ty Cobb .60 1.50
3 Grover C. Alexander .10 .30
4 Walter Johnson .30 .75
5 Bill Klem .10 .30
6 Ty Cobb .60 1.50
7 Mickey Cochrane .10 .30
8 Paul Waner .10 .30
9 Joe Cronin .10 .30
10 Dizzy Dean .20 .50
11 Leo Durocher .10 .30
12 Jimmy Foxx .20 .50
(Jimmie)
13 Babe Ruth .75 2.00
14 Mike Gonzalez .05 .15
Frank Frisch
Clyde Ellsworth Wares
15 Carl Hubbell .10 .30
16 Miller Huggins .05 .15
17 Lou Gehrig .60 1.50
18 Connie McGillicuddy/(Connie Mack) .20 .50
19 Heinie Manush .10 .30
20 Babe Ruth .75 2.00
22 Pepper Martin .05 .15
23 Christy Mathewson .20 .50
24 Ty Cobb .60 1.50
25 Bucky Harris .10 .30
26 Waite Hoyt .10 .30
27 Rube Marquard .10 .30
28 Joe McCarthy .10 .30
29 John McGraw .20 .50
30 Tris Speaker .20 .50
31 Bill Terry .10 .30
32 Christy Mathewson .30 .75
33 Casey Stengel .30 .75
34 Bob Meusel .10 .30
35 Rube Waddell .10 .30
36 Mel Ott .20 .50
37 Roger Peckinpaugh .05 .15
38 Pie Traynor .20 .50
39 Chief Bender .10 .30
40 Jack Coombs .05 .15
41 Ty Cobb .60 1.50
42 Harry Heilmann .10 .30
43 Charlie Gehringer .10 .30
44 Rogers Hornsby .30 .75
45 Lefty Gomez .10 .30
46 Christy Mathewson .30 .75
47 Lefty Grove .20 .50
48 Babe Ruth .75 2.00
49 Fred Merkle .05 .15
50 Babe Ruth .75 2.00
51 Herb Pennock .10 .30
52 Lou Gehrig .60 1.50
53 Fred Clarke .10 .30
54 Babe Ruth .75 2.00
55 Honus Wagner .30 .75
56 Hack Wilson .10 .30
57 Lou Gehrig .60 1.50
58 Lloyd Waner .10 .30
59 Charles Martin Conlon .05 .15
60 Charles Conlon .05 .15
Margie Conlon
NNO Set Number Card .05 .15

1987 Conlon Series 2

The second series of 60 Charles Martin Conlon standard-size sepia toned photo cards was produced by World Wide Sports in conjunction with The Sporting News. Reportedly 12,000 sets were produced. The photos were selected and background information written by Paul MacFarlane of The Sporting News.

COMPLETE SET (60) 5.00 12.00
1 Lou Gehrig .60 1.50
2 Lefty Gomez .15 .40
3 Christy Mathewson .30 .75
4 Grover Alexander .20 .50
5 Ty Cobb .60 1.50
6 Walter Johnson .30 .75
7 Charles(Babe) Adams .02 .10
8 Nick Altrock .08 .25
9 Al Schacht .08 .25
10 Hugh Critz .02 .10
11 Henry Cullop .02 .10
12 Jacob Daubert .02 .10
13 William Donovan .02 .10
14 Chick Hafey .08 .25
15 Bill Hallahan .02 .10
16 Fred Haney .02 .10
17 Charles Hartnett .08 .25
18 Walter Henline .02 .10
19 Edwin Rommel .02 .10
20 Babe Pinelli .02 .10
21 Robert Meusel .08 .25
22 Emil Meusel .02 .10
23 Smead Jolley .02 .10
24 Ike Boone .02 .10
25 Earl Webb .02 .10
26 Charles Comiskey .15 .40
27 Eddie Collins .15 .40
28 George(Buck) Weaver .15 .40
29 Eddie Cicotte .15 .40
30 Sam Crawford .08 .25
31 Charlie Dressen .02 .10
32 Arthur Fletcher .02 .10
33 Hugh Duffy .08 .25
34 Ira Flagstead .02 .10
35 Harry Hooper .08 .25
36 George Lewis .02 .10
37 Jimmie Dykes .02 .10
38 Goose Goslin .08 .25
39 Hank Gowdy .02 .10
40 Charlie Grimm .02 .10
41 Mark Koenig .02 .10
42 James Hogan .02 .10
43 William Jacobson .02 .10
44 Fielder Jones .02 .10
45 George Kelly .08 .25
46 Adolpho Luque .02 .10
47 Rabbit Maranville .08 .25
48 Carl Mays .02 .10
49 Edward Plank .08 .25
50 Hubert Pruett .02 .10
51 John(Picus) Quinn .02 .10
52 Charles(Flint) Rhem .02 .10
53 Amos Rusie .08 .25
54 Edd Roush .08 .25
55 Ray Schalk .08 .25
56 Ernie Shore .02 .10
57 Joe Wood .15 .40
58 George Sisler .15 .40
59 Jim Thorpe .60 1.50
60 Earl Whitehill .02 .10

1988 Conlon American All-Stars

This set of 24 Charles Martin Conlon photo cards was produced by World Wide Sports in conjunction with The Sporting News. The cards are standard size and are in a sepia tone. The photos (members of the 1933 American League All-Star team) were selected and background information written by Paul MacFarlane of The Sporting News. These cards are unnumbered and hence are listed below in alphabetical order. American League is indicated in the lower right corner of each card's reverse. In the upper right corner of each card's obverse is printed "1933 American All Stars."

COMPLETE SET (24) 2.50 6.00
1 Luke Appling .10 .30
2 Earl Averill .10 .30
3 Tommy Bridges .05 .15
4 Ben Chapman .05 .15
5 Mickey Cochrane .10 .30
6 Joe Cronin .10 .30
7 Alvin Crowder .05 .15
8 Bill Dickey .15 .40
9 James Emory Foxx .30 .75
10 Lou Gehrig .60 1.50
11 Charlie Gehringer .10 .30
12 Lefty Gomez .10 .30
13 Lefty Grove .25 .60
14 Mel Harder .05 .15
15 Pinky Higgins .05 .15
16 Urban Hodapp .05 .15
17 Roy Johnson .05 .15
18 Joe Kuhel .05 .15
19 Tony Lazzeri .10 .30
20 Heinie Manush .10 .30
21 Babe Ruth .75 2.00
22 Al Simmons .10 .30
23 Evar Swanson .05 .15
24 Earl Whitehill .05 .15

1988 Conlon Hardee's/Coke

This six-card standard-size sepia tone set was issued in 18 central Indiana Hardee's restaurants over a six-week period, a different card per purchase per week. The set features the vintage photography of Charles Martin Conlon, except for the Cool Papa Bell photo which was not shot by Conlon. The card backs contain biographical information, Hardee's logo and a Coca Cola Classic logo. The cards are also copyrighted by The Sporting News.

COMPLETE SET (6) 2.00 5.00
1 Cool Papa Bell .30 .75
2 Ty Cobb .75 2.00
3 Lou Gehrig .75 2.00
4 Connie Mack .30 .75
5 Casey Stengel .30 .75
6 Rube Waddell .20 .50

1988 Conlon National All-Stars

This set of 24 Charles Martin Conlon photo cards was produced by World Wide Sports in conjunction with The Sporting News. The cards are standard size, and are in a sepia tone. The photos (members of the 1933 National League All-Star team) were selected and background information written by Paul MacFarlane of The Sporting News. These cards are unnumbered and hence are listed below in alphabetical order. National League is indicated in the lower right corner of each card's reverse. In the upper right corner of each card's obverse is printed "1933 National All Stars."

COMPLETE SET (24) 2.00 5.00
1 Wally Berger .05 .15
2 Guy Bush .05 .15
3 Ripper Collins .05 .15
4 Spud Davis .05 .15
5 Dizzy Dean .20 .50
6 Johnny Frederick .05 .15
7 Larry French .05 .15
8 Frankie Frisch .10 .30
9 Chick Fullis .05 .15
10 Chick Hafey .10 .30
11 Carl Hubbell .20 .50
12 Chuck Klein .10 .30
13 Fred Lindstrom .10 .30
14 Pepper Martin .10 .30
15 Joe Medwick .10 .30
16 Tony Piet .05 .15
17 Wes Schulmerich .05 .15
18 Hal Schumacher .05 .15
19 Riggs Stephenson .10 .30
20 Bill Terry .20 .50
21 Pie Traynor .20 .50
22 Arky Vaughan .10 .30
23 Paul Waner .20 .50
24 Lon Warneke .05 .15

1988 Conlon Negro All-Stars

This set of 12 photo cards was produced by World Wide Sports in conjunction with The Sporting News. The cards are standard size, and are in a sepia tone. The photos (Negro League All Stars from 1933) were selected and background information written by Paul MacFarlane of The Sporting News. Despite the stylistic similarity of this set with the other Conlon sets, the photos for this set were not taken by Charles Martin Conlon. These cards are unnumbered and hence are listed below in alphabetical order. Negro League is indicated in the lower right corner of each card's reverse. In the upper right corner of each card's obverse is printed "1933 Negro All Stars." The photo quality on some of the cards is very poor suggesting that the original photo or negative may have been enlarged to an excessive degree.

COMPLETE SET (12) 2.00 5.00
1 Cool Papa Bell .30 .75
2 Oscar Charleston .20 .50
3 Martin DiHigo .20 .50
4 Rube Foster .20 .50
5 Josh Gibson .40 1.00
6 Judy Johnson .20 .50
7 Buck Leonard .20 .50
8 John Henry Lloyd .20 .50
9 Dave Malarcher .08 .25
10 Satchel Paige .40 1.00
11 Willie Wells .20 .50
12 Smoky Joe Williams .20 .50

1988 Conlon Series 3

This third series of 30 Charles Martin Conlon photo cards was produced by World Wide Sports in conjunction with The Sporting News. The cards are standard size, and are in a sepia tone. The photos were selected and background information written by Paul MacFarlane of The Sporting News. These cards are unnumbered and hence are listed below in alphabetical order. Series 3 is indicated in the lower right corner of each card's reverse. A black and white logo for the "Baseball Immortals" and The Conlon Collection is over-printed in the lower left corner of each obverse.

COMPLETE SET (30) 2.50 6.00
1 Ace Adams .05 .15
2 Grover C. Alexander .20 .50
3 Elden Auker .05 .15
4 Jack Barry .05 .15
5 Wally Berger .05 .15
6 Ben Chapman .05 .15
7 Mickey Cochrane .10 .30
8 Frankie Crosetti .05 .15
9 Paul Dean .05 .15
10 Leo Durocher .20 .50
11 Wes Ferrell .10 .30
12 Hank Gowdy .05 .15
13 Andy High .05 .15
14 Rogers Hornsby .30 .75
15 Carl Hubbell .10 .30
16 Joe Judge .05 .15
17 Tony Lazzeri .10 .30
18 Pepper Martin .10 .30
19 Lee Meadows .05 .15
20 Johnny Murphy .05 .15
21 Steve O'Neil .05 .15
22 Ed Plank .10 .30
23 Jack(Picus) Quinn .05 .15
24 Charley Root .05 .15
25 Babe Ruth .75 2.00
26 Fred Snodgrass .05 .15
27 Tris Speaker .20 .50
28 Bill Terry .20 .50
29 Jeff Tesreau .05 .15
30 George Toporcer .05 .15

1988 Conlon Series 4

This fourth series of 30 Charles Martin Conlon photo cards was produced by World Wide Sports in conjunction with The Sporting News. The cards are standard size, and are in a sepia tone. The photos were selected and background information written by Paul MacFarlane of The Sporting News. These cards are unnumbered and hence are listed below in alphabetical order. Series 4 is indicated in the lower right corner of each card's reverse. A black and white logo for the "Baseball Immortals" and The Conlon Collection is over-printed in the lower left corner of each obverse.

COMPLETE SET (30) 2.50 6.00
1 Dale Alexander .05 .15
2 Morris Badgro .05 .15
3 Dick Bartell .05 .15
4 Max Bishop .05 .15
5 Hal Chase .10 .30
6 Ty Cobb .60 1.50
7 Nick Cullop .05 .15
8 Dizzy Dean .30 .75
9 Charlie Dressen .05 .15
10 Jimmy Dykes .05 .15
11 Art Fletcher .05 .15
12 Charlie Grimm .05 .15
13 Lefty Grove .20 .50
14 Baby Doll Jacobson .05 .15
15 Bill Klem UMP .10 .30
16 Mark Koenig .05 .15
17 Duffy Lewis .05 .15
18 Carl Mays .05 .15
19 Fred Merkle .05 .15
20 Greasy Neale .10 .30
21 Mel Ott .20 .50
22 Babe Pinelli .05 .15
23 Flint Rhem .05 .15
24 Slim Sallee UER/(Misspelled Salee .05 .15
on card back)
25 Al Simmons .10 .30
26 George Sisler .10 .30
27 Riggs Stephenson .05 .15
28 Jim Thorpe .60 1.50
29 Bill Wambsganss .05 .15
30 Cy Young .20 .50

1988 Conlon Series 5

This fifth series of 30 Charles Martin Conlon photo cards was produced by World Wide Sports in conjunction with The Sporting News. The cards are standard size, and are in a sepia tone. The photos were selected and background information written by Paul MacFarlane of The Sporting News. These cards are unnumbered and hence are listed below in alphabetical order. Series 5 is indicated in the lower right corner of each card's reverse. A black and white logo for the "Baseball Immortals" and The Conlon Collection is over-printed in the lower left corner of each obverse.

COMPLETE SET (30) 2.50 6.00
1 Nick Altrock .10 .30
2 Del Baker .05 .15
3 Moe Berg .40 1.00
4 Zeke Bonura .05 .15
5 Eddie Collins .20 .50
6 Hughie Critz .05 .15
7 George Dauss .05 .15
8 Joe Dugan .05 .15
9 Howard Ehmke .05 .15
10 James Emory Foxx .30 .75
11 Frankie Frisch .10 .30
12 Lou Gehrig .60 1.50
13 Charlie Gehringer .20 .50
14 Kid Gleason .10 .30
15 Lefty Gomez .20 .50
16 Babe Herman .10 .30
17 Bill James .05 .15
18 Joe Kuhel .05 .15
19 Dolf Luque .10 .30
20 John McGraw .20 .50
21 Stuffy McInnis .05 .15
22 Bob Meusel .05 .15
23 Lefty O'Doul .05 .15
24 Hub Pruett .05 .15
25 Paul Richards .05 .15
26 Bob Shawkey .05 .15
27 Gabby Street .05 .15
28 Johnny Tobin .05 .15
29 Rube Waddell .10 .30
30 Billy Werber .05 .15

1991 Conlon TSN

This 330-card standard-size set was issued in black and white and again featured the photography of Charles Conlon. The set was produced by MegaCards in conjunction with The Sporting News. The set was available in both packs as well as factory set form. The card backs contain pertinent information relevant to the front of the cards whether it is career statistics or all-time leaders format or the special cards commemorating the great teams of the first part of the twentieth century.

COMPLETE SET (330) 10.00 25.00
1 Rogers Hornsby HOF .15 .40
2 Jimmie Foxx HOF .15 .40
3 Dizzy Dean HOF .15 .40
4 Rabbit Maranville HOF .07 .20
5 Paul Waner HOF .07 .20
6 Lloyd Waner HOF .07 .20
7 Mel Ott HOF .10 .30
8 Honus Wagner HOF .15 .40
9 Walter Johnson HOF .15 .40
10 Carl Hubbell HOF .08 .25
11 Frank Frisch HOF .07 .20
12 Kiki Cuyler HOF .07 .20
13 Red Ruffing HOF .07 .20
14 Hank Greenberg HOF .10 .30
15 Johnny Evers HOF .07 .20
16 Hugh Jennings HOF .07 .20
17 Dave Bancroft HOF .07 .20
18 Joe Medwick HOF .07 .20
19 Ted Lyons HOF .07 .20
20 Chief Bender HOF .07 .20
21 Eddie Collins HOF .07 .20
22 Jim Bottomley HOF .07 .20
23 Lefty Grove HOF .10 .30
24 Max Carey HOF .07 .20
25 Burleigh Grimes HOF .07 .20
26 Ross Youngs HOF .07 .20
27 Ernie Lombardi HOF .07 .20
28 Joe McCarthy HOF .07 .20
29 Hack Wilson HOF .08 .25
30 Chuck Klein HOF .07 .20
31 Earl Averill HOF .07 .20
32 Grover C. Alexander HOF .10 .30
33 Chick Hafey HOF .07 .20
34 Bill McKechnie HOF .07 .20
35 Bob Feller HOF .10 .30
36 Pie Traynor HOF .07 .20
37 Casey Stengel HOF .10 .30
38 Arky Vaughan HOF .07 .20
39 Eppa Rixey HOF .07 .20
40 Joe Sewell HOF .07 .20
41 Red Faber HOF .07 .20
42 Travis Jackson HOF .07 .20
43 Jesse Haines HOF .07 .20
44 Tris Speaker HOF .08 .25
45 Connie Mack HOF .08 .25
46 Connie Mack HOF .08 .25
47 Connie Mack HOF .08 .25
48 Ray Schalk HOF .07 .20
49 Al Simmons HOF .07 .20
50 Joe Cronin HOF .07 .20
51 Mickey Cochrane HOF .08 .25
52 Harry Heilmann HOF .07 .20
53 Johnny Mize HOF .08 .25
54 Sam Rice HOF .07 .20
55 Edd Roush HOF .07 .20
56 Enos Slaughter HOF .07 .20
57 Christy Mathewson HOF .15 .40
58 Fred Lindstrom HOF .07 .20
59 Gabby Hartnett HOF .07 .20
60 George Kelly HOF .07 .20
61 Bucky Harris HOF .07 .20
62 Goose Goslin HOF .07 .20
63 Heinie Manush HOF .07 .20
64 Bill Terry HOF .08 .25
65 John McGraw HOF .08 .25
66 George Sisler HOF .07 .20
67 Lefty Gomez HOF .08 .25
68 Joe Judge .02 .10
69 Tommy Thevenow .01 .05
70 Charlie Gelbert .01 .05
71 Jackie Hayes .01 .05
72 Bob Fothergill .01 .05
73 Adam Comorosky .01 .05
74 Earl Smith .01 .05
75 Sam Gray .01 .05
76 Pete Appleton .01 .05
77 Gene Moore .01 .05
78 Art Jorgens .01 .05
79 Bill Knickerbocker .01 .05
80 Carl Reynolds .01 .05
81 Ski Melillo .01 .05
82 Johnny Burnett .01 .05
83 Jake Powell .01 .05
84 Johnny Murphy .02 .10
85 Roy Parmelee .01 .05
86 Jimmy Ripple .01 .05
87 Gee Walker .01 .05
88 George Earnshaw .02 .10
89 Billy Southworth .01 .05
90 Wally Moses .01 .05
91 Rube Walberg .01 .05
92 Jimmy Dykes .02 .10
93 Charlie Root .01 .05
94 Johnny Cooney .01 .05
95 Charlie Grimm .05 .15
96 Bob Johnson .02 .10
97 Jack Scott .01 .05
98 Rip Radcliff .01 .05
99 Fritz Ostermueller .01 .05
100 Julie Wera '27NY .01 .05
101 Miller Huggins '27NY .07 .20
102 Ray Morehart '27NY .01 .05
103 Benny Bengough '27NY .02 .10
104 Dutch Ruether '27NY .01 .05
105 Earle Combs '27NY .07 .20
106 Myles Thomas '27NY .01 .05
107 Ben Paschal '27NY .01 .05
108 Cedric Durst '27NY .01 .05
109 Wilcy Moore '27NY .01 .05
110 Babe Ruth '27NY .40 1.00
111 Lou Gehrig '27NY .30 .75
112 Joe Dugan '27NY .02 .10
113 Tony Lazzeri '27NY .07 .20
114 Urban Shocker '27NY .01 .05
115 Waite Hoyt '27NY .07 .20
116 Charley O'Leary '27NY .01 .05
117 Art Fletcher '27NY .01 .05
118 Pat Collins '27NY .01 .05
119 Joe Giard '27NY .01 .05
120 Herb Pennock '27NY .07 .20
121 Mike Gazella '27NY .01 .05
122 Bob Meusel '27NY .05 .15
123 George Pipgras '27NY .01 .05
124 Johnny Grabowski '27NY .01 .05
125 Mark Koenig '27NY .02 .10
126 Stan Hack .02 .10
127 Earl Whitehill .01 .05
128 Bill Lee .01 .05
129 Gus Mancuso .01 .05
130 Ray Blades .01 .05
131 Jack Burns .01 .05
132 Clint Brown .01 .05
133 Bill Dietrich .01 .05
134 Cy Blanton .01 .05
135 Harry Hooper/'16 Champs .07 .20
136 Chick Shorten/'16 Champs .01 .05
137 Tilly Walker/'16 Champs .01 .05
138 Rube Foster/'16 Champs .01 .05
139 Jack Barry/'16 Champs .01 .05
140 Sad Sam Jones/'16 Champs .02 .10
141 Ernie Shore/'16 Champs .01 .05
142 Dutch Leonard/'16 Champs .01 .05
143 Herb Pennock/'16 Champs .07 .20
144 Hal Janvrin/'16 Champs .01 .05
145 Babe Ruth/'16 Champs .40 1.00
146 Duffy Lewis/'16 Champs .01 .05
147 Larry Gardner/'16 Champs .01 .05
148 Doc Hoblitzel/'16 Champs .01 .05
149 Everett Scott/'16 Champs .01 .05
150 Carl Mays/'16 Champs .02 .10
151 Bert Niehoff '16LL .01 .05
152 Burt Shotton '16LL .01 .05
153 Red Ames '16LL .01 .05
154 Cy Williams '16LL .01 .05
155 Bill Hinchman '16LL .01 .05
156 Bob Shawkey '16LL .01 .05
157 Wally Pipp '16LL .05 .15
158 George J. Burns '16LL .01 .05
159 Bob Veach '16LL .01 .05
160 Hal Chase '16LL .01 .05
161 Tom Hughes '16LL .01 .05
162 Del Pratt '16LL .01 .05
163 Heinie Groh '16LL .01 .05
164 Zack Wheat '16LL .07 .20
165 Lefty O'Doul Story .01 .05
166 Willie Kamm Story .01 .05
167 Paul Waner Story .07 .20
168 Fred Snodgrass Story .01 .05
169 Babe Herman Story .05 .15
170 Al Bridwell Story .01 .05
171 Chief Meyers Story .01 .05
172 Hans Lobert Story .01 .05
173 Rube Bressler Story .01 .05
174 Sad Sam Jones Story .02 .10
175 Bob O'Farrell Story .01 .05
176 Specs Toporcer Story .01 .05
177 Earl McNeely Story .01 .05
178 Jack Knott Story .01 .05
179 Heinie Mueller .01 .05
180 Tommy Bridges .01 .05
181 Lloyd Brown .01 .05
182 Larry Benton .01 .05
183 Max Bishop .01 .05
184 Moe Berg .20 .50
185 Cy Perkins .01 .05
186 Steve O'Neill .01 .05
187 Glenn Myatt .01 .05
188 Joe Kuhel .01 .05
189 Marty McManus .01 .05
190 Red Lucas .01 .05

191 Stuffy McInnis .01 .05
192 Bing Miller .01 .05
193 Luke Sewell .02 .10
194 Bill Sherdel .01 .05
195 Hal Rhyne .01 .05
196 Guy Bush .01 .05
197 Pete Fox .01 .05
198 Wes Ferrell .05 .15
199 Roy Johnson .01 .05
200 Bill Wambsganss .02 .10
Triple Play
201 George H. Burns .01 .05
Triple Play
202 Clarence Mitchell .01 .05
Triple Play
203 Neal Ball .01 .05
Triple Play
204 Johnny Neun .01 .05
Triple Play
205 Homer Summa .01 .05
Triple Play
206 Ernie Padgett .01 .05
Triple Play
207 Walter Holke .01 .05
Triple Play
208 Glenn Wright .01 .05
Triple Play
209 Hank Gowdy .02 .10
210 Zack Taylor .01 .05
211 Ben Cantwell .01 .05
212 Frank Demaree .01 .05
213 Paul Derringer .02 .10
214 Bill Hallahan .01 .05
215 Danny MacFayden .01 .05
216 Harry Rice .01 .05
217 Bob Smith .01 .05
218 Riggs Stephenson .05 .15
219 Pat Malone .01 .05
220 Bennie Tate .01 .05
221 Joe Vosmik .01 .05
222 George Watkins .01 .05
223 Jimmie Wilson .01 .05
224 George Uhle .01 .05
225 Mel Ott TRIV .10 .30
226 Nick Altrock TRIV .01 .05
227 Red Ruffing TRIV .07 .20
228 Joe Krakauskas TRIV .01 .05
229 Wally Berger TRIV .02 .10
230 Bobo Newsom .05 .15
231 Lon Warneke .02 .10
232 Frank Snyder .01 .05
233 Myril Hoag .01 .05
234 Mel Almada .01 .05
235 Ivey Wingo .01 .05
236 Jimmy Austin .01 .05
237 Zeke Bonura .01 .05
238 Russ Wrightstone .01 .05
239 Al Todd .01 .05
240 Rabbit Warstler .01 .05
241 Sammy West .01 .05
242 Art Reinhart .01 .05
243 Lefty Stewart .01 .05
244 Johnny Gooch .01 .05
245 Bubbles Hargrave .01 .05
246 George Harper .01 .05
247 Sarge Connally .01 .05
248 Garland Braxton .01 .05
249 Wally Schang .02 .10
250 Ty Cobb ATL .30 .75
251 Rogers Hornsby ATL .15 .40
252 Rube Marquard ATL .07 .20
253 Carl Hubbell ATL .08 .25
254 Joe Wood ATL .02 .10
255 Lefty Grove ATL .10 .30
256 Schoolboy Rowe ATL .02 .10
257 General Crowder ATL .01 .05
258 Walter Johnson ATL .15 .40
259 Chick Hafey ATL .07 .20
260 Fred Fitzsimmons ATL .02 .10
261 Earl Webb ATL .02 .10
262 Earle Combs ATL .07 .20
263 Ed Konetchy ATL .01 .05
264 Taylor Douthit ATL .01 .05
265 Lloyd Waner ATL .07 .20
266 Mickey Cochrane ATL .08 .25
267 Hack Wilson ATL .08 .25
268 Pie Traynor ATL .07 .20
269 Spud Davis ATL .01 .05
270 Heinie Manush ATL .07 .20
271 Pinky Higgins ATL .01 .05
272 Addie Joss ATL .07 .20
273 Ed Walsh ATL .07 .20
274 Pepper Martin ATL .05 .15
275 Joe Sewell ATL .07 .20
276 Dutch Leonard ATL .02 .10
277 Gavvy Cravath ATL .02 .10
278 Oral Hildebrand .01 .05
279 Ray Kremer .01 .05
280 Frankie Pytlak .01 .05
281 Sammy Byrd .01 .05
282 Curt Davis .01 .05
283 Lew Fonseca .01 .05
284 Muddy Ruel .01 .05
285 Moose Solters .01 .05
286 Fred Schulte .01 .05
287 Jack Quinn .02 .10
288 Pinky Whitney .01 .05
289 John Stone .01 .05
290 Hughie Critz .01 .05
291 Ira Flagstead .01 .05
292 George Grantham .01 .05
293 Sammy Hale .01 .05
294 Shanty Hogan .01 .05
295 Ossie Bluege .01 .05
296 Debs Garms .01 .05
297 Barney Friberg .01 .05
298 Ed Brandt .01 .05
299 Rollie Hemsley .01 .05
300 Chuck Klein MVP .07 .20
301 Mort Cooper MVP .01 .05
302 Jim Bottomley MVP .07 .20
303 Jimmie Foxx MVP .15 .40
304 Fred Schulte MVP .01 .05
305 Frank Frisch MVP .07 .20
306 Frank McCormick MVP .02 .10
307 Jake Daubert MVP .02 .10
308 Roger Peckinpaugh MVP .01 .05
309 George H. Burns MVP .01 .05
310 Lou Gehrig MVP .30 .75
311 Al Simmons MVP .07 .20
312 Eddie Collins MVP .07 .20
313 Gabby Hartnett MVP .07 .20
314 Joe Cronin MVP .07 .20
315 Paul Waner MVP .07 .20
316 Bob O'Farrell MVP .01 .05
317 Larry Doyle MVP .02 .10
318 Lyn Lary .01 .05
319 Jakie May .01 .05
320 Roy Spencer .01 .05
321 Dick Coffman .01 .05
322 Pete Donohue .01 .05
323 Mule Haas .01 .05
324 Doc Farrell .01 .05
325 Flint Rhem .01 .05
326 Firpo Marberry .01 .05
327 Charles Conlon .01 .05
328 Checklist 1-110 .01 .05
329 Checklist 111-220 .01 .05
330 Checklist 221-330 .01 .05

1991-92 Conlon TSN Prototypes

In conjunction with The Sporting News, Megacards issued various prototype cards to preview their soon to be released regular issue sets. All the cards were standard size. The 1991 Conlon prototypes from the first series were not marked as prototypes, and neither did they have the Major League Baseball logo and the Curtis Management logo on their backs. Their numbering was identical with the regular issue cards, with the exception of Dean (number 3 in the regular issue). The production run was reported to be very limited for these first series cards. The 1991 Conlon Color Babe Ruth prototype has the word "prototype" on its reverse. The 50,000 color Ruth prototype cards produced were distributed to collectors and dealers at the 12th National Sports Collectors Convention in Anaheim in July, 1991. Moreover, five prototypes for the second series (1992 Conlon Collection) were distributed at the same time. The production run was announced to be 20,000 for each card, with the exception of Joe Jackson (67,000). All these cards are marked "prototype" on their backs, and with the exception of the Mathewson card, also bear different card numbers from the regular issues. In general, some subtle differences in photos are found with some of the prototype cards. The second series prototypes show a 1992 copyright on the card back. The Cobb and Jackson cards have a computer color-enhanced photo with white and dark blue borders, while the other cards have black and white photos with white and black borders.

COMPLETE SET (16) 25.00 60.00
13 Ty Cobb 3.00 8.00
Color (Card 250)
14 Joe Jackson 3.00 8.00
Color Card 444 in
regular set prototype
34 Dizzy Dean 3.00 8.00
111 Lou Gehrig 4.00 10.00
145 Babe Ruth Color DP 6.00 15.00
250 Ty Cobb 4.00 10.00
331 Christy Mathewson 1.25 3.00
Prototype on back
400 Joe Jackson DP/(Prototype on back) 2.00 5.00
450 Hughie Jennings .60 1.50
Prototype on back
500 Ty Cobb 2.00 5.00
Prototype on back
520 Goose Goslin .60 1.50
Prototype on back
661 Bill Terry 1.00 2.50
662 Lefty Gomez 1.00 2.50
664 Frank Frisch .60 1.50
710 Red Faber .60 1.50
905 Lena Blackburne .40 1.00

1992 Conlon TSN

This 330-card standard-size set is numbered in continuation of the previous year's issue and again features the photography of Charles Conlon. The fronts have either posed or action black and white player photos, enframed by a white line on a black card face. A caption in a diagonal stripe cuts across the upper right corner of the picture. The player's name, team, position, and year the photos were taken appear below the pictures in white lettering. The back has biography, statistics, and career summary. The cards are numbered on the back. Special subsets include No-Hitters (331-372), Two Sports (393-407), Great Stories (421-440), Why Not in Hall of Fame (441-450), Hall of Fame (459-474), 75 Years Ago Highlights (483-492), Triple Crown Winners (525-537), Everyday Heroes (538-550), Nicknames (551-566), Trivia (581-601), and St. Louis Cardinals 1892-1992 (618-657). The set was available in packs as well as in a factory set. Four special gold-border cards previewing the 1993 Conlon Sporting News set were available exclusively in the factory sets. Also randomly inserted in the wax packs were a limited number of personally autographed (but not certified) cards of Bobby Doerr, Bob Feller, Marty Marion, Johnny Mize, Enos Slaughter, and Johnny Vander Meer. These autographed cards range in value from 15.00 to 30.00.

COMPLETE SET (330) 8.00 20.00
COMP.FACT SET (300)
331 Christy Mathewson .15 .40
332 Hooks Wiltse .01 .05
333 Nap Rucker .01 .05
334 Red Ames .01 .05
335 Chief Bender .07 .20
336 Joe Wood .02 .10
337 Ed Walsh .07 .20
338 George Mullin .01 .05
339 Earl Hamilton .01 .05
340 Jeff Tesreau .01 .05
341 Jim Scott .01 .05
342 Rube Marquard .07 .20
343 Claude Hendrix .01 .05
344 Jimmy Lavender .01 .05
345 Joe Bush .02 .10
346 Dutch Leonard .02 .10
347 Fred Toney .01 .05
348 Hippo Vaughn .01 .05
349 Ernie Koob .01 .05
350 Bob Groom .01 .05
351 Ernie Shore .02 .10
352 Hod Eller .01 .05
353 Walter Johnson .15 .40
354 Charles Robertson .01 .05
355 Jesse Barnes .01 .05
356 Sad Sam Jones .02 .10
357 Howard Ehmke .01 .05
358 Jesse Haines .07 .20
359 Ted Lyons .07 .20
360 Carl Hubbell .08 .25
361 Wes Ferrell .05 .15
362 Bobby Burke .01 .05
363 Daffy Dean .02 .10
364 Bobo Newsom .05 .15
365 Vern Kennedy .01 .05
366 Bill Dietrich .01 .05
367 Johnny VanderMeer .05 .15
368 Johnny VanderMeer .05 .15
369 Monte Pearson .01 .05
370 Bob Feller .10 .30
371 Lon Warneke .02 .10
372 Jim Tobin .01 .05
373 Earl Moore .01 .05
374 Bill Dineen .01 .05
375 Mal Eason .01 .05
376 George Mogridge .01 .05
377 Dazzy Vance .07 .20
378 Tex Carleton .01 .05
379 Clyde Shoun .01 .05
380 Frankie Hayes .01 .05
381 Benny Frey .01 .05
382 Hank Johnson .01 .05
383 Red Kress .01 .05
384 Johnny Allen .01 .05
385 Hal Trosky .02 .10
386 Gene Robertson .01 .05
387 Pep Young .01 .05
388 George Selkirk .02 .10
389 Ed Wells .01 .05
390 Jim Weaver .01 .05
391 George McQuinn .01 .05
392 Hans Lobert .01 .05
393 Evar Swanson .01 .05
394 Ernie Nevers .08 .25
395 Jim Levey .01 .05
396 Hugo Bezdek .01 .05
397 Walt French .01 .05
398 Charlie Berry .02 .10
399 Frank Grube .01 .05
400 Chuck Dressen .02 .10
401 Greasy Neale .02 .10
402 Ernie Vick .01 .05
403 Jim Thorpe .40 1.00
404 Wally Gilbert .01 .05
405 Luke Urban .01 .05
406 Pid Purdy .01 .05
407 Ab Wright .01 .05
408 Billy Urbanski .01 .05
409 Carl Fischer .01 .05
410 Jack Warner .01 .05
411 Bill Cissell .01 .05
412 Merv Shea .01 .05
413 Dolf Luque .02 .10
414 Johnny Bassler .01 .05
415 Odell Hale .01 .05
416 Larry French .01 .05
417 Curt Walker .01 .05
418 Dusty Cooke .01 .05
419 Phil Todt .01 .05
420 Poison Andrews .01 .05
421 Billy Herman .07 .20
422 Tris Speaker .08 .25
423 Al Simmons .07 .20
424 Hack Wilson .08 .25
425 Ty Cobb .30 .75
426 Babe Ruth .40 1.00
427 Ernie Lombardi .07 .20
428 Dizzy Dean .15 .40
429 Lloyd Waner .07 .20
430 Hank Greenberg .10 .30
431 Lefty Grove .10 .30
432 Mickey Cochrane .08 .25
433 Burleigh Grimes .07 .20
434 Pie Traynor .07 .20
435 Johnny Mize .08 .25
436 Sam Rice .07 .20
437 Goose Goslin .07 .20
438 Chuck Klein .07 .20
439 Connie Mack .08 .25
440 Jim Bottomley .07 .20
441 Riggs Stephenson .05 .15
442 Ken Williams .05 .15
443 Babe Adams .02 .10
444 Joe Jackson .40 1.00
445 Hal Newhouser .07 .20
446 Wes Ferrell .05 .15
447 Lefty O'Doul .02 .10
448 Wally Schang .02 .10
449 Sherry Magee .02 .10
450 Mike Donlin .02 .10
451 Doc Cramer .02 .10
452 Dick Bartell .01 .05
453 Earle Mack .01 .05
454 Jumbo Brown .01 .05
455 Johnnie Heving .01 .05
456 Percy Jones .01 .05
457 Ted Blankenship .01 .05
458 Al Wingo .01 .05
459 Roger Bresnahan .07 .20
460 Bill Klem .08 .25
461 Charlie Gehringer .08 .25
462 Stan Coveleski .07 .20
463 Eddie Plank .07 .20
464 Clark Griffith .07 .20
465 Herb Pennock .07 .20
466 Earle Combs .07 .20
467 Bobby Doerr .07 .20
468 Waite Hoyt .07 .20
469 Tommy Connolly .07 .20
470 Harry Hooper .07 .20
471 Rick Ferrell .07 .20
472 Billy Evans .05 .15
473 Billy Herman .07 .20
474 Bill Dickey .08 .25
475 Luke Appling .07 .20
476 Babe Pinelli .02 .10
477 Eric McNair .01 .05
478 Sherriff Blake .01 .05
479 Val Picinich .01 .05
480 Fred Heimach .01 .05
481 Jack Graney .01 .05
482 Reb Russell .01 .05
483 Red Faber .07 .20
484 Benny Kauff .02 .10
485 Pants Rowland .01 .05
486 Bobby Veach .01 .05
487 Jim Bagby Sr. .01 .05
488 Pol Perritt .01 .05
489 Buck Herzog .01 .05
490 Art Fletcher .01 .05
491 Walter Holke .01 .05
492 Art Nehf .02 .10
493 Fresco Thompson .01 .05
494 Jimmy Welsh .01 .05
495 Ossie Vitt .01 .05
496 Ownie Carroll .01 .05
497 Ken O'Dea .01 .05
498 Fred Frankhouse .01 .05
499 Jewel Ens .01 .05
500 Morrie Arnovich .01 .05
501 Wally Gerber .01 .05
502 Kiddo Davis .01 .05
503 Buddy Myer .01 .05
504 Sam Leslie .01 .05
505 Cliff Bolton .01 .05
506 Dixie Walker .02 .10
507 Jack Smith .01 .05
508 Bump Hadley .01 .05
509 Buck Crouse .01 .05
510 Joe Glenn .01 .05
511 Chad Kimsey .01 .05
512 Lou Finney .01 .05
513 Roxie Lawson .01 .05
514 Chuck Fullis .01 .05
515 Earl Sheely .01 .05
516 George Gibson .01 .05
517 Johnny Broaca .01 .05
518 Bibb Falk .01 .05
519 Don Hurst .01 .05
520 Grover Hartley .01 .05
521 Don Heffner .01 .05
522 Harvey Hendrick .01 .05
523 Allen Sothoron .01 .05
524 Tony Piet .01 .05
525 Ty Cobb .30 .75
526 Jimmie Foxx .15 .40
527 Rogers Hornsby .15 .40
528 Nap Lajoie .15 .40
529 Lou Gehrig .30 .75
530 Heinie Zimmerman .01 .05
531 Chuck Klein .07 .20
532 Hugh Duffy .07 .20
533 Lefty Grove .10 .30
534 Grover C. Alexander .10 .30
535 Amos Rusie .07 .20
536 Lefty Gomez .08 .25
537 Bucky Walters .05 .15
538 Johnny Hodapp .01 .05
539 Bruce Campbell .01 .05
540 Hod Lisenbee .01 .05
541 Jack Fournier .01 .05
542 Jim Tabor .01 .05
543 Johnny Burnett .01 .05
544 Roy Hartzell .01 .05
545 Doc Gautreau .01 .05
546 Emil Yde .01 .05
547 Bob Johnson .02 .10
548 Joe Hauser .01 .05
549 Ed Reulbach .01 .05
550 Mel Almada .01 .05
551 Mickey Cochrane .08 .25
552 Carl Hubbell .08 .25
553 Charlie Gehringer .08 .25
554 Al Simmons .07 .20
555 Mordecai Brown .07 .20
556 Hugh Jennings .07 .20
557 Kid Elberfeld .01 .05
558 Casey Stengel .10 .30
559 Al Schacht .02 .10
560 Jimmie Foxx .15 .40
561 George Kelly .07 .20
562 Lloyd Waner .07 .20
563 Paul Waner .07 .20
564 Walter Johnson .15 .40
565 Home Run Baker .07 .20
566 Roy Hughes .01 .05
567 Lew Riggs .01 .05
568 John Whitehead .01 .05
569 Elam Vangilder .01 .05
570 Billy Zitzmann .01 .05
571 Walter Schmidt .01 .05
572 Jackie Tavener .01 .05
573 Joe Genewich .01 .05
574 Johnny Marcum .01 .05
575 Fred Hoffmann .01 .05
576 Red Rolfe .02 .10
577 Vic Sorrell .01 .05
578 Pete Scott .01 .05
579 Tommy Thomas .01 .05
580 Al Smith .01 .05
581 Butch Henline .01 .05
582 Eddie Collins .07 .20
583 Earle Combs .07 .20
584 John McGraw .08 .25
585 Hack Wilson .08 .25
586 Gabby Hartnett .07 .20
587 Kiki Cuyler .07 .20
588 Bill Terry .08 .25
589 Joe McCarthy .07 .20
590 Hank Greenberg .10 .30
591 Tris Speaker .08 .25
592 Bill McKechnie .07 .20
593 Bucky Harris .07 .20
594 Herb Pennock .07 .20
595 George Sisler .07 .20
596 Fred Lindstrom .07 .20
597 Earl Averill .07 .20
598 Dave Bancroft .07 .20
599 Connie Mack .08 .25
600 Joe Cronin .07 .20
601 Ken Ash .01 .05
602 Al Spohrer .01 .05
603 Roy Mahaffey .01 .05
604 Frank O'Rourke .01 .05
605 Lil Stoner .01 .05
606 Frank Gabler .01 .05
607 Tom Padden .01 .05
608 Art Shires .01 .05
609 Sherry Smith .01 .05
610 Phil Weintraub .01 .05
611 Russ Van Atta .01 .05
612 Jo Jo White .01 .05
613 Cliff Melton .01 .05
614 Jimmy Ring .01 .05
615 Heinie Sand .01 .05
616 Dale Alexander .01 .05
617 Kent Greenfield .01 .05
618 Eddie Dyer .01 .05
619 Bill Sherdel .01 .05
620 Max Lanier .01 .05
621 Bob O'Farrell .01 .05
622 Rogers Hornsby .15 .40
623 Bill Beckman .01 .05
624 Mort Cooper .01 .05
625 Bill DeLancey .01 .05
626 Marty Marion .02 .10
627 Billy Southworth .01 .05
628 Johnny Mize .08 .25
629 Joe Medwick .07 .20
630 Grover C. Alexander .10 .30
631 Daffy Dean .02 .10
632 Hi Bell .01 .05
633 Walker Cooper .01 .05
634 Frank Frisch .07 .20
635 Dizzy Dean .15 .40
636 Don Gutteridge .01 .05
637 Pepper Martin .05 .15
638 Ed Konetchy .01 .05
639 Bill Hallahan .01 .05
640 Lon Warneke .02 .10
641 Terry Moore .02 .10
642 Enos Slaughter .07 .20
643 Heinie Mueller .01 .05
644 Specs Toporcer .01 .05
645 Jim Bottomley .07 .20
646 Ray Blades .01 .05
647 Jesse Haines .07 .20
648 Andy High .01 .05
649 Miller Huggins .07 .20
650 Ernie Orsatti .01 .05
651 Les Bell .01 .05
652 Gabby Street .01 .05
653 Wally Roettger .01 .05
654 Syl Johnson .01 .05
655 Mike Gonzalez .01 .05
656 Ripper Collins .01 .05
657 Chick Hafey .07 .20
658 Checklist 331-440 .01 .05
659 Checklist 441-550 .01 .05
660 Checklist 551-660 .01 .05

1992 Conlon TSN 13th National

In conjunction with The Sporting News, Megacards issued various prototype cards during 1992 to preview their soon to be released regular issue sets. All the cards were standard size. These cards were given away as promotional items at the 13th National Sports Collectors Convention in Atlanta and therefore have "13th National" stamped on their backs.

COMPLETE SET (4) 4.00 10.00
400 Joe Jackson DP/(13th National) 2.00 5.00
663 Babe Ruth (BW)/(13th National) 3.00 8.00
775 Chief Meyers/(13th National) .40 1.00
800 Hippo Vaughn/(13th National) .40 1.00

1992 Conlon TSN All-Star Program

In 1992 several gold-foil edition black and white Conlon Collection cards were released to preview the 1993 Conlon Collection. Cards 661G-664G feature four players who played in the first All-Star Game in 1933. Reportedly 34,000 of each of these cards were produced exclusively for and inserted (one per program) in the 1992 All-Star Game program. These standard-size cards have the same design typical of other Conlon issues, only that the vintage black and white player photos are framed in gold foil.

COMPLETE SET (4) 8.00 20.00
661G Bill Terry 2.00 5.00
662G Lefty Gomez 2.00 5.00
663G Babe Ruth 4.00 10.00
664G Frankie Frisch 1.25 3.00

1992-93 Conlon TSN Color Inserts

All the cards in this 22-card standard-size set were previously released in black and white in the 1991 or 1992 Conlon regular issue sets. Released on two different occasions, cards 1-6 and 7-12 were issued exclusively as a bonus to collectors who purchased Megacards' hobby accessory products (plastic sheets, card frames, and card sleeves) through retail outlets. The announced production figures for cards 1-6 were 250,000 of each card. For cards 7-12, the announced production run was 252,000 of each card. Cards 13-20 were randomly inserted in 1993 Conlon counter packs and blister packs, with an announced production run of 100,000 of each card. Cards 21-22 were available only through a special send-away offer on the backs of Conlon counter packs and blister packs; 75,000 of each card were produced. There were 60,000 cards of Bob Feller (23) produced exclusively for the Sports Collectors Digest 1993 Price Guide and bound inside copies of that book. The fronts display color player portraits inside a white picture frame on a navy blue card face. A diagonal graphic across the upper right corner of the picture gives the year the player was inducted into the Hall of Fame. The black and white backs are accented in navy blue and provide biography, career statistics, and career summary. The corresponding card number of the black and white regular issue card is given on the line after each player's name.

COMPLETE SET (23) 20.00 50.00
COMMON CARD (1-6) .40 1.00
COMMON CARD (7-12) .40 1.00
COMMON CARD (13-20) .80 2.00
COMMON CARD (21-22) 2.40 6.00
COMMON CARD (23) 2.00 5.00
1 Jim Bottomley .40 1.00
Card 22
2 Lefty Grove .75 2.00
Card 23
3 Lou Gehrig 1.50 4.00
Card 111
4 Babe Ruth 2.50 6.00
Card 145
5 Casey Stengel .75 2.00
Card 37
6 Rube Marquard .40 1.00
Card 252
7 Walter Johnson .75 2.00
Card 353
8 Lou Gehrig 1.50 4.00
Card 310
9 Christy Mathewson .75 2.00
Card 331
10 Ty Cobb 1.50 4.00
Card 250
11 Mel Ott .75 2.00
Card 225
12 Carl Hubbell .40 1.00
Card 253
13 Al Simmons .75 2.00
Card 49
14 Connie Mack 1.25 3.00
Card 47
15 Grover C. Alexander 1.25 3.00
Card 32
16 Jimmie Foxx 1.25 3.00
Card 303
17 Lloyd Waner .75 2.00
Card 6
18 Tris Speaker 1.25 3.00
Card 422
19 Dizzy Dean 1.50 4.00
Card 3
20 Rogers Hornsby 1.50 4.00
Card 1
21 Joe Jackson 2.50 6.00
Card 444
22 Jim Thorpe 2.50 6.00
Card 403
23 Bob Feller 2.00 5.00

1992-93 Conlon TSN Gold Inserts

Several gold-foil edition black and white Conlon Collection standard-size cards were released to preview the 1993 Conlon Collection. Card numbers 665, 770, 820, and 880 were included in 1992 Conlon factory sets; reportedly 90,000 of each card were produced. The factory set cases distributed through hobby dealers also included two additional cards (667 and 730) as a bonus (roughly a dozen of each per case), with a stated production run of 20,000 for each card. Card 1000G, of which 100,000 were produced, was inserted in the 65-card jumbo packs sold only at Toys 'R' Us. Likewise, 100,000 of card 934G were produced and inserted into packs sold only at Eckerd's Drugs. The cards have the same design typical of other Conlon issues, only that the vintage black and white player photos are framed in gold foil.

COMPLETE SET (8) 5.00 12.00
665 Carl Hubbell .60 1.50
667 Charlie Gehringer SP 1.00 2.50
730 Luke Appling SP
(Old Aches and Pains) 1.00 2.50
770 Tommy Henrich .40 1.00
820 John McGraw .75 2.00
880 Gabby Hartnett .60 1.50
934G Walter Johnson 2.00 5.00
and Nolan Ryan
1000G Ty Cobb DP 1.25 3.00

1993 Conlon Masters BW

The 1993 Conlon Collection Master Series premier issue consists of nine cards subtitled "The Best There Was". The set production was limited to 25,000, and each set includes a certificate of authenticity with the serial number. The oversize cards measure approximately 8" by 10" and feature the photography of Charles Martin Conlon, the greatest sports photographer of his time. The Sporting News acquired Conlon's work in 1945, and from this archive, Megacards created the Master Series. With the exception of the Johnson and Gehrig card (3), the horizontal backs have a black-and-white close-up player shot on the left. Each set was accompanied by a certificate of authenticity that gave the set number out of a production run of 25,000. By returning the original certificate of authenticity along with 9.95, the collector received a protective portfolio to display the cards and a new deluxe certificate. The portfolio and the cards carried a suggested retail price of 29.95.

COMPLETE SET (9) 12.50 30.00
1 The Best There Was/1905 to 1942 .75 2.00
2 Babe Ruth 4.00 10.00
Outfield
3 Walter Johnson 1.50 4.00
Pitcher
Lou Gehrig
First base
4 Honus Wagner 1.50 4.00
Shortstop
5 Mickey Cochrane 1.00 2.50
Catcher
6 Tris Speaker 1.00 2.50
Outfield
7 Ty Cobb 2.00 5.00
Outfield
8 Rogers Hornsby/2nd Base 1.50 4.00
9 Pie Traynor/3rd Base 1.00 2.50

1993 Conlon Masters Color

The 1993 Conlon Collection Color Master Series premier issue consists of nine cards. The set production was limited to 25,000, and each set includes a certificate of authenticity with the serial number. The oversize cards measure approximately 8" by 10" and feature the photography of Charles Martin Conlon, the greatest sports photographer of his time. The Sporting News acquired Conlon's work in 1945, and from this archive, Megacards created the Master Series. Using 1993 technology, one special card (3) features Nolan Ryan transported back in time to Yankee Stadium in 1927 in a fantasy conversation with Walter Johnson. Each set was accompanied by a certificate of authenticity that gave the set number out of a production run of 25,000. By returning the original certificate of authenticity along with 9.95, the collector received a protective portfolio to display the cards and a new deluxe certificate. The portfolio and the cards retailed for 29.95.

COMPLETE SET (9) 10.00 25.00
1 Title Card .60 1.50
2 Nap Lajoie 1.25 3.00
3 Nolan Ryan 4.00 10.00
Walter Johnson
4 Hilltop Park .60 1.50
home of the Highlanders
5 Babe Ruth 5.00 12.00
6 Frank Baker 1.25 3.00
7 John McGraw MG 1.50 4.00
8 John McGraw 1.25 3.00
Wilbert Robinson
Christy Mathewson
9 Hughie Jennings MG 1.25 3.00

1993 Conlon TSN Prototypes

These two cards are colorized prototypes, with same design as the regular 888 and 934 from the 1993 Conlon TSN set. The production run for each of these two cards was 52,000.

COMPLETE SET 4.00 10.00
888 Babe Ruth 2.00 5.00
934 Walter Johnson 2.00 5.00
with Nolan Ryan

1993 Conlon TSN

The third 330-card standard-size set of The Sporting News Conlon Collection again features turn-of-the-century to World War II-era players photographed by Charles Conlon, including more than 100 cards of Hall of Famers. Cards from a subset displaying computer color-enhanced photos were randomly inserted in the counter box packs and blister packs. The set contains several subsets continuing from last year's issue and some new subsets unique to this year's set: Game of the Century: 1933 All-Star Game (661-689), Spitballers (702-712), Accused Spitballers (717-725), Nicknames (730-741), Great Stories (751-770), Native Americans: American Indians who played big-league ball (771-777), League Leaders (795-798 and 801-805), Great Managers (817-848), Great Backstops (861-880), Against All Odds (881-894), Trivia (905-918), Nolan Ryan: compares eight Hall of Famers to Ryan (928-935), and First Cards: players for whom cards have never been done before (945-987). The set closes with checklist cards (988-990). The set was also available as a factory set in a special commemorative tin and in the form of three 110-card uncut sheets.

COMPLETE SET (330) 15.00 40.00
COMP.FACT (330) 15.00 40.00
661 Bill Terry .08 .25
662 Lefty Gomez .08 .25
663 Babe Ruth .60 1.50
664 Frank Frisch .08 .25
665 Carl Hubbell .08 .25
666 Al Simmons .08 .25
667 Charlie Gehringer .08 .25
668 Earl Averill .08 .25
669 Lefty Grove .15 .40
670 Pie Traynor .08 .25
671 Chuck Klein .08 .25
672 Paul Waner .08 .25
673 Lou Gehrig .40 1.00
674 Rick Ferrell .08 .25
675 Gabby Hartnett .08 .25
676 Joe Cronin .08 .25
677 Chick Hafey .08 .25
678 Jimmy Dykes .02 .10
679 Sammy West .01 .05
680 Pepper Martin .05 .15
681 Lefty O'Doul .02 .10
682 General Crowder .01 .05
683 Jimmie Wilson .01 .05
684 Dick Bartell .01 .05
685 Bill Hallahan .01 .05
686 Wally Berger .02 .10
687 Lon Warneke .02 .10
688 Ben Chapman .01 .05
689 Woody English .01 .05
690 Jimmy Reese .02 .10
691 Wattie Holm .01 .05
692 Charlie Jamieson .01 .05
693 Tom Zachary .01 .05
694 Blondy Ryan .01 .05
695 Sparky Adams .01 .05
696 Bill Hunnefield .01 .05
697 Lee Meadows .01 .05
698 Tom Carey .01 .05
699 Johnny Rawlings .01 .05
700 Ken Holloway .01 .05
701 Lance Richbourg .01 .05
702 Ray Fisher .01 .05
703 Ed Walsh .08 .25
704 Dick Rudolph .01 .05
705 Ray Caldwell .01 .05
706 Burleigh Grimes .08 .25
707 Stan Coveleski .08 .25
708 George Hildebrand .01 .05
709 Jack Quinn .02 .10
710 Red Faber .08 .25
711 Urban Shocker .02 .10
712 Dutch Leonard .02 .10
713 Lou Koupal .01 .05
714 Jimmy Wasdell .01 .05
715 Johnny Lindell .01 .05
716 Don Padgett .01 .05

717 Nelson Potter .01 .05
718 Schoolboy Rowe .02 .10
719 Dave Danforth .01 .05
720 Claude Passeau .01 .05
721 Harry Kelley .01 .05
722 Johnny Allen .01 .05
723 Tommy Bridges .02 .10
724 Bill Lee .01 .05
725 Fred Frankhouse .01 .05
726 Johnny McCarthy .01 .05
727 Rip Russell .01 .05
728 Emory(Topper) Rigney .01 .05
729 Howie Shanks .01 .05
730 Luke Appling .08 .25
731 Bill Byron UMP .01 .05
732 Earle Combs .08 .25
733 Hank Greenberg .15 .40
734 Walter(Boom Boom) Beck .01 .05
735 Sloppy Thurston .01 .05
736 Hack Wilson .08 .25
737 Bill McGowan UMP .08 .25
738 Zeke Bonura .02 .10
739 Tom Baker .01 .05
740 Bill(Baby Doll) Jacobson .01 .05
741 Kiki Cuyler .08 .25
742 George Blaeholder .01 .05
743 Dee Miles .01 .05
744 Lee Handley .01 .05
745 Shano Collins .01 .05
746 Rosy Ryan .01 .05
747 Aaron Ward .01 .05
748 Monte Pearson .01 .05
749 Jake Early .01 .05
750 Bill Atwood .01 .05
751 Mark Koenig .02 .10
752 Buddy Hassett .01 .05
753 Davy Jones .01 .05
754 Honus Wagner .20 .50
755 Bill Dickey .08 .25
756 Max Butcher .01 .05
757 Waite Hoyt .08 .25
758 Walter Johnson .20 .50
759 Howard Ehmke .01 .05
760 Bobo Newsom .05 .15
761 Tony Lazzeri .08 .25
762 Tony Lazzeri .08 .25
763 Spud Chandler .02 .10
764 Kirby Higbe .01 .05
765 Paul Richards .02 .10
766 Rogers Hornsby .15 .40
767 Joe Vosmik .01 .05
768 Jesse Haines .08 .25
769 Bucky Walters .05 .15
770 Tommy Henrich .05 .15
771 Jim Thorpe .50 1.25
772 Euel Moore .01 .05
773 Rudy York .02 .10
774 Chief Bender .08 .25
775 Chief Meyers .01 .05
776 Bob Johnson .02 .10
777 Roy Johnson .01 .05
778 Dick Porter .01 .05
779 Ethan Allen .02 .10
780 Slim Sallee .01 .05
781 Beau Bell .01 .05
782 Jigger Statz .01 .05
783 Dutch Henry .01 .05
784 Larry Woodall .01 .05
785 Phil Collins .01 .05
786 Joe Sewell .08 .25
787 Billy Herman .08 .25
788 Rube Oldring .01 .05
789 Bill Walker .01 .05
790 Joe Schultz .01 .05
791 Fred Maguire .01 .05
792 Claude Willoughby .01 .05
793 Alex Ferguson .01 .05
794 Johnny Morrison .01 .05
795 Tris Speaker .08 .25
796 Ty Cobb .40 1.00
797 Max Carey .08 .25
798 George Sisler .08 .25
799 Charlie Hollocher .01 .05
800 Hippo Vaughn .01 .05
801 Sad Sam Jones .02 .10
802 Harry Hooper .08 .25
803 Gavvy Cravath .02 .10
804 Walter Johnson .08 .25
805 Jake Daubert .02 .10
806 Clyde Milan .02 .10
807 Hugh McQuillan .01 .05
808 Fred Brickell .01 .05
809 Joe Stripp .01 .05
810 Johnny Hodapp .01 .05
811 Johnny Vergez .01 .05
812 Lonny Frey .01 .05
813 Bill Regan .01 .05
814 Babe Young .01 .05
815 Charlie Robertson .01 .05
816 Walt Judnich .01 .05
817 Joe Tinker .08 .25
818 Johnny Evers .08 .25
819 Frank Chance .08 .25
820 John McGraw .08 .25
821 Charles Grimm .05 .15
822 Ted Lyons .08 .25
823 Joe McCarthy MG .08 .25
824 Connie Mack MG .08 .25
825 George Gibson .01 .05
826 Steve O'Neill .01 .05
827 Tris Speaker .08 .25
828 Bill Carrigan .01 .05
829 Casey Stengel .15 .40
830 Miller Huggins .08 .25
831 Bill McKechnie MG .08 .25
832 Chuck Dressen .02 .10
833 Gabby Street .01 .05
834 Mel Ott .15 .40
835 Frank Frisch .08 .25
836 George Sisler .08 .25
837 Nap Lajoie .15 .40
838 Ty Cobb .40 1.00
839 Billy Southworth MG .01 .05
840 Clark Griffith .08 .25
841 Bill Terry .08 .25
842 Rogers Hornsby .15 .40
843 Joe Cronin .08 .25
844 Al Lopez .08 .25
845 Bucky Harris MG .08 .25
846 Wilbert Robinson MG .08 .25
847 Hughie Jennings .08 .25
848 Jimmie Dykes .02 .10
849 Roy Cullenbine .01 .05
850 Eddie Moore .01 .05
851 Jack Rothrock .01 .05
852 Bill Lamar .01 .05
853 Monte Weaver .01 .05
854 Ival Goodman .01 .05
855 Hank Severeid .01 .05
856 Fred Haney .01 .05
857 Joe Shaute .01 .05
858 Smead Jolley .01 .05
859 Dib Williams .01 .05
860 Benny Bengough .02 .10
861 Rick Ferrell .08 .25
862 Bob O'Farrell .01 .05
863 Spud Davis .01 .05
864 Frankie Hayes .01 .05
865 Muddy Ruel .01 .05
866 Mickey Cochrane .10 .30
867 Johnny Kling .01 .05
868 Ivey Wingo .01 .05
869 Bill Dickey .10 .30
870 Frank Snyder .01 .05
871 Roger Bresnahan .08 .25
872 Wally Schang .02 .10
873 Al Lopez .08 .25
874 Jimmie Wilson .01 .05
875 Val Picinich .01 .05
876 Steve O'Neill .01 .05
877 Ernie Lombardi .08 .25
878 Johnny Bassler .01 .05
879 Ray Schalk .08 .25
880 Gabby Hartnett .08 .25
881 Bruce Campbell .01 .05
882 Red Ruffing .08 .25
883 Mordecai Brown .08 .25
884 Jimmy Archer .01 .05
885 Dave Keefe .01 .05
886 Nate Andrews .01 .05
887 Sam Rice .08 .25
888 Babe Ruth .50 1.25
889 Chick Hafey .08 .25
890 Oscar Melillo .01 .05
891 Joe Wood .02 .10
892 Johnny Evers .08 .25
893 Specs Toporcer .01 .05
894 Myril Hoag .01 .05
895 Bob Weiland .01 .05
896 Joe Marty .01 .05
897 Sherry Magee .01 .05
898 Danny Taylor .01 .05
899 Willie Kamm .01 .05
900 Jimmy Sheckard .01 .05
901 Syl Johnson .01 .05
902 Steve Sundra .01 .05
903 Doc Cramer .02 .10
904 Hub Pruett .01 .05
905 Lena Blackburne .01 .05
906 Eppa Rixey .08 .25
907 Goose Goslin .08 .25
908 George Kelly .08 .25
909 Jim Bottomley .08 .25
910 Christy Mathewson .20 .50
911 Tony Lazzeri .08 .25
912 Johnny Mostil .01 .05
913 Bobby Doerr .08 .25
914 Rabbit Maranville .08 .25
915 Harry Heilmann .08 .25
916 Bobby Wallace .08 .25
917 Jimmie Foxx .15 .40
918 Johnny Mize .08 .25
919 Jack Bentley .01 .05
920 Al Schacht .05 .15
921 Ed Coleman .01 .05
922 Dode Paskert .01 .05
923 Hod Ford .01 .05
924 Randy Moore .01 .05
925 Milt Shoffner .01 .05
926 Dick Siebert .01 .05
927 Tony Kaufmann .01 .05
928 Dizzy Dean with Nolan Ryan .50 1.25
929 Dazzy Vance with Nolan Ryan .30 .75
930 Lefty Grove with Nolan Ryan .40 1.00
931 Rube Waddell with Nolan Ryan .40 1.00
932 Grover C. Alexander with Nolan Ryan .40 1.00
933 Bob Feller with Nolan Ryan .40 1.00
934 Walter Johnson with Nolan Ryan .75 2.00
935 Ted Lyons with Nolan Ryan .40 1.00
936 Jim Bagby Jr. .01 .05
937 Joe Sugden CO .01 .05
938 Earl Grace .01 .05
939 Jeff Heath .01 .05
940 Ken Williams .05 .15
941 Marv Owen .01 .05
942 Roy Weatherly .01 .05
943 Ed Morgan .01 .05
944 Johnny Rizzo .01 .05
945 Archie McKain .01 .05
946 Bob Garbark .01 .05
947 Bob Osborn .01 .05
948 Johnny Podgajny .01 .05
949 Joe Evans .01 .05
950 Tony Rensa .01 .05
951 John Humphries .01 .05
952 Merritt(Sugar) Cain .01 .05
953 Roy(Snipe) Hansen .01 .05
954 Johnny Niggeling .01 .05
955 Hal Wiltse .01 .05
956 Alex Carrasquel .02 .10
957 George Grant .01 .05
958 Lefty Weinert .01 .05
959 Erv Brame .01 .05
960 Ray Harrell .01 .05
961 Ed Linke .01 .05
962 Sam Gibson .01 .05
963 Johnny Watwood .01 .05
964 Doc Prothro .01 .05
965 Julio Bonetti .01 .05
966 Lefty Mills .01 .05
967 Chick Galloway .01 .05
968 Hal Kelleher .01 .05
969 Chief Hogsett .01 .05
970 Ed Heusser .01 .05
971 Ed Baecht .01 .05
972 Jack Saltzgaver .01 .05
973 Leroy Herrmann .01 .05
974 Belve Bean .01 .05
975 Harry(Socks) Seibold .01 .05
976 Vic Keen .01 .05
977 Bill Barrett .01 .05
978 Pat McNulty .01 .05
979 George Turbeville .01 .05
980 Eddie Phillips .01 .05
981 Garland Buckeye .01 .05
982 Vic Frasier .01 .05
983 Gordon Rhodes .01 .05
984 Red Barnes .01 .05
985 Jim Joe Edwards .01 .05
986 Herschel Bennett .01 .05
987 Carmen Hill .01 .05
988 Checklist 661-770 .01 .05
989 Checklist 771-880 .01 .05
990 Checklist 881-990 .01 .05

1994 Conlon TSN Promos

Issued to herald the release of the 330-card 1994 Conlon The Sporting News set, these eight standard-size promos feature black-bordered and white-line-framed black-and-white player photos on their fronts. The player's name, team, position, and year appear in white lettering within the lower black margin. The white and black back carries the player's name, biography, statistics, and career highlights. The faint "For Promotional Use Only" disclaimer appears obliquely. The production run for card numbers 991, 1050, 1105, 1140, 1190, and 1230 was 26,000; for card numbers 1030 and 1170, production was reportedly 52,000.

COMPLETE SET (8) 4.00 10.00
991 Pepper Martin .40 1.00
1030 Joe Jackson DP 1.25 3.00
1050 Pie Traynor .75 2.00
1105 Carl Hubbell .75 2.00
1140 Lefty Grove .75 2.00
1170 Dizzy Dean and-Daffy Dean DP .75 2.00
1190 Bill Klem .60 1.50
1230 Mark Koenig .40 1.00

1994 Conlon TSN

This fourth 330-card standard-size set of The Sporting News Conlon Collection again features the work of noted sports photographer Charles Conlon. The fronts feature black-and-white vintage player photos inside a white frame on a black card face. Subset cards are marked by their title in a black diagonal that cuts across the top right corner. The backs carry biography, statistics, and extended career summary and highlights. Topical subsets featured are Great Stories (991-1007), Hall of Fame (1008-1018), Black Sox Scandal (1019-1042), Nicknames (1050-1066), 1934 All-Star Game (1075-1113), In Memoriam (1121-1128), 1929 Athletics (1135-1159), Double Play Combo (1164-1166), Brothers (1169-1180), Umpires (1185-1212), All-Time Leaders (1217-1223), Switch-Hitters (1229-1237), Trivia (1247-1257), Action (1266-1274), First Card (1282-1317), and Checklists (1318-1320). The cards are numbered on the back in continuation of the previous year's issue. Card 1000 is the famous photo of Ty Cobb sliding. The 1994 Conlon set was issued in 12-card foil packs instead of the 15-card foil packs used in previous years. Reportedly 10,000 gold-bordered burgundy cards were produced for every card in the set. Each foil pack contained one of these cards, while two were inserted in each blister pack. According to Megacards, no more than 200,000 of each card were produced. The set was also available in factory set form.

COMPLETE SET (330) 12.50 30.00
COMPLETE FACT.SET (330) 12.50 30.00
991 Pepper Martin .07 .20
992 Joe Sewell .08 .25
993 Edd Roush .08 .25
994 Rick Ferrell .08 .25
995 Johnny Broaca .02 .10
996 Luke Sewell .05 .15
997 Burleigh Grimes .08 .25
998 Hack Wilson .08 .25
999 Lefty Grove .15 .40
1000 Ty Cobb .50 1.25
1001 John McGraw .08 .25
1002 Eddie Plank .08 .25
1003 Sad Sam Jones .05 .15
1004 Jim Bottomley .08 .25
1005 Hank Greenberg .20 .50
1006 Lloyd Waner .08 .25
1007 Wilcy Moore .02 .10
1008 Luke Appling .08 .25
1009 Hal Newhouser .08 .25
1010 Al Lopez .08 .25
1011 Ty Cobb .50 1.25
1012 Kid Nichols .08 .25
1013 Ed Walsh .08 .25
1014 Hugh Duffy .08 .25
1015 Rube Marquard .08 .25
1016 Addie Joss .08 .25
1017 Bobby Wallace .08 .25
1018 Willie Keeler .08 .25
1019 Jake Daubert .05 .15
1020 Slim Sallee .02 .10
1021 Dolf Luque .05 .15
1022 Ivey Wingo .02 .10
1023 Edd Roush .08 .25
1024 Bill Rariden .02 .10
1025 Sherry Magee .02 .10
1026 Pat Duncan .02 .10
1027 Hod Eller .02 .10
1028 Greasy Neale .05 .15
1029 Buck Weaver .08 .25
1030 Joe Jackson .60 1.50
1031 Chick Gandil .08 .25
1032 Swede Risberg .08 .25
1033 Ray Schalk .08 .25
1034 Eddie Cicotte .07 .20
1035 Bill James .02 .10
1036 Nemo Leibold .02 .10
1037 Dickie Kerr .07 .20
1038 Kid Gleason MG .05 .15
1039 Fred McMullin .02 .10
1040 Eddie Collins .08 .25
1041 Sox Pitchers Lefty Williams Bill James Ed Cicot .07 .20
1042 Sox Outfielders Nemo Leibold Happy Felsch Shano .08 .25
1043 Ken Keltner .05 .15
1044 Charlie Berry .05 .15
1045 Rube Lutzke .02 .10
1046 Johnny Schulte .02 .10
1047 Johnny Welch .02 .10
1048 Jack Russell .02 .10
1049 Red Murray .02 .10
1050 Pie Traynor .08 .25
1051 Mike Donlin .05 .15
1052 Gabby Hartnett .08 .25
1053 Tony Lazzeri .08 .25
1054 Hack Miller .02 .10
1055 Dazzy Vance .08 .25
1056 Bill Carrigan .02 .10
1057 Johnny Murphy .05 .15
1058 Cliff Heathcote .02 .10
1059 Joe Dugan .05 .15
1060 Rabbit Maranville .08 .25
1061 Tommy Henrich .07 .20
1062 Roy Parmelee .02 .10
1063 Lefty Gomez .08 .25
1064 Ernie Lombardi .08 .25
1065 Dave Bancroft .08 .25
1066 Bill McKechnie MG .08 .25
1067 Buddy Hassett .02 .10
1068 Spud Chandler .05 .15
1069 Roy Hughes .02 .10
1070 Hooks Dauss .02 .10
1071 Joe Hauser .02 .10
1072 Spud Davis .02 .10
1073 Max Butcher .02 .10
1074 Lou Chiozza .02 .10
1075 Polo Grounds 1934 All-Star Game .02 .10
1076 Charlie Gehringer .08 .25
1077 Heinie Manush .08 .25
1078 Red Ruffing .08 .25
1079 Mel Harder .05 .15
1080 Babe Ruth .75 2.00
1081 Ben Chapman .02 .10
1082 Lou Gehrig .40 1.00
1083 Jimmie Foxx .20 .50
1084 Al Simmons .08 .25
1085 Joe Cronin .08 .25
1086 Bill Dickey .08 .25
1087 Mickey Cochrane .08 .25
1088 Lefty Gomez .08 .25
1089 Earl Averill Sr. .08 .25
1090 Sammy West .02 .10
1091 Frank Frisch P-MG .08 .25
1092 Billy Herman .08 .25
1093 Pie Traynor .08 .25
1094 Joe Medwick .08 .25
1095 Chuck Klein .08 .25
1096 Kiki Cuyler .08 .25
1097 Mel Ott .20 .50
1098 Wally Berger .05 .15
1099 Paul Waner .08 .25
1100 Bill Terry .08 .25
1101 Travis Jackson .08 .25
1102 Arky Vaughan .08 .25
1103 Gabby Hartnett .08 .25
1104 Al Lopez .08 .25
1105 Carl Hubbell .08 .25
1106 Lon Warneke .05 .15
1107 Van Lingle Mungo .05 .15
1108 Pepper Martin .07 .20
1109 Dizzy Dean .25 .60
1110 Fred Frankhouse .02 .10
1111 Bob Quinn J.G. Taylor Spink Mrs. J.G. Taylor Spi .02 .10
1112 Mrs. Joseph Gilleaudeau Joseph Gilleaudeau Mrs. .02 .10
1113 Bill Hinchman Edward Keller .02 .10
1114 Vic Aldridge .02 .10
1115 Pinky Higgins .02 .10
1116 Hal Carlson .02 .10
1117 Fred Fitzsimmons .05 .15
1118 Bucky Walters .07 .20
1119 Nick Altrock .02 .10
1120 Chuck Dressen .05 .15
1121 Mark Koenig .05 .15
1122 Charlie Gehringer .08 .25
1123 Vern Kennedy .02 .10
1124 Harlond Clift .02 .10
1125 Babe Phelps .02 .10
1126 Johnny Mize .08 .25
1127 Hal Schumacher .05 .15
1128 Ethan Allen .05 .15
1129 Bill Wambsganss .02 .10
1130 Freddy Leach .02 .10
1131 Bud Clancy .02 .10
1132 Stuffy Stewart .02 .10
1133 Bill Brubaker .02 .10
1134 Les Mann .02 .10
1135 Howard Ehmke .02 .10
1136 Al Simmons .08 .25
1137 George Earnshaw .05 .15
1138 Mule Haas .02 .10
1139 Bing Miller .02 .10
1140 Lefty Grove .20 .50
1141 Joe Boley .02 .10
1142 Eddie Collins .08 .25
1143 Walter French .02 .10
1144 Eric McNair .02 .10
1145 Bill Shores .02 .10
1146 Mickey Cochrane .08 .25
1147 Homer Summa .02 .10
1148 Jack Quinn .05 .15
1149 Max Bishop .02 .10
1150 Jimmy Dykes .05 .15
1151 Rube Walberg .02 .10
1152 Jimmie Foxx .20 .50
1153 George H. Burns .02 .10
1154 Doc Cramer .05 .15
1155 Sammy Hale .02 .10
1156 Eddie Rommel .02 .10
1157 Cy Perkins .02 .10
1158 Jim Cronin .02 .10
1159 Connie Mack MG .08 .25
1160 Ray Kolp .02 .10
1161 Clyde Manion .02 .10
1162 Frank Grube .02 .10
1163 Steve Swetonic .02 .10
1164 Joe Tinker .08 .25
1165 Johnny Evers .08 .25
1166 Frank Chance .08 .25
1167 Emerson Dickman .02 .10
1168 Jack Tobin .02 .10
1169 Wes Ferrell Rick Ferrell .07 .20
1170 Dizzy Dean Daffy Dean .08 .25
1171 Tony Cuccinello Al Cuccinello .02 .10
1172 Harry Coveleski Stan Coveleski .05 .15
1173 Bob Johnson Roy Johnson .02 .10
1174 Andy High Hugh High .02 .10
1175 Luke Sewell Joe Sewell .07 .20
1176 Johnnie Heving Joe Heving .02 .10
1177 Al Wingo Ivy Wingo .02 .10
1178 Red Killefer Bill Killefer .02 .10
1179 Bubbles Hargrave Pinky Hargrave .02 .10
1180 Paul Waner Lloyd Waner .07 .20
1181 Johnny VanderMeer .07 .20
1182 Jo Jo Moore .02 .10
1183 Bobby Burke .02 .10
1184 Johnny Moore .02 .10
1185 Jack Egan UMP .02 .10
1186 Tommy Connolly UMP .08 .25
1187 Silk O'Loughlin UMP .02 .10
1188 Beans Reardon UMP .05 .15
1189 Charles Moran UMP .02 .10
1190 Bill Klem UMP .08 .25
1191 Dolly Stark UMP .05 .15
1192 Albert Orth UMP .02 .10
1193 Kitty Bransfield UMP .02 .10
1194 Roy Van Graflan UMP .02 .10
1195 Bob Hart UMP .02 .10
1196 Jocko Conlan UMP .08 .25
1197 Babe Pinelli UMP .05 .15
1198 John Sheridan UMP .02 .10
1199 Dick Nallin UMP .02 .10
1200 Bill Dineen UMP .02 .10
1201 Hank O'Day UMP .05 .15
1202 Cy Rigler UMP .02 .10
1203 Bob Emslie UMP .02 .10
1204 Charles Pfirman UMP .02 .10
1205 Harry Geisel UMP .02 .10
1206 Ernest Quigley UMP .02 .10
1207 Red Ormsby UMP .02 .10
1208 George Hildebrand UMP .02 .10
1209 George Moriarty UMP .05 .15
1210 Billy Evans UMP .07 .20
1211 Brick Owens UMP .02 .10
1212 Bill McGowan UMP .08 .25
1213 Kirby Higbe .02 .10
1214 Taylor Douthit .02 .10
1215 Del Baker .02 .10
1216 Al Demaree .02 .10
1217 Connie Mack MG .08 .25
1218 Nap Lajoie .20 .50
1219 Honus Wagner .25 .60
1220 Christy Mathewson .25 .60
1221 Sam Crawford .08 .25
1222 Tris Speaker .08 .25
1223 Grover C. Alexander .20 .50
1224 Joe Bowman .02 .10
1225 Johnny Rigney .02 .10
1226 Earl Webb .05 .15
1227 Whitey Moore .02 .10
1228 Bruce Campbell .02 .10
1229 Lu Blue .02 .10
1230 Mark Koenig .05 .15
1231 Wally Schang .05 .15
1232 Max Carey .08 .25
1233 Frank Frisch .08 .25
1234 Donie Bush .02 .10
1235 George Davis .02 .10
1236 Billy Rogell .02 .10
1237 Ripper Collins .02 .10
1238 Dick Burrus .02 .10
1239 Evar Swanson .02 .10
1240 Woody English .02 .10
1241 Joe Harris .02 .10
1242 Harry McCurdy .02 .10
1243 Dick Bartell .02 .10
1244 Tommy Thompson .02 .10
1245 Babe Adams .05 .15
1246 Art Nehf .05 .15
1247 Jack Graney .02 .10
1248 Ted Lyons .08 .25
1249 Lou Gehrig .50 1.25
1250 Mickey Welch .08 .25
1251 Red Faber .08 .25
1252 Joe McGinnity .08 .25
1253 Rogers Hornsby .20 .50
1254 Mel Ott .20 .50
1255 Walter Johnson .25 .60
1256 Sam Rice .08 .25
1257 Jim Tobin .02 .10
1258 Roger Peckinpaugh .05 .15
1259 George Stovall .02 .10
1260 Fred Merkle .05 .15
1261 Rip Collins .02 .10
1262 Carl Lind .02 .10
1263 Nap Rucker .02 .10
1264 Sloppy Thurston .02 .10
1265 Alex Metzler .02 .10
1266 Charles M.Conlon .02 .10
1267 Lew McCarty IA Sherry Magee .02 .10
1268 B.A. Daniels IA .02 .10
1269 Benny Kauff IA .05 .15
1270 Heinie Groh IA .05 .15
1271 Fritz Mollwitz IA .02 .10
1272 George H. Burns IA .02 .10
1273 Lee Magee IA .02 .10
1274 Bill Killefer IA .02 .10
1275 Jack Warhop .02 .10
1276 Dutch Leonard .05 .15
1277 General Crowder .02 .10
1278 Chet Laabs .02 .10
1279 Joe Bush .05 .15
1280 Rube Bressler .02 .10
1281 Bob Brown .02 .10
1282 Bernie DeViveiros .02 .10
1283 Les Tietje .02 .10
1284 Charlie Devens .02 .10
1285 Elliott Bigelow .02 .10
1286 Johnny Dickshot .02 .10
1287 Buster Chatham .02 .10
1288 Walter Beall .02 .10
1289 Dick Attreau .02 .10
1290 Bunny Brief .02 .10
1291 Jim Gleeson .02 .10
1292 Wally Shaner .02 .10
1293 Pat Crawford .02 .10
1294 Manny Salvo .02 .10
1295 Cal Dorsett .02 .10
1296 Rusty Peters .02 .10
1297 Johnny Couch .02 .10
1298 Dutch Ulrich .02 .10
1299 Jim Bivin .02 .10
1300 Paul Strand .02 .10
1301 Johnny Lanning .02 .10
1302 Bill Brenzel .02 .10
1303 Don Songer .02 .10
1304 Dutch Levsen .02 .10
1305 Otto Bluege .02 .10
1306 Fabian Gaffke .02 .10
1307 Flash Archdeacon .02 .10
1308 Tiny Chaplin .02 .10
1309 Larry Rosenthal .02 .10
1310 Bill Bagwell .02 .10
1311 Joe Dawson .02 .10
1312 Johnny Sturm .02 .10
1313 Haskell Billings .02 .10
1314 Whitey Wilshere .02 .10
1315 Asby Asbjornson .02 .10
1316 Hank Steinbacher .02 .10
1317 Stan Baumgartner .02 .10
1318 Checklist 991-1100 .02 .10
1319 Checklist 1101-1210 .02 .10
1320 Checklist 1211-1320 .02 .10

1994 Conlon TSN Burgundy

*STARS: 1.5X TO 4X BASIC CARDS

1994 Conlon TSN Color Inserts

COMPLETE SET (16) 15.00 40.00
COMMON CARD (24-28) .60 1.50
COMMON CARD (29-33) .80 2.00
COMMON CARD (34-37) .60 1.50
COMMON CARD (38-39) 1.20 3.00
24 Hal Newhouser Card 445 .75 2.00
25 Hugh Jennings Card 556 .60 1.50
26 Red Faber .60 1.50
27 Enos Slaughter Card 710 .75 2.00
28 Johnny Mize Card 56 .75 2.00
29 Pie Traynor Card 628 1.25 3.00
30 Walter Johnson Card 268 Nolan Ryan 2.50 6.00
31 Lou Gehrig Card 529 2.50 6.00
32 Benny Bengough Card 860 .75 2.00
33 Babe Ruth Card 888 3.00 8.00
34 Charlie Gehringer Card 667 .75 2.00
35 Babe Ruth Card 426 3.00 8.00
36 Bill Dickey Card 869 1.00 2.50
37 Three Finger Brown Card 883 .60 1.50
38 Ray Schalk Card 48 1.25 3.00
39 Homerun Baker Card 565 1.50 4.00

1995 Conlon TSN Prototypes

COMPLETE SET 8.00 20.00
3C Babe Ruth/100th Anniversary 2.00 5.00
1337 Bob Feller 1.25 3.00
1357 Tris Speaker .75 2.00
1397 Charles Comisky OWN .75 2.00
1404 Gabby Hartnett .75 2.00
1421 Lou Gehrig 1.50 4.00
1425 Lou Boudreau .75 2.00
1464 Ray Chapman .40 1.00
1475 Bill Dickey .75 2.00
1500 Rabbit Maranville .60 1.50
1535 Babe Ruth 2.00 5.00

1995 Conlon TSN

The 1995 Conlon Collection set consists of 110 standard-size cards. This continuation of the Conlon Collection set was supposed to be released in two 110-card series (February and August respectively), but the second series (nor any sets after that) was never released because of the baseball strike. This was the first year that the Conlon Collection did not consist of 330 cards. The set continues to feature the work of noted sports photographer Charles Conlon. No more than 50,000 sets were printed, with a suggested retail price of $19.95 per series. As a special tribute to Conlon and the 100th Anniversary of Babe Ruth's birth, Megacards teamed with Topps to produce a 100th Birthday Card. The card was issued in two forms: a sepia-tone version for 1995 Topps regular series (number 3) and an color-enhanced version (number 3C) inserted in each 1995 Conlon complete set. On the fronts, each black-and-white photo has a gold foil inner border and a forest green outer border. Topical subsets featured are Veterans of World War I and II (1321-1350), '75 Champs (1354-1367), Great Stories (1371-1378), Nicknames (1382-1390), Behind the Scenes (1394-1400), Great Games (1404-1412), and Beating the Odds (1416-1429). Also groups of three "Generic" cards are scattered throughout the set (1351-1352, 1368-1370, 1379-1381, 1391-1393, 1401-1403, 1413-1415).

COMPLETE FACT. SET (110) 75.00 150.00
1321 Grover C. Alexander .60 1.50
1322 Christy Mathewson .60 1.50
1323 Eddie Grant .20 .50
1324 Gabby Street .20 .50
1325 Hank Gowdy .20 .50
1326 Jack Bentley .20 .50
1327 Eppa Rixey .40 1.00
1328 Bob Shawkey .30 .75
1329 Rabbit Maranville .40 1.00
1330 Casey Stengel .60 1.50
1331 Herb Pennock .40 1.00
1332 Eddie Collins Sr. .40 1.00
1333 Buddy Hassett .20 .50
1334 Andy Cohen .20 .50
1335 Hank Greenberg .60 1.50
1336 Andy High .20 .50
1337 Bob Feller .60 1.50
1338 George Earnshaw .30 .75
1339 Jack Knott .20 .50
1340 Larry French .20 .50
1341 Skippy Roberge .20 .50
1342 Boze Berger .20 .50
1343 Bill Posedel .20 .50
1344 Kirby Higbe .20 .50
1345 Bob Neighbors .20 .50
1346 Hugh Mulcahy .20 .50
1347 Harry Walker .20 .50
1348 Buddy Lewis .20 .50
1349 Cecil Travis .20 .50
1350 Moe Berg 1.50 4.00
1351 Nixey Callahan .20 .50
1352 Heinie Peitz .20 .50
1353 Doc White .20 .50
1354 Joe Wood Game 1 .40 1.00
1355 Larry Gardner Game 2 .20 .50
1356 Steve O'Neill Game 3 .20 .50
1357 Tris Speaker Game 4 .60 1.50
1358 Bill Wambsganss Game 5 .20 .50
1359 George H. Burns Game 6 .20 .50
1360 Charlie Jamieson Game 7 .20 .50
1361 Les Nunamaker .20 .50
1362 Stan Coveleski .40 1.00
1363 Joe Sewell .40 1.00
1364 Jim Bagby Sr. .20 .50
1365 Duster Mails .20 .50
1366 Jack Graney .20 .50
1367 Elmer Smith .20 .50
1368 Tommy Leach .20 .50
1369 Russ Ford .20 .50
1370 Harry M. Wolter .20 .50
1371 Dazzy Vance .40 1.00
1372 Germany Schaefer .30 .75
1373 Elbie Fletcher .20 .50
1374 Clark Griffith .40 1.00
1375 Al Simmons .40 1.00
1376 Billy Jurges .20 .50
1377 Earl Averill Sr. .40 1.00
1378 Bill Klem .40 1.00
1379 Armando Marsans .20 .50
1380 Mike Gonzalez .20 .50
1381 Jack Fournier .20 .50
1382 Burleigh Grimes .40 1.00
1383 Arlie Latham .20 .50
1384 Ray Schalk .40 1.00
1385 Goose Goslin .40 1.00
1386 Joe Hauser .20 .50
1387 Dixie Walker .30 .75
1388 Jesse Burkett .20 .50
1389 Cliff Melton .20 .50
1390 Gee Walker .20 .50
1391 Tony Cuccinello .20 .50
1392 Vern Kennedy .20 .50
1393 Tuck Stainback .20 .50
1394 Ed Barrow .30 .75
1395 Ford C. Frick .30 .75
1396 Ban Johnson August Herrmann .30 .75
1397 Charles Comiskey .30 .75
1398 Jacob Ruppert Joe McCarthy .30 .75
1399 Branch Rickey .40 1.00
1400 Jack Kieran Moe Berg .40 1.00

1401 Mike Ryba .20 .50
1402 Stan Spence .20 .50
1403 Red Barrett .20 .50
1404 Gabby Hartnett .40 1.00
1405 Babe Ruth 3.00 8.00
1406 Fred Merkle .30 .75
1407 Claude Passeau .20 .50
1408 Joe Wood .40 1.00
1409 Cliff Heathcote .20 .50
1410 Walt Cruise .20 .50
1411 Cookie Lavagetto .20 .50
1412 Tony Lazzeri .40 1.00
1413 Atley Donald .20 .50
1414 Ken Raffensberger .20 .50
1415 Dizzy Trout .20 .50
1416 Augie Galan .20 .50
1417 Monty Stratton .20 .50
1418 Claude Passeau .20 .50
1419 Oscar Grimes .20 .50
1420 Rollie Hemsley .20 .50
1421 Lou Gehrig 2.50 6.00
1422 Tom Sunkel .20 .50
1423 Tris Speaker .40 1.00
1424 Chick Fewster .20 .50
1425 Lou Boudreau .40 1.00
1426 Hank Leiber .20 .50
1427 Eddie Mayo .20 .50
1428 Charley Gelbert .20 .50
1429 Jackie Hayes .20 .50
1430 Checklist .20 .50
NNO Babe Ruth/100th Birthday 3.00 8.00

1995 Conlon TSN Griffey Jr.

COMPLETE SET (8) 5.00 12.50
1 Ken Griffey Jr. 1.25 3.00
Babe Ruth
2 Ken Griffey Jr. 1.25 3.00
Lou Gehrig
3 Ken Griffey Jr. 1.00 2.50
Ty Cobb
4 Ken Griffey Jr. .75 2.00
Jimmie Foxx
5 Ken Griffey Jr. .75 2.00
Mel Ott
6 Ken Griffey Jr. 1.25 3.00
Shoeless Joe Jackson
7 Ken Griffey Jr. .75 2.00
Tris Speaker
8 Ken Griffey Jr. .50 1.25
Jim(Sunny) Bottomley

1995 Conlon TSN Club Members Promos

Issued to herald the release of the 1995 Conlon series, these two standard-size promos feature black-bordered and white-line-framed black-and-white player photos on their fronts. The player's name, team, position, and year appear in white lettering within the lower black margin. The white and black back carries the player's name, biography, statistics, and career highlights. The faint "Club Members Promo" disclaimer is printed diagonally across the back.

COMPLETE SET 2.00 5.00
1387 Rabbit Maranville .75 2.00
1435 Bob Feller 1.25 3.00

1939 Coombs Mobil Booklets

This six-booklet set features tips by Jack Coombs, one of the greatest of all pitchers, on how the stars play the national game. Each pamphlet consists of eight fold-out pages and displays black-and-white photos of players demonstrating the instructions written by Jack Coombs on the various aspects of playing the game. When all six pamphlets were collected, the coupons on the back page of each were to be mailed in with the official contest entry blank printed in booklet No. 6 for a chance to win a trip to two World Series games for that season.

COMPLETE SET (6) 15.00 30.00
COMMON CARD (1-6) 2.50 5.00

1998 Joey Cora Bookmarks

These four small bookmarks feature Joey Cora, who was extremely popular in the Seattle area. The fronts have action photos of Cora while the back makes up a small puzzle. We have sequenced the cards from top to bottom as they appear. These bookmarks were produced by Strategic Pro Marketing.

COMPLETE SET (4) 1.50 4.00
COMMON CARD (1-4) .40 1.00

1979-83 Coral-Lee Postcards

Little is known about this set. Seven of these postcards usually come together as a group and feature players in both game and non-game situations in photos taken by famous photographers such as Annie Leibovitz. Any additional information on these is greatly appreciated. We have sequenced these in alphabetical order. In addition, there have been several recently discovered Coral-Lee Postcards issued after 1981, any further information on those is appreciated as well. The Rose card was apparently issued a couple of years earlier.

COMPLETE SET 15.00 40.00
1 Dave Lopes .60 1.50
2 Billy Martin MG .75 2.00
3 Willie Mays 2.00 5.00
Ronald Reagan PRES
Ed Stack
4 Pete Rose 2.50 6.00
Issued in 1979
5 George Steinbrenner OWN 3.00 8.00
Billy Martin MG
Reggie J
6 Fernando Valenzuela 1.25 3.00
Jose Lopez Portillo PRES
Nan
7 Dave Winfield UER 2.00 5.00
Name spelled Windfield
8 Carl Yastrzemski 1.50 4.00
Jimmy Carter PRES
9 Bobby Grich .60 1.50
Card numbered as number 8 on back
10 Reggie Jackson 2.00 5.00
Angels
11 Joe Morgan 1.25 3.00
Phillies
12 Rod Carew 1.25 3.00
Angels
13 Lou Piniella .75 2.00
Batting

1993 Costacos Brothers Poster Cards Promos

These cards measure approximately 4" by 6 1/4" and features a color image of the players. The fronts make it look like these were later issued as posters. Since these cards are unnumbered, we have sequenced thm in alphabetical order.

1 Albert Belle 2.00 5.00
2 Kirby Puckett 4.00 10.00

1993-94 Costacos Brothers Poster Cards

COMPLETE SET (18) 10.00 20.00
6 Travis Fryman .20 .50
Eye of the Tiger
18 Frank Thomas 1.25 3.00
The Big Hurt

1910-19 Coupon T213

The catalog designation T213, like its predecessor T212, actually contains three separate sets. Set 1 was issued about 1910 and consists of brown-captioned designs taken directly from the T206 set. Set 2 cards are also T206 designs, but with pale blue captions. They were produced in 1914-1915 and contain many team changes and Federal League affiliations. Set 3 cards were produced in 1919 and are physically slightly smaller than the the other two sets. Set 1 cards are printed on heavy paper; set 2 cards are printed on cardboard and have a glossy surface, which has resulted in a distinctive type of surface cracking. Each card in Set 1 and 2 measures 1 1/2" by 2 5/8" whereas Set 3 cards are only 1 3/8" by 2 9/16". The "Coupon" brand of cigarettes was manufactured by a branch of the American Tobacco Company located in New Orleans. The different sets can also be distinguished by their back titles, Set 1 (Coupon Mild Cigarettes), Set 2 (Mild and Sweet Coupon Cigarettes 20 for 5 cents), and Set 3 (Coupon Cigarettes 16 for 10 cts.).

COMMON TYPE 1 (1-68) 400.00 800.00
COMMON TYPE 2 (69-255) 400.00 800.00
COMMON TYPE 3 (256-325) 250.00 500.00
1 Harry Bay/Nashville 500.00 1000.00
2 Beals Becker 400.00 800.00
3 Chief Bender 600.00 1200.00
4 William H. Bernhard/Nashville 500.00 1000.00
5 Ted Breitenstein/New Orleans 500.00 1000.00
6 Bobby Byrne 400.00 800.00
7 William J. Campbell 400.00 800.00
8 Max Carey/Memphis 600.00 1200.00
9 Frank Chance 750.00 1500.00
10 Chappy Charles 400.00 800.00
11 Hal Chase (portrait) 500.00 1000.00
12 Hal Chase (throwing) 500.00 1000.00
13 Ty Cobb 4000.00 8000.00
14 Cranston/Memphis 400.00 800.00
15 Birdie Cree 400.00 800.00
16 Bill Donovan 400.00 800.00
17 Mickey Doolan 400.00 800.00
18 Jean Dubuc 400.00 800.00
19 Joe Dunn 400.00 800.00
20 Roy Ellam/Nashville 500.00 1000.00
21 Clyde Engle 400.00 800.00
22 Johnny Evers 750.00 1500.00
23 Art Fletcher 400.00 800.00
24 Charles Fritz/New Orleans 500.00 1000.00
25 Edward Greminger/Montgomery 500.00 1000.00
26 Hart/Little Rock 500.00 1000.00
27 Hart/Montgomery 500.00 1000.00
28 Topsy Hartsel 400.00 800.00
29 Charles Hickman/Mobile 500.00 1000.00
30 Danny Hoffman 400.00 800.00
31 Harry Howell 400.00 800.00
32 Miller Huggins/portrait 600.00 1200.00
33 Miller Huggins/yelling 600.00 1200.00
34 George Hunter 400.00 800.00
35 Dutch Jordan/Atlanta 500.00 1000.00
36 Ed Killian 400.00 800.00
37 Otto Knabe 400.00 800.00
38 Frank LaPorte 400.00 800.00
39 Ed Lennox 400.00 800.00
40 Harry Lentz/Little Rock 500.00 1000.00
41 Rube Marquard 600.00 1200.00
42 Doc Marshall 400.00 800.00
43 Christy Mathewson 1500.00 3000.00
44 George McBride 400.00 800.00
45 Pryor McElveen 400.00 800.00
46 Matty McIntyre 400.00 800.00
47 Michael Mitchell 400.00 800.00
48 Carlton Molesworth/Birmingham 500.00 1000.00
49 Mike Mowrey 400.00 800.00
50 Hy Myers/batting 400.00 800.00
51 Hy Myers/fielding 400.00 800.00
52 Dode Paskert 400.00 800.00
53 Hub Perdue/Nashville 500.00 1000.00
54 Archie Persons/Montgomery 500.00 1000.00
55 Edward Reagan/New Orleans 500.00 1000.00
56 Robert Rhoades 400.00 800.00
57 Isaac Rockenfeld/New Orleans 500.00 1000.00
58 Claude Rossman 400.00 800.00
59 Boss Schmidt 400.00 800.00
60 Sid Smith/Atlanta 500.00 1000.00
61 Charles Starr 400.00 800.00
62 Gabby Street 400.00 800.00
63 Ed Summers 400.00 800.00
64 William Sweeney 400.00 800.00
65 Chester Thomas 400.00 800.00
66 Woodie Thornton/Mobile 500.00 1000.00
67 Ed Willett 400.00 800.00
68 Owen Wilson 400.00 800.00
69 Red Ames/Cincinnati 500.00 1000.00
70 Red Ames/St. Louis 500.00 1000.00
71 Frank Baker/New York Amer. 750.00 1500.00
72 Frank Baker/Philadelphia 750.00 1500.00
73 Frank Baker/Phila. 750.00 1500.00
74 Cy Barger 400.00 800.00
75 Chief Bender/trees/Baltimore Fed. 750.00 1500.00
76 Chief Bender/no trees
Baltimore Fed. 750.00 1500.00
77 Chief Bender/trees
Philadelphia Amer. 750.00 1500.00
78 Chief Bender/no trees
Philadelphia Amer. 750.00 1500.00
79 Chief Bender/trees
Philadelphia Nat. 750.00 1500.00
80 Chief Bender/no trees
Philadelphia Nat. 750.00 1500.00
81 Bill Bradley 400.00 800.00
82 Roger Bresnahan/Chicago 750.00 1500.00
83 Roger Bresnahan/Toledo 750.00 1500.00
84 Al Bridwell/St. Louis 400.00 800.00
85 Al Bridwell/Nashville 400.00 800.00
86 Mordecai Brown/Chicago 750.00 1500.00
87 Mordecai Brown/St. Louis Fed. 750.00 1500.00
88 Bobby Byrne 400.00 800.00
89 Howie Camnitz/hands over
Pittsburgh Fed. 400.00 800.00
90 Howie Camnitz/arm at side
Pittsburgh Fed. 400.00 800.00
91 Howie Camnitz/Savannah 400.00 800.00
92 William J. Campbell 400.00 800.00
93 Frank Chance/Los Angeles/batting 750.00 1500.00
94 Frank Chance/Los Angeles/portrait 750.00 1500.00
95 Frank Chance
New York Amer./batting 750.00 1500.00
96 Frank Chance
New York Amer./portrait 750.00 1500.00
97 William Chappelle/Brooklyn 400.00 800.00
98 William Chappelle/Cleveland 400.00 800.00
99 Hal Chase/Buffalo Fed./portrait 600.00 1200.00
100 Hal Chase/Buffalo Fed.
holding cup 600.00 1200.00
101 Hal Chase/Buffalo Fed./throwing 600.00 1200.00
102 Hal Chase/Chicago Amer./portrait 600.00 1200.00
103 Hal Chase/Chicago Amer.
holding cup) 600.00 1200.00
104 Hal Chase/Chicago Amer.
throwing 600.00 1200.00
105 Ty Cobb Batting 10000.00 20000.00
106 Ty Cobb Portrait 10000.00 20000.00
107 Eddie Collins
Chicago Amer./with A 750.00 1500.00
108 Eddie Collins/Chicago Amer.
without A 750.00 1500.00
109 Eddie Collins/Philadelphia/with A 750.00 1500.00
110 Doc Crandall/St. Louis Amer. 400.00 800.00
111 Doc Crandall/St. Louis Fed. 400.00 800.00
112 Sam Crawford 750.00 1500.00
113 Birdie Cree 400.00 800.00
114 Harry Davis/Philadelphia 400.00 800.00
115 Harry Davis/Phila. 400.00 800.00
116 Ray Demmitt 400.00 800.00
117 Josh Devore/Philadelphia 400.00 800.00
118 Josh Devore/Chillicothe 400.00 800.00
119 Mike Donlin/New York Nat. 500.00 1000.00
120 Mike Donlin/.300 Batter/7 Years 750.00 1500.00
121 Mike Donlin/Name spelled
Dohlin on card 750.00 1500.00
122 Bill Donovan 400.00 800.00
123 Mickey Doolan (batting)
Baltimore Fed. 400.00 800.00
124 Mickey Doolan (fielding)
Chicago Nat. 400.00 800.00
125 Mickey Doolan (batting)
Baltimore Fed. 400.00 800.00
126 Mickey Doolan (fielding)
Chicago Nat. 400.00 800.00
127 Tom Downey 400.00 800.00
128 Larry Doyle/batting 500.00 1000.00
129 Larry Doyle/portrait 500.00 1000.00
130 Jean Dubuc 400.00 800.00
131 Jack Dunn 400.00 800.00
132 Kid Elberfeld/Brooklyn 750.00 1500.00
133 Kid Elberfeld/Chattanooga 750.00 1500.00
134 Steve Evans 400.00 800.00
135 Johnny Evers 750.00 1500.00
136 Russ Ford 400.00 800.00
137 Art Fromme 400.00 800.00
138 Chick Gandil/Cleveland 750.00 1500.00
139 Chick Gandil/Washington 750.00 1500.00
140 Rube Geyer 400.00 800.00
141 Clark Griffith 750.00 1500.00
142 Bob Groom 400.00 800.00
143 Buck Herzog/with B 400.00 800.00
144 Buck Herzog/without B 400.00 800.00
145 Doc Hoblitzell/Boston Amer. 400.00 800.00
146 Doc Hoblitzell/Boston Fed. 400.00 800.00
147 Doc Hoblitzell/Cincinnati 400.00 800.00
148 Solly Hofman 400.00 800.00
149 Danny Hofmann 400.00 800.00
150 Miller Huggins/portrait 750.00 1500.00
151 Miller Huggins/yelling 750.00 1500.00
152 John Hummel/Brooklyn 400.00 800.00
153 John Hummel/Brooklyn Nat. 400.00 800.00
154 Hugh Jennings/yelling 750.00 1500.00
155 Hugh Jennings/dancing 750.00 1500.00
156 Walter Johnson 2500.00 5000.00
157 Tim Jordan/Ft. Worth 400.00 800.00
158 Tim Jordan/Toronto 400.00 800.00
159 Joe Kelley/New York Amer. 750.00 1500.00
160 Joe Kelley/Toronto 750.00 1500.00
161 Otto Knabe 400.00 800.00
162 Ed Konetchy/Boston Nat. 400.00 800.00
163 Ed Konetchy/Pittsburgh Fed. 400.00 800.00
164 Ed Konetchy/Pittsburgh Nat. 400.00 800.00
165 Harry Krause 400.00 800.00
166 Nap Lajoie/Cleveland 1250.00 2500.00
167 Nap Lajoie/Philadelphia 1250.00 2500.00
168 Nap Lajoie/Phila. 1250.00 2500.00
169 Tommy Leach/Chicago 400.00 800.00
170 Tommy Leach/Cincinnati 400.00 800.00
171 Tommy Leach/Rochester 400.00 800.00
172 Ed Lennox 400.00 800.00
173 Sherry Magee/Boston 500.00 1000.00
174 Sherry Magee/Philadelphia 500.00 1000.00
175 Sherry Magee/Phila. 500.00 1000.00
176 Rube Marquard/Brooklyn/pitching 750.00 1500.00
177 Rube Marquard/Brooklyn/portrait 750.00 1500.00
178 Rube Marquard/New York/pitching 750.00 1500.00
179 Rube Marquard/New York/portrait 750.00 1500.00
180 Christy Mathewson Dark Cap 2500.00 5000.00
181 John McGraw/portrait 750.00 1500.00
182 John McGraw/glove on hip 750.00 1500.00
183 Larry McLean 400.00 800.00
184 George McQuillan/Philadelphia 400.00 800.00
185 George McQuillan/Phila. 400.00 800.00
186 George McQuillan/Pittsburgh 400.00 800.00
187 Fred Merkle 500.00 1000.00
188 Chief Meyers/Brooklyn
T206-249 pose 500.00 1000.00
189 Chief Meyers/Brooklyn/fielding 500.00 1000.00
190 Chief Meyers/New York
T206-249 pose 500.00 1000.00
191 Chief Meyers/New York/fielding 500.00 1000.00
192 Dots Miller 400.00 800.00
193 Michael Mitchell 400.00 800.00
194 Mike Mowrey/Brooklyn 400.00 800.00
195 Mike Mowrey/Pittsburgh Fed. 400.00 800.00
196 Mike Mowrey/Pittsburgh Nat. 400.00 800.00
197 George Mullin/Indianapolis 400.00 800.00
198 George Mullin/Newark 400.00 800.00
199 Danny Murphy 400.00 800.00
200 Red Murray/Chicago 400.00 800.00
201 Red Murray/Kansas City 400.00 800.00
202 Red Murray/New York 400.00 800.00
203 Tom Needham 400.00 800.00
204 Rebel Oakes 400.00 800.00
205 Rube Oldring/Philadelphia 500.00 1000.00
206 Rube Oldring/Phila. 500.00 1000.00
207 Dode Paskert/Philadelphia 400.00 800.00
208 Dode Paskert/Phila. 400.00 800.00
209 William Purtell 400.00 800.00
210 Jack Quinn/Baltimore 500.00 1000.00
211 Jack Quinn/Vernon 500.00 1000.00
212 Ed Reulbach/Brooklyn Fed. 500.00 1000.00
213 Ed Reulbach/Pittsburgh 500.00 1000.00
214 Ed Reulbach/Brooklyn Nat. 500.00 1000.00
215 Nap Rucker/Brooklyn 500.00 1000.00
216 Nap Rucker/Brooklyn Nat. 500.00 1000.00
217 Dick Rudolph 400.00 800.00
218 Germany Schaefer/Kansas City 500.00 1000.00
219 Germany Schaefer/New York 500.00 1000.00
220 Germany Schaefer/Washington 500.00 1000.00
221 Admiral Schlei/portrait 400.00 800.00
222 Admiral Schlei/batting 400.00 800.00
223 Boss Schmidt 400.00 800.00
224 Frank Schulte 500.00 1000.00
225 Nig Smith 400.00 800.00
226 Tris Speaker 750.00 1500.00
227 George Stovall 400.00 800.00
228 Gabby Street/catching 400.00 800.00
229 Gabby Street/portrait 400.00 800.00
230 Ed Summers 400.00 800.00
231 Ed Sweeney/Boston 500.00 1000.00
232 Ed Sweeney/Chicago 500.00 1000.00
233 Ed Sweeney/New York 500.00 1000.00
234 Ed Sweeney/Richmond 500.00 1000.00
235 Chester Thomas/Philadelphia 400.00 800.00
236 Chester Thomas/Phila. 400.00 800.00
237 Joe Tinker/Chicago Fed.
bat on shoulder 750.00 1500.00
238 Joe Tinker/Chicago Fed./swinging 750.00 1500.00
239 Joe Tinker/Chicago Nat.
bat on shoulder 750.00 1500.00
240 Joe Tinker/Chicago Nat.
swinging 750.00 1500.00
241 Honus Wagner 400.00 800.00
242 Jack Warhop/New York 400.00 800.00
243 Jack Warhop/St. Louis 400.00 800.00
244 Zack Wheat/Brooklyn 750.00 1500.00
245 Zack Wheat/Brooklyn Nat. 750.00 1500.00
246 Kaiser Wilhelm 400.00 800.00
247 Ed Willett/Memphis 400.00 800.00
248 Ed Willett/St. Louis 400.00 800.00
249 Owen Wilson/St. Louis 400.00 800.00
250 Hooks Wiltse/Brooklyn Fed.
pitching 400.00 800.00
251 Hooks Wiltse/Brooklyn Fed./portrait 400.00 800.00
252 Hooks Wiltse/Jersey City/pitching 400.00 800.00
253 Hooks Wiltse/Jersey City/portrait 400.00 800.00
254 Hooks Wiltse/New York/pitching 400.00 800.00
255 Hooks Wiltse/New York/portrait 400.00 800.00
256 Heinie Zimmerman 400.00 800.00
257 Red Ames 250.00 500.00
258 Frank Baker/New York Amer. 500.00 1000.00
259 Chief Bender 500.00 1000.00
260 Chief Bender 500.00 1000.00
261 Roger Bresnahan/Toledo 500.00 1000.00
262 Al Bridwell 250.00 500.00
263 Mordecai Brown 500.00 1000.00
264 Bobby Byrne/St.Louis Nat. 250.00 500.00
265 Frank Chance 500.00 1000.00
266 Frank Chance 500.00 1000.00
267 Hal Chase/N.Y. Nat. 400.00 800.00
268 Hal Chase/N.Y. Nat. 400.00 800.00
269 Hal Chase/N.Y. Nat. 400.00 800.00
270 Ty Cobb Detroit 7500.00 15000.00
271 Ty Cobb Detroit 7500.00 15000.00
272 Eddie Collins/Chicago Amer. 500.00 1000.00
273 Sam Crawford 500.00 1000.00
274 Harry Davis/Philadelphia Amer. 250.00 500.00
275 Mike Donlin 300.00 600.00
276 Bill Donovan/Jersey City 250.00 500.00
277 Mickey Doolan/Reading 250.00 500.00
278 Mickey Doolan/Reading 250.00 500.00
279 Larry Doyle/N.Y. Nat. 300.00 600.00
280 Larry Doyle/N.Y. Nat. 300.00 600.00
281 Jean Dubuc/N.Y. Nat. 250.00 500.00
282 Jack Dunn/Baltimore 300.00 600.00
283 Kid Elberfeld 250.00 500.00
284 Johnny Evers 500.00 1000.00
285 Chick Gandil/Chicago Amer. 500.00 1000.00
286 Clark Griffith/Washington 500.00 1000.00
287 Buck Herzog/Boston Nat. 250.00 500.00
288 Doc Hoblitzell/Boston Amer. 250.00 500.00
289 Miller Huggins/N.Y. Amer. 500.00 1000.00
290 Miller Huggins/N.Y. Amer. 500.00 1000.00
291 John Hummel 250.00 500.00
292 Hugh Jennings MG/Detroit 500.00 1000.00
293 Hugh Jennings MG/Detroit 500.00 1000.00
294 Walter Johnson/Washington 1500.00 3000.00
295 Tim Jordan 250.00 500.00
296 Kelley/N.Y. Amer. 500.00 1000.00
297 Ed Konetchy/Brooklyn 250.00 500.00
298 Nap Lajoie 750.00 1500.00
299 Sherry Magee/Cincinnati 300.00 600.00
300 Rube Marquard/Brooklyn 500.00 1000.00
301 Rube Marquard/Brooklyn 500.00 1000.00
302 Christy Mathewson
New York Nat. 1000.00 2000.00
303 John McGraw MG/New York Nat. 500.00 1000.00
304 John McGraw MG/New York Nat. 500.00 1000.00
305 George McQuillan/Boston Nat. 250.00 500.00
306 Fred Merkle/Chicago Nat. 300.00 600.00
307 Dots Miller/St. Louis Nat. 250.00 500.00
308 Mike Mowrey/Brooklyn 250.00 500.00
309 Hy Myers/New Haven 250.00 500.00
310 Hy Myers/Brooklyn 250.00 500.00
311 Dode Paskert/Chicago Nat. 250.00 500.00
312 Jack Quinn/N.Y. Nat. 300.00 600.00
313 Ed Reulbach 300.00 600.00
314 Nap Rucker 300.00 600.00
315 Dick Rudolph/Boston Nat. 250.00 500.00
316 Germany Schaeffer 250.00 500.00
317 Frank Schulte/Binghamton 300.00 600.00
318 Tris Speaker/Cleveland 750.00 1500.00
319 Gabby Street/Nashville 250.00 500.00
320 Gabby Street/Nashville 250.00 500.00
321 Ed Sweeney/Pittsburg 300.00 600.00
322 Ira Thomas 250.00 500.00
323 Joe Tinker 500.00 1000.00
324 Zack Wheat/Brooklyn 500.00 1000.00
325 Hooks Wiltse 250.00 500.00
326 Heinie Zimmerman/N.Y. Nat. 250.00 500.00

1914 Cracker Jack

The cards in this 144-card set measure approximately 2 1/4" by 3". This "Series of colored pictures of Famous Ball Players and Managers" was issued in packages of Cracker Jack in 1914. The cards have tinted photos set against red backgrounds and many are commonly found with caramel stains. The set contains American, National, and Federal League players. The company claims to have printed 15 million cards as noted on the backs. Most of the cards were issued in both 1914 and 1915, but each year can easily be distinguished from the other by the notation of the number of cards in the series as printed on the back (144 for 1914 and 176 for 1915) and by the orientation of the text on the back of the cards. For 1914, the cardback text is right side up when the card is turned over but will be upside down for the 1915 release. Team names are included below for some players to show more specific differences between the 1914 and 1915 issues on those cards.

COMPLETE SET (144) 60000.00 120000.00
1 Otto Knabe 300.00 600.00
2 Frank Baker 750.00 1500.00
3 Joe Tinker 1000.00 2000.00
4 Larry Doyle 200.00 400.00
5 Ward Miller 200.00 400.00
6 Eddie Plank 750.00 1500.00
7 Eddie Collins 750.00 1500.00
8 Rube Oldring 200.00 400.00
9 Artie Hoffman 200.00 400.00
10 John McInnis 200.00 400.00
11 George Stovall 200.00 400.00
12 Connie Mack MG 750.00 1500.00
13 Art Wilson 200.00 400.00
14 Sam Crawford 750.00 1500.00
15 Reb Russell 200.00 400.00
16 Howie Camnitz 200.00 400.00
17 Roger Bresnahan 750.00 1500.00
17B Roger Bresnahan NNO 2000.00 4000.00
18 Johnny Evers 750.00 1500.00
19 Chief Bender 750.00 1500.00
20 Cy Falkenberg 200.00 400.00
21 Heinie Zimmerman 200.00 400.00
22 Joe Wood 1250.00 2500.00
23 Charles Comiskey 750.00 1500.00
24 George Mullen 200.00 400.00
25 Michael Simon 200.00 400.00
26 James Scott 200.00 400.00
27 Bill Carrigan 200.00 400.00
28 Jack Barry 200.00 400.00
29 Vean Gregg 200.00 400.00
30 Ty Cobb 5000.00 10000.00
31 Heinie Wagner 200.00 400.00
32 Mordecai Brown 750.00 1500.00
33 Amos Strunk 200.00 400.00
34 Ira Thomas 300.00 600.00
35 Harry Hooper 750.00 1500.00
36 Ed Walsh 750.00 1500.00
37 Grover C. Alexander 2000.00 4000.00
38 Red Dooin 200.00 400.00
39 Chick Gandil 750.00 1500.00
40 Jimmy Austin 200.00 400.00
41 Tommy Leach 200.00 400.00
42 Al Bridwell 200.00 400.00
43 Rube Marquard 750.00 1500.00
44 Jeff (Charles) Tesreau 200.00 400.00
45 Fred Luderus 200.00 400.00
46 Bob Groom 200.00 400.00
47 Josh Devore 200.00 400.00
48 Harry Lord 300.00 600.00
49 John Miller 200.00 400.00
50 John Hummell 200.00 400.00
51 Nap Rucker 200.00 400.00
52 Zach Wheat 750.00 1500.00
53 Otto Miller 200.00 400.00
54 Marty O'Toole 200.00 400.00
55 Dick Hoblitzel 200.00 400.00
56 Clyde Milan 200.00 400.00
57 Walter Johnson 2000.00 4000.00
58 Wally Schang 200.00 400.00
59 Harry Gessler 200.00 400.00
60 Rollie Zeider 300.00 600.00
61 Ray Schalk 1000.00 2000.00
62 Jay Cashion 300.00 600.00
63 Babe Adams 200.00 400.00
64 Jimmy Archer 200.00 400.00
65 Tris Speaker 750.00 1500.00
66 Napoleon Lajoie 1250.00 2500.00
67 Otis Crandall 200.00 400.00
68 Honus Wagner 4000.00 8000.00
69 John McGraw 750.00 1500.00
70 Fred Clarke 600.00 1200.00
71 Chief Meyers 200.00 400.00
72 John Boehling 200.00 400.00
73 Max Carey 750.00 1500.00
74 Frank Owens 200.00 400.00
75 Miller Huggins 600.00 1200.00
76 Claude Hendrix 200.00 400.00
77 Hughie Jennings MG 750.00 1500.00
78 Fred Merkle 200.00 400.00
79 Ping Bodie 200.00 400.00
80 Ed Ruelbach 200.00 400.00
81 Jim Delahanty 200.00 400.00
82 Gavvy Cravath 200.00 400.00
83 Russ Ford 200.00 400.00
84 Elmer E. Knetzer 200.00 400.00
85 Buck Herzog 200.00 400.00
86 Burt Shotton 200.00 400.00
87 Forrest Cady 200.00 400.00
88 Christy Mathewson 20000.00 50000.00
89 Lawrence Cheney 200.00 400.00
90 Frank Smith 200.00 400.00
91 Roger Peckinpaugh 200.00 400.00
92 Al Demaree 200.00 400.00
93 Del Pratt 200.00 400.00
94 Eddie Cicotte 750.00 1500.00
95 Ray Keating 200.00 400.00
96 Beals Becker 200.00 400.00
97 John (Rube) Benton 200.00 400.00
98 Frank LaPorte 200.00 400.00
99 Frank Chance 2000.00 4000.00
100 Thomas Seaton 200.00 400.00
101 Frank Schulte 200.00 400.00
102 Ray Fisher 200.00 400.00
103 Joe Jackson 10000.00 20000.00
104 Vic Saier 200.00 400.00
105 James Lavender 200.00 400.00
106 Joe Birmingham 200.00 400.00
107 Tom Downey 200.00 400.00
108 Sherry Magee 200.00 400.00
109 Fred Blanding 200.00 400.00
110 Bob Bescher 200.00 400.00
111 Jim Callahan 200.00 400.00
112 Ed Sweeney 200.00 400.00
113 George Suggs 200.00 400.00
114 George Moriarity 200.00 400.00
115 Addison Brennan 200.00 400.00
116 Rollie Zeider 200.00 400.00
117 Ted Easterly 200.00 400.00
118 Ed Konetchy 200.00 400.00
119 George Perring 200.00 400.00
120 Mike Doolan 200.00 400.00
121 Hub Perdue 200.00 400.00
122 Owen Bush 200.00 400.00
123 Slim Sallee 200.00 400.00
124 Earl Moore 200.00 400.00
125 Bert Niehoff 200.00 400.00
126 Walter Blair 200.00 400.00
127 Butch Schmidt 200.00 400.00
128 Steve Evans 200.00 400.00
129 Ray Caldwell 200.00 400.00
130 Ivy Wingo 200.00 400.00
131 George Baumgardner 200.00 400.00
132 Les Nunamaker 200.00 400.00
133 Branch Rickey MG 1000.00 2000.00
134 Armando Marsans 200.00 400.00
135 Bill Killefer 200.00 400.00
136 Rabbit Maranville 750.00 1500.00
137 William Rariden 200.00 400.00
138 Hank Gowdy 200.00 400.00
139 Rebel Oakes 200.00 400.00
140 Danny Murphy 200.00 400.00
141 Cy Barger 200.00 400.00
142 Eugene Packard 200.00 400.00
143 Jake Daubert 200.00 400.00
144 James C. Walsh 400.00 800.00

1915 Cracker Jack

The cards in this 176-card set measure approximately 2 1/4" by 3". The cards were available in boxes of Cracker Jack or from the company for "100 Cracker Jack coupons, or one coupon and 25 cents." An album was available for "50 coupons or one coupon and 10 cents." Most of the cards were issued in both 1914 and 1915, but each year can easily be distinguished from the other by the notation of the number of cards in the series as printed on the back (144 for 1914 and 176 for 1915) and by the orientation of the text on the back of the cards. For 1914, the cardback text is right side up when the card is turned over but will be upside down for the 1915 release. The 1915 Cracker Jack cards are noticeably easier to find than the 1914 Cracker Jack cards due to the mail-in offer, although neither set is plentiful. The set essentially duplicates E145-1 (1914 Cracker Jack) except for some additional cards and new poses. Players in the Federal League are indicated by FED in the checklist below.

COMPLETE SET (176) 25000.00 60000.00
COMMON CARD (1-144) 100.00 200.00
COMMON CARD(145-176) 125.00 250.00
1 Otto Knabe 300.00 600.00
2 Frank Baker 500.00 1000.00
3 Joe Tinker 400.00 800.00
4 Larry Doyle 125.00 250.00
5 Ward Miller 100.00 200.00
6 Eddie Plank 750.00 1500.00
7 Eddie Collins 400.00 800.00
8 Rube Oldring 100.00 200.00
9 Artie Hoffman 100.00 200.00
10 John McInnis 100.00 200.00
11 George Stovall 100.00 200.00
12 Connie Mack MG 400.00 800.00
13 Art Wilson 100.00 200.00
14 Sam Crawford 400.00 800.00
15 Reb Russell 100.00 200.00
16 Howie Camnitz 100.00 200.00
17 Roger Bresnahan 300.00 600.00
18 Johnny Evers 400.00 800.00
19 Chief Bender 400.00 800.00
20 Cy Falkenberg 100.00 200.00
21 Heinie Zimmerman 100.00 200.00
22 Joe Wood 500.00 1000.00
23 Charles Comiskey 500.00 1000.00
24 George Mullen 100.00 200.00
25 Michael Simon 100.00 200.00
26 James Scott 100.00 200.00
27 Bill Carrigan 100.00 200.00
28 Jack Barry 125.00 250.00
29 Vean Gregg 100.00 200.00
30 Ty Cobb 3000.00 6000.00
31 Heinie Wagner 100.00 200.00
32 Mordecai Brown 500.00 1000.00
33 Amos Strunk 100.00 200.00
34 Ira Thomas 100.00 200.00
35 Harry Hooper 300.00 600.00
36 Ed Walsh 400.00 800.00
37 Grover C. Alexander 1000.00 2000.00
38 Red Dooin 100.00 200.00
39 Chick Gandil 400.00 800.00
40 Jimmy Austin 125.00 250.00
41 Tommy Leach 100.00 200.00
42 Al Bridwell 100.00 200.00
43 Rube Marquard 300.00 600.00
44 Jeff (Charles) Tesreau 100.00 200.00
45 Fred Luderus 100.00 200.00
46 Bob Groom 100.00 200.00
47 Josh Devore 100.00 200.00
48 Steve O'Neill 100.00 200.00
49 John Miller 100.00 200.00
50 John Hummell 100.00 200.00
51 Nap Rucker 100.00 200.00
52 Zach Wheat 300.00 600.00
53 Otto Miller 100.00 200.00
54 Marty O'Toole 100.00 200.00
55 Dick Hoblitzel 100.00 200.00
56 Clyde Milan 100.00 200.00
57 Walter Johnson 1500.00 3000.00
58 Wally Schang 100.00 200.00
59 Harry Gessler 100.00 200.00
60 Oscar Dugey 100.00 200.00
61 Ray Schalk 400.00 800.00
62 Willie Mitchell 100.00 200.00
63 Babe Adams 100.00 200.00
64 Jimmy Archer 100.00 200.00
65 Tris Speaker 750.00 1500.00
66 Napoleon Lajoie 600.00 1200.00
67 Otis Crandall 100.00 200.00
68 Honus Wagner 3000.00 6000.00
69 John McGraw MG 400.00 800.00
70 Fred Clarke 300.00 600.00
71 Chief Meyers 125.00 250.00
72 John Boehling 100.00 200.00
73 Max Carey 400.00 800.00
74 Frank Owens 100.00 200.00
75 Miller Huggins 300.00 600.00
76 Claude Hendrix 100.00 200.00
77 Hughie Jennings MG 300.00 600.00
78 Fred Merkle 100.00 200.00
79 Ping Bodie 100.00 200.00
80 Ed Ruelbach 100.00 200.00
81 Jim Delahanty 100.00 200.00
82 Gavvy Cravath 100.00 200.00
83 Russ Ford 100.00 200.00
84 Elmer E. Knetzer 100.00 200.00
85 Buck Herzog 100.00 200.00
86 Burt Shotton 100.00 200.00
87 Forrest Cady 100.00 200.00
88 Christy Mathewson 1750.00 3500.00
89 Lawrence Cheney 100.00 200.00
90 Frank Smith 100.00 200.00
91 Roger Peckinpaugh 100.00 200.00
92 Al Demaree 100.00 200.00
93 Del Pratt 125.00 250.00
94 Eddie Cicotte 450.00 900.00
95 Ray Keating 100.00 200.00
96 Beals Becker 125.00 250.00
97 John (Rube) Benton 100.00 200.00
98 Frank LaPorte 100.00 200.00
99 Hal Chase 250.00 500.00
100 Thomas Seaton 100.00 200.00
101 Frank Schulte 100.00 200.00
102 Ray Fisher 100.00 200.00
103 Joe Jackson 7500.00 15000.00
104 Vic Saier 100.00 200.00
105 James Lavender 100.00 200.00
106 Joe Birmingham 100.00 200.00
107 Thomas Downey 100.00 200.00
108 Sherry Magee 100.00 200.00
109 Fred Blanding 100.00 200.00
110 Bob Bescher 100.00 200.00
111 Herbie Moran 100.00 200.00
112 Ed Sweeney 100.00 200.00
113 George Suggs 100.00 200.00
114 George Moriarity 100.00 200.00
115 Addison Brennan 100.00 200.00
116 Rollie Zeider 100.00 200.00
117 Ted Easterly 100.00 200.00
118 Ed Konetchy 100.00 200.00
119 George Perring 100.00 200.00
120 Mike Doolan 100.00 200.00
121 Hub Perdue 100.00 200.00
122 Owen Bush 100.00 200.00
123 Slim Sallee 100.00 200.00
124 Earl Moore 100.00 200.00
125 Bert Niehoff 100.00 200.00
126 Walter Blair 100.00 200.00
127 Butch Schmidt 100.00 200.00
128 Steve Evans 100.00 200.00
129 Ray Caldwell 100.00 200.00
130 Ivy Wingo 100.00 200.00
131 Geo. Baumgardner 100.00 200.00
132 Les Nunamaker 100.00 200.00
133 Branch Rickey MG 600.00 1200.00
134 Armando Marsans 125.00 250.00
135 William Killefer 100.00 200.00
136 Rabbit Maranville 300.00 600.00
137 William Rariden 100.00 200.00
138 Hank Gowdy 100.00 200.00
139 Rebel Oakes 100.00 200.00
140 Danny Murphy 100.00 200.00
141 Cy Barger 100.00 200.00
142 Eugene Packard 100.00 200.00
143 Jake Daubert 100.00 200.00
144 James C. Walsh 100.00 200.00
145 Ted Cather 125.00 250.00
146 George Tyler 125.00 250.00
147 Lee Magee 125.00 250.00
148 Owen Wilson 125.00 250.00
149 Hal Janvrin 125.00 250.00
150 Doc Johnston 125.00 250.00
151 George Whitted 125.00 250.00
152 George McQuillen 125.00 250.00
153 Bill James 125.00 250.00
154 Dick Rudolph 125.00 250.00
155 Joe Connolly 125.00 250.00
156 Jean Dubuc 125.00 250.00
157 George Kaiserling 125.00 250.00
158 Fritz Maisel 125.00 250.00
159 Heinie Groh 125.00 250.00
160 Benny Kauff 125.00 250.00
161 Edd Roush 500.00 1000.00
162 George Stallings MG 125.00 250.00
163 Bert Whaling 125.00 250.00
164 Bob Shawkey 125.00 250.00
165 Eddie Murphy 125.00 250.00
166 Joe Bush 125.00 250.00
167 Clark Griffith 300.00 600.00
168 Vin Campbell 125.00 250.00
169 Raymond Collins 125.00 250.00
170 Hans Lobert 125.00 250.00
171 Earl Hamilton 125.00 250.00
172 Erskine Mayer 125.00 250.00
173 Tilly Walker 125.00 250.00
174 Robert Veach 125.00 250.00

175 Joseph Benz 125.00 250.00
176 Hippo Vaughn 300.00 600.00

1982 Cracker Jack

The cards in this 16-card set measure 2 1/2" by 3 1/2"; cards came in two sheets of eight cards, plus an advertising card with a title in the center, which measured approximately 7 1/2" by 10 1/2". Cracker Jack reentered the baseball card market for the first time since 1915 to promote the first "Old Timers Baseball Classic" held July 19, 1982. The color player photos have a Cracker Jack border and have either green (NL) or red (AL) frame lines and name panels. The Cracker Jack logo appears on both sides of each card, with AL players numbered 1-8 and NL players numbered 9-16. Of the 16 ballplayers pictured, five did not appear at the game. At first, the two sheets were available only through the mail but are now commonly found in hobby circles. The set was prepared for Cracker Jack by Topps. The prices below reflect individual card prices; the price for complete panels would be about the same as the sum of the card prices for those players on the panel due to the easy availability of uncut sheets.

COMPLETE SET (16) 4.00 10.00
1 Larry Doby .30 .75
2 Bob Feller .40 1.00
3 Whitey Ford .40 1.00
4 Al Kaline .40 1.00
5 Harmon Killebrew .20 .50
6 Mickey Mantle 2.00 5.00
7 Tony Oliva .08 .25
8 Brooks Robinson .40 1.00
9 Hank Aaron 1.25 3.00
10 Ernie Banks .60 1.50
11 Ralph Kiner .20 .50
12 Ed Mathews .20 .50
13 Willie Mays 1.25 3.00
14 Robin Roberts .30 .75
15 Duke Snider .60 1.50
16 Warren Spahn .30 .75

1993 Cracker Jack 1915 Reprints

To commemorate its 100th anniversary, Cracker Jack issued a 24-card set of miniature replicas of its 1915 set. One mini-card was inserted into each specially marked single, triple, and value-pack box. A mini-card holder album and a fact booklet that includes each player's lifetime stats were available for 6.95 through a mail-in offer. The album features room for 72 cards implying that Cracker Jack would like to continue this series into future years as well. Each minicard measures approximately 1 1/4" by 1 3/4" and features on its front a white-bordered color portrait of the player on a brick-colored background. The player's name, team, and league appear in the white margin below the picture and "Cracker Jack Ball Players" appears at the top. The white back displays the player's name, team, and league at the top, along with his card number from the 1915 set, followed below by a biography.

COMPLETE SET (24) 10.00 25.00
1 Ty Cobb 1.25 3.00
2 Joe Jackson 1.25 3.00
3 Honus Wagner .60 1.50
4 Christy Mathewson .50 1.25
5 Walter Johnson .60 1.50
6 Tris Speaker .40 1.00
7 Grover Alexander .40 1.00
8 Nap Lajoie .40 1.00
9 Rube Marquard .20 .50
10 Connie Mack MG .30 .75
11 Johnny Evers .30 .75
12 Branch Rickey .20 .50
13 Fred Clarke MG .20 .50
14 Harry Hooper .20 .50
15 Zack Wheat .20 .50
16 Joe Tinker .20 .50
17 Eddie Collins .40 1.00
18 Mordecai Brown .20 .50
19 Eddie Plank .20 .50
20 Rabbit Maranville .20 .50
21 John McGraw MG .30 .75
22 Miller Huggins .20 .50
23 Ed Walsh .20 .50
24 Joe Bush .08 .25

1997 Cracker Jack

This 20-card set was distributed in Cracker Jack boxes and measures approximately 1 5/16" by 1 3/4". The fronts feature color action player photos in white borders. The backs carry player information and statistics.

COMPLETE SET (20) 10.00 25.00
1 Jeff Bagwell .50 1.25
2 Chuck Knoblauch .20 .50
3 Cal Ripken 2.00 5.00
4 Chipper Jones 1.00 2.50
5 Derek Jeter 2.00 5.00
6 Barry Larkin .40 1.00
7 Bernie Williams .40 1.00
8 Barry Bonds 1.00 2.50
9 Kenny Lofton .20 .50
10 Gary Sheffield .50 1.25
11 Sammy Sosa .60 1.50
12 Paul Molitor .50 1.25
13 Andreas Galarraga .40 1.00
14 Ivan Rodriguez .40 1.00
15 Mike Piazza 1.25 3.00
16 Andy Pettitte .20 .50
17 Tom Glavine .40 1.00
18 Albert Belle .08 .25
19 Mark McGwire .75 2.00
20 Mo Vaughn .08 .25

2002 Cracker Jack

COMPLETE SET (30) 10.00 25.00
1 Roger Clemens .60 1.50
2 Pedro Martinez .50 1.25
3 Carlos Delgado .40 1.00
4 Jeff Conine .08 .25
5 Greg Vaughn .08 .25
6 Jim Thome .40 1.00
7 Brad Radke .08 .25
8 Frank Thomas .40 1.00
9 Steve Sparks .08 .25
10 Carlos Beltran .40 1.00
11 Ichiro Suzuki 1.00 2.50
12 Mark Mulder .30 .75
13 Troy Glaus .40 1.00
14 Alex Rodriguez .50 1.50
15 Chipper Jones .60 1.50
16 Bobby Abreu .40 1.00
17 Mike Piazza .60 1.50
18 Cliff Floyd .40 1.00
19 Vladimir Guerrero .60 1.50
20 Jeff Bagwell .50 1.25
21 Albert Pujols 1.25 3.00
22 Sammy Sosa .40 1.00
23 Richie Sexson .30 .75
24 Sean Casey .20 .50
25 Brian Giles .30 .75
26 Randy Johnson .50 1.25
27 Barry Bonds .60 1.50
28 Kevin Brown .20 .50
29 Phil Nevin .08 .25
30 Todd Helton .40 1.00

2003 Cracker Jack All-Stars

COMPLETE SET (32) 6.00 15.00
1 Roberto Alomar .30 .75
2 Jeff Bagwell .30 .75
3 Tony Batista .20 .50
4 Bret Boone .20 .50
5 Ellis Burks .20 .50
6 Ellis Burks .20 .50
7 A.J. Burnett .20 .50
8 Pat Burrell .20 .50
9 Sean Casey .20 .50
10 Carlos Delgado .20 .50
11 Damion Easley .20 .50
12 Jason Giambi .20 .50
13 Brian Giles .20 .50
14 Troy Glaus .20 .50
15 Shawn Green .20 .50
16 Ben Grieve .20 .50
17 Vladimir Guerrero .30 .75
18 Todd Helton .30 .75
19 Torii Hunter .20 .50
20 Randy Johnson .50 1.25
21 Chipper Jones .50 1.25
22 Ryan Klesko .20 .50
23 Paul Konerko .30 .75
24 Pedro Martinez .30 .75
25 Mark Mulder .20 .50
26 Robb Nen .20 .50
27 Rafael Palmeiro .30 .75
28 Albert Pujols .60 1.50
29 Ben Sheets .20 .50
30 Sammy Sosa .50 1.25
31 All Star Logo .20 .50
32 Cracker Jack Logo .20 .50

2005 Cracker Jack Ballpark Legends

COMPLETE SET (10) 5.00 12.00
1 Lou Brock .60 1.50
2 Roy Campanella .60 1.50
3 Ty Cobb 1.50 4.00
4 Joe Jackson 1.25 3.00
5 Walter Johnson .60 1.50
6 Thurman Munson .60 1.50
7 Satchel Paige 1.00 2.50
8 George Sisler .60 1.50
9 Honus Wagner .60 1.50
10 Cy Young .60 1.50

2006 Cracker Jack Ballpark Legends II

COMPLETE SET (10) 4.00 10.00
1 Johnny Bench 1.00 2.50
2 Orlando Cepeda .60 1.50
3 Rollie Fingers .60 1.50
4 Ferguson Jenkins .60 1.50
5 Harmon Killebrew 1.00 2.50
6 Juan Marichal .60 1.50
7 Jim Palmer .60 1.50
8 Gaylord Perry .60 1.50
9 Brooks Robinson .60 1.50
10 Ozzie Smith 1.25 3.00

1976 Crane Discs

Produced by MSA, these discs were distributed by a wide variety of advertisers and can be found in various regions of the country. There are many different versions of this set, however, we are only pricing the Crane version. Several players changed teams during the printing of this set, however only the more commonly found version is included in the complete set price. These sets are unnumbered and sequenced in alphabetical order. Some of the other sponsors include Buchmans, Carousel (of which many different locations are known), Dairy Isle, Isaly, Orbakers, Red Barn, Safelon and Towne Club. All multiplier values are notated before.

COMPLETE SET (70) 15.00 40.00
*BLANKBACK DISCS: SAME VALUE AS BASIC DISCS
BUCHMANS DISCS: 1.25X BASIC DISCS
*CAROUSEL: 3X BASIC DISCS
*DAIRY ISLE: 2X BASIC DISCS
*ISALYS: SAME VALUE AS BASIC DISCS
*ORBAKERS: 1.25X BASIC DISCS
*RED BARN: 15X BASIC DISCS
*SAFELON: 2X BASIC DISCS
*TOWNE CLUB: 1.25X BASIC DISCS
1 Hank Aaron 1.25 3.00
2 Johnny Bench .75 2.00
3 Vida Blue .12 .30
4 Larry Bowa .10 .25
5 Lou Brock .75 2.00
6 Jeff Burroughs .10 .25
7 John Candelaria .10 .25
8 Jose Cardenal .10 .25
9 Rod Carew .75 2.00
10 Steve Carlton .75 2.00
11 Dave Cash .10 .25
12 Cesar Cedeno .12 .30
13 Ron Cey .12 .30
14 Carlton Fisk 1.00 2.50
15 Tito Fuentes .10 .25
16 Steve Garvey .40 1.00
17 Ken Griffey .12 .30
18 Don Gullett .10 .25
19 Willie Horton .10 .25
20 Al Hrabosky .10 .25
21 Catfish Hunter .75 2.00
22A Reggie Jackson 2.50 6.00
Oakland Athletics
22B Reggie Jackson .75 2.00
Baltimore Orioles
23 Randy Jones .10 .25
24 Jim Kaat .25 .60
25 Don Kessinger .10 .25
26 Dave Kingman .25 .60
27 Jerry Koosman .12 .30
28 Mickey Lolich .12 .30
29 Greg Luzinski .25 .60
30 Fred Lynn .25 .60
31 Bill Madlock .12 .30
32A Carlos May .40 1.00
Chicago White Sox
32B Carlos May .10 .25
New York Yankees
33 John Mayberry .10 .25
34 Bake McBride .10 .25
35 Doc Medich .10 .25
36A Andy Messersmith .40 1.00
Los Angeles Dodgers
36B Andy Messersmith .10 .25
Atlanta Braves
37 Rick Monday .10 .25
38 John Montefusco .10 .25
39 Jerry Morales .10 .25
40 Joe Morgan .75 2.00
41 Thurman Munson .75 2.00
42 Bobby Murcer .25 .60
43 Al Oliver .25 .60
44 Jim Palmer .75 2.00
45 Dave Parker .40 1.00
46 Tony Perez .40 1.00
47 Jerry Reuss .10 .25
48 Brooks Robinson .75 2.00
49 Frank Robinson .75 2.00
50 Steve Rogers .10 .25
51 Pete Rose 1.00 2.50
52 Nolan Ryan 2.00 5.00
53 Manny Sanguillen .10 .25
54 Mike Schmidt 1.25 3.00
55 Tom Seaver 1.00 2.50
56 Ted Simmons .25 .60
57 Reggie Smith .12 .30
58 Willie Stargell .75 2.00
59 Rusty Staub .25 .60
60 Rennie Stennett .10 .25
61 Don Sutton .75 2.00
62A Andre Thornton .40 1.00
Chicago Cubs
62B Andre Thornton .10 .25
Montreal Expos
63 Luis Tiant .25 .60
64 Joe Torre .40 1.00
65 Mike Tyson .10 .25
66 Bob Watson .12 .30
67 Wilbur Wood .10 .25
68 Jimmy Wynn .10 .25
69 Carl Yastrzemski .75 2.00
70 Richie Zisk .10 .25

1998 Crown Royale

The 1998 Crown Royale set (produced by Pacific) consists of 144 standard size cards. The six-card hobby-only packs retailed for a suggested price of $5.99. The card fronts feature game-action color photos of today's top baseball stars on the distinctively unique horizontal, die cut Crown Royale design. The featured player's name is printed across the bottom of the card along with the the team name. The release date was September, 1998. Orlando Hernandez is the most notable Rookie Card in this set.

COMPLETE SET (144) 40.00 100.00
1 Garret Anderson .40 1.00
2 Jim Edmonds .40 1.00
3 Darin Erstad .40 1.00
4 Tim Salmon .60 1.50
5 Jarrod Washburn .40 1.00
6 Dave Dellucci RC 1.00 2.50
7 Travis Lee .40 1.00
8 Devon White .40 1.00
9 Matt Williams .40 1.00
10 Andres Galarraga .40 1.00
11 Tom Glavine .60 1.50
12 Andruw Jones .60 1.50
13 Chipper Jones 1.00 2.50
14 Ryan Klesko .40 1.00
15 Javy Lopez .40 1.00
16 Greg Maddux 1.50 4.00
17 Walt Weiss .40 1.00
18 Roberto Alomar .60 1.50
19 Harold Baines .40 1.00
20 Eric Davis .40 1.00
21 Mike Mussina .60 1.50
22 Rafael Palmeiro .60 1.50
23 Cal Ripken 3.00 8.00
24 Nomar Garciaparra 1.50 4.00
25 Pedro Martinez .60 1.50
26 Troy O'Leary .40 1.00
27 Mo Vaughn .40 1.00
28 Tim Wakefield .40 1.00
29 Mark Grace .60 1.50
30 Mickey Morandini .40 1.00
31 Sammy Sosa 1.00 2.50
32 Kerry Wood .50 1.25
33 Albert Belle .40 1.00
34 Mike Caruso .40 1.00
35 Ray Durham .40 1.00
36 Frank Thomas 1.00 2.50
37 Robin Ventura .40 1.00
38 Bret Boone .40 1.00
39 Sean Casey .40 1.00
40 Barry Larkin .60 1.50
41 Reggie Sanders .40 1.00
42 Sandy Alomar Jr. .40 1.00
43 David Justice .40 1.00
44 Kenny Lofton .40 1.00
45 Manny Ramirez .60 1.50
46 Jim Thome .60 1.50
47 Omar Vizquel .60 1.50
48 Jaret Wright .40 1.00
49 Dante Bichette .40 1.00
50 Ellis Burks .40 1.00
51 Vinny Castilla .40 1.00
52 Todd Helton .60 1.50
53 Larry Walker .40 1.00
54 Tony Clark .40 1.00
55 Damion Easley .40 1.00
56 Bobby Higginson .40 1.00
57 Cliff Floyd .40 1.00
58 Livan Hernandez .40 1.00
59 Derrek Lee .60 1.50
60 Edgar Renteria .40 1.00
61 Moises Alou .40 1.00
62 Jeff Bagwell .60 1.50
63 Derek Bell .40 1.00
64 Craig Biggio .60 1.50
65 Johnny Damon .60 1.50
66 Jeff King .40 1.00
67 Hal Morris .40 1.00
68 Dean Palmer .40 1.00
69 Bobby Bonilla .40 1.00
70 Eric Karros .40 1.00
71 Raul Mondesi .40 1.00
72 Gary Sheffield .40 1.00
73 Jeromy Burnitz .40 1.00
74 Jeff Cirillo .40 1.00
75 Marquis Grissom .40 1.00
76 Fernando Vina .40 1.00
77 Marty Cordova .40 1.00
78 Pat Meares .40 1.00
79 Paul Molitor .40 1.00
80 Terry Steinbach .40 1.00
81 Todd Walker .40 1.00
82 Brad Fullmer .40 1.00
83 Vladimir Guerrero 1.00 2.50
84 Carl Pavano .40 1.00
85 Rondell White .40 1.00
86 Carlos Baerga .40 1.00
87 Hideo Nomo 1.00 2.50
88 John Olerud .40 1.00
89 Rey Ordonez .40 1.00
90 Mike Piazza 1.50 4.00
91 Masato Yoshii RC .60 1.50
92 Orlando Hernandez RC 2.00 5.00
93 Hideki Irabu .40 1.00
94 Derek Jeter 2.50 6.00
95 Chuck Knoblauch .40 1.00
96 Ricky Ledee .40 1.00
97 Tino Martinez .60 1.50
98 Paul O'Neill .60 1.50
99 Bernie Williams .60 1.50
100 Jason Giambi .40 1.00
101 Ben Grieve .40 1.00
102 Rickey Henderson 1.00 2.50
103 Matt Stairs .40 1.00
104 Bob Abreu .40 1.00
105 Doug Glanville .40 1.00
106 Scott Rolen .60 1.50
107 Curt Schilling .40 1.00
108 Jose Guillen .40 1.00
109 Jason Kendall .40 1.00
110 Jason Schmidt .40 1.00
111 Kevin Young .40 1.00
112 Delino DeShields .40 1.00
113 Brian Jordan .40 1.00
114 Ray Lankford .40 1.00
115 Mark McGwire 2.50 6.00
116 Tony Gwynn 1.25 3.00
117 Wally Joyner .40 1.00
118 Ruben Rivera .40 1.00
119 Greg Vaughn .40 1.00
120 Rich Aurilia .40 1.00
121 Barry Bonds 2.50 6.00
122 Bill Mueller .40 1.00
123 Robb Nen .40 1.00
124 Jay Buhner .40 1.00
125 Ken Griffey Jr. 2.00 5.00
126 Edgar Martinez .60 1.50
127 Shane Monahan .40 1.00
128 Alex Rodriguez 1.50 4.00
129 David Segui .40 1.00
130 Rolando Arrojo RC .60 1.50
131 Wade Boggs .60 1.50
132 Quinton McCracken .40 1.00
133 Fred McGriff .60 1.50
134 Bobby Smith .40 1.00
135 Will Clark .60 1.50
136 Juan Gonzalez .40 1.00
137 Rusty Greer .40 1.00
138 Ivan Rodriguez .60 1.50
139 Aaron Sele .40 1.00
140 John Wetteland .40 1.00
141 Jose Canseco .60 1.50
142 Roger Clemens 2.00 5.00
143 Carlos Delgado .40 1.00
144 Shawn Green .40 1.00

1998 Crown Royale All-Stars

COMPLETE SET (20) 125.00 250.00
STATED ODDS 1:25
1 Roberto Alomar 2.50 6.00
2 Cal Ripken 12.50 30.00
3 Kenny Lofton 1.50 4.00
4 Jim Thome 2.50 6.00
5 Derek Jeter 10.00 25.00
6 David Wells 2.50 6.00
7 Ken Griffey Jr. 8.00 20.00
8 Alex Rodriguez 6.00 15.00
9 Juan Gonzalez 1.50 4.00
10 Ivan Rodriguez 2.50 6.00
11 Gary Sheffield 1.50 4.00
12 Chipper Jones 4.00 10.00
13 Greg Maddux 6.00 15.00
14 Walt Weiss 1.50 4.00
15 Larry Walker 1.50 4.00
16 Craig Biggio 2.50 6.00
17 Mike Piazza 6.00 15.00
18 Mark McGwire 10.00 25.00
19 Tony Gwynn 5.00 12.00
20 Barry Bonds 10.00 25.00

1998 Crown Royale Cramer's Choice Premiums

COMPLETE SET (10) 40.00 100.00
ONE PER BOX
CRAMER AU'S RANDOM IN BOXES
CRAMER AU'S PR.RUN 10 SERIAL #'d SETS
CRAMER AU'S TOO SCARCE TO PRICE
1 Cal Ripken 8.00 20.00
2 Ken Griffey Jr. 5.00 12.00
3 Alex Rodriguez 4.00 10.00
4 Juan Gonzalez 1.00 2.50
5 Travis Lee 1.00 2.50
6 Chipper Jones 2.50 6.00
7 Greg Maddux 4.00 10.00
8 Kerry Wood 1.25 3.00
9 Mark McGwire 6.00 15.00
10 Tony Gwynn 3.00 8.00

1998 Crown Royale Diamond Knights

COMPLETE SET (25) 15.00 40.00
1 Andres Galarraga .20 .50
2 Chipper Jones .50 1.25
3 Greg Maddux .75 2.00
4 Cal Ripken 1.50 4.00
5 Nomar Garciaparra .75 2.00
6 Mo Vaughn .20 .50
7 Kerry Wood .25 .60
8 Frank Thomas .50 1.25
9 Vinny Castilla .20 .50
10 Jeff Bagwell .30 .75
11 Craig Biggio .30 .75
12 Paul Molitor .20 .50
13 Mike Piazza .75 2.00
14 Orlando Hernandez 1.00 2.50
15 Derek Jeter 1.25 3.00
16 Ricky Ledee .20 .50
17 Mark McGwire 1.25 3.00
18 Tony Gwynn .60 1.50
19 Barry Bonds 1.25 3.00
20 Ken Griffey Jr. 1.00 2.50
21 Alex Rodriguez .75 2.00
22 Wade Boggs .30 .75
23 Juan Gonzalez .20 .50
24 Ivan Rodriguez .30 .75
25 Jose Canseco .30 .75

1998 Crown Royale Firestone on Baseball

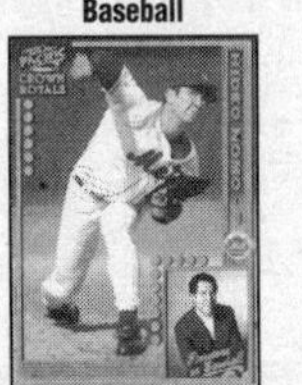

COMPLETE SET (26) 100.00 200.00
STATED ODDS 2:25
FIRESTONE SIGNED 300 OF CARD 26
FIRESTONE ALSO SIGNED 8 OF EACH 1-25
FIRESTONE AU'S TOO
SCARCE TO PRICE 2.50 6.00
COMP.SET EXCLUDES FIRESTONE AU'S 2.50 6.00
1 Travis Lee 1.00 2.50
2 Chipper Jones 2.50 6.00
3 Greg Maddux 4.00 10.00
4 Cal Ripken 8.00 20.00
5 Nomar Garciaparra 4.00 10.00
6 Mo Vaughn 1.00 2.50
7 Kerry Wood 1.25 3.00
8 Frank Thomas 2.50 6.00
9 Manny Ramirez 1.50 4.00
10 Larry Walker 1.00 2.50
11 Gary Sheffield 1.00 2.50
12 Paul Molitor 1.00 2.50
13 Hideo Nomo 2.50 6.00
14 Mike Piazza 4.00 10.00
15 Ben Grieve 1.00 2.50
16 Mark McGwire 6.00 15.00
17 Tony Gwynn 3.00 8.00
18 Barry Bonds 6.00 15.00
19 Ken Griffey Jr. 5.00 12.00
20 Randy Johnson 1.50 4.00
21 Alex Rodriguez 4.00 10.00
22 Wade Boggs 1.50 4.00
23 Juan Gonzalez 1.00 2.50
24 Ivan Rodriguez 1.50 4.00
25 Roger Clemens 5.00 12.00
26 R.Firestone 2.00 5.00
T.Gwynn
26A Roy Firestone AU300 15.00 40.00

1998 Crown Royale Home Run Fever

COMPLETE SET (10) 60.00 150.00
STATED ODDS 1:73
STATED PRINT RUN 374 SERIAL #'d SETS
1 Andres Galarraga 6.00 15.00
2 Sammy Sosa 10.00 25.00
3 Albert Belle 4.00 10.00
4 Jim Thome 6.00 15.00
5 Mark McGwire 15.00 40.00
6 Greg Vaughn 4.00 10.00
7 Ken Griffey Jr. 20.00 50.00
8 Alex Rodriguez 12.00 30.00
9 Juan Gonzalez 4.00 10.00
10 Jose Canseco 6.00 15.00

1998 Crown Royale Pillars of the Game

COMPLETE SET (25) 10.00 25.00
1 Jim Edmonds .20 .50
2 Travis Lee .20 .50
3 Chipper Jones .50 1.25
4 G.Maddux .75 2.00
Glavine
Smoltz
5 Cal Ripken 1.50 4.00
6 Nomar Garciaparra .75 2.00
7 Roberto Alomar .30 .75
8 Sammy Sosa .50 1.25
9 Kerry Wood .25 .60
10 Frank Thomas .50 1.25
11 Jim Thome .30 .75
12 Larry Walker .20 .50
13 Moises Alou .20 .50
14 Raul Mondesi .20 .50
15 Mike Piazza .75 2.00
16 Hideki Irabu .20 .50
17 Bernie Williams .30 .75
18 Ben Grieve .20 .50
19 Scott Rolen .30 .75
20 Mark McGwire 1.25 3.00
21 Tony Gwynn .60 1.50
22 Ken Griffey Jr. 1.00 2.50
23 Alex Rodriguez .75 2.00
24 Juan Gonzalez .20 .50
25 Roger Clemens 1.00 2.50

1999 Crown Royale

The 1999 Crown Royale set (produced by Pacific) was issued in one series totalling 144 cards and distributed exclusively to hobby dealers in six-card packs with a suggested retail price of $5.99. The set features color action player photos printed on die-cut dual-foiled card stock. The set also includes 18 short-printed rookies and prospects with an insertion rate of 1:8 packs. Notable Rookie Cards include Freddy Garcia.

COMPLETE SET (144) 20.00 50.00
COMP.SET w/o SP's (126) 12.50 30.00
COMMON CARD (1-144) .20 .50
COMMON PROSPECT SP .75 2.00
PROSPECT SP ODDS 1:8
SP's: 17/35/55/56/58/61/67/69/80/82/85
SP's: 101/105/113/114/118/127/144
1 Jim Edmonds .30 .75
2 Darin Erstad .20 .50
3 Troy Glaus .20 .50
4 Tim Salmon .20 .50
5 Mo Vaughn .20 .50
6 Jay Bell .20 .50
7 Steve Finley .20 .50
8 Randy Johnson .50 1.25
9 Travis Lee .20 .50
10 Matt Williams .20 .50
11 Andruw Jones .20 .50
12 Chipper Jones .50 1.25
13 Brian Jordan .20 .50
14 Ryan Klesko .20 .50
15 Javy Lopez .20 .50
16 Greg Maddux .60 1.50
17 Randall Simon SP .75 2.00
18 Albert Belle .20 .50
19 Will Clark .30 .75
20 Delino DeShields .20 .50
21 Mike Mussina .30 .75
22 Cal Ripken 1.50 4.00
23 Nomar Garciaparra .30 .75
24 Pedro Martinez .30 .75
25 Jose Offerman .20 .50
26 John Valentin .20 .50
27 Mark Grace .30 .75
28 Lance Johnson .20 .50
29 Henry Rodriguez .20 .50
30 Sammy Sosa .50 1.25
31 Kerry Wood .20 .50
32 Mike Caruso .20 .50
33 Ray Durham .20 .50
34 Magglio Ordonez .30 .75
35 Brian Simmons SP .75 2.00
36 Frank Thomas .50 1.25
37 Mike Cameron .20 .50
38 Barry Larkin .30 .75
39 Greg Vaughn .20 .50
40 Dmitri Young .20 .50
41 Roberto Alomar .30 .75
42 Sandy Alomar Jr. .20 .50
43 David Justice .20 .50
44 Kenny Lofton .20 .50
45 Manny Ramirez .50 1.25
46 Jim Thome .30 .75
47 Dante Bichette .20 .50
48 Vinny Castilla .20 .50
49 Todd Helton .30 .75
50 Larry Walker .30 .75
51 Tony Clark .20 .50
52 Damion Easley .20 .50
53 Bob Higginson .20 .50
54 Brian Hunter .20 .50
55 Gabe Kapler SP .75 2.00
56 Jeff Weaver SP RC .75 2.00
57 Cliff Floyd .20 .50
58 Alex Gonzalez SP .75 2.00
59 Mark Kotsay .20 .50
60 Derrek Lee .20 .50
61 Preston Wilson SP .75 2.00
62 Moises Alou .20 .50
63 Jeff Bagwell .30 .75
64 Derek Bell .20 .50
65 Craig Biggio .30 .75
66 Ken Caminiti .20 .50
67 Carlos Beltran SP 1.25 3.00
68 Johnny Damon .30 .75
69 Carlos Febles SP .75 2.00
70 Jeff King .20 .50
71 Kevin Brown .20 .50
72 Todd Hundley .20 .50
73 Eric Karros .20 .50
74 Raul Mondesi .20 .50
75 Gary Sheffield .20 .50
76 Jeromy Burnitz .20 .50
77 Jeff Cirillo .20 .50
78 Marquis Grissom .20 .50
79 Fernando Vina .20 .50
80 Chad Allen SP RC .75 2.00
81 Matt Lawton .20 .50
82 Doug Mientkiewicz SP RC 1.25 3.00
83 Brad Radke .20 .50
84 Todd Walker .20 .50
85 Michael Barrett SP .75 2.00
86 Brad Fullmer .20 .50
87 Vladimir Guerrero .30 .75
88 Wilton Guerrero .20 .50
89 Ugueth Urbina .20 .50
90 Bobby Bonilla .20 .50
91 Rickey Henderson .50 1.25
92 Rey Ordonez .20 .50
93 Mike Piazza .50 1.25
94 Robin Ventura .20 .50
95 Roger Clemens .60 1.50
96 Orlando Hernandez .20 .50
97 Derek Jeter 1.25 3.00
98 Chuck Knoblauch .20 .50
99 Tino Martinez .20 .50
100 Bernie Williams .30 .75
101 Eric Chavez SP .75 2.00
102 Jason Giambi .20 .50
103 Ben Grieve .20 .50
104 Tim Raines .30 .75
105 Marlon Anderson SP .75 2.00
106 Doug Glanville .20 .50
107 Scott Rolen .30 .75
108 Curt Schilling .20 .50
109 Brian Giles .20 .50
110 Jose Guillen .20 .50
111 Jason Kendall .20 .50
112 Kevin Young .20 .50
113 J.D. Drew SP .75 2.00
114 Jose Jimenez SP .75 2.00
115 Ray Lankford .20 .50
116 Mark McGwire .75 2.00
117 Fernando Tatis .20 .50
118 Matt Clement SP .75 2.00
119 Tony Gwynn .50 1.25
120 Trevor Hoffman .30 .75
121 Wally Joyner .20 .50
122 Reggie Sanders .20 .50
123 Barry Bonds .75 2.00
124 Ellis Burks .20 .50
125 Jeff Kent .20 .50
126 J.T. Snow .20 .50
127 Freddy Garcia SP RC 2.00 5.00
128 Ken Griffey Jr. 1.00 2.50
129 Edgar Martinez .30 .75
130 Alex Rodriguez .60 1.50
131 David Segui .20 .50
132 Rolando Arrojo .20 .50
133 Wade Boggs .30 .75
134 Jose Canseco .30 .75
135 Quinton McCracken .20 .50
136 Fred McGriff .30 .75
137 Juan Gonzalez .20 .50
138 Rusty Greer .20 .50
139 Rafael Palmeiro .30 .75
140 Ivan Rodriguez .30 .75
141 Jose Cruz Jr. .20 .50
142 Carlos Delgado .20 .50
143 Shawn Green .20 .50
144 Roy Halladay SP 1.25 3.00

1999 Crown Royale Limited

*LTD: 6X TO 15X BASIC
*LTD SP: 1.5X TO 4X BASIC SP
RANDOM INSERTS IN PACKS
STATED PRINT RUN 99 SERIAL #'d SETS

1999 Crown Royale Opening Day

*OPENING DAY: 8X TO 20X BASIC
*OPENING DAY SP: 2X TO 5X BASIC SP
STATED ODDS 1:25 HOBBY
STATED PRINT RUN 72 SERIAL #'d SETS

1999 Crown Royale Century 21

COMPLETE SET (10) 15.00 40.00
STATED ODDS 1:25
1 Cal Ripken 5.00 12.00
2 Nomar Garciaparra 1.00 2.50
3 Sammy Sosa 1.50 4.00
4 Frank Thomas 1.50 4.00
5 Mike Piazza 1.50 4.00
6 J.D. Drew .60 1.50
7 Mark McGwire 2.50 6.00
8 Tony Gwynn 1.50 4.00
9 Ken Griffey Jr. 3.00 8.00
10 Alex Rodriguez 2.00 5.00

1999 Crown Royale Cramer's Choice Premiums

COMPLETE SET (10) 25.00 60.00
ONE PREMIUM PER BOX
*DARK BLUE: 2.5X TO 6X PREMIUMS
DARK BLUE PRINT RUN 35 SERIAL #'d SETS
GOLD PRINT RUN 10 SERIAL #'d SETS
NO GOLD PRICING DUE TO SCARCITY
*GREEN: 3X TO 8X PREMIUMS
GREEN PRINT RUN 30 SERIAL #'d SETS
*LIGHT BLUE: 5X TO 12X PREMIUMS
LIGHT BLUE PRINT RUN 20 SERIAL #'d SETS
PURPLE AU PRINT RUN 1 SERIAL #'d SET
PURPLE AU'S NOT PRICED DUE TO SCARCITY
PURPLE AU'S SIGNED BY MIKE CRAMER
*RED: 4X TO 10X PREMIUMS
RED PRINT RUN 25 SERIAL #'d SETS
PARALLELS ARE RANDOM IN PACKS
BASIC PREMIUMS LISTED BELOW!
1 Cal Ripken 8.00 20.00
2 Nomar Garciaparra 1.50 4.00
3 Sammy Sosa 2.50 6.00
4 Frank Thomas 2.50 6.00
5 Mike Piazza 2.50 6.00
6 Derek Jeter 6.00 15.00
7 J.D. Drew 1.00 2.50
8 Mark McGwire 4.00 10.00
9 Tony Gwynn 2.50 6.00
10 Ken Griffey Jr. 5.00 12.00

1999 Crown Royale Gold Crown Die Cut Premiums

COMPLETE SET (6) 12.50 30.00
STATED ODDS 6:10 BOXES
STATED PRINT RUN 1036 SERIAL #'d SETS
1 Cal Ripken 6.00 15.00
2 Mike Piazza 2.00 5.00
3 Ken Griffey Jr. 4.00 10.00
4 Tony Gwynn 2.00 5.00
5 Mark McGwire 3.00 8.00
6 J.D. Drew .75 2.00

1999 Crown Royale Living Legends

COMPLETE SET (10) 30.00 80.00
RANDOM INSERTS IN PACKS
STATED PRINT RUN 375 SERIAL #'d SETS
1 Greg Maddux 4.00 10.00
2 Cal Ripken 10.00 25.00
3 Nomar Garciaparra 2.00 5.00
4 Sammy Sosa 3.00 8.00
5 Frank Thomas 3.00 8.00

6 Mike Piazza 3.00 8.00
7 Mark McGwire 5.00 12.00
8 Tony Gwynn 3.00 8.00
9 Ken Griffey Jr. 6.00 15.00
10 Alex Rodriguez 4.00 10.00

1999 Crown Royale Master Performers

COMPLETE SET (20) 20.00 50.00
STATED ODDS 2:25
1 Chipper Jones 1.25 3.00
2 Greg Maddux 1.50 4.00
3 Cal Ripken 4.00 10.00
4 Nomar Garciaparra .75 2.00
5 Sammy Sosa 1.25 3.00
6 Frank Thomas 1.25 3.00
7 Raul Mondesi .50 1.25
8 Vladimir Guerrero .75 2.00
9 Mike Piazza 1.25 3.00
10 Roger Clemens 1.50 4.00
11 Derek Jeter 3.00 8.00
12 Scott Rolen .75 2.00
13 J.D. Drew .50 1.25
14 Mark McGwire 2.00 5.00
15 Tony Gwynn 1.25 3.00
16 Barry Bonds 2.00 5.00
17 Ken Griffey Jr. 2.50 6.00
18 Alex Rodriguez 1.50 4.00
19 Juan Gonzalez .50 1.25
20 Ivan Rodriguez .75 2.00

1999 Crown Royale Pillars of the Game

COMPLETE SET (25) 10.00 25.00
ONE PER PACK
1 Mo Vaughn .20 .50
2 Chipper Jones .50 1.25
3 Greg Maddux .60 1.50
4 Albert Belle .20 .50
5 Cal Ripken 1.50 4.00
6 Nomar Garciaparra .30 .75
7 Sammy Sosa .50 1.25
8 Frank Thomas .50 1.25
9 Manny Ramirez .50 1.25
10 Jeff Bagwell .30 .75
11 Raul Mondesi .20 .50
12 Vladimir Guerrero .30 .75
13 Mike Piazza .50 1.25
14 Roger Clemens .60 1.50
15 Derek Jeter 1.25 3.00
16 Bernie Williams .30 .75
17 Ben Grieve .20 .50
18 J.D. Drew .20 .50
19 Mark McGwire .75 2.00
20 Tony Gwynn .50 1.25
21 Barry Bonds .75 2.00
22 Ken Griffey Jr. 1.00 2.50
23 Alex Rodriguez .60 1.50
24 Juan Gonzalez .20 .50
25 Ivan Rodriguez .30 .75

1999 Crown Royale Pivotal Players

COMPLETE SET (25) 10.00 25.00
ONE PER PACK
1 Mo Vaughn .20 .50
2 Chipper Jones .50 1.25
3 Greg Maddux .60 1.50
4 Albert Belle .20 .50
5 Cal Ripken 1.50 4.00
6 Nomar Garciaparra .30 .75
7 Sammy Sosa .50 1.25
8 Frank Thomas .50 1.25
9 Manny Ramirez .50 1.25
10 Craig Biggio .30 .75
11 Raul Mondesi .20 .50
12 Vladimir Guerrero .30 .75
13 Mike Piazza .50 1.25
14 Roger Clemens .60 1.50
15 Derek Jeter 1.25 3.00
16 Bernie Williams .30 .75
17 Ben Grieve .20 .50
18 Scott Rolen .30 .75
19 J.D. Drew .20 .50
20 Mark McGwire .75 2.00
21 Tony Gwynn .50 1.25
22 Ken Griffey Jr. 1.00 2.50
23 Alex Rodriguez .60 1.50
24 Juan Gonzalez .20 .50
25 Ivan Rodriguez .30 .75

1999 Crown Royale Pivotal Players FanFest

1 Mo Vaughn 8.00 20.00
2 Chipper Jones 20.00 50.00
3 Greg Maddux 25.00 60.00
4 Albert Belle 8.00 20.00
5 Cal Ripken 60.00 150.00
6 Nomar Garciaparra 12.00 30.00
7 Sammy Sosa 20.00 50.00
8 Frank Thomas 20.00 50.00
9 Manny Ramirez 20.00 50.00
10 Craig Biggio 12.00 30.00
11 Raul Mondesi 8.00 20.00
12 Vladimir Guerrero 12.00 30.00
13 Mike Piazza 20.00 50.00
14 Roger Clemens 25.00 60.00
15 Derek Jeter 50.00 125.00
16 Bernie Williams 12.00 30.00
17 Ben Grieve 8.00 20.00
18 Scott Rolen 12.00 30.00
19 J.D. Drew 8.00 20.00
20 Mark McGwire 30.00 80.00
21 Tony Gwynn 20.00 50.00
22 Ken Griffey Jr. 40.00 100.00
23 Alex Rodriguez 25.00 60.00
24 Juan Gonzalez 8.00 20.00
25 Ivan Rodriguez 12.00 30.00

1999 Crown Royale Player's Choice

ese cards, which parallel the regular Crown Royale rds were issued by Pacific to be given away at the ayers Choice award ceremony. The cards have a layers Choice" stamp on them and are skip mbered to match their number from the basic 1999 wn Royale set. These cards were produced in ying quantities so we have put the print run next to players name.

COMPLETE SET 100.00 200.00
8 Randy Johnson/43 10.00 25.00
10 Matt Williams/40 4.00 10.00
16 Greg Maddux/24 12.00 30.00
22 Cal Ripken/156 30.00 80.00
30 Sammy Sosa/193 10.00 25.00
41 Roberto Alomar/79 6.00 15.00
61 Preston Wilson/31 4.00 10.00
67 Carlos Beltran/68 6.00 15.00
91 Rickey Henderson/57 10.00 25.00
127 Freddy Garcia/47 10.00 25.00
139 Rafael Palmeiro/52 6.00 15.00

2000 Crown Royale

COMPLETE SET (144) 30.00 60.00
COMMON CARD (1-144) .15 .40
COMMON ROOKIE SP .40 1.00
SP's: 3/4/11/25/34/58/64/69/74/80/82/83
SP's: 91/97/103/104/105/111/114/115/119
SP's: 126/131/137/138
1 Darin Erstad .15 .40
2 Troy Glaus .15 .40
3 Adam Kennedy SP .40 1.00
4 Derrick Turnbow SP RC .40 1.00
5 Mo Vaughn .15 .40
6 Erubiel Durazo .15 .40
7 Steve Finley .15 .40
8 Randy Johnson .40 1.00
9 Travis Lee .15 .40
10 Matt Williams .15 .40
11 Rafael Furcal SP .60 1.50
12 Andres Galarraga .25 .60
13 Andruw Jones .15 .40
14 Chipper Jones .40 1.00
15 Javy Lopez .15 .40
16 Greg Maddux .50 1.25
17 Albert Belle .15 .40
18 Will Clark .25 .60
19 Mike Mussina .25 .60
20 Cal Ripken 1.25 3.00
21 Carl Everett .15 .40
22 Nomar Garciaparra .25 .60
23 Pedro Martinez .25 .60
24 Jason Varitek .40 1.00
25 Scott Downs SP RC .40 1.00
26 Mark Grace .25 .60
27 Sammy Sosa .40 1.00
28 Kerry Wood .15 .40
29 Ray Durham .15 .40
30 Paul Konerko .15 .40
31 Carlos Lee .15 .40
32 Magglio Ordonez .25 .60
33 Frank Thomas .40 1.00
34 Rob Bell SP .40 1.00
35 Sean Casey .15 .40
36 Ken Griffey Jr. .75 2.00
37 Barry Larkin .25 .60
38 Pokey Reese .15 .40
39 Roberto Alomar .25 .60
40 David Justice .15 .40
41 Kenny Lofton .15 .40
42 Manny Ramirez .40 1.00
43 Richie Sexson .15 .40
44 Jim Thome .25 .60
45 Rolando Arrojo .15 .40
46 Jeff Cirillo .15 .40
47 Tom Goodwin .15 .40
48 Todd Helton .25 .60
49 Larry Walker .25 .60
50 Tony Clark .15 .40
51 Juan Encarnacion .15 .40
52 Juan Gonzalez .15 .40
53 Hideo Nomo .40 1.00
54 Dean Palmer .15 .40
55 Cliff Floyd .15 .40
56 Alex Gonzalez .15 .40
57 Mike Lowell .15 .40
58 Brad Penny SP .40 1.00
59 Preston Wilson .15 .40
60 Moises Alou .15 .40
61 Jeff Bagwell .25 .60
62 Craig Biggio .25 .60
63 Roger Cedeno .15 .40
64 Julio Lugo SP .40 1.00
65 Carlos Beltran .25 .60
66 Johnny Damon .25 .60
67 Jermaine Dye .15 .40
68 Carlos Febles .15 .40
69 Mark Quinn SP .40 1.00
70 Kevin Brown .15 .40
71 Shawn Green .15 .40
72 Eric Karros .15 .40
73 Gary Sheffield .15 .40
74 Kevin Barker SP .40 1.00
75 Ron Belliard .15 .40
76 Jeromy Burnitz .15 .40
77 Geoff Jenkins .15 .40
78 Jacque Jones .15 .40
79 Corey Koskie .15 .40
80 Matt LeCroy SP .40 1.00
81 Brad Radke .15 .40
82 Peter Bergeron SP .40 1.00
83 Matt Blank SP .40 1.00
84 Vladimir Guerrero .25 .60
85 Hideki Irabu .15 .40
86 Rondell White .15 .40
87 Edgardo Alfonzo .15 .40
88 Mike Hampton .15 .40
89 Rickey Henderson .40 1.00
90 Rey Ordonez .15 .40
91 Jay Payton SP .40 1.00
92 Mike Piazza .40 1.00
93 Roger Clemens .50 1.25
94 Orlando Hernandez .15 .40
95 Derek Jeter 1.00 2.50
96 Tino Martinez .15 .40
97 Alfonso Soriano SP 1.00 2.50
98 Bernie Williams .25 .60
99 Eric Chavez .15 .40
100 Jason Giambi .15 .40
101 Ben Grieve .15 .40
102 Tim Hudson .25 .60
103 Terrence Long SP .40 1.00
104 Mark Mulder SP .40 1.00
105 Adam Piatt SP .40 1.00
106 Bobby Abreu .15 .40
107 Doug Glanville .15 .40
108 Mike Lieberthal .15 .40
109 Scott Rolen .25 .60
110 Brian Giles .15 .40
111 Chad Hermansen SP .40 1.00
112 Jason Kendall .15 .40
113 Warren Morris .15 .40
114 Rick Ankiel SP .60 1.50
115 Justin Brunette SP RC .40 1.00
116 J.D. Drew .15 .40
117 Mark McGwire .60 1.50
118 Fernando Tatis .15 .40
119 Wiki Gonzalez SP .40 1.00
120 Tony Gwynn .40 1.00
121 Trevor Hoffman .25 .60
122 Ryan Klesko .15 .40
123 Barry Bonds .60 1.50
124 Ellis Burks .15 .40
125 Jeff Kent .15 .40
126 Calvin Murray SP .40 1.00
127 J.T. Snow .15 .40
128 Freddy Garcia .15 .40
129 John Olerud .15 .40
130 Alex Rodriguez .50 1.25
131 Kazuhiro Sasaki SP RC 1.00 2.50
132 Jose Canseco .25 .60
133 Vinny Castilla .15 .40
134 Fred McGriff .25 .60
135 Greg Vaughn .15 .40
136 Gabe Kapler .15 .40
137 Mike Lamb SP RC UER .40 1.00
138 Ruben Mateo SP .40 1.00
139 Rafael Palmeiro .25 .60
140 Ivan Rodriguez .25 .60
141 Tony Batista .15 .40
142 Carlos Delgado .15 .40
143 Raul Mondesi .15 .40
144 Shannon Stewart .15 .40

2000 Crown Royale Limited

*STARS: 4X TO 10X BASIC CARDS
*SP's: 1.5X TO 4X BASIC SP's
STATED PRINT RUN 144 SERIAL #'d SETS

2000 Crown Royale Platinum Blue

*STARS: 5X TO 12X BASIC CARDS
*SP's: 2X TO 5X BASIC SP RC's
STATED PRINT RUN 75 SERIAL #'d SETS

2000 Crown Royale Premiere Date

*STARS: 3X TO 8X BASIC CARDS
*SP's: 1.2X TO 3X BASIC SP's
STATED ODDS 1:25 HOBBY
STATED PRINT RUN 121 SERIAL #' SETS

2000 Crown Royale Red

COMPLETE SET (144) 150.00 300.00
*STARS: 1X TO 2.5X BASIC CARDS
*SP's: .4X TO 1X BASIC SP's
RED ARE BASE CARDS IN RETAIL PACKS

2000 Crown Royale Rookie 499

COMPLETE SET (25) 50.00 120.00
*ROOKIE 499's: .75X TO 2X BASIC SP's
*ROOKIE 499 RC's: .75X TO 2X BASIC SP RC's
STATED PRINT RUN 499 SERIAL #'d SETS

2000 Crown Royale Card-Supials

COMPLETE SET (20) 15.00 40.00
STATED ODDS 2:25
1 Randy Johnson 1.00 2.50
2 Chipper Jones 1.00 2.50
3 Cal Ripken 3.00 8.00
4 Nomar Garciaparra .60 1.50
5 Sammy Sosa 1.00 2.50
6 Frank Thomas 1.00 2.50
7 Ken Griffey Jr. 2.00 5.00
8 Manny Ramirez 1.00 2.50
9 Larry Walker .60 1.50
10 Juan Gonzalez .40 1.00
11 Jeff Bagwell .60 1.50
12 Shawn Green .40 1.00
13 Vladimir Guerrero .60 1.50
14 Mike Piazza 1.00 2.50
15 Derek Jeter 2.50 6.00
16 Scott Rolen .60 1.50
17 Mark McGwire 1.50 4.00
18 Tony Gwynn 1.00 2.50
19 Alex Rodriguez 1.25 3.00
20 Ivan Rodriguez .60 1.50

2000 Crown Royale Card-Supials Minis

COMPLETE SET (20) 6.00 15.00
STATED ODDS 2:25
1 Erubiel Durazo .40 1.00
2 Andruw Jones .40 1.00
3 Matt Riley .40 1.00
4 Jason Varitek 1.00 2.50
5 Kerry Wood .40 1.00
6 Magglio Ordonez .60 1.50
7 Sean Casey .40 1.00
8 Richie Sexson .40 1.00
9 Ben Petrick .40 1.00
10 Juan Encarnacion .40 1.00
11 Lance Berkman .60 1.50
12 Eric Gagne .60 1.50
13 Peter Bergeron .40 1.00
14 Edgardo Alfonzo .40 1.00
15 Alfonso Soriano 1.00 2.50
16 Bob Abreu .40 1.00
17 Rick Ankiel .60 1.50
18 Ben Davis .40 1.00
19 Freddy Garcia .40 1.00
20 Ruben Mateo .40 1.00

2000 Crown Royale Cramer's Choice Premiums

COMPLETE SET (10) 15.00 40.00
ONE PREMIUM PER HOBBY BOX
*AQUA: 3X TO 8X BASIC PREMIUMS
AQUA PRINT RUN 20 SERIAL #'d SETS
*BLUE: 1.5X TO 4X BASIC PREMIUMS
BLUE PRINT RUN 35 SERIAL #'d SETS
GOLD PRINT RUN 10 SERIAL #'d SETS
NO GOLD PRICING DUE TO SCARCITY
*GREEN: 2X TO 5X BASIC PREMIUMS
GREEN PRINT RUN 30 SERIAL #'d SETS
PURPLE AU PRINT RUN 1 SERIAL #'d SET
PURPLE AU NO PRICE DUE TO SCARCITY
*RED: 2.5X TO 6X BASIC PREMIUMS
RED PRINT RUN 25 SERIAL #'d SETS
BASIC PREMIUMS LISTED BELOW!
1 Cal Ripken 5.00 12.00
2 Nomar Garciaparra 1.00 2.50
3 Ken Griffey Jr. 3.00 8.00
4 Sammy Sosa 1.50 4.00
5 Mike Piazza 1.50 4.00
6 Derek Jeter 4.00 10.00
7 Rick Ankiel 1.00 2.50
8 Mark McGwire 2.50 6.00
9 Tony Gwynn 1.50 4.00
10 Alex Rodriguez 2.00 5.00

2000 Crown Royale Feature Attractions

COMPLETE SET (25) 8.00 20.00
STATED ODDS 1:1 HOBBY, 1:2 RETAIL
*EXCL.SHOW: 30X TO 80X BASIC FEATURE
EXCL.SHOW RANDOM INSERTS IN PACKS
EXCL.SHOW PRINT RUN 20 SERIAL #'d SETS
1 Erubiel Durazo .15 .40
2 Chipper Jones .40 1.00
3 Greg Maddux .50 1.25
4 Cal Ripken 1.25 3.00
5 Nomar Garciaparra .25 .60
6 Pedro Martinez .25 .60
7 Sammy Sosa .40 1.00
8 Frank Thomas .40 1.00
9 Ken Griffey Jr. .75 2.00
10 Manny Ramirez .40 1.00
11 Larry Walker .25 .60
12 Juan Gonzalez .15 .40
13 Jeff Bagwell .25 .60
14 Carlos Beltran .25 .60
15 Shawn Green .15 .40
16 Vladimir Guerrero .25 .60
17 Mike Piazza .40 1.00
18 Roger Clemens .50 1.25
19 Derek Jeter 1.00 2.50
20 Ben Grieve .15 .40
21 Rick Ankiel .25 .60
22 Mark McGwire .60 1.50
23 Tony Gwynn .40 1.00
24 Alex Rodriguez .50 1.25
25 Ivan Rodriguez .25 .60

2000 Crown Royale Final Numbers

COMPLETE SET (25) 8.00 20.00
STATED ODDS 1:1
HOLO.PRINT RUN 10 SERIAL #'d SETS
HOLO.NO PRICING DUE TO SCARCITY
1 Randy Johnson .40 1.00
2 Andruw Jones .15 .40
3 Chipper Jones .40 1.00
4 Cal Ripken 1.25 3.00
5 Nomar Garciaparra .25 .60
6 Pedro Martinez .25 .60
7 Sammy Sosa .40 1.00
8 Ken Griffey Jr. .75 2.00
9 Sean Casey .15 .40
10 Manny Ramirez .40 1.00
11 Larry Walker .25 .60
12 Jeff Bagwell .25 .60
13 Craig Biggio .25 .60
14 Shawn Green .15 .40
15 Vladimir Guerrero .25 .60
16 Mike Piazza .40 1.00
17 Derek Jeter 1.00 2.50
18 Bernie Williams .25 .60
19 Scott Rolen .25 .60
20 Mark McGwire .60 1.50
21 Tony Gwynn .40 1.00
22 Barry Bonds .60 1.50
23 Alex Rodriguez .50 1.25
24 Jose Canseco .25 .60
25 Ivan Rodriguez .25 .60

2000 Crown Royale Final Numbers FanFest

STATED PRINT RUN 20 SER.#'d SETS
NO PRICING DUE TO SCARCITY

2000 Crown Royale Premiums

COMPLETE SET (6) 12.50 30.00
STATED ODDS 6:10 HOBBY BOXES
1 Cal Ripken 5.00 12.00
2 Nomar Garciaparra 1.00 2.50
3 Ken Griffey Jr. 3.00 8.00
4 Alex Rodriguez 2.00 5.00
5 Mark McGwire 2.50 6.00
6 Derek Jeter 4.00 10.00

2000 Crown Royale Proofs

COMPLETE SET (36) 20.00 50.00
STATED ODDS 1:25
*SERIAL 50: 2X TO 5X BASIC PROOFS
SERIAL 50 RANDOM INSERTS IN PACKS
SERIAL 50 PRINT RUN 50 SERIAL #'d SETS
1 Erubiel Durazo .40 1.00
2 Randy Johnson 1.00 2.50
3 Chipper Jones 1.00 2.50
4 Greg Maddux 1.25 3.00
5 Cal Ripken 3.00 8.00
6 Nomar Garciaparra .60 1.50
7 Pedro Martinez .60 1.50
8 Sammy Sosa 1.00 2.50
9 Frank Thomas 1.00 2.50
10 Sean Casey .40 1.00
11 Ken Griffey Jr. 2.00 5.00
12 Manny Ramirez 1.00 2.50
13 Jim Thome .60 1.50
14 Larry Walker .60 1.50
15 Juan Gonzalez .40 1.00
16 Jeff Bagwell .60 1.50
17 Craig Biggio .60 1.50
18 Carlos Beltran .60 1.50
19 Shawn Green .40 1.00
20 Vladimir Guerrero .60 1.50
21 Edgardo Alfonzo .40 1.00
22 Mike Piazza 1.00 2.50
23 Roger Clemens 1.25 3.00
24 Derek Jeter 2.50 6.00
25 Alfonso Soriano 1.00 2.50
26 Bernie Williams .60 1.50
27 Ben Grieve .40 1.00
28 Rick Ankiel .60 1.50
29 Mark McGwire 1.50 4.00
30 Tony Gwynn 1.00 2.50
31 Barry Bonds 1.50 4.00
32 Alex Rodriguez 1.25 3.00
33 Jose Canseco .60 1.50
34 Vinny Castilla .40 1.00
35 Ivan Rodriguez .60 1.50
36 Rafael Palmeiro .60 1.50

2000 Crown Royale Sweet Spot Signatures

1 Adam Kennedy 6.00 15.00
2 Trot Nixon 4.00 10.00
3 Magglio Ordonez 6.00 15.00
4 Sean Casey 6.00 15.00
5 Gookie Dawkins 4.00 10.00
6 Todd Helton 6.00 15.00
7 Ben Petrick 4.00 10.00
8 Jeff Weaver 6.00 15.00
9 Preston Wilson 6.00 15.00
10 Lance Berkman 6.00 15.00
11 Roger Cedeno 4.00 10.00
12 Eric Gagne 6.00 15.00
13 Kevin Barker 4.00 10.00
14 Kyle Peterson 4.00 10.00
15 Tony Armas Jr. 4.00 10.00
16 Peter Bergeron 4.00 10.00
17 Alfonso Soriano 8.00 20.00
18 Ben Grieve 4.00 10.00
19 Ramon Hernandez 4.00 10.00
20 Brian Giles 6.00 15.00
21 Chad Hermansen 4.00 10.00
22 Warren Morris 4.00 10.00
23 Rick Ankiel 4.00 10.00
24 Chad Hutchinson 4.00 10.00
25 Ben Davis 4.00 10.00
26 Freddy Garcia 6.00 15.00
27 Gabe Kapler 6.00 15.00
28 Ruben Mateo 4.00 10.00
29 Billy Koch 6.00 15.00
30 Vernon Wells 6.00 15.00

2018 Crown Royale Heirs to the Throne Materials

*BLUE/49-99: .5X TO 1.2X BASIC
*BLUE/25: .6X TO 1.5X BASIC
*GOLD/49-149: .5X TO 1.2X BASIC
*HOLO GLD/49: .5X TO 1.2X BASIC
*HOLO GLD/25: .6X TO 1.5X BASIC
*RED/25: .6X TO 1.5X BASIC
INSERTED IN '18 CHRONICLES PACKS
1 Cody Bellinger 5.00 12.00
2 Joey Gallo 2.00 5.00
3 Addison Russell 2.00 5.00
4 Ian Happ 2.00 5.00
5 Nomar Mazara 1.50 4.00
6 Michael Conforto 2.00 5.00
7 Dansby Swanson 2.50 6.00
8 Matt Olson 2.50 6.00
9 Trea Turner 2.00 5.00
10 Byron Buxton 2.50 6.00
11 Alex Bregman 2.50 6.00
12 Aaron Nola 2.00 5.00
13 Yoan Moncada 2.50 6.00
14 Andrew Benintendi 3.00 8.00
15 Luis Severino 2.00 5.00
16 Corey Seager 2.50 6.00
17 Carlos Correa 2.50 6.00
18 Gary Sanchez 2.50 6.00
19 Bryce Harper 4.00 10.00
20 Rougned Odor 2.00 5.00

1907 Cubs A.C. Dietsche Postcards PC765

This set of black and white Dietsche postcards was issued in 1907 and feature Chicago Cubs only. Cards have been seen with and without the player's name on the front. There is no current price differential for either variation.

COMPLETE SET 2000.00 4000.00
1 Mordecai Brown 200.00 400.00
2 Frank Chance 250.00 500.00
3 Johnny Evers 250.00 500.00
4 Arthur F. Hoffman 100.00 200.00
5 John Kling 125.00 250.00
6 Carl Lundgren 100.00 200.00
7 Patrick J. Moran 100.00 200.00
8 Orvall Overall 125.00 250.00
9 John A. Pfeister 100.00 200.00
10 Ed Reulbach 125.00 250.00
11 Frank Schulte 125.00 250.00
12 James T. Sheckard 100.00 200.00
13 Harry Steinfeldt 125.00 250.00
14 James Slagle 100.00 200.00
15 Joseph B. Tinker 250.00 500.00

1907 Cubs G.F. Grignon Co. PC775

This rather interesting postcard set measures 3 1/2" by 5 1/2", was issued in 1907 and features a Chicago Cub player in a circle in the upper right corner of the front of the card. These cards have green backgrounds featuring a teddy bear in different poses. There is also a head shot in the upper right corner blending comic and photo art. Cards are known to come with an ad for the Boston Oyster House, a popular Chicago restaurant at the time.

COMPLETE SET (16) 1000.00 2000.00
1 Mordecai Brown 300.00 600.00
2 Frank Chance 400.00 800.00
3 Johnny Evers 400.00 800.00
4 Arthur Hoffman 150.00 300.00
5 John Kling 200.00 400.00
6 Carl Lundgren 150.00 300.00
7 Pat Moran 200.00 400.00
8 Orvall Overall 200.00 400.00
9 Jack Pfiester 150.00 300.00
10 Ed Reulbach 200.00 400.00
11 Frank Schulte 200.00 400.00
12 Jimmy Sheckard 150.00 300.00
13 James Slagle 150.00 300.00
14 Harry Steinfeldt 150.00 300.00
15 Jack Taylor 150.00 300.00
16 Joe Tinker 400.00 800.00

1908 Cubs Postcards

An unknown Chicago Publisher using a logo of a dollar sign inside a shield produced an attractive set of Cubs players on a gray background in 1908. The known cards in this set are listed below any additions to this checklist are appreciated.

COMPLETE SET (4) 400.00 800.00
1 Frank Chance 200.00 400.00
2 Artie Hoffman 75.00 150.00
3 John Kling 100.00 200.00
4 Harry Steinfeldt 100.00 200.00

1930 Cubs Blue Ribbon Malt

These photographs, which measure 6 1/4" by 8 3/4" and feature fascimile autographs are surrounded by plain white borders. Both Chicago teams were produced; howeverm we have seperated the two teams included in this set. The cards have black backs and are therefore sequenced in alphabetical order. It is possible that other cards may be in the set so all additional information is appreciated. These cards were sent out in special envelopes which included an advertising drawing of Charlie Grimm.

COMPLETE SET 900.00 1800.00
1 Clyde Beck 40.00 80.00
2 Les Bell 40.00 80.00
3 Clarence Blair 40.00 80.00
4 Fred Blake 40.00 80.00
5 Jimmy Burke CO 40.00 80.00
6 Guy Bush 40.00 80.00
7 Hal Carlson 40.00 80.00
8 Kiki Cuyler 75.00 150.00
9 Woody English 50.00 100.00
10 Charlie Grimm 60.00 120.00
11 Gabby Hartnett 100.00 200.00
12 Cliff Heathcote 40.00 80.00
13 Rogers Hornsby 125.00 250.00
14 Pat Malone 40.00 80.00
15 Joe McCarthy MG 75.00 150.00
16 Malcolm Moss 40.00 80.00
17 Lynn Nelson 40.00 80.00
18 Bob Osborn 40.00 80.00
19 Bobby Smith 40.00 80.00
19 Charlie Root 50.00 100.00
20 Ray Schalk CO 75.00 150.00
21 John Schulte 40.00 80.00
22 Al Shealy 40.00 80.00
23 Riggs Stephenson 60.00 120.00
24 Dan Taylor 40.00 80.00
25 Zach Taylor 40.00 80.00
26 Charles Tolson 40.00 80.00
27 Hal Totten ANN 40.00 80.00
28 Hack Wilson 75.00 150.00

1930 Cubs Team Issue

This 21-card set of the Chicago Cubs features black-and-white player photos with facsimile autographs. The backs are blank. The cards are all 3 1/2" high but have various widths ranging from 1 3/8" to 3". The cards are unnumbered and checklisted below in alphabetical order. A few uncut sheets of this set have survivied.

COMPLETE SET (21) 250.00 500.00
1 Clyde Beck 10.00 25.00
2 Les Bell 10.00 25.00
3 Clarence Blair 10.00 25.00
4 John Blake 10.00 25.00
5 Woody English 15.00 40.00
6 Doc Farrell 10.00 25.00
7 Gabby Hartnett 40.00 80.00
8 Clifton Heathcote 10.00 25.00
9 Rogers Hornsby 60.00 120.00
10 George Kelly 20.00 50.00
11 Pat Malone 10.00 25.00
12 Joe McCarthy MG 20.00 50.00
13 Bob Osborn 10.00 25.00
14 Jesse Petty 10.00 25.00
15 Charlie Root 15.00 40.00
16 Ray Schalk CO 20.00 50.00
17 John Schulte 10.00 25.00
18 Al Shealy 10.00 25.00
19 Zack Taylor 10.00 25.00
20 Bud Teachout 10.00 25.00
21 Hack Wilson 30.00 60.00

1931 Cubs Team Issue

These 31 photos feature players and club personnel involved with the 1931 Chicago Cubs. They measure approximately 6" by 9 1/2" and all the photos have a facsimile autograph as well. All of this is surrounded by white borders. The backs are black and we have sequenced the photos in alphabetical order.

COMPLETE SET (31) 350.00 700.00
1 Ed Baecht 10.00 25.00
2 Clyde Beck 10.00 25.00
3 Les Bell 10.00 25.00
4 Clarence Blair 10.00 25.00
5 Sheriff Blake 15.00 40.00
6 Guy Bush 15.00 40.00
7 KiKi Cuyler 10.00 25.00
8 Margaret Donahue 15.00 40.00
9 Woody English 20.00 50.00
10 Earl Grace 30.00 60.00
11 Charlie Grimm 10.00 25.00
12 Gabby Hartnett 60.00 120.00
13 Rollie Hemsley 15.00 40.00
14 Rogers Hornsby 10.00 25.00
15 Billy Jurges 10.00 25.00
16 Bob Lewis TS 10.00 25.00
17 Andy Lotshaw TR 10.00 25.00
18 Pat Malone 10.00 25.00
19 Jakie May 15.00 40.00
20 John Moore 20.00 50.00
21 Charley O'Leary 10.00 25.00
22 Charlie Root 10.00 25.00
23 Ray Schalk 20.00 50.00
24 John Seys FO 10.00 25.00
25 Bob Smith 10.00 25.00
26 Riggs Stephenson 10.00 25.00
27 Les Sweetland 10.00 25.00
28 Dan Taylor 15.00 40.00
29 Zack Taylor 10.00 25.00
30 Bud Teachout
31 William Veeck PRES 30.00 60.00
32 W.M. Walker FO 15.00 40.00
33 Lon Warneke 15.00 40.00
34 Hack Wilson
35 Phil Wrigley FO
36 William Wrigley OWN

1932 Cubs Denby Postcards

* USE $250 FOR COMMONS* This eight-card postcard set features members of the 1932 Chicago Cubs. The borderless fronts feature a player's photo with a facsimile autograph while the backs promote the use of Denby Cigars. Since these postcards are unnumbered, we have sequenced them in alphabetical order.

1932 Cubs Team Issue

These 35 photos feature members of the 1932 Chicago Cubs. The photos are shot against a black background and feature a player photo and a facsimile signature. The cards measure approximately 6" by 9" are unnumbered and we have sequenced them in alphabetical order. This set was issued late in the season as Mark Koenig who only spent the last part of the season with the Cubs was included.

COMPLETE SET (35) 200.00 450.00
1 Guy Bush 10.00 25.00
2 Gilly Campbell
3 Red Corriden CO 6.00 15.00
4 Kiki Cuyler 30.00 60.00
5 Frank Demaree 6.00 15.00
6 Margaret Donahue 6.00 15.00
7 Woody English 10.00 25.00
8 Burleigh Grimes 30.00 60.00
9 Charlie Grimm 12.50 30.00
10 Marv Gudat 6.00 15.00
11 Stanley Hack 10.00 25.00
12 Gabby Hartnett 40.00 80.00
13 Rollie Helmsley 6.00 15.00
14 Billy Herman 30.00 60.00
15 Leroy Herrmann 6.00 15.00
16 Billy Jurges 10.00 25.00
17 Mark Koenig 10.00 25.00
18 Bob Lewis 6.00 15.00
19 Pat Malone 6.00 15.00
20 Jake May 6.00 15.00
21 Johnny Moore 6.00 15.00
22 Charley O'Leary CO 6.00 15.00
23 Lance Richbourg 6.00 15.00
24 Charlie Root 10.00 25.00
25 John Seys 6.00 15.00
26 Bob Smith 6.00 15.00
27 Riggs Stephenson 12.50 30.00
28 Harry Taylor
29 Zack Taylor 6.00 15.00
30 Bud Tinning 6.00 15.00
31 William Veeck GM 10.00 25.00
32 W.M. Walker 6.00 15.00
33 Lon Warneke 10.00 25.00
34 Phil Wrigley 10.00 25.00
35 William Wrigley OWN 10.00 25.00

1933 Cubs Team Issue

1 Guy Bush
2 Gilly Campbell
3 Red Corriden
4 Kiki Cuyler
5 Frank Demaree
6 Margaret Donahue
7 Woody English
8 Burleigh Grimes
9 Charlie Grimm
10 Gabby Hartnett
11 Harvey Hendrick
12 Roy Henshaw
13 Babe Herman
14 Billy Herman
15 Billy Jurges
16 Mark Koenig
17 Bob Lewis
18 Pat Malone
19 Charlie Root
20 John Seys
21 Riggs Stephenson
22 John Schulte
23 Zack Taylor
24 Bud Tinning
25 William Veeck
26 W.M. Walker
27 Lon Warneke
28 Phil Wrigley
29 William Wrigley

1936 Cubs Team Issue

This 32-card set of the Chicago Cubs measures approximately 6" by 9" and is printed on black paper with a facimile autograph in white. The backs are blank. The cards are unnumbered and checklisted below in alphabetical order.

COMPLETE SET (32) 225.00 450.00
1 Clay Bryant 6.00 15.00
2 Tex Carleton 6.00 15.00
3 Phil Cavarretta 12.50 30.00
4 John Corriden CO 6.00 15.00
5 Frank Demaree 6.00 15.00
6 Margaret Donahue 6.00 15.00
7 Woody English 6.00 15.00
8 Larry French 8.00 20.00
9 Augie Galan 8.00 20.00
10 Johnny Gill 6.00 15.00
11 Charlie Grimm MG 10.00 25.00
12 Stanley Hack 12.50 30.00
13 Leo Gabby Hartnett 20.00 50.00
14 Roy Henshaw 6.00 15.00
15 Billy Herman 20.00 50.00
16 Roy Johnson 6.00 15.00
17 Bill Jurges 10.00 25.00
18 Chuck Klein 20.00 50.00
19 Fabian Kowalick 6.00 15.00
20 Bill Lee 6.00 15.00
21 Robert Lewis TS 6.00 15.00
22 Gene Lillard 6.00 15.00
23 Andy Lotshaw TR 6.00 15.00
24 Jim O'Dea 6.00 15.00
25 Charlie Root 10.00 25.00
26 John Seys 6.00 15.00
27 Clyde Shoun 6.00 15.00
28 Tuck Stainback 6.00 15.00
29 Riggs Stephenson 12.50 30.00
30 Lon Warneke 6.00 15.00
31 Charles Weber 6.00 15.00
32 Wrigley Field 30.00 60.00

1939 Cubs Team Issue

This set of the Chicago Cubs measures approximately 6 1/2" by 9". The black and white photos display fascimile autographs. The backs are blank. The cards are unnumbered and are checklisted below in alphabetical order.

COMPLETE SET (25)	200.00	400.00
1 Dick Bartell	10.00	25.00
2 Clay Bryant	6.00	15.00
3 Phil Cavarretta	10.00	25.00
4 John Corriden	6.00	15.00
5 Dizzy Dean	40.00	80.00
6 Larry French	8.00	20.00
7 Augie Galan	10.00	25.00
8 Bob Garbark	6.00	15.00
9 Jim Gleeson	6.00	15.00
10 Stanley Hack	10.00	25.00
11 Leo Hartnett	30.00	60.00
12 Billy Herman	30.00	60.00
13 Roy Johnson	6.00	15.00
14 Bill Lee	8.00	20.00
15 Hank Lieber	6.00	15.00
16 Gene Lillard	6.00	15.00
17 Gus Mancuso	6.00	15.00
18 Bobby Mattick	8.00	20.00
19 Vance Page	6.00	15.00
20 Claude Passeau	10.00	25.00
21 Carl Reynolds	6.00	15.00
22 Charlie Root	10.00	25.00
23 Glen Rip Russell	6.00	15.00
24 Jack Russell	6.00	15.00
25 E. Whitehill	6.00	15.00

1941 Cubs Team Issue

These photos measure approximately 6 1/2" by 9". They feature members of the 1941 Chicago Cubs. The set is dated by the appearence of Greek George. The backs are blank and we have sequenced them in alphabetical order. This set was issued twice so there are more than the normal amount of players in this set due to roster manipluations during the season.

COMPLETE SET (25)	125.00	250.00
1 Phil Cavarretta	10.00	25.00
2 Dom Dallessandro	5.00	12.00
3 Paul Erickson	5.00	12.00
4 Larry French	8.00	20.00
5 Augie Galan	8.00	20.00
6 Greek George	5.00	12.00
7 Charlie Gilbert	5.00	12.00
8 Stan Hack	8.00	20.00
9 Johnny Hudson	5.00	12.00
10 Bill Lee	8.00	20.00
11 Hank Leiber	5.00	12.00
12 Clyde McCullough	5.00	12.00
13 Jake Mooty	5.00	12.00
14 Bill Myers	5.00	12.00
15 Bill Nicholson	10.00	25.00
16 Lou Novikoff	6.00	15.00
17 Vern Olsen	5.00	12.00
18 Vance Page	5.00	12.00
19 Claude Passeau	8.00	20.00
20 Tot Pressnell	5.00	12.00
21 Charlie Root	8.00	20.00
22 Bob Scheffing	5.00	12.00
23 Lou Stringer	5.00	12.00
24 Bob Sturgeon	5.00	12.00
25 Cubs Staff Dick Spalding CO Jimmie Wilson CO	15.00	40.00

1942 Cubs Team Issue

These 25 photos were issued by the Chicago Cubs. The black and white blank back photos measure 6 1/2" by 9". Since they are unnumbered we have sequenced them in alphabetical order.

COMPLETE SET (25)	125.00	250.00
1 Hiram Bithorn	5.00	12.00
2 Phil Cavarretta	8.00	20.00
3 Dom Dallessandro	5.00	12.00
4 Paul Erickson	5.00	12.00
5 Bill Fleming	5.00	12.00
6 Charlie Gilbert	5.00	12.00
7 Stanley Hack	8.00	20.00
8 Edward Hanyzewski	5.00	12.00
9 Chico Hernandez	5.00	12.00
10 Bill Lee	6.00	15.00
11 Peanuts Lowrey	5.00	12.00
12 Clyde McCullough	5.00	12.00
13 Jake Mooty	5.00	12.00
14 Lennie Merullo	5.00	12.00
15 Bill Nicholson	10.00	25.00
16 Louie Novikoff	5.00	12.00
17 Vern Olsen	5.00	12.00
18 Claude Passeau	8.00	20.00
19 Tot Pressnell	5.00	12.00
20 Glen Russell	5.00	12.00
21 Bob Scheffing	5.00	12.00
22 John Schmitz	5.00	12.00
23 Lou Stringer	5.00	12.00
24 Bob Sturgeon	5.00	12.00
25 Coaches Card Ki Ki Cuyler Jimmie Wilson Dick Sp	15.00	40.00

1943 Cubs Team Issue

This set of photographs measure approximately 6 1/2" by 9". They feature members of the 1943 Chicago Cubs. The black and white photos also feature fascimile autographs. The backs are blank and we have sequenced this set in alphabetical order.

COMPLETE SET (24)	125.00	250.00
1 Dick Barrett	5.00	12.00
2 Heinz Becker	5.00	12.00
3 Hi Bithorn	5.00	12.00
4 Phil Cavarretta	10.00	25.00
5 Dom Dallessandro	5.00	12.00
6 Paul Derringer	8.00	20.00
7 Paul Erickson	5.00	12.00
8 Bill Fleming	5.00	12.00
9 Stan Hack	8.00	20.00
10 Ed Hanyzewski	5.00	12.00
11 Chico Hernandez	5.00	12.00
12 Bill Lee	5.00	12.00
13 Peanuts Lowery	6.00	15.00
14 Stu Martin	5.00	12.00
15 Clyde McCullough	5.00	12.00
16 Lennie Merullo	5.00	12.00
17 Bill Nicholson	10.00	25.00
18 Lou Novikoff	5.00	12.00
19 Claude Passeau	8.00	20.00
20 Ray Prim	5.00	12.00
21 Eddie Stanky	10.00	25.00
22 Al Todd	5.00	12.00
23 Lon Warneke	8.00	20.00
24 Hank Wyse	5.00	12.00
25 Kiki Cuyler CO Jimmie Wilson CO Dick Spalding CO	15.00	40.00

1944 Cubs Team Issue

These 1944 Chicago Cub team photos are printed on thin paper stock and measure approximately 6" by 8 1/2". The photos feature a black and white head and shoulders shot, with white borders and the player's autograph inscribed across the picture. The backs are blank. The photos are unnumbered and checklisted below in alphabetical order.

COMPLETE SET (25)	150.00	300.00
1 Heinz Becker	6.00	15.00
2 John Burrows	6.00	15.00
3 Phil Cavarretta	10.00	25.00
4 Dom Dallessandro	6.00	15.00
6 Paul Derringer	10.00	25.00
7 Roy Easterwood	6.00	15.00
8 Paul Erickson	6.00	15.00
9 Bill Fleming	6.00	15.00
10 Jimmie Foxx	30.00	60.00
11 Ival Goodman	6.00	15.00
12 Edward Hanyzewski	6.00	15.00
13 William Holm	6.00	15.00
14 Don Johnson	6.00	15.00
15 Garth Mann	6.00	15.00
16 Lennie Merullo	6.00	15.00
17 John Miklos	6.00	15.00
18 Bill Nicholson	10.00	25.00
19 Lou Novikoff	8.00	20.00
20 Andy Pafko	10.00	25.00
21 Eddie Sauer	6.00	15.00
22 William Schuster	6.00	15.00
23 Eddie Stanky	12.50	30.00
24 Hy Vandenberg	6.00	15.00
25 Hank Wyse	6.00	15.00
26 Tony York	6.00	15.00

1950 Cubs Greats Brace

These 18 photos were issued by noted Chicago photographer George Brace and honored some of the leading players in Cub history. The fronts have a photo of the player along with how long they were in the majors and what years they spent with the Cubs. The backs are blank so we have sequenced this set in alphabetical order.

COMPLETE SET (18)	75.00	150.00
1 Grover C. Alexander	6.00	12.00
2 Cap Anson	6.00	12.00
3 Mordecai Browne	6.00	12.00
4 Frank Chance	6.00	12.00
5 John Evers	6.00	12.00
6 Charlie Grimm	5.00	10.00
7 Stan Hack	4.00	8.00
8 Gabby Hartnett	6.00	12.00
9 Billy Herman	6.00	12.00
10 Charlie Hollocher	3.00	6.00
11 Billy Jurges	4.00	8.00
12 Johnny Kling	3.00	6.00
13 Joe McCarthy MG	5.00	10.00
14 Ed Reulbach	4.00	8.00
15 Albert Spalding	6.00	12.00
16 Joe Tinker	6.00	12.00
17 Hippo Vaughn	3.00	6.00
18 Hack Wilson	6.00	12.00

1952 Cubs Ben Bey

These 8" by 11" photos were issued by Ben Bey and featured members of the Chicago Cubs. The front has a player photo as well as a fascimile signature. The back has the notation; "courtesy of Ben Bey, Lucky Fan WBKB Chicago." Since the photos are unnumbered we have sequenced them in alphabetical order. It is possible that there are more photos in this set so please send any additions you might have.

COMPLETE SET (26)	60.00	120.00
1 Frank Baumholtz	2.50	5.00
2 Bob Borkowski	2.50	5.00
3 Smoky Burgess	3.00	6.00
4 Phil Cavaretta	4.00	8.00
5 Chuck Connors	5.00	10.00
6 Jack Cusick	2.50	5.00
7 Bruce Edwards	2.50	5.00
8 Dee Fondy	2.50	5.00
9 Joe Hatten	2.50	5.00
10 Gene Hermanski	2.50	5.00
11 Frank Hiller	2.50	5.00
12 Ransom Jackson	2.50	5.00
13 Hal Jeffcoat	2.50	5.00
14 Bob Kelly	2.50	5.00
15 John Klippstein	2.50	5.00
16 Dutch Leonard	2.50	5.00
17 Turk Lown	2.50	5.00
18 Cal McLish	2.50	5.00
19 Eddie Miksis	2.50	5.00
20 Paul Minner	2.50	5.00
21 Bob Ramazzotti	2.50	5.00
22 Bob Rush	2.50	5.00
23 Hank Sauer	5.00	10.00
24 Bob Schultz	2.50	5.00
25 Bill Serena	2.50	5.00
26 Roy Smalley	2.50	5.00

1960 Cubs Jay Publishing

This 12-card set of the Chicago Cubs measures approximately 5" by 7" and features black-and-white player photos in a white border. These cards were packaged 12 to a packet. The backs are blank. The cards are unnumbered and checklisted below in alphabetical order.

COMPLETE SET (12)	15.00	40.00
1 George Altman	.75	2.00
2 Bob Anderson	.75	2.00
3 Richie Ashburn	2.50	6.00
4 Ernie Banks	5.00	12.00
5 Moe Drabowsky	.75	2.00
6 Don Elston	.75	2.00
7 Glen Hobbie	.75	2.00
8 Dale Long	.75	2.00
9 Walt Moryn	.75	2.00
10 Sam Taylor	.75	2.00
11 Tony Taylor	.75	2.00
12 Frank Thomas	1.25	3.00

1961 Cubs Jay Publishing

This 12-card set of the Chicago Cubs measures approximately 5" by 7". The fronts feature black-and-white posed player photos with the player's and team name printed below in the white border. These cards were packaged 12 in a packet. The backs are blank. The cards are unnumbered and checklisted below in alphabetical order. Ron Santo appears in his Rookie Card year.

COMPLETE SET	8.00	20.00
1 George Altman	.75	2.00
2 Bob Anderson	.75	2.00
3 Richie Ashburn	2.50	6.00
4 Ernie Banks	5.00	12.00
5 Ed Bouchee	.75	2.00
6 Dick Ellsworth	.75	2.00
7 Don Elston	.75	2.00
8 Glen Hobbie	.75	2.00
9 Jerry Kindall	.75	2.00
10 Ron Santo	2.50	6.00
11 Moe Thacker	.75	2.00
12 Don Zimmer	1.50	4.00

1962 Cubs Jay Publishing

This 12-card set of the Chicago Cubs measures approximately 5" by 7". The fronts feature black-and-white posed player photos with the player's and team name printed below in the white border. These cards were packaged 12 in a packet. The backs are blank. The cards are unnumbered and checklisted below in alphabetical order.

COMPLETE SET (12)	15.00	40.00
1 George Altman	.75	2.00
2 Bob Anderson	.75	2.00
3 Ernie Banks	5.00	12.00
4 Don Cardwell	.75	2.00
5 Jack Curtis	.75	2.00
6 Don Elston	.75	2.00
7 Glen Hobbie	.75	2.00
8 Ken Hubbs	2.00	5.00
9 Ron Santo	2.00	5.00
10 Barney Schultz	.75	2.00
11 Sam Taylor	.75	2.00
12 Billy Williams	3.00	8.00

1963 Cubs Jay Publishing

This 12-card set of the Chicago Cubs measures approximately 5" by 7". The fronts feature black-and-white posed player photos with the player's and team name printed below in the white border. These cards were packaged 12 in a packet. The backs are blank. The cards are unnumbered and checklisted below in alphabetical order.

COMPLETE SET (12)	15.00	40.00
1 Ernie Banks	5.00	12.00
2 Dick Bertell	.75	2.00
3 Lou Brock	5.00	12.00
4 Bob Buhl	.75	2.00
5 Dick Ellsworth	.75	2.00
6 Glen Hobbie	.75	2.00
7 Larry Jackson	.75	2.00
8 Bob Kennedy CO	.75	2.00
9 Lindy McDaniel	.75	2.00
10 Andre Rodgers	.75	2.00
11 Ron Santo	2.00	5.00
12 Billy Williams	3.00	8.00

1964 Cubs Jay Publishing

This 12-card set of the Chicago Cubs measures approximately 5" by 7". The fronts feature black-and-white posed player photos with the player's and team name printed below in the white border. These cards were packaged 12 in a packet. The backs are blank. The cards are unnumbered and checklisted below in alphabetical order.

COMPLETE SET (12)	15.00	40.00
1 Ernie Banks	5.00	12.00
2 Dick Bertell	.75	2.00
3 Lou Brock	4.00	10.00
4 Bob Buhl	.75	2.00
5 Don Elston	.75	2.00
6 Ken Hubbs	2.00	5.00
7 Larry Jackson	.75	2.00
8 Don Landrum	.75	2.00
9 Lindy McDaniel	.75	2.00
10 Andre Rodgers	.75	2.00
11 Ron Santo	2.00	5.00
12 Billy Williams	3.00	8.00

1965 Cubs Announcers

Issued to promote the announcers of the 1965 Chicago Cubs. These two postcards feature both announcers.

COMPLETE SET	6.00	15.00
1 Lou Boudreau Vince Lloyd Color photo in the dugout	2.00	5.00
2 Lou Bourdreau Vince Lloyd Black and White Photo, on the field	4.00	10.00

1965 Cubs Jay Publishing

This 12-card set of the Chicago Cubs measures approximately 5" by 7". The fronts feature black-and-white posed player photos with the player's and team name printed below in the white border. These cards were packaged 12 in a packet. The backs are blank. The cards are unnumbered and checklisted below in alphabetical order.

COMPLETE SET (12)	15.00	40.00
1 George Altman	.75	2.00
2 Ernie Banks	5.00	12.00
3 Dick Bertell	.75	2.00
4 Ernie Broglio	.75	2.00
5 Bob Buhl	.75	2.00
6 Lou Burdette	1.25	3.00
7 Dick Ellsworth	.75	2.00
8 Larry Jackson	.75	2.00
9 Bob Kennedy CO	.75	2.00
10 Ron Santo	2.00	5.00
11 Jim Stewart	.75	2.00
12 Billy Williams	3.00	8.00

1966 Cubs Team Issue

These 12 cards feature members of the 1966 Chicago Cubs, who by finishing last, enabled the New York Mets to finally not finish in the cellar. The cards are unnumbered and we have sequenced them in alphabetical order.

COMPLETE SET (12)	15.00	40.00
1 Ted Abernathy	.75	2.00
2 George Altman	1.25	3.00
3 Ernie Banks	4.00	10.00
4 Glenn Beckert	1.25	3.00
5 Ernie Broglio	.75	2.00
6 Leo Durocher	2.00	5.00
7 Dick Ellsworth	.75	2.00
8 Larry Jackson	.75	2.00
9 Chris Krug	.75	2.00
10 Harvey Kuenn	1.25	3.00
11 Ron Santo	2.00	5.00
12 Billy Williams	2.00	5.00

1968 Cubs Pro's Pizza

This 12-card set measures 4 3/4: in diameter and featured members of the Chicago Cubs. Only the Cubs players are included in this listing.

COMPLETE SET (12)	1250.00	2500.00
1 Joe Amalfitano	100.00	200.00
2 Ernie Banks	350.00	700.00
3 Glenn Beckert	125.00	250.00
4 John Boccabella	100.00	200.00
5 Bill Hands	100.00	200.00
6 Ken Holtzman	100.00	200.00
7 Randy Hundley	100.00	200.00
8 Fergie Jenkins	200.00	400.00
9 Don Kessinger	150.00	300.00
10 Adolfo Phillips	100.00	200.00
11 Ron Santo	300.00	600.00
12 Billy Williams	200.00	400.00

1969 Cubs Bumper Stickers

This six-sticker set of the Chicago Cubs measures approximately 7 7/8" by 4" and features color player head photos printed at the end of a baseball bat drawing. Two versions of this set were issued with either "Cub Power" or "Dunkin Donuts" printed inside a ball that looked as if it was being hit by the bat. The stickers are unnumbered and checklisted below in alphabetical order.

COMPLETE SET (6)	50.00	100.00
1 Ernie Banks	15.00	40.00
2 Glenn Beckert	5.00	12.00
3 Randy Hundley	5.00	12.00
4 Don Kessinger	5.00	12.00
5 Ron Santo	10.00	25.00
6 Billy Williams	10.00	25.00

1969 Cubs Jewel Tea

This 20-card set of the Chicago Cubs measures approximately 6" by 9" and were given away over a five week period in 1969. The white-bordered fronts feature color player action and posed photos with a facsimile autograph across the picture. The backs are blank. The cards are unnumbered and checklisted below in alphabetical order.

COMPLETE SET (20)	20.00	50.00
1 Ted Abernathy	.60	1.50
2 Hank Aguirre	.60	1.50
3 Ernie Banks	4.00	10.00
4 Glenn Beckert	.75	2.00
5 Bill Hands	.60	1.50
6 Jim Hickman	.60	1.50
7 Kenny Holtzman	.75	2.00
8 Randy Hundley	.75	2.00
9 Fergie Jenkins	3.00	8.00
10 Don Kessinger	1.00	2.50
11 Rich Nye	.60	1.50
12 Paul Popovich	.60	1.50
13 Jim Qualls	.60	1.50
14 Phil Regan	.60	1.50
15 Ron Santo	1.25	3.00
16 Dick Selma	.60	1.50
17 Willie Smith	.60	1.50
18 Al Spangler	.60	1.50
19 Billy Williams	2.50	6.00
20 Don Young	.60	1.50

1969 Cubs Photos

These photos feature members of the 1969 Chicago Cubs, best known as the team which lost a huge lead so the Miracle Mets could win the pennant. These photos are unnumbered and we have sequenced them in alphabetical order.

COMPLETE SET (12)	12.50	30.00
1 Ted Abernathy	.60	1.50
2 Ernie Banks	3.00	8.00
3 Glenn Beckert	.60	1.50
4 Leo Durocher MG	1.25	3.00
5 Ken Holtzman	.75	2.00
6 Randy Hundley	.75	2.00
7 Ferguson Jenkins	2.00	5.00
8 Don Kessinger	1.00	2.50
9 Phil Regan	.60	1.50
10 Ron Santo	1.25	3.00
11 Al Spangler	.60	1.50
12 Billy Williams	2.00	5.00

1969 Cubs Team Issue Color

This 10-card set of the Chicago Cubs measures approximately 7" by 8 3/4" with the fronts featuring white-bordered color player photos. The player's name and team is printed in black in the white margin below the picture. The backs are blank. The cards are unnumbered and checklisted below in alphabetical order.

COMPLETE SET	12.50	30.00
1 Ernie Banks	3.00	8.00
2 Glenn Beckert	.60	1.50
3 Ken Holtzman	.75	2.00
4 Randy Hundley	1.00	2.50
5 Ferguson Jenkins	2.00	5.00
6 Don Kessinger	1.00	2.50
7 Phil Regan	.60	1.50
8 Ron Santo	1.25	3.00
9 Willie Smith	.60	1.50
10 Billy Williams	2.00	5.00

1970 Cubs Dunkin Donuts

This set of six bumper stickers (apparently commemorating the Cubs near-miss in 1969) was produced and distributed by Dunkin Donuts. The stickers are approximately 4 1/16" by 8 1/16" and are in color. Each sticker features a facsimile autograph in the upper left hand corner. The stickers are unnumbered and are listed below in alphabetical order. according to the player's name.

COMPLETE SET (6)	40.00	80.00
1 Ernie Banks	15.00	40.00
2 Glenn Beckert	1.25	3.00
3 Randy Hundley	1.25	3.00
4 Don Kessinger	8.00	20.00
5 Ron Santo	10.00	25.00
6 Billy Williams	6.00	15.00

1972 Cubs Chi-Foursome

These 11" by 14" drawings feature Chicago Cubs players. The attractive color drawings also have a facimilie signature. The backs are blank and we have sequenced this set in alphabetical order.

COMPLETE SET (8)	6.00	15.00
1 Ernie Banks	2.00	5.00
2 Glenn Beckert	.40	1.00
3 Fergie Jenkins	1.00	2.50
4 Don Kessinger	.40	1.00
5 Milt Pappas	.40	1.00
6 Joe Pepitone	.75	2.00
7 Ron Santo	1.00	2.50
8 Billy Williams	1.00	2.50

1972 Cubs Team Issue

These 12 photos feature members of the 1972 Chicago Cubs. The photos measure approximately 4 1/4" by 7". The black and white photos are surrounded by white borders and feature a facsimile autograph. The backs are blank and we have sequenced this set in alphabetical order.

COMPLETE SET (12)	12.50	30.00
1 Ernie Banks CO	2.50	6.00
2 Glenn Beckert	.75	2.00
3 Bill Hands	.60	1.50
4 Jim Hickman	.60	1.50
5 Randy Hundley	.75	2.00
6 Fergie Jenkins	2.00	5.00
7 Don Kessinger	.75	2.00
8 Rick Monday	1.00	2.50
9 Milt Pappas	.60	1.50
10 Joe Pepitone	.75	2.00
11 Ron Santo	1.25	3.00
12 Billy Williams	2.00	5.00

1973 Cubs Jewel

These blank-backed photos, which measure approximately 6" by 9", feature members of the 1973 Chicago Cubs. These fronts have white borders which surround a full-color player portrait as well as a fascimile autograph. These cards are unnumbered, so we have sequenced them in alphabetical order.

COMPLETE SET	6.00	15.00
1 Jack Aker	.20	.50
2 Glenn Beckert	.40	1.00
3 Jose Cardenal	.40	1.00
4 Carmen Fanzone	.20	.50
5 Jim Hickman	.20	.50
6 Burt Hooton	.20	.50
7 Randy Hundley	.40	1.00
8 Fergie Jenkins	1.25	3.00
9 Don Kessinger	.40	1.00
10 Bob Locker	.20	.50
11 Rick Monday	.40	1.00
12 Milt Pappas	.40	1.00
13 Rick Reuschel	.75	2.00
14 Ken Rudolph	.20	.50
15 Ron Santo	1.00	2.50
16 Billy Williams	1.25	3.00

1974 Cubs 1938 Bra-Mac

These 29 photos, which measure 3 1/2" by 5" feature members of the 1938 Chicago Cubs and were issued by Bra-Mac using negatives they had in their massive photo file.

COMPLETE SET	10.00	25.00
1 Phil Cavaretta	.60	1.50
2 Bob Garbark	.20	.50
3 Jack Russell	.20	.50
4 Tony Lazzeri	.75	2.00
5 Dizzy Dean	1.25	3.00
6 Coaker Triplett	.20	.50
7 Ken O'Dea	.20	.50
8 Larry French	.40	1.00
9 Stan Hack	.40	1.00
10 Gabby Hartnett	.75	2.00
11 Bill Lee	.60	1.50
12 Kirby Higbe	.40	1.00
13 Bobby Mattick	.40	1.00
14 Tex Carleton	.20	.50
15 Charlie Root	.40	1.00
16 Bob Logan	.20	.50
17 Steve Mesner	.20	.50
18 Newt Kimball	.20	.50
19 Clay Bryant	.20	.50
20 Rip Collins	.40	1.00
21 Augie Galan	.40	1.00
22 Frank Demaree	.20	.50
23 Al Epperly	.20	.50
24 Billy Herman	.75	2.00
25 Jim Asbell	.20	.50
26 Carl Reynolds	.20	.50
27 Vance Page	.20	.50
28 Billy Jurges	.40	1.00
29 Joe Marty	.20	.50

1974 Cubs Team Issue

These blank-backed photos, which measure approximately 7" by 9", feature members of the 1974 Chicago Cubs. The fronts have full color photos surrounded by white borders with the players name and team on the bottom. Since these photos are unnumbered, we have sequenced them in alphabetical order.

COMPLETE SET	3.00	8.00
1 Ray Burris	.20	.50
2 Jose Cardenal	.30	.75
3 Carmen Fanzone	.20	.50
4 Vic Harris	.20	.50
5 Burt Hooton UER Spelled Houton	.30	.75
6 Don Kessinger	.20	.50
7 Bill Madlock	.60	1.50
8 George Mitterwald	.20	.50
9 Rick Monday	.30	.75
10 Jerry Morales	.20	.50
11 Steve Stone	.30	.75
12 Billy Williams	.75	2.00

1976 Cubs TCMA 1938

These cards were issued by TCMA and feature members of the pennant winning 1938 Chicago Cubs. These cards are unnumbered and we have sequenced them in alphabetical order.

COMPLETE SET (33)	8.00	20.00
1 Jim Asbell	.20	.50
2 Clay Bryant	.20	.50
3 Tex Carleton	.20	.50
4 Phil Cavaretta	.40	1.00
5 Ripper Collins	.20	.50
6 Red Corriden	.20	.50
7 Dizzy Dean	1.25	3.00
8 Frank Demaree	.20	.50
9 Al Epperly	.20	.50
10 Larry French	.30	.75
11 Augie Galan	.30	.75
12 Bob Garbark	.20	.50
13 Charlie Grimm MG	.60	1.50
14 Stan Hack	.40	1.00
15 Gabby Hartnett P MG	.75	2.00
16 Billy Herman	.75	2.00
17 Kirby Higbe	.30	.75
18 Roy Johnson CO	.20	.50
19 Billy Jurges	.30	.75
20 Newt Kimball	.20	.50
21 Tony Lazzeri	.75	2.00
22 Bill Lee	.20	.50
23 Bob Logan	.20	.50
24 Joe Marty	.20	.50
25 Bobby Mattick	.30	.75
26 Steve Mesner	.20	.50
27 Ken O'Dea	.20	.50
28 Vance Page	.20	.50
29 Carl Reynolds	.20	.50
30 Charlie Root	.30	.75
31 Jack Russell	.20	.50
32 Coaker Triplett	.20	.50
33 Chicago Cub Unidentified Player	.20	.50

1976 Cubs Tribune

These 26 cards were issued by the Chicago Tribune and features the members of the 1976 Cubs. They are unnumbered and we have sequenced them in alphabetical order. This set features a "pre-rookie card" of Hall of Famer Bruce Sutter.

COMPLETE SET	10.00	25.00
1 Larry Biittner	.40	1.00
2 Bill Bonham	.40	1.00
3 Pete Broberg	.40	1.00
4 Ray Burris	.40	1.00
5 Jose Cardenal	.60	1.50
6 Gene Clines	.40	1.00
7 Bobby Darwin	.40	1.00
8 Ivan DeJesus	.40	1.00
9 Herman Franks MG	.40	1.00
10 Greg Gross	.40	1.00
11 Willie Hernandez	1.00	2.50
12 Mick Kelleher	.40	1.00
13 Mike Krukow	.40	1.00
14 George Mitterwald	.40	1.00
15 Donnie Moore	.40	1.00
16 Jerry Morales	.40	1.00
17 Bobby Murcer	.75	2.00
18 Steve Ontiveros	.40	1.00
19 Steve Renko	.40	1.00
20 Rick Reuschel	.75	2.00
21 Dave Rosello	.40	1.00
22 Bruce Sutter	4.00	10.00
23 Steve Swisher	.40	1.00
24 Jim Todd	.40	1.00
25 Manny Trillo	.60	1.50
26 Joe Wallis	.40	1.00

1977 Cubs All-Time TCMA

This 13-card set features black-and-white photos with wide white and thin black borders of Chicago Cubs players considered to be the best at their respective positions.The backs carry the checklist for the set. The cards are unnumbered and checklisted below in alphabetical order.

COMPLETE SET (13)	3.00	8.00
1 Ernie Banks	.60	1.50
2 Kiki Cuyler	.30	.75
3 Larry French	.20	.50
4 Charlie Grimm	.20	.50
5 Charlie Grimm MG	.20	.50
6 Gabby Hartnett	.30	.75
7 Billy Herman	.30	.75
8 Rogers Hornsby	.60	1.50
9 Emil Kush	.20	.50
10 Charlie Root	.20	.50
11 Ron Santo	.40	1.00
12 Billy Williams	.40	1.00
13 Hack Wilson	.30	.75

1977 Cubs Jewel Tea

This 16-card set of the Chicago Cubs measures approximately 5 7/8" by 9". The white-bordered fronts feature color player head photos with a facsimile autograph. The backs are blank. The cards are unnumbered and checklisted below in alphabetical order.

COMPLETE SET (16)	6.00	15.00
1 Larry Biittner	.30	.75
2 Bill Bonham	.30	.75
3 Bill Buckner	.60	1.50
4 Ray Burris	.30	.75
5 Jose Cardenal	.30	.75
6 Gene Clines	.30	.75
7 Ivan DeJesus	.30	.75
8 Willie Hernandez	.60	1.50
9 Mike Krukow	.30	.75
10 George Mitterwald	.30	.75
11 Jerry Morales	.30	.75
12 Bobby Murcer	.40	1.00
13 Steve Ontiveros	.30	.75
14 Rick Reuschel	.40	1.00
15 Bruce Sutter	2.00	5.00
16 Manny Trillo	.40	1.00

1980 Cubs Greats TCMA

This 12-card standard-size set honors some all-time Chicago Cubs greats. The fronts have a player photo, his name and position. The backs have vital statistics, career totals and a brief biography.

COMPLETE SET (12)	2.00	5.00
1 Billy Williams	.40	1.00
2 Charlie Root	.20	.50
3 Ron Santo	.30	.75
4 Larry French	.08	.25
5 Gabby Hartnett	.40	1.00
6 Emil Kush	.08	.25
7 Charlie Grimm	.20	.50
8 Kiki Cuyler	.30	.75
9 Billy Herman	.30	.75
10 Hack Wilson	.30	.75
11 Rogers Hornsby	.40	1.00
12 Ernie Banks	.60	1.50

1980 Cubs Sun Times

Measuring approximately 7" by 11" when neatly cut, these newspaper "inserts" feature a black and white photo of the player on top along with biographical information on the left and year by year statistics on the right. Since these are unnumbered, we have sequenced them in alphabetical order. The Lee Smith cut predates his Rookie Card by two years.

COMPLETE SET	10.00	25.00
1 Larry Biittner	.40	1.00
2 Tim Blackwell	.40	1.00
3 Bill Buckner	.75	2.00
4 Doug Capilla	.40	1.00
5 Bill Caudill	.40	1.00
6 Ivan DeJesus	.40	1.00
7 Steve Dillard	.40	1.00
8 Jesus Figueroa	.40	1.00
9 Barry Foote	.40	1.00
10 Ken Henderson	.40	1.00
11 Dave Kingman	1.25	3.00
12 Mike Krukow	.40	1.00
13 Dennis Lamp	.40	1.00
14 Jerry Martin	.40	1.00
15 Lynn McGlothen	.40	1.00
16 Lenny Randle	.40	1.00
17 Rick Reuschel	.60	1.50
18 Lee Smith	2.00	5.00
19 Scot Thompson	.40	1.00
20 Dick Tidrow	.40	1.00
21 Mike Tyson	.40	1.00
22 Mike Vail	.40	1.00

1981 Cubs Tribune

These photos were inserted daily into the Chicago Tribune and featured members of the 1981 Chicago Cubs. Most of the newspaper cutout is dedicated to the players photo while the bottom of the section featured biographical information about the player and career stats. We have sequenced what we have information on in alphabetical order but this information is incomplete so any additional help is appreciated.

COMPLETE SET	1.25	3.00
1 Larry Biittner	.20	.50
2 Bill Caudill	.20	.50
3 Jesus Figueroa	.20	.50
4 Ken Henderson	.20	.50
5 Willie Hernandez	.40	1.00
6 Mick Kelleher	.20	.50
7 Mike O'Berry	.20	.50

1982 Cubs Red Lobster

The cards in this 28-card set measure 2 1/4" by 3 1/2". This set of Chicago Cubs players was co-produced by the Cubs and Chicago-area Red Lobster restaurants and was introduced as a promotional giveaway on August 20, 1982, at Wrigley Field. The cards contain borderless color photos of 25 players, manager Lee Elia, the coaching staff, and a team picture. A facsimile autograph appears on the front, and the cards run in sequence by uniform number. While the coaches have a short biographical sketch on back, the player cards simply list the individual's professional record. The key card in the set is obviously Ryne Sandberg's as it predates his Donruss, Fleer, and Topps Rookie Cards by one year. Lee Smith also appears in this set in his Rookie Card year.

COMPLETE SET (28)	50.00	100.00
1 Larry Bowa	.30	.75
4 Lee Elia MG	.20	.50
6 Keith Moreland	.30	.75
7 Jody Davis	.40	1.00
10 Leon Durham	.30	.75
15 Junior Kennedy	.20	.50
17 Bump Wills	.20	.50
18 Scot Thompson	.20	.50
21 Jay Johnstone	.40	1.00
22 Bill Buckner	.50	1.25
23 Ryne Sandberg	30.00	60.00
24 Jerry Morales	.20	.50
25 Gary Woods	.20	.50
28 Steve Henderson	.20	.50
29 Bob Molinaro	.20	.50
31 Fergie Jenkins	1.50	4.00
33 Al Ripley	.20	.50
34 Randy Martz	.20	.50
36 Mike Proly	.20	.50
37 Ken Kravec	.20	.50
38 Willie Hernandez	.40	1.00
39 Bill Campbell	.20	.50
41 Dick Tidrow	.20	.50
46 Lee Smith	3.00	8.00
47 Doug Bird	.20	.50
48 Dickie Noles	.20	.50
NNO Team Picture	1.50	4.00
NNO0 Coaches Card	.40	1.00

John Vukovich
Gordy MacKenzie
Bill

1983 Cubs Thorn Apple Valley

This set of 27 Chicago Cubs features full-color action photos on the front and was sponsored by Thorn Apple Valley. The cards measure approximately 2 1/4" by 3 1/2". The backs provide year-by-year statistics. The cards are unnumbered except for uniform number; they are listed below by uniform with the special cards listed at the end. The card of Joe Carter predates his Donruss Rookie Card by one year.

COMPLETE SET (27) 12.50 30.00
1 Larry Bowa .20 .50
6 Keith Moreland .08 .25
7 Jody Davis .20 .50
10 Leon Durham .20 .50
11 Ron Cey .30 .75
16 Steve Lake .08 .25
20 Thad Bosley .08 .25
21 Jay Johnstone .20 .50
22 Bill Buckner .30 .75
23 Ryne Sandberg 6.00 15.00
24 Jerry Morales .08 .25
25 Gary Woods .08 .25
27 Mel Hall .20 .50
29 Tom Veryzer .08 .25
30 Chuck Rainey .08 .25
31 Fergie Jenkins .75 2.00
32 Craig Lefferts .08 .25
33 Joe Carter 5.00 10.00
34 Steve Trout .08 .25
36 Mike Proly .08 .25
39 Bill Campbell .08 .25
41 Warren Brusstar .08 .25
44 Dick Ruthven .08 .25
46 Lee Smith 1.25 3.00
48 Dickie Noles .08 .25
NNO Manager .08 .25
Coaches
Lee Elia MG
Ruben Amaro
Billy C
NNO Team Photo .40 1.00

1984 Cubs Brickhouse Playing Cards

This 58-card set features black-and-white photos in white borders with rounded corners of top players who have played with the Chicago Cubs at some time during their careers. The backs display a picture of Jack Brickhouse in a circle with crossed baseball bats behind it on a blue background with red and white printing. The cards are checklisted below in playing card order by suits and assigned numbers to aces (1), jacks (11), queens (12), and kings (13).

COMPLETE SET (58) 5.00 12.00
1C Lon Warneke .02 .10
1D Burt Hooten .02 .10
1H Jack Brickhouse .02 .10
1S Leon Durham .02 .10
2C Augie Galan .08 .25
2D Fergie Jenkins .30 .75
2H 1876 Champions .02 .10
2S Keith Moreland .02 .10
3C 1935 Pennant Winning Cubs .02 .10
3D Ron Santo .20 .50
3H Cap Anson .50 1.25
3S Gary Matthews .02 .10
4C Dizzy Dean .60 1.50
4D Ken Holtzman .02 .10
4H Joe Tinker .20 .50
Evans
Frank Leroy Chance
Harry Stein
4S Bob Dernier .02 .10
5C Gabby Hartnett .30 .75
5D 1969 Cubs .02 .10
5H Ed Reulbach .08 .25
5S Eastern Division Champs 1984 .02 .10
6C Billy Herman .30 .75
6D Billy Williams .40 1.00
6H Mordecai Brown .30 .75
6S Ryne Sandberg 1.25 3.00
7C Charlie Root .02 .10
7D Ken Hubbs .20 .50
7H Jim HIPPO Vaughn .02 .10
7S Jim Frey MG .02 .10
8C Charlie Grimm .08 .25
8D Don Cardwell .02 .10
8H Joe McCarthy .20 .50
8S Rick Sutcliffe .02 .10
C Andy Pafko .02 .10
D Lou Boudreau .20 .50
H Jimmy Cooney .02 .10
S Jody Davis .02 .10
0C Stan Hack .02 .10
0D Dale Long .02 .10
0H Rogers Hornsby .40 1.00
0S Dallas Green GM .02 .10
1C Phil Cavarretta .20 .50
1D Sam Jones .02 .10
H Hack Wilson .20 .50
S Bill Madlock .08 .25
C 1945 N.L. Champs .02 .10
D Ernie Banks 1.00 2.50
H Hack Wilson .75 2.00
Babe Ruth
Lou Gehrig
S Rick Reuschel .02 .10
C Bill Nicholson .02 .10
D Hank Sauer .02 .10
H Babe Ruth 1.50 4.00
S Milt Pappas .02 .10
0 Joker .02 .10
Hey Hey! And Holy Cow!
0 Joker .02 .10
Ron Cey
0 Moments in History/1945-1972 .02 .10
0 Moments in History/1876-1925 .02 .10
0 Moments in History/1972-1984 .02 .10
0 Moments in History/1927-1945 .02 .10

1984 Cubs Chicago Tribune

1984 Chicago Tribune set was issued in the sports ...ion of the newspaper and features 34 Chicago Cub ...ers. The posed color headshots measure 3 1/4" by 4 5/8" and have blue borders. Next to the photo in a section of equal dimensions appears player information, including position, date of birth, playing experience, baseball career and Major-league playing record. The pictures are unnumbered and checklisted below in alphabetical order.

COMPLETE SET (34) 10.00 25.00
1 Ruben Amaro CO .20 .50
2 Rich Bordi .20 .50
3 Thad Bosley .20 .50
4 Larry Bowa .40 1.00
5 Warren Brusstar .20 .50
6 Ron Cey .40 1.00
7 Billy Connors CO .20 .50
8 Henry Cotto .20 .50
9 Jody Davis .30 .75
10 Bob Dernier .20 .50
11 Dennis Eckersley .75 2.00
12 George Frazier .20 .50
13 Jim Frey MG .20 .50
14 Ron Hassey .20 .50
15 Richie Hebner .30 .75
16 Steve Lake .20 .50
17 Davey Lopes .30 .75
18 Gary Matthews .40 1.00
19 Keith Moreland .20 .50
20 Johnny Oates CO .20 .50
21 Dave Owen .20 .50
22 Rick Reuschel .40 1.00
23 Dan Rohn .20 .50
24 Dick Ruthven .20 .50
25 Ryne Sandberg 3.00 8.00
26 Scott Sanderson .20 .50
27 Lee Smith .60 1.50
28 Tim Stoddard .20 .50
29 Rick Sutcliffe .40 1.00
30 Steve Trout .20 .50
31 Tom Veryzer .20 .50
32 John Vukovich CO .20 .50
33 Gary Woods .20 .50
34 Don Zimmer CO .30 .75

1984 Cubs Jewel

These 16 blank backed cards feature members of the 1984 Chicago White Sox. The fronts have the players photo against a blue background with a fascimile autograph on the bottom and the MLBPA logo in the upper left. These cards are unnumbered so we have sequenced them in alphabetical order.

COMPLETE SET (16) 6.00 15.00
1 Larry Bowa .50 1.00
2 Ron Cey .50 1.00
3 Bob Dernier .20 .50
4 Jody Davis .20 .50
5 Leon Durham .20 .50
6 Dennis Eckersley 1.00 2.50
7 Richie Hebner .20 .50
8 Gary Matthews .50 1.00
9 Keith Moreland .20 .50
10 Ryne Sandberg 2.00 5.00
11 Scott Sanderson .20 .50
12 Lee Smith .75 2.00
13 Tim Stoddard .20 .50
14 Rick Sutcliffe .75 2.00
15 Steve Trout .20 .50
16 Gary Woods .20 .50

1984 Cubs Seven-Up

This 28-card set was sponsored by 7-Up. The cards are in full color and measure approximately 2 1/4" by 3 1/2". The card backs are printed in black on white card stock. This set is tougher to find than the other similar Cubs sets since the Cubs were more successful (on the field) in 1984 winning their division, that is, virtually all of the cards printed were distributed during the "Baseball Card Day" promotion (August 12th) which was much better attended that year. There actually were two additional cards produced (in limited quantities) later which some collectors consider part of this set; these late issue cards show four Cubs rookies on each card.

COMPLETE SET (28) 12.50 30.00
1 Larry Bowa .40 1.00
6 Keith Moreland .20 .50
7 Jody Davis .40 1.00
10 Leon Durham .40 1.00
11 Ron Cey .60 1.50
15 Ron Hassey .20 .50
18 Richie Hebner .40 1.00
19 Dave Owen .20 .50
20 Bob Dernier .20 .50
21 Jay Johnstone .60 1.50
23 Ryne Sandberg 6.00 15.00
24 Scott Sanderson .20 .50
25 Gary Woods .20 .50
27 Thad Bosley .20 .50
28 Henry Cotto .20 .50
34 Steve Trout .20 .50
36 Gary Matthews .60 1.50
39 George Frazier .20 .50
40 Rick Sutcliffe .75 2.00
41 Warren Brusstar .20 .50
42 Rich Bordi .20 .50
43 Dennis Eckersley 1.50 4.00
44 Dick Ruthven .20 .50
46 Lee Smith 1.25 3.00
47 Rick Reuschel .60 1.50
49 Tim Stoddard .20 .50
NNO Coaches Card .20 .50
Ruben Amaro
Billy Connors
Johnny O
NNO Jim Frey MG .20 .50

1984 Cubs Sun Times

Measuring approximately 6 1/2" by 4 1/2" when cut out neatly, these inserts feature members of the 1984 Chicago Cubs. The left side features biographical information, career highlights and statistics while the right side featues a player photo. Since these are unnumbered, we have sequenced these in alphabetical order. This list may be incomplete, so any additions are appreciated.

COMPLETE SET 8.00 20.00
1 Thad Bosley .40 1.00
2 Larry Bowa .50 1.25
3 Warren Brusstar .40 1.00
4 Ron Cey .60 1.50
5 Henry Cotto .40 1.00
6 Leon Durham .50 1.25
7 Bob Dernier .50 1.25
8 Jay Johnstone .50 1.25
9 Gary Matthews .50 1.25
10 Keith Moreland .50 1.25
11 Scott Sanderson .40 1.00
12 Ryne Sandberg 1.50 4.00
13 Lee Smith .75 2.00
14 Tim Stoddard .40 1.00
15 Steve Trout .40 1.00
16 Gary Woods .40 1.00

1984 Cubs Unocal

Unocal 76 sponsored this set of 16 color paintings by several different artists. The paintings have white borders and are printed on 11" by 8 1/2" glossy paper. They capture memorable events and players in Chicago Cub history. The backs have an extended caption. The paintings are unnumbered and checklisted below in alphabetical order.

COMPLETE SET (16) 6.00 15.00
1 Billy Williams .60 1.50
2 Gold Glove Winners .60 1.50
Bob Dernier
Ryne Sandberg
Er
3 MVP Award Winners 1.00 2.50
Rogers Hornsby
Gabby Hartnett#
4 Ernie Banks 1.25 3.00
5 Fergie Jenkins .60 1.50
6 Great Cub Catchers .40 1.00
Gabby Hartnett
Randy Hundley#
7 Great Infields .75 2.00
Frank Chance
Johnny Evers
Joe Ti
8 Great Managers .40 1.00
Frank Chance
Joe McCarthy
Charli
9 Great Relief Pitchers .30 .75
Don Elston
Lindy McDaniel#
10 Jim Frey .20 .50
Post-Game Victory Lap/9/30/84
11 Memorable High Scoring Games .20 .50
12 '84 Cubs Award Winners .60 1.50
Ryne Sandberg
Rick Sutcli
13 '84 Clincher at Pittsburgh .20 .50
14 Rick Sutcliffe .30 .75
Sensational 16-1
15 Ryne Sandberg .60 1.50
23-Jun-84
16 Wrigley Field .20 .50

1985 Cubs Lion Photo

This 27-card set of the Chicago Cubs measures approximately 3 1/2" by 5". The fronts feature color player portraits on a blue background with a white border. The player's name is printed in blue in the wide bottom margin. The white backs carry sponsor information. The cards are unnumbered and checklisted below in alphabetical order.

COMPLETE SET (27) 5.00 12.00
1 Larry Bowa .30 .75
2 Thad Bosley .20 .50
3 Warren Brusstar .20 .50
4 Ron Cey .40 1.00
5 Jody Davis .20 .50
6 Brian Dayett .20 .50
7 Bob Dernier .20 .50
8 Shawon Dunston .60 1.50
9 Leon Durham .20 .50
10 Dennis Eckersley .75 2.00
11 Ray Fontenot .20 .50
12 George Frazier .20 .50
13 Jim Frey MG .20 .50
14 Steve Lake .20 .50
15 Davey Lopes .30 .75
16 Gary Matthews .30 .75
17 Keith Moreland .20 .50
18 Dick Ruthven .20 .50
19 Ryne Sandberg 1.25 3.00
20 Scott Sanderson .20 .50
21 Lee Smith .60 1.50
22 Lary Sorensen .20 .50
23 Chris Speier .20 .50
24 Rick Sutcliffe .40 1.00
25 Steve Trout .20 .50
26 Gary Woods .20 .50
27 Don Zimmer CO .30 .75

1985 Cubs Seven-Up

This 28-card set was distributed on August 14th at Wrigley Field for the game against the Expos. The cards measure 2 1/2" by 3 1/2" and were distributed wrapped in cellophane. The cards are unnumbered except for uniform number. The card backs are printed in black on white with a 7-Up logo in the upper right hand corner.

COMPLETE SET (28) 6.00 15.00
1 Larry Bowa .20 .50
6 Keith Moreland .08 .25
7 Jody Davis .20 .50
10 Leon Durham .20 .50
11 Ron Cey .30 .75
15 Davey Lopes .20 .50
16 Steve Lake .08 .25
18 Rich Hebner .20 .50
20 Bob Dernier .08 .25
21 Scott Sanderson .08 .25
22 Billy Hatcher .08 .25
23 Ryne Sandberg 3.00 8.00
24 Brian Dayett .08 .25
25 Gary Woods .08 .25
27 Thad Bosley .08 .25
28 Chris Speier .08 .25
31 Ray Fontenot .08 .25
34 Steve Trout .08 .25
36 Gary Matthews .30 .75
39 George Frazier .08 .25
40 Rick Sutcliffe .30 .75
41 Warren Brusstar .08 .25
42 Lary Sorensen .08 .25
43 Dennis Eckersley 1.00 2.50
44 Dick Ruthven .08 .25
46 Lee Smith .60 1.50
NNO Jim Frey MG .08 .25
NNO Cubs Coaching Staff .20 .50
Ruben Amaro
Billy Connors
J

1986 Cubs Gatorade

This 28-card set was given out at Wrigley Field on the Cubs' special "baseball card" promotion held July 17th for the game against the Giants. The set was sponsored by Gatorade. The cards are unnumbered except for uniform number. Card backs feature blue print on white card stock. The cards measure approximately 2 7/8" by 4 1/4" and are in full color.

COMPLETE SET (28) 5.00 12.00
4 Gene Michael MG .08 .25
6 Keith Moreland .08 .25
7 Jody Davis .20 .50
10 Leon Durham .20 .50
11 Ron Cey .30 .75
12 Shawon Dunston .20 .50
15 Davey Lopes .20 .50
16 Terry Francona .20 .50
18 Steve Christmas .08 .25
19 Manny Trillo .08 .25
20 Bob Dernier .08 .25
21 Scott Sanderson .08 .25
22 Jerry Mumphrey .08 .25
23 Ryne Sandberg 2.50 6.00
27 Thad Bosley .08 .25
28 Chris Speier .08 .25
29 Steve Lake .08 .25
31 Ray Fontenot .08 .25
34 Steve Trout .08 .25
36 Gary Matthews .20 .50
39 George Frazier .08 .25
40 Rick Sutcliffe .30 .75
43 Dennis Eckersley .75 2.00
46 Lee Smith .60 1.50
48 Jay Baller .08 .25
49 Jamie Moyer 1.00 2.50
50 Guy Hoffman .08 .25
NNO Coaches Card .20 .50
Ruben Amaro
Billy Connors
Johnny O

1986 Cubs Unocal

This set of 20 color action player photos was sponsored by Unocal 76. They are bordered in black and are printed on (approximately) 8 1/2" by 11" glossy paper sheets. A color headshot is superimposed on each front. The backs contain extensive player information, including biography, performance in the 1985 season, complete Major League statistics, and career summary. The player photos are unnumbered and checklisted below in alphabetical order.

COMPLETE SET (20) 4.00 10.00
1 Jay Baller .08 .25
2 Thad Bosley .08 .25
3 Ron Cey .30 .75
4 Jody Davis .20 .50
5 Bob Dernier .08 .25
6 Shawon Dunston .20 .50
7 Leon Durham .08 .25
8 Dennis Eckersley .75 2.00
9 Ray Fontenot .08 .25
10 George Frazier .08 .25
11 Davey Lopes .20 .50
12 Gary Matthews .20 .50
13 Keith Moreland .08 .25
14 Jerry Mumphrey .08 .25
15 Ryne Sandberg 2.00 5.00
16 Scott Sanderson .08 .25
17 Lee Smith .60 1.50
18 Rick Sutcliffe .30 .75
19 Manny Trillo .08 .25
20 Steve Trout .08 .25

1987 Cubs 1907 TCMA

This nine-card standard-size set features some of the 1907 Chicago Cubs stars. The fronts have player photo and identification, while the backs have vital statistics, a biography and 1907 stats.

COMPLETE SET (9) 2.00 5.00
1 Harry Steinfeldt .20 .50
2 Three-Finger Brown .40 1.00
3 Ed Reulbach .20 .50
4 Johnny Kling .20 .50
5 Orvie Overall .08 .25
6 Joe Tinker .40 1.00
7 Wildfire Schulte .30 .75
8 Frank Chance P MG .40 1.00
9 Johnny Evers .40 1.00

1987 Cubs Canon

This 38 card set features members of the 1987 Chicago Cubs. The fronts have a player photo with his name under the photo. At the bottom are the words "Canon" and "Chicago Cubs" The backs are blank so we have sequenced this set in alphabetical order. An early Greg Maddux item is in this set.

COMPLETE SET (38) 8.00 20.00
1 Glenn Brummer .20 .50
2 Phil Claussen .20 .50
3 Jody Davis .30 .75
4 Ron Davis .20 .50
5 Andre Dawson 1.25 3.00
6 Brian Dayett .20 .50
7 Bob Dernier .20 .50
8 Frank DiPino .20 .50
9 Shawon Dunston .20 .50
10 Leon Durham .30 .75
11 John Fierro TR .20 .50
12 Dallas Green GM .30 .75
13 Les Lancaster .20 .50
14 Frank Lucchesi CO .20 .50
15 Ed Lynch .20 .50
16 Greg Maddux 5.00 12.00
17 David Martinez .60 1.50
18 Gary Matthews .40 1.00
19 Gene Michael MG .20 .50
20 Keith Moreland .20 .50
21 Jamie Moyer 1.00 2.50
22 Jerry Mumphrey .20 .50
23 Dickie Noles .20 .50
24 Johnny Oates CO .20 .50
25 Jimmy Piersall ANN .40 1.00
26 Ryne Sandberg 2.00 5.00
27 Scott Sanderson .20 .50
28 Bob Searles .20 .50
29 Lee Smith .60 1.50
30 Jim Snyder CO .20 .50
31 Herm Starrette CO .20 .50
32 Jim Sundberg .20 .50
33 Rick Sutcliffe .40 1.00
34 Manny Trillo .20 .50
35 Steve Trout .20 .50
36 John Vukovich CO .20 .50
37 Chico Walker .20 .50
38 Billy Williams CO .60 1.50

1987 Cubs David Berg

This 26-card set was given out at Wrigley Field on the Cubs' special "baseball card" promotion held July 29th. The set was sponsored by David Berg Pure Beef Hot Dogs. The cards are unnumbered except for uniform number. Card backs feature red and blue print on white card stock. The cards measure approximately 2 7/8" by 4 1/4" and are in full color. The set features Greg Maddux in his Rookie Card year.

COMPLETE SET (26) 75.00 150.00
1 Dave Martinez .40 1.00
4 Gene Michael MG .08 .25
6 Keith Moreland .08 .25
7 Jody Davis .20 .50
8 Andre Dawson .75 2.00
10 Leon Durham .20 .50
11 Jim Sundberg .20 .50
12 Shawon Dunston .30 .75
19 Manny Trillo .20 .50
20 Bob Dernier .08 .25
21 Scott Sanderson .08 .25
22 Jerry Mumphrey .08 .25
23 Ryne Sandberg 2.00 5.00
24 Brian Dayett .08 .25
29 Chico Walker .08 .25
31 Greg Maddux 40.00 100.00
33 Frank DiPino .08 .25
34 Steve Trout .08 .25
36 Gary Matthews .30 .75
37 Ed Lynch .08 .25
39 Ron Davis .08 .25
40 Rick Sutcliffe .30 .75
46 Lee Smith .60 1.50
47 Dickie Noles .08 .25
49 Jamie Moyer .60 1.50
NNO Coaching Staff .20 .50
Johnny Oates
Jim Snyder
Herm Sta

1988 Cubs Canon

This blank-backed set, measuring 3 1/2" by 5 1/2" features members of the 1988 Chicago Cubs. The photos which were sponsored by Canon, are black and white and feature posed photos of the featured players surrounded by white borders. Since the photos are not numbered, we have sequenced them in alphabetical order.

COMPLETE SET
1 Joe Altobelli CO .20 .50
2 Chuck Cottier CO .20 .50
3 Larry Cox .20 .50
4 Jody Davis .20 .50
5 Andre Dawson .75 2.00
6 Frank DiPino .20 .50
7 Shawon Dunston .30 .75
8 Leon Durham .20 .50
9 Rich Gossage .60 1.50
10 Drew Hall .20 .50
11 Darrin Jackson .20 .50
12 Les Lancaster .20 .50
13 Vance Law .20 .50
14 Greg Maddux 2.00 5.00
15 David Martinez .20 .50
16 Jose Martinez .20 .50
17 Jerry Mumphrey .20 .50
18 Al Nipper .20 .50
19 Rafael Palmeiro .75 2.00
20 Dick Pole CO .20 .50
21 Ryne Sandberg 1.50 4.00
22 Calvin Schiraldi .20 .50
23 Jim Sundberg .20 .50
24 Rick Sutcliffe .40 1.00
25 Don Zimmer MG .30 .75

1988 Cubs David Berg

This 27-card set was given out at Wrigley Field with every paid admission on the Cubs' special "baseball card" promotion held August 24th. The set was sponsored by David Berg Pure Beef Hot Dogs and the Venture store chain. The cards are unnumbered except for uniform number. Card backs feature primarily black print on white card stock. The cards measure approximately 2 7/8" by 4 1/4" and are in full color. Mark Grace makes an early card appearance in this set.

COMPLETE SET (27) 6.00 15.00
2 Vance Law .08 .25
4 Don Zimmer MG .20 .50
7 Jody Davis .20 .50
8 Andre Dawson .60 1.50
9 Damon Berryhill .08 .25
12 Shawon Dunston .30 .75
17 Mark Grace 2.00 5.00
18 Angel Salazar .08 .25
19 Manny Trillo .08 .25
21 Scott Sanderson .08 .25
22 Jerry Mumphrey .08 .25
23 Ryne Sandberg 1.50 4.00
24 Gary Varsho .08 .25
25 Rafael Palmeiro 1.25 3.00
28 Mitch Webster .08 .25
30 Darrin Jackson .08 .25
31 Greg Maddux 2.50 6.00
32 Calvin Schiraldi .08 .25
33 Frank DiPino .08 .25
37 Pat Perry .08 .25
40 Rick Sutcliffe .30 .75
41 Jeff Pico .08 .25
45 Al Nipper .08 .25
49 Jamie Moyer .60 1.50
50 Les Lancaster .08 .25
54 Rich Gossage .30 .75
NNO Cubs Coaching Staff .08 .25
Joe Altobelli
Chuck Cottier#

1988 Cubs Donruss Team Book

The 1988 Donruss Cubs Team Book set features 27 cards (three pages with nine cards on each page) plus a large full-page puzzle of Stan Musial. Cards are in full color and are standard size. The set was distributed as a four-page book; although the puzzle page was perforated, the card pages were not. The cover of the "Team Collection" book is primarily bright red. Card fronts are very similar in design to the 1988 Donruss regular issue. The card numbers on the backs are the same for those players that are the same as in the regular Donruss set; the new players pictured are numbered on the back as "NEW." The book is usually sold intact. When cut from the book into individual cards, these cards are distinguishable from the regular 1988 Donruss cards since these have a 1988 copyright on the back whereas the regular issue has a 1987 copyright on the back.

COMPLETE SET (27) 2.50 6.00
40 Mark Grace RR 1.00 2.50
68 Rick Sutcliffe .02 .10
119 Jody Davis .02 .10
146 Shawon Dunston .02 .10
169 Jamie Moyer .30 .75
191 Leon Durham .02 .10
242 Ryne Sandberg .40 1.00
269 Andre Dawson .30 .75
315 Paul Noce .02 .10
324 Rafael Palmeiro .40 1.00
438 Dave Martinez .02 .10
447 Jerry Mumphrey .02 .10
488 Jim Sundberg .02 .10
516 Manny Trillo .02 .10
539 Greg Maddux 1.50 4.00
561 Les Lancaster .02 .10
570 Frank DiPino .02 .10
639 Damon Berryhill .02 .10
646 Scott Sanderson .02 .10
NEW Mike Bielecki .02 .10
NEW Rich Gossage .08 .25
NEW Drew Hall .02 .10
NEW Darrin Jackson .08 .25
NEW Vance Law .02 .10
NEW Al Nipper .02 .10
NEW Angel Salazar .02 .10
NEW Calvin Schiraldi .02 .10

1988 Cubs Vance Law Smokey

These cards which measure 3 3/4" by 5 1/2" feature Cub player Vance Law. He is in several different poses.

COMPLETE SET (4) 1.50 4.00
1 Vance Law .60 1.50
Smokey Bear
2 Vance Law .50 1.25
Fielding
3 Vance Law .50 1.25
Batting
4 Smokey Bear .40 1.00

1989 Cubs Marathon

The 1989 Marathon Cubs set features 25 cards measuring approximately 2 3/4" by 4 1/4". The fronts are green and white, and feature facsimile autographs. The backs show black and white mug shots and career stats. The set was given away at the August 10, 1989 Cubs' home game. The cards are numbered by the players' uniform numbers.

COMPLETE SET (25) 8.00 20.00
2 Vance Law .08 .25
4 Don Zimmer MG .20 .50
7 Joe Girardi .30 .75
8 Andre Dawson .75 2.00
9 Damon Berryhill .08 .25
10 Lloyd McClendon .08 .25
12 Shawon Dunston .30 .75
15 Domingo Ramos .08 .25
17 Mark Grace 2.00 5.00
18 Dwight Smith .20 .50
19 Curt Wilkerson .08 .25
20 Jerome Walton .30 .75
21 Scott Sanderson .08 .25
23 Ryne Sandberg 2.00 5.00
28 Mitch Williams .20 .50
31 Greg Maddux 3.00 8.00
32 Calvin Schiraldi .08 .25
33 Mitch Webster .08 .25
36 Mike Bielecki .08 .25
39 Paul Kilgus .08 .25
40 Rick Sutcliffe .30 .75
41 Jeff Pico .08 .25
44 Steve Wilson .08 .25
50 Les Lancaster .08 .25
NNO Cubs Coaches .08 .25
Joe Altobelli
Chuck Cottier
Larry

1990 Cubs Marathon

The Marathon Oil Chicago Cubs set contains 28 cards measuring approximately 2 7/8" by 4 1/4" which was given away at the August 17th Cubs' home game. Since the cards are unnumbered, the set is checklisted alphabetically below.

COMPLETE SET (28) 5.00 12.00
1 Paul Assenmacher .08 .25
2 Mike Bielecki .08 .25
3 Shawn Boskie .08 .25
4 Dave Clark .08 .25
5 Doug Dascenzo .08 .25
6 Andre Dawson .60 1.50
7 Shawon Dunston .30 .75
8 Joe Girardi .20 .50
9 Mark Grace .30 .75
10 Mike Harkey .08 .25
11 Les Lancaster .08 .25
12 Bill Long .08 .25
13 Greg Maddux 1.50 4.00
14 Lloyd McClendon .08 .25
15 Jeff Pico .08 .25
16 Domingo Ramos .08 .25
17 Luis Salazar .08 .25
18 Ryne Sandberg 1.25 3.00
19 Dwight Smith .08 .25
20 Rick Sutcliffe .30 .75
21 Hector Villanueva .08 .25
22 Jerome Walton .08 .25
23 Curtis Wilkerson .08 .25
24 Mitch Williams .20 .50
25 Steve Wilson .08 .25
26 Marvell Wynne .08 .25
27 Don Zimmer MG .20 .50
28 Cubs Coaches .08 .25
Joe Altobelli
Jose Martinez
Phil R

1990 Cubs Topps TV

This Cubs team set contains 66 standard-size cards. Cards numbered 1-35 were with the parent club, while cards 36-66 were in the farm system. The key card in this set is Greg Maddux

COMPLETE FACT. SET (66) 60.00 120.00
1 Don Zimmer MG .20 .50
2 Joe Altobelli CO .08 .25
3 Chuck Cottier CO .08 .25
4 Jose Martinez CO .08 .25
5 Dick Pole CO .08 .25
6 Phil Roof CO .08 .25
7 Paul Assenmacher .08 .25
8 Mike Bielecki .08 .25
9 Mike Harkey .08 .25
10 Joe Kraemer .08 .25
11 Les Lancaster .08 .25
12 Greg Maddux 30.00 80.00
13 Jose Nunez .08 .25
14 Jeff Pico .08 .25
15 Rick Sutcliffe .20 .50
16 Dean Wilkins .08 .25
17 Mitch Williams .08 .25
18 Steve Wilson .08 .25
19 Damon Berryhill .08 .25
20 Joe Girardi .60 1.50
21 Rick Wrona .08 .25
22 Shawon Dunston .20 .50
23 Mark Grace 8.00 20.00
24 Domingo Ramos .08 .25
25 Luis Salazar .08 .25
26 Ryne Sandberg 20.00 50.00
27 Greg Smith .08 .25
28 Curtis Wilkerson .08 .25
29 Dave Clark .08 .25
30 Doug Dascenzo .08 .25
31 Andre Dawson 3.00 8.00
32 Lloyd McClendon .08 .25
33 Dwight Smith .08 .25
34 Jerome Walton .08 .25
35 Marvell Wynne .08 .25
36 Alex Arias .08 .25
37 Bob Bafia .08 .25
38 Brad Bierley .08 .25
39 Shawn Boskie .08 .25
40 Danny Clay .08 .25
41 Rusty Crockett .08 .25
42 Earl Cunningham .08 .25
43 Len Damian .08 .25
44 Darrin Duffy .08 .25
45 Ty Griffin .08 .25
46 Brian Guinn .08 .25
47 Phil Hannon .08 .25
48 Phil Harrison .08 .25
49 Jeff Hearron .08 .25
50 Greg Kallevig .08 .25
51 Ced Landrum .08 .25
52 Bill Long .08 .25
53 Derrick May .08 .25
54 Ray Mullino .08 .25
55 Erik Pappas .08 .25
56 Steve Parker .08 .25
57 Dave Pavlas .08 .25
58 Laddie Renfroe .08 .25
59 Jeff Small .08 .25
60 Doug Strange .08 .25
61 Gary Varsho .08 .25
62 Hector Villanueva .08 .25
63 Rick Wilkins .08 .25
64 Dana Williams .08 .25
65 Bill Wrona .08 .25
66 Fernando Zarranz .08 .25

1991 Cubs Marathon

This 28-card set was produced by Marathon Oil, and its company logo appears at the bottom of card back. The cards were given away at the Cubs' home game against Montreal Expos on August 14, 1991. The oversized cards measure approximately 2 7/8" by 4 1/4" and feature on the fronts color action player photos with white borders. The set can also be found with blank backs. The cards are skip-numbered by uniform number and checklisted below accordingly.

COMPLETE SET (28) 5.00 12.00
7 Joe Girardi .20 .50
8 Andre Dawson .40 1.00
9 Damon Berryhill .08 .25
10 Luis Salazar .08 .25
11 George Bell .08 .25
12 Shawon Dunston .20 .50
16 Jose Vizcaino .20 .50
17 Mark Grace .40 1.00
18 Dwight Smith .08 .25
19 Hector Villanueva .08 .25
20 Jerome Walton .08 .25
22 Mike Harkey .08 .25
23 Ryne Sandberg 1.25 3.00
24 Chico Walker .08 .25

29 Doug Dascenzo .08 .25
30 Bob Scanlan .08 .25
31 Greg Maddux 1.50 4.00
32 Danny Jackson .08 .25
33 Chuck McElroy .08 .25
36 Mike Bielecki .08 .25
40 Rick Sutcliffe .20 .50
41 Jim Essian MG .08 .25
42 Dave Smith .08 .25
45 Paul Assenmacher .08 .25
47 Shawn Boskie .08 .25
50 Les Lancaster .08 .25
51 Heathcliff Slocumb .20 .50
NNO Coaches Card .08 .25
Joe Altobelli
Chuck Cottier
Jose M

1991 Cubs Vine Line

This 36-card set was issued as insert sheets in the Cubs' Vine Line fan news magazine. Each sheet measures approximately 7 1/2" by 10 1/2" and features nine different player cards. After perforation, the cards measure the standard size. The cards are unnumbered and checklisted below in alphabetical order.

COMPLETE SET (36) 8.00 20.00
1 Paul Assenmacher .08 .25
2 Joe Altobelli CO .08 .25
3 George Bell .08 .25
4 Damon Berryhill .08 .25
5 Mike Bielecki .08 .25
6 Shawn Boskie .08 .25
7 Chuck Cottier CO .08 .25
8 Doug Dascenzo .08 .25
9 Andre Dawson .75 2.00
10 Shawon Dunston .30 .75
11 Joe Girardi .08 .25
12 Mark Grace 1.00 2.50
13 Mike Harkey .08 .25
14 Danny Jackson .08 .25
15 Ferguson Jenkins CO .60 1.50
16 Les Lancaster .08 .25
17 Greg Maddux 3.00 8.00
18 Jose Martinez CO .08 .25
19 Chuck McElroy .08 .25
20 Erik Pappas .08 .25
21 Dick Pole CO .08 .25
22 Phil Roof CO .08 .25
23 Ryne Sandberg 2.00 5.00
24 Luis Salazar .08 .25
25 Gary Scott .08 .25
26 Heathcliff Slocumb .20 .50
27 Dave Smith .20 .50
28 Dwight Smith .08 .25
29 Rick Sutcliffe .30 .75
30 Hector Villanueva .08 .25
31 Jose Vizcaino .20 .50
32 Chico Walker .08 .25
33 Jerome Walton .08 .25
34 Steve Wilson .08 .25
35 Don Zimmer MG .20 .50
36 Most Valuable Players .60 1.50
Ryne Sandberg
Andre Dawson

1992 Cubs Marathon

This 28-card set was produced by Marathon Oil, and its company logo appears at the bottom of the card back. The cards measure approximately 2 7/8" by 4 1/4". The cards are skip-numbered on the back by uniform number and checklisted below accordingly.

COMPLETE SET (28) 5.00 12.00
1 Doug Strange .08 .25
5 Jim Lefebvre MG .08 .25
6 Rey Sanchez .08 .25
7 Joe Girardi .20 .50
8 Andre Dawson .40 1.00
10 Luis Salazar .08 .25
12 Shawon Dunston .20 .50
16 Jose Vizcaino .20 .50
17 Mark Grace .75 2.00
18 Dwight Smith .08 .25
19 Hector Villanueva .08 .25
20 Jerome Walton .08 .25
21 Sammy Sosa 1.50 4.00
23 Ryne Sandberg 1.00 2.50
27 Derrick May .08 .25
29 Doug Dascenzo .08 .25
30 Bob Scanlan .08 .25
31 Greg Maddux 1.50 4.00
32 Danny Jackson .08 .25
34 Ken Patterson .08 .25
35 Chuck McElroy .08 .25
36 Mike Morgan .08 .25
38 Jeff D. Robinson .08 .25
42 Dave Smith .20 .50
45 Paul Assenmacher .08 .25
47 Shawn Boskie .08 .25
49 Frank Castillo .08 .25
NNO Coaches Card .20 .50
Tom Trebelhorn
Jose Martinez
Billy

1992 Cubs Old Style

This 28-card set measures the standard size and features sepia-tone player photos with tan borders. The cards are unnumbered and checklisted below in alphabetical order.

COMPLETE SET (28) 6.00 15.00
1 Grover C. Alexander .60 1.50
2 Cap Anson .40 1.00
3 Ernie Banks 1.25 3.00
4 Mordecai Brown .30 .75
5 Phil Cavarretta .20 .50
6 Frank Chance .40 1.00
7 Kiki Cuyler .30 .75
8 Johnny Evers .40 1.00
9 Charlie Grimm .20 .50
10 Stan Hack .10 .25
11 Gabby Hartnett .30 .75
12 Billy Herman .30 .75
13 Rogers Hornsby .60 1.50
14 Ken Hubbs .20 .50
15 Randy Hundley .08 .25
16 Ferguson Jenkins .40 1.00
17 Bill Lee .08 .25
18 Andy Pafko .08 .25
19 Rick Reuschel .08 .25
20 Charlie Root .08 .25
21 Ron Santo .30 .75
22 Hank Sauer .08 .25
23 Riggs Stephenson .20 .50
24 Bruce Sutter .20 .50
25 Joe Tinker .40 1.00
26 Jim(Hippo) Vaughn .08 .25
27 Billy Williams .60 1.50
28 Hack Wilson .40 1.00

1992 Cubs U.S. Playing Cards

This 54-card set was issued in its own box and featured members of the 1992 Chicago Cubs. These cards have rounded borders and feature color posed and action player photos against a white background. The set is checklists below in playing card ortder and assigned numbers to Aces (1), Jacks (11), Queens (12) and Kings (13).

COMP.FACT SET (54) 2.50 6.00
1C George Bell .02 .10
1D Greg Maddux .40 1.00
1H Andre Dawson .15 .40
1S Ryne Sandberg .30 .75
2C Gary Scott .01 .05
2D Shawn Boskie .01 .05
2H Dwight Smith .01 .05
2S Frank Castillo .01 .05
3C Jose Vizcaino .02 .10
3D Ced Landrum .01 .05
3H Rick Wilkins .01 .05
3S Mike Harkey .01 .05
4C Heathcliff Slocumb .01 .05
4D Gary Scott .01 .05
4H Doug Dascenzo .01 .05
4S Dave Smith .01 .05
5C Danny Jackson .01 .05
5D Ced Landrum .01 .05
5H Bob Scanlan .01 .05
5S Les Lancaster .01 .05
6C Shawn Boskie .01 .05
6D Jose Vizcaino .01 .05
6H Chico Walker .01 .05
6S Hector Villanueva .01 .05
7C Luis Salazar .01 .05
7D Mike Harkey .01 .05
7H Paul Assenmacher .01 .05
7S Shawon Dunston .02 .10
8C Chuck McElroy .01 .05
8D Jerome Walton .01 .05
8H Mark Grace .20 .50
8S Heathcliff Slocumb .01 .05
9C Andre Dawson .15 .40
9D George Bell .02 .10
9H Ryne Sandberg .30 .75
9S Greg Maddux .40 1.00
10C Dave Smith .01 .05
10D Frank Castillo .01 .05
10H Danny Jackson .01 .05
10S Dwight Smith .01 .05
11C Hector Villanueva .01 .05
11D Rick Wilkins .01 .05
11H Jerome Walton .01 .05
11S Bob Scanlan .01 .05
12C Doug Dascenzo .01 .05
12D Les Lancaster .01 .05
12H Chico Walker .01 .05
12S Luis Salazar .01 .05
13C Shawon Dunston .02 .10
13D Paul Assenmacher .01 .05
13H Chuck McElroy .01 .05
13S Mark Grace .20 .50

1993 Cubs Marathon

This 32-card set was produced by Marathon Oil, and its company logo appears at the bottom of the card back. The cards measure approximately 2 7/8" by 4 1/4". The backs present biographical and statistical information. The cards are checklisted below in alphabetical order.

COMPLETE SET (32) 5.00 12.00
1 Paul Assenmacher .08 .25
2 Jose Bautista .08 .25
3 Steve Buechele .08 .25
4 Frank Castillo .08 .25
5 Billy Connors CO .08 .25
6 Chuck Cottier CO .08 .25
7 Mark Grace 1.00 2.50
8 Jose Guzman .08 .25
9 Mike Harkey .08 .25
10 Greg Hibbard .08 .25
11 Doug Jennings .08 .25
12 Steve Lake .08 .25
13 Jim Lefebvre MG .08 .25
14 Candy Maldonado .08 .25
15 Jose Martinez CO .08 .25
16 Derrick May .08 .25
17 Mike Morgan .08 .25
18 Randy Myers .30 .75
19 Tony Muser CO .08 .25
20 Dan Plesac .08 .25
21 Ryne Sandberg 1.50 4.00
22 Rey Sanchez .08 .25
23 Bob Scanlan .08 .25
24 Dan Simonds .08 .25
25 Dwight Smith .08 .25
26 Sammy Sosa 1.50 4.00
27 Tom Trebelhorn CO .08 .25
28 Jose Vizcaino .20 .50
29 Rick Wilkins .08 .25
30 Billy Williams CO .40 1.00
31 Willie Wilson .08 .25
32 Eric Yelding .08 .25

1993 Cubs Old Style Billy Williams

These four standard-size cards feature on their red, white, and blue-bordered fronts black-and-white action shots (except for number 1 below, which carries a posed color photo) of Billy Williams. His first and last name appear in white lettering in blue boxes above and below his image, respectively. The white backs are framed in red and blue lines and carry career highlights. The cards are unnumbered.

COMPLETE SET (4) 4.00 10.00
COMMON CARD (1-4) 1.20 3.00

1993 Cubs Rolaids

This four-card standard-size set is subtitled "All-Time Cubs Relief Pitchers" and was given away at Wrigley Field on Sept. 4, 1993. The cards are unnumbered and checklisted below in alphabetical order.

COMPLETE SET (4) 1.50 4.00
1 Randy Myers .50 1.25
2 Lee Smith .50 1.25
3 Bruce Sutter .75 2.00
4 Mitch Williams .40 1.00

1993 Cubs Stadium Club

This 30-card standard-size set features the 1993 Chicago Cubs. The set was issued in hobby (plastic box) and retail (blister) form.

COMP. FACT SET (30) 1.50 4.00
1 Ryne Sandberg .75 2.00
2 Sammy Sosa .60 1.50
3 Greg Hibbard .02 .10
4 Candy Maldonado .02 .10
5 Willie Wilson .08 .25
6 Dan Plesac .02 .10
7 Steve Buechele .02 .10
8 Mark Grace .40 1.00
9 Shawon Dunston .08 .25
10 Steve Lake .02 .10
11 Dwight Smith .02 .10
12 Derrick May .02 .10
13 Paul Assenmacher .02 .10
14 Mike Harkey .02 .10
15 Lance Dickson .02 .10
16 Randy Myers .08 .25
17 Mike Morgan .02 .10
18 Chuck McElroy .02 .10
19 Jose Guzman .02 .10
20 Jose Vizcaino .08 .25
21 Frank Castillo .02 .10
22 Bob Scanlan .02 .10
23 Rick Wilkins .02 .10
24 Rey Sanchez .02 .10
25 Phil Dauphin .02 .10
26 Jim Bullinger .02 .10
27 Jessie Hollins .02 .10
28 Matt Walbeck .02 .10
29 Fernando Ramsey .02 .10
30 Jose Bautista .02 .10

1994 Cubs WGN/Pepsi

These 5" by 7" cards featured members of the 1994 Chicago Cubs. There was supposed to be a series of 30 cards which were sponsored by WGN Television Station, Pepsi Cola, and Taco Bell. However, due to the strike of 1994 it is actually unknown if the entire set as planned was actually released. Any additions to this checklist are very appreciated. The fronts feature a black-and-white player photo with a gray border and sponsor logos. The backs display information about the player as well as some of his favorite things and people.

COMPLETE SET 8.00 20.00
1 Mark Grace .60 1.50
2 Chicago Cubs 1984 .30 .75
3 Ryne Sandberg 1.00 2.50
4 Randy Myers .30 .75
5 Rick Wilkins .20 .50
6 Tom Trebelhorn MG .20 .50
7 Mike Morgan .20 .50
8 Ernie Banks 1.50 4.00
9 Steve Stone .30 .75
10 Steve Trachsel .30 .75
11 Jose Guzman .20 .50
12 Sammy Sosa 2.00 5.00
13 Steve Buechele .20 .50
14 Jose Bautista .20 .50
17 Glenallen Hill .20 .50
19 Ron Santo .60 1.50
20 Shawon Dunston .30 .75
21 Tuffy Rhodes .20 .50
22 Thom Brennaman ANN .20 .50
24 Ryne Sandberg GAME .60 1.50
29 Jack Brickhouse ANN .30 .75

1995 Cubs Gatorade

This set, which measures 2 7/8" by 4 1/4" feature members of the 1995 Chicago Cubs. The fronts have full color photos surrounded by white borders with the player's name, uniform number and position on the bottom. The backs have biographical information and year by year statistics. Since these cards are unnumbered, we have sequenced them in alphabetical order.

COMPLETE SET 6.00 15.00
1 Scott Bullett .20 .50
2 Jim Bullinger .20 .50
3 Larry Casian .20 .50
4 Frank Castillo .20 .50
5 Shawon Dunston .30 .75
6 Kevin Foster .20 .50
7 Rich Garces .20 .50
8 Luis Gonzalez .60 1.50
9 Mark Grace .75 2.00
10 Jose Guzman .20 .50
11 Jose Hernandez .20 .50
12 Howard Johnson .30 .75
13 Brian McRae .20 .50
14 Randy Myers .30 .75
15 Chris Nabholz .20 .50
16 Jaime Navarro .20 .50
17 Mike Perez .20 .50
18 Jim Riggleman MG .20 .50
19 Rey Sanchez .20 .50
20 Scott Servais .20 .50
21 Sammy Sosa .75 2.00
22 Ozzie Timmons .20 .50
23 Steve Trachsel .30 .75
24 Turk Wendell .20 .50
25 Anthony Young .20 .50
26 Todd Zeile .20 .50
27 Dave Bialas CO .40 1.00
Fergie Jenkins CO
Tony Muser CO
Mako Oliveras CO
Dan Radison CO
Billy Williams CO

1995 Cubs Police

These 16 cards were issued by the Illinois State Police and feature members of the 1995 Chicago Cubs. There are black and white photos on the front and the bottom of the card has the Illinois State Police logo as well as the Cub logo. The back has vital statistics as well as having six ways to prevent conflicts. Since the cards are unnumbered we have sequenced them in alphabetical order. There is a possibility there are more cards in this set so any additions to this checklist are appreciated.

COMPLETE SET 4.00 10.00
1 Dave Bialas .08 .25
2 Scott Bullett .08 .25
3 Jim Bullinger .08 .25
4 Larry Casian .08 .25
5 Frank Castillo .08 .25
6 Shawon Dunston .20 .50
7 Kevin Foster .08 .25
8 Mark Grace .60 1.50
9 Jose Guzman .08 .25
10 Jose Hernandez .08 .25
11 Bryan Hickerson .08 .25
12 Fergie Jenkins CO .40 1.00
13 Howard Johnson .20 .50
14 Brian McRae .08 .25
15 Tony Muser CO .08 .25
16 Randy Myers .20 .50
17 Jaime Navarro .08 .25
18 Chris Nabholz .08 .25
19 Mako Oliveras .08 .25
20 Mike Perez .08 .25
21 Todd Pratt .08 .25
22 Dan Radison .08 .25
23 Jim Riggleman MG .08 .25
24 Rey Sanchez .08 .25
25 Sammy Sosa .75 2.00
26 Ozzie Timmons .08 .25
27 Steve Trachsel .08 .25
28 Mike Walker .08 .25
29 Turk Wendell .08 .25
30 Billy Williams CO .40 1.00
31 Anthony Young .08 .25
32 Todd Zeile .20 .50

1996 Cubs Convention

These black and white photos were given out to fans attending the 1996 Cubs Convention so attendees could have an item for players to sign. The fronts have a player photo along with the Chicago Cubs logo and the player name on top. Inset in the photo is the logo for the Cubs Convention. The horizontal backs feature information about the player as well as his career stats. This checklist is incomplete so any additions are appreciated.

COMPLETE SET 2.00 5.00
1 Mark Grace 1.00 2.50
2 Randy Hundley .40 1.00
3 Steve Stone .60 1.50

1996 Cubs Fleer

These 20 standard-size cards feature the same design as the regular Fleer issue, except they are UV coated, use silver foil and are numbered "x of 20". The team set packs were available at retail locations and hobby shops in 10-card packs for a suggested retail price of $1.99.

COMPLETE SET (20) 2.00 5.00
1 Terry Adams .02 .10
2 Jim Bullinger .02 .10
3 Frank Castillo .02 .10
4 Kevin Foster .02 .10
5 Leo Gomez .02 .10
6 Luis Gonzalez .20 .50
7 Mark Grace .30 .75
8 Jose Hernandez .02 .10
9 Robin Jennings .02 .10
10 Doug Jones .02 .10
11 Brooks Kieschnick .02 .10
12 Brian McRae .02 .10
13 Jaime Navarro .02 .10
14 Rey Sanchez .02 .10
15 Ryne Sandberg .40 1.00
16 Scott Servais .02 .10
17 Sammy Sosa .30 .75
18 Steve Trachsel .02 .10
19 Logo card .02 .10
20 Checklist .02 .10

1996 Cubs Gatorade

This 27-card postcard size set features members of the 1996 Chicago Cubs. The fronts have red borders surrounding an action photo of the player. The backs have the players vital statistics as well as complete season and career statistics.

COMPLETE SET (27)
1 Terry Adams .20 .50
2 Kent Bottenfield .20 .50
3 Scott Bullett .20 .50
4 Jim Bullinger .20 .50
5 Mike Campbell .20 .50
6 Frank Castillo .20 .50
7 Doug Glanville .20 .50
8 Leo Gomez .20 .50
9 Luis Gonzalez .60 1.50
10 Mark Grace .75 2.00
11 Jose Hernandez .20 .50
12 Dave Magadan .20 .50
13 Brian McRae .20 .50
14 Rodney Myers .20 .50
15 Jaime Navarro .20 .50
16 Bob Patterson .20 .50
17 Rey Sanchez .20 .50
18 Ryne Sandberg 1.25 3.00
19 Scott Servais .20 .50
20 Terry Shumpert .20 .50
21 Sammy Sosa .75 2.00
22 Tanyon Sturtze .20 .50
23 Amaury Telemaco .20 .50
24 Steve Trachsel .20 .50
25 Turk Wendell .20 .50
26 Jim Riggleman MG .20 .50
27 Dave Bialas CO .30 .75
Fergie Jenkins CO
Tony Muser CO/

1997 Cubs Gatorade

This 26 card postcard size set features members of the 1997 Chicago Cubs. The cards are unnumbered and we have sequenced them in alphabetical order. The fronts have green borders surrounding an action photo of the player. The backs have the players vital statistics as well as complete season and career statistics.

COMPLETE SET (26) 4.00 10.00
1 Terry Adams .08 .25
2 Kent Bottenfield .08 .25
3 Brant Brown .08 .25
4 Dave Clark .08 .25
5 Shawon Dunston .20 .50
6 Kevin Foster .08 .25
7 Doug Glanville .20 .50
8 Jeremi Gonzalez .08 .25
9 Mark Grace .60 1.50
10 Dave Hansen .08 .25
11 Jose Hernandez .08 .25
12 Tyler Houston .08 .25
13 Brian McRae .08 .25
14 Kevin Orie .08 .25
15 Bob Patterson .08 .25
16 Jim Riggleman MG .08 .25
17 Mel Rojas .08 .25
18 Rey Sanchez .08 .25
19 Ryne Sandberg .75 2.00
20 Scott Servais .08 .25
21 Sammy Sosa .50 1.25
22 Kevin Tapani .08 .25
23 Ramon Tatis .08 .25
24 Steve Traschel .08 .25
25 Turk Wendell .08 .25
26 Dave Bialas CO .20 .50
Rick Kranitz CO
Jeff Pentland CO#

1998 Cubs Fan Convention

These 30 cards were issued during the 1998 Cubs Fan Convention and featured players and other members of the Cubs organization past and present. The fronts have the players name on top along with 2 Cubs logos. The 13th Cubs Convention logo is also on the front along with a photo(s) of the people involved. The cards are unnumbered so we have sequenced the individual cards alphabetically and the multi-player card in alphabetical order of the headline on the top. The backs have biographical information and statistics where appropriate.

COMPLETE SET (30) 10.00 25.00
1 Terry Adams .20 .50
2 Ernie Banks 1.00 2.50
3 Jack Brickhouse ANN .40 1.00
4 Harry Caray ANN .60 1.50
5 Andre Dawson .60 1.50
6 Mark Grace .60 1.50
7 Kevin Orie .20 .50
8 Jim Riggleman MG .20 .50
9 Ron Santo .60 1.50
10 Scott Servais .20 .50
11 Sammy Sosa 1.00 2.50
12 Rick Sutcliffe .20 .50
13 Steve Trachsel .20 .50
14 Billy Williams .60 1.50
15 Carmen Fanzone .20 .50
Paul Reuschel
Alumni Club
16 Oscar Gamble .20 .50
Larry Bowa
Alumni Club
17 Randy Hundley .20 .50
Jody Davis
Behind the Plate
18 Pat Hughes .20 .50
Josh Lewin
Booth Banter
19 Mike Hubbard .20 .50
Tyler Houston
Catching Corps
20 Mike Bielecki .20 .50
Vance Law/89ers
21 Kerry Wood 1.50 4.00
Pat Cline
Future Stars
22 Kevin Foster .20 .50
Marc Pisciotta
Flame Throwers
23 Robin Jennings .20 .50
Rodney Myers
Hot Prospects
24 Mark Clark .20 .50
Jeremi Gonzalez
Mound Mates
25 Jeff Blauser .20 .50
Mickey Morandini
New Cubs
26 Dick Selma .20 .50
Willie Smith/1969 Cubs
27 Glenn Beckert UER .40 1.00
Don Kessinger/1969 Infield
GI
28 Milt Pappas .20 .50
Don Cardwell
No-hit Hurlers
29 Andy Pafko .30 .75
Gary Matthews
Outfield Greats
30 Bob Patterson .20 .50
Kevin Tapani
Veteran Hurlers

1998 Cubs Sosa ComEd

This one card standard-size set was among items given out by the Cubs to honor Sammy Sosa's 66 homer season. An action shot of Sosa is framed by blue borders with the words 'Slammin' Sammy" on top and the Cubs logo and 1998 on the bottom. The back features biographical information as well as highlights from the 1998 season.

1 Sammy Sosa 2.00 5.00

1999 Cubs Old Style All-Century Team

These 21 standard-size cards were issued over three different Cub games. They were issued in seven card packs sequenced in alphabetical order except for the Frank Chance manager card being included in the third pack. Since the cards are unnumbered we have sequenced them in alphabetical order.

COMPLETE SET (21) 10.00 25.00
1 Grover Alexander .60 1.50
2 Ernie Banks .60 1.50
3 Mordecai Brown .60 1.50
4 Phil Cavaretta .30 .75
5 Frank Chance MG .60 1.50
P
6 Andre Dawson .40 1.00
7 Mark Grace .60 1.50
8 Charlie Grimm .30 .75
9 Stan Hack .30 .75
10 Gabby Hartnett .60 1.50
11 Billy Herman .30 .75
12 Fergie Jenkins .60 1.50
13 Andy Pafko .20 .50
14 Ryne Sandberg .60 1.50
15 Ron Santo .40 1.00
16 Lee Smith .30 .75
17 Sammy Sosa .75 2.00
18 Bruce Sutter .60 1.50
19 Joe Tinker .60 1.50
20 Billy Williams .60 1.50
21 Hack Wilson .60 1.50

2000 Cubs Sosa Commemorative

1 Sammy Sosa 4.00 10.00

2001 Cubs Topps 50th Anniversary

COMPLETE SET (10) 32.00 80.00
1 Ernie Banks 58 4.80 12.00
2 Andre Dawson 88 3.20 8.00
3 Fergie Jenkins 71 4.00 10.00
4 Andy Pafko 52 2.00 5.00
5 Ryne Sandberg 84 4.80 12.00
6 Ron Santo 61 4.80 12.00
7 Sammy Sosa 98 5.00 12.00
8 Rick Sutcliffe 85 2.00 5.00
9 Bruce Sutter 79 4.00 10.00
10 Billy Williams 72 4.80 12.00

2001 Cubs Topps 50th Anniversary Autographs

COMPLETE SET (10) 320.00 800.00
1 Ernie Banks 58 60.00 150.00
2 Andre Dawson 88 32.00 80.00
3 Fergie Jenkins 71 40.00 100.00
4 Andy Pafko 52 20.00 50.00
5 Ryne Sandberg 84 48.00 120.00
6 Ron Santo 61 50.00 120.00
7 Sammy Sosa 98 60.00 150.00
8 Rick Sutcliffe 85 20.00 50.00
9 Bruce Sutter 79 40.00 100.00
10 Billy Williams 72 40.00 100.00

2002 Cubs Topps Best Moments

COMPLETE SET (12) 30.00 60.00
1 Ernie Banks 6.00 15.00
1954 Topps
April 21st
2 Kerry Wood 3.00 8.00
1998 Topps
May 6th
3 Don Cardwell 2.00 5.00
1961 Topps
May 7th
4 Billy Williams 5.00 12.00
1961 Topps
June 19th
5 Bill Buckner 2.00 5.00
1980 Topps
June 24th
6 Ken Hubbs 2.00 5.00
1962 Topps
June 26th
7 Dave Kingman 2.00 5.00
1979 Topps
July 25th
8 Sammy Sosa 5.00 12.00
2002 Topps
August 16th
9 Ken Holtzman 2.00 5.00
1969 Topps
September 1st
10 Milt Pappas 2.00 5.00
1972 Topps
September 2nd
11 Mark Prior 3.00 8.00
2002 Topps
September 9th
12 Lee Smith 3.00 8.00
1984 Topps
September 28th

2003 Cubs Santo

1 Ron Santo 5.00 10.00

2003 Cubs Sweepstakes

COMPLETE SET 15.00 30.00
1 Sammy Sosa 1.25 3.00
2 Billy Williams 1.00 2.50
3 Mark Prior 1.50 4.00
4 Jody Davis .40 1.00
5 Ron Santo 1.00 2.50
6 Ryne Sandberg 1.50 4.00
7 Corey Patterson .40 1.00
8 Dusty Baker MG .60 1.50
9 Ernie Banks 2.00 5.00
10 Kerry Wood 1.00 2.50
11 Fergie Jenkins 1.00 2.50

2003 Cubs Topps

COMPLETE SET 15.00 30.00
1 Steve Stone 2.00 5.00
2 Bobby Hill 1.50 4.00
3 Hee Seop Choi 2.00 5.00
4 Glenn Beckert 2.00 5.00
5 Bill Madlock 2.50 6.00
6 Ron Santo 4.00 10.00

2004 Cubs Scratchoff

COMPLETE SET (22) 15.00 40.00
1 Greg Maddux 2.00 5.00
16-Apr
2 1908 World Series .40 1.00
17-Apr
3 Dusty Baker MG .40 1.00
24-Apr
4 Ernie Banks 2.00 5.00
25-Apr
5 Mark Prior 1.50 4.00
4-May
6 Kerry Wood .60 1.50
6-May
7 Ron Santo 1.50 4.00
7-May
8 Sammy Sosa 1.25 3.00
8-May
9 Fergie Jenkins 1.25 3.00
18-May
10 Billy Williams 1.25 3.00
20-May
11 Rick Sutcliffe .40 1.00
1-Jun
12 Ernie Banks 2.00 5.00
20-Jun
13 Ryne Sandberg 2.00 5.00
30-Jun
14 Bill Buckner .40 1.00
21-Jul
15 Rick Sutcliffe .60 1.50
11-Aug
16 Kerry Wood .75 2.00
12-Aug
17 Andy Pafko .40 1.00
25-Aug
18 Mark Prior 1.50 4.00
26-Aug
19 Ryne Sandberg 2.00 5.00
8-Sep
20 Andre Dawson 1.00 2.50
10-Sep
21 Sammy Sosa 1.25 3.00
15-Sep
22 Ron Santo 1.50 4.00
29-Sep

2004 Cubs Topps

COMPLETE SET (2) 2.50 6.00
1 Shawon Dunston 1.25 3.00
19-May
2 Mark Prior 2.00 5.00
6-Jun

2005 Cubs Donruss Team Heroes National

COMPLETE SET (6)
1 Kerry Wood .75 2.00
2 Aramis Ramirez .75 2.00
3 Mark Prior 1.25 3.00
4 Nomar Garciaparra 1.25 3.00
5 Greg Maddux 1.25 3.00
6 Derrek Lee 1.00 2.50

2005 Cubs Giveaway Cards

COMPLETE SET
1 Carlos Zambrano 1.00 2.50
10-Apr
2 Billy Williams 1.50 4.00
23-Apr
3 Ernie Banks 2.00 5.00
24-Apr
4 Kerry Wood 1.00 2.50
25-Apr
5 Hack Wilson 1.00 2.50
6-May
6 Dusty Baker MG .60 1.50
7-May
7 Corey Patterson .40 1.00
9-May
8 Aramis Ramirez .75 2.00
10-May
9 Kerry Wood 1.00 2.50
20-May
10 Gabby Hartnett 1.00 2.50
24-May
11 Ryne Sandberg 1.50 4.00
25-May
12 Mark Prior 1.25 3.00
26-May
13 Billy Williams 1.50 4.00
29-May
14 Mark Prior 1.25 3.00
8-Jun
15 Nomar Garciaparra 1.00 2.50
10-Jun
16 Ron Santo 1.50 4.00
13-Jun
17 Carlos Zambrano 1.00 2.50
29-Jun
18 Mia Hamm 3.00 8.00
3-Jul
19 Ron Santo 1.50 4.00
17-Jul
20 Bruce Sutter 1.25 3.00
26-Jul
21 Derrek Lee 1.00 2.50
31-Jul
22 Aramis Ramirez .75 2.00
9-Aug
23 Ryne Sandberg 1.50 4.00
14-Aug
24 Greg Maddux 2.00 5.00
22-Aug
25 Nomar Garciaparra 1.00 2.50
31-Aug
26 Fergie Jenkins 1.25 3.00
13-Sep
27 Nomar Garciaparra 1.00 2.50
14-Sep

2006 Cubs Topps

COMPLETE SET (14) 3.00 8.00
CHC1 Kerry Wood .12 .30
CHC2 Mark Prior .20 .50
CHC3 Greg Maddux .40 1.00
CHC4 Carlos Zambrano .20 .50
CHC5 Michael Barrett .12 .30

CHC6 Derrek Lee .12 .30
CHC7 Jerry Hairston Jr. .12 .30
CHC8 Ronny Cedeno .12 .30
CHC9 Todd Walker .12 .30
CHC10 Aramis Ramirez .12 .30
CHC11 Ryan Dempster .12 .30
CHC12 Jacque Jones .12 .30
CHC13 Glendon Rusch .12 .30
CHC14 Juan Pierre .12 .30

2006 Cubs Upper Deck

COMPLETE SET (13) 2.50 6.00

2007 Cubs Topps

COMPLETE SET (14) 3.00 8.00
CHC1 Alfonso Soriano .20 .50
CHC2 Daryle Ward .12 .30
CHC3 Matt Murton .12 .30
CHC4 Jacque Jones .12 .30
CHC5 Rich Hill .12 .30
CHC6 Michael Barrett .12 .30
CHC7 Scott Moore .12 .30
CHC8 Ted Lilly .12 .30
CHC9 Aramis Ramirez .12 .30
CHC10 Mark Prior .20 .50
CHC11 Derek Lee .12 .30
CHC12 Mark DeRosa .12 .30
CHC13 Kerry Wood .12 .30
CHC14 Carlos Zambrano .20 .50

2008 Cubs Topps

COMPLETE SET (14) 3.00 8.00
CHC1 Alfonso Soriano .20 .50
CHC2 Geovany Soto .30 .75
CHC3 Matt Murton .12 .30
CHC4 Kerry Wood .12 .30
CHC5 Rich Hill .12 .30
CHC6 Carlos Marmol .20 .50
CHC7 Ryan Theriot .12 .30
CHC8 Ted Lilly .12 .30
CHC9 Aramis Ramirez .12 .30
CHC10 Jason Marquis .12 .30
CHC11 Derrek Lee .12 .30
CHC12 Mark DeRosa .12 .30
CHC13 Felix Pie .12 .30
CHC14 Carlos Zambrano .20 .50

2009 Cubs Topps

CHC1 Alfonso Soriano .25 .60
CHC2 Carlos Zambrano .25 .60
CHC3 Geovany Soto .25 .60
CHC4 Rich Harden .15 .40
CHC5 Kosuke Fukudome .25 .60
CHC6 Milton Bradley .15 .40
CHC7 Mike Fontenot .15 .40
CHC8 Ted Lilly .15 .40
CHC9 Aramis Ramirez .15 .40
CHC10 Reed Johnson .15 .40
CHC11 Derrek Lee .15 .40
CHC12 Jeff Samardzija .25 .60
CHC13 Ryan Dempster .15 .40
CHC14 Ryan Theriot .15 .40
CHC15 Wrigley Field .15 .40

2010 Cubs Topps

CHC1 Alfonso Soriano .25 .60
CHC2 Ted Lilly .15 .40
CHC3 Kevin Gregg .15 .40
CHC4 Ryan Dempster .15 .40
CHC5 Mike Fontenot .15 .40
CHC6 Jeff Samardzija .15 .40
CHC7 Jeff Baker .15 .40
CHC8 Ryan Theriot .15 .40
CHC9 Tyler Colvin .25 .60
CHC10 Kosuke Fukudome .25 .60
CHC11 Geovany Soto .25 .60
CHC12 Carlos Marmol .25 .60
CHC13 Derrek Lee .15 .40
CHC14 Aramis Ramirez .15 .40
CHC15 Carlos Zambrano .25 .60
CHC16 Randy Wells .15 .40
CHC17 Marlon Byrd .15 .40

2011 Cubs Topps

CHC1 Starlin Castro .25 .60
CHC2 Marlon Byrd .15 .40
CHC3 Aramis Ramirez .15 .40
CHC4 Tyler Colvin .15 .40
CHC5 Kerry Wood .15 .40
CHC6 Ryan Dempster .15 .40
CHC7 Carlos Pena .25 .60
CHC8 Carlos Marmol .25 .60
CHC9 Andrew Cashner .15 .40
CHC10 Carlos Silva .15 .40
CHC11 Blake DeWitt .15 .40
CHC12 Kosuke Fukudome .25 .60
CHC13 Alfonso Soriano .25 .60
CHC14 Geovany Soto .25 .60
CHC15 Matt Garza .15 .40
CHC16 Carlos Zambrano .25 .60
CHC17 Wrigley Field .15 .40

2012 Cubs Topps

CHC1 Starlin Castro .30 .75
CHC2 Reed Johnson .25 .60
CHC3 Alfonso Soriano .30 .75
CHC4 Ryan Dempster .25 .60
CHC5 Darwin Barney .25 .60
CHC6 Kerry Wood .25 .60
CHC7 Marlon Byrd .25 .60
CHC8 Matt Garza .25 .60
CHC9 Geovany Soto .30 .75
CHC10 Randy Wells .25 .60
CHC11 Carlos Marmol .25 .60
CHC12 Bryan LaHair .25 .60
CHC13 Anthony Rizzo .50 1.25
CHC14 David DeJesus .25 .60
CHC15 Paul Maholm .25 .60
CHC16 Ian Stewart .25 .60
CHC17 Wrigley Field .15 .40

2013 Cubs Topps

COMPLETE SET (17) 3.00 8.00
CHC1 Anthony Rizzo .30 .75
CHC2 Starlin Castro .15 .40
CHC3 Alfonso Soriano .30 .75
CHC4 Matt Garza .25 .60
CHC5 Scott Feldman .25 .60
CHC6 Carlos Marmol .25 .60
CHC7 Scott Baker .15 .40
CHC8 David DeJesus .15 .40
CHC9 Jeff Samardzija .25 .60
CHC10 Tony Campana .15 .40
CHC11 Darwin Barney .15 .40
CHC12 Wellington Castillo .15 .40
CHC13 Edwin Jackson .15 .40
CHC14 Brett Jackson .25 .60
CHC15 Travis Wood .15 .40
CHC16 Ian Stewart .25 .60
CHC17 Wrigley Field .15 .40

2014 Cubs Topps

COMPLETE SET (17) 3.00 8.00
CHC1 Anthony Rizzo .30 .75
CHC2 Starlin Castro .15 .40
CHC3 Mike Olt .15 .40
CHC4 Junior Lake .15 .40
CHC5 Nate Schierholtz .15 .40
CHC6 Kyuji Fujikawa .20 .50
CHC7 Carlos Villanueva .15 .40
CHC8 Jake Arrieta .20 .50
CHC9 Jeff Samardzija .15 .40
CHC10 Luis Valbuena .15 .40
CHC11 Darwin Barney .15 .40
CHC12 Wellington Castillo .15 .40
CHC13 Edwin Jackson .15 .40
CHC14 Justin Ruggiano .15 .40
CHC15 Travis Wood .15 .40
CHC16 Jose Veras .15 .40
CHC17 Wrigley Field .15 .40

2015 Cubs Topps

COMPLETE SET (17) 3.00 8.00
CHC1 Anthony Rizzo .30 .75
CHC2 Junior Lake .15 .40
CHC3 Starlin Castro .15 .40
CHC4 Brian Schlitter .15 .40
CHC5 Travis Wood .15 .40
CHC6 Javier Baez 1.25 3.00
CHC7 Jorge Soler .25 .60
CHC8 Miguel Montero .15 .40
CHC9 Mike Olt .15 .40
CHC10 Chris Coghlan .15 .40
CHC11 Dexter Fowler .20 .50
CHC12 Jon Lester .20 .50
CHC13 Jake Arrieta .20 .50
CHC14 Jason Hammel .20 .50
CHC15 Hector Rondon .15 .40
CHC16 Tsuyoshi Wada .15 .40
CHC17 Kyle Hendricks .25 .60

2016 Cubs Topps

COMPLETE SET (17) 3.00 8.00
CC1 Kris Bryant .30 .75
CC2 Kyle Schwarber .50 1.25
CC3 Jorge Soler .25 .60
CC4 Addison Russell .25 .60
CHC5 Ben Zobrist .20 .50
CC6 Anthony Rizzo .30 .75
CC7 Javier Baez .30 .75
CC8 Jon Lester .20 .50
CC9 Jake Arrieta .20 .50
CC10 Kyle Hendricks .25 .60
CC11 Jason Hammel .20 .50
CC12 Hector Rondon .15 .40
CC13 Miguel Montero .15 .40
CC14 Jason Heyward .20 .50
CC15 Chris Coghlan .15 .40
CC16 John Lackey .20 .50
CC17 Travis Wood .15 .40

2017 Cubs Topps

COMPLETE SET (17) 3.00 8.00
CHC1 Kris Bryant .30 .75
CHC2 Willson Contreras .25 .60
CHC3 Kyle Hendricks .25 .60
CHC4 Jon Lester .20 .50
CHC5 Ben Zobrist .20 .50
CHC6 Kyle Schwarber .25 .60
CHC7 Anthony Rizzo .30 .75
CHC8 Wade Davis .15 .40
CHC9 Jason Heyward .20 .50
CHC10 John Lackey .20 .50
CHC11 Javier Baez .30 .75
CHC12 Jake Arrieta .20 .50
CHC13 Addison Russell .25 .60
CHC14 Jon Jay .15 .40
CHC15 Hector Rondon .15 .40
CHC16 Pedro Strop .15 .40
CHC17 Koji Uehara .15 .40

2018 Cubs Topps

COMPLETE SET (17) 2.50 6.00
CC1 Kris Bryant .30 .75
CC2 Ian Happ .20 .50
CC3 Anthony Rizzo .30 .75
CC4 Kyle Schwarber .25 .60
CC5 Jon Lester .20 .50
CC6 Mike Montgomery .15 .40
CC7 Addison Russell .20 .50
CC8 Jose Quintana .15 .40
CC9 Javier Baez .30 .75
CC10 Jason Heyward .20 .50
CC11 Tommy La Stella .15 .40
CC12 Brandon Morrow .15 .40
CC13 Ben Zobrist .20 .50
CC14 Kyle Hendricks .25 .60
CC15 Albert Almora Jr. .20 .50
CC16 Willson Contreras .25 .60
CC17 Carl Edwards Jr.

2019 Cubs Topps

COMPLETE SET (17) 2.50 6.00
CC1 Javier Baez .30 .75
CC2 Anthony Rizzo .30 .75
CC3 Kris Bryant .30 .75
CC4 Jon Lester .20 .50
CC5 Kyle Schwarber .25 .60
CC6 Kyle Hendricks .25 .60
CC7 Willson Contreras .20 .50
CC8 Ben Zobrist .20 .50
CC9 Jason Heyward .20 .50
CC10 Albert Almora Jr. .20 .50
CC11 Ian Happ .20 .50
CC12 David Bote .20 .50
CC13 Cole Hamels .20 .50
CC14 Yu Darvish .25 .60
CC15 Jose Quintana .15 .40
CC16 Mike Montgomery .15 .40
CC17 Brandon Morrow .15 .40

2020 Cubs Topps

CHC1 Javier Baez .30 .75
CHC2 Kris Bryant .30 .75
CHC3 Jon Lester .20 .50
CHC4 Anthony Rizzo .30 .75
CHC5 Willson Contreras .25 .60
CHC6 Kyle Hendricks .25 .60
CHC7 Jose Quintana .15 .40
CHC8 Kyle Schwarber .25 .60
CHC9 Jason Heyward .20 .50
CHC10 Craig Kimbrel .20 .50
CHC11 David Bote .20 .50
CHC12 Ian Happ .20 .50
CHC13 Ben Zobrist .20 .50
CHC14 Albert Almora .20 .50
CHC15 Nico Hoerner .60 1.50
CHC16 Nicholas Castellanos .25 .60
CHC17 Yu Darvish .25 .60

2017 Cubs Topps National Baseball Card Day

COMPLETE SET (10) 8.00 20.00
CC1 Anthony Rizzo 1.25 3.00
CC2 Jake Arrieta .75 2.00
CC3 Javier Baez 1.25 3.00
CC4 Kris Bryant 1.25 3.00
CC5 Kyle Schwarber 1.00 2.50
CC6 Ben Zobrist .75 2.00
CC7 Addison Russell 1.00 2.50
CC8 Jon Lester .75 2.00
CC9 Kyle Hendricks 1.00 2.50
CC10 Ryne Sandberg 2.00 5.00

2013 Cubs Topps Archives

1 Ernie Banks 1.25 3.00
2 Fergie Jenkins 1.00 2.50
3 Ron Santo .75 2.00
4 Don Kessinger .50 1.25
5 Shawon Dunston .75 2.00
6 Starlin Castro .75 2.00
7 Bobby Murcer .50 1.25
8 Andre Dawson 1.00 2.50
9 Fergie Jenkins 1.00 2.50
10 Sammy Sosa 1.25 3.00
11 Jeff Samardzija .75 2.00
12 Anthony Rizzo 1.50 4.00
13 Starlin Castro .75 2.00
14 Ernie Banks 1.25 3.00
15 Darwin Barney .75 2.00
16 Billy Williams 1.00 2.50
17 Mark Grace 1.00 2.50
18 Starlin Castro .75 2.00
19 Andre Dawson 1.00 2.50
20 Ernie Banks 1.25 3.00
21 Dave Kingman .75 2.00
22 Aramis Ramirez .75 2.00
23 Ryne Sandberg 2.50 6.00
24 Glenn Beckert .75 2.00
25 Kerry Wood .75 2.00
26 Ron Santo .75 2.00
27 Steve Stone .75 2.00
28 Greg Maddux 1.50 4.00
29 Jeff Samardzija .75 2.00
30 Mark Grace 1.00 2.50
31 Greg Maddux 1.50 4.00
32 Jon Lieber .50 1.25
33 Randy Hundley .50 1.25
34 Kerry Wood .75 2.00
35 Don Kessinger .50 1.25
36 Alfonso Soriano 1.00 2.50
37 Rick Sutcliffe .50 1.25
38 Sammy Sosa 1.25 3.00
39 Bill Buckner .75 2.00
40 Ryne Sandberg 2.50 6.00
41 Billy Williams 1.00 2.50
42 Bruce Sutter 1.00 2.50
43 Dennis Eckersley 1.00 2.50
44 Anthony Rizzo 1.50 4.00
45 Ryne Sandberg 2.50 6.00
46 Billy Williams 1.00 2.50
47 Starlin Castro .75 2.00
48 Rick Reuschel .50 1.25
49 Ernie Banks 1.25 3.00
50 Jeff Samardzija .75 2.00
51 Mark Grace 1.00 2.50
52 Glenn Beckert .75 2.00
53 Rick Sutcliffe .50 1.25
54 Darwin Barney .75 2.00
55 Andy Pafko .50 1.25
56 Hank Sauer .50 1.25
57 Rick Monday .75 2.00
58 Jeff Samardzija .75 2.00
59 Ernie Banks 1.25 3.00
60 Jose Cardenal .75 2.00
61 Bruce Sutter 1.00 2.50
62 Lee Smith .75 2.00
63 Ken Holtzman .50 1.25
64 Jerome Walton .75 2.00
65 Scott Sanderson .50 1.25
66 Sammy Sosa 1.25 3.00
67 Ivan DeJesus .75 2.00
68 Ryne Sandberg 2.50 6.00
69 Larry Bowa .75 2.00
70 Milt Pappas .50 1.25
71 Billy Williams 1.00 2.50
72 Sammy Sosa 1.25 3.00
73 Keith Moreland .75 2.00
74 Greg Maddux 1.50 4.00
75 Bruce Sutter 1.00 2.50
76 Ernie Banks 1.25 3.00
77 Fergie Jenkins 1.00 2.50
78 Gene Baker .75 2.00
79 Greg Maddux 1.50 4.00
80 Rick Sutcliffe .50 1.25
81 Jorge Soler 30.00 80.00
Albert Almora
Javier Baez
82 Steve Trachsel .50 1.25

2013 Cubs Topps Archives Season Ticket Holder

1 Ernie Banks 1.25 3.00
2 Fergie Jenkins 1.00 2.50
3 Ron Santo .75 2.00
4 Don Kessinger .50 1.25
5 Shawon Dunston .75 2.00
6 Starlin Castro .75 2.00
7 Bobby Murcer .50 1.25
8 Andre Dawson 1.00 2.50
9 Fergie Jenkins 1.00 2.50
10 Sammy Sosa 1.25 3.00
11 Jeff Samardzija .75 2.00
12 Anthony Rizzo 1.50 4.00
13 Starlin Castro .75 2.00
14 Ernie Banks 1.25 3.00
15 Darwin Barney .75 2.00
16 Billy Williams 1.00 2.50
17 Mark Grace 1.00 2.50
18 Starlin Castro .75 2.00
19 Andre Dawson 1.00 2.50
20 Ernie Banks 1.25 3.00
21 Dave Kingman .75 2.00
22 Aramis Ramirez .75 2.00
23 Ryne Sandberg 2.50 6.00
24 Glenn Beckert .75 2.00
25 Kerry Wood .75 2.00
26 Ron Santo .75 2.00
27 Steve Stone .75 2.00
28 Greg Maddux 1.50 4.00
29 Jeff Samardzija .75 2.00
30 Mark Grace 1.00 2.50
31 Greg Maddux 1.50 4.00
32 Jon Lieber .50 1.25
33 Randy Hundley .50 1.25
34 Kerry Wood .75 2.00
35 Don Kessinger .50 1.25
36 Alfonso Soriano 1.00 2.50
37 Rick Sutcliffe .50 1.25
38 Sammy Sosa 1.25 3.00
39 Bill Buckner .75 2.00
40 Ryne Sandberg 2.50 6.00
41 Billy Williams 1.00 2.50
42 Bruce Sutter 1.00 2.50
43 Dennis Eckersley 1.00 2.50
44 Anthony Rizzo 1.50 4.00
45 Ryne Sandberg 2.50 6.00
46 Billy Williams 1.00 2.50
47 Starlin Castro .75 2.00
48 Rick Reuschel .50 1.25
49 Ernie Banks 1.25 3.00
50 Jeff Samardzija .75 2.00
51 Mark Grace 1.00 2.50
52 Glenn Beckert .75 2.00
53 Rick Sutcliffe .50 1.25
54 Darwin Barney .75 2.00
55 Andy Pafko .50 1.25
56 Hank Sauer .50 1.25
57 Rick Monday .75 2.00
58 Jeff Samardzija .75 2.00
59 Ernie Banks 1.25 3.00
60 Jose Cardenal .75 2.00
61 Bruce Sutter 1.00 2.50
62 Lee Smith .75 2.00
63 Ken Holtzman .50 1.25
64 Jerome Walton .75 2.00
65 Scott Sanderson .50 1.25
66 Sammy Sosa 1.25 3.00
67 Ivan DeJesus .75 2.00
68 Ryne Sandberg 2.50 6.00
69 Larry Bowa .75 2.00
70 Milt Pappas .50 1.25
71 Billy Williams 1.00 2.50
72 Sammy Sosa 1.25 3.00
73 Keith Moreland .75 2.00
74 Greg Maddux 1.50 4.00
75 Bruce Sutter 1.00 2.50
76 Ernie Banks 1.25 3.00
77 Fergie Jenkins 1.00 2.50
78 Gene Baker .75 2.00
79 Greg Maddux 1.50 4.00
80 Rick Sutcliffe .50 1.25
81 Jorge Soler 30.00 80.00
Albert Almora
Javier Baez
82 Steve Trachsel .50 1.25

2008 Cubs Topps Gift Set

1 Lou Piniella MG .15 .40
2 Carlos Zambrano POTM .25 .60
3 Alfonso Soriano .25 .60
4 Alfonso Soriano
Aramis Ramirez/Derrek Lee .25 .60
5 Carlos Zambrano .25 .60
6 Geovany Soto .40 1.00
7 Rich Hill .15 .40
8 Aramis Ramirez .15 .40
9 Alfonso Soriano POTM .25 .60
10 Ted Lilly/Rich Hill/Sean Marshall .15 .40
11 Ted Lilly .15 .40
12 Derrek Lee .15 .40
13 Alfonso Soriano Cubs Clinch .25 .60
14 Kerry Wood .15 .40
15 Alan Trammell CO .25 .60
16 Carlos Zambrano 1000th K .25 .60
17 Ryan Theriot .15 .40
18 Jason Marquis .15 .40
19 Rich Hill/Carlos Zambrano/Ted Lilly .25 .60
20 Felix Pie .15 .40
21 Aramis Ramirez/Alfonso Soriano .25 .60
22 Michael Wuertz .15 .40
23 Derrek Lee/Aramis Ramirez
Alfonso Soriano .25 .60
24 Derrek Lee Hit Streak .15 .40
25 Mark DeRosa .15 .40
26 Matt Sinatro CO .15 .40
27 Carlos Marmol .25 .60
28 Rich Hill Dominates .15 .40
29 Mike Fontenot .15 .40
30 Jon Lieber .15 .40
31 Carlos Zambrano
Ted Lilly/Jason Marquis .25 .60
32 Henry Blanco .15 .40
33 Bob Howry .15 .40
34 Mike Quade CO .15 .40
35 Derrek Lee 7 In A Row .15 .40
36 Matt Murton .15 .40
37 Sean Marshall .15 .40
38 Derrek Lee .15 .40
Alfonso Soriano
Aramis Ramirez
39 Ronny Cedeno .15 .40
40 Ryan Dempster .15 .40
41 Larry Rothschild CO .15 .40
42 Aramis Ramirez 200th HR .15 .40
43 Sam Fuld .50 1.25
44 Neal Cotts .15 .40
45 Carlos Zambrano/Ted Lilly/Rich Hill .25 .60
46 Ted Lilly K'S 10 .15 .40
47 Aramis Ramirez
Derrek Lee/Mark DeRosa .15 .40
48 Daryle Ward .15 .40
49 Aramis Ramirez
Derrek Lee/Carlos Marmol .25 .60
50 Kevin Hart .15 .40
51 Gerald Perry CO .15 .40
52 Angel Guzman .15 .40
53 Alfonso Soriano Goes Yard .25 .60
54 Scott Eyre .15 .40
55 Wrigley Field .15 .40

1996 CUI Metal Cards Griffey

This metal card set was issued in a tin box with a suggested retail price of $9.95. The fronts feature color player photos of Ken Griffey Jr. on a blue and green background. The backs carry information about different phases of his life. The cards are unnumbered and checklisted below according to what is taking place on the card.

COMPLETE SET (5) 4.00 10.00
COMMON CARD (1-4) 1.25 3.00
NNO Ken Griffey Jr. Tin 1.00 2.50

1996 CUI Metal Cards Ripken

This metal card set was issued in a tin-holder with a suggested retail price of $9.95 and was primarily sold in retail outlets such as K-Mart. The fronts feature color action photos of Cal Ripken Jr. with the backs displaying something about his life. The cards are unnumbered.

COMPLETE SET (5) 4.00 10.00
COMMON CARD (1-4) 1.00 2.50
NNO Cal Ripken Tin Box .75 2.00

2005 Daigle/Finch

1 Casey Daigle 5.00 10.00
Jennie Finch

1976 Dallas Convention

This nine-card slightly oversized set features local Dallas players and was issued in conjunction with the annual Dallas Sports Card Convention hosted by noted hobbyist Gervise Ford. Mr. Ford also produced the set with "Life of the Southwest Insurance Co.".

COMPLETE SET (9) .75 2.00
1 Paul Aube .10 .25
2 Jodie Beeler .10 .25
3 Edward Borom/(Red) .10 .25
4 Sal Gliatto .10 .25
5 Richard Herrscher .10 .25
6 Joe Kotrany .10 .25
7 Joe Macko .10 .25
8 Frank Murray .10 .25
9 Ron Samford .10 .25

1985 Dallas National Collectors Convention

This 12-card set was issued by First Base Sports Nostalgia Shop in Dallas, Texas, to commemorate a bid for the Dallas National Collectors Convention. The black-and-white cards measure approximately 2" by 2 1/2" and include various photos relating to their National Convention bid including a photo of the proposed 1986 Convention hosts (Jim Beckett, Wayne Grove, and Gervise Ford) along with Dallas Maverick star Brad Davis, a shot of the Dallas Marriott, Market Hall and several Baseball legends who were guests of honor of the convention. The backs list the subject of the card front with a brief description and the First Base Sports Nostalgia Shop address.

COMPLETE SET (12) 4.00 10.00
1 Stan Musial 1.00 2.50
2 Ted Williams 1.25 3.00
3 Bob Gibson .40 1.00
4 Brooks Robinson .40 1.00
5 Warren Spahn .40 1.00
6 Enos Slaughter .40 1.00
7 The Famous Chicken .20 .50
8 Lou Brock .30 .75
9 Market Hall/(1986 Dallas Natl. .08 .25
Convention Facili
10 Texas Ranger .08 .25
Scoreboard
11 Dallas Marriott .08 .25
Market Center
12 Hosts .60 1.50
Jim Beckett
Wayne Grove
Brad Davis (Dalla

1954 Dan-Dee

DALE MITCHELL

The cards in this 29-card set measure approximately 2 1/2" by 3 5/8". Most of the cards marketed by Dan Dee in bags of potato chips in 1954 depict players from the Cleveland Indians or Pittsburgh Pirates. The Pittsburgh Pirates players in the set are much tougher to find than the Cleveland Indians players. The pictures used for New York Yankees players were also employed in the Briggs and Stahl-Meyer sets. Dan Dee cards have a waxed surface, but are commonly found with product stains. Paul Smith and Walker Cooper are considered the known scarcities. The catalog designation for this set is F342. These unnumbered cards are listed below in alphabetical order.

COMPLETE SET (29) 5000.00 10000.00
COMMON CARD (1-29) 50.00 100.00
COMMON PIRATE CARD 50.00 100.00
COMMON PIRATE SP'S 250.00 500.00
1 Bobby Avila 60.00 120.00
2 Hank Bauer 60.00 120.00
3 Walker Cooper SP/Pittsburgh Pirates 300.00 600.00
4 Larry Doby 100.00 200.00
5 Luke Easter 60.00 120.00
6 Bob Feller 150.00 300.00
7 Bob Friend/Pittsburgh Pirates 100.00 200.00
8 Mike Garcia 60.00 120.00
9 Sid Gordon/Pittsburgh Pirates 75.00 150.00
10 Jim Hegan 50.00 100.00
11 Gil Hodges 125.00 250.00
12 Art Houtteman 50.00 100.00
13 Monte Irvin 100.00 200.00
14 Paul LaPalme/Pittsburgh Pirates 60.00 120.00
15 Bob Lemon 100.00 200.00
16 Al Lopez MG 75.00 150.00
17 Mickey Mantle 1500.00 2500.00
18 Dale Mitchell 50.00 100.00
19 Phil Rizzuto 200.00 400.00
20 Curt Roberts/Pittsburgh Pirates 60.00 120.00
21 Al Rosen 75.00 150.00
22 Red Schoendienst 100.00 200.00
23 Paul Smith SP/Pittsburgh Pirates 500.00 1000.00
24 Duke Snider 250.00 500.00
25 George Strickland 50.00 100.00
26 Max Surkont/Pittsburgh Pirates 60.00 120.00
27 Frank Thomas/Pittsburgh Pirates 150.00 300.00
28 Wally Westlake 50.00 100.00
29 Early Wynn 100.00 200.00

1910 Darby Chocolates E271

These 34 cards listed below are what are known of this very scarce set. A major help in cataloguing this set was a find of 22 cards in 1982. Some new cards are always being discovered. We understand that this checklist may be incomplete therefore verified copies of unlisted cards are appreciated. Uncut complete boxes are more desirable when found and are worth a little more than twice the value of the combined cards.

COMPLETE SET (34) 15000.00 35000.00
1 Jimmy Archer 1000.00 2000.00
2 Chief Bender 2000.00 4000.00
3 Bob Bescher 1000.00 2000.00
4 Roger Bresnahan 2000.00 4000.00
5 Al Bridwell 1000.00 2000.00
6 Mordecai Brown 2000.00 4000.00
7 Eddie Cicotte 2000.00 4000.00
8 Fred Clarke 2000.00 4000.00
9 Ty Cobb Batting 6000.00 15000.00
10 Ty Cobb Fielding 6000.00 15000.00
11 King Cole 1000.00 2000.00
12 Eddie Collins 2500.00 5000.00
13 Wid Conroy 1000.00 2000.00
14 Sam Crawford 2000.00 4000.00
15 Bill Dahlen 1000.00 2000.00
16 Bill Donovan 1000.00 2000.00
17 Patsy Dougherty 1000.00 2000.00
18 Kid Elberfeld 1000.00 2000.00
19 Johnny Evers 2000.00 4000.00
20 Buck Herzog 1000.00 2000.00
21 Hugh Jennings MG 2000.00 4000.00
22 Walter Johnson 5000.00 10000.00
23 Ed Konetchy 1000.00 2000.00
24 Tommy Leach 1000.00 2000.00
25 Fred Luderus 1000.00 2000.00
Sic, Luderous
26 John McGraw MG 2500.00 5000.00
27 Mike Mowrey 1000.00 2000.00
28 Jack Powell 1000.00 2000.00
29 Slim Sallee 1000.00 2000.00
30 Jimmy Sheckard 1000.00 2000.00
Sic, Scheckard
31 Fred Snodgrass 1250.00 2500.00
32 Tris Speaker 2500.00 5000.00
33 Charlie Suggs 1000.00 2000.00
34 Fred Tenney 1000.00 2000.00
35 Jim Vaughn 1000.00 2000.00
36 Honus Wagner 1250.00 3000.00

2004 DAV

COMMON CARD .25 .60
1 Robby Hammock .25 .60
2 Austin Kearns .25 .60
3 Larry Bigbie .25 .60
4 Wes Helms .25 .60
5 Scott Podsednik .25 .60
6 Ben Sheets .25 .60
7 Brian Giles .25 .60
8 Joel Pineiro .25 .60
9 Dan Wilson .25 .60
10 Ron Gardenhire MG .25 .60
11 Eddie Guardado .25 .60
12 Raul Ibanez .40 1.00
13 Hank Blalock .25 .60
14 Mark Teixeira .40 1.00
15 Michael Young .25 .60
16 Danys Baez .25 .60
17 Jose Cruz Jr. .25 .60
18 Robert Fick .25 .60
19 Toby Hall .25 .60
20 Tino Martinez .40 1.00
21 Mike Maroth .25 .60
22 Lou Piniella MG .25 .60
23 Damian Rolls .25 .60
24 Doug Waechter .25 .60
25 Victor Zambrano .25 .60
26 Don Zimmer CO .25 .60
27 J.D. Drew .25 .60
28 Horacio Ramirez .25 .60
29 Jeff Kent .25 .60
30 John Thomson .25 .60
31 Johnny Estrada .25 .60
32 Rafael Furcal .25 .60
33 John Smoltz .60 1.50
34 Chipper Jones .60 1.50
35 Marcus Giles .25 .60
36 Andruw Jones .25 .60
37 Josh Beckett .25 .60
38 Miguel Cabrera .60 1.50
39 Hee Seop Choi .25 .60
40 Brad Penny .25 .60
41 Juan Pierre .25 .60
42 Dontrelle Willis .25 .60

2005 DAV

COMMON CARD .25 .60
1 Ron Gardenhire MG .25 .60
2 Mike Maroth .25 .60
3 Bobby Cox MG .25 .60
4 Adam LaRoche .25 .60
5 Bobby Dews CO .25 .60
6 Chipper Jones .60 1.50
7 Chris Reitsma .25 .60
8 Eddie Perez .25 .60
9 Fredi Gonzales CO .25 .60
10 Glenn Hubbard CO .25 .60
11 Horacio Ramirez .25 .60
12 John Smoltz .60 1.50
13 John Thomson .25 .60
14 Johnny Estrada .25 .60
15 Andruw Jones .25 .60
16 Julio Franco .25 .60
17 Kevin Gryboski .25 .60
18 Leo Mazzone CO .25 .60
19 Marcus Giles .25 .60
20 Mike Hampton .25 .60
21 Nick Green .25 .60
22 Rafael Furcal .25 .60
23 Roman Colon .25 .60
24 Terry Pendleton CO .25 .60
25 Tom Martin .25 .60
26 Wily Mo Pena .25 .60
27 Ichiro Suzuki .75 2.00
28 Adrian Beltre .60 1.50
29 Richie Sexson .25 .60
30 Jamie Moyer .25 .60
31 B.J. Surhoff .25 .60
32 Tony Clark .25 .60
33 Jake Peavy .25 .60
34 Craig Counsell .25 .60
35 Roger Clemens .75 2.00
36 Roy Oswalt .40 1.00
37 Lance Berkman .40 1.00
38 Lyle Overbay .25 .60
39 Carlos Lee .25 .60
40 Brady Clark .25 .60
41 Doug Davis .25 .60
42 Josh Beckett .25 .60
43 A.J. Burnett .25 .60
44 Jeff Conine .25 .60
45 Al Leiter .25 .60
46 Paul LoDuca .25 .60
47 Mike Lowell .25 .60
48 Juan Pierre .25 .60
49 Dontrelle Willis .25 .60
50 Mark Teixeira .40 1.00
51 Michael Young .25 .60
52 Hank Blalock .25 .60
53 B.J. Upton .40 1.00
54 Hideo Nomo .60 1.50
55 Doug Waechter .25 .60
56 Jonny Gomes .25 .60
57 Delmon Young .60 1.50
58 Toby Hall .25 .60
59 Nick Green .25 .60
60 Travis Lee .25 .60
61 Julio Lugo .25 .60
62 Alex S. Gonzalez .25 .60
63 Casey Fossum .25 .60
64 Eduardo Perez .25 .60
65 Mark Hendrickson .25 .60
66 Jorge Cantu .25 .60
67 Carl Crawford .40 1.00
68 Scott Kazmir .60 1.50
69 Aubrey Huff .25 .60
70 Damon Hollins .25 .60
71 Danys Baez .25 .60
72 Bob Horner .25 .60
73 Dale Murphy .60 1.50
74 David Justice .25 .60
75 Eddie Mathews .60 1.50
76 Francisco Cabrera .25 .60
77 Fred McGriff .40 1.00
78 Gene Garber .25 .60
79 Glenn Hubbard .25 .60
80 Greg Olson .25 .60
81 Hank Aaron 1.25 3.00
82 Jeff Blauser .25 .60
83 Mark Lemke .25 .60
84 Phil Niekro .40 1.00
85 Ron Gant .25 .60
86 Steve Avery .25 .60
87 Warren Spahn .40 1.00

2006 DAV

COMMON CARD .25 .60
1 Eric Byrnes .25 .60
2 Tony Clark .25 .60
3 Orlando Hudson .25 .60
4 Conor Jackson .40 1.00
5 Rich Aurilia .25 .60
6 Gapper MASCOT .25 .60
7 Jason LaRue .25 .60
8 Felipe Lopez .25 .60
9 Ron Gardenhire MG .25 .60
10 Miguel Cabrera .60 1.50
11 Jeremy Hermida .25 .60
12 Mike Jacobs .25 .60
13 Sergio Mitre .25 .60
14 Miguel Olivo .25 .60
15 Hanley Ramirez .40 1.00
16 Dan Uggla .40 1.00
17 Jason Vargas .25 .60
18 Josh Willingham .40 1.00
19 Dontrelle Willis .25 .60
20 Darin Erstad .25 .60
21 Chone Figgins .25 .60
22 John Lackey .40 1.00
23 Chris Capuano .25 .60
24 Bill Hall .25 .60
25 Corey Koskie .25 .60
26 Geoff Jenkins .25 .60
27 Mike Scioscia MG .25 .60
28 Felipe Alou MG .25 .60
29 Moises Alou .25 .60
30 Armando Benitez .25 .60
31 Barry Bonds 1.00 2.50
32 Ray Durham .25 .60
33 Pedro Feliz .25 .60
34 Mike Matheny .25 .60
35 Lance Niekro .25 .60
36 Jason Schmidt .25 .60
37 Omar Vizquel .40 1.00
38 Randy Winn .25 .60
39 Tim Worrell .25 .60
40 Raul Ibanez .40 1.00
41 Kenji Johjima .60 1.50
42 Jeremy Reed .25 .60
43 Jarrod Washburn .25 .60

44 Dave Roberts .40 1.00
45 Mike Cameron .25 .60
46 Alfonso Soriano .40 1.00
47 Brian Schneider .25 .60
48 Chad Cordero .25 .60
49 Frank Robinson MG .40 1.00
50 John Patterson .25 .60
51 Jose Guillen .25 .60
52 Jose Vidro .25 .60
53 Livan Hernandez .25 .60
54 Marlon Byrd .25 .60
55 Nick Johnson .25 .60
56 Ramon Ortiz .25 .60
57 Royce Clayton .25 .60
58 Jeff Conine .25 .60
59 Ryan Zimmerman .75 2.00
60 Tony Armas Jr. .25 .60
61 Rocco Baldelli .25 .60
62 Jorge Cantu .25 .60
63 Carl Crawford .40 1.00
64 Casey Fossum .25 .60
65 Joey Gathright .25 .60
66 Jonny Gomes .25 .60
67 Toby Hall .25 .60
68 Travis Harper .25 .60
69 Mark Hendrickson .25 .60
70 Damon Hollins .25 .60
71 Aubrey Huff .25 .60
72 Scott Kazmir .40 1.00
73 Travis Lee .25 .60
74 Julio Lugo .25 .60
75 Joe Maddon MG .25 .60
76 Seth McClung .25 .60
77 Chad Orvella .25 .60
78 Doug Waechter .25 .60
79 Ty Wigginton .25 .60
80 Mark Teixeira .40 1.00
81 Michael Young .25 .60
82 Craig Biggio .40 1.00
83 Morgan Ensberg .25 .60
84 Mike Maroth .25 .60

2008 DAV

COMMON CARD .25 .60
9 Dusty Baker MG .25 .60
10 Francisco Cordero .25 .60
11 Edwin Encarnacion .60 1.50
12 Adam Dunn .40 1.00
56 Barry Zito .40 1.00
61 Bengie Molina .25 .60
117 Chris Duncan .25 .60
130 Yadier Molina .75 2.00
133 Albert Pujols .75 2.00

2010 DAV

COMMON CARD .25 .60
1 Bronson Arroyo .25 .60
2 Johnny Cueto .40 1.00
3 Brandon Phillips .40 1.00
6 Matt Cain .40 1.00
9 Tim Lincecum .40 1.00
10 Bengie Molina .25 .60
11 Edgar Renteria .25 .60
12 Aaron Rowand .25 .60
13 Jonathan Sanchez .25 .60
14 Pablo Sandoval .40 1.00
15 Juan Uribe .25 .60
16 Barry Zito .40 1.00
17 Ichiro Suzuki .75 2.00
18 Felix Hernandez .40 1.00
21 Chone Figgins .25 .60
22 Cliff Lee .40 1.00
23 Jose Lopez .25 .60
25 Austin Jackson .40 1.00
28 Willie Horton .25 .60
29 Joel Zumaya .25 .60
30 Mario Impemba .25 .60
32 Rick Porcello .40 1.00
33 Ryan Perry .25 .60
35 Joe Blanton .25 .60
36 Roy Halladay .40 1.00
37 Cole Hamels .50 1.25
38 Ryan Howard .50 1.25
39 Raul Ibanez .40 1.00
40 Brad Lidge .25 .60
44 Placido Polanco .25 .60
45 Jimmy Rollins .40 1.00
47 Chase Utley .40 1.00
50 Jamie Moyer .25 .60
50 Michael Cuddyer .25 .60
51 Francisco Liriano .25 .60
53 Jim Thome .40 1.00
55 Justin Morneau .40 1.00
56 Joe Mauer .50 1.25
58 Jon Rauch .25 .60
59 Orlando Hudson .25 .60
60 John Baker .25 .60
61 Anibal Sanchez .25 .60
65 Hanley Ramirez .40 1.00
67 Clay Hensley .25 .60
68 Josh Johnson .40 1.00
72 Ricky Nolasco .25 .60
76 Cody Ross .25 .60
77 Mike Stanton 2.00 5.00
78 Taylor Tankersley .25 .60
79 Dan Uggla .25 .60
80 Chris Volstad .25 .60
81 Tim Wood .25 .60
83 Mike Adams .25 .60
84 Heath Bell .25 .60
85 Everth Cabrera .25 .60
86 Kevin Correia .25 .60
87 David Eckstein .25 .60
88 Jon Garland .25 .60
89 Adrian Gonzalez .50 1.25
91 Tony Gwynn Jr. .25 .60
92 Scott Hairston .25 .60
93 Chase Headley .25 .60
94 Mat Latos .40 1.00
95 Clayton Richard .25 .60
96 Yorvit Torrealba .25 .60
122 Mitchell Boggs .25 .60
123 Chris Carpenter .40 1.00
125 Jaime Garcia .40 1.00
126 Blake Hawksworth .25 .60
127 Kyle McClellan .25 .60
129 Jason Motte .25 .60
130 Dennys Reyes .25 .60
131 Adam Wainwright .40 1.00
132 Jason LaRue .25 .60
133 Yadier Molina .75 2.00
134 David Freese .40 1.00
135 Felipe Lopez .25 .60
136 Aaron Miles .25 .60
137 Albert Pujols .75 2.00
139 Skip Schumaker .25 .60
140 Matt Holliday .60 1.50
141 Jon Jay .40 1.00
142 Colby Rasmus .40 1.00
143 Nick Stavinoha .25 .60
145 Tyler Greene .25 .60
146 Jeff Suppan .25 .60
148 Evan Longoria .40 1.00
150 Matt Garza .25 .60
152 Lance Cormier .25 .60
154 John Jaso .25 .60
155 Reid Brignac .25 .60
155 Reid Brignac .25 .60
156 Carlos Pena .40 1.00
157 Carl Crawford .40 1.00
160 Andy Sonnanstine .25 .60
162 Joe Maddon MG .25 .60
163 Jeff Niemann .25 .60
167 Kelly Shoppach .25 .60
168 Jason Bartlett .25 .60
170 B.J. Upton .40 1.00
174 Rocco Baldelli .25 .60
176 Chad Qualls .25 .60

1982 Davco Hall of Fame Boxes

This 25-card set features color drawings of Hall of Fame Baseball Stars measuring approximately 4 1/4" by 7 1/4". The fronts carry both an action drawing of the player and a drawn portrait with blue borders and a red, white, and blue facsimile ribbon around the top and sides of the picture. The player's name and why he is in the Hall of Fame is printed below. The backs are blank. The cards are unnumbered and checklisted below in alphabetical order.

COMPLETE SET (25) 12.50 30.00
1 Hank Aaron 1.25 3.00
2 Grover C. Alexander .60 1.50
3 Roy Campanella 1.00 2.50
4 Ty Cobb 1.25 3.00
5 Joe DiMaggio 1.50 4.00
6 Bob Feller .60 1.50
7 Jimmy Foxx (Jimmie) 1.00 2.50
8 Frank Frisch .40 1.00
9 Lou Gehrig 1.25 3.00
10 Bob Gibson .60 1.50
11 Hank Greenberg 1.00 2.50
12 Rogers Hornsby .75 2.00
13 Walter Johnson 1.00 2.50
14 Sandy Koufax 1.00 2.50
15 Mickey Mantle 2.00 5.00
16 Christy Mathewson .75 2.00
17 Willie Mays 1.25 3.00
18 Stan Musial 1.00 2.50
19 Jackie Robinson 1.25 3.00
20 Babe Ruth 2.00 5.00
21 Tris Speaker .60 1.50
22 Pie Traynor .60 1.50
23 Honus Wagner .75 2.00
24 Ted Williams 1.25 3.00
25 Cy Young 1.00 2.50

2000 Eric Davis Colon Cancer

1 Eric Davis .40 1.00

1993 Leon Day Commemorative Card

Published by Hieronimus and Co., this card measures 2 1/2" by 3 1/2" and features a portrait of Leon Day on a white background by artist Gary Cieradkowski Jr. The player's name appears in a black-and-white banner that includes drawings of a glove, bat, ball and face mask. The back is printed in black ink and carries biography and career highlights.

1 Leon Day 4.00 10.00

1970 Dayton Daily News M137

These 3 3/4" by 3 1/2" cards were issued inside issues of the Dayton Daily News. The newsprint-stock cards were issued on successive days and were numbered in that order. Tony Perez, card number 11, has been seen with a light or dark cap. There is no pricing difference for either card. The Dave Concepcion card predates his Topps Rookie Card by one year.

COMPLETE SET 300.00 600.00
COMMON CARD (61-160) 1.25 3.00
1 Pete Rose 8.00 20.00
2 Johnny Bench 4.00 10.00
3 Maury Wills 2.00 5.00
4 Harmon Killebrew 2.50 6.00
5 Frank Robinson 3.00 8.00
6 Willie Mays 6.00 15.00
7 Hank Aaron 6.00 15.00
8 Tom Seaver 4.00 10.00
9 Sam McDowell 1.50 4.00
10 Rico Petrocelli 1.50 4.00
11 Tony Perez Dark Cap 2.50 6.00
11A Tony Perez White Cap 2.50 6.00
12 Hoyt Wilhelm 2.50 6.00
13 Alex Johnson 1.00 2.50
14 Gary Nolan 1.00 2.50
15 Al Kaline 3.00 8.00
16 Bob Gibson 3.00 8.00
17 Larry Dierker 1.00 2.50
18 Ernie Banks 3.00 8.00
19 Lee May 1.50 4.00
20 Claude Osteen 1.00 2.50
21 Tony Horton 1.00 2.50
22 Mack Jones 1.00 2.50
23 Wally Bunker 1.00 2.50
24 Bill Hands 1.00 2.50
25 Bobby Tolan 1.00 2.50
26 Jim Wynn 1.50 4.00
27 Tom Haller 1.00 2.50
28 Carl Yastrzemski 3.00 8.00
29 Jim Merritt 1.00 2.50
30 Tony Oliva 2.00 5.00
31 Reggie Jackson 8.00 20.00
32 Bob Clemente 12.50 30.00
33 Tommy Helms 1.00 2.50
34 Boog Powell 2.00 5.00
35 Mickey Lolich 1.50 4.00
36 Frank Howard 1.50 4.00
37 Jim McGlothlin 1.00 2.50
38 Rusty Staub 1.50 4.00
39 Mel Stottlemyre 1.50 4.00
40 Rico Carty 1.00 2.50
41 Nate Colbert 1.00 2.50
42 Wayne Granger 1.00 2.50
43 Mike Hegan 1.00 2.50
44 Jerry Koosman 1.50 4.00
45 Jim Perry 1.00 2.50
46 Pat Corrales 1.00 2.50
47 Dick Bosman 1.00 2.50
48 Bert Campaneris 1.50 4.00
49 Larry Hisle 1.00 2.50
50 Bernie Carbo 1.00 2.50
51 Wilbur Wood 1.00 2.50
52 Dave McNally 1.50 4.00
53 Andy Messersmith 1.50 4.00
54 Jimmy Stewart 1.00 2.50
55 Luis Aparicio 2.50 6.00
56 Mike Cuellar 1.00 2.50
57 Bill Grabarkewitz 1.00 2.50
58 Dick Dietz 1.00 2.50
59 Dave Concepcion 2.50 6.00
60 Gary Gentry 1.00 2.50
61 Don Money 1.25 3.00
62 Rod Carew 4.00 10.00
63 Denis Menke 1.25 3.00
64 Hal McRae 1.50 4.00
65 Felipe Alou 1.50 4.00
66 Richie Hebner 1.25 3.00
67 Don Sutton 2.50 6.00
68 Wayne Simpson 1.25 3.00
69 Art Shamsky 1.25 3.00
70 Luis Tiant 2.00 5.00
71 Clay Carroll 1.25 3.00
72 Jim Hickman 1.25 3.00
73 Clarence Gaston 1.25 3.00
74 Angel Bravo 1.25 3.00
75 Jim Hunter 2.50 6.00
76 Lou Piniella 2.00 5.00
77 Jim Bunning 2.50 6.00
78 Don Gullett 1.25 3.00
80 Richie Allen 2.00 5.00
81 Jim Bouton 1.50 4.00
82 Jim Palmer 4.00 10.00
83 Woody Woodward 1.25 3.00
84 Tom Agee 1.25 3.00
85 Carlos May 1.25 3.00
86 Ray Washburn 1.25 3.00
87 Denny McLain 1.50 4.00
88 Lou Brock 4.00 10.00
89 Ken Henderson 1.25 3.00
90 Roy White 1.50 4.00
91 Chris Cannizzaro 1.25 3.00
92 Willie Horton 1.50 4.00
93 Jose Cardenal 1.25 3.00
94 Jim Fregosi 1.50 4.00
95 Richie Hebner 1.25 3.00
96 Tony Conigliaro 2.00 5.00
97 Tony Cloninger 1.25 3.00
98 Mike Epstein 1.25 3.00
99 Ty Cline 1.25 3.00
100 Tommy Harper 1.25 3.00
101 Jose Azcue 1.25 3.00
102a Ray Fosse 1.25 3.00
102b Glenn Beckert 1.25 3.00
103 not issued
104 Gerry Moses 1.25 3.00
105 Bud Harrelson 1.25 3.00
106 Joe Torre 2.50 6.00
107 Dave Johnson 1.50 4.00
108 Don Kessinger 1.50 4.00
109 Bill Freehan 1.50 4.00
110 Sandy Alomar 1.25 3.00
111 Matty Alou 1.25 3.00
112 Joe Morgan 2.50 6.00
113 John Odom 1.25 3.00
114 Amos Otis 1.50 4.00
115 Jay Johnstone 1.25 3.00
116 Ron Perranoski 1.25 3.00
117 Manny Mota 1.25 3.00
118 Billy Conigliaro 1.25 3.00
119 Leo Cardenas 1.25 3.00
120 Rich Reese 1.25 3.00
121 Ron Santo 2.00 5.00
122 Gene Michael 1.25 3.00
123 Milt Pappas 1.25 3.00
124 Joe Pepitone 1.50 4.00
125 Jose Cardenal 1.25 3.00
126 Jim Northrup 1.50 4.00
127 Wes Parker 1.25 3.00
128 Fritz Peterson 1.25 3.00
129 Phil Regan 1.25 3.00
130 John Callison 1.25 3.00
131 Cookie Rojas 1.25 3.00
132 Claude Raymond 1.25 3.00
133 Darrell Chaney 1.25 3.00
134 Gary Peters 1.25 3.00
135 Del Unser 1.25 3.00
136 Joey Foy 1.25 3.00
137 Luke Walker 1.25 3.00
138 Bill Mazeroski 2.50 6.00
139 Tony Taylor 1.25 3.00
140 Leron Lee 1.25 3.00
141 Jesus Alou 1.50 4.00
142 Donn Clendenon 1.25 3.00
143 Merv Rettenmund 1.25 3.00
144 Bob Moose 1.25 3.00
145 Jim Kaat 2.00 5.00
146 Randy Hundley 1.25 3.00
147 Jim McAndrew 1.25 3.00
148 Manny Sanguillen 1.25 3.00
149 Bob Allison 1.25 3.00
150 Jim Maloney 1.25 3.00
151 Don Buford 1.25 3.00
152 Gene Alley 1.25 3.00
153 Cesar Tovar 1.25 3.00
154 Brooks Robinson 4.00 10.00
155 Milt Wilcox 1.25 3.00
156 Willie Stargell 2.50 6.00
157 Paul Blair 1.25 3.00
158 Andy Etchebarren 1.25 3.00
159 Mark Belanger 1.25 3.00
160 Elrod Hendricks 1.25 3.00

1971 Dell Today's Team Stamps

This set of stamps consists of 600 stamps contained in 25 stamp books (each containing 24 stamps) labeled Today's 1971 Team. The stamps are usually found still in the team albums. The value of each album intact with all its stamps would be the sum of the prices of all the individual player stamps inside the album. Stamps are unnumbered but are presented here in alphabetical order by team, Atlanta Braves (1-24), Chicago Cubs (25-48), Cincinnati Reds (49-72), Houston Astros (73-96), Los Angeles Dodgers (97-120), Montreal Expos (121-144), New York Mets (145-168), Philadelphia Phillies (169-192), Pittsburgh Pirates (193-216), San Diego Padres (217-240), San Francisco Giants (241-264), St. Louis Cardinals (265-288), Baltimore Orioles AL (289-312), Boston Red Sox (313-336), California Angels (337-360), Chicago White Sox (361-384), Cleveland Indians (385-408), Detroit Tigers (409-432), Kansas City Royals (433-456), Milwaukee Brewers (457-480), Minnesota Twins (481-504), New York Yankees (505-528), Oakland A's (529-552), Washington Senators (553-576) and All-Stars (577-600).

COMPLETE SET (576) 100.00 200.00
1 Hank Aaron 1.50 4.00
2 Tommy Aaron .08 .20
3 Hank Allen .08 .20
4 Clete Boyer .12 .30
5 Oscar Brown .08 .20
6 Rico Carty .08 .20
7 Orlando Cepeda .40 1.00
8 Bob Didier .08 .20
9 Ralph Garr .08 .20
10 Gil Garrido .08 .20
11 Ron Herbel .08 .20
12 Sonny Jackson .08 .20
13 Pat Jarvis .08 .20
14 Larry Jaster .08 .20
15 Hal King .08 .20
16 Mike Lum .08 .20
17 Felix Millan .08 .20
18 Jim Nash .08 .20
19 Phil Niekro .50 1.25
20 Bob Priddy .08 .20
21 Ron Reed .08 .20
22 George Stone .08 .20
23 Cecil Upshaw .08 .20
24 Hoyt Wilhelm .40 1.00
25 Ernie Banks .75 2.00
26 Glenn Beckert .08 .20
27 Danny Breeden .08 .20
28 Johnny Callison .08 .20
29 Jim Colborn .08 .20
30 Joe Decker .08 .20
31 Bill Hands .08 .20
32 Jim Hickman .08 .20
33 Ken Holtzman .08 .20
34 Randy Hundley .08 .20
35 Fergie Jenkins .40 1.00
36 Don Kessinger .08 .20
37 J.C. Martin .08 .20
38 Bob Miller .08 .20
39 Milt Pappas .08 .20
40 Joe Pepitone .08 .20
41 Juan Pizarro .08 .20
42 Paul Popovich .08 .20
43 Phil Regan .08 .20
44 Roberto Rodriguez .08 .20
45 Ken Rudolph .08 .20
46 Ron Santo .15 .40
47 Hector Torres .08 .20
48 Billy Williams .50 1.25
49 Johnny Bench .75 2.00
50 Angel Bravo .08 .20
51 Bernie Carbo .08 .20
52 Clay Carroll .08 .20
53 Darrel Chaney .08 .20
54 Ty Cline .08 .20
55 Tony Cloninger .08 .20
56 Dave Concepcion .15 .40
57 Pat Corrales .08 .20
58 Greg Garrett .08 .20
59 Wayne Granger .08 .20
60 Don Gullett .08 .20
61 Tommy Helms .08 .20
62 Lee May .08 .20
63 Jim McGlothlin .08 .20
64 Hal McRae .08 .20
65 Jim Merritt .08 .20
66 Gary Nolan .08 .20
67 Tony Perez .40 1.00
68 Pete Rose 1.25 3.00
69 Wayne Simpson .08 .20
70 Jimmy Stewart .08 .20
71 Bobby Tolan .08 .20
72 Woody Woodward .08 .20
73 Jesus Alou .08 .20
74 Jack Billingham .08 .20
75 Ron Cook .08 .20
76 George Culver .08 .20
77 Larry Dierker .08 .20
78 Jack DiLauro .08 .20
79 Johnny Edwards .08 .20
80 Fred Gladding .08 .20
81 Tom Griffin .08 .20
82 Skip Guinn .08 .20
83 Jack Hiatt .08 .20
84 Denver Lemaster .08 .20
85 Marty Martinez .08 .20
86 John Mayberry .08 .20
87 Denis Menke .08 .20
88 Norm Miller .08 .20
89 Joe Morgan .40 1.00
90 Doug Rader .08 .20
91 Jim Ray .08 .20
92 Scipio Spinks .08 .20
93 Bob Watkins .08 .20
94 Bob Watson .12 .30
95 Don Wilson .08 .20
96 Jim Wynn .12 .30
97 Rich Allen .15 .40
98 Jim Brewer .08 .20
99 Bill Buckner .15 .40
100 Willie Crawford .08 .20
101 Willie Davis .12 .30
102 Al Downing .08 .20
103 Steve Garvey .50 1.25
104 Billy Grabarkewitz .08 .20
105 Tom Haller .08 .20
106 Jim LeFebvre .08 .20
107 Pete Mikkelsen .08 .20
108 Joe Moeller .08 .20
109 Manny Mota .08 .20
110 Claude Osteen .08 .20
111 Wes Parker .08 .20
112 Jose Pena .08 .20
113 Bill Russell .08 .20
114 Duke Sims .08 .20
115 Bill Singer .08 .20
116 Mike Strahler .08 .20
117 Bill Sudakis .08 .20
118 Don Sutton .50 1.25
119 Jeff Torborg .08 .20
120 Maury Wills .40 1.00
121 Bob Bailey .08 .20
122 John Bateman .08 .20
123 John Boccabella .08 .20
124 Ron Brand .08 .20
125 Boots Day .08 .20
126 Jim Fairey .08 .20
127 Ron Fairly .08 .20
128 Jim Gosger .08 .20
129 Don Hahn .08 .20
130 Ron Hunt .08 .20
131 Mack Jones .08 .20
132 Jose Laboy .08 .20
133 Mike Marshall .08 .20
134 Dan McGinn .08 .20
135 Carl Morton .08 .20
136 John O'Donoghue .08 .20
137 Adolpho Phillips .08 .20
138 Claude Raymond .08 .20
139 Steve Renko .08 .20
140 Marv Staehle .08 .20
141 Rusty Staub .15 .40
142 Bill Stoneman .08 .20
143 Gary Sutherland .08 .20
144 Bobby Wine .08 .20
145 Tommy Agee .08 .20
146 Bob Aspromonte .08 .20
147 Ken Boswell .08 .20
148 Dean Chance .08 .20
149 Donn Clendenon .08 .20
150 Duffy Dyer .08 .20
151 Dan Frisella .08 .20
152 Wayne Garrett .08 .20
153 Gary Gentry .08 .20
154 Jerry Grote .08 .20
155 Bud Harrelson .12 .30
156 Cleon Jones .08 .20
157 Jerry Koosman .15 .40
158 Ed Kranepool .08 .20
159 Dave Marshall .08 .20
160 Jim McAndrew .08 .20
161 Tug McGraw .15 .40
162 Nolan Ryan 4.00 10.00
163 Ray Sadecki .08 .20
164 Tom Seaver .75 2.00
165 Art Shamsky .08 .20
166 Ron Swoboda .08 .20
167 Ron Taylor .08 .20
168 Al Weis .08 .20
169 Larry Bowa .15 .40
170 Johnny Briggs .08 .20
171 Byron Browne .08 .20
172 Jim Bunning .40 1.00
173 Billy Champion .08 .20
174 Mike Compton .08 .20
175 Denny Doyle .08 .20
176 Roger Freed .08 .20
177 Woody Fryman .08 .20
178 Oscar Gamble .08 .20
179 Terry Harmon .08 .20
180 Larry Hisle .08 .20
181 Joe Hoerner .08 .20
182 Deron Johnson .08 .20
183 Barry Lersch .08 .20
184 Tim McCarver .15 .40
185 Don Money .08 .20
186 Mike Ryan .08 .20
187 Dick Selma .08 .20
188 Chris Short .08 .20
189 Ron Stone .08 .20
190 Tony Taylor .08 .20
191 Rick Wise .08 .20
192 Billy Wilson .08 .20
193 Gene Alley .08 .20
194 Steve Blass .08 .20
195 Nelson Briles .08 .20
196 Jim Campanis .08 .20
197 Dave Cash .08 .20
198 Roberto Clemente 2.50 6.00
199 Vic Davalillo .08 .20
200 Dock Ellis .08 .20
201 Jim Grant .08 .20
202 Dave Giusti .08 .20
203 Richie Hebner .08 .20
204 Jackie Hernandez .08 .20
205 Johnny Jeter .08 .20
206 Lou Marone .08 .20
207 Jose Martinez .08 .20
208 Bill Mazeroski .30 .75
209 Bob Moose .08 .20
210 Al Oliver .15 .40
211 Jose Pagan .08 .20
212 Bob Robertson .08 .20
213 Manny Sanguillen .08 .20
214 Willie Stargell .40 1.00
215 Bob Veale .08 .20
216 Luke Walker .08 .20
217 Jose Arcia .08 .20
218 Bob Barton .08 .20
219 Fred Beene .08 .20
220 Ollie Brown .08 .20
221 Dave Campbell .12 .30
222 Chris Cannizzaro .08 .20
223 Nate Colbert .08 .20
224 Mike Corkins .08 .20
225 Tommy Dean .08 .20
226 Al Ferrara .08 .20
227 Rod Gaspar .08 .20
228 Clarence Gaston .08 .20
229 Enzo Hernandez .08 .20
230 Clay Kirby .08 .20
231 Don Mason .08 .20
232 Ivan Murrell .08 .20
233 Gerry Nyman .08 .20
234 Tom Phoebus .08 .20
235 Dave Roberts .08 .20
236 Gary Ross .08 .20
237 Al Santorini .08 .20
238 Al Severinsen .08 .20
239 Ron Slocum .08 .20
240 Ed Spiezio .08 .20
241 Bobby Bonds .15 .40
242 Ron Bryant .08 .20
243 Don Carrithers .08 .20
244 John Cumberland .08 .20
245 Mike Davison .08 .20
246 Dick Dietz .08 .20
247 Tito Fuentes .08 .20
248 Russ Gibson .08 .20
249 Jim Ray Hart .08 .20
250 Bob Heise .08 .20
251 Ken Henderson .08 .20
252 Steve Huntz .08 .20
253 Frank Johnson .08 .20
254 Jerry Johnson .08 .20
255 Hal Lanier .08 .20
256 Juan Marichal .40 1.00
257 Willie Mays 1.50 4.00
258 Willie McCovey .60 1.50
259 Don McMahon .08 .20
260 Jackie Moyer .08 .20
261 Gaylord Perry .50 1.25
262 Frank Reberger .08 .20
263 Rich Robertson .08 .20
264 Bernie Williams .08 .20
265 Matty Alou .12 .30
266 Jim Beauchamp .08 .20
267 Frank Bertaina .08 .20
268 Lou Brock .60 1.50
269 George Brunet .08 .20
270 Jose Cardenal .08 .20
271 Steve Carlton .60 1.50
272 Moe Drabowsky .08 .20
273 Bob Gibson .60 1.50
274 Joe Hague .08 .20
275 Julian Javier .08 .20
276 Leron Lee .08 .20
277 Frank Linzy .08 .20
278 Dal Maxvill .08 .20
279 Gerry McNertney .08 .20
280 Fred Norman .08 .20
281 Milt Ramirez .08 .20
282 Dick Schofield .08 .20
283 Mike Shannon .08 .20
284 Ted Sizemore .08 .20
285 Bob Stinson .08 .20
286 Carl Taylor .08 .20
287 Joe Torre .30 .75
288 Mike Torrez .08 .20
289 Mark Belanger .08 .20
290 Paul Blair .08 .20
291 Don Buford .08 .20
292 Terry Crowley .08 .20
293 Mike Cuellar .08 .20
294 Clay Dalrymple .08 .20
295 Pat Dobson .08 .20
296 Andy Etchebarren .08 .20
297 Dick Hall .08 .20
298 Jim Hardin .08 .20
299 Elrod Hendricks .08 .20
300 Grant Jackson .08 .20
301 Dave Johnson .15 .40
302 Dave Leonhard .08 .20
303 Marcelino Lopez .08 .20
304 Dave McNally .08 .20
305 Curt Motton .08 .20
306 Jim Palmer .60 1.50
307 Boog Powell .12 .30
308 Merv Rettenmund .08 .20
309 Brooks Robinson .60 1.50
310 Frank Robinson .60 1.50
311 Pete Richert .08 .20
312 Chico Salmon .08 .20
313 Luis Aparicio .40 1.00
314 Bobby Bolin .08 .20
315 Ken Brett .08 .20
316 Billy Conigliaro .08 .20
317 Ray Culp .08 .20
318 Mike Fiore .08 .20
319 John Kennedy .08 .20
320 Cal Koonce .08 .20
321 Joe Lahoud .08 .20
322 Bill Lee .08 .20
323 Jim Lonborg .08 .20
324 Sparky Lyle .15 .40
325 Mike Nagy .08 .20
326 Don Pavletich .08 .20
327 Gary Peters .08 .20
328 Rico Petrocelli .12 .30
329 Vicente Romo .08 .20
330 Tom Satriano .08 .20
331 George Scott .12 .30
332 Sonny Siebert .08 .20
333 Reggie Smith .15 .40
334 Jarvis Tatum .08 .20
335 Ken Tatum .08 .20
336 Carl Yastrzemski .75 2.00
337 Sandy Alomar .08 .20
338 Jose Azcue .08 .20
339 Ken Berry .08 .20
340 Gene Brabender .08 .20
341 Billy Cowan .08 .20
342 Tony Conigliaro .15 .40
343 Eddie Fisher .08 .20
344 Jim Fregosi .12 .30
345 Tony Gonzales .08 .20
346 Alex Johnson .08 .20
347 Fred Lasher .08 .20
348 Jim Maloney .08 .20
349 Rudy May .08 .20
350 Ken McMullen .08 .20
351 Andy Messersmith .08 .20
352 Gerry Moses .08 .20
353 Syd O'Brien .08 .20
354 Mel Queen .08 .20
355 Roger Repoz .08 .20
356 Archie Reynolds .08 .20
357 Chico Ruiz .08 .20
358 Jim Spencer .08 .20
359 Clyde Wright .08 .20
360 Billy Wynne .08 .20
361 Mike Andrews .08 .20
362 Luis Alvarado .08 .20
363 Tom Egan .08 .20
364 Steve Hamilton .08 .20
365 Ed Herrmann .08 .20
366 Joel Horlen .08 .20
367 Tommy John .15 .40
368 Bart Johnson .08 .20
369 Jay Johnstone .08 .20
370 Duane Josephson .08 .20
371 Pat Kelly .08 .20
372 Bobby Knoop .08 .20
373 Carlos May .08 .20
374 Lee Maye .08 .20
375 Tom McCraw .08 .20
376 Bill Melton .08 .20
377 Rich Morales .08 .20
378 Tom Murphy .08 .20
379 Don O'Riley .08 .20
380 Rick Reichardt .08 .20
381 Bill Robinson .08 .20
382 Bob Spence .08 .20
383 Walt Williams .08 .20
384 Wilbur Wood .08 .20
385 Rick Austin .08 .20
386 Buddy Bradford .08 .20
387 Larry Brown .08 .20
388 Lou Camilli .08 .20
389 Vince Colbert .08 .20
390 Ray Fosse .08 .20
391 Alan Foster .08 .20
392 Roy Foster .08 .20
393 Rich Hand .08 .20
394 Steve Hargan .08 .20
395 Ken Harrelson .15 .40
396 Jack Heidemann .08 .20
397 Phil Hennigan .08 .20
398 Dennis Higgins .08 .20
399 Chuck Hinton .08 .20
400 Tony Horton .08 .20
401 Ray Lamb .08 .20
402 Eddie Leon .08 .20
403 Sam McDowell .12 .30
404 Graig Nettles .15 .40
405 Mike Paul .08 .20
406 Vada Pinson .15 .40
407 Ken Suarez .08 .20
408 Ted Uhlaender .08 .20
409 Eddie Brinkman .08 .20
410 Gates Brown .08 .20
411 Ike Brown .08 .20
412 Les Cain .08 .20
413 Norm Cash .15 .40
414 Joe Coleman .08 .20
415 Bill Freehan .12 .30
416 Cesar Gutierrez .08 .20
417 John Hiller .08 .20
418 Willie Horton .12 .30
419 Dalton Jones .08 .20
420 Al Kaline .60 1.50
421 Mike Kilkenny .08 .20
422 Mickey Lolich .15 .40
423 Dick McAuliffe .08 .20
424 Joe Niekro .15 .40
425 Jim Northrup .08 .20
426 Daryl Patterson .08 .20
427 Jimmie Price .08 .20
428 Bob Reed .08 .20
429 Aurelio Rodriguez .08 .20
430 Fred Scherman .08 .20
431 Mickey Stanley .08 .20
432 Tom Timmerman .08 .20
433 Ted Abernathy .08 .20
434 Wally Bunker .08 .20
435 Tom Burgmeier .08 .20
436 Bill Butler .08 .20
437 Bruce Dal Canton .08 .20
438 Dick Drago .08 .20
439 Bobby Floyd .08 .20
440 Gail Hopkins .08 .20
441 Joe Keough .08 .20
442 Ed Kirkpatrick .08 .20
443 Tom Matchick .08 .20
444 Jerry May .08 .20
445 Aurelio Monteagudo .08 .20
446 Dave Morehead .08 .20
447 Bob Oliver .08 .20
448 Amos Otis .08 .20
449 Fred Patek .08 .20
450 Lou Piniella .15 .40
451 Cookie Rojas .08 .20
452 Jim Rooker .08 .20
453 Paul Schaal .08 .20
454 Rich Severson .08 .20
455 George Spriggs .08 .20
456 Carl Taylor .08 .20
457 Dave Baldwin .08 .20
458 Ted Savage .08 .20
459 Dick Ellsworth .08 .20
460 John Gelnar .08 .20
461 Tommy Harper .08 .20
462 Mike Hegan .08 .20
463 Bob Humphreys .08 .20
464 Andy Kosco .08 .20
465 Lew Krausse .08 .20

Card	Low	High
466 Ted Kubiak	.08	.20
467 Skip Lockwood	.08	.20
468 Dave May	.08	.20
469 Bob Meyer	.08	.20
470 John Morris	.08	.20
471 Marty Pattin	.08	.20
472 Roberto Pena	.08	.20
473 Ellie Rodriguez	.08	.20
474 Phil Roof	.08	.20
475 Ken Sanders	.08	.20
476 Russ Snyder	.08	.20
477 Bill Tillman	.08	.20
478 Bill Voss	.08	.20
479 Danny Walton	.08	.20
480 Floyd Wicker	.08	.20
481 Brant Alyea	.08	.20
482 Bert Blyleven	.15	.40
483 Dave Boswell	.08	.20
484 Leo Cardenas	.08	.20
485 Rod Carew	.75	2.00
486 Tom Hall	.08	.20
487 Jim Holt	.08	.20
488 Jim Kaat	.15	.40
489 Harmon Killebrew	.40	1.00
490 Charlie Manuel	.08	.20
491 George Mitterwald	.08	.20
492 Tony Oliva	.15	.40
493 Ron Perranoski	.08	.20
494 Jim Perry	.08	.20
495 Frank Quilici	.08	.20
496 Rich Reese	.08	.20
497 Rick Renick	.08	.20
498 Danny Thompson	.08	.20
499 Luis Tiant	.12	.30
500 Tom Tischinski	.08	.20
501 Cesar Tovar	.08	.20
502 Stan Williams	.08	.20
503 Dick Woodson	.08	.20
504 Bill Zepp	.08	.20
505 Jack Aker	.08	.20
506 Stan Bahnsen	.08	.20
507 Curt Blefary	.08	.20
508 Bill Burbach	.08	.20
509 Danny Cater	.08	.20
510 Horace Clarke	.08	.20
511 John Ellis	.08	.20
512 Jake Gibbs	.08	.20
513 Ron Hansen	.08	.20
514 Mike Kekich	.08	.20
515 Jerry Kenney	.08	.20
516 Ron Klimkowski	.08	.20
517 Steve Kline	.08	.20
518 Mike McCormick	.08	.20
519 Lindy McDaniel	.08	.20
520 Gene Michael	.08	.20
521 Thurman Munson	.75	2.00
522 Bobby Murcer	.15	.40
523 Fritz Peterson	.08	.20
524 Mel Stottlemyre	.15	.40
525 Pete Ward	.08	.20
526 Gary Waslewski	.08	.20
527 Roy White	.12	.30
528 Ron Woods	.08	.20
529 Felipe Alou	.15	.40
530 Sal Bando	.12	.30
531 Vida Blue	.15	.40
532 Bert Campaneris	.12	.30
533 Ron Clark	.08	.20
534 Chuck Dobson	.08	.20
535 Dave Duncan	.08	.20
536 Frank Fernandez	.08	.20
537 Rollie Fingers	.40	1.00
538 Dick Green	.08	.20
539 Steve Hovley	.08	.20
540 Jim Hunter	.60	1.50
541 Reggie Jackson	1.25	3.00
542 Marcel Lachemann	.08	.20
543 Paul Lindblad	.08	.20
544 Bob Locker	.08	.20
545 Don Mincher	.08	.20
546 Rick Monday	.12	.30
547 John Odom	.08	.20
548 Jim Roland	.08	.20
549 Joe Rudi	.12	.30
550 Diego Segui	.08	.20
551 Bob Stickels	.08	.20
552 Gene Tenace	.08	.20
553 Bernie Allen	.08	.20
554 Dick Bosman	.08	.20
555 Jackie Brown	.08	.20
556 Paul Casanova	.08	.20
557 Casey Cox	.08	.20
558 Tim Cullen	.08	.20
559 Mike Epstein	.08	.20
560 Curt Flood	.15	.40
561 Joe Foy	.08	.20
562 Jim French	.08	.20
563 Bill Gogolewski	.08	.20
564 Tom Grieve	.12	.30
565 Joe Grzenda	.08	.20
566 Frank Howard	.15	.40
567 Joe Janeski	.08	.20
568 Darold Knowles	.08	.20
569 Elliott Maddox	.08	.20
570 Denny McLain	.15	.40
571 Dave Nelson	.08	.20
572 Horacio Pina	.08	.20
573 Jim Shellenback	.08	.20
574 Ed Stroud	.08	.20
575 Del Unser	.08	.20
576 Don Wert	.08	.20
577 Hank Aaron	1.50	4.00
578 Luis Aparicio	.40	1.00
579 Ernie Banks	.75	2.00
580 Johnny Bench	.75	2.00
581 Rico Carty	.08	.20
582 Roberto Clemente	2.50	6.00
583 Bob Gibson	.50	1.25
584 Willie Horton	.12	.30
585 Frank Howard	.15	.40
586 Reggie Jackson	1.25	3.00
587 Fergie Jenkins	.40	1.00
588 Alex Johnson	.08	.20
589 Al Kaline	.60	1.50
590 Harmon Killebrew	.40	1.00
591 Willie Mays	1.50	4.00
592 Sam McDowell	.08	.20
593 Denny McLain	.15	.40
594 Boog Powell	.15	.40
595 Brooks Robinson	.60	1.50
596 Frank Robinson	.60	1.50
597 Pete Rose	1.25	3.00
598 Tom Seaver	.75	2.00
599 Rusty Staub	.15	.40
600 Carl Yastrzemski	.75	2.00

1933 DeLong

The cards in this 24-card set measure approximately 2" by 3". The 1933 Delong Gum set of 24 multi-colored cards was, along with the 1933 Goudey Big League series, one of the first baseball card sets issued with chewing gum. It was the only card set issued by this company. The reverse text was written by Austen Lake, who also wrote the sports tips found on the Diamond Stars series which began in 1934, leading to speculation that Delong was bought out by National Chicle.

Card	Low	High
COMPLETE SET (24)	6000.00	15000.00
1 Marty McManus	200.00	400.00
2 Al Simmons	250.00	500.00
3 Oscar Melillo	150.00	300.00
4 Bill Terry	300.00	600.00
5 Charlie Gehringer	300.00	600.00
6 Mickey Cochrane	500.00	1000.00
7 Lou Gehrig	4000.00	8000.00
8 Kiki Cuyler	400.00	800.00
9 Bill Urbanski	150.00	300.00
10 Lefty O'Doul	250.00	500.00
11 Fred Lindstrom	300.00	600.00
12 Pie Traynor	400.00	800.00
13 Rabbit Maranville	300.00	600.00
14 Lefty Gomez	400.00	800.00
15 Riggs Stephenson	200.00	400.00
16 Lon Warneke	150.00	300.00
17 Pepper Martin	200.00	400.00
18 Jimmy Dykes	200.00	400.00
19 Chick Hafey	300.00	600.00
20 Joe Vosmik	150.00	300.00
21 Jimmie Foxx	600.00	1200.00
22 Chuck Klein	300.00	600.00
23 Lefty Grove	500.00	1000.00
24 Goose Goslin	400.00	800.00

1991 Denny's Holograms

The 1991 Denny's Grand Slam hologram baseball card set was produced by Upper Deck. The 26-card standard-size set contains one player from each major league team, who was selected on the basis of the number and circumstances of his grand slam home runs. These cards were available at Denny's only with the purchase of a meal from the restaurant's Grand Slam menu; each card came sealed in a plastic bag that prevents prior identification. It is estimated that two million cards were printed. In 1991, if the contest card was a winner, the collector was entitled to a free meal. By the end of the contest, almost half the teams had hit grand slams during the length of the contest. So many teams hit grand slams in that time frame which caused Denny's never to run that aspect of the promotion again.

Card	Low	High
COMPLETE SET (26)	8.00	20.00
1 Ellis Burks	.30	.75
2 Cecil Fielder	.20	.50
3 Will Clark	.40	1.00
4 Eric Davis	.20	.50
5 Dave Parker	.20	.50
6 Kelly Gruber	.08	.25
7 Kent Hrbek	.20	.50
8 Don Mattingly	1.50	4.00
9 Brook Jacoby	.08	.25
10 Mark McGwire	1.50	4.00
11 Howard Johnson	.08	.25
12 Tim Wallach	.08	.25
13 Ricky Jordan	.08	.25
14 Andre Dawson	.40	1.00
15 Eddie Murray	.60	1.50
16 Danny Tartabull	.08	.25
17 Bobby Bonilla	.08	.25
18 Benito Santiago	.20	.50
19 Alvin Davis	.08	.25
20 Cal Ripken	3.00	8.00
21 Ruben Sierra	.20	.50
22 Pedro Guerrero	.08	.25
23 Wally Joyner	.20	.50
24 Craig Biggio	.40	1.00
25 Dave Justice	.20	.50
26 Tim Raines	.20	.50

1935 Al Demaree Die Cuts R304

These cards are drawings which were produced approximately in 1935; other cards may exist in this scarce set. The cards measure 1" x 4 1/2". This listing may be incomplete. All additions are welcome and appreciated. A few cards have not yet been discovered with the tab that would enable us to ID the card numbers. They are listed at the end as NNO's

Card	Low	High
COMPLETE SET	2500.00	50000.00
3 Earle Combs	400.00	800.00
4 Babe Ruth	2000.00	4000.00
5 Sam Byrd	200.00	400.00
6 Tony Lazzeri	300.00	600.00
7 Frank Crosetti	250.00	500.00
9 Lou Gehrig	1500.00	3000.00
11 Mule Haas	200.00	400.00
12 Evar Swanson	200.00	400.00
13 Merv Shea	200.00	400.00
14 Al Simmons throwing	300.00	600.00
15 Minter Hayes	200.00	400.00
16 Al Simmons batting	300.00	600.00
17 Jimmy Dykes	250.00	500.00
18 Luke Appling	300.00	600.00
19 Ted Lyons	300.00	600.00
20 Red Kress	200.00	400.00
21 Gee Walker	200.00	400.00
23 Gordon Stanley/(Mickey) Cochrane/(catcher unifor	400.00	800.00
24 Gordon Stanley/(Mickey) Cochrane/(batting - poss	400.00	800.00
25 Pete Fox	200.00	400.00
26 Firpo Marberry	200.00	400.00
28 Mickey Owen	200.00	400.00
35 Joe Vosmik	200.00	400.00
40 Oral Hildebrand	200.00	400.00
41 Jack Burns	200.00	400.00
45 Ray Pepper	200.00	400.00
46 Bruce Campbell	200.00	400.00
48 Art Scharein	200.00	400.00
49 George Blaeholder	200.00	400.00
50 Rogers Hornsby	1000.00	2000.00
54 Jimmie Foxx	600.00	1200.00
56 Dib Williams	200.00	400.00
57 Lou Finney	200.00	400.00
59 Bob Johnson	250.00	500.00
60 Roy Mahaffey	200.00	400.00
61 Ossie Bluege	200.00	400.00
64 Joe Cronin	300.00	600.00
66 Buddy Myer	200.00	400.00
67 Earl Whitehill	200.00	400.00
71 Ed Morgan	200.00	400.00
73 Rick Ferrell	400.00	800.00
74 Carl Reynolds	200.00	400.00
76 Bill Cissell	200.00	400.00
77 Johnny Hodapp	200.00	400.00
78 Dusty Cooke	200.00	400.00
79 Lefty Grove	400.00	800.00
82 Gus Mancuso	200.00	400.00
83 Kiddo Davis	200.00	400.00
84 Blondy Ryan	200.00	400.00
86 Travis Jackson	300.00	600.00
87 Mel Ott	600.00	1200.00
89 Bill Terry	400.00	800.00
90 Carl Hubbell	600.00	1200.00
91 Tony Cuccinello	200.00	400.00
92 Al Lopez	400.00	800.00
94 John Frederick	200.00	400.00
96 Hack Wilson	400.00	800.00
97 Danny Taylor	200.00	400.00
99 Johnny Frederick	200.00	400.00
100 Sam Leslie	200.00	400.00
101 Sparky Adams	200.00	400.00
107 Syl Johnson	200.00	400.00
108 Jim Bottomley	300.00	600.00
110 Adam Comorosky	200.00	400.00
112 Harvey Hendrick	200.00	400.00
115 Don Hurst	200.00	400.00
117 Prince Oana	200.00	400.00
118 Ed Holley	200.00	400.00
121 Spud Davis	200.00	400.00
122 George Watkins	200.00	400.00
123 Frankie Frisch	300.00	600.00
125 Rip Collins	200.00	400.00
126 Dizzy Dean	600.00	1200.00
127 Pepper Martin	250.00	500.00
128 Joe Medwick	300.00	600.00
129 Leo Durocher	300.00	600.00
130 Ernie Orsatti	200.00	400.00
132 Shanty Hogan	200.00	400.00
137 Wally Berger	250.00	500.00
138 Hal Lee	200.00	400.00
139 Rabbit Maranville	400.00	800.00
141 Gus Suhr	200.00	400.00
142 Earl Grace	200.00	400.00
144 Arky Vaughan	400.00	800.00
147 Lloyd Waner	400.00	800.00
148 Paul Waner	600.00	1200.00
149 Pie Traynor	600.00	1200.00
151 Kiki Cuyler	400.00	800.00
152 Gabby Hartnett	300.00	600.00
154 Chuck Klein	300.00	600.00
156 Woody English	250.00	500.00
158 Billy Herman	300.00	600.00
160 Charlie Grimm	250.00	500.00
162 Bill Klem UMP	300.00	600.00
167 George Hildebrand UMP	200.00	400.00
NNO Willie Kamm	200.00	400.00
NNO Roy Mahaffey	200.00	400.00
NNO Bob Johnson	200.00	400.00
NNO Pinky Higgins	200.00	400.00
NNO Roy Johnson	200.00	400.00
102A Mark Koenig	200.00	400.00
102B Ernie Lombardi	400.00	800.00
133A Wes Schulmerich	200.00	400.00
133B Randy Moore	200.00	400.00

1992 Denny's Holograms

This 26-card standard-size set of holographic cards was produced by Upper Deck for Denny's. The set features one player from each major league team, who was selected on the basis of the number and circumstances of his grand slam home runs. With each order of a Grand Slam meal, the customer received one hologram card.

Card	Low	High
COMPLETE SET (26)	6.00	15.00
1 Marquis Grissom	.08	.25
2 Ken Caminiti	.20	.50
3 Fred McGriff	.30	.75
4 Felix Jose	.08	.25
5 Jack Clark	.20	.50
6 Albert Belle	.20	.50
7 Sid Bream	.08	.25
8 Robin Ventura	.30	.75
9 Cal Ripken	2.50	6.00
10 Ryne Sandberg	1.25	3.00
11 Paul O'Neill	.30	.75
12 Luis Polonia	.08	.25
13 Cecil Fielder	.20	.50
14 Kal Daniels	.08	.25
15 Brian McRae	.08	.25
16 Howard Johnson	.08	.25
17 Greg Vaughn	.20	.50
18 Dale Murphy	.40	1.00
19 Kent Hrbek	.20	.50
20 Barry Bonds	1.25	3.00
21 Matt Nokes	.08	.25
22 Jose Canseco	.60	1.50
23 Jay Buhner	.20	.50
24 Will Clark	.50	1.25
25 Ruben Sierra	.20	.50
26 Joe Carter	.20	.50

1993 Denny's Holograms

This 28-card standard-size set of holographic cards was produced by Upper Deck for Denny's. The set features one player from each major league team who was selected on the basis of the number and circumstances of his grand slam home runs. With each order of a Grand Slam meal and a Coca-Cola Classic, the customer received one lithogram card. The set ordering follows alphabetical order of team nicknames.

Card	Low	High
COMPLETE SET (28)	6.00	15.00
1 Chili Davis	.20	.50
2 Eric Anthony	.08	.25
3 Rickey Henderson	.60	1.50
4 Joe Carter	.20	.50
5 Terry Pendleton	.08	.25
6 Robin Yount	.50	1.25
7 Ray Lankford	.20	.50
8 Ryne Sandberg	.75	2.00
9 Darryl Strawberry	.20	.50
10 Marquis Grissom	.08	.25
11 Will Clark	.50	1.25
12 Albert Belle	.08	.25
13 Edgar Martinez	.30	.75
14 Benito Santiago	.20	.50
15 Eddie Murray	.40	1.00
16 Cal Ripken	1.50	4.00
17 Gary Sheffield	.50	1.25
18 Dave Hollins	.08	.25
19 Andy Van Slyke	.08	.25
20 Juan Gonzalez	.30	.75
21 John Valentin	.08	.25
22 Joe Oliver	.08	.25
23 Dante Bichette	.20	.50
24 Wally Joyner	.20	.50
25 Cecil Fielder	.20	.50
26 Kirby Puckett	.50	1.25
27 Robin Ventura	.30	.75
28 Danny Tartabull	.08	.25

1994 Denny's Holograms

This 28-card standard-size set of holographic cards was produced by Upper Deck for Denny's and features a star player from each of the 28 Major League baseball teams. With each order of any "Classic Hits" entree, the customer received one hologram card in a blue poly pack. There was also a Reggie Jackson Hologram printed. The Jackson card was a contest giveaway for each participating Denny's.

Card	Low	High
COMP FACT. SET (29)	20.00	50.00
COMPLETE SET (28)	6.00	15.00
1 Jim Abbott	.20	.50
2 Roberto Alomar	.30	.75
3 Kevin Appier	.08	.25
4 Jeff Bagwell	.50	1.25
5 Albert Belle	.08	.25
6 Barry Bonds	.60	1.50
7 Bobby Bonilla	.08	.25
8 Lenny Dykstra	.20	.50
9 Cal Eldred	.08	.25
10 Cecil Fielder	.20	.50
11 Andres Galarraga	.40	1.00
12 Ken Griffey Jr.	.75	2.00
13 Juan Gonzalez	.40	1.00
14 Tony Gwynn	.60	1.50
15 Rickey Henderson	.50	1.25
16 Kent Hrbek	.20	.50
17 David Justice	.40	1.00
18 Mike Piazza	.75	2.00
19 Jose Rijo	.08	.25
20 Cal Ripken	1.25	3.00
21 Tim Salmon	.30	.75
22 Ryne Sandberg	.60	1.50
23 Gary Sheffield	.40	1.00
24 Ozzie Smith	.60	1.50
25 Frank Thomas	.30	.75
26 Andy Van Slyke	.20	.50
27 Mo Vaughn	.08	.25
28 Larry Walker	.40	1.00
XX Reggie Jackson Issued in Giveaway sets	15.00	40.00

1995 Denny's Holograms

This 28-card standard-size set of holographic cards. was produced by Upper Deck for Denny's and features a star player from each of the 28 Major League baseball teams. With each order of an "Classic Hits" entree and a non-alcoholic beverage, the customer received one hologram card in a blue poly pack. Also guests at the restaurants could enter a sweepstakes drawing for a complete set of cards, to be given away by each participating restaurant at the end of the promotion after September 30.

Card	Low	High
COMPLETE SET (28)	6.00	15.00
1 Roberto Alomar	.30	.75
2 Moises Alou	.20	.50
3 Jeff Bagwell	.50	1.25
4 Albert Belle	.08	.25
5 Jason Bere	.08	.25
6 Roger Clemens	.75	2.00
7 Darren Daulton	.20	.50
8 Cecil Fielder	.20	.50
9 Andres Galarraga	.20	.50
10 Juan Gonzalez	.30	.75
11 Ken Griffey Jr.	1.00	2.50
12 Tony Gwynn	.60	1.50
13 Barry Larkin	.40	1.00
14 Greg Maddux	.60	1.50
15 Don Mattingly	.75	2.00
16 Mark McGwire	.60	1.50
17 Orlando Merced	.08	.25
18 Jeff Montgomery	.08	.25
19 Rafael Palmeiro	.30	.75
20 Mike Piazza	.75	2.00
21 Kirby Puckett	.50	1.25
22 Bret Saberhagen	.20	.50
23 Tim Salmon	.30	.75
24 Gary Sheffield	.50	1.25
25 Ozzie Smith	.60	1.50
26 Sammy Sosa	.40	1.00
27 Greg Vaughn	.08	.25
28 Matt Williams	.30	.75

1996 Denny's Holograms

This 28-card set was produced by Pinnacle for Denny's and features a star player from each of the Major League baseball teams. The fronts feature a full motion hologram player image. The backs carry player information. By ordering anything on the menu, a customer could buy two packs. Each Denny's also sponsored a drawing to win all 48 cards (the regular set and both insert sets).

Card	Low	High
COMPLETE SET (28)	5.00	12.00
1 Greg Maddux	.60	1.50
2 Cal Ripken	1.25	3.00
3 Frank Thomas	.10	.30
4 Albert Belle	.02	.10
5 Mo Vaughn	.02	.10
6 Jeff Bagwell	.30	.75
7 Jay Buhner	.07	.20
8 Barry Bonds	.60	1.50
9 Ryne Sandberg	.60	1.50
10 Hideo Nomo	.60	1.50
11 Kirby Puckett	.30	.75
12 Gary Sheffield	.40	1.00
13 Barry Larkin	.15	.40
14 Wade Boggs	.40	1.00
15 Tony Gwynn	.60	1.50
16 Tim Salmon	.07	.20
17 Jason Isringhausen	.10	.30
18 Cecil Fielder	.07	.20
19 Dante Bichette	.02	.10
20 Ozzie Smith	.60	1.50
21 Ivan Rodriguez	.40	1.00
22 Kevin Appier	.02	.10
23 Joe Carter	.07	.20
24 Moises Alou	.07	.20
25 Mark McGwire	.60	1.50
26 Kevin Seitzer	.02	.10
27 Darren Daulton	.07	.20
28 Jay Bell	.02	.10

1996 Denny's Holograms Grand Slam

Card	Low	High
COMPLETE SET (10)	12.00	30.00
*ARTIST PROOF: 5X BASIC CARDS		
1 Cal Ripken	4.00	10.00
2 Frank Thomas	1.00	2.50
3 Mike Piazza	2.50	6.00
4 Tony Gwynn	2.00	5.00
5 Sammy Sosa	1.25	3.00
6 Barry Bonds	2.00	5.00
7 Jeff Bagwell	1.25	3.00
8 Albert Belle	.40	1.00
9 Mo Vaughn	.40	1.00
10 Kirby Puckett	1.00	2.50

1997 Denny's Holograms

This 29-card set was produced by Pinnacle for Denny's Restaurants and features a star player from each of the Major League baseball teams. Card number 29 is a commemorative Jackie Robinson card and card number 30 was only distributed in the Cleveland area. The fronts feature 3-D lenticular color player photos. The backs carry a 3-D hologram and player statistics. By purchasing any entree and non-alcoholic beverage, a collector could purchase a card for 59 cents. A significant portion of the proceeds went to support Denny's national charity, Save the Children. The complete set price does not include the regional Larry Doby card

Card	Low	High
COMPLETE SET (29)	10.00	25.00
1 Tim Salmon	.20	.50
2 Rafael Palmeiro	.40	1.00
3 Mo Vaughn	.08	.25
4 Frank Thomas	.40	1.00
5 Dave Justice	.40	1.00
6 Travis Fryman	.20	.50
7 Johnny Damon	.60	1.50
8 John Jaha	.08	.25
9 Chuck Knoblauch	.20	.50
10 Mark McGwire	1.00	2.50
11 Alex Rodriguez	1.25	3.00
12 Juan Gonzalez	.30	.75
13 Roger Clemens	1.00	2.50
14 Derek Jeter	2.00	5.00
15 Andruw Jones	1.00	2.50
16 Sammy Sosa	.60	1.50
17 Barry Larkin	.40	1.00
18 Dante Bichette	.20	.50
19 Jeff Bagwell	.50	1.25
20 Mike Piazza	1.25	3.00
21 Gary Sheffield	.50	1.25
22 Vladimir Guerrero	.75	2.00
23 Todd Hundley	.08	.25
24 Jason Kendall	.30	.75
25 Ray Lankford	.20	.50
26 Ken Caminiti	.20	.50
27 Barry Bonds	1.00	2.50
28 Scott Rolen	.40	1.00
29 Jackie Robinson 50th Anniversary Commemorative	2.00	5.00
30 Larry Doby 50th Anniversary	1.00	2.50

1986 DeSa Commemorative

This one-card set measures approximately 4" by 6" and commemorates Baseball player Joe DeSa. The front features a color player photo with a red border and the words "Joe DeSa Remembered" printed in white at the top. The back displays information about the player and career statistics.

Card	Low	High
1 Joe DeSa	1.25	3.00

1979 Detroit Convention

This 20 card 3 1/2" by 5" set was issued to commemorate the 10th annual Detroit show. The cards are reproductions of photos provided by various fans and the Detroit Tigers. An interesting mix of players and media members are commemorated in this set. The cards are unnumbered so we have sequenced them in alphabetical order. The set was originally available for $3.

Card	Low	High
COMPLETE SET	4.00	10.00
1 Gates Brown	.20	.50
2 Norm Cash	.60	1.50
3 Al Cicotte	.20	.50
4 Roy Cullenbine	.30	.75
5 Gene Desautels	.20	.50
6 Hoot Evers	.20	.50
7 Joe Falls Columnist	.20	.50
8 Joe Ginsberg	.20	.50
9 Ernie Harwell ANN	.40	1.00
10 Ray Herbert	.20	.50
11 John Hiller	.20	.50
12 Billy Hoeft	.20	.50
13 Ralph Houk MG	.30	.75
14 Cliff Kachline Writer	.20	.50
15 George Kell	.60	1.50
16 Ron LeFlore	.20	.50
17 Barney McCosky	.20	.50
18 Jim Northrup	.20	.50
19 Dick Radatz	.20	.50
20 Tom Timmerman	.20	.50

1935 Detroit Free Press

This newsprint set of the 1935 Detroit Tigers and one boxer measures approximately 9" by 11" and was within the "The Detroit Free Press." The cards are unnumbered and checklisted below in alphabetical order. One boxer -- Joe Lewis is known to be issued as part of this set.

Card	Low	High
COMPLETE SET	162.50	325.00
1 Eldon Auker	5.00	10.00
2 Del Baker	5.00	10.00
3 Tommy Bridges	7.50	15.00
4 Flea Clifton	5.00	10.00
5 Mickey Cochrane	12.50	25.00
6 General Crowder	5.00	10.00
7 Frank Deljack	5.00	10.00
8 Carl Fischer	5.00	10.00
9 Pete Fox	5.00	10.00
10 Charlie Gehringer	10.00	20.00
11 Goose Goslin	10.00	20.00
12 Hank Greenberg	12.50	25.00
13 Luke Hamlin	5.00	10.00
14 Ray Hayworth	5.00	10.00
15 Chief Hogsett	5.00	10.00
17 Firpo Marberry	5.00	10.00
18 Marvin Owen	5.00	10.00
19 Cy Perkins	5.00	10.00
20 Billie Rogell	5.00	10.00
21 Schoolboy Rowe	7.50	15.00
22 Geinie Schuble	5.00	10.00
23 Victor Sorrell	5.00	10.00
24 Joe Sullivan	5.00	10.00
25 Gee Walker	5.00	10.00
26 Jo-Jo White	5.00	10.00

1998 Devil Rays Pinnacle

This 26-card set was produced by Pinnacle to commemorate the Devil Rays first team and was distributed in a Collector's Edition box. The fronts feature color action player photos in a blue, purple, and gray-spotted white border. The backs carry a small player head shot and player information. Only 3000 of the set were produced with the boxes serially numbered.

Card	Low	High
COMPLETE SET (26)	1.25	3.00
1 Wilson Alvarez	.08	.25
2 Rolando Arrojo	.30	.75
3 Dan Carlson	.02	.10
4 Rick Gorecki	.02	.10
5 Roberto Hernandez	.08	.25
6 Albie Lopez	.02	.10
7 Jim Mecir	.02	.10
8 Tony Saunders	.02	.10
9 Dennis Springer	.02	.10
10 Ramon Tatis	.02	.10
11 Esteban Yan	.02	.10
12 Mike Difelice	.02	.10
13 John Flaherty	.02	.10
14 Wade Boggs	.40	1.00
15 Miguel Cairo	.08	.25
16 Aaron Ledesma	.02	.10
17 Fred McGriff	.20	.50
18 Bobby Smith	.02	.10
19 Paul Sorrento	.02	.10
20 Kevin Stocker	.02	.10
21 Rich Butler	.02	.10
22 Mike Kelly	.02	.10
23 Dave Martinez	.02	.10
24 Quinton McCracken	.02	.10
25 Bubba Trammell	.02	.10
NNO Team Logo CL	.02	.10

1998-99 Devil Rays Postcards

These 4" by 6" blank-backed color postcards have a player photo with the sponsoring information of St Anthony's Health Care on the bottom. The photos were credited to Robert Rogers. It is believed that some of these cards were issued during the 1999 season, thus we are listing this as a split-year set.

Card	Low	High
COMPLETE SET	6.00	15.00
1 Scott Aldred	.08	.25
2 Wilson Alvarez	.08	.25
3 Rolando Arrojo	.40	1.00
4 Wade Boggs	.75	2.00
5 Rich Butler	.08	.25
6 Miguel Cairo	.20	.50
7 Jose Canseco	.75	2.00
8 Dan Carlson	.08	.25
9 Mike DiFelice	.08	.25
10 Dave Eiland	.08	.25
11 Vaughn Eshelman	.08	.25
12 John Flaherty	.08	.25
13 Orlando Gomez CO	.08	.25
14 Rick Gorecki	.08	.25
15 Billy Hatcher CO	.08	.25
16 Steve Henderson CO	.08	.25
17 Roberto Hernandez	.20	.50
18 Frank Howard CO	.20	.50
19 Mike Kelly	.08	.25
20 Chuck LaMar GM	.08	.25
21 Aaron Ledesma	.08	.25
22 Albie Lopez	.08	.25
23 Joe Magrane CO	.08	.25
24 Dave Martinez	.08	.25
25 Quinton McCracken	.08	.25
26 Fred McGriff	.30	.75
27 Jim Mecir	.08	.25
28 Jim Morris	.75	2.00
29 Vincent Naimoli OWN	.08	.25
30 Bryan Rekar	.08	.25
31 Greg Riddoch CO	.08	.25
32 Larry Rothschild MG	.08	.25
33 Ryan Rupe	.08	.25
34 Julio Santana	.08	.25
35 Tony Saunders	.08	.25
36 Bobby Smith	.08	.25
37 Paul Sorrento	.08	.25
38 Jeff Sparks	.08	.25
39 Dennis Springer	.08	.25
40 Dewayne Staats ANN	.08	.25
41 Kevin Stocker	.08	.25
42 Bubba Trammell	.08	.25
43 Terrell Wade	.08	.25
44 Dan Wheeler	.08	.25
45 Rick White	.08	.25
46 Randy Williams	.08	.25
47 Rick Williams CO	.08	.25
48 Randy Winn	.30	.75
49 Esteban Yan	.08	.25

2000 Devil Rays Verizon

Card	Low	High
COMPLETE SET (28)	4.00	10.00
1 Wilson Alvarez	.20	.50
2 Miguel Cairo	.20	.50
3 Jose Canseco	.60	1.25
4 Vinny Castilla	.20	.50
5 Steve Cox	.10	.25
6 Mike DiFelice	.10	.25
7 John Flaherty	.10	.25
8 Jose Guillen	.40	1.00
9 Ozzie Guillen	.30	.75
10 Juan Guzman	.10	.25
11 Roberto Hernandez	.20	.50
12 Russ Johnson	.10	.25
13 Albie Lopez	.10	.25
14 Felix Martinez	.10	.25
15 Fred McGriff	.30	.75
16 Raymond Mascot	.10	.25
17 Brian Rekar	.10	.25
18 Larry Rothschild MG	.10	.25
19 Steve Traschel	.10	.25
20 Bubba Trammell	.10	.25
21 Greg Vaughn	.20	.50
22 Rick White	.10	.25
23 Gerald Williams	.10	.25
24 Randy Winn	.20	.50
25 Esteban Yan	.10	.25
26 Jose Cardenal CO Bill Fischer CO Orlando Gomez C	.10	.25
27 Wade Boggs GTE Reading	.60	1.50
28 Header Card	.10	.25

2001 Devil Rays Team Issue

Card	Low	High
COMPLETE SET (51)	6.00	15.00
1 Brent Abernathy	.10	.25
2 Wilson Alvarez	.10	.25
3 Nick Bierbrodt	.10	.25
4 Wade Boggs CO	.40	1.00
5 Terry Collins CO	.10	.25
6 Jesus Colome	.10	.25
7 Steve Cox	.10	.25
8 Doug Creek	.10	.25
9 Doug Creek	.10	.25
10 Mike DiFelice	.10	.25
11 Bill Fischer CO	.10	.25
12 John Flaherty	.10	.25
13 Chris Gomez	.10	.25
14 Ben Grieve	.20	.50
15 Jose Guillen	.40	1.00
16 Juan Guzman	.10	.25
17 Toby Hall	.30	.75
18 Toby Hall	.30	.75
19 Josh Hamilton	.20	.50
20 Travis Harper	.10	.25
21 Billy Hatcher CO	.10	.25
22 Frank Howard CO	.20	.50
23 Aubrey Huff	.40	1.00
24 Russ Johnson	.10	.25
25 Russ Johnson	.10	.25
26 Joe Kennedy	.20	.50
27 Albie Lopez	.10	.25
28 Felix Martinez	.10	.25
29 Fred McGriff	.30	.75
30 Hal McRae MGR	.10	.25
31 Travis Phelps	.10	.25
32 Bryan Rekar	.10	.25
33 Damian Rolls	.10	.25
34 Ryan Rupe	.10	.25
35 Alex Sanchez	.10	.25
36 Jared Sandberg	.10	.25
37 Bobby Seay	.10	.25
38 Jason Standridge	.10	.25
39 Tanyon Sturtze	.10	.25
40 Tanyon Sturtze	.10	.25
41 Jason Tyner	.10	.25
42 Jason Tynor	.10	.26
43 Greg Vaughn	.20	.50
44 Jeff Wallace	.10	.25
45 Dan Wheeler	.10	.25
46 Matt White	.10	.25
47 Gerald Williams	.10	.25
48 Paul Wilson	.10	.25
49 Randy Winn	.20	.50
50 Esteban Yan	.10	.25
51 Victor Zambrano	.10	.25

2003 Devil Rays Baldelli DAV

Card	Low	High
NNO Rocco Baldelli	1.25	3.00

2004 Devil Rays Team Issue

Card	Low	High
COMPLETE SET		
1 Danny Baez	.40	1.00
2 Rocco Baldelli	.60	1.50
3 Rob Bell	.20	.50
4 Geoff Blum	.20	.50
5 Dewon Brazelton	.20	.50
6 Lance Carter	.20	.50
7 Carl Crawford	.75	2.00
8 Jose Cruz Jr.	.30	.75
9 Lee Elia CO	.20	.50
10 Robert Fick	.20	.50
11 Brook Fordyce	.20	.50
12 Jonny Gomes	.30	.75
13 John Halama	.20	.50
14 Toby Hall	.20	.50
15 Travis Harper	.20	.50
16 Mark Hendrickson	.20	.50
17 Chuck Hernandez	.20	.50
18 Aubrey Huff	.60	1.50
19 Scott Kazmir	1.00	2.50

20 Julio Lugo .20 .50
21 Tino Martinez .40 1.00
22 Seth McClung .20 .50
23 John McLaren CO .20 .50
24 Trever Miller .20 .50
25 Eduardo Perez .20 .50
26 Lou Piniella MG .30 .75
27 Rey Sanchez .20 .50
28 Bobby Seay .20 .50
29 Matt Sinatro CO .20 .50
30 Jason Standridge .20 .50
31 B.J. Upton 1.25 3.00
32 Doug Waechter .20 .50
33 Victor Zambrano .20 .50
34 Don Zimmer CO .30 .75

2006 Devil Rays Topps

COMPLETE SET (14) 3.00 8.00
TDR1 Rocco Baldelli .12 .30
TDR2 Scott Kazmir .20 .50
TDR3 Aubrey Huff .12 .30
TDR4 Jorge Cantu .12 .30
TDR5 Julio Lugo .12 .30
TDR6 Danys Baez .12 .30
TDR7 Jonny Gomes .12 .30
TDR8 Doug Waechter .12 .30
TDR9 B.J. Upton .12 .30
TDR10 Carl Crawford .20 .50
TDR11 Sean Burroughs .12 .30
TDR12 Nick Green .12 .30
TDR13 Mark Hendrickson .12 .30
TDR14 Toby Hall .12 .30

2007 Devil Rays Topps

COMPLETE SET (14) 3.00 8.00
TBD1 Delmon Young .20 .50
TBD2 Carl Crawford .20 .50
TBD3 Casey Fossum .12 .30
TBD4 Ben Zobrist .20 .50
TBD5 Dioner Navarro .12 .30
TBD6 James Shields .12 .30
TBD7 Scott Kazmir .20 .50
TBD8 B.J. Upton .12 .30
TBD9 Jorge Cantu .12 .30
TBD10 Greg Norton .12 .30
TBD11 Seth McClung .12 .30
TBD12 Jonny Gomes .12 .30
TBD13 Ty Wigginton .12 .30
TBD14 Rocco Baldelli .12 .30

1967 Dexter Press

This 228-card set was produced by Dexter Press and issued in team sets as a premium by the Coca-Cola Bottling Co. Eighteen Major League teams participated in the promotion. The set measures approximately 5 1/2" by 7" and features glossy color waist-to-cap player photos in a white border with a black facsimile autograph at the top. The white backs display player biographical details and career highlights printed in blue. An all-star set was also produced with these players' cards differentiated from their regular cards in the team sets by the lengthier biographies on the back. The cards are unnumbered and checklisted below in alphabetical order. Paul Schaal was also issued as a sample print. This card is considered a SP and is not included in the checklist.

COMPLETE SET (228) 400.00 800.00
1 Hank Aaron 8.00 20.00
2 Tommie Agee 1.50 4.00
3 Jack Aker 1.25 3.00
4 Bernie Allen 1.25 3.00
5 Richie Allen 2.00 5.00
6 Gene Alley 1.25 3.00
7 Bob Allison 1.50 4.00
8 Felipe Alou 2.00 5.00
9 Jesus Alou 1.50 4.00
10 Matty Alou 1.50 4.00
11 George Altman 1.25 3.00
12 Max Alvis 1.25 3.00
13 Luis Aparicio 4.00 10.00
14 Bob Aspromonte 1.25 3.00
15 Joe Azcue 1.25 3.00
16 Bob Bailey 1.25 3.00
17 Ernie Banks 6.00 15.00
18 John Bateman 1.25 3.00
19 Earl Battey 1.25 3.00
20 Glenn Beckert 1.25 3.00
21 Gary Bell 1.25 3.00
22 Ken Berry 1.25 3.00
23 Wade Blasingame 1.25 3.00
24 Curt Blefary 1.25 3.00
25 John Boccabella 1.25 3.00
26 Dave Boswell 1.25 3.00
27 Jim Bouton 1.50 4.00
28 Clete Boyer 1.50 4.00
29 Ken Boyer 2.00 5.00
30 Ed Bressoud 1.25 3.00
31 John Briggs 1.25 3.00
32 Ed Brinkman 1.25 3.00
33 Larry Brown 1.25 3.00
34 Ollie Brown 1.25 3.00
35 Bob Bruce 1.25 3.00
36 Don Buford 1.25 3.00
37 Wally Bunker 1.25 3.00
38 Jim Bunning 4.00 10.00
39 Jim Bunning AS 2.00 5.00
40 Johnny Callison 1.50 4.00
41 Bert Campaneris 1.25 3.00
42 Leo Cardenas 1.25 3.00
43 Paul Casanova 1.25 3.00
44 Norm Cash 2.00 5.00
45 Danny Cater 1.25 3.00
46 Dean Chance 1.25 3.00
47 Ed Charles 1.25 3.00
48 Ossie Chavarria 1.25 3.00
49 Horace Clarke 1.25 3.00
50 Roberto Clemente 10.00 25.00
51 Roberto Clemente AS 5.00 12.00
52 Donn Clendenon 1.25 3.00
53 Ty Cline 1.25 3.00
54 Tony Cloninger 1.25 3.00
55 Rocky Colavito 3.00 8.00
56 Gordy Coleman 1.25 3.00
57 Ray Culp 1.25 3.00
58 Clay Dalrymple 1.25 3.00
59 Vic Davalillo 1.25 3.00
60 Jim Davenport 1.25 3.00
61 Ron Davis 1.25 3.00
62 Tommy Davis 1.50 4.00
63 Willie Davis 1.50 4.00
64 Willie Davis AS 1.50 4.00
65 Don Demeter 1.25 3.00
66 Larry Dierker 1.25 3.00
67 Al Downing 1.25 3.00
68 Johnny Edwards 1.25 3.00
69 Andy Etchebarren 1.25 3.00
70 Ron Fairly 1.50 4.00
71 Dick Farrell 1.25 3.00
72 Bill Fischer 1.25 3.00
73 Eddie Fisher 1.25 3.00
74 Jack Fisher 1.25 3.00
75 Joe Foy 1.25 3.00
76 Bill Freehan 1.50 4.00
77 Woodie Fryman 1.25 3.00
78 Tito Fuentes 1.25 3.00
79 Dave Giusti 1.25 3.00
80 Pedro Gonzalez 1.25 3.00
81 Mudcat Grant 1.25 3.00
82 Dick Green 1.25 3.00
83 Dick Groat 1.50 4.00
84 Jerry Grote 1.25 3.00
85 Tom Haller 1.25 3.00
86 Jack Hamilton 1.25 3.00
87 Steve Hamilton 1.25 3.00
88 Ron Hansen 1.25 3.00
89 Tommy Harper 1.25 3.00
90 Ken Harrelson 1.50 4.00
91 Chuck Harrison 1.25 3.00
92 Jim Hart 1.25 3.00
93 Tommy Helms 1.25 3.00
94 Mike Hershberger 1.25 3.00
95 Chuck Hinton 1.25 3.00
96 Ken Holtzman 1.25 3.00
97 Joe Horlen 1.25 3.00
98 Willie Horton 1.50 4.00
99 Elston Howard 2.00 5.00
100 Frank Howard 2.00 5.00
101 Randy Hundley 1.25 3.00
102 Ron Hunt 1.25 3.00
103 Larry Jackson 1.25 3.00
104 Sonny Jackson 1.25 3.00
105 Tommy John 2.00 5.00
106 Davey Johnson 1.50 4.00
107 Deron Johnson 1.25 3.00
108 Ken Johnson 1.25 3.00
109 Lou Johnson 1.25 3.00
110 Cleon Jones 1.25 3.00
111 Dalton Jones 1.25 3.00
112 Al Kaline 6.00 15.00
113 Al Kaline AS 3.00 8.00
114 John Kennedy 1.25 3.00
115 Harmon Killebrew 6.00 15.00
116 Harmon Killebrew AS 3.00 8.00
117 Jim King 1.25 3.00
118 Cal Koonce 1.25 3.00
119 Ed Kranepool 1.25 3.00
120 Lew Krausse 1.25 3.00
121 Jim Landis 1.25 3.00
122 Hal Lanier 1.25 3.00
123 Vern Law 1.25 3.00
124 Jim Lefebvre 1.25 3.00
125 Johnny Lewis 1.25 3.00
126 Don Lock 1.25 3.00
127 Bob Locker 1.25 3.00
128 Mickey Lolich 3.00 8.00
129 Jim Lonborg 1.50 4.00
130 Jerry Lumpe 1.25 3.00
131 Jim Maloney 1.25 3.00
132 Mickey Mantle 50.00 100.00
133 Eddie Mathews 6.00 15.00
134 Willie Mays 12.50 30.00
135 Willie Mays AS 6.00 15.00
136 Bill Mazeroski 3.00 8.00
137 Dick McAuliffe 1.25 3.00
138 Bill McCool 1.25 3.00
139 Mike McCormick 1.25 3.00
140 Willie McCovey 4.00 10.00
141 Tommy McCraw 1.25 3.00
142 Sam McDowell 1.25 3.00
143 Ken McMullen 1.25 3.00
144 Dave McNally 1.25 3.00
145 Jerry McNertney 1.25 3.00
146 Dennis Menke 1.25 3.00
147 Jim Merritt 1.25 3.00
148 Joe Morgan 4.00 10.00
149 Manny Mota 1.50 4.00
150 Jim Nash 1.25 3.00
151 Dick Nen 1.25 3.00
152 Joe Nossek 1.25 3.00
153 Tony Oliva 2.00 5.00
154 Gene Oliver 1.25 3.00
155 Phil Ortega 1.25 3.00
156 Claude Osteen 1.25 3.00
157 Jim O'Toole 1.25 3.00
158 Jim Pagliaroni 1.25 3.00
159 Jim Palmer 6.00 15.00
160 Milt Pappas 1.25 3.00
161 Wes Parker 1.25 3.00
162 Joe Pepitone 1.50 4.00
163 Joe Pepitone AS 1.25 3.00
164 Ron Perranoski 1.25 3.00
165 Gaylord Perry 4.00 10.00
166 Fritz Peterson 1.25 3.00
167 Rico Petrocelli 1.50 4.00
168 Adolfo Phillips 1.25 3.00
169 Vada Pinson 2.00 5.00
170 Johnny Podres 1.50 4.00
171 Boog Powell 2.00 5.00
172 Phil Regan 1.25 3.00
173 Roger Repoz 1.25 3.00
174 Pete Richert 1.25 3.00
175 Brooks Robinson 6.00 15.00
176 Brooks Robinson AS 3.00 8.00
177 Frank Robinson 6.00 15.00
178 Frank Robinson AS 3.00 8.00
179 Cookie Rojas 1.25 3.00
180 Rich Rollins 1.25 3.00
181 Phil Roof 1.25 3.00
182 Pete Rose 8.00 20.00
183 Jose Santiago 1.25 3.00
184 Ron Santo 4.00 10.00
185 Ron Santo AS 2.00 5.00
186 Bob Saverine 1.25 3.00
187 George Scott 1.25 3.00
188 Art Shamsky 1.25 3.00
189 Bob Shaw 1.25 3.00
190 Chris Short 1.25 3.00
191 Norman Siebern 1.25 3.00
192 Moose Skowron 1.50 4.00
193 Charley Smith 1.25 3.00
194 George Smith 1.25 3.00
195 Russ Snyder 1.25 3.00
196 Joe Sparma 1.25 3.00
197 Willie Stargell 4.00 10.00
198 Rusty Staub 2.00 5.00
199 John Stephenson 1.25 3.00
200 Mel Stottlemyre 1.50 4.00
201 Don Sutton 4.00 10.00
202 Ron Swoboda 1.25 3.00
203 Jose Tartabull 1.25 3.00
204 Tony Taylor 1.25 3.00
205 Lee Thomas 1.25 3.00
206 Luis Tiant 2.00 5.00
207 Bob Tillman 1.25 3.00
208 Joe Torre 2.50 6.00
209 Joe Torre AS 2.00 5.00
210 Tom Tresh 1.50 4.00
211 Ted Uhlaender 1.25 3.00
212 Sandy Valdespino 1.25 3.00
213 Fred Valentine 1.25 3.00
214 Bob Veale 1.25 3.00
215 Zoilo Versalles 1.25 3.00
216 Leon Wagner 1.25 3.00
217 Pete Ward 1.25 3.00
218 Don Wert 1.25 3.00
219 Bill White 2.00 5.00
220 Roy White 1.25 3.00
221 Fred Whitfield 1.25 3.00
222 Dave Wickersham 1.25 3.00
223 Billy Williams 4.00 10.00
224 Maury Wills 2.00 5.00
225 Earl Wilson 1.25 3.00
226 Woody Woodward 1.25 3.00
227 Carl Yastrzemski 6.00 15.00
228 Carl Yastrzemski AS 3.00 8.00

1968 Dexter Press

This 77-card set, which measures approximately 3 1/2" by 5 1/2", has beautiful full-color photos on the front of the card with biographical and career information on the back of the card. There are no year by year statistical lines on the back of the card. Dexter Press is another name for cards which the Coca-Cola Company helped to distribute during the mid sixties. The backs of the cards have a facsimile autograph. Dexter Press was located in West Nyack, New York. These unnumbered cards are listed below in alphabetical order.

COMPLETE SET (77) 400.00 800.00
1 Hank Aaron 20.00 50.00
2 Jerry Adair 2.50 6.00
3 Richie Allen 4.00 10.00
4 Bob Allison 3.00 8.00
5 Felipe Alou 4.00 10.00
6 Jesus Alou 2.50 6.00
7 Mike Andrews 2.50 6.00
8 Bob Aspromonte 2.50 6.00
9 Johnny Bateman 2.50 6.00
10 Mark Belanger 2.50 6.00
11 Gary Bell 2.50 6.00
12 Paul Blair 2.50 6.00
13 Curt Blefary 2.50 6.00
14 Bobby Bolin 2.50 6.00
15 Ken Boswell 2.50 6.00
16 Clete Boyer 3.00 8.00
17 Ron Brand 2.50 6.00
18 Darrell Brandon 2.50 6.00
19 Don Buford 2.50 6.00
20 Rod Carew 20.00 50.00
21 Clay Carroll 2.50 6.00
22 Rico Carty 3.00 8.00
23 Dean Chance 2.50 6.00
24 Roberto Clemente 75.00 150.00
25 Tony Cloninger 2.50 6.00
26 Mike Cuellar 2.50 6.00
27 Jim Davenport 2.50 6.00
28 Ron Davis 2.50 6.00
29 Moe Drabowsky 2.50 6.00
30 Dick Ellsworth 2.50 6.00
31 Andy Etchebarren 2.50 6.00
32 Joe Foy 2.50 6.00
33 Bill Freehan 3.00 8.00
34 Jim Fregosi 3.00 8.00
35 Julio Gotay 2.50 6.00
36 Dave Giusti 2.50 6.00
37 Jim Ray Hart 2.50 6.00
38 Jack Hiatt 2.50 6.00
39 Ron Hunt 2.50 6.00
40 Sonny Jackson 2.50 6.00
41 Pat Jarvis 2.50 6.00
42 Davey Johnson 3.00 8.00
43 Ken Johnson 2.50 6.00
44 Dalton Jones 2.50 6.00
45 Jim Kaat 4.00 10.00
46 Harmon Killebrew 10.00 25.00
47 Denny Lemaster 2.50 6.00
48 Frank Linzy 2.50 6.00
49 Jim Lonborg 3.00 8.00
50 Juan Marichal 10.00 25.00
51 Willie Mays 40.00 80.00
52 Bill Mazeroski 5.00 12.00
53 Mike McCormick 3.00 8.00
54 Dave McNally 3.00 8.00
55 Denis Menke 2.50 6.00
56 Joe Morgan 8.00 20.00
57 Dave Morehead 2.50 6.00
58 Phil Niekro 8.00 20.00
59 Russ Nixon 2.50 6.00
60 Tony Oliva 4.00 10.00
61 Gaylord Perry 8.00 20.00
62 Rico Petrocelli 3.00 8.00
63 Tom Phoebus 2.50 6.00
64 Boog Powell 3.00 8.00
65 Brooks Robinson 10.00 25.00
66 Frank Robinson 10.00 25.00
67 Rich Rollins 2.50 6.00
68 John Roseboro 2.50 6.00
69 Ray Sadecki 2.50 6.00
70 George Scott 2.50 6.00
71 Rusty Staub 4.00 10.00
72 Cesar Tovar 2.50 6.00
73 Joe Torre 5.00 12.00
74 Ted Uhlaender 2.50 6.00
75 Woody Woodward 2.50 6.00
76 John Wyatt 2.50 6.00
77 Jimmy Wynn 3.00 8.00

2003 Diamond Action

COMPLETE SET 10.00 20.00
1 Richie Ashburn .40 1.00
2 Ernie Banks .60 1.50
3 Yogi Berra .75 2.00
4 Smoky Burgess .20 .50
5 Phil Cavarretta .20 .50
6 Frank Crosetti .20 .50
7 Don Demeter .10 .25
8 Sam Dente .10 .25
9 Joe DiMaggio 1.25 3.00
10 Jim Gilliam .20 .50
11 Don Hoak .10 .25
12 Eddie Kasko .10 .25
13 Dale Long .10 .25
14 Roger Maris .75 2.00
15 Eddie Mathews .60 1.50
16 Lee Maye .10 .25
17 Willie Mays 1.00 2.50
18 Roy McMillan .10 .25
19 Wally Moon .20 .50
20 Bobby Richardson .30 .75
21 Jackie Robinson 1.00 2.50
22 Bill Serena .10 .25
23 Birdie Tebbetts .10 .25
24 Tom Tresh .20 .50
25 Gee Walker .10 .25
26 Vic Wertz .10 .25
27 Maury Wills .30 .75
28 Ed Yost .10 .25

1982-83 Diamond Classics

These very attractive cards measure 2 1/2" by 3 3/4" and feature drawings of all-time stars on the front. The drawings cover almost all the front of the cards. The backs give a history of the player as well as some important statistics. Upon release, the 1st series was offered for $8 plus postage. The second series was available for $10 upon release. These cards were produced from original art work and distributed by collector Steve Mitchell.

COMPLETE SET (110) 30.00 60.00
1 Joe DiMaggio .75 2.00
2 Enos Slaughter .08 .25
3 Smokey Joe Wood .08 .25
4 Roy Campanella .20 .50
5 Charlie Gehringer .08 .25
6 Carl Hubbell .20 .50
7 Rogers Hornsby .20 .50
8 Arky Vaughan .08 .25
9 Al Simmons .08 .25
10 Wally Berger .02 .10
11 Sam Rice .08 .25
12 Dizzy Dean .20 .50
13 Babe Ruth 1.25 3.00
14 Frankie Frisch .08 .25
15 George Kell .08 .25
16 Pee Wee Reese .20 .50
17 Earl Averill .08 .25
18 Willie Mays .60 1.50
19 Frank Baker .08 .25
20 Hack Wilson .08 .25
21 Ted Williams .75 2.00
22 Chuck Klein .08 .25
23 Bill Dickey .08 .25
24 Johnny Mize .08 .25
25 Luke Appling .08 .25
26 Duke Snider .20 .50
27 Wahoo Sam Crawford .20 .50
28 Waite Hoyt .08 .25
29 Eddie Collins .20 .50
30 Warren Spahn .20 .50
31 Satchel Paige .40 1.00
32 Ernie Lombardi .08 .25
33 Dom DiMaggio .08 .25
34 Joe Garagiola .20 .50
35 Lou Gehrig .75 2.00
36 Burleigh Grimes .08 .25
37 Walter Johnson .20 .50
38 Bill Terry .08 .25
39 Ty Cobb .75 2.00
40 Pie Traynor .08 .25
41 Ted Lyons .08 .25
42 Richie Ashburn .20 .50
43 Lefty Grove .20 .50
44 Edd Roush .08 .25
45 Phil Rizzuto .20 .50
46 Stan Musial .40 1.00
47 Bob Feller .20 .50
48 Jackie Robinson .75 2.00
49 Hank Greenberg .20 .50
50 Mel Ott .20 .50
51 Joe Cronin .08 .25
52 Lefty O'Doul .08 .25
53 Indian Bob Johnson .02 .10
54 Kiki Cuyler .08 .25
55 Mickey Mantle 1.25 3.00
56 Ernie Banks .40 1.00
57 Stan Coveleskie .08 .25
58 Vince DiMaggio .08 .25
59 Jim Bottomley .08 .25
60 Sandy Koufax .40 1.00
61 Doc Cramer .02 .10
62 Ted Kluszewski .20 .50
63 Zeke Bonura .02 .10
64 Spud Davis .02 .10
65 Jackie Jensen .02 .10
66 Honus Wagner .30 .75
67 Brooks Robinson .20 .50
68 Dazzy Vance .08 .25
69 George Uhle .02 .10
70 Juan Marichal .20 .50
71 Bobo Newsom .02 .10
72 Billy Herman .08 .25
73 Al Rosen .08 .25
74 Roberto Clemente .75 2.00
75 George Case .02 .10
76 Bill Nicholson .02 .10
77 Tommy Bridges .02 .10
78 Rabbit Maranville .08 .25
79 Bob Lemon .08 .25
80 Heinie Groh .02 .10
81 Tris Speaker .20 .50
82 Hank Aaron .60 1.50
83 Whitey Ford .20 .50
84 Guy Bush .02 .10
85 Jimmie Foxx .20 .50
86 Marty Marion .08 .25
87 Hal Newhouser .08 .25
88 George Kelly .08 .25
89 Harmon Killebrew .20 .50
90 Willie McCovey .20 .50
91 Mel Harder .02 .10
92 Vada Pinson .08 .25
93 Luis Aparicio .20 .50
94 Grover Alexander .20 .50
95 Joe Kuhel .02 .10
96 Casey Stengel .20 .50
97 Joe Sewell .08 .25
98 Red Lucas .02 .10
99 Luke Sewell .02 .10
100 Charlie Grimm .02 .10
101 Cecil Travis .02 .10
102 Travis Jackson .08 .25
103 Lou Boudreau .08 .25
104 Nap Rucker .02 .10
105 Chief Bender .08 .25
106 Riggs Stephenson .02 .10
107 Red Ruffing .08 .25
108 Robin Roberts .20 .50
109 Harland Clift .02 .10
110 Ralph Kiner .20 .50
XX Certificate Card .02 .10
NNO Checklist Card .02 .10

1958 Diamond Gallery

These photos which were inserted into copies of the NY Daily News feature leading players in baseball at that time. It is believed that these photos were actually issued over a course of a few seasons and any additions to this checklist is appreciated. There are probably many additions to this checklist so any further information is very appreciated.

COMPLETE SET 15.00 30.00
COMMON CARD
1 Gus Bell 5.00 10.00
2 Nellie Fox 10.00 20.00
Brooks Lawrence

1979 Diamond Greats

This 400-card set features black-and-white player portraits with the player's name, life-time statistics, team name, and playing position printed in black in the white margins. The backs are blank.

COMPLETE SET (400) 60.00 120.00
1 Joe DiMaggio 2.50 6.00
2 Ben Chapman .10 .25
3 Joe Dugan .10 .25
4 Bob Shawkey .20 .50
5 Joe Sewell .30 .75
6 George Pipgras .10 .25
7 George Selkirk .10 .25
8 Babe Dahlgren .10 .25
9 Spud Chandler .20 .50
10 Duffy Lewis .10 .25
11 Lefty Gomez .40 1.00
12 Atley Donald .10 .25
13 Whitey Witt .10 .25
14 Marius Russo .10 .25
15 Buddy Rosar .10 .25
16 Russ Van Atta .10 .25
17 Johnny Lindell .10 .25
18 Bobby Brown .20 .50
19 Tony Kubek .20 .50
20 Joe Beggs .10 .25
21 Don Larsen .20 .50
22 Andy Carey .10 .25
23 Johnny Kucks .10 .25
24 Elston Howard .20 .50
25 Roger Maris .75 2.00
26 Rube Marquard .40 1.00
27 Sam Leslie .10 .25
28 Freddy Leach .10 .25
29 Fred Fitzsimmons .20 .50
30 Bill Terry .40 1.00
31 Joe Moore .10 .25
32 Waite Hoyt .30 .75
33 Travis Jackson .30 .75
34 Gus Mancuso .10 .25
35 Carl Hubbell .60 1.50
36 Bill Voiselle .10 .25
37 Hank Leiber .10 .25
38 Burgess Whitehead .10 .25
39 Johnny Mize .40 1.00
40 Bill Lohrman .10 .25
41 Bill Rigney .10 .25
42 Cliff Melton .10 .25
43 Willard Marshall .10 .25
44 Wes Westrum .10 .25
45 Monte Irvin .40 1.00
46 Marv Grissom .10 .25
47 Clyde Castleman .10 .25
48 Harry Gumbert .10 .25
49 Daryl Spencer .10 .25
50 Willie Mays 2.00 5.00
51 Sam West .10 .25
52 Fred Schulte .10 .25
53 Cecil Travis .10 .25
54 Tommy Thomas .10 .25
55 Dutch Leonard .10 .25
56 Jimmy Wasdell .10 .25
57 Doc Cramer .20 .50
58 Harland Clift .20 .50
59 Ken Chase .10 .25
60 Buddy Lewis .10 .25
61 Ossie Bluege .10 .25
62 Chuck Stobbs .10 .25
63 Jimmy DeShong .10 .25
64 Roger Wolff .10 .25
65 Luke Sewell .10 .25
66 Sid Hudson .10 .25
67 Jack Russell .10 .25
68 Walt Masterson .10 .25
69 George Myatt .10 .25
70 Monte Weaver .10 .25
71 Cliff Bolton .10 .25
72 Ray Scarborough .10 .25
73 Albie Pearson .10 .25
74 Gil Coan .10 .25
75 Roy Sievers .20 .50
76 Burleigh Grimes .30 .75
77 Charlie Hargreaves .10 .25
78 Babe Herman .20 .50
79 Fred Frankhouse .10 .25
80 Al Lopez .30 .75
81 Lonny Frey .10 .25
82 Dixie Walker .10 .25
83 Kirby Higbe .10 .25
84 Bobby Bragan .10 .25
85 Leo Durocher .30 .75
86 Woody English .10 .25
87 Preacher Roe .10 .25
88 Vic Lombardi .10 .25
89 Clyde Sukeforth .10 .25
90 Pee Wee Reese 1.00 2.50
91 Joe Hatten .10 .25
92 Gene Hermanski .10 .25
93 Ray Benge .10 .25
94 Duke Snider 1.00 2.50
95 Walter Alston MG .30 .75
96 Don Drysdale .75 2.00
97 Andy Pafko .20 .50
98 Don Zimmer .20 .50
99 Carl Erskine .20 .50
100 Dick Williams .20 .50
101 Charlie Grimm .20 .50
102 Clarence Blair .10 .25
103 Johnny Moore .10 .25
104 Clay Bryant .10 .25
105 Billy Herman .30 .75
106 Hy Vandenberg .10 .25
107 Lennie Merullo .10 .25
108 Hank Wyse .10 .25
109 Dom Dallessandro .10 .25
110 Al Epperly .10 .25
111 Bill Nicholson .10 .25
112 Vern Olsen .10 .25
113 Johnny Schmitz .10 .25
114 Bob Scheffing .10 .25
115 Bob Rush .10 .25
116 Roy Smalley .10 .25
117 Ransom Jackson .10 .25
118 Cliff Chambers .10 .25
119 Harry Chiti .10 .25
120 Johnny Klippstein .10 .25
121 Gene Baker .10 .25
122 Walt Moryn .10 .25
123 Dick Littlefield .10 .25
124 Bob Speake .10 .25
125 Hank Sauer .10 .25
126 Monty Stratton .20 .50
127 Johnny Kerr .10 .25
128 Milt Gaston .10 .25
129 Eddie Smith .10 .25
130 Larry Rosenthal .10 .25
131 Orval Grove .10 .25
132 Johnny Hodapp .10 .25
133 Johnny Rigney .10 .25
134 Willie Kamm .10 .25
135 Ed Lopat .20 .50
136 Smead Jolley .10 .25
137 Ralph Hodgin .10 .25
138 Ollie Bejma .10 .25
139 Zeke Bonura .10 .25
140 Al Hollingsworth .10 .25
141 Thurman Tucker .10 .25
142 Cass Michaels .10 .25
143 Bill Wight .10 .25
144 Don Lenhardt .10 .25
145 Sammy Esposito .10 .25
146 Jack Harshman .10 .25
147 Turk Lown .10 .25
148 Jim Landis .10 .25
149 Bob Shaw .10 .25
150 Minnie Minoso .30 .75
151 Les Bell .10 .25
152 Taylor Douthit .10 .25
153 Jack Rothrock .10 .25
154 Terry Moore .20 .50
155 Max Lanier .10 .25
156 Don Gutteridge .10 .25
157 Stu Martin .10 .25
158 Stan Musial .75 2.00
159 Frank Crespi .10 .25
160 Johnny Hopp .10 .25
161 Ernie Koy .10 .25
162 Joe Garagiola .40 1.00
163 Joe Orengo .10 .25
164 Ed Kazak .10 .25
165 Howie Krist .10 .25
166 Enos Slaughter .30 .75
167 Ray Sanders .10 .25
168 Walker Cooper .10 .25
169 Nippy Jones .10 .25
170 Dick Sisler .10 .25
171 Harvey Haddix .10 .25
172 Solly Hemus .10 .25
173 Ray Jablonski .10 .25
174 Alex Grammas .10 .25
175 Joe Cunningham .20 .50
176 Debs Garms .10 .25
177 Chief Hogsett .10 .25
178 Alan Strange .10 .25
179 Rick Ferrell .30 .75
180 Jack Kramer .10 .25
181 Jack Knott .10 .25
182 Bob Harris .10 .25
183 Billy Hitchcock .10 .25
184 Jim Walkup .10 .25
185 Roy Cullenbine .10 .25
186 Bob Muncrief .10 .25
187 Chet Laabs .10 .25
188 Vern Kennedy .10 .25
189 Bill Trotter .10 .25
190 Denny Galehouse .10 .25
191 Al Zarilla .10 .25
192 Hank Arft .10 .25
193 Nelson Potter .10 .25
194 Ray Coleman .10 .25
195 Bob Dillinger .20 .50
196 Dick Kokos .10 .25
197 Bob Cain .10 .25
198 Virgil Trucks .10 .25
199 Duane Pillette .10 .25
200 Bob Turley .20 .50
201 Wally Berger .20 .50
202 John Lanning .10 .25
203 Buck Jordan .10 .25
204 Jim Turner .10 .25
205 Johnny Cooney .10 .25
206 Hank Majeski .10 .25
207 Phil Masi .10 .25
208 Tony Cuccinello .10 .25
209 Whitey Wietelman .10 .25
210 Lou Fette .10 .25
211 Vince Di Maggio .10 .25
212 Huck Betts .10 .25
213 Red Barrett .10 .25
214 Pinkey Whitney .10 .25
215 Tommy Holmes .20 .50
216 Ray Berres .10 .25
217 Mike Sandlock .10 .25
218 Max Macon .10 .25
219 Sibby Sisti .10 .25
220 Johnny Beazley .10 .25
221 Bill Posedel .10 .25
222 Connie Ryan .10 .25
223 Del Crandall .10 .25
224 Bob Addis .10 .25
225 Warren Spahn .60 1.50
227 Dom DiMaggio .20 .50
228 Emerson Dickman .10 .25
229 Bobby Doerr .30 .75
230 Tony Lupien .10 .25
231 Roy Partee .10 .25
232 Stan Spence .10 .25
233 Jim Bagby .10 .25
234 Buster Mills .10 .25
235 Fabian Gaffke .10 .25
236 George Metkovich .10 .25
237 Tom McBride .10 .25
238 Charlie Wagner .10 .25
239 Eddie Pellegrini .10 .25
240 Harry Dorish .10 .25
241 Ike Delock .10 .25
242 Mel Parnell .10 .25
243 Matt Batts .10 .25
244 Gene Stephens .10 .25
245 Milt Bolling .10 .25
246 Charlie Maxwell .10 .25
247 Willard Nixon .10 .25
248 Sammy White .10 .25
249 Dick Gernert .10 .25
250 Rico Petrocelli .10 .25
251 Edd Roush .30 .75
252 Mark Koenig .20 .50
253 Jimmy Outlaw .10 .25
254 Ethan Allen .10 .25
255 Tony Freitas .10 .25
256 Frank McCormick .10 .25
257 Bucky Walters .20 .50
258 Harry Craft .10 .25
259 Nate Andrews .10 .25
260 Ed Lukon .10 .25
261 Elmer Riddle .10 .25
262 Lee Grissom .10 .25
263 Johnny Vander Meer .20 .50
264 Eddie Joost .10 .25
265 Kermit Wahl .10 .25
266 Ival Goodman .10 .25
267 Clyde Vollmer .10 .25
268 Grady Hatten .10 .25
269 Ted Kluszewski .40 1.00
270 Johnny Pramesa .10 .25
271 Joe Black .20 .50
272 Roy McMillan .10 .25
273 Wally Post .10 .25
274 Joe Nuxhall .10 .25
275 Jerry Lynch .10 .25
276 Stan Coveleski .30 .75
277 Bill Wambsganss .20 .50
278 Bruce Campbell .10 .25
279 George Uhle .10 .25
280 Earl Averill .30 .75
281 Whit Wyatt .10 .25
282 Oscar Grimes .10 .25
283 Roy Weatherly .10 .25
284 Joe Dobson .10 .25
285 Bob Feller .75 2.00
286 Jim Hegan .10 .25
287 Mel Harder .20 .50
288 Ken Keltner .10 .25
289 Red Embree .10 .25
290 Al Milnar .10 .25
291 Lou Boudreau .40 1.00
292 Ed Klieman .10 .25
293 Steve Gromek .10 .25
294 George Strickland .10 .25
295 Gene Woodling .10 .25
296 Hank Edwards .10 .25
297 Don Mossi .20 .50
298 Eddie Robinson .10 .25
299 Sam Dente .10 .25
300 Herb Score .20 .50
301 Dolf Camilli .20 .50
302 Jack Warner .10 .25
303 Ike Pearson .10 .25
304 Johnny Peacock .10 .25
305 Gene Corbett .10 .25
306 Walt Millies .10 .25
307 Vance Dinges .10 .25
308 Joe Marty .10 .25
309 Hugh Mulcahey .10 .25
310 Boom Boom Beck .10 .25
311 Charley Schanz .10 .25
312 John Bolling .10 .25
313 Danny Litwhiler .10 .25
314 Emil Verban .10 .25

315 Andy Seminick .10 .25
316 John Antonelli .10 .25
317 Robin Roberts .75 2.00
318 Richie Ashburn .40 1.00
319 Curt Simmons .10 .25
320 Murry Dickson .10 .25
321 Jim Greengrass .10 .25
322 Gene Freese .10 .25
323 Bobby Morgan .10 .25
324 Don Demeter .10 .25
325 Eddie Sawyer .10 .25
326 Bob Johnson .10 .25
327 Ace Parker .30 .75
328 Joe Hauser .10 .25
329 Walt French .10 .25
330 Tom Ferrick .10 .25
331 Bill Werber .10 .25
332 Walt Masters .10 .25
333 Les McCrabb .10 .25
334 Ben McCoy .10 .25
335 Eric Tipton .10 .25
336 Al Rubeling .10 .25
337 Nick Etten .10 .25
338 Carl Scheib .10 .25
339 Dario Lodigiani .10 .25
340 Earle Brucker .10 .25
341 Al Brancato .10 .25
342 Lou Limmer .10 .25
343 Elmer Valo .10 .25
344 Bob Hooper .10 .25
345 Joe Astroth .10 .25
346 Pete Suder .10 .25
347 Dave Philley .10 .25
348 Gus Zernial .10 .25
349 Bobby Shantz .10 .25
350 Joe DeMaestri .10 .25
351 Fred Lindstrom .30 .75
352 Red Lucas .10 .25
353 Clyde Barnhart .10 .25
354 Nick Strincevich .10 .25
355 Lloyd Waner .30 .75
356 Guy Bush .10 .25
357 Joe Bowman .10 .25
358 Al Todd .10 .25
359 Mace Brown .10 .25
360 Larry French .10 .25
361 Elbie Fletcher .10 .25
362 Woody Jensen .10 .25
363 Rip Sewell .10 .25
364 Johnny Dickshot .10 .25
365 Pete Coscarart .10 .25
366 Bud Hafey .10 .25
367 Ken Heintzelman .10 .25
368 Wally Westlake .10 .25
369 Frank Gustine .10 .25
370 Smokey Burgess .20 .50
371 Vernon Law .20 .50
372 Dick Groat .20 .50
373 Bob Skinner .10 .25
374 Don Cardwell .10 .25
375 Bob Friend .10 .25
376 Frank O'Rourke .10 .25
377 Birdie Tebbetts .10 .25
378 Charlie Gehringer .40 1.00
379 Eldon Auker .10 .25
380 Tuck Stainback .10 .25
381 Chet Morgan .10 .25
382 Johnny Lipon .10 .25
383 Paul Richards .10 .25
384 Johnny Gorsica .10 .25
385 Ray Hayworth .10 .25
386 Jimmy Bloodworth .10 .25
387 Gene Desautels .10 .25
388 Jo Jo White .10 .25
389 Boots Poffenberger .10 .25
390 Barney McCoskey .10 .25
391 Dick Wakefield .10 .25
392 Johnny Groth .10 .25
393 Steve Souchock .10 .25
394 George Vico .10 .25
395 Hal Newhouser .30 .75
396 Ray Herbert .10 .25
397 Jim Bunning .40 1.00
398 Frank Lary .10 .25
399 Harvey Kuenn .20 .50
400 Eddie Mathews .75 2.00

1911 Diamond Gum Pins

This set of 29 (the number of pins known at this time) pins is described on each pin as "Free with Diamond Gum." The border of each pin is blue. Since the pins are unnumbered they are ordered below in alphabetical order. The player's name and team are given on the front of the pin on either side of the black and white player photo. Each pin measures approximately 7/8" in diameter.

COMPLETE SET 4000.00 8000.00
1 Babe Adams 75.00 150.00
2 Frank Baker 125.00 250.00
3 Chief Bender 125.00 250.00
4 Mordecai Brown 125.00 250.00
5 Donie Bush 75.00 150.00
6 Bill Carrigan 75.00 150.00
7 Frank Chance 150.00 300.00
8 Hal Chase 125.00 250.00
9 Ty Cobb 750.00 1500.00
10 Eddie Collins 150.00 300.00
11 Harry Davis 75.00 150.00
12 Red Dooin 75.00 150.00
13 Larry Doyle 87.50 175.00
14 Johnny Evers 125.00 250.00
15 Miller Huggins 125.00 250.00
16 Hugh Jennings 125.00 250.00
17 Napoleon Lajoie 200.00 400.00
18 Harry Lord 75.00 150.00
19 C.Mathewson 300.00 600.00
20 Dots Miller 75.00 150.00
21 G.Mullen (Mullin) 75.00 150.00
22 Danny Murphy 75.00 150.00
23 Orval Overall 75.00 150.00
24 Eddie Plank 150.00 300.00
25 H.Simmons Roch. 75.00 150.00
26 Ira Thomas 75.00 150.00
27 Joe Tinker 150.00 300.00
28 Honus Wagner 250.00 500.00
29 Cy Young 200.00 400.00

2002 Diamond Kings Samples

*SAMPLES: 1.5X TO 4X BASIC DK'S
ONE PER BECKETT ISSUE 206 AND 208

2002 Diamond Kings Samples Gold

*GOLD SAMPLES: 1X TO 2.5X BASIC SAMPLES

2002 Diamond Kings

COMP.LOW SET (150) 100.00 200.00
COMP.LOW w/o SP's (100) 20.00 50.00
COMP.UPDATE SET (10) 15.00 40.00
COMMON CARD (1-100) .20 .50
COMMON PROSPECT (101-150) 1.50 4.00
COMMON RETIRED (101-150) 1.50 4.00
101-150 STATED ODDS 1:3
COMMON CARD (151-160) 1.50 4.00
151-160 STATED ODDS 1:10 HOB, 1:12 RET
151-160 DIST.IN DONRUSS ROOKIES PACKS
1 Vladimir Guerrero .50 1.25
2 Adam Dunn .20 .50
3 Tsuyoshi Shinjo .20 .50
4 Adrian Beltre .20 .50
5 Troy Glaus .20 .50
6 Albert Pujols 1.00 2.50
7 Trot Nixon .20 .50
8 Alex Rodriguez .60 1.50
9 Tom Glavine .30 .75
10 Alfonso Soriano .20 .50
11 Todd Helton .30 .75
12 Joe Torre .30 .75
13 Tim Hudson .20 .50
14 Andruw Jones .30 .75
15 Shawn Green .20 .50
16 Aramis Ramirez .20 .50
17 Shannon Stewart .20 .50
18 Barry Bonds 1.25 3.00
19 Sean Casey .20 .50
20 Barry Larkin .30 .75
21 Scott Rolen .30 .75
22 Barry Zito .20 .50
23 Sammy Sosa .50 1.25
24 Bartolo Colon .20 .50
25 Ryan Klesko .20 .50
26 Ben Grieve .20 .50
27 Roy Oswalt .20 .50
28 Kazuhiro Sasaki .20 .50
29 Roger Clemens 1.00 2.50
30 Bernie Williams .30 .75
31 Roberto Alomar .30 .75
32 Bobby Abreu .20 .50
33 Robert Fick .20 .50
34 Bret Boone .20 .50
35 Rickey Henderson .50 1.25
36 Brian Giles .20 .50
37 Richie Sexson .20 .50
38 Bud Smith .20 .50
39 Richard Hidalgo .20 .50
40 C.C. Sabathia .20 .50
41 Rich Aurilia .20 .50
42 Carlos Beltran .20 .50
43 Raul Mondesi .20 .50
44 Carlos Delgado .20 .50
45 Randy Johnson .50 1.25
46 Chan Ho Park .20 .50
47 Rafael Palmeiro .30 .75
48 Chipper Jones .50 1.25
49 Phil Nevin .20 .50
50 Cliff Floyd .20 .50
51 Pedro Martinez .30 .75
52 Craig Biggio .30 .75
53 Paul LoDuca .20 .50
54 Cristian Guzman .20 .50
55 Pat Burrell .20 .50
56 Curt Schilling .20 .50
57 Orlando Cabrera .20 .50
58 Darin Erstad .20 .50
59 Omar Vizquel .30 .75
60 Derek Jeter 1.25 3.00
61 Nomar Garciaparra .75 2.00
62 Edgar Martinez .30 .75
63 Moises Alou .20 .50
64 Eric Chavez .20 .50
65 Mike Sweeney .20 .50
66 Frank Thomas .50 1.25
67 Mike Piazza .75 2.00
68 Gary Sheffield .20 .50
69 Mike Mussina .30 .75
70 Greg Maddux .75 2.00
71 Juan Gonzalez .20 .50
72 Hideo Nomo .50 1.25
73 Miguel Tejada .20 .50
74 Ichiro Suzuki 1.00 2.50
75 Matt Morris .20 .50
76 Ivan Rodriguez .30 .75
77 Mark Mulder .20 .50
78 J.D. Drew .20 .50
79 Mark Grace .30 .75
80 Jason Giambi .20 .50
81 Mark Buehrle .20 .50
82 Jose Vidro .20 .50
83 Manny Ramirez .30 .75
84 Jeff Bagwell .30 .75
85 Maggio Ordonez .20 .50
86 Ken Griffey Jr. 1.00 2.50
87 Luis Gonzalez .20 .50
88 Jim Edmonds .20 .50
89 Larry Walker .20 .50
90 Jim Thome .30 .75
91 Lance Berkman .20 .50
92 Jorge Posada .30 .75
93 Kevin Brown .20 .50
94 Joe Mays .20 .50
95 Kerry Wood .20 .50
96 Mark Ellis .20 .50
97 Austin Kearns .20 .50
98 Jorge De La Rosa RC .20 .50
99 Brandon Berger .20 .50
100 Ryan Ludwick .20 .50
101 Marlon Byrd SP 1.50 4.00
102 Brandon Backe SP RC 1.50 4.00
103 Juan Cruz SP 1.50 4.00
104 Anderson Machado SP RC 1.50 4.00
105 So Taguchi SP RC 1.50 4.00
106 Dewon Brazelton SP 1.50 4.00
107 Josh Beckett SP 1.50 4.00
108 John Buck SP 1.50 4.00
109 Jorge Padilla SP RC 1.50 4.00
110 Hee Seop Choi SP 1.50 4.00
111 Angel Berroa SP 1.50 4.00
112 Mark Teixeira SP 2.00 5.00
113 Victor Martinez SP 2.00 5.00
114 Kazuhisa Ishii SP RC 1.50 4.00
115 Dennis Tankersley SP 1.50 4.00
116 Wilson Valdez SP RC 1.50 4.00
117 Antonio Perez SP 1.50 4.00
118 Ed Rogers SP 1.50 4.00
119 Wilson Betemit SP 1.50 4.00
120 Mike Rivera SP 1.50 4.00
121 Mark Prior SP 1.25 3.00
122 Roberto Clemente SP 3.00 8.00
123 Roberto Clemente SP 3.00 8.00
124 Roberto Clemente SP 3.00 8.00
125 Roberto Clemente SP 3.00 8.00
126 Roberto Clemente SP 3.00 8.00
127 Babe Ruth SP 4.00 10.00
128 Ted Williams SP 3.00 8.00
129 Andre Dawson SP 1.50 4.00
130 Eddie Murray SP 2.00 5.00
131 Juan Marichal SP 1.50 4.00
132 Kirby Puckett SP 2.00 5.00
133 Alan Trammell SP 1.50 4.00
134 Bobby Doerr SP 1.50 4.00
135 Carlton Fisk SP 1.50 4.00
136 Eddie Mathews SP 2.00 5.00
137 Mike Schmidt SP 4.00 10.00
138 Catfish Hunter SP 1.50 4.00
139 Nolan Ryan SP 5.00 12.00
140 George Brett SP 4.00 10.00
141 Gary Carter SP 1.50 4.00
142 Paul Molitor SP 1.50 4.00
143 Lou Gehrig SP 2.50 6.00
144 Ryne Sandberg SP 4.00 10.00
145 Tony Gwynn SP 2.50 6.00
146 Ron Santo SP 1.50 4.00
147 Cal Ripken SP 6.00 15.00
148 Al Kaline SP 2.00 5.00
149 Bo Jackson SP 2.00 5.00
150 Don Mattingly SP 4.00 10.00
151 Chris Snelling RC 1.50 4.00
152 Satoru Komiyama RC 1.50 4.00
153 Oliver Perez RC 1.50 4.00
154 Kirk Saarloos RC 1.50 4.00
155 Rene Reyes RC 1.50 4.00
156 Runelvys Hernandez RC 1.50 4.00
157 Rodrigo Rosario RC 1.50 4.00
158 Jason Simontacchi RC 1.50 4.00
159 Miguel Asencio RC 1.50 4.00
160 Aaron Cook RC 1.50 4.00

2002 Diamond Kings Bronze Foil

*BRONZE 1-100: 1.5X TO 4X BASIC
*BRONZE 101-121: .4X TO 1X BASIC
*BRONZE 122-150: .4X TO 1X BASIC
*BRONZE 151-160: 1X TO 2.5X BASIC
1-150 STATED ODDS 1:6
151-160 STATED ODDS 1:128 HOB, 1:256 RET
151-160 DIST.IN DONRUSS ROOKIES PACKS
BRONZE CARDS FEATURE WHITE FRAMES

2002 Diamond Kings Gold Foil

*GOLD 1-100: 6X TO 15X BASIC
*GOLD 101-121: 1.5X TO 4X BASIC
*GOLD 122-150: 2.5X TO 6X BASIC
*GOLD 151-160: 1.5X TO 4X BASIC
1-150 RANDOM INSERTS IN PACKS
151-160 RANDOM IN DONRUSS ROOK.PACKS
STATED PRINT RUN 100 SERIAL #'d SETS
GOLD CARDS FEATURE BLACK FRAMES

2002 Diamond Kings Silver Foil

*SILVER 1-100: 3X TO 8X BASIC
*SILVER 101-121: .75X TO 2X BASIC
*SILVER 122-150: 1.25X TO 3X BASIC
*SILVER 151-160: 1.25X TO 3X BASIC
1-150 RANDOM INSERTS IN PACKS
151-160 RANDOM IN DONRUSS ROOK.PACKS
1-150 PRINT RUN 400 SERIAL #'d SETS
151-160 PRINT RUN 250 SERIAL #'d SETS
SILVER CARDS FEATURE GREY FRAMES

2002 Diamond Kings Diamond Cut Collection

APPROXIMATELY ONE PER HOBBY BOX
PRINT RUNS B/WN 100-500 COPIES PER
DC1 Vladimir Guerrero AU/400 10.00 25.00
DC2 Mark Prior AU/400 10.00 25.00
DC3 Victor Martinez AU/500 5.00 12.00
DC4 Marlon Byrd AU/500 4.00 10.00
DC5 Bud Smith AU/400 4.00 10.00
DC6 Joe Mays AU/500 4.00 10.00
DC7 Troy Glaus AU/500 6.00 15.00
DC8 Ron Santo AU/500 12.00 30.00
DC9 Roy Oswalt AU/500 6.00 15.00
DC10 Angel Berroa AU/500 4.00 10.00
DC11 Mark Buehrle AU/500 6.00 15.00
DC12 John Buck AU/500 4.00 10.00
DC13 Barry Larkin AU/250 20.00 50.00
DC14 Gary Carter AU/250 10.00 25.00
DC15 Mark Teixeira AU/300 8.00 20.00
DC16 Alan Trammell AU/500 8.00 20.00
DC17 Kazuhisa Ishii AU/100 10.00 25.00
DC18 Rafael Palmeiro AU/125 12.50 30.00
DC19 Austin Kearns AU/500 4.00 10.00
DC20 Joe Torre AU/125 30.00 60.00
DC21 J.D. Drew AU/400 6.00 15.00
DC22 So Taguchi AU/400 12.00 30.00
DC23 Juan Marichal AU/500 6.00 15.00
DC24 Bobby Doerr AU/500 8.00 20.00
DC25 Carlos Beltran AU/500 8.00 20.00
DC26 Robert Fick AU/500 4.00 10.00
DC27 Albert Pujols AU/200 60.00 150.00
DC28 Shannon Stewart AU/500 6.00 15.00
DC29 Antonio Perez AU/500 4.00 10.00
DC30 Wilson Betemit AU/500 4.00 10.00
DC31 Alex Rodriguez Jsy/500 6.00 15.00
DC32 Curt Schilling Jsy/500 3.00 8.00
DC33 George Brett Jsy/300 10.00 25.00
DC34 Hideo Nomo Jsy/100 6.00 15.00
DC35 Ivan Rodriguez Jsy/500 4.00 10.00
DC36 Don Mattingly Jsy/200 10.00 25.00
DC37 Joe Mays Jsy/500 3.00 8.00
DC38 Lance Berkman Jsy/400 3.00 8.00
DC39 Tony Gwynn Jsy/500 6.00 15.00
DC40 Darin Erstad Jsy/400 3.00 8.00
DC41 Adrian Beltre Jsy/400 3.00 8.00
DC42 Frank Thomas Jsy/500 5.00 12.00
DC43 Cal Ripken Jsy/300 12.00 30.00
DC44 Jose Vidro Jsy/500 3.00 8.00
DC45 Randy Johnson Jsy/300 5.00 12.00
DC46 Carlos Delgado Jsy/500 3.00 8.00
DC47 Roger Clemens Jsy/400 6.00 15.00
DC48 Luis Gonzalez Jsy/500 3.00 8.00
DC49 Marlon Byrd Jsy/500 3.00 8.00
DC50 Carlton Fisk Jsy/500 4.00 10.00
DC51 Manny Ramirez Jsy/500 4.00 10.00
DC52 Vladimir Guerrero Jsy/500 4.00 10.00
DC53 Barry Larkin Jsy/500 4.00 10.00
DC54 Aramis Ramirez Jsy/500 3.00 8.00
DC55 Todd Helton Jsy/300 4.00 10.00
DC56 Carlos Beltran Jsy/250 3.00 8.00
DC57 Jeff Bagwell Jsy/250 4.00 10.00
DC58 Larry Walker Jsy/500 3.00 8.00
DC59 Al Kaline Jsy/200 6.00 15.00
DC60 Chipper Jones Jsy/500 4.00 10.00
DC61 Bernie Williams Jsy/500 4.00 10.00
DC62 Bud Smith Jsy/500 3.00 8.00
DC63 Edgar Martinez Jsy/500 4.00 10.00
DC64 Pedro Martinez Jsy/500 4.00 10.00
DC65 Andre Dawson Jsy/200 3.00 8.00
DC66 Mike Piazza Jsy/100 10.00 25.00
DC67 Barry Zito Jsy/500 3.00 8.00
DC68 Bo Jackson Jsy/300 6.00 15.00
DC69 Nolan Ryan Jsy/400 10.00 25.00
DC70 Troy Glaus Jsy/500 3.00 8.00
DC71 Jorge Posada Jsy/500 4.00 10.00
DC72 Ted Williams Jsy/100 50.00 100.00
DC73 N.Garciaparra Jsy/500 6.00 15.00
DC74 Catfish Hunter Jsy/100 6.00 15.00
DC75 Gary Carter Jsy/500 3.00 8.00
DC76 Craig Biggio Jsy/500 4.00 10.00
DC77 Andruw Jones Jsy/500 4.00 10.00
DC78 Rickey Henderson Jsy/300 4.00 10.00
DC79 Greg Maddux Jsy/400 6.00 15.00
DC80 Kerry Wood Jsy/500 3.00 8.00
DC81 Alex Rodriguez Bat/500 6.00 15.00
DC82 Don Mattingly Bat/425 10.00 25.00
DC83 Craig Biggio Bat/500 6.00 15.00
DC84 Kazuhisa Ishii Bat/375 4.00 10.00
DC85 Eddie Murray Bat/500 6.00 15.00
DC86 Carlton Fisk Bat/500 6.00 15.00
DC87 Tsuyoshi Shinjo Bat/500 4.00 10.00
DC88 Bo Jackson Bat/500 6.00 15.00
DC89 Eddie Mathews Bat/100 10.00 25.00
DC90 Chipper Jones Bat/500 6.00 15.00
DC91 Adam Dunn Bat/375 4.00 10.00
DC92 Tony Gwynn Bat/200 6.00 15.00
DC93 Kirby Puckett Bat/500 12.00 30.00
DC94 Andre Dawson Bat/500 4.00 10.00
DC95 Bernie Williams Bat/500 6.00 15.00
DC96 Rob Clemente Bat/300 40.00 100.00
DC97 Babe Ruth Bat/100 75.00 150.00
DC98 Roberto Alomar Bat/500 6.00 15.00
DC99 Frank Thomas Bat/500 6.00 15.00
DC100 So Taguchi Bat/500 4.00 10.00

2002 Diamond Kings DK Originals

COMPLETE SET (15) 75.00 150.00
RANDOM INSERTS IN PACKS
STATED PRINT RUN 1000 SERIAL #'d SETS
DK1 Alex Rodriguez 4.00 10.00
DK2 Kazuhisa Ishii 3.00 8.00
DK3 Pedro Martinez 3.00 8.00
DK4 Nomar Garciaparra 5.00 12.00
DK5 Albert Pujols 6.00 15.00
DK6 Chipper Jones 3.00 8.00
DK7 So Taguchi 3.00 8.00
DK8 Jeff Bagwell 3.00 8.00
DK9 Vladimir Guerrero 3.00 8.00
DK10 Derek Jeter 8.00 20.00
DK11 Sammy Sosa 3.00 8.00
DK12 Ichiro Suzuki 6.00 15.00
DK13 Barry Bonds 8.00 20.00
DK14 Jason Giambi 3.00 8.00
DK15 Mike Piazza 5.00 12.00

2002 Diamond Kings Heritage Collection

COMPLETE SET (25) 100.00 200.00
STATED ODDS 1:23 HOBBY, 1:46 RETAIL
HC1 Lou Gehrig 4.00 10.00
HC2 Nolan Ryan 6.00 15.00
HC3 Ryne Sandberg 4.00 10.00
HC4 Ted Williams 5.00 12.00
HC5 Roberto Clemente 6.00 15.00
HC6 Mike Schmidt 5.00 12.00
HC7 Roger Clemens 5.00 12.00
HC8 Kirby Puckett 2.00 5.00
HC9 Andre Dawson 1.50 4.00
HC10 Carlton Fisk 1.50 4.00
HC11 Don Mattingly 5.00 12.00
HC12 Juan Marichal 1.50 4.00
HC13 George Brett 5.00 12.00
HC14 Bo Jackson 2.00 5.00
HC15 Eddie Mathews 2.00 5.00
HC16 Randy Johnson 2.00 5.00
HC17 Alan Trammell 1.50 4.00
HC18 Tony Gwynn 3.00 8.00
HC19 Paul Molitor 1.50 4.00
HC20 Barry Bonds 6.00 15.00
HC21 Eddie Murray 2.00 5.00
HC22 Catfish Hunter 1.50 4.00
HC23 Rickey Henderson 2.00 5.00
HC24 Cal Ripken 8.00 20.00
HC25 Babe Ruth 6.00 15.00

2002 Diamond Kings Recollection Autographs

RANDOM INSERTS IN PACKS
PRINT RUNS B/WN 2-110 COPIES PER
NO PRICING ON QTY OF 48 OR LESS
47 Alan Trammell 88 DK/110 15.00 40.00

2002 Diamond Kings T204

COMPLETE SET (25) 50.00 120.00
RANDOM INSERTS IN PACKS
STATED PRINT RUN 1000 SERIAL #'d SETS
RC1 Vladimir Guerrero 2.00 5.00
RC2 Jeff Bagwell 2.00 5.00
RC3 Barry Bonds 5.00 12.00
RC4 Rickey Henderson 3.00 8.00
RC5 Mike Piazza 3.00 8.00
RC6 Derek Jeter 8.00 20.00
RC7 Kazuhisa Ishii 2.00 5.00
RC8 Ichiro Suzuki 4.00 10.00
RC9 Chipper Jones 3.00 8.00
RC10 Sammy Sosa 3.00 8.00
RC11 Don Mattingly 6.00 15.00
RC12 Shawn Green 1.25 3.00
RC13 Nomar Garciaparra 2.00 5.00
RC14 Luis Gonzalez 1.25 3.00
RC15 Albert Pujols 6.00 15.00
RC16 Cal Ripken 10.00 25.00
RC17 Todd Helton 2.00 5.00
RC18 Hideo Nomo 3.00 8.00
RC19 Alex Rodriguez 4.00 10.00
RC20 So Taguchi 2.00 5.00
RC21 Lance Berkman 2.00 5.00
RC22 Tony Gwynn 3.00 8.00
RC23 Roger Clemens 4.00 10.00
RC24 Jason Giambi 1.25 3.00
RC25 Ken Griffey Jr. 6.00 15.00

2002 Diamond Kings Timeline

COMPLETE SET (10) 60.00 120.00
STATED ODDS 1:60 HOBBY, 1:120 RETAIL
TL1 L.Gehrig D.Mattingly 6.00 15.00
TL2 H.Nomo I.Suzuki 4.00 10.00
TL3 C.Ripken A.Rodriguez 6.00 15.00
TL4 M.Schmidt S.Rolen 5.00 12.00
TL5 I.Suzuki A.Pujols 5.00 12.00
TL6 C.Schilling R.Johnson 4.00 10.00
TL7 C.Jones E.Mathews 4.00 10.00
TL8 L.Gehrig C.Ripken 8.00 20.00
TL9 D.Jeter R.Clemens 6.00 15.00
TL10 K.Ishii S.Taguchi 4.00 10.00

2002 Diamond Kings Hawaii

*PARALLEL 20'S RANDOMLY INSERTED INTO PACKS
*PARALLEL: NO PRICING DUE TO SCARCITY
*BLUE PORT: RANDOMLY INSERTED INTO PACKS
*BLUE PORT: SERIAL #'D TO 1 OR 5
*BLUE PORT: NO PRICING DUE TO SCARCITY

2003 Diamond Kings Samples

*SAMPLES: 1.5X TO 4X BASIC CARDS

2003 Diamond Kings Samples Gold

*GOLD SAMPLES: 4X TO 10X BASIC CARDS

2003 Diamond Kings

COMP.LO SET (176) 60.00 150.00
COMP.LO SET w/o SP's (150) 20.00 50.00
COMMON CARD (1-150) .20 .50
COMMON CARD (151-158) .40 1.00
151-158 STATED ODDS 1:6
COMMON CARD (159-175) .40 1.00
159-175 STATED ODDS 1:6
COMMON CARD (176) 1.50 4.00
COMMON CARD (177-201) 1.50 4.00
177-201 STATED ODDS 1:24 DLP R/T
CARD 190 DOES NOT EXIST
1 Darin Erstad .20 .50
2 Garret Anderson .20 .50
3 Troy Glaus .20 .50
4 David Eckstein .20 .50
5 Jarrod Washburn .20 .50
6 Adam Kennedy .20 .50
7 Jay Gibbons .20 .50
8 Tony Batista .20 .50
9 Melvin Mora .20 .50
10 Rodrigo Lopez .20 .50
11 Manny Ramirez .50 1.25
12 Pedro Martinez .30 .75
13 Nomar Garciaparra .30 .75
14 Rickey Henderson .50 1.25
15 Johnny Damon .30 .75
16 Derek Lowe .20 .50
17 Cliff Floyd .20 .50
18 Frank Thomas .50 1.25
19 Magglio Ordonez .30 .75
20 Paul Konerko .30 .75
21 Mark Buehrle .30 .75
22 C.C. Sabathia .30 .75
23 Omar Vizquel .30 .75
24 Jim Thome .30 .75
25 Ellis Burks .20 .50
26 Robert Fick .20 .50
27 Bobby Higginson .20 .50
28 Randall Simon .20 .50
29 Carlos Pena .30 .75
30 Carlos Beltran .30 .75
31 Paul Byrd .20 .50
32 Raul Ibanez .30 .75
33 Mike Sweeney .20 .50
34 Torii Hunter .20 .50
35 Corey Koskie .20 .50
36 A.J. Pierzynski .20 .50
37 Cristian Guzman .20 .50
38 Jacque Jones .20 .50
39 Derek Jeter 1.25 3.00
40 Bernie Williams .30 .75
41 Roger Clemens .60 1.50
42 Mike Mussina .30 .75
43 Jorge Posada .30 .75
44 Alfonso Soriano .30 .75
45 Jason Giambi .20 .50
46 Robin Ventura .20 .50
47 David Wells .20 .50
48 Tim Hudson .30 .75
49 Barry Zito .30 .75
50 Mark Mulder .20 .50
51 Miguel Tejada .30 .75
52 Eric Chavez .20 .50
53 Jermaine Dye .20 .50
54 Ichiro Suzuki .60 1.50
55 Edgar Martinez .30 .75
56 John Olerud .20 .50
57 Dan Wilson .20 .50
58 Joel Pineiro .20 .50
59 Kazuhiro Sasaki .20 .50
60 Freddy Garcia .20 .50
61 Aubrey Huff .20 .50
62 Steve Cox .20 .50
63 Randy Winn .20 .50
64 Alex Rodriguez .60 1.50
65 Juan Gonzalez .20 .50
66 Rafael Palmeiro .30 .75
67 Ivan Rodriguez .30 .75
68 Kenny Rogers .20 .50
69 Carlos Delgado .20 .50
70 Eric Hinske .20 .50
71 Roy Halladay .30 .75
72 Vernon Wells .20 .50
73 Shannon Stewart .20 .50
74 Curt Schilling .30 .75
75 Randy Johnson .50 1.25
76 Luis Gonzalez .20 .50
77 Mark Grace .30 .75
78 Junior Spivey .20 .50
79 Greg Maddux .60 1.50
80 Tom Glavine .30 .75
81 John Smoltz .50 1.25
82 Chipper Jones .50 1.25
83 Gary Sheffield .20 .50
84 Andruw Jones .20 .50
85 Kerry Wood .20 .50
86 Fred McGriff .30 .75
87 Sammy Sosa .50 1.25
88 Mark Prior .30 .75
89 Ken Griffey Jr. 1.00 2.50
90 Barry Larkin .30 .75
91 Adam Dunn .30 .75
92 Sean Casey .20 .50
93 Austin Kearns .20 .50
94 Aaron Boone .20 .50
95 Larry Walker .30 .75
96 Todd Helton .30 .75
97 Jason Jennings .20 .50
98 Jay Payton .20 .50
99 Josh Beckett .20 .50
100 Mike Lowell .20 .50
101 A.J. Burnett .20 .50
102 Jeff Bagwell .30 .75
103 Craig Biggio .30 .75
104 Lance Berkman .30 .75
105 Roy Oswalt .30 .75
106 Wade Miller .20 .50
107 Shawn Green .20 .50
108 Adrian Beltre .50 1.25
109 Hideo Nomo .50 1.25
110 Kazuhisa Ishii .20 .50
111 Odalis Perez .20 .50
112 Paul Lo Duca .20 .50
113 Ben Sheets .20 .50
114 Richie Sexson .20 .50
115 Jose Hernandez .20 .50
116 Vladimir Guerrero .30 .75
117 Jose Vidro .20 .50
118 Tomo Ohka .20 .50
119 Andres Galarraga .30 .75
120 Bartolo Colon .20 .50
121 Mike Piazza .50 1.25
122 Roberto Alomar .30 .75
123 Mo Vaughn .20 .50
124 Al Leiter .20 .50
125 Edgardo Alfonzo .20 .50
126 Pat Burrell .20 .50
127 Bobby Abreu .20 .50
128 Mike Lieberthal .20 .50
129 Vicente Padilla .20 .50
130 Marlon Byrd .20 .50
131 Jason Kendall .20 .50
132 Brian Giles .20 .50
133 Aramis Ramirez .20 .50
134 Kip Wells .20 .50
135 Ryan Klesko .20 .50
136 Phil Nevin .20 .50
137 Brian Lawrence .20 .50
138 Sean Burroughs .20 .50
139 Mark Kotsay .20 .50
140 Barry Bonds .75 2.00
141 Jeff Kent .20 .50
142 Benito Santiago .20 .50
143 Kirk Rueter .20 .50
144 Jason Schmidt .20 .50
145 Jim Edmonds .30 .75
146 J.D. Drew .20 .50
147 Albert Pujols .60 1.50
148 Tino Martinez .30 .75
149 Matt Morris .20 .50
150 Scott Rolen .30 .75
151 Joe Borchard ROO .40 1.00
152 Cliff Lee ROO 2.50 6.00
153 Brian Tallet ROO .40 1.00
154 Freddy Sanchez ROO .40 1.00
155 Chone Figgins ROO .40 1.00
156 Kevin Cash ROO .40 1.00
157 Justin Wayne ROO .40 1.00
158 Ben Kozlowski ROO .40 1.00
159 Babe Ruth RET 2.50 6.00
160 Jackie Robinson RET 1.00 2.50
161 Ozzie Smith RET 1.25 3.00
162 Lou Gehrig RET 2.00 5.00
163 Stan Musial RET 1.50 4.00
164 Mike Schmidt RET 1.50 4.00
165 Carlton Fisk RET .60 1.50
166 George Brett RET 2.00 5.00
167 Dale Murphy RET 1.00 2.50
168 Cal Ripken RET 3.00 8.00
169 Tony Gwynn RET 1.00 2.50
170 Don Mattingly RET 2.00 5.00
171 Jack Morris RET .60 1.50
172 Ty Cobb RET 1.50 4.00
173 Nolan Ryan RET 3.00 8.00
174 Ryne Sandberg RET 2.00 5.00
175 Thurman Munson RET 1.00 2.50
176 Jose Contreras ROO RC 1.00 2.50
177 Hideki Matsui ROO RC 2.00 5.00
178 Jeremy Bonderman ROO RC 1.50 4.00
179 Brandon Webb ROO RC 1.25 3.00
180 Adam Loewen ROO RC .40 1.00
181 Chien-Ming Wang ROO RC 1.50 4.00
182 Hong-Chih Kuo ROO RC 2.00 5.00
183 Clint Barmes ROO RC 1.00 2.50
184 Guillermo Quiroz ROO RC .40 1.00
185 Edgar Gonzalez ROO RC .40 1.00
186 Todd Wellemeyer ROO RC .40 1.00
187 Dan Haren ROO RC 2.00 5.00
188 Dustin McGowan ROO RC .40 1.00
189 Preston Larrison ROO RC .40 1.00
191 Kevin Youkilis ROO RC 2.50 6.00
192 Bubba Nelson ROO RC .40 1.00
193 Chris Burke ROO RC .40 1.00
194 J.D. Durbin ROO RC .40 1.00
195 Ryan Howard ROO RC 3.00 8.00
196 Jason Kubel ROO RC 1.25 3.00
197 Brendan Harris ROO RC .40 1.00
198 Brian Bruney ROO RC .40 1.00
199 Ramon Nivar ROO RC .40 1.00
200 Rickie Weeks ROO RC 1.25 3.00
201 Delmon Young ROO RC 2.50 6.00

2003 Diamond Kings Bronze Foil

*BRONZE 1-150: 1.5X TO 4X BASIC
*BRONZE 151-158: .75X TO 2X BASIC
*BRONZE 159-175: .75X TO 2X BASIC
*BRZ 177-189/191-201: .75X TO 2X BASIC
1-176 RANDOM INSERTS IN PACKS
177-201 RANDOM IN DLP R/T PACKS
177-201 PRINT RUN 200 SERIAL #'d SETS
BRONZE CARDS FEATURE WHITE FRAMES

2003 Diamond Kings Gold Foil

*GOLD 1-150: 4X TO 10X BASIC
*GOLD 151-158: 2X TO 5X BASIC
*GOLD 159-175: 2X TO 5X BASIC
*GOLD 176: 2X TO 5X BASIC
*GOLD 177-201: 2X TO 5X BASIC
1-176 RANDOM INSERTS IN PACKS
177-201 RANDOM IN DLP R/T PACKS
1-176 PRINT RUN 100 SERIAL #'d SETS
177-201 PRINT RUN 50 SERIAL #'d SETS
GOLD CARDS FEATURE BLACK FRAMES

2003 Diamond Kings Silver Foil

*SILVER 1-150: 2.5X TO 6X BASIC
*SILVER 151-158: 1.25X TO 3X BASIC
*SILVER 159-175: 1.25X TO 3X BASIC
*SILVER 176: 1.25X TO 3X BASIC
*SILVER 177-201: 1.25X TO 3X BASIC
1-176 RANDOM INSERTS IN PACKS
177-201 RANDOM IN DLP R/T PACKS
1-176 PRINT RUN 400 SERIAL #'d SETS
177-201 PRINT RUN 100 SERIAL #'d SETS
SILVER CARDS FEATURE GREY FRAMES

2003 Diamond Kings Diamond Cut Collection

STATED PRINT RUNS LISTED BELOW
DC1 Barry Zito AU/75 10.00 25.00
DC2 Edgar Martinez AU/125 12.00 30.00
DC3 Jay Gibbons AU/150 10.00 25.00
DC4 Joe Borchard AU/150 10.00 25.00
DC5 Marlon Byrd AU/150 10.00 25.00
DC6 Adam Dunn AU/150 6.00 15.00
DC7 Torii Hunter AU/150 6.00 15.00
DC9 Wade Miller AU/150 10.00 25.00
DC10 Alfonso Soriano AU/100 10.00 25.00
DC11 Brian Lawrence AU/150 10.00 25.00
DC12 Cliff Floyd AU/100 12.50 30.00
DC13 Dale Murphy AU/75 10.00 25.00
DC14 Jack Morris AU/150 12.50 30.00
DC15 Eric Hinske AU/150 10.00 25.00
DC16 Jason Jennings AU/150 10.00 25.00
DC17 Mark Buehrle AU/150 30.00 60.00
DC18 Mark Prior AU/150 6.00 15.00
DC19 Mark Mulder AU/150 12.50 30.00
DC20 Mike Sweeney AU/150 12.50 30.00
DC21 Nolan Ryan AU/50 50.00 100.00
DC22 Don Mattingly AU/75 40.00 80.00
DC23 Andruw Jones AU/75 10.00 25.00
DC24 Aubrey Huff AU/150 10.00 25.00
DC26 Nolan Ryan Jsy/250 20.00 50.00
DC27 Ozzie Smith Jsy/400 6.00 15.00
DC28 Rickey Henderson Jsy/300 4.00 10.00
DC29 Jack Morris Jsy/500 3.00 8.00
DC30 George Brett Jsy/350 10.00 25.00
DC31 Cal Ripken Jsy/300 15.00 40.00
DC32 Ryne Sandberg Jsy/450 10.00 25.00
DC33 Don Mattingly Jsy/400 8.00 20.00
DC34 Tony Gwynn Jsy/400 6.00 15.00
DC35 Dale Murphy Jsy/350 4.00 10.00
DC36 Carlton Fisk Jsy/400 4.00 10.00
DC38 Lou Gehrig Jsy/50 150.00 250.00
DC39 Garret Anderson Jsy/450 3.00 8.00
DC40 Pedro Martinez Jsy/400 4.00 10.00
DC41 Nomar Garciaparra Jsy/350 6.00 15.00
DC42 Maggio Ordonez Jsy/450 3.00 8.00
DC43 C.C. Sabathia Jsy/500 3.00 8.00
DC44 Omar Vizquel Jsy/250 6.00 15.00
DC45 Jim Thome Jsy/500 4.00 10.00
DC46 Torii Hunter Jsy/500 3.00 8.00
DC47 Roger Clemens Jsy/500 6.00 15.00
DC48 Alfonso Soriano Jsy/400 3.00 8.00
DC49 Tim Hudson Jsy/500 3.00 8.00
DC50 Barry Zito Jsy/350 3.00 8.00
DC51 Mark Mulder Jsy/500 3.00 8.00
DC52 Miguel Tejada Jsy/400 3.00 8.00
DC53 John Olerud Jsy/350 3.00 8.00
DC54 Alex Rodriguez Jsy/500 6.00 15.00
DC55 Rafael Palmeiro Jsy/500 4.00 10.00
DC56 Curt Schilling Jsy/500 3.00 8.00
DC57 Randy Johnson Jsy/400 4.00 10.00
DC58 Greg Maddux Jsy/350 6.00 15.00
DC59 John Smoltz Jsy/400 4.00 10.00
DC60 Chipper Jones Jsy/450 4.00 10.00
DC61 Andruw Jones Jsy/500 4.00 10.00
DC62 Kerry Wood Jsy/500 3.00 8.00
DC63 Mark Prior Jsy/500 4.00 10.00
DC64 Adam Dunn Jsy/350 3.00 8.00
DC65 Larry Walker Jsy/500 3.00 8.00

DC66 Todd Helton Jsy/500 4.00 10.00
DC67 Jeff Bagwell Jsy/500 4.00 10.00
DC68 Roy Oswalt Jsy/500 3.00 8.00
DC69 Hideo Nomo Jsy/150 6.00 15.00
DC70 Kazuhisa Ishii Jsy/250 4.00 10.00
DC71 Vladimir Guerrero Jsy/500 4.00 10.00
DC72 Mike Piazza Jsy/500 6.00 15.00
DC73 Joe Borchard Jsy/500 3.00 8.00
DC74 Ryan Klesko Jsy/500 3.00 8.00
DC75 Shawn Green Jsy/500 3.00 8.00
DC76 George Brett Bat/350 8.00 20.00
DC77 Ozzie Smith Bat/450 6.00 15.00
DC78 Cal Ripken Bat/150 20.00 50.00
DC79 Don Mattingly Bat/400 8.00 20.00
DC80 Babe Ruth Bat/50 50.00 120.00
DC81 Dale Murphy Bat/350 4.00 10.00
DC82 Rickey Henderson Bat/500 4.00 10.00
DC83 Ivan Rodriguez Bat/500 4.00 10.00
DC84 Marlon Byrd Bat/500 3.00 8.00
DC85 Eric Chavez Bat/500 3.00 8.00
DC86 Nomar Garciaparra Bat/500 6.00 15.00
DC87 Alex Rodriguez Bat/500 6.00 15.00
DC88 Vladimir Guerrero Bat/500 4.00 10.00
DC89 Paul Lo Duca Bat/500 3.00 8.00
DC90 Richie Sexson Bat/500 3.00 8.00
DC91 Mike Piazza Bat/350 6.00 15.00
DC92 J.D. Drew Bat/500 3.00 8.00
DC93 Juan Gonzalez Bat/500 3.00 8.00
DC94 Pat Burrell Bat/500 3.00 8.00
DC95 Adam Dunn Bat/250 4.00 10.00
DC96 Mike Schmidt Bat/500 8.00 20.00
DC97 Ryne Sandberg Bat/500 8.00 20.00
DC98 Edgardo Alfonzo Bat/500 3.00 8.00
DC99 Andruw Jones Bat/500 4.00 10.00
DC100 Carlos Beltran Bat/500 3.00 8.00
DC101 Jeff Bagwell Bat/500 4.00 10.00
DC102 Lance Berkman Bat/500 3.00 8.00
DC103 Luis Gonzalez Bat/500 3.00 8.00
DC104 Carlos Delgado Bat/500 3.00 8.00
DC105 Jim Edmonds Bat/250 4.00 10.00
DC106 Alf Soriano Hat-Jsy/75 10.00 25.00
DC107 Greg Maddux Jsy-AU/50 100.00 200.00
DC109 Adam Dunn Bat-AU/50 6.00 15.00
DC110 R.Henderson Jsy-Bat/50 10.00 25.00

2003 Diamond Kings DK Evolution

STATED ODDS 1:18 HOBBY, 1:36 RETAIL
DK1 Cal Ripken 3.00 8.00
DK2 Ichiro Suzuki 1.25 3.00
DK3 Randy Johnson 1.00 2.50
DK4 Pedro Martinez .60 1.50
DK5 Nolan Ryan 3.00 8.00
DK6 Derek Jeter 2.50 6.00
DK7 Kerry Wood .40 1.00
DK8 Alex Rodriguez 1.25 3.00
DK9 Magglio Ordonez .60 1.50
DK10 Greg Maddux 1.25 3.00
DK11 Todd Helton .60 1.50
DK12 Sammy Sosa 1.00 2.50
DK13 Lou Gehrig 2.00 5.00
DK14 Lance Berkman .60 1.50
DK15 Barry Zito .60 1.50
DK16 Barry Bonds 1.50 4.00
DK17 Tom Glavine .60 1.50
DK18 Shawn Green .40 1.00
DK19 Roger Clemens 1:25 3.00
DK20 Nomar Garciaparra .60 1.50
DK21 Tony Gwynn 1.00 2.50
DK22 Vladimir Guerrero .60 1.50
DK23 Albert Pujols 1.25 3.00
DK24 Chipper Jones 1.00 2.50
DK25 Alfonso Soriano .60 1.50

2003 Diamond Kings Heritage Collection

STATED ODDS 1:23
25 Vladimir Guerrero .60 1.50
HC1 Ozzie Smith 1.25 3.00
HC2 Lou Gehrig 2.00 5.00
HC3 Stan Musial 1.50 4.00
HC4 Mike Schmidt 1.50 4.00
HC5 Carlton Fisk .60 1.50
HC6 George Brett 2.00 5.00
HC7 Dale Murphy 1.00 2.50
HC8 Cal Ripken 3.00 8.00
HC9 Tony Gwynn 1.00 2.50
HC10 Don Mattingly 2.00 5.00
HC11 Jack Morris .60 1.50
HC12 Ty Cobb 1.50 4.00
HC13 Nolan Ryan 3.00 8.00
HC14 Ryne Sandberg 2.00 5.00
HC15 Thurman Munson 1.00 2.50
HC16 Ichiro Suzuki 1.25 3.00
HC17 Derek Jeter 2.50 6.00
HC18 Greg Maddux 1.25 3.00
HC19 Sammy Sosa 1.00 2.50
HC20 Pedro Martinez .60 1.50
HC21 Alex Rodriguez 1.25 3.00
HC22 Roger Clemens 1.25 3.00
HC23 Barry Bonds 1.50 4.00
HC24 Lance Berkman .60 1.50

2003 Diamond Kings HOF Heroes Reprints

STATED ODDS 1:43 HOBBY, 1:67 RETAIL
1 Bob Feller 1.50 4.00
2 Al Kaline 1.50 4.00
3 Lou Boudreau 1.50 4.00
4 Duke Snider 1.50 4.00
5 Jackie Robinson 2.50 6.00
6 Early Wynn 1.50 4.00
7 Yogi Berra 2.50 6.00
8 Stan Musial 4.00 10.00
9 Ty Cobb 4.00 10.00
10 Ted Williams 5.00 12.00

2003 Diamond Kings Recollection Autographs

SEE BECKETT.COM FOR PRINT RUNS
NO PRICING ON QTY OF 40 OR LESS
2 Brandon Berger 02 DK/99 6.00 15.00
9 Mark Buehrle 02 DK/73 15.00 40.00

2003 Diamond Kings Team Timeline

RANDOM INSERTS IN PACKS
STATED PRINT RUN 1000 SERIAL #'d SETS
TT1 N.Ryan 6.00 15.00
R.Oswalt
TT2 D.Murphy 2.00 5.00
C.Jones
TT3 S.Musial 3.00 8.00
J.Edmonds
TT4 G.Brett 4.00 10.00
M.Sweeney
TT5 T.Gwynn 2.00 5.00
R.Klesko
TT6 C.Fisk 1.25 3.00
M.Ordonez
TT7 M.Schmidt 3.00 8.00
P.Burrell
TT8 D.Mattingly 4.00 10.00
B.Williams
TT9 R.Sandberg 4.00 10.00
K.Wood
TT10 L.Gehrig 4.00 10.00
A.Soriano

2003 Diamond Kings Team Timeline Jerseys

RANDOM INSERTS IN PACKS
STATED PRINT RUN 100 SERIAL #'d SETS
CARDS FEATURE TWO JERSEY SWATCHES
TT1 N.Ryan/R.Oswalt 30.00 60.00
TT2 D.Murphy/C.Jones 10.00 25.00
TT3 S.Musial/J.Edmonds 20.00 50.00
TT4 G.Brett/M.Sweeney 40.00 80.00
TT5 T.Gwynn/R.Klesko 10.00 25.00
TT6 C.Fisk/M.Ordonez 10.00 25.00
TT7 M.Schmidt/P.Burrell 40.00 80.00
TT8 D.Mattingly/B.Williams 15.00 40.00
TT9 R.Sandberg/K.Wood 10.00 25.00
TT10 L.Gehrig/A.Soriano/50 150.00 250.00

2003 Diamond Kings Atlantic City National

PRINT RUN 5 SERIAL #'d SETS

2003 Diamond Kings Chicago Collection

DIST.AT MARCH 03 SUN TIMES SHOW
STATED PRINT RUN 5 SERIAL #'d SETS
NO PRICING DUE TO SCARCITY

2003 Diamond Kings Heritage Collection Hawaii

DISTRIBUTED AT 2003 HAWAII CONFERENCE
STATED PRINT RUN 20 SERIAL #'d SETS
NO PRICING DUE TO SCARCITY

2003 Diamond Kings Team Timeline Hawaii

*HAWAII: 2X TO 5X BASIC TIMELINE
DISTRIBUTED AT 2003 HAWAII CONFERENCE
STATED PRINT RUN 50 SERIAL #'d SETS

2003 Diamond Kings HOF Heroes Reprints Hawaii

*HAWAII: 1X TO 2.5X BASIC HOF REPRINTS
DISTRIBUTED AT 2003 HAWAII CONFERENCE
STATED PRINT RUN 50 SERIAL #'d SETS

2004 Diamond Kings

COMPLETE SET w/Sepia (200) 75.00 200.00
COMPLETE SET (175) 30.00 80.00
COMP.SET w/o SP's (150) 15.00 40.00
COMMON CARD (1-150) .20 .50
COMMON CARD (151-175) .40 1.00
151-175 RANDOM INSERTS IN PACKS
1 Alex Rodriguez .60 1.50
2 Andruw Jones .20 .50
3 Nomar Garciaparra .30 .75
4 Kerry Wood .20 .50
5 Magglio Ordonez .30 .75
6 Victor Martinez .30 .75
7 Jeremy Bonderman .20 .50
8 Josh Beckett .20 .50
9 Jeff Kent .20 .50
10 Carlos Beltran .30 .75
11 Hideo Nomo .50 1.25
12 Richie Sexson .20 .50
13 Jose Vidro .20 .50
14 Jae Weong Seo .20 .50
15 Alfonso Soriano .30 .75
16 Barry Zito .30 .75
17 Brett Myers .20 .50
18 Brian Giles .20 .50
19 Edgar Martinez .30 .75
20 Jim Edmonds .30 .75
21 Rocco Baldelli .20 .50
22 Mark Teixeira .30 .75
23 Carlos Delgado .20 .50
24 Julius Matos .20 .50
25 Jose Reyes .30 .75
26 Marlon Byrd .20 .50
27 Albert Pujols .60 1.50
28 Vernon Wells .20 .50
29 Garret Anderson .20 .50
30 Jerome Williams .20 .50
31 Chipper Jones .50 1.25
32 Rich Harden .20 .50
33 Manny Ramirez .50 1.25
34 Derek Jeter 1.25 3.00
35 Brandon Webb .20 .50
36 Mark Prior .30 .75
37 Roy Halladay .30 .75
38 Frank Thomas .50 1.25
39 Rafael Palmeiro .30 .75
40 Adam Dunn .30 .75
41 Aubrey Huff .20 .50
42 Todd Helton .30 .75
43 Matt Morris .20 .50
44 Dontrelle Willis .20 .50
45 Lance Berkman .30 .75
46 Mike Sweeney .20 .50
47 Kazuhisa Ishii .20 .50
48 Torii Hunter .20 .50
49 Vladimir Guerrero .30 .75
50 Mike Piazza .50 1.25
51 Alexis Rios .20 .50
52 Shannon Stewart .20 .50
53 Eric Hinske .20 .50
54 Jason Jennings .20 .50
55 Jason Giambi .20 .50
56 Brandon Claussen .20 .50
57 Joe Thurston .20 .50
58 Ramon Nivar .20 .50
59 Jay Gibbons .20 .50
60 Eric Chavez .20 .50
61 Jimmy Gobble .20 .50
62 Walter Young .20 .50
63 Mark Grace .30 .75
64 Austin Kearns .20 .50
65 Bob Abreu .20 .50
66 Hee Seop Choi .20 .50
67 Brandon Phillips .20 .50
68 Rickie Weeks .20 .50
69 Luis Gonzalez .20 .50
70 Mariano Rivera .60 1.50
71 Jason Lane .20 .50
72 Xavier Nady .20 .50
73 Runelvys Hernandez .20 .50
74 Aramis Ramirez .20 .50
75 Ichiro Suzuki .60 1.50
76 Cliff Lee .30 .75
77 Chris Snelling .20 .50
78 Ryan Wagner .20 .50
79 Miguel Tejada .30 .75
80 Juan Gonzalez .20 .50
81 Joe Borchard .20 .50
82 Gary Sheffield .20 .50
83 Wade Miller .20 .50
84 Jeff Bagwell .30 .75
85 Ryan Church .20 .50
86 Adrian Beltre .50 1.25
87 Jeff Baker .20 .50
88 Adam Loewen .20 .50
89 Bernie Williams .30 .75
90 Pedro Martinez .30 .75
91 Carlos Rivera .20 .50
92 Junior Spivey .20 .50
93 Tim Hudson .30 .75
94 Troy Glaus .20 .50
95 Ken Griffey Jr. 1.00 2.50
96 Alexis Gomez .20 .50
97 Antonio Perez .20 .50
98 Dan Haren .20 .50
99 Ivan Rodriguez .30 .75
100 Randy Johnson .50 1.25
101 Lyle Overbay .20 .50
102 Oliver Perez .20 .50
103 Miguel Cabrera .50 1.25
104 Scott Rolen .30 .75
105 Roger Clemens .60 1.50
106 Brian Tallet .20 .50
107 Nic Jackson .20 .50
108 Angel Berroa .20 .50
109 Hank Blalock .20 .50
110 Ryan Klesko .20 .50
111 Jose Castillo .20 .50
112 Paul Konerko .30 .75
113 Greg Maddux .60 1.50
114 Mark Mulder .20 .50
115 Pat Burrell .20 .50
116 Garrett Atkins .20 .50
117 Jeremy Guthrie .20 .50
118 Orlando Cabrera .20 .50
119 Nick Johnson .20 .50
120 Tom Glavine .30 .75
121 Morgan Ensberg .20 .50
122 Sean Casey .20 .50
123 Orlando Hudson .20 .50
124 Hideki Matsui .75 2.00
125 Craig Biggio .30 .75
126 Adam LaRoche .20 .50
127 Hong-Chih Kuo .20 .50
128 Paul LoDuca .20 .50
129 Shawn Green .20 .50
130 Luis Castillo .20 .50
131 Joe Crede .20 .50
132 Ken Harvey .20 .50
133 Freddy Sanchez .20 .50
134 Roy Oswalt .30 .75
135 Curt Schilling .30 .75
136 Alfredo Amezaga .20 .50
137 Chien-Ming Wang .75 2.00
138 Barry Larkin .30 .75
139 Trot Nixon .20 .50
140 Jim Thome .30 .75
141 Bret Boone .20 .50
142 Jacque Jones .20 .50
143 Travis Hafner .20 .50
144 Sammy Sosa .50 1.25
145 Mike Mussina .30 .75
146 Vinny Chulk .20 .50
147 Chad Gaudin .20 .50
148 Delmon Young .30 .75
149 Mike Lowell .20 .50
150 Rickey Henderson .50 1.25
151 Roger Clemens FB 1.25 3.00
152 Mark Grace FB .60 1.50
153 Rickey Henderson FB 1.00 2.50
154 Alex Rodriguez FB 1.25 3.00
155 Rafael Palmeiro FB .60 1.50
156 Greg Maddux FB 1.25 3.00
157 Mike Piazza FB 1.00 2.50
158 Mike Mussina FB .60 1.50
159 Dale Murphy LGD 1.00 2.50
160 Cal Ripken LGD 3.00 8.00
161 Carl Yastrzemski LGD 1.00 2.50
162 Marty Marion LGD .40 1.00
163 Don Mattingly LGD 2.00 5.00
164 Robin Yount LGD 1.00 2.50
165 Andre Dawson LGD .60 1.50
166 Jim Palmer LGD .60 1.50
167 George Brett LGD 2.00 5.00
168 Whitey Ford LGD .60 1.50
169 Roy Campanella LGD 1.00 2.50
170 Roger Maris LGD 1.00 2.50
171 Duke Snider LGD .60 1.50
172 Steve Carlton LGD .60 1.50
173 Stan Musial LGD 1.50 4.00
174 Nolan Ryan LGD 3.00 8.00
175 Deion Sanders LGD .60 1.50

2004 Diamond Kings Sepia

*SEPIA: .75X TO 2X BASIC
RANDOM INSERTS IN PACKS

2004 Diamond Kings Bronze

*BRONZE 1-150: 3X TO 8X BASIC
*BRONZE 151-175: 1.25X TO 3X BASIC
RANDOM INSERTS IN PACKS
STATED PRINT RUN 100 SERIAL #'d SETS

2004 Diamond Kings Bronze Sepia

*BRONZE SEPIA: 1.25X TO 3X BASIC
RANDOM INSERTS IN PACKS
STATED PRINT RUN 100 SERIAL #'d SETS

2004 Diamond Kings Silver

*SILVER 1-150: 5X TO 12X BASIC
*SILVER 151-175: 2X TO 5X BASIC
RANDOM INSERTS IN PACKS
STATED PRINT RUN 50 SERIAL #'d SETS

2004 Diamond Kings Silver Sepia

*SILVER SEPIA: 2X TO 5X BASIC
RANDOM INSERTS IN PACKS
STATED PRINT RUN 50 SERIAL #'d SETS

2004 Diamond Kings Framed Platinum Grey

STATED PRINT RUN 1 SERIAL #'d SET
NO PRICING DUE TO SCARCITY

2004 Diamond Kings Framed Bronze

*FRAMED BRZ 1-150: 1.5X TO 4X BASIC
*FRAMED BRZ 151-175: .75X TO 2X BASIC
STATED ODDS 1:6

2004 Diamond Kings Framed Bronze Sepia

*FRAMED BRZ.SEPIA: .75X TO 2X BASIC
STATED ODDS 1:6

2004 Diamond Kings Framed Gold

*FRAMED GOLD 1-150: 10X TO 25X BASIC
*FRAMED GOLD 150-175: 4X TO 10X BASIC
RANDOM INSERTS IN PACKS
STATED PRINT RUN 25 SERIAL #'d SETS

2004 Diamond Kings Framed Gold Sepia

*FRAMED GOLD SEPIA: 4X TO 10X BASIC
RANDOM INSERTS IN PACKS
STATED PRINT RUN 25 SERIAL #'d SETS

2004 Diamond Kings Framed Platinum Black

STATED PRINT RUN 1 SERIAL #'d SET
NO PRICING DUE TO SCARCITY

2004 Diamond Kings Framed Platinum Black Sepia

STATED PRINT RUN 1 SERIAL #'d SET
NO PRICING DUE TO SCARCITY

2004 Diamond Kings Framed Platinum Grey Sepia

STATED PRINT RUN 1 SERIAL #'d SET
NO PRICING DUE TO SCARCITY

2004 Diamond Kings Framed Platinum White

STATED PRINT RUN 1 SERIAL #'d SET
NO PRICING DUE TO SCARCITY

2004 Diamond Kings Framed Platinum White Sepia

STATED PRINT RUN 1 SERIAL #'d SET
NO PRICING DUE TO SCARCITY

2004 Diamond Kings Framed Silver

*FRAMED SLV 1-150: 4X TO 10X BASIC
*FRAMED SLV 151-175: 1.5X TO 4X BASIC
RANDOM INSERTS IN PACKS
STATED PRINT RUN 100 SERIAL #'d SETS

2004 Diamond Kings Framed Silver Sepia

*FRAMED SLV SEPIA: 1.5X TO 4X BASIC
RANDOM INSERTS IN PACKS
STATED PRINT RUN 100 SERIAL #'d SETS

2004 Diamond Kings DK Combos Bronze

RANDOM INSERTS IN PACKS
PRINT RUNS B/WN 1-30 COPIES PER
NO PRICING ON QTY OF 10 OR LESS
26 Marlon Byrd Bat-Jsy/30 12.50 30.00
32 Rich Harden Jsy-Jsy/15 20.00 50.00
35 Brandon Webb Bat-Jsy/15 15.00 40.00
41 Aubrey Huff Bat-Jsy/15 20.00 50.00
53 Eric Hinske Bat-Jsy/30 12.50 30.00
57 Joe Thurston Bat-Jsy/25 12.50 30.00
59 Jay Gibbons Jsy-Jsy/15 15.00 40.00
62 Walter Young Bat-Bat/15 15.00 40.00
65 Bob Abreu Bat-Jsy/15 20.00 50.00
71 Jason Lane Bat-Hat/15 20.00 50.00
73 Run Hernandez Jsy-Jsy/15 15.00 40.00
74 Aramis Ramirez Bat-Bat/15 40.00 80.00
77 Chris Snelling Bat-Bat/15 15.00 40.00
81 Joe Borchard Bat-Jsy/15 15.00 40.00
92 Junior Spivey Bat-Jsy/15 15.00 40.00
98 Dan Haren Bat-Jsy/15 15.00 40.00
101 Lyle Overbay Bat-Jsy/30 12.50 30.00
103 Miguel Cabrera Bat-Jsy/30 40.00 80.00
108 Angel Berroa Bat-Pants/30 12.50 30.00
109 Hank Blalock Bat-Jsy/30 15.00 40.00
111 Jose Castillo Bat-Bat/15 15.00 40.00
121 Morgan Ensberg Bat-Jsy/30 15.00 40.00
123 Orlando Hudson Bat-Jsy/30 12.50 30.00
126 Adam LaRoche Bat-Bat/30 12.50 30.00
127 Hong-Chih Kuo Bat-Bat/15 75.00 150.00
130 Luis Castillo Bat-Jsy/30 12.50 30.00
133 Freddy Sanchez Bat-Bat/15 15.00 40.00
136 Alfredo Amezaga Bat-Jsy/15 15.00 40.00
143 Travis Hafner Bat-Jsy/30 15.00 40.00
147 Chad Gaudin Jsy-Jsy/25 12.50 30.00

2004 Diamond Kings DK Combos Gold

PRINT RUNS B/WN 1-5 COPIES PER
NO PRICING DUE TO SCARCITY

2004 Diamond Kings DK Combos Gold Sepia

STATED PRINT RUN 1 SERIAL #'d SET
NO PRICING DUE TO SCARCITY

2004 Diamond Kings DK Combos Silver

RANDOM INSERTS IN PACKS
PRINT RUNS B/WN 1-15 COPIES PER
NO PRICING ON QTY OF 10 OR LESS
26 Marlon Byrd Bat-Jsy/15 15.00 40.00
101 Lyle Overbay Bat-Jsy/15 15.00 40.00
103 Miguel Cabrera Bat-Jsy/15 50.00 100.00
108 Angel Berroa Bat-Pants/15 15.00 40.00
109 Hank Blalock Bat-Jsy/15 20.00 50.00
121 Morgan Ensberg Bat-Jsy/15 20.00 50.00
123 Orlando Hudson Bat-Jsy/15 15.00 40.00
126 Adam LaRoche Bat-Bat/15 15.00 40.00
130 Luis Castillo Bat-Jsy/15 15.00 40.00
143 Travis Hafner Bat-Jsy/15 20.00 50.00

2004 Diamond Kings DK Combos Framed Bronze

RANDOM INSERTS IN PACKS
PRINT RUNS B/WN 1-25 COPIES PER
NO PRICING ON QTY OF 10 OR LESS
26 Marlon Byrd Bat-Jsy/25 10.00 25.00
35 Brandon Webb Bat-Jsy/25 10.00 25.00
53 Eric Hinske Bat-Jsy/25 10.00 25.00
57 Joe Thurston Bat-Jsy/25 10.00 25.00
59 Jay Gibbons Jsy-Jsy/25 10.00 25.00
62 Walter Young Bat-Bat/25 10.00 25.00
65 Bob Abreu Bat-Jsy/25 15.00 40.00
71 Jason Lane Bat-Hat/25 15.00 40.00
74 Aramis Ramirez Bat-Bat/25 20.00 50.00
77 Chris Snelling Bat-Bat/25 10.00 25.00
81 Joe Borchard Bat-Jsy/25 10.00 25.00
92 Junior Spivey Bat-Jsy/25 10.00 25.00
97 Antonio Perez Bat-Pants/25 10.00 25.00
98 Dan Haren Bat-Jsy/25 10.00 25.00
101 Lyle Overbay Bat-Jsy/25 10.00 25.00
103 Miguel Cabrera Bat-Jsy/25 30.00 60.00
107 Nic Jackson Bat-Bat/25 10.00 25.00
108 Angel Berroa Bat-Pants/25 10.00 25.00
109 Hank Blalock Bat-Jsy/25 15.00 40.00
110 Ryan Klesko Bat-Jsy/15 20.00 50.00
111 Jose Castillo Bat-Bat/25 10.00 25.00
112 Paul Konerko Bat-Jsy/15 30.00 60.00
121 Morgan Ensberg Bat-Jsy/25 15.00 40.00
123 Orlando Hudson Bat-Jsy/25 10.00 25.00
126 Adam LaRoche Bat-Bat/25 10.00 25.00
127 Hong-Chih Kuo Bat-Bat/25 20.00 50.00
130 Luis Castillo Bat-Jsy/25 10.00 25.00
133 Freddy Sanchez Bat-Bat/15 12.50 30.00
136 Alfredo Amezaga Bat-Jsy/15 12.50 30.00
143 Travis Hafner Bat-Jsy/15 20.00 50.00
147 Chad Gaudin Jsy-Jsy/25 10.00 25.00

2004 Diamond Kings DK Combos Framed Bronze Sepia

PRINT RUNS B/WN 1-5 COPIES PER
NO PRICING DUE TO SCARCITY

2004 Diamond Kings DK Combos Framed Platinum Grey

STATED PRINT RUN 1 SERIAL #'d SET
NO PRICING DUE TO SCARCITY

2004 Diamond Kings DK Combos Framed Silver

RANDOM INSERTS IN PACKS
PRINT RUNS B/WN 1-15 COPIES PER
NO PRICING ON QTY OF 10 OR LESS
110 Ryan Klesko Bat-Jsy/15 20.00 50.00

2004 Diamond Kings DK Combos Framed Silver Sepia

PRINT RUNS B/WN 1-5 COPIES PER
NO PRICING DUE TO SCARCITY

2004 Diamond Kings DK Materials Bronze

PRINT RUNS B/WN 1-150 COPIES PER
NO PRICING ON QTY OF 5 OR LESS
1 Alex Rodriguez Bat-Jsy/150 10.00 25.00
2 Andruw Jones Bat-Jsy/150 6.00 15.00
3 Nomar Garciaparra Bat-Jsy/150 10.00 25.00
4 Kerry Wood Bat-Jsy/150 4.00 10.00
5 Magglio Ordonez Bat-Jsy/150 4.00 10.00
6 Victor Martinez Bat-Bat/100 4.00 10.00
7 Jeremy Bonderman Jsy-Jsy/30 6.00 15.00
8 Josh Beckett Bat-Jsy/150 4.00 10.00
9 Jeff Kent Bat-Jsy/150 4.00 10.00
10 Carlos Beltran Bat-Jsy/150 4.00 10.00
11 Hideo Nomo Bat-Jsy/150 8.00 20.00
12 Richie Sexson Bat-Jsy/150 4.00 10.00
13 Jose Vidro Bat-Jsy/50 4.00 10.00
14 Jae Seo Jsy-Jsy/100 4.00 10.00
15 Alfonso Soriano Bat-Jsy/150 4.00 10.00
16 Barry Zito Bat-Jsy/100 4.00 10.00
17 Brett Myers Jsy-Jsy/30 6.00 15.00
18 Brian Giles Bat-Bat/100 4.00 10.00
19 Edgar Martinez Bat-Jsy/150 6.00 15.00
20 Jim Edmonds Bat-Jsy/150 4.00 10.00
21 Rocco Baldelli Bat-Jsy/100 4.00 10.00
22 Mark Teixeira Bat-Jsy/100 6.00 15.00
23 Carlos Delgado Bat-Jsy/150 4.00 10.00
25 Jose Reyes Bat-Jsy/100 4.00 10.00
26 Marlon Byrd Bat-Jsy/100 4.00 10.00
27 Albert Pujols Bat-Jsy/150 10.00 25.00
28 Vernon Wells Bat-Jsy/150 4.00 10.00
29 Garret Anderson Bat-Jsy/15 10.00 25.00
30 Jerome Williams Jsy-Jsy/100 4.00 10.00
31 Chipper Jones Bat-Jsy/150 8.00 20.00
32 Rich Harden Jsy-Jsy/100 4.00 10.00
33 Manny Ramirez Bat-Jsy/150 6.00 15.00
34 Derek Jeter Base-Base/100 12.50 30.00
35 Brandon Webb Bat-Jsy/100 4.00 10.00
36 Mark Prior Bat-Jsy/100 6.00 15.00
37 Roy Halladay Jsy-Jsy/100 4.00 10.00
38 Frank Thomas Bat-Jsy/150 8.00 20.00
39 Rafael Palmeiro Bat-Jsy/150 6.00 15.00
40 Adam Dunn Bat-Jsy/150 4.00 10.00
41 Aubrey Huff Bat-Jsy/30 6.00 15.00
42 Todd Helton Bat-Jsy/150 6.00 15.00
43 Matt Morris Jsy-Jsy/100 4.00 10.00
44 Dontrelle Willis Bat-Jsy/100 6.00 15.00
45 Lance Berkman Bat-Jsy/150 4.00 10.00
46 Mike Sweeney Bat-Jsy/100 4.00 10.00
47 Kazuhisa Ishii Bat-Jsy/100 4.00 10.00
48 Torii Hunter Bat-Jsy/100 4.00 10.00
49 Vladimir Guerrero Bat-Jsy/100 8.00 20.00
50 Mike Piazza Bat-Jsy/150 10.00 25.00
51 Alexis Rios Bat-Bat/150 4.00 10.00
52 Shannon Stewart Bat-Bat/100 4.00 10.00
53 Eric Hinske Bat-Jsy/100 4.00 10.00
54 Jason Jennings Bat-Jsy/150 4.00 10.00
55 Jason Giambi Bat-Jsy/150 4.00 10.00
57 Joe Thurston Bat-Jsy/150 4.00 10.00
58 Ramon Nivar Bat-Jsy/100 4.00 10.00
59 Jay Gibbons Jsy-Jsy/100 4.00 10.00
60 Eric Chavez Bat-Jsy/150 4.00 10.00
62 Walter Young Bat-Bat/100 4.00 10.00
63 Mark Grace Bat-Jsy/150 6.00 15.00
64 Austin Kearns Bat-Jsy/150 4.00 10.00
65 Bob Abreu Bat-Jsy/150 4.00 10.00
66 Hee Seop Choi Bat-Jsy/100 4.00 10.00
67 Brandon Phillips Bat-Bat/100 4.00 10.00
68 Rickie Weeks Bat-Bat/100 4.00 10.00
69 Luis Gonzalez Bat-Jsy/150 4.00 10.00
70 Mariano Rivera Jsy-Jsy/100 8.00 20.00
71 Jason Lane Bat-Hat/15 10.00 25.00
73 Run Hernandez Jsy-Jsy/30 6.00 15.00
75 Ichiro Suzuki Ball-Base/15 50.00 100.00
77 Chris Snelling Bat-Bat/30 6.00 15.00
79 Miguel Tejada Bat-Jsy/150 4.00 10.00
80 Juan Gonzalez Bat-Jsy/150 4.00 10.00
81 Joe Borchard Bat-Jsy/15 10.00 25.00
82 Gary Sheffield Bat-Jsy/150 4.00 10.00
83 Wade Miller Bat-Jsy/50 4.00 10.00
84 Jeff Bagwell Bat-Jsy/150 6.00 15.00
86 Adrian Beltre Bat-Jsy/100 4.00 10.00
87 Jeff Baker Bat-Bat/100 4.00 10.00
89 Bernie Williams Bat-Jsy/150 6.00 15.00
90 Pedro Martinez Bat-Jsy/100 6.00 15.00
92 Junior Spivey Bat-Jsy/100 4.00 10.00
93 Tim Hudson Bat-Jsy/150 4.00 10.00
94 Troy Glaus Bat-Jsy/100 4.00 10.00
95 Ken Griffey Jr. Base-Base/100 8.00 20.00
96 Alexis Gomez Bat-Bat/30 6.00 15.00
97 Antonio Perez Bat-Pants/100 4.00 10.00
98 Dan Haren Bat-Jsy/100 4.00 10.00
99 Ivan Rodriguez Bat-Jsy/150 6.00 15.00
100 Randy Johnson Bat-Jsy/100 8.00 20.00
101 Lyle Overbay Bat-Jsy/100 4.00 10.00
103 Miguel Cabrera Bat-Jsy/100 6.00 15.00
104 Scott Rolen Bat-Jsy/100 6.00 15.00
105 Roger Clemens Bat-Jsy/100 12.50 30.00
107 Nic Jackson Bat-Bat/100 4.00 10.00
108 Angel Berroa Bat-Pants/30 6.00 15.00
109 Hank Blalock Bat-Jsy/100 4.00 10.00
110 Ryan Klesko Bat-Jsy/100 4.00 10.00
111 Jose Castillo Bat-Bat/100 4.00 10.00
112 Paul Konerko Bat-Jsy/100 4.00 10.00
113 Greg Maddux Bat-Jsy/100 10.00 25.00
114 Mark Mulder Bat-Jsy/100 4.00 10.00
115 Pat Burrell Bat-Jsy/100 4.00 10.00
116 Garrett Atkins Jsy-Jsy/100 4.00 10.00
118 Orlando Cabrera Bat-Jsy/100 4.00 10.00
119 Nick Johnson Bat-Jsy/100 4.00 10.00
120 Tom Glavine Bat-Jsy/100 6.00 15.00
121 Morgan Ensberg Bat-Jsy/100 4.00 10.00
122 Sean Casey Bat-Hat/15 10.00 25.00
123 Orlando Hudson Bat-Jsy/100 4.00 10.00
124 Hideki Matsui Ball-Base/15 40.00 80.00
125 Craig Biggio Bat-Jsy/100 6.00 15.00
126 Adam LaRoche Bat-Bat/100 4.00 10.00
127 Hong-Chih Kuo Bat-Bat/100 4.00 10.00
128 Paul LoDuca Bat-Jsy/100 4.00 10.00
129 Shawn Green Bat-Jsy/100 4.00 10.00
130 Luis Castillo Bat-Jsy/100 4.00 10.00
132 Ken Harvey Bat-Bat/100 4.00 10.00
133 Freddy Sanchez Bat-Bat/100 4.00 10.00
134 Roy Oswalt Bat-Jsy/100 4.00 10.00
135 Curt Schilling Bat-Jsy/100 6.00 15.00
136 Alfredo Amezaga Bat-Jsy/15 10.00 25.00
138 Barry Larkin Bat-Jsy/15 15.00 40.00
139 Trot Nixon Bat-Bat/100 4.00 10.00
140 Jim Thome Bat-Jsy/100 6.00 15.00
141 Bret Boone Bat-Jsy/100 4.00 10.00
142 Jacque Jones Bat-Jsy/100 4.00 10.00
143 Travis Hafner Bat-Jsy/100 4.00 10.00
144 Sammy Sosa Bat-Jsy/100 8.00 20.00
145 Mike Mussina Bat-Jsy/100 6.00 15.00
147 Chad Gaudin Jsy-Jsy/100 4.00 10.00
149 Mike Lowell Bat-Jsy/100 4.00 10.00
150 R.Henderson Bat-Jsy/100 6.00 15.00
151 R.Clemens FB Bat-Jsy/100 12.50 30.00
152 Mark Grace FB Bat-Jsy/15 10.00 25.00
153 R.Henderson FB Bat-Jsy/30 12.50 30.00
154 A.Rodriguez FB Bat-Jsy/100 10.00 25.00
155 R.Palmeiro FB Bat-Jsy/100 6.00 15.00
156 G.Maddux FB Bat-Bat/100 10.00 25.00
157 Mike Piazza FB Bat-Jsy/100 10.00 25.00
158 M.Mussina FB Bat-Jsy/100 6.00 15.00
159 Dale Murphy LGD Bat-Jsy/30 10.00 25.00
160 Cal Ripken LGD Bat-Jsy/100 8.00 20.00
161 C.Yaz LGD Bat-Jsy/100 10.00 25.00
162 M.Marion LGD Jsy-Jsy/30 6.00 15.00
163 D.Mattingly LGD Bat-Jsy/100 15.00 40.00
164 R.Yount LGD Bat-Jsy/100 8.00 20.00
165 A.Dawson LGD Bat-Jsy/30 6.00 15.00
167 George Brett LGD Bat-Jsy/30 12.00 30.00
168 W.Ford LGD Jsy-Pants/30 10.00 25.00
169 R.Campy LGD Bat-Pants/15 20.00 50.00
170 R.Maris LGD Bat-Jsy/15 60.00 120.00
172 S.Carlton LGD Bat-Jsy/100 4.00 10.00
173 Stan Musial LGD Bat-Jsy/30 20.00 50.00
174 Nolan Ryan LGD Bat-Jsy/30 30.00 60.00
175 D.Sanders LGD Bat-Jsy/100 6.00 15.00

2004 Diamond Kings DK Materials Bronze Sepia

RANDOM INSERTS IN PACKS
PRINT RUNS B/WN 4-50 COPIES PER
NO PRICING ON QTY OF 5 OR LESS
151 R.Clemens FB Bat-Jsy/30 20.00 50.00
152 Mark Grace FB Bat-Jsy/15 10.00 25.00
153 R.Henderson FB Bat-Jsy/15 20.00 50.00
154 A.Rodriguez FB Bat-Jsy/30 20.00 50.00
155 R.Palmeiro FB Bat-Jsy/50 6.00 15.00
156 G.Maddux FB Bat-Bat/50 15.00 40.00
157 Mike Piazza FB Bat-Jsy/50 15.00 40.00
158 M.Mussina FB Bat-Jsy/50 6.00 15.00
159 Dale Murphy LGD Bat-Jsy/15 15.00 40.00
160 Cal Ripken LGD Bat-Jsy/50 6.00 15.00
161 C.Yaz LGD Bat-Jsy/50 15.00 40.00
162 M.Marion LGD Jsy-Jsy/15 10.00 25.00
163 D.Mattingly LGD Bat-Jsy/50 20.00 50.00
164 R.Yount LGD Bat-Jsy/50 10.00 25.00
165 A.Dawson LGD Bat-Jsy/15 10.00 25.00
167 G.Brett LGD Bat-Jsy/15 20.00 50.00
168 W.Ford LGD Jsy-Pants/15 15.00 40.00
169 R.Campy LGD Bat-Pants/15 20.00 50.00
170 R.Maris LGD Bat-Jsy/15 60.00 120.00
172 S.Carlton LGD Bat-Jsy/50 4.00 10.00
173 Stan Musial LGD Bat-Jsy/15 40.00 80.00
174 Nolan Ryan LGD Bat-Jsy/15 15.00 40.00
175 D.Sanders LGD Bat-Jsy/50 6.00 15.00

2004 Diamond Kings DK Materials Gold

RANDOM INSERTS IN PACKS
PRINT RUNS B/WN 1-50 COPIES PER
NO PRICING ON QTY OF 5 OR LESS
1 Alex Rodriguez Bat-Jsy/25 20.00 50.00
2 Andruw Jones Bat-Jsy/25 10.00 25.00
3 Nomar Garciaparra Bat-Jsy/25 20.00 50.00
4 Kerry Wood Bat-Jsy/25 6.00 15.00
5 Magglio Ordonez Bat-Jsy/25 6.00 15.00
6 Victor Martinez Bat-Bat/50 4.00 10.00
8 Josh Beckett Bat-Jsy/25 6.00 15.00
9 Jeff Kent Bat-Jsy/25 6.00 15.00
10 Carlos Beltran Bat-Jsy/25 6.00 15.00
11 Hideo Nomo Bat-Jsy/25 12.50 30.00
12 Richie Sexson Bat-Jsy/25 6.00 15.00
13 Jose Vidro Bat-Jsy/25 6.00 15.00
14 Jae Seo Jsy-Jsy/25 6.00 15.00
15 Alfonso Soriano Bat-Jsy/25 6.00 15.00
16 Barry Zito Bat-Jsy/25 6.00 15.00
18 Brian Giles Bat-Bat/25 6.00 15.00
19 Edgar Martinez Bat-Jsy/25 10.00 25.00
20 Jim Edmonds Bat-Jsy/25 6.00 15.00
21 Rocco Baldelli Bat-Jsy/25 6.00 15.00
22 Mark Teixeira Bat-Jsy/25 10.00 25.00
25 Jose Reyes Bat-Jsy/25 6.00 15.00
26 Marlon Byrd Bat-Jsy/25 6.00 15.00
27 Albert Pujols Bat-Jsy/25 15.00 40.00
28 Vernon Wells Bat-Jsy/25 6.00 15.00
30 Jerome Williams Jsy-Jsy/50 4.00 10.00
31 Chipper Jones Bat-Jsy/25 12.50 30.00
32 Rich Harden Jsy-Jsy/50 4.00 10.00
33 Manny Ramirez Bat-Jsy/25 10.00 25.00
34 Derek Jeter Base-Base/50 15.00 40.00
35 Brandon Webb Bat-Jsy/50 4.00 10.00
36 Mark Prior Bat-Jsy/25 10.00 25.00
37 Roy Halladay Jsy-Jsy/25 6.00 15.00
38 Frank Thomas Bat-Jsy/25 12.50 30.00
39 Rafael Palmeiro Bat-Jsy/50 6.00 15.00
40 Adam Dunn Bat-Jsy/25 6.00 15.00
42 Todd Helton Bat-Jsy/25 10.00 25.00
43 Matt Morris Jsy-Jsy/25 6.00 15.00
44 Dontrelle Willis Bat-Jsy/25 10.00 25.00
45 Lance Berkman Bat-Jsy/25 6.00 15.00
46 Mike Sweeney Bat-Jsy/25 6.00 15.00
47 Kazuhisa Ishii Bat-Jsy/25 6.00 15.00
48 Torii Hunter Bat-Jsy/25 6.00 15.00
49 Vladimir Guerrero Bat-Jsy/25 12.50 30.00
50 Mike Piazza Bat-Jsy/25 20.00 50.00
51 Alexis Rios Bat-Bat/25 6.00 15.00
52 Shannon Stewart Bat-Bat/50 4.00 10.00
53 Eric Hinske Bat-Jsy/50 4.00 10.00
54 Jason Jennings Bat-Jsy/25 6.00 15.00
55 Jason Giambi Bat-Jsy/25 6.00 15.00
57 Joe Thurston Bat-Jsy/50 4.00 10.00
58 Ramon Nivar Bat-Jsy/50 4.00 10.00
59 Jay Gibbons Jsy-Jsy/25 6.00 15.00
60 Eric Chavez Bat-Jsy/25 6.00 15.00
62 Walter Young Bat-Bat/50 4.00 10.00
63 Mark Grace Bat-Jsy/25 10.00 25.00
64 Austin Kearns Bat-Jsy/25 6.00 15.00
65 Bob Abreu Bat-Jsy/25 6.00 15.00
66 Hee Seop Choi Bat-Jsy/25 6.00 15.00
67 Brandon Phillips Bat-Bat/50 4.00 10.00
68 Rickie Weeks Bat-Bat/50 4.00 10.00
69 Luis Gonzalez Bat-Jsy/25 6.00 15.00
70 Mariano Rivera Jsy-Jsy/50 10.00 25.00
79 Miguel Tejada Bat-Jsy/50 4.00 10.00
80 Juan Gonzalez Bat-Jsy/25 6.00 15.00
82 Gary Sheffield Bat-Jsy/25 6.00 15.00
84 Jeff Bagwell Bat-Jsy/25 10.00 25.00
86 Adrian Beltre Bat-Jsy/25 6.00 15.00
87 Jeff Baker Bat-Bat/50 4.00 10.00
89 Bernie Williams Bat-Jsy/25 10.00 25.00
90 Pedro Martinez Bat-Jsy/25 10.00 25.00
92 Junior Spivey Bat-Jsy/25 6.00 15.00
93 Tim Hudson Bat-Jsy/25 6.00 15.00
94 Troy Glaus Bat-Jsy/25 6.00 15.00
95 Ken Griffey Jr. Base-Base/50 12.50 30.00
97 Antonio Perez Bat-Pants/50 4.00 10.00
98 Dan Haren Bat-Jsy/25 6.00 15.00
99 Ivan Rodriguez Bat-Jsy/25 10.00 25.00
100 Randy Johnson Bat-Jsy/25 12.50 30.00
101 Lyle Overbay Bat-Jsy/50 4.00 10.00
103 Miguel Cabrera Bat-Jsy/25 10.00 25.00
104 Scott Rolen Bat-Jsy/25 10.00 25.00
105 Roger Clemens Bat-Jsy/25 20.00 50.00
107 Nic Jackson Bat-Bat/30 6.00 15.00
109 Hank Blalock Bat-Jsy/25 6.00 15.00
110 Ryan Klesko Bat-Jsy/25 6.00 15.00
111 Jose Castillo Bat-Bat/50 4.00 10.00
112 Paul Konerko Bat-Jsy/25 6.00 15.00
113 Greg Maddux Bat-Jsy/25 20.00 50.00
114 Mark Mulder Bat-Jsy/25 6.00 15.00
115 Pat Burrell Bat-Jsy/25 6.00 15.00
116 Garrett Atkins Jsy-Jsy/50 4.00 10.00
118 Orlando Cabrera Bat-Jsy/25 6.00 15.00
119 Nick Johnson Bat-Jsy/25 6.00 15.00
120 Tom Glavine Bat-Jsy/25 10.00 25.00
121 Morgan Ensberg Bat-Jsy/25 6.00 15.00
123 Orlando Hudson Bat-Jsy/25 6.00 15.00
125 Craig Biggio Bat-Jsy/25 10.00 25.00
126 Adam LaRoche Bat-Bat/50 4.00 10.00
127 Hong-Chih Kuo Bat-Bat/50 4.00 10.00
128 Paul LoDuca Bat-Jsy/25 6.00 15.00
129 Shawn Green Bat-Jsy/25 6.00 15.00
130 Luis Castillo Bat-Jsy/25 6.00 15.00
132 Ken Harvey Bat-Bat/50 4.00 10.00
133 Freddy Sanchez Bat-Bat/50 4.00 10.00
134 Roy Oswalt Bat-Jsy/50 4.00 10.00
135 Curt Schilling Bat-Jsy/25 10.00 25.00
139 Trot Nixon Bat-Bat/25 6.00 15.00
140 Jim Thome Bat-Jsy/25 10.00 25.00
142 Jacque Jones Bat-Jsy/50 4.00 10.00

143 Travis Hafner Bat-Jsy/50 4.00 10.00
144 Sammy Sosa Bat-Jsy/25 12.50 30.00
145 Mike Mussina Bat-Jsy/50 6.00 15.00
147 Chad Gaudin Jsy-Jsy/25 6.00 15.00
149 Mike Lowell Bat-Jsy/25 6.00 15.00
150 R.Henderson Bat-Jsy/25 10.00 25.00
151 R.Clemens FB Bat-Jsy/25 10.00 25.00
154 A.Rodriguez FB Bat-Jsy/25 20.00 50.00
155 R.Palmeiro FB Bat-Jsy/50 10.00 25.00
156 G.Maddux FB Bat-Bat/50 15.00 40.00
157 Mike Piazza FB Bat-Jsy/50 15.00 40.00
158 M.Mussina FB Bat-Jsy/50 10.00 25.00
160 Cal Ripken LGD Bat-Jsy/50 12.00 30.00
161 C.Yaz LGD Bat-Jsy/50 15.00 40.00
163 D.Mattingly LGD Bat-Jsy/50 20.00 50.00
164 R.Yount LGD Bat-Jsy/50 10.00 25.00
172 S.Carlton LGD Bat-Jsy/50 4.00 10.00
175 D.Sanders LGD Bat-Jsy/50 6.00 15.00

2004 Diamond Kings DK Materials Gold Sepia

RANDOM INSERTS IN PACKS
PRINT RUNS B/WN 1-15 COPIES PER
NO PRICING ON QTY OF 5 OR LESS
155 R.Palmeiro FB Bat-Jsy/15 15.00 40.00
156 G.Maddux FB Bat-Bat/15 30.00 60.00
157 Mike Piazza FB Bat-Jsy/15 30.00 60.00
158 M.Mussina FB Bat-Jsy/15 15.00 40.00
160 Cal Ripken LGD Bat-Jsy/15 25.00 60.00
161 C.Yaz LGD Bat-Jsy/15 40.00 80.00
163 D.Mattingly LGD Bat-Jsy/15 50.00 100.00
164 R.Yount LGD Bat-Jsy/15 15.00 40.00
172 S.Carlton LGD Bat-Jsy/15 10.00 25.00
175 D.Sanders LGD Bat-Jsy/15 15.00 40.00

2004 Diamond Kings DK Materials Platinum

STATED PRINT RUN 1 SERIAL #'d SET
NO PRICING DUE TO SCARCITY

2004 Diamond Kings DK Materials Platinum Sepia

STATED PRINT RUN 1 SERIAL #'d SET
NO PRICING DUE TO SCARCITY

2004 Diamond Kings DK Materials Silver

RANDOM INSERTS IN PACKS
PRINT RUNS B/WN 1-50 COPIES PER
NO PRICING ON QTY OF 6 OR LESS
1 Alex Rodriguez Bat-Jsy/50 15.00 40.00
2 Andruw Jones Bat-Jsy/50 6.00 15.00
3 Nomar Garciaparra Bat-Jsy/50 15.00 40.00
4 Kerry Wood Bat-Jsy/50 4.00 10.00
5 Magglio Ordonez Bat-Jsy/50 4.00 10.00
6 Victor Martinez Bat-Bat/50 4.00 10.00
7 Jeremy Bonderman Jsy-Jsy/15 10.00 25.00
8 Josh Beckett Bat-Jsy/50 4.00 10.00
9 Jeff Kent Bat-Jsy/50 4.00 10.00
10 Carlos Beltran Bat-Jsy/50 4.00 10.00
11 Hideo Nomo Bat-Jsy/50 10.00 25.00
12 Richie Sexson Bat-Jsy/50 4.00 10.00
13 Jose Vidro Bat-Jsy/30 6.00 15.00
14 Jae Seo Jsy-Jsy/50 4.00 10.00
15 Alfonso Soriano Bat-Jsy/50 4.00 10.00
16 Barry Zito Bat-Jsy/50 4.00 10.00
17 Brett Myers Jsy-Jsy/15 10.00 25.00
18 Brian Giles Bat-Bat/50 4.00 10.00
19 Edgar Martinez Bat-Jsy/50 6.00 15.00
20 Jim Edmonds Bat-Jsy/50 4.00 10.00
21 Rocco Baldelli Bat-Jsy/50 4.00 10.00
22 Mark Teixeira Bat-Jsy/50 6.00 15.00
23 Carlos Delgado Bat-Jsy/50 4.00 10.00
25 Jose Reyes Bat-Jsy/50 4.00 10.00
26 Marlon Byrd Bat-Jsy/50 4.00 10.00
27 Albert Pujols Bat-Jsy/50 12.50 30.00
28 Vernon Wells Bat-Jsy/50 4.00 10.00
30 Jerome Williams Jsy-Jsy/50 4.00 10.00
31 Chipper Jones Bat-Jsy/50 10.00 25.00
32 Rich Harden Jsy-Jsy/50 4.00 10.00
33 Manny Ramirez Bat-Jsy/50 6.00 15.00
34 Derek Jeter Base-Base/50 15.00 40.00
35 Brandon Webb Bat-Jsy/50 4.00 10.00
36 Mark Prior Bat-Jsy/50 6.00 15.00
37 Roy Halladay Jsy-Jsy/50 4.00 10.00
38 Frank Thomas Bat-Jsy/50 10.00 25.00
39 Rafael Palmeiro Bat-Jsy/50 6.00 15.00
40 Adam Dunn Bat-Jsy/50 4.00 10.00
41 Aubrey Huff Bat-Jsy/15 10.00 25.00
42 Todd Helton Bat-Jsy/50 6.00 15.00
43 Matt Morris Jsy-Jsy/50 4.00 10.00
44 Dontrelle Willis Bat-Jsy/50 6.00 15.00
45 Lance Berkman Bat-Jsy/50 4.00 10.00
46 Mike Sweeney Bat-Jsy/50 4.00 10.00
47 Kazuhisa Ishii Bat-Jsy/50 4.00 10.00
48 Torii Hunter Bat-Jsy/50 4.00 10.00
49 Vladimir Guerrero Bat-Jsy/50 10.00 25.00
50 Mike Piazza Bat-Jsy/50 15.00 40.00
51 Alexis Rios Bat-Bat/50 4.00 10.00
52 Shannon Stewart Bat-Bat/50 4.00 10.00
53 Eric Hinske Bat-Jsy/50 4.00 10.00
54 Jason Jennings Bat-Jsy/50 4.00 10.00
55 Jason Giambi Bat-Jsy/50 4.00 10.00
57 Joe Thurston Bat-Jsy/50 4.00 10.00
58 Ramon Nivar Bat-Jsy/50 4.00 10.00
59 Jay Gibbons Jsy-Jsy/50 4.00 10.00
60 Eric Chavez Bat-Jsy/50 4.00 10.00
62 Walter Young Bat-Bat/50 4.00 10.00
63 Mark Grace Bat-Jsy/50 6.00 15.00
64 Austin Kearns Bat-Jsy/50 4.00 10.00
65 Bob Abreu Bat-Jsy/50 4.00 10.00
66 Hee Seop Choi Bat-Jsy/50 4.00 10.00
67 Brandon Phillips Bat-Bat/50 4.00 10.00
68 Rickie Weeks Bat-Bat/50 4.00 10.00
69 Luis Gonzalez Bat-Jsy/50 4.00 10.00
70 Mariano Rivera Jsy-Jsy/50 10.00 25.00
73 Run Hernandez Jsy-Jsy/15 10.00 25.00
77 Chris Snelling Bat-Bat/15 10.00 25.00
79 Miguel Tejada Bat-Jsy/50 4.00 10.00
80 Juan Gonzalez Bat-Jsy/50 4.00 10.00
82 Gary Sheffield Bat-Jsy/50 4.00 10.00
84 Jeff Bagwell Bat-Jsy/50 6.00 15.00
86 Adrian Beltre Bat-Jsy/50 4.00 10.00
87 Jeff Baker Bat-Bat/50 4.00 10.00
89 Bernie Williams Bat-Jsy/50 6.00 15.00
90 Pedro Martinez Bat-Jsy/50 6.00 15.00
92 Junior Spivey Bat-Jsy/50 4.00 10.00
93 Tim Hudson Bat-Jsy/50 4.00 10.00
94 Troy Glaus Bat-Jsy/50 4.00 10.00
95 Ken Griffey Jr. Base-Base/50 12.50 30.00
96 Alexis Gomez Bat-Bat/15 10.00 25.00
97 Antonio Perez Bat-Pants/50 4.00 10.00
98 Dan Haren Bat-Jsy/50 4.00 10.00
99 Ivan Rodriguez Bat-Jsy/50 6.00 15.00
100 Randy Johnson Bat-Jsy/50 10.00 25.00
101 Lyle Overbay Bat-Jsy/50 4.00 10.00
103 Miguel Cabrera Bat-Jsy/50 6.00 15.00
104 Scott Rolen Bat-Jsy/50 6.00 15.00
105 Roger Clemens Bat-Jsy/50 15.00 40.00
107 Nic Jackson Bat-Bat/50 4.00 10.00
109 Hank Blalock Bat-Jsy/50 4.00 10.00
110 Ryan Klesko Bat-Jsy/50 4.00 10.00
111 Jose Castillo Bat-Bat/50 4.00 10.00
112 Paul Konerko Bat-Jsy/50 4.00 10.00
113 Greg Maddux Bat-Jsy/50 15.00 40.00
114 Mark Mulder Bat-Jsy/50 4.00 10.00
115 Pat Burrell Bat-Jsy/50 4.00 10.00
116 Garrett Atkins Jsy-Jsy/50 4.00 10.00
118 Orlando Cabrera Bat-Jsy/50 4.00 10.00
119 Nick Johnson Bat-Jsy/50 4.00 10.00
120 Tom Glavine Bat-Jsy/50 6.00 15.00
121 Morgan Ensberg Bat-Jsy/50 4.00 10.00
123 Orlando Hudson Bat-Jsy/50 4.00 10.00
125 Craig Biggio Bat-Jsy/50 6.00 15.00
126 Adam LaRoche Bat-Bat/50 4.00 10.00
127 Hong-Chih Kuo Bat-Bat/50 4.00 10.00
128 Paul LoDuca Bat-Jsy/50 4.00 10.00
129 Shawn Green Bat-Jsy/50 4.00 10.00
130 Luis Castillo Bat-Jsy/50 4.00 10.00
132 Ken Harvey Bat-Bat/50 4.00 10.00
133 Freddy Sanchez Bat-Bat/50 4.00 10.00
134 Roy Oswalt Bat-Jsy/50 4.00 10.00
135 Curt Schilling Bat-Jsy/50 6.00 15.00
139 Trot Nixon Bat-Bat/50 4.00 10.00
140 Jim Thome Bat-Jsy/50 6.00 15.00
141 Bret Boone Bat-Jsy/50 4.00 10.00
142 Jacque Jones Bat-Jsy/50 4.00 10.00
143 Travis Hafner Bat-Jsy/50 4.00 10.00
144 Sammy Sosa Bat-Jsy/50 10.00 25.00
145 Mike Mussina Bat-Jsy/50 6.00 15.00
147 Chad Gaudin Jsy-Jsy/50 4.00 10.00
149 Mike Lowell Bat-Jsy/50 4.00 10.00
150 R.Henderson Bat-Jsy/50 8.00 20.00
151 R.Clemens FB Bat-Jsy/50 8.00 20.00
153 R.Henderson FB Bat-Jsy/15 20.00 50.00
154 A.Rodriguez FB Bat-Jsy/30 20.00 50.00
155 R.Palmeiro FB Bat-Jsy/50 6.00 15.00
156 G.Maddux FB Bat-Bat/50 15.00 40.00
157 Mike Piazza FB Bat-Jsy/50 15.00 40.00
158 M.Mussina FB Bat-Jsy/50 6.00 15.00
160 Cal Ripken LGD Bat-Jsy/50 12.00 30.00
161 C.Yaz LGD Bat-Jsy/50 15.00 40.00
162 M.Marion LGD Jsy-Jsy/15 10.00 25.00
163 D.Mattingly LGD Bat-Jsy/50 20.00 50.00
164 R.Yount LGD Bat-Jsy/50 10.00 25.00
165 A.Dawson LGD Bat-Jsy/15 10.00 25.00
167 G.Brett LGD Bat-Jsy/15 20.00 50.00
168 W.Ford LGD Jsy-Pants/15 15.00 40.00
172 S.Carlton LGD Bat-Jsy/50 4.00 10.00
173 Stan Musial LGD Bat-Jsy/15 40.00 80.00
174 Nolan Ryan LGD Bat-Jsy/15 15.00 40.00
175 D.Sanders LGD Bat-Jsy/50 6.00 15.00

2004 Diamond Kings DK Materials Silver Sepia

RANDOM INSERTS IN PACKS
PRINT RUNS B/WN 1-30 COPIES PER
NO PRICING ON QTY OF 6 OR LESS
151 R.Clemens FB Bat-Jsy/15 12.00 30.00
154 A.Rodriguez FB Bat-Jsy/15 30.00 60.00
155 R.Palmeiro FB Bat-Jsy/30 10.00 25.00
156 G.Maddux FB Bat-Bat/30 20.00 50.00
157 Mike Piazza FB Bat-Jsy/30 20.00 50.00
158 M.Mussina FB Bat-Jsy/30 10.00 25.00
160 Cal Ripken LGD Bat-Jsy/30 15.00 40.00
161 C.Yaz LGD Bat-Jsy/30 20.00 50.00
163 D.Mattingly LGD Bat-Jsy/30 30.00 60.00
164 R.Yount LGD Bat-Jsy/30 12.50 30.00
172 S.Carlton LGD Bat-Jsy/30 6.00 15.00
175 D.Sanders LGD Bat-Jsy/30 10.00 25.00

2004 Diamond Kings DK Materials Framed Bronze

RANDOM INSERTS IN PACKS
PRINT RUNS B/WN 1-100 COPIES PER
NO PRICING ON QTY OF 10 OR LESS
1 Alex Rodriguez Bat-Jsy/100 10.00 25.00
2 Andruw Jones Bat-Jsy/100 6.00 15.00
3 Nomar Garciaparra Bat-Jsy/100 10.00 25.00
4 Kerry Wood Bat-Jsy/100 4.00 10.00
5 Magglio Ordonez Bat-Jsy/100 4.00 10.00
6 Victor Martinez Bat-Bat/100 4.00 10.00
7 Jeremy Bonderman Jsy-Jsy/25 6.00 15.00
8 Josh Beckett Bat-Jsy/100 4.00 10.00
9 Jeff Kent Bat-Jsy/100 4.00 10.00
10 Carlos Beltran Bat-Jsy/100 4.00 10.00
11 Hideo Nomo Bat-Jsy/100 8.00 20.00
12 Richie Sexson Bat-Jsy/100 4.00 10.00
13 Jose Vidro Bat-Jsy/50 4.00 10.00
14 Jae Seo Jsy-Jsy/100 4.00 10.00
15 Alfonso Soriano Bat-Jsy/100 4.00 10.00
16 Barry Zito Bat-Jsy/100 4.00 10.00
17 Brett Myers Jsy-Jsy/25 6.00 15.00
18 Brian Giles Bat-Bat/100 4.00 10.00
19 Edgar Martinez Bat-Jsy/100 6.00 15.00
20 Jim Edmonds Bat-Jsy/100 4.00 10.00
21 Rocco Baldelli Bat-Jsy/100 4.00 10.00
22 Mark Teixeira Bat-Jsy/100 6.00 15.00
23 Carlos Delgado Bat-Jsy/100 4.00 10.00
25 Jose Reyes Bat-Jsy/100 4.00 10.00
26 Marlon Byrd Bat-Jsy/100 4.00 10.00
27 Albert Pujols Bat-Jsy/100 10.00 25.00
28 Vernon Wells Bat-Jsy/100 4.00 10.00
29 Garret Anderson Bat-Jsy/25 6.00 15.00
30 Jerome Williams Jsy-Jsy/100 4.00 10.00
31 Chipper Jones Bat-Jsy/100 8.00 20.00
32 Rich Harden Jsy-Jsy/100 4.00 10.00
33 Manny Ramirez Bat-Jsy/100 6.00 15.00
34 Derek Jeter Base-Base/100 12.50 30.00
35 Brandon Webb Bat-Jsy/100 4.00 10.00
36 Mark Prior Bat-Jsy/100 6.00 15.00
37 Roy Halladay Jsy-Jsy/75 4.00 10.00
38 Frank Thomas Bat-Jsy/100 8.00 20.00
39 Rafael Palmeiro Bat-Jsy/100 6.00 15.00
40 Adam Dunn Bat-Jsy/100 4.00 10.00
41 Aubrey Huff Bat-Jsy/25 6.00 15.00
42 Todd Helton Bat-Jsy/100 6.00 15.00
43 Matt Morris Jsy-Jsy/100 4.00 10.00
44 Dontrelle Willis Bat-Jsy/100 6.00 15.00
45 Lance Berkman Bat-Jsy/100 4.00 10.00
46 Mike Sweeney Bat-Jsy/100 4.00 10.00
47 Kazuhisa Ishii Bat-Jsy/100 4.00 10.00
48 Torii Hunter Bat-Jsy/100 4.00 10.00
49 Vladimir Guerrero Bat-Jsy/100 8.00 20.00
50 Mike Piazza Bat-Jsy/100 10.00 25.00
51 Alexis Rios Bat-Bat/100 4.00 10.00
52 Shannon Stewart Bat-Bat/100 4.00 10.00
53 Eric Hinske Bat-Jsy/100 4.00 10.00
54 Jason Jennings Bat-Jsy/100 4.00 10.00
55 Jason Giambi Bat-Jsy/100 4.00 10.00
57 Joe Thurston Bat-Jsy/100 4.00 10.00
58 Ramon Nivar Bat-Jsy/100 4.00 10.00
59 Jay Gibbons Jsy-Jsy/100 4.00 10.00
60 Eric Chavez Bat-Jsy/100 4.00 10.00
62 Walter Young Bat-Bat/100 4.00 10.00
63 Mark Grace Bat-Jsy/100 6.00 15.00
64 Austin Kearns Bat-Jsy/50 4.00 10.00
65 Bob Abreu Bat-Jsy/100 4.00 10.00
66 Hee Seop Choi Bat-Jsy/100 4.00 10.00
67 Brandon Phillips Bat-Bat/100 4.00 10.00
68 Rickie Weeks Bat-Bat/100 4.00 10.00
69 Luis Gonzalez Bat-Jsy/100 4.00 10.00
70 Mariano Rivera Jsy-Jsy/100 8.00 20.00
71 Jason Lane Bat-Hat/25 6.00 15.00
73 Run Hernandez Jsy-Jsy/50 4.00 10.00
75 Ichiro Suzuki Ball-Base/25 40.00 80.00
77 Chris Snelling Bat-Bat/25 6.00 15.00
79 Miguel Tejada Bat-Jsy/100 4.00 10.00
80 Juan Gonzalez Bat-Jsy/100 10.00 25.00
81 Joe Borchard Bat-Jsy/25 6.00 15.00
82 Gary Sheffield Bat-Jsy/100 4.00 10.00
83 Wade Miller Bat-Jsy/25 6.00 15.00
84 Jeff Bagwell Bat-Jsy/100 6.00 15.00
86 Adrian Beltre Bat-Jsy/100 4.00 10.00
87 Jeff Baker Bat-Bat/100 4.00 10.00
89 Bernie Williams Bat-Jsy/100 6.00 15.00
90 Pedro Martinez Bat-Jsy/100 6.00 15.00
92 Junior Spivey Bat-Jsy/100 4.00 10.00
93 Tim Hudson Bat-Jsy/100 4.00 10.00
94 Troy Glaus Bat-Jsy/100 4.00 10.00
95 Ken Griffey Jr. Base-Base/100 8.00 20.00
96 Alexis Gomez Bat-Bat/30 6.00 15.00
97 Antonio Perez Bat-Pants/100 4.00 10.00
98 Dan Haren Bat-Jsy/100 4.00 10.00
99 Ivan Rodriguez Bat-Jsy/100 6.00 15.00
100 Randy Johnson Bat-Jsy/100 8.00 20.00
101 Lyle Overbay Bat-Jsy/100 4.00 10.00
103 Miguel Cabrera Bat-Jsy/100 6.00 15.00
104 Scott Rolen Bat-Jsy/100 6.00 15.00
105 Roger Clemens Bat-Jsy/100 12.50 30.00
107 Nic Jackson Bat-Bat/100 4.00 10.00
108 Angel Berroa Bat-Pants/25 6.00 15.00
109 Hank Blalock Bat-Jsy/100 4.00 10.00
110 Ryan Klesko Bat-Jsy/100 4.00 10.00
111 Jose Castillo Bat-Bat/100 4.00 10.00
112 Paul Konerko Bat-Jsy/50 4.00 10.00
113 Greg Maddux Bat-Jsy/100 10.00 25.00
114 Mark Mulder Bat-Jsy/100 4.00 10.00
115 Pat Burrell Bat-Jsy/100 4.00 10.00
116 Garrett Atkins Jsy-Jsy/100 4.00 10.00
118 Orlando Cabrera Bat-Jsy/100 4.00 10.00
120 Tom Glavine Bat-Jsy/100 6.00 15.00
121 Morgan Ensberg Bat-Jsy/100 4.00 10.00
122 Sean Casey Bat-Hat/25 6.00 15.00
123 Orlando Hudson Bat-Jsy/100 4.00 10.00
124 Hideki Matsui Ball-Base/25 30.00 60.00
125 Craig Biggio Bat-Jsy/25 10.00 25.00
126 Adam LaRoche Bat-Bat/100 4.00 10.00
127 Hong-Chih Kuo Bat-Bat/100 4.00 10.00
128 Paul LoDuca Bat-Jsy/100 4.00 10.00
129 Shawn Green Bat-Jsy/100 4.00 10.00
130 Luis Castillo Bat-Jsy/100 4.00 10.00
132 Ken Harvey Bat-Bat/100 4.00 10.00
133 Freddy Sanchez Bat-Bat/100 4.00 10.00
134 Roy Oswalt Bat-Jsy/100 4.00 10.00
135 Curt Schilling Bat-Jsy/100 6.00 15.00
136 Alfredo Amezaga Bat-Jsy/25 6.00 15.00
138 Barry Larkin Bat-Jsy/25 10.00 25.00
139 Trot Nixon Bat-Bat/100 4.00 10.00
140 Jim Thome Bat-Jsy/100 6.00 15.00
141 Bret Boone Bat-Jsy/100 4.00 10.00
142 Jacque Jones Bat-Jsy/100 4.00 10.00
143 Travis Hafner Bat-Jsy/100 4.00 10.00
144 Sammy Sosa Bat-Jsy/100 8.00 20.00
145 Mike Mussina Bat-Jsy/100 6.00 15.00
147 Chad Gaudin Jsy-Jsy/50 4.00 10.00
149 Mike Lowell Bat-Jsy/100 4.00 10.00
150 R.Henderson Bat-Jsy/100 6.00 15.00
151 R.Clemens FB Bat-Jsy/25 20.00 50.00
152 Mark Grace FB Bat-Jsy/25 6.00 15.00
153 R.Henderson FB Bat-Jsy/25 12.50 30.00
154 A.Rodriguez FB Bat-Jsy/25 20.00 50.00
155 R.Palmeiro FB Bat-Jsy/100 6.00 15.00
156 G.Maddux FB Bat-Bat/100 10.00 25.00
157 Mike Piazza FB Bat-Jsy/100 10.00 25.00
158 M.Mussina FB Bat-Jsy/100 6.00 15.00
159 Dale Murphy LGD Bat-Jsy/25 10.00 25.00
160 Cal Ripken LGD Bat-Jsy/100 8.00 20.00
161 C.Yaz LGD Bat-Jsy/100 10.00 25.00
162 M.Marion LGD Jsy-Jsy/25 6.00 15.00
163 D.Mattingly LGD Bat-Jsy/100 15.00 40.00
164 R.Yount LGD Bat-Jsy/100 8.00 20.00
165 A.Dawson LGD Bat-Jsy/25 6.00 15.00
167 George Brett LGD Bat-Jsy/25 30.00 60.00
168 W.Ford LGD Jsy-Pants/25 10.00 25.00
169 R.Campy LGD Bat-Pants/25 12.50 30.00
170 R. Maris LGD Bat-Jsy/25 50.00 100.00
172 S.Carlton LGD Bat-Jsy/100 4.00 10.00
173 Stan Musial LGD Bat-Jsy/25 20.00 50.00
174 Nolan Ryan LGD Bat-Jsy/25 30.00 60.00
175 D.Sanders LGD Bat-Jsy/100 6.00 15.00

2004 Diamond Kings DK Materials Framed Bronze Sepia

RANDOM INSERTS IN PACKS
PRINT RUNS B/WN 4-50 COPIES PER
NO PRICING ON QTY OF 5 OR LESS
151 R.Clemens FB Bat-Jsy/25 20.00 50.00
152 Mark Grace FB Bat-Jsy/25 6.00 15.00
153 R.Henderson FB Bat-Jsy/25 12.50 30.00
154 A.Rodriguez FB Bat-Jsy/25 20.00 50.00
155 R.Palmeiro FB Bat-Jsy/50 6.00 15.00
156 G.Maddux FB Bat-Bat/50 15.00 40.00
157 Mike Piazza FB Bat-Jsy/50 15.00 40.00
158 M.Mussina FB Bat-Jsy/50 6.00 15.00
159 Dale Murphy LGD Bat-Jsy/15 15.00 40.00
160 Cal Ripken LGD Bat-Jsy/50 12.00 30.00
161 C.Yaz LGD Bat-Jsy/50 15.00 40.00
162 M.Marion LGD Jsy-Jsy/15 10.00 25.00
163 D.Mattingly LGD Bat-Jsy/50 20.00 50.00
164 R.Yount LGD Bat-Jsy/50 10.00 25.00
165 A.Dawson LGD Bat-Jsy/15 10.00 25.00
167 G.Brett LGD Bat-Jsy/15 50.00 100.00
168 W.Ford LGD Jsy-Pants/15 15.00 40.00
169 R.Campy LGD Bat-Pants/15 20.00 50.00
170 R.Maris LGD Bat-Jsy/15 60.00 120.00
172 S.Carlton LGD Bat-Jsy/15 10.00 25.00
173 Stan Musial LGD Bat-Jsy/15 40.00 80.00
174 Nolan Ryan LGD Bat-Jsy/15 50.00 100.00
175 D.Sanders LGD Bat-Jsy/50 6.00 15.00

2004 Diamond Kings DK Materials Framed Silver

RANDOM INSERTS IN PACKS
PRINT RUNS B/WN 1-75 COPIES PER
NO PRICING ON QTY OF 10 OR LESS
1 Alex Rodriguez Bat-Jsy/25 20.00 50.00
2 Andruw Jones Bat-Jsy/25 10.00 25.00
3 Nomar Garciaparra Bat-Jsy/25 20.00 50.00
4 Kerry Wood Bat-Jsy/25 6.00 15.00
5 Magglio Ordonez Bat-Jsy/25 6.00 15.00
6 Victor Martinez Bat-Bat/50 4.00 10.00
8 Josh Beckett Bat-Jsy/25 6.00 15.00
9 Jeff Kent Bat-Jsy/25 6.00 15.00
10 Carlos Beltran Bat-Jsy/25 6.00 15.00
11 Hideo Nomo Bat-Jsy/25 12.50 30.00
12 Richie Sexson Bat-Jsy/25 6.00 15.00
13 Jose Vidro Bat-Jsy/25 6.00 15.00
14 Jae Seo Jsy-Jsy/25 6.00 15.00
15 Alfonso Soriano Bat-Jsy/25 6.00 15.00
16 Barry Zito Bat-Jsy/25 6.00 15.00
18 Brian Giles Bat-Bat/25 6.00 15.00
19 Edgar Martinez Bat-Jsy/25 10.00 25.00
20 Jim Edmonds Bat-Jsy/25 6.00 15.00
21 Rocco Baldelli Bat-Jsy/25 6.00 15.00
22 Mark Teixeira Bat-Jsy/25 10.00 25.00
23 Carlos Delgado Bat-Jsy/25 6.00 15.00
25 Jose Reyes Bat-Jsy/25 6.00 15.00
26 Marlon Byrd Bat-Jsy/50 4.00 10.00
27 Albert Pujols Bat-Jsy/25 15.00 40.00
28 Vernon Wells Bat-Jsy/25 6.00 15.00
29 Garret Anderson Bat-Jsy/25 6.00 15.00
31 Chipper Jones Bat-Jsy/25 12.50 30.00
32 Rich Harden Jsy-Jsy/50 4.00 10.00
33 Manny Ramirez Bat-Jsy/25 10.00 25.00
34 Derek Jeter Base-Base/50 15.00 40.00
35 Brandon Webb Bat-Jsy/50 4.00 10.00
36 Mark Prior Bat-Jsy/25 10.00 25.00
38 Frank Thomas Bat-Jsy/25 12.50 30.00
39 Rafael Palmeiro Bat-Jsy/50 6.00 15.00
40 Adam Dunn Bat-Jsy/25 6.00 15.00
42 Todd Helton Bat-Jsy/25 10.00 25.00
43 Matt Morris Jsy-Jsy/25 6.00 15.00
44 Dontrelle Willis Bat-Jsy/25 10.00 25.00
45 Lance Berkman Bat-Jsy/25 6.00 15.00
47 Kazuhisa Ishii Bat-Jsy/25 6.00 15.00
48 Torii Hunter Bat-Jsy/25 6.00 15.00
49 Vladimir Guerrero Bat-Jsy/25 12.50 30.00
50 Mike Piazza Bat-Jsy/50 15.00 40.00
51 Alexis Rios Bat-Bat/50 4.00 10.00
52 Shannon Stewart Bat-Bat/50 4.00 10.00
53 Eric Hinske Bat-Jsy/50 4.00 10.00
54 Jason Jennings Bat-Jsy/25 6.00 15.00
55 Jason Giambi Bat-Jsy/25 6.00 15.00
57 Joe Thurston Bat-Jsy/50 4.00 10.00
58 Ramon Nivar Bat-Jsy/50 4.00 10.00
59 Jay Gibbons Jsy-Jsy/25 6.00 15.00
60 Eric Chavez Bat-Jsy/25 6.00 15.00
62 Walter Young Bat-Bat/50 4.00 10.00
63 Mark Grace Bat-Jsy/25 10.00 25.00
64 Austin Kearns Bat-Jsy/25 6.00 15.00
65 Bob Abreu Bat-Jsy/25 6.00 15.00
66 Hee Seop Choi Bat-Jsy/25 6.00 15.00
67 Brandon Phillips Bat-Bat/50 4.00 10.00
68 Rickie Weeks Bat-Bat/50 4.00 10.00
69 Luis Gonzalez Bat-Jsy/25 6.00 15.00
70 Mariano Rivera Jsy-Jsy/75 10.00 25.00
71 Jason Lane Bat-Hat/25 6.00 15.00
79 Miguel Tejada Bat-Jsy/50 4.00 10.00
80 Juan Gonzalez Bat-Jsy/25 6.00 15.00
81 Joe Borchard Bat-Jsy/25 6.00 15.00
82 Gary Sheffield Bat-Jsy/25 6.00 15.00
83 Wade Miller Bat-Jsy/25 6.00 15.00
84 Jeff Bagwell Bat-Jsy/25 10.00 25.00
86 Adrian Beltre Bat-Jsy/25 6.00 15.00
87 Jeff Baker Bat-Bat/50 4.00 10.00
89 Bernie Williams Bat-Jsy/25 10.00 25.00
90 Pedro Martinez Bat-Jsy/25 10.00 25.00
92 Junior Spivey Bat-Jsy/25 6.00 15.00
93 Tim Hudson Bat-Jsy/25 6.00 15.00
94 Troy Glaus Bat-Jsy/25 6.00 15.00
95 Ken Griffey Jr. Base-Base/50 12.50 30.00
97 Antonio Perez Bat-Pants/50 4.00 10.00
98 Dan Haren Bat-Jsy/50 4.00 10.00
99 Ivan Rodriguez Bat-Jsy/25 10.00 25.00
100 Randy Johnson Bat-Jsy/25 12.50 30.00
101 Lyle Overbay Bat-Jsy/50 4.00 10.00
103 Miguel Cabrera Bat-Jsy/25 10.00 25.00
104 Scott Rolen Bat-Jsy/25 10.00 25.00
105 Roger Clemens Bat-Jsy/25 20.00 50.00
107 Nic Jackson Bat-Bat/50 4.00 10.00
108 Angel Berroa Bat-Pants/25 6.00 15.00
109 Hank Blalock Bat-Jsy/25 6.00 15.00
110 Ryan Klesko Bat-Jsy/25 6.00 15.00
111 Jose Castillo Bat-Bat/50 4.00 10.00
112 Paul Konerko Bat-Jsy/25 6.00 15.00
113 Greg Maddux Bat-Jsy/25 20.00 50.00
114 Mark Mulder Bat-Jsy/25 6.00 15.00
115 Pat Burrell Bat-Jsy/25 6.00 15.00
116 Garrett Atkins Jsy-Jsy/50 4.00 10.00
118 Orlando Cabrera Bat-Jsy/25 6.00 15.00
119 Nick Johnson Bat-Jsy/25 6.00 15.00
120 Tom Glavine Bat-Jsy/25 10.00 25.00
121 Morgan Ensberg Bat-Jsy/25 6.00 15.00
122 Sean Casey Bat-Hat/25 6.00 15.00
123 Orlando Hudson Bat-Jsy/25 6.00 15.00
125 Craig Biggio Bat-Jsy/25 10.00 25.00
126 Adam LaRoche Bat-Bat/50 4.00 10.00
127 Hong-Chih Kuo Bat-Bat/50 4.00 10.00
128 Paul LoDuca Bat-Jsy/25 6.00 15.00
129 Shawn Green Bat-Jsy/25 6.00 15.00
130 Luis Castillo Bat-Jsy/25 6.00 15.00
132 Ken Harvey Bat-Bat/50 4.00 10.00
133 Freddy Sanchez Bat-Bat/50 4.00 10.00
134 Roy Oswalt Bat-Jsy/50 4.00 10.00
135 Curt Schilling Bat-Jsy/25 10.00 25.00
136 Alfredo Amezaga Bat-Jsy/25 6.00 15.00
138 Barry Larkin Bat-Jsy/25 10.00 25.00
139 Trot Nixon Bat-Bat/25 6.00 15.00
140 Jim Thome Bat-Jsy/25 10.00 25.00
141 Bret Boone Bat-Jsy/50 4.00 10.00
142 Jacque Jones Bat-Jsy/50 4.00 10.00
143 Travis Hafner Bat-Jsy/50 4.00 10.00
144 Sammy Sosa Bat-Jsy/25 12.50 30.00
145 Mike Mussina Bat-Jsy/50 6.00 15.00
147 Chad Gaudin Jsy-Jsy/25 6.00 15.00
149 Mike Lowell Bat-Jsy/25 6.00 15.00
150 R.Henderson Bat-Jsy/25 10.00 25.00
151 R.Clemens FB Bat-Jsy/15 30.00 60.00
152 Mark Grace FB Bat-Jsy/15 10.00 25.00
153 R.Henderson FB Bat-Jsy/15 10.00 25.00
154 A.Rodriguez FB Bat-Jsy/15 30.00 60.00
155 R.Palmeiro FB Bat-Jsy/50 6.00 15.00
156 G.Maddux FB Bat-Bat/50 15.00 40.00
157 Mike Piazza FB Bat-Jsy/50 15.00 40.00
158 M.Mussina FB Bat-Jsy/50 6.00 15.00
159 Dale Murphy LGD Bat-Jsy/15 15.00 40.00
160 Cal Ripken LGD Bat-Jsy/50 12.00 30.00
161 C.Yaz LGD Bat-Jsy/50 15.00 40.00
162 M.Marion LGD Jsy-Jsy/15 10.00 25.00
163 D.Mattingly LGD Bat-Jsy/50 12.50 30.00
164 R.Yount LGD Bat-Jsy/50 10.00 25.00
165 A.Dawson LGD Bat-Jsy/15 10.00 25.00
167 G.Brett LGD Bat-Jsy/15 50.00 100.00
168 W.Ford LGD Jsy-Pants/15 15.00 40.00
169 R.Campy LGD Bat-Pants/15 20.00 50.00
170 R.Maris LGD Bat-Jsy/15 60.00 120.00
172 S.Carlton LGD Bat-Jsy/50 4.00 10.00
173 Stan Musial LGD Bat-Jsy/15 40.00 80.00
174 Nolan Ryan LGD Bat-Jsy/15 15.00 40.00
175 D.Sanders LGD Bat-Jsy/50 6.00 15.00

2004 Diamond Kings DK Signatures Bronze

RANDOM INSERTS IN PACKS
PRINT RUNS B/WN 1-200 COPIES PER
NO PRICING ON QTY OF 10 OR LESS
6 Victor Martinez/200 6.00 15.00
13 Jose Vidro/200 4.00 10.00
14 Jae Seo/200 6.00 15.00
17 Brett Myers/200 6.00 15.00
19 Edgar Martinez/25 15.00 40.00
26 Marlon Byrd/200 4.00 10.00
32 Rich Harden/200 6.00 15.00
35 Brandon Webb/25 6.00 15.00
41 Aubrey Huff/100 6.00 15.00
44 Dontrelle Willis/15 20.00 50.00
48 Torii Hunter/100 6.00 15.00
51 Alexis Rios/200 6.00 15.00
52 Shannon Stewart/200 6.00 15.00
53 Eric Hinske/25 6.00 15.00
54 Jason Jennings/15 10.00 25.00
56 Brandon Claussen/200 4.00 10.00
57 Joe Thurston/200 4.00 10.00
58 Ramon Nivar/100 4.00 10.00
59 Jay Gibbons/25 6.00 15.00
61 Jimmy Gobble/100 4.00 10.00
62 Walter Young/200 4.00 10.00
67 Brandon Phillips/100 4.00 10.00
68 Rickie Weeks/30 5.00 12.00
71 Jason Lane/200 6.00 15.00
73 Runelvys Hernandez/50 5.00 12.00
74 Aramis Ramirez/100 6.00 15.00
76 Cliff Lee/200 5.00 12.00
77 Chris Snelling/200 4.00 10.00
78 Ryan Wagner/100 4.00 10.00
81 Joe Borchard/200 4.00 10.00
85 Ryan Church/200 6.00 15.00
87 Jeff Baker/100 4.00 10.00
88 Adam Loewen/100 4.00 10.00
91 Carlos Rivera/100 4.00 10.00
92 Junior Spivey/25 6.00 15.00
96 Alexis Gomez/200 4.00 10.00
97 Antonio Perez/46 5.00 12.00
98 Dan Haren/100 4.00 10.00
101 Lyle Overbay/200 4.00 10.00
102 Oliver Perez/200 6.00 15.00
103 Miguel Cabrera/100 15.00 40.00
106 Brian Tallet/200 4.00 10.00
107 Nic Jackson/200 4.00 10.00
108 Angel Berroa/25 6.00 15.00
109 Hank Blalock/25 10.00 25.00
111 Jose Castillo/200 4.00 10.00
114 Mark Mulder/25 10.00 25.00
116 Garrett Atkins/100 4.00 10.00
117 Jeremy Guthrie/200 4.00 10.00
118 Orlando Cabrera/75 8.00 20.00
121 Morgan Ensberg/200 6.00 15.00
123 Orlando Hudson/100 4.00 10.00
126 Adam LaRoche/100 4.00 10.00
127 Hong-Chih Kuo/25 40.00 80.00
130 Luis Castillo/25 6.00 15.00
131 Joe Crede/100 6.00 15.00
132 Ken Harvey/200 4.00 10.00
133 Freddy Sanchez/50 6.00 15.00
136 Alfredo Amezaga/90 4.00 10.00
137 Chien-Ming Wang/25 125.00 200.00
139 Trot Nixon/15 12.50 30.00
142 Jacque Jones/25 10.00 25.00
143 Travis Hafner/200 6.00 15.00
146 Vinny Chulk/200 4.00 10.00
147 Chad Gaudin/100 4.00 10.00
148 Delmon Young/25 15.00 40.00
149 Mike Lowell/25 10.00 25.00
162 Marty Marion LGD/15 12.50 30.00

2004 Diamond Kings DK Signatures Bronze Sepia

PRINT RUNS B/WN 1-15 COPIES PER
NO PRICING ON QTY OF 1 OR LESS
162 Marty Marion LGD/15 12.50 30.00

2004 Diamond Kings DK Signatures Gold

RANDOM INSERTS IN PACKS
PRINT RUNS B/WN 1-50 COPIES PER
NO PRICING ON QTY OF 12 OR LESS
26 Marlon Byrd/15 10.00 25.00
32 Rich Harden/50 8.00 20.00
51 Alexis Rios/50 8.00 20.00
56 Brandon Claussen/50 5.00 12.00
57 Joe Thurston/50 5.00 12.00
62 Walter Young/50 5.00 12.00
71 Jason Lane/40 8.00 20.00
77 Chris Snelling/50 5.00 12.00
81 Joe Borchard/50 5.00 12.00
85 Ryan Church/50 8.00 20.00
96 Alexis Gomez/50 5.00 12.00
101 Lyle Overbay/50 5.00 12.00
102 Oliver Perez/50 8.00 20.00
106 Brian Tallet/50 5.00 12.00
107 Nic Jackson/50 5.00 12.00
121 Morgan Ensberg/48 8.00 20.00
146 Vinny Chulk/50 5.00 12.00

2004 Diamond Kings DK Signatures Platinum

STATED PRINT RUN 1 SERIAL #'d SET
NO PRICING DUE TO SCARCITY

2004 Diamond Kings DK Signatures Silver

RANDOM INSERTS IN PACKS
PRINT RUNS B/WN 1-100 COPIES PER
NO PRICING ON QTY OF 10 OR LESS
6 Victor Martinez/49 8.00 20.00
13 Jose Vidro/20 8.00 20.00
14 Jae Seo/80 6.00 15.00
17 Brett Myers/90 6.00 15.00
19 Edgar Martinez/15 40.00 80.00
26 Marlon Byrd/100 4.00 10.00
32 Rich Harden/100 6.00 15.00
35 Brandon Webb/15 10.00 25.00
41 Aubrey Huff/40 10.00 25.00
48 Torii Hunter/30 10.00 25.00
51 Alexis Rios/100 6.00 15.00
52 Shannon Stewart/30 10.00 25.00
53 Eric Hinske/15 10.00 25.00
56 Brandon Claussen/100 4.00 10.00
57 Joe Thurston/100 4.00 10.00
58 Ramon Nivar/30 6.00 15.00
59 Jay Gibbons/15 10.00 25.00
61 Jimmy Gobble/30 6.00 15.00
62 Walter Young/100 4.00 10.00
67 Brandon Phillips/30 6.00 15.00
68 Rickie Weeks/20 10.00 25.00
71 Jason Lane/100 6.00 15.00
73 Runelvys Hernandez/30 6.00 15.00
74 Aramis Ramirez/30 10.00 25.00
76 Cliff Lee/100 6.00 15.00
77 Chris Snelling/100 4.00 10.00
78 Ryan Wagner/30 6.00 15.00
81 Joe Borchard/100 4.00 10.00
85 Ryan Church/100 6.00 15.00
87 Jeff Baker/30 6.00 15.00
88 Adam Loewen/30 6.00 15.00
92 Junior Spivey/15 10.00 25.00
96 Alexis Gomez/100 4.00 10.00
97 Antonio Perez/15 10.00 25.00
98 Dan Haren/30 6.00 15.00
101 Lyle Overbay/100 4.00 10.00
102 Oliver Perez/100 6.00 15.00
103 Miguel Cabrera/30 25.00 50.00
106 Brian Tallet/100 4.00 10.00
107 Nic Jackson/100 4.00 10.00
109 Hank Blalock/30 10.00 25.00
111 Jose Castillo/100 4.00 10.00
114 Mark Mulder/15 12.50 30.00
116 Garrett Atkins/30 6.00 15.00
117 Jeremy Guthrie/30 6.00 15.00
118 Orlando Cabrera/15 12.50 30.00
121 Morgan Ensberg/50 8.00 20.00
123 Orlando Hudson/30 6.00 15.00
126 Adam LaRoche/30 6.00 15.00
127 Hong-Chih Kuo/15 60.00 120.00
130 Luis Castillo/15 10.00 25.00
131 Joe Crede/35 6.00 15.00
132 Ken Harvey/30 6.00 15.00
133 Freddy Sanchez/15 10.00 25.00
136 Alfredo Amezaga/30 6.00 15.00
137 Chien-Ming Wang/15 150.00 250.00
143 Travis Hafner/30 10.00 25.00
146 Vinny Chulk/100 4.00 10.00
147 Chad Gaudin/30 6.00 15.00
149 Mike Lowell/15 12.50 30.00

2004 Diamond Kings DK Signatures Framed Bronze

PRINT RUNS B/WN 1-50 COPIES PER
NO PRICING ON QTY OF 10 OR LESS
6 Victor Martinez/50 8.00 20.00
13 Jose Vidro/25 8.00 20.00
14 Jae Seo/50 8.00 20.00
17 Brett Myers/25 10.00 25.00
19 Edgar Martinez/25 30.00 60.00
21 Rocco Baldelli/25 10.00 25.00
26 Marlon Byrd/50 5.00 12.00
28 Vernon Wells/25 10.00 25.00
32 Rich Harden/50 8.00 20.00
35 Brandon Webb/25 8.00 20.00
40 Adam Dunn/25 15.00 40.00
41 Aubrey Huff/25 10.00 25.00
44 Dontrelle Willis/25 15.00 40.00
48 Torii Hunter/25 10.00 25.00
51 Alexis Rios/50 8.00 20.00
52 Shannon Stewart/25 10.00 25.00
53 Eric Hinske/25 8.00 20.00
54 Jason Jennings/25 8.00 20.00
56 Brandon Claussen/50 5.00 12.00
57 Joe Thurston/50 5.00 12.00
58 Ramon Nivar/25 8.00 20.00
59 Jay Gibbons/25 8.00 20.00
61 Jimmy Gobble/50 5.00 12.00
62 Walter Young/50 5.00 12.00
65 Bob Abreu/25 10.00 25.00
67 Brandon Phillips/50 5.00 12.00
68 Rickie Weeks/25 10.00 25.00
71 Jason Lane/25 10.00 25.00
73 Runelvys Hernandez/25 8.00 20.00
74 Aramis Ramirez/25 10.00 25.00
76 Cliff Lee/50 20.00 50.00
77 Chris Snelling/50 5.00 12.00
78 Ryan Wagner/25 8.00 20.00
81 Joe Borchard/50 5.00 12.00
85 Ryan Church/50 8.00 20.00
87 Jeff Baker/25 8.00 20.00
88 Adam Loewen/25 8.00 20.00
91 Carlos Rivera/50 5.00 12.00
94 Troy Glaus/25 15.00 40.00
96 Alexis Gomez/50 5.00 12.00
97 Antonio Perez/25 8.00 20.00
98 Dan Haren/25 8.00 20.00
101 Lyle Overbay/50 5.00 12.00
102 Oliver Perez/50 8.00 20.00
103 Miguel Cabrera/50 20.00 50.00
106 Brian Tallet/50 5.00 12.00
107 Nic Jackson/50 5.00 12.00
108 Angel Berroa/25 8.00 20.00
109 Hank Blalock/25 10.00 25.00
111 Jose Castillo/50 5.00 12.00
112 Paul Konerko/15 20.00 50.00
114 Mark Mulder/25 10.00 25.00
116 Garrett Atkins/50 5.00 12.00
117 Jeremy Guthrie/25 8.00 20.00
118 Orlando Cabrera/25 10.00 25.00
121 Morgan Ensberg/50 8.00 20.00
123 Orlando Hudson/50 5.00 12.00
126 Adam LaRoche/50 5.00 12.00
127 Hong-Chih Kuo/25 40.00 80.00
130 Luis Castillo/25 8.00 20.00
131 Joe Crede/50 8.00 20.00
132 Ken Harvey/25 8.00 20.00
133 Freddy Sanchez/25 8.00 20.00
134 Roy Oswalt/20 10.00 25.00
136 Alfredo Amezaga/25 8.00 20.00
137 Chien-Ming Wang/25 125.00 200.00
139 Trot Nixon/25 10.00 25.00
142 Jacque Jones/25 10.00 25.00
143 Travis Hafner/25 10.00 25.00
146 Vinny Chulk/50 5.00 12.00
147 Chad Gaudin/25 8.00 20.00
148 Delmon Young/25 15.00 40.00
149 Mike Lowell/25 10.00 25.00
162 Marty Marion LGD/25 10.00 25.00

2004 Diamond Kings DK Signatures Framed Bronze Sepia

RANDOM INSERTS IN PACKS
PRINT RUNS B/WN 1-25 COPIES PER
NO PRICING ON QTY OF 1 OR LESS
162 Marty Marion LGD/25 10.00 25.00

2004 Diamond Kings DK Signatures Framed Silver

RANDOM INSERTS IN PACKS
PRINT RUNS B/WN 1-25 COPIES PER
NO PRICING ON QTY OF 10 OR LESS
6 Victor Martinez/15 12.50 30.00
14 Jae Seo/15 12.50 30.00
21 Rocco Baldelli/15 12.50 30.00
26 Marlon Byrd/15 10.00 25.00
32 Rich Harden/25 10.00 25.00
35 Brandon Webb/15 10.00 25.00
51 Alexis Rios/25 10.00 25.00
56 Brandon Claussen/25 8.00 20.00
57 Joe Thurston/25 8.00 20.00
58 Ramon Nivar/15 10.00 25.00
59 Jay Gibbons/15 10.00 25.00
61 Jimmy Gobble/15 10.00 25.00
62 Walter Young/25 8.00 20.00
67 Brandon Phillips/15 10.00 25.00
73 Runelvys Hernandez/15 10.00 25.00
76 Cliff Lee/15 30.00 60.00
77 Chris Snelling/25 8.00 20.00
81 Joe Borchard/25 8.00 20.00
85 Ryan Church/25 10.00 25.00
91 Carlos Rivera/15 10.00 25.00
96 Alexis Gomez/25 8.00 20.00
101 Lyle Overbay/25 8.00 20.00
102 Oliver Perez/25 10.00 25.00
106 Brian Tallet/25 8.00 20.00
107 Nic Jackson/25 8.00 20.00
111 Jose Castillo/15 10.00 25.00
121 Morgan Ensberg/15 12.50 30.00
123 Orlando Hudson/15 10.00 25.00
126 Adam LaRoche/15 10.00 25.00
130 Luis Castillo/15 10.00 25.00
133 Freddy Sanchez/15 10.00 25.00
136 Alfredo Amezaga/15 10.00 25.00
137 Chien-Ming Wang/15 150.00 250.00
146 Vinny Chulk/25 8.00 20.00
147 Chad Gaudin/15 10.00 25.00
149 Mike Lowell/15 12.50 30.00

2004 Diamond Kings Diamond Cut Bats

RANDOM INSERTS IN PACKS
PRINT RUNS B/WN 1-100 COPIES PER
NO PRICING ON QTY OF 1 OR LESS
DC1 Alex Rodriguez/100 5.00 12.00
DC2 Nomar Garciaparra/100 2.50 6.00
DC3 Hideo Nomo/100 4.00 10.00
DC4 Alfonso Soriano/100 2.50 6.00
DC6 Edgar Martinez/100 2.50 6.00
DC7 Rocco Baldelli/100 1.50 4.00
DC8 Mark Teixeira/100 2.50 6.00
DC9 Albert Pujols/100 5.00 12.00
DC10 Vernon Wells/100 1.50 4.00
DC11 Garret Anderson/100 1.50 4.00
DC14 Brandon Webb/100 1.50 4.00
DC15 Mark Prior/100 2.50 6.00
DC16 Rafael Palmeiro/100 2.50 6.00
DC17 Adam Dunn/100 2.50 6.00
DC18 Dontrelle Willis/100 1.50 4.00
DC19 Kazuhisa Ishii/100 1.50 4.00
DC20 Torii Hunter/100 1.50 4.00
DC21 Vladimir Guerrero/100 2.50 6.00
DC22 Mike Piazza/100 4.00 10.00
DC23 Jason Giambi/100 1.50 4.00
DC26 Bob Abreu/100 1.50 4.00
DC27 Hee Seop Choi/100 1.50 4.00
DC28 Rickie Weeks/100 1.50 4.00
DC30 Troy Glaus/100 1.50 4.00
DC31 Ivan Rodriguez/100 2.50 6.00
DC32 Hank Blalock/100 1.50 4.00
DC33 Greg Maddux/100 5.00 12.00
DC34 Nick Johnson/100 1.50 4.00
DC35 Shawn Green/100 1.50 4.00
DC36 Sammy Sosa/100 4.00 10.00
DC37 Dale Murphy/50 5.00 12.00
DC38 Cal Ripken/50 15.00 40.00
DC39 Carl Yastrzemski/100 4.00 10.00
DC41 Don Mattingly/100 8.00 20.00

DC43 George Brett/50 10.00 25.00
DC46 Steve Carlton/50 3.00 8.00
DC47 Stan Musial/25 12.00 30.00
DC48 Nolan Ryan/50 15.00 40.00
DC49 Deion Sanders/50 3.00 8.00
DC50 Roberto Clemente/25 30.00 80.00

2004 Diamond Kings Diamond Cut Combos Material

RANDOM INSERTS IN PACKS
PRINT RUNS B/WN 1-50 COPIES PER
NO PRICING ON QTY OF 8 OR LESS
DC1 Alex Rodriguez Bat-Jsy/50 15.00 40.00
DC2 Nomar Garciaparra Bat-Jsy/50 15.00 40.00
DC3 Hideo Nomo Bat-Jsy/25 15.00 40.00
DC4 Alfonso Soriano Bat-Jsy/50 6.00 15.00
DC6 Edgar Martinez Bat-Jsy/25 15.00 40.00
DC7 Rocco Baldelli Bat-Jsy/25 10.00 25.00
DC8 Mark Teixeira Bat-Jsy/25 15.00 40.00
DC9 Albert Pujols Bat-Jsy/50 8.00 20.00
DC10 Vernon Wells Bat-Jsy/25 10.00 25.00
DC11 Garret Anderson Bat-Jsy/25 10.00 25.00
DC14 Brandon Webb Bat-Jsy/25 10.00 25.00
DC15 Mark Prior Bat-Jsy/50 10.00 25.00
DC16 Rafael Palmeiro Bat-Jsy/25 15.00 40.00
DC17 Adam Dunn Bat-Jsy/25 10.00 25.00
DC18 Dontrelle Willis Bat-Jsy/25 15.00 40.00
DC19 Kazuhisa Ishii Bat-Jsy/25 10.00 25.00
DC20 Torii Hunter Bat-Jsy/25 10.00 25.00
DC21 Vladimir Guerrero Bat-Jsy/25 15.00 40.00
DC22 Mike Piazza Bat-Jsy/50 15.00 40.00
DC23 Jason Giambi Bat-Jsy/25 10.00 25.00
DC26 Bob Abreu Bat-Jsy/50 6.00 15.00
DC27 Hee Seop Choi Bat-Jsy/50 6.00 15.00
DC30 Troy Glaus Bat-Jsy/25 10.00 25.00
DC31 Ivan Rodriguez Bat-Jsy/25 15.00 40.00
DC32 Hank Blalock Bat-Jsy/25 10.00 25.00
DC33 Greg Maddux Bat-Jsy/50 15.00 40.00
DC34 Nick Johnson Bat-Jsy/25 10.00 25.00
DC35 Shawn Green Bat-Jsy/25 10.00 25.00
DC36 Sammy Sosa Bat-Jsy/50 10.00 25.00
DC41 Don Mattingly Bat-Jsy/23 40.00 80.00
DC42 Jim Palmer Jsy-Jsy/22 12.50 30.00
DC44 Whitey Ford Jsy-Pants/16 20.00 50.00
DC46 Steve Carlton Bat-Jsy/32 10.00 25.00
DC48 Nolan Ryan Bat-Jsy/34 12.00 30.00
DC49 Deion Sanders Bat-Jsy/24 20.00 50.00

2004 Diamond Kings Diamond Cut Combos Signature

RANDOM INSERTS IN PACKS
PRINT RUNS B/WN 1-32 COPIES PER
NO PRICING ON QTY OF 10 OR LESS
DC40 Marty Marion Jsy/25 15.00 40.00
DC41 Don Mattingly Jsy/23 20.00 50.00
DC42 Jim Palmer Jsy/22 15.00 40.00
DC44 Whitey Ford Jsy/16 40.00 80.00
DC46 Steve Carlton Jsy/32 15.00 40.00

2004 Diamond Kings Diamond Cut Jerseys

RANDOM INSERTS IN PACKS
PRINT RUNS B/WN 10-100 COPIES PER
NO PRICING ON QTY OF 10 OR LESS
DC1 Alex Rodriguez/100 10.00 25.00
DC2 Nomar Garciaparra/100 10.00 25.00
DC3 Hideo Nomo/50 10.00 25.00
DC4 Alfonso Soriano/100 4.00 10.00
DC5 Brett Myers/50 6.00 15.00
DC6 Edgar Martinez/100 6.00 15.00
DC7 Rocco Baldelli/100 4.00 10.00
DC8 Mark Teixeira/100 6.00 15.00
DC9 Albert Pujols/100 12.50 30.00
DC10 Vernon Wells/100 4.00 10.00
DC11 Garret Anderson/50 6.00 15.00
DC12 Jerome Williams/100 4.00 10.00
DC13 Rich Harden/100 4.00 10.00
DC14 Brandon Webb/100 4.00 10.00
DC15 Mark Prior/100 6.00 15.00
DC16 Rafael Palmeiro/100 6.00 15.00
DC17 Adam Dunn/100 4.00 10.00
DC18 Dontrelle Willis/100 6.00 15.00
DC19 Kazuhisa Ishii/100 4.00 10.00
DC20 Torii Hunter/100 4.00 10.00
DC21 Vladimir Guerrero/50 10.00 25.00
DC22 Mike Piazza/100 10.00 25.00
DC23 Jason Giambi/100 4.00 10.00
DC25 Ramon Nivar/100 4.00 10.00
DC26 Bob Abreu/100 4.00 10.00
DC27 Hee Seop Choi/100 4.00 10.00
DC30 Troy Glaus/100 4.00 10.00
DC31 Ivan Rodriguez/100 6.00 15.00
DC32 Hank Blalock/100 4.00 10.00
DC33 Greg Maddux/100 10.00 25.00
DC34 Nick Johnson/100 4.00 10.00
DC35 Shawn Green/100 4.00 10.00
DC36 Sammy Sosa/100 6.00 15.00
DC37 Dale Murphy/50 10.00 25.00
DC38 Cal Ripken/50 30.00 60.00
DC39 Carl Yastrzemski/100 10.00 25.00
DC40 Marty Marion/50 6.00 15.00
DC41 Don Mattingly/100 12.50 30.00
DC42 Jim Palmer/25 10.00 25.00
DC43 George Brett/50 15.00 40.00
DC44 Whitey Ford/25 15.00 40.00
DC46 Steve Carlton/50 6.00 15.00
DC48 Nolan Ryan/50 20.00 50.00
DC49 Deion Sanders/50 10.00 25.00

2004 Diamond Kings Diamond Cut Signatures

RANDOM INSERTS IN PACKS
PRINT RUNS B/WN 1-50 COPIES PER
NO PRICING ON QTY OF 10 OR LESS
DC7 Rocco Baldelli/25 10.00 25.00
DC8 Mark Teixeira/25 15.00 40.00
DC13 Rich Harden/50 8.00 20.00
DC14 Brandon Webb/50 6.00 15.00
DC20 Torii Hunter/25 15.00 40.00
DC24 Ryan Wagner/50 6.00 15.00
DC25 Ramon Nivar/50 6.00 15.00
DC28 Rickie Weeks/50 8.00 20.00
DC29 Adam Loewen/50 6.00 15.00
DC32 Hank Blalock/25 10.00 25.00
DC40 Marty Marion/25 10.00 25.00
DC41 Don Mattingly/23 60.00 120.00
DC42 Jim Palmer/22 12.50 30.00
DC44 Whitey Ford/16 20.00 50.00
DC46 Steve Carlton/32 10.00 25.00
DC48 Nolan Ryan/34 75.00 150.00

2004 Diamond Kings Gallery of Stars

STATED ODDS 1:37
G1 Nolan Ryan 4.00 10.00
G2 Cal Ripken 4.00 10.00
G3 George Brett 2.50 6.00
G4 Don Mattingly 2.50 6.00
G5 Deion Sanders .75 2.00
G6 Mike Piazza 1.25 3.00
G7 Hideo Nomo 1.25 3.00
G8 Rickey Henderson 1.25 3.00
G9 Roger Clemens 1.50 4.00
G10 Greg Maddux 1.50 4.00
G11 Albert Pujols 1.50 4.00
G12 Alex Rodriguez 1.50 4.00
G13 Dale Murphy 1.25 3.00
G14 Mark Prior .75 2.00
G15 Dontrelle Willis .50 1.25

2004 Diamond Kings Gallery of Stars Signatures

RANDOM INSERTS IN PACKS
PRINT RUNS B/WN 1-10 COPIES PER
NO PRICING DUE TO SCARCITY

2004 Diamond Kings Heritage Collection

RANDOM INSERTS IN PACKS
HC1 Dale Murphy 1.25 3.00
HC2 Cal Ripken 4.00 10.00
HC3 Carl Yastrzemski 1.25 3.00
HC4 Don Mattingly 2.50 6.00
HC5 Jim Palmer .75 2.00
HC6 Andre Dawson .75 2.00
HC7 Roy Campanella 1.25 3.00
HC8 George Brett 2.50 6.00
HC9 Duke Snider .75 2.00
HC10 Marty Marion .50 1.25
HC11 Deion Sanders .75 2.00
HC12 Whitey Ford .75 2.00
HC13 Stan Musial 2.00 5.00
HC14 Nolan Ryan 4.00 10.00
HC15 Steve Carlton .75 2.00
HC16 Robin Yount 1.25 3.00
HC17 Albert Pujols 1.50 4.00
HC18 Alex Rodriguez 1.50 4.00
HC19 Mike Piazza 1.25 3.00
HC20 Roger Clemens 1.50 4.00
HC21 Hideo Nomo 1.25 3.00
HC22 Mark Prior .75 2.00
HC23 Roger Maris 1.25 3.00
HC24 Greg Maddux 1.50 4.00
HC25 Mark Grace .75 2.00

2004 Diamond Kings Heritage Collection Bats

RANDOM INSERTS IN PACKS
PRINT RUNS B/WN 1-50 COPIES PER
NO PRICING ON QTY OF 1 OR LESS
HC1 Dale Murphy/50 10.00 25.00
HC2 Cal Ripken/50 12.00 30.00
HC3 Carl Yastrzemski/50 12.00 30.00
HC4 Don Mattingly/50 12.00 30.00
HC6 Andre Dawson/25 10.00 25.00
HC7 Roy Campanella/25 10.00 25.00
HC8 George Brett/25 12.00 30.00
HC11 Deion Sanders/50 10.00 25.00
HC13 Stan Musial/25 20.00 50.00
HC14 Nolan Ryan/25 15.00 40.00
HC15 Steve Carlton/25 10.00 25.00
HC16 Robin Yount/50 10.00 25.00
HC17 Albert Pujols/50 10.00 25.00
HC18 Alex Rodriguez/50 12.50 30.00
HC19 Mike Piazza/50 10.00 25.00
HC20 Roger Clemens/50 10.00 25.00
HC21 Hideo Nomo/50 10.00 25.00
HC22 Mark Prior/50 10.00 25.00
HC23 Roger Maris/25 12.00 30.00
HC24 Greg Maddux/50 12.50 30.00
HC25 Mark Grace/50 10.00 25.00

2004 Diamond Kings Heritage Collection Jerseys

RANDOM INSERTS IN PACKS
PRINT RUNS B/WN 10-50 COPIES PER
NO PRICING ON QTY OF 10 OR LESS
HC1 Dale Murphy/50 10.00 25.00
HC2 Cal Ripken/50 30.00 60.00
HC3 Carl Yastrzemski/50 12.50 30.00
HC4 Don Mattingly/50 15.00 40.00
HC6 Andre Dawson/25 10.00 25.00
HC7 Roy Campanella Pants/25 15.00 40.00
HC8 George Brett/25 30.00 60.00
HC10 Marty Marion/50 6.00 15.00
HC11 Deion Sanders/50 10.00 25.00
HC12 Whitey Ford/25 15.00 40.00
HC14 Nolan Ryan/25 30.00 60.00
HC15 Steve Carlton/25 10.00 25.00
HC16 Robin Yount/50 10.00 25.00
HC17 Albert Pujols/50 15.00 40.00
HC18 Alex Rodriguez/50 15.00 40.00
HC19 Mike Piazza/50 12.50 30.00
HC20 Roger Clemens/50 12.50 30.00
HC21 Hideo Nomo/50 10.00 25.00
HC22 Mark Prior/50 10.00 25.00
HC23 Roger Maris/25 40.00 80.00
HC24 Greg Maddux/50 12.50 30.00
HC25 Mark Grace/50 10.00 25.00

2004 Diamond Kings Heritage Collection Signatures

RANDOM INSERTS IN PACKS
PRINT RUNS B/WN 1-16 COPIES PER
NO PRICING ON QTY OF 10 OR LESS
HC12 Whitey Ford/16 20.00 50.00

2004 Diamond Kings HOF Heroes

RANDOM INSERTS IN PACKS
PRINT RUNS B/WN 100-1000 COPIES PER
1 George Brett #45/1000 2.50 6.00
2 George Brett #45/500 4.00 10.00
3 George Brett #45/250 6.00 15.00
4 Mike Schmidt #46/1000 2.00 5.00
5 Mike Schmidt #46/250 5.00 12.00
6 Nolan Ryan #47/1000 4.00 10.00
7 Nolan Ryan #47/500 6.00 15.00
8 Nolan Ryan #47/250 10.00 25.00
9 Roberto Clemente #48/1000 3.00 8.00
10 Roberto Clemente #48/500 5.00 12.00
11 Roberto Clemente #48/250 8.00 20.00
12 Roberto Clemente #48/100 12.00 30.00
13 Carl Yastrzemski #49/1000 1.25 3.00
14 Robin Yount #50/1000 1.25 3.00
15 Whitey Ford #51/1000 .75 2.00
16 Duke Snider #52/1000 .75 2.00
17 Duke Snider #52/250 2.00 5.00
18 Carlton Fisk #53/1000 .75 2.00
19 Ozzie Smith #54/1000 1.50 4.00
20 Kirby Puckett #55/1000 1.25 3.00
21 Bobby Doerr #56/1000 .75 2.00
22 Frank Robinson #57/1000 .75 2.00
23 Ralph Kiner #58/1000 .75 2.00
24 Al Kaline #59/1000 1.25 3.00
25 Bob Feller #60/1000 .75 2.00
26 Yogi Berra #61/1000 1.25 3.00
27 Stan Musial #62/1000 2.00 5.00
28 Stan Musial #62/500 3.00 8.00
29 Stan Musial #62/250 5.00 12.00
30 Jim Palmer #63/1000 .75 2.00
31 Johnny Bench #64/1000 1.25 3.00
32 Steve Carlton #65/1000 .75 2.00
33 Gary Carter #66/1000 .75 2.00
34 Roy Campanella #67/1000 1.25 3.00
35 Roy Campanella #67/250 3.00 8.00

2004 Diamond Kings HOF Heroes Bats

RANDOM INSERTS IN PACKS
PRINT RUNS B/WN 1-25 COPIES PER
NO PRICING ON QTY OF 5 OR LESS
1 George Brett #45/25 20.00 50.00
2 George Brett #45/25 20.00 50.00
3 George Brett #45/25 20.00 50.00
4 Mike Schmidt #46/25 20.00 50.00
5 Mike Schmidt #46/25 20.00 50.00
6 Nolan Ryan #47/25 30.00 60.00
7 Nolan Ryan #47/25 30.00 60.00
8 Nolan Ryan #47/25 30.00 60.00
13 Carl Yastrzemski #49/25 20.00 50.00
14 Robin Yount #50/25 15.00 40.00
18 Carlton Fisk #53/25 15.00 40.00
19 Ozzie Smith #54/25 20.00 50.00
20 Kirby Puckett #55/25 15.00 40.00
21 Bobby Doerr #56/25 10.00 25.00
22 Frank Robinson #57/25 10.00 25.00
23 Ralph Kiner #58/25 10.00 25.00
24 Al Kaline #59/25 15.00 40.00
31 Johnny Bench #64/25 15.00 40.00
32 Steve Carlton #65/25 10.00 25.00
33 Gary Carter #66/25 10.00 25.00
34 Roy Campanella #67/25 15.00 40.00
35 Roy Campanella #67/25 15.00 40.00

2004 Diamond Kings HOF Heroes Combos

RANDOM INSERTS IN PACKS
PRINT RUNS B/WN 1-25 COPIES PER
NO PRICING ON QTY OF 10 OR LESS
1 George Brett #45 Bat-Jsy/25 15.00 40.00
2 George Brett #45 Bat-Jsy/25 15.00 40.00
3 George Brett #45 Bat-Jsy/25 15.00 40.00
4 Mike Schmidt #46 Bat-Jsy/25 30.00 60.00
5 Mike Schmidt #46 Bat-Jsy/25 30.00 60.00
6 Nolan Ryan #47 Bat-Jsy/25 40.00 80.00
7 Nolan Ryan #47 Bat-Jsy/25 40.00 80.00
8 Nolan Ryan #47 Bat-Jsy/25 40.00 80.00
13 C.Yastrzemski #49 Bat-Jsy/25 30.00 60.00
14 Robin Yount #50 Bat-Jsy/25 20.00 50.00
15 Whitey Ford #51 Jsy-Pants/25 12.00 30.00
18 Carlton Fisk #53 Bat-Jsy/25 20.00 50.00
19 Ozzie Smith #54 Bat-Jsy/25 30.00 60.00
20 Kirby Puckett #55 Bat-Jsy/25 20.00 50.00
21 Bobby Doerr #56 Bat-Jsy/25 12.50 30.00
23 Ralph Kiner #58 Bat-Bat/25 12.50 30.00
24 Al Kaline #59 Bat-Jsy/25 20.00 50.00
32 Steve Carlton #65 Bat-Jsy/25 12.50 30.00
33 Gary Carter #66 Bat-Jsy/25 12.50 30.00
34 R.Campy #67 Bat-Pants/25 20.00 50.00
35 R.Campy #67 Bat-Pants/25 20.00 50.00

2004 Diamond Kings HOF Heroes Jerseys

RANDOM INSERTS IN PACKS
PRINT RUNS B/WN 1-25 COPIES PER
NO PRICING ON QTY OF 10 OR LESS
1 George Brett #45/25 20.00 50.00
2 George Brett #45/25 20.00 50.00
3 George Brett #45/25 20.00 50.00
4 Mike Schmidt #46/25 20.00 50.00
5 Mike Schmidt #46/25 20.00 50.00
6 Nolan Ryan #47/25 30.00 60.00
7 Nolan Ryan #47/25 30.00 60.00
8 Nolan Ryan #47/25 30.00 60.00
13 Carl Yastrzemski #49/25 20.00 50.00
14 Robin Yount #50/25 15.00 40.00
15 Whitey Ford #51/25 15.00 40.00
18 Carlton Fisk #53/25 15.00 40.00
19 Ozzie Smith #54/25 20.00 50.00
20 Kirby Puckett #55/25 15.00 40.00
21 Bobby Doerr #56/25 10.00 25.00
24 Al Kaline #59/25 15.00 40.00
32 Steve Carlton #65/25 10.00 25.00
33 Gary Carter #66/25 10.00 25.00
34 Roy Campanella #67 Pants/25 15.00 40.00
35 Roy Campanella #67 Pants/25 15.00 40.00

2004 Diamond Kings HOF Heroes Signatures

RANDOM INSERTS IN PACKS
PRINT RUNS B/WN 4-32 COPIES PER
NO PRICING ON QTY OF 10 OR LESS
14 Robin Yount #50/19 50.00 100.00
15 Whitey Ford #51/16 20.00 50.00
22 Frank Robinson #57/20 20.00 50.00
25 Bob Feller #60/19 12.50 30.00
30 Jim Palmer #63/22 12.50 30.00
32 Steve Carlton #65/32 10.00 25.00

2004 Diamond Kings Recollection Autographs

PRINT RUNS B/WN 1-159 COPIES PER
NO PRICING ON QTY OF 14 OR LESS
6 Clint Barmes 03 DK Black/82 5.00 12.00
7 Clint Barmes 03 DK Blue/72 6.00 15.00
8 Carlos Beltran 02 DK/23 10.00 25.00
9 Carlos Beltran 03 DK/99 6.00 15.00
10 Adrian Beltre 02 DK/40 8.00 20.00
19 Chris Burke 03 DK/150 6.00 15.00
20 Marlon Byrd 02 DK/23 6.00 15.00
21 Marlon Byrd 03 DK/100 4.00 10.00
24 Kevin Cash 03 DK/103 4.00 10.00
25 Jose Cruz 85 DK/59 5.00 12.00
26 J.D. Durbin 03 DK/151 4.00 10.00
27 Jim Edmonds 03 DK/24 15.00 40.00
29 Bob Feller 03 DK HOF/18 15.00 40.00
32 Julio Franco 87 DK/25 10.00 25.00
33 Freddy Garcia 03 DK/50 8.00 20.00
34 Jay Gibbons 03 DK/100 4.00 10.00
39 Brendan Harris 03 DK/150 4.00 10.00
42 Ru.Hernandez 02 DK/100 4.00 10.00
43 Eric Hinske 03 DK/20 6.00 15.00
44 Tim Hudson 02 DK/25 15.00 40.00
45 Tim Hudson 03 DK/25 15.00 40.00
46 Aubrey Huff 03 DK/99 6.00 15.00
49 Jason Jennings 03 DK/50 5.00 12.00
50 Tommy John 88 DK Black/62 8.00 20.00
52 Howard Johnson 90 DK/52 5.00 12.00
54 Austin Kearns 02 DK/25 6.00 15.00
55 Austin Kearns 03 DK/25 6.00 15.00
59 P.Larrison 03 DK Black/74 8.00 20.00
60 Pr.Larrison 03 DK Blue/77 8.00 20.00
67 Dustin McGowan 03 DK/159 4.00 10.00
69 Melvin Mora 03 DK/101 6.00 15.00
71 Jack Morris 03 DK/60 8.00 20.00
72 Jack Morris 03 DK Her/19 15.00 40.00
74 Dale Murphy 03 DK Blue/47 12.50 30.00
77 Dale Murphy 03 DK Time/18 30.00 60.00
82 Magglio Ordonez 03 DK/25 15.00 40.00
85 Dave Parker 82 DK/20 10.00 25.00
86 Dave Parker 90 DK/18 15.00 40.00
88 Jorge Posada 02 DK/25 75.00 150.00
89 Mark Prior 03 DK/25 10.00 25.00
92 Mike Rivera 02 DK/24 6.00 15.00
97 Ivan Rodriguez 03 DK/22 30.00 60.00
100 Rodrigo Rosario 02 DK/50 5.00 12.00
105 Ron Santo 02 DK/29 15.00 40.00
106 Richie Sexson 02 DK/25 10.00 25.00
107 Richie Sexson 03 DK/25 10.00 25.00
109 Chris Snelling 02 DK/46 5.00 12.00
119 Shannon Stewart 02 DK/50 8.00 20.00
120 S.Stewart 03 DK Black/92 6.00 15.00
126 G.Thomas 82 DK Black/22 6.00 15.00
127 G.Thomas 82 DK Blue/20 6.00 15.00
128 Alan Trammell 02 DK/29 10.00 25.00
129 Alan Trammell 02 DK Her/25 10.00 25.00
130 Robin Ventura 03 DK/25 10.00 25.00
131 Jose Vidro 03 DK/25 6.00 15.00
132 Rickie Weeks 03 DK/52 12.50 30.00
133 Kevin Youkilis 03 DK/153 6.00 15.00

2004 Diamond Kings Team Timeline

STATED ODDS 1:29
TT1 D.Sanders A.Jones .75 2.00
TT2 R.Weeks R.Yount 1.25 3.00
TT3 D.Mattingly W.Ford 2.50 6.00
TT4 C.Jones D.Murphy 1.25 3.00
TT5 N.Garciaparra B.Doerr .75 2.00
TT6 M.Prior S.Sosa 1.25 3.00
TT7 H.Nomo K.Ishii 1.25 3.00
TT8 A.Dawson M.Grace .75 2.00
TT9 R.Clemens C.Yastrzemski 1.50 4.00
TT10 M.Mussina C.Ripken 4.00 10.00
TT11 S.Musial A.Pujols 2.00 5.00
TT12 J.Palmer M.Mussina .75 2.00
TT13 M.Marion S.Musial 2.00 5.00
TT14 G.Brett M.Sweeney 2.50 6.00
TT15 R.Clemens R.Maris 1.50 4.00
TT16 D.Snider S.Green .75 2.00
TT17 J.Thome M.Schmidt 2.00 5.00
TT18 N.Ryan A.Rodriguez 4.00 10.00
TT19 R.Campanella M.Piazza 1.25 3.00

2004 Diamond Kings Team Timeline Bats

RANDOM INSERTS IN PACKS
STATED PRINT RUN 25 SERIAL #'d SETS
SNIDER/GREEN PRINT 1 SERIAL #'d CARD
SNIDER/GREEN TOO SCARCE TO PRICE
TT1 D.Sanders/A.Jones 12.50 30.00
TT2 R.Weeks/R.Yount 20.00 50.00
TT3 D.Mattingly/W.Ford 50.00 100.00
TT4 C.Jones/D.Murphy 30.00 60.00
TT5 N.Garciaparra/B.Doerr 20.00 50.00
TT6 M.Prior/S.Sosa 20.00 50.00
TT7 H.Nomo/K.Ishii 30.00 60.00
TT8 A.Dawson/M.Grace 12.50 30.00
TT9 R.Clemens/C.Yastrzemski 30.00 60.00
TT10 M.Mussina/C.Ripken 60.00 120.00
TT11 S.Musial/A.Pujols 50.00 100.00
TT12 J.Palmer/M.Mussina 12.50 30.00
TT14 G.Brett/M.Sweeney 20.00 50.00
TT15 R.Clemens/R.Maris 25.00 60.00
TT17 J.Thome/M.Schmidt 30.00 60.00
TT18 N.Ryan/A.Rodriguez 40.00 80.00
TT19 R.Campanella/M.Piazza 30.00 60.00

2004 Diamond Kings Team Timeline Jerseys

PRINT RUNS B/WN 10-25 COPIES PER
NO PRICING ON QTY OF 10 OR LESS
PRIME PRINT RUN 1 SERIAL #'d SET
NO PRIME PRICING DUE TO SCARCITY
RANDOM INSERTS IN PACKS
R.WEEKS IS A BAT SWATCH
R.CAMPANELLA IS A PANTS SWATCH
TT1 D.Sanders/A.Jones/25 12.50 30.00
TT2 R.Weeks/R.Yount/25 20.00 50.00
TT3 D.Mattingly/W.Ford/25 15.00 40.00
TT4 C.Jones/D.Murphy/25 30.00 60.00
TT5 N.Garciaparra/B.Doerr/25 20.00 50.00
TT6 M.Prior/S.Sosa/25 20.00 50.00
TT7 H.Nomo/K.Ishii/25 30.00 60.00
TT8 A.Dawson/M.Grace/25 12.50 30.00
TT9 R.Clemens/C.Yastrzemski/25 30.00 60.00
TT10 M.Mussina/C.Ripken/25 60.00 120.00
TT14 G.Brett/M.Sweeney/25 20.00 50.00
TT15 R.Clemens/R.Maris/25 50.00 100.00
TT17 J.Thome/M.Schmidt/25 30.00 60.00
TT18 N.Ryan/A.Rodriguez/25 40.00 80.00
TT19 R.Campy Pants/M.Piazza/25 30.00 60.00

2004 Diamond Kings Timeline

STATED ODDS 1:92
T1 Roger Clemens 1.50 4.00
T2 Mark Grace .75 2.00
T3 Mike Mussina .75 2.00
T4 Mike Piazza 1.25 3.00
T5 Nolan Ryan 4.00 10.00
T6 Rickey Henderson 1.25 3.00

2004 Diamond Kings Timeline Bats

RANDOM INSERTS IN PACKS
STATED PRINT RUN 25 SERIAL #'d SETS
T1 Roger Clemens Sox-Yanks 20.00 50.00
T2 Mark Grace Cubs-D'backs 15.00 40.00
T3 Mike Mussina O's-Yanks 15.00 40.00
T4 Mike Piazza Dodgers-Mets 20.00 50.00
T5 Nolan Ryan Astros-Rangers 20.00 50.00
T6 Rickey Henderson A's-Dodgers 15.00 40.00

2004 Diamond Kings Timeline Jerseys

STATED PRINT RUN 25 SERIAL #'d SETS
PRIME PRINT RUN 1 SERIAL #'d SET
NO PRIME PRICING DUE TO SCARCITY
RANDOM INSERTS IN PACKS
T1 Roger Clemens Sox-Yanks 12.00 30.00
T2 Mark Grace Cubs-D'backs 20.00 50.00
T3 Mike Mussina O's-Yanks 20.00 50.00
T4 Mike Piazza Dodgers-Mets 30.00 60.00
T5 Nolan Ryan Astros-Rangers 50.00 100.00
T6 Rickey Henderson A's-Dodgers 20.00 50.00

2005 Diamond Kings

COMPLETE SET (450) 50.00 120.00
COMP.SERIES 1 SET (300) 30.00 80.00
COMP.SERIES 2 SET (150) 15.00 40.00
COMMON CARD .20 .50
COMMON RC .20 .50
COMMON RETIRED .20 .50
COMP.SET DOES NOT CONTAIN ANY SP's
1 Garret Anderson .20 .50
2 Vladimir Guerrero .30 .75
3 Jose Guillen .20 .50
4 Troy Glaus .20 .50
5 Tim Salmon .20 .50
6 Casey Kotchman .20 .50
7 Chone Figgins .20 .50
8 Robb Quinlan .20 .50
9 Francisco Rodriguez .30 .75
10 Troy Percival .20 .50
11 Randy Johnson .50 1.25
12 Brandon Webb .30 .75
13 Richie Sexson .20 .50
14 Shea Hillenbrand .20 .50
15 Chad Tracy .20 .50
16 Alex Cintron .20 .50
17 Luis Gonzalez .20 .50
18 Rafael Furcal .20 .50
19 Andruw Jones .20 .50
20 Marcus Giles .20 .50
21 John Smoltz .50 1.25
22 Adam LaRoche .20 .50
23 Russ Ortiz .20 .50
24 J.D. Drew .20 .50
25 Chipper Jones .50 1.25
26 Nick Green .20 .50
27 Rafael Palmeiro O's .30 .75
28 Miguel Tejada .30 .75
29 Javy Lopez .20 .50
30 Luis Matos .20 .50
31 Larry Bigbie .20 .50
32 Rodrigo Lopez .20 .50
33 Brian Roberts .20 .50
34 Melvin Mora .20 .50
35 Adam Loewen .20 .50
36 Manny Ramirez .50 1.25
37 Jason Varitek .50 1.25
38 Trot Nixon .20 .50
39 Curt Schilling .30 .75
40 Keith Foulke .20 .50
41 Pedro Martinez .30 .75
42 Johnny Damon .30 .75
43 Kevin Youkilis .20 .50
44 Orlando Cabrera Sox .20 .50
45 Abe Alvarez .20 .50
46 David Ortiz .50 1.25
47 Kerry Wood .20 .50
48 Mark Prior .30 .75
49 Aramis Ramirez .20 .50
50 Greg Maddux Cubs .60 1.50
51 Carlos Zambrano .30 .75
52 Derrek Lee .20 .50
53 Corey Patterson .20 .50
54 Moises Alou .20 .50
55 Matt Clement .20 .50
56 Sammy Sosa .50 1.25
57 Nomar Garciaparra Cubs .30 .75
58 Todd Walker .20 .50
59 Angel Guzman .20 .50
60 Magglio Ordonez .30 .75
61 Carlos Lee .20 .50
62 Joe Crede .20 .50
63 Paul Konerko .30 .75
64 Shingo Takatsu .20 .50
65 Frank Thomas .50 1.25
66 Freddy Garcia .20 .50
67 Aaron Rowand .20 .50
68 Jose Contreras .20 .50
69 Adam Dunn .30 .75
70 Austin Kearns .20 .50
71 Barry Larkin .30 .75
72 Ken Griffey Jr. 1.00 2.50
73 Ryan Wagner .20 .50
74 Sean Casey .20 .50
75 Danny Graves .20 .50
76 C.C. Sabathia .30 .75
77 Jody Gerut .20 .50
78 Omar Vizquel .30 .75
79 Victor Martinez .30 .75
80 Matt Lawton .20 .50
81 Jake Westbrook .20 .50
82 Kazuhito Tadano .20 .50
83 Travis Hafner .20 .50
84 Todd Helton .30 .75
85 Preston Wilson .20 .50
86 Matt Holliday .50 1.25
87 Jeromy Burnitz .20 .50
88 Vinny Castilla .20 .50
89 Jeremy Bonderman .20 .50
90 Ivan Rodriguez Tigers .30 .75
91 Carlos Guillen .20 .50
92 Brandon Inge .20 .50
93 Rondell White .20 .50
94 Dontrelle Willis .20 .50
95 Miguel Cabrera .50 1.25
96 Josh Beckett .20 .50
97 Mike Lowell .20 .50
98 Luis Castillo .20 .50
99 Juan Pierre .20 .50
100 Paul LoDuca Marlins .20 .50
101 Guillermo Mota .20 .50
102 Craig Biggio .30 .75
103 Lance Berkman .30 .75
104 Roy Oswalt .30 .75
105 Roger Clemens Astros .60 1.50
106 Jeff Kent .20 .50
107 Morgan Ensberg .20 .50
108 Jeff Bagwell .30 .75
109 Carlos Beltran Astros .30 .75
110 Angel Berroa .20 .50
111 Mike Sweeney .20 .50
112 Jeremy Affeldt .20 .50
113 Zack Greinke .60 1.50
114 Juan Gonzalez .20 .50
115 Andres Blanco .20 .50
116 Shawn Green .20 .50
117 Milton Bradley .20 .50
118 Adrian Beltre .50 1.25
119 Hideo Nomo .50 1.25
120 Steve Finley .20 .50
121 Eric Gagne .20 .50
122 Brad Penny Dgr .20 .50
123 Scott Podsednik .20 .50
124 Ben Sheets .20 .50
125 Lyle Overbay .20 .50
126 Junior Spivey .20 .50
127 Bill Hall .20 .50
128 Rickie Weeks .20 .50
129 Jacque Jones .20 .50
130 Torii Hunter .20 .50
131 Johan Santana .30 .75
132 Lew Ford .20 .50
133 Joe Mauer .40 1.00
134 Justin Morneau .30 .75
135 Jason Kubel .20 .50
136 Jose Vidro .20 .50
137 Chad Cordero .20 .50
138 Brad Wilkerson .20 .50
139 Nick Johnson .20 .50
140 Livan Hernandez .20 .50
141 Tom Glavine .30 .75
142 Jae Weong Seo .20 .50
143 Jose Reyes .30 .75
144 Al Leiter .20 .50
145 Mike Piazza .50 1.25
146 Kazuo Matsui .20 .50
147 Richard Hidalgo Mets .20 .50
148 David Wright .40 1.00
149 Mariano Rivera .60 1.50
150 Mike Mussina .30 .75
151 Alex Rodriguez .60 1.50
152 Derek Jeter 1.25 3.00
153 Jorge Posada .30 .75
154 Jason Giambi .20 .50
155 Gary Sheffield .20 .50
156 Bubba Crosby .20 .50
157 Javier Vazquez .20 .50
158 Kevin Brown .20 .50
159 Tom Gordon .20 .50
160 Esteban Loaiza Yanks .20 .50
161 Hideki Matsui .75 2.00
162 Eric Chavez .20 .50
163 Mark Mulder .20 .50
164 Barry Zito .30 .75
165 Tim Hudson .30 .75
166 Jermaine Dye .20 .50
167 Octavio Dotel .20 .50
168 Bobby Crosby .20 .50
169 Mark Kotsay .20 .50
170 Scott Hatteberg .20 .50
171 Jim Thome Phils .30 .75
172 Bobby Abreu .20 .50
173 Kevin Millwood .20 .50
174 Mike Lieberthal .20 .50
175 Jimmy Rollins .30 .75
176 Chase Utley .30 .75
177 Randy Wolf .20 .50
178 Craig Wilson .20 .50
179 Jason Kendall .20 .50
180 Jack Wilson .20 .50
181 Jose Castillo .20 .50
182 Rob Mackowiak .20 .50
183 Oliver Perez .20 .50
184 Jason Bay .20 .50
185 Sean Burroughs .20 .50
186 Jay Payton .20 .50
187 Brian Giles .20 .50
188 Akinori Otsuka .20 .50
189 Jake Peavy .20 .50
190 Phil Nevin .20 .50
191 Mark Loretta .20 .50
192 Khalil Greene .20 .50
193 Trevor Hoffman .30 .75
194 Freddy Guzman .20 .50
195 Jerome Williams .20 .50
196 Jason Schmidt .20 .50
197 Todd Linden .20 .50
198 Merkin Valdez .20 .50
199 J.T. Snow .20 .50
200 A.J. Pierzynski .20 .50
201 Edgar Martinez .30 .75
202 Ichiro Suzuki .60 1.50
203 Raul Ibanez .30 .75
204 Bret Boone .20 .50
205 Shigetoshi Hasegawa .20 .50
206 Miguel Olivo .20 .50
207 Bucky Jacobsen .20 .50
208 Jamie Moyer .20 .50
209 Jim Edmonds .30 .75
210 Scott Rolen .30 .75
211 Edgar Renteria .20 .50
212 Dan Haren .20 .50
213 Matt Morris .20 .50
214 Albert Pujols .60 1.50
215 Larry Walker Cards .30 .75
216 Jason Isringhausen .20 .50
217 Chris Carpenter .30 .75
218 Jason Marquis .20 .50
219 Jeff Suppan .20 .50
220 Aubrey Huff .20 .50
221 Carl Crawford .30 .75
222 Rocco Baldelli .20 .50
223 Fred McGriff .30 .75
224 Dewon Brazelton .20 .50
225 B.J. Upton .30 .75
226 Joey Gathright .20 .50
227 Scott Kazmir .50 1.25
228 Hank Blalock .20 .50
229 Mark Teixeira .30 .75
230 Michael Young .20 .50
231 Adrian Gonzalez .40 1.00
232 Laynce Nix .20 .50
233 Alfonso Soriano Rgr .30 .75
234 Rafael Palmeiro Rgr .30 .75
235 Kevin Mench .20 .50
236 David Dellucci .20 .50
237 Francisco Cordero .20 .50
238 Kenny Rogers .20 .50
239 Roy Halladay .30 .75
240 Carlos Delgado .20 .50
241 Alexis Rios .20 .50
242 Vernon Wells .20 .50
243 Yadier Molina 2.00 5.00
244 Rene Rivera .20 .50
245 Logan Kensing .20 .50
246 Gavin Floyd .20 .50
247 Russ Adams .20 .50
248 Dioner Navarro .20 .50
249 Ryan Howard .40 1.00
250 Ryan Church .20 .50
251 Jeff Francis .20 .50
252 John VanBenschoten .20 .50
253 Yhency Brazoban .20 .50
254 Dave Krynzel .20 .50
255 Victor Diaz .20 .50
256 Jairo Garcia .20 .50
257 Scott Proctor .20 .50
258 Shawn Hill .20 .50
259 Jeff Baker .20 .50
260 Matt Peterson .20 .50
261 Josh Kroeger .20 .50
262 Grady Sizemore .30 .75
263 Clint Nageotte .20 .50
264 Andy Green .20 .50
265 Justin Verlander RC 4.00 10.00
266 Jim Thome Indians .30 .75
267 Larry Walker Rockies .30 .75
268 Ivan Rodriguez Rgr .30 .75
269 Brad Penny Marlins .20 .50
270 Carlos Beltran Royals .30 .75
271 Paul LoDuca Dgr .20 .50
272 Orlando Cabrera Expos .20 .50
273 Nomar Garciaparra Sox .30 .75
274 Esteban Loaiza Sox .20 .50
275 Richard Hidalgo Astros .20 .50
276 John Olerud .20 .50
277 Greg Maddux Braves .60 1.50
278 Roger Clemens Yanks .60 1.50
279 Alfonso Soriano Yanks .30 .75
280 Dale Murphy .50 1.25
281 Cal Ripken 1.50 4.00
282 Dwight Evans .30 .75
283 Ron Santo .30 .75
284 Andre Dawson .30 .75
285 Harold Baines .30 .75
286 Jack Morris .30 .75
287 Kirk Gibson .20 .50
288 Bo Jackson .50 1.25
289 Orel Hershiser .20 .50
290 Maury Wills .20 .50
291 Tony Oliva .20 .50
292 Darryl Strawberry .20 .50
293 Roger Maris .50 1.25
294 Don Mattingly 1.00 2.50
295 Rickey Henderson .50 1.25
296 Dave Stewart .20 .50
297 Dave Parker .20 .50
298 Steve Garvey .20 .50

299 Matt Williams .20 .50
300 Keith Hernandez .20 .50
301 John Lackey .30 .75
302 Vladimir Guerrero Angels .30 .75
303 Garret Anderson .20 .50
304 Dallas McPherson .20 .50
305 Orlando Cabrera .20 .50
306 Steve Finley Angels .20 .50
307 Luis Gonzalez .20 .50
308 Randy Johnson D'backs .50 1.25
309 Scott Hairston .20 .50
310 Shawn Green .20 .50
311 Troy Glaus .20 .50
312 Javier Vazquez .20 .50
313 Russ Ortiz .20 .50
314 Chipper Jones .50 1.25
315 Johnny Estrada .20 .50
316 Andruw Jones .20 .50
317 Tim Hudson .30 .75
318 Danny Kolb .20 .50
319 Jay Gibbons .20 .50
320 Melvin Mora .20 .50
321 Rafael Palmeiro O's .30 .75
322 Val Majewski .20 .50
323 David Ortiz .50 1.25
324 Manny Ramirez .50 1.25
325 Edgar Renteria .20 .50
326 Matt Clement .20 .50
327 Curt Schilling Sox .30 .75
328 Sammy Sosa Cubs .50 1.25
329 Mark Prior .30 .75
330 Greg Maddux .60 1.50
331 Nomar Garciaparra .30 .75
332 Frank Thomas .50 1.25
333 Mark Buehrle .30 .75
334 Jermaine Dye .20 .50
335 Scott Podsednik .20 .50
336 Sean Casey .20 .50
337 Adam Dunn .30 .75
338 Ken Griffey Jr. 1.00 2.50
339 Travis Hafner .20 .50
340 Victor Martinez .30 .75
341 Cliff Lee .30 .75
342 Todd Helton .30 .75
343 Preston Wilson .20 .50
344 Ivan Rodriguez Tigers .30 .75
345 Dmitri Young .20 .50
346 Nate Robertson .20 .50
347 Miguel Cabrera .50 1.25
348 Jeff Bagwell .30 .75
349 Andy Pettitte .30 .75
350 Roger Clemens Astros .60 1.50
351 Ken Harvey .20 .50
352 Denny Bautista .20 .50
353 Hideo Nomo .50 1.25
354 Kazuhisa Ishii .20 .50
355 Edwin Jackson .20 .50
356 J.D. Drew .20 .50
357 Jeff Kent .20 .50
358 Geoff Jenkins .20 .50
359 Carlos Lee .20 .50
360 Shannon Stewart .20 .50
361 Joe Nathan .20 .50
362 Johan Santana .30 .75
363 Mike Piazza Mets .50 1.25
364 Kazuo Matsui .20 .50
365 Carlos Beltran .30 .75
366 Pedro Martinez .30 .75
367 Ambiorix Concepcion RC .20 .50
368 Hideki Matsui .75 2.00
369 Bernie Williams .30 .75
370 Gary Sheffield Yanks .20 .50
371 Randy Johnson Yanks .50 1.25
372 Jaret Wright .20 .50
373 Carl Pavano .20 .50
374 Derek Jeter 1.25 3.00
375 Alex Rodriguez .60 1.50
376 Eric Byrnes .20 .50
377 Rich Harden .20 .50
378 Mark Mulder A's .20 .50
379 Nick Swisher .30 .75
380 Eric Chavez .20 .50
381 Jason Kendall .20 .50
382 Marlon Byrd .20 .50
383 Pat Burrell .20 .50
384 Brett Myers .20 .50
385 Jim Thome .30 .75
386 Jason Bay .20 .50
387 Jake Peavy .20 .50
388 Moises Alou .20 .50
389 Omar Vizquel .30 .75
390 Travis Blackley .20 .50
391 Jose Lopez .20 .50
392 Jeremy Reed .20 .50
393 Adrian Beltre .50 1.25
394 Richie Sexson .20 .50
395 Wladimir Balentien RC .30 .75
396 Ichiro Suzuki .60 1.50
397 Albert Pujols .60 1.50
398 Scott Rolen Cards .30 .75
399 Mark Mulder Cards .20 .50
400 David Eckstein .20 .50
401 Delmon Young .50 1.25
402 Aubrey Huff .20 .50
403 Alfonso Soriano .30 .75
404 Hank Blalock .20 .50
405 Richard Hidalgo .20 .50
406 Vernon Wells .20 .50
407 Orlando Hudson .20 .50
408 Alexis Rios .20 .50
409 Shea Hillenbrand .20 .50
410 Jose Guillen .20 .50
411 Vinny Castilla .20 .50
412 Jose Vidro .20 .50
413 Nick Johnson .20 .50
414 Livan Hernandez .20 .50
415 Miguel Tejada .30 .75
416 Gary Sheffield Braves .20 .50
417 Curt Schilling D'backs .30 .75
418 Rafael Palmeiro Rgr .30 .75
419 Scott Rolen Phils .30 .75
420 Aramis Ramirez .20 .50
421 Vladimir Guerrero Expos .30 .75
422 Steve Finley D'backs .20 .50
423 Roger Clemens Sox .60 1.50
424 Mike Piazza Dgr .50 1.25
425 Ivan Rodriguez M's .30 .75
426 David Justice .20 .50
427 Mark Grace .30 .75
428 Alan Trammell .30 .75
429 Bert Blyleven .30 .75
430 Dwight Gooden .20 .50
431 Deion Sanders .30 .75
432 Joe Torre MG .30 .75
433 Jose Canseco .30 .75
434 Tony Gwynn .60 1.50
435 Will Clark .30 .75
436 Marty Marion .20 .50
437 Nolan Ryan 1.50 4.00
438 Billy Martin .30 .75
439 Carlos Delgado .20 .50
440 Magglio Ordonez .30 .75
441 Sammy Sosa O's .50 1.25
442 Keiichi Yabu RC .20 .50
443 Yuniesky Betancourt RC .75 2.00
444 Jeff Niemann RC .50 1.25
445 Brandon McCarthy RC .30 .75
446 Phil Humber RC .50 1.25
447 Tadahito Iguchi RC .30 .75
448 Cal Ripken 1.50 4.00
449 Ryne Sandberg 1.00 2.50
450 Willie Mays 1.00 2.50

2005 Diamond Kings B/W

*B/W: .6X TO 1.5X BASIC
SER.2 STATED ODDS 1:2

2005 Diamond Kings Bronze

*BRONZE 1-300: 2X TO 5X BASIC
*BRONZE 1-300: 1.25X TO 3X BASIC RC's
1-300 INSERT ODDS 10 PER SER.1 BOX
1-300 PRINT RUN 100 SERIAL #'d SETS
*BRONZE 301-450: 2.5X TO 6X BASIC
*BRONZE 301-450: 1.5X TO 4X BASIC RC's
301-450 INSERT ODDS 12 PER SER.2 BOX
301-450 PRINT RUN 50 SERIAL #'d SETS

2005 Diamond Kings Bronze B/W

*BRONZE B/W: 2X TO 5X BASIC
OVERALL INSERT ODDS 12 PER SER.2 BOX
STATED PRINT RUN 100 SERIAL #'d SETS

2005 Diamond Kings Gold

*GOLD 1-300: 4X TO 10X BASIC
1-300 INSERT ODDS 10 PER SER.1 BOX
1-300 PRINT RUN 25 SERIAL #'d SETS
NO PRICING ON CARD 265 VERLANDER
301-450 INSERT ODDS 12 PER SER.2 BOX
301-450 PRINT RUN 10 SERIAL #'d SETS
301-450 NO PRICING DUE TO SCARCITY

2005 Diamond Kings Gold B/W

*GOLD B/W: 4X TO 10X BASIC
OVERALL INSERT ODDS 12 PER SER.2 BOX
STATED PRINT RUN 25 SERIAL #'d SETS

2005 Diamond Kings Silver

*SILVER 1-300: 2.5X TO 6X BASIC
*SILVER 1-300: 1.5X TO 4X BASIC RC's
1-300 INSERT ODDS 10 PER SER.1 BOX
1-300 PRINT RUN 50 SERIAL #'d SETS
*SILVER: 4X TO 10X BASIC
301-450 INSERT ODDS 12 PER SER.2 BOX
301-450 PRINT RUN 25 SERIAL #'d SETS
301-450 NO RC PRICING DUE TO SCARCITY

2005 Diamond Kings Silver B/W

*SILVER B/W: 2.5X TO 6X BASIC
OVERALL INSERT ODDS 12 PER SER.2 BOX
STATED PRINT RUN 50 SERIAL #'d SETS

2005 Diamond Kings Framed Black

*BLACK: 5X TO 12X BASIC
STATED PRINT RUN 25 SERIAL #'d SETS
NO RC PRICING DUE TO SCARCITY
PLATINUM PRINT RUN 1 SERIAL #'d SET
NO PLAT.PRICING DUE TO SCARCITY
OVERALL INSERT ODDS 10 PER SER.1 BOX
OVERALL INSERT ODDS 12 PER SER.2 BOX

2005 Diamond Kings Framed Black B/W

*BLACK: 5X TO 12X BASIC
STATED PRINT RUN 25 SERIAL #'d SETS
PLATINUM PRINT RUN 1 SERIAL #'d SET
NO PLAT.PRICING DUE TO SCARCITY
OVERALL INSERT ODDS 12 PER SER.2 BOX

2005 Diamond Kings Framed Blue

*BLUE: 2.5X TO 6X BASIC
*BLUE: 1.5X TO 4X BASIC RC's
STATED PRINT RUN 100 SERIAL #'d SETS
PLATINUM PRINT RUN 1 SERIAL #'d SET
NO PLAT.PRICING DUE TO SCARCITY
1-300 INSERT ODDS 10 PER SER.1 BOX
301-450 INSERT ODDS 12 PER SER.2 BOX

2005 Diamond Kings Framed Blue B/W

*BLUE B/W: 2.5X TO 6X BASIC
STATED PRINT RUN 100 SERIAL #'d SETS
PLATINUM PRINT RUN 1 SERIAL #'d SET
NO PLAT.PRICING DUE TO SCARCITY
OVERALL INSERT ODDS 12 PER SER.2 BOX

2005 Diamond Kings Framed Green

*GREEN: 3X TO 8X BASIC
*GREEN: 2X TO 5X BASIC RC's
STATED PRINT RUN 50 SERIAL #'d SETS
PLATINUM PRINT RUN 1 SERIAL #'d SET
NO PLAT.PRICING DUE TO SCARCITY
1-300 INSERT ODDS 10 PER SER.1 BOX
301-450 INSERT ODDS 12 PER SER.2 BOX

2005 Diamond Kings Framed Green B/W

*GREEN B/W: 3X TO 8X BASIC
STATED PRINT RUN 50 SERIAL #'d SETS
PLATINUM PRINT RUN 1 SERIAL #'d SET
NO PLAT.PRICING DUE TO SCARCITY
OVERALL INSERT ODDS 12 PER SER.2 BOX

2005 Diamond Kings Framed Red

*RED: 1X TO 2.5X BASIC
*RED: .6X TO 1.5X BASIC RC's
1-300 SER.1 STATED ODDS 1:3
301-450 SER.2 STATED ODDS 1:3
PLAT.1-300: INSERTS 10 PER SER.1 BOX
PLAT.301-450: INSERTS 12 PER SER.2 BOX
PLATINUM PRINT RUN 1 SERIAL #'d SET
NO PLAT.PRICING DUE TO SCARCITY

2005 Diamond Kings Framed Red B/W

*RED: 1X TO 2.5X BASIC
OVERALL FRAMED RED ODDS 1:3
PLAT: INSERT ODDS 12 PER SER.2 BOX
PLATINUM PRINT RUN 1 SERIAL #'d SET
NO PLAT.PRICING DUE TO SCARCITY

2005 Diamond Kings Materials Bronze

OVERALL AU-GU ODDS 1:6
PRINT RUNS B/WN 10-200 COPIES PER
NO PRICING ON QTY OF 10 OR LESS
1 G.Anderson Bat-Jsy/200 2.50 6.00
2 Vlad Guerrero Bat-Jsy/200 4.00 10.00
4 Troy Glaus Bat-Jsy/200 2.50 6.00
5 Tim Salmon Bat-Jsy/200 3.00 8.00
7 Chone Figgins Bat-Jsy/200 2.50 6.00
10 Troy Percival Jsy-Jsy/200 2.50 6.00
12 B.Webb Bat-Pants/200 2.50 6.00
13 Richie Sexson Bat-Bat/200 2.50 6.00
17 Luis Gonzalez Jsy-Jsy/200 2.50 6.00
18 Rafael Furcal Bat-Jsy/200 2.50 6.00
19 Andruw Jones Bat-Jsy/200 3.00 8.00
21 John Smoltz Jsy-Jsy/200 3.00 8.00
24 J.D. Drew Bat-Bat/200 2.50 6.00
25 Chipper Jones Bat-Jsy/200 4.00 10.00
27 R.Palmeiro O's Bat-Jsy/200 3.00 8.00
28 Miguel Tejada Bat-Jsy/200 2.50 6.00
29 Javy Lopez Bat-Jsy/25 5.00 12.00
30 Luis Matos Jsy-Jsy/100 3.00 8.00
31 Larry Bigbie Jsy-Jsy/200 2.50 6.00
32 Rodrigo Lopez Jsy-Jsy/200 2.50 6.00
34 Melvin Mora Bat-Jsy/200 2.50 6.00
36 Manny Ramirez Bat-Jsy/200 3.00 8.00
38 Trot Nixon Bat-Bat/200 3.00 8.00
39 Curt Schilling Bat-Jsy/200 3.00 8.00
41 Pedro Martinez Bat-Jsy/200 3.00 8.00
42 Johnny Damon Bat-Bat/200 3.00 8.00
43 Kevin Youkilis Bat-Bat/200 2.50 6.00
46 David Ortiz Bat-Jsy/200 4.00 10.00
47 Kerry Wood Jsy-Pants/200 2.50 6.00
48 Mark Prior Bat-Jsy/200 3.00 8.00
49 Aramis Ramirez Bat-Jsy/200 2.50 6.00
50 G.Madd Cubs Bat-Jsy/100 6.00 15.00
51 C.Zambrano Jsy-Jsy/200 2.50 6.00
52 Derrek Lee Bat-Bat/200 3.00 8.00
54 Moises Alou Bat-Bat/200 2.50 6.00
56 Sammy Sosa Bat-Jsy/200 4.00 10.00
57 N.G'parra Cubs Bat-Bat/200 4.00 10.00
60 M.Ordonez Bat-Jsy/200 2.50 6.00
61 Carlos Lee Bat-Jsy/200 2.50 6.00
62 Joe Crede Bat-Bat/200 2.50 6.00
65 Frank Thomas Bat-Jsy/200 4.00 10.00
69 Adam Dunn Bat-Jsy/200 2.50 6.00
70 Austin Kearns Bat-Bat/200 2.50 6.00
74 Sean Casey Jsy-Pants/200 2.50 6.00
76 C.C. Sabathia Jsy-Jsy/200 2.50 6.00
77 Jody Gerut Bat-Jsy/200 2.50 6.00
78 Omar Vizquel Bat-Jsy/200 3.00 8.00
79 Victor Martinez Bat-Jsy/200 2.50 6.00
80 Matt Lawton Bat-Bat/200 2.50 6.00
84 Todd Helton Bat-Jsy/200 3.00 8.00
85 Preston Wilson Bat-Jsy/200 2.50 6.00
90 I.Rod Tigers Bat-Jsy/200 3.00 8.00
92 Brandon Inge Bat-Jsy/200 2.50 6.00
94 Dontrelle Willis Jsy-Jsy/200 2.50 6.00
95 Miguel Cabrera Bat-Jsy/200 3.00 8.00
96 Josh Beckett Bat-Bat/100 3.00 8.00
97 Mike Lowell Bat-Jsy/100 3.00 8.00
98 Luis Castillo Bat-Bat/200 2.50 6.00
99 Juan Pierre Bat-Bat/200 2.50 6.00
100 P.LoDuca M's Bat-Bat/200 2.50 6.00
102 Craig Biggio Bat-Pants/200 3.00 8.00
103 L.Berkman Bat-Jsy/200 2.50 6.00
104 Roy Oswalt Jsy-Jsy/200 2.50 6.00
105 R.Clem Astros Bat-Jsy/200 5.00 12.00
106 Jeff Kent Bat-Jsy/100 3.00 8.00
108 Jeff Bagwell Bat-Jsy/200 3.00 8.00
109 C.Belt Astros Bat-Jsy/200 2.50 6.00
110 Angel Berroa Bat-Bat/200 2.50 6.00
111 Mike Sweeney Bat-Jsy/200 2.50 6.00
112 J.Affeldt Pants-Pants/200 2.50 6.00
114 Juan Gonzalez Bat-Jsy/200 2.50 6.00
116 Shawn Green Bat-Jsy/200 2.50 6.00
118 Adrian Beltre Bat-Jsy/200 2.50 6.00
119 Hideo Nomo Bat-Jsy/200 4.00 10.00
123 S.Podsednik Jsy-Jsy/200 2.50 6.00
124 Ben Sheets Bat-Pants/200 2.50 6.00
125 Lyle Overbay Jsy-Jsy/200 2.50 6.00
126 Junior Spivey Jsy-Jsy/200 2.50 6.00
127 Bill Hall Bat-Jsy/200 2.50 6.00
129 Jacque Jones Bat-Jsy/200 2.50 6.00
130 Torii Hunter Bat-Jsy/200 2.50 6.00
131 Johan Santana Jsy-Jsy/200 4.00 10.00
132 Lew Ford Bat-Jsy/200 2.50 6.00
136 Jose Vidro Bat-Jsy/200 2.50 6.00
138 Brad Wilkerson Bat-Bat/100 3.00 8.00
139 Nick Johnson Bat-Bat/100 3.00 8.00
140 L.Hernandez Jsy-Jsy/25 5.00 12.00
141 Tom Glavine Bat-Bat/200 3.00 8.00
143 Jose Reyes Bat-Jsy/200 2.50 6.00
144 Al Leiter Jsy-Jsy/200 2.50 6.00
145 Mike Piazza Jsy-Jsy/100 5.00 12.00
146 Kazuo Matsui Bat-Jsy/200 2.50 6.00
147 R.Hidalgo Mets Bat-Bat/200 2.50 6.00
149 Mariano Rivera Jsy-Jsy/100 5.00 12.00
150 Mike Mussina Bat-Jsy/200 3.00 8.00
153 Jorge Posada Bat-Jsy/200 3.00 8.00
154 Jason Giambi Bat-Jsy/200 2.50 6.00
155 Gary Sheffield Bat-Jsy/200 2.50 6.00
158 Kevin Brown Bat-Bat/100 3.00 8.00
160 E.Loaiza Yanks Bat-Bat/100 3.00 8.00
161 H.Matsui Jsy-Pants/200 6.00 15.00
162 Eric Chavez Bat-Jsy/200 2.50 6.00
163 Mark Mulder Bat-Bat/25 5.00 12.00
164 Barry Zito Bat-Jsy/200 2.50 6.00
165 Tim Hudson Bat-Jsy/200 2.50 6.00
166 Jermaine Dye Bat-Jsy/200 2.50 6.00
168 Bobby Crosby Jsy-Jsy/200 2.50 6.00
171 J.Thome Phils Bat-Jsy/200 3.00 8.00
172 Bobby Abreu Jsy-Jsy/200 2.50 6.00
173 Kevin Millwood Jsy-Jsy/200 2.50 6.00
178 Craig Wilson Bat-Jsy/200 2.50 6.00
180 Jack Wilson Bat-Bat/200 2.50 6.00
181 Jose Castillo Bat-Bat/200 2.50 6.00
184 Jason Bay Bat-Jsy/200 2.50 6.00
185 S.Burroughs Bat-Jsy/200 2.50 6.00
187 Brian Giles Bat-Bat/100 3.00 8.00
193 Trevor Hoffman Jsy-Jsy/200 2.50 6.00
199 J.T. Snow Jsy-Jsy/25 5.00 12.00
200 A.J. Pierzynski Jsy-Jsy/100 3.00 8.00
201 Edgar Martinez Bat-Bat/200 3.00 8.00
204 Bret Boone Jsy-Jsy/200 2.50 6.00
208 Jamie Moyer Jsy-Jsy/50 4.00 10.00
209 Jim Edmonds Bat-Jsy/200 2.50 6.00
210 Scott Rolen Bat-Jsy/200 3.00 8.00
211 Edgar Renteria Bat-Jsy/200 2.50 6.00
212 Dan Haren Bat-Jsy/100 3.00 8.00
213 Matt Morris Jsy-Jsy/100 3.00 8.00
214 Albert Pujols Jsy-Jsy/200 8.00 20.00
215 L.Walker Cards Bat-Bat/200 3.00 8.00
220 Aubrey Huff Bat-Bat/100 3.00 8.00
221 Carl Crawford Jsy-Jsy/200 2.50 6.00
222 Rocco Baldelli Bat-Jsy/200 2.50 6.00
223 Fred McGriff Bat-Jsy/200 3.00 8.00
224 D.Brazelton Jsy-Jsy/200 2.50 6.00
225 B.J. Upton Bat-Bat/200 3.00 8.00
226 Joey Gathright Bat-Jsy/200 2.50 6.00
228 Hank Blalock Bat-Jsy/100 3.00 8.00
229 Mark Teixeira Bat-Jsy/200 3.00 8.00
230 Michael Young Bat-Jsy/200 2.50 6.00
232 Laynce Nix Bat-Jsy/200 2.50 6.00
233 A.Soriano Rgr Bat-Jsy/200 2.50 6.00
234 R.Palmeiro Rgr Bat-Jsy/200 3.00 8.00
235 Kevin Mench Bat-Jsy/200 2.50 6.00
236 David Dellucci Jsy-Jsy/200 4.00 10.00
237 F.Cordero Jsy-Jsy/200 2.50 6.00
239 Roy Halladay Jsy-Jsy/200 2.50 6.00
240 Carlos Delgado Bat-Jsy/200 2.50 6.00
242 Vernon Wells Bat-Jsy/200 2.50 6.00
267 L.Walk Rockies Jsy-Jsy/200 2.50 6.00
268 I.Rodriguez Rgr Jsy-Jsy/200 3.00 8.00
269 B.Penny M's Bat-Jsy/200 2.50 6.00
270 C.Belt Royals Bat-Jsy/200 2.50 6.00
271 P.LoDuca Dgr Bat-Jsy/200 2.50 6.00
273 N.G'parra Sox Bat-Bat/100 5.00 12.00
274 E.Loaiza Sox Bat-Bat/100 3.00 8.00
275 R.Hidal Astros Jkt-Pants/200 2.50 6.00
276 John Olerud Bat-Jsy/200 2.50 6.00
277 G.Madd Braves Jsy-Jsy/200 5.00 12.00
278 R.Clem Yanks Bat-Jsy/200 5.00 12.00
279 A.Sor Yanks Bat-Jsy/200 2.50 6.00
280 Dale Murphy Jsy-Jsy/200 4.00 10.00
281 Cal Ripken Bat-Jsy/200 12.50 30.00
282 Dwight Evans Bat-Jsy/200 4.00 10.00
283 Ron Santo Bat-Bat/200 4.00 10.00
284 Andre Dawson Bat-Jsy/100 4.00 10.00
285 Harold Baines Bat-Jsy/200 3.00 8.00
286 Jack Morris Jsy-Jsy/100 4.00 10.00
287 Kirk Gibson Bat-Jsy/200 3.00 8.00
288 Bo Jackson Bat-Jsy/200 5.00 12.00
289 Orel Hershiser Jsy-Jsy/50 5.00 12.00
291 Tony Oliva Bat-Jsy/200 3.00 8.00
292 D.Strawberry Bat-Jsy/100 4.00 10.00
293 Roger Maris Bat-Jsy/100 20.00 50.00
294 Don Mattingly Bat-Jsy/100 10.00 25.00
295 R.Henderson Bat-Jsy/100 8.00 20.00
297 Dave Parker Bat-Jsy/200 3.00 8.00
298 Steve Garvey Bat-Jsy/200 3.00 8.00
299 Matt Williams Jsy-Jsy/200 3.00 8.00
300 K.Hernandez Bat-Jsy/200 3.00 8.00
302 V.Guer Angels Jsy-Jsy/200 4.00 10.00
303 G.Anderson Bat-Jsy/200 2.50 6.00
307 Luis Gonzalez Jsy-Jsy/200 2.50 6.00
310 Shawn Green Bat-Bat/200 2.50 6.00
311 Troy Glaus Bat-Bat/200 2.50 6.00
314 Chipper Jones Jsy-Jsy/100 5.00 12.00
315 Johnny Estrada Jsy-Jsy/200 2.50 6.00
316 Andruw Jones Bat-Jsy/200 3.00 8.00
319 Jay Gibbons Bat-Bat/200 2.50 6.00
320 Melvin Mora Jsy-Jsy/200 2.50 6.00
321 R.Palmeiro O's Bat-Jsy/200 3.00 8.00
323 David Ortiz Bat-Jsy/200 4.00 10.00
324 M.Ramirez Bat-Jsy/200 3.00 8.00
327 C.Schill Sox Jsy-Jsy/200 3.00 8.00
328 S.Sosa Cubs Bat-Jsy/100 5.00 12.00
329 Mark Prior Bat-Jsy/200 3.00 8.00
330 Greg Maddux Jsy-Jsy/25 10.00 25.00
332 F.Thomas Bat-Pants/200 4.00 10.00
333 Mark Buehrle Bat-Jsy/200 2.50 6.00
336 Sean Casey Bat-Jsy/200 2.50 6.00
337 Adam Dunn Bat-Jsy/200 2.50 6.00
339 Travis Hafner Jsy-Jsy/100 3.00 8.00
340 Victor Martinez Bat-Jsy/100 3.00 8.00
341 Cliff Lee Jsy-Jsy/200 2.50 6.00
342 Todd Helton Bat-Jsy/25 6.00 15.00
343 P.Wilson Jsy-Jsy/200 2.50 6.00
344 I.Rod Tigers Bat-Jsy/200 3.00 8.00
347 M.Cabrera Bat-Jsy/200 3.00 8.00
348 Jeff Bagwell Bat-Jsy/200 3.00 8.00
349 Andy Pettitte Bat-Jsy/200 3.00 8.00
350 R.Clem Astros Bat-Jsy/100 6.00 15.00
351 Ken Harvey Jsy-Jsy/200 2.50 6.00
353 Hideo Nomo Bat-Jsy/200 4.00 10.00
354 Kazuhisa Ishii Jsy-Jsy/200 2.50 6.00
355 E.Jackson Jsy-Jsy/200 2.50 6.00
356 J.D. Drew Bat-Bat/200 2.50 6.00
357 Jeff Kent Bat-Bat/25 5.00 12.00
358 G.Jenkins Jsy-Pants/200 2.50 6.00
359 Carlos Lee Bat-Bat/200 2.50 6.00
360 S.Stewart Jsy-Jsy/200 2.50 6.00
362 J.Santana Jsy-Jsy/100 4.00 10.00
363 M.Piaz Mets Bat-Jsy/100 5.00 12.00
364 Kazuo Matsui Bat-Jsy/100 3.00 8.00
366 P.Martinez Bat-Bat/100 4.00 10.00
368 Hideki Matsui Bat-Jsy/100 6.00 15.00
369 B.Williams Bat-Jsy/200 3.00 8.00
370 G.Shef Yanks Bat-Jsy/100 3.00 8.00
371 R.John Yanks Bat-Bat/25 8.00 20.00
378 M.Mulder A's Bat-Bat/50 4.00 10.00
380 Eric Chavez Jsy-Jsy/100 3.00 8.00
382 Marlon Byrd Bat-Jsy/200 2.50 6.00
383 Pat Burrell Jsy-Jsy/200 2.50 6.00
385 Jim Thome Bat-Bat/200 3.00 8.00
388 Moises Alou Bat-Bat/200 2.50 6.00
393 Adrian Beltre Bat-Bat/50 4.00 10.00
394 R.Sexson Bat-Bat/200 2.50 6.00
397 Albert Pujols Bat-Jsy/200 8.00 20.00
398 S.Rolen Cards Bat-Jsy/200 3.00 8.00
401 D.Young Bat-Bat/200 3.00 8.00
402 Aubrey Huff Bat-Bat/50 4.00 10.00
403 A.Soriano Bat-Jsy/200 2.50 6.00
404 Hank Blalock Bat-Jsy/200 2.50 6.00
405 R.Hidalgo Bat-Bat/200 2.50 6.00
406 Vernon Wells Jsy-Jsy/200 2.50 6.00
407 O.Hudson Bat-Bat/200 2.50 6.00
415 M.Tejada Jsy-Jsy/200 2.50 6.00
416 G.Shef Braves Bat-Bat/200 2.50 6.00
417 C.Schil D'back J-J/200 2.50 6.00
418 R.Palm Rgr Bat-Pants/50 5.00 12.00
419 S.Rolen Phils Bat-Jsy/200 3.00 8.00
420 A.Ramirez Jsy-Jsy/200 2.50 6.00
421 V.Guer Expos Bat-Bat/200 4.00 10.00
422 S.Finley D'backs J-J/200 2.50 6.00
423 R.Clem Sox Bat-Jsy/200 5.00 12.00
424 M.Piaz Dgr Jsy-Jsy/200 4.00 10.00
425 I.Rod M's Bat-Jsy/200 3.00 8.00
426 David Justice Jsy-Jsy/200 5.00 12.00
427 Mark Grace Bat-Jsy/25 8.00 20.00
428 Alan Trammell Bat-Jsy/100 4.00 10.00
430 D.Gooden Bat-Jsy/200 3.00 8.00
431 D.Sanders Bat-Jsy/200 4.00 10.00
432 Joe Torre MG Bat-Bat/100 5.00 12.00
433 Jose Canseco Jsy-Jsy/100 6.00 15.00
434 T.Gwynn Bat-Pants/200 5.00 12.00
435 Will Clark Bat-Jsy/100 5.00 12.00
437 Nolan Ryan Bat-Jsy/50 12.50 30.00
438 Billy Martin Jsy-Pants/200 4.00 10.00
439 C.Delgado Bat-Bat/100 3.00 8.00
440 M.Ordonez Bat-Bat/200 2.50 6.00
441 S.Sosa O's Bat-Bat/25 8.00 20.00
449 R.Sandberg Bat-Jsy/100 8.00 20.00

2005 Diamond Kings Materials Bronze B/W

*BRZ B/W p/r 100: .5X TO 1.2X BRZ p/r 200
*BRZ B/W p/r 100: .4X TO 1X BRZ p/r 100
*BRZ B/W p/r 50: .6X TO 1.5X BRZ p/r 200
*BRZ B/W p/r 50: .5X TO 1.2X BRZ p/r 100
OVERALL AU-GU ODDS 1:6
PRINT RUNS B/WN 10-100 COPIES PER
NO PRICING ON QTY OF 10
73 Ryan Wagner Jsy-Jsy/100 3.00 8.00

2005 Diamond Kings Materials Gold

*GOLD p/r 50: .6X TO 1.5X BRZ p/r 200
*GOLD p/r 50: .5X TO 1.2X BRZ p/r 100
*GOLD p/r 50: .4X TO 1X BRZ p/r 50
*GOLD p/r 50: .3X TO .8X BRZ p/r 25
*GOLD p/r 25: .75X TO 2X BRZ p/r 200
*GOLD p/r 25: .6X TO 1.5X BRZ p/r 100
*GOLD p/r 25: .5X TO 1.2X BRZ p/r 50
*GOLD p/r 25: .4X TO 1X BRZ p/r 25
OVERALL AU-GU ODDS 1:6
PRINT RUNS B/WN 25-50 COPIES PER
6 C.Kotchman Jsy-Jsy/50 4.00 10.00
9 Francisco Rodriguez Jsy-Jsy/50 4.00 10.00
11 Randy Johnson Bat-Bat/25 8.00 20.00
20 Marcus Giles Jsy-Jsy/50 4.00 10.00
26 Nick Green Bat-Jsy/50 4.00 10.00
33 Brian Roberts Jsy-Jsy/50 4.00 10.00
55 Matt Clement Jsy-Jsy/50 4.00 10.00
73 Ryan Wagner Jsy-Jsy/50 4.00 10.00
89 J.Bonderman Jsy-Jsy/50 4.00 10.00
107 Morgan Ensberg Jsy-Jsy/50 4.00 10.00

2005 Diamond Kings Materials Gold B/W

*GOLD B/W p/r 50: .6X TO 1.5X BRZ p/r 200
*GOLD B/W p/r 50: .5X TO 1.2X BRZ p/r 100
*GOLD B/W p/r 25: .75X TO 2X BRZ p/r 200
OVERALL AU-GU ODDS 1:6
PRINT RUNS B/WN 25-50 COPIES PER
11 Randy Johnson Bat-Bat/25 8.00 20.00
73 Ryan Wagner Jsy-Jsy/50 4.00 10.00

2005 Diamond Kings Materials Platinum

OVERALL AU-GU ODDS 1:6
STATED PRINT RUN 1 SERIAL #'d SET
NO PRICING DUE TO SCARCITY

2005 Diamond Kings Materials Platinum B/W

OVERALL AU-GU ODDS 1:6
STATED PRINT RUN 1 SERIAL #'d SET
NO PRICING DUE TO SCARCITY

2005 Diamond Kings Materials Silver

*SILV p/r 100: .5X TO 1.2X BRZ p/r 200
*SILV p/r 100: .4X TO 1X BRZ p/r 100
*SILV p/r 100: .25X TO .6X BRZ p/r 25
*SILV p/r 50: .6X TO 1.5X BRZ p/r 200
*SILV p/r 50: .5X TO 1.2X BRZ p/r 100
*SILV p/r 50: .4X TO 1X BRZ p/r 50
*SILV p/r 25: .6X TO 1.5X BRZ p/r 100
*SILV p/r 25: .5X TO 1.2X BRZ p/r 50
*SILV p/r 25: .4X TO 1X BRZ p/r 25
OVERALL AU-GU ODDS 1:6
PRINT RUNS B/WN 1-100 COPIES PER
NO PRICING ON QTY OF 10 OR LESS
6 C.Kotchman Jsy-Jsy/100 3.00 8.00
9 F.Rodriguez Jsy-Jsy/100 3.00 8.00
11 Randy Johnson Bat-Bat/25 8.00 20.00
20 Marcus Giles Jsy-Jsy/100 3.00 8.00
26 Nick Green Bat-Jsy/100 3.00 8.00
33 Brian Roberts Jsy-Jsy/100 3.00 8.00
37 Jason Varitek Bat-Bat/50 6.00 15.00
55 Matt Clement Jsy-Jsy/100 3.00 8.00
71 Barry Larkin Bat-Bat/50 5.00 12.00
73 Ryan Wagner Jsy-Jsy/100 3.00 8.00
83 Travis Hafner Jsy-Jsy/50 4.00 10.00
89 J.Bonderman Jsy-Jsy/100 3.00 8.00
107 Morgan Ensberg Jsy-Jsy/100 3.00 8.00

2005 Diamond Kings Materials Silver B/W

*SILV B/W p/r 100: .5X TO 1.2X BRZ p/r 200
*SILV B/W p/r 100: .4X TO 1X BRZ p/r 100
*SILV B/W p/r 50: .6X TO 1.5X BRZ p/r 200
*SILV B/W p/r 50: .5X TO 1.2X BRZ p/r 100
*SILV B/W p/r 25: .75X TO 2X BRZ p/r 200
*SILV B/W p/r 25: .6X TO 1.5X BRZ p/r 100
OVERALL AU-GU ODDS 1:6
PRINT RUNS B/WN 25-100 COPIES PER
11 Randy Johnson Bat-Bat/25 8.00 20.00
73 Ryan Wagner Jsy-Jsy/100 3.00 8.00

2005 Diamond Kings Materials Framed Black

1-300 PRINT RUN 10 SERIAL #'d SETS
301-450 PRINT RUN 1 SERIAL #'d SET
PLATINUM PRINT RUN 1 SERIAL #'d SET
OVERALL AU-GU ODDS 1:6
NO PRICING DUE TO SCARCITY

2005 Diamond Kings Materials Framed Black B/W

STATED PRINT RUN 1 SERIAL #'d SET
PLATINUM PRINT RUN 1 SERIAL #'d SET
OVERALL AU-GU ODDS 1:6
NO PRICING DUE TO SCARCITY

2005 Diamond Kings Materials Framed Blue

*BLUE p/r 100: .5X TO 1.2X BRZ p/r 200
*BLUE p/r 100: .4X TO 1X BRZ p/r 100
*BLUE p/r 100: .3X TO .8X BRZ p/r 50
*BLUE p/r 100: .25X TO .6X BRZ p/r 25
*BLUE p/r 50: .6X TO 1.5X BRZ p/r 200
*BLUE p/r 50: .5X TO 1.2X BRZ p/r 100
*BLUE p/r 50: .4X TO 1X BRZ p/r 50
*BLUE p/r 50: .3X TO .8X BRZ p/r 25
*BLUE p/r 25: .75X TO 2X BRZ p/r 200
*BLUE p/r 25: .4X TO 1X BRZ p/r 25
1-300 PRINT RUN 50 SERIAL #'d SETS
301-450 PRINT RUNS B/WN 1-100 PER
301-450 NO PRICE ON QTY OF 10 OR LESS
PLATINUM PRINT RUN 1 SERIAL #'d SET
NO PLAT.PRICING DUE TO SCARCITY
OVERALL AU-GU ODDS 1:6 PACKS

2005 Diamond Kings Materials Framed Blue B/W

*BLUE B/W p/r 25: .75X TO 2X BRZ p/r 200
*BLUE B/W p/r 25: .6X TO 1.5X BRZ p/r 100
STATED PRINT RUN 25 SERIAL #'d SETS
PLATINUM PRINT RUN 1 SERIAL #'d SET
NO PLAT.PRICING DUE TO SCARCITY
OVERALL AU-GU ODDS 1:6
73 Ryan Wagner Jsy-Jsy/25 5.00 12.00

2005 Diamond Kings Materials Framed Green

*GREEN p/r 25: .75X TO 2X BRZ p/r 200
*GREEN p/r 25: .6X TO 1.5X BRZ p/r 100
*GREEN p/r 25: .5X TO 1.2X BRZ p/r 50
*GREEN p/r 25: .4X TO 1X BRZ p/r 25
1-300 PRINT RUN 25 SERIAL #'d SETS
301-450 PRINT RUNS B/WN 1-25 PER
301-450 NO PRICES ON QTY OF 10 OR LESS
PLATINUM PRINT RUN 1 SERIAL #'d SET
NO PLAT.PRICING DUE TO SCARCITY
OVERALL AU-GU ODDS 1:6
11 Randy Johnson Bat-Jsy 8.00 20.00

2005 Diamond Kings Materials Framed Green B/W

*GRN B/W p/r 25: .75X TO 2X BRZ p/r 200
*GRN B/W p/r 25: .6X TO 1.5X BRZ p/r 100
STATED PRINT RUN 25 SERIAL #'d SETS
PLATINUM PRINT RUN 1 SERIAL #'d SET
NO PLAT.PRICING DUE TO SCARCITY
OVERALL AU-GU ODDS 1:6
73 Ryan Wagner Jsy-Jsy/25 5.00 12.00

2005 Diamond Kings Materials Framed Red

*RED p/r 200: .4X TO 1X BRZ p/r 200
*RED p/r 200: .3X TO .8X BRZ p/r 100
*RED p/r 100: .5X TO 1.2X BRZ p/r 200
*RED p/r 100: .4X TO 1X BRZ p/r 100
*RED p/r 100: .3X TO .8X BRZ p/r 50
*RED p/r 100: .25X TO .6X BRZ p/r 25
*RED p/r 50: .6X TO 1.5X BRZ p/r 200
*RED p/r 50: .5X TO 1.2X BRZ p/r 100
*RED p/r 50: .4X TO 1X BRZ p/r 50
*RED p/r 50: .3X TO .8X BRZ p/r 25
*RED p/r 25: .75X TO 2X BRZ p/r 200
*RED p/r 25: .6X TO 1.5X BRZ p/r 100
*RED p/r 25: .4X TO 1X BRZ p/r 25
PRINT RUNS B/WN 25-100 COPIES PER
PLATINUM PRINT RUN 1 SERIAL #'d SET
NO PLAT.PRICING DUE TO SCARCITY
OVERALL AU-GU ODDS 1:6
6 C.Kotchman Jsy-Jsy/100 3.00 8.00
9 F.Rodriguez Jsy-Jsy/100 3.00 8.00
11 Randy Johnson Bat-Bat/50 6.00 15.00
20 Marcus Giles Jsy-Jsy/100 3.00 8.00
26 Nick Green Bat-Jsy/100 3.00 8.00
33 Brian Roberts Jsy-Jsy/100 3.00 8.00
37 Jason Varitek Bat-Bat/25 8.00 20.00
55 Matt Clement Jsy-Jsy/100 3.00 8.00
71 Barry Larkin Bat-Bat/100 4.00 10.00
73 Ryan Wagner Jsy-Jsy/100 3.00 8.00
83 Travis Hafner Jsy-Jsy/50 4.00 10.00
89 J.Bonderman Jsy-Jsy/100 3.00 8.00
107 Morg Ensberg Jsy-Jsy/100 3.00 8.00
190 Phil Nevin Jsy-Jsy/50 4.00 10.00
195 Jerome Williams Jsy-Jsy/50 4.00 10.00
266 J.Thome Indians Bat-Bat/25 6.00 15.00
272 O.Cabrera Expos Bat-Jsy/50 4.00 10.00
290 Maury Wills Jsy-Jsy/25 5.00 12.00
365 Carlos Beltran Bat-Bat/25 5.00 12.00
412 Jose Vidro Bat-Jsy/25 5.00 12.00

2005 Diamond Kings Materials Framed Red B/W

*RED B/W p/r 100: .5X TO 1.2X BRZ p/r 200
*RED B/W p/r 100: .4X TO 1X BRZ p/r 100
*RED B/W p/r 50: .6X TO 1.5X BRZ p/r 200
*RED B/W p/r 50: .5X TO 1.2X BRZ p/r 100
*RED B/W p/r 25: .6X TO 1.5X BRZ p/r 100
PRINT RUNS B/WN 25-100 COPIES PER
PLATINUM PRINT RUN 1 SERIAL #'d SET
NO PLAT.PRICING DUE TO SCARCITY
OVERALL AU-GU ODDS 1:6
73 Ryan Wagner Jsy-Jsy/100 3.00 8.00

2005 Diamond Kings Signature Black

OVERALL AU-GU ODDS 1:6
STATED PRINT RUN 1 SERIAL #'d SET
NO PRICING DUE TO SCARCITY

2005 Diamond Kings Signature Bronze

OVERALL AU-GU ODDS 1:6
PRINT RUNS B/WN 1-100 COPIES PER
NO PRICING ON QTY OF 10 OR LESS
NO RC YR PRICING ON QTY OF 25 OR LESS
3 Jose Guillen/100 6.00 15.00
5 Tim Salmon/100 10.00 25.00
6 Casey Kotchman/100 6.00 15.00
7 Chone Figgins/100 6.00 15.00
8 Robb Quinlan/100 4.00 10.00
9 Francisco Rodriguez/50 12.50 30.00
10 Troy Percival/50 8.00 20.00
14 Shea Hillenbrand/100 6.00 15.00
15 Chad Tracy/100 4.00 10.00
16 Alex Cintron/100 4.00 10.00
22 Adam LaRoche/50 5.00 12.00
23 Russ Ortiz/50 5.00 12.00
26 Nick Green/100 4.00 10.00
30 Luis Matos/100 4.00 10.00
31 Larry Bigbie/100 6.00 15.00
32 Rodrigo Lopez/100 4.00 10.00
33 Brian Roberts/100 6.00 15.00
34 Melvin Mora/100 6.00 15.00
40 Keith Foulke/50 12.50 30.00
43 Kevin Youkilis/100 4.00 10.00
44 Orlando Cabrera Sox/50 8.00 20.00
45 Abe Alvarez/100 6.00 15.00
51 Carlos Zambrano/50 12.50 30.00
58 Todd Walker/50 5.00 12.00
59 Angel Guzman/100 4.00 10.00
61 Carlos Lee/100 6.00 15.00
73 Ryan Wagner/100 4.00 10.00
75 Danny Graves/100 4.00 10.00
76 C.C. Sabathia/50 8.00 20.00
77 Jody Gerut/100 4.00 10.00
79 Victor Martinez/50 8.00 20.00
82 Kazuhito Tadano/100 6.00 15.00
83 Travis Hafner/100 6.00 15.00
89 Jeremy Bonderman/100 6.00 15.00
92 Brandon Inge/100 4.00 10.00
101 Guillermo Mota/50 5.00 12.00
107 Morgan Ensberg/100 6.00 15.00
112 Jeremy Affeldt/100 4.00 10.00
117 Milton Bradley/100 6.00 15.00
122 Brad Penny Dgr/100 4.00 10.00
123 Scott Podsednik/50 12.50 30.00
125 Lyle Overbay/100 4.00 10.00
127 Bill Hall/100 4.00 10.00
132 Lew Ford/100 4.00 10.00
135 Jason Kubel/100 4.00 10.00
137 Chad Cordero/100 6.00 15.00
140 Livan Hernandez/25 10.00 25.00
156 Bubba Crosby/100 4.00 10.00
159 Tom Gordon/25 10.00 25.00
160 Esteban Loaiza Yanks/100 6.00 15.00
166 Jermaine Dye/50 8.00 20.00
167 Octavio Dotel/50 8.00 20.00
168 Bobby Crosby/100 6.00 15.00
174 Mike Lieberthal/100 6.00 15.00
177 Randy Wolf/100 6.00 15.00
178 Craig Wilson/100 4.00 10.00
180 Jack Wilson/100 6.00 15.00
181 Jose Castillo/100 4.00 10.00
184 Jason Bay/100 6.00 15.00
186 Jay Payton/50 5.00 12.00
189 Jake Peavy/50 4.00 10.00
194 Freddy Guzman/100 4.00 10.00
197 Todd Linden/50 5.00 12.00
198 Merkin Valdez/100 6.00 15.00
203 Raul Ibanez/100 10.00 25.00
206 Miguel Olivo/100 4.00 10.00
207 Bucky Jacobsen/100 4.00 10.00
208 Jamie Moyer/50 8.00 20.00
212 Dan Haren/100 4.00 10.00
219 Jeff Suppan/100 6.00 15.00
220 Aubrey Huff/50 8.00 20.00
221 Carl Crawford/25 10.00 25.00
224 Dewon Brazelton/100 4.00 10.00
226 Joey Gathright/100 4.00 10.00
227 Scott Kazmir/25 10.00 25.00
230 Michael Young/50 8.00 20.00
231 Adrian Gonzalez/100 10.00 25.00
232 Laynce Nix/100 4.00 10.00
236 David Dellucci/100 12.50 30.00
237 Francisco Cordero/100 6.00 15.00
241 Alexis Rios/100 6.00 15.00
248 Dioner Navarro/100 6.00 15.00
253 Yhency Brazoban/100 4.00 10.00
257 Scott Proctor/100 4.00 10.00
260 Matt Peterson/100 4.00 10.00
269 Brad Penny Marlins/50 5.00 12.00
272 Orlando Cabrera Expos/50 8.00 20.00
274 Esteban Loaiza Sox/100 6.00 15.00
284 Andre Dawson/50 8.00 20.00
285 Harold Baines/100 6.00 15.00
286 Jack Morris/100 6.00 15.00
290 Maury Wills/100 6.00 15.00
292 Darryl Strawberry/100 6.00 15.00
297 Dave Parker/100 6.00 15.00
299 Matt Williams/25 15.00 40.00
303 Garret Anderson/50 8.00 20.00
304 Dallas McPherson/100 4.00 10.00
305 Orlando Cabrera/25 10.00 25.00
306 Steve Finley Angels/50 8.00 20.00
313 Russ Ortiz/50 5.00 12.00
315 Johnny Estrada/100 4.00 10.00
317 Tim Hudson/25 15.00 40.00
318 Danny Kolb/100 4.00 10.00
319 Jay Gibbons/50 5.00 12.00
320 Melvin Mora/50 8.00 20.00
325 Edgar Renteria/50 8.00 20.00
333 Mark Buehrle/50 10.00 25.00
336 Sean Casey/25 10.00 25.00

339 Travis Hafner/50 8.00 20.00
340 Victor Martinez/50 8.00 20.00
341 Cliff Lee/100 10.00 25.00
343 Preston Wilson/50 8.00 20.00
351 Ken Harvey/100 4.00 10.00
355 Edwin Jackson/100 4.00 10.00
359 Carlos Lee/100 6.00 15.00
360 Shannon Stewart/25 10.00 25.00
361 Joe Nathan/100 6.00 15.00
376 Eric Byrnes/100 4.00 10.00
377 Rich Harden/100 6.00 15.00
378 Mark Mulder A's/25 10.00 25.00
380 Eric Chavez/25 10.00 25.00
382 Marlon Byrd/100 4.00 10.00
384 Brett Myers/100 6.00 15.00
386 Jason Bay/50 8.00 20.00
387 Jake Peavy/50 12.50 30.00
402 Aubrey Huff/50 8.00 20.00
407 Orlando Hudson/25 6.00 15.00
410 Jose Guillen/25 10.00 25.00
429 Bert Blyleven/50 8.00 20.00
430 Dwight Gooden/50 8.00 20.00
436 Marty Marion/50 8.00 20.00

2005 Diamond Kings Signature Bronze B/W

*BRZ B/W p/r 100: .4X TO 1X BRZ p/r 100
*BRZ B/W p/r 50: .4X TO 1X BRZ p/r 50
*BRZ B/W p/r 25: .4X TO 1X BRZ p/r 25
OVERALL AU-GU ODDS 1:6
PRINT RUNS B/WN 1-100 COPIES PER
NO PRICING ON QTY OF 10 OR LESS
185 Sean Burroughs/25 6.00 15.00

2005 Diamond Kings Signature Gold

*GOLD p/r 50: .5X TO 1.2X BRZ p/r 100
*GOLD p/r 25: .6X TO 1.5X BRZ p/r 100
*GOLD p/r 25: .5X TO 1.2X BRZ p/r 50
*GOLD p/r 25: .4X TO 1X BRZ p/r 25
OVERALL AU-GU ODDS 1:6
PRINT RUNS B/WN 1-50 COPIES PER
NO PRICING ON QTY OF 10 OR LESS
115 Andres Blanco/25 6.00 15.00
325 Edgar Renteria/25 10.00 25.00

2005 Diamond Kings Signature Gold B/W

*GOLD B/W p/r 25: .6X TO 1.5X BRZ p/r 100
OVERALL AU-GU ODDS 1:6
PRINT RUNS B/WN 1-25 COPIES PER
NO PRICING ON QTY OF 10 OR LESS
185 Sean Burroughs/25 6.00 15.00

2005 Diamond Kings Signature Platinum

OVERALL AU-GU ODDS 1:6
STATED PRINT RUN 1 SERIAL #'d SET
NO PRICING DUE TO SCARCITY

2005 Diamond Kings Signature Platinum B/W

OVERALL AU-GU ODDS 1:6
STATED PRINT RUN 1 SERIAL #'d SET
NO PRICING DUE TO SCARCITY

2005 Diamond Kings Signature Silver

*SILV p/r 100: .4X TO 1X BRZ p/r 100
*SILV p/r 50: .5X TO 1.2X BRZ p/r 100
*SILV p/r 50: .4X TO 1X BRZ p/r 50
*SILV p/r 25: .6X TO 1.5X BRZ p/r 100
*SILV p/r 25: .5X TO 1.2X BRZ p/r 50
*SILV p/r 25: .4X TO 1X BRZ p/r 25
OVERALL AU-GU ODDS 1:6
PRINT RUNS B/WN 1-100 COPIES PER
NO PRICING ON QTY OF 10 OR LESS
115 Andres Blanco/50 5.00 12.00

2005 Diamond Kings Signature Silver B/W

*SILV B/W p/r 50: .5X TO 1.2X BRZ p/r 100
*SILV B/W p/r 25: .6X TO 1.5X BRZ p/r 100
OVERALL AU-GU ODDS 1:6
PRINT RUNS B/WN 1-50 COPIES PER
NO PRICING ON QTY OF 10 OR LESS

2005 Diamond Kings Signature Framed Blue

*BLUE p/r 50: .5X TO 1.2X BRZ p/r 100
*BLUE p/r 25: .6X TO 1.5X BRZ p/r 100
PRINT RUNS B/WN 1-50 COPIES PER
NO PRICING ON QTY OF 10 OR LESS
PLATINUM PRINT RUN 1 SERIAL #'d SET
NO PLAT.PRICING DUE TO SCARCITY
OVERALL AU-GU ODDS 1:6
115 Andres Blanco/25 6.00 15.00

2005 Diamond Kings Signature Framed Blue B/W

*BLUE B/W p/r 50: .5X TO 1.2X BRZ p/r 100
*BLUE B/W p/r 25: .6X TO 1.5X BRZ p/r 100
PRINT RUNS B/WN 1-50 COPIES PER
NO PRICING ON QTY OF 10 OR LESS
PLATINUM PRINT RUN 1 SERIAL #'d SET
NO PLAT.PRICING DUE TO SCARCITY
OVERALL AU-GU ODDS 1:6

2005 Diamond Kings Signature Framed Green

*GRN p/r 25: .6X TO 1.5X BRZ p/r 100
PRINT RUNS B/WN 1-25 COPIES PER
NO PRICING ON QTY OF 10 OR LESS
PLATINUM PRINT RUN 1 SERIAL #'d SET
NO PLATINUM PRICING DUE TO SCARCITY
OVERALL AU-GU ODDS 1:6

2005 Diamond Kings Signature Framed Green B/W

*GREEN B/W p/r 25: .6X TO 1.5X BRZ p/r 100
PRINT RUNS B/WN 1-25 COPIES PER
NO PRICING ON QTY OF 10 OR LESS
PLATINUM PRINT RUN 1 SERIAL #'d SET
NO PLAT.PRICING DUE TO SCARCITY
OVERALL AU-GU ODDS 1:6

2005 Diamond Kings Signature Framed Red

*RED p/r 100: .4X TO 1X BRZ p/r 100
*RED p/r 50: .5X TO 1.2X BRZ p/r 100
*RED p/r 50: .4X TO 1X BRZ p/r 50
*RED p/r 25: .6X TO 1.5X BRZ p/r 100
*RED p/r 25: .5X TO 1.2X BRZ p/r 50
*RED p/r 25: .4X TO 1X BRZ p/r 25
PRINT RUNS B/WN 1-100 COPIES PER
NO PRICING ON QTY OF 14 OR LESS
PLATINUM PRINT RUN 1 SERIAL #'d SET
NO PLAT.PRICING DUE TO SCARCITY
OVERALL AU-GU ODDS 1:6

2005 Diamond Kings Signature Framed Red B/W

*RED B/W p/r 100: .4X TO 1X BRZ p/r 100
*RED B/W p/r 50: .5X TO 1.2X BRZ p/r 100
*RED B/W p/r 50: .4X TO 1X BRZ p/r 50
*RED B/W p/r 25: .6X TO 1.5X BRZ p/r 100
*RED B/W p/r 25: .5X TO 1.2X BRZ p/r 50
*RED B/W p/r 25: .4X TO 1X BRZ p/r 25
PRINT RUNS B/WN 1-100 COPIES PER
NO PRICING ON QTY OF 10 OR LESS
PLATINUM PRINT RUN 1 SERIAL #'d SET
NO PLAT.PRICING DUE TO SCARCITY
OVERALL AU-GU ODDS 1:6

2005 Diamond Kings Signature Materials Black

OVERALL AU-GU ODDS 1:6
STATED PRINT RUN 1 SERIAL #'d SET
NO PRICING DUE TO SCARCITY

2005 Diamond Kings Signature Materials Bronze

OVERALL AU-GU ODDS 1:6
PRINT RUNS B/WN 1-200 COPIES PER
NO PRICING ON QTY OF 10 OR LESS
1 Garret Anderson Bat-Jsy/50 10.00 25.00
7 Chone Figgins Bat-Jsy/200 6.00 15.00
18 Rafael Furcal Bat-Jsy/50 10.00 25.00
19 Andruw Jones Bat-Jsy/25 20.00 50.00
31 Larry Bigbie Jsy-Jsy/200 6.00 15.00
32 Rodrigo Lopez Jsy-Jsy/200 4.00 10.00
38 Trot Nixon Jsy-Jsy/100 12.50 30.00
46 David Ortiz Bat-Jsy/100 15.00 40.00
48 Mark Prior Bat-Jsy/25 15.00 40.00
49 A.Ramirez Bat-Jsy/100 8.00 20.00
51 C.Zambrano Jsy-Jsy/200 6.00 15.00
52 Derrek Lee Bat-Bat/100 12.50 30.00
61 Carlos Lee Bat-Jsy/100 5.00 12.00
76 C.C. Sabathia Jsy-Jsy/100 12.50 30.00
78 Omar Vizquel Jsy-Jsy/25 20.00 50.00
95 Miguel Cabrera Bat-Jsy/25 30.00 60.00
109 C.Belt Astros Bat-Jsy/50 10.00 25.00
112 J.Affeldt Pants-Pants/100 5.00 12.00
127 Bill Hall Bat-Bat/100 5.00 12.00
129 Jacque Jones Bat-Jsy/50 10.00 25.00
131 Johan Santana Jsy-Jsy/50 15.00 40.00
132 Lew Ford Bat-Jsy/200 4.00 10.00
139 Nick Johnson Bat-Bat/50 10.00 25.00
153 Jorge Posada Bat-Jsy/25 75.00 150.00
162 Eric Chavez Bat-Jsy/25 12.50 30.00
178 Craig Wilson Bat-Jsy/200 4.00 10.00
185 S.Burroughs Bat-Jsy/100 5.00 12.00
201 Edgar Martinez Bat-Bat/25 20.00 50.00
211 Edgar Renteria Bat-Jsy/50 10.00 25.00
221 Carl Crawford Jsy-Jsy/200 6.00 15.00
229 Mark Teixeira Bat-Jsy/25 20.00 50.00
230 Michael Young Bat-Jsy/100 8.00 20.00
232 Laynce Nix Bat-Jsy/200 4.00 10.00
233 A.Soriano Rgr Bat-Jsy/25 12.50 30.00
239 Roy Halladay Jsy-Jsy/25 30.00 80.00
269 B.Penny M's Bat-Jsy/100 5.00 12.00
280 Dale Murphy Jsy-Jsy/50 15.00 40.00
282 Dwight Evans Bat-Jsy/50 15.00 40.00
283 Ron Santo Bat-Bat/100 15.00 40.00
284 Andre Dawson Bat-Jsy/100 8.00 20.00
286 Jack Morris Jsy-Jsy/100 8.00 20.00
287 Kirk Gibson Bat-Jsy/25 12.50 30.00
289 Orel Hershiser Jsy-Jsy/25 12.50 30.00
291 Tony Oliva Bat-Jsy/100 8.00 20.00
294 Don Mattingly Bat-Jsy/25 40.00 80.00
297 Dave Parker Bat-Jsy/100 8.00 20.00
298 Steve Garvey Bat-Jsy/50 10.00 25.00
300 K.Hernandez Bat-Jsy/100 8.00 20.00
303 G.Anderson Bat-Jsy/50 10.00 25.00
315 Johnny Estrada Jsy-Jsy/50 6.00 15.00
319 Jay Gibbons Bat-Bat/50 6.00 15.00
320 Melvin Mora Jsy-Jsy/50 10.00 25.00
323 David Ortiz Jsy-Jsy/25 30.00 60.00
333 Mark Buehrle Jsy-Jsy/25 15.00 40.00
339 Travis Hafner Jsy-Jsy/25 12.50 30.00
340 Victor Martinez Jsy-Jsy/25 12.50 30.00
341 Cliff Lee Jsy-Jsy/25 10.00 25.00
343 P.Wilson Bat-Jsy/25 12.50 30.00
351 Ken Harvey Jsy-Jsy/25 8.00 20.00
382 Marlon Byrd Bat-Jsy/50 6.00 15.00
401 Delmon Young Bat-Bat/25 20.00 50.00
407 O.Hudson Bat-Bat/25 8.00 20.00
419 S.Rolen Phils Bat-Jsy/25 20.00 50.00
428 Alan Trammell Bat-Jsy/25 12.50 30.00
430 D.Gooden Bat-Jsy/25 12.50 30.00
434 Tony Gwynn Bat-Jsy/25 30.00 60.00

2005 Diamond Kings Signature Materials Bronze B/W

*BRZ B/W p/r 100: .5X TO 1.2X BRZ p/r 200
*BRZ B/W p/r 50: .5X TO 1.2X BRZ p/r 100
*BRZ B/W p/r 25: .75X TO 2X BRZ p/r 200
*BRZ B/W p/r 25: .6X TO 1.5X BRZ p/r 100
OVERALL AU-GU ODDS 1:6
PRINT RUNS B/WN 1-100 COPIES PER
NO PRICING ON QTY OF 10 OR LESS
73 Ryan Wagner Jsy-Jsy/50 6.00 15.00
97 Mike Lowell Jsy-Jsy/25 8.00 20.00
136 Jose Vidro Bat-Bat/50 6.00 15.00
180 Jack Wilson Bat-Bat/100 5.00 12.00
271 P.Lo Duca Dgr Bat-Bat/25 12.50 30.00
285 Harold Baines Bat-Jsy/50 10.00 25.00

2005 Diamond Kings Signature Materials Gold

*GOLD p/r 50: .6X TO 1.5X BRZ p/r 200
*GOLD p/r 50: .5X TO 1.2X BRZ p/r 100
*GOLD p/r 50: .4X TO 1X BRZ p/r 50
*GOLD p/r 25: .5X TO 1.2X BRZ p/r 50
*GOLD p/r 25: .4X TO 1X BRZ p/r 25
OVERALL AU-GU ODDS 1:6
PRINT RUNS B/WN 1-50 COPIES PER
NO PRICING ON QTY OF 10 OR LESS
104 Roy Oswalt Jsy-Jsy/50 10.00 25.00
285 Harold Baines Bat-Jsy/50 10.00 25.00
299 Matt Williams Jsy-Jsy/25 20.00 50.00

2005 Diamond Kings Signature Materials Gold B/W

*GOLD B/W p/r 25: .75X TO 2X BRZ p/r 200
*GOLD B/W p/r 25: .6X TO 1.5X BRZ p/r 100
OVERALL AU-GU ODDS 1:6
PRINT RUNS B/WN 1-25 COPIES PER
NO PRICING ON QTY OF 10 OR LESS
73 Ryan Wagner Jsy-Jsy/25 8.00 20.00
97 Mike Lowell Jsy-Jsy/25 8.00 20.00
136 Jose Vidro Bat-Bat/25 8.00 20.00
180 Jack Wilson Bat-Bat/25 8.00 20.00
271 P.Lo Duca Dgr Bat-Bat/25 12.50 30.00
285 Harold Baines Bat-Jsy/25 12.50 30.00

2005 Diamond Kings Signature Materials Silver

*SILV p/r 100: .5X TO 1.2X BRZ p/r 200
*SILV p/r 100: .4X TO 1X BRZ p/r 100
*SILV p/r 50: .5X TO 1.2X BRZ p/r 100
*SILV p/r 50: .4X TO 1X BRZ p/r 50
*SILV p/r 25: .5X TO 1.2X BRZ p/r 50
*SILV p/r 25: .4X TO 1X BRZ p/r 25
OVERALL AU-GU ODDS 1:6
PRINT RUNS B/WN 1-100 COPIES PER
NO PRICING ON QTY OF 10 OR LESS
104 Roy Oswalt Jsy-Jsy/50 10.00 25.00
285 Harold Baines Bat-Jsy/50 10.00 25.00
299 Matt Williams Jsy-Jsy/25 20.00 50.00
354 Kazuhisa Ishii Jsy-Jsy/25 12.50 30.00

2005 Diamond Kings Signature Materials Silver B/W

*SILV B/W p/r 50: .6X TO 1.5X BRZ p/r 200
*SILV B/W p/r 50: .5X TO 1.2X BRZ p/r 100
*SILV B/W p/r 25: .75X TO 2X BRZ p/r 200
*SILV B/W p/r 25: .6X TO 1.5X BRZ p/r 100
OVERALL AU-GU ODDS 1:6
PRINT RUNS B/WN 1-50 COPIES PER
NO PRICING ON QTY OF 10 OR LESS
73 Ryan Wagner Jsy-Jsy/50 6.00 15.00
97 Mike Lowell Jsy-Jsy/25 8.00 20.00
136 Jose Vidro Bat-Bat/50 6.00 15.00
180 Jack Wilson Bat-Bat/50 6.00 15.00
271 P.Lo Duca Dgr Bat-Bat/25 12.50 30.00
285 Harold Baines Bat-Jsy/25 12.50 30.00

2005 Diamond Kings Signature Materials Framed Black

PRINT RUNS B/WN 1-10 COPIES PER
PLATINUM PRINT RUN 1 SERIAL #'d SET
OVERALL AU-GU ODDS 1:6
NO PRICING DUE TO SCARCITY

2005 Diamond Kings Signature Materials Framed Black B/W

STATED PRINT RUN 1 SERIAL #'d SET
PLATINUM PRINT RUN 1 SERIAL #'d SET
OVERALL AU-GU ODDS 1:6
NO PRICING DUE TO SCARCITY

2005 Diamond Kings Signature Materials Framed Blue

*BLUE p/r 50: .6X TO 1.5X BRZ p/r 200
*BLUE p/r 50: .5X TO 1.2X BRZ p/r 100
*BLUE p/r 50: .4X TO 1X BRZ p/r 50
*BLUE p/r 25: .5X TO 1.2X BRZ p/r 50
PRINT RUNS B/WN 1-50 COPIES PER
NO PRICING ON QTY OF 10 OR LESS
PLATINUM PRINT RUN 1 SERIAL #'d SET
NO PLAT.PRICING DUE TO SCARCITY
OVERALL AU-GU ODDS 1:6

2005 Diamond Kings Signature Materials Framed Blue B/W

*BLUE B/W p/r 25: .75X TO 2X BRZ p/r 200
*BLUE B/W p/r 25: .6X TO 1.5X BRZ p/r 100
PRINT RUNS B/WN 1-25 COPIES PER
NO PRICING ON QTY OF 10 OR LESS
PLATINUM PRINT RUN 1 SERIAL #'d SET
NO PLAT.PRICING DUE TO SCARCITY
OVERALL AU-GU ODDS 1:6
73 Ryan Wagner Jsy-Jsy/25 8.00 20.00
97 Mike Lowell Jsy-Jsy/25 8.00 20.00
180 Jack Wilson Bat-Bat/25 8.00 20.00
271 P.Lo Duca Dgr Bat-Bat/25 12.50 30.00

2005 Diamond Kings Signature Materials Framed Green

*GRN p/r 25: .75X TO 2X BRZ p/r 200
*GRN p/r 25: .6X TO 1.5X BRZ p/r 100
*GRN p/r 25: .5X TO 1.2X BRZ p/r 50
PRINT RUNS B/WN 1-25 COPIES PER
NO PRICING ON QTY OF 10 OR LESS
PLATINUM PRINT RUN 1 SERIAL #'d SET
NO PLAT.PRICING DUE TO SCARCITY
OVERALL AU-GU ODDS 1:6
299 Matt Williams Jsy-Jsy/25 20.00 50.00

2005 Diamond Kings Signature Materials Framed Green B/W

*GREEN B/W p/r 25: .75X TO 2X BRZ p/r 200
*GREEN B/W p/r 25: .6X TO 1.5X BRZ p/r 100
PRINT RUNS B/WN 1-25 COPIES PER
NO PRICING ON QTY OF 10 OR LESS
PLATINUM PRINT RUN 1 SERIAL #'d SET
NO PLAT.PRICING DUE TO SCARCITY
OVERALL AU-GU ODDS 1:6
73 Ryan Wagner Jsy-Jsy/25 8.00 20.00
97 Mike Lowell Jsy-Jsy/25 8.00 20.00
180 Jack Wilson Bat-Bat/25 8.00 20.00
271 P.Lo Duca Dgr Bat-Bat/25 12.50 30.00
285 Harold Baines Bat-Jsy/25 12.50 30.00

2005 Diamond Kings Signature Materials Framed Red

*RED p/r 100: .5X TO 1.2X BRZ p/r 200
*RED p/r 100: .4X TO 1X BRZ p/r 100
*RED p/r 50: .5X TO 1.2X BRZ p/r 100
*RED p/r 50: .4X TO 1X BRZ p/r 50
*RED p/r 25: .5X TO 1.2X BRZ p/r 50
PRINT RUNS B/WN 1-100 COPIES PER
NO PRICING ON QTY OF 10 OR LESS
PLATINUM PRINT RUN 1 SERIAL #'d SET
NO PLAT.PRICING DUE TO SCARCITY
OVERALL AU-GU ODDS 1:6

2005 Diamond Kings Signature Materials Framed Red B/W

*RED B/W p/r 25: .75X TO 2X BRZ p/r 200
*RED B/W p/r 25: .6X TO 1.5X BRZ p/r 100
PRINT RUNS B/WN 1-50 COPIES PER
NO PRICING ON QTY OF 10 OR LESS
PLATINUM PRINT RUN 1 SERIAL #'d SET
NO PLAT.PRICING DUE TO SCARCITY
OVERALL AU-GU ODDS 1:6

2005 Diamond Kings Diamond Cuts Bat

*BAT p/r 200: .4X TO 1X JSY p/r 200
*BAT p/r 200: .4X TO 1X JSY p/r 100
*BAT p/r 200: .3X TO .8X JSY p/r 50
*BAT p/r 100: .5X TO 1.2X JSY p/r 200
*BAT p/r 100: .3X TO .8X JSY p/r 50
*BAT p/r 50: .6X TO 1.5X JSY p/r 200
*BAT p/r 50: .5X TO 1.2X JSY p/r 100
*BAT p/r 50: .4X TO 1X JSY p/r 50
OVERALL AU-GU ODD 1:6
PRINT RUNS B/WN 50-200 COPIES PER
DC16 Derrek Lee/200 2.50 6.00
DC47 Tim Salmon/200 2.50 6.00
DC49 Torii Hunter/200 2.00 5.00

2005 Diamond Kings Diamond Cuts Combos

*COMBO p/r 200: .5X TO 1.2X JSY p/r 200
*COMBO p/r 100: .6X TO 1.5X JSY p/r 200
*COMBO p/r 100: .5X TO 1.2X JSY p/r 100
*COMBO p/r 100: .4X TO 1X JSY p/r 50
*COMBO p/r 50: .75X TO 2X JSY p/r 200
*COMBO p/r 50: .6X TO 1.5X JSY p/r 100
*COMBO p/r 50: .5X TO 1.2X JSY p/r 50
PRINT RUNS B/WN 25-200 COPIES PER
PRIME PRINT RUN 1 SERIAL #'d SET
NO PRIME PRICING DUE TO SCARCITY
OVERALL AU-GU ODDS 1:6
DC49 Torii Hunter Bat-Jsy/25 5.00 12.00

2005 Diamond Kings Diamond Cuts Jersey

PRINT RUNS B/WN 50-200 COPIES PER
PRIME PRINT RUN 1 SERIAL #'d SET
NO PRIME PRICING DUE TO SCARCITY
OVERALL AU-GU ODDS 1:6
DC1 Adam Dunn/50 3.00 8.00
DC2 Adrian Beltre/200 2.00 5.00
DC3 Alfonso Soriano/50 3.00 8.00
DC4 Andruw Jones/200 2.50 6.00
DC5 Andy Pettitte/100 3.00 8.00
DC6 Aramis Ramirez/200 2.00 5.00
DC7 Brian Giles/200 2.00 5.00
DC8 C.C. Sabathia/200 2.00 5.00
DC9 Carl Crawford/200 2.00 5.00
DC10 Carlos Beltran/200 2.00 5.00
DC11 Carlos Lee/200 2.00 5.00
DC12 Craig Wilson/200 2.00 5.00
DC13 Curt Schilling/50 4.00 10.00
DC14 Darin Erstad/200 2.00 5.00
DC17 Fred McGriff/200 2.50 6.00
DC18 Greg Maddux/50 6.00 15.00
DC19 Ivan Rodriguez/200 2.50 6.00
DC20 Jason Bay/200 2.00 5.00
DC21 Jason Giambi/200 2.00 5.00
DC22 Jay Gibbons/100 2.50 6.00
DC23 Jeff Kent/200 2.00 5.00
DC24 John Olerud/200 2.00 5.00
DC25 Juan Gonzalez Pants/200 2.00 5.00
DC26 Junior Spivey/200 2.00 5.00
DC27 Kazuhisa Ishii/200 2.00 5.00
DC28 Kevin Brown/200 2.00 5.00
DC29 Larry Walker Rockies/200 2.00 5.00
DC30 Lyle Overbay/200 2.00 5.00
DC31 Mark Teixeira/100 3.00 8.00
DC32 Melvin Mora/200 2.00 5.00
DC33 Michael Young/200 2.00 5.00
DC34 Miguel Tejada/200 2.00 5.00
DC35 Mike Mussina/100 3.00 8.00
DC36 Paul LoDuca/50 3.00 8.00
DC37 Preston Wilson/200 2.00 5.00
DC38 Randy Johnson/200 3.00 8.00
DC39 Richie Sexson/200 2.00 5.00
DC40 Roger Clemens/50 6.00 15.00
DC41 Scott Rolen/50 4.00 10.00
DC42 Sean Burroughs/200 2.00 5.00
DC43 Sean Casey/200 2.00 5.00
DC44 Shannon Stewart/100 2.50 6.00
DC45 Shawn Green/200 2.00 5.00
DC46 Steve Finley/200 2.00 5.00
DC48 Tom Glavine/200 2.50 6.00
DC50 Travis Hafner/100 2.50 6.00

2005 Diamond Kings Diamond Cuts Signature

*SIG p/r 100: .3X TO .8X SIG.JSY p/r 100
*SIG p/r 100: .25X TO .6X SIG.JSY p/r 50
*SIG p/r 50: .3X TO .8X SIG.JSY p/r 50
*SIG p/r 25: .5X TO 1.2X SIG.JSY p/r 100
*SIG p/r 25: .3X TO .8X SIG.JSY p/r 25
OVERALL AU-GU ODDS 1:6
PRINT RUNS B/WN 1-100 COPIES PER
NO PRICING ON QTY OF 10 OR LESS
DC20 Jason Bay/100 6.00 15.00
DC22 Jay Gibbons/100 4.00 10.00
DC47 Tim Salmon/100 10.00 25.00

2005 Diamond Kings Diamond Cuts Signature Bat

*SIG.BAT p/r 100: .4X TO 1X SIG.JSY p/r 100
*SIG.BAT p/r 50: .5X TO 1.2X SIG.JSY p/r 100
*SIG.BAT p/r 25: .4X TO 1X SIG.JSY p/r 25
OVERALL AU-GU ODDS 1:6
PRINT RUNS B/WN 1-100 COPIES PER
NO PRICING ON QTY OF 10 OR LESS
DC10 Carlos Beltran/50 10.00 25.00
DC16 Derrek Lee/100 12.50 30.00
DC17 Fred McGriff/25 10.00 25.00
DC22 Jay Gibbons/100 5.00 12.00
DC49 Torii Hunter/25 10.00 25.00
DC53 Carlos Beltran/25 12.50 30.00

2005 Diamond Kings Diamond Cuts Signature Combos

*SIG.COM p/r 100: .4X TO 1X SIG.JSY p/r 100
*SIG.COM p/r 50: .5X TO 1.2X SIG.JSY p/r 100
*SIG.COM p/r 25: .6X TO 1.5X SIG.JSY p/r 100
*SIG.COM p/r 25: .5X TO 1.2X SIG.JSY p/r 50
*SIG.COM p/r 25: .4X TO 1X SIG.JSY p/r 25
PRINT RUNS B/WN 1-100 COPIES PER
NO PRICING ON QTY OF 10 OR LESS
PRIME PRINT RUN 1 SERIAL #'d SET
NO PRIME PRICING DUE TO SCARCITY
OVERALL AU-GU ODDS 1:6
DC1 Adam Dunn Bat-Jsy/25 20.00 50.00
DC17 Fred McGriff Bat-Jsy/25 30.00 60.00
DC22 Jay Gibbons Bat-Bat/50 6.00 15.00
DC25 Juan Gonzalez Bat-Jsy/100 8.00 20.00
DC49 Torii Hunter Bat-Jsy/25 6.00 15.00
DC51 Aramis Ramirez Jsy-Jsy/24 12.50 30.00
DC54 Craig Biggio Bat-Pants/25 20.00 50.00

2005 Diamond Kings Diamond Cuts Signature Jersey

PRINT RUNS B/WN 5-100 COPIES PER
NO PRICING ON QTY OF 10 OR LESS
PRIME PRINT RUN 1 SERIAL #'d SET
NO PRIME PRICING DUE TO SCARCITY
OVERALL AU-GU ODDS 1:6
DC2 Adrian Beltre/100 8.00 20.00
DC6 Aramis Ramirez/100 8.00 20.00
DC8 C.C. Sabathia/100 8.00 20.00
DC9 Carl Crawford/50 8.00 20.00
DC11 Carlos Lee/100 8.00 20.00
DC12 Craig Wilson/100 5.00 12.00
DC30 Lyle Overbay/100 5.00 12.00
DC31 Mark Teixeira/25 20.00 50.00
DC32 Melvin Mora/50 10.00 25.00
DC33 Michael Young/100 8.00 20.00
DC36 Paul LoDuca/25 12.50 30.00
DC42 Sean Burroughs/50 6.00 15.00
DC43 Sean Casey/25 12.50 30.00
DC44 Shannon Stewart/25 12.50 30.00
DC46 Steve Finley/25 12.50 30.00
DC50 Travis Hafner/50 10.00 25.00
DC56 Johan Santana/25 20.00 50.00
DC57 Mark Mulder/25 10.00 25.00
DC60 Victor Martinez/25 12.50 30.00

2005 Diamond Kings Gallery of Stars

SER.2 STATED ODDS 1:8
GS1 Andre Dawson .75 2.00
GS2 Bob Feller .75 2.00
GS3 Bobby Doerr .75 2.00
GS4 C.C. Sabathia .75 2.00
GS5 Carl Crawford .75 2.00
GS6 Dale Murphy 1.25 3.00
GS7 Danny Kolb .50 1.25
GS8 Darryl Strawberry .50 1.25
GS9 Dave Parker .50 1.25
GS10 David Ortiz 1.25 3.00
GS11 Dwight Gooden .50 1.25
GS12 Garret Anderson .50 1.25
GS13 Jack Morris .75 2.00
GS14 Jacque Jones .50 1.25
GS15 Jim Palmer .75 2.00
GS16 Johan Santana .75 2.00
GS17 Ken Harvey .50 1.25
GS18 Lyle Overbay .50 1.25
GS19 Marty Marion .50 1.25
GS20 Melvin Mora .50 1.25
GS21 Michael Young .50 1.25
GS22 Miguel Cabrera 1.25 3.00
GS23 Preston Wilson .50 1.25
GS24 Sean Casey .50 1.25
GS25 Victor Martinez .75 2.00

2005 Diamond Kings Gallery of Stars Bat

*BAT p/r 200: .3X TO .8X JSY p/r 100
*BAT p/r 100: .4X TO 1X JSY p/r 100
*BAT p/r 100: .3X TO .8X JSY p/r 50
*BAT p/r 100: .25X TO .6X JSY p/r 25
*BAT p/r 50: .5X TO 1.2X JSY p/r 100
OVERALL AU-GU ODDS 1:6
PRINT RUNS B/WN 50-200 COPIES PER

2005 Diamond Kings Gallery of Stars Combos

*COMBO p/r 200: .4X TO 1X JSY p/r 100
*COMBO p/r 100: .5X TO 1.2X JSY p/r 100
*COMBO p/r 100: .4X TO 1X JSY p/r 50
*COMBO p/r 100: .3X TO .8X JSY p/r 25
*COMBO p/r 50: .6X TO 1.5X JSY p/r 100
*COMBO p/r 50: .5X TO 1.2X JSY p/r 50
PRINT RUNS B/WN 50-200 COPIES PER
PRIME PRINT RUN 1 SERIAL #'d SET
NO PRIME PRICING DUE TO SCARCITY
OVERALL AU-GU ODDS 1:6

2005 Diamond Kings Gallery of Stars Jersey

PRINT RUNS B/WN 25-100 COPIES PER
PRIME PRINT RUN 1 SERIAL #'d SET
NO PRIME PRICING DUE TO SCARCITY
OVERALL AU-GU ODDS 1:6
GS1 Andre Dawson/100 3.00 8.00
GS2 Bob Feller Pants/50 5.00 12.00
GS3 Bobby Doerr Pants/100 3.00 8.00
GS4 C.C. Sabathia/100 2.50 6.00
GS5 Carl Crawford/100 2.50 6.00
GS6 Dale Murphy/100 4.00 10.00
GS8 Darryl Strawberry/25 5.00 12.00
GS9 Dave Parker/100 3.00 8.00
GS10 David Ortiz/100 3.00 8.00
GS11 Dwight Gooden/25 5.00 12.00
GS12 Garret Anderson/50 3.00 8.00
GS13 Jack Morris/100 3.00 8.00
GS14 Jacque Jones/100 2.50 6.00
GS15 Jim Palmer Pants/50 4.00 10.00
GS17 Ken Harvey/100 2.50 6.00
GS18 Lyle Overbay/100 2.50 6.00
GS20 Melvin Mora/100 2.50 6.00
GS21 Michael Young/100 2.50 6.00
GS22 Miguel Cabrera/100 3.00 8.00
GS23 Preston Wilson/100 2.50 6.00
GS24 Sean Casey/100 2.50 6.00
GS25 Victor Martinez/25 4.00 10.00

2005 Diamond Kings Gallery of Stars Signature

*SIG p/r 100: .3X TO .8X SIG.JSY p/r 100
*SIG p/r 100: .25X TO .6X SIG.JSY p/r 50
*SIG p/r 100: .2X TO .5X SIG.JSY p/r 25
*SIG p/r 50: .4X TO 1X SIG.JSY p/r 100
*SIG p/r 50: .25X TO .6X SIG.JSY p/r 25
*SIG p/r 25: .5X TO 1.2X SIG.JSY p/r 100
*SIG p/r 25: .3X TO .8X SIG.JSY p/r 25
OVERALL AU-GU ODDS 1:6
PRINT RUNS B/WN 5-100 COPIES PER
NO PRICING ON QTY OF 10 OR LESS
GS7 Danny Kolb/100 4.00 10.00
GS8 Darryl Strawberry/100 6.00 15.00

2005 Diamond Kings Gallery of Stars Signature Bat

*BAT p/r 200: .3X TO .8X SIG.JSY p/r 100
*BAT p/r 100: .3X TO .8X SIG.JSY p/r 50
*BAT p/r 100: .25X TO .6X SIG.JSY p/r 25
*BAT p/r 50: .3X TO .8X SIG.JSY p/r 25
*BAT p/r 25: .6X TO 1.5X SIG.JSY p/r 100
*BAT p/r 25: .4X TO 1X SIG.JSY p/r 25
OVERALL AU-GU ODDS 1:6
PRINT RUNS B/WN 25-200 COPIES PER
GS21 Michael Young/100 8.00 20.00
GS22 Miguel Cabrera/50 20.00 50.00

2005 Diamond Kings Gallery of Stars Signature Combos

*SIG.COM p/r 200: .5X TO 1.2X SIG.JSYp/r100
*SIG.COM p/r 100: .4X TO 1X SIG.JSY p/r 100
*SIG.COM p/r 100: .3X TO .8X SIG.JSY p/r 50
*SIG.COM p/r 50: .4X TO 1X SIG.JSY p/r 50
*SIG.COM p/r 50: .3X TO .8X SIG.JSY p/r 25
*SIG.COM p/r 25: .6X TO 1.5X SIG.JSY p/r 100
*SIG.COM p/r 25: .4X TO 1X SIG.JSY p/r 25
PRINT RUNS B/WN 25-200 COPIES PER
PRIME PRINT RUN 1 SERIAL #'d SET
NO PRIME PRICING DUE TO SCARCITY
OVERALL AU-GU ODDS 1:6
GS21 Michael Young Bat-Jsy/50 10.00 25.00
GS22 Miguel Cabrera Bat-Jsy/50 30.00 60.00

2005 Diamond Kings Gallery of Stars Signature Jersey

PRINT RUNS B/WN 25-100 COPIES PER
PRIME PRINT RUN 1 SERIAL #'d SET
NO PRIME PRICING DUE TO SCARCITY
OVERALL AU-GU ODDS 1:6
GS1 Andre Dawson/25 12.50 30.00
GS2 Bob Feller Pants/50 15.00 40.00
GS3 Bobby Doerr Pants/100 8.00 20.00
GS4 C.C. Sabathia/100 8.00 20.00
GS5 Carl Crawford/50 10.00 25.00
GS6 Dale Murphy/50 10.00 25.00
GS9 Dave Parker/100 8.00 20.00
GS10 David Ortiz/50 20.00 50.00
GS11 Dwight Gooden/50 10.00 25.00
GS12 Garret Anderson/50 10.00 25.00
GS13 Jack Morris/50 10.00 25.00
GS14 Jacque Jones/25 12.50 30.00
GS15 Jim Palmer Pants/25 12.50 30.00
GS17 Ken Harvey/100 5.00 12.00
GS18 Lyle Overbay/100 5.00 12.00
GS19 Marty Marion/25 12.50 30.00
GS20 Melvin Mora/100 8.00 20.00
GS24 Sean Casey/25 12.50 30.00
GS25 Victor Martinez/100 8.00 20.00

2005 Diamond Kings Heritage Collection

1-25 STATED ODDS 1:21 SER.1 PACKS
26-35 STATED ODDS 1:76 SER.2 PACKS
HC1 Andre Dawson .60 1.50
HC2 Bob Gibson .60 1.50
HC3 Cal Ripken 3.00 8.00
HC4 Dale Murphy 1.00 2.50
HC5 Darryl Strawberry .40 1.00
HC6 Dennis Eckersley .60 1.50
HC7 Don Mattingly 2.00 5.00
HC8 Duke Snider .60 1.50
HC9 Dwight Gooden .40 1.00
HC10 Eddie Murray .60 1.50
HC11 Frank Robinson .60 1.50
HC12 Gary Carter .60 1.50
HC13 George Brett 2.00 5.00
HC14 Harmon Killebrew 1.00 2.50
HC15 Jack Morris .60 1.50
HC16 Jim Palmer .60 1.50
HC17 Lou Brock .60 1.50
HC18 Mike Schmidt 1.50 4.00
HC19 Nolan Ryan 3.00 8.00
HC20 Ozzie Smith 1.25 3.00
HC21 Phil Niekro .60 1.50
HC22 Rod Carew .60 1.50
HC23 Rollie Fingers .60 1.50
HC24 Steve Carlton .60 1.50
HC25 Tony Gwynn 1.25 3.00
HC26 Curt Schilling .60 1.50
HC27 Bobby Doerr .60 1.50
HC28 Edgar Martinez .60 1.50
HC29 Jim Thorpe 1.50 4.00
HC30 Mark Grace .60 1.50
HC31 Matt Williams .60 1.50
HC32 Paul Molitor 1.00 2.50
HC33 Robin Yount 1.00 2.50
HC34 Ryne Sandberg 2.00 5.00
HC35 Will Clark .60 1.50

2005 Diamond Kings Heritage Collection Bat

*BAT p/r 100: .4X TO 1X JSY p/r 100
*BAT p/r 100: .3X TO .8X JSY p/r 50
*BAT p/r 50: .5X TO 1.2X JSY p/r 100
*BAT p/r 50: .4X TO 1X JSY p/r 50
*BAT p/r 50: .3X TO .8X JSY p/r 25
OVERALL AU-GU ODDS 1:6
PRINT RUNS B/WN 50-100 COPIES PER
HC11 Frank Robinson/50 4.00 10.00

2005 Diamond Kings Heritage Collection Combos

*COMBO p/r 100: .5X TO 1.2X JSY p/r 100
*COMBO p/r 100: .4X TO 1X JSY p/r 50
*COMBO p/r 50: .6X TO 1.5X JSY p/r 100
*COMBO p/r 50: .5X TO 1.2X JSY p/r 50
*COMBO p/r 25: .75X TO 2X JSY p/r 100
*COMBO p/r 25: .6X TO 1.5X JSY p/r 50
PRINT RUNS B/WN 25-100 COPIES PER
PRIME PRINT RUN 1 SERIAL #'d SET
NO PRIME PRICING DUE TO SCARCITY
OVERALL AU-GU ODDS 1:6

2005 Diamond Kings Heritage Collection Jersey

PRINT RUNS B/WN 25-100 COPIES PER
PRIME PRINT RUN 1 SERIAL #'d SET
NO PRIME PRICING DUE TO SCARCITY
OVERALL AU-GU ODDS 1:6
HC1 Andre Dawson/100 3.00 8.00
HC2 Bob Gibson/50 4.00 10.00
HC3 Cal Ripken/100 15.00 40.00
HC4 Dale Murphy/100 5.00 12.00
HC5 Darryl Strawberry/25 3.00 8.00
HC6 Dennis Eckersley/100 3.00 8.00
HC7 Don Mattingly/100 10.00 25.00
HC8 Duke Snider/50 4.00 10.00
HC9 Dwight Gooden/100 2.00 5.00
HC10 Eddie Murray/100 3.00 8.00
HC12 Gary Carter/100 3.00 8.00
HC13 George Brett/50 12.00 30.00
HC14 Harmon Killebrew/100 5.00 12.00
HC15 Jack Morris/100 3.00 8.00
HC16 Jim Palmer/100 3.00 8.00
HC17 Lou Brock/100 3.00 8.00
HC18 Mike Schmidt Jkt/100 8.00 20.00
HC19 Nolan Ryan/100 15.00 40.00
HC20 Ozzie Smith Pants/100 6.00 15.00
HC21 Phil Niekro/50 4.00 10.00
HC22 Rod Carew/100 3.00 8.00
HC23 Rollie Fingers/50 4.00 10.00
HC24 Steve Carlton/50 4.00 10.00
HC25 Tony Gwynn/100 6.00 15.00

2005 Diamond Kings Heritage Collection Signature

*SIG p/r 50: .4X TO 1X SIG.JSY p/r 100
*SIG p/r 25: .5X TO 1.2X SIG.JSY p/r 100
*SIG p/r 25: .4X TO 1X SIG.JSY p/r 50
OVERALL AU-GU ODDS 1:6
PRINT RUNS B/WN 1-50 COPIES PER
NO PRICING ON QTY OF 10 OR LESS

2005 Diamond Kings Heritage Collection Signature Bat

*SIG.BAT p/r 100: .4X TO 1X SIG.JSY p/r 100
*SIG.BAT p/r 50: .5X TO 1.2X SIG.JSY p/r 100
*SIG.BAT p/r 50: .4X TO 1X SIG.JSY p/r 50
*SIG.BATp/r20-25: .5X TO 1.2X SIG.JSYp/r50
*SIG.BAT p/r 20-25: .4X TO 1X SIG.JSY p/r 25
OVERALL AU-GU ODDS 1:6
PRINT RUNS B/WN 5-100 COPIES PER
NO PRICING ON QTY OF 10 OR LESS
HC11 Frank Robinson/25 20.00 50.00
HC25 Tony Gwynn/25 30.00 60.00

2005 Diamond Kings Heritage Collection Signature Combos

*SIG.COM p/r 100: .4X TO 1X SIG.JSY p/r 100
*SIG.COM p/r 50: .5X TO 1.2X SIG.JSY p/r 100
*SIG.COM p/r 50: .4X TO 1X SIG.JSY p/r 50
*SIG.COM p/r 50: .3X TO .8X SIG.JSY p/r 25
*SIG.COM p/r 25: .6X TO 1.5X SIG.JSY p/r 100
*SIG.COM p/r 25: .5X TO 1.2X SIG.JSY p/r 50
*SIG.COM p/r 25: .4X TO 1X SIG.JSY p/r 25
PRINT RUNS B/WN 5-100 COPIES PER
NO PRICING ON QTY OF 10 OR LESS
PRIME PRINT RUN 1 SERIAL #'d SET
NO PRIME PRICING DUE TO SCARCITY
OVERALL AU-GU ODDS 1:6
HC25 Tony Gwynn Bat-Jsy/25 30.00 60.00

2005 Diamond Kings Heritage Collection Signature Jersey

PRINT RUNS B/WN 5-100 COPIES PER
NO PRICING ON QTY OF 10 OR LESS
PRIME PRINT RUN 1 SERIAL #'d SET
NO PRIME PRICING DUE TO SCARCITY
OVERALL AU-GU ODDS 1:6
HC1 Andre Dawson/100 8.00 20.00
HC2 Bob Gibson/25 20.00 50.00
HC4 Dale Murphy/50 15.00 40.00
HC5 Darryl Strawberry Pants/100 8.00 20.00
HC6 Dennis Eckersley/50 10.00 25.00
HC7 Don Mattingly/25 40.00 80.00
HC8 Duke Snider/50 15.00 40.00
HC9 Dwight Gooden/100 8.00 20.00
HC11 Frank Robinson/25 12.00 30.00
HC12 Gary Carter/50 10.00 25.00
HC14 Harmon Killebrew/50 30.00 60.00
HC15 Jack Morris/100 8.00 20.00
HC16 Jim Palmer/25 12.50 30.00
HC17 Lou Brock/50 15.00 40.00
HC20 Ozzie Smith/25 15.00 40.00
HC21 Phil Niekro/25 12.50 30.00
HC22 Rod Carew/25 20.00 50.00
HC23 Rollie Fingers/25 12.50 30.00
HC24 Steve Carlton/25 12.50 30.00
HC27 Bobby Doerr Pants/25 12.50 30.00
HC28 Edgar Martinez/25 20.00 50.00
HC31 Matt Williams/25 20.00 50.00
HC35 Will Clark/25 20.00 50.00

2005 Diamond Kings HOF Heroes

1-50 STATED ODDS 1:5 SER.1 PACKS
51-100 STATED ODDS 1:7 SER.2 PACKS
NON CANVAS RANDOM IN PACKS
NON-CANVAS PRINT RUN 20 SETS
NON-CANVAS PRINT RUN INFO BY DONRUSS
NO NON-CANVAS PRICING AVAILABLE
*BRONZE 1-50: .75X TO 2X BASIC
*BRONZE 51-100: 1X TO 2.5X BASIC
BRONZE 1-50 PRINT RUN 100 #'d SETS
BRONZE 51-100 PRINT RUN 50 #'d SETS
*GOLD 1-50: 1.5X TO 4X BASIC
GOLD 1-50 PRINT RUN 25 #'d SETS
GOLD 51-100 PRINT RUN 10 #'d SETS
GOLD 51-100 NO PRICING AVAILABLE
PLATINUM PRINT RUN 1 SERIAL #'d SET
NO PLATINUM PRICING DUE TO SCARCITY
*SILVER 1-50: 1.25X TO 3X BASIC
*SILVER 51-100: 2X TO 5X BASIC
SILVER 1-50 PRINT RUN 50 #'d SETS
SILVER 51-100 PRINT RUN 25 #'d SETS
*FRAME BLK: 2X TO 5X BASIC
FRAME BLK PRINT RUN 25 #'d SETS
FRAME BLK PLAT.PRINT RUN 1 #'d SET
NO FRAME BLK PLAT.PRICING AVAIL.
*FRAME BLUE: 1X TO 2.5X BASIC
FRAME BLUE PRINT RUN 100 #'d SETS
FRAME BLUE PLAT.PRINT RUN 1 #'d SET
NO FRAME BLUE PLAT.PRICING AVAIL.
*FRAME GRN: 1.25X TO 3X BASIC
FRAME GRN PRINT RUN 50 #'d SETS
FRAME GRN PLAT.PRINT RUN 1 #'d SET
NO FRAME GRN PLAT.PRICING AVAIL.
*FRAME RED: .6X TO 1.5X BASIC
FRAME RED STATED ODDS 1:18
FRAME RED PLAT.PRINT RUN 1 #'d SET
NO FRAME RED PLAT.PRICING AVAIL.

OVERALL INSERT ODDS 10 PER SER.1 BOX
OVERALL INSERT ODDS 12 PER SER.2 BOX
HH1 Phil Niekro .75 2.00
HH2 Brooks Robinson .75 2.00
HH3 Jim Palmer .75 2.00
HH4 Carl Yastrzemski 1.50 4.00
HH5 Ted Williams 2.50 6.00
HH6 Duke Snider .75 2.00
HH7 Burleigh Grimes .75 2.00
HH8 Don Sutton .50 1.25
HH9 Nolan Ryan 4.00 10.00
HH10 Fergie Jenkins .75 2.00
HH11 Carlton Fisk .75 2.00
HH12 Tom Seaver .75 2.00
HH13 Bob Feller .75 2.00
HH14 Nolan Ryan 4.00 10.00
HH15 George Brett 2.50 6.00
HH16 Warren Spahn .75 2.00
HH17 Paul Molitor 1.25 3.00
HH18 Rod Carew .75 2.00
HH19 Harmon Killebrew 1.25 3.00
HH20 Monte Irvin .75 2.00
HH21 Gary Carter .75 2.00
HH22 Phil Rizzuto .75 2.00
HH23 Babe Ruth 3.00 8.00
HH24 Reggie Jackson .75 2.00
HH25 Mike Schmidt 2.00 5.00
HH26 Roberto Clemente 3.00 8.00
HH27 Juan Marichal .75 2.00
HH28 Willie McCovey .75 2.00
HH29 Stan Musial 2.00 5.00
HH30 Ozzie Smith 1.50 4.00
HH31 Dennis Eckersley .75 2.00
HH32 Phil Niekro .75 2.00
HH33 Jim Palmer .75 2.00
HH34 Carl Yastrzemski 1.50 4.00
HH35 Duke Snider .75 2.00
HH36 Don Sutton .75 2.00
HH37 Nolan Ryan 4.00 10.00
HH38 Carlton Fisk .75 2.00
HH39 Tom Seaver .75 2.00
HH40 Bob Feller .75 2.00
HH41 Nolan Ryan 4.00 10.00
HH42 George Brett 2.50 6.00
HH43 Harmon Killebrew 1.25 3.00
HH44 Gary Carter .75 2.00
HH45 Mike Schmidt 2.00 5.00
HH46 Stan Musial 2.00 5.00
HH47 Ozzie Smith 1.50 4.00
HH48 Dennis Eckersley .75 2.00
HH49 Fergie Jenkins .75 2.00
HH50 Brooks Robinson .75 2.00
HH51 Eddie Murray .75 2.00
HH52 Frank Robinson .75 2.00
HH53 Carlton Fisk .75 2.00
HH54 Ted Williams 2.50 6.00
HH55 Rod Carew .75 2.00
HH56 Ernie Banks 1.25 3.00
HH57 Luis Aparicio .75 2.00
HH58 Johnny Bench 1.25 3.00
HH59 Al Kaline 1.25 3.00
HH60 George Kell .75 2.00
HH61 Robin Yount 1.25 3.00
HH62 Nolan Ryan 4.00 10.00
HH63 Whitey Ford .75 2.00
HH64 Reggie Jackson .75 2.00
HH65 Babe Ruth 3.00 8.00
HH66 Rollie Fingers .75 2.00
HH67 Steve Carlton .75 2.00
HH68 Robin Roberts .75 2.00
HH69 Ralph Kiner .75 2.00
HH70 Willie Stargell .75 2.00
HH71 Roberto Clemente 3.00 8.00
HH72 Gaylord Perry .75 2.00
HH73 Bob Gibson .75 2.00
HH74 Lou Brock .75 2.00
HH75 Frankie Frisch .75 2.00
HH76 Eddie Murray .75 2.00
HH77 Frank Robinson .75 2.00
HH78 Carlton Fisk .75 2.00
HH79 Ted Williams 2.50 6.00
HH80 Rod Carew .75 2.00
HH81 Ernie Banks 1.25 3.00
HH82 Luis Aparicio .75 2.00
HH83 Johnny Bench 1.25 3.00
HH84 Al Kaline 1.25 3.00
HH85 Willie Mays 2.50 6.00
HH86 Robin Yount 1.25 3.00
HH87 Nolan Ryan 4.00 10.00
HH88 Whitey Ford .75 2.00
HH89 Reggie Jackson .75 2.00
HH90 Babe Ruth 3.00 8.00
HH91 Rollie Fingers .75 2.00
HH92 Steve Carlton .75 2.00
HH93 Wade Boggs Yanks .75 2.00
HH94 Wade Boggs Sox .75 2.00
HH95 Willie Stargell .75 2.00
HH96 Roberto Clemente 3.00 8.00
HH97 Gaylord Perry .75 2.00
HH98 Bob Gibson .75 2.00
HH99 Lou Brock .75 2.00
HH100 Frankie Frisch .75 2.00

2005 Diamond Kings HOF Heroes Materials Bronze

OVERALL AU-GU ODDS 1:6 PACKS
PRINT RUNS B/WN 1-100 COPIES PER
NO PRICING ON QTY OF 10 OR LESS
HH1 Phil Niekro Bat-Jsy/100 3.00 8.00
HH2 B.Robinson Bat-Jsy/100 3.00 8.00
HH3 Jim Palmer Jsy-Pants/100 3.00 8.00
HH4 C.Yastrzemski Bat-Pants/50 8.00 20.00
HH6 Duke Snider Jsy-Pants/50 4.00 10.00
HH7 B.Grimes Pants-Pants/25 20.00 50.00
HH8 Don Sutton Jsy-Jsy/100 3.00 8.00
HH9 Nolan Ryan Bat-Jkt/50 12.00 30.00
HH10 F.Jenkins Pants-Pants/100 3.00 8.00
HH11 Carlton Fisk Bat-Jkt/100 3.00 8.00
HH12 Tom Seaver Jsy-Pants/50 4.00 10.00
HH13 Bob Feller Pants-Pants/25 5.00 12.00
HH14 Nolan Ryan Bat-Jsy/50 12.00 30.00
HH15 George Brett Bat-Bat/25 15.00 40.00
HH16 W.Spahn Jsy-Pants/25 5.00 12.00
HH17 Paul Molitor Bat-Jsy/100 5.00 12.00
HH18 Rod Carew Bat-Jsy/50 4.00 10.00
HH19 H.Killebrew Bat-Jsy/50 6.00 15.00
HH21 Gary Carter Bat-Jsy/100 3.00 8.00
HH23 Babe Ruth Bat-Pants/25 150.00 400.00
HH24 R.Jackson Bat-Jkt/100 3.00 8.00
HH25 Mike Schmidt Bat-Jkt/50 10.00 25.00
HH26 R.Clemente Bat-Bat/50 15.00 40.00
HH27 J.Marichal Pants-Pants/25 5.00 12.00
HH28 W.McCovey Jsy-Pants/100 3.00 8.00
HH29 Stan Musial Bat-Bat/25 12.00 30.00
HH30 Ozzie Smith Bat-Pants/100 6.00 15.00
HH31 D.Eckersley Jsy-Jsy/100 3.00 8.00
HH32 Phil Niekro Bat-Jsy/100 3.00 8.00
HH33 Jim Palmer Jsy-Pants/25 5.00 12.00
HH34 C.Yaz Bat-Pants/25 10.00 25.00
HH35 Duke Snider Jsy-Pants/25 5.00 12.00
HH36 Don Sutton Jsy-Jsy/100 3.00 8.00
HH37 Nolan Ryan Bat-Jkt/25 15.00 40.00
HH38 Carlton Fisk Bat-Jkt/100 3.00 8.00
HH39 Tom Seaver Bat-Jsy/25 5.00 12.00
HH40 Bob Feller Pants-Pants/25 5.00 12.00
HH41 Nolan Ryan Bat-Jkt/25 15.00 40.00
HH42 George Brett Bat-Bat/25 15.00 40.00
HH43 H.Killebrew Bat-Jsy/25 8.00 20.00
HH44 Gary Carter Bat-Jsy/100 3.00 8.00
HH45 Mike Schmidt Bat-Jsy/25 12.00 30.00
HH46 Stan Musial Bat-Bat/25 12.00 30.00
HH47 Ozzie Smith Bat-Pants/100 6.00 15.00
HH48 D.Eckersley Jsy-Jsy/100 3.00 8.00
HH49 F.Jenkins Pants-Pants/25 5.00 12.00
HH50 B.Robinson Bat-Jsy/25 5.00 12.00
HH51 Eddie Murray Bat-Pants/50 4.00 10.00
HH52 Frank Robinson Bat-Bat/50 4.00 10.00
HH53 Carlton Fisk Bat-Bat/50 4.00 10.00
HH54 Ted Williams Bat-Bat/50 25.00 60.00
HH55 Rod Carew Bat-Jkt Jsy/50 4.00 10.00
HH56 Ernie Banks Bat-Pants/50 6.00 15.00
HH57 Luis Aparicio Bat-Bat/50 4.00 10.00
HH58 Johnny Bench Bat-Jsy/50 6.00 15.00
HH59 Al Kaline Bat-Bat/25 8.00 20.00
HH61 Robin Yount Bat-Jsy/50 6.00 15.00
HH62 Nolan Ryan Bat-Jsy/25 15.00 40.00
HH63 Whitey Ford Jsy-Jsy/25 5.00 12.00
HH64 R.Jackson Pants-Pants/50 4.00 10.00
HH65 Babe Ruth Bat-Pants/25 150.00 400.00
HH66 Rollie Fingers Jsy-Jsy/50 4.00 10.00
HH67 Steve Carlton Bat-Jsy/50 4.00 10.00
HH70 Willie Stargell Bat-Jsy/50 4.00 10.00
HH71 R.Clemente Bat-Bat/25 20.00 50.00
HH72 Gaylord Perry Jsy-Jsy/50 4.00 10.00
HH73 Bob Gibson Jsy-Jsy/25 5.00 12.00
HH74 Lou Brock Bat-Jsy/50 4.00 10.00
HH75 Frankie Frisch Jkt-Jkt/50 8.00 20.00
HH76 Eddie Murray Bat-Bat/50 4.00 10.00
HH77 Frank Robinson Bat-Bat/50 4.00 10.00
HH78 Carlton Fisk Bat-Bat/50 4.00 10.00
HH79 Ted Williams Bat-Bat/25 30.00 80.00
HH80 Rod Carew Bat-Jkt/50 4.00 10.00
HH81 Ernie Banks Bat-Jsy/25 8.00 20.00
HH82 Luis Aparicio Bat-Bat/50 4.00 10.00
HH83 Johnny Bench Bat-Jsy/50 6.00 15.00
HH86 Robin Yount Bat-Jsy/50 6.00 15.00
HH87 Nolan Ryan Bat-Jsy/25 15.00 40.00
HH88 Whitey Ford Jsy-Jsy/25 5.00 12.00
HH89 R.Jackson Pants-Pants/50 4.00 10.00
HH91 Rollie Fingers Jsy-Jsy/50 4.00 10.00
HH92 Steve Carlton Bat-Jsy/50 4.00 10.00
HH95 Willie Stargell Jsy-Jsy/50 4.00 10.00
HH97 Gaylord Perry Jsy-Jsy/50 4.00 10.00
HH99 Lou Brock Bat-Jsy/50 4.00 10.00
HH100 Frankie Frisch Jkt-Jkt/50 8.00 20.00

2005 Diamond Kings HOF Heroes Materials Gold

*GOLD p/r 25: .6X TO 1.5X BRZ p/r 100
*GOLD p/r 25: .5X TO 1.2X BRZ p/r 50
*GOLD p/r 25: .4X TO 1X BRZ p/r 25
OVERALL AU-GU ODDS 1:6
PRINT RUNS B/WN 1-25 COPIES PER
NO PRICING ON QTY OF 10 OR LESS
HH96 R.Clemente Bat-Bat/25 20.00 50.00
HH98 Bob Gibson Jsy-Jsy/25 5.00 12.00

2005 Diamond Kings HOF Heroes Materials Silver

*SILV p/r 50: .5X TO 1.2X BRZ p/r 100
*SILV p/r 50: .4X TO 1X BRZ p/r 50
*SILV p/r 50: .3X TO .8X BRZ p/r 25
*SILV p/r 25: .6X TO 1.5X BRZ p/r 100
*SILV p/r 25: .5X TO 1.2X BRZ p/r 50
*SILV p/r 25: .4X TO 1X BRZ p/r 25
OVERALL AU-GU ODDS 1:6
PRINT RUNS B/WN 10-50 COPIES PER
NO PRICING ON QTY OF 10
HH65 Babe Ruth Pants-Pants/25 150.00 400.00

2005 Diamond Kings HOF Heroes Materials Framed Blue

*BLUE p/r 25: .6X TO 1.5X BRZ p/r 100
*BLUE p/r 25: .5X TO 1.2X BRZ p/r 50
*BLUE p/r 25: .4X TO 1X BRZ p/r 25
PRINT RUNS B/WN 1-25 COPIES PER
NO PRICING ON QTY OF 10 OR LESS
PLATINUM PRINT RUN 1 SERIAL #'d SET
NO PLAT.PRICING DUE TO SCARCITY
OVERALL AU-GU ODDS 1:6
HH65 Babe Ruth Pants-Pants/25 150.00 400.00

2005 Diamond Kings HOF Heroes Materials Framed Red

*RED p/r 50: .5X TO 1.2X BRZ p/r 100
*RED p/r 50: .4X TO 1X BRZ p/r 50
*RED p/r 50: .3X TO .8X BRZ p/r 25
*RED p/r 25: .6X TO 1.5X BRZ p/r 100
*RED p/r 25: .5X TO 1.2X BRZ p/r 50
*RED p/r 25: .4X TO 1X BRZ p/r 25
PRINT RUNS B/WN 5-50 COPIES PER
NO PRICING ON QTY OF 10 OR LESS
PLATINUM PRINT RUN 1 SERIAL #'d SET
NO PLATINUM PRICING DUE TO SCARCITY
OVERALL AU-GU ODDS 1:6
HH5 Ted Williams Bat-Jsy/50 25.00 60.00
HH65 Babe Ruth Pants-Pants/50 125.00 300.00
HH90 Babe Ruth Bat-Pants/50 125.00 300.00
HH96 R.Clemente Bat-Bat/50 15.00 40.00

2005 Diamond Kings HOF Heroes Signature Bronze

OVERALL AU-GU ODDS 1:6
PRINT RUNS B/WN 1-25 COPIES PER
NO PRICING ON QTY OF 10 OR LESS
HH13 Bob Feller/25 15.00 40.00
HH40 Bob Feller/25 15.00 40.00
HH52 Frank Robinson/25 15.00 40.00
HH57 Luis Aparicio/25 10.00 25.00
HH59 Al Kaline/25 25.00 50.00
HH60 George Kell/25 15.00 40.00
HH66 Rollie Fingers/25 10.00 25.00
HH67 Steve Carlton/25 10.00 25.00
HH68 Robin Roberts/25 10.00 25.00
HH69 Ralph Kiner/25 20.00 50.00
HH72 Gaylord Perry/25 10.00 25.00
HH74 Lou Brock/25 15.00 40.00
HH82 Luis Aparicio/25 10.00 25.00
HH84 Al Kaline/25 12.00 30.00
HH91 Rollie Fingers/25 10.00 25.00
HH92 Steve Carlton/25 10.00 25.00
HH93 Wade Boggs Yanks/25 15.00 40.00
HH94 Wade Boggs Sox/25 15.00 40.00
HH97 Gaylord Perry/25 10.00 25.00
HH99 Lou Brock/25 15.00 40.00

2005 Diamond Kings HOF Heroes Signature Framed Black

STATED PRINT RUN 1 SERIAL #'d SET
PLATINUM PRINT RUN 1 SERIAL #'d SET
OVERALL AU-GU ODDS 1:6
NO PRICING DUE TO SCARCITY

2005 Diamond Kings HOF Heroes Signature Framed Blue

PRINT RUNS B/WN 1-10 COPIES PER
PLATINUM PRINT RUN 1 SERIAL #'d SET
OVERALL AU-GU ODDS 1:6
NO PRICING DUE TO SCARCITY

2005 Diamond Kings HOF Heroes Signature Framed Green

PRINT RUNS B/WN 1-10 COPIES PER
PLATINUM PRINT RUN 1 SERIAL #'d SET
OVERALL AU-GU ODDS 1:6
NO PRICING DUE TO SCARCITY

2005 Diamond Kings HOF Heroes Signature Framed Red

*SILV p/r 25: .4X TO 1X BRZ p/r 25
PRINT RUNS B/WN 1-25 COPIES PER
NO PRICING ON QTY OF 10 OR LESS
PLATINUM PRINT RUN 1 SERIAL #'d SET
NO PLAT.PRICING DUE TO SCARCITY
OVERALL AU-GU ODDS 1:6

2005 Diamond Kings HOF Heroes Signature Materials Bronze

OVERALL AU-GU ODDS 1:6 -
PRINT RUNS B/WN 5-50 COPIES PER
NO PRICING ON QTY OF 10 OR LESS
HH2 B.Robinson Bat-Jsy/25 20.00 50.00
HH3 Jim Palmer Jsy-Pants/25 12.50 30.00
HH6 Duke Snider Jsy-Pants/25 20.00 50.00
HH8 Don Sutton Jsy-Jsy/25 12.50 30.00
HH10 F.Jenkins Pants-Pants/25 12.50 30.00
HH13 Bob Feller Pants-Pants/50 15.00 40.00
HH18 Rod Carew Bat-Jsy/50 15.00 40.00
HH19 H.Killebrew Bat-Jsy/25 40.00 80.00
HH21 Gary Carter Bat-Jsy/50 20.00 50.00
HH27 J.Marichal Pants-Pants/25 12.50 30.00
HH28 W.McCovey Jsy-Pants/25 20.00 50.00
HH29 Stan Musial Bat-Bat/25 50.00 100.00
HH30 Ozzie Smith Bat-Pants/25 30.00 60.00
HH31 D.Eckersley Jsy-Jsy/25 12.50 30.00
HH32 Phil Niekro Bat-Jsy/25 12.50 30.00
HH33 Jim Palmer Jsy-Pants/25 12.50 30.00
HH35 Duke Snider Jsy-Pants/25 20.00 50.00
HH36 Don Sutton Jsy-Jsy/25 12.50 30.00
HH40 Bob Feller Pants-Pants/50 15.00 40.00
HH43 H.Killebrew Bat-Jsy/50 30.00 60.00
HH44 Gary Carter Bat-Jsy/50 15.00 40.00
HH47 Ozzie Smith Bat-Pants/25 30.00 60.00
HH48 D.Eckersley Jsy-Jsy/50 10.00 25.00
HH49 F.Jenkins Pants-Pants/25 12.50 30.00
HH50 B.Robinson Bat-Jsy/25 20.00 50.00
HH61 Robin Yount Bat-Jsy/25 30.00 60.00
HH66 Rollie Fingers Jsy-Jsy/50 10.00 25.00
HH72 Gaylord Perry Jsy-Jsy/50 10.00 25.00
HH74 Lou Brock Jsy-Jsy/50 15.00 40.00
HH80 Rod Carew Bat-Jsy/50 15.00 40.00
HH99 Lou Brock Bat-Jsy/25 20.00 50.00

2005 Diamond Kings HOF Heroes Signature Materials Gold

*GOLD: p/r 25: .5X TO 1.2X BRZ p/r 50
*GOLD: p/r 25: .4X TO 1X BRZ p/r 25
OVERALL AU-GU ODDS 1:6
PRINT RUNS B/WN 5-25 COPIES PER
NO PRICING ON QTY OF 10 OR LESS
HH91 Rollie Fingers Jsy-Jsy/25 12.50 30.00

2005 Diamond Kings HOF Heroes Signature Materials Platinum

OVERALL AU-GU ODDS 1:6
STATED PRINT RUN 1 SERIAL #'d SET
NO PRICING DUE TO SCARCITY

2005 Diamond Kings HOF Heroes Signature Materials Silver

*SILV p/r 50: .4X TO 1X BRZ p/r 50
*SILV p/r 25: .5X TO 1.2X BRZ p/r 50
*SILV p/r 25: .4X TO 1X BRZ p/r 25
OVERALL AU-GU ODDS 1:6
PRINT RUNS B/WN 5-50 COPIES PER
NO PRICING ON QTY OF 10 OR LESS
HH91 Rollie Fingers Jsy-Jsy/50 10.00 25.00

2005 Diamond Kings HOF Heroes Signature Materials Framed Black

PRINT RUNS B/WN 5-10 COPIES PER
PLATINUM PRINT RUN 1 SERIAL #'d SET
OVERALL AU-GU ODDS 1:6
NO PRICING DUE TO SCARCITY

2005 Diamond Kings HOF Heroes Signature Materials Framed Blue

*BLUE p/r 25: .5X TO 1.2X BRZ p/r 50
*BLUE p/r 25: .4X TO 1X BRZ p/r 25
PRINT RUNS B/WN 5-25 COPIES PER
NO PRICING ON QTY OF 10 OR LESS
PLATINUM PRINT RUN 1 SERIAL #'d SET
NO PLAT.PRICING DUE TO SCARCITY
OVERALL AU-GU ODDS 1:6
HH53 Carlton Fisk Bat-Jsy/25 12.50 30.00
HH55 Rod Carew Bat-Jkt/25 20.00 50.00
HH58 Johnny Bench Bat-Jsy/25 30.00 60.00
HH62 Nolan Ryan Bat-Jsy/25 100.00 175.00
HH63 Whitey Ford Jsy-Jsy/25 20.00 50.00
HH64 R.Jackson Bat-Pants/25 30.00 60.00
HH67 Steve Carlton Bat-Jsy/25 12.50 30.00
HH77 Frank Robinson Bat-Bat/25 20.00 50.00
HH78 Carlton Fisk Bat-Bat/25 12.50 30.00
HH83 Johnny Bench Bat-Jsy/25 30.00 60.00
HH86 Robin Yount Bat-Jsy/25 30.00 60.00
HH87 Nolan Ryan Bat-Jsy/25 60.00 120.00
HH88 Whitey Ford Jsy-Jsy/25 20.00 50.00
HH89 R.Jackson Bat-Pants/25 30.00 60.00
HH91 Rollie Fingers Jsy-Jsy/25 12.50 30.00
HH92 Steve Carlton Jsy-Pants/25 12.50 30.00

2005 Diamond Kings HOF Heroes Signature Materials Framed Green

PRINT RUNS B/WN 5-10 COPIES PER
PLATINUM PRINT RUN 1 SERIAL #'d SET
OVERALL AU-GU ODDS 1:6
NO PRICING DUE TO SCARCITY

2005 Diamond Kings HOF Heroes Signature Materials Framed Red

*RED p/r 50: .4X TO 1X BRZ p/r 50
*RED p/r 25: .5X TO 1.2X BRZ p/r 50
*RED p/r 25: .4X TO 1X BRZ p/r 25
PRINT RUNS B/WN 5-50 COPIES PER
NO PRICING ON QTY OF 10 OR LESS
PLATINUM PRINT RUN 1 SERIAL #'d SET
NO PLAT.PRICING DUE TO SCARCITY
OVERALL AU-GU ODDS 1:6
HH91 Rollie Fingers Jsy-Jsy/50 10.00 25.00

2005 Diamond Kings HOF Sluggers

RANDOM INSERTS IN SER.2 PACKS
HS1 Duke Snider .75 2.00
HS2 Eddie Murray .75 2.00
HS3 Frank Robinson .75 2.00
HS4 George Brett 2.50 6.00
HS5 Harmon Killebrew 1.25 3.00
HS6 Mike Schmidt 2.00 5.00
HS7 Reggie Jackson .75 2.00
HS8 Roberto Clemente 3.00 8.00
HS9 Stan Musial 2.00 5.00
HS10 Willie Mays 2.50 6.00

2005 Diamond Kings HOF Sluggers Bat

*BAT p/r 50: .4X TO 1X JSY p/r 25
*BAT p/r 50: .3X TO .8X JSY p/r 25
OVERALL AU-GU ODDS 1:6
PRINT RUNS B/WN 10-50 COPIES PER
NO PRICING ON QTY OF 10
HS3 Frank Robinson/50 4.00 10.00
HS4 George Brett/50 10.00 25.00
HS8 Roberto Clemente/50 20.00 50.00

2005 Diamond Kings HOF Sluggers Combos

*COMBO p/r 50: .5X TO 1.2X JSY p/r 50
*COMBO p/r 25: .6X TO 1.5X JSY p/r 50
OVERALL AU-GU ODDS 1:6
PRINT RUNS B/WN 5-50 COPIES PER
NO PRICING ON QTY OF 10 OR LESS
HS4 George Brett Bat-Hat/50 12.50 30.00

2005 Diamond Kings HOF Sluggers Jersey

OVERALL AU-GU ODDS 1:6
PRINT RUNS B/WN 5-50 COPIES PER
NO PRICING ON QTY OF 5
10 Willie Mays Pants/50 12.50 30.00
HS1 Duke Snider Pants/25 6.00 15.00
HS2 Eddie Murray/50 6.00 15.00
HS5 Harmon Killebrew/25 8.00 20.00
HS6 Mike Schmidt/50 10.00 25.00
HS7 Reggie Jackson Pants/50 5.00 12.00
HS9 Stan Musial Pants/25 12.50 30.00

2005 Diamond Kings Masters of the Game

RANDOM INSERTS IN SER.2 PACKS
MG1 Albert Pujols 1.50 4.00
MG2 Cal Ripken 4.00 10.00
MG3 Don Mattingly 2.50 6.00
MG4 Greg Maddux 1.50 4.00
MG5 Jim Thorpe 2.00 5.00
MG6 Nolan Ryan 4.00 10.00
MG7 Randy Johnson 1.25 3.00
MG8 Roberto Clemente 3.00 8.00
MG9 Roger Clemens 1.50 4.00
MG10 Willie Mays 2.50 6.00

2005 Diamond Kings Masters of the Game Bat

*BAT p/r 100: .3X TO .8X JSY p/r 50
*BAT p/r 50: .3X TO .8X JSY p/r 25
*BAT p/r 25: .4X TO 1X JSY p/r 25
OVERALL AU-GU ODDS 1:6
PRINT RUNS B/WN 25-100 COPIES PER
MG8 Roberto Clemente/50 20.00 50.00

2005 Diamond Kings Masters of the Game Combos

*COMBO p/r 50: .5X TO 1.2X JSY p/r 50
*COMBO p/r 25: .5X TO 1.2X JSY p/r 25
OVERALL AU-GU ODDS 1:6
PRINT RUNS B/WN 25-50 COPIES PER

2005 Diamond Kings Masters of the Game Jersey

OVERALL AU-GU ODDS 1:6
PRINT RUNS B/WN 25-50 COPIES PER
MG1 Albert Pujols/50 10.00 25.00
MG2 Cal Ripken/50 15.00 40.00
MG3 Don Mattingly/25 12.50 30.00
MG4 Greg Maddux/50 6.00 15.00
MG5 Jim Thorpe/25 100.00 250.00
MG6 Nolan Ryan/50 10.00 25.00
MG7 Randy Johnson/25 6.00 15.00
MG9 Roger Clemens/50 6.00 15.00
MG10 Willie Mays Pants/25 15.00 40.00

2005 Diamond Kings Team Timeline

1-25 STATED ODDS 1:21 SER.1 PACKS
26-30 RANDOM INSERTS IN SER.2 PACKS
TT1 A.Pujols 2.00 5.00
S.Rolen
TT2 R.Clemens 2.00 5.00
A.Pettitte
TT3 T.Hudson 1.00 2.50
M.Mulder
TT4 H.Blalock 1.00 2.50
M.Teixeira
TT5 M.Cabrera 1.50 4.00
M.Lowell
TT6 G.Maddux 2.00 5.00
S.Sosa
TT7 M.Tejada 5.00 12.00
C.Ripken
TT8 V.Guerrero 1.00 2.50
R.Jackson
TT9 M.Schmidt 2.50 6.00
J.Thome
TT10 C.Jones 2.00 5.00
G.Maddux
TT11 G.Brett 3.00 8.00
K.Harvey
TT12 D.Mattingly 3.00 8.00
H.Matsui
TT13 T.Hunter 1.00 2.50
J.Santana
TT14 C.Delgado .60 1.50
V.Wells
TT15 T.Helton 1.00 2.50
L.Walker
TT16 D.Snider 1.50 4.00
A.Beltre
TT17 A.Kaline 1.50 4.00
I.Rodriguez
TT18 R.Palmeiro 1.00 2.50
E.Murray
TT19 M.Ramirez 2.00 5.00
C.Yastrzemski
TT20 R.Kiner 1.00 2.50
J.Bay
TT21 J.Bench 1.50 4.00
A.Dunn
TT22 R.Yount 1.50 4.00
L.Overbay
TT23 N.Ryan 5.00 12.00
R.Johnson
TT24 G.Carter 1.50 4.00
M.Piazza
TT25 C.Fisk 1.50 4.00
F.Thomas
TT26 N.Ryan 5.00 12.00
M.Piazza
TT27 R.Clemens 2.00 5.00
J.Bagwell
TT28 C.Ripken 5.00 12.00
S.Sosa
TT29 W.Mays 3.00 8.00
J.Thorpe
TT30 A.Pujols 2.50 6.00
S.Musial

2005 Diamond Kings Team Timeline Materials Bat

*BAT p/r 75-100: .4X TO 1X JSY p/r 100
*BAT p/r 50: .5X TO 1.2X JSY p/r 100
*BAT p/r 50: .3X TO .8X JSY p/r 25
*BAT p/r 25: .6X TO 1.5X JSY p/r 100
*BAT p/r 25: .5X TO 1.2X JSY p/r 50
*BAT p/r 25: .4X TO 1X JSY p/r 25
OVERALL AU-GU ODDS 1:6
PRINT RUNS B/WN 25-100 COPIES PER
TT5 M.Cabrera/M.Lowell/100 6.00 15.00
TT17 A.Kaline/I.Rodriguez/25 12.50 30.00
TT28 C.Ripken/S.Sosa/50 12.00 30.00

2005 Diamond Kings Team Timeline Materials Jersey

PRINT RUNS B/WN 25-100 COPIES PER
PRIME PRINT RUN 1 SERIAL #'d SET
NO PRIME PRICING DUE TO SCARCITY
OVERALL AU-GU ODDS 1:6
TT1 A.Pujols/S.Rolen/100 12.00 30.00
TT2 R.Clemens/A.Pettitte/100 10.00 25.00
TT3 T.Hudson/M.Mulder/100 5.00 12.00
TT4 H.Blalock/M.Teixeira/100 6.00 15.00
TT7 M.Tejada/C.Ripken/100 20.00 50.00
TT8 V.Guerrero/R.Jackson/100 8.00 20.00
TT9 Schmidt Jkt/Thome/100 15.00 40.00
TT10 C.Jones/G.Maddux/100 15.00 40.00
TT12 D.Matt Jkt/H.Matsui/100 20.00 50.00
TT14 C.Delgado/V.Wells/100 5.00 12.00
TT15 T.Helton/L.Walker/100 6.00 15.00
TT16 D.Snider/A.Beltre/100 5.00 12.00
TT18 R.Palmeiro/E.Murray/100 8.00 20.00
TT19 M.Ramirez/C.Yaz/100 10.00 25.00
TT21 J.Bench/A.Dunn/100 8.00 20.00
TT22 R.Yount/L.Overbay/100 8.00 20.00
TT23 N.Ryan/R.Johnson/100 15.00 40.00
TT24 G.Carter/M.Piazza/100 8.00 20.00
TT25 C.Fisk/F.Thomas/100 8.00 20.00
TT26 N.Ryan/M.Piazza/50 10.00 25.00
TT27 R.Clemens/J.Bagwell/25 10.00 25.00
TT29 W.Mays/J.Thorpe/25 125.00 200.00
TT30 A.Pujols/S.Musial/25 25.00 60.00

2005 Diamond Kings Timeline

1-25 STATED ODDS 1:21 SER.1 PACKS
26-30 RANDOM INSERTS IN SER.2 PACKS
T1 Roger Clemens Sox-Yanks 2.00 5.00
T2 Nolan Ryan Angels-Astros 5.00 12.00
T3 Carlos Beltran Royals-Astros 1.00 2.50
T4 Ivan Rodriguez Rgr-M's 1.00 2.50
T5 Jim Thome Indians-Phils 1.00 2.50
T6 Mike Piazza Dgr-Mets 1.50 4.00
T7 Miguel Tejada A's-O's 1.00 2.50
T8 Rafael Palmeiro O's-Rgr 1.00 2.50
T9 Greg Maddux Braves-Cubs 2.00 5.00
T10 Tom Glavine Braves-Mets 1.00 2.50
T11 Vlad Guerrero Expos-Angels 1.00 2.50
T12 Curt Schilling D'backs-Sox 1.00 2.50
T13 Mike Mussina O's-Yanks 1.00 2.50
T14 Rickey Henderson A's-Dgr 1.50 4.00
T15 Scott Rolen Phils-Cards 1.00 2.50
T16 Alfonso Soriano Yanks-Rgr 1.00 2.50
T17 Gary Sheffield Braves-Yanks .60 1.50
T18 Carlton Fisk R.Sox-W.Sox 1.00 2.50
T19 Aramis Ramirez Pirates-Cubs .60 1.50
T20 Mark Grace Cubs-D'backs 1.00 2.50
T21 Jason Giambi A's-Yanks .60 1.50
T22 Juan Gonzalez Rgr-Royals .60 1.50
T23 Brad Penny M's-Dgr .60 1.50
T24 N.Garciaparra Sox-Cubs 1.00 2.50
T25 Larry Walker Rockies-Cards 1.00 2.50
T26 Curt Schilling Phils-D'backs 1.00 2.50
T27 R.Jackson Angels-Yanks 1.00 2.50
T28 Gary Carter Expos-Mets 1.00 2.50
T29 Roger Clemens Sox-Astros 2.00 5.00
T30 Nolan Ryan Mets-Astros 5.00 12.00

2005 Diamond Kings Timeline Materials Bat

*BAT p/r 100: .5X TO 1.2X JSY p/r 200
*BAT p/r 100: .4X TO 1X JSY p/r 100
*BAT p/r 50: .4X TO 1X JSY p/r 50
*BAT p/r 50: .3X TO .8X JSY p/r 25
*BAT p/r 25: .6X TO 1.5X JSY p/r 100
*BAT p/r 25: .5X TO 1.2X JSY p/r 50
OVERALL AU-GU ODDS 1:6
PRINT RUNS B/WN 25-100 COPIES PER
T5 J.Thome Indians-Phils/25 10.00 25.00
T10 T.Glavine Braves-Mets/100 6.00 15.00
T17 G.Sheff Braves-Yanks/100 5.00 12.00
T20 M.Grace Cubs-D'backs/100 6.00 15.00
T25 L.Walk Rockies-Cards/100 5.00 12.00

2005 Diamond Kings Timeline Materials Jersey

PRINT RUNS B/WN 25-200 COPIES PER
PRIME PRINT RUN 1 SERIAL #'d SET
NO PRIME PRICING DUE TO SCARCITY
OVERALL AU-GU ODDS 1:6
T1 R.Clemens Sox-Yanks/50 12.50 30.00
T2 N.Ryan Angels-Astros/50 25.00 60.00
T3 C.Belt Royals-Astros/100 5.00 12.00
T4 I.Rodriguez Rgr-M's/200 5.00 12.00
T6 M.Piazza Dgr-Mets/100 8.00 20.00
T7 M.Tejada A's-O's/100 5.00 12.00
T8 R.Palmeiro O's-Rgr/100 6.00 15.00
T9 G.Madd Braves-Cubs/50 12.50 30.00
T11 V.Guer Expos-Angels/100 8.00 20.00
T12 C.Schilling D'backs-Sox/100 6.00 15.00
T13 M.Mussina O's-Yanks/100 6.00 15.00
T14 R.Henderson A's-Dgr/100 10.00 25.00
T15 S.Rolen Phils-Cards/100 6.00 15.00
T16 A.Soriano Yanks-Rgr/50 6.00 15.00
T18 C.Fisk R.Sox-W.Sox/100 6.00 15.00
T19 A.Ramirez Pirates-Cubs/100 5.00 12.00
T21 J.Giambi A's-Yanks/100 5.00 12.00
T22 J.Gonzalez Rgr-Royals/100 5.00 12.00
T26 C.Schill Phils-D'backs/50 6.00 15.00
T27 R.Jack Ang-Yank Pants/50 10.00 25.00
T28 G.Carter Expos-Mets/25 10.00 25.00
T29 R.Clemens Sox-Astros/50 12.50 30.00
T30 N.Ryan Mets-Astros/25 30.00 80.00

2005 Diamond Kings Hawaii

ISSUED AT 05 HAWAII TRADE CONFERENCE
STATED PRINT RUN 10 SERIAL #'d SETS
NO PRICING DUE TO SCARCITY

2015 Diamond Kings

COMP.SET w/o SP's (200) 15.00 40.00
SPs RANDOMLY INSERTED
1 Adam Jones .25 .60
2 Adam Wainwright .25 .60
3 Adrian Beltre .30 .75
4 Adrian Gonzalez .25 .60
5 Al Simmons .25 .60
6 Albert Pujols .40 1.00
7 Alex Gordon .25 .60
8 Alexei Ramirez .25 .60
9 Andrew McCutchen .30 .75
10 Anthony Rendon .30 .75
11 Anthony Rizzo .40 1.00
12 Aroldis Chapman .30 .75
13 Babe Ruth .75 2.00
14 Bill Dickey .20 .50
15 Billy Butler .20 .50
16 Bob Feller .25 .60
17 Bobby Murcer .20 .50
18 Bobby Thomson .25 .60
19 Brock Holt .20 .50
20 Bryce Harper .50 1.25
21 Buster Posey .40 1.00
22 Cal Ripken 1.00 2.50
23 Carl Furillo .20 .50
24 Carlos Gomez .20 .50
25 Charlie Blackmon .30 .75
26 Charlie Gehringer .20 .50
27 Chase Utley .25 .60
28 Chris Davis .20 .50
29 Chris Sale .30 .75
30 Clayton Kershaw .50 1.25
31 Collin McHugh .20 .50
32 Corey Kluber .25 .60
33 Dallas Keuchel .25 .60
34 Danny Santana .20 .50
35 Dave Bancroft .20 .50
36 David Ortiz .30 .75
37 David Wright .25 .60
38 Devin Mesoraco .20 .50
39 Don Drysdale .25 .60
40 Duke Snider .25 .60
41 Dustin Pedroia .30 .75
42 Eddie Mathews .30 .75
43 Edwin Encarnacion .30 .75
44 Elston Howard .20 .50
45 Eric Hosmer .25 .60
46 Evan Gattis .20 .50
47 Evan Longoria .25 .60
48 Felix Hernandez .25 .60
49 Frank Chance .25 .60
50 Frankie Frisch .25 .60
51 Freddie Freeman .40 1.00
52 Gabby Hartnett .20 .50
53 Garrett Richards .25 .60
54 Gary Carter .25 .60
55 George Brett .60 1.50
56 George Kelly .20 .50
57 George Springer .25 .60
58 Giancarlo Stanton .30 .75
59 Gil Hodges .25 .60
60 Gil McDougald .20 .50
61 Gregory Polanco .25 .60
62 Harmon Killebrew .30 .75
63 Herb Pennock .25 .60
64 Honus Wagner .30 .75
65 Ichiro Suzuki .40 1.00
66 Jacoby Ellsbury .25 .60
67 Jake Arrieta .25 .60
68 Jason Heyward .25 .60
69 Jim Gilliam .20 .50
70 Jimmie Foxx .30 .75
71 Joe Cronin .20 .50
72 Joe DiMaggio .60 1.50
73 Joe Jackson .40 1.00
74 Joe Mauer .25 .60
75 Johnny Cueto .25 .60
76 Jonathan Lucroy .25 .60
77 Jose Abreu .30 .75
78 Jose Altuve .25 .60
79 Jose Bautista .25 .60
80 Jose Fernandez .30 .75
81 Josh Donaldson .25 .60
82 Jon Lester .25 .60
83 Justin Upton .25 .60
84 Ken Boyer .20 .50
85 Kirby Puckett .30 .75
86 Kyle Seager .20 .50
87 Lefty Gomez .20 .50
88 Lefty O'Doul .20 .50
89 Lefty Williams .20 .50
90 Leo Durocher .20 .50
91 Lloyd Waner .25 .60
92 Lou Gehrig .60 1.50
93 Luke Appling .25 .60
94 Madison Bumgarner .25 .60
95 Manny Machado .30 .75
96 Mark McGwire .50 1.25
97 Masahiro Tanaka .25 .60
98 Matt Adams .20 .50
99 Matt Shoemaker .25 .60
100 Max Scherzer .30 .75
101 Mel Ott .30 .75
102 Michael Brantley .25 .60
103 Mike Trout 1.50 4.00
104 Miller Huggins .20 .50
105 Miguel Cabrera .30 .75
106 Mookie Betts .60 1.50
107 Nap Lajoie .30 .75
108 Nellie Fox .25 .60
109 Nelson Cruz .30 .75
110 Nolan Ryan 1.00 2.50
111 Paul Goldschmidt .30 .75
112 Paul Waner .25 .60
113 Pee Wee Reese .25 .60
114 Rickey Henderson .30 .75
115 Roberto Clemente .75 2.00
116 Robinson Cano .25 .60
117 Roger Maris .30 .75
118 Rogers Hornsby .25 .60
119 Ron Santo .25 .60
120 Ryan Braun .25 .60
121 Salvador Perez .25 .60
122 Sam Crawford .25 .60
123 Shelby Miller .25 .60
124 Sonny Gray .25 .60
125 Stan Musial .50 1.25
126 Starling Marte .25 .60
127 Stephen Strasburg .30 .75
128 Ted Kluszewski .25 .60
129 Ted Williams .60 1.50
130 Thurman Munson .30 .75
131 Todd Frazier .20 .50
132 Tommy Henrich .20 .50
133 Tony Gwynn .30 .75
134 Tony Lazzeri .25 .60
135 Tris Speaker .25 .60
136 Troy Tulowitzki .30 .75
137 Ty Cobb .50 1.25
138 Victor Martinez .25 .60
139 Walter Alston .25 .60
140 Warren Spahn .25 .60
141 Wei-Yin Chen .20 .50
142 Whitey Ford .25 .60
143 Willie Kamm .20 .50
144 Willie Keeler .20 .50
145 Willie Stargell .25 .60
146 Xander Bogaerts .30 .75
147 Yadier Molina .40 1.00
148 Yasiel Puig .30 .75
149 Yoenis Cespedes .25 .60
150 Yu Darvish .30 .75
151A Andy Wilkins RC .25 .60
151B Andy Wilkins SP .40 1.00
Black jsy
152A Anthony Ranaudo RC .25 .60
152B Anthony Ranaudo SP .40 1.00
No ball
153 Brandon Finnegan RC .25 .60
154 Buck Farmer RC .25 .60
155A Christian Walker RC .50 1.25
155B Walker SP Bat back .75 2.00
156A Cory Spangenberg RC .25 .60
156B Cory Spangenberg SP .40 1.00
Batting
157A Dalton Pompey RC .30 .75
157B Dalton Pompey SP .50 1.25
White jsy
158A Daniel Norris RC .25 .60
158B Daniel Norris SP .40 1.00
Leg up
159A Dilson Herrera RC .30 .75
159B Dilson Herrera SP .50 1.25
Batting
160 Edwin Escobar RC .25 .60
161 Gary Brown RC .25 .60
162A Jake Lamb RC .40 1.00
162B Jake Lamb SP .60 1.50
Bat Back
163 James McCann RC .40 1.00
164A Javier Baez RC 2.00 5.00
164B Javier Baez SP 3.00 8.00
Looking up
165A Joc Pederson RC 1.00 2.50
165B Joc Pederson SP 1.50 4.00
Bunting
166A Jorge Soler RC .40 1.00
166B Jorge Soler SP .60 1.50
Facing left
167A Kendall Graveman RC .25 .60
167B Kendall Graveman SP .40 1.00
Leg up

168A Kennys Vargas RC .25 .60
168B Kennys Vargas SP .40 1.00
Black jsy
169 Lane Adams RC .25 .60
170A Maikel Franco RC .30 .75
170B Franco SP Swing .50 1.25
171 Matt Barnes RC .25 .60
172 Matt Clark RC .25 .60
173 Matt Szczur RC .30 .75
174A Michael Taylor RC .25 .60
174B Michael Taylor SP .40 1.00
White jsy
175A Mike Foltynewicz RC .25 .60
175B Mike Foltynewicz SP .40 1.00
Ball above head
176 R.J. Alvarez RC .25 .60
177A Rusney Castillo RC .30 .75
177B Rusney Castillo SP .50 1.25
Purple sleeves
178 Ryan Rua RC .25 .60
179A Rymer Liriano RC .25 .60
179B Rymer Liriano SP .40 1.00
Facing right
180A Steven Moya RC .30 .75
180B Steven Moya SP .50 1.25
Facing left
181 Terrance Gore RC .25 .60
182 Trevor May RC .25 .60
183A Yorman Rodriguez RC .25 .60
183B Yorman Rodriguez SP .40 1.00
Black jsy
184 Andrew Chafin RC .25 .60
185 Bryce Brentz RC .25 .60
186 Carson Smith RC .25 .60
187 Daniel Corcino RC .25 .60
188 Melvin Mercedes RC .25 .60
189 Alexander Claudio RC .25 .60
190 Bryan Mitchell RC .25 .60
191 Carlos Rivero RC .25 .60
192 Chris Bassitt RC .25 .60
193 Eric Jokisch RC .25 .60
194 Jose Pirela RC .25 .60
195 Kyle Lobstein RC .25 .60
196 Kyle Ryan RC .25 .60
197 Lisalverto Bonilla RC .25 .60
198 Nick Tropeano RC .25 .60
199 Phil Klein RC .25 .60
200 Tomas Telis RC .25 .60

2015 Diamond Kings Framed Blue

*FRMD BLUE: 2X TO 5X BASIC
*FRMD BLUE RC: 1.5X TO 4X BASIC RC
RANDOM INSERTS IN PACKS
STATED PRINT RUN 99 SER.#'d SETS

2015 Diamond Kings Framed Red

*FRMD RED: 1.2X TO 3X BASIC
*FRMD RED RC: 1X TO 2.5X BASIC RC
RANDOM INSERTS IN PACKS

2015 Diamond Kings Gold

*GOLD: 5X TO 12X BASIC
*GOLD: RC: 4X TO 10X BASIC RC
RANDOM INSERTS IN PACKS
STATED PRINT RUN 25 SER.#'d SETS

2015 Diamond Kings Rookie Sapphire

*SAPPHIRE 1.5X TO 4X BASIC SP
RANDOM INSERTS IN PACKS
STATED PRINT RUN 25 SER.#'d SETS

2015 Diamond Kings Silver

*SILVER: 2X TO 5X BASIC
*SILVER: RC: 1.5X TO 4X BASIC RC
RANDOM INSERTS IN PACKS
STATED PRINT RUN 99 SER.#'d SETS

2015 Diamond Kings Aficionado

COMPLETE SET (20) 12.00 30.00
RANDOM INSERTS IN PACKS
*SAPPHIRE/25: 1.5X TO 4X BASIC
1 Mike Trout 3.00 8.00
2 Yasiel Puig .60 1.50
3 Clayton Kershaw 1.00 2.50
4 Bryce Harper 1.00 2.50
5 Yu Darvish .60 1.50
6 Madison Bumgarner .50 1.25
7 Buster Posey .75 2.00
8 Jose Abreu .60 1.50
9 Masahiro Tanaka .50 1.25
10 Ichiro Suzuki .75 2.00
11 Giancarlo Stanton .60 1.50
12 Corey Kluber .50 1.25
13 Yasmany Tomas .50 1.25
14 Rusney Castillo .50 1.25
15 David Ortiz .60 1.50
16 Miguel Cabrera .60 1.50
17 Andrew McCutchen .60 1.50
18 Yadier Molina .75 2.00
19 David Wright .50 1.25
20 Freddie Freeman .75 2.00

2015 Diamond Kings Also Known As

COMPLETE SET (20) 12.00 30.00
RANDOM INSERTS IN PACKS
*SAPPHIRE/25: 1.5X TO 4X BASIC
1 Nolan Ryan 2.00 5.00
2 Frank Thomas .60 1.50
3 Mariano Rivera .75 2.00
4 Babe Ruth 1.50 4.00
5 Lou Gehrig 1.25 3.00
6 Yasiel Puig .60 1.50
7 Ty Cobb 1.00 2.50
8 Honus Wagner .60 1.50
9 Tris Speaker .50 1.25
10 Rogers Hornsby .50 1.25
11 Frank Chance .50 1.25
12 Sam Crawford .50 1.25
13 Reggie Jackson .50 1.25
14 Joe Jackson .75 2.00
15 Stan Musial 1.00 2.50
16 Albert Pujols .75 2.00
17 Mike Trout 3.00 8.00
18 David Ortiz .60 1.50
19 Tony Gwynn .60 1.50
20 Johnny Bench .60 1.50

2015 Diamond Kings Diamond Cuts Signatures

RANDOM INSERTS IN PACKS
PRINT RUNS B/WN 1-99 COPIES PER
NO PRICING ON QTY 15 OR LESS
1 Stan Musial/99 20.00 50.00
2 Bobby Thomson/99 25.00 60.00
3 Johnny Pesky/99 10.00 25.00
7 Lou Boudreau/49 12.00 30.00
11 Rick Ferrell/25 25.00 60.00
14 Harmon Killebrew/49 15.00 40.00
15 Ralph Kiner/99 12.00 30.00

2015 Diamond Kings DK Materials Silver

RANDOM INSERTS IN PACKS
PRINT RUNS B/WN 10-99 COPIES PER
NO PRICING ON QTY 10
*BLUE p/r 25: .6X TO 1.5X BASE p/r 49-99
*BLUE p/r 25: .4X TO 1X BASE p/r 25
*RED p/r 49-99: .4X TO 1X BASE p/r 49-99
*RED p/r 49-99: .25X TO .6X BASE p/r 25
*RED p/r 25: .6X TO 1.5X BASE p/r 49-99
*RED p/r 25: .4X TO 1X BASE p/r 25
1 Adam Jones/99 3.00 8.00
3 Adrian Beltre/99 4.00 10.00
4 Adrian Gonzalez/99 3.00 8.00
6 Albert Pujols/49 5.00 12.00
7 Alex Gordon/99 3.00 8.00
8 Alexei Ramirez/99 3.00 8.00
9 Andrew McCutchen/99 10.00 25.00
10 Anthony Rendon/25 6.00 15.00
11 Anthony Rizzo/99 5.00 12.00
12 Aroldis Chapman/99 4.00 10.00
15 Billy Butler/99 2.50 6.00
19 Brock Holt/25 4.00 10.00
21 Buster Posey/49 10.00 25.00
24 Carlos Gomez/99 2.50 6.00
27 Chase Utley/99 3.00 8.00
28 Chris Davis/49 2.50 6.00
29 Chris Sale/49 4.00 10.00
30 Clayton Kershaw/49 6.00 15.00
33 Dallas Keuchel/99 3.00 8.00
34 Danny Santana/99 2.50 6.00
36 David Ortiz/99 4.00 10.00
37 David Wright/49 3.00 8.00
38 Devin Mesoraco/99 2.50 6.00
41 Dustin Pedroia/99 4.00 10.00
43 Edwin Encarnacion/99 4.00 10.00
45 Eric Hosmer/99 4.00 10.00
46 Evan Gattis/99 2.50 6.00
47 Evan Longoria/49 3.00 8.00
48 Felix Hernandez/25 5.00 12.00
51 Freddie Freeman/49 5.00 12.00
53 Garrett Richards/49 3.00 8.00
57 George Springer/99 3.00 8.00
58 Giancarlo Stanton/49 4.00 10.00
61 Gregory Polanco/25 5.00 12.00
62 Harmon Killebrew/25 6.00 15.00
63 Herb Pennock/25 15.00 40.00
66 Jacoby Ellsbury/25 5.00 12.00
74 Joe Mauer/49 3.00 8.00
75 Johnny Cueto/99 3.00 8.00
77 Jose Abreu/25 6.00 15.00
78 Jose Altuve/99 3.00 8.00
79 Jose Bautista/99 3.00 8.00
80 Jose Fernandez/25 6.00 15.00
81 Josh Donaldson/99 3.00 8.00
83 Justin Upton/99 3.00 8.00
86 Kyle Seager/25 4.00 10.00
94 Madison Bumgarner/49 3.00 8.00
95 Manny Machado/25 6.00 15.00
97 Masahiro Tanaka/25 5.00 12.00
98 Matt Adams/99 2.50 6.00
100 Max Scherzer/99 4.00 10.00
102 Michael Brantley/99 3.00 8.00
103 Mike Trout/49 20.00 50.00
105 Miguel Cabrera/99 4.00 10.00
106 Mookie Betts/99 8.00 20.00
109 Nelson Cruz/99 4.00 10.00
111 Paul Goldschmidt/49 4.00 10.00
116 Robinson Cano/99 3.00 8.00
120 Ryan Braun/99 3.00 8.00
121 Salvador Perez/99 3.00 8.00
123 Shelby Miller/99 3.00 8.00
124 Sonny Gray/99 3.00 8.00
126 Starling Marte/49 3.00 8.00
127 Stephen Strasburg/25 6.00 15.00
136 Troy Tulowitzki/49 4.00 10.00
138 Victor Martinez/99 3.00 8.00
141 Wei-Yin Chen/25 4.00 10.00
146 Xander Bogaerts/25 6.00 15.00
147 Yadier Molina/25 12.00 30.00
148 Yasiel Puig/25 6.00 15.00
150 Yu Darvish/99 4.00 10.00
201 Aaron Sanchez/99 3.00 8.00
202 Addison Russell/25 10.00 25.00
203 Archie Bradley/99 2.50 6.00
204 Barry Bonds/99 10.00 25.00
205 Billy Hamilton/99 3.00 8.00
206 Byron Buxton/99 12.00 30.00
207 Corey Seager/99 5.00 12.00
208 Deven Marrero/99 2.50 6.00
209 Francisco Lindor/99 4.00 10.00
210 Hunter Harvey/99 2.50 6.00
211 Jacob deGrom/99 8.00 20.00
212 Jake Marisnick/99 2.50 6.00
213 Jameson Taillon/99 3.00 8.00
214 Jesse Winker/99 5.00 12.00
215 Jonathan Gray/99 2.50 6.00
216 Kevin Plawecki/99 2.50 6.00
217 Kolten Wong/99 3.00 8.00
218 Kyle Zimmer/99 2.50 6.00
219 Luis Severino/99 4.00 10.00
220 Nick Castellanos/99 4.00 10.00
221 Peter O'Brien/99 4.00 10.00
223 Robert Stephenson/99 2.50 6.00
224 Travis d'Arnaud/99 3.00 8.00

2015 Diamond Kings DK Minis

RANDOM INSERTS IN PACKS
1 Adam Jones 1.25 3.00
2 Adam Wainwright 1.25 3.00
3 Adrian Beltre 1.50 4.00
4 Adrian Gonzalez 1.25 3.00
5 Al Simmons 1.25 3.00
6 Albert Pujols 2.00 5.00
7 Alex Gordon 1.25 3.00
8 Alexei Ramirez 1.25 3.00
9 Andrew McCutchen 1.50 4.00
10 Anthony Rendon 1.50 4.00
11 Anthony Rizzo 2.00 5.00
12 Aroldis Chapman 1.50 4.00
13 Babe Ruth 4.00 10.00
14 Bill Dickey 1.00 2.50
15 Billy Butler 1.00 2.50
16 Bob Feller 1.25 3.00
17 Bobby Murcer 1.00 2.50
18 Bobby Thomson 1.25 3.00
19 Brock Holt 1.00 2.50
20 Bryce Harper 2.50 6.00
21 Buster Posey 2.00 5.00
22 Cal Ripken 6.00 15.00
23 Carl Furillo 1.00 2.50
24 Carlos Gomez 1.00 2.50
26 Charlie Gehringer 1.00 2.50
27 Chase Utley 1.25 3.00
28 Chris Davis 1.00 2.50
29 Chris Sale 1.50 4.00
30 Clayton Kershaw 2.50 6.00
32 Corey Kluber 1.25 3.00
33 Dallas Keuchel 1.25 3.00
34 Danny Santana 1.00 2.50
35 Dave Bancroft 1.00 2.50
36 David Ortiz 1.50 4.00
37 David Wright 1.25 3.00
38 Devin Mesoraco 1.00 2.50
39 Don Drysdale 1.25 3.00
40 Duke Snider 1.25 3.00
41 Dustin Pedroia 1.50 4.00
42 Eddie Mathews 1.50 4.00
43 Edwin Encarnacion 1.50 4.00
44 Elston Howard 1.00 2.50
45 Eric Hosmer 1.25 3.00
46 Evan Gattis 1.00 2.50
47 Evan Longoria 1.25 3.00
48 Felix Hernandez 1.25 3.00
49 Frank Chance 1.25 3.00
50 Frankie Frisch 1.25 3.00
51 Freddie Freeman 2.00 5.00
52 Gabby Hartnett 1.00 2.50
53 Garrett Richards 1.25 3.00
54 Gary Carter 1.25 3.00
55 George Brett 3.00 8.00
56 George Kelly 1.00 2.50
57 George Springer 1.25 3.00
58 Giancarlo Stanton 1.50 4.00
59 Gil Hodges 1.25 3.00
60 Gil McDougald 1.00 2.50
61 Gregory Polanco 1.25 3.00
62 Harmon Killebrew 1.50 4.00
63 Herb Pennock 1.25 3.00
64 Honus Wagner 1.50 4.00
65 Ichiro Suzuki 2.00 5.00
66 Jacoby Ellsbury 1.25 3.00
68 Jason Heyward 1.25 3.00
69 Jim Gilliam 1.00 2.50
70 Jimmie Foxx 1.50 4.00
71 Joe Cronin 1.00 2.50
72 Joe DiMaggio 3.00 8.00
73 Joe Jackson 2.00 5.00
74 Joe Mauer 1.25 3.00
75 Johnny Cueto 1.25 3.00
76 Jonathan Lucroy 1.25 3.00
77 Jose Abreu 1.50 4.00
78 Jose Altuve 1.25 3.00
79 Jose Bautista 1.25 3.00
80 Jose Fernandez 1.50 4.00
81 Josh Donaldson 1.25 3.00
82 Jon Lester 1.25 3.00
83 Justin Upton 1.25 3.00
84 Ken Boyer 1.00 2.50
85 Kirby Puckett 1.50 4.00
86 Kyle Seager 1.00 2.50
87 Lefty Gomez 1.00 2.50
88 Lefty O'Doul 1.00 2.50
89 Lefty Williams 1.00 2.50
90 Leo Durocher 1.00 2.50
91 Lloyd Waner 1.25 3.00
92 Lou Gehrig 3.00 8.00
93 Luke Appling 1.25 3.00
94 Madison Bumgarner 1.25 3.00
95 Manny Machado 1.50 4.00
96 Mark McGwire 2.50 6.00
97 Masahiro Tanaka 1.25 3.00
98 Matt Adams 1.00 2.50
99 Matt Shoemaker 1.25 3.00
100 Max Scherzer 1.50 4.00
101 Mel Ott 1.50 4.00
102 Michael Brantley 1.25 3.00
103 Mike Trout 8.00 20.00
104 Miller Huggins 1.00 2.50
105 Miguel Cabrera 1.50 4.00
106 Mookie Betts 3.00 8.00
107 Nap Lajoie 1.50 4.00
108 Nellie Fox 1.25 3.00
109 Nelson Cruz 1.50 4.00
110 Nolan Ryan 5.00 12.00
111 Paul Goldschmidt 1.50 4.00
112 Paul Waner 1.25 3.00
113 Pee Wee Reese 1.25 3.00
114 Rickey Henderson 1.50 4.00
115 Roberto Clemente 4.00 10.00
116 Robinson Cano 1.25 3.00
117 Roger Maris 1.50 4.00
118 Rogers Hornsby 1.25 3.00
119 Ron Santo 1.25 3.00
120 Ryan Braun 1.25 3.00
121 Salvador Perez 1.25 3.00
122 Sam Crawford 1.25 3.00
123 Shelby Miller 1.25 3.00
124 Sonny Gray 1.25 3.00
125 Stan Musial 2.50 6.00
126 Starling Marte 1.25 3.00
127 Stephen Strasburg 1.50 4.00
128 Ted Kluszewski 1.25 3.00
129 Ted Williams 3.00 8.00
130 Thurman Munson 1.50 4.00
132 Tommy Henrich 1.00 2.50
133 Tony Gwynn 1.50 4.00
134 Tony Lazzeri 1.25 3.00
135 Tris Speaker 1.25 3.00
136 Troy Tulowitzki 1.50 4.00
137 Ty Cobb 2.50 6.00
138 Victor Martinez 1.25 3.00
139 Walter Alston 1.25 3.00
140 Warren Spahn 1.25 3.00
141 Wei-Yin Chen 1.00 2.50
142 Whitey Ford 1.25 3.00
143 Willie Kamm 1.00 2.50
144 Willie Keeler 1.00 2.50
145 Willie Stargell 1.25 3.00
146 Xander Bogaerts 1.50 4.00
147 Yadier Molina 2.00 5.00
148 Yasiel Puig 1.50 4.00
149 Yoenis Cespedes 1.25 3.00
150 Yu Darvish 1.50 4.00
151 Andy Wilkins 1.00 2.50
152 Anthony Ranaudo 1.00 2.50
153 Brandon Finnegan 1.00 2.50
159 Dilson Herrera 1.25 3.00
160 Edwin Escobar 1.00 2.50
161 Gary Brown 1.00 2.50
162 Jake Lamb 1.50 4.00
164 Javier Baez 8.00 20.00
165 Joc Pederson 4.00 10.00
166 Jorge Soler 1.50 4.00
168 Kennys Vargas 1.00 2.50
170 Maikel Franco 1.25 3.00
171 Matt Barnes 1.00 2.50
173 Matt Szczur 1.25 3.00
174 Michael Taylor 1.00 2.50
175 Mike Foltynewicz 1.00 2.50
176 R.J. Alvarez 1.00 2.50
177 Rusney Castillo 1.25 3.00
178 Ryan Rua 1.00 2.50
179 Rymer Liriano 1.00 2.50
180 Steven Moya 1.25 3.00
182 Trevor May 1.00 2.50
183 Yorman Rodriguez 1.00 2.50
201 Aaron Sanchez 1.25 3.00
202 Addison Russell 3.00 8.00
203 Archie Bradley 1.00 2.50
204 Barry Bonds 2.50 6.00
205 Billy Hamilton 1.25 3.00
206 Byron Buxton 5.00 12.00
207 Corey Seager 5.00 12.00
208 Deven Marrero 1.00 2.50
209 Francisco Lindor 8.00 20.00
210 Hunter Harvey 1.00 2.50
211 Jacob deGrom 3.00 8.00
212 Jake Marisnick 1.00 2.50
213 Jameson Taillon 1.25 3.00
214 Jesse Winker 4.00 10.00
215 Jonathan Gray 1.00 2.50
216 Kevin Plawecki 1.00 2.50
217 Kolten Wong 1.25 3.00
218 Kyle Zimmer 1.00 2.50
219 Luis Severino 1.25 3.00
220 Nick Castellanos 1.50 4.00
221 Peter O'Brien 1.50 4.00
222 Robert Refsnyder 1.25 3.00
223 Robert Stephenson 1.00 2.50
224 Travis d'Arnaud 1.25 3.00
231 Yasmany Tomas 1.25 3.00
232 Todd Frazier 1.00 2.50
233 Randy Johnson 1.50 4.00
234 Craig Biggio 1.25 3.00
235 Frank Thomas 1.50 4.00
236 Frankie Crosetti 1.00 2.50
237 Greg Maddux 2.00 5.00
238 Raisel Iglesias 1.25 3.00
239A Kris Bryant 6.00 15.00
Facing Left
239B Kris Bryant 6.00 15.00
Facing Right
240 Mariano Rivera 2.00 5.00
241 Matt Kemp 1.25 3.00
242 Pedro Martinez 1.25 3.00

2015 Diamond Kings DK Minis Framed Materials

RANDOM INSERTS IN PACKS
PRINT RUNS B/WN 5-99 COPIES PER
NO PRICING ON QTY 15 OR LESS
5 Al Simmons/25 10.00 25.00
6 Albert Pujols/25 8.00 20.00
9 Andrew McCutchen/49 10.00 25.00
14 Bill Dickey/49 6.00 15.00
16 Bob Feller/25 8.00 20.00
20 Bryce Harper/49 10.00 25.00
22 Cal Ripken/49 12.00 30.00
23 Carl Furillo/49 6.00 15.00
26 Charlie Gehringer/25 12.00 30.00
29 Chris Sale/49 4.00 10.00
30 Clayton Kershaw/49 6.00 15.00
39 Don Drysdale/49 8.00 20.00
40 Duke Snider/49 3.00 8.00
42 Eddie Mathews/49 6.00 15.00
44 Elston Howard/49 5.00 12.00
48 Felix Hernandez/49 3.00 8.00
50 Frankie Frisch/25 15.00 40.00
51 Freddie Freeman/49 5.00 12.00
52 Gabby Hartnett/49 20.00 50.00
55 George Brett/49 15.00 40.00
56 George Kelly/49 15.00 40.00
57 George Springer/49 3.00 8.00
58 Giancarlo Stanton/49 4.00 10.00
59 Gil Hodges/99 8.00 20.00
65 Ichiro Suzuki/49 5.00 12.00
73 Joe Jackson/25 100.00 200.00
77 Jose Abreu/25 6.00 15.00
88 Lefty O'Doul/49 50.00 100.00
90 Leo Durocher/25 15.00 40.00
91 Lloyd Waner/49 6.00 15.00
92 Lou Gehrig/25 40.00 100.00
94 Madison Bumgarner/49 3.00 8.00
96 Mark McGwire/49 6.00 15.00
97 Masahiro Tanaka/49 10.00 25.00
101 Mel Ott/25 20.00 50.00
102 Michael Brantley/49 6.00 15.00
103 Mike Trout/49 15.00 40.00
104 Miller Huggins/25 12.00 30.00
105 Miguel Cabrera/49 6.00 15.00
106 Mookie Betts/49 8.00 20.00
107 Nap Lajoie/25 40.00 80.00
108 Nellie Fox/25 10.00 25.00
110 Nolan Ryan/49 25.00 60.00
111 Paul Goldschmidt/49 4.00 10.00
112 Paul Waner/25 12.00 30.00
113 Pee Wee Reese/49 6.00 15.00
114 Rickey Henderson/49 5.00 12.00
115 Roberto Clemente/25 40.00 100.00
116 Robinson Cano/49 3.00 8.00
117 Roger Maris/49 10.00 25.00
118 Rogers Hornsby/25 30.00 60.00
119 Ron Santo/49 3.00 8.00
122 Sam Crawford/25 15.00 40.00
124 Sonny Gray/49 3.00 8.00
125 Stan Musial/49 12.00 30.00
129 Ted Williams/49 20.00 50.00
130 Thurman Munson/49 12.00 30.00
132 Tommy Henrich/49 6.00 15.00
133 Tony Gwynn/49 4.00 10.00
134 Tony Lazzeri/25 10.00 25.00
135 Tris Speaker/25 10.00 25.00
136 Troy Tulowitzki/49 4.00 10.00
137 Ty Cobb/25 40.00 100.00
139 Walter Alston/49 6.00 15.00
144 Willie Keeler/49 10.00 25.00
148 Yasiel Puig/49 4.00 10.00
150 Yu Darvish/49 4.00 10.00
161 Gary Brown/49 2.50 6.00
164 Javier Baez/49 20.00 50.00
165 Joc Pederson/49 10.00 25.00
166 Jorge Soler/49 4.00 10.00
168 Kennys Vargas/49 2.50 6.00
170 Maikel Franco/49 3.00 8.00
174 Michael Taylor/49 2.50 6.00
177 Rusney Castillo/49 3.00 8.00
180 Steven Moya/49 3.00 8.00
204 Barry Bonds/49 10.00 25.00
206 Byron Buxton/49 12.00 30.00
207 Corey Seager/49 12.00 30.00
209 Francisco Lindor/49 20.00 50.00
211 Jacob deGrom/49 8.00 20.00
219 Luis Severino/49 3.00 8.00
235 Frank Thomas/49 15.00 40.00
236 Frankie Crosetti/49 8.00 20.00
240 Mariano Rivera/49 5.00 12.00
243 Pedro Martinez/49 3.00 8.00
245 Randy Johnson/49 8.00 20.00

2015 Diamond Kings DK Minis Materials

RANDOM INSERTS IN PACKS
PRINT RUNS B/WN 10-99 COPIES PER
NO PRICING ON QTY 10
*PRIME/25: .5X TO 1.2X BASE p/r 49-99
*PRIME/25: .4X TO 1X BASE p/r 25
1 Adam Jones/99 3.00 8.00
3 Adrian Beltre/99 4.00 10.00
4 Adrian Gonzalez/99 3.00 8.00
7 Alex Gordon/99 3.00 8.00
8 Alexei Ramirez/99 3.00 8.00
10 Anthony Rendon/99 4.00 10.00
11 Anthony Rizzo/99 5.00 12.00
12 Aroldis Chapman/99 4.00 10.00
15 Billy Butler/99 2.50 6.00
17 Bobby Murcer/99 8.00 20.00
18 Bobby Thomson/99 6.00 15.00
19 Brock Holt/49 2.50 6.00
21 Buster Posey/99 5.00 12.00
24 Carlos Gomez/99 2.50 6.00
27 Chase Utley/99 3.00 8.00
28 Chris Davis/99 2.50 6.00
33 Dallas Keuchel/99 3.00 8.00
34 Danny Santana/49 2.50 6.00
36 David Ortiz/99 4.00 10.00
37 David Wright/99 3.00 8.00
38 Devin Mesoraco/99 2.50 6.00
41 Dustin Pedroia/99 4.00 10.00
43 Edwin Encarnacion/99 4.00 10.00
45 Eric Hosmer/99 3.00 8.00
46 Evan Gattis/99 2.50 6.00
47 Evan Longoria/49 3.00 8.00
53 Garrett Richards/49 3.00 8.00
54 Gary Carter/99 6.00 15.00
60 Gil McDougald/99 6.00 15.00
61 Gregory Polanco/99 6.00 15.00
62 Harmon Killebrew/99 4.00 10.00
66 Jacoby Ellsbury/99 3.00 8.00
68 Jason Heyward/99 3.00 8.00
69 Jim Gilliam/99 2.50 6.00
74 Joe Mauer/99 3.00 8.00
75 Johnny Cueto/99 3.00 8.00
78 Jose Altuve/99 3.00 8.00
79 Jose Bautista/99 3.00 8.00
81 Josh Donaldson/99 3.00 8.00
83 Justin Upton/99 3.00 8.00
84 Ken Boyer/99 2.50 6.00
85 Kirby Puckett/99 15.00 40.00
89 Lefty Williams/99 12.00 30.00
93 Luke Appling/25 8.00 20.00
95 Manny Machado/99 4.00 10.00
98 Matt Adams/99 2.50 6.00
100 Max Scherzer/99 4.00 10.00
109 Nelson Cruz/99 4.00 10.00
120 Ryan Braun/99 3.00 8.00
121 Salvador Perez/99 3.00 8.00
123 Shelby Miller/99 3.00 8.00
126 Starling Marte/99 3.00 8.00
127 Stephen Strasburg/99 4.00 10.00
128 Ted Kluszewski/99 3.00 8.00
138 Victor Martinez/99 3.00 8.00
142 Whitey Ford/99 3.00 8.00
143 Willie Kamm/99 5.00 12.00
145 Willie Stargell/99 8.00 20.00
146 Xander Bogaerts/99 4.00 10.00
147 Yadier Molina/99 6.00 15.00
151 Andy Wilkins/99 2.50 6.00
152 Anthony Ranaudo/99 2.50 6.00
153 Brandon Finnegan/99 2.50 6.00
159 Dilson Herrera/99 3.00 8.00
160 Edwin Escobar/99 2.50 6.00
162 Jake Lamb/99 4.00 10.00
171 Matt Barnes/99 2.50 6.00
173 Matt Szczur/99 3.00 8.00
175 Mike Foltynewicz/99 2.50 6.00
176 R.J. Alvarez/99 2.50 6.00
178 Ryan Rua/25 4.00 10.00
179 Rymer Liriano/99 2.50 6.00
182 Trevor May/99 2.50 6.00
183 Yorman Rodriguez/99 2.50 6.00
201 Aaron Sanchez/99 3.00 8.00
202 Addison Russell/99 4.00 10.00
203 Archie Bradley/99 2.50 6.00
205 Billy Hamilton/99 3.00 8.00
208 Deven Marrero/99 2.50 6.00
210 Hunter Harvey/99 2.50 6.00
212 Jake Marisnick/99 2.50 6.00
213 Jameson Taillon/99 3.00 8.00
214 Jesse Winker/99 5.00 12.00
215 Jonathan Gray/99 2.50 6.00
216 Kevin Plawecki/99 2.50 6.00
217 Kolten Wong/99 3.00 8.00
218 Kyle Zimmer/99 2.50 6.00
220 Nick Castellanos/99 4.00 10.00
221 Peter O'Brien/99 4.00 10.00
223 Robert Stephenson/99 2.50 6.00
224 Travis d'Arnaud/99 3.00 8.00
234 Craig Biggio/49 3.00 8.00
237 Greg Maddux/99 5.00 12.00
247 Wei-Yin Chen/99 2.50 6.00

2015 Diamond Kings DK Originals

COMPLETE SET (20) 10.00 25.00
RANDOM INSERTS IN PACKS
*SAPPHIRE/25: 1.5X TO 4X BASIC
1 Mike Trout 3.00 8.00
2 Yasiel Puig .60 1.50
3 Clayton Kershaw 1.00 2.50
4 Bryce Harper 1.00 2.50
5 Yu Darvish .60 1.50
6 Madison Bumgarner .50 1.25
7 Buster Posey .75 2.00
8 Jose Abreu .60 1.50
9 Masahiro Tanaka .50 1.25
10 Ichiro Suzuki .75 2.00
11 Giancarlo Stanton .60 1.50
12 Corey Kluber .50 1.25
13 Yasmany Tomas .50 1.25
14 Rusney Castillo .50 1.25
15 Dustin Pedroia .60 1.50
16 Miguel Cabrera .60 1.50
17 Andrew McCutchen .60 1.50
18 Yadier Molina .75 2.00
19 Robinson Cano .50 1.25
20 Jacob deGrom 1.25 3.00

2015 Diamond Kings DK Signature Materials Framed Blue

*FRMD BLUE: .6X TO 1.5X BASIC
RANDOM INSERTS IN PACKS
PRINT RUNS B/WN 5-25 COPIES PER
NO PRICING ON QTY 15 OR LESS
1 Adam Jones/25 12.00 30.00
4 Adrian Gonzalez/25 12.00 3.00
10 Anthony Rendon/25 12.00 30.00
11 Anthony Rizzo/25 20.00 50.00
29 Chris Sale/25 12.00 30.00
36 David Ortiz/25 30.00 80.00
203 Archie Bradley/25 6.00 15.00
206 Byron Buxton/25 25.00 60.00

2015 Diamond Kings DK Signature Materials Framed Red

*FRMD RED: .5X TO 1.2X BASIC
RANDOM INSERTS IN PACKS
PRINT RUNS B/WN 5-99 COPIES PER
NO PRICING ON QTY 15 OR LESS
1 Adam Jones/75 10.00 25.00
4 Adrian Gonzalez/49 10.00 25.00
10 Anthony Rendon/75 10.00 25.00
11 Anthony Rizzo/49 15.00 40.00
36 David Ortiz/49 25.00 60.00
203 Archie Bradley/49 5.00 12.00
225 Carlos Rodon/75 12.00 30.00
226 D.J. Peterson/49 5.00 12.00

2015 Diamond Kings DK Signature Materials Silver

RANDOM INSERTS IN PACKS
PRINT RUNS B/WN 10-299 COPIES PER
NO PRICING ON QTY 10 OR LESS
15 Billy Butler/99 4.00 10.00
19 Brock Holt/299 4.00 10.00
33 Dallas Keuchel/299 5.00 12.00
34 Danny Santana/299 4.00 10.00
201 Aaron Sanchez/299 5.00 12.00
202 Addison Russell/199 12.00 30.00
207 Corey Seager/299 20.00 50.00
208 Deven Marrero/99 6.00 15.00
209 Francisco Lindor/99 30.00 80.00
210 Hunter Harvey/99 4.00 10.00
211 Jacob deGrom/99 25.00 60.00
212 Jake Marisnick/99 4.00 10.00
213 Jameson Taillon/99 5.00 12.00
214 Jesse Winker/99 6.00 15.00
215 Jonathan Gray/99 4.00 10.00
216 Kevin Plawecki/99 4.00 10.00
217 Kolten Wong/99 5.00 12.00
218 Kyle Zimmer/99 4.00 10.00
219 Luis Severino/99 5.00 12.00
220 Nick Castellanos/99 6.00 15.00
221 Peter O'Brien/99 6.00 15.00
223 Robert Stephenson/99 4.00 10.00
228 Kendall Graveman/299 4.00 10.00
230 Kris Bryant/99 40.00 100.00

2015 Diamond Kings HOF Heroes Materials Framed Blue

RANDOM INSERTS IN PACKS
PRINT RUNS B/WN 1-25 COPIES PER
NO PRICING ON QTY 10 OR LESS
4 Bob Feller/25 15.00 40.00
5 Charlie Gehringer/25 12.00 30.00

2015 Diamond Kings HOF Heroes Signature Materials Framed Blue

*FRMD BLUE: .5X TO 1.2X BASIC
RANDOM INSERTS IN PACKS
PRINT RUNS B/WN 8-25 COPIES PER
NO PRICING ON QTY 10 OR LESS
14 Carlton Fisk/25 12.00 30.00

2015 Diamond Kings HOF Heroes Signature Materials Framed Red

RANDOM INSERTS IN PACKS
PRINT RUNS B/WN 15-49 COPIES PER
NO PRICING ON QTY 15
10 Al Kaline/49 25.00 50.00
11 Andre Dawson/49 10.00 25.00
12 Billy Williams/49 10.00 25.00
13 Brooks Robinson/49 20.00 50.00
17 Bert Blyleven/49 15.00 40.00
18 Barry Larkin/49 25.00 60.00
19 Bob Gibson/25 20.00 50.00

2015 Diamond Kings HOF Sluggers

COMPLETE SET (20) 10.00 25.00
RANDOM INSERTS IN PACKS
*SAPPHIRE/25: 1.5X TO 4X BASIC
1 Babe Ruth 1.50 4.00
2 Frank Robinson .50 1.25
3 Harmon Killebrew .60 1.50
4 Reggie Jackson .50 1.25
5 Frank Thomas .60 1.50
6 Eddie Mathews .60 1.50
7 Mel Ott .60 1.50
8 Eddie Murray .50 1.25
9 Lou Gehrig 1.25 3.00
10 Stan Musial 1.00 2.50
11 Willie Stargell .50 1.25
12 Carl Yastrzemski 1.00 2.50
13 Andre Dawson .50 1.25
14 Cal Ripken 2.00 5.00
15 Billy Williams .50 1.25
16 Duke Snider .50 1.25
17 Al Kaline .60 1.50
18 Johnny Bench .60 1.50
19 Ty Cobb 1.00 2.50
20 Jimmie Foxx .60 1.50

2015 Diamond Kings Masters of the Game Materials

RANDOM INSERTS IN PACKS
PRINT RUNS B/WN 10-99 COPIES PER
NO PRICING ON QTY 10
1 Nap Lajoie/25 30.00 60.00
5 Chuck Klein/99 10.00 25.00
6 Lou Gehrig/25 30.00 80.00
7 Frank Robinson/99 4.00 10.00
8 Carl Yastrzemski/49 15.00 40.00
9 Miguel Cabrera/99 5.00 12.00
11 Bob Feller/99 6.00 15.00
12 Steve Carlton/99 4.00 10.00
13 Dwight Gooden/99 3.00 8.00
14 Roger Clemens/99 6.00 15.00
15 Pedro Martinez/99 4.00 10.00
16 Randy Johnson/99 5.00 12.00
17 Clayton Kershaw/99 8.00 20.00
18 Mike Trout/99 15.00 40.00
19 Tony Gwynn/99 5.00 12.00
20 Ken Griffey Jr./99 6.00 15.00

2015 Diamond Kings Rookie Signature Materials Silver

RANDOM INSERTS IN PACKS
PRINT RUNS B/WN 99-299 COPIES PER
*FRMD RED/99: .5X TO 1.2X BASIC
*FRMD RED/25: .6X TO 1.5X BASIC
*BLUE/25: .6X TO 1.5X BASIC
151 Andy Wilkins/299 4.00 10.00
152 Anthony Ranaudo/299 4.00 10.00
153 Brandon Finnegan/299 4.00 10.00
157 Dalton Pompey/299 5.00 12.00
159 Dilson Herrera/299 5.00 12.00
160 Edwin Escobar/299 4.00 10.00
161 Gary Brown/299 4.00 10.00
162 Jake Lamb/299 6.00 15.00
164 Javier Baez/299 12.00 30.00
165 Joc Pederson/299 6.00 15.00
166 Jorge Soler/299 6.00 15.00
168 Kennys Vargas/299 4.00 10.00
170 Maikel Franco/299 6.00 15.00
171 Matt Barnes/299 4.00 10.00
173 Matt Szczur/299 5.00 12.00
174 Michael Taylor/299 4.00 10.00
175 Mike Foltynewicz/299 4.00 10.00
176 R.J. Alvarez/299 4.00 10.00
177 Rusney Castillo/299 5.00 12.00
178 Ryan Rua/99 4.00 10.00
179 Rymer Liriano/299 4.00 10.00
180 Steven Moya/299 5.00 12.00
182 Trevor May/299 4.00 10.00
183 Yorman Rodriguez/299 4.00 10.00

2015 Diamond Kings Sketches and Swatches

RANDOM INSERTS IN PACKS
PRINT RUNS B/WN 5-99 COPIES PER
NO PRICING ON QTY 5
*PRIME/25: .5X TO 1.2X BASIC
2 Chris Sale/25 12.00 30.00
3 Dustin Pedroia/25 20.00 50.00
4 Freddie Freeman/49 12.00 30.00
5 Jose Abreu/25 10.00 25.00
7 Paul Goldschmidt/25 12.00 30.00
8 Sonny Gray/25 12.00 30.00
9 Troy Tulowitzki/25 20.00 50.00
10 Jacob deGrom/25 30.00 80.00
11 Brock Holt/99 8.00 20.00
13 Anthony Rendon/49 12.00 30.00
14 Starling Marte/25 20.00 50.00
15 Matt Adams/25 6.00 15.00
17 Eric Hosmer/25 20.00 50.00
18 Edwin Encarnacion/25 10.00 25.00
19 Dallas Keuchel/99 12.00 30.00
20 Adrian Gonzalez/49 8.00 20.00

2015 Diamond Kings Sovereign Signatures Materials

RANDOM INSERTS IN PACKS
PRINT RUNS B/WN 5-99 COPIES PER
NO PRICING ON QTY 15 OR LESS
*PRIME/25: .6X TO 1.5X BASIC
10 Anthony Rizzo/49 12.00 30.00
11 Danny Santana/99 6.00 15.00
19 Adam Jones/49 12.00 30.00

2015 Diamond Kings Studio Portraits Materials Silver

RANDOM INSERTS IN PACKS
PRINT RUNS B/WN 25-99 COPIES PER
1 Yu Darvish/99 4.00 10.00
2 Yasiel Puig/99 10.00 25.00
3 Mike Trout/99 15.00 40.00
4 Bryce Harper/99 8.00 20.00
5 Clayton Kershaw/49 8.00 20.00
6 Madison Bumgarner/99 6.00 15.00
7 Masahiro Tanaka/25 10.00 25.00

8 Ichiro Suzuki/99 8.00 20.00
9 Albert Pujols/99 5.00 12.00
10 David Ortiz/99 4.00 10.00
11 Yadier Molina/99 5.00 12.00
12 Andrew McCutchen/99 10.00 25.00
13 Hyun-Jin Ryu/99 3.00 8.00
14 Jose Bautista/99 3.00 8.00
15 Edwin Encarnacion/99 4.00 10.00
16 Giancarlo Stanton/99 4.00 10.00
17 Felix Hernandez/99 3.00 8.00
18 Miguel Cabrera/99 8.00 20.00
19 Jose Abreu/25 6.00 15.00
20 Robinson Cano/99 3.00 8.00
21 Buster Posey/99 10.00 25.00
22 Paul Goldschmidt/99 4.00 10.00
23 Stephen Strasburg/99 4.00 10.00
24 Evan Longoria/99 3.00 8.00
25 Troy Tulowitzki/99 4.00 10.00

2015 Diamond Kings Studio Portraits Signature Materials Silver

RANDOM INSERTS IN PACKS
PRINT RUNS B/WN 25-99 COPIES PER
*FRMD RED: .4X TO 1X BASIC
1 Andy Wilkins/99 4.00 10.00
2 Anthony Ranaudo/99 4.00 10.00
3 Dalton Pompey/99 5.00 12.00
4 Dilson Herrera/99 5.00 12.00
5 Gary Brown/99 4.00 10.00
6 Jake Lamb/99 6.00 15.00
7 Javier Baez/99 15.00 40.00
8 Joc Pederson/99 15.00 40.00
9 Jorge Soler/99 15.00 40.00
10 Kennys Vargas/99 4.00 10.00
11 Maikel Franco/99 5.00 12.00
12 Matt Barnes/99 4.00 10.00
13 Matt Szczur/99 5.00 12.00
14 Michael Taylor/99 4.00 10.00
15 Mike Foltynewicz/99 4.00 10.00
16 R.J. Alvarez/99 4.00 10.00
17 Rusney Castillo/99 5.00 12.00
19 Rymer Liriano/99 4.00 10.00
20 Steven Moya/99 5.00 12.00
21 Trevor May/99 4.00 10.00
22 Yorman Rodriguez/99 4.00 10.00
23 Edwin Escobar/99 4.00 10.00
25 Kris Bryant/49 75.00 150.00

2015 Diamond Kings Timeline Materials

RANDOM INSERTS IN PACKS
PRINT RUNS B/WN 10-99 COPIES PER
NO PRICING ON QTY 10
*PRIME/25: .75X TO 2X BASIC
2 Abreu/deGrom/25 12.00 30.00
3 Kershaw/Trout/49 20.00 50.00
4 Posey/Bumgarner/99 12.00 30.00
7 Kershaw/Verlander/25 10.00 25.00
9 Castillo/Abreu/25 6.00 15.00
10 Soler/Baez/99 6.00 15.00
11 Pederson/Puig/99 12.00 30.00
12 D.Ortiz/K.Vargas/99 6.00 15.00
13 Harper/Taylor/99 6.00 15.00
15 Suzuki/Tanaka/25 15.00 40.00
16 Johnson/Martinez/99 10.00 25.00
18 Seager/Pederson/49 20.00 50.00
19 Buxton/Vargas/99 20.00 50.00
20 Russell/Bryant/49 20.00 50.00

2016 Diamond Kings

COMP.SET w/o SP (185) 20.00 50.00
1 Babe Ruth .75 2.00
2 Bill Dickey .20 .50
3 Billy Martin .25 .60
4 Frank Chance .25 .60
5 George Kelly .20 .50
6 Gil Hodges .25 .60
7A Honus Wagner .30 .75
7B Honus Wagner SP w/Glove .75 2.00
8 Jimmie Foxx .30 .75
9A Joe DiMaggio .60 1.50
9B DMggo SP Empty stnd 1.50 4.00
10 Joe Jackson .40 1.00
11 Lefty Gomez .20 .50
12 Leo Durocher .20 .50
13A Lou Gehrig .60 1.50
13B Gehrig SP Green 1.50 4.00
14 Luke Appling .25 .60
15 Mel Ott .30 .75
16 Pee Wee Reese .25 .60
17A Roberto Clemente .75 2.00
17B Clmnte SP SP Green 2.00 5.00
18 Roger Maris .30 .75
19 Rogers Hornsby .25 .60
20 Stan Musial .50 1.25
21A Ted Williams .60 1.50
21B Wllms SP Blk slvs 1.50 4.00
22 Tony Lazzeri .25 .60
23A Ty Cobb .50 1.25
23B Cobb SP Bat on shldr 1.25 3.00
24 Walter O'Malley .20 .50
25 Don Hoak .20 .50
26 Earl Averill .20 .50
27 Elston Howard .20 .50
28 Frankie Crosetti .20 .50
29 Frankie Frisch .25 .60
30 Gabby Hartnett .20 .50
31 Gil McDougald .20 .50
32 Goose Goslin .25 .60
33 Bob Meusel .20 .50
34 Bob Turley .20 .50
35 Chuck Klein .20 .50
36 Dom DiMaggio .20 .50
37 Harry Brecheen .20 .50
38 Heinie Groh .20 .50
39 Jake Daubert .20 .50
40 Jim Bottomley .20 .50
41 John McGraw .25 .60
42 Johnny Sain .20 .50
43 Moose Skowron .20 .50
44 Roger Bresnahan .25 .60
45 Tom Yawkey .20 .50
46A Kirby Puckett .30 .75
46B Kirby Puckett SP No bat .75 2.00
47 Jim Gilliam .20 .50
48 Miller Huggins .20 .50
49 Nap Lajoie .30 .75
50 Lefty O'Doul .20 .50
51 Adam Jones .25 .60
52 Adam Wainwright .25 .60
53 Adrian Beltre .30 .75
54 Adrian Gonzalez .25 .60
55 Albert Pujols .40 1.00
56 Andrew McCutchen .30 .75
57 Anthony Rendon .30 .75
58 Anthony Rizzo .40 1.00
59A Bryce Harper .50 1.25
59B Harper SP Thrwng 1.25 3.00
60 Buster Posey .40 1.00
61 Chris Davis .20 .50
62 Clayton Kershaw .50 1.25
63 Dallas Keuchel .25 .60
64 David Ortiz .30 .75
65 David Wright .25 .60
66 Dustin Pedroia .30 .75
67 Edwin Encarnacion .30 .75
68 Eric Hosmer .25 .60
69 Evan Gattis .20 .50
70 Evan Longoria .25 .60
71 Felix Hernandez .25 .60
72 Freddie Freeman .40 1.00
73 Garrett Richards .25 .60
74 George Springer .25 .60
75 Giancarlo Stanton .30 .75
76 Ichiro Suzuki .40 1.00
77 Jake Arrieta .25 .60
78 Jason Heyward .25 .60
79 Joe Mauer .25 .60
80 Jonathan Lucroy .25 .60
81 Jose Abreu .30 .75
82 Jose Altuve .25 .60
83 Jose Bautista .25 .60
84 Josh Donaldson .25 .60
85 Justin Upton .25 .60
86 Madison Bumgarner .25 .60
87 Manny Machado .30 .75
88 Max Scherzer .30 .75
89 Michael Brantley .25 .60
90 Miguel Cabrera .30 .75
91A Mike Trout 1.50 4.00
91B Trout SP Swngng 4.00 10.00
92 Mookie Betts .60 1.50
93 Nelson Cruz .30 .75
94 Paul Goldschmidt .30 .75
95 Robinson Cano .25 .60
96 Salvador Perez .25 .60
97 Sonny Gray .25 .60
98 Starling Marte .25 .60
99 Stephen Strasburg .30 .75
100 Todd Frazier .20 .50
101 Troy Tulowitzki .30 .75
102 Wei-Yin Chen .20 .50
103 Xander Bogaerts .30 .75
104 Yadier Molina .40 1.00
105 Yoenis Cespedes .30 .75
106 Yu Darvish .30 .75
107 Matt Kemp .25 .60
108 David Price .25 .60
109A Kris Bryant .40 1.00
109B Bryant SP Blue slvs 1.00 2.50
110 Yasmany Tomas .20 .50
111 Rusney Castillo .20 .50
112 Jorge Soler .30 .75
113 Joc Pederson .25 .60
114 Maikel Franco .25 .60
115 Noah Syndergaard .25 .60
116 Prince Fielder .25 .60
117 Zack Greinke .30 .75
118 Chris Archer .20 .50
119 Corey Kluber .25 .60
120 Matt Carpenter .30 .75
121 Michael Taylor .20 .50
122 Carlos Correa .30 .75
123 Vladimir Guerrero .25 .60
124 A.J. Pollock .20 .50
125 Nolan Arenado .50 1.25
126 Ken Griffey Jr. .60 1.50
127 George Brett .60 1.50
128 Cal Ripken 1.00 2.50
129 Nolan Ryan 1.00 2.50
130 Rickey Henderson .30 .75
131 Mariano Rivera .40 1.00
132 Dave Winfield .25 .60
133 Jung-Ho Kang .20 .50
134 Roger Clemens .40 1.00
135 Bob Gibson .25 .60
136 Addison Russell .30 .75
137 James McCann .25 .60
138 Dalton Pompey .25 .60
139 Joey Gallo .25 .60
140 Carlos Rodon .30 .75
141A Kyle Schwarber RC .75 2.00
141B Schwrbr SP Bttng 1.50 4.00
142A Corey Seager RC 2.50 6.00
142B Seager SP Bttng 5.00 12.00
143A Miguel Sano RC .40 1.00
143B Sano SP Drk jsy .75 2.00
144A Michael Conforto RC .30 .75
144B Conforto SP Gry jsy .60 1.50
145A Stephen Piscotty RC .40 1.00
145B Piscotty SP Swngng .75 2.00
146 Trea Turner RC .75 2.00
147 Aaron Nola RC .50 1.25
148 Ketel Marte RC .50 1.25
149 Raul Mondesi RC .50 1.25
150 Henry Owens RC .30 .75
151 Greg Bird RC .30 .75
152 Richie Shaffer RC .25 .60
153 Brandon Drury RC .40 1.00
154 Kaleb Cowart RC .25 .60
155 Travis Jankowski RC .25 .60
156 Colin Rea RC .25 .60
157 Dariel Alvarez RC .25 .60
158 Zach Davies RC .30 .75
159 Rob Refsnyder RC .30 .75
160 Peter O'Brien RC .25 .60
161 Brian Johnson RC .25 .60
162 Kyle Waldrop RC .30 .75
163 Luis Severino RC .30 .75
164 Jose Peraza RC .30 .75
165 Jonathan Gray RC .25 .60
166 Hector Olivera RC .30 .75
167 Max Kepler RC .40 1.00
168 Carl Edwards Jr. RC .30 .75
169 Tom Murphy RC .25 .60
170 Mac Williamson RC .25 .60
171 Gary Sanchez RC .75 2.00
172 Miguel Almonte RC .25 .60
173 Michael Reed RC .25 .60
174 Jorge Lopez RC .25 .60
175 Zach Lee RC .25 .60
176 Elias Diaz RC .25 .60
177 Luke Jackson RC .25 .60
178 John Lamb RC .25 .60
179 Pedro Severino RC .25 .60
180 Alex Dickerson RC .25 .60
181 Brian Ellington RC .25 .60
182 Socrates Brito RC .25 .60
183 Kelby Tomlinson RC .25 .60
184 Trayce Thompson RC .40 1.00
185 Frankie Montas RC .30 .75

2016 Diamond Kings Artist's Proofs

*AP 1-140: 2.5X TO 6X BASIC
*AP SP: 1X TO 2.5X BASIC
*AP 141-185: 2X TO 5X BASIC
RANDOM INSERTS IN PACKS
STATED PRINT RUN 99 SER.#'d SETS

2016 Diamond Kings Artist's Proofs Silver

*AP SILVER 1-140: 4X TO 10X BASIC
*AP SILVER SP: 1.5X TO 4X BASIC
*AP SILVER 141-185: 3X TO 8X BASIC
RANDOM INSERTS IN PACKS
STATED PRINT RUN 25 SER.#'d SETS

2016 Diamond Kings Framed

*FRMD 1-140: 1.2X TO 3X BASIC
*FRMD SP: .5X TO 1.2X BASIC
*FRMD 141-185: 1X TO 2.5X BASIC
RANDOM INSERTS IN PACKS

2016 Diamond Kings Framed Blue

*FRMD BLUE 1-140: 2.5X TO 6X BASIC
*FRMD BLUE SP: 1X TO 2.5X BASIC
*FRMD BLUE 141-185: 2X TO 5X BASIC
RANDOM INSERTS IN PACKS
STATED PRINT RUN 99 SER.#'d SETS

2016 Diamond Kings Framed Red

*FRMD RED 1-140: 2.5X TO 6X BASIC
*FRMD RED SP: 1X TO 2.5X BASIC
*FRMD RED 141-185: 2X TO 5X BASIC
RANDOM INSERTS IN PACKS
STATED PRINT RUN 99 SER.#'d SETS

2016 Diamond Kings Aficionado

COMPLETE SET (20) 10.00 25.00
RANDOM INSERTS IN PACKS
*SAPPHIRE/25: 2.5X TO 6X BASIC
A1 Albert Pujols .60 1.50
A2 Josh Donaldson .40 1.00
A3 Jake Arrieta .40 1.00
A4 Dallas Keuchel .40 1.00
A5 Joey Votto .50 1.25
A6 Chris Davis .30 .75
A7 Paul Goldschmidt .50 1.25
A8 Kris Bryant .60 1.50
A9 Carlos Correa .50 1.25
A10 Nolan Arenado .75 2.00
A11 Jose Bautista .40 1.00
A12 Gerrit Cole .50 1.25
A13 Adam Wainwright .40 1.00
A14 Felix Hernandez .40 1.00
A15 Jacob deGrom 1.00 2.50
A16 Adrian Beltre .50 1.25
A17 Todd Frazier .30 .75
A18 Dee Gordon .30 .75
A19 Nelson Cruz .50 1.25
A20 A.J. Pollock .30 .75

2016 Diamond Kings Diamond Cuts Signatures

RANDOM INSERTS IN PACKS
PRINT RUNS B/WN 1-99 COPIES PER
NO PRICING ON QTY 20 OR LESS
EXCHANGE DEADLINE 10/6/2017
DCJP Johnny Pesky/99 8.00 20.00
DCSM Stan Musial/99 20.00 50.00

2016 Diamond Kings Diamond Deco Materials

RANDOM INSERTS IN PACKS
PRINT RUNS B/WN 15-99 COPIES PER
NO PRICING ON QTY 20 OR LESS
*PRIME/25: .75X TO 2X BASIC
DDBB Byron Buxton/99 6.00 15.00
DDCS Corey Seager/49 12.00 30.00
DDGM Greg Maddux/25 10.00 25.00
DDIS Ichiro Suzuki/25
DDJD Josh Donaldson/25 10.00 25.00
DDKB Kris Bryant/25
DDKG Ken Griffey Jr./49 25.00 60.00
DDKS Kyle Schwarber/99 8.00 20.00
DDMC Michael Conforto/99 10.00 20.00
DDMS Mike Schmidt/25 10.00 25.00
DDMS Miguel Sano/99 6.00 15.00
DDMT Mike Trout/25 25.00 60.00
DDRH Rickey Henderson/25 15.00 40.00
DDSP Stephen Piscotty/49
DDVG Vladimir Guerrero/25
DDYM Yoan Moncada/25 15.00 40.00
DDYM Yadier Molina/25 6.00 15.00

2016 Diamond Kings DK Jumbo Materials Silver

RANDOM INSERTS IN PACKS
PRINT RUNS B/WN 5-99 COPIES PER
NO PRICING ON QTY 15 OR LESS
DKJMBH Bryce Harper/25 6.00 15.00
DKJMCC Carlos Correa/25 20.00 50.00
DKJMDK Dallas Keuchel/25 4.00 10.00
DKJMJD Josh Donaldson/25 6.00 15.00
DKJMKB Kris Bryant/99 5.00 12.00
DKJMKG Ken Griffey Jr./25

2016 Diamond Kings DK Jumbo Materials Framed

RANDOM INSERTS IN PACKS
PRINT RUNS B/WN 5-99 COPIES PER
NO PRICING ON QTY 15 OR LESS
DKJMBH Bryce Harper/25 6.00 15.00
DKJMDK Dallas Keuchel/49 3.00 8.00
DKJMDO David Ortiz/25 10.00 25.00
DKJMJD Josh Donaldson/25 6.00 15.00
DKJMKB Kris Bryant/99 5.00 12.00
DKJMKG Ken Griffey Jr./49

2016 Diamond Kings DK Jumbo Materials Framed Blue

RANDOM INSERTS IN PACKS
PRINT RUNS B/WN 3-25 COPIES PER
NO PRICING ON QTY 10 OR LESS
DKJMDK Dallas Keuchel/25 4.00 10.00
DKJMKB Kris Bryant/25 6.00 15.00
DKJMKG Ken Griffey Jr./25

2016 Diamond Kings DK Materials Silver

RANDOM INSERTS IN PACKS
PRINT RUNS B/WN 5-99 COPIES PER
NO PRICING ON QTY 15 OR LESS
9 Adam Wainwright/99 2.50 6.00
10 Adrian Beltre/25 4.00 10.00
11 Adrian Gonzalez/25 3.00 8.00
12 Albert Pujols/25 10.00 25.00
13 Andrew McCutchen/49 8.00 20.00
14 Bryce Harper/25 12.00 30.00
15 Buster Posey/25 8.00 20.00
18 Dallas Keuchel/99 2.50 6.00
19 David Ortiz/25 4.00 10.00
20 David Wright/25 3.00 8.00
21 Dustin Pedroia/25 4.00 10.00
22 Edwin Encarnacion/25 4.00 10.00
24 Felix Hernandez/25 3.00 8.00
25 Freddie Freeman/25 5.00 12.00
26 George Springer/99 2.50 6.00
27 Giancarlo Stanton/25 4.00 10.00
32 Jose Altuve/49 2.50 6.00
33 Jose Bautista/25 3.00 8.00
36 Madison Bumgarner/25 3.00 8.00
39 Miguel Cabrera/25 4.00 10.00
42 Nelson Cruz/25 4.00 10.00
45 Salvador Perez/25 3.00 8.00
46 Sonny Gray/25 3.00 8.00
47 Starling Marte/25 3.00 8.00
49 Xander Bogaerts/99 6.00 15.00
51 Yu Darvish/25 4.00 10.00
52 Matt Kemp/25 3.00 8.00
53 David Price/25 3.00 8.00
54 Kris Bryant/99 4.00 10.00
55 Yasmany Tomas/49 2.00 5.00
57 Jorge Soler/25 4.00 10.00
58 Joc Pederson/25 3.00 8.00
59 Maikel Franco/49 4.00 10.00
60 Noah Syndergaard/25 3.00 8.00
61 Prince Fielder/25 3.00 8.00
62 Chris Archer/25 2.50 6.00
63 Matt Carpenter/25 4.00 10.00
64 Michael Taylor/49 2.00 5.00
65 Carlos Correa/99 6.00 15.00
66 Vladimir Guerrero/25 3.00 8.00
67 A.J. Pollock/99 2.00 5.00
68 Ken Griffey Jr./49 8.00 20.00
70 Jung-Ho Kang/99 5.00 12.00
71 Addison Russell/99 3.00 8.00
72 James McCann/25 12.00 30.00
73 Dalton Pompey/49 2.50 6.00
75 Carlos Rodon/49 3.00 8.00
76 Lucas Giolito/99 3.00 8.00
77 Yoan Moncada/49 8.00 20.00
78 Tyler Glasnow/25 10.00 25.00
79 Dansby Swanson/99 5.00 12.00
80 Blake Snell/99 2.50 6.00
82 Nomar Mazara/99 5.00 12.00
83 Aaron Judge/99 10.00 25.00
84 Wei-Chieh Huang/25 2.50 6.00
85 Alex Bregman/99 6.00 15.00
86 Josh Bell/25 5.00 12.00
87 Willy Adames/25 4.00 10.00
88 Brett Phillips/99 2.00 5.00
89 Jameson Taillon/49 2.50 6.00
90 Rafael Devers/99 4.00 10.00

2016 Diamond Kings DK Materials Bronze

RANDOM INSERTS IN PACKS
PRINT RUNS B/WN 3-49 COPIES PER
NO PRICING ON QTY 15 OR LESS
DKMAB Alex Bregman/49 6.00 15.00
DKMAJ Aaron Judge/49 10.00 25.00
DKMAM Andrew McCutchen/25 10.00 25.00
DKMAP A.J. Pollock/49 2.00 5.00
DKMAR Addison Russell/49 3.00 8.00
DKMAW Adam Wainwright/49 2.50 6.00
DKMBP Brett Phillips/49 2.00 5.00
DKMBS Blake Snell/49 2.50 6.00
DKMCC Carlos Correa/49 6.00 15.00
DKMCR Carlos Rodon/25 4.00 10.00
DKMDP Dalton Pompey/25 3.00 8.00
DKMDS Dansby Swanson/49 5.00 12.00
DKMJK Jung-Ho Kang/49 5.00 12.00
DKMJT Jameson Taillon/25 3.00 8.00
DKMKB Kris Bryant/49 4.00 10.00
DKMLG Lucas Giolito/49 3.00 8.00
DKMMF Maikel Franco/25 5.00 12.00
DKMNM Nomar Mazara/49 5.00 12.00
DKMRD Rafael Devers/49 4.00 10.00
DKMXB Xander Bogaerts/49 6.00 15.00
DKMYM Yoan Moncada/25 10.00 25.00
DKMYT Yasmany Tomas/25 2.50 6.00

2016 Diamond Kings DK Materials Framed

RANDOM INSERTS IN PACKS
PRINT RUNS B/WN 5-99 COPIES PER
NO PRICING ON QTY 15 OR LESS
DKMAB Adrian Beltre/49 3.00 8.00
DKMAB Alex Bregman/99 6.00 15.00
DKMAG Adrian Gonzalez/25 3.00 8.00
DKMAJ Aaron Judge/99 10.00 25.00
DKMAM Andrew McCutchen/99 8.00 20.00
DKMAP Albert Pujols/25 10.00 25.00
DKMAP A.J. Pollock/99 2.00 5.00
DKMAR Addison Russell/99 3.00 8.00
DKMAW Adam Wainwright/99 2.50 6.00
DKMBH Bryce Harper/25 12.00 30.00
DKMBP Buster Posey/25 8.00 20.00
DKMBP Brett Phillips/99 2.00 5.00
DKMBS Blake Snell/99 2.50 6.00
DKMCA Chris Archer/49 2.00 5.00
DKMCC Carlos Correa/99 6.00 15.00
DKMCK Clayton Kershaw/25 6.00 15.00
DKMCR Carlos Rodon/99 3.00 8.00
DKMDK Dallas Keuchel/99 2.50 6.00
DKMDO David Ortiz/49 3.00 8.00
DKMDP Dustin Pedroia/49 3.00 8.00
DKMDP Dalton Pompey/99 2.50 6.00
DKMDP David Price/49 2.50 6.00
DKMDS Dansby Swanson/99 5.00 12.00
DKMDW David Wright/99 2.50 6.00
DKMEE Edwin Encarnacion/49 3.00 8.00
DKMEH Eric Hosmer/25 3.00 8.00
DKMFF Freddie Freeman/49 4.00 10.00
DKMFH Felix Hernandez/25 3.00 8.00
DKMGS George Springer/99 2.50 6.00
DKMGS Giancarlo Stanton/49 3.00 8.00
DKMIS Ichiro Suzuki/25 12.00 30.00
DKMJA Jake Arrieta/25 3.00 8.00
DKMJA Jose Abreu/25 4.00 10.00
DKMJA Jose Altuve/99 2.50 6.00
DKMJB Jose Bautista/49 2.50 6.00
DKMJB Josh Bell/99 4.00 10.00
DKMJD Josh Donaldson/25 3.00 8.00
DKMJG Joey Gallo/25 3.00 8.00
DKMJK Jung-Ho Kang/99 5.00 121.00
DKMJM James McCann/25 12.00 30.00
DKMJM Joe Mauer/25 3.00 8.00
DKMJP Joc Pederson/49 2.50 6.00
DKMJS Jorge Soler/49 3.00 8.00
DKMJT Jameson Taillon/99 2.50 6.00
DKMKB Kris Bryant/99 4.00 10.00
DKMKG Ken Griffey Jr./99 8.00 20.00
DKMLG Lucas Giolito/99 3.00 8.00
DKMMB Michael Brantley/25 3.00 8.00
DKMMB Madison Bumgarner/25 3.00 8.00
DKMMC Miguel Cabrera/49 3.00 8.00
DKMMC Matt Carpenter/49 3.00 8.00
DKMMF Maikel Franco/99 4.00 10.00
DKMMK Matt Kemp/49 2.50 6.00
DKMMM Manny Machado/49 6.00 15.00
DKMMT Mike Trout/25 20.00 50.00
DKMMT Michael Taylor/99 2.00 5.00
DKMNC Nelson Cruz/49 3.00 8.00
DKMNM Nomar Mazara/99 5.00 12.00
DKMNS Noah Syndergaard/49 2.50 6.00
DKMPF Prince Fielder/49 2.50 6.00
DKMPG Paul Goldschmidt/49 3.00 8.00
DKMRC Robinson Cano/25 3.00 8.00
DKMRC Rusney Castillo/25 2.50 6.00
DKMRD Rafael Devers/99 4.00 10.00
DKMSG Sonny Gray/25 3.00 8.00
DKMSM Starling Marte/49 2.50 6.00
DKMSM Stan Musial/25 10.00 25.00
DKMSP Salvador Perez/49 2.50 6.00
DKMTG Tyler Glasnow/25 10.00 25.00
DKMVG Vladimir Guerrero/49 2.50 6.00
DKMWA Willy Adames/49 3.00 8.00
DKMWH Wei-Chieh Huang/25 2.50 6.00
DKMXB Xander Bogaerts/99 6.00 15.00
DKMYD Yu Darvish/49 3.00 8.00
DKMYM Yadier Molina/25 5.00 12.00
DKMYM Yoan Moncada/99 8.00 20.00
DKMYT Yasmany Tomas/49 2.00 5.00

2016 Diamond Kings DK Materials Framed Blue

RANDOM INSERTS IN PACKS
PRINT RUNS B/WN 5-25 COPIES PER
NO PRICING ON QTY 15 OR LESS
DKMAB Adrian Beltre/25 4.00 10.00
DKMAB Alex Bregman/25 8.00 20.00
DKMAJ Aaron Judge/25 12.00 30.00
DKMAM Andrew McCutchen/25 10.00 25.00
DKMAP A.J. Pollock/25 2.50 6.00
DKMAR Addison Russell/25 4.00 10.00
DKMAW Adam Wainwright/25 3.00 8.00
DKMBP Brett Phillips/25 2.50 6.00
DKMBS Blake Snell/25 3.00 8.00
DKMCC Carlos Correa/25 8.00 20.00
DKMDK Dallas Keuchel/25 3.00 8.00
DKMDO David Ortiz/25 4.00 10.00
DKMDP Dalton Pompey/25 3.00 8.00
DKMDS Dansby Swanson/25 6.00 15.00
DKMEE Edwin Encarnacion/25 4.00 10.00
DKMFF Freddie Freeman/25 5.00 12.00
DKMJA Jose Altuve/25 3.00 8.00
DKMJB Jose Bautista/25 3.00 8.00
DKMJB Josh Bell/25 5.00 12.00
DKMJK Jung-Ho Kang/25 6.00 15.00
DKMJP Joc Pederson/25 3.00 8.00
DKMKB Kris Bryant/25 5.00 12.00
DKMKG Ken Griffey Jr./25 10.00 25.00
DKMLG Lucas Giolito/25 4.00 10.00
DKMMF Maikel Franco/25 5.00 12.00
DKMMT Michael Taylor/25 2.50 6.00
DKMNM Nomar Mazara/25 6.00 15.00
DKMPF Prince Fielder/25 3.00 8.00
DKMRD Rafael Devers/25 5.00 12.00
DKMSP Salvador Perez/25 3.00 8.00
DKMXB Xander Bogaerts/25 8.00 20.00
DKMYM Yoan Moncada/25 10.00 25.00
DKMYT Yasmany Tomas/25 2.50 6.00

2016 Diamond Kings DK Materials Signatures Silver

RANDOM INSERTS IN PACKS
PRINT RUNS B/WN 5-299 COPIES PER
NO PRICING ON QTY 20 OR LESS
EXCHANGE DEADLINE 10/6/2017
*BRONZE/99: .4X TO 1X p/r 49-99
*BRONZE/99: .5X TO 1.2X p/r 199-299
*BRONZE/25: .5X TO 1.2X p/r 49-99
*BRONZE/25: .6X TO 1.5X p/r 199-299
DKSAJ Aaron Judge/199 60.00 150.00
DKSAP A.J. Pollock/49 4.00 10.00
DKSAR Addison Russell/49 15.00 40.00
DKSBP Brett Phillips/199 5.00 12.00
DKSBS Blake Snell/199 4.00 10.00
DKSCR Carlos Rodon/25 8.00 20.00
DKSDP Dalton Pompey/49 5.00 12.00
DKSEG Evan Gattis/49 4.00 10.00
DKSGS George Springer/49 8.00 20.00
DKSJA Jake Arrieta/49 EXCH 25.00 60.00
DKSJA Jose Abreu/99 12.00 30.00
DKSJB Josh Bell/99 8.00 20.00
DKSJG Joey Gallo/25 12.00 30.00
DKSJH Jason Heyward/49 5.00 12.00
DKSJK Jung-Ho Kang/49 15.00 40.00
DKSJM James McCann/299 6.00 15.00
DKSJP Joc Pederson/199 10.00 25.00
DKSJS Jorge Soler/199 6.00 15.00
DKSKB Kris Bryant/25 60.00 150.00
DKSLG Lucas Giolito/199 6.00 15.00
DKSMB Michael Brantley/99 5.00 12.00
DKSMB Mookie Betts/299 40.00 100.00
DKSMC Matt Carpenter/99 8.00 20.00
DKSMF Maikel Franco/299 4.00 10.00
DKSMT Michael Taylor/199 3.00 8.00
DKSNS Noah Syndergaard/25 10.00 25.00
DKSSG Sonny Gray/99 5.00 12.00
DKSTF Todd Frazier/49 8.00 20.00
DKSTG Tyler Glasnow/25 15.00 40.00
DKSWH Wei-Chieh Huang/199 3.00 8.00
DKSXB Xander Bogaerts/49 15.00 40.00

2016 Diamond Kings DK Materials Signatures Framed

*FRAMED/49-99: .4X TO 1X p/r 49-99
*FRAMED/49-99: .5X TO 1.2X p/r 199-299
*FRAMED/25: .4X TO 1X p/r 25
*FRAMED/25: .5X TO 1.2X p/r 49-99
*FRAMED/25: .6X TO 1.5X p/r 199-299
RANDOM INSERTS IN PACKS
PRINT RUNS B/WN 5-99 COPIES PER
NO PRICING ON QTY 20 OR LESS
EXCHANGE DEADLINE 10/6/2017
DKSDK Dallas Keuchel/49 8.00 20.00
DKSGR Garrett Richards/99 5.00 12.00
DKSMS Max Scherzer/25
DKSRC Rusney Castillo/49 4.00 10.00

2016 Diamond Kings DK Materials Signatures Framed Blue

*FRM BLUE/49: .4X TO 1X p/r 49-99
*FRM BLUE/49: .5X TO 1.2X p/r 199-299
*FRM BLUE/25: .4X TO 1X p/r 25
*FRM BLUE/25: .5X TO 1.2X p/r 49-99
*FRM BLUE/25: .6X TO 1.5X p/r 199-299
RANDOM INSERTS IN PACKS
PRINT RUNS B/WN 5-49 COPIES PER
NO PRICING ON QTY 15 OR LESS
EXCHANGE DEADLINE 10/6/2017
DKSGR Garrett Richards/25 6.00 15.00
DKSRC Rusney Castillo/25 5.00 12.00

2016 Diamond Kings DK Minis

RANDOM INSERTS IN PACKS
*BLACK/25: .75X TO 2X BASIC
1 Babe Ruth 3.00 8.00
2 Bill Dickey .75 2.00
3 Billy Martin 1.00 2.50
4 Frank Chance 1.00 2.50
5 George Kelly .75 2.00
6 Gil Hodges 1.00 2.50
7 Honus Wagner 1.25 3.00
8 Jimmie Foxx 1.25 3.00
9 Joe DiMaggio 2.50 6.00
10 Joe Jackson 1.50 4.00
11 Lefty Gomez .75 2.00
12 Leo Durocher .75 2.00
13 Lou Gehrig 2.50 6.00
14 Luke Appling 1.00 2.50
15 Mel Ott 1.25 3.00
16 Pee Wee Reese 1.00 2.50
17 Roberto Clemente 3.00 8.00
18 Roger Maris 1.25 3.00
19 Rogers Hornsby 1.00 2.50
20 Stan Musial 2.00 5.00
21 Ted Williams 2.50 6.00
22 Tony Lazzeri 1.00 2.50
23 Ty Cobb 2.00 5.00
24 Walter O'Malley .75 2.00
25 Don Hoak .75 2.00
26 Earl Averill .75 2.00
27 Elston Howard .75 2.00
28 Frankie Crosetti .75 2.00
29 Frankie Frisch 1.00 2.50
30 Gabby Hartnett .75 2.00
31 Gil McDougald .75 2.00
32 Goose Goslin 1.00 2.50
33 Bob Meusel .75 2.00
34 Bob Turley .75 2.00
35 Chuck Klein .75 2.00
36 Dom DiMaggio .75 2.00
37 Harry Brecheen .75 2.00
38 Heinie Groh .75 2.00
39 Jake Daubert .75 2.00
40 Jim Bottomley .75 2.00
41 John McGraw 1.00 2.50
42 Johnny Sain .75 2.00
43 Moose Skowron .75 2.00
44 Roger Bresnahan 1.00 2.50
45 Tom Yawkey .75 2.00
46 Kirby Puckett 1.25 3.00
47 Jim Gilliam .75 2.00
48 Miller Huggins .75 2.00
49 Nap Lajoie 1.25 3.00
50 Lefty O'Doul .75 2.00
51 Adam Jones 1.00 2.50
52 Adam Wainwright 1.00 2.50
53 Adrian Beltre 1.25 3.00
54 Adrian Gonzalez 1.00 2.50
55 Albert Pujols 1.50 4.00
56 Andrew McCutchen 1.25 3.00
57 Anthony Rendon 1.25 3.00
58 Anthony Rizzo 1.50 4.00
59 Bryce Harper 2.00 5.00
60 Buster Posey 1.50 4.00
61 Chris Davis .75 2.00
62 Clayton Kershaw 2.00 5.00
63 Dallas Keuchel 1.00 2.50
64 David Ortiz 1.25 3.00
65 David Wright 1.00 2.50
66 Dustin Pedroia 1.25 3.00
67 Edwin Encarnacion 1.25 3.00
68 Eric Hosmer 1.00 2.50
69 Evan Gattis .75 2.00
70 Evan Longoria 1.00 2.50
71 Felix Hernandez 1.00 2.50
72 Freddie Freeman 1.50 4.00
73 Garrett Richards 1.00 2.50
74 George Springer 1.00 2.50
75 Giancarlo Stanton 1.25 3.00
76 Ichiro Suzuki 1.50 4.00
77 Jake Arrieta 1.00 2.50
78 Jason Heyward 1.00 2.50
79 Joe Mauer 1.00 2.50
80 Jonathan Lucroy 1.00 2.50
81 Jose Abreu 1.25 3.00
82 Jose Altuve 1.00 2.50
83 Jose Bautista 1.00 2.50
84 Josh Donaldson 1.00 2.50
85 Justin Upton 1.00 2.50
86 Madison Bumgarner 1.00 2.50
87 Manny Machado 1.25 3.00
88 Max Scherzer 1.25 3.00
89 Michael Brantley 1.00 2.50
90 Miguel Cabrera 1.25 3.00
91 Mike Trout 6.00 15.00
92 Mookie Betts 2.50 6.00
93 Nelson Cruz 1.25 3.00
94 Paul Goldschmidt 1.25 3.00
95 Robinson Cano 1.00 2.50
96 Salvador Perez 1.00 2.50
97 Sonny Gray 1.00 2.50
98 Starling Marte 1.00 2.50
99 Stephen Strasburg 1.25 3.00
100 Todd Frazier .75 2.00
101 Troy Tulowitzki 1.25 3.00
102 Wei-Yin Chen .75 2.00
103 Xander Bogaerts 1.25 3.00
104 Yadier Molina 1.50 4.00
105 Yoenis Cespedes 1.25 3.00
106 Yu Darvish 1.25 3.00
107 Matt Kemp 1.00 2.50
108 David Price 1.00 2.50
109 Kris Bryant 1.50 4.00
110 Yasmany Tomas .75 2.00
111 Rusney Castillo .75 2.00
112 Jorge Soler 1.25 3.00
113 Joc Pederson 1.00 2.50
114 Maikel Franco 1.00 2.50
115 Noah Syndergaard 1.00 2.50
116 Prince Fielder 1.00 2.50
117 Zack Greinke 1.25 3.00
118 Chris Archer .75 2.00
119 Corey Kluber 1.00 2.50
120 Matt Carpenter 1.25 3.00
121 Michael Taylor .75 2.00
122 Carlos Correa 1.25 3.00
123 Vladimir Guerrero 1.00 2.50
124 A.J. Pollock .75 2.00
125 Nolan Arenado 2.00 5.00
126 Ken Griffey Jr. 2.50 6.00
127 George Brett 2.50 6.00
128 Cal Ripken 4.00 10.00
129 Nolan Ryan 4.00 10.00
130 Rickey Henderson 1.25 3.00
131 Mariano Rivera 1.50 4.00
132 Dave Winfield 1.00 2.50
133 Jung-Ho Kang .75 2.00
134 Roger Clemens 1.50 4.00
135 Bob Gibson 1.00 2.50
136 Addison Russell 1.25 3.00
137 James McCann 1.00 2.50
138 Dalton Pompey 1.00 2.50
139 Joey Gallo 1.00 2.50
140 Carlos Rodon 1.25 3.00
141 Kyle Schwarber 2.50 6.00
142 Corey Seager 8.00 20.00
143 Miguel Sano 1.25 3.00
144 Michael Conforto 1.00 2.50
145 Stephen Piscotty 1.25 3.00
146 Trea Turner 2.50 6.00
147 Aaron Nola 1.50 4.00
148 Ketel Marte 1.50 4.00
149 Raul Mondesi 1.50 4.00
150 Henry Owens 1.00 2.50
151 Greg Bird 1.00 2.50
152 Richie Shaffer .75 2.00
153 Brandon Drury 1.25 3.00
154 Kaleb Cowart .75 2.00
155 Travis Jankowski .75 2.00
156 Colin Rea .75 2.00
157 Dariel Alvarez .75 2.00
158 Zach Davies 1.00 2.50
159 Rob Refsnyder 1.00 2.50
160 Peter O'Brien .75 2.00
161 Brian Johnson .75 2.00
162 Kyle Waldrop 1.00 2.50
163 Luis Severino 1.00 2.50
164 Jose Peraza 1.00 2.50
165 Jonathan Gray .75 2.00
166 Hector Olivera 1.00 2.50
167 Max Kepler 1.25 3.00
168 Carl Edwards Jr. 1.00 2.50
169 Tom Murphy .75 2.00
170 Mac Williamson .75 2.00
171 Gary Sanchez 2.50 6.00
172 Miguel Almonte .75 2.00
173 Michael Reed .75 2.00
174 Jorge Lopez .75 2.00
175 Zach Lee .75 2.00
176 Elias Diaz .75 2.00
177 Luke Jackson .75 2.00
178 John Lamb .75 2.00
179 Pedro Severino .75 2.00
180 Alex Dickerson .75 2.00
181 Brian Ellington .75 2.00
182 Socrates Brito .75 2.00
183 Kelby Tomlinson .75 2.00
184 Trayce Thompson 1.25 3.00
185 Frankie Montas 1.00 2.50
186 Lucas Giolito 1.25 3.00
187 Yoan Moncada 2.00 5.00
188 Tyler Glasnow 3.00 8.00
189 Dansby Swanson 3.00 8.00
190 Blake Snell 1.00 2.50
191 Nomar Mazara 1.25 3.00
192 Aaron Judge 6.00 15.00
193 Wei-Chieh Huang .75 2.00
194 Alex Bregman 4.00 10.00
195 Josh Bell 1.50 4.00
196 Willy Adames 1.25 3.00
197 Brett Phillips .75 2.00
198 Jameson Taillon 1.00 2.50

199 Rafael Devers 2.50 6.00
200 Ken Griffey Jr. 2.50 6.00
201 Frank Robinson 1.00 2.50
202 Andy Pettitte 1.00 2.50
203 Omar Vizquel 1.00 2.50
204 Rickey Henderson 1.25 3.00
205 Johnny Bench 1.25 3.00
206 Greg Maddux 1.50 4.00
207 Randy Johnson 1.25 3.00
208 Roger Clemens 1.50 4.00

2016 Diamond Kings DK Minis Materials

RANDOM INSERTS IN PACKS
PRINT RUNS B/WN 5-99 COPIES PER
NO PRICING ON QTY 15 OR LESS
*PRIME/25: .75X TO 2X BASIC
51 Adam Jones/25 3.00 8.00
54 Adrian Gonzalez/25 3.00 8.00
57 Anthony Rendon/49 3.00 8.00
58 Anthony Rizzo/99 4.00 10.00
65 David Wright/49 2.50 6.00
67 Edwin Encarnacion/99 3.00 8.00
68 Eric Hosmer/49 2.50 6.00
69 Evan Gattis/25 2.50 6.00
72 Freddie Freeman/25 5.00 12.00
73 Garrett Richards/25 3.00 8.00
78 Jason Heyward/25 3.00 8.00
85 Justin Upton/25 3.00 8.00
88 Max Scherzer/25 4.00 10.00
89 Michael Brantley/25 3.00 8.00
92 Mookie Betts/25 8.00 20.00
93 Nelson Cruz/25 4.00 10.00
96 Salvador Perez/25 3.00 8.00
97 Sonny Gray/49 2.50 6.00
98 Starling Marte/25 3.00 8.00
100 Todd Frazier/25 2.50 6.00
102 Wei-Yin Chen/25 2.50 6.00
103 Xander Bogaerts/25 10.00 25.00
106 Yu Darvish/25 4.00 10.00
107 Matt Kemp/49 2.50 6.00
110 Yasmany Tomas/99 2.00 5.00
114 Maikel Franco/99 2.50 6.00
116 Prince Fielder/99 2.50 6.00
118 Chris Archer/25 2.50 6.00
120 Matt Carpenter/25 4.00 10.00
121 Michael Taylor/99 2.00 5.00
124 A.J. Pollock/99 2.00 5.00
136 Addison Russell/99 3.00 8.00
137 James McCann/99 10.00 25.00
138 Dalton Pompey/25 3.00 8.00
139 Joey Gallo/99 2.50 6.00
140 Carlos Rodon/99 3.00 8.00
143 Miguel Sano/99 3.00 8.00
144 Michael Conforto/99 4.00 10.00
145 Stephen Piscotty/49 3.00 8.00
146 Trea Turner/99 6.00 15.00
147 Aaron Nola/99 4.00 10.00
148 Ketel Marte/99 4.00 10.00
149 Raul Mondesi/99 4.00 10.00
151 Greg Bird/25 3.00 8.00
152 Richie Shaffer/99 2.00 5.00
153 Brandon Drury/99 3.00 8.00
154 Kaleb Cowart/99 2.00 5.00
157 Dariel Alvarez/25 2.50 6.00
158 Zach Davies/99 2.50 6.00
159 Rob Refsnyder/99 2.50 6.00
160 Peter O'Brien/99 2.00 5.00
161 Brian Johnson/99 2.00 5.00
162 Kyle Waldrop/49 2.50 6.00
163 Luis Severino/99 2.50 6.00
164 Jose Peraza/99 2.50 6.00
165 Jonathan Gray/99 2.00 5.00
170 Mac Williamson/99 2.00 5.00
171 Gary Sanchez/99 6.00 15.00
173 Michael Reed/25 2.50 6.00
186 Lucas Giolito/99 3.00 8.00
188 Tyler Glasnow/99 8.00 20.00
189 Dansby Swanson/99 6.00 15.00

2016 Diamond Kings DK Minis Materials Framed

RANDOM INSERTS IN PACKS
PRINT RUNS B/WN 5-99 COPIES PER
NO PRICING ON QTY 20 OR LESS
6 Gil Hodges/99 5.00 12.00
12 Leo Durocher/99 6.00 15.00
14 Luke Appling/99 6.00 15.00
15 Mel Ott/99 10.00 25.00
16 Pee Wee Reese/99 6.00 15.00
18 Roger Maris/99 12.00 30.00
19 Rogers Hornsby/25 20.00 50.00
20 Stan Musial/49 10.00 25.00
22 Tony Lazzeri/49 10.00 25.00
25 Don Hoak/99 6.00 15.00
26 Earl Averill/49
27 Elston Howard/99 6.00 15.00
28 Frankie Crosetti/99 6.00 15.00
29 Frankie Frisch/25
31 Gil McDougald/99 6.00 15.00
32 Goose Goslin/99 15.00 40.00
33 Bob Meusel/49 20.00 50.00
34 Bob Turley/99 4.00 10.00
35 Chuck Klein/25 15.00 40.00
37 Harry Brecheen/49 12.00 30.00
38 Heinie Groh/99 8.00 20.00
39 Jake Daubert/49 10.00 25.00
40 Jim Bottomley/25 10.00 25.00
41 John McGraw/25
42 Johnny Sain/99 5.00 12.00
43 Moose Skowron/99 5.00 12.00
44 Roger Bresnahan/49 12.00 30.00
45 Tom Yawkey/99 6.00 15.00
46 Kirby Puckett/99 20.00 50.00
47 Jim Gilliam/99 2.00 5.00
48 Miller Huggins/99 10.00 25.00
50 Lefty O'Doul/99 12.00 30.00
52 Adam Wainwright/99 2.50 6.00
55 Albert Pujols/99 4.00 10.00
56 Andrew McCutchen/99 12.00 30.00
59 Bryce Harper/49 10.00 25.00
60 Buster Posey/99 5.00 12.00
62 Clayton Kershaw/99 6.00 15.00
63 Dallas Keuchel/99 2.50 6.00
64 David Ortiz/99 6.00 15.00
71 Felix Hernandez/99 2.50 6.00
75 Giancarlo Stanton/99 3.00 8.00
76 Ichiro Suzuki/25 20.00 50.00
77 Jake Arrieta/99 3.00 8.00
81 Jose Abreu/99 3.00 8.00
82 Jose Altuve/99 6.00 15.00
83 Jose Bautista/99 2.50 6.00
84 Josh Donaldson/99 2.50 6.00
86 Madison Bumgarner/99 5.00 12.00
87 Manny Machado/99 8.00 20.00
90 Miguel Cabrera/99 10.00 25.00
91 Mike Trout/25 20.00 50.00
94 Paul Goldschmidt/99 3.00 8.00
101 Troy Tulowitzki/99 3.00 8.00
104 Yadier Molina/25 4.00 10.00
108 David Price/99 3.00 8.00
109 Kris Bryant/99 8.00 20.00
113 Joc Pederson/99 3.00 8.00
115 Noah Syndergaard/99 4.00 10.00
122 Carlos Correa/99 12.00 30.00
123 Vladimir Guerrero/99 2.50 6.00
126 Ken Griffey Jr./99 10.00 25.00
127 George Brett/99 12.00 30.00
128 Cal Ripken/99 8.00 20.00
129 Nolan Ryan/99 10.00 25.00
130 Rickey Henderson/99 6.00 15.00
131 Mariano Rivera/49 10.00 25.00
132 Dave Winfield/99 6.00 15.00
133 Jung-Ho Kang/99 8.00 20.00
134 Roger Clemens/99 6.00 15.00
135 Bob Gibson/25 10.00 25.00
141 Kyle Schwarber/99 10.00 25.00
142 Corey Seager/99 6.00 15.00

2016 Diamond Kings DK Minis Signatures

RANDOM INSERTS IN PACKS
PRINT RUNS B/WN 5-99 COPIES PER
NO PRICING ON QTY 15 OR LESS
EXCHANGE DEADLINE 10/6/2017
DMSCK Clayton Kershaw/49 40.00 100.00
DMSDG Dwight Gooden/25 10.00 25.00
DMSJC Jose Canseco/99 12.00 30.00
DMSLC Lorenzo Cain/25 10.00 25.00

2016 Diamond Kings DK Minis Signatures Framed

*FRMD/25-49: .5X TO 1.2X BASIC
RANDOM INSERTS IN PACKS
PRINT RUNS B/WN 5-49 COPIES PER
NO PRICING ON QTY 15 OR LESS
EXCHANGE DEADLINE 10/6/2017
DMSBP Buster Posey/25 60.00 120.00
DMSKB Kris Bryant/49 75.00 150.00

2016 Diamond Kings DK Originals

COMPLETE SET (20) 10.00 25.00
RANDOM INSERTS IN PACKS
*SAPPHIRE/25: 2.5X TO 6X BASIC
DKO1 Mike Trout 2.50 6.00
DKO2 Buster Posey .60 1.50
DKO3 Bryce Harper .75 2.00
DKO4 Clayton Kershaw .75 2.00
DKO5 Jake Arrieta .40 1.00
DKO6 Giancarlo Stanton .50 1.25
DKO7 Josh Donaldson .40 1.00
DKO8 Albert Pujols .60 1.50
DKO9 Kris Bryant .60 1.50
DKO10 Carlos Correa .50 1.25
DKO11 Ken Griffey Jr. 1.00 2.50
DKO12 George Brett 1.00 2.50
DKO13 Cal Ripken 1.50 4.00
DKO14 Rickey Henderson .50 1.25
DKO15 Nolan Ryan 1.50 4.00
DKO16 Kirby Puckett .50 1.25
DKO17 Pete Rose 1.00 2.50
DKO18 Frank Thomas .50 1.25
DKO19 Bo Jackson .50 1.25
DKO20 Mariano Rivera .60 1.50

2016 Diamond Kings Elements of Royalty Material Signatures Framed

RANDOM INSERTS IN PACKS
STATED PRINT RUN 49 SER.#'d SETS
EXCHANGE DEADLINE 10/6/2017
ERDE Dennis Eckersley 8.00 20.00
ERFT Frank Thomas 25.00 60.00
ERJP Jim Palmer

2016 Diamond Kings Elements of Royalty Material Signatures Framed Blue

RANDOM INSERTS IN PACKS
PRINT RUNS B/WN 3-25 COPIES PER
NO PRICING ON QTY 10 OR LESS
EXCHANGE DEADLINE 10/6/2017
ERPR Pete Rose/25 30.00 80.00

2016 Diamond Kings Elements of Royalty Materials Silver

RANDOM INSERTS IN PACKS
PRINT RUNS B/WN 5-99 COPIES PER
NO PRICING ON QTY 10 OR LESS
*FRAMED/99: .4X TO 1X BASIC
*FRAMED/25: .5X TO 1.2X BASIC
*FRM BLUE/25: .5X TO 1.2X BASIC
ERBM Billy Martin/99 6.00 15.00
EREH Elston Howard/99 5.00 12.00
ERGH Gil Hodges/99 6.00 15.00
ERLA Luke Appling/99 6.00 15.00
ERLD Leo Durocher/99 5.00 12.00
ERMO Mel Ott/99 6.00 15.00
ERPR Pee Wee Reese/99 6.00 15.00
ERRM Roger Maris/99 15.00 40.00
ERTL Tony Lazzeri/99 8.00 20.00

2016 Diamond Kings Expressionists

COMPLETE SET (20) 8.00 20.00
RANDOM INSERTS IN PACKS
*SAPPHIRE/25: 2.5X TO 6X BASIC
E1 Robinson Cano .40 1.00
E2 Ken Griffey Jr. 1.00 2.50
E3 Randy Johnson .50 1.25
E4 Andy Pettitte .40 1.00
E5 Troy Tulowitzki .50 1.25
E6 Jose Bautista .40 1.00
E7 Alex Gordon .40 1.00
E8 Felix Hernandez .40 1.00
E9 Andrew McCutchen .50 1.25
E10 Yadier Molina .60 1.50
E11 David Ortiz .50 1.25
E12 Salvador Perez .40 1.00
E13 Ozzie Smith .60 1.50
E14 Justin Upton .40 1.00
E15 Kris Bryant .60 1.50
E16 Rickey Henderson .50 1.25
E17 Addison Russell .50 1.25
E18 Miguel Sano .50 1.25
E19 Gregory Polanco .40 1.00
E20 David Wright .40 1.00

2016 Diamond Kings Heritage Collection

COMPLETE SET (20) 8.00 20.00
RANDOM INSERTS IN PACKS
*SAPPHIRE/25: 2.5X TO 6X BASIC
HC1 Robin Yount .50 1.25
HC2 Brooks Robinson .40 1.00
HC3 Frank Robinson .40 1.00
HC4 Reggie Jackson .40 1.00
HC5 Steve Carlton .40 1.00
HC6 Johnny Bench .50 1.25
HC7 Jose Canseco .40 1.00
HC8 Will Clark .40 1.00
HC9 Paul Molitor .50 1.25
HC10 Greg Maddux .60 1.50
HC11 Gaylord Perry .40 1.00
HC12 Orlando Cepeda .40 1.00
HC13 Jim Palmer .40 1.00
HC14 Tim Raines .40 1.00
HC15 Andre Dawson .40 1.00
HC16 Eddie Murray .40 1.00
HC17 Mike Schmidt .75 2.00
HC18 Ryne Sandberg 1.00 2.50
HC19 Lou Brock .40 1.00
HC20 Dennis Eckersley .40 1.00

2016 Diamond Kings Limited Lithos Material Signatures Silver

RANDOM INSERTS IN PACKS
PRINT RUNS B/WN 5-99 COPIES PER
NO PRICING ON QTY 15 OR LESS
EXCHANGE DEADLINE 10/6/2017
*FRM BLUE/25: .4X TO 1X BASIC p/r 25
1 Jose Canseco/99 10.00 25.00
3 Juan Gonzalez/25 12.00 30.00
6 Rollie Fingers/25 20.00 50.00
8 Tim Raines/99 10.00 25.00

2016 Diamond Kings Limited Lithos Material Signatures Framed

*FRAMED/99: .4X TO 1X BASIC p/r 99
*FRAMED/49: .3X TO .8X BASIC p/r 25
*FRAMED/25: .5X TO 1.2X BASIC p/r 99
RANDOM INSERTS IN PACKS
PRINT RUNS B/WN 1-25 COPIES PER
NO PRICING ON QTY 15 OR LESS
EXCHANGE DEADLINE 10/6/2017
5 Paul Molitor/25

2016 Diamond Kings Limited Lithos Materials Silver

RANDOM INSERTS IN PACKS
PRINT RUNS B/WN 15-99 COPIES PER
NO PRICING ON QTY 15
*FRAMED/99: .4X TO 1X BASIC
*FRM BLUE/25: .5X TO 1.2X BASIC
1 Kyle Schwarber/99 6.00 15.00
2 Corey Seager/99 20.00 50.00
3 Miguel Sano/99 3.00 8.00
4 Michael Conforto/99 2.50 6.00
5 Stephen Piscotty/25 5.00 12.00
6 Trea Turner/99 4.00 10.00
7 Aaron Nola/99 4.00 10.00
8 Raul Mondesi/99 4.00 10.00
10 Luis Severino/99 2.50 6.00

2016 Diamond Kings Masters of the Game Materials

RANDOM INSERTS IN PACKS
PRINT RUNS B/WN 5-99 COPIES PER
NO PRICING ON QTY 15 OR LESS
MGBH Bryce Harper/25 8.00 20.00
MGCF Carlton Fisk/99 4.00 10.00
MGCR Cal Ripken/99 15.00 40.00
MGFT Frank Thomas/99 6.00 15.00
MGGB George Brett/99 6.00 15.00
MGJB Johnny Bench/99 6.00 15.00
MGJD Josh Donaldson/99 4.00 10.00
MGJS John Smoltz/99 6.00 15.00
MGKP Kirby Puckett/99 6.00 15.00
MGLG Lou Gehrig/25 40.00 100.00
MGMR Mariano Rivera/99 5.00 12.00
MGNR Nolan Ryan/99 8.00 20.00
MGRJ Reggie Jackson/99 4.00 10.00
MGRM Roger Maris/99 10.00 25.00
MGRS Ryne Sandberg/99 6.00 15.00
MGWF Whitey Ford/99 10.00 25.00

2016 Diamond Kings Memorable Feats

COMPLETE SET (20) 8.00 20.00
RANDOM INSERTS IN PACKS
*SAPPHIRE/25: 2.5X TO 6X BASIC
MF1 Babe Ruth 1.25 3.00
MF2 Roberto Clemente 1.25 3.00
MF3 Lou Gehrig 1.00 2.50
MF4 Ty Cobb .75 2.00
MF5 Honus Wagner .50 1.25
MF6 Jimmie Foxx .50 1.25
MF7 Joe Jackson .60 1.50
MF8 Roger Maris .50 1.25
MF9 Stan Musial .75 2.00
MF10 Ted Williams 1.00 2.50
MF11 Rogers Hornsby .40 1.00
MF12 Mel Ott .50 1.25
MF13 Bill Dickey .30 .75
MF14 Walter O'Malley .30 .75
MF15 Gil Hodges .40 1.00
MF16 Tony Lazzeri .40 1.00
MF17 Nap Lajoie .50 1.25
MF18 Frankie Frisch .30 .75
MF19 Elston Howard .30 .75
MF20 Hack Wilson .40 1.00

2016 Diamond Kings Rookie Material Signatures Silver

RANDOM INSERTS IN PACKS
PRINT RUNS B/WN 49-99
EXCHANGE DEADLINE 10/6/2017
*BRNZE/49-99: .5X TO 1.2X p/r 299
*BRNZE/49-99: .4X TO 1X p/r 49-99
*FRMD/99: .5X TO 1.2X p/r 299
*FRMD/99: .4X TO 1X p/r 49-99
RSAN Aaron Nola/299 8.00 20.00
RSBD Brandon Drury/299 6.00 15.00
RSBJ Brian Johnson/299 4.00 10.00
RSCS Corey Seager/299 25.00 60.00
RSDA Dariel Alvarez/299 4.00 10.00
RSJP Jose Peraza/299 5.00 12.00
RSKC Kaleb Cowart/299 4.00 10.00
RSKM Ketel Marte/299 8.00 20.00
RSKS Michael Reed/99 10.00 25.00
RSKS Kyle Schwarber/299 20.00 50.00
RSKW Kyle Waldrop/299 5.00 12.00
RSMS Miguel Sano/299 6.00 15.00
RSMW Mac Williamson/299 4.00 10.00
RSPO Peter O'Brien/299 4.00 10.00
RSRR Rob Refsnyder/299 5.00 12.00
RSRS Richie Shaffer/299 4.00 10.00
RSSP Stephen Piscotty/299 6.00 15.00
RSTM Tom Murphy/49 5.00 12.00
RSTT Trea Turner/299 12.00 30.00

2016 Diamond Kings Rookie Material Signatures Framed Blue

*FRMD BLUE: .5X TO 1.2X p/r 299
*FRMD BLUE: .4X TO 1X p/r 49-99
RANDOM INSERTS IN PACKS
STATED PRINT RUN 49 SER.#'d SETS
EXCHANGE DEADLINE 10/6/2017
RSLS Luis Severino

2016 Diamond Kings Sketches And Swatches

RANDOM INSERTS IN PACKS
PRINT RUNS B/WN 10-99 COPIES PER
NO PRICING ON QTY 15 OR LESS
EXCHANGE DEADLINE 10/6/2017
*PRIME/25: .4X TO 1X BASIC p/r 25
*PRIME/25: .5X TO 1.2X BASIC p/r 99
SASCS Chris Sale/49 12.00 30.00
SASDS Dansby Swanson/25
SASJF Jose Fernandez/49 6.00 15.00
SASJK Jung-Ho Kang/49 20.00 50.00
SASJP Joe Panik/99 5.00 12.00
SASJP Joc Pederson/99 8.00 20.00
SASLC Lorenzo Cain/49 20.00 50.00
SASMS Miguel Sano/25 12.00 30.00
SASRC Rusney Castillo/99 4.00 10.00
SASSP Stephen Piscotty/99 6.00 15.00
SASTT Trea Turner/99 12.00 30.00

2016 Diamond Kings Sovereign Material Signatures

RANDOM INSERTS IN PACKS
PRINT RUNS B/WN 5-99 COPIES PER
NO PRICING ON QTY 20 OR LESS
EXCHANGE DEADLINE 10/6/2017
SSAP Andy Pettitte/25 10.00 25.00
SSDG Dwight Gooden/25 12.00 30.00
SSFL Fred Lynn/99 4.00 10.00
SSMG Mark Grace/49 10.00 25.00
SSPM Paul Molitor/99 10.00 25.00
SSRP Rafael Palmeiro/99 6.00 15.00

2016 Diamond Kings Studio Portraits Material Signatures Silver

RANDOM INSERTS IN PACKS
PRINT RUNS B/WN 15-99 COPIES PER
NO PRICING ON QTY 15
EXCHANGE DEADLINE 10/6/2017
*FRAMED/99: .4X TO 1X BASIC
SPSAN Aaron Nola/99 10.00 25.00
SPSDA Dariel Alvarez/99 4.00 10.00
SPSKC Kaleb Cowart/99 4.00 10.00
SPSKM Ketel Marte/99 8.00 20.00
SPSKS Kyle Schwarber/99 15.00 40.00
SPSMS Miguel Sano/99 10.00 25.00
SPSPO Peter O'Brien/99 4.00 10.00
SPSRR Rob Refsnyder/99 5.00 12.00
SPSRS Richie Shaffer/99 4.00 10.00
SPSSP Stephen Piscotty/99 10.00 25.00
SPSTT Trea Turner/99 8.00 20.00

2016 Diamond Kings Studio Portraits Material Signatures Framed Blue

*FRM BLUE: .5X TO 1.2X BASIC
RANDOM INSERTS IN PACKS
PRINT RUNS B/WN 10-25 COPIES PER
NO PRICING ON QTY 10
EXCHANGE DEADLINE 10/6/2017
SPSLS Luis Severino/25 12.00 30.00

2016 Diamond Kings Studio Portraits Materials Silver

RANDOM INSERTS IN PACKS
PRINT RUNS B/WN 49-99 COPIES PER
*FRAMED/99: .4X TO 1X BASIC
*FRM BLUE/25: .5X TO 1.2X BASIC
SPAG Alex Gordon 4.00 10.00
SPAJ Adam Jones 4.00 10.00
SPAR Anthony Rizzo 6.00 15.00
SPAR Alex Rodriguez 5.00 12.00
SPCG Carlos Gonzalez 4.00 10.00
SPDG Dee Gordon 3.00 8.00
SPGC Gerrit Cole 5.00 12.00
SPJD Jacob deGrom 10.00 25.00
SPJM J.D. Martinez 5.00 12.00
SPJV Joey Votto 5.00 12.00
SPLC Lorenzo Cain 3.00 8.00
SPMH Matt Harvey 4.00 10.00
SPMS Max Scherzer 5.00 12.00

2017 Diamond Kings

COMPLETE SET (200) 60.00 150.00
1 Babe Ruth .75 2.00
2A Bill Dickey .20 .50
2B Bill Dickey VAR .60 1.50
Catchers equipment
3 Billy Herman .20 .50
4 Billy Martin .25 .60
5 Harry Brecheen .20 .50
6 Carl Erskine .20 .50
7 Carl Furillo .20 .50
8A Don Larsen .20 .50
8B Don Larsen VAR .60 1.50
Standing
9 Grover Alexander .25 .60
10A Ernie Banks .30 .75
10B Ernie Banks VAR 1.00 2.50
Face showing
11 George Kelly .20 .50
12 Harry Hooper .20 .50
13 Herb Pennock .25 .60
14 Honus Wagner .30 .75
15A Jackie Robinson .30 .75
15B Jackie Robinson VAR 1.00 2.50
42 on front
16 Jim Thorpe .50 1.25
17 Joe Cronin .20 .50
18A Joe DiMaggio .60 1.50
18B DiMaggio VAR Face lft 2.00 5.00
19 Joe Jackson .40 1.00
20 Kiki Cuyler .25 .60
21 Lefty Gomez .20 .50
22 Leo Durocher .20 .50
23 Lloyd Waner .25 .60
24 Lou Gehrig .60 1.50
25 Luke Appling .20 .50
26 Max Carey .20 .50
27A Kirby Puckett .30 .75
27B Kirby Puckett VAR 1.00 2.50
Throwback jersey
28 Nellie Fox .25 .60
29 Paul Waner .25 .60
30A Pee Wee Reese .25 .60
30B Pee Wee Reese VAR .75 2.00
Batting
31A Roberto Clemente .75 2.00
31B Clmnte VAR Solid jrsy 2.50 6.00
32 Roger Maris .30 .75
33A Stan Musial .50 1.25
33B Musial VAR Red belt 1.50 4.00
34 Ted Lyons .20 .50
35 Ted Williams .60 1.50
36 Tommy Henrich .20 .50
37 Ty Cobb .50 1.25
38 Tony Lazzeri .25 .60
39A Hack Wilson .25 .60
39B Hack Wilson VAR .75 2.00
Standing with bat
40 Earl Averill .20 .50
41 Nap Lajoie .30 .75
42 Goose Goslin .25 .60
43 Jim Bottomley .20 .50
44 Harry Walker .20 .50
45 Gabby Hartnett .20 .50
46 Heinie Groh .20 .50
47 Johnny Pesky .20 .50
48 John McGraw .25 .60
49 Moose Skowron .20 .50
50 Chuck Klein .20 .50
51 Paul Goldschmidt .30 .75
52 Freddie Freeman .40 1.00
53 Mark Trumbo .20 .50
54A Mookie Betts .60 1.50
54B Betts VAR Face lft 2.00 5.00
55A Kris Bryant .40 1.00
55B Bryant VAR No glss 1.25 3.00
56A Anthony Rizzo .40 1.00
56B Rizzo VAR Solid jrsy 1.25 3.00
57 Jake Arrieta .25 .60
58 Kyle Schwarber .30 .75
59 Jose Abreu .30 .75
60 Joey Votto .30 .75
61 Francisco Lindor .30 .75
62A Corey Kluber .25 .60
62B Corey Kluber VAR .75 2.00
Facing forward
63 Trevor Story .30 .75
64 Nolan Arenado .50 1.25
65 Justin Verlander .30 .75
66A Jose Altuve .25 .60
66B Altuve Ornge jrsy .75 2.00
67A Mike Trout 1.50 4.00
67B Trout VAR Red jrsy 5.00 12.00
68 Albert Pujols .40 1.00
69A Corey Seager .30 .75
69B Seager VAR Pre-swing 1.00 2.50
70 Clayton Kershaw .50 1.25
71 Christian Yelich .40 1.00
72 Ryan Braun .25 .60
73 Brian Dozier .30 .75
74 Yoenis Cespedes .30 .75
75 Didi Gregorius .25 .60
76 Khris Davis .30 .75
77 Maikel Franco .25 .60
78 Andrew McCutchen .30 .75
79 Wil Myers .25 .60
80A Madison Bumgarner .25 .60
80B Bmgrnr VAR Grey jrsy .75 2.00
81 Robinson Cano .25 .60
82 Stephen Piscotty .25 .60
83 Carlos Martinez .25 .60
84 Evan Longoria .25 .60
85 Adrian Beltre .30 .75
86 Cole Hamels .25 .60
87A Josh Donaldson .25 .60
87B Josh Donaldson VAR .75 2.00
Leg up
88 Edwin Encarnacion .30 .75
89 Bryce Harper .50 1.25
90A Daniel Murphy .25 .60
90B Daniel Murphy VAR .75 2.00
Red jersey
91 Don Mattingly .60 1.50
92 Al Oliver .20 .50
93 Andy Pettitte .25 .60
94 Chipper Jones .30 .75
95 Curt Schilling .25 .60
96 Fergie Jenkins .25 .60
97 Craig Biggio .25 .60
98 Brooks Robinson .25 .60
99 Larry Doby .25 .60
100 Billy Williams .25 .60
101 A.J. Pollock SP .60 1.50
102 Addison Russell SP 1.00 2.50
103 Anthony Rendon SP 1.00 2.50
104 Carlos Gonzalez SP .75 2.00
105 Charlie Blackmon SP 1.00 2.50
106 Chris Davis SP .60 1.50
107 Chris Sale SP 1.00 2.50
108 Eric Hosmer SP .75 2.00
109 Gerrit Cole SP 1.00 2.50
110 Gregory Polanco SP .75 2.00
111 Hanley Ramirez SP
112 J.D. Martinez SP 1.00 2.50
113 Jacob deGrom SP 2.00 5.00
114 Jason Kipnis SP .75 2.00
115 Jon Lester SP .75 2.00
116 Jonathan Villar SP .60 1.50
117 Kyle Hendricks SP 1.00 2.50
118 Kyle Seager SP .60 1.50
119 Matt Carpenter SP 1.00 2.50
120 Miguel Cabrera SP 1.00 2.50
121 Miguel Sano SP .75 2.00
122 Rougned Odor SP .75 2.00
123 Stephen Strasburg SP 1.00 2.50
124 Trea Turner SP .75 2.00
125 Nelson Cruz SP 1.00 2.50
126A Yoan Moncada RC 1.25 3.00
126B Mncda VAR Legs sprd 2.00 5.00
127A Alex Reyes RC .50 1.25
127B Reyes VAR Tan glv .75 2.00
128 Tyler Glasnow RC 1.50 4.00
129A Dansby Swanson RC 1.00 2.50
129B Swnsn VAR Back: Hype 1.50 4.00
130 Alex Bregman RC 2.00 5.00
131A Andrew Benintendi RC 1.25 3.00
131B Bnntndi VAR Blue jrsy 2.00 5.00
132 Orlando Arcia RC .60 1.50
133 David Dahl RC .50 1.25
134 Jose De Leon RC .40 1.00
135 Joe Musgrove RC 1.25 3.00
136 Josh Bell RC 1.00 2.50
137 Manuel Margot RC .40 1.00
138 Aaron Judge RC 5.00 12.00
139 David Paulino RC .50 1.25
140 Reynaldo Lopez RC .40 1.00
141 Jeff Hoffman RC .40 1.00
142 Braden Shipley RC .40 1.00
143 Hunter Renfroe RC .50 1.25
144 Jorge Alfaro RC .50 1.25
145A Carson Fulmer RC .40 1.00
145B Carson Fulmer VAR .60 1.50
Throwback
146 Luke Weaver RC .50 1.25
147 Raimel Tapia RC .50 1.25
148 Adalberto Mejia RC .40 1.00
149 Gavin Cecchini RC .40 1.00
150 Renato Nunez RC .75 2.00
151 Jacoby Jones RC .50 1.25
152 Yohander Mendez RC .40 1.00
153 Chad Pinder RC .40 1.00
154 Carson Kelly RC .50 1.25
155 Trey Mancini RC .75 2.00
156 Jose Rondon RC .40 1.00
157 Teoscar Hernandez RC 1.50 4.00
158 Ryon Healy RC .50 1.25
159 Erik Gonzalez RC .40 1.00
160 Roman Quinn RC .40 1.00
161 Matt Olson RC 2.00 5.00
162 Rio Ruiz RC .40 1.00
163 German Marquez RC .60 1.50
164 Jharel Cotton RC .40 1.00
165 Jake Thompson RC .40 1.00
166 Mitch Haniger RC .60 1.50
167 Robert Gsellman RC .40 1.00
168 Jordan Patterson RC .40 1.00
169 Hunter Dozier RC .40 1.00
170 Carlos Asuaje RC .40 1.00
171 Adam Plutko RC .40 1.00
172 Koda Glover RC .40 1.00
173 Austin Brice RC .40 1.00
174 Gabriel Ynoa RC .40 1.00
175 Jake Esch RC .40 1.00

2017 Diamond Kings Artist's Proof Blue

*FRM.BLUE: 3X TO 8X BASIC
*FRM.BLUE RC: 1.5X TO 4X BASIC RC
*FRM.BLUE SP: 1X TO 2.5X BASIC SP
*FRM.BLUE VAR: 1X TO 2.5X BASIC VAR
STATED PRINT RUN 25 SER.#'d SETS
27A Kirby Puckett 20.00 50.00
27B Puckett VAR Thrwbck jrsy 20.00 50.00
31A Roberto Clemente 12.00 30.00
31B Clmnte VAR Solid jrsy 12.00 30.00

2017 Diamond Kings Artist's Proof Gold

*AP GOLD: 2X TO 5X BASIC
*AP GOLD RC: 1X TO 2.5X BASIC RC
*AP GOLD SP: .6X TO 1.5X BASIC SP
*AP GOLD VAR: .6X TO 1.5X BASIC VAR
STATED PRINT RUN 99 SER.#'d SETS
27A Kirby Puckett 8.00 20.00
27B Puckett VAR Thrwbck jrsy 8.00 20.00
31A Roberto Clemente 8.00 20.00
31B Clmnte VAR Solid jrsy 8.00 20.00

2017 Diamond Kings Framed Brown

*FRM.BRWN: 2.5X TO 6X BASIC
*FRM.BRWN RC: 1.2X TO 3X BASIC RC
*FRM.BRWN SP: .75X TO 2X BASIC SP
*FRM.BRWN VAR: .75X TO 2X BASIC VAR
STATED PRINT RUN 49 SER.#'d SETS
27A Kirby Puckett 15.00 40.00
27B Puckett VAR Thrwbck jrsy 15.00 40.00
31A Roberto Clemente 10.00 25.00
31B Clmnte VAR Solid jrsy 10.00 25.00

2017 Diamond Kings Framed Green

*FRM.GRN: 1.5X TO 4X BASIC
*FRM.GRN RC: .75X TO 2X BASIC RC
*FRM.GRN SP: .5X TO 1.2X BASIC SP
*FRM.GRN VAR: .5X TO 1.2X BASIC VAR

2017 Diamond Kings Framed Grey

*FRM.GREY: 1.2X TO 3X BASIC
*FRM.GREY RC: .6X TO 1.5X BASIC RC
*FRM.GREY SP: .4X TO 1X BASIC SP
*FRM.GREY VAR: .4X TO 1X BASIC VAR

2017 Diamond Kings Framed Red

*FRM.RED: 2X TO 5X BASIC
*FRM.RED RC: 1X TO 2.5X BASIC RC
*FRM.RED SP: .6X TO 1.5X BASIC SP
*FRM.RED VAR: .6X TO 1.5X BASIC VAR
STATED PRINT RUN 99 SER.#'d SETS
27A Kirby Puckett 8.00 20.00
27B Puckett VAR Thrwbck jrsy 8.00 20.00
31A Roberto Clemente 8.00 20.00
31B Clmnte VAR Solid jrsy 8.00 20.00

2017 Diamond Kings Aurora

COMPLETE SET (20) 10.00 25.00
*HOLO BLUE/25: 1.5X TO 4X BASIC
A1 Brian Dozier .60 1.50
A2 Charlie Blackmon .60 1.50
A3 Clayton Kershaw 1.00 2.50
A4 Corey Seager .60 1.50
A5 Edwin Encarnacion .60 1.50
A6 Joey Votto .60 1.50
A7 Jon Lester .50 1.25
A8 Jonathan Villar .40 1.00
A9 Jose Altuve .50 1.25
A10 Josh Donaldson .50 1.25
A11 Justin Verlander .60 1.50
A12 Kris Bryant .75 2.00
A13 Madison Bumgarner .50 1.25
A14 Max Scherzer .60 1.50
A15 Miguel Cabrera .60 1.50
A16 Mike Trout 3.00 8.00
A17 Mookie Betts 1.25 3.00
A18 Nolan Arenado 1.00 2.50
A19 Paul Goldschmidt .60 1.50
A20 Robinson Cano .50 1.25

2017 Diamond Kings Bat Kings

RANDOM INSERTS IN PACKS
PRINT RUNS B/WN 10-99 COPIES PER
NO PRICING ON QTY 15 OR LESS
*GOLD/49: .5X TO 1.2X BASIC
*GOLD/25: .6X TO 1.5X BASIC
*BLUE/25: .6X TO 1.5X BASIC
BKAP Albert Pujols/49 6.00 15.00
BKCB Craig Biggio/49 4.00 10.00
BKCC Carlos Correa/99 4.00 10.00
BKCS Corey Seager/99 10.00 25.00
BKCY Christian Yelich/99 5.00 12.00
BKDM Don Mattingly/25 12.00 30.00
BKI Ichiro/25 12.00 30.00
BKIR Ivan Rodriguez/99 3.00 8.00
BKJB Jose Bautista/99 5.00 12.00
BKJB Johnny Bench/49 4.00 10.00
BKJC Joe Carter/49 3.00 8.00
BKKG Ken Griffey Jr./25 15.00 40.00
BKMC Miguel Cabrera/25 6.00 15.00
BKMN Mike Napoli/49 3.00 8.00
BKMT Mike Trout/99 15.00 40.00
BKRS Ryne Sandberg/49 10.00 25.00
BKSM Stan Musial/25 10.00 25.00
BKTC Rod Carew/49 4.00 10.00
BKTH Todd Helton/49 4.00 10.00
BKTS Trevor Story/99 4.00 10.00
BKTT Trea Turner/99 3.00 8.00
BKWB Wade Boggs/25
BKYT Yasmany Tomas/99 2.50 6.00

2017 Diamond Kings Bat Kings Signatures

RANDOM INSERTS IN PACKS
PRINT RUNS B/WN 7-99 COPIES PER
NO PRICING ON QTY 15 OR LESS
*GOLD/49: .5X TO 1.2X BASIC
*GOLD/25: .6X TO 1.5X BASIC
*BLUE/25: .6X TO 1.5X BASIC
BKSDF David Freese/20 8.00 20.00
BKSDS Darryl Strawberry/20 15.00 40.00
BKSEB Ernie Banks/25 25.00 60.00
BKSFF Freddie Freeman/20
BKSHR Hanley Ramirez/25 6.00 15.00
BKSMF Maikel Franco/49 5.00 12.00
BKSMN Mike Napoli/99 8.00 20.00
BKSPA Pedro Alvarez/25 6.00 15.00
BKSPM Paul Molitor/20 12.00 30.00
BKSTT Trea Turner/49 10.00 25.00
BKSYS Yangervis Solarte/99 3.00 8.00

2017 Diamond Kings Diamond Cuts Signatures

RANDOM INSERTS IN PACKS
PRINT RUNS B/WN 5-99 COPIES PER
NO PRICING ON QTY 15 OR LESS
*BLUE/25: .6X TO 1.5X BASIC
DCGC Gary Carter/99 12.00 30.00
DCGC Gary Carter/99 12.00 30.00
DCHK Harmon Killebrew/25 20.00 50.00
DCHK Harmon Killebrew/25 20.00 50.00
DCRK Ralph Kiner/25 20.00 50.00
DCRK Ralph Kiner/25 20.00 50.00
DCSM Stan Musial/25 20.00 50.00
DCSM Stan Musial/25 20.00 50.00

2017 Diamond Kings Diamond Cuts Signatures Holo Gold

*GOLD/49: .5X TO 1.2X BASIC
PRINT RUNS B/WN 4-49 COPIES PER
NO PRICING ON QTY 15 OR LESS
DCJP Johnny Pesky/20 20.00 50.00

2017 Diamond Kings Diamond Deco Materials

RANDOM INSERTS IN PACKS
PRINT RUNS B/WN 7-99 COPIES PER
NO PRICING ON QTY 7
*GOLD/49: .5X TO 1.2X BASIC
*GOLD/25: .6X TO 1.5X BASIC
*BLUE/25: .6X TO 1.5X BASIC
2 Willson Contreras/99 4.00 10.00
3 Francisco Lindor/99 6.00 15.00
5 Trea Turner/99 3.00 8.00
6 Corey Seager/99 6.00 15.00
7 Kyle Schwarber/99 4.00 10.00
8 Tony Gwynn/49 20.00 50.00
9 Kirby Puckett/25 40.00 100.00
10 Ken Griffey Jr./49 12.00 30.00

2017 Diamond Kings DK Materials

*SILVER/99: .4X TO 1X BASIC
*SILVER/49: .5X TO 1.2X BASIC

*SILVER/25: .6X TO 1.5X BASIC
*GOLD/49: .5X TO 1.2X BASIC
*GOLD/25: .6X TO 1.5X BASIC
*BLUE/25: .6X TO 1.5X BASIC
DKMAA Anthony Alford 2.50 6.00
DKMAB Adrian Beltre 4.00 10.00
DKMAG Adrian Gonzalez 3.00 8.00
DKMAJ Adam Jones 3.00 8.00
DKMAM Austin Meadows 6.00 15.00
DKMAM Andrew McCutchen 6.00 15.00
DKMAR Addison Russell 4.00 10.00
DKMAW Adam Wainwright 3.00 8.00
DKMBA Brian Anderson 3.00 8.00
DKMBH Bryce Harper 6.00 15.00
DKMBH Brent Honeywell 3.00 8.00
DKMBJ Bo Jackson 6.00 15.00
DKMBM Billy Martin 5.00 12.00
DKMBP Buster Posey 5.00 12.00
DKMBR Babe Ruth 250.00 400.00
DKMBZ Bradley Zimmer 3.00 8.00
DKMCA Chris Archer 2.50 6.00
DKMCB Cody Bellinger 8.00 20.00
DKMCB Charlie Blackmon 4.00 10.00
DKMCC Carlos Correa 4.00 10.00
DKMCH Cole Hamels 3.00 8.00
DKMCJ Chipper Jones 5.00 12.00
DKMCK Clayton Kershaw 5.00 12.00
DKMCS Chris Sale 4.00 10.00
DKMCS Curt Schilling 3.00 8.00
DKMCS Corey Seager 6.00 15.00
DKMCY Christian Yelich 5.00 12.00
DKMDM Daniel Murphy 3.00 8.00
DKMDM Don Mattingly 6.00 15.00
DKMDP David Price 3.00 8.00
DKMDW Dave Winfield 3.00 8.00
DKMEA Elvis Andrus 3.00 8.00
DKMEB Ernie Banks 8.00 20.00
DKMEJ Eloy Jimenez 5.00 12.00
DKMFB Franklin Barreto 2.50 6.00
DKMFF Freddie Freeman 5.00 12.00
DKMFH Felix Hernandez 3.00 8.00
DKMFL Francisco Lindor 5.00 12.00
DKMFM Francis Martes 2.50 6.00
DKMFT Frank Thomas 5.00 12.00
DKMGH Gabby Hartnett 20.00 50.00
DKMGS Giancarlo Stanton 4.00 10.00
DKMHB Harold Baines 3.00 8.00
DKMHG Heinie Groh 6.00 15.00
DKMIH Ian Happ 5.00 12.00
DKMJA Jose Altuve 3.00 8.00
DKMJA Jake Arrieta 3.00 8.00
DKMJB Jackie Bradley Jr. 4.00 10.00
DKMJB Javier Baez 5.00 12.00
DKMJC Joe Carter 2.50 6.00
DKMJC Joe Cronin 8.00 20.00
DKMJC Johnny Cueto 3.00 8.00
DKMJD Josh Donaldson 3.00 8.00
DKMJK Jason Kipnis 3.00 8.00
DKMJM J.D. Martinez 4.00 10.00
DKMJP Jose Peraza 3.00 8.00
DKMJP Jorge Posada 3.00 8.00
DKMJR Jose Ramirez 3.00 8.00
DKMJV Joey Votto 4.00 10.00
DKMJV Justin Verlander 4.00 10.00
DKMKB Kris Bryant 5.00 12.00
DKMKB Kris Bryant 5.00 12.00
DKMKC Kiki Cuyler 8.00 20.00
DKMKG Ken Griffey Jr. 5.00 12.00
DKMKL Corey Kluber 3.00 8.00
DKMKM Kenta Maeda 3.00 8.00
DKMKS Kyle Schwarber 4.00 10.00
DKMLG Lou Gehrig 50.00 120.00
DKMMB Mookie Betts 8.00 20.00
DKMMB Madison Bumgarner 3.00 8.00
DKMMC Matt Carpenter 4.00 10.00
DKMMC Miguel Cabrera 4.00 10.00
DKMMC Max Carey
DKMMF Michael Fulmer 2.50 6.00
DKMMM Manny Machado 4.00 10.00
DKMMS Max Scherzer 4.00 10.00
DKMMT Mike Trout 15.00 40.00
DKMMT Mike Trout 15.00 40.00
DKMMT Masahiro Tanaka 3.00 8.00
DKMNA Nolan Arenado 6.00 15.00
DKMNG Nick Gordon 2.50 6.00
DKMNG Nomar Garciaparra 3.00 8.00
DKMNS Noah Syndergaard 3.00 8.00
DKMRC Robinson Cano 3.00 8.00
DKMRM Roger Maris
DKMRO Rougned Odor 3.00 8.00
DKMRP Rick Porcello 3.00 8.00
DKMTL Tony Lazzeri 25.00 60.00
DKMTO Tyler O'Neill 3.00 8.00
DKMTS Trevor Story 4.00 10.00
DKMTT Trea Turner 3.00 8.00
DKMTT Tim Tebow 5.00 12.00
DKMXB Xander Bogaerts 4.00 10.00
DKMYD Yu Darvish 4.00 10.00
DKMYM Yadier Molina 6.00 15.00
DKMJTR J.T. Realmuto 4.00 10.00

2017 Diamond Kings DK Originals

COMPLETE SET (25) 6.00 15.00
*HOLO BLUE/25: 1.5X TO 4X BASIC
DO1 Anthony Rizzo .75 2.00
DO2 Corey Kluber .50 1.25
DO3 Corey Seager .60 1.50
DO4 Daniel Murphy .50 1.25
DO5 Freddie Freeman .75 2.00
DO6 Jose Altuve .50 1.25
DO7 Josh Donaldson .50 1.25
DO8 Kris Bryant .75 2.00
DO9 Manny Machado .60 1.50
DO10 Max Scherzer .60 1.50
DO11 Mike Trout 3.00 8.00
DO12 Mookie Betts 1.25 3.00
DO13 Rick Porcello .50 1.25
DO14 Bill Mazeroski .50 1.25
DO15 Dave Winfield .50 1.25
DO16 Jim Palmer .50 1.25
DO17 Mike Schmidt 1.00 2.50
DO18 Ozzie Smith .75 2.00
DO19 Paul Molitor .60 1.50
DO20 Pedro Martinez .50 1.25
DO21 Reggie Jackson .50 1.25
DO22 Robin Yount .60 1.50
DO23 Ryne Sandberg 1.25 3.00
DO24 Tony Gwynn .60 1.50
DO25 Wade Boggs .50 1.25

2017 Diamond Kings DK Rookie Signature Materials

*SILVER/99: .4X TO 1X BASIC
*SILVER/49: .5X TO 1.2X BASIC
*GOLD/49: .5X TO 1.2X BASIC
*GOLD/25: .6X TO 1.5X BASIC
RANDOM INSERTS IN PACKS
PRINT RUNS B/WN 99-299 COPIES PER
RSAB Andrew Benintendi/299 30.00 80.00
RSAJ Aaron Judge/299 75.00 200.00
RSAM Adalberto Mejia/299 3.00 8.00
RSAR Alex Reyes/299 8.00 20.00
RSAX Alex Bregman/299 15.00 40.00
RSBS Braden Shipley/299 3.00 8.00
RSCF Carson Fulmer/299 3.00 8.00
RSCK Carson Kelly/299 4.00 10.00
RSCP Chad Pinder/299 3.00 8.00
RSDD David Dahl/99 4.00 10.00
RSDD David Dahl/299 4.00 10.00
RSDP David Paulino/299 4.00 10.00
RSDS Dansby Swanson/299 5.00 12.00
RSEG Erik Gonzalez/299 3.00 8.00
RSGC Gavin Cecchini/299 3.00 8.00
RSHR Hunter Renfroe/299 4.00 10.00
RSJA Jorge Alfaro/299 6.00 15.00
RSJB Josh Bell/299 10.00 25.00
RSJC Jharel Cotton/299 8.00 20.00
RSJDL Jose De Leon/299 3.00 8.00
RSJH Jeff Hoffman/299 3.00 8.00
RSJJ Jacoby Jones/299 4.00 10.00
RSJM Joe Musgrove/299 10.00 25.00
RSJT Jake Thompson/299 3.00 8.00
RSLW Luke Weaver/299 4.00 10.00
RSMM Manuel Margot/299 5.00 12.00
RSMO Matt Olson/299 6.00 15.00
RSRH Ryon Healy/299 4.00 10.00
RSRL Reynaldo Lopez/299 3.00 8.00
RSRQ Roman Quinn/299 3.00 8.00
RSRT Raimel Tapia/299 5.00 12.00
RSTG Tyler Glasnow/299 8.00 20.00
RSTH Teoscar Hernandez/299 12.00 30.00
RSTM Trey Mancini/299 15.00 40.00
RSYM1 Yoan Moncada/242 15.00 40.00
RSYM2 Yoan Moncada/299 15.00 40.00
RSYO Yohander Mendez/299 3.00 8.00

2017 Diamond Kings DK Rookie Signature Materials Holo Blue

*BLUE/25: .6X TO 1.5X BASIC
PRINT RUNS B/WN 5-25 COPIES PER
NO PRICING ON QTY 10 OR LESS
RSAB Andrew Benintendi/25 100.00 250.00

2017 Diamond Kings DK Signature Materials

RANDOM INSERTS IN PACKS
PRINT RUNS B/WN 10-299 COPIES PER
NO PRICING ON QTY 10
*BLUE/25: .6X TO 1.5X BASIC
DKSAB Adrian Beltre/49 25.00 60.00
DKSAD Aledmys Diaz/299 4.00 10.00
DKSAM Austin Meadows/299 6.00 15.00
DKSAS Aaron Sanchez/99 10.00 25.00
DKSBB Bill Buckner/99 4.00 10.00
DKSBK Charlie Blackmon/49 6.00 15.00
DKSBN Brandon Nimmo/299 4.00 10.00
DKSCB Cody Bellinger/99 40.00 100.00
DKSCH Cole Hamels/25 10.00 25.00
DKSCK Corey Kluber/49 6.00 15.00
DKSCO Corey Seager/49 30.00 80.00
DKSCR Cameron Rupp/199 3.00 8.00
DKSCS Cory Spangenberg/199 3.00 8.00
DKSDW David Wright/25 12.00 30.00
DKSEH Eric Hosmer/49 12.00 30.00
DKSEJ Eloy Jimenez/299 15.00 40.00
DKSEL Evan Longoria/25 15.00 40.00
DKSGS George Springer/49 10.00 25.00
DKSJA Jake Arrieta/25 20.00 50.00
DKSJC John Cusack/49 20.00 50.00
DKSJH Jason Heyward/20 10.00 25.00
DKSJM Joe Mauer/25 8.00 20.00
DKSJP Joe Panik/199 4.00 10.00
DKSJR Jose Ramirez/49 5.00 12.00
DKSJS Jorge Soler/149 5.00 12.00
DKSJU Julio Urias/49 10.00 25.00
DKSKG Kendall Graveman/199 3.00 8.00
DKSKS Kyle Schwarber/49 20.00 50.00
DKSKY Kyle Seager/199 5.00 12.00
DKSLS Luis Severino/99 8.00 20.00
DKSMB Michael Brantley/49 6.00 15.00
DKSMF Mike Foltynewicz/299 3.00 8.00
DKSMM Manny Machado/99 15.00 40.00
DKSMS Max Scherzer/49 20.00 50.00
DKSMS Matt Szczur/299 4.00 10.00
DKSNC Nelson Cruz/25 8.00 20.00
DKSNS Noah Syndergaard/49 12.00 30.00
DKSOA Ozhaino Albies/299 12.00 30.00
DKSRB Robert Stephenson/199 3.00 8.00
DKSRS Richie Shaffer/199 3.00 8.00
DKSSZ Gary Sanchez/99 40.00 100.00
DKSTR Tanner Roark/99 3.00 8.00
DKSTT Trea Turner/149 12.00 30.00
DKSWR Wilin Rosario/199 3.00 8.00
DKSXB Xander Bogaerts/49 20.00 50.00
DKSYM Yadier Molina/49 30.00 80.00
DKSYT Yasmany Tomas/49 4.00 10.00

2017 Diamond Kings DK Signature Materials Holo Gold

*GOLD/49: .5X TO 1.2X BASIC
*GOLD/20-25: .6X TO 1.5X BASIC
PRINT RUNS B/WN 5-49 COPIES PER
NO PRICING ON QTY 15 OR LESS
DKSTS Trevor Story/49 12.00 30.00

2017 Diamond Kings DK Signature Materials Holo Silver

*SILVER/99: .4X TO 1X BASIC
*SILVER/49: .5X TO 1.2X BASIC
*SILVER/20-25: .6X TO 1.5X BASIC
PRINT RUNS B/WN 7-99 COPIES PER
NO PRICING ON QTY 15 OR LESS
DKSGT Gleyber Torres/25 60.00 150.00
DKSSG Sonny Gray/20 6.00 15.00
DKSTS Trevor Story/99 10.00 25.00

2017 Diamond Kings Heritage Collection

COMPLETE SET (28) 10.00 25.00
*HOLO BLUE/25: 1.5X TO 4X BASIC
HC1 Al Kaline .60 1.50
HC2 Bill Mazeroski .50 1.25
HC3 Bob Feller .50 1.25
HC4 Bruce Sutter .50 1.25
HC5 Cal Ripken 2.00 5.00
HC6 Carlton Fisk .50 1.25
HC7 Catfish Hunter .50 1.25
HC8 Frank Thomas .60 1.50
HC9 George Brett 1.25 3.00
HC10 Jim Bunning .50 1.25
HC11 Jim Rice .50 1.25
HC12 Joe Morgan .50 1.25
HC13 John Smoltz .60 1.50
HC14 Juan Marichal .50 1.25
HC15 Ken Griffey Jr. 1.25 3.00
HC16 Kirby Puckett .60 1.50
HC17 Mike Piazza .60 1.50
HC18 Nolan Ryan 2.00 5.00
HC19 Ozzie Smith .75 2.00
HC20 Phil Niekro .50 1.25
HC21 Eddie Murray .50 1.25
HC22 Rickey Henderson .60 1.50
HC23 Rod Carew .50 1.25
HC24 Rollie Fingers .50 1.25
HC25 Tony Gwynn .60 1.50
HC26 Tony Perez .50 1.25
HC27 Wade Boggs .50 1.25
HCWM Willie McCovey .50 1.25

2017 Diamond Kings Heritage Collection Material Signatures

RANDOM INSERTS IN PACKS
PRINT RUNS B/WN 7-49 COPIES PER
NO PRICING ON QTY 15 OR LESS
*GOLD/25: .5X TO 1.2X BASIC
HCMSBB Bill Buckner/25 12.00 30.00
HCMSCD Carlos Delgado/25 6.00 15.00
HCMSGP Gaylord Perry/49 8.00 20.00
HCMSWB Wade Boggs/25 20.00 50.00

2017 Diamond Kings Jersey Kings

RANDOM INSERTS IN PACKS
PRINT RUNS B/WN 10-99 COPIES PER
NO PRICING ON QTY 15 OR LESS
*GOLD/49: .5X TO 1.2X BASIC
*GOLD/25: .6X TO 1.5X BASIC
*BLUE/25: .6X TO 1.5X BASIC
JKAD Aledmys Diaz/49 5.00 12.00
JKAG Adrian Gonzalez/49 4.00 10.00
JKBD Brandon Drury/99 2.50 6.00
JKCB Charlie Blackmon/99 4.00 10.00
JKCH Cole Hamels/99 3.00 8.00
JKDM Daniel Murphy/99 3.00 8.00
JKGS Giancarlo Stanton/49 5.00 12.00
JKGS Gary Sanchez/99 8.00 20.00
JKHP Herb Pennock/49 6.00 15.00
JKID Ian Desmond/99 2.50 6.00
JKKP Kirby Puckett/25 40.00 100.00
JKKS Kyle Schwarber/99 4.00 10.00
JKMC Matt Carpenter/49 5.00 12.00
JKMF Michael Fulmer/99 2.50 6.00
JKMM Manny Machado/49 5.00 12.00
JKNM Nomar Mazara/99 2.50 6.00
JKSP Stephen Piscotty/99 3.00 8.00
JKTA Tim Anderson/99 4.00 10.00
JKTR Tim Raines/49 4.00 10.00
JKTT Trea Turner/99 3.00 8.00
JKHSK Hyun Soo Kim/49 4.00 10.00
JKPWR Pee Wee Reese/49 6.00 15.00
JKSHO Seung-Hwan Oh/49 5.00 12.00

2017 Diamond Kings Jersey Kings Signatures

RANDOM INSERTS IN PACKS
PRINT RUNS B/WN 7-99 COPIES PER
NO PRICING ON QTY 15 OR LESS
*GOLD/49: .5X TO 1.2X BASIC
*GOLD/25: .6X TO 1.5X BASIC
*BLUE/25: .6X TO 1.5X BASIC
JKSAG Alex Gordon/20 12.00 30.00
JKSBD Brian Dozier/25 15.00 40.00
JKSBF Brandon Finnegan/99 8.00 20.00
JKSBG Brett Gardner/49 6.00 15.00
JKSDP David Price/25 10.00 25.00
JKSDT Devon Travis/99 3.00 8.00
JKSGR Garrett Richards/25 6.00 15.00
JKSGS Gary Sanchez/25 40.00 100.00
JKSHI Hisashi Iwakuma/25 6.00 15.00
JKSJK Jason Kipnis/25 10.00 25.00
JKSJL Jake Lamb/99 4.00 10.00
JKSJP Joe Panik/99 4.00 10.00
JKSJR J.T. Realmuto/99 20.00 50.00
JKSJS Jonathan Schoop/25 15.00 40.00
JKSMB Matt Barnes/99 3.00 8.00
JKSMC Matt Carpenter/25 10.00 25.00
JKSMF Maikel Franco/99 4.00 10.00
JKSMS Marcus Semien/79
JKSNC Nick Castellanos/25
JKSRG Randal Grichuk/99 8.00 20.00
JKSSM Steven Matz/99 3.00 8.00
JKSSS Steven Souza/49 5.00 12.00
JKSTK Tom Koehler/49 4.00 10.00
JKSTT Trea Turner/49 15.00 40.00
JKSWB Wade Boggs/25 20.00 50.00

2017 Diamond Kings Limited Lithos Signature Materials

RANDOM INSERTS IN PACKS
PRINT RUNS B/WN 7-99 COPIES PER
NO PRICING ON QTY 15 OR LESS
*BLUE/25: .6X TO 1.5X BASIC
LLAN Aaron Nola/99 4.00 10.00
LLBB Bill Buckner/25 8.00 20.00
LLDS Darryl Strawberry/25 15.00 40.00
LLEM Edgar Martinez/25 20.00 50.00
LLGS George Springer/25 12.00 30.00
LLMC Matt Carpenter/25 10.00 25.00
LLMG Mark Grace/25 20.00 50.00
LLMS Matt Szczur/99 4.00 10.00
LLMT Michael Taylor/99 3.00 8.00
LLRS Ross Stripling/49 4.00 10.00
LLSM Steven Matz/99 3.00 8.00
LLWC Willson Contreras/99 15.00 40.00

2017 Diamond Kings Limited Lithos Signature Materials Holo Gold

*GOLD/49: .5X TO 1.2X BASIC
PRINT RUNS B/WN 5-49 COPIES PER
NO PRICING ON QTY 15 OR LESS
LLTS Trevor Story/49 12.00 30.00

2017 Diamond Kings Memorable Moment

COMPLETE SET (18) 10.00 25.00
*HOLO BLUE/25: 1.5X TO 4X BASIC
MM1 Babe Ruth 1.50 4.00
MM2 Nolan Ryan 2.00 5.00
MM3 Grover Alexander .50 1.25
MM4 Ernie Banks .60 1.50
MM5 Honus Wagner .60 1.50
MM6 Jackie Robinson .60 1.50
MM7 Jim Bottomley .40 1.00
MM8 Joe DiMaggio 1.25 3.00
MM9 Kirby Puckett .60 1.50
MM10 Lefty Gomez .40 1.00
MM11 Lou Gehrig 1.25 3.00
MM12 Luke Appling .50 1.25
MM13 Reggie Jackson .50 1.25
MM14 Nellie Fox .50 1.25
MM15 Paul Waner .50 1.25
MM16 Roberto Clemente 1.50 4.00
MM17 Ted Williams 1.25 3.00
MM18 Ty Cobb 1.00 2.50

2017 Diamond Kings Sketches and Swatches

RANDOM INSERTS IN PACKS
PRINT RUNS B/WN 7-99 COPIES PER
NO PRICING ON QTY 15 OR LESS
*GOLD/49: .5X TO 1.2X BASIC
*GOLD/20-25: .6X TO 1.5X BASIC
*BLUE/25: .6X TO 1.5X BASIC
SSAG Andres Galarraga/25 10.00 25.00
SSAG Adrian Gonzalez/20 5.00 12.00
SSAJ Andruw Jones/49 8.00 20.00
SSBC Bert Campaneris/99 5.00 12.00
SSBW Bernie Williams/25 20.00 50.00
SSCB Charlie Blackmon/25 8.00 20.00
SSCD Chris Davis/20
SSCH Cole Hamels/20 10.00 25.00
SSDS Don Sutton/25 6.00 15.00
SSDW David Wright/20 12.00 30.00
SSEE Edwin Encarnacion/25 12.00 30.00
SSEL Evan Longoria/20 15.00 40.00
SSJA Jose Abreu/20 6.00 15.00
SSJB Jeff Bagwell/20
SSJR Jose Ramirez/25 6.00 15.00
SSJS Jonathan Schoop/25 15.00 40.00
SSJT Josh Tomlin/99 3.00 8.00
SSKW Kerry Wood/25
SSLC Lorenzo Cain/25 10.00 25.00
SSNS Noah Syndergaard/20 15.00 40.00
SSRP Rafael Palmeiro/20
SSTL Tommy Lasorda/20 40.00 100.00

2017 Diamond Kings Studio Portraits Materials

RANDOM INSERTS IN PACKS
PRINT RUNS B/WN 7-99 COPIES PER
NO PRICING ON QTY 15 OR LESS
*GOLD/49: .5X TO 1.2X BASIC
*GOLD/25: .6X TO 1.5X BASIC
*BLUE/25: .6X TO 1.5X BASIC
SPMBF Bob Feller/49 6.00 15.00
SPMCK Corey Kluber/99 3.00 8.00
SPMCR Cal Ripken/99 10.00 25.00
SPMDG Dwight Gooden/99 4.00 10.00
SPMFL Francisco Lindor/99 6.00 15.00
SPMGB George Brett/25 15.00 40.00
SPMGC Gary Carter/99 5.00 15.00
SPMJB Javier Baez/99 5.00 12.00
SPMJR Jim Rice/49 5.00 12.00
SPMKB Kris Bryant/99 5.00 12.00
SPMMT Mike Trout/25 25.00 60.00
SPMNR Nolan Ryan/25 20.00 50.00
SPMPM Paul Molitor/99 6.00 15.00
SPMRA Roberto Alomar/49 4.00 10.00
SPMRJ Reggie Jackson/49 8.00 20.00

2017 Diamond Kings Ted Williams Collection

COMPLETE SET (3) 4.00 10.00
*HOLO BLUE/25: 1.2X TO 3X BASIC
1 Ted Williams 1.50 4.00
2 Ted Williams 1.50 4.00
3 Ted Williams 1.50 4.00

2017 Diamond Kings Ted Williams Collection Materials

RANDOM INSERTS IN PACKS
PRINT RUNS B/WN 25-99 COPIES PER
*GOLD/49: .5X TO 1.2X BASIC
*GOLD/25: .6X TO 1.5X BASIC
*BLUE/25: .6X TO 1.5X BASIC
TWCM1 Ted Williams/25 40.00 100.00
TWCM2 Ted Williams/99 25.00 60.00
TWCM3 Ted Williams/49 30.00 80.00

2018 Diamond Kings

COMPLETE SET (150)
1 Babe Ruth .75 2.00
2 Honus Wagner .30 .75
3 Stan Musial .50 1.25
4 Lou Gehrig .60 1.50
5 Bobby Thomson .25 .60
6 George Kelly .30 .75
7 Mickey Mantle 1.00 2.50
8 Harry Hooper .20 .50
9 Ted Williams .60 1.50
10 Joe Cronin .20 .50
11 Joe DiMaggio .60 1.50
12 Kiki Cuyler .25 .60
13 Lloyd Waner .25 .60
14 Luke Appling .25 .60
15 Max Carey .20 .50
16 Carl Furillo .20 .50
17 Nellie Fox .25 .60
18 Paul Waner .25 .60
19 Roberto Clemente .75 2.00
20 Roger Maris .30 .75
21 Ted Lyons .20 .50
22 Tommy Henrich .20 .50
23 Pee Wee Reese .25 .60
24 Don Larsen .20 .50
25 Ernie Banks .30 .75
26 Herb Pennock .25 .60
27 Lefty Gomez .20 .50
28 Jackie Robinson .30 .75
29 Jim Thorpe .50 1.25
30 Joe Jackson .40 1.00
31 Leo Durocher .20 .50
32 Gabby Hartnett .20 .50
33 Tony Lazzeri .25 .60
34 Ty Cobb .50 1.25
35 Billy Herman .20 .50
36 Carl Erskine .20 .50
37 Chuck Klein .20 .50
38 Earl Averill .20 .50
39 Dom DiMaggio .20 .50
40 John McGraw .25 .60
41 Goose Goslin .25 .60
42 Grover Alexander .25 .60
43 Hack Wilson .25 .60
44 Harry Brecheen .20 .50
45 Harry Walker .20 .50
46 Heinie Groh .20 .50
47 Jim Bottomley .20 .50
48 Johnny Pesky .20 .50
49 Frank Thomas .30 .75
50 Kirby Puckett .30 .75
51 Moose Skowron .20 .50
52 Luis Severino .25 .60
53 Alex Bregman .30 .75
54 Trey Mancini .25 .60
55 Paul DeJong .30 .75
56 Max Scherzer .30 .75
57 Chris Sale .30 .75
58 George Springer .25 .60
59 Carlos Correa .30 .75
60 Sam Crawford .25 .60
61 Paul Goldschmidt .30 .75
62 Mookie Betts .60 1.50
63 Kris Bryant .40 1.00
64 Anthony Rizzo .40 1.00
65 Francisco Lindor .30 .75
66 Corey Kluber .25 .60
67 Nolan Arenado .50 1.25
68 Justin Verlander .30 .75
69 Jose Altuve .25 .60
70 Mike Trout 1.50 4.00
71 Corey Seager .30 .75
72 Clayton Kershaw .50 1.25
73 Shohei Ohtani RC 10.00 25.00
74 Andrew McCutchen .30 .75
75 Robinson Cano .25 .60
76 Shohei Ohtani RC 10.00 25.00
77 Josh Donaldson .25 .60
78 Bryce Harper .50 1.25
79 Buster Posey .40 1.00
80 Aaron Judge .75 2.00
81 Andrew Benintendi .30 .75
82 Cody Bellinger .60 1.50
83 Anthony Banda RC .40 1.00
84 Luiz Gohara RC .40 1.00
85 Max Fried RC 1.50 4.00
86 Lucas Sims RC .40 1.00
87 Anthony Santander RC .40 1.00
88 Victor Caratini RC .50 1.25
89 Nicky Delmonico RC .40 1.00
90 Tyler Mahle RC .50 1.25
91 Greg Allen RC .40 1.00
92 Ryan McMahon RC 1.00 2.50
93 Dillon Peters RC .40 1.00
94 Brandon Woodruff RC 1.25 3.00
95 Dominic Smith RC .50 1.25
96 Chris Flexen RC .40 1.00
97 Tyler Wade RC .50 1.25
98 J.P. Crawford RC .40 1.00
99 Nick Williams RC .50 1.25
100 Victor Robles RC 1.00 2.50
101 Ozzie Albies SP RC 2.50 6.00
102 Austin Hays SP RC 1.25 3.00
103 Chance Sisco SP RC 1.00 2.50
104 Rafael Devers SP RC 2.50 6.00
105 Francisco Mejia SP RC 1.00 2.50
106 J.D. Davis SP RC 1.00 2.50
107 Cameron Gallagher SP RC .75 2.00
108 Walker Buehler SP RC 4.00 10.00
109 Alex Verdugo SP RC 1.25 3.00
110 Kyle Farmer SP RC .75 2.00
111 Brian Anderson SP RC 1.00 2.50
112 Mitch Garver SP RC .75 2.00
113 Zack Granite SP RC .75 2.00
114 Felix Jorge SP RC .75 2.00
115 Tomas Nido SP RC .75 2.00
116 Amed Rosario SP RC 1.00 2.50
117 Clint Frazier SP RC 1.50 4.00
118 Miguel Andujar SP RC 3.00 8.00
119 Dustin Fowler SP RC .75 2.00
120 Paul Blackburn SP RC .75 2.00
121 Rhys Hoskins SP RC 3.00 8.00
122 Thyago Vieira SP RC .75 2.00
123 Reyes Moronta SP RC .75 2.00
124 Jack Flaherty SP RC 3.00 8.00
125 Harrison Bader SP RC 1.25 3.00
126 Willie Calhoun SP RC 1.25 3.00
127 Richard Urena SP RC .75 2.00
128 Erick Fedde SP RC .75 2.00
129 Andrew Stevenson SP RC .75 2.00
130 Odubel Herrera SP .50 1.25
131 Evan Longoria SP .50 1.25
132 David Ortiz SP .60 1.50
133 Manny Machado SP .60 1.50
134 Jose Ramirez SP .50 1.25
135 George Brett SP 1.25 3.00
136 Nolan Ryan SP 2.00 5.00
137 J.D. Martinez SP .60 1.50
138 Ichiro SP .75 2.00
139 Shohei Ohtani SP 10.00 25.00
140 Dustin Pedroia SP .60 1.50
141 Giancarlo Stanton SP .60 1.50
142 Brooks Robinson SP .50 1.25
143 Freddie Freeman SP .75 2.00
144 Noah Syndergaard SP .50 1.25
145 Shohei Ohtani SP 10.00 25.00
146 Madison Bumgarner SP .50 1.25
147 Josh Bell SP .50 1.25
148 Joey Votto SP .60 1.50
149 Manuel Margot SP .40 1.00
150 Charlie Blackmon SP .60 1.50

2018 Diamond Kings Artist Proof Blue

*AP BLUE: 4X TO 10X BASIC
*AP BLUE RC: 2X TO 5X BASIC
*AP BLUE SP: 2X TO 5X BASIC
*AP BLUE SP RC: 1X TO 2.5X BASIC
RANDOM INSERTS IN PACKS
STATED PRINT RUN 25 SER. #'D SETS

2018 Diamond Kings Artist Proof Gold

*AP GOLD: 2X TO 5X BASIC
*AP GOLD RC: 1X TO 2.5X BASIC
*AP GOLD SP: 1X TO 2.5X BASIC
*AP GOLD SP RC: .5X TO 1.2X BASIC
RANDOM INSERTS IN PACKS
STATED PRINT RUN 99 SER. #'D SETS

2018 Diamond Kings Artist Proof Red

*AP RED: 1.5X TO 4X BASIC
*AP RED RC: ..75X TO 2X BASIC
*AP RED SP: .75X TO 2X BASIC
*AP RED SP RC: .4X TO 1X BASIC
RANDOM INSERTS IN PACKS

2018 Diamond Kings Blue Frame

*BLUE FRAME: 1.5X TO 4X BASIC
*BLUE FRAME RC: ..75X TO 2X BASIC
*BLUE FRAME SP: .75X TO 2X BASIC
*BLUE FRAME SP RC: .4X TO 1X BASIC
RANDOM INSERTS IN PACKS

2018 Diamond Kings Brown Frame

*BRWN FRAME: 2.5X TO 6X BASIC
*BRWN FRAME RC: 1.2X TO 3X BASIC
*BRWN FRAME SP: 1.2X TO 3X BASIC
*BRWN FRAME SP RC: .6X TO 1.5X BASIC
RANDOM INSERTS IN PACKS
STATED PRINT RUN 49 SER. #'D SETS

2018 Diamond Kings Gray Frame

*GRAY FRAME: 2X TO 5X BASIC
*GRAY FRAME RC: 1X TO 2.5X BASIC
*GRAY FRAME SP: 1X TO 2.5X BASIC
*GRAY FRAME SP RC: .5X TO 1.2X BASIC
STATED PRINT RUN 99 SER. #'D SETS

2018 Diamond Kings Red Frame

*RED FRAME: 1.5X TO 4X BASIC
*RED FRAME RC: ..75X TO 2X BASIC
*RED FRAME SP: .75X TO 2X BASIC
*RED FRAME SP RC: .4X TO 1X BASIC
RANDOM INSERTS IN PACKS

2018 Diamond Kings Black and White Variations

*AP RED: .75X TO 2X BASIC
*BLUE FRAME: .75X TO 2X BASIC
*RED FRAME: .75X TO 2X BASIC
*AP GOLD/99: 1X TO 2.5X BASIC
*GRAY FRAME/99: 1X TO 2.5X BASIC
*BRN FRAME/49: 1.2X TO 3X BASIC
*AP BLUE/25: 1.5X TO 4X BASIC
RANDOM INSERTS IN PACKS
73 Shohei Ohtani 10.00 25.00
76 Shohei Ohtani 10.00 25.00
100 Victor Robles 1.00 2.50
104 Rafael Devers 1.25 3.00
105 Francisco Mejia .50 1.25
108 Walker Buehler 1.50 4.00
116 Amed Rosario .50 1.25
117 Clint Frazier .75 2.00
118 Miguel Andujar 1.50 4.00
121 Rhys Hoskins 1.50 4.00

2018 Diamond Kings Name Variations

*AP RED: .75X TO 2X BASIC
*BLUE FRAME: .75X TO 2X BASIC
*RED FRAME: .75X TO 2X BASIC
*AP GOLD/99: 1X TO 2.5X BASIC
*GRAY FRAME/99: 1X TO 2.5X BASIC
*BRN FRAME/49: 1.2X TO 3X BASIC
*AP BLUE/25: 1.5X TO 4X BASIC
RANDOM INSERTS IN PACKS
1 Babe Ruth 1.50 4.00
2 Honus Wagner .60 1.50
7 Mickey Mantle 2.00 5.00
9 Ted Williams 1.25 3.00
25 Ernie Banks .60 1.50
49 Frank Thomas .60 1.50
73 Shohei Ohtani 10.00 25.00
76 Shohei Ohtani 10.00 25.00
80 Aaron Judge 1.50 4.00
136 Nolan Ryan 2.00 5.00

2018 Diamond Kings Photo Variations

RANDOM INSERTS IN PACKS
*AP RED: .75X TO 2X BASIC
*BLUE FRAME: .75X TO 2X BASIC
*RED FRAME: .75X TO 2X BASIC
*AP GOLD/99: 1X TO 2.5X BASIC
*GRAY FRAME/99: 1X TO 2.5X BASIC
*BRN FRAME/49: 1.2X TO 3X BASIC
*AP BLUE/25: 1.5X TO 4X BASIC
2 Honus Wagner .60 1.50
3 Stan Musial 1.00 2.50
4 Lou Gehrig 1.25 3.00
7 Mickey Mantle 2.00 5.00
8 Harry Hooper .40 1.00
9 Ted Williams 1.25 3.00
10 Joe Cronin .40 1.00
11 Joe DiMaggio 1.25 3.00
13 Lloyd Waner .50 1.25
18 Paul Waner .50 1.25
19 Roberto Clemente 1.50 4.00
20 Roger Maris .60 1.50
23 Pee Wee Reese .50 1.25
25 Ernie Banks .60 1.50
27 Lefty Gomez .40 1.00
28 Jackie Robinson .60 1.50
30 Joe Jackson .75 2.00
35 Ty Cobb 1.00 2.50
73 Shohei Ohtani 10.00 25.00
76 Shohei Ohtani 10.00 25.00

2018 Diamond Kings Sepia Variations

*AP RED: .75X TO 2X BASIC
*BLUE FRAME: .75X TO 2X BASIC
*RED FRAME: .75X TO 2X BASIC
*AP GOLD/99: 1X TO 2.5X BASIC
*GRAY FRAME/99: 1X TO 2.5X BASIC
*BRN FRAME/49: 1.2X TO 3X BASIC
*AP BLUE/25: 1.5X TO 4X BASIC
RANDOM INSERTS IN PACKS
65 Francisco Lindor .60 1.50
69 Jose Altuve .50 1.25
70 Mike Trout 3.00 8.00
73 Shohei Ohtani 10.00 25.00
76 Shohei Ohtani 10.00 25.00
78 Bryce Harper 1.00 2.50
79 Buster Posey .75 2.00
80 Aaron Judge 1.50 4.00
81 Andrew Benintendi .60 1.50
82 Cody Bellinger 1.25 3.00

2018 Diamond Kings '82 DK Materials Signatures

RANDOM INSERTS IN PACKS
PRINT RUNS B/WN 10-99 COPIES PER
NO PRICING ON QTY 15 OR LESS
*HOLO BLUE/25: .6X TO 1.5X BASE p/r 99
*HOLO GOLD/49: .5X TO 1.2X BASE p/r 99
*HOLO GOLD/25: .5X TO 1.2X BASE p/r 49
4 Nolan Ryan/49 50.00 120.00
5 Reggie Jackson/49 30.00 80.00
6 Dennis Eckersley/25 12.00 30.00
8 Josh Donaldson/25 8.00 20.00
9 Shohei Ohtani/99 300.00 600.00
10 Joey Votto/49 15.00 40.00
11 Josh Tomlin/99 10.00 25.00
12 Tommy Lasorda/99 30.00 80.00
13 Mark Grace/20 15.00 40.00
14 Max Scherzer/49 25.00 60.00
16 Ryne Sandberg/99 20.00 50.00
17 Terry Francona/25 15.00 40.00
18 Wade Boggs/99 12.00 30.00
19 Roberto Alomar/99 10.00 25.00
20 Frank Thomas/25 30.00 80.00

2018 Diamond Kings '82 DK Signatures

RANDOM INSERTS IN PACKS
STATED PRINT RUN 50 SER.#'d SETS
DKSSO1 Shohei Ohtani 800.00 1200.00
DKSSO2 Shohei Ohtani 800.00 1200.00

2018 Diamond Kings Aurora

COMPLETE SET (10)
RANDOM INSERTS IN PACKS
1 George Springer .40 1.00
2 Yadier Molina .60 1.50
3 Mookie Betts 1.00 2.50
4 Francisco Lindor .50 1.25
5 Andrew McCutchen .50 1.25
6 Carlos Correa .50 1.25
7 Buster Posey .60 1.50
8 Albert Pujols .60 1.50
9 Ichiro .60 1.50
10 Shohei Ohtani 8.00 20.00

2018 Diamond Kings Aurora Holo Blue

*HOLO BLUE: 2X TO 5X BASIC
RANDOM INSERTS IN PACKS
STATED PRINT RUN 25 SER.#'d SET
10 Shohei Ohtani 50.00 120.00

2018 Diamond Kings Bat Kings

RANDOM INSERTS IN PACKS
*HOLO BLUE/25: .75X TO 2X BASIC
*HOLO GOLD/49: .6X TO 1.5X BASIC
*HOLO GOLD/25: .75X TO 2X BASIC
*HOLO SILVER/99: .5X TO 1.2X BASIC
*HOLO SILVER/49: .6X TO 1.5X BASIC
*HOLO SILVER/25: .75X TO 2X BASIC
1 George Brett 6.00 15.00
2 Cal Ripken 15.00 40.00
3 Ted Williams 40.00 100.00
4 Manny Ramirez 3.00 8.00
5 Gary Sheffield 2.00 5.00
6 Barry Larkin 2.50 6.00
7 Alex Rodriguez 4.00 10.00
8 Babe Ruth 75.00 200.00
9 Pee Wee Reese 5.00 12.00
10 Mickey Mantle 25.00 60.00
12 Stan Musial 15.00 40.00
13 Harry Hooper
14 Joe Cronin
15 Ernie Banks 3.00 8.00
16 Heinie Groh 6.00 15.00
17 Sam Crawford 10.00 25.00
18 Kiki Cuyler 12.00 30.00
19 George Kelly 8.00 20.00
20 Frank Thomas 5.00 12.00
21 Rod Carew 2.50 6.00
22 George Springer 2.50 6.00
23 Giancarlo Stanton 3.00 8.00
24 Logan Morrison 2.00 5.00
25 Joey Votto 3.00 8.00

2018 Diamond Kings Diamond Cuts Signatures

RANDOM INSERTS IN PACKS
PRINT RUNS B/WN 2-25 COPIES PER
NO PRICING ON QTY 5 OR LESS
2 Gary Carter/25 20.00 50.00
3 Al Barlick/25 15.00 40.00
5 Bobby Thomson/25 12.00 30.00
17 Buck Leonard/25 10.00 25.00

2018 Diamond Kings Diamond Deco Materials

RANDOM INSERTS IN PACKS
*HOLO BLUE/25: .75X TO 2X BASIC
2 Tony Gwynn 10.00 25.00
3 Don Mattingly 15.00 40.00
4 Aaron Judge 12.00 30.00
5 Cody Bellinger 5.00 12.00
6 Alex Bregman 5.00 12.00
7 Andrew Benintendi 3.00 8.00
10 Alex Rodriguez 6.00 15.00

2018 Diamond Kings Diamond Deco Materials Holo Gold

*HOLO GOLD/49: .6X TO 1.5X BASIC
*HOLO GOLD/25: .75X TO 2X BASIC
RANDOM INSERTS IN PACKS
PRINT RUNS B/WN 5-49 COPIES PER
NO PRICING ON QTY 5

8 Ken Griffey Jr./25	40.00	100.00
9 Mike Trout/25	25.00	60.00

2018 Diamond Kings Diamond Deco Materials Holo Silver

*HOLO SILVER/99: .5X TO 1.2X BASIC
*HOLO SILVER/49: .6X TO 1.5X BASIC
RANDOM INSERTS IN PACKS
PRINT RUNS B/WN 49-99 COPIES PER

8 Ken Griffey Jr./49	30.00	80.00
9 Mike Trout/49	20.00	50.00

2018 Diamond Kings Diamond Material Cuts Signatures

RANDOM INSERTS IN PACKS
PRINT RUNS B/WN X-X COPIES PER
NO PRICING ON QTY X OR LESS

3 Gary Carter/49	12.00	30.00
4 Lloyd Waner/25	30.00	80.00
5 Stan Musial/25	25.00	60.00

2018 Diamond Kings DK Jumbo Materials Signatures

RANDOM INSERTS IN PACKS
PRINT RUNS B/WN 15-75 COPIES PER
NO PRICING ON QTY 15 OR LESS

1 Dwight Gooden/49	8.00	20.00
2 Eric Hosmer/49	5.00	12.00
3 Kyle Schwarber/49	12.00	30.00
5 Mariano Rivera/25	60.00	150.00
11 Wade Boggs/49	15.00	40.00
12 Paul Goldschmidt/75	10.00	25.00
13 Noah Syndergaard/49	5.00	12.00
14 Mike Napoli/25	5.00	12.00
15 Mike Piazza/75	20.00	50.00
17 Addison Russell/49	5.00	12.00
18 Brandon Belt/25	6.00	15.00
19 Edgar Martinez/49	10.00	25.00
20 George Springer/49	5.00	12.00

2018 Diamond Kings DK Jumbo Materials Signatures Holo Gold

*HOLO GOLD/49: .5X TO 1.2X BASE p/r 75
*HOLO GOLD/25: .5X TO 1.2X BASE p/r 49
RANDOM INSERTS IN PACKS
PRINT RUNS B/WN 5-49 COPIES PER
NO PRICING ON QTY 15 OR LESS

7 Ronald Acuna/25	100.00	250.00

2018 Diamond Kings DK Jumbo Rookie Materials Signatures

RANDOM INSERTS IN PACKS
PRINT RUNS B/WN 49-99 COPIES PER
*HOLO GOLD/25: .6X TO 1.5X BASE p/r 99

1 Max Fried/99	12.00	30.00
2 Ozzie Albies/99	10.00	25.00
3 Austin Hays/99	5.00	12.00
4 Shohei Ohtani/49	350.00	700.00
5 Rafael Devers/99	12.00	30.00
6 Francisco Mejia/99	4.00	10.00
7 Walker Buehler/99	15.00	40.00
8 Alex Verdugo/99	5.00	12.00
9 Kyle Farmer/99	6.00	15.00
10 Zack Granite/99	3.00	8.00
11 Anthony Banda/99	3.00	8.00
12 Amed Rosario/99	4.00	10.00
13 Clint Frazier/99	6.00	15.00
14 Miguel Andujar/99	20.00	50.00
15 J.P. Crawford/99	3.00	8.00
16 Nick Williams/99	4.00	10.00
17 Rhys Hoskins/99	25.00	60.00
18 Harrison Bader/99	5.00	12.00
19 Willie Calhoun/99	5.00	12.00
20 Victor Robles/99	8.00	20.00

2018 Diamond Kings DK Materials

RANDOM INSERTS IN PACKS

1 Anthony Banda	2.00	5.00
2 Luiz Gohara	2.00	5.00
3 Max Fried	8.00	20.00
4 Ozzie Albies	5.00	12.00
5 Lucas Sims	2.00	5.00
6 Austin Hays	3.00	8.00
7 Chance Sisco	2.50	6.00
8 Anthony Santander	2.00	5.00
9 Rafael Devers	5.00	12.00
10 Victor Caratini	2.50	6.00
11 Nicky Delmonico	2.00	5.00
12 Tyler Mahle	2.50	6.00
13 Francisco Mejia	2.50	6.00
14 Greg Allen	2.00	5.00
15 Ryan McMahon	5.00	12.00
16 J.D. Davis	2.50	6.00
17 Cameron Gallagher	2.00	5.00
18 Walker Buehler	5.00	12.00
19 Alex Verdugo	3.00	8.00
20 Kyle Farmer	2.00	5.00
21 Brian Anderson	2.50	6.00
22 Dillon Peters	2.00	5.00
23 Brandon Woodruff	6.00	15.00
24 Mitch Garver	2.00	5.00
25 Zack Granite	2.00	5.00
26 Felix Jorge	2.00	5.00
27 Tomas Nido	2.00	5.00
28 Greg Bird	2.50	6.00
29 Chris Flexen	2.00	5.00
30 Amed Rosario	2.50	6.00
31 Clint Frazier	4.00	10.00
32 Miguel Andujar	5.00	12.00
33 Tyler Wade	2.50	6.00
34 Dustin Fowler	2.00	5.00
35 Paul Blackburn	2.00	5.00
36 J.P. Crawford	2.00	5.00
37 Nick Williams	2.50	6.00
38 Rhys Hoskins	5.00	12.00
39 Thyago Vieira	2.00	5.00
40 Reyes Moronta	2.00	5.00
41 Jack Flaherty	4.00	10.00
42 Harrison Bader	3.00	8.00
43 Willie Calhoun	3.00	8.00
44 Richard Urena	2.00	5.00
45 Victor Robles	4.00	10.00
46 Erick Fedde	2.00	5.00
47 Andrew Stevenson	2.00	5.00
48 Mark McGwire	5.00	12.00
49 Ernie Banks	3.00	8.00
50 Herb Pennock	6.00	15.00
52 Leo Durocher	6.00	15.00
53 Lou Gehrig	60.00	150.00
54 Pee Wee Reese	5.00	12.00
55 Tony Lazzeri	12.00	30.00
56 Babe Ruth	75.00	200.00
57 Billy Martin	5.00	12.00
58 Carl Furillo		
59 George Kelly	8.00	20.00
60 Harry Hooper		
61 Joe Cronin		
62 Joe DiMaggio	15.00	40.00
63 Kiki Cuyler	12.00	30.00
64 Lloyd Waner		
65 Luke Appling	4.00	10.00
66 Max Carey		
67 Mickey Mantle	25.00	60.00
70 Roger Maris		
71 Stan Musial	15.00	40.00
73 Ted Williams	40.00	100.00
74 Tommy Henrich	5.00	12.00
75 Mike Trout	15.00	40.00
76 Ken Griffey Jr.	8.00	20.00
77 Gary Sheffield	2.00	5.00
78 Aaron Judge	10.00	25.00
80 Reggie Jackson	5.00	12.00
81 Andrew Benintendi	4.00	10.00
82 Jose Altuve	2.50	6.00
83 Cody Bellinger	4.00	10.00
84 Adrian Beltre	3.00	8.00
85 Addie Joss		
86 Justin Turner	3.00	8.00
87 Shohei Ohtani	10.00	25.00
88 Marcell Ozuna	3.00	8.00
89 Mookie Betts	5.00	12.00
90 Joey Votto	3.00	8.00
91 Clayton Kershaw	5.00	12.00
92 Corey Kluber	2.50	6.00
93 Max Scherzer	3.00	8.00
94 Jose Abreu	3.00	8.00
95 Lorenzo Cain	2.00	5.00
96 Andrew McCutchen	3.00	8.00
97 Dallas Keuchel	2.50	6.00
99 Albert Pujols	4.00	10.00

2018 Diamond Kings DK Materials Holo Blue

*HOLO BLUE/25: .75X TO 2X BASIC
RANDOM INSERTS IN PACKS
PRINT RUNS B/WN 3-25 COPIES PER
NO PRICING ON QTY 10 OR LESS

79 Giancarlo Stanton/25	6.00	15.00

2018 Diamond Kings DK Materials Holo Gold

*HOLO GOLD/49: .6X TO 1.5X BASIC
*HOLO GOLD/20-25: .75X TO 2X BASIC
RANDOM INSERTS IN PACKS
PRINT RUNS B/WN 5-49 COPIES PER
NO PRICING ON QTY 15 OR LESS

79 Giancarlo Stanton/49	5.00	12.00
100 Mike Piazza/25	6.00	15.00

2018 Diamond Kings DK Materials Holo Silver

*HOLO SILVER/99: .5X TO 1.2X BASIC
*HOLO SILVER/49: .6X TO 1.5X BASIC
*HOLO SILVER/25: .75X TO 2X BASIC
RANDOM INSERTS IN PACKS
PRINT RUNS B/WN 7-99 COPIES PER
NO PRICING ON QTY 15 OR LESS

79 Giancarlo Stanton/99	4.00	10.00
100 Mike Piazza/99	4.00	10.00

2018 Diamond Kings DK Materials Signatures

RANDOM INSERTS IN PACKS
PRINT RUNS B/WN 10-299 COPIES PER
NO PRICING ON QTY 15 OR LESS
*HOLO BLUE/25: .6X TO 1.5X BASE p/r 75-299
*HOLO GOLD/49: .5X TO 1.2X BASE p/r 75-299
*HOLO GOLD/25: .6X TO 1.5X BASE p/r 75-299
*HOLO SLVR/99: .4X TO 1X BASE p/r 75-299
*HOLO SLVR/49: .5X TO 1.2X BASE p/r 75-299
*HOLO SLVR/25: .5X TO 1.2X BASE p/r 49

1 Rafael Palmeiro/49	12.00	30.00
2 Rickey Henderson/99	20.00	50.00
3 David Dahl/99	3.00	8.00
4 Roger Clemens/75	15.00	40.00
5 Ryne Sandberg/99	20.00	50.00
6 Stephen Piscotty/49		
7 Todd Helton/99	8.00	20.00
8 Trea Turner/25	6.00	15.00
9 Trey Mancini/49	5.00	12.00
10 Wil Myers/30	6.00	15.00
11 Byron Buxton/35	8.00	20.00
12 Carlos Gonzalez/25	10.00	25.00
13 Cole Hamels/99	4.00	10.00
14 Craig Kimbrel/49	10.00	25.00
15 Eric Hosmer/49	12.00	30.00
17 Fergie Jenkins/99	4.00	10.00
18 Maikel Franco/299	4.00	10.00
19 Alex Bregman/150	12.00	30.00
20 Derek Fisher/299	3.00	8.00
21 Franklin Barreto/299	3.00	8.00
22 Jordan Montgomery/166	3.00	8.00
23 Ian Happ/196	4.00	10.00
24 Matt Olson/299	5.00	12.00
25 Ryon Healy/49	8.00	20.00
26 Bradley Zimmer/49	4.00	10.00
28 Jake Thompson/299	3.00	8.00
29 Antonio Senzatela/150	3.00	8.00
30 Joe Musgrove/299	5.00	12.00
31 Juan Gonzalez/299	5.00	12.00
32 Gary Sheffield/99	6.00	15.00
33 Yoenis Cespedes/75	8.00	20.00
34 Gerrit Cole/99	12.00	30.00
35 Jason Kipnis/49	5.00	12.00
36 Luke Weaver/299	4.00	10.00
37 Reynaldo Lopez/226	4.00	10.00
38 Carson Kelly/299	3.00	8.00
39 Jeff Hoffman/299	3.00	8.00

2018 Diamond Kings DK Originals Materials

RANDOM INSERTS IN PACKS

1 Carlos Gonzalez	2.50	6.00
2 Joey Gallo	2.50	6.00
3 Cody Bellinger	4.00	10.00
4 Aaron Judge	10.00	25.00
5 Andrew Benintendi	4.00	10.00
6 Josh Bell	2.50	6.00
7 Alex Bregman	3.00	8.00
8 Charlie Blackmon	3.00	8.00
9 Joey Votto	3.00	8.00
11 J.D. Martinez	3.00	8.00
12 Rhys Hoskins	5.00	12.00
13 Nolan Arenado	5.00	12.00
14 Manny Machado	3.00	8.00
15 Gary Sanchez	4.00	10.00
16 Paul Goldschmidt	3.00	8.00
17 Anthony Rizzo	4.00	10.00
18 Jose Abreu	3.00	8.00
19 Ozzie Albies	5.00	12.00
20 Victor Robles	4.00	10.00
21 Rafael Devers	5.00	12.00
22 Clint Frazier	4.00	10.00
23 Amed Rosario	2.50	6.00
24 Greg Bird	2.50	6.00
25 J.P. Crawford	2.00	5.00
26 Miguel Andujar	5.00	12.00
27 Chance Sisco	2.50	6.00
28 Kyle Farmer	2.00	5.00
29 Jonathan Schoop	2.00	5.00
30 Ryan Zimmerman	2.50	6.00
31 Corey Kluber	2.50	6.00
32 Stephen Strasburg	3.00	8.00
33 Luis Severino	2.50	6.00
34 Clayton Kershaw	5.00	12.00
35 Chris Sale	3.00	8.00
36 Max Scherzer	3.00	8.00
37 Craig Kimbrel	2.50	6.00
38 Kirby Puckett	12.00	30.00
39 Dom DiMaggio		
40 Mickey Mantle	25.00	60.00

2018 Diamond Kings DK Originals Materials Holo Blue

*HOLO BLUE/25: .75X TO 2X BASIC
RANDOM INSERTS IN PACKS
PRINT RUNS B/WN 3-25 COPIES PER
NO PRICING ON QTY 10 OR LESS

10 Giancarlo Stanton/25	6.00	15.00

2018 Diamond Kings DK Originals Materials Holo Gold

*HOLO GOLD/49: .6X TO 1.5X BASIC
*HOLO GOLD/25: .75X TO 2X BASIC
RANDOM INSERTS IN PACKS
PRINT RUNS B/WN 5-49 COPIES PER
NO PRICING ON QTY 15 OR LESS

10 Giancarlo Stanton/49	5.00	12.00
14 Manny Machado/25	6.00	15.00

2018 Diamond Kings DK Originals Materials Holo Silver

*HOLO SILVER/99: .5X TO 1.2X BASIC
*HOLO SILVER/49: .6X TO 1.5X BASIC
*HOLO SILVER/25: .75X TO 2X BASIC
RANDOM INSERTS IN PACKS
PRINT RUNS B/WN 25-99 COPIES PER

10 Giancarlo Stanton/99	4.00	10.00
14 Manny Machado/49	5.00	12.00

2018 Diamond Kings DK Rookie Materials Signatures

RANDOM INSERTS IN PACKS
PRINT RUNS B/WN 99-299 COPIES PER
*HOLO GOLD/25: .6X TO 1.5X BASE
*HOLO SILVER/49: .5X TO 1.2X BASE

1 Anthony Banda/299	3.00	8.00
2 Luiz Gohara/199	6.00	15.00
3 Max Fried/299	12.00	30.00
4 Ozzie Albies/299	20.00	50.00
5 Lucas Sims/299	3.00	8.00
6 Austin Hays/299	5.00	12.00
7 Chance Sisco/299	4.00	10.00
8 Anthony Santander/299	3.00	8.00
9 Rafael Devers/299	10.00	25.00
10 Victor Caratini/299	4.00	10.00
11 Nicky Delmonico/299	3.00	8.00
12 Tyler Mahle/299	4.00	10.00
13 Francisco Mejia/299	4.00	10.00
14 Greg Allen/299	3.00	8.00
15 Ryan McMahon/299	8.00	20.00
16 J.D. Davis/299	4.00	10.00
17 Cameron Gallagher/199	3.00	8.00
18 Walker Buehler/299	12.00	30.00
19 Alex Verdugo/299	6.00	15.00
20 Kyle Farmer/199	6.00	15.00
21 Brian Anderson/299	4.00	10.00
22 Dillon Peters/299	3.00	8.00
23 Brandon Woodruff/299	10.00	25.00
24 Mitch Garver/299	3.00	8.00
25 Zack Granite/299	3.00	8.00
26 Felix Jorge/299	3.00	8.00
27 Tomas Nido/299	3.00	8.00
28 Ozzie Albies/299	20.00	50.00
29 Chris Flexen/299	3.00	8.00
30 Amed Rosario/299	4.00	10.00
31 Clint Frazier/299	6.00	15.00
32 Miguel Andujar/299	12.00	30.00
33 Tyler Wade/299	4.00	10.00
34 Dustin Fowler/299	3.00	8.00
35 Paul Blackburn/299	3.00	8.00
36 J.P. Crawford/199	3.00	8.00
37 Nick Williams/299	4.00	10.00
38 Rhys Hoskins/299	10.00	50.00
39 Thyago Vieira/299	3.00	8.00
40 Reyes Moronta/299	3.00	8.00
41 Jack Flaherty/299	12.00	30.00
42 Harrison Bader/299	5.00	12.00
43 Willie Calhoun/299	5.00	12.00
44 Richard Urena/299	3.00	8.00
45 Victor Robles/299	8.00	20.00
46 Erick Fedde/299	3.00	8.00
47 Andrew Stevenson/299	3.00	8.00
48 Shohei Ohtani/99	300.00	600.00

2018 Diamond Kings DK Rookie Signatures

RANDOM INSERTS IN PACKS
*HOLO SILVER/49: .5X TO 1.2X BASIC
*HOLO GOLD/25: .6X TO 1.5X BASIC

1 Anthony Banda	3.00	8.00
2 Luiz Gohara	3.00	8.00
3 Max Fried	12.00	30.00
4 Ozzie Albies	6.00	15.00
5 Lucas Sims	3.00	8.00
6 Austin Hays	4.00	10.00
7 Chance Sisco	4.00	10.00
8 Anthony Santander	3.00	8.00
9 Rafael Devers	5.00	12.00
10 Victor Caratini	4.00	10.00
11 Nicky Delmonico	3.00	8.00
12 Tyler Mahle	4.00	10.00
13 Francisco Mejia	4.00	10.00
14 Greg Allen	3.00	8.00
15 Ryan McMahon	8.00	20.00
16 J.D. Davis	4.00	10.00
17 Cameron Gallagher	3.00	8.00
18 Walker Buehler	8.00	20.00
19 Alex Verdugo	5.00	12.00
20 Kyle Farmer	3.00	8.00
21 Brian Anderson	4.00	10.00
22 Dillon Peters	3.00	8.00
23 Brandon Woodruff	10.00	25.00
24 Mitch Garver	3.00	8.00
25 Zack Granite	3.00	8.00
26 Felix Jorge	3.00	8.00
27 Tomas Nido	3.00	8.00
28 Dominic Smith	4.00	10.00
29 Chris Flexen	3.00	8.00
30 Amed Rosario	4.00	10.00
31 Clint Frazier	5.00	12.00
32 Miguel Andujar	20.00	50.00
33 Tyler Wade	4.00	10.00
34 Dustin Fowler	3.00	8.00
35 Paul Blackburn	3.00	8.00
36 J.P. Crawford	3.00	8.00
37 Nick Williams	4.00	10.00
38 Rhys Hoskins	15.00	40.00
39 Thyago Vieira	3.00	8.00
40 Reyes Moronta	3.00	8.00
41 Jack Flaherty	10.00	25.00
42 Harrison Bader	5.00	12.00
43 Willie Calhoun	5.00	12.00
44 Richard Urena	3.00	8.00
45 Victor Robles	6.00	15.00
46 Erick Fedde	3.00	8.00
47 Shohei Ohtani	125.00	300.00

2018 Diamond Kings DK Rookie Signatures Purple

*PURPLE/20: .6X TO 1.5X BASIC
RANDOM INSERTS IN PACKS
PRINT RUNS B/WN 10-20 COPIES PER
NO PRICING ON QTY 10

2018 Diamond Kings DK Signatures

RANDOM INSERTS IN PACKS
*HOLO BLUE/25: .6X TO 1.5X BASIC
*HOLO GOLD/49: .5X TO 1.2X BASIC
*HOLO GOLD/25: .6X TO 1.5X BASIC
*HOLO SILVER/49-99: .5X TO 1.2X BASIC
*HOLO SILVER/25: .6X TO 1.5X BASIC
*PURPLE/20: .6X TO 1.5X BASIC

1 Wade Boggs	10.00	25.00
2 Bob Gibson	12.00	30.00
3 David Dahl	3.00	8.00
4 Jose Abreu	4.00	10.00
SAJ Aaron Judge	60.00	150.00
6 Jose Altuve	12.00	30.00
7 Adam Frazier	3.00	8.00
8 Andre Dawson	6.00	15.00
9 Bill Mazeroski	12.00	30.00
10 Aaron Hicks	5.00	12.00
11 Bert Blyleven	4.00	10.00
12 Al Kaline	15.00	40.00
13 Jacoby Jones	4.00	10.00
14 Josh Bell	4.00	10.00
15 Raimel Tapia	3.00	8.00
16 Mike Foltynewicz	3.00	8.00
17 Carson Fulmer	3.00	8.00
18 Yasmany Tomas	3.00	8.00
19 Luke Weaver	4.00	10.00
20 Gavin Cecchini	3.00	8.00
21 Joe Musgrove	5.00	12.00
22 Tyler Glasnow	5.00	12.00
23 Matt Olson	5.00	12.00
24 Odubel Herrera	8.00	20.00
25 Ivan Rodriguez	10.00	25.00
26 Tom Glavine	6.00	15.00
27 Dansby Swanson	8.00	20.00
28 Sean Newcomb	4.00	10.00
29 Matt Carpenter	5.00	12.00
30 Chris Taylor	5.00	12.00
31 Brooks Robinson	12.00	30.00
32 Manuel Margot	3.00	8.00
33 Luis Robert	20.00	50.00
34 Justin Turner	15.00	40.00
35 Ozzie Smith	15.00	40.00
36 David Ortiz	20.00	50.00
37 Braden Shipley	3.00	8.00
38 Willie McGee	8.00	20.00
39 Adam Duvall	4.00	10.00
40 Chipper Jones	30.00	80.00
41 Chris Sale		
42 Corey Seager	8.00	20.00
43 Darrell Evans	3.00	8.00
44 Darryl Strawberry	5.00	12.00
45 George Springer	10.00	25.00
46 Ian Kinsler	4.00	10.00
47 Jacob deGrom		
48 Johnny Damon	5.00	12.00
49 Josh Donaldson		
50 Kyle Seager	3.00	8.00
51 Manny Machado	15.00	40.00
52 Michael Kopech	12.00	30.00
53 Carlos Correa	15.00	40.00

2018 Diamond Kings DK Triple Materials Signatures

RANDOM INSERTS IN PACKS
PRINT RUNS B/WN 10-150 COPIES PER
NO PRICING ON QTY 10
*HOLO GOLD/25: .6X TO 1.5X BASE p/r 97
*HOLO SILVER/99: .4X TO 1X BASE p/r 150
*HOLO SILVER/49: .5X TO 1.2X BASE p/r 97-99
*HOLO SILVER/25: .5X TO 1.2X BASE p/r 49

1 Yoan Moncada/150	10.00	25.00
2 Craig Kimbrel/49	10.00	25.00
3 Don Mattingly/99	20.00	50.00
4 Greg Maddux/49	25.00	60.00
5 Nomar Mazara/97	3.00	8.00
6 Josh Donaldson/25	8.00	20.00
7 Barry Larkin/99	20.00	50.00
8 Joe Torre/49	12.00	30.00
9 Kyle Schwarber/99	8.00	20.00
10 Lou Brock/49	20.00	50.00
12 Shohei Ohtani/49	250.00	500.00
13 Nomar Garciaparra/49	20.00	50.00

2018 Diamond Kings Gallery of Stars

COMPLETE SET (18)
RANDOM INSERTS IN PACKS

1 Daniel Murphy	.40	1.00
2 Justin Turner	.50	1.25
3 Jose Ramirez	.40	1.00
4 Nolan Arenado	.75	2.00
5 Alex Bregman	.50	1.25
6 Miguel Cabrera	.50	1.25
7 Paul Goldschmidt	.50	1.25
8 Brian Dozier	.40	1.00
9 Joey Gallo	.40	1.00
10 J.D. Martinez	.50	1.25
11 Shohei Ohtani	8.00	20.00
12 Chris Sale	.50	1.25
13 Jacob deGrom	1.00	2.50
14 Willie Stargell	.40	1.00
15 Tony Gwynn	.50	1.25
16 Reggie Jackson	.40	1.00
17 Ozzie Smith	.60	1.50
18 Orlando Cepeda	.40	1.00

2018 Diamond Kings Gallery of Stars Holo Blue

*HOLO BLUE: 2X TO 5X BASIC
RANDOM INSERTS IN PACKS
STATED PRINT RUN 25 SER.#'d SET

11 Shohei Ohtani	50.00	120.00
16 Reggie Jackson	10.00	25.00
17 Ozzie Smith	10.00	25.00

2018 Diamond Kings Jersey Kings

RANDOM INSERTS IN PACKS
*HOLO BLUE/25: .75X TO 2X BASIC
*HOLO GOLD/49: .6X TO 1.5X BASIC
*HOLO GOLD/20-25: .75X TO 2X BASIC
*HOLO SILVER/99: .5X TO 1.2X BASIC
*HOLO SILVER/49: .6X TO 1.5X BASIC
*HOLO SILVER/25: .75X TO 2X BASIC

1 George Springer	2.50	6.00
2 Kris Bryant	6.00	15.00
3 Bryce Harper	5.00	12.00
4 Carlos Correa	3.00	8.00
5 Harmon Killebrew	5.00	12.00
6 George Brett	6.00	15.00
7 Johnny Bench	6.00	15.00
8 Ryne Sandberg	5.00	12.00
9 Juan Gonzalez	2.00	5.00
10 Greg Maddux	4.00	10.00
11 Yoenis Cespedes	3.00	8.00
12 Jeff Bagwell	2.50	6.00
13 Matt Carpenter	3.00	8.00
14 Marcell Ozuna	3.00	8.00
15 Babe Ruth	75.00	200.00
16 Lou Gehrig	60.00	150.00
17 Ted Williams	40.00	100.00
18 Jackie Robinson	25.00	60.00
19 Leo Durocher	6.00	15.00
20 Gabby Hartnett	8.00	20.00
21 Tony Gwynn	3.00	8.00
22 Aaron Judge	10.00	25.00
23 Cody Bellinger	4.00	10.00
24 Jose Altuve	2.50	6.00
25 Justin Turner	3.00	8.00

2018 Diamond Kings Mickey Mantle Collection

COMPLETE SET (8)
*HOLO BLUE/25: 1.5X TO 4X BASIC

1 Mickey Mantle	1.50	4.00
2 Mickey Mantle	1.50	4.00
3 Mickey Mantle	1.50	4.00
4 Mickey Mantle	1.50	4.00
5 Mickey Mantle	1.50	4.00
6 Mickey Mantle	1.50	4.00
7 Mickey Mantle	1.50	4.00
8 Mickey Mantle	1.50	4.00

2018 Diamond Kings Past and Present

COMPLETE SET (15)
RANDOM INSERTS IN PACKS
*HOLO BLUE/25: 1X TO 2.5X BASIC

1 Judge/Ruth	1.00	2.50
2 Bobby Doerr Dustin Pedroia	.40	1.00
3 Gonzalez/Bellinger	.75	2.00
4 Brooks Robinson Manny Machado	.40	1.00
5 Verlander/Ryan	1.25	3.00
6 Frank Thomas Jose Abreu	.40	1.00
7 J.Ramriez/R.Alomar	.30	.75
8 Mantle/Trout	2.00	5.00
9 Biggio/Altuve	.30	.75
10 Ruth/Ohtani	6.00	15.00
11 Rizo/Banks	.50	1.25
12 Lindor/Brock	.40	1.00
13 Juan Marichal Madison Bumgarner	.30	.75
14 Benintendi/Lynn	.40	1.00
15 Sanchez/Posada	.40	1.00

2018 Diamond Kings Portraits

COMPLETE SET (15)
RANDOM INSERTS IN PACKS

1 Ken Griffey Jr.	1.00	2.50
2 David Ortiz	.50	1.25
3 Cal Ripken	1.50	4.00
4 Chipper Jones	.50	1.25
5 George Brett	1.00	2.50
6 Nolan Ryan	1.50	4.00
7 Mickey Mantle	1.50	4.00
8 Tony Gwynn	.50	1.25
9 Ty Cobb	.75	2.00
10 Ted Williams	1.00	2.50
11 Honus Wagner	.50	1.25
12 Jackie Robinson	.50	1.25
13 Greg Maddux	.60	1.50
14 Joe Morgan	.40	1.00
15 Shohei Ohtani	8.00	20.00

2018 Diamond Kings Portraits Holo Blue

*HOLO BLUE: 2X TO 5X BASIC
RANDOM INSERTS IN PACKS
STATED PRINT RUN 25 SER.#'d SET

15 Shohei Ohtani	50.00	120.00

2018 Diamond Kings Recollection Buyback Autographs

RANDOM INSERTS IN PACKS
PRINT RUNS B/WN 1-30 COPIES PER
NO PRICING ON QTY 10 OR LESS

102 Jeff Bagwell/23	20.00	50.00
119 Matt Carpenter/30	10.00	25.00

2018 Diamond Kings Royalty

RANDOM INSERTS IN PACKS
*HOLO BLUE/25: 4X TO 10X BASIC

1 Babe Ruth	1.25	3.00

2018 Diamond Kings The 500

RANDOM INSERTS IN PACKS
*HOLO BLUE/25: 2X TO 5X BASIC

1 Albert Pujols	.60	1.50
2 Alex Rodriguez	.60	1.50
3 Babe Ruth	1.25	3.00
4 Mark McGwire	.75	2.00
5 David Ortiz	.50	1.25
6 Eddie Mathews	.50	1.25
7 Eddie Murray	.40	1.00
8 Ernie Banks	.50	1.25
9 Frank Thomas	.50	1.25
10 Gary Sheffield	.30	.75
11 Harmon Killebrew	.50	1.25
12 Ken Griffey Jr.	1.00	2.50
13 Manny Ramirez	.50	1.25
14 Mickey Mantle	1.50	4.00
15 Rafael Palmeiro	.40	1.00
16 Reggie Jackson	.40	1.00
17 Ted Williams	1.00	2.50
18 Willie McCovey	.40	1.00

2018 Diamond Kings Trophy Club

COMPLETE SET (15)
RANDOM INSERTS IN PACKS
*HOLO BLUE/25: 1.5X TO 4X BASIC

1 George Springer	.40	1.00
2 Aaron Judge	1.25	3.00
3 Cody Bellinger	1.00	2.50
4 Corey Seager	.50	1.25
5 Justin Verlander	.50	1.25
6 Corey Kluber	.40	1.00
7 Max Scherzer	.50	1.25
8 Clayton Kershaw	.75	2.00
9 Mickey Mantle	1.50	4.00
10 Kris Bryant	.60	1.50
11 Mike Trout	2.50	6.00
12 Bryce Harper	.75	2.00
13 Dallas Keuchel	.40	1.00
14 Josh Donaldson	.40	1.00
15 Carlos Correa	.50	1.25

2019 Diamond Kings

1 Stan Musial	.50	1.25
2 Hank Greenberg	.30	.75
3 Babe Ruth	.75	2.00
4 Roger Maris	.30	.75
5 Roberto Clemente	.75	2.00
6 Mel Ott	.30	.75
7 Walter Alston	.25	.60
8 Mickey Cochrane	.25	.60
9 Eddie Stanky	.20	.50
10 Joe Wood	.20	.50
11 Al Simmons	.25	.60
12 Tris Speaker	.25	.60
13 Grover Alexander	.25	.60
14 Rogers Hornsby	.25	.60
15 Mickey Mantle	1.00	2.50
16 Lou Gehrig	.60	1.50
17 Yogi Berra	.30	.75
18 Carl Erskine	.20	.50
19 Joe DiMaggio	.60	1.50
20 Jimmie Foxx	.30	.75
21 Satchel Paige	.30	.75
22 Ted Williams	.60	1.50
23 Carl Hubbell	.25	.60
24 Christy Mathewson	.30	.75
25 Joe Jackson	.40	1.00
26 Ty Cobb	.50	1.25
27 Honus Wagner	.30	.75
28 Joe Sewell	.25	.60
29 Jackie Robinson	.30	.75
30 Charlie Keller	.20	.50
31 Enyel De Los Santos RC	.40	1.00
32 Brad Keller RC	.40	1.00
33 Nolan Ryan	1.00	2.50
34 Miguel Cabrera	.30	.75
35 Brandon Lowe RC	.60	1.50
36 Chipper Jones	.30	.75
37 Tony Gwynn	.30	.75
38 Jose Altuve	.25	.60
39 J.D. Martinez	.30	.75
40 Ronald Acuna Jr.	1.50	4.00
41 Kiki Cuyler	.25	.60
42 Max Scherzer	.30	.75
43 Corbin Burnes RC	3.00	8.00
44 Roger Clemens	.40	1.00
45 Kevin Kramer RC	.50	1.25
46 Khris Davis	.30	.75
47 Paul Goldschmidt	.30	.75
48 Johnny Bench	.30	.75
49 Jacob deGrom	.60	1.50
50 Michael Kopech RC	1.25	3.00
51 Walker Buehler	.40	1.00
52 Garrett Hampson RC	.60	1.50
53 Kyle Freeland	.25	.60
54 Jeff McNeil RC	1.00	2.50
55 Luis Severino	.25	.60
56 Brooks Robinson	.25	.60
57 Ramon Laureano RC	.75	2.00
58 Jake Bauers RC	.60	1.50
59 Andrew Benintendi	.30	.75
60 Alex Bregman	.30	.75
61 Kolby Allard RC	.60	1.50
62 Kevin Newman RC	.60	1.50
63 Josh James RC	.60	1.50
64 Ryan O'Hearn RC	.40	1.00
65 Juan Soto	1.00	2.50
66 Justus Sheffield	.30	.75
67 Aaron Judge	.75	2.00
68 Chris Shaw RC	.40	1.00
69 Dakota Hudson RC	.50	1.25
70 Giancarlo Stanton	.30	.75
71 Joey Votto	.30	.75
72 Sean Reid-Foley RC	.40	1.00
73 Matt Carpenter	.30	.75
74 Al Kaline	.30	.75
75 Salvador Perez	.25	.60
76 Kyle Wright RC	.60	1.50
77 Cedric Mullins RC	.75	2.00
78 Jonathan Loaisiga RC	.50	1.25
79 Jacob Nix RC	.50	1.25
80 Ichiro	.40	1.00
81 Ozzie Albies	.30	.75
82 Luis Urias RC	.60	1.50
83 Sam Crawford	.25	.60
84 Chris Sale	.30	.75
85 Rickey Henderson	.30	.75
86 Corey Kluber	.25	.60
87 Aaron Nola	.25	.60
88 Justin Verlander	.30	.75
89 Rhys Hoskins	.40	1.00
90 David Fletcher RC	1.25	3.00
91 Vladimir Guerrero	.25	.60
92 Pee Wee Reese	.25	.60
93 Freddie Freeman	.40	1.00
94 Jonathan Davis RC	.50	1.25
95 Mookie Betts	.60	1.50
96 Bryse Wilson RC	.50	1.25
97 Cionel Perez RC	.40	1.00
98 Chance Adams RC	.40	1.00
99 Christin Stewart RC	.50	1.25
100 Miguel Andujar	.30	.75
101 Framber Valdez SP SP RC	.60	1.50
102 Noah Syndergaard SP	.50	1.25
103 Touki Toussaint SP RC	.75	2.00
104 Patrick Wisdom SP RC	.60	1.50
105 Ryne Sandberg SP	1.25	3.00
106 Ryan Borucki SP RC	.60	1.50
107 Nolan Arenado SP	1.00	2.50
108 Luis Ortiz SP RC	.60	1.50
109 Steven Duggar SP RC	.75	2.00
110 Kirby Puckett SP	.60	1.50
111 Stephen Gonsalves SP RC	.60	1.50
112 Yusei Kikuchi SP RC	1.00	2.50
113 Ken Griffey Jr. SP	1.25	3.00
114 Jake Cave SP RC	.75	2.00
115 Albert Pujols SP	.75	2.00
116 Jesus Aguilar SP	.50	1.25
117 Taylor Ward SP RC	.60	1.50
118 Kyle Tucker SP RC	1.50	4.00
119 Dennis Santana SP RC	.60	1.50
120 Danny Jansen SP RC	.60	1.50
121 Cal Ripken SP	2.00	5.00
122 Reese McGuire SP RC	1.00	2.50
123 Bob Gibson SP	.50	1.25
124 Shohei Ohtani SP	1.00	2.50
125 Mariano Rivera SP	.75	2.00
126 Matt Chapman SP	.60	1.50
127 Yadier Molina SP	.75	2.00
128 Adrian Beltre SP	.60	1.50
129 Paul Waner SP	.50	1.25
130 Jose Ramirez SP	.50	1.25
131 Caleb Ferguson SP RC	.75	2.00
132 Larry Doby SP	.50	1.25
133 Mike Trout SP	3.00	8.00
134 Daniel Ponce de Leon SP RC	1.00	2.50
135 Anthony Rizzo SP	.75	2.00
136 J.T. Realmuto SP	.60	1.50
137 George Brett SP	1.25	3.00
138 Christian Yelich SP	.75	2.00
139 Kris Bryant SP	.75	2.00
140 Myles Straw SP RC	1.00	2.50
141 Rowdy Tellez SP RC	1.00	2.50
142 Clayton Kershaw SP	1.00	2.50
143 Bryce Harper SP	1.00	2.50
144 Gleyber Torres SP	1.25	3.00
145 Francisco Lindor SP	.60	1.50
146 Blake Snell SP	.50	1.25
147 Trevor Story SP	.60	1.50
148 Frank Thomas SP	.60	1.50
149 Manny Machado SP	.60	1.50
150 Javier Baez SP	.75	2.00

2019 Diamond Kings Artist Proof

*AP: 1.2X TO 3X BASIC
*AP RC: ..6X TO 1.5X BASIC
*AP SP: ..6X TO 1.5X BASIC
*AP SP RC: .4X TO 1X BASIC
RANDOM INSERTS IN PACKS

2019 Diamond Kings Artist Proof Blue

*AP BLUE: 1.5X TO 4X BASIC
*AP BLUE RC: ..75X TO 2X BASIC
*AP BLUE SP: .75X TO 2X BASIC
*AP BLUE SP RC: .5X TO 1.2X BASIC
RANDOM INSERTS IN PACKS

2019 Diamond Kings Blue Frame

*BLUE FRAME: 1.5X TO 4X BASIC
*BLUE FRAME RC: .75X TO 2X BASIC
*BLUE FRAME SP: .75X TO 2X BASIC
*BLUE FRAME SP RC: .5X TO 1.2X BASIC
RANDOM INSERTS IN PACKS

2019 Diamond Kings Plum Frame

*PLUM FRAME: 1.2X TO 3X BASIC
*PLUM FRAME RC: .6X TO 1.5X BASIC
*PLUM FRAME SP: .6X TO 1.5X BASIC

*PLUM FRAME SP RC: .4X TO 1X BASIC
RANDOM INSERTS IN PACKS

2019 Diamond Kings Red Frame
*RED FRAME: 1.5X TO 4X BASIC
*RED FRAME RC: .75X TO 2X BASIC
*RED FRAME SP: .75X TO 2X BASIC
*RED FRAME SP RC: .5X TO 1.2X BASIC
RANDOM INSERTS IN PACKS

2019 Diamond Kings Variations
RANDOM INSERTS IN PACKS
*AP: .6X TO 1.5X BASIC
*PLUM FRAME: .6X TO 1.5X BASIC
*AP BLUE: .75X TO 2X BASIC
*BLUE FRAME: .75X TO 2X BASIC
*RED FRAME: .75X TO 2X BASIC
21 Satchel Paige .60 1.50
22 Wade Boggs .50 1.25
26 Ty Cobb 1.00 2.50
33 Nolan Ryan 2.00 5.00
43 Gleyber Torres 1.25 3.00
44 Javier Baez .75 2.00
60 Alex Bregman .60 1.50
64 Ryan O'Hearn .40 1.00
65 Juan Soto 2.00 5.00
80 Ichiro .75 2.00
81 Ozzie Albies .60 1.50
85 Rickey Henderson .60 1.50
91 Vladimir Guerrero .50 1.25
95 Mookie Betts 1.25 3.00
105 Ryne Sandberg 1.25 3.00
112 Yusei Kikuchi .60 1.50
124 Shohei Ohtani 1.00 2.50
130 Jose Ramirez .50 1.25
139 Kris Bryant .75 2.00
144 Gleyber Torres 1.25 3.00

2019 Diamond Kings '02 DK Retro
RANDOM INSERTS IN PACKS
*AP: .75X TO 2X BASIC
*PLUM FRAME: .75X TO 2X BASIC
*AP BLUE: 1X TO 2.5X BASIC
*BLUE FRAME: 1X TO 2.5X BASIC
*RED FRAME: 1X TO 2.5X BASIC
1 Randy Johnson .50 1.25
2 Pedro Martinez .40 1.00
3 Jason Giambi .30 .75
4 Miguel Tejada .30 .75
5 Ichiro .60 1.50
6 Albert Pujols .60 1.50
7 Paul Goldschmidt .50 1.25
8 Giancarlo Stanton .50 1.25
9 Joey Votto .50 1.25
10 Mookie Betts 1.00 2.50

2019 Diamond Kings '03 DK Retro
RANDOM INSERTS IN PACKS
*AP: .75X TO 2X BASIC
*PLUM FRAME: .75X TO 2X BASIC
*AP BLUE: 1X TO 2.5X BASIC
*BLUE FRAME: 1X TO 2.5X BASIC
*RED FRAME: 1X TO 2.5X BASIC
1 Alex Rodriguez .60 1.50
2 Hideki Matsui .50 1.25
3 Dontrelle Willis .30 .75
4 Jose Reyes .40 1.00
5 Miguel Cabrera .50 1.25
6 Max Scherzer .50 1.25
7 Freddie Freeman .60 1.50
8 Vladimir Guerrero Jr. 2.00 5.00
9 Jose Ramirez .40 1.00
10 Mike Trout 2.50 6.00

2019 Diamond Kings '04 DK Retro
RANDOM INSERTS IN PACKS
*AP: .75X TO 2X BASIC
*PLUM FRAME: .75X TO 2X BASIC
*AP BLUE: 1X TO 2.5X BASIC
*BLUE FRAME: 1X TO 2.5X BASIC
*RED FRAME: 1X TO 2.5X BASIC
1 David Wright .40 1.00
2 Vladimir Guerrero .40 1.00
3 Roger Clemens .60 1.50
4 Zack Greinke .50 1.25
5 Adrian Beltre .50 1.25
6 Justin Verlander .50 1.25
7 Anthony Rizzo .60 1.50
8 Clayton Kershaw .75 2.00
9 Bryce Harper .75 2.00
10 Francisco Lindor .50 1.25

2019 Diamond Kings '19 Diamond Kings
RANDOM INSERTS IN PACKS
*HOLO BLUE/25: 1.5X TO 4X BASIC
1 Babe Ruth 1.25 3.00
2 Joe Jackson .60 1.50
3 Jake Daubert .30 .75
4 Eddie Collins .40 1.00
5 Frank Baker .50 1.25
6 Honus Wagner .50 1.25
7 Ty Cobb .75 2.00
8 Tris Speaker .40 1.00
9 Walter Johnson .50 1.25
10 Eddie Cicotte .30 .75
11 Bob Shawkey .30 .75
12 Sam Rice .40 1.00
13 George Sisler .40 1.00
14 Lefty Williams .30 .75
15 Harry Heilmann .40 1.00

2019 Diamond Kings Diamond Cuts
RANDOM INSERTS IN PACKS
EXCHANGE DEADLINE 10/10/2020
8 Harmon Killebrew 25.00 60.00
10 Gary Carter 25.00 60.00
12 Elmer Flick

2019 Diamond Kings Diamond Cuts Materials
RANDOM INSERTS IN PACKS
EXCHANGE DEADLINE 10/10/2020
*HOLO BLUE/25: .6X TO 1.5X BASIC
1 Gary Carter 20.00 50.00
4 Harmon Killebrew 20.00 50.00

2019 Diamond Kings Diamond Deco
RANDOM INSERTS IN PACKS
2 Tony Gwynn 10.00 25.00
3 Mookie Betts 6.00 15.00
4 Ken Griffey Jr. 10.00 25.00
5 Ronald Acuna Jr. 8.00 20.00
6 Shohei Ohtani 5.00 12.00
7 Juan Soto 4.00 10.00
8 Rhys Hoskins 6.00 15.00
10 Max Muncy 2.50 6.00
11 Justin Verlander 3.00 8.00
12 Jesus Aguilar 2.50 6.00
13 Buster Posey 4.00 10.00
14 Michael Brantley 2.50 6.00
15 Noah Syndergaard 2.50 6.00
16 Jose Ramirez 2.50 6.00
17 Rickey Henderson 15.00 40.00
18 Reggie Jackson 6.00 15.00

2019 Diamond Kings Diamond Deco Holo Blue
*HOLO BLUE/25: .75X TO 2X BASIC
RANDOM INSERTS IN PACKS
PRINT RUNS B/WN 10-25 COPIES PER
NO PRICING ON QTY 15 OR LESS
9 Willie McCovey/25 12.00 30.00

2019 Diamond Kings DK 205
RANDOM INSERTS IN PACKS
*HOLO GOLD: .6X TO 1.5X BASIC
1 Cal Ripken 1.50 4.00
2 Aaron Judge 1.25 3.00
3 Ken Griffey Jr. 1.00 2.50
4 Mike Trout 2.50 6.00
5 Kirby Puckett .50 1.25
6 Shohei Ohtani .75 2.00
7 Justin Verlander .50 1.25
8 Javier Baez .60 1.50
9 Nolan Arenado .75 2.00
10 Ronald Acuna Jr. 2.50 6.00
11 Nolan Ryan 1.50 4.00
12 Christian Yelich .60 1.50
13 Max Scherzer .50 1.25
14 Gleyber Torres 1.00 2.50
15 Mike Piazza .50 1.25
16 Frank Thomas .50 1.25
17 Jacob deGrom 1.00 2.50
18 Blake Snell .40 1.00
19 Juan Soto 1.50 4.00
20 Mookie Betts 1.00 2.50
21 Jose Altuve .40 1.00
22 Clayton Kershaw .75 2.00
23 Anthony Rizzo .60 1.50
24 Bryce Harper .75 2.00
25 Mickey Mantle 1.50 4.00

2019 Diamond Kings DK 205 Holo Blue
*HOLO BLUE: 1.5X TO 4X BASIC
RANDOM INSERTS IN PACKS
STATED PRINT RUN 25 SER.#'d SETS
1 Cal Ripken 12.00 30.00
3 Ken Griffey Jr. 20.00 50.00
4 Mike Trout 10.00 25.00
11 Nolan Ryan 10.00 25.00
16 Frank Thomas 10.00 25.00

2019 Diamond Kings DK 205 Signatures
RANDOM INSERTS IN PACKS
EXCHANGE DEADLINE 10/10/2020
*HOLO BLUE/25: .6X TO 1.5X BASIC
*HOLO GOLD/49: .5X TO 1.2X BASIC
*HOLO GOLD/25: .6X TO 1.5X BASIC
*HOLO SLVR/49-99: .5X TO 1.2X BASIC
*HOLO SLVR/25: .6X TO 1.5X BASIC
2 Aaron Judge 50.00 120.00
3 Cal Ripken 25.00 60.00
4 Shohei Ohtani 50.00 120.00
5 Gleyber Torres 15.00 40.00
6 Juan Soto 10.00 25.00
7 Jacob deGrom 25.00 60.00
8 Ronald Acuna Jr. 40.00 100.00
9 Nolan Arenado 25.00 60.00
10 Ken Griffey Jr. 75.00 200.00
11 Clayton Kershaw 15.00 40.00
12 Frank Thomas 15.00 40.00
13 Nolan Ryan 40.00 100.00
14 Kyle Tucker 6.00 15.00
15 Michael Kopech 8.00 20.00
16 Bobby Richardson 12.00 30.00
17 Paul Goldschmidt 25.00 60.00
18 Francisco Lindor 10.00 25.00
19 Alex Bregman 15.00 40.00
20 Freddie Freeman 10.00 25.00

2019 Diamond Kings DK Flashbacks
RANDOM INSERTS IN PACKS
1 Albert Pujols .60 1.50
2 Miguel Cabrera .50 1.25
3 Tony Gwynn .50 1.25
4 Cal Ripken 1.50 4.00
5 Greg Maddux .60 1.50
6 Mark McGwire .75 2.00
7 Roger Clemens .60 1.50
8 Vladimir Guerrero .40 1.00
9 Kirby Puckett .50 1.25
10 Adrian Beltre .50 1.25
11 Frank Thomas .50 1.25
12 Nolan Ryan 1.50 4.00
13 Larry Walker .40 1.00
14 Alex Rodriguez .60 1.50
15 Jason Giambi .30 .75
16 Mike Piazza .50 1.25
17 Chipper Jones .50 1.25
18 Randy Johnson .50 1.25
19 Pedro Martinez .40 1.00
20 Wade Boggs .40 1.00

2019 Diamond Kings DK Flashbacks Holo Blue
*HOLO BLUE: 1.5X TO 4X BASIC
RANDOM INSERTS IN PACKS
STATED PRINT RUN 25 SER.#'d SETS
3 Tony Gwynn 8.00 20.00
4 Cal Ripken 12.00 30.00
11 Frank Thomas 10.00 25.00
12 Nolan Ryan 10.00 25.00
17 Chipper Jones 8.00 20.00

2019 Diamond Kings DK Jumbo Material Signatures
RANDOM INSERTS IN PACKS
EXCHANGE DEADLINE 10/10/2020
1 Robin Yount 20.00 50.00
2 Vladimir Guerrero Jr. 60.00 150.00
3 Addison Russell 4.00 10.00
4 Rickey Henderson 25.00 60.00
5 David Ortiz 20.00 50.00
6 Carlos Correa 12.00 30.00
7 Aaron Judge 50.00 120.00
8 Max Muncy 8.00 20.00
9 Rhys Hoskins 15.00 40.00
10 Nick Williams 3.00 8.00
12 Victor Robles 10.00 25.00
13 Gleyber Torres 15.00 40.00
14 Fernando Tatis Jr. 40.00 100.00
15 Trevor Story 8.00 20.00
16 Eloy Jimenez 20.00 50.00
17 Andrew Benintendi 10.00 25.00
18 Justin Turner 8.00 20.00
19 Edgar Martinez 12.00 30.00
20 Albert Pujols 40.00 100.00

2019 Diamond Kings DK Jumbo Material Signatures Holo Blue
*HOLO BLUE: .6X TO 1.5X BASIC
RANDOM INSERTS IN PACKS
PRINT RUNS B/WN 3-25 COPIES PER
NO PRICING ON QTY 15 OR LESS
EXCHANGE DEADLINE 10/10/2020
11 Yoan Moncada/25 25.00 60.00

2019 Diamond Kings DK Material Signatures
RANDOM INSERTS IN PACKS
EXCHANGE DEADLINE 10/10/2020
1 Brad Keller 3.00 8.00
2 Brandon Lowe 8.00 20.00
3 Bryse Wilson 4.00 10.00
4 Caleb Ferguson 4.00 10.00
5 Cedric Mullins 10.00 25.00
6 Chance Adams 3.00 8.00
7 Chris Shaw 3.00 8.00
8 Christin Stewart 4.00 10.00
9 Cionel Perez 3.00 8.00
10 Corbin Burnes 10.00 25.00
11 Dakota Hudson 4.00 10.00
12 Daniel Ponce de Leon 5.00 12.00
13 Danny Jansen 3.00 8.00
14 David Fletcher 10.00 25.00
15 Dennis Santana 3.00 8.00
16 Eloy Jimenez 12.00 30.00
18 Fernando Tatis Jr. 60.00 150.00
19 Framber Valdez 3.00 8.00
20 Garrett Hampson 5.00 12.00
21 Jacob Nix 4.00 10.00
22 Jake Bauers 5.00 12.00
23 Jake Cave 4.00 10.00
24 Jeff McNeil 15.00 40.00
25 Jonathan Davis 4.00 10.00
26 Jonathan Loaisiga 6.00 15.00
27 Josh James 5.00 12.00
28 Justus Sheffield 6.00 15.00
29 Kevin Kramer 4.00 10.00
30 Kevin Newman 5.00 12.00
31 Kolby Allard 5.00 12.00
32 Kyle Tucker 8.00 20.00
33 Kyle Wright 5.00 12.00
34 Luis Ortiz 3.00 8.00
35 Luis Urias 5.00 12.00
36 Michael Kopech 8.00 20.00
37 Myles Straw 5.00 12.00
39 Patrick Wisdom 3.00 8.00
40 Ramon Laureano 12.00 30.00
41 Reese McGuire 5.00 12.00
42 Rowdy Tellez 5.00 12.00
43 Ryan Borucki 3.00 8.00
44 Ryan O'Hearn 3.00 8.00
45 Sean Reid-Foley 3.00 8.00
46 Stephen Gonsalves 3.00 8.00
47 Steven Duggar 4.00 10.00
48 Taylor Ward 3.00 8.00
49 Touki Toussaint 4.00 10.00
50 Vladimir Guerrero Jr. 30.00 80.00
51 Eddie Murray 12.00 30.00
52 Byron Buxton 5.00 12.00
53 Masahiro Tanaka 40.00 100.00
54 Clayton Kershaw 40.00 100.00
55 Gary Sanchez 15.00 40.00
56 Clint Frazier 10.00 25.00
57 Willie McCovey 20.00 50.00
58 Joey Votto 20.00 50.00
59 Xander Bogaerts 10.00 25.00
60 Larry Walker 12.00 30.00

2019 Diamond Kings DK Material Signatures Holo Blue
*HOLO BLUE: .6X TO 1.5X BASIC
RANDOM INSERTS IN PACKS
PRINT RUNS B/WN 5-25 COPIES PER
NO PRICING ON QTY 15 OR LESS
EXCHANGE DEADLINE 10/10/2020
17 Enyel De Los Santos/25 5.00 12.00

2019 Diamond Kings DK Materials
RANDOM INSERTS IN PACKS
1 Brad Keller 2.00 5.00
2 Brandon Lowe 3.00 8.00
3 Bryse Wilson 2.50 6.00
4 Caleb Ferguson 2.50 6.00
5 Cedric Mullins 4.00 10.00
6 Chance Adams 2.00 5.00
7 Chris Shaw 2.00 5.00
8 Christin Stewart 2.50 6.00
9 Cionel Perez 2.00 5.00
10 Corbin Burnes 5.00 12.00
11 Dakota Hudson 2.50 6.00
12 Daniel Ponce de Leon 3.00 8.00
13 Danny Jansen 2.00 5.00
14 David Fletcher 6.00 15.00
15 Dennis Santana 2.00 5.00
16 Eloy Jimenez 8.00 20.00
17 Enyel De Los Santos 2.00 5.00
18 Fernando Tatis Jr. 4.00 10.00
19 Framber Valdez 2.00 5.00
20 Garrett Hampson 3.00 8.00
21 Jacob Nix 2.50 6.00
22 Jake Bauers 3.00 8.00
23 Jake Cave 2.50 6.00
24 Jeff McNeil 5.00 12.00
25 Jonathan Davis 2.50 6.00
26 Jonathan Loaisiga 2.50 6.00
27 Josh James 3.00 8.00
28 Justus Sheffield 3.00 8.00
29 Kevin Kramer 2.50 6.00
30 Kevin Newman 3.00 8.00
31 Kolby Allard 3.00 8.00
32 Kyle Tucker 4.00 10.00
33 Kyle Wright 3.00 8.00
34 Luis Ortiz 2.00 5.00
35 Luis Urias 3.00 8.00
36 Michael Kopech 6.00 15.00
37 Myles Straw 3.00 8.00
38 Nick Senzel 5.00 12.00
39 Patrick Wisdom 2.00 5.00
40 Ramon Laureano 4.00 10.00
41 Reese McGuire 3.00 8.00
42 Rowdy Tellez 3.00 8.00
43 Ryan Borucki 2.00 5.00
44 Ryan O'Hearn 2.00 5.00
45 Sean Reid-Foley 2.00 5.00
46 Stephen Gonsalves 2.00 5.00
47 Steven Duggar 2.50 6.00
48 Taylor Ward 2.00 5.00
49 Touki Toussaint 2.50 6.00
50 Vladimir Guerrero Jr. 6.00 15.00
51 Charlie Keller 3.00 8.00
52 Eddie Stanky 3.00 8.00
75 Patrick Corbin 2.50 6.00
76 Robinson Cano 2.50 6.00
77 Cal Ripken 6.00 15.00
78 Jonathan Schoop 2.00 5.00
80 Craig Kimbrel 2.50 6.00
81 Dallas Keuchel 2.50 6.00
82 Daniel Murphy 2.50 6.00
83 Ronald Acuna Jr. 5.00 12.00
84 Juan Soto 4.00 10.00
85 George Brett 8.00 20.00
87 Harvey Kuenn 2.00 5.00
89 Ichiro 4.00 10.00
91 Adrian Beltre 3.00 8.00
92 Frank Thomas 3.00 8.00
93 Paul Molitor 5.00 12.00
94 Willie McCovey 5.00 12.00
95 Al Kaline 4.00 10.00
98 Alex Rodriguez 4.00 10.00
99 Joe Morgan 2.50 6.00

2019 Diamond Kings DK Materials Holo Blue
*HOLO BLUE/25: .75X TO 2X BASIC
RANDOM INSERTS IN PACKS
PRINT RUNS B/WN 3-25 COPIES PER
NO PRICING ON QTY 15 OR LESS
2 Brandon Lowe/25 6.00 15.00
97 Rickey Henderson/25 12.00 30.00

2019 Diamond Kings DK Materials Holo Gold
*HOLO GOLD/49: .6X TO 1.5X BASIC
*HOLO GOLD/20-25: .75X TO 2X BASIC
RANDOM INSERTS IN PACKS
PRINT RUNS B/WN 4-49 COPIES PER
NO PRICING ON QTY 15 OR LESS
2 Brandon Lowe/49 5.00 12.00
61 Stan Musial/25 10.00 25.00
62 Ted Williams/25 40.00 100.00
64 Yogi Berra/20 6.00 15.00
65 Ernie Banks/25 6.00 15.00
86 Catfish Hunter/25 5.00 12.00
90 Nolan Ryan/25 25.00 60.00
96 Lee Smith/49 4.00 10.00
97 Rickey Henderson/49 10.00 25.00

2019 Diamond Kings DK Materials Holo Silver
*HOLO SLVR/60-99: .5X TO 1.2X BASIC
*HOLO SLVR/49: .6X TO 1.5X BASIC
*HOLO SLVR/20-25: .75X TO 2X BASIC
RANDOM INSERTS IN PACKS
PRINT RUNS B/WN 10-99 COPIES PER
NO PRICING ON QTY 15 OR LESS
2 Brandon Lowe/99 4.00 10.00
57 Mickey Mantle/25 40.00 100.00
66 Jackie Robinson/25 30.00 80.00
86 Catfish Hunter/49 4.00 10.00
90 Nolan Ryan/49 20.00 50.00
96 Lee Smith/99 3.00 8.00
97 Rickey Henderson/99 8.00 20.00

2019 Diamond Kings DK Signatures
RANDOM INSERTS IN PACKS
EXCHANGE DEADLINE 10/10/2020
*HOLO GOLD/35-49: .5X TO 1.2X BASIC
*HOLO GOLD/25: .6X TO 1.5X BASIC
*HOLO SLVR/49-99: .5X TO 1.2X BASIC
*HOLO SLVR/20-25: .6X TO 1.5X BASIC
1 Brad Keller 2.50 6.00
2 Brandon Lowe 6.00 15.00
3 Bryse Wilson 3.00 8.00
4 Caleb Ferguson 3.00 8.00
5 Cedric Mullins 8.00 20.00
6 Chance Adams 2.50 6.00
7 Chris Shaw 2.50 6.00
8 Christin Stewart 3.00 8.00
9 Cionel Perez 2.50 6.00
10 Corbin Burnes 8.00 20.00
11 Dakota Hudson 3.00 8.00
12 Daniel Ponce de Leon 4.00 10.00
13 Danny Jansen 2.50 6.00
14 David Fletcher 8.00 20.00
15 Dennis Santana 2.50 6.00
16 Eloy Jimenez 15.00 40.00
18 Fernando Tatis Jr. 50.00 120.00
19 Framber Valdez 2.50 6.00
20 Garrett Hampson 4.00 10.00
21 Jacob Nix 3.00 8.00
22 Jake Bauers 4.00 10.00
23 Jake Cave 3.00 8.00
24 Jeff McNeil 10.00 25.00
25 Jonathan Davis 3.00 8.00
26 Jonathan Loaisiga 3.00 8.00
27 Josh James 4.00 10.00
28 Justus Sheffield 4.00 10.00
29 Kevin Kramer 3.00 8.00
30 Kevin Newman 4.00 10.00
31 Kolby Allard 4.00 10.00
32 Kyle Tucker 5.00 12.00
33 Kyle Wright 4.00 10.00
34 Luis Ortiz 2.50 6.00
35 Luis Urias 4.00 10.00
36 Michael Kopech 8.00 20.00
37 Myles Straw 4.00 10.00
39 Patrick Wisdom 2.50 6.00
40 Ramon Laureano 6.00 15.00
41 Reese McGuire 4.00 10.00
42 Rowdy Tellez 4.00 10.00
43 Ryan Borucki 2.50 6.00
44 Ryan O'Hearn 2.50 6.00
45 Sean Reid-Foley 2.50 6.00
46 Stephen Gonsalves 2.50 6.00
47 Steven Duggar 3.00 8.00
48 Taylor Ward 2.50 6.00
49 Touki Toussaint 3.00 8.00
50 Vladimir Guerrero Jr. 30.00 80.00
51 Vin Scully 100.00 250.00
52 Ronald Acuna Jr. 40.00 100.00
53 Gleyber Torres 15.00 40.00
54 Rafael Devers 10.00 25.00
55 Rhys Hoskins 8.00 20.00
56 Ozzie Albies 6.00 15.00
57 Juan Soto 15.00 40.00
58 Miguel Andujar 6.00 15.00
59 Walker Buehler 12.00 30.00
60 Shohei Ohtani 50.00 120.00
61 Cody Bellinger 40.00 100.00
62 Victor Robles 5.00 12.00
63 Willy Adames 2.50 6.00
64 David Bote 6.00 15.00
65 Harrison Bader 3.00 8.00
66 Ryan McMahon 4.00 10.00
67 Yusei Kikuchi 12.00 30.00
68 Anthony Rizzo 15.00 40.00
69 Trea Turner 6.00 15.00
70 Yoan Moncada 4.00 10.00

2019 Diamond Kings DK Signatures Holo Blue
*HOLO BLUE/25: .6X TO 1.5X BASIC
RANDOM INSERTS IN PACKS
PRINT RUNS BW/N 10-25 COPIES PER
NO PRICING ON QTY 10
EXCHANGE DEADLINE 10/10/2020
17 Enyel De Los Santos/25 4.00 10.00

2019 Diamond Kings Downtown
RANDOM INSERTS IN PACKS
1 Shohei Ohtani 30.00 80.00
2 Javier Baez 20.00 50.00
3 Christian Yelich 20.00 50.00
4 Mookie Betts 30.00 80.00
5 Mike Trout 80.00 200.00
6 Matt Carpenter 15.00 40.00
7 Alex Bregman 30.00 80.00
8 Aaron Judge 40.00 100.00
9 Nolan Arenado 25.00 60.00
10 Francisco Lindor 15.00 40.00

2019 Diamond Kings Gallery of Stars
RANDOM INSERTS IN PACKS
1 Jose Altuve .50 1.25
2 Ronald Acuna Jr. 3.00 8.00
3 Walker Buehler .75 2.00
4 Andrew Benintendi .60 1.50
5 Alex Bregman .60 1.50
6 Juan Soto 2.00 5.00
7 Aaron Judge 1.50 4.00
8 Ichiro .75 2.00
9 Aaron Nola .50 1.25
10 Nolan Arenado 1.00 2.50
11 Ken Griffey Jr. 1.25 3.00
12 Shohei Ohtani 1.00 2.50
13 Mike Trout 3.00 8.00
14 Clayton Kershaw 1.00 2.50
15 Christian Yelich .75 2.00

2019 Diamond Kings Gallery of Stars Holo Blue
*HOLO BLUE: 1.5X TO 4X BASIC
RANDOM INSERTS IN PACKS
STATED PRINT RUN 25 SER.#'d SETS
11 Ken Griffey Jr. 20.00 50.00
13 Mike Trout 10.00 25.00

2019 Diamond Kings Heirs to the Throne
RANDOM INSERTS IN PACKS
1 Chris Sale .50 1.25
Pedro Martinez
2 Josh Donaldson 2.00 5.00
Vladimir Guerrero Jr.
3 Aaron Judge 1.25 3.00
Babe Ruth
4 Ichiro .75 2.00
Shohei Ohtani
5 Eloy Jimenez 1.25 3.00
Frank Thomas
6 Mickey Mantle 2.50 6.00
Mike Trout
7 Forrest Whitley 1.50 4.00
Nolan Ryan
8 Bryce Harper 1.50 4.00
Juan Soto
9 Luis Severino .60 1.50
Roger Clemens
10 Blake Snell .40 1.00
David Price
11 Javier Baez 1.00 2.50
Ryne Sandberg
12 Adrian Beltre .50 1.25
Matt Chapman
13 Craig Biggio .40 1.00
Jose Altuve
14 Brooks Robinson .75 2.00
Nolan Arenado
15 Vladimir Guerrero 2.00 5.00
Vladimir Guerrero Jr.

2019 Diamond Kings Heirs to the Throne Holo Blue
*HOLO BLUE: 1.5X TO 4X BASIC
RANDOM INSERTS IN PACKS
STATED PRINT RUN 25 SER.#'d SETS
5 Jimenez/Thomas 10.00 25.00

2019 Diamond Kings HOF Heroes
RANDOM INSERTS IN PACKS
*HOLO GOLD: .6X TO 1.5X BASIC
*HOLO BLUE/25: 1.5X TO 4X BASIC
1 Honus Wagner .50 1.25
2 Joe DiMaggio 1.00 2.50
3 Roberto Clemente 1.25 3.00
4 Stan Musial .75 2.00
5 Ted Williams 1.00 2.50
6 Yogi Berra .50 1.25
7 Mariano Rivera .60 1.50
8 Jackie Robinson .50 1.25
9 Mel Ott .50 1.25
10 Ty Cobb .75 2.00

2019 Diamond Kings Jersey Kings
RANDOM INSERTS IN PACKS
*HOLO BLUE/20-25: .75X TO 2X BASIC
1 Shohei Ohtani 5.00 12.00
2 Ichiro 4.00 10.00
4 Jacob deGrom 6.00 15.00
5 Christian Yelich 4.00 10.00
6 Juan Gonzalez 2.00 5.00
7 Tony Gwynn 3.00 8.00
8 Aaron Judge 6.00 15.00
9 Gleyber Torres 4.00 10.00
10 Max Muncy 2.50 6.00
11 Charlie Blackmon 3.00 8.00
12 Alex Rodriguez 4.00 10.00
13 Rhys Hoskins 4.00 10.00
14 Starling Marte 2.50 6.00
15 Frank Thomas 3.00 8.00
16 Whit Merrifield 3.00 8.00
17 Patrick Corbin 2.50 6.00
18 Michael Brantley 2.50 6.00
19 Pee Wee Reese 6.00 15.00

2019 Diamond Kings Joe Jackson Collection
RANDOM INSERTS IN PACKS
*HOLO GOLD: .6X TO 1.5X BASIC
*HOLO BLUE/25: 1.5X TO 4X BASIC
1 Joe Jackson .60 1.50
2 Joe Jackson .60 1.50
3 Joe Jackson .60 1.50
4 Joe Jackson .60 1.50
5 Joe Jackson .60 1.50

2019 Diamond Kings Masters of the Game
RANDOM INSERTS IN PACKS
*HOLO GOLD: .6X TO 1.5X BASIC
1 Mookie Betts 1.00 2.50
2 Max Scherzer .50 1.25
3 Mike Trout 2.50 6.00
4 Clayton Kershaw .75 2.00
5 Matt Chapman .50 1.25
6 Justin Verlander .50 1.25
7 Francisco Lindor .50 1.25
8 Christian Yelich .60 1.50
9 Jose Ramirez .40 1.00
10 Javier Baez .60 1.50
11 Alex Bregman .50 1.25
12 Nolan Arenado .75 2.00
13 Aaron Nola .40 1.00
14 Freddie Freeman .60 1.50
15 Jacob deGrom 1.00 2.50

2019 Diamond Kings Masters of the Game Holo Blue
*HOLO BLUE: 1.5X TO 4X BASIC
RANDOM INSERTS IN PACKS
STATED PRINT RUN 25 SER.#'d SETS
3 Mike Trout 10.00 25.00

2019 Diamond Kings Portraits
RANDOM INSERTS IN PACKS
1 Rickey Henderson .50 1.25
2 Gleyber Torres 1.00 2.50
3 Albert Pujols .60 1.50
4 Mariano Rivera .60 1.50
5 Yadier Molina .60 1.50
6 Jose Ramirez .40 1.00
7 George Brett 1.00 2.50
8 Kris Bryant .60 1.50
9 Bryce Harper .75 2.00
10 Francisco Lindor .50 1.25
11 Trevor Story .50 1.25
12 Javier Baez .60 1.50
13 Robinson Cano .40 1.00
14 Mookie Betts 1.00 2.50
15 Noah Syndergaard .40 1.00

2019 Diamond Kings Portraits Holo Blue
*HOLO BLUE: 1.5X TO 4X BASIC
RANDOM INSERTS IN PACKS
STATED PRINT RUN 25 SER.#'d SETS
1 Rickey Henderson 10.00 25.00
7 George Brett 8.00 20.00

2019 Diamond Kings Recollection Buyback Autographs
RANDOM INSERTS IN PACKS
PRINT RUNS B/WN 1-23 COPIES PER
NO PRICING ON QTY 15 OR LESS
EXCHANGE DEADLINE 10/10/2020
4 Joey Votto/23 12.00 30.00

2019 Diamond Kings Retro '83 DK Material Signatures
RANDOM INSERTS IN PACKS
EXCHANGE DEADLINE 10/10/2020
1 Randy Johnson
2 Dave Concepcion 10.00 25.00
3 Vladimir Guerrero 15.00 40.00
4 John Smoltz 15.00 40.00
6 Frank Robinson 15.00 40.00
7 Mike Mussina 20.00 50.00
9 Kirk Gibson
10 Steve Garvey
11 Larry Walker 12.00 30.00
12 Dale Murphy 15.00 40.00
13 Wade Boggs 15.00 40.00
14 David Ortiz 20.00 50.00
15 Ivan Rodriguez 15.00 40.00
16 Dave Winfield 12.00 30.00
17 Luis Aparicio 10.00 25.00
19 Edgar Martinez 12.00 30.00
20 George Brett 50.00 120.00

2019 Diamond Kings Retro '83 DK Material Signatures Holo Blue
*HOLO BLUE: .6X TO 1.5X BASIC
RANDOM INSERTS IN PACKS
PRINT RUNS B/WN 10-25 COPIES PER
NO PRICING ON QTY 15 OR LESS
EXCHANGE DEADLINE 10/10/2020
8 Lee Smith/25 10.00 25.00

2019 Diamond Kings Squires
RANDOM INSERTS IN PACKS
*HOLO GOLD: .6X TO 1.5X BASIC
*HOLO BLUE/25: 1.5X TO 4X BASIC
1 Shohei Ohtani .75 2.00
2 Miguel Andujar .50 1.25
3 Gleyber Torres 1.00 2.50
4 Ronald Acuna Jr. 2.50 6.00
5 Juan Soto 1.50 4.00
6 Walker Buehler .60 1.50
7 Jack Flaherty .50 1.25
8 Vladimir Guerrero Jr. 2.00 5.00
9 Eloy Jimenez 1.25 3.00
10 Victor Robles .60 1.50
11 Kyle Tucker .75 2.00
12 Forrest Whitley .50 1.25
13 Jo Adell 1.25 3.00
14 Royce Lewis .60 1.50
15 Fernando Tatis Jr. 5.00 12.00
16 Nick Senzel 1.00 2.50
17 Brendan Rodgers .50 1.25
18 Ozzie Albies .50 1.25
19 Alex Verdugo .40 1.00
20 Sean Newcomb .30 .75

2019 Diamond Kings Team Heroes
RANDOM INSERTS IN PACKS
*HOLO GOLD: .6X TO 1.5X BASIC
*HOLO BLUE/25: 1.5X TO 4X BASIC
1 Mookie Betts 1.00 2.50
2 Alex Bregman .50 1.25
3 Aaron Judge 1.25 3.00
4 Matt Chapman .50 1.25
5 Christian Yelich .60 1.50
6 Javier Baez .60 1.50
7 Clayton Kershaw .75 2.00
8 Jose Ramirez .40 1.00
9 Nolan Arenado .75 2.00
10 Ronald Acuna Jr. 2.50 6.00
11 Blake Snell .40 1.00
12 Felix Hernandez .40 1.00
13 Yadier Molina .60 1.50
14 Starling Marte .40 1.00
15 Juan Soto 1.50 4.00
16 David Peralta .30 .75
17 Shohei Ohtani .75 2.00
18 Aaron Nola .40 1.00
19 Joe Mauer .40 1.00
20 Jacob deGrom 1.00 2.50
21 Justin Smoak .30 .75
22 Madison Bumgarner .40 1.00
23 Adrian Beltre .50 1.25
24 Joey Votto .50 1.25
25 Eric Hosmer .40 1.00
26 Miguel Cabrera .50 1.25
27 J.T. Realmuto .50 1.25
28 Jose Abreu .50 1.25
29 Whit Merrifield .50 1.25
30 Adam Jones .40 1.00

2019 Diamond Kings The 300
RANDOM INSERTS IN PACKS
1 Grover Alexander .40 1.00
2 Christy Mathewson .50 1.25
3 Warren Spahn .40 1.00
4 Greg Maddux .60 1.50
5 Roger Clemens .60 1.50
6 Early Wynn .40 1.00
7 Randy Johnson .50 1.25
8 Nolan Ryan 1.50 4.00
9 Tom Seaver .40 1.00
10 Tom Glavine .40 1.00

2019 Diamond Kings The 300 Holo Blue
*HOLO BLUE: 1.5X TO 4X BASIC
RANDOM INSERTS IN PACKS
STATED PRINT RUN 25 SER.#'d SETS
8 Nolan Ryan 10.00 25.00

2019 Diamond Kings Babe Ruth Collection
RANDOM INSERTS IN PACKS
*HOLO GOLD: .6X TO 1.5X BASIC
*HOLO BLUE/25: 1.5X TO 4X BASIC
BR1 Babe Ruth 1.25 3.00
BR2 Babe Ruth 1.25 3.00
BR3 Babe Ruth 1.25 3.00
BR4 Babe Ruth 1.25 3.00
BR5 Babe Ruth 1.25 3.00

2019 Diamond Kings Babe Ruth DK Materials Holo Blue
RANDOM INSERTS IN PACKS
STATED PRINT RUN 25 SER.#'d SETS
1 Babe Ruth

2019 Diamond Kings Bat Kings
RANDOM INSERTS IN PACKS
1 Mike Trout 12.00 30.00
3 Christian Yelich 4.00 10.00
4 Reggie Jackson 2.50 6.00
5 Juan Soto 4.00 10.00
6 Kris Bryant 4.00 10.00
7 Nick Senzel 5.00 12.00
8 Kirk Gibson 2.00 5.00
9 Matt Chapman 3.00 8.00
10 Alex Bregman 3.00 8.00
11 Dave Winfield 2.50 6.00
12 Eddie Murray 5.00 12.00
13 Ken Griffey Sr. 2.00 5.00

14 Luis Aparicio 2.50 6.00
15 Willie Stargell 2.50 6.00
17 Jimmie Foxx
20 Joe Jackson

2019 Diamond Kings Bat Kings Holo Blue

*HOLO BLUE/25: .75X TO 2X BASIC
RANDOM INSERTS IN PACKS
PRINT RUNS B/WN 15-25 COPIES PER
NO PRICING ON QTY 15 OR LESS
16 Roberto Clemente/25 60.00 150.00
17 Jimmie Foxx/25 15.00 40.00
18 Roger Maris/25
19 Tris Speaker/25 12.00 30.00
20 Joe Jackson/25 40.00 100.00

2020 Diamond Kings

RANDOM INSERTS IN PACKS
1 Joe Sewell .25 .60
2 Honus Wagner .30 .75
3 Mel Ott .30 .75
4 Walter Alston .25 .60
5 Don Larsen .20 .50
6 Roger Maris .30 .75
7 Mule Suttles .30 .75
8 Joe McCarthy .20 .50
9 Mickey Cochrane .25 .60
10 Joe Jackson .40 1.00
11 Stan Musial .50 1.25
12 Yogi Berra .30 .75
13 Ty Cobb .50 1.25
14 Satchel Paige .30 .75
15 Babe Ruth .75 2.00
16 Tris Speaker .25 .60
17 Christy Mathewson .30 .75
18 Lou Gehrig .60 1.50
19 Carl Hubbell .25 .60
20 Joe DiMaggio .60 1.50
21 Hank Greenberg .30 .75
22 Roberto Clemente .75 2.00
23 Harvey Kuenn .20 .50
24 Carl Erskine .20 .50
25 Charlie Keller .20 .50
26 Jimmie Foxx .30 .75
27 Jackie Robinson .30 .75
28 Joe Cronin .20 .50
29 Joe Wood .20 .50
30 Eddie Stanky .20 .50
31 Grover Alexander .25 .60
32 Rogers Hornsby .25 .60
33 Mickey Mantle 1.00 2.50
34 Ted Williams .60 1.50
35 Bill Terry .20 .50
36 Dom DiMaggio .20 .50
37 Elston Howard .20 .50
38 Frank Baker .30 .75
39 Goose Goslin .25 .60
40 Hack Wilson .25 .60
41 Johnny Pesky .20 .50
42 Bert Blyleven .25 .60
43 Billy Williams .25 .60
44 Cal Ripken 1.00 2.50
45 Eddie Mathews .30 .75
46 Frank Thomas .30 .75
47 Harmon Killebrew .30 .75
48 Adbert Alzolay RC .50 1.25
49 Zack Collins RC .50 1.25
50 Josh Rojas RC .40 1.00
51 Zac Gallen RC 1.00 2.50
52 Yu Chang RC .60 1.50
53 Cody Bellinger .60 1.50
54 Aristides Aquino RC 1.00 2.50
55 Logan Allen RC .40 1.00
56 Larry Walker .25 .60
57 Clayton Kershaw .50 1.25
58 Yordan Alvarez RC 4.00 10.00
59 Joey Votto .30 .75
60 Patrick Sandoval RC .60 1.50
61 Sam Hilliard RC .60 1.50
62 Tony Gonsolin RC 1.50 4.00
63 Yonathan Daza RC .50 1.25
64 Dylan Cease RC .60 1.50
65 Willi Castro RC .60 1.50
66 Bryce Harper .50 1.25
67 Jordan Yamamoto RC .40 1.00
68 Domingo Leyba RC .50 1.25
69 Ketel Marte .25 .60
70 Danny Mendick RC .50 1.25
71 Keston Hiura .40 1.00
72 Kris Bryant .40 1.00
73 Dustin May RC 1.25 3.00
74 Pete Alonso .75 2.00
75 Jake Rogers RC .40 1.00
76 Gavin Lux RC 2.00 5.00
77 Paul Goldschmidt .30 .75
78 Curt Schilling .25 .60
79 Bryan Abreu RC .40 1.00
80 Javier Baez .40 1.00
81 Isan Diaz RC .60 1.50
82 Pete Rose .60 1.50
83 Christian Yelich .40 1.00
84 Matt Thaiss RC .50 1.25
85 Travis Demeritte RC .60 1.50
86 Josh Bell .25 .60
87 Madison Bumgarner .25 .60
88 Aaron Civale RC .75 2.00
89 Anthony Rizzo .40 1.00
90 Nico Hoerner RC 1.50 4.00
91 Edwin Rios RC 1.00 2.50
92 Randy Johnson .30 .75
93 Tyrone Taylor RC .40 1.00
94 Bobby Bradley RC .40 1.00
95 Luis Robert RC 3.00 8.00
96 Buster Posey .40 1.00
97 Aaron Nola .25 .60
98 Brian Anderson .20 .50
99 Abraham Toro .25 .60
100 Jack Flaherty .30 .75
101 Tres Barrera SP .75 2.00
102 Sean Murphy SP RC 1.00 2.50
103 Albert Pujols SP .75 2.00
104 Mookie Betts SP 1.25 3.00
105 Adrian Morejon SP RC .60 1.50
106 Kyle Seager SP .40 1.00
107 Jose Altuve SP .50 1.25
108 Jonathan Hernandez SP RC .60 1.50
109 Reggie Jackson SP .50 1.25
110 Ronald Bolanos SP .40 1.00
111 Michael King SP RC 1.00 2.50
112 Tony Gwynn SP .60 1.50
113 Donnie Walton SP RC 1.50 4.00
114 Mike Trout SP 3.00 8.00
115 Ozzie Smith SP .75 2.00
116 Aaron Judge SP 1.50 4.00
117 Ronald Acuna Jr. SP 2.50 6.00
118 Johnny Bench SP .60 1.50
119 Mike Piazza SP .60 1.50
120 Randy Arozarena SP RC 5.00 12.00
121 Billy Williams SP .50 1.25
122 Joe Palumbo SP RC .60 1.50
123 Miguel Cabrera SP .60 1.50
124 Joey Gallo SP .60 1.50
125 Justin Dunn SP RC .75 2.00
126 Manny Machado SP .60 1.50
127 Trent Grisham SP RC 2.50 6.00
128 A.J. Puk SP RC 1.00 2.50
129 Whit Merrifield SP .60 1.50
130 Brusdar Graterol SP RC 1.00 2.50
131 Jake Fraley SP RC .75 2.00
132 Jose Berrios SP .50 1.25
133 T.J. Zeuch SP RC .60 1.50
134 Francisco Lindor SP .60 1.50
135 Vladimir Guerrero Jr. SP 1.00 2.50
136 Nolan Ryan SP 2.00 5.00
137 Fernando Tatis Jr. SP 3.00 8.00
138 Trevor Story SP .60 1.50
139 Nick Solak SP RC 2.50 6.00
140 Anthony Kay SP RC .60 1.50
141 Juan Soto SP 2.00 5.00
142 Joe Morgan SP .50 1.25
143 Ken Griffey Jr. SP 1.25 3.00
144 Bo Bichette SP RC 5.00 12.00
145 Mauricio Dubon SP RC .75 2.00
146 Sheldon Neuse SP RC .75 2.00
147 Justin Verlander SP .60 1.50
148 Kirby Puckett SP .60 1.50
149 Nolan Arenado SP 1.00 2.50
150 Jaylin Davis SP RC 1.00 2.50
151 Lewis Thorpe SP RC .60 1.50
152 Jesus Luzardo SP RC 1.25 3.00
153 Rico Garcia SP .60 1.50
154 Michel Baez SP RC .60 1.50
155 Deivy Grullon SP .40 1.00
156 Logan Webb SP RC 1.00 2.50
157 Kyle Lewis SP RC 5.00 12.00
158 Eloy Jimenez SP 1.25 3.00
159 Trey Mancini SP .60 1.50
160 Blake Snell SP .50 1.25
161 Sam Crawford SP .50 1.25
162 Brendan McKay SP RC 1.00 2.50
163 Nap Lajoie SP .60 1.50
164 Jose Ramirez SP .50 1.25
165 Shohei Ohtani SP 1.00 2.50
166 Ryne Sandberg SP 1.25 3.00
167 Sam Rice SP .50 1.25
168 Ichiro SP .75 2.00
169 Andres Munoz SP RC 1.00 2.50
170 Brock Burke SP RC .60 1.50

2020 Diamond Kings Artist Proof Gold

*AP GOLD 1-100: 2.5X TO 6X BASIC
*AP GOLD 1-100 RC: 1.2X TO 3X BASIC RC
*AP GOLD 101-170 SP: 1.2X TO 3X BASIC SP
*AP GOLD 101-170 SP RC: .8X TO 2X BASIC
RANDOM INSERTS IN PACKS
STATED PRINT RUN 49 SER. #'d SETS
22 Roberto Clemente 10.00 25.00
44 Cal Ripken 12.00 30.00
47 Harmon Killebrew 12.00 30.00
76 Gavin Lux 20.00 50.00
114 Mike Trout SP 20.00 50.00
143 Ken Griffey Jr. SP 12.00 30.00

2020 Diamond Kings Aficionado

RANDOM INSERTS IN PACKS
*BLUE: 1.5X TO 4X BASIC
1 Kirby Puckett .50 1.25
2 Mike Piazza .50 1.25
3 Cal Ripken 1.50 4.00
4 Nolan Arenado .75 2.00
5 Miguel Cabrera .50 1.25
6 Bryce Harper .75 2.00
7 Mike Trout 2.50 6.00
8 Ichiro .60 1.50
9 Jose Altuve .40 1.00
10 Anthony Rizzo .60 1.50
11 Mookie Betts 1.00 2.50
12 Rhys Hoskins .60 1.50
13 Justin Verlander .50 1.25
14 Pete Alonso 1.25 3.00
15 Gleyber Torres 1.00 2.50

2020 Diamond Kings All-Time Diamond Kings

RANDOM INSERTS IN PACKS
1 Tony Gwynn .50 1.25
2 Larry Walker .40 1.00
3 Mel Ott .50 1.25
4 Randy Johnson .50 1.25
5 Jackie Robinson .50 1.25
6 Craig Biggio .40 1.00
7 Rickey Henderson .50 1.25
8 Nolan Ryan 1.50 4.00
9 Mike Trout 2.50 6.00
10 Ken Griffey Jr. 1.00 2.50
11 Stan Musial .75 2.00
12 Robin Yount .50 1.25
13 Ryne Sandberg 1.00 2.50
14 Pete Rose 1.00 2.50
15 Roberto Clemente 1.25 3.00
16 Harmon Killebrew .50 1.25
17 Bob Feller .40 1.00
18 Frank Thomas .50 1.25
19 George Brett 1.00 2.50
20 Ty Cobb .75 2.00
21 Chipper Jones .50 1.25
22 Vladimir Guerrero .40 1.00
23 Mike Piazza .50 1.25
24 Richie Ashburn .40 1.00
25 Miguel Cabrera .50 1.25
26 Babe Ruth 1.25 3.00
27 Evan Longoria .40 1.00
28 Ted Williams 1.00 2.50
29 Roberto Alomar .40 1.00
30 Cal Ripken 1.50 4.00

2020 Diamond Kings All-Time Diamond Kings Artist Proof Blue

*AP BLUE: 1X TO 2.5X BASIC
RANDOM INSERTS IN PACKS
10 Ken Griffey Jr. 5.00 12.00

2020 Diamond Kings All-Time Diamond Kings Artist Proof Gold

*AP GOLD: 1.5X TO 4X BASIC
RANDOM INSERTS IN PACKS
STATED PRINT RUN 49 COPIES PER
7 Rickey Henderson 10.00 25.00
9 Mike Trout 15.00 40.00
10 Ken Griffey Jr. 25.00 60.00
11 Stan Musial 8.00 20.00
12 Robin Yount 6.00 15.00
15 Roberto Clemente 10.00 25.00
24 Richie Ashburn 10.00 25.00

2020 Diamond Kings All-Time Diamond Kings Blue Frame

*BLUE: 1X TO 2.5X BASIC
RANDOM INSERTS IN PACKS
10 Ken Griffey Jr. 5.00 12.00

2020 Diamond Kings All-Time Diamond Kings Gray Frame

*GRAY: 1X TO 2.5X BASIC
RANDOM INSERTS IN PACKS
10 Ken Griffey Jr. 5.00 12.00

2020 Diamond Kings All-Time Diamond Kings Litho Proof

*LITHO: 2.5X TO 6X BASIC
RANDOM INSERTS IN PACKS
STATED PRINT RUN 25 COPIES PER
7 Rickey Henderson 15.00 40.00
9 Mike Trout 25.00 60.00
10 Ken Griffey Jr. 40.00 100.00
11 Stan Musial 12.00 30.00
12 Robin Yount 10.00 25.00
15 Roberto Clemente 15.00 40.00
23 Mike Piazza 10.00 25.00
24 Richie Ashburn 15.00 40.00
30 Cal Ripken 20.00 50.00

2020 Diamond Kings All-Time Diamond Kings Plum Frame

*PLUM: 1X TO 2.5X BASIC
RANDOM INSERTS IN PACKS
10 Ken Griffey Jr. 5.00 12.00

2020 Diamond Kings All-Time Diamond Kings Red Frame

*RED: 1X TO 2.5X BASIC
RANDOM INSERTS IN PACKS
10 Ken Griffey Jr. 5.00 12.00

2020 Diamond Kings Artist's Palette

RANDOM INSERTS IN PACKS
*BLUE: 1.5X TO 4X BASIC
1 Ken Griffey Jr. 1.00 2.50
2 Ronald Acuna Jr. 2.00 5.00
3 Vladimir Guerrero Jr. .75 2.00
4 Francisco Lindor .50 1.25
5 Javier Baez .60 1.50
6 Mike Trout 2.50 6.00
7 Yadier Molina .60 1.50
8 Yordan Alvarez 3.00 8.00
9 Fernando Tatis Jr. 2.50 6.00
10 Aaron Judge 1.25 3.00

2020 Diamond Kings Bat Kings

RANDOM INSERTS IN PACKS
1 Joe DiMaggio
2 Joe Jackson 10.00 25.00
3 Roger Maris
4 Hank Greenberg 12.00 30.00
5 Honus Wagner
6 Joe Sewell 2.50 6.00
7 Mike Trout 12.00 30.00
8 Ronald Acuna Jr. 5.00 12.00
9 Alex Bregman 3.00 8.00
10 Eugenio Suarez 2.50 6.00
11 Ozzie Albies 3.00 8.00
12 Eddie Murray 6.00 15.00
13 Manny Machado 3.00 8.00
14 Anthony Rizzo 4.00 10.00
15 Whit Merrifield 3.00 8.00
16 Rickey Henderson 3.00 8.00
17 Gary Carter 6.00 15.00
18 Dave Concepcion 2.00 5.00
19 Orlando Cepeda 4.00 10.00
20 Kirby Puckett 6.00 15.00
21 Fernando Tatis Jr. 12.00 30.00
22 Vladimir Guerrero Jr. 4.00 10.00
23 Paul Molitor 6.00 15.00
24 Matt Chapman 3.00 8.00
25 J.D. Martinez 3.00 8.00
26 Trevor Story 3.00 8.00
27 Eloy Jimenez 4.00 10.00
28 Mookie Betts 6.00 15.00
29 Rhys Hoskins 4.00 10.00
30 Trea Turner 2.50 6.00
31 Yordan Alvarez 3.00 8.00
32 Jose Ramirez 2.50 6.00
33 Carl Yastrzemski 6.00 15.00
34 Doc Cramer 3.00 8.00
35 Pete Rose 10.00 25.00
36 Reggie Jackson 5.00 12.00
37 Richie Ashburn 4.00 10.00
38 Robin Yount
39 Tris Speaker
40 Wade Boggs 4.00 10.00

2020 Diamond Kings Bat Kings Holo Blue

*BLUE/25: .8X TO 2X BASIC
RANDOM INSERTS IN PACKS
PRINT RUN BTW 10-25 COPIES PER
NO PRICING QTY 15 OR LESS
7 Mike Trout/25 40.00 100.00
11 Ozzie Albies/25 10.00 25.00
14 Anthony Rizzo/25 15.00 40.00
23 Paul Molitor/25 15.00 40.00
35 Pete Rose/25 20.00 50.00
36 Reggie Jackson/25 12.00 30.00
37 Richie Ashburn/25 40.00 100.00

2020 Diamond Kings Bat Kings Purple

RANDOM INSERTS IN PACKS
STATED PRINT RUN 20 COPIES PER
1 Joe DiMaggio 20.00 50.00
2 Joe Jackson 30.00 80.00
3 Roger Maris 15.00 40.00
5 Honus Wagner 30.00 80.00
7 Mike Trout 40.00 100.00
11 Ozzie Albies 10.00 25.00
14 Anthony Rizzo 15.00 40.00
23 Paul Molitor 15.00 40.00
35 Pete Rose 20.00 50.00
36 Reggie Jackson 12.00 30.00
37 Richie Ashburn 40.00 100.00

2020 Diamond Kings DK 206

RANDOM INSERTS IN PACKS
1 Ken Griffey Jr. 1.00 2.50
2 Aaron Judge 1.25 3.00
3 Anthony Rizzo .60 1.50
4 Bryce Harper .75 2.00
5 Cal Ripken 1.50 4.00
6 Mookie Betts 1.00 2.50
7 Nolan Ryan 1.50 4.00
8 Ronald Acuna Jr. 2.00 5.00
9 Shohei Ohtani .75 2.00
10 Frank Thomas .50 1.25
11 Javier Baez .60 1.50
12 Jose Altuve .40 1.00
13 Justin Verlander .50 1.25
14 Kirby Puckett .50 1.25
15 Yordan Alvarez 3.00 8.00
16 Mickey Mantle 1.50 4.00
17 Mike Trout 2.50 6.00
18 Pete Alonso 1.25 3.00
19 Vladimir Guerrero Jr. .75 2.00
20 George Brett 1.00 2.50

2020 Diamond Kings DK 206 Holo Blue

*BLUE: 1.5X TO 4X BASIC
RANDOM INSERTS IN PACKS
STATED PRINT RUN 99 COPIES PER
1 Ken Griffey Jr. 15.00 40.00
17 Mike Trout 15.00 40.00
19 Vladimir Guerrero Jr. 10.00 25.00
20 George Brett 10.00 25.00

2020 Diamond Kings DK 206 Signatures

RANDOM INSERTS IN PACKS
EXCHANGE DEADLINE 12/10/2021
7 Yordan Alvarez 25.00 60.00

2020 Diamond Kings DK 206 Signatures Holo Blue

RANDOM INSERTS IN PACKS
PRINT RUN BTW 5-25 COPIES PER
NO PRICING QTY 15 OR LESS
EXCHANGE DEADLINE 12/10/2021
3 Ronald Acuna Jr./25 75.00 200.00
5 Frank Thomas/25 60.00 150.00
6 Jose Altuve/25 20.00 50.00
8 Pete Alonso/25 60.00 150.00

2020 Diamond Kings DK 206 Signatures Holo Gold

*GOLD/35-50: .6X TO 1.5X BASIC
*GOLD/25: .8X TO 2X BASIC
RANDOM INSERTS IN PACKS
PRINT RUN BTW 10-50 COPIES PER
NO PRICING QTY 15 OR LESS
EXCHANGE DEADLINE 12/10/2021
2 Nolan Ryan/25 75.00 200.00
3 Ronald Acuna Jr./50
5 Frank Thomas/50 50.00 120.00
6 Jose Altuve/35 15.00 40.00
8 Pete Alonso/50 40.00 100.00

2020 Diamond Kings DK 206 Signatures Holo Silver

*SLVR/99: .5X TO 1.2X BASIC
RANDOM INSERTS IN PACKS
PRINT RUN BTW 15-99 COPIES PER
NO PRICING QTY 15 OR LESS
EXCHANGE DEADLINE 12/10/2021
5 Frank Thomas/99 40.00 100.00
8 Pete Alonso/99 30.00 80.00

2020 Diamond Kings DK 206 Signatures Purple

*PRPL/20: .8X TO 2X BASIC
RANDOM INSERTS IN PACKS
PRINT RUN BTW 10-20 COPIES PER
NO PRICING QTY 15 OR LESS
EXCHANGE DEADLINE 12/10/2021
2 Nolan Ryan/20 75.00 200.00
3 Ronald Acuna Jr./20 75.00 200.00
4 Shohei Ohtani/20
5 Frank Thomas/20 60.00 150.00
6 Jose Altuve/20 20.00 50.00
8 Pete Alonso/20 60.00 150.00

2020 Diamond Kings DK Material Signatures

RANDOM INSERTS IN PACKS
EXCHANGE DEADLINE 12/10/2021
1 Josh Rojas 6.00 15.00
2 Matt Thaiss 4.00 10.00
3 Logan Allen 3.00 8.00
4 Kyle Lewis 30.00 80.00
5 Jesus Luzardo 6.00 15.00
6 Brendan McKay 5.00 12.00
7 Tony Gonsolin 5.00 12.00
8 Andres Munoz 5.00 12.00
9 Yonathan Daza 6.00 15.00
10 Yu Chang 5.00 12.00
11 Logan Webb 5.00 12.00
12 Michel Baez 3.00 8.00
13 Tyrone Taylor 3.00 8.00
14 Dylan Cease 5.00 12.00
15 Patrick Sandoval 5.00 12.00
16 Jaylin Davis 4.00 10.00
17 Sean Murphy 5.00 12.00
18 Jake Fraley 4.00 10.00
19 Jordan Yamamoto 3.00 8.00
20 Ronald Bolanos 3.00 8.00
21 Mauricio Dubon 4.00 10.00
22 Dustin May 10.00 25.00
23 Isan Diaz 5.00 12.00
24 Randy Arozarena 40.00 100.00
25 Michael King 5.00 12.00
26 Zac Gallen 8.00 20.00
27 Jake Rogers 3.00 8.00
28 Donnie Walton 4.00 10.00
29 Danny Mendick 4.00 10.00
30 Deivy Grullon 3.00 8.00
31 Brusdar Graterol 10.00 25.00
32 Bryan Abreu 3.00 8.00
33 Bo Bichette 25.00 60.00
34 Aristides Aquino 10.00 25.00
35 T.J. Zeuch 3.00 8.00
36 Lewis Thorpe 3.00 8.00
37 Justin Dunn 4.00 10.00
38 Joe Palumbo 3.00 8.00
39 Abraham Toro 4.00 10.00
40 Adrian Morejon 3.00 8.00
41 Rico Garcia 5.00 12.00
42 Willi Castro 5.00 12.00
43 Jonathan Hernandez 3.00 8.00
44 Adbert Alzolay 4.00 10.00
45 Yordan Alvarez 30.00 80.00
46 Anthony Kay 3.00 8.00
47 Domingo Leyba 4.00 10.00
48 Gavin Lux 15.00 40.00
49 Tres Barrera 6.00 15.00
50 Bobby Bradley 6.00 15.00
51 Trent Grisham 10.00 25.00
52 Sheldon Neuse 4.00 10.00
53 Nick Solak 6.00 15.00
54 Nico Hoerner 8.00 20.00
55 Zack Collins 4.00 10.00
56 Aaron Civale 6.00 15.00
57 Travis Demeritte 3.00 8.00
58 Sam Hilliard 5.00 12.00
59 Edwin Rios 6.00 15.00
60 A.J. Puk 6.00 15.00
61 Brock Burke 3.00 8.00

2020 Diamond Kings DK Material Signatures Gold

*GOLD: .5X TO 1.2X BASIC
RANDOM INSERTS IN PACKS
PRINT RUN BTW 15-49 COPIES PER
NO PRICING QTY 15 OR LESS
EXCHANGE DEADLINE 12/10/2021
45 Yordan Alvarez/49 60.00 150.00

2020 Diamond Kings DK Material Signatures Purple

RANDOM INSERTS IN PACKS
PRINT RUN BTW 15-20 COPIES PER
NO PRICING QTY 15 OR LESS
EXCHANGE DEADLINE 12/10/2021
6 Brendan McKay/20 12.00 30.00
45 Yordan Alvarez/20 75.00 200.00

2020 Diamond Kings DK Materials

RANDOM INSERTS IN PACKS
*SILVER/99: .5X TO 1.2X BASIC
*GOLD/50: .6X TO 1.5X BASIC
1 Josh Rojas 2.00 5.00
2 Matt Thaiss 2.50 6.00
3 Logan Allen 2.00 5.00
4 Kyle Lewis 8.00 20.00
5 Jesus Luzardo 5.00 12.00
6 Brendan McKay 3.00 8.00
7 Tony Gonsolin 8.00 20.00
8 Andres Munoz 3.00 8.00
9 Yonathan Daza 2.50 6.00
10 Yu Chang 3.00 8.00
11 Logan Webb 3.00 8.00
12 Michel Baez 2.00 5.00
13 Tyrone Taylor 2.00 5.00
14 Dylan Cease 3.00 8.00
15 Patrick Sandoval 3.00 8.00
16 Jaylin Davis 3.00 8.00
17 Sean Murphy 3.00 8.00
18 Jake Fraley 2.50 6.00
19 Jordan Yamamoto 2.00 5.00
20 Ronald Bolanos 2.00 5.00
21 Mauricio Dubon 2.50 6.00
22 Dustin May 5.00 12.00
23 Isan Diaz 3.00 8.00
24 Randy Arozarena 6.00 15.00
25 Michael King 3.00 8.00
26 Zac Gallen 5.00 12.00
27 Jake Rogers 2.00 5.00
28 Donnie Walton 5.00 12.00
29 Danny Mendick 2.50 6.00
30 Deivy Grullon 2.00 5.00
31 Brusdar Graterol 3.00 8.00
32 Bryan Abreu 2.00 5.00
33 Bo Bichette 4.00 10.00
34 Aristides Aquino 5.00 12.00
35 T.J. Zeuch 2.00 5.00
36 Lewis Thorpe 2.00 5.00
37 Justin Dunn 2.50 6.00
38 Joe Palumbo 2.00 5.00
39 Abraham Toro 2.50 6.00
40 Adrian Morejon 2.00 5.00
41 Rico Garcia 3.00 8.00
42 Willi Castro 3.00 8.00
43 Jonathan Hernandez 2.00 5.00
44 Adbert Alzolay 2.50 6.00
45 Yordan Alvarez 6.00 15.00
46 Anthony Kay 2.00 5.00
47 Domingo Leyba 2.50 6.00
48 Gavin Lux 10.00 25.00
49 Tres Barrera 4.00 10.00
50 Bobby Bradley 2.00 5.00
51 Trent Grisham 8.00 20.00
52 Sheldon Neuse 2.50 6.00
53 Nick Solak 8.00 20.00
54 Nico Hoerner 5.00 12.00
55 Zack Collins 2.50 6.00
56 Aaron Civale 4.00 10.00
57 Travis Demeritte 3.00 8.00
58 Sam Hilliard 3.00 8.00
59 Edwin Rios 5.00 12.00
60 A.J. Puk 3.00 8.00
61 Brock Burke 2.00 5.00
62 Mule Suttles 5.00 12.00
63 Babe Ruth 100.00 250.00
64 Jackie Robinson 20.00 50.00
65 Jimmie Foxx 12.00 30.00
66 Ty Cobb 20.00 50.00
67 Lou Gehrig 40.00 100.00
68 Mel Ott
69 Charlie Keller
70 Mickey Mantle 25.00 60.00
71 Roberto Clemente 60.00 150.00
72 Roger Maris
73 Ted Williams
74 Yogi Berra
75 Tris Speaker
76 Walter Alston 4.00 10.00
77 Eddie Stanky 2.00 5.00
78 Harvey Kuenn
79 Joe Cronin
80 Joe McCarthy 2.00 5.00
81 Ken Griffey Jr. 10.00 25.00
82 Mike Trout 12.00 30.00
83 Juan Soto 4.00 10.00
84 Ronald Acuna Jr. 8.00 20.00
85 Aaron Judge 5.00 12.00
86 Vladimir Guerrero Jr. 4.00 10.00
87 Pete Alonso 8.00 20.00
88 Walker Buehler 4.00 10.00
89 Eloy Jimenez 4.00 10.00
91 Nolan Arenado 5.00 12.00
92 Rafael Devers 4.00 10.00
93 Kris Bryant 10.00 25.00
94 Shohei Ohtani 8.00 20.00
95 Alex Bregman 3.00 8.00
96 Justin Verlander 3.00 8.00
97 Stephen Strasburg 3.00 8.00
98 Mookie Betts 6.00 15.00
99 Max Scherzer 3.00 8.00
100 Javier Baez 8.00 20.00

2020 Diamond Kings DK Materials Holo Blue

*BLUE/25: .8X TO 2X BASIC
RANDOM INSERTS IN PACKS
PRINT RUN BTW 3-25 COPIES PER
NO PRICING QTY 15 OR LESS
82 Mike Trout/25 40.00 100.00
83 Juan Soto/25 10.00 25.00
85 Aaron Judge/25 20.00 50.00
87 Pete Alonso/25 15.00 40.00

2020 Diamond Kings DK Originals

RANDOM INSERTS IN PACKS
*BLUE: 1.5X TO 4X BASIC
1 Alex Bregman .50 1.25
2 Clayton Kershaw .75 2.00
3 Anthony Rizzo .60 1.50
4 Mel Ott .50 1.25
5 Joe DiMaggio 1.00 2.50
6 Ted Williams 1.00 2.50
7 Anthony Rendon .50 1.25
8 Keston Hiura .60 1.50
9 Justin Verlander .50 1.25
10 Ty Cobb .75 2.00

2020 Diamond Kings DK Originals Signatures

RANDOM INSERTS IN PACKS
EXCHANGE DEADLINE 12/10/2021
5 Curt Schilling
8 Alec Bohm 15.00 40.00
12 Luis Robert 60.00 150.00
13 Jose Abreu 4.00 10.00
15 Barry Larkin 12.00 30.00
17 Keith Hernandez 10.00 25.00
19 Anthony Rizzo
21 Trevor Hoffman EXCH 8.00 20.00
23 Corey Seager 4.00 10.00
24 Josh Donaldson 3.00 8.00
27 Blake Snell 3.00 8.00
28 Luis Severino 6.00 15.00
29 Andre Dawson
30 Walker Buehler EXCH 8.00 20.00

2020 Diamond Kings DK Originals Signatures Holo Blue

*BLUE/25: .8X TO 2X BASIC
RANDOM INSERTS IN PACKS
PRINT RUN BTW 10-25 COPIES PER
NO PRICING QTY 15 OR LESS
EXCHANGE DEADLINE 12/10/2021
1 Vladimir Guerrero Jr./25 40.00 100.00
2 Alan Trammell/25 25.00 60.00
3 Kenny Lofton/25 20.00 50.00
7 Xander Bogaerts/25 20.00 50.00
9 Forrest Whitley/25 8.00 20.00
10 Ben Zobrist/25 10.00 25.00
16 Dale Murphy/25 20.00 50.00
18 Aaron Judge/25 EXCH 40.00 100.00
20 J.D. Martinez/25 15.00 40.00
22 Kyle Hendricks/25 20.00 50.00
26 David Wright/25 20.00 50.00

2020 Diamond Kings DK Originals Signatures Holo Gold

*GOLD/30-50: .6X TO 1.5X BASIC
*GOLD/25: .8X TO 2X BASIC
RANDOM INSERTS IN PACKS
PRINT RUN BTW 15-50 COPIES PER
NO PRICING QTY 15 OR LESS
EXCHANGE DEADLINE 12/10/2021
1 Vladimir Guerrero Jr./50 30.00 80.00
2 Alan Trammell/50 20.00 50.00
3 Kenny Lofton/50
4 Clayton Kershaw/25 40.00 100.00
7 Xander Bogaerts/50 12.00 30.00
9 Forrest Whitley/50 6.00 15.00
11 John Smoltz/25 15.00 40.00
14 Jose Ramirez/25
16 Dale Murphy/50 15.00 40.00
20 J.D. Martinez/50 12.00 30.00
22 Kyle Hendricks/50 15.00 40.00
26 David Wright/50 15.00 40.00

2020 Diamond Kings DK Originals Signatures Holo Silver

*SLVR/75-99: .5X TO 1.2X BASIC
*SLVR/49-50: .6X TO 1.5X BASIC
*SLVR/25: .8X TO 2X BASIC
RANDOM INSERTS IN PACKS
PRINT RUN BTW 25-99 COPIES PER
EXCHANGE DEADLINE 12/10/2021
1 Vladimir Guerrero Jr./99 25.00 60.00
4 Clayton Kershaw/49 25.00 60.00
9 Forrest Whitley/99 5.00 12.00
11 John Smoltz/50 12.00 30.00
14 Jose Ramirez/75
16 Dale Murphy/99 12.00 30.00
19 Anthony Rizzo/25 15.00 40.00
20 J.D. Martinez/99 10.00 25.00
22 Kyle Hendricks/99 12.00 30.00
26 David Wright/99 12.00 30.00

2020 Diamond Kings DK Originals Signatures Purple

*PRPL: .8X TO 2X BASIC
RANDOM INSERTS IN PACKS
STATED PRINT RUN 25 COPIES PER
EXCHANGE DEADLINE 12/10/2021
1 Vladimir Guerrero Jr. 40.00 100.00
2 Alan Trammell 25.00 60.00
3 Kenny Lofton 20.00 50.00
4 Clayton Kershaw 40.00 100.00
5 Curt Schilling 20.00 50.00
6 Steve Garvey 30.00 80.00
7 Xander Bogaerts 20.00 50.00
9 Forrest Whitley 8.00 20.00
10 Ben Zobrist 10.00 25.00
11 John Smoltz 15.00 40.00
14 Jose Ramirez
16 Dale Murphy 20.00 50.00
18 Aaron Judge EXCH 40.00 100.00
19 Anthony Rizzo 15.00 40.00
20 J.D. Martinez 15.00 40.00
22 Kyle Hendricks 20.00 50.00
25 Josh Hader 6.00 15.00
26 David Wright 20.00 50.00

2020 Diamond Kings DK Quad Material Signatures

RANDOM INSERTS IN PACKS
EXCHANGE DEADLINE 12/10/2021
3 Yordan Alvarez 25.00 60.00
4 Bo Bichette 40.00 100.00
5 Cody Bellinger 50.00 120.00
6 Rickey Henderson 40.00 100.00
7 Chipper Jones 40.00 100.00
9 Frank Robinson 15.00 40.00
11 Eloy Jimenez
13 Mike Soroka 15.00 40.00
14 Gleyber Torres 30.00 80.00
15 Omar Vizquel 15.00 40.00
17 Jose Berrios 8.00 20.00
18 Brendan McKay 10.00 25.00
19 Chris Sale 10.00 25.00

2020 Diamond Kings DK Quad Material Signatures Gold

*GOLD/49: .5X TO 1.2X BASIC
*GOLD/25: .6X TO 1.5X BASIC
RANDOM INSERTS IN PACKS
PRINT RUN BTW 25-50 COPIES PER
EXCHANGE DEADLINE 12/10/2021
1 Aaron Judge/49
2 Ken Griffey Jr./25 300.00 600.00
3 Yordan Alvarez/49 60.00 150.00
8 Shohei Ohtani/49 50.00 120.00
10 Ronald Acuna Jr./49 75.00 200.00
11 Eloy Jimenez/49
12 Xander Bogaerts/49 20.00 50.00

2020 Diamond Kings DK Quad Material Signatures Holo Blue

*BLUE/23-25: .6X TO 1.5X BASIC
RANDOM INSERTS IN PACKS
PRINT RUN BTW 15-25 COPIES PER
NO PRICING QTY 15 OR LESS
EXCHANGE DEADLINE 12/10/2021
1 Aaron Judge/25 50.00 120.00
3 Yordan Alvarez/25 75.00 200.00
7 Chipper Jones/25 75.00 200.00
8 Shohei Ohtani/25 75.00 200.00
10 Ronald Acuna Jr./25 100.00 250.00
11 Eloy Jimenez/25 40.00 100.00
12 Xander Bogaerts/25 40.00 100.00
16 Scooter Gennett/25 15.00 40.00
19 Chris Sale/25 20.00 50.00

2020 Diamond Kings DK Quad Material Signatures Purple

*PRPL/20: .6X TO 1.5X BASIC
RANDOM INSERTS IN PACKS
PRINT RUN BTW 10-20 COPIES PER
NO PRICING QTY 15 OR LESS
EXCHANGE DEADLINE 12/10/2021
1 Aaron Judge/20 50.00 120.00
3 Yordan Alvarez/20 75.00 200.00
7 Chipper Jones/20 75.00 200.00
8 Shohei Ohtani/20 75.00 200.00
10 Ronald Acuna Jr./20 100.00 250.00
11 Eloy Jimenez/20 40.00 100.00
12 Xander Bogaerts/20 40.00 100.00
16 Scooter Gennett/20 15.00 40.00
19 Chris Sale/20 20.00 50.00

2020 Diamond Kings DK Quad Materials

RANDOM INSERTS IN PACKS
1 Jeff McNeil 4.00 10.00
2 Yordan Alvarez 6.00 15.00
3 Pete Alonso 6.00 15.00
4 Tony Gwynn 6.00 15.00
5 Aristides Aquino 5.00 12.00
6 Bo Bichette 10.00 25.00
7 Brendan McKay 3.00 8.00
8 Gavin Lux 10.00 25.00
9 Dustin May 6.00 15.00
10 Fernando Tatis Jr. 8.00 20.00
11 Eloy Jimenez 4.00 10.00
12 Mookie Betts 12.00 30.00
13 Shohei Ohtani 5.00 12.00
14 Hyun-Jin Ryu 2.50 6.00
15 Jacob deGrom 6.00 15.00
16 Gerrit Cole 5.00 12.00
17 Buster Posey 8.00 20.00
18 Miguel Cabrera 6.00 15.00
19 Adrian Beltre 3.00 8.00
20 Max Scherzer 3.00 8.00
21 Clayton Kershaw 6.00 15.00
22 Yadier Molina 8.00 20.00
23 David Ortiz 5.00 12.00

24 Justin Verlander 3.00 8.00
25 Robinson Cano 2.50 6.00

2020 Diamond Kings DK Quad Materials Holo Blue

*BLUE: .8X TO 2X BASIC
RANDOM INSERTS IN PACKS
STATED PRINT RUN 25 COPIES PER
3 Pete Alonso 15.00 40.00

2020 Diamond Kings DK Signatures

RANDOM INSERTS IN PACKS
EXCHANGE DEADLINE 12/10/2021
1 Josh Rojas 2.50 6.00
2 Matt Thaiss 3.00 8.00
3 Logan Allen 2.50 6.00
4 Kyle Lewis 10.00 25.00
5 Jesus Luzardo
6 Brendan McKay 10.00 25.00
7 Tony Gonsolin 10.00 25.00
8 Andres Munoz 4.00 10.00
9 Yonathan Daza 3.00 8.00
10 Yu Chang 4.00 10.00
11 Logan Webb 5.00 12.00
12 Michel Baez 2.50 6.00
13 Tyrone Taylor 2.50 6.00
14 Dylan Cease 4.00 10.00
15 Patrick Sandoval 4.00 10.00
16 Jaylin Davis 4.00 10.00
17 Sean Murphy 4.00 10.00
18 Jake Fraley 3.00 8.00
19 Jordan Yamamoto 2.50 6.00
20 Ronald Bolanos 2.50 6.00
21 Mauricio Dubon
22 Dustin May 8.00 20.00
23 Isan Diaz 4.00 10.00
24 Randy Arozarena 40.00 100.00
25 Michael King 4.00 10.00
26 Zac Gallen 4.00 10.00
27 Jake Rogers 2.50 6.00
28 Donnie Walton 6.00 15.00
29 Danny Mendick 3.00 8.00
30 Deivy Grullon 2.50 6.00
31 Brusdar Graterol 4.00 10.00
32 Bryan Abreu 2.50 6.00
33 Bo Bichette 20.00 50.00
34 Aristides Aquino 6.00 15.00
35 T.J. Zeuch 2.50 6.00
36 Lewis Thorpe 2.50 6.00
37 Justin Dunn 3.00 8.00
38 Joe Palumbo 2.50 6.00
39 Abraham Toro 3.00 8.00
40 Adrian Morejon 2.50 6.00
41 Rico Garcia 4.00 10.00
42 Willi Castro 5.00 12.00
43 Jonathan Hernandez 2.50 6.00
44 Adbert Alzolay 3.00 8.00
45 Yordan Alvarez 40.00 100.00
46 Anthony Kay 2.50 6.00
47 Domingo Leyba 3.00 8.00
48 Gavin Lux 25.00 60.00
49 Tres Barrera 5.00 12.00
50 Bobby Bradley 5.00 12.00
51 Trent Grisham 6.00 15.00
52 Sheldon Neuse 3.00 8.00
53 Nick Solak 5.00 12.00
54 Nico Hoerner 10.00 25.00
55 Zack Collins 3.00 8.00
56 Aaron Civale 5.00 12.00
57 Travis Demeritte 3.00 8.00
58 Sam Hilliard 4.00 10.00
59 Edwin Rios 6.00 15.00
60 A.J. Puk 4.00 10.00
61 Brock Burke 2.50 6.00
62 Yoshitomo Tsutsugo EXCH 20.00 50.00

2020 Diamond Kings DK Signatures Holo Gold

*GOLD/25: .8X TO 2X BASIC
RANDOM INSERTS IN PACKS
PRINT RUN BTW 10-25 COPIES PER
NO PRICING QTY 15 OR LESS
EXCHANGE DEADLINE 12/10/2021
48 Gavin Lux/25 60.00 150.00

2020 Diamond Kings DK Signatures Holo Silver

*SLVR/49: .6X TO 1.5X BASIC
RANDOM INSERTS IN PACKS
PRINT RUN BTW 15-49 COPIES PER
NO PRICING QTY 15 OR LESS
EXCHANGE DEADLINE 12/10/2021

2020 Diamond Kings DK Signatures Purple

*PRPL/20: .8X TO 2X BASIC
RANDOM INSERTS IN PACKS
PRINT RUN BTW 5-20 COPIES PER
NO PRICING QTY 15 OR LESS
EXCHANGE DEADLINE 12/10/2021
48 Gavin Lux/20 60.00 150.00

2020 Diamond Kings Downtown

RANDOM INSERTS IN PACKS
1 Mike Trout 100.00 250.00
2 Aaron Judge 100.00 250.00
3 Cody Bellinger 20.00 50.00
4 Yordan Alvarez 60.00 150.00
5 Fernando Tatis Jr. 150.00 400.00
6 Anthony Rendon 10.00 25.00
7 Yadier Molina 25.00 60.00
8 Rafael Devers 25.00 60.00
9 Anthony Rizzo 40.00 100.00
10 Bo Bichette 100.00 250.00
11 Wander Franco 30.00 80.00
12 Luis Robert 400.00 800.00
13 Jo Adell 25.00 60.00
14 Aristides Aquino 30.00 80.00
15 Gleyber Torres 40.00 100.00
16 Ronald Acuna Jr. 40.00 100.00
17 Pete Alonso 75.00 200.00
18 Juan Soto 40.00 100.00
19 Bryce Harper 30.00 80.00
20 Vladimir Guerrero Jr. 15.00 40.00

2020 Diamond Kings Gallery of Stars

RANDOM INSERTS IN PACKS
*BLUE: 1.5X TO 4X BASIC
1 Aaron Judge 1.25 3.00
2 Mookie Betts 1.00 2.50
3 Vladimir Guerrero Jr. .75 2.00
4 Francisco Lindor .50 1.25
5 Jose Altuve .40 1.00
6 Mike Trout 2.50 6.00
7 Shohei Ohtani .75 2.00
8 Ronald Acuna Jr. 2.00 5.00
9 Juan Soto 1.50 4.00
10 Pete Alonso 1.25 3.00
11 Bryce Harper .75 2.00
12 Javier Baez .60 1.50
13 Cody Bellinger 1.00 2.50
14 Christian Yelich .60 1.50
15 Fernando Tatis Jr. 2.50 6.00

2020 Diamond Kings In The Zone

RANDOM INSERTS IN PACKS
*BLUE: 1.5X TO 4X BASIC
1 Tony Gwynn .50 1.25
2 Reggie Jackson 1.00 2.50
3 Tim Anderson .50 1.25
4 Roger Maris .50 1.25
5 Matt Chapman .50 1.25
6 Alex Rodriguez .60 1.50
7 Pedro Martinez .40 1.00
8 Manny Machado .50 1.25
9 Shohei Ohtani .75 2.00
10 Juan Soto 1.50 4.00
11 Christian Yelich .60 1.50
12 Anthony Rendon .50 1.25
13 Jose Ramirez .40 1.00
14 Gerrit Cole .75 2.00
15 George Brett 1.20 3.00

2020 Diamond Kings Jersey Kings

RANDOM INSERTS IN PACKS
1 Stan Musial 8.00 20.00
2 Satchel Paige 25.00 60.00
3 Jorge Polanco 2.50 6.00
4 Yordan Alvarez 5.00 12.00
5 Pete Alonso 5.00 12.00
6 Ken Griffey Jr. 10.00 25.00
7 Mike Trout 12.00 30.00
8 Mickey Mantle 25.00 60.00
9 Nolan Arenado 5.00 12.00
10 Aaron Judge 5.00 12.00
11 Jose Altuve 2.50 6.00
12 Juan Soto 10.00 25.00
13 Miguel Cabrera 6.00 15.00
14 Jose Abreu 5.00 12.00
15 Andrew Benintendi 3.00 8.00
16 Frank Thomas 5.00 12.00
17 Elroy Face 2.00 5.00
18 Tim Anderson 3.00 8.00
19 J.D. Martinez 3.00 8.00
20 Anthony Rizzo 4.00 10.00
21 Giancarlo Stanton 3.00 8.00
22 Freddie Freeman 4.00 10.00
23 Kris Bryant 4.00 10.00
24 Craig Biggio 2.50 6.00
25 Aaron Nola 2.50 6.00
26 Max Muncy 2.50 6.00
27 Larry Walker 2.50 6.00
28 Lou Gehrig 40.00 100.00
29 Jackie Robinson 20.00 50.00
30 Babe Ruth 100.00 250.00
31 Ted Williams
32 Gil McDougald
33 Elston Howard
34 Kirby Puckett 12.00 30.00
35 Joe McCarthy 2.00 5.00

2020 Diamond Kings Jersey Kings Holo Blue

*BLUE: .8X TO 2X BASIC
RANDOM INSERTS IN PACKS
STATED PRINT RUN 25 COPIES PER
6 Ken Griffey Jr. 40.00 100.00
7 Mike Trout 50.00 120.00
10 Aaron Judge 15.00 40.00
16 Frank Thomas 25.00 60.00
20 Anthony Rizzo 15.00 40.00
29 Jackie Robinson 50.00 120.00
30 Babe Ruth 125.00 300.00
31 Ted Williams 50.00 120.00

2020 Diamond Kings Jersey Kings Purple

*PURPLE/19-20: .8X TO 2X BASIC
RANDOM INSERTS IN PACKS
PRINT RUN BTW 8-20 COPIES PER
NO PRICING QTY 15 OR LESS
6 Ken Griffey Jr./20 40.00 100.00
7 Mike Trout/20 50.00 120.00
10 Aaron Judge/20 15.00 40.00
16 Frank Thomas/20 25.00 60.00
20 Anthony Rizzo/20 15.00 40.00
29 Jackie Robinson/20 50.00 120.00
30 Babe Ruth/20 125.00 300.00
31 Ted Williams/20 50.00 120.00

2020 Diamond Kings Litho Proof

*LITHO 1-100: 4X TO 10X BASIC
*LITHO 1-100 RC: 2X TO 5X BASIC RC
*LITHO 101-170 SP: 2X TO 5X BASIC SP
*LITHO 101-170 SP RC: 1.2X TO 3X BASIC
RANDOM INSERTS IN PACKS
STATED PRINT RUN 25 SER. #'d SETS
22 Roberto Clemente 15.00 40.00
44 Cal Ripken 20.00 50.00
47 Harmon Killebrew 20.00 50.00
58 Yordan Alvarez 30.00 80.00
76 Gavin Lux 30.00 80.00
114 Mike Trout SP 30.00 80.00
143 Ken Griffey Jr. SP 20.00 50.00

2020 Diamond Kings Pixel Art

RANDOM INSERTS IN PACKS 3.00 8.00
1 Mookie Betts 12.00 30.00
2 Juan Soto 20.00 50.00
3 Jose Altuve 6.00 15.00
4 Javier Baez 10.00 25.00
5 Shohei Ohtani 15.00 40.00
6 Clayton Kershaw 8.00 20.00
7 Yoshitomo Tsutsugo 8.00 20.00
8 Miguel Cabrera 20.00 50.00
9 Manny Machado 10.00 25.00
10 Yadier Molina 8.00 20.00
11 Ketel Marte 4.00 10.00
12 Francisco Lindor 5.00 12.00
13 Ozzie Albies 5.00 12.00
14 Isan Diaz 5.00 12.00
15 Joey Votto 12.00 30.00
16 Josh Bell 4.00 10.00
17 Kirby Puckett 40.00 100.00
18 Josh Donaldson 10.00 25.00
19 Trey Mancini 5.00 12.00
20 Trevor Story 5.00 12.00

2020 Diamond Kings The 3000

RANDOM INSERTS IN PACKS
*BLUE: 1.5X TO 4X BASIC
1 George Brett 1.00 2.50
2 Honus Wagner .50 1.25
3 Roberto Clemente 3.00 8.00
4 Al Kaline .50 1.25
5 Ty Cobb .75 2.00
6 Tris Speaker .40 1.00
7 Stan Musial .75 2.00
8 Pete Rose 1.00 2.50
9 Paul Molitor .50 1.25
10 Nap Lajoie .50 1.25
11 Eddie Murray .40 1.00
12 Albert Pujols .60 1.50
13 Cal Ripken 1.50 4.00
14 Tony Gwynn .50 1.25
15 Ichiro .60 1.50

2021 Diamond Kings

RANDOM INSERTS IN PACKS
1 Charlie Keller .20 .50
2 Eddie Stanky .20 .50
3 Harvey Kuenn .20 .50
4 Joe Cronin .20 .50
5 Joe Sewell .25 .60
6 Babe Ruth .75 2.00
7 Pete Rose .60 1.50
8 Hank Greenberg .30 .75
9 Honus Wagner .30 .75
10 Joe DiMaggio .60 1.50
11 Mickey Mantle 1.00 2.50
12 Satchel Paige .30 .75
13 Ted Williams .60 1.50
14 Walter Johnson .30 .75
15 Carl Erskine .20 .50
16 Christy Mathewson .30 .75
17 George Sisler .20 .50
18 Jackie Robinson .30 .75
19 Joe Jackson .40 1.00
20 Lou Gehrig .60 1.50
21 Mickey Cochrane .25 .60
22 Rogers Hornsby .25 .60
23 Ty Cobb .50 1.25
24 Harmon Killebrew .30 .75
25 Joe Morgan .25 .60
26 Lou Brock .25 .60
27 Ryne Sandberg .60 1.50
28 Frank Thomas .30 .75
29 Vladimir Guerrero .25 .60
30 Tony Gwynn .30 .75
31 Andy Young RC 1.00 2.50
32 Pavin Smith RC .60 1.50
33 Ian Anderson RC 2.50 6.00
34 William Contreras RC .50 1.25
35 Keegan Akin RC .40 1.00
36 Bobby Dalbec RC 3.00 8.00
37 Brailyn Marquez RC 2.00 5.00
38 Garrett Crochet RC .60 1.50
39 Luis Gonzalez RC .40 1.00
40 Jose Garcia RC 1.50 4.00
41 Daniel Johnson RC .60 1.50
42 Casey Mize RC 3.00 8.00
43 Isaac Paredes RC 1.50 4.00
44 Cristian Javier RC 1.00 2.50
45 Edward Olivares RC 1.00 2.50
46 Jahmai Jones RC .40 1.00
47 Keibert Ruiz RC 1.25 3.00
48 Braxton Garrett RC .40 1.00
49 Jesus Sanchez RC 1.25 3.00
50 Monte Harrison RC .60 1.50
51 Sixto Sanchez RC 2.00 5.00
52 Alex Kirilloff RC 1.50 4.00
53 Ryan Jeffers RC .75 2.00
54 Andres Gimenez RC 1.00 2.50
55 Clarke Schmidt RC .60 1.50
56 Estevan Florial RC .60 1.50
57 Adonis Medina RC .60 1.50
58 Mickey Moniak RC 1.00 2.50
59 Spencer Howard RC 1.25 3.00
60 Ke'Bryan Hayes RC 4.00 10.00
61 Jorge Mateo RC .50 1.25
62 Luis Patino RC 1.50 4.00
63 Joey Bart RC 1.25 3.00
64 Dylan Carlson RC 3.00 8.00
65 Shane McClanahan RC .50 1.25
66 Leody Taveras RC 1.25 3.00
67 Sherten Apostel RC 1.25 3.00
68 Nate Pearson RC 2.00 5.00
69 Wil Crowe RC .40 1.00
70 DJ LeMahieu .30 .75
71 Marcell Ozuna .30 .75
72 Yu Darvish .30 .75
73 Lucas Giolito .25 .60
74 Roberto Clemente .75 2.00
75 Brandon Lowe .25 .60
76 Aaron Judge .75 2.00
77 Bo Bichette .75 2.00
78 Luis Robert 1.00 2.50
79 Jose Ramirez .25 .60
80 Miguel Cabrera .30 .75
81 Alex Bregman .30 .75
82 Vladimir Guerrero Jr. .50 1.25
83 Mike Trout 1.50 4.00
84 Freddie Freeman .40 1.00
85 Bryce Harper .50 1.25
86 Pete Alonso .75 2.00
87 Juan Soto 1.00 2.50
88 Kris Bryant .40 1.00
89 Paul Goldschmidt .30 .75
90 Joey Votto .30 .75
91 Christian Yelich .40 1.00
92 Shane Bieber .30 .75
93 Cody Bellinger .60 1.50
94 Kohei Arihara RC .40 1.00
95 Walker Buehler .40 1.00
96 Fernando Tatis Jr. 1.50 4.00
97 Buster Posey .40 1.00
98 Trevor Story .30 .75
99 Ha-Seong Kim RC .75 2.00
100 Manny Machado .30 .75
101 Roger Maris SP .60 1.50
102 Stan Musial SP 1.00 2.50
103 Walter Alston SP .50 1.25
104 Yogi Berra SP .60 1.50
105 Carl Hubbell SP .50 1.25
106 Eddie Collins SP .50 1.25
107 Grover Alexander SP .50 1.25
108 Jimmie Foxx SP .50 1.25
109 Joe Wood SP .40 1.00
110 Mel Ott SP .60 1.50
111 Pee Wee Reese SP .50 1.25
112 Tris Speaker SP .50 1.25
113 Kirby Puckett SP .60 1.50
114 Al Kaline SP .60 1.50
115 Bob Gibson SP .50 1.25
116 Sandy Koufax SP 1.25 3.00
117 Tom Seaver SP .50 1.25
118 George Brett SP 2.00 5.00
119 Cal Ripken SP 2.00 5.00
120 Daulton Varsho SP RC 1.50 4.00
121 Cristian Pache SP RC 6.00 15.00
122 Tucker Davidson SP RC .60 1.50
123 Dean Kremer SP RC .75 2.00
124 Ryan Mountcastle SP RC 6.00 15.00
125 Tanner Houck SP RC 1.00 2.50
126 Dane Dunning SP RC 2.00 5.00
127 Jonathan Stiever SP RC .60 1.50
128 Nick Madrigal SP RC 5.00 12.00
129 Tyler Stephenson SP RC 3.00 8.00
130 Triston McKenzie SP RC 2.00 5.00
131 Daz Cameron SP RC .60 1.50
132 Tarik Skubal SP RC 3.00 8.00
133 Brady Singer SP RC 3.00 8.00
134 Kris Bubic SP RC 1.00 2.50
135 Jo Adell SP RC RC 4.00 10.00
136 Zach McKinstry SP RC 8.00 20.00
137 Jazz Chisholm SP RC 2.50 6.00
138 Lewin Diaz SP RC .60 1.50
139 Nick Neidert SP RC 1.00 2.50
140 Trevor Rogers SP RC 1.50 4.00
141 Brent Rooker SP RC .75 2.00
142 Travis Blankenhorn SP RC 1.25 3.00
143 David Peterson SP RC 1.25 3.00
144 Deivi Garcia SP RC 5.00 12.00
145 Daulton Jefferies SP RC .60 1.50
146 Alec Bohm SP RC 6.00 15.00
147 Rafael Marchan SP RC .75 2.00
148 Jared Oliva SP RC 1.50 4.00
149 Jake Cronenworth SP RC 4.00 10.00
150 Luis Campusano SP RC .60 1.50
151 Ryan Weathers SP RC .60 1.50
152 Evan White SP RC 4.00 10.00
153 Josh Fleming SP RC .60 1.50
154 Anderson Tejeda SP RC 1.50 4.00
155 Sam Huff SP RC 1.25 3.00
156 Alejandro Kirk SP RC 1.50 4.00
157 Luis V. Garcia SP RC 3.00 8.00
158 Kyle Lewis SP 1.50 4.00
159 Rafael Devers SP .75 2.00
160 Mookie Betts SP 1.25 3.00
161 Jose Abreu SP .60 1.50
162 Francisco Lindor SP .60 1.50
163 Matt Chapman SP .60 1.50
164 Jose Altuve SP .50 1.25
165 Shohei Ohtani SP 1.00 2.50
166 Ronald Acuna Jr. SP 2.50 6.00
167 Jacob deGrom SP 1.25 3.00
168 Max Scherzer SP .60 1.50
169 Javier Baez SP .75 2.00
170 Trevor Bauer SP 2.00 5.00

2021 Diamond Kings Artist Proof Gold

*AP GOLD 1-100: 2.5X TO 6X BASIC
*AP GOLD 1-100 RC: 1.2X TO 3X BASIC RC
*AP GOLD 101-170 SP: 1.2X TO 3X BASIC SP
*AP GOLD 101-170 SP RC: .8X TO 2X BASIC
RANDOM INSERTS IN PACKS
STATED PRINT RUN 49 SER. #'d SETS
104 Yogi Berra SP 8.00 20.00
110 Mel Ott SP 4.00 10.00

2021 Diamond Kings Aficionado

RANDOM INSERTS IN PACKS
*BLUE/99: 1.5X TO 4X BASIC
*SILVER/25: 2.5X TO 6X BASIC
1 Tris Speaker .40 1.00
2 Carl Hubbell .40 1.00
3 Hank Greenberg .50 1.25
4 Mickey Cochrane .40 1.00
5 Alex Bregman .50 1.25
6 Jose Abreu .50 1.25
7 Gerrit Cole .75 2.00
8 Vladimir Guerrero Jr. .75 2.00
9 Randy Arozarena 5.00 12.00
10 Xander Bogaerts 1.00 2.50
11 Freddie Freeman 1.25 3.00
12 Dylan Carlson 4.00 10.00
13 Nate Pearson 1.50 4.00
14 DJ LeMahieu .50 1.25
15 Anthony Rendon .50 1.25

2021 Diamond Kings Artist's Palette

RANDOM INSERTS IN PACKS
*BLUE/99: 1.5X TO 4X BASIC
*SILVER/25: 2.5X TO 6X BASIC
1 Pee Wee Reese 2.00 5.00
2 Pete Alonso 1.25 3.00
3 Juan Soto 3.00 8.00
4 Yordan Alvarez 2.00 5.00
5 Shohei Ohtani 4.00 10.00
6 Blake Snell .40 1.00
7 Kyle Lewis 3.00 8.00
8 Joey Gallo .50 1.25
9 Shane Bieber .50 1.25
10 Jo Adell 2.00 5.00
11 Joey Bart 1.00 2.50
12 Casey Mize 2.50 6.00
13 Anthony Rizzo .60 1.50
14 Charlie Blackmon .50 1.25
15 Jack Flaherty .50 1.25

2021 Diamond Kings Bat Kings

RANDOM INSERTS IN PACKS
*PURPLE/20: .8X TO 2X BASIC
1 Al Simmons
2 Alan Trammell 8.00 20.00
3 Harry Heilmann 8.00 20.00
4 Alex Rodriguez 4.00 10.00
5 Anthony Rizzo 4.00 10.00
6 Barry Larkin 4.00 10.00
7 Bill Mazeroski 6.00 15.00
8 Bob Meusel
9 Bobby Doerr 10.00 25.00
10 Charlie Keller 6.00 15.00
11 Chipper Jones 6.00 15.00
12 David Ortiz 8.00 20.00
13 Doc Cramer 3.00 8.00
14 Don Hoak 4.00 10.00
15 Giancarlo Stanton 3.00 8.00
16 Ivan Rodriguez 5.00 12.00
17 Jimmie Foxx 15.00 40.00
18 Joe Jackson
19 Tris Speaker 10.00 25.00
20 Jose Canseco 2.50 6.00
21 Keith Hernandez 15.00 40.00
22 Kris Bryant 4.00 10.00
23 Lance Berkman 2.50 6.00
24 Lou Whitaker 12.00 30.00
25 Mark McGwire 8.00 20.00
26 Miguel Cabrera 3.00 8.00
27 Mike Schmidt 12.00 30.00
28 Mike Piazza 3.00 8.00
29 Paul Molitor 10.00 25.00
30 Pee Wee Reese
31 Ralph Kiner 4.00 10.00
32 Roberto Clemente 50.00 120.00
33 Wally Pipp
34 Frank Thomas 8.00 20.00
35 Whit Merrifield 3.00 8.00

2021 Diamond Kings Bat Kings Holo Platinum Blue

*BLUE: .8X TO 2X BASIC
RANDOM INSERTS IN PACKS
STATED PRINT RUN 25 COPIES PER
1 Al Simmons 10.00 25.00
33 Wally Pipp 20.00 50.00

2021 Diamond Kings Debut Diamond Kings

*AP BLUE: 1X TO 2.5X BASIC
*BLUE: 1X TO 2.5X BASIC
*GRAY: 1X TO 2.5X BASIC
*PLUM: 1X TO 2.5X BASIC
*RED: 1X TO 2.5X BASIC
*AP GOLD/49: 1.5X TO 4X BASIC
*LITHO/25: 2.5X TO 6X BASIC
RANDOM INSERTS IN PACKS
1 Daulton Varsho .75 2.00
2 Cristian Pache 3.00 8.00
3 Ryan Mountcastle 3.00 8.00
4 Bobby Dalbec 2.50 6.00
5 Brailyn Marquez 1.50 4.00
6 Nick Madrigal 2.50 6.00
7 Tyler Stephenson 1.50 4.00
8 Triston McKenzie 1.00 2.50
9 Ryan Castellani .50 1.25
10 Casey Mize 2.50 6.00
11 Cristian Javier .75 2.00
12 Brady Singer 1.50 4.00
13 Jo Adell 2.00 5.00
14 Keibert Ruiz 1.00 2.50
15 Sixto Sanchez 1.50 4.00
16 Drew Rasmussen .50 1.25
17 Alex Kirilloff 1.25 3.00
18 Andres Gimenez .75 2.00
19 Deivi Garcia 2.50 6.00
20 Daulton Jefferies .30 .75
21 Alec Bohm 3.00 8.00
22 Ke'Bryan Hayes 3.00 8.00
23 Jake Cronenworth 3.00 8.00
24 Joey Bart 1.00 2.50
25 Evan White 2.00 5.00
26 Dylan Carlson 2.50 6.00
27 Shane McClanahan .40 1.00
28 Sam Huff .60 1.50
29 Nate Pearson 1.50 4.00
30 Luis V. Garcia 1.50 4.00

2021 Diamond Kings DK Material Signatures

RANDOM INSERTS IN PACKS
EXCHANGE DEADLINE 10/28/2022
1 Andy Young 8.00 20.00
2 Cristian Pache 20.00 50.00
3 William Contreras 12.00 30.00
4 Ryan Mountcastle 20.00 50.00
5 Brailyn Marquez 15.00 40.00
6 Jonathan Stiever 3.00 8.00
7 Jose Garcia 12.00 30.00
8 Triston McKenzie 8.00 20.00
9 Isaac Paredes 12.00 30.00
10 Brady Singer 15.00 40.00
11 Jahmai Jones 3.00 8.00
12 Zach McKinstry 15.00 40.00
13 Jesus Sanchez 10.00 25.00
14 Nick Neidert 5.00 12.00
15 Alex Kirilloff 15.00 40.00
16 Travis Blankenhorn 6.00 15.00
17 Clarke Schmidt 5.00 12.00
18 Daulton Jefferies 3.00 8.00
19 Mickey Moniak 8.00 20.00
20 Jared Oliva 8.00 20.00
21 Jorge Mateo 4.00 10.00
22 Ryan Weathers 8.00 20.00
23 Dylan Carlson 25.00 60.00
24 Anderson Tejeda 8.00 20.00
25 Sherten Apostel 10.00 25.00
26 Luis V. Garcia 15.00 40.00
27 Daulton Varsho 8.00 20.00
28 Tucker Davidson 3.00 8.00
29 Bobby Dalbec 25.00 60.00
30 Garrett Crochet 10.00 25.00
31 Tyler Stephenson 8.00 20.00
32 Daz Cameron 12.00 30.00
33 Edward Olivares 8.00 20.00
34 Keibert Ruiz 10.00 25.00
35 Lewin Diaz 3.00 8.00
36 Trevor Rogers 8.00 20.00
37 Andres Gimenez 8.00 20.00
38 Estevan Florial 5.00 12.00
39 Rafael Marchan 4.00 10.00
40 Jake Cronenworth 20.00 50.00
41 Joey Bart 15.00 40.00
42 Shane McClanahan 4.00 10.00
43 Alejandro Kirk 8.00 20.00
44 Pavin Smith 10.00 25.00
45 Keegan Akin 3.00 8.00
46 Luis Gonzalez 3.00 8.00
47 Casey Mize 25.00 60.00
48 Kris Bubic 5.00 12.00
49 Jazz Chisholm 12.00 30.00
50 Brent Rooker 4.00 10.00
51 Deivi Garcia 25.00 60.00
52 Spencer Howard 10.00 25.00
53 Luis Patino 12.00 30.00
54 Leody Taveras 10.00 25.00
55 Wil Crowe 3.00 8.00
56 Ian Anderson 15.00 40.00
57 Tanner Houck 5.00 12.00
58 Nick Madrigal 15.00 40.00
59 Tarik Skubal 6.00 15.00
60 Jo Adell EXCH 25.00 60.00
61 Monte Harrison 5.00 12.00
62 Ryan Jeffers 6.00 15.00
63 Adonis Medina 5.00 12.00
64 Ke'Bryan Hayes 20.00 50.00
65 Evan White 20.00 50.00
66 Sam Huff 6.00 15.00
67 Dean Kremer 4.00 10.00
68 Daniel Johnson 5.00 12.00
69 Braxton Garrett 3.00 8.00
70 David Peterson 6.00 15.00
71 Luis Campusano 3.00 8.00
72 Nate Pearson 8.00 20.00
73 Dane Dunning 10.00 25.00
74 Sixto Sanchez 15.00 40.00
75 Josh Fleming 3.00 8.00
76 Cristian Javier 8.00 20.00
77 Alec Bohm 30.00 80.00

2021 Diamond Kings DK Material Signatures Gold

*GOLD/99: .5X TO 1.2X BASIC
RANDOM INSERTS IN PACKS
STATED PRINT RUN 99 SER.#'d SETS
EXCHANGE DEADLINE 10/28/2022
15 Alex Kirilloff 40.00 100.00

2021 Diamond Kings DK Material Signatures Holo Platinum Blue

*BLUE/25: .6X TO 1.5X BASIC
RANDOM INSERTS IN PACKS
STATED PRINT RUN 25 SER.#'d SETS
EXCHANGE DEADLINE 10/28/2022
15 Alex Kirilloff 50.00 120.00

2021 Diamond Kings DK Material Signatures Purple

*PURPLE/20: .6X TO 1.5X BASIC
RANDOM INSERTS IN PACKS
PRINT RUNS B/WN 10-20 COPIES PER
NO PRICING ON QTY 15 OR LESS
EXCHANGE DEADLINE 10/28/2022
15 Alex Kirilloff/20 50.00 120.00

2021 Diamond Kings DK Materials

RANDOM INSERTS IN PACKS
*BLUE/25: .8X TO 2X BASIC
1 Andy Young 5.00 12.00
2 Cristian Pache 10.00 25.00
3 William Contreras 2.50 6.00
4 Ryan Mountcastle 20.00 50.00
5 Brailyn Marquez 2.50 6.00
6 Jonathan Stiever 2.00 5.00
7 Jose Garcia 8.00 20.00
8 Triston McKenzie 4.00 10.00
9 Isaac Paredes 8.00 20.00
10 Brady Singer 10.00 25.00
11 Jahmai Jones 2.00 5.00
12 Zach McKinstry 10.00 25.00
13 Jesus Sanchez 6.00 15.00
14 Nick Neidert 3.00 8.00
15 Alex Kirilloff 8.00 20.00
16 Travis Blankenhorn 4.00 10.00
17 Clarke Schmidt 3.00 8.00
18 Daulton Jefferies 2.00 5.00
19 Mickey Moniak 5.00 12.00
20 Jared Oliva 5.00 12.00
21 Jorge Mateo 2.50 6.00
22 Ryan Weathers 2.00 5.00
23 Dylan Carlson 15.00 40.00
24 Anderson Tejeda 5.00 12.00
25 Sherten Apostel 6.00 15.00
26 Luis V. Garcia 10.00 25.00
27 Daulton Varsho 5.00 12.00
28 Tucker Davidson 2.00 5.00
29 Bobby Dalbec 6.00 15.00
30 Garrett Crochet 3.00 8.00
31 Tyler Stephenson 4.00 10.00
32 Daz Cameron 2.00 5.00
33 Edward Olivares 5.00 12.00
34 Keibert Ruiz 6.00 15.00
35 Lewin Diaz 2.00 5.00
36 Trevor Rogers 5.00 12.00
37 Andres Gimenez 5.00 12.00
38 Estevan Florial 8.00 20.00
39 Rafael Marchan 2.50 6.00
40 Jake Cronenworth 12.00 30.00
41 Joey Bart 2.50 6.00
42 Shane McClanahan 2.50 6.00
43 Alejandro Kirk 5.00 12.00
44 Pavin Smith 3.00 8.00
45 Keegan Akin 2.00 5.00
46 Luis Gonzalez 2.00 5.00
47 Casey Mize 15.00 40.00
48 Kris Bubic 3.00 8.00
49 Jazz Chisholm 8.00 20.00
50 Brent Rooker 2.50 6.00
51 Deivi Garcia 15.00 40.00
52 Spencer Howard 6.00 15.00
53 Luis Patino 8.00 20.00
54 Leody Taveras 6.00 15.00
55 Wil Crowe 2.00 5.00
56 Ian Anderson 8.00 20.00
57 Tanner Houck 3.00 8.00
58 Nick Madrigal 15.00 40.00
59 Tarik Skubal 10.00 25.00
60 Jo Adell 12.00 30.00
61 Monte Harrison 3.00 8.00
62 Ryan Jeffers 4.00 10.00
63 Adonis Medina 3.00 8.00
64 Ke'Bryan Hayes 20.00 50.00
65 Evan White 12.00 30.00
66 Sam Huff 2.00 5.00
67 Dean Kremer 2.50 6.00
68 Daniel Johnson 3.00 8.00
69 Braxton Garrett 2.00 5.00
70 David Peterson 4.00 10.00
71 Luis Campusano 2.00 5.00
72 Nate Pearson 6.00 15.00
73 Dane Dunning 6.00 15.00
74 Sixto Sanchez 10.00 25.00
75 Josh Fleming 2.00 5.00
76 Cristian Javier 5.00 12.00
77 Alec Bohm 20.00 50.00
78 Aaron Judge 8.00 20.00
79 Babe Ruth
80 Greg Maddux 8.00 20.00
81 Ronald Acuna Jr. 12.00 30.00
82 Brandon Woodruff 3.00 8.00
83 Brian Anderson 2.00 5.00
84 Clint Frazier 2.50 6.00
85 Dakota Hudson 2.50 6.00
86 Erick Fedde 2.00 5.00
87 Jesse Winker 3.00 8.00
88 Kyle Tucker 3.00 8.00
89 Mike Trout 15.00 40.00
90 Joe Cronin 10.00 25.00
91 Harvey Kuenn 5.00 12.00
92 Heinie Groh 2.00 5.00
93 Ozzie Albies 6.00 15.00
94 Pablo Sandoval 2.50 6.00
95 Roberto Alomar 2.50 6.00
96 Stan Musial 12.00 30.00
97 Eloy Jimenez 3.00 8.00
98 Kyle Lewis 8.00 20.00
99 Yordan Alvarez 8.00 20.00
100 Tim Raines 2.50 6.00

2021 Diamond Kings DK Materials Holo Gold

*GOLD/50: .6X TO 1.5X BASIC
*GOLD/25: .8X TO 2X BASIC
RANDOM INSERTS IN PACKS
PRINT RUNS B/WN 5-50 COPIES PER
89 Mike Trout/25 50.00 120.00

2021 Diamond Kings DK Materials Holo Silver

*SILVER/99: .5X TO 1.2X BASIC
*SILVER/50: .6X TO 1.5X BASIC
*SILVER/25: .8X TO 2X BASIC
RANDOM INSERTS IN PACKS
PRINT RUNS B/WN 7-99 COPIES PER
89 Mike Trout/50 40.00 100.00

2021 Diamond Kings DK Quad Material Signatures

RANDOM INSERTS IN PACKS
EXCHANGE DEADLINE 10/28/2022
*GOLD/99: .5X TO 1.2X BASIC
*GOLD/20-25: .6X TO 1.5X BASIC
1 Mike Schmidt
2 Will Clark
3 Adrian Beltre
4 Robin Yount
5 Sammy Sosa
6 Dale Murphy
7 Eddie Murray
8 Luis Aparicio
9 Miguel Tejada
10 Tom Glavine
11 Brendan McKay 4.00 10.00
12 Rhys Hoskins
13 Jeff Bagwell 30.00 80.00

2021 Diamond Kings DK Quad Material Signatures Holo Platinum Blue

*BLUE/25: .6X TO 1.5X BASIC
RANDOM INSERTS IN PACKS
PRINT RUNS B/WN 5-25 COPIES PER
NO PRICING ON QTY 15 OR LESS
EXCHANGE DEADLINE 10/28/2022
11 Brendan McKay/25 10.00 25.00

2021 Diamond Kings DK Quad Materials

RANDOM INSERTS IN PACKS
*BLUE/25: .8X TO 2X BASIC
1 Albert Pujols 8.00 20.00
2 Andrew Benintendi 3.00 8.00
3 Lou Gehrig
4 Jim Thome
5 Mickey Mantle
6 Rogers Hornsby
7 Yu Darvish 3.00 8.00
8 Christian Yelich 4.00 10.00
9 Charlie Blackmon 3.00 8.00
10 Corbin Burnes 3.00 8.00
11 Forrest Whitley 3.00 8.00
12 Hoyt Wilhelm
13 Ivan Rodriguez 2.50 6.00
14 Kevin Kiermaier 2.50 6.00
15 Kolten Wong 2.50 6.00
16 Greg Maddux 10.00 25.00
17 Michael Conforto 2.50 6.00
18 Miguel Cabrera 6.00 15.00
19 Mike Piazza 3.00 8.00
20 Pablo Sandoval 2.50 6.00
21 Phil Niekro 6.00 15.00
22 Ramon Laureano 2.50 6.00
23 Rickey Henderson 10.00 25.00
24 Rougned Odor 2.50 6.00
25 Tony Gwynn 8.00 20.00
26 Victor Robles 4.00 10.00
27 Isan Diaz 3.00 8.00
28 Jose Berrios 2.50 6.00
29 Raisel Iglesias 2.00 5.00
30 Tim Anderson 3.00 8.00

2021 Diamond Kings DK Signatures
*SILVER/99: .5X TO 1.2X BASIC
*GOLD/50: .6X TO 1.5X BASIC
*BLUE/25: .8X TO 2X BASIC
*PURPLE/20: .8X TO 2X BASIC
RANDOM INSERTS IN PACKS
EXCHANGE DEADLINE 10/28/2022
1 Andy Young 6.00 15.00
2 Alec Bohm 25.00 60.00
3 William Contreras 5.00 12.00
4 Josh Fleming 2.50 6.00
5 Brailyn Marquez 12.00 30.00
6 Dane Dunning 8.00 20.00
7 Triston McKenzie 8.00 20.00
8 Luis Campusano 2.50 6.00
9 Brady Singer 12.00 30.00
10 Daniel Johnson 4.00 10.00
11 Zach McKinstry 20.00 50.00
12 Jesus Sanchez 8.00 20.00
13 Alex Kirilloff 25.00 60.00
14 Clarke Schmidt 4.00 10.00
15 Daulton Jefferies 2.50 6.00
16 Mickey Moniak 6.00 15.00
17 Jared Oliva 6.00 15.00
18 Jorge Mateo 3.00 8.00
19 Ryan Weathers 2.50 6.00
20 Sam Huff 5.00 12.00
21 Luis V. Garcia 12.00 30.00
22 Ke'Bryan Hayes 20.00 50.00
23 Bobby Dalbec 20.00 50.00
24 Jo Adell EXCH 15.00 40.00
25 Tyler Stephenson 12.00 30.00
26 Nick Madrigal 15.00 40.00
27 Edward Olivares 6.00 15.00
28 Ian Anderson 15.00 40.00
29 Lewin Diaz 2.50 6.00
30 Leody Taveras 8.00 20.00
31 Estevan Florial 15.00 40.00
32 Jake Cronenworth 15.00 40.00
33 Joey Bart 8.00 20.00
34 Shane McClanahan 3.00 8.00
35 Alejandro Kirk 6.00 15.00
36 Casey Mize 20.00 50.00
37 Jazz Chisholm 10.00 25.00
38 Deivi Garcia 20.00 50.00
39 Spencer Howard 8.00 20.00
40 Dylan Carlson 20.00 50.00
41 Wil Crowe 2.50 6.00
42 Daulton Varsho 6.00 15.00
43 Tanner Houck 4.00 10.00
44 Garrett Crochet 4.00 10.00
45 Tarik Skubal 12.00 30.00
46 Daz Cameron 12.00 30.00
47 Ryan Jeffers 5.00 12.00
48 Keibert Ruiz 8.00 20.00
49 Evan White 15.00 40.00
50 Andres Gimenez 6.00 15.00
51 Kohei Arihara 2.50 6.00
52 Ha-Seong Kim 5.00 12.00
53 David Peterson 5.00 12.00
54 Isaac Paredes 10.00 25.00
55 Nate Pearson 12.00 30.00
56 Jose Garcia 10.00 25.00
57 Sixto Sanchez 12.00 30.00
58 Ryan Mountcastle 25.00 60.00
59 Cristian Javier 6.00 15.00
60 Cristian Pache 25.00 60.00

2021 Diamond Kings Downtown
RANDOM INSERTS IN PACKS
1 Kris Bryant 50.00 120.00
2 Fernando Tatis Jr. 200.00 500.00
3 Mookie Betts 75.00 200.00
4 Mike Trout 250.00 600.00
5 Christian Yelich 30.00 80.00
6 Bryce Harper 50.00 120.00
7 Ronald Acuna Jr. 150.00 400.00
8 Juan Soto 125.00 300.00
9 Bo Bichette 100.00 250.00
10 Pete Alonso 60.00 150.00
11 Manny Machado 50.00 120.00
12 Jo Adell 50.00 120.00
13 Dylan Carlson 75.00 200.00
14 Cristian Pache 60.00 150.00
15 Joey Bart 40.00 100.00
16 Nick Madrigal 30.00 80.00
17 Francisco Lindor 50.00 120.00
18 Jose Altuve 40.00 100.00
19 Miguel Cabrera 75.00 200.00
20 Cody Bellinger 50.00 120.00

2021 Diamond Kings Elegance
RANDOM INSERTS IN PACKS
1 Nolan Arenado 2.00 5.00
2 Mickey Mantle 3.00 8.00
3 Jackie Robinson .50 1.25
4 Tim Anderson .50 1.25
5 Carlos Correa .50 1.25
6 Trea Turner .40 1.00
7 Manny Machado 2.00 5.00
8 Mookie Betts 2.00 5.00
9 Bo Bichette 1.25 3.00
10 Cristian Pache 3.00 8.00

2021 Diamond Kings Elegance Holo Blue
*BLUE: 1.5X TO 4X BASIC
RANDOM INSERTS IN PACKS
STATED PRINT RUN 99 COPIES PER
8 Mookie Betts 10.00 25.00

2021 Diamond Kings Elegance Holo Silver
*SILVER: 2.5X TO 6X BASIC
RANDOM INSERTS IN PACKS
STATED PRINT RUN 25 COPIES PER
8 Mookie Betts 15.00 40.00

2021 Diamond Kings Gallery of Stars
RANDOM INSERTS IN PACKS
1 Aaron Judge 1.25 3.00
2 Christy Mathewson .50 1.25
3 Satchel Paige .50 1.25
4 Honus Wagner .50 1.25
5 Jimmie Foxx .40 1.00
6 Lou Gehrig 2.00 5.00
7 Roger Maris .50 1.25
8 Francisco Lindor .50 1.25
9 Mike Trout 3.00 8.00
10 Ronald Acuna Jr. 2.00 5.00
11 Bryce Harper 2.00 5.00
12 Kris Bryant .60 1.50
13 Mookie Betts 1.00 2.50
14 Fernando Tatis Jr. 3.00 8.00
15 Christian Yelich .60 1.50

2021 Diamond Kings Gallery of Stars Holo Blue
*BLUE: 1.5X TO 4X BASIC
RANDOM INSERTS IN PACKS
STATED PRINT RUN 99 COPIES PER
13 Mookie Betts 8.00 20.00

2021 Diamond Kings Gallery of Stars Holo Silver
*SILVER: 2.5X TO 6X BASIC
RANDOM INSERTS IN PACKS
STATED PRINT RUN 25 COPIES PER
13 Mookie Betts 12.00 30.00

2021 Diamond Kings Jersey Kings
RANDOM INSERTS IN PACKS
1 Adam Wainwright 2.50 6.00
2 Al Kaline 8.00 20.00
3 Andrew McCutchen 3.00 8.00
4 Ken Griffey Jr.
5 Willie Stargell 6.00 15.00
6 Yadier Molina 6.00 15.00
7 Bob Lemon
8 Brandon Lowe 2.50 6.00
9 Buster Posey 4.00 10.00
10 Cal Ripken
11 Catfish Hunter
12 Sandy Koufax
13 Chris Sale 5.00 12.00
14 Clayton Kershaw 10.00 25.00
15 Curt Schilling 4.00 10.00
16 David Wright 2.50 6.00
17 Duke Snider
18 Dwight Gooden 2.00 5.00
19 Earl Weaver 5.00 12.00
20 Eduardo Rodriguez 2.00 5.00
21 Fernando Tatis Jr. 12.00 30.00
22 Frankie Frisch
23 A.J. Puk 3.00 8.00
24 Gary Carter 8.00 20.00
25 George Brett
26 Harold Baines 2.50 6.00
27 Randy Arozarena 5.00 121.00
28 Joe Torre 2.50 6.00
29 Joey Gallo 3.00 8.00
30 Jose Abreu 3.00 8.00
31 Kirby Puckett 12.00 30.00
32 Mariano Rivera 6.00 15.00
33 Randy Johnson
34 Rod Carew 5.00 12.00
35 Ryne Sandberg 10.00 25.00

2021 Diamond Kings Jersey Kings Holo Platinum Blue
*BLUE: .8X TO 2X BASIC
RANDOM INSERTS IN PACKS
STATED PRINT RUN 25 COPIES PER
4 Ken Griffey Jr. 20.00 50.00
7 Bob Lemon 12.00 30.00
22 Frankie Frisch 8.00 20.00

2021 Diamond Kings Legacy Lithographs
RANDOM INSERTS IN PACKS
*BLUE/99: 1.5X TO 4X BASIC
*SILVER/25: 2.5X TO 6X BASIC
1 Lou Gehrig 1.00 2.50
2 Joe DiMaggio 1.00 2.50
3 Mike Schmidt .75 2.00
4 Rogers Hornsby .40 1.00
5 Randy Johnson .50 1.25
6 Ozzie Smith .60 1.50
7 Johnny Bench .50 1.25
8 Trevor Hoffman .40 1.00
9 Buster Posey .60 1.50
10 Clayton Kershaw .75 2.00
11 Rickey Henderson .50 1.25
12 Eddie Mathews .50 1.25
13 Reggie Jackson .40 1.00
14 Vladimir Guerrero .40 1.00
15 George Sisler .30 .75
16 Joe Wood .30 .75
17 Walter Johnson .50 1.25
18 David Ortiz .50 1.25
19 Yogi Berra .50 1.25
20 Mike Piazza .50 1.25

2021 Diamond Kings Litho Proof
*LITHO 1-100: 4X TO 10X BASIC
*LITHO 1-100 RC: 2X TO 5X BASIC RC
*LITHO 101-170 SP: 2X TO 5X BASIC SP
*LITHO 101-170 SP RC: 1.2X TO 3X BASIC
RANDOM INSERTS IN PACKS
STATED PRINT RUN 25 SER. #'d SETS
104 Yogi Berra SP 12.00 30.00
110 Mel Ott SP 6.00 15.00

2021 Diamond Kings Signature Portraits
*SILVER/99: .5X TO 1.2X BASIC
*SILVER/25: .8X TO 2X BASIC
*GOLD/49: .6X TO 1.5X BASIC
*BLUE/25: .8X TO 2X BASIC
*PURPLE/20: .8X TO 2X BASIC
RANDOM INSERTS IN PACKS
EXCHANGE DEADLINE 10/28/2022
1 Tommy Lasorda
2 Willie McCovey
3 Bob Gibson
4 Orlando Cepeda
5 Bud Selig
6 Nolan Ryan
7 Cal Ripken
8 Ken Griffey Jr.
9 Roger Clemens
10 Wade Boggs
11 Sandy Koufax
12 Ryne Sandberg
13 Fernando Tatis Jr. 60.00 150.00
14 Andrew McCutchen
15 Pete Alonso
16 Rafael Palmeiro
17 Lance Berkman
18 Bill Mazeroski
19 Josh Donaldson
20 Goose Gossage

2021 Diamond Kings Signed Lithographs
*SILVER/99: .5X TO 1.2X BASIC
*SILVER/25: .8X TO 2X BASIC
*GOLD/50: .6X TO 1.5X BASIC
*BLUE/25: .8X TO 2X BASIC
*PURPLE/20: .8X TO 2X BASIC
RANDOM INSERTS IN PACKS
EXCHANGE DEADLINE 10/28/2022
1 Dave Winfield
2 Phil Niekro
3 Juan Marichal
4 Mike Piazza
5 Fergie Jenkins
6 Trevor Hoffman
7 Brooks Robinson
8 Ozzie Smith
9 Aaron Judge 60.00 150.00
10 Sammy Sosa
11 David Ortiz 20.00 50.00
12 Vladimir Guerrero Jr.
13 Nolan Arenado
14 Alex Bregman
15 Juan Soto
16 Bartolo Colon
17 Kyle Lewis 10.00 25.00
18 Clayton Kershaw
19 Randy Johnson
20 Rickey Henderson

2021 Diamond Kings The Art of Hitting
RANDOM INSERTS IN PACKS
*BLUE/99: 1.5X TO 4X BASIC
*SILVER/25: 2.5X TO 6X BASIC
1 Ted Williams 1.00 2.50
2 Joe Jackson 2.00 5.00
3 Ty Cobb .75 2.00
4 Stan Musial .75 2.00
5 Mel Ott .50 1.25
6 Tony Gwynn 4.00 10.00
7 Miguel Cabrera .50 1.25
8 Albert Pujols 2.00 5.00
9 Jose Altuve .40 1.00
10 Ichiro .60 1.50

2021 Diamond Kings The Club
RANDOM INSERTS IN PACKS
*BLUE/99: 1.5X TO 4X BASIC
*SILVER/25: 2.5X TO 6X BASIC
1 Babe Ruth 2.00 5.00
2 Alex Rodriguez 2.00 5.00
3 Ken Griffey Jr. 2.50 6.00
4 Harmon Killebrew 2.00 5.00
5 Mark McGwire .75 2.00
6 Sammy Sosa .50 1.25
7 Jim Thome .40 1.00
8 Rod Carew 2.00 5.00
9 Ichiro .60 1.50
10 Cal Ripken 3.00 8.00
11 Pete Rose 4.00 10.00
12 Greg Maddux .60 1.50
13 Nolan Ryan 1.50 4.00
14 Justin Verlander .50 1.25
15 Albert Pujols 1.50 4.00

1993 Diamond Marks Prototypes
This eight-bookmark prototype set was a collaboration of Barry Colla and Terry Smith. It was produced to gain approval from MLB, and reportedly less than 600 of each card was printed. Dealers who responded to the initial promotional offer from Card Collectors Co., the principal distributor, were given one prototype card with their order. The bookmarks measure approximately 2 1/2" by 5" and feature black-bordered color player shots, some action, others posed, on their fronts. The backs also state "1993 Prototype." The bookmarks are unnumbered and checklisted below in alphabetical order.
COMPLETE SET (8) 75.00 150.00
1 Roberto Alomar 6.00 15.00
2 Will Clark 8.00 20.00
3 Dennis Eckersley 6.00 15.00
4 Juan Gonzalez 6.00 15.00
5 Ken Griffey Jr. 15.00 40.00
6 Kirby Puckett 12.50 30.00
7 Ryne Sandberg 10.00 25.00
8 Frank Thomas 8.00 20.00

1993 Diamond Marks
This 120-card bookmark set was a collaboration of Barry Colla and Terry Smith. Ten bookmarks and an ad card came in each cello pack. A total production run of only 2,500 cases were produced, and no factory sets were issued. The bookmarks measure approximately 2 1/2" by 5" and feature black-bordered color player shots, some action. others posed, on their fronts. The bookmarks are unnumbered and checklisted below in alphabetical order.
COMPLETE SET (120) 8.00 20.00
1 Roberto Alomar .40 1.00
2 Sandy Alomar Jr. .20 .50
3 Moises Alou .20 .50
4 Brady Anderson .20 .50
5 Steve Avery .08 .25
6 Carlos Baerga .08 .25
7 Jeff Bagwell .50 1.25
8 Derek Bell .08 .25
9 Jay Bell .08 .25
10 Albert Belle .20 .50
11 Dante Bichette .20 .50
12 Craig Biggio .30 .75
13 Wade Boggs .50 1.25
14 Barry Bonds 1.00 2.50
15 Bobby Bonilla .08 .25
16 Pat Borders .08 .25
17 Daryl Boston .08 .25
18 George Brett 1.00 2.50
19 John Burkett .08 .25
20 Brett Butler .20 .50
21 Ken Caminiti .30 .75
22 Jose Canseco .50 1.25
23 Joe Carter .20 .50
24 Will Clark .40 1.00
25 Roger Clemens 1.00 2.50
26 Chad Curtis .08 .25
27 Darren Daulton .20 .50
28 Eric Davis .20 .50
29 Andre Dawson .30 .75
30 Delino DeShields .08 .25
31 Orestes Destrade .08 .25
32 Gary DiSarcina .08 .25
33 Len Dykstra .20 .50
34 Dennis Eckersley .50 1.25
35 Cecil Fielder .20 .50
36 Andres Galarraga .30 .75
37 Ron Gant .20 .50
38 Tom Glavine .40 1.00
39 Luis Gonzalez .40 1.00
40 Juan Gonzalez .40 1.00
41 Dwight Gooden .20 .50
42 Mark Grace .30 .75
43 Mike Greenwell .08 .25
44 Ken Griffey Jr. 1.25 3.00
45 Marquis Grissom .20 .50
46 Juan Guzman .08 .25
47 Tony Gwynn 1.00 2.50
48 Darryl Hamilton .08 .25
49 Charlie Hayes .08 .25
50 Rickey Henderson .50 1.25
51 Orel Hershiser .20 .50
52 Dave Hollins .08 .25
53 Kent Hrbek .20 .50
54 Bo Jackson .40 1.00
55 Gregg Jefferies .08 .25
56 Howard Johnson .08 .25
57 Wally Joyner .20 .50
58 David Justice .30 .75
59 Eric Karros .30 .75
60 Roberto Kelly .08 .25
61 Chuck Knoblauch .20 .50
62 John Kruk .20 .50
63 Barry Larkin .40 1.00
64 Pat Listach .08 .25
65 Kenny Lofton .30 .75
66 Mike Macfarlane .08 .25
67 Al Martin .08 .25
68 Dennis Martinez .20 .50
69 Edgar Martinez .20 .50
70 Ramon Martinez .08 .25
71 Don Mattingly 1.00 2.50
72 Fred McGriff .30 .75
73 Mark McGwire 1.00 2.50
74 Brian McRae .08 .25
75 Orlando Merced .08 .25
76 Kevin Mitchell .20 .50
77 Paul Molitor .50 1.25
78 Eddie Murray .50 1.25
79 Mike Mussina .40 1.00
80 Randy Myers .08 .25
81 Pete O'Brien .08 .25
82 John Olerud .20 .50
83 Tom Pagnozzi .08 .25
84 Terry Pendleton .08 .25
85 Tony Phillips .08 .25
86 Mike Piazza 1.25 3.00
87 Kirby Puckett .50 1.25
88 Jose Rijo .08 .25
89 Cal Ripken 2.00 5.00
90 Ivan Rodriguez .50 1.25
91 Nolan Ryan 2.00 5.00
92 Tim Salmon .40 1.00
93 Ryne Sandberg .75 2.00
94 Deion Sanders .30 .75
95 Reggie Sanders .20 .50
96 Benito Santiago .20 .50
97 Gary Sheffield .50 1.25
98 Ruben Sierra .20 .50
99 Ozzie Smith 1.00 2.50
100 John Smoltz .40 1.00
101 J.T. Snow .40 1.00
102 Terry Steinbach .08 .25
103 Dave Stewart .20 .50
104 Darryl Strawberry .20 .50
105 B.J. Surhoff .20 .50
106 Danny Tartabull .08 .25
107 Mickey Tettleton .08 .25
108 Frank Thomas .50 1.25
109 Alan Trammell .40 1.00
110 David Valle .08 .25
111 Andy Van Slyke .08 .25
112 Mo Vaughn .20 .50
113 Robin Ventura .30 .75
114 Jose Vizcaino .08 .25
115 Larry Walker .40 1.00
116 Walt Weiss .08 .25
117 Matt Williams .30 .75
118 Dave Winfield .50 1.25
119 Robin Yount .50 1.25
120 Todd Zeile .08 .25

1993 Diamond Marks Art
Complimenting the 120-card bookmark set, this eight-bookmark art card set was a collaboration of Barry Colla and Terry Smith. One of the special art cards is included in each 48-pack carton. The bookmark art cards measure approximately 2 1/2" by 5" and feature black-bordered fanciful color player paintings by Terry Smith on their fronts. The bookmarks are unnumbered and checklisted below in alphabetical order. There are reports in the hobby that no more than 3,000 of each card were produced.
COMPLETE SET (8) 75.00 150.00
1 Roberto Alomar 4.00 10.00
2 Barry Bonds 10.00 25.00
3 Ken Griffey Jr. 12.50 30.00
4 David Justice 2.50 6.00
5 John Olerud 2.00 5.00
6 Nolan Ryan 20.00 50.00
7 Frank Thomas 4.00 10.00
8 Robin Yount 6.00 15.00

1934 Diamond Match Co. Silver Border
Issued in 1934, the 200-cover Silver-Bordered set includes many of the day's premier ballplayers. Each cover features four different background colors, red, green, blue and orange. Charlie Grimm is shown in two different poses. Players are listed in alphabetical order. All color variations are equally valued. The complete set price includes both Grimm covers. Complete matchbooks can sell for 60 to 100 percent higher.
COMPLETE SET (200) 1500.00 3000.00
1 Earl Adams 6.00 15.00
2 Ethan Allen 6.00 15.00
3 Eldon Auker 6.00 15.00
4 Del Baker 6.00 15.00
5 Dick Bartell 6.00 15.00
6 Walter Beck 6.00 15.00
7 Herman Bell 6.00 15.00
8 Ray Benge 6.00 15.00
9 Larry Benton 6.00 15.00
10 Louis Berger 6.00 15.00
11 Wally Berger 8.00 20.00
12 Ray Berres 6.00 15.00
13 Charlie Berry 6.00 15.00
14 Walter Betts 20.00 50.00
15 Ralph Birkofer 6.00 15.00
16 George Blaeholder 6.00 15.00
17 Jim Bottomley 6.00 15.00
18 Ralph Boyle 6.00 15.00
19 Ed Brandt 6.00 15.00
20 Don Brennan 6.00 15.00
21 Jack Burns 6.00 15.00
22 Guy Bush 6.00 15.00
23 Dolph Camilli 8.00 20.00
24 Ben Cantwell 6.00 15.00
25 Tex Carleton 6.00 15.00
26 Owen Carroll 6.00 15.00
27 Louis Chiozza 6.00 15.00
28 Watson Clark 6.00 15.00
29 James A. Collins 8.00 20.00
30 Phil Collins 6.00 15.00
31 Edward Connolly 6.00 15.00
32 Raymond Coombs 6.00 15.00
33 Roger Doc Cramer 8.00 20.00
34 Cliff Crawford 6.00 15.00
35 Hugh Critz 6.00 15.00
36 General Crowder 6.00 15.00
37 Tony Cuccinello 6.00 15.00
38 Kiki Cuyler 20.00 50.00
39 Virgil Davis 6.00 15.00
40 Dizzy Dean 12.50 30.00
41 Paul Dean 12.50 30.00
42 Edward Delker 6.00 15.00
43 Paul Derringer 12.50 30.00
44 Gene DeSautel 6.00 15.00
45 Bill Dietrich 6.00 15.00
46 Frank F. Doljack 6.00 15.00
47 Edward Durham 6.00 15.00
48 Leo Durocher 10.00 25.00
49 Jim Elliott 6.00 15.00
50 Woody English 6.00 15.00
51 Woody English 6.00 15.00
52 Rick Ferrell 12.50 30.00
53 Wes Ferrell 10.00 25.00
54 Charles Fischer 6.00 15.00
55 Freddy Fitzsimmons 8.00 20.00
56 Lew Fonseca 8.00 20.00
57 Fred Frankhouse 6.00 15.00
58 John Frederick 6.00 15.00
59 Benny Frey 6.00 15.00
60 Linus Frey 6.00 15.00
61 Frankie Frisch 15.00 40.00
62 Chick Fullis 6.00 15.00
63 Augie Galan 6.00 15.00
64 Milton Galatzer 6.00 15.00
65 Dennis Galehouse 6.00 15.00
66 Milton Gaston 6.00 15.00
67 Charlie Gehringer 20.00 50.00
68 Edward Gharrity 6.00 15.00
69 George Gibson 6.00 15.00
70 Isidore Goldstein 75.00 150.00
71 Hank Gowdy 6.00 15.00
72 Earl Grace 6.00 15.00
73 Charlie Grimm 12.50 30.00
74 Charlie Grimm 12.50 30.00
75 Frank Grube 6.00 15.00
76 Richard Gyselman 6.00 15.00
77 Stan Hack 6.00 15.00
78 Bump Hadley 6.00 15.00
79 Chick Hafey 6.00 15.00
80 Harold Haid 6.00 15.00
81 Jesse Haines 6.00 15.00
82 Odell Hale 6.00 15.00
83 Bill Hallahan 6.00 15.00
84 Luke Hamlin 6.00 15.00
85 Roy Hansen 6.00 15.00
86 Mel Harder 8.00 20.00
87 William Harris 6.00 15.00
88 Gabby Hartnett 12.50 30.00
89 Harvey Hendrick 6.00 15.00
90 Babe Herman 8.00 20.00
91 Billy Herman 10.00 25.00
92 Shanty Hogan 6.00 15.00
93 Chief Hogsett 6.00 15.00
94 Waite Hoyt 20.00 50.00
95 Carl Hubbell 30.00 60.00
96 Si Johnson 6.00 15.00
97 Syl Johnson 6.00 15.00
98 Roy Joiner 6.00 15.00
99 Baxter Jordan 6.00 15.00
100 Arndt Jorgens 6.00 15.00
101 Billy Jurges 8.00 20.00
102 Vern Kennedy 6.00 15.00
103 John Kerr 6.00 15.00
104 Chuck Klein 10.00 25.00
105 Ted Kleinhans 6.00 15.00
106 Bill Klem UMP 12.50 30.00
107 Robert Kline 6.00 15.00
108 William Knickerbocker 6.00 15.00
109 Jack Knott 6.00 15.00
110 Mark Koenig 8.00 20.00
111 William Lawrence 6.00 15.00
112 Thornton Lee 6.00 15.00
113 Bill Lee 6.00 15.00
114 Dutch Leonard 6.00 15.00
115 Ernie Lombardi 30.00 60.00
116 Al Lopez 20.00 50.00
117 Red Lucas 6.00 15.00
118 Ted Lyons 8.00 20.00
119 Daniel MacFayden 6.00 15.00
120 Ed. Majeski 6.00 15.00
121 Leroy Mahaffey 6.00 15.00
122 Pat Malone 6.00 15.00
123 Leo Mangum 6.00 15.00
124 Rabbit Maranville 12.50 30.00
125 Charles Marrow 6.00 15.00
126 Bill McKechnie MG 12.50 30.00
127 Justin McLaughlin 6.00 15.00
128 Marty McManus 6.00 15.00
129 Eric McNair 6.00 15.00
130 Joe Medwick 12.50 30.00
131 Jim Mooney 6.00 15.00
132 Joe Moore 6.00 15.00
133 John Moore 6.00 15.00
134 Randy Moore 6.00 15.00
135 Joe Morrisey 6.00 15.00
136 Joseph Mowrey 6.00 15.00
137 Fred Muller 6.00 15.00
138 Van Lingle Mungo 10.00 25.00
139 Glenn Myatt 6.00 15.00
140 Lynn Nelson 6.00 15.00
141 Prince Oana 30.00 60.00
142 Lefty O'Doul 12.50 30.00
143 Robert O'Farrell 6.00 15.00
144 Ernest Orsatti 6.00 15.00
145 Fritz Ostermueller 6.00 15.00
146 Mel Ott 12.50 30.00
147 Roy Parmelee 6.00 15.00
148 Ralph Perkins 6.00 15.00
149 Frank Pytlak 6.00 15.00
150 Ernest Quigley 6.00 15.00
151 George Rensa 6.00 15.00
152 Harry Rice 6.00 15.00
153 Walter Roettger 8.00 20.00
154 William Rogell 6.00 15.00
155 Edwin Rommel 6.00 15.00
156 Charlie Root 4.00 10.00
157 John Rothrock 6.00 15.00
158 Jack Russell 6.00 15.00
159 Blondy Ryan 6.00 15.00
160 Al Schacht CO 8.00 20.00
161 Wes Schultmerick 6.00 15.00
162 Rip Sewell 6.00 15.00
163 Gordon Slade 6.00 15.00
164 Bob Smith 6.00 15.00
165 Moose Solters 6.00 15.00
166 Glenn Spencer 6.00 15.00
167 Al Spohrer 6.00 15.00
168 George Stainback 8.00 20.00
169 Dolly Stark 12.50 30.00
170 Casey Stengel MG 30.00 60.00
171 Riggs Stephenson 12.50 30.00
172 Walter Stewart 6.00 15.00
173 Lin Storti 6.00 15.00
174 Allyn Stout 6.00 15.00
175 Joe Stripp 6.00 15.00
176 Gus Suhr 8.00 20.00
177 Billy Sullivan Jr. 6.00 15.00
178 Benny Tate 6.00 15.00
179 Danny Taylor 6.00 15.00
180 Tommy Thevenow 6.00 15.00
181 Bud Tinning 6.00 15.00
182 Cecil Travis 6.00 15.00
183 Forest Twogood 6.00 15.00
184 Bill Urbanski 6.00 15.00
185 Dazzy Vance 12.50 30.00
186 Arthur Veltman 6.00 15.00
187 John Vergez 6.00 15.00
188 Gee Walker 6.00 15.00
189 Bill Walker 8.00 20.00
190 Lloyd Waner 10.00 25.00
191 Paul Waner 10.00 25.00
192 Lon Warneke 8.00 20.00
193 Rabbit Warstler 6.00 15.00
194 Bill Werber 8.00 20.00
195 Jo Jo White 6.00 15.00
196 Pinky Whitney 6.00 15.00
197 Jimmy Wilson 6.00 15.00
198 Hack Wilson 75.00 150.00
199 Ralph Winegarner 6.00 15.00
200 Thomas Zachary 8.00 20.00

1935 Diamond Match Co. Series 2
The Second baseball set was issued circa 1935 by the Diamond Match Company. Each cover in the 24-cover set features a black border on the front and a brief player biography on the reverse. Covers are either green, red or blue in color. A crossed-bat design appears on the front-side of each cover. Players are listed in alphabetical order. Complete matchbooks are valued at fifty percent higher.
COMPLETE SET (24) 750.00 1500.00
1 Ethan Allen (red) 30.00 60.00
2 Wally Berger (red) 30.00 60.00
3 Tommy Carey (blue) 20.00 40.00
4 Louis Chiozza (blue) 20.00 40.00
5 Dizzy Dean (green) 75.00 150.00
6 Frankie Frisch (red) 50.00 100.00
7 Charlie Grimm (blue) 40.00 80.00
8 Chick Hafey (red) 40.00 80.00
9 Francis Hogan (red) 20.00 40.00
10 Carl Hubbell (green) 50.00 100.00
11 Chuck Klein (green) 50.00 100.00
12 Ernie Lombardi (blue) 40.00 80.00
13 Al Lopez (blue) 50.00 100.00
14 Rabbit Maranville (green) 50.00 100.00
15 Joe Moore (red) 20.00 40.00
16 Van Lingle Mungo (green) 30.00 60.00
17 Mel Ott (blue) 60.00 120.00
18 Gordon Slade (green) 20.00 40.00
19 Casey Stengel MG (green) 60.00 120.00
20 Tommy Thevenow (red) 20.00 40.00
21 Lloyd Waner (red) 50.00 100.00
22 Paul Waner (green) 50.00 100.00
23 Lon Warneke (blue) 30.00 60.00
24 James Wilson (blue) 20.00 40.00

1935-36 Diamond Match Co. Series 3 Type 1
This set was released over two years (1935-36) by the Diamond Match Company. This set varies from the First and Second set in that the saddle has the "ball" with the players name and team only. Covers come in red, green and blue. Players are listed in alphabetical order. Complete matchbooks are valued fifty percent higher.
COMPLETE SET (151) 900.00 1800.00
1 Ethan Allen 6.00 15.00
2 Melo Almada 6.00 15.00
3 Eldon Auker 6.00 15.00
4 Dick Bartell 6.00 15.00
5 Aloysius Bejma 6.00 15.00
6 Ollie Bejma 6.00 15.00
7 Roy Bell 6.00 15.00
8 Louis Berger 6.00 15.00
9 Wally Berger 8.00 20.00
10 Ralph Birkofer 6.00 15.00
11 Max Bishop 6.00 15.00
12 George Blaeholder 6.00 15.00
13 Zeke Bonura 8.00 20.00
14 Jim Bottomley 15.00 40.00
15 Ed Brandt 6.00 15.00
16 Don Brennan 6.00 15.00
17 Lloyd Brown 6.00 15.00
18 Walter Brown 6.00 15.00
19 Claiborne Bryant 6.00 15.00
20 Jim Bucher 6.00 15.00
21 John Burnett 6.00 15.00
22 Irving Burns 6.00 15.00
23 Merritt Cain 6.00 15.00
24 Ben Cantwell 6.00 15.00
25 Tommy Carey 6.00 15.00
26 Tex Carleton 6.00 15.00
27 Joseph Cascarella 6.00 15.00
28 Thomas Casey 6.00 15.00
29 George Caster 6.00 15.00
30 Phil Cavaretta 12.50 30.00
31 Louis Chiozza 6.00 15.00
32 Edward Cihocki 6.00 15.00
33 Herman E. Clifton 6.00 15.00
34 Richard Coffman 6.00 15.00
35 Edward Coleman 6.00 15.00
36 James A. Collins 8.00 20.00
37 Jocko Conlon 12.50 30.00
38 Roger Cramer 8.00 20.00
39 Hugh Critz 6.00 15.00
40 Alvin Crowder 6.00 15.00
41 Tony Cuccinello 6.00 15.00
42 Kiki Cuyler 15.00 40.00
43 Virgil Davis 6.00 15.00
44 Dizzy Dean 30.00 60.00
45 Paul Derringer 8.00 20.00
46 James DeShong 6.00 15.00
47 Billy Dietrich 6.00 15.00
48 Leo Durocher 20.00 50.00
49 George Earnshaw 10.00 25.00
50 Woody English 6.00 15.00
51 Louis Finney 6.00 15.00
52 Charles Fischer 6.00 15.00
53 Freddy Fitzsimmons 10.00 25.00
54 Linus Frey 6.00 15.00
55 Frankie Frisch 20.00 50.00
56 Augie Galan 8.00 20.00
57 Milton Galatzer 15.00 40.00
58 Dennis Galehouse 6.00 15.00
59 Debs Garms 6.00 15.00
60 Angelo Giuliani 6.00 15.00
61 Earl Grace 6.00 15.00
62 Charlie Grimm 12.50 30.00
63 Frank Grube 6.00 15.00
64 Stan Hack 12.50 30.00
65 Bump Hadley 6.00 15.00
66 Odell Hale 6.00 15.00
67 Bill Hallahan 6.00 15.00
68 Roy Hanson 6.00 15.00
69 Mel Harder 8.00 20.00
70 Gabby Hartnett 15.00 40.00
71 Clyde Hatter 6.00 15.00
72 Raymond Hayworth 6.00 15.00
73 Babe Herman 12.50 30.00
74 Gordon Hinkle 6.00 15.00
75 George Hockette 6.00 15.00
76 James Holbrook 6.00 15.00
77 Alex Hooks 6.00 15.00
78 Waite Hoyt 12.50 30.00
79 Carl Hubbell 15.00 40.00
80 Roy Joiner 6.00 15.00
81 Sam Jones 8.00 20.00
82 Baxter Jordan 6.00 15.00
83 Arndt Jorgens 6.00 15.00
84 Billy Jurges 8.00 20.00
85 Willie Kamm 8.00 20.00
86 Vern Kennedy 6.00 15.00
87 John Kerr 6.00 15.00
88 Chuck Klein 15.00 40.00
89 Ted Kleinhans 6.00 15.00
90 William Knickerbocker 6.00 15.00
91 Jack Knott 6.00 15.00
92 Mark Koenig 8.00 20.00
93 Fabian Kowalik 6.00 15.00
94 Red Kress 6.00 15.00
95 Bill Lee 6.00 15.00
96 Louis Legett 6.00 15.00
97 Dutch Leonard 6.00 15.00
98 Fred Lindstrom 12.50 30.00
99 Edward Linke 6.00 15.00
100 Ernie Lombardi 12.50 30.00
101 Al Lopez 15.00 40.00
102 John Marcum 6.00 15.00
103 Bill McKechnie MG 12.50 30.00
104 Eric McNair 6.00 15.00
105 Joe Medwick 15.00 40.00
106 Oscar Melillo 6.00 15.00
107 John Michaels 6.00 15.00
108 Joe Moore 6.00 15.00
109 John Moore 6.00 15.00
110 Wally Moses 8.00 20.00
111 Joseph Milligan 6.00 15.00
112 Van Lingle Mungo 10.00 25.00
113 Glenn Myatt 6.00 15.00
114 James O'Dea 6.00 15.00
115 Ernest Orsatti 6.00 15.00
116 Fred Ostermueller 6.00 15.00
117 Mel Ott 20.00 50.00
118 LeRoy Parmelee 6.00 15.00
119 Monte Pearson 6.00 15.00
120 Raymond Pepper 6.00 15.00
121 Raymond Phelps 6.00 15.00
122 George Pipgras 6.00 15.00
123 Frank Pytlak 6.00 15.00
124 Gordon Rhodes 6.00 15.00
125 Charlie Root 8.00 20.00
126 John Rothrock 6.00 15.00
127 Muddy Ruel 6.00 15.00

128 Jack Saltzgaver	6.00	15.00
129 Fred Schulte	6.00	15.00
130 George Selkirk	8.00	20.00
131 Mervyn Shea	6.00	15.00
132 Al Spoher	6.00	15.00
133 George Stainback	6.00	15.00
134 Casey Stengel MG	20.00	50.00
135 Walter Stephenson	6.00	15.00
136 Lee Stine	6.00	15.00
137 John Stone	6.00	15.00
138 Gus Suhr	6.00	15.00
139 Tommy Thevenow	6.00	15.00
140 Fay Thomas	6.00	15.00
141 Leslie Tietje	6.00	15.00
142 Bill Urbanski	6.00	15.00
143 William Walker	6.00	15.00
144 Lloyd Waner	15.00	40.00
145 Paul Waner	15.00	40.00
146 Lon Warneke	8.00	20.00
147 Harold Warstler	6.00	15.00
148 Bill Werber	8.00	20.00
149 Vernon Wiltshere	6.00	15.00
150 James Wilson	6.00	15.00
151 Ralph Winegarner	6.00	15.00

1936 Diamond Match Co. Series 3 Type 2

This 23-player set was issued by the Diamond Match Company around 1936. Each player's cover is featured in three different colors, red, green and blue, All player photos, except "Dizzy" Dean, feature head and shoulders shot. The set was released with two different colors of ink, brown and black. All players are listed in alphabetical order. Complete matchbooks are valued fifty percent higher.

COMPLETE SET (23)	100.00	200.00
1 Claiborne Bryant	4.00	8.00
2 Tex Carleton	4.00	8.00
3 Phil Cavaretta	6.00	12.00
4 James A. Collins	5.00	10.00
5 Curt Davis	4.00	8.00
6 Dizzy Dean	12.50	25.00
7 Frank Demaree	4.00	8.00
8 Larry French	4.00	8.00
9 Linus Frey	4.00	8.00
10 Augie Galan	5.00	10.00
11 Bob Garbark	4.00	8.00
12 Stan Hack	6.00	12.00
13 Gabby Hartnett	10.00	20.00
14 Billy Herman	10.00	20.00
15 Billy Jurges	5.00	10.00
16 Bill Lee	4.00	8.00
17 Joe Marty	4.00	8.00
18 James O'Dea	4.00	8.00
19 LeRoy Parmelee	4.00	8.00
20 Charlie Root	5.00	10.00
21 Clyde Shoun	4.00	8.00
22 George Stainback	5.00	10.00
23 Paul Waner	10.00	20.00

1936 Diamond Match Co. Series 4

This is by far the smallest matchcover set released by the Diamond Match Company during the 1930's. The set is similar to the Third Baseball set other than the players team name shows under his name on the back. All of the covers minus Charlie Grimm were printed using brown ink. The three different Grimm cover feature black ink. The players are listed in alphabetical order. Complete matchbooks are valued fifty percent higher.

COMPLETE SET (12)	75.00	150.00
1 Tommy Carey	4.00	10.00
2 Tony Cuccinello	4.00	10.00
3 Freddy Fitzsimmons	5.00	12.00
4 Frankie Frisch	12.50	30.00
5 Charlie Grimm (3)	8.00	20.00
6 Carl Hubbell	10.00	25.00
7 Baxter Jordan	4.00	10.00
8 Chuck Klein	10.00	25.00
9 Al Lopez	8.00	20.00
10 Joe Medwick	8.00	20.00
11 Van Lingle Mungo	6.00	15.00
12 Mel Ott	12.50	30.00

1934-36 Diamond Stars

The cards in this 108-card set measure approximately 2 3/8" by 2 7/8". The Diamond Stars set, produced by National Chicle from 1934-36, is also commonly known by its catalog designation, R327. The year of production can be determined by the statistics contained on the back of the card. There are 170 possible front/back combinations counting blue (B) and green (G) backs over all three years. The last twelve cards are repeat players and are quite scarce. The checklist below lists the year(s) and back color(s) for the cards. Cards 32 through 72 were issued only in 1935 with green ink on back. Cards 73 through 84 were issued three ways: 35B, 35G, and 36B. Card numbers 85 through 108 were issued only in 1936 with blue ink on back. The complete set price below refers to the set of all variations listed explicitly below. A blank-backed proof sheet of 12 additional (never-issued) cards was discovered in 1980.

COMPLETE SET (119)	9000.00	15000.00
COMMON CARD (1-31)	30.00	50.00
COMMON CARD (32-84)	35.00	60.00
COMMON CARD (85-96)	60.00	100.00
COMMON CARD (97-108)	125.00	200.00
WRAPPER (1-CENT, BLUE)	200.00	250.00
WRAPPER (1-CENT, YEL.)	150.00	200.00
WRAPPER (1-CENT, CLR.)	150.00	200.00
1 Lefty Grove (34G, 35G)	800.00	1500.00
2A Simmons w/Sox (34G,35G)	90.00	150.00
2B Al Simmons w/o Sox (36B)	125.00	200.00
3 Rabbit Maranville (34G,35G)	90.00	150.00
4 Buddy Myer (34G,35G,36B)	35.00	60.00
5 T.Bridges (34G,35G,36B)	35.00	60.00
6 Max Bishop (34G,35G)	35.00	60.00
7 Lew Fonseca (34G,35G)	35.00	60.00
8 Joe Vosmik XRC (34G,35G,36B)	30.00	50.00
9 M.Cochrane (34G,35G,36B)	200.00	400.00
10A L.Mahaffey w/A's(34G,35G)	30.00	50.00
10B L.Mahaffey w/o A's (36B)	50.00	80.00
11 Bill Dickey (34G, 35G)	200.00	400.00
12A Fred Walker XRC (34G)	50.00	80.00
12B Fred Walker (35G)	50.00	80.00
12C Fred Walker (36B)	60.00	100.00
13 G.Blaeholder (34G,35G)	30.00	50.00
14 Bill Terry (34G,35G)	100.00	175.00
15A Dick Bartell (34G)	60.00	100.00
15B Dick Bartell (35G)	50.00	80.00
16 L.Waner (34G,35G,36B)	125.00	250.00
17 Frankie Frisch (34G,35G)	150.00	300.00
18 Chick Hafey XRC (34G,35G)	100.00	200.00
19 Van Mungo XRC (34G,35G)	50.00	80.00
20 Frank Hogan (34G,35G)	35.00	60.00
21A Johnny Vergez (34G)	50.00	80.00
21B Johnny Vergez (35G)	35.00	60.00
22 J.Wilson (34G,35G,36B)	35.00	60.00
23 Bill Hallahan (34G,35G)	30.00	50.00
24 Earl Adams (34G,35G)	30.00	50.00
25 Wally Berger (35G)	35.00	60.00
26 P.Martin (35G,36B)	50.00	80.00
27 Pie Traynor (35G)	90.00	150.00
28 Al Lopez (35G)	90.00	150.00
29 Red Rolfe (35G)	50.00	80.00
30A Manush W/sleeve (35G)	90.00	150.00
30B H.Manush no W (36B)	125.00	200.00
31A Kiki Cuyler (35G)	75.00	125.00
31B Kiki Cuyler (36B)	100.00	175.00
32 Sam Rice (35G)	75.00	125.00
33 Schoolboy Rowe (35G)	50.00	80.00
34 Stan Hack (35G)	50.00	80.00
35 Earl Averill (35G)	75.00	125.00
36A Earnie Lombardi (35G)	175.00	300.00
36B Ernie Lombardi (35G)	125.00	200.00
37 Billy Urbanski (35G)	35.00	60.00
38 Ben Chapman (35G)	50.00	80.00
39 Carl Hubbell (35G)	125.00	200.00
40 Blondy Ryan (35G)	35.00	60.00
41 Harvey Hendrick XRC (35G)	35.00	60.00
42 Jimmy Dykes (35G)	50.00	80.00
43 Ted Lyons (35G)	75.00	125.00
44 Rogers Hornsby (35G)	150.00	300.00
45 Jo Jo White XRC (35G)	35.00	60.00
46 Red Lucas (35G)	35.00	60.00
47 Bob Bolton XRC (35G)	35.00	60.00
48 Rick Ferrell (35G)	75.00	125.00
49 Buck Jordan (35G)	35.00	60.00
50 Mel Ott (35G)	150.00	300.00
51 John Whitehead XRC (35G)	35.00	60.00
52 Tuck Stainback XRC (35G)	35.00	60.00
53 Oscar Melillo (35G)	35.00	60.00
54A Hank Greenburg (35G)	600.00	1200.00
54B Hank Greenberg (35G)	300.00	600.00
55 Tony Cuccinello (35G)	50.00	80.00
56 Gus Suhr (35G)	35.00	60.00
57 Cy Blanton (35G)	35.00	60.00
58 Glenn Myatt (35G)	35.00	60.00
59 Jim Bottomley (35G)	75.00	125.00
60 Red Ruffing (35G)	90.00	150.00
61 Bill Werber (35G)	50.00	80.00
62 Fred Frankhouse (35G)	35.00	60.00
63 Travis Jackson (35G)	75.00	125.00
64 Jimmie Foxx (35G)	250.00	500.00
65 Zeke Bonura (35G)	35.00	60.00
66 Ducky Medwick (35G)	125.00	200.00
67 Marvin Owen (35G)	50.00	80.00
68 Sam Leslie (35G)	35.00	60.00
69 Earl Grace (35G)	35.00	60.00
70 Hal Trosky (35G)	50.00	80.00
71 Ossie Bluege (35G)	50.00	80.00
72 Tony Piet (35G)	35.00	60.00
73 F.Ostermueller (35G,35B,36B)	50.00	80.00
74 Tony Lazzeri (35G,35B,36B)	125.00	200.00
75 Jack Burns (35G,35B,36B)	50.00	80.00
76 Billy Rogell (35G,35B,36B)	50.00	80.00
77 C.Gehringer (35G,35B,36B)	150.00	300.00
78 Joe Kuhel (35G,35B,36B)	50.00	80.00
79 W.Hudlin (35G,35B,36B)	50.00	80.00
80 Lou Chiozza XRC (35G,35B,36B)	50.00	80.00
81 Bill Delancey XRC (35G,35B,36B)	35.00	60.00
82A Babich w/Dodgers(35G,35B)	50.00	80.00
82B John Babich wo/Dod. (36B)	75.00	125.00
83 P.Waner (35G,35B,36B)	90.00	150.00
84 Sam Byrd (35G,35B,36B)	50.00	80.00
85 Moose Solters (36B)	60.00	100.00
86 Frank Crosetti (36B)	90.00	150.00
87 Steve O'Neill MG (36B)	75.00	125.00
88 George Selkirk XRC (36B)	75.00	125.00
89 Joe Stripp (36B)	75.00	125.00
90 Ray Hayworth (36B)	75.00	125.00
91 Bucky Harris MG XRC (36B)	125.00	200.00
92 Ethan Allen (36B)	60.00	100.00
93 General Crowder (36B)	60.00	100.00
94 Wes Ferrell (36B)	90.00	150.00
95 Luke Appling (36B)	150.00	250.00
96 Lew Riggs XRC (36B)	60.00	100.00
97 Al Lopez (36B)	250.00	400.00
98 Schoolboy Rowe (36B)	125.00	200.00
99 Pie Traynor (36B)	300.00	500.00
100 Earl Averill (36B)	250.00	400.00
101 Dick Bartell (36B)	125.00	200.00
102 Van Lingle Mungo (36B)	150.00	250.00
103 Bill Dickey (36B)	400.00	700.00
104 Red Rolfe (36B)	125.00	200.00
105 Ernie Lombardi (36B)	250.00	400.00
106 Red Lucas (36B)	125.00	200.00
107 Stan Hack (36B)	125.00	200.00
108 Wally Berger (36B)	175.00	300.00

1993 Diamond Stars Extension Set

This 36-card set measures 2 3/8" by 2 7/8" and was issued by The Chicle Fantasy Company. These cards did not exist in 1936, but might have, had the National Chicle Co. of Cambridge, Mass. not been on the verge of bankruptcy. Only 108 of a proposed 240 cards were issued from 1934-36. These 36 cards are an idealized version of what might have been. The colorful fronts feature art by D'August Roth Martin and are edged in white. The back carries a descriptive summary of the player's career with biography below. The cards are arranged alphabetically and are numbered on their backs, beginning with number 121. Additionally, three cards (1-3) are included that feature Negro League stars.

COMPLETE SET (36)	4.00	10.00
COMMON PLAYER (N1-N3)	.20	.50
COMMON PLAYER (121-153)	.10	.25
121 Moe Berg	.60	1.50
122 Harlond Clift	.08	.25
123 Joe Cronin MG	.30	.75
124 Dizzy Dean	.30	.75
125 Paul Dean	.20	.50
126 Joe DiMaggio	.75	2.00
127 Leo Durocher	.30	.75
128 Bob Feller	.40	1.00
129 Carl Fisher	.08	.25
130 Lou Gehrig	.75	2.00
131 Bump Hadley	.08	.25
132 Jesse Haines	.20	.50
133 Bad News Hale	.08	.25
134 Gabby Hartnett	.30	.75
135 Babe Herman	.20	.50
136 Billy Herman	.30	.75
137 Waite Hoyt	.30	.75
138 Bob Johnson	.20	.50
139 Chuck Klein	.30	.75
140 Mike Kreevich	.08	.25
141 Fred Lindstrom	.20	.50
142 Connie Mack MG	.30	.75
143 Joe McCarthy MG	.30	.75
144 Bill McKechnie MG	.20	.50
145 Johnny Mize	.30	.75
146 Johnny Moore	.08	.25
147 Hugh Mulcahy	.08	.25
148 Buck Newsom	.20	.50
149 Al Smith	.08	.25
150 Casey Stengel MG	.30	.75
151 Arky Vaughan	.30	.75
152 Gee Walker	.08	.25
153 Kenesaw M. Landis COMM	.20	.50
N1 Cool Papa Bell	.20	.50
N2 Josh Gibson	.30	.75
N3 Satchel Paige	.30	.75
NNO Title card	.20	.50

1981 Diamond Stars Continuation Den's

These 2 1/2" by 3" cards feature reproductions of cards which were prepared by Diamond Stars but never printed. These cards were on a twelve-card sheet and continue the numbering of already existing Diamond Stars cards. This set was created and produced by Denny Eckes. Hobbyist Mike Galella was involved in bringing this sheet to the public. These cards were originally available from the producer for $3.

COMPLETE SET (12)	12.50	30.00
109 Benny Frey	.75	2.00
110 Pete Fox	.75	2.00
111 Phil Cavaretta	1.25	3.00
112 Goose Goslin	2.00	5.00
113 Mel Harder	1.25	3.00
114 Doc Cramer	1.25	3.00
115 Gene Moore	.75	2.00
116 Rip Collins	.75	2.00
117 Linus Frey	.75	2.00
118 Lefty Gomez	2.50	6.00
119 Jim Bottomley Rogers Hornsby	2.50	6.00
120 Lon Warneke	1.25	3.00

1998 Diamondbacks McDaddy

This 24 card standard-size set was issued by the McDonald restaurant chain in the Arizona area and features members of the Arizona Diamondbacks in their inagural season. The cards are unnumbered so we have sequenced them in alphabetical order.

COMPLETE SET (24)	2.50	6.00
1 Joel Adamson	.08	.25
2 Brian Anderson	.08	.25
3 Tony Batista	.10	.25
4 Jay Bell	.08	.25
5 Andy Benes	.08	.25
6 Yamil Benitez	.08	.25
7 Willie Blair	.08	.25
8 Brent Brede	.08	.25
9 Omar Daal	.08	.25
10 David Dellucci	.30	.75
11 Jorge Fabregas	.08	.25
12 Andy Fox	.08	.25
13 Karim Garcia	.08	.25
14 Travis Lee	.30	.75
15 Damian Miller	.20	.50
16 Gregg Olson	.08	.25
17 Felix Rodriguez	.08	.25
18 Buck Showalter MG	.20	.50
19 Clint Sodowsky	.08	.25
20 Andy Stankiewicz	.08	.25
21 Kelly Stinnett	.08	.25
22 Jeff Suppan	.08	.25
23 Devon White	.08	.25
24 Matt Williams	.30	.75

1998 Diamondbacks Pinnacle

This 26-card set was produced by Pinnacle to commemorate the Diamondbacks first team and was distributed in a Collector's Edition box. The fronts feature color action player photos in a green, purple, and white border. The backs carry a small player head shot and player information. Only 3000 of the set were produced with the boxes serially numbered.

COMPLETE SET (26)	2.50	6.00
1 Chris Clemons	.08	.25
2 Brian Anderson	.08	.25
3 Andy Benes	.08	.25
4 Willie Blair	.08	.25
5 Scott Brow	.08	.25
6 Omar Daal	.08	.25
7 Barry Manuel	.08	.25
8 Gregg Olson	.08	.25
9 Felix Rodriguez	.08	.25
10 Clint Sodowsky	.08	.25
11 Russ Springer	.08	.25
12 Jeff Suppan	.08	.25
13 Jorge Fabregas	.08	.25
14 Kelly Stinnett	.08	.25
15 Tony Batista	.08	.25
16 Jay Bell	.08	.25
17 Andy Fox	.08	.25
18 Travis Lee	.30	.75
19 Matt Williams	.30	.75
20 Yamil Benitez	.08	.25
21 Brent Brede	.08	.25
22 David Dellucci	.30	.75
23 Karim Garcia	.08	.25
24 Chris Jones	.08	.25
25 Devon White	.08	.25
NNO Team Logo CL	.08	.25

1999 Diamondbacks Pepsi Fleer

This set features members of the Arizona Diamond Backs and the players photos is situated against a red, white and blue background with the players name and uniform number in the background. The Pepsi logo in in the bottom left while the Fleer logo is on the upper right. The back has a player photo, some information and complete statistics. The Steve Finley card was pulled early during the run and was only available at the ballpark. The cards were issued in three card packs with one checklist so the checklist should be considered a Double print. Kelly Stinnett and Omar Daal apparently are among the toughest ones to acquire from the packs.

COMPLETE SET (15)	4.00	10.00
1 Jay Bell	.08	.25
2 Andy Benes	.08	.25
3 Randy Johnson	.75	2.00
4 Matt Williams	.30	.75
5 Steve Finley	2.00	5.00
6 Todd Stottlemyre	.08	.25
7 Omar Daal	.08	.25
8 Travis Lee	.08	.25
9 Armando Reynoso	.08	.25
10 Gregg Olson	.08	.25
11 Tony Batista	.08	.25
12 Greg Swindell	.08	.25
13 Greg Colbrunn	.08	.25
14 Damian Miller	.20	.50
15 Kelly Stinnett	.08	.25
NNO Checklist	.08	.25

2000 Diamondbacks Circle K

COMPLETE SET (4)	16.00	40.00
1 Greg Colbrunn	2.00	5.00
2 Randy Johnson	10.00	25.00
3 Matt Mantei	2.40	6.00
4 Damian Miller	2.00	5.00

2000 Diamondbacks Keebler

COMPLETE SET (28)	12.00	30.00
1 Buck Showalter MG	.40	1.00
2 Randy Johnson	2.00	6.00
3 Luis Gonzalez	1.20	3.00
4 Todd Stottlemyre	.40	1.00
5 Matt Williams	.80	2.00
6 Curt Schilling	1.20	3.00
7 Jay Bell	.40	1.00
8 Steve Finley	.80	2.00
9 Brian Anderson	.40	1.00
10 Tony Womack	.40	1.00
11 Mike Morgan	.40	1.00
12 Damian Miller	.60	1.50
13 Greg Swindell	.40	1.00
14 Greg Colbrunn	.40	1.00
15 Dan Plesac	.40	1.00
16 Craig Counsell	.40	1.00
17 Russ Springer	.40	1.00
18 Kelly Stinnett	.40	1.00
19 Alex Cabrera	.40	1.00
20 Matt Mantei	.40	1.00
21 Danny Klassen	.40	1.00
22 Hanley Frias	.40	1.00
23 Byung-Hyun Kim	.80	2.00
24 Jason Conti	.40	1.00
25 Danny Bautista	.40	1.00
26 Eurbiel Durazo	.60	1.50
27 Armando Reynoso	.40	1.00
28 Brian Butterfield CO Mark Connor CO Dwayne Murph	.40	1.00

2000 Diamondbacks Pepsi Upper Deck

COMPLETE SET (15)	2.00	5.00
1 Jay Bell	.20	.50
2 Matt Mantei	.20	.50
3 Greg Swindell	.20	.50
4 Matt Williams	.20	.50
5 Erubiel Durazo	.20	.50
6 Todd Stottlemyre	.20	.50
7 Randy Johnson	.50	1.25
8 Tony Womack	.20	.50
9 Greg Colbrunn	.20	.50
10 Brian Anderson	.20	.50
11 Omar Daal	.20	.50
12 Travis Lee	.20	.50
13 Steve Finley	.20	.50
14 Luis Gonzalez	.20	.50
15 Kelly Stinnett	.20	.50

2001 Diamondbacks Keebler

COMPLETE SET (28)	4.80	12.00
1 Bob Brenly MG	.10	.25
2 Randy Johnson	.80	2.50
3 Luis Gonzalez	.50	1.25
4 Curt Schilling	.60	1.50
5 Matt Williams	.30	.75
6 Todd Stottlemyre	.10	.25
7 Jay Bell	.10	.25
8 Steve Finley	.30	.75
9 Mark Grace	.40	1.00
10 Brian Anderson	.10	.25
11 Tony Womack	.10	.25
12 Damian Miller	.20	.50
13 Russ Springer	.10	.25
14 Greg Colbrunn	.10	.25
15 Craig Counsell	.10	.25
16 Greg Swindell	.10	.25
17 Reggie Sanders	.20	.50
18 Matt Mantei	.10	.25
19 Danny Bautista	.10	.25
20 Mike Morgan	.10	.25
21 Erubiel Durazo	.20	.50
22 Troy Brohawn	.10	.25
23 Byung-Hyun Kim	.30	.75
24 David Dellucci	.30	.75
25 Robert Ellis	.10	.25
26 Rod Barajas	.30	.75
27 Armando Reynoso	.10	.25
28 Bob Melvin CO Dwayne Murphy CO Eddie Rodriguez CO Glenn Sherlock CO Chris Speier CO Bob Welch	.10	.25

2001 Diamondbacks Upper Deck Pepsi

COMPLETE SET	4.80	12.00
1 Randy Johnson	1.20	4.00
2 Matt Williams	.40	1.00
3 Greg Colbrunn	.20	.50
4 Mark Grace	.60	1.50
5 Armando Reynoso	.20	.50
6 Matt Mantei	.20	.50
7 Curt Schilling	1.00	2.50
8 Jay Bell	.20	.50
9 Reggie Sanders	.30	.75
10 Steve Finley	.40	1.00
11 Todd Stottlemyre	.20	.50
12 Greg Swindell	.20	.50
13 Luis Gonzalez	.60	1.50
14 Brian Anderson	.20	.50
15 Tony Womack	.20	.50

2002 Diamondbacks ALS

1 Curt Schilling Lou Gehrig	2.00	5.00

2002 Diamondbacks Keebler

COMPLETE SET (28)	4.00	10.00
1 Bob Brenly MG	.20	.50
2 Luis Gonzalez	.50	1.25
3 Randy Johnson	1.00	2.50
4 Curt Schilling	.60	1.50
5 Matt Williams	.30	.75
6 Todd Stottlemyre	.08	.25
7 Jay Bell	.08	.25
8 Steve Finley	.30	.75
9 Mark Grace	.40	1.00
10 Brian Anderson	.08	.25
11 Tony Womack	.08	.25
12 Damian Miller	.20	.50
13 Erubiel Durazo	.20	.50
14 Craig Counsell	.08	.25
15 David Dellucci	.30	.75
16 Greg Swindell	.08	.25
17 Greg Colbrunn	.08	.25
18 Rick Helling	.08	.25
19 Danny Bautista	.08	.25
20 Mike Morgan	.08	.25
21 Rod Barajas	.20	.50
22 Byung-Hyun Kim	.30	.75
23 Mike Myers	.08	.25
24 Jose Guillen	.30	.75
25 Miguel Batista	.08	.25
26 Junior Spivey	.08	.25
27 Quinton McCracken	.08	.25
28 Chuck Kniffin CO Bob Melvin CO Dwayne Murphy CO Eddie Rodriguez CO Glenn Sherlock CO Robin Yount CO	.08	.25

2003 Diamondbacks Keebler

COMPLETE SET	7.50	15.00
1 Bob Brenly MG	.10	.25
2 Luis Gonzalez	.50	1.25
3 Randy Johnson	.75	2.00
4 Curt Schilling	.75	2.00
5 Danny Bautista	.10	.25
6 Matt Mantei	.10	.25
7 Craig Counsell	.20	.50
8 Steve Finley	.30	.75
9 Mark Grace	.40	1.00
10 Alex Cintron	.10	.25
11 Tony Womack	.10	.25
12 Chad Moeller	.10	.25
13 Shea Hillenbrand	.20	.50
14 Miguel Batista	.10	.25
15 David Dellucci	.30	.75
16 Elmer Dessens	.10	.25
17 Lyle Overbay	.40	1.00
18 Mike Myers	.10	.25
19 Quinton McCracken	.10	.25
20 Rod Barajas	.30	.75
21 Junior Spivey	.10	.25
22 Stephen Randolph	.10	.25
23 Carlos Baerga	.10	.25
24 Mike Koplove	.10	.25
25 Brandon Webb	1.25	3.00
26 Oscar Villarreal	.10	.25
27 Bret Prinz	.10	.25
28 Mark Davis CO Chuck Kniffin CO Dwayne Murphy CO#	.30	.75

2006 Diamondbacks Topps

COMPLETE SET (14)	3.00	8.00
ARZ1 Luis Gonzalez	.12	.30
ARZ2 Shawn Green	.12	.30
ARZ3 Brandon Webb	.20	.50
ARZ4 Orlando Hudson	.12	.30
ARZ5 Tony Clark	.12	.30
ARZ6 Chad Tracy	.12	.30
ARZ7 Conor Jackson	.20	.50
ARZ8 Russ Ortiz	.12	.30
ARZ9 Claudio Vargas	.12	.30
ARZ10 Brad Halsey	.12	.30
ARZ11 Miguel Batista	.12	.30
ARZ12 Craig Counsell	.12	.30
ARZ13 Orlando Hernandez	.12	.30
ARZ14 Johnny Estrada	.12	.30

2007 Diamondbacks Topps

COMPLETE SET (14)	3.00	8.00
ARI1 Brandon Webb	.20	.50
ARI2 Chad Tracy	.12	.30
ARI3 Eric Byrnes	.12	.30
ARI4 Livan Hernandez	.12	.30
ARI5 Jose Valverde	.12	.30
ARI6 Conor Jackson	.12	.30
ARI7 Miguel Montero	.12	.30
ARI8 Orlando Hudson	.12	.30
ARI9 Chris Snyder	.12	.30
ARI10 Carlos Quentin	.12	.30
ARI11 Stephen Drew	.12	.30
ARI12 Doug Davis	.12	.30
ARI13 Chris Young	.12	.30
ARI14 Randy Johnson	.30	.75

2008 Diamondbacks Topps

COMPLETE SET (14)	3.00	8.00
ARI1 Brandon Webb	.20	.50
ARI2 Mark Reynolds	.12	.30
ARI3 Eric Byrnes	.12	.30
ARI4 Chris Burke	.12	.30
ARI5 Dan Haren	.12	.30
ARI6 Conor Jackson	.12	.30
ARI7 Micah Owings	.12	.30
ARI8 Orlando Hudson	.12	.30
ARI9 Chris Snyder	.12	.30
ARI10 Justin Upton	.20	.50
ARI11 Stephen Drew	.12	.30
ARI12 Doug Davis	.12	.30
ARI13 Chris Young	.12	.30
ARI14 Randy Johnson	.30	.75

2009 Diamondbacks Topps

ARI1 Brandon Webb	.25	.60
ARI2 Justin Upton	.25	.60
ARI3 Dan Haren	.15	.40
ARI4 Felipe Lopez	.15	.40
ARI5 Stephen Drew	.15	.40
ARI6 Miguel Montero	.15	.40
ARI7 Chris Young	.15	.40
ARI8 Eric Byrnes	.15	.40
ARI9 Max Scherzer	.40	1.00
ARI10 Chad Qualls	.15	.40
ARI11 Conor Jackson	.15	.40
ARI12 Mark Reynolds	.15	.40
ARI13 Chris Snyder	.15	.40
ARI14 Doug Davis	.15	.40
ARI15 Baxter The Bobcat	.15	.40

2010 Diamondbacks Topps

ARI1 Justin Upton	.25	.60
ARI2 Edwin Jackson	.15	.40
ARI3 Brandon Allen	.15	.40
ARI4 Kelly Johnson	.15	.40
ARI5 Eric Byrnes	.15	.40
ARI6 Stephen Drew	.15	.40
ARI7 Chris Young	.15	.40
ARI8 Chad Tracy	.15	.40
ARI9 Gerardo Parra	.15	.40
ARI10 Mark Reynolds	.15	.40
ARI11 Ryan Roberts	.15	.40
ARI12 Dan Haren	.15	.40
ARI13 Brandon Webb	.25	.60
ARI14 Miguel Montero	.15	.40
ARI15 Conor Jackson	.15	.40
ARI16 Augie Ojeda	.15	.40
ARI17 Chad Qualls	.15	.40

2011 Diamondbacks Topps

ARI1 Justin Upton	.25	.60
ARI2 Stephen Drew	.15	.40
ARI3 Barry Enright	.15	.40
ARI4 Daniel Hudson	.15	.40
ARI5 Kelly Johnson	.15	.40
ARI6 Ian Kennedy	.15	.40
ARI7 Melvin Mora	.15	.40
ARI8 Miguel Montero	.15	.40
ARI9 Gerardo Parra	.15	.40
ARI10 Joe Saunders	.15	.40
ARI11 Chris Young	.15	.40
ARI12 Juan Miranda	.15	.40
ARI13 Xavier Nady	.15	.40
ARI14 Juan Gutierrez	.15	.40
ARI15 J.J. Putz	.15	.40
ARI16 Zach Duke	.15	.40
ARI17 Chase Field	.15	.40

2012 Diamondbacks Topps

ARZ1 Justin Upton	.30	.75
ARZ2 Chris Young	.25	.60
ARZ3 Stephen Drew	.25	.60
ARZ4 Lyle Overbay	.25	.60
ARZ5 Ryan Roberts	.25	.60
ARZ6 Daniel Hudson	.25	.60
ARZ7 Gerardo Parra	.25	.60
ARZ8 J.J. Putz	.25	.60
ARZ9 Paul Goldschmidt	.40	1.00
ARZ10 Ian Kennedy	.25	.60
ARZ11 Miguel Montero	.25	.60
ARZ12 Willie Bloomquist	.25	.60
ARZ13 Jason Kubel	.25	.60
ARZ14 Trevor Cahill	.25	.60
ARZ15 Aaron Hill	.25	.60
ARZ16 Josh Collmenter	.30	.75
ARZ17 Chase Field	.15	.40

2013 Diamondbacks Topps

ARI1 Ian Kennedy	.15	.40
ARI2 Gerardo Parra	.15	.40
ARI3 Wade Miley	.15	.40
ARI4 Trevor Cahill	.15	.40
ARI5 Paul Goldschmidt	.40	1.00
ARI6 Miguel Montero	.25	.60
ARI7 Jason Kubel	.25	.60
ARI8 J.J. Putz	.25	.60
ARI9 Martin Prado	.15	.40
ARI10 Patrick Corbin	.20	.50
ARI11 Brandon McCarthy	.15	.40
ARI12 Adam Eaton	.25	.60
ARI13 Aaron Hill	.25	.60
ARI14 Didi Gregorius	.60	1.50
ARI15 Cody Ross	.25	.60
ARI16 Tyler Skaggs	.25	.60
ARI17 Chase Field	.15	.40

2014 Diamondbacks Topps

COMPLETE SET (17)	3.00	8.00
ARI1 Paul Goldschmidt	.25	.60
ARI2 Gerardo Parra	.15	.40
ARI3 Wade Miley	.15	.40
ARI4 Trevor Cahill	.15	.40
ARI5 Addison Reed	.15	.40
ARI6 Miguel Montero	.15	.40
ARI7 Brad Ziegler	.15	.40
ARI8 Chris Owings	.15	.40
ARI9 Martin Prado	.15	.40
ARI10 Patrick Corbin	.20	.50
ARI11 Brandon McCarthy	.15	.40
ARI12 A.J. Pollock	.20	.50
ARI13 Aaron Hill	.15	.40
ARI14 Didi Gregorius	.20	.50
ARI15 Cody Ross	.15	.40
ARI16 Mark Trumbo	.15	.40
ARI17 Chase Field	.15	.40

2015 Diamondbacks Topps

COMPLETE SET (17)	3.00	8.00
AD1 Paul Goldschmidt	.25	.60
AD2 Trevor Cahill	.15	.40
AD3 Chris Owings	.15	.40
AD4 Aaron Hill	.15	.40
AD5 Jake Lamb	.25	.60
AD6 Tuffy Gosewisch	.15	.40
AD7 Patrick Corbin	.20	.50
AD8 David Peralta	.15	.40
AD9 Addison Reed	.15	.40
AD10 Cody Ross	.15	.40
AD11 A.J. Pollock	.20	.50
AD12 Mark Trumbo	.15	.40
AD13 Bronson Arroyo	.15	.40
AD14 Jeremy Hellickson	.15	.40
AD15 Daniel Hudson	.15	.40
AD16 Josh Collmenter	.15	.40
AD17 Brad Ziegler	.15	.40

2016 Diamondbacks Topps

COMPLETE SET (17)	3.00	8.00
ARI1 Paul Goldschmidt	.25	.60
ARI2 Wellington Castillo	.15	.40
ARI3 Chris Owings	.15	.40
ARI4 Nick Ahmed	.15	.40
ARI5 Jake Lamb	.20	.50
ARI6 David Peralta	.15	.40
ARI7 A.J. Pollock	.15	.40
ARI8 Shelby Miller	.20	.50
ARI9 Yasmany Tomas	.15	.40
ARI10 Patrick Corbin	.20	.50
ARI11 Rubby De La Rosa	.15	.40
ARI12 Zack Greinke	.25	.60
ARI13 Brad Ziegler	.15	.40
ARI14 Daniel Hudson	.15	.40
ARI15 Aaron Hill	.15	.40
ARI16 Socrates Brito	.15	.40
ARI17 Tuffy Gosewisch	.15	.40

2017 Diamondbacks Topps

COMPLETE SET (17)	3.00	8.00
ARI1 Paul Goldschmidt	.25	.60
ARI2 Archie Bradley	.15	.40
ARI3 Yasmany Tomas	.15	.40
ARI4 Fernando Rodney	.15	.40
ARI5 A.J. Pollock	.15	.40
ARI6 Patrick Corbin	.20	.50
ARI7 Jake Lamb	.20	.50
ARI8 Shelby Miller	.20	.50
ARI9 Jake Barrett	.15	.40
ARI10 Taijuan Walker	.15	.40
ARI11 David Peralta	.15	.40
ARI12 Jeff Mathis	.20	.50
ARI13 Brandon Drury	.15	.40
ARI14 Braden Shipley	.15	.40
ARI15 Zack Greinke	.25	.60
ARI16 Robbie Ray	.15	.40
ARI17 Chris Owings	.15	.40

2018 Diamondbacks Topps

COMPLETE SET (17)	2.00	5.00
AD1 Paul Goldschmidt	.25	.60
AD2 David Peralta	.15	.40
AD3 Chris Owings	.15	.40
AD4 Brandon Drury	.15	.40
AD5 Jeff Mathis	.20	.50
AD6 Robbie Ray	.15	.40
AD7 Zack Godley	.15	.40
AD8 Jake Lamb	.20	.50
AD9 J.D. Martinez	.25	.60
AD10 Nick Ahmed	.15	.40
AD11 Zack Greinke	.25	.60
AD12 Shelby Miller	.20	.50
AD13 A.J. Pollock	.15	.40
AD14 Taijuan Walker	.15	.40
AD15 Patrick Corbin	.20	.50
AD16 Yasmany Tomas	.15	.40
AD17 Archie Bradley	.15	.40

2019 Diamondbacks Topps

COMPLETE SET (17)	2.00	5.00
AD1 Zack Greinke	.25	.60
AD2 Jake Lamb	.20	.50
AD3 Ketel Marte	.20	.50
AD4 Nick Ahmed	.15	.40
AD5 Taijuan Walker	.15	.40
AD6 Zack Godley	.15	.40
AD7 Steven Souza Jr.	.20	.50
AD8 Eduardo Escobar	.15	.40
AD9 Jarrod Dyson	.15	.40
AD10 David Peralta	.15	.40
AD11 Alex Avila	.20	.50
AD12 Robbie Ray	.15	.40
AD13 Luke Weaver	.15	.40
AD14 Carson Kelly	.15	.40
AD15 Archie Bradley	.15	.40
AD16 Ildemaro Vargas	.15	.40
AD17 Andrew Chafin	.15	.40

2020 Diamondbacks Topps

AZ1 Ketel Marte	.20	.50
AZ2 Eduardo Escobar	.15	.40
AZ3 Josh Rojas	.15	.40
AZ4 Stephen Vogt	.20	.50
AZ5 Christian Walker	.20	.50
AZ6 Archie Bradley	.15	.40
AZ7 Carson Kelly	.15	.40
AZ8 Nick Ahmed	.15	.40
AZ9 Andrew Chafin	.15	.40
AZ10 Zac Gallen	.40	1.00
AZ11 Robbie Ray	.15	.40
AZ12 David Peralta	.15	.40
AZ13 Mike Leake	.15	.40
AZ14 Merrill Kelly	.15	.40
AZ15 Luke Weaver	.15	.40
AZ16 Jake Lamb	.20	.50
AZ17 Yoan Lopez	.15	.40

2017 Diamondbacks Topps National Baseball Card Day

COMPLETE SET (10)	5.00	12.00
AD1 A.J. Pollock	.60	1.50

AD2 Zack Greinke 1.00 2.50
AD3 Taijuan Walker .60 1.50
AD4 David Peralta .60 1.50
AD5 Paul Goldschmidt 1.00 2.50
AD6 Jake Lamb .75 2.00
AD7 Fernando Rodney .60 1.50
AD8 Yasmany Tomas .60 1.50
AD9 Patrick Corbin .75 2.00
AD10 Randy Johnson 1.00 2.50

1924 Diaz Cigarettes

These 136 cards measure 1 3/4" by 2 1/4" with a white band on the top and the bottom. The team name is on the top while the players name is on the bottom. The middle has a player portrait. The back of the card has some information in Spanish Interestingly enough, all the players in this set are pitchers.

COMPLETE SET (136) 25000.00 50000.00
1 Walter Johnson 1250.00 2500.00
2 Waite Hoyt 500.00 1000.00
3 Grover Alexander 750.00 1500.00
4 Tom Sheehan 300.00 600.00
5 Pete Donohue 300.00 600.00
6 Herb Pennock 500.00 1000.00
7 Adolfo Luque 400.00 800.00
8 Carl Mays 400.00 800.00
9 Fred Marberry 350.00 700.00
10 Red Faber 500.00 1000.00
11 William Piercy 300.00 600.00
12 Curt Fullerton 300.00 600.00
13 Sloppy Thurston 300.00 600.00
14 Rube Walberg 300.00 600.00
15 Fred Heimach 300.00 600.00
16 Sherry Smith 300.00 600.00
17 Warren Ogden 300.00 600.00
18 Ernest Osborne 300.00 600.00
19 Dutch Ruether 300.00 600.00
20 Burleigh Grimes 500.00 1000.00
21 Joe Genewich 300.00 600.00
22 Vic Aldridge 300.00 600.00
23 Arnold Stone 300.00 600.00
24 Les Howe 300.00 600.00
25 George Murry 300.00 600.00
26 Herman Pillette 300.00 600.00
27 John Couch 300.00 600.00
28 Tony Kaufmann 300.00 600.00
29 Frank May 300.00 600.00
30 Howard Ehmke 350.00 700.00
31 Bob Hasty 300.00 600.00
32 Dazzy Vance 600.00 1200.00
33 Gorham Leverette 300.00 600.00
34 Bryan Harris 300.00 600.00
35 Paul Schreiber 300.00 600.00
36 Dewey Hinkle 300.00 600.00
37 Byron Yarrison 300.00 600.00
38 Jesse Haines 400.00 800.00
39 Earl Hamilton 300.00 600.00
40 Wilbur Cooper 350.00 700.00
41 Tom Long 300.00 600.00
42 Alex Ferguson 300.00 600.00
43 Chet Ross 300.00 600.00
44 Jack Quinn 350.00 700.00
45 Ray Kolp 300.00 600.00
46 Art Nehf 350.00 700.00
47 Hugh McQuillan 300.00 600.00
48 George Uhle 350.00 700.00
49 Ed Rommel 350.00 700.00
50 Ted Lyons 500.00 1000.00
51 Roy Meeker 300.00 600.00
52 John Stuart 300.00 600.00
53 Joe Oeschger 300.00 600.00
54 Wayland Dean 300.00 600.00
55 Guy Morton 300.00 600.00
56 Bill Doak 300.00 600.00
57 Ed Pfeffer 300.00 600.00
58 Sam Gray 300.00 600.00
59 Lou North 300.00 600.00
60 Godfrey Brogan 300.00 600.00
61 Jimmy Ring 300.00 600.00
62 Rube Marquard 500.00 1000.00
63 Bert Lewis 300.00 600.00
64 Frank Henry 300.00 600.00
65 Dennis Burns 300.00 600.00
66 Roline Naylor 300.00 600.00
67 Walt Huntzinger 300.00 600.00
68 Stan Baumgartner 300.00 600.00
69 Virgil Barnes 300.00 600.00
70 Clarence Mitchell 300.00 600.00
71 Lee Meadows 300.00 600.00
72 Charles Clazner 300.00 600.00
73 Jesse Barnes 300.00 600.00
74 Sam Jones 350.00 700.00
75 Dennis Gearin 300.00 600.00
76 Tom Zachary 350.00 700.00
77 Larry Benton 300.00 600.00
78 Jess Winter 300.00 600.00
79 Red Ruffing 600.00 1200.00
80 John Cooney 300.00 600.00
81 Joe Bush 350.00 700.00
82 William Harris 300.00 600.00
83 Joe Shaute 300.00 600.00
84 George Pipgras 350.00 700.00
85 Eppa Rixey 500.00 1000.00
86 Bill Sherdel 300.00 600.00
87 John Benton 300.00 600.00
88 Art Decatur 300.00 600.00
89 Harry Shriver 300.00 600.00
90 John Morrison 300.00 600.00
91 Walter Betts 300.00 600.00
92 Oscar Roettger 300.00 600.00
93 Bob Shawkey 500.00 1000.00
94 Mike Cvengros 300.00 600.00
95 Leo Dickerman 300.00 600.00
96 Phillip Weinert 300.00 600.00
97 Nicholas Dumovich 300.00 600.00
98 Herb McQuaid 300.00 600.00
99 Tim McNamara 300.00 600.00
100 Alan Russell 300.00 600.00
101 Ted Blankenship 300.00 600.00
102 Howard Baldwin 300.00 600.00
103 Frank Davis 300.00 600.00
104 James Edwards 300.00 600.00
105 Hub Pruett 350.00 700.00
106 Dick Rudolph 300.00 600.00
107 Allan Sothoron 300.00 600.00
108 Claude Jonnard 300.00 600.00
109 Joubert Davenport 300.00 600.00
110 Paul Zahnser 300.00 600.00
111 John Bentley 300.00 600.00
112 Wilfred Ryan 300.00 600.00
113 George Metevier 300.00 600.00
114 John Watson 300.00 600.00
115 Syl Johnson 300.00 600.00
116 Oscar Fuhr 300.00 600.00
117 Warren Collins 300.00 600.00
118 Stan Covelskie 500.00 1000.00
119 Dave Danforth 300.00 600.00
120 Elam Van Gilder 300.00 600.00
121 Bert Cole 300.00 600.00
122 Ken Holoway 300.00 600.00
123 Charles Robertson 300.00 600.00
124 Ed Wells 300.00 600.00
125 George Davis 300.00 600.00
126 William Bayne 300.00 600.00
127 Urban Shocker 400.00 800.00
128 Slim McGrew 300.00 600.00
129 Philip Bedgood 300.00 600.00
130 Fred Wingfield 300.00 600.00
131 George Modridge 300.00 600.00
132 Joe Martina 300.00 600.00
133 Byron Speece 300.00 600.00
134 Hal Carlson 300.00 600.00
135 Wilbur Hubbell 300.00 600.00
136 Milt Gaston 300.00 600.00

1951 DiMaggio Yankee Clipper Shoes

This one card set, which measures approximately 2 1/2" by 3 1/2" was issued as part of the shoe purchase. These cards were supposed to be tied to the shoe strings. The front has a batting portrait shot of DiMaggio set against a green background while the back a bullet point assortment of career highlights

1 Joe DiMaggio 25.00 50.00

1972-87 DiMaggio Bowery Bank

This one-card standard-size set was actually released three times. The first time was is 1972, the second was in 1979 and third was in 1987. We have priced the 1987 version here. The 1979 version is valued at $25 and the 1972 version is at $50. The front features a full-color photo of Dimaggio framed by the words Yankees on top and his name and position on the bottom. The horizontal backs has his career numbers, a brief biography and his vital statistics.

1 Joe DiMaggio 5.00 12.00

1972-83 Dimanche/Derniere Heure

The blank-backed photo sheets in this multi-sport set measure approximately 8 1/2" by 11" and feature white-bordered color sports star photos from Dimanche Derniere Heure, a Montreal newspaper. The player's name, position and biographical information appear within the lower white margin. All text is in French. A white vinyl album was available for storing the photo sheets. Printed on the album's spine are the words, "Mes Vedettes du Sport" (My Stars of Sport).The photos are unnumbered and are checklisted below in alphabetical order according to sport or team as follows: Montreal Expos baseball players (1-117; National League baseball players (118-130); Montreal Canadiens hockey players (131-177); wrestlers (178-202); prize fighters (203-204); auto racing drivers (205-208); women's golf (209); Patof the circus clown (210); and CFL (211-278).

1 Santo Alcala 1.00 2.00
2 Bill Almon 1.00 2.00
3 Bill Atkinson 1.00 2.00
4 Stan Bahnsen 1.00 2.00
5 Bob Bailey 1.00 2.00
6 Greg Bargar 1.00 2.00
7 Tony Bernazard 1.00 2.00
8 Tim Blackwell 1.00 2.00
9 Dennis Blair 1.00 2.00
10 John Boccabella 1.25 2.50
11 Jim Brewer CO 1.00 2.00
12 Hal Breeden 1.00 2.00
13 Dave Bristol CO 1.00 2.00
14 Jackie Brown 1.25 2.50
15 Ray Burris 1.00 2.00
16 Don Carrithers 1.00 2.00
17 Gary Carter 7.50 15.00
18 Dave Cash 1.00 2.00
19 Jim Cox 1.00 2.00
20 Warren Cromartie 1.00 2.00
21 Terry Crowley 1.00 2.00
22 Willie Davis 1.50 3.00
23 Andre Dawson 5.00 10.00
24 Boots Day 1.00 2.00
25 Don Demola 1.00 2.00
26 Larry Doby CO 2.00 4.00
27 Hal Dues 1.00 2.00
28 Duffy Dyer 1.00 2.00
29 Jim Fairey 1.00 2.00
30 Ron Fairly 1.50 3.00
31 Jim Fanning MG 1.00 2.00
32 Doug Flynn 1.00 2.00
33 Tim Foli 1.25 2.50
34 Barry Foote 1.00 2.00
35 Barry Foote/(Wearing chest protector and shin 1.00 2.00
36 Terry Francona 1.25 2.50
37 Pepe Frias 1.00 2.00
38 Woodie Fryman 1.00 2.00
39 Woodie Fryman 1.25 2.50
Jeff Reardon
40 Mike Garman 1.00 2.00
41 Wayne Garrett 1.00 2.00
42 Ross Grimsley 1.00 2.00
43 Bill Gullickson 1.00 2.00
44 Ed Herrmann 1.00 2.00
45 Terry Humphrey 1.00 2.00
46 Ron Hunt 1.25 2.50
47 Tommy Hutton 1.00 2.00
48 Bob James 1.00 2.00
49 Wallace Johnson 1.00 2.00
50 Mike Jorgensen 1.00 2.00
51 Joe Kerrigan 1.00 2.00
52 Darold Knowles 1.00 2.00
53 Coco Laboy 1.25 2.50
54 Charles Lea 1.00 2.00
55 Bill Lee 1.25 2.50
56 Ron LeFlore 1.25 2.50
57 Larry Lintz 1.00 2.00
58 Bryan Little 1.00 2.00
59 Ken Macha 1.00 2.00
60 Jerry Manuel 1.25 2.50
61 Mike Marshall 1.50 3.00
62 Clyde Mashore 1.00 2.00
63 Jim Mason 1.00 2.00
64 Gene Mauch MG 1.50 3.00
65 Rudy May 1.00 2.00
66 Ernie McAnally 1.00 2.00
67 Tim McCarver 2.00 4.00
68 Cal McLish CO 1.00 2.00
69 Sam Mejias 1.00 2.00
70 John Milner 1.00 2.00
71 John Montague 1.00 2.00
72 Willie Montanez 1.00 2.00
73 Balor Moore 1.00 2.00
74 Jose Morales 1.00 2.00
75 Dan Norman 1.00 2.00
76 Fred Norman 1.00 2.00
77 Al Oliver 2.00 4.00
78 David Palmer 1.00 2.00
79 Stan Papi 1.00 2.00
80 Larry Parrish 1.25 2.50
81 Tony Perez 2.00 4.00
82 Tim Raines 2.00 4.00
83 Tim Raines 2.00 4.00
Andre Dawson
Warren Cromartie
84 Bobby Ramos 1.00 2.00
85 Bob Reece 1.00 2.00
86 Steve Renko 1.00 2.00
87 Steve Rogers 1.50 3.00
88 Angel Salazar 1.00 2.00
89 Scott Sanderson 1.00 2.00
90 Dan Schatzeder 1.00 2.00
91 Rodney Scott 1.00 2.00
92 Norm Sherry CO 1.00 2.00
93 Ken Singleton 1.25 2.50
94 Tony Solaita 1.00 2.00
95 Elias Sosa 1.00 2.00
96 Chris Speier 1.00 2.00
97 Don Stanhouse 1.00 2.00
98 Mike Stenhouse 1.00 2.00
99 Bill Stoneman 1.25 2.50
100 John Strohmayer 1.00 2.00
101 John Tamargo 1.00 2.00
102 Frank Taveres 1.00 2.00
103 Chuck Taylor 1.00 2.00
104 Jeff Terpko 1.00 2.00
105 Hector Torres 1.00 2.00
106 Mike Torrez 1.25 2.50
107 Wayne Twitchell 1.00 2.00
108 Del Unser 1.00 2.00
109 Ellis Valentine 1.00 2.00
110 Mickey Vernon CO 1.25 2.50
111 Bill Virdon MG 1.25 2.50
112 Tom Walker 1.00 2.00
113 Tim Wallach 1.00 2.00
114 Dan Warthen 1.00 2.00
115 Jerry White 1.00 2.00
116 Dick Williams MG 1.50 3.00
117 Bobby Wine 1.00 2.00
118 Jim Wohlford 1.00 2.00
119 Ron Woods 1.00 2.00
120 Joel Youngblood 1.00 2.00
121 Hank Aaron 5.00 10.00
122 Johnny Bench 3.00 6.00
123 Larry Bowa 1.25 2.50
124 Steve Carlton 2.00 4.00
125 Roberto Clemente 5.00 10.00
126 Willie Davis 1.00 2.00
127 Bob Gibson 2.00 4.00
128 Ferguson Jenkins 2.00 4.00
129 Willie McCovey 2.00 4.00
130 Willie Montanez 1.00 2.00
131 Pete Rose 4.00 8.00
132 Willie Stargell 2.00 4.00
133 Rusty Staub 1.50 3.00
Mike Jorgensen

1988 Disney World Series

These two cards were issued during the 1988 season and featured three star members of various teams. The fronts have the players pictured with Mickey Mouse and the backs have the name of the team, the names of the Disney Palaces and are sponsored by Delta.

COMPLETE SET (3) 5.00 12.00
1 Kevin Bass 4.00 10.00
Nolan Ryan
Mike Scott
2 Jack Clark 2.00 5.00
Don Mattingly
Willie Randolph
3 Dave LaPoint .40 1.00
Greg Walker
Harold Baines

1937 Dixie Lids Small

This unnumbered set of lids is actually a combined sport and non-sport set with 24 different lids. The lids are found in more than one size, approximately 2 11/16" in diameter as well as 2 5/16" in diameter. The 1937 lids are distinguished from the 1938 Dixie Lids by the fact that the 1937 lids are printed in black or wine-colored ink where the 1938 lids are printed in blue ink. In the checklist below only the sports subjects are checklisted; non-sport subjects (celebrities) included in this 24-card set are Gene Autry, Freddie Bartholomew, Bill Boyd, Johnny Mack Brown, Madeleine Carroll, Nelson Eddy, Clark Gable, Jean Harlow, Carole Lombard, Myrna Loy, Fred MacMurray, Ken Maynard, Merle Oberon, Eleanor Powell, William Powell, Luisa Rainer, Charles Starrett and Robert Taylor. The catalog designation is F7-1.

COMPLETE SPORT (6) 175.00 350.00
*LARGE: .6X TO 1.5X SMALL
2 Charles Gehringer 50.00 100.00
3 Charles Hartnett 40.00 80.00
4 Carl Hubbell 60.00 120.00
5 Joe Medwick 40.00 80.00

1937 Dixie Premiums

COMPLETE SPORT SET (6) 175.00 350.00
2 Charles Gehringer 50.00 100.00
3 Charles Hartnett 40.00 80.00
4 Carl Hubbell 50.00 100.00
5 Joe Medwick 40.00 80.00

1938 Dixie Lids Small

This unnumbered set of lids is actually a combined sport and non-sport set with 24 different lids. The lids are found in more than one size, approximately 2 11/16" in diameter as well as 2 5/16" in diameter. The catalog designation is F7-1. The 1938 lids are distinguished from the 1937 Dixie Lids by the fact that the 1938 lids are printed in blue ink whereas the 1938 lids are printed in black or wine-colored ink. In the checklist below only the sports subjects are checklisted; non-sport subjects (celebrities) included in this 24 card set are Don Ameche, Annabella, Gene Autry, Warner Baxter, William Boyd, Bobby Breen, Gary Cooper, Alice Fay, Sonja Henie, Tommy Kelly, June Lang, Colonel Tim McCoy, Tyrone Power, Tex Ritter, Simone Simon, Bob Steele, The Three Musquiteers and Jane Withers.

COMPLETE SPORT SET (6) 250.00 500.00
*LARGE: .6X TO 1.5X SMALL
2 Bob Feller 40.00 80.00
3 Jimmie Foxx 40.00 80.00
4 Carl Hubbell 40.00 80.00
mouth open
5 Wally Moses 20.00 40.00

1938 Dixie Premiums

COMPLETE SET (6) 375.00 750.00
2 Bob Feller 50.00 100.00
3 Jimmie Foxx 50.00 100.00
4 Carl Hubbell 50.00 100.00
5 Wally Moses 25.00 50.00

1952 Dixie Lids

This scarce 24-lid set features all baseball subjects each measuring 2 11/16". The 1952 set was released very late in the year and in only one size; it is undoubtedly the toughest Dixie baseball set. The lids are found with a blue tint. The catalog designation for this set is F7-2A. Lids found with the tab removed would suffer an approximate 25 percent in value. The asterisked lids below are those that were only available in 1952. The 50s Dixie Lids are distinguished from the 30's lids also by the fact that the 50s lids have the circular picture portion abruptly squared off near the bottom end of the lid where the player's name appears.

COMPLETE SET (24) 3000.00 6000.00
1 Richie Ashburn 300.00 600.00
2 Tommy Byrne 150.00 300.00
3 Chico Carrasquel 125.00 250.00
4 Pete Castiglione 125.00 250.00
5 Walker Cooper 150.00 300.00
6 Billy Cox 125.00 250.00
7 Ferris Fain 125.00 250.00
8 Bobby Feller 350.00 700.00
9 Nellie Fox 250.00 500.00
10 Monte Irvin 250.00 500.00
11 Ralph Kiner 250.00 500.00
12 Cass Michaels 125.00 250.00
13 Don Mueller 125.00 250.00
14 Mel Parnell 125.00 250.00
15 Allie Reynolds 175.00 350.00
16 Preacher Roe 175.00 350.00
17 Connie Ryan 125.00 250.00
18 Hank Sauer 150.00 300.00
19 Al Schoendienst 250.00 500.00
20 Andy Seminick 150.00 300.00
21 Bobby Shantz 150.00 300.00
22 Enos Slaughter 250.00 500.00
23 Virgil Trucks 125.00 250.00
24 Gene Woodling 150.00 300.00

1952 Dixie Premiums

The catalog designation is F7-2A. The 1952 Dixie Cup Baseball Premiums contain 1951 statistics. There are 24 (sepia-tinted) black and white photos each measuring approximately 8" by 10". Each photo has a facsimile autograph at the bottom. These large premium photos are blank backed and were printed on thick paper stock.

COMPLETE SET (24) 1000.00 2000.00
1 Richie Ashburn 125.00 250.00
2 Tommy Byrne 40.00 80.00
3 Chico Carrasquel 40.00 80.00
4 Pete Castiglione 40.00 80.00
5 Walker Cooper 40.00 80.00
6 Billy Cox 40.00 80.00
7 Ferris Fain 40.00 80.00
8 Bob Feller 150.00 300.00
9 Nellie Fox 200.00 400.00
10 Monte Irvin 100.00 200.00
11 Ralph Kiner 100.00 200.00
12 Cass Michaels 40.00 80.00
13 Don Mueller 40.00 80.00
14 Mel Parnell 40.00 80.00
15 Allie Reynolds 60.00 120.00
16 Preacher Roe 60.00 120.00
17 Connie Ryan 40.00 80.00
18 Hank Sauer 50.00 100.00
19 Al Schoendienst 100.00 200.00
20 Andy Seminick 40.00 80.00
21 Bobby Shantz 50.00 100.00
22 Enos Slaughter 100.00 200.00
23 Virgil Trucks 40.00 80.00
24 Gene Woodling 50.00 100.00

1953 Dixie Lids

This 24-lid set features all baseball subjects each measuring 2 11/16". There are many different back types in existence. The lids are found with a wine tint. The catalog designation for this set is F7-2. Lids found without the tab attached are considered good condition at best. There is also a smaller size variation, 2 5/16" in diameter. These smaller lids are worth an additional 50 percent more than the prices listed below.

COMPLETE SET (24) 1200.00 2400.00
1 Richie Ashburn 100.00 200.00
2 Chico Carrasquel 40.00 80.00
3 Billy Cox 40.00 80.00
4 Ferris Fain 40.00 80.00
5 Nellie Fox 100.00 200.00
6A Sid Gordon 100.00 200.00
Boston Braves
6B Sid Gordon 40.00 80.00
Milwaukee Braves
7 Warren Hacker 40.00 80.00
8 Monte Irvin 100.00 200.00
9 Jackie Jensen 75.00 150.00
10 Ralph Kiner 100.00 200.00
11 Ted Kluszewski 100.00 200.00
12 Bob Lemon 100.00 200.00
13 Don Mueller 40.00 80.00
14 Mel Parnell 40.00 80.00
15 Jerry Priddy 40.00 80.00
16 Allie Reynolds 75.00 150.00
17 Preacher Roe 75.00 150.00
18 Hank Sauer 40.00 80.00
19 Al Schoendienst 100.00 200.00
20 Bobby Shantz 40.00 80.00
21 Enos Slaughter 100.00 200.00
22A Warren Spahn 175.00 350.00
Boston Braves
22B Warren Spahn 175.00 350.00
Milwaukee Braves
23A Virgil Trucks 40.00 80.00
Chicago White Sox
23B Virgil Trucks 40.00 80.00
St. Louis Browns
24 Gene Woodling 40.00 80.00

1953 Dixie Premiums

The catalog designation is F7-2A. The 1953 Dixie Cup Baseball Premiums contain 1952 statistics. There are 24 (sepia-tinted) black and white photos each measuring approximately 8" by 10". Each photo has a facsimile autograph at the bottom. These large premium photos are blank backed and were printed on thick paper stock.

COMPLETE SET (24) 800.00 1600.00
1 Richie Ashburn 100.00 200.00
2 Chico Carrasquel 30.00 60.00
3 Billy Cox 40.00 80.00
4 Ferris Fain 30.00 60.00
5 Nellie Fox 175.00 350.00
6 Sid Gordon 30.00 60.00
7 Warren Hacker 30.00 60.00
8 Monte Irvin 75.00 150.00
9 Jack Jensen 50.00 100.00
10 Ralph Kiner 75.00 150.00
11 Ted Kluszewski 60.00 120.00
12 Bob Lemon 75.00 150.00
13 Don Mueller 30.00 60.00
14 Mel Parnell 30.00 60.00
15 Jerry Priddy 30.00 60.00
16 Allie Reynolds 50.00 100.00
17 Preacher Roe 75.00 150.00
18 Hank Sauer 40.00 80.00
19 Al Schoendienst 60.00 120.00
20 Bobby Shantz 40.00 80.00
21 Enos Slaughter 60.00 120.00
22 Warren Spahn 100.00 200.00
23 Virgil Trucks 30.00 60.00
24 Gene Woodling 40.00 80.00

1954 Dixie Lids

This 18 lid set features all baseball subjects each measuring 2 11/16". There are many different back types in existence. The lids are typically found with a brown sepia tint. The catalog designation for this set is F7-4. Lids found without the tab attached are considered good condition at best. This year is distinguishable by the fact that the lids say "Get Dixie Lid 3-D Starviewer. Send 25 cents, this lid, name, address, to DIXIE, Box 630, New York 17, N.Y." around the border on the front. The lids have an "L" or "R" on the tab, which distinguished which side of the 3-D viewer was to be used for that particular card. The lids are also seen in a small (2 5/16") and large (3 3/16") size; these variations carry approximately double the prices below.

COMPLETE SET (18) 500.00 1000.00
1 Richie Ashburn 60.00 120.00
2 Clint Courtney 30.00 60.00
3 Sid Gordon 30.00 60.00
4 Billy Hoeft - 30.00 60.00
5 Monte Irvin 60.00 120.00
6 Jackie Jensen 50.00 100.00
7 Ralph Kiner 60.00 120.00
8 Ted Kluszewski 60.00 120.00
9 Gil McDougald 50.00 100.00
10 Minnie Minoso 50.00 100.00
11 Danny O'Connell 30.00 60.00
12 Mel Parnell 30.00 60.00
13 Preacher Roe 50.00 100.00
14 Al Rosen 40.00 80.00
15 Al Schoendienst 40.00 80.00
16 Enos Slaughter 60.00 120.00
17 Gene Woodling 30.00 60.00
18 Gus Zernial 30.00 60.00

1991 Doc The Video

This one-card set features a color portrait photo of Dwight Gooden on the front posed with video equipment while the back has another photo of Gooden; seasonal and career stats; biographical information as well as an informational blurb.

COMPLETE SET (1)
1 Dwight Gooden 4.00 10.00

1969-72 Dodge Promo Postcards

These postcards were issued by the car maker, Dodge to promote some of their lines of cars. These cards feature players involved in the 1968 World Series and feature a player photo as well as a photo of the card being promoted. The back is blank except for a brief description of the player as well as how it relates to the "Dodge car" pictured on the front. The cards are unnumbered so we have sequenced them in alphabetical order.

COMPLETE SET (4) 15.00 40.00
1 Lou Brock 4.00 10.00
2 Bill Freehan 3.00 8.00
3 Joe Garagiola 4.00 10.00
4 Mickey Lolich 3.00 8.00

1909 Dodgers Daily Eagle Supplement

These supplments to the Brooklyn Daily Eagle are sepia toned photos and measure approximately 7" by 9 1/2" and feature members of the Brooklyn Dodgers. Since the photos are unnumbered, we have sequenced them in alphabetical order. Also, it is possible that there are more cards in this set so any additions to this checklist is appreciated.

COMPLETE SET 250.00 500.00
1 George Bell 50.00 100.00
2 George Hunter 50.00 100.00
3 Doc Scanlon 50.00 100.00
4 Kaiser Wilhelm 50.00 100.00
5 Harry McIntire 50.00 100.00
Jimmy Pastorious

1940 Dodgers Team Issue

These photos measure approximately 6 1/2" by 9". They feature members of the 1940 Brooklyn Dodgers. The photos take up nearly all of the card except for a small white border. There is also a facsimile signature of each player. The backs are blank and we have sequenced them in alphabetical order. Pee Wee Reese appears in his rookie season in this set.

COMPLETE SET (25) 150.00 300.00
1 Dolph Camilli 7.50 15.00
2 Tex Carleton 5.00 10.00
3 Hugh Casey 6.00 12.00
4 Pete Coscarart 5.00 10.00
5 Curt Davis 5.00 10.00
6 Leo Durocher 10.00 20.00
7 Fred Fitzsimmons 6.00 12.00
8 Herman Franks 5.00 10.00
9 Joe Gallagher 5.00 10.00
10 Charlie Gilbert 5.00 10.00
11 Luke Hamlin 5.00 10.00
12 Johnny Hudson 5.00 10.00
13 Newt Kimball 5.00 10.00
14 Cookie Lavagetto 6.00 12.00
15 Gus Mancuso 5.00 10.00
16 Joe Medwick 10.00 20.00
17 Van Lingle Mungo 6.00 12.00
18 Babe Phelps 5.00 10.00
19 Tot Pressnell 5.00 10.00
20 Pee Wee Reese 25.00 50.00
21 Vito Tamulis 5.00 10.00
22 Joe Vosmik 5.00 10.00
23 Dixie Walker 7.50 15.00
24 Jimmy Wasdell 5.00 10.00
25 Whit Wyatt 6.00 12.00

1941 Dodgers Team Issue

These are blank-backed, white-bordered, 6 1/2" X 9" black-and-white photos. The photos have fascimile autographs, are unnumbered and checklisted below in alphabetical order.

COMPLETE SET (28) 125.00 250.00
1 Mace Brown 5.00 10.00
2 Dolph Camilli 7.50 15.00
3 Tex Carleton 5.00 10.00
4 Hugh Casey 5.00 10.00
5 Pete Coscarart 5.00 10.00
6 Curt Davis 5.00 10.00
7 Leo Durocher MG 15.00 30.00
8 Fred Fitzsimmons 6.00 12.00
9 Herman Franks 5.00 10.00
10 Joe Gallagher 5.00 10.00
10 Jimmy Wasdell 5.00 10.00
11 Charlie Gilbert 5.00 10.00
11 Kemp Wicker 5.00 10.00
12 Luke Hamlin 5.00 10.00
13 Johnny Hudson 5.00 10.00
14 Newill Kimball 5.00 10.00
15 Cookie Lavagetto 6.00 12.00
16 Gus Mancuso 6.00 12.00
17 Joe Medwick 15.00 30.00
18 Van Mungo 7.50 15.00
19 Babe Phelps 5.00 10.00
20 Tot Pressnell 5.00 10.00
21 Pee Wee Reese 20.00 40.00
22 Lew Riggs 5.00 10.00
23 Bill Swift 5.00 10.00
24 Vito Tamulis 5.00 10.00
25 Joe Vosmik 5.00 10.00
26 Dixie Walker 7.50 15.00
27 Jimmy Wasdell 5.00 10.00
28 Whit Wyatt 5.00 10.00

1942 Dodgers Team Issue

This 25-card set of the Brooklyn Dodgers measures approximately 6 1/2" by 9" and features black-and-white player portraits with a facsimile autograph. The cards are unnumbered and checklisted below in alphabetical order.

COMPLETE SET (25) 125.00 250.00
1 Johnny Allen 5.00 10.00
2 Frenchy Bordagaray 5.00 10.00
3 Dolph Camilli 6.00 12.00
4 Hugh Casey 5.00 10.00
5 Curt Davis 5.00 10.00
6 Leo Durocher 10.00 20.00
7 Larry French 6.00 12.00
8 Augie Galan 5.00 10.00
9 Ed Head 5.00 10.00
10 Billy Herman 10.00 20.00
11 Kirby Higbe 6.00 12.00
12 Alex Kampouris 5.00 10.00
13 Newell Kimball 5.00 10.00
14 Joe Medwick 10.00 20.00
15 Mickey Owen 6.00 12.00
16 Pee Wee Reese 10.00 20.00
17 Pete Reiser 7.50 15.00
18 Lew Riggs 5.00 10.00
19 Johnny Rizzo 5.00 10.00
20 Schoolboy Rowe 6.00 12.00
21 Bill Sullivan 5.00 10.00
22 Arky Vaughn 10.00 20.00
23 Dixie Walker 7.50 15.00
24 Les Webber 5.00 10.00
25 Whitlow Wyatt 6.00 12.00

1943 Dodgers Team Issue

This set of the Brooklyn Dodgers measures approximately 6 1/2" by 9". The black-and-white player photos display fascimile autographs. The backs are blank. The cards are unnumbered and checklisted below in alphabetical order.

COMPLETE SET (25) 100.00 200.00
1 Johnny Allen 6.00 12.00
2 Frenchy Bordagaray 5.00 10.00
3 Bob Bragan 6.00 12.00
4 Dolph Camilli 7.50 15.00
5 John Cooney 5.00 10.00
6 John Corriden 5.00 10.00
7 Curt Davis 5.00 10.00
8 Leo Durocher 10.00 20.00
9 Fred Fitzimmons 6.00 12.00
10 Augie Galan 6.00 12.00
11 Al Glossop 5.00 10.00
12 Ed Head 5.00 10.00
13 Billy Herman 10.00 20.00
14 Kirby Higbe 6.00 12.00
15 Max Macon 5.00 10.00
16 Joe Medwick 10.00 20.00
17 Rube Melton 5.00 10.00
18 Dee Moore 5.00 10.00
19 B. Newsom 7.50 15.00
20 Mickey Owen 6.00 12.00
21 Arky Vaughan 10.00 20.00
22 Dixie Walker 7.50 15.00
23 Paul Waner 10.00 20.00
24 Les Webber 5.00 10.00
25 Whitlow Wyatt 5.00 10.00

1943 Dodgers War Bonds

Issued in conjunction with a war bonds drive in 1943, this card, which measure 2 1/2" by 4 3/8" features a team photo of the 1943 Brooklyn Dodgers. Because of the nature of how it was issued, not many of these cards have survived.

1 Brooklyn Dodgers 250.00 500.00

1946 Dodgers Team Issue

This 25-card set of the Brooklyn Dodgers measures approximately 6 1/2" by 9" and features black-and-white player portraits with white borders. The backs are blank. The cards are unnumbered and checklisted below in alphabetical order.

COMPLETE SET (25) 125.00 250.00
1 Ferrell(Andy) Anderson 4.00 8.00
2 Henry Behrman 4.00 8.00
3 Ralph Branca 7.50 15.00
4 Hugh Casey 4.00 8.00
5 Leo Durocher 7.50 15.00
6 Carl Furillo 7.50 15.00
7 Augie Galan 5.00 10.00
8 Hal Gregg 4.00 8.00
9 Joe Hatten 4.00 8.00
10 Ed Head 4.00 8.00
11 Billy Herman 7.50 15.00
12 Gene Hermanski 4.00 8.00
13 Art Herring 4.00 8.00
14 Kirby Higbe 5.00 10.00
15 Cookie Lavagetto 6.00 12.00
16 Vic Lombardi 4.00 8.00
17 Pee Wee Reese 15.00 30.00
18 Pete Reiser 6.00 12.00
19 Stan Rojek 4.00 8.00
20 Mike Sandlock 4.00 8.00
21 Eddie Stanky 7.50 15.00
22 Ed Stevens 4.00 8.00
23 Dixie Walker 6.00 12.00
24 Les Webber 4.00 8.00
25 Dick Whitman 4.00 8.00

1947 Dodgers Team Issue

This 25-card set of the Brooklyn Dodgers measures approximately 6 1/2" by 9" and features black-and-white player portraits with white borders and facsimile autographs. The backs are blank. The cards are unnumbered and checklisted below in alphabetical order. Carl Furillo, Gil Hodges and Duke Snider are featured in this set, two years before their Rookie Cards. Jackie Robinson is featured in this set as well during his rookie season.

COMPLETE SET (25) 150.00 300.00
1 Ray Blades 4.00 8.00
2 Bob Bragan 5.00 10.00
3 Ralph Branca 6.00 12.00
4 Tommy Brown 4.00 8.00
5 Hugh Casey 4.00 8.00
6 Eddie Chandler 4.00 8.00
7 Carl Furillo 12.50 25.00
8 Hal Gregg 4.00 8.00
9 Joe Hatten 4.00 8.00
10 Gene Hermanski 4.00 8.00
11 Gil Hodges 15.00 30.00
12 John Jorgensen 4.00 8.00
13 Clyde King 4.00 8.00
14 Vic Lombardi 4.00 8.00
15 Rube Melton 4.00 8.00
16 Eddie Miksis 4.00 8.00
17 Pee Wee Reese 7.50 15.00
18 Pete Reiser 6.00 12.00
19 Jackie Robinson 50.00 100.00
20 Stan Fojek 4.00 8.00
21 B.E. Shotton 4.00 8.00
22 Duke Snider 20.00 40.00
23 Eddie Stanky 6.00 12.00
24 Harry Taylor 4.00 8.00
25 Dixie Walker 5.00 10.00

1948 Dodgers Team Issue

This 26-card set of the Brooklyn Dodgers measures approximately 6 1/2" by 9" and features black-and-white player portraits with white borders. The backs are blank. The cards are unnumbered and checklisted below in alphabetical order. This set can be dated to 1948 with the inclusion of Preston Ward in his only season in Brooklyn.

COMPLETE SET (26) 150.00 300.00
1 Rex Barney 5.00 10.00
2 Ray Blades 4.00 8.00
3 Bob Bragan 5.00 10.00
4 Ralph Branca 6.00 12.00
5 Tommy Brown 4.00 8.00
6 Hugh Casey 4.00 8.00
7 Billy Cox 6.00 12.00
8 Leo Durocher 7.50 15.00
9 Bruce Edwards 4.00 8.00
10 Carl Furillo 6.00 12.00
11 Joe Hatten 4.00 8.00
12 Gene Hermanski 4.00 8.00
13 Gil Hodges 12.50 25.00
14 John Jorgensen 4.00 8.00

15 Don Lund	4.00	8.00
16 Eddie Miksis	4.00	8.00
17 Jake Pitler	4.00	8.00
18 Pee Wee Reese	20.00	40.00
19 Pete Reiser	6.00	12.00
20 Jackie Robinson	30.00	60.00
21 Preacher Roe	6.00	12.00
22 B.E. Shotton	4.00	8.00
23 Clyde Sukeforth	4.00	8.00
24 Harry Taylor	4.00	8.00
25 Arky Vaughan	7.50	15.00
26 Preston Ward	4.00	8.00

1949 Dodgers Team Issue

This 25-card set of the Brooklyn Dodgers measures approximately 6 1/2" by 9" and features black-and-white player portraits with white borders. The backs are blank. The cards are unnumbered and checklisted below in alphabetical order. Roy Campanella is featured in his Rookie Card year. Don Newcombe is featured in this set a year prior to his Rookie Card. The Dodgers, Giants, Red Sox and Yankees Team Issue sets were all available at time of issue from Harry M Stevens for 68 cents per set.

COMPLETE SET (25)	200.00	400.00
1 Jack Banta	5.00	10.00
2 Rex Barney	6.00	12.00
3 Ralph Branca	7.50	15.00
4 Tommy Brown	5.00	10.00
5 Roy Campanella	25.00	50.00
6 Billy Cox	7.50	15.00
7 Bruce Edwards	5.00	10.00
8 Carl Furillo	10.00	20.00
9 Joe Hatten	5.00	10.00
10 Gene Hermanski	5.00	10.00
11 Gil Hodges	10.00	20.00
12 Johnny Hopp	5.00	10.00
13 Spider Jorgensen	5.00	10.00
14 Mike McCormick	5.00	10.00
15 Eddie Miksis	5.00	10.00
16 Don Newcombe	10.00	20.00
17 Erv Palica	5.00	10.00
18 Jake Pitler CO	5.00	10.00
19 Pee Wee Reese	25.00	50.00
20 Jackie Robinson	40.00	80.00
21 Preacher Roe	5.00	10.00
22 Burt Shotton MG	5.00	10.00
23 Duke Snider	25.00	50.00
24 Milt Stock CO	5.00	10.00
25 Clyde Sukeforth CO	5.00	10.00

1955 Dodgers Golden Stamps

This 32-stamp set features color photos of the Brooklyn Dodgers and measures approximately 2" by 2 5/8". The stamps are designed to be placed in a 32-page album which measures approximately 8 3/8" by 10 15/16". The album contains black-and-white drawings of players with statistics and life stories. The stamps are unnumbered and listed below according to where they fall in the album. Sandy Koufax appears in what was both his rookie and Rookie Card season.

COMPLETE SET (32)	100.00	200.00
1 Walt Alston MG	6.00	12.00
2 Don Newcombe	2.00	4.00
3 Carl Erskine	2.00	4.00
4 Johnny Podres	2.00	4.00
5 Billy Loes	1.25	2.50
6 Russ Meyer	1.25	2.50
7 Jim Hughes	1.25	2.50
8 Sandy Koufax	40.00	80.00
9 Joe Black	1.50	3.00
10 Karl Spooner	1.25	2.50
11 Clem Labine	1.50	3.00
12 Roy Campanella	10.00	20.00
13 Gil Hodges	6.00	12.00
14 Jim Gilliam	2.50	5.00
15 Jackie Robinson	20.00	40.00
16 Pee Wee Reese	10.00	20.00
17 Duke Snider	10.00	20.00
18 Carl Furillo	2.50	5.00
19 Sandy Amoros	2.00	4.00
20 Frank Kellert	1.25	2.50
21 Don Zimmer	2.00	4.00
22 Al Walker	1.25	2.50
23 Tom Lasorda	10.00	20.00
24 Ed Roebuck	1.25	2.50
25 Don Hoak	1.25	2.50
26 George Shuba	1.50	3.00
27 Billy Herman CO	2.00	4.00
28 Jake Pitler CO	1.25	2.50
29 Joe Becker CO	1.25	2.50
30 Doc Wendler	1.50	3.00
Carl Furillo		
31 Charlie Di Giovanna	1.25	2.50
32 Ebbets Field	10.00	20.00
XX Album	2.50	5.00

1956 Dodgers Team Issue

Issued the year after the Brooklyn Dodgers won their only World Series, these 12 black and white blank-backed photos, which measure 5" by 7" feature some of the key members of the 1956 Brooklyn Dodgers. The pack was issued in an envelope which cost 25 cents upon release in 1956. Since these photos are unnumbered, we have sequenced them in alphabetical order.

COMPLETE SET (12)	75.00	150.00
1 Walt Alston MG	5.00	10.00
2 Roy Campanella	10.00	20.00
3 Carl Erskine	4.00	8.00
4 Carl Furillo	4.00	8.00
5 Gil Hodges	7.50	15.00
6 Randy Jackson	2.50	5.00
7 Clem Labine	3.00	6.00
8 Don Newcombe	4.00	8.00
9 Johnny Podres	4.00	8.00
10 Pee Wee Reese	10.00	20.00
11 Jackie Robinson	12.50	25.00
12 Duke Snider	10.00	20.00

1958 Dodgers Bell Brand

The 1958 Bell Brand Potato Chips set of ten unnumbered cards features members of the Los Angeles Dodgers exclusively. Each card has a 1/4" green border, and the Gino Cimoli, Johnny Podres, Pee Wee Reese and Duke Snider cards are more difficult to find; they are marked with an SP (short printed) in the checklist below. The cards measure approximately 3" by 4". This set marks the first year for the Dodgers in Los Angeles and includes a Campanella card despite the fact that he never played for the team in California. The catalog designation for this set is F339-1. Cards found still inside the original cellophane wrapper are valued at double the prices below. According to printed reports, the promotion went badly for Bell Brand and much of the product was destroyed. The cards were found in both 29 cent and 49 cent packages.

COMPLETE SET (10)	3000.00	6000.00
COMMON CARD (1-10)	100.00	200.00
COMMON SP	200.00	400.00
1 Roy Campanella	400.00	800.00
2 Gino Cimoli SP	200.00	400.00
3 Don Drysdale	250.00	500.00
4 Jim Gilliam	100.00	200.00
5 Gil Hodges	200.00	400.00
6 Sandy Koufax	500.00	1000.00
7 Johnny Podres SP	300.00	600.00
8 Pee Wee Reese SP	400.00	800.00
9 Duke Snider SP	600.00	1200.00
10 Don Zimmer	100.00	200.00

1958 Dodgers Jay Publishing

This 12-card set of the Los Angeles Dodgers measures approximately 5" by 7" and features black-and-white player photos in a white border. These cards were packaged 12 to a packet. The backs are blank. The cards are unnumbered and checklisted below in alphabetical order.

COMPLETE SET (12)	37.50	75.00
1 Walt Alston MG	2.50	5.00
2 Roy Campanella	7.50	15.00
3 Gino Cimoli	1.50	3.00
4 Don Drysdale	5.00	10.00
5 Carl Furillo	2.50	5.00
6 Gil Hodges	5.00	10.00
7 Clem Labine	1.50	3.00
8 Charley Neal	1.50	3.00
9 Don Newcombe	2.50	5.00
10 Johnny Podres	2.50	5.00
11 Pee Wee Reese	7.50	15.00
12 Duke Snider	5.00	10.00

1958 Dodgers Team Issue

This 25-card set features black-and-white photos of the Los Angeles Dodgers in white borders. The backs are blank. The set could originally be obtained through the mail for $1. Later on this set was also sold at the park for $1 and due to lack of early sales was later reduced to $.50. The cards are unnumbered and checklisted below in alphabetical order.

COMPLETE SET (25)	62.50	125.00
1 Walt Alston MG	3.00	6.00
2 Joe Becker CO	1.50	3.00
3 Don Bessent	1.50	3.00
4 Roger Craig	2.50	5.00
5 Charlie Dressen CO	2.50	5.00
6 Don Drysdale	5.00	10.00
7 Carl Erskine	2.50	5.00
8 Carl Furillo	2.50	5.00
9 Junior Gilliam	2.50	5.00
10 Gil Hodges	5.00	10.00
11 Randy Jackson	1.50	3.00
12 Sandy Koufax	10.00	20.00
13 Clem Labine	2.50	5.00
14 Danny McDevitt	1.50	3.00
15 Greg Mulleavy CO	1.50	3.00
16 Charlie Neal	1.50	3.00
17 Don Newcombe	2.50	5.00
18 Joe Pignatano	1.50	3.00
19 Johnny Podres	2.50	5.00
20 Pee Wee Reese	5.00	10.00
21 Ed Roebuck	1.50	3.00
22 Duke Snider	5.00	10.00
23 Elmer Valo	2.00	4.00
24 Rube Walker	1.50	3.00
25 Don Zimmer	2.50	5.00

1958 Dodgers Volpe

Printed on heavy paper stock, these blank-backed reproductions of artist Nicholas Volpe's charcoal portraits of the 1958 Los Angeles Dodgers were issued in two sizes, 2 5/8" by 3 3/4" and 8" by 10". The player's name appears near the bottom. The smaller size was sold by mail at a cost of 50 cents a protrait. The larger size was also sold by mail by the club for $1.00 a card. The portraits are unnumbered and checklisted below in alphabetical order.

COMPLETE SET (12)	200.00	400.00
1 Walter Alston	15.00	30.00
2 Gino Cimolli	12.50	25.00
3 Don Drysdale	30.00	60.00
4 Carl Erskine	12.50	25.00
5 Carl Furillo	15.00	30.00
6 Jim Gilliam	15.00	30.00
7 Gil Hodges	30.00	60.00
8 Clem Labine	12.50	25.00
9 Don Newcombe	15.00	30.00
10 Johnny Podres	15.00	30.00
11 Pee Wee Reese	40.00	80.00
12 Duke Snider	40.00	80.00

1959 Dodgers Morrell

The cards in this 12-card set measure 2 1/2" by 3 1/2". The 1959 Morrell Meats set of full color, unnumbered cards features Los Angeles Dodger players only. The photos used are the same as those selected for the Dodger team issue postcards in 1959. The Morrell Meats logo is on the backs of the cards. The Clem Labine card actually features a picture of Stan Williams and the Norm Larker card actually features a picture of Joe Pignatano as indicated in the checklist below. The catalog designation is F172-1.

COMPLETE SET (12)	750.00	1250.00
1 Don Drysdale	75.00	150.00
2 Carl Furillo	60.00	120.00
3 Jim Gilliam	60.00	120.00
4 Gil Hodges	75.00	150.00
5 Sandy Koufax	150.00	300.00
6 Clem Labine UER/(Photo actually Stan Williams)	40.00	80.00
7 Norm Larker UER/(Photo actually Joe Pignatano)	40.00	80.00
8 Charlie Neal	40.00	80.00
9 Johnny Podres	60.00	120.00
10 John Roseboro	50.00	100.00
11 Duke Snider	150.00	300.00
12 Don Zimmer	50.00	100.00

1959 Dodgers Postcards

These 12 postcards were issued by the Dodgers during the 1959 season and feature some of the leading players from the team. The cards have color photos on the front and brown printing on the back and were produced by the H.S. Crocker Co. in LA. A couple of the players are misidentified and we have notated them as such.

COMPLETE SET (12)	100.00	200.00
901 Duke Snider	12.50	25.00
902 Gil Hodges	10.00	20.00
903 Johnny Podres	6.00	12.00
904 Carl Furillo	6.00	12.00
905 Don Drysdale	12.50	25.00
906 Sandy Koufax	25.00	50.00
907 Jim Gilliam	6.00	12.00
908 Don Zimmer	6.00	12.00
909 Charlie Neal	5.00	10.00
910 Norm Larker UER	5.00	10.00
911 Clem Labine	6.00	12.00
912 John Roseboro	5.00	10.00

1959 Dodgers Team Issue

This 26-card set of the Los Angeles Dodgers measures approximately 5" by 7" and features black-and-white player photos in a white border. The backs are blank. The cards are unnumbered and checklisted below in alphabetical order.

COMPLETE SET (26)	37.50	75.00
1 Walter Alston MG	3.00	6.00
2 Don Bessent	1.50	3.00
3 Roger Craig	1.50	3.00
4 Charlie Dressen CO	1.50	3.00
5 Don Drysdale	5.00	10.00
6 Carl Erskine	2.50	5.00
7 Ron Fairly	2.50	5.00
8 Carl Furillo	2.50	5.00
9 Junior Gilliam	2.50	5.00
10 Gil Hodges	3.00	6.00
11 Fred Kipp	1.50	3.00
12 Sandy Koufax	7.50	15.00
13 Clem Labine	2.00	4.00
14 Norm Larker	1.50	3.00
15 Bob Lillis	1.50	3.00
16 Danny McDevitt	1.50	3.00
17 Wally Moon	1.50	3.00
18 Greg Mulleavy CO	1.50	3.00
19 Charlie Neal	1.50	3.00
20 Joe Pignatano	1.50	3.00
21 Johnny Podres	2.50	5.00
22 Pee Wee Reese	3.00	6.00
23 Rip Repulski	1.50	3.00
24 John Roseboro	1.50	3.00
25 Duke Snider	3.00	6.00
26 Don Zimmer	2.00	4.00

1959 Dodgers Volpe

Issued on thin paper stock, these blank-backed reproductions of artist Nicholas Volpe's charcoal portraits of the 1959 Dodgers measure approximately 8" by 10". The player's name appears near the bottom. The portraits are unnumbered and checklisted below in alphabetical order. The Campanella portrait has his career stats on the back.

COMPLETE SET (15)	125.00	250.00
1 Walter Alston MG	10.00	25.00
2 Roy Campnella TRIB	12.50	30.00
3 Don Drysdale	12.50	30.00
4 Carl Erskine	10.00	25.00
5 Carl Furillo	10.00	25.00
6 Jim Gilliam	10.00	25.00
7 Gil Hodges	12.50	30.00
8 Clem Labine	8.00	20.00
9 Wally Moon	8.00	20.00
10 Don Newcombe	10.00	25.00
11 Johnny Podres	8.00	20.00
12 Pee Wee Reese CO	15.00	40.00
13 Rip Repulski	8.00	20.00
14 Vin Scully ANN	8.00	20.00
Jerry Doggett ANN		
15 Duke Snider	15.00	40.00

1960 Dodgers Bell Brand

The 1960 Bell Brand Potato Chips set of 20 full color, numbered cards features Los Angeles Dodgers only. Because these cards, measuring approximately 2 1/2" by 3 1/2", were issued in packages of potato chips, many cards suffered from stains. Clem Labine, Johnny Klippstein, and Walt Alston are somewhat more difficult to obtain than other cards in the set; they are marked with SP (short printed) in the checklist below. The catalog designation for this set is F339-2.

COMPLETE SET (20)	500.00	1000.00
COMMON CARD (1-20)	8.00	20.00
COMMON SP	50.00	100.00
1 Norm Larker	8.00	20.00
2 Duke Snider	50.00	100.00
3 Danny McDevitt	8.00	20.00
4 Jim Gilliam	12.50	30.00
5 Rip Repulski	8.00	20.00
6 Clem Labine SP	60.00	120.00
7 John Roseboro	8.00	20.00
8 Carl Furillo	10.00	25.00
9 Sandy Koufax	100.00	200.00
10 Joe Pignatano	8.00	20.00
11 Chuck Essegian	8.00	20.00
12 John Klippstein SP	50.00	100.00
13 Ed Roebuck	8.00	20.00
14 Don Demeter	8.00	20.00
15 Roger Craig	10.00	25.00
16 Stan Williams	8.00	20.00
17 Don Zimmer	10.00	25.00
18 Walt Alston SP MG	75.00	150.00
19 Johnny Podres	12.50	30.00
20 Maury Wills	15.00	40.00

1960 Dodgers Jay Publishing

This set of the Los Angeles Dodgers measures approximately 5" by 7" and features black-and-white player photos in a white border. The backs are blank. These cards were originally packaged 12 to a packet. The set is more than 12 cards as changes during the season necessitated a second printing. The cards are unnumbered and checklisted below in alphabetical order.

COMPLETE SET (16)	20.00	50.00
1 Roger Craig	1.25	3.00
2 Don Demeter	1.25	3.00
3 Don Drysdale	2.50	6.00
4 Ron Fairly	1.50	4.00
5 Junior Gilliam	2.00	5.00
6 Gil Hodges	2.50	6.00
7 Frank Howard	2.00	5.00
8 Norm Larker	1.25	3.00
9 Wally Moon	1.50	4.00
10 Charlie Neal	1.25	3.00
11 Johnny Podres	2.00	5.00
12 John Roseboro	1.50	4.00
13 Larry Sherry	1.25	3.00
14 Duke Snider	2.50	6.00
15 Stan Williams	1.25	3.00
16 Maury Wills	2.00	5.00

1960 Dodgers Morrell

The cards in this 12-card set measure 2 1/2" by 3 1/2". The 1960 Morrell Meats set of full color, unnumbered cards is similar in format to the 1959 Morrell set but can be distinguished from the 1959 set by a red heart which appears in the Morrell logo on the back. The photos used are the same as those selected for the Dodger team issue postcards in 1960. The Furillo, Hodges, and Snider cards received limited distribution and are hence more scarce. The catalog designation is F172-2. The cards were printed in Japan.

COMPLETE SET (12)	600.00	1200.00
COMMON CARD (1-12)	12.50	30.00
COMMON SP	60.00	120.00
1 Walt Alston MG	40.00	80.00
2 Roger Craig	15.00	40.00
3 Don Drysdale	60.00	120.00
4 Carl Furillo SP	60.00	120.00
5 Gil Hodges SP	125.00	250.00
6 Sandy Koufax	150.00	300.00
7 Wally Moon	12.50	30.00
8 Charlie Neal	12.50	30.00
9 Johnny Podres	20.00	50.00
10 John Roseboro	12.50	30.00
11 Larry Sherry	12.50	30.00
12 Duke Snider SP	200.00	400.00

1960 Dodgers Postcards

These 12 postcards feature members of the 1960 Los Angeles Dodgers. These cards are unnumbered and we have sequenced them in alphabetical order. The Furillo card is very scarce as he was released midway through the season and this card is therefored presumed no longer circulated after that point. We are considering the Furillo card a SP

COMPLETE SET (12)	30.00	60.00
COMMON PLAYER (1-10)	1.00	2.50
COMMON SP	4.00	10.00
1 Walt Alston MG	2.00	5.00
2 Roger Craig	1.25	3.00
3 Don Drysdale	3.00	8.00
4 Carl Furillo SP	4.00	10.00
5 Gil Hodges	2.00	5.00
6 Sandy Koufax	4.00	10.00
7 Wally Moon	1.25	3.00
8 Charlie Neal	1.00	2.50
9 Johnny Podres	1.50	4.00
10 Johnny Roseboro	1.25	3.00
11 Larry Sherry	1.00	2.50
12 Duke Snider	3.00	8.00

1960 Dodgers Team Issue

These 20 blank-backed, black-and-white photos of the 1960 Dodgers have white borders around posed player shots and measure approximately 5" by 7". The pictures came in a manila envelope that carried the year of issue. The player's facsimile autograph appears in the margin below each photo. The photos are unnumbered and checklisted below in alphabetical order.

COMPLETE SET (20)	40.00	80.00
1 Walter Alston MG	2.00	5.00
2 Bob Bragan CO	1.00	2.50
3 Roger Craig	1.25	3.00
4 Don Demeter	1.00	2.50
5 Don Drysdale	3.00	8.00
6 Chuck Essegian	1.00	2.50
7 Jim Gilliam	1.50	4.00
8 Gil Hodges	3.00	8.00
9 Frank Howard	1.50	4.00
10 Sandy Koufax	6.00	15.00
11 Norm Larker	1.00	2.50
12 Wally Moon	1.00	2.50
13 Charlie Neal	1.00	2.50
14 Johnny Podres	1.50	4.00
15 Pete Reiser CO	1.00	2.50
16 John Roseboro	1.25	3.00
17 Larry Sherry	1.25	3.00
18 Duke Snider	3.00	8.00
19 Stan Williams	1.00	2.50
20 Maury Wills	2.00	5.00

1960 Dodgers Union Oil

The set contains 23, 16-page unnumbered booklets which describe and give more detailed biographies of the player on the front covers. These booklets were given away at Union Oil gas stations and covered members of the 1960 Los Angeles Dodgers. The back page of the booklets had the Dodger schedule on it along with an ad for Union Oil. They are sometimes referenced as "Meet the Dodger Family" booklets. Each booklet measures approximately 5 3/8" by 7 1/2".

COMPLETE SET (23)	40.00	80.00
1 Walt Alston MG	2.00	5.00
2 Roger Craig	1.25	3.00
3 Tom Davis	1.50	4.00
4 Don Demeter	.75	2.00
5 Don Drysdale	4.00	10.00
6 Chuck Essegian	.75	2.00
7 Jim Gilliam	1.50	4.00
8 Gil Hodges	4.00	10.00
9 Frank Howard	1.50	4.00
10 Sandy Koufax	8.00	20.00
11 Norm Larker	.75	2.00
12 Wally Moon	1.25	3.00
13 Charlie Neal	.75	2.00
14 Johnny Podres	1.50	4.00
15 Ed Roebuck	.75	2.00
16 John Roseboro	1.25	3.00
17 Larry Sherry	.75	2.00
18 Norm Sherry	.75	2.00
19 Duke Snider	4.00	10.00
20 Stan Williams	.75	2.00
21 Maury Wills	2.00	5.00
22 Dodger Broadcasters/(Vin Scully and Jerry Dogget	1.25	3.00
23 Dodger Coaches	.75	2.00
Greg Mulleavy CO		
Joe Becker CO		
B		

1961 Dodgers Bell Brand

The 1961 Bell Brand Potato Chips set of 20 full color cards features Los Angeles Dodger players only and is numbered by the uniform numbers of the players. The cards are slightly smaller (approximately 2 7/16" by 3 1/2") than the 1960 Bell Brand cards and are on thinner paper stock. The catalog designation is F339-3.

COMPLETE SET (20)	250.00	500.00
3 Willie Davis	12.50	30.00
4 Duke Snider	50.00	100.00
5 Norm Larker	8.00	20.00
8 John Roseboro	10.00	25.00
9 Wally Moon	10.00	25.00
11 Bob Lillis	8.00	20.00
12 Tommy Davis	12.50	30.00
14 Gil Hodges	15.00	40.00
16 Don Demeter	8.00	20.00
19 Jim Gilliam	12.50	30.00
22 John Podres	12.50	30.00
24 Walt Alston MG	15.00	40.00
30 Maury Wills	15.00	40.00
32 Sandy Koufax	75.00	150.00
34 Norm Sherry	8.00	20.00
37 Ed Roebuck	8.00	20.00
38 Roger Craig	10.00	25.00
40 Stan Williams	8.00	20.00
43 Charlie Neal	8.00	20.00
51 Larry Sherry	8.00	20.00

1961 Dodgers Jay Publishing

This 12-card set of the Los Angeles Dodgers measures approximately 5" by 7". The fronts feature black-and-white posed player portraits with the player's and team name printed below in the white border. The backs are blank. The cards are unnumbered and checklisted below in alphabetical order.

COMPLETE SET (11)	15.00	40.00
1 Walt Alston MG	2.00	5.00
2 Don Drysdale	3.00	8.00
3 Junior Gilliam	1.50	4.00
4 Frank Howard	1.50	4.00
5 Norm Larker	.75	2.00
6 Wally Moon	.75	2.00
7 Charlie Neal	.75	2.00
8 Johnny Podres	1.50	4.00
9 John Roseboro	.75	2.00
10 Larry Sherry	.75	2.00
11 Stan Williams	.75	2.00
12 Maury Wills	2.00	5.00

1961 Dodgers Morrell

The cards in this six-card set measure 2 1/2" by 3 1/2". The 1961 Morrell Meats set of full color, unnumbered cards features Los Angeles Dodger players only and contains statistical information on the backs of the cards in brown print. The catalog designation is F172-3.

COMPLETE SET (6)	600.00	1200.00
1 Tommy Davis	50.00	100.00
2 Don Drysdale	150.00	300.00
3 Frank Howard	60.00	120.00
4 Sandy Koufax	300.00	600.00
5 Norm Larker	40.00	80.00
6 Maury Wills	75.00	150.00

1961 Dodgers Union Oil

The set contains 24, 16-page unnumbered booklets which describe and give more detailed biographies of the player on the front covers. These booklets were given away by Union Oil at gas stations and covered members of the 1961 Los Angeles Dodgers. The back page of the booklets had the Dodger schedule on it along with an ad for Union Oil. They are sometimes referenced as "Meet the Dodger Family" booklets. Each booklet measures approximately 5 3/8" by 7 1/2".

COMPLETE SET (24)	50.00	100.00
1 Walt Alston MG	2.00	5.00
2 Roger Craig	1.50	4.00
3 Tommy Davis	1.50	4.00
4 Willie Davis	1.50	4.00
5 Don Drysdale	4.00	10.00
6 Dick Farrell	.75	2.00
7 Ron Fairly	1.25	3.00
8 Jim Gilliam	1.50	4.00
9 Gil Hodges	4.00	10.00
10 Frank Howard	2.00	5.00
11 Sandy Koufax	8.00	20.00
12 Norm Larker	.75	2.00
13 Wally Moon	1.25	3.00
14 Charlie Neal	.75	2.00
15 Ron Perranoski	1.25	3.00
16 Johnny Podres	1.50	4.00
17 John Roseboro	1.25	3.00
18 Larry Sherry	.75	2.00
19 Norm Sherry	.75	2.00
20 Duke Snider	4.00	10.00
21 Daryl Spencer	.75	2.00
22 Stan Williams	.75	2.00
23 Maury Wills	2.00	5.00
24 Dodger Broadcasters/(Vin Scully and Jerry Dogget	1.25	3.00

1962 Dodgers Bell Brand

The 1962 Bell Brand Potato Chips set of 20 full color cards features Los Angeles Dodger players only and is numbered by the uniform numbers of the players. These cards were printed on a high quality glossy paper, much better than the previous two years, virtually eliminating the grease stains. This set is distinguished by a 1962 Home schedule on the backs of the cards. The cards measure 2 7/16" by 3 1/2", the same size as the year before. The catalog designation is F339-4.

COMPLETE SET (20)	500.00	1000.00
3 Willie Davis	20.00	50.00
4 Duke Snider	75.00	150.00
6 Ron Fairly	15.00	40.00
8 John Roseboro	15.00	40.00
9 Wally Moon	15.00	40.00
12 Tommy Davis	20.00	50.00
16 Ron Perranoski	15.00	40.00
19 Jim Gilliam	20.00	50.00
20 Daryl Spencer	12.50	30.00
22 John Podres	20.00	50.00
24 Walt Alston MG	30.00	60.00
25 Frank Howard	20.00	50.00
30 Maury Wills	30.00	60.00
32 Sandy Koufax	125.00	250.00
34 Norm Sherry	12.50	30.00
37 Ed Roebuck	12.50	30.00
40 Stan Williams	12.50	30.00
51 Larry Sherry	12.50	30.00
53 Don Drysdale	50.00	100.00
56 Lee Walls	12.50	30.00

1962 Dodgers Jay Publishing

This 12-card set of the Los Angeles Dodgers measures approximately 5" by 7". The fronts feature black-and-white posed player photos with the player's and team name printed below in the white border. These cards were packaged 12 in a packet. The backs are blank. The cards are unnumbered and checklisted below in alphabetical order.

COMPLETE SET (12)	30.00	60.00
1 Walt Alston MG	2.00	5.00
2 Don Drysdale	3.00	8.00
3 Ron Fairly	1.25	3.00
4 Jim Gilliam	1.50	4.00
5 Frank Howard	1.25	3.00
6 Sandy Koufax	6.00	15.00
7 Wally Moon	1.00	2.50
8 John Podres	1.25	3.00
9 John Roseboro	1.25	3.00
10 Duke Snider	3.00	8.00
11 Stan Williams	1.00	2.50
12 Maury Wills	2.00	5.00

1962-65 Dodgers Postcards

These ten cards were printed by "Plastic Chrome" and distributed by Mitock and Sons Postcards. All the photos were taken at Dodger Stadium. The backs are red and black with a sketch of Dodgers Stadium on the back in the early cards. These same cards were issued through 1965 so it is really difficult to tell the years apart. We are using the last three numbers printed on the postcard to identify the card number.

COMPLETE SET (10)	40.00	80.00
315 Willie Davis	3.00	8.00
316 Larry Sherry	2.00	5.00
317 Ron Perranoski	2.00	5.00
318 Sandy Koufax	8.00	20.00
319 Frank Howard	4.00	10.00
320 Tommy Davis	2.50	6.00
321 Don Drysdale	6.00	15.00
322 John Roseboro	2.50	6.00
323 Ron Fairly	2.00	5.00
324 Maury Wills	4.00	10.00

1962 Dodgers Volpe

These cards measure 8 3/4" by 11". This set, like many others of the period, were drawn by noted sports artist Nicholas Volpe. They were issued by Union Oil Co/Phillips 76. The backs have a brief biography of Volpe. This set was released one per week during the 1962 season.

COMPLETE SET (24)	125.00	250.00
1 Sandy Koufax	15.00	40.00
2 Wally Moon	3.00	8.00
3 Don Drysdale	8.00	20.00
4 Jim Gilliam	5.00	12.00
5 Larry Sherry	3.00	8.00
6 John Roseboro	4.00	10.00
7 Willie Davis	4.00	10.00
8 Norm Sherry	3.00	8.00
9 Lee Walls	3.00	8.00
10 Stan Williams	3.00	8.00
11 Tommy Davis	4.00	10.00
12 Ron Fairly	4.00	10.00
13 Larry Burright	3.00	8.00
14 Duke Snider	8.00	20.00
15 Ron Perranoski	3.00	8.00
16 Maury Wills	6.00	15.00
17 Frank Howard	5.00	12.00
18 Joe Moeller	3.00	8.00
19 Ed Roebuck	3.00	8.00
20 Andy Carey	3.00	8.00
21 Johnny Podres	5.00	12.00
22 Daryl Spencer	3.00	8.00
23 Doug Camilli	3.00	8.00
24 Tim Harkness	3.00	8.00

1963 Dodgers Jay Publishing

The 1963 Dodgers Jay set consists of 13 cards produced by Jay Publishing. The Skowron card establishes the year of the set, since 1963 was Skowron's only year with the Dodgers. The cards measure approximately 4 3/4" by 7 1/4" and are printed on thin photographic paper stock. The white fronts feature a black-and-white player portrait with the player's name and the team name below. The backs are blank. The cards are packaged 12 to a packet. The cards are unnumbered and checklisted below in alphabetical order. As far as we can tell, the Bill Skowron card was added and the Wally Moon card not issued in the second printing.

COMPLETE SET (13)	20.00	50.00
1 Walt Alston MG	2.00	5.00
2 Tom Davis	1.25	3.00
3 Willie Davis	1.25	3.00
4 Don Drysdale	3.00	8.00
5 Ron Fairly	1.25	3.00
6 Jim Gilliam	1.25	3.00
7 Frank Howard	1.50	4.00
8 Sandy Koufax	6.00	15.00
9 Wally Moon	1.25	3.00
10 Johnny Podres	1.25	3.00
11 John Roseboro	1.00	2.50
12 Bill Skowron	1.25	3.00
13 Maury Wills	2.00	5.00

1964 Dodgers Heads Up

This ten-card blank-backed set was issued in 1964 as a way to further merchandise some of the Los Angeles stars. This set features a large full-color head shot of a player which came with instructiions on how to push out the players face and the rest of the torso. The whole cardboard sheet measures approximately 7 1/4" by 8 1/2". There was a quantity of these items found in the late 1980's. Since these are unnummbered, they are checklisted below alphabetically.

COMPLETE SET (10)	15.00	40.00
1 Tom Davis	1.25	3.00
2 Willie Davis	1.25	3.00
3 Don Drysdale	3.00	8.00
4 Ron Fairly	1.25	3.00
5 Frank Howard	1.50	4.00
6 Sandy Koufax	6.00	15.00
7 Joe Moeller	1.00	2.50
8 Ron Perranoski	1.00	2.50
9 John Roseboro	1.25	3.00
10 Maury Wills	2.00	5.00

1964 Dodgers Jay Publishing

This 12-card set of the Los Angeles Dodgers measures approximately 5" by 7". The fronts feature black-and-white posed player photos with the player's and team name printed below in the white border. These cards were packaged 12 to a packet. The backs are blank. The cards are unnumbered and checklisted below in alphabetical order.

COMPLETE SET (12)	20.00	50.00
1 Walt Alston MG	2.00	5.00
2 Tom Davis	1.25	3.00
3 Willie Davis	1.25	3.00
4 Don Drysdale	3.00	8.00
5 Ron Fairly	1.25	3.00
6 Jim Gilliam	1.50	4.00
7 Frank Howard	1.50	4.00
8 Sandy Koufax	6.00	15.00
9 Wally Moon	1.00	2.50
10 John Podres	1.50	4.00
11 John Roseboro	1.00	2.50
12 Maury Wills	2.00	5.00

1964 Dodgers Volpe

This set which measure approximately 8 1/2" by 11" features members of the L.A. Dodgers and were drawn by noted sports artist Nicholas Volpe. These posters were distributed at local Union 76 gas stations. The drawings featured a large full-size facial shot while the background had the player dressed in street clothes.

COMPLETE SET	100.00	200.00
1 Willie Davis	4.00	10.00
2 Tommy Davis	6.00	15.00
3 Don Drysdale	8.00	20.00
4 Ron Fairly	4.00	10.00
5 Jim Gilliam	4.00	10.00
6 Frank Howard	6.00	15.00
7 Sandy Koufax	12.50	30.00
8 Bob Miller	3.00	8.00
9 Joe Moeller	3.00	8.00
10 Wally Moon	4.00	10.00
11 Phil Ortega	3.00	8.00
12 Wes Parker	5.00	12.00
13 Ron Perranoski	3.00	8.00
14 Johnny Podres	4.00	10.00
15 John Roseboro	4.00	10.00
16 Dick Tracewski	3.00	8.00
17 Lee Walls	3.00	8.00
18 Maury Wills	6.00	15.00

1965 Dodgers Jay Publishing

These 12 cards feature members of the World Champion Los Angeles Dodgers. They were issued in a pack as a 12 card set and the cards are unnumbered and checklisted below in alphabetical order. This set was issued twice to correct the Tommy and Willie Davis misidentifications.

COMPLETE SET (14)	30.00	60.00
1 Walter Alston MG	2.00	5.00
2A Tommy Davis ERR	2.00	5.00
Photo is Willie Davis		
2B Tommy Davis COR	2.00	5.00
3A Willie Davis ERR	2.00	5.00
Photo is Tommy Davis		
3B Willie Davis COR	2.00	5.00
4 Don Drysdale	3.00	8.00
5 Ron Fairly	1.25	3.00
6 Lou Johnson	1.00	2.50
7 Sandy Koufax	6.00	15.00
8 Jim Lefebvre	1.25	3.00
9 Claude Osteen	1.00	2.50
10 Wes Parker	1.25	3.00
11 John Roseboro	1.25	3.00
12 Maury Wills	2.00	5.00

1965 Dodgers Team Issue

These 21 blank-backed, black-and-white photos of the 1965 Los Angeles Dodgers have white borders around posed player shots and measure approximately 5" by 7". The player's facsimile autograph appears in the bottom margin on each photo. The pictures came in an undated manila envelope. The year of issue was determined to be 1965 because that was Dick Tracewski's last year with the Dodgers and Lou Johnson's first. The photos are unnumbered and checklisted below in alphabetical order.

COMPLETE SET (21)	30.00	60.00
1 Walter Alston MG	1.50	4.00
2 Willie Crawford	.60	1.50
3 Tommy Davis	1.25	3.00
4 Willie Davis	1.25	3.00
5 Don Drysdale	2.50	6.00
6 Ron Fairly	.75	2.00
7 Derrell Griffith	.60	1.50
8 Lou Johnson	.60	1.50
9 John Kennedy	.60	1.50
10 Sandy Koufax	6.00	15.00
11 Bob Miller	.60	1.50
12 Nate Oliver	.60	1.50
13 Claude Osteen	.75	2.00
14 Wes Parker	.75	2.00
15 Ron Perranoski	.75	2.00
16 Johnny Podres	1.25	3.00

17 John Purdin	.60	1.50
18 Howie Reed	.60	1.50
19 John Roseboro	.75	2.00
20 Dick Tracewski	.60	1.50
21 Maury Wills	1.50	4.00

1970 Dodgers Team Issue

These blank-backed cards featured members of the 1970 Los Angeles Dodgers. The fronts have a player photo with the fascimile autograph on the bottom. These photos were sold in a special envelope which said 20 individual pictures 50 cents and photo of the stadium and a drawing on the envelope. Since these cards are unnumbered, we have sequenced them in alphabetical order.

COMPLETE SET	15.00	40.00
1 Walt Alston MG	1.25	3.00
2 Jim Brewer	.75	2.00
3 Willie Crawford	.75	2.00
4 Willie Davis	1.00	2.50
5 Alan Foster	.75	2.00
6 Len Gabrielson	.75	2.00
7 Bill Grabarkewitz	.75	2.00
8 Tom Haller	.75	2.00
9 Andy Kosco	.75	2.00
10 Ray Lamb	.75	2.00
11 Jim Lefebvre	.75	2.00
12 Joe Moeller	.75	2.00
13 Manny Mota	1.00	2.50
14 Fred Norman	.75	2.00
15 Claude Osteen	.75	2.00
16 Wes Parker	.75	2.00
17 Bill Singer	.75	2.00
18 Ted Sizemore	.75	2.00
19 Bill Sudakis	.75	2.00
20 Maury Wills	1.50	4.00

1971 Dodgers Photos

These photos featured the members of the 1971 Los Angeles Dodgers. They are unnumbered and are therefore sequenced alphabetically. It is possible there are more photos so any additions to this list is appreciated.

COMPLETE SET	15.00	40.00
1 Walt Alston MG	2.00	5.00
2 Bill Buckner	1.50	4.00
3 Jim Brewer	.75	2.00
4 Willie Crawford	.75	2.00
5 Bill Grabarkewitz	.75	2.00
6 Jim Lefebvre	1.25	3.00
7 Pete Mikkelsen	.75	2.00
8 Joe Moeller	.75	2.00
9 Manny Mota	1.25	3.00
10 Danny Ozark CO	.75	2.00
11 Jose Pena	.75	2.00
12 Bill Russell	1.50	4.00
13 Duke Sims	.75	2.00
14 Bill Singer	1.25	3.00
15 Mike Strahler	.75	2.00
16 Billy Sudakis	.75	2.00
17 Don Sutton	2.50	6.00
18 Bobby Valentine	1.50	4.00

1971 Dodgers Ticketron

The 1971 Ticketron Los Angeles Dodgers set is a 20-card set with cards measuring approximately 4" by 6". This set has a 1971 Garvey rookie year card as well as 18 other players including Richie Allen in his only year as a Dodger. The fronts are beautiful full-color photos which also have a facsimile autograph on the front and are borderless while the backs contain an advertisement for Ticketron, the 1971 Dodger home schedule and a list of promotional events scheduled for 1971. These unnumbered cards are listed in alphabetical order for convenience.

COMPLETE SET (20)	30.00	60.00
1 Richie Allen	2.00	5.00
2 Walt Alston MG	2.00	5.00
3 Jim Brewer	.75	2.00
4 Willie Crawford	.75	2.00
5 Willie Davis	1.25	3.00
6 Steve Garvey	6.00	15.00
7 Bill Grabarkewitz	.75	2.00
8 Jim Lefebvre	1.25	3.00
9 Pete Mikkelsen	.75	2.00
10 Joe Moeller	.75	2.00
11 Manny Mota	1.25	3.00
12 Claude Osteen	1.25	3.00
13 Wes Parker	1.25	3.00
14 Bill Russell	1.50	4.00
15 Duke Sims	.75	2.00
16 Bill Singer	.75	2.00
17 Bill Sudakis	.75	2.00
18 Don Sutton	3.00	8.00
19 Maury Wills	2.00	5.00
20 Vic Scully ANN and Jerry Doggett ANN	1.50	4.00

1972 Dodgers McDonald's

These borderless discs have color player photos on the front. The backs have the player's name, some biographical information and the 1971 statistics. Since these discs are unnumbered, we have sequenced them in alphabetical order. These items are also known as photoballs.

COMPLETE SET	100.00	200.00
1 Walter Alston MG	6.00	15.00
2 Red Adams CO	4.00	10.00
3 Willie Crawford	4.00	10.00
4 Willie Davis	5.00	12.00
5 Al Downing	4.00	10.00
6 Jim Gilliam CO	5.00	12.00
7 Jim LeFebvre	4.00	10.00
8 Pete Mikkelsen	4.00	10.00
9 Manny Mota	5.00	12.00
10 Wes Parker	5.00	12.00
11 Claude Osteen	4.00	10.00
12 Bill Russell	4.00	10.00
13 Duke Sims	4.00	10.00
14 Bill Sudakis	4.00	10.00
15 Don Sutton	8.00	20.00
16 Bobby Valentine	6.00	15.00
17 Maury Wills	8.00	20.00

1973 Dodgers 1941 TCMA

This 32-card set features blue tinted photos of the 1941 National League Champion Brooklyn Dodgers. The backs carry player information. The cards are unnumbered and checklisted below alphabetically.

COMPLETE SET (32)	12.50	30.00
1 John Allen	.40	1.00
2 Mace Brown	.40	1.00
3 Adolf Camilli	.75	2.00
4 Hugh Casey	.60	1.50
5 Curtis Davis	.40	1.00
6 Thomas Drake	.40	1.00
7 Leo Durocher	1.50	4.00
8 Fred Fitzsimmons	1.00	2.50
9 Herman Franks	.40	1.00
10 August Galan	.60	1.50
11 Angelo Giuliani	.40	1.00
12 Luke Hamlin	.40	1.00
13 William Herman	1.00	2.50
14 Walter Higby	.40	1.00
15 Alex Kampouris	.40	1.00
16 Newell Kimball	.40	1.00
17 Cookie Lavagetto	.60	1.50
18 Joseph Medwick	1.00	2.50
19 Van Lingle Mungo	.60	1.50
20 N.L. Champion Card	.40	1.00
21 Mickey Owen	.40	1.00
22 Babe Phelps	.40	1.00
23 Pee Wee Reese	2.00	5.00
24 Harold Reiser	.60	1.50
25 Lewis Riggs	.40	1.00
26 William Swift	.40	1.00
27 Vitautis Tamulis	.40	1.00
28 Joseph Vosmik	.40	1.00
29 Dixie Walker	.75	2.00
30 Paul Waner	1.25	3.00
31 James Wasdell	.40	1.00
32 John Wyatt	.60	1.50

1973 Dodgers Postcards

These fifteen cards were created by Kolor View Press and were distributed by Mitock and Sonds. The fronts show clear photographs and the backs are in black print and all these cards are labeled KV5251. Since these cards are unnumbered, we have sequenced them in alphabetical order.

COMPLETE SET	12.50	30.00
1 Bill Buckner	1.00	2.50
2 Ron Cey	1.50	4.00
3 Willie Davis	1.00	2.50
4 Joe Ferguson	.75	2.00
5 Tommy John	1.25	3.00
6 Lee Lacy	.75	2.00
7 Tom Lasorda CO	1.50	4.00
8 Davey Lopes	1.25	3.00
9 Andy Messersmith	.75	2.00
10 Manny Mota	1.00	2.50
11 Claude Osteen	.75	2.00
12 Tom Paciorek	.75	2.00
13 Bill Russell	.75	2.00
14 Don Sutton	1.50	4.00
15 Steve Yeager	1.00	2.50

1973 Dodgers Team Issue

These 20 5" by 7" blank-backed black and white photos with fascimile autographs on the bottom feature members of the 1973 Los Angeles Dodgers. They were sold at the ballpark for 50 cents for the 20 photos. Since the photos are unnumbered, we have sequenced them in alphabetical order.

COMPLETE SET (20)	6.00	15.00
1 Walt Alston MG	.60	1.50
2 Red Adams CO	.20	.50
3 Jim Brewer	.20	.50
4 Bill Buckner	.40	1.00
5 Ron Cey	.60	1.50
6 Willie Davis	.30	.75
7 Joe Ferguson	.20	.50
8 Steve Garvey	1.25	3.00
9 Jim Gilliam CO	.30	.75
10 Charlie Hough	.30	.75
11 Tommy John	.60	1.50
12 Lee Lacy	.20	.50
13 Tom Lasorda CO	.60	1.50
14 Davey Lopes	.40	1.00
15 Manny Mota	.20	.50
16 Tom Paciorek	.20	.50
17 Doug Rau	.20	.50
18 Pete Richert	.20	.50
19 Bill Russell	.20	.50
20 Don Sutton	.75	2.00

1974 Dodgers 1952 TCMA Black/White Red Names

This 40-card set features players from the 1952 Brooklyn Dodgers team. The player photos can be found in three different color variations: blue and white photos with red names, black and white photos with red names, and blue and white photos with black names. The backs carry player information.

COMPLETE SET (40)	20.00	50.00
1 1952 Cover Card	.60	1.50
2 Cal Abrams	.40	1.00
3 Sandy Amoros	.60	1.50
4 Joe Black	1.00	2.50
5 Rocky Bridges	.40	1.00
6 Ralph Branca	.60	1.50
7 Roy Campanella	2.00	5.00
8 Billy Cox	.75	2.00
9 Chuck Dressen MG	.60	1.50
10 Carl Furillo	1.00	2.50
11 Jim Hughes	.40	1.00
12 Billy Herman CO	.60	1.50
13 Carl Erskine	1.00	2.50
14 Gil Hodges	1.25	3.00
15 Thomas Holmes	.40	1.00
16 Richard Williams	.60	1.50
17 Clyde King	.40	1.00
18 Stephen Lembo	.40	1.00
19 Ken Lehman	.40	1.00
20 Joe Landrum	.40	1.00
21 Clem Labine	.75	2.00
22 Ray Moore	.40	1.00
23 Bob Morgan	.40	1.00
24 Ron Negray	.40	1.00
25 Rocky Nelson	.40	1.00
26 Jake Pitler CO	.40	1.00
27 Billy Loes	.40	1.00
28 Cookie Lavagetto	.40	1.00
29 Andy Pafko	.60	1.50
30 Bud Podbielan	.40	1.00
31 Preacher Roe	1.00	2.50
32 John Rutherford	.40	1.00
33 Harold Reese	1.25	3.00
34 Jackie Robinson	2.00	5.00
35 George Shuba	.40	1.00
36 Johnny Schmitz	.40	1.00
37 Duke Snider	1.25	3.00
38 Chris Van Cuyk	.40	1.00
39 Ben Wade	.40	1.00
40 Rube Walker	.40	1.00

1974 Dodgers 1890 Program TCMA

This 16-card set contains copies of information included in the 1890 Brooklyn Dodgers programs. The cards measure approximately 4" by 4 1/4" and feature black-and-white player photos with artistically designed borders. The backs carry a paragraph about the player. The cards are unnumbered and checklisted below in alphabetical order.

COMPLETE SET (16)	3.00	8.00
1 Oyster Burns	.30	.75
2 Doc Bushong	.30	.75
3 Robert Lee Caruthers	.60	1.50
4 Robert H. Clark	.20	.50
5 Hubbert Collins	.20	.50
6 John S. Corkhill	.20	.50
7 Thomas P. Daly	.20	.50
8 Dave Foutz	.20	.50
9 Michael F. Hughes	.20	.50
10 Thomas J. Lovett	.20	.50
11 Bill McGunnigle MG	.20	.50
12 Wm. D. O'Brien	.20	.50
13 George Burton Pinkney	.20	.50
14 George J. Smith	.20	.50
15 George T. Stallings	.30	.75
16 Wm. H. Terry	.20	.50

1975 Dodgers All-Time TCMA

This 12-card set features black-and-white photos with white borders of all-time Dodgers great players. The cards are unnumbered and checklisted below in alphabetical order.

COMPLETE SET (12)	8.00	20.00
1 Walter Alston	.20	.50
2 Roy Campanella	.75	2.00
3 Hugh Casey	.20	.50
4 Don Drysdale	.75	2.00
5 Junior Gilliam	.40	1.00
6 Gil Hodges	.75	2.00
7 Sandy Koufax	1.25	3.00
8 Pee Wee Reese	1.00	2.50
9 Jackie Robinson	2.00	5.00
10 Duke Snider	1.25	3.00
11 Dixie Walker	.40	1.00
12 Zack Wheat	.60	1.50

1975 Dodgers Postcards

These 15 postcards were issued by Kolor View Press and featured members of the 1975 Dodgers. The fronts feature full-color photos while the backs were issued in black print. The Garvey card has the line "1974 National League MVP" added to the back. These cards are numbered with the prefix "KV7813" and we have used the final number in that sequence as our numbering of this set.

COMPLETE SET (15)	8.00	20.00
1 Bill Buckner	.60	1.50
2 Jim Wynn	.60	1.50
3 Henry Cruz	.40	1.00
4 Rick Auerbach	.40	1.00
5 Bill Russell	.40	1.00
6 Tom Paciorek	.40	1.00
7 Steve Yeager	.60	1.50
8 Don Sutton	1.00	2.50
9 Mike Marshall	.60	1.50
10 Ron Cey	.75	2.00
11 Rick Rhoden	.40	1.00
13 Joe Ferguson	.40	1.00
15 Davey Lopes	.75	2.00
31 Doug Rau	.40	1.00
57 Willie Crawford	.40	1.00

1976 Dodgers Photo Album

Issued as a photo album, but with easily perforated photos, which measure approximately 5 1/4" by 8 1/2" when seperated, these pictures feature members of the 1976 Los Angeles Dodgers. Since the photos were issued in alphabetical order, we have notated these photos in that order as well.

COMPLETE SET	12.50	30.00
1 Rick Auerbach	.40	1.00
2 Dusty Baker	.75	2.00
3 Bill Buckner	.60	1.50
4 Ron Cey	.40	1.00
5 Henry Cruz	.40	1.00
6 Al Downing	.40	1.00
7 Steve Garvey	1.00	2.50
8 Ed Goodson	.40	1.00
9 Burt Hooton	.40	1.00
10 Charlie Hough	.60	1.50
11 Tommy John	1.00	2.50
12 Lee Lacy	.40	1.00
13 Davey Lopes	.60	1.50
14 Manny Mota	.40	1.00
15 Doug Rau	.40	1.00
16 Rick Rhoden	.40	1.00
17 Ellie Rodriguez	.40	1.00
18 Bill Russell	.40	1.00
19 Ted Sizemore	.40	1.00
20 Reggie Smith	.60	1.50
21 Elias Sosa	.40	1.00
22 Don Sutton	1.25	3.00
23 Stan Wall	.40	1.00
24 Danny Walton	.40	1.00
25 Steve Yeager	.40	1.00
26 Walt Alston MG	.75	2.00
27 Red Adams CO Monty Basgall CO	.40	1.00
28 Jim Gilliam CO Tom Lasorda CO	.75	2.00

1976 Dodgers Postcards

This 10-card set of the Los Angeles Dodgers measures approximately 3 1/2" by 5 1/2" and features borderless color player photos with a facsimile player autograph printed in white. The backs carry a postcard format.

COMPLETE SET (10)	5.00	12.00
1 Walt Alston	.75	2.00
2 Ron Cey	.75	2.00
3 Tommy John	.75	2.00
4 Davey Lopes	.60	1.50
5 Charlie Hough	.50	1.25
6 Steve Garvey	1.25	3.00
7 Mike Marshall	.40	1.00
8 Joe Ferguson	.40	1.00
9 Dusty Baker	.60	1.50
10 Burt Hooton	.40	1.00

1977-78 Dodgers Photos

This 15-card set of the Los Angeles Dodgers features color player photos in white borders measuring approximately 8" by 10" and with a facsimile autograph. The backs are blank. There is no way to tell if the set was produced in 1977 or 1978. It could be either year. The cards are unnumbered and checklisted below in alphabetical order.

COMPLETE SET (15)	15.00	40.00
1 Ron Cey	.75	2.00
2 Steve Garvey	2.00	5.00
3 Burt Hooton	.75	2.00
4 Charlie Hough	1.25	3.00
5 Tommy John	1.50	4.00
6 Tom Lasorda MG	2.00	5.00
7 Davey Lopes	1.25	3.00
8 Rick Monday	.75	2.00
9 Manny Mota	1.25	3.00
10 Johnny Oates	.75	2.00
11 Doug Rau	.75	2.00
12 Rick Rhoden	.75	2.00
13 Bill Russell	.75	2.00
14 Reggie Smith	1.25	3.00
15 Steve Yeager	.75	2.00

1978 Dodgers 1941 TCMA

This 43-card set features blue-and-white action photos of the 1941 National League Champion Brooklyn Dodgers in white borders. The backs carry player information. Cards numbers 39 and 40 are oversized and measure 5" by 3".

COMPLETE SET (43)	6.00	15.00
1 Mickey Owen	.10	.25
2 Pee Wee Reese	.75	2.00
3 Hugh Casey	.10	.25
4 Larry French	.10	.25
5 Tom Drake	.10	.25
6 Ed Albasta	.10	.25
7 Tommy Tatum	.10	.25
8 Paul Waner	.60	1.50
9 Van Lingle Mungo	.20	.50
10 Bill Swift	.10	.25
11 Dolph Camilli	.30	.75
12 Pete Coscarart	.10	.25
13 Vito Tamulis	.10	.25
14 Johnny Allen	.10	.25
15 Lee Grissom	.10	.25
16 Billy Herman	.40	1.00
17 Joe Vosmik	.10	.25
18 Babe Phelps	.10	.25
19 Mace Brown	.10	.25
20 Freddie Fitzsimmons	.20	.50
21 Tony Giuliani	.10	.25
22 Lew Riggs	.10	.25
23 Jimmy Wasdell	.10	.25
24 Herman Franks	.10	.25
25 Alex Kampouris	.10	.25
26 Kirby Higby	.10	.25
27 Ducky Medwick	.40	1.00
28 Newt Kimball	.10	.25
29 Curt Davis	.10	.25
30 Augie Galan	.10	.25
31 Luke Hamlin	.10	.25
32 Cookie Lavagetto	.10	.25
33 Joe Gallagher	.10	.25
34 Whit Wyatt	.20	.50
35 Dixie Walker	.30	.75
36 Pete Reiser	.40	1.00
37 Leo Durocher MG	.40	1.00
38 Pee Wee Reese Ducky Medwick	.60	1.50
39 Dixie Walker Joe Medwick Dolph Camilli Pete Reiser		
40 Joe Medwick Billy Herman Pee Wee Reese Pete Reiser Mickey Owen Whit Wyatt		
41 Kemp Wicker	.10	.25
42 George Pfister CO	.10	.25
43 Chuck Dressen CO	.10	.25

1979 Dodgers Blue

This 15-card standard-size set features full-bleed posed color player photos. The backs are white and carry the slogan "Go Dodger Blue," the player's name, uniform number, batting and throwing preference and a player profile. The cards are unnumbered and checklisted below in alphabetical order.

COMPLETE SET (15)	4.00	10.00
1 Dusty Baker	.40	1.00
2 Ron Cey	.40	1.00
3 Terry Forster	.20	.50
4 Steve Garvey	.60	1.50
5 Burt Hooton	.20	.50
6 Charlie Hough	.30	.75
7 Tom Lasorda MG	.60	1.50
8 Davey Lopes	.40	1.00
9 Rick Monday	.30	.75
10 Manny Mota	.30	.75
11 Doug Rau	.20	.50
12 Bill Russell	.20	.50
13 Reggie Smith	.40	1.00
14 Don Sutton	.60	1.50
15 Steve Yeager	.30	.75

1979 Dodgers Postcards

These were the only new postcards issued of Dodger players in 1979. Other than Bob Welch who was playing his first full season, most of the other players were acquired from other teams.

COMPLETE SET	1.25	3.00
1 Joe Ferguson	.20	.50
2 Charlie Hough	.30	.75
3 Andy Messersmith	.20	.50
4 Derrel Thomas	.20	.50
5 Gary Thomasson	.20	.50
6 Bob Welch	.40	1.00

1980 Dodgers Greats TCMA

This 12-card standard-size set features some leading all-time Brooklyn Dodgers. The fronts have a player photo in the middle with the words "All-Time Dodgers" on top and his name on the bottom. The backs have vital statistics, a biography as well as career totals.

COMPLETE SET (12)	3.00	8.00
1 Gil Hodges	.40	1.00
2 Jim Gilliam	.20	.50
3 Pee Wee Reese	.60	1.50
4 Jackie Robinson	1.00	2.50
5 Sandy Koufax	.75	2.00
6 Zach Wheat	.20	.50
7 Dixie Walker	.20	.50
8 Hugh Casey	.08	.25
9 Dazzy Vance	.20	.50
10 Duke Snider	.60	1.50
11 Roy Campanella	.60	1.50
12 Walter Alston MG	.20	.50

1980 Dodgers Police

The cards in this 30-card set measure approximately 2 13/16" by 4 1/8". The full color 1980 Police Los Angeles Dodgers set features the player's name, uniform number, position, and biographical data on the fronts in addition to the photo. The backs feature Tips from the Dodgers, the LAPD logo, and the Dodgers' logo. The cards are listed below according to uniform number.

COMPLETE SET (30)	5.00	12.00
5 Johnny Oates	.08	.25
6 Steve Garvey	.40	1.00
7 Steve Yeager	.20	.50
8 Reggie Smith	.30	.75
9 Gary Thomasson	.08	.25
10 Ron Cey	.30	.75
12 Dusty Baker	.30	.75
13 Joe Ferguson	.08	.25
15 Davey Lopes	.30	.75
16 Rick Monday	.20	.50
18 Bill Russell	.08	.25
20 Don Sutton	.60	1.50
21 Jay Johnstone	.20	.50
23 Teddy Martinez	.08	.25
27 Joe Beckwith	.08	.25
28 Pedro Guerrero	.50	1.25
29 Don Stanhouse	.08	.25
30 Derrel Thomas	.08	.25
31 Doug Rau	.08	.25
34 Ken Brett	.08	.25
35 Bob Welch	.20	.50
37 Robert Castillo	.08	.25
38 Dave Goltz	.08	.25
41 Jerry Reuss	.20	.50
43 Rick Sutcliffe	.60	1.50
44 Mickey Hatcher	.08	.25
46 Burt Hooton	.20	.50
49 Charlie Hough	.30	.75
51 Terry Forster	.20	.50
NNO Team Card	.20	.50

1980 Dodgers TCMA 1959

This 40-card standard-size set features members of the 1959 Los Angeles Dodgers, who became the first team to win a World Series while playing on the West Coast. The cards have white blue with Dodger Blue borders inside them. There is a player photo and his name and position are on the bottom. The horizontal backs have vital stats as well as a blurb about the player and his 1959 and career stats

COMPLETE SET (40)	10.00	25.00
1 Joe Pignatano	.08	.25
2 Carl Furillo	.30	.75
3 Bob Lillis	.08	.25
4 Chuck Essegian	.08	.25
5 Dick Gray	.08	.25
6 Rip Repulski	.08	.25
7 Jim Baxes	.08	.25
8 Frank Howard	.40	1.00
9 Solly Drake	.08	.25
10 Sandy Amoros	.08	.25
11 Norm Sherry	.08	.25
12 Tommy Davis	.20	.50
13 Jim Gilliam	.20	.50
14 Duke Snider	.60	1.50
15 Maury Wills	.40	1.00
16 Don Demeter	.08	.25
17 Wally Moon	.20	.50
18 John Roseboro	.20	.50
19 Ron Fairly	.20	.50
20 Norm Larker	.08	.25
21 Charlie Neal	.08	.25
22 Don Zimmer	.30	.75
23 Chuck Dressen CO	.08	.25
24 Gil Hodges	.40	1.00
25 Joe Becker CO	.08	.25
26 Walter Alston MG	.40	1.00
27 Greg Mulleavy	.08	.25
28 Don Drysdale	.60	1.50
29 Johnny Podres	.08	.25
30 Sandy Koufax	1.00	2.50
31 Roger Craig	.08	.25
32 Danny McDevitt	.08	.25
33 Bill Harris	.08	.25
34 Larry Sherry	.08	.25
35 Stan Williams	.08	.25
36 Clem Labine	.20	.50
37 Chuck Churn	.08	.25
38 Johnny Klippstein	.08	.25
39 Carl Erskine	.20	.50
40 Fred Kipp	.08	.25

1981 Dodgers

This 12-card set of the Los Angeles Dodgers measures approximately 8" by 10" and features white-bordered color action player photos with a facsimile autograph on the front. The backs are blank. The cards are unnumbered and checklisted below in alphabetical order.

COMPLETE SET (12)	4.00	10.00
1 Dusty Baker	.40	1.00
2 Ron Cey	.40	1.00
3 Terry Forster	.20	.50
4 Steve Garvey	.75	2.00
5 Pedro Guerrero	.60	1.50
6 Burt Hooton	.20	.50
7 Davey Lopes	.40	1.00
8 Rick Monday	.30	.75
9 Jerry Reuss	.40	1.00
10 Don Sutton	1.00	2.50
11 Derrel Thomas	.20	.50
12 Fernando Valenzuela	1.25	3.00

1981 Dodgers Photos

These photos feature members of the World Champion 1981 Los Angeles Dodgers. They are unnumbered so we have sequenced them alphabetically.

COMPLETE SET	10.00	25.00
1 Dusty Baker	.40	1.00
2 Monty Basgall CO	.20	.50
3 Joe Beckwith	.20	.50
4 Robert Castillo	.20	.50
5 Ron Cey	.40	1.00
6 Mark Cresse CO	.20	.50
7 Joe Ferguson	.20	.50
8 Terry Forster	.20	.50
9 Pepe Frias	.20	.50
10 Steve Garvey	.60	1.50
11 Dave Goltz	.20	.50
12 Pedro Guerrero	.60	1.50
13 Burt Hooten	.20	.50
14 Steve Howe	.20	.50
15 Jay Johnstone	.30	.75
16 Ken Landreaux	.20	.50
17 Tommy Lasorda MG	.60	1.50
18 Rudy Law	.20	.50
19 Davey Lopes	.40	1.00
20 Rick Monday	.30	.75
21 Manny Mota CO	.20	.50
22 Danny Ozark CO	.20	.50
23 Ron Perranoski CO	.20	.50
24 Jerry Reuss	.30	.75
25 Bill Russell	.30	.75
26 Mike Scioscia	.75	2.00
27 Reggie Smith	.30	.75
28 Dave Stewart	.60	1.50
29 Rick Sutcliffe	.40	1.00
30 Derrel Thomas	.20	.50
31 Fernando Valenzuela	.75	2.00
32 Bob Welch	.40	1.00
33 Steve Yeager	.30	.75

1981 Dodgers Police

The cards in this 32-card set measure approximately 2 13/16" by 4 1/8". The full color set of 1981 Los Angeles Dodgers features the player's name, number, position and a line stating that the LAPD salutes the 1981 Dodgers, in addition to the player's photo. The backs feature the LAPD logo and short narratives, attributable to the player on the front of the card, revealing police associated tips. The cards of Ken Landreaux and Dave Stewart are reported to be more difficult to obtain than other cards in this set due to the fact that they are replacements for Stanhouse (released 4/17/81) and Hatcher (traded for Landreaux 3/30/81). The complete set price below refers to all 32 cards, i.e., including the variations. The Dave Stewart card pre-dates his Rookie Card.

COMPLETE SET (32)	8.00	20.00
COMMON CARD	.10	.25
COMMON SP	1.00	2.50
2 Tom Lasorda MG	.40	1.00
3 Rudy Law	.08	.25
6 Steve Garvey	.40	1.00
7 Steve Yeager	.20	.50
8 Reggie Smith	.30	.75
10 Ron Cey	.30	.75
12 Dusty Baker	.30	.75
13 Joe Ferguson	.08	.25
14 Mike Scioscia		1.25
15 Davey Lopes	.30	.75
16 Rick Monday	.20	.50
18 Bill Russell	.08	.25
21 Jay Johnstone	.20	.50
26 Don Stanhouse	.08	.25
27 Joe Beckwith	.08	.25
28 Pedro Guerrero	.40	1.00
30 Derrel Thomas	.08	.25
34 Fernando Valenzuela		1.25
35 Bob Welch	.30	.75
36 Pepe Frias	.08	.25
37 Robert Castillo	.08	.25
38 Dave Goltz	.08	.25
41 Jerry Reuss	.20	.50
43 Rick Sutcliffe	.40	1.00
44A Mickey Hatcher	.08	.25
44B Ken Landreaux SP	1.00	2.50
46 Burt Hooton	.20	.50
48 Dave Stewart SP	2.00	5.00
51 Terry Forster	.08	.25
57 Steve Howe	.08	.25
NNO Team Photo Checklist	.20	.50
NNO Coaching Staff Monty Basgall Tom Lasorda MG Dan	.20	.50

1981 Dodgers Postcards

This 11-card set of the Los Angeles Dodgers measures approximately 3 1/2" by 5 1/2" and features borderless color player photos with a facsimile autograph. The backs display a postcard format. The cards are unnumbered and checklisted below in alphabetical order.

COMPLETE SET (11)	4.00	10.00
1 Dusty Baker	.40	1.00
2 Steve Garvey	.60	1.50
3 Pedro Guerrero	.60	1.50
4 Steve Howe	.20	.50
5 Ken Landreaux	.20	.50
6 Davey Lopes	.40	1.00
7 Jerry Reuss	.40	1.00
8 Mike Scioscia	.75	2.00
9 Fernando Valenzuela	.75	2.00
10 Bob Welch	.40	1.00
11 Steve Yeager	.30	.75

1982 Dodgers Builders Emporium

This seven-card set of the Los Angeles Dodgers was sponsored by Builders Emporium. The fronts feature black-and-white player action pictures with a small black-and-white head photo of the player on the left. The player's name, team, and sponsor name are printed below this small photo. The backs are blank. The cards are unnumbered and checklisted below in alphabetical order.

COMPLETE SET (7)	3.00	8.00
1 Dusty Baker	.60	1.50
2 Ron Cey	.60	1.50
3 Steve Garvey	.75	2.00
4 Pedro Guerrero	.50	1.25
5 Tommy Lasorda MG	.75	2.00
6 Jerry Reuss	.50	1.25
7 Steve Sax	.75	2.00

1982 Dodgers Police

The cards in this 30-card set measure approximately 2 13/16" by 4 1/8". The 1982 Los Angeles Dodgers police set depicts the players and events of the 1981 season. There is a World Series trophy card, three cards commemorating the Division, League, and World Series wins, one manager card, and 25 player cards. The obverses have brilliant color photos set on white, and the player cards are numbered according to the uniform number of the individual. The reverses contain biographical material, information about stadium events, and a safety feature emphasizing "the team that wouldn't quit." According to published reports, 4.5 million cards were produced for this promotion.

COMPLETE SET (30)	4.00	10.00
2 Tom Lasorda MG	.40	1.00
6 Steve Garvey	.40	1.00
7 Steve Yeager	.20	.50
8 Mark Belanger	.08	.25
10 Ron Cey	.40	1.00
12 Dusty Baker	.30	.75
14 Mike Scioscia	.30	.75
16 Rick Monday	.20	.50
18 Bill Russell	.08	.25
21 Jay Johnstone	.20	.50
26 Alejandro Pena	.08	.25
28 Pedro Guerrero	.30	.75
30 Derrel Thomas	.08	.25
31 Jorge Orta	.08	.25
34 Fernando Valenzuela	.40	1.00
35 Bob Welch	.30	.75
38 Dave Goltz	.08	.25
40 Ron Roenicke	.08	.25
41 Jerry Reuss	.20	.50
44 Ken Landreaux	.08	.25
46 Burt Hooton	.20	.50
48 Dave Stewart	.40	1.00
49 Tom Niedenfuer	.08	.25
51 Terry Forster	.08	.25
52 Steve Sax	.40	1.00
57 Steve Howe	.08	.25
NNO World Series Trophy (Checklist back)	.20	.50
NNO World Series Commemorative	.08	.25
NNO NL Champions	.08	.25
NNO Division Champs	.08	.25

1982 Dodgers Postcards

These postcards feature members of the 1982 Los Angeles Dodgers. These cards are unnumbered and we have sequenced them in alphabetical order.

COMPLETE SET (10)	2.50	6.00
1 Terry Forster	.20	.50
2 Steve Garvey	.60	1.50
3 Pedro Guerrero	.30	.75
4 Steve Howe	.20	.50
5 Tom Lasorda MG	.60	1.50
6 Tom Neidenfuer	.20	.50
7 Steve Sax	.60	1.50
8 Mike Scioscia	.40	1.00
9 Bob Welch	.30	.75
10 Steve Yeager	.30	.75

1982 Dodgers Union Oil Volpe

Artist Nicholas Volpe drew members of the Dodgers for a Union Oil giveaway. These color portraits are painted in pastel; one portrait a week was given away at the stations. The cards measure 8 1/2" x 11" and the backs contain statistics and other biographical inforamtion. An album which contained 20 plastic sheets to hold these cards was sold by the Dodgers for $6.

COMPLETE SET	15.00	40.00
1 Dusty Baker	.40	1.00
2 Mark Belanger	.20	.50
3 Ron Cey	.40	1.00
4 Terry Forster	.20	.50
5 Steve Garvey	.60	1.50
6 Pedro Guerrero	.40	1.00
7 Burt Hooton	.20	.50
8 Steve Howe	.20	.50
9 Ken Landreaux	.20	.50
10 Tom Lasorda MG	.60	1.50
11 Mike Marshall	.30	.75
12 Rick Monday	.30	.75
13 Jose Morales	.20	.50
14 Tom Niedenfuer	.20	.50
15 Jorge Orta	.20	.50
16 Jerry Reuss	.30	.75
17 Ron Roenicke	.20	.50
18 Bill Russell	.20	.50
19 Steve Sax	.60	1.50
20 Mike Scioscia	.40	1.00
21 Vin Scully ANN	.60	1.50
22 Dave Stewart	.60	1.50
23 Derrell Thomas	.20	.50
24 Fernando Valenzuela	.60	1.50
25 Bob Welch	.30	.75
26 Steve Yeager	.30	.75

1983 Dodgers Boys of Summer TCMA

This set of the Los Angeles Dodgers was issued on October 8, 1983. The cards were distributed on sheets measuring approximately 10" by 3 1/2". The fronts feature two color or black-and-white action player photos with a picture of Ebbets Field in the middle. The backs carry the pictured players' names. There maybe more cards in the set and any confirmed additions would be appreciated. The cards are unnumbered and checklisted below in alphabetical order.

COMPLETE SET 6.00 15.00
1 Clem Labine 4.00 10.00
Jackie Robinson
2 Sal Maglie 2.00 5.00
George Shuba

1983 Dodgers Police

The cards in this 30-card set measure approximately 2 13/16" by 4 1/8". The full color Police Los Angeles Dodgers set of 1983 features the player's name and uniform number on the front along with the Dodger's logo, the year, and the player's photo. The backs feature a small insert portrait picture of the player, player biographies, and career statistics. The logo of the Los Angeles Police Department, the sponsor of the set, is found on the backs of the cards.

COMPLETE SET (30) 3.00 8.00
2 Tom Lasorda MG .40 1.00
3 Steve Sax .20 .50
5 Mike Marshall .08 .25
7 Steve Yeager .20 .50
12 Dusty Baker .30 .75
14 Mike Scioscia .30 .75
16 Rick Monday .20 .50
17 Greg Brock .08 .25
18 Bill Russell .20 .50
20 Candy Maldonado .20 .50
21 Ricky Wright .08 .25
22 Mark Bradley .08 .25
23 Dave Sax .08 .25
26 Alejandro Pena .08 .25
27 Joe Beckwith .08 .25
28 Pedro Guerrero .30 .75
30 Derrel Thomas .08 .25
34 Fernando Valenzuela .40 1.00
35 Bob Welch .30 .75
38 Pat Zachry .08 .25
40 Ron Roenicke .08 .25
41 Jerry Reuss .20 .50
43 Jose Morales .08 .25
44 Ken Landreaux .08 .25
46 Burt Hooton .08 .25
47 Larry White .08 .25
48 Dave Stewart .40 1.00
49 Tom Niedenfuer .08 .25
57 Steve Howe .08 .25
NNO Coaching Staff .08 .25
Ron Perranoski
Joe Amalfitano
Mo

1983 Dodgers Postcards

These postcards feature members of the 1983 Los Angeles Dodgers. These cards are unnumbered and checklisted below in alphabetical order.

COMPLETE SET 4.00 10.00
1 Dusty Baker .40 1.00
2 Greg Brock .20 .50
3 Pedro Guerrero .40 1.00
4 Burt Hooton .20 .50
5 Steve Howe .20 .50
6 Ken Landreaux .20 .50
7 Tommy Lasorda MG .60 1.50
8 Mike Marshall .20 .50
9 Rick Monday .30 .75
10 Manny Mota CO .30 .75
11 Tom Neidenfuer .20 .50
12 Jerry Reuss .30 .75
13 Bill Russell .20 .50
14 Steve Sax .30 .75
15 Mike Scioscia .40 1.00
16 Dave Stewart .30 .75
17 Derrel Thomas .20 .50
18 Fernando Valenzuela .60 1.50
19 Bob Welch .30 .75
20 Steve Yeager .30 .75

1984 Dodgers Coke

These 30 postcards, which measure 3 1/2" by 5 1/4" were issued by the Los Angeled Dodgers. The fronts have the player photo and his name. The backs have a message to Dodger fans, a facsimile autograph and the Coke logo. Some cards were issued with blank backs. Since these cards are unnumbered, we have sequenced them in alphabetical order.

COMPLETE SET 6.00 15.00
1 Joe Amalfitano CO .20 .50
2 Dave Anderson .20 .50
3 Bob Bailor .20 .50
4 Monty Basgall CO .20 .50
5 Greg Brock .20 .50
6 Mark Cresse CO .20 .50
7 Carlos Diaz .20 .50
8 Pedro Guerrero .40 1.00
9 Orel Hershiser .75 2.00
10 Rick Honeycutt .20 .50
11 Burt Hooton .20 .50
12 Ken Landreaux .20 .50
13 Rafael Landestoy .20 .50
14 Tom Lasorda MG .60 1.50
15 Candy Maldonado .20 .50
16 Mike Marshall .20 .50
17 Manny Mota CO .20 .50
18 Jose Morales .20 .50
19 Tom Niedenfuer .20 .50
20 Alejandro Pena .20 .50
21 Ron Perranoski CO .20 .50
22 Jerry Reuss .30 .75
23 German Rivera .20 .50
24 Bill Russell .20 .50
25 Steve Sax .30 .75
26 Mike Scioscia .40 1.00
27 Bob Welch .30 .75
28 Terry Whitfield .20 .50
29 Steve Yeager .30 .75
30 Pat Zachry .20 .50

1984 Dodgers Police

The cards in this 30-card set measure 2 13/16" by 4 1/8". For the fifth straight year, the Los Angeles Police Department sponsored a set of Dodger baseball cards. The set is numbered by player uniform number, which is featured on both the fronts and backs of the cards. The set features an early card of Orel Hershiser predating his Rookie Cards issued the following year.

COMPLETE SET (30) 3.00 8.00
2 Tom Lasorda MG .40 1.00
3 Steve Sax .30 .75
5 Mike Marshall .08 .25
7 Steve Yeager .20 .50
9 Greg Brock .08 .25
10 Dave Anderson .08 .25
14 Mike Scioscia .30 .75
16 Rick Monday .20 .50
17 Rafael Landestoy .08 .25
18 Bill Russell .20 .50
20 Candy Maldonado .08 .25
21 Bob Bailor .08 .25
25 German Rivera .08 .25
26 Alejandro Pena .08 .25
27 Carlos Diaz .08 .25
28 Pedro Guerrero .30 .75
31 Jack Fimple .08 .25
34 Fernando Valenzuela .40 1.00
35 Bob Welch .30 .75
38 Pat Zachry .08 .25
40 Rick Honeycutt .08 .25
41 Jerry Reuss .20 .50
43 Jose Morales .08 .25
44 Ken Landreaux .08 .25
45 Terry Whitfield .08 .25
46 Burt Hooton .20 .50
49 Tom Niedenfuer .08 .25
55 Orel Hershiser 1.50 4.00
56 Richard Rodas .08 .25
NNO Coaching Staff .08 .25
Monty Basgall
Joe Amalfitano
Mar

1984 Dodgers Smokey

This four-card set was not widely distributed and has not proven to be very popular with collectors. Cards were supposedly distributed by fire agencies in Southern California at fairs, mall displays, and special events. Cards measure approximately 5" by 7" and feature a color picture of Smokey the Bear with a Dodger. The cards were printed on relatively thin card stock; printing on the back is black on white.

COMPLETE SET (4) 8.00 20.00
1 Ken Landreaux 2.00 5.00
with Smokey
2 Tom Niedenfuer 2.00 5.00
with Smokey
3 Steve Sax 2.50 6.00
with Smokey
4 Smokey the Bear/(Batting pose) 1.50 4.00

1984 Dodgers Union Oil

Distributed by Union Oil, this 16-card set measures approximately 8 1/2" by 11" and features color drawings of some of the great moments in Dodgers history. The backs carry text discribing the significance of the drawing. A variety of artists drew these posters. An album was also available to contain these oversized cards.

COMPLETE SET (16) 8.00 20.00
1 Record-Setting Infield .40 1.00
2 Roy Campanella 2.00 5.00
Tribute
3 Willie Davis/31-Game Hitting Streak .60 1.50
4 Don Drysdale/58 2/3
Scoreless Inning Streak 1.25 3.00
5 Manny Mota/145th Pinch Hit .60 1.50
6 Jerry Reuss .60 1.50
Bill Singer
No-Hitters
7 The Tenth Player .40 1.00
8 Dusty Baker .75 2.00
Ron Cey
Steve Garvey
Reggie Smith/
9 Fernando Valenzuela 1.00 2.50
Cy Young Award Season 1981
10 Bob Welch .60 1.50
Strikes Out Reggie Jackson
11 Maury Wills/104th Stolen Base-1962 1.00 2.50
12 1959 World Championship .40 1.00
13 1963 World Championship .40 1.00
14 1965 World Championship .40 1.00
15 1977 NLCS .40 1.00
16 1981 World Championship .40 1.00

1985 Dodgers Coke Postcards

This 34-card set was sponsored by Coke, and the company logo appears on the back of the cards. These oversized cards measure approximately 3 1/2" by 5 1/2". The front design features glossy color player photos, bordered in white and with the player's name below the pictures. Except for the sponsor's logo, the backs are blank. The cards are unnumbered and checklisted below in alphabetical order.

COMPLETE SET (34) 8.00 20.00
1 Joe Amalfitano CO .20 .50
2 Dave Anderson .20 .50
3 Bob Bailor .20 .50
4 Monty Basgall CO .20 .50
5 Tom Brennan .20 .50
6 Greg Brock .20 .50
7 Bobby Castillo .20 .50
8 Mark Cresse CO .20 .50
9 Carlos Diaz .20 .50
10 Mariano Duncan .60 1.50
11 Pedro Guerrero .60 1.50
12 Orel Hershiser .75 2.00
13 Rick Honeycutt .20 .50
14 Steve Howe .20 .50
15 Ken Howell .20 .50
16 Jay Johnstone .40 1.00
17 Ken Landreaux .20 .50
18 Tom Lasorda MG .75 2.00
19 Candy Maldonado .20 .50
20 Mike Marshall .20 .50
21 Manny Mota CO .40 1.00
22 Tom Niedenfuer .20 .50
23 Al Oliver .60 1.50
24 Alejandro Pena .20 .50
25 Ron Perranoski CO .20 .50
26 Jerry Reuss .40 1.00
27 R.J. Reynolds .20 .50
28 Bill Russell .20 .50
29 Steve Sax .40 1.00
30 Mike Scioscia .60 1.50
31 Fernando Valenzuela .60 1.50
32 Bob Welch .40 1.00
33 Terry Whitfield .20 .50
34 Steve Yeager .40 1.00

1986 Dodgers Coke Postcards

This 33-card Dodger set was sponsored by Coke, and the company logo appears on the back of the cards. The oversized cards measure approximately 3 1/2" by 5 1/2". The front design features glossy color player photos (mostly action), bordered in white and with the player's name below the picture. The backs are blank except for a small Coca-Cola logo. The cards are unnumbered and checklisted below in alphabetical order.

COMPLETE SET (33) 6.00 15.00
1 Joe Amalfitano CO .20 .50
2 Dave Anderson .20 .50
3 Monty Basgall CO .20 .50
4 Greg Brock .20 .50
5 Enos Cabell .20 .50
6 Cesar Cedeno .30 .75
7 Mark Cresse CO .20 .50
8 Mariano Duncan .40 1.00
9 Carlos Diaz .20 .50
10 Pedro Guerrero .40 1.00
11 Orel Hershiser 1.00 2.50
12 Ben Hines TR .20 .50
13 Rick Honeycutt .20 .50
14 Ken Howell .20 .50
15 Ken Landreaux .20 .50
16 Tom Lasorda MG .60 1.50
17 Bill Madlock .30 .75
18 Mike Marshall .20 .50
19 Len Matuszek .20 .50
20 Manny Mota CO .30 .75
21 Tom Niedenfuer .20 .50
22 Alejandro Pena .20 .50
23 Ron Perranoski CO .20 .50
24 Dennis Powell .20 .50
25 Jerry Reuss .30 .75
26 Bill Russell .20 .50
27 Steve Sax .30 .75
28 Mike Scioscia .40 1.00
29 Franklin Stubbs
30 Alex Trevino .20 .50
31 Fernando Valenzuela .40 1.00
32 Ed VandeBerg .20 .50
33 Bob Welch .30 .75
34 Terry Whitfield .20 .50

1986 Dodgers Police

This 30-card set features full-color cards each measuring 2 13/16" by 4 1/8". The cards are unnumbered except for uniform numbers. The backs give a safety tip as well as a short capsule biography. The sets were given away at Dodger Stadium on May 18th.

COMPLETE SET (30) 2.50 6.00
2 Tom Lasorda MG .40 1.00
3 Steve Sax .30 .75
5 Mike Marshall .08 .25
9 Greg Brock .08 .25
10 Dave Anderson .08 .25
12 Bill Madlock .20 .50
14 Mike Scioscia .30 .75
17 Len Matuszek .08 .25
18 Bill Russell .08 .25
22 Franklin Stubbs .08 .25
23 Enos Cabell .08 .25
25 Mariano Duncan .30 .75
26 Alejandro Pena .08 .25
27 Carlos Diaz .08 .25
28 Pedro Guerrero .30 .75
29 Alex Trevino .08 .25
31 Ed VandeBerg .08 .25
34 Fernando Valenzuela .30 .75
35 Bob Welch .30 .75
40 Rick Honeycutt .08 .25
41 Jerry Reuss .20 .50
43 Ken Howell .08 .25
44 Ken Landreaux .08 .25
45 Terry Whitfield .08 .25
48 Dennis Powell .08 .25
49 Tom Niedenfuer .08 .25
51 Reggie Williams .08 .25
55 Orel Hershiser .40 1.00
NNO Coaching Staff .08 .25
Don McMahon
Mark Cresse
Ben Hine
NNO Team Photo/(Checklist back) .20 .50

1986 Dodgers Union Oil Photos

This 24-card set features color photos of the 1986 Los Angeles Dodgers and measures approximately 8 1/2" by 11". Player information is printed on the backs. The cards are unnumbered and checklisted below in alphabetical order.

COMPLETE SET (24) 4.00 10.00
1 Dave Anderson .08 .25
2 Greg Brock .08 .25
3 Enos Cabell .08 .25
4 Carlos Diaz .08 .25
5 Mariano Duncan .20 .50
6 Pedro Guerrero .30 .75
7 Orel Hershiser .40 1.00
8 Rick Honeycutt .08 .25
9 Ken Howell .08 .25
10 Tommy Lasorda MG .40 1.00
11 Ken Landreaux .08 .25
12 Bill Madlock .20 .50
13 Mike Marshall .08 .25
14 Tom Niedenfuer .08 .25
15 Jerry Reuss .20 .50
16 Bill Russell .08 .25
17 Steve Sax .20 .50
18 Mike Scioscia .30 .75
19 Franklin Stubbs .08 .25
20 Alex Trevino .08 .25
21 Fernando Valenzuela .30 .75
22 Ed Vandeberg .08 .25
23 Bob Welch .20 .50
24 Reggie Williams .08 .25

1987 Dodgers 1955 TCMA

This nine-card standard-size set feature members of the 1955 Brooklyn Dodgers. That team was the only Brooklyn Dodger team to win the World Series. The fronts have player photos, while the backs have information about the players as well as their 1955 statistics.

COMPLETE SET (9) 2.00 5.00
1 Duke Snider .30 .75
Walter Alston MG
2 Roy Campanella .40 1.00
3 Jackie Robinson .75 2.00
4 Carl Furillo .30 .75
5 Gil Hodges .40 1.00
6 Pee Wee Reese .30 .75
Jim Gilliam
7 Don Newcombe .30 .75
8 Ed Roebuck .08 .25
Clem Labine
9 Carl Erskine .20 .50

1987 Dodgers Mother's

This set consists of 28 full-color, rounded-corner cards each measuring 2 1/2" by 3 1/2". Starter sets (only 20 cards but also including a certificate for eight more cards) were given out at the ballpark and collectors were encouraged to trade to fill in the rest of their set. Cards were originally given out at Dodger Stadium on August 9th. Photos were taken by Barry Colla. The sets were reportedly given out free to all game attendees 14 years of age and under.

COMPLETE SET (28) 3.00 8.00
1 Tom Lasorda MG .40 1.00
2 Pedro Guerrero .30 .75
3 Steve Sax .30 .75
4 Fernando Valenzuela .30 .75
5 Mike Marshall .08 .25
6 Orel Hershiser .40 1.00
7 Mariano Duncan .08 .25
8 Bill Madlock .20 .50
9 Bob Welch .20 .50
10 Mike Scioscia .30 .75
11 Mike Ramsey .08 .25
12 Matt Young .08 .25
13 Franklin Stubbs .08 .25
14 Tom Niedenfuer .08 .25
15 Reggie Williams .08 .25
16 Rick Honeycutt .08 .25
17 Dave Anderson .08 .25
18 Alejandro Pena .08 .25
19 Ken Howell .08 .25
20 Len Matuszek .10 .25
21 Tim Leary .08 .25
22 Tracy Woodson .08 .25
23 Alex Trevino .08 .25
24 Ken Landreaux .08 .25
25 Mickey Hatcher .08 .25
26 Brian Holton .08 .25
27 Dodgers' Coaches .08 .25
28 Checklist Card .08 .25

1987 Dodgers Photos

These photos feature members of the 1987 Los Angeles Dodgers. The photos are unnumbered so we have sequenced them in alphabetical order.

COMPLETE SET 4.00 10.00
1 Dave Anderson .20 .50
2 Mariano Duncan .20 .50
3 Pedro Guerrero .40 1.00
4 Orel Hershiser .40 1.00
5 Brian Holton .20 .50
6 Rick Honeycutt .20 .50
7 Ken Howell .20 .50
8 Tommy Larsorda MG .60 1.50
9 Tim Leary .20 .50
10 Len Matuszek .20 .50
11 Alejandro Pena .20 .50
12 Steve Sax .30 .75
13 Mike Scioscia .40 1.00
14 Franklin Stubbs .20 .50
15 Alex Trevino .20 .50
16 Fernando Valenzuela .40 1.00
17 Matt Young .20 .50

1987 Dodgers Police

This 30-card set features full-color cards each measuring approximately 2 13/16" by 4 1/8". The cards are unnumbered except for uniform numbers. The backs give a safety tip as well as a short capsule biography. Cards were given away at Dodger Stadium on April 24th and later during the summer by LAPD officers at a rate of two cards per week.

COMPLETE SET (30) 2.50 6.00
1 Tom Lasorda MG .40 1.00
2 Steve Sax .20 .50
3 Mike Marshall .08 .25
4 Dave Anderson .08 .25
5 Bill Madlock .20 .50
6 Mike Scioscia .30 .75
7 Gilberto Reyes .08 .25
8 Len Matuszek .08 .25
9 Reggie Williams .08 .25
10 Franklin Stubbs .08 .25
11 Tim Leary .08 .25
12 Mariano Duncan .08 .25
13 Alejandro Pena .08 .25
14 Pedro Guerrero .30 .75
15 Alex Trevino .08 .25
16 Jeff Hamilton .08 .25
17 Fernando Valenzuela .30 .75
18 Bob Welch .30 .75
19 Matt Young .08 .25
20 Rick Honeycutt .08 .25
21 Jerry Reuss .20 .50
22 Ken Howell .08 .25
23 Ken Landreaux .08 .25
24 Ralph Bryant .08 .25
25 Jose Gonzalez .08 .25
26 Tom Niedenfuer .08 .25
27 Brian Holton .08 .25
28 Orel Hershiser .40 1.00
29 Coaching Staff .20 .50
Ron Perranoski
Tom Lasorda
Joe A
30 Dodgers Stadium/(25th Anniversary) .08 .25

1987 Dodgers Smokey All-Stars

This 40-card set was issued by the U.S. Forestry Service to commemorate the Los Angeles Dodgers selected for the All-Star game over the past 25 years. The cards measure approximately 2 1/2" by 3 3/4" and have full-color fronts. The card fronts are distinguished by their thick silver borders and the bats, balls, and stadium design layout. The 25th anniversary logo for Dodger Stadium is in the lower right corner of each card. The set numbering is alphabetical by subject's name.

COMPLETE SET (40) 6.00 15.00
1 Walt Alston MG .40 1.00
2 Dusty Baker .30 .75
3 Jim Brewer .08 .25
4 Ron Cey .30 .75
5 Tommy Davis .20 .50
6 Willie Davis .20 .50
7 Don Drysdale .60 1.50
8 Steve Garvey .40 1.00
9 Bill Grabarkewitz .08 .25
10 Pedro Guerrero .30 .75
11 Tom Haller .08 .25
12 Orel Hershiser .30 .75
13 Burt Hooton .08 .25
14 Steve Howe .08 .25
15 Tommy John .30 .75
16 Sandy Koufax .75 2.00
17 Tom Lasorda MG .40 1.00
18 Jim Lefebvre .08 .25
19 Davey Lopes .20 .50
20 Mike G. Marshall .08 .25
21 Mike A. Marshall .08 .25
22 Andy Messersmith .08 .25
23 Rick Monday .08 .25
24 Manny Mota .20 .50
25 Claude Osteen .08 .25
26 Johnny Podres .20 .50
27 Phil Regan .08 .25
28 Jerry Reuss .08 .25
29 Rick Rhoden .08 .25
30 John Roseboro .20 .50
31 Bill Russell .20 .50
32 Steve Sax .20 .50
33 Bill Singer .08 .25
34 Reggie Smith .20 .50
35 Don Sutton .50 1.25
36 Fernando Valenzuela .30 .75
37 Bob Welch .20 .50
38 Maury Wills .30 .75
39 Jim Wynn .08 .25
40 Checklist Card .08 .25

1988 Dodgers Mother's

This set consists of 28 full-color, rounded-corner cards each measuring 2 1/2" by 3 1/2". Starter sets (only 20 cards but also including a certificate for eight more cards) were given out at the ballpark and collectors were encouraged to trade to fill in the rest of their set. Cards were originally given out at Dodger Stadium on July 31st. Photos were taken by Barry Colla. The sets were reportedly given out free to the first 25,000 game attendees 14 years of age and under.

COMPLETE SET (28) 4.00 10.00
1 Tom Lasorda MG .40 1.00
2 Pedro Guerrero .30 .75
3 Steve Sax .20 .50
4 Fernando Valenzuela .30 .75
5 Mike Marshall .08 .25
6 Orel Hershiser .30 .75
7 Alfredo Griffin .08 .25
8 Kirk Gibson .40 1.00
9 Don Sutton .40 1.00
10 Mike Scioscia .30 .75
11 Franklin Stubbs .08 .25
12 Mike Davis .08 .25
13 Jesse Orosco .20 .50
14 John Shelby .08 .25
15 Rick Dempsey .20 .50
16 Jay Howell .08 .25
17 Dave Anderson .08 .25
18 Alejandro Pena .08 .25
19 Jeff Hamilton .08 .25
20 Danny Heep .08 .25
21 Tim Leary .08 .25
22 Brad Havens .08 .25
23 Tim Belcher .20 .50
24 Ken Howell .08 .25
25 Mickey Hatcher .08 .25
26 Brian Holton .08 .25
27 Mike Devereaux .08 .25
28 Checklist Card .08 .25
Joe Ferguson CO
Mark Cresse CO
R

1988 Dodgers Police

This 30-card set features full-color cards each measuring approximately 2 13/16" by 4 1/8". The cards are unnumbered except for uniform numbers. The backs give a safety tip as well as a short capsule biography. Cards were given during the summer by LAPD officers. The set is very similar to the 1987 set, the 1988 set is distinguished by the fact that it does not have the 25th anniversary (of Dodger Stadium) logo on the card front.

COMPLETE SET (30) 2.50 6.00
2 Tom Lasorda MG .40 1.00
3 Steve Sax .20 .50
5 Mike Marshall .08 .25
7 Alfredo Griffin .08 .25
9 Mickey Hatcher .08 .25
10 Dave Anderson .08 .25
12 Danny Heep .08 .25
14 Mike Scioscia .30 .75
20 Don Sutton .40 1.00
21 Tito Landrum and/17 Len Matuszek .08 .25
22 Franklin Stubbs .08 .25
23 Kirk Gibson .40 1.00
25 Mariano Duncan .08 .25
26 Alejandro Pena .08 .25
27 Mike Sharperson and/52}Tim Crews .08 .25
28 Pedro Guerrero .30 .75
29 Alex Trevino .08 .25
31 John Shelby .08 .25
33 Jeff Hamilton .08 .25
34 Fernando Valenzuela .30 .75
37 Mike Davis .08 .25
41 Brad Havens .08 .25
43 Ken Howell .08 .25
47 Jesse Orosco .20 .50
49 Tim Belcher and/57}Shawn Hillegas .08 .25
50 Jay Howell .08 .25
51 Brian Holton .08 .25
54 Tim Leary .08 .25
55 Orel Hershiser .40 1.00
NNO Tom Lasorda MG .40 1.00
and Coaches

1988 Dodgers Rini Postcards 1

This set of 36 postcards measures 3 1/2" by 5 1/2" and showcases the Brooklyn Dodgers. On a blue background, the horizontal fronts feature color drawings by Susan Rini. There were three subsets in the first series, with 12 cards each. The cards are numbered on the back as "X of 12." Suffixes (A, B, and C) have been arbitrarily assigned to the card numbers below to distinguish between the three subsets.

COMPLETE SET (36) 6.00 15.00
1A Dodgers Sym-Phony Band .20 .50
1B Tom Lasorda .75 2.00
1C Carl Erskine .60 1.50
2A Sandy Amoros .20 .50
2B Carl Furillo .60 1.50
2C Ebbets Field .20 .50
3A Don Newcombe .60 1.50
3B Roger Craig .30 .75
3C Jackie Robinson 1.50 4.00
4A Duke Snider 1.25 3.00
4B Andy Pafko .30 .75
4C Red Barber .40 1.00
Leo Durocher
5A Harold(Pee Wee) Reese 1.25 3.00
5B George Shuba .20 .50
5C Red Barber .40 1.00
6A Johnny Podres .60 1.50
6B Jackie Robinson .75 2.00
Branch Rickey
6C Leo Durocher .75 2.00
7A Ralph Branca .30 .75
7B Clem Labine .60 1.50
7C Gil Hodges .75 2.00
8A Don Drysdale .75 2.00
8B Larry Mac Phail .30 .75
8C Mickey Owen .20 .50
9A Roy Campanella 1.25 3.00
9B Chuck Connors .60 1.50
9C Preacher Roe .60 1.50
10A Harry Lavagetto/(Cookie) .20 .50
10B Walter O'Malley .40 1.00
10C Cal Abrams .20 .50
11A Sal Maglie .40 1.00
11B Carl Erskine .60 1.50
11C Harry Lavagetto/(Cookie) .30 .75
12A Clyde King .20 .50
12B Eddie Miksis .20 .50
12C Gene Hermanski .20 .50

1988 Dodgers Smokey

This 32-card set was issued by the U.S. Forestry Service as a perforated sheet that could be separated into individual cards. The set commemorates Los Angeles Dodgers who hold various team and league records, i.e., "L.A. Dodgers Record-Breakers." The cards measure approximately 2 1/2" by 4" and have full-color fronts. The card fronts are distinguished by their thick light blue borders and the bats, balls, and stadium design layout. The sheets of cards were distributed at the Dodgers' Smokey Bear Day game on September 9th.

COMPLETE SET (32) 5.00 12.00
1 Walter Alston MG .30 .75
2 John Roseboro .08 .25
3 Frank Howard .20 .50
4 Sandy Koufax .75 2.00
5 Manny Mota .20 .50
6 Sandy Koufax .30 .75
Jerry Reuss
Bill Singer
7 Maury Wills .30 .75
8 Tommy Davis .20 .50
9 Phil Regan .08 .25
10 Wes Parker .08 .25
11 Don Drysdale .50 1.25
12 Willie Davis .20 .50
13 Bill Russell .20 .50
14 Jim Brewer .08 .25
15 Steve Garvey .30 .75
Davey Lopes&
Bill Russell& and
Ro
16 Mike Marshall .08 .25
17 Steve Garvey .40 1.00
18 Davey Lopes .20 .50
19 Burt Hooton .08 .25
20 Jim Wynn .08 .25
21 Dusty Baker .20 .50
Ron Cey
Steve Garvey and
Reggie
22 Dusty Baker .30 .75
23 Tommy Lasorda MG .40 1.00
24 Fernando Valenzuela .30 .75
25 Steve Sax .20 .50
26 Dodger Stadium .08 .25
27 Ron Cey .20 .50
28 Pedro Guerrero .20 .50
29 Mike Marshall .08 .25
30 Don Sutton .50 1.25
NNO Checklist Card .20 .50
NNO Smokey Bear .08 .25

1989 Dodgers Mother's

The 1989 Mother's Los Angeles Dodgers set contains 28 standard-size cards with rounded corners. The fronts have borderless color photos, and the horizontally oriented backs have biographical information. Starter sets containing 20 of these cards were given away at a Dodgers home game during the 1989 season.

COMPLETE SET (28) 3.00 8.00
1 Tom Lasorda MG .40 1.00
2 Eddie Murray .50 1.25
3 Mike Scioscia .20 .50
4 Fernando Valenzuela .30 .75
5 Mike Marshall .08 .25
6 Orel Hershiser .30 .75
7 Alfredo Griffin .08 .25
8 Kirk Gibson .30 .75
9 John Tudor .08 .25
10 Willie Randolph .20 .50
11 Franklin Stubbs .08 .25
12 Mike Davis .08 .25
13 Mike Morgan .08 .25
14 John Shelby .08 .25
15 Rick Dempsey .20 .50
16 Jay Howell .08 .25
17 Dave Anderson .08 .25
18 Alejandro Pena .08 .25
19 Jeff Hamilton .08 .25
20 Ricky Horton .08 .25
21 Tim Leary .08 .25
22 Ray Searage .08 .25
23 Tim Belcher .08 .25
24 Tim Crews .08 .25
25 Mickey Hatcher .08 .25
26 Mariano Duncan .08 .25
27 Dodgers Coaches .08 .25
Joe Amalfitano
Manny Mota
Joe F
28 Checklist Card .08 .25
World Championship
Trophy

1989 Dodgers Police

The 1989 Police Los Angeles Dodgers set contains 30 cards measuring approximately 2 5/8" by 4 1/4". The fronts have color photos with white borders; the backs feature safety tips and biographical information. The unnumbered cards were given away by various Los Angeles-area police departments. The cards were also issued as an uncut, perforated sheet to children (age 14 and under) at Dodger Stadium on Baseball Card Night, May 5, 1989.

COMPLETE SET (30) 2.50 6.00
1 Dodger Coaches/(Unnumbered) .20 .50
Ben Hines
Ron Perra
2 Tom Lasorda MG .40 1.00
3 Jeff Hamilton .08 .25
4 Mike Marshall .08 .25
5 Alfredo Griffin .08 .25
6 Mickey Hatcher .08 .25
7 Dave Anderson .08 .25
8 Willie Randolph .20 .50
9 Mike Scioscia .30 .75
10 Rick Dempsey .20 .50
11 Mike Davis .08 .25
12 Tracy Woodson .08 .25
13 Franklin Stubbs .08 .25
14 Kirk Gibson .30 .75
15 Mariano Duncan .08 .25
16 Alejandro Pena .08 .25
17 Mike Sharperson .08 .25
18 Ricky Horton .08 .25
19 John Tudor .08 .25
20 John Shelby .08 .25
21 Eddie Murray .50 1.25
22 Fernando Valenzuela .30 .75
23 Mike Morgan .08 .25
24 Ramon Martinez .40 1.00
25 Tim Belcher .08 .25
26 Jay Howell .08 .25
27 Tim Crews .08 .25
28 Tim Leary .08 .25
29 Orel Hershiser .30 .75
30 Ray Searage .08 .25

1989 Dodgers Smokey Greats

The 1989 Smokey Dodger Greats set contains 104 standard-size cards. The fronts and backs have white and blue borders. The backs are vertically oriented and feature career totals and fire prevention cartoons. The set depicts notable Dodgers of all eras, and was distributed in perforated sheet format. Cards 1-36 are ordered alphabetically and (except for number 31) depict Dodger members of the Hall of Fame. Cards 37-64 (except for number 57) represent Brooklyn Dodgers whereas cards 65-101 represent Los Angeles Dodgers. The last three cards in the set (102-104) are Hall of Famers apparently overlooked in the first group.

COMPLETE SET (104) 8.00 20.00
COMMON PLAYER (1-100) .04 .10
COMMON PLAYER (101-104) .12 .30
1 Walter Alston MG .20 .50
2 David Bancroft .14 .40
3 Dan Brouthers .14 .40
4 Roy Campanella .40 1.00
5 Max Carey .14 .35
6 Hazen(Kiki) Cuyler .14 .40
7 Don Drysdale .30 .75
8 Burleigh Grimes .14 .35
9 Billy Herman .14 .40
10 Waite Hoyt .14 .35
11 Hughie Jennings .14 .40
12 Willie Keeler .14 .35
13 Joseph Kelley .14 .40
14 George Kelly .14 .35
15 Sandy Koufax .60 1.50
16 Heinie Manush .14 .40
17 Juan Marichal .20 .50
18 Rabbit Maranville .14 .35
19 Rube Marquard .14 .40
20 Thomas McCarthy .14 .35
21 Joseph McGinnity .14 .40
22 Joe Medwick .14 .35

23 Pee Wee Reese .30 .75
24 Frank Robinson .30 .75
25 Jackie Robinson .75 2.00
26 Babe Ruth 1.25 3.00
27 Duke Snider .40 1.00
28 Casey Stengel .30 .75
29 Dazzy Vance .14 .40
30 Arky Vaughan .14 .35
31 Mike Scioscia .02 .10
32 Lloyd Waner .14 .40
33 John Montgemery Ward .14 .35
34 Zack Wheat .14 .40
35 Hoyt Wilhelm .14 .35
36 Hack Wilson .14 .40
37 Tony Cuccinello .02 .10
38 Al Lopez .14 .40
39 Leo Durocher .14 .40
40 Cookie Lavagetto .02 .10
41 Babe Phelps .02 .10
42 Dolph Camilli .07 .20
43 Whitlow Wyatt .02 .10
44 Mickey Owen .02 .10
45 Van Mungo .02 .10
46 Pete Coscarart .02 .10
47 Pete Reiser .07 .20
48 Augie Galan .02 .10
49 Dixie Walker .07 .20
50 Kirby Higbe .02 .10
51 Ralph Branca .07 .20
52 Bruce Edwards .02 .10
53 Eddie Stanky .07 .20
54 Gil Hodges .14 .35
55 Don Newcombe .07 .20
56 Preacher Roe .07 .20
57 Willie Randolph .07 .20
58 Carl Furillo .07 .20
59 Charlie Dressen .02 .10
60 Carl Erskine .07 .20
61 Clem Labine .02 .10
62 Gino Cimoli .02 .10
63 Johnny Podres .07 .20
64 Johnny Roseboro .02 .10
65 Wally Moon .07 .20
66 Charlie Neal .02 .10
67 Norm Larker .02 .10
68 Stan Williams .02 .10
69 Maury Wills .14 .40
70 Tommy Davis .07 .20
71 Jim Lefebvre .02 .10
72 Phil Regan .02 .10
73 Claude Osteen .02 .10
74 Tom Haller .02 .10
75 Bill Singer .02 .10
76 Bill Grabarkewitz .02 .10
77 Willie Davis .07 .20
78 Don Sutton .14 .40
79 Jim Brewer .02 .10
80 Manny Mota .07 .20
81 Bill Russell .02 .10
82 Ron Cey .07 .20
83 Steve Garvey .14 .40
84 Mike G. Marshall .02 .10
85 Andy Messersmith .02 .10
86 Jimmy Wynn .02 .10
87 Rick Rhoden .02 .10
88 Reggie Smith .07 .20
89 Jay Howell .02 .10
90 Rick Monday .07 .20
91 Tommy John .07 .20
92 Bob Welch .07 .20
93 Dusty Baker .07 .20
94 Pedro Guerrero .07 .20
95 Burt Hooton .02 .10
96 Davey Lopes .07 .20
97 Fernando Valenzuela .14 .40
98 Steve Howe .02 .10
99 Steve Sax .07 .20
100 Orel Hershiser .15 .40
101 Mike A. Marshall .10 .30
102 Ernie Lombardi .30 .75
103 Fred Lindstrom .30 .75
104 Wilbert Robinson .30 .75

1989 Dodgers Stamps St. Vincent

This 18-stamp set was issued by the government of the Caribbean Island of St. Vincent and distributed by Empire of America Federal Savings Bank. The stamps were designed to be placed in a commemorative folder with the 1989 Dodgers team photo printed in the center section. Two players' photos appear on most of the stamps. The stamps are unnumbered and checklisted below in alphabetical order according to the name of the player on the left of the stamp.

COMPLETE SET (18) 4.00 10.00
1 Dave Anderson .20 .50
Alfredo Griffin
2 Tim Belcher .20 .50
Tim Crews
3 Coaches Stamp .20 .50
4 Kal Daniels .20 .50
Mike Marshall
5 Mike Davis .40 1.00
Kirk Gibson
6 Jeff Hamilton .20 .50
Franklin Stubbs
7 Lenny Harris .30 .75
Chris Gwynn
Billy Bean
8 Orel Hershiser .30 .75
Mike Morgan
9 Jay Howell .20 .50
Alejandro Pena
10 Tom Lasorda MG .30 .75
Jose Gonzalez
11 Eddie Murray .60 1.50
Willie Randolph
12 Mike Scioscia .20 .50
Rick Dempsey
13 Ray Searage .20 .50
John Tudor
14 Mike Sharperson .20 .50
Mickey Hatcher
15 Fernando Valenzuela .30 .75
John Shelby
16 John Wetteland .50 1.25
Ramon Martinez
17 Stadium Stamp .20 .50
18 Team Logo .20 .50

1990 Dodgers Mother's

The 1990 Mother's Cookies Los Angeles Dodgers set contains 28 standard-size cards issued with rounded corners and beautiful full color fronts with biographical information on the back. These Dodgers cards were given away at Chavez Ravine to all fans fourteen and under at the August 19th game. They were distributed in 20-card random packets at the game and eight more at the redemption booths. However, both groups of cards were random and there was no guarantee of getting a complete set in the cards. The promotional idea was that the only way one could finish the set was to trade for them. The redemption for eight more cards was done at the 22nd Annual Labor Day card show at the Anaheim Convention Center.

COMPLETE SET (28) 3.00 8.00
1 Tom Lasorda MG .40 1.00
2 Fernando Valenzuela .30 .75
3 Kal Daniels .08 .25
4 Mike Scioscia .30 .75
5 Eddie Murray .50 1.25
6 Mickey Hatcher .08 .25
7 Juan Samuel .08 .25
8 Alfredo Griffin .08 .25
9 Tim Belcher .08 .25
10 Hubie Brooks .08 .25
11 Jose Gonzalez .08 .25
12 Orel Hershiser .30 .75
13 Kirk Gibson .30 .75
14 Chris Gwynn .08 .25
15 Jay Howell .08 .25
16 Rick Dempsey .20 .50
17 Ramon Martinez .20 .50
18 Lenny Harris .08 .25
19 John Wetteland .40 1.00
20 Mike Sharperson .08 .25
21 Mike Morgan .08 .25
22 Ray Searage .08 .25
23 Jeff Hamilton .08 .25
24 Jim Gott .08 .25
25 John Shelby .08 .25
26 Tim Crews .08 .25
27 Don Aase .08 .25
28 Dodger Coaches .08 .25
Joe Ferguson
Ron Perranoski
Mark

1990 Dodgers Police

This 30-card set measures approximately 2 13/16" by 4 1/8" and was distributed by both the Los Angeles Police Department and at a pre-season Dodger-Angel exhibition game. This set also commemorated the 100th anniversary of the Dodgers existence. The front has a full-color photo of the player on the front while the back has a brief profile of the player with an anti-crime message. This set is checklisted below by uniform number.

COMPLETE SET (30) 2.50 6.00
2 Tommy Lasorda MG .40 1.00
3 Jeff Hamilton .08 .25
7 Alfredo Griffin .08 .25
9 Mickey Hatcher .08 .25
10 Juan Samuel .08 .25
12 Willie Randolph .20 .50
14 Mike Scioscia .30 .75
15 Chris Gwynn .08 .25
17 Rick Dempsey .08 .25
21 Hubie Brooks .08 .25
22 Franklin Stubbs .08 .25
23 Kirk Gibson .30 .75
27 Mike Sharperson .08 .25
28 Kal Daniels .08 .25
29 Lenny Harris .08 .25
31 John Shelby .08 .25
33 Eddie Murray .50 1.25
34 Fernando Valenzuela .30 .75
35 Jim Gott .08 .25
36 Mike Morgan .08 .25
38 Jose Gonzalez .08 .25
39 Jim Neidlinger .08 .25
46 Mike Hartley .08 .25
48 Ramon Martinez
49 Tim Belcher .08 .25
50 Jay Howell .08 .25
52 Tim Crews .08 .25
55 Orel Hershiser .30 .75
57 John Wetteland .40 1.00
59 Ray Searage .08 .25
NNO Coaches Card .20 .50
Ben Hines
Ron Perranowski
Mark Cre

1990 Dodgers Target

The 1990 Target Dodgers is one of the largest sets ever made. This (more than) 1000-card set features cards each measuring approximately 2" by 3" individually and was issued in large perforated sheets of 15 cards. Players in the set played at one time or another for one of the Dodgers franchises. As such many of the players in the set are older and relatively unknown to today's younger collectors. The set was apparently intended to be arranged in alphabetical order. There were several numbers not used (408, 458, 463, 792, 902, 907, 969, 996, 1031, 1054, 1061, and 1098) as well as a few instances of duplicated numbers.

COMPLETE SET (1096) 50.00 120.00
1 Bert Abbey .20 .50
2 Cal Abrams .20 .50
3 Hank Aguirre .20 .50
4 Eddie Ainsmith .20 .50
5 Ed Albosta .20 .50
6 Luis Alcaraz .20 .50
7 Doyle Alexander .20 .50
8 Dick Allen .25 .60
9 Frank Allen .20 .50
10 Johnny Allen .20 .50
11 Mel Almada .20 .50
12 Walt Alston .30 .75
13 Ed Amelung .20 .50
14 Sandy Amoros .20 .50
15 Dave Anderson .20 .50
16 Ferrell Anderson .20 .50
17 John Anderson .20 .50
18 Stan Andrews .20 .50
19 Bill Antonello .20 .50
20 Jimmy Archer .20 .50
21 Bob Aspromonte .20 .50
22 Rick Auerbach .20 .50
23 Charlie Babb .20 .50
24 Johnny Babich .20 .50
25 Bob Bailey .20 .50
26 Bob Bailor .20 .50
27 Dusty Baker .25 .60
28 Tom Baker .20 .50
29 Dave Bancroft .25 .60
30 Dan Bankhead .20 .50
31 Jack Banta .20 .50
32 Jim Barbieri .20 .50
33 Red Barkley .20 .50
34 Jesse Barnes .20 .50
35 Rex Barney .20 .50
36 Billy Barnie .20 .50
37 Bob Barrett .20 .50
38 Jim Baxes .20 .50
39 Billy Bean .25 .60
40 BoomBoom Beck .20 .50
41 Joe Beckwith .20 .50
42 Hank Behrman .20 .50
43 Mark Belanger .20 .50
44 Wayne Belardi .20 .50
45 Tim Belcher .20 .50
46 George Bell .20 .50
47 Ray Benge .20 .50
48 Moe Berg .75 2.00
49 Bill Bergen .20 .50
50 Ray Berres .20 .50
51 Don Bessent .20 .50
52 Steve Bilko .20 .50
53 Jack Billingham .20 .50
54 Babe Birrer .20 .50
55 Del Bissonette .20 .50
56 Joe Black .20 .50
57 Lu Blue .20 .50
58 George Boehler .20 .50
59 Sammy Bohne .20 .50
60 John Bolling .20 .50
61 Ike Boone .20 .50
62 Frenchy Bordagaray .20 .50
63 Ken Boyer .25 .60
64 Buzz Boyle .20 .50
65 Mark Bradley .20 .50
66 Bobby Bragan .20 .50
67 Ralph Branca .25 .60
68 Ed Brandt .20 .50
69 Sid Bream .20 .50
70 Marv Breeding .20 .50
71 Tom Brennan .20 .50
72 William Brennan .20 .50
73 Rube Bressler .20 .50
74 Ken Brett .20 .50
75 Jim Brewer .20 .50
76 Tony Brewer .20 .50
77 Rocky Bridges .20 .50
78 Greg Brock .20 .50
79 Dan Brouthers .25 .60
80 Eddie Brown .20 .50
81 Elmer Brown .20 .50
82 Lindsay Brown .20 .50
83 Lloyd Brown .20 .50
84 Mace Brown .20 .50
85 Tommy Brown .20 .50
86 Pete Browning .25 .60
87 Ralph Bryant .20 .50
88 Jim Bucher .20 .50
89 Bill Buckner .25 .60
90 Jim Bunning .25 .60
91 Jack Burdock .20 .50
92 Glenn Burke .20 .50
93 Buster Burrell .20 .50
94 Larry Burright .20 .50
95 Doc Bushong .20 .50
96 Max Butcher .20 .50
97 Johnny Butler .20 .50
98 Enos Cabell .20 .50
99 Leon Cadore .20 .50
100 Bruce Caldwell .20 .50
101 Dick Calmus .20 .50
102 Dolf Camilli .20 .50
103 Doug Camilli .20 .50
104 Roy Campanella 2.00 5.00
105 Al Campanis .20 .50
106 Jim Campanis .20 .50
107A Leo Callahan .20 .50
107B Gilly Campbell .20 .50
108 Jimmy Canavan .20 .50
109 Chris Cannizzaro .20 .50
110 Guy Cantrell .20 .50
111 Ben Cantwell .20 .50
112 Andy Carey .20 .50
113 Max Carey .25 .60
114 Tex Carleton .20 .50
115 Ownie Carroll .20 .50
116 Bob Caruthers .20 .50
117 Doc Casey .20 .50
118 Hugh Casey .20 .50
119 Bobby Castillo .20 .50
120 Cesar Cedeno .20 .50
121 Ron Cey .25 .60
122 Ed Chandler .20 .50
123 Ben Chapman .20 .50
124 Larry Cheney .20 .50
125 Bob Chipman .20 .50
126 Chuck Churn .20 .50
127 Gino Cimoli .20 .50
128 Moose Clabaugh .20 .50
129 Bud Clancy .20 .50
130 Bob Clark .20 .50
131 Watty Clark .20 .50
132 Alta Cohen .20 .50
133 Rocky Colavito .30 .75
134 Jackie Collum .20 .50
135 Chuck Connors .60 1.50
136 Jack Coombs .25 .60
137 Johnny Cooney .20 .50
138 Tommy Corcoran .20 .50
139 Pop Corkhill .20 .50
140 John Corriden .20 .50
141 Pete Coscarart .20 .50
142 Wes Covington .20 .50
143 Billy Cox .20 .50
144 Roger Craig .20 .50
145 Cannonball Crane .20 .50
146 Willie Crawford .20 .50
147 Tim Crews .20 .50
148 John Cronin .20 .50
149 Lave Cross .20 .50
150 Bill Crouch .20 .50
151 Don Crow .20 .50
152 Henry Cruz .20 .50
153 Tony Cuccinello .20 .50
154 Roy Cullenbine .20 .50
155 George Culver .20 .50
156 Nick Cullop .20 .50
157 George Cutshaw .20 .50
158 Kiki Cuyler .25 .60
159 Bill Dahlen .20 .50
160 Babe Dahlgren .20 .50
161 Jack Dalton .20 .50
162 Tom Daly .20 .50
163 Cliff Dapper .20 .50
164 Bob Darnell .20 .50
165 Bobby Darwin .20 .50
166 Jake Daubert .20 .50
167 Vic Davalillo .20 .50
168 Curt Davis .20 .50
169 Mike Davis .20 .50
170 Ron Davis .20 .50
171 Tommy Davis .25 .60
172 Willie Davis .20 .50
173 Pea Ridge Day .20 .50
174 Tommy Dean .20 .50
175 Hank DeBerry .20 .50
176 Art Decatur .20 .50
177 Raoul(Rod) Dedeaux .30 .75
178 Ivan DeJesus .20 .50
179 Don Demeter .20 .50
180 Gene DeMontreville .20 .50
181 Rick Dempsey .20 .50
182 Eddie Dent .20 .50
183 Mike Devereaux .20 .50
184 Carlos Diaz .20 .50
185 Dick Dietz .20 .50
186 Pop Dillon .20 .50
187 Bill Doak .20 .50
188 John Dobbs .20 .50
189 George Dockins .20 .50
190 Cozy Dolan .20 .50
191 Patsy Donovan .20 .50
192 Wild Bill Donovan .20 .50
193 Mickey Doolan .20 .50
194 Jack Doscher .20 .50
195 Phil Douglas .20 .50
196 Snooks Dowd .20 .50
197 Al Downing .20 .50
198 Red Downs .20 .50
199 Jack Doyle .20 .50
200 Solly Drake .20 .50
201 Tom Drake .20 .50
202 Chuck Dressen .20 .50
203 Don Drysdale 1.00 2.50
204 Clise Dudley .20 .50
205 Mariano Duncan .20 .50
206 Jack Dunn .20 .50
207 Bull Durham .20 .50
208 Leo Durocher .30 .75
209 Billy Earle .20 .50
210 George Earnshaw .20 .50
211 Ox Eckhardt .20 .50
212 Bruce Edwards .20 .50
213 Hank Edwards .20 .50
214 Dick W. Egan .20 .50
215 Harry Eisenstat .20 .50
216 Kid Elberfeld .20 .50
217 Jumbo Elliot .20 .50
218 Don Elston .20 .50
219 Gil English .20 .50
220 Johnny Enzmann .20 .50
221 Al Epperly .20 .50
222 Carl Erskine .25 .60
223 Tex Erwin .20 .50
224 Cecil Espy .20 .50
225 Chuck Essegian .20 .50
226 Dude Esterbrook .20 .50
227 Red Evans .20 .50
228 Bunny Fabrique .20 .50
229 Jim Fairey .20 .50
230 Ron Fairly .20 .50
231 George Fallon .20 .50
232 Turk Farrell .20 .50
233 Duke Farrel .20 .50
234 Jim Faulkner .20 .50
235 Alex Ferguson .20 .50
236 Joe Ferguson .20 .50
237 Chico Fernandez .20 .50
238 Sid Fernandez .20 .50
239 Al Ferrara .20 .50
240 Wes Ferrell .25 .60
241 Lou Fette .20 .50
242 Chick Fewster .20 .50
243 Jack Fimple .20 .50
244 Neal Mickey Finn .20 .50
245 Bob Fisher .20 .50
246 Freddie Fitzsimmons .20 .50
247 Tim Flood .20 .50
248 Jake Flowers .20 .50
249 Hod Ford .20 .50
250 Terry Forster .20 .50
251 Alan Foster .20 .50
252 Jack Fournier .20 .50
253 Dave Foutz .20 .50
254 Art Fowler .20 .50
255 Fred Frankhouse .20 .50
256 Herman Franks .20 .50
257 Johnny Frederick .20 .50
258 Larry French .20 .50
259 Lonny Frey .20 .50
260 Pepe Frias .20 .50
261 Charlie Fuchs .20 .50
262 Carl Furillo .25 .60
263 Len Gabrielson .20 .50
264 Augie Galan .20 .50
265 Joe Gallagher .20 .50
266 Phil Gallivan .20 .50
267 Balvino Galvez .20 .50
268 Mike Garman .20 .50
269 Phil Garner .20 .50
270 Steve Garvey .30 .75
271 Ned Garvin .20 .50
272 Hank Gastright .20 .50
273 Sid Gautreaux .20 .50
274 Jim Gentile .20 .50
275 Greek George .20 .50
276 Ben Geraghty .20 .50
277 Gus Getz .20 .50
278 Bob Giallombardo .20 .50
279 Kirk Gibson .25 .60
280 Charlie Gilbert .20 .50
281 Jim Gilliam .20 .50
282 Al Gionfriddo .20 .50
283 Tony Giuliani .20 .50
284 Al Glossop .20 .50
285 John Gochnaur .20 .50
286 Jim Golden .20 .50
287 Dave Goltz .20 .50
288 Jose Gonzalez .20 .50
289 Johnny Gooch .20 .50
290 Ed Goodson .20 .50
291 Billy Grabarkewitz .20 .50
292 Jack Graham .20 .50
293 Mudcat Grant .20 .50
294 Dick Gray .20 .50
295 Kent Greenfield .20 .50
296 Hal Gregg .20 .50
297 Alfredo Griffin .20 .50
298 Mike Griffin .20 .50
299 Derrell Griffith .20 .50
300 Tommy Griffith .20 .50
301 Burleigh Grimes .25 .60
302 Lee Grissom .20 .50
303 Jerry Grote .20 .50
304 Pedro Guerrero .25 .60
305 Brad Gulden .20 .50
306 Ad Gumbert .20 .50
307 Chris Gwynn .20 .50
308 Bert Haas .20 .50
309 John Hale .20 .50
310 Tom Haller .20 .50
311 Bill Hallman .20 .50
312 Jeff Hamilton .20 .50
313 Luke Hamlin .20 .50
314 Ned Hanlon .25 .60
315 Gerald Hannahs .20 .50
316 Charlie Hargreaves .20 .50
317 Tim Harkness .20 .50
318 Harry Harper .20 .50
319 Joe Harris .20 .50
320 Lenny Harris .20 .50
321 Bill F. Hart .20 .50
322 Buddy Hassett .20 .50
323 Mickey Hatcher .20 .50
324 Joe Hatten .20 .50
325 Phil Haugstad .20 .50
326 Brad Havens .20 .50
327 Ray Hayworth .20 .50
328 Ed Head .20 .50
329 Danny Heep .20 .50
330 Fred Heimach .20 .50
331 Harvey Hendrick .20 .50
332 Weldon Henley .20 .50
333 Butch Henline .20 .50
334 Dutch Henry .20 .50
335 Roy Henshaw .20 .50
336 Babe Herman .25 .60
337 Billy Herman .25 .60
338 Gene Hermanski .20 .50
339 Enzo Hernandez .20 .50
340 Art Herring .20 .50
341 Orel Hershiser .25 .60
342 Dave J. Hickman .20 .50
343 Jim Hickman .20 .50
344 Kirby Higbe .20 .50
345 Andy High .20 .50
346 George Hildebrand .20 .50
347 Hunkey Hines .20 .50
348 Don Hoak .20 .50
349 Oris Hockett .20 .50
350 Gil Hodges 1.00 2.50
351 Glenn Hoffman .20 .50
352 Al Hollingsworth .20 .50
353 Tommy Holmes .20 .50
354 Brian Holton .20 .50
355 Rick Honeycutt .20 .50
356 Burt Hooton .20 .50
357 Gail Hopkins .20 .50
358 Johnny Hopp .20 .50
359 Charlie Hough .25 .60
360 Frank Howard .25 .60
361 Steve Howe .20 .50
362 Dixie Howell .20 .50
363 Harry Howell .20 .50
364 Jay Howell .20 .50
365 Ken Howell .20 .50
366 Waite Hoyt .25 .60
367 Johnny Hudson .20 .50
368 Jim J. Hughes .20 .50
369 Jim R. Hughes .20 .50
370 Mickey Hughes .20 .50
371 John Hummel .20 .50
372 Ron Hunt .20 .50
373 Willard Hunter .20 .50
374 Ira Hutchinson .20 .50
375 Tom Hutton .20 .50
376 Charlie Irwin .20 .50
377 Fred Jacklitsch .20 .50
378 Randy Jackson .20 .50
379 Merwin Jacobson .20 .50
380 Cleo James .20 .50
381 Hal Janvrin .20 .50
382 Roy Jarvis .20 .50
383 George Jeffcoat .20 .50
384 Jack Jenkins .20 .50
385 Hughie Jennings .25 .60
386 Tommy John .25 .60
387 Lou Johnson .20 .50
388 Fred Ivy Johnston .20 .50
389 Jimmy Johnston .20 .50
390 Jay Johnstone .25 .60
391 Fielder Jones .20 .50
392 Oscar Jones .20 .50
393 Tim Jordan .20 .50
394 Spider Jorgensen .20 .50
395 Von Joshua .20 .50
396 Bill Joyce .20 .50
397 Joe Judge .20 .50
398 Alex Kampouris .20 .50
399 Willie Keeler .25 .60
400 Mike Kekich .20 .50
401 John Kelleher .20 .50
402 Frank Kellert .20 .50
403 Joe Kelley .25 .60
404 George Kelly .25 .60
405 Bob Kennedy .20 .50
406 Brickyard Kennedy .20 .50
407 John Kennedy .20 .50
409 Newt Kimball .20 .50
410 Clyde King .20 .50
411 Enos Kirkpatrick .20 .50
412 Frank Kitson .20 .50
413 Johnny Klippstein .20 .50
414 Elmer Klumpp .20 .50
415 Len Koenecke .20 .50
416 Ed Konetchy .20 .50
417 Andy Kosco .20 .50
418 Sandy Koufax 4.00 10.00
419 Ernie Koy .20 .50
420 Charlie Kress .20 .50
421 Bill Krueger .20 .50
422 Ernie Krueger .20 .50
423 Clem Labine .20 .50
424 Candy LaChance .20 .50
425 Lee Lacy .20 .50
426 Lerrin LaGrow .20 .50
427 Bill Lamar .20 .50
428 Wayne LaMaster .20 .50
429 Ray Lamb .20 .50
430 Rafael Landestoy .20 .50
431 Ken Landreaux .20 .50
432 Tito Landrum .20 .50
433 Norm Larker .20 .50
434 Lyn Lary .20 .50
435 Tom Lasorda 1.00 2.50
436 Cookie Lavagetto .20 .50
437 Rudy Law .20 .50
438 Tony Lazzeri .25 .60
439 Tim Leary .20 .50
440 Bob Lee .20 .50
441 Hal Lee .20 .50
442 Leron Lee .20 .50
443 Jim Lefebvre .20 .50
444 Ken Lehman .20 .50
445 Don LeJohn .20 .50
446 Steve Lembo .20 .50
447 Ed Lennox .20 .50
448 Dutch Leonard .20 .50
449 Jeffery Leonard .20 .50
450 Sam Leslie .20 .50
451 Dennis Lewallyn .20 .50
452 Bob Lillis .20 .50
453 Jim Lindsey .20 .50
454 Fred Lindstrom .25 .60
455 Billy Loes .20 .50
456 Bob Logan .20 .50
457 Bill Lohrman .20 .50
459 Vic Lombardi .20 .50
460 Davey Lopes .25 .60
461 Al Lopez .25 .60
462 Ray Lucas .20 .50
464 Harry Lumley .20 .50
465 Don Lund .20 .50
466 Dolf Luque .25 .60
467 Jim Lyttle .20 .50
468 Max Macon .20 .50
469 Bill Madlock .25 .60
470 Lee Magee .20 .50
471 Sal Maglie .25 .60
472 George Magoon .20 .50
473 Duster Mails .20 .50
474 Candy Maldonado .20 .50
475 Tony Malinosky .20 .50
476 Lew Malone .20 .50
477 Al Mamaux .20 .50
478 Gus Mancuso .20 .50
479 Charlie Manuel .20 .50
480 Heinie Manush .25 .60
481 Rabbit Maranville .25 .60
482 Juan Marichal .30 .75
483 Rube Marquard .25 .60
484 Bill Marriott .20 .50
485 Buck Marrow .20 .50
486 Mike A. Marshall .20 .50
487 Mike G. Marshall .20 .50
488 Morrie Martin .20 .50
489 Ramon Martinez .25 .60
490 Teddy Martinez .20 .50
491 Earl Mattingly .20 .50
492 Len Matuszek .20 .50
493 Gene Mauch .20 .50
494 Al Maul .20 .50
495 Carmen Mauro .20 .50
496 Alvin McBean .20 .50
497 Bill McCarren .20 .50
498 Jack McCarthy .20 .50
499 Tommy McCarthy .25 .60
500 Lew McCarty .20 .50
501 Mike J. McCormick .20 .50
502 Judge McCreedie .20 .50
503 Tom McCreery .20 .50
504 Danny McDevitt .20 .50
505 Chappie McFarland .20 .50
506 Joe McGinnity .25 .60
507 Bob McGraw .20 .50
508 Deacon McGuire .20 .50
509 Bill McGunnigle .20 .50
510 Harry McIntire .20 .50
511 Cal McLish .20 .50
512 Ken McMullen .20 .50
513 Doug McWeeny .20 .50
514 Joe Medwick .25 .60
515 Rube Melton .20 .50
516 Fred Merkle .20 .50
517 Orlando Mercado .20 .50
518 Andy Messersmith .20 .50
519 Irish Meusel .20 .50
520 Benny Meyer .20 .50
521 Russ Meyer .20 .50
522 Chief Meyers .20 .50
523 Gene Michael .20 .50
524 Pete Mikkelsen .20 .50
525 Eddie Miksis .20 .50
526 Johnny Miljus .20 .50
527 Bob Miller .20 .50
528 Larry Miller .20 .50
Wearing a N.Y. Mets uniform
529 Otto Miller .20 .50
530 Ralph Miller .20 .50
531 Walt Miller .20 .50
532 Wally Millies .20 .50
533 Bob Milliken .20 .50
534 Buster Mills .20 .50
535 Paul Minner .20 .50
536 Bobby Mitchell .20 .50
537 Clarence Mitchell .20 .50
538 Dale Mitchell .20 .50
539 Fred Mitchell .20 .50
540 Johnny Mitchell .20 .50
541 Joe Moeller .20 .50
542 Rick Monday .20 .50
543 Wally Moon .20 .50
544 Cy Moore .20 .50
545 Dee Moore .20 .50
546 Eddie Moore .20 .50
547 Gene Moore .20 .50
548 Randy Moore .20 .50
549 Ray Moore .20 .50
550 Jose Morales .20 .50
551 Bobby Morgan .20 .50
552 Eddie Morgan .20 .50
553 Mike Morgan .20 .50
554 Johnny Morrison .20 .50
555 Walt Moryn .20 .50
556 Ray Moss .20 .50
557 Manny Mota .20 .50
558 Joe Mulvey .20 .50
559 Van Lingle Mungo .20 .50
560 Les Munns .20 .50
561 Mike Munoz .20 .50
562 Simmy Murch .20 .50
563 Eddie Murray .75 2.00
564 Hy Myers .20 .50
565 Sam Nahem .20 .50
566 Earl Naylor .20 .50
567 Charlie Neal .20 .50
568 Ron Negray .20 .50
569 Bernie Neis .20 .50
570 Rocky Nelson .20 .50
571 Dick Nen .20 .50
572 Don Newcombe .25 .60
573 Bobo Newsom .25 .60
574 Doc Newton .20 .50
575 Tom Niedenfuer .20 .50
576 Otho Nitcholas .20 .50
577 Al Nixon .20 .50
578 Jerry Nops .20 .50
579 Irv Noren .20 .50
580 Fred Norman .20 .50
581 Bill North .20 .50
582 Johnny Oates .20 .50
583 Bob O'Brien .20 .50
584 John O'Brien .20 .50
585 Lefty O'Doul .25 .60
586 Joe Oeschger .20 .50
587 Al Oliver .25 .60
588 Nate Oliver .20 .50
589 Luis Olmo .20 .50
590 Ivy Olson .20 .50
591 Mickey O'Neil .20 .50
592 Joe Orengo .20 .50
593 Jesse Orosco .20 .50
594 Frank O'Rourke .20 .50
595 Jorge Orta .20 .50
596 Phil Ortega .20 .50
597 Claude Osteen .20 .50
598 Fritz Ostermueller .20 .50
599 Mickey Owen .20 .50
600 Tom Paciorek .20 .50
601 Don Padgett .20 .50
602 Andy Pafko .20 .50
603 Erv Palica .20 .50
604 Ed Palmquist .20 .50
605 Wes Parker .20 .50
606 Jay Partridge .20 .50
607 Camilo Pascual .20 .50
608 Kevin Pasley .20 .50
609 Dave Patterson .20 .50
610 Harley Payne .20 .50
611 Johnny Peacock .20 .50
612 Hal Peck .20 .50
613 Stu Pederson .20 .50
614 Alejandro Pena .20 .50
615 Jose Pena .20 .50
616 Jack Perconte .20 .50
617 Charlie Perkins .20 .50
618 Ron Perranoski .20 .50
619 Jim Peterson .20 .50
620 Jesse Petty .20 .50
621 Jeff Pfeffer .20 .50
622 Babe Phelps .20 .50
623 Val Picinich .20 .50
624 Joe Pignatano .20 .50
625 George Pinkney .20 .50
626 Ed Pipgras .20 .50
627 Bud Podbielan .20 .50
628 Johnny Podres .20 .50
629 Boots Poffenberger .20 .50
630 Nick Polly .20 .50
631 Paul Popovich .20 .50
632 Bill Posedel .20 .50
633 Boog Powell .25 .60
634 Dennis Powell .20 .50
635 Paul Ray Powell .20 .50
636 Ted Power .20 .50
637 Tot Pressnell .20 .50
638 John Purdin .20 .50
639 Jack Quinn .20 .50
640 Marv Rackley .20 .50
641 Jack Radtke .20 .50
642 Pat Ragan .20 .50
643 Ed Rakow .20 .50
644 Bob Ramazzotti .20 .50
645 Willie Ramsdell .20 .50
646 Mike James Ramsey .20 .50
647 Mike Jeffery Ramsey .20 .50
648 Willie Randolph .20 .50

649 Doug Rau .20 .50
650 Lance Rautzhan .20 .50
651 Howie Reed .20 .50
652 Pee Wee Reese 1.25 3.00
653 Phil Regan .20 .50
654 Bill Reidy .20 .50
655 Bobby Reis .20 .50
656 Pete Reiser .25 .60
657 Rip Repulski .20 .50
658 Ed Reulbach .20 .50
659 Jerry Reuss .20 .50
660 R.J. Reynolds .20 .50
661 Billy Rhiel .20 .50
662 Rick Rhoden .20 .50
663 Paul Richards .20 .50
664 Danny Richardson .20 .50
665 Pete Richert .20 .50
666 Harry Riconda .20 .50
667 Joe Riggert .20 .50
668 Lew Riggs .20 .50
669 Jimmy Ripple .20 .50
670 Lou Ritter .20 .50
671 German Rivera .20 .50
672 Johnny Rizzo .20 .50
673 Jim Roberts .20 .50
674 Earl Robinson .20 .50
675 Frank Robinson 1.25 3.00
676 Jackie Robinson 4.00 10.00
677A Wilbert Robinson .30 .75
678 Rich Rodas .20 .50
678B Sergio Robles .20 .50
679 Ellie Rodriguez .20 .50
680 Preacher Roe .25 .60
681 Ed Roebuck .20 .50
682 Ron Roenicke .20 .50
683 Oscar Roettger .20 .50
684 Lee Rogers .20 .50
685 Packy Rogers .20 .50
686 Stan Rojek .20 .50
687 Vicente Romo .20 .50
688 Johnny Roseboro .20 .50
689 Goody Rosen .20 .50
690 Don Ross .20 .50
691 Ken Rowe .20 .50
692 Schoolboy Rowe .20 .50
693 Luther Roy .20 .50
694 Jerry Royster .20 .50
695 Nap Rucker .20 .50
696 Dutch Ruether .20 .50
697 Bill Russell .25 .60
698 Jim Russell .20 .50
699 John Russell UER/(Photo actually .20 .50
current catcher
700 Johnny Rutherford .20 .50
701 John Ryan .20 .50
702 Rosy Ryan .20 .50
703 Mike Sandlock .20 .50
704 Ted Savage .20 .50
705 Dave Sax .20 .50
706 Steve Sax .20 .50
707 Bill Sayles .20 .50
708 Bill Schardt .20 .50
709 Johnny Schmitz .20 .50
710 Dick Schofield .20 .50
711 Howie Schultz .20 .50
712 Ferdie Schupp .20 .50
713 Mike Scioscia .25 .60
714 Dick Scott .20 .50
715 Tom Seats .20 .50
716 Jimmy Sebring .20 .50
717 Larry See .20 .50
718 Dave Sells .20 .50
719 Greg Shanahan .20 .50
720 Mike Sharperson .20 .50
721 Joe Shaute .20 .50
722 Merv Shea .20 .50
723 Jimmy Sheckard .20 .50
724 Jack Sheehan .20 .50
725 John Shelby .20 .50
726 Vince Sherlock .20 .50
727 Larry Sherry .20 .50
728 Norm Sherry .20 .50
729 Bill Shindle .20 .50
730 Craig Shipley .20 .50
731 Bart Shirley .20 .50
732 Steve Shirley .20 .50
733 Burt Shotton .20 .50
734 George Shuba .20 .50
735 Dick Siebert .20 .50
736 Joe Simpson .20 .50
737 Duke Sims .20 .50
738 Bill Singer .20 .50
739 Fred Sington .20 .50
740 Ted Sizemore .20 .50
741 Frank Skaff .20 .50
742 Bill Skowron .20 .50
743 Gordon Slade .20 .50
744 Dwain Lefty Sloat .20 .50
745 Charley Smith .20 .50
746 Dick Smith .20 .50
Wearing a N.Y> Mets uniform
747 George Smith .20 .50
748 Germany Smith .20 .50
749 Jack Smith .20 .50
750 Reggie Smith .20 .50
751 Sherry Smith .20 .50
752 Harry Smythe .20 .50
753 Duke Snider 2.00 5.00
754 Eddie Solomon .20 .50
755 Elias Sosa .20 .50
756 Daryl Spencer .20 .50
757 Roy Spencer .20 .50
758 Karl Spooner .20 .50
759 Eddie Stack .20 .50
760 Tuck Stainback .20 .50
761 George Stallings .20 .50
762 Jerry Standaert .20 .50
763 Don Stanhouse .20 .50
764 Eddie Stanky .20 .50
765 Dolly Stark .20 .50
766 Jigger Statz .20 .50
767 Casey Stengel .75 2.00
768 Jerry Stephenson .20 .50
769 Ed Stevens .20 .50
770 Dave Stewart .25 .60
771 Stuffy Stewart .20 .50
772 Bob Stinson .20 .50
773 Milt Stock .20 .50
774 Harry Stovey .20 .50
775 Mike Strahler .20 .50
776 Sammy Strang .20 .50
777 Elmer Stricklett .20 .50
778 Joe Stripp .20 .50
779 Dick Stuart .20 .50
Wearing a N.Y. Mets uniform
780 Franklin Stubbs .20 .50
781 Bill Sudakis .20 .50
782 Clyde Sukeforth .20 .50
783 Billy Sullivan .20 .50
784 Tom Sunkel .20 .50
785 Rick Sutcliffe .20 .50
786 Don Sutton .60 1.50
787 Bill Swift .20 .50
788 Vito Tamulis .20 .50
789 Danny Taylor .20 .50
790 Harry Taylor .20 .50
791 Zack Taylor .20 .50
793 Chuck Templeton .20 .50
794 Wayne Terwilliger .20 .50
795 Derrel Thomas .20 .50
796 Fay Thomas .20 .50
797 Gary Thomasson .20 .50
798 Don Thompson .20 .50
799 Fresco Thompson .20 .50
800 Tim Thompson .20 .50
801 Hank Thormahlen .20 .50
802 Sloppy Thurston .20 .50
803 Cotton Tierney .20 .50
804 Al Todd .20 .50
805 Bert Tooley .20 .50
806 Jeff Torborg .20 .50
807 Dick Tracewski .20 .50
808 Nick Tremark .20 .50
809 Alex Trevino .20 .50
810 Tommy Tucker .20 .50
811 John Tudor .20 .50
812 Mike Vail .20 .50
813 Rene Valdes .20 .50
814 Bobby Valentine .20 .50
815 Fernando Valenzuela .25 .60
816 Elmer Valo .20 .50
817 Dazzy Vance .25 .60
818 Sandy Vance .20 .50
819 Chris Van Cuyk .20 .50
820 Ed VandeBerg .20 .50
821 Arky Vaughan .25 .60
822 Zoilo Versalles .20 .50
823 Joe Vosmik .20 .50
824 Ben Wade .20 .50
825 Dixie Walker .25 .60
826 Rube Walker .20 .50
827 Stan Wall .20 .50
828 Lee Walls .20 .50
829 Danny Walton .20 .50
830 Lloyd Waner .25 .60
831 Paul Waner .25 .60
832 Chuck Ward .20 .50
833 John Monte Ward .25 .60
834 Preston Ward .20 .50
835 Jack Warner .20 .50
836 Tommy Warren .20 .50
837 Carl Warwick .20 .50
838 Jimmy Wasdell .20 .50
839 Ron Washington .25 .60
840 George Watkins .20 .50
841 Hank Webb .20 .50
842 Les Webber .20 .50
843 Gary Weiss .20 .50
844 Bob Welch .25 .60
845 Brad Wellman .20 .50
846 John Werhas .20 .50
847 Max West .20 .50
848 Gus Weyhing .20 .50
849 Mack Wheat .20 .50
850 Zack Wheat .25 .60
851 Ed Wheeler .20 .50
852 Larry White .20 .50
853 Myron White .20 .50
854 Terry Whitfield .20 .50
855 Dick Whitman .20 .50
856 Possum Whitted .20 .50
857 Kemp Wicker .20 .50
858 Hoyt Wilhelm .25 .60
859 Kaiser Wilhelm .20 .50
860 Nick Willhite .20 .50
861 Dick Williams .20 .50
862 Reggie Williams .20 .50
863 Stan Williams .20 .50
864 Woody Williams .20 .50
865 Maury Wills .30 .75
866 Hack Wilson .25 .60
867 Robert Wilson .20 .50
868 Gordon Windhorn .20 .50
869 Jim Winford .20 .50
870 Lave Winham .20 .50
871 Tom Winsett .20 .50
872 Hank Winston .20 .50
873 Whitey Witt .20 .50
874 Pete Wojey .20 .50
875 Tracy Woodson .20 .50
876 Clarence Wright .20 .50
877 Glenn Wright .20 .50
878 Ricky Wright .20 .50
879 Whit Wyatt .20 .50
880 Jimmy Wynn .20 .50
881 Joe Yeager .20 .50
882 Steve Yeager .20 .50
883 Matt Young .20 .50
884 Tom Zachary .20 .50
885 Pat Zachry .20 .50
886 Geoff Zahn .20 .50
887 Don Zimmer .25 .60
888 Morrie Aderholt .20 .50
889 Raleigh Aitchison .20 .50
890 Whitey Alperman .20 .50
891 Orlando Alvarez .20 .50
892 Pat Ankenman .20 .50
893 Ed Appleton .20 .50
894 Doug Baird .20 .50
895 Lady Baldwin .20 .50
896 Win Ballou .20 .50
897 Bob Barr .20 .50
898 Boyd Bartley .20 .50
899 Eddie Basinski .20 .50
900 Erve Beck .20 .50
901 Ralph Birkofer .20 .50
903 Joe Bradshaw .20 .50
904 Bruce Brubaker .20 .50
905 Oyster Burns .20 .50
906 John Butler .20 .50
908 Kid Carsey .20 .50
909 Pete Cassidy .20 .50
910 Tom Catterson .20 .50
911 Glenn Chapman .20 .50
912 Paul Chervinko .20 .50
913 George Cisar .20 .50
914 Wally Clement .20 .50
915 Bill Collins .20 .50
916 Chuck Corgan .20 .50
917 Dick Cox .20 .50
918 George Crable .20 .50
919 Sam Crane .20 .50
920 Cliff Curtis .20 .50
921 Fats Dantonio .20 .50
922 Con Daily .20 .50
923 Jud Daley .20 .50
924 Jake Daniel .20 .50
925 Kal Daniels .20 .50
926 Dan Daub .20 .50
927 Lindsay Deal .20 .50
928 Artie Dede .20 .50
929 Pat Deisel .20 .50
930 Bert Delmas .20 .50
931 Rube Dessau .20 .50
932 Leo Dickerman .20 .50
933 John Douglas .20 .50
934 Red Downey .20 .50
935 Carl Doyle .20 .50
936 John Duffie .20 .50
937 Dick Durning .20 .50
938 Red Durrett .20 .50
939 Mal Eason .20 .50
940 Charlie Ebbetts .25 .60
941 Rube Ehardt .20 .50
942 Rowdy Elliot .20 .50
943 Bones Ely .20 .50
944 Woody English .20 .50
945 Roy Evans .20 .50
946 Gus Felix .20 .50
947 Bill Fischer .20 .50
948 Jeff Fischer .20 .50
949 Chauncey Fisher .20 .50
950 Tom Fitzsimmons .20 .50
951 Darrin Fletcher .20 .50
952 Wes Flowers .20 .50
953 Howard Freigau .20 .50
954 Nig Fuller .20 .50
955 John Gaddy .20 .50
956 Welcome Gaston .20 .50
957 Frank Gatins .20 .50
958 Pete Gilbert .20 .50
959 Wally Gilbert .20 .50
960 Carden Gillenwater .20 .50
961 Roy Gleason .20 .50
962 Harvey Green .20 .50
963 Nelson Greene .20 .50
964 John Grim .20 .50
965 Dan Griner .20 .50
966 George Haddock .20 .50
967 Bill Hall .20 .50
968 Johnny Hall .20 .50
970 Pat Hanifin .20 .50
971 Bill Harris .20 .50
972 Bill W. Hart .20 .50
973 Chris Hartje .20 .50
974 Mike Hartley .20 .50
975 Gil Hatfield .20 .50
976 Chris Haughey .20 .50
977 Hugh Hearne .20 .50
978 Mike Hechinger .20 .50
979 Jake Hehl .20 .50
980 Bob Higgins .20 .50
981 Still Bill Hill .20 .50
982 Shawn Hillegas .20 .50
983 Wally Hood .20 .50
984 Lefty Hopper .20 .50
985 Ricky Horton .20 .50
986 Ed Householder .20 .50
987 Bill Hubbell .20 .50
988 Al Humphrey .20 .50
989 Bernie Hungling .20 .50
990 George Hunter .20 .50
991 Pat Hurley .20 .50
992 Joe Hutcheson .20 .50
993 Roy Hutson .20 .50
994 Bert Inks .20 .50
995 Dutch Jordan .20 .50
997 Frank Kane .20 .50
998 Chet Kehn .20 .50
999 Maury Kent .20 .50
1000 Tom Kinslow .20 .50
1001 Fred Kipp .20 .50
1002 Joe Klugman .20 .50
1003 Elmer Knetzer .20 .50
1004 Barney Koch .20 .50
1005 Jim Korwan .20 .50
1006 Joe Koukalik .20 .50
1007 Lou Koupal .20 .50
1008 Joe Kustus .20 .50
1009 Frank Lamanske .20 .50
1010 Tacks Latimer .20 .50
1011 Bill Leard .20 .50
1012 Phil Lewis .20 .50
1013 Mickey Livingston .20 .50
1014 Dick Loftus .20 .50
1015 Charlie Loudenslager .20 .50
1016 Tom Lovett .20 .50
1017 Charlie Malay .20 .50
1018 Mal Mallette .20 .50
1019 Ralph Mauriello .20 .50
1020 Bill McCabe .20 .50
1021 Gene McCann .20 .50
1022 Mike W. McCormick .20 .50
1023 Terry McDermott .20 .50
1024 John McDougal .20 .50
1025 Pryor McElveen .20 .50
1026 Dan McGann .20 .50
1027 Pat McGlothin .20 .50
1028 Doc McJames .20 .50
1029 Kit McKenna .20 .50
1030 Sadie McMahon .20 .50
1032 Tommy McMillan .20 .50
1033 Glenn Mickens .20 .50
1034 Don Miles .20 .50
1035 Hack Miller .20 .50
1036 John Miller .20 .50
1037 Lemmie Miller .20 .50
1038 George Mohart .20 .50
1039 Gary Moore .20 .50
1040 Herbie Moran .20 .50
1041 Earl Mossor .20 .50
1042 Glen Moulder .20 .50
1043 Billy Mullen .20 .50
1044 Hub Northen .20 .50
1045 Curly Onis .20 .50
1046 Tiny Osborne .20 .50
1047 Jim Pastorius .20 .50
1048 Art Parks .20 .50
1049 Chink Outen .20 .50
1050 Jimmy Pattison .20 .50
1051 Norman Plitt .20 .50
1052 Doc Reisling .20 .50
1053 Gilberto Reyes .20 .50
1055 Lou Rochelli .20 .50
1056 Jim Romano .20 .50
1057 Max Rosenfeld .20 .50
1058 Andy Rush .20 .50
1059 Jack Ryan .20 .50
1060 Jack Savage .20 .50
1062 Ray Schmandt .20 .50
1063 Henry Schmidt .20 .50
1064 Charlie Schmutz .20 .50
1065 Joe Schultz .20 .50
1066 Ray Searage .20 .50
1067 Elmer Sexauer .20 .50
1068 George Sharrott .20 .50
1069 Tommy Sheehan .20 .50
1070 Red Sheridan .20 .50
1071 George Shoch .20 .50
1072 Broadway Aleck Smith .20 .50
1073 Hap Smith .20 .50
1074 Red Smith .20 .50
1075 Tony Smith .20 .50
1076 Gene Snyder .20 .50
1077 Denny Sothern .20 .50
1078 Bill Steele .20 .50
1079 Elmer Steele .20 .50
1080 Farmer Steelman .20 .50
1081 Dutch Stryker .20 .50
1082 Tommy Tatum .20 .50
1083 Joe Tepsic .20 .50
1084 Adonis Terry .20 .50
1085 Ray Thomas .20 .50
1086 George Treadway .20 .50
1087 Overton Tremper .20 .50
1088 Ty Tyson .20 .50
1089 Rube Vickers .20 .50
1090 Jose Vizcaino .25 .60
1091 Bull Wagner .20 .50
1092 Butts Wagner .20 .50
1093 Rube Ward .20 .50
1094 John Wetteland .25 .60
1095 Eddie Wilson .20 .50
1096 Tex Wilson .20 .50
1097 Zeke Wrigley .20 .50
1099 Rube Yarrison .20 .50
1100 Earl Yingling .20 .50
1101 Chink Zachary .20 .50
1102 Lefty Davis .20 .50
1103 Bob Hall .20 .50
1104 Darby O'Brien .20 .50
1105 Larry LeJeune .20 .50
1144 Hub Northen .20 .50

1991 Dodgers Mother's

The 1991 Mother's Cookies Los Angeles Dodgers set contains 28 standard-size cards with rounded corners.

COMPLETE SET (28) 3.00 8.00
1 Tom Lasorda MG .40 1.00
2 Darryl Strawberry .20 .50
3 Kal Daniels .08 .25
4 Mike Scioscia .30 .75
5 Eddie Murray .50 1.25
6 Brett Butler .30 .75
7 Juan Samuel .08 .25
8 Alfredo Griffin .08 .25
9 Tim Belcher .08 .25
10 Ramon Martinez .20 .50
11 Jose Gonzalez .08 .25
12 Orel Hershiser .30 .75
13 Bob Ojeda .08 .25
14 Chris Gwynn .08 .25
15 Jay Howell .08 .25
16 Gary Carter .50 1.25
17 Kevin Gross .08 .25
18 Lenny Harris .08 .25
19 Mike Hartley .08 .25
20 Mike Sharperson .08 .25
21 Mike Morgan .08 .25
22 John Candelaria .08 .25
23 Jeff Hamilton .08 .25
24 Jim Gott .08 .25
25 Barry Lyons .08 .25
26 Tim Crews .08 .25
27 Stan Javier .08 .25
28 Checklist Card .08 .25
Joe Ferguson CO
Ben Hines CO
Mar

1991 Dodgers Photos

These photos were issued and feature members of the 1991 Los Angeles Dodgers. They are sequenced in manager and coach order and then alphabetical order by player.

COMPLETE SET 8.00 20.00
1 Tommy Lasorda MG .60 1.50
2 Joe Amalfitano CO .20 .50
3 Mark Cresse CO .20 .50
4 Manny Mota CO .30 .75
5 Ron Perranoski CO .20 .50
6 Bill Russell CO .30 .75
7 Tim Belcher .20 .50
8 John Canderlaria .20 .50
9 Gary Carter .75 2.00
10 Kal Daniels .20 .50
11 Butch Davis .20 .50
12 Chris Gwynn .20 .50
13 Carlos Hernandez .20 .50
14 Orel Hershiser .40 1.00
15 Jay Howell .20 .50
16 Stan Javier .20 .50
17 Eric Karros .75 2.00
18 Ramon Martinez .30 .75
19 Mike Morgan .20 .50
20 Eddie Murray .75 2.00
21 Jose Offerman .20 .50
22 Bob Ojeda .20 .50
23 Juan Samuel .20 .50
24 Henry Rodriguez .30 .75
25 Mike Scioscia .40 1.00
26 Zakary Shinall .20 .50
27 Greg Smith .20 .50
28 Darryl Strawberry .30 .75
29 Dave Walsh .20 .50
30 Mitch Webster .20 .50
31 John Wetteland .40 1.00

1991 Dodgers Police

This 30-card set was sponsored by the Los Angeles Police Department and its Crime Prevention Advisory Council. The cards measure approximately 2 13/16" by 4 1/8". The cards are skip-numbered by uniform number on the fronts.

COMPLETE SET (30) 2.50 6.00
3 Jeff Hamilton .08 .25
5 Stan Javier .08 .25
7 Alfredo Griffin .08 .25
10 Juan Samuel .08 .25
12 Gary Carter .50 1.25
14 Mike Scioscia .30 .75
15 Chris Gwynn .08 .25
17 Bob Ojeda .08 .25
22 Brett Butler .30 .75
25 Dennis Cook .08 .25
27 Mike Sharperson .08 .25
28 Kal Daniels .08 .25
29 Lenny Harris .08 .25
30 Jose Offerman .08 .25
31 Jim Neidlinger .08 .25
33 Eddie Murray .50 1.25
35 Jim Gott .08 .25
36 Mike Morgan .08 .25
38 Jose Gonzalez .08 .25
40 Barry Lyons .08 .25
44 Darryl Strawberry .20 .50
45 Kevin Gross .08 .25
46 Mike Hartley .08 .25
48 Ramon Martinez .20 .50
49 Tim Belcher .08 .25
50 Jay Howell .08 .25
52 Tim Crews .08 .25
54 John Candelaria .08 .25
55 Orel Hershiser .20 .50
NNO Coaches Card .20 .50
Ben Hines
Ron Perranoski
Mark Cres

1991 Dodgers Rini Postcards 2

This set of 12 postcards measures 3 1/2" by 5 1/2" and showcases the Brooklyn Dodgers. On a blue background, the horizontal fronts feature color drawings by Susan Rini. The cards are numbered on the back as "X of 12."

COMPLETE SET (12) 2.00 5.00
1 Charley Dressen .20 .50
2 Johnny Roseboro .20 .50
3 Eddie Stanky .20 .50
4 Goodwin(Goody) Rosen .08 .25
5 Ed Head .08 .25
6 Dick Williams .20 .50
7 Clarence(Bud) Podbielan .08 .25
8 Erv Palica .08 .25
9 Augie Galan .08 .25
10 Billy Loes .20 .50
11 Billy Cox .20 .50
12 Phil Phifer .08 .25

1991 Dodgers Rini Postcards 3

This set of 12 postcards measures 3 1/2" by 5 1/2" and showcases the Brooklyn Dodgers. On a blue background, the horizontal fronts feature color drawings by Susan Rini. The cards are numbered on the back as "X of 12."

COMPLETE SET (12) 2.00 5.00
1 Joe Black .20 .50
2 Jack Banta .08 .25
3 Whitlow Wyatt .08 .25
4 Gino Cimoli .08 .25
5 Dolph Camilli .20 .50
6 Dan Bankhead .08 .25
7 Henry Behrman .08 .25
8 Pete Reiser .30 .75
9 Chris Van Cuyk .08 .25
10 James(Junior) Gilliam .30 .75
11 Don Zimmer .20 .50
12 Ed Roebuck .08 .25

1991 Dodgers Rini Postcards 4

This set of 12 postcards measures 3 1/2" by 5 1/2" and showcases the Brooklyn Dodgers. On a blue background, the horizontal fronts feature color drawings by Susan Rini. The cards are numbered on the back as "X of 12."

COMPLETE SET (12) 2.00 5.00
1 Billy Herman .40 1.00
2 Rube Walker .08 .25
3 Tommy Brown .08 .25
4 Charles Neal .08 .25
5 Kirby Higbe .20 .50
6 Bruce Edwards .08 .25
7 Joe Hatten .08 .25
8 Rex Barney .08 .25
9 Al Gionfriddo .08 .25
10 Luis Olmo .08 .25
11 Dixie Walker .30 .75
12 Walter Alston .40 1.00

1991 Dodgers St. Vincent

This 18-stamp set was issued by the government of the Caribbean Island of St. Vincent. The stamps were designed to be placed in a commemorative folder with the 1989 Dodgers team photo printed in the center section. Two players' photos appear on all of the player stamps. Manager and coaches share stamps as well. The stamps are unnumbered and checklisted below in alphabetical order according to the name of the player on the left of the stamp.

COMPLETE SET (18) 4.00 10.00
1 Stan Javier .20 .50
Alfredo Griffin
2 Gary Carter .30 .75
Juan Samuel
3 Mike Scioscia .20 .50
Chris Gwynn
4 Bob Ojeda .20 .50
Mitch Webster
5 Dodger Stadium .20 .50
6 Brett Butler .20 .50
Mike Sharperson
7 Joe Amalfitano .20 .50
Ben Hines
Manny Mota
Ron Perrano
8 Kal Daniels .20 .50
Lenny Harris
9 Dan Opperman .20 .50
Jim Neidlinger
Carlos Hernandez
He
10 Jose Offerman .20 .50
Roger McDowell
11 Eddie Murray .30 .75
Jim Gott
12 Mike Morgan .20 .50
Dave Hansen
13 Darryl Strawberry .20 .50
Kevin Gross
14 Tommy Lasorda MG .30 .75
Jeff Hamilton
15 Ramon Martinez .30 .75
Tim Belcher
16 Jay Howell .20 .50
Tim Crews
17 John Candelaria .30 .75
Orel Hershiser
18 Zak Shinall .30 .75

1992 Dodgers Mother's

The 1992 Mother's Cookies Los Angeles Dodgers set contains 28 standard size cards with rounded corners.

COMPLETE SET (28) 4.00 10.00
1 Tom Lasorda MG .40 1.00
2 Brett Butler .30 .75
3 Tom Candiotti .08 .25
4 Eric Davis .30 .75
5 Lenny Harris .08 .25
6 Orel Hershiser .30 .75
7 Ramon Martinez .20 .50
8 Jose Offerman .08 .25
9 Mike Scioscia .30 .75
10 Darryl Strawberry .20 .50
11 Todd Benzinger .08 .25
12 John Candelaria .08 .25
13 Tim Crews .08 .25
14 Kal Daniels .08 .25
15 Jim Gott .08 .25
16 Kevin Gross .08 .25
17 Dave Hansen .08 .25
18 Carlos Hernandez .08 .25
19 Jay Howell .08 .25
20 Stan Javier .08 .25
21 Eric Karros .40 1.00
22 Roger McDowell .08 .25
23 Bob Ojeda .08 .25
24 Juan Samuel .08 .25
25 Mike Sharperson .08 .25
26 Mitch Webster .08 .25
27 Steve Wilson .08 .25
28 Checklist Card .08 .25
Mark Cresse CO
Ron Perranoski CO#

1992 Dodgers Police

This 30-card standard size set was given out as a promotion at the ball park and was sponsored by the Los Angeles Police Department and D.A.R.E. California. The set, which commemorates the 30th anniversary of Dodger Stadium, features color action photos with rounded corners on a white card face with a navy blue stripe bordering the photos. The cards are skip-numbered by uniform number on the front and back.

COMPLETE SET (30) 2.50 6.00
2 Tommy Lasorda MG .40 1.00
3 Jeff Hamilton .08 .25
5 Stan Javier .08 .25
10 Juan Samuel .08 .25
14 Mike Scioscia .30 .75
15 Dave Hansen .08 .25
17 Bob Ojeda .08 .25
20 Mitch Webster .08 .25
22 Brett Butler .30 .75
23 Eric Karros .40 1.00
27 Mike Sharperson .08 .25
28 Kal Daniels .08 .25
29 Lenny Harris .08 .25
30 Jose Offerman .08 .25
31 Roger McDowell .08 .25
33 Eric Davis .30 .75
35 Jim Gott .08 .25
36 Todd Benzinger .08 .25
38 Steve Wilson .08 .25
41 Carlos Hernandez .08 .25
44 Darryl Strawberry .20 .50
46 Kevin Gross .08 .25
48 Ramon Martinez .20 .50
49 Tom Candiotti .08 .25
50 Jay Howell .08 .25
52 Tim Crews .08 .25
54 John Candelaria .08 .25
55 Orel Hershiser .20 .50
57 Kip Gross .08 .25
NNO Coaching Staff .20 .50
Ben Hines
Ron Perranoski
Tommy L

1992 Dodgers Smokey

This set measures 3 1/2" by 5 1/2". The cards are numbered in various sequences but the last two numbers are always 92 since that was the year of issue.

COMPLETE SET (30) 6.00 15.00
10092 Stan Javier .20 .50
10192 Roger McDowell .20 .50
10292 Jose Offerman .20 .50
10392 Bob Ojeda .20 .50
10492 Juan Samuel .20 .50
10592 Mike Sharperson .20 .50
10692 Mitch Webster .20 .50
4192 Dodger Coaches .20 .50
4292 Brett Butler .40 1.00
4392 Eric Davis .40 1.00
4492 Orel Hershiser .30 .75
4592 Ramon Martinez .30 .75
4692 Darryl Strawberry .30 .75
4792 Tom Candiotti .20 .50
4892 Jim Gott .20 .50
4992 Eric Karros .60 1.50
5092 Tom Lasorda .60 1.50
5192 Mike Scioscia .40 1.00
5292 Steve Wilson .20 .50
5392 Dave Anderson .20 .50
5492 Todd Benzinger .20 .50
5592 John Candelaria .20 .50
5692 Tim Crews .20 .50
5792 Kal Daniels .20 .50
5892 Kevin Gross .20 .50
5992 Kip Gross .20 .50
9692 Dave Hansen .20 .50
9792 Lenny Harris .20 .50
9892 Carlos Hernandez .20 .50
9992 Jay Howell .20 .50

1992 Dodgers Stamps Trak Auto

This 32-stamp set salutes the Los Angeles Dodgers All-Stars from 1962 through 1992. They were presented by Trak Auto and Valvoline. The stamps were designed to go into a folder making a frameable print. The stamps are listed below in chronological order according to their all-star years.

COMPLETE SET (32) 4.00 10.00
1 Johnny Podres .07 .20
John Roseboro
2 Tommy Davis .20 .50
Maury Wills
3 Don Drysdale .30 .75
4 Sandy Koufax .60 1.50
5 Jim Lefebvre .07 .20
Phil Regan
6 Walter Alston MG .20 .50
7 Tom Haller .07 .20
8 Bill Singer .07 .20
9 Bill Grabarkewitz .07 .20
Claude Osteen
10 Willie Davis .10 .30
11 Don Sutton .20 .50
12 Jim Brewer .07 .20
Manny Mota
13 Mike Marshall .07 .20
Jimmy Wynn
14 Ron Cey .10 .30
Andy Messersmith
15 Rick Rhoden .07 .20
Bill Russell
16 Steve Garvey .20 .50
Reggie Smith
17 Tommy John .07 .20
Rick Monday
18 Tommy Lasorda MG .20 .50
19 Jerry Reuss .10 .30
Bob Welch
20 Burt Hooton .07 .20
Davey Lopes
21 Dusty Baker .10 .30
Steve Howe
22 Tommy Lasorda CO .20 .50
23 Mike Marshall .07 .20
24 Fernando Valenzuela .10 .30
25 Steve Sax .07 .20
26 Pedro Guerrero .10 .30
27 Orel Hershiser .20 .50
28 Jay Howell .07 .20
Willie Randolph
29 Ramon Martinez .20 .50
Mike Scioscia
30 1991 All-Stars .10 .30
Brett Butler
Mike Morgan
31 Mike Sharperson .07 .20
32 Special Stamp .07 .20

1993 Dodgers Mother's

The 1993 Mother's Cookies Dodgers set consists of 28 standard-size cards with rounded corners.

COMPLETE SET (28) 6.00 15.00
1 Tommy Lasorda MG .40 1.00
2 Eric Karros .40 1.00
3 Brett Butler .30 .75
4 Mike Piazza 3.00 8.00
5 Jose Offerman .08 .25
6 Tim Wallach .20 .50
7 Eric Davis .20 .50
8 Darryl Strawberry .20 .50
9 Jody Reed .08 .25
10 Orel Hershiser .30 .75
11 Tom Candiotti .08 .25
12 Ramon Martinez .20 .50
13 Lenny Harris .08 .25
14 Mike Sharperson .08 .25
15 Omar Daal .08 .25
16 Pedro Martinez 1.50 4.00
17 Jim Gott .08 .25
18 Carlos Hernandez .08 .25
19 Kevin Gross .08 .25
20 Cory Snyder .08 .25

21 Todd Worrell	.20	.50
22 Mitch Webster	.08	.25
23 Steve Wilson	.08	.25
24 Dave Hansen	.08	.25
25 Roger McDowell	.08	.25
26 Pedro Astacio	.20	.50
27 Rick Trlicek	.08	.25
28 Checklist	.08	.25
Coaches		
Joe Ferguson		
Ben Hines		
Manny		

1993 Dodgers Police

This 30-card standard size set was sponsored by the Los Angeles Police Department, the L.A. Dodgers, and D.A.R.E. Other than the uniform numbers on front and back, the cards are unnumbered and checklisted below in alphabetical order.

COMPLETE SET (30)	3.00	8.00
1 Pedro Astacio	.40	1.00
2 Brett Butler	.30	.75
3 Tom Candiotti	.08	.25
4 Eric Davis	.20	.50
5 Tom Goodwin	.20	.50
6 Jim Gott	.08	.25
7 Kevin Gross	.08	.25
8 Kip Gross	.08	.25
9 Dave Hansen	.08	.25
10 Lenny Harris	.08	.25
11 Carlos Hernandez	.08	.25
12 Orel Hershiser	.30	.75
13 Eric Karros	.40	1.00
14 Tommy Lasorda MG	.40	1.00
15 Pedro Martinez	.75	2.00
16 Ramon Martinez	.20	.50
17 Roger McDowell	.08	.25
18 Jose Offerman	.08	.25
19 Lance Parrish	.20	.50
20 Mike Piazza	1.25	3.00
21 Jody Reed	.08	.25
22 Henry Rodriguez	.20	.50
23 Mike Sharperson	.08	.25
24 Cory Snyder	.08	.25
25 Darryl Strawberry	.20	.50
26 Tim Wallach	.20	.50
27 Mitch Webster	.08	.25
28 Steve Wilson	.08	.25
29 Todd Worrell	.20	.50
30 Coaches Card	.20	.50
Joe Amalfitano		
Ron Perranoski		
Ben		

1993 Dodgers Stadium Club

This 30-card standard-size set features the 1993 Los Angeles Dodgers. The set was issued in hobby (plastic box) and retail (blister) form.

COMP.FACT SET (30)	3.00	8.00
1 Darryl Strawberry	.08	.25
2 Pedro Martinez	1.00	2.50
3 Jody Reed	.02	.10
4 Carlos Hernandez	.02	.10
5 Kevin Gross	.02	.10
6 Mike Piazza	1.25	3.00
7 Jim Gott	.02	.10
8 Eric Karros	.20	.50
9 Mike Sharperson	.02	.10
10 Ramon Martinez	.08	.25
11 Tim Wallach	.02	.10
12 Pedro Astacio	.08	.25
13 Lenny Harris	.02	.10
14 Brett Butler	.08	.25
15 Raul Mondesi	.30	.75
16 Todd Worrell	.08	.25
17 Jose Offerman	.02	.10
18 Mitch Webster	.02	.10
19 Tom Candiotti	.02	.10
20 Eric Davis	.08	.25
21 Michael Moore	.02	.10
22 Billy Ashley	.02	.10
23 Orel Hershiser	.08	.25
24 Roger Cedeno	.30	.75
25 Roger McDowell	.02	.10
26 Mike James	.02	.10
27 Steve Wilson	.02	.10
28 Todd Hollandsworth	.08	.25
29 Cory Snyder	.02	.10
30 Todd Williams	.02	.10

1994 Dodgers Daily News

This 18-card set was issued by the Daily News and appeared on a page of their Sports section on certain dates. Originally a 25-card set was planned, but the baseball strike interfered. The cards feature large color action photos of the Los Angeles Dodgers which take up about 3/4 of the page with the pictured player's position and statistics, team schedule information, and the rules to a contest for Dodgers home game tickets taking up the rest of the page.

COMPLETE SET (18)	10.00	25.00
1 Raul Mondesi	1.00	2.50
2 Orel Hershiser	.75	2.00
3 Henry Rodriguez	.40	1.00
4 Tim Wallach	.60	1.50
5 Tom Candiotti	.40	1.00
6 Delino DeShields	.60	1.50
7 Ramon Martinez	.60	1.50
8 Brett Butler	.75	2.00
9 Kevin Gross	.40	1.00
10 Eric Karros	1.00	2.50
11 Pedro Astacio	.60	1.50
12 Cory Snyder	.40	1.00
13 Todd Worrell	.60	1.50
14 Mike Piazza	2.00	5.00
15 Roger McDowell	.40	1.00
16 Chris Gwynn	.40	1.00
17 Jim Gott	.40	1.00
18 Mitch Webster	.40	1.00

1994 Dodgers Mother's

The 1994 Mother's Cookies Dodgers set consists of 28 standard-size cards with rounded corners. A blank slot for the player's autograph rounds out lthe back.

COMPLETE SET (28)	6.00	15.00
1 Tommy Lasorda MG	.40	1.00
2 Mike Piazza	2.50	6.00
3 Delino DeShields	.20	.50
4 Eric Karros	.30	.75
5 Jose Offerman	.08	.25
6 Brett Butler	.30	.75
7 Orel Hershiser	.30	.75
8 Henry Rodriguez	.08	.25
9 Raul Mondesi	1.50	4.00
10 Tim Wallach	.20	.50
11 Ramon Martinez	.20	.50
12 Mitch Webster	.08	.25
13 Todd Worrell	.20	.50
14 Jeff Treadway	.08	.25
15 Tom Candiotti	.08	.25
16 Pedro Astacio	.20	.50
17 Chris Gwynn	.08	.25
18 Jim Gott	.08	.25
19 Omar Daal	.08	.25
20 Cory Snyder	.08	.25
21 Kevin Gross	.08	.25
22 Dave Hansen	.08	.25
23 Al Osuna	.08	.25
24 Darren Dreifort	.30	.75
25 Roger McDowell	.08	.25
26 Carlos Hernandez	.08	.25
27 Gary Wayne	.08	.25
28 Checklist	.08	.25
Coaches/		

1994 Dodgers Police

As part of an annual promotion, this 30-card standard-size set was given out at the home game vs. the Pirates on May 27, 1994. All fans in attendance were given a perforated, uncut sheet of the 30-card set. The set was also available as individual cards. The cards are unnumbered and checklisted below in alphabetical order.

COMPLETE SET (30)	2.50	6.00
1 Billy Ashley	.08	.25
2 Pedro Astacio	.20	.50
3 Rafael Bournigal	.08	.25
4 Brett Butler	.30	.75
5 Tom Candiotti	.08	.25
6 Delino DeShields	.20	.50
7 Darren Dreifort	.08	.25
8 Jim Gott	.08	.25
9 Kevin Gross	.08	.25
10 Chris Gwynn	.08	.25
11 Dave Hansen	.08	.25
12 Carlos Hernandez	.08	.25
13 Orel Hershiser	.30	.75
14 Chan Ho Park	.40	1.00
15 Tommy Lasorda MG	.40	1.00
16 Eric Karros	.30	.75
17 Ramon Martinez	.20	.50
18 Roger McDowell	.08	.25
19 Raul Mondesi	.40	1.00
20 Jose Offerman	.08	.25
21 Mike Piazza	1.00	2.50
22 Tom Prince	.08	.25
23 Henry Rodriguez	.08	.25
24 Cory Snyder	.08	.25
25 Jeff Treadway	.08	.25
26 Tim Wallach	.20	.50
27 Gary Wayne	.08	.25
28 Mitch Webster	.08	.25
29 Todd Worrell	.20	.50
30 Coaches	.20	.50
Mark Cresse		
Manny Mota		
Bill Russell		
Re		

1995 Dodgers Mother's

The 1995 Mother's Cookies Los Angeles Dodgers set consists of 28 standard-size cards with rounded corners. A rookie year card of Hideo Nomo is in this set.

COMPLETE SET (28)	6.00	15.00
1 Tommy Lasorda MG	.40	1.00
2 Mike Piazza	1.25	3.00
3 Raul Mondesi	.40	1.00
4 Ramon Martinez	.20	.50
5 Eric Karros	.30	.75
6 Roberto Kelly	.08	.25
7 Tim Wallach	.20	.50
8 Jose Offerman	.08	.25
9 Delino DeShields	.20	.50
10 Dave Hansen	.08	.25
11 Pedro Astacio	.20	.50
12 Mitch Webster	.08	.25
13 Hideo Nomo	3.00	8.00
14 Billy Ashley	.08	.25
15 Chris Gwynn	.08	.25
16 Todd Hollandsworth	.08	.25
17 Omar Daal	.08	.25
18 Todd Worrell	.20	.50
19 Todd Williams	.08	.25
20 Carlos Hernandez	.08	.25
21 Tom Candiotti	.08	.25
22 Antonio Osuna	.08	.25
23 Ismael Valdes	.20	.50
24 Rudy Seanez	.08	.25
25 Joey Eischen	.08	.25
26 Greg Hansell	.08	.25
27 Rick Parker	.08	.25
28 Coaches	.08	.25
Checklist		

1995 Dodgers Police

As part of an annual promotion, this 30-card standard-size set was given out at the home game vs. Atlanta on April 30, 1995. All fans in attendance were given a perforated, uncut sheet of this 30-card set. (40,785 sets were handed out.) The fronts feature color action player photos with blue borders. The team logo appears in the lower left, with the player's name inside a yellow bar next to it, while the player's uniform number is printed inside a baseball in the upper left corner. The backs carry player biography and a safety tip, along with the LAPD and D.A.R.E. logos. The cards are unnumbered and checklisted below in alphabetical order. The key card in this set is a rookie year card of international sensation Hideo Nomo.

COMPLETE SET (30)	4.00	10.00
1 Billy Ashley	.08	.25
2 Pedro Astacio	.08	.25
3 Rafael Bournigal	.08	.25
4 Tom Candiotti	.08	.25
5 Ron Coomer	.08	.25
6 Omar Daal	.08	.25
7 Delino DeShields	.08	.25
8 Greg Hansell	.08	.25
9 Dave Hansen	.08	.25
10 Carlos Hernandez	.08	.25
11 Todd Hollandsworth	.08	.25
12 Eric Karros	.40	1.00
13 Tommy Lasorda MG	.40	1.00
14 Ramon Martinez	.20	.50
15 Raul Mondesi	.40	1.00
16 Hideo Nomo	2.00	5.00
17 Jose Offerman	.08	.25
18 Al Osuna	.08	.25
19 Antonio Osuna	.08	.25
20 Chan Ho Park	.08	.25
21 Mike Piazza	1.00	2.50
22 Eddie Pye	.08	.25
23 Henry Rodriguez	.08	.25
24 Rudy Seanez	.08	.25
25 Jeff Treadway	.08	.25
26 Ismael Valdes	.20	.50
27 Tim Wallach	.20	.50
28 Todd Williams	.08	.25
29 Todd Worrell	.20	.50
30 Coaches	.20	.50

1995 Dodgers ROYs

Consisting of 14 standard-size cards, this team-issued boxed set features all 14 Dodger National League Rookie of the Year winners. The set was not sold but was made available to Dodger season ticket holders and preseason mail order customers. The cards are chromium-plated and feature on their fronts player action cutouts on colorful background designs. The words "Limited Edition," the year the player received the award, and his name are printed on bars superposed on the picture. The horizontal backs carry an oval-shaped portrait, biography, player profile, and statistics, all on a color background (red, green, turquoise, or purple) that varies from card to card. The cards are numbered on the back "X of 14."

COMPLETE SET (14)	100.00	200.00
1 Jackie Robinson	25.00	60.00
2 Don Newcombe	5.00	12.00
3 Joe Black	3.00	8.00
4 Jim Gilliam	4.00	10.00
5 Frank Howard	4.00	10.00
6 Jim Lefebvre	3.00	8.00
7 Ted Sizemore	3.00	8.00
8 Rick Sutcliffe	3.00	8.00
9 Steve Howe	3.00	8.00
10 Fernando Valenzuela	5.00	12.00
11 Steve Sax	4.00	10.00
12 Eric Karros	5.00	12.00
13 Mike Piazza	20.00	50.00
14 Raul Mondesi	6.00	15.00

1995 Dodgers Rookie of the Year Pogs

Issued by the Los Angeles Dodgers along with the World Pog Federation, these Pogs feature the Dodgers who were the Rookie of the Year for the Dodgers either in Brooklyn or in Los Angeles. The pogs feature the player's name and photo on the front and the back has an interesting one-liner fact about the player along with his stats the year he won the award

COMPLETE SET (14)	2.00	5.00
1 Jackie Robinson	.60	1.50
2 Don Newcombe	.30	.75
3 Joe Black	.08	.25
4 Jim Gilliam	.08	.25
5 Frank Howard	.08	.25
6 Jim Lefebvre	.02	.10
7 Ted Sizemore	.02	.10
8 Rick Sutcliffe	.08	.25
9 Steve Howe	.02	.10
10 Fernando Valenzuela	.30	.75
11 Steve Sax	.08	.25
12 Eric Karros	.20	.50
13 Mike Piazza	.60	1.50
14 Raul Mondesi	.08	.25

1996 Dodgers Fleer

These 20 standard-size cards feature the same design as the regular Fleer issue, except they are UV coated, use silver foil and are numbered "x of 20". The team set packs were available at retail locations and hobby shops in 10-card packs for a suggested retail price of $1.99.

COMPLETE SET (20)	2.00	5.00
1 Mike Blowers	.02	.10
2 Brett Butler	.10	.30
3 Tom Candiotti	.02	.10
4 Roger Cedeno	.02	.10
5 Delino DeShields	.02	.10
6 Chad Fonville	.02	.10
7 Greg Gagne	.02	.10
8 Karim Garcia	.02	.10
9 Todd Hollandsworth	.02	.10
10 Eric Karros	.10	.30
11 Ramon Martinez	.07	.20
12 Raul Mondesi	.07	.20
13 Hideo Nomo	.30	.75
14 Antonio Osuna	.02	.10
15 Chan Ho Park	.02	.10
16 Mike Piazza	.75	2.00
17 Ismael Valdes	.02	.10
18 Todd Worrell	.07	.20
19 Logo card	.02	.10
20 Checklist	.02	.10

1996 Dodgers Mother's

This 28-card set consists of borderless posed color player portraits in stadium settings.

COMPLETE SET (28)	5.00	12.00
1 Tommy Lasorda MG	.40	1.00
2 Mike Piazza	1.25	3.00
3 Hideo Nomo	.75	2.00
4 Raul Mondesi	.20	.50
5 Eric Karros	.30	.75
6 Delino DeShields	.20	.50
7 Greg Gagne	.08	.25
8 Brett Butler	.30	.75
9 Todd Hollandsworth	.08	.25
10 Mike Blowers	.08	.25
11 Ismael Valdes	.20	.50
12 Pedro Astacio	.20	.50
13 Billy Ashley	.08	.25
14 Tom Candiotti	.08	.25
15 Dave Hansen	.08	.25
16 Joey Eischen	.08	.25
17 Milt Thompson	.08	.25
18 Chan Ho Park	.08	.25
19 Antonio Osuna	.08	.25
20 Carlos Hernandez	.08	.25
21 Ramon Martinez	.20	.50
22 Scott Radinsky	.08	.25
23 Chad Fonville	.08	.25
24 Darren Hall	.08	.25
25 Todd Worrell	.20	.50
26 Mark Guthrie	.08	.25
27 Roger Cedeno	.08	.25
28 Coaches Card CL	.08	.25
Joe Amalfitano		
Mark Cresse		
Mann		

1996 Dodgers Police

This 30-card set was distributed as a perforated sheet. The fronts feature color action player photos in blue borders while the backs carry player biography and a safety tip. The cards are unnumbered and checklisted below in alphabetical order.

COMPLETE SET (30)	3.00	8.00
1 Billy Ashley	.02	.10
2 Pedro Astacio	.02	.10
3 Mike Blowers	.02	.10
4 Mike Busch	.02	.10
5 Brett Butler	.10	.30
6 Tom Candiotti	.02	.10
7 Roger Cedeno	.02	.10
8 Coaches/	.02	.10
9 John Cummings	.02	.10
10 Delino DeShields	.07	.20
11 Joey Eischen	.02	.10
12 Chad Fonville	.02	.10
13 Greg Gagne	.02	.10
14 Karim Garcia	.02	.10
15 Mark Guthrie	.02	.10
16 Darren Hall	.02	.10
17 Dave Hansen	.02	.10
18 Carlos Hernandez	.02	.10
19 Todd Hollandsworth	.02	.10
20 Garey Ingram	.02	.10
21 Eric Karros	.10	.30
22 Tommy Lasorda CO	.20	.50
23 Ramon Martinez	.07	.20
24 Raul Mondesi	.07	.20
25 Hideo Nomo	.40	1.00
26 Antonio Osuna	.02	.10
27 Mike Piazza	1.50	4.00
28 Milt Thompson	.02	.10
29 Ismael Valdes	.07	.20
30 Todd Worrell	.07	.20

1996 Dodgers Rookies of the Year

This standard-size card was issued as a one-card set premium to Los Angeles Dodger season ticket holders. The card features the five consecutive Rookie of the Years the Dodgers had from 1992 through 1996. The front features a head shot of all five players while the back gives a quick stat line of how the player did in the year they won the honor.

1 Eric Karros	2.00	5.00
Mike Piazza		
Raul Mondesi		
Hideo Nomo		

1997 Dodgers DWP Magnets

This five-card set features action color player photos printed on die-cut magnets. The magnets are unnumbered and checklisted below in alphabetical order.

COMPLETE SET (5)	5.00	12.00
1 Todd Hollandsworth	.40	1.00
2 Eric Karros	1.25	3.00
3 Raul Mondesi	.60	1.50
4 Hideo Nomo	1.50	4.00
5 Mike Piazza	2.50	6.00

1997 Dodgers Fan Appreciation

This three-card set features perforated color action, photos of three Dodgers players distributed on a sheet measuring 8 1/2" by 11" that displayed savings on team merchandise. The backs of the player cards carry player information and questions and answers from about that player. The cards are unnumbered and checklisted below in alphabetical order.

COMPLETE SET (3)	1.50	4.00
1 Hideo Nomo	.60	1.50
2 Chan Ho Park	.20	.50
3 Mike Piazza	1.00	2.50

1997 Dodgers Mother's

This 28-card set of the Los Angeles Dodgers sponsored by Mother's Cookies consists of posed color player photos with rounded corners.

COMPLETE SET (28)	5.00	12.00
1 Bill Russell MG	.20	.50
2 Eric Karros	.30	.75
3 Mike Piazza	1.00	2.50
4 Raul Mondesi	.20	.50
5 Hideo Nomo	.75	2.00
6 Todd Hollandsworth	.08	.25
7 Greg Gagne	.08	.25
8 Brett Butler	.30	.75
9 Ramon Martinez	.20	.50
10 Todd Zeile	.20	.50
11 Ismael Valdes	.20	.50
12 Chip Hale	.08	.25
13 Tom Candiotti	.08	.25
14 Billy Ashley	.08	.25
15 Chan Ho Park	.08	.25
16 Wayne Kirby	.08	.25
17 Mark Guthrie	.08	.25
18 Juan Castro	.08	.25
19 Todd Worrell	.20	.50
20 Tom Prince	.08	.25
21 Scott Radinsky	.08	.25
22 Pedro Astacio	.20	.50
23 Wilton Guerrero	.08	.25
24 Darren Hall	.08	.25
25 Darren Dreifort	.08	.25
26 Nelson Liriano	.08	.25
27 Coaches Card	.20	.50
Joe Amalfitano		
Mark Cresse		
Manny M		
28 Checklist	.08	.25

1997 Dodgers Police

This 30-card set features color action player photos in white borders. The backs carry biographical information and a safety tip. The cards are unnumbered and checklisted below in alphabetical order.

COMPLETE SET (30)	3.00	8.00
1 Billy Ashley	.08	.25
2 Pedro Astacio	.20	.50
3 Brett Butler	.30	.75
4 Tom Candiotti	.08	.25
5 Juan Castro	.08	.25
6 Darren Dreifort	.08	.25
7 Chad Fonville	.08	.25
8 Greg Gagne	.08	.25
9 Karim Garcia	.08	.25
10 Wilton Guerrero	.08	.25
11 Mark Guthrie	.08	.25
12 Chip Hale	.08	.25
13 Darren Hall	.08	.25
14 Todd Hollandsworth	.08	.25
15 Eric Karros	.30	.75
16 Wayne Kirby	.08	.25
17 Nelson Liriano	.08	.25
18 Ramon Martinez	.20	.50
19 Raul Mondesi	.40	1.00
20 Hideo Nomo	.75	2.00
21 Antonio Osuna	.08	.25
22 Chan Ho Park	.08	.25
23 Mike Piazza	1.25	3.00
24 Tom Prince	.08	.25
25 Scott Radinsky	.08	.25
26 Bill Russell	.08	.25
27 Ismael Valdes	.20	.50
28 Todd Worrell	.20	.50
29 Todd Zeile	.20	.50
30 Coaches Card	.08	.25
Joe Amalfitano		
Mark Cresse		
Manny M		

1997 Dodgers Score

This 15-card set of the Los Angeles Dodgers was issued in five-card packs with a suggested retail price of $1.30 each. The fronts feature color player photos with special team specific color foil stamping. The backs carry player information. Only 100 cases were made for each team. Platinum parallel cards were inserted at a rate of 1:6, Premier parallel cards at a rate of 1:31.

COMPLETE SET (15)	2.00	5.00
*PLATINUM: 5X BASIC CARDS		
*PREMIER: 20X BASIC CARDS		
1 Ismael Valdes	.08	.25
2 Mike Piazza	1.25	3.00
3 Todd Hollandsworth	.08	.25
4 Delino DeShields	.20	.50
5 Chan Ho Park	.08	.25
6 Roger Cedeno	.08	.25
7 Raul Mondesi	.20	.50
8 Darren Dreifort	.08	.25
9 Jim Bruske	.08	.25
10 Greg Gagne	.08	.25
11 Chad Curtis	.08	.25
12 Ramon Martinez	.20	.50
13 Brett Butler	.20	.50
14 Eric Karros	.40	1.00
15 Hideo Nomo	.60	1.50

1997 Dodgers Topps Rookies of the Year

This six-card set honors five recent National League Rookies of the Year who have all been from the Los Angeles Dodgers. The fronts feature the player's rookie card reproduced on special foil board with the N.L. Rookie of the Year stamp. The backs carry player information. Jackie Robinson's 1952 Topps card with a Rookie of the Year designation has been reproduced to celebrate his being chosen as the very first Rookie of the Year recipient. The cards are listed below according to the year in which the player received the Rookie of the Year award.

COMPLETE SET (6)	15.00	40.00
1 Jackie Robinson	6.00	15.00
2 Eric Karros	1.25	3.00
3 Mike Piazza	5.00	12.00
4 Raul Mondesi	1.25	3.00
5 Hideo Nomo	2.00	5.00
6 Todd Hollandsworth	.75	2.00

1998 Dodgers Fan Appreciation

This three-card set features perforated color action photos of three Dodgers players distributed on a sheet measuring 8 1/2" by 11" that displayed savings on team merchandise. The backs of the player cards carry player information and questions and answers from "Doctor Baseball." The cards are unnumbered and checklisted below in alphabetical order.

COMPLETE SET (4)	2.00	5.00
1 Comp Sheet	2.00	5.00
2 Eric Karros	.75	2.00
3 Raul Mondesi	.75	2.00
4 Gary Sheffield	1.25	3.00

1998 Dodgers Kids Clubhouse

These five cards feature action shots from when various Dodger stars achieved a feat worth noting. The front feature footage from that event while the back has biographical information about the player as well as a description about the event and its significance.

COMPLETE SET (5)	4.00	10.00
1 Eric Karros	1.00	2.50
2 Raul Mondesi	.60	1.50
3 Ramon Martinez	.60	1.50
4 Hideo Nomo	1.25	3.00
5 Mike Piazza	1.25	3.00
XX Raul Mondesi	.40	1.00
Membership Card		

1998 Dodgers Magnets

These four magnets were issued to honor the four players who were active with the Los Angeles Dodgers in 1998 who had appeared in an All-Star game while playing for the Dodgers at one time. Since the Magnets are unnumbered we have sequenced them in alphabetical order.

COMPLETE SET (4)	2.50	6.00
1 Ramon Martinez	.60	1.50
2 Raul Mondesi	.60	1.50
3 Jeff Shaw	.40	1.00
4 Gary Sheffield	1.50	4.00

1998 Dodgers Mother's

This 28-card set of the Los Angeles Dodgers sponsored by Mother's Cookies consists of posed color player photos with rounded corners.

COMPLETE SET (28)	4.00	10.00
1 Glenn Hoffman MG	.08	.25
2 Eric Karros	.40	1.00
3 Bobby Bonilla	.20	.50
4 Raul Mondesi	.20	.50
5 Gary Sheffield	.50	1.25
6 Ramon Martinez	.20	.50
7 Charles Johnson	.08	.25
8 Jose Vizcaino	.08	.25
9 Scott Radinsky	.08	.25
10 Jim Eisenreich	.08	.25
11 Ismael Valdes	.08	.25
12 Eric Young	.20	.50
13 Chan Ho Park	.08	.25
14 Roger Cedeno	.08	.25
15 Antonio Osuna	.08	.25
16 Dave Mlicki	.08	.25
17 Mark Guthrie	.08	.25
18 Juan Castro	.08	.25
19 Darren Dreifort	.08	.25
20 Tom Prince	.08	.25
21 Jeff Shaw	.08	.25
22 Alex Cora	.08	.25
23 Matt Luke	.08	.25
24 Darren Hall	.08	.25
25 Trenidad Hubbard	.08	.25
26 Jim Bruske	.08	.25
27 Tripp Cromer	.08	.25
28 Coaches Card CL	.08	.25
Joe Amalfitano		
Mickey Hatcher		
C		

1998 Dodgers Police

This 30 card standard-size set was issued by the LA Police department and featured members of the 1998 Dodgers Police set. The cards were also available in strips of six along with the purchase of a kids meal at Dodger Stadium. The cards are not numbered so we have sequenced them alphabetically.

COMPLETE SET (30)	4.00	10.00
1 Jim Bruske	.08	.25
2 Juan Castro	.08	.25
3 Roger Cedeno	.08	.25
4 Tripp Cromer	.08	.25
5 Mike Devereaux	.08	.25
6 Darren Dreifort	.08	.25
7 Wilton Guerrero	.08	.25
8 Mark Guthrie	.08	.25
9 Darren Hall	.08	.25
10 Todd Hollandsworth	.08	.25
11 Thomas Howard	.08	.25
12 Trenidad Hubbard	.08	.25
13 Eric Karros	.30	.75
14 Paul Konerko	.75	2.00
15 Frank Lankford	.08	.25
16 Matt Luke	.08	.25
17 Ramon Martinez	.20	.50
18 Raul Mondesi	.20	.50
19 Hideo Nomo	.50	1.25
20 Antonio Osuna	.08	.25
21 Chan Ho Park	.08	.25
22 Mike Piazza	.75	2.00
23 Tom Prince	.08	.25
24 Scott Radinsky	.08	.25
25 Bill Russell MG	.08	.25
26 Ismael Valdes	.20	.50
27 Jose Vizcaino	.08	.25
28 Eric Young	.20	.50
29 Todd Zeile	.20	.50
30 Coaches Card	.08	.25
Joe Amalfitano		
Mark Cresse		
Glenn G		

1998 Dodgers Score

This 15-card set was issued in special retail packs and features color photos of the Los Angeles Dodgers team. The backs carry player information. A special platinum parallel set was also issued and randomly inserted in packs.

COMPLETE SET (15)	3.00	8.00
*PLATINUM: 5X BASIC CARDS		
1 Hideo Nomo	.50	1.25
2 Mike Piazza	1.25	3.00
3 Wilton Guerrero	.08	.25
4 Greg Gagne	.08	.25
5 Brett Butler	.20	.50
6 Todd Hollandsworth	.08	.25
7 Roger Cedeno	.08	.25
8 Chan Ho Park	.08	.25
9 Todd Worrell	.08	.25
10 Ramon Martinez	.20	.50
11 Ismael Valdes	.08	.25
12 Eric Karros	.30	.75
13 Raul Mondesi	.20	.50
14 Todd Zeile	.20	.50
15 Billy Ashley	.08	.25

1999 Dodgers Keebler

This 28 card standard-size set features members of the 1999 Los Angeles Dodgers. The borderless cards are similar to the old Mother Cookie sets and the players photo are in the top half with the the Dodgers Logo and player's name on the bottom in a combination of red, white and blue. The back has biographical data. Similar to the old Mother's promotions, 20 different cards and eight cards of one number were handed out at a selected game and collectors were encouraged to trade for the missing numbers they needed.

COMPLETE SET (28)	4.00	10.00
1 Davey Johnson MG	.20	.50
2 Eric Karros	.20	.50
3 Gary Sheffield	.50	1.25
4 Raul Mondesi	.20	.50
5 Kevin Brown	.20	.50
6 Mark Grudzielanek	.08	.25
7 Todd Hollandsworth	.08	.25
8 Todd Hundley	.20	.50
9 Jeff Shaw	.08	.25
10 Pedro Borbon Jr.	.08	.25
11 Chan Ho Park	.08	.25
12 Jose Vizcaino	.08	.25
13 Devon White	.08	.25
14 Darren Dreifort	.08	.25
15 Osan Masaoka	.08	.25
16 Dave Hansen	.08	.25
17 Adrian Beltre	.60	1.50
18 Ismael Valdes	.08	.25
19 Alan Mills	.08	.25
20 Eric Young	.20	.50
21 Mike Maddux	.08	.25
22 Carlos Perez	.08	.25
23 Tripp Cromer	.08	.25
24 Jamie Arnold	.08	.25
25 Angel Pena	.08	.25
26 Trenidad Hubbard	.08	.25
27 Doug Bochtler	.08	.25
28 Rick Dempsey CO	.08	.25
Claude Osteen CO		
Rick Down CO		
M		

1999 Dodger Kids

These three standard-size cards were originally issued as part of a three-card sheet. The fronts feature player drawings, similar to the 1953 Topps set design. The backs are written in a way similar the early 1950's Bowman sets. Since the cards are unnumbered, we have sequenced them in alphabetical order

COMPLETE SET (3)	1.50	4.00
1 Adrian Beltre	.75	2.00
2 Kevin Brown	.40	1.00
3 Eric Karros	.40	1.00

1999 Dodgers Police

This set measures the standard-size when torn off the perforated strips it was issued on. Since the only numerical identification is the uniform number in the upper left corner, we have sequenced this set alphabetically.

COMPLETE SET (30)	4.00	10.00
1 Adrian Beltre	.60	1.50
2 Pedro Borbon	.08	.25
3 Kevin Brown	.20	.50
4 Jacob Brumfield	.08	.25
5 Juan Castro	.08	.25
6 Tripp Cromer	.08	.25
7 Darren Dreifort	.08	.25
8 Mark Grudzielanek	.08	.25
9 Dave Hansen	.08	.25
10 Todd Hollandsworth	.08	.25
11 Todd Hundley	.20	.50
12 Davey Johnson MG	.20	.50
13 Eric Karros	.20	.50
14 Paul LoDuca	.40	1.00
15 Osan Masaoka	.08	.25
16 Alan Mills	.08	.25
17 Raul Mondesi	.20	.50
18 Antonio Osuna	.08	.25
19 Chan Ho Park	.08	.25
20 Angel Pena	.08	.25
21 Carlos Perez	.08	.25
22 Adam Riggs	.08	.25
23 Jeff Shaw	.08	.25
24 Gary Sheffield	.60	1.50
25 Ismael Valdes	.20	.50
26 Jose Vizcaino	.08	.25
27 Devon White	.08	.25
28 Rick Wilkins	.08	.25
29 Eric Young	.20	.50
30 Glenn Hoffman CO	.08	.25
Rick Down CO		
Rick Dempsey CO		
C		

2000 Dodgers Keebler

COMPLETE SET (28)	4.00	10.00
1 Davey Johnson MG	.20	.50
2 Eric Karros	.30	.75
3 Gary Sheffield	.50	1.25
4 Kevin Brown	.40	1.00
5 Shawn Green		1.25
6 Mark Grudzielanek	.20	.50
7 Todd Hollandsworth	.10	.25
8 Todd Hundley	.20	.50
9 Jeff Shaw	.20	.50
10 Adrian Beltre	.60	1.50
11 Chan Ho Park	.10	.25
12 Jose Vizcaino	.10	.25
13 Devon White	.10	.25
14 Darren Dreifort	.10	.25
15 Onan Masaoka	.10	.25
16 Dave Hansen	.10	.25
17 Kevin Elster	.10	.25
18 Antonio Osuna	.10	.25
19 Geronimo Berroa	.10	.25
20 Orel Hershiser	.20	.50
21 Chad Kreuter	.10	.25
22 Carlos Perez	.10	.25
23 F.P. Santangelo	.10	.25

24 Terry Adams	.10	.25
25 Alex Cora	.10	.25
26 Matt Herges	.10	.25
27 Mike Fetters	.10	.25
28 Rick Dempsey CO	.10	.25
Claude Osteen CO		
Rick Down CO		
M		

2000 Dodgers Kids

COMPLETE SET (3)	1.50	4.00
1 Shawn Green	.60	1.50
2 Eric Karros	.40	1.00
3 Gary Sheffield	.75	2.00

2000 Dodgers Police

COMPLETE SET (30)	4.00	10.00
1 Terry Adams	.10	.25
2 Adrian Beltre	.60	1.50
3 Kevin Brown	.30	.75
4 Alex Cora	.10	.25
5 Darren Dreifort	.10	.25
6 Kevin Elster	.10	.25
7 Mike Fetters	.10	.25
8 Eric Gagne	.10	.25
9 Shawn Green		1.25
10 Mark Grudzielanek	.20	.50
11 Dave Hansen	.10	.25
12 Orel Hershiser	.20	.50
13 Todd Hollandsworth	.10	.25
14 Todd Hundley	.20	.50
15 Eric Karros	.30	.75
16 Chad Kreuter	.10	.25
17 Paul Loduca	.40	1.00
18 Onan Masaoka	.10	.25
19 Alan Mills	.10	.25
20 Gregg Olson	.10	.25
21 Antonio Osuna	.10	.25
22 Chan Ho Park	.10	.25
23 Angel Pena	.10	.25
24 Carlos Perez	.10	.25
25 F.P. Santangelo	.10	.25
26 Jeff Shaw	.10	.25
27 Gary Sheffield	.50	1.25
28 Jose Vizcaino	.10	.25
29 Devon White	.10	.25
30 Rick Down CO	.10	.25
Manny Mota CO		
Jim Tracy CO		
Glenn H		

2001 Dodgers Fan Appreciation

COMPLETE SET	1.60	4.00
1 Paul LoDuca	.60	1.50
2 Chan Ho Park	.20	.50
3 Gary Sheffield	.75	2.00

2001 Dodgers Keebler

COMPLETE SET	4.00	10.00
1 Jim Tracy MG	.10	.25
2 Eric Karros	.20	.50
3 Shawn Green	.40	1.00
4 Kevin Brown	.20	.50
5 Gary Sheffield	.50	1.25
6 Mark Grudzielanek	.20	.50
7 Darren Dreifort	.10	.25
8 Dave Hansen	.10	.25
9 Jeff Shaw	.10	.25
10 Chad Kreuter	.10	.25
11 Chan Ho Park	.10	.25
12 Adrian Beltre	.60	1.50
13 Marquis Grissom	.20	.50
14 Alex Cora	.10	.25
15 Tom Goodwin	.10	.25
16 Gregg Olson	.10	.25
17 Andy Ashby	.10	.25
18 Paul LoDuca	.40	1.00
19 Luke Prokopec	.10	.25
20 Mike Fetters	.10	.25
21 Giovanni Carrara	.10	.25
22 Chris Donnels	.10	.25
23 Matt Herges	.10	.25
24 Jeff Reboulet	.10	.25
25 Terry Adams	.10	.25
26 Hiram Bocachica	.10	.25
27 Jesse Orosco	.20	.50
28 Travis Barbary CO	.10	.25
Jack Clark CO		
Jim Colborn CO/		

2001 Dodgers Police

COMPLETE SET (30)	4.80	12.00
1 Terry Adams	.10	.25
2 Andy Ashby	.10	.25
3 Bruce Aven	.10	.25
4 Adrian Beltre	.60	1.50
5 Hiram Bocachica	.10	.25
6 Tim Bogar	.10	.25
7 Kevin Brown	.20	.50
8 Alex Cora	.10	.25
9 Chris Donnels	.10	.25
10 Darren Dreifort	.10	.25
11 Mike Fetters	.10	.25
12 Eric Gagne	.10	.25
13 Tom Goodwin	.10	.25
14 Shawn Green	.50	1.25
15 Marquis Grissom	.20	.50
16 Mark Grudzielanek	.10	.25
17 Dave Hansen	.10	.25
18 Matt Herges	.10	.25
19 Eric Karros	.20	.50
20 Chad Kreuter	.10	.25
21 Paul LoDuca	.40	1.00
22 Onan Masaoka	.10	.25
23 Jose Nunez	.10	.25
24 Gregg Olson	.10	.25
25 Chan Ho Park	.10	.25
26 Angel Pena	.10	.25
27 Jeff Reboulet	.10	.25
28 Jeff Shaw	.20	.50
29 Gary Sheffield	.50	1.25
30 Jack Clark CO	.10	.25
Jim Lett CO		
Jim Riggleman CO		
Mann		

2001 Dodgers Upper Deck Collectibles

COMP.FACT SET (21)	5.00	12.00
LA1 Gary Sheffield	.50	1.25
LA2 Shawn Green	.60	1.50
LA3 Kevin Brown	.40	1.00
LA4 Adrian Beltre	.60	1.50
LA5 Eric Karros	.30	.75
LA6 Darren Dreifort	.08	.25
LA7 Chan Ho Park	.08	.25
LA8 Alex Cora	.08	.25
LA9 Mark Grudzielanek	.08	.25
LA10 Paul LoDuca	.40	1.00
LA11 Dave Hansen	.08	.25
LA12 Tom Goodwin	.08	.25
LA13 Ramon Martinez	.08	.25
LA14 Luke Prokopec	.08	.25
LA15 Chad Krueter	.08	.25
LA16 Jeff Shaw	.08	.25
LA17 Erig Gagne	1.25	3.00
LA18 Andy Ashby	.08	.25
LA19 F.P. Santangelo	.08	.25
LA20 Mike Fetters	.08	.25
LA21 Gary Sheffield	1.25	3.00
Eric Karros		
Kevin Brown		
Adrian B		

2002 Dodgers Keebler

COMPLETE SET	5.00	12.00
1 Jim Tracy MG	.08	.25
2 Eric Karros	.20	.50
3 Shawn Green	.50	1.25
4 Kevin Brown	.20	.50
5 Paul Lo Duca	.40	1.00
6 Mark Grudzielanek	.20	.50
7 Brian Jordan	.20	.50
8 Kazuhisa Ishii	.40	1.00
9 Dave Hansen	.08	.25
10 Chad Kreuter	.08	.25
11 Hideo Nomo	.40	1.00
12 Adrian Beltre	.60	1.50
13 Marquis Grissom	.20	.50
14 Eric Gagne	.60	1.50
15 Odalis Perez	.30	.75
16 Dave Roberts	.08	.25
17 Omar Daal	.08	.25
18 Alex Cora	.08	.25
19 Andy Ashby	.08	.25
20 Hiram Bocachica	.08	.25
21 Darren Dreifort	.08	.25
22 Jesse Orosco	.20	.50
23 Cesar Izturis	.20	.50
24 Terry Mulholland	.08	.25
25 Jeff Reboulet	.08	.25
26 Paul Quantrill	.20	.50
27 Giovanni Carrara	.08	.25
28 Jack Clark CO	.08	.25
Jim Colborn CO		
Robert Flippo CO		
G		

2002 Dodgers Police

COMPLETE SET	5.00	12.00
1 Andy Ashby	.08	.25
2 Adrian Beltre	.60	1.50
3 Hiram Bocachica	.08	.25
4 Jeff Branson	.08	.25
5 Kevin Brown	.20	.50
6 Giovanni Carrara	.08	.25
7 Alex Cora	.08	.25
8 Omar Daal	.08	.25
9 Darren Dreifort	.08	.25
10 Eric Gagne	.60	1.50
11 Shawn Green	.60	1.50
12 Marquis Grissom	.20	.50
13 Mark Grudzielanek	.20	.50
14 Dave Hansen	.08	.25
15 Phil Hiatt	.08	.25
16 Kazuhisa Ishii	.40	1.00
17 Cesar Izturis	.08	.25
18 Brian Jordan	.20	.50
19 Eric Karros	.30	.75
20 Mike Kinkade	.08	.25
21 Chad Kreuter	.08	.25
22 Paul LoDuca	.40	1.00
23 Terry Mulholland	.08	.25
24 Hideo Nomo	.60	1.50
25 Jesse Orosco	.20	.50
26 Odalis Perez	.20	.50
27 Paul Quantrill	.08	.25
28 Jeff Reboulet	.08	.25
29 Dave Roberts	.08	.25
30 Jim Tracy MG	.08	.25
Jack Clark CO		
Jim Lett CO		
Jim Rigg		

2003 Dodgers Fan Appreciation

COMPLETE SET (3)	2.00	5.00
1 Eric Gagne	1.25	3.00
2 Paul LoDuca	.75	2.00
3 Hideo Nomo	1.00	2.50

2003 Dodgers Keebler

COMPLETE SET (28)	5.00	12.00
1 Jim Tracy MG	.10	.25
2 Shawn Green	.50	1.25
3 Paul Lo Duca	.40	1.00
4 Kevin Brown	.40	1.00
5 Adrian Beltre	.60	1.50
6 Eric Gagne	.60	1.50
7 Brian Jordan	.20	.50
8 Kazuhisa Ishii	.30	.75
9 Fred McGriff	.30	.75
10 Dave Roberts	.10	.25
11 Hideo Nomo	.50	1.25
12 Alex Cora	.10	.25
13 Paul Quantrill	.10	.25
14 Darren Dreifort	.10	.25
15 Odalis Perez	.20	.50
16 Cesar Izturis	.20	.50
17 Todd Hundley	.10	.25
18 Daryle Ward	.10	.25
19 Paul Shuey	.10	.25
20 Guillermo Mota	.10	.25
21 Andy Ashby	.10	.25
22 Tom Martin	.10	.25
23 Jason Romano	.10	.25
24 Jolbert Cabrera	.10	.25
25 Mike Kinkade	.10	.25
26 Ron Coomer	.10	.25
27 David Ross	.10	.25
28 Jack Clark CO	.10	.25
Jim Colborn CO		
Robert Flippo CO		
G		

2003 Dodgers Police

COMPLETE SET (30)	4.00	10.00
1 Victor Alvarez	.10	.25
2 Andy Ashby	.10	.25
3 Adrian Beltre	.60	1.50
4 Troy Brohawn	.10	.25
5 Kevin Brown	.20	.50
6 Jolbert Cabrera	.10	.25
7 Chin-Feng Chen	.40	1.00
8 Ron Coomer	.10	.25
9 Alex Cora	.10	.25
10 Darren Dreifort	.10	.25
11 Eric Gagne	.60	1.50
12 Shawn Green	.50	1.25
13 Chad Hermansen	.10	.25
14 Todd Hundley	.10	.25
15 Kazuhisa Ishii	.20	.50
16 Cesar Izturis	.10	.25
17 Brian Jordan	.20	.50
18 Mike Kinkade	.10	.25
19 Paul Lo Duca	.40	1.00
20 Fred McGriff	.30	.75
21 Guillermo Mota	.10	.25
22 Hideo Nomo	.50	1.25
23 Odalis Perez	.20	.50
24 Paul Quantrill	.10	.25
25 Dave Roberts	.10	.25
26 David Ross	.10	.25
27 Wilkin Ruan	.10	.25
28 Paul Shuey	.10	.25
29 Daryle Ward	.10	.25
30 Jack Clark CO	.10	.25
Jim Lett CO		
Jim Riggleman CO		
Mann		

2004 Dodgers Fleer

COMPLETE SET	4.00	10.00
1 Hideo Nomo	.50	1.25
2 Paul LoDuca	.40	1.00
3 Alex Cora	.10	.25
4 Paul Shuey	.10	.25
5 Juan Encarnacion	.20	.50
6 Steve Colyer	.10	.25
7 Joe Thurston	.10	.25
8 Shawn Green	.40	1.00
9 Edwin Jackson	.40	1.00
10 Dave Roberts	.10	.25
11 Guillermo Mota	.10	.25
12 Jolbert Cabrera	.10	.25
13 Darren Dreifort	.10	.25
14 David Ross	.10	.25
15 Eric Gagne	.60	1.50
16 Adrian Beltre	.60	1.50
17 Cesar Izturis	.20	.50
18 Robin Ventura	.20	.50
19 Wilson Alvarez	.10	.25
20 Bubba Trammell	.10	.25
21 Wilkin Ruan	.10	.25

2004 Dodgers Program Inserts

COMPLETE SET (3)	3.00	8.00
1 Adrian Beltre	1.25	3.00
Odalis Perez		
Dave Roberts		
Derek J		
2 Eric Gagne	1.25	3.00
Milton Bradley		
Kazuhisa Ishii		
Marian		
3 Cesar Izturis	1.00	2.50
Shawn Green		
Paul LoDuca		
Alex Rodr		

2006 Dodgers Topps

COMPLETE SET (14)	3.00	8.00
LAD1 Eric Gagne	.12	.30
LAD2 Rafael Furcal	.12	.30
LAD3 Jeff Kent	.12	.30
LAD4 Cesar Izturis	.12	.30
LAD5 Kenny Lofton	.12	.30
LAD6 J.D. Drew	.12	.30
LAD7 Jose Cruz Jr.	.12	.30
LAD8 Bill Mueller	.12	.30
LAD9 Brett Tomko	.12	.30
LAD10 Derek Lowe	.12	.30
LAD11 Brad Penny	.12	.30
LAD12 Odalis Perez	.12	.30
LAD13 Jayson Werth	.20	.50
LAD14 Nomar Garciaparra	.20	.50

2007 Dodgers Topps

COMPLETE SET (14)	3.00	8.00
LAD1 Rafael Furcal	.12	.30
LAD2 Jonathan Broxton	.12	.30
LAD3 Derek Lowe	.12	.30
LAD4 Brad Penny	.12	.30
LAD5 Takashi Saito	.12	.30
LAD6 Andre Ethier	.20	.50
LAD7 Juan Pierre	.12	.30
LAD8 Jeff Kent	.12	.30
LAD9 Randy Wolf	.12	.30
LAD10 Chad Billingsley	.20	.50
LAD11 Jason Schmidt	.12	.30
LAD12 Russell Martin	.12	.30
LAD13 Wilson Betemit	.12	.30
LAD14 Luis Gonzalez	.12	.30

2008 Dodgers Topps

COMPLETE SET (14)	3.00	8.00
LAD1 Russell Martin	.12	.30
LAD2 Matt Kemp	.25	.60
LAD3 Derek Lowe	.12	.30
LAD4 Brad Penny	.12	.30
LAD5 Andruw Jones	.12	.30
LAD6 Andre Ethier	.20	.50
LAD7 Juan Pierre	.12	.30
LAD8 Jeff Kent	.12	.30
LAD9 James Loney	.12	.30
LAD10 Chad Billingsley	.20	.50
LAD11 Jason Schmidt	.12	.30
LAD12 Rafael Furcal	.12	.30
LAD13 Jonathan Broxton	.12	.30
LAD14 Joe Torre	.20	.50

2009 Dodgers Topps

LAD1 Russell Martin	.15	.40
LAD2 Clayton Kershaw	.60	1.50
LAD3 Jonathan Broxton	.15	.40
LAD4 Rafael Furcal	.15	.40
LAD5 Andre Ethier	.25	.60
LAD6 Chad Billingsley	.25	.60
LAD7 Matt Kemp	.30	.75
LAD8 Juan Pierre	.15	.40
LAD9 James Loney	.15	.40
LAD10 Hiroki Kuroda	.15	.40
LAD11 Blake DeWitt	.15	.40
LAD12 Casey Blake	.15	.40
LAD13 Mark Loretta	.15	.40
LAD14 Hong-Chih Kuo	.15	.40
LAD15 Joe Torre	.25	.60

2010 Dodgers Topps

LAD1 Manny Ramirez	.40	1.00
LAD2 James Loney	.15	.40
LAD3 Ronald Belisario	.15	.40
LAD4 Clayton Kershaw	.60	1.50
LAD5 Jonathan Broxton	.15	.40
LAD6 Casey Blake	.15	.40
LAD7 Matt Kemp	.30	.75
LAD8 Andre Ethier	.25	.60
LAD9 Ronnie Belliard	.15	.40
LAD10 Chad Billingsley	.25	.60
LAD11 Russell Martin	.15	.40
LAD12 Rafael Furcal	.15	.40
LAD13 George Sherrill	.15	.40
LAD14 Hiroki Kuroda	.15	.40
LAD15 Mark Loretta	.15	.40
LAD16 Hong-Chih Kuo	.15	.40
LAD17 Blake DeWitt	.15	.40

2011 Dodgers Topps

LAD1 Andre Ethier	.25	.60
LAD2 Chad Billingsley	.25	.60
LAD3 Clayton Kershaw	.60	1.50
LAD4 Rafael Furcal	.15	.40
LAD5 Matt Kemp	.30	.75
LAD6 Hiroki Kuroda	.15	.40
LAD7 Ted Lilly	.15	.40
LAD8 Rod Barajas	.15	.40
LAD9 Vicente Padilla	.15	.40
LAD10 Jay Gibbons	.15	.40
LAD11 Jon Garland	.15	.40
LAD12 James Loney	.15	.40
LAD13 Hong-Chih Kuo	.15	.40
LAD14 Casey Blake	.15	.40
LAD15 Juan Uribe	.15	.40
LAD16 Jonathan Broxton	.15	.40
LAD17 Dodger Stadium	.15	.40

2012 Dodgers Topps

LAD1 Matt Kemp	.30	.75
LAD2 Jerry Sands	.25	.60
LAD3 Mark Ellis	.25	.60
LAD4 Juan Uribe	.25	.60
LAD5 Juan Rivera	.25	.60
LAD6 Ted Lilly	.25	.60
LAD7 Andre Ethier	.30	.75
LAD8 Clayton Kershaw	.60	1.50
LAD9 James Loney	.25	.60
LAD10 Kenley Jansen	.30	.75
LAD11 Aaron Harang	.25	.60
LAD12 Tony Gwynn Jr.	.25	.60
LAD13 Dee Gordon	.25	.60
LAD14 Chad Billingsley	.25	.60
LAD15 Javy Guerra	.25	.60
LAD16 Nathan Eovaldi	.30	.75
LAD17 Dodger Stadium	.15	.40

2013 Dodgers Topps

COMPLETE SET (17)	3.00	8.00
LAD1 Adrian Gonzalez	.30	.75
LAD2 Matt Kemp	.20	.50
LAD3 Clayton Kershaw	.40	1.00
LAD4 Andre Ethier	.20	.50
LAD5 Carl Crawford	.20	.50
LAD6 Hanley Ramirez	.20	.50
LAD7 Mark Ellis	.25	.60
LAD8 A.J. Ellis	.25	.60
LAD9 Zack Greinke	.25	.60
LAD10 Kenley Jansen	.20	.50
LAD11 Josh Beckett	.15	.40
LAD12 Chad Billingsley	.20	.50
LAD13 Dee Gordon	.25	.60
LAD14 Ted Lilly	.15	.40
LAD15 Brandon League	.15	.40
LAD16 Luis Cruz	.15	.40
LAD17 Dodger Stadium	.15	.40

2014 Dodgers Topps

COMPLETE SET (17)	3.00	8.00
LAD1 Adrian Gonzalez	.20	.50
LAD2 Matt Kemp	.20	.50
LAD3 Clayton Kershaw	.40	1.00
LAD4 Brian Wilson	.25	.60
LAD5 Kenley Jansen	.20	.50
LAD6 Hanley Ramirez	.20	.50
LAD7 Yasiel Puig	.25	.60
LAD8 A.J. Ellis	.15	.40
LAD9 Zack Greinke	.25	.60
LAD10 Carl Crawford	.20	.50
LAD11 Josh Beckett	.15	.40
LAD12 Chad Billingsley	.20	.50
LAD13 Andre Ethier	.20	.50
LAD14 Juan Uribe	.15	.40
LAD15 Hyun-Jin Ryu	.20	.50
LAD16 Dan Haren	.15	.40
LAD17 Dodger Stadium	.15	.40

2015 Dodgers Topps

COMPLETE SET (17)	3.00	8.00
LAD1 Clayton Kershaw	.40	1.00
LAD2 Andre Ethier	.20	.50
LAD3 Yimi Garcia	.15	.40
LAD4 Adrian Gonzalez	.20	.50
LAD5 Zack Greinke	.25	.60
LAD6 A.J. Ellis	.15	.40
LAD7 Carl Crawford	.20	.50
LAD8 Brandon League	.15	.40
LAD9 Joc Pederson	.60	1.50
LAD10 Yasiel Puig	.25	.60
LAD11 Hyun-Jin Ryu	.20	.50
LAD12 Yasmani Grandal	.15	.40
LAD13 Jimmy Rollins	.20	.50
LAD14 Howie Kendrick	.15	.40
LAD15 Juan Uribe	.15	.40
LAD16 Kenley Jansen	.20	.50
LAD17 Brandon McCarthy	.15	.40

2016 Dodgers Topps

COMPLETE SET (17)	3.00	8.00
LAD1 Clayton Kershaw	.40	1.00
LAD2 Carl Crawford	.20	.50
LAD3 Joc Pederson	.20	.50
LAD4 Yasmani Grandal	.15	.40
LAD5 Adrian Gonzalez	.20	.50
LAD6 Frankie Montas	.20	.50
LAD7 Chase Utley	.20	.50
LAD8 Corey Seager	1.50	4.00
LAD9 Justin Turner	.25	.60
LAD10 Andre Ethier	.20	.50
LAD11 Yasiel Puig	.25	.60
LAD12 Hyun-Jin Ryu	.20	.50
LAD13 Kenley Jansen	.20	.50
LAD14 Brett Anderson	.15	.40
LAD15 Scott Kazmir	.15	.40
LAD16 Alex Wood	.15	.40
LAD17 Scott Van Slyke	.15	.40

2017 Dodgers Topps

COMPLETE SET (17)	3.00	8.00
LAD1 Clayton Kershaw	.40	1.00
LAD2 Andre Ethier	.20	.50
LAD3 Alex Wood	.15	.40
LAD4 Joc Pederson	.20	.50
LAD5 Scott Van Slyke	.15	.40
LAD6 Yasmani Grandal	.15	.40
LAD7 Enrique Hernandez	.25	.60
LAD8 Kenta Maeda	.20	.50
LAD9 Chase Utley	.20	.50
LAD10 Julio Urias	.25	.60
LAD11 Kenley Jansen	.20	.50
LAD12 Trayce Thompson	.20	.50
LAD13 Corey Seager	.25	.60
LAD14 Justin Turner	.25	.60
LAD15 Andrew Toles	.15	.40
LAD16 Rich Hill	.15	.40
LAD17 Adrian Gonzalez	.20	.50

2018 Dodgers Topps

COMPLETE SET (17)	2.50	6.00
LD1 Clayton Kershaw	.40	1.00
LD2 Alex Wood	.15	.40
LD3 Julio Urias	.25	.60
LD4 Yasmani Grandal	.15	.40
LD5 Logan Forsythe	.15	.40
LD6 Joc Pederson	.20	.50
LD7 Cody Bellinger	.50	1.25
LD8 Kenta Maeda	.20	.50
LD9 Hyun-jin Ryu	.20	.50
LD10 Kenley Jansen	.20	.50
LD11 Corey Seager	.25	.60
LD12 Rich Hill	.15	.40
LD13 Justin Turner	.25	.60
LD14 Chris Taylor	.20	.50
LD15 Yu Darvish	.25	.60
LD16 Matt Kemp	.20	.50
LD17 Yasiel Puig	.25	.60

2019 Dodgers Topps

COMPLETE SET (17)	2.50	6.00
LD1 Clayton Kershaw	.40	1.00
LD2 Cody Bellinger	.50	1.25
LD3 Walker Buehler	.30	.75
LD4 Justin Turner	.25	.60
LD5 Pedro Baez	.15	.40
LD6 Max Muncy	.20	.50
LD7 Corey Seager	.25	.60
LD8 Enrique Hernandez	.25	.60
LD9 Rich Hill	.15	.40
LD10 Ross Stripling	.15	.40
LD11 Kenta Maeda	.20	.50
LD12 Joc Pederson	.20	.50
LD13 Chris Taylor	.20	.50
LD14 Julio Urias	.25	.60
LD15 David Freese	.15	.40
LD16 Kenley Jansen	.20	.50
LD17 Austin Barnes	.15	.40

2020 Dodgers Topps

LAD1 Cody Bellinger	.50	1.25
LAD2 Clayton Kershaw	.40	1.00
LAD3 Corey Seager	.25	.60
LAD4 Justin Turner	.25	.60
LAD5 Walker Buehler	.30	.75
LAD6 Max Muncy	.20	.50
LAD7 Joc Pederson	.20	.50
LAD8 Gavin Lux	.75	2.00
LAD9 Will Smith	.25	.60
LAD10 Kenta Maeda	.20	.50
LAD11 Kenley Jansen	.20	.50
LAD12 A.J. Pollock	.15	.40
LAD13 Enrique Hernandez	.25	.60
LAD14 Alex Verdugo	.20	.50
LAD15 Dodger Stadium	.15	.40
LAD16 Chris Taylor	.20	.50
LAD17 Dustin May	.50	1.25

2017 Dodgers Topps National Baseball Card Day

COMPLETE SET (10)	6.00	15.00
LAD1 Clayton Kershaw	1.50	4.00
LAD2 Adrian Gonzalez	.75	2.00
LAD3 Kenley Jansen	.75	2.00
LAD4 Kenta Maeda	.75	2.00
LAD5 Corey Seager	1.00	2.50
LAD6 Julio Urias	1.00	2.50
LAD7 Justin Turner	1.00	2.50
LAD8 Joc Pederson	.75	2.00
LAD9 Rich Hill	.60	1.50
LAD10 Mike Piazza	1.00	2.50

2008 Dodgers Topps Gift Set

1 Joe Torre MG	.25	.60
2 Russ Martin Award Winner	.15	.40
3 Russell Martin	.15	.40
4 Jeff Kent/Russell Martin/James Loney	.15	.40
5 Chad Billingsley	.25	.60
6 Rafael Furcal	.15	.40
7 Brad Penny	.15	.40
8 Tony Abreu	.15	.40
9 Jeff Kent 2B-HR	.15	.40
10 Brad Penny Chad Billingsley/Derek Lowe	.25	.60
11 Derek Lowe	.15	.40
12 Andruw Jones	.15	.40
13 Brad Penny/Takashi Saito/Russ Martin	.15	.40
14 Scott Proctor	.15	.40
15 Bob Schaefer CO	.15	.40
16 Chin-Lung Hu Futures Game	.15	.40
17 Matt Kemp	.30	.75
18 Jason Schmidt	.15	.40
19 Derek Lowe/Chad Billingsley Brad Penny	.25	.60
20 Juan Pierre	.15	.40
21 Chin-Lung Hu/James Loney	.15	.40
22 Takashi Saito	.15	.40
23 Jeff Kent/Russel Martin/Juan Pierre	.15	.40
24 Brad Penny K'S 14	.15	.40
25 Andre Ethier	.25	.60
26 Mariano Duncan CO	.15	.40
27 Rudy Seanez	.15	.40
28 James Loney 32 RBI	.15	.40
29 James Loney	.15	.40
30 Esteban Loaiza	.15	.40
31 Brad Penny Chad Billingsley/Derek Lowe	.25	.60
32 Gary Bennett	.15	.40
33 Jon Meloan	.25	.60
34 Larry Bowa CO	.15	.40
35 Jon Broxton No HRs	.15	.40
36 Chin-Lung Hu	.15	.40
37 Jonathan Broxton	.15	.40
38 Juan Pierre Russell Martin/Rafael Furcal	.15	.40
39 Andy LaRoche	.15	.40
40 Hiroki Kuroda	.40	1.00
41 Joe Beimel	.15	.40
42 Takashi Saito 47 Saves	.15	.40
43 Delwyn Young	.15	.40
44 Yhency Brazoban	.15	.40
45 Brad Penny/Derek Lowe Chad Billingsley	.25	.60
46 Joe Beimel GPs By Lefty	.15	.40
47 Russell Martin/Jeff Kent/Luis Gonzalez	.15	.40
48 Mark Sweeney	.15	.40
49 Rick Honeycutt CO	.15	.40
50 Blake DeWitt	.25	.60
51 Mike Easler CO	.15	.40
52 Jeff Kent	.15	.40
53 Derek Lowe 12+	.15	.40
54 Jason Repko	.15	.40
55 Dodger Stadium	.15	.40

1955-62 Don Wingfield

This set of black and white and color postcards was first issued in 1955 and consists of three diffferent types. Type 1 postcards consist of Washington Senatos only and feature the player's name - Washington Nationals, copyright 1955 - Don Wingfield, Griffith Stadium, Washington, D.C., at the base of the front. The type 2 postcards feature players from many teams and present the player's name on the back down the center of the card. The type 3 postcard is in color and consists of but one card (Killebrew). Multiple player poses of several of the Type 2 postcards exist. Cards 1-9 are Type 1 card, Cards 10-43 are Type 2 and Card 44 is Type 3.

COMPLETE SET (43)	250.00	500.00
1 Jim Busby	10.00	20.00
2 Charley Dressen MG	25.00	50.00
3 Ed Fitzgerald	25.00	50.00
4 Bob Porterfield	10.00	20.00
5 Roy Sievers	25.00	50.00
6 Chuck Stobbs	25.00	50.00
7 Dean Stone	25.00	50.00
8 Mickey Vernon	25.00	50.00
9 Eddie Yost	25.00	50.00
10 Ted Abernathy	10.00	20.00
11 Bob Allison (2)	10.00	20.00
12 Ernie Banks	30.00	60.00
13 Earl Battey	10.00	20.00
14 Norm Cash	15.00	30.00
15 Jim Coates	10.00	20.00
16 Rocky Colavito	20.00	40.00
17 Chuck Cottier	10.00	20.00
18 Bennie Daniels	10.00	20.00
19 Dan Dobbek	10.00	20.00
20 Nellie Fox	20.00	40.00
21 Jim Gentile	10.00	20.00
22 Gene Green	10.00	20.00
23 Steve Hamilton	10.00	20.00
24 Ken Hamlin	10.00	20.00
25 Rudy Hernandez	10.00	20.00
26 Ed Hobaugh	10.00	20.00
27 Elston Howard	20.00	40.00
28 Bob Johnson	10.00	20.00
29 Russ Kemmerer	10.00	20.00
30 Harmon Killebrew (3)	25.00	50.00
31 Dale Long	10.00	20.00
32 Mickey Mantle	60.00	120.00
33 Roger Maris	30.00	60.00
34 Willie Mays	40.00	80.00
35 Stan Musial	40.00	80.00
36 Claude Osteen	10.00	20.00
37 Ken Retzer	10.00	20.00
38 Brooks Robinson	25.00	50.00
39 Dick Rudolph	10.00	20.00
40 Dave Stenhouse	10.00	20.00
41 Jose Valdivielso	10.00	20.00
42 Gene Woodling	15.00	30.00
43 Bud Zipfel	10.00	20.00
44 Harmon Killebrew	25.00	50.00

1981 Donruss Test

These cards were issued in very limited quantities and were distributed as part of a test to see how collectors liked the original design for the 1981 Donruss set. According to published reports somewhere between 400 and 500 each of these cards were produced for this test. These were issued either seperately or as part of a three card strip

COMPLETE SET (3)	15.00	40.00
1 George Brett	8.00	20.00
2 Reggie Jackson	8.00	20.00
3 Test Photo	.40	1.00
4 Uncut Strip	15.00	40.00

1981 Donruss

In 1981 Donruss launched itself into the baseball card market with a 600-card set. Wax packs contained 15 cards as well as a piece of gum. This would be the only year that Donruss was allowed to have any confectionary product in their packs. The standard-size cards are printed on thin stock and more than one pose exists for several popular players. Numerous errors of the first print run were later corrected by the company. These are marked P1 and P2 in our checklist below. According to published reports at the time, approximately 500 sets were made available in uncut sheet form. The key Rookie Cards in this set are Danny Ainge, Tim Raines, and Jeff Reardon.

COMPLETE SET (605)	20.00	50.00
COMMON CARD (1-605)	.02	.10
COMMON RC	.05	.15
1 Ozzie Smith	1.25	3.00
2 Rollie Fingers	.08	.25
3 Rick Wise	.02	.10
4 Gene Richards	.02	.10
5 Alan Trammell	.20	.50
6 Tom Brookens	.02	.10
7A Duffy Dyer P1	.08	.25
7B Duffy Dyer P2	.02	.10
8 Mark Fidrych	.08	.25
9 Dave Rozema	.02	.10
10 Ricky Peters RC	.02	.10
11 Mike Schmidt	1.00	2.50
12 Willie Stargell	.20	.50
13 Tim Foli	.02	.10
14 Manny Sanguillen	.08	.25
15 Grant Jackson	.02	.10
16 Eddie Solomon	.02	.10
17 Omar Moreno	.02	.10
18 Joe Morgan	.20	.50
19 Rafael Landestoy	.02	.10
20 Bruce Bochy	.02	.10
21 Joe Sambito	.02	.10
22 Manny Trillo	.02	.10
23A Dave Smith P1	.20	.50
23B Dave Smith P2 RC	.20	.50
24 Terry Puhl	.02	.10
25 Bump Wills	.02	.10
26A John Ellis P1 ERR	.20	.50
26B John Ellis P2 COR	.08	.25
27 Jim Kern	.02	.10
28 Richie Zisk	.02	.10
29 John Mayberry	.02	.10
30 Bob Davis	.02	.10
31 Jackson Todd	.02	.10
32 Alvis Woods	.02	.10
33 Steve Carlton	.20	.50
34 Lee Mazzilli	.08	.25
35 John Stearns	.02	.10
36 Roy Lee Jackson RC	.02	.10
37 Mike Scott	.08	.25
38 Lamar Johnson	.02	.10
39 Kevin Bell	.02	.10
40 Ed Farmer	.02	.10
41 Ross Baumgarten	.02	.10
42 Leo Sutherland RC	.02	.10
43 Dan Meyer	.02	.10
44 Ron Reed	.02	.10
45 Mario Mendoza	.02	.10
46 Rick Honeycutt	.02	.10
47 Glenn Abbott	.02	.10
48 Leon Roberts	.02	.10
49 Rod Carew	.20	.50
50 Bert Campaneris	.08	.25
51A Tom Donahue P1 ERR	.08	.25
51B Tom Donohue P2 RC	.02	.10
52 Dave Frost	.02	.10
53 Ed Halicki	.02	.10
54 Dan Ford	.02	.10
55 Garry Maddox	.02	.10
56A Steve Garvey P1 25HR	.08	.25
56B Steve Garvey P2 21HR	.08	.25
57 Bill Russell	.08	.25
58 Don Sutton	.08	.25
59 Reggie Smith	.08	.25
60 Rick Monday	.08	.25
61 Ray Knight	.08	.25
62 Johnny Bench	.40	1.00
63 Mario Soto	.08	.25
64 Doug Bair	.02	.10
65 George Foster	.08	.25
66 Jeff Burroughs	.08	.25
67 Keith Hernandez	.08	.25
68 Tom Herr	.02	.10
69 Bob Forsch	.02	.10
70 John Fulgham	.02	.10
71A Bobby Bonds P1 ERR	.40	1.00
71B Bobby Bonds P2 COR	.20	.50
72A Rennie Stennett P1	.08	.25
72B Rennie Stennett P2	.02	.10
73 Joe Strain	.02	.10
74 Ed Whitson	.02	.10
75 Tom Griffin	.02	.10
76 Billy North	.02	.10
77 Gene Garber	.02	.10
78 Mike Hargrove	.02	.10
79 Dave Rosello	.02	.10
80 Ron Hassey	.02	.10
81 Sid Monge	.02	.10
82A Joe Charboneau P1	.40	1.00
82B Joe Charboneau P2 RC	.40	1.00
83 Cecil Cooper	.08	.25
84 Sal Bando	.08	.25
85 Moose Haas	.02	.10
86 Mike Caldwell	.02	.10
87A Larry Hisle P1	.08	.25
87B Larry Hisle P2	.02	.10
88 Luis Gomez	.02	.10
89 Larry Parrish	.02	.10
90 Gary Carter	.20	.50
91 Bill Gullickson RC	.20	.50
92 Fred Norman	.02	.10

93 Tommy Hutton .02 .10
94 Carl Yastrzemski .60 1.50
95 Glenn Hoffman RC .02 .10
96 Dennis Eckersley .20 .50
97A Tom Burgmeier P1 .08 .25
97B Tom Burgmeier P2 .02 .10
98 Win Remmerswaal RC .02 .10
99 Bob Horner .08 .25
100 George Brett 1.00 2.50
101 Dave Chalk .02 .10
102 Dennis Leonard .02 .10
103 Renie Martin .02 .10
104 Amos Otis .08 .25
105 Graig Nettles .08 .25
106 Eric Soderholm .02 .10
107 Tommy John .08 .25
108 Tom Underwood .02 .10
109 Lou Piniella .08 .25
110 Mickey Klutts .02 .10
111 Bobby Murcer .08 .25
112 Eddie Murray .60 1.50
113 Rick Dempsey .02 .10
114 Scott McGregor .02 .10
115 Ken Singleton .08 .25
116 Gary Roenicke .02 .10
117 Dave Revering .02 .10
118 Mike Norris .02 .10
119 Rickey Henderson 2.50 6.00
120 Mike Heath .02 .10
121 Dave Cash .02 .10
122 Randy Jones .08 .25
123 Eric Rasmussen .02 .10
124 Jerry Mumphrey .02 .10
125 Richie Hebner .02 .10
126 Mark Wagner .02 .10
127 Jack Morris .20 .50
128 Dan Petry .02 .10
129 Bruce Robbins .02 .10
130 Champ Summers .02 .10
131 Pete Rose 1.25 3.00
131B Pete Rose P2 .75 2.00
132 Willie Stargell .20 .50
133 Ed Ott .02 .10
134 Jim Bibby .02 .10
135 Bert Blyleven .08 .25
136 Dave Parker .08 .25
137 Bill Robinson .02 .10
138 Enos Cabell .02 .10
139 Dave Bergman .02 .10
140 J.R. Richard .08 .25
141 Ken Forsch .02 .10
142 Larry Bowa UER .08 .25
143 Frank LaCorte UER .02 .10
144 Denny Walling .02 .10
145 Buddy Bell .08 .25
146 Fergie Jenkins .08 .25
147 Dannny Darwin .08 .25
148 John Grubb .02 .10
149 Alfredo Griffin .02 .10
150 Jerry Garvin .02 .10
151 Paul Mirabella RC .02 .10
152 Rick Bosetti .02 .10
153 Dick Ruthven .02 .10
154 Frank Taveras .02 .10
155 Craig Swan .02 .10
156 Jeff Reardon RC .40 1.00
157 Steve Henderson .02 .10
158 Jim Morrison .02 .10
159 Glenn Borgmann .02 .10
160 LaMarr Hoyt RC .20 .50
161 Rich Wortham .02 .10
162 Thad Bosley .02 .10
163 Julio Cruz .02 .10
164A Del Unser P1 .08 .25
164B Del Unser P2 .02 .10
165 Jim Anderson .02 .10
166 Jim Beattie .02 .10
167 Shane Rawley .02 .10
168 Joe Simpson .02 .10
169 Rod Carew .20 .50
170 Fred Patek .02 .10
171 Frank Tanana .08 .25
172 Alfredo Martinez RC .02 .10
173 Chris Knapp .02 .10
174 Joe Rudi .08 .25
175 Greg Luzinski .08 .25
176 Steve Garvey .20 .50
177 Joe Ferguson .02 .10
178 Bob Welch .08 .25
179 Dusty Baker .08 .25
180 Rudy Law .02 .10
181 Dave Concepcion .08 .25
182 Johnny Bench .40 1.00
183 Mike LaCoss .02 .10
184 Ken Griffey .08 .25
185 Dave Collins .02 .10
186 Brian Asselstine .02 .10
187 Garry Templeton .08 .25
188 Mike Phillips .02 .10
189 Pete Vuckovich .02 .10
190 John Urrea .02 .10
191 Tony Scott .02 .10
192 Darrell Evans .08 .25
193 Milt May .02 .10
194 Bob Knepper .02 .10
195 Randy Moffitt .02 .10
196 Larry Herndon .02 .10
197 Rick Camp .02 .10
198 Andre Thornton .08 .25
199 Tom Veryzer .02 .10
200 Gary Alexander .02 .10
201 Rick Waits .02 .10
202 Rick Manning .02 .10
203 Paul Molitor .40 1.00
204 Jim Gantner .02 .10
205 Paul Mitchell .02 .10
206 Reggie Cleveland .02 .10
207 Sixto Lezcano .02 .10
208 Bruce Benedict .02 .10
209 Rodney Scott .02 .10
210 John Tamargo .02 .10
211 Bill Lee .08 .25
212 Andre Dawson .20 .50
213 Rowland Office .02 .10
214 Carl Yastrzemski .60 1.50
215 Jerry Remy .02 .10
216 Mike Torrez .02 .10
217 Skip Lockwood .02 .10
218 Fred Lynn .08 .25
219 Chris Chambliss .08 .25
220 Willie Aikens .02 .10
221 John Wathan .02 .10
222 Dan Quisenberry .02 .10
223 Willie Wilson .08 .25
224 Clint Hurdle .02 .10
225 Bob Watson .02 .10
226 Jim Spencer .02 .10
227 Ron Guidry .08 .25
228 Reggie Jackson .40 1.00
229 Oscar Gamble .02 .10
230 Jeff Cox RC .02 .10
231 Luis Tiant .08 .25
232 Rich Dauer .02 .10
233 Dan Graham .02 .10
234 Mike Flanagan .02 .10
235 John Lowenstein .02 .10
236 Benny Ayala .02 .10
237 Wayne Gross .02 .10
238 Rick Langford .02 .10
239 Tony Armas .08 .25
240A Bob Lacy P1 ERR .20 .50
240B Bob Lacey P2 COR .02 .10
241 Gene Tenace .08 .25
242 Bob Shirley .02 .10
243 Gary Lucas RC .02 .10
244 Jerry Turner .02 .10
245 John Wockenfuss .02 .10
246 Stan Papi .02 .10
247 Milt Wilcox .02 .10
248 Dan Schatzeder .02 .10
249 Steve Kemp .02 .10
250 Jim Lentine RC .02 .10
251 Pete Rose 1.25 3.00
252 Bill Madlock .08 .25
253 Dale Berra .02 .10
254 Kent Tekulve .02 .10
255 Enrique Romo .02 .10
256 Mike Easler .02 .10
257 Chuck Tanner MG .02 .10
258 Art Howe .02 .10
259 Alan Ashby .02 .10
260 Nolan Ryan 2.00 5.00
261A Vern Ruhle P1 ERR .20 .50
261B Vern Ruhle P2 COR .08 .25
262 Bob Boone .08 .25
263 Cesar Cedeno .08 .25
264 Jeff Leonard .08 .25
265 Pat Putnam .02 .10
266 Jon Matlack .02 .10
267 Dave Rajsich .02 .10
268 Billy Sample .02 .10
269 Damaso Garcia RC .02 .10
270 Tom Buskey .02 .10
271 Joey McLaughlin .02 .10
272 Barry Bonnell .02 .10
273 Tug McGraw .08 .25
274 Mike Jorgensen .02 .10
275 Pat Zachry .02 .10
276 Neil Allen .02 .10
277 Joel Youngblood .02 .10
278 Greg Pryor .02 .10
279 Britt Burns RC .02 .10
280 Rich Dotson RC .02 .10
281 Chet Lemon .08 .25
282 Rusty Kuntz RC .02 .10
283 Ted Cox .02 .10
284 Sparky Lyle .08 .25
285 Larry Cox .02 .10
286 Floyd Bannister .02 .10
287 Byron McLaughlin .02 .10
288 Rodney Craig .02 .10
289 Bobby Grich .08 .25
290 Dickie Thon .02 .10
291 Mark Clear .02 .10
292 Dave Lemanczyk .02 .10
293 Jason Thompson .02 .10
294 Rick Miller .02 .10
295 Lonnie Smith .08 .25
296 Ron Cey .08 .25
297 Steve Yeager .08 .25
298 Bobby Castillo .02 .10
299 Manny Mota .08 .25
300 Jay Johnstone .02 .10
301 Dan Driessen .02 .10
302 Joe Nolan .02 .10
303 Paul Householder RC .02 .10
304 Harry Spilman .02 .10
305 Cesar Geronimo .02 .10
306A Gary Mathews P1 ERR .20 .50
306B Gary Matthews P2 COR .08 .25
307 Ken Reitz .02 .10
308 Ted Simmons .08 .25
309 John Littlefield RC .02 .10
310 George Frazier .02 .10
311 Dane Iorg .02 .10
312 Mike Ivie .02 .10
313 Dennis Littlejohn .02 .10
314 Gary Lavelle .02 .10
315 Jack Clark .08 .25
316 Jim Wohlford .02 .10
317 Rick Matula .02 .10
318 Toby Harrah .08 .25
319A Dwane Kuiper P1 ERR .08 .25
319B Duane Kuiper P2 COR .02 .10
320 Len Barker .08 .25
321 Victor Cruz .02 .10
322 Dell Alston .02 .10
323 Robin Yount .60 1.50
324 Charlie Moore .02 .10
325 Lary Sorensen .02 .10
326A Gorman Thomas P1 .20 .50
326B Gorman Thomas P2 .08 .25
327 Bob Rodgers MG .02 .10
328 Phil Niekro .08 .25
329 Chris Speier .02 .10
330A Steve Rodgers P1 .08 .25
330B Steve Rogers P2 COR .08 .25
331 Woodie Fryman .02 .10
332 Warren Cromartie .02 .10
333 Jerry White .02 .10
334 Tony Perez .20 .50
335 Carlton Fisk .20 .50
336 Dick Drago .02 .10
337 Steve Renko .02 .10
338 Jim Rice .08 .25
339 Jerry Royster .02 .10
340 Frank White .08 .25
341 Jamie Quirk .02 .10
342A Paul Spittorff P1 ERR .08 .25
342B Paul Splittorff P2 COR .02 .10
343 Marty Pattin .02 .10
344 Pete LaCock .02 .10
345 Willie Randolph .08 .25
346 Rick Cerone .02 .10
347 Rich Gossage .08 .25
348 Reggie Jackson .40 1.00
349 Ruppert Jones .02 .10
350 Dave McKay .02 .10
351 Yogi Berra CO .40 1.00
352 Doug DeCinces .02 .10
353 Jim Palmer .20 .50
354 Tippy Martinez .02 .10
355 Al Bumbry .02 .10
356 Earl Weaver MG .08 .25
357A Bob Picciolo P1 ERR .08 .25
357B Rob Picciolo P2 COR .02 .10
358 Matt Keough .02 .10
359 Dwayne Murphy .02 .10
360 Brian Kingman .02 .10
361 Bill Fahey .02 .10
362 Steve Mura .02 .10
363 Dennis Kinney RC .02 .10
364 Dave Winfield .20 .50
365 Lou Whitaker .20 .50
366 Lance Parrish .08 .25
367 Tim Corcoran .02 .10
368 Pat Underwood .02 .10
369 Al Cowens .02 .10
370 Sparky Anderson MG .08 .25
371 Pete Rose 1.25 3.00
372 Phil Garner .08 .25
373 Steve Nicosia .02 .10
374 John Candelaria .08 .25
375 Don Robinson .02 .10
376 Lee Lacy .02 .10
377 John Milner .02 .10
378 Craig Reynolds .02 .10
379A Luis Pujois P1 ERR .08 .25
379B Luis Pujols P2 COR .02 .10
380 Joe Niekro .02 .10
381 Joaquin Andujar .08 .25
382 Keith Moreland RC .02 .10
383 Jose Cruz .08 .25
384 Bill Virdon MG .02 .10
385 Jim Sundberg .08 .25
386 Doc Medich .02 .10
387 Al Oliver .08 .25
388 Jim Norris .02 .10
389 Bob Bailor .02 .10
390 Ernie Whitt .02 .10
391 Otto Velez .02 .10
392 Roy Howell .02 .10
393 Bob Walk RC .20 .50
394 Doug Flynn .02 .10
395 Pete Falcone .02 .10
396 Tom Hausman .02 .10
397 Elliott Maddox .02 .10
398 Mike Squires .02 .10
399 Marvis Foley RC .02 .10
400 Steve Trout .02 .10
401 Wayne Nordhagen .02 .10
402 Tony LaRussa MG .08 .25
403 Bruce Bochte .02 .10
404 Bake McBride .08 .25
405 Jerry Narron .02 .10
406 Rob Dressler .02 .10
407 Dave Heaverlo .02 .10
408 Tom Paciorek .02 .10
409 Carney Lansford .08 .25
410 Brian Downing .08 .25
411 Don Aase .02 .10
412 Jim Barr .02 .10
413 Don Baylor .08 .25
414 Jim Fregosi MG .02 .10
415 Dallas Green MG .02 .10
416 Dave Lopes .08 .25
417 Jerry Reuss .02 .10
418 Rick Sutcliffe .08 .25
419 Derrel Thomas .02 .10
420 Tom Lasorda MG .20 .50
421 Charlie Leibrandt RC .20 .50
422 Tom Seaver .40 1.00
423 Ron Oester .02 .10
424 Junior Kennedy .02 .10
425 Tom Seaver .40 1.00
426 Bobby Cox MG .08 .25
427 Leon Durham RC .20 .50
428 Terry Kennedy .02 .10
429 Silvio Martinez .02 .10
430 George Hendrick .08 .25
431 Red Schoendienst MG .20 .50
432 Johnnie LeMaster .02 .10
433 Vida Blue .08 .25
434 John Montefusco .02 .10
435 Terry Whitfield .02 .10
436 Dave Bristol MG .02 .10
437 Dale Murphy .20 .50
438 Jerry Dybzinski RC .02 .10
439 Jorge Orta .02 .10
440 Wayne Garland .02 .10
441 Miguel Dilone .02 .10
442 Dave Garcia MG .02 .10
443 Don Money .02 .10
444A Buck Martinez P1 ERR .08 .25
444B Buck Martinez P2 COR .02 .10
445 Jerry Augustine .02 .10
446 Ben Oglivie .08 .25
447 Jim Slaton .02 .10
448 Doyle Alexander .02 .10
449 Tony Bernazard .02 .10
450 Scott Sanderson .02 .10
451 David Palmer .02 .10
452 Stan Bahnsen .02 .10
453 Dick Williams MG .02 .10
454 Rick Burleson .02 .10
455 Gary Allenson .02 .10
456 Bob Stanley .02 .10
457A John Tudor ERR .40 1.00
457B John Tudor RC .40 1.00
458 Dwight Evans .20 .50
459 Glenn Hubbard .02 .10
460 U.L. Washington .02 .10
461 Larry Gura .02 .10
462 Rich Gale .02 .10
463 Hal McRae .08 .25
464 Jim Frey MG RC .02 .10
465 Bucky Dent .08 .25
466 Dennis Werth RC .02 .10
467 Ron Davis .02 .10
468 Reggie Jackson .40 1.00
469 Bobby Brown .02 .10
470 Mike Davis RC .20 .50
471 Gaylord Perry .08 .25
472 Mark Belanger .02 .10
473 Jim Palmer .20 .50
474 Sammy Stewart .02 .10
475 Tim Stoddard .02 .10
476 Steve Stone .02 .10
477 Jeff Newman .02 .10
478 Steve McCatty .02 .10
479 Billy Martin MG .20 .50
480 Mitchell Page .02 .10
481 Steve Carlton CY .08 .25
482 Bill Buckner .08 .25
483A Ivan DeJesus P1 ERR .08 .25
483B Ivan DeJesus P2 COR .02 .10
484 Cliff Johnson .02 .10
485 Lenny Randle .02 .10
486 Larry Milbourne .02 .10
487 Roy Smalley .02 .10
488 John Castino .02 .10
489 Ron Jackson .02 .10
490A Dave Roberts P1 .08 .25
490B Dave Roberts P2 .02 .10
491 George Brett MVP .60 1.50
492 Mike Cubbage .02 .10
493 Rob Wilfong .02 .10
494 Danny Goodwin .02 .10
495 Jose Morales .02 .10
496 Mickey Rivers .02 .10
497 Mike Edwards .02 .10
498 Mike Sadek .02 .10
499 Lenn Sakata .02 .10
500 Gene Michael MG .02 .10
501 Dave Roberts .02 .10
502 Steve Dillard .02 .10
503 Jim Essian .02 .10
504 Rance Mulliniks .02 .10
505 Darrell Porter .02 .10
506 Joe Torre MG .08 .25
507 Terry Crowley .02 .10
508 Bill Travers .02 .10
509 Nelson Norman .02 .10
510 Bob McClure .02 .10
511 Steve Howe RC .20 .50
512 Dave Rader .02 .10
513 Mick Kelleher .02 .10
514 Kiko Garcia .02 .10
515 Larry Biittner .02 .10
516A Willie Norwood P1 .08 .25
516B Willie Norwood P2 .02 .10
517 Bo Diaz .02 .10
518 Juan Beniquez .02 .10
519 Scot Thompson .02 .10
520 Jim Tracy RC .40 1.00
521 Carlos Lezcano RC .02 .10
522 Joe Amalfitano MG .02 .10
523 Preston Hanna .02 .10
524A Ray Burris P1 .08 .25
524B Ray Burris P2 .02 .10
525 Broderick Perkins .02 .10
526 Mickey Hatcher .02 .10
527 John Goryl MG .02 .10
528 Dick Davis .02 .10
529 Butch Wynegar .02 .10
530 Sal Butera RC .02 .10
531 Jerry Koosman .08 .25
532A Geoff Zahn P1 .08 .25
532B Geoff Zahn P2 .02 .10
533 Dennis Martinez .08 .25
534 Gary Thomasson .02 .10
535 Steve Macko .02 .10
536 Jim Kaat .08 .25
537 G.Brett/R.Carew .60 1.50
538 Tim Raines RC 1.00 2.50
539 Keith Smith .02 .10
540 Ken Macha .02 .10
541 Burt Hooton .02 .10
542 Butch Hobson .02 .10
543 Bill Stein .02 .10
544 Dave Stapleton RC .02 .10
545 Bob Pate RC .02 .10
546 Doug Corbett RC .02 .10
547 Darrell Jackson .02 .10
548 Pete Redfern .02 .10
549 Roger Erickson .02 .10
550 Al Hrabosky .08 .25
551 Dick Tidrow .02 .10
552 Dave Ford .02 .10
553 Dave Kingman .08 .25
554A Mike Vail P1 .08 .25
554B Mike Vail P2 .02 .10
555A Jerry Martin P1 .08 .25
555B Jerry Martin P2 .02 .10
556A Jesus Figueroa P1 .08 .25
556B Jesus Figueroa P2 RC .02 .10
557 Don Stanhouse .02 .10
558 Barry Foote .02 .10
559 Tim Blackwell .02 .10
560 Bruce Sutter .20 .50
561 Rick Reuschel .08 .25
562 Lynn McGlothen .02 .10
563A Bob Owchinko P1 .08 .25
563B Bob Owchinko P2 .02 .10
564 John Verhoeven .02 .10
565 Ken Landreaux .02 .10
566A Glen Adams P1 ERR .08 .25
566B Glenn Adams P2 COR .02 .10
567 Hosken Powell .02 .10
568 Dick Noles .02 .10
569 Danny Ainge RC 1.25 3.00
570 Bobby Mattick MG RC .02 .10
571 Joe Lefebvre RC .02 .10
572 Bobby Clark .02 .10
573 Dennis Lamp .02 .10
574 Randy Lerch .02 .10
575 Mookie Wilson RC 1.25 3.00
576 Ron LeFlore .08 .25
577 Jim Dwyer .02 .10
578 Bill Castro .02 .10
579 Greg Minton .02 .10
580 Mark Littell .02 .10
581 Andy Hassler .02 .10
582 Dave Stieb .08 .25
583 Ken Oberkfell .02 .10
584 Larry Bradford .02 .10
585 Fred Stanley .02 .10
586 Bill Caudill .02 .10
587 Doug Capilla .02 .10
588 George Riley RC .02 .10
589 Willie Hernandez .02 .10
590 Mike Schmidt MVP 1.00 2.50
591 Steve Stone CY .02 .10
592 Rick Sofield .02 .10
593 Bombo Rivera .02 .10
594 Gary Ward .02 .10
595A Dave Edwards P1 .08 .25
595B Dave Edwards P2 .02 .10
596 Mike Proly .02 .10
597 Tommy Boggs .02 .10
598 Greg Gross .02 .10
599 Elias Sosa .02 .10
600 Pat Kelly .02 .10
601A Checklist 1-120 P1 .08 .25
601B Checklist 1-120 P2 .20 .50
602 Checklist 121-240 NNO .08 .25
603A Checklist 241-360 P1 .08 .25
603B Checklist 241-360 P2 .08 .25
604A Checklist 361-480 P1 .08 .25
604B Checklist 361-480 P2 .08 .25
605A Checklist 481-600 P1 .08 .25
605B Checklist 481-600 P2 .08 .25

1982 Donruss

The 1982 Donruss set contains 653 numbered standard-size cards and seven unnumbered checklists. The first 26 cards of this set are entitled Diamond Kings (DK) and feature the artwork of Dick Perez of Perez-Steele Galleries. The set was marketed with puzzle pieces in 15-card packs rather than with bubble gum. Those 15-card packs with an 30 cent SRP were issued 36 packs to a box and 20 boxes to a case. There are 63 pieces to the puzzle, which, when put together, make a collage of Babe Ruth entitled "Hall of Fame Diamond King." The card stock in this year's Donruss cards is considerably thicker than the 1981 cards. The seven unnumbered checklist cards are arbitrarily assigned numbers 654 through 660 and are listed at the end of the list below. Notable Rookie Cards in this set include Brett Butler, Cal Ripken Jr., Lee Smith and Dave Stewart.

COMPLETE SET (660) 20.00 50.00
COMP.FACT.SET (660) 20.00 50.00
COMP.RUTH PUZZLE 5.00 10.00
1 Pete Rose DK 1.00 2.50
2 Gary Carter DK .07 .20
3 Steve Garvey DK .07 .20
4 Vida Blue DK .07 .20
5 Alan Trammell DK COR .07 .20
5A Alan Trammel DK ERR Name misspelled .07 .20
6 Len Barker DK .02 .10
7 Dwight Evans DK .15 .40
8 Rod Carew DK .15 .40
9 George Hendrick DK .07 .20
10 Phil Niekro DK .07 .20
11 Richie Zisk DK .02 .10
12 Dave Parker DK .07 .20
13 Nolan Ryan DK 1.50 4.00
14 Ivan DeJesus DK .02 .10
15 George Brett DK .75 2.00
16 Tom Seaver DK .15 .40
17 Dave Kingman DK .07 .20
18 Dave Winfield DK .07 .20
19 Mike Norris DK .02 .10
20 Carlton Fisk DK .15 .40
21 Ozzie Smith DK .60 1.50
22 Roy Smalley DK .02 .10
23 Buddy Bell DK .07 .20
24 Ken Singleton DK .07 .20
25 John Mayberry DK .02 .10
26 Gorman Thomas DK .07 .20
27 Earl Weaver MG .07 .20
28 Rollie Fingers .07 .20
29 Sparky Anderson MG .07 .20
30 Dennis Eckersley .15 .40
31 Dave Winfield .07 .20
32 Burt Hooton .02 .10
33 Rick Waits .02 .10
34 George Brett .75 2.00
35 Steve McCatty .02 .10
36 Steve Rogers .07 .20
37 Bill Stein .02 .10
38 Steve Renko .02 .10
39 Mike Squires .02 .10
40 George Hendrick .07 .20
41 Bob Knepper .02 .10
42 Steve Carlton .15 .40
43 Larry Biittner .02 .10
44 Chris Welsh .02 .10
45 Steve Nicosia .02 .10
46 Jack Clark .07 .20
47 Chris Chambliss .07 .20
48 Ivan DeJesus .02 .10
49 Lee Mazzilli .07 .20
50 Julio Cruz .02 .10
51 Pete Redfern .02 .10
52 Dave Stieb .07 .20
53 Doug Corbett .02 .10
54 Jorge Bell RC George Bell .40 1.00
55 Joe Simpson .02 .10
56 Rusty Staub .07 .20
57 Hector Cruz .02 .10
58 Claudell Washington .02 .10
59 Enrique Romo .02 .10
60 Gary Lavelle .02 .10
61 Tim Flannery .02 .10
62 Joe Nolan .02 .10
63 Larry Bowa .07 .20
64 Sixto Lezcano .02 .10
65 Joe Sambito .02 .10
66 Bruce Kison .02 .10
67 Wayne Nordhagen .02 .10
68 Woodie Fryman .02 .10
69 Billy Sample .02 .10
70 Amos Otis .07 .20
71 Matt Keough .02 .10
72 Toby Harrah .07 .20
73 Dave Righetti RC .60 1.50
74 Carl Yastrzemski .50 1.25
75 Bob Welch .07 .20
76 Alan Trammell COR .07 .20
76A Alan Trammel ERR Name misspelled .07 .20
77 Rick Dempsey .02 .10
78 Paul Molitor .07 .20
79 Dennis Martinez .07 .20
80 Jim Slaton .02 .10
81 Champ Summers .02 .10
82 Carney Lansford .07 .20
83 Barry Foote .02 .10
84 Steve Garvey .07 .20
85 Rick Manning .02 .10
86 John Wathan .02 .10
87 Brian Kingman .02 .10
88 Andre Dawson UER Middle name Fernando should be Nolan .07 .20
89 Jim Kern .02 .10
90 Bobby Grich .07 .20
91 Bob Forsch .02 .10
92 Art Howe .02 .10
93 Marty Bystrom .02 .10
94 Ozzie Smith .60 1.50
95 Dave Parker .07 .20
96 Doyle Alexander .02 .10
97 Al Hrabosky .02 .10
98 Frank Taveras .02 .10
99 Tim Blackwell .02 .10
100 Floyd Bannister .02 .10
101 Alfredo Griffin .02 .10
102 Dave Engle .02 .10
103 Mario Soto .07 .20
104 Ross Baumgarten .02 .10
105 Ken Singleton .07 .20
106 Ted Simmons .07 .20
107 Jack Morris .07 .20
108 Bob Watson .02 .10
109 Dwight Evans .15 .40
110 Tom Lasorda MG .15 .40
111 Bert Blyleven .07 .20
112 Dan Quisenberry .02 .10
113 Rickey Henderson 1.00 2.50
114 Gary Carter .07 .20
115 Brian Downing .07 .20
116 Al Oliver .07 .20
117 LaMarr Hoyt .02 .10
118 Cesar Cedeno .07 .20
119 Keith Moreland .02 .10
120 Bob Shirley .02 .10
121 Terry Kennedy .02 .10
122 Frank Pastore .02 .10
123 Gene Garber .02 .10
124 Tony Pena .07 .20
125 Allen Ripley .02 .10
126 Randy Martz .02 .10
127 Richie Zisk .02 .10
128 Mike Scott .07 .20
129 Lloyd Moseby .02 .10
130 Rob Wilfong .02 .10
131 Tim Stoddard .02 .10
132 Gorman Thomas .07 .20
133 Dan Petry .02 .10
134 Bob Stanley .02 .10
135 Lou Piniella .07 .20
136 Pedro Guerrero .07 .20
137 Len Barker .02 .10
138 Rich Gale .02 .10
139 Wayne Gross .02 .10
140 Tim Wallach RC .40 1.00
141 Gene Mauch MG .02 .10
142 Doc Medich .02 .10
143 Tony Bernazard .02 .10
144 Bill Virdon MG .02 .10
145 John Littlefield .02 .10
146 Dave Bergman .02 .10
147 Dick Davis .02 .10
148 Tom Seaver .30 .75
149 Matt Sinatro .02 .10
150 Chuck Tanner MG .02 .10
151 Leon Durham .02 .10
152 Gene Tenace .07 .20
153 Al Bumbry .02 .10
154 Mark Brouhard .02 .10
155 Rick Peters .02 .10
156 Jerry Remy .02 .10
157 Rick Reuschel .07 .20
158 Steve Howe .02 .10
159 Alan Bannister .02 .10
160 U.L. Washington .02 .10
161 Rick Langford .02 .10
162 Bill Gullickson .02 .10
163 Mark Wagner .02 .10
164 Geoff Zahn .02 .10
165 Ron LeFlore .07 .20
166 Dane Iorg .02 .10
167 Joe Niekro .02 .10
168 Pete Rose 1.00 2.50
169 Dave Collins .02 .10
170 Rick Wise .02 .10
171 Jim Bibby .02 .10
172 Larry Herndon .02 .10
173 Bob Horner .07 .20
174 Steve Dillard .02 .10
175 Mookie Wilson .07 .20
176 Dan Meyer .02 .10
177 Fernando Arroyo .02 .10
178 Jackson Todd .02 .10
179 Darrell Jackson .02 .10
180 Alvis Woods .02 .10
181 Jim Anderson .02 .10
182 Dave Kingman .07 .20
183 Steve Henderson .02 .10
184 Brian Asselstine .02 .10
185 Rod Scurry .02 .10
186 Fred Breining .02 .10
187 Danny Boone .02 .10
188 Junior Kennedy .02 .10
189 Sparky Lyle .07 .20
190 Whitey Herzog MG .07 .20
191 Dave Smith .02 .10
192 Ed Ott .02 .10
193 Greg Luzinski .07 .20
194 Bill Lee .07 .20
195 Don Zimmer MG .07 .20
196 Hal McRae .07 .20
197 Mike Norris .02 .10
198 Duane Kuiper .02 .10
199 Rick Cerone .02 .10
200 Jim Rice .07 .20
201 Steve Yeager .07 .20
202 Tom Brookens .02 .10
203 Jose Morales .02 .10
204 Roy Howell .02 .10
205 Tippy Martinez .02 .10
206 Moose Haas .02 .10
207 Al Cowens .02 .10
208 Dave Stapleton .02 .10
209 Bucky Dent .07 .20
210 Ron Cey .07 .20
211 Jorge Orta .02 .10
212 Jamie Quirk .02 .10
213 Jeff Jones .02 .10
214 Tim Raines .15 .40
215 Jon Matlack .02 .10
216 Rod Carew .15 .40
217 Jim Kaat .07 .20
218 Joe Pittman .02 .10
219 Larry Christenson .02 .10
220 Juan Bonilla RC .05 .15
221 Mike Easler .02 .10
222 Vida Blue .07 .20
223 Rick Camp .02 .10
224 Mike Jorgensen .02 .10
225 Jody Davis RC .02 .10
226 Mike Parrott .02 .10
227 Jim Clancy .02 .10
228 Hosken Powell .02 .10
229 Tom Hume .02 .10
230 Britt Burns .02 .10
231 Jim Palmer .07 .20
232 Bob Rodgers MG .02 .10
233 Milt Wilcox .02 .10
234 Dave Revering .02 .10
235 Mike Torrez .02 .10
236 Robert Castillo .02 .10
237 Von Hayes RC .20 .50
238 Renie Martin .02 .10
239 Dwayne Murphy .02 .10
240 Rodney Scott .02 .10
241 Fred Patek .02 .10
242 Mickey Rivers .02 .10
243 Steve Trout .02 .10
244 Jose Cruz .07 .20
245 Manny Trillo .02 .10
246 Lary Sorensen .02 .10
247 Dave Edwards .02 .10
248 Dan Driessen .02 .10
249 Tommy Boggs .02 .10
250 Dale Berra .02 .10
251 Ed Whitson .02 .10
252 Lee Smith RC .75 2.00
253 Tom Paciorek .02 .10
254 Pat Zachry .02 .10
255 Luis Leal .02 .10
256 John Castino .02 .10
257 Rich Dauer .02 .10
258 Cecil Cooper .07 .20
259 Dave Rozema .02 .10
260 John Tudor .07 .20
261 Jerry Mumphrey .02 .10
262 Jay Johnstone .02 .10
263 Bo Diaz .02 .10
264 Dennis Leonard .02 .10
265 Jim Spencer .02 .10
266 John Milner .02 .10
267 Don Aase .02 .10
268 Jim Sundberg .07 .20
269 Lamar Johnson .02 .10
270 Frank LaCorte .02 .10
271 Barry Evans .02 .10
272 Enos Cabell .02 .10
273 Del Unser .02 .10
274 George Foster .07 .20
275 Brett Butler RC .40 1.00
276 Lee Lacy .02 .10
277 Ken Reitz .02 .10
278 Keith Hernandez .07 .20
279 Doug DeCinces .02 .10
280 Charlie Moore .02 .10
281 Lance Parrish .07 .20
282 Ralph Houk MG .02 .10
283 Rich Gossage .07 .20
284 Jerry Reuss .02 .10
285 Mike Stanton .02 .10
286 Frank White .07 .20
287 Bob Owchinko .02 .10
288 Scott Sanderson .02 .10
289 Bump Wills .02 .10
290 Dave Frost .02 .10
291 Chet Lemon .07 .20
292 Tito Landrum .02 .10
293 Vern Ruhle .02 .10
294 Mike Schmidt .75 2.00
295 Sam Mejias .02 .10
296 Gary Lucas .02 .10
297 John Candelaria .02 .10
298 Jerry Martin .02 .10

299 Dale Murphy .15 .40
300 Mike Lum .02 .10
301 Tom Hausman .02 .10
302 Glenn Abbott .02 .10
303 Roger Erickson .02 .10
304 Otto Velez .02 .10
305 Danny Goodwin .02 .10
306 John Mayberry .02 .10
307 Lenny Randle .02 .10
308 Bob Bailor .02 .10
309 Jerry Morales .02 .10
310 Rufino Linares .02 .10
311 Kent Tekulve .02 .10
312 Joe Morgan .07 .20
313 John Urrea .02 .10
314 Paul Householder .02 .10
315 Garry Maddox .02 .10
316 Mike Ramsey .02 .10
317 Alan Ashby .02 .10
318 Bob Clark .02 .10
319 Tony LaRussa MG .07 .20
320 Charlie Lea .02 .10
321 Danny Darwin .02 .10
322 Cesar Geronimo .02 .10
323 Tom Underwood .02 .10
324 Andre Thornton .02 .10
325 Rudy May .02 .10
326 Frank Tanana .07 .20
327 Dave Lopes .07 .20
328 Richie Hebner .02 .10
329 Mike Flanagan .02 .10
330 Mike Caldwell .02 .10
331 Scott McGregor .02 .10
332 Jerry Augustine .02 .10
333 Stan Papi .02 .10
334 Rick Miller .02 .10
335 Graig Nettles .07 .20
336 Dusty Baker .07 .20
337 Dave Garcia MG .02 .10
338 Larry Gura .02 .10
339 Cliff Johnson .02 .10
340 Warren Cromartie .02 .10
341 Steve Comer .02 .10
342 Rick Burleson .02 .10
343 John Martin RC .05 .15
344 Craig Reynolds .02 .10
345 Mike Proly .02 .10
346 Ruppert Jones .02 .10
347 Omar Moreno .02 .10
348 Greg Minton .02 .10
349 Rick Mahler .02 .10
350 Alex Trevino .02 .10
351 Mike Krukow .02 .10
352A Shane Rawley ERR .15 .40
Photo actually
Jim Anderson
352B Shane Rawley COR .02 .10
353 Garth Iorg .02 .10
354 Pete Mackanin .02 .10
355 Paul Moskau .02 .10
356 Richard Dotson .02 .10
357 Steve Stone .02 .10
358 Larry Hisle .02 .10
359 Aurelio Lopez .02 .10
360 Oscar Gamble .02 .10
361 Tom Burgmeier .02 .10
362 Terry Forster .07 .20
363 Joe Charboneau .07 .20
364 Ken Brett .02 .10
365 Tony Armas .07 .20
366 Chris Speier .02 .10
367 Fred Lynn .07 .20
368 Buddy Bell .07 .20
369 Jim Essian .02 .10
370 Terry Puhl .02 .10
371 Greg Gross .02 .10
372 Bruce Sutter .15 .40
373 Joe Lefebvre .02 .10
374 Ray Knight .07 .20
375 Bruce Benedict .02 .10
376 Tim Foli .02 .10
377 Al Holland .02 .10
378 Ken Kravec .02 .10
379 Jeff Burroughs .02 .10
380 Pete Falcone .02 .10
381 Ernie Whitt .02 .10
382 Brad Havens .02 .10
383 Terry Crowley .02 .10
384 Don Money .02 .10
385 Dan Schatzeder .02 .10
386 Gary Allenson .02 .10
387 Yogi Berra CO .30 .75
388 Ken Landreaux .02 .10
389 Mike Hargrove .02 .10
390 Darryl Motley .02 .10
391 Dave McKay .02 .10
392 Stan Bahnsen .02 .10
393 Ken Forsch .02 .10
394 Mario Mendoza .02 .10
395 Jim Morrison .02 .10
396 Mike Ivie .02 .10
397 Broderick Perkins .02 .10
398 Darrell Evans .07 .20
399 Ron Reed .02 .10
400 Johnny Bench .30 .75
401 Steve Bedrosian RC .20 .50
402 Bill Robinson .02 .10
403 Bill Buckner .07 .20
404 Ken Oberkfell .02 .10
405 Cal Ripken RC 15.00 40.00
406 Jim Gantner .02 .10
407 Kirk Gibson .30 .75
408 Tony Perez .15 .40
409 Tommy John UER .07 .20
Text says 52-56 as
Yankee, should be
52-26
410 Dave Stewart RC .60 1.50
411 Dan Spillner .02 .10
412 Willie Aikens .02 .10
413 Mike Heath .02 .10
414 Ray Burris .02 .10
415 Leon Roberts .02 .10
416 Mike Witt .20 .50
417 Bob Molinaro .02 .10
418 Steve Braun .02 .10
419 Nolan Ryan UER 1.50 4.00
420 Tug McGraw .07 .20
421 Dave Concepcion .07 .20
422A Juan Eichelberger .15 .40
ERR Photo actually
Gary Lucas
422B Juan Eichelberger .02 .10
COR
423 Rick Rhoden .02 .10
424 Frank Robinson MG .15 .40
425 Eddie Miller .02 .10
426 Bill Caudill .02 .10
427 Doug Flynn .02 .10
428 Larry Andersen UER .02 .10
Misspelled Anderson
on card front
429 Al Williams .02 .10
430 Jerry Garvin .02 .10
431 Glenn Adams .02 .10
432 Barry Bonnell .02 .10
433 Jerry Narron .02 .10
434 John Stearns .02 .10
435 Mike Tyson .02 .10
436 Glenn Hubbard .02 .10
437 Eddie Solomon .02 .10
438 Jeff Leonard .02 .10
439 Randy Bass .20 .50
440 Mike LaCoss .02 .10
441 Gary Matthews .07 .20
442 Mark Littell .02 .10
443 Don Sutton .07 .20
444 John Harris .02 .10
445 Vada Pinson CO .07 .20
446 Elias Sosa .02 .10
447 Charlie Hough .07 .20
448 Willie Wilson, .07 .20
449 Fred Stanley .02 .10
450 Tom Veryzer .02 .10
451 Ron Davis .02 .10
452 Mark Clear .02 .10
453 Bill Russell .07 .20
454 Lou Whitaker .07 .20
455 Dan Graham .02 .10
456 Reggie Cleveland .02 .10
457 Sammy Stewart .02 .10
458 Pete Vuckovich .02 .10
459 John Wockenfuss .02 .10
460 Glenn Hoffman .02 .10
461 Willie Randolph .07 .20
462 Fernando Valenzuela .30 .75
463 Ron Hassey .02 .10
464 Paul Splittorff .02 .10
465 Rob Picciolo .02 .10
466 Larry Parrish .02 .10
467 Johnny Grubb .02 .10
468 Dan Ford .02 .10
469 Silvio Martinez .02 .10
470 Kiko Garcia .02 .10
471 Bob Boone .07 .20
472 Luis Salazar .02 .10
473 Randy Niemann UER .02 .10
Card says Pirate, but in an Astro uniform
474 Tom Griffin .02 .10
475 Phil Niekro .07 .20
476 Hubie Brooks .02 .10
477 Dick Tidrow .02 .10
478 Jim Beattie .02 .10
479 Damaso Garcia .02 .10
480 Mickey Hatcher .02 .10
481 Joe Price .02 .10
482 Ed Farmer .02 .10
483 Eddie Murray .30 .75
484 Ben Oglivie .07 .20
485 Kevin Saucier .02 .10
486 Bobby Murcer .07 .20
487 Bill Campbell .02 .10
488 Reggie Smith .07 .20
489 Wayne Garland .02 .10
490 Jim Wright .02 .10
491 Billy Martin MG .15 .40
492 Jim Fanning MG .02 .10
493 Don Baylor .07 .20
494 Rick Honeycutt .02 .10
495 Carlton Fisk .15 .40
496 Denny Walling .02 .10
497 Bake McBride .07 .20
498 Darrell Porter .02 .10
499 Gene Richards .02 .10
500 Ron Oester .02 .10
501 Ken Dayley .02 .10
502 Jason Thompson .02 .10
503 Milt May .02 .10
504 Doug Bird .02 .10
505 Bruce Bochte .02 .10
506 Neil Allen .02 .10
507 Joey McLaughlin .02 .10
508 Butch Wynegar .02 .10
509 Gary Roenicke .02 .10
510 Robin Yount .50 1.25
511 Dave Tobik .02 .10
512 Rich Gedman .20 .50
513 Gene Nelson .02 .10
514 Rick Monday .07 .20
515 Miguel Dilone .02 .10
516 Clint Hurdle .02 .10
517 Jeff Newman .02 .10
518 Grant Jackson .02 .10
519 Andy Hassler .02 .10
520 Pat Putnam .02 .10
521 Greg Pryor .02 .10
522 Tony Scott .02 .10
523 Steve Mura .02 .10
524 Johnnie LeMaster .02 .10
525 Dick Ruthven .02 .10
526 John McNamara MG .02 .10
527 Larry McWilliams .02 .10
528 Johnny Ray RC .20 .50
529 Pat Tabler .02 .10
530 Tom Herr .02 .10
531A San Diego Chicken .40 1.00
ERR Without TM
531B San Diego Chicken .40 1.00
COR With TM
532 Sal Butera .02 .10
533 Mike Griffin .02 .10
534 Kelvin Moore .02 .10
535 Reggie Jackson .15 .40
536 Ed Romero .02 .10
537 Derrel Thomas .02 .10
538 Mike O'Berry .02 .10
539 Jack O'Connor .02 .10
540 Bob Ojeda RC .20 .50
541 Roy Lee Jackson .02 .10
542 Lynn Jones .02 .10
543 Gaylord Perry .07 .20
544A Phil Garner ERR .07 .20
Reverse negative
544B Phil Garner COR .07 .20
545 Garry Templeton .07 .20
546 Rafael Ramirez .02 .10
547 Jeff Reardon .07 .20
548 Ron Guidry .07 .20
549 Tim Laudner .02 .10
550 John Henry Johnson .02 .10
551 Chris Bando .02 .10
552 Bobby Brown .02 .10
553 Larry Bradford .02 .10
554 Scott Fletcher RC .20 .50
555 Jerry Royster .02 .10
556 Shooty Babitt UER .02 .10
Spelled Babbitt
on front
557 Kent Hrbek RC .40 1.00
558 Ron Guidry .07 .20
Tommy John
559 Mark Bomback .02 .10
560 Julio Valdez .02 .10
561 Buck Martinez .02 .10
562 Mike A. Marshall RC .20 .50
563 Rennie Stennett .02 .10
564 Steve Crawford .02 .10
565 Bob Babcock .02 .10
566 Johnny Podres CO .07 .20
567 Paul Serna .02 .10
568 Harold Baines .07 .20
569 Dave LaRoche .02 .10
570 Lee May .02 .10
571 Gary Ward .02 .10
572 John Denny .02 .10
573 Roy Smalley .02 .10
574 Bob Brenly RC .40 1.00
575 Reggie Jackson .07 .20
Dave Winfield
576 Luis Pujols .02 .10
577 Butch Hobson .02 .10
578 Harvey Kuenn MG .02 .10
579 Cal Ripken Sr. CO .07 .20
580 Juan Berenguer .02 .10
581 Benny Ayala .02 .10
582 Vance Law .02 .10
583 Rick Leach .02 .10
584 George Frazier .02 .10
585 P.Rose/M.Schmidt .60 1.50
586 Joe Rudi .07 .20
587 Juan Beniquez .02 .10
588 Luis DeLeon .02 .10
589 Craig Swan .02 .10
590 Dave Chalk .02 .10
591 Billy Gardner MG .02 .10
592 Sal Bando .07 .20
593 Bert Campaneris .07 .20
594 Steve Kemp .02 .10
595A Randy Lerch ERR .15 .40
Braves
595B Randy Lerch COR .02 .10
Brewers
596 Bryan Clark RC .05 .15
597 Dave Ford .02 .10
598 Mike Scioscia .07 .20
599 John Lowenstein .02 .10
600 Rene Lachemann MG .02 .10
601 Mick Kelleher .02 .10
602 Ron Jackson .02 .10
603 Jerry Koosman .07 .20
604 Dave Goltz .02 .10
605 Ellis Valentine .02 .10
606 Lonnie Smith .02 .10
607 Joaquin Andujar .07 .20
608 Garry Hancock .02 .10
609 Jerry Turner .02 .10
610 Bob Bonner .02 .10
611 Jim Dwyer .02 .10
612 Terry Bulling .02 .10
613 Joel Youngblood .02 .10
614 Larry Milbourne .02 .10
615 Gene Roof UER .02 .10
Name on front
is Phil Roof
616 Keith Drumwright .02 .10
617 Dave Rosello .02 .10
618 Rickey Keeton .02 .10
619 Dennis Lamp .02 .10
620 Sid Monge .02 .10
621 Jerry White .02 .10
622 Luis Aguayo .02 .10
623 Jamie Easterly .02 .10
624 Steve Sax RC .40 1.00
625 Dave Roberts .02 .10
626 Rick Bosetti .02 .10
627 Terry Francona RC 1.25 3.00
628 Tom Seaver .30 .75
Johnny Bench
629 Paul Mirabella .02 .10
630 Rance Mulliniks .02 .10
631 Kevin Hickey RC .05 .15
632 Reid Nichols .02 .10
633 Dave Geisel .02 .10
634 Ken Griffey .07 .20
635 Bob Lemon MG .15 .40
636 Orlando Sanchez .02 .10
637 Bill Almon .02 .10
638 Danny Ainge .07 .20
639 Willie Stargell .15 .40
640 Bob Sykes .02 .10
641 Ed Lynch .02 .10
642 John Ellis .02 .10
643 Fergie Jenkins .07 .20
644 Lenn Sakata .02 .10
645 Julio Gonzalez .02 .10
646 Jesse Orosco .02 .10
647 Jerry Dybzinski .02 .10
648 Tommy Davis CO .07 .20
649 Ron Gardenhire RC .20 .50
650 Felipe Alou CO .07 .20
651 Harvey Haddix CO .07 .20
652 Willie Upshaw .20 .50
653 Bill Madlock .07 .20
654A DK Checklist 1-26 .15 .40
ERR Unnumbered
With Trammel
654B DK Checklist 1-26 .07 .20
COR Unnumbered
With Trammell
655 Checklist 27-130 .07 .20
Unnumbered
656 Checklist 131-234 .07 .20
Unnumbered
657 Checklist 235-338 .07 .20
Unnumbered
658 Checklist 339-442 .07 .20
Unnumbered
659 Checklist 443-544 .07 .20
Unnumbered
660 Checklist 545-653 .07 .20
Unnumbered

1982 Donruss Babe Ruth Puzzle

1 Ruth Puzzle 1-3 .20 .50
4 Ruth Puzzle 4-6 .20 .50
7 Ruth Puzzle 7-10 .20 .50
10 Ruth Puzzle 10-12 .20 .50
13 Ruth Puzzle 13-15 .20 .50
16 Ruth Puzzle 16-18 .20 .50
19 Ruth Puzzle 19-21 .20 .50
22 Ruth Puzzle 22-24 .20 .50
25 Ruth Puzzle 25-27 .20 .50
28 Ruth Puzzle 28-30 .20 .50
31 Ruth Puzzle 29-31 .20 .50
34 Ruth Puzzle 34-36 .20 .50
37 Ruth Puzzle 37-39 .20 .50
40 Ruth Puzzle 40-42 .20 .50
43 Ruth Puzzle 43-45 .20 .50
46 Ruth Puzzle 46-48 .20 .50
49 Ruth Puzzle 49-51 .20 .50
52 Ruth Puzzle 52-54 .20 .50
55 Ruth Puzzle 55-57 .20 .50
58 Ruth Puzzle 58-60 .20 .50
61 Ruth Puzzle 61-63 .20 .50

1983 Donruss

The 1983 Donruss baseball set leads off with a 26-card Diamond Kings (DK) series. Of the remaining 634 standard-size cards, two are combination cards, one portrays the San Diego Chicken, one shows the completed Ty Cobb puzzle, and seven are unnumbered checklist cards. The seven unnumbered checklist cards are arbitrarily assigned numbers 654 through 660 and are listed at the end of the list below. All cards measure the standard size. Card fronts feature full color photos around a framed white broder. Several printing variations are available but the complete set price below includes only the more common of each variation pair. Cards were issued in 15-card packs which included a three-piece Ty Cobb puzzle panel (21 different panels were needed to complete the puzzle). Notable Rookie Cards include Wade Boggs, Tony Gwynn and Ryne Sandberg.

COMPLETE SET (660) 25.00 60.00
COMP.FACT.SET (660) 30.00 80.00
COMP.COBB PUZZLE 2.00 5.00
1 Fernando Valenzuela DK .07 .20
2 Rollie Fingers DK .07 .20
3 Reggie Jackson DK .15 .40
4 Jim Palmer DK .07 .20
5 Jack Morris DK .07 .20
6 George Foster DK .07 .20
7 Jim Sundberg DK .07 .20
8 Willie Stargell DK .15 .40
9 Dave Stieb DK .07 .20
10 Joe Niekro DK .02 .10
11 Rickey Henderson DK .60 1.50
12 Dale Murphy DK .15 .40
13 Toby Harrah DK .07 .20
14 Bill Buckner DK .07 .20
15 Willie Wilson DK .07 .20
16 Steve Carlton DK .15 .40
17 Ron Guidry DK .07 .20
18 Steve Rogers DK .07 .20
19 Kent Hrbek DK .07 .20
20 Keith Hernandez DK .07 .20
21 Floyd Bannister DK .02 .10
22 Johnny Bench DK .30 .75
23 Britt Burns DK .02 .10
24 Joe Morgan DK .07 .20
25 Carl Yastrzemski DK .30 .75
26 Terry Kennedy DK .02 .10
27 Gary Roenicke .02 .10
28 Dwight Bernard .02 .10
29 Pat Underwood .02 .10
30 Gary Allenson .02 .10
31 Ron Guidry .07 .20
32 Burt Hooton .02 .10
33 Chris Bando .02 .10
34 Vida Blue .07 .20
35 Rickey Henderson .60 1.50
36 Ray Burris .02 .10
37 John Butcher .02 .10
38 Don Aase .02 .10
39 Jerry Koosman .07 .20
40 Bruce Sutter .15 .40
41 Jose Cruz .07 .20
42 Pete Rose 1.00 2.50
43 Cesar Cedeno .07 .20
44 Floyd Chiffer .02 .10
45 Larry McWilliams .02 .10
46 Alan Fowlkes .02 .10
47 Dale Murphy .15 .40
48 Doug Bird .02 .10
49 Hubie Brooks .02 .10
50 Floyd Bannister .02 .10
51 Jack O'Connor .02 .10
52 Steve Senteney .02 .10
53 Gary Gaetti RC .40 1.00
54 Damaso Garcia .02 .10
55 Gene Nelson .02 .10
56 Mookie Wilson .07 .20
57 Allen Ripley .02 .10
58 Bob Horner .07 .20
59 Tony Pena .02 .10
60 Gary Lavelle .02 .10
61 Tim Lollar .02 .10
62 Frank Pastore .02 .10
63 Garry Maddox .02 .10
64 Bob Forsch .02 .10
65 Harry Spilman .02 .10
66 Geoff Zahn .02 .10
67 Salome Barojas .02 .10
68 David Palmer .02 .10
69 Charlie Hough .07 .20
70 Dan Quisenberry .02 .10
71 Tony Armas .07 .20
72 Rick Sutcliffe .07 .20
73 Steve Balboni .02 .10
74 Jerry Remy .02 .10
75 Mike Scioscia .07 .20
76 John Wockenfuss .02 .10
77 Jim Palmer .07 .20
78 Rollie Fingers .07 .20
79 Joe Nolan .02 .10
80 Pete Vuckovich .02 .10
81 Rick Leach .02 .10
82 Rick Miller .02 .10
83 Graig Nettles .07 .20
84 Ron Cey .07 .20
85 Miguel Dilone .02 .10
86 John Wathan .02 .10
87 Kelvin Moore .02 .10
88A Byrn Smith ERR .07 .20
Sic, Bryn
88B Bryn Smith FDC COR .15 .40
89 Dave Hostetler RC .02 .10
90 Rod Carew .15 .40
91 Lonnie Smith .02 .10
92 Bob Knepper .02 .10
93 Marty Bystrom .02 .10
94 Chris Welsh .02 .10
95 Jason Thompson .02 .10
96 Tom O'Malley .02 .10
97 Phil Niekro .07 .20
98 Neil Allen .02 .10
99 Bill Buckner .07 .20
100 Ed VandeBerg .02 .10
101 Jim Clancy .02 .10
102 Robert Castillo .02 .10
103 Bruce Berenyi .02 .10
104 Carlton Fisk .15 .40
105 Mike Flanagan .02 .10
106 Cecil Cooper .07 .20
107 Jack Morris .07 .20
108 Mike Morgan .02 .10
109 Luis Aponte .02 .10
110 Pedro Guerrero .07 .20
111 Len Barker .02 .10
112 Willie Wilson .07 .20
113 Dave Beard .02 .10
114 Mike Gates .02 .10
115 Reggie Jackson .15 .40
116 George Wright RC .20 .50
117 Vance Law .02 .10
118 Nolan Ryan 1.50 4.00
119 Mike Krukow .02 .10
120 Ozzie Smith .50 1.25
121 Broderick Perkins .02 .10
122 Tom Seaver .30 .75
123 Chris Chambliss .07 .20
124 Chuck Tanner MG .02 .10
125 Johnnie LeMaster .02 .10
126 Mel Hall RC .20 .50
127 Bruce Bochte .02 .10
128 Charlie Puleo .02 .10
129 Luis Leal .02 .10
130 John Pacella .02 .10
131 Glenn Gulliver .02 .10
132 Don Money .02 .10
133 Dave Rozema .02 .10
134 Bruce Hurst .02 .10
135 Rudy May .02 .10
136 Tom Lasorda MG .15 .40
137 Dan Spillner UER .02 .10
Photo actually
Ed Whitson
138 Jerry Martin .02 .10
139 Mike Norris .02 .10
140 Al Oliver .07 .20
141 Daryl Sconiers .02 .10
142 Lamar Johnson .02 .10
143 Harold Baines .07 .20
144 Alan Ashby .02 .10
145 Garry Templeton .07 .20
146 Al Holland .02 .10
147 Bo Diaz .02 .10
148 Dave Concepcion .07 .20
149 Rick Camp .02 .10
150 Jim Morrison .02 .10
151 Randy Martz .02 .10
152 Keith Hernandez .07 .20
153 John Lowenstein .02 .10
154 Mike Caldwell .02 .10
155 Milt Wilcox .02 .10
156 Rich Gedman .02 .10
157 Rich Gossage .07 .20
158 Jerry Reuss .02 .10
159 Ron Hassey .02 .10
160 Larry Gura .02 .10
161 Dwayne Murphy .02 .10
162 Woodie Fryman .02 .10
163 Steve Comer .02 .10
164 Ken Forsch .02 .10
165 Dennis Lamp .02 .10
166 David Green RC .20 .50
167 Terry Puhl .02 .10
168 Mike Schmidt .75 2.00
169 Eddie Milner .02 .10
170 John Curtis .02 .10
171 Don Robinson .02 .10
172 Rich Gale .02 .10
173 Steve Bedrosian .02 .10
174 Willie Hernandez .02 .10
175 Ron Gardenhire .02 .10
176 Jim Beattie .02 .10
177 Tim Laudner .02 .10
178 Buck Martinez .02 .10
179 Kent Hrbek .07 .20
180 Alfredo Griffin .02 .10
181 Larry Andersen .02 .10
182 Pete Falcone .02 .10
183 Jody Davis .02 .10
184 Glenn Hubbard .02 .10
185 Dale Berra .02 .10
186 Greg Minton .02 .10
187 Gary Lucas .02 .10
188 Dave Van Gorder .02 .10
189 Bob Dernier .02 .10
190 Willie McGee RC .60 1.50
191 Dickie Thon .02 .10
192 Bob Boone .07 .20
193 Britt Burns .02 .10
194 Jeff Reardon .07 .20
195 Jon Matlack .02 .10
196 Don Slaught RC .20 .50
197 Fred Stanley .02 .10
198 Rick Manning .02 .10
199 Dave Righetti .07 .20
200 Dave Stapleton .02 .10
201 Steve Yeager .07 .20
202 Enos Cabell .02 .10
203 Sammy Stewart .02 .10
204 Moose Haas .02 .10
205 Lenn Sakata .02 .10
206 Charlie Moore .02 .10
207 Alan Trammell .07 .20
208 Jim Rice .07 .20
209 Roy Smalley .02 .10
210 Bill Russell .07 .20
211 Andre Thornton .02 .10
212 Willie Aikens .02 .10
213 Dave McKay .02 .10
214 Tim Blackwell .02 .10
215 Buddy Bell .07 .20
216 Doug DeCinces .02 .10
217 Tom Herr .02 .10
218 Frank LaCorte .02 .10
219 Steve Carlton .15 .40
220 Terry Kennedy .02 .10
221 Mike Easler .02 .10
222 Jack Clark .07 .20
223 Gene Garber .02 .10
224 Scott Holman .02 .10
225 Mike Proly .02 .10
226 Terry Bulling .02 .10
227 Jerry Garvin .02 .10
228 Ron Davis .02 .10
229 Tom Hume .02 .10
230 Marc Hill .02 .10
231 Dennis Martinez .07 .20
232 Jim Gantner .02 .10
233 Larry Pashnick .02 .10
234 Dave Collins .02 .10
235 Tom Burgmeier .02 .10
236 Ken Landreaux .02 .10
237 John Denny .02 .10
238 Hal McRae .07 .20
239 Matt Keough .02 .10
240 Doug Flynn .02 .10
241 Fred Lynn .07 .20
242 Billy Sample .02 .10
243 Tom Paciorek .02 .10
244 Joe Sambito .02 .10
245 Sid Monge .02 .10
246 Ken Oberkfell .02 .10
247 Joe Pittman UER .02 .10
Photo actually
Juan Eichelberger
248 Mario Soto .07 .20
249 Claudell Washington .02 .10
250 Rick Rhoden .02 .10
251 Darrell Evans .07 .20
252 Steve Henderson .02 .10
253 Manny Castillo .02 .10
254 Craig Swan .02 .10
255 Joey McLaughlin .02 .10
256 Pete Redfern .02 .10
257 Ken Singleton .07 .20
258 Robin Yount .50 1.25
259 Elias Sosa .02 .10
260 Bob Ojeda .02 .10
261 Bobby Murcer .07 .20
262 Candy Maldonado RC .20 .50
263 Rick Waits .02 .10
264 Greg Pryor .02 .10
265 Bob Owchinko .02 .10
266 Chris Speier .02 .10
267 Bruce Kison .02 .10
268 Mark Wagner .02 .10
269 Steve Kemp .02 .10
270 Phil Garner .07 .20
271 Gene Richards .02 .10
272 Renie Martin .02 .10
273 Dave Roberts .02 .10
274 Dan Driessen .02 .10
275 Rufino Linares .02 .10
276 Lee Lacy .02 .10
277 Ryne Sandberg RC 8.00 20.00
278 Darrell Porter .02 .10
279 Cal Ripken 4.00 10.00
280 Jamie Easterly .02 .10
281 Bill Fahey .02 .10
282 Glenn Hoffman .02 .10
283 Willie Randolph .07 .20
284 Fernando Valenzuela .07 .20
285 Alan Bannister .02 .10
286 Paul Splittorff .02 .10
287 Joe Rudi .07 .20
288 Bill Gullickson .02 .10
289 Danny Darwin .02 .10
290 Andy Hassler .02 .10
291 Ernesto Escarrega .02 .10
292 Steve Mura .02 .10
293 Tony Scott .02 .10
294 Manny Trillo .02 .10
295 Greg Harris .02 .10
296 Luis DeLeon .02 .10
297 Kent Tekulve .02 .10
298 Atlee Hammaker .02 .10
299 Bruce Benedict .02 .10
300 Fergie Jenkins .07 .20
301 Dave Kingman .07 .20
302 Bill Caudill .02 .10
303 John Castino .02 .10
304 Ernie Whitt .02 .10
305 Randy Johnson RC .02 .10
306 Garth Iorg .02 .10
307 Gaylord Perry .07 .20
308 Ed Lynch .02 .10
309 Keith Moreland .02 .10
310 Rafael Ramirez .02 .10
311 Bill Madlock .07 .20
312 Milt May .02 .10
313 John Montefusco .02 .10
314 Wayne Krenchicki .02 .10
315 George Vukovich .02 .10
316 Joaquin Andujar .07 .20
317 Craig Reynolds .02 .10
318 Rick Burleson .02 .10
319 Richard Dotson .02 .10
320 Steve Rogers .07 .20
321 Dave Schmidt .02 .10
322 Bud Black RC .20 .50
323 Jeff Burroughs .02 .10
324 Von Hayes .02 .10
325 Butch Wynegar .02 .10
326 Carl Yastrzemski .50 1.25
327 Ron Roenicke .02 .10
328 Howard Johnson RC .40 1.00
329 Rick Dempsey UER .02 .10
Posing as a left-
handed batter
330A Jim Slaton .02 .10
Bio printed
black on white
330B Jim Slaton .07 .20
Bio printed
black on yellow
331 Benny Ayala .02 .10
332 Ted Simmons .07 .20
333 Lou Whitaker .07 .20
334 Chuck Rainey .02 .10
335 Lou Piniella .07 .20
336 Steve Sax .07 .20
337 Toby Harrah .07 .20
338 George Brett .75 2.00
339 Dave Lopes .07 .20
340 Gary Carter .07 .20
341 John Grubb .02 .10
342 Tim Foli .02 .10
343 Jim Kaat .07 .20
344 Mike LaCoss .02 .10
345 Larry Christenson .02 .10
346 Juan Bonilla .02 .10
347 Omar Moreno .02 .10
348 Chili Davis .07 .20
349 Tommy Boggs .02 .10
350 Rusty Staub .07 .20
351 Bump Wills .02 .10
352 Rick Sweet .02 .10
353 Jim Gott RC .20 .50
354 Terry Felton .02 .10
355 Jim Kern .02 .10
356 Bill Almon UER .02 .10
Expos
Mets in 1980,
not Padres
Mets
357 Tippy Martinez .02 .10
358 Roy Howell .02 .10
359 Dan Petry .02 .10
360 Jerry Mumphrey .02 .10
361 Mark Clear .02 .10
362 Mike Marshall .02 .10
363 Lary Sorensen .02 .10
364 Amos Otis .07 .20
365 Rick Langford .02 .10
366 Brad Mills .02 .10
367 Brian Downing .07 .20
368 Mike Richardt .02 .10
369 Aurelio Rodriguez .02 .10
370 Dave Smith .02 .10
371 Tug McGraw .07 .20
372 Doug Bair .02 .10
373 Ruppert Jones .02 .10
374 Alex Trevino .02 .10
375 Ken Dayley .02 .10
376 Rod Scurry .02 .10
377 Bob Brenly .02 .10
378 Scot Thompson .02 .10
379 Julio Cruz .02 .10
380 John Stearns .02 .10
381 Dale Murray .02 .10
382 Frank Viola RC .60 1.50
383 Al Bumbry .02 .10
384 Ben Oglivie .07 .20
385 Dave Tobik .02 .10
386 Bob Stanley .02 .10
387 Andre Robertson .02 .10
388 Jorge Orta .02 .10
389 Ed Whitson .02 .10
390 Don Hood .02 .10
391 Tom Underwood .02 .10
392 Tim Wallach .07 .20
393 Steve Renko .02 .10
394 Mickey Rivers .02 .10
395 Greg Luzinski .07 .20
396 Art Howe .02 .10
397 Alan Wiggins .02 .10
398 Jim Barr .02 .10
399 Ivan DeJesus .02 .10
400 Tom Lawless .02 .10
401 Bob Walk .02 .10
402 Jimmy Smith .02 .10
403 Lee Smith .15 .40
404 George Hendrick .07 .20
405 Eddie Murray .30 .75
406 Marshall Edwards .02 .10
407 Lance Parrish .07 .20
408 Carney Lansford .07 .20

409 Dave Winfield .07 .20
410 Bob Welch .07 .20
411 Larry Milbourne .02 .10
412 Dennis Leonard .02 .10
413 Dan Meyer .02 .10
414 Charlie Lea .02 .10
415 Rick Honeycutt .02 .10
416 Mike Witt .02 .10
417 Steve Trout .02 .10
418 Glenn Brummer .02 .10
419 Denny Walling .02 .10
420 Gary Matthews .07 .20
421 Charlie Leibrandt UER .02 .10
Liebrandt on
front of card
422 Juan Eichelberger UER .02 .10
Photo actually
Joe Pittma
423 Cecilio Guante UER .02 .10
Listed as Matt
on card
424 Bill Laskey .02 .10
425 Jerry Royster .02 .10
426 Dickie Noles .02 .10
427 George Foster .07 .20
428 Mike Moore RC .20 .50
429 Gary Ward .02 .10
430 Barry Bonnell .02 .10
431 Ron Washington RC .10 .25
432 Rance Mulliniks .02 .10
433 Mike Stanton .02 .10
434 Jesse Orosco .02 .10
435 Larry Bowa .07 .20
436 Biff Pocoroba .02 .10
437 Johnny Ray .02 .10
438 Joe Morgan .07 .20
439 Eric Show RC .20 .50
440 Larry Biittner .02 .10
441 Greg Gross .02 .10
442 Gene Tenace .07 .20
443 Danny Heep .02 .10
444 Bobby Clark .02 .10
445 Kevin Hickey .02 .10
446 Scott Sanderson .02 .10
447 Frank Tanana .07 .20
448 Cesar Geronimo .02 .10
449 Jimmy Sexton .02 .10
450 Mike Hargrove .02 .10
451 Doyle Alexander .02 .10
452 Dwight Evans .15 .40
453 Terry Forster .07 .20
454 Tom Brookens .02 .10
455 Rich Dauer .02 .10
456 Rob Picciolo .02 .10
457 Terry Crowley .02 .10
458 Ned Yost .02 .10
459 Kirk Gibson .07 .20
460 Reid Nichols .02 .10
461 Oscar Gamble .02 .10
462 Dusty Baker .07 .20
463 Jack Perconte .02 .10
464 Frank White .07 .20
465 Mickey Klutts .02 .10
466 Warren Cromartie .02 .10
467 Larry Parrish .02 .10
468 Bobby Grich .07 .20
469 Dane Iorg .02 .10
470 Joe Niekro .02 .10
471 Ed Farmer .02 .10
472 Tim Flannery .02 .10
473 Dave Parker .07 .20
474 Jeff Leonard .02 .10
475 Al Hrabosky .02 .10
476 Ron Hodges .02 .10
477 Leon Durham .02 .10
478 Jim Essian .02 .10
479 Roy Lee Jackson .02 .10
480 Brad Havens .02 .10
481 Joe Price .02 .10
482 Tony Bernazard .02 .10
483 Scott McGregor .02 .10
484 Paul Molitor .07 .20
485 Mike Ivie .02 .10
486 Ken Griffey .07 .20
487 Dennis Eckersley .15 .40
488 Steve Garvey .07 .20
489 Mike Fischlin .02 .10
490 U.L. Washington .02 .10
491 Steve McCatty .02 .10
492 Roy Johnson .02 .10
493 Don Baylor .07 .20
494 Bobby Johnson .02 .10
495 Mike Squires .02 .10
496 Bert Roberge .02 .10
497 Dick Ruthven .02 .10
498 Tito Landrum .02 .10
499 Sixto Lezcano .02 .10
500 Johnny Bench .30 .75
501 Larry Whisenton .02 .10
502 Manny Sarmiento .02 .10
503 Fred Breining .02 .10
504 Bill Campbell .02 .10
505 Todd Cruz .02 .10
506 Bob Bailor .02 .10
507 Dave Stieb .07 .20
508 Al Williams .02 .10
509 Dan Ford .02 .10
510 Gorman Thomas .07 .20
511 Chet Lemon .07 .20
512 Mike Torrez .02 .10
513 Shane Rawley .02 .10
514 Mark Belanger .02 .10
515 Rodney Craig .02 .10
516 Onix Concepcion .02 .10
517 Mike Heath .02 .10
518 Andre Dawson UER .07 .20
Middle name Fernando,
should be Nolan
519 Luis Sanchez .02 .10
520 Terry Bogener .02 .10
521 Rudy Law .02 .10
522 Ray Knight .07 .20
523 Joe Lefebvre .02 .10
524 Jim Wohlford .02 .10
525 Julio Franco RC 2.50 6.00
526 Ron Oester .02 .10
527 Rick Mahler .02 .10
528 Steve Nicosia .02 .10
529 Junior Kennedy .02 .10
530A Whitey Herzog MG .07 .20
Bio printed
black on white
530B Whitey Herzog MG .07 .20
Bio printed
black on yellow
531A Don Sutton .07 .20
Blue border
on photo
531B Don Sutton .07 .20
Green border
on photo
532 Mark Brouhard .02 .10
533A Sparky Anderson MG .07 .20
Bio printed
black on white
533B Sparky Anderson MG .07 .20
Bio printed
black on yellow
534 Roger LaFrancois .02 .10
535 George Frazier .02 .10
536 Tom Niedenfuer .02 .10
537 Ed Glynn .02 .10
538 Lee May .02 .10
539 Bob Kearney .02 .10
540 Tim Raines .07 .20
541 Paul Mirabella .02 .10
542 Luis Tiant .07 .20
543 Ron LeFlore .07 .20
544 Dave LaPoint .02 .10
545 Randy Moffitt .02 .10
546 Luis Aguayo .02 .10
547 Brad Lesley .05 .15
548 Luis Salazar .02 .10
549 John Candelaria .02 .10
550 Dave Bergman .02 .10
551 Bob Watson .02 .10
552 Pat Tabler .02 .10
553 Brent Gaff .02 .10
554 Al Cowens .02 .10
555 Tom Brunansky .07 .20
556 Lloyd Moseby .02 .10
557A Pascual Perez ERR .75 2.00
557B Pascual Perez COR .07 .20
Braves in glove
558 Willie Upshaw .02 .10
559 Richie Zisk .02 .10
560 Pat Zachry .02 .10
561 Jay Johnstone .02 .10
562 Carlos Diaz RC .05 .15
563 John Tudor .07 .20
564 Frank Robinson MG .15 .40
565 Dave Edwards .02 .10
566 Paul Householder .02 .10
567 Ron Reed .02 .10
568 Mike Ramsey .02 .10
569 Kiko Garcia .02 .10
570 Tommy John .07 .20
571 Tony LaRussa MG .07 .20
572 Joel Youngblood .02 .10
573 Wayne Tolleson .02 .10
574 Keith Creel .02 .10
575 Billy Martin MG .15 .40
576 Jerry Dybzinski .02 .10
577 Rick Cerone .02 .10
578 Tony Perez .15 .40
579 Greg Brock .02 .10
580 Glenn Wilson .20 .50
581 Tim Stoddard .02 .10
582 Bob McClure .02 .10
583 Jim Dwyer .02 .10
584 Ed Romero .02 .10
585 Larry Herndon .02 .10
586 Wade Boggs RC 8.00 20.00
587 Jay Howell .02 .10
588 Dave Stewart .07 .20
589 Bert Blyleven .07 .20
590 Dick Howser MG .02 .10
591 Wayne Gross .02 .10
592 Terry Francona .07 .20
593 Don Werner .02 .10
594 Bill Stein .02 .10
595 Jesse Barfield .07 .20
596 Bob Molinaro .02 .10
597 Mike Vail .02 .10
598 Tony Gwynn RC 12.00 30.00
599 Gary Rajsich .02 .10
600 Jerry Ujdur .02 .10
601 Cliff Johnson .02 .10
602 Jerry White .02 .10
603 Bryan Clark .02 .10
604 Joe Ferguson .02 .10
605 Guy Sularz .02 .10
606A Ozzie Virgil .07 .20
Green border
on photo
606B Ozzie Virgil .07 .20
Orange border
on photo
607 Terry Harper .02 .10
608 Harvey Kuenn MG .02 .10
609 Jim Sundberg .07 .20
610 Willie Stargell .15 .40
611 Reggie Smith .07 .20
612 Rob Wilfong .02 .10
613 Joe Niekro .07 .20
Phil Niekro
614 Lee Elia MG .02 .10
615 Mickey Hatcher .02 .10
616 Jerry Hairston .02 .10
617 John Martin .02 .10
618 Wally Backman .02 .10
619 Storm Davis RC .20 .50
620 Alan Knicely .02 .10
621 John Stuper .02 .10
622 Matt Sinatro .02 .10
623 Geno Petralli .20 .50
624 Duane Walker RC .02 .10
625 Dick Williams MG .02 .10
626 Pat Corrales MG .02 .10
627 Vern Ruhle .02 .10
628 Joe Torre MG .07 .20
629 Anthony Johnson .02 .10
630 Steve Howe .02 .10
631 Gary Woods .02 .10
632 LaMarr Hoyt .02 .10
633 Steve Swisher .02 .10
634 Terry Leach .02 .10
635 Jeff Newman .02 .10
636 Brett Butler .07 .20
637 Gary Gray .02 .10
638 Lee Mazzilli .07 .20
639A Ron Jackson ERR 8.00 20.00
639B Ron Jackson COR .02 .10
Angels in glove,
red border
on photo
639C Ron Jackson COR .15 .40
Angels in glove,
green border
on photo
640 Juan Beniquez .02 .10
641 Dave Rucker .02 .10
642 Luis Pujols .02 .10
643 Rick Monday .07 .20
644 Hosken Powell .02 .10
645 The Chicken .15 .40
646 Dave Engle .02 .10
647 Dick Davis .02 .10
648 Frank Robinson .15 .40
Vida Blue
Joe Morgan
649 Al Chambers .02 .10
650 Jesus Vega .02 .10
651 Jeff Jones .02 .10
652 Marvis Foley .02 .10
653 Ty Cobb Puzzle Card .30 .75
654A Dick Perez .15 .40
Diamond
King Checklist 1-26
Unnumbered ERR
Word 'checklist'
omitted from back
654B Dick Perez .15 .40
Diamond
King Checklist 1-26
Unnumbered COR
Word 'checklist'
is on back
655 Checklist 27-130 .02 .10
Unnumbered
656 Checklist 131-234 .02 .10
Unnumbered
657 Checklist 235-338 .02 .10
Unnumbered
658 Checklist 339-442 .02 .10
Unnumbered
659 Checklist 443-544 .02 .10
Unnumbered
660 Checklist 545-653 .02 .10
Unnumbered

1983 Donruss Mickey Mantle Puzzle

1 Mantle Puzzle 1-3 .10 .25
4 Mantle Puzzle 4-6 .10 .25
7 Mantle Puzzle 7-9 .10 .25
10 Mantle Puzzle 10-12 .10 .25
13 Mantle Puzzle 13-15 .10 .25
16 Mantle Puzzle 16-18 .10 .25
19 Mantle Puzzle 19-21 .10 .25
22 Mantle Puzzle 22-24 .10 .25
25 Mantle Puzzle 25-27 .10 .25
28 Mantle Puzzle 28-30 .10 .25
31 Mantle Puzzle 31-33 .10 .25
34 Mantle Puzzle 34-36 .10 .25
37 Mantle Puzzle 37-39 .10 .25
40 Mantle Puzzle 40-42 .10 .25
43 Mantle Puzzle 43-45 .10 .25
46 Mantle Puzzle 46-48 .10 .25
49 Mantle Puzzle 49-51 .10 .25
52 Mantle Puzzle 52-54 .10 .25
55 Mantle Puzzle 55-57 .10 .25
58 Mantle Puzzle 58-60 .10 .25
61 Mantle Puzzle 61-63 .10 .25

1983 Donruss Ty Cobb Puzzle

1 Cobb Puzzle 1-3 .10 .25
4 Cobb Puzzle 4-6 .10 .25
7 Cobb Puzzle 7-10 .10 .25
10 Cobb Puzzle 10-12 .10 .25
13 Cobb Puzzle 13-15 .10 .25
16 Cobb Puzzle 16-18 .10 .25
19 Cobb Puzzle 19-21 .10 .25
22 Cobb Puzzle 22-24 .10 .25
25 Cobb Puzzle 25-27 .10 .25
28 Cobb Puzzle 28-30 .10 .25
31 Cobb Puzzle 29-31 .10 .25
34 Cobb Puzzle 34-36 .10 .25
37 Cobb Puzzle 37-39 .10 .25
40 Cobb Puzzle 40-42 .10 .25
43 Cobb Puzzle 43-45 .10 .25
46 Cobb Puzzle 46-48 .10 .25
49 Cobb Puzzle 49-51 .10 .25
52 Cobb Puzzle 52-54 .10 .25
55 Cobb Puzzle 55-57 .10 .25
58 Cobb Puzzle 58-60 .10 .25
61 Cobb Puzzle 61-63 .10 .25

1983 Donruss Action All-Stars

COMPLETE SET (60) 3.00 8.00
COMP.MANTLE PUZZLE 6.00 15.00
1 Eddie Murray .25 .60
2 Dwight Evans .02 .10
3A Reggie Jackson ERR
(Red screen on back 1.25 3.00
covers so
3B Reggie Jackson COR .20 .50
4 Greg Luzinski .02 .10
5 Larry Herndon .01 .05
6 Al Oliver .02 .10
7 Bill Buckner .02 .10
8 Jason Thompson .01 .05
9 Andre Dawson .15 .40
10 Greg Minton .01 .05
11 Terry Kennedy .01 .05
12 Phil Niekro .15 .40
13 Willie Wilson .01 .05
14 Johnny Bench .20 .50
15 Ron Guidry .02 .10
16 Hal McRae .01 .05
17 Damaso Garcia .01 .05
18 Gary Ward .01 .05
19 Cecil Cooper .02 .10
20 Keith Hernandez .02 .10
21 Ron Cey .02 .10
22 Rickey Henderson .20 .50
23 Nolan Ryan 1.25 3.00
24 Steve Carlton .15 .40
25 John Stearns .01 .05
26 Jim Sundberg .01 .05
27 Joaquin Andujar .01 .05
28 Gaylord Perry .10 .30
29 Jack Clark .02 .10
30 Bill Madlock .02 .10
31 Pete Rose .30 .75
32 Mookie Wilson .02 .10
33 Rollie Fingers .10 .30
34 Lonnie Smith .01 .05
35 Tony Pena .02 .10
36 Dave Winfield .15 .40
37 Tim Lollar .01 .05
38 Rod Carew .15 .40
39 Toby Harrah .01 .05
40 Buddy Bell .02 .10
41 Bruce Sutter .07 .20
42 George Brett .50 1.25
43 Carlton Fisk .20 .50
44 Carl Yastrzemski .20 .50
45 Dale Murphy .07 .20
46 Bob Horner .01 .05
47 Dave Concepcion .02 .10
48 Dave Stieb .01 .05
49 Kent Hrbek .02 .10
50 Lance Parrish .02 .10
51 Joe Niekro .01 .05
52 Cal Ripken 1.25 3.00
53 Fernando Valenzuela .02 .10
54 Richie Zisk .01 .05
55 Leon Durham .01 .05
56 Robin Yount .20 .50
57 Mike Schmidt .30 .75
58 Gary Carter .20 .50
59 Fred Lynn .02 .10
60 Checklist Card .01 .05

1983 Donruss HOF Heroes

COMPLETE SET (44) 4.00 10.00
1 Ty Cobb .40 1.00
2 Walter Johnson .15 .40
3 Christy Mathewson .15 .40
4 Josh Gibson .15 .40
5 Honus Wagner .30 .75
6 Jackie Robinson .50 1.25
7 Mickey Mantle 1.00 2.50
8 Luke Appling .01 .05
9 Ted Williams .40 1.00
10 Johnny Mize .05 .15
11 Satchel Paige .15 .40
12 Lou Boudreau .01 .05
13 Jimmie Foxx .05 .15
14 Duke Snider .15 .40
15 Monte Irvin .05 .15
16 Hank Greenberg .08 .25
17 Roberto Clemente .50 1.25
18 Al Kaline .15 .40
19 Frank Robinson .15 .40
20 Joe Cronin .05 .15
21 Burleigh Grimes .01 .05
22 The Waner Brothers .01 .05
Paul Waner
Lloyd Waner
23 Grover Alexander .05 .15
24 Yogi Berra .15 .40
25 Cool Papa Bell .05 .15
26 Bill Dickey .05 .15
27 Cy Young .08 .25
28 Charlie Gehringer .01 .05
29 Dizzy Dean .15 .40
30 Bob Lemon .05 .15
31 Red Ruffing .01 .05
32 Stan Musial .30 .75
33 Carl Hubbell .08 .25
34 Hank Aaron .30 .75
35 John McGraw .01 .05
36 Bob Feller .15 .40
37 Casey Stengel .15 .40
38 Ralph Kiner .05 .15
39 Roy Campanella .15 .40
40 Mel Ott .05 .15
41 Robin Roberts .05 .15
42 Early Wynn .01 .05
43 Mantle Puzzle Card 1.00 2.50
44 Checklist Card .01 .05

1984 Donruss

The 1984 Donruss set contains a total of 660 standard-size cards; however, only 658 are numbered. The first 26 cards in the set are again Diamond Kings (DK). A new feature, Rated Rookies (RR), was introduced with this set with Bill Madden's 20 selections comprising numbers 27 through 46. Two "Living Legend" cards designated A (featuring Gaylord Perry and Rollie Fingers) and B (featuring Johnny Bench and Carl Yastrzemski) were issued as bonus cards in wax packs, but were not issued in the factory sets sold to hobby dealers. The seven unnumbered checklist cards are arbitrarily assigned numbers 652 through 658 and are listed at the end of the list below. The attractive card front designs changed considerably from the previous two years. This set has since grown in stature to be recognized as one of the finest produced in the 1980's. The backs contain statistics and are printed in green and black ink. The cards, issued amongst other ways in 15 card packs which had a 30 cent SRP, were distributed with a three-piece puzzle panel of Duke Snider. There are no extra variation cards included in the complete set price below. The variation cards apparently resulted from a different printing for the factory sets as the Darling and Stenhouse no number variations as well as the Perez-Steele errors were corrected in the factory sets which were released later in the year. The factory sets were shipped 15 to a case. The Diamond King cards found in packs spelled Perez-Steele as Perez-Steel. Rookie Cards in this set include Joe Carter, Don Mattingly, Darryl Strawberry, and Andy Van Slyke. The Joe Carter card is almost never found well centered.

COMPLETE SET (660) 60.00 120.00
COMP.FACT.SET (658) 100.00 175.00
COMP.SNIDER PUZZLE 2.00 5.00
1 Robin Yount DK COR 1.00 2.50
1A Robin Yount DK ERR 2.00 5.00
2 Dave Concepcion DK .30 .75
COR
2A Dave Concepcion DK .30 .75
ERR Perez Steel
3 Dwayne Murphy DK .08 .25
COR
3A Dwayne Murphy DK .08 .25
ERR Perez Steel
4 John Castino DK COR .08 .25
4A John Castino DK ERR .08 .25
Perez Steel
5 Leon Durham DK COR .30 .75
5A Leon Durham DK ERR .08 .25
Perez Steel
6 Rusty Staub DK COR .30 .75
6A Rusty Staub DK ERR .30 .75
Perez Steel
7 Jack Clark DK COR .30 .75
7A Jack Clark DK ERR .30 .75
Perez Steel
8 Dave Dravecky DK .08 .25
COR
8A Dave Dravecky DK .08 .25
ERR Perez Steel
9 Al Oliver DK COR .30 .75
9A Al Oliver DK ERR .30 .75
Perez Steel
10 Dave Righetti DK .30 .75
COR
10A Dave Righetti DK .30 .75
ERR Perez Steel
11 Hal McRae DK COR .30 .75
11A Hal McRae DK ERR .30 .75
Perez Steel
12 Ray Knight DK COR .30 .75
12A Ray Knight DK ERR .30 .75
Perez Steel
13 Bruce Sutter DK COR .60 1.50
13A Bruce Sutter DK ERR .60 1.50
Perez Steel
14 Bob Horner DK COR .30 .75
14A Bob Horner DK ERR .30 .75
Perez Steel
15 Lance Parrish DK .30 .75
COR
15A Lance Parrish DK .30 .75
ERR Perez Steel
16 Matt Young DK COR .30 .75
16A Matt Young DK ERR .30 .75
Perez Steel
17 Fred Lynn DK COR .30 .75
17A Fred Lynn DK ERR .30 .75
Perez Steel
A's logo on back
18 Ron Kittle DK COR .08 .25
18A Ron Kittle DK ERR .08 .25
Perez Steel
19 Jim Clancy DK COR .08 .25
19A Jim Clancy DK ERR .08 .25
Perez Steel
20 Bill Madlock DK COR .30 .75
20A Bill Madlock DK ERR .30 .75
Perez Steel
21 Larry Parrish DK .08 .25
COR
21A Larry Parrish DK .08 .25
ERR Perez Steel
22 Eddie Murray DK COR 1.25 3.00
22A Eddie Murray DK ERR 1.25 3.00
23 Mike Schmidt DK COR 2.00 5.00
23A Mike Schmidt DK ERR 2.00 5.00
24 Pedro Guerrero DK .30 .75
COR
24A Pedro Guerrero DK .30 .75
ERR Perez Steel
25 Andre Thornton DK .08 .25
COR
25A Andre Thornton DK .08 .25
ERR Perez Steel
26 Wade Boggs DK COR 1.25 3.00
26A Wade Boggs DK ERR 1.25 3.00
27 Joel Skinner RC .08 .25
28 Tommy Dunbar RC .08 .25
29A Mike Stenhouse RC .08 .25
ERR No number on back
29B M.Stenhouse RR COR 1.25 3.00
30A Ron Darling RC .75 2.00
ERR No number on back
30B Ron Darling RR COR 1.25 3.00
Numbered on back
31 Dion James RC .08 .25
32 Tony Fernandez RC .75 2.00
33 Angel Salazar RC .08 .25
34 Kevin McReynolds RC .75 2.00
35 Dick Schofield RC .40 1.00
36 Brad Komminsk RC .08 .25
37 Tim Teufel RR RC .40 1.00
38 Doug Frobel RC .08 .25
39 Greg Gagne RC .40 1.00
40 Mike Fuentes RC .08 .25
41 Joe Carter RR RC 5.00 12.00
42 Mike C. Brown RC .08 .25
Angels OF
43 Mike Jeffcoat RC .08 .25
44 Sid Fernandez RC ! .75 2.00
45 Brian Dayett RC .08 .25
46 Chris Smith RC .08 .25
47 Eddie Murray 1.25 3.00
48 Robin Yount 2.00 5.00
49 Lance Parrish .60 1.50
50 Jim Rice .30 .75
51 Dave Winfield .30 .75
52 Fernando Valenzuela .30 .75
53 George Brett 3.00 8.00
54 Rickey Henderson 2.00 5.00
55 Gary Carter .30 .75
56 Buddy Bell .30 .75
57 Reggie Jackson .60 1.50
58 Harold Baines .30 .75
59 Ozzie Smith 2.00 5.00
60 Nolan Ryan UER 4.00 10.00
61 Pete Rose 4.00 10.00
62 Ron Oester .08 .25
63 Steve Garvey .30 .75
64 Jason Thompson .08 .25
65 Jack Clark .30 .75
66 Dale Murphy .60 1.50
67 Leon Durham .08 .25
68 Darryl Strawberry RC 10.00 25.00
69 Richie Zisk .08 .25
70 Kent Hrbek .30 .75
71 Dave Stieb .30 .75
72 Ken Schrom .08 .25
73 George Bell .30 .75
74 John Moses .08 .25
75 Ed Lynch .08 .25
76 Chuck Rainey .08 .25
77 Biff Pocoroba .08 .25
78 Cecilio Guante .08 .25
79 Jim Barr .08 .25
80 Kurt Bevacqua .08 .25
81 Tom Foley .08 .25
82 Joe Lefebvre .08 .25
83 Andy Van Slyke RC 1.50 4.00
84 Bob Lillis MG .08 .25
85 Ricky Adams .08 .25
86 Jerry Hairston .08 .25
87 Bob James .08 .25
88 Joe Altobelli MG .08 .25
89 Ed Romero .08 .25
90 John Grubb .08 .25
91 John Henry Johnson .08 .25
92 Juan Espino .08 .25
93 Candy Maldonado .08 .25
94 Andre Thornton .08 .25
95 Onix Concepcion .08 .25
96 Donnie Hill UER .08 .25
Listed as P,
should be 2B
97 Andre Dawson UER .30 .75
Wrong middle name,
should be Nolan
98 Frank Tanana .30 .75
99 Curtis Wilkerson .08 .25
100 Larry Gura .08 .25
101 Dwayne Murphy .08 .25
102 Tom Brennan .08 .25
103 Dave Righetti .30 .75
104 Steve Sax .08 .25
105 Dan Petry .30 .75
106 Cal Ripken 5.00 12.00
107 Paul Molitor UER .30 .75
'83 stats should
say .270 BA, 608 AB,
and 164 hits
108 Fred Lynn .30 .75
109 Neil Allen .08 .25
110 Joe Niekro .08 .25
111 Steve Carlton .60 1.50
112 Terry Kennedy .08 .25
113 Bill Madlock .30 .75
114 Chili Davis .30 .75
115 Jim Gantner .08 .25
116 Tom Seaver 1.25 3.00
117 Bill Buckner .30 .75
118 Bill Caudill .08 .25
119 Jim Clancy .08 .25
120 John Castino .08 .25
121 Dave Concepcion .30 .75
122 Greg Luzinski .30 .75
123 Mike Boddicker .08 .25
124 Pete Ladd .08 .25
125 Juan Berenguer .08 .25
126 John Montefusco .08 .25
127 Ed Jurak .08 .25
128 Tom Niedenfuer .08 .25
129 Bert Blyleven .30 .75
130 Bud Black .08 .25
131 Gorman Heimueller .08 .25
132 Dan Schatzeder .08 .25
133 Ron Jackson .08 .25
134 Tom Henke RC .75 2.00
135 Kevin Hickey .08 .25
136 Mike Scott .30 .75
137 Bo Diaz .08 .25
138 Glenn Brummer .08 .25
139 Sid Monge .08 .25
140 Rich Gale .08 .25
141 Brett Butler .30 .75
142 Brian Harper RC .40 1.00
143 John Rabb .08 .25
144 Gary Woods .08 .25
145 Pat Putnam .08 .25
146 Jim Acker .08 .25
147 Mickey Hatcher .08 .25
148 Todd Cruz .08 .25
149 Tom Tellmann .08 .25
150 John Wockenfuss .08 .25
151 Wade Boggs UER 3.00 8.00
152 Don Baylor .30 .75
153 Bob Welch .30 .75
154 Alan Bannister .08 .25
155 Willie Aikens .08 .25
156 Jeff Burroughs .08 .25
157 Bryan Little .08 .25
158 Bob Boone .30 .75
159 Dave Hostetler .08 .25
160 Jerry Dybzinski .08 .25
161 Mike Madden .08 .25
162 Luis DeLeon .08 .25
163 Willie Hernandez .08 .25
164 Frank Pastore .08 .25
165 Rick Camp .08 .25
166 Lee Mazzilli .30 .75
167 Scot Thompson .08 .25
168 Bob Forsch .08 .25
169 Mike Flanagan .08 .25
170 Rick Manning .08 .25
171 Chet Lemon .30 .75
172 Jerry Remy .08 .25
173 Ron Guidry .30 .75
174 Pedro Guerrero .30 .75
175 Willie Wilson .30 .75
176 Carney Lansford .30 .75
177 Al Oliver .30 .75
178 Jim Sundberg .30 .75
179 Bobby Grich .30 .75
180 Rich Dotson .08 .25
181 Joaquin Andujar .30 .75
182 Jose Cruz .30 .75
183 Mike Schmidt 3.00 8.00
184 Gary Redus RC .40 1.00
185 Garry Templeton .30 .75
186 Tony Pena .08 .25
187 Greg Minton .08 .25
188 Phil Niekro .30 .75
189 Ferguson Jenkins .30 .75
190 Mookie Wilson .30 .75
191 Jim Beattie .08 .25
192 Gary Ward .08 .25
193 Jesse Barfield .30 .75
194 Pete Filson .08 .25
195 Roy Lee Jackson .08 .25
196 Rick Sweet .08 .25
197 Jesse Orosco .08 .25
198 Steve Lake .08 .25
199 Ken Dayley .08 .25
200 Manny Sarmiento .08 .25
201 Mark Davis .08 .25
202 Tim Flannery .08 .25
203 Bill Scherrer .08 .25
204 Al Holland .08 .25
205 Dave Von Ohlen .08 .25
206 Mike LaCoss .08 .25
207 Juan Beniquez .08 .25
208 Juan Agosto .08 .25
209 Bobby Ramos .08 .25
210 Al Bumbry .08 .25
211 Mark Brouhard .08 .25
212 Howard Bailey .08 .25
213 Bruce Hurst .08 .25
214 Bob Shirley .08 .25
215 Pat Zachry .08 .25
216 Julio Franco 1.25 3.00
217 Mike Armstrong .08 .25
218 Dave Beard .08 .25
219 Steve Rogers .30 .75
220 John Butcher .08 .25
221 Mike Smithson .08 .25
222 Frank White .30 .75
223 Mike Heath .08 .25
224 Chris Bando .08 .25
225 Roy Smalley .08 .25
226 Dusty Baker .30 .75
227 Lou Whitaker .30 .75
228 John Lowenstein .08 .25
229 Ben Oglivie .30 .75
230 Doug DeCinces .08 .25
231 Lonnie Smith .08 .25
232 Ray Knight .30 .75
233 Gary Matthews .30 .75
234 Juan Bonilla .08 .25
235 Rod Scurry .08 .25
236 Atlee Hammaker .08 .25
237 Mike Caldwell .08 .25
238 Keith Hernandez .30 .75
239 Larry Bowa .30 .75
240 Tony Bernazard .08 .25
241 Damaso Garcia .08 .25
242 Tom Brunansky .08 .25
243 Dan Driessen .08 .25
244 Ron Kittle .08 .25
245 Tim Stoddard .08 .25
246 Bob L. Gibson RC/(Brewers Pitcher).08 .25
247 Marty Castillo .08 .25
248 Don Mattingly RC 40.00 100.00
249 Jeff Newman .08 .25
250 Alejandro Pena RC .75 2.00
251 Toby Harrah .30 .75
252 Cesar Geronimo .08 .25
253 Tom Underwood .08 .25
254 Doug Flynn .08 .25
255 Andy Hassler .08 .25
256 Odell Jones .08 .25
257 Rudy Law .08 .25
258 Harry Spilman .08 .25
259 Marty Bystrom .08 .25
260 Dave Rucker .08 .25
261 Ruppert Jones .08 .25
262 Jeff R. Jones/(Reds OF) .08 .25
263 Gerald Perry .40 1.00
264 Gene Tenace .30 .75
265 Brad Wellman .08 .25
266 Dickie Noles .08 .25
267 Jamie Allen .08 .25
268 Jim Gott .08 .25
269 Ron Davis .08 .25
270 Benny Ayala .08 .25
271 Ned Yost .08 .25
272 Dave Rozema .08 .25
273 Dave Stapleton .08 .25
274 Lou Piniella .30 .75
275 Jose Morales .08 .25
276 Broderick Perkins .08 .25
277 Butch Davis RC .08 .25
278 Tony Phillips RC .75 2.00
279 Jeff Reardon .30 .75
280 Ken Forsch .08 .25
281 Pete O'Brien RC .40 1.00
282 Tom Paciorek .08 .25
283 Frank LaCorte .08 .25
284 Tim Lollar .08 .25
285 Greg Gross .08 .25
286 Alex Trevino .08 .25
287 Gene Garber .08 .25
288 Dave Parker .30 .75
289 Lee Smith .30 .75
290 Dave LaPoint .08 .25
291 John Shelby .08 .25
292 Charlie Moore .08 .25
293 Alan Trammell .30 .75

294 Tony Armas .30 .75
295 Shane Rawley .08 .25
296 Greg Brock .08 .25
297 Hal McRae .30 .75
298 Mike Davis .08 .25
299 Tim Raines .30 .75
300 Bucky Dent .30 .75
301 Tommy John .30 .75
302 Carlton Fisk .60 1.50
303 Darrell Porter .08 .25
304 Dickie Thon .08 .25
305 Garry Maddox .08 .25
306 Cesar Cedeno .30 .75
307 Gary Lucas .08 .25
308 Johnny Ray .08 .25
309 Andy McGaffigan .08 .25
310 Claudell Washington .08 .25
311 Ryne Sandberg 5.00 12.00
312 George Foster .30 .75
313 Spike Owen RC .40 1.00
314 Gary Gaetti .60 1.50
315 Willie Upshaw .08 .25
316 Al Williams .08 .25
317 Jorge Orta .08 .25
318 Orlando Mercado .08 .25
319 Junior Ortiz .08 .25
320 Mike Proly .08 .25
321 Randy Johnson UER .08 .25
'72-'82 stats are
from Twins' Randy John-
son, '83 stats are from
Braves' Randy Johnson
322 Jim Morrison .08 .25
323 Max Venable .08 .25
324 Tony Gwynn 5.00 12.00
325 Duane Walker .08 .25
326 Ozzie Virgil .08 .25
327 Jeff Lahti .08 .25
328 Bill Dawley .08 .25
329 Rob Wilfong .08 .25
330 Marc Hill .08 .25
331 Ray Burris .08 .25
332 Allan Ramirez .08 .25
333 Chuck Porter .08 .25
334 Wayne Krenchicki .08 .25
335 Gary Allenson .08 .25
336 Bobby Meacham .08 .25
337 Joe Beckwith .08 .25
338 Rick Sutcliffe .30 .75
339 Mark Huismann .08 .25
340 Tim Conroy .08 .25
341 Scott Sanderson .08 .25
342 Larry Biittner .08 .25
343 Dave Stewart .30 .75
344 Darryl Motley .08 .25
345 Chris Codiroli .08 .25
346 Rich Behenna .08 .25
347 Andre Robertson .08 .25
348 Mike Marshall .08 .25
349 Larry Herndon .30 .75
350 Rich Dauer .08 .25
351 Cecil Cooper .30 .75
352 Rod Carew .60 1.50
353 Willie McGee .30 .75
354 Phil Garner .30 .75
355 Joe Morgan .30 .75
356 Luis Salazar .08 .25
357 John Candelaria .08 .25
358 Bill Laskey .08 .25
359 Bob McClure .08 .25
360 Dave Kingman .30 .75
361 Ron Cey .30 .75
362 Matt Young RC .40 1.00
363 Lloyd Moseby .08 .25
364 Frank Viola .60 1.50
365 Eddie Milner .08 .25
366 Floyd Bannister .08 .25
367 Dan Ford .08 .25
368 Moose Haas .08 .25
369 Doug Bair .08 .25
370 Ray Fontenot .08 .25
371 Luis Aponte .08 .25
372 Jack Fimple .08 .25
373 Neal Heaton .08 .25
374 Greg Pryor .08 .25
375 Wayne Gross .08 .25
376 Charlie Lea .08 .25
377 Steve Lubratich .08 .25
378 Jon Matlack .08 .25
379 Julio Cruz .08 .25
380 John Mizerock .08 .25
381 Kevin Gross RC .40 1.00
382 Mike Ramsey .08 .25
383 Doug Gwosdz .08 .25
384 Kelly Paris .08 .25
385 Pete Falcone .08 .25
386 Milt May .08 .25
387 Fred Breining .08 .25
388 Craig Lefferts RC .08 .25
389 Steve Henderson .08 .25
390 Randy Moffitt .08 .25
391 Ron Washington .08 .25
392 Gary Roenicke .08 .25
393 Tom Candiotti RC .75 2.00
394 Larry Pashnick .08 .25
395 Dwight Evans .60 1.50
396 Rich Gossage .30 .75
397 Derrel Thomas .08 .25
398 Juan Eichelberger .08 .25
399 Leon Roberts .08 .25
400 Dave Lopes .30 .75
401 Bill Gullickson .08 .25
402 Geoff Zahn .08 .25
403 Billy Sample .08 .25
404 Mike Squires .08 .25
405 Craig Reynolds .08 .25
406 Eric Show .08 .25
407 John Denny .08 .25
408 Dann Bilardello .08 .25
409 Bruce Benedict .08 .25
410 Kent Tekulve .08 .25
411 Mel Hall .30 .75
412 John Stuper .08 .25
413 Rick Dempsey .08 .25
414 Don Sutton .30 .75
415 Jack Morris .30 .75
416 John Tudor .30 .75
417 Willie Randolph .30 .75
418 Jerry Reuss .08 .25
419 Don Slaught .30 .75
420 Steve McCatty .08 .25
421 Tim Wallach .08 .25
422 Larry Parrish .08 .25
423 Brian Downing .30 .75
424 Britt Burns .08 .25
425 David Green .08 .25
426 Jerry Mumphrey .08 .25
427 Ivan DeJesus .08 .25
428 Mario Soto .30 .75
429 Gene Richards .08 .25
430 Dale Berra .08 .25
431 Darrell Evans .30 .75
432 Glenn Hubbard .08 .25
433 Jody Davis .08 .25
434 Danny Heep .08 .25
435 Ed Nunez RC .08 .25
436 Bobby Castillo .08 .25
437 Ernie Whitt .08 .25
438 Scott Ullger .08 .25
439 Doyle Alexander .08 .25
440 Domingo Ramos .08 .25
441 Craig Swan .08 .25
442 Warren Brusstar .08 .25
443 Len Barker .08 .25
444 Mike Easler .08 .25
445 Renie Martin .08 .25
446 Dennis Rasmussen RC .40 1.00
447 Ted Power .08 .25
448 Charles Hudson .08 .25
449 Danny Cox RC .40 1.00
450 Kevin Bass .08 .25
451 Daryl Sconiers .08 .25
452 Scott Fletcher .08 .25
453 Bryn Smith .08 .25
454 Jim Dwyer .08 .25
455 Rob Picciolo .08 .25
456 Enos Cabell .08 .25
457 Dennis Boyd .30 .75
458 Butch Wynegar .08 .25
459 Burt Hooton .08 .25
460 Ron Hassey .08 .25
461 Danny Jackson RC .40 1.00
462 Bob Kearney .08 .25
463 Terry Francona .30 .75
464 Wayne Tolleson .08 .25
465 Mickey Rivers .08 .25
466 John Wathan .08 .25
467 Bill Almon .08 .25
468 George Vukovich .08 .25
469 Steve Kemp .08 .25
470 Ken Landreaux .08 .25
471 Milt Wilcox .08 .25
472 Tippy Martinez .08 .25
473 Ted Simmons .30 .75
474 Tim Foli .08 .25
475 George Hendrick .30 .75
476 Terry Puhl .08 .25
477 Von Hayes .08 .25
478 Bobby Brown .08 .25
479 Lee Lacy .08 .25
480 Joel Youngblood .08 .25
481 Jim Slaton .08 .25
482 Mike Fitzgerald .08 .25
483 Keith Moreland .08 .25
484 Ron Roenicke .08 .25
485 Luis Leal .08 .25
486 Bryan Oelkers .08 .25
487 Bruce Berenyi .08 .25
488 LaMarr Hoyt .08 .25
489 Joe Nolan .08 .25
490 Marshall Edwards .08 .25
491 Mike Laga .30 .75
492 Rick Cerone .08 .25
493 Rick Miller UER .08 .25
Listed as Mike
on card front
494 Rick Honeycutt .08 .25
495 Mike Hargrove .08 .25
496 Joe Simpson .08 .25
497 Keith Atherton .08 .25
498 Chris Welsh .08 .25
499 Bruce Kison .08 .25
500 Bobby Johnson .08 .25
501 Jerry Koosman .30 .75
502 Frank DiPino .08 .25
503 Tony Perez .60 1.50
504 Ken Oberkfell .08 .25
505 Mark Thurmond .08 .25
506 Joe Price .08 .25
507 Pascual Perez .08 .25
508 Marvell Wynne .40 1.00
509 Mike Krukow .08 .25
510 Dick Ruthven .08 .25
511 Al Cowens .08 .25
512 Cliff Johnson .08 .25
513 Randy Bush .08 .25
514 Sammy Stewart .08 .25
515 Bill Schroeder .08 .25
516 Aurelio Lopez .30 .75
517 Mike C. Brown .08 .25
518 Graig Nettles .30 .75
519 Dave Sax .08 .25
520 Jerry Willard .08 .25
521 Paul Splittorff .08 .25
522 Tom Burgmeier .08 .25
523 Chris Speier .08 .25
524 Bobby Clark .08 .25
525 George Wright .08 .25
526 Dennis Lamp .08 .25
527 Tony Scott .08 .25
528 Ed Whitson .08 .25
529 Ron Reed .08 .25
530 Charlie Puleo .08 .25
531 Jerry Royster .08 .25
532 Don Robinson .08 .25
533 Steve Trout .08 .25
534 Bruce Sutter .60 1.50
535 Bob Horner ! .30 .75
536 Pat Tabler .08 .25
537 Chris Chambliss .30 .75
538 Bob Ojeda .08 .25
539 Alan Ashby .08 .25
540 Jay Johnstone .08 .25
541 Bob Dernier .08 .25
542 Brook Jacoby .40 1.00
543 U.L. Washington .08 .25
544 Danny Darwin .08 .25
545 Kiko Garcia .08 .25
546 Vance Law UER .08 .25
Listed as P
on card front
547 Tug McGraw .30 .75
548 Dave Smith .08 .25
549 Len Matuszek .08 .25
550 Tom Hume .08 .25
551 Dave Dravecky .08 .25
552 Rick Rhoden .08 .25
553 Duane Kuiper .08 .25
554 Rusty Staub .30 .75
555 Bill Campbell .08 .25
556 Mike Torrez .08 .25
557 Dave Henderson .30 .75
558 Len Whitehouse .08 .25
559 Barry Bonnell .08 .25
560 Rick Lysander .08 .25
561 Garth Iorg .08 .25
562 Bryan Clark .08 .25
563 Brian Giles .08 .25
564 Vern Ruhle .08 .25
565 Steve Bedrosian .08 .25
566 Larry McWilliams .08 .25
567 Jeff Leonard UER .08 .25
Listed as P
on card front
568 Alan Wiggins .08 .25
569 Jeff Russell RC .40 1.00
570 Salome Barojas .08 .25
571 Dane Iorg .08 .25
572 Bob Knepper .08 .25
573 Gary Lavelle .08 .25
574 Gorman Thomas .30 .75
575 Manny Trillo .08 .25
576 Jim Palmer .30 .75
577 Dale Murray .08 .25
578 Tom Brookens .30 .75
579 Rich Gedman .08 .25
580 Bill Doran RC .40 1.00
581 Steve Yeager .30 .75
582 Dan Spillner .08 .25
583 Dan Quisenberry .08 .25
584 Rance Mulliniks .08 .25
585 Storm Davis .08 .25
586 Dave Schmidt .08 .25
587 Bill Russell .30 .75
588 Pat Sheridan .08 .25
589 Rafael Ramirez .08 .25
UER (A's on front)
590 Bud Anderson .08 .25
591 George Frazier .08 .25
592 Lee Tunnell .08 .25
593 Kirk Gibson 1.25 3.00
594 Scott McGregor .08 .25
595 Bob Bailor .08 .25
596 Tom Herr .08 .25
597 Luis Sanchez .08 .25
598 Dave Engle .08 .25
599 Craig McMurtry .08 .25
600 Carlos Diaz .08 .25
601 Tom O'Malley .08 .25
602 Nick Esasky .08 .25
603 Ron Hodges .08 .25
604 Ed VandeBerg .08 .25
605 Alfredo Griffin .08 .25
606 Glenn Hoffman .08 .25
607 Hubie Brooks .08 .25
608 Richard Barnes UER .08 .25
Photo actually
Neal Heaton
609 Greg Walker .40 1.00
610 Ken Singleton .30 .75
611 Mark Clear .08 .25
612 Buck Martinez .08 .25
613 Ken Griffey .30 .75
614 Reid Nichols .08 .25
615 Doug Sisk .08 .25
616 Bob Brenly .08 .25
617 Joey McLaughlin .08 .25
618 Glenn Wilson .30 .75
619 Bob Stoddard .08 .25
620 Lenn Sakata UER .08 .25
Listed as Len
on card front
621 Mike Young RC .08 .25
622 John Stefero .08 .25
623 Carmelo Martinez .08 .25
624 Dave Bergman .08 .25
625 Runnin' Reds UER 1.25 3.00
Sic, Redbirds
David Green
Willie McGee
Lonnie Smith
Ozzie Smith
626 Rudy May .08 .25
627 Matt Keough .08 .25
628 Jose DeLeon RC .40 1.00
629 Jim Essian .08 .25
630 Darnell Coles RC .40 1.00
631 Mike Warren .08 .25
632 Del Crandall MG .08 .25
633 Dennis Martinez .30 .75
634 Mike Moore .08 .25
635 Lary Sorensen .08 .25
636 Ricky Nelson .08 .25
637 Omar Moreno .08 .25
638 Charlie Hough .30 .75
639 Dennis Eckersley ! .60 1.50
640 Walt Terrell .08 .25
641 Denny Walling .08 .25
642 Dave Anderson RC .08 .25
643 Jose Oquendo RC .40 1.00
644 Bob Stanley .08 .25
645 Dave Geisel .08 .25
646 Scott Garrelts .08 .25
647 Gary Pettis .08 .25
648 Duke Snider .60 1.50
Puzzle Card
649 Johnnie LeMaster .08 .25
650 Dave Collins .08 .25
651 The Chicken .60 1.50
652 DK Checklist 1-26 .30 .75
Unnumbered
653 Checklist 27-130 .08 .25
Unnumbered
654 Checklist 131-234 .08 .25
Unnumbered
655 Checklist 235-338 .08 .25
Unnumbered
656 Checklist 339-442 .08 .25
Unnumbered
657 Checklist 443-546 .08 .25
Unnumbered
658 Checklist 547-651 .08 .25
Unnumbered
A Living Legends A 1.00 2.50
B Living Legends B 2.00 5.00

1984 Donruss Duke Snider Puzzle

1 Snider Puzzle 1-3 .10 .25
4 Snider Puzzle 4-6 .10 .25
7 Snider Puzzle 7-10 .10 .25
10 Snider Puzzle 10-12 .10 .25
13 Snider Puzzle 13-15 .10 .25
16 Snider Puzzle 16-18 .10 .25
19 Snider Puzzle 19-21 .10 .25
22 Snider Puzzle 22-24 .10 .25
25 Snider Puzzle 25-27 .10 .25
28 Snider Puzzle 28-30 .10 .25
31 Snider Puzzle 29-31 .10 .25
34 Snider Puzzle 34-36 .10 .25
37 Snider Puzzle 37-39 .10 .25
40 Snider Puzzle 40-42 .10 .25
43 Snider Puzzle 43-45 .10 .25
46 Snider Puzzle 46-48 .10 .25
49 Snider Puzzle 49-51 .10 .25
52 Snider Puzzle 52-54 .10 .25
55 Snider Puzzle 55-57 .10 .25
58 Snider Puzzle 58-60 .10 .25
61 Snider Puzzle 61-63 .10 .25

1984 Donruss Ted Williams Puzzle

1 Williams Puzzle 1-3 .10 .25
4 Williams Puzzle 4-6 .10 .25
7 Williams Puzzle 7-10 .10 .25
10 Williams Puzzle 10-12 .10 .25
13 Williams Puzzle 13-15 .10 .25
16 Williams Puzzle 16-18 .10 .25
19 Williams Puzzle 19-21 .10 .25
22 Williams Puzzle 22-24 .10 .25
25 Williams Puzzle 25-27 .10 .25
28 Williams Puzzle 28-30 .10 .25
31 Williams Puzzle 29-31 .10 .25
34 Williams Puzzle 34-36 .10 .25
37 Williams Puzzle 37-39 .10 .25
40 Williams Puzzle 40-42 .10 .25
43 Williams Puzzle 43-45 .10 .25
46 Williams Puzzle 46-48 .10 .25
49 Williams Puzzle 49-51 .10 .25
52 Williams Puzzle 52-54 .10 .25
55 Williams Puzzle 55-57 .10 .25
58 Williams Puzzle 58-60 .10 .25
61 Williams Puzzle 61-63 .10 .25

1984 Donruss Action All-Stars

COMPLETE SET (60) 3.00 8.00
COMP.WILLIAMS PUZZLE 12.50 25.00
1 Gary Lavelle .01 .05
2 Willie McGee .10 .30
3 Tony Pena .01 .05
4 Lou Whitaker .07 .20
5 Robin Yount .15 .40
6 Doug DeCinces .01 .05
7 John Castino .01 .05
8 Terry Kennedy .01 .05
9 Rickey Henderson .30 1.00
10 Bob Horner .01 .05
11 Harold Baines .02 .10
12 Buddy Bell .02 .10
13 Fernando Valenzuela .02 .10
14 Nolan Ryan 1.00 2.50
15 Andre Thornton .01 .05
16 Gary Redus .01 .05
17 Pedro Guerrero .02 .10
18 Andre Dawson .10 .30
19 Dave Stieb .01 .05
20 Cal Ripken 1.00 2.50
21 Ken Griffey .02 .10
22 Wade Boggs .30 1.00
23 Keith Hernandez .02 .10
24 Steve Carlton .20 .50
25 Hal McRae .01 .05
26 John Lowenstein .01 .05
27 Fred Lynn .02 .10
28 Bill Buckner .02 .10
29 Chris Chambliss .01 .05
30 Richie Zisk .01 .05
31 Jack Clark .02 .10
32 George Hendrick .01 .05
33 Bill Madlock .02 .10
34 Lance Parrish .07 .20
35 Paul Molitor .20 .50
36 Reggie Jackson .20 .50
37 Kent Hrbek .02 .10
38 Steve Garvey .02 .10
39 Carney Lansford .02 .10
40 Dale Murphy .10 .30
41 Greg Luzinski .02 .10
42 Larry Parrish .01 .05
43 Ryne Sandberg .50 1.25
44 Dickie Thon .01 .05
45 Bert Blyleven .02 .10
46 Ron Oester .01 .05
47 Dusty Baker .02 .10
48 Steve Rogers .01 .05
49 Jim Clancy .01 .05
50 Eddie Murray .25 .60
51 Ron Guidry .02 .10
52 Jim Rice .02 .10
53 Tom Seaver .20 .50
54 Pete Rose .30 .75
55 George Brett .50 1.25
56 Dan Quisenberry .01 .05
57 Mike Schmidt .25 .60
58 Ted Simmons .02 .10
59 Dave Righetti .01 .05
60 Checklist Card .01 .05

1984 Donruss Champions

COMPLETE SET (60) 5.00 12.00
1 Babe Ruth GC .75 2.00
2 George Foster .02 .10
3 Dave Kingman .02 .10
4 Jim Rice .02 .10
5 Gorman Thomas .01 .05
6 Ben Oglivie .01 .05
7 Jeff Burroughs .01 .05
8 Hank Aaron GC .30 .75
9 Reggie Jackson .20 .50
10 Carl Yastrzemski .20 .50
11 Mike Schmidt .25 .60
12 Graig Nettles .02 .10
13 Greg Luzinski .02 .10
14 Ted Williams GC .60 1.50
15 George Brett .50 1.25
16 Wade Boggs .20 .50
17 Hal McRae .01 .05
18 Bill Buckner .02 .10
19 Eddie Murray .25 .60
20 Rogers Hornsby GC .20 .50
21 Rod Carew .15 .40
22 Bill Madlock .02 .10
23 Lonnie Smith .01 .05
24 Cecil Cooper .02 .10
25 Ken Griffey .02 .10
26 Ty Cobb GC .40 1.00
27 Pete Rose .30 .75
28 Rusty Staub .02 .10
29 Tony Perez .02 .10
30 Al Oliver .02 .10
31 Cy Young GC .20 .50
32 Gaylord Perry .15 .40
33 Ferguson Jenkins .15 .40
34 Phil Niekro .15 .40
35 Jim Palmer .15 .40
36 Tommy John .02 .10
37 Walter Johnson GC .20 .50
38 Steve Carlton .15 .40
39 Nolan Ryan 1.00 2.50
40 Tom Seaver .15 .40
41 Don Sutton .15 .40
42 Bert Blyleven .02 .10
43 Frank Robinson GC .15 .40
44 Joe Morgan .15 .40
45 Rollie Fingers .10 .30
46 Keith Hernandez .02 .10
47 Robin Yount .10 .30
48 Cal Ripken 1.00 2.50
49 Dale Murphy .10 .30
50 Mickey Mantle GC 1.25 3.00
51 Johnny Bench .20 .50
52 Carlton Fisk .20 .50
53 Tug McGraw .02 .10
54 Paul Molitor .20 .50
55 Carl Hubbell GC .10 .30
56 Steve Garvey .02 .10
57 Dave Parker .02 .10
58 Gary Carter .20 .50
59 Fred Lynn .02 .10
60 Checklist Card .01 .05

1985 Donruss

The 1985 Donruss set consists of 660 standard-size cards. The wax packs, packed 36 packs to a box and 20 boxes to a case, contained 15 cards and a Lou Gehrig puzzle panel. The fronts feature full color photos framed by jet black borders (making the cards condition sensitive). The first 26 cards of the set feature Diamond Kings (DK), for the fourth year in a row; the artwork on the Diamond Kings was again produced by the Perez-Steele Galleries. Cards 27-46 feature Rated Rookies (RR). The unnumbered checklist cards are arbitrarily numbered below as numbers 654 through 660. Rookie Cards in this set include Roger Clemens, Eric Davis, Shawon Dunston, Dwight Gooden, Orel Hershiser, Jimmy Key, Terry Pendleton, Kirby Puckett and Bret Saberhagen.

COMPLETE SET (660) 20.00 50.00
COMP.FACT.SET (660) 30.00 60.00
COMP.GEHRIG PUZZLE 1.50 4.00
1 Ryne Sandberg DK .50 1.25
2 Doug DeCinces DK .05 .15
3 Richard Dotson DK .05 .15
4 Bert Blyleven DK .15 .40
5 Lou Whitaker DK .15 .40
6 Dan Quisenberry DK .05 .15
7 Don Mattingly DK 1.00 2.50
8 Carney Lansford DK .15 .40
9 Frank Tanana DK .15 .40
10 Willie Upshaw DK .05 .15
11 C.Washington DK .05 .15
12 Mike Marshall DK .05 .15
13 Joaquin Andujar DK .15 .40
14 Cal Ripken DK 1.00 2.50
15 Jim Rice DK .15 .40
16 Don Sutton DK .15 .40
17 Frank Viola DK .15 .40
18 Alvin Davis DK .15 .40
19 Mario Soto DK .15 .40
20 Jose Cruz DK .15 .40
21 Charlie Lea DK .05 .15
22 Jesse Orosco DK .05 .15
23 Juan Samuel DK .05 .15
24 Tony Pena DK .05 .15
25 Tony Gwynn DK .50 1.25
26 Bob Brenly DK .05 .15
27 Danny Tartabull RC .40 1.00
28 Mike Bielecki RC .08 .25
29 Steve Lyons RC .20 .50
30 Jeff Reed RC .08 .25
31 Tony Brewer RC .08 .25
32 John Morris RC .08 .25
33 Daryl Boston RC .08 .25
34 Al Pulido RC .08 .25
35 Steve Kiefer RC .08 .25
36 Larry Sheets RC .08 .25
37 Scott Bradley RC .08 .25
38 Calvin Schiraldi RC .20 .50
39 Shawon Dunston RC .40 1.00
40 Charlie Mitchell RC .08 .25
41 Billy Hatcher RC .20 .50
42 Russ Stephans RC .08 .25
43 Alejandro Sanchez RC .08 .25
44 Steve Jeltz RC .08 .25
45 Jim Traber RC .08 .25
46 Doug Loman RC .08 .25
47 Eddie Murray .50 1.25
48 Robin Yount .75 2.00
49 Lance Parrish .15 .40
50 Jim Rice .15 .40
51 Dave Winfield .15 .40
52 Fernando Valenzuela .15 .40
53 George Brett 1.25 3.00
54 Dave Kingman .15 .40
55 Gary Carter .15 .40
56 Buddy Bell .15 .40
57 Reggie Jackson .30 .75
58 Harold Baines .15 .40
59 Ozzie Smith .75 2.00
60 Nolan Ryan UER 2.50 6.00
61 Mike Schmidt 1.25 3.00
62 Dave Parker .15 .40
63 Tony Gwynn 1.00 2.50
64 Tony Pena .05 .15
65 Jack Clark .15 .40
66 Dale Murphy .30 .75
67 Ryne Sandberg 1.00 2.50
68 Keith Hernandez .15 .40
69 Alvin Davis RC* .20 .50
70 Kent Hrbek .15 .40
71 Willie Upshaw .05 .15
72 Dave Engle .05 .15
73 Alfredo Griffin .05 .15
74A Jack Perconte .05 .15
Career Highlights
takes four lines
74B Jack Perconte .05 .15
Career Highlights
takes three lines
75 Jesse Orosco .05 .15
76 Jody Davis .05 .15
77 Bob Horner .15 .40
78 Larry McWilliams .05 .15
79 Joel Youngblood .05 .15
80 Alan Wiggins .05 .15
81 Ron Oester .05 .15
82 Ozzie Virgil .05 .15
83 Ricky Horton .05 .15
84 Bill Doran .05 .15
85 Rod Carew .30 .75
86 LaMarr Hoyt .05 .15
87 Tim Wallach .05 .15
88 Mike Flanagan .05 .15
89 Jim Sundberg .15 .40
90 Chet Lemon .15 .40
91 Bob Stanley .05 .15
92 Willie Randolph .15 .40
93 Bill Russell .15 .40
94 Julio Franco .15 .40
95 Dan Quisenberry .05 .15
96 Bill Caudill .05 .15
97 Bill Gullickson .05 .15
98 Danny Darwin .05 .15
99 Curtis Wilkerson .05 .15
100 Bud Black .05 .15
101 Tony Phillips .05 .15
102 Tony Bernazard .05 .15
103 Jay Howell .05 .15
104 Burt Hooton .05 .15
105 Milt Wilcox .05 .15
106 Rich Dauer .05 .15
107 Don Sutton .15 .40
108 Mike Witt .05 .15
109 Bruce Sutter .15 .40
110 Enos Cabell .05 .15
111 John Denny .05 .15
112 Dave Dravecky .05 .15
113 Marvell Wynne .05 .15
114 Johnnie LeMaster .05 .15
115 Chuck Porter .05 .15
116 John Gibbons RC .05 .15
117 Keith Moreland .05 .15
118 Darnell Coles .05 .15
119 Dennis Lamp .05 .15
120 Ron Davis .05 .15
121 Nick Esasky .05 .15
122 Vance Law .05 .15
123 Gary Roenicke .05 .15
124 Bill Schroeder .05 .15
125 Dave Rozema .05 .15
126 Bobby Meacham .05 .15
127 Marty Barrett .05 .15
128 R.J. Reynolds .05 .15
129 Ernie Camacho UER .05 .15
Photo actually
Rich Thompson
130 Jorge Orta .05 .15
131 Lary Sorensen .05 .15
132 Terry Francona .15 .40
133 Fred Lynn .15 .40
134 Bob Jones .05 .15
135 Jerry Hairston .05 .15
136 Kevin Bass .05 .15
137 Garry Maddox .05 .15
138 Dave LaPoint .05 .15
139 Kevin McReynolds .15 .40
140 Wayne Krenchicki .05 .15
141 Rafael Ramirez .05 .15
142 Rod Scurry .05 .15
143 Greg Minton .05 .15
144 Tim Stoddard .05 .15
145 Steve Henderson .05 .15
146 George Bell .15 .40
147 Dave Meier .05 .15
148 Sammy Stewart .05 .15
149 Mark Brouhard .05 .15
150 Larry Herndon .05 .15
151 Oil Can Boyd .05 .15
152 Brian Dayett .05 .15
153 Tom Niedenfuer .05 .15
154 Brook Jacoby .05 .15
155 Onix Concepcion .05 .15
156 Tim Conroy .05 .15
157 Joe Hesketh .05 .15
158 Brian Downing .15 .40
159 Tommy Dunbar .05 .15
160 Marc Hill .05 .15
161 Phil Garner .15 .40
162 Jerry Davis .05 .15
163 Bill Campbell .05 .15
164 John Franco RC .40 1.00
165 Len Barker .05 .15
166 Benny Distefano .05 .15
167 George Frazier .05 .15
168 Tito Landrum .05 .15
169 Cal Ripken 2.00 5.00
170 Cecil Cooper .15 .40
171 Alan Trammell .15 .40
172 Wade Boggs .50 1.25
173 Don Baylor .15 .40
174 Pedro Guerrero .15 .40
175 Frank White .15 .40
176 Rickey Henderson .60 1.50
177 Charlie Lea .05 .15
178 Pete O'Brien .05 .15
179 Doug DeCinces .05 .15
180 Ron Kittle .05 .15
181 George Hendrick .15 .40
182 Joe Niekro .05 .15
183 Juan Samuel .05 .15
184 Mario Soto .15 .40
185 Rich Gossage .15 .40
186 Johnny Ray .05 .15
187 Bob Brenly .05 .15
188 Craig McMurtry .05 .15
189 Leon Durham .05 .15
190 Dwight Gooden RC 1.25 3.00
191 Barry Bonnell .05 .15
192 Tim Teufel .05 .15
193 Dave Stieb .15 .40
194 Mickey Hatcher .05 .15
195 Jesse Barfield .15 .40
196 Al Cowens .05 .15
197 Hubie Brooks .05 .15
198 Steve Trout .05 .15
199 Glenn Hubbard .05 .15
200 Bill Madlock .15 .40
201 Jeff D. Robinson .05 .15
202 Eric Show .05 .15
203 Dave Concepcion .15 .40
204 Ivan DeJesus .05 .15
205 Neil Allen .05 .15
206 Jerry Mumphrey .05 .15
207 Mike C. Brown .05 .15
208 Carlton Fisk .30 .75
209 Bryn Smith .05 .15
210 Tippy Martinez .05 .15
211 Dion James .05 .15
212 Willie Hernandez .05 .15
213 Mike Easler .05 .15
214 Ron Guidry .15 .40
215 Rick Honeycutt .05 .15
216 Brett Butler .15 .40
217 Larry Gura .05 .15
218 Ray Burris .05 .15
219 Steve Rogers .15 .40
220 Frank Tanana UER .15 .40
Bats Left listed
twice on card back
221 Ned Yost .05 .15
222 B.Saberhagen RC UER .60 1.50
223 Mike Davis .05 .15
224 Bert Blyleven .15 .40
225 Steve Kemp .05 .15
226 Jerry Reuss .05 .15
227 Darrell Evans UER .15 .40
80 homers in 1980
228 Wayne Gross .05 .15
229 Jim Gantner .05 .15
230 Bob Boone .15 .40
231 Lonnie Smith .05 .15
232 Frank DiPino .05 .15
233 Jerry Koosman .15 .40
234 Graig Nettles .15 .40
235 John Tudor .15 .40
236 John Rabb .05 .15
237 Rick Manning .05 .15
238 Mike Fitzgerald .05 .15
239 Gary Matthews .15 .40
240 Jim Presley .20 .50
241 Dave Collins .05 .15
242 Gary Gaetti .15 .40
243 Dann Bilardello .05 .15
244 Rudy Law .05 .15
245 John Lowenstein .05 .15
246 Tom Tellmann .05 .15
247 Howard Johnson .15 .40
248 Ray Fontenot .05 .15
249 Tony Armas .15 .40
250 Candy Maldonado .05 .15
251 Mike Jeffcoat .05 .15
252 Dane Iorg .05 .15
253 Bruce Bochte .05 .15
254 Pete Rose Expos 1.50 4.00
255 Don Aase .05 .15
256 George Wright .05 .15
257 Britt Burns .05 .15
258 Mike Scott .15 .40
259 Len Matuszek .05 .15
260 Dave Rucker .05 .15
261 Craig Lefferts .05 .15
262 Jay Tibbs .05 .15
263 Bruce Benedict .05 .15
264 Don Robinson .05 .15
265 Gary Lavelle .05 .15
266 Scott Sanderson .05 .15
267 Matt Young .05 .15
268 Ernie Whitt .05 .15
269 Houston Jimenez .05 .15
270 Ken Dixon .05 .15
271 Pete Ladd .05 .15
272 Juan Berenguer .05 .15

273 Roger Clemens RC 12.00 30.00
274 Rick Cerone .05 .15
275 Dave Anderson .05 .15
276 George Vukovich .05 .15
277 Greg Pryor .05 .15
278 Mike Warren .05 .15
279 Bob James .05 .15
280 Bobby Grich .15 .40
281 Mike Mason RC .08 .25
282 Ron Reed .05 .15
283 Alan Ashby .05 .15
284 Mark Thurmond .05 .15
285 Joe Lefebvre .05 .15
286 Ted Power .05 .15
287 Chris Chambliss .15 .40
288 Lee Tunnell .05 .15
289 Rich Bordi .05 .15
290 Glenn Brummer .05 .15
291 Mike Boddicker .05 .15
292 Rollie Fingers .15 .40
293 Lou Whitaker .15 .40
294 Dwight Evans .30 .75
295 Don Mattingly 2.00 5.00
296 Mike Marshall .05 .15
297 Willie Wilson .15 .40
298 Mike Heath .05 .15
299 Tim Raines .15 .40
300 Larry Parrish .05 .15
301 Geoff Zahn .05 .15
302 Rich Dotson .05 .15
303 David Green .05 .15
304 Jose Cruz .15 .40
305 Steve Carlton .15 .40
306 Gary Redus .05 .15
307 Steve Garvey .15 .40
308 Jose DeLeon .05 .15
309 Randy Lerch .05 .15
310 Claudell Washington .05 .15
311 Lee Smith .15 .40
312 Darryl Strawberry .50 1.25
313 Jim Beattie .05 .15
314 John Butcher .05 .15
315 Damaso Garcia .05 .15
316 Mike Smithson .05 .15
317 Luis Leal .05 .15
318 Ken Phelps .05 .15
319 Wally Backman .05 .15
320 Ron Cey .15 .40
321 Brad Komminsk .05 .15
322 Jason Thompson .05 .15
323 Frank Williams .05 .15
324 Tim Lollar .05 .15
325 Eric Davis RC 1.25 3.00
326 Von Hayes .05 .15
327 Andy Van Slyke .30 .75
328 Craig Reynolds .05 .15
329 Dick Schofield .05 .15
330 Scott Fletcher .05 .15
331 Jeff Reardon .15 .40
332 Rick Dempsey .05 .15
333 Ben Oglivie .15 .40
334 Dan Petry .05 .15
335 Jackie Gutierrez .05 .15
336 Dave Righetti .15 .40
337 Alejandro Pena .05 .15
338 Mel Hall .05 .15
339 Pat Sheridan .05 .15
340 Keith Atherton .05 .15
341 David Palmer .05 .15
342 Gary Ward .05 .15
343 Dave Stewart .15 .40
344 Mark Gubicza RC .20 .50
345 Carney Lansford .15 .40
346 Jerry Willard .05 .15
347 Ken Griffey .15 .40
348 Franklin Stubbs .05 .15
349 Aurelio Lopez .05 .15
350 Al Bumbry .05 .15
351 Charlie Moore .05 .15
352 Luis Sanchez .05 .15
353 Darrell Porter .05 .15
354 Bill Dawley .05 .15
355 Charles Hudson .05 .15
356 Garry Templeton .15 .40
357 Cecilio Guante .05 .15
358 Jeff Leonard .05 .15
359 Paul Molitor .15 .40
360 Ron Gardenhire .05 .15
361 Larry Bowa .15 .40
362 Bob Kearney .05 .15
363 Garth Iorg .05 .15
364 Tom Brunansky .05 .15
365 Brad Gulden .05 .15
366 Greg Walker .05 .15
367 Mike Young .05 .15
368 Rick Waits .05 .15
369 Doug Bair .05 .15
370 Bob Shirley .05 .15
371 Bob Ojeda .05 .15
372 Bob Welch .15 .40
373 Neal Heaton .05 .15
374 Danny Jackson UER .05 .15
Photo actually
Frank Wills
375 Donnie Hill .05 .15
376 Mike Stenhouse .05 .15
377 Bruce Kison .05 .15
378 Wayne Tolleson .05 .15
379 Floyd Bannister .05 .15
380 Vern Ruhle .05 .15
381 Tim Corcoran .05 .15
382 Kurt Kepshire .05 .15
383 Bobby Brown .05 .15
384 Dave Van Gorder .05 .15
385 Rick Mahler .05 .15
386 Lee Mazzilli .15 .40
387 Bill Laskey .05 .15
388 Thad Bosley .05 .15
389 Al Chambers .05 .15
390 Tony Fernandez .15 .40
391 Ron Washington .05 .15
392 Bill Swaggerty .05 .15
393 Bob L. Gibson .05 .15
394 Marty Castillo .05 .15
395 Steve Crawford .05 .15
396 Clay Christiansen .05 .15
397 Bob Bailor .05 .15
398 Mike Hargrove .05 .15
399 Charlie Leibrandt .05 .15
400 Tom Burgmeier .05 .15
401 Razor Shines .05 .15
402 Rob Wilfong .05 .15
403 Tom Henke .15 .40
404 Al Jones .05 .15
405 Mike LaCoss .05 .15
406 Luis DeLeon .05 .15
407 Greg Gross .05 .15
408 Tom Hume .05 .15
409 Rick Camp .05 .15
410 Milt May .05 .15
411 Henry Cotto RC .08 .25
412 David Von Ohlen .05 .15
413 Scott McGregor .05 .15
414 Ted Simmons .15 .40
415 Jack Morris .15 .40
416 Bill Buckner .15 .40
417 Butch Wynegar .05 .15
418 Steve Sax .05 .15
419 Steve Balboni .05 .15
420 Dwayne Murphy .05 .15
421 Andre Dawson .15 .40
422 Charlie Hough .15 .40
423 Tommy John .15 .40
424A Tom Seaver ERR .30 .75
Photo actually
Floyd Bannister
424B Tom Seaver COR 4.00 10.00
425 Tom Herr .05 .15
426 Terry Puhl .05 .15
427 Al Holland .05 .15
428 Eddie Milner .05 .15
429 Terry Kennedy .05 .15
430 John Candelaria .05 .15
431 Manny Trillo .05 .15
432 Ken Oberkfell .05 .15
433 Rick Sutcliffe .15 .40
434 Ron Darling .15 .40
435 Spike Owen .05 .15
436 Frank Viola .15 .40
437 Lloyd Moseby .05 .15
438 Kirby Puckett RC 10.00 25.00
439 Jim Clancy .05 .15
440 Mike Moore .05 .15
441 Doug Sisk .05 .15
442 Dennis Eckersley .30 .75
443 Gerald Perry .05 .15
444 Dale Berra .05 .15
445 Dusty Baker .15 .40
446 Ed Whitson .05 .15
447 Cesar Cedeno .15 .40
448 Rick Schu .05 .15
449 Joaquin Andujar .15 .40
450 Mark Bailey .05 .15
451 Ron Romanick .05 .15
452 Julio Cruz .05 .15
453 Miguel Dilone .05 .15
454 Storm Davis .05 .15
455 Jaime Cocanower .05 .15
456 Barbaro Garbey .05 .15
457 Rich Gedman .05 .15
458 Phil Niekro .15 .40
459 Mike Scioscia .15 .40
460 Pat Tabler .05 .15
461 Darryl Motley .05 .15
462 Chris Codiroli .05 .15
463 Doug Flynn .05 .15
464 Billy Sample .05 .15
465 Mickey Rivers .05 .15
466 John Wathan .05 .15
467 Bill Krueger .05 .15
468 Andre Thornton .05 .15
469 Rex Hudler .05 .15
470 Sid Bream RC .20 .50
471 Kirk Gibson .15 .40
472 John Shelby .05 .15
473 Moose Haas .05 .15
474 Doug Corbett .05 .15
475 Willie McGee .15 .40
476 Bob Knepper .05 .15
477 Kevin Gross .05 .15
478 Carmelo Martinez .05 .15
479 Kent Tekulve .05 .15
480 Chili Davis .15 .40
481 Bobby Clark .05 .15
482 Mookie Wilson .15 .40
483 Dave Owen .05 .15
484 Ed Nunez .05 .15
485 Rance Mulliniks .05 .15
486 Ken Schrom .05 .15
487 Jeff Russell .05 .15
488 Tom Paciorek .05 .15
489 Dan Ford .05 .15
490 Mike Caldwell .05 .15
491 Scottie Earl .05 .15
492 Jose Rijo RC .40 1.00
493 Bruce Hurst .05 .15
494 Ken Landreaux .05 .15
495 Mike Fischlin .05 .15
496 Don Slaught .05 .15
497 Steve McCatty .05 .15
498 Gary Lucas .05 .15
499 Gary Pettis .05 .15
500 Marvis Foley .05 .15
501 Mike Squires .05 .15
502 Jim Pankovits .05 .15
503 Luis Aguayo .05 .15
504 Ralph Citarella .05 .15
505 Bruce Bochy .05 .15
506 Bob Owchinko .05 .15
507 Pascual Perez .05 .15
508 Lee Lacy .05 .15
509 Atlee Hammaker .05 .15
510 Bob Dernier .05 .15
511 Ed VandeBerg .05 .15
512 Cliff Johnson .05 .15
513 Len Whitehouse .05 .15
514 Dennis Martinez .15 .40
515 Ed Romero .05 .15
516 Rusty Kuntz .05 .15
517 Rick Miller .05 .15
518 Dennis Rasmussen .05 .15
519 Steve Yeager .15 .40
520 Chris Bando .05 .15
521 U.L. Washington .05 .15
522 Curt Young .05 .15
523 Angel Salazar .05 .15
524 Curt Kaufman .05 .15
525 Odell Jones .05 .15
526 Juan Agosto .05 .15
527 Denny Walling .05 .15
528 Andy Hawkins .05 .15
529 Sixto Lezcano .05 .15
530 Skeeter Barnes RC .08 .25
531 Randy Johnson .05 .15
532 Jim Morrison .05 .15
533 Warren Brusstar .05 .15
534A Terry Pendleton RC .40 1.00
ERR Wrong first name as Jeff
534B Terry Pendleton COR .40 1.00
535 Vic Rodriguez .05 .15
536 Bob McClure .05 .15
537 Dave Bergman .05 .15
538 Mark Clear .05 .15
539 Mike Pagliarulo .05 .15
540 Terry Whitfield .05 .15
541 Joe Beckwith .05 .15
542 Jeff Burroughs .05 .15
543 Dan Schatzeder .05 .15
544 Donnie Scott .05 .15
545 Jim Slaton .05 .15
546 Greg Luzinski .15 .40
547 Mark Salas .05 .15
548 Dave Smith .05 .15
549 John Wockenfuss .05 .15
550 Frank Pastore .05 .15
551 Tim Flannery .05 .15
552 Rick Rhoden .05 .15
553 Mark Davis .05 .15
554 Jeff Dedmon .05 .15
555 Gary Woods .05 .15
556 Danny Heep .05 .15
557 Mark Langston RC .40 1.00
558 Darrell Brown .05 .15
559 Jimmy Key RC .40 1.00
560 Rick Lysander .05 .15
561 Doyle Alexander .05 .15
562 Mike Stanton .05 .15
563 Sid Fernandez .15 .40
564 Richie Hebner .05 .15
565 Alex Trevino .05 .15
566 Brian Harper .05 .15
567 Dan Gladden RC .20 .50
568 Luis Salazar .05 .15
569 Tom Foley .05 .15
570 Larry Andersen .05 .15
571 Danny Cox .05 .15
572 Joe Sambito .05 .15
573 Juan Beniquez .05 .15
574 Joel Skinner .05 .15
575 Randy St.Claire .05 .15
576 Floyd Rayford .05 .15
577 Roy Howell .05 .15
578 John Grubb .05 .15
579 Ed Jurak .05 .15
580 John Montefusco .05 .15
581 Orel Hershiser RC 1.25 3.00
582 Tom Waddell .05 .15
583 Mark Huismann .05 .15
584 Joe Morgan .15 .40
585 Jim Wohlford .05 .15
586 Dave Schmidt .05 .15
587 Jeff Kunkel .05 .15
588 Hal McRae .15 .40
589 Bill Almon .05 .15
590 Carmelo Castillo .05 .15
591 Omar Moreno .05 .15
592 Ken Howell .05 .15
593 Tom Brookens .05 .15
594 Joe Nolan .05 .15
595 Willie Lozado .05 .15
596 Tom Nieto .05 .15
597 Walt Terrell .05 .15
598 Al Oliver .15 .40
599 Shane Rawley .05 .15
600 Denny Gonzalez .05 .15
601 Mark Grant .05 .15
602 Mike Armstrong .05 .15
603 George Foster .15 .40
604 Dave Lopes .15 .40
605 Salome Barojas .05 .15
606 Roy Lee Jackson .05 .15
607 Pete Filson .05 .15
608 Duane Walker .05 .15
609 Glenn Wilson .05 .15
610 Rafael Santana .05 .15
611 Roy Smith .05 .15
612 Ruppert Jones .05 .15
613 Joe Cowley .05 .15
614 Al Nipper UER .05 .15
Photo actually
Mike Brown
615 Gene Nelson .05 .15
616 Joe Carter .50 1.25
617 Ray Knight .15 .40
618 Chuck Rainey .05 .15
619 Dan Driessen .05 .15
620 Daryl Sconiers .05 .15
621 Bill Stein .05 .15
622 Roy Smalley .05 .15
623 Ed Lynch .05 .15
624 Jeff Stone RC .05 .15
625 Bruce Berenyi .05 .15
626 Kelvin Chapman .05 .15
627 Joe Price .05 .15
628 Steve Bedrosian .05 .15
629 Vic Mata .05 .15
630 Mike Krukow .05 .15
631 Phil Bradley .20 .50
632 Jim Gott .05 .15
633 Randy Bush .05 .15
634 Tom Browning RC .20 .50
635 Lou Gehrig .50 1.25
Puzzle Card
636 Reid Nichols .05 .15
637 Dan Pasqua RC .20 .50
638 German Rivera .05 .15
639 Don Schulze .05 .15
640A Mike Jones .05 .15
Career Highlights,
takes five lines
640B Mike Jones .05 .15
Career Highlights,
takes four lines
641 Pete Rose 1.50 4.00
642 Wade Rowdon .05 .15
643 Jerry Narron .05 .15
644 Darrell Miller .05 .15
645 Tim Hulett RC .08 .25
646 Andy McGaffigan .05 .15
647 Kurt Bevacqua .05 .15
648 John Russell .05 .15
649 Ron Robinson .05 .15
650 Donnie Moore .05 .15
651A Two for the Title YL .75 2.00
651B Two for the Title WL 2.00 5.00
652 Tim Laudner .05 .15
653 Steve Farr RC .20 .50
654 DK Checklist 1-26 .05 .15
Unnumbered
655 Checklist 27-130 .05 .15
Unnumbered
656 Checklist 131-234 .05 .15
Unnumbered
657 Checklist 235-338 .05 .15
Unnumbered
658 Checklist 339-442 .05 .15
Unnumbered
659 Checklist 443-546 .05 .15
Unnumbered
660 Checklist 547-653 .05 .15
Unnumbered

1985 Donruss Lou Gehrig Puzzle

1 Gehrig Puzzle 1-3 .10 .25
4 Gehrig Puzzle 4-6 .10 .25
7 Gehrig Puzzle 7-9 .10 .25
10 Gehrig Puzzle 10-12 .10 .25
13 Gehrig Puzzle 13-15 .10 .25
16 Gehrig Puzzle 16-18 .10 .25
19 Gehrig Puzzle 19-21 .10 .25
22 Gehrig Puzzle 22-24 .10 .25
25 Gehrig Puzzle 25-27 .10 .25
28 Gehrig Puzzle 28-30 .10 .25
31 Gehrig Puzzle 31-33 .10 .25
34 Gehrig Puzzle 34-36 .10 .25
37 Gehrig Puzzle 37-39 .10 .25
40 Gehrig Puzzle 40-42 .10 .25
43 Gehrig Puzzle 43-45 .10 .25
46 Gehrig Puzzle 46-48 .10 .25
49 Gehrig Puzzle 49-51 .10 .25
52 Gehrig Puzzle 52-54 .10 .25
55 Gehrig Puzzle 55-57 .10 .25
58 Gehrig Puzzle 58-60 .10 .25
61 Gehrig Puzzle 61-63 .10 .25

1985 Donruss Wax Box Cards

COMPLETE SET (4) 1.50 4.00
PC1 Dwight Gooden .40 1.00
PC2 Ryne Sandberg 1.25 3.00
PC3 Ron Kittle .08 .25
PUZ Lou Gehrig .30 .75
Puzzle Card

1985 Donruss Action All-Stars

COMPLETE SET (60) 3.00 8.00
1 Tim Raines .02 .10
2 Jim Gantner .01 .05
3 Mario Soto .01 .05
4 Spike Owen .01 .05
5 Lloyd Moseby .01 .05
6 Damaso Garcia .01 .05
7 Cal Ripken 1.00 2.50
8 Dan Quisenberry .01 .05
9 Eddie Murray .25 .60
10 Tony Pena .02 .10
11 Buddy Bell .02 .10
12 Dave Winfield .15 .40
13 Ron Kittle .01 .05
14 Rich Gossage .02 .10
15 Dwight Evans .02 .10
16 Alvin Davis .01 .05
17 Mike Schmidt .25 .60
18 Pascual Perez .01 .05
19 Tony Gwynn .75 2.00
20 Nolan Ryan 1.00 2.50
21 Robin Yount .15 .40
22 Mike Marshall .01 .05
23 Brett Butler .02 .10
24 Ryne Sandberg .30 .75
25 Dale Murphy .10 .30
26 George Brett .50 1.25
27 Jim Rice .02 .10
28 Ozzie Smith .40 1.00
29 Larry Parrish .01 .05
30 Jack Clark .02 .10
31 Manny Trillo .01 .05
32 Dave Kingman .07 .20
33 Geoff Zahn .01 .05
34 Pedro Guerrero .02 .10
35 Dave Parker .02 .10
36 Rollie Fingers .15 .40
37 Fernando Valenzuela .07 .20
38 Wade Boggs .20 .50
39 Reggie Jackson .20 .50
40 Kent Hrbek .02 .10
41 Keith Hernandez .02 .10
42 Lou Whitaker .02 .10
43 Tom Herr .01 .05
44 Alan Trammell .07 .20
45 Butch Wynegar .01 .05
46 Leon Durham .01 .05
47 Dwight Gooden .20 .50
48 Don Mattingly .60 1.50
49 Phil Niekro .15 .40
50 Johnny Ray .01 .05
51 Doug DeCinces .01 .05
52 Willie Upshaw .01 .05
53 Lance Parrish .02 .10
54 Jody Davis .01 .05
55 Steve Carlton .15 .40
56 Juan Samuel .01 .05
57 Gary Carter .20 .50
58 Harold Baines .10 .30
59 Eric Show .01 .05
60 Checklist Card .01 .05

1985 Donruss Highlights

COMPLETE SET (56) 6.00 15.00
1 Tom Seaver .30 .75
2 Rollie Fingers .20 .50
3 Mike Davis .02 .10
4 Charlie Leibrandt .02 .10
5 Dale Murphy .20 .50
6 Fernando Valenzuela .07 .20
7 Larry Bowa .07 .20
8 Dave Concepcion .07 .20
9 Tony Perez .20 .50
10 Pete Rose .60 1.50
11 George Brett .60 1.50
12 Dave Stieb .02 .10
13 Dave Parker .07 .20
14 Andy Hawkins .02 .10
15 Andy Hawkins .02 .10
16 Von Hayes .02 .10
17 Rickey Henderson .30 .75
18 Jay Howell .02 .10
19 Pedro Guerrero .07 .20
20 John Tudor .02 .10
21 Keith Hernandez .20 .50
and Gary Carter:
Marathon Game I
22 Nolan Ryan 2.00 5.00
23 LaMarr Hoyt .02 .10
24 Oddibe McDowell .02 .10
25 George Brett .60 1.50
26 Bret Saberhagen .20 .50
27 Keith Hernandez .07 .20
28 Fernando Valenzuela .07 .20
29 Willie McGee and .07 .20
Vince Coleman: Record
Setting B
30 Tom Seaver .20 .50
31 Rod Carew .20 .50
32 Dwight Gooden .30 .75
33 Dwight Gooden .30 .75
34 Eddie Murray .20 .50
35 Don Baylor .07 .20
36 Don Mattingly .60 1.50
37 Dave Righetti .07 .20
38 Willie McGee .07 .20
39 Shane Rawley .02 .10
40 Pete Rose .60 1.50
41 Andre Dawson .20 .50
42 Rickey Henderson .30 .75
43 Tom Browning .07 .20
44 Don Mattingly .60 1.50
45 Don Mattingly .60 1.50
46 Charlie Leibrandt .02 .10
47 Gary Carter .20 .50
48 Dwight Gooden .30 .75
49 Wade Boggs .30 .75
50 Phil Niekro .20 .50
51 Darrell Evans .07 .20
52 Willie McGee .10 .30
53 Dave Winfield .20 .50
54 Vince Coleman .07 .20
55 Ozzie Guillen .20 .50
NNO Checklist Card .02 .10

1985 Donruss HOF Sluggers

COMPLETE SET (8) 4.00 10.00
1 Babe Ruth 1.25 3.00
2 Ted Williams .75 2.00
3 Lou Gehrig .75 2.00
4 Johnny Mize .20 .50
5 Stan Musial .30 .75
6 Mickey Mantle 1.25 3.00
7 Hank Aaron .60 1.50
8 Frank Robinson .20 .50

1985 Donruss Super DK's

COMPLETE SET (28) 5.00 12.00
1 Ryne Sandberg .75 2.00
2 Doug DeCinces .08 .25
3 Richard Dotson .08 .25
4 Bert Blyleven .20 .50
5 Lou Whitaker .30 .75
6 Dan Quisenberry .08 .25
7 Don Mattingly 1.25 3.00
8 Carney Lansford .20 .50
9 Frank Tanana .08 .25
10 Willie Upshaw .08 .25
11 Claudell Washington .08 .25
12 Mike Marshall .08 .25
13 Joaquin Andujar .08 .25
14 Cal Ripken 2.00 5.00
15 Jim Rice .20 .50
16 Don Sutton .40 1.00
17 Frank Viola .20 .50
18 Alvin Davis .08 .25
19 Mario Soto .08 .25
20 Jose Cruz .08 .25
21 Charlie Lea .08 .25
22 Jesse Orosco .20 .50
23 Juan Samuel .08 .25
24 Tony Pena .20 .50
25 Tony Gwynn 1.25 3.00
26 Bob Brenly .08 .25
NNO Checklist Card .08 .25
NNO Dick Perez/(History of DK's) .08 .25

1986 Donruss

The 1986 Donruss set consists of 660 standard-size cards. Wax packs, packed 36 packs to a box and 20 boxes to a case, contained 15 cards plus a Hank Aaron puzzle panel. The card fronts feature blue borders, the standard team logo, player's name, position, and Donruss logo. The first 26 cards of the set are Diamond Kings (DK), for the fifth year in a row; the artwork on the Diamond Kings was again produced by the Perez-Steele Galleries. Cards 27-46 again feature Rated Rookies (RR). The unnumbered checklist cards are arbitrarily numbered below as numbers 654 through 660. Rookie Cards in this set include Jose Canseco, Darren Daulton, Len Dykstra, Cecil Fielder, Andres Galarraga, Fred McGriff and Paul O'Neill.

COMPLETE SET (660) 15.00 40.00
COMP.FACT.SET (660) 15.00 40.00
COMP.AARON PUZZLE .75 2.00
1 Kirk Gibson DK .08 .25
2 Goose Gossage DK .08 .25
3 Willie McGee DK .08 .25
4 George Bell DK .08 .25
5 Tony Armas DK .08 .25
6 Chili Davis DK .08 .25
7 Cecil Cooper DK .08 .25
8 Mike Boddicker DK .05 .15
9 Dave Lopes DK .08 .25
10 Bill Doran DK .05 .15
11 Bret Saberhagen DK .08 .25
12 Brett Butler DK .08 .25
13 Harold Baines DK .08 .25
14 Mike Davis DK .05 .15
15 Tony Perez DK .20 .50
16 Willie Randolph DK .08 .25
17 Bob Boone DK .08 .25
18 Orel Hershiser DK .20 .50
19 Johnny Ray DK .05 .15
20 Gary Ward DK .05 .15
21 Rick Mahler DK .05 .15
22 Phil Bradley DK .05 .15
23 Jerry Koosman DK .08 .25
24 Tom Brunansky DK .05 .15
25 Andre Dawson DK .05 .15
26 Dwight Gooden DK .30 .75
27 Kal Daniels RC .20 .50
28 Fred McGriff RC 3.00 8.00
29 Cory Snyder .05 .15
30 Jose Guzman RC .05 .15
31 Ty Gainey RC .05 .15
32 Johnny Abrego RC .05 .15
33A Andres Galarraga RC .60 1.50
33B Andre`s Galarraga RC .60 1.50
34 Dave Shipanoff RC .05 .15
35 Mark McLemore RC .40 1.00
36 Marty Clary RC .05 .15
37 Paul O'Neill RC 1.50 4.00
38 Danny Tartabull .08 .25
39 Jose Canseco RC 10.00 25.00
40 Juan Nieves RC .05 .15
41 Lance McCullers RC .05 .15
42 Rick Surhoff RC .05 .15
43 Todd Worrell RC .20 .50
44 Bob Kipper RC .05 .15
45 John Habyan RC .05 .15
46 Mike Woodard RC .05 .15
47 Mike Boddicker .05 .15
48 Robin Yount .50 1.25
49 Lou Whitaker .08 .25
50 Oil Can Boyd .05 .15
51 Rickey Henderson .30 .75
52 Mike Marshall .05 .15
53 George Brett .75 2.00
54 Dave Kingman .08 .25
55 Hubie Brooks .05 .15
56 Oddibe McDowell .05 .15
57 Doug DeCinces .05 .15
58 Britt Burns .05 .15
59 Ozzie Smith .50 1.25
60 Jose Cruz .08 .25
61 Mike Schmidt .75 2.00
62 Pete Rose 1.00 2.50
63 Steve Garvey .08 .25
64 Tony Pena .05 .15
65 Chili Davis .08 .25
66 Dale Murphy .20 .50
67 Ryne Sandberg .60 1.50
68 Gary Carter .08 .25
69 Alvin Davis .05 .15
70 Kent Hrbek .08 .25
71 George Bell .08 .25
72 Kirby Puckett .75 2.00
73 Lloyd Moseby .05 .15
74 Bob Kearney .05 .15
75 Dwight Gooden .30 .75
76 Gary Matthews .08 .25
77 Rick Mahler .05 .15
78 Benny Distefano .05 .15
79 Jeff Leonard .05 .15
80 Kevin McReynolds .08 .25
81 Ron Oester .05 .15
82 John Russell .05 .15
83 Tommy Herr .05 .15
84 Jerry Mumphrey .05 .15
85 Ron Romanick .05 .15
86 Daryl Boston .05 .15
87 Andre Dawson .08 .25
88 Eddie Murray .30 .75
89 Dion James .05 .15
90 Chet Lemon .08 .25
91 Bob Stanley .05 .15
92 Willie Randolph .08 .25
93 Mike Scioscia .08 .25
94 Tom Waddell .05 .15
95 Danny Jackson .05 .15
96 Mike Davis .05 .15
97 Mike Fitzgerald .05 .15
98 Gary Ward .05 .15
99 Pete O'Brien .05 .15
100 Bret Saberhagen .08 .25
101 Alfredo Griffin .05 .15
102 Brett Butler .08 .25
103 Ron Guidry .08 .25
104 Jerry Reuss .05 .15
105 Jack Morris .08 .25
106 Rick Dempsey .05 .15
107 Ray Burris .05 .15
108 Brian Downing .08 .25
109 Willie McGee .08 .25
110 Bill Doran .05 .15
111 Kent Tekulve .05 .15
112 Tony Gwynn .50 1.25
113 Marvell Wynne .05 .15
114 David Green .05 .15
115 Jim Gantner .05 .15
116 George Foster .08 .25
117 Steve Trout .05 .15
118 Mark Langston .08 .25
119 Tony Fernandez .05 .15
120 John Butcher .05 .15
121 Ron Robinson .05 .15
122 Dan Spillner .05 .15
123 Mike Young .05 .15
124 Paul Molitor .08 .25
125 Kirk Gibson .08 .25
126 Ken Griffey .08 .25
127 Tony Armas .08 .25
128 Mariano Duncan RC .20 .50
129 Pat Tabler .05 .15
130 Frank White .08 .25
131 Carney Lansford .08 .25
132 Vance Law .05 .15
133 Dick Schofield .05 .15
134 Wayne Tolleson .05 .15
135 Greg Walker .05 .15
136 Denny Walling .05 .15
137 Ozzie Virgil .05 .15
138 Ricky Horton .05 .15
139 LaMarr Hoyt .05 .15
140 Wayne Krenchicki .05 .15
141 Glenn Hubbard .05 .15
142 Cecilio Guante .05 .15
143 Mike Krukow .05 .15
144 Lee Smith .08 .25
145 Edwin Nunez .05 .15
146 Dave Stieb .08 .25
147 Mike Smithson .05 .15
148 Ken Dixon .05 .15
149 Danny Darwin .05 .15
150 Chris Pittaro .05 .15
151 Bill Buckner .08 .25
152 Mike Pagliarulo .05 .15
153 Bill Russell .08 .25
154 Brook Jacoby .05 .15
155 Pat Sheridan .05 .15
156 Mike Gallego RC .05 .15
157 Jim Wohlford .05 .15
158 Gary Pettis .05 .15
159 Toby Harrah .08 .25
160 Richard Dotson .05 .15
161 Bob Knepper .05 .15
162 Dave Dravecky .05 .15
163 Greg Gross .05 .15
164 Eric Davis .30 .75
165 Gerald Perry .05 .15
166 Rick Rhoden .05 .15
167 Keith Moreland .05 .15
168 Jack Clark .08 .25
169 Storm Davis .05 .15
170 Cecil Cooper .08 .25
171 Alan Trammell .08 .25
172 Roger Clemens 2.00 5.00
173 Don Mattingly 1.00 2.50
174 Pedro Guerrero .08 .25
175 Willie Wilson .08 .25
176 Dwayne Murphy .05 .15
177 Tim Raines .08 .25
178 Larry Parrish .05 .15
179 Mike Witt .05 .15
180 Harold Baines .08 .25
181 Vince Coleman UER RC .40 1.00
182 Jeff Heathcock .05 .15
183 Steve Carlton .08 .25
184 Mario Soto .08 .25
185 Goose Gossage .08 .25
186 Johnny Ray .05 .15
187 Dan Gladden .05 .15
188 Bob Horner .08 .25
189 Rick Sutcliffe .08 .25
190 Keith Hernandez .08 .25
191 Phil Bradley .05 .15
192 Tom Brunansky .05 .15
193 Jesse Barfield .08 .25
194 Frank Viola .08 .25
195 Willie Upshaw .05 .15
196 Jim Beattie .05 .15
197 Darryl Strawberry .20 .50
198 Ron Cey .08 .25
199 Steve Bedrosian .05 .15
200 Steve Kemp .05 .15
201 Manny Trillo .05 .15
202 Garry Templeton .08 .25
203 Dave Parker .08 .25
204 John Denny .05 .15
205 Terry Pendleton .08 .25
206 Terry Puhl .05 .15
207 Bobby Grich .08 .25
208 Ozzie Guillen RC .75 2.00
209 Jeff Reardon .08 .25
210 Cal Ripken 1.25 3.00
211 Bill Schroeder .05 .15
212 Dan Petry .05 .15
213 Jim Rice .08 .25
214 Dave Righetti .08 .25
215 Fernando Valenzuela .08 .25
216 Julio Franco .08 .25
217 Darryl Motley .05 .15
218 Dave Collins .05 .15
219 Tim Wallach .05 .15
220 George Wright .05 .15
221 Tommy Dunbar .05 .15
222 Steve Balboni .05 .15
223 Jay Howell .05 .15
224 Joe Carter .08 .25
225 Ed Whitson .05 .15
226 Orel Hershiser .30 .75
227 Willie Hernandez .05 .15
228 Lee Lacy .05 .15
229 Rollie Fingers .08 .25
230 Bob Boone .08 .25
231 Joaquin Andujar .08 .25
232 Craig Reynolds .05 .15
233 Shane Rawley .05 .15
234 Eric Show .05 .15
235 Jose DeLeon .05 .15
236 Jose Uribe .05 .15
237 Moose Haas .05 .15
238 Wally Backman .05 .15
239 Dennis Eckersley .20 .50
240 Mike Moore .05 .15
241 Damaso Garcia .05 .15
242 Tim Teufel .05 .15
243 Dave Concepcion .08 .25

244 Floyd Bannister .05 .15
245 Fred Lynn .08 .25
246 Charlie Moore .05 .15
247 Walt Terrell .05 .15
248 Dave Winfield .08 .25
249 Dwight Evans .20 .50
250 Dennis Powell .05 .15
251 Andre Thornton .05 .15
252 Onix Concepcion .05 .15
253 Mike Heath .05 .15
254A David Palmer ERR/(Position 2B) .05 .15
254B David Palmer COR/(Position P) .20 .50
255 Donnie Moore .05 .15
256 Curtis Wilkerson .05 .15
257 Julio Cruz .05 .15
258 Nolan Ryan 1.50 4.00
259 Jeff Stone .05 .15
260 John Tudor .08 .25
261 Mark Thurmond .05 .15
262 Jay Tibbs .05 .15
263 Rafael Ramirez .05 .15
264 Larry McWilliams .05 .15
265 Mark Davis .05 .15
266 Bob Dernier .05 .15
267 Matt Young .05 .15
268 Jim Clancy .05 .15
269 Mickey Hatcher .05 .15
270 Sammy Stewart .05 .15
271 Bob L. Gibson .05 .15
272 Nelson Simmons .05 .15
273 Rich Gedman .05 .15
274 Butch Wynegar .05 .15
275 Ken Howell .05 .15
276 Mel Hall .05 .15
277 Jim Sundberg .08 .25
278 Chris Codiroli .05 .15
279 Herm Winningham .05 .15
280 Rod Carew .20 .50
281 Don Slaught .05 .15
282 Scott Fletcher .05 .15
283 Bill Dawley .05 .15
284 Andy Hawkins .05 .15
285 Glenn Wilson .05 .15
286 Nick Esasky .05 .15
287 Claudell Washington .05 .15
288 Lee Mazzilli .08 .25
289 Jody Davis .05 .15
290 Darrell Porter .05 .15
291 Scott McGregor .05 .15
292 Ted Simmons .08 .25
293 Aurelio Lopez .05 .15
294 Marty Barrett .05 .15
295 Dale Berra .05 .15
296 Greg Brock .05 .15
297 Charlie Leibrandt .05 .15
298 Bill Krueger .05 .15
299 Bryn Smith .05 .15
300 Burt Hooton .05 .15
301 Stu Cliburn .05 .15
302 Luis Salazar .05 .15
303 Ken Dayley .05 .15
304 Frank DiPino .05 .15
305 Von Hayes .05 .15
306 Gary Redus .05 .15
307 Craig Lefferts .05 .15
308 Sammy Khalifa .05 .15
309 Scott Garrelts .05 .15
310 Rick Cerone .05 .15
311 Shawon Dunston .08 .25
312 Howard Johnson .08 .25
313 Jim Presley .05 .15
314 Gary Gaetti .08 .25
315 Luis Leal .05 .15
316 Mark Salas .05 .15
317 Bill Caudill .05 .15
318 Dave Henderson .05 .15
319 Rafael Santana .05 .15
320 Leon Durham .05 .15
321 Bruce Sutter .08 .25
322 Jason Thompson .05 .15
323 Bob Brenly .05 .15
324 Carmelo Martinez .05 .15
325 Eddie Milner .05 .15
326 Juan Samuel .05 .15
327 Tom Nieto .05 .15
328 Dave Smith .05 .15
329 Urbano Lugo .05 .15
330 Joel Skinner .05 .15
331 Bill Gullickson .05 .15
332 Floyd Rayford .05 .15
333 Ben Oglivie .08 .25
334 Lance Parrish .08 .25
335 Jackie Gutierrez .05 .15
336 Dennis Rasmussen .05 .15
337 Terry Whitfield .05 .15
338 Neal Heaton .05 .15
339 Jorge Orta .05 .15
340 Donnie Hill .05 .15
341 Joe Hesketh .05 .15
342 Charlie Hough .08 .25
343 Dave Rozema .05 .15
344 Greg Pryor .05 .15
345 Mickey Tettleton RC .20 .50
346 George Vukovich .05 .15
347 Don Baylor .08 .25
348 Carlos Diaz .05 .15
349 Barbaro Garbey .05 .15
350 Larry Sheets .05 .15
351 Teddy Higuera RC* .20 .50
352 Juan Beniquez .05 .15
353 Bob Forsch .05 .15
354 Mark Bailey .05 .15
355 Larry Andersen .05 .15
356 Terry Kennedy .05 .15
357 Don Robinson .05 .15
358 Jim Gott .05 .15
359 Earnie Riles .05 .15
360 John Christensen .05 .15
361 Ray Fontenot .05 .15
362 Spike Owen .05 .15
363 Jim Acker .05 .15
364 Ron Davis .05 .15
365 Tom Hume .05 .15
366 Carlton Fisk .20 .50
367 Nate Snell .05 .15
368 Rick Manning .05 .15
369 Darrell Evans .08 .25
370 Ron Hassey .05 .15
371 Wade Boggs .20 .50
372 Rick Honeycutt .05 .15
373 Chris Bando .05 .15
374 Bud Black .05 .15
375 Steve Henderson .05 .15
376 Charlie Lea .05 .15
377 Reggie Jackson .20 .50
378 Dave Schmidt .05 .15
379 Bob James .05 .15
380 Glenn Davis .05 .15
381 Tim Corcoran .05 .15
382 Danny Cox .05 .15
383 Tim Flannery .05 .15
384 Tom Browning .05 .15
385 Rick Camp .05 .15
386 Jim Morrison .05 .15
387 Dave LaPoint .05 .15
388 Dave Lopes .08 .25
389 Al Cowens .05 .15
390 Doyle Alexander .05 .15
391 Tim Laudner .05 .15
392 Don Aase .05 .15
393 Jaime Cocanower .05 .15
394 Randy O'Neal .05 .15
395 Mike Easler .05 .15
396 Scott Bradley .05 .15
397 Tom Niedenfuer .05 .15
398 Jerry Willard .05 .15
399 Lonnie Smith .05 .15
400 Bruce Bochte .05 .15
401 Terry Francona .08 .25
402 Jim Slaton .05 .15
403 Bill Stein .05 .15
404 Tim Hulett .05 .15
405 Alan Ashby .05 .15
406 Tim Stoddard .05 .15
407 Garry Maddox .05 .15
408 Ted Power .05 .15
409 Len Barker .05 .15
410 Denny Gonzalez .05 .15
411 George Frazier .05 .15
412 Andy Van Slyke .20 .50
413 Jim Dwyer .05 .15
414 Paul Householder .05 .15
415 Alejandro Sanchez .05 .15
416 Steve Crawford .05 .15
417 Dan Pasqua .05 .15
418 Enos Cabell .05 .15
419 Mike Jones .05 .15
420 Steve Kiefer .05 .15
421 Tim Burke .05 .15
422 Mike Mason .05 .15
423 Ruppert Jones .05 .15
424 Jerry Hairston .05 .15
425 Tito Landrum .05 .15
426 Jeff Calhoun .05 .15
427 Don Carman .05 .15
428 Tony Perez .20 .50
429 Jerry Davis .05 .15
430 Bob Walk .05 .15
431 Brad Wellman .05 .15
432 Terry Forster .08 .25
433 Billy Hatcher .05 .15
434 Clint Hurdle .05 .15
435 Ivan Calderon RC* .20 .50
436 Pete Filson .05 .15
437 Tom Henke .08 .25
438 Dave Engle .05 .15
439 Tom Filer .05 .15
440 Gorman Thomas .08 .25
441 Rick Aguilera RC .20 .50
442 Scott Sanderson .05 .15
443 Jeff Dedmon .05 .15
444 Joe Orsulak RC* .20 .50
445 Atlee Hammaker .05 .15
446 Jerry Royster .05 .15
447 Buddy Bell .08 .25
448 Dave Rucker .05 .15
449 Ivan DeJesus .05 .15
450 Jim Pankovits .05 .15
451 Jerry Narron .05 .15
452 Bryan Little .05 .15
453 Gary Lucas .05 .15
454 Dennis Martinez .08 .25
455 Ed Romero .05 .15
456 Bob Melvin .05 .15
457 Glenn Hoffman .05 .15
458 Bob Shirley .05 .15
459 Bob Welch .08 .25
460 Carmen Castillo .05 .15
461 Dave Leeper OF .05 .15
462 Tim Birtsas .05 .15
463 Randy St.Claire .05 .15
464 Chris Welsh .05 .15
465 Greg Harris .05 .15
466 Lynn Jones .05 .15
467 Dusty Baker .08 .25
468 Roy Smith .05 .15
469 Andre Robertson .05 .15
470 Ken Landreaux .05 .15
471 Dave Bergman .05 .15
472 Gary Roenicke .05 .15
473 Pete Vuckovich .05 .15
474 Kirk McCaskill RC .20 .50
475 Jeff Lahti .05 .15
476 Mike Scott .08 .25
477 Darren Daulton RC .40 1.00
478 Graig Nettles .08 .25
479 Bill Almon .05 .15
480 Greg Minton .05 .15
481 Randy Ready .05 .15
482 Len Dykstra RC .60 1.50
483 Thad Bosley .05 .15
484 Harold Reynolds RC .60 1.50
485 Al Oliver .08 .25
486 Roy Smalley .05 .15
487 John Franco .08 .25
488 Juan Agosto .05 .15
489 Al Pardo .05 .15
490 Bill Wegman RC .05 .15
491 Frank Tanana .08 .25
492 Brian Fisher RC .05 .15
493 Mark Clear .05 .15
494 Len Matuszek .05 .15
495 Ramon Romero .05 .15
496 John Wathan .05 .15
497 Rob Picciolo .05 .15
498 U.L. Washington .05 .15
499 John Candelaria .05 .15
500 Duane Walker .05 .15
501 Gene Nelson .05 .15
502 John Mizerock .05 .15
503 Luis Aguayo .05 .15
504 Kurt Kepshire .05 .15
505 Ed Wojna .05 .15
506 Joe Price .05 .15
507 Milt Thompson RC .20 .50
508 Junior Ortiz .05 .15
509 Vida Blue .08 .25
510 Steve Engel .05 .15
511 Karl Best .05 .15
512 Cecil Fielder RC .75 2.00
513 Frank Eufemia .05 .15
514 Tippy Martinez .05 .15
515 Billy Joe Robidoux .05 .15
516 Bill Scherrer .05 .15
517 Bruce Hurst .05 .15
518 Rich Bordi .05 .15
519 Steve Yeager .08 .25
520 Tony Bernazard .05 .15
521 Hal McRae .08 .25
522 Jose Rijo .08 .25
523 Mitch Webster .05 .15
524 Jack Howell .05 .15
525 Alan Bannister .05 .15
526 Ron Kittle .05 .15
527 Phil Garner .08 .25
528 Kurt Bevacqua .05 .15
529 Kevin Gross .05 .15
530 Bo Diaz .05 .15
531 Ken Oberkfell .05 .15
532 Rick Reuschel .08 .25
533 Ron Meridith .05 .15
534 Steve Braun .05 .15
535 Wayne Gross .05 .15
536 Ray Searage .05 .15
537 Tom Brookens .05 .15
538 Al Nipper .05 .15
539 Billy Sample .05 .15
540 Steve Sax .05 .15
541 Dan Quisenberry .05 .15
542 Tony Phillips .05 .15
543 Floyd Youmans .05 .15
544 Steve Buechele RC .20 .50
545 Craig Gerber .05 .15
546 Joe DeSa .05 .15
547 Brian Harper .05 .15
548 Kevin Bass .05 .15
549 Tom Foley .05 .15
550 Dave Van Gorder .05 .15
551 Bruce Bochy .05 .15
552 R.J. Reynolds .05 .15
553 Chris Brown RC .05 .15
554 Bruce Benedict .05 .15
555 Warren Brusstar .05 .15
556 Danny Heep .05 .15
557 Darnell Coles .05 .15
558 Greg Gagne .05 .15
559 Ernie Whitt .05 .15
560 Ron Washington .05 .15
561 Jimmy Key .08 .25
562 Bill Swift .05 .15
563 Ron Darling .08 .25
564 Dick Ruthven .05 .15
565 Zane Smith .05 .15
566 Sid Bream .05 .15
567A Joel Youngblood ERR/(Position P).05 .15
567B Joel Youngblood COR/(Position IF).20 .50
568 Mario Ramirez .05 .15
569 Tom Runnells .05 .15
570 Rick Schu .05 .15
571 Bill Campbell .05 .15
572 Dickie Thon .05 .15
573 Al Holland .05 .15
574 Reid Nichols .05 .15
575 Bert Roberge .05 .15
576 Mike Flanagan .05 .15
577 Tim Leary .05 .15
578 Mike Laga .05 .15
579 Steve Lyons .05 .15
580 Phil Niekro .08 .25
581 Gilberto Reyes .05 .15
582 Jamie Easterly .05 .15
583 Mark Gubicza .05 .15
584 Stan Javier RC .20 .50
585 Bill Laskey .05 .15
586 Jeff Russell .05 .15
587 Dickie Noles .05 .15
588 Steve Farr .05 .15
589 Steve Ontiveros RC .05 .15
590 Mike Hargrove .05 .15
591 Marty Bystrom .05 .15
592 Franklin Stubbs .05 .15
593 Larry Herndon .05 .15
594 Bill Swaggerty .05 .15
595 Carlos Ponce .05 .15
596 Pat Perry .05 .15
597 Ray Knight .08 .25
598 Steve Lombardozzi .05 .15
599 Brad Havens .05 .15
600 Pat Clements .05 .15
601 Joe Niekro .05 .15
602 Hank Aaron Puzzle .30 .75
603 Dwayne Henry .05 .15
604 Mookie Wilson .08 .25
605 Buddy Biancalana .05 .15
606 Rance Mulliniks .05 .15
607 Alan Wiggins .05 .15
608 Joe Cowley .05 .15
609 Tom Seaver .20 .50
609B Tom Seaver YL .75 2.00
610 Neil Allen .05 .15
611 Don Sutton .08 .25
612 Fred Toliver .05 .15
613 Jay Baller .05 .15
614 Marc Sullivan .05 .15
615 John Grubb .05 .15
616 Bruce Kison .05 .15
617 Bill Madlock .08 .25
618 Chris Chambliss .08 .25
619 Dave Stewart .08 .25
620 Tim Lollar .05 .15
621 Gary Lavelle .05 .15
622 Charles Hudson .05 .15
623 Joel Davis .05 .15
624 Joe Johnson .05 .15
625 Sid Fernandez .05 .15
626 Dennis Lamp .05 .15
627 Terry Harper .05 .15
628 Jack Lazorko .05 .15
629 Roger McDowell RC* .20 .50
630 Mark Funderburk .05 .15
631 Ed Lynch .05 .15
632 Rudy Law .05 .15
633 Roger Mason RC .05 .15
634 Mike Felder RC .05 .15
635 Ken Schrom .05 .15
636 Bob Ojeda .05 .15
637 Ed VandeBerg .05 .15
638 Bobby Meacham .05 .15
639 Cliff Johnson .05 .15
640 Garth Iorg .05 .15
641 Dan Driessen .05 .15
642 Mike Brown OF .05 .15
643 John Shelby .05 .15
644 Pete Rose RB .30 .75
645 The Knuckle Brothers .08 .25
646 Jesse Orosco .05 .15
647 Billy Beane RC .40 1.00
648 Cesar Cedeno .08 .25
649 Bert Blyleven .08 .25
650 Max Venable .05 .15
651 Fleet Feet .05 .15
Vince Coleman
Willie McGee
652 Calvin Schiraldi .05 .15
653 Pete Rose KING .30 .75
654 Diamond Kings CL
1-26/(Unnumbered) .05 .15
655A CL 1: 27-130/(Unnumbered)
(45 Beane ERR) .05 .15
655B CL 1: 27-130/(Unnumbered)
(45 Habyan COR) .05 .15
656 CL 2: 131-234/(Unnumbered) .05 .15
657 CL 3: 235-338/(Unnumbered) .05 .15
658 CL 4: 339-442/(Unnumbered) .05 .15
659 CL 5: 443-546/(Unnumbered) .05 .15
660 CL 6: 547-653/(Unnumbered) .05 .15

1986 Donruss Hank Aaron Puzzle

1 Aaron Puzzle 1-3 .10 .25
4 Aaron Puzzle 4-6 .10 .25
7 Aaron Puzzle 7-10 .10 .25
10 Aaron Puzzle 10-12 .10 .25
13 Aaron Puzzle 13-15 .10 .25
16 Aaron Puzzle 16-18 .10 .25
19 Aaron Puzzle 19-21 .10 .25
22 Aaron Puzzle 22-24 .10 .25
25 Aaron Puzzle 25-27 .10 .25
28 Aaron Puzzle 28-30 .10 .25
31 Aaron Puzzle 29-31 .10 .25
34 Aaron Puzzle 34-36 .10 .25
37 Aaron Puzzle 37-39 .10 .25
40 Aaron Puzzle 40-42 .10 .25
43 Aaron Puzzle 43-45 .10 .25
46 Aaron Puzzle 46-48 .10 .25
49 Aaron Puzzle 49-51 .10 .25
52 Aaron Puzzle 52-54 .10 .25
55 Aaron Puzzle 55-57 .10 .25
58 Aaron Puzzle 58-60 .10 .25
61 Aaron Puzzle 61-63 .10 .25

1986 Donruss Wax Box Cards

COMPLETE SET (4) .40 1.00
PC4 Kirk Gibson .15 .40
PC5 Willie Hernandez .02 .10
PC6 Doug DeCinces .02 .10
PUZ Hank Aaron .30 .75
Puzzle Card

1986 Donruss Rookies

The 1986 Donruss "The Rookies" set features 56 full-color standard-size cards plus a 15-piece puzzle of Hank Aaron. The set was distributed through hobby dealers, packed in 60-set cases, in a small green, cellophane wrapped factory box. Although the set was wrapped in cellophane, the top card was number one Joyner, resulting in a percentage of the Joyner cards arriving in less than perfect condition. Donruss fixed the problem after it was called to their attention and even went so far as to include a customer service phone number in their second printing. Card fronts are similar in design to the 1986 Donruss regular issue except for the presence of "The Rookies" logo in the lower left corner and a bluish green border instead of a blue border. The key extended Rookie Cards in this set are Barry Bonds, Bobby Bonilla, Will Clark, Bo Jackson, Wally Joyner and John Kruk.

COMP.FACT.SET (56) 10.00 25.00
1 Wally Joyner XRC .40 1.00
2 Tracy Jones .05 .15
3 Allan Anderson XRC .05 .15
4 Ed Correa .05 .15
5 Reggie Williams .05 .15
6 Charlie Kerfeld .05 .15
7 Andres Galarraga .60 1.50
8 Bob Tewksbury XRC .20 .50
9 Al Newman XRC .08 .25
10 Andres Thomas .05 .15
11 Barry Bonds XRC 8.00 20.00
12 Juan Nieves .05 .15
13 Mark Eichhorn .05 .15
14 Dan Plesac XRC .20 .50
15 Cory Snyder .05 .15
16 Kelly Gruber .05 .15
17 Kevin Mitchell XRC .40 1.00
18 Steve Lombardozzi .05 .15
19 Mitch Williams XRC .20 .50
20 John Cerutti .05 .15
21 Todd Worrell .20 .50
22 Jose Canseco 1.50 4.00
23 Pete Incaviglia XRC .20 .50
24 Jose Guzman .05 .15
25 Scott Bailes .05 .15
26 Greg Mathews .05 .15
27 Eric King .05 .15
28 Paul Assenmacher .20 .50
29 Jeff Sellers .05 .15
30 Bobby Bonilla XRC .40 1.00
31 Doug Drabek XRC .40 1.00
32 Will Clark XRC .75 2.00
33 Bip Roberts XRC .20 .50
34 Jim Deshaies XRC .05 .15
35 Mike LaValliere XRC .20 .50
36 Scott Bankhead .05 .15
37 Dale Sveum .05 .15
38 Bo Jackson XRC 2.50 6.00
39 Robby Thompson XRC .20 .50
40 Eric Plunk .05 .15
41 Bill Bathe .05 .15
42 John Kruk XRC .60 1.50
43 Andy Allanson XRC .05 .15
44 Mark Portugal XRC .20 .50
45 Danny Tartabull .08 .25
46 Bob Kipper .05 .15
47 Gene Walter .05 .15
48 Rey Quinones UER
(Misspelled Quinonez) .05 .15
49 Bobby Witt XRC .20 .50
50 Bill Mooneyham .05 .15
51 John Cangelosi .05 .15
52 Ruben Sierra XRC .60 1.50
53 Rob Woodward .05 .15
54 Ed Hearn XRC .05 .15
55 Joel McKeon .05 .15
56 Checklist 1-56 .05 .15

1986 Donruss All-Stars

COMPLETE SET (60) 2.50 6.00
1 Tony Gwynn .50 1.25
2 Tommy Herr .01 .05
3 Steve Garvey .07 .20
4 Dale Murphy .07 .20
5 Darryl Strawberry .02 .10
6 Graig Nettles .02 .10
7 Terry Kennedy .01 .05
8 Ozzie Smith .30 .75
9 LaMarr Hoyt .01 .05
10 Rickey Henderson .25 .60
11 Lou Whitaker .02 .10
12 George Brett .40 1.00
13 Eddie Murray .20 .50
14 Cal Ripken .75 2.00
15 Dave Winfield .20 .50
16 Jim Rice .02 .10
17 Carlton Fisk .20 .50
18 Jack Morris .02 .10
19 Jose Cruz .01 .05
20 Tim Raines .02 .10
21 Nolan Ryan .75 2.00
22 Tony Pena .02 .10
23 Jack Clark .02 .10
24 Dave Parker .02 .10
25 Tim Wallach .01 .05
26 Ozzie Virgil .01 .05
27 Fernando Valenzuela .02 .10
28 Dwight Gooden .07 .20
29 Glenn Wilson .01 .05
30 Garry Templeton .01 .05
31 Goose Gossage .02 .10
32 Ryne Sandberg .30 .75
33 Jeff Reardon .01 .05
34 Pete Rose .20 .50
35 Scott Garrelts .01 .05
36 Willie McGee .02 .10
37 Ron Darling .01 .05
38 Dick Williams MG .01 .05
39 Paul Molitor .20 .50
40 Damaso Garcia .01 .05
41 Phil Bradley .01 .05
42 Dan Petry .01 .05
43 Willie Hernandez .01 .05
44 Tom Brunansky .01 .05
45 Alan Trammell .07 .20
46 Donnie Moore .01 .05
47 Wade Boggs .20 .50
48 Ernie Whitt .01 .05
49 Harold Baines .02 .10
50 Don Mattingly .30 .75
51 Gary Ward .01 .05
52 Bert Blyleven .02 .10
53 Jimmy Key .02 .10
54 Cecil Cooper .02 .10
55 Dave Stieb .01 .05
56 Rich Gedman .01 .05
57 Jay Howell .01 .05
58 Sparky Anderson MG .01 .05
59 Minneapolis Metrodome .01 .05
NNO Checklist Card .01 .05

1986 Donruss All-Star Box

COMPLETE SET (4) .75 2.00
PC7 Wade Boggs .40 1.00
PC8 Lee Smith .20 .50
PC9 Cecil Cooper .08 .25
PUZ Hank Aaron .30 .75
Puzzle Card

1986 Donruss Highlights

COMP.FACT.SET (56) 2.00 5.00
DISTRIBUTED IN FACTORY SET ONLY
1 Will Clark .40 1.00
2 Jose Rijo .02 .10
3 George Brett .25 .60
4 Mike Schmidt .15 .40
5 Roger Clemens .75 2.00
6 Roger Clemens .75 2.00
7 Kirby Puckett .20 .50
8 Dwight Gooden .15 .40
9 Johnny Ray .02 .10
10 M.Mantle .75 2.00
R.Jackson
11 Wade Boggs .08 .25
12 Don Aase .02 .10
13 Wade Boggs .08 .25
14 Jeff Reardon .02 .10
15 Hubie Brooks .02 .10
16 Don Sutton .15 .40
17 Roger Clemens .75 2.00
18 Roger Clemens .75 2.00
19 Kent Hrbek .05 .15
20 Rick Rhoden .02 .10
21 Kevin Bass .02 .10
22 Bob Horner .02 .10
23 Wally Joyner .08 .25
24 Darryl Strawberry .08 .25
25 Fernando Valenzuela .05 .15
26 Roger Clemens .75 2.00
27 Jack Morris .05 .15
28 Scott Fletcher .02 .10
29 Todd Worrell .05 .15
30 Eric Davis .15 .40
31 Bert Blyleven .05 .15
32 Bobby Doerr .08 .25
33 Ernie Lombardi .05 .15
34 Willie McCovey .05 .15
35 Steve Carlton .05 .15
36 Mike Schmidt .15 .40
37 Juan Samuel .02 .10
38 Mike Witt .02 .10
39 Doug DeCinces .02 .10
40 Bill Gullickson .02 .10
41 Dale Murphy .08 .25
42 Joe Carter .15 .40
43 Bo Jackson .50 1.25
44 Joe Cowley .02 .10
45 Jim Deshaies .02 .10
46 Mike Scott .02 .10
47 Bruce Hurst .02 .10
48 Don Mattingly .25 .60
49 Mike Krukow .02 .10
50 Steve Sax .02 .10
51 John Cangelosi .02 .10
52 Dave Righetti .02 .10
53 Don Mattingly .25 .60
54 Todd Worrell .05 .15
55 Jose Canseco 1.25 3.00
56 Checklist Card .02 .10

1986 Donruss Pop-Ups

COMPLETE SET (18) 2.00 5.00
1 Tony Gwynn .60 1.50
2 Tommy Herr .01 .05
3 Steve Garvey .07 .20
4 Dale Murphy .10 .30
5 Darryl Strawberry .02 .10
6 Graig Nettles .02 .10
7 Terry Kennedy .01 .05
8 Ozzie Smith .40 1.00
9 LaMarr Hoyt .01 .05
10 Rickey Henderson .20 .50
11 Lou Whitaker .02 .10
12 George Brett .50 1.25
13 Eddie Murray .25 .60
14 Cal Ripken 1.00 2.50
15 Dave Winfield .20 .50
16 Jim Rice .02 .10
17 Carlton Fisk .20 .50
18 Jack Morris .02 .10

1986 Donruss Super DK's

COMPLETE SET (27) 5.00 12.00
1 Kirk Gibson .20 .50
2 Goose Gossage .20 .50
3 Willie McGee .20 .50
4 George Bell .08 .25
5 Tony Armas .08 .25
6 Chili Davis .20 .50
7 Cecil Cooper .08 .25
8 Mike Boddicker .08 .25
9 Dave Lopes .08 .25
10 Bill Doran .08 .25
11 Bret Saberhagen .20 .50
12 Brett Butler .20 .50
13 Harold Baines .30 .75
14 Mike Davis .08 .25
15 Tony Perez .40 1.00
16 Willie Randolph .20 .50
17 Bob Boone .20 .50
18 Orel Hershiser .30 .75
19 Johnny Ray .08 .25
20 Gary Ward .08 .25
21 Rick Mahler .08 .25
22 Phil Bradley .08 .25
23 Jerry Koosman .20 .50
24 Tom Brunansky .08 .25
25 Andre Dawson .30 .75
26 Dwight Gooden .40 1.00
27 Pete Rose 1.00 2.50
King of Kings
NNO Checklist Card .08 .25
NNO Aaron Large Puzzle .40 1.00

1987 Donruss

This set consists of 660 standard-size cards. Cards were primarily distributed in 15-card wax packs, rack packs and a factory set. All packs included a Roberto Clemente puzzle panel and the factory sets contained a complete puzzle.The regular-issue cards feature a black and gold border on the front. The backs of the cards in the factory sets are oriented differently than cards taken from wax packs, giving the appearance that one version or the other is upside down when sorting from the card backs. There are no premiums or discounts for either version. The popular Diamond King subset returns for the sixth consecutive year. Some of the Diamond King (1-26) selections are repeats from prior years; Perez-Steele Galleries had indicated in 1987 that a five-year rotation would be maintained in order to avoid depleting the pool of available worthy "kings" on some of the teams. The rich selection of Rookie Cards in this set include Barry Bonds, Bobby Bonilla, Kevin Brown, Will Clark, David Cone, Chuck Finley, Bo Jackson, Wally Joyner, Barry Larkin, Greg Maddux and Rafael Palmeiro.

COMPLETE SET (660) 15.00 40.00
COMP.FACT.SET (660) 20.00 50.00
COMP.CLEMENTE PUZZLE .60 1.50
1 Wally Joyner DK .15 .40
2 Roger Clemens DK .75 2.00
3 Dale Murphy DK .08 .25
4 Darryl Strawberry DK .05 .15
5 Ozzie Smith DK .25 .60
6 Jose Canseco DK .40 1.00
7 Charlie Hough DK .05 .15
8 Brook Jacoby DK .02 .10
9 Fred Lynn DK .05 .15
10 Rick Rhoden DK .02 .10
11 Chris Brown DK .02 .10
12 Von Hayes DK .02 .10
13 Jack Morris DK .05 .15
14A Kevin McReynolds DK ERR .15 .40
14B Kevin McReynolds DK .02 .10
COR
15 George Brett DK .40 1.00
16 Ted Higuera DK .02 .10
17 Hubie Brooks DK .02 .10
18 Mike Scott DK .05 .15
19 Kirby Puckett DK .30 .75
20 Dave Winfield DK .05 .15
21 Lloyd Moseby DK .02 .10
22A Eric Davis DK ERR .15 .40
22B Eric Davis DK COR .08 .25
23 Jim Presley DK .02 .10
24 Keith Moreland DK .02 .10
25A Greg Walker DK ERR .15 .40
No color in DK banner on card back
25B Greg Walker DK COR .02 .10
DK banner on back colored yellow
26 Steve Sax DK .02 .10
27 DK Checklist 1-26 .02 .10
28 B.J. Surhoff RC .25 .60
29 Randy Myers RC .25 .60
30 Ken Gerhart RC .05 .15
31 Benito Santiago .05 .15
32 Greg Swindell RC .15 .40
33 Mike Birkbeck RC .05 .15
34 Terry Steinbach RC .25 .60
35 Bo Jackson RC 8.00 20.00
36 Greg Maddux RC 6.00 15.00
37 Jim Lindeman RC .05 .15
38 Devon White RC .25 .60
39 Eric Bell RC .05 .15
40 Willie Fraser RC .05 .15
41 Jerry Browne RC .05 .15
42 Chris James RC * .05 .15
43 Rafael Palmeiro RC 2.00 5.00
44 Pat Dodson RC .05 .15
45 Duane Ward RC * .15 .40
46 Mark McGwire 5.00 12.00
47 Bruce Fields UER RC .05 .15
48 Eddie Murray .15 .40
49 Ted Higuera .02 .10
50 Kirk Gibson .05 .15
51 Oil Can Boyd .02 .10
52 Don Mattingly .50 1.25
53 Pedro Guerrero .05 .15
54 George Brett .40 1.00
55 Jose Rijo .05 .15
56 Tim Raines .05 .15
57 Ed Correa .02 .10
58 Mike Witt .02 .10
59 Greg Walker .02 .10
60 Ozzie Smith .25 .60
61 Glenn Davis .02 .10
62 Glenn Wilson .02 .10
63 Tom Browning .02 .10
64 Tony Gwynn .25 .60
65 R.J. Reynolds .02 .10
66 Will Clark RC .60 1.50
67 Ozzie Virgil .02 .10
68 Rick Sutcliffe .05 .15
69 Gary Carter .05 .15
70 Mike Moore .02 .10
71 Bert Blyleven .05 .15
72 Tony Fernandez .02 .10
73 Kent Hrbek .05 .15
74 Lloyd Moseby .02 .10
75 Alvin Davis .02 .10
76 Keith Hernandez .05 .15
77 Ryne Sandberg .30 .75
78 Dale Murphy .08 .25
79 Sid Bream .02 .10
80 Chris Brown .02 .10
81 Steve Garvey .05 .15
82 Mario Soto .05 .15
83 Shane Rawley .02 .10
84 Willie McGee .05 .15
85 Jose Cruz .05 .15
86 Brian Downing .05 .15
87 Ozzie Guillen .08 .25
88 Hubie Brooks .02 .10
89 Cal Ripken .60 1.50
90 Juan Nieves .02 .10
91 Lance Parrish .05 .15
92 Jim Rice .05 .15
93 Ron Guidry .05 .15
94 Fernando Valenzuela .05 .15
95 Andy Allanson RC .02 .10
96 Willie Wilson .05 .15
97 Jose Canseco .40 1.00
98 Jeff Reardon .05 .15
99 Bobby Witt RC .15 .40
100 Checklist 28-133 .02 .10
101 Jose Guzman .02 .10
102 Steve Balboni .02 .10
103 Tony Phillips .02 .10
104 Brook Jacoby .02 .10
105 Dave Winfield .05 .15
106 Orel Hershiser .08 .25
107 Lou Whitaker .05 .15
108 Fred Lynn .05 .15
109 Bill Wegman .02 .10
110 Donnie Moore .02 .10
111 Jack Clark .05 .15
112 Bob Knepper .02 .10
113 Von Hayes .02 .10
114 Bip Roberts RC .15 .40
115 Tony Pena .02 .10
116 Scott Garrelts .02 .10
117 Paul Molitor .05 .15
118 Darryl Strawberry .05 .15
119 Shawon Dunston .02 .10
120 Jim Presley .02 .10
121 Jesse Barfield .05 .15
122 Gary Gaetti .05 .15

123 Kurt Stillwell .02 .10
124 Joel Davis .02 .10
125 Mike Boddicker .02 .10
126 Robin Yount .25 .60
127 Alan Trammell .05 .15
128 Dave Righetti .05 .15
129 Dwight Evans .08 .25
130 Mike Scioscia .05 .15
131 Julio Franco .05 .15
132 Bret Saberhagen .05 .15
133 Mike Davis .02 .10
134 Joe Hesketh .02 .10
135 Wally Joyner RC .25 .60
136 Don Slaught .02 .10
137 Daryl Boston .02 .10
138 Nolan Ryan .75 2.00
139 Mike Schmidt .40 1.00
140 Tommy Herr .02 .10
141 Garry Templeton .05 .15
142 Kal Daniels .02 .10
143 Billy Sample .02 .10
144 Johnny Ray .02 .10
145 Robby Thompson RC * .15 .40
146 Bob Dernier .02 .10
147 Danny Tartabull .02 .10
148 Ernie Whitt .02 .10
149 Kirby Puckett .30 .75
150 Mike Young .02 .10
151 Ernest Riles .02 .10
152 Frank Tanana .05 .15
153 Rich Gedman .02 .10
154 Willie Randolph .05 .15
155 Bill Madlock .05 .15
156 Joe Carter .05 .15
157 Danny Jackson .02 .10
158 Carney Lansford .05 .15
159 Bryn Smith .02 .10
160 Gary Pettis .02 .10
161 Oddibe McDowell .02 .10
162 John Cangelosi .02 .10
163 Mike Scott .05 .15
164 Eric Show .02 .10
165 Juan Samuel .02 .10
166 Nick Esasky .02 .10
167 Zane Smith .02 .10
168 Mike C. Brown OF .02 .10
169 Keith Moreland .02 .10
170 John Tudor .05 .15
171 Ken Dixon .02 .10
172 Jim Gantner .02 .10
173 Jack Morris .05 .15
174 Bruce Hurst .02 .10
175 Dennis Rasmussen .02 .10
176 Mike Marshall .02 .10
177 Dan Quisenberry .02 .10
178 Eric Plunk .02 .10
179 Tim Wallach .02 .10
180 Steve Buechele .02 .10
181 Don Sutton .05 .15
182 Dave Schmidt .02 .10
183 Terry Pendleton .05 .15
184 Jim Deshaies RC * .05 .15
185 Steve Bedrosian .02 .10
186 Pete Rose .50 1.25
187 Dave Dravecky .02 .10
188 Rick Reuschel .05 .15
189 Dan Gladden .02 .10
190 Rick Mahler .02 .10
191 Thad Bosley .02 .10
192 Ron Darling .05 .15
193 Matt Young .02 .10
194 Tom Brunansky .02 .10
195 Dave Stieb .05 .15
196 Frank Viola .05 .15
197 Tom Henke .02 .10
198 Karl Best .02 .10
199 Dwight Gooden .08 .25
200 Checklist 134-239 .02 .10
201 Steve Trout .02 .10
202 Rafael Ramirez .02 .10
203 Bob Walk .02 .10
204 Roger Mason .02 .10
205 Terry Kennedy .02 .10
206 Ron Oester .02 .10
207 John Russell .02 .10
208 Greg Mathews .02 .10
209 Charlie Kerfeld .02 .10
210 Reggie Jackson .08 .25
211 Floyd Bannister .02 .10
212 Vance Law .02 .10
213 Rich Bordi .02 .10
214 Dan Plesac .02 .10
215 Dave Collins .02 .10
216 Bob Stanley .02 .10
217 Joe Niekro .02 .10
218 Tom Niedenfuer .02 .10
219 Brett Butler .05 .15
220 Charlie Leibrandt .02 .10
221 Steve Ontiveros .02 .10
222 Tim Burke .02 .10
223 Curtis Wilkerson .02 .10
224 Pete Incaviglia RC * .15 .40
225 Lonnie Smith .02 .10
226 Chris Codiroli .02 .10
227 Scott Bailes .02 .10
228 Rickey Henderson .15 .40
229 Ken Howell .02 .10
230 Darnell Coles .02 .10
231 Don Aase .02 .10
232 Tim Leary .02 .10
233 Bob Boone .05 .15
234 Ricky Horton .02 .10
235 Mark Bailey .02 .10
236 Kevin Gross .02 .10
237 Lance McCullers .02 .10
238 Cecilio Guante .02 .10
239 Bob Melvin .02 .10
240 Billy Joe Robidoux .02 .10
241 Roger McDowell .02 .10
242 Leon Durham .02 .10
243 Ed Nunez .02 .10
244 Jimmy Key .05 .15
245 Mike Smithson .02 .10
246 Bo Diaz .02 .10
247 Carlton Fisk .08 .25
248 Larry Sheets .02 .10
249 Juan Castillo RC .05 .15
250 Eric King .02 .10
251 Doug Drabek RC .25 .60
252 Wade Boggs .08 .25
253 Mariano Duncan .02 .10
254 Pat Tabler .02 .10
255 Frank White .05 .15
256 Alfredo Griffin .02 .10
257 Floyd Youmans .02 .10
258 Rob Wilfong .02 .10
259 Pete O'Brien .02 .10
260 Tim Hulett .02 .10
261 Dickie Thon .02 .10
262 Darren Daulton .05 .15
263 Vince Coleman .02 .10
264 Andy Hawkins .02 .10
265 Eric Davis .08 .25
266 Andres Thomas .02 .10
267 Mike Diaz .02 .10
268 Chili Davis .05 .15
269 Jody Davis .02 .10
270 Phil Bradley .02 .10
271 George Bell .05 .15
272 Keith Atherton .02 .10
273 Storm Davis .02 .10
274 Rob Deer .02 .10
275 Walt Terrell .02 .10
276 Roger Clemens .75 2.00
277 Mike Easler .02 .10
278 Steve Sax .02 .10
279 Andre Thornton .02 .10
280 Jim Sundberg .05 .15
281 Bill Bathe .02 .10
282 Jay Tibbs .02 .10
283 Dick Schofield .02 .10
284 Mike Mason .02 .10
285 Jerry Hairston .02 .10
286 Bill Doran .02 .10
287 Tim Flannery .02 .10
288 Gary Redus .02 .10
289 John Franco .05 .15
290 Paul Assenmacher .15 .40
291 Joe Orsulak .02 .10
292 Lee Smith .05 .15
293 Mike Laga .02 .10
294 Rick Dempsey .02 .10
295 Mike Felder .02 .10
296 Tom Brookens .02 .10
297 Al Nipper .02 .10
298 Mike Pagliarulo .02 .10
299 Franklin Stubbs .02 .10
300 Checklist 240-345 .02 .10
301 Steve Farr .02 .10
302 Bill Mooneyham .02 .10
303 Andres Galarraga .05 .15
304 Scott Fletcher .02 .10
305 Jack Howell .02 .10
306 Russ Morman .02 .10
307 Todd Worrell .02 .10
308 Dave Smith .02 .10
309 Jeff Stone .02 .10
310 Ron Robinson .02 .10
311 Bruce Bochy .02 .10
312 Jim Winn .02 .10
313 Mark Davis .02 .10
314 Jeff Dedmon .02 .10
315 Jamie Moyer RC .40 1.00
316 Wally Backman .02 .10
317 Ken Phelps .02 .10
318 Steve Lombardozzi .02 .10
319 Rance Mulliniks .02 .10
320 Tim Laudner .02 .10
321 Mark Eichhorn .02 .10
322 Lee Guetterman .02 .10
323 Sid Fernandez .02 .10
324 Jerry Mumphrey .02 .10
325 David Palmer .02 .10
326 Bill Almon .02 .10
327 Candy Maldonado .02 .10
328 John Kruk RC .40 1.00
329 John Denny .02 .10
330 Milt Thompson .02 .10
331 Mike LaValliere RC * .15 .40
332 Alan Ashby .02 .10
333 Doug Corbett .02 .10
334 Ron Karkovice RC .15 .40
335 Mitch Webster .02 .10
336 Lee Lacy .02 .10
337 Glenn Braggs RC .05 .15
338 Dwight Lowry .02 .10
339 Don Baylor .05 .15
340 Brian Fisher .02 .10
341 Reggie Williams .02 .10
342 Tom Candiotti .02 .10
343 Rudy Law .02 .10
344 Curt Young .02 .10
345 Mike Fitzgerald .02 .10
346 Ruben Sierra RC .40 1.00
347 Mitch Williams RC * .15 .40
348 Jorge Orta .02 .10
349 Mickey Tettleton .02 .10
350 Ernie Camacho .02 .10
351 Ron Kittle .02 .10
352 Ken Landreaux .02 .10
353 Chet Lemon .05 .15
354 John Shelby .02 .10
355 Mark Clear .02 .10
356 Doug DeCinces .02 .10
357 Ken Dayley .02 .10
358 Phil Garner .05 .15
359 Steve Jeltz .02 .10
360 Ed Whitson .02 .10
361 Barry Bonds RC 5.00 12.00
362 Vida Blue .05 .15
363 Cecil Cooper .05 .15
364 Bob Ojeda .02 .10
365 Dennis Eckersley .08 .25
366 Mike Morgan .02 .10
367 Willie Upshaw .02 .10
368 Allan Anderson RC .02 .10
369 Bill Gullickson .02 .10
370 Bobby Thigpen RC .15 .40
371 Juan Beniquez .02 .10
372 Charlie Moore .02 .10
373 Dan Petry .02 .10
374 Rod Scurry .02 .10
375 Tom Seaver .08 .25
376 Ed VandeBerg .02 .10
377 Tony Bernazard .02 .10
378 Greg Pryor .02 .10
379 Dwayne Murphy .02 .10
380 Andy McGaffigan .02 .10
381 Kirk McCaskill .02 .10
382 Greg Harris .02 .10
383 Rich Dotson .02 .10
384 Craig Reynolds .02 .10
385 Greg Gross .02 .10
386 Tito Landrum .02 .10
387 Craig Lefferts .02 .10
388 Dave Parker .05 .15
389 Bob Horner .05 .15
390 Pat Clements .02 .10
391 Jeff Leonard .02 .10
392 Chris Speier .02 .10
393 John Moses .02 .10
394 Garth Iorg .02 .10
395 Greg Gagne .02 .10
396 Nate Snell .02 .10
397 Bryan Clutterbuck .02 .10
398 Darrell Evans .05 .15
399 Steve Crawford .02 .10
400 Checklist 346-451 .02 .10
401 Phil Lombardi .02 .10
402 Rick Honeycutt .02 .10
403 Ken Schrom .02 .10
404 Bud Black .02 .10
405 Donnie Hill .02 .10
406 Wayne Krenchicki .02 .10
407 Chuck Finley RC .25 .60
408 Toby Harrah .05 .15
409 Steve Lyons .02 .10
410 Kevin Bass .02 .10
411 Marvell Wynne .02 .10
412 Ron Roenicke .02 .10
413 Tracy Jones .02 .10
414 Gene Garber .02 .10
415 Mike Bielecki .02 .10
416 Frank DiPino .02 .10
417 Andy Van Slyke .08 .25
418 Jim Dwyer .02 .10
419 Ben Oglivie .05 .15
420 Dave Bergman .02 .10
421 Joe Sambito .02 .10
422 Bob Tewksbury RC * .15 .40
423 Len Matuszek .02 .10
424 Mike Kingery RC .05 .15
425 Dave Kingman .05 .15
426 Al Newman RC .02 .10
427 Gary Ward .02 .10
428 Ruppert Jones .02 .10
429 Harold Baines .05 .15
430 Pat Perry .02 .10
431 Terry Puhl .02 .10
432 Don Carman .02 .10
433 Eddie Milner .02 .10
434 LaMarr Hoyt .02 .10
435 Rick Rhoden .02 .10
436 Jose Uribe .02 .10
437 Ken Oberkfell .02 .10
438 Ron Davis .02 .10
439 Jesse Orosco .02 .10
440 Scott Bradley .02 .10
441 Randy Bush .02 .10
442 John Cerutti .02 .10
443 Roy Smalley .02 .10
444 Kelly Gruber .02 .10
445 Bob Kearney .02 .10
446 Ed Hearn RC .02 .10
447 Scott Sanderson .02 .10
448 Bruce Benedict .02 .10
449 Junior Ortiz .02 .10
450 Mike Aldrete .02 .10
451 Kevin McReynolds .02 .10
452 Rob Murphy .02 .10
453 Kent Tekulve .02 .10
454 Curt Ford .02 .10
455 Dave Lopes .05 .15
456 Bob Grich .05 .15
457 Jose DeLeon .02 .10
458 Andre Dawson .05 .15
459 Mike Flanagan .02 .10
460 Joey Meyer .05 .15
461 Chuck Cary .02 .10
462 Bill Buckner .05 .15
463 Bob Shirley .02 .10
464 Jeff Hamilton .02 .10
465 Phil Niekro .05 .15
466 Mark Gubicza .02 .10
467 Jerry Willard .02 .10
468 Bob Sebra .02 .10
469 Larry Parrish .02 .10
470 Charlie Hough .05 .15
471 Hal McRae .05 .15
472 Dave Leiper .02 .10
473 Mel Hall .02 .10
474 Dan Pasqua .02 .10
475 Bob Welch .05 .15
476 Johnny Grubb .02 .10
477 Jim Traber .02 .10
478 Chris Bosio RC .15 .40
479 Mark McLemore .05 .15
480 John Morris .02 .10
481 Billy Hatcher .02 .10
482 Dan Schatzeder .02 .10
483 Rich Gossage .05 .15
484 Jim Morrison .02 .10
485 Bob Brenly .02 .10
486 Bill Schroeder .02 .10
487 Mookie Wilson .05 .15
488 Dave Martinez RC .15 .40
489 Harold Reynolds .05 .15
490 Jeff Hearron .02 .10
491 Mickey Hatcher .02 .10
492 Barry Larkin RC 1.50 4.00
493 Bob James .02 .10
494 John Habyan .02 .10
495 Jim Adduci .02 .10
496 Mike Heath .02 .10
497 Tim Stoddard .02 .10
498 Tony Armas .05 .15
499 Dennis Powell .02 .10
500 Checklist 452-557 .02 .10
501 Chris Bando .02 .10
502 David Cone RC .40 1.00
503 Jay Howell .02 .10
504 Tom Foley .02 .10
505 Ray Chadwick .02 .10
506 Mike Loynd RC .05 .15
507 Neil Allen .02 .10
508 Danny Darwin .02 .10
509 Rick Schu .02 .10
510 Jose Oquendo .02 .10
511 Gene Walter .02 .10
512 Terry McGriff .02 .10
513 Ken Griffey .05 .15
514 Benny Distefano .02 .10
515 Terry Mulholland RC .15 .40
516 Ed Lynch .02 .10
517 Bill Swift .02 .10
518 Manny Lee .02 .10
519 Andre David .02 .10
520 Scott McGregor .02 .10
521 Rick Manning .02 .10
522 Willie Hernandez .02 .10
523 Marty Barrett .02 .10
524 Wayne Tolleson .02 .10
525 Jose Gonzalez RC .05 .15
526 Cory Snyder .02 .10
527 Buddy Biancalana .02 .10
528 Moose Haas .02 .10
529 Wilfredo Tejada .02 .10
530 Stu Cliburn .02 .10
531 Dale Mohorcic .02 .10
532 Ron Hassey .02 .10
533 Ty Gainey .02 .10
534 Jerry Royster .02 .10
535 Mike Maddux RC .02 .10
536 Ted Power .02 .10
537 Ted Simmons .05 .15
538 Rafael Belliard RC .15 .40
539 Chico Walker .02 .10
540 Bob Forsch .02 .10
541 John Stefero .02 .10
542 Dale Sveum .02 .10
543 Mark Thurmond .02 .10
544 Jeff Sellers .02 .10
545 Joel Skinner .02 .10
546 Alex Trevino .02 .10
547 Randy Kutcher .02 .10
548 Joaquin Andujar .05 .15
549 Casey Candaele .02 .10
550 Jeff Russell .02 .10
551 John Candelaria .02 .10
552 Joe Cowley .02 .10
553 Danny Cox .02 .10
554 Denny Walling .02 .10
555 Bruce Ruffin RC .05 .15
556 Buddy Bell .05 .15
557 Jimmy Jones RC .05 .15
558 Bobby Bonilla RC .25 .60
559 Jeff D. Robinson .02 .10
560 Ed Olwine .02 .10
561 Glenallen Hill RC .15 .40
562 Lee Mazzilli .05 .15
563 Mike G. Brown P .02 .10
564 George Frazier .02 .10
565 Mike Sharperson RC .05 .15
566 Mark Portugal RC * .15 .40
567 Rick Leach .02 .10
568 Mark Langston .02 .10
569 Rafael Santana .02 .10
570 Manny Trillo .02 .10
571 Cliff Speck .02 .10
572 Bob Kipper .02 .10
573 Kelly Downs RC .05 .15
574 Randy Asadoor .02 .10
575 Dave Magadan RC .15 .40
576 Marvin Freeman RC .05 .15
577 Jeff Lahti .02 .10
578 Jeff Calhoun .02 .10
579 Gus Polidor .02 .10
580 Gene Nelson .02 .10
581 Tim Teufel .02 .10
582 Odell Jones .02 .10
583 Mark Ryal .02 .10
584 Randy O'Neal .02 .10
585 Mike Greenwell RC .15 .40
586 Ray Knight .05 .15
587 Ralph Bryant .02 .10
588 Carmen Castillo .02 .10
589 Ed Wojna .02 .10
590 Stan Javier .02 .10
591 Jeff Musselman .02 .10
592 Mike Stanley RC .15 .40
593 Darrell Porter .02 .10
594 Drew Hall .02 .10
595 Rob Nelson .02 .10
596 Bryan Oelkers .02 .10
597 Scott Nielsen .02 .10
598 Brian Holton .02 .10
599 Kevin Mitchell RC * .25 .60
600 Checklist 558-660 .02 .10
601 Jackie Gutierrez .02 .10
602 Barry Jones .02 .10
603 Jerry Narron .02 .10
604 Steve Lake .02 .10
605 Jim Pankovits .02 .10
606 Ed Romero .02 .10
607 Dave LaPoint .02 .10
608 Don Robinson .02 .10
609 Mike Krukow .02 .10
610 Dave Valle RC ** .05 .15
611 Len Dykstra .05 .15
612 Roberto Clemente PUZ .20 .50
613 Mike Trujillo .02 .10
614 Damaso Garcia .02 .10
615 Neal Heaton .02 .10
616 Juan Berenguer .02 .10
617 Steve Carlton .05 .15
618 Gary Lucas .02 .10
619 Geno Petralli .02 .10
620 Rick Aguilera .02 .10
621 Fred McGriff .30 .75
622 Dave Henderson .02 .10
623 Dave Clark RC .05 .15
624 Angel Salazar .02 .10
625 Randy Hunt .02 .10
626 John Gibbons .02 .10
627 Kevin Brown RC .60 1.50
628 Bill Dawley .02 .10
629 Aurelio Lopez .02 .10
630 Charles Hudson .02 .10
631 Ray Soff .02 .10
632 Ray Hayward .02 .10
633 Spike Owen .02 .10
634 Glenn Hubbard .02 .10
635 Kevin Elster RC .15 .40
636 Mike LaCoss .02 .10
637 Dwayne Henry .02 .10
638 Rey Quinones .02 .10
639 Jim Clancy .02 .10
640 Larry Andersen .02 .10
641 Calvin Schiraldi .02 .10
642 Stan Jefferson .02 .10
643 Marc Sullivan .02 .10
644 Mark Grant .02 .10
645 Cliff Johnson .02 .10
646 Howard Johnson .05 .15
647 Dave Sax .02 .10
648 Dave Stewart .05 .15
649 Danny Heep .02 .10
650 Joe Johnson .02 .10
651 Bob Brower .02 .10
652 Rob Woodward .02 .10
653 John Mizerock .02 .10
654 Tim Pyznarski .02 .10
655 Luis Aquino .02 .10
656 Mickey Brantley .02 .10
657 Doyle Alexander .02 .10
658 Sammy Stewart .02 .10
659 Jim Acker .02 .10
660 Pete Ladd .02 .10

1987 Donruss Roberto Clemente Puzzle

1 Clemente Puzzle 1-3 .10 .25
4 Clemente Puzzle 4-6 .10 .25
7 Clemente Puzzle 7-10 .10 .25
10 Clemente Puzzle 10-12 .10 .25
13 Clemente Puzzle 13-15 .10 .25
16 Clemente Puzzle 16-18 .10 .25
19 Clemente Puzzle 19-21 .10 .25
22 Clemente Puzzle 22-24 .10 .25
25 Clemente Puzzle 25-27 .10 .25
28 Clemente Puzzle 28-30 .10 .25
31 Clemente Puzzle 31-33 .10 .25
34 Clemente Puzzle 34-36 .10 .25
37 Clemente Puzzle 37-39 .10 .25
40 Clemente Puzzle 40-42 .10 .25
43 Clemente Puzzle 43-45 .10 .25
46 Clemente Puzzle 46-48 .10 .25
49 Clemente Puzzle 49-51 .10 .25
52 Clemente Puzzle 52-54 .10 .25
55 Clemente Puzzle 55-57 .10 .25
58 Clemente Puzzle 58-60 .10 .25
61 Clemente Puzzle 61-63 .10 .25

1987 Donruss Wax Box Cards

COMPLETE SET (4) .75 2.00
PC10 Dale Murphy .20 .50
PC11 Jeff Reardon .08 .25
PC12 Jose Canseco .50 1.25
PUZ Roberto Clemente/(Puzzle Card) .30 .75

1987 Donruss Rookies

The 1987 Donruss "The Rookies" set features 56 full-color standard-size cards plus a 15-piece puzzle of Roberto Clemente. The set was distributed in factory set form packaged in a small green and black box through hobby dealers. Card fronts are similar in design to the 1987 Donruss regular issue except for the presence of "The Rookies" logo in the lower left corner and a green border instead of a black border. The key extended Rookie Cards in this set are Ellis Burks and Matt Williams. The second Donruss-issued cards of Greg Maddux and Rafael Palmeiro are also in this set. Because it's the first card in the set (of which came in a tightly-sealed cello wrap, the Mark McGwire card is quite condition sensitive.

COMP.FACT.SET (56) 10.00 25.00
1 Mark McGwire 5.00 12.00
2 Eric Bell .05 .15
3 Mark Williamson .02 .10
4 Mike Greenwell .15 .40
5 Ellis Burks XRC .25 .60
6 DeWayne Buice .02 .10
7 Mark McLemore .08 .25
8 Devon White .25 .60
9 Willie Fraser .05 .15
10 Les Lancaster .02 .10
11 Ken Williams .02 .10
12 Matt Nokes XRC .15 .40
13 Jeff M. Robinson .02 .10
14 Bo Jackson 2.50 6.00
15 Kevin Seitzer XRC .15 .40
16 Bill Ripken XRC .15 .40
17 B.J. Surhoff .25 .60
18 Chuck Crim .02 .10
19 Mike Birkbeck .05 .15
20 Chris Bosio .15 .40
21 Les Straker .02 .10
22 Mark Davidson .02 .10
23 Gene Larkin XRC .15 .40
24 Ken Gerhart .02 .10
25 Luis Polonia XRC .15 .40
26 Terry Steinbach .25 .60
27 Mickey Brantley .02 .10
28 Mike Stanley .15 .40
29 Jerry Browne .05 .15
30 Todd Benzinger XRC .15 .40
31 Fred McGriff .60 1.50
32 Mike Henneman XRC .15 .40
33 Casey Candaele .02 .10
34 Dave Magadan .15 .40
35 David Cone .40 1.00
36 Mike Jackson XRC .15 .40
37 John Mitchell XRC .05 .15
38 Mike Dunne .02 .10
39 John Smiley XRC .15 .40
40 Joe Magrane XRC .05 .15
41 Jim Lindeman .05 .15
42 Shane Mack .02 .10
43 Stan Jefferson .02 .10
44 Benito Santiago .08 .25
45 Matt Williams XRC 1.00 2.50
46 Dave Meads .02 .10
47 Rafael Palmeiro 2.00 5.00
48 Bill Long .02 .10
49 Bob Brower .02 .10
50 James Steels .02 .10
51 Paul Noce .02 .10
52 Greg Maddux 5.00 12.00
53 Jeff Musselman .02 .10
54 Brian Holton .02 .10
55 Chuck Jackson .02 .10
56 Checklist 1-56 .02 .10
RC Roberto Clemente Puzzle 1.25 3.00

1987 Donruss All-Stars

COMPLETE SET (60) 2.50 6.00
1 Wally Joyner .10 .30
2 Dave Winfield .20 .50
3 Lou Whitaker .02 .10
4 Kirby Puckett .30 .75
5 Cal Ripken .75 2.00
6 Rickey Henderson .20 .50
7 Wade Boggs .20 .50
8 Roger Clemens .30 .75
9 Lance Parrish .02 .10
10 Dick Howser MG .01 .05
11 Keith Hernandez .02 .10
12 Darryl Strawberry .02 .10
13 Ryne Sandberg .20 .50
14 Dale Murphy .10 .30
15 Ozzie Smith .30 .75
16 Tony Gwynn .40 1.00
17 Mike Schmidt .20 .50
18 Dwight Gooden .02 .10
19 Gary Carter .20 .50
20 Whitey Herzog MG .02 .10
21 Jose Canseco .20 .50
22 John Franco .02 .10
23 Jesse Barfield .01 .05
24 Rick Rhoden .01 .05
25 Harold Baines .07 .20
26 Sid Fernandez .01 .05
27 George Brett .40 1.00
28 Steve Sax .01 .05
29 Jim Presley .01 .05
30 Dave Smith .01 .05
31 Eddie Murray .20 .50
32 Mike Scott .01 .05
33 Don Mattingly .40 1.00
34 Dave Parker .02 .10
35 Tony Fernandez .01 .05
36 Tim Raines .07 .20
37 Brook Jacoby .01 .05
38 Chili Davis .02 .10
39 Rich Gedman .01 .05
40 Kevin Bass .01 .05
41 Frank White .02 .10
42 Glenn Davis .01 .05
43 Willie Hernandez .01 .05
44 Chris Brown .01 .05
45 Jim Rice .02 .10
46 Tony Pena .02 .10
47 Don Aase .01 .05
48 Hubie Brooks .01 .05
49 Charlie Hough .01 .05
50 Jody Davis .01 .05
51 Mike Witt .01 .05
52 Jeff Reardon .02 .10
53 Ken Schrom .01 .05
54 Fernando Valenzuela .02 .10
55 Dave Righetti .01 .05
56 Shane Rawley .01 .05
57 Ted Higuera .01 .05
58 Mike Krukow .01 .05
59 Lloyd Moseby .01 .05
60 Checklist Card .01 .05

1987 Donruss All-Star Box

COMPLETE SET (4) 1.00 2.50
PC13 Mike Scott .08 .25
PC14 Roger Clemens .50 1.25
PC15 Mike Krukow .08 .25
PUZ Roberto Clemente Puzzle Card .40 1.00

1987 Donruss Highlights

COMP.FACT.SET (56) 4.00 10.00
ISSUED ONLY IN FACTORY SET FORM
1 Juan Nieves .02 .10
2 Mike Schmidt .15 .40
3 Eric Davis .08 .25
4 Sid Fernandez .02 .10
5 Brian Downing .02 .10
6 Bret Saberhagen .05 .15
7 Tim Raines .05 .15
8 Eric Davis .08 .25
9 Steve Bedrosian .02 .10
10 Larry Parrish .02 .10
11 Jim Clancy .02 .10
12 Tony Gwynn .15 .40
13 Orel Hershiser .08 .25
14 Wade Boggs .08 .25
15 Steve Ontiveros .02 .10
16 Tim Raines .05 .15
17 Don Mattingly .30 .75
18 Ray Dandridge .05 .15
19 Jim Hunter .08 .25
20 Billy Williams .05 .15
21 Bo Diaz .02 .10
22 Floyd Youmans .02 .10
23 Don Mattingly .30 .75
24 Frank Viola .02 .10
25 Bobby Witt .05 .15
26 Kevin Seitzer .15 .40
27 Mark McGwire 1.00 2.50
28 Andre Dawson .05 .15
29 Paul Molitor .05 .15
30 Kirby Puckett .30 .75
31 Andre Dawson .05 .15
32 Doug Drabek .15 .40
33 Dwight Evans .08 .25
34 Mark Langston .02 .10
35 Wally Joyner .08 .25
36 Vince Coleman .02 .10
37 Eddie Murray .15 .40
38 Cal Ripken .30 .75
39 F.McGriff R.Ducey E.Whitt .05 .15
40 M.McGwire J.Canseco 2.50 6.00
41 Bob Boone .05 .15
42 Darryl Strawberry .05 .15
43 Howard Johnson .02 .10
44 Wade Boggs .08 .25
45 Benito Santiago .05 .15
46 Mark McGwire 1.00 2.50
47 Kevin Seitzer .15 .40
48 Don Mattingly .30 .75
49 Darryl Strawberry .05 .15
50 Pascual Perez .02 .10
51 Alan Trammell .05 .15
52 Doyle Alexander .02 .10
53 Nolan Ryan .40 1.00
54 Mark McGwire 1.00 2.50
55 Benito Santiago .05 .15
56 Checklist 1-56 .02 .10

1987 Donruss Opening Day

This innovative set of 272 standard-size cards features a card for each of the players in the starting line-ups of all the teams on Opening Day 1987. The set was packaged in a specially designed box. Cards are very similar in design to the 1987 regular Donruss issue except that these "OD" cards have a maroon border instead of a black border. Teams in the same city share a checklist card. A 15-piece puzzle of Roberto Clemente is also included with every complete set. The error on Barry Bonds (picturing Johnny Ray by mistake) was corrected very early in the press run; supposedly less than one percent of the sets have the error. Players in this set in their Rookie Card year include Will Clark, Bo Jackson, Wally Joyner and Barry Larkin.

COMP.FACT.SET (272) 12.50 30.00
163A LISTED IN NEAR MINT CONDITION
1 Doug DeCinces .02 .10
2 Mike Witt .02 .10
3 George Hendrick .05 .15
4 Dick Schofield .02 .10
5 Devon White .25 .60
6 Butch Wynegar .02 .10
7 Wally Joyner .08 .25
8 Mark McLemore .05 .15
9 Brian Downing .05 .15
10 Gary Pettis .02 .10
11 Bill Doran .02 .10
12 Phil Garner .05 .15
13 Jose Cruz .05 .15
14 Kevin Bass .02 .10
15 Mike Scott .05 .15
16 Glenn Davis .02 .10
17 Alan Ashby .02 .10
18 Billy Hatcher .02 .10
19 Craig Reynolds .02 .10
20 Carney Lansford .05 .15
21 Mike Davis .02 .10
22 Reggie Jackson .08 .25
23 Mickey Tettleton .02 .10
24 Jose Canseco .60 1.50
25 Rob Nelson .02 .10
26 Tony Phillips .02 .10
27 Dwayne Murphy .02 .10
28 Alfredo Griffin .02 .10
29 Curt Young .02 .10
30 Willie Upshaw .02 .10
31 Mike Sharperson .02 .10
32 Rance Mulliniks .02 .10
33 Ernie Whitt .02 .10
34 Jesse Barfield .05 .15
35 Tony Fernandez .02 .10
36 Lloyd Moseby .02 .10
37 Jimmy Key .05 .15
38 Fred McGriff .30 .75
39 George Bell .05 .15
40 Dale Murphy .08 .25
41 Rick Mahler .02 .10
42 Ken Griffey .05 .15
43 Andres Thomas .02 .10
44 Dion James .02 .10
45 Ozzie Virgil .02 .10
46 Ken Oberkfell .02 .10
47 Gary Roenicke .02 .10
48 Glenn Hubbard .02 .10
49 Bill Schroeder .02 .10
50 Greg Brock .02 .10
51 Billy Joe Robidoux .02 .10
52 Glenn Braggs .05 .15
53 Jim Gantner .02 .10
54 Paul Molitor .05 .15
55 Dale Sveum .02 .10
56 Ted Higuera .02 .10
57 Rob Deer .02 .10
58 Robin Yount .25 .60
59 Jim Lindeman .05 .15
60 Vince Coleman .02 .10
61 Tommy Herr .02 .10
62 Terry Pendleton .05 .15
63 John Tudor .05 .15
64 Tony Pena .02 .10
65 Ozzie Smith .25 .60
66 Tito Landrum .02 .10
67 Jack Clark .05 .15
68 Bob Dernier .02 .10
69 Rick Sutcliffe .05 .15
70 Andre Dawson .05 .15
71 Keith Moreland .02 .10
72 Jody Davis .02 .10
73 Brian Dayett .02 .10
74 Leon Durham .02 .10
75 Ryne Sandberg .30 .75
76 Shawon Dunston .02 .10
77 Mike Marshall .02 .10

78 Bill Madlock .05 .15
79 Orel Hershiser .08 .25
80 Mike Ramsey .02 .10
81 Ken Landreaux .02 .10
82 Mike Scioscia .05 .15
83 Franklin Stubbs .02 .10
84 Mariano Duncan .02 .10
85 Steve Sax .02 .10
86 Mitch Webster .02 .10
87 Reid Nichols .02 .10
88 Tim Wallach .02 .10
89 Floyd Youmans .02 .10
90 Andres Galarraga .05 .15
91 Hubie Brooks .02 .10
92 Jeff Reed .02 .10
93 Alonzo Powell .02 .10
94 Vance Law .02 .10
95 Bob Brenly .02 .10
96 Will Clark .75 2.00
97 Chili Davis .05 .15
98 Mike Krukow .02 .10
99 Jose Uribe .02 .10
100 Chris Brown .02 .10
101 Robby Thompson .15 .40
102 Candy Maldonado .02 .10
103 Jeff Leonard .02 .10
104 Tom Candiotti .02 .10
105 Chris Bando .02 .10
106 Cory Snyder .02 .10
107 Pat Tabler .02 .10
108 Andre Thornton .02 .10
109 Joe Carter .05 .15
110 Tony Bernazard .02 .10
111 Julio Franco .05 .15
112 Brook Jacoby .02 .10
113 Brett Butler .05 .15
114 Donell Nixon .02 .10
115 Alvin Davis .02 .10
116 Mark Langston .02 .10
117 Harold Reynolds .05 .15
118 Ken Phelps .02 .10
119 Mike Kingery .05 .15
120 Dave Valle .05 .15
121 Rey Quinones .02 .10
122 Phil Bradley .02 .10
123 Jim Presley .02 .10
124 Keith Hernandez .05 .15
125 Kevin McReynolds .02 .10
126 Rafael Santana .02 .10
127 Bob Ojeda .02 .10
128 Darryl Strawberry .05 .15
129 Mookie Wilson .05 .15
130 Gary Carter .05 .15
131 Tim Teufel .02 .10
132 Howard Johnson .05 .15
133 Cal Ripken .60 1.50
134 Rick Burleson .02 .10
135 Fred Lynn .05 .15
136 Eddie Murray .15 .40
137 Ray Knight .05 .15
138 Alan Wiggins .02 .10
139 John Shelby .02 .10
140 Mike Boddicker .02 .10
141 Ken Gerhart .02 .10
142 Terry Kennedy .02 .10
143 Steve Garvey .05 .15
144 Marvell Wynne .02 .10
145 Kevin Mitchell .08 .25
146 Tony Gwynn .25 .60
147 Joey Cora .15 .40
148 Benito Santiago .05 .15
149 Eric Show .02 .10
150 Garry Templeton .05 .15
151 Carmelo Martinez .02 .10
152 Von Hayes .02 .10
153 Lance Parrish .05 .15
154 Milt Thompson .02 .10
155 Mike Easler .02 .10
156 Juan Samuel .02 .10
157 Steve Jeltz .02 .10
158 Glenn Wilson .02 .10
159 Shane Rawley .02 .10
160 Mike Schmidt .40 1.00
161 Andy Van Slyke .08 .25
162 Johnny Ray .02 .10
163A B.Bonds ERR J.Ray 250.00 600.00
163B Barry Bonds COR 6.00 15.00
164 Junior Ortiz .02 .10
165 Rafael Belliard .15 .40
166 Bob Patterson .02 .10
167 Bobby Bonilla .25 .60
168 Sid Bream .02 .10
169 Jim Morrison .02 .10
170 Jerry Browne .05 .15
171 Scott Fletcher .02 .10
172 Ruben Sierra .40 1.00
173 Larry Parrish .02 .10
174 Pete O'Brien .02 .10
175 Pete Incaviglia .15 .40
176 Don Slaught .02 .10
177 Oddibe McDowell .02 .10
178 Charlie Hough .05 .15
179 Steve Buechele .02 .10
180 Bob Stanley .02 .10
181 Wade Boggs .08 .25
182 Jim Rice .05 .15
183 Bill Buckner .05 .15
184 Dwight Evans .08 .25
185 Spike Owen .02 .10
186 Don Baylor .05 .15
187 Marc Sullivan .02 .10
188 Marty Barrett .02 .10
189 Dave Henderson .02 .10
190 Bo Diaz .02 .10
191 Barry Larkin .75 2.00
192 Kal Daniels .02 .10
193 Terry Francona .05 .15
194 Tom Browning .02 .10
195 Ron Oester .02 .10
196 Buddy Bell .05 .15
197 Eric Davis .08 .25
198 Dave Parker .05 .15
199 Steve Balboni .02 .10
200 Danny Tartabull .02 .10
201 Ed Hearn .02 .10
202 Buddy Biancalana .02 .10
203 Danny Jackson .02 .10
204 Frank White .05 .15
205 Bo Jackson 2.50 6.00
206 George Brett .40 1.00
207 Kevin Seitzer .05 .15
208 Willie Wilson .05 .15
209 Orlando Mercado .02 .10
210 Darrell Evans .05 .15
211 Larry Herndon .02 .10
212 Jack Morris .05 .15
213 Chet Lemon .05 .15
214 Mike Heath .02 .10
215 Darnell Coles .02 .10
216 Alan Trammell .05 .15
217 Terry Harper .02 .10
218 Lou Whitaker .05 .15
219 Gary Gaetti .05 .15
220 Tom Nieto .02 .10
221 Kirby Puckett .30 .75
222 Tom Brunansky .02 .10
223 Greg Gagne .02 .10
224 Dan Gladden .02 .10
225 Mark Davidson .02 .10
226 Bert Blyleven .05 .15
227 Steve Lombardozzi .02 .10
228 Kent Hrbek .05 .15
229 Gary Redus .02 .10
230 Ivan Calderon .02 .10
231 Tim Hulett .02 .10
232 Carlton Fisk .08 .25
233 Greg Walker .02 .10
234 Ron Karkovice .15 .40
235 Ozzie Guillen .08 .25
236 Harold Baines .05 .15
237 Donnie Hill .02 .10
238 Rich Dotson .02 .10
239 Mike Pagliarulo .02 .10
240 Joel Skinner .02 .10
241 Don Mattingly .50 1.25
242 Gary Ward .02 .10
243 Dave Winfield .05 .15
244 Dan Pasqua .02 .10
245 Wayne Tolleson .02 .10
246 Willie Randolph .05 .15
247 Dennis Rasmussen .02 .10
248 Rickey Henderson .15 .40
249 Angels Logo .01 .05
250 Astros Logo .01 .05
251 A's Logo .01 .05
252 Blue Jays Logo .01 .05
253 Braves Logo .01 .05
254 Brewers Logo .01 .05
255 Cardinals Logo .01 .05
256 Dodgers Logo .01 .05
257 Expos Logo .01 .05
258 Giants Logo .01 .05
259 Indians Logo .01 .05
260 Mariners Logo .01 .05
261 Orioles Logo .01 .05
262 Padres Logo .01 .05
263 Phillies Logo .01 .05
264 Pirates Logo .01 .05
265 Rangers Logo .01 .05
266 Red Sox Logo .01 .05
267 Reds Logo .01 .05
268 Royals Logo .01 .05
269 Tigers Logo .01 .05
270 Twins Logo .01 .05
271 Chicago Logos .01 .05
272 New York Logos .01 .05

1987 Donruss Pop-Ups

COMPLETE SET (20) 2.00 5.00
1 Wally Joyner .10 .30
2 Dave Winfield .15 .40
3 Lou Whitaker .02 .10
4 Kirby Puckett .30 .75
5 Cal Ripken .75 2.00
6 Rickey Henderson .20 .50
7 Wade Boggs .20 .50
8 Roger Clemens .50 1.25
9 Lance Parrish .02 .10
10 Dick Howser MG .01 .05
11 Keith Hernandez .02 .10
12 Darryl Strawberry .02 .10
13 Ryne Sandberg .20 .50
14 Dale Murphy .10 .30
15 Ozzie Smith .30 .75
16 Tony Gwynn .40 1.00
17 Mike Schmidt .20 .50
18 Dwight Gooden .07 .20
19 Gary Carter .15 .40
20 Whitey Herzog MG .02 .10

1987 Donruss Super DK's

COMPLETE SET (26) 5.00 12.00
1 Wally Joyner .60 1.50
2 Roger Clemens 1.00 2.50
3 Dale Murphy .60 1.50
4 Darryl Strawberry .30 .75
5 Ozzie Smith .75 2.00
6 Jose Canseco 1.00 2.50
7 Charlie Hough .20 .50
8 Brook Jacoby .20 .50
9 Fred Lynn .30 .75
10 Rick Rhoden .20 .50
11 Chris Brown .20 .50
12 Von Hayes .20 .50
13 Jack Morris .30 .75
14 Kevin McReynolds .20 .50
15 George Brett 1.25 3.00
16 Ted Higuera .20 .50
17 Hubie Brooks .20 .50
18 Mike Scott .20 .50
19 Kirby Puckett 1.00 2.50
20 Dave Winfield .75 2.00
21 Lloyd Moseby .20 .50
22 Eric Davis .40 1.00
23 Jim Presley .20 .50
24 Keith Moreland .20 .50
25 Greg Walker .20 .50
26 Steve Sax .20 .50
NNO Roberto Clemente Large Puzzle .60 1.50
NNO DK Checklist 1-26 .20 .50

1988 Donruss

This set consists of 660 standard-size cards. For the seventh straight year, wax packs consisted of 15 cards plus a puzzle panel (featuring Stan Musial this time around). Cards were also distributed in rack packs and retail and hobby factory sets. Card fronts feature a distinctive black and blue border on the front. The card front border design pattern of the factory set card fronts is oriented differently from that of the regular wax pack cards. No premium or discount exists for either version. Subsets include Diamond Kings (1-27) and Rated Rookies (28-47). Cards marked as SP (short printed) from 648-660 are more difficult to find than the other 13 SP's in the lower 600s. These 26 cards listed as SP were apparently pulled from the printing sheet to make room for the 26 Bonus MVP cards. Six of the checklist cards were done two different ways to reflect the inclusion or exclusion of the Bonus MVP cards in the wax packs. In the checklist below, the A variations (for the checklist cards) are from the wax packs and the B variations are from the factory-collated sets. The key Rookie Cards in this set are Roberto Alomar, Jay Bell, Jay Buhner, Ellis Burks, Ken Caminiti, Tom Glavine, Mark Grace and Matt Williams. There was also a Kirby Puckett card issued as the package back of Donruss blister packs; it uses a different photo from both of Kirby's regular and Bonus MVP cards and is unnumbered on the back.

COMPLETE SET (660) 4.00 10.00
COMP.FACT.SET (660) 6.00 15.00
COMMON CARD (1-660) .01 .05
COMMON SP (648-660) .02 .10
1 Mark McGwire DK .30 .75
2 Tim Raines DK .02 .10
3 Benito Santiago DK .02 .10
4 Alan Trammell DK .02 .10
5 Danny Tartabull DK .01 .05
6 Ron Darling DK .02 .10
7 Paul Molitor DK .02 .10
8 Devon White DK .02 .10
9 Andre Dawson DK .01 .05
10 Julio Franco DK .02 .10
11 Scott Fletcher DK .01 .05
12 Tony Fernandez DK .01 .05
13 Shane Rawley DK .01 .05
14 Kal Daniels DK .01 .05
15 Jack Clark DK .02 .10
16 Dwight Evans DK .05 .15
17 Tommy John DK .02 .10
18 Andy Van Slyke DK .05 .15
19 Gary Gaetti DK .02 .10
20 Mark Langston DK .01 .05
21 Will Clark DK .07 .20
22 Glenn Hubbard DK .01 .05
23 Billy Hatcher DK .01 .05
24 Bob Welch DK .02 .10
25 Ivan Calderon DK .01 .05
26 Cal Ripken DK .15 .40
27 DK Checklist 1-26 .01 .05
28 Mackey Sasser RC .08 .25
29 Jeff Treadway RC .08 .25
30 Mike Campbell RR RC .01 .05
31 Lance Johnson RC .08 .25
32 Nelson Liriano RR RC .01 .05
33 Shawn Abner RR .01 .05
34 Roberto Alomar RC .75 2.00
35 Shawn Hillegas RR RC .01 .05
36 Joey Meyer RR .01 .05
37 Kevin Elster RR .01 .05
38 Jose Lind RC .08 .25
39 Kirt Manwaring RC .08 .25
40 Mark Grace RC .75 2.00
41 Jody Reed RC .08 .25
42 John Farrell RR RC .02 .10
43 Al Leiter RC .30 .75
44 Gary Thurman RR RC .01 .05
45 Vicente Palacios RR RC .01 .05
46 Eddie Williams RC .02 .10
47 Jack McDowell RC .15 .40
48 Ken Dixon .01 .05
49 Mike Birkbeck .01 .05
50 Eric King .01 .05
51 Roger Clemens .40 1.00
52 Pat Clements .01 .05
53 Fernando Valenzuela .02 .10
54 Mark Gubicza .01 .05
55 Jay Howell .01 .05
56 Floyd Youmans .01 .05
57 Ed Correa .01 .05
58 DeWayne Buice .01 .05
59 Jose DeLeon .01 .05
60 Danny Cox .01 .05
61 Nolan Ryan .40 1.00
62 Steve Bedrosian .01 .05
63 Tom Browning .01 .05
64 Mark Davis .01 .05
65 R.J. Reynolds .01 .05
66 Kevin Mitchell .02 .10
67 Ken Oberkfell .01 .05
68 Rick Sutcliffe .02 .10
69 Dwight Gooden .02 .10
70 Scott Bankhead .01 .05
71 Bert Blyleven .02 .10
72 Jimmy Key .02 .10
73 Les Straker .01 .05
74 Jim Clancy .01 .05
75 Mike Moore .01 .05
76 Ron Darling .02 .10
77 Ed Lynch .01 .05
78 Dale Murphy .05 .15
79 Doug Drabek .01 .05
80 Scott Garrelts .01 .05
81 Ed Whitson .01 .05
82 Rob Murphy .01 .05
83 Shane Rawley .01 .05
84 Greg Mathews .01 .05
85 Jim Deshaies .01 .05
86 Mike Witt .01 .05
87 Donnie Hill .01 .05
88 Jeff Reed .01 .05
89 Mike Boddicker .01 .05
90 Ted Higuera .01 .05
91 Walt Terrell .01 .05
92 Bob Stanley .01 .05
93 Dave Righetti .02 .10
94 Orel Hershiser .02 .10
95 Chris Bando .01 .05
96 Bret Saberhagen .02 .10
97 Curt Young .01 .05
98 Tim Burke .01 .05
99 Charlie Hough .02 .10
100A Checklist 28-137 .01 .05
100B Checklist 28-133 .01 .05
101 Bobby Witt .01 .05
102 George Brett .20 .50
103 Mickey Tettleton .01 .05
104 Scott Bailes .01 .05
105 Mike Pagliarulo .01 .05
106 Mike Scioscia .02 .10
107 Tom Brookens .01 .05
108 Ray Knight .02 .10
109 Dan Plesac .01 .05
110 Wally Joyner .02 .10
111 Bob Forsch .01 .05
112 Mike Scott .02 .10
113 Kevin Gross .01 .05
114 Benito Santiago .02 .10
115 Bob Kipper .01 .05
116 Mike Krukow .01 .05
117 Chris Bosio .01 .05
118 Sid Fernandez .01 .05
119 Jody Davis .01 .05
120 Mike Morgan .01 .05
121 Mark Eichhorn .01 .05
122 Jeff Reardon .02 .10
123 John Franco .02 .10
124 Richard Dotson .01 .05
125 Eric Bell .01 .05
126 Juan Nieves .01 .05
127 Jack Morris .02 .10
128 Rick Rhoden .01 .05
129 Rich Gedman .01 .05
130 Ken Howell .01 .05
131 Brook Jacoby .01 .05
132 Danny Jackson .01 .05
133 Gene Nelson .01 .05
134 Neal Heaton .01 .05
135 Willie Fraser .01 .05
136 Jose Guzman .01 .05
137 Ozzie Guillen .02 .10
138 Bob Knepper .01 .05
139 Mike Jackson RC* .08 .25
140 Joe Magrane RC* .08 .25
141 Jimmy Jones .01 .05
142 Ted Power .01 .05
143 Ozzie Virgil .01 .05
144 Felix Fermin .01 .05
145 Kelly Downs .01 .05
146 Shawon Dunston .01 .05
147 Scott Bradley .01 .05
148 Dave Stieb .02 .10
149 Frank Viola .02 .10
150 Terry Kennedy .01 .05
151 Bill Wegman .01 .05
152 Matt Nokes RC* .08 .25
153 Wade Boggs .05 .15
154 Wayne Tolleson .01 .05
155 Mariano Duncan .01 .05
156 Julio Franco .02 .10
157 Charlie Leibrandt .01 .05
158 Terry Steinbach .02 .10
159 Mike Fitzgerald .01 .05
160 Jack Lazorko .01 .05
161 Mitch Williams .01 .05
162 Greg Walker .01 .05
163 Alan Ashby .01 .05
164 Tony Gwynn .10 .30
165 Bruce Ruffin .01 .05
166 Ron Robinson .01 .05
167 Zane Smith .01 .05
168 Junior Ortiz .01 .05
169 Jamie Moyer .02 .10
170 Tony Pena .01 .05
171 Cal Ripken .30 .75
172 B.J. Surhoff .02 .10
173 Lou Whitaker .02 .10
174 Ellis Burks RC .15 .40
175 Ron Guidry .02 .10
176 Steve Sax .01 .05
177 Danny Tartabull .01 .05
178 Carney Lansford .02 .10
179 Casey Candaele .01 .05
180 Scott Fletcher .01 .05
181 Mark McLemore .01 .05
182 Ivan Calderon .01 .05
183 Jack Clark .02 .10
184 Glenn Davis .01 .05
185 Luis Aguayo .01 .05
186 Bo Diaz .01 .05
187 Stan Jefferson .01 .05
188 Sid Bream .01 .05
189 Bob Brenly .01 .05
190 Dion James .01 .05
191 Leon Durham .01 .05
192 Jesse Orosco .01 .05
193 Alvin Davis .01 .05
194 Gary Gaetti .02 .10
195 Fred McGriff .07 .20
196 Steve Lombardozzi .01 .05
197 Rance Mulliniks .01 .05
198 Rey Quinones .01 .05
199 Gary Carter .02 .10
200A Checklist 138-247 .01 .05
200B Checklist 134-239 .01 .05
201 Keith Moreland .01 .05
202 Ken Griffey .02 .10
203 Tommy Gregg .01 .05
204 Will Clark .07 .20
205 John Kruk .02 .10
206 Buddy Bell .02 .10
207 Von Hayes .01 .05
208 Tommy Herr .01 .05
209 Craig Reynolds .01 .05
210 Gary Pettis .01 .05
211 Harold Baines .02 .10
212 Vance Law .01 .05
213 Ken Gerhart .01 .05
214 Jim Gantner .01 .05
215 Chet Lemon .02 .10
216 Dwight Evans .05 .15
217 Don Mattingly .25 .60
218 Franklin Stubbs .01 .05
219 Pat Tabler .01 .05
220 Bo Jackson .07 .20
221 Tony Phillips .01 .05
222 Tim Wallach .01 .05
223 Ruben Sierra .02 .10
224 Steve Buechele .01 .05
225 Frank White .02 .10
226 Alfredo Griffin .01 .05
227 Greg Swindell .01 .05
228 Willie Randolph .02 .10
229 Mike Marshall .01 .05
230 Alan Trammell .02 .10
231 Eddie Murray .07 .20
232 Dale Sveum .01 .05
233 Dick Schofield .01 .05
234 Jose Oquendo .01 .05
235 Bill Doran .01 .05
236 Milt Thompson .01 .05
237 Marvell Wynne .01 .05
238 Bobby Bonilla .02 .10
239 Chris Speier .01 .05
240 Glenn Braggs .01 .05
241 Wally Backman .01 .05
242 Ryne Sandberg .15 .40
243 Phil Bradley .01 .05
244 Kelly Gruber .01 .05
245 Tom Brunansky .01 .05
246 Ron Oester .01 .05
247 Bobby Thigpen .01 .05
248 Fred Lynn .02 .10
249 Paul Molitor .02 .10
250 Darrell Evans .02 .10
251 Gary Ward .01 .05
252 Bruce Hurst .01 .05
253 Bob Welch .02 .10
254 Joe Carter .02 .10
255 Willie Wilson .02 .10
256 Mark McGwire .60 1.50
257 Mitch Webster .01 .05
258 Brian Downing .02 .10
259 Mike Stanley .01 .05
260 Carlton Fisk .05 .15
261 Billy Hatcher .01 .05
262 Glenn Wilson .01 .05
263 Ozzie Smith .10 .30
264 Randy Ready .01 .05
265 Kurt Stillwell .01 .05
266 David Palmer .01 .05
267 Mike Diaz .01 .05
268 Robby Thompson .01 .05
269 Andre Dawson .02 .10
270 Lee Guetterman .01 .05
271 Willie Upshaw .01 .05
272 Randy Bush .01 .05
273 Larry Sheets .01 .05
274 Rob Deer .01 .05
275 Kirk Gibson .07 .20
276 Marty Barrett .01 .05
277 Rickey Henderson .07 .20
278 Pedro Guerrero .02 .10
279 Brett Butler .02 .10
280 Kevin Seitzer .01 .05
281 Mike Davis .01 .05
282 Andres Galarraga .02 .10
283 Devon White .02 .10
284 Pete O'Brien .01 .05
285 Jerry Hairston .01 .05
286 Kevin Bass .01 .05
287 Carmelo Martinez .01 .05
288 Juan Samuel .01 .05
289 Kal Daniels .01 .05
290 Albert Hall .01 .05
291 Andy Van Slyke .05 .15
292 Lee Smith .02 .10
293 Vince Coleman .01 .05
294 Tom Niedenfuer .01 .05
295 Robin Yount .10 .30
296 Jeff M. Robinson .01 .05
297 Todd Benzinger RC* .08 .25
298 Dave Winfield .02 .10
299 Mickey Hatcher .01 .05
300A Checklist 248-357 .01 .05
300B Checklist 240-345 .01 .05
301 Bud Black .01 .05
302 Jose Canseco .20 .50
303 Tom Foley .01 .05
304 Pete Incaviglia .01 .05
305 Bob Boone .02 .10
306 Bill Long .01 .05
307 Willie McGee .02 .10
308 Ken Caminiti RC .75 2.00
309 Darren Daulton .02 .10
310 Tracy Jones .01 .05
311 Greg Booker .01 .05
312 Mike LaValliere .01 .05
313 Chili Davis .02 .10
314 Glenn Hubbard .01 .05
315 Paul Noce .01 .05
316 Keith Hernandez .02 .10
317 Mark Langston .01 .05
318 Keith Atherton .01 .05
319 Tony Fernandez .01 .05
320 Kent Hrbek .02 .10
321 John Cerutti .01 .05
322 Mike Kingery .01 .05
323 Dave Magadan .01 .05
324 Rafael Palmeiro .15 .40
325 Jeff Dedmon .01 .05
326 Barry Bonds .75 2.00
327 Jeffrey Leonard .01 .05
328 Tim Flannery .01 .05
329 Dave Concepcion .02 .10
330 Mike Schmidt .20 .50
331 Bill Dawley .01 .05
332 Larry Andersen .01 .05
333 Jack Howell .01 .05
334 Ken Williams .01 .05
335 Bryn Smith .01 .05
336 Bill Ripken RC* .08 .25
337 Greg Brock .01 .05
338 Mike Heath .01 .05
339 Mike Greenwell .01 .05
340 Claudell Washington .01 .05
341 Jose Gonzalez .01 .05
342 Mel Hall .01 .05
343 Jim Eisenreich .01 .05
344 Tony Bernazard .01 .05
345 Tim Raines .02 .10
346 Bob Brower .01 .05
347 Larry Parrish .01 .05
348 Thad Bosley .01 .05
349 Dennis Eckersley .05 .15
350 Cory Snyder .01 .05
351 Rick Cerone .01 .05
352 John Shelby .01 .05
353 Larry Herndon .01 .05
354 John Habyan .01 .05
355 Chuck Crim .01 .05
356 Gus Polidor .01 .05
357 Ken Dayley .01 .05
358 Danny Darwin .01 .05
359 Lance Parrish .02 .10
360 James Steels .01 .05
361 Al Pedrique .01 .05
362 Mike Aldrete .01 .05
363 Juan Castillo .01 .05
364 Len Dykstra .02 .10
365 Luis Quinones .01 .05
366 Jim Presley .01 .05
367 Lloyd Moseby .01 .05
368 Kirby Puckett .07 .20
369 Eric Davis .02 .10
370 Gary Redus .01 .05
371 Dave Schmidt .01 .05
372 Mark Clear .01 .05
373 Dave Bergman .01 .05
374 Charles Hudson .01 .05
375 Calvin Schiraldi .01 .05
376 Alex Trevino .01 .05
377 Tom Candiotti .01 .05
378 Steve Farr .01 .05
379 Mike Gallego .01 .05
380 Andy McGaffigan .01 .05
381 Kirk McCaskill .01 .05
382 Oddibe McDowell .01 .05
383 Floyd Bannister .01 .05
384 Denny Walling .01 .05
385 Don Carman .01 .05
386 Todd Worrell .01 .05
387 Eric Show .01 .05
388 Dave Parker .02 .10
389 Rick Mahler .01 .05
390 Mike Dunne .01 .05
391 Candy Maldonado .01 .05
392 Bob Dernier .01 .05
393 Dave Valle .01 .05
394 Ernie Whitt .01 .05
395 Juan Berenguer .01 .05
396 Mike Young .01 .05
397 Mike Felder .01 .05
398 Willie Hernandez .01 .05
399 Jim Rice .02 .10
400A Checklist 358-467 .01 .05
400B Checklist 346-451 .01 .05
401 Tommy John .02 .10
402 Brian Holton .01 .05
403 Carmen Castillo .01 .05
404 Jamie Quirk .01 .05
405 Dwayne Murphy .01 .05
406 Jeff Parrett .01 .05
407 Don Sutton .02 .10
408 Jerry Browne .01 .05
409 Jim Winn .01 .05
410 Dave Smith .01 .05
411 Shane Mack .01 .05
412 Greg Gross .01 .05
413 Nick Esasky .01 .05
414 Damaso Garcia .01 .05
415 Brian Fisher .01 .05
416 Brian Dayett .01 .05
417 Curt Ford .01 .05
418 Mark Williamson .01 .05
419 Bill Schroeder .01 .05
420 Mike Henneman RC* .08 .25
421 John Marzano .01 .05
422 Ron Kittle .01 .05
423 Matt Young .01 .05
424 Steve Balboni .01 .05
425 Luis Polonia RC* .08 .25
426 Randy St.Claire .01 .05
427 Greg Harris .01 .05
428 Johnny Ray .01 .05
429 Ray Searage .01 .05
430 Ricky Horton .01 .05
431 Gerald Young .01 .05
432 Rick Schu .01 .05
433 Paul O'Neill .05 .15
434 Rich Gossage .02 .10
435 John Cangelosi .01 .05
436 Mike LaCoss .01 .05
437 Gerald Perry .01 .05
438 Dave Martinez .01 .05
439 Darryl Strawberry .02 .10
440 John Moses .01 .05
441 Greg Gagne .01 .05
442 Jesse Barfield .02 .10
443 George Frazier .01 .05
444 Garth Iorg .01 .05
445 Ed Nunez .01 .05
446 Rick Aguilera .01 .05
447 Jerry Mumphrey .01 .05
448 Rafael Ramirez .01 .05
449 John Smiley RC* .08 .25
450 Atlee Hammaker .01 .05
451 Lance McCullers .01 .05
452 Guy Hoffman .01 .05
453 Chris James .01 .05
454 Terry Pendleton .02 .10
455 Dave Meads .01 .05
456 Bill Buckner .02 .10
457 John Pawlowski .01 .05
458 Bob Sebra .01 .05
459 Jim Dwyer .01 .05
460 Jay Aldrich .01 .05
461 Frank Tanana .02 .10
462 Oil Can Boyd .01 .05
463 Dan Pasqua .01 .05
464 Tim Crews RC .08 .25
465 Andy Allanson .01 .05
466 Bill Pecota RC* .02 .10
467 Steve Ontiveros .01 .05
468 Hubie Brooks .01 .05
469 Paul Kilgus .01 .05
470 Dale Mohorcic .01 .05
471 Dan Quisenberry .01 .05
472 Dave Stewart .02 .10
473 Dave Clark .01 .05
474 Joel Skinner .01 .05
475 Dave Anderson .01 .05
476 Dan Petry .01 .05
477 Carl Nichols .01 .05
478 Ernest Riles .01 .05
479 George Hendrick .02 .10
480 John Morris .01 .05
481 Manny Hernandez .01 .05
482 Jeff Stone .01 .05
483 Chris Brown .01 .05
484 Mike Bielecki .01 .05
485 Dave Dravecky .01 .05
486 Rick Manning .01 .05
487 Bill Almon .01 .05
488 Jim Sundberg .02 .10
489 Ken Phelps .01 .05
490 Tom Henke .01 .05
491 Dan Gladden .01 .05
492 Barry Larkin .05 .15
493 Fred Manrique .01 .05
494 Mike Griffin .01 .05
495 Mark Knudson .01 .05
496 Bill Madlock .02 .10
497 Tim Stoddard .01 .05
498 Sam Horn RC .02 .10
499 Tracy Woodson RC .02 .10
500A Checklist 468-577 .01 .05
500B Checklist 452-557 .01 .05
501 Ken Schrom .01 .05
502 Angel Salazar .01 .05
503 Eric Plunk .01 .05
504 Joe Hesketh .01 .05
505 Greg Minton .01 .05
506 Geno Petralli .01 .05
507 Bob James .01 .05
508 Robbie Wine .01 .05
509 Jeff Calhoun .01 .05
510 Steve Lake .01 .05
511 Mark Grant .01 .05
512 Frank Williams .01 .05
513 Jeff Blauser RC .08 .25
514 Bob Walk .01 .05
515 Craig Lefferts .01 .05
516 Manny Trillo .01 .05
517 Jerry Reed .01 .05
518 Rick Leach .01 .05
519 Mark Davidson .01 .05
520 Jeff Ballard RC .01 .05
521 Dave Stapleton RC .01 .05
522 Pat Sheridan .01 .05
523 Al Nipper .01 .05
524 Steve Trout .01 .05
525 Jeff Hamilton .01 .05
526 Tommy Hinzo .01 .05
527 Lonnie Smith .01 .05
528 Greg Cadaret .01 .05
529 Bob McClure UER/(Rob~ on front) .01 .05
530 Chuck Finley .02 .10
531 Jeff Russell .01 .05
532 Steve Lyons .01 .05
533 Terry Puhl .01 .05
534 Eric Nolte .01 .05
535 Kent Tekulve .01 .05
536 Pat Pacillo .01 .05
537 Charlie Puleo .01 .05
538 Tom Prince .01 .05
539 Greg Maddux .40 1.00
540 Jim Lindeman .01 .05
541 Pete Stanicek RC .01 .05
542 Steve Kiefer .01 .05
543A Jim Morrison ERR (No decimal before lifetime ave .05 .15
543B Jim Morrison COR .01 .05
544 Spike Owen .01 .05
545 Jay Buhner RC .20 .50
546 Mike Devereaux RC .08 .25
547 Jerry Don Gleaton .01 .05
548 Jose Rijo .02 .10
549 Dennis Martinez .02 .10
550 Mike Loynd .01 .05
551 Darrell Miller .01 .05
552 Dave LaPoint .01 .05
553 John Tudor .02 .10
554 Rocky Childress .01 .05
555 Wally Ritchie .01 .05
556 Terry McGriff .01 .05
557 Dave Leiper .01 .05
558 Jeff D. Robinson .01 .05
559 Jose Uribe UER .01 .05
560 Ted Simmons .02 .10
561 Les Lancaster .01 .05
562 Keith Miller RC .08 .25
563 Harold Reynolds .02 .10
564 Gene Larkin RC* .08 .25
565 Cecil Fielder .02 .10
566 Roy Smalley .01 .05
567 Duane Ward .01 .05
568 Bill Wilkinson .01 .05
569 Howard Johnson .02 .10
570 Frank DiPino .01 .05
571 Pete Smith RC .02 .10
572 Darnell Coles .01 .05
573 Don Robinson .01 .05
574 Rob Nelson UER/(Career 0 RBI& but 1 RBI in '87) .01 .05
575 Dennis Rasmussen .01 .05

576 Steve Jeltz UER/(Photo actually Juan .01 .05
Samuel; Sam
577 Tom Pagnozzi RC .02 .10
578 Ty Gainey .01 .05
579 Gary Lucas .01 .05
580 Ron Hassey .01 .05
581 Herm Winningham .01 .05
582 Rene Gonzales RC .02 .10
583 Brad Komminsk .01 .05
584 Doyle Alexander .01 .05
585 Jeff Sellers .01 .05
586 Bill Gullickson .01 .05
587 Tim Belcher .01 .05
588 Doug Jones RC .08 .25
589 Melido Perez RC .08 .25
590 Rick Honeycutt .01 .05
591 Pascual Perez .01 .05
592 Curt Wilkerson .01 .05
593 Steve Howe .01 .05
594 John Davis RC .01 .05
595 Storm Davis .01 .05
596 Sammy Stewart .01 .05
597 Neil Allen .01 .05
598 Alejandro Pena .01 .05
599 Mark Thurmond .01 .05
600A Checklist 578-660 .01 .05
BC1-BC26
600B Checklist 558-660 .01 .05
601 Jose Mesa RC .08 .25
602 Don August .01 .05
603 Terry Leach SP .02 .10
604 Tom Newell .01 .05
605 Randall Byers SP .02 .10
606 Jim Gott .01 .05
607 Harry Spilman .01 .05
608 John Candelaria .01 .05
609 Mike Brumley .01 .05
610 Mickey Brantley .01 .05
611 Jose Nunez SP .02 .10
612 Tom Nieto .01 .05
613 Rick Reuschel .02 .10
614 Lee Mazzilli SP .02 .10
615 Scott Lusader .01 .05
616 Bobby Meacham .01 .05
617 Kevin McReynolds SP .02 .10
618 Gene Garber .01 .05
619 Barry Lyons SP .02 .10
620 Randy Myers .02 .10
621 Donnie Moore .01 .05
622 Domingo Ramos .01 .05
623 Ed Romero .01 .05
624 Greg Myers RC .08 .25
625 The Ripken Family .15 .40
626 Pat Perry .01 .05
627 Andres Thomas SP .02 .10
628 Matt Williams RC .30 .75
629 Dave Hengel .01 .05
630 Jeff Musselman SP .02 .10
631 Tim Laudner .01 .05
632 Bob Ojeda SP .02 .10
633 Rafael Santana .01 .05
634 Wes Gardner .01 .05
635 Roberto Kelly SP RC .08 .25
636 Mike Flanagan SP .02 .10
637 Jay Bell RC .15 .40
638 Bob Melvin .01 .05
639 Damon Berryhill RC .08 .25
640 David Wells RC .40 1.00
641 Stan Musial Puzzle .07 .20
642 Doug Sisk .01 .05
643 Keith Hughes RC .01 .05
644 Tom Glavine RC 1.25 3.00
645 Al Newman .01 .05
646 Scott Sanderson .01 .05
647 Scott Terry .01 .05
648 Tim Teufel SP .02 .10
649 Garry Templeton SP .02 .10
650 Manny Lee SP .02 .10
651 Roger McDowell SP .02 .10
652 Mookie Wilson SP .02 .10
653 David Cone .02 .10
654 Ron Gant RC .15 .40
655 Joe Price SP .02 .10
656 George Bell SP .02 .10
657 Gregg Jefferies RC .08 .25
658 Todd Stottlemyre RC .08 .25
659 Geronimo Berroa RC .08 .25
660 Jerry Royster SP .02 .10
XX Kirby Puckett .50 1.25
Blister Pack

1988 Donruss Bonus MVP's

COMPLETE SET (26) 1.25 3.00
RANDOM INSERTS IN PACKS
BC1 Cal Ripken .30 .75
BC2 Eric Davis .02 .10
BC3 Paul Molitor .02 .10
BC4 Mike Schmidt .20 .50
BC5 Ivan Calderon .01 .05
BC6 Tony Gwynn .10 .30
BC7 Wade Boggs .05 .15
BC8 Andy Van Slyke .05 .15
BC9 Joe Carter .02 .10
BC10 Andre Dawson .02 .10
BC11 Alan Trammell .02 .10
BC12 Mike Scott .02 .10
BC13 Wally Joyner .02 .10
BC14 Dale Murphy SP .05 .15
BC15 Kirby Puckett SP .07 .20
BC16 Pedro Guerrero SP .02 .10
BC17 Kevin Seitzer SP .01 .05
BC18 Tim Raines SP .02 .10
BC19 George Bell SP .02 .10
BC20 Darryl Strawberry SP .02 .10
BC21 Don Mattingly SP .25 .60
BC22 Ozzie Smith SP .10 .30
BC23 Mark McGwire SP .60 1.50
BC24 Will Clark SP .07 .20
BC25 Alvin Davis SP .01 .05
BC26 Ruben Sierra SP .02 .10

1988 Donruss Rookies

The 1988 Donruss "The Rookies" set features 56 standard-size full-color cards plus a 15-piece puzzle of Stan Musial. This set was distributed exclusively in factory set form in a small, cellophane-wrapped, green and black through hobby dealers. Card fronts are similar in design to the 1988 Donruss regular issue except for the presence of "The Rookies" logo in the lower right corner and a green and black border instead of a blue and black border on the fronts. Extended Rookie Cards in this set include Brady Anderson, Edgar Martinez, and Walt Weiss. Notable early cards were issued of Roberto Alomar, Mark Grace and Jay Buhner.

COMP.FACT.SET (56) 4.00 10.00
1 Mark Grace .75 2.00
2 Mike Campbell .05 .15
3 Todd Frohwirth .05 .15
4 Dave Stapleton .05 .15
5 Shawn Abner .05 .15
6 Jose Cecena .05 .15
7 Dave Gallagher .05 .15
8 Mark Parent XRC .05 .15
9 Cecil Espy XRC .05 .15
10 Pete Smith .05 .15
11 Jay Buhner .40 1.00
12 Pat Borders XRC .20 .50
13 Doug Jennings XRC .05 .15
14 Brady Anderson XRC .30 .75
15 Pete Stanicek .05 .15
16 Roberto Kelly .20 .50
17 Jeff Treadway .05 .15
18 Walt Weiss XRC* .30 .75
19 Paul Gibson .05 .15
20 Tim Crews .05 .15
21 Melido Perez .05 .15
22 Steve Peters .05 .15
23 Craig Worthington .05 .15
24 John Trautwein .05 .15
25 DeWayne Vaughn .05 .15
26 David Wells .60 1.50
27 Al Leiter .40 1.00
28 Tim Belcher .05 .15
29 Johnny Paredes .05 .15
30 Chris Sabo XRC .15 .40
31 Damon Berryhill .05 .15
32 Randy Milligan XRC* .08 .25
33 Gary Thurman .05 .15
34 Kevin Elster .05 .15
35 Roberto Alomar 1.50 4.00
36 Edgar Martinez XRC 2.50 6.00
37 Todd Stottlemyre .05 .15
38 Joey Meyer .05 .15
39 Carl Nichols .05 .15
40 Jack McDowell .30 .75
41 Jose Bautista XRC .08 .25
42 Sil Campusano .05 .15
43 John Dopson .05 .15
44 Jody Reed .20 .50
45 Darrin Jackson XRC* .08 .25
46 Mike Capel .05 .15
47 Ron Gant .30 .75
48 John Davis .05 .15
49 Kevin Coffman .05 .15
50 Cris Carpenter XRC .08 .25
51 Mackey Sasser .05 .15
52 Luis Alicea XRC .20 .50
53 Bryan Harvey XRC .10 .30
54 Steve Ellsworth .05 .15
55 Mike Macfarlane XRC .20 .50
56 Checklist 1-56 .05 .15

1988 Donruss Stan Musial Puzzle

1 Musial Puzzle 1-3 .10 .25
4 Musial Puzzle 4-6 .10 .25
7 Musial Puzzle 7-10 .10 .25
10 Musial Puzzle 10-12 .10 .25
13 Musial Puzzle 13-15 .10 .25
16 Musial Puzzle 16-18 .10 .25
19 Musial Puzzle 19-21 .10 .25
22 Musial Puzzle 22-24 .10 .25
25 Musial Puzzle 25-27 .10 .25
28 Musial Puzzle 28-30 .10 .25
31 Musial Puzzle 31-33 .10 .25
34 Musial Puzzle 34-36 .10 .25
37 Musial Puzzle 37-39 .10 .25
40 Musial Puzzle 40-42 .10 .25
43 Musial Puzzle 43-45 .10 .25
46 Musial Puzzle 46-48 .10 .25
49 Musial Puzzle 49-51 .10 .25
52 Musial Puzzle 52-54 .10 .25
55 Musial Puzzle 55-57 .10 .25
58 Musial Puzzle 58-60 .10 .25
61 Musial Puzzle 61-63 .10 .25

1988 Donruss All-Stars

COMPLETE SET (64) 3.00 8.00
1 Don Mattingly .40 1.00
2 Dave Winfield .20 .50
3 Willie Randolph .02 .10
4 Rickey Henderson .20 .50
5 Cal Ripken 1.00 2.50
6 George Bell .01 .05
7 Wade Boggs .20 .50
8 Bret Saberhagen .02 .10
9 Terry Kennedy .01 .05
10 John McNamara MG .01 .05
11 Jay Howell .01 .05
12 Harold Baines .07 .20
13 Harold Reynolds .02 .10
14 Bruce Hurst .01 .05
15 Kirby Puckett .40 1.00
16 Matt Nokes .01 .05
17 Pat Tabler .01 .05
18 Dan Plesac .01 .05
19 Mark McGwire .75 2.00
20 Mike Witt .01 .05
21 Larry Parrish .01 .05
22 Alan Trammell .07 .20
23 Dwight Evans .02 .10
24 Jack Morris .02 .10
25 Tony Fernandez .01 .05
26 Mark Langston .01 .05
27 Kevin Seitzer .01 .05
28 Tom Henke .01 .05
29 Dave Righetti .01 .05
30 Oakland Stadium .01 .05
31 Wade Boggs/(Top AL Vote Getter) .20 .50
32 AL Checklist UER .01 .05
33 Jack Clark .01 .05
34 Darryl Strawberry .02 .10
35 Ryne Sandberg .30 .75
36 Andre Dawson .10 .30
37 Ozzie Smith .40 1.00
38 Eric Davis .02 .10
39 Mike Schmidt .30 .75
40 Mike Scott .01 .05
41 Gary Carter .20 .50
42 Davey Johnson MG .01 .05
43 Rick Sutcliffe .01 .05
44 Willie McGee .02 .10
45 Hubie Brooks .01 .05
46 Dale Murphy .10 .30
47 Bo Diaz .01 .05
48 Pedro Guerrero .01 .05
49 Keith Hernandez .02 .10
50 Ozzie Virgil UER/(Phillies logo .01 .05
on card back&
w
51 Tony Gwynn .50 1.25
52 Rick Reuschel UER/(Pirates logo .01 .05
on card back)
53 John Franco .02 .10
54 Jeffrey Leonard .01 .05
55 Juan Samuel .01 .05
56 Orel Hershiser .02 .10
57 Tim Raines .02 .10
58 Sid Fernandez .01 .05
59 Tim Wallach .01 .05
60 Lee Smith .02 .10
61 Steve Bedrosian .01 .05
62 Tim Raines .02 .10
63 Ozzie Smith/(Top NL Vote Getter) .40 1.00
64 NL Checklist .01 .05

1988 Donruss Baseball's Best

This innovative set of 336 standard-size cards was released by Donruss very late in the 1988 season to be sold in large national retail chains as a complete packaged set. The set was packaged in a specially designed box. Cards are very similar in design to the 1988 regular Donruss issue except that these cards have orange and black borders instead of blue and black borders. The set is also sometimes referred to as the Halloween set because of the orange box and design of the cards. Six (2 1/2" by 3 1/2") 15-piece puzzles of Stan Musial are also included with every complete set.

COMP.FACT.SET (336) 10.00 25.00
1 Don Mattingly .40 1.00
2 Ron Gant .20 .50
3 Bob Boone .07 .20
4 Mark Grace .75 2.00
5 Andy Allanson .02 .10
6 Kal Daniels .02 .10
7 Floyd Bannister .02 .10
8 Alan Ashby .02 .10
9 Marty Barrett .02 .10
10 Tim Belcher .02 .10
11 Harold Baines .07 .20
12 Hubie Brooks .02 .10
13 Doyle Alexander .02 .10
14 Gary Carter .20 .50
15 Glenn Braggs .02 .10
16 Steve Bedrosian .02 .10
17 Barry Bonds .50 1.00
18 Bert Blyleven .07 .20
19 Tom Brunansky .02 .10
20 John Candelaria .02 .10
21 Shawn Abner .02 .10
22 Jose Canseco .20 .50
23 Brett Butler .07 .20
24 Scott Bradley .02 .10
25 Ivan Calderon .02 .10
26 Rich Gossage .07 .20
27 Brian Downing .07 .20
28 Jim Rice .07 .20
29 Dion James .02 .10
30 Terry Kennedy .02 .10
31 George Bell .02 .10
32 Scott Fletcher .02 .10
33 Bobby Bonilla .07 .20
34 Tim Burke .02 .10
35 Darrell Evans .07 .20
36 Mike Davis .02 .10
37 Shawon Dunston .02 .10
38 Kevin Bass .02 .10
39 George Brett .50 1.25
40 David Cone .15 .40
41 Ron Darling .02 .10
42 Roberto Alomar .75 2.00
43 Dennis Eckersley .20 .50
44 Vince Coleman .02 .10
45 Sid Bream .02 .10
46 Gary Gaetti .07 .20
47 Phil Bradley .02 .10
48 Jim Clancy .02 .10
49 Jack Clark .07 .20
50 Mike Krukow .02 .10
51 Henry Cotto .02 .10
52 Rich Dotson .02 .10
53 Jim Gantner .02 .10
54 John Franco .07 .20
55 Pete Incaviglia .02 .10
56 Joe Carter .15 .40
57 Roger Clemens .30 1.00
58 Gerald Perry .02 .10
59 Jack Howell .02 .10
60 Vance Law .02 .10
61 Jay Bell .20 .50
62 Eric Davis .07 .20
63 Gene Garber .07 .20
64 Glenn Davis .02 .10
65 Wade Boggs .20 .50
66 Kirk Gibson .07 .20
67 Carlton Fisk .20 .50
68 Casey Candaele .02 .10
69 Mike Heath .02 .10
70 Kevin Elster .02 .10
71 Greg Brock .02 .10
72 Don Carman .02 .10
73 Doug Drabek .07 .20
74 Greg Gagne .07 .20
75 Danny Cox .02 .10
76 Rickey Henderson .20 .50
77 Chris Brown .02 .10
78 Terry Steinbach .07 .20
79 Will Clark .20 .50
80 Mickey Brantley .02 .10
81 Ozzie Guillen .07 .20
82 Greg Maddux .50 1.25
83 Kirk McCaskill .02 .10
84 Dwight Evans .07 .20
85 Ozzie Virgil .02 .10
86 Mike Morgan .02 .10
87 Tony Fernandez .07 .20
88 Jose Guzman .02 .10
89 Mike Dunne .02 .10
90 Andres Galarraga .15 .40
91 Mike Henneman .07 .20
92 Alfredo Griffin .02 .10
93 Rafael Palmeiro .30 .75
94 Jim Deshaies .02 .10
95 Mark Gubicza .02 .10
96 Dwight Gooden .07 .20
97 Howard Johnson .02 .10
98 Mark Davis .02 .10
99 Dave Stewart .07 .20
100 Joe Magrane .02 .10
101 Brian Fisher .02 .10
102 Kent Hrbek .07 .20
103 Kevin Gross .02 .10
104 Tom Henke .02 .10
105 Mike Pagliarulo .02 .10
106 Kelly Downs .02 .10
107 Alvin Davis .02 .10
108 Willie Randolph .07 .20
109 Rob Deer .02 .10
110 Bo Diaz .02 .10
111 Paul Kilgus .02 .10
112 Tom Candiotti .02 .10
113 Dale Murphy .15 .40
114 Rick Mahler .02 .10
115 Wally Joyner .10 .30
116 Ryne Sandberg .20 .50
117 John Farrell .02 .10
118 Nick Esasky .02 .10
119 Bo Jackson .15 .40
120 Bill Doran .02 .10
121 Ellis Burks .30 .75
122 Pedro Guerrero .02 .10
123 Dave LaPoint .02 .10
124 Neal Heaton .02 .10
125 Willie Hernandez .02 .10
126 Roger McDowell .02 .10
127 Ted Higuera .02 .10
128 Von Hayes .02 .10
129 Mike LaValliere .02 .10
130 Dan Gladden .02 .10
131 Willie McGee .07 .20
132 Al Leiter .20 .50
133 Mark Grant .02 .10
134 Bob Welch .02 .10
135 Dave Dravecky .07 .20
136 Mark Langston .02 .10
137 Dan Pasqua .02 .10
138 Rick Sutcliffe .07 .20
139 Dan Petry .02 .10
140 Rich Gedman .02 .10
141 Ken Griffey .07 .20
142 Eddie Murray .20 .50
143 Jimmy Key .07 .20
144 Dale Mohorcic .02 .10
145 Jose Lind .02 .10
146 Dennis Martinez .07 .20
147 Chet Lemon .02 .10
148 Orel Hershiser .07 .20
149 Dave Martinez .02 .10
150 Billy Hatcher .02 .10
151 Charlie Leibrandt .02 .10
152 Keith Hernandez .07 .20
153 Kevin McReynolds .02 .10
154 Tony Gwynn .30 1.00
155 Stan Javier .02 .10
156 Tony Pena .07 .20
157 Andy Van Slyke .07 .20
158 Gene Larkin .02 .10
159 Chris James .02 .10
160 Fred McGriff .30 .75
161 Rick Rhoden .02 .10
162 Scott Garrelts .02 .10
163 Mike Campbell .02 .10
164 Dave Righetti .02 .10
165 Paul Molitor .20 .50
166 Danny Jackson .02 .10
167 Pete O'Brien .02 .10
168 Julio Franco .07 .20
169 Mark McGwire .75 2.00
170 Zane Smith .02 .10
171 Johnny Ray .02 .10
172 Les Lancaster .02 .10
173 Mel Hall .02 .10
174 Tracy Jones .02 .10
175 Kevin Seitzer .02 .10
176 Bob Knepper .02 .10
177 Mike Greenwell .02 .10
178 Mike Marshall .02 .10
179 Melido Perez .02 .10
180 Tim Raines .07 .20
181 Jack Morris .07 .20
182 Darryl Strawberry .07 .20
183 Robin Yount .20 .50
184 Lance Parrish .02 .10
185 Darnell Coles .02 .10
186 Kirby Puckett .20 .50
187 Terry Pendleton .07 .20
188 Don Slaught .02 .10
189 Jimmy Jones .02 .10
190 Dave Parker .07 .20
191 Mike Aldrete .02 .10
192 Mike Moore .02 .10
193 Greg Walker .02 .10
194 Calvin Schiraldi .02 .10
195 Dick Schofield .02 .10
196 Jody Reed .07 .20
197 Pete Smith .02 .10
198 Cal Ripken .75 2.00
199 Lloyd Moseby .02 .10
200 Ruben Sierra .07 .20
201 R.J. Reynolds .02 .10
202 Bryn Smith .02 .10
203 Gary Pettis .02 .10
204 Steve Sax .02 .10
205 Frank DiPino .02 .10
206 Mike Scott UER .02 .10
1977 Jackson losses
say 1.10, should be 1
207 Kurt Stillwell .02 .10
208 Mookie Wilson .07 .20
209 Lee Mazzilli .07 .20
210 Lance McCullers .02 .10
211 Rick Honeycutt .02 .10
212 John Tudor .02 .10
213 Jim Gott .02 .10
214 Frank Viola .02 .10
215 Juan Samuel .02 .10
216 Jesse Barfield .02 .10
217 Claudell Washington .02 .10
218 Rick Reuschel .07 .20
219 Jim Presley .02 .10
220 Tommy John .07 .20
221 Dan Plesac .02 .10
222 Barry Larkin .15 .40
223 Mike Stanley .02 .10
224 Cory Snyder .02 .10
225 Andre Dawson .15 .40
226 Ken Oberkfell .02 .10
227 Devon White .07 .20
228 Jamie Moyer .20 .50
229 Brook Jacoby .02 .10
230 Rob Murphy .02 .10
231 Bret Saberhagen .07 .20
232 Nolan Ryan .75 2.00
233 Bruce Hurst .02 .10
234 Jesse Orosco .07 .20
235 Bobby Thigpen .02 .10
236 Pascual Perez .02 .10
237 Matt Nokes .07 .20
238 Bob Ojeda .02 .10
239 Joey Meyer .02 .10
240 Shane Rawley .02 .10
241 Jeff Robinson .02 .10
242 Jeff Reardon .07 .20
243 Ozzie Smith .20 .50
244 Dave Winfield .20 .50
245 John Kruk .08 .25
246 Carney Lansford .07 .20
247 Candy Maldonado .02 .10
248 Ken Phelps .02 .10
249 Ken Williams .15 .40
250 Al Nipper .02 .10
251 Mark McLemore .02 .10
252 Lee Smith .07 .20
253 Albert Hall .02 .10
254 Billy Ripken .02 .10
255 Kelly Gruber .02 .10
256 Charlie Hough .07 .20
257 John Smiley .02 .10
258 Tim Wallach .02 .10
259 Frank Tanana .07 .20
260 Mike Scioscia .07 .20
261 Damon Berryhill .02 .10
262 Dave Smith .07 .20
263 Willie Wilson .02 .10
264 Len Dykstra .07 .20
265 Randy Myers .10 .30
266 Keith Moreland .02 .10
267 Eric Plunk .02 .10
268 Todd Worrell .07 .20
269 Bob Walk .02 .10
270 Keith Atherton .02 .10
271 Mike Schmidt .20 .50
272 Mike Flanagan .02 .10
273 Rafael Santana .02 .10
274 Robby Thompson .02 .10
275 Rey Quinones .02 .10
276 Cecilio Guante .02 .10
277 B.J. Surhoff .10 .30
278 Chris Sabo .02 .10
279 Mitch Williams .02 .10
280 Greg Swindell .02 .10
281 Alan Trammell .10 .30
282 Storm Davis .02 .10
283 Chuck Finley .10 .30
284 Dave Stieb .02 .10
285 Scott Bailes .02 .10
286 Larry Sheets .02 .10
287 Danny Tartabull .02 .10
288 Checklist Card .02 .10
289 Todd Benzinger .02 .10
290 John Shelby .02 .10
291 Steve Lyons .07 .20
292 Mitch Webster .02 .10
293 Walt Terrell .02 .10
294 Pete Stanicek .02 .10
295 Chris Bosio .02 .10
296 Milt Thompson .02 .10
297 Fred Lynn .07 .20
298 Juan Berenguer .02 .10
299 Ken Dayley .02 .10
300 Joel Skinner .02 .10
301 Benito Santiago .07 .20
302 Ron Hassey .02 .10
303 Jose Uribe .02 .10
304 Harold Reynolds .07 .20
305 Dale Sveum .02 .10
306 Glenn Wilson .02 .10
307 Mike Witt .02 .10
308 Ron Robinson .02 .10
309 Denny Walling .02 .10
310 Joe Orsulak .02 .10
311 David Wells .60 1.50
312 Steve Buechele .02 .10
313 Jose Oquendo .02 .10
314 Floyd Youmans .02 .10
315 Lou Whitaker .07 .20
316 Fernando Valenzuela .07 .20
317 Mike Boddicker .02 .10
318 Gerald Young .02 .10
319 Frank White .07 .20
320 Bill Wegman .02 .10
321 Tom Niedenfuer .02 .10
322 Ed Whitson .02 .10
323 Curt Young .02 .10
324 Greg Mathews .02 .10
325 Doug Jones .15 .40
326 Tommy Herr .02 .10
327 Kent Tekulve .02 .10
328 Rance Mulliniks .02 .10
329 Checklist Card .02 .10
330 Craig Lefferts .02 .10
331 Franklin Stubbs .02 .10
332 Rick Cerone .02 .10
333 Dave Schmidt .02 .10
334 Larry Parrish .02 .10
335 Tom Browning .02 .10
336 Checklist Card .02 .10

1988 Donruss Pop-Ups

COMPLETE SET (20) 2.00 5.00
1 Don Mattingly .50 1.25
2 Dave Winfield .15 .40
3 Willie Randolph .02 .10
4 Rickey Henderson .25 .60
5 Cal Ripken .75 2.00
6 George Bell .01 .05
7 Wade Boggs .20 .50
8 Bret Saberhagen .02 .10
9 Terry Kennedy .01 .05
10 John McNamara MG .01 .05
11 Jack Clark .02 .10
12 Darryl Strawberry .02 .10
13 Ryne Sandberg .20 .50
14 Andre Dawson .10 .30
15 Ozzie Smith .30 .75
16 Eric Davis .02 .10
17 Mike Schmidt .20 .50
18 Mike Scott .01 .05
19 Gary Carter .15 .40
20 Davey Johnson MG .01 .05

1988 Donruss Super DK's

COMPLETE SET (26) 6.00 15.00
1 Mark McGwire 1.25 3.00
2 Tim Raines .30 .75
3 Benito Santiago .30 .75
4 Alan Trammell .40 1.00
5 Danny Tartabull .20 .50
6 Ron Darling .20 .50
7 Paul Molitor .75 2.00
8 Devon White .30 .75
9 Andre Dawson .60 1.50
10 Julio Franco .30 .75
11 Scott Fletcher .20 .50
12 Tony Fernandez .20 .50
13 Shane Rawley .20 .50
14 Kal Daniels .20 .50
15 Jack Clark .30 .75
16 Dwight Evans .30 .75
17 Tommy John .30 .75
18 Andy Van Slyke .30 .75
19 Gary Gaetti .30 .75
20 Mark Langston .20 .50
21 Will Clark .75 2.00
22 Glenn Hubbard .20 .50
23 Billy Hatcher .20 .50
24 Bob Welch .20 .50
25 Ivan Calderon .20 .50
26 Cal Ripken 2.00 5.00

1989 Donruss

This set consists of 660 standard-size cards. The cards were primarily issued in 15-card wax packs, rack packs and hobby and retail factory sets. Each wax pack also contained a puzzle panel (featuring Warren Spahn this year). The wax packs were issued 36 packs to a box and 20 boxes to a case. The cards feature a distinctive black side border with an alternating coating. Subsets include Diamond Kings (1-27) and Rated Rookies (28-47). There are two variations that occur throughout most of the set. On the card backs "Denotes Led League" can be found with one asterisk to the left or with an asterisk on each side. On the card fronts the horizontal lines on the left and right borders can be glossy or non-glossy. Since both of these variation types are relatively minor and seem equally common, there is no premium value for either type. Rather than short-printing 26 cards in order to make room for printing the Bonus MVP's this year, Donruss apparently chose to double print 106 cards. These double prints are listed below by DP. Rookie Cards in this set include Sandy Alomar Jr., Brady Anderson, Dante Bichette, Craig Biggio, Ken Griffey Jr., Randy Johnson, Curt Schilling, Gary Sheffield and John Smoltz. Similar to the 1988 Donruss set, a special card was issued on blister packs, and features the card number as "Bonus Card".

COMPLETE SET (660) 10.00 25.00
COMP.FACT.SET (672) 10.00 25.00
1 Mike Greenwell DK .01 .05
2 Bobby Bonilla DK DP .01 .05
3 Pete Incaviglia DK .01 .05
4 Chris Sabo DK DP .02 .10
5 Robin Yount DK .15 .40
6 Tony Gwynn DK DP .05 .15
7 Carlton Fisk DK UER .05 .15
OF on back
8 Cory Snyder DK .01 .05
9 David Cone DK UER .02 .10
'hurdlers'
10 Kevin Seitzer DK .01 .05
11 Rick Reuschel DK .01 .05
12 Johnny Ray DK .01 .05
13 Dave Schmidt DK .01 .05
14 Andres Galarraga DK .02 .10
15 Kirk Gibson DK .02 .10
16 Fred McGriff DK .05 .15
17 Mark Grace DK .08 .25
18 Jeff M. Robinson DK .01 .05
19 Vince Coleman DK DP .01 .05
20 Dave Henderson DK .01 .05
21 Harold Reynolds DK .02 .10
22 Gerald Perry DK .01 .05
23 Frank Viola DK .02 .10
24 Steve Bedrosian DK .01 .05
25 Glenn Davis DK .01 .05
26 Don Mattingly DK UER .10 .30
27 DK Checklist 1-26 DP .01 .05
28 Sandy Alomar Jr. RC .15 .40
29 Steve Searcy RR .01 .05
30 Cameron Drew RR .01 .05
31 Gary Sheffield RR RC .60 1.50
32 Erik Hanson RR RC .08 .25
33 Ken Griffey Jr. RR RC 6.00 15.00
34 Greg W. Harris RR RC .02 .10
35 Gregg Jefferies RR .01 .05
36 Luis Medina RR .01 .05
37 Carlos Quintana RR RC .02 .10
38 Felix Jose RR RC .02 .10
39 Cris Carpenter RR RC* .02 .10
40 Ron Jones RR .02 .10
41 Dave West RR RC .02 .10
42 R.Johnson RC RR UER 1.00 2.50
43 Mike Harkey RR RC .02 .10
44 Pete Harnisch RC .08 .25
45 Tom Gordon RR DP RC .20 .50
46 Gregg Olson RC RR DP .08 .25
47 Alex Sanchez RC .01 .05
48 Ruben Sierra .02 .10
49 Rafael Palmeiro .08 .25
50 Ron Gant .02 .10
51 Cal Ripken .30 .75
52 Wally Joyner .02 .10
53 Gary Carter .02 .10
54 Andy Van Slyke .05 .15
55 Robin Yount .15 .40
56 Pete Incaviglia .01 .05
57 Greg Brock .01 .05
58 Melido Perez .01 .05
59 Craig Lefferts .01 .05
60 Gary Pettis .01 .05
61 Danny Tartabull .01 .05
62 Guillermo Hernandez .01 .05
63 Ozzie Smith .15 .40
64 Gary Gaetti .02 .10
65 Mark Davis .01 .05
66 Lee Smith .02 .10
67 Dennis Eckersley .05 .15
68 Wade Boggs .05 .15
69 Mike Scott .02 .10
70 Fred McGriff .05 .15
71 Tom Browning .01 .05
72 Claudell Washington .01 .05
73 Mel Hall .01 .05
74 Don Mattingly .25 .60
75 Steve Bedrosian .01 .05
76 Juan Samuel .01 .05
77 Mike Scioscia .02 .10
78 Dave Righetti .02 .10
79 Alfredo Griffin .01 .05
80 Eric Davis UER .02 .10
165 games in 1988,
should be 135
81 Juan Berenguer .01 .05
82 Todd Worrell .01 .05
83 Joe Carter .02 .10
84 Steve Sax .01 .05
85 Frank White .02 .10
86 John Kruk .02 .10
87 Rance Mulliniks .01 .05
88 Alan Ashby .01 .05
89 Charlie Leibrandt .01 .05
90 Frank Tanana .02 .10
91 Jose Canseco .08 .25
92 Barry Bonds .60 1.50
93 Harold Reynolds .02 .10
94 Mark McLemore .01 .05
95 Mark McGwire .40 1.00
96 Eddie Murray .08 .25
97 Tim Raines .02 .10
98 Robby Thompson .01 .05
99 Kevin McReynolds .01 .05
100 Checklist 28-137 .01 .05
101 Carlton Fisk .05 .15
102 Dave Martinez .01 .05
103 Glenn Braggs .01 .05
104 Dale Murphy .05 .15
105 Ryne Sandberg .15 .40
106 Dennis Martinez .02 .10
107 Pete O'Brien .01 .05
108 Dick Schofield .01 .05
109 Henry Cotto .01 .05
110 Mike Marshall .01 .05
111 Keith Moreland .01 .05
112 Tom Brunansky .01 .05
113 Kelly Gruber UER .01 .05
Wrong birthdate
114 Brook Jacoby .01 .05
115 Keith Brown .01 .05
116 Matt Nokes .01 .05
117 Keith Hernandez .02 .10
118 Bob Forsch .01 .05
119 Bert Blyleven UER .02 .10
120 Willie Wilson .01 .05
121 Tommy Gregg .01 .05
122 Jim Rice .02 .10
123 Bob Knepper .01 .05
124 Danny Jackson .01 .05
125 Eric Plunk .01 .05
126 Brian Fisher .01 .05
127 Mike Pagliarulo .01 .05
128 Tony Gwynn .10 .30
129 Lance McCullers .01 .05
130 Andres Galarraga .02 .10
131 Jose Uribe .01 .05
132 Kirk Gibson UER .02 .10
Wrong birthdate
133 David Palmer .01 .05
134 R.J. Reynolds .01 .05
135 Greg Walker .01 .05
136 Kirk McCaskill UER .01 .05
Wrong birthdate
137 Shawon Dunston .01 .05
138 Andy Allanson .01 .05
139 Rob Murphy .01 .05
140 Mike Aldrete .01 .05
141 Terry Kennedy .01 .05
142 Scott Fletcher .01 .05
143 Steve Balboni .01 .05
144 Bret Saberhagen .02 .10
145 Ozzie Virgil .01 .05
146 Dale Sveum .01 .05

147 Darryl Strawberry .02 .10
148 Harold Baines .02 .10
149 George Bell .02 .10
150 Dave Parker .02 .10
151 Bobby Bonilla .02 .10
152 Mookie Wilson .02 .10
153 Ted Power .01 .05
154 Nolan Ryan .40 1.00
155 Jeff Reardon .02 .10
156 Tim Wallach .01 .05
157 Jamie Moyer .02 .10
158 Rich Gossage .02 .10
159 Dave Winfield .02 .10
160 Von Hayes .01 .05
161 Willie McGee .02 .10
162 Rich Gedman .01 .05
163 Tony Pena .01 .05
164 Mike Morgan .01 .05
165 Charlie Hough .02 .10
166 Mike Stanley .01 .05
167 Andre Dawson .02 .10
168 Joe Boever .01 .05
169 Pete Stanicek .01 .05
170 Bob Boone .02 .10
171 Ron Darling .02 .10
172 Bob Walk .01 .05
173 Rob Deer .01 .05
174 Steve Buechele .01 .05
175 Ted Higuera .01 .05
176 Ozzie Guillen .02 .10
177 Candy Maldonado .01 .05
178 Doyle Alexander .01 .05
179 Mark Gubicza .01 .05
180 Alan Trammell .02 .10
181 Vince Coleman .01 .05
182 Kirby Puckett .08 .25
183 Chris Brown .01 .05
184 Marty Barrett .01 .05
185 Stan Javier .01 .05
186 Mike Greenwell .01 .05
187 Billy Hatcher .01 .05
188 Jimmy Key .02 .10
189 Nick Esasky .01 .05
190 Don Slaught .01 .05
191 Cory Snyder .01 .05
192 John Candelaria .01 .05
193 Mike Schmidt .20 .50
194 Kevin Gross .01 .05
195 John Tudor .02 .10
196 Neil Allen .01 .05
197 Orel Hershiser .02 .10
198 Kal Daniels .01 .05
199 Kent Hrbek .02 .10
200 Checklist 138-247 .01 .05
201 Joe Magrane .01 .05
202 Scott Bailes .01 .05
203 Tim Belcher .01 .05
204 George Brett .25 .60
205 Benito Santiago .02 .10
206 Tony Fernandez .01 .05
207 Gerald Young .01 .05
208 Bo Jackson .08 .25
209 Chet Lemon .02 .10
210 Storm Davis .01 .05
211 Doug Drabek .01 .05
212 Mickey Brantley UER .01 .05
Photo actually
Nelson Simmons
213 Devon White .02 .10
214 Dave Stewart .02 .10
215 Dave Schmidt .01 .05
216 Bryn Smith .01 .05
217 Brett Butler .02 .10
218 Bob Ojeda .01 .05
219 Steve Rosenberg .01 .05
220 Hubie Brooks .01 .05
221 B.J. Surhoff .02 .10
222 Rick Mahler .01 .05
223 Rick Sutcliffe .02 .10
224 Neal Heaton .01 .05
225 Mitch Williams .01 .05
226 Chuck Finley .02 .10
227 Mark Langston .01 .05
228 Jesse Orosco .01 .05
229 Ed Whitson .01 .05
230 Terry Pendleton .02 .10
231 Lloyd Moseby .01 .05
232 Greg Swindell .01 .05
233 John Franco .02 .10
234 Jack Morris .02 .10
235 Howard Johnson .02 .10
236 Glenn Davis .01 .05
237 Frank Viola .02 .10
238 Kevin Seitzer .01 .05
239 Gerald Perry .01 .05
240 Dwight Evans .05 .15
241 Jim Deshaies .01 .05
242 Bo Diaz .01 .05
243 Carney Lansford .02 .10
244 Mike LaValliere .01 .05
245 Rickey Henderson .08 .25
246 Roberto Alomar .08 .25
247 Jimmy Jones .01 .05
248 Pascual Perez .01 .05
249 Will Clark .05 .15
250 Fernando Valenzuela .02 .10
251 Shane Rawley .01 .05
252 Sid Bream .01 .05
253 Steve Lyons .01 .05
254 Brian Downing .02 .10
255 Mark Grace .08 .25
256 Tom Candiotti .01 .05
257 Barry Larkin .05 .15
258 Mike Krukow .01 .05
259 Billy Ripken .01 .05
260 Cecilio Guante .01 .05
261 Scott Bradley .01 .05
262 Floyd Bannister .01 .05
263 Pete Smith .01 .05
264 Jim Gantner UER .01 .05
Wrong birthdate
265 Roger McDowell .01 .05
266 Bobby Thigpen .01 .05
267 Jim Clancy .01 .05
268 Terry Steinbach .02 .10
269 Mike Dunne .01 .05
270 Dwight Gooden .02 .10
271 Mike Heath .01 .05
272 Dave Smith .01 .05
273 Keith Atherton .01 .05
274 Tim Burke .01 .05
275 Damon Berryhill .01 .05
276 Vance Law .01 .05
277 Rich Dotson .01 .05
278 Lance Parrish .02 .10
279 Denny Walling .01 .05
280 Roger Clemens .40 1.00
281 Greg Mathews .01 .05
282 Tom Niedenfuer .01 .05
283 Paul Kilgus .01 .05
284 Jose Guzman .01 .05
285 Calvin Schiraldi .01 .05
286 Charlie Puleo UER .01 .05
Career ERA 4.24,
should be 4.23
287 Joe Orsulak .01 .05
288 Jack Howell .01 .05
289 Kevin Elster .01 .05
290 Jose Lind .01 .05
291 Paul Molitor .02 .10
292 Cecil Espy .01 .05
293 Bill Wegman .01 .05
294 Dan Pasqua .01 .05
295 Scott Garrelts UER .01 .05
Wrong birthdate
296 Walt Terrell .01 .05
297 Ed Hearn .01 .05
298 Lou Whitaker .02 .10
299 Ken Dayley .01 .05
300 Checklist 248-357 .01 .05
301 Tommy Herr .01 .05
302 Mike Brumley .01 .05
303 Ellis Burks .02 .10
304 Curt Young UER .01 .05
Wrong birthdate
305 Jody Reed .01 .05
306 Bill Doran .01 .05
307 David Wells .02 .10
308 Ron Robinson .01 .05
309 Rafael Santana .01 .05
310 Julio Franco .02 .10
311 Jack Clark .02 .10
312 Chris James .01 .05
313 Milt Thompson .01 .05
314 John Shelby .01 .05
315 Al Leiter .08 .25
316 Mike Davis .01 .05
317 Chris Sabo RC .15 .40
318 Greg Gagne .01 .05
319 Jose Oquendo .01 .05
320 John Farrell .01 .05
321 Franklin Stubbs .01 .05
322 Kurt Stillwell .01 .05
323 Shawn Abner .01 .05
324 Mike Flanagan .01 .05
325 Kevin Bass .01 .05
326 Pat Tabler .01 .05
327 Mike Henneman .01 .05
328 Rick Honeycutt .01 .05
329 John Smiley .01 .05
330 Rey Quinones .01 .05
331 Johnny Ray .01 .05
332 Bob Welch .02 .10
333 Larry Sheets .01 .05
334 Jeff Parrett .01 .05
335 Rick Reuschel UER .02 .10
For Don Robinson&
should be Jeff
336 Randy Myers .02 .10
337 Ken Williams .01 .05
338 Andy McGaffigan .01 .05
339 Joey Meyer .01 .05
340 Dion James .01 .05
341 Les Lancaster .01 .05
342 Tom Foley .01 .05
343 Geno Petralli .01 .05
344 Dan Petry .01 .05
345 Alvin Davis .01 .05
346 Mickey Hatcher .01 .05
347 Marvell Wynne .01 .05
348 Danny Cox .01 .05
349 Dave Stieb .02 .10
350 Jay Bell .02 .10
351 Jeff Treadway .01 .05
352 Luis Salazar .01 .05
353 Len Dykstra .02 .10
354 Juan Agosto .01 .05
355 Gene Larkin .01 .05
356 Steve Farr .01 .05
357 Paul Assenmacher .01 .05
358 Todd Benzinger .01 .05
359 Larry Andersen .01 .05
360 Paul O'Neill .05 .15
361 Ron Hassey .01 .05
362 Jim Gott .01 .05
363 Ken Phelps .01 .05
364 Tim Flannery .01 .05
365 Randy Ready .01 .05
366 Nelson Santovenia .01 .05
367 Kelly Downs .01 .05
368 Danny Heep .01 .05
369 Phil Bradley .01 .05
370 Jeff D. Robinson .01 .05
371 Ivan Calderon .01 .05
372 Mike Witt .01 .05
373 Greg Maddux .20 .50
374 Carmen Castillo .01 .05
375 Jose Rijo .02 .10
376 Joe Price .01 .05
377 Rene Gonzales .01 .05
378 Oddibe McDowell .01 .05
379 Jim Presley .01 .05
380 Brad Wellman .01 .05
381 Tom Glavine .08 .25
382 Dan Plesac .01 .05
383 Wally Backman .01 .05
384 Dave Gallagher .01 .05
385 Tom Henke .01 .05
386 Luis Polonia .01 .05
387 Junior Ortiz .01 .05
388 David Cone .02 .10
389 Dave Bergman .01 .05
390 Danny Darwin .01 .05
391 Dan Gladden .01 .05
392 John Dopson .01 .05
393 Frank DiPino .01 .05
394 Al Nipper .01 .05
395 Willie Randolph .02 .10
396 Don Carman .01 .05
397 Scott Terry .01 .05
398 Rick Cerone .01 .05
399 Tom Pagnozzi .01 .05
400 Checklist 358-467 .01 .05
401 Mickey Tettleton .01 .05
402 Curtis Wilkerson .01 .05
403 Jeff Russell .01 .05
404 Pat Perry .01 .05
405 Jose Alvarez RC .02 .10
406 Rick Schu .01 .05
407 Sherman Corbett RC .01 .05
408 Dave Magadan .01 .05
409 Bob Kipper .01 .05
410 Don August .01 .05
411 Bob Brower .01 .05
412 Chris Bosio .01 .05
413 Jerry Reuss .01 .05
414 Atlee Hammaker .01 .05
415 Jim Walewander .01 .05
416 Mike Macfarlane RC * .08 .25
417 Pat Sheridan .01 .05
418 Pedro Guerrero .02 .10
419 Allan Anderson .01 .05
420 Mark Parent RC .01 .05
421 Bob Stanley .01 .05
422 Mike Gallego .01 .05
423 Bruce Hurst .01 .05
424 Dave Meads .01 .05
425 Jesse Barfield .02 .10
426 Rob Dibble RC .15 .40
427 Joel Skinner .01 .05
428 Ron Kittle .01 .05
429 Rick Rhoden .01 .05
430 Bob Dernier .01 .05
431 Steve Jeltz .01 .05
432 Rick Dempsey .01 .05
433 Roberto Kelly .01 .05
434 Dave Anderson .01 .05
435 Herm Winningham .01 .05
436 Al Newman .01 .05
437 Jose DeLeon .01 .05
438 Doug Jones .01 .05
439 Brian Holton .01 .05
440 Jeff Montgomery .01 .05
441 Dickie Thon .01 .05
442 Cecil Fielder .02 .10
443 John Fishel RC .01 .05
444 Jerry Don Gleaton .01 .05
445 Paul Gibson .01 .05
446 Walt Weiss .01 .05
447 Glenn Wilson .01 .05
448 Mike Moore .01 .05
449 Chili Davis .02 .10
450 Dave Henderson .01 .05
451 Jose Bautista RC .02 .10
452 Rex Hudler .01 .05
453 Bob Brenly .01 .05
454 Mackey Sasser .01 .05
455 Daryl Boston .01 .05
456 Mike R. Fitzgerald .01 .05
457 Jeffrey Leonard .01 .05
458 Bruce Sutter .02 .10
459 Mitch Webster .01 .05
460 Joe Hesketh .01 .05
461 Bobby Witt .01 .05
462 Stu Cliburn .01 .05
463 Scott Bankhead .01 .05
464 Ramon Martinez RC .08 .25
465 Dave Leiper .01 .05
466 Luis Alicea RC * .08 .25
467 John Cerutti .01 .05
468 Ron Washington .01 .05
469 Jeff Reed .01 .05
470 Jeff M. Robinson .01 .05
471 Sid Fernandez .01 .05
472 Terry Puhl .01 .05
473 Charlie Lea .01 .05
474 Israel Sanchez .01 .05
475 Bruce Benedict .01 .05
476 Oil Can Boyd .01 .05
477 Craig Reynolds .01 .05
478 Frank Williams .01 .05
479 Greg Cadaret .01 .05
480 Randy Kramer .01 .05
481 Dave Eiland .01 .05
482 Eric Show .01 .05
483 Garry Templeton .02 .10
484 Wallace Johnson .01 .05
485 Kevin Mitchell .02 .10
486 Tim Crews .01 .05
487 Mike Maddux .01 .05
488 Dave LaPoint .01 .05
489 Fred Manrique .01 .05
490 Greg Minton .01 .05
491 Doug Dascenzo UER .01 .05
Photo actually
Damon Berryhill
492 Willie Upshaw .01 .05
493 Jack Armstrong RC * .08 .25
494 Kirt Manwaring .01 .05
495 Jeff Ballard .01 .05
496 Jeff Kunkel .01 .05
497 Mike Campbell .01 .05
498 Gary Thurman .01 .05
499 Zane Smith .01 .05
500 Checklist 468-577 DP .01 .05
501 Mike Birkbeck .01 .05
502 Terry Leach .01 .05
503 Shawn Hillegas .01 .05
504 Manny Lee .01 .05
505 Doug Jennings RC .01 .05
506 Ken Oberkfell .01 .05
507 Tim Teufel .01 .05
508 Tom Brookens .01 .05
509 Rafael Ramirez .01 .05
510 Fred Toliver .01 .05
511 Brian Holman RC * .02 .10
512 Mike Bielecki .01 .05
513 Jeff Pico .01 .05
514 Charles Hudson .01 .05
515 Bruce Ruffin .01 .05
516 L.McWilliams UER .01 .05
New Richland, should
be North Richland
517 Jeff Sellers .01 .05
518 John Costello RC .01 .05
519 Brady Anderson RC .15 .40
520 Craig McMurtry .01 .05
521 Ray Hayward DP .01 .05
522 Drew Hall DP .01 .05
523 Mark Lemke DP RC .15 .40
524 Oswald Peraza DP RC .01 .05
525 Bryan Harvey DP RC * .08 .25
526 Rick Aguilera DP .01 .05
527 Tom Prince DP .01 .05
528 Mark Clear DP .01 .05
529 Jerry Browne DP .01 .05
530 Juan Castillo DP .01 .05
531 Jack McDowell DP .02 .10
532 Chris Speier DP .01 .05
533 Darrell Evans DP .02 .10
534 Luis Aquino DP .01 .05
535 Eric King DP .01 .05
536 Ken Hill DP RC .08 .25
537 Randy Bush DP .01 .05
538 Shane Mack DP .01 .05
539 Tom Bolton DP .01 .05
540 Gene Nelson DP .01 .05
541 Wes Gardner DP .01 .05
542 Ken Caminiti DP .05 .15
543 Duane Ward DP .01 .05
544 Norm Charlton DP RC .08 .25
545 Hal Morris DP RC .08 .25
546 Rich Yett DP .01 .05
547 Hensley Meulens DP RC .02 .10
548 Greg A. Harris DP .01 .05
549 Darren Daulton DP .02 .10
Posing as right-
handed hitter
550 Jeff Hamilton DP .01 .05
551 Luis Aguayo DP .01 .05
552 Tim Leary DP .01 .05
553 Ron Oester DP .01 .05
554 Steve Lombardozzi DP .01 .05
555 Tim Jones DP .01 .05
556 Bud Black DP .01 .05
557 Alejandro Pena DP .01 .05
558 Jose DeJesus DP .01 .05
559 Dennis Rasmussen DP .01 .05
560 Pat Borders DP RC* .08 .25
561 Craig Biggio DP RC 1.25 3.00
562 Luis DeLosSantos DP .01 .05
563 Fred Lynn DP .02 .10
564 Todd Burns DP .01 .05
565 Felix Fermin DP .01 .05
566 Darnell Coles DP .01 .05
567 Willie Fraser DP .01 .05
568 Glenn Hubbard DP .01 .05
569 Craig Worthington DP .01 .05
570 Johnny Paredes DP .01 .05
571 Don Robinson DP .01 .05
572 Barry Lyons DP .01 .05
573 Bill Long DP .01 .05
574 Tracy Jones DP .01 .05
575 Juan Nieves DP .01 .05
576 Andres Thomas DP .01 .05
577 Rolando Roomes DP .01 .05
578 Luis Rivera UER DP .01 .05
Wrong birthdate
579 Chad Kreuter DP RC .08 .25
580 Tony Armas DP .02 .10
581 Jay Buhner .02 .10
582 Ricky Horton DP .01 .05
583 Andy Hawkins DP .01 .05
584 Sil Campusano .01 .05
585 Dave Clark .01 .05
586 Van Snider DP .01 .05
587 Todd Frohwirth DP .01 .05
588 Warren Spahn Puzzle DP .05 .15
589 William Brennan .01 .05
590 German Gonzalez .01 .05
591 Ernie Whitt DP .01 .05
592 Jeff Blauser .01 .05
593 Spike Owen DP .01 .05
594 Matt Williams .08 .25
595 Lloyd McClendon DP .01 .05
596 Steve Ontiveros .01 .05
597 Scott Medvin .01 .05
598 Hipolito Pena DP .01 .05
599 Jerald Clark DP RC .02 .10
600A CL 578-660 DP .01 .05
635 Curt Schilling
600B CL 578-660 DP .01 .05
635 Curt Schilling;
MVP's not listed
on checklist card
600C CL 578-660 DP .01 .05
635 Curt Schilling;
MVP's listed
following 660
601 Carmelo Martinez DP .01 .05
602 Mike LaCoss .01 .05
603 Mike Devereaux .01 .05
604 Alex Madrid DP .01 .05
605 Gary Redus DP .01 .05
606 Lance Johnson .01 .05
607 Terry Clark DP .01 .05
608 Manny Trillo DP .01 .05
609 Scott Jordan RC .08 .25
610 Jay Howell DP .01 .05
611 Francisco Melendez .01 .05
612 Mike Boddicker .01 .05
613 Kevin Brown DP .08 .25
614 Dave Valle .01 .05
615 Tim Laudner DP .01 .05
616 Andy Nezelek UER .01 .05
Wrong birthdate
617 Chuck Crim .01 .05
618 Jack Savage DP .01 .05
619 Adam Peterson .01 .05
620 Todd Stottlemyre .01 .05
621 Lance Blankenship RC .02 .10
622 Miguel Garcia DP .01 .05
623 Keith A. Miller DP .01 .05
624 Ricky Jordan DP RC* .08 .25
625 Ernest Riles DP .01 .05
626 John Moses DP .01 .05
627 Nelson Liriano DP .01 .05
628 Mike Smithson DP .01 .05
629 Scott Sanderson .01 .05
630 Dale Mohorcic .01 .05
631 Marvin Freeman DP .01 .05
632 Mike Young DP .01 .05
633 Dennis Lamp .01 .05
634 Dante Bichette DP RC .15 .40
635 Curt Schilling DP RC 1.50 4.00
636 Scott May DP .01 .05
637 Mike Schooler .01 .05
638 Rick Leach .01 .05
639 Tom Lampkin UER .01 .05
Throws Left, should
be Throws Right
640 Brian Meyer .01 .05
641 Brian Harper .01 .05
642 John Smoltz RC .60 1.50
643 Jose Canseco .08 .25
40-40 Club
644 Bill Schroeder .01 .05
645 Edgar Martinez .08 .25
646 Dennis Cook RC .08 .25
647 Barry Jones .01 .05
648 Orel Hershiser .02 .10
59 and Counting
649 Rod Nichols .01 .05
650 Jody Davis .01 .05
651 Bob Milacki .01 .05
652 Mike Jackson .01 .05
653 Derek Lilliquist RC .02 .10
654 Paul Mirabella .01 .05
655 Mike Diaz .01 .05
656 Jeff Musselman .01 .05
657 Jerry Reed .01 .05
658 Kevin Blankenship .01 .05
659 Wayne Tolleson .01 .05
660 Eric Hetzel .01 .05
BC Jose Canseco .75 2.00
Blister Pack

1989 Donruss Bonus MVP's

COMPLETE SET (26) .60 1.50
RANDOM INSERTS IN PACKS
BC1 Kirby Puckett .08 .25
BC2 Mike Scott .02 .10
BC3 Joe Carter .02 .10
BC4 Orel Hershiser .02 .10
BC5 Jose Canseco .08 .25
BC6 Darryl Strawberry .02 .10
BC7 George Brett .25 .60
BC8 Andre Dawson .02 .10
BC9 Paul Molitor UER .02 .10
Brewers logo missing
the word Milwaukee
BC10 Andy Van Slyke .05 .15
BC11 Dave Winfield .02 .10
BC12 Kevin Gross .01 .05
BC13 Mike Greenwell .01 .05
BC14 Ozzie Smith .15 .40
BC15 Cal Ripken .30 .75
BC16 Andres Galarraga .02 .10
BC17 Alan Trammell .02 .10
BC18 Kal Daniels .01 .05
BC19 Fred McGriff .05 .15
BC20 Tony Gwynn .10 .30
BC21 Wally Joyner DP .02 .10
BC22 Will Clark DP .05 .15
BC23 Ozzie Guillen .02 .10
BC24 Gerald Perry DP .01 .05
BC25 Alvin Davis DP .01 .05
BC26 Ruben Sierra .02 .10

1989 Donruss Grand Slammers

COMPLETE SET (12) .75 2.00
ONE PER CELLO PACK
ONE SET PER FACTORY SET
1 Jose Canseco .08 .25
2 Mike Marshall .01 .05
3 Walt Weiss .01 .05
4 Kevin McReynolds .01 .05
5 Mike Greenwell .01 .05
6 Dave Winfield .02 .10
7 Mark McGwire .40 1.00
8 Keith Hernandez .02 .10
9 Franklin Stubbs .01 .05
10 Danny Tartabull .01 .05
11 Jesse Barfield .02 .10
12 Ellis Burks .02 .10

1989 Donruss Rookies

The 1989 Donruss Rookies set contains 56 standard-size cards. The cards were distributed exclusively in factory set form in small, emerald green, cellophane-wrapped boxes through hobby dealers. The cards are almost identical in design to regular 1989 Donruss except for the green borders. Rookie Cards in this set include Jim Abbott, Steve Finley, Kenny Rogers and Deion Sanders. Ken Griffey Jr. and Randy Johnson are also featured on a card within the set.

COMP.FACT.SET (56) 6.00 15.00
1 Gary Sheffield .75 2.00
2 Gregg Jefferies .02 .10
3 Ken Griffey Jr. ! 6.00 15.00
4 Tom Gordon .08 .25
5 Billy Spiers RC .08 .25
6 Deion Sanders RC .60 1.50
7 Donn Pall .01 .05
8 Steve Carter RC .01 .05
9 Francisco Oliveras .01 .05
10 Steve Wilson RC .02 .10
11 Bob Geren RC .01 .05
12 Tony Castillo RC .02 .10
13 Kenny Rogers RC 1.00 2.50
14 Carlos Martinez RC .02 .10
15 Edgar Martinez .08 .25
16 Jim Abbott RC .40 1.00
17 Torey Lovullo RC .02 .10
18 Mark Carreon .01 .05
19 Geronimo Berroa .01 .05
20 Luis Medina .01 .05
21 Sandy Alomar Jr. .05 .15
22 Bob Milacki .01 .05
23 Joe Girardi RC .15 .40
24 German Gonzalez .01 .05
25 Craig Worthington .01 .05
26 Jerome Walton RC .08 .25
27 Gary Wayne .01 .05
28 Tim Jones .01 .05
29 Dante Bichette .05 .15
30 Alexis Infante RC .01 .05
31 Ken Hill .08 .25
32 Dwight Smith RC .08 .25
33 Luis de los Santos .01 .05
34 Eric Yelding .01 .05
35 Gregg Olson .08 .25
36 Phil Stephenson .01 .05
37 Ken Patterson .01 .05
38 Rick Wrona .01 .05
39 Mike Brumley .01 .05
40 Cris Carpenter .01 .05
41 Jeff Brantley RC .08 .25
42 Ron Jones .01 .05
43 R.Johnson UER 1.00 2.50
44 Kevin Brown .08 .25
45 Ramon Martinez .02 .10
46 Greg W.Harris .01 .05
47 Steve Finley RC .30 .75
48 Randy Kramer .01 .05
49 Erik Hanson .02 .10
50 Matt Merullo .01 .05
51 Mike Devereaux .01 .05
52 Clay Parker .01 .05
53 Omar Vizquel RC .40 1.00
54 Derek Lilliquist .01 .05
55 Junior Felix RC .02 .10
56 Checklist 1-56 .01 .05

1989 Donruss Warren Spahn Puzzle

1 Spahn Puzzle 1-3 .10 .25
4 Spahn Puzzle 4-6 .10 .25
7 Spahn Puzzle 7-10 .10 .25
10 Spahn Puzzle 10-12 .10 .25
13 Spahn Puzzle 13-15 .10 .25
16 Spahn Puzzle 16-18 .10 .25
19 Spahn Puzzle 19-21 .10 .25
22 Spahn Puzzle 22-24 .10 .25
25 Spahn Puzzle 25-27 .10 .25
28 Spahn Puzzle 28-30 .10 .25
31 Spahn Puzzle 31-33 .10 .25
34 Spahn Puzzle 34-36 .10 .25
37 Spahn Puzzle 37-39 .10 .25
40 Spahn Puzzle 40-42 .10 .25
43 Spahn Puzzle 43-45 .10 .25
46 Spahn Puzzle 46-48 .10 .25
49 Spahn Puzzle 49-51 .10 .25
52 Spahn Puzzle 52-54 .10 .25
55 Spahn Puzzle 55-57 .10 .25
58 Spahn Puzzle 58-60 .10 .25
61 Spahn Puzzle 61-63 .10 .25

1989 Donruss All-Stars

COMPLETE SET (64) 3.00 8.00
1 Mark McGwire .50 1.25
2 Jose Canseco .20 .50
3 Paul Molitor .20 .50
4 Rickey Henderson .25 .60
5 Cal Ripken .75 2.00
6 Dave Winfield .08 .25
7 Wade Boggs .08 .25
8 Frank Viola .01 .05
9 Terry Steinbach .02 .10
10 Tom Kelly MG .01 .05
11 George Brett .40 1.00
12 Doyle Alexander .01 .05
13 Gary Gaetti .02 .10
14 Roger Clemens .40 1.00
15 Mike Greenwell .01 .05
16 Dennis Eckersley .20 .50
17 Carney Lansford .02 .10
18 Mark Gubicza .01 .05
19 Tim Laudner .01 .05
20 Doug Jones .01 .05
21 Don Mattingly .40 1.00
22 Dan Plesac .01 .05
23 Kirby Puckett .20 .50
24 Jeff Reardon .02 .10
25 Johnny Ray .01 .05
26 Jeff Russell .01 .05
27 Harold Reynolds .02 .10
28 Dave Stieb .01 .05
29 Kurt Stillwell .01 .05
30 Jose Canseco/(Top AL Vote Getter) .02 .10
31 Terry Steinbach/(All-Star Game MVP) .01 .05
32 AL Checklist 1-32 .01 .05
33 Will Clark .15 .40
34 Darryl Strawberry .02 .10
35 Ryne Sandberg .40 1.00
36 Andre Dawson .07 .20
37 Ozzie Smith .40 1.00
38 Vince Coleman .01 .05
39 Bobby Bonilla .01 .05
40 Dwight Gooden .02 .10
41 Gary Carter .15 .40
42 Whitey Herzog MG .01 .05
43 Shawon Dunston .01 .05
44 David Cone .05 .15
45 Andres Galarraga .07 .20
46 Mark Davis .01 .05
47 Barry Larkin .07 .20
48 Kevin Gross .01 .05
49 Vance Law .01 .05
50 Orel Hershiser .02 .10
51 Willie McGee .02 .10
52 Danny Jackson .01 .05
53 Rafael Palmeiro .15 .40
54 Bob Knepper .01 .05
55 Lance Parrish .01 .05
56 Greg Maddux .60 1.50
57 Gerald Perry .01 .05
58 Bob Walk .01 .05
59 Chris Sabo .01 .05
60 Todd Worrell .01 .05
61 Andy Van Slyke .02 .10
62 Ozzie Smith/(Top AL Vote Getter) .20 .50
63 Riverfront Stadium .01 .05
64 NL Checklist 33-64 .01 .05

1989 Donruss Baseball's Best

The 1989 Donruss Baseball's Best set contains 336 standard-size glossy cards. The fronts are green and yellow, and the backs feature career highlight information. The backs are green, and feature vertically oriented career stats. The cards were distributed as a set in a blister pack through various retail and department store chains. The Sammy Sosa card in this set is the only major league licensed card issued of him in 1989. In addition, early cards of Ken Griffey Jr. and Randy Johnson are featured in this set.

COMP.FACT.SET (336) 20.00 50.00
1 Don Mattingly .60 1.50
2 Tom Glavine .25 .60
3 Bert Blyleven .08 .25
4 Andre Dawson .08 .25
5 Pete O'Brien .05 .15
6 Eric Davis .08 .25
7 George Brett .60 1.50
8 Glenn Davis .05 .15
9 Ellis Burks .08 .25
10 Kirk Gibson .08 .25
11 Carlton Fisk .15 .40
12 Andres Galarraga .08 .25
13 Alan Trammell .08 .25
14 Dwight Gooden .08 .25
15 Paul Molitor .08 .25
16 Roger McDowell .05 .15
17 Doug Drabek .05 .15
18 Kent Hrbek .08 .25
19 Vince Coleman .05 .15
20 Steve Sax .05 .15
21 Roberto Alomar .25 .60
22 Carney Lansford .08 .25
23 Will Clark .15 .40
24 Alvin Davis .05 .15
25 Bobby Thigpen .05 .15
26 Ryne Sandberg .40 1.00
27 Devon White .08 .25
28 Mike Greenwell .05 .15
29 Dale Murphy .15 .40
30 Jeff Ballard .05 .15
31 Kelly Gruber .05 .15
32 Julio Franco .08 .25
33 Bobby Bonilla .08 .25
34 Tim Wallach .05 .15
35 Lou Whitaker .08 .25
36 Jay Howell .05 .15
37 Greg Maddux .50 1.25
38 Bill Doran .05 .15
39 Danny Tartabull .05 .15
40 Darryl Strawberry .08 .25
41 Ron Darling .08 .25
42 Tony Gwynn .30 .75
43 Mark McGwire 1.00 2.50
44 Ozzie Smith .40 1.00
45 Andy Van Slyke .15 .40
46 Juan Berenguer .05 .15
47 Von Hayes .05 .15
48 Tony Fernandez .05 .15
49 Eric Plunk .05 .15
50 Ernest Riles .05 .15
51 Harold Reynolds .08 .25
52 Andy Hawkins .05 .15
53 Robin Yount .40 1.00
54 Danny Jackson .05 .15
55 Nolan Ryan 1.00 2.50
56 Joe Carter .08 .25
57 Jose Canseco .25 .60
58 Jody Davis .05 .15
59 Lance Parrish .08 .25
60 Mitch Williams .05 .15
61 Brook Jacoby .05 .15
62 Tom Browning .05 .15
63 Kurt Stillwell .05 .15
64 Rafael Ramirez .05 .15
65 Roger Clemens 1.00 2.50
66 Mike Scioscia .08 .25
67 Dave Gallagher .05 .15
68 Mark Langston .05 .15
69 Chet Lemon .08 .25
70 Kevin McReynolds .05 .15
71 Rob Deer .05 .15
72 Tommy Herr .05 .15
73 Barry Bonds 1.25 3.00
74 Frank Viola .08 .25
75 Pedro Guerrero .08 .25
76 Dave Righetti UER/(ML total of 7 .05 .15
wins incorrect)
77 Bruce Hurst .05 .15
78 Rickey Henderson .25 .60
79 Robby Thompson .05 .15
80 Randy Johnson 3.00 8.00
81 Harold Baines .08 .25
82 Calvin Schiraldi .05 .15
83 Kirk McCaskill .05 .15
84 Lee Smith .08 .25
85 John Smoltz 1.50 4.00
86 Mickey Tettleton .05 .15
87 Jimmy Key .08 .25
88 Rafael Palmeiro .25 .60
89 Sid Bream .05 .15
90 Dennis Martinez .08 .25
91 Frank Tanana .08 .25
92 Eddie Murray .25 .60
93 Shawon Dunston .05 .15
94 Mike Scott .05 .15
95 Bret Saberhagen .08 .25
96 David Cone .08 .25
97 Kevin Elster .05 .15
98 Jack Clark .08 .25
99 Dave Stewart .08 .25
100 Jose Oquendo .05 .15
101 Jose Lind .05 .15
102 Gary Gaetti .08 .25
103 Ricky Jordan .20 .50
104 Fred McGriff .15 .40
105 Don Slaught .05 .15

Card	Low	High
106 Jose Uribe	.05	.15
107 Jeffrey Leonard	.05	.15
108 Lee Guetterman	.05	.15
109 Chris Bosio	.05	.15
110 Barry Larkin	.15	.40
111 Ruben Sierra	.08	.25
112 Greg Swindell	.05	.15
113 Gary Sheffield	1.50	4.00
114 Lonnie Smith	.05	.15
115 Chili Davis	.08	.25
116 Damon Berryhill	.05	.15
117 Tom Candiotti	.05	.15
118 Kal Daniels	.05	.15
119 Mark Gubicza	.05	.15
120 Jim Deshaies	.05	.15
121 Dwight Evans	.15	.40
122 Mike Morgan	.05	.15
123 Dan Pasqua	.05	.15
124 Bryn Smith	.05	.15
125 Doyle Alexander	.05	.15
126 Howard Johnson	.08	.25
127 Chuck Crim	.05	.15
128 Darren Daulton	.08	.25
129 Jeff Robinson	.05	.15
130 Kirby Puckett	.25	.60
131 Joe Magrane	.05	.15
132 Jesse Barfield	.08	.25
133 Mark Davis UER/(Photo actually Dave Leiper)	.05	.15
134 Dennis Eckersley	.15	.40
135 Mike Krukow	.05	.15
136 Jay Buhner	.08	.25
137 Ozzie Guillen	.08	.25
138 Rick Sutcliffe	.08	.25
139 Wally Joyner	.08	.25
140 Wade Boggs	.15	.40
141 Jeff Treadway	.05	.15
142 Cal Ripken	.75	2.00
143 Dave Stieb	.08	.25
144 Pete Incaviglia	.05	.15
145 Bob Walk	.05	.15
146 Nelson Santovenia	.05	.15
147 Mike Heath	.05	.15
148 Willie Randolph	.08	.25
149 Paul Kilgus	.05	.15
150 Billy Hatcher	.05	.15
151 Steve Farr	.05	.15
152 Gregg Jefferies	.05	.15
153 Randy Myers	.08	.25
154 Garry Templeton	.08	.25
155 Walt Weiss	.05	.15
156 Terry Pendleton	.08	.25
157 John Smiley	.05	.15
158 Greg Gagne	.05	.15
159 Len Dykstra	.08	.25
160 Nelson Liriano	.05	.15
161 Alvaro Espinoza	.05	.15
162 Rick Reuschel	.08	.25
163 Omar Vizquel UER	.75	2.00
164 Clay Parker	.05	.15
165 Dan Plesac	.05	.15
166 John Franco	.08	.25
167 Scott Fletcher	.05	.15
168 Cory Snyder	.05	.15
169 Bo Jackson	.25	.60
170 Tommy Gregg	.05	.15
171 Jim Abbott	.75	2.00
172 Jerome Walton	.20	.50
173 Doug Jones	.05	.15
174 Todd Benzinger	.05	.15
175 Frank White	.08	.25
176 Craig Biggio	1.25	3.00
177 John Dopson	.05	.15
178 Alfredo Griffin	.05	.15
179 Melido Perez	.05	.15
180 Tim Burke	.05	.15
181 Matt Nokes	.05	.15
182 Gary Carter	.08	.25
183 Ted Higuera	.05	.15
184 Ken Howell	.05	.15
185 Rey Quinones	.05	.15
186 Wally Backman	.05	.15
187 Tom Brunansky	.05	.15
188 Steve Balboni	.05	.15
189 Marvell Wynne	.05	.15
190 Dave Henderson	.05	.15
191 Don Robinson	.05	.15
192 Ken Griffey Jr.	6.00	15.00
193 Ivan Calderon	.05	.15
194 Mike Bielecki	.05	.15
195 Johnny Ray	.05	.15
196 Rob Murphy	.05	.15
197 Andres Thomas	.05	.15
198 Phil Bradley	.05	.15
199 Junior Felix	.08	.25
200 Jeff Russell	.05	.15
201 Mike LaValliere	.05	.15
202 Kevin Gross	.05	.15
203 Keith Moreland	.05	.15
204 Mike Marshall	.05	.15
205 Dwight Smith	.20	.50
206 Jim Clancy	.05	.15
207 Kevin Seitzer	.05	.15
208 Keith Hernandez	.08	.25
209 Bob Ojeda	.05	.15
210 Ed Whitson	.05	.15
211 Tony Phillips	.05	.15
212 Milt Thompson	.05	.15
213 Randy Kramer	.05	.15
214 Randy Bush	.05	.15
215 Randy Ready	.05	.15
216 Duane Ward	.05	.15
217 Jimmy Jones	.05	.15
218 Scott Garrelts	.05	.15
219 Scott Bankhead	.05	.15
220 Lance McCullers	.05	.15
221 B.J. Surhoff	.08	.25
222 Chris Sabo	.30	.75
223 Steve Buechele	.05	.15
224 Joel Skinner	.05	.15
225 Orel Hershiser	.08	.25
226 Derek Lilliquist	.08	.25
227 Claudell Washington	.05	.15
228 Lloyd McClendon	.05	.15
229 Felix Fermin	.05	.15
230 Paul O'Neill	.15	.40
231 Charlie Leibrandt	.05	.15
232 Dave Smith	.05	.15
233 Bob Stanley	.05	.15
234 Tim Belcher	.05	.15
235 Eric King	.05	.15
236 Spike Owen	.05	.15
237 Mike Henneman	.05	.15
238 Juan Samuel	.05	.15
239 Greg Brock	.05	.15
240 John Kruk	.08	.25
241 Glenn Wilson	.05	.15
242 Jeff Reardon	.08	.25
243 Todd Worrell	.05	.15
244 Dave LaPoint	.05	.15
245 Walt Terrell	.05	.15
246 Mike Moore	.05	.15
247 Kelly Downs	.05	.15
248 Dave Valle	.05	.15
249 Ron Kittle	.05	.15
250 Steve Wilson	.08	.25
251 Dick Schofield	.05	.15
252 Marty Barrett	.05	.15
253 Dion James	.05	.15
254 Bob Milacki	.05	.15
255 Ernie Whitt	.05	.15
256 Kevin Brown	.25	.60
257 R.J. Reynolds	.05	.15
258 Tim Raines	.08	.25
259 Frank Williams	.05	.15
260 Jose Gonzalez	.05	.15
261 Mitch Webster	.05	.15
262 Ken Caminiti	.15	.40
263 Bob Boone	.08	.25
264 Dave Magadan	.05	.15
265 Rick Aguilera	.05	.15
266 Chris James	.05	.15
267 Bob Welch	.08	.25
268 Ken Dayley	.05	.15
269 Junior Ortiz	.05	.15
270 Allan Anderson	.05	.15
271 Steve Jeltz	.05	.15
272 George Bell	.08	.25
273 Roberto Kelly	.05	.15
274 Brett Butler	.08	.25
275 Mike Schooler	.08	.25
276 Ken Phelps	.05	.15
277 Glenn Braggs	.05	.15
278 Jose Rijo	.08	.25
279 Bobby Witt	.05	.15
280 Jerry Browne	.05	.15
281 Kevin Mitchell	.08	.25
282 Craig Worthington	.05	.15
283 Greg Minton	.05	.15
284 Nick Esasky	.05	.15
285 John Farrell	.05	.15
286 Rick Mahler	.05	.15
287 Tom Gordon	.40	1.00
288 Gerald Young	.05	.15
289 Jody Reed	.05	.15
290 Jeff Hamilton	.05	.15
291 Gerald Perry	.05	.15
292 Hubie Brooks	.05	.15
293 Bo Diaz	.05	.15
294 Terry Puhl	.05	.15
295 Jim Gantner	.05	.15
296 Jeff Parrett	.05	.15
297 Mike Boddicker	.05	.15
298 Dan Gladden	.05	.15
299 Tony Pena	.05	.15
300 Checklist Card	.05	.15
301 Tom Henke	.05	.15
302 Pascual Perez	.05	.15
303 Steve Bedrosian	.05	.15
304 Ken Hill	.20	.50
305 Jerry Reuss	.05	.15
306 Jim Eisenreich	.05	.15
307 Jack Howell	.05	.15
308 Rick Cerone	.05	.15
309 Tim Leary	.05	.15
310 Joe Orsulak	.05	.15
311 Jim Dwyer	.05	.15
312 Geno Petralli	.05	.15
313 Rick Honeycutt	.05	.15
314 Tom Foley	.05	.15
315 Kenny Rogers	1.25	3.00
316 Mike Flanagan	.05	.15
317 Bryan Harvey	.05	.15
318 Billy Ripken	.05	.15
319 Jeff Montgomery	.05	.15
320 Erik Hanson	.20	.50
321 Brian Downing	.08	.25
322 Gregg Olson	.20	.50
323 Terry Steinbach	.08	.25
324 Sammy Sosa	4.00	10.00
325 Gene Harris	.05	.15
326 Mike Devereaux	.05	.15
327 Dennis Cook	.20	.50
328 David Wells	.08	.25
329 Checklist Card	.05	.15
330 Kirt Manwaring	.05	.15
331 Jim Presley	.05	.15
332 Checklist Card	.05	.15
333 Chuck Finley	.08	.25
334 Rob Dibble	.30	.75
335 Cecil Espy	.05	.15
336 Dave Parker	.08	.25

1989 Donruss Pop-Ups

Card	Low	High
COMPLETE SET (20)	2.00	5.00
1 Mark McGwire	.75	2.00
2 Jose Canseco	.20	.50
3 Paul Molitor	.20	.50
4 Rickey Henderson	.30	1.00
5 Cal Ripken	1.25	3.00
6 Dave Winfield	.20	.50
7 Wade Boggs	.20	.50
8 Frank Viola	.02	.10
9 Terry Steinbach	.02	.10
10 Tom Kelly MG	.02	.10
33 Will Clark	.20	.50
34 Darryl Strawberry	.07	.20
35 Ryne Sandberg	.40	1.00
36 Andre Dawson	.15	.40
37 Ozzie Smith	.40	1.00
38 Vince Coleman	.02	.10
39 Bobby Bonilla	.07	.20
40 Dwight Gooden	.07	.20
41 Gary Carter	.20	.50
42 Whitey Herzog MG	.02	.10

1989 Donruss Super DK's

Card	Low	High
COMPLETE SET (26)	6.00	15.00
1 Mike Greenwell	.02	.10
2 Bobby Bonilla	.07	.20
3 Pete Incaviglia	.02	.10
4 Chris Sabo	.02	.10
5 Robin Yount	.40	1.00
6 Tony Gwynn	1.50	4.00
7 Carlton Fisk	1.25	3.00
8 Cory Snyder	.02	.10
9 David Cone	.10	.30
10 Kevin Seitzer	.02	.10
11 Rick Reuschel	.02	.10
12 Johnny Ray	.02	.10
13 Dave Schmidt	.02	.10
14 Andres Galarraga	.15	.40
15 Kirk Gibson	.07	.20
16 Fred McGriff	.40	1.00
17 Mark Grace	1.50	4.00
18 Jeff M. Robinson	.02	.10
19 Vince Coleman	.02	.10
20 Dave Henderson	.02	.10
21 Harold Reynolds	.07	.20
22 Gerald Perry	.02	.10
23 Frank Viola	.02	.10
24 Steve Bedrosian	.02	.10
25 Glenn Davis	.02	.10
26 Don Mattingly	2.00	5.00

1989 Donruss Traded

Card	Low	High
COMP.FACT.SET (56)	1.25	3.00
1 Jeffrey Leonard	.02	.10
2 Jack Clark	.07	.20
3 Kevin Gross	.02	.10
4 Tommy Herr	.02	.10
5 Bob Boone	.07	.20
6 Rafael Palmeiro	.20	.50
7 John Dopson	.02	.10
8 Willie Randolph	.07	.20
9 Chris Brown	.02	.10
10 Wally Backman	.02	.10
11 Steve Ontiveros	.02	.10
12 Eddie Murray	.20	.50
13 Lance McCullers	.02	.10
14 Spike Owen	.02	.10
15 Rob Murphy	.02	.10
16 Pete O'Brien	.02	.10
17 Ken Williams	.02	.10
18 Nick Esasky	.02	.10
19 Nolan Ryan	.60	1.50
20 Brian Holton	.02	.10
21 Mike Moore	.02	.10
22 Joel Skinner	.02	.10
23 Steve Sax	.02	.10
24 Rick Mahler	.02	.10
25 Mike Aldrete	.02	.10
26 Jesse Orosco	.02	.10
27 Dave LaPoint	.02	.10
28 Walt Terrell	.02	.10
29 Eddie Williams	.02	.10
30 Mike Devereaux	.02	.10
31 Julio Franco	.07	.20
32 Jim Clancy	.02	.10
33 Felix Fermin	.02	.10
34 Curt Wilkerson	.02	.10
35 Bert Blyleven	.07	.20
36 Mel Hall	.02	.10
37 Eric King	.02	.10
38 Mitch Williams	.02	.10
39 Jamie Moyer	.07	.20
40 Rick Rhoden	.02	.10
41 Phil Bradley	.02	.10
42 Paul Kilgus	.02	.10
43 Milt Thompson	.02	.10
44 Jerry Browne	.02	.10
45 Bruce Hurst	.02	.10
46 Claudell Washington	.02	.10
47 Todd Benzinger	.02	.10
48 Steve Balboni	.02	.10
49 Oddibe McDowell	.02	.10
50 Charles Hudson	.02	.10
51 Ron Kittle	.02	.10
52 Andy Hawkins	.02	.10
53 Tom Brookens	.02	.10
54 Tom Niedenfuer	.02	.10
55 Jeff Parrett	.02	.10
56 Checklist Card	.02	.10

1989 Donruss Blue Chips

Card	Low	High
COMPLETE SET (12)		
1 Jose Canseco		
2 Mike Marshall		
3 Walt Weiss		
4 Kevin McReynolds		
5 Mike Greenwell		
6 Dave Winfield		
7 Mark McGwire		
8 Keith Hernandez		
9 Franklin Stubbs		
10 Danny Tartabull		
11 Jesse Barfield		
12 Ellis Burks		

1990 Donruss Previews

Card	Low	High
COMPLETE SET (12)	200.00	400.00
1 Todd Zeile/(Not shown as Rated Rookie on front)	6.00	15.00
2 Ben McDonald	4.00	10.00
3 Bo Jackson	15.00	40.00
4 Will Clark	20.00	50.00
5 Dave Stewart	6.00	15.00
6 Kevin Mitchell	4.00	10.00
7 Nolan Ryan	60.00	120.00
8 Howard Johnson	4.00	10.00
9 Tony Gwynn	30.00	80.00
10 Jerome Walton/(Shown ready to bunt)	4.00	10.00
11 Wade Boggs	20.00	50.00
12 Kirby Puckett	15.00	40.00

1990 Donruss

The 1990 Donruss set contains 716 standard-size cards. Cards were issued in wax packs and hobby and retail factory sets. The card fronts feature bright red borders. Subsets include Diamond Kings (1-27) and Rated Rookies (28-47). The set was the largest ever produced by Donruss, unfortunately it also had a large number of errors which were corrected after the cards were released. Most of these feature minor printing flaws and insignificant variations that collectors have found unworthy of price differentials. There are several double-printed cards indicated in our checklist with the set indicated with a "DP" coding. Rookie Cards of note include Juan Gonzalez, David Justice, John Olerud, Dean Palmer, Sammy Sosa, Larry Walker and Bernie Williams.

Card	Low	High
COMPLETE SET (716)	6.00	15.00
COMP.FACT.SET (728)	6.00	15.00
COMP.YAZ PUZZLE	.40	1.00
1 Bo Jackson DK	.05	.15
2 Steve Sax DK	.01	.05
3A Ruben Sierra DK ERR No small line on top border on card back	.02	.10
3B Ruben Sierra DK COR	.02	.10
4 Ken Griffey Jr. DK	.20	.50
5 Mickey Tettleton DK	.01	.05
6 Dave Stewart DK	.01	.05
7 Jim Deshaies DK DP	.01	.05
8 John Smoltz DK	.08	.25
9 Mike Bielecki DK	.01	.05
10A Brian Downing DK ERR	.05	.15
10B Brian Downing DK COR	.01	.05
11 Kevin Mitchell DK	.01	.05
12 Kelly Gruber DK	.01	.05
13 Joe Magrane DK	.01	.05
14 John Franco DK	.02	.10
15 Ozzie Guillen DK	.02	.10
16 Lou Whitaker DK	.01	.05
17 John Smiley DK	.01	.05
18 Howard Johnson DK	.01	.05
19 Willie Randolph DK	.02	.10
20 Chris Bosio DK	.01	.05
21 Tommy Herr DK DP	.01	.05
22 Dan Gladden DK	.01	.05
23 Ellis Burks DK	.02	.10
24 Pete O'Brien DK	.01	.05
25 Bryn Smith DK	.01	.05
26 Ed Whitson DK DP	.01	.05
27 DK Checklist 1-27 DP Comments on Perez-Steele on back	.01	.05
28 Robin Ventura	.08	.25
29 Todd Zeile RR	.02	.10
30 Sandy Alomar Jr.	.02	.10
31 Kent Mercker RC	.08	.25
32 Ben McDonald RC UER Middle name Benard not Benjamin	.08	.25
33A Juan Gonzalez RevNg RC	.75	2.00
33B Juan Gonzalez COR RC	.40	1.00
34 Eric Anthony RC	.02	.10
35 Mike Fetters RC	.08	.25
36 Marquis Grissom RC	.15	.40
37 Greg Vaughn	.01	.05
38 Brian DuBois RC	.02	.10
39 Steve Avery RR UER Born in MI, not NJ	.01	.05
40 Mark Gardner RC	.02	.10
41 Andy Benes	.02	.10
42 Delino DeShields RC	.08	.25
43 Scott Coolbaugh RC	.02	.10
44 Pat Combs DP	.01	.05
45 Alex Sanchez DP	.01	.05
46 Kelly Mann DP RC	.02	.10
47 Julio Machado RC	.02	.10
48 Pete Incaviglia	.01	.05
49 Shawon Dunston	.01	.05
50 Jeff Treadway	.01	.05
51 Jeff Ballard	.01	.05
52 Claudell Washington	.01	.05
53 Juan Samuel	.01	.05
54 John Smiley	.01	.05
55 Rob Deer	.01	.05
56 Geno Petralli	.01	.05
57 Chris Bosio	.01	.05
58 Carlton Fisk	.05	.15
59 Kirt Manwaring	.01	.05
60 Chet Lemon	.01	.05
61 Bo Jackson	.08	.25
62 Doyle Alexander	.01	.05
63 Pedro Guerrero	.01	.05
64 Allan Anderson	.01	.05
65 Greg W. Harris	.01	.05
66 Mike Greenwell	.01	.05
67 Walt Weiss	.01	.05
68 Wade Boggs	.05	.15
69 Jim Clancy	.01	.05
70 Junior Felix	.01	.05
71 Barry Larkin	.05	.15
72 Dave LaPoint	.01	.05
73 Joel Skinner	.01	.05
74 Jesse Barfield	.01	.05
75 Tommy Herr	.01	.05
76 Ricky Jordan	.01	.05
77 Eddie Murray	.08	.25
78 Steve Sax	.01	.05
79 Tim Belcher	.01	.05
80 Danny Jackson	.01	.05
81 Kent Hrbek	.02	.10
82 Milt Thompson	.01	.05
83 Brook Jacoby	.01	.05
84 Mike Marshall	.01	.05
85 Kevin Seitzer	.01	.05
86 Tony Gwynn	.10	.30
87 Dave Stieb	.02	.10
88 Dave Smith	.01	.05
89 Bret Saberhagen	.02	.10
90 Alan Trammell	.02	.10
91 Tony Phillips	.01	.05
92 Doug Drabek	.01	.05
93 Jeffrey Leonard	.01	.05
94 Wally Joyner	.02	.10
95 Carney Lansford	.02	.10
96 Cal Ripken	.30	.75
97 Andres Galarraga	.02	.10
98 Kevin Mitchell	.01	.05
99 Howard Johnson	.01	.05
100A Checklist 28-129	.01	.05
100B Checklist 28-125	.01	.05
101 Melido Perez	.01	.05
102 Spike Owen	.01	.05
103 Paul Molitor	.02	.10
104 Geronimo Berroa	.01	.05
105 Ryne Sandberg	.15	.40
106 Bryn Smith	.01	.05
107 Steve Buechele	.01	.05
108 Jim Abbott	.05	.15
109 Alvin Davis	.01	.05
110 Lee Smith	.02	.10
111 Roberto Alomar	.05	.15
112 Rick Reuschel	.01	.05
113A Kelly Gruber ERR Born 2/22	.01	.05
113B Kelly Gruber COR Born 2/26; corrected in factory sets	.01	.05
114 Joe Carter	.02	.10
115 Jose Rijo	.01	.05
116 Greg Minton	.01	.05
117 Bob Ojeda	.01	.05
118 Glenn Davis	.01	.05
119 Jeff Reardon	.02	.10
120 Kurt Stillwell	.01	.05
121 John Smoltz	.08	.25
122 Dwight Evans	.05	.15
123 Eric Yelding RC	.01	.05
124 John Franco	.02	.10
125 Jose Canseco	.05	.15
126 Barry Bonds	.40	1.00
127 Lee Guetterman	.01	.05
128 Jack Clark	.02	.10
129 Dave Valle	.01	.05
130 Hubie Brooks	.01	.05
131 Ernest Riles	.01	.05
132 Mike Morgan	.01	.05
133 Steve Jeltz	.01	.05
134 Jeff D. Robinson	.01	.05
135 Ozzie Guillen	.02	.10
136 Chili Davis	.02	.10
137 Mitch Webster	.01	.05
138 Jerry Browne	.01	.05
139 Bo Diaz	.01	.05
140 Robby Thompson	.01	.05
141 Craig Worthington	.01	.05
142 Julio Franco	.02	.10
143 Brian Holman	.01	.05
144 George Brett	.25	.60
145 Tom Glavine	.05	.15
146 Robin Yount	.15	.40
147 Gary Carter	.02	.10
148 Ron Kittle	.01	.05
149 Tony Fernandez	.01	.05
150 Dave Stewart	.02	.10
151 Gary Gaetti	.02	.10
152 Kevin Elster	.01	.05
153 Gerald Perry	.01	.05
154 Jesse Orosco	.01	.05
155 Wally Backman	.01	.05
156 Dennis Martinez	.02	.10
157 Rick Sutcliffe	.02	.10
158 Greg Maddux	.15	.40
159 Andy Hawkins	.01	.05
160 John Kruk	.02	.10
161 Jose Oquendo	.01	.05
162 John Dopson	.01	.05
163 Joe Magrane	.01	.05
164 Bill Ripken	.01	.05
165 Fred Manrique	.01	.05
166 Nolan Ryan UER	.40	1.00
167 Damon Berryhill	.01	.05
168 Dale Murphy	.05	.15
169 Mickey Tettleton	.01	.05
170A Kirk McCaskill ERR Born 4/19	.01	.05
170B Kirk McCaskill COR Born 4/9; corrected in factory sets	.01	.05
171 Dwight Gooden	.02	.10
172 Jose Lind	.01	.05
173 B.J. Surhoff	.02	.10
174 Ruben Sierra	.02	.10
175 Dan Plesac	.01	.05
176 Dan Pasqua	.01	.05
177 Kelly Downs	.01	.05
178 Matt Nokes	.01	.05
179 Luis Aquino	.01	.05
180 Frank Tanana	.01	.05
181 Tony Pena	.01	.05
182 Dan Gladden	.01	.05
183 Bruce Hurst	.01	.05
184 Roger Clemens	.40	1.00
185 Mark McGwire	.40	1.00
186 Rob Murphy	.01	.05
187 Jim Deshaies	.01	.05
188 Fred McGriff	.08	.25
189 Rob Dibble	.02	.10
190 Don Mattingly	.25	.60
191 Felix Fermin	.01	.05
192 Roberto Kelly	.01	.05
193 Dennis Cook	.01	.05
194 Darren Daulton	.02	.10
195 Alfredo Griffin	.01	.05
196 Eric Plunk	.01	.05
197 Orel Hershiser	.02	.10
198 Paul O'Neill	.05	.15
199 Randy Bush	.01	.05
200A Checklist 130-231	.01	.05
200B Checklist 126-223	.01	.05
201 Ozzie Smith	.15	.40
202 Pete O'Brien	.01	.05
203 Jay Howell	.01	.05
204 Mark Gubicza	.01	.05
205 Ed Whitson	.01	.05
206 George Bell	.01	.05
207 Mike Scott	.01	.05
208 Charlie Leibrandt	.01	.05
209 Mike Heath	.01	.05
210 Dennis Eckersley	.02	.10
211 Mike LaValliere	.01	.05
212 Darnell Coles	.01	.05
213 Lance Parrish	.01	.05
214 Mike Moore	.01	.05
215 Steve Finley	.02	.10
216 Tim Raines	.02	.10
217A Scott Garrelts ERR Born 10/20	.01	.05
217B Scott Garrelts COR Born 10/30; corrected in factory sets	.01	.05
218 Kevin McReynolds	.01	.05
219 Dave Gallagher	.01	.05
220 Tim Wallach	.01	.05
221 Chuck Crim	.01	.05
222 Lonnie Smith	.01	.05
223 Andre Dawson	.02	.10
224 Nelson Santovenia	.01	.05
225 Rafael Palmeiro	.05	.15
226 Devon White	.02	.10
227 Harold Reynolds	.02	.10
228 Ellis Burks	.05	.15
229 Mark Parent	.01	.05
230 Will Clark	.05	.15
231 Jimmy Key	.02	.10
232 John Farrell	.01	.05
233 Eric Davis	.02	.10
234 Johnny Ray	.01	.05
235 Darryl Strawberry	.02	.10
236 Bill Doran	.01	.05
237 Greg Gagne	.01	.05
238 Jim Eisenreich	.01	.05
239 Tommy Gregg	.01	.05
240 Marty Barrett	.01	.05
241 Rafael Ramirez	.01	.05
242 Chris Sabo	.01	.05
243 Dave Henderson	.01	.05
244 Andy Van Slyke	.05	.15
245 Alvaro Espinoza	.01	.05
246 Garry Templeton	.01	.05
247 Gene Harris	.01	.05
248 Kevin Gross	.01	.05
249 Brett Butler	.02	.10
250 Willie Randolph	.02	.10
251 Roger McDowell	.01	.05
252 Rafael Belliard	.01	.05
253 Steve Rosenberg	.01	.05
254 Jack Howell	.01	.05
255 Marvell Wynne	.01	.05
256 Tom Candiotti	.01	.05
257 Todd Benzinger	.01	.05
258 Don Robinson	.01	.05
259 Phil Bradley	.01	.05
260 Cecil Espy	.01	.05
261 Scott Bankhead	.01	.05
262 Frank White	.02	.10
263 Andres Thomas	.01	.05
264 Glenn Braggs	.01	.05
265 David Cone	.02	.10
266 Bobby Thigpen	.01	.05
267 Nelson Liriano	.01	.05
268 Terry Steinbach	.01	.05
269 Kirby Puckett UER Back doesn't consider Joe Torre's .363 in '71	.08	.25
270 Gregg Jefferies	.02	.10
271 Jeff Blauser	.01	.05
272 Cory Snyder	.01	.05
273 Roy Smith	.01	.05
274 Tom Foley	.01	.05
275 Mitch Williams	.01	.05
276 Paul Kilgus	.01	.05
277 Don Slaught	.01	.05
278 Von Hayes	.01	.05
279 Vince Coleman	.01	.05
280 Mike Boddicker	.01	.05
281 Ken Dayley	.01	.05
282 Mike Devereaux	.01	.05
283 Kenny Rogers	.02	.10
284 Jeff Russell	.01	.05
285 Jerome Walton	.01	.05
286 Derek Lilliquist	.01	.05
287 Joe Orsulak	.01	.05
288 Dick Schofield	.01	.05
289 Ron Darling	.01	.05
290 Bobby Bonilla	.02	.10
291 Jim Gantner	.01	.05
292 Bobby Witt	.01	.05
293 Greg Brock	.01	.05
294 Ivan Calderon	.01	.05
295 Steve Bedrosian	.01	.05
296 Mike Henneman	.01	.05
297 Tom Gordon	.02	.10
298 Lou Whitaker	.02	.10
299 Terry Pendleton	.02	.10
300A Checklist 232-333	.01	.05
300B Checklist 224-321	.01	.05
301 Juan Berenguer	.01	.05
302 Mark Davis	.01	.05
303 Nick Esasky	.01	.05
304 Rickey Henderson	.08	.25
305 Rick Cerone	.01	.05
306 Craig Biggio	.08	.25
307 Duane Ward	.01	.05
308 Tom Browning	.01	.05
309 Walt Terrell	.01	.05
310 Greg Swindell	.01	.05
311 Dave Righetti	.01	.05
312 Mike Maddux	.01	.05
313 Len Dykstra	.02	.10
314 Jose Gonzalez	.01	.05
315 Steve Balboni	.01	.05
316 Mike Scioscia	.01	.05
317 Ron Oester	.01	.05
318 Gary Wayne	.01	.05
319 Todd Worrell	.01	.05
320 Doug Jones	.01	.05
321 Jeff Hamilton	.01	.05
322 Danny Tartabull	.01	.05
323 Chris James	.01	.05
324 Mike Flanagan	.01	.05
325 Gerald Young	.01	.05
326 Bob Boone	.02	.10
327 Frank Williams	.01	.05
328 Dave Parker	.02	.10
329 Sid Bream	.01	.05
330 Mike Schooler	.01	.05
331 Bert Blyleven	.02	.10
332 Bob Welch	.01	.05
333 Bob Milacki	.01	.05
334 Tim Burke	.01	.05
335 Jose Uribe	.01	.05
336 Randy Myers	.02	.10
337 Eric King	.01	.05
338 Mark Langston	.01	.05
339 Teddy Higuera	.01	.05
340 Oddibe McDowell	.01	.05
341 Lloyd McClendon	.01	.05
342 Pascual Perez	.01	.05
343 Kevin Brown UER Signed is misspelled as signeed on back	.02	.10
344 Chuck Finley	.02	.10
345 Erik Hanson	.01	.05
346 Rich Gedman	.01	.05
347 Bip Roberts	.01	.05
348 Matt Williams	.02	.10
349 Tom Henke	.01	.05
350 Brad Komminsk	.01	.05
351 Jeff Reed	.01	.05
352 Brian Downing	.01	.05
353 Frank Viola	.01	.05
354 Terry Puhl	.01	.05
355 Brian Harper	.01	.05
356 Steve Farr	.01	.05
357 Joe Boever	.01	.05
358 Danny Heep	.01	.05
359 Larry Andersen	.01	.05
360 Rolando Roomes	.01	.05
361 Mike Gallego	.01	.05
362 Bob Kipper	.01	.05
363 Clay Parker	.01	.05
364 Mike Pagliarulo	.01	.05
365 Ken Griffey Jr. UER	.40	1.00
366 Rex Hudler	.01	.05
367 Pat Sheridan	.01	.05
368 Kirk Gibson	.02	.10
369 Jeff Parrett	.01	.05
370 Bob Walk	.01	.05
371 Ken Patterson	.01	.05
372 Bryan Harvey	.01	.05
373 Mike Bielecki	.01	.05
374 Tom Magrann RC	.01	.05
375 Rick Mahler	.01	.05
376 Craig Lefferts	.01	.05
377 Gregg Olson	.02	.10
378 Jamie Moyer	.02	.10
379 Randy Johnson	.20	.50
380 Jeff Montgomery	.02	.10
381 Marty Clary	.01	.05
382 Bill Spiers	.01	.05
383 Dave Magadan	.01	.05
384 Greg Hibbard RC	.02	.10
385 Ernie Whitt	.01	.05
386 Rick Honeycutt	.01	.05
387 Dave West	.01	.05
388 Keith Hernandez	.02	.10
389 Jose Alvarez	.01	.05
390 Albert Belle	.08	.25
391 Rick Aguilera	.02	.10
392 Mike Fitzgerald	.01	.05
393 Dwight Smith	.01	.05
394 Steve Wilson	.01	.05
395 Bob Geren	.01	.05
396 Randy Ready	.01	.05
397 Ken Hill	.02	.10
398 Jody Reed	.01	.05
399 Tom Brunansky	.01	.05
400A Checklist 334-435	.01	.05
400B Checklist 322-419	.01	.05
401 Rene Gonzales	.01	.05
402 Harold Baines	.02	.10
403 Cecilio Guante	.01	.05
404 Joe Girardi	.05	.15
405A Sergio Valdez ERR RC	.01	.05
405B Sergio Valdez COR RC	.01	.05
406 Mark Williamson	.01	.05
407 Glenn Hoffman	.01	.05
408 Jeff Innis RC	.01	.05
409 Randy Kramer	.01	.05
410 Charlie O'Brien	.01	.05
411 Charlie Hough	.02	.10
412 Gus Polidor	.01	.05
413 Ron Karkovice	.01	.05
414 Trevor Wilson	.01	.05
415 Kevin Ritz RC	.01	.05
416 Gary Thurman	.01	.05
417 Jeff M. Robinson	.01	.05
418 Scott Terry	.01	.05
419 Tim Laudner	.01	.05
420 Dennis Rasmussen	.01	.05
421 Luis Rivera	.01	.05
422 Jim Corsi	.01	.05
423 Dennis Lamp	.01	.05
424 Ken Caminiti	.02	.10
425 David Wells	.02	.10
426 Norm Charlton	.01	.05
427 Deion Sanders	.08	.25
428 Dion James	.01	.05
429 Chuck Cary	.01	.05
430 Ken Howell	.01	.05
431 Steve Lake	.01	.05
432 Kal Daniels	.01	.05
433 Lance McCullers	.01	.05
434 Lenny Harris	.01	.05
435 Scott Scudder	.01	.05
436 Gene Larkin	.01	.05
437 Dan Quisenberry	.01	.05
438 Steve Olin RC	.08	.25
439 Mickey Hatcher	.01	.05
440 Willie Wilson	.01	.05
441 Mark Grant	.01	.05
442 Mookie Wilson	.02	.10
443 Alex Trevino	.01	.05
444 Pat Tabler	.01	.05
445 Dave Bergman	.01	.05
446 Todd Burns	.01	.05
447 R.J. Reynolds	.01	.05
448 Jay Buhner	.02	.10
449 Lee Stevens	.02	.10

450 Ron Hassey .01 .05
451 Bob Melvin .01 .05
452 Dave Martinez .01 .05
453 Greg Litton .01 .05
454 Mark Carreon .01 .05
455 Scott Fletcher .01 .05
456 Otis Nixon .01 .05
457 Tony Fossas RC .01 .05
458 John Russell .01 .05
459 Paul Assenmacher .01 .05
460 Zane Smith .01 .05
461 Jack Daugherty RC .01 .05
462 Rich Monteleone .01 .05
463 Greg Briley .01 .05
464 Mike Smithson .01 .05
465 Benito Santiago .02 .10
466 Jeff Brantley .01 .05
467 Jose Nunez .01 .05
468 Scott Bailes .01 .05
469 Ken Griffey Sr. .02 .10
470 Bob McClure .01 .05
471 Mackey Sasser .01 .05
472 Glenn Wilson .01 .05
473 Kevin Tapani RC .08 .25
474 Bill Buckner .01 .05
475 Ron Gant .02 .10
476 Kevin Romine .01 .05
477 Juan Agosto .01 .05
478 Herm Winningham .01 .05
479 Storm Davis .01 .05
480 Jeff King .01 .05
481 Kevin Mmahat RC .01 .05
482 Carmelo Martinez .01 .05
483 Omar Vizquel .08 .25
484 Jim Dwyer .01 .05
485 Bob Knepper .01 .05
486 Dave Anderson .01 .05
487 Ron Jones .01 .05
488 Jay Bell .02 .10
489 Sammy Sosa RC 1.00 2.50
490 Kent Anderson .01 .05
491 Domingo Ramos .01 .05
492 Dave Clark .01 .05
493 Tim Birtsas .01 .05
494 Ken Oberkfell .01 .05
495 Larry Sheets .01 .05
496 Jeff Kunkel .01 .05
497 Jim Presley .01 .05
498 Mike Macfarlane .01 .05
499 Pete Smith .01 .05
500A Checklist 436-537 DP .01 .05
500B Checklist 420-517 .01 .05
501 Gary Sheffield .08 .25
502 Terry Bross RC .01 .05
503 Jerry Kutzler RC .01 .05
504 Lloyd Moseby .01 .05
505 Curt Young .01 .05
506 Al Newman .01 .05
507 Keith Miller .01 .05
508 Mike Stanton RC .08 .25
509 Rich Yett .01 .05
510 Tim Drummond RC .01 .05
511 Joe Hesketh .01 .05
512 Rick Wrona .01 .05
513 Luis Salazar .01 .05
514 Hal Morris .01 .05
515 Terry Mulholland .01 .05
516 John Morris .01 .05
517 Carlos Quintana .01 .05
518 Frank DiPino .01 .05
519 Randy Milligan .01 .05
520 Chad Kreuter .01 .05
521 Mike Jeffcoat .01 .05
522 Mike Harkey .01 .05
523A Andy Nezelek ERR .01 .05
Wrong birth year
523B Andy Nezelek COR .05 .15
Finally corrected
in factory sets
524 Dave Schmidt .01 .05
525 Tony Armas .01 .05
526 Barry Lyons .01 .05
527 Rick Reed RC .08 .25
528 Jerry Reuss .01 .05
529 Dean Palmer RC .08 .25
530 Jeff Peterek RC .01 .05
531 Carlos Martinez .01 .05
532 Atlee Hammaker .01 .05
533 Mike Brumley .01 .05
534 Terry Leach .01 .05
535 Doug Strange RC .01 .05
536 Jose DeLeon .01 .05
537 Shane Rawley .01 .05
538 Joey Cora .02 .10
539 Eric Hetzel .01 .05
540 Gene Nelson .01 .05
541 Wes Gardner .01 .05
542 Mark Portugal .01 .05
543 Al Leiter .08 .25
544 Jack Armstrong .01 .05
545 Greg Cadaret .01 .05
546 Rod Nichols .01 .05
547 Luis Polonia .01 .05
548 Charlie Hayes .01 .05
549 Dickie Thon .01 .05
550 Tim Crews .01 .05
551 Dave Winfield .02 .10
552 Mike Davis .01 .05
553 Ron Robinson .01 .05
554 Carmen Castillo .01 .05
555 John Costello .01 .05
556 Bud Black .01 .05
557 Rick Dempsey .01 .05
558 Jim Acker .01 .05
559 Eric Show .01 .05
560 Pat Borders .01 .05
561 Danny Darwin .01 .05
562 Rick Luecken RC .01 .05
563 Edwin Nunez .01 .05
564 Felix Jose .01 .05
565 John Cangelosi .01 .05
566 Bill Swift .01 .05
567 Bill Schroeder .01 .05
568 Stan Javier .01 .05
569 Jim Traber .01 .05
570 Wallace Johnson .01 .05
571 Donell Nixon .01 .05
572 Sid Fernandez .01 .05
573 Lance Johnson .01 .05
574 Andy McGaffigan .01 .05
575 Mark Knudson .01 .05
576 Tommy Greene RC .02 .10
577 Mark Grace .05 .15
578 Larry Walker RC .40 1.00
579 Mike Stanley .01 .05
580 Mike Witt DP .01 .05
581 Scott Bradley .01 .05
582 Greg A. Harris .01 .05
583A Kevin Hickey ERR .08 .25
583B Kevin Hickey COR .01 .05
584 Lee Mazzilli .01 .05
585 Jeff Pico .01 .05
586 Joe Oliver .01 .05
587 Willie Fraser DP .01 .05
588 Carl Yastrzemski .08 .25
Puzzle Card DP
589 Kevin Bass DP .01 .05
590 John Moses DP .01 .05
591 Tom Pagnozzi DP .01 .05
592 Tony Castillo DP .01 .05
593 Jerald Clark DP .01 .05
594 Dan Schatzeder .01 .05
595 Luis Quinones DP .01 .05
596 Pete Harnisch DP .01 .05
597 Gary Redus .01 .05
598 Mel Hall .01 .05
599 Rick Schu .01 .05
600A Checklist 538-639 .01 .05
600B Checklist 518-617 .01 .05
601 Mike Kingery DP .01 .05
602 Terry Kennedy DP .01 .05
603 Mike Sharperson DP .01 .05
604 Don Carman DP .01 .05
605 Jim Gott .01 .05
606 Donn Pall DP .01 .05
607 Rance Mulliniks .01 .05
608 Curt Wilkerson DP .01 .05
609 Mike Felder DP .01 .05
610 Guillermo Hernandez DP .01 .05
611 Candy Maldonado DP .01 .05
612 Mark Thurmond DP .01 .05
613 Rick Leach DP RC .01 .05
614 Jerry Reed DP .01 .05
615 Franklin Stubbs .01 .05
616 Billy Hatcher DP .01 .05
617 Don August DP .01 .05
618 Tim Teufel .01 .05
619 Shawn Hillegas DP .01 .05
620 Manny Lee .01 .05
621 Gary Ward DP .01 .05
622 Mark Guthrie DP RC .01 .05
623 Jeff Musselman DP .01 .05
624 Mark Lemke DP .01 .05
625 Fernando Valenzuela .02 .10
626 Paul Sorrento DP RC .08 .25
627 Glenallen Hill DP .01 .05
628 Les Lancaster DP .01 .05
629 Vance Law DP .01 .05
630 Randy Velarde DP .01 .05
631 Todd Frohwirth DP .01 .05
632 Willie McGee .02 .10
633 Dennis Boyd DP .01 .05
634 Cris Carpenter DP .01 .05
635 Brian Holton .01 .05
636 Tracy Jones DP .01 .05
637A Terry Steinbach AS .01 .05
Recent Major
League Performance
637B Terry Steinbach AS .01 .05
All-Star Game
Performance
638 Brady Anderson .02 .10
639A Jack Morris ERR .02 .10
Card front shows
black line crossing
J in Jack
639B Jack Morris COR .02 .10
640 Jaime Navarro .01 .05
641 Darrin Jackson .01 .05
642 Mike Dyer RC .01 .05
643 Mike Schmidt .20 .50
644 Henry Cotto .01 .05
645 John Cerutti .01 .05
646 Francisco Cabrera .01 .05
647 Scott Sanderson .01 .05
648 Brian Meyer .01 .05
649 Ray Searage .01 .05
650A Bo Jackson AS .08 .25
Recent Major
League Performance
650B Bo Jackson AS .08 .25
All-Star Game
Performance
651 Steve Lyons .01 .05
652 Mike LaCoss .01 .05
653 Ted Power .01 .05
654A Howard Johnson AS .01 .05
Recent Major
League Performance
654B Howard Johnson AS .01 .05
All-Star Game
Performance
655 Mauro Gozzo RC .01 .05
656 Mike Blowers RC .02 .10
657 Paul Gibson .01 .05
658 Neal Heaton .01 .05
659 N.Ryan 5000K COR .20 .50
659A Nolan Ryan 5000K .60 1.50
660A Harold Baines AS .30 .75
660B Harold Baines AS .40 1.00
660C Harold Baines AS .08 .25
Black line behind
star on front;
Recent Major
League Performance
660D Harold Baines AS .01 .05
Black line behind
star on front;
All-Star Game
Performance
661 Gary Pettis .01 .05
662 Clint Zavaras RC .01 .05
663A Rick Reuschel AS .01 .05
Recent Major
League Performance
663B Rick Reuschel AS .01 .05
All-Star Game
Performance
664 Alejandro Pena .01 .05
665 Nolan Ryan KING COR .20 .50
665A N.Ryan KING .60 1.50
665C N.Ryan KING ERR .30 .75
666 Ricky Horton .01 .05
667 Curt Schilling .40 1.00
668 Bill Landrum .01 .05
669 Todd Stottlemyre .02 .10
670 Tim Leary .01 .05
671 John Wetteland .08 .25
672 Calvin Schiraldi .01 .05
673A Ruben Sierra AS .01 .05
Recent Major
League Performance
673B Ruben Sierra AS .01 .05
All-Star Game
Performance
674A Pedro Guerrero AS .01 .05
Recent Major
League Performance
674B Pedro Guerrero AS .01 .05
All-Star Game
Performance
675 Ken Phelps .01 .05
676A Cal Ripken AS .15 .40
676B Cal Ripken AS .30 .75
677 Denny Walling .01 .05
678 Goose Gossage .02 .10
679 Gary Mielke RC .01 .05
680 Bill Bathe .01 .05
681 Tom Lawless .01 .05
682 Xavier Hernandez RC .01 .05
683A Kirby Puckett AS .05 .15
Recent Major
League Performance
683B Kirby Puckett AS .05 .15
All-Star Game
Performance
684 Mariano Duncan .01 .05
685 Ramon Martinez .01 .05
686 Tim Jones .01 .05
687 Tom Filer .01 .05
688 Steve Lombardozzi .01 .05
689 Bernie Williams RC .60 1.50
690 Chip Hale RC .01 .05
691 Beau Allred RC .01 .05
692A Ryne Sandberg AS .08 .25
Recent Major
League Performance
692B Ryne Sandberg AS .08 .25
All-Star Game
Performance
693 Jeff Huson RC .02 .10
694 Curt Ford .01 .05
695A Eric Davis AS .01 .05
Recent Major
League Performance
695B Eric Davis AS .01 .05
All-Star Game
Performance
696 Scott Lusader .01 .05
697A Mark McGwire AS .20 .50
697B Mark McGwire AS .20 .50
698 Steve Cummings RC .01 .05
699 George Canale RC .01 .05
700A Checklist 640-715 .08 .25
and BC1-BC26
700B Checklist 640-716 .02 .10
and BC1-BC26
700C Checklist 618-716 .01 .05
701A Julio Franco AS .01 .05
Recent Major
League Performance
701B Julio Franco AS .01 .05
All-Star Game
Performance
702 Dave Wayne Johnson RC .01 .05
703A Dave Stewart AS ERR .01 .05
703B Dave Stewart AS COR .01 .05
704 Dave Justice RC .20 .50
705 Tony Gwynn AS .05 .15
All-Star Game
Performance
705A Tony Gwynn AS .05 .15
Recent Major
League Performance
706 Greg Myers .01 .05
707A Will Clark AS .05 .15
Recent Major
League Performance
707B Will Clark AS .05 .15
All-Star Game
Performance
708A Benito Santiago AS .01 .05
Recent Major
League Performance
708B Benito Santiago AS .01 .05
All-Star Game
Performance
709 Larry McWilliams .01 .05
710A Ozzie Smith AS .08 .25
Recent Major
League Performance
710B Ozzie Smith AS Perf .08 .25
711 John Olerud RC .20 .50
712A Wade Boggs AS .02 .10
Recent Major
League Performance
712B Wade Boggs AS .02 .10
All-Star Game
Performance
713 Gary Eave RC .01 .05
714 Bob Tewksbury .01 .05
715A Kevin Mitchell AS .01 .05
Recent Major
League Performance
715B Kevin Mitchell AS .01 .05
All-Star Game
Performance
716 Bart Giamatti MEM .08 .25

1990 Donruss Bonus MVP's

COMPLETE SET (26) .60 1.50
RANDOM INSERTS IN PACKS
BC1 Bo Jackson .08 .25
BC2 Howard Johnson .01 .05
BC3 Dave Stewart .02 .10
BC4 Tony Gwynn .10 .30
BC5 Orel Hershiser .02 .10
BC6 Pedro Guerrero .01 .05
BC7 Tim Raines .02 .10
BC8 Kirby Puckett .08 .25
BC9 Alvin Davis .01 .05
BC10 Ryne Sandberg .15 .40
BC11 Kevin Mitchell .01 .05
BC12A J.Smoltz ERR Glavine .05 .15
BC12B John Smoltz COR .08 .25
BC13 George Bell .01 .05
BC14 Julio Franco .02 .10
BC15 Paul Molitor .02 .10
BC16 Bobby Bonilla .02 .10
BC17 Mike Greenwell .01 .05
BC18 Cal Ripken .30 .75
BC19 Carlton Fisk .05 .15
BC20 Chili Davis .02 .10
BC21 Glenn Davis .01 .05
BC22 Steve Sax .01 .05
BC23 Eric Davis DP .02 .10
BC24 Greg Swindell DP .01 .05
BC25 Von Hayes DP .01 .05
BC26 Alan Trammell .02 .10

1990 Donruss Carl Yastrzemski Puzzle

1 Yastrzemski Puzzle 1-3 .10 .25
4 Yastrzemski Puzzle 4-6 .10 .25
7 Yastrzemski Puzzle 7-10 .10 .25
10 Yastrzemski Puzzle 10-12 .10 .25
13 Yastrzemski Puzzle 13-15 .10 .25
16 Yastrzemski Puzzle 16-18 .10 .25
19 Yastrzemski Puzzle 19-21 .10 .25
22 Yastrzemski Puzzle 22-24 .10 .25
25 Yastrzemski Puzzle 25-27 .10 .25
28 Yastrzemski Puzzle 28-30 .10 .25
31 Yastrzemski Puzzle 31-33 .10 .25
34 Yastrzemski Puzzle 34-36 .10 .25
37 Yastrzemski Puzzle 37-39 .10 .25
40 Yastrzemski Puzzle 40-42 .10 .25
43 Yastrzemski Puzzle 43-45 .10 .25
46 Yastrzemski Puzzle 46-48 .10 .25
49 Yastrzemski Puzzle 49-51 .10 .25
52 Yastrzemski Puzzle 52-54 .10 .25
55 Yastrzemski Puzzle 55-57 .10 .25
58 Yastrzemski Puzzle 58-60 .10 .25
61 Yastrzemski Puzzle 61-63 .10 .25
NNO Complete Puzzle 1.00 2.50

1990 Donruss Grand Slammers

COMPLETE SET (12) .60 1.50
ONE SET PER FACTORY SET
1 Matt Williams .02 .10
2 Jeffrey Leonard .01 .05
3 Chris James .01 .05
4 Mark McGwire .40 1.00
5 Dwight Evans .05 .15
6 Will Clark .05 .15
7 Mike Scioscia .01 .05
8 Todd Benzinger .01 .05
9 Fred McGriff .08 .25
10 Kevin Bass .01 .05
11 Jack Clark .02 .10
12 Bo Jackson .08 .25

1990 Donruss Rookies

The 1990 Donruss Rookies set marked the fifth consecutive year that Donruss issued a boxed set at season's end honoring the best rookies of the season. This set, which used the 1990 Donruss design but featured a green border, was issued exclusively through the Donruss dealer network to hobby dealers. This 56-card, standard size set came in its own box and the words "The Rookies" are featured prominently on the front of the cards. There are no notable Rookie Cards in this set.

COMP.FACT.SET (56) .75 2.00
1 Sandy Alomar Jr. .02 .10
2 John Olerud .20 .50
3 Pat Combs .01 .05
4 Brian DuBois .01 .05
5 Felix Jose .01 .05
6 Delino DeShields .08 .25
7 Mike Stanton .01 .05
8 Mike Munoz RC .01 .05
9 Craig Grebeck RC .02 .10
10 Joe Kraemer RC .01 .05
11 Jeff Huson .01 .05
12 Bill Sampen RC .01 .05
13 Brian Bohanon RC .02 .10
14 David Justice .20 .50
15 Robin Ventura .08 .25
16 Greg Vaughn .02 .10
17 Wayne Edwards RC .01 .05
18 Shawn Boskie RC .02 .10
19 Carlos Baerga RC .08 .25
20 Mark Gardner .01 .05
21 Kevin Appier .02 .10
22 Mike Harkey .01 .05
23 Tim Layana RC .01 .05
24 Glenallen Hill .01 .05
25 Jerry Kutzler .01 .05
26 Mike Blowers .02 .10
27 Scott Ruskin RC .01 .05
28 Dana Kiecker RC .01 .05
29 Willie Blair RC .02 .10
30 Ben McDonald .01 .05
31 Todd Zeile .02 .10
32 Scott Coolbaugh RC .01 .05
33 Xavier Hernandez .01 .05
34 Mike Hartley RC .01 .05
35 Kevin Tapani .08 .25
36 Kevin Wickander .01 .05
37 Carlos Hernandez RC .08 .25
38 Brian Traxler RC .02 .10
39 Marty Brown .01 .05
40 Scott Radinsky RC .02 .10
41 Julio Machado .01 .05
42 Steve Avery .01 .05
43 Mark Lemke .01 .05
44 Alan Mills RC .02 .10
45 Marquis Grissom .08 .25
46 Greg Olson (C) RC .02 .10
47 Dave Hollins RC .08 .25
48 Jerald Clark .01 .05
49 Eric Anthony .01 .05
50 Tim Drummond .01 .05
51 John Burkett .01 .05
52 Brent Knackert RC .02 .10
53 Jeff Shaw .01 .05
54 John Orton RC .02 .10
55 Terry Shumpert RC .01 .05
56 Checklist 1-56 .01 .05

1990 Donruss Aqueous Test

1 Bo Jackson DK 20.00 50.00
3 Ruben Sierra DK 12.50 30.00
6 Dave Stewart DK 10.00 25.00
9 Mike Bielecki DK 10.00 25.00
16 Lou Whitaker DK 12.50 30.00
18 Howard Johnson DK 10.00 25.00
22 Dan Gladden DK 10.00 25.00
30 Sandy Alomar Jr RR 10.00 25.00
32 Ben McDonald RR 10.00 25.00
33 Juan Gonzalez RR 50.00 120.00
34 Eric Anthony RR 10.00 25.00
35 Mike Fetters RR 10.00 25.00
48 Pete Incaviglia 10.00 25.00
51 Jeff Ballard 10.00 25.00
52 Claudell Washington 10.00 25.00
55 Rob Deer 10.00 25.00
56 Geno Petralli 10.00 25.00
57 Chris Bosio 10.00 25.00
60 Chet Lemon 10.00 25.00
65 Greg Harris 10.00 25.00
71 Barry Larkin 20.00 50.00
72 Dave LaPoint 10.00 25.00
77 Eddie Murray 30.00 80.00
78 Steve Sax 10.00 25.00
79 Tim Belcher 10.00 25.00
81 Kent Hrbek 12.50 30.00
83 Brook Jacoby 10.00 25.00
85 Kevin Seitzer 10.00 25.00
86 Tony Gwynn 40.00 100.00
89 Bret Saberhagen 12.50 30.00
91 Tony Phillips 10.00 25.00
93 Jeff Leonard 10.00 25.00
94 Wally Joyner 10.00 25.00
95 Carney Lansford 12.50 30.00
96 Cal Ripken Jr. 75.00 600.00
98 Kevin Mitchell 10.00 25.00
100 Checklist 10.00 25.00
102 Spike Owen 10.00 25.00
103 Paul Molitor 25.00 60.00
105 Ryne Sandberg 40.00 100.00
107 Steve Buechele 10.00 25.00
108 Jim Abbott 15.00 40.00
109 Alvin Davis 10.00 25.00
112 Rick Reuschel 12.50 30.00
114 Joe Carter 12.50 30.00
117 Bobby Ojeda 10.00 25.00
118 Glenn Davis 10.00 25.00
120 Kurt Stillwell 10.00 25.00
125 Jose Canseco 25.00 60.00
126 Barry Bonds 50.00 120.00
129 Dave Valle 10.00 25.00
132 Mike Morgan 10.00 25.00
134 Jeff Robinson 10.00 25.00
139 Bo Diaz 10.00 25.00
140 Robby Thompson 10.00 25.00
141 Craig Worthington 10.00 25.00
146 Robin Yount 25.00 60.00
147 Gary Carter 25.00 60.00
148 Ron Kittle 10.00 25.00
149 Tony Fernandez 12.50 30.00
154 Jesse Orosco 12.50 30.00
155 Wally Backman 10.00 25.00
158 Greg Maddux 50.00 120.00
162 John Dopson 10.00 25.00
164 Bill Ripken 10.00 25.00
165 Fred Manrique 10.00 25.00
166 Nolan Ryan 75.00 200.00
167 Damon Berryhill 10.00 25.00
168 Dale Murphy 20.00 50.00
169 Mickey Tettleton 10.00 25.00
170 Kirk McCaskill 10.00 25.00
171 Dwight Gooden 12.50 30.00
172 Jose Lind 10.00 25.00
173 B.J. Surhoff 12.50 30.00
174 Ruben Sierra 12.50 30.00
175 Dan Plesac 10.00 25.00
176 Dan Pasqua 10.00 25.00
177 Kelly Downs 10.00 25.00
178 Matt Nokes 10.00 25.00
179 Luis Aquino 10.00 25.00
180 Frank Tanana 12.50 30.00
181 Tony Pena 10.00 25.00
182 Dan Gladden 10.00 25.00
183 Bruce Hurst 10.00 25.00
184 Roger Clemens 40.00 100.00
185 Mark McGwire 50.00 120.00
186 Rob Murphy 10.00 25.00
187 Jim Deshaies 10.00 25.00
188 Fred McGriff 20.00 50.00
189 Rob Dibble 10.00 25.00
190 Don Mattingly 40.00 100.00
191 Felix Fermin 10.00 25.00
192 Roberto Kelly 10.00 25.00
193 Dennis Cook 10.00 25.00
194 Darren Daulton 10.00 25.00
195 Alfredo Griffin 10.00 25.00
196 Eric Plunk 10.00 25.00
197 Orel Hershiser 12.50 30.00
198 Paul O'Neill 15.00 40.00
199 Randy Bush 10.00 25.00
201 Ozzie Smith 30.00 80.00
202 Pete O'Brien 10.00 25.00
203 Jay Howell 10.00 25.00
204 Mark Gubicza 10.00 25.00
205 Ed Whitson 10.00 25.00
206 George Bell 10.00 25.00
207 Mike Scott 10.00 25.00
208 Charlie Liebrandt 10.00 25.00
209 Mike Heath 10.00 25.00
210 Dennis Eckersley 15.00 40.00
211 Mike LaValliere 10.00 25.00
212 Darnell Coles 10.00 25.00
213 Lance Parrish 10.00 25.00
214 Mike Moore 10.00 25.00
215 Steve Finley 12.50 30.00
216 Tim Raines 12.50 30.00
217 Scott Garrelts 10.00 25.00
218 Kevin McReynolds 10.00 25.00
219 Dave Gallagher 10.00 25.00
220 Tim Wallach 10.00 25.00
221 Chuck Crim 10.00 25.00
222 Lonnie Smith 12.50 30.00
223 Andre Dawson 30.00 80.00
224 Nelson Santovenia 10.00 25.00
225 Rafael Palmeiro 20.00 50.00
226 Devon White 10.00 25.00
227 Harold Reynolds 12.50 30.00
228 Ellis Burks 12.50 30.00
229 Mark Parent 10.00 25.00
230 Will Clark 25.00 60.00
231 Jimmy Key 10.00 25.00
232 John Farrell 10.00 25.00
233 Eric Davis 12.50 30.00
234 Johnny Ray 10.00 25.00
235 Darryl Strawberry 12.50 30.00
236 Bill Doran 10.00 25.00
237 Greg Gagne 10.00 25.00
238 Jim Eisenreich 10.00 25.00
239 Tommy Gregg 10.00 25.00
240 Marty Barrett 10.00 25.00
241 Rafael Ramirez 10.00 25.00
242 Chris Sabo 10.00 25.00
243 Dave Henderson 10.00 25.00
245 Alvaro Espinoza 10.00 25.00
246 Garry Templeton 10.00 25.00
247 Gene Harris 10.00 25.00
248 Kevin Gross 10.00 25.00
249 Brett Butler 12.50 30.00
250 Willie Randolph 12.50 30.00
251 Roger McDowell 10.00 25.00
252 Rafael Belliard 10.00 25.00
253 Steve Rosenberg 10.00 25.00
254 Jack Howell 10.00 25.00
255 Marvell Wynne 10.00 25.00
256 Tom Candiotti 10.00 25.00
257 Todd Benzinger 10.00 25.00
258 Don Robinson 10.00 25.00
259 Phil Bradley 10.00 25.00
260 Cecil Espy 10.00 25.00
261 Scott Bankhead 10.00 25.00
262 Rafael Belliard 10.00 25.00
262 Frank White 12.50 30.00
263 Andres Thomas 10.00 25.00
264 Glenn Braggs 10.00 25.00
265 David Cone 15.00 40.00
266 Bobby Thigpen 10.00 25.00
267 Nelson Liriano 10.00 25.00
268 Terry Steinbach 10.00 25.00
269 Kirby Puckett 40.00 100.00
270 Gregg Jefferies 10.00 25.00
271 Jeff Blauser 10.00 25.00
272 Cory Snyder 10.00 25.00
273 Roy Smith 10.00 25.00
274 Tom Foley 10.00 25.00
275 Mitch Williams 10.00 25.00
276 Paul Kilgus 10.00 25.00
277 Don Slaught 10.00 25.00
278 Von Hayes 10.00 25.00
279 Vince Coleman 10.00 25.00
280 Mike Boddicker 10.00 25.00
281 Ken Dayley 10.00 25.00
282 Mike Devereaux 10.00 25.00
BC1 Bo Jackson MVP 20.00 50.00
BC3 Dave Stewart MVP 12.50 30.00
BC6 Pedro Guerrero MVP 12.50 30.00
BC7 Tim Raines MVP 12.50 30.00
BC8 Kirby Puckett MVP 40.00 100.00
BC9 Alvin Davis MVP 10.00 25.00

1990 Donruss Best AL

The 1990 Donruss Best of the American League set consists of 144 standard-size cards. This was Donruss' latest version of what had been titled the previous two years as Baseball's Best. In 1990, the sets were split into National and American League and marketed separately. The front design was similar to the regular issue Donruss set except for the front borders being blue while the backs have complete major and minor league statistics as compared to the regular Donruss cards which only cover the past five major-league seasons. An early Sammy Sosa card is featured within this set.

COMP.FACT.SET (144) 15.00 40.00
1 Ken Griffey Jr. .60 1.50
2 Bob Milacki .05 .15
3 Mike Boddicker .05 .15
4 Bert Blyleven .07 .20
5 Carlton Fisk .10 .30
6 Greg Swindell .05 .15
7 Alan Trammell .07 .20
8 Mark Davis .05 .15
9 Chris Bosio .05 .15
10 Gary Gaetti .07 .20
11 Matt Nokes .05 .15
12 Dennis Eckersley .07 .20
13 Kevin Brown .07 .20
14 Tom Henke .05 .15
15 Mickey Tettleton .05 .15
16 Jody Reed .05 .15
17 Mark Langston .05 .15
18 Melido Perez UER .05 .15
Listed as an Expo
rather than White Sox
19 John Farrell .05 .15
20 Tony Phillips .05 .15
21 Bret Saberhagen .07 .20
22 Robin Yount .30 .75
23 Kirby Puckett .20 .50
24 Steve Sax .05 .15
25 Dave Stewart .07 .20
26 Alvin Davis .05 .15
27 Geno Petralli .05 .15
28 Mookie Wilson .07 .20
29 Jeff Ballard .05 .15
30 Ellis Burks .07 .20
31 Wally Joyner .07 .20
32 Bobby Thigpen .05 .15
33 Keith Hernandez .07 .20
34 Jack Morris .07 .20
35 George Brett .50 1.25
36 Dan Plesac .05 .15
37 Brian Harper .05 .15
38 Don Mattingly .50 1.25
39 Dave Henderson .05 .15
40 Scott Bankhead UER .05 .15
Ashboro misspelled
as Ashboro on card
41 Rafael Palmeiro .10 .30
42 Jimmy Key .07 .20
43 Gregg Olson .05 .15
44 Tony Pena .05 .15
45 Jack Howell .05 .15
46 Eric King .05 .15
47 Cory Snyder .05 .15
48 Frank Tanana .07 .20
49 Nolan Ryan .60 1.50
50 Bob Boone .07 .20
51 Dave Parker .07 .20
52 Allan Anderson .05 .15
53 Tim Leary .05 .15
54 Mark McGwire .60 1.50
55 Dave Valle .05 .15
56 Fred McGriff .10 .30
57 Cal Ripken .60 1.50
58 Roger Clemens .60 1.50
59 Lance Parrish .07 .20
60 Robin Ventura .20 .50
61 Doug Jones .05 .15
62 Lloyd Moseby .05 .15
63 Bo Jackson .20 .50
64 Paul Molitor .07 .20
65 Kent Hrbek .07 .20
66 Mel Hall .05 .15
67 Bob Welch .07 .20
68 Erik Hanson .05 .15
69 Harold Baines .07 .20
70 Junior Felix .05 .15
71 Craig Worthington .05 .15
72 Jeff Reardon .07 .20
73 Johnny Ray .05 .15
74 Ozzie Guillen .07 .20
75 Brook Jacoby .05 .15
76 Chet Lemon .05 .15
77 Mark Gubicza .05 .15
78 B.J. Surhoff .07 .20
79 Rick Aguilera .07 .20
80 Pascual Perez .05 .15
81 Jose Canseco .10 .30
82 Mike Schooler .05 .15
83 Jeff Huson .05 .15
84 Kelly Gruber .05 .15
85 Randy Milligan .05 .15
86 Wade Boggs .10 .30
87 Dave Winfield .07 .20
88 Scott Fletcher .05 .15
89 Tom Candiotti .05 .15
90 Mike Heath .05 .15
91 Kevin Seitzer .05 .15
92 Ted Higuera .05 .15
93 Kevin Tapani .20 .50
94 Roberto Kelly .05 .15
95 Walt Weiss .05 .15
96 Checklist Card .05 .15
97 Sandy Alomar Jr. .07 .20
98 Pete O'Brien .05 .15
99 Jeff Russell .05 .15
100 John Olerud .60 1.50
101 Pete Harnisch .05 .15
102 Dwight Evans .10 .30
103 Chuck Finley .07 .20
104 Sammy Sosa 2.50 6.00
105 Mike Henneman .05 .15
106 Kurt Stillwell .05 .15
107 Greg Vaughn .05 .15
108 Dan Gladden .05 .15
109 Jesse Barfield .05 .15
110 Willie Randolph .07 .20
111 Randy Johnson .30 .75
112 Julio Franco .07 .20
113 Tony Fernandez .05 .15
114 Ben McDonald .05 .15
115 Mike Greenwell .05 .15
116 Luis Polonia .05 .15
117 Carney Lansford .07 .20
118 Bud Black .05 .15
119 Lou Whitaker .07 .20
120 Jim Eisenreich .05 .15
121 Gary Sheffield .20 .50
122 Shane Mack .05 .15
123 Alvaro Espinoza .05 .15
124 Rickey Henderson .20 .50
125 Jeffrey Leonard .05 .15
126 Gary Pettis .05 .15
127 Dave Stieb .07 .20
128 Danny Tartabull .05 .15
129 Joe Orsulak .05 .15
130 Tom Brunansky .05 .15
131 Dick Schofield .05 .15
132 Candy Maldonado .05 .15
133 Cecil Fielder .07 .20
134 Terry Shumpert .05 .15
135 Greg Gagne .05 .15
136 Dave Righetti .07 .20
137 Terry Steinbach .05 .15
138 Harold Reynolds .07 .20
139 George Bell .05 .15
140 Carlos Quintana .05 .15
141 Ivan Calderon .05 .15
142 Greg Brock .05 .15
143 Ruben Sierra .07 .20
144 Checklist Card .05 .15

1990 Donruss Best NL

The 1990 Donruss Best of the National League set consists of 144 standard-size cards. This was Donruss' latest version of what had been titled the previous two years as Baseball's Best. In 1990, the sets were split into National and American League and marketed separately. The front design was similar to the regular issue Donruss set except for the front borders being blue while the backs have complete major and minor league statistics as compared to the regular Donruss cards which only cover the past five major-league seasons. An early Larry Walker card is featured within this set.

Card	Low	High
COMP.FACT.SET (144)	3.00	8.00
1 Eric Davis	.07	.20
2 Tom Glavine	.10	.30
3 Mike Bielecki	.05	.15
4 Jim Deshaies	.05	.15
5 Mike Scioscia	.05	.15
6 Spike Owen	.05	.15
7 Dwight Gooden	.07	.20
8 Ricky Jordan	.05	.15
9 Doug Drabek	.05	.15
10 Bryn Smith	.05	.15
11 Tony Gwynn	.25	.60
12 John Burkett	.05	.15
13 Nick Esasky	.05	.15
14 Greg Maddux	.30	.75
15 Joe Oliver	.05	.15
16 Mike Scott	.05	.15
17 Tim Belcher	.05	.15
18 Kevin Gross	.05	.15
19 Howard Johnson	.05	.15
20 Darren Daulton	.07	.20
21 John Smiley	.05	.15
22 Ken Dayley	.05	.15
23 Craig Lefferts	.05	.15
24 Will Clark	.10	.30
25 Greg Olson	.05	.15
26 Ryne Sandberg	.25	.60
27 Tom Browning	.05	.15
28 Eric Anthony	.05	.15
29 Juan Samuel	.05	.15
30 Dennis Martinez	.07	.20
31 Kevin Elster	.05	.15
32 Tom Herr	.05	.15
33 Sid Bream	.05	.15
34 Terry Pendleton	.07	.20
35 Roberto Alomar	.10	.30
36 Kevin Bass	.05	.15
37 Jim Presley	.05	.15
38 Les Lancaster	.05	.15
39 Paul O'Neill	.10	.30
40 Dave Smith	.05	.15
41 Kirk Gibson	.07	.20
42 Tim Burke	.05	.15
43 David Cone	.07	.20
44 Ken Howell	.05	.15
45 Barry Bonds	.60	1.50
46 Joe Magrane	.05	.15
47 Andy Benes	.07	.20
48 Gary Carter	.07	.20
49 Pat Combs	.05	.15
50 John Smoltz	.20	.50
51 Mark Grace	.10	.30
52 Barry Larkin	.10	.30
53 Danny Darwin	.05	.15
54 Orel Hershiser	.07	.20
55 Tim Wallach	.05	.15
56 Dave Magadan	.05	.15
57 Roger McDowell	.05	.15
58 Bill Landrum	.05	.15
59 Jose DeLeon	.05	.15
60 Bip Roberts	.05	.15
61 Matt Williams	.07	.20
62 Dale Murphy	.10	.30
63 Dwight Smith	.05	.15
64 Chris Sabo	.05	.15
65 Glenn Davis	.05	.15
66 Jay Howell	.05	.15
67 Andres Galarraga	.07	.20
68 Frank Viola	.07	.20
69 John Kruk	.07	.20
70 Bobby Bonilla	.07	.20
71 Todd Zeile	.07	.20
72 Joe Carter	.07	.20
73 Robby Thompson	.05	.15
74 Jeff Blauser	.05	.15
75 Mitch Williams	.05	.15
76 Rob Dibble	.07	.20
77 Rafael Ramirez	.05	.15
78 Eddie Murray	.20	.50
79 Dave Martinez	.05	.15
80 Darryl Strawberry	.07	.20
81 Dickie Thon	.05	.15
82 Jose Lind	.05	.15
83 Ozzie Smith	.30	.75
84 Bruce Hurst	.05	.15
85 Kevin Mitchell	.05	.15
86 Lonnie Smith	.05	.15
87 Joe Girardi	.05	.15
88 Randy Myers	.07	.20
89 Craig Biggio	.20	.50
90 Fernando Valenzuela	.07	.20
91 Larry Walker	.75	2.00
92 John Franco	.07	.20
93 Dennis Cook	.05	.15
94 Bob Walk	.05	.15
95 Pedro Guerrero	.07	.20
96 Checklist Card	.05	.15
97 Andre Dawson	.07	.20
98 Ed Whitson	.05	.15
99 Steve Bedrosian	.05	.15
100 Oddibe McDowell	.05	.15
101 Todd Benzinger	.05	.15
102 Bill Doran	.05	.15
103 Alfredo Griffin	.05	.15
104 Tim Raines	.07	.20
105 Sid Fernandez	.05	.15
106 Charlie Hayes	.05	.15
107 Mike LaValliere	.05	.15
108 Jose Oquendo	.05	.15
109 Jack Clark	.07	.20
110 Scott Garrelts	.05	.15
111 Ron Gant	.07	.20
112 Shawon Dunston	.05	.15
113 Mariano Duncan	.05	.15
114 Eric Yelding	.05	.15
115 Hubie Brooks	.05	.15
116 Delino DeShields	.07	.20
117 Gregg Jefferies	.05	.15
118 Len Dykstra	.07	.20
119 Andy Van Slyke	.10	.30
120 Lee Smith	.07	.20
121 Benito Santiago	.07	.20
122 Jose Uribe	.05	.15
123 Jeff Treadway	.05	.15
124 Jerome Walton	.05	.15
125 Billy Hatcher	.05	.15
126 Ken Caminiti	.07	.20
127 Kal Daniels	.05	.15
128 Marquis Grissom	.20	.50
129 Kevin McReynolds	.05	.15
130 Wally Backman	.05	.15
131 Willie McGee	.07	.20
132 Terry Kennedy	.05	.15
133 Garry Templeton	.05	.15
134 Lloyd McClendon	.05	.15
135 Daryl Boston	.05	.15
136 Jay Bell	.07	.20
137 Mike Pagliarulo	.05	.15
138 Vince Coleman	.05	.15
139 Brett Butler	.07	.20
140 Von Hayes	.05	.15
141 Ramon Martinez	.05	.15
142 Jack Armstrong	.05	.15
143 Franklin Stubbs	.05	.15
144 Checklist Card	.05	.15

1990 Donruss Learning Series

Card	Low	High
COMPLETE SET (55)	15.00	40.00
1 George Brett DK	1.00	2.50
2 Kevin Mitchell	.02	.10
3 Andy Van Slyke	.07	.20
4 Benito Santiago	.07	.20
5 Gary Carter	.40	1.00
6 Jose Canseco	.50	1.25
7 Rickey Henderson	.50	1.25
8 Ken Griffey Jr.	2.00	5.00
9 Ozzie Smith	1.00	2.50
10 Dwight Gooden	.07	.20
11 Ryne Sandberg DK	1.00	2.50
12 Don Mattingly	1.00	2.50
13 Ozzie Guillen	.07	.20
14 Dave Righetti	.02	.10
15 Rick Dempsey	.02	.10
16 Tom Herr	.02	.10
17 Julio Franco	.07	.20
18 Von Hayes	.02	.10
19 Cal Ripken	3.00	8.00
20 Alan Trammell	.30	.75
21 Wade Boggs	.40	1.00
22 Glenn Davis	.02	.10
23 Will Clark	.60	1.50
24 Nolan Ryan	3.00	8.00
25 George Bell	.02	.10
26 Cecil Fielder	.20	.50
27 Gregg Olson	.02	.10
28 Tim Wallach	.02	.10
29 Ron Darling	.02	.10
30 Kelly Gruber	.02	.10
31 Shawn Boskie	.02	.10
32 Mike Greenwell	.02	.10
33 Dave Parker	.07	.20
34 Joe Magrane	.02	.10
35 Dave Stewart	.07	.20
36 Kent Hrbek	.07	.20
37 Robin Yount	.40	1.00
38 Bo Jackson	.20	.50
39 Fernando Valenzuela	.07	.20
40 Sandy Alomar Jr.	.07	.20
41 Lance Parrish	.02	.10
42 Candy Maldonado	.02	.10
43 Mike LaValliere	.02	.10
44 Jim Abbott	.07	.20
45 Edgar Martinez	.10	.30
46 Kirby Puckett	.40	1.00
47 Delino DeShields	.20	.50
48 Tony Gwynn	1.00	2.50
49 Carlton Fisk	.40	1.00
50 Mike Scott	.02	.10
51 Barry Larkin	.30	.75
52 Andre Dawson	.20	.50
53 Tom Glavine	.30	.75
54 Tom Browning	.02	.10
55 Checklist Card	.02	.10

1990 Donruss Super DK's

Card	Low	High
COMPLETE SET (26)	12.50	30.00
1 Bo Jackson	.40	1.00
2 Steve Sax	.08	.25
3 Ruben Sierra	.20	.50
4 Ken Griffey Jr.	5.00	12.00
5 Mickey Tettleton	.20	.50
6 Dave Stewart	.20	.50
7 Jim Deshaies	.08	.25
8 John Smoltz	.30	.75
9 Mike Bielecki	.08	.25
10 Brian Downing	.08	.25
11 Kevin Mitchell	.08	.25
12 Kelly Gruber	.08	.25
13 Joe Magrane	.08	.25
14 John Franco	.20	.50
15 Ozzie Guillen	.08	.25
16 Lou Whitaker	.20	.50
17 John Smiley	.08	.25
18 Howard Johnson	.08	.25
19 Willie Randolph	.20	.50
20 Chris Bosio	.08	.25
21 Tommy Herr	.08	.25
22 Dan Gladden	.08	.25
23 Ellis Burks	.30	.75
24 Pete O'Brien	.08	.25
25 Bryn Smith	.08	.25
26 Ed Whitson	.08	.25
NNO Nolan Ryan King of Kings	6.00	15.00

1991 Donruss Previews

Card	Low	High
COMPLETE SET (12)	125.00	250.00
1 Dave Justice	5.00	12.00
2 Doug Drabek	2.00	5.00
3 Scott Chiamparino	2.00	5.00
4 Ken Griffey Jr.	20.00	50.00
5 Bob Welch	2.00	5.00
6 Tino Martinez	5.00	12.00
7 Nolan Ryan	15.00	40.00
8 Dwight Gooden	3.00	8.00
9 Ryne Sandberg	20.00	50.00
10 Barry Bonds	15.00	40.00
11 Jose Canseco	8.00	20.00
12 Eddie Murray	8.00	20.00

1991 Donruss

The 1991 Donruss set was issued in two series of 386 and 384 for a total of 770 standard-size cards. This set marked the first time Donruss issued cards in multiple series. The second series was issued approximately three months after the first series was issued. Cards were issued in wax packs and factory sets. As a separate promotion, wax packs were also given away with six and 12-packs of Coke and Diet Coke. First series cards feature blue borders and second series green borders with some stripes and the players name in white against a red background. Subsets include Diamond Kings (1-27), Rated Rookies (28-47/413-432), AL All-Stars (48-56), MVP's (387-412) and NL All-Stars (433-441). There were also special cards to honor the award winners and the heroes of the World Series. On cards 60, 70, 127, 182, 239, 294, 355, 368, and 377, the border stripes are red and yellow. There are no notable Rookie Cards in this set.

Card	Low	High
COMPLETE SET (770)	3.00	8.00
COMP.FACT.w/LEAF PREV	4.00	10.00
COMP.FACT.w/STUDIO PREV	4.00	10.00
SUBSET CARDS HALF VALUE OF BASE CARDS		
COMP.STARGELL PUZZLE	.40	1.00
1 Dave Stieb DK	.01	.05
2 Craig Biggio DK	.02	.10
3 Cecil Fielder DK	.01	.05
4 Barry Bonds DK	.20	.50
5 Barry Larkin DK	.02	.10
6 Dave Parker DK	.01	.05
7 Len Dykstra DK	.01	.05
8 Bobby Thigpen DK	.01	.05
9 Roger Clemens DK	.15	.40
10 Ron Gant DK UER	.02	.10
11 Delino DeShields DK	.01	.05
12 Roberto Alomar DK UER	.02	.10
13 Sandy Alomar Jr. DK	.01	.05
14 Ryne Sandberg DK UER	.08	.25
15 Ramon Martinez DK	.01	.05
16 Edgar Martinez DK	.05	.15
17 Dave Magadan DK	.01	.05
18 Matt Williams DK	.01	.05
19 Rafael Palmeiro DK UER	.02	.10
20 Bob Welch DK	.01	.05
21 Dave Righetti DK	.01	.05
22 Brian Harper DK	.01	.05
23 Gregg Olson DK	.01	.05
24 Kurt Stillwell DK	.01	.05
25 Pedro Guerrero DK UER	.01	.05
26 Chuck Finley DK UER	.02	.10
27 DK Checklist 1-27	.01	.05
28 Tino Martinez RR	.08	.25
29 Mark Lewis RR	.01	.05
30 Bernard Gilkey RR	.01	.05
31 Hensley Meulens RR	.01	.05
32 Derek Bell RR	.02	.10
33 Jose Offerman RR	.01	.05
34 Terry Bross RR	.01	.05
35 Leo Gomez RR	.01	.05
36 Derrick May RR	.01	.05
37 Kevin Morton RR RC	.01	.05
38 Moises Alou RR	.02	.10
39 Julio Valera RR	.01	.05
40 Milt Cuyler RR	.01	.05
41 Phil Plantier RR RC	.08	.25
42 Scott Chiamparino RR	.01	.05
43 Ray Lankford RR	.02	.10
44 Mickey Morandini RR	.01	.05
45 Dave Hansen RR	.01	.05
46 Kevin Belcher RR RC	.01	.05
47 Darrin Fletcher RR	.01	.05
48 Steve Sax AS	.01	.05
49 Ken Griffey Jr. AS	.10	.30
50A Jose Canseco AS ERR	.02	.10
50B Jose Canseco AS COR	.05	.15
51 Sandy Alomar Jr. AS	.01	.05
52 Cal Ripken AS	.15	.40
53 Rickey Henderson AS	.05	.15
54 Bob Welch AS	.01	.05
55 Wade Boggs AS	.02	.10
56 Mark McGwire AS	.15	.40
57A Jack McDowell ERR	.08	.25
57B Jack McDowell COR	.20	.50
58 Jose Lind	.01	.05
59 Alex Fernandez	.01	.05
60 Pat Combs	.01	.05
61 Mike Walker	.01	.05
62 Juan Samuel	.01	.05
63 Mike Blowers UER	.01	.05
64 Mark Guthrie	.01	.05
65 Mark Salas	.01	.05
66 Tim Jones	.01	.05
67 Tim Leary	.01	.05
68 Andres Galarraga	.02	.10
69 Bob Milacki	.01	.05
70 Tim Belcher	.01	.05
71 Todd Zeile	.01	.05
72 Jerome Walton	.01	.05
73 Kevin Seitzer	.01	.05
74 Jerald Clark	.01	.05
75 John Smoltz UER	.05	.15
76 Mike Henneman	.01	.05
77 Ken Griffey Jr.	.25	.60
78 Jim Abbott	.05	.15
79 Gregg Jefferies	.01	.05
80 Kevin Reimer	.01	.05
81 Roger Clemens	.30	.75
82 Mike Fitzgerald	.01	.05
83 Bruce Hurst UER	.01	.05
84 Eric Davis	.02	.10
85 Paul Molitor	.02	.10
86 Will Clark	.05	.15
87 Mike Bielecki	.01	.05
88 Bret Saberhagen	.02	.10
89 Nolan Ryan	.40	1.00
90 Bobby Thigpen	.01	.05
91 Dickie Thon	.01	.05
92 Duane Ward	.01	.05
93 Luis Polonia	.01	.05
94 Terry Kennedy	.01	.05
95 Kent Hrbek	.02	.10
96 Danny Jackson	.01	.05
97 Sid Fernandez	.01	.05
98 Jimmy Key	.02	.10
99 Franklin Stubbs	.01	.05
100 Checklist 28-103	.01	.05
101 R.J. Reynolds	.01	.05
102 Dave Stewart	.02	.10
103 Dan Pasqua	.01	.05
104 Dan Plesac	.01	.05
105 Mark McGwire	.30	.75
106 John Farrell	.01	.05
107 Don Mattingly	.25	.60
108 Carlton Fisk	.05	.15
109 Ken Oberkfell	.01	.05
110 Darrel Akerfelds	.01	.05
111 Gregg Olson	.01	.05
112 Mike Scioscia	.01	.05
113 Bryn Smith	.01	.05
114 Bob Geren	.01	.05
115 Tom Candiotti	.01	.05
116 Kevin Tapani	.01	.05
117 Jeff Treadway	.01	.05
118 Alan Trammell	.02	.10
119 Pete O'Brien UER	.01	.05
120 Joel Skinner	.01	.05
121 Mike LaValliere	.01	.05
122 Dwight Evans	.05	.15
123 Jody Reed	.01	.05
124 Lee Guetterman	.01	.05
125 Tim Burke	.01	.05
126 Dave Johnson	.01	.05
127 Fernando Valenzuela UER	.02	.10
128 Jose DeLeon	.01	.05
129 Andre Dawson	.02	.10
130 Gerald Perry	.01	.05
131 Greg W. Harris	.01	.05
132 Tom Glavine	.05	.15
133 Lance McCullers	.01	.05
134 Randy Johnson	.10	.30
135 Lance Parrish UER	.02	.10
136 Mackey Sasser	.01	.05
137 Geno Petralli	.01	.05
138 Dennis Lamp	.01	.05
139 Dennis Martinez	.02	.10
140 Mike Pagliarulo	.01	.05
141 Hal Morris	.01	.05
142 Dave Parker	.02	.10
143 Brett Butler	.02	.10
144 Paul Assenmacher	.01	.05
145 Mark Gubicza	.01	.05
146 Charlie Hough	.02	.10
147 Sammy Sosa	.08	.25
148 Randy Ready	.01	.05
149 Kelly Gruber	.01	.05
150 Devon White	.02	.10
151 Gary Carter	.02	.10
152 Gene Larkin	.01	.05
153 Chris Sabo	.01	.05
154 David Cone	.02	.10
155 Todd Stottlemyre	.01	.05
156 Glenn Wilson	.01	.05
157 Bob Walk	.01	.05
158 Mike Gallego	.01	.05
159 Greg Hibbard	.01	.05
160 Chris Bosio	.01	.05
161 Mike Moore	.01	.05
162 Jerry Browne UER	.01	.05
163 Steve Sax UER	.01	.05
164 Melido Perez	.01	.05
165 Danny Darwin	.01	.05
166 Roger McDowell	.01	.05
167 Bill Ripken	.01	.05
168 Mike Sharperson	.01	.05
169 Lee Smith	.02	.10
170 Matt Nokes	.01	.05
171 Jesse Orosco	.01	.05
172 Rick Aguilera	.02	.10
173 Jim Presley	.01	.05
174 Lou Whitaker	.02	.10
175 Harold Reynolds	.02	.10
176 Brook Jacoby	.01	.05
177 Wally Backman	.01	.05
178 Wade Boggs	.05	.15
179 Chuck Cary UER	.01	.05
180 Tom Foley	.01	.05
181 Pete Harnisch	.01	.05
182 Mike Morgan	.01	.05
183 Bob Tewksbury	.01	.05
184 Joe Girardi	.01	.05
185 Storm Davis	.01	.05
186 Ed Whitson	.01	.05
187 Steve Avery UER	.01	.05
188 Lloyd Moseby	.01	.05
189 Scott Bankhead	.01	.05
190 Mark Langston	.01	.05
191 Kevin McReynolds	.01	.05
192 Julio Franco	.02	.10
193 John Dopson	.01	.05
194 Dennis Boyd	.01	.05
195 Bip Roberts	.01	.05
196 Billy Hatcher	.01	.05
197 Edgar Diaz	.01	.05
198 Greg Litton	.01	.05
199 Mark Grace	.05	.15
200 Checklist 104-179	.01	.05
201 George Brett	.25	.60
202 Jeff Russell	.01	.05
203 Ivan Calderon	.01	.05
204 Ken Howell	.01	.05
205 Tom Henke	.01	.05
206 Bryan Harvey	.01	.05
207 Steve Bedrosian	.01	.05
208 Al Newman	.01	.05
209 Randy Myers	.01	.05
210 Daryl Boston	.01	.05
211 Manny Lee	.01	.05
212 Dave Smith	.01	.05
213 Don Slaught	.01	.05
214 Walt Weiss	.01	.05
215 Donn Pall	.01	.05
216 Jaime Navarro	.01	.05
217 Willie Randolph	.02	.10
218 Rudy Seanez	.01	.05
219 Jim Leyritz	.01	.05
220 Ron Karkovice	.01	.05
221 Ken Caminiti	.02	.10
222 Von Hayes	.01	.05
223 Cal Ripken	.30	.75
224 Lenny Harris	.01	.05
225 Milt Thompson	.01	.05
226 Alvaro Espinoza	.01	.05
227 Chris James	.01	.05
228 Dan Gladden	.01	.05
229 Jeff Blauser	.01	.05
230 Mike Heath	.01	.05
231 Omar Vizquel	.05	.15
232 Doug Jones	.01	.05
233 Jeff King	.01	.05
234 Luis Rivera	.01	.05
235 Ellis Burks	.02	.10
236 Greg Cadaret	.01	.05
237 Dave Martinez	.01	.05
238 Mark Williamson	.01	.05
239 Stan Javier	.01	.05
240 Ozzie Smith	.15	.40
241 Shawn Boskie	.01	.05
242 Tom Gordon	.01	.05
243 Tony Gwynn	.10	.30
244 Tommy Gregg	.01	.05
245 Jeff M. Robinson	.01	.05
246 Keith Comstock	.01	.05
247 Jack Howell	.01	.05
248 Keith Miller	.01	.05
249 Bobby Witt	.01	.05
250 Rob Murphy UER	.01	.05
251 Spike Owen	.01	.05
252 Garry Templeton	.01	.05
253 Glenn Braggs	.01	.05
254 Ron Robinson	.01	.05
255 Kevin Mitchell	.01	.05
256 Les Lancaster	.01	.05
257 Mel Stottlemyre Jr.	.01	.05
258 Kenny Rogers UER	.02	.10
259 Lance Johnson	.01	.05
260 John Kruk	.02	.10
261 Fred McGriff	.05	.15
262 Dick Schofield	.01	.05
263 Trevor Wilson	.01	.05
264 David West	.01	.05
265 Scott Scudder	.01	.05
266 Dwight Gooden	.02	.10
267 Willie Blair	.01	.05
268 Mark Portugal	.01	.05
269 Doug Drabek	.01	.05
270 Dennis Eckersley	.02	.10
271 Eric King	.01	.05
272 Robin Yount	.15	.40
273 Carney Lansford	.02	.10
274 Carlos Baerga	.01	.05
275 Dave Righetti	.02	.10
276 Scott Fletcher	.01	.05
277 Eric Yelding	.01	.05
278 Charlie Hayes	.01	.05
279 Jeff Ballard	.01	.05
280 Orel Hershiser	.02	.10
281 Jose Oquendo	.01	.05
282 Mike Witt	.01	.05
283 Mitch Webster	.01	.05
284 Greg Gagne	.01	.05
285 Greg Olson	.01	.05
286 Tony Phillips UER	.01	.05
287 Scott Bradley	.01	.05
288 Cory Snyder	.01	.05
289 Jay Bell UER	.02	.10
290 Kevin Romine	.01	.05
291 Jeff D. Robinson	.01	.05
292 Steve Frey UER	.01	.05
293 Craig Worthington	.01	.05
294 Tim Crews	.01	.05
295 Joe Magrane	.01	.05
296 Hector Villanueva	.01	.05
297 Terry Shumpert	.01	.05
298 Joe Carter	.02	.10
299 Kent Mercker UER	.01	.05
300 Checklist 180-255	.01	.05
301 Chet Lemon	.01	.05
302 Mike Schooler	.01	.05
303 Dante Bichette	.02	.10
304 Kevin Elster	.01	.05
305 Jeff Huson	.01	.05
306 Greg A. Harris	.01	.05
307 Marquis Grissom UER	.02	.10
308 Calvin Schiraldi	.01	.05
309 Mariano Duncan	.01	.05
310 Bill Spiers	.01	.05
311 Scott Garrelts	.01	.05
312 Mitch Williams	.01	.05
313 Mike Macfarlane	.01	.05
314 Kevin Brown	.02	.10
315 Robin Ventura	.02	.10
316 Darren Daulton	.02	.10
317 Pat Borders	.01	.05
318 Mark Eichhorn	.01	.05
319 Jeff Brantley	.01	.05
320 Shane Mack	.01	.05
321 Rob Dibble	.02	.10
322 John Franco	.02	.10
323 Junior Felix	.01	.05
324 Casey Candaele	.01	.05
325 Bobby Bonilla	.02	.10
326 Dave Henderson	.01	.05
327 Wayne Edwards	.01	.05
328 Mark Knudson	.01	.05
329 Terry Steinbach	.01	.05
330 Colby Ward UER RC	.01	.05
331 Oscar Azocar	.01	.05
332 Scott Radinsky	.01	.05
333 Eric Anthony	.01	.05
334 Steve Lake	.01	.05
335 Bob Melvin	.01	.05
336 Kal Daniels	.01	.05
337 Tom Pagnozzi	.01	.05
338 Alan Mills	.01	.05
339 Steve Olin	.01	.05
340 Juan Berenguer	.01	.05
341 Francisco Cabrera	.01	.05
342 Dave Bergman	.01	.05
343 Henry Cotto	.01	.05
344 Sergio Valdez	.01	.05
345 Bob Patterson	.01	.05
346 John Marzano	.01	.05
347 Dana Kiecker	.01	.05
348 Dion James	.01	.05
349 Hubie Brooks	.01	.05
350 Bill Landrum	.01	.05
351 Bill Sampen	.01	.05
352 Greg Briley	.01	.05
353 Paul Gibson	.01	.05
354 Dave Eiland	.01	.05
355 Steve Finley	.02	.10
356 Bob Boone	.02	.10
357 Steve Buechele	.01	.05
358 Chris Hoiles FDC	.01	.05
359 Larry Walker	.08	.25
360 Frank DiPino	.01	.05
361 Mark Grant	.01	.05
362 Dave Magadan	.01	.05
363 Robby Thompson	.01	.05
364 Lonnie Smith	.01	.05
365 Steve Farr	.01	.05
366 Dave Valle	.01	.05
367 Tim Naehring	.01	.05
368 Jim Acker	.01	.05
369 Jeff Reardon UER	.02	.10
370 Tim Teufel	.01	.05
371 Juan Gonzalez	.08	.25
372 Luis Salazar	.01	.05
373 Rick Honeycutt	.01	.05
374 Greg Maddux	.15	.40
375 Jose Uribe UER	.01	.05
376 Donnie Hill	.01	.05
377 Don Carman	.01	.05
378 Craig Grebeck	.01	.05
379 Willie Fraser	.01	.05
380 Glenallen Hill	.01	.05
381 Joe Oliver	.01	.05
382 Randy Bush	.01	.05
383 Alex Cole	.01	.05
384 Norm Charlton	.01	.05
385 Gene Nelson	.01	.05
386 Checklist 256-331	.01	.05
387 Rickey Henderson MVP	.05	.15
388 Lance Parrish MVP	.01	.05
389 Fred McGriff MVP	.02	.10
390 Dave Parker MVP	.01	.05
391 Candy Maldonado MVP	.01	.05
392 Ken Griffey Jr. MVP	.10	.30
393 Gregg Olson MVP	.01	.05
394 Rafael Palmeiro MVP	.02	.10
395 Roger Clemens MVP	.15	.40
396 George Brett MVP	.08	.25
397 Cecil Fielder MVP	.01	.05
398 Brian Harper MVP UER	.01	.05
399 Bobby Thigpen MVP	.01	.05
400 Roberto Kelly MVP UER	.01	.05
401 Danny Darwin MVP	.01	.05
402 Dave Justice MVP	.01	.05
403 Lee Smith MVP	.01	.05
404 Ryne Sandberg MVP	.08	.25
405 Eddie Murray MVP	.05	.15
406 Tim Wallach MVP	.01	.05
407 Kevin Mitchell MVP	.01	.05
408 D. Strawberry MVP	.01	.05
409 Joe Carter MVP	.01	.05
410 Len Dykstra MVP	.01	.05
411 Doug Drabek MVP	.01	.05
412 Chris Sabo MVP	.01	.05
413 Paul Marak RR RC	.01	.05
414 Tim McIntosh RR	.01	.05
415 Brian Barnes RR RC	.02	.10
416 Eric Gunderson RR	.01	.05
417 Mike Gardiner RR RC	.01	.05
418 Steve Carter RR	.01	.05
419 Gerald Alexander RR RC	.01	.05
420 Rich Garces RR RC	.02	.10
421 Chuck Knoblauch RR	.02	.10
422 Scott Aldred RR	.01	.05
423 Wes Chamberlain RR RC	.08	.25
424 Lance Dickson RR RC	.02	.10
425 Greg Colbrunn RR RC	.08	.25
426 Rich DeLucia RR UER RC	.01	.05
427 Jeff Conine RR RC	.15	.40
428 Steve Decker RR RC	.01	.05
429 Turner Ward RR RC	.08	.25
430 Mo Vaughn RR	.02	.10
431 Steve Chitren RR RC	.01	.05
432 Mike Benjamin RR	.01	.05
433 Ryne Sandberg AS	.08	.25
434 Len Dykstra AS	.01	.05
435 Andre Dawson AS	.01	.05
436A Mike Scioscia AS White	.01	.05
436B Mike Scioscia AS Yellow	.01	.05
437 Ozzie Smith AS	.08	.25
438 Kevin Mitchell AS	.01	.05
439 Jack Armstrong AS	.01	.05
440 Chris Sabo AS	.01	.05
441 Will Clark AS	.02	.10
442 Mel Hall	.01	.05
443 Mark Gardner	.01	.05
444 Mike Devereaux	.01	.05
445 Kirk Gibson	.02	.10
446 Terry Pendleton	.02	.10
447 Mike Harkey	.01	.05
448 Jim Eisenreich	.01	.05
449 Benito Santiago	.02	.10
450 Oddibe McDowell	.01	.05
451 Cecil Fielder	.02	.10
452 Ken Griffey Sr.	.02	.10
453 Bert Blyleven	.02	.10
454 Howard Johnson	.01	.05
455 Monty Fariss UER	.01	.05
456 Tony Pena	.01	.05
457 Tim Raines	.02	.10
458 Dennis Rasmussen	.01	.05
459 Luis Quinones	.01	.05
460 B.J. Surhoff	.02	.10
461 Ernest Riles	.01	.05
462 Rick Sutcliffe	.02	.10
463 Danny Tartabull	.01	.05
464 Pete Incaviglia	.01	.05
465 Carlos Martinez	.01	.05
466 Ricky Jordan	.01	.05
467 John Cerutti	.01	.05
468 Dave Winfield	.02	.10
469 Francisco Oliveras	.01	.05
470 Roy Smith	.01	.05
471 Barry Larkin	.05	.15
472 Ron Darling	.01	.05
473 David Wells	.02	.10
474 Glenn Davis	.01	.05
475 Neal Heaton	.01	.05
476 Ron Hassey	.01	.05
477 Frank Thomas	.08	.25
478 Greg Vaughn	.01	.05
479 Todd Burns	.01	.05
480 Candy Maldonado	.01	.05
481 Dave LaPoint	.01	.05
482 Alvin Davis	.01	.05
483 Mike Scott	.01	.05
484 Dale Murphy	.05	.15
485 Ben McDonald	.01	.05
486 Jay Howell	.01	.05
487 Vince Coleman	.01	.05
488 Alfredo Griffin	.01	.05
489 Sandy Alomar Jr.	.01	.05
490 Kirby Puckett	.08	.25
491 Andres Thomas	.01	.05
492 Jack Morris	.02	.10
493 Matt Young	.01	.05
494 Greg Myers	.01	.05
495 Barry Bonds	.40	1.00
496 Scott Cooper UER	.01	.05
497 Dan Schatzeder	.01	.05
498 Jesse Barfield	.01	.05
499 Jerry Goff	.01	.05
500 Checklist 332-408	.01	.05
501 Anthony Telford RC	.01	.05
502 Eddie Murray	.08	.25
503 Omar Olivares RC	.08	.25
504 Ryne Sandberg	.15	.40
505 Jeff Montgomery	.01	.05
506 Mark Parent	.01	.05
507 Ron Gant	.02	.10
508 Frank Tanana	.01	.05
509 Jay Buhner	.02	.10
510 Max Venable	.01	.05
511 Wally Whitehurst	.01	.05
512 Gary Pettis	.01	.05
513 Tom Brunansky	.01	.05
514 Tim Wallach	.01	.05
515 Craig Lefferts	.01	.05
516 Tim Layana	.01	.05
517 Darryl Hamilton	.01	.05
518 Rick Reuschel	.01	.05
519 Steve Wilson	.01	.05
520 Kurt Stillwell	.01	.05
521 Rafael Palmeiro	.05	.15
522 Ken Patterson	.01	.05
523 Len Dykstra	.02	.10
524 Tony Fernandez	.01	.05
525 Kent Anderson	.01	.05
526 Mark Leonard RC	.01	.05
527 Allan Anderson	.01	.05
528 Tom Browning	.01	.05
529 Frank Viola	.02	.10
530 John Olerud	.02	.10
531 Juan Agosto	.01	.05
532 Zane Smith	.01	.05
533 Scott Sanderson	.01	.05
534 Barry Jones	.01	.05
535 Mike Felder	.01	.05
536 Jose Canseco	.05	.15
537 Felix Fermin	.01	.05
538 Roberto Kelly	.01	.05
539 Brian Holman	.01	.05
540 Mark Davidson	.01	.05
541 Terry Mulholland	.01	.05
542 Randy Milligan	.01	.05
543 Jose Gonzalez	.01	.05
544 Craig Wilson RC	.01	.05
545 Mike Hartley	.01	.05
546 Greg Swindell	.01	.05
547 Gary Gaetti	.02	.10
548 Dave Justice	.02	.10
549 Steve Searcy	.01	.05
550 Erik Hanson	.01	.05
551 Dave Stieb	.01	.05
552 Andy Van Slyke	.05	.15
553 Mike Greenwell	.01	.05
554 Kevin Maas	.01	.05
555 Delino DeShields	.02	.10
556 Curt Schilling	.08	.25
557 Ramon Martinez	.01	.05
558 Pedro Guerrero	.02	.10
559 Dwight Smith	.01	.05
560 Mark Davis	.01	.05
561 Shawn Abner	.01	.05
562 Charlie Leibrandt	.01	.05
563 John Shelby	.01	.05
564 Bill Swift	.01	.05
565 Mike Fetters	.01	.05
566 Alejandro Pena	.01	.05
567 Ruben Sierra	.02	.10
568 Carlos Quintana	.01	.05
569 Kevin Gross	.01	.05
570 Derek Lilliquist	.01	.05
571 Jack Armstrong	.01	.05
572 Greg Brock	.01	.05
573 Mike Kingery	.01	.05
574 Greg Smith	.01	.05
575 Brian McRae RC	.08	.25
576 Jack Daugherty	.01	.05
577 Ozzie Guillen	.02	.10
578 Joe Boever	.01	.05
579 Luis Sojo	.01	.05
580 Chili Davis	.02	.10
581 Don Robinson	.01	.05
582 Brian Harper	.01	.05

583 Paul O'Neill .05 .15
584 Bob Ojeda .01 .05
585 Mookie Wilson .02 .10
586 Rafael Ramirez .01 .05
587 Gary Redus .01 .05
588 Jamie Quirk .01 .05
589 Shawn Hillegas .01 .05
590 Tom Edens RC .01 .05
591 Joe Klink .01 .05
592 Charles Nagy .01 .05
593 Eric Plunk .01 .05
594 Tracy Jones .01 .05
595 Craig Biggio .05 .15
596 Jose DeJesus .01 .05
597 Mickey Tettleton .01 .05
598 Chris Gwynn .01 .05
599 Rex Hudler .01 .05
600 Checklist 409-506 .01 .05
601 Jim Gott .01 .05
602 Jeff Manto .01 .05
603 Nelson Liriano .01 .05
604 Mark Lemke .01 .05
605 Clay Parker .01 .05
606 Edgar Martinez .05 .15
607 Mark Whiten .01 .05
608 Ted Power .01 .05
609 Tom Bolton .01 .05
610 Tom Herr .01 .05
611 Andy Hawkins UER .01 .05
612 Scott Ruskin .01 .05
613 Ron Kittle .01 .05
614 John Wetteland .02 .10
615 Mike Perez RC .02 .10
616 Dave Clark .01 .05
617 Brent Mayne .01 .05
618 Jack Clark .02 .10
619 Marvin Freeman .01 .05
620 Edwin Nunez .01 .05
621 Russ Swan .01 .05
622 Johnny Ray .01 .05
623 Charlie O'Brien .01 .05
624 Joe Bitker RC .01 .05
625 Mike Marshall .01 .05
626 Otis Nixon .01 .05
627 Andy Benes .01 .05
628 Ron Oester .01 .05
629 Ted Higuera .01 .05
630 Kevin Bass .01 .05
631 Damon Berryhill .01 .05
632 Bo Jackson .08 .25
633 Brad Arnsberg .01 .05
634 Jerry Willard .01 .05
635 Tommy Greene .01 .05
636 Bob MacDonald RC .01 .05
637 Kirk McCaskill .01 .05
638 John Burkett .01 .05
639 Paul Abbott RC .01 .05
640 Todd Benzinger .01 .05
641 Todd Hundley .01 .05
642 George Bell .01 .05
643 Javier Ortiz .01 .05
644 Sid Bream .01 .05
645 Bob Welch .01 .05
646 Phil Bradley .01 .05
647 Bill Krueger .01 .05
648 Rickey Henderson .08 .25
649 Kevin Wickander .01 .05
650 Steve Balboni .01 .05
651 Gene Harris .01 .05
652 Jim Deshaies .01 .05
653 Jason Grimsley .01 .05
654 Joe Orsulak .01 .05
655 Jim Poole .01 .05
656 Felix Jose .01 .05
657 Denis Cook .01 .05
658 Tom Brookens .01 .05
659 Junior Ortiz .01 .05
660 Jeff Parrett .01 .05
661 Jerry Don Gleaton .01 .05
662 Brent Knackert .01 .05
663 Rance Mulliniks .01 .05
664 John Smiley .01 .05
665 Larry Andersen .01 .05
666 Willie McGee .02 .10
667 Chris Nabholz .01 .05
668 Brady Anderson .02 .10
669 Darren Holmes UER RC .08 .25
670 Ken Hill .01 .05
671 Gary Varsho .01 .05
672 Bill Pecota .01 .05
673 Fred Lynn .01 .05
674 Kevin D. Brown .01 .05
675 Dan Petry .01 .05
676 Mike Jackson .01 .05
677 Wally Joyner .02 .10
678 Danny Jackson .01 .05
679 Bill Haselman RC .01 .05
680 Mike Boddicker .01 .05
681 Mel Rojas .01 .05
682 Roberto Alomar .05 .15
683 Dave Justice ROY .01 .05
684 Chuck Crim .01 .05
685 Matt Williams .02 .10
686 Shawon Dunston .01 .05
687 Jeff Schulz RC .01 .05
688 John Barfield .01 .05
689 Gerald Young .01 .05
690 Luis Gonzalez RC .20 .50
691 Frank Wills .01 .05
692 Chuck Finley .02 .10
693 Sandy Alomar Jr. ROY .01 .05
694 Tim Drummond .01 .05
695 Herm Winningham .01 .05
696 Darryl Strawberry .02 .10
697 Al Leiter .02 .10
698 Karl Rhodes .01 .05
699 Stan Belinda .01 .05
700 Checklist 507-604 .01 .05
701 Lance Blankenship .01 .05
702 Willie Stargell PUZ .05 .15
703 Jim Gantner .01 .05
704 Reggie Harris .01 .05
705 Rob Ducey .01 .05
706 Tim Hulett .01 .05
707 Atlee Hammaker .01 .05
708 Xavier Hernandez .01 .05
709 Chuck McElroy .01 .05
710 John Mitchell .01 .05
711 Carlos Hernandez .01 .05
712 Geronimo Pena .01 .05
713 Jim Neidlinger RC .01 .05
714 John Orton .01 .05
715 Terry Leach .01 .05
716 Mike Stanton .01 .05
717 Walt Terrell .01 .05
718 Luis Aquino .01 .05
719 Bud Black UER .01 .05
720 Bob Kipper .01 .05
721 Jeff Gray RC .01 .05
722 Jose Rijo .01 .05
723 Curt Young .01 .05
724 Jose Vizcaino .01 .05
725 Randy Tomlin RC .02 .10
726 Junior Noboa .01 .05
727 Bob Welch CY .01 .05
728 Gary Ward .01 .05
729 Rob Deer UER .01 .05
730 David Segui .01 .05
731 Mark Carreon .01 .05
732 Vicente Palacios .01 .05
733 Sam Horn .01 .05
734 Howard Farmer .01 .05
735 Ken Dayley UER .01 .05
736 Kelly Mann .01 .05
737 Joe Grahe RC .02 .10
738 Kelly Downs .01 .05
739 Jimmy Kremers .01 .05
740 Kevin Appier .02 .10
741 Jeff Reed .01 .05
742 Jose Rijo WS .01 .05
743 Dave Rohde .01 .05
744 L.Dykstra/D.Murphy UER .05 .15
745 Paul Sorrento .01 .05
746 Thomas Howard .01 .05
747 Matt Stark RC .01 .05
748 Harold Baines .02 .10
749 Doug Dascenzo .01 .05
750 Doug Drabek CY .01 .05
751 Gary Sheffield .02 .10
752 Terry Lee RC .01 .05
753 Jim Vatcher RC .01 .05
754 Lee Stevens .01 .05
755 Randy Veres .01 .05
756 Bill Doran .01 .05
757 Gary Wayne .01 .05
758 Pedro Munoz RC .02 .10
759 Chris Hammond FDC .01 .05
760 Checklist 605-702 .01 .05
761 Rickey Henderson MVP .05 .15
762 Barry Bonds MVP .20 .50
763 Billy Hatcher WS UER .01 .05
764 Julio Machado .01 .05
765 Jose Mesa .01 .05
766 Willie Randolph WS .01 .05
767 Scott Erickson .01 .05
768 Travis Fryman .02 .10
769 Rich Rodriguez RC .01 .05
770 Checklist 703-770 .01 .05
BC1-BC22
793 Bozo T. Clown

1991 Donruss Bonus Cards

COMPLETE SET (22) .60 1.50
RANDOM INSERTS IN PACKS
BC1 M.Langston/M.Witt .01 .05
BC2 Randy Johnson .10 .30
BC3 Nolan Ryan NH .40 1.00
BC4 Dave Stewart .02 .10
BC5 Cecil Fielder .02 .10
BC6 Carlton Fisk .05 .15
BC7 Ryne Sandberg .15 .40
BC8 Gary Carter .02 .10
BC9 Mark McGwire UER .30 .75
BC10 Bo Jackson .08 .25
BC11 Fernando Valenzuela .02 .10
BC12A Andy Hawkins ERR .01 .05
BC12B Andy Hawkins COR .01 .05
BC13 Melido Perez .01 .05
BC14 Terry Mulholland UER .01 .05
BC15 Nolan Ryan 300W .40 1.00
BC16 Delino DeShields .02 .10
BC17 Cal Ripken .30 .75
BC18 Eddie Murray .08 .25
BC19 George Brett .25 .60
BC20 Bobby Thigpen .01 .05
BC21 Dave Stieb .01 .05
BC22 Willie McGee .02 .10

1991 Donruss Elite

RANDOM INSERTS IN PACKS
STATED PRINT RUN 10,000 SERIAL #'d SETS
1 Barry Bonds 12.00 30.00
2 George Brett 20.00 50.00
3 Jose Canseco 12.00 30.00
4 Andre Dawson 10.00 25.00
5 Doug Drabek 12.00 30.00
6 Cecil Fielder 12.00 30.00
7 Rickey Henderson 20.00 50.00
8 Matt Williams 10.00 25.00
L1 Nolan Ryan LGD/7500 40.00 100.00
S1 Ryne Sandberg AU/5000 100.00 250.00

1991 Donruss Grand Slammers

COMPLETE SET (14) .75 2.00
ONE SET PER FACTORY SET
1 Joe Carter .02 .10
2 Bobby Bonilla .02 .10
3 Kal Daniels .01 .05
4 Jose Canseco .05 .15
5 Barry Bonds .40 1.00
6 Jay Buhner .02 .10
7 Cecil Fielder .02 .10
8 Matt Williams .02 .10
9 Andres Galarraga .02 .10
10 Luis Polonia .01 .05
11 Mark McGwire .30 .75
12 Ron Karkovice .01 .05
13 Darryl Strawberry UER .02 .10
14 Mike Greenwell .01 .05

1991 Donruss Willie Stargell Puzzle

1 Stargell Puzzle 1-3 .10 .25
4 Stargell Puzzle 4-6 .10 .25
7 Stargell Puzzle 7-10 .10 .25
10 Stargell Puzzle 10-12 .10 .25
13 Stargell Puzzle 13-15 .10 .25
16 Stargell Puzzle 16-18 .10 .25
19 Stargell Puzzle 19-21 .10 .25
22 Stargell Puzzle 22-24 .10 .25
25 Stargell Puzzle 25-27 .10 .25
28 Stargell Puzzle 28-30 .10 .25
31 Stargell Puzzle 29-31 .10 .25
34 Stargell Puzzle 34-36 .10 .25
37 Stargell Puzzle 37-39 .10 .25
40 Stargell Puzzle 40-42 .10 .25
43 Stargell Puzzle 43-45 .10 .25
46 Stargell Puzzle 46-48 .10 .25
49 Stargell Puzzle 49-51 .10 .25
52 Stargell Puzzle 52-54 .10 .25
55 Stargell Puzzle 55-57 .10 .25
58 Stargell Puzzle 58-60 .10 .25
61 Stargell Puzzle 61-63 .10 .25

1991 Donruss Rookies

The 56-card 1991 Donruss Rookies set was issued exclusively in factory set form through hobby dealers. The cards measure the standard size and a mini puzzle featuring Hall of Famer Willie Stargell was included with the set. The fronts feature color action player photos, with white and red borders. Rookie Cards include Jeff Bagwell and Ivan Rodriguez.

COMP.FACT.SET (56) 2.00 5.00
1 Pat Kelly RC .02 .10
2 Rich DeLucia .02 .10
3 Wes Chamberlain .02 .10
4 Scott Leius .02 .10
5 Darryl Kile .08 .25
6 Milt Cuyler .02 .10
7 Todd Van Poppel RC .02 .10
8 Ray Lankford .08 .25
9 Brian R.Hunter RC .08 .25
10 Tony Perezchica .02 .10
11 Ced Landrum RC .02 .10
12 Dave Burba RC .08 .25
13 Ramon Garcia RC .02 .10
14 Ed Sprague .02 .10
15 Warren Newson RC .02 .10
16 Paul Faries RC .02 .10
17 Luis Gonzalez .20 .50
18 Charles Nagy .02 .10
19 Chris Hammond .02 .10
20 Frank Castillo RC .08 .25
21 Pedro Munoz .02 .10
22 Orlando Merced RC .02 .10
23 Jose Melendez RC .02 .10
24 Kirk Dressendorfer RC .02 .10
25 Heathcliff Slocumb RC .08 .25
26 Doug Simons RC .02 .10
27 Mike Timlin RC .08 .25
28 Jeff Fassero RC .08 .25
29 Mark Leiter RC .02 .10
30 Jeff Bagwell RC .60 1.50
31 Brian McRae .08 .25
32 Mark Whiten .02 .10
33 Ivan Rodriguez RC .75 2.00
34 Wade Taylor RC .02 .10
35 Darren Lewis FDC .02 .10
36 Mo Vaughn .08 .25
37 Mike Remlinger .02 .10
38 Rick Wilkins RC .02 .10
39 Chuck Knoblauch .08 .25
40 Kevin Morton .02 .10
41 Carlos Rodriguez RC .02 .10
42 Mark Lewis .02 .10
43 Brent Mayne .02 .10
44 Chris Haney RC .02 .10
45 Denis Boucher RC .02 .10
46 Mike Gardiner .02 .10
47 Jeff Johnson RC .02 .10
48 Dean Palmer .08 .25
49 Chuck McElroy .02 .10
50 Chris Jones RC .02 .10
51 Scott Kamieniecki RC .02 .10
52 Al Osuna RC .02 .10
53 Rusty Meacham RC .02 .10
54 Chito Martinez RC .02 .10
55 Reggie Jefferson .02 .10
56 Checklist 1-56 .02 .10

1991 Donruss Super DK's

COMPLETE SET (26) 15.00 40.00
1 Dave Stieb .30 .75
2 Craig Biggio 1.00 2.50
3 Cecil Fielder .30 .75
4 Barry Bonds 4.00 10.00
5 Barry Larkin .60 1.50
6 Dave Parker .30 .75
7 Len Dykstra .30 .75
8 Bobby Thigpen .20 .50
9 Roger Clemens 3.00 8.00
10 Ron Gant .30 .75
11 Delino DeShields .30 .75
12 Roberto Alomar .60 1.50
13 Sandy Alomar Jr. .30 .75
14 Ryne Sandberg 2.50 6.00
15 Ramon Martinez .30 .75
16 Edgar Martinez .40 1.00
17 Dave Magadan .20 .50
18 Matt Williams .40 1.00
19 Rafael Palmeiro .60 1.50
20 Bob Welch .20 .50
21 Dave Righetti .20 .50
22 Brian Harper .20 .50
23 Gregg Olson .20 .50
24 Kurt Stillwell .20 .50
25 Pedro Guerrero .20 .50
26 Chuck Finley .30 .75

1992 Donruss Previews

COMPLETE SET (12) 100.00 200.00
1 Wade Boggs 6.00 15.00
2 Barry Bonds 10.00 25.00
3 Will Clark 5.00 12.00
4 Andre Dawson 5.00 12.00
5 Dennis Eckersley 6.00 15.00
6 Robin Ventura 3.00 8.00
7 Ken Griffey Jr. 15.00 40.00
8 Kelly Gruber 2.00 5.00
9 Ryan Klesko 4.00 10.00
10 Cal Ripken 20.00 50.00
11 Nolan Ryan 20.00 50.00
12 Todd Van Poppel 2.00 5.00

1992 Donruss

The 1992 Donruss set contains 784 standard-size cards issued in two separate series of 396. Cards were issued in first and second series foil wrapped packs in addition to hobby and retail factory sets. One of 21 different puzzle panels featuring Hall of Famer Rod Carew was inserted into each pack. The basic card design features glossy color player photos with white borders. Two-toned blue stripes overlay the top and bottom of the picture. Subsets include Rated Rookies (1-20, 397-421], All-Stars (21-30/422-431) and Highlights (33, 94, 154, 215, 276, 434, 495, 555, 616, 677). The only notable Rookie Card in the set features Scott Brosius.

COMPLETE SET (784) 4.00 10.00
COMP.HOBBY SET (788) 4.00 10.00
COMP.RETAIL SET (788) 4.00 10.00
COMPLETE SERIES 1 (396) 2.00 5.00
COMPLETE SERIES 2 (388) 2.00 5.00
COMP.CAREW PUZZLE .40 1.00
1 Mark Wohlers RR .01 .05
2 Wil Cordero .01 .05
3 Kyle Abbott RR .01 .05
4 Dave Nilsson .01 .05
5 Kenny Lofton .05 .15
6 Luis Mercedes RR .01 .05
7 Roger Salkeld RR .01 .05
8 Eddie Zosky RR .01 .05
9 Todd Van Poppel .01 .05
10 Frank Seminara RR RC .02 .10
11 Andy Ashby .01 .05
12 Reggie Jefferson RR .01 .05
13 Ryan Klesko .02 .10
14 Carlos Garcia .01 .05
15 John Ramos RR .01 .05
16 Eric Karros .02 .10
17 Patrick Lennon RR .01 .05
18 Eddie Taubensee RR RC .08 .25
19 Roberto Hernandez RR .01 .05
20 D.J. Dozier RR .01 .05
21 Dave Henderson AS .01 .05
22 Cal Ripken AS .15 .40
23 Wade Boggs AS .02 .10
24 Ken Griffey Jr. AS .10 .30
25 Jack Morris AS .01 .05
26 Danny Tartabull AS .01 .05
27 Cecil Fielder AS .01 .05
28 Roberto Alomar AS .02 .10
29 Sandy Alomar Jr. AS .01 .05
30 Rickey Henderson AS .05 .15
31 Ken Hill .01 .05
32 John Habyan .01 .05
33 Otis Nixon HL .01 .05
34 Tim Wallach .01 .05
35 Cal Ripken .30 .75
36 Gary Carter .02 .10
37 Juan Agosto .01 .05
38 Doug Dascenzo .01 .05
39 Kirk Gibson .02 .10
40 Benito Santiago .02 .10
41 Otis Nixon .01 .05
42 Andy Allanson .01 .05
43 Brian Holman .01 .05
44 Dick Schofield .01 .05
45 Dave Magadan .01 .05
46 Rafael Palmeiro .05 .15
47 Jody Reed .01 .05
48 Ivan Calderon .01 .05
49 Greg W. Harris .01 .05
50 Chris Sabo .01 .05
51 Paul Molitor .02 .10
52 Robby Thompson .01 .05
53 Dave Smith .01 .05
54 Mark Davis .01 .05
55 Kevin Brown .02 .10
56 Donn Pall .01 .05
57 Len Dykstra .02 .10
58 Roberto Alomar .05 .15
59 Jeff D. Robinson .01 .05
60 Willie McGee .02 .10
61 Jay Buhner .02 .10
62 Mike Pagliarulo .01 .05
63 Paul O'Neill .05 .15
64 Hubie Brooks .01 .05
65 Kelly Gruber .01 .05
66 Ken Caminiti .02 .10
67 Gary Redus .01 .05
68 Harold Baines .02 .10
69 Charlie Hough .02 .10
70 B.J. Surhoff .02 .10
71 Walt Weiss .01 .05
72 Shawn Hillegas .01 .05
73 Roberto Kelly .01 .05
74 Jeff Ballard .01 .05
75 Craig Biggio .05 .15
76 Pat Combs .01 .05
77 Jeff M. Robinson .01 .05
78 Tim Belcher .01 .05
79 Cris Carpenter .01 .05
80 Checklist 1-79 .01 .05
81 Steve Avery .01 .05
82 Chris James .01 .05
83 Brian Harper .01 .05
84 Charlie Leibrandt .01 .05
85 Mickey Tettleton .01 .05
86 Pete O'Brien .01 .05
87 Danny Darwin .01 .05
88 Bob Walk .01 .05
89 Jeff Reardon .02 .10
90 Bobby Rose .01 .05
91 Danny Jackson .01 .05
92 John Morris .01 .05
93 Bud Black .01 .05
94 Tommy Greene HL .01 .05
95 Rick Aguilera .02 .10
96 Gary Gaetti .02 .10
97 David Cone .02 .10
98 John Olerud .02 .10
99 Joel Skinner .01 .05
100 Jay Bell .02 .10
101 Bob Milacki .01 .05
102 Norm Charlton .01 .05
103 Chuck Crim .01 .05
104 Terry Steinbach .01 .05
105 Juan Samuel .01 .05
106 Steve Howe .01 .05
107 Rafael Belliard .01 .05
108 Joey Cora .01 .05
109 Tommy Greene .01 .05
110 Gregg Olson .01 .05
111 Frank Tanana .01 .05
112 Lee Smith .02 .10
113 Greg A. Harris .01 .05
114 Dwayne Henry .01 .05
115 Chili Davis .02 .10
116 Kent Mercker .01 .05
117 Brian Barnes .01 .05
118 Rich DeLucia .01 .05
119 Andre Dawson .02 .10
120 Carlos Baerga .01 .05
121 Mike LaValliere .01 .05
122 Jeff Gray .01 .05
123 Bruce Hurst .01 .05
124 Alvin Davis .01 .05
125 John Candelaria .01 .05
126 Matt Nokes .01 .05
127 George Bell .01 .05
128 Bret Saberhagen .02 .10
129 Jeff Russell .01 .05
130 Jim Abbott .05 .15
131 Bill Gullickson .01 .05
132 Todd Zeile .01 .05
133 Dave Winfield .02 .10
134 Wally Whitehurst .01 .05
135 Matt Williams .02 .10
136 Tom Browning .01 .05
137 Marquis Grissom .02 .10
138 Erik Hanson .01 .05
139 Rob Dibble .02 .10
140 Don August .01 .05
141 Tom Henke .01 .05
142 Dan Pasqua .01 .05
143 George Brett .25 .60
144 Jerald Clark .01 .05
145 Robin Ventura .02 .10
146 Dale Murphy .05 .15
147 Dennis Eckersley .02 .10
148 Eric Yelding .01 .05
149 Mario Diaz .01 .05
150 Casey Candaele .01 .05
151 Steve Olin .01 .05
152 Luis Salazar .01 .05
153 Kevin Maas .01 .05
154 Nolan Ryan HL .20 .50
155 Barry Jones .01 .05
156 Chris Hoiles .01 .05
157 Bob Ojeda .01 .05
158 Pedro Guerrero .02 .10
159 Paul Assenmacher .01 .05
160 Checklist 80-157 .01 .05
161 Mike Macfarlane .01 .05
162 Craig Lefferts .01 .05
163 Brian Hunter .01 .05
164 Alan Trammell .02 .10
165 Ken Griffey Jr. .20 .50
166 Lance Parrish .02 .10
167 Brian Downing .01 .05
168 John Barfield .01 .05
169 Jack Clark .02 .10
170 Chris Nabholz .01 .05
171 Tim Teufel .01 .05
172 Chris Hammond .01 .05
173 Robin Yount .15 .40
174 Dave Righetti .02 .10
175 Joe Girardi .01 .05
176 Mike Boddicker .01 .05
177 Dean Palmer .02 .10
178 Greg Hibbard .01 .05
179 Randy Ready .01 .05
180 Devon White .02 .10
181 Mark Eichhorn .01 .05
182 Mike Felder .01 .05
183 Joe Klink .01 .05
184 Steve Bedrosian .01 .05
185 Barry Larkin .05 .15
186 John Franco .02 .10
187 Ed Sprague .01 .05
188 Mark Portugal .01 .05
189 Jose Lind .01 .05
190 Bob Welch .01 .05
191 Alex Fernandez .01 .05
192 Gary Sheffield .02 .10
193 Rickey Henderson .08 .25
194 Rod Nichols .01 .05
195 Scott Kamieniecki .01 .05
196 Mike Flanagan .01 .05
197 Steve Finley .02 .10
198 Darren Daulton .02 .10
199 Leo Gomez .01 .05
200 Mike Morgan .01 .05
201 Bob Tewksbury .01 .05
202 Sid Bream .01 .05
203 Sandy Alomar Jr. .01 .05
204 Greg Gagne .01 .05
205 Juan Berenguer .01 .05
206 Cecil Fielder .02 .10
207 Randy Johnson .08 .25
208 Tony Pena .01 .05
209 Doug Drabek .01 .05
210 Wade Boggs .05 .15
211 Bryan Harvey .01 .05
212 Jose Vizcaino .01 .05
213 Alonzo Powell .01 .05
214 Will Clark .05 .15
215 Rickey Henderson HL .05 .15
216 Jack Morris .02 .10
217 Junior Felix .01 .05
218 Vince Coleman .01 .05
219 Jimmy Key .02 .10
220 Alex Cole .01 .05
221 Bill Landrum .01 .05
222 Randy Milligan .01 .05
223 Jose Rijo .01 .05
224 Greg Vaughn .01 .05
225 Dave Stewart .02 .10
226 Lenny Harris .01 .05
227 Scott Sanderson .01 .05
228 Jeff Blauser .01 .05
229 Ozzie Guillen .02 .10
230 John Kruk .02 .10
231 Bob Melvin .01 .05
232 Milt Cuyler .01 .05
233 Felix Jose .01 .05
234 Ellis Burks .02 .10
235 Pete Harnisch .01 .05
236 Kevin Tapani .01 .05
237 Terry Pendleton .02 .10
238 Mark Gardner .01 .05
239 Harold Reynolds .02 .10
240 Checklist 158-237 .01 .05
241 Mike Harkey .01 .05
242 Felix Fermin .01 .05
243 Barry Bonds .40 1.00
244 Roger Clemens .20 .50
245 Dennis Rasmussen .01 .05
246 Jose DeLeon .01 .05
247 Orel Hershiser .02 .10
248 Mel Hall .01 .05
249 Rick Wilkins .01 .05
250 Tom Gordon .01 .05
251 Kevin Reimer .01 .05
252 Luis Polonia .01 .05
253 Mike Henneman .01 .05
254 Tom Pagnozzi .01 .05
255 Chuck Finley .02 .10
256 Mackey Sasser .01 .05
257 John Burkett .01 .05
258 Hal Morris .01 .05
259 Larry Walker .05 .15
260 Bill Swift .01 .05
261 Joe Oliver .01 .05
262 Julio Machado .01 .05
263 Todd Stottlemyre .01 .05
264 Matt Merullo .01 .05
265 Brent Mayne .01 .05
266 Thomas Howard .01 .05
267 Lance Johnson .01 .05
268 Terry Mulholland .01 .05
269 Rick Honeycutt .01 .05
270 Luis Gonzalez .02 .10
271 Jose Guzman .01 .05
272 Jimmy Jones .01 .05
273 Mark Lewis .01 .05
274 Rene Gonzales .01 .05
275 Jeff Johnson .01 .05
276 Dennis Martinez HL .01 .05
277 Delino DeShields .01 .05
278 Sam Horn .01 .05
279 Kevin Gross .01 .05
280 Jose Oquendo .01 .05
281 Mark Grace .05 .15
282 Mark Gubicza .01 .05
283 Fred McGriff .05 .15
284 Ron Gant .02 .10
285 Lou Whitaker .02 .10
286 Edgar Martinez .05 .15
287 Ron Tingley .01 .05
288 Kevin McReynolds .01 .05
289 Ivan Rodriguez .08 .25
290 Mike Gardiner .01 .05
291 Chris Haney .01 .05
292 Darrin Jackson .01 .05
293 Bill Doran .01 .05
294 Ted Higuera .01 .05
295 Jeff Brantley .01 .05
296 Les Lancaster .01 .05
297 Jim Eisenreich .01 .05
298 Ruben Sierra .02 .10
299 Scott Radinsky .01 .05
300 Jose DeJesus .01 .05
301 Mike Timlin .01 .05
302 Luis Sojo .01 .05
303 Kelly Downs .01 .05
304 Scott Bankhead .01 .05
305 Pedro Munoz .01 .05
306 Scott Scudder .01 .05
307 Kevin Elster .01 .05
308 Duane Ward .01 .05
309 Darryl Kile .02 .10
310 Orlando Merced .01 .05
311 Dave Henderson .01 .05
312 Tim Raines .02 .10
313 Mark Lee .01 .05
314 Mike Gallego .01 .05
315 Charles Nagy .01 .05
316 Jesse Barfield .01 .05
317 Todd Frohwirth .01 .05
318 Al Osuna .01 .05
319 Darrin Fletcher .01 .05
320 Checklist 238-316 .01 .05
321 David Segui .01 .05
322 Stan Javier .01 .05
323 Bryn Smith .01 .05
324 Jeff Treadway .01 .05
325 Mark Whiten .01 .05
326 Kent Hrbek .02 .10
327 David Justice .02 .10
328 Tony Phillips .01 .05
329 Rob Murphy .01 .05
330 Kevin Morton .01 .05
331 John Smiley .01 .05
332 Luis Rivera .01 .05
333 Wally Joyner .02 .10
334 Heathcliff Slocumb .01 .05
335 Rick Cerone .01 .05
336 Mike Remlinger .01 .05
337 Mike Moore .01 .05
338 Lloyd McClendon .01 .05
339 Al Newman .01 .05
340 Kirk McCaskill .01 .05
341 Howard Johnson .01 .05
342 Greg Myers .01 .05
343 Kal Daniels .01 .05
344 Bernie Williams .05 .15
345 Shane Mack .01 .05
346 Gary Thurman .01 .05
347 Dante Bichette .02 .10
348 Mark McGwire .25 .60
349 Travis Fryman .02 .10
350 Ray Lankford .02 .10
351 Mike Jeffcoat .01 .05
352 Jack McDowell .01 .05
353 Mitch Williams .01 .05
354 Mike Devereaux .01 .05
355 Andres Galarraga .02 .10
356 Henry Cotto .01 .05
357 Scott Bailes .01 .05
358 Jeff Bagwell .08 .25
359 Scott Leius .01 .05
360 Zane Smith .01 .05
361 Bill Pecota .01 .05
362 Tony Fernandez .01 .05
363 Glenn Braggs .01 .05
364 Bill Spiers .01 .05
365 Vicente Palacios .01 .05
366 Tim Burke .01 .05
367 Randy Tomlin .01 .05
368 Kenny Rogers .02 .10
369 Brett Butler .02 .10
370 Pat Kelly .01 .05
371 Bip Roberts .01 .05
372 Gregg Jefferies .01 .05
373 Kevin Bass .01 .05
374 Ron Karkovice .01 .05
375 Paul Gibson .01 .05
376 Bernard Gilkey .01 .05
377 Dave Gallagher .01 .05
378 Bill Wegman .01 .05
379 Pat Borders .01 .05
380 Ed Whitson .01 .05
381 Gilberto Reyes .01 .05
382 Russ Swan .01 .05
383 Andy Van Slyke .05 .15
384 Wes Chamberlain .01 .05
385 Steve Chitren .01 .05
386 Greg Olson .01 .05
387 Brian McRae .01 .05
388 Rich Rodriguez .01 .05
389 Steve Decker .01 .05
390 Chuck Knoblauch .02 .10
391 Bobby Witt .01 .05
392 Eddie Murray .08 .25
393 Juan Gonzalez .05 .15
394 Scott Ruskin .01 .05
395 Jay Howell .01 .05
396 Checklist 317-396 .01 .05
397 Royce Clayton RR .01 .05
398 John Jaha RR RC .08 .25
399 Dan Wilson RR .01 .05
400 Archie Corbin .01 .05
401 Barry Manuel RR .01 .05
402 Kim Batiste RR .01 .05
403 Pat Mahomes RR RC .08 .25
404 Dave Fleming .01 .05
405 Jeff Juden RR .01 .05
406 Jim Thome .08 .25
407 Sam Militello RR .01 .05
408 Jeff Nelson RR RC .15 .40
409 Anthony Young .01 .05
410 Tino Martinez RR .05 .15
411 Jeff Mutis RR .01 .05
412 Rey Sanchez RR RC .08 .25
413 Chris Gardner RR .01 .05
414 John Vander Wal RR .01 .05
415 Reggie Sanders .02 .10
416 Brian Williams RR RC .02 .10
417 Mo Sanford RR .01 .05
418 David Weathers RR RC .15 .40
419 Hector Fajardo RR RC .02 .10
420 Steve Foster RR .01 .05
421 Lance Dickson RR .01 .05
422 Andre Dawson AS .01 .05
423 Ozzie Smith AS .08 .25
424 Chris Sabo AS .01 .05
425 Tony Gwynn AS .05 .15
426 Tom Glavine AS .02 .10
427 Bobby Bonilla AS .01 .05
428 Will Clark AS .02 .10
429 Ryne Sandberg AS .08 .25
430 Benito Santiago AS .01 .05
431 Ivan Calderon AS .01 .05
432 Ozzie Smith .15 .40
433 Tim Leary .01 .05
434 Bret Saberhagen HL .01 .05
435 Mel Rojas .01 .05
436 Ben McDonald .01 .05
437 Tim Crews .01 .05
438 Rex Hudler .01 .05
439 Chico Walker .01 .05
440 Kurt Stillwell .01 .05
441 Tony Gwynn .10 .30
442 John Smoltz .05 .15
443 Lloyd Moseby .01 .05
444 Mike Schooler .01 .05
445 Joe Grahe .01 .05
446 Dwight Gooden .02 .10
447 Oil Can Boyd .01 .05
448 John Marzano .01 .05
449 Bret Barberie .01 .05
450 Mike Maddux .01 .05
451 Jeff Reed .01 .05
452 Dale Sveum .01 .05
453 Jose Uribe .01 .05
454 Bob Scanlan .01 .05
455 Kevin Appier .02 .10
456 Jeff Huson .01 .05
457 Ken Patterson .01 .05
458 Ricky Jordan .01 .05
459 Tom Candiotti .01 .05
460 Lee Stevens .01 .05
461 Rod Beck RC .08 .25
462 Dave Valle .01 .05
463 Scott Erickson .01 .05
464 Chris Jones .01 .05
465 Mark Carreon .01 .05
466 Rob Ducey .01 .05
467 Jim Corsi .01 .05
468 Jeff King .01 .05
469 Curt Young .01 .05

470 Bo Jackson .08 .25
471 Chris Bosio .01 .05
472 Jamie Quirk .01 .05
473 Jesse Orosco .01 .05
474 Alvaro Espinoza .01 .05
475 Joe Orsulak .01 .05
476 Checklist 397-477 .01 .05
477 Gerald Young .01 .05
478 Wally Backman .01 .05
479 Juan Bell .01 .05
480 Mike Scioscia .01 .05
481 Omar Olivares .01 .05
482 Francisco Cabrera .01 .05
483 Greg Swindell UER (Shown on Indians& but listed .01 .05
484 Terry Leach .01 .05
485 Tommy Gregg .01 .05
486 Scott Aldred .01 .05
487 Greg Briley .01 .05
488 Phil Plantier .01 .05
489 Curtis Wilkerson .01 .05
490 Tom Brunansky .01 .05
491 Mike Fetters .01 .05
492 Frank Castillo .01 .05
493 Joe Boever .01 .05
494 Kirt Manwaring .01 .05
495 Wilson Alvarez HL .01 .05
496 Gene Larkin .01 .05
497 Gary DiSarcina .01 .05
498 Frank Viola .02 .10
499 Manuel Lee .01 .05
500 Albert Belle .02 .10
501 Stan Belinda .01 .05
502 Dwight Evans .05 .15
503 Eric Davis .02 .10
504 Darren Holmes .01 .05
505 Mike Bordick .01 .05
506 Dave Hansen .01 .05
507 Lee Guetterman .01 .05
508 Keith Mitchell .01 .05
509 Melido Perez .01 .05
510 Dickie Thon .01 .05
511 Mark Williamson .01 .05
512 Mark Salas .01 .05
513 Milt Thompson .01 .05
514 Mo Vaughn .02 .10
515 Jim Deshaies .01 .05
516 Rich Garces .01 .05
517 Lonnie Smith .01 .05
518 Spike Owen .01 .05
519 Tracy Jones .01 .05
520 Greg Maddux .15 .40
521 Carlos Martinez .01 .05
522 Neal Heaton .01 .05
523 Mike Greenwell .01 .05
524 Andy Benes .01 .05
525 Jeff Schaefer UER .01 .05
526 Mike Sharperson .01 .05
527 Wade Taylor .01 .05
528 Jerome Walton .01 .05
529 Storm Davis .01 .05
530 Jose Hernandez RC .08 .25
531 Mark Langston .01 .05
532 Rob Deer .01 .05
533 Geronimo Pena .01 .05
534 Juan Guzman .01 .05
535 Pete Schourek .01 .05
536 Todd Benzinger .01 .05
537 Billy Hatcher .01 .05
538 Tom Foley .01 .05
539 Dave Cochrane .01 .05
540 Mariano Duncan .01 .05
541 Edwin Nunez .01 .05
542 Rance Mulliniks .01 .05
543 Carlton Fisk .05 .15
544 Luis Aquino .01 .05
545 Ricky Bones .01 .05
546 Craig Grebeck .01 .05
547 Charlie Hayes .01 .05
548 Jose Canseco .05 .15
549 Andujar Cedeno .01 .05
550 Geno Petralli .01 .05
551 Javier Ortiz .01 .05
552 Rudy Seanez .01 .05
553 Rich Gedman .01 .05
554 Eric Plunk .01 .05
555 N.Ryan G.Gossage HL .15 .40
556 Checklist 478-555 .01 .05
557 Greg Colbrunn .01 .05
558 Chito Martinez .01 .05
559 Darryl Strawberry .02 .10
560 Luis Alicea .01 .05
561 Dwight Smith .01 .05
562 Terry Shumpert .01 .05
563 Jim Vatcher .01 .05
564 Deion Sanders .05 .15
565 Walt Terrell .01 .05
566 Dave Burba .01 .05
567 Dave Howard .01 .05
568 Todd Hundley .01 .05
569 Jack Daugherty .01 .05
570 Scott Cooper .01 .05
571 Bill Sampen .01 .05
572 Jose Melendez .01 .05
573 Freddie Benavides .01 .05
574 Jim Gantner .01 .05
575 Trevor Wilson .01 .05
576 Ryne Sandberg .15 .40
577 Kevin Seitzer .01 .05
578 Gerald Alexander .01 .05
579 Mike Huff .01 .05
580 Von Hayes .01 .05
581 Derek Bell .02 .10
582 Mike Stanley .01 .05
583 Kevin Mitchell .01 .05
584 Mike Jackson .01 .05
585 Dan Gladden .01 .05
586 Ted Power UER/(Wrong year given for.01 .05 signing with
587 Jeff Innis .01 .05
588 Bob MacDonald .01 .05
589 Jose Tolentino .01 .05
590 Bob Patterson .01 .05
591 Scott Brosius RC .15 .40
592 Frank Thomas .08 .25
593 Darryl Hamilton .01 .05
594 Kirk Dressendorfer .01 .05
595 Jeff Shaw .01 .05
596 Don Mattingly .25 .60
597 Glenn Davis .01 .05
598 Andy Mota .01 .05
599 Jason Grimsley .01 .05
600 Jim Poole .01 .05
601 Jim Gott .01 .05
602 Stan Royer .01 .05
603 Marvin Freeman .01 .05
604 Denis Boucher .01 .05
605 Denny Neagle .02 .10
606 Mark Lemke .01 .05
607 Jerry Don Gleaton .01 .05
608 Brent Knackert .01 .05
609 Carlos Quintana .01 .05
610 Bobby Bonilla .02 .10
611 Joe Hesketh .01 .05
612 Daryl Boston .01 .05
613 Shawon Dunston .01 .05
614 Danny Cox .01 .05
615 Darren Lewis .01 .05
616 Mercker/Pena/Wohlers UER .01 .05
617 Kirby Puckett .08 .25
618 Franklin Stubbs .01 .05
619 Chris Donnels .01 .05
620 David Wells UER .02 .10
621 Mike Aldrete .01 .05
622 Bob Kipper .01 .05
623 Anthony Telford .01 .05
624 Randy Myers .01 .05
625 Willie Randolph .02 .10
626 Joe Slusarski .01 .05
627 John Wetteland .02 .10
628 Greg Cadaret .01 .05
629 Tom Glavine .05 .15
630 Wilson Alvarez .01 .05
631 Wally Ritchie .01 .05
632 Mike Mussina .08 .25
633 Mark Leiter .01 .05
634 Gerald Perry .01 .05
635 Matt Young .01 .05
636 Checklist 556-635 .01 .05
637 Scott Hemond .01 .05
638 David West .01 .05
639 Jim Clancy .01 .05
640 Doug Piatt UER/(Not born in 1955 as.01 .05 on card; inc
641 Omar Vizquel .05 .15
642 Rick Sutcliffe .02 .10
643 Glenallen Hill .01 .05
644 Gary Varsho .01 .05
645 Tony Fossas .01 .05
646 Jack Howell .01 .05
647 Jim Campanis .01 .05
648 Chris Gwynn .01 .05
649 Jim Leyritz .01 .05
650 Chuck McElroy .01 .05
651 Sean Berry .01 .05
652 Donald Harris .01 .05
653 Don Slaught .01 .05
654 Rusty Meacham .01 .05
655 Scott Terry .01 .05
656 Ramon Martinez .01 .05
657 Keith Miller .01 .05
658 Ramon Garcia .01 .05
659 Milt Hill .01 .05
660 Steve Frey .01 .05
661 Bob McClure .01 .05
662 Ced Landrum .01 .05
663 Doug Henry RC .02 .10
664 Candy Maldonado .01 .05
665 Carl Willis .01 .05
666 Jeff Montgomery .01 .05
667 Craig Shipley .01 .05
668 Warren Newson .01 .05
669 Mickey Morandini .01 .05
670 Brook Jacoby .01 .05
671 Ryan Bowen .01 .05
672 Bill Krueger .01 .05
673 Rob Mallicoat .01 .05
674 Doug Jones .01 .05
675 Scott Livingstone .01 .05
676 Danny Tartabull .01 .05
677 Joe Carter HL .01 .05
678 Cecil Espy .01 .05
679 Randy Velarde .01 .05
680 Bruce Ruffin .01 .05
681 Ted Wood .01 .05
682 Dan Plesac .01 .05
683 Eric Bullock .01 .05
684 Junior Ortiz .01 .05
685 Dave Hollins .01 .05
686 Dennis Martinez .02 .10
687 Larry Andersen .01 .05
688 Doug Simons .01 .05
689 Tim Spehr .01 .05
690 Calvin Jones .01 .05
691 Mark Guthrie .01 .05
692 Alfredo Griffin .01 .05
693 Joe Carter .02 .10
694 Terry Mathews .01 .05
695 Pascual Perez .01 .05
696 Gene Nelson .01 .05
697 Gerald Williams .01 .05
698 Chris Cron .01 .05
699 Steve Buechele .01 .05
700 Paul McClellan .01 .05
701 Jim Lindeman .01 .05
702 Francisco Oliveras .01 .05
703 Rob Maurer RC .01 .05
704 Pat Hentgen .01 .05
705 Jaime Navarro .01 .05
706 Mike Magnante RC .02 .10
707 Nolan Ryan .40 1.00
708 Bobby Thigpen .01 .05
709 John Cerutti .01 .05
710 Steve Wilson .01 .05
711 Hensley Meulens .01 .05
712 Rheal Cormier .01 .05
713 Scott Bradley .01 .05
714 Mitch Webster .01 .05
715 Roger Mason .01 .05
716 Checklist 636-716 .01 .05
717 Jeff Fassero .01 .05
718 Cal Eldred .01 .05
719 Sid Fernandez .01 .05
720 Bob Zupcic RC .02 .10
721 Jose Offerman .01 .05
722 Cliff Brantley .01 .05
723 Ron Darling .01 .05
724 Dave Stieb .01 .05
725 Hector Villanueva .01 .05
726 Mike Hartley .01 .05
727 Arthur Rhodes .01 .05
728 Randy Bush .01 .05
729 Steve Sax .01 .05
730 Dave Otto .01 .05
731 John Wehner .01 .05
732 Dave Martinez .01 .05
733 Ruben Amaro .01 .05
734 Billy Ripken .01 .05
735 Steve Farr .01 .05
736 Shawn Abner .01 .05
737 Gil Heredia RC .08 .25
738 Ron Jones .01 .05
739 Tony Castillo .01 .05
740 Sammy Sosa .08 .25
741 Julio Franco .02 .10
742 Tim Naehring .01 .05
743 Steve Wapnick .01 .05
744 Craig Wilson .01 .05
745 Darrin Chapin .01 .05
746 Chris George .01 .05
747 Mike Simms .01 .05
748 Rosario Rodriguez .01 .05
749 Skeeter Barnes .01 .05
750 Roger McDowell .01 .05
751 Dann Howitt .01 .05
752 Paul Sorrento .01 .05
753 Braulio Castillo .01 .05
754 Yorkis Perez .01 .05
755 Willie Fraser .01 .05
756 Jeremy Hernandez RC .02 .10
757 Curt Schilling .05 .15
758 Steve Lyons .01 .05
759 Dave Anderson .01 .05
760 Willie Banks .01 .05
761 Mark Leonard .01 .05
762 Jack Armstrong/(Listed on Indians&.01 .05 but shown on
763 Scott Servais .01 .05
764 Ray Stephens .01 .05
765 Junior Noboa .01 .05
766 Jim Olander .01 .05
767 Joe Magrane .01 .05
768 Lance Blankenship .01 .05
769 Mike Humphreys .01 .05
770 Jarvis Brown .01 .05
771 Damon Berryhill .01 .05
772 Alejandro Pena .01 .05
773 Jose Mesa .01 .05
774 Gary Cooper .01 .05
775 Carney Lansford .02 .10
776 Mike Bielecki/(Shown on Cubs& .01 .05 but listed on Brav
777 Charlie O'Brien .01 .05
778 Carlos Hernandez .01 .05
779 Howard Farmer .01 .05
780 Mike Stanton .01 .05
781 Reggie Harris .01 .05
782 Xavier Hernandez .01 .05
783 Bryan Hickerson RC .02 .10
784 Checklist 717-784 and BC1-BC8 .01 .05

1992 Donruss Bonus Cards

COMPLETE SET (8) .75 2.00
RANDOM INSERTS IN FOIL PACKS
BC1 Cal Ripken MVP .30 .75
BC2 Terry Pendleton MVP .02 .10
BC3 Roger Clemens CY .20 .50
BC4 Tom Glavine CY .05 .15
BC5 Chuck Knoblauch ROY .02 .10
BC6 Jeff Bagwell ROY .08 .25
BC7 Colorado Rockies .01 .05
BC8 Florida Marlins .01 .05

1992 Donruss Diamond Kings

COMPLETE SET (27) 8.00 20.00
COMPLETE SERIES 1 (14) 8.00 20.00
COMPLETE SERIES 2 (13) 2.00 4.00
RANDOM INSERTS IN PACKS
DK1 Paul Molitor .30 .75
DK2 Will Clark .50 1.25
DK3 Joe Carter .30 .75
DK4 Julio Franco .30 .75
DK5 Cal Ripken 2.50 6.00
DK6 David Justice .30 .75
DK7 George Bell .15 .40
DK8 Frank Thomas .75 2.00
DK9 Wade Boggs .50 1.25
DK10 Scott Sanderson .15 .40
DK11 Jeff Bagwell .75 2.00
DK12 John Kruk .30 .75
DK13 Felix Jose .15 .40
DK14 Harold Baines .30 .75
DK15 Dwight Gooden .30 .75
DK16 Brian McRae .15 .40
DK17 Jay Bell .30 .75
DK18 Brett Butler .30 .75
DK19 Hal Morris .15 .40
DK20 Mark Langston .15 .40
DK21 Scott Erickson .15 .40
DK22 Randy Johnson .75 2.00
DK23 Greg Swindell .15 .40
DK24 Dennis Martinez .30 .75
DK25 Tony Phillips .15 .40
DK26 Fred McGriff .50 1.25
DK27 Checklist 1-26 DP/(Dick Perez) .15 .40

1992 Donruss Elite

RANDOM INSERTS IN PACKS
STATED PRINT RUN 10,000 SERIAL #'d SETS
9 Wade Boggs 15.00 40.00
10 Joe Carter 10.00 25.00
11 Will Clark 12.50 30.00
12 Dwight Gooden 15.00 40.00
13 Ken Griffey Jr. 75.00 200.00
14 Tony Gwynn 15.00 40.00
15 Howard Johnson 20.00 50.00
16 Terry Pendleton 10.00 25.00
17 Kirby Puckett 20.00 50.00
18 Frank Thomas 25.00 60.00
L2 R.Henderson LGD/7500 30.00 80.00
S2 Cal Ripken AU/5000 175.00 350.00

1992 Donruss Rod Carew Puzzle

1 Carew Puzzle 1-3 .10 .25
4 Carew Puzzle 4-6 .10 .25
7 Carew Puzzle 7-10 .10 .25
10 Carew Puzzle 10-12 .10 .25
13 Carew Puzzle 13-15 .10 .25
16 Carew Puzzle 16-18 .10 .25
19 Carew Puzzle 19-21 .10 .25
22 Carew Puzzle 22-24 .10 .25
25 Carew Puzzle 25-27 .10 .25
28 Carew Puzzle 28-30 .10 .25
31 Carew Puzzle 31-33 .10 .25
34 Carew Puzzle 34-36 .10 .25
37 Carew Puzzle 37-39 .10 .25
40 Carew Puzzle 40-42 .10 .25
43 Carew Puzzle 43-45 .10 .25
46 Carew Puzzle 46-48 .10 .25
49 Carew Puzzle 49-51 .10 .25
52 Carew Puzzle 52-54 .10 .25
55 Carew Puzzle 55-57 .10 .25
58 Carew Puzzle 58-60 .10 .25
61 Carew Puzzle 61-63 .10 .25

1992 Donruss Update

COMPLETE SET (22) 20.00 50.00
FOUR PER RETAIL FACTORY SET
U1 Pat Listach .60 1.50
U2 Andy Stankiewicz .40 1.00
U3 Brian Jordan 1.00 2.50
U4 Dan Walters RR .40 1.00
U5 Chad Curtis .60 1.50
U6 Kenny Lofton .60 1.50
U7 Mark McGwire HL 4.00 10.00
U8 Eddie Murray HL 1.50 4.00
U9 Jeff Reardon HL .60 1.50
U10 Frank Viola .60 1.50
U11 Gary Sheffield .60 1.50
U12 George Bell .40 1.00
U13 Rick Sutcliffe .60 1.50
U14 Wally Joyner .60 1.50
U15 Kevin Seitzer .40 1.00
U16 Bill Krueger .40 1.00
U17 Danny Tartabull .40 1.00
U18 Dave Winfield .60 1.50
U19 Gary Carter .60 1.50
U20 Bobby Bonilla .60 1.50
U21 Cory Snyder .40 1.00
U22 Bill Swift .40 1.00

1992 Donruss Rookies

After six years of issuing "The Rookies" as a 56-card boxed set, Donruss expanded it to a 132-card standard-size set and distributed the cards in hobby and retail foil packs. The card design is the same as the 1992 Donruss regular issue except that the two-tone blue color bars have been replaced by green, as in the previous six Donruss Rookies sets. The cards are arranged in alphabetical order and numbered on the back. Rookie Cards in this set include Jeff Kent, Manny Ramirez and Eric Young. In addition an early card of Pedro Martinez is featured.

COMPLETE SET (132) 4.00 10.00
1 Kyle Abbott .01 .05
2 Troy Afenir .01 .05
3 Rich Amaral RC .02 .10
4 Ruben Amaro .01 .05
5 Billy Ashley RC .02 .10
6 Pedro Astacio RC .08 .25
7 Jim Austin .01 .05
8 Robert Ayrault .01 .05
9 Kevin Baez .01 .05
10 Esteban Beltre .01 .05
11 Brian Bohanon .01 .05
12 Kent Bottenfield RC .08 .25
13 Jeff Branson .01 .05
14 Brad Brink .01 .05
15 John Briscoe .01 .05
16 Doug Brocail RC .02 .10
17 Rico Brogna .01 .05
18 J.T. Bruett .01 .05
19 Jacob Brumfield .01 .05
20 Jim Bullinger .01 .05
21 Kevin Campbell .01 .05
22 Pedro Castellano RC .02 .10
23 Mike Christopher .01 .05
24 Archi Cianfrocco RC .02 .10
25 Mark Clark RC .02 .10
26 Craig Colbert .01 .05
27 Victor Cole RC .01 .05
28 Steve Cooke RC .02 .10
29 Tim Costo .01 .05
30 Chad Curtis RC .08 .25
31 Doug Davis .01 .05
32 Gary DiSarcina .01 .05
33 John Doherty RC .02 .10
34 Mike Draper .01 .05
35 Monty Fariss .01 .05
36 Bien Figueroa .01 .05
37 John Flaherty RC .01 .05
38 Tim Fortugno .01 .05
39 Eric Fox RC .02 .10
40 Jeff Frye RC .02 .10
41 Ramon Garcia .01 .05
42 Brent Gates RC .02 .10
43 Tom Goodwin .01 .05
44 Buddy Groom RC .02 .10
45 Jeff Grotewold .01 .05
46 Juan Guerrero .01 .05
47 Johnny Guzman RC .02 .10
48 Shawn Hare RC .02 .10
49 Ryan Hawblitzel RC .02 .10
50 Bert Hefferman .01 .05
51 Butch Henry .01 .05
52 Cesar Hernandez RC .02 .10
53 Vince Horsman .01 .05
54 Steve Hosey .01 .05
55 Pat Howell .01 .05
56 Peter Hoy .01 .05
57 Jonathan Hurst RC .02 .10
58 Mark Hutton RC .02 .10
59 Shawn Jeter RC .02 .10
60 Joel Johnston .01 .05
61 Jeff Kent RC 1.00 2.50
62 Kurt Knudsen RC .02 .10
63 Kevin Koslofski .01 .05
64 Danny Leon .01 .05
65 Jesse Levis .01 .05
66 Tom Marsh RC .01 .05
67 Ed Martel .01 .05
68 Al Martin RC .08 .25
69 Pedro Martinez .75 2.00
70 Derrick May .01 .05
71 Matt Maysey .01 .05
72 Russ McGinnis .01 .05
73 Tim McIntosh .01 .05
74 Jim McNamara .01 .05
75 Jeff McNeely .01 .05
76 Rusty Meacham .01 .05
77 Tony Menendez .01 .05
78 Henry Mercedes .01 .05
79 Paul Miller .01 .05
80 Joe Millette .01 .05
81 Blas Minor .01 .05
82 Dennis Moeller .01 .05
83 Raul Mondesi .02 .10
84 Rob Natal .01 .05
85 Troy Neel RC .02 .10
86 David Nied RC .02 .10
87 Jerry Nielson .01 .05
88 Donovan Osborne .01 .05
89 John Patterson RC .02 .10
90 Roger Pavlik RC .02 .10
91 Dan Peltier .01 .05
92 Jim Pena .01 .05
93 William Pennyfeather .01 .05
94 Mike Perez .01 .05
95 Hipolito Pichardo RC .02 .10
96 Greg Pirkl RC .02 .10
97 Harvey Pulliam .01 .05
98 Manny Ramirez RC 1.50 4.00
99 Pat Rapp RC .02 .10
100 Jeff Reboulet .01 .05
101 Darren Reed .01 .05
102 Shane Reynolds RC .08 .25
103 Bill Risley .01 .05
104 Ben Rivera .01 .05
105 Henry Rodriguez .01 .05
106 Rico Rossy .01 .05
107 Johnny Ruffin .01 .05
108 Steve Scarsone .01 .05
109 Tim Scott .01 .05
110 Steve Shifflett .01 .05
111 Dave Silvestri .01 .05
112 Matt Stairs RC .08 .25
113 William Suero .01 .05
114 Jeff Tackett .01 .05
115 Eddie Taubensee .02 .10
116 Rick Trlicek RC .02 .10
117 Scooter Tucker .01 .05
118 Shane Turner .01 .05
119 Julio Valera .01 .05
120 Paul Wagner RC .02 .10
121 Tim Wakefield RC 1.25 3.00
122 Mike Walker .01 .05
123 Bruce Walton .01 .05
124 Lenny Webster .01 .05
125 Bob Wickman .08 .25
126 Mike Williams RC .08 .25
127 Kerry Woodson .01 .05
128 Eric Young RC .08 .25
129 Kevin Young RC .08 .25
130 Pete Young .01 .05
131 Checklist 1-66 .01 .05
132 Checklist 67-132 .01 .05

1992 Donruss Rookies Phenoms

COMP.FOIL SET (12) 12.50 30.00
COMP.JUMBO SET (8) 5.00 10.00
COMMON FOIL (BC1-BC12) .40 1.00
FOIL: RANDOM INSERTS IN PACKS
COMMON JUMBO (BC13-BC20) .40 1.00
JUMBOS: ONE PER JUMBO PACK
BC1 Moises Alou .60 1.50
BC2 Bret Boone .60 1.50
BC3 Jeff Conine .60 1.50
BC4 Dave Fleming .40 1.00
BC5 Tyler Green .40 1.00
BC6 Eric Karros .60 1.50
BC7 Pat Listach .60 1.50
BC8 Kenny Lofton .60 1.50
BC9 Mike Piazza 6.00 15.00
BC10 Tim Salmon .60 1.50
BC11 Andy Stankiewicz .40 1.00
BC12 Dan Walters .40 1.00
BC13 Ramon Caraballo .40 1.00
BC14 Brian Jordan .60 1.50
BC15 Ryan Klesko .60 1.50
BC16 Sam Militello .40 1.00
BC17 Frank Seminara .40 1.00
BC18 Salomon Torres .40 1.00
BC19 John Valentin .60 1.50
BC20 Wil Cordero .40 1.00

1992 Donruss Coke Ryan

COMPLETE SET (26) 4.00 10.00
COMMON PLAYER (1-26) .20 .50

1992 Donruss Cracker Jack I

COMPLETE SET (36) 4.00 10.00
1 Dennis Eckersley .20 .50
2 Jeff Bagwell .40 1.00
3 Jim Abbott .02 .10
4 Steve Avery .01 .05
5 Kelly Gruber .01 .05
6 Ozzie Smith .40 1.00
7 Lance Dickson .01 .05
8 Robin Yount .20 .50
9 Brett Butler .02 .10
10 Sandy Alomar Jr. .02 .10
11 Travis Fryman .02 .10
12 Ken Griffey Jr. .75 2.00
13 Cal Ripken 1.00 2.50
14 Will Clark .08 .25
15 Nolan Ryan 1.00 2.50
16 Tony Gwynn .40 1.00
17 Roger Clemens .50 1.25
18 Wes Chamberlain .01 .05
19 Barry Larkin .07 .20
20 Brian McRae .01 .05
21 Marquis Grissom .02 .10
22 Cecil Fielder .02 .10
23 Dwight Gooden .02 .10
24 Chuck Knoblauch .07 .20
25 Jose Canseco .20 .50
26 Terry Pendleton .01 .05
27 Ivan Rodriguez .40 1.00
28 Ryne Sandberg .20 .50
29 Kent Hrbek .02 .10
30 Ramon Martinez .02 .10
31 Todd Zeile .02 .10
32 Hal Morris .01 .05
33 Robin Ventura .07 .20
34 Doug Drabek .01 .05
35 Frank Thomas .20 .50
36 Don Mattingly .50 1.25

1992 Donruss Cracker Jack II

COMPLETE SET (36) 2.50 6.00
1 Craig Biggio .05 .15
2 Tom Glavine .02 .10
3 David Justice .08 .25
4 Lee Smith .02 .10
5 Mark Grace .08 .25
6 Andre Dawson .08 .25
7 Darryl Strawberry .02 .10
8 Eric Davis .02 .10
9 Ivan Calderon .01 .05
10 Royce Clayton .01 .05
11 Matt Williams .05 .15
12 Fred McGriff .05 .15
13 Len Dykstra .02 .10
14 Barry Bonds .40 1.00
15 Reggie Sanders .02 .10
16 Chris Sabo .01 .05
17 Howard Johnson .01 .05
18 Bobby Bonilla .01 .05
19 Rickey Henderson .30 .75
20 Mark Langston .01 .05
21 Joe Carter .02 .10
22 Paul Molitor .20 .50
23 Glenallen Hill .01 .05
24 Edgar Martinez .05 .15
25 Gregg Olson .01 .05
26 Ruben Sierra .02 .10
27 Julio Franco .02 .10
28 Phil Plantier .01 .05
29 Wade Boggs .15 .40
30 George Brett .40 1.00
31 Alan Trammell .05 .15
32 Kirby Puckett .20 .50
33 Scott Erickson .01 .05
34 Jack McDowell .05 .15
35 Matt Nokes .01 .05
36 Danny Tartabull .01 .05

1992 Donruss McDonald's

COMPLETE SET (33) 6.00 15.00
COMMON PLAYER (1-26) .04 .10
COMMON PLAYER (G1-G6) .20 .50
1 Cal Ripken 1.00 2.50
2 Frank Thomas .20 .50
3 George Brett .50 1.25
4 Roberto Kelly .02 .10
5 Nolan Ryan 1.00 2.50
6 Ryne Sandberg .30 .75
7 Darryl Strawberry .07 .20
8 Len Dykstra .07 .20
9 Fred McGriff .10 .30
10 Roger Clemens .50 1.25
11 Sandy Alomar Jr. .07 .20
12 Robin Yount .20 .50
13 Jose Canseco .30 .75
14 Jimmy Key .07 .20
15 Barry Larkin .15 .40
16 Dennis Martinez .07 .20
17 Andy Van Slyke .07 .20
18 Will Clark .15 .40
19 Mark Langston .02 .10
20 Cecil Fielder .07 .20
21 Kirby Puckett .20 .50
22 Ken Griffey Jr. 1.00 2.50
23 David Justice .15 .40
24 Jeff Bagwell .40 1.00
25 Howard Johnson .02 .10
26 Ozzie Smith .30 .75
G1 Roberto Alomar .75 2.00
G2 Joe Carter .30 .75
G3 Kelly Gruber .20 .50
G4 Jack Morris .30 .75
G5 Tom Henke .20 .50
G6 Devon White .20 .50
GAU Roberto Alomar AU 15.00 40.00
NNO Checklist Card SP .02 .10

1992 Donruss Super DK's

COMPLETE SET (27) 250.00 500.00
COMPLETE SERIES 1 (14) 150.00 400.00
COMPLETE SERIES 2 (13) 40.00 100.00
RANDOM INSERTS IN PACKS
DK1 Paul Molitor 12.50 30.00
DK2 Will Clark 10.00 25.00
DK3 Joe Carter 4.00 10.00
DK4 Julio Franco 4.00 10.00
DK5 Cal Ripken 60.00 150.00
DK6 David Justice 5.00 12.00
DK7 George Bell 3.00 8.00
DK8 Frank Thomas 20.00 50.00
DK9 Wade Boggs 15.00 40.00
DK10 Scott Sanderson 3.00 8.00
DK11 Jeff Bagwell 25.00 60.00
DK12 John Kruk 4.00 10.00
DK13 Felix Jose 3.00 8.00
DK14 Harold Baines 5.00 12.00
DK15 Dwight Gooden 4.00 10.00
DK16 Brian McRae 3.00 8.00
DK17 Jay Bell 3.00 8.00
DK18 Brett Butler 4.00 10.00
DK19 Hal Morris 3.00 8.00
DK20 Mark Langston 3.00 8.00
DK21 Scott Erickson 3.00 8.00
DK22 Randy Johnson 15.00 40.00
DK23 Greg Swindell 3.00 8.00
DK24 Dennis Martinez 4.00 10.00
DK25 Tony Phillips 3.00 8.00
DK26 Fred McGriff 5.00 12.00
DK27 Checklist 1-26 DP/(Dick Perez) 3.00 8.00

1993 Donruss Previews

COMPLETE SET (22) 30.00 80.00
1 Tom Glavine 1.25 3.00
2 Ryne Sandberg 3.00 8.00
3 Barry Larkin 1.25 3.00
4 Jeff Bagwell 2.50 6.00
5 Eric Karros .60 1.50
6 Larry Walker 1.25 3.00
7 Eddie Murray 2.00 5.00
8 Darren Daulton .60 1.50
9 Andy Van Slyke .60 1.50
10 Gary Sheffield 1.50 4.00
11 Will Clark 1.25 3.00
12 Cal Ripken 6.00 15.00
13 Roger Clemens 4.00 10.00
14 Frank Thomas 2.00 5.00
15 Cecil Fielder .60 1.50
16 George Brett 3.00 8.00
17 Robin Yount 1.50 4.00
18 Don Mattingly 3.00 8.00
19 Dennis Eckersley 1.50 4.00
20 Ken Griffey Jr. 8.00 20.00
21 Jose Canseco 1.25 3.00
22 Roberto Alomar 1.25 3.00

1993 Donruss

The 792-card 1993 Donruss set was issued in two series, each with 396 standard-size cards. Cards were distributed in foil packs. The basic card fronts feature glossy color action photos with white borders. At the bottom of the picture, the team logo appears in a team color-coded diamond with the player's name in a color-coded bar extending to the right. A Rated Rookies (RR) subset, sprinkled throughout the set, spotlights 20 young prospects. There are no key Rookie Cards in this set.

COMPLETE SET (792) 12.50 30.00
COMPLETE SERIES 1 (396) 6.00 15.00
COMPLETE SERIES 2 (396) 6.00 15.00
1 Craig Lefferts .02 .10
2 Kent Mercker .02 .10
3 Phil Plantier .02 .10
4 Alex Arias .02 .10
5 Julio Valera .02 .10
6 Dan Wilson .07 .20
7 Frank Thomas .20 .50
8 Eric Anthony .02 .10
9 Derek Lilliquist .02 .10
10 Rafael Bournigal .02 .10
11 Manny Alexander .02 .10
12 Bret Barberie .02 .10
13 Mickey Tettleton .02 .10
14 Anthony Young .02 .10
15 Tim Spehr .02 .10
16 Bob Ayrault .02 .10
17 Bill Wegman .02 .10
18 Jay Bell .07 .20
19 Rick Aguilera .02 .10
20 Todd Zeile .02 .10
21 Steve Farr .02 .10
22 Andy Benes .02 .10
23 Lance Blankenship .02 .10
24 Ted Wood .02 .10
25 Omar Vizquel .10 .30
26 Steve Avery .02 .10
27 Brian Bohanon .02 .10
28 Rick Wilkins .02 .10
29 Devon White .07 .20
30 Bobby Ayala RC .02 .10
31 Leo Gomez .02 .10
32 Mike Simms .02 .10
33 Ellis Burks .07 .20
34 Steve Wilson .02 .10
35 Jim Abbott .10 .30
36 Tim Wallach .02 .10
37 Wilson Alvarez .02 .10
38 Daryl Boston .02 .10
39 Sandy Alomar Jr. .02 .10
40 Mitch Williams .02 .10
41 Rico Brogna .02 .10
42 Gary Varsho .02 .10
43 Kevin Appier .07 .20
44 Eric Wedge RC .02 .10
45 Dante Bichette .07 .20
46 Jose Oquendo .02 .10
47 Mike Trombley .02 .10
48 Dan Walters .02 .10
49 Gerald Williams .02 .10
50 Bud Black .02 .10
51 Bobby Witt .02 .10
52 Mark Davis .02 .10
53 Shawn Barton RC .02 .10
54 Paul Assenmacher .02 .10
55 Kevin Reimer .02 .10
56 Billy Ashley .02 .10
57 Eddie Zosky .02 .10
58 Chris Sabo .02 .10
59 Billy Ripken .02 .10
60 Scooter Tucker .02 .10
61 Tim Wakefield .20 .50
62 Mitch Webster .02 .10
63 Jack Clark .07 .20
64 Mark Gardner .02 .10
65 Lee Stevens .02 .10
66 Todd Hundley .02 .10

67 Bobby Thigpen .02 .10
68 Dave Hollins .02 .10
69 Jack Armstrong .02 .10
70 Alex Cole .02 .10
71 Mark Carreon .02 .10
72 Todd Worrell .02 .10
73 Steve Shifflett .02 .10
74 Jerald Clark .02 .10
75 Paul Molitor .07 .20
76 Larry Carter RC .02 .10
77 Rich Rowland .02 .10
78 Damon Berryhill .02 .10
79 Willie Banks .02 .10
80 Hector Villanueva .02 .10
81 Mike Gallego .02 .10
82 Tim Belcher .02 .10
83 Mike Bordick .02 .10
84 Craig Biggio .10 .30
85 Lance Parrish .07 .20
86 Brett Butler .07 .20
87 Mike Timlin .02 .10
88 Brian Barnes .02 .10
89 Brady Anderson .07 .20
90 D.J. Dozier .02 .10
91 Frank Viola .07 .20
92 Darren Daulton .07 .20
93 Chad Curtis .02 .10
94 Zane Smith .02 .10
95 George Bell .02 .10
96 Rex Hudler .02 .10
97 Mark Whiten .02 .10
98 Tim Teufel .02 .10
99 Kevin Ritz .02 .10
100 Jeff Brantley .02 .10
101 Jeff Conine .07 .20
102 Vinny Castilla .20 .50
103 Greg Vaughn .02 .10
104 Steve Buechele .02 .10
105 Darren Reed .02 .10
106 Bip Roberts .02 .10
107 John Habyan .02 .10
108 Scott Servais .02 .10
109 Walt Weiss .02 .10
110 J.T.Snow RC .10 .30
111 Jay Buhner .07 .20
112 Darryl Strawberry .07 .20
113 Roger Pavlik .02 .10
114 Chris Nabholz .02 .10
115 Pat Borders .02 .10
116 Pat Howell .02 .10
117 Gregg Olson .02 .10
118 Curt Schilling .07 .20
119 Roger Clemens .40 1.00
120 Victor Cole .02 .10
121 Gary DiSarcina .02 .10
122 Checklist 1-80 .02 .10
Gary Carter and
Kirt Manwaring
123 Steve Sax .02 .10
124 Chuck Carr .02 .10
125 Mark Lewis .02 .10
126 Tony Gwynn .25 .60
127 Travis Fryman .07 .20
128 Dave Burba .02 .10
129 Wally Joyner .07 .20
130 John Smoltz .10 .30
131 Cal Eldred .02 .10
132 Checklist 81-159
(Roberto Alomar and .07 .20
Devon White
133 Arthur Rhodes .02 .10
134 Jeff Blauser .02 .10
135 Scott Cooper .02 .10
136 Doug Strange .02 .10
137 Luis Sojo .02 .10
138 Jeff Branson .02 .10
139 Alex Fernandez .02 .10
140 Ken Caminiti .07 .20
141 Charles Nagy .02 .10
142 Tom Candiotti .02 .10
143 Willie Greene .02 .10
144 John Vander Wal .02 .10
145 Kurt Knudsen .02 .10
146 John Franco .07 .20
147 Eddie Pierce RC .02 .10
148 Kim Batiste .02 .10
149 Darren Holmes .02 .10
150 Steve Cooke .02 .10
151 Terry Jorgensen .02 .10
152 Mark Clark .02 .10
153 Randy Velarde .02 .10
154 Greg W. Harris .02 .10
155 Kevin Campbell .02 .10
156 John Burkett .02 .10
157 Kevin Mitchell .02 .10
158 Deion Sanders .10 .30
159 Jose Canseco .10 .30
160 Jeff Hartsock .02 .10
161 Tom Quinlan RC .02 .10
162 Tim Pugh RC .02 .10
163 Glenn Davis .02 .10
164 Shane Reynolds .02 .10
165 Jody Reed .02 .10
166 Mike Sharperson .02 .10
167 Scott Lewis .02 .10
168 Dennis Martinez .07 .20
169 Scott Radinsky .02 .10
170 Dave Gallagher .02 .10
171 Jim Thome .10 .30
172 Terry Mulholland .02 .10
173 Milt Cuyler .02 .10
174 Bob Patterson .02 .10
175 Jeff Montgomery .02 .10
176 Tim Salmon .10 .30
177 Franklin Stubbs .02 .10
178 Donovan Osborne .02 .10
179 Jeff Reboulet .02 .10
180 Jeremy Hernandez .02 .10
181 Charlie Hayes .02 .10
182 Matt Williams .07 .20
183 Mike Raczka .02 .10
184 Francisco Cabrera .02 .10
185 Rich DeLucia .02 .10
186 Sammy Sosa .20 .50
187 Ivan Rodriguez .10 .30
188 Bret Boone .07 .20

189 Juan Guzman .02 .10
190 Tom Browning .02 .10
191 Randy Milligan .02 .10
192 Steve Finley .07 .20
193 John Patterson RR .02 .10
194 Kip Gross .02 .10
195 Tony Fossas .02 .10
196 Ivan Calderon .02 .10
197 Junior Felix .02 .10
198 Pete Schourek .02 .10
199 Craig Grebeck .02 .10
200 Juan Bell .02 .10
201 Glenallen Hill .02 .10
202 Danny Jackson .02 .10
203 John Kiely .02 .10
204 Bob Tewksbury .02 .10
205 Kevin Koslofski .02 .10
206 Craig Shipley .02 .10
207 John Jaha .02 .10
208 Royce Clayton .02 .10
209 Mike Piazza 1.25 3.00
210 Ron Gant .07 .20
211 Scott Erickson .02 .10
212 Doug Dascenzo .02 .10
213 Andy Stankiewicz .02 .10
214 Geronimo Berroa .02 .10
215 Dennis Eckersley .07 .20
216 Al Osuna .02 .10
217 Tino Martinez .10 .30
218 Henry Rodriguez .02 .10
219 Ed Sprague .02 .10
220 Ken Hill .02 .10
221 Chito Martinez .02 .10
222 Bret Saberhagen .07 .20
223 Mike Greenwell .02 .10
224 Mickey Morandini .02 .10
225 Chuck Finley .07 .20
226 Denny Neagle .07 .20
227 Kirk McCaskill .02 .10
228 Rheal Cormier .02 .10
229 Paul Sorrento .02 .10
230 Darrin Jackson .02 .10
231 Rob Deer .02 .10
232 Bill Swift .02 .10
233 Kevin McReynolds .02 .10
234 Terry Pendleton .07 .20
235 Dave Nilsson .02 .10
236 Chuck McElroy .02 .10
237 Derek Parks .02 .10
238 Norm Charlton .02 .10
239 Matt Nokes .02 .10
240 Juan Guerrero .02 .10
241 Jeff Parrett .02 .10
242 Ryan Thompson .02 .10
243 Dave Fleming .02 .10
244 Dave Hansen .02 .10
245 Monty Fariss .02 .10
246 Archi Cianfrocco .02 .10
247 Pat Hentgen .02 .10
248 Bill Pecota .02 .10
249 Ben McDonald .02 .10
250 Cliff Brantley .02 .10
251 John Valentin .02 .10
252 Jeff King .02 .10
253 Reggie Williams .02 .10
254 Checklist 160-238 .02 .10
Sammy Sosa
Damon Berryhill
255 Ozzie Guillen .07 .20
256 Mike Perez .02 .10
257 Thomas Howard .02 .10
258 Kurt Stillwell .02 .10
259 Mike Henneman .02 .10
260 Steve Decker .02 .10
261 Brent Mayne .02 .10
262 Otis Nixon .02 .10
263 Mark Kiefer .02 .10
264 Checklist 239-317 .10 .30
Don Mattingly
Mike Bordick CL
265 Richie Lewis RC .02 .10
266 Pat Gomez RC .02 .10
267 Scott Taylor .02 .10
268 Shawon Dunston .02 .10
269 Greg Myers .02 .10
270 Tim Costo .02 .10
271 Greg Hibbard .02 .10
272 Pete Harnisch .02 .10
273 Dave Mlicki .02 .10
274 Orel Hershiser .07 .20
275 Sean Berry RR .02 .10
276 Doug Simons .02 .10
277 John Doherty .02 .10
278 Eddie Murray .20 .50
279 Chris Haney .02 .10
280 Stan Javier .02 .10
281 Jaime Navarro .02 .10
282 Orlando Merced .02 .10
283 Kent Hrbek .07 .20
284 Bernard Gilkey .02 .10
285 Russ Springer .02 .10
286 Mike Maddux .02 .10
287 Eric Fox .02 .10
288 Mark Leonard .02 .10
289 Tim Leary .02 .10
290 Brian Hunter .02 .10
291 Donald Harris .02 .10
292 Bob Scanlan .02 .10
293 Turner Ward .02 .10
294 Hal Morris .02 .10
295 Jimmy Poole .02 .10
296 Doug Jones .02 .10
297 Tony Pena .02 .10
298 Ramon Martinez .02 .10
299 Tim Fortugno .02 .10
300 Marquis Grissom .07 .20
301 Lance Johnson .02 .10
302 Jeff Kent .20 .50
303 Reggie Jefferson .02 .10
304 Wes Chamberlain .02 .10
305 Shawn Hare .02 .10
306 Mike LaValliere .02 .10
307 Gregg Jefferies .02 .10
308 Troy Neel .02 .10
309 Pat Listach .02 .10
310 Geronimo Pena .02 .10

311 Pedro Munoz .02 .10
312 Guillermo Velasquez .02 .10
313 Roberto Kelly .02 .10
314 Mike Jackson .02 .10
315 Rickey Henderson .20 .50
316 Mark Lemke .02 .10
317 Erik Hanson .02 .10
318 Derrick May .02 .10
319 Geno Petralli .02 .10
320 Melvin Nieves .02 .10
321 Doug Linton .02 .10
322 Rob Dibble .07 .20
323 Chris Hoiles .02 .10
324 Jimmy Jones .02 .10
325 Dave Staton .02 .10
326 Pedro Martinez .40 1.00
327 Paul Quantrill .02 .10
328 Greg Colbrunn .02 .10
329 Hilly Hathaway RC .02 .10
330 Jeff Innis .02 .10
331 Ron Karkovice .02 .10
332 Keith Shepherd RC .02 .10
333 Alan Embree .02 .10
334 Paul Wagner .02 .10
335 Dave Haas .02 .10
336 Ozzie Canseco .02 .10
337 Bill Sampen .02 .10
338 Rich Rodriguez .02 .10
339 Dean Palmer .07 .20
340 Greg Litton .02 .10
341 Jim Tatum RC .02 .10
342 Todd Haney RC .02 .10
343 Larry Casian .02 .10
344 Ryne Sandberg .30 .75
345 Sterling Hitchcock RC .07 .20
346 Chris Hammond .02 .10
347 Vince Horsman .02 .10
348 Butch Henry .02 .10
349 Dann Howitt .02 .10
350 Roger McDowell .02 .10
351 Jack Morris .07 .20
352 Bill Krueger .02 .10
353 Cris Colon .02 .10
354 Joe Vitko .02 .10
355 Willie McGee .07 .20
356 Jay Baller .02 .10
357 Pat Mahomes .02 .10
358 Roger Mason .02 .10
359 Jerry Nielsen .02 .10
360 Tom Pagnozzi .02 .10
361 Kevin Baez .02 .10
362 Tim Scott .02 .10
363 Domingo Martinez RC .02 .10
364 Kirt Manwaring .02 .10
365 Rafael Palmeiro .10 .30
366 Ray Lankford .07 .20
367 Tim McIntosh .02 .10
368 Jessie Hollins .02 .10
369 Scott Leius .02 .10
370 Bill Doran .02 .10
371 Sam Militello .02 .10
372 Ryan Bowen .02 .10
373 Dave Henderson .02 .10
374 Dan Smith .02 .10
375 Steve Reed RC .02 .10
376 Jose Offerman .02 .10
377 Kevin Brown .07 .20
378 Darrin Fletcher .02 .10
379 Duane Ward .02 .10
380 Wayne Kirby .02 .10
381 Steve Scarsone .02 .10
382 Mariano Duncan .02 .10
383 Ken Ryan RC .02 .10
384 Lloyd McClendon .02 .10
385 Brian Holman .02 .10
386 Braulio Castillo .02 .10
387 Danny Leon .02 .10
388 Omar Olivares .02 .10
389 Kevin Wickander .02 .10
390 Fred McGriff .10 .30
391 Phil Clark .02 .10
392 Darren Lewis .02 .10
393 Phil Hiatt .02 .10
394 Mike Morgan .02 .10
395 Shane Mack .02 .10
396 Checklist 318-396/(Dennis Eckersley.07 .20
and Art Kusn
397 David Segui .02 .10
398 Rafael Belliard .02 .10
399 Tim Naehring .02 .10
400 Frank Castillo .02 .10
401 Joe Grahe .02 .10
402 Reggie Sanders .07 .20
403 Roberto Hernandez .02 .10
404 Luis Gonzalez .07 .20
405 Carlos Baerga .02 .10
406 Carlos Hernandez .02 .10
407 Pedro Astacio .02 .10
408 Mel Rojas .02 .10
409 Scott Livingstone .02 .10
410 Chico Walker .02 .10
411 Brian McRae .02 .10
412 Ben Rivera .02 .10
413 Ricky Bones .02 .10
414 Andy Van Slyke .10 .30
415 Chuck Knoblauch .07 .20
416 Luis Alicea .02 .10
417 Bob Wickman .02 .10
418 Doug Brocail .02 .10
419 Scott Brosius .07 .20
420 Rod Beck .02 .10
421 Edgar Martinez .10 .30
422 Ryan Klesko .07 .20
423 Nolan Ryan .75 2.00
424 Rey Sanchez .02 .10
425 Roberto Alomar .10 .30
426 Barry Larkin .10 .30
427 Mike Mussina .10 .30
428 Jeff Bagwell .10 .30
429 Mo Vaughn .07 .20
430 Eric Karros .07 .20
431 John Orton .02 .10
432 Wil Cordero .02 .10
433 Jack McDowell .02 .10
434 Howard Johnson .02 .10
435 Albert Belle .07 .20

436 John Kruk .07 .20
437 Skeeter Barnes .02 .10
438 Don Slaught .02 .10
439 Rusty Meacham .02 .10
440 Tim Laker RC .02 .10
441 Robin Yount .30 .75
442 Brian Jordan .07 .20
443 Kevin Tapani .02 .10
444 Gary Sheffield .07 .20
445 Rich Monteleone .02 .10
446 Will Clark .10 .30
447 Jerry Browne .02 .10
448 Jeff Treadway .02 .10
449 Mike Schooler .02 .10
450 Mike Harkey .02 .10
451 Julio Franco .07 .20
452 Kevin Young .07 .20
453 Kelly Gruber .02 .10
454 Jose Rijo .02 .10
455 Mike Devereaux .02 .10
456 Andujar Cedeno .02 .10
457 Damion Easley RR .02 .10
458 Kevin Gross .02 .10
459 Matt Young .02 .10
460 Matt Stairs .02 .10
461 Luis Polonia .02 .10
462 Dwight Gooden .07 .20
463 Warren Newson .02 .10
464 Jose DeLeon .02 .10
465 Jose Mesa .02 .10
466 Danny Cox .02 .10
467 Dan Gladden .02 .10
468 Gerald Perry .02 .10
469 Mike Boddicker .02 .10
470 Jeff Gardner .02 .10
471 Doug Henry .02 .10
472 Mike Benjamin .02 .10
473 Dan Peltier .02 .10
474 Mike Stanton .02 .10
475 John Smiley .02 .10
476 Dwight Smith .02 .10
477 Jim Leyritz .02 .10
478 Dwayne Henry .02 .10
479 Mark McGwire .50 1.25
480 Pete Incaviglia .02 .10
481 Dave Cochrane .02 .10
482 Eric Davis .07 .20
483 John Olerud .07 .20
484 Kent Bottenfield .02 .10
485 Mark McLemore .02 .10
486 Dave Magadan .02 .10
487 John Marzano .02 .10
488 Ruben Amaro .02 .10
489 Rob Ducey .02 .10
490 Stan Belinda .02 .10
491 Dan Pasqua .02 .10
492 Joe Magrane .02 .10
493 Brook Jacoby .02 .10
494 Gene Harris .02 .10
495 Mark Leiter .02 .10
496 Bryan Hickerson .02 .10
497 Tom Gordon .02 .10
498 Pete Smith .02 .10
499 Chris Bosio .02 .10
500 Shawn Boskie .02 .10
501 Dave West .02 .10
502 Milt Hill .02 .10
503 Pat Kelly .02 .10
504 Joe Boever .02 .10
505 Terry Steinbach .02 .10
506 Butch Huskey .02 .10
507 David Valle .02 .10
508 Mike Scioscia .02 .10
509 Kenny Rogers .07 .20
510 Moises Alou .07 .20
511 David Wells .07 .20
512 Mackey Sasser .02 .10
513 Todd Frohwirth .02 .10
514 Ricky Jordan .02 .10
515 Mike Gardiner .02 .10
516 Gary Redus .02 .10
517 Gary Gaetti .07 .20
518 Cal Ripken Jr. .02 .10
Kenny Lofton CL
519 Carlton Fisk .10 .30
520 Ozzie Smith .30 .75
521 Rod Nichols .02 .10
522 Benito Santiago .07 .20
523 Bill Gullickson .02 .10
524 Robby Thompson .02 .10
525 Mike Macfarlane .02 .10
526 Sid Bream .02 .10
527 Darryl Hamilton .02 .10
528 Checklist .02 .10
529 Jeff Tackett .02 .10
530 Greg Olson .02 .10
531 Bob Zupcic .02 .10
532 Mark Grace .10 .30
533 Steve Frey .02 .10
534 Dave Martinez .02 .10
535 Robin Ventura .07 .20
536 Casey Candaele .02 .10
537 Kenny Lofton .07 .20
538 Jay Howell .02 .10
539 Fernando Ramsey RC .02 .10
540 Larry Walker .07 .20
541 Cecil Fielder .07 .20
542 Lee Guetterman .02 .10
543 Keith Miller .02 .10
544 Len Dykstra .07 .20
545 B.J. Surhoff .07 .20
546 Bob Walk .02 .10
547 Brian Harper .02 .10
548 Lee Smith .07 .20
549 Danny Tartabull .02 .10
550 Frank Seminara .02 .10
551 Henry Mercedes .02 .10
552 Dave Righetti .07 .20
553 Ken Griffey Jr. .40 1.00
554 Tom Glavine .10 .30
555 Juan Gonzalez .07 .20
556 Jim Bullinger .02 .10
557 Derek Bell .02 .10
558 Cesar Hernandez .02 .10
559 Cal Ripken .60 1.50
560 Eddie Taubensee .02 .10

561 John Flaherty .02 .10
562 Todd Benzinger .02 .10
563 Hubie Brooks .02 .10
564 Delino DeShields .02 .10
565 Tim Raines .07 .20
566 Sid Fernandez .02 .10
567 Steve Olin .02 .10
568 Tommy Greene .02 .10
569 Buddy Groom .02 .10
570 Randy Tomlin .02 .10
571 Hipolito Pichardo .02 .10
572 Rene Arocha RC .07 .20
573 Mike Fetters .02 .10
574 Felix Jose .02 .10
575 Gene Larkin .02 .10
576 Bruce Hurst .02 .10
577 Bernie Williams .10 .30
578 Trevor Wilson .02 .10
579 Bob Welch .02 .10
580 David Justice .07 .20
581 Randy Johnson .20 .50
582 Jose Vizcaino .02 .10
583 Jeff Huson .02 .10
584 Rob Maurer .02 .10
585 Todd Stottlemyre .02 .10
586 Joe Oliver .02 .10
587 Bob Milacki .02 .10
588 Rob Murphy .02 .10
589 Greg Pirkl .02 .10
590 Lenny Harris .02 .10
591 Luis Rivera .02 .10
592 John Wetteland .07 .20
593 Mark Langston .02 .10
594 Bobby Bonilla .07 .20
595 Esteban Beltre .02 .10
596 Mike Hartley .02 .10
597 Felix Fermin .02 .10
598 Carlos Garcia .02 .10
599 Frank Tanana .02 .10
600 Pedro Guerrero .07 .20
601 Terry Shumpert .02 .10
602 Wally Whitehurst .02 .10
603 Kevin Seitzer .02 .10
604 Chris James .02 .10
605 Greg Gohr .02 .10
606 Mark Wohlers .02 .10
607 Kirby Puckett .20 .50
608 Greg Maddux .30 .75
609 Don Mattingly .50 1.25
610 Greg Cadaret .02 .10
611 Dave Stewart .07 .20
612 Mark Portugal .02 .10
613 Pete O'Brien .02 .10
614 Bob Ojeda .02 .10
615 Joe Carter .07 .20
616 Pete Young .02 .10
617 Sam Horn .02 .10
618 Vince Coleman .02 .10
619 Wade Boggs .10 .30
620 Todd Pratt RC .07 .20
621 Ron Tingley .02 .10
622 Doug Drabek .02 .10
623 Scott Hemond .02 .10
624 Tim Jones .02 .10
625 Dennis Cook .02 .10
626 Jose Melendez .02 .10
627 Mike Munoz .02 .10
628 Jim Pena .02 .10
629 Gary Thurman .02 .10
630 Charlie Leibrandt .02 .10
631 Scott Fletcher .02 .10
632 Andre Dawson .07 .20
633 Greg Gagne .02 .10
634 Greg Swindell .02 .10
635 Kevin Maas .02 .10
636 Xavier Hernandez .02 .10
637 Ruben Sierra .07 .20
638 Dmitri Young .07 .20
639 Harold Reynolds .07 .20
640 Tom Goodwin .02 .10
641 Todd Burns .02 .10
642 Jeff Fassero .02 .10
643 Dave Winfield .07 .20
644 Willie Randolph .07 .20
645 Luis Mercedes .02 .10
646 Dale Murphy .10 .30
647 Danny Darwin .02 .10
648 Dennis Moeller .02 .10
649 Chuck Crim .02 .10
650 Carlos Baerga CL .02 .10
651 Shawn Abner .02 .10
652 Tracy Woodson .02 .10
653 Scott Scudder .02 .10
654 Tom Lampkin .02 .10
655 Alan Trammell .07 .20
656 Cory Snyder .02 .10
657 Chris Gwynn .02 .10
658 Lonnie Smith .02 .10
659 Jim Austin .02 .10
660 Rob Picciolo .02 .10
Tony Gwynn
Gary Sheffield CL
661 Tim Hulett .02 .10
662 Marvin Freeman .02 .10
663 Greg A. Harris .02 .10
664 Heathcliff Slocumb .02 .10
665 Mike Butcher .02 .10
666 Steve Foster .02 .10
667 Donn Pall .02 .10
668 Darryl Kile .07 .20
669 Jesse Levis .02 .10
670 Jim Gott .02 .10
671 Mark Hutton .02 .10
672 Brian Drahman .02 .10
673 Chad Kreuter .02 .10
674 Tony Fernandez .02 .10
675 Jose Lind .02 .10
676 Kyle Abbott .02 .10
677 Dan Plesac .02 .10
678 Barry Bonds .60 1.50
679 Chili Davis .07 .20
680 Stan Royer .02 .10
681 Scott Kamieniecki .02 .10
682 Carlos Martinez .02 .10
683 Mike Moore .02 .10
684 Candy Maldonado .02 .10

685 Jeff Nelson .02 .10
686 Lou Whitaker .07 .20
687 Jose Guzman .02 .10
688 Manuel Lee .02 .10
689 Bob MacDonald .02 .10
690 Scott Bankhead .02 .10
691 Alan Mills .02 .10
692 Brian Williams .02 .10
693 Tom Brunansky .02 .10
694 Lenny Webster .02 .10
695 Greg Briley .02 .10
696 Paul O'Neill .10 .30
697 Joey Cora .02 .10
698 Charlie O'Brien .02 .10
699 Junior Ortiz .02 .10
700 Ron Darling .02 .10
701 Tony Phillips .02 .10
702 William Pennyfeather .02 .10
703 Mark Gubicza .02 .10
704 Steve Hosey .02 .10
705 Henry Cotto .02 .10
706 David Hulse RC .02 .10
707 Mike Pagliarulo .02 .10
708 Dave Stieb .02 .10
709 Melido Perez .02 .10
710 Jimmy Key .07 .20
711 Jeff Russell .02 .10
712 David Cone .07 .20
713 Russ Swan .02 .10
714 Mark Guthrie .02 .10
715 Mark Grace .02 .10
Bip Roberts CL
716 Al Martin .02 .10
717 Randy Knorr .02 .10
718 Mike Stanley .02 .10
719 Rick Sutcliffe .07 .20
720 Terry Leach .02 .10
721 Chipper Jones .20 .50
722 Jim Eisenreich .02 .10
723 Tom Henke .02 .10
724 Jeff Frye .02 .10
725 Harold Baines .07 .20
726 Scott Sanderson .02 .10
727 Tom Foley .02 .10
728 Bryan Harvey .02 .10
729 Tom Edens .02 .10
730 Eric Young .02 .10
731 Dave Weathers .02 .10
732 Spike Owen .02 .10
733 Scott Aldred .02 .10
734 Cris Carpenter .02 .10
735 Dion James .02 .10
736 Joe Girardi .02 .10
737 Nigel Wilson .02 .10
738 Scott Chiamparino .02 .10
739 Jeff Reardon .07 .20
740 Willie Blair .02 .10
741 Jim Corsi .02 .10
742 Ken Patterson .02 .10
743 Andy Ashby .02 .10
744 Rob Natal .02 .10
745 Kevin Bass .02 .10
746 Freddie Benavides .02 .10
747 Chris Donnels .02 .10
748 Kerry Woodson .02 .10
749 Calvin Jones .02 .10
750 Gary Scott .02 .10
751 Joe Orsulak .02 .10
752 Armando Reynoso .02 .10
753 Monty Fariss .02 .10
754 Billy Hatcher .02 .10
755 Denis Boucher .02 .10
756 Walt Weiss .02 .10
757 Mike Fitzgerald .02 .10
758 Rudy Seanez .02 .10
759 Bret Barberie .02 .10
760 Mo Sanford .02 .10
761 Pedro Castellano .02 .10
762 Chuck Carr .02 .10
763 Steve Howe .02 .10
764 Andres Galarraga .07 .20
765 Jeff Conine .07 .20
766 Ted Power .02 .10
767 Butch Henry .02 .10
768 Steve Decker .02 .10
769 Storm Davis .02 .10
770 Vinny Castilla .20 .50
771 Junior Felix .02 .10
772 Walt Terrell .02 .10
773 Brad Ausmus .20 .50
774 Jamie McAndrew .02 .10
775 Milt Thompson .02 .10
776 Charlie Hayes .02 .10
777 Jack Armstrong .02 .10
778 Dennis Rasmussen .02 .10
779 Darren Holmes .02 .10
780 Alex Arias .02 .10
781 Randy Bush .02 .10
782 Javy Lopez .10 .30
783 Dante Bichette .07 .20
784 John Johnstone RC .02 .10
785 Rene Gonzales .02 .10
786 Alex Cole .02 .10
787 Jeromy Burnitz .07 .20
788 Michael Huff .02 .10
789 Anthony Telford .02 .10
790 Jerald Clark .02 .10
791 Joel Johnston .02 .10
792 David Nied .02 .10

1993 Donruss Diamond Kings

COMPLETE SET (31) 12.50 30.00
COMPLETE SERIES 1 (15) 8.00 20.00
COMPLETE SERIES 2 (16) 4.00 10.00
RANDOM INSERTS IN FOIL PACKS
DK1 Ken Griffey Jr. 2.50 6.00
DK2 Ryne Sandberg 2.00 5.00
DK3 Roger Clemens 2.50 6.00
DK4 Kirby Puckett 1.25 3.00
DK5 Bill Swift .25 .60
DK6 Larry Walker .50 1.25
DK7 Juan Gonzalez .50 1.25
DK8 Wally Joyner .50 1.25
DK9 Andy Van Slyke .75 2.00
DK10 Robin Ventura .50 1.25
DK11 Bip Roberts .25 .60
DK12 Roberto Kelly .25 .60
DK13 Carlos Baerga .25 .60
DK14 Orel Hershiser .50 1.25
DK15 Cecil Fielder .50 1.25
DK16 Robin Yount 2.00 5.00
DK17 Darren Daulton .50 1.25
DK18 Mark McGwire 3.00 8.00
DK19 Tom Glavine .75 2.00
DK20 Roberto Alomar .75 2.00
DK21 Gary Sheffield .50 1.25
DK22 Bob Tewksbury .25 .60
DK23 Brady Anderson .50 1.25
DK24 Craig Biggio .75 2.00
DK25 Eddie Murray 1.25 3.00
DK26 Luis Polonia .25 .60
DK27 Nigel Wilson .25 .60
DK28 David Nied .25 .60
DK29 Pat Listach ROY .25 .60
DK30 Eric Karros .50 1.25
DK31 Checklist 1-31 .40 1.00

1993 Donruss Elite

RANDOM INSERTS IN PACKS
STATED PRINT RUN 10,000 SERIAL #'d SETS
19 Fred McGriff 8.00 20.00
20 Ryne Sandberg 8.00 20.00
21 Eddie Murray 8.00 20.00
22 Paul Molitor 5.00 12.00
23 Barry Larkin 8.00 20.00
24 Don Mattingly 10.00 25.00
25 Dennis Eckersley 5.00 12.00
26 Roberto Alomar 8.00 20.00
27 Edgar Martinez 8.00 20.00
28 Gary Sheffield 5.00 12.00
29 Darren Daulton 5.00 12.00
30 Larry Walker 5.00 12.00
31 Barry Bonds 20.00 50.00
32 Andy Van Slyke 12.00 30.00
33 Mark McGwire 10.00 25.00
34 Cecil Fielder 8.00 20.00
35 Dave Winfield 5.00 12.00
36 Juan Gonzalez 5.00 12.00
L3 Robin Yount Legend 10.00 25.00
S3 Will Clark AU/5000 50.00 100.00

1993 Donruss Long Ball Leaders

COMPLETE SET (18) 25.00 60.00
COMPLETE SERIES 1 (9) 12.50 30.00
COMPLETE SERIES 2 (9) 12.50 30.00
RANDOM INSERTS IN 26-CARD JUMBOS
LL1 Rob Deer .40 1.00
LL2 Fred McGriff 1.25 3.00
LL3 Albert Belle .75 2.00
LL4 Mark McGwire 5.00 12.00
LL5 David Justice .75 2.00
LL6 Jose Canseco 1.25 3.00
LL7 Kent Hrbek .75 2.00
LL8 Roberto Alomar 1.25 3.00
LL9 Ken Griffey Jr. 4.00 10.00
LL10 Frank Thomas 2.00 5.00
LL11 Darryl Strawberry .75 2.00
LL12 Felix Jose .40 1.00
LL13 Cecil Fielder .75 2.00
LL14 Juan Gonzalez .75 2.00
LL15 Ryne Sandberg 3.00 8.00
LL16 Gary Sheffield .75 2.00
LL17 Jeff Bagwell 1.25 3.00
LL18 Larry Walker .75 2.00

1993 Donruss MVPs

COMPLETE SET (26) 10.00 25.00
COMPLETE SERIES 1 (13) 4.00 10.00
COMPLETE SERIES 2 (13) 8.00 20.00
ONE PER 23-CARD JUMBO PACK
1 Luis Polonia .15 .40
2 Frank Thomas .75 2.00
3 George Brett 2.00 5.00
4 Paul Molitor .30 .75
5 Don Mattingly 2.00 5.00
6 Roberto Alomar .50 1.25
7 Terry Pendleton .30 .75
8 Eric Karros .30 .75
9 Larry Walker .30 .75
10 Eddie Murray .75 2.00
11 Darren Daulton .30 .75
12 Ray Lankford .30 .75
13 Will Clark .50 1.25
14 Cal Ripken 2.50 6.00
15 Roger Clemens 1.50 4.00
16 Carlos Baerga .15 .40
17 Cecil Fielder .30 .75
18 Kirby Puckett .75 2.00
19 Mark McGwire 2.00 5.00
20 Ken Griffey Jr. 1.50 4.00
21 Juan Gonzalez .30 .75
22 Ryne Sandberg 1.25 3.00
23 Bip Roberts .15 .40
24 Jeff Bagwell .50 1.25
25 Barry Bonds 2.50 6.00
26 Gary Sheffield .30 .75

1993 Donruss Spirit of the Game

COMPLETE SET (20) 8.00 20.00
COMPLETE SERIES 1 (10) 3.00 8.00
COMPLETE SERIES 2 (10) 5.00 12.00
RANDOM INSERTS IN FOIL/JUMBO PACKS
SG1 M.Bordick .20 .50
D.Winfield
SG2 David Justice .40 1.00
SG3 Roberto Alomar .60 1.50
SG4 Dennis Eckersley .40 1.00
SG5 J.Gonzalez .60 1.50
J.Canseco
SG6 G.Bell 1.00 2.50
F.Thomas
SG7 W.Boggs .60 1.50
L.Polonia

SG8 Will Clark .60 1.50
SG9 Bip Roberts .20 .50
SG10 Fielder .20 .50
Deer
Tettleton
SG11 Kenny Lofton .40 1.00
SG12 G.Sheffield 1.00 2.50
F.McGriff
SG13 G.Gagne .20 .50
B.Larkin
SG14 Ryne Sandberg 1.50 4.00
SG15 C.Baerga .20 .50
G.Gaetti
SG16 Danny Tartabull .20 .50
SG17 Brady Anderson .40 1.00
SG18 Frank Thomas 1.00 2.50
SG19 Kevin Gross .20 .50
SG20 Robin Yount 1.50 4.00

1993 Donruss Elite Dominators

COMP.UNSIGNED SET (20) 125.00 250.00
1 Ryne Sandberg 10.00 25.00
2 Fred McGriff 2.00 5.00
3 Greg Maddux 8.00 20.00
4 Ron Gant 1.50 4.00
5 Dave Justice 6.00 15.00
6 Don Mattingly 8.00 20.00
7 Tim Salmon 4.00 10.00
8 Mike Piazza 8.00 20.00
9 John Olerud 1.50 4.00
10 Nolan Ryan 20.00 50.00
11 Juan Gonzalez 2.50 6.00
12 Ken Griffey Jr. 30.00 80.00
13 Frank Thomas 15.00 40.00
14 Tom Glavine 2.00 5.00
15 George Brett 10.00 25.00
16 Barry Bonds 8.00 20.00
17 Albert Belle 3.00 8.00
18 Paul Molitor 3.00 8.00
19 Cal Ripken 6.00 15.00
20 Roberto Alomar 6.00 15.00
AU6 Don Mattingly AU 50.00 120.00
AU10 Nolan Ryan AU 40.00 100.00
AU11 Juan Gonzalez AU 20.00 50.00
AU18 Paul Molitor AU 15.00 40.00

1993 Donruss Elite Supers

COMPLETE SET (20) 75.00 150.00
1 Fred McGriff 1.50 4.00
2 Ryne Sandberg 6.00 15.00
3 Eddie Murray 8.00 20.00
4 Paul Molitor 4.00 10.00
5 Barry Larkin 4.00 10.00
6 Don Mattingly 6.00 15.00
7 Dennis Eckersley 3.00 8.00
8 Roberto Alomar 2.00 5.00
9 Edgar Martinez 1.50 4.00
10 Gary Sheffield 3.00 8.00
11 Darren Daulton 1.00 2.50
12 Larry Walker 4.00 10.00
13 Barry Bonds 8.00 20.00
14 Andy Van Slyke 6.00 15.00
15 Mark McGwire 8.00 20.00
16 Cecil Fielder 1.00 2.50
17 Dave Winfield 5.00 12.00
18 Juan Gonzalez 2.00 5.00
19 Frank Thomas 8.00 20.00
20 Nolan Ryan 15.00 40.00

1993 Donruss Masters of the Game

COMPLETE SET (16) 8.00 20.00
1 Frank Thomas 1.25 3.00
2 Nolan Ryan 4.00 10.00
3 Gary Sheffield 1.25 3.00
4 Fred McGriff .75 2.00
5 Ryne Sandberg 1.50 4.00
6 Cal Ripken 4.00 10.00
7 Jose Canseco 1.00 2.50
8 Ken Griffey Jr. 3.00 8.00
9 Will Clark 1.00 2.50
10 Roberto Alomar 1.00 2.50
11 Juan Gonzalez 1.00 2.50
12 David Justice 1.00 2.50
13 Kirby Puckett 1.25 3.00
14 Barry Bonds 2.00 5.00
15 Robin Yount 1.25 3.00
16 Deion Sanders .75 2.00

1994 Donruss Promos

COMPLETE SET (12) 25.00 60.00
COMMON PLAYER (1-10) .40 1.00
COMMON SP 6.00 15.00
1 Barry Bonds 2.50 6.00
1SE Barry Bonds SP 8.00 20.00
2 Darren Daulton .40 1.00
3 John Olerud .40 1.00
4 Frank Thomas 1.50 4.00
4SE Frank Thomas SP 6.00 15.00
5 Mike Piazza 2.50 6.00
6 Tim Salmon .40 1.00
7 Ken Griffey Jr. 5.00 12.00
8 Fred McGriff .60 1.50
9 Don Mattingly 2.00 5.00
10 Gary Sheffield 1.00 2.50

1994 Donruss

The 1994 Donruss set was issued in two separate series of 330 standard-size cards for a total of 660. Cards were issued in foil wrapped packs. The fronts feature borderless color player action photos on front. There are no notable Rookie Cards in this set.

COMPLETE SET (660) 12.50 30.00
COMPLETE SERIES 1 (330) 6.00 15.00
COMPLETE SERIES 2 (330) 6.00 15.00
1 Nolan Ryan Salute 1.50 4.00
2 Mike Piazza .60 1.50
3 Moises Alou .10 .30
4 Ken Griffey Jr. .60 1.50
5 Gary Sheffield .10 .30
6 Roberto Alomar .20 .50
7 John Kruk .10 .30
8 Gregg Olson .05 .15
9 Gregg Jefferies .05 .15
10 Tony Gwynn .40 1.00
11 Chad Curtis .05 .15
12 Craig Biggio .20 .50
13 John Burkett .05 .15
14 Carlos Baerga .05 .15
15 Robin Yount .50 1.25
16 Dennis Eckersley .10 .30
17 Dwight Gooden .10 .30
18 Ryne Sandberg .50 1.25
19 Rickey Henderson .30 .75
20 Jack McDowell .05 .15
21 Jay Bell .10 .30
22 Kevin Brown .10 .30
23 Robin Ventura .10 .30
24 Paul Molitor .10 .30
25 David Justice .10 .30
26 Rafael Palmeiro .20 .50
27 Cecil Fielder .10 .30
28 Chuck Knoblauch .10 .30
29 Dave Hollins .05 .15
30 Jimmy Key .10 .30
31 Mark Langston .05 .15
32 Darryl Kile .10 .30
33 Ruben Sierra .10 .30
34 Ron Gant .10 .30
35 Ozzie Smith .50 1.25
36 Wade Boggs .20 .50
37 Marquis Grissom .10 .30
38 Will Clark .20 .50
39 Kenny Lofton .10 .30
40 Cal Ripken 1.00 2.50
41 Steve Avery .05 .15
42 Mo Vaughn .10 .30
43 Brian McRae .05 .15
44 Mickey Tettleton .05 .15
45 Barry Larkin .20 .50
46 Charlie Hayes .05 .15
47 Kevin Appier .10 .30
48 Robby Thompson .05 .15
49 Juan Gonzalez .10 .30
50 Paul O'Neill .20 .50
51 Marcos Armas .05 .15
52 Mike Butcher .05 .15
53 Ken Caminiti .10 .30
54 Pat Borders .05 .15
55 Pedro Munoz .05 .15
56 Tim Belcher .05 .15
57 Paul Assenmacher .05 .15
58 Damon Berryhill .05 .15
59 Ricky Bones .05 .15
60 Rene Arocha .05 .15
61 Shawn Boskie .05 .15
62 Pedro Astacio .05 .15
63 Frank Bolick .05 .15
64 Bud Black .05 .15
65 Sandy Alomar Jr. .05 .15
66 Rich Amaral .05 .15
67 Luis Aquino .05 .15
68 Kevin Baez .05 .15
69 Mike Devereaux .05 .15
70 Andy Ashby .05 .15
71 Larry Andersen .05 .15
72 Steve Cooke .05 .15
73 Mario Diaz .05 .15
74 Rob Deer .05 .15
75 Bobby Ayala .05 .15
76 Freddie Benavides .05 .15
77 Stan Belinda .05 .15
78 John Doherty .05 .15
79 Willie Banks .05 .15
80 Spike Owen .05 .15
81 Mike Bordick .05 .15
82 Chili Davis .10 .30
83 Luis Gonzalez .10 .30
84 Ed Sprague .05 .15
85 Jeff Reboulet .05 .15
86 Jason Bere .05 .15
87 Mark Hutton .05 .15
88 Jeff Blauser .05 .15
89 Cal Eldred .05 .15
90 Bernard Gilkey .05 .15
91 Frank Castillo .05 .15
92 Jim Gott .05 .15
93 Greg Colbrunn .05 .15
94 Jeff Brantley .05 .15
95 Jeremy Hernandez .05 .15
96 Norm Charlton .05 .15
97 Alex Arias .05 .15
98 John Franco .10 .30
99 Chris Hoiles .05 .15
100 Brad Ausmus .20 .50
101 Wes Chamberlain .05 .15
102 Mark Dewey .05 .15
103 Benji Gil .05 .15
104 John Dopson .05 .15
105 John Smiley .05 .15
106 David Nied .05 .15
107 George Brett Salute .75 2.00
108 Kirk Gibson .10 .30
109 Larry Casian .05 .15
110 Ryne Sandberg CL .30 .75
111 Brent Gates .05 .15
112 Damion Easley .05 .15
113 Pete Harnisch .05 .15
114 Danny Cox .05 .15
115 Kevin Tapani .05 .15
116 Roberto Hernandez .05 .15
117 Domingo Jean .05 .15
118 Sid Bream .05 .15
119 Doug Henry .05 .15
120 Omar Olivares .05 .15
121 Mike Harkey .05 .15
122 Carlos Hernandez .05 .15
123 Jeff Fassero .05 .15
124 Dave Burba .05 .15
125 Wayne Kirby .05 .15
126 John Cummings .05 .15
127 Bret Barberie .05 .15
128 Todd Hundley .05 .15
129 Tim Hulett .05 .15
130 Phil Clark .05 .15
131 Danny Jackson .05 .15
132 Tom Foley .05 .15
133 Donald Harris .05 .15
134 Scott Fletcher .05 .15
135 Johnny Ruffin .05 .15
136 Jerald Clark .05 .15
137 Billy Brewer .05 .15
138 Dan Gladden .05 .15
139 Eddie Guardado .10 .30
140 Cal Ripken CL .30 .75
141 Scott Hemond .05 .15
142 Steve Frey .05 .15
143 Xavier Hernandez .05 .15
144 Mark Eichhorn .05 .15
145 Ellis Burks .10 .30
146 Jim Leyritz .05 .15
147 Mark Lemke .05 .15
148 Pat Listach .05 .15
149 Donovan Osborne .05 .15
150 Glenallen Hill .05 .15
151 Orel Hershiser .10 .30
152 Darrin Fletcher .05 .15
153 Royce Clayton .05 .15
154 Derek Lilliquist .05 .15
155 Mike Felder .05 .15
156 Jeff Conine .10 .30
157 Ryan Thompson .05 .15
158 Ben McDonald .05 .15
159 Ricky Gutierrez .05 .15
160 Terry Mulholland .05 .15
161 Carlos Garcia .05 .15
162 Tom Henke .05 .15
163 Mike Greenwell .05 .15
164 Thomas Howard .05 .15
165 Joe Girardi .05 .15
166 Hubie Brooks .05 .15
167 Greg Gohr .05 .15
168 Chip Hale .05 .15
169 Rick Honeycutt .05 .15
170 Hilly Hathaway .05 .15
171 Todd Jones .05 .15
172 Tony Fernandez .05 .15
173 Bo Jackson .30 .75
174 Bobby Munoz .05 .15
175 Greg McMichael .05 .15
176 Graeme Lloyd .05 .15
177 Tom Pagnozzi .05 .15
178 Derrick May .05 .15
179 Pedro Martinez .30 .75
180 Ken Hill .05 .15
181 Bryan Hickerson .05 .15
182 Jose Mesa .05 .15
183 Dave Fleming .05 .15
184 Henry Cotto .05 .15
185 Jeff Kent .20 .50
186 Mark McLemore .05 .15
187 Trevor Hoffman .20 .50
188 Todd Pratt .05 .15
189 Blas Minor .05 .15
190 Charlie Leibrandt .05 .15
191 Tony Pena .05 .15
192 Larry Luebbers RC .05 .15
193 Greg W. Harris .05 .15
194 David Cone .10 .30
195 Bill Gullickson .05 .15
196 Brian Harper .05 .15
197 Steve Karsay .05 .15
198 Greg Myers .05 .15
199 Mark Portugal .05 .15
200 Pat Hentgen .05 .15
201 Mike LaValliere .05 .15
202 Mike Stanley .05 .15
203 Kent Mercker .05 .15
204 Dave Nilsson .05 .15
205 Erik Pappas .05 .15
206 Mike Morgan .05 .15
207 Roger McDowell .05 .15
208 Mike Lansing .10 .30
209 Kirt Manwaring .05 .15
210 Randy Milligan .05 .15
211 Erik Hanson .05 .15
212 Orestes Destrade .05 .15
213 Mike Maddux .05 .15
214 Alan Mills .05 .15
215 Tim Mauser .05 .15
216 Ben Rivera .05 .15
217 Don Slaught .05 .15
218 Bob Patterson .05 .15
219 Carlos Quintana .05 .15
220 Tim Raines CL .05 .15
221 Hal Morris .05 .15
222 Darren Holmes .05 .15
223 Chris Gwynn .05 .15
224 Chad Kreuter .05 .15
225 Mike Hartley .05 .15
226 Scott Lydy .05 .15
227 Eduardo Perez .05 .15
228 Greg Swindell .05 .15
229 Al Leiter .10 .30
230 Scott Radinsky .05 .15
231 Bob Wickman .05 .15
232 Otis Nixon .05 .15
233 Kevin Reimer .05 .15
234 Geronimo Pena .05 .15
235 Kevin Roberson .05 .15
236 Jody Reed .05 .15
237 Kirk Rueter .05 .15
238 Willie McGee .10 .30
239 Charles Nagy .05 .15
240 Tim Leary .05 .15
241 Carl Everett .10 .30
242 Charlie O'Brien .05 .15
243 Mike Pagliarulo .05 .15
244 Kerry Taylor .05 .15
245 Kevin Stocker .05 .15
246 Joel Johnston .05 .15
247 Geno Petralli .05 .15
248 Jeff Russell .05 .15
249 Joe Oliver .05 .15
250 Roberto Mejia .05 .15
251 Chris Haney .05 .15
252 Bill Krueger .05 .15
253 Shane Mack .05 .15
254 Terry Steinbach .05 .15
255 Luis Polonia .05 .15
256 Eddie Taubensee .05 .15
257 Dave Stewart .10 .30
258 Tim Raines .10 .30
259 Bernie Williams .20 .50
260 John Smoltz .20 .50
261 Kevin Seitzer .05 .15
262 Bob Tewksbury .05 .15
263 Bob Scanlan .05 .15
264 Henry Rodriguez .05 .15
265 Tim Scott .05 .15
266 Scott Sanderson .05 .15
267 Eric Plunk .05 .15
268 Edgar Martinez .20 .50
269 Charlie Hough .10 .30
270 Joe Orsulak .05 .15
271 Harold Reynolds .10 .30
272 Tim Teufel .05 .15
273 Bobby Thigpen .05 .15
274 Randy Tomlin .05 .15
275 Gary Redus .05 .15
276 Ken Ryan .05 .15
277 Tim Pugh .05 .15
278 Jayhawk Owens .05 .15
279 Phil Hiatt .05 .15
280 Alan Trammell .10 .30
281 David McCarty .05 .15
282 Bob Welch .05 .15
283 J.T.Snow .10 .30
284 Brian Williams .05 .15
285 Devon White .10 .30
286 Steve Sax .05 .15
287 Tony Tarasco .05 .15
288 Bill Spiers .05 .15
289 Allen Watson .05 .15
290 Rickey Henderson CL .20 .50
291 Jose Vizcaino .05 .15
292 Darryl Strawberry .10 .30
293 John Wetteland .10 .30
294 Bill Swift .05 .15
295 Jeff Treadway .05 .15
296 Tino Martinez .20 .50
297 Richie Lewis .05 .15
298 Bret Saberhagen .10 .30
299 Arthur Rhodes .05 .15
300 Guillermo Velasquez .05 .15
301 Milt Thompson .05 .15
302 Doug Strange .05 .15
303 Aaron Sele .05 .15
304 Bip Roberts .05 .15
305 Bruce Ruffin .05 .15
306 Jose Lind .05 .15
307 David Wells .10 .30
308 Bobby Witt .05 .15
309 Mark Wohlers .05 .15
310 B.J. Surhoff .10 .30
311 Mark Whiten .05 .15
312 Turk Wendell .05 .15
313 Raul Mondesi .10 .30
314 Brian Turang RC .05 .15
315 Chris Hammond .05 .15
316 Tim Bogar .05 .15
317 Brad Pennington .05 .15
318 Tim Worrell .05 .15
319 Mitch Williams .05 .15
320 Rondell White .10 .30
321 Frank Viola .10 .30
322 Manny Ramirez .30 .75
323 Gary Wayne .05 .15
324 Mike Macfarlane .05 .15
325 Russ Springer .05 .15
326 Tim Wallach .05 .15
327 Salomon Torres .05 .15
328 Omar Vizquel .20 .50
329 Andy Tomberlin RC .05 .15
330 Chris Sabo .05 .15
331 Mike Mussina .20 .50
332 Andy Benes .05 .15
333 Darren Daulton .10 .30
334 Orlando Merced .05 .15
335 Mark McGwire .75 2.00
336 Dave Winfield .10 .30
337 Sammy Sosa .30 .75
338 Eric Karros .10 .30
339 Greg Vaughn .05 .15
340 Don Mattingly .75 2.00
341 Frank Thomas .30 .75
342 Fred McGriff .20 .50
343 Kirby Puckett .30 .75
344 Roberto Kelly .05 .15
345 Wally Joyner .10 .30
346 Andres Galarraga .10 .30
347 Bobby Bonilla .10 .30
348 Benito Santiago .10 .30
349 Barry Bonds .75 2.00
350 Delino DeShields .05 .15
351 Albert Belle .10 .30
352 Randy Johnson .30 .75
353 Tim Salmon .20 .50
354 John Olerud .10 .30
355 Dean Palmer .10 .30
356 Roger Clemens .60 1.50
357 Jim Abbott .20 .50
358 Mark Grace .20 .50
359 Ozzie Guillen .10 .30
360 Lou Whitaker .10 .30
361 Jose Rijo .05 .15
362 Jeff Montgomery .05 .15
363 Chuck Finley .10 .30
364 Tom Glavine .20 .50
365 Jeff Bagwell .20 .50
366 Joe Carter .10 .30
367 Ray Lankford .10 .30
368 Ramon Martinez .05 .15
369 Jay Buhner .10 .30
370 Matt Williams .10 .30
371 Larry Walker .10 .30
372 Jose Canseco .20 .50
373 Lenny Dykstra .10 .30
374 Bryan Harvey .05 .15
375 Andy Van Slyke .20 .50
376 Ivan Rodriguez .20 .50
377 Kevin Mitchell .05 .15
378 Travis Fryman .10 .30
379 Duane Ward .05 .15
380 Greg Maddux .50 1.25
381 Scott Servais .05 .15
382 Greg Olson .05 .15
383 Rey Sanchez .05 .15
384 Tom Kramer .05 .15
385 David Valle .05 .15
386 Eddie Murray .30 .75
387 Kevin Higgins .05 .15
388 Dan Wilson .05 .15
389 Todd Frohwirth .05 .15
390 Gerald Williams .05 .15
391 Hipolito Pichardo .05 .15
392 Pat Meares .05 .15
393 Luis Lopez .05 .15
394 Ricky Jordan .05 .15
395 Bob Walk .05 .15
396 Sid Fernandez .05 .15
397 Todd Worrell .05 .15
398 Darryl Hamilton .05 .15
399 Randy Myers .05 .15
400 Rod Brewer .05 .15
401 Lance Blankenship .05 .15
402 Steve Finley .10 .30
403 Phil Leftwich RC .05 .15
404 Juan Guzman .05 .15
405 Anthony Young .05 .15
406 Jeff Gardner .05 .15
407 Ryan Bowen .05 .15
408 Fernando Valenzuela .10 .30
409 David West .05 .15
410 Kenny Rogers .10 .30
411 Bob Zupcic .05 .15
412 Eric Young .05 .15
413 Bret Boone .10 .30
414 Danny Tartabull .05 .15
415 Bob MacDonald .05 .15
416 Ron Karkovice .05 .15
417 Scott Cooper .05 .15
418 Dante Bichette .10 .30
419 Tripp Cromer .05 .15
420 Billy Ashley .05 .15
421 Roger Smithberg .05 .15
422 Dennis Martinez .10 .30
423 Mike Blowers .05 .15
424 Darren Lewis .05 .15
425 Junior Ortiz .05 .15
426 Butch Huskey .05 .15
427 Jimmy Poole .05 .15
428 Walt Weiss .05 .15
429 Scott Bankhead .05 .15
430 Deion Sanders .20 .50
431 Scott Bullett .05 .15
432 Jeff Huson .05 .15
433 Tyler Green .05 .15
434 Billy Hatcher .05 .15
435 Bob Hamelin .05 .15
436 Reggie Sanders .10 .30
437 Scott Erickson .05 .15
438 Steve Reed .05 .15
439 Randy Velarde .05 .15
440 Tony Gwynn CL .20 .50
441 Terry Leach .05 .15
442 Danny Bautista .05 .15
443 Kent Hrbek .10 .30
444 Rick Wilkins .05 .15
445 Tony Phillips .05 .15
446 Dion James .05 .15
447 Joey Cora .05 .15
448 Andre Dawson .10 .30
449 Pedro Castellano .05 .15
450 Tom Gordon .05 .15
451 Rob Dibble .10 .30
452 Ron Darling .05 .15
453 Chipper Jones .30 .75
454 Joe Grahe .05 .15
455 Domingo Cedeno .05 .15
456 Tom Edens .05 .15
457 Mitch Webster .05 .15
458 Jose Bautista .05 .15
459 Troy O'Leary .05 .15
460 Todd Zeile .05 .15
461 Sean Berry .05 .15
462 Brad Holman RC .05 .15
463 Dave Martinez .05 .15
464 Mark Lewis .05 .15
465 Paul Carey .05 .15
466 Jack Armstrong .05 .15
467 David Telgheder .05 .15
468 Gene Harris .05 .15
469 Danny Darwin .05 .15
470 Kim Batiste .05 .15
471 Tim Wakefield .20 .50
472 Craig Lefferts .05 .15
473 Jacob Brumfield .05 .15
474 Lance Painter .05 .15
475 Milt Cuyler .05 .15
476 Melido Perez .05 .15
477 Derek Parks .05 .15
478 Gary DiSarcina .05 .15
479 Steve Bedrosian .05 .15
480 Eric Anthony .05 .15
481 Julio Franco .10 .30
482 Tommy Greene .05 .15
483 Pat Kelly .05 .15
484 Nate Minchey .05 .15
485 William Pennyfeather .05 .15
486 Harold Baines .10 .30
487 Howard Johnson .05 .15
488 Angel Miranda .05 .15
489 Scott Sanders .05 .15
490 Shawon Dunston .05 .15
491 Mel Rojas .05 .15
492 Jeff Nelson .05 .15
493 Archi Cianfrocco .05 .15
494 Al Martin .05 .15
495 Mike Gallego .05 .15
496 Mike Henneman .05 .15
497 Armando Reynoso .05 .15
498 Mickey Morandini .05 .15
499 Rick Renteria .05 .15
500 Rick Sutcliffe .10 .30
501 Bobby Jones .05 .15
502 Gary Gaetti .10 .30
503 Rick Aguilera .05 .15
504 Todd Stottlemyre .05 .15
505 Mike Mohler .05 .15
506 Mike Stanton .05 .15
507 Jose Guzman .05 .15
508 Kevin Rogers .05 .15
509 Chuck Carr .05 .15
510 Chris Jones .05 .15
511 Brent Mayne .05 .15
512 Greg Harris .05 .15
513 Dave Henderson .05 .15
514 Eric Hillman .05 .15
515 Dan Peltier .05 .15
516 Craig Shipley .05 .15
517 John Valentin .05 .15
518 Wilson Alvarez .05 .15
519 Andujar Cedeno .05 .15
520 Troy Neel .05 .15
521 Tom Candiotti .05 .15
522 Matt Mieske .05 .15
523 Jim Thome .20 .50
524 Lou Frazier .05 .15
525 Mike Jackson .05 .15
526 Pedro A.Martinez RC .05 .15
527 Roger Pavlik .05 .15
528 Kent Bottenfield .05 .15
529 Felix Jose .05 .15
530 Mark Guthrie .05 .15
531 Steve Farr .05 .15
532 Craig Paquette .05 .15
533 Doug Jones .05 .15
534 Luis Alicea .05 .15
535 Cory Snyder .05 .15
536 Paul Sorrento .05 .15
537 Nigel Wilson .05 .15
538 Jeff King .05 .15
539 Willie Greene .05 .15
540 Kirk McCaskill .05 .15
541 Al Osuna .05 .15
542 Greg Hibbard .05 .15
543 Brett Butler .10 .30
544 Jose Valentin .05 .15
545 Wil Cordero .05 .15
546 Chris Bosio .05 .15
547 Jamie Moyer .10 .30
548 Jim Eisenreich .05 .15
549 Vinny Castilla .10 .30
550 Dave Winfield CL .05 .15
551 John Roper .05 .15
552 Lance Johnson .05 .15
553 Scott Kamieniecki .05 .15
554 Mike Moore .05 .15
555 Steve Buechele .05 .15
556 Terry Pendleton .10 .30
557 Todd Van Poppel .05 .15
558 Rob Butler .05 .15
559 Zane Smith .05 .15
560 David Hulse .05 .15
561 Tim Costo .05 .15
562 John Habyan .05 .15
563 Terry Jorgensen .05 .15
564 Matt Nokes .05 .15
565 Kevin McReynolds .05 .15
566 Phil Plantier .05 .15
567 Chris Turner .05 .15
568 Carlos Delgado .20 .50
569 John Jaha .05 .15
570 Dwight Smith .05 .15
571 John Vander Wal .05 .15
572 Trevor Wilson .05 .15
573 Felix Fermin .05 .15
574 Marc Newfield .05 .15
575 Jeromy Burnitz .10 .30
576 Leo Gomez .05 .15
577 Curt Schilling .10 .30
578 Kevin Young .05 .15
579 Jerry Spradlin RC .05 .15
580 Curt Leskanic .05 .15
581 Carl Willis .05 .15
582 Alex Fernandez .05 .15
583 Mark Holzemer .05 .15
584 Domingo Martinez .05 .15
585 Pete Smith .05 .15
586 Brian Jordan .10 .30
587 Kevin Gross .05 .15
588 J.R. Phillips .05 .15
589 Chris Nabholz .05 .15
590 Bill Wertz .05 .15
591 Derek Bell .05 .15
592 Brady Anderson .10 .30
593 Matt Turner .05 .15
594 Pete Incaviglia .05 .15
595 Greg Gagne .05 .15
596 John Flaherty .05 .15
597 Scott Livingstone .05 .15
598 Rod Bolton .05 .15
599 Mike Perez .05 .15
600 Roger Clemens CL .30 .75
601 Tony Castillo .05 .15
602 Henry Mercedes .05 .15
603 Mike Fetters .05 .15
604 Rod Beck .05 .15
605 Damon Buford .05 .15
606 Matt Whiteside .05 .15
607 Shawn Green .30 .75
608 Midre Cummings .05 .15
609 Jeff McNeely .05 .15
610 Danny Sheaffer .05 .15
611 Paul Wagner .05 .15
612 Torey Lovullo .05 .15
613 Javier Lopez .10 .30
614 Mariano Duncan .05 .15
615 Doug Brocail .05 .15
616 Dave Hansen .05 .15
617 Ryan Klesko .10 .30
618 Eric Davis .10 .30
619 Scott Ruffcorn .05 .15
620 Mike Trombley .05 .15
621 Jaime Navarro .05 .15
622 Rheal Cormier .05 .15
623 Jose Offerman .05 .15
624 David Segui .05 .15
625 Robb Nen .10 .30
626 Dave Gallagher .05 .15
627 Julian Tavarez RC .10 .30
628 Chris Gomez .05 .15
629 Jeffrey Hammonds .05 .15
630 Scott Brosius .10 .30
631 Willie Blair .05 .15
632 Doug Drabek .05 .15
633 Bill Wegman .05 .15
634 Jeff McKnight .05 .15
635 Rich Rodriguez .05 .15
636 Steve Trachsel .05 .15
637 Buddy Groom .05 .15
638 Sterling Hitchcock .05 .15
639 Chuck McElroy .05 .15
640 Rene Gonzales .05 .15
641 Dan Plesac .05 .15
642 Jeff Branson .05 .15
643 Darrell Whitmore .05 .15
644 Paul Quantrill .05 .15
645 Rich Rowland .05 .15
646 Curtis Pride RC .10 .30
647 Erik Plantenberg RC .05 .15
648 Albie Lopez .05 .15
649 Rich Batchelor RC .05 .15
650 Lee Smith .10 .30
651 Cliff Floyd .10 .30
652 Pete Schourek .05 .15
653 Reggie Jefferson .05 .15
654 Bill Haselman .05 .15
655 Steve Hosey .05 .15
656 Mark Clark .05 .15
657 Mark Davis .05 .15
658 Dave Magadan .05 .15
659 Candy Maldonado .05 .15
660 Mark Langston CL .05 .15

1994 Donruss Special Edition

COMPLETE SET (100) 8.00 20.00
*STARS: .75X TO 2X BASIC CARDS
ONE PER PACK/TWO PER JUMBO
NUMBERS 51-100 CORRESPOND TO 331-380

1994 Donruss Anniversary '84

COMPLETE SET (10) 12.50 30.00
RANDOM INSERTS IN SER.1 HOBBY PACKS
1 Joe Carter .75 2.00
2 Robin Yount 3.00 8.00
3 George Brett 5.00 12.00
4 Rickey Henderson 2.00 5.00
5 Nolan Ryan 10.00 25.00
6 Cal Ripken 6.00 15.00
7 Wade Boggs 1.25 3.00
8 Don Mattingly 5.00 12.00
9 Ryne Sandberg 3.00 8.00
10 Tony Gwynn 2.50 6.00

1994 Donruss Award Winner Jumbos

COMPLETE SET (10) 30.00 80.00
COMPLETE SERIES 1 (5) 25.00 60.00
COMPLETE SERIES 2 (5) 8.00 20.00
ONE PER JUMBO BOX OR CDN FOIL BOX
STATED PRINT RUN 10,000 SERIAL #'d SETS
1 Barry Bonds 8.00 20.00
2 Greg Maddux 5.00 12.00
3 Mike Piazza 6.00 15.00
4 Barry Bonds 8.00 20.00
5 Kirby Puckett 3.00 8.00
6 Frank Thomas 3.00 8.00
7 Jack McDowell CY .60 1.50
8 Tim Salmon 2.00 5.00
9 Juan Gonzalez 1.25 3.00
10 Paul Molitor WS MVP 2.50 6.00

1994 Donruss Diamond Kings

COMPLETE SET (30) 20.00 50.00
COMPLETE SERIES 1 (15) 10.00 25.00
COMPLETE SERIES 2 (15) 10.00 25.00
STATED ODDS 1:9
*JUMBO DK's: .75X TO 2X BASIC DK'S
ONE JUMBO DK PER RETAIL BOX
DK1 Barry Bonds 2.50 6.00
DK2 Mo Vaughn .40 1.00
DK3 Steve Avery .20 .50
DK4 Tim Salmon .60 1.50
DK5 Rick Wilkins .20 .50
DK6 Brian Harper .20 .50
DK7 Andres Galarraga .40 1.00
DK8 Albert Belle .40 1.00
DK9 John Kruk .40 1.00
DK10 Ivan Rodriguez .60 1.50
DK11 Tony Gwynn 1.25 3.00
DK12 Brian McRae .20 .50
DK13 Bobby Bonilla .40 1.00
DK14 Ken Griffey Jr. 2.00 5.00
DK15 Mike Piazza 2.00 5.00
DK16 Don Mattingly 2.50 6.00
DK17 Barry Larkin .60 1.50
DK18 Ruben Sierra .40 1.00
DK19 Orlando Merced .20 .50
DK20 Greg Vaughn .20 .50
DK21 Gregg Jefferies .20 .50
DK22 Cecil Fielder .40 1.00
DK23 Moises Alou .40 1.00
DK24 John Olerud .40 1.00
DK25 Gary Sheffield .40 1.00
DK26 Mike Mussina .60 1.50
DK27 Jeff Bagwell .60 1.50
DK28 Frank Thomas 1.00 2.50
DK29 Dave Winfield .40 1.00
DK30 Checklist .20 .50

1994 Donruss Dominators

COMPLETE SET (20) 15.00 40.00
COMPLETE SERIES 1 (10) 8.00 20.00
COMPLETE SERIES 2 (10) 8.00 20.00
RANDOM INSERTS IN PACKS
*JUMBOS: .75X TO 2X BASIC DOM.
ONE JUMBO DOMINATOR PER HOBBY BOX
A1 Cecil Fielder .40 1.00
A2 Barry Bonds 2.50 6.00
A3 Fred McGriff .60 1.50
A4 Matt Williams .40 1.00
A5 Joe Carter .40 1.00
A6 Juan Gonzalez .40 1.00
A7 Jose Canseco .60 1.50
A8 Ron Gant .40 1.00
A9 Ken Griffey Jr. 2.00 5.00
A10 Mark McGwire 2.50 6.00
B1 Tony Gwynn 1.25 3.00
B2 Frank Thomas 1.00 2.50
B3 Paul Molitor .40 1.00
B4 Edgar Martinez .60 1.50
B5 Kirby Puckett 1.00 2.50
B6 Ken Griffey Jr. 2.00 5.00
B7 Barry Bonds 2.50 6.00

B8 Willie McGee .40 1.00
B9 Len Dykstra .40 1.00
B10 John Kruk .40 1.00

1994 Donruss Elite

COMPLETE SET (12) 30.00 80.00
COMPLETE SERIES 1 (6) 15.00 40.00
COMPLETE SERIES 2 (6) 15.00 40.00
RANDOM INSERTS IN HOBBY/RETAIL PACKS
STATED PRINT RUN 10,000 SERIAL #'d SETS
37 Frank Thomas 6.00 15.00
38 Tony Gwynn 4.00 10.00
39 Tim Salmon 1.50 4.00
40 Albert Belle 1.50 4.00
41 John Kruk 2.00 5.00
42 Juan Gonzalez 2.50 6.00
43 John Olerud 1.50 4.00
44 Barry Bonds 8.00 20.00
45 Ken Griffey Jr. 15.00 40.00
46 Mike Piazza 4.00 10.00
47 Jack McDowell 2.00 5.00
48 Andres Galarraga 2.50 6.00

1994 Donruss Long Ball Leaders

COMPLETE SET (10) 12.50 30.00
RANDOM INSERTS IN SER.2 HOBBY PACKS
1 Cecil Fielder .60 1.50
2 Dean Palmer .60 1.50
3 Andres Galarraga .60 1.50
4 Bo Jackson 1.50 4.00
5 Ken Griffey Jr. 3.00 8.00
6 David Justice .60 1.50
7 Mike Piazza 3.00 8.00
8 Frank Thomas 1.50 4.00
9 Barry Bonds 4.00 10.00
10 Juan Gonzalez .60 1.50

1994 Donruss MVPs

COMPLETE SET (28) 25.00 60.00
COMPLETE SERIES 1 (14) 6.00 15.00
COMPLETE SERIES 2 (14) 20.00 50.00
ONE PER JUMBO PACK
1 David Justice .60 1.50
2 Mark Grace 1.00 2.50
3 Jose Rijo .30 .75
4 Andres Galarraga .60 1.50
5 Bryan Harvey .30 .75
6 Jeff Bagwell 1.00 2.50
7 Mike Piazza 3.00 8.00
8 Moises Alou .60 1.50
9 Bobby Bonilla .60 1.50
10 Len Dykstra .60 1.50
11 Jeff King .30 .75
12 Gregg Jefferies .30 .75
13 Tony Gwynn 2.00 5.00
14 Barry Bonds 4.00 10.00
15 Cal Ripken 5.00 12.00
16 Mo Vaughn .60 1.50
17 Tim Salmon 1.00 2.50
18 Frank Thomas 1.50 4.00
19 Albert Belle .60 1.50
20 Cecil Fielder .60 1.50
21 Wally Joyner .60 1.50
22 Greg Vaughn .30 .75
23 Kirby Puckett 1.50 4.00
24 Don Mattingly 4.00 10.00
25 Ruben Sierra .60 1.50
26 Ken Griffey Jr. 3.00 8.00
27 Juan Gonzalez .60 1.50
28 John Olerud .60 1.50

1994 Donruss Spirit of the Game

COMPLETE SET (10) 15.00 40.00
COMPLETE SERIES 1 (5) 10.00 25.00
COMPLETE SERIES 2 (5) 8.00 20.00
RANDOM INSERTS IN MAG.JUMBO PACKS
*JUMBOS: .75X TO 2X BASIC SOG
ONE JUMBO SPIRIT PER MAG.JUMBO BOX
JUMBO PRINT RUN 10,000 SERIAL #'d SETS
1 John Olerud .75 2.00
2 Barry Bonds 5.00 12.00
3 Ken Griffey Jr. 4.00 10.00
4 Mike Piazza 4.00 10.00
5 Juan Gonzalez .75 2.00
6 Frank Thomas 2.00 5.00
7 Tim Salmon 1.25 3.00
8 David Justice .75 2.00
9 Don Mattingly 5.00 12.00
10 Len Dykstra .75 2.00

1995 Donruss

The 1995 Donruss set consists of 550 standard-size cards. The first series had 330 cards while 220 cards comprised the second series. The fronts feature borderless color action player photos. A second, smaller color player photo in a homeplate shape with team color-coded borders appears in the lower left corner. There are no key Rookie Cards in this set. To preview the product prior to its public release, Donruss printed up additional quantities of cards 5, 8, 20, 42, 55, 275, 331 and 340 and mailed them to dealers and hobby media.

COMPLETE SET (550) 12.50 30.00
COMPLETE SERIES 1 (330) 8.00 20.00
COMPLETE SERIES 2 (220) 4.00 10.00
1 David Justice .10 .30
2 Rene Arocha .05 .15
3 Sandy Alomar Jr. .05 .15
4 Luis Lopez .05 .15
5 Mike Piazza .50 1.25
6 Bobby Jones .05 .15
7 Damion Easley .05 .15
8 Barry Bonds .75 2.00
9 Mike Mussina .20 .50
10 Kevin Seitzer .05 .15
11 John Smiley .05 .15
12 Wm.VanLandingham .05 .15
13 Ron Darling .05 .15
14 Walt Weiss .05 .15
15 Mike Lansing .05 .15
16 Allen Watson .05 .15
17 Aaron Sele .05 .15
18 Randy Johnson .30 .75
19 Dean Palmer .10 .30
20 Jeff Bagwell .20 .50
21 Curt Schilling .10 .30
22 Darrell Whitmore .05 .15
23 Steve Trachsel .05 .15
24 Dan Wilson .05 .15
25 Steve Finley .10 .30
26 Bret Boone .10 .30
27 Charles Johnson .10 .30
28 Mike Stanton .05 .15
29 Ismael Valdes .05 .15
30 Salomon Torres .05 .15
31 Eric Anthony .05 .15
32 Spike Owen .05 .15
33 Joey Cora .05 .15
34 Robert Eenhoorn .05 .15
35 Rick White .05 .15
36 Omar Vizquel .20 .50
37 Carlos Delgado .10 .30
38 Eddie Williams .05 .15
39 Shawon Dunston .05 .15
40 Darrin Fletcher .05 .15
41 Leo Gomez .05 .15
42 Juan Gonzalez .10 .30
43 Luis Alicea .05 .15
44 Ken Ryan .05 .15
45 Lou Whitaker .10 .30
46 Mike Blowers .05 .15
47 Willie Blair .05 .15
48 Todd Van Poppel .05 .15
49 Roberto Alomar .20 .50
50 Ozzie Smith .50 1.25
51 Sterling Hitchcock .05 .15
52 Mo Vaughn .10 .30
53 Rick Aguilera .05 .15
54 Kent Mercker .05 .15
55 Don Mattingly .75 2.00
56 Bob Scanlan .05 .15
57 Wilson Alvarez .05 .15
58 Jose Mesa .05 .15
59 Scott Kamieniecki .05 .15
60 Todd Jones .05 .15
61 John Kruk .10 .30
62 Mike Stanley .05 .15
63 Tino Martinez .20 .50
64 Eddie Zambrano .05 .15
65 Todd Hundley .05 .15
66 Jamie Moyer .10 .30
67 Rich Amaral .05 .15
68 Jose Valentin .05 .15
69 Alex Gonzalez .05 .15
70 Kurt Abbott .05 .15
71 Delino DeShields .05 .15
72 Brian Anderson .05 .15
73 John Vander Wal .05 .15
74 Turner Ward .05 .15
75 Tim Raines .10 .30
76 Mark Acre .05 .15
77 Jose Offerman .05 .15
78 Jimmy Key .10 .30
79 Mark Whiten .05 .15
80 Mark Gubicza .05 .15
81 Darren Hall .05 .15
82 Travis Fryman .10 .30
83 Cal Ripken 1.00 2.50
84 Geronimo Berroa .05 .15
85 Bret Barberie .05 .15
86 Andy Ashby .05 .15
87 Steve Avery .05 .15
88 Rich Becker .05 .15
89 John Valentin .05 .15
90 Glenallen Hill .05 .15
91 Carlos Garcia .05 .15
92 Dennis Martinez .10 .30
93 Pat Kelly .05 .15
94 Orlando Miller .05 .15
95 Felix Jose .05 .15
96 Mike Kingery .05 .15
97 Jeff Kent .10 .30
98 Pete Incaviglia .05 .15
99 Chad Curtis .05 .15
100 Thomas Howard .05 .15
101 Hector Carrasco .05 .15
102 Tom Pagnozzi .05 .15
103 Danny Tartabull .05 .15
104 Donnie Elliott .05 .15
105 Danny Jackson .05 .15
106 Steve Dunn .05 .15
107 Roger Salkeld .05 .15
108 Jeff King .05 .15
109 Cecil Fielder .10 .30
110 Paul Molitor CL .05 .15
111 Denny Neagle .10 .30
112 Troy Neel .05 .15
113 Rod Beck .05 .15
114 Alex Rodriguez .75 2.00
115 Joey Eischen .05 .15
116 Tom Candiotti .05 .15
117 Ray McDavid .05 .15
118 Vince Coleman .05 .15
119 Pete Harnisch .05 .15
120 David Nied .05 .15
121 Pat Rapp .05 .15
122 Sammy Sosa .30 .75
123 Steve Reed .05 .15
124 Jose Oliva .05 .15
125 Ricky Bottalico .05 .15
126 Jose DeLeon .05 .15
127 Pat Hentgen .05 .15
128 Will Clark .20 .50
129 Mark Dewey .05 .15
130 Greg Vaughn .05 .15
131 Darren Dreifort .05 .15
132 Ed Sprague .05 .15
133 Lee Smith .10 .30
134 Charles Nagy .05 .15
135 Phil Plantier .05 .15
136 Jason Jacome .05 .15
137 Jose Lima .05 .15
138 J.R. Phillips .05 .15
139 J.T. Snow .10 .30
140 Michael Huff .05 .15
141 Billy Brewer .05 .15
142 Jeromy Burnitz .10 .30
143 Ricky Bones .05 .15
144 Carlos Rodriguez .05 .15
145 Luis Gonzalez .10 .30
146 Mark Lemke .05 .15
147 Al Martin .05 .15
148 Mike Bordick .05 .15
149 Robb Nen .10 .30
150 Wil Cordero .05 .15
151 Edgar Martinez .20 .50
152 Gerald Williams .05 .15
153 Esteban Beltre .05 .15
154 Mike Moore .05 .15
155 Mark Langston .05 .15
156 Mark Clark .05 .15
157 Bobby Ayala .05 .15
158 Rick Wilkins .05 .15
159 Bobby Munoz .05 .15
160 Brett Butler CL .05 .15
161 Scott Erickson .05 .15
162 Paul Molitor .10 .30
163 Jon Lieber .05 .15
164 Jason Grimsley .05 .15
165 Norberto Martin .05 .15
166 Javier Lopez .10 .30
167 Brian McRae .05 .15
168 Gary Sheffield .10 .30
169 Marcus Moore .05 .15
170 John Hudek .05 .15
171 Kelly Stinnett .05 .15
172 Chris Gomez .05 .15
173 Rey Sanchez .05 .15
174 Juan Guzman .05 .15
175 Chan Ho Park .10 .30
176 Terry Shumpert .05 .15
177 Steve Ontiveros .05 .15
178 Brad Ausmus .10 .30
179 Tim Davis .05 .15
180 Billy Ashley .05 .15
181 Vinny Castilla .10 .30
182 Bill Spiers .05 .15
183 Randy Knorr .05 .15
184 Brian L.Hunter .05 .15
185 Pat Meares .05 .15
186 Steve Buechele .05 .15
187 Kirt Manwaring .05 .15
188 Tim Naehring .05 .15
189 Matt Mieske .05 .15
190 Josias Manzanillo .05 .15
191 Greg McMichael .05 .15
192 Chuck Carr .05 .15
193 Midre Cummings .05 .15
194 Darryl Strawberry .10 .30
195 Greg Gagne .05 .15
196 Steve Cooke .05 .15
197 Woody Williams .05 .15
198 Ron Karkovice .05 .15
199 Phil Leftwich .05 .15
200 Jim Thome .20 .50
201 Brady Anderson .10 .30
202 Pedro A.Martinez .05 .15
203 Steve Karsay .05 .15
204 Reggie Sanders .10 .30
205 Bill Risley .05 .15
206 Jay Bell .10 .30
207 Kevin Brown .10 .30
208 Tim Scott .05 .15
209 Lenny Dykstra .10 .30
210 Willie Greene .05 .15
211 Jim Eisenreich .05 .15
212 Cliff Floyd .10 .30
213 Otis Nixon .05 .15
214 Eduardo Perez .05 .15
215 Manuel Lee .05 .15
216 Armando Benitez .05 .15
217 Dave McCarty .05 .15
218 Scott Livingstone .05 .15
219 Chad Kreuter .05 .15
220 Don Mattingly CL .40 1.00
221 Brian Jordan .10 .30
222 Matt Whiteside .05 .15
223 Jim Edmonds .20 .50
224 Tony Gwynn .40 1.00
225 Jose Lind .05 .15
226 Marvin Freeman .05 .15
227 Ken Hill .05 .15
228 David Hulse .05 .15
229 Joe Hesketh .05 .15
230 Roberto Petagine .05 .15
231 Jeffrey Hammonds .05 .15
232 John Jaha .05 .15
233 John Burkett .05 .15
234 Hal Morris .05 .15
235 Tony Castillo .05 .15
236 Ryan Bowen .05 .15
237 Wayne Kirby .05 .15
238 Brent Mayne .05 .15
239 Jim Bullinger .05 .15
240 Mike Lieberthal .10 .30
241 Barry Larkin .20 .50
242 David Segui .05 .15
243 Jose Bautista .05 .15
244 Hector Fajardo .05 .15
245 Orel Hershiser .10 .30
246 James Mouton .05 .15
247 Scott Leius .05 .15
248 Tom Glavine .20 .50
249 Danny Bautista .05 .15
250 Jose Mercedes .05 .15
251 Marquis Grissom .10 .30
252 Charlie Hayes .05 .15
253 Ryan Klesko .10 .30
254 Vicente Palacios .05 .15
255 Matias Carrillo .05 .15
256 Gary DiSarcina .05 .15
257 Kirk Gibson .10 .30
258 Garey Ingram .05 .15
259 Alex Fernandez .05 .15
260 John Mabry .05 .15
261 Chris Howard .05 .15
262 Miguel Jimenez .05 .15
263 Heathcliff Slocumb .05 .15
264 Albert Belle .10 .30
265 Dave Clark .05 .15
266 Joe Orsulak .05 .15
267 Joey Hamilton .05 .15
268 Mark Portugal .05 .15
269 Kevin Tapani .05 .15
270 Sid Fernandez .05 .15
271 Steve Dreyer .05 .15
272 Denny Hocking .05 .15
273 Troy O'Leary .05 .15
274 Milt Cuyler .05 .15
275 Frank Thomas .30 .75
276 Jorge Fabregas .05 .15
277 Mike Gallego .05 .15
278 Mickey Morandini .05 .15
279 Roberto Hernandez .05 .15
280 Henry Rodriguez .05 .15
281 Garret Anderson .10 .30
282 Bob Wickman .05 .15
283 Gar Finnvold .05 .15
284 Paul O'Neill .20 .50
285 Royce Clayton .05 .15
286 Chuck Knoblauch .10 .30
287 Johnny Ruffin .05 .15
288 Dave Nilsson .05 .15
289 David Cone .10 .30
290 Chuck McElroy .05 .15
291 Kevin Stocker .05 .15
292 Jose Rijo .05 .15
293 Sean Berry .05 .15
294 Ozzie Guillen .10 .30
295 Chris Hoiles .05 .15
296 Kevin Foster .05 .15
297 Jeff Frye .05 .15
298 Lance Johnson .05 .15
299 Mike Kelly .05 .15
300 Ellis Burks .10 .30
301 Roberto Kelly .05 .15
302 Dante Bichette .10 .30
303 Alvaro Espinoza .05 .15
304 Alex Cole .05 .15
305 Rickey Henderson .30 .75
306 Dave Weathers .05 .15
307 Shane Reynolds .05 .15
308 Bobby Bonilla .10 .30
309 Junior Felix .05 .15
310 Jeff Fassero .05 .15
311 Darren Lewis .05 .15
312 John Doherty .05 .15
313 Scott Servais .05 .15
314 Rick Helling .05 .15
315 Pedro Martinez .20 .50
316 Wes Chamberlain .05 .15
317 Bryan Eversgerd .05 .15
318 Trevor Hoffman .10 .30
319 John Patterson .05 .15
320 Matt Walbeck .05 .15
321 Jeff Montgomery .05 .15
322 Mel Rojas .05 .15
323 Eddie Taubensee .05 .15
324 Ray Lankford .10 .30
325 Jose Vizcaino .05 .15
326 Carlos Baerga .05 .15
327 Jack Voigt .05 .15
328 Julio Franco .10 .30
329 Brent Gates .05 .15
330 Kirby Puckett CL .20 .50
331 Greg Maddux .50 1.25
332 Jason Bere .05 .15
333 Bill Wegman .05 .15
334 Tuffy Rhodes .05 .15
335 Kevin Young .05 .15
336 Andy Benes .05 .15
337 Pedro Astacio .05 .15
338 Reggie Jefferson .05 .15
339 Tim Belcher .05 .15
340 Ken Griffey Jr. .60 1.50
341 Mariano Duncan .05 .15
342 Andres Galarraga .10 .30
343 Rondell White .10 .30
344 Cory Bailey .05 .15
345 Bryan Harvey .05 .15
346 John Franco .10 .30
347 Greg Swindell .05 .15
348 David West .05 .15
349 Fred McGriff .20 .50
350 Jose Canseco .20 .50
351 Orlando Merced .05 .15
352 Rheal Cormier .05 .15
353 Carlos Pulido .05 .15
354 Terry Steinbach .05 .15
355 Wade Boggs .20 .50
356 B.J. Surhoff .10 .30
357 Rafael Palmeiro .20 .50
358 Anthony Young .05 .15
359 Tom Brunansky .05 .15
360 Todd Stottlemyre .05 .15
361 Chris Turner .05 .15
362 Joe Boever .05 .15
363 Jeff Blauser .05 .15
364 Derek Bell .05 .15
365 Matt Williams .10 .30
366 Jeremy Hernandez .05 .15
367 Joe Girardi .05 .15
368 Mike Devereaux .05 .15
369 Jim Abbott .20 .50
370 Manny Ramirez .20 .50
371 Kenny Lofton .10 .30
372 Mark Smith .05 .15
373 Dave Fleming .05 .15
374 Dave Stewart .10 .30
375 Roger Pavlik .05 .15
376 Hipolito Pichardo .05 .15
377 Bill Taylor .05 .15
378 Robin Ventura .10 .30
379 Bernard Gilkey .05 .15
380 Kirby Puckett .30 .75
381 Steve Howe .05 .15
382 Devon White .10 .30
383 Roberto Mejia .05 .15
384 Darrin Jackson .05 .15
385 Mike Morgan .05 .15
386 Rusty Meacham .05 .15
387 Bill Swift .05 .15
388 Lou Frazier .05 .15
389 Andy Van Slyke .20 .50
390 Brett Butler .10 .30
391 Bobby Witt .05 .15
392 Jeff Conine .10 .30
393 Tim Hyers .05 .15
394 Terry Pendleton .10 .30
395 Ricky Jordan .05 .15
396 Eric Plunk .05 .15
397 Melido Perez .05 .15
398 Darryl Kile .10 .30
399 Mark McLemore .05 .15
400 Greg W.Harris .05 .15
401 Jim Leyritz .05 .15
402 Doug Strange .05 .15
403 Tim Salmon .20 .50
404 Terry Mulholland .05 .15
405 Robby Thompson .05 .15
406 Ruben Sierra .10 .30
407 Tony Phillips .05 .15
408 Moises Alou .10 .30
409 Felix Fermin .05 .15
410 Pat Listach .05 .15
411 Kevin Bass .05 .15
412 Ben McDonald .05 .15
413 Scott Cooper .05 .15
414 Jody Reed .05 .15
415 Deion Sanders .20 .50
416 Ricky Gutierrez .05 .15
417 Gregg Jefferies .05 .15
418 Jack McDowell .05 .15
419 Al Leiter .10 .30
420 Tony Longmire .05 .15
421 Paul Wagner .05 .15
422 Geronimo Pena .05 .15
423 Ivan Rodriguez .20 .50
424 Kevin Gross .05 .15
425 Kirk McCaskill .05 .15
426 Greg Myers .05 .15
427 Roger Clemens .60 1.50
428 Chris Hammond .05 .15
429 Randy Myers .05 .15
430 Roger Mason .05 .15
431 Bret Saberhagen .10 .30
432 Jeff Reboulet .05 .15
433 John Olerud .10 .30
434 Bill Gullickson .05 .15
435 Eddie Murray .30 .75
436 Pedro Munoz .05 .15
437 Charlie O'Brien .05 .15
438 Jeff Nelson .05 .15
439 Mike Macfarlane .05 .15
440 Don Mattingly CL .40 1.00
441 Derrick May .05 .15
442 John Roper .05 .15
443 Darryl Hamilton .05 .15
444 Dan Miceli .05 .15
445 Tony Eusebio .05 .15
446 Jerry Browne .05 .15
447 Wally Joyner .10 .30
448 Brian Harper .05 .15
449 Scott Fletcher .05 .15
450 Bip Roberts .05 .15
451 Pete Smith .05 .15
452 Chili Davis .10 .30
453 Dave Hollins .05 .15
454 Tony Pena .05 .15
455 Butch Henry .05 .15
456 Craig Biggio .20 .50
457 Zane Smith .05 .15
458 Ryan Thompson .05 .15
459 Mike Jackson .05 .15
460 Mark McGwire .75 2.00
461 John Smoltz .20 .50
462 Steve Scarsone .05 .15
463 Greg Colbrunn .05 .15
464 Shawn Green .10 .30
465 David Wells .10 .30
466 Jose Hernandez .05 .15
467 Chip Hale .05 .15
468 Tony Tarasco .05 .15
469 Kevin Mitchell .05 .15
470 Billy Hatcher .05 .15
471 Jay Buhner .10 .30
472 Ken Caminiti .10 .30
473 Tom Henke .05 .15
474 Todd Worrell .05 .15
475 Mark Eichhorn .05 .15
476 Bruce Ruffin .05 .15
477 Chuck Finley .10 .30
478 Marc Newfield .05 .15
479 Paul Shuey .05 .15
480 Bob Tewksbury .05 .15
481 Ramon J.Martinez .05 .15
482 Melvin Nieves .05 .15
483 Todd Zeile .05 .15
484 Benito Santiago .10 .30
485 Stan Javier .05 .15
486 Kirk Rueter .05 .15
487 Andre Dawson .10 .30
488 Eric Karros .10 .30
489 Dave Magadan .05 .15
490 Joe Carter CL .05 .15
491 Randy Velarde .05 .15
492 Larry Walker .10 .30
493 Cris Carpenter .05 .15
494 Tom Gordon .05 .15
495 Dave Burba .05 .15
496 Darren Bragg .05 .15
497 Darren Daulton .10 .30
498 Don Slaught .05 .15
499 Pat Borders .05 .15
500 Lenny Harris .05 .15
501 Joe Ausanio .05 .15
502 Alan Trammell .10 .30
503 Mike Fetters .05 .15
504 Scott Ruffcorn .05 .15
505 Rich Rowland .05 .15
506 Juan Samuel .05 .15
507 Bo Jackson .30 .75
508 Jeff Branson .05 .15
509 Bernie Williams .20 .50
510 Paul Sorrento .05 .15
511 Dennis Eckersley .10 .30
512 Pat Mahomes .05 .15
513 Rusty Greer .10 .30
514 Luis Polonia .05 .15
515 Willie Banks .05 .15
516 John Wetteland .10 .30
517 Mike LaValliere .05 .15
518 Tommy Greene .05 .15
519 Mark Grace .20 .50
520 Bob Hamelin .05 .15
521 Scott Sanderson .05 .15
522 Joe Carter .10 .30
523 Jeff Brantley .05 .15
524 Andrew Lorraine .05 .15
525 Rico Brogna .05 .15
526 Shane Mack .05 .15
527 Mark Wohlers .05 .15
528 Scott Sanders .05 .15
529 Chris Bosio .05 .15
530 Andujar Cedeno .05 .15
531 Kenny Rogers .10 .30
532 Doug Drabek .05 .15
533 Curt Leskanic .05 .15
534 Craig Shipley .05 .15
535 Craig Grebeck .05 .15
536 Cal Eldred .05 .15
537 Mickey Tettleton .05 .15
538 Harold Baines .10 .30
539 Tim Wallach .05 .15
540 Damon Buford .05 .15
541 Lenny Webster .05 .15
542 Kevin Appier .10 .30
543 Raul Mondesi .10 .30
544 Eric Young .05 .15
545 Russ Davis .05 .15
546 Mike Benjamin .05 .15
547 Mike Greenwell .05 .15
548 Scott Brosius .10 .30
549 Brian Dorsett .05 .15
550 Chili Davis CL .05 .15

1995 Donruss Press Proofs

COMPLETE SET (550) 400.00 600.00
*STARS: 6X TO 15X BASIC CARDS
SER.1 ODDS 1:20 H/R, 1:18 JUM, 1:24 MAG
SER.2 ODDS 1:24 H/R, 1:18 JUM, 1:24 MAG
STATED PRINT RUN 2000 SETS

1995 Donruss Promos

1 Frank Thomas 1.00 2.50
2 Barry Bonds 1.50 4.00
3 Hideo Nomo 1.00 2.50
4 Ken Griffey Jr. 2.00 5.00
5 Cal Ripken Jr. 3.00 8.00
6 Manny Ramirez .60 1.50
7 Mike Piazza 1.00 2.50
8 Greg Maddux 1.50 4.00

1995 Donruss All-Stars

COMPLETE SET (18) 75.00 150.00
COMPLETE SERIES AL (9) 40.00 100.00
COMPLETE SERIES NL (9) 25.00 60.00
STATED ODDS 1:8 JUMBO
AL1 Jimmy Key 1.25 3.00
AL2 Ivan Rodriguez 2.00 5.00
AL3 Frank Thomas 3.00 8.00
AL4 Roberto Alomar 2.00 5.00
AL5 Wade Boggs 2.00 5.00
AL6 Cal Ripken 10.00 25.00
AL7 Joe Carter 1.25 3.00
AL8 Ken Griffey Jr. 6.00 15.00
AL9 Kirby Puckett 3.00 8.00
NL1 Greg Maddux 5.00 12.00
NL2 Mike Piazza 5.00 12.00
NL3 Gregg Jefferies .60 1.50
NL4 Mariano Duncan .60 1.50
NL5 Matt Williams 1.25 3.00
NL6 Ozzie Smith 5.00 12.00
NL7 Barry Bonds 8.00 20.00
NL8 Tony Gwynn 4.00 10.00
NL9 David Justice 1.25 3.00

1995 Donruss Bomb Squad

COMPLETE SET (6) 5.00 12.00
SER.1 STATED ODDS 1:24 RET, 1:16 MAG
1 K.Griffey 1.50 4.00
M.Williams
2 F.Thomas .75 2.00
J.Bagwell
3 B.Bonds 2.00 5.00
A.Belle
4 J.Canseco .50 1.25
F.McGriff
5 C.Fielder .30 .75
A.Galarraga
6 J.Carter .30 .75
K.Mitchell

1995 Donruss Diamond Kings

COMPLETE SET (29) 20.00 50.00
COMPLETE SERIES 1 (14) 8.00 20.00
COMPLETE SERIES 2 (15) 15.00 30.00
STATED ODDS 1:10 H/R, 1:9 JUM, 1:10 MAG
DK1 Frank Thomas 1.25 3.00
DK2 Jeff Bagwell .75 2.00
DK3 Chili Davis .50 1.25
DK4 Dante Bichette .50 1.25
DK5 Ruben Sierra .50 1.25
DK6 Jeff Conine .50 1.25
DK7 Paul O'Neill .75 2.00
DK8 Bobby Bonilla .50 1.25
DK9 Joe Carter .50 1.25
DK10 Moises Alou .50 1.25
DK11 Kenny Lofton .50 1.25
DK12 Matt Williams .50 1.25
DK13 Kevin Seitzer .25 .60
DK14 Sammy Sosa 1.25 3.00
DK15 Scott Cooper .25 .60
DK16 Raul Mondesi .50 1.25
DK17 Will Clark .75 2.00
DK18 Lenny Dykstra .50 1.25
DK19 Kirby Puckett 1.25 3.00
DK20 Hal Morris .25 .60
DK21 Travis Fryman .50 1.25
DK22 Greg Maddux 2.00 5.00
DK23 Rafael Palmeiro .75 2.00
DK24 Tony Gwynn 1.50 4.00
DK25 David Cone .50 1.25
DK26 Al Martin .25 .60
DK27 Ken Griffey Jr. 2.50 6.00
DK28 Gregg Jefferies .25 .60
DK29 Checklist .25 .60

1995 Donruss Dominators

COMPLETE SET (9) 10.00 25.00
SER.2 STATED ODDS 1:24 HOBBY
1 Maddux 1.25 3.00
Cone
Mussina
2 Piazza 1.25 3.00
Rodriguez
Daulton
3 Thomas .75 2.00
Bagwell
McGriff
4 Alomar .50 1.25
Baerga
Biggio
5 Ventura .30 .75
Fryman
Williams
6 Ripken 2.50 6.00
Larkin
Cordero
7 Bonds 2.00 5.00
Alou
Belle
8 Griffey 1.50 4.00
Lofton
Grissom
9 Gwynn 1.00 2.50
Puckett
O'Neill

1995 Donruss Elite

COMPLETE SET (12) 40.00 100.00
COMPLETE SERIES 1 (6) 20.00 50.00
COMPLETE SERIES 2 (6) 20.00 50.00
SER.1 ODDS 1:210 H/R, 1:120 J, 1:210 M
SER.2 ODDS 1:180 H/R, 1:120 J, 1:180 M
STATED PRINT RUN 10,000 SERIAL #'d SETS
49 Jeff Bagwell 3.00 8.00
50 Paul O'Neill 3.00 8.00
51 Greg Maddux 6.00 15.00
52 Mike Piazza 5.00 12.00
53 Matt Williams 2.00 5.00
54 Ken Griffey Jr. 6.00 15.00
55 Frank Thomas 5.00 12.00
56 Barry Bonds 8.00 20.00
57 Kirby Puckett 5.00 12.00
58 Fred McGriff 3.00 8.00
59 Jose Canseco 3.00 8.00
60 Albert Belle 2.00 5.00

1995 Donruss Long Ball Leaders

COMPLETE SET (8) 8.00 20.00
SER.1 STATED ODDS 1:24 HOBBY
1 Frank Thomas 1.00 2.50
2 Fred McGriff .60 1.50
3 Ken Griffey Jr. 2.00 5.00
4 Matt Williams .40 1.00
5 Mike Piazza 1.50 4.00
6 Jose Canseco .60 1.50
7 Barry Bonds 2.50 6.00
8 Jeff Bagwell .60 1.50

1995 Donruss Mound Marvels

COMPLETE SET (8) 8.00 20.00
SER.2 STATED ODDS 1:16 RET/MAG
1 Greg Maddux 2.50 6.00
2 David Cone .60 1.50
3 Mike Mussina 1.00 2.50
4 Bret Saberhagen .60 1.50
5 Jimmy Key .60 1.50
6 Doug Drabek .30 .75
7 Randy Johnson 1.50 4.00
8 Jason Bere .30 .75

1995 Donruss Top of the Order

This 360-card standard-size set was distributed as a Major League Baseball Card Game. The cards were packaged in 80-card starter decks with other cards available in booster packs. The fronts carry player action photos with the player's name, team, position, and other player information needed to play the game. The green backs carry the card logo. The first 180 cards feature players in the American League with the National League represented by the second 180 cards. The cards are unnumbered and checklisted below in alphabetical order within each team. There are three levels of scarcity for these cards; common, uncommon and rare. All cards have been given either a designation of C (for common), U (for uncommon) or R (for rare).

COMPLETE SET (360) 250.00 500.00
COMMON CARD (1-360) .04 .10
UNCOMMON CARD (1-360) .20 .50
RARE CARD (1-360) .40 1.00
1 Brady Anderson C .07 .20
2 Harold Baines U .30 .75
3 Bret Barberie U .20 .50
4 Armando Benitez C .07 .20
5 Bobby Bonilla U .20 .50
6 Scott Erickson C .02 .10
7 Leo Gomez C .02 .10
8 Curtis Goodwin R .40 1.00
9 Jeffrey Hammonds C .07 .20
10 Chris Hoiles C .02 .10
11 Doug Jones C .02 .10
12 Ben McDonald U .20 .50
13 Mike Mussina U 1.00 2.50
14 Rafael Palmeiro R 1.00 2.50
15 Cal Ripken Jr. R 15.00 40.00
16 Rick Aguilera C .07 .20
17 Luis Alicea C .02 .10
18 Jose Canseco U 1.00 2.50
19 Roger Clemens C .50 1.25
20 Mike Greenwell U .20 .50
21 Erik Hanson C .02 .10
22 Mike Macfarlane C .02 .10
23 Tim Naehring R .40 1.00
24 Troy O'Leary U .20 .50
25 Ken Ryan C .02 .10
26 Aaron Sele C .30 .75
27 Lee Tinsley U .20 .50
28 John Valentin R .40 1.00
29 Mo Vaughn R .40 1.00
30 Jim Abbott C .07 .20
31 Mike Butcher C .02 .10
32 Chili Davis R .60 1.50
33 Gary DiSarcina R .40 1.00
34 Damion Easley C .02 .10
35 Jim Edmonds R 1.00 2.50
36 Chuck Finley U .30 .75
37 Mark Langston C .02 .10

38 Greg Myers C .02 .10
39 Spike Owen C .02 .10
40 Troy Percival R .60 1.50
41 Tony Phillips U .20 .50
42 Tim Salmon R .75 2.00
43 Lee Smith R .60 1.50
44 J.T. Snow U .30 .75
45 Jason Bere C .02 .10
46 Mike Devereaux U .20 .50
47 Ray Durham C .30 .75
48 Alex Fernandez C .02 .10
49 Ozzie Guillen R .60 1.50
50 Roberto Hernandez C .07 .20
51 Lance Johnson U .20 .50
52 Ron Karkovice C .02 .10
53 Tim Raines U .30 .75
54 Frank Thomas R 3.00 8.00
55 Robin Ventura U .60 1.50
56 Sandy Alomar R .60 1.50
57 Carlos Baerga R .40 1.00
58 Albert Belle R .60 1.50
59 Kenny Lofton R .75 2.00
60 Dennis Martinez C .07 .20
61 Jose Mesa U .20 .50
62 Eddie Murray R 1.00 2.50
63 Charles Nagy C .02 .10
64 Tony Pena C .07 .20
65 Eric Plunk R .40 1.00
66 Manny Ramirez R 3.00 8.00
67 Paul Sorrento C .02 .10
68 Jim Thome R 1.00 2.50
69 Omar Vizquel C .07 .20
70 Danny Bautista C .02 .10
71 Joe Boever C .02 .10
72 Chad Curtis C .02 .10
73 Cecil Fielder U .30 .75
74 John Flaherty U .20 .50
75 Travis Fryman U .30 .75
76 Kirk Gibson C .07 .20
77 Chris Gomez C .02 .10
78 Mike Henneman R .40 1.00
79 Bob Higginson C .30 .75
80 Alan Trammell U .40 1.00
81 Lou Whitaker R .60 1.50
82 Kevin Appier R .60 1.50
83 Billy Brewer C .02 .10
84 Vince Coleman R .40 1.00
85 Gary Gaetti C .07 .20
86 Greg Gagne C .02 .10
87 Tom Goodwin R .40 1.00
88 Tom Gordon C .07 .20
89 Mark Gubicza C .02 .10
90 Bob Hamelin C .02 .10
91 Phil Hiatt C .02 .10
92 Wally Joyner R .40 1.00
93 Brent Mayne C .02 .10
94 Jeff Montgomery C .02 .10
95 Ricky Bones C .02 .10
96 Mike Fetters C .02 .10
97 Darryl Hamilton C .02 .10
98 Pat Listach C .02 .10
99 Matt Mieske C .02 .10
100 Dave Nilsson C .02 .10
101 Joe Oliver U .20 .50
102 Kevin Seitzer U .20 .50
103 B.J. Surhoff U .30 .75
104 Jose Valentin C .02 .10
105 Greg Vaughn C .07 .20
106 Bill Wegman C .02 .10
107 Alex Cole U .20 .50
108 Marty Cordova C .07 .20
109 Chuck Knoblauch R .60 1.50
110 Scott Leius C .02 .10
111 Pat Meares C .02 .10
112 Pedro Munoz C .02 .10
113 Kirby Puckett R 8.00 20.00
114 Scott Stahoviak C .02 .10
115 Mike Trombley C .02 .10
116 Matt Walbeck C .02 .10
117 Wade Boggs R 2.50 6.00
118 David Cone U .40 1.00
119 Tony Fernandez C .07 .20
120 Don Mattingly R 8.00 20.00
121 Jack McDowell C .02 .10
122 Paul O'Neill U .30 .75
123 Melido Perez C .02 .10
124 Luis Polonia C .02 .10
125 Ruben Sierra C .07 .20
126 Mike Stanley C .02 .10
127 Randy Velarde C .02 .10
128 John Wetteland R .60 1.50
129 Bob Wickman C .02 .10
130 Bernie Williams C .15 .40
131 Gerald Williams C .02 .10
132 Geronimo Berroa C .02 .10
133 Mike Bordick U .20 .50
134 Scott Brosius C .07 .20
135 Dennis Eckersley C .20 .50
136 Brent Gates C .02 .10
137 Rickey Henderson U 1.50 4.00
138 Stan Javier C .02 .10
139 Mark McGwire R 12.50 30.00
140 Steve Ontiveros U .20 .50
141 Terry Steinbach C .02 .10
142 Todd Stottlemyre R .40 1.00
143 Danny Tartabull C .02 .10
144 Bobby Ayala R .40 1.00
145 Andy Benes U .20 .50
146 Mike Blowers C .02 .10
147 Jay Buhner U .30 .75
148 Joey Cora U .20 .50
149 Alex Diaz C .02 .10
150 Ken Griffey Jr. R 10.00 25.00
151 Randy Johnson R 2.00 5.00
152 Edgar Martinez R .75 2.00
153 Tino Martinez U .40 1.00
154 Bill Risley R .40 1.00
155 Alex Rodriguez C 1.25 3.00
156 Dan Wilson C .02 .10
157 Will Clark R 1.00 2.50
158 Jeff Frye U .20 .50
159 Benji Gil C .02 .10
160 Juan Gonzalez C .30 .75
161 Rusty Greer C .07 .20
162 Mark McLemore R .40 1.00
163 Otis Nixon U .20 .50
164 Dean Palmer R .60 1.50
165 Ivan Rodriguez R 4.00 10.00
166 Kenny Rogers C .07 .20
167 Jeff Russell C .02 .10
168 Mickey Tettleton C .02 .10
169 Bob Tewksbury C .02 .10
170 Bobby Witt C .02 .10
171 Roberto Alomar R 1.00 2.50
172 Joe Carter R .60 1.50
173 Alex Gonzalez C .02 .10
174 Candy Maldonado C .02 .10
175 Paul Molitor C .20 .50
176 John Olerud C .07 .20
177 Lance Parrish C .07 .20
178 Ed Sprague C .02 .10
179 Devon White C .02 .10
180 Woody Williams C .02 .10
181 Steve Avery C .02 .10
182 Jeff Blauser C .02 .10
183 Tom Glavine U .60 1.50
184 Marquis Grissom R .40 1.00
185 Chipper Jones C .60 1.50
186 David Justice R 1.00 2.50
187 Ryan Klesko U .30 .75
188 Mark Lemke C .02 .10
189 Javy Lopez C .15 .40
190 Greg Maddux R 10.00 25.00
191 Fred McGriff R .75 2.00
192 Greg McMichael U .20 .50
193 John Smoltz R .60 1.50
194 Mark Wohlers R .40 1.00
195 Jim Bullinger U .20 .50
196 Shawon Dunston R .40 1.00
197 Kevin Foster C .02 .10
198 Luis Gonzalez C .20 .50
199 Mark Grace R 1.00 2.50
200 Brian McRae R .40 1.00
201 Randy Myers R .60 1.50
202 Jaime Navarro U .20 .50
203 Rey Sanchez U .20 .50
204 Scott Servais C .02 .10
205 Sammy Sosa R 8.00 20.00
206 Steve Trachsel U .30 .75
207 Todd Zeile C .07 .20
208 Bret Boone R .75 2.00
209 Jeff Branson U .20 .50
210 Jeff Brantley R .60 1.50
211 Hector Carrasco C .02 .10
212 Ron Gant R .60 1.50
213 Lenny Harris C .02 .10
214 Barry Larkin R 1.00 2.50
215 Darren Lewis C .02 .10
216 Hal Morris C .02 .10
217 Mark Portugal C .02 .10
218 Jose Rijo U .20 .50
219 Reggie Sanders R .60 1.50
220 Pete Schourek U .20 .50
221 John Smiley C .02 .10
222 Eddie Taubensee C .02 .10
223 David Wells C .10 .30
224 Jason Bates C .02 .10
225 Dante Bichette R .60 1.50
226 Vinny Castilla U .30 .75
227 Andres Galarraga R 1.00 2.50
228 Joe Girardi U .20 .50
229 Mike Kingery C .02 .10
230 Steve Reed R .40 1.00
231 Bruce Ruffin U .20 .50
232 Bret Saberhagen U .20 .50
233 Bill Swift C .02 .10
234 Larry Walker R 1.00 2.50
235 Walt Weiss C .02 .10
236 Eric Young C .02 .10
237 Kurt Abbott C .02 .10
238 John Burkett C .07 .20
239 Chuck Carr C .02 .10
240 Greg Colbrunn C .02 .10
241 Jeff Conine R .40 1.00
242 Andre Dawson C .15 .40
243 Chris Hammond R .40 1.00
244 Charles Johnson C .07 .20
245 Robb Nen C .07 .20
246 Terry Pendleton U .30 .75
247 Gary Sheffield R 1.50 4.00
248 Quilvio Veras C .02 .10
249 Jeff Bagwell U 1.50 4.00
250 Derek Bell R .40 1.00
251 Craig Biggio U .60 1.50
252 Doug Drabek C .02 .10
253 Tony Eusebio U .20 .50
254 John Hudek C .02 .10
255 Brian L. Hunter U .20 .50
256 Todd Jones R .60 1.50
257 Dave Magadan U .20 .50
258 Orlando Miller C .02 .10
259 James Mouton C .02 .10
260 Shane Reynolds C .02 .10
261 Greg Swindell C .02 .10
262 Billy Ashley C .02 .10
263 Tom Candiotti U .20 .50
264 Delino DeShields C .07 .20
265 Eric Karros R .60 1.50
266 Roberto Kelly C .02 .10
267 Ramon Martinez C .07 .20
268 Raul Mondesi R .60 1.50
269 Hideo Nomo R 15.00 40.00
270 Jose Offerman U .20 .50
271 Mike Piazza R 10.00 25.00
272 Kevin Tapani C .02 .10
273 Ismael Valdes U .20 .50
274 Tim Wallach C .02 .10
275 Todd Worrell R .40 1.00
276 Moises Alou R .60 1.50
277 Sean Berry U .20 .50
278 Wil Cordero U .20 .50
279 Jeff Fassero C .02 .10
280 Darrin Fletcher C .02 .10
281 Mike Lansing C .02 .10
282 Pedro Martinez R 3.00 8.00
283 Carlos Perez U .20 .50
284 Mel Rojas U .20 .50
285 Tim Scott R .40 1.00
286 David Segui U .30 .75
287 Tony Tarasco U .20 .50
288 Rondell White C .07 .20
289 Rico Brogna C .02 .10
290 Brett Butler C .07 .20
291 John Franco C .07 .20
292 Pete Harnisch C .02 .10
293 Todd Hundley C .07 .20
294 Bobby Jones C .02 .10
295 Jeff Kent C .15 .40
296 Joe Orsulak U .20 .50
297 Ryan Thompson U .20 .50
298 Jose Vizcaino C .02 .10
299 Ricky Bottalico U .20 .50
300 Darren Daulton C .07 .20
301 Mariano Duncan U .20 .50
302 Lenny Dykstra U .30 .75
303 Jim Eisenreich U .30 .75
304 Tyler Green U .20 .50
305 Charlie Hayes U .20 .50
306 Dave Hollins C .02 .10
307 Gregg Jefferies C .02 .10
308 Mickey Morandini U .20 .50
309 Curt Schilling R 2.00 5.00
310 Heathcliff Slocumb U .20 .50
311 Kevin Stocker C .02 .10
312 Jay Bell C .02 .10
313 Jacob Brumfield C .02 .10
314 Dave Clark U .20 .50
315 Carlos Garcia C .02 .10
316 Mark Johnson C .02 .10
317 Jeff King C .02 .10
318 Nelson Liriano U .20 .50
319 Al Martin U .20 .50
320 Orlando Merced U .20 .50
321 Dan Miceli U .20 .50
322 Denny Neagle C .07 .20
323 Mark Parent C .02 .10
324 Dan Plesac R .40 1.00
325 Scott Cooper C .02 .10
326 Bernard Gilkey R .40 1.00
327 Tom Henke R .40 1.00
328 Ken Hill C .02 .10
329 Danny Jackson C .02 .10
330 Brian Jordan R .60 1.50
331 Ray Lankford U .30 .75
332 John Mabry U .20 .50
333 Jose Oquendo C .02 .10
334 Tom Pagnozzi C .02 .10
335 Ozzie Smith U 2.00 5.00
336 Andy Ashby U .20 .50
337 Brad Ausmus U .20 .50
338 Ken Caminiti U .40 1.00
339 Andujar Cedeno C .02 .10
340 Steve Finley R .60 1.50
341 Tony Gwynn R 8.00 20.00
342 Joey Hamilton C .02 .10
343 Trevor Hoffman C .07 .20
344 Jody Reed C .02 .10
345 Bip Roberts R .40 1.00
346 Eddie Williams C .02 .10
347 Rod Beck U .30 .75
348 Mike Benjamin U .20 .50
349 Barry Bonds R 8.00 20.00
350 Royce Clayton C .02 .10
351 Glenallen Hill C .02 .10
352 Kirt Manwaring C .02 .10
353 Terry Mulholland C .02 .10
354 John Patterson C .02 .10
355 J.R. Phillips C .02 .10
356 Deion Sanders R .60 1.50
357 Steve Scarsone U .20 .50
358 Robby Thompson C .02 .10
359 William VanLandingham C .02 .10
360 Matt Williams R .75 2.00

1996 Donruss Samples

COMPLETE SET (8) 6.00 15.00
1 Frank Thomas .50 1.25
2 Barry Bonds 1.00 2.50
3 Hideo Nomo .40 1.00
4 Ken Griffey Jr. 1.50 4.00
5 Cal Ripken 2.00 5.00
6 Manny Ramirez .50 1.25
7 Mike Piazza 1.25 3.00
8 Greg Maddux 1.00 2.50

1996 Donruss

The 1996 Donruss set was issued in two series of 330 and 220 cards respectively, for a total of 550. The 12-card packs had a suggested retail price of $1.79. The full-bleed fronts feature full-color action photos with the player's name is in white ink in the upper right. The horizontal backs feature season and career stats, text, vital stats and another photo. Rookie Cards in this set include Mike Cameron.

COMPLETE SET (550) 15.00 40.00
COMPLETE SERIES 1 (330) 10.00 25.00
COMPLETE SERIES 2 (220) 6.00 15.00
SUBSET CARDS HALF VALUE OF BASE CARDS
1 Frank Thomas .30 .75
2 Jason Bates .10 .30
3 Steve Sparks .10 .30
4 Scott Servais .10 .30
5 Angelo Encarnacion RC .10 .30
6 Scott Sanders .10 .30
7 Billy Ashley .10 .30
8 Alex Rodriguez .60 1.50
9 Sean Bergman .10 .30
10 Brad Radke .10 .30
11 Andy Van Slyke .20 .50
12 Joe Girardi .10 .30
13 Mark Grudzielanek .10 .30
14 Rick Aguilera .10 .30
15 Randy Veres .10 .30
16 Tim Bogar .10 .30
17 Dave Veres .10 .30
18 Kevin Stocker .10 .30
19 Marquis Grissom .10 .30
20 Will Clark .20 .50
21 Jay Bell .10 .30
22 Allen Battle .10 .30
23 Frank Rodriguez .10 .30
24 Terry Steinbach .10 .30
25 Gerald Williams .10 .30
26 Sid Roberson .10 .30
27 Greg Zaun .10 .30
28 Ozzie Timmons .10 .30
29 Vaughn Eshelman .10 .30
30 Ed Sprague .10 .30
31 Gary DiSarcina .10 .30
32 Joe Boever .10 .30
33 Steve Avery .10 .30
34 Brad Ausmus .10 .30
35 Kirt Manwaring .10 .30
36 Gary Sheffield .10 .30
37 Jason Bere .10 .30
38 Jeff Manto .10 .30
39 David Cone .10 .30
40 Manny Ramirez .20 .50
41 Sandy Alomar Jr. .10 .30
42 Curtis Goodwin .10 .30
43 Tino Martinez .20 .50
44 Woody Williams .10 .30
45 Dean Palmer .10 .30
46 Hipolito Pichardo .10 .30
47 Jason Giambi .10 .30
48 Lance Johnson .10 .30
49 Bernard Gilkey .10 .30
50 Kirby Puckett .30 .75
51 Tony Fernandez .10 .30
52 Alex Gonzalez .10 .30
53 Bret Saberhagen .10 .30
54 Lyle Mouton .10 .30
55 Brian McRae .10 .30
56 Mark Gubicza .10 .30
57 Sergio Valdez .10 .30
58 Darrin Fletcher .10 .30
59 Steve Parris .10 .30
60 Johnny Damon .20 .50
61 Rickey Henderson .30 .75
62 Darrell Whitmore .10 .30
63 Roberto Petagine .10 .30
64 Trenidad Hubbard .10 .30
65 Heathcliff Slocumb .10 .30
66 Steve Finley .10 .30
67 Mariano Rivera .60 1.50
68 Brian L.Hunter .10 .30
69 Jamie Moyer .10 .30
70 Ellis Burks .10 .30
71 Pat Kelly .10 .30
72 Mickey Tettleton .10 .30
73 Garret Anderson .10 .30
74 Andy Pettitte .20 .50
75 Glenallen Hill .10 .30
76 Brent Gates .10 .30
77 Lou Whitaker .10 .30
78 David Segui .10 .30
79 Dan Wilson .10 .30
80 Pat Listach .10 .30
81 Jeff Bagwell .20 .50
82 Ben McDonald .10 .30
83 John Valentin .10 .30
84 John Jaha .10 .30
85 Pete Schourek .10 .30
86 Bryce Florie .10 .30
87 Brian Jordan .10 .30
88 Ron Karkovice .10 .30
89 Al Leiter .10 .30
90 Tony Longmire .10 .30
91 Nelson Liriano .10 .30
92 David Bell .10 .30
93 Kevin Gross .10 .30
94 Tom Candiotti .10 .30
95 Dave Martinez .10 .30
96 Greg Myers .10 .30
97 Rheal Cormier .10 .30
98 Chris Hammond .10 .30
99 Randy Myers .10 .30
100 Bill Pulsipher .10 .30
101 Jason Isringhausen .10 .30
102 Dave Stevens .10 .30
103 Roberto Alomar .20 .50
104 Bob Higginson .10 .30
105 Eddie Murray .30 .75
106 Matt Walbeck .10 .30
107 Mark Wohlers .10 .30
108 Jeff Nelson .10 .30
109 Tom Goodwin .10 .30
110 Cal Ripken CL .50 1.25
111 Rey Sanchez .10 .30
112 Hector Carrasco .10 .30
113 B.J. Surhoff .10 .30
114 Dan Miceli .10 .30
115 Dean Hartgraves .10 .30
116 John Burkett .10 .30
117 Gary Gaetti .10 .30
118 Ricky Bones .10 .30
119 Mike Macfarlane .10 .30
120 Bip Roberts .10 .30
121 Dave Mlicki .10 .30
122 Chili Davis .10 .30
123 Mark Whiten .10 .30
124 Herbert Perry .10 .30
125 Butch Henry .10 .30
126 Derek Bell .10 .30
127 Al Martin .10 .30
128 John Franco .10 .30
129 W. VanLandingham .10 .30
130 Mike Bordick .10 .30
131 Mike Mordecai .10 .30
132 Robby Thompson .10 .30
133 Greg Colbrunn .10 .30
134 Domingo Cedeno .10 .30
135 Chad Curtis .10 .30
136 Jose Hernandez .10 .30
137 Scott Klingenbeck .10 .30
138 Ryan Klesko .10 .30
139 John Smiley .10 .30
140 Charlie Hayes .10 .30
141 Jay Buhner .10 .30
142 Doug Drabek .10 .30
143 Roger Pavlik .10 .30
144 Todd Worrell .10 .30
145 Cal Ripken 1.00 2.50
146 Steve Reed .10 .30
147 Chuck Finley .10 .30
148 Mike Blowers .10 .30
149 Orel Hershiser .10 .30
150 Allen Watson .10 .30
151 Ramon Martinez .10 .30
152 Melvin Nieves .10 .30
153 Tripp Cromer .10 .30
154 Yorkis Perez .10 .30
155 Stan Javier .10 .30
156 Mel Rojas .10 .30
157 Aaron Sele .10 .30
158 Eric Karros .10 .30
159 Robb Nen .10 .30
160 Raul Mondesi .10 .30
161 John Wetteland .10 .30
162 Tim Scott .10 .30
163 Kenny Rogers .10 .30
164 Melvin Bunch .10 .30
165 Rod Beck .10 .30
166 Andy Benes .10 .30
167 Lenny Dykstra .10 .30
168 Orlando Merced .10 .30
169 Tomas Perez .10 .30
170 Xavier Hernandez .10 .30
171 Ruben Sierra .10 .30
172 Alan Trammell .10 .30
173 Mike Fetters .10 .30
174 Wilson Alvarez .10 .30
175 Erik Hanson .10 .30
176 Travis Fryman .10 .30
177 Jim Abbott .20 .50
178 Bret Boone .10 .30
179 Sterling Hitchcock .10 .30
180 Pat Mahomes .10 .30
181 Mark Acre .10 .30
182 Charles Nagy .10 .30
183 Rusty Greer .10 .30
184 Mike Stanley .10 .30
185 Jim Bullinger .10 .30
186 Shane Andrews .10 .30
187 Brian Keyser .10 .30
188 Tyler Green .10 .30
189 Mark Grace .20 .50
190 Bob Hamelin .10 .30
191 Luis Ortiz .10 .30
192 Joe Carter .10 .30
193 Eddie Taubensee .10 .30
194 Brian Anderson .10 .30
195 Edgardo Alfonzo .10 .30
196 Pedro Munoz .10 .30
197 David Justice .10 .30
198 Trevor Hoffman .10 .30
199 Bobby Ayala .10 .30
200 Tony Eusebio .10 .30
201 Jeff Russell .10 .30
202 Mike Hampton .10 .30
203 Walt Weiss .10 .30
204 Joey Hamilton .10 .30
205 Roberto Hernandez .10 .30
206 Greg Vaughn .10 .30
207 Felipe Lira .10 .30
208 Harold Baines .10 .30
209 Tim Wallach .10 .30
210 Manny Alexander .10 .30
211 Tim Laker .10 .30
212 Chris Haney .10 .30
213 Brian Maxcy .10 .30
214 Eric Young .10 .30
215 Darryl Strawberry .10 .30
216 Barry Bonds .75 2.00
217 Tim Naehring .10 .30
218 Scott Brosius .10 .30
219 Reggie Sanders .10 .30
220 Eddie Murray CL .20 .50
221 Luis Alicea .10 .30
222 Albert Belle .10 .30
223 Benji Gil .10 .30
224 Dante Bichette .10 .30
225 Bobby Bonilla .10 .30
226 Todd Stottlemyre .10 .30
227 Jim Edmonds .10 .30
228 Todd Jones .10 .30
229 Shawn Green .10 .30
230 Javier Lopez .10 .30
231 Ariel Prieto .10 .30
232 Tony Phillips .10 .30
233 James Mouton .10 .30
234 Jose Oquendo .10 .30
235 Royce Clayton .10 .30
236 Chuck Carr .10 .30
237 Doug Jones .10 .30
238 Mark McLemore .10 .30
239 Bill Swift .10 .30
240 Scott Leius .10 .30
241 Russ Davis .10 .30
242 Ray Durham .10 .30
243 Matt Mieske .10 .30
244 Brent Mayne .10 .30
245 Thomas Howard .10 .30
246 Troy O'Leary .10 .30
247 Jacob Brumfield .10 .30
248 Mickey Morandini .10 .30
249 Todd Hundley .10 .30
250 Chris Bosio .10 .30
251 Omar Vizquel .20 .50
252 Mike Lansing .10 .30
253 John Mabry .10 .30
254 Mike Perez .10 .30
255 Delino DeShields .10 .30
256 Wil Cordero .10 .30
257 Mike James .10 .30
258 Todd Van Poppel .10 .30
259 Joey Cora .10 .30
260 Andre Dawson .10 .30
261 Jerry DiPoto .10 .30
262 Rick Krivda .10 .30
263 Glenn Dishman .10 .30
264 Mike Mimbs .10 .30
265 John Ericks .10 .30
266 Jose Canseco .20 .50
267 Jeff Branson .10 .30
268 Curt Leskanic .10 .30
269 Jon Nunnally .10 .30
270 Scott Stahoviak .10 .30
271 Jeff Montgomery .10 .30
272 Hal Morris .10 .30
273 Esteban Loaiza .10 .30
274 Rico Brogna .10 .30
275 Dave Winfield .10 .30
276 J.R. Phillips .10 .30
277 Todd Zeile .10 .30
278 Tom Pagnozzi .10 .30
279 Mark Lemke .10 .30
280 Dave Magadan .10 .30
281 Greg McMichael .10 .30
282 Mike Morgan .10 .30
283 Moises Alou .10 .30
284 Dennis Martinez .10 .30
285 Jeff Kent .10 .30
286 Mark Johnson .10 .30
287 Darren Lewis .10 .30
288 Brad Clontz .10 .30
289 Chad Fonville .10 .30
290 Paul Sorrento .10 .30
291 Lee Smith .10 .30
292 Tom Glavine .20 .50
293 Antonio Osuna .10 .30
294 Kevin Foster .10 .30
295 Sandy Martinez .10 .30
296 Mark Leiter .10 .30
297 Julian Tavarez .10 .30
298 Mike Kelly .10 .30
299 Joe Oliver .10 .30
300 John Flaherty .10 .30
301 Don Mattingly .75 2.00
302 Pat Meares .10 .30
303 John Doherty .10 .30
304 Joe Vitiello .10 .30
305 Vinny Castilla .10 .30
306 Jeff Brantley .10 .30
307 Mike Greenwell .10 .30
308 Midre Cummings .10 .30
309 Curt Schilling .10 .30
310 Ken Caminiti .10 .30
311 Scott Erickson .10 .30
312 Carl Everett .10 .30
313 Charles Johnson .10 .30
314 Alex Diaz .10 .30
315 Jose Mesa .10 .30
316 Mark Carreon .10 .30
317 Carlos Perez .10 .30
318 Ismael Valdes .10 .30
319 Frank Castillo .10 .30
320 Tom Henke .10 .30
321 Spike Owen .10 .30
322 Joe Orsulak .10 .30
323 Paul Menhart .10 .30
324 Pedro Borbon .10 .30
325 Paul Molitor CL .10 .30
326 Jeff Cirillo .10 .30
327 Edwin Hurtado .10 .30
328 Orlando Miller .10 .30
329 Steve Ontiveros .10 .30
330 Kirby Puckett CL .20 .50
331 Scott Bullett .10 .30
332 Andres Galarraga .10 .30
333 Cal Eldred .10 .30
334 Sammy Sosa .30 .75
335 Don Slaught .10 .30
336 Jody Reed .10 .30
337 Roger Cedeno .10 .30
338 Ken Griffey Jr. .60 1.50
339 Todd Hollandsworth .10 .30
340 Mike Trombley .10 .30
341 Gregg Jefferies .10 .30
342 Larry Walker .10 .30
343 Pedro Martinez .20 .50
344 Dwayne Hosey .10 .30
345 Terry Pendleton .10 .30
346 Pete Harnisch .10 .30
347 Tony Castillo .10 .30
348 Paul Quantrill .10 .30
349 Fred McGriff .20 .50
350 Ivan Rodriguez .20 .50
351 Butch Huskey .10 .30
352 Ozzie Smith .50 1.25
353 Marty Cordova .10 .30
354 John Wasdin .10 .30
355 Wade Boggs .20 .50
356 Dave Nilsson .10 .30
357 Rafael Palmeiro .20 .50
358 Luis Gonzalez .10 .30
359 Reggie Jefferson .10 .30
360 Carlos Delgado .10 .30
361 Orlando Palmeiro .10 .30
362 Chris Gomez .10 .30
363 John Smoltz .20 .50
364 Marc Newfield .10 .30
365 Matt Williams .10 .30
366 Jesus Tavarez .10 .30
367 Bruce Ruffin .10 .30
368 Sean Berry .10 .30
369 Randy Velarde .10 .30
370 Tony Pena .10 .30
371 Jim Thome .20 .50
372 Jeffrey Hammonds .10 .30
373 Bob Wolcott .10 .30
374 Juan Guzman .10 .30
375 Juan Gonzalez .10 .30
376 Michael Tucker .10 .30
377 Doug Johns .10 .30
378 Mike Cameron RC .25 .60
379 Ray Lankford .10 .30
380 Jose Parra .10 .30
381 Jimmy Key .10 .30
382 John Olerud .10 .30
383 Kevin Ritz .10 .30
384 Tim Raines .10 .30
385 Rich Amaral .10 .30
386 Keith Lockhart .10 .30
387 Steve Scarsone .10 .30
388 Cliff Floyd .10 .30
389 Rich Aude .10 .30
390 Hideo Nomo .30 .75
391 Geronimo Berroa .10 .30
392 Pat Rapp .10 .30
393 Dustin Hermanson .10 .30
394 Greg Maddux .50 1.25
395 Darren Daulton .10 .30
396 Kenny Lofton .10 .30
397 Ruben Rivera .10 .30
398 Billy Wagner .10 .30
399 Kevin Brown .10 .30
400 Mike Kingery .10 .30
401 Bernie Williams .20 .50
402 Otis Nixon .10 .30
403 Damion Easley .10 .30
404 Paul O'Neill .20 .50
405 Deion Sanders .20 .50
406 Dennis Eckersley .10 .30
407 Tony Clark .10 .30
408 Rondell White .10 .30
409 Luis Sojo .10 .30
410 David Hulse .10 .30
411 Shane Reynolds .10 .30
412 Chris Hoiles .10 .30
413 Lee Tinsley .10 .30
414 Scott Karl .10 .30
415 Ron Gant .10 .30
416 Brian Johnson .10 .30
417 Jose Oliva .10 .30
418 Jack McDowell .10 .30
419 Paul Molitor .10 .30
420 Ricky Bottalico .10 .30
421 Paul Wagner .10 .30
422 Terry Bradshaw .10 .30
423 Bob Tewksbury .10 .30
424 Mike Piazza .50 1.25
425 Luis Andujar .10 .30
426 Mark Langston .10 .30
427 Stan Belinda .10 .30
428 Kurt Abbott .10 .30
429 Shawon Dunston .10 .30
430 Bobby Jones .10 .30
431 Jose Vizcaino .10 .30
432 Matt Lawton RC .15 .40
433 Pat Hentgen .10 .30
434 Cecil Fielder .10 .30
435 Carlos Baerga .10 .30
436 Rich Becker .10 .30
437 Chipper Jones .30 .75
438 Bill Risley .10 .30
439 Kevin Appier .10 .30
440 Wade Boggs CL .10 .30
441 Jaime Navarro .10 .30
442 Barry Larkin .20 .50
443 Jose Valentin .10 .30
444 Bryan Rekar .10 .30
445 Rick Wilkins .10 .30
446 Quilvio Veras .10 .30
447 Greg Gagne .10 .30
448 Mark Kiefer .10 .30
449 Bobby Witt .10 .30
450 Andy Ashby .10 .30
451 Alex Ochoa .10 .30
452 Jorge Fabregas .10 .30
453 Gene Schall .10 .30
454 Ken Hill .10 .30
455 Tony Tarasco .10 .30
456 Donnie Wall .10 .30
457 Carlos Garcia .10 .30
458 Ryan Thompson .10 .30
459 Marvin Benard RC .15 .40
460 Jose Herrera .10 .30
461 Jeff Blauser .10 .30
462 Chris Hook .10 .30
463 Jeff Conine .10 .30
464 Devon White .10 .30
465 Danny Bautista .10 .30
466 Steve Trachsel .10 .30
467 C.J. Nitkowski .10 .30
468 Mike Devereaux .10 .30
469 David Wells .10 .30
470 Jim Eisenreich .10 .30
471 Edgar Martinez .20 .50
472 Craig Biggio .20 .50
473 Jeff Frye .10 .30
474 Karim Garcia .10 .30
475 Jimmy Haynes .10 .30
476 Darren Holmes .10 .30
477 Tim Salmon .20 .50
478 Randy Johnson .30 .75
479 Eric Plunk .10 .30
480 Scott Cooper .10 .30
481 Chan Ho Park .10 .30
482 Ray McDavid .10 .30
483 Mark Petkovsek .10 .30
484 Greg Swindell .10 .30
485 George Williams .10 .30
486 Yamil Benitez .10 .30
487 Tim Wakefield .10 .30
488 Kevin Tapani .10 .30
489 Derrick May .10 .30
490 Ken Griffey Jr. CL .40 1.00
491 Derek Jeter .75 2.00
492 Jeff Fassero .10 .30
493 Benito Santiago .10 .30
494 Tom Gordon .10 .30
495 Jamie Brewington RC .10 .30
496 Vince Coleman .10 .30
497 Kevin Jordan .10 .30
498 Jeff King .10 .30
499 Mike Simms .10 .30
500 Jose Rijo .10 .30
501 Denny Neagle .10 .30
502 Jose Lima .10 .30
503 Kevin Seitzer .10 .30
504 Alex Fernandez .10 .30
505 Mo Vaughn .10 .30
506 Phil Nevin .10 .30
507 J.T. Snow .10 .30
508 Andujar Cedeno .10 .30
509 Ozzie Guillen .10 .30
510 Mark Clark .10 .30
511 Mark McGwire .75 2.00
512 Jeff Reboulet .10 .30
513 Armando Benitez .10 .30
514 LaTroy Hawkins .10 .30
515 Brett Butler .10 .30
516 Tavo Alvarez .10 .30
517 Chris Snopek .10 .30
518 Mike Mussina .20 .50
519 Darryl Kile .10 .30
520 Wally Joyner .10 .30
521 Willie McGee .10 .30
522 Kent Mercker .10 .30
523 Mike Jackson .10 .30

524 Troy Percival .10 .30
525 Tony Gwynn .40 1.00
526 Ron Coomer .10 .30
527 Darryl Hamilton .10 .30
528 Phil Plantier .10 .30
529 Norm Charlton .10 .30
530 Craig Paquette .10 .30
531 Dave Burba .10 .30
532 Mike Henneman .10 .30
533 Terrell Wade .10 .30
534 Eddie Williams .10 .30
535 Robin Ventura .10 .30
536 Chuck Knoblauch .10 .30
537 Les Norman .10 .30
538 Brady Anderson .10 .30
539 Roger Clemens .60 1.50
540 Mark Portugal .10 .30
541 Mike Matheny .10 .30
542 Jeff Parrett .10 .30
543 Roberto Kelly .10 .30
544 Damon Buford .10 .30
545 Chad Ogea .10 .30
546 Jose Offerman .10 .30
547 Brian Barber .10 .30
548 Danny Tartabull .10 .30
549 Duane Singleton .10 .30
550 Tony Gwynn CL .20 .50

1996 Donruss Press Proofs

*STARS: 6X TO 15X BASIC CARDS
*ROOKIES: 4X TO 10X BASIC CARDS
SER.1 STATED ODDS 1:12
SER.2 STATED ODDS 1:10
STATED PRINT RUN 2000 SETS
50 Kirby Puckett 12.50 30.00

1996 Donruss Diamond Kings

COMPLETE SET (31) 20.00 50.00
COMPLETE SERIES 1 (14) 10.00 25.00
COMPLETE SERIES 2 (17) 10.00 25.00
SER.1 STATED ODDS 1:60
SER.2 STATED ODDS 1:30
STATED PRINT RUN 10,000 SERIAL #'d SETS
1 Frank Thomas 1.25 3.00
2 Mo Vaughn .50 1.25
3 Manny Ramirez .75 2.00
4 Mark McGwire 2.50 6.00
5 Juan Gonzalez .50 1.25
6 Roberto Alomar .75 2.00
7 Tim Salmon .50 1.25
8 Barry Bonds 2.00 5.00
9 Tony Gwynn 1.25 3.00
10 Reggie Sanders .50 1.25
11 Larry Walker .75 2.00
12 Pedro Martinez .75 2.00
13 Jeff King .50 1.25
14 Mark Grace .75 2.00
15 Greg Maddux 2.00 5.00
16 Don Mattingly 2.50 6.00
17 Gregg Jefferies .50 1.25
18 Chad Curtis .50 1.25
19 Jason Isringhausen .50 1.25
20 B.J. Surhoff .50 1.25
21 Jeff Conine .50 1.25
22 Kirby Puckett 1.25 3.00
23 Derek Bell .50 1.25
24 Wally Joyner .50 1.25
25 Brian Jordan .50 1.25
26 Edgar Martinez .75 2.00
27 Hideo Nomo 1.25 3.00
28 Mike Mussina .75 2.00
29 Eddie Murray 1.25 3.00
30 Cal Ripken 5.00 12.00
31 Checklist .50 1.25

1996 Donruss Elite

COMPLETE SET (12) 40.00 100.00
COMPLETE SERIES 1 (6) 20.00 50.00
COMPLETE SERIES 2 (6) 25.00 60.00
SER.1 STATED ODDS 1:140
SER.2 STATED ODDS 1:75
STATED PRINT RUN 10,000 SERIAL #'d SETS
61 Cal Ripken 12.50 30.00
62 Hideo Nomo 4.00 10.00
63 Reggie Sanders 1.50 4.00
64 Mo Vaughn 1.50 4.00
65 Tim Salmon 2.50 6.00
66 Chipper Jones 4.00 10.00
67 Manny Ramirez 2.50 6.00
68 Greg Maddux 6.00 15.00
69 Frank Thomas 4.00 10.00
70 Ken Griffey Jr. 15.00 40.00
71 Dante Bichette 1.50 4.00
72 Tony Gwynn 5.00 12.00

1996 Donruss Freeze Frame

COMPLETE SET (8) 40.00 100.00
SER.2 STATED ODDS 1:60
STATED PRINT RUN 5000 SERIAL #'d SETS
1 Frank Thomas 4.00 10.00
2 Ken Griffey Jr. 8.00 20.00
3 Cal Ripken 12.50 30.00
4 Hideo Nomo 4.00 10.00
5 Greg Maddux 6.00 15.00
6 Albert Belle 1.50 4.00
7 Chipper Jones 4.00 10.00
8 Mike Piazza 6.00 15.00

1996 Donruss Hit List

COMPLETE SET (16) 20.00 50.00
COMPLETE SERIES 1 (8) 10.00 25.00
COMPLETE SERIES 2 (8) 10.00 25.00
SER.1 STATED ODDS 1:105
SER.2 STATED ODDS 1:60
STATED PRINT RUN 10,000 SERIAL #'d SETS
1 Tony Gwynn 1.50 4.00
2 Ken Griffey Jr. 3.00 8.00
3 Will Clark 1.00 2.50
4 Mike Piazza 1.50 4.00
5 Carlos Baerga .60 1.50
6 Mo Vaughn .60 1.50
7 Mark Grace 1.00 2.50
8 Kirby Puckett 1.50 4.00
9 Frank Thomas 1.50 4.00
10 Barry Bonds 2.50 6.00
11 Jeff Bagwell 1.00 2.50
12 Edgar Martinez 1.00 2.50
13 Tim Salmon .60 1.50
14 Wade Boggs 1.00 2.50
15 Don Mattingly 3.00 8.00
16 Eddie Murray 1.00 2.50

1996 Donruss Long Ball Leader

COMPLETE SET (8) 15.00 40.00
SER.1 STATED ODDS 1:96 RETAIL
STATED PRINT RUN 5000 SERIAL #'d SETS
1 Barry Bonds 3.00 8.00
2 Ryan Klesko .75 2.00
3 Mark McGwire 3.00 8.00
4 Raul Mondesi .75 2.00
5 Cecil Fielder .75 2.00
6 Ken Griffey Jr. 4.00 10.00
7 Larry Walker 1.25 3.00
8 Frank Thomas 2.00 5.00

1996 Donruss Power Alley

COMPLETE SET (10) 15.00 40.00
SER.1 STATED ODDS 1:92 HOBBY
STATED PRINT RUN 4500 SERIAL #'d SETS
*DC'S: 3X TO 8X BASIC POWER ALLEY
DC SER.1 ODDS 1:920 HOBBY
DC PRINT RUN 500 SERIAL #'d SETS
1 Frank Thomas 2.00 5.00
2 Barry Bonds 3.00 8.00
3 Reggie Sanders .75 2.00
4 Albert Belle .75 2.00
5 Tim Salmon .75 2.00
6 Dante Bichette .75 2.00
7 Mo Vaughn .75 2.00
8 Jim Edmonds .75 2.00
9 Manny Ramirez 1.25 3.00
10 Ken Griffey Jr. 4.00 10.00

1996 Donruss Pure Power

COMPLETE SET (8) 30.00 80.00
RANDOM INSERTS IN SER.2 RETAIL PACKS
STATED PRINT RUN 5000 SETS
1 Raul Mondesi 2.00 5.00
2 Barry Bonds 12.50 30.00
3 Albert Belle 2.00 5.00
4 Frank Thomas 5.00 12.00
5 Mike Piazza 8.00 20.00
6 Dante Bichette 2.00 5.00
7 Manny Ramirez 3.00 8.00
8 Mo Vaughn 2.00 5.00

1996 Donruss Round Trippers

COMPLETE SET (10) 12.50 30.00
SER.2 STATED ODDS 1:55 HOBBY
STATED PRINT RUN 5000 SERIAL #'d SETS
1 Albert Belle 1.50 4.00
2 Barry Bonds 10.00 25.00
3 Jeff Bagwell 2.50 6.00
4 Tim Salmon 2.50 6.00
5 Mo Vaughn 1.50 4.00
6 Ken Griffey Jr. 8.00 20.00
7 Mike Piazza 6.00 15.00
8 Cal Ripken 12.50 30.00
9 Frank Thomas 4.00 10.00
10 Dante Bichette 1.50 4.00

1996 Donruss Showdown

COMPLETE SET (8) 20.00 50.00
SER.1 STATED ODDS 1:105
STATED PRINT RUN 10,000 SERIAL #'d SETS
1 F.Thomas 3.00 8.00
H.Nomo
2 B.Bonds 4.00 10.00
R.Johnson
3 K.Griffey Jr. 6.00 15.00
G.Maddux
4 T.Gwynn 4.00 10.00
R.Clemens
5 M.Piazza 4.00 10.00
M.Mussina
6 C.Ripken 10.00 25.00
P.Martinez
7 T.Wakefield 1.25 3.00
M.Williams
8 M.Ramirez 2.00 5.00
C.Perez

1997 Donruss

The 1997 Donruss set was issued in two separate series of 270 and 180 cards respectively. Both first series and Update cards were distributed in 10-card packs carrying a suggested retail price of $1.99 each. Card fronts feature color action player photos while the backs carry another color player photo with player information and career statistics. The following subsets are included within the set: Checklists (267-270/448-450), Rookies (353-397), Hit List (398-422), King of the Hill (423-437) and Interleague Showdown (438-447). Rookie Cards in this set include Jose Cruz Jr., Brian Giles and Hideki Irabu.

COMPLETE SET (450) 20.00 50.00
COMPLETE SERIES 1 (270) 10.00 25.00
COMPLETE UPDATE (180) 10.00 25.00
SUBSET CARDS HALF VALUE OF BASE CARDS
1 Juan Gonzalez .10 .30
2 Jim Edmonds .10 .30
3 Tony Gwynn .40 1.00
4 Andres Galarraga .10 .30
5 Joe Carter .10 .30
6 Raul Mondesi .10 .30
7 Greg Maddux .50 1.25
8 Travis Fryman .10 .30
9 Brian Jordan .10 .30
10 Henry Rodriguez .10 .30
11 Manny Ramirez .20 .50
12 Mark McGwire .75 2.00
13 Marc Newfield .10 .30
14 Craig Biggio .20 .50
15 Sammy Sosa .30 .75
16 Brady Anderson .10 .30
17 Wade Boggs .20 .50
18 Charles Johnson .10 .30
19 Matt Williams .10 .30
20 Denny Neagle .10 .30
21 Ken Griffey Jr. .60 1.50
22 Robin Ventura .10 .30
23 Barry Larkin .20 .50
24 Todd Zeile .10 .30
25 Chuck Knoblauch .10 .30
26 Todd Hundley .10 .30
27 Roger Clemens .60 1.50
28 Michael Tucker .10 .30
29 Rondell White .10 .30
30 Osvaldo Fernandez .10 .30
31 Ivan Rodriguez .20 .50
32 Alex Fernandez .10 .30
33 Jason Isringhausen .10 .30
34 Chipper Jones .30 .75
35 Paul O'Neill .20 .50
36 Hideo Nomo .30 .75
37 Roberto Alomar .20 .50
38 Derek Bell .10 .30
39 Paul Molitor .10 .30
40 Andy Benes .10 .30
41 Steve Trachsel .10 .30
42 J.T. Snow .10 .30
43 Jason Kendall .10 .30
44 Alex Rodriguez .50 1.25
45 Joey Hamilton .10 .30
46 Carlos Delgado .10 .30
47 Jason Giambi .10 .30
48 Larry Walker .10 .30
49 Derek Jeter .75 2.00
50 Kenny Lofton .10 .30
51 Devon White .10 .30
52 Matt Mieske .10 .30
53 Melvin Nieves .10 .30
54 Jose Canseco .20 .50
55 Tino Martinez .20 .50
56 Rafael Palmeiro .20 .50
57 Edgardo Alfonzo .10 .30
58 Jay Buhner .10 .30
59 Shane Reynolds .10 .30
60 Steve Finley .10 .30
61 Bobby Higginson .10 .30
62 Dean Palmer .10 .30
63 Terry Pendleton .10 .30
64 Marquis Grissom .10 .30
65 Mike Stanley .10 .30
66 Moises Alou .10 .30
67 Ray Lankford .10 .30
68 Marty Cordova .10 .30
69 John Olerud .10 .30
70 David Cone .10 .30
71 Benito Santiago .10 .30
72 Ryne Sandberg .50 1.25
73 Rickey Henderson .30 .75
74 Roger Cedeno .10 .30
75 Wilson Alvarez .10 .30
76 Tim Salmon .20 .50
77 Orlando Merced .10 .30
78 Vinny Castilla .10 .30
79 Ismael Valdes .10 .30
80 Dante Bichette .10 .30
81 Kevin Brown .10 .30
82 Andy Pettitte .20 .50
83 Scott Stahoviak .10 .30
84 Mickey Tettleton .10 .30
85 Jack McDowell .10 .30
86 Tom Glavine .20 .50
87 Gregg Jefferies .10 .30
88 Chili Davis .10 .30
89 Randy Johnson .30 .75
90 John Mabry .10 .30
91 Billy Wagner .10 .30
92 Jeff Cirillo .10 .30
93 Trevor Hoffman .10 .30
94 Juan Guzman .10 .30
95 Geronimo Berroa .10 .30
96 Bernard Gilkey .10 .30
97 Danny Tartabull .10 .30
98 Johnny Damon .20 .50
99 Charlie Hayes .10 .30
100 Reggie Sanders .10 .30
101 Robby Thompson .10 .30
102 Bobby Bonilla .10 .30
103 Reggie Jefferson .10 .30
104 John Smoltz .20 .50
105 Jim Thome .20 .50
106 Ruben Rivera .10 .30
107 Darren Oliver .10 .30
108 Mo Vaughn .10 .30
109 Roger Pavlik .10 .30
110 Terry Steinbach .10 .30
111 Jermaine Dye .10 .30
112 Mark Grudzielanek .10 .30
113 Rick Aguilera .10 .30
114 Jamey Wright .10 .30
115 Eddie Murray .30 .75
116 Brian L. Hunter .10 .30
117 Hal Morris .10 .30
118 Tom Pagnozzi .10 .30
119 Mike Mussina .20 .50
120 Mark Grace .20 .50
121 Cal Ripken 1.00 2.50
122 Tom Goodwin .10 .30
123 Paul Sorrento .10 .30
124 Jay Bell .10 .30
125 Todd Hollandsworth .10 .30
126 Edgar Martinez .20 .50
127 George Arias .10 .30
128 Greg Vaughn .10 .30
129 Roberto Hernandez .10 .30
130 Delino DeShields .10 .30
131 Bill Pulsipher .10 .30
132 Joey Cora .10 .30
133 Mariano Rivera .30 .75
134 Mike Piazza .50 1.25
135 Carlos Baerga .10 .30
136 Jose Mesa .10 .30
137 Will Clark .20 .50
138 Frank Thomas .30 .75
139 John Wetteland .10 .30
140 Shawn Estes .10 .30
141 Garret Anderson .10 .30
142 Andre Dawson .10 .30
143 Eddie Taubensee .10 .30
144 Ryan Klesko .10 .30
145 Rocky Coppinger .10 .30
146 Jeff Bagwell .20 .50
147 Donovan Osborne .10 .30
148 Greg Myers .10 .30
149 Brant Brown .10 .30
150 Kevin Elster .10 .30
151 Bob Wells .10 .30
152 Wally Joyner .10 .30
153 Rico Brogna .10 .30
154 Dwight Gooden .10 .30
155 Jermaine Allensworth .10 .30
156 Ray Durham .10 .30
157 Cecil Fielder .10 .30
158 John Burkett .10 .30
159 Gary Sheffield .10 .30
160 Albert Belle .10 .30
161 Tomas Perez .10 .30
162 David Doster .10 .30
163 John Valentin .10 .30
164 Danny Graves .10 .30
165 Jose Paniagua .10 .30
166 Brian Giles RC .60 1.50
167 Barry Bonds .75 2.00
168 Sterling Hitchcock .10 .30
169 Bernie Williams .20 .50
170 Fred McGriff .20 .50
171 George Williams .10 .30
172 Amaury Telemaco .10 .30
173 Ken Caminiti .10 .30
174 Ron Gant .10 .30
175 Dave Justice .10 .30
176 James Baldwin .10 .30
177 Pat Hentgen .10 .30
178 Ben McDonald .10 .30
179 Tim Naehring .10 .30
180 Jim Eisenreich .10 .30
181 Ken Hill .10 .30
182 Paul Wilson .10 .30
183 Marvin Benard .10 .30
184 Alan Benes .10 .30
185 Ellis Burks .10 .30
186 Scott Servais .10 .30
187 David Segui .10 .30
188 Scott Brosius .10 .30
189 Jose Offerman .10 .30
190 Eric Davis .10 .30
191 Brett Butler .10 .30
192 Curtis Pride .10 .30
193 Yamil Benitez .10 .30
194 Chan Ho Park .10 .30
195 Bret Boone .10 .30
196 Omar Vizquel .20 .50
197 Orlando Miller .10 .30
198 Ramon Martinez .10 .30
199 Harold Baines .10 .30
200 Eric Young .10 .30
201 Fernando Vina .10 .30
202 Alex Gonzalez .10 .30
203 Fernando Valenzuela .10 .30
204 Steve Avery .10 .30
205 Ernie Young .10 .30
206 Kevin Appier .10 .30
207 Randy Myers .10 .30
208 Jeff Suppan .10 .30
209 James Mouton .10 .30
210 Russ Davis .10 .30
211 Al Martin .10 .30
212 Troy Percival .10 .30
213 Al Leiter .10 .30
214 Dennis Eckersley .10 .30
215 Mark Johnson .10 .30
216 Eric Karros .10 .30
217 Royce Clayton .10 .30
218 Tony Phillips .10 .30
219 Tim Wakefield .10 .30
220 Alan Trammell .10 .30
221 Eduardo Perez .10 .30
222 Butch Huskey .10 .30
223 Tim Belcher .10 .30
224 Jamie Moyer .10 .30
225 F.P. Santangelo .10 .30
226 Rusty Greer .10 .30
227 Jeff Brantley .10 .30
228 Mark Langston .10 .30
229 Ray Montgomery .10 .30
230 Rich Becker .10 .30
231 Ozzie Smith .50 1.25
232 Rey Ordonez .10 .30
233 Ricky Otero .10 .30
234 Mike Cameron .10 .30
235 Mike Sweeney .10 .30
236 Mark Lewis .10 .30
237 Luis Gonzalez .10 .30
238 Marcus Jensen .10 .30
239 Ed Sprague .10 .30
240 Jose Valentin .10 .30
241 Jeff Frye .10 .30
242 Charles Nagy .10 .30
243 Carlos Garcia .10 .30
244 Mike Hampton .10 .30
245 B.J. Surhoff .10 .30
246 Wilton Guerrero .10 .30
247 Frank Rodriguez .10 .30
248 Gary Gaetti .10 .30
249 Lance Johnson .10 .30
250 Darren Bragg .10 .30
251 Darryl Hamilton .10 .30
252 John Jaha .10 .30
253 Craig Paquette .10 .30
254 Jaime Navarro .10 .30
255 Shawn Dunston .10 .30
256 Mark Loretta .10 .30
257 Tim Belk .10 .30
258 Jeff Darwin .10 .30
259 Ruben Sierra .10 .30
260 Chuck Finley .10 .30
261 Darryl Strawberry .10 .30
262 Shannon Stewart .10 .30
263 Pedro Martinez .20 .50
264 Neifi Perez .10 .30
265 Jeff Conine .10 .30
266 Orel Hershiser .10 .30
267 Eddie Murray CL .20 .50
268 Paul Molitor CL .10 .30
269 Barry Bonds CL .40 1.00
270 Mark McGwire CL .40 1.00
271 Matt Williams .10 .30
272 Todd Zeile .10 .30
273 Roger Clemens .60 1.50
274 Michael Tucker .10 .30
275 J.T. Snow .10 .30
276 Kenny Lofton .10 .30
277 Jose Canseco .20 .50
278 Marquis Grissom .10 .30
279 Moises Alou .10 .30
280 Benito Santiago .10 .30
281 Willie McGee .10 .30
282 Chili Davis .10 .30
283 Ron Coomer .10 .30
284 Orlando Merced .10 .30
285 Delino DeShields .10 .30
286 John Wetteland .10 .30
287 Darren Daulton .10 .30
288 Lee Stevens .10 .30
289 Albert Belle .10 .30
290 Sterling Hitchcock .10 .30
291 David Justice .10 .30
292 Eric Davis .10 .30
293 Brian Hunter .10 .30
294 Darryl Hamilton .10 .30
295 Steve Avery .10 .30
296 Joe Vitiello .10 .30
297 Jaime Navarro .10 .30
298 Eddie Murray .30 .75
299 Randy Myers .10 .30
300 Francisco Cordova .10 .30
301 Javier Lopez .10 .30
302 Geronimo Berroa .10 .30
303 Jeffrey Hammonds .10 .30
304 Deion Sanders .20 .50
305 Jeff Fassero .10 .30
306 Curt Schilling .10 .30
307 Robb Nen .10 .30
308 Mark McLemore .10 .30
309 Jimmy Key .10 .30
310 Quilvio Veras .10 .30
311 Bip Roberts .10 .30
312 Esteban Loaiza .10 .30
313 Andy Ashby .10 .30
314 Sandy Alomar Jr. .10 .30
315 Shawn Green .10 .30
316 Luis Castillo .10 .30
317 Benji Gil .10 .30
318 Otis Nixon .10 .30
319 Aaron Sele .10 .30
320 Brad Ausmus .10 .30
321 Troy O'Leary .10 .30
322 Terrell Wade .10 .30
323 Jeff King .10 .30
324 Kevin Seitzer .10 .30
325 Mark Wohlers .10 .30
326 Edgar Renteria .10 .30
327 Dan Wilson .10 .30
328 Brian McRae .10 .30
329 Rod Beck .10 .30
330 Julio Franco .10 .30
331 Dave Nilsson .10 .30
332 Glenallen Hill .10 .30
333 Kevin Elster .10 .30
334 Joe Girardi .10 .30
335 David Wells .10 .30
336 Jeff Blauser .10 .30
337 Darryl Kile .10 .30
338 Jeff Kent .10 .30
339 Jim Leyritz .10 .30
340 Todd Stottlemyre .10 .30
341 Tony Clark .10 .30
342 Chris Hoiles .10 .30
343 Mike Lieberthal .10 .30
344 Matt Lawton .10 .30
345 Alex Ochoa .10 .30
346 Chris Snopek .10 .30
347 Rudy Pemberton .10 .30
348 Eric Owens .10 .30
349 Joe Randa .10 .30
350 John Olerud .10 .30
351 Steve Karsay .10 .30
352 Mark Whiten .10 .30
353 Bob Abreu .20 .50
354 Bartolo Colon .10 .30
355 Vladimir Guerrero .30 .75
356 Darin Erstad .10 .30
357 Scott Rolen .20 .50
358 Andruw Jones .20 .50
359 Scott Spiezio .10 .30
360 Karim Garcia .10 .30
361 Hideki Irabu RC .15 .40
362 Nomar Garciaparra .50 1.25
363 Dmitri Young .10 .30
364 Bubba Trammell RC .15 .40
365 Kevin Orie .10 .30
366 Jose Rosado .10 .30
367 Jose Guillen .10 .30
368 Brooks Kieschnick .10 .30
369 Pokey Reese .10 .30
370 Glendon Rusch .10 .30
371 Jason Dickson .10 .30
372 Todd Walker .10 .30
373 Justin Thompson .10 .30
374 Todd Greene .10 .30
375 Jeff Suppan .10 .30
376 Trey Beamon .10 .30
377 Damon Mashore .10 .30
378 Wendell Magee .10 .30
379 Shigetoshi Hasegawa RC .20 .50
380 Bill Mueller RC .50 1.25
381 Chris Widger .10 .30
382 Tony Graffanino .10 .30
383 Derrek Lee .20 .50
384 Brian Moehler RC .15 .40
385 Quinton McCracken .10 .30
386 Matt Morris .10 .30
387 Marvin Benard .10 .30
388 Deivi Cruz RC .15 .40
389 Javier Valentin .10 .30
390 Todd Dunwoody .10 .30
391 Derrick Gibson .10 .30
392 Raul Casanova .10 .30
393 George Arias .10 .30
394 Tony Womack RC .15 .40
395 Antone Williamson .10 .30
396 Jose Cruz Jr. RC .15 .40
397 Desi Relaford .10 .30
398 Frank Thomas HIT .20 .50
399 Ken Griffey Jr. HIT .40 1.00
400 Cal Ripken HIT .50 1.25
401 Chipper Jones HIT .20 .50
402 Mike Piazza HIT .30 .75
403 Gary Sheffield HIT .10 .30
404 Alex Rodriguez HIT .30 .75
405 Wade Boggs HIT .10 .30
406 Juan Gonzalez HIT .10 .30
407 Tony Gwynn HIT .20 .50
408 Edgar Martinez HIT .10 .30
409 Jeff Bagwell HIT .10 .30
410 Larry Walker HIT .10 .30
411 Kenny Lofton HIT .10 .30
412 Manny Ramirez HIT .10 .30
413 Mark McGwire HIT .40 1.00
414 Roberto Alomar HIT .10 .30
415 Derek Jeter HIT .40 1.00
416 Brady Anderson HIT .10 .30
417 Paul Molitor HIT .10 .30
418 Dante Bichette HIT .10 .30
419 Jim Edmonds HIT .10 .30
420 Mo Vaughn HIT .10 .30
421 Barry Bonds HIT .40 1.00
422 Rusty Greer HIT .10 .30
423 Greg Maddux KING .30 .75
424 Andy Pettitte KING .10 .30
425 John Smoltz KING .10 .30
426 Randy Johnson KING .20 .50
427 Hideo Nomo KING .10 .30
428 Roger Clemens KING .30 .75
429 Tom Glavine KING .10 .30
430 Pat Hentgen KING .10 .30
431 Kevin Brown KING .10 .30
432 Mike Mussina KING .10 .30
433 Alex Fernandez KING .10 .30
434 Kevin Appier KING .10 .30
435 David Cone KING .10 .30
436 Jeff Fassero KING .10 .30
437 John Wetteland KING .10 .30
438 B.Bonds .40 1.00
I.Rodriguez IS
439 K.Griffey Jr. .40 1.00
A.Galarraga IS
440 F.McGriff .10 .30
R.Palmeiro IS
441 B.Larkin .20 .50
J.Thome IS
442 S.Sosa .20 .50
A.Belle IS
443 B.Williams .10 .30
T.Hundley IS
444 C.Knoblauch .10 .30
B.Jordan IS
445 M.Vaughn .10 .30
J.Conine IS
446 K.Caminiti .10 .30
J.Giambi IS
447 R.Mondesi .10 .30
T.Salmon IS
448 Cal Ripken CL .50 1.25
449 Greg Maddux CL .30 .75
450 Ken Griffey Jr. CL .40 1.00

1997 Donruss Gold Press Proofs

*STARS: 10X TO 25X BASIC CARDS
*ROOKIES: 3X TO 8X BASIC CARDS
SER.1 STATED ODDS 1:32
SER.2 STATED ODDS 1:64
STATED PRINT RUN 500 SETS

1997 Donruss Silver Press Proofs

*STARS: 4X TO 10X BASIC CARDS
*ROOKIES: 1.25X TO 3X BASIC CARDS
SER.1 STATED ODDS 1:8
SER.2 STATED ODDS 1:16
STATED PRINT RUN 2000 SETS

1997 Donruss Armed and Dangerous

COMPLETE SET (15) 15.00 40.00
SER.1 STATED ODDS 1:58 HOBBY
STATED PRINT RUN 5000 SERIAL #'d SETS
1 Ken Griffey Jr. 3.00 8.00
2 Raul Mondesi .60 1.50
3 Chipper Jones 1.50 4.00
4 Ivan Rodriguez 1.00 2.50
5 Randy Johnson 1.50 4.00
6 Alex Rodriguez 2.00 5.00
7 Larry Walker 1.00 2.50
8 Cal Ripken 5.00 12.00
9 Kenny Lofton .60 1.50
10 Barry Bonds 2.50 6.00
11 Derek Jeter 4.00 10.00
12 Charles Johnson .60 1.50
13 Greg Maddux 2.50 6.00
14 Roberto Alomar 1.00 2.50
15 Barry Larkin 1.00 2.50

1997 Donruss Diamond Kings

COMPLETE SET (10) 12.50 30.00
SER.1 STATED ODDS 1:45
STATED PRINT RUN 9500 SERIAL #'d SETS
*CANVAS: 2X TO 5X BASIC DK'S
CANVAS: RANDOM INS.IN SER.1 PACKS
CANVAS PRINT RUN 500 SERIAL #'d SETS
EACH CARD #1982 WINS ORIGINAL ART
1 Ken Griffey Jr. 4.00 10.00
2 Cal Ripken 6.00 15.00
3 Mo Vaughn .75 2.00
4 Chuck Knoblauch .75 2.00
5 Jeff Bagwell 1.25 3.00
6 Henry Rodriguez .75 2.00
7 Mike Piazza 2.00 5.00
8 Ivan Rodriguez 1.25 3.00
9 Frank Thomas 2.00 5.00
10 Chipper Jones 2.00 5.00

1997 Donruss Dominators

COMPLETE SET (20) 30.00 80.00
RANDOM INSERTS IN UPDATE PACKS
1 Frank Thomas 1.50 4.00
2 Ken Griffey Jr. 3.00 8.00
3 Greg Maddux 2.50 6.00
4 Cal Ripken 5.00 12.00
5 Alex Rodriguez 2.50 6.00
6 Albert Belle .60 1.50
7 Mark McGwire 4.00 10.00
8 Juan Gonzalez .60 1.50
9 Chipper Jones 1.50 4.00
10 Hideo Nomo 1.50 4.00
11 Roger Clemens 3.00 8.00
12 John Smoltz 1.00 2.50
13 Mike Piazza 2.50 6.00
14 Sammy Sosa 1.50 4.00
15 Matt Williams .60 1.50
16 Kenny Lofton .60 1.50
17 Barry Larkin 1.00 2.50
18 Rafael Palmeiro 1.00 2.50
19 Ken Caminiti .60 1.50
20 Gary Sheffield .60 1.50

1997 Donruss Elite Insert Promos

COMPLETE SET (12) 40.00 100.00
1 Frank Thomas 3.00 8.00
2 Paul Molitor 2.50 6.00
3 Sammy Sosa 4.00 10.00
4 Barry Bonds 4.00 10.00
5 Chipper Jones 4.00 10.00
6 Alex Rodriguez 6.00 15.00
7 Ken Griffey Jr. 5.00 12.00
8 Jeff Bagwell 2.50 6.00
9 Cal Ripken 8.00 20.00
10 Mo Vaughn .75 2.00
11 Mike Piazza 6.00 15.00
12 Juan Gonzalez 2.00 5.00

1997 Donruss Elite Inserts

COMPLETE SET (12) 125.00 250.00
SER.1 STATED ODDS 1:144
STATED PRINT RUN 2500 SERIAL #'d SETS
1 Frank Thomas 4.00 10.00
2 Paul Molitor 4.00 10.00
3 Sammy Sosa 2.50 6.00
4 Barry Bonds 6.00 15.00
5 Chipper Jones 4.00 10.00
6 Alex Rodriguez 5.00 12.00
7 Ken Griffey Jr. 8.00 20.00
8 Jeff Bagwell 2.50 6.00
9 Cal Ripken 12.00 30.00
10 Mo Vaughn 1.50 4.00
11 Mike Piazza 4.00 10.00
12 Juan Gonzalez 1.50 4.00

1997 Donruss Franchise Features

COMPLETE SET (15) 20.00 50.00
RANDOM INSERTS IN UPDATE PACKS
STATED PRINT RUN 3000 SERIAL #'d SETS
1 K.Griffey Jr. 3.00 8.00
A.Jones
2 F.Thomas 1.50 4.00
D.Erstad
3 A.Rodriguez 2.00 5.00
N.Garciaparra
4 C.Knoblauch .60 1.50
W.Guerrero
5 J.Gonzalez .60 1.50
B.Trammell
6 C.Jones 1.50 4.00
T.Walker
7 B.Bonds 2.50 6.00
V.Guerrero
8 M.McGwire 2.50 6.00
D.Young
9 M.Piazza 1.50 4.00
M.Sweeney
10 M.Vaughn .60 1.50
T.Clark
11 G.Sheffield .60 1.50
J.Guillen
12 K.Lofton .60 1.50
S.Stewart
13 C.Ripken 5.00 12.00
S.Rolen
14 D.Jeter 4.00 10.00
P.Reese
15 T.Gwynn 1.50 4.00
B.Abreu

1997 Donruss Longball Leaders

COMPLETE SET (15) 30.00 80.00
RANDOM INSERTS IN SER.1 RETAIL PACKS
STATED PRINT RUN 5000 SERIAL #'d SETS
1 Frank Thomas 2.50 6.00
2 Albert Belle 1.00 2.50
3 Mo Vaughn 1.00 2.50
4 Brady Anderson 1.00 2.50
5 Greg Vaughn 1.00 2.50
6 Ken Griffey Jr. 5.00 12.00
7 Jay Buhner 1.00 2.50
8 Juan Gonzalez 1.00 2.50
9 Mike Piazza 4.00 10.00
10 Jeff Bagwell 1.50 4.00
11 Sammy Sosa 2.50 6.00
12 Mark McGwire 6.00 15.00
13 Cecil Fielder 1.00 2.50
14 Ryan Klesko 1.00 2.50
15 Jose Canseco 1.50 4.00

1997 Donruss Power Alley

RANDOM INSERTS IN UPDATE PACKS
GREEN PRINT RUN 3750 SERIAL #'d SETS
BLUE PRINT RUN 1750 SERIAL #'d SETS
GOLD PRINT RUN 750 SERIAL #'d SETS
*GREEN DC's: 2X TO 5X BASIC GREEN
*BLUE DC's: 1.25X TO 3X BASIC BLUE
*GOLD DC's: .75X TO 2X BASIC GOLD
DIE CUTS: RANDOM INS.IN UPDATE PACKS
DIE CUTS PRINT RUN 250 SERIAL #'d SETS
1 Frank Thomas G 6.00 15.00
2 Ken Griffey Jr. G 25.00 60.00
3 Cal Ripken G 12.00 30.00
4 Jeff Bagwell B 2.50 6.00
5 Mike Piazza B 6.00 15.00
6 Andruw Jones GR 1.50 4.00
7 Alex Rodriguez G 10.00 25.00
8 Albert Belle GR 1.00 2.50
9 Mo Vaughn GR 1.00 2.50
10 Chipper Jones B 4.00 10.00
11 Juan Gonzalez B 1.50 4.00
12 Ken Caminiti GR 1.00 2.50
13 Manny Ramirez GR 1.50 4.00
14 Mark McGwire GR 6.00 15.00
15 Kenny Lofton B 1.50 4.00
16 Barry Bonds GR 6.00 15.00
17 Gary Sheffield GR 1.00 2.50
18 Tony Gwynn GR 3.00 8.00
19 Vladimir Guerrero B 4.00 10.00
20 Ivan Rodriguez B 2.50 6.00
21 Paul Molitor B 1.50 4.00
22 Sammy Sosa GR 2.50 6.00
23 Matt Williams GR 1.00 2.50
24 Derek Jeter GR 6.00 15.00

1997 Donruss Rated Rookies

COMPLETE SET (30) 15.00 40.00
RANDOM INSERTS IN SER.1 PACKS

WRAPPER ODDS 1:6
1 Jason Thompson .75 2.00
2 LaTroy Hawkins .75 2.00
3 Scott Rolen 1.25 3.00
4 Trey Beamon .75 2.00
5 Kimera Bartee .75 2.00
6 Nerio Rodriguez .75 2.00
7 Jeff D'Amico .75 2.00
8 Quinton McCracken .75 2.00
9 John Wasdin .75 2.00
10 Robin Jennings .75 2.00
11 Steve Gibralter .75 2.00
12 Tyler Houston .75 2.00
13 Tony Clark .75 2.00
14 Ugueth Urbina .75 2.00
15 Karim Garcia .75 2.00
16 Raul Casanova .75 2.00
17 Brooks Kieschnick .75 2.00
18 Luis Castillo .75 2.00
19 Edgar Renteria .75 2.00
20 Andruw Jones 1.25 3.00
21 Chad Mottola .75 2.00
22 Mac Suzuki .75 2.00
23 Justin Thompson .75 2.00
24 Darin Erstad .75 2.00
25 Todd Walker .75 2.00
26 Todd Greene .75 2.00
27 Vladimir Guerrero 2.00 5.00
28 Darren Dreifort .75 2.00
29 John Burke .75 2.00
30 Damon Mashore .75 2.00

1997 Donruss Ripken The Only Way I Know

COMPLETE SET (9) 40.00 100.00
COMMON CARD (1-9) 6.00 12.00
RANDOM INSERTS IN UPDATE PACKS
STATED PRINT RUN 5000 SERIAL #'d SETS
COMMON CARD (10) 10.00 20.00
CARD #10 DIST.ONLY W/RIPKEN'S BOOK
10A Cal Ripken BOOK AU/2131 100.00 200.00

1997 Donruss Rocket Launchers

COMPLETE SET (15) 12.50 30.00
1 Frank Thomas 1.50 4.00
2 Albert Belle .60 1.50
3 Chipper Jones 1.50 4.00
4 Mike Piazza 1.50 4.00
5 Mo Vaughn .60 1.50
6 Juan Gonzalez .60 1.50
7 Fred McGriff 1.00 2.50
8 Jeff Bagwell 1.00 2.50
9 Matt Williams .60 1.50
10 Gary Sheffield .60 1.50
11 Barry Bonds 2.50 6.00
12 Manny Ramirez 1.00 2.50
13 Henry Rodriguez .60 1.50
14 Jason Giambi .60 1.50
15 Cal Ripken 5.00 12.00

1997 Donruss Rookie Diamond Kings

COMPLETE SET (10) 15.00 40.00
STATED PRINT RUN 9500 SERIAL #'d SETS
*CANVAS: 1.25X TO 3X BASIC DK'S
CANVAS PRINT RUN 500 SERIAL #'d SETS
RANDOM INSERTS IN UPDATE PACKS
1 Andruw Jones 2.50 6.00
2 Vladimir Guerrero 4.00 10.00
3 Scott Rolen 2.50 6.00
4 Todd Walker 1.50 4.00
5 Bartolo Colon 1.50 4.00
6 Jose Guillen 1.50 4.00
7 Nomar Garciaparra 6.00 15.00
8 Darin Erstad 1.50 4.00
9 Dmitri Young 1.50 4.00
10 Wilton Guerrero 1.50 4.00

1997 Donruss Update Ripken Info Card

1 Cal Ripken Jr. 1.25 3.00

1998 Donruss

The 1998 Donruss set was issued in two series (series one numbers 1-170, series two numbers 171-420) and was distributed in 10-card packs with a suggested retail price of $1.99. The fronts feature color player photos with player information on the backs. The set contains the topical subsets: Fan Club (156-165), Hit List (346-375), The Untouchables (376-385), Spirit of the Game (386-415) and Checklists (416-420). Each Fan Club card carried instructions on how the fan could vote for their favorite players to be included in the 1998 Donruss Update set. Rookie Cards include Kevin Millwood and Magglio Ordonez. Sadly, after an eighteen year run, this was the last Donruss set to be issued due to card manufacturer Pinnacle's bankruptcy in 1998. In 2001, however, Donruss/Playoff procured a license to produce baseball cards and the Donruss brand was reinstituted after a two year break.

COMPLETE SET (420) 20.00 50.00
COMPLETE SERIES 1 (170) 8.00 20.00
COMPLETE UPDATE (250) 12.50 30.00
1 Paul Molitor .08 .25
2 Juan Gonzalez .08 .25
3 Darryl Kile .08 .25
4 Randy Johnson .25 .60
5 Tom Glavine .15 .40
6 Pat Hentgen .08 .25
7 David Justice .08 .25
8 Kevin Brown .15 .40
9 Mike Mussina .15 .40
10 Ken Caminiti .08 .25
11 Todd Hundley .08 .25
12 Frank Thomas .25 .60
13 Ray Lankford .08 .25
14 Justin Thompson .08 .25
15 Jason Dickson .08 .25
16 Kenny Lofton .08 .25
17 Ivan Rodriguez .15 .40
18 Pedro Martinez .15 .40
19 Brady Anderson .08 .25
20 Barry Larkin .15 .40
21 Chipper Jones .25 .60
22 Tony Gwynn .30 .75
23 Roger Clemens .50 1.25
24 Sandy Alomar Jr. .08 .25
25 Tino Martinez .15 .40
26 Jeff Bagwell .15 .40
27 Shawn Estes .08 .25
28 Ken Griffey Jr. .50 1.25
29 Javier Lopez .08 .25
30 Denny Neagle .08 .25
31 Mike Piazza .40 1.00
32 Andres Galarraga .08 .25
33 Larry Walker .08 .25
34 Alex Rodriguez .40 1.00
35 Greg Maddux .40 1.00
36 Albert Belle .08 .25
37 Barry Bonds .60 1.50
38 Mo Vaughn .08 .25
39 Kevin Appier .08 .25
40 Wade Boggs .15 .40
41 Garret Anderson .08 .25
42 Jeffrey Hammonds .08 .25
43 Marquis Grissom .08 .25
44 Jim Edmonds .08 .25
45 Brian Jordan .08 .25
46 Raul Mondesi .08 .25
47 John Valentin .08 .25
48 Brad Radke .08 .25
49 Ismael Valdes .08 .25
50 Matt Stairs .08 .25
51 Matt Williams .08 .25
52 Reggie Jefferson .08 .25
53 Alan Benes .08 .25
54 Charles Johnson .08 .25
55 Chuck Knoblauch .08 .25
56 Edgar Martinez .15 .40
57 Nomar Garciaparra .40 1.00
58 Craig Biggio .15 .40
59 Bernie Williams .15 .40
60 David Cone .08 .25
61 Cal Ripken .75 2.00
62 Mark McGwire .60 1.50
63 Roberto Alomar .15 .40
64 Fred McGriff .15 .40
65 Eric Karros .08 .25
66 Robin Ventura .08 .25
67 Darin Erstad .08 .25
68 Michael Tucker .08 .25
69 Jim Thome .15 .40
70 Mark Grace .15 .40
71 Lou Collier .08 .25
72 Karim Garcia .08 .25
73 Alex Fernandez .08 .25
74 J.T. Snow .08 .25
75 Reggie Sanders .08 .25
76 John Smoltz .15 .40
77 Tim Salmon .15 .40
78 Paul O'Neill .15 .40
79 Vinny Castilla .08 .25
80 Rafael Palmeiro .15 .40
81 Jaret Wright .08 .25
82 Jay Buhner .08 .25
83 Brett Butler .08 .25
84 Todd Greene .08 .25
85 Scott Rolen .15 .40
86 Sammy Sosa .25 .60
87 Jason Giambi .08 .25
88 Carlos Delgado .08 .25
89 Deion Sanders .15 .40
90 Wilton Guerrero .08 .25
91 Andy Pettitte .15 .40
92 Brian Giles .08 .25
93 Dmitri Young .08 .25
94 Ron Coomer .08 .25
95 Mike Cameron .08 .25
96 Edgardo Alfonzo .08 .25
97 Jimmy Key .08 .25
98 Ryan Klesko .08 .25
99 Andy Benes .08 .25
100 Derek Jeter .60 1.50
101 Jeff Fassero .08 .25
102 Neifi Perez .08 .25
103 Hideo Nomo .25 .60
104 Andruw Jones .15 .40
105 Todd Helton .15 .40
106 Livan Hernandez .08 .25
107 Brett Tomko .08 .25
108 Shannon Stewart .08 .25
109 Bartolo Colon .08 .25
110 Matt Morris .08 .25
111 Miguel Tejada .25 .60
112 Pokey Reese .08 .25
113 Fernando Tatis .08 .25
114 Todd Dunwoody .08 .25
115 Jose Cruz Jr. .08 .25
116 Chan Ho Park .08 .25
117 Kevin Young .08 .25
118 Rickey Henderson .25 .60
119 Hideki Irabu .08 .25
120 Francisco Cordova .08 .25
121 Al Martin .08 .25
122 Tony Clark .08 .25
123 Curt Schilling .08 .25
124 Rusty Greer .08 .25
125 Jose Canseco .15 .40
126 Edgar Renteria .08 .25
127 Todd Walker .08 .25
128 Wally Joyner .08 .25
129 Bill Mueller .08 .25
130 Jose Guillen .08 .25
131 Manny Ramirez .15 .40
132 Bobby Higginson .08 .25
133 Kevin Orie .08 .25
134 Will Clark .15 .40
135 Dave Nilsson .08 .25
136 Jason Kendall .08 .25
137 Ivan Cruz .08 .25
138 Gary Sheffield .08 .25
139 Bubba Trammell .08 .25
140 Vladimir Guerrero .25 .60
141 Dennis Reyes .08 .25
142 Bobby Bonilla .08 .25
143 Ruben Rivera .08 .25
144 Ben Grieve .08 .25
145 Moises Alou .08 .25
146 Tony Womack .08 .25
147 Eric Young .08 .25
148 Paul Konerko .08 .25
149 Dante Bichette .08 .25
150 Joe Carter .08 .25
151 Rondell White .08 .25
152 Chris Holt .08 .25
153 Shawn Green .08 .25
154 Mark Grudzielanek .08 .25
155 Jermaine Dye .08 .25
156 Ken Griffey Jr. FC .30 .75
157 Frank Thomas FC .15 .40
158 Chipper Jones FC .15 .40
159 Mike Piazza FC .25 .60
160 Cal Ripken FC .40 1.00
161 Greg Maddux FC .25 .60
162 Juan Gonzalez FC .08 .25
163 Alex Rodriguez FC .25 .60
164 Mark McGwire FC .30 .75
165 Derek Jeter FC .30 .75
166 Larry Walker CL .08 .25
167 Tony Gwynn CL .15 .40
168 Tino Martinez CL .08 .25
169 Scott Rolen CL .08 .25
170 Nomar Garciaparra CL .25 .60
171 Mike Sweeney .08 .25
172 Dustin Hermanson .08 .25
173 Darren Dreifort .08 .25
174 Ron Gant .08 .25
175 Todd Hollandsworth .08 .25
176 John Jaha .08 .25
177 Kerry Wood .08 .25
178 Chris Stynes .08 .25
179 Kevin Elster .08 .25
180 Derek Bell .08 .25
181 Darryl Strawberry .08 .25
182 Damion Easley .08 .25
183 Jeff Cirillo .08 .25
184 John Thomson .08 .25
185 Dan Wilson .08 .25
186 Jay Bell .08 .25
187 Bernard Gilkey .08 .25
188 Marc Valdes .08 .25
189 Ramon Martinez .08 .25
190 Charles Nagy .08 .25
191 Derek Lowe .08 .25
192 Andy Benes .08 .25
193 Delino DeShields .08 .25
194 Ryan Jackson RC .08 .25
195 Kenny Lofton .08 .25
196 Chuck Knoblauch .08 .25
197 Andres Galarraga .08 .25
198 Jose Canseco .15 .40
199 John Olerud .08 .25
200 Lance Johnson .08 .25
201 Darryl Kile .08 .25
202 Luis Castillo .08 .25
203 Joe Carter .08 .25
204 Dennis Eckersley .08 .25
205 Steve Finley .08 .25
206 Esteban Loaiza .08 .25
207 Ryan Christenson RC .08 .25
208 Deivi Cruz .08 .25
209 Mariano Rivera .25 .60
210 Mike Judd RC .10 .30
211 Billy Wagner .08 .25
212 Scott Spiezio .08 .25
213 Russ Davis .08 .25
214 Jeff Suppan .08 .25
215 Doug Glanville .08 .25
216 Dmitri Young .08 .25
217 Rey Ordonez .08 .25
218 Cecil Fielder .08 .25
219 Masato Yoshii RC .10 .30
220 Raul Casanova .08 .25
221 Rolando Arrojo RC .10 .30
222 Ellis Burks .08 .25
223 Butch Huskey .08 .25
224 Brian Hunter .08 .25
225 Marquis Grissom .08 .25
226 Kevin Brown .15 .40
227 Joe Randa .08 .25
228 Henry Rodriguez .08 .25
229 Omar Vizquel .15 .40
230 Fred McGriff .15 .40
231 Matt Williams .08 .25
232 Moises Alou .08 .25
233 Travis Fryman .08 .25
234 Wade Boggs .15 .40
235 Pedro Martinez .15 .40
236 Rickey Henderson .25 .60
237 Bubba Trammell .08 .25
238 Mike Caruso .08 .25
239 Wilson Alvarez .08 .25
240 Geronimo Berroa .08 .25
241 Eric Milton .08 .25
242 Scott Erickson .08 .25
243 Todd Erdos RC .08 .25
244 Bobby Hughes .08 .25
245 Dave Hollins .08 .25
246 Dean Palmer .08 .25
247 Carlos Baerga .08 .25
248 Jose Silva .08 .25
249 Jose Cabrera RC .08 .25
250 Tom Evans .08 .25
251 Marty Cordova .08 .25
252 Hanley Frias RC .08 .25
253 Javier Valentin .08 .25
254 Mario Valdez .08 .25
255 Joey Cora .08 .25
256 Mike Lansing .08 .25
257 Jeff Kent .08 .25
258 Dave Dellucci RC .20 .50
259 Curtis King RC .08 .25
260 David Segui .08 .25
261 Royce Clayton .08 .25
262 Jeff Blauser .08 .25
263 Manny Aybar RC .08 .25
264 Mike Cather RC .08 .25
265 Todd Zeile .08 .25
266 Richard Hidalgo .08 .25
267 Dante Powell .08 .25
268 Mike DeJean RC .08 .25
269 Ken Cloude .08 .25
270 Danny Klassen .08 .25
271 Sean Casey .08 .25
272 A.J. Hinch .08 .25
273 Rich Butler RC .08 .25
274 Ben Ford RC .08 .25
275 Billy McMillon .08 .25
276 Wilson Delgado .08 .25
277 Orlando Cabrera .08 .25
278 Geoff Jenkins .08 .25
279 Enrique Wilson .08 .25
280 Derrek Lee .15 .40
281 Marc Pisciotta RC .08 .25
282 Abraham Nunez .08 .25
283 Aaron Boone .08 .25
284 Brad Fullmer .08 .25
285 Rob Stanifer RC .08 .25
286 Preston Wilson .08 .25
287 Greg Norton .08 .25
288 Bobby Smith .08 .25
289 Josh Booty .08 .25
290 Russell Branyan .08 .25
291 Jeremi Gonzalez .08 .25
292 Michael Coleman .08 .25
293 Cliff Politte .08 .25
294 Eric Ludwick .08 .25
295 Rafael Medina .08 .25
296 Jason Varitek .25 .60
297 Ron Wright .08 .25
298 Mark Kotsay .08 .25
299 David Ortiz .30 .75
300 Frank Catalanotto RC .20 .50
301 Robinson Checo .08 .25
302 Kevin Millwood RC .30 .75
303 Jacob Cruz .08 .25
304 Javier Vazquez .08 .25
305 Magglio Ordonez RC 1.00 2.50
306 Kevin Witt .08 .25
307 Derrick Gibson .08 .25
308 Shane Monahan .08 .25
309 Brian Rose .08 .25
310 Bobby Estalella .08 .25
311 Felix Heredia .08 .25
312 Desi Relaford .08 .25
313 Esteban Yan RC .10 .30
314 Ricky Ledee .08 .25
315 Steve Woodard .08 .25
316 Pat Watkins .08 .25
317 Damian Moss .08 .25
318 Bob Abreu .08 .25
319 Jeff Abbott .08 .25
320 Miguel Cairo .08 .25
321 Rigo Beltran RC .08 .25
322 Tony Saunders .08 .25
323 Randall Simon .08 .25
324 Hiram Bocachica .08 .25
325 Richie Sexson .08 .25
326 Karim Garcia .08 .25
327 Mike Lowell RC .50 1.25
328 Pat Cline .08 .25
329 Matt Clement .08 .25
330 Scott Elarton .08 .25
331 Manuel Barrios RC .08 .25
332 Bruce Chen .08 .25
333 Juan Encarnacion .08 .25
334 Travis Lee .08 .25
335 Wes Helms .08 .25
336 Chad Fox RC .08 .25
337 Donnie Sadler .08 .25
338 Carlos Mendoza RC .08 .25
339 Damian Jackson .08 .25
340 Julio Ramirez RC .08 .25
341 John Halama RC .10 .30
342 Edwin Diaz .08 .25
343 Felix Martinez .08 .25
344 Eli Marrero .08 .25
345 Carl Pavano .08 .25
346 Vladimir Guerrero HL .15 .40
347 Barry Bonds HL .30 .75
348 Darin Erstad HL .08 .25
349 Albert Belle HL .08 .25
350 Kenny Lofton HL .08 .25
351 Mo Vaughn HL .08 .25
352 Jose Cruz Jr. HL .08 .25
353 Tony Clark HL .08 .25
354 Roberto Alomar HL .08 .25
355 Manny Ramirez HL .08 .25
356 Paul Molitor HL .08 .25
357 Jim Thome HL .08 .25
358 Tino Martinez HL .08 .25
359 Tim Salmon HL .08 .25
360 David Justice HL .08 .25
361 Raul Mondesi HL .08 .25
362 Mark Grace HL .08 .25
363 Craig Biggio HL .08 .25
364 Larry Walker HL .08 .25
365 Mark McGwire HL .30 .75
366 Juan Gonzalez HL .08 .25
367 Derek Jeter HL .30 .75
368 Chipper Jones HL .15 .40
369 Frank Thomas HL .15 .40
370 Alex Rodriguez HL .15 .40
371 Mike Piazza HL .15 .40
372 Tony Gwynn HL .15 .40
373 Jeff Bagwell HL .08 .25
374 Nomar Garciaparra HL .25 .60
375 Ken Griffey Jr. HL .30 .75
376 Livan Hernandez UN .08 .25
377 Chan Ho Park UN .08 .25
378 Mike Mussina UN .08 .25
379 Andy Pettitte UN .08 .25
380 Greg Maddux UN .25 .60
381 Hideo Nomo UN .15 .40
382 Roger Clemens UN .25 .60
383 Randy Johnson UN .15 .40
384 Pedro Martinez UN .08 .25
385 Jaret Wright UN .08 .25
386 Ken Griffey Jr. SG .30 .75
387 Todd Helton SG .08 .25
388 Paul Konerko SG .08 .25
389 Cal Ripken SG .40 1.00
390 Larry Walker SG .08 .25
391 Ken Caminiti SG .08 .25
392 Jose Guillen SG .08 .25
393 Jim Edmonds SG .08 .25
394 Barry Larkin SG .08 .25
395 Bernie Williams SG .08 .25
396 Tony Clark SG .08 .25
397 Jose Cruz Jr. SG .08 .25
398 Ivan Rodriguez SG .08 .25
399 Darin Erstad SG .08 .25
400 Scott Rolen SG .08 .25
401 Mark McGwire SG .30 .75
402 Andruw Jones SG .08 .25
403 Juan Gonzalez SG .08 .25
404 Derek Jeter SG .30 .75
405 Chipper Jones SG .15 .40
406 Greg Maddux SG .25 .60
407 Frank Thomas SG .15 .40
408 Alex Rodriguez SG .25 .60
409 Mike Piazza SG .25 .60
410 Tony Gwynn SG .15 .40
411 Jeff Bagwell SG .08 .25
412 Nomar Garciaparra SG .25 .60
413 Hideo Nomo SG .15 .40
414 Barry Bonds SG .30 .75
415 Ben Grieve SG .08 .25
416 Barry Bonds CL .30 .75
417 Mark McGwire CL .30 .75
418 Roger Clemens CL .25 .60
419 Livan Hernandez CL .08 .25
420 Ken Griffey Jr. CL .30 .75

1998 Donruss Gold Press Proofs

*STARS: 10X TO 25X BASIC CARDS
*ROOKIES: 5X TO 12X BASIC CARDS
RANDOM INSERTS IN PACKS
STATED PRINT RUN 500 SETS

1998 Donruss Silver Press Proofs

*STARS: 5X TO 12X BASIC CARDS
*ROOKIES: 3X TO 6X BASIC CARDS
RANDOM INSERTS IN PACKS
STATED PRINT RUN 1500 SETS

1998 Donruss Crusade Green

RANDOM INSERTS IN SEVERAL BRANDS
STATED PRINT RUN 250 SERIAL #'d SETS
D SUFFIX ON DONRUSS DISTRIBUTION
L SUFFIX ON LEAF DISTRIBUTION
U SUFFIX ON DON.UPDATE DISTRIBUTION
ALL CTA CARDS ARE UNNUMBERED ERRORS
1 Tim Salmon 10.00 25.00
2 Garret Anderson 6.00 15.00
3 Jim Edmonds CTA 6.00 15.00
4 Darin Erstad CTA 6.00 15.00
5 Jason Dickson 6.00 15.00
6 Todd Greene 6.00 15.00
7 Roberto Alomar CTA 10.00 25.00
8 Cal Ripken 50.00 100.00
9 Rafael Palmeiro CTA 10.00 25.00
10 Brady Anderson 6.00 15.00
11 Mike Mussina 10.00 25.00
12 Mo Vaughn CTA 6.00 15.00
13 Nomar Garciaparra 15.00 40.00
14 Frank Thomas CTA 12.50 30.00
15 Albert Belle CTA 6.00 15.00
16 Mike Cameron 6.00 15.00
17 Robin Ventura 6.00 15.00
18 Manny Ramirez 10.00 25.00
19 Jim Thome CTA 10.00 25.00
20 Sandy Alomar Jr. 6.00 15.00
21 David Justice 6.00 15.00
22 Matt Williams 6.00 15.00
23 Tony Clark 6.00 15.00
24 Bubba Trammell 6.00 15.00
25 Justin Thompson 6.00 15.00
26 Bobby Higginson 6.00 15.00
27 Kevin Appier 6.00 15.00
28 Paul Molitor 6.00 15.00
29 Chuck Knoblauch CTA 6.00 15.00
30 Todd Walker 6.00 15.00
31 Bernie Williams 10.00 25.00
32 Derek Jeter CTA 40.00 80.00
33 Tino Martinez 10.00 25.00
34 Andy Pettitte 10.00 25.00
35 Wade Boggs CTA 10.00 25.00
36 Hideki Irabu 6.00 15.00
37 Jose Canseco 10.00 25.00
38 Jason Giambi 6.00 15.00
39 Ken Griffey Jr. 100.00 200.00
40 Alex Rodriguez CTA 20.00 50.00
41 Randy Johnson 12.50 30.00
42 Edgar Martinez 10.00 25.00
43 Jay Buhner CTA 6.00 15.00
44 Juan Gonzalez CTA 6.00 15.00
45 Will Clark 15.00 40.00
46 Ivan Rodriguez 10.00 25.00
47 Rusty Greer 6.00 15.00
48 Roger Clemens 20.00 50.00
49 Carlos Delgado 6.00 15.00
50 Shawn Green 6.00 15.00
51 Jose Cruz Jr. 6.00 15.00
52 Kenny Lofton 6.00 15.00
53 Chipper Jones 30.00 60.00
54 Andruw Jones CTA 10.00 25.00
55 Greg Maddux 20.00 50.00
56 John Smoltz CTA 10.00 25.00
57 Tom Glavine 10.00 25.00
58 Javier Lopez 6.00 15.00
59 Fred McGriff 10.00 25.00
60 Mark Grace 10.00 25.00
61 Sammy Sosa CTA 12.50 30.00
62 Kevin Orie 6.00 15.00
63 Barry Larkin CTA 10.00 25.00
64 Pokey Reese 6.00 15.00
65 Deion Sanders 10.00 25.00
66 Andres Galarraga 6.00 15.00
67 Larry Walker 6.00 15.00
68 Dante Bichette CTA 6.00 15.00
69 Neifi Perez 6.00 15.00
70 Eric Young 6.00 15.00
71 Todd Helton 10.00 25.00
72 Gary Sheffield CTA 6.00 15.00
73 Moises Alou 6.00 15.00
74 Bobby Bonilla 6.00 15.00
75 Kevin Brown 10.00 25.00
76 Ben Grieve 6.00 15.00
77 Jeff Bagwell CTA 10.00 25.00
78 Craig Biggio 10.00 25.00
79 Mike Piazza 20.00 50.00
80 Raul Mondesi 6.00 15.00
81 Hideo Nomo CTA 12.50 30.00
82 Wilton Guerrero 6.00 15.00
83 Rondell White CTA 6.00 15.00
84 Vladimir Guerrero CTA 12.50 30.00
85 Pedro Martinez 10.00 25.00
86 Edgardo Alfonzo 6.00 15.00
87 Todd Hundley CTA 6.00 15.00
88 Scott Rolen 10.00 25.00
89 Francisco Cordova 6.00 15.00
90 Jose Guillen 6.00 15.00
91 Jason Kendall 6.00 15.00
92 Ray Lankford 6.00 15.00
93 Mark McGwire CTA 40.00 80.00
94 Matt Morris 6.00 15.00
95 Alan Benes 6.00 15.00
96 Brian Jordan CTA 6.00 15.00
97 Tony Gwynn 15.00 40.00
98 Ken Caminiti CTA 6.00 15.00
99 Barry Bonds CTA 40.00 80.00
100 Shawn Estes 6.00 15.00

1998 Donruss Crusade Purple

*PURPLE: 1X TO 2.5X GREEN
RANDOM INSERTS IN PACKS
STATED PRINT RUN 100 SERIAL #'d SETS

1998 Donruss Crusade Red

RANDOM INSERTS IN PACKS
STATED PRINT RUN 25 SERIAL #'d SETS
NO PRICING DUE TO SCARCITY

1998 Donruss Diamond Kings

COMPLETE SET (20) 25.00 60.00
RANDOM INSERTS IN PACKS
STATED PRINT RUN 9500 SERIAL #'d SETS
*CANVAS: 1.25X TO 3X BASIC DIAM.KINGS
CANVAS: RANDOM INSERTS IN PACKS
CANVAS PRINT RUN 500 SERIAL #'d SETS
1 Cal Ripken 5.00 12.00
2 Greg Maddux 2.00 5.00
3 Ivan Rodriguez 1.00 2.50
4 Tony Gwynn 1.50 4.00
5 Paul Molitor 1.50 4.00
6 Kenny Lofton .60 1.50
7 Andy Pettitte 1.00 2.50
8 Darin Erstad .60 1.50
9 Randy Johnson 1.50 4.00
10 Derek Jeter 4.00 10.00
11 Hideo Nomo 1.50 4.00
12 David Justice .60 1.50
13 Bernie Williams 1.00 2.50
14 Roger Clemens 2.00 5.00
15 Barry Larkin 1.00 2.50
16 Andruw Jones .60 1.50
17 Mike Piazza 1.50 4.00
18 Frank Thomas 1.50 4.00
19 Alex Rodriguez 2.00 5.00
20 Ken Griffey Jr. 3.00 8.00
S20 Frank Thomas Sample 1.50 4.00

1998 Donruss Dominators

COMPLETE SET (30) 60.00 120.00
RANDOM INSERTS IN UPDATE PACKS
1 Roger Clemens 3.00 8.00
2 Tony Clark .60 1.50
3 Darin Erstad .60 1.50
4 Jeff Bagwell 1.00 2.50
5 Ken Griffey Jr 3.00 8.00
6 Andruw Jones 1.00 2.50
7 Juan Gonzalez .60 1.50
8 Ivan Rodriguez 1.00 2.50
9 Randy Johnson 1.50 4.00
10 Tino Martinez 1.00 2.50
11 Mark McGwire 4.00 10.00
12 Chuck Knoblauch .60 1.50
13 Jim Thome 1.00 2.50
14 Alex Rodriguez 2.50 6.00
15 Hideo Nomo 1.50 4.00
16 Jose Cruz Jr. .60 1.50
17 Chipper Jones 1.50 4.00
18 Tony Gwynn 2.00 5.00
19 Barry Bonds 4.00 10.00
20 Mo Vaughn .60 1.50
21 Cal Ripken 5.00 12.00
22 Greg Maddux 2.50 6.00
23 Manny Ramirez 1.00 2.50
24 Andres Galarraga .60 1.50
25 Vladimir Guerrero 1.50 4.00
26 Albert Belle .60 1.50
27 Nomar Garciaparra 2.50 6.00
28 Kenny Lofton .60 1.50
29 Mike Piazza 2.50 6.00
30 Frank Thomas 1.50 4.00

1998 Donruss Elite Inserts

COMPLETE SET (20) 50.00 100.00
RANDOM INSERTS IN UPDATE PACKS
STATED PRINT RUN 2500 SERIAL #'d SETS
1 Jeff Bagwell 1.50 4.00
2 Andruw Jones 1.00 2.50
3 Ken Griffey Jr. 5.00 12.00
4 Derek Jeter 6.00 15.00
5 Juan Gonzalez 1.00 2.50
6 Mark McGwire 4.00 10.00
7 Ivan Rodriguez 1.50 4.00
8 Paul Molitor 2.50 6.00
9 Hideo Nomo 2.50 6.00
10 Mo Vaughn 1.00 2.50
11 Chipper Jones 2.50 6.00
12 Nomar Garciaparra 1.50 4.00
13 Mike Piazza 2.50 6.00
14 Frank Thomas 2.50 6.00
15 Greg Maddux 3.00 8.00
16 Cal Ripken 8.00 20.00
17 Alex Rodriguez 3.00 8.00
18 Jose Cruz Jr. 1.00 2.50
19 Barry Bonds 4.00 10.00
20 Tony Gwynn 2.50 6.00

1998 Donruss FANtasy Team

COMPLETE SET (20) 75.00 150.00
1ST TEAM 1-10 PRINT 1750 SERIAL #'d SETS
2ND TEAM 11-20 PRINT 3750 SERIAL #'d SETS
*1ST TEAM DC's: .75X TO 2X BASIC FANTASY
*2ND TEAM DC's: 1X TO 2.5X BASIC FANTASY
DIE CUTS PRINT RUN 250 SERIAL #'d SETS
RANDOM INSERTS IN UPDATE PACKS
1 Frank Thomas 2.00 5.00
2 Ken Griffey Jr. 4.00 10.00
3 Cal Ripken 6.00 15.00
4 Jose Cruz Jr. .75 2.00
5 Travis Lee .75 2.00
6 Greg Maddux 2.50 6.00
7 Alex Rodriguez 2.50 6.00
8 Mark McGwire 3.00 8.00
9 Chipper Jones 2.00 5.00
10 Andruw Jones .75 2.00
11 Mike Piazza 1.50 4.00
12 Tony Gwynn 1.50 4.00
13 Larry Walker 1.00 2.50
14 Nomar Garciaparra 1.00 2.50
15 Jaret Wright .60 1.50
16 Livan Hernandez .60 1.50
17 Roger Clemens 2.00 5.00
18 Derek Jeter 4.00 10.00
19 Scott Rolen 1.00 2.50
20 Jeff Bagwell 1.00 2.50

1998 Donruss Longball Leaders

COMPLETE SET (24) 12.00 30.00
RANDOM INSERTS IN PACKS
STATED PRINT RUN 5000 SERIAL #'d SETS
1 Ken Griffey Jr. 2.00 5.00
2 Mark McGwire 1.50 4.00
3 Tino Martinez .40 1.00
4 Barry Bonds 1.50 4.00
5 Frank Thomas 1.00 2.50
6 Albert Belle .40 1.00
7 Mike Piazza 1.00 2.50
8 Chipper Jones 1.00 2.50
9 Vladimir Guerrero .60 1.50
10 Matt Williams .40 1.00
11 Sammy Sosa 1.00 2.50
12 Tim Salmon .40 1.00
13 Raul Mondesi .40 1.00
14 Jeff Bagwell .60 1.50
15 Mo Vaughn .40 1.00
16 Manny Ramirez 1.00 2.50
17 Jim Thome .60 1.50
18 Jim Edmonds .60 1.50
19 Tony Clark .40 1.00
20 Nomar Garciaparra .60 1.50
21 Juan Gonzalez .40 1.00
22 Scott Rolen .60 1.50
23 Larry Walker .60 1.50
24 Andres Galarraga .60 1.50

1998 Donruss MLB 99

COMPLETE SET (20) 4.00 10.00
UPDATE STATED ODDS 1:2
1 Cal Ripken .75 2.00
2 Nomar Garciaparra .40 1.00
3 Barry Bonds .60 1.50
4 Mike Mussina .15 .40
5 Pedro Martinez .15 .40
6 Derek Jeter .60 1.50
7 Andruw Jones .15 .40
8 Kenny Lofton .08 .25
9 Gary Sheffield .08 .25
10 Raul Mondesi .08 .25
11 Jeff Bagwell .15 .40
12 Tim Salmon .15 .40
13 Tom Glavine .15 .40
14 Ben Grieve .08 .25
15 Matt Williams .08 .25
16 Juan Gonzalez .08 .25
17 Mark McGwire .60 1.50
18 Bernie Williams .15 .40
19 Andres Galarraga .08 .25
20 Jose Cruz Jr. .08 .25

1998 Donruss Production Line On-Base

RANDOM INSERTS IN PRE-PRICED PACKS
PRINT RUN BASED ON PLAYER STATS
1 Frank Thomas/456 8.00 20.00
2 Edgar Martinez/456 5.00 12.00
3 Roberto Alomar/390 5.00 12.00
4 Chuck Knoblauch/390 3.00 8.00
5 Mike Piazza/431 12.50 30.00
6 Barry Larkin/440 5.00 12.00
7 Kenny Lofton/409 3.00 8.00
8 Jeff Bagwell/425 5.00 12.00
9 Barry Bonds/446 20.00 50.00
10 Rusty Greer/405 3.00 8.00
11 Gary Sheffield/424 3.00 8.00
12 Mark McGwire/393 20.00 50.00
13 Chipper Jones/371 8.00 20.00
14 Tony Gwynn/409 10.00 25.00
15 Craig Biggio/415 5.00 12.00
16 Mo Vaughn/420 3.00 8.00
17 Bernie Williams/408 5.00 12.00
18 Ken Griffey Jr./382 20.00 50.00
19 Brady Anderson/393 3.00 8.00
20 Derek Jeter/370 20.00 50.00

1998 Donruss Production Line Power Index

RANDOM INSERTS IN HOBBY PACKS
PRINT RUN BASED ON PLAYER STATS
1 Frank Thomas/1067 4.00 10.00
2 Mark McGwire/1039 10.00 25.00
3 Barry Bonds/1031 10.00 25.00
4 Jeff Bagwell/1017 2.50 6.00
5 Ken Griffey Jr./1028 12.00 30.00
6 Alex Rodriguez/846 6.00 15.00
7 Chipper Jones/850 4.00 10.00
8 Mike Piazza/1070 6.00 15.00
9 Mo Vaughn/980 1.50 4.00
10 Brady Anderson/863 1.50 4.00
11 Manny Ramirez/953 2.50 6.00
12 Albert Belle/823 1.50 4.00
13 Jim Thome/1001 2.50 6.00
14 Bernie Williams/952 2.50 6.00
15 Scott Rolen/846 2.50 6.00
16 Vladimir Guerrero/833 4.00 10.00
17 Larry Walker/1172 1.50 4.00
18 David Justice/1013 1.50 4.00
19 Tino Martinez/948 2.50 6.00
20 Tony Gwynn/957 5.00 12.00

1998 Donruss Production Line Slugging

RANDOM INSERTS IN RETAIL PACKS
PRINT RUN BASED ON PLAYER STATS
1 Mark McGwire/646 15.00 40.00
2 Ken Griffey Jr./646 15.00 40.00

3 Andres Galarraga/585 2.50 6.00
4 Barry Bonds/585 15.00 40.00
5 Juan Gonzalez/589 2.50 6.00
6 Mike Piazza/638 10.00 25.00
7 Jeff Bagwell/592 4.00 10.00
8 Manny Ramirez/538 4.00 10.00
9 Jim Thome/579 4.00 10.00
10 Mo Vaughn/560 2.50 6.00
11 Larry Walker/720 2.50 6.00
12 Tino Martinez/577 4.00 10.00
13 Frank Thomas/611 6.00 15.00
14 Tim Salmon/517 4.00 10.00
15 Raul Mondesi/541 2.50 6.00
16 Alex Rodriguez/496 10.00 25.00
17 Nomar Garciaparra/534 10.00 25.00
18 Jose Cruz Jr./499 2.50 6.00
19 Tony Clark/500 2.50 6.00
20 Cal Ripken/402 20.00 50.00

1998 Donruss Rated Rookies

COMPLETE SET (30) 15.00 40.00
*MEDALISTS: 2.5X TO 6X BASIC RR
MEDALIST PRINT RUN 250 SETS
RANDOM INSERTS IN PACKS
1 Mark Kotsay .75 2.00
2 Neifi Perez .75 2.00
3 Paul Konerko .75 2.00
4 Jose Cruz Jr. .75 2.00
5 Hideki Irabu .75 2.00
6 Mike Cameron .75 2.00
7 Jeff Suppan .75 2.00
8 Kevin Orie .75 2.00
9 Pokey Reese .75 2.00
10 Todd Dunwoody .75 2.00
11 Miguel Tejada 2.00 5.00
12 Jose Guillen .75 2.00
13 Bartolo Colon .75 2.00
14 Derrek Lee 1.25 3.00
15 Antone Williamson .75 2.00
16 Wilton Guerrero .75 2.00
17 Jaret Wright .75 2.00
18 Todd Helton 1.25 3.00
19 Shannon Stewart .75 2.00
20 Nomar Garciaparra 3.00 8.00
21 Brett Tomko .75 2.00
22 Fernando Tatis .75 2.00
23 Raul Ibanez .75 2.00
24 Dennis Reyes .75 2.00
25 Bobby Estalella .75 2.00
26 Lou Collier .75 2.00
27 Bubba Trammell .75 2.00
28 Ben Grieve .75 2.00
29 Ivan Cruz .75 2.00
30 Karim Garcia .75 2.00

1998 Donruss Rookie Diamond Kings

COMPLETE SET (12) 12.50 30.00
STATED PRINT RUN 9500 SERIAL #'d SETS
*CANVAS: 1.25X TO 3X BASIC ROOK.DK'S
CANVAS PRINT RUN 500 SERIAL #'d SETS
RANDOM INSERTS IN UPDATE PACKS
1 Travis Lee 1.50 4.00
2 Fernando Tatis 1.50 4.00
3 Livan Hernandez 1.50 4.00
4 Todd Helton 2.50 6.00
5 Derrek Lee 2.50 6.00
6 Jaret Wright 1.50 4.00
7 Ben Grieve 1.50 4.00
8 Paul Konerko 1.50 4.00
9 Jose Cruz Jr. 1.50 4.00
10 Mark Kotsay 1.50 4.00
11 Todd Greene 1.50 4.00
12 Brad Fullmer 1.50 4.00

1998 Donruss Signature Series Previews

RANDOM INSERTS IN UPDATE PACKS
ALOU/CASEY/JENKINS/JETER/WILSON
WERE NOT PUBLICLY RELEASED
NO PRICING ON QTY OF 25 OR LESS
1 Sandy Alomar Jr./96 * 15.00 40.00
2 Moises Alou 10.00 25.00
3 Andy Benes/135 * 15.00 40.00
4 Russell Branyan/188 * 15.00 40.00
5 Sean Casey 8.00 20.00
6 Tony Clark/188 * 10.00 25.00
7 Juan Encarnacion/193 * 20.00 50.00
8 Brad Fullmer/396 * 8.00 20.00
9 Juan Gonzalez/108 * 20.00 50.00
10 Ben Grieve/100 * 15.00 40.00
11 Todd Helton/101 * 20.00 50.00
12 Richard Hidalgo/380 * 6.00 15.00
13 A.J. Hinch/400 * 6.00 15.00
14 Damian Jackson/15 *
15 Geoff Jenkins 60.00 120.00
16 Derek Jeter SP
17 Chipper Jones/112 * 30.00 80.00
18 Chuck Knoblauch/98 * 12.00 30.00
19 Travis Lee/101 * 10.00 25.00
20 Mike Lowell/450 * 6.00 15.00
21 Greg Maddux/92 * 250.00 400.00
22 Kevin Millwood/395 * 12.50 30.00
23 Magglio Ordonez/420 * 6.00 15.00
24 David Ortiz/393 * 25.00 60.00
25 Rafael Palmeiro/107 * 8.00 20.00
26 Cal Ripken/22 *
27 Alex Rodriguez/23 *
28 Curt Schilling/100 * 50.00 100.00
29 Randall Simon/380 * 6.00 15.00
30 Fernando Tatis/400 * 6.00 15.00
31 Miguel Tejada/375 * 6.00 15.00
32 Robin Ventura/95 * 20.00 50.00
33 Dan Wilson * 15.00 40.00
34 Kerry Wood/373 * 15.00 40.00

1998 Donruss Days

As a special mid-season promotion, Donruss/Leaf distributed these special Donruss Days cards to selected hobby shops in fourteen different areas of the nation. To obtain these cards, collectors had to redeem a special exchange card of which was handed out at local ballparks upon entrance into the stadium. Each hobby shop was supplied with a complete selection of all fourteen players, but received larger supplies of their local stars. Collectors were free to choose any player they wished until supplies ran out. The cards are somewhat similar in design to standard 1998 Donruss but have been upgraded with 20 point cardboard stock and foil fronts. According to Donruss representatives, no more than 10,000 of any of these cards were produced.

COMPLETE SET (14) 6.00 15.00
1 Frank Thomas .30 .75
2 Tony Clark .08 .25
3 Ivan Rodriguez .30 .75
4 David Justice .08 .25
5 Nomar Garciaparra .75 2.00
6 Mark McGwire 1.00 2.50
7 Travis Lee .08 .25
8 Cal Ripken 1.25 3.00
9 Jeff Bagwell .30 .75
10 Barry Bonds .60 1.50
11 Ken Griffey Jr. 1.00 2.50
12 Derek Jeter 1.25 3.00
13 Raul Mondesi .08 .25
14 Greg Maddux .75 2.00

2001 Donruss

COMP.SET w/o SP's (150) 10.00 25.00
COMMON CARD (1-150) .10 .30
COMMON CARD (151-200) 3.00 8.00
151-200 RANDOM INSERTS IN PACKS
151-200 PRINT RUN 2001 SERIAL #'d SETS
COMMON CARD (201-220) 1.00 2.50
FAN CLUB 201-220 APPX. ONE PER BOX
EXCHANGE DEADLINE 05/01/03
BASEBALL'S BEST COUPON 1:720
COUPON EXCHANGE DEADLINE 01/20/02
1 Alex Rodriguez .40 1.00
2 Barry Bonds .75 2.00
3 Cal Ripken 1.00 2.50
4 Chipper Jones .30 .75
5 Derek Jeter .75 2.00
6 Troy Glaus .10 .30
7 Frank Thomas .30 .75
8 Greg Maddux .50 1.25
9 Ivan Rodriguez .20 .50
10 Jeff Bagwell .20 .50
11 Jose Canseco .20 .50
12 Todd Helton .20 .50
13 Ken Griffey Jr. .60 1.50
14 Manny Ramirez Sox .20 .50
15 Mark McGwire .75 2.00
16 Mike Piazza .50 1.25
17 Nomar Garciaparra .50 1.25
18 Pedro Martinez .20 .50
19 Randy Johnson .30 .75
20 Rick Ankiel .10 .30
21 Rickey Henderson .30 .75
22 Roger Clemens .60 1.50
23 Sammy Sosa .30 .75
24 Tony Gwynn .40 1.00
25 Vladimir Guerrero .30 .75
26 Eric Davis .10 .30
27 Roberto Alomar .10 .30
28 Mark Mulder .10 .30
29 Pat Burrell .10 .30
30 Harold Baines .10 .30
31 Carlos Delgado .10 .30
32 J.D. Drew .10 .30
33 Jim Edmonds .10 .30
34 Darin Erstad .10 .30
35 Jason Giambi .10 .30
36 Tom Glavine .20 .50
37 Juan Gonzalez .10 .30
38 Mark Grace .20 .50
39 Shawn Green .10 .30
40 Tim Hudson .10 .30
41 Andruw Jones .20 .50
42 David Justice .10 .30
43 Jeff Kent .10 .30
44 Barry Larkin .20 .50
45 Pokey Reese .10 .30
46 Mike Mussina .20 .50
47 Hideo Nomo .30 .75
48 Rafael Palmeiro .20 .50
49 Adam Piatt .10 .30
50 Scott Rolen .20 .50
51 Gary Sheffield .10 .30
52 Bernie Williams .20 .50
53 Bob Abreu .10 .30
54 Edgardo Alfonzo .10 .30
55 Jermaine Clark RC .20 .50
56 Albert Belle .10 .30
57 Craig Biggio .20 .50
58 Andres Galarraga .10 .30
59 Edgar Martinez .20 .50
60 Fred McGriff .20 .50
61 Magglio Ordonez .10 .30
62 Jim Thome .20 .50
63 Matt Williams .10 .30
64 Kerry Wood .10 .30
65 Moises Alou .10 .30
66 Brady Anderson .10 .30
67 Garret Anderson .10 .30
68 Tony Armas Jr. .10 .30
69 Tony Batista .10 .30
70 Jose Cruz Jr. .10 .30
71 Carlos Beltran .10 .30
72 Adrian Beltre .10 .30
73 Kris Benson .10 .30
74 Lance Berkman .10 .30
75 Kevin Brown .10 .30
76 Jay Buhner .10 .30
77 Jeromy Burnitz .10 .30
78 Ken Caminiti .10 .30
79 Sean Casey .10 .30
80 Luis Castillo .10 .30
81 Eric Chavez .10 .30
82 Jeff Cirillo .10 .30
83 Bartolo Colon .10 .30
84 David Cone .10 .30
85 Freddy Garcia .10 .30
86 Johnny Damon .20 .50
87 Ray Durham .10 .30
88 Jermaine Dye .10 .30
89 Juan Encarnacion .10 .30
90 Terrence Long .10 .30
91 Carl Everett .10 .30
92 Steve Finley .10 .30
93 Cliff Floyd .10 .30
94 Brad Fullmer .10 .30
95 Brian Giles .10 .30
96 Luis Gonzalez .10 .30
97 Rusty Greer .10 .30
98 Jeffrey Hammonds .10 .30
99 Mike Hampton .10 .30
100 Orlando Hernandez .10 .30
101 Richard Hidalgo .10 .30
102 Geoff Jenkins .10 .30
103 Jacque Jones .10 .30
104 Brian Jordan .10 .30
105 Gabe Kapler .10 .30
106 Eric Karros .10 .30
107 Jason Kendall .10 .30
108 Adam Kennedy .10 .30
109 Byung-Hyun Kim .10 .30
110 Ryan Klesko .10 .30
111 Chuck Knoblauch .10 .30
112 Paul Konerko .10 .30
113 Carlos Lee .10 .30
114 Kenny Lofton .10 .30
115 Javy Lopez .10 .30
116 Tino Martinez .20 .50
117 Ruben Mateo .10 .30
118 Kevin Millwood .10 .30
119 Ben Molina .10 .30
120 Raul Mondesi .10 .30
121 Trot Nixon .10 .30
122 John Olerud .10 .30
123 Paul O'Neill .20 .50
124 Chan Ho Park .10 .30
125 Andy Pettitte .20 .50
126 Jorge Posada .20 .50
127 Mark Quinn .10 .30
128 Aramis Ramirez .10 .30
129 Mariano Rivera .30 .75
130 Tim Salmon .20 .50
131 Curt Schilling .10 .30
132 Richie Sexson .10 .30
133 John Smoltz .20 .50
134 J.T. Snow .10 .30
135 Jay Payton .10 .30
136 Shannon Stewart .10 .30
137 B.J. Surhoff .10 .30
138 Mike Sweeney .10 .30
139 Fernando Tatis .10 .30
140 Miguel Tejada .10 .30
141 Jason Varitek .30 .75
142 Greg Vaughn .10 .30
143 Mo Vaughn .10 .30
144 Robin Ventura .10 .30
145 Jose Vidro .10 .30
146 Omar Vizquel .20 .50
147 Larry Walker .10 .30
148 David Wells .10 .30
149 Rondell White .10 .30
150 Preston Wilson .10 .30
151 Brent Abernathy RR 3.00 8.00
152 Cory Aldridge RR RC 3.00 8.00
153 Gene Altman RR RC 3.00 8.00
154 Josh Beckett RR 4.00 10.00
155 Wilson Betemit RR RC 4.00 10.00
156 Albert Pujols RR/500 RC 100.00 250.00
157 Joe Crede RR 4.00 10.00
158 Jack Cust RR 3.00 8.00
159 Ben Sheets RR/500 15.00 40.00
160 Alex Escobar RR 3.00 8.00
161 Adrian Hernandez RR RC 3.00 8.00
162 Pedro Feliz RR 3.00 8.00
163 Nate Frese RR RC 3.00 8.00
164 Carlos Garcia RR RC 3.00 8.00
165 Marcus Giles RR 3.00 8.00
166 Alexis Gomez RR RC 3.00 8.00
167 Jason Hart RR 3.00 8.00
168 Eric Hinske RR RC 4.00 10.00
169 Cesar Izturis RR 3.00 8.00
170 Nick Johnson RR 3.00 8.00
171 Mike Young RR 4.00 10.00
172 Brian Lawrence RR RC 3.00 8.00
173 Steve Lomasney RR 3.00 8.00
174 Nick Maness RR 3.00 8.00
175 Jose Mieses RR RC 3.00 8.00
176 Greg Miller RR RC 3.00 8.00
177 Eric Munson RR 3.00 8.00
178 Xavier Nady RR 3.00 8.00
179 Blaine Neal RR RC 3.00 8.00
180 Abraham Nunez RR 3.00 8.00
181 Jose Ortiz RR 3.00 8.00
182 Jeremy Owens RR RC 3.00 8.00
183 Pablo Ozuna RR 3.00 8.00
184 Corey Patterson RR 3.00 8.00
185 Carlos Pena RR 3.00 8.00
186 Wily Mo Pena RR 3.00 8.00
187 Timo Perez RR 3.00 8.00
188 Adam Pettyjohn RR RC 3.00 8.00
189 Luis Rivas RR 3.00 8.00
190 Jackson Melian RR RC 3.00 8.00
191 Wilken Ruan RR RC 3.00 8.00
192 Duaner Sanchez RR RC 3.00 8.00
193 Alfonso Soriano RR 4.00 10.00
194 Rafael Soriano RR RC 3.00 8.00
195 Ichiro Suzuki RR RC 15.00 40.00
196 Billy Sylvester RR RC 3.00 8.00
197 Juan Uribe RR RC 4.00 10.00
198 Eric Valent RR 3.00 8.00
199 Carlos Valderrama RR RC 3.00 8.00
200 Matt White RR RC 3.00 8.00
201 Alex Rodriguez FC 2.00 5.00
202 Barry Bonds FC 4.00 10.00
203 Cal Ripken FC 5.00 12.00
204 Chipper Jones FC 1.50 4.00
205 Derek Jeter FC 4.00 10.00
206 Troy Glaus FC 1.00 2.50
207 Frank Thomas FC 1.50 4.00
208 Greg Maddux FC 2.50 6.00
209 Ivan Rodriguez FC 1.00 2.50
210 Jeff Bagwell FC 1.00 2.50
211 Todd Helton FC 1.00 2.50
212 Ken Griffey Jr. FC 3.00 8.00
213 Manny Ramirez Sox FC 1.00 2.50
214 Mark McGwire FC 4.00 10.00
215 Mike Piazza FC 2.50 6.00
216 Pedro Martinez FC 1.00 2.50
217 Sammy Sosa FC 1.50 4.00
218 Tony Gwynn FC 2.00 5.00
219 Vladimir Guerrero FC 1.50 4.00
220 Nomar Garciaparra FC 2.50 6.00
NNO BB Best Coupon .75 2.00
NNO The Rookies Coupon .20 .50

2001 Donruss Stat Line Career

*1-150 P/R b/wn 251-400: 2.5X TO 6X
*1-150 P/R b/wn 201-250: 2.5X TO 6X
*1-150 P/R b/wn 151-200: 3X TO 8X
*1-150 P/R b/wn 121-150: 3X TO 8X
*1-150 P/R b/wn 81-120: 4X TO 10X
*1-150 P/R b/wn 66-80: 5X TO 12X
*1-150 P/R b/wn 51-65: 5X TO 12X
*1-150 P/R b/wn 36-50: 6X TO 15X
*1-150 P/R b/wn 26-35: 8X TO 20X
*201-220 P/R b/wn 251-400 .5X TO 1.2X
*201-220 P/R b/wn 201-250 .5X TO 1.2X
*201-220 P/R b/wn 151-200 .6X TO 1.5X
*201-220 P/R b/wn 121-150 .6X TO 1.5X
*201-220 P/R b/wn 81-120 .75X TO 2X
*201-220 P/R b/wn 36-50 1.25X TO 3X
SEE BECKETT.COM FOR PRINT RUNS
NO PRICING ON QTY OF 25 OR LESS
EXCHANGE DEADLINE 05/01/03
152 Cory Aldridge RR/33 4.00 10.00
153 Gene Altman RR/351 .75 2.00
154 Josh Beckett RR/212 1.00 2.50
156 Albert Pujols RR/154 100.00 250.00
157 Joe Crede RR/357 1.25 3.00
158 Jack Cust RR/66 2.00 5.00
159 Ben Sheets RR/159 6.00 15.00
160 Alex Escobar RR/45 3.00 8.00
161 Adrian Hernandez RR/86 2.00 5.00
162 Pedro Feliz RR/286 .75 2.00
163 Nate Frese RR/119 2.00 5.00
164 Carlos Garcia RR/106 2.00 5.00
165 Marcus Giles RR/320 .75 2.00
166 Alexis Gomez RR/34 4.00 10.00
167 Jason Hart RR/303 .75 2.00
168 Eric Hinske RR/332 1.00 2.50
169 Cesar Izturis RR/60 2.50 6.00
170 Nick Johnson RR/308 .75 2.00
171 Mike Young RR/37 5.00 12.00
172 Brian Lawrence RR/281 .75 2.00
173 Steve Lomasney RR/229 1.00 2.50
175 Jose Mieses RR/265 .75 2.00
176 Greg Miller RR/328 .75 2.00
179 Blaine Neal RR/296 .75 2.00
180 Abraham Nunez RR/38 3.00 8.00
182 Jeremy Owens RR/273 .75 2.00
183 Pablo Ozuna RR/333 .75 2.00
185 Carlos Pena RR/52 2.50 6.00
186 Wily Mo Pena RR/114 2.00 5.00
187 Timo Perez RR/49 3.00 8.00
189 Luis Rivas RR/310 .75 2.00
190 Jackson Melian RR/26 4.00 10.00
191 Wilken Ruan RR/215 1.00 2.50
193 Alfonso Soriano RR/50 3.00 8.00
195 Ichiro Suzuki RR/106 60.00 150.00
197 Juan Uribe RR/157 1.25 3.00
198 Eric Valent RR/342 .75 2.00
200 Matt White RR/31 4.00 10.00

2001 Donruss Stat Line Season

*1-150 P/R b/wn 151-200: 3X TO 8X
*1-150 P/R b/wn 121-150: 3X TO 8X
*1-150 P/R b/wn 81-120: 4X TO 10X
*1-150 P/R b/wn 66-80: 5X TO 12X
*1-150 P/R b/wn 51-65: 5X TO 12X
*1-150 P/R b/wn 36-50: 6X TO 15X
*1-150 P/R b/wn 26-35: 8X TO 20X
*201-220 P/R b/wn 151-200 .6X TO 1.5X
*201-220 P/R b/wn 121-150 .6X TO 1.5X
*201-220 P/R b/wn 81-120 .75X TO 2X
*201-220 P/R b/wn 66-80 1X TO 2.5X
*201-220 P/R b/wn 36-50 1.25X TO 3X
*201-220 P/R b/wn 26-35 1.5X TO 4X
SEE BECKETT.COM FOR PRINT RUNS
NO PRICING ON QTY OF 25 OR LESS
151-200 NO PRICING ON QTY OF 25 OR LESS
EXCHANGE DEADLINE 05/01/03
151 Brent Abernathy RR/130 1.50 4.00
152 Cory Aldridge RR/100 2.00 5.00
154 Josh Beckett RR/61 2.50 6.00
155 Wilson Betemit RR/89 6.00 15.00
156B Albert Pujols RR AU 300.00 800.00
158 Jack Cust RR/131 1.50 4.00
159B Ben Sheets RR AU 30.00 60.00
160 Alex Escobar RR/126 1.50 4.00
163 Nate Frese RR/126 1.50 4.00
165 Marcus Giles RR/133 1.50 4.00
166 Alexis Gomez RR/117 2.00 5.00
167 Jason Hart RR/31 4.00 10.00
169 Cesar Izturis RR/95 2.00 5.00
170 Nick Johnson RR/145 1.50 4.00
171 Mike Young RR/155 2.00 5.00
172 Brian Lawrence RR/165 1.25 3.00
174 Nick Maness RR/127 1.50 4.00
179 Blaine Neal RR/65 2.50 6.00
180 Abraham Nunez RR/51 2.50 6.00
185 Carlos Pena RR/117 2.00 5.00
188 Adam Pettyjohn RR/68 2.00 5.00
190 Jackson Melian RR/73 2.00 5.00
191 Wilken Ruan RR/165 1.25 3.00
192 Duaner Sanchez RR/121 1.50 4.00
194 Rafael Soriano RR/90 2.00 5.00
195 Ichiro Suzuki RR/153 50.00 120.00
199 Carlos Valderrama RR/137 1.50 4.00
200 Matt White RR/126 1.50 4.00

2001 Donruss 1999 Retro

COMPLETE SET (100) 75.00 150.00
COMP.SET w/o SP's (80) 20.00 50.00
COMMON CARD (1-80) .25 .60
1-80 ONE PER 1999 RETRO HOBBY PACK
COMMON CARD (81-100) 2.00 5.00
81-100 RANDOM IN '99 RETRO HOBBY PACKS
81-100 PRINT RUN 1999 SERIAL #'d SETS
1 Ken Griffey Jr. 1.25 3.00
2 Nomar Garciaparra 1.00 2.50
3 Alex Rodriguez .75 2.00
4 Mark McGwire 1.50 4.00
5 Sammy Sosa .60 1.50
6 Chipper Jones .60 1.50
7 Mike Piazza 1.00 2.50
8 Barry Larkin .40 1.00
9 Andruw Jones .40 1.00
10 Albert Belle .25 .60
11 Jeff Bagwell .40 1.00
12 Tony Gwynn .75 2.00
13 Manny Ramirez .40 1.00
14 Mo Vaughn .25 .60
15 Barry Bonds 1.50 4.00
16 Frank Thomas .60 1.50
17 Vladimir Guerrero .60 1.50
18 Derek Jeter 1.50 4.00
19 Randy Johnson .60 1.50
20 Greg Maddux 1.00 2.50
21 Pedro Martinez .40 1.00
22 Cal Ripken 2.00 5.00
23 Ivan Rodriguez .40 1.00
24 Matt Williams .25 .60
25 Javy Lopez .25 .60
26 Tim Salmon .40 1.00
27 Raul Mondesi .25 .60
28 Todd Helton .40 1.00
29 Magglio Ordonez .25 .60
30 Sean Casey .25 .60
31 Jeromy Burnitz .25 .60
32 Jeff Kent .25 .60
33 Jim Edmonds .25 .60
34 Jim Thome .40 1.00
35 Dante Bichette .25 .60
36 Larry Walker .25 .60
37 Will Clark .40 1.00
38 Omar Vizquel .40 1.00
39 Mike Mussina .40 1.00
40 Eric Karros .25 .60
41 Kenny Lofton .25 .60
42 David Justice .25 .60
43 Craig Biggio .40 1.00
44 J.D. Drew .25 .60
45 Rickey Henderson .60 1.50
46 Bernie Williams .40 1.00
47 Brian Giles .25 .60
48 Paul O'Neill .40 1.00
49 Orlando Hernandez .25 .60
50 Jason Giambi .25 .60
51 Curt Schilling .25 .60
52 Scott Rolen .40 1.00
53 Mark Grace .40 1.00
54 Moises Alou .25 .60
55 Jason Kendall .25 .60
56 Ray Lankford .25 .60
57 Kerry Wood .25 .60
58 Gary Sheffield .25 .60
59 Ruben Mateo .25 .60
60 Darin Erstad .25 .60
61 Troy Glaus .25 .60
62 Jose Canseco .40 1.00
63 Wade Boggs .40 1.00
64 Tom Glavine .40 1.00
65 Gabe Kapler .25 .60
66 Juan Gonzalez .25 .60
67 Rafael Palmeiro .40 1.00
68 Richie Sexson .25 .60
69 Carl Everett .25 .60
70 David Wells .25 .60
71 Carlos Delgado .25 .60
72 Eric Davis .25 .60
73 Shawn Green .25 .60
74 Andres Galarraga .25 .60
75 Edgar Martinez .40 1.00
76 Roberto Alomar .40 1.00
77 John Olerud .25 .60
78 Luis Gonzalez .25 .60
79 Kevin Brown .25 .60
80 Roger Clemens 1.25 3.00
81 Josh Beckett SP 3.00 8.00
82 Alfonso Soriano SP 3.00 8.00
83 Alex Escobar SP 2.00 5.00
84 Pat Burrell SP 2.00 5.00
85 Eric Chavez SP 2.00 5.00
86 Erubiel Durazo SP 2.00 5.00
87 Abraham Nunez SP 2.00 5.00
88 Carlos Pena SP 2.00 5.00
89 Nick Johnson SP 2.00 5.00
90 Eric Munson SP 2.00 5.00
91 Corey Patterson SP 2.00 5.00
92 Wily Mo Pena SP 2.00 5.00
93 Rafael Furcal SP 2.00 5.00
94 Eric Valent SP 2.00 5.00
95 Mark Mulder SP 2.00 5.00
96 Chad Hutchinson SP 2.00 5.00
97 Freddy Garcia SP 2.00 5.00
98 Tim Hudson SP 2.00 5.00
99 Rick Ankiel SP 2.00 5.00
100 Kip Wells SP 2.00 5.00

2001 Donruss 1999 Retro Stat Line Career

*1-80 P/R b/wn 251-400: 1.25X TO 3X
*1-80 P/R b/wn 201-250: 1.25X TO 3X
*1-80 P/R b/wn 151-200: 1.5X TO 4X
*1-80 P/R b/wn 121-150: 1.5X TO 4X
*1-80 P/R b/wn 81-120: 2X TO 5X
*1-80 P/R b/wn 66-80: 2.5X TO 6X
*1-80 P/R b/wn 51-65: 2.5X TO 6X
*1-80 P/R b/wn 36-50: 3X TO 8X
*1-80 P/R b/wn 26-35: 4X TO 10X
SEE BECKETT.COM FOR PRINT RUNS
NO PRICING ON QTY OF 25 OR LESS
81-100 NO PRICING ON QTY OF 25 OR LESS
82 Alfonso Soriano/113 1.50 4.00
83 Alex Escobar/181 1.00 2.50
84 Pat Burrell/303 .75 2.00
85 Eric Chavez/314 .75 2.00
86 Erubiel Durazo/147 1.25 3.00
87 Abraham Nunez/106 1.50 4.00
88 Carlos Pena/46 2.50 6.00
89 Nick Johnson/259 .75 2.00
90 Eric Munson/392 .75 2.00
91 Corey Patterson/117 1.50 4.00
92 Wily Mo Pena/247 .75 2.00
93 Rafael Furcal/137 1.25 3.00
94 Eric Valent/53 2.00 5.00
95 Mark Mulder/340 .75 2.00
97 Freddy Garcia/397 .75 2.00
99 Rick Ankiel/222 .75 2.00
100 Kip Wells/371 .75 2.00

2001 Donruss 1999 Retro Stat Line Season

*1-80 P/R b/wn 251-400: 1.25X TO 3X
*1-80 P/R b/wn 201-250: 1.25X TO 3X
*1-80 P/R b/wn 151-200: 1.5X TO 4X
*1-80 P/R b/wn 121-150: 1.5X TO 4X
*1-80 P/R b/wn 81-120: 2X TO 5X
*1-80 P/R b/wn 66-80: 2.5X TO 6X
*1-80 P/R b/wn 51-65: 2.5X TO 6X
*1-80 P/R b/wn 36-50: 3X TO 8X
*1-80 P/R b/wn 26-35: 4X TO 10X
PLEASE SEE BECKETT.COM FOR PRINT RUNS
NO PRICING ON QTY OF 25 OR LESS
81-100 NO PRICING ON QTY OF 25 OR LESS
81 Josh Beckett/178 1.00 2.50
83 Alex Escobar/27 3.00 8.00
85 Eric Chavez/33 3.00 8.00
87 Abraham Nunez/95 1.50 4.00
88 Carlos Pena/319 .75 2.00
93 Rafael Furcal/88 1.50 4.00
95 Mark Mulder/113 1.50 4.00
96 Chad Hutchinson/51 2.00 5.00
98 Tim Hudson/152 1.00 2.50
100 Kip Wells/135 1.00 2.50

2001 Donruss 1999 Retro Diamond Kings

COMPLETE SET (5) 30.00 60.00
STATED PRINT RUN 2,500 SERIAL #'d SETS
*STUDIO: .75X TO 2X BASIC RETRO DK
STUDIO PRINT RUN 250 SERIAL #'d SETS
1 Scott Rolen 4.00 10.00
2 Sammy Sosa 4.00 10.00
3 Juan Gonzalez 4.00 10.00
4 Ken Griffey Jr. 6.00 15.00
5 Derek Jeter 8.00 20.00

2001 Donruss 2000 Retro

COMPLETE SET (100) 125.00 250.00
COMP.SET w/o SP's (80) 40.00 80.00
COMMON CARD (1-80) .25 .60
1-80 ONE PER 2000 RETRO RETAIL PACK
COMMON CARD (81-100) 2.00 5.00
81-100 RANDOM IN 2000 RETRO RETAIL
81-100 PRINT RUN 2000 SERIAL #'d SETS
1 Vladimir Guerrero .60 1.50
2 Alex Rodriguez .75 2.00
3 Ken Griffey Jr. 1.25 3.00
4 Nomar Garciaparra 1.00 2.50
5 Mike Piazza 1.00 2.50
6 Mark McGwire 1.50 4.00
7 Sammy Sosa .60 1.50
8 Chipper Jones .60 1.50
9 Jim Edmonds .25 .60
10 Tony Gwynn .75 2.00
11 Andruw Jones .40 1.00
12 Albert Belle .25 .60
13 Jeff Bagwell .40 1.00
14 Manny Ramirez .40 1.00
15 Mo Vaughn .25 .60
16 Barry Bonds 1.50 4.00
17 Frank Thomas .60 1.50
18 Ivan Rodriguez .40 1.00
19 Derek Jeter 3.00 8.00
20 Randy Johnson .60 1.50
21 Greg Maddux 1.00 2.50
22 Pedro Martinez .40 1.00
23 Cal Ripken 2.00 5.00
24 Mark Grace .40 1.00
25 Javy Lopez .25 .60
26 Ray Durham .25 .60
27 Todd Helton .40 1.00
28 Magglio Ordonez .25 .60
29 Sean Casey .25 .60
30 Darin Erstad .25 .60
31 Barry Larkin .40 1.00
32 Will Clark .40 1.00
33 Jim Thome .40 1.00
34 Dante Bichette .25 .60
35 Larry Walker .25 .60
36 Ken Caminiti .25 .60
37 Omar Vizquel .40 1.00
38 Miguel Tejada .25 .60
39 Eric Karros .25 .60
40 Gary Sheffield .25 .60
41 Jeff Cirillo .25 .60
42 Rondell White .25 .60
43 Rickey Henderson .60 1.50
44 Bernie Williams .40 1.00
45 Brian Giles .25 .60
46 Paul O'Neill .40 1.00
47 Orlando Hernandez .25 .60
48 Ben Grieve .25 .60
49 Jason Giambi .25 .60
50 Curt Schilling .25 .60
51 Scott Rolen .40 1.00
52 Bobby Abreu .25 .60
53 Jason Kendall .25 .60
54 Fernando Tatis .25 .60
55 Jeff Kent .25 .60
56 Mike Mussina .40 1.00
57 Troy Glaus .25 .60
58 Jose Canseco .40 1.00
59 Wade Boggs .40 1.00
60 Fred McGriff .25 .60
61 Juan Gonzalez .25 .60
62 Rafael Palmeiro .40 1.00
63 Rusty Greer .25 .60
64 Carl Everett .25 .60
65 David Wells .25 .60
66 Carlos Delgado .25 .60
67 Shawn Green .25 .60
68 David Justice .25 .60
69 Edgar Martinez .40 1.00
70 Andres Galarraga .25 .60
71 Roberto Alomar .40 1.00
72 Jermaine Dye .25 .60
73 John Olerud .25 .60
74 Luis Gonzalez .25 .60
75 Craig Biggio .40 1.00
76 Kevin Millwood .25 .60
77 Kevin Brown .25 .60
78 John Smoltz .40 1.00
79 Roger Clemens 1.25 3.00
80 Mike Hampton .25 .60
81 Tomas De La Rosa SP 2.00 5.00
82 C.C. Sabathia 6.00 15.00
83 Ryan Christenson SP 2.00 5.00
84 Pedro Feliz SP 2.00 5.00
85 Jose Ortiz SP 2.00 5.00
86 Xavier Nady SP 2.00 5.00
87 Julio Zuleta SP 2.00 5.00
88 Jason Hart SP 2.00 5.00
89 Keith Ginter SP 2.00 5.00
90 Brent Abernathy SP 2.00 5.00
91 Timo Perez SP 2.00 5.00
92 Juan Pierre SP 2.00 5.00
93 Tike Redman SP 2.00 5.00
94 Mike Lamb SP 2.00 5.00
95A Ben Sheets 6.00 15.00
95B Ichiro Suzuki 25.00 60.00
96 Kazuhiro Sasaki SP 2.00 5.00
97 Barry Zito SP 3.00 8.00
98 Adam Bernero SP 2.00 5.00
99 Chad Durbin SP 2.00 5.00
100 Matt Ginter SP 2.00 5.00

2001 Donruss 2000 Retro Stat Line Career

*1-80 P/R b/wn 201-400: 1.2X TO 3X
*1-80 P/R b/wn 121-200: 1.5X TO 4X
*1-80 P/R b/wn 81-120: 2X TO 5X
*1-80 P/R b/wn 51-80: 2.5X TO 6X
*1-80 P/R b/wn 36-50: 3X TO 8X
*1-80 P/R b/wn 26-35: 4X TO 10X
19 Derek Jeter/63 20.00 50.00
81 Tomas De La Rosa/76 2.00 5.00
84 Pedro Feliz/45 2.00 5.00
85 Jose Ortiz/90 1.50 4.00
86 Xavier Nady/175 1.00 2.50
87 Julio Zuleta/295 .75 2.00
89 Keith Ginter/188 1.00 2.50
90 Brent Abernathy/254 .75 2.00
92 Juan Pierre/104 1.50 4.00
93 Tike Redman/151 1.00 2.50
94 Mike Lamb/240 .75 2.00
95A Ben Sheets/300 1.25 3.00
95B Ichiro Suzuki/159 12.00 30.00
96 Kazuhiro Sasaki/229 .75 2.00
98 Adam Bernero/254 .75 2.00
100 Matt Ginter/300 .75 2.00

2001 Donruss 2000 Retro Stat Line Season

*1-80 P/R b/wn 201-400: 1.2X TO 3X
*1-80 P/R b/wn 121-200: 1.5X TO 4X,
*1-80 P/R b/wn 81-120: 2X TO 5X
*1-80 P/R b/wn 51-80: 2.5X TO 6X
*1-80 P/R b/wn 36-50: 3X TO 8X
*1-80 P/R b/wn 26-35: 4X TO 10X
19 Derek Jeter/37 30.00 80.00
81 Tomas De La Rosa/122 1.00 2.50
82 C.C. Sabathia/76 10.00 25.00
83 Ryan Christenson/56 2.00 5.00
85 Jose Ortiz/107 1.50 4.00
88 Jason Hart/168 1.00 2.50
90 Brent Abernathy/168 1.00 2.50
92 Juan Pierre/187 1.00 2.50
93 Tike Redman/143 1.00 2.50
94 Mike Lamb/177 1.00 2.50
96 Kazuhiro Sasaki/34 3.00 8.00
97 Barry Zito/97 1.50 4.00
98 Adam Bernero/80 2.00 5.00
100 Matt Ginter/66 2.00 5.00

2001 Donruss 2000 Retro Diamond Kings

COMPLETE SET (5) 30.00 60.00
STATED PRINT RUN 2,500 SERIAL #'d SETS
*STUDIO: .75X TO 2X BASIC RETRO DK
STUDIO PRINT RUN 250 SERIAL #'d SETS
DK1 Frank Thomas 4.00 10.00
DK2 Greg Maddux 5.00 12.00
DK3 Alex Rodriguez 4.00 10.00
DK4 Jeff Bagwell 4.00 10.00
DK5 Manny Ramirez 4.00 10.00

2001 Donruss 2000 Retro Diamond Kings Studio Series Autograph

STATED PRINT RUN 50 SERIAL #'d SETS
DK3 Alex Rodriguez 100.00 200.00

2001 Donruss All-Time Diamond Kings

COMPLETE SET (10) 15.00 40.00
STATED PRINT RUN 2,500 SERIAL #'d SETS
*STUDIO: 1X TO 2.5X BASIC ALL-TIME DK
STUDIO PRINT RUN 200 SERIAL #'d SETS
STUDIO CARDS ARE SERIAL #'d 51-250
ATDK1 Willie Mays 3.00 8.00
ATDK1 Frank Robinson 1.00 2.50
ATDK2 Harmon Killebrew 1.50 4.00
ATDK3 Mike Schmidt 2.50 6.00
ATDK4 Reggie Jackson 1.25 3.00
ATDK5 Nolan Ryan 5.00 12.00
ATDK6 George Brett 3.00 8.00
ATDK7 Tom Seaver 1.00 2.50
ATDK8 Hank Aaron 3.00 8.00
ATDK10 Stan Musial 2.50 6.00

2001 Donruss All-Time Diamond Kings Studio Series Autograph

STATED PRINT RUN 50 SERIAL #'d SETS
AU CARDS ARE #'d 1/250 TO 50/250
MAYS & F.ROBINSON BOTH #'d ATDK-1
CARD ATDK-9 DOES NOT EXIST
ATDK1 Willie Mays 150.00 300.00
ATDK1 Frank Robinson 40.00 80.00
ATDK2 Harmon Killebrew 75.00 150.00
ATDK3 Mike Schmidt 100.00 175.00
ATDK4 Reggie Jackson 60.00 120.00
ATDK5 Nolan Ryan 150.00 250.00
ATDK6 George Brett 125.00 200.00
ATDK7 Tom Seaver 50.00 120.00
ATDK8 Hank Aaron 150.00 250.00
ATDK10 Stan Musial 75.00 150.00

2001 Donruss Anniversary Originals Autograph

PRINT RUNS B/WN 2-250 COPIES PER
NO PRICING ON QTY OF 25 OR LESS
PRICES REFER TO BGS 7 AND BGS 8 CARDS

8743 Rafael Palmeiro/250 8.00 20.00
8834 Roberto Alomar/250 20.00 50.00
88644 Tom Glavine/250 30.00 60.00

2001 Donruss Bat Kings

STATED PRINT RUN 250 SERIAL #'d SETS
BK1 Ivan Rodriguez 10.00 25.00
BK2 Tony Gwynn 15.00 40.00
BK3 Barry Bonds 10.00 25.00
BK4 Todd Helton 10.00 25.00
BK5 Troy Glaus 10.00 25.00
BK6 Mike Schmidt 10.00 25.00
BK7 Reggie Jackson 10.00 25.00
BK8 Harmon Killebrew 10.00 25.00
BK9 Frank Robinson 10.00 25.00
BK10 Hank Aaron 50.00 100.00

2001 Donruss Bat Kings Autograph

STATED PRINT RUN 50 SERIAL #'d SETS
BK1 Ivan Rodriguez 60.00 120.00
BK2 Tony Gwynn 75.00 150.00
BK3 Barry Bonds NO AUTO 30.00 60.00
BK4 Todd Helton 15.00 40.00
BK5 Troy Glaus 50.00 100.00
BK6 Mike Schmidt 100.00 175.00
BK7 Reggie Jackson 30.00 80.00
BK8 Harmon Killebrew 75.00 150.00
BK9 Frank Robinson 75.00 200.00
BK10 Hank Aaron 175.00 300.00

2001 Donruss Diamond Kings Hawaii Promo

COMPLETE SET (1) 100.00 200.00
HDK1 Alex Rodriguez SAMPLE 3.00 8.00
HDK1 Alex Rodriguez AU/100 100.00 200.00
HDK1 Alex Rodriguez 3.00 8.00

2001 Donruss Diamond Kings

COMPLETE SET (20) 30.00 60.00
STATED PRINT RUN 2,500 SERIAL #'d SETS
*STUDIO: .75X TO 2X BASIC DK
STUDIO NO AU PLAYER PRINT 250 #'d SETS
STUDIO AU PLAYER PRINT 200 #'d SETS
DK1 Alex Rodriguez 2.00 5.00
DK2 Cal Ripken 5.00 12.00
DK3 Mark McGwire 2.50 6.00
DK4 Ken Griffey Jr. 3.00 8.00
DK5 Derek Jeter 4.00 10.00
DK6 Nomar Garciaparra 1.00 2.50
DK7 Mike Piazza 1.50 4.00
DK8 Roger Clemens 2.50 6.00
DK9 Greg Maddux 2.50 6.00
DK10 Chipper Jones 1.50 4.00
DK11 Tony Gwynn 1.50 4.00
DK12 Barry Bonds 2.50 6.00
DK13 Sammy Sosa 1.00 2.50
DK14 Vladimir Guerrero 1.50 4.00
DK15 Frank Thomas 1.50 4.00
DK16 Troy Glaus .60 1.50
DK17 Todd Helton 1.00 2.50
DK18 Ivan Rodriguez 1.00 2.50
DK19 Pedro Martinez 1.00 2.50
DK20 Carlos Delgado .60 1.50

2001 Donruss Diamond Kings Studio Series Autograph

STATED PRINT RUN 50 SERIAL #'d SETS
SKIP-NUMBERED 11 CARD SET
DK1 Alex Rodriguez 25.00 60.00
DK2 Cal Ripken 150.00 300.00
DK8 Roger Clemens 100.00 175.00
DK9 Greg Maddux 100.00 200.00
DK10 Chipper Jones 60.00 150.00
DK11 Tony Gwynn 30.00 80.00
DK14 Vladimir Guerrero 15.00 40.00
DK16 Troy Glaus 12.00 30.00
DK17 Todd Helton 50.00 100.00
DK18 Ivan Rodriguez 20.00 50.00

2001 Donruss Diamond Kings Reprints

COMPLETE SET (20) 100.00 200.00
STATED PRINT RUNS LISTED BELOW
DKR1 Rod Carew/1982 4.00 10.00
DKR2 Nolan Ryan/1982 10.00 25.00
DKR3 Tom Seaver/1982 4.00 10.00
DKR4 Carlton Fisk/1982 4.00 10.00
DKR5 Reggie Jackson/1983 4.00 10.00
DKR6 Steve Carlton/1983 4.00 10.00
DKR7 Johnny Bench/1983 4.00 10.00
DKR8 Joe Morgan/1983 4.00 10.00
DKR9 Mike Schmidt/1984 8.00 20.00
DKR10 Wade Boggs/1984 4.00 10.00
DKR11 Cal Ripken/1985 10.00 25.00
DKR12 Tony Gwynn/1985 5.00 12.00
DKR13 Andre Dawson/1986 4.00 10.00
DKR14 Ozzie Smith/1987 6.00 15.00
DKR15 George Brett/1987 8.00 20.00
DKR16 Dave Winfield/1987 4.00 10.00
DKR17 Paul Molitor/1988 4.00 10.00
DKR18 Will Clark/1988 6.00 15.00
DKR19 Robin Yount/1989 4.00 10.00
DKR20 Ken Griffey Jr./1989 8.00 20.00

2001 Donruss Diamond Kings Reprints Autographs

STATED PRINT RUNS LISTED BELOW
DKR1 Rod Carew/82 20.00 50.00
DKR2 Nolan Ryan/82 50.00 120.00
DKR3 Tom Seaver/82 40.00 100.00
DKR4 Carlton Fisk/82 20.00 50.00
DKR5 Reggie Jackson/83 40.00 80.00
DKR6 Steve Carlton/83 10.00 25.00
DKR7 Johnny Bench/83 40.00 80.00
DKR8 Joe Morgan/83 20.00 50.00
DKR9 Mike Schmidt/84 75.00 150.00
DKR10 Wade Boggs/84 20.00 50.00
DKR11 Cal Ripken/85 90.00 150.00
DKR12 Tony Gwynn/85 50.00 100.00
DKR13 Andre Dawson/86 10.00 25.00
DKR14 Ozzie Smith/87 30.00 60.00
DKR15 George Brett/87 60.00 120.00
DKR16 Dave Winfield/87 10.00 25.00
DKR17 Paul Molitor/88 10.00 25.00
DKR18 Will Clark/88 60.00 120.00
DKR19 Robin Yount/89 40.00 80.00
DKR20 Ken Griffey Jr./89 NO AU 20.00 50.00

2001 Donruss Elite Series

COMPLETE SET (20) 75.00 150.00
STATED PRINT RUN 2,500 SERIAL #'d SETS
*DOMINATORS: 6X TO 15X BASIC ELITE
DOMINATORS PRINT RUN 25 SERIAL #'d SETS
ES1 Vladimir Guerrero 2.00 5.00
ES2 Cal Ripken 6.00 15.00
ES3 Greg Maddux 3.00 8.00
ES4 Alex Rodriguez 2.50 6.00
ES5 Barry Bonds 5.00 12.00
ES6 Chipper Jones 2.00 5.00
ES7 Derek Jeter 5.00 12.00
ES8 Ivan Rodriguez 1.50 4.00
ES9 Ken Griffey Jr. 4.00 10.00
ES10 Mark McGwire 5.00 12.00
ES11 Mike Piazza 3.00 8.00
ES12 Nomar Garciaparra 3.00 8.00
ES13 Pedro Martinez 1.50 4.00
ES14 Randy Johnson 2.00 5.00
ES15 Roger Clemens 4.00 10.00
ES16 Sammy Sosa 2.00 5.00
ES17 Tony Gwynn 2.50 6.00
ES18 Darin Erstad 1.50 4.00
ES19 Andruw Jones 1.50 4.00
ES20 Bernie Williams 1.50 4.00

2001 Donruss Jersey Kings

STATED PRINT RUN 250 SERIAL #'d SETS
JK1 Vladimir Guerrero 4.00 10.00
JK2 Cal Ripken 12.50 30.00
JK3 Greg Maddux 8.00 20.00
JK4 Chipper Jones 4.00 10.00
JK5 Roger Clemens 10.00 25.00
JK6 George Brett 8.00 20.00
JK7 Tom Seaver 4.00 10.00
JK8 Nolan Ryan 12.50 30.00
JK9 Stan Musial 5.00 12.00
JK10 Ozzie Smith 6.00 15.00

2001 Donruss Jersey Kings Autograph

STATED PRINT RUN 50 SERIAL #'d SETS
JK1 Vladimir Guerrero 75.00 150.00
JK2 Cal Ripken 175.00 300.00
JK3 Greg Maddux 60.00 150.00
JK4 Chipper Jones 75.00 150.00
JK5 Roger Clemens 125.00 200.00
JK6 George Brett 125.00 200.00
JK7 Tom Seaver 60.00 150.00
JK8 Nolan Ryan 150.00 250.00
JK9 Stan Musial 125.00 200.00
JK10 Ozzie Smith 75.00 150.00

2001 Donruss Longball Leaders

COMPLETE SET (20) 75.00 150.00
STATED PRINT RUN 1000 SERIAL #'d SETS
SEASONAL PRINT RUN BASED ON '00 HR'S
LL1 Vladimir Guerrero 3.00 8.00
LL2 Alex Rodriguez 4.00 10.00
LL3 Barry Bonds 8.00 20.00
LL4 Troy Glaus 1.50 4.00
LL5 Frank Thomas 3.00 8.00
LL6 Jeff Bagwell 2.00 5.00
LL7 Todd Helton 2.00 5.00
LL8 Ken Griffey Jr. 6.00 15.00
LL9 Manny Ramirez Sox 2.00 5.00
LL10 Mike Piazza 5.00 12.00
LL11 Sammy Sosa 3.00 8.00
LL12 Carlos Delgado 1.50 4.00
LL13 Jim Edmonds 1.50 4.00
LL14 Jason Giambi 1.50 4.00
LL15 David Justice 1.50 4.00
LL16 Rafael Palmeiro 2.00 5.00
LL17 Gary Sheffield 1.50 4.00
LL18 Jim Thome 2.00 5.00
LL19 Tony Batista 1.50 4.00
LL20 Richard Hidalgo 1.50 4.00

2001 Donruss Production Line

COMPLETE SET (60) 200.00 400.00
COMMON SLG (21-40) 1.25 3.00
COMMON PI (41-60) 1.00 2.50
STATED PRINT RUNS LISTED BELOW
*DIE CUT OBP 1-20: .75X TO 2X BASIC PL
*DIE CUT SLG 21-40: 1X TO 2.5X BASIC PL
*DIE CUT PI 41-60: 1.25X TO 3X BASIC PL
DIE CUT PRINT RUN 100 SERIAL #'d SETS
PL1 Jason Giambi OBP/476 1.50 4.00
PL2 Carlos Delgado OBP/470 1.50 4.00
PL3 Todd Helton OBP/463 2.50 6.00
PL4 Manny Ramirez Sox OBP/457 2.50 6.00
PL5 Barry Bonds OBP/440 10.00 25.00
PL6 Gary Sheffield OBP/438 1.50 4.00
PL7 Frank Thomas OBP/436 4.00 10.00
PL8 Nomar Garciaparra OBP/434 6.00 15.00
PL9 Brian Giles OBP/432 1.50 4.00
PL10 Edgardo Alfonzo OBP/425 1.50 4.00
PL11 Jeff Kent OBP/424 1.50 4.00
PL12 Jeff Bagwell OBP/424 2.50 6.00
PL13 Edgar Martinez OBP/423 2.50 6.00
PL14 Alex Rodriguez OBP/420 5.00 12.00
PL15 Luis Castillo OBP/418 1.50 4.00
PL16 Will Clark OBP/418 2.50 6.00
PL17 Jorge Posada OBP/417 2.50 6.00
PL18 Derek Jeter OBP/416 10.00 25.00
PL19 Bob Abreu OBP/416 1.50 4.00
PL20 Moises Alou OBP/416 1.50 4.00
PL21 Todd Helton SLG/698 2.00 5.00
PL22 Manny Ramirez Sox SLG/697 2.00 5.00
PL23 Barry Bonds SLG/688 8.00 20.00
PL24 Carlos Delgado SLG/664 1.25 3.00
PL25 Vladimir Guerrero SLG/664 3.00 8.00
PL26 Jason Giambi SLG/647 1.25 3.00
PL27 Gary Sheffield SLG/643 1.25 3.00
PL28 Richard Hidalgo SLG/636 1.25 3.00
PL29 Sammy Sosa SLG/634 3.00 8.00
PL30 Frank Thomas SLG/625 3.00 8.00
PL31 Moises Alou SLG/623 1.25 3.00
PL32 Jeff Bagwell SLG/615 2.00 5.00
PL33 Mike Piazza SLG/614 5.00 12.00
PL34 Alex Rodriguez SLG/606 4.00 10.00
PL35 Troy Glaus SLG/604 1.25 3.00
PL36 N.Garciaparra SLG/599 5.00 12.00
PL37 Jeff Kent SLG/596 1.25 3.00
PL38 Brian Giles SLG/594 1.25 3.00
PL39 Geoff Jenkins SLG/588 1.25 3.00
PL40 Carl Everett SLG/587 1.25 3.00
PL41 Todd Helton PI/1161 1.50 4.00
PL42 Manny Ramirez Sox PI/1154 1.50 4.00
PL43 Carlos Delgado PI/1134 1.00 2.50
PL44 Barry Bonds PI/1128 6.00 15.00
PL45 Jason Giambi PI/1123 1.00 2.50
PL46 Gary Sheffield PI/1081 1.00 2.50
PL47 Vladimir Guerrero PI/1074 2.50 6.00
PL48 Frank Thomas PI/1061 2.50 6.00
PL49 Sammy Sosa PI/1040 2.50 6.00
PL50 Moises Alou PI/1039 1.00 2.50
PL51 Jeff Bagwell PI/1039 1.50 4.00
PL52 Nomar Garciaparra PI/1033 4.00 10.00
PL53 Richard Hidalgo PI/1027 1.00 2.50
PL54 Alex Rodriguez PI/1026 3.00 8.00
PL55 Brian Giles PI/1026 1.00 2.50
PL56 Jeff Kent PI/1020 1.00 2.50
PL57 Mike Piazza PI/1012 4.00 10.00
PL58 Troy Glaus PI/1008 1.00 2.50
PL59 Edgar Martinez PI/1002 1.50 4.00
PL60 Jim Edmonds PI/994 1.50 4.00

2001 Donruss Recollection Autographs

A-ROD RANDOM INSERTS IN PACKS
BONDS AVAIL.VIA BAT KING AU EXCH
ALL A.ROD'S ARE EXCH CARDS
NO PRICING ON QTY OF 25 OR LESS
RC3 A.Rodriguez 01 Retro/30 60.00 120.00
RC4 A.Rodriguez 01 Don/40 60.00 120.00

2001 Donruss Rookie Reprints

COMPLETE SET (40) 150.00 300.00
STATED PRINT RUNS LISTED BELOW
PARALLEL PRINT RUN BASED ON RC YEAR
RR1 Cal Ripken/1982 10.00 25.00
RR2 Wade Boggs/1983 2.00 5.00
RR3 Tony Gwynn/1983 5.00 12.00
RR4 Ryne Sandberg/1983 6.00 15.00
RR5 Don Mattingly/1984 10.00 25.00
RR6 Joe Carter/1984 2.00 5.00
RR7 Roger Clemens/1985 8.00 20.00
RR8 Kirby Puckett/1985 3.00 8.00
RR9 Orel Hershiser/1985 2.00 5.00
RR10 Andres Galarraga/1986 2.00 5.00
RR11 Jose Canseco/1986 2.00 5.00
RR12 Fred McGriff/1986 2.00 5.00
RR13 Paul O'Neill/1986 2.00 5.00
RR14 Mark McGwire/1987 8.00 20.00
RR15 Barry Bonds/1987 8.00 20.00
RR16 Kevin Brown/1987 2.00 5.00
RR17 David Cone/1987 2.00 5.00
RR18 Rafael Palmeiro/1987 2.00 5.00
RR19 Barry Larkin/1987 2.00 5.00
RR20 Bo Jackson/1987 3.00 8.00
RR21 Greg Maddux/1987 5.00 12.00
RR22 Roberto Alomar/1988 2.00 5.00
RR23 Mark Grace/1988 2.00 5.00
RR24 David Wells/1988 2.00 5.00
RR25 Tom Glavine/1988 2.00 5.00
RR26 Matt Williams/1988 2.00 5.00
RR27 Ken Griffey Jr./1989 6.00 15.00
RR28 Randy Johnson/1989 3.00 8.00
RR29 Gary Sheffield/1989 2.00 5.00
RR30 Craig Biggio/1989 2.00 5.00
RR31 Curt Schilling/1989 2.00 5.00
RR32 Larry Walker/1990 2.00 5.00
RR33 Bernie Williams/1990 2.00 5.00
RR34 Sammy Sosa/1990 3.00 8.00
RR35 Juan Gonzalez/1990 2.00 5.00
RR36 David Justice/1990 2.00 5.00
RR37 Ivan Rodriguez/1991 2.00 5.00
RR38 Jeff Bagwell/1991 2.00 5.00
RR39 Jeff Kent/1992 2.00 5.00
RR39 Manny Ramirez/1992 2.00 5.00

2001 Donruss Rookie Reprints Autograph

STATED PRINT RUNS LISTED BELOW
SKIP-NUMBERED 18 CARD SET
RR1 Cal Ripken/82 200.00 400.00
RR2 Wade Boggs/83 30.00 60.00
RR3 Tony Gwynn/83 50.00 100.00
RR4 Ryne Sandberg/83 125.00 250.00
RR5 Don Mattingly/84 60.00 120.00
RR6 Joe Carter/84 15.00 40.00
RR7 Roger Clemens/85 175.00 300.00
RR8 Kirby Puckett/85 100.00 200.00
RR9 Orel Hershiser/85 30.00 60.00
RR10 Andres Galarraga/86 30.00 60.00
RR15 Barry Bonds/87 150.00 300.00
RR16 Kevin Brown/87 15.00 40.00
RR17 David Cone/87 15.00 40.00
RR18 Rafael Palmeiro/87 30.00 60.00
RR20 Bo Jackson/87 100.00 200.00
RR21 Greg Maddux/87 75.00 200.00
RR22 Roberto Alomar/88 30.00 60.00
RR24 Luis Gonzalez/91 15.00 40.00
RR25 Tom Glavine/88 50.00 120.00
RR28 Randy Johnson/89 150.00 300.00
RR29 Gary Sheffield/89 40.00 80.00
RR31 Curt Schilling/89 30.00 80.00
RR35 Juan Gonzalez/90 30.00 60.00
RR36 David Justice/90 15.00 40.00
RR37 Ivan Rodriguez/91 30.00 60.00
RR39 Manny Ramirez/92 75.00 150.00

2001 Donruss Rookies

COMP.FACT.SET (106) 30.00 60.00
COMP.SET w/o SP's (105) 10.00 25.00
ONE SET PER COUPON VIA MAIL
COUPON ODDS 1:72 '01 DONRUSS PACKS
COUPON EXCHANGE DEADLINE 01/20/02
R1 Adam Dunn .30 .75
R2 Ryan Drese RC .30 .75
R3 Bud Smith RC .15 .40
R4 Tsuyoshi Shinjo RC .30 .75
R5 Roy Oswalt .40 1.00
R6 Wilmy Caceres RC .20 .50
R7 Willie Harris RC .20 .50
R8 Andres Torres RC .15 .40
R9 Brandon Knight RC .15 .40
R10 Horacio Ramirez RC .30 .75
R11 Benito Baez RC .15 .40
R12 Jeremy Affeldt RC .20 .50
R13 Ryan Jensen RC .20 .50
R14 Casey Fossum RC .15 .40
R15 Ramon Vazquez RC .20 .50
R16 Dustan Mohr RC .20 .50
R17 Saul Rivera RC .20 .50
R18 Zach Day RC .20 .50
R19 Erik Hiljus RC .15 .40
R20 Cesar Crespo RC .15 .40
R21 Wilson Guzman RC .20 .50
R22 Travis Hafner RC 2.00 5.00
R23 Grant Balfour RC .15 .40
R24 Johnny Estrada RC .30 .75
R25 Morgan Ensberg RC .75 2.00
R26 Jack Wilson RC .30 .75
R27 Aubrey Huff .20 .50
R28 Endy Chavez RC .30 .75
R29 Delvin James RC .15 .40
R30 Michael Cuddyer .15 .40
R31 Jason Michaels RC .20 .50
R32 Martin Vargas RC .20 .50
R33 Donaldo Mendez RC .15 .40
R34 Jorge Julio RC .20 .50
R35 Tim Spooneybarger RC .20 .50
R36 Kurt Ainsworth .15 .40
R37 Josh Fogg RC .20 .50
R38 Brian Reith RC .15 .40
R39 Rick Bauer RC .15 .40
R40 Tim Redding .15 .40
R41 Erick Almonte RC .15 .40
R42 Juan A.Pena RC .15 .40
R43 Ken Harvey .15 .40
R44 David Brous RC .15 .40
R45 Kevin Olsen RC .20 .50
R46 Henry Mateo RC .15 .40
R47 Nick Neugebauer .15 .40
R48 Mike Penney RC .20 .50
R49 Jay Gibbons RC .30 .75
R50 Tim Christman RC .15 .40
R51 Brandon Duckworth RC .15 .40
R52 Brett Jodie RC .15 .40
R53 Christian Parker RC .15 .40
R54 Carlos Hernandez .15 .40
R55 Brandon Larson RC .15 .40
R56 Nick Punto RC .20 .50
R57 Elpidio Guzman RC .15 .40
R58 Joe Beimel RC .15 .40
R59 Junior Spivey RC .30 .75
R60 Will Ohman RC .20 .50
R61 Brandon Lyon RC .15 .40
R62 Stubby Clapp RC .15 .40
R63 Justin Duchscherer RC .20 .50
R64 Jimmy Rollins .20 .50
R65 David Williams RC .15 .40
R66 Craig Monroe RC 1.00 2.50
R67 Jose Acevedo RC .15 .40
R68 Jason Jennings .15 .40
R69 Josh Phelps .15 .40
R70 Brian Roberts RC .75 2.00
R71 Claudio Vargas RC .15 .40
R72 Adam Johnson .15 .40
R73 Bart Miadich RC .15 .40
R74 Juan Rivera .15 .40
R75 Brad Voyles RC .15 .40
R76 Nate Cornejo .15 .40
R77 Juan Moreno RC .20 .50
R78 Brian Rogers RC .15 .40
R79 Ricardo Rodriguez RC .20 .50
R80 Geronimo Gil RC .15 .40
R81 Joe Kennedy RC .30 .75
R82 Kevin Joseph RC .20 .50
R83 Josue Perez RC .20 .50
R84 Victor Zambrano RC .30 .75
R85 Josh Towers RC .30 .75
R86 Mike Rivera RC .20 .50
R87 Mark Prior RC 2.00 5.00
R88 Juan Cruz RC .20 .50
R89 Dewon Brazelton RC .20 .50
R90 Angel Berroa RC .30 .75
R91 Mark Teixeira RC 4.00 10.00
R92 Cody Ransom RC .15 .40
R93 Angel Santos RC .15 .40
R94 Corky Miller RC .15 .40
R95 Brandon Berger RC .15 .40
R96 Corey Patterson UPD .15 .40
R97 Albert Pujols UPD 12.00 30.00
R98 Josh Beckett UPD .30 .75
R99 C.C. Sabathia UPD .20 .50
R100 Alfonso Soriano UPD .30 .75
R101 Ben Sheets UPD .30 .75
R102 Rafael Soriano UPD .20 .50
R103 Wilson Betemit UPD .75 2.00
R104 Ichiro Suzuki UPD 6.00 15.00
R105 Jose Ortiz UPD .15 .40

2001 Donruss Rookies Diamond Kings

COMPLETE SET (5) 30.00 60.00
ONE DK PER ROOKIES FACTORY SET
RDK1 C.C. Sabathia DK 3.00 8.00
RDK2 Tsuyoshi Shinjo DK 4.00 10.00
RDK3 Albert Pujols DK 15.00 40.00
RDK4 Roy Oswalt DK 4.00 10.00
RDK5 Ichiro Suzuki DK 12.00 30.00

2002 Donruss Samples

*SAMPLES: 1.5X TO 4X BASIC CARDS
ONE PER SEALED BBCM 204
*GOLD SAMPLES: 1.5X TO 4X LISTED PRICE

2002 Donruss

COMPLETE SET (220) 50.00 100.00
COMP.SET w/o SP'S (150) 10.00 25.00
COMMON CARD (1-150) .10 .30
COMMON CARD (151-200) 1.25 3.00
151-200 STATED ODDS 1:4
COMMON CARD (201-220) .60 1.50
201-220 STATED ODDS 1:8
1 Alex Rodriguez .40 1.00
2 Barry Bonds .75 2.00
3 Derek Jeter .75 2.00
4 Robert Fick .10 .30
5 Juan Pierre .10 .30
6 Torii Hunter .10 .30
7 Todd Helton .20 .50
8 Cal Ripken 1.00 2.50
9 Manny Ramirez .20 .50
10 Johnny Damon .20 .50
11 Mike Piazza .50 1.25
12 Nomar Garciaparra .50 1.25
13 Pedro Martinez .20 .50
14 Brian Giles .10 .30
15 Albert Pujols .60 1.50
16 Roger Clemens .60 1.50
17 Sammy Sosa .30 .75
18 Vladimir Guerrero .30 .75
19 Tony Gwynn .40 1.00
20 Pat Burrell .10 .30
21 Carlos Delgado .10 .30
22 Tino Martinez .20 .50
23 Jim Edmonds .10 .30
24 Jason Giambi .10 .30
25 Tom Glavine .20 .50
26 Mark Grace .20 .50
27 Tony Armas Jr. .10 .30
28 Andruw Jones .20 .50
29 Ben Sheets .10 .30
30 Jeff Kent .10 .30
31 Barry Larkin .20 .50
32 Joe Mays .10 .30
33 Mike Mussina .20 .50
34 Hideo Nomo .30 .75
35 Rafael Palmeiro .20 .50
36 Scott Brosius .10 .30
37 Scott Rolen .20 .50
38 Gary Sheffield .10 .30
39 Bernie Williams .20 .50
40 Bob Abreu .10 .30
41 Edgardo Alfonzo .10 .30
42 C.C. Sabathia .10 .30
43 Jeremy Giambi .10 .30
44 Craig Biggio .20 .50
45 Andres Galarraga .10 .30
46 Edgar Martinez .20 .50
47 Fred McGriff .20 .50
48 Magglio Ordonez .10 .30
49 Jim Thome .20 .50
50 Matt Williams .10 .30
51 Kerry Wood .10 .30
52 Moises Alou .10 .30
53 Brady Anderson .10 .30
54 Garret Anderson .10 .30
55 Juan Gonzalez .10 .30
56 Bret Boone .10 .30
57 Jose Cruz Jr. .10 .30
58 Carlos Beltran .10 .30
59 Adrian Beltre .10 .30
60 Joe Kennedy .10 .30
61 Lance Berkman .10 .30
62 Kevin Brown .10 .30
63 Tim Hudson .10 .30
64 Jeromy Burnitz .10 .30
65 Jarrod Washburn .10 .30
66 Sean Casey .10 .30
67 Eric Chavez .10 .30
68 Bartolo Colon .10 .30
69 Freddy Garcia .10 .30
70 Jermaine Dye .10 .30
71 Terrence Long .10 .30
72 Cliff Floyd .10 .30
73 Luis Gonzalez .10 .30
74 Ichiro Suzuki .60 1.50
75 Mike Hampton .10 .30
76 Richard Hidalgo .10 .30
77 Geoff Jenkins .10 .30
78 Gabe Kapler .10 .30
79 Ken Griffey Jr. .60 1.50
80 Jason Kendall .10 .30
81 Josh Towers .10 .30
82 Ryan Klesko .10 .30
83 Paul Konerko .10 .30
84 Carlos Lee .10 .30
85 Kenny Lofton .10 .30
86 Josh Beckett .10 .30
87 Raul Mondesi .10 .30
88 Trot Nixon .10 .30
89 John Olerud .10 .30
90 Paul O'Neill .20 .50
91 Chan Ho Park .10 .30
92 Andy Pettitte .20 .50
93 Jorge Posada .20 .50
94 Mark Quinn .10 .30
95 Aramis Ramirez .10 .30
96 Curt Schilling .10 .30
97 Richie Sexson .10 .30
98 John Smoltz .20 .50
99 Wilson Betemit .10 .30
100 Shannon Stewart .10 .30
101 Alfonso Soriano .10 .30
102 Mike Sweeney .10 .30
103 Miguel Tejada .10 .30
104 Greg Vaughn .10 .30
105 Robin Ventura .10 .30
106 Jose Vidro .10 .30
107 Larry Walker .10 .30
108 Preston Wilson .10 .30
109 Corey Patterson .10 .30
110 Mark Mulder .10 .30
111 Tony Clark .10 .30
112 Roy Oswalt .10 .30
113 Jimmy Rollins .10 .30
114 Kazuhiro Sasaki .10 .30
115 Barry Zito .10 .30
116 Javier Vazquez .10 .30
117 Mike Cameron .10 .30
118 Phil Nevin .10 .30
119 Bud Smith .10 .30
120 Cristian Guzman .10 .30
121 Al Leiter .10 .30
122 Brad Radke .10 .30
123 Bobby Higginson .10 .30
124 Robert Person .10 .30
125 Adam Dunn .10 .30
126 Ben Grieve .10 .30
127 Rafael Furcal .10 .30
128 Jay Gibbons .10 .30
129 Paul LoDuca .10 .30
130 Wade Miller .10 .30
131 Tsuyoshi Shinjo .10 .30
132 Eric Milton .10 .30
133 Rickey Henderson .30 .75
134 Roberto Alomar .20 .50
135 Darin Erstad .10 .30
136 J.D. Drew .10 .30
137 Shawn Green .10 .30
138 Randy Johnson .30 .75
139 Austin Kearns .10 .30
140 Jose Canseco .20 .50
141 Jeff Bagwell .20 .50
142 Greg Maddux .50 1.25
143 Mark Buehrle .10 .30
144 Ivan Rodriguez .20 .50
145 Frank Thomas .30 .75
146 Rich Aurilia .10 .30
147 Troy Glaus .10 .30
148 Ryan Dempster .10 .30
149 Chipper Jones .30 .75
150 Matt Morris .10 .30
151 Marlon Byrd RR 1.25 3.00
152 Ben Howard RR RC 1.25 3.00
153 Brandon Backe RR RC 1.25 3.00
154 Jorge De La Rosa RR RC 1.25 3.00
155 Corky Miller RR 1.25 3.00
156 Dennis Tankersley RR 1.25 3.00
157 Kyle Kane RR RC 1.25 3.00
158 Justin Duchscherer RR 1.25 3.00
159 Brian Mallette RR RC 1.25 3.00
160 Chris Baker RR RC 1.25 3.00
161 Jason Lane RR 1.25 3.00
162 Hee Seop Choi RR 1.25 3.00
163 Juan Cruz RR 1.25 3.00
164 Rodrigo Rosario RR RC 1.25 3.00
165 Matt Guerrier RR 1.25 3.00
166 Anderson Machado RR RC 1.25 3.00
167 Geronimo Gil RR 1.25 3.00
168 Dewon Brazelton RR 1.25 3.00
169 Mark Prior RR 1.50 4.00
170 Bill Hall RR 1.25 3.00
171 Jorge Padilla RR RC 1.25 3.00
172 Jose Cueto RR 1.25 3.00
173 Allan Simpson RR RC 1.25 3.00
174 Doug Devore RR RC 1.25 3.00
175 Josh Pearce RR 1.25 3.00
176 Angel Berroa RR 1.25 3.00
177 Steve Bechler RR RC 1.25 3.00
178 Antonio Perez RR 1.25 3.00
179 Mark Teixeira RR 1.50 4.00
180 Erick Almonte RR 1.25 3.00
181 Orlando Hudson RR 1.25 3.00
182 Michael Rivera RR 1.25 3.00
183 Raul Chavez RR RC 1.25 3.00
184 Juan Pena RR 1.25 3.00
185 Travis Hughes RR RC 1.25 3.00
186 Ryan Ludwick RR 1.25 3.00
187 Ed Rogers RR 1.25 3.00
188 Andy Pratt RR RC 1.25 3.00
189 Nick Neugebauer RR 1.25 3.00
190 Tom Shearn RR RC 1.25 3.00
191 Eric Cyr RR 1.25 3.00
192 Victor Martinez RR 1.50 4.00
193 Brandon Berger RR 1.25 3.00
194 Erik Bedard RR 1.25 3.00
195 Fernando Rodney RR 1.25 3.00
196 Joe Thurston RR 1.25 3.00
197 John Buck RR 1.25 3.00
198 Jeff Deardorff RR 1.25 3.00
199 Ryan Jamison RR 1.25 3.00
200 Alfredo Amezaga RR 1.25 3.00
201 Luis Gonzalez FC .60 1.50
202 Roger Clemens FC 2.00 5.00
203 Barry Zito FC .60 1.50
204 Bud Smith FC .60 1.50
205 Magglio Ordonez FC .60 1.50
206 Kerry Wood FC .60 1.50
207 Freddy Garcia FC .60 1.50
208 Adam Dunn FC .60 1.50
209 Curt Schilling FC .60 1.50
210 Lance Berkman FC .60 1.50
211 Rafael Palmeiro FC .60 1.50
212 Ichiro Suzuki FC 2.00 5.00
213 Bob Abreu FC .60 1.50
214 Mark Mulder FC .60 1.50
215 Roy Oswalt FC .60 1.50
216 Mike Sweeney FC .60 1.50
217 Paul LoDuca FC .60 1.50
218 Aramis Ramirez FC .60 1.50
219 Randy Johnson FC 1.00 2.50
220 Albert Pujols FC 2.00 5.00

2002 Donruss Autographs

RANDOM INSERTS IN PACKS
SEE BECKETT.COM FOR PRINT RUNS
SKIP-NUMBERED 19-CARD SET
NO PRICING ON QTY OF 25 OR LESS
203 Barry Zito FC/200 15.00 40.00
204 Bud Smith FC/200 10.00 25.00
205 Magglio Ordonez FC/200 10.00 25.00
206 Kerry Wood FC/200 15.00 40.00
207 Freddy Garcia FC/200 10.00 25.00
208 Adam Dunn FC/200 15.00 40.00
210 Lance Berkman FC/175 15.00 40.00
213 Bob Abreu FC/200 10.00 25.00
214 Mark Mulder FC/200 10.00 25.00
215 Roy Oswalt FC/200 10.00 25.00
216 Mike Sweeney FC/200 10.00 25.00
217 Paul LoDuca FC/200 10.00 25.00
218 Aramis Ramirez FC/200 10.00 25.00
220 Albert Pujols FC/200 150.00 250.00

2002 Donruss Stat Line Career

*1-150 P/R b/wn 251-400: 2.5X TO 6X
*1-150 P/R b/wn 201-250: 2.5X TO 6X
*1-150 P/R b/wn 151-200: 3X TO 8X
*1-150 P/R b/wn 121-150: 3X TO 8X
*1-150 P/R b/wn 81-120: 4X TO 10X
*1-150 P/R b/wn 66-80: 5X TO 12X
*1-150 P/R b/wn 51-65: 5X TO 12X
*1-150 P/R b/wn 36-50: 6X TO 15X
*201-220 P/R b/wn 251-400 .5X TO 1.2X
*201-220 P/R b/wn 201-250 .6X TO 1.5X
*201-220 P/R b/wn 151-200 .75X TO 2X
*201-220 P/R b/wn 121-150 1X TO 2.5X
*201-220 P/R b/wn 51-65 1.5X TO 4X
SEE BECKETT.COM FOR PRINT RUNS
NO PRICING ON QTY OF 25 OR LESS
151 Marlon Byrd RR/232 1.00 2.50
152 Ben Howard RR/283 .75 2.00
153 Brandon Backe RR/94 2.00 5.00
154 Jorge De La Rosa RR/54 2.50 6.00
155 Corky Miller RR/184 1.25 3.00
156 Dennis Tankersley RR/253 .75 2.00
157 Kyle Kane RR/179 1.25 3.00
159 Brian Mallette RR/273 .75 2.00
160 Chris Baker RR/270 .75 2.00
161 Jason Lane RR/302 .75 2.00
162 Hee Seop Choi RR/286 .75 2.00
163 Juan Cruz RR/322 .75 2.00
164 Rodrigo Rosario RR/313 .75 2.00
165 Matt Guerrier RR/280 .75 2.00
166 Anderson Machado RR/252 .75 2.00
167 Geronimo Gil RR/293 .75 2.00
168 Dewon Brazelton RR/335 .75 2.00
169 Mark Prior RR/303 1.25 3.00
170 Bill Hall RR/373 .75 2.00
171 Jorge Padilla RR/273 .75 2.00
172 Jose Cueto RR/156 1.25 3.00
173 Allan Simpson RR/204 1.00 2.50
174 Doug Devore RR/287 .75 2.00
175 Josh Pearce RR/315 .75 2.00
176 Angel Berroa RR/268 .75 2.00
178 Antonio Perez RR/143 1.50 4.00
179 Mark Teixeira RR/165 2.00 5.00
181 Orlando Hudson RR/283 .75 2.00
182 Michael Rivera RR/333 .75 2.00
183 Raul Chavez RR/253 .75 2.00
184 Juan Pena RR/293 .75 2.00
185 Travis Hughes RR/174 1.25 3.00
186 Ryan Ludwick RR/264 .75 2.00
187 Ed Rogers RR/270 .75 2.00
188 Andy Pratt RR/203 1.00 2.50
190 Tom Shearn RR/251 .75 2.00
191 Eric Cyr RR/161 1.25 3.00
192 Victor Martinez RR/305 1.25 3.00
193 Brandon Berger RR/313 .75 2.00
194 Erik Bedard RR/279 .75 2.00
195 Fernando Rodney RR/309 .75 2.00
196 Joe Thurston RR/284 .75 2.00
197 John Buck RR/271 .75 2.00
198 Jeff Deardorff RR/201 1.00 2.50
199 Ryan Jamison RR/273 .75 2.00
200 Alfredo Amezaga RR/290 .75 2.00

2002 Donruss Stat Line Season

*1-150 P/R b/wn 151-200: 3X TO 8X
*1-150 P/R b/wn 121-150: 3X TO 8X
*1-150 P/R b/wn 81-120: 4X TO 10X
*1-150 P/R b/wn 66-80: 5X TO 12X
*1-150 P/R b/wn 51-65: 5X TO 12X
*1-150 P/R b/wn 36-50: 6X TO 15X
*1-150 P/R b/wn 26-35: 8X TO 20X
*201-220 P/R b/wn 81-120 1.25X TO 3X
*201-220 P/R b/wn 66-80 1.5X TO 4X
*201-220 P/R b/wn 51-65 1.5X TO 4X
*201-220 P/R b/wn 36-50 2X TO 5X
*201-220 P/R b/wn 26-35 2.5X TO 6X
SEE BECKETT.COM FOR PRINT RUNS
NO PRICING ON QTY OF 25 OR LESS
151 Marlon Byrd RR/89 2.00 5.00
152 Ben Howard RR/29 4.00 10.00
153 Brandon Backe RR/39 3.00 8.00
154 Jorge De La Rosa RR/32 4.00 10.00
156 Dennis Tankersley RR/30 4.00 10.00
157 Kyle Kane RR/75 2.50 6.00
159 Brian Mallette RR/94 2.00 5.00
160 Chris Baker RR/121 1.50 4.00
161 Jason Lane RR/38 3.00 8.00
162 Hee Seop Choi RR/45 3.00 8.00
163 Juan Cruz RR/39 3.00 8.00
164 Rodrigo Rosario RR/131 1.50 4.00
165 Matt Guerrier RR/118 2.00 5.00
166 Anderson Machado RR/36 3.00 8.00
170 Bill Hall RR/65 2.50 6.00
171 Jorge Padilla RR/66 2.50 6.00
172 Jose Cueto RR/62 2.50 6.00
173 Allan Simpson RR/77 2.50 6.00
174 Doug Devore RR/74 2.50 6.00
175 Josh Pearce RR/132 1.50 4.00
176 Angel Berroa RR/63 2.50 6.00
177 Steve Bechler RR/135 1.50 4.00
178 Antonio Perez RR/143 1.50 4.00
181 Orlando Hudson RR/79 2.50 6.00
184 Juan Pena RR/106 2.00 5.00
185 Travis Hughes RR/86 2.00 5.00
186 Ryan Ludwick RR/103 2.00 5.00
187 Ed Rogers RR/54 2.50 6.00
188 Andy Pratt RR/132 1.50 4.00
190 Tom Shearn RR/136 1.50 4.00
191 Eric Cyr RR/131 1.50 4.00
192 Victor Martinez RR/57 4.00 10.00
194 Erik Bedard RR/137 1.50 4.00
195 Fernando Rodney RR/52 2.50 6.00
196 Joe Thurston RR/46 3.00 8.00
197 John Buck RR/73 2.50 6.00
198 Jeff Deardorff RR/100 2.00 5.00
199 Ryan Jamison RR/95 2.00 5.00
200 Alfredo Amezaga RR/37 3.00 8.00

2002 Donruss All-Time Diamond Kings

STATED PRINT RUN 2500 SERIAL #'d SETS
*STUDIO: 1X TO 2.5X BASIC ALL-TIME DK
STUDIO PRINT RUN 250 SERIAL #'d SETS
1 Ted Williams 6.00 15.00
2 Cal Ripken 12.50 30.00
3 Lou Gehrig 6.00 15.00
4 Babe Ruth 10.00 25.00
5 Roberto Clemente 8.00 20.00
6 Don Mattingly 10.00 25.00
7 Kirby Puckett 4.00 10.00
8 Stan Musial 6.00 15.00
9 Yogi Berra 4.00 10.00
10 Ernie Banks 4.00 10.00

2002 Donruss Bat Kings

1-3 PRINT RUN 250 SERIAL #'d SETS
4-5 PRINT RUN 125 SERIAL #'d SETS
*STUDIO 1-3: .75X TO 2X BASIC BAT KING
STUDIO 1-3 PRINT RUN 50 SERIAL #'d SETS
STUDIO 4-5 PRINT RUN 25 SERIAL #'d SETS
1 Jason Giambi 6.00 15.00
2 Alex Rodriguez 10.00 25.00
3 Mike Piazza 10.00 25.00
4 Roberto Clemente/125 25.00 60.00
5 Babe Ruth/125 50.00 100.00

2002 Donruss Diamond Kings Inserts

STATED PRINT RUN 2500 SERIAL #'d SETS
*STUDIO: .75X TO 2X BASIC DK'S
STUDIO PRINT RUN 250 SERIAL #'d SETS
DK1 Nomar Garciaparra 5.00 12.00
DK2 Shawn Green 4.00 10.00
DK3 Randy Johnson 4.00 10.00
DK4 Derek Jeter 8.00 20.00
DK5 Carlos Delgado 4.00 10.00
DK6 Roger Clemens 6.00 15.00
DK7 Jeff Bagwell 4.00 10.00
DK8 Vladimir Guerrero 4.00 10.00
DK9 Luis Gonzalez 4.00 10.00
DK10 Mike Piazza 5.00 12.00
DK11 Ichiro Suzuki 6.00 15.00
DK12 Pedro Martinez 4.00 10.00
DK13 Todd Helton 4.00 10.00
DK14 Sammy Sosa 4.00 10.00
DK15 Ivan Rodriguez 4.00 10.00
DK16 Barry Bonds 8.00 20.00
DK17 Albert Pujols 6.00 15.00
DK18 Jim Thome 4.00 10.00
DK19 Alex Rodriguez 4.00 10.00
DK20 Jason Giambi 4.00 10.00

2002 Donruss Elite Series

RANDOM INSERTS IN PACKS
STATED PRINT RUN 2500 SERIAL #'d SETS
1 Barry Bonds 5.00 12.00
2 Lance Berkman 1.50 4.00
3 Jason Giambi 1.50 4.00
4 Nomar Garciaparra 3.00 8.00
5 Curt Schilling 1.50 4.00
6 Vladimir Guerrero 2.00 5.00
7 Shawn Green 1.50 4.00
8 Troy Glaus 1.50 4.00
9 Jeff Bagwell 1.50 4.00
10 Manny Ramirez 1.50 4.00
11 Eric Chavez 1.50 4.00
12 Carlos Delgado 1.50 4.00
13 Mike Sweeney 1.50 4.00
14 Todd Helton 1.50 4.00
15 Luis Gonzalez 1.50 4.00
16 Enos Slaughter LGD 1.50 4.00
17 Frank Robinson LGD 1.50 4.00
17A Frank Robinson LGD AU/375 10.00 25.00
18 Bob Gibson LGD 1.50 4.00
19 Warren Spahn LGD 1.50 4.00
20 Whitey Ford LGD 1.50 4.00

2002 Donruss Elite Series Signatures

RANDOM INSERTS IN PACKS
STATED PRINT RUNS LISTED BELOW
SKIP-NUMBERED 18-CARD SET
NO PRICING ON QTY OF 25 OR LESS
16 Enos Slaughter LGD/250 15.00 40.00
17 Frank Robinson LGD/250 12.00 30.00
18 Bob Gibson LGD/250 15.00 40.00
19 Warren Spahn LGD/250 15.00 40.00
20 Whitey Ford LGD/250 15.00 40.00

2002 Donruss Jersey Kings

1-12 PRINT RUN 250 SERIAL #'d SETS
13-15 PRINT RUN 125 SERIAL #'d SETS
*STUDIO 1-12: .75X TO 2X BASIC JSY KINGS
STUDIO 1-12 PRINT RUN 50 SERIAL #'d SETS
STUDIO 13-15 PRINT RUN 25 SERIAL #'d SETS
STUDIO 13-15 TOO SCARCE TO PRICE
1 Alex Rodriguez 5.00 12.00
2 Jason Giambi 1.50 4.00
3 Carlos Delgado 1.50 4.00
4 Barry Bonds 6.00 15.00
5 Randy Johnson 4.00 10.00
6 Jim Thome 2.50 6.00
7 Shawn Green 1.50 4.00
8 Pedro Martinez 2.50 6.00
9 Jeff Bagwell 2.50 6.00
10 Vladimir Guerrero 2.50 6.00
11 Ivan Rodriguez 2.50 6.00
12 Nomar Garciaparra 2.50 6.00
13 Don Mattingly/125 10.00 25.00
14 Ted Williams/125 10.00 25.00
15 Lou Gehrig/125 75.00 150.00

2002 Donruss Longball Leaders

STATED PRINT RUN 1000 SERIAL #'d SETS
SEASONAL PRINT RUN BASED ON '01 HR'S
1 Barry Bonds 8.00 20.00
2 Sammy Sosa 3.00 8.00
3 Luis Gonzalez 1.50 4.00
4 Alex Rodriguez 4.00 10.00
5 Shawn Green 1.50 4.00
6 Todd Helton 2.00 5.00
7 Jim Thome 2.00 5.00
8 Rafael Palmeiro 2.00 5.00
9 Richie Sexson 1.50 4.00
10 Troy Glaus 1.50 4.00
11 Manny Ramirez 2.00 5.00
12 Phil Nevin 1.50 4.00
13 Jeff Bagwell 2.00 5.00
14 Carlos Delgado 1.50 4.00
15 Jason Giambi 1.50 4.00
16 Chipper Jones 3.00 8.00
17 Larry Walker 1.50 4.00
18 Albert Pujols 6.00 15.00
19 Brian Giles 1.50 4.00
20 Bret Boone 1.50 4.00

2002 Donruss Production Line

COMMON OBP (1-20) 1.50 4.00
COMMON SLG (21-40) 1.25 3.00
COMMON OPS (41-60) 1.00 2.50
STATED PRINT RUNS LISTED BELOW
*DIE CUT OBP 1-20: .75X TO 2X BASIC PL
*DIE CUT SLG 21-40: 1X TO 2.5X BASIC PL
*DIE CUT OPS 41-60: 1.25X TO 3X BASIC PL
DIE CUT PRINT RUN 100 SERIAL #'d SETS
DC's ARE 1ST 100 #'d OF EACH PLAYER
1 Barry Bonds OBP/415* 10.00 25.00
2 Jason Giambi OBP/377* 1.50 4.00
3 Larry Walker OBP/349* 1.50 4.00
4 Sammy Sosa OBP/337* 4.00 10.00
5 Todd Helton OBP/332* 2.50 6.00
6 Lance Berkman OBP/330* 1.50 4.00
7 Luis Gonzalez OBP/329* 1.50 4.00
8 Chipper Jones OBP/327* 4.00 10.00
9 Edgar Martinez OBP/323* 2.50 6.00
10 Gary Sheffield OBP/317* 1.50 4.00
11 Jim Thome OBP/316* 2.50 6.00
12 Roberto Alomar OBP/315* 2.50 6.00
13 J.D. Drew OBP/314* 1.50 4.00
14 Jim Edmonds OBP/310* 1.50 4.00
15 Carlos Delgado OBP/308* 1.50 4.00
16 Manny Ramirez OBP/305* 2.50 6.00
17 Brian Giles OBP/304* 1.50 4.00
18 Albert Pujols OBP/303* 8.00 20.00
19 John Olerud OBP/301* 1.50 4.00
20 Alex Rodriguez OBP/299* 5.00 12.00
21 Barry Bonds SLG/763* 8.00 20.00
22 Sammy Sosa SLG/637* 4.00 10.00
23 Luis Gonzalez SLG/588* 1.25 3.00
24 Todd Helton SLG/585* 2.00 5.00
25 Larry Walker SLG/562* 1.25 3.00
26 Jason Giambi SLG/560* 1.25 3.00
27 Jim Thome SLG/524* 2.00 5.00
28 Alex Rodriguez SLG/522* 4.00 10.00
29 Lance Berkman SLG/520* 1.25 3.00
30 J.D. Drew SLG/513* 1.25 3.00
31 Albert Pujols SLG/510* 6.00 15.00
32 Manny Ramirez SLG/509* 2.00 5.00
33 Chipper Jones SLG/505* 3.00 8.00
34 Shawn Green SLG/498* 1.25 3.00
35 Brian Giles SLG/490* 1.25 3.00
36 Juan Gonzalez SLG/490* 1.25 3.00
37 Phil Nevin SLG/488* 1.25 3.00
38 Gary Sheffield SLG/483* 1.25 3.00
39 Bret Boone SLG/478* 1.25 3.00
40 Cliff Floyd SLG/478* 1.25 3.00
41 Barry Bonds OPS/1278* 6.00 15.00
42 Sammy Sosa OPS/1074* 4.00 10.00
43 Jason Giambi OPS/1037* 1.00 2.50
44 Todd Helton OPS/1017* 1.50 4.00
45 Luis Gonzalez OPS/1017* 1.00 2.50
46 Larry Walker OPS/1011* 1.00 2.50
47 Lance Berkman OPS/950* 1.00 2.50
48 Jim Thome OPS/940* 1.50 4.00
49 Chipper Jones OPS/932* 2.50 6.00
50 J.D. Drew OPS/927* 1.00 2.50
51 Alex Rodriguez OPS/921* 3.00 8.00
52 Manny Ramirez OPS/914* 1.50 4.00
53 Albert Pujols OPS/913* 5.00 12.00
54 Gary Sheffield OPS/900* 1.00 2.50
55 Brian Giles OPS/894* 1.00 2.50
56 Phil Nevin OPS/876* 1.00 2.50
57 Jim Edmonds OPS/874* 1.00 2.50
58 Shawn Green OPS/870* 1.00 2.50
59 Cliff Floyd OPS/868* 1.00 2.50
60 Edgar Martinez OPS/866* 1.50 4.00

2002 Donruss Recollection Autographs

RANDOM INSERTS IN PACKS
STATED PRINT RUNS LISTED BELOW
NO PRICING ON QTY OF 40 OR LESS
8 Gary Carter 87/100 10.00 25.00
9 Gary Carter 89/100 10.00 25.00
24 Steve Garvey 87/75 8.00 20.00
46 Tom Seaver 87/60 30.00 80.00
47 Don Sutton 87/200 10.00 25.00

2002 Donruss Rookie Year Materials Bats

STATED PRINT RUN 250 SERIAL #'d SETS
ERA PRINT RUNS BASED ON ROOKIE YR
1 Barry Bonds 20.00 50.00
2 Cal Ripken 15.00 40.00
3 Kirby Puckett 20.00 50.00
4 Johnny Bench 15.00 40.00

2002 Donruss Rookie Year Materials Bats ERA

RANDOM INSERTS IN PACKS
STATED PRINT RUNS LISTED BELOW
1 Barry Bonds/86 20.00 50.00
2 Cal Ripken/81 10.00 25.00
3 Kirby Puckett/84 25.00 50.00
4 Johnny Bench/68 40.00 80.00

2002 Donruss Rookie Year Materials Jersey

RANDOM INSERTS IN PACKS
1-4 PRINT RUN 250 SERIAL #'d SETS
5-6 PRINT RUN 50 SERIAL #'d SETS
1 Nomar Garciaparra 10.00 25.00
2 Randy Johnson 10.00 25.00
3 Ivan Rodriguez 10.00 25.00
4 Vladimir Guerrero 10.00 25.00
5 Stan Musial/50 40.00 80.00
6 Yogi Berra/50 40.00 80.00

2002 Donruss Rookies

COMPLETE SET (110) 10.00 25.00
1 Kazuhisa Ishii RC .20 .50
2 P.J. Bevis RC .15 .40
3 Jason Simontacchi RC .15 .40
4 John Lackey .08 .25
5 Travis Driskill RC .15 .40
6 Carl Sadler RC .15 .40
7 Tim Kalita RC .15 .40
8 Nelson Castro RC .15 .40
9 Francis Beltran RC .15 .40
10 So Taguchi RC .20 .50
11 Ryan Bukvich RC .15 .40
12 Brian Fitzgerald RC .15 .40
13 Kevin Frederick RC .15 .40
14 Chone Figgins RC .60 1.50
15 Marlon Byrd .08 .25
16 Ron Calloway RC .15 .40
17 Jason Lane .15 .40
18 Satoru Komiyama RC .15 .40
19 John Ennis RC .15 .40
20 Juan Brito RC .15 .40
21 Gustavo Chacin RC .30 .75
22 Josh Bard RC .15 .40
23 Brett Myers .15 .40
24 Mike Smith RC .15 .40
25 Eric Hinske .08 .25
26 Jake Peavy .20 .50
27 Todd Donovan RC .15 .40
28 Luis Ugueto RC .15 .40
29 Corey Thurman RC .15 .40
30 Takahito Nomura RC .15 .40
31 Andy Shibilo RC .15 .40
32 Mike Crudale RC .15 .40
33 Earl Snyder RC .15 .40
34 Brian Tallet RC .15 .40
35 Miguel Asencio RC .15 .40
36 Felix Escalona RC .15 .40
37 Drew Henson .08 .25
38 Steve Kent RC .15 .40
39 Rene Reyes RC .15 .40
40 Edwin Almonte RC .15 .40
41 Chris Snelling RC .25 .60
42 Franklyn German RC .15 .40
43 Jeriome Robertson RC .15 .40
44 Colin Young RC .15 .40
45 Jeremy Lambert RC .15 .40
46 Kirk Saarloos RC .15 .40
47 Matt Childers RC .15 .40
48 Justin Wayne .08 .25
49 Jose Valverde RC .15 .40
50 Wily Mo Pena .15 .40
51 Victor Alvarez RC .15 .40
52 Julius Matos RC .15 .40
53 Aaron Cook RC .15 .40
54 Jeff Austin RC .15 .40
55 Adrian Burnside RC .15 .40
56 Brandon Puffer RC .15 .40
57 Jeremy Hill RC .15 .40
58 Jaime Cerda RC .15 .40
59 Aaron Guiel RC .15 .40
60 Ron Chiavacci .08 .25
61 Kevin Cash RC .15 .40
62 Elio Serrano RC .15 .40
63 Julio Mateo RC .15 .40
64 Cam Esslinger RC .15 .40
65 Ken Huckaby RC .15 .40
66 Will Nieves RC .15 .40
67 Luis Martinez RC .15 .40
68 Scotty Layfield RC .15 .40
69 Jeremy Guthrie RC .30 .75
70 Hansel Izquierdo RC .15 .40
71 Shane Nance RC .15 .40
72 Jeff Baker RC .40 1.00
73 Cliff Bartosh RC .15 .40
74 Mitch Wylie RC .15 .40
75 Oliver Perez RC .30 .75
76 Matt Thornton RC .15 .40
77 John Foster RC .15 .40
78 Joe Borchard .08 .25
79 Eric Junge RC .15 .40
80 Jorge Sosa RC .20 .50
81 Runelvys Hernandez RC .15 .40
82 Kevin Mench .08 .25
83 Ben Kozlowski RC .15 .40
84 Trey Hodges RC .15 .40
85 Reed Johnson RC .30 .75
86 Eric Eckenstahler RC .15 .40
87 Franklin Nunez RC .15 .40
88 Victor Martinez .30 .75
89 Kevin Gryboski RC .15 .40
90 Jason Jennings .08 .25
91 Jim Rushford RC .15 .40
92 Jeremy Ward RC .15 .40
93 Adam Walker RC .15 .40
94 Freddy Sanchez RC .75 2.00
95 Wilson Valdez RC .15 .40
96 Lee Gardner RC .15 .40
97 Eric Good RC .15 .40
98 Hank Blalock .20 .50
99 Mark Corey RC .15 .40
100 Jason Davis RC .15 .40
101 Mike Gonzalez RC .15 .40
102 David Ross RC .25 .60
103 Tyler Yates RC .15 .40
104 Cliff Lee RC 1.50 4.00
105 Mike Moriarty RC .15 .40
106 Josh Hancock RC .20 .50
107 Jason Beverlin RC .15 .40
108 Clay Condrey RC .15 .40
109 Shawn Sedlacek RC .15 .40
110 Sean Burroughs .08 .25

2002 Donruss Rookies Autographs

STATED PRINT RUNS LISTED BELOW
NO PRICING ON QTY OF 25 OR LESS
2 P.J. Bevis/50 10.00 25.00
9 Francis Beltran/100 4.00 10.00
13 Kevin Frederick/100 4.00 10.00
14 Chone Figgins/100 10.00 25.00
15 Marlon Byrd/100 4.00 10.00
17 Jason Lane/100 6.00 15.00
19 John Ennis/100 4.00 10.00
22 Josh Bard/100 4.00 10.00
25 Eric Hinske/100 4.00 10.00
28 Luis Ugueto/100 4.00 10.00
29 Corey Thurman/100 4.00 10.00
30 Takahito Nomura/100 10.00 25.00
33 Earl Snyder/100 4.00 10.00
34 Brian Tallet/100 4.00 10.00
37 Drew Henson/50 6.00 15.00
39 Rene Reyes/50 10.00 25.00
40 Edwin Almonte/50 10.00 25.00
41 Chris Snelling/50 12.50 30.00
42 Franklyn German/100 4.00 10.00
45 Jeremy Lambert/100 4.00 10.00
46 Kirk Saarloos/50 6.00 15.00
47 Matt Childers/100 4.00 10.00
50 Wily Mo Pena/100 6.00 15.00
51 Victor Alvarez/100 4.00 10.00
61 Kevin Cash/100 4.00 10.00
62 Elio Serrano/100 4.00 10.00
64 Cam Esslinger/100 4.00 10.00
69 Jeremy Guthrie/100 6.00 15.00
71 Shane Nance/100 4.00 10.00
72 Jeff Baker/100 10.00 25.00
76 Matt Thornton/100 4.00 10.00
78 Joe Borchard/100 4.00 10.00
82 Kevin Mench/100 6.00 15.00
83 Ben Kozlowski/100 4.00 10.00
84 Trey Hodges/100 4.00 10.00
85 Reed Johnson/100 6.00 15.00
88 Victor Martinez/100 15.00 40.00
90 Jason Jennings/100 4.00 10.00
95 Wilson Valdez/100 4.00 10.00
97 Eric Good/100 4.00 10.00
98 Hank Blalock/100 6.00 15.00
104 Cliff Lee/100 20.00 50.00
110 Sean Burroughs/50 6.00 15.00

2002 Donruss Rookies Crusade

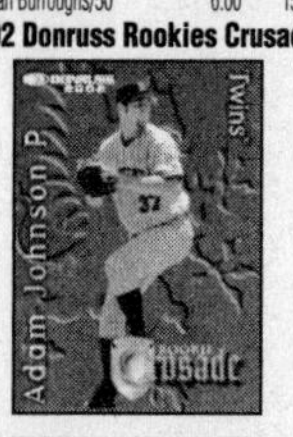

STATED PRINT RUN 1500 SERIAL #'d SETS
1 Corky Miller 1.50 4.00
2 Jack Cust 1.50 4.00
3 Erik Bedard 1.50 4.00
4 Andres Torres 1.50 4.00
5 Geronimo Gil 1.50 4.00
6 Rafael Soriano 1.50 4.00
7 Johnny Estrada 1.50 4.00
8 Steve Bechler 1.50 4.00
9 Adam Johnson 1.50 4.00
10 So Taguchi 1.50 4.00
11 Dee Brown 1.50 4.00
12 Kevin Frederick 1.50 4.00
13 Allan Simpson 1.50 4.00
14 Ricardo Rodriguez 1.50 4.00
15 Jason Hart 1.50 4.00
16 Matt Childers 1.50 4.00
17 Jason Jennings 1.50 4.00
18 Anderson Machado 1.50 4.00
19 Fernando Rodney 1.50 4.00
20 Brandon Larson 1.50 4.00
21 Satoru Komiyama 1.50 4.00
22 Francis Beltran 1.50 4.00
23 Joe Thurston 1.50 4.00
24 Josh Pearce 1.50 4.00
25 Carlos Hernandez 1.50 4.00
26 Ben Howard 1.50 4.00
27 Wilson Valdez 1.50 4.00
28 Victor Alvarez 1.50 4.00
29 Cesar Izturis 1.50 4.00
30 Endy Chavez 1.50 4.00
31 Michael Cuddyer 1.50 4.00
32 Bobby Hill 1.50 4.00
33 Willie Harris 1.50 4.00
34 Joe Crede 1.50 4.00
35 Jorge Padilla 1.50 4.00
36 Brandon Backe 1.50 4.00
37 Franklyn German 1.50 4.00
38 Xavier Nady 1.50 4.00
39 Raul Chavez 1.50 4.00
40 Shane Nance 1.50 4.00
41 Brandon Claussen 1.50 4.00
42 Tom Shearn 1.50 4.00
43 Freddy Sanchez 3.00 8.00
44 Chone Figgins 2.00 5.00
45 Cliff Lee 3.00 8.00
46 Brian Mallette 1.50 4.00
47 Mike Rivera 1.50 4.00
48 Elio Serrano 1.50 4.00
49 Rodrigo Rosario 1.50 4.00
50 Earl Snyder 1.50 4.00

2002 Donruss Rookies Crusade Autographs

COMMON CARD p/r 300+ 4.00 10.00
COMMON ROOKIE p/r 300+ 4.00 10.00
COMMON CARD p/r 150-250 4.00 10.00
COMMON CARD p/r 100 4.00 10.00
STATED PRINT RUNS LISTED BELOW
NO PRICING ON QTY OF 25 OR LESS
1 Corky Miller/500 4.00 10.00
2 Jack Cust/500 4.00 10.00
3 Erik Bedard/100 4.00 10.00
4 Andres Torres/500 4.00 10.00
5 Geronimo Gil/500 4.00 10.00
6 Rafael Soriano/500 4.00 10.00
7 Johnny Estrada/400 4.00 10.00
8 Steve Bechler/500 4.00 10.00
9 Adam Johnson/500 4.00 10.00
11 Dee Brown/500 4.00 10.00
12 Kevin Frederick/150 4.00 10.00
13 Allan Simpson/150 4.00 10.00
14 Ricardo Rodriguez/500 4.00 10.00
15 Jason Hart/500 4.00 10.00
16 Matt Childers/150 4.00 10.00
17 Jason Jennings/500 4.00 10.00
18 Anderson Machado/500 4.00 10.00
19 Fernando Rodney/500 4.00 10.00
20 Brandon Larson/400 4.00 10.00
22 Francis Beltran/500 4.00 10.00
23 Joe Thurston/500 4.00 10.00
24 Josh Pearce/500 4.00 10.00
25 Carlos Hernandez/500 4.00 10.00
26 Ben Howard/500 4.00 10.00
27 Wilson Valdez/500 4.00 10.00
28 Victor Alvarez/500 4.00 10.00
29 Cesar Izturis/500 4.00 10.00
30 Endy Chavez/500 4.00 10.00
31 Michael Cuddyer/375 4.00 10.00
32 Bobby Hill/250 4.00 10.00
33 Willie Harris/300 4.00 10.00
34 Joe Crede/100 4.00 10.00
35 Jorge Padilla/475 4.00 10.00
36 Brandon Backe/350 6.00 15.00
37 Franklyn German/500 4.00 10.00
38 Xavier Nady/500 4.00 10.00
39 Raul Chavez/500 4.00 10.00
40 Shane Nance/500 4.00 10.00
41 Brandon Claussen/150 4.00 10.00
42 Tom Shearn/500 4.00 10.00
44 Chone Figgins/500 6.00 15.00
45 Cliff Lee/500 15.00 40.00
46 Brian Mallette/150 4.00 10.00
47 Mike Rivera/400 4.00 10.00
48 Elio Serrano/500 4.00 10.00
49 Rodrigo Rosario/100 4.00 10.00
50 Earl Snyder/100 4.00 10.00

2002 Donruss Rookies Phenoms

RANDOM INSERTS IN PACKS
STATED PRINT RUN 1000 SERIAL #'d SETS
1 Kazuhisa Ishii 2.00 5.00
2 Eric Hinske 2.00 5.00
3 Jason Lane 2.00 5.00
4 Victor Martinez 3.00 8.00
5 Mark Prior 2.00 5.00
6 Antonio Perez 2.00 5.00
7 John Buck 2.00 5.00
8 Joe Borchard 2.00 5.00
9 Alexis Gomez 2.00 5.00
10 Sean Burroughs 2.00 5.00
11 Carlos Pena 2.00 5.00
12 Bill Hall 2.00 5.00
13 Alfredo Amezaga 2.00 5.00
14 Ed Rogers 2.00 5.00
15 Mark Teixeira 3.00 8.00
16 Chris Snelling 2.50 6.00
17 Nick Johnson 2.00 5.00
18 Angel Berroa 2.00 5.00
19 Orlando Hudson 2.00 5.00
20 Drew Henson 2.00 5.00
21 Austin Kearns 2.00 5.00
22 Dewon Brazelton 2.00 5.00
23 Dennis Tankersley 2.00 5.00
24 Josh Beckett 2.00 5.00
25 Marlon Byrd 2.00 5.00

2002 Donruss Rookies Phenoms Autographs

COMMON CARD p/r 300+ 4.00 10.00
COMMON CARD p/r 150-250 4.00 10.00
STATED PRINT RUNS LISTED BELOW
NO PRICING ON QTY OF 25 OR LESS
2 Eric Hinske/500 4.00 10.00
3 Jason Lane/500 6.00 15.00
4 Victor Martinez/225 10.00 25.00
5 Mark Prior/100 10.00 25.00
6 Antonio Perez/500 4.00 10.00
7 John Buck/100 4.00 10.00
8 Joe Borchard/100 4.00 10.00
9 Alexis Gomez/400 4.00 10.00
10 Sean Burroughs/150 4.00 10.00
11 Carlos Pena/150 4.00 10.00
12 Bill Hall/200 6.00 15.00
13 Alfredo Amezaga/500 4.00 10.00
14 Ed Rogers/500 4.00 10.00
15 Mark Teixeira/100 10.00 25.00
16 Chris Snelling/100 8.00 20.00
17 Nick Johnson/250 6.00 15.00
18 Angel Berroa/500 4.00 10.00
19 Orlando Hudson/400 4.00 10.00
20 Drew Henson/500 4.00 10.00
21 Austin Kearns/75 4.00 10.00
22 Dewon Brazelton/350 4.00 10.00
23 Dennis Tankersley/100 4.00 10.00
24 Josh Beckett/125 10.00 25.00
25 Marlon Byrd/500 4.00 10.00

2003 Donruss Samples

*SAMPLES: 1.5X TO 4X BASIC CARDS
ONE PER BBCM MAGAZINE

2003 Donruss

COMPLETE SET (400) 25.00 50.00
COMMON CARD (71-400) .10 .30
COMMON CARD (1-20) .10 .30
COMMON CARD (21-70) .20 .50
1 Vladimir Guerrero DK .20 .50
2 Derek Jeter DK .75 2.00
3 Adam Dunn DK .20 .50
4 Greg Maddux DK .40 1.00
5 Lance Berkman DK .20 .50
6 Ichiro Suzuki DK .40 1.00
7 Mike Piazza DK .30 .75
8 Alex Rodriguez DK .40 1.00
9 Tom Glavine DK .20 .50
10 Randy Johnson DK .30 .75
11 Nomar Garciaparra DK .20 .50
12 Jason Giambi DK .12 .30
13 Sammy Sosa DK .30 .75
14 Barry Zito DK .20 .50
15 Chipper Jones DK .30 .75
16 Magglio Ordonez DK .20 .50
17 Larry Walker DK .20 .50
18 Alfonso Soriano DK .20 .50
19 Curt Schilling DK .20 .50
20 Barry Bonds DK .50 1.25
21 Joe Borchard RR .20 .50
22 Chris Snelling RR .20 .50
23 Brian Tallet RR .20 .50
24 Cliff Lee RR 1.25 3.00
25 Freddy Sanchez RR .20 .50
26 Chone Figgans RR .20 .50
27 Kevin Cash RR .20 .50
28 Josh Bard RR .20 .50
29 Jeriome Robertson RR .20 .50
30 Jeremy Hill RR .20 .50
31 Shane Nance RR .20 .50
32 Jake Peavy RR .20 .50
33 Trey Hodges RR .20 .50
34 Eric Eckenstahler RR .20 .50
35 Jim Rushford RR .20 .50
36 Oliver Perez RR .20 .50
37 Kirk Saarloos RR .20 .50
38 Hank Blalock RR .20 .50
39 Francisco Rodriguez RR .30 .75
40 Runelvys Hernandez RR .20 .50
41 Aaron Cook RR .20 .50
42 Josh Hancock RR .20 .50
43 P.J. Bevis RR .20 .50
44 Jon Adkins RR .20 .50
45 Tim Kalita RR .20 .50
46 Nelson Castro RR .20 .50
47 Colin Young RR .20 .50
48 Adrian Burnside RR .20 .50
49 Luis Martinez RR .20 .50
50 Pete Zamora RR .20 .50
51 Todd Donovan RR .20 .50
52 Jeremy Ward RR .20 .50
53 Wilson Valdez RR .20 .50
54 Eric Good RR .20 .50
55 Jeff Baker RR .20 .50
56 Mitch Wylie RR .20 .50
57 Ron Calloway RR .20 .50
58 Jose Valverde RR .20 .50
59 Jason Davis RR .20 .50
60 Scotty Layfield RR .20 .50
61 Matt Thornton RR .20 .50
62 Adam Walker RR .20 .50
63 Gustavo Chacin RR .20 .50
64 Ron Chiavacci RR .20 .50
65 Wiki Nieves RR .20 .50
66 Cliff Bartosh RR .20 .50
67 Mike Gonzalez RR .20 .50
68 Justin Wayne RR .20 .50
69 Eric Junge RR .20 .50
70 Ben Kozlowski RR .20 .50
71 Darin Erstad .12 .30
72 Garret Anderson .12 .30
73 Troy Glaus .12 .30
74 David Eckstein .12 .30
75 Adam Kennedy .12 .30
76 Kevin Appier .12 .30
77 Jarrod Washburn .12 .30
78 Scott Spiezio .12 .30
79 Tim Salmon .12 .30
80 Ramon Ortiz .12 .30
81 Bengie Molina .12 .30
82 Brad Fullmer .12 .30
83 Troy Percival .12 .30
84 David Segui .12 .30
85 Jay Gibbons .12 .30
86 Tony Batista .12 .30
87 Scott Erickson .12 .30
88 Jeff Conine .12 .30
89 Melvin Mora .12 .30
90 Buddy Groom .12 .30
91 Rodrigo Lopez .12 .30
92 Marty Cordova .12 .30
93 Geronimo Gil .12 .30
94 Kenny Lofton .12 .30
95 Shea Hillenbrand .12 .30
96 Manny Ramirez .30 .75
97 Pedro Martinez .20 .50
98 Nomar Garciaparra .20 .50
99 Rickey Henderson .30 .75
100 Johnny Damon .20 .50
101 Trot Nixon .12 .30
102 Derek Lowe .12 .30
103 Hee Seop Choi .12 .30
104 Mark Teixeira .20 .50
105 Tim Wakefield .20 .50
106 Jason Varitek .30 .75
107 Frank Thomas .30 .75
108 Joe Crede .12 .30
109 Magglio Ordonez .20 .50
110 Ray Durham .12 .30
111 Mark Buehrle .20 .50
112 Paul Konerko .20 .50
113 Jose Valentin .12 .30
114 Carlos Lee .12 .30
115 Royce Clayton .12 .30
116 C.C. Sabathia .20 .50
117 Ellis Burks .12 .30
118 Omar Vizquel .20 .50
119 Jim Thome .20 .50
120 Matt Lawton .12 .30
121 Travis Fryman .12 .30
122 Earl Snyder .12 .30
123 Ricky Gutierrez .12 .30
124 Einar Diaz .12 .30
125 Danys Baez .12 .30
126 Robert Fick .12 .30
127 Bobby Higginson .12 .30
128 Steve Sparks .12 .30
129 Mike Rivera .12 .30
130 Wendell Magee .12 .30
131 Randall Simon .12 .30
132 Carlos Pena .20 .50
133 Mark Redman .12 .30
134 Juan Acevedo .12 .30
135 Mike Sweeney .12 .30
136 Aaron Guiel .12 .30
137 Carlos Beltran .20 .50
138 Joe Randa .12 .30
139 Paul Byrd .12 .30
140 Shawn Sedlacek .12 .30
141 Raul Ibanez .20 .50
142 Michael Tucker .12 .30
143 Torii Hunter .12 .30
144 Jacque Jones .12 .30
145 David Ortiz .30 .75
146 Corey Koskie .12 .30
147 Brad Radke .12 .30
148 Doug Mientkiewicz .12 .30
149 A.J. Pierzynski .12 .30
150 Dustan Mohr .12 .30
151 Michael Cuddyer .12 .30
152 Eddie Guardado .12 .30
153 Cristian Guzman .12 .30
154 Derek Jeter .75 2.00
155 Bernie Williams .20 .50
156 Roger Clemens .40 1.00
157 Mike Mussina .20 .50
158 Jorge Posada .20 .50
159 Alfonso Soriano .20 .50
160 Jason Giambi .12 .30
161 Robin Ventura .12 .30
162 Andy Pettitte .20 .50
163 David Wells .12 .30
164 Nick Johnson .12 .30
165 Jeff Weaver .12 .30
166 Raul Mondesi .12 .30
167 Rondell White .12 .30
168 Tim Hudson .20 .50
169 Barry Zito .20 .50
170 Mark Mulder .12 .30
171 Miguel Tejada .20 .50
172 Eric Chavez .12 .30
173 Billy Koch .12 .30
174 Jermaine Dye .12 .30
175 Scott Hatteberg .12 .30
176 Terrence Long .12 .30
177 David Justice .12 .30
178 Ramon Hernandez .12 .30
179 Ted Lilly .12 .30
180 Ichiro Suzuki .40 1.00
181 Edgar Martinez .20 .50
182 Mike Cameron .12 .30
183 John Olerud .12 .30
184 Bret Boone .12 .30
185 Dan Wilson .12 .30
186 Freddy Garcia .12 .30
187 Jamie Moyer .12 .30
188 Carlos Guillen .12 .30
189 Ruben Sierra .12 .30
190 Kazuhiro Sasaki .12 .30
191 Mark McLemore .12 .30
192 John Halama .12 .30
193 Joel Pineiro .12 .30
194 Jeff Cirillo .12 .30
195 Rafael Soriano .12 .30
196 Ben Grieve .12 .30
197 Aubrey Huff .12 .30
198 Steve Cox .12 .30
199 Toby Hall .12 .30
200 Randy Winn .12 .30
201 Brent Abernathy .12 .30
202 Chris Gomez .12 .30
203 John Flaherty .12 .30
204 Paul Wilson .12 .30
205 Chan Ho Park .20 .50
206 Alex Rodriguez .40 1.00
207 Juan Gonzalez .12 .30
208 Rafael Palmeiro .20 .50
209 Ivan Rodriguez .20 .50
210 Rusty Greer .12 .30
211 Kenny Rogers .12 .30
212 Ismael Valdes .12 .30
213 Frank Catalanotto .12 .30
214 Hank Blalock .12 .30
215 Michael Young .12 .30
216 Kevin Mench .12 .30
217 Herbert Perry .12 .30
218 Gabe Kapler .12 .30
219 Carlos Delgado .12 .30
220 Shannon Stewart .12 .30
221 Eric Hinske .12 .30
222 Roy Halladay .20 .50
223 Felipe Lopez .12 .30
224 Vernon Wells .12 .30
225 Josh Phelps .12 .30
226 Jose Cruz .12 .30
227 Curt Schilling .20 .50
228 Randy Johnson .30 .75
229 Luis Gonzalez .12 .30
230 Mark Grace .20 .50
231 Junior Spivey .12 .30
232 Tony Womack .12 .30
233 Matt Williams .12 .30
234 Steve Finley .12 .30
235 Byung-Hyun Kim .12 .30
236 Craig Counsell .12 .30
237 Greg Maddux .40 1.00
238 Tom Glavine .20 .50
239 John Smoltz .30 .75
240 Chipper Jones .30 .75
241 Gary Sheffield .12 .30
242 Andruw Jones .12 .30
243 Vinny Castilla .12 .30
244 Damian Moss .12 .30
245 Rafael Furcal .12 .30
246 Javy Lopez .12 .30
247 Kevin Millwood .12 .30
248 Kerry Wood .12 .30
249 Fred McGriff .20 .50
250 Sammy Sosa .30 .75
251 Alex Gonzalez .12 .30
252 Corey Patterson .12 .30
253 Moises Alou .12 .30
254 Juan Cruz .12 .30
255 Jon Lieber .12 .30
256 Matt Clement .12 .30
257 Mark Prior .20 .50
258 Ken Griffey Jr. .60 1.50
259 Barry Larkin .20 .50
260 Adam Dunn .20 .50
261 Sean Casey .12 .30
262 Jose Rijo .12 .30
263 Elmer Dessens .12 .30
264 Austin Kearns .12 .30
265 Corky Miller .12 .30
266 Todd Walker .12 .30
267 Chris Reitsma .12 .30
268 Ryan Dempster .12 .30
269 Aaron Boone .12 .30
270 Danny Graves .12 .30
271 Brandon Larson .12 .30
272 Larry Walker .20 .50
273 Todd Helton .20 .50
274 Juan Uribe .12 .30
275 Juan Pierre .12 .30
276 Mike Hampton .12 .30
277 Todd Zeile .12 .30
278 Todd Hollandsworth .12 .30
279 Jason Jennings .12 .30
280 Josh Beckett .12 .30
281 Mike Lowell .12 .30
282 Derrek Lee .12 .30
283 A.J. Burnett .12 .30
284 Luis Castillo .12 .30
285 Tim Raines .12 .30
286 Preston Wilson .12 .30
287 Juan Encarnacion .12 .30
288 Charles Johnson .12 .30
289 Jeff Bagwell .20 .50
290 Craig Biggio .20 .50
291 Lance Berkman .20 .50
292 Daryle Ward .12 .30
293 Roy Oswalt .20 .50
294 Richard Hidalgo .12 .30
295 Octavio Dotel .12 .30
296 Wade Miller .12 .30
297 Julio Lugo .12 .30
298 Billy Wagner .12 .30
299 Shawn Green .12 .30
300 Adrian Beltre .30 .75
301 Paul Lo Duca .12 .30
302 Eric Karros .12 .30
303 Kevin Brown .12 .30
304 Hideo Nomo .30 .75
305 Odalis Perez .12 .30
306 Eric Gagne .12 .30

307 Brian Jordan .12 .30
308 Cesar Izturis .12 .30
309 Mark Grudzielanek .12 .30
310 Kazuhisa Ishii .12 .30
311 Geoff Jenkins .12 .30
312 Richie Sexson .12 .30
313 Jose Hernandez .12 .30
314 Ben Sheets .12 .30
315 Ruben Quevedo .12 .30
316 Jeffrey Hammonds .12 .30
317 Alex Sanchez .12 .30
318 Eric Young .12 .30
319 Takahito Nomura .12 .30
320 Vladimir Guerrero .20 .50
321 Jose Vidro .12 .30
322 Orlando Cabrera .12 .30
323 Michael Barrett .12 .30
324 Javier Vazquez .12 .30
325 Tony Armas Jr. .12 .30
326 Andres Galarraga .20 .50
327 Tomo Ohka .12 .30
328 Bartolo Colon .12 .30
329 Fernando Tatis .12 .30
330 Brad Wilkerson .12 .30
331 Masato Yoshii .12 .30
332 Mike Piazza .30 .75
333 Jeromy Burnitz .12 .30
334 Roberto Alomar .20 .50
335 Mo Vaughn .12 .30
336 Al Leiter .12 .30
337 Pedro Astacio .12 .30
338 Edgardo Alfonzo .12 .30
339 Armando Benitez .12 .30
340 Timo Perez .12 .30
341 Jay Payton .12 .30
342 Roger Cedeno .12 .30
343 Rey Ordonez .12 .30
344 Steve Trachsel .12 .30
345 Satoru Komiyama .12 .30
346 Scott Rolen .20 .50
347 Pat Burrell .12 .30
348 Bobby Abreu .12 .30
349 Mike Lieberthal .12 .30
350 Brandon Duckworth .12 .30
351 Jimmy Rollins .20 .50
352 Marlon Anderson .12 .30
353 Travis Lee .12 .30
354 Vicente Padilla .12 .30
355 Randy Wolf .12 .30
356 Jason Kendall .12 .30
357 Brian Giles .12 .30
358 Aramis Ramirez .12 .30
359 Pokey Reese .12 .30
360 Kip Wells .12 .30
361 Josh Fogg .12 .30
362 Mike Williams .12 .30
363 Jack Wilson .12 .30
364 Craig Wilson .12 .30
365 Kevin Young .12 .30
366 Ryan Klesko .12 .30
367 Phil Nevin .12 .30
368 Brian Lawrence .12 .30
369 Mark Kotsay .12 .30
370 Brett Tomko .12 .30
371 Trevor Hoffman .20 .50
372 Deivi Cruz .12 .30
373 Bubba Trammell .12 .30
374 Sean Burroughs .12 .30
375 Barry Bonds .50 1.25
376 Jeff Kent .12 .30
377 Rich Aurilia .12 .30
378 Tsuyoshi Shinjo .12 .30
379 Benito Santiago .12 .30
380 Kirk Rueter .12 .30
381 Livan Hernandez .12 .30
382 Russ Ortiz .12 .30
383 David Bell .12 .30
384 Jason Schmidt .12 .30
385 Reggie Sanders .12 .30
386 J.T. Snow .12 .30
387 Robb Nen .12 .30
388 Ryan Jensen .12 .30
389 Jim Edmonds .20 .50
390 J.D. Drew .12 .30
391 Albert Pujols .40 1.00
392 Fernando Vina .12 .30
393 Tino Martinez .12 .30
394 Edgar Renteria .12 .30
395 Matt Morris .12 .30
396 Woody Williams .12 .30
397 Jason Isringhausen .12 .30
398 Placido Polanco .12 .30
399 Eli Marrero .12 .30
400 Jason Simontacchi .12 .30

2003 Donruss Chicago Collection

DISTRIBUTED AT CHICAGO SPORTSFEST
STATED PRINT RUN 5 SERIAL #'d SETS
NO PRICING DUE TO SCARCITY

2003 Donruss Stat Line Career

*STAT LINE 1-20: 2.5X TO 6X BASIC
*21-70 P/R b/wn 251-400: 1.25X TO 3X
*21-70 P/R b/wn 201-250: 1.25X TO 3X
*21-70 P/R b/wn 151-200 1.5X TO 4X
*21-70 P/R b/wn 121-150: 2X TO 5X
*21-70 P/R b/wn 81-120: 2.5X TO 6X
*21-70 P/R b/wn 51-65: 3X TO 8X
*21-70 P/R b/wn 36-50: 4X TO 10X
*21-70 P/R b/wn 26-35: 5X TO 12X
*71-400 P/R b/wn 251-400: 1.25X TO 3X
*71-400 P/R b/wn 201-250: 2.5X TO 6X
*71-400 P/R b/wn 151-200 3X TO 8X
*71-400 P/R b/wn 121-150: 3X TO 8X
*71-400 P/R b/wn 81-120: 4X TO 10X
*71-400 P/R b/wn 66-80: 5X TO 12X
*71-400 P/R b/wn 51-65: 5X TO 12X
*71-400 P/R b/wn 36-50: 6X TO 15X
*71-400 P/R b/wn 26-35: 8X TO 20X
SEE BECKETT.COM FOR FOR PRINT RUNS
NO PRICING ON QTY OF 25 OR LESS

2003 Donruss Stat Line Season

*1-20 P/R b/wn 121-150 3X TO 8X
*1-20 P/R b/wn 81-120 4X TO 10X
*1-20 P/R b/wn 66-80 5X TO 12X
*1-20 P/R b/wn 51-65 5X TO 12X
*1-20 P/R b/wn 36-50 6X TO 15X
*1-20 P/R b/wn 26-35 8X TO 20X
*21-70 P/R b/wn 81-120 2.5X TO 6X
*21-70 P/R b/wn 66-80 3X TO 8X
*21-70 P/R b/wn 51-65 3X TO 8X
*21-70 P/R b/wn 36-50 4X TO 10X
*21-70 P/R b/wn 26-35 5X TO 12X
*71-400 P/R b/wn 81-120 4X TO 10X
*71-400 P/R b/wn 66-80 5X TO 12X
*71-400 P/R b/wn 51-65 5X TO 12X
*71-400 P/R b/wn 36-50 6X TO 15X
*71-400 P/R b/wn 26-35 8X TO 20X
SEE BECKETT.COM FOR PRINT RUNS
NO PRICING ON QTY OF 25 OR LESS

2003 Donruss All-Stars

STATED ODDS 1:12 RETAIL
1 Ichiro Suzuki 1.25 3.00
2 Alex Rodriguez 1.25 3.00
3 Nomar Garciaparra .60 1.50
4 Derek Jeter 2.50 6.00
5 Manny Ramirez 1.00 2.50
6 Barry Bonds 1.50 4.00
7 Adam Dunn .60 1.50
8 Mike Piazza 1.00 2.50
9 Sammy Sosa 1.00 2.50
10 Todd Helton .60 1.50

2003 Donruss Anniversary 1983

COMPLETE SET (20) 20.00 50.00
STATED ODDS 1:12
1 Dale Murphy 1.00 2.50
2 Jim Palmer .60 1.50
3 Nolan Ryan 3.00 8.00
4 Ozzie Smith 1.25 3.00
5 Tom Seaver .60 1.50
6 Mike Schmidt 1.50 4.00
7 Steve Carlton .60 1.50
8 Robin Yount 1.00 2.50
9 Ryne Sandberg 2.00 5.00
10 Cal Ripken 3.00 8.00
11 Fernando Valenzuela .40 1.00
12 Andre Dawson .60 1.50
13 George Brett 2.00 5.00
14 Eddie Murray .60 1.50
15 Dave Winfield .60 1.50
16 Johnny Bench 1.00 2.50
17 Wade Boggs .60 1.50
18 Tony Gwynn 1.00 2.50
19 San Diego Chicken .40 1.00
20 Ty Cobb 1.50 4.00

2003 Donruss Bat King

1-10 PRINT RUN 250 SERIAL #'d SETS
11-20 PRINT RUN 100 SERIAL #'d SETS
*STUDIO 1-10: .75X TO 2X BASIC BAT KING
STUDIO 1-10 PRINT RUN 50 SERIAL #'d SETS
STUDIO 11-20 PRINT RUN 25 SERIAL #'d SETS
STUDIO 11-20 NO PRICING DUE TO SCARCITY
1 Scott Rolen 99 DK/250 8.00 20.00
2 Frank Thomas 00 DK/250 8.00 20.00
3 Chipper Jones 01 DK/250 8.00 20.00
4 Ivan Rodriguez 01 DK/250 8.00 20.00
5 Stan Musial 01 ATDK/100 20.00 50.00
6 Nomar Garciaparra 02 DK/250 10.00 25.00
7 Vladimir Guerrero 03 DK/250 8.00 20.00
8 Adam Dunn 03 DK/250 6.00 15.00
9 Lance Berkman 03 DK/250 6.00 15.00
10 Magglio Ordonez 03 DK/250 6.00 15.00
12 Manny Ramirez 95 DK/100 10.00 25.00
13 Mike Piazza 94 DK/100 15.00 40.00
14 Alex Rodriguez 97 DK/100 15.00 40.00
15 Todd Helton 97 RDK/100 10.00 25.00
16 Andre Dawson 85 DK/100 8.00 20.00
17 Cal Ripken 87 DK/100 25.00 60.00
18 Tony Gwynn 88 DK/100 12.50 30.00
19 Don Mattingly 02 ATDK/100 15.00 40.00
20 Ryne Sandberg 90 DK/100 12.00 30.00

2003 Donruss Diamond Kings Inserts

STATED PRINT RUN 2500 SERIAL #'d SETS
*STUDIO: .75X TO 2X BASIC DK
STUDIO PRINT RUN 250 SERIAL #'d SETS
DK1 Vladimir Guerrero 1.00 2.50
DK2 Derek Jeter 4.00 10.00
DK3 Adam Dunn 1.00 2.50
DK4 Greg Maddux 2.00 5.00
DK5 Lance Berkman 1.00 2.50
DK6 Ichiro Suzuki 2.00 5.00
DK7 Mike Piazza 1.50 4.00
DK8 Alex Rodriguez 2.00 5.00
DK9 Tom Glavine 1.00 2.50
DK10 Randy Johnson 1.50 4.00
DK11 Nomar Garciaparra 1.00 2.50
DK12 Jason Giambi .60 1.50
DK13 Sammy Sosa 1.50 4.00
DK14 Barry Zito 1.00 2.50
DK15 Chipper Jones 1.50 4.00
DK16 Magglio Ordonez 1.00 2.50
DK17 Larry Walker 1.00 2.50
DK18 Alfonso Soriano 1.00 2.50
DK19 Curt Schilling 1.00 2.50
DK20 Barry Bonds 2.50 6.00

2003 Donruss Elite Series

STATED PRINT RUN 2500 SERIAL #'d SETS
DOMINATORS PR.RUN 25 SERIAL #'d SETS
DOMINATORS NO PRICE DUE TO SCARCITY
1 Alex Rodriguez 1.25 3.00
2 Barry Bonds 1.50 4.00
3 Ichiro Suzuki 1.25 3.00
4 Vladimir Guerrero .60 1.50
5 Randy Johnson 1.00 2.50
6 Pedro Martinez .60 1.50
7 Adam Dunn .60 1.50
8 Sammy Sosa 1.00 2.50
9 Jim Edmonds .60 1.50
10 Greg Maddux 1.25 3.00
11 Kazuhisa Ishii .40 1.00
12 Jason Giambi .40 1.00
13 Nomar Garciaparra .60 1.50
14 Tom Glavine .60 1.50
15 Todd Helton .60 1.50

2003 Donruss Gamers

STATED PRINT RUN 500 SERIAL #'d SETS
*JSY NUM: .6X TO 1.5X BASIC
JSY NUM PRINT RUN 100 SERIAL #'d SETS
*POSITION: .6X TO 1.5X BASIC
POSITION PRINT RUN 100 SERIAL #'d SETS
PRIME PRINT RUN 25 SERIAL #'d SETS
NO PRIME PRICING DUE TO SCARCITY
REWARDS PRINT RUN 10 SERIAL #'d SETS
NO REWARDS PRICING DUE TO SCARCITY
1 Nomar Garciaparra 6.00 15.00
2 Alex Rodriguez 4.00 10.00
3 Mike Piazza 4.00 10.00
4 Greg Maddux 4.00 10.00
5 Roger Clemens 6.00 15.00
6 Sammy Sosa 3.00 8.00
7 Randy Johnson 3.00 8.00
8 Albert Pujols 6.00 15.00
9 Alfonso Soriano 2.00 5.00
10 Chipper Jones 3.00 8.00
11 Mark Prior 3.00 8.00
12 Hideo Nomo 3.00 8.00
13 Adam Dunn 2.00 5.00
14 Juan Gonzalez 2.00 5.00
15 Vladimir Guerrero 3.00 8.00
16 Pedro Martinez 3.00 8.00
17 Jim Thome 3.00 8.00
18 Brandon Webb/200 4.00 10.00
19 Mike Mussina 3.00 8.00
20 Mark Teixeira 3.00 8.00
21 Barry Larkin 3.00 8.00
22 Ivan Rodriguez 3.00 8.00
23 Hank Blalock 2.00 5.00
24 Rafael Palmeiro 3.00 8.00
25 Curt Schilling 2.00 5.00
26 Troy Glaus 2.00 5.00
27 Bernie Williams 3.00 8.00
28 Scott Rolen 3.00 8.00
29 Torii Hunter 2.00 5.00
30 Nick Johnson 2.00 5.00
31 Kazuhisa Ishii 2.00 5.00
32 Shawn Green 2.00 5.00
33 Jeff Bagwell 3.00 8.00
34 Lance Berkman 3.00 8.00
35 Roy Oswalt 2.00 5.00
36 Kerry Wood 2.00 5.00
37 Todd Helton 3.00 8.00
38 Manny Ramirez 3.00 8.00
39 Andruw Jones 3.00 8.00
40 Frank Thomas 3.00 8.00
41 Gary Sheffield 2.00 5.00
42 Magglio Ordonez 2.00 5.00
43 Mike Sweeney 2.00 5.00
44 Carlos Beltran 2.00 5.00
45 Richie Sexson 2.00 5.00
46 Jeff Kent 2.00 5.00
47 Carlos Delgado 2.00 5.00
48 Vernon Wells 2.00 5.00
49 Dontrelle Willis 3.00 8.00
50 Jae Weong Seo 2.00 5.00

2003 Donruss Gamers Autographs

PRINT RUNS B/WN 5-50 COPIES PER
NO PRICING ON QTY OF 25 OR LESS
20 Mark Teixeira/50 10.00 25.00
23 Hank Blalock/50 12.50 30.00
29 Torii Hunter/50 12.50 30.00
35 Roy Oswalt/50 12.50 30.00
43 Mike Sweeney/50 12.50 30.00
48 Vernon Wells/30 15.00 40.00
49 Dontrelle Willis/50 6.00 15.00
50 Jae Weong Seo/50 12.50 30.00

2003 Donruss Jersey Kings

1-10 PRINT RUN 250 SERIAL #'d SETS
11-20 PRINT RUN 100 SERIAL #'d SETS
*STUDIO 1-10: .75X TO 2X BASIC JSY KINGS
STUDIO 1-10 PRINT RUN 50 SERIAL #'d SETS
STUDIO 11-20 PRINT RUN 25 SERIAL #'d SETS
STUDIO 11-20 NO PRICE DUE TO SCARCITY
1 Juan Gonzalez 99 DK/250 6.00 15.00
2 Greg Maddux 00 DK/250 8.00 20.00
3 Nomar Garciaparra 01 DK/250 10.00 25.00
4 Troy Glaus 01 DK/250 6.00 15.00
5 Reggie Jackson 01 ATDK/100 10.00 25.00
6 Alex Rodriguez 01 DK/250 10.00 25.00
7 Alfonso Soriano 03 DK/250 6.00 15.00
8 Curt Schilling 03 DK/250 6.00 15.00
9 Vladimir Guerrero 03 DK/250 6.00 15.00
10 Adam Dunn 03 DK/250 6.00 15.00
11 Mark Grace 88 DK/100 10.00 25.00
12 Roger Clemens 90 DK/100 15.00 40.00
13 Jeff Bagwell 91 DK/100 10.00 25.00
14 Tom Glavine 92 DK/100 10.00 25.00
15 Mike Piazza 94 DK/100 12.50 30.00
16 Rod Carew 82 DK/100 10.00 25.00
17 Rickey Henderson 82 DK/100 10.00 25.00
18 Mike Schmidt 83 DK/100 15.00 40.00
19 Cal Ripken 85 DK/100 40.00 80.00
20 Dale Murphy 86 DK/100 10.00 25.00

2003 Donruss Longball Leaders

STATED PRINT RUN 1000 SERIAL #'d SETS
*SEASON SUM: 1.5X TO 4X BASIC LL
SEASON PRINT RUN BASED ON 02 HR'S
1 Alex Rodriguez 2.00 5.00
2 Alfonso Soriano 1.00 2.50
3 Rafael Palmeiro 1.00 2.50
4 Jim Thome 1.00 2.50
5 Jason Giambi .60 1.50
6 Sammy Sosa 1.50 4.00
7 Barry Bonds 2.50 6.00
8 Lance Berkman 1.00 2.50
9 Shawn Green .60 1.50
10 Vladimir Guerrero 1.00 2.50

2003 Donruss Production Line

STATED PRINT RUNS LISTED BELOW
*DIE CUT OPS: 1.25X TO 3X BASIC PL
*DIE CUT OBP/SLG: 1X TO 2.5X BASIC PL
*DIE CUT AVG/TB: .75X TO 2X BASIC PL
DIE CUT PRINT RUN 100 SERIAL #'d SETS
1 Alex Rodriguez OPS/1015 2.00 5.00
2 Jim Thome OPS/1122 1.00 2.50
3 Lance Berkman OPS/982 1.00 2.50
4 Barry Bonds OPS/1381 2.50 6.00
5 Sammy Sosa OPS/993 1.50 4.00
6 Vladimir Guerrero OPS/1010 1.00 2.50
7 Barry Bonds OBP/582 3.00 8.00
8 Jason Giambi OBP/435 .75 2.00
9 Vladimir Guerrero OBP/417 1.25 3.00
10 Adam Dunn OBP/400 1.25 3.00
11 Chipper Jones OBP/435 2.00 5.00
12 Todd Helton OBP/429 1.25 3.00
13 Rafael Palmeiro SLG/571 1.25 3.00
14 Sammy Sosa SLG/594 2.00 5.00
15 Alex Rodriguez SLG/623 2.50 6.00
16 Larry Walker SLG/602 1.25 3.00
17 Lance Berkman SLG/578 1.25 3.00
18 Alfonso Soriano SLG/547 1.25 3.00
19 Ichiro Suzuki AVG/321 2.50 6.00
20 Mike Sweeney AVG/340 .75 2.00
21 Manny Ramirez AVG/349 2.00 5.00
22 Larry Walker AVG/338 1.25 3.00
23 Barry Bonds AVG/370 3.00 8.00
24 Jim Edmonds AVG/311 1.25 3.00
25 Alfonso Soriano TB/381 1.25 3.00
26 Jason Giambi TB/335 .75 2.00
27 Miguel Tejada TB/336 1.25 3.00
28 Brian Giles TB/309 .75 2.00
29 Vladimir Guerrero TB/364 1.25 3.00
30 Pat Burrell TB/319 .75 2.00

2003 Donruss Recollection Autographs

RANDOM INSERTS IN PACKS
SEE BECKETT.COM FOR CHECKLIST
NO PRICING DUE TO SCARCITY

2003 Donruss Timber and Threads

STATED PRINT RUNS LISTED BELOW
1 Al Kaline Bat/125 10.00 25.00
2 Alex Rodriguez Bat/350 8.00 20.00
3 Carlos Delgado Bat/250 4.00 10.00
4 Cliff Floyd Bat/250 4.00 10.00
5 Eddie Mathews Bat/125 10.00 25.00
6 Edgar Martinez Bat/125 10.00 25.00
7 Ernie Banks Bat/50 15.00 40.00
8 Ivan Rodriguez Bat/125 10.00 25.00
9 J.D. Drew Bat/125 6.00 15.00
10 Jorge Posada Bat/300 6.00 15.00
11 Lou Brock Bat/125 10.00 25.00
12 Mike Piazza Bat/125 10.00 25.00
13 Mike Schmidt Bat/125 15.00 40.00
14 Reggie Jackson Bat/125 10.00 25.00
15 Rickey Henderson Bat/125 10.00 25.00
16 Robin Yount Bat/125 10.00 25.00
17 Rod Carew Bat/125 10.00 25.00
18 Scott Rolen Bat/125 10.00 25.00
19 Shawn Green Bat/200 4.00 10.00
20 Willie Stargell Bat/125 10.00 25.00
21 Alex Rodriguez Jsy/175 12.50 30.00
22 Andruw Jones Jsy/275 6.00 15.00
23 Brooks Robinson Jsy/150 10.00 25.00
24 Chipper Jones Jsy/150 10.00 25.00
25 Greg Maddux Jsy/175 8.00 20.00
26 Hideo Nomo Jsy/300 15.00 40.00
27 Ivan Rodriguez Jsy/225 6.00 15.00
28 Jack Morris Jsy/150 6.00 15.00
29 J.D. Drew Jsy/150 6.00 15.00
30 Jeff Bagwell Jsy/500 6.00 15.00
31 Jim Thome Jsy/200 6.00 15.00
32 John Smoltz Jsy/175 6.00 15.00
33 John Olerud Jsy/450 4.00 10.00
34 Kerry Wood Jsy/200 4.00 10.00
36 Larry Walker Jsy/500 4.00 10.00
37 Magglio Ordonez Jsy/150 6.00 15.00
38 Manny Ramirez Jsy/500 6.00 15.00
39 Mike Piazza Jsy/300 6.00 15.00
40 Mike Sweeney Jsy/200 4.00 10.00
41 Nomar Garciaparra Jsy/200 10.00 25.00
42 Paul Konerko Jsy/500 4.00 10.00
43 Pedro Martinez Jsy/175 6.00 15.00
44 Randy Johnson Jsy/175 6.00 15.00
45 Roger Clemens Jsy/350 10.00 25.00
46 Shawn Green Jsy/250 4.00 10.00
47 Todd Helton Jsy/175 6.00 15.00
48 Tom Glavine Jsy/225 6.00 15.00
49 Tony Gwynn Jsy/150 10.00 25.00
50 Vladimir Guerrero Jsy/450 6.00 15.00

2003 Donruss Rookies

COMPLETE SET (65) 8.00 20.00
COMMON CARD (1-65) .10 .25
COMMON RC .10 .25
1 Jeremy Bonderman RC .40 1.00
2 Adam Loewen RC .10 .25
3 Dan Haren RC .50 1.25
4 Jose Contreras RC .25 .60
5 Hideki Matsui RC .50 1.25
6 Arnie Munoz RC .10 .25
7 Miguel Cabrera 1.25 3.00
8 Andrew Brown RC .10 .25
9 Josh Hall RC .10 .25
10 Josh Stewart RC .10 .25
11 Clint Barmes RC .25 .60
12 Luis Ayala RC .10 .25
13 Brandon Webb RC .30 .75
14 Greg Aquino RC .10 .25
15 Chien-Ming Wang RC .40 1.00
16 Rickie Weeks RC .30 .75
17 Edgar Gonzalez RC .10 .25
18 Dontrelle Willis .10 .25
19 Bo Hart RC .10 .25
20 Rosman Garcia RC .10 .25
21 Jeremy Griffiths RC .10 .25
22 Craig Brazell RC .10 .25
23 Daniel Cabrera RC .15 .40
24 Fernando Cabrera RC .10 .25
25 Termel Sledge RC .10 .25
26 Ramon Nivar RC .10 .25
27 Rob Hammock RC .10 .25
28 Francisco Rosario RC .10 .25
29 Cory Stewart RC .10 .25
30 Felix Sanchez RC .10 .25
31 Jorge Cordova RC .10 .25
32 Rocco Baldelli .10 .25
33 Beau Kemp RC .10 .25
34 Mike Nakamura RC .10 .25
35 Rett Johnson RC .10 .25
36 Guillermo Quiroz RC .10 .25
37 Hong-Chih Kuo RC .50 1.25
38 Ian Ferguson RC .10 .25
39 Franklin Perez RC .10 .25
40 Tim Olson RC .10 .25
41 Jerome Williams .10 .25
42 Rich Fischer RC .10 .25
43 Phil Seibel RC .10 .25
44 Aaron Looper RC .10 .25
45 Jae Weong Seo .10 .25
46 Chad Gaudin RC .10 .25
47 Matt Kata RC .10 .25
48 Ryan Wagner RC .10 .25
49 Michel Hernandez RC .10 .25
50 Diegomar Markwell RC .10 .25
51 Doug Waechter RC .10 .25
52 Mike Nicolas RC .10 .25
53 Prentice Redman RC .10 .25
54 Shane Bazzell RC .10 .25
55 Delmon Young RC .60 1.50
56 Brian Stokes RC .10 .25
57 Matt Bruback RC .10 .25
58 Nook Logan RC .10 .25
59 Oscar Villarreal RC .10 .25
60 Pete LaForest RC .10 .25
61 Shea Hillenbrand .10 .25
62 Aramis Ramirez .10 .25
63 Aaron Boone .10 .25
64 Roberto Alomar .15 .40
65 Rickey Henderson .25 .60

2003 Donruss Rookies Autographs

PRINT RUNS B/WN 10-1000 COPIES PER
NO PRICING ON QTY OF 25 OR LESS
1 Jeremy Bonderman/50 20.00 50.00
2 Adam Loewen/500 6.00 15.00
3 Dan Haren/100 10.00 25.00
4 Jose Contreras/100 12.50 30.00
6 Arnie Munoz/584 4.00 10.00
7 Miguel Cabrera/50 60.00 120.00
8 Andrew Brown/584 6.00 15.00
9 Josh Hall/1000 4.00 10.00
10 Josh Stewart/300 4.00 10.00
11 Clint Barmes/129 6.00 15.00
12 Luis Ayala/1000 4.00 10.00
13 Brandon Webb/100 12.50 30.00
14 Greg Aquino/1000 4.00 10.00
15 Chien-Ming Wang/100 60.00 120.00
17 Edgar Gonzalez/400 4.00 10.00
19 Bo Hart/150 4.00 10.00
20 Rosman Garcia/250 4.00 10.00
21 Jeremy Griffiths/812 4.00 10.00
22 Craig Brazell/205 4.00 10.00
23 Daniel Cabrera/383 10.00 25.00
24 Fernando Cabrera/1000 4.00 10.00
25 Termel Sledge/250 4.00 10.00
26 Ramon Nivar/100 4.00 10.00
27 Rob Hammock/201 4.00 10.00
29 Cory Stewart/1000 4.00 10.00
30 Felix Sanchez/1000 4.00 10.00
31 Jorge Cordova/1000 4.00 10.00
33 Beau Kemp/1000 4.00 10.00
34 Mike Nakamura/1000 4.00 10.00
35 Rett Johnson/1000 4.00 10.00
36 Guillermo Quiroz/90 4.00 10.00
37 Hong-Chih Kuo/50 100.00 200.00
38 Ian Ferguson/1000 4.00 10.00
39 Franklin Perez/1000 4.00 10.00
40 Tim Olson/150 4.00 10.00
41 Jerome Williams/50 6.00 15.00
42 Rich Fischer/734 4.00 10.00
43 Phil Seibel/1000 4.00 10.00
44 Aaron Looper/513 4.00 10.00
45 Jae Weong Seo/50 10.00 25.00
47 Matt Kata/203 4.00 10.00
48 Ryan Wagner/100 4.00 10.00
50 Diegomar Markwell/1000 4.00 10.00
51 Doug Waechter/583 6.00 15.00
52 Mike Nicolas/1000 4.00 10.00
53 Prentice Redman/425 4.00 10.00
54 Shane Bazzell/1000 4.00 10.00
55 Delmon Young/75 100.00 200.00
56 Brian Stokes/1000 4.00 10.00
57 Matt Bruback/513 4.00 10.00
58 Nook Logan/150 6.00 15.00
59 Oscar Villarreal/150 6.00 15.00
60 Pete LaForest/250 4.00 10.00

2003 Donruss Rookies Stat Line Career

*SLC P/R b/wn 201+: 3X TO 8X
*SLC P/R b/wn 121-200: 4X TO 10X
*SLC P/R b/wn 81-120: 5X TO 12X
*SLC P/R b/wn 66-80: 6X TO 15X
*SLC P/R b/wn 51-65: 6X TO 15X
*SLC RC's P/R b/wn 201+: 4X TO 10X
*SLC RC's P/R b/wn 121-200: 4X TO 10X
*SLC RC's P/R b/wn 81-120: 4X TO 10X
*SLC RC's P/R b/wn 66-80: 5X TO 12X
*SLC RC's P/R b/wn 51-65: 5X TO 12X
*SLC RC's P/R b/wn 36-50: 6X TO 15X
*SLC RC's P/R b/wn 26-35: 8X TO 20X
PRINT RUNS B/WN 1-245 COPIES PER
NO PRICING ON QTY OF 25 OR LESS

2003 Donruss Rookies Stat Line Season

*SLS P/R b/wn 201+: 3X TO 8X
*SLS P/R b/wn 121-200: 4X TO 10X
*SLS P/R b/wn 66-80: 6X TO 15X
*SLS P/R b/wn 36-50: 8X TO 20X
*SLS P/R b/wn 26-35: 10X TO 25X
*SLS RC's P/R b/wn 81-120: 4X TO 10X
*SLS RC's P/R b/wn 66-80: 5X TO 12X
*SLS RC's P/R b/wn 51-65: 5X TO 12X
*SLS RC's P/R b/wn 36-50: 6X TO 15X
*SLS RC's P/R b/wn 26-35: 8X TO 20X
PRINT RUNS B/WN 1-130 COPIES PER
NO PRICING ON QTY OF 25 OR LESS

2003 Donruss Rookies Recollection Autographs

RANDOM INSERTS IN DLP R/T PACKS
PRINT RUNS B/WN 1-75 COPIES PER
NO PRICING ON QTY OF 5 OR LESS
7 Jack McDowell 88/75 10.00 25.00

2004 Donruss

COMPLETE SET (400) 40.00 100.00
COMP.SET w/o SP's (300) 10.00 25.00
COMMON CARD (71-370) .12 .30
COMMON CARD (1-25/371-400) .25 .60
COMMON CARD (26-70) .60 1.50
1-70/370-400 RANDOM INSERTS IN PACKS
1 Derek Jeter DK 1.50 4.00
2 Greg Maddux DK .75 2.00
3 Albert Pujols DK .75 2.00
4 Ichiro Suzuki DK .75 2.00
5 Alex Rodriguez DK .75 2.00
6 Roger Clemens DK .75 2.00
7 Andruw Jones DK .25 .60
8 Barry Bonds DK 1.00 2.50
9 Jeff Bagwell DK .40 1.00
10 Randy Johnson DK .60 1.50
11 Scott Rolen DK .40 1.00
12 Lance Berkman DK .40 1.00
13 Barry Zito DK .40 1.00
14 Manny Ramirez DK .60 1.50
15 Carlos Delgado DK .25 .60
16 Alfonso Soriano DK .40 1.00
17 Todd Helton DK .40 1.00
18 Mike Mussina DK .40 1.00
19 Austin Kearns DK .25 .60
20 Nomar Garciaparra DK .40 1.00
21 Chipper Jones DK .60 1.50
22 Mark Prior DK .40 1.00
23 Jim Thome DK .40 1.00
24 Vladimir Guerrero DK .40 1.00
25 Pedro Martinez DK .40 1.00
26 Sergio Mitre RR .60 1.50
27 Adam Loewen RR .60 1.50
28 Alfredo Gonzalez RR .60 1.50
29 Miguel Ojeda RR .60 1.50
30 Rosman Garcia RR .60 1.50
31 Arnie Munoz RR .60 1.50
32 Andrew Brown RR .60 1.50
33 Josh Hall RR .60 1.50
34 Josh Stewart RR .60 1.50
35 Clint Barmes RR 1.00 2.50
36 Brandon Webb RR .60 1.50
37 Chien-Ming Wang RR 2.50 6.00
38 Edgar Gonzalez RR .60 1.50
39 Alejandro Machado RR .60 1.50
40 Jeremy Griffiths RR .60 1.50
41 Craig Brazell RR .60 1.50
42 Daniel Cabrera RR .60 1.50
43 Fernando Cabrera RR .60 1.50
44 Termel Sledge RR .60 1.50
45 Rob Hammock RR .60 1.50
46 Francisco Rosario RR .60 1.50
47 Francisco Cruceta RR .60 1.50
48 Rett Johnson RR .60 1.50
49 Guillermo Quiroz RR .60 1.50
50 Hong-Chih Kuo RR .60 1.50
51 Ian Ferguson RR .60 1.50
52 Tim Olson RR .60 1.50
53 Todd Wellemeyer RR .60 1.50
54 Rich Fischer RR .60 1.50
55 Phil Seibel RR .60 1.50
56 Joe Valentine RR .60 1.50
57 Matt Kata RR .60 1.50
58 Michael Hessman RR .60 1.50
59 Michel Hernandez RR .60 1.50
60 Doug Waechter RR .60 1.50
61 Prentice Redman RR .60 1.50
62 Nook Logan RR .60 1.50
63 Oscar Villarreal RR .60 1.50
64 Pete LaForest RR .60 1.50
65 Matt Bruback RR .60 1.50
66 Dan Haren RR .60 1.50
67 Greg Aquino RR .60 1.50
68 Lew Ford RR .60 1.50
69 Jeff Duncan RR .60 1.50
70 Ryan Wagner RR .60 1.50
71 Bengie Molina .12 .30
72 Brad Fullmer .12 .30
73 Darin Erstad .12 .30
74 David Eckstein .12 .30
75 Garret Anderson .12 .30
76 Jarrod Washburn .12 .30
77 Kevin Appier .12 .30
78 Scott Spiezio .12 .30
79 Tim Salmon .12 .30
80 Troy Glaus .12 .30
81 Troy Percival .12 .30
82 Jason Johnson .12 .30
83 Jay Gibbons .12 .30
84 Melvin Mora .12 .30
85 Sidney Ponson .12 .30
86 Tony Batista .12 .30
87 Bill Mueller .12 .30
88 Byung-Hyun Kim .12 .30
89 David Ortiz .30 .75
90 Derek Lowe .12 .30
91 Johnny Damon .20 .50
92 Casey Fossum .12 .30
93 Manny Ramirez .30 .75
94 Nomar Garciaparra .20 .50
95 Pedro Martinez .20 .50
96 Todd Walker .12 .30
97 Trot Nixon .12 .30
98 Bartolo Colon .12 .30
99 Carlos Lee .12 .30
100 D'Angelo Jimenez .12 .30
101 Esteban Loaiza .12 .30
102 Frank Thomas .30 .75
103 Joe Crede .12 .30
104 Jose Valentin .12 .30
105 Magglio Ordonez .20 .50
106 Mark Buehrle .20 .50
107 Paul Konerko .20 .50
108 Brandon Phillips .12 .30
109 C.C Sabathia .20 .50
110 Ellis Burks .12 .30
111 Jeremy Guthrie .12 .30
112 Josh Bard .12 .30
113 Matt Lawton .12 .30
114 Milton Bradley .12 .30
115 Omar Vizquel .20 .50
116 Travis Hafner .12 .30
117 Bobby Higginson .12 .30
118 Carlos Pena .20 .50
119 Dmitri Young .12 .30
120 Eric Munson .12 .30
121 Jeremy Bonderman .12 .30
122 Nate Cornejo .12 .30
123 Omar Infante .12 .30
124 Ramon Santiago .12 .30
125 Angel Berroa .12 .30
126 Carlos Beltran .20 .50
127 Desi Relaford .12 .30
128 Jeremy Affeldt .12 .30
129 Joe Randa .12 .30
130 Ken Harvey .12 .30
131 Mike MacDougal .12 .30
132 Michael Tucker .12 .30
133 Mike Sweeney .12 .30
134 Raul Ibanez .20 .50
135 Runelvys Hernandez .12 .30
136 A.J. Pierzynski .12 .30
137 Brad Radke .12 .30
138 Corey Koskie .12 .30
139 Cristian Guzman .12 .30
140 Doug Mientkiewicz .12 .30
141 Dustan Mohr .12 .30
142 Jacque Jones .12 .30
143 Kenny Rogers .12 .30
144 Bobby Kielty .12 .30
145 Kyle Lohse .12 .30
146 Luis Rivas .12 .30
147 Torii Hunter .12 .30
148 Alfonso Soriano .20 .50
149 Andy Pettitte .20 .50
150 Bernie Williams .20 .50
151 David Wells .12 .30
152 Derek Jeter .75 2.00
153 Hideki Matsui .50 1.25
154 Jason Giambi .12 .30
155 Jorge Posada .20 .50
156 Jose Contreras .12 .30
157 Mike Mussina .20 .50
158 Nick Johnson .12 .30
159 Robin Ventura .12 .30
160 Roger Clemens .40 1.00
161 Barry Zito .20 .50
162 Chris Singleton .12 .30
163 Eric Byrnes .12 .30
164 Eric Chavez .12 .30
165 Erubiel Durazo .12 .30
166 Keith Foulke .12 .30
167 Mark Ellis .12 .30
168 Miguel Tejada .20 .50
169 Mark Mulder .12 .30
170 Ramon Hernandez .12 .30
171 Ted Lilly .12 .30
172 Terrence Long .12 .30
173 Tim Hudson .20 .50
174 Bret Boone .12 .30
175 Carlos Guillen .12 .30
176 Dan Wilson .12 .30
177 Edgar Martinez .20 .50
178 Freddy Garcia .12 .30
179 Gil Meche .12 .30
180 Ichiro Suzuki .40 1.00
181 Jamie Moyer .12 .30
182 Joel Pineiro .12 .30
183 John Olerud .12 .30
184 Mike Cameron .12 .30
185 Randy Winn .12 .30
186 Ryan Franklin .12 .30
187 Kazuhiro Sasaki .12 .30
188 Aubrey Huff .12 .30
189 Carl Crawford .20 .50
190 Joe Kennedy .12 .30
191 Marlon Anderson .12 .30
192 Rey Ordonez .12 .30
193 Rocco Baldelli .12 .30
194 Toby Hall .12 .30
195 Travis Lee .12 .30
196 Alex Rodriguez .40 1.00
197 Carl Everett .12 .30
198 Chan Ho Park .20 .50
199 Einar Diaz .12 .30
200 Hank Blalock .12 .30
201 Ismael Valdes .12 .30
202 Juan Gonzalez .12 .30
203 Mark Teixeira .20 .50
204 Mike Young .12 .30
205 Rafael Palmeiro .20 .50
206 Carlos Delgado .12 .30
207 Kelvim Escobar .12 .30
208 Eric Hinske .12 .30
209 Frank Catalanotto .12 .30
210 Josh Phelps .12 .30
211 Orlando Hudson .12 .30
212 Roy Halladay .20 .50
213 Shannon Stewart .12 .30
214 Vernon Wells .12 .30
215 Carlos Baerga .12 .30
216 Curt Schilling .20 .50
217 Junior Spivey .12 .30
218 Luis Gonzalez .12 .30
219 Lyle Overbay .12 .30
220 Mark Grace .20 .50
221 Matt Williams .12 .30
222 Randy Johnson .30 .75
223 Shea Hillenbrand .12 .30
224 Steve Finley .12 .30
225 Andruw Jones .12 .30
226 Chipper Jones .30 .75
227 Gary Sheffield .12 .30
228 Greg Maddux .40 1.00
229 Javy Lopez .12 .30
230 John Smoltz .30 .75
231 Marcus Giles .12 .30
232 Mike Hampton .12 .30
233 Rafael Furcal .12 .30
234 Robert Fick .12 .30
235 Russ Ortiz .12 .30
236 Alex Gonzalez .12 .30
237 Carlos Zambrano .20 .50
238 Corey Patterson .12 .30
239 Hee Seop Choi .12 .30
240 Kerry Wood .12 .30
241 Mark Bellhorn .12 .30
242 Mark Prior .20 .50
243 Moises Alou .12 .30

244 Sammy Sosa .30 .75
245 Aaron Boone .12 .30
246 Adam Dunn .20 .50
247 Austin Kearns .12 .30
248 Barry Larkin .20 .50
249 Felipe Lopez .12 .30
250 Jose Guillen .12 .30
251 Ken Griffey Jr. .60 1.50
252 Jason LaRue .12 .30
253 Scott Williamson .12 .30
254 Sean Casey .12 .30
255 Shawn Chacon .12 .30
256 Chris Stynes .12 .30
257 Jason Jennings .12 .30
258 Jay Payton .12 .30
259 Jose Hernandez .12 .30
260 Larry Walker .20 .50
261 Preston Wilson .12 .30
262 Ronnie Belliard .12 .30
263 Todd Helton .20 .50
264 A.J. Burnett .12 .30
265 Alex Gonzalez .12 .30
266 Brad Penny .12 .30
267 Derrek Lee .12 .30
268 Ivan Rodriguez .20 .50
269 Josh Beckett .12 .30
270 Juan Encarnacion .12 .30
271 Juan Pierre .12 .30
272 Luis Castillo .12 .30
273 Mike Lowell .12 .30
274 Todd Hollandsworth .12 .30
275 Billy Wagner .12 .30
276 Brad Ausmus .12 .30
277 Craig Biggio .20 .50
278 Jeff Bagwell .20 .50
279 Jeff Kent .12 .30
280 Lance Berkman .20 .50
281 Richard Hidalgo .12 .30
282 Roy Oswalt .20 .50
283 Wade Miller .12 .30
284 Adrian Beltre .30 .75
285 Brian Jordan .12 .30
286 Cesar Izturis .12 .30
287 Dave Roberts .20 .50
288 Eric Gagne .12 .30
289 Fred McGriff .12 .30
290 Hideo Nomo .30 .75
291 Kazuhisa Ishii .12 .30
292 Kevin Brown .12 .30
293 Paul Lo Duca .12 .30
294 Shawn Green .12 .30
295 Ben Sheets .12 .30
296 Geoff Jenkins .12 .30
297 Rey Sanchez .12 .30
298 Richie Sexson .12 .30
299 Wes Helms .12 .30
300 Brad Wilkerson .12 .30
301 Claudio Vargas .12 .30
302 Endy Chavez .12 .30
303 Fernando Tatis .12 .30
304 Javier Vazquez .12 .30
305 Jose Vidro .12 .30
306 Michael Barrett .12 .30
307 Orlando Cabrera .12 .30
308 Tony Armas Jr. .12 .30
309 Vladimir Guerrero .20 .50
310 Zach Day .12 .30
311 Al Leiter .12 .30
312 Cliff Floyd .12 .30
313 Jae Weong Seo .12 .30
314 Jeromy Burnitz .12 .30
315 Mike Piazza .30 .75
316 Mo Vaughn .12 .30
317 Roberto Alomar .20 .50
318 Roger Cedeno .12 .30
319 Tom Glavine .20 .50
320 Jose Reyes .20 .50
321 Bobby Abreu .12 .30
322 Brett Myers .12 .30
323 David Bell .12 .30
324 Jim Thome .20 .50
325 Jimmy Rollins .20 .50
326 Kevin Millwood .12 .30
327 Marlon Byrd .12 .30
328 Mike Lieberthal .12 .30
329 Pat Burrell .12 .30
330 Randy Wolf .12 .30
331 Aramis Ramirez .12 .30
332 Brian Giles .12 .30
333 Jason Kendall .12 .30
334 Kenny Lofton .12 .30
335 Kip Wells .12 .30
336 Kris Benson .12 .30
337 Randall Simon .12 .30
338 Reggie Sanders .12 .30
339 Albert Pujols .40 1.00
340 Edgar Renteria .12 .30
341 Fernando Vina .12 .30
342 J.D. Drew .12 .30
343 Jim Edmonds .20 .50
344 Matt Morris .12 .30
345 Mike Matheny .12 .30
346 Scott Rolen .20 .50
347 Tino Martinez .20 .50
348 Woody Williams .12 .30
349 Brian Lawrence .12 .30
350 Mark Kotsay .12 .30
351 Mark Loretta .12 .30
352 Ramon Vazquez .12 .30
353 Rondell White .12 .30
354 Ryan Klesko .12 .30
355 Sean Burroughs .12 .30
356 Trevor Hoffman .20 .50
357 Xavier Nady .12 .30
358 Andres Galarraga .20 .50
359 Barry Bonds .50 1.25
360 Benito Santiago .12 .30
361 Deivi Cruz .12 .30
362 Edgardo Alfonzo .12 .30
363 J.T. Snow .12 .30
364 Jason Schmidt .12 .30
365 Kirk Rueter .12 .30
366 Kurt Ainsworth .12 .30
367 Marquis Grissom .12 .30
368 Ray Durham .12 .30
369 Rich Aurilia .12 .30
370 Tim Worrell .12 .30
371 Troy Glaus TC .25 .60
372 Melvin Mora TC .25 .60
373 Nomar Garciaparra TC .40 1.00
374 Magglio Ordonez TC .40 1.00
375 Omar Vizquel TC .40 1.00
376 Dmitri Young TC .25 .60
377 Mike Sweeney TC .25 .60
378 Torii Hunter TC .25 .60
379 Derek Jeter TC 1.50 4.00
380 Barry Zito TC .40 1.00
381 Ichiro Suzuki TC .75 2.00
382 Rocco Baldelli TC .25 .60
383 Alex Rodriguez TC .75 2.00
384 Carlos Delgado TC .25 .60
385 Randy Johnson TC .60 1.50
386 Greg Maddux TC .75 2.00
387 Sammy Sosa TC .60 1.50
388 Ken Griffey Jr. TC 1.25 3.00
389 Todd Helton TC .40 1.00
390 Ivan Rodriguez TC .40 1.00
391 Jeff Bagwell TC .40 1.00
392 Hideo Nomo TC .60 1.50
393 Richie Sexson TC .25 .60
394 Vladimir Guerrero TC .40 1.00
395 Mike Piazza TC .60 1.50
396 Jim Thome TC .40 1.00
397 Jason Kendall TC .25 .60
398 Albert Pujols TC .75 2.00
399 Ryan Klesko TC .25 .60
400 Barry Bonds TC 1.00 2.50

2004 Donruss Autographs

RANDOM INSERTS IN PACKS
#'d CARD PRINTS B/WN 5-141 COPIES PER
NO PRICING ON QTY OF 12 OR LESS
51 Ian Ferguson 4.00 10.00
106 Mark Buehrle/141 12.50 30.00
112 Josh Bard 4.00 10.00
123 Omar Infante 4.00 10.00
172 Terrence Long 4.00 10.00
188 Aubrey Huff/143 6.00 15.00
194 Toby Hall 4.00 10.00
217 Junior Spivey/132 4.00 10.00
234 Robert Fick 4.00 10.00
349 Brian Lawrence 4.00 10.00

2004 Donruss Press Proofs Black

STATED PRINT RUN 10 SERIAL #'d SETS
NO PRICING DUE TO SCARCITY

2004 Donruss Press Proofs Blue

*PP BLUE 71-370: 4X TO 10X BASIC
*PP BLUE 1-25/371-400: 1.5X TO 4X BASIC
*PP BLUE 26-70: .75X TO 2X BASIC
RANDOM INSERTS IN RETAIL PACKS
STATED PRINT RUN 100 SERIAL #'d SETS

2004 Donruss Press Proofs Gold

STATED PRINT RUN 25 SERIAL #'d SETS
NO PRICING DUE TO SCARCITY

2004 Donruss Press Proofs Red

*PP RED 71-370: 2.5X TO 6X BASIC
*PP RED 1-25/371-400: 1X TO 2.5X BASIC
*PP RED 26-70: .5X TO 1.2X BASIC
STATED ODDS 1:12 RETAIL

2004 Donruss Stat Line Career

*71-370 p/r 200-443 2.5X TO 6X
*71-370 p/r 121-200: 3X TO 8X
*71-370 p/r 81-120: 4X TO 10X
*71-370 p/r 66-80: 5X TO 12X
*71-370 p/r 51-65: 5X TO 12X
*71-370 p/r 36-50: 6X TO 15X
*71-370 p/r 26-35: 8X TO 20X
*1-25/371-400 p/r 200-500: 1X TO 2.5X
*1-25/371-400 p/r 121-200: 1.25X TO 3X
*1-25/371-400 p/r 81-120: 1.5X TO 4X
*1-25/371-400 p/r 66-80: 2X TO 5X
*1-25/371-400 p/r 51-65: 2X TO 5X
*1-25/371-400 p/r 36-50: 2.5X TO 6X
*1-25/371-400 p/r 26-35: 3X TO 8X
*26-70 p/r 200-491: .5X TO 1.2X
*26-70 p/r 121-200: .6X TO 1.5X
*26-70 p/r 81-120: .75X TO 2X
*26-70 p/r 66-80: 1X TO 2.5X
*26-70 p/r 51-65: 1X TO 2.5X
*26-70 p/r 36-50: 1.25X TO 3X
*26-70 p/r 26-35: 1.5X TO 4X
RANDOM INSERTS IN PACKS
PRINT RUNS B/WN 6-500 COPIES PER
NO PRICING ON QTY OF 25 OR LESS

2004 Donruss Stat Line Season

*71-370 p/r 121-193: 3X TO 8X
*71-370 p/r 81-120: 4X TO 10X
*71-370 p/r 66-80: 5X TO 12X
*71-370 p/r 51-65: 5X TO 12X
*71-370 p/r 36-50: 6X TO 15X
*71-370 p/r 26-35: 8X TO 20X
*1-25/371-400 p/r 201-225:1X TO 2.5X
*1-25/371-400 p/r 121-200: 1.25X TO 3X
*1-25/371-400 p/r 81-120: 1.5X TO 4X
*1-25/371-400 p/r 66-80: 2X TO 5X
*1-25/371-400 p/r 51-65: 2X TO 5X
*1-25/371-400 p/r 36-50: 2.5X TO 6X
*1-25/371-400 p/r 26-35: 3X TO 8X
*26-70 p/r 201-261: .5X TO 1.2X
*26-70 p/r 121-200: .6X TO 1.5X
*26-70 p/r 81-120: .75X TO 2X
*26-70 p/r 66-80: 1X TO 2.5X
*26-70 p/r 51-65: 1X TO 2.5X
*26-70 p/r 36-50: 1.25X TO 3X
*26-70 p/r 26-35: 1.5X TO 4X
RANDOM INSERTS IN PACKS
PRINT RUNS B/WN 1-261 COPIES PER
NO PRICING ON QTY OF 25 OR LESS

2004 Donruss All-Stars American League

STATED PRINT RUN 1000 SERIAL #'d SETS
*BLACK: .6X TO 1.5X BASIC
BLACK PRINT RUN 250 SERIAL #'d SETS
RANDOM INSERTS IN PACKS
1 Alex Rodriguez 2.00 5.00
2 Roger Clemens 2.00 5.00
3 Ichiro Suzuki 2.00 5.00
4 Barry Zito 1.00 2.50
5 Garret Anderson .60 1.50
6 Derek Jeter 4.00 10.00
7 Manny Ramirez 1.50 4.00
8 Pedro Martinez 1.00 2.50
9 Alfonso Soriano 1.00 2.50
10 Carlos Delgado .60 1.50

2004 Donruss All-Stars National League

STATED PRINT RUN 1000 SERIAL #'d SETS
*BLACK: .6X TO 1.5X BASIC
BLACK PRINT RUN 250 SERIAL #'d SETS
RANDOM INSERTS IN PACKS
1 Barry Bonds 2.50 6.00
2 Andruw Jones .60 1.50
3 Scott Rolen 1.00 2.50
4 Austin Kearns .60 1.50
5 Mark Prior 1.00 2.50
6 Vladimir Guerrero 1.00 2.50
7 Jeff Bagwell 1.00 2.50
8 Mike Piazza 1.50 4.00
9 Albert Pujols 2.00 5.00
10 Randy Johnson 1.50 4.00

2004 Donruss Bat Kings

1-4 PRINT RUN 250 SERIAL #'d SETS
5-8 PRINT RUN 100 SERIAL #'d SETS
*STUDIO 1-4: .75X TO 2X BASIC
STUDIO 1-4 PRINT RUN 50 SERIAL #'d SETS
STUDIO 5-8 PRINT RUN 25 SERIAL #'d SETS
STUDIO 5-8 NO PRICING DUE TO SCARCITY
1 Alex Rodriguez 03 8.00 20.00
2 Albert Pujols 03 10.00 25.00
3 Chipper Jones 03 6.00 15.00
4 Lance Berkman 03 4.00 10.00
5 Cal Ripken 88 20.00 50.00
6 George Brett 87 15.00 40.00
7 Don Mattingly 89 15.00 40.00
8 Roberto Clemente 02 50.00 100.00

2004 Donruss Craftsmen

STATED PRINT RUN 2000 SERIAL #'d SETS
*BLACK: 1X TO 2.5X BASIC
BLACK PRINT RUN 275 SERIAL #'d SETS
*MASTER: 1.25X TO 3X BASIC
MASTER PRINT RUN 150 SERIAL #'d SETS
RANDOM INSERTS IN PACKS
1 Alex Rodriguez 1.25 3.00
2 Mark Prior .60 1.50
3 Ichiro Suzuki 1.25 3.00
4 Barry Bonds 1.50 4.00
5 Ken Griffey Jr. 2.00 5.00
6 Alfonso Soriano .60 1.50
7 Mike Piazza 1.00 2.50
8 Chipper Jones 1.00 2.50
9 Derek Jeter 2.50 6.00
10 Randy Johnson 1.00 2.50
11 Sammy Sosa 1.00 2.50
12 Roger Clemens 1.25 3.00
13 Nomar Garciaparra .60 1.50
14 Greg Maddux 1.25 3.00
15 Albert Pujols 1.25 3.00

2004 Donruss Diamond Kings Inserts

STATED PRINT RUN 2500 SERIAL #'d SETS
*BLACK: .75X TO 2X BASIC
BLACK PRINT RUN 100 SERIAL #'d SETS
*STUDIO: .6X TO 1.5X BASIC
STUDIO PRINT RUN 250 SERIAL #'d SETS
DK1 Derek Jeter 5.00 12.00
DK2 Greg Maddux 2.50 6.00
DK3 Albert Pujols 2.50 6.00
DK4 Ichiro Suzuki 2.50 6.00
DK5 Alex Rodriguez 2.50 6.00
DK6 Roger Clemens 2.50 6.00
DK7 Andruw Jones .75 2.00
DK8 Barry Bonds 3.00 8.00
DK9 Jeff Bagwell 1.25 3.00
DK10 Randy Johnson 2.00 5.00
DK11 Scott Rolen 1.25 3.00
DK12 Lance Berkman 1.25 3.00
DK13 Barry Zito 1.25 3.00
DK14 Manny Ramirez 2.00 5.00
DK15 Carlos Delgado .75 2.00
DK16 Alfonso Soriano 1.25 3.00
DK17 Todd Helton 1.25 3.00
DK18 Mike Mussina 1.25 3.00
DK19 Austin Kearns .75 2.00
DK20 Nomar Garciaparra 1.25 3.00
DK21 Chipper Jones 2.00 5.00
DK22 Mark Prior 1.25 3.00
DK23 Jim Thome 1.25 3.00
DK24 Vladimir Guerrero 1.25 3.00
DK25 Pedro Martinez 1.25 3.00

2004 Donruss Elite Series

RANDOM INSERTS IN PACKS
STATED PRINT RUN 1500 SERIAL #'d SETS
*BLACK: 1X TO 2.5X BASIC
BLACK PRINT RUN 150 SERIAL #'d SETS
DOMINATORS PRINT 25 SERIAL #'d SETS
DOMINATORS NO PRICE DUE TO SCARCITY
1 Albert Pujols 2.00 5.00
2 Barry Zito 1.00 2.50
3 Gary Sheffield .60 1.50
4 Mike Mussina 1.00 2.50
5 Lance Berkman 1.00 2.50
6 Alfonso Soriano 1.00 2.50
7 Randy Johnson 1.50 4.00
8 Nomar Garciaparra 1.00 2.50
9 Austin Kearns .60 1.50
10 Manny Ramirez 1.50 4.00
11 Mark Prior 1.00 2.50
12 Alex Rodriguez 2.00 5.00
13 Derek Jeter 4.00 10.00
14 Barry Bonds 2.50 6.00
15 Roger Clemens 2.00 5.00

2004 Donruss Inside View

RANDOM INSERTS IN PACKS
STATED PRINT RUN 1250 SERIAL #'d SETS
1 Derek Jeter 3.00 8.00
2 Greg Maddux 1.50 4.00
3 Albert Pujols 1.50 4.00
4 Ichiro Suzuki 1.50 4.00
5 Alex Rodriguez 1.50 4.00
6 Roger Clemens 1.50 4.00
7 Andruw Jones .50 1.25
8 Barry Bonds 2.00 5.00
9 Jeff Bagwell .75 2.00
10 Randy Johnson 1.25 3.00
11 Scott Rolen .75 2.00
12 Lance Berkman .75 2.00
13 Barry Zito .75 2.00
14 Manny Ramirez 1.25 3.00
15 Carlos Delgado .50 1.25
16 Alfonso Soriano .75 2.00
17 Todd Helton .75 2.00
18 Mike Mussina .75 2.00
19 Austin Kearns .50 1.25
20 Nomar Garciaparra .75 2.00
21 Chipper Jones 1.25 3.00
22 Mark Prior .75 2.00
23 Jim Thome .75 2.00
24 Vladimir Guerrero .75 2.00
25 Pedro Martinez .75 2.00

2004 Donruss Jersey Kings

1-6 PRINT RUN 250 SERIAL #'d SETS
7-12 PRINT RUN 100 SERIAL #'d SETS
*STUDIO 1-6: .75X TO 2X BASIC JSY KINGS
STUDIO 1-6 PRINT RUN 50 SERIAL #'d SETS
STUDIO 7-12 PRINT RUN 25 SERIAL #'d SETS
STUDIO 7-12 NO PRICING DUE TO SCARCITY
1 Alfonso Soriano 03 2.00 5.00
2 Sammy Sosa 03 3.00 8.00
3 Roger Clemens 03 4.00 10.00
4 Nomar Garciaparra 03 2.00 5.00
5 Mark Prior 03 2.00 5.00
6 Vladimir Guerrero 03 2.00 5.00
7 Don Mattingly 89 6.00 15.00
8 Roberto Clemente 02 40.00 100.00
9 George Brett 87 6.00 15.00
10 Nolan Ryan 01 10.00 25.00
11 Cal Ripken 01 15.00 40.00
12 Mike Schmidt 01 5.00 12.00

2004 Donruss Longball Leaders

STATED PRINT RUN 1500 SERIAL #'d SETS
*BLACK: .75X TO 2X BASIC LL
BLACK PRINT RUN 250 SERIAL #'d SETS
*DIE CUT: 1.25X TO 3X BASIC LL
DIE CUT PRINT RUN 50 SERIAL #'d SETS
1 Barry Bonds 2.00 5.00
2 Alfonso Soriano .75 2.00
3 Adam Dunn .75 2.00
4 Alex Rodriguez 1.50 4.00
5 Jim Thome .75 2.00
6 Garret Anderson .50 1.25
7 Juan Gonzalez .50 1.25
8 Jeff Bagwell .75 2.00
9 Gary Sheffield .50 1.25
10 Sammy Sosa 1.25 3.00

2004 Donruss Mound Marvels

STATED PRINT RUN 750 SERIAL #'d SETS
*BLACK: .75X TO 2X BASIC MM
BLACK PRINT RUN 175 SERIAL #'d SETS
RANDOM INSERTS IN PACKS
1 Mark Prior 1.25 3.00
2 Curt Schilling 1.25 3.00
3 Mike Mussina 1.25 3.00
4 Kevin Brown .75 2.00
5 Pedro Martinez 1.25 3.00
6 Mark Mulder .75 2.00
7 Kerry Wood .75 2.00
8 Greg Maddux 2.50 6.00
9 Kevin Millwood .75 2.00
10 Barry Zito 1.25 3.00
11 Roger Clemens 2.50 6.00
12 Randy Johnson 2.00 5.00
13 Hideo Nomo 2.00 5.00
14 Tim Hudson 1.25 3.00
15 Tom Glavine 1.25 3.00

2004 Donruss Power Alley Red

STATED PRINT RUN 2500 SERIAL #'d SETS
BLACK DC PRINT RUN 1 SERIAL #'d SET
BLACK DC NO PRICING DUE TO SCARCITY
*BLUE: .6X TO 1.5X BASIC RED
BLUE PRINT RUN 1000 SERIAL #'d SETS
*BLUE DC: 1.25X TO 3X BASIC RED
BLUE DC PRINT RUN 100 SERIAL #'d SETS
GREEN PRINT RUN 25 SERIAL #'d SETS
GREEN NO PRICING DUE TO SCARCITY
GREEN DC 5 SERIAL #'d SETS
GREEN DC NO PRICING DUE TO SCARCITY
*PURPLE: 1X TO 2.5X BASIC RED
PURPLE PRINT RUN 250 SERIAL #'d SETS
PURPLE DC PRINT RUN 25 SERIAL #'d SETS
PURPLE DC NO PRICING DUE TO SCARCITY
*RED DC: 1X TO 2.5X BASIC RED
RED DC PRINT RUN 250 SERIAL #'d SETS
*YELLOW: 1.25X TO 3X BASIC RED
YELLOW PRINT RUN 100 SERIAL #'d SETS
YELLOW DC PRINT RUN 10 SERIAL #'d SETS
YELLOW DC NO PRICING DUE TO SCARCITY
1 Albert Pujols 1.25 3.00
2 Mike Piazza 1.00 2.50
3 Carlos Delgado .40 1.00
4 Barry Bonds 1.50 4.00
5 Jim Edmonds .60 1.50
6 Nomar Garciaparra .60 1.50
7 Alfonso Soriano .60 1.50
8 Alex Rodriguez 1.25 3.00
9 Lance Berkman .60 1.50
10 Scott Rolen .60 1.50
11 Manny Ramirez 1.00 2.50
12 Rafael Palmeiro .60 1.50
13 Sammy Sosa 1.00 2.50
14 Adam Dunn .60 1.50
15 Andruw Jones .40 1.00
16 Jim Thome .60 1.50
17 Jason Giambi .40 1.00
18 Jeff Bagwell .60 1.50
19 Juan Gonzalez .40 1.00
20 Austin Kearns .40 1.00

2004 Donruss Production Line Average

PRINT RUNS B/WN 300-359 COPIES PER
*BLACK: .75X TO 2X BASIC AVG
BLACK PRINT RUN 35 SERIAL #'d SETS
*DIE CUT: .5X TO 1.2X BASIC AVG
DIE CUT PRINT RUN 100 SERIAL #'d SETS
1 Gary Sheffield/330 1.00 2.50
2 Ichiro Suzuki/312 3.00 8.00
3 Todd Helton/358 1.50 4.00
4 Manny Ramirez/325 2.50 6.00
5 Garret Anderson/315 1.00 2.50
6 Barry Bonds/341 4.00 10.00
7 Albert Pujols/359 3.00 8.00
8 Derek Jeter/324 6.00 15.00
9 Nomar Garciaparra/301 1.50 4.00
10 Hank Blalock/300 1.00 2.50

2004 Donruss Production Line OBP

PRINT RUNS B/WN 396-529 COPIES PER
*BLACK: 1X TO 2.5X BASIC OBP
BLACK PRINT RUN 40 SERIAL #'d SETS
*DIE CUT: .6X TO 1.5X BASIC OBP
DIE CUT PRINT RUN 100 SERIAL #'d SETS
1 Todd Helton/458 1.25 3.00
2 Albert Pujols/439 2.50 6.00
3 Larry Walker/422 1.25 3.00
4 Barry Bonds/529 3.00 8.00
5 Chipper Jones/402 2.00 5.00
6 Manny Ramirez/427 2.00 5.00
7 Gary Sheffield/419 .75 2.00
8 Lance Berkman/412 1.25 3.00
9 Alex Rodriguez/396 2.50 6.00
10 Jason Giambi/412 .75 2.00

2004 Donruss Production Line OPS

PRINT RUNS B/WN 910-1278 COPIES PER
*BLACK: .75X TO 2X BASIC OPS
BLACK PRINT RUN 125 SERIAL #'d SETS
*DIE CUT: .75X TO 2X BASIC OPS
DIE CUT PRINT RUN 100 SERIAL #'d SETS
1 Albert Pujols/1106 2.00 5.00
2 Barry Bonds/1278 2.50 6.00
3 Gary Sheffield/1023 .60 1.50
4 Todd Helton/1088 1.00 2.50
5 Scott Rolen/910 1.00 2.50
6 Manny Ramirez/1014 1.50 4.00
7 Alex Rodriguez/995 2.00 5.00
8 Jim Thome/958 1.00 2.50
9 Jason Giambi/939 .60 1.50
10 Frank Thomas/952 1.50 4.00

2004 Donruss Production Line Slugging

PRINT RUNS B/WN 541-749 COPIES PER
*BLACK: .75X TO 2X BASIC SLG
BLACK PRINT RUN 75 SERIAL #'d SETS
*DIE CUT: .6X TO 1.5X BASIC SLG
DIE CUT PRINT RUN 100 SERIAL #'d SETS
1 Alex Rodriguez/600 2.50 6.00
2 Frank Thomas/562 2.00 5.00
3 Garret Anderson/541 .75 2.00
4 Albert Pujols/667 2.50 6.00
5 Sammy Sosa/553 2.00 5.00
6 Gary Sheffield/604 .75 2.00
7 Manny Ramirez/587 2.00 5.00
8 Jim Edmonds/617 1.25 3.00
9 Barry Bonds/749 3.00 8.00
10 Todd Helton/630 1.25 3.00

2004 Donruss Recollection Autographs

PRINT RUNS B/WN 1-100 COPIES PER
NO PRICING ON QTY OF 50 OR LESS
27 John Candelaria 88 Black/83 6.00 15.00
39 Jack Clark 87/67 8.00 20.00
40 Jack Clark 88/75 6.00 15.00
69 Sid Fernandez 86/52 8.00 20.00
72 Sid Fernandez 88/58 8.00 20.00
83 George Foster 83/50 8.00 20.00
84 George Foster 84/70 8.00 20.00
85 George Foster 85/50 8.00 20.00
86 George Foster 86/83 6.00 15.00
91 Cliff Lee 03/100 8.00 20.00
92 Terrence Long 01/90 4.00 10.00
93 Melvin Mora 03/50 8.00 20.00
100 Jesse Orosco 86 Blue/65 5.00 12.00
102 Jesse Orosco 87 Blue/90 4.00 10.00
115 Jose Vidro 01/89 4.00 10.00

2004 Donruss Timber and Threads

STATED ODDS 1:40
*STUDIO: .75X TO 2X BASIC TT
STUDIO RANDOM INSERTS IN PACKS
STUDIO PRINT RUN 50 SERIAL #'d SETS
1 Adam Dunn Jsy 3.00 8.00
2 Alex Rodriguez Blue Jsy 6.00 15.00
3 Alex Rodriguez White Jsy 6.00 15.00
4 Andruw Jones Jsy 4.00 10.00
5 Austin Kearns Jsy 3.00 8.00
6 Carlos Beltran Jsy 3.00 8.00
7 Carlos Lee Jsy 3.00 8.00
8 Frank Thomas Jsy 4.00 10.00
9 Greg Maddux Jsy 4.00 10.00
10 Hideo Nomo Jsy 4.00 10.00
11 Jeff Bagwell Jsy 4.00 10.00
12 Lance Berkman Jsy 3.00 8.00
13 Magglio Ordonez Jsy 3.00 8.00
14 Mike Sweeney Jsy 3.00 8.00
15 Randy Johnson Jsy 4.00 10.00
16 Rocco Baldelli Jsy 3.00 8.00
17 Roger Clemens Jsy 6.00 15.00
18 Sammy Sosa Jsy 4.00 10.00
19 Shawn Green Jsy 3.00 8.00
20 Tom Glavine Jsy 4.00 10.00
21 Adam Dunn Bat 3.00 8.00
22 Andruw Jones Bat 4.00 10.00
23 Bobby Abreu Bat 3.00 8.00
24 Hank Blalock Bat 3.00 8.00
25 Ivan Rodriguez Bat 4.00 10.00
26 Jim Edmonds Bat 3.00 8.00
27 Josh Phelps Bat 3.00 8.00
28 Juan Gonzalez Bat 3.00 8.00
29 Lance Berkman Bat 3.00 8.00
30 Larry Walker Bat 3.00 8.00
31 Magglio Ordonez Bat 3.00 8.00
32 Manny Ramirez Bat 4.00 10.00
33 Mike Piazza Bat 4.00 10.00
34 Nomar Garciaparra Bat 6.00 15.00
35 Paul Lo Duca Bat 3.00 8.00
36 Roberto Alomar Bat 4.00 10.00
37 Rocco Baldelli Bat 3.00 8.00
38 Sammy Sosa Bat 4.00 10.00
39 Vernon Wells Bat 3.00 8.00
40 Vladimir Guerrero Bat 4.00 10.00

2004 Donruss Timber and Threads Autographs

RANDOM INSERTS IN PACKS
PRINT RUNS B/WN 5-50 COPIES PER
NO PRICING ON QTY OF 34 OR LESS
23 Bobby Abreu Bat/50 10.00 25.00
24 Hank Blalock Bat/50 10.00 25.00
27 Josh Phelps Bat/50 10.00 25.00
35 Paul Lo Duca Bat/50 10.00 25.00
40 Vladimir Guerrero Bat/50 30.00 60.00

2004 Donruss-Playoff Hawaii Fans of the Game Gandolfini

FG1 James Gandolfini/300

2005 Donruss

COMPLETE SET (400) 40.00 100.00
COMP.SET w/o SP's (300) 10.00 25.00
COMMON CARD (71-370) .10 .30
COMMON (1-25/371-400) .40 1.00
COMMON CARD (26-70) .75 2.00
1-25 STATED ODDS 1:6
26-70 STATED ODDS 1:6
371-400 STATED ODDS 1:6
1 Garret Anderson DK .40 1.00
2 Vladimir Guerrero DK .60 1.50
3 Manny Ramirez DK 1.00 2.50
4 Kerry Wood DK .40 1.00
5 Sammy Sosa DK 1.00 2.50
6 Magglio Ordonez DK .60 1.50
7 Adam Dunn DK .60 1.50
8 Todd Helton DK .60 1.50
9 Josh Beckett DK .40 1.00
10 Miguel Cabrera DK 1.00 2.50
11 Lance Berkman DK .60 1.50
12 Carlos Beltran DK .60 1.50
13 Shawn Green DK .40 1.00
14 Roger Clemens DK 1.25 3.00
15 Mike Piazza DK 1.00 2.50
16 Alex Rodriguez DK 1.25 3.00
17 Derek Jeter DK 2.50 6.00
18 Mark Mulder DK .40 1.00
19 Jim Thome DK .60 1.50
20 Albert Pujols DK 1.25 3.00
21 Scott Rolen DK .60 1.50
22 Aubrey Huff DK .40 1.00
23 Alfonso Soriano DK .60 1.50
24 Hank Blalock DK .40 1.00
25 Vernon Wells DK .40 1.00
26 Kazuo Matsui RR .75 2.00
27 B.J. Upton RR 1.25 3.00
28 Charles Thomas RR .75 2.00
29 Akinori Otsuka RR .75 2.00
30 David Aardsma RR .75 2.00
31 Travis Blackley RR .75 2.00
32 Brad Halsey RR .75 2.00
33 David Wright RR 1.50 4.00
34 Kazuhito Tadano RR .75 2.00
35 Casey Kotchman RR .75 2.00
36 Khalil Greene RR .75 2.00
37 Adrian Gonzalez RR 1.50 4.00
38 Zack Greinke RR 2.50 6.00
39 Chad Cordero RR .75 2.00
40 Scott Kazmir RR 2.00 5.00
41 Jeremy Guthrie RR 1.25 3.00
42 Noah Lowry RR .75 2.00
43 Chase Utley RR 1.25 3.00
44 Billy Traber RR .75 2.00
45 Aarom Baldiris RR .75 2.00
46 Abe Alvarez RR .75 2.00
47 Angel Chavez RR .75 2.00
48 Joe Mauer RR 1.50 4.00
49 Joey Gathright RR .75 2.00
50 John Gall RR .75 2.00
51 Ronald Belisario RR .75 2.00
52 Ryan Wing RR .75 2.00
53 Scott Proctor RR .75 2.00
54 Yadier Molina RR 15.00 40.00
55 Carlos Hines RR .75 2.00
56 Frankie Francisco RR .75 2.00
57 Graham Koonce RR .75 2.00
58 Jake Woods RR .75 2.00
59 Jason Bartlett RR .75 2.00
60 Mike Rouse RR .75 2.00
61 Phil Stockman RR .75 2.00
62 Renyel Pinto RR .75 2.00
63 Roberto Novoa RR .75 2.00
64 Ryan Meaux RR .75 2.00
65 Dave Crouthers RR .75 2.00
66 Justin Knoedler RR .75 2.00
67 Justin Leone RR .75 2.00
68 Nick Regilio RR .75 2.00
69 Mike Gosling RR .75 2.00
70 Onil Joseph RR .75 2.00
71 Bartolo Colon .12 .30
72 Brad Fullmer .12 .30
73 Chone Figgins .12 .30
74 Darin Erstad .12 .30
75 Francisco Rodriguez .20 .50
76 Garret Anderson .12 .30
77 Jarrod Washburn .12 .30
78 John Lackey .20 .50
79 Jose Guillen .12 .30
80 Robb Quinlan .12 .30
81 Tim Salmon .12 .30
82 Troy Glaus .12 .30
83 Troy Percival .12 .30
84 Vladimir Guerrero .20 .50
85 Brandon Webb .20 .50
86 Casey Fossum .12 .30
87 Luis Gonzalez .12 .30
88 Randy Johnson .30 .75
89 Richie Sexson .12 .30
90 Robby Hammock .12 .30
91 Roberto Alomar .20 .50
92 Adam LaRoche .12 .30
93 Andruw Jones .12 .30
94 Bubba Nelson .12 .30
95 Chipper Jones .30 .75
96 J.D. Drew .12 .30
97 John Smoltz .30 .75
98 Johnny Estrada .12 .30
99 Marcus Giles .12 .30
100 Mike Hampton .12 .30
101 Nick Green .12 .30
102 Rafael Furcal .12 .30
103 Russ Ortiz .12 .30
104 Adam Loewen .12 .30
105 Brian Roberts .12 .30
106 Javy Lopez .12 .30
107 Jay Gibbons .12 .30
108 L.Bigbie UER Roberts .12 .30
109 Luis Matos .12 .30
110 Melvin Mora .12 .30
111 Miguel Tejada .20 .50
112 Rafael Palmeiro .20 .50
113 Rodrigo Lopez .12 .30
114 Sidney Ponson .12 .30
115 Bill Mueller .12 .30
116 Byung-Hyun Kim .12 .30
117 Curt Schilling .20 .50
118 David Ortiz .30 .75
119 Derek Lowe .12 .30
120 Doug Mientkiewicz .12 .30
121 Jason Varitek .30 .75
122 Johnny Damon .20 .50
123 Keith Foulke .12 .30
124 Kevin Youkilis .12 .30
125 Manny Ramirez .30 .75
126 Orlando Cabrera .12 .30
127 Pedro Martinez .20 .50
128 Trot Nixon .12 .30
129 Aramis Ramirez .12 .30
130 Carlos Zambrano .20 .50
131 Corey Patterson .12 .30
132 Derrek Lee .12 .30
133 Greg Maddux .40 1.00
134 Kerry Wood .12 .30
135 Mark Prior .20 .50
136 Matt Clement .12 .30
137 Moises Alou .12 .30
138 Nomar Garciaparra .20 .50
139 Sammy Sosa .30 .75
140 Todd Walker .12 .30
141 Angel Guzman .12 .30
142 Billy Koch .12 .30
143 Carlos Lee .12 .30
144 Frank Thomas .30 .75
145 Maggio Ordonez .20 .50
146 Mark Buehrle .20 .50
147 Paul Konerko .20 .50
148 Wilson Valdez .12 .30
149 Adam Dunn .20 .50
150 Austin Kearns .12 .30
151 Barry Larkin .20 .50
152 Benito Santiago .12 .30
153 Jason LaRue .12 .30
154 Ken Griffey Jr. .60 1.50
155 Ryan Wagner .12 .30
156 Sean Casey .12 .30
157 Brandon Phillips .12 .30
158 Brian Tallet .12 .30
159 C.C. Sabathia .20 .50
160 Cliff Lee .20 .50
161 Jeremy Guthrie .20 .50
162 Jody Gerut .12 .30
163 Matt Lawton .12 .30
164 Omar Vizquel .20 .50
165 Travis Hafner .12 .30
166 Victor Martinez .20 .50
167 Charles Johnson .12 .30
168 Garrett Atkins .12 .30
169 Jason Jennings .12 .30
170 Jay Payton .12 .30
171 Jeromy Burnitz .12 .30
172 Joe Kennedy .12 .30
173 Larry Walker .20 .50
174 Preston Wilson .12 .30
175 Todd Helton .20 .50
176 Vinny Castilla .12 .30
177 Bobby Higginson .12 .30
178 Brandon Inge .12 .30
179 Carlos Guillen .12 .30
180 Carlos Pena .20 .50
181 Craig Monroe .12 .30
182 Dmitri Young .12 .30
183 Eric Munson .12 .30
184 Fernando Vina .12 .30
185 Ivan Rodriguez .20 .50
186 Jeremy Bonderman .12 .30
187 Rondell White .12 .30
188 A.J. Burnett .12 .30
189 Dontrelle Willis .12 .30
190 Guillermo Mota .12 .30
191 Hee Seop Choi .12 .30
192 Jeff Conine .12 .30
193 Josh Beckett .12 .30
194 Juan Encarnacion .12 .30
195 Juan Pierre .12 .30
196 Luis Castillo .12 .30
197 Miguel Cabrera .30 .75
198 Mike Lowell .12 .30
199 Paul Lo Duca .12 .30
200 Andy Pettitte .20 .50
201 Brad Ausmus .12 .30
202 Carlos Beltran .20 .50
203 Chris Burke .12 .30
204 Craig Biggio .20 .50
205 Jeff Bagwell .20 .50
206 Jeff Kent .12 .30

207 Lance Berkman .20 .50
208 Morgan Ensberg .12 .30
209 Octavio Dotel .12 .30
210 Roger Clemens .40 1.00
211 Roy Oswalt .20 .50
212 Tim Redding .12 .30
213 Angel Berroa .12 .30
214 Juan Gonzalez .12 .30
215 Ken Harvey .12 .30
216 Mike Sweeney .12 .30
217 Adrian Beltre .30 .75
218 Brad Penny .12 .30
219 Eric Gagne .12 .30
220 Hideo Nomo .30 .75
221 Hong-Chih Kuo .12 .30
222 Jeff Weaver .12 .30
223 Kazuhisa Ishii .12 .30
224 Milton Bradley .12 .30
225 Shawn Green .12 .30
226 Steve Finley .12 .30
227 Danny Kolb .12 .30
228 Geoff Jenkins .12 .30
229 Junior Spivey .12 .30
230 Lyle Overbay .12 .30
231 Rickie Weeks .12 .30
232 Scott Podsednik .12 .30
233 Brad Radke .12 .30
234 Corey Koskie .12 .30
235 Cristian Guzman .12 .30
236 Dustan Mohr .12 .30
237 Eddie Guardado .12 .30
238 J.D. Durbin .12 .30
239 Jacque Jones .12 .30
240 Joe Nathan .12 .30
241 Johan Santana .20 .50
242 Lew Ford .12 .30
243 Michael Cuddyer .12 .30
244 Shannon Stewart .12 .30
245 Torii Hunter .12 .30
246 Brad Wilkerson .12 .30
247 Carl Everett .12 .30
248 Jeff Fassero .12 .30
249 Jose Vidro .12 .30
250 Livan Hernandez .12 .30
251 Michael Barrett .12 .30
252 Tony Batista .12 .30
253 Zach Day .12 .30
254 Al Leiter .12 .30
255 Cliff Floyd .12 .30
256 Jae Weong Seo .12 .30
257 John Olerud .12 .30
258 Jose Reyes .20 .50
259 Mike Cameron .12 .30
260 Mike Piazza .30 .75
261 Richard Hidalgo .12 .30
262 Tom Glavine .20 .50
263 Vance Wilson .12 .30
264 Alex Rodriguez .40 1.00
265 Armando Benitez .12 .30
266 Bernie Williams .20 .50
267 Bubba Crosby .12 .30
268 Chien-Ming Wang .50 1.25
269 Derek Jeter .75 2.00
270 Esteban Loaiza .12 .30
271 Gary Sheffield .12 .30
272 Hideki Matsui .50 1.25
273 Jason Giambi .12 .30
274 Javier Vazquez .12 .30
275 Jorge Posada .20 .50
276 Jose Contreras .12 .30
277 Kenny Lofton .12 .30
278 Kevin Brown .12 .30
279 Mariano Rivera .40 1.00
280 Mike Mussina .20 .50
281 Barry Zito .20 .50
282 Bobby Crosby .12 .30
283 Eric Byrnes .12 .30
284 Eric Chavez .12 .30
285 Erubiel Durazo .12 .30
286 Jermaine Dye .12 .30
287 Mark Kotsay .12 .30
288 Mark Mulder .12 .30
289 Rich Harden .12 .30
290 Tim Hudson .20 .50
291 Billy Wagner .12 .30
292 Bobby Abreu .12 .30
293 Brett Myers .12 .30
294 Eric Milton .12 .30
295 Jim Thome .20 .50
296 Jimmy Rollins .20 .50
297 Kevin Millwood .12 .30
298 Marlon Byrd .12 .30
299 Mike Lieberthal .12 .30
300 Pat Burrell .12 .30
301 Randy Wolf .12 .30
302 Craig Wilson .12 .30
303 Jack Wilson .12 .30
304 Jacob Cruz .12 .30
305 Jason Bay .12 .30
306 Jason Kendall .12 .30
307 Jose Castillo .12 .30
308 Kip Wells .12 .30
309 Brian Giles .12 .30
310 Brian Lawrence .12 .30
311 Chris Oxspring .12 .30
312 David Wells .12 .30
313 Freddy Guzman .12 .30
314 Jake Peavy .12 .30
315 Mark Loretta .12 .30
316 Ryan Klesko .12 .30
317 Sean Burroughs .12 .30
318 Trevor Hoffman .20 .50
319 Xavier Nady .12 .30
320 A.J. Pierzynski .12 .30
321 Edgardo Alfonzo .12 .30
322 J.T. Snow .12 .30
323 Jason Schmidt .12 .30
324 Jerome Williams .12 .30
325 Kirk Rueter .12 .30
326 Bret Boone .12 .30
327 Bucky Jacobsen .12 .30
328 Edgar Martinez .20 .50
329 Freddy Garcia .12 .30
330 Ichiro Suzuki .40 1.00
331 Jamie Moyer .12 .30
332 Joel Pineiro .12 .30
333 Scott Spiezio .12 .30
334 Shigetoshi Hasegawa .12 .30
335 Albert Pujols .40 1.00
336 Edgar Renteria .12 .30
337 Jason Isringhausen .12 .30
338 Jim Edmonds .20 .50
339 Matt Morris .12 .30
340 Mike Matheny .12 .30
341 Reggie Sanders .12 .30
342 Scott Rolen .20 .50
343 Woody Williams .12 .30
344 Jeff Suppan .12 .30
345 Aubrey Huff .12 .30
346 Carl Crawford .20 .50
347 Chad Gaudin .12 .30
348 Delmon Young .30 .75
349 Dewon Brazelton .12 .30
350 Jose Cruz Jr. .12 .30
351 Rocco Baldelli .12 .30
352 Tino Martinez .20 .50
353 Toby Hall .12 .30
354 Alfonso Soriano .20 .50
355 Brian Jordan .12 .30
356 Francisco Cordero .12 .30
357 Hank Blalock .12 .30
358 Kenny Rogers .12 .30
359 Kevin Mench .12 .30
360 Laynce Nix .12 .30
361 Mark Teixeira .20 .50
362 Michael Young .12 .30
363 Alex S. Gonzalez .12 .30
364 Alexis Rios .12 .30
365 Carlos Delgado .12 .30
366 Eric Hinske .12 .30
367 Frank Catalanotto .12 .30
368 Josh Phelps .12 .30
369 Roy Halladay .20 .50
370 Vernon Wells .12 .30
371 Vladimir Guerrero TC .60 1.50
372 Randy Johnson TC 1.00 2.50
373 Chipper Jones TC 1.00 2.50
374 Miguel Tejada TC .60 1.50
375 Pedro Martinez TC .60 1.50
376 Sammy Sosa TC 1.00 2.50
377 Frank Thomas TC 1.00 2.50
378 Ken Griffey Jr. TC 2.00 5.00
379 Victor Martinez TC .60 1.50
380 Todd Helton TC .60 1.50
381 Ivan Rodriguez TC .60 1.50
382 Miguel Cabrera TC 1.00 2.50
383 Roger Clemens TC 1.25 3.00
384 Ken Harvey TC .40 1.00
385 Eric Gagne TC .40 1.00
386 Lyle Overbay TC .40 1.00
387 Shannon Stewart TC .40 1.00
388 Brad Wilkerson TC .40 1.00
389 Mike Piazza TC 1.00 2.50
390 Alex Rodriguez TC 1.25 3.00
391 Mark Mulder TC .40 1.00
392 Jim Thome TC .60 1.50
393 Jack Wilson TC .40 1.00
394 Khalil Greene TC .40 1.00
395 Jason Schmidt TC .40 1.00
396 Ichiro Suzuki TC 1.25 3.00
397 Albert Pujols TC 1.25 3.00
398 Rocco Baldelli TC .40 1.00
399 Alfonso Soriano TC .60 1.50
400 Vernon Wells TC .40 1.00

2005 Donruss 25th Anniversary

*25th ANN 71-370: 10X TO 25X BASIC
*25th ANN 1-25/371-400: 4X TO 10X BASIC
*25th ANN 26-70: 2X TO 5X BASIC
RANDOM INSERTS IN PACKS
STATED PRINT RUN 25 SERIAL #'d SETS

2005 Donruss Press Proofs Black

STATED PRINT RUN 10 SERIAL #'d SETS
NO PRICING DUE TO SCARCITY

2005 Donruss Press Proofs Blue

*BLUE 71-370: 4X TO 10X BASIC
*BLUE 1-25/371-400: 1.5X TO 4X BASIC
*BLUE 26-70: .75X TO 2X BASIC
RANDOM INSERTS IN PACKS
STATED PRINT RUN 100 SERIAL #'d SETS

2005 Donruss Press Proofs Gold

*GOLD 71-370: 10X TO 25X BASIC
*GOLD 1-25/371-400: 4X TO 10X BASIC
*GOLD 26-70: 2X TO 5X BASIC
RANDOM INSERTS IN PACKS
STATED PRINT RUN 25 SERIAL #'d SETS

2005 Donruss Press Proofs Red

*RED 71-370: 2.5X TO 6X BASIC
*RED 1-25/371-400: 1X TO 2.5X BASIC
*RED 26-70: .5X TO 1.2X BASIC
RANDOM INSERTS IN PACKS
STATED PRINT RUN 200 SERIAL #'d SETS

2005 Donruss Stat Line Career

*71-370 p/r 200-394 2.5X TO 6X
*71-370 p/r 121-200: 3X TO 8X
*71-370 p/r 81-120: 4X TO 10X
*71-370 p/r 51-80: 5X TO 12X
*71-370 p/r 36-50: 6X TO 15X
*71-370 p/r 26-35: 8X TO 20X
*71-370 p/r 16-25: 10X TO 25X
*1-25/371-400 p/r 200-574:1X TO 2.5X
*1-25/371-400 p/r 121-200: 1.25X TO 3X
*1-25/371-400 p/r 81-120: 1.5X TO 4X
*1-25/371-400 p/r 51-80: 2X TO 5X
*1-25/371-400 p/r 36-50: 2.5X TO 6X
*1-25/371-400 p/r 26-35: 3X TO 8X
*26-70 p/r 200-263: .5X TO 1.2X
*26-70 p/r 121-200: .6X TO 1.5X
*26-70 p/r 81-120: .75X TO 2X
*26-70 p/r 51-80: 1X TO 2.5X
*26-70 p/r 36-50: 1.25X TO 3X
*26-70 p/r 26-35: 1.5X TO 4X
*26-70 p/r 16-25: 2X TO 5X
RANDOM INSERTS IN PACKS
PRINT RUNS B/WN 6-500 COPIES PER
NO PRICING ON QTY OF 15 OR LESS

2005 Donruss Stat Line Season

*71-370 p/r 121-158: 3X TO 8X
*71-370 p/r 81-120: 4X TO 10X
*71-370 p/r 51-80: 5X TO 12X
*71-370 p/r 36-50: 6X TO 15X
*71-370 p/r 26-35: 8X TO 20X
*71-370 p/r 16-25: 10X TO 25X
*1-25/371-400 p/r 81-120: 1.5X TO 4X
*1-25/371-400 p/r 51-80: 2X TO 5X
*1-25/371-400 p/r 36-50: 2.5X TO 6X
*1-25/371-400 p/r 26-35: 3X TO 8X
*1-25/371-400 p/r 16-25: 4X TO 10X
*26-70 p/r 121-200: .6X TO 1.5X
*26-70 p/r 81-120: .75X TO 2X
*26-70 p/r 51-80: 1X TO 2.5X
*26-70 p/r 36-50: 1.25X TO 3X
*26-70 p/r 26-35: 1.5X TO 4X
*26-70 p/r 16-25: 2X TO 5X
RANDOM INSERTS IN PACKS
PRINT RUNS B/WN 1-158 COPIES PER
NO PRICING ON QTY OF 15 OR LESS

2005 Donruss Autographs

RANDOM INSERTS IN PACKS
80 Robb Quinlan 4.00 10.00
101 Nick Green 4.00 10.00
141 Angel Guzman 4.00 10.00
148 Wilson Valdez 4.00 10.00
172 Joe Kennedy 4.00 10.00
178 Brandon Inge 6.00 15.00
181 Craig Monroe 4.00 10.00
263 Vance Wilson 4.00 10.00
304 Jacob Cruz 4.00 10.00
327 Bucky Jacobsen 4.00 10.00
344 Jeff Suppan 6.00 15.00

2005 Donruss '85 Reprints

RANDOM INSERTS IN PACKS
STATED PRINT RUN 1985 SERIAL #'d SETS
1 Eddie Murray 1.25 3.00
2 George Brett 4.00 10.00
3 Nolan Ryan 6.00 15.00
4 Mike Schmidt 3.00 8.00
5 Tony Gwynn 2.50 6.00
7 Cal Ripken 6.00 15.00
8 Dwight Gooden .75 2.00
9 Roger Clemens 2.50 6.00
10 Don Mattingly 4.00 10.00
11 Kirby Puckett 2.00 5.00
12 Orel Hershiser .75 2.00

2005 Donruss '85 Reprints Material

RANDOM INSERTS IN PACKS
STATED PRINT RUN 85 SERIAL #'d SETS
1 Eddie Murray Jsy 10.00 25.00
2 George Brett Jsy 15.00 40.00
3 Nolan Ryan Jkt 15.00 40.00
4 Mike Schmidt Jkt 15.00 40.00
5 Tony Gwynn Jsy 10.00 25.00
7 Cal Ripken Jsy 30.00 60.00
8 Dwight Gooden Jsy 6.00 15.00
9 Roger Clemens Jsy 15.00 40.00
10 Don Mattingly Jsy 15.00 40.00
11 Kirby Puckett Jsy 10.00 25.00
12 Orel Hershiser Jsy 6.00 15.00

2005 Donruss All-Stars AL

STATED PRINT RUN 1000 SERIAL #'d SETS
*GOLD: .75X TO 2X BASIC
GOLD PRINT RUN 100 SERIAL #'d SETS
RANDOM INSERTS IN PACKS
1 Alex Rodriguez 2.50 6.00
2 Alfonso Soriano 1.25 3.00
3 Curt Schilling 1.25 3.00
4 Derek Jeter 5.00 12.00
5 Hank Blalock .75 2.00
6 Hideki Matsui 3.00 8.00
7 Ichiro Suzuki 2.50 6.00
8 Ivan Rodriguez 1.25 3.00
9 Jason Giambi .75 2.00
10 Manny Ramirez 2.00 5.00
11 Mark Mulder .75 2.00
12 Michael Young .75 2.00
13 Tim Hudson 1.25 3.00
14 Victor Martinez 1.25 3.00
15 Vladimir Guerrero 1.25 3.00

2005 Donruss All-Stars NL

STATED PRINT RUN 1000 SERIAL #'d SETS
*GOLD: .75X TO 2X BASIC
GOLD PRINT RUN 100 SERIAL #'d SETS
RANDOM INSERTS IN PACKS
1 Albert Pujols 2.50 6.00
2 Ben Sheets .75 2.00
3 Edgar Renteria .75 2.00
4 Eric Gagne .75 2.00
5 Jack Wilson .75 2.00
6 Jason Schmidt .75 2.00
7 Jeff Kent .75 2.00
8 Jim Thome 1.25 3.00
9 Ken Griffey Jr. 4.00 10.00
10 Mike Piazza 2.00 5.00
11 Roger Clemens 2.50 6.00
12 Sammy Sosa 2.00 5.00
13 Scott Rolen 1.25 3.00
14 Sean Casey .75 2.00
15 Todd Helton 1.25 3.00

2005 Donruss Bat Kings

RANDOM INSERTS IN PACKS
PRINT RUNS B/WN 100-250 COPIES PER
1 Garret Anderson/250 3.00 8.00
2 Vladimir Guerrero/250 4.00 10.00
3 Cal Ripken/100 30.00 60.00
4 Manny Ramirez/250 4.00 10.00
5 Kerry Wood/250 3.00 8.00
6 Sammy Sosa/250 4.00 10.00
7 Magglio Ordonez/250 3.00 8.00
8 Adam Dunn/250 3.00 8.00
9 Todd Helton/250 4.00 10.00
10 Josh Beckett/250 3.00 8.00
11 Miguel Cabrera/250 4.00 10.00
12 Lance Berkman/250 3.00 8.00
13 Carlos Beltran/250 3.00 8.00
14 Shawn Green/250 3.00 8.00
15 Roger Clemens/100 8.00 20.00
16 Mike Piazza/250 4.00 10.00
17 Nolan Ryan/100 8.00 20.00
18 Mark Mulder/250 3.00 8.00
19 Jim Thome/250 4.00 10.00
20 Albert Pujols/250 8.00 20.00
21 Scott Rolen/250 4.00 10.00
22 Aubrey Huff/250 3.00 8.00
23 Alfonso Soriano/250 3.00 8.00

2005 Donruss Bat Kings Signatures

PRINT RUNS B/WN 5-10 COPIES PER
NO PRICING DUE TO SCARCITY

2005 Donruss Craftsmen

STATED PRINT RUN 2000 SERIAL #'d SETS
*BLACK: 1.25X TO 3X BASIC
BLACK PRINT RUN 100 SERIAL #'d SETS
*MASTER: 1X TO 2.5X BASIC
MASTER PRINT RUN 250 SERIAL #'d SETS
MASTER BLACK PRINT RUN 10 #'d SETS
NO MASTER BLACK PRICING AVAILABLE
RANDOM INSERTS IN PACKS
1 Albert Pujols 1.25 3.00
2 Alex Rodriguez 1.25 3.00
3 Alfonso Soriano .60 1.50
4 Andruw Jones .40 1.00
5 Carlos Beltran .60 1.50
6 Derek Jeter 2.50 6.00
7 Greg Maddux 1.25 3.00
8 Hank Blalock .40 1.00
9 Ichiro Suzuki 1.25 3.00
10 Jeff Bagwell .60 1.50
11 Jim Thome .60 1.50
12 Josh Beckett .40 1.00
13 Ken Griffey Jr. 2.00 5.00
14 Manny Ramirez 1.00 2.50
15 Mark Mulder .40 1.00
16 Mark Prior .60 1.50
17 Mark Teixeira .60 1.50
18 Miguel Tejada .60 1.50
19 Mike Mussina .60 1.50
20 Mike Piazza 1.00 2.50
21 Nomar Garciaparra .60 1.50
22 Pedro Martinez .60 1.50
23 Rafael Palmeiro .60 1.50
24 Randy Johnson 1.00 2.50
25 Roger Clemens 1.25 3.00
26 Sammy Sosa 1.00 2.50
27 Scott Rolen .60 1.50
28 Tim Hudson .60 1.50
29 Vernon Wells .40 1.00
30 Vladimir Guerrero .60 1.50

2005 Donruss Diamond Kings Inserts

STATED PRINT RUN 2005 SERIAL #'d SETS
*STUDIO: 1X TO 2.5X BASIC
STUDIO PRINT RUN 250 SERIAL #'d SETS
*STUDIO BLACK: 1.25X TO 3X BASIC
STUDIO BLACK PRINT RUN 100 #'d SETS
RANDOM INSERTS IN PACKS
DK1 Garret Anderson .40 1.00
DK2 Vladimir Guerrero .60 1.50
DK3 Manny Ramirez 1.00 2.50
DK4 Kerry Wood .40 1.00
DK5 Sammy Sosa 1.00 2.50
DK6 Magglio Ordonez .60 1.50
DK7 Adam Dunn .60 1.50
DK8 Todd Helton .60 1.50
DK9 Josh Beckett .40 1.00
DK10 Miguel Cabrera 1.00 2.50
DK11 Lance Berkman .60 1.50
DK12 Carlos Beltran .60 1.50
DK13 Shawn Green .40 1.00
DK14 Roger Clemens 1.25 3.00
DK15 Mike Piazza 1.00 2.50
DK16 Alex Rodriguez 1.25 3.00
DK17 Derek Jeter 2.50 6.00
DK18 Mark Mulder .40 1.00
DK19 Jim Thome .60 1.50
DK20 Albert Pujols 1.25 3.00
DK21 Scott Rolen .60 1.50
DK22 Aubrey Huff .40 1.00
DK23 Alfonso Soriano .60 1.50
DK24 Hank Blalock .40 1.00
DK25 Vernon Wells .40 1.00

2005 Donruss Elite Series

STATED PRINT RUN 1500 SERIAL #'d SETS
*BLACK: .75X TO 2X BASIC
BLACK PRINT RUN 100 SERIAL #'d SETS
*DOMINATOR: .6X TO 1.5X BASIC
DOMINATOR PRINT RUN 250 #'d SETS
*DOM.BLACK: 1.5X TO 4X BASIC
DOM.BLACK PRINT RUN 25 #'d SETS
RANDOM INSERTS IN PACKS
1 Albert Pujols 2.00 5.00
2 Alex Rodriguez 2.00 5.00
3 Alfonso Soriano 1.00 2.50
4 Derek Jeter 4.00 10.00
5 Hank Blalock .60 1.50
6 Ichiro Suzuki 2.00 5.00
7 Ivan Rodriguez 1.00 2.50
8 Jim Thome 1.00 2.50
9 Ken Griffey Jr. 3.00 8.00
10 Manny Ramirez 1.50 4.00
11 Mark Mulder .60 1.50
12 Mark Prior 1.00 2.50
13 Michael Young .60 1.50
14 Miguel Cabrera 1.50 4.00
15 Miguel Tejada 1.00 2.50
16 Mike Piazza 1.50 4.00
17 Nomar Garciaparra 1.00 2.50
18 Rafael Palmeiro 1.00 2.50
19 Randy Johnson 1.50 4.00
20 Roger Clemens 2.00 5.00
21 Sammy Sosa 1.50 4.00
22 Scott Rolen 1.00 2.50
23 Tim Hudson 1.00 2.50
24 Todd Helton 1.00 2.50
25 Vladimir Guerrero 1.00 2.50

2005 Donruss Fans of the Game

COMPLETE SET (5) 4.00 10.00
RANDOM INSERTS IN PACKS
1 Jesse Ventura 1.25 3.00
2 John C. McGinley .75 2.00
3 Susie Essman .75 2.00
4 Dean Cain .75 2.00
5 Meat Loaf 1.25 3.00

2005 Donruss Fans of the Game Autographs

RANDOM INSERTS IN PACKS
SP PRINT RUNS PROVIDED BY DONRUSS
SP'S ARE NOT SERIAL-NUMBERED
1 Jesse Ventura 25.00 50.00
2 John C. McGinley SP/300 12.00 30.00
3 Susie Essman 20.00 50.00
4 Dean Cain SP/250 40.00 80.00
5 Meat Loaf 25.00 60.00

2005 Donruss Inside View

NO PRICING DUE TO SCARCITY
NOT INTENDED FOR PUBLIC RELEASE

2005 Donruss Jersey Kings

RANDOM INSERTS IN PACKS
PRINT RUNS B/WN 100-250 COPIES PER
1 Garret Anderson/250 3.00 8.00
2 Vladimir Guerrero/250 4.00 10.00
3 Cal Ripken/100 30.00 60.00
4 Manny Ramirez/250 4.00 10.00
5 Kerry Wood/250 3.00 8.00
6 Sammy Sosa/250 4.00 10.00
7 Magglio Ordonez/250 3.00 8.00
8 Adam Dunn/250 3.00 8.00
9 Todd Helton/250 4.00 10.00
10 Josh Beckett/250 3.00 8.00
11 Miguel Cabrera/250 4.00 10.00
12 Lance Berkman/250 3.00 8.00
13 Carlos Beltran/250 3.00 8.00
14 Shawn Green/250 3.00 8.00
15 Roger Clemens/250 6.00 15.00
16 Mike Piazza/250 4.00 10.00
17 Nolan Ryan/100 20.00 50.00
18 Mark Mulder/250 3.00 8.00
19 Jim Thome/250 4.00 10.00
20 Albert Pujols/250 6.00 15.00
21 Scott Rolen/250 4.00 10.00
22 Aubrey Huff/250 3.00 8.00
23 Alfonso Soriano/250 3.00 8.00
24 Hank Blalock/250 3.00 8.00
25 Vernon Wells/250 3.00 8.00

2005 Donruss Jersey Kings Signatures

PRINT RUNS B/WN 5-10 COPIES PER
NO PRICING DUE TO SCARCITY

2005 Donruss Longball Leaders

STATED PRINT RUN 1500 SERIAL #'d SETS
*BLACK: .75X TO 2X BASIC
BLACK PRINT RUN 250 SERIAL #'d SETS
*DIE CUT: 1.25X TO 3X BASIC
DIE CUT PRINT RUN 50 SERIAL #'d SETS
BLACK DC PRINT RUN 10 SERIAL #'d SETS
NO BLACK DC PRICING DUE TO SCARCITY
RANDOM INSERTS IN PACKS
1 Adam Dunn .75 2.00
2 Adrian Beltre 1.25 3.00
3 Albert Pujols 1.50 4.00
4 Alex Rodriguez 1.50 4.00
5 David Ortiz 1.25 3.00
6 Hank Blalock .50 1.25
7 J.D. Drew .50 1.25
8 Jeromy Burnitz .50 1.25
9 Jim Edmonds .75 2.00
10 Jim Thome .75 2.00
11 Manny Ramirez 1.25 3.00
12 Mark Teixeira .75 2.00
13 Moises Alou .50 1.25
14 Paul Konerko .75 2.00
15 Steve Finley .50 1.25

2005 Donruss Mound Marvels

STATED PRINT RUN 1000 SERIAL #'d SETS
BLACK PRINT RUN 10 SERIAL #'d SETS
NO BLACK PRICING DUE TO SCARCITY
RANDOM INSERTS IN PACKS
1 Curt Schilling 1.00 2.50
2 Dontrelle Willis .60 1.50
3 Eric Gagne .60 1.50
4 Greg Maddux 2.00 5.00
5 John Smoltz 1.50 4.00
6 Kenny Rogers .60 1.50
7 Kerry Wood .60 1.50
8 Mariano Rivera 2.00 5.00
9 Mark Mulder .60 1.50
10 Mark Prior 1.00 2.50
11 Mike Mussina 1.00 2.50
12 Pedro Martinez 1.00 2.50
13 Randy Johnson 1.50 4.00
14 Roger Clemens 2.00 5.00
15 Tim Hudson 1.00 2.50

2005 Donruss Power Alley Red

STATED PRINT RUN 2500 SERIAL #'d SETS
BLACK PRINT RUN 10 SERIAL #'d SETS
NO BLACK PRICING DUE TO SCARCITY
BLACK DC PRINT RUN 5 SERIAL #'d SETS
NO BLACK DC PRICING DUE TO SCARCITY
*BLUE: .6X TO 1.5X RED
BLUE PRINT RUN 1000 SERIAL #'d SETS
*BLUE DC: 1.25X TO 3X RED
BLUE DC PRINT RUN 100 SERIAL #'d SETS
*GREEN: 2.5X TO 6X RED
GREEN PRINT RUN 25 SERIAL #'d SETS
GREEN DC PRINT RUN 10 SERIAL #'d SETS
NO GREEN DC PRICING DUE TO SCARCITY
*PURPLE: 1X TO 2.5X RED
PURPLE PRINT RUN 250 SERIAL #'d SETS
*PURPLE DC: 1.5X TO 4X RED
PURPLE DC PRINT RUN 50 SERIAL #'d SETS
*RED DC: 1X TO 2.5X RED
RED DC PRINT RUN 250 SERIAL #'d SETS
*YELLOW: 1.25X TO 3X RED
YELLOW PRINT RUN 100 SERIAL #'d SETS
*YELLOW DC: 2.5X TO 6X RED
YELLOW DC PRINT RUN 25 #'d SETS
1 Adam Dunn .60 1.50
2 Adrian Beltre 1.00 2.50
3 Albert Pujols 1.25 3.00
4 Alex Rodriguez 1.25 3.00
5 Alfonso Soriano .60 1.50
6 Gary Sheffield .40 1.00
7 Hank Blalock .40 1.00
8 Hideki Matsui 1.50 4.00
9 J.D. Drew .40 1.00
10 Jeromy Burnitz .40 1.00
11 Jim Edmonds .60 1.50
12 Jim Thome .60 1.50
13 Ken Griffey Jr. 2.00 5.00
14 Manny Ramirez 1.00 2.50
15 Mark Teixeira .60 1.50
16 Miguel Cabrera 1.00 2.50
17 Miguel Tejada .60 1.50
18 Mike Lowell .40 1.00
19 Mike Piazza 1.00 2.50
20 Moises Alou .40 1.00
21 Paul Konerko .60 1.50
22 Sammy Sosa 1.00 2.50
23 Scott Rolen .60 1.50
24 Todd Helton .60 1.50
25 Vladimir Guerrero .60 1.50

2005 Donruss Production Line BA

PRINT RUNS B/WN 324-372 COPIES PER
*BLACK: 1X TO 2.5X BASIC PL
BLACK PRINT RUN 25 SERIAL #'d SETS
*DIE CUT: .5X TO 1.2X BASIC PL
DIE CUT PRINT RUN 100 SERIAL #'d SETS
BLACK DC PRINT RUN 10 SERIAL #'d SETS
NO BLACK DC PRICING DUE TO SCARCITY
RANDOM INSERTS IN PACKS
1 Ichiro Suzuki/372 3.00 8.00
2 Ivan Rodriguez/334 1.50 4.00
3 Juan Pierre/326 1.00 2.50
4 Adrian Beltre/334 2.50 6.00
5 Albert Pujols/331 3.00 8.00
6 Mark Loretta/335 1.00 2.50
7 Melvin Mora/340 1.00 2.50
8 Sean Casey/324 1.00 2.50
9 Todd Helton/347 1.50 4.00
10 Vladimir Guerrero/337 1.50 4.00

2005 Donruss Production Line OBP

RANDOM INSERTS IN PACKS
PRINT RUNS B/WN 397-469 COPIES PER
*BLACK: 1.25X TO 3X BASIC PL
BLACK PRINT RUN 25 SERIAL #'d SETS
*DIE CUT: .6X TO 1.5X BASIC PL
DIE CUT PRINT RUN 100 SERIAL #'d SETS
BLACK DC PRINT RUN 10 SERIAL #'d SETS
NO BLACK DC PRICING DUE TO SCARCITY
RANDOM INSERTS IN PACKS
1 Albert Pujols/415 2.50 6.00
2 Bobby Abreu/428 .75 2.00
3 Lance Berkman/450 1.25 3.00
4 J.D. Drew/436 .75 2.00
5 Jorge Posada/400 1.25 3.00
6 Ichiro Suzuki/414 2.50 6.00
7 Manny Ramirez/397 2.00 5.00
8 Melvin Mora/419 .75 2.00
9 Todd Helton/469 1.25 3.00
10 Travis Hafner/410 .75 2.00

2005 Donruss Production Line OPS

RANDOM INSERTS IN PACKS
PRINT RUNS B/WN 977-1088 COPIES PER
*BLACK: 1X TO 2.5X BASIC PL
BLACK PRINT RUN 50 SERIAL #'d SETS
*DIE CUT: .75X TO 2X BASIC PL
DIE CUT PRINT RUN 100 SERIAL #'d SETS
*BLACK DC: 1.5X TO 4X BASIC PL
BLACK DC PRINT RUN 25 SERIAL #'d SETS
RANDOM INSERTS IN PACKS
1 Albert Pujols/1072 2.00 5.00
2 David Ortiz/983 1.50 4.00
3 Adrian Beltre/1017 1.50 4.00
4 J.D. Drew/1006 .60 1.50
5 Jim Thome/977 1.00 2.50
6 Lance Berkman/1016 1.00 2.50
7 Manny Ramirez/1009 1.50 4.00
8 Scott Rolen/1007 1.00 2.50
9 Todd Helton/1088 1.00 2.50
10 Travis Hafner/993 .60 1.50

2005 Donruss Production Line Slugging

PRINT RUNS B/WN 569-657 COPIES PER
*BLACK: .75X TO 2X BASIC PL
BLACK PRINT RUN 50 SERIAL #'d SETS
*DIE CUT: .6X TO 1.5X BASIC PL
DIE CUT PRINT RUN 100 SERIAL #'d SETS
*BLACK DC: 1.2X TO 3X BASIC PL
BLACK DC PRINT RUN 25 SERIAL #'d SETS
RANDOM INSERTS IN PACKS
1 Adrian Beltre/629 2.00 5.00
2 Albert Pujols/657 2.50 6.00
3 Todd Helton/620 1.25 3.00
4 J.D. Drew/569 .75 2.00
5 Jim Edmonds/643 1.25 3.00
6 Jim Thome/581 1.25 3.00
7 Vladimir Guerrero/598 1.25 3.00
8 Manny Ramirez/613 2.00 5.00
9 Scott Rolen/598 1.25 3.00
10 Travis Hafner/583 .75 2.00

2005 Donruss Rookies

STATED ODDS 1:23
BLACK PRINT RUN 10 SERIAL #'d SETS
NO BLACK PRICING DUE TO SCARCITY
*BLUE: .5X TO 1.2X BASIC
BLUE PRINT RUN 100 SERIAL #'d SETS
*GOLD: 1.25X TO 3X BASIC
GOLD PRINT RUN 25 SERIAL #'d SETS
*RED: .4X TO 1X BASIC
RED PRINT RUN 200 SERIAL #'d SETS
1 Fernando Nieve .40 1.00
2 Frankie Francisco .40 1.00
3 Jorge Vasquez .40 1.00
4 Travis Blackley .40 1.00
5 Joey Gathright .40 1.00
6 Kazuhito Tadano .40 1.00
7 Edwin Moreno .40 1.00
8 Lance Cormier .40 1.00
9 Justin Knoedler .40 1.00
10 Orlando Rodriguez .40 1.00
11 Renyel Pinto .40 1.00
12 Justin Leone .40 1.00
13 Dennis Sarfate .40 1.00
14 Sam Narron .40 1.00
15 Yadier Molina 8.00 20.00
16 Carlos Vasquez .40 1.00
17 Ryan Wing .40 1.00
18 Brad Halsey .40 1.00
19 Ryan Meaux .40 1.00
20 Michael Wuertz .40 1.00
21 Shawn Camp .40 1.00
22 Ruddy Yan .40 1.00
23 Don Kelly .40 1.00
24 Jake Woods .40 1.00
25 Colby Miller .40 1.00
26 Abe Alvarez .40 1.00
27 Mike Rouse .40 1.00
28 Phil Stockman .40 1.00
29 Kevin Cave .40 1.00
30 Chris Shelton .40 1.00
31 Tim Bittner .40 1.00
32 Mariano Gomez .40 1.00
33 Angel Chavez .40 1.00
34 Carlos Hines .40 1.00
35 Aarom Baldiris .40 1.00
36 Kazuo Matsui .40 1.00
37 Nick Regilio .40 1.00
38 Ivan Ochoa .40 1.00
39 Graham Koonce .40 1.00
40 Merkin Valdez .40 1.00
41 Greg Dobbs .40 1.00
42 Chris Oxspring .40 1.00
43 Dave Crouthers .40 1.00
44 Freddy Guzman .40 1.00
45 Akinori Otsuka .40 1.00
46 Jesse Crain .40 1.00
47 Casey Daigle .40 1.00
48 Roberto Novoa .40 1.00
49 Eddy Rodriguez .40 1.00
50 Jason Bartlett .40 1.00

2005 Donruss Rookies Stat Line Career

*SLC p/r 201-316: .4X TO 1X
*SLC p/r 121-200: .4X TO 1X
*SLC p/r 81-120: .5X TO 1.2X
*SLC p/r 51-80: .6X TO 1.5X
*SLC p/r 36-50: .75X TO 2X
*SLC p/r 26-35: 1X TO 2.5X
*SLC p/r 16-25: 1.25X TO 3X
RANDOM INSERTS IN DLP R/T PACKS
PRINT RUNS B/WN 1-316 COPIES PER
NO PRICING ON QTY OF 15 OR LESS

2005 Donruss Rookies Stat Line Season

*SLS p/r 121-200: .4X TO 1X
*SLS p/r 81-120: .5X TO 1.2X
*SLS p/r 51-80: .6X TO 1.5X
*SLS p/r 36-50: .75X TO 2X
*SLS p/r 26-35: 1X TO 2.5X
*SLS p/r 16-25: 1.25X TO 3X
RANDOM INSERTS IN DLP R/T PACKS
PRINT RUNS B/WN 1-188 COPIES PER
NO PRICING ON QTY OF 15 OR LESS

2005 Donruss Rookies Autographs

COMMON SP 4.00 10.00
RANDOM INSERTS IN PACKS
6/12/14/21/36/40-41/44-47 DO NOT EXIST
SP INFO PROVIDED BY DONRUSS
1 Fernando Nieve 3.00 8.00
2 Frankie Francisco 3.00 8.00
3 Jorge Vasquez 3.00 8.00
4 Travis Blackley 3.00 8.00
5 Joey Gathright 4.00 10.00
7 Edwin Moreno 3.00 8.00
8 Lance Cormier 3.00 8.00
9 Justin Knoedler 3.00 8.00
10 Orlando Rodriguez 3.00 8.00
11 Renyel Pinto 3.00 8.00
13 Dennis Sarfate 3.00 8.00
15 Yadier Molina 75.00 200.00
17 Ryan Wing SP 4.00 10.00
18 Brad Halsey 4.00 10.00
19 Ryan Meaux 3.00 8.00
20 Michael Wuertz 3.00 8.00
22 Ruddy Yan 3.00 8.00
23 Don Kelly 3.00 8.00
24 Jake Woods 3.00 8.00
25 Colby Miller 3.00 8.00
26 Abe Alvarez 4.00 10.00
27 Mike Rouse SP 4.00 10.00
28 Phil Stockman 3.00 8.00
29 Kevin Cave 3.00 8.00
30 Chris Shelton SP 10.00 25.00
31 Tim Bittner 3.00 8.00
32 Mariano Gomez 3.00 8.00
33 Angel Chavez 3.00 8.00
34 Carlos Hines 3.00 8.00
35 Aarom Baldiris 3.00 8.00
37 Nick Regilio 3.00 8.00
38 Ivan Ochoa 3.00 8.00
39 Graham Koonce 3.00 8.00
42 Chris Oxspring 3.00 8.00
43 Dave Crouthers 3.00 8.00
48 Roberto Novoa 3.00 8.00
49 Eddy Rodriguez 3.00 8.00
50 Jason Bartlett 3.00 8.00

2005 Donruss Timber and Threads Bat

RANDOM INSERTS IN PACKS
1 Albert Pujols 6.00 15.00
2 Alfonso Soriano 3.00 8.00
3 Andre Dawson 3.00 8.00
4 Austin Kearns 3.00 8.00
5 Brad Penny 3.00 8.00
6 Carlos Beltran 3.00 8.00
7 Carlos Lee 3.00 8.00
8 Chipper Jones 4.00 10.00
9 Dale Murphy 4.00 10.00

10 Don Mattingly 8.00 20.00
11 Frank Thomas 4.00 10.00
12 Garret Anderson 3.00 8.00
13 Gary Carter 3.00 8.00
14 Hank Blalock 3.00 8.00
15 Jacque Jones 3.00 8.00
17 Jay Gibbons 3.00 8.00
18 Jeff Bagwell 4.00 10.00
20 Jermaine Dye 3.00 8.00
21 Jim Thome 4.00 10.00
22 Jose Vidro 3.00 8.00
23 Lance Berkman 3.00 8.00
24 Laynce Nix 3.00 8.00
25 Magglio Ordonez 3.00 8.00
26 Marcus Giles 3.00 8.00
27 Mark Prior 4.00 10.00
28 Mark Teixeira 4.00 10.00
29 Melvin Mora 3.00 8.00
30 Michael Young 3.00 8.00
31 Miguel Cabrera 4.00 10.00
32 Mike Lowell 3.00 8.00
33 Roy Oswalt 3.00 8.00
34 Sammy Sosa 4.00 10.00
35 Scott Rolen 4.00 10.00
36 Sean Burroughs 3.00 8.00
37 Sean Casey 3.00 8.00
38 Shannon Stewart 3.00 8.00
39 Torii Hunter 3.00 8.00
40 Travis Hafner 3.00 8.00

2005 Donruss Timber and Threads Bat Signature

PRINT RUNS B/WN 5-10 COPIES PER
NO PRICING DUE TO SCARCITY

2005 Donruss Timber and Threads Combo

*COMBO: .6X TO 1.5X BAT
RANDOM INSERTS IN PACKS

2005 Donruss Timber and Threads Combo Signature

PRINT RUNS B/WN 5-10 COPIES PER
NO PRICING DUE TO SCARCITY

2005 Donruss Timber and Threads Jersey

*JSY: .4X TO 1X BAT
RANDOM INSERTS IN PACKS
19 Jeremy Bonderman 3.00 8.00

2005 Donruss Timber and Threads Jersey Signature

PRINT RUNS B/WN 5-10 COPIES PER
NO PRICING DUE TO SCARCITY

2014 Donruss

COMP.FACT.SET (356) 50.00 100.00
1 Bryce Harper DK 1.50 4.00
2 Mike Trout DK 5.00 12.00
3 Derek Jeter DK 2.50 6.00
4 Yasiel Puig DK 1.00 2.50
5 Chris Davis DK .60 1.50
6 Jose Bautista DK .75 2.00
7 Freddie Freeman DK 1.25 3.00
8 Eric Hosmer DK .75 2.00
9 Miguel Cabrera DK 1.00 2.50
10 Andrew McCutchen DK 1.00 2.50
11 Paul Goldschmidt DK 1.00 2.50
12 Adrian Beltre DK 1.00 2.50
13 David Ortiz DK 1.00 2.50
14 Buster Posey DK 1.25 3.00
15 David Wright DK .75 2.00
16 Jason Kipnis DK .75 2.00
17 Evan Longoria DK .75 2.00
18 Giancarlo Stanton DK 1.00 2.50
19 Chase Utley DK .75 2.00
20 Chris Sale DK 1.00 2.50
21 Joe Mauer DK .75 2.00
22 Anthony Rizzo DK 1.25 3.00
23 Jay Bruce DK .75 2.00
24 Jean Segura DK .75 2.00
25 Yadier Molina DK 1.25 3.00
26 Chris Carter DK .60 1.50
27 Josh Donaldson DK .75 2.00
28 Felix Hernandez DK .75 2.00
29 Troy Tulowitzki DK 1.00 2.50
30 Chase Headley DK .60 1.50
31 Michael Choice RC .50 1.25
32 Billy Hamilton RC .60 1.50
33 Nick Castellanos RC 1.50 4.00
34 Taijuan Walker RC .50 1.25
35 Kolten Wong RC .60 1.50
36 Travis d'Arnaud RC .60 1.50
37 Jonathan Schoop RC .50 1.25
38 Cameron Rupp RC .50 1.25
39 James Paxton RC .75 2.00
40 Tim Beckham RC .75 2.00
41 J.R. Murphy RC .50 1.25
42 Erik Johnson RC .50 1.25
43 Wilmer Flores RC .60 1.50
44 Xander Bogaerts RC 1.50 4.00
45 Tommy Medica RC .50 1.25
46 Jayson Werth .20 .50
47 Alex Gordon .20 .50
48 Allen Craig .20 .50
49 Buster Posey .30 .75
50 Prince Fielder .20 .50
51 Yadier Molina .30 .75
52 Justin Morneau .20 .50
53 Jacoby Ellsbury .20 .50
54 Ryan Zimmerman .20 .50
55 Michael Cuddyer .15 .40
56 Evan Longoria .20 .50
57 Justin Upton .20 .50
58 Chris Johnson .15 .40
59 Ichiro Suzuki .40 1.00
60 Joe Mauer .20 .50
61 Billy Butler .15 .40
62 Chase Utley UER .20 .50
Chase Headley name on back
63 Adam Dunn .20 .50
64 Brandon Phillips .15 .40
65 Joey Votto .25 .60
66 Jason Heyward .20 .50
67 Robinson Cano .20 .50
68 David Wright .20 .50
69 Clayton Kershaw .40 1.00
70 Troy Tulowitzki .25 .60
71 Kris Medlen .20 .50
72 Elvis Andrus .20 .50
73 Paul Konerko .20 .50
74 Josh Hamilton .20 .50
75 Felix Hernandez .20 .50
76 Nick Markakis .20 .50
77 Craig Kimbrel .20 .50
78 Max Scherzer .25 .60
79 Carlos Beltran .20 .50
80 Mike Napoli .15 .40
81 Travis Wood .15 .40
82 Adam Jones .20 .50
83 Jose Altuve .20 .50
84 Edwin Encarnacion .25 .60
85 Dustin Pedroia .25 .60
86 Shin-Soo Choo .20 .50
87 Hunter Pence .20 .50
88 Torii Hunter .15 .40
89 James Shields .15 .40
90 Yu Darvish .25 .60
91 Justin Verlander .25 .60
92 Adrian Gonzalez .20 .50
93 Matt Holliday .25 .60
94 Roy Halladay .20 .50
95 Albert Pujols .30 .75
96 Matt Carpenter .25 .60
97 Josh Donaldson .20 .50
98 Jason Kipnis .20 .50
99 Mark Trumbo .15 .40
100 Alfonso Soriano .20 .50
101 Carlos Gonzalez .20 .50
102 Adam Wainwright .20 .50
103 Jose Fernandez .25 .60
104 Jean Segura .20 .50
105 Evan Gattis .15 .40
106 Aroldis Chapman .25 .60
107 Nick Swisher .20 .50
108 Chris Sale .25 .60
109 Chris Carter .15 .40
110 Matt Harvey .20 .50
111 Cliff Lee .20 .50
112 Mike Trout 1.25 3.00
113 Everth Cabrera .15 .40
114 Matt Moore .20 .50
115 Andrew McCutchen .25 .60
116 Jordan Zimmermann .20 .50
117 Freddie Freeman .30 .75
118 Wei-Yin Chen .15 .40
119 Anthony Rizzo .30 .75
120 Jon Lester .20 .50
121 Starlin Castro .15 .40
122 Gerardo Parra .15 .40
123 Ian Kennedy .15 .40
124 Stephen Strasburg .25 .60
125 Manny Machado .25 .60
126 Chase Headley .15 .40
127 Paul Goldschmidt .25 .60
128 Miguel Cabrera .25 .60
129 Adrian Beltre .25 .60
130 J.J. Hardy .15 .40
131 Eric Hosmer .20 .50
132 Giancarlo Stanton .25 .60
133 Hyun-Jin Ryu .20 .50
134 Shane Victorino .20 .50
135 R.A. Dickey .20 .50
136 Jhonny Peralta .15 .40
137 Alex Rodriguez .30 .75
138 Victor Martinez .20 .50
139 Shelby Miller .20 .50
140 Jose Reyes .20 .50
141 Jose Iglesias .20 .50
142 Yan Gomes .15 .40
143 Bryce Harper .40 1.00
144 Colby Rasmus .20 .50
145 Chris Archer .15 .40
146 Wil Myers .15 .40
147 Matt Kemp .20 .50
148 Pedro Alvarez .15 .40
149 Raul Ibanez .20 .50
150 Brandon Moss .15 .40
151 Marlon Byrd .15 .40
152 Zack Greinke .25 .60
153 Domonic Brown .20 .50
154 Derek Jeter .60 1.50
155 Yoenis Cespedes .25 .60
156 Kendrys Morales .15 .40
157 Hanley Ramirez .20 .50
158 Mitch Moreland .15 .40
159 Pablo Sandoval .20 .50
160 CC Sabathia .20 .50
161 Ian Kinsler .20 .50
162 Hisashi Iwakuma .20 .50
163 Michael Young .15 .40
164 Curtis Granderson .20 .50
165 Jered Weaver .20 .50
166 Zack Wheeler .20 .50
167 Glen Perkins .15 .40
168 Hiroki Kuroda .15 .40
169 Kyle Lohse .15 .40
170 Yasiel Puig .25 .60
171 C.J. Wilson .15 .40
172 Matt Wieters .25 .60
173 Trevor Bauer .30 .75
174 Aramis Ramirez .15 .40
175 Jay Bruce .20 .50
176 Carl Crawford .20 .50
177 B.J. Upton .20 .50
178 A.J. Pierzynski .15 .40
179 Chris Davis .15 .40
180 Jose Bautista .20 .50
181 David Ortiz .25 .60
182 Starling Marte .20 .50
183 Tim Lincecum .20 .50
184 Mariano Rivera .30 .75
185 Todd Helton .20 .50
186 Roberto Alomar .20 .50
187 Rickey Henderson .25 .60
188 Reggie Jackson .20 .50
189 Ozzie Smith .30 .75
190 Nolan Ryan .75 2.00
191 Mike Piazza .25 .60
192 Pete Rose .50 1.25
193 Nomar Garciaparra .20 .50
194 Chipper Jones .25 .60
195 Johnny Bench .25 .60
196 Ken Griffey Jr. .50 1.25
197 Frank Thomas .25 .60
198 Cal Ripken Jr. .75 2.00
199 George Brett .50 1.25
200 Don Mattingly .50 1.25
201A Tanaka English RC 10.00 25.00
201B Tanaka Japanese 60.00 120.00
202 Jose Abreu 8.00 20.00
203 Yordano Ventura 1.50 4.00
204 Stephen Strasburg DK 1.00 2.50
205 Albert Pujols DK 1.25 3.00
206 Masahiro Tanaka DK 2.00 5.00
207 Clayton Kershaw DK 1.50 4.00
208 Manny Machado DK 1.00 2.50
209 Edwin Encarnacion DK 1.00 2.50
210 Justin Upton DK .75 2.00
211 Yordano Ventura DK .75 2.00
212 Max Scherzer DK 1.00 2.50
213 Starling Marte DK .75 2.00
214 Mark Trumbo DK .60 1.50
215 Yu Darvish DK 1.00 2.50
216 Koji Uehara DK .60 1.50
217 Brandon Belt DK .75 2.00
218 Matt Harvey DK .75 2.00
219 Yan Gomes DK .60 1.50
220 Wil Myers DK .60 1.50
221 Jose Fernandez DK 1.00 2.50
222 Cliff Lee DK .75 2.00
223 Jose Abreu DK 5.00 12.00
224 Brian Dozier DK .75 2.00
225 Starlin Castro DK .60 1.50
226 Joey Votto DK 1.00 2.50
227 Carlos Gomez DK .60 1.50
228 Michael Wacha DK .75 2.00
229 Jose Altuve DK .75 2.00
230 Yoenis Cespedes DK 1.00 2.50
231 Robinson Cano DK .75 2.00
232 Carlos Gonzalez DK .75 2.00
233 Jedd Gyorko DK .60 1.50
234 Jose Abreu RC 4.00 10.00
235 Masahiro Tanaka RC 1.50 4.00
236 Alex Guerrero RC .60 1.50
237 Yordano Ventura RC .60 1.50
238 Rougned Odor RC 1.25 3.00
239 Nick Martinez RC .50 1.25
240 Oscar Taveras RC .60 1.50
241 Tucker Barnhart RC .50 1.25
242 Matt Davidson RC .60 1.50
243 Marcus Semien RC 2.50 6.00
244 Chris Owings RC .50 1.25
245 Yangervis Solarte RC .50 1.25
246 Wei-Chung Wang RC .50 1.25
247 Jimmy Nelson RC .50 1.25
248 Christian Bethancourt RC .50 1.25
249 George Springer RC 2.00 5.00
250 Jake Marisnick RC .50 1.25
251 Enny Romero RC .50 1.25
252 Chad Bettis RC .50 1.25
253 Erisbel Arruebarrena RC .50 1.25
254 Jon Singleton RC .60 1.50
255 David Holmberg RC .50 1.25
256 C.J. Cron RC .50 1.25
257 David Hale RC .50 1.25
258 Jose Ramirez RC 4.00 10.00
259 Patrick Corbin .20 .50
260 Paul Goldschmidt .25 .60
261 Wade Miley .15 .40
262 Alex Wood .15 .40
263 Andrelton Simmons .15 .40
264 Freddie Freeman .30 .75
265 Julio Teheran .20 .50
266 Chris Davis .15 .40
267 Chris Tillman .15 .40
268 Jonathan Schoop .15 .40
269 Nelson Cruz .25 .60
270 Clay Buchholz .15 .40
271 David Ortiz .25 .60
272 Grady Sizemore .20 .50
273 Koji Uehara .15 .40
274 Xander Bogaerts .50 1.25
275 Emilio Bonifacio .15 .40
276 Alejandro De Aza .15 .40
277 Alexei Ramirez .20 .50
278 Avisail Garcia .20 .50
279 Chris Sale .25 .60
280 Erik Johnson .15 .40
281 Billy Hamilton .20 .50
282 Joey Votto .25 .60
283 Johnny Cueto .20 .50
284 Mat Latos .20 .50
285 Tony Cingrani .20 .50
286 Carlos Santana .20 .50
287 Justin Masterson .15 .40
288 Michael Brantley .20 .50
289 Nolan Arenado .40 1.00
290 Troy Tulowitzki .25 .60
291 Wilin Rosario .15 .40
292 Anibal Sanchez .15 .40
293 Austin Jackson .15 .40
294 Miguel Cabrera .25 .60
295 Nick Castellanos .50 1.25
296 Jason Castro .15 .40
297 Greg Holland .15 .40
298 Norichika Aoki .15 .40
299 Salvador Perez .20 .50
300 Kole Calhoun .15 .40
301 Mike Trout 1.25 3.00
302 Tyler Skaggs .15 .40
303 Dee Gordon .15 .40
304 Kenley Jansen .20 .50
305 Yasiel Puig .25 .60
306 Adeiny Hechavarria .15 .40
307 Christian Yelich .30 .75
308 Jose Fernandez .25 .60
309 Marcell Ozuna .25 .60
310 Carlos Gomez .15 .40
311 Ryan Braun .20 .50
312 Khris Davis .25 .60
313 Yovani Gallardo .15 .40
314 Brian Dozier .20 .50
315 Oswaldo Arcia .15 .40
316 Travis d'Arnaud .20 .50
317 Brian McCann .20 .50
318 Derek Jeter .60 1.50
319 Jed Lowrie .15 .40
320 Sonny Gray .20 .50
321 Carlos Ruiz .15 .40
322 Cole Hamels .20 .50
323 Ryan Howard .20 .50
324 Andrew McCutchen .25 .60
325 Francisco Liriano .15 .40
326 Gerrit Cole .25 .60
327 Andrew Cashner .15 .40
328 Jedd Gyorko .15 .40
329 Yonder Alonso .15 .40
330 Brandon Belt .20 .50
331 Buster Posey .30 .75
332 Madison Bumgarner .20 .50
333 Matt Cain .20 .50
334 James Paxton .25 .60
335 Robinson Cano .20 .50
336 Kolten Wong .20 .50
337 Lance Lynn .15 .40
338 Matt Adams .15 .40
339 Michael Wacha .20 .50
340 Trevor Rosenthal .20 .50
341 Yadier Molina .30 .75
342 Alex Cobb .15 .40
343 Ben Zobrist .20 .50
344 David Price .20 .50
345 Evan Longoria .20 .50
346 Yunel Escobar .15 .40
347 Alex Rios .20 .50
348 Jurickson Profar .20 .50
349 Leonys Martin .15 .40
350 Shin-Soo Choo .20 .50
351 Yu Darvish .25 .60
352 Brett Lawrie .20 .50
353 Jose Bautista .20 .50
354 Anthony Rendon .25 .60
355 Bryce Harper .40 1.00
356 Doug Fister .15 .40
357 Gio Gonzalez .20 .50
358 Ian Desmond .15 .40

2014 Donruss Press Proofs Silver

*SILVER DK: 1.2X TO 3X BASIC
*SILVER RC: 1.5X TO 4X BASIC
*SILVER VET: 5X TO 12X BASIC
STATED PRINT RUN 199 SER.#'d SETS
2 Mike Trout DK 12.00 30.00
112 Mike Trout 12.00 30.00
196 Ken Griffey Jr. 10.00 25.00
198 Cal Ripken Jr. 10.00 25.00
223 Jose Abreu DK 8.00 20.00
234 Jose Abreu 8.00 20.00
301 Mike Trout 10.00 25.00

2014 Donruss Press Proofs Gold

*GOLD DK: 1.5X TO 4X BASIC
*GOLD RC: 2X TO 5X BASIC
*GOLD VET: 6X TO 15X BASIC
STATED PRINT RUN 99 SER.#'d SETS
2 Mike Trout DK 15.00 40.00
112 Mike Trout 15.00 40.00
196 Ken Griffey Jr. 12.00 30.00
198 Cal Ripken Jr. 15.00 40.00
223 Jose Abreu DK 10.00 25.00
234 Jose Abreu 10.00 25.00
301 Mike Trout 12.00 30.00

2014 Donruss Stat Line Career

*CAR.DK p/r 251-400: 1X TO 2.5X BASIC
*CAR.DK p/r 100-248: 1.2X TO 3X BASIC
*CAR.DK p/r 51-99: 1.5X TO 4X BASIC
*CAR.DK p/r 26-50: 2X TO 5X BASIC
*CAR.RC p/r 251-400: 1.2X TO 3X BASIC
*CAR.RC p/r 51-99: 2X TO 5X BASIC
*CAR.RC p/r 26-50: 2.5X TO 6X BASIC
*CAR.VET p/r 251-400: 4X TO 10X BASIC
*CAR.VET p/r 100-248: 5X TO 12X BASIC
*CAR.VET p/r 51-99: 6X TO 15X BASIC
*CAR.VET p/r 26-50: 8X TO 20X BASIC
*CAR.VET p/r 20-25: 10X TO 25X BASIC
*CAR.VET p/r 17-19: 12X TO 30X BASIC
PRINT RUNS B/WN 4-400 COPIES PER
NO PRICING ON QTY 4
223 Jose Abreu DK/184 6.00 15.00
234 Jose Abreu/184 6.00 15.00

2014 Donruss Stat Line Season

*SEA.DK p/r 251-400: 1X TO 2.5X BASIC
*SEA.DK p/r 100-248: 1.2X TO 3X BASIC
*SEA.DK p/r 51-99: 1.5X TO 4X BASIC
*SEA.DK p/r 26-50: 2X TO 5X BASIC
*SEA.DK p/r 20-25: 2.5X TO 6X BASIC
*SEA.DK p/r 17-19: 3X TO 8X BASIC
*SEA.RC p/r 251-400: 1.2X TO 3X BASIC
*SEA.RC p/r 100-248: 1.5X TO 4X BASIC
*SEA.RC p/r 20-25: 3X TO 8X BASIC
*SEA.VET p/r 251-400: 4X TO 10X BASIC
*SEA.VET p/r 100-248: 5X TO 12X BASIC
*SEA.VET p/r 51-99: 6X TO 15X BASIC
*SEA.VET p/r 26-50: 8X TO 20X BASIC
*SEA.VET p/r 20-25: 10X TO 25X BASIC
*SEA.VET p/r 17-19: 12X TO 30X BASIC
PRINT RUNS B/WN 3-400 COPIES PER
NO PRICING ON QTY 13 OR LESS
223 Jose Abreu DK/37 20.00 50.00
234 Jose Abreu/33 20.00 50.00

2014 Donruss Bat Kings

RANDOM INSERTS IN PACKS
1 Hunter Pence 3.00 8.00
2 Ryan Howard 3.00 8.00
3 Shelby Miller 3.00 8.00
4 Robinson Cano 3.00 8.00
5 Mark Teixeira 3.00 8.00
6 Ichiro Suzuki 8.00 20.00
7 Jose Bautista 3.00 8.00
8 Justin Upton 3.00 8.00
9 David Wright 3.00 8.00
10 Ike Davis 2.50 6.00
11 Jay Bruce 3.00 8.00
12 Didi Gregorius 3.00 8.00
13 Logan Morrison 2.50 6.00
14 Devin Mesoraco 2.50 6.00
15 Hanley Ramirez 3.00 8.00
16 Dustin Ackley 2.50 6.00
17 Jose Reyes 3.00 8.00
18 Adam Jones 3.00 8.00
19 Derek Jeter 10.00 25.00
20 Alex Rodriguez 5.00 12.00
21 Yasiel Puig 6.00 15.00
22 Mike Trout 20.00 50.00
23 Albert Pujols 5.00 12.00
24 Adrian Gonzalez 3.00 8.00
25 Anthony Rizzo 5.00 12.00
26 B.J. Upton 3.00 8.00
27 Brandon Phillips 2.50 6.00
28 Christian Yelich 5.00 12.00
29 Edwin Encarnacion 4.00 10.00
30 Evan Gattis 2.50 6.00
31 Gerardo Parra 2.50 6.00
32 Miguel Cabrera 5.00 12.00
33 Jurickson Profar 3.00 8.00
34 Mike Napoli 2.50 6.00
35 Justin Morneau 3.00 8.00
36 David Freese 2.50 6.00
37 Starling Marte 3.00 8.00
38 Adam Dunn 3.00 8.00
39 Carl Crawford 3.00 8.00
40 Giancarlo Stanton 4.00 10.00
41 Dustin Pedroia 4.00 10.00
42 Evan Longoria 3.00 8.00
43 Jacoby Ellsbury 5.00 12.00
44 Joey Votto 4.00 10.00
45 Joe Mauer 3.00 8.00
46 Matt Kemp 3.00 8.00
47 Michael Bourn 2.50 6.00
48 Melky Cabrera 2.50 6.00
49 Nelson Cruz 4.00 10.00
50 Pedro Alvarez 2.50 6.00

2014 Donruss Bat Kings Studio Series

*STUDIO: .75X TO 2X BASIC
RANDOM INSERTS IN PACKS
STATED PRINT RUN 25 SER.#'d SETS

2014 Donruss Breakout Hitters

1 Chris Davis .60 1.50
2 Eric Hosmer .75 2.00
3 Josh Donaldson .75 2.00
4 Chris Johnson .60 1.50
5 Matt Carpenter 1.00 2.50
6 Paul Goldschmidt 1.00 2.50
7 Jean Segura .75 2.00
8 Yasiel Puig 1.00 2.50
9 Yadier Molina 1.25 3.00
10 Wil Myers .60 1.50
11 Jose Altuve .75 2.00
12 Jason Kipnis .75 2.00
13 Austin Jackson .60 1.50
14 Manny Machado 1.00 2.50
15 Allen Craig .75 2.00
16 Carlos Gomez .60 1.50
17 Ian Desmond .60 1.50
18 Anthony Rizzo 1.25 3.00
19 Starling Marte .75 2.00
20 Domonic Brown .75 2.00
21 Kyle Seager .60 1.50
22 Chris Carter .60 1.50
23 Pedro Alvarez .60 1.50
24 Denard Span .60 1.50
25 Giancarlo Stanton 1.00 2.50
26 Andrelton Simmons .60 1.50
27 Anthony Rendon 1.00 2.50
28 Edwin Encarnacion 1.00 2.50
29 Freddie Freeman 1.25 3.00
30 Mike Trout 5.00 12.00
31 Jedd Gyorko .60 1.50
32 Evan Gattis .60 1.50
33 Matt Adams .60 1.50
34 Jed Lowrie .60 1.50
35 Brandon Moss .60 1.50

2014 Donruss Breakout Pitchers

1 Max Scherzer 1.00 2.50
2 Homer Bailey .60 1.50
3 Jarrod Parker .60 1.50
4 Gerrit Cole 1.00 2.50
5 Hisashi Iwakuma .75 2.00
6 Craig Kimbrel .75 2.00
7 Yu Darvish 1.00 2.50
8 Matt Harvey .75 2.00
9 Patrick Corbin .75 2.00
10 Rick Porcello .75 2.00
11 Jose Fernandez 1.00 2.50
12 Madison Bumgarner .75 2.00
13 Jordan Zimmermann .75 2.00
14 Chris Sale 1.00 2.50
15 Derek Holland .60 1.50
16 Shelby Miller .75 2.00
17 David Price .75 2.00
18 Aroldis Chapman 1.00 2.50
19 Mike Leake .60 1.50
20 Andrew Cashner .60 1.50
21 Matt Moore .75 2.00
22 Mat Latos .75 2.00
23 A.J. Griffin .60 1.50
24 Adam Wainwright .75 2.00
25 Kris Medlen .75 2.00
26 Stephen Strasburg 1.00 2.50
27 Wade Miley .60 1.50
28 Travis Wood .60 1.50
29 Hyun-Jin Ryu .75 2.00
30 Dillon Gee .60 1.50
31 Anibal Sanchez .60 1.50
32 Martin Perez .75 2.00
33 Julio Teheran .75 2.00
34 Gio Gonzalez .75 2.00
35 Alex Cobb .60 1.50

2014 Donruss Diamond King Box Toppers

1 David Price 2.50 6.00
2 David Ortiz 3.00 8.00
3 Edwin Encarnacion 3.00 8.00
4 Max Scherzer 3.00 8.00
5 Matt Harvey 2.50 6.00
6 Nick Castellanos 5.00 12.00
7 Mike Zunino 2.00 5.00
8 Chris Sale 3.00 8.00
9 Cal Ripken Jr. 10.00 25.00
10 Craig Biggio 2.50 6.00
11 Evan Longoria 2.50 6.00
12 David Wright 2.50 6.00
13 Mike Trout 15.00 40.00
14 Jordan Zimmermann 2.50 6.00
15 Josh Donaldson 2.50 6.00
16 Ken Griffey Jr. 6.00 15.00
17 Jurickson Profar 2.50 6.00
18 Stephen Strasburg 3.00 8.00
19 Paul Goldschmidt 3.00 8.00
20 Kris Medlen 2.50 6.00
21 Manny Machado 3.00 8.00
22 Mark Trumbo 2.00 5.00
23 Chris Davis 2.00 5.00
24 Yoenis Cespedes 3.00 8.00
25 Gerrit Cole 3.00 8.00

2014 Donruss Diamond King Box Toppers Signatures

EXCHANGE DEADLINE 8/26/2015
3 Edwin Encarnacion EXCH 12.00 30.00
5 Matt Harvey EXCH 60.00 120.00
7 Mike Zunino 12.00 30.00
14 Jordan Zimmermann 8.00 20.00
17 Jurickson Profar EXCH 20.00 50.00
23 Chris Davis 40.00 80.00
24 Yoenis Cespedes 30.00 60.00
25 Gerrit Cole 30.00 60.00

2014 Donruss Elite Dominator

STATED PRINT RUN 999 SER.#'d SETS
1A Jered Weaver 1.50 4.00
1B Adrian Beltre 2.00 5.00
2A Chris Davis 1.25 3.00
2B Adrian Gonzalez 1.50 4.00
3A Stephen Strasburg 2.00 5.00
3B Brandon Belt 1.50 4.00
4A Jose Bautista 1.50 4.00
4B Clayton Kershaw 3.00 8.00
5A Miguel Cabrera 2.00 5.00
5B Cliff Lee 1.50 4.00
6A Matt Harvey 1.50 4.00
6B David Ortiz 2.00 5.00
7A Jarrod Parker 1.25 3.00
7B David Wright 1.50 4.00
8A Yasiel Puig 2.00 5.00
8B Derek Jeter 5.00 12.00
9A Robinson Cano 1.50 4.00
9B Eric Hosmer 1.50 4.00
10A Jose Fernandez 2.00 5.00
10B Felix Hernandez 1.50 4.00
11A Prince Fielder 1.50 4.00
11B Giancarlo Stanton 2.00 5.00
12A David Price 1.50 4.00
12B Hyun-Jin Ryu 1.50 4.00
13A Yoenis Cespedes 2.00 5.00
13B Ichiro Suzuki 3.00 8.00
14A Matt Kemp 1.50 4.00
14B Joe Mauer 1.50 4.00
15A James Shields 1.25 3.00
15B Joey Votto 2.00 5.00
16A Pablo Sandoval 1.50 4.00
16B Jose Abreu 10.00 25.00
17A Mark Trumbo 1.25 3.00
17B Josh Donaldson 1.50 4.00
18A Carlos Gonzalez 1.50 4.00
18B Madison Bumgarner 1.50 4.00
19A Edwin Encarnacion 2.00 5.00
19B Max Scherzer 2.00 5.00
20A Chad Billingsley 1.50 4.00
20B Masahiro Tanaka 4.00 10.00
21A Will Clark 1.50 4.00
21B Mike Trout 10.00 25.00
22A Craig Biggio 1.50 4.00
22B Nick Castellanos 4.00 10.00
23A Ken Griffey Jr. 4.00 10.00
23B Paul Goldschmidt 2.00 5.00
24A Mike Mussina 1.50 4.00
24B Ryan Braun 1.50 4.00
25A Tom Glavine 1.50 4.00
25B Sonny Gray 1.50 4.00
26A Tony Gwynn 2.00 5.00
26B Starling Marte 1.50 4.00
27A Pedro Martinez 1.50 4.00
27B Troy Tulowitzki 2.00 5.00
28A Curt Schilling 1.50 4.00
28B Wil Myers 1.25 3.00
29A Nolan Ryan 6.00 15.00
29B Yadier Molina 2.50 6.00
30A Jeff Bagwell 1.50 4.00
30B Yordano Ventura 1.50 4.00

2014 Donruss Game Gear

1 Derek Jeter 10.00 25.00
2 Buster Posey 6.00 15.00
3 Chris Davis 2.00 5.00
4 Bryce Harper 8.00 20.00
5 Drew Smyly 2.00 5.00
6 Hunter Pence 2.50 6.00
7 Paul Goldschmidt 3.00 8.00
8 Matt Wieters 3.00 8.00
9 Curtis Granderson 2.50 6.00
10 Jordan Lyles 2.00 5.00
11 Andy Dirks 2.00 5.00
12 Dillon Gee 2.00 5.00
13 Logan Morrison 2.00 5.00
14 Joey Votto 5.00 12.00
15 Brad Ziegler 2.00 5.00
16 Ian Kinsler 2.50 6.00
17 Dan Uggla 2.00 5.00
18 CC Sabathia 2.50 6.00
19 Chris Perez 2.00 5.00
20 Eric Hosmer 2.50 6.00
21 Jonathon Niese 2.00 5.00
22 Cliff Lee 2.50 6.00
23 Dustin Pedroia 3.00 8.00
24 Starlin Castro 2.00 5.00
25 Matt Moore 2.50 6.00
26 Josh Reddick 2.00 5.00
27 Devin Mesoraco 2.00 5.00
28 Austin Jackson 2.00 5.00
29 Madison Bumgarner 5.00 12.00
30 Jarrod Parker 2.00 5.00
31 Andrew McCutchen 3.00 8.00
32 Kendrys Morales 2.00 5.00
33 Paul Konerko 2.50 6.00
34 Johan Santana 2.50 6.00
35 Adrian Beltre 3.00 8.00
36 Leonys Martin 2.00 5.00
37 Felix Hernandez 2.50 6.00
38 Aroldis Chapman 3.00 8.00
39 Domonic Brown 2.50 6.00
40 Tim Hudson 2.50 6.00
41 Ike Davis 2.00 5.00
42 Brett Gardner 2.50 6.00
43 Matt Kemp 2.50 6.00
44 Edwin Encarnacion 3.00 8.00
45 Pedro Alvarez 2.00 5.00
46 Will Middlebrooks 2.00 5.00
47 Yoenis Cespedes 3.00 8.00
48 Anthony Rizzo 4.00 10.00
49 David Ortiz 5.00 12.00
50 Yasiel Puig 20.00 50.00

2014 Donruss Game Gear Prime

*PRIME: 1X TO 2.5X BASIC
PRINT RUNS B/WN 2-25 COPIES PER
NO PRICING ON QTY 10 OR LESS

2014 Donruss Hall Worthy

1 Mariano Rivera 1.50 4.00
2 Derek Jeter 3.00 8.00
3 Albert Pujols 1.50 4.00
4 Ichiro Suzuki 2.00 5.00
5 Carlos Beltran 1.00 2.50
6 Randy Johnson 1.25 3.00
7 Tim Hudson 1.00 2.50
8 Todd Helton 1.00 2.50
9 Roy Halladay 1.00 2.50
10 David Ortiz 1.25 3.00
11 Adrian Beltre 1.00 2.50
12 Miguel Cabrera 1.25 3.00
13 Johan Santana 1.00 2.50
14 Paul Konerko 1.00 2.50
15 CC Sabathia 1.00 2.50

2014 Donruss Jersey Kings

RANDOM INSERTS IN PACKS
1 Albert Pujols 5.00 12.00
2 Alex Rodriguez 5.00 12.00
3 David Ortiz 4.00 10.00
4 Brett Jackson 2.50 6.00
5 Joe Mauer 3.00 8.00
6 Miguel Cabrera 5.00 12.00
7 Mike Zunino 2.50 6.00
8 Neftali Feliz 2.50 6.00
9 Rick Porcello 3.00 8.00
10 Robinson Cano 3.00 8.00
11 Torii Hunter 2.50 6.00
12 Yovani Gallardo 2.50 6.00
13 Adrian Beltre 4.00 10.00
14 A.J. Burnett 2.50 6.00
15 Drew Smyly 2.50 6.00
16 Dustin Pedroia 4.00 10.00
17 Zoilo Almonte 3.00 8.00
18 Will Middlebrooks 2.50 6.00
19 Prince Fielder 3.00 8.00
20 Patrick Corbin 3.00 8.00
21 Matt Wieters 4.00 10.00
22 Matt Harvey 5.00 12.00
23 Justin Wilson 2.50 6.00
24 Derek Jeter 8.00 20.00
25 Alfonso Soriano 3.00 8.00
26 Derrick Robinson 2.50 6.00
27 Kyle Kendrick 2.50 6.00
28 Hanley Ramirez 3.00 8.00
29 Jose Fernandez 4.00 10.00
30 Ivan Nova 3.00 8.00
31 Jason Heyward 3.00 8.00
32 Nick Swisher 3.00 8.00
33 Russell Martin 2.50 6.00
34 Brandon Barnes 2.50 6.00
35 Pablo Sandoval 3.00 8.00
36 Zack Cozart 2.50 6.00
37 Nick Markakis 3.00 8.00
38 Alex Avila 3.00 8.00
39 Mike Napoli 2.50 6.00
40 Christian Yelich 5.00 12.00
41 Evan Longoria 3.00 8.00
42 Jeff Samardzija 2.50 6.00
43 Jose Reyes 3.00 8.00
44 John Mayberry 2.50 6.00
45 Robbie Ross 2.50 6.00
46 Aaron Hicks 3.00 8.00
47 Junior Lake 2.50 6.00
48 Jimmy Rollins 3.00 8.00
49 Kyle Seager 2.50 6.00
50 Michael Morse 2.50 6.00

2014 Donruss Jersey Kings Studio Series

*STUDIO: .75X TO 2X BASIC
RANDOM INSERTS IN PACKS
PRINT RUNS B/WN 3-25 COPIES PER
NO PRICING ON QTY 15 OR LESS

2014 Donruss National Convention Rated Rookies

201 Masahiro Tanaka 2.00 5.00
202 Jose Abreu 5.00 12.00
203 Yordano Ventura 3.00 8.00

2014 Donruss No No's

1 Nolan Ryan 4.00 10.00
2 Tim Lincecum 1.00 2.50
3 Homer Bailey .75 2.00
4 Dwight Gooden .75 2.00
5 Johan Santana 1.00 2.50
6 Jered Weaver 1.00 2.50
7 Roy Halladay 1.00 2.50
8 Justin Verlander 1.25 3.00
9 Mark Buehrle 1.00 2.50
10 Randy Johnson 1.25 3.00

2014 Donruss Power Plus

COMPLETE SET (12) 6.00 15.00
1 Mike Trout 3.00 8.00
2 Rickey Henderson .60 1.50
3 Josh Hamilton .50 1.25
4 Andrew McCutchen .60 1.50
5 Bryce Harper 1.00 2.50
6 Alex Rodriguez .75 2.00
7 Carlos Beltran .50 1.25
8 Alfonso Soriano .50 1.25
9 Joe Morgan .50 1.25
10 Ryne Sandberg 1.25 3.00
11 Yasiel Puig .60 1.50
12 Matt Kemp .50 1.25

2014 Donruss Power Plus Signatures

PRINT RUNS B/WN 5-25 COPIES PER
NO PRICING ON QTY 10 OR LESS
EXCHANGE DEADLINE 8/26/2015
3 Edwin Encarnacion/15 5.00 12.00
7 Alex Rios/25 10.00 25.00
10 Carlos Gomez/25 EXCH 15.00 40.00

11 Jason Kipnis/25 10.00 25.00
12 Starling Marte/25 EXCH 6.00 15.00
13 David Wright/15 60.00 120.00
14 Jose Canseco/25 150.00 250.00

2014 Donruss Recollection Buyback Autographs

PRINT RUNS B/WN 3-86 COPIES PER
NO PRICING ON QTY 10 OR LESS
EXCHANGE DEADLINE 8/26/2015
1 Tim Raines/45 12.00 30.00
179 Dusty Baker 81 Donruss/20 10.00 25.00
3 Alan Trammell/23 40.00 100.00
11 Ron Darling/18 EXCH 25.00 60.00
12 Don Mattingly/20 EXCH 100.00 200.00
13 Dusty Baker 84 Donruss/20 15.00 40.00
14 Darryl Strawberry 84 Donruss/26 30.00 80.00
293 Alan Trammell 84 Donruss/25 60.00 120.00
18 Eric Davis/40 EXCH 50.00 100.00
21 Vince Coleman 86 Donruss/66 10.00 25.00
24 Fred McGriff 86 Donruss/40 20.00 50.00
26 Wally Joyner 86 Donruss/48 30.00 60.00
30 Mark Grace 88 Donruss/86 15.00 40.00
32 Tom Glavine 88 Donruss/20 60.00 120.00
34 Craig Biggio 89 Donruss/50 15.00 40.00
667 Gregg Jefferies 88 Donruss/99 30.00 80.00

2014 Donruss Signatures

EXCHANGE DEADLINE 8/26/2015
1 Billy Hamilton 4.00 10.00
2 Dave Parker 5.00 12.00
3 Wil Myers 3.00 8.00
4 Jason Kipnis 3.00 8.00
5 Mike Zunino 3.00 8.00
6 Manny Machado 15.00 40.00
7 Bucky Dent 3.00 8.00
8 Kris Medlen 4.00 10.00
9 Chris Sale 5.00 12.00
10 Dusty Baker 3.00 8.00
11 Oscar Gamble 3.00 8.00
12 Willie Horton 3.00 8.00
13 Brandon Barnes 3.00 8.00
14 Martin Prado 3.00 8.00
15 Brandon Maurer 3.00 8.00
16 Alex Wilson 3.00 8.00
17 Andrew Brown 3.00 8.00
18 Starling Marte EXCH 4.00 10.00
19 Chris Rusin 3.00 8.00
20 Jordan Zimmermann 4.00 10.00
21 Evan Gattis EXCH 8.00 20.00
22 Mitch Moreland 3.00 8.00
23 Josh Donaldson 6.00 15.00
24 Bruce Rondon 3.00 8.00
25 Asdrubal Cabrera 4.00 10.00
26 Troy Glaus 8.00 20.00
27 James Shields 5.00 12.00
30 Didi Gregorius 4.00 10.00
31 Reymond Fuentes 3.00 8.00
32 Ivan Nova 4.00 10.00
33 Kevin Gausman 5.00 12.00
34 Jay Bruce 4.00 10.00
35 Michael Choice 3.00 8.00
36 Daniel Nava 6.00 15.00
38 Lance Lynn 6.00 15.00
39 Taijuan Walker 3.00 8.00
40 Xander Bogaerts 12.00 30.00
41 Kolten Wong 4.00 10.00
42 Jurickson Profar 8.00 20.00
43 Mike Napoli 3.00 8.00
44 Zack Wheeler 6.00 15.00
45 Vinnie Pestano 3.00 8.00
46 Michael Morse 3.00 8.00
47 Jay Buhner 4.00 10.00
48 Oscar Taveras 4.00 10.00
50 Miguel Sano 4.00 10.00

2014 Donruss Studio

1A Yasiel Puig 2.50 6.00
1B Adrian Beltre 2.50 6.00
2A Ichiro Suzuki 4.00 10.00
2B Albert Pujols 3.00 8.00
3A Andrew McCutchen 2.50 6.00
3B Chris Sale 2.50 6.00
4A Bryce Harper 4.00 10.00
4B Derek Jeter 6.00 15.00
5A Mike Trout 12.00 30.00
5B Dustin Pedroia 2.50 6.00
6A Chris Davis 1.50 4.00
6B Evan Longoria 2.00 5.00
7A Clayton Kershaw 4.00 10.00
7B Felix Hernandez 2.00 5.00
8A Buster Posey 3.00 8.00
8B Freddie Freeman 3.00 8.00
9A Yadier Molina 3.00 8.00
9B Giancarlo Stanton 2.50 6.00
10A David Ortiz 2.50 6.00
10B Joey Votto 2.50 6.00
11A Yu Darvish 2.50 6.00
11B Jose Abreu 6.00 15.00
12A Stephen Strasburg 2.50 6.00
12B Jose Bautista 2.00 5.00
13 Jose Fernandez 2.50 6.00
14 Masahiro Tanaka 5.00 12.00
15 Max Scherzer 2.50 6.00
16 Miguel Cabrera 2.50 6.00
17 Paul Goldschmidt 2.50 6.00
18 Robinson Cano 2.00 5.00
19 Troy Tulowitzki 2.50 6.00
20 Wil Myers 1.50 4.00

2014 Donruss Team MVPs

1 Buster Posey 2.50 6.00
2 Miguel Cabrera 2.00 5.00
3 Justin Verlander 2.00 5.00
4 Joey Votto 2.00 5.00
5 Josh Hamilton 1.50 4.00
6 Albert Pujols 2.50 6.00
7 Joe Mauer 1.50 4.00
8 Dustin Pedroia 2.00 5.00
9 Ryan Howard 1.50 4.00
10 Ichiro Suzuki 3.00 8.00
11 Chipper Jones 2.00 5.00
12 Ken Griffey Jr. 6.00 15.00
13 Frank Thomas 2.00 5.00
14 Dennis Eckersley 1.50 4.00
15 Cal Ripken Jr. 6.00 15.00
16 Rickey Henderson 2.00 5.00
17 Kirk Gibson 1.25 3.00
18 Roger Clemens 2.50 6.00
19 Don Mattingly 6.00 15.00
20 Dale Murphy 2.00 5.00
21 Robin Yount 2.00 5.00
22 Mike Schmidt 3.00 8.00
23 George Brett 4.00 10.00
24 Dave Parker 1.25 3.00
25 Rod Carew 1.50 4.00
26 Joe Morgan 1.50 4.00
27 Pete Rose 4.00 10.00
28 Reggie Jackson 1.50 4.00
29 Miguel Cabrera 2.00 5.00
30 Andrew McCutchen 2.00 5.00

2014 Donruss The Elite Series

STATED PRINT RUN 999 SER.#'d SETS
1A Brandon Phillips 1.50 4.00
1B Albert Pujols 3.00 8.00
2A Kris Medlen 2.00 5.00
2B Andrew McCutchen 2.50 6.00
3A David Ortiz 2.50 6.00
3B Bryce Harper 4.00 10.00
4A Mike Trout 12.00 30.00
4B Buster Posey 3.00 8.00
5A Evan Gattis 1.50 4.00
5B Carlos Beltran 2.00 5.00
6A Paul Konerko 2.00 5.00
6B Carlos Gomez 1.50 4.00
7A Yasiel Puig 2.50 6.00
7B Carlos Gonzalez 2.00 5.00
8A David Wright 2.00 5.00
8B Chris Archer 1.50 4.00
9A Paul Goldschmidt 2.50 6.00
9B Chris Davis 1.50 4.00
10A Jay Bruce 2.00 5.00
10B Chris Sale 2.50 6.00
11A Manny Machado 2.50 6.00
11B Derek Jeter 6.00 15.00
12A Adam Jones 2.00 5.00
12B Domonic Brown 2.00 5.00
13A Gerrit Cole 2.50 6.00
13B Edwin Encarnacion 2.50 6.00
14A Mariano Rivera 3.00 8.00
14B Evan Longoria 2.00 5.00
15A Stephen Strasburg 2.50 6.00
15B Freddie Freeman 3.00 8.00
16A Paul O'Neill 2.00 5.00
16B Hanley Ramirez 2.00 5.00
17A Cal Ripken Jr. 6.00 15.00
17B Jose Abreu 6.00 15.00
18A Johnny Damon 2.00 5.00
18B Jose Bautista 2.00 5.00
19A Chipper Jones 2.50 6.00
19B Jose Fernandez 2.50 6.00
20A Ozzie Smith 3.00 8.00
20B Jurickson Profar 2.00 5.00
21 Justin Verlander 2.50 6.00
22 Masahiro Tanaka 6.00 15.00
23 Miguel Cabrera 2.50 6.00
24 Nick Castellanos 5.00 12.00
25 Pablo Sandoval 2.00 5.00
26 Prince Fielder 2.00 5.00
27 Robinson Cano 2.00 5.00
28 Xander Bogaerts 5.00 12.00
29 Yordano Ventura 2.00 5.00
30 Yu Darvish 2.50 6.00

2014 Donruss The Rookies

42-100 ISSUED IN THE ROOKIES BOX SET
1 Michael Choice .40 1.00
2 Billy Hamilton .50 1.25
3 Nick Castellanos 1.25 3.00
4 Taijuan Walker .40 1.00
5 Kolten Wong .50 1.25
6 Travis d'Arnaud .50 1.25
7 Wilmer Flores .50 1.25
8 Xander Bogaerts 1.25 3.00
9 Tommy Medica .40 1.00
10 Tim Beckham .60 1.50
11 Cameron Rupp .40 1.00
12 Max Stassi .40 1.00
13 Tanner Roark .40 1.00
14 Enny Romero .40 1.00
15 Jonathan Schoop .40 1.00
16 Erik Johnson .40 1.00
17 Jose Abreu 3.00 8.00
18 Masahiro Tanaka 1.25 3.00
19 Alex Guerrero .50 1.25
20 Yordano Ventura .50 1.25
21 Abraham Almonte .40 1.00
22 Nick Martinez .40 1.00
23 Tyler Collins .40 1.00
24 Tucker Barnhart .40 1.00
25 Matt Davidson .50 1.25
26 Marcus Semien 2.00 5.00
27 Chris Owings .40 1.00
28 Yangervis Solarte .40 1.00
29 Wei-Chung Wang .40 1.00
30 Jimmy Nelson .40 1.00
31 Christian Bethancourt .40 1.00
32 George Springer 1.50 4.00
33 Jake Marisnick .40 1.00
34 Onelki Garcia .40 1.00
35 Chad Bettis .40 1.00
36 Ethan Martin .40 1.00
37 Brian Flynn .40 1.00
38 David Holmberg .40 1.00
39 Heath Hembree .75 2.00
40 David Hale .40 1.00
41 Jose Ramirez 3.00 8.00
42 Oscar Taveras .50 1.25
43 Gregory Polanco .60 1.50
44 Eddie Butler .40 1.00
45 Andrew Heaney .40 1.00
46 Rougned Odor 1.00 2.50
47 Marcus Stroman .60 1.50
48 Rafael Montero .40 1.00
49 Garin Cecchini .40 1.00
50 Mookie Betts 10.00 25.00
51 Jon Singleton .50 1.25
52 James Paxton .60 1.50
53 C.J. Cron .40 1.00
54 J.R. Murphy .40 1.00
55 Marco Gonzales .60 1.50
56 Kyle Parker .50 1.25
57 Anthony DeSclafani .40 1.00
58 Robbie Ray .40 1.00
59 Corey Knebel .40 1.00
60 Chris Withrow .40 1.00
61 Luis Sardinas .40 1.00
62 Eugenio Suarez 1.50 4.00
63 Jace Peterson .40 1.00
64 Carlos Contreras .40 1.00
65 Ryan Goins .50 1.25
66 Burch Smith .40 1.00
67 Aaron Altherr .40 1.00
68 Tommy La Stella .40 1.00
69 Danny Santana .50 1.25
70 Joe Panik .60 1.50
71 Matt Stites .40 1.00
72 Stolmy Pimentel .40 1.00
73 J.T. Realmuto 2.50 6.00
74 Jacob deGrom 12.00 30.00
75 Randal Grichuk .60 1.50
76 Kevin Kiermaier .60 1.50
77 Steven Souza .50 1.25
78 Jorge Polanco 1.00 2.50
79 Adrian Nieto .40 1.00
80 Erisbel Arruebarrena .40 1.00
81 Chase Whitley .40 1.00
82 Odrisamer Despaigne .40 1.00
83 Roenis Elias .40 1.00
84 Matt Shoemaker .60 1.50
85 Domingo Santana .60 1.50
86 Arismendy Alcantara .40 1.00
87 Nick Ahmed .40 1.00
89 Carlos Sanchez .40 1.00
90 C.C. Lee .40 1.00
91 Zach Walters .40 1.00
92 Enrique Hernandez .75 2.00
93 David Peralta .60 1.50
94 James Jones .40 1.00
95 Andrew Susac .50 1.25
96 Aaron Sanchez .40 1.00
97 Chris Taylor 2.00 5.00
98 Shane Greene 1.25 3.00
99 Jesse Hahn .50 1.25
100 Chase Anderson .40 1.00

2014 Donruss The Rookies Press Proofs Gold

*GOLD PROOF: 2.5X TO 6X BASIC
STATED PRINT RUN 99 SER.#'d SETS
RANDOM INSERTS IN PACKS
17 Jose Abreu 8.00 20.00

2014 Donruss The Rookies Press Proofs Silver

*SILVER PROOF: 2X TO 5X BASIC
STATED PRINT RUN 199 SER.#'d SETS
RANDOM INSERTS IN PACKS
17 Jose Abreu 6.00 15.00

2014 Donruss The Rookies Stat Line Career

*CAREER p/r 308-400: 1.5X TO 4X BASIC
*CAREER p/r 102-184: 2X TO 5X BASIC
*CAREER p/r 62-99: 2.5X TO 6X BASIC
*CAREER p/r 36-48: 3X TO 8X BASIC
*CAREER p/r 23: 4X TO 10X BASIC
RANDOM INSERTS IN PACKS
PRINT RUNS B/WN 23-400 COPIES PER
17 Jose Abreu/184 6.00 15.00

2014 Donruss The Rookies Stat Line Season

*SEASON p/r 116-180: 2X TO 5X BASIC
*SEASON p/r 67-77: 2.5X TO 6X BASIC
*SEASON p/r 31-44: 3X TO 8X BASIC
*SEASON p/r 21-24: 4X TO 10X BASIC
*SEASON p/r 15-19: 5X TO 12X BASIC
RANDOM INSERTS IN PACKS
PRINT RUNS B/WN 11-180 COPIES PER
NO PRICING ON QTY 12 OR LESS
17 Jose Abreu/37 10.00 25.00

2014 Donruss The Rookies Autographs

INSERTED IN THE ROOKIES UPDATE BOXES
1 Michael Choice 3.00 8.00
3 Nick Castellanos 10.00 25.00
4 Taijuan Walker 3.00 8.00
5 Kolten Wong 4.00 10.00
8 Xander Bogaerts 10.00 25.00
11 Cameron Rupp 3.00 8.00
17 Jose Abreu 25.00 60.00
19 Alex Guerrero 4.00 10.00
21 Abraham Almonte 3.00 8.00
22 Nick Martinez 3.00 8.00
23 Tyler Collins 3.00 8.00
24 Tucker Barnhart 3.00 8.00
26 Marcus Semien 15.00 40.00
27 Chris Owings 3.00 8.00
28 Yangervis Solarte 3.00 8.00
30 Jimmy Nelson 3.00 8.00
32 George Springer 8.00 20.00
33 Jake Marisnick 3.00 8.00
41 Jose Ramirez 20.00 50.00
42 Oscar Taveras 4.00 10.00
43 Gregory Polanco 5.00 12.00
44 Eddie Butler 3.00 8.00
45 Andrew Heaney 3.00 8.00
46 Rougned Odor 8.00 20.00
47 Marcus Stroman 5.00 12.00
48 Rafael Montero 3.00 8.00
49 Garin Cecchini 3.00 8.00
50 Mookie Betts 50.00 80.00
51 Jon Singleton 4.00 10.00
52 James Paxton 5.00 12.00
53 C.J. Cron 3.00 8.00
54 J.R. Murphy 3.00 8.00
56 Kyle Parker 4.00 10.00
57 Anthony DeSclafani 3.00 8.00
58 Robbie Ray 3.00 8.00
59 Corey Knebel 3.00 8.00
61 Luis Sardinas 3.00 8.00
62 Eugenio Suarez 10.00 25.00
63 Jace Peterson 3.00 8.00
64 Carlos Contreras 3.00 8.00
65 Ryan Goins 4.00 10.00
66 Burch Smith 3.00 8.00
67 Aaron Altherr 3.00 8.00
68 Tommy La Stella 3.00 8.00
69 Danny Santana 4.00 10.00
70 Joe Panik 5.00 12.00
72 Stolmy Pimentel 3.00 8.00
73 J.T. Realmuto 25.00 60.00
74 Jacob deGrom 150.00 400.00
75 Randal Grichuk 5.00 12.00
76 Kevin Kiermaier 8.00 20.00
77 Steven Souza 4.00 10.00
79 Adrian Nieto 3.00 8.00
80 Erisbel Arruebarrena 3.00 8.00
81 Chase Whitley 3.00 8.00
82 Odrisamer Despaigne 3.00 8.00
83 Roenis Elias 3.00 8.00
84 Matt Shoemaker 5.00 12.00
85 Domingo Santana 5.00 12.00
86 Arismendy Alcantara 3.00 8.00
87 Nick Ahmed 3.00 8.00
88 Christian Vazquez 10.00 25.00
89 Carlos Sanchez 3.00 8.00
90 C.C. Lee 3.00 8.00
92 Enrique Hernandez 8.00 20.00
94 James Jones 3.00 8.00
95 Andrew Susac 4.00 10.00
96 Aaron Sanchez 3.00 8.00
97 Chris Taylor 8.00 20.00
98 Shane Greene 5.00 12.00
99 Jesse Hahn 4.00 10.00
100 Chase Anderson 3.00 8.00

2015 Donruss

SPs RANDOMLY INSERTED
1 Paul Goldschmidt DK 1.00 2.50
2 Freddie Freeman DK 1.25 3.00
3 Adam Jones DK .75 2.00
4 Dustin Pedroia DK 1.00 2.50
5 Anthony Rizzo DK 1.25 3.00
6 Jose Abreu DK 1.00 2.50
7 Johnny Cueto DK .75 2.00
8 Corey Kluber DK .75 2.00
9 Nolan Arenado DK 1.50 4.00
10A Victor Martinez DK .75 2.00
10B Alex Gordon .20 .50
10C Gordon SP Back in KC 5.00 12.00
11 George Springer DK .75 2.00
12 Alex Gordon DK .75 2.00
13 Mike Trout DK 5.00 12.00
14 Clayton Kershaw DK 1.50 4.00
15 Giancarlo Stanton DK 1.00 2.50
16 Ryan Braun DK .75 2.00
17 Joe Mauer DK .75 2.00
18 David Wright DK .75 2.00
19 Jacoby Ellsbury DK .75 2.00
20 Sonny Gray DK .75 2.00
21 Ryan Howard DK .75 2.00
22 Gerrit Cole DK 1.00 2.50
23 Andrew Cashner DK .60 1.50
24 Madison Bumgarner DK .75 2.00
25 Felix Hernandez DK .75 2.00
26 Adam Wainwright DK .75 2.00
27 James Loney DK .60 1.50
28 Adrian Beltre DK 1.00 2.50
29 Jose Reyes DK .75 2.00
30 Jordan Zimmermann DK .75 2.00
31 Rusney Castillo RC .60 1.50
32 Joc Pederson RC 2.00 5.00
33 Dalton Pompey RC .60 1.50
34 Daniel Norris RC .50 1.25
35 Javier Baez RC 4.00 10.00
36 Kennys Vargas (RC) .50 1.25
37 Jorge Soler RC .75 2.00
38 Michael Taylor RC .50 1.25
39 Mike Foltynewicz RC .50 1.25
40 Brandon Finnegan RC .50 1.25
41 Maikel Franco RC .60 1.50
42 Yorman Rodriguez RC .50 1.25
43 Christian Walker RC 1.00 2.50
44 Jake Lamb RC .75 2.00
45 Rymer Liriano RC .50 1.25*
46 Paul Goldschmidt .25 .60
47 Mark Trumbo .15 .40
48 Patrick Corbin .20 .50
49 Alex Wood .15 .40
50 Freddie Freeman .30 .75
51 Jason Heyward .20 .50
52 Justin Upton .20 .50
53 Julio Teheran .20 .50
54 Nelson Cruz .25 .60
55 Chris Davis .15 .40
56 Adam Jones .20 .50
57 Wei-Yin Chen .15 .40
58 Chris Tillman .15 .40
59 David Ortiz .25 .60
60 Dustin Pedroia .25 .60
61 Yoenis Cespedes .20 .50
62 Xander Bogaerts .25 .60
63 Anthony Rizzo .30 .75
64 Junior Lake .15 .40
65 Starlin Castro .15 .40
66 Jake Arrieta .20 .50
67A Jose Abreu .25 .60
67B J.Abreu SP ROY 2.50 6.00
68 Chris Sale .25 .60
69 Alexei Ramirez .20 .50
70 Adam Eaton .15 .40
71 Joey Votto .25 .60
72 Todd Frazier .15 .40
73 Devin Mesoraco .15 .40
74 Billy Hamilton .20 .50
75 Johnny Cueto .20 .50
76 Aroldis Chapman .25 .60
77 Michael Brantley .20 .50
78 Corey Kluber .20 .50
79 Carlos Santana .20 .50
80 Yan Gomes .15 .40
81 Troy Tulowitzki .25 .60
82 Corey Dickerson .15 .40
83 Charlie Blackmon .25 .60
84 Nolan Arenado .40 1.00
85 Justin Morneau .20 .50
86 Justin Verlander .25 .60
87A Miguel Cabrera .25 .60
87B Cabrera SP Marlins 2.50 6.00
88 Victor Martinez .20 .50
89 Max Scherzer .25 .60
90 David Price .20 .50
91 Dallas Keuchel .20 .50
92 Chris Carter .15 .40
93 George Springer .20 .50
94 Jose Altuve .20 .50
95 Eric Hosmer .20 .50
96 James Shields .15 .40
97 Alex Gordon .20 .50
98 Yordano Ventura .20 .50
99 Salvador Perez .20 .50
100A Mike Trout 1.25 3.00
100B Trout SP Rev Neg 15.00 40.00
100C Trout SP Fldng 15.00 40.00
100D Trout SP MVP 12.00 30.00
101 Albert Pujols .30 .75
102 Matt Shoemaker .20 .50
103 Jered Weaver .20 .50
104A Clayton Kershaw .40 1.00
104B Kershaw SP MVP 4.00 10.00
105 Adrian Gonzalez .20 .50
106A Yasiel Puig .25 .60
106B Puig SP White borders 6.00 15.00
107 Matt Kemp .20 .50
108 Zack Greinke .25 .60
109 Dee Gordon .15 .40
110 Giancarlo Stanton .25 .60
111 Marcell Ozuna .25 .60
112 Henderson Alvarez .15 .40
113 Jose Fernandez .25 .60
114 Ryan Braun .20 .50
115 Carlos Gomez .15 .40
116 Jonathan Lucroy .20 .50
117 Francisco Rodriguez .20 .50
118 Joe Mauer .20 .50
119 Brian Dozier .20 .50
120 Danny Santana .15 .40
121 Phil Hughes .15 .40
122 David Wright .20 .50
123 Zack Wheeler .20 .50
124 Matt Harvey .20 .50
125 Bartolo Colon .15 .40
126A Ichiro .30 .75
126B Ichiro SP Mariners 3.00 8.00
127 Brett Gardner .20 .50
128 Jacoby Ellsbury .20 .50
129A Masahiro Tanaka .20 .50
129B Tanaka SP No logo 2.00 5.00
130 David Robertson .20 .50
131 Josh Donaldson .20 .50
132 Sonny Gray .20 .50
133 Scott Kazmir .15 .40
134 Jon Lester .20 .50
135 Ryan Howard .20 .50
136 Jimmy Rollins .20 .50
137 Chase Utley .20 .50
138 Cole Hamels .20 .50
139 Gregory Polanco .20 .50
140A Andrew McCutchen .25 .60
140B McCutchen SP B/W 10.00 25.00
141 Neil Walker .15 .40
142 Starling Marte .20 .50
143 Edinson Volquez .15 .40
144 Gerrit Cole .25 .60
145 Seth Smith .15 .40
146 Everth Cabrera .15 .40
147 Ian Kennedy .15 .40
148A Buster Posey .30 .75
148B Posey SP Dynasty 3.00 8.00
149 Hunter Pence .20 .50
150 Madison Bumgarner .20 .50
151 Pablo Sandoval .20 .50
152 Brandon Belt .20 .50
153 Robinson Cano .20 .50
154 Kyle Seager .15 .40
155 Mike Zunino .15 .40
156 Felix Hernandez .20 .50
157 Hisashi Iwakuma .20 .50
158 Matt Adams .15 .40
159 Kolten Wong .20 .50
160 Yadier Molina .30 .75
161 Adam Wainwright .20 .50
162 Matt Carpenter .25 .60
163 Matt Holliday .25 .60
164 Evan Longoria .20 .50
165 Kevin Kiermaier .20 .50
166 Alex Cobb .15 .40
167 James Loney .15 .40
168 Adrian Beltre .25 .60
169 Yu Darvish .25 .60
170 Leonys Martin .15 .40
171 Rougned Odor .20 .50
172 Edwin Encarnacion .25 .60
173 Jose Bautista .20 .50
174 Melky Cabrera .15 .40
175 R.A. Dickey .20 .50
176A Bryce Harper .40 1.00
176B Harper SP Mohawk 10.00 25.00
177 Anthony Rendon .25 .60
178 Jordan Zimmermann .20 .50
179 Doug Fister .15 .40
180 Stephen Strasburg .25 .60
181 Rickey Henderson .25 .60
182 Mike Piazza .25 .60
183 Willie McCovey .20 .50
184 Mark McGwire .40 1.00
185A Frank Thomas .25 .60
185B Thomas SP NNOF 12.00 30.00
186 Frank Robinson .20 .50
187A Kirby Puckett .25 .60
187B Puckett SP Puck 10.00 25.00
188A Mariano Rivera .30 .75
188B Rivera SP B/W 10.00 25.00
189 George Brett .50 1.25
190 Wade Boggs .20 .50
191 Ryne Sandberg .50 1.25
192A Pete Rose .50 1.25
192B Rose SP '81 Design 20.00 50.00
193 Tony Gwynn .25 .60
194A Bo Jackson .25 .60
194B Jackson SP B/W 10.00 25.00
195 Ernie Banks .25 .60
196 Mike Trout 81 6.00 15.00
197 Miguel Cabrera 81 1.25 3.00
198 Andrew McCutchen 81 1.25 3.00
199 Albert Pujols 81 1.50 4.00
200 Yu Darvish 81 1.25 3.00
201 Bryce Harper 81 2.00 5.00
202 Jose Abreu 81 1.25 3.00
203 Masahiro Tanaka 81 1.00 2.50
204 Robinson Cano 81 1.00 2.50
205 Madison Bumgarner 81 1.00 2.50
206 Adam Wainwright 81 1.00 2.50
207 Yasiel Puig 81 1.25 3.00
208 Giancarlo Stanton 81 1.25 3.00
209 Evan Longoria 81 1.00 2.50
210 Yadier Molina 81 1.50 4.00
211 Joe Mauer 81 1.00 2.50
212 David Wright 81 1.00 2.50
213 Dustin Pedroia 81 1.25 3.00
214 Felix Hernandez 81 1.00 2.50
215 Clayton Kershaw 81 2.00 5.00
216 Chris Sale 81 1.25 3.00
217 Buster Posey 81 1.50 4.00
218 Alex Gordon 81 1.00 2.50
219 Freddie Freeman 81 1.50 4.00
220 David Ortiz 81 1.25 3.00
221 Ichiro 81 1.50 4.00
222 Nelson Cruz 81 1.25 3.00
223 Jose Bautista 81 1.00 2.50
224 Johnny Cueto 81 1.00 2.50
225 Ryan Howard 81 1.00 2.50
226 Eric Hosmer 81 1.00 2.50
227 Josh Donaldson 81 1.00 2.50
228 Troy Tulowitzki 81 1.25 3.00
229 Corey Kluber 81 1.00 2.50
230 Max Scherzer 81 1.25 3.00
231 Jose Altuve 81 1.00 2.50
232 Manny Machado 81 1.25 3.00
233 Yordano Ventura 81 1.00 2.50
234 Billy Hamilton 81 1.00 2.50
235 Adrian Beltre 81 1.25 3.00
236 Reggie Jackson 81 1.00 2.50
237 Johnny Bench 81 1.25 3.00
238 Cal Ripken 81 4.00 10.00
239 Bob Gibson 81 1.00 2.50
240 George Brett 81 2.50 6.00
241 Ozzie Smith 81 1.50 4.00
242 Don Mattingly 81 2.50 6.00
243 Greg Maddux 81 1.50 4.00
244 Ken Griffey Jr. 81 2.50 6.00
245 Nolan Ryan 81 4.00 10.00

2015 Donruss '81 Press Proofs Bronze

*PLAT.BRONZE: .6X TO 1.5X BASIC
RANDOM INSERTS IN PACKS
STATED PRINT RUN 299 SER.#'d SETS

2015 Donruss '81 Press Proofs Platinum Blue

*PLAT.BLUE: .75X TO 2X BASIC
RANDOM INSERTS IN PACKS
STATED PRINT RUN 199 SER.#'d SETS

2015 Donruss Press Proofs Gold

*GOLD DK: 1.2X TO 3X BASIC
*GOLD RC: 1.5X TO 4X BASIC
*GOLD VET: 5X TO 12X BASIC
RANDOM INSERTS IN PACKS
STATED PRINT RUN 99 SER.#'d SETS

2015 Donruss Press Proofs Silver

*SILVER DK: .75X TO 2X BASIC
*SILVER RC: 1X TO 2.5X BASIC
*SILVER VET: 3X TO 8X BASIC
RANDOM INSERTS IN PACKS
STATED PRINT RUN 199 SER.#'d SETS

2015 Donruss Stat Line Career

*CAR DK p/r 280-400: .6X TO 1.5X
*CAR DK p/r 154-230: .75X TO 2X
*CAR DK p/r 106-121: 1X TO 2.5X
*CAR DK p/r 63-71: 1.2X TO 3X
*CAR RR p/r 274-400: .75X TO 2X
*CAR RR p/r 150: 1X TO 2.5X
*CAR RR p/r 100: 1.2X TO 3X
*CAR RR p/r 19: 2.5X TO 6X
*CAR p/r 262-400: 2.5X TO 6X
*CAR p/r 136-248: 3X TO 8X
*CAR p/r 82-122: 4X TO 10X
*CAR p/r 50-73: 5X TO 12X
*CAR p/r 27: 6X TO 15X
*CAR p/r 17-23: 8X TO 20X
RANDOM INSERTS IN PACKS
PRINT RUNS B/WN 5-400 COPIES PER
NO PRICING ON QTY 15 OR LESS

2015 Donruss Stat Line Season

*SEA DK p/r 255-400: .6X TO 1.5X
*SEA DK p/r 138-248: .75X TO 2X
*SEA DK p/r 81-107: 1X TO 2.5X
*SEA DK p/r 29-36: 1.5X TO 4X
*SEA DK p/r 18-20: 2X TO 5X
*SEA RR p/r 255-400: .75X TO 2X
*SEA RR p/r 126-231: 1X TO 2.5X
*SEA RR p/r 84-106: 1.2X TO 3X
*SEA RR p/r 59: 1.5X TO 4X
*SEA RR p/r 30-46: 2X TO 5X
*SEA p/r 252-400: 2.5X TO 6X
*SEA p/r 130-246: 3X TO 8X
*SEA p/r 78-116: 4X TO 10X
*SEA p/r 53-70: 5X TO 12X
*SEA p/r 26-49: 6X TO 15X
*SEA p/r 16-25: 8X TO 20X
RANDOM INSERTS IN PACKS
PRINT RUNS B/WN 7-400 COPIES PER
NO PRICING ON QTY 15 OR LESS

2015 Donruss All Time Diamond Kings

RANDOM INSERTS IN PACKS
*SILVER/49: 3X TO 8X BASIC
1 Ken Griffey Jr. 2.50 6.00
2 Cal Ripken 4.00 10.00
3 Nolan Ryan 4.00 10.00
4 Frank Thomas 1.25 3.00
5 Greg Maddux 1.50 4.00
6 Pete Rose 2.50 6.00
7 George Brett 2.50 6.00
8 Robin Yount 1.25 3.00
9 Rickey Henderson 1.25 3.00
10 Kirby Puckett 1.25 3.00
11 Ozzie Smith 1.50 4.00
12 Tony Gwynn 1.25 3.00
13 Johnny Bench 1.25 3.00
14 Reggie Jackson 1.00 2.50
15 Ryne Sandberg 2.50 6.00
16 Willie McCovey 1.00 2.50
17 Brooks Robinson 1.00 2.50
18 Wade Boggs 1.00 2.50
19 Ernie Banks 1.25 3.00
20 Carl Yastrzemski 2.00 5.00
21 Mariano Rivera 1.50 4.00
22 Mike Piazza 1.25 3.00
23 Frank Robinson 1.00 2.50
24 Bob Gibson 1.00 2.50
25 Jim Palmer 1.00 2.50
26 Chipper Jones 1.25 3.00
27 Don Mattingly 2.50 6.00
28 Bo Jackson 1.25 3.00
29 Mark McGwire 2.00 5.00
30 Paul Molitor 1.25 3.00

2015 Donruss Bat Kings

RANDOM INSERTS IN PACKS
*STUDIO/25: .6X TO 1.5X BASIC
1 Albert Pujols 4.00 10.00
2 Brandon Belt 2.50 6.00
3 Evan Gattis 2.00 5.00
4 Carlos Beltran 2.50 6.00
5 Carlos Gonzalez 2.50 6.00
6 B.J. Upton 2.50 6.00
7 David Ortiz 3.00 8.00
8 Devin Mesoraco 2.00 5.00
9 Dustin Pedroia 3.00 8.00
10 Edwin Encarnacion 3.00 8.00
11 Evan Longoria 2.50 6.00
12 Gerardo Parra 2.00 5.00
13 Hanley Ramirez 2.50 6.00
14 Jacoby Ellsbury 2.50 6.00
15 Jose Bautista 2.50 6.00
16 Jose Reyes 2.50 6.00
17 Josh Donaldson 2.50 6.00
18 Justin Upton 2.50 6.00
19 Mark Teixeira 2.50 6.00
20 Matt Kemp 2.50 6.00
21 Mike Napoli 2.00 5.00
22 Nelson Cruz 3.00 8.00
23 Pedro Alvarez 2.00 5.00
24 Prince Fielder 2.50 6.00
25 Robinson Cano 2.50 6.00
26 Ryan Howard 2.50 6.00
27 Ryan Zimmerman 2.50 6.00
28 Troy Tulowitzki 3.00 8.00
29 Wil Myers 2.50 6.00
30 Adrian Gonzalez 2.50 6.00
31 Andrew McCutchen 3.00 8.00
32 Brandon Phillips 2.00 5.00
33 David Wright 2.50 6.00
34 George Springer 2.50 6.00
35 Hunter Pence 2.50 6.00
36 Joe Mauer 2.50 6.00
37 Joey Votto 3.00 8.00
38 Matt Adams 2.00 5.00
39 Melky Cabrera 2.00 5.00
40 Yasiel Puig 3.00 8.00
41 Giancarlo Stanton 3.00 8.00
42 Miguel Cabrera 3.00 8.00
43 Starlin Castro 2.00 5.00
44 Starling Marte 2.50 6.00
45 Mike Trout 6.00 15.00

2015 Donruss Elite Inserts

COMPLETE SET (36) 10.00 25.00
RANDOM INSERTS IN PACKS
*STAT.GLD/49: 1.5X TO 4X BASIC
*STAT.RED/25: 2.5X TO 6X BASIC
1 Patrick Corbin .50 1.25
2 Jason Heyward .50 1.25
3 Wei-Yin Chen .40 1.00
4 Yoenis Cespedes .50 1.25
5 Jose Abreu .60 1.50
6 Anthony Rizzo .75 2.00
7 Johnny Cueto .50 1.25
8 Corey Kluber .50 1.25
9 Nolan Arenado 1.00 2.50
10 Victor Martinez .50 1.25
11 Jose Altuve .50 1.25
12 Alex Gordon .50 1.25
13 Jered Weaver .50 1.25
14 Dee Gordon .40 1.00
15 Henderson Alvarez .40 1.00
16 Jonathan Lucroy .50 1.25
17 Brian Dozier .50 1.25
18 Zack Wheeler .50 1.25
19 Jacoby Ellsbury .50 1.25
20 Sonny Gray .50 1.25
21 Jimmy Rollins .50 1.25
22 Neil Walker .40 1.00
23 Matt Adams .40 1.00
24 Hisashi Iwakuma .50 1.25
25 Hunter Pence .50 1.25
26 Everth Cabrera .40 1.00
27 James Loney .40 1.00
28 Leonys Martin .40 1.00
29 R.A. Dickey .50 1.25
30 Anthony Rendon .60 1.50
31 Greg Holland .40 1.00
32 Francisco Lindor 3.00 8.00
33 Yasmany Tomas .50 1.25
34 Carlos Correa 2.00 5.00
35 Byron Buxton 2.00 5.00
36 Kris Bryant 4.00 10.00

2015 Donruss Elite Inserts Dominator

RANDOM INSERTS IN PACKS
STATED PRINT RUN 999 SER.#'d SETS
1 Freddie Freeman 2.00 5.00
2 Adam Jones 1.25 3.00
3 Yoenis Cespedes 1.25 3.00
4 Chris Sale 1.50 4.00
5 Andrew McCutchen 1.50 4.00
6 Buster Posey 2.00 5.00
7 Robinson Cano 1.25 3.00
8 Adam Wainwright 1.25 3.00
9 Bryce Harper 2.50 6.00
10 Jose Altuve 1.25 3.00
11 Salvador Perez 1.25 3.00
12 Albert Pujols 2.00 5.00
13 Ryan Howard 1.25 3.00
14 Yu Darvish 1.50 4.00
15 Javier Baez 8.00 20.00
16 Nolan Arenado 2.50 6.00
17 Zack Greinke 1.50 4.00
18 Mike Trout 8.00 20.00
19 Ichiro 2.00 5.00
20 Rusney Castillo 1.25 3.00
21 Kennys Vargas 1.00 2.50

22 Jorge Soler 1.50 4.00
23 Joc Pederson 4.00 10.00
24 Maikel Franco 1.25 3.00
25 Michael Taylor 1.00 2.50

2015 Donruss Hot off the Press

*HP DK: .6X TO 1.5X BASIC
*HP RC: .75X TO 2X BASIC
*SP VET: 2.5X TO 6X BASIC
*SP 81: .5X TO 1.2X BASIC
RANDOM INSERTS IN PACKS

2015 Donruss Jersey Kings

RANDOM INSERTS IN PACKS
*STUDIO/25: 1X TO 2.5X BASIC
1 Andrew McCutchen 4.00 10.00
2 Aaron Hicks 2.50 6.00
3 Adam Eaton 2.00 5.00
4 Anthony Rizzo 4.00 10.00
5 Billy Hamilton 2.50 6.00
6 Brad Ziegler 2.00 5.00
7 Brandon Belt 2.50 6.00
8 Brian Dozier 2.50 6.00
9 Bryce Harper 5.00 12.00
10 Carl Crawford 2.50 6.00
11 Carlos Gomez 2.00 5.00
12 Chase Headley 2.00 5.00
13 Chris Perez 2.00 5.00
14 Dallas Keuchel 2.50 6.00
15 Dan Uggla 2.00 5.00
16 David Ortiz 3.00 8.00
17 Dee Gordon 2.00 5.00
18 Dexter Fowler 2.50 6.00
19 Dillon Gee 2.00 5.00
20 Evan Longoria 2.50 6.00
21 Felix Hernandez 2.50 6.00
22 Ian Kinsler 2.50 6.00
23 Hunter Pence 2.50 6.00
24 Jackie Bradley Jr. 3.00 8.00
25 Jacoby Ellsbury 2.50 6.00
26 Albert Pujols 4.00 10.00
27 Jason Heyward 2.50 6.00
28 Jake Odorizzi 2.00 5.00
29 Jay Bruce 2.50 6.00
30 Jon Lester 2.50 6.00
31 Aramis Ramirez 2.00 5.00
32 Prince Fielder 2.50 6.00
33 Jason Kipnis 2.50 6.00
35 Josh Hamilton 2.50 6.00
36 Leonys Martin 2.00 5.00
37 Mark Trumbo 2.00 5.00
38 Matt Adams 2.00 5.00
39 Yovani Gallardo 2.00 5.00
40 Victor Martinez 2.50 6.00
41 Torii Hunter 2.00 5.00
42 Shane Victorino 2.50 6.00
43 Robinson Cano 2.50 6.00
44 Patrick Corbin 2.50 6.00
45 Nelson Cruz 3.00 8.00

2015 Donruss Long Ball Leaders

RANDOM INSERTS IN PACKS
*RED/99: 1.2X TO 3X BASIC
*GREEN/25: 2X TO 5X BASIC
1 Mike Trout 6.00 15.00
2 Giancarlo Stanton 1.25 3.00
3 David Ortiz 1.25 3.00
4 Justin Upton 1.00 2.50
5 Hanley Ramirez 1.00 2.50
6 Paul Goldschmidt 1.25 3.00
7 C.J. Cron .75 2.00
8 Anthony Rizzo 1.50 4.00
9 George Springer 1.00 2.50
10 Alex Gordon 1.00 2.50
11 Ian Desmond .75 2.00
12 Edwin Encarnacion 1.25 3.00
13 Hunter Pence 1.00 2.50
14 Buster Posey 1.50 4.00
15 Yasiel Puig 1.25 3.00

2015 Donruss Preferred Black

*BLACK: 1.5X TO 4X BASIC
RANDOM INSERTS IN PACKS
STATED PRINT RUN 99 SER.#'d SETS
2 George Brett 10.00 25.00
5 Kirby Puckett 10.00 25.00

2015 Donruss Preferred Bronze

COMPLETE SET (40) 10.00 25.00
RANDOM INSERTS IN PACKS
1 Ken Griffey Jr. 1.25 3.00
2 George Brett 1.25 3.00
3 Cal Ripken 2.00 5.00
4 Nolan Ryan 2.00 5.00
5 Kirby Puckett .60 1.50
6 Javier Baez 3.00 8.00
7 Kennys Vargas .40 1.00
8 Joc Pederson 1.50 4.00
9 Rusney Castillo .50 1.25
10 Dalton Pompey .50 1.25
11 Maikel Franco .50 1.25
12 Jorge Soler .60 1.50
13 Michael Taylor .40 1.00
14 Daniel Norris .40 1.00
15 Brandon Finnegan .40 1.00
16 Rymer Liriano .40 1.00
17 Mike Foltynewicz .40 1.00
18 Mike Trout 3.00 8.00
19 Ichiro .75 2.00
20 Clayton Kershaw 1.00 2.50
21 Jose Abreu .60 1.50
22 Yu Darvish .60 1.50
23 Bryce Harper 1.00 2.50
24 Chris Sale .60 1.50
25 Giancarlo Stanton .60 1.50
26 Masahiro Tanaka .50 1.25
27 George Springer .50 1.25
28 Eric Hosmer .50 1.25
29 Buster Posey .75 2.00
30 Felix Hernandez .50 1.25
31 Miguel Cabrera .60 1.50
32 Yasiel Puig .60 1.50
33 Adam Wainwright .50 1.25
34 Jose Altuve .50 1.25
35 David Ortiz .60 1.50
36 Francisco Lindor 3.00 8.00
37 Yasmany Tomas .50 1.25
38 Carlos Correa 2.00 5.00
39 Byron Buxton 2.00 5.00
40 Kris Bryant 4.00 10.00

2015 Donruss Preferred Cut to the Chase Bronze

*BRONZE: 2.5X TO 6X BASIC
RANDOM INSERTS IN PACKS
STATED PRINT RUN 49 SER.#'d SETS
2 George Brett 15.00 40.00
5 Kirby Puckett 15.00 40.00

2015 Donruss Preferred Cut to the Chase Gold

*GOLD: 3X TO 8X BASIC
RANDOM INSERTS IN PACKS
STATED PRINT RUN 25 SER.#'d SETS
2 George Brett 20.00 50.00
5 Kirby Puckett 20.00 50.00

2015 Donruss Preferred Gold

*GOLD: 1X TO 2.5X BASIC
RANDOM INSERTS IN PACKS
STATED PRINT RUN 299 SER.#'d SETS
2 George Brett 6.00 15.00
5 Kirby Puckett 6.00 15.00

2015 Donruss Preferred Red

*RED: 1.2X TO 3X BASIC
RANDOM INSERTS IN PACKS
STATED PRINT RUN 199 SER.#'d SETS
2 George Brett 8.00 20.00
5 Kirby Puckett 8.00 20.00

2015 Donruss Production Line Blue

RANDOM INSERTS IN PACKS
PRINT RUNS B/WN 427-581 COPIES PER
*RED: .75X TO 2X BASIC
*GREEN: 2.5X TO 6X BASIC
1 Jose Abreu/581 1.50 4.00
2 Giancarlo Stanton/555 1.50 4.00
3 Victor Martinez/565 1.25 3.00
4 Adrian Gonzalez/482 1.25 3.00
5 Adrian Beltre/492 1.50 4.00
6 Miguel Cabrera/524 1.50 4.00
7 Mike Trout/561 8.00 20.00
8 Adam LaRoche/455 1.00 2.50
9 Andrew McCutchen/542 1.50 4.00
10 Anthony Rizzo/527 2.00 5.00
11 Nelson Cruz/525 1.50 4.00
12 Jose Bautista/524 1.25 3.00
13 Chris Carter/491 1.00 2.50
14 David Ortiz/517 1.50 4.00
15 Albert Pujols/466 2.00 5.00
16 Justin Upton/491 1.25 3.00
17 Yoenis Cespedes/450 1.25 3.00
18 Carlos Santana/427 1.25 3.00
19 Freddie Freeman/461 2.00 5.00
20 Buster Posey/490 2.00 5.00

2015 Donruss Rated Rookies Die Cut Silver

RANDOM INSERTS IN PACKS
STATED PRINT RUN 750 SER.#'d SETS
*GOLD/25: 1X TO 2.5X BASIC
1 Rusney Castillo 1.50 4.00
2 Joc Pederson 5.00 12.00
3 Javier Baez 10.00 25.00
4 Jorge Soler 2.00 5.00
5 Maikel Franco 1.50 4.00
6 Kennys Vargas 1.25 3.00
7 Michael Taylor 1.25 3.00
8 Mike Foltynewicz 1.25 3.00
9 Daniel Norris 1.25 3.00
10 Dalton Pompey 1.50 4.00

2015 Donruss Signature Series

RANDOM INSERTS IN PACKS
1 Christian Walker 5.00 12.00
2 Rusney Castillo 3.00 8.00
3 Yasmany Tomas 3.00 8.00
4 Matt Barnes 2.50 6.00
5 Brandon Finnegan 2.50 6.00
6 Daniel Norris 2.50 6.00
7 Kendall Graveman 2.50 6.00
8 Yorman Rodriguez 2.50 6.00
9 Gary Brown 2.50 6.00
10 R.J. Alvarez 2.50 6.00
11 Dalton Pompey 3.00 8.00
14 Lane Adams 2.50 6.00
15 Joc Pederson 10.00 25.00
16 Steven Moya 3.00 8.00
17 Cory Spangenberg 2.50 6.00
18 Andy Wilkins 2.50 6.00
19 Terrance Gore 2.50 6.00
21 Dilson Herrera 3.00 8.00
23 Jorge Soler 4.00 10.00
24 Matt Szczur 3.00 8.00
25 Buck Farmer 2.50 6.00
26 Michael Taylor 2.50 6.00
28 Trevor May 2.50 6.00
29 Jake Lamb 4.00 10.00
30 Javier Baez 25.00 60.00
31 Mike Foltynewicz 2.50 6.00
32 Kennys Vargas 2.50 6.00
33 Anthony Ranaudo 2.50 6.00
34 Matt Carpenter 4.00 10.00
35 David Price 12.00 30.00
36 Alex Wood 2.50 6.00
37 Dante Bichette 2.50 6.00
38 Fernando Rodney 2.50 6.00
39 Ron Gant 2.50 6.00
40 Adam Eaton 2.50 6.00
41 Shane Victorino 3.00 8.00
42 Anthony Rendon 6.00 15.00
43 Max Scherzer 6.00 15.00
44 Daniel Murphy 3.00 8.00
45 Adam Jones 6.00 15.00
46 Adrian Beltre 6.00 15.00
48 Jered Weaver 3.00 8.00
49 Prince Fielder 6.00 15.00
50 R.A. Dickey 3.00 8.00
51 Victor Martinez 3.00 8.00
52 Brian McCann 3.00 8.00
53 David Freese 2.50 6.00
54 Gerrit Cole 4.00 10.00
55 Jason Kipnis 3.00 8.00
56 Wilin Rosario 2.50 6.00
57 Tanner Roark 2.50 6.00
58 Wil Myers 3.00 8.00
59 Matt den Dekker 2.50 6.00
60 Norichika Aoki 2.50 6.00
61 Junior Lake 2.50 6.00
62 Ehire Adrianza 2.50 6.00
64 Stephen Strasburg 10.00 25.00
65 Manny Machado 12.00 30.00
66 Evan Longoria 3.00 8.00
67 Alexi Ogando 2.50 6.00
69 Anthony Rizzo 12.00 30.00
70 Bob Horner 2.50 6.00
71 Bret Saberhagen 3.00 8.00
72 Curt Schilling 8.00 20.00
73 Jeff Conine 2.50 6.00
74 Jose Abreu 25.00 60.00
75 Mark Grace 10.00 25.00
76 Edgar Martinez 4.00 10.00
77 Paul Konerko 8.00 20.00
78 Kevin Millar 4.00 10.00
79 Willie McGee 10.00 25.00
80 Ryan Goins 4.00 10.00
81 Chuck Knoblauch 10.00 25.00
82 Archie Bradley 2.50 6.00
83 Danny Salazar 3.00 8.00
84 Darin Ruf 2.50 6.00
85 Harold Reynolds 3.00 8.00
86 John Franco 2.50 6.00
87 Fred McGriff 3.00 8.00
88 Steve Garvey 8.00 20.00
89 Kevin Mitchell 2.50 6.00
90 Steve Finley 2.50 6.00
91 Lance Parrish 2.50 6.00
93 Rob Dibble 4.00 10.00
94 Michael Young 2.50 6.00

2015 Donruss Signature Series Blue

*BLUE p/r 99: .5X TO 1.2X BASIC
*BLUE p/r 49: .6X TO 1.5X BASIC
*BLUE p/r 25: .75X TO 2X BASIC
RANDOM INSERTS IN PACKS
PRINT RUNS B/WN 15-99 COPIES PER
NO PRICING ON QTY 15 OR LESS

2015 Donruss Signature Series Green

*GREEN: .75X TO 2X BASIC
RANDOM INSERTS IN PACKS
PRINT RUNS B/WN 5-25 COPIES PER
NO PRICING ON QTY 15 OR LESS
12 Maikel Franco/25 6.00 15.00
32 Kennys Vargas/25 20.00 50.00

2015 Donruss Signature Series Red

*GREEN p/r 49: .6X TO 1.5X BASIC
*GREEN p/r 25-29: .75X TO 2X BASIC
RANDOM INSERTS IN PACKS
PRINT RUNS B/WN 10-49 COPIES PER
NO PRICING ON QTY 15 OR LESS

2015 Donruss Studio

RANDOM INSERTS IN PACKS
1 Yordano Ventura 1.25 3.00
2 Kennys Vargas 1.00 2.50
3 Javier Baez 8.00 20.00
4 Matt Shoemaker 1.25 3.00
5 Jorge Soler 1.50 4.00
6 Rusney Castillo 1.25 3.00
7 Jose Altuve 1.25 3.00
8 Joc Pederson 4.00 10.00
9 Michael Taylor 1.00 2.50
10 Pablo Sandoval 1.25 3.00

2015 Donruss The Elite Series

RANDOM INSERTS IN PACKS
STATED PRINT RUN 999 SER.#'d SET
1 Mark Trumbo 1.25 3.00
2 Javier Baez 3.00 8.00
3 Dustin Pedroia 2.00 5.00
4 Troy Tulowitzki 2.00 5.00
5 Max Scherzer 2.00 5.00
6 Rusney Castillo 1.50 4.00
7 Salvador Perez 1.50 4.00
8 Chase Utley 1.50 4.00
9 Madison Bumgarner 1.50 4.00
10 Adrian Beltre 2.00 5.00
11 Starling Marte 1.50 4.00
12 Clayton Kershaw 3.00 8.00
13 Giancarlo Stanton 2.00 5.00
14 Justin Upton 1.50 4.00
15 Josh Donaldson 1.50 4.00
16 Yadier Molina 2.50 6.00
17 Ichiro 2.50 6.00
18 Ryan Braun 1.50 4.00
19 Matt Harvey 1.50 4.00
20 Joey Votto 2.00 5.00
21 Kennys Vargas 1.25 3.00
22 Michael Taylor 1.25 3.00
23 Jorge Soler 2.00 5.00
24 Joc Pederson 5.00 12.00
25 Maikel Franco 1.50 4.00

2015 Donruss The Rookies

RANDOM INSERTS IN PACKS
*GOLD/99: 1X TO 2.5X
*SILVER/199: .75X TO 2X
*CAR p/r 276-400: .6X TO 1.5X
*CAR p/r 150: .75X TO 2X
*CAR p/r 100 : 1X TO 2.5X
*CAR p/r 19 : 2X TO 5X
*SEA p/r 255-400: .6X TO 1.5X
*SEA p/r 126-231: .75X TO 2X
*SEA p/r 84-106 : 1X TO 2.5X
*SEA p/r 59 : 1.2X TO 3X
*SEA p/r 30-46 : 1.5X TO 4X
1 Rusney Castillo .75 2.00
2 Joc Pederson 2.50 6.00
3 Javier Baez 5.00 12.00
4 Jorge Soler 1.00 2.50
5 Maikel Franco .75 2.00
6 Anthony Ranaudo .60 1.50
7 Michael Taylor .60 1.50
8 Mike Foltynewicz .60 1.50
9 Daniel Norris .60 1.50
10 Dalton Pompey .75 2.00
11 Brandon Finnegan .60 1.50
12 Yorman Rodriguez .60 1.50
13 Christian Walker 1.25 3.00
14 Jake Lamb 1.00 2.50
15 Rymer Liriano .60 1.50

2015 Donruss Tony Gwynn Tribute

COMPLETE SET (5) 5.00 12.00
RANDOM INSERTS IN PACKS
*RED/99: 2X TO 5X BASIC
*GREEN/25: 4X TO 10X BASIC
1 Tony Gwynn 1.25 3.00
2 Tony Gwynn 1.25 3.00
3 Tony Gwynn 1.25 3.00
4 Tony Gwynn 1.25 3.00
5 Tony Gwynn 1.25 3.00

2015 Donruss USA Collegiate National Team

RANDOM INSERTS IN PACKS
*RED/49: 1.2X TO 3X BASIC
*GOLD/25: 2X TO 5X BASIC
1 James Kaprielian .60 1.50
2 Jake Lemoine .60 1.50
3 Ryan Burr .60 1.50
4 Carson Fulmer .60 1.50
5 DJ Stewart .75 2.00
6 Chris Okey .60 1.50
7 Alex Bregman 3.00 8.00
8 Dansby Swanson 4.00 10.00
9 Blake Trahan .60 1.50
10 Thomas Eshelman .60 1.50
11 Kyle Funkhouser .75 2.00
12 A.J. Minter .75 2.00
13 Nicholas Banks .60 1.50
14 Zack Collins .75 2.00
15 Mark Mathias .75 2.00
16 Bryan Reynolds 2.00 5.00
17 Taylor Ward 1.00 2.50
18 Justin Garza .60 1.50
19 Tyler Jay .60 1.50
20 Tate Matheny .60 1.50
21 Trey Killian .60 1.50
22 Andrew Moore .75 2.00
23 Christin Stewart .75 2.00
24 Dillon Tate .75 2.00

2016 Donruss

COMP.SET w/o SPs (150) 10.00 25.00
SPs RANDOMLY INSERTED
COMP.SET ARE CARD 46-195
1 A.J. Pollock DK .60 1.50
2 Nick Markakis DK .75 2.00
3 Manny Machado DK 1.00 2.50
4 Xander Bogaerts DK 1.00 2.50
5 Jake Arrieta DK .75 2.00
6 Chris Sale DK 1.00 2.50
7 Todd Frazier DK .60 1.50
8 Michael Brantley DK .75 2.00
9 Carlos Gonzalez DK .75 2.00
10 Miguel Cabrera DK 1.00 2.50
11 Jose Altuve DK .75 2.00
12 Eric Hosmer DK .75 2.00
13 Albert Pujols DK 1.25 3.00
14 Zack Greinke DK 1.00 2.50
15 Jose Fernandez DK 1.00 2.50
16 Adam Lind DK .75 2.00
17 Brian Dozier DK .75 2.00
18 Jacob deGrom DK 2.00 5.00
19 Alex Rodriguez DK 1.25 3.00
20 Billy Burns DK .60 1.50
21 Odubel Herrera DK .75 2.00
22 Andrew McCutchen DK 1.00 2.50
23 Matt Kemp DK .75 2.00
24 Buster Posey DK 1.25 3.00
25 Nelson Cruz DK 1.00 2.50
26 Yadier Molina DK 1.25 3.00
27 Evan Longoria DK .75 2.00
28 Prince Fielder DK .75 2.00
29 Josh Donaldson DK .75 2.00
30 Bryce Harper DK 1.50 4.00
31 Kyle Schwarber RR RC 1.50 4.00
32 Corey Seager RR RC 5.00 12.00
33 Trea Turner RR RC 1.50 4.00
34 Rob Refsnyder RR RC .60 1.50
35 Miguel Sano RR RC .75 2.00
36 Stephen Piscotty RR RC .75 2.00
37 Aaron Nola RR RC 1.00 2.50
38 Michael Conforto RR RC .60 1.50
39 Ketel Marte RR RC 1.00 2.50
40 Luis Severino RR RC .60 1.50
41 Greg Bird RR RC .60 1.50
42 Hector Olivera RR RC .60 1.50
43 Jose Peraza RR RC .60 1.50
44 Henry Owens RR RC .60 1.50
45 Richie Shaffer RR RC .50 1.25
46 Edwin Encarnacion .25 .60
47A Josh Donaldson .20 .50
47B Donaldson SP MVP 1.50 4.00
47C Dnldsn SP Nickname 1.50 4.00
48 Robinson Cano .20 .50
49 David Price .20 .50
50 Sonny Gray .20 .50
51 Dallas Keuchel .20 .50
52 Jake Arrieta .20 .50
53 Clayton Kershaw .40 1.00
54 Zack Greinke .25 .60
55 Jose Bautista .20 .50
56 Paul Goldschmidt .25 .60
57A Bryce Harper .40 1.00
57B Harper SP MVP 3.00 8.00
58 Joey Votto .25 .60
59A Carlos Correa .25 .60
59B Correa SP ROY 2.00 5.00
60A Kris Bryant .30 .75
60B Bryant SP ROY 2.50 6.00
61 Andrew McCutchen .25 .60
62 Albert Pujols .30 .75
63 Prince Fielder .20 .50
64 Buster Posey .30 .75
65 Dee Gordon .15 .40
66 Nolan Arenado .40 1.00
67 Miguel Cabrera .25 .60
68 Jose Altuve .20 .50
69 Xander Bogaerts .25 .60
70 Nelson Cruz .25 .60
71 Carlos Gonzalez .20 .50
72 Manny Machado .25 .60
73 Kevin Kiermaier .20 .50
74 Brandon Crawford .20 .50
75 Starling Marte .20 .50
76 A.J. Pollock .15 .40
77 Kole Calhoun .15 .40
78 Alcides Escobar .20 .50
79 Kevin Pillar .15 .40
80 Andrelton Simmons .15 .40
81 Lorenzo Cain .15 .40
82 Yadier Molina .30 .75
83A Mike Trout 1.25 3.00
83B Trout SP Hat off 10.00 25.00
83C Trout SP Nickname 10.00 25.00
84 David Ortiz .25 .60
85 Yoenis Cespedes .25 .60
86 Todd Frazier .15 .40
87 Anthony Rizzo .30 .75
88 Jose Abreu .25 .60
89 Matt Carpenter .25 .60
90 Adrian Gonzalez .20 .50
91 Chris Davis .15 .40
92 Kendrys Morales .15 .40
93 J.D. Martinez .25 .60
94 Collin McHugh .15 .40
95 Madison Bumgarner .20 .50
96 Gerrit Cole .25 .60
97 Michael Wacha .20 .50
98 Colby Lewis .15 .40
99 Jacob deGrom .50 1.25
100 Max Scherzer .25 .60
101 Ian Kinsler .20 .50
102 Ben Revere .15 .40
103 Charlie Blackmon .25 .60
104 Adam Eaton .15 .40
105 Jason Kipnis .20 .50
106 Joc Pederson .20 .50
107 Francisco Lindor .25 .60
108 Chris Sale .25 .60
109 Billy Hamilton .20 .50
110 Billy Burns .15 .40
111 Ryan Braun .20 .50
112 Jason Heyward .20 .50
113 Eddie Rosario .20 .50
114 Dexter Fowler .20 .50
115 Brian Dozier .20 .50
116 Curtis Granderson .20 .50
117 Shin-Soo Choo .20 .50
118 Mookie Betts .50 1.25
119 Kyle Seager .15 .40
120 Mark Melancon .15 .40
121 Trevor Rosenthal .20 .50
122 Jeurys Familia .20 .50
123 Corey Kluber .20 .50
124 Francisco Liriano .15 .40
125 Jon Lester .20 .50
126 Carlos Carrasco .15 .40
127 Carlos Martinez .20 .50
128 Cole Hamels .20 .50
129 Adrian Beltre .25 .60
130 James Shields .15 .40
131 Yordano Ventura .20 .50
132 Eric Hosmer .20 .50
133 Adam Wainwright .20 .50
134 Hisashi Iwakuma .20 .50
135 Chris Heston .15 .40
136 Alex Rodriguez .30 .75
137 Felix Hernandez .20 .50
138 CC Sabathia .20 .50
139 Aroldis Chapman .25 .60
140 Adam Jones .20 .50
141 Jonathan Lucroy .20 .50
142 Evan Longoria .20 .50
143 Troy Tulowitzki .25 .60
144 Matt Holliday .25 .60
145 Matt Duffy .15 .40
146 Pedro Alvarez .15 .40
147 Giancarlo Stanton .25 .60
148 Brian McCann .20 .50
149 Ichiro .30 .75
150 Evan Gattis .15 .40
151 Ted Giannoulas .25 .60
152 Chris Archer .15 .40
153 Johnny Cueto .20 .50
154 Stephen Strasburg .25 .60
155 Wei-Yin Chen .15 .40
156 Jose Fernandez .25 .60
157 Yasmany Tomas .15 .40
158 Addison Russell .25 .60
159 Maikel Franco .20 .50
160 Noah Syndergaard .20 .50
161 Jung-Ho Kang .15 .40
162 Rusney Castillo .15 .40
163 Carlos Rodon .25 .60
164 Odubel Herrera .20 .50
165 Yu Darvish .25 .60
166 Michael Taylor .15 .40
167 Jorge Soler .25 .60
168 Eduardo Rodriguez .15 .40
169 Delino DeShields Jr. .15 .40
170 David Wright .20 .50
171 Steven Matz .15 .40
172 Salvador Perez .20 .50
173 DJ LeMahieu .25 .60
174 Justin Upton .20 .50
175 Bo Jackson .25 .60
176 Mariano Rivera .30 .75
177 Ryne Sandberg .50 1.25
178A Kirby Puckett .25 .60
178B Puckett SP HOF 01 2.00 5.00
179A Ken Griffey Jr. .50 1.25
179B Griffey SP SEA 4.00 10.00
179C Grffy SP Nickname 4.00 10.00
180 Frank Thomas .25 .60
181A Cal Ripken .75 2.00
181B Rpkn SP Nickname 6.00 15.00
182A George Brett .50 1.25
182B Brett SP 80 MVP 4.00 10.00
183 Nolan Ryan .75 2.00
184 Rickey Henderson .25 .60
185 Carl Yastrzemski .40 1.00
186A Don Mattingly .50 1.25
186B Mttngly SP Nickname 4.00 10.00
187A Pete Rose .50 1.25
187B Rose SP Nickname 4.00 10.00
188 Pedro Martinez .20 .50
189 Craig Biggio .20 .50
190 John Smoltz .25 .60
191A Omar Vizquel .20 .50
191B Vzql SP Nickname 1.50 4.00
192 Andres Galarraga .20 .50
193 Checklist .15 .40
194 Checklist .15 .40
195 Checklist .15 .40

2016 Donruss Black Border

*BLK BRD DK: .75X TO 2X BASIC
*BLK BRD RR: 1X TO 2.5X BASIC
*BLK BRD VET: 3X TO 8X BASIC
RANDOM INSERTS IN PACKS
STATED PRINT RUN 199 SER.#'d SETS

2016 Donruss Pink Border

*PINK DK: .6X TO 1.5X BASIC
*PINK RR: .75X TO 2X BASIC
*PINK VET: 2.5X TO 6X BASIC
RANDOM INSERTS IN PACKS

2016 Donruss Press Proof Gold

*GLD PROOF DK: 1X TO 2.5X BASIC
*GLD PROOF RR: 1.2X TO 3X BASIC
*GLD PROOF VET: 4X TO 10X BASIC
RANDOM INSERTS IN PACKS
STATED PRINT RUN 99 SER.#'d SETS

2016 Donruss Stat Line Career

*CAR DK p/r 261-400: .6X TO 1.5X
*CAR DK p/r 166: .75X TO 2X
*CAR DK p/r 101-118: 1X TO 2.5X
*CAR RR p/r 351-400: .75X TO 2X
*CAR RR p/r 120: 1.2X TO 3X
*CAR RR p/r 63: 1.5X TO 4X
*CAR p/r 261-500: 2.5X TO 6X
*CAR p/r 126-243: 3X TO 8X
*CAR p/r 100-125: 4X TO 10X
*CAR p/r 42-58: 5X TO 12X
RANDOM INSERTS IN PACKS
PRINT RUNS B/WN 13-500 COPIES PER
NO PRICING ON QTY 13

2016 Donruss Stat Line Season

*SEA DK p/r 274-338: .6X TO 1.5X
*SEA DK p/r 166-236: .75X TO 2X
*SEA DK p/r 81-122: 1X TO 2.5X
*SEA DK p/r 38-45: 1.2X TO 3X
*SEA DK p/r 26-35: 1.5X TO 4X
*SEA DK p/r 20-23: 2X TO 5X
*SEA RR p/r 253-400: .75X TO 2X
*SEA RR p/r 50-68: 1.5X TO 4X
*SEA p/r 252-400: 2.5X TO 6X
*SEA p/r 130-248: 3X TO 8X
*SEA p/r 98-112: 4X TO 10X
*SEA p/r 36-70: 5X TO 12X
*SEA p/r 26-35: 6X TO 15X
*SEA p/r 20-25: 8X TO 20X
RANDOM INSERTS IN PACKS
PRINT RUNS B/WN 10-400 COPIES PER
NO PRICING ON QTY 19 OR LESS

2016 Donruss Test Proof Black

*PROOF BLK DK: 2X TO 5X BASIC
*PROOF BLK RR: 2.5X TO 6X BASIC
*PROOF BLK VET: 8X TO 20X BASIC
RANDOM INSERTS IN PACKS
STATED PRINT RUN 25 SER.#'d SETS

2016 Donruss Test Proof Cyan

*PROOF CYAN DK: 1.2X TO 3X BASIC
*PROOF CYAN RR: 1.5X TO 4X BASIC
*PROOF CYAN VET: 5X TO 12X BASIC
RANDOM INSERTS IN PACKS
STATED PRINT RUN 49 SER.#'d SETS

2016 Donruss '82

COMPLETE SET (50) 10.00 25.00
RANDOM INSERTS IN PACKS
*PINK: 1.5X TO 4X BASIC
*HOLMTRC/299: 1.2X TO 3X BASIC
*HOLOVIEW/199: 1.2X TO 3X BASIC
*BLK BRDR/99: 2.5X TO 6X BASIC
*CYAN/49: 2.5X TO 6X BASIC
*GLD PRF/49: 2.5X TO 6X BASIC
*BLCK PRF/25: 6X TO 15X BASIC
1 Mike Trout 2.50 6.00
2 Josh Donaldson .40 1.00
3 Lorenzo Cain .30 .75
4 David Price .40 1.00
5 Sonny Gray .40 1.00
6 Dallas Keuchel .40 1.00
7 Jake Arrieta .40 1.00
8 Clayton Kershaw .75 2.00
9 Zack Greinke .50 1.25
10 Yadier Molina .60 1.50
11 Paul Goldschmidt .50 1.25
12 Bryce Harper .75 2.00
13 Joey Votto .50 1.25
14 Carlos Correa .50 1.25
15 Kris Bryant .60 1.50
16 Andrew McCutchen .50 1.25
17 Matt Harvey .40 1.00
18 Prince Fielder .40 1.00
19 Buster Posey .60 1.50
20 Dee Gordon .30 .75
21 Nolan Arenado .75 2.00
22 Brandon Crawford .40 1.00
23 Madison Bumgarner .40 1.00
24 Miguel Cabrera .50 1.25
25 Jose Altuve .40 1.00
26 Xander Bogaerts .50 1.25
27 Nelson Cruz .50 1.25
28 Carlos Gonzalez .40 1.00
29 Eric Hosmer .40 1.00
30 Manny Machado .50 1.25
31 Kevin Kiermaier .40 1.00
32 Adrian Beltre .50 1.25
33 Starling Marte .40 1.00
34 A.J. Pollock .30 .75
35 Jason Heyward .40 1.00
36 Kole Calhoun .30 .75
37 Alcides Escobar .40 1.00
38 Kevin Pillar .30 .75
39 Jacob deGrom 1.00 2.50
40 Andrelton Simmons .30 .75
41 Cal Ripken 1.50 4.00
42 Kirby Puckett .50 1.25
43 George Brett 1.00 2.50
44 Ken Griffey Jr. 1.00 2.50
45 Nolan Ryan 1.50 4.00
46 Pete Rose 1.00 2.50
47 Rickey Henderson .50 1.25
48 Robin Yount .50 1.25
49 Frank Thomas .50 1.25
50 Steve Carlton .40 1.00

2016 Donruss Back to the Future Materials

RANDOM INSERTS IN PACKS
*GREEN/49-99: .5X TO 1.2X BASIC
*GREEN/25: .6X TO 1.5X BASIC
BFAB Adrian Beltre 3.00 8.00
BFAG Adrian Gonzalez 2.50 6.00
BFAR Alex Rodriguez 4.00 10.00
BFCB Carlos Beltran 2.50 6.00
BFCG Curtis Granderson 2.50 6.00
BFCG Carlos Gomez 2.00 5.00
BFCL Cliff Lee 2.50 6.00
BFCU Chase Utley 2.50 6.00
BFIK Ian Kinsler 2.50 6.00
BFJA Jake Arrieta 2.50 6.00
BFJC Johnny Cueto 2.50 6.00
BFJD Josh Donaldson 2.50 6.00
BFJL Jon Lester 2.50 6.00
BFJS Jeff Samardzija 2.00 5.00
BFJU Justin Upton 2.50 6.00
BFMC Miguel Cabrera 3.00 8.00
BFMK Matt Kemp 2.50 6.00
BFMS Max Scherzer 3.00 8.00
BFNC Nelson Cruz 3.00 8.00
BFNC Nelson Cruz 3.00 8.00
BFNS Nick Swisher 2.50 6.00
BFPF Prince Fielder 2.50 6.00
BFRC Robinson Cano 2.50 6.00
BFTT Troy Tulowitzki 3.00 8.00
BFYC Yoenis Cespedes 3.00 8.00

2016 Donruss Bat Kings

RANDOM INSERTS IN PACKS
*GREEN/49-99: .5X TO 1.2X BASIC
*GREEN/25: .6X TO 1.5X BASIC
*RED/49-199: .5X TO 1.2X BASIC
*RED/25: .6X TO 1.5X BASIC
*STUDIO/25: .6X TO 1.5X BASIC
BKI Ichiro 4.00 10.00
BKAG Adrian Gonzalez 2.50 6.00
BKAJ Adam Jones 2.50 6.00
BKAM Andrew McCutchen 3.00 8.00
BKAP Albert Pujols 4.00 10.00
BKAR Anthony Rizzo 4.00 10.00
BKAR Alex Rodriguez 4.00 10.00
BKBB Billy Burns 2.00 5.00
BKBH Bryce Harper 5.00 12.00
BKBM Brian McCann 2.50 6.00
BKCB Craig Biggio 2.50 6.00
BKCC Carlos Correa 5.00 12.00
BKCG Carlos Gomez 2.00 5.00
BKDO David Ortiz 3.00 8.00
BKDW Dave Winfield 2.50 6.00
BKER Eddie Rosario 2.50 6.00
BKGB George Brett 4.00 10.00
BKJA Jose Abreu 3.00 8.00
BKJB Jose Bautista 2.50 6.00
BKJB Javier Baez 4.00 10.00
BKJD Josh Donaldson 2.50 6.00
BKJH Josh Harrison 2.00 5.00
BKJP Joc Pederson 2.50 6.00
BKJS Jorge Soler 3.00 8.00
BKJV Joey Votto 3.00 8.00
BKKB Kris Bryant 6.00 15.00
BKKK Kevin Kiermaier 2.50 6.00
BKKW Kolten Wong 2.50 6.00
BKLM Logan Morrison 2.00 5.00
BKMB Mookie Betts 6.00 15.00
BKMB Michael Brantley 2.50 6.00
BKMC Matt Carpenter 3.00 8.00
BKMC Miguel Cabrera 3.00 8.00
BKMF Maikel Franco 2.50 6.00
BKMM Manny Machado 3.00 8.00
BKMN Mike Napoli 2.00 5.00
BKMT Mike Trout 8.00 20.00
BKNC Nelson Cruz 3.00 8.00
BKPF Prince Fielder 2.50 6.00
BKRC Robinson Cano 2.50 6.00
BKRH Rickey Henderson 6.00 15.00
BKVG Vladimir Guerrero 2.50 6.00
BKYT Yasmany Tomas 2.00 5.00
BKJHK Jung-Ho Kang 2.00 5.00

2016 Donruss Elite Dominators

RANDOM INSERTS IN PACKS
STATED PRINT RUN 999 SER.#'d SETS
ED1 Carlos Correa 1.00 2.50
ED2 Lorenzo Cain .60 1.50
ED3 Mike Trout 5.00 12.00
ED4 Kris Bryant 1.25 3.00
ED5 Giancarlo Stanton 1.00 2.50
ED6 Miguel Cabrera 1.00 2.50
ED7 Dee Gordon .60 1.50
ED8 Bryce Harper 1.50 4.00
ED9 Eric Hosmer .75 2.00
ED10 Nolan Arenado 1.50 4.00
ED11 Josh Donaldson .75 2.00
ED12 Corey Seager 6.00 15.00
ED13 Jake Arrieta .75 2.00
ED14 Dallas Keuchel .75 2.00
ED15 Madison Bumgarner .75 2.00
ED16 Buster Posey 1.25 3.00
ED 17 Alcides Escobar .75 2.00
ED18 Clayton Kershaw 1.50 4.00
ED19 Xander Bogaerts 1.00 2.50
ED20 Noah Syndergaard .75 2.00
ED21 Matt Duffy .60 1.50
ED22 Ichiro 1.25 3.00
ED23 Andrew McCutchen 1.00 2.50
ED24 Salvador Perez .75 2.00
ED25 Joey Votto 1.00 2.50

2016 Donruss Elite Series

RANDOM INSERTS IN PACKS
STATED PRINT RUN 999 SER.#'d SETS
ES1 Jacob deGrom 2.00 5.00
ES2 Mike Moustakas .75 2.00
ES3 Troy Tulowitzki 1.00 2.50
ES4 Jose Altuve .75 2.00
ES5 Manny Machado 1.00 2.50
ES6 Anthony Rizzo 1.25 3.00
ES7 Kevin Kiermaier .75 2.00
ES8 Brandon Crawford .75 2.00
ES9 A.J. Pollock .60 1.50

ES10 Paul Goldschmidt 1.00 2.50
ES11 Matt Harvey .75 2.00
ES12 Nelson Cruz 1.00 2.50
ES13 Kendrys Morales .60 1.50
ES14 Prince Fielder .75 2.00
ES15 Carlos Correa 1.00 2.50
ES16 Kyle Schwarber 2.00 5.00
ES17 Luis Severino .75 2.00
ES18 Corey Seager 6.00 15.00
ES19 Stephen Piscotty 1.00 2.50
ES20 Miguel Sano 1.00 2.50
ES21 Mike Trout 5.00 12.00
ES22 Bryce Harper 1.50 4.00
ES23 Carlos Gomez .60 1.50
ES24 Adam Jones .75 2.00
ES25 Robinson Cano .75 2.00

2016 Donruss Jersey Kings

RANDOM INSERTS IN PACKS
*GREEN/49-99: .5X TO 1.2X BASIC
*GREEN/25: .6X TO 1.5X BASIC
*RED/49-199: .5X TO 1.2X BASIC
*RED/25: .6X TO 1.5X BASIC
*STUDIO/25: .6X TO 1.5X BASIC
JKAB Archie Bradley 2.00 5.00
JKAC Aroldis Chapman 3.00 8.00
JKAJ Adam Jones 2.50 6.00
JKAM Andrew McCutchen 3.00 8.00
JKAP A.J. Pollock 2.00 5.00
JKAR Addison Russell 3.00 8.00
JKBB Byron Buxton 3.00 8.00
JKBD Brian Dozier 2.50 6.00
JKBH Bryce Harper 5.00 12.00
JKCA Chris Archer 2.00 5.00
JKCG Carlos Gonzalez 2.50 6.00
JKCK Clayton Kershaw 5.00 12.00
JKCR Cal Ripken 8.00 20.00
JKCS Chris Sale 3.00 8.00
JKDG Dee Gordon 2.00 5.00
JKDK Dallas Keuchel 2.50 6.00
JKEE Edwin Encarnacion 3.00 8.00
JKEH Eric Hosmer 2.50 6.00
JKFH Felix Hernandez 2.50 6.00
JKFL Francisco Lindor 3.00 8.00
JKGC Gerrit Cole 3.00 8.00
JKGS George Springer 2.50 6.00
JKJA Jose Altuve 2.50 6.00
JKJB Javier Baez 4.00 10.00
JKJB Jeff Bagwell 2.50 6.00
JKJD Josh Donaldson 2.50 6.00
JKJG Juan Gonzalez 2.00 5.00
JKJS Jorge Soler 3.00 8.00
JKKB Kris Bryant 6.00 15.00
JKKG Ken Griffey Jr. 6.00 15.00
JKLC Lorenzo Cain 2.00 5.00
JKMB Michael Brantley 2.50 6.00
JKMC Miguel Cabrera 3.00 8.00
JKMF Maikel Franco 2.50 6.00
JKMH Matt Harvey 2.50 6.00
JKMT Masahiro Tanaka 2.50 6.00
JKMT Michael Taylor 2.00 5.00
JKMT Mike Trout 15.00 40.00
JKNR Nolan Ryan 4.00 10.00
JKPS Pablo Sandoval 2.50 6.00
JKRH Rickey Henderson 3.00 8.00
JKSG Sonny Gray 2.50 6.00
JKSS Steven Souza 2.50 6.00
JKYT Yasmany Tomas 2.00 5.00

2016 Donruss Masters of the Game

COMPLETE SET (10) 3.00 8.00
RANDOM INSERTS IN PACKS
*BLUE/199: 1.5X TO 4X BASIC
*RED/99: 3X TO 8X BASIC
MG1 Rickey Henderson .50 1.25
MG2 Roger Clemens .60 1.50
MG3 Juan Gonzalez .30 .75
MG4 Frank Thomas .50 1.25
MG5 Steve Carlton .40 1.00
MG6 Mariano Rivera .60 1.50
MG7 Mark McGwire .75 2.00
MG8 Randy Johnson .50 1.25
MG9 Ken Griffey Jr. 1.00 2.50
MG10 Cal Ripken 1.50 4.00

2016 Donruss New Breed Autographs

RANDOM INSERTS IN PACKS
EXCHANGE DEADLINE 9/2/2017
*GREEN: .5X TO 1.2X BASIC
NBAC A.J. Cole 3.00 8.00
NBAR Anthony Ranaudo 3.00 8.00
NBBF Brandon Finnegan 3.00 8.00
NBBF Buck Farmer 3.00 8.00
NBCS Cory Spangenberg 3.00 8.00
NBDH Dilson Herrera 4.00 10.00
NBDN Daniel Norris 3.00 8.00
NBEE Edwin Escobar 3.00 8.00
NBGB Gary Brown 3.00 8.00
NBJL Jake Lamb 4.00 10.00
NBJM James McCann 4.00 10.00
NBKG Kendall Graveman 3.00 8.00
NBLA Lane Adams 3.00 8.00
NBMB Matt Barnes 3.00 8.00
NBMC Miguel Castro 3.00 8.00
NBMF Mike Foltynewicz 3.00 8.00
NBMS Matt Szczur 4.00 10.00
NBMT Michael Taylor 3.00 8.00
NBRA R.J. Alvarez 3.00 8.00
NBRL Rymer Liriano 3.00 8.00
NBRR Ryan Rua 3.00 8.00
NBSM Steven Moya 3.00 8.00
NBTG Terrance Gore 3.00 8.00
NBTM Trevor May 3.00 8.00
NBYR Yorman Rodriguez 3.00 8.00

2016 Donruss Power Alley

COMPLETE SET (10) 4.00 10.00
RANDOM INSERTS IN PACKS
*DISCO/299: 1X TO 2.5X BASIC
*BLUE/199: 1.2X TO 3X BASIC
*RED/99: 1.5X TO 4X BASIC
PA1 Bryce Harper .75 2.00
PA2 Mike Trout 2.50 6.00
PA3 Josh Donaldson .40 1.00
PA4 Carlos Correa .50 1.25
PA5 Miguel Sano .50 1.25
PA6 Giancarlo Stanton .50 1.25
PA7 Madison Bumgarner .40 1.00
PA8 Kyle Schwarber 1.00 2.50
PA9 Eric Hosmer .40 1.00
PA10 Jose Bautista .40 1.00

2016 Donruss Preferred Pairings Signatures Red

2 Schwarber/Seager/25 75.00 200.00
3 Gonzalez/IRod/25 20.00 50.00
5 Clemens/Vlad/25 25.00 60.00
6 Ripken/Brett/25 125.00 250.00

2016 Donruss Promising Pros Materials

RANDOM INSERTS IN PACKS
*GREEN/99: .5X TO 1.2X BASIC
*GREEN/25: .6X TO 1.5X BASIC
PPMAJ Aaron Judge 15.00 40.00
PPMAN Aaron Nola 4.00 10.00
PPMBS Rafael Devers 4.00 10.00
PPMBS Blake Snell 2.50 6.00
PPMCS Corey Seager 5.00 12.00
PPMGB Greg Bird 2.50 6.00
PPMJG Jonathan Gray 2.00 5.00
PPMKM Ketel Marte 4.00 10.00
PPMKS Kyle Schwarber 5.00 12.00
PPMLG Lucas Giolito 3.00 8.00
PPMLS Luis Severino 2.50 6.00
PPMMC Michael Conforto 4.00 10.00
PPMMO Matt Olson 4.00 10.00
PPMMS Miguel Sano 3.00 8.00
PPMNM Nomar Mazara 3.00 8.00
PPMOB Peter O'Brien 2.00 5.00
PPMRM Raul Mondesi 4.00 10.00
PPMRR Rob Refsnyder 2.50 6.00
PPMRS Richie Shaffer 2.00 5.00
PPMSP Stephen Piscotty 3.00 8.00
PPMTB Tyler Beede 2.50 6.00
PPMTM Tom Murphy 2.00 5.00
PPMTT Trea Turner 4.00 10.00
PPMWH Wei-Chieh Huang 2.00 5.00
PPMYM Yoan Moncada 5.00 12.00

2016 Donruss Promising Pros Materials Signatures

RANDOM INSERTS IN PACKS
PRINT RUNS B/WN 25-199 COPIES PER
EXCHANGE DEADLINE 9/2/2017
*GREEN/99: .5X TO 1.2X BASIC
PPMSAJ Aaron Judge/199 75.00 200.00
PPMSAN Aaron Nola/199 6.00 15.00
PPMSBS Blake Snell/199 4.00 10.00
PPMSCS Corey Seager/25 20.00 50.00
PPMSJG Jonathan Gray/99 3.00 8.00
PPMSKS Kyle Schwarber/25 30.00 80.00
PPMSLG Lucas Giolito/99 8.00 20.00
PPMSLS Luis Severino/25 10.00 25.00
PPMSMO Matt Olson/199 8.00 20.00
PPMSPO Peter O'Brien/199 3.00 8.00
PPMSRR Rob Refsnyder/199 6.00 15.00
PPMSRS Richie Shaffer/199 3.00 8.00
PPMSSP Stephen Piscotty/199 10.00 25.00
PPMSTB Tyler Beede/199 4.00 10.00
PPMSTM Tom Murphy/99 3.00 8.00
PPMSTT Trea Turner/199 10.00 25.00
PPMSWH Wei-Chieh Huang/199 3.00 8.00
PPMSYM Yoan Moncada/99 8.00 20.00

2016 Donruss Rated Rookies Die-Cut Blue

RANDOM INSERTS IN PACKS
STATED PRINT RUN 999 SER.#'d SETS
*RED/299: .5X TO 1.2X BASIC
*GREEN/99: .75X TO 2X BASIC
*BLACK/25: 1.5X TO 4X BASIC
RRDCAN Aaron Nola 2.00 5.00
RRDCCS Corey Seager 10.00 25.00
RRDCGB Greg Bird 1.25 3.00
RRDCHO Hector Olivera 1.25 3.00
RRDCKS Kyle Schwarber 3.00 8.00
RRDCLS Luis Severino 1.25 3.00
RRDCMC Michael Conforto 1.25 3.00
RRDCMS Miguel Sano 1.50 4.00
RRDCRR Rob Refsnyder 1.25 3.00
RRDCSP Stephen Piscotty 1.50 4.00

2016 Donruss San Diego Chicken Silhouette Materials

RANDOM INSERTS IN PACKS
STATED PRINT RUN 82 SER.#'d SETS
*GREEN/25: .5X TO 1.2X BASIC
1 Ted Giannoulas 30.00 80.00

2016 Donruss San Diego Chicken Silhouette Materials Autographs

RANDOM INSERTS IN PACKS
STATED PRINT RUN 82 SER.#'d SETS
*GREEN/25: .6X TO 1.5X BASIC
1 Ted Giannoulas 40.00 100.00

2016 Donruss Signature Series

RANDOM INSERTS IN PACKS
EXCHANGE DEADLINE 9/2/2017
SGSAG Andres Galarraga 8.00 20.00
SGSAN Aaron Nola 8.00 20.00
SGSBD Brandon Drury 4.00 10.00
SGSBE Brian Ellington 2.50 6.00
SGSBJ Brian Johnson 2.50 6.00
SGSBP Buster Posey 25.00 60.00
SGSCB Craig Biggio 10.00 25.00
SGSCE Carl Edwards Jr. 3.00 8.00
SGSCK Corey Kluber 3.00 8.00
SGSCL Clayton Kershaw 25.00 60.00
SGSCS Corey Seager 12.00 30.00
SGSCY Carl Yastrzemski 25.00 60.00
SGSDM Don Mattingly 20.00 50.00
SGSDO David Ortiz 20.00 50.00
SGSDP David Peralta 2.50 6.00
SGSDV Dave Winfield 6.00 15.00
SGSDW David Wright 3.00 8.00
SGSED Elias Diaz 2.50 6.00
SGSEL Evan Longoria 6.00 15.00
SGSFM Frankie Montas 3.00 8.00
SGSGS George Springer 5.00 12.00
SGSHO Henry Owens 4.00 10.00
SGSJG Juan Gonzalez 4.00 10.00
SGSJA Jake Arrieta 12.00 30.00
SGSJA Jose Abreu 12.00 30.00
SGSJC Jose Canseco 8.00 20.00
SGSJD Josh Donaldson 12.00 30.00
SGSJF Jeurys Familia 3.00 8.00
SGSJG Jonathan Gray 2.50 6.00
SGSJJ Jimmy Wynn 2.50 6.00
SGSJL John Lamb 2.50 6.00
SGSJP Joc Pederson 3.00 8.00
SGSJP Jose Peraza
SGSJS Jorge Soler 4.00 10.00
SGSJW Jered Weaver 3.00 8.00
SGSKB Kris Bryant 30.00 80.00
SGSKG Ken Griffey Jr. 60.00 150.00
SGSKS Kyle Schwarber 15.00 40.00
SGSKT Kelby Tomlinson 2.50 6.00
SGSKW Kyle Waldrop 3.00 8.00
SGSLA Luis Aparicio 8.00 20.00
SGSLS Luis Severino 10.00 25.00
SGSMD Matt Duffy 2.50 6.00
SGSMF Maikel Franco 3.00 8.00
SGSMK Max Kepler 4.00 10.00
SGSMM Mark McGwire 40.00 100.00
SGSMO Mariano Rivera 40.00 100.00
SGSMR Michael Reed 2.50 6.00
SGSMW Mac Williamson 2.50 6.00
SGSNK Nathan Karns 2.50 6.00
SGSNS Nick Swisher 3.00 8.00
SGSOV Omar Vizquel EXCH 8.00 20.00
SGSPF Prince Fielder 3.00 8.00
SGSPM Pedro Martinez 20.00 50.00
SGSPO Peter O'Brien 2.50 6.00
SGSPR Pete Rose 10.00 25.00
SGSRC Roger Clemens 20.00 50.00
SGSRD R.A. Dickey 3.00 8.00
SGSRI Raul Ibanez 3.00 8.00
SGSRS Richie Shaffer 4.00 10.00
SGSRU Rusney Castillo 2.50 6.00
SGSSB Socrates Brito 2.50 6.00
SGSSM Steven Matz 2.50 6.00
SGSSP Stephen Piscotty 4.00 10.00
SGSSS Stephen Strasburg 12.00 30.00
SGSTD Tyler Duffey 2.50 6.00
SGSTJ Travis Jankowski 2.50 6.00
SGSTM Tom Murphy 2.50 6.00
SGSTR Trea Turner 6.00 15.00
SGSTT Trayce Thompson 4.00 10.00
SGSTT Troy Tulowitzki 6.00 15.00
SGSVG Vladimir Guerrero 8.00 20.00
SGSWB Wade Boggs 15.00 40.00
SGSYM Yadier Molina 30.00 80.00
SGSYT Yasmany Tomas 4.00 10.00
SGSZG Zack Godley 2.50 6.00

2016 Donruss Signature Series Blue

*BLUE/99-199: .5X TO 1.2X BASIC
2016 Donruss Signature Series Blue
*BLUE/25: .75X TO 2X BASIC
RANDOM INSERTS IN PACKS
PRINT RUNS B/WN 20-199 COPIES PER
EXCHANGE DEADLINE 9/2/2017
SGSDA Dariel Alvarez/199 3.00 8.00
SGSOH Odubel Herrera/199 8.00 20.00
SGSRM Raul Mondesi/199 5.00 12.00

2016 Donruss Signature Series Green

*GREEN/25: .75X TO 2X BASIC
RANDOM INSERTS IN PACKS
PRINT RUNS B/WN 7-25 COPIES PER
NO PRICING ON QTY 15 OR LESS
EXCHANGE DEADLINE 9/2/2017
SGSDA Dariel Alvarez/25 5.00 12.00
SGSOH Odubel Herrera/25 12.00 30.00
SGSRM Raul Mondesi/25 8.00 20.00

2016 Donruss Signature Series Orange

*ORANGE/49: .6X TO 1.5X BASIC
*ORANGE/25: .75X TO 2X BASIC
RANDOM INSERTS IN PACKS
PRINT RUNS B/WN 10-49 COPIES PER
NO PRICING ON QTY 15 OR LESS
EXCHANGE DEADLINE 9/2/2017
SGSDA Dariel Alvarez/49 4.00 10.00
SGSOH Odubel Herrera/49 10.00 25.00
SGSRM Raul Mondesi/49 6.00 15.00
SGSRR Rob Refsnyder/49 6.00 15.00

2016 Donruss Signature Series Red

*RED/99: .5X TO 1.2X BASIC
*RED/49: .6X TO 1.5X BASIC
*RED/25: .75X TO 2X BASIC
RANDOM INSERTS IN PACKS
PRINT RUNS B/WN 15-99 COPIES PER
NO PRICING ON QTY 15
EXCHANGE DEADLINE 9/2/2017
SGSDA Dariel Alvarez/99 3.00 8.00
SGSOH Odubel Herrera/99 8.00 20.00
SGSRM Raul Mondesi/99 5.00 12.00
SGSRR Rob Refsnyder/99 5.00 12.00

2016 Donruss Signifcant Signatures Blue

RANDOM INSERTS IN PACKS
STATED PRINT RUN 99 SER.#'d SETS
EXCHANGE DEADLINE 9/2/2017
*RED/49: .5X TO 1.2X BASIC
*ORANGE/25: .6X TO 1.5X BASIC
SIGDN Don Newcombe 10.00 25.00
SIGAK Al Kaline 20.00 50.00
SIGJP Jim Palmer 8.00 20.00
SIGSC Steve Carlton 8.00 20.00
SIGGP Gaylord Perry 8.00 20.00

2016 Donruss Studio

RANDOM INSERTS IN PACKS
*RED/199: .75X TO 2X BASIC
*GLD PRF/99: 1X TO 2.5X BASIC
*CYAN/49: 1.2X TO 3X BASIC
*BLCK PRF/25: 1.5X TO 4X BASIC
S1 Kris Bryant .75 2.00
S2 Byron Buxton .60 1.50
S3 Michael Taylor .40 1.00
S4 Miguel Sano .60 1.50
S5 Corey Seager 4.00 10.00
S6 Kyle Schwarber 1.25 3.00
S7 Trea Turner 1.25 3.00
S8 Stephen Piscotty .60 1.50
S9 Luis Severino .50 1.25
S10 Michael Conforto .50 1.25

2016 Donruss Studio Signatures Blue

RANDOM INSERTS IN PACKS
PRINT RUNS B/WN 49-99 COPIES PER
EXCHANGE DEADLINE 9/2/2017
*RED/49: .5X TO 1.2X BASIC
*ORANGE/25: .6X TO 1.5X BASIC
SSCS Corey Seager/49 30.00 80.00
SSKB Kris Bryant/99 50.00 120.00
SSKS Kyle Schwarber/49 30.00 80.00
SSMT Michael Taylor/99

2016 Donruss The Prospects

COMPLETE SET (15) 10.00 25.00
RANDOM INSERTS IN PACKS
*CAREER: 1X TO 2.5X BASIC
*STAT/270-289: 1X TO 2.5X BASIC
*STAT/131-175: 1.2X TO 3X BASIC
*STAT/88: 1.5X TO 4X BASIC
*STAT/34-49: 2X TO 5X BASIC
*BLK BRDR/199: 1.2X TO 3X BASIC
*GLD PRF/99: 1.5X TO 4X BASIC
*CYAN PRF/49: 2X TO 5X BASIC
*BLCK PRF/25: 2.5X TO 6X BASIC
TP1 Lucas Giolito .50 1.25
TP2 Julio Urias 1.00 2.50
TP3 Yoan Moncada .75 2.00
TP4 Tyler Glasnow 1.25 3.00
TP5 Brendan Rodgers .50 1.25
TP6 Dansby Swanson 1.25 3.00
TP7 Orlando Arcia .40 1.00
TP8 Rafael Devers 1.00 2.50
TP9 Blake Snell .40 1.00
TP10 A.J. Reed .30 .75
TP11 Jose Berrios .50 1.25
TP12 Bradley Zimmer .50 1.25
TP13 Alex Reyes .40 1.00
TP14 Nomar Mazara .50 1.25
TP15 Josh Bell .60 1.50

2016 Donruss The Rookies

COMPLETE SET (15) 10.00 25.00
RANDOM INSERTS IN PACKS
*CAREER: 1X TO 2.5X BASIC
*STAT/253-337: 1X TO 2.5X BASIC
*STAT/56-68: 1.2X TO 3X BASIC
*BLK BRDR/199: 1.2X TO 3X BASIC
*GLD PRF/99: 1.5X TO 4X BASIC
*CYAN PRF/49: 2X TO 5X BASIC
*BLCK PRF/25: 2.5X TO 6X BASIC
TR1 Kyle Schwarber 1.00 2.50
TR2 Corey Seager 3.00 8.00
TR3 Trea Turner 1.00 2.50
TR4 Rob Refsnyder .40 1.00
TR5 Miguel Sano .50 1.25
TR6 Stephen Piscotty .50 1.25
TR7 Aaron Nola .60 1.50
TR8 Michael Conforto .40 1.00
TR9 Ketel Marte .60 1.50
TR10 Luis Severino .40 1.00
TR11 Greg Bird .40 1.00
TR12 Hector Olivera .40 1.00
TR13 Jose Peraza .40 1.00
TR14 Henry Owens .40 1.00
TR15 Richie Shaffer .30 .75

2016 Donruss USA Collegiate National Team

COMPLETE SET (24) 10.00 25.00
RANDOM INSERTS IN PACKS
*DISCO/299: .75X TO 2X BASIC
*BLUE/199: 1X TO 2.5X BASIC
*RED/99: 1.2X TO 3X BASIC
USA1 Buddy Reed .50 1.25
USA2 Robert Tyler .40 1.00
USA3 KJ Harrison .75 2.00
USA4 Bobby Dalbec 4.00 10.00
USA5 JJ Schwarz .50 1.25
USA6 Stephen Nogosek .40 1.00
USA7 Ryan Howard .40 1.00
USA8 Nick Banks .40 1.00
USA9 Bryson Brigman .40 1.00
USA10 Zack Burdi .50 1.25
USA11 Brendan McKay 1.00 2.50
USA12 A.J. Puk .60 1.50
USA13 Corey Ray .50 1.25
USA14 Matt Thaiss .40 1.00
USA15 Anfernee Grier .50 1.25
USA16 Garrett Hampson .75 2.00
USA17 Ryan Hendrix .40 1.00
USA18 Tanner Houck 1.00 2.50
USA19 Zach Jackson .50 1.25
USA20 Daulton Jefferies .50 1.25
USA21 Anthony Kay .40 1.00
USA22 Chris Okey .40 1.00
USA23 Mike Shawaryn .50 1.25
USA24 Logan Shore .50 1.25

2017 Donruss

COMP.SET w/o SPs (150) 10.00 25.00
196-245 INSERTED IN '17 CHRONICLES
SPs RANDOMLY INSERTED
COMP.SET ARE CARD 46-195
1 Paul Goldschmidt DK .60 1.50
2 Freddie Freeman DK .75 2.00
3 Mark Trumbo DK .40 1.00
4 Jackie Bradley Jr. DK .60 1.50
5 Anthony Rizzo DK .75 2.00
6 Jose Abreu DK .60 1.50
7 Joey Votto DK .60 1.50
8 Corey Kluber DK .60 1.50
9 Nolan Arenado DK 1.00 2.50
10 Justin Verlander DK .60 1.50
11 Carlos Correa DK .60 1.50
12 Salvador Perez DK .60 1.50
13 Mike Trout DK 3.00 8.00
14 Corey Seager DK .60 1.50
15 Christian Yelich DK .75 2.00
16 Jonathan Villar DK .40 1.00
17 Miguel Sano DK .50 1.25
18 Noah Syndergaard DK .50 1.25
19 Masahiro Tanaka DK .50 1.25
20 Khris Davis DK .60 1.50
21 Maikel Franco DK .50 1.25
22 Gregory Polanco DK .50 1.25
23 Wil Myers DK .50 1.25
24 Madison Bumgarner DK .50 1.25
25 Robinson Cano DK .50 1.25
26 Stephen Piscotty DK .50 1.25
27 Brad Miller DK .50 1.25
28 Rougned Odor DK .50 1.25
29 Edwin Encarnacion DK .60 1.50
30 Daniel Murphy DK .50 1.25
31 Yoan Moncada RR RC 1.25 3.00
32 David Dahl RR RC .50 1.25
33 Dansby Swanson RR RC 1.00 2.50
34 Andrew Benintendi RR RC 1.25 3.00
35 Alex Reyes RR RC .50 1.25
36 Tyler Glasnow RR RC 1.50 4.00
37 Josh Bell RR RC 1.00 2.50
38 Aaron Judge RR RC 10.00 25.00
39 Jose De Leon RR RC .40 1.00
40 Jeff Hoffman RR RC .40 1.00
41 Hunter Renfroe RR RC .50 1.25
42 Carson Fulmer RR RC .40 1.00
43 Alex Bregman RR RC 2.00 5.00
44 Orlando Arcia RR RC .60 1.50
45 Manny Margot RR RC .40 1.00
46 Paul Goldschmidt .25 .60
47 Jean Segura .20 .50
48 Zack Greinke .25 .60
49 Jake Lamb .20 .50
50 Yasmany Tomas .15 .40
51 Freddie Freeman .30 .75
52 Matt Kemp .20 .50
53 Nick Markakis .20 .50
54 Mark Trumbo .15 .40
55 Chris Davis .15 .40
56 Adam Jones .20 .50
57A Manny Machado .25 .60
57B Manny Machado SP 1.00 2.50
Hakuna Machado
58 Zach Britton .20 .50
59A Mookie Betts .50 1.25
59B Mookie Betts SP 2.00 5.00
back of jersey
60 Xander Bogaerts .25 .60
61 Dustin Pedroia .25 .60
62 Jackie Bradley Jr. .25 .60
63 Rick Porcello .20 .50
64 David Price .20 .50
65 Hanley Ramirez .20 .50
66 Jake Arrieta .20 .50
67 Javier Baez .30 .75
68A Kris Bryant .30 .75
68B Kris Bryant SP 1.25 3.00
black and white
68C Kris Bryant SP 1.25 3.00
MVP
68D Kris Bryant SP 1.25 3.00
Throwback Uniform
69 Kyle Hendricks .25 .60
70A Anthony Rizzo .30 .75
70B Anthony Rizzo SP 1.25 3.00
Rizz
71 Ben Zobrist .20 .50
72 Addison Russell .25 .60
73 Jon Lester .20 .50
74 Kyle Schwarber .25 .60
75 Todd Frazier .15 .40
76 Melky Cabrera .15 .40
77 Chris Sale .25 .60
78 Jose Abreu .25 .60
79 Joey Votto .25 .60
80 Adam Duvall .20 .50
81 Dan Straily .15 .40
82 Jay Bruce .20 .50
83 Corey Kluber .20 .50
84 Francisco Lindor .25 .60
85 Jose Ramirez .20 .50
86 Mike Napoli .15 .40
87 Trevor Bauer .30 .75
88 Tyler Naquin .25 .60
89A Nolan Arenado .40 1.00
89B Nolan Arenado SP 1.50 4.00
Grey Jersey
90 Trevor Story .25 .60
91 Charlie Blackmon .25 .60
92 D.J. LeMahieu .25 .60
93A Miguel Cabrera .25 .60
93B Miguel Cabrera SP 1.00 2.50
Miggy
94 Ian Kinsler .20 .50
95 Justin Verlander .25 .60
96A Michael Fulmer .15 .40
96B Michael Fulmer SP .60 1.50
ROY
97A Jose Altuve .20 .50
97B Altve SP Gigante .75 2.00
98 Carlos Correa .25 .60
99 George Springer .20 .50
100 Evan Gattis .15 .40
101 Eric Hosmer .20 .50
102 Salvador Perez .20 .50
103 Kendrys Morales .15 .40
104A Mike Trout 1.25 3.00
104B Mike Trout SP 5.00 12.00
Clapping
104C Mike Trout SP 5.00 12.00
MVP
105 Albert Pujols .30 .75
106A Corey Seager .25 .60
106B Corey Seager SP 1.00 2.50
ROY
107 Justin Turner .25 .60
108 Clayton Kershaw .40 1.00
109 Kenta Maeda .20 .50
110 Kenley Jansen .20 .50
111 Joc Pederson .20 .50
112 Adrian Gonzalez .20 .50
113 Christian Yelich .30 .75
114 Dee Gordon .15 .40
115 Marcell Ozuna .20 .50
116 Giancarlo Stanton .25 .60
117 Ryan Braun .20 .50
118 Jonathan Villar .15 .40
119 Chris Carter .15 .40
120 Brian Dozier .25 .60
121 Miguel Sano .20 .50
122 Noah Syndergaard .20 .50
123 Yoenis Cespedes .25 .60
124 Jacob deGrom .50 1.25
125 Curtis Granderson .20 .50
126 Gary Sanchez .25 .60
127 Starlin Castro .15 .40
128 Masahiro Tanaka .20 .50
129 Khris Davis .25 .60
130 Marcus Semien .20 .50
131 Odubel Herrera .20 .50
132 Maikel Franco .20 .50
133 Freddy Galvis .15 .40
134 Starling Marte .20 .50
135 Andrew McCutchen .25 .60
136 Gregory Polanco .20 .50
137 Jung-Ho Kang .15 .40
138 Wil Myers .20 .50
139 Alex Dickerson .15 .40
140 Madison Bumgarner .20 .50
141 Buster Posey .30 .75
142 Johnny Cueto .20 .50
143 Brandon Belt .20 .50
144 Kyle Seager .15 .40
145 Robinson Cano .20 .50
146 Nelson Cruz .25 .60
147 Hisashi Iwakuma .20 .50
148 Felix Hernandez .20 .50
149 Matt Holliday .25 .60
150 Stephen Piscotty .20 .50
151 Randal Grichuk .15 .40
152 Yadier Molina .30 .75
153 Matt Carpenter .25 .60
154 Carlos Martinez .20 .50
155 Evan Longoria .20 .50
156 Brad Miller .20 .50
157 Jake Odorizzi .15 .40
158 Adrian Beltre .25 .60
159 Cole Hamels .20 .50
160 Ian Desmond .15 .40
161 Rougned Odor .20 .50
162 Elvis Andrus .20 .50
163 Nomar Mazara .15 .40
164 Edwin Encarnacion .25 .60
165A Josh Donaldson .20 .50
165B Josh Donaldson SP .75 2.00
Bringer of Rain
166 J.A. Happ .20 .50
167 Aaron Sanchez .20 .50
168 Devon Travis .15 .40
169 Troy Tulowitzki .25 .60
170 Jose Bautista .20 .50
171 Bryce Harper .40 1.00
172 Max Scherzer .25 .60
173A Daniel Murphy .20 .50
173B Daniel Murphy SP .75 2.00
Murphy
Black and White
174 Wilson Ramos .15 .40
175 Trea Turner .20 .50
176 Mark Melancon .15 .40
177A Cal Ripken .75 2.00
177B Cal Ripken SP 3.00 8.00
Hall of Fame 2007
178A Dave Winfield .20 .50
178B Dave Winfield SP .75 2.00
12 Time All Star
179A Duke Snider .20 .50
179B Duke Snider SP .75 2.00
The Duke of Flatbush
180A Frank Thomas .25 .60
180B Frank Thomas SP 1.00 2.50
1993 MVP
Black and White
181 Jim Palmer .20 .50
182A Johnny Bench .25 .60
182B Johnny Bench SP 1.00 2.50
Little General
183 Ken Griffey Jr. .50 1.25
184 Kirby Puckett .25 .60
185A Nolan Ryan .75 2.00
185B Nolan Ryan .75 2.00
The Express
186A Pete Rose .50 1.25
186B Pete Rose SP 2.00 5.00
Charlie Hustle
187 Roberto Alomar .20 .50
188A Ryne Sandberg .50 1.25
188B Ryne Sandberg SP 2.00 5.00
Ryno
189 Tom Seaver .20 .50
190 Tony Gwynn .25 .60
191A Wade Boggs .20 .50
191B Wade Boggs SP .75 2.00
Chicken Man
192 Willie McCovey .20 .50
193A Willie Stargell .20 .50
193B Willie Stargell SP .75 2.00
Pops
194 Yu Darvish .25 .60
195 Carlos Gonzalez .20 .50
196 Cody Bellinger RR RC 6.00 15.00
197 Christian Arroyo RR RC .60 1.50
198 Ryon Healy RR RC .50 1.25
199 Mitch Haniger RR RC .60 1.50
200 Antonio Senzatela RR RC .40 1.00
201 Ian Happ RR RC .75 2.00
202 Trey Mancini RR RC .75 2.00
203 Jordan Montgomery RR RC .60 1.50
204 Bradley Zimmer RR RC .50 1.25
205 Jorge Bonifacio RR RC .40 1.00
206 Lewis Brinson RR RC .60 1.50
207 Jacoby Jones RR RC .50 1.25
208 Derek Fisher RR RC .50 1.25
209 Erik Gonzalez RR RC .40 1.00
210 Sam Travis RR RC .50 1.25
211 Franklin Barreto RR RC .40 1.00
212 Dinelson Lamet RR RC .40 1.00
213 Andrew Toles RR RC .40 1.00
214 Chad Pinder RR RC .40 1.00
215 Kyle Freeland RR RC .50 1.25
216 Yandy Diaz RR RC .75 2.00
217 Yulieski Gurriel RR RC .60 1.50
218 Magneuris Sierra RR RC .40 1.00
219 Marco Hernandez RR RC .40 1.00
220 Anthony Alford RR RC .40 1.00
221 Brock Stewart RR RC .40 1.00
222 Carson Kelly RR RC .50 1.25
223 Adam Frazier RR RC .40 1.00
224 Gavin Cecchini RR RC .40 1.00
225 Guillermo Heredia RR RC .60 1.50
226 German Marquez RR RC .60 1.50
227 Francis Martes RR RC .40 1.00
228 Matt Chapman RR RC 1.25 3.00
229 Hunter Dozier RR RC .40 1.00
230 Josh Hader RR RC .50 1.25
231 Luke Weaver RR RC .50 1.25
232 Jorge Alfaro RR RC .50 1.25
233 Matt Olson RR RC 2.00 5.00
234 Raimel Tapia RR RC .50 1.25
235 Teoscar Hernandez RR RC 1.50 4.00
236 Amir Garrett RR RC .40 1.00
237 Dan Vogelbach RR RC .60 1.50
238 Jharel Cotton RR RC .40 1.00
239 Roman Quinn RR RC .40 1.00
240 T.J. Rivera RR RC .60 1.50
241 Renato Nunez RR RC .75 2.00
242 Braden Shipley RR RC .40 1.00
243 Bruce Maxwell RR RC .40 1.00
244 Robert Gsellman RR RC .40 1.00
245 Paul DeJong RR RC 1.25 3.00

2017 Donruss Cyan Back

*CYAN BACK DK: .75X TO 2X BASIC
*CYAN BACK RR: .75X TO 2X BASIC
*CYAN BACK SP: .5X TO 1.2X BASIC
RANDOM INSERTS IN PACKS
196-245 INSERTED IN '17 CHRONICLES

2017 Donruss Gray Border

*GRAY DK: 1X TO 2.5X BASIC
*GRAY RR: 1X TO 2.5X BASIC
*GRAY VET: 2.5X TO 6X BASIC
*GRAY SP: .6X TO 1.5X BASIC
RANDOM INSERTS IN PACKS
196-245 INSERTED IN '17 CHRONICLES
STATED PRINT RUN 199 SER.#'d SETS
184 Kirby Puckett 8.00 20.00

2017 Donruss Magenta Back

*MAGENTA BACK: 2.5X TO 6X BASIC

2017 Donruss Pink Border

*PINK DK: 2X TO 5X BASIC
*PINK RR: 2X TO 5X BASIC
*PINK VET: 5X TO 12X BASIC
*PINK SP: 1.2X TO 3X BASIC
RANDOM INSERTS IN PACKS
196-245 INSERTED IN '17 CHRONICLES
STATED PRINT RUN 25 SER.#'d SETS
184 Kirby Puckett 25.00 60.00

2017 Donruss Press Proof Gold

*PROOF GLD DK: 1.5X TO 4X BASIC
*PROOF GLD RR: 1.5X TO 4X BASIC
*PROOF GLD VET: 4X TO 10X BASIC
*PROOF GLD SP: 1X TO 2.5X BASIC
RANDOM INSERTS IN PACKS
196-245 INSERTED IN '17 CHRONICLES
STATED PRINT RUN 99 SER.#'d SETS
184 Kirby Puckett 12.00 30.00

2017 Donruss Stat Line Career

*CAR p/r 126-515: 2X TO 5X BASIC
*CAR p/r 102-121: 2.5X TO 6X BASIC
RANDOM INSERTS IN PACKS
PRINT RUNS B/WN 102-515 COPIES PER
184 Kirby Puckett/318 6.00 15.00

2017 Donruss Stat Line Season

*SEA p/r 254-500: 2X TO 5X BASIC
*SEA p/r 127-234: 2.5X TO 6X BASIC
*SEA p/r 100-121: 3X TO 8X BASIC
*SEA p/r 51-98: 4X TO 10X BASIC
*SEA p/r 36-48: 5X TO 12X BASIC
*SEA p/r 26-34: 6X TO 15X BASIC
*SEA p/r 20-25: 8X TO 20X BASIC
RANDOM INSERTS IN PACKS
PRINT RUNS B/WN 14-500 COPIES PER
NO PRICING ON QTY 14
184 Kirby Puckett/234 8.00 20.00

2017 Donruss '83 Retro Materials

*GOLD/50-99: .5X TO 1.2X BASIC
*GOLD/25: .6X TO 1.5X BASIC
1 Ken Griffey Jr. 10.00 25.00
2 George Brett 5.00 12.00
3 Ryne Sandberg 6.00 15.00
4 Cal Ripken 8.00 20.00
5 Wade Boggs 4.00 10.00
6 Tony Gwynn 5.00 12.00
7 Gary Carter 2.50 6.00
8 Robin Yount 3.00 8.00
9 Lou Brock 4.00 10.00
10 Fergie Jenkins 2.50 6.00

2017 Donruss '83 Retro Signatures

*BLUE/49-99: .5X TO 1.2X BASIC
*RED/49: .5X TO 1.2X BASIC
*BLUE/20-25: .6X TO 1.5X BASIC
2017 Donruss New Breed Autographs Gold
*RED/25: .6X TO 1.5X BASIC
1 Omar Vizquel 6.00 15.00
2 Andres Galarraga 6.00 15.00
3 Wade Boggs 12.00 30.00
5 Ryne Sandberg 15.00 40.00
6 Todd Helton 6.00 15.00
7 George Springer 10.00 25.00
8 Cole Hamels
9 Manny Machado 20.00 50.00
10 Xander Bogaerts 12.00 30.00
11 Brian Dozier 4.00 10.00
12 Jose Ramirez 10.00 25.00
13 Anthony Rizzo 20.00 50.00
14 Evan Longoria 8.00 20.00
15 Jason Kipnis 8.00 20.00
17 Adam Eaton 4.00 10.00
18 Adrian Beltre 25.00 60.00
20 Edgar Renteria 5.00 12.00
22 Noah Syndergaard 10.00 25.00
23 Khris Davis 4.00 10.00

2017 Donruss '83 Retro Variations

*CAR p/r 282-500: 1.2X TO 3X
*CAR p/r 126-241: 1.5X TO 4X
*CAR p/r 102-117: 2X TO 5X
*SEA p/r 251-500: 1.2X TO 3X
*SEA p/r 140-210: 1.5X TO 4X
*SEA p/r 100-124: 2X TO 5X

*SEA p/r 73-98: 2.5X TO 6X
*SEA p/r 36-47: 3X TO 8X
*SEA p/r 28-34: 4X TO 10X
*SEA p/r 24-25: 5X TO 12X
*MGNTA BCK: 1X TO 2.5X BASIC
*GRAY/199: 1.5X TO 4X BASIC
*GOLD PP/99: 2.5X TO 6X BASIC
*AQS PP/49: 2.5X TO 6X BASIC
*PINK/25: 5X TO 12X BASIC
RV1 Paul Goldschmidt .40 1.00
RV2 Freddie Freeman .50 1.25
RV3 Mark Trumbo .25 .60
RV4 Mookie Betts .75 2.00
RV5 Kris Bryant .50 1.25
RV6 Kyle Hendricks .40 1.00
RV7 Todd Frazier .25 .60
RV8 Joey Votto .40 1.00
RV9 Corey Kluber .30 .75
RV10 Francisco Lindor .40 1.00
RV11 Nolan Arenado .60 1.50
RV12 Justin Verlander .40 1.00
RV13 Jose Altuve .30 .75
RV14 Eric Hosmer .30 .75
RV15 Mike Trout 2.00 5.00
RV16 Albert Pujols .50 1.25
RV17 Clayton Kershaw .60 1.50
RV18 Corey Seager .40 1.00
RV19 Christian Yelich .50 1.25
RV20 Ryan Braun .30 .75
RV21 Brian Dozier .40 1.00
RV22 Noah Syndergaard .30 .75
RV23 Masahiro Tanaka .30 .75
RV24 Khris Davis .40 1.00
RV25 Maikel Franco .30 .75
RV26 Andrew McCutchen .40 1.00
RV27 Wil Myers .30 .75
RV28 Madison Bumgarner .30 .75
RV29 Johnny Cueto .30 .75
RV30 Kyle Seager .25 .60
RV31 Robinson Cano .30 .75
RV32 Nelson Cruz .40 1.00
RV33 Stephen Piscotty .30 .75
RV34 Matt Carpenter .40 1.00
RV35 Evan Longoria .30 .75
RV36 Adrian Beltre .40 1.00
RV37 Rougned Odor .30 .75
RV38 Cole Hamels .30 .75
RV39 Josh Donaldson .30 .75
RV40 Daniel Murphy .30 .75
RV41 Mike Piazza .40 1.00
RV42 Pedro Martinez .30 .75
RV43 Robin Yount .40 1.00
RV44 Eddie Murray .30 .75
RV45 Ozzie Smith .50 1.25
RV46 Harmon Killebrew .40 1.00
RV47 Joe Morgan .30 .75
RV48 Goose Gossage .30 .75
RV49 Craig Biggio .30 .75
RV50 Brooks Robinson .30 .75

2017 Donruss All Stars

STATED PRINT RUN 999 SER.#'d SETS
*SILVER/349: .5X TO 1.2X BASIC
*BLUE/249: .6X TO 1.5X BASIC
*RED/149: .6X TO 1.5X BASIC
*GOLD/99: 1X TO 2.5X BASIC
*BLACK/25: 2X TO 5X BASIC
AS1 Addison Russell 1.00 2.50
AS2 Bryce Harper 1.50 4.00
AS3 Chris Sale 1.00 2.50
AS4 Eric Hosmer .75 2.00
AS5 Johnny Cueto .75 2.00
AS6 Jose Altuve .75 2.00
AS7 Kris Bryant 1.25 3.00
AS8 Manny Machado 1.00 2.50
AS9 Marcell Ozuna 1.00 2.50
AS10 Mike Trout 5.00 12.00
AS11 Mookie Betts 2.00 5.00
AS12 Yoenis Cespedes 1.00 2.50

2017 Donruss American Pride

RANDOM INSERTS IN PACKS
STATED PRINT RUN 999 SER.#'d SETS
*SILVER/349: .5X TO 1.2X BASIC
*BLUE/249: .6X TO 1.5X BASIC
*RED/149: .6X TO 1.5X BASIC
*GOLD/99: 1X TO 2.5X BASIC
*BLACK/25: 2X TO 5X BASIC
AP1 Darren McCaughan .75 2.00
AP2 Seth Beer 2.50 6.00
AP3 J.B. Bukauskas 1.00 2.50
AP4 Jake Burger 1.25 3.00
AP5 Tyler Johnson .75 2.00
AP6 Alex Faedo 1.00 2.50
AP7 TJ Friedl .60 1.50
AP8 Dalton Guthrie 1.00 2.50
AP9 Devin Hairston .75 2.00
AP10 KJ Harrison 1.00 2.50
AP11 Keston Hiura 3.00 8.00
AP12 Tanner Houck 3.00 8.00
AP13 Jeren Kendall 1.25 3.00
AP14 Alex Lange 1.00 2.50
AP15 Brendan McKay 2.50 6.00
AP16 Glenn Otto .60 1.50
AP17 David Peterson 1.25 3.00
AP18 Mike Rivera .60 1.50
AP19 Evan Skoug .75 2.00
AP20 Ricky Tyler Thomas .60 1.50
AP21 Taylor Walls .60 1.50
AP22 Tim Cate .75 2.00
AP23 Evan White 1.50 4.00
AP24 Kyle Wright 2.00 5.00

2017 Donruss Aqueous Test Proof

*AQUEOUS PROOF DK: 1.5X TO 4X BASIC
*AQUEOUS PROOF RR: 1.5X TO 4X BASIC
*AQUEOUS PROOF VET: 4X TO 10X BASIC
*AQUEOUS PROOF SP: 1X TO 2.5X BASIC
RANDOM INSERTS IN PACKS
196-245 INSERTED IN '17 CHRONICLES
STATED PRINT RUN 49 SER.#'d SETS
184 Kirby Puckett 15.00 40.00

2017 Donruss Back to the Future Materials

*GOLD/49-99: .5X TO 1.2X BASIC
*GOLD/25: .6X TO 1.5X BASIC
BFMAC Aroldis Chapman 3.00 8.00
BFMCB Carlos Beltran 2.50 6.00
BFMCS CC Sabathia 2.50 6.00
BFMDM Daniel Murphy 2.50 6.00
BFMDP David Price 2.50 6.00
BFMHP Hunter Pence 2.50 6.00
BFMJD Josh Donaldson 2.50 6.00
BFMJL Jon Lester 2.50 6.00
BFMMC Miguel Cabrera 3.00 8.00
BFMMK Matt Kemp 2.50 6.00
BFMMM Matt Moore 2.50 6.00
BFMMS Max Scherzer 3.00 8.00
BFMMT Mark Trumbo 2.00 5.00
BFMRC Robinson Cano 2.50 6.00
BFMRP Rick Porcello 2.50 6.00

2017 Donruss Diamond Collection Memorabilia

*GOLD/20-25: .6X TO 1.5X BASIC
DCAD Alex Dickerson 2.00 5.00
DCAJ Aaron Judge 12.00 30.00
DCAM Adalberto Mejia 2.00 5.00
DCAN Aaron Nola 2.50 6.00
DCAP Albert Pujols 4.00 10.00
DCAR A.J. Reed 2.00 5.00
DCAR Addison Russell 3.00 8.00
DCAX Alex Reyes 2.50 6.00
DCBB Bill Buckner 2.00 5.00
DCBD Brandon Drury 2.00 5.00
DCBE Brian Ellington 2.00 5.00
DCBH Bryce Harper 5.00 12.00
DCBJ Bo Jackson 3.00 8.00
DCBJ Brian Johnson 2.00 5.00
DCBL Barry Larkin 2.50 6.00
DCBN Brandon Nimmo 2.50 6.00
DCBP Byung-ho Park 2.00 5.00
DCCC Carlos Correa 3.00 8.00
DCCC C.J. Cron 2.00 5.00
DCCE Carl Edwards Jr. 2.00 5.00
DCCF Carson Fulmer 2.00 5.00
DCCK Carson Kelly 2.50 6.00
DCCK Corey Kluber 2.50 6.00
DCCK Clayton Kershaw 4.00 10.00
DCCR Colin Rea 2.00 5.00
DCCS Corey Seager 4.00 10.00
DCCY Christian Yelich 4.00 10.00
DCDD David Dahl 2.50 6.00
DCDP David Paulino 2.50 6.00
DCEL Evan Longoria 2.50 6.00
DCEM Eddie Murray 2.50 6.00
DCFF Freddie Freeman 4.00 10.00
DCFL Francisco Lindor 3.00 8.00
DCGB George Brett 5.00 12.00
DCGB Greg Bird 2.50 6.00
DCGC Gavin Cecchini 2.00 5.00
DCGC Gary Carter 2.50 6.00
DCGM Greg Maddux 4.00 10.00
DCGS Giancarlo Stanton 3.00 8.00
DCGS Gary Sanchez 5.00 12.00
DCGS George Springer 2.50 6.00
DCHR Hanley Ramirez 2.50 6.00
DCJB Javier Baez 4.00 10.00
DCJB Jay Bruce 2.50 6.00
DCJE Jacoby Ellsbury 2.50 6.00
DCJG Jonathan Gray 2.00 5.00
DCJJ Jacoby Jones 2.50 6.00
DCJL Jake Lamb 2.50 6.00
DCJM J.D. Martinez 3.00 8.00
DCJP Joe Panik 2.50 6.00
DCJP Joc Pederson 2.50 6.00
DCJT Jameson Taillon 2.50 6.00
DCJV Joey Votto 3.00 8.00
DCJV Justin Verlander 3.00 8.00
DCKB Kris Bryant 4.00 10.00
DCKG Kirk Gibson 2.00 5.00
DCKM Ketel Marte 2.50 6.00
DCKS Kyle Schwarber 5.00 12.00
DCLG Lucas Giolito 2.50 6.00
DCLS Luis Severino 2.50 6.00
DCMB Madison Bumgarner 2.50 6.00
DCMC Michael Conforto 2.50 6.00
DCMF Michael Fulmer 2.00 5.00
DCMK Max Kepler 2.50 6.00
DCMN Mike Napoli 2.00 5.00
DCMO Matt Olson 4.00 10.00
DCMP Mike Piazza 3.00 8.00
DCMS Mike Schmidt 5.00 12.00
DCMS Miguel Sano 2.50 6.00
DCMT Mike Trout 15.00 40.00
DCMW Mac Williamson 2.00 5.00
DCNA Nolan Arenado 5.00 12.00
DCOA Orlando Arcia 3.00 8.00
DCOH Orel Hershiser 2.00 5.00
DCPO Peter O'Brien 2.00 5.00
DCPR Pete Rose 5.00 12.00
DCRC Robinson Cano 2.50 6.00
DCRO Rougned Odor 2.50 6.00
DCRR Rob Refsnyder 2.00 5.00
DCRS Ryne Sandberg 6.00 15.00
DCRT Raimel Tapia 2.50 6.00
DCRY Robin Yount 3.00 8.00
DCSM Starling Marte 2.50 6.00
DCSP Stephen Piscotty 2.50 6.00
DCTA Tim Anderson 3.00 8.00
DCTD Tyler Duffey 2.00 5.00
DCTF Todd Frazier 2.00 5.00
DCTG Tony Gwynn 3.00 8.00
DCTH Todd Helton 2.50 6.00
DCTJ Travis Jankowski 2.00 5.00
DCTS Trevor Story 3.00 8.00
DCTT Trayce Thompson 2.50 6.00
DCTT Trea Turner 2.50 6.00
DCWC Willson Contreras 3.00 8.00
DCWC Will Clark 4.00 10.00
DCXB Xander Bogaerts 3.00 8.00
DCYM Yadier Molina 4.00 10.00
DCYM Yoan Moncada 3.00 8.00
DCZG Zack Godley 2.00 5.00

2017 Donruss Dominators

RANDOM INSERTS IN PACKS
STATED PRINT RUN 999 SER.#'d SETS
*SILVER/349: .5X TO 1.2X BASIC
*BLUE/249: .6X TO 1.5X BASIC
*RED/149: .6X TO 1.5X BASIC
*GOLD/99: 1X TO 2.5X BASIC
*BLACK/25: 2X TO 5X BASIC
D1 Kris Bryant 1.25 3.00
D2 Mike Trout 5.00 12.00
D3 Mookie Betts 2.00 5.00
D4 Jose Altuve .75 2.00
D5 D.J. LeMahieu 1.00 2.50
D6 Daniel Murphy .75 2.00
D7 Mark Trumbo .60 1.50
D8 Joey Votto 1.00 2.50
D9 Brian Dozier 1.00 2.50
D10 Max Scherzer 1.00 2.50
D11 Justin Verlander 1.00 2.50
D12 Rick Porcello .75 2.00
D13 Jon Lester .75 2.00
D14 Corey Kluber .75 2.00
D15 Miguel Cabrera 1.00 2.50
D16 Nolan Arenado 1.50 4.00
D17 Corey Seager 1.00 2.50
D18 Edwin Encarnacion 1.00 2.50
D19 Jean Segura .75 2.00
D20 Josh Donaldson .75 2.00
D21 Charlie Blackmon 1.00 2.50
D22 Robinson Cano .75 2.00
D23 Khris Davis 1.00 2.50
D24 Kyle Hendricks 1.00 2.50
D25 Jonathan Villar .60 1.50

2017 Donruss Elite Series

RANDOM INSERTS IN PACKS
STATED PRINT RUN 999 SER.#'d SETS
*SILVER/349: .5X TO 1.2X BASIC
*BLUE/249: .6X TO 1.5X BASIC
*RED/149: .6X TO 1.5X BASIC
*GOLD/99: 1X TO 2.5X BASIC
*BLACK/25: 2X TO 5X BASIC
ES1 Wil Myers .75 2.00
ES2 Freddie Freeman 1.25 3.00
ES3 Kris Bryant 1.25 3.00
ES4 Clayton Kershaw 1.50 4.00
ES5 Bryce Harper 1.50 4.00
ES6 Dustin Pedroia 1.00 2.50
ES7 Xander Bogaerts 1.00 2.50
ES8 Todd Frazier .60 1.50
ES9 Hanley Ramirez .75 2.00
ES10 Ian Kinsler .75 2.00
ES11 Manny Machado 1.00 2.50
ES12 Anthony Rizzo 1.25 3.00
ES13 Adrian Beltre 1.00 2.50
ES14 Kyle Seager .60 1.50
ES15 Tyler Naquin 1.00 2.50
ES16 Madison Bumgarner .75 2.00
ES17 Chris Sale 1.00 2.50
ES18 Gary Sanchez 1.00 2.50
ES19 Trevor Story 1.00 2.50
ES20 Trea Turner .75 2.00
ES21 Kenta Maeda .75 2.00
ES22 Buster Posey 1.25 3.00
ES23 Christian Yelich 1.25 3.00
ES24 Mike Trout 5.00 12.00
ES25 Jose Ramirez .75 2.00

2017 Donruss Masters of the Game

RANDOM INSERTS IN PACKS
STATED PRINT RUN 999 SER.#'d SETS
*SILVER/349: .5X TO 1.2X BASIC
*BLUE/249: .6X TO 1.5X BASIC
*RED/149: .6X TO 1.5X BASIC
*GOLD/99: 1X TO 2.5X BASIC
*BLACK/25: 2X TO 5X BASIC
MGCR Cal Ripken 3.00 8.00
MGFV Fernando Valenzuela .60 1.50
MGGB George Brett 2.00 5.00
MGLB Lou Brock .75 2.00
MGMM Mike Mussina .75 2.00
MGMP Mike Piazza 1.00 2.50
MGOS Ozzie Smith 1.25 3.00
MGPM Pedro Martinez .75 2.00
MGRC Rod Carew .75 2.00
MGRJ Reggie Jackson .75 2.00

2017 Donruss New Breed Autographs

*GOLD/99: .5X TO 1.2X BASIC
*GOLD/25: .6X TO 1.5X BASIC
NBAD Aledmys Diaz 10.00 25.00
NBAR A.J. Reed 2.50 6.00
NBBE Brett Eibner 2.50 6.00
NBBJ Brian Johnson 2.50 6.00
NBBN Brandon Nimmo 3.00 8.00
NBDA Dariel Alvarez 2.50 6.00
NBDR Daniel Robertson 2.50 6.00
NBFM Frankie Montas 5.00 12.00
NBGB Greg Bird 3.00 8.00
NBGM Greg Mahle 2.50 6.00
NBJB Jose Berrios 3.00 8.00
NBJE Jerad Eickhoff 2.50 6.00
NBJP Jose Peraza 3.00 8.00
NBJU Julio Urias 12.00 30.00
NBKM Ketel Marte 3.00 8.00
NBKW Kyle Waldrop
NBLJ Luke Jackson 2.50 6.00
NBMK Max Kepler 3.00 8.00
NBMS Mallex Smith 2.50 6.00
NBOA Ozhaino Albies 10.00 25.00
NBPS Pedro Severino 2.50 6.00
NBRS Ross Stripling 2.50 6.00
NBTT Trayce Thompson 3.00 8.00
NBZG Zack Godley 2.50 6.00

2017 Donruss Promising Pros Materials

*GOLD/49-99: .5X TO 1.2X BASIC
*GOLD/25: .6X TO 1.5X BASIC
PPMAD Aledmys Diaz 4.00 10.00
PPMAR A.J. Reed 2.00 5.00
PPMBE Brett Eibner 2.00 5.00
PPMBE Brian Ellington 2.00 5.00
PPMBN Brandon Nimmo 2.50 6.00
PPMDL Dae-ho Lee 3.00 8.00
PPMFM Frankie Montas 2.00 5.00
PPMGB Greg Bird 2.50 6.00
PPMGM Greg Mahle 2.00 5.00
PPMHK Hyun-soo Kim 2.50 6.00
PPMHO Henry Owens 2.00 5.00
PPMJB Jose Berrios 2.50 6.00
PPMJE Jerad Eickhoff 2.00 5.00
PPMJP Jose Peraza 2.50 6.00
PPMJR Joey Rickard 2.00 5.00
PPMJU Julio Urias 3.00 8.00
PPMKM Ketel Marte 2.50 6.00
PPMLJ Luke Jackson 2.00 5.00
PPMMS Mallex Smith 2.00 5.00
PPMPS Pedro Severino 2.00 5.00
PPMRS Ross Stripling 2.00 5.00
PPMSO Seung-Hwan Oh 4.00 10.00
PPMTT Trayce Thompson 2.50 6.00
PPMTW Tyler White 2.00 5.00
PPMWM Whit Merrifield 3.00 8.00

2017 Donruss Promising Pros Materials Signatures

PPMSAA Anthony Alford 3.00 8.00
PPMSAM Austin Meadows 8.00 20.00
PPMSBA Brian Anderson 4.00 10.00
PPMSBH Brent Honeywell 4.00 10.00
PPMSBZ Bradley Zimmer 5.00 12.00
PPMSCB Cody Bellinger 25.00 60.00
PPMSCF Clint Frazier 5.00 12.00
PPMSCS Christin Stewart
PPMSEJ Eloy Jimenez 12.00 30.00
PPMSFB Franklin Barreto 4.00 10.00
PPMSIH Ian Happ 12.00 30.00
PPMSJC Jeimer Candelario 6.00 15.00
PPMSJT Jake Thompson 3.00 8.00
PPMSLS Lucas Sims 5.00 12.00
PPMSMC Matt Chapman 10.00 25.00
PPMSNM Nomar Mazara 3.00 8.00
PPMSRD Rafael Devers 25.00 60.00
PPMSSN Sean Newcomb 4.00 10.00
PPMSTT Tyrone Taylor 3.00 8.00
PPMSTT Tim Tebow 40.00 100.00
PPMSWC Willson Contreras 8.00 20.00

2017 Donruss Promising Pros Materials Signatures Gold

*GOLD/40-99: .5X TO 1.2X BASIC
*GOLD/25: .6X TO 1.5X BASIC
PRINT RUNS B/WN 10-99 COPIES PER
NO PRICING ON QTY 10
PPMSJM Jorge Mateo/40 8.00 20.00

2017 Donruss San Diego Chicken Triple Material

1 Ted Giannoulas/83 20.00 50.00

2017 Donruss San Diego Chicken Triple Material Signatures

STATED PRINT RUN 83 SER.#'d SETS
1 Ted Giannoulas/83 50.00 120.00

2017 Donruss Signature Series

SOME ISSUED IN'17 CHRONICLES
*BLUE/49-199: .5X TO 1.2X BASIC
*BLUE/25-35: .6X TO 1.5X BASIC
*GOLD/49: .5X TO 1.2X BASIC
*GOLD/20-25: .6X TO 1.5X BASIC
*PURPLE/25: .6X TO 1.5X BASIC
*RED/49-99: .5X TO 1.2X BASIC
*RED/20-35: .6X TO 1.5X BASIC
CHRON.EXCH.DEADLINE 5/22/2019
1 Cody Bellinger
2 Ian Happ 6.00 15.00
3 Mitch Haniger 4.00 10.00
4 Sam Travis 3.00 8.00
6 Adam Frazier 2.50 6.00
7 Derek Fisher 3.00 8.00
8 Franklin Barreto 2.50 6.00
9 Jorge Bonifacio 2.50 6.00
10 Dinelson Lamet 2.50 6.00
12 Lewis Brinson 4.00 10.00
13 Magneuris Sierra 2.50 6.00
14 Juan Gonzalez 6.00 15.00
15 Andrew Toles 2.50 6.00
16 Bradley Zimmer 3.00 8.00
17 Antonio Senzatela 2.50 6.00
18 Brock Stewart 2.50 6.00
19 Yandy Diaz 5.00 12.00
20 Hunter Dozier 2.50 6.00
SSRR Rio Ruiz 2.50 6.00
22 Reggie Jackson 20.00 50.00
SS2RY Rhys Hoskins 6.00 15.00
24 Rickey Henderson 25.00 60.00
25 Wade Boggs 12.00 30.00
26 Adrian Beltre
27 Alex Rodriguez 30.00 80.00
28 Aaron Sanchez 3.00 8.00
29 Carlos Gonzalez 3.00 8.00
30 Jonathan Lucroy 3.00 8.00
31 Anthony Rizzo 25.00 60.00
32 David Ortiz 20.00 50.00
33 Hunter Pence 4.00 10.00
34 Ian Kinsler 3.00 8.00
35 Jonathan Villar 2.50 6.00
36 Rougned Odor 3.00 8.00
37 Frank Thomas
38 Jose Canseco 6.00 15.00
39 Alfonso Soriano 4.00 10.00
40 Ozzie Smith 12.00 30.00
41 Amed Rosario 4.00 10.00
42 Ozzie Albies 12.00 30.00
SS2GS George Springer 8.00 20.00
44 Jake Lamb 3.00 8.00
45 Charlie Blackmon 5.00 12.00
46 Logan Morrison 2.50 6.00
47 Ervin Santana 2.50 6.00
48 Lance McCullers 2.50 6.00
49 Craig Kimbrel 5.00 12.00
50 Kevin Pillar 2.50 6.00
SSAB Alex Bregman 15.00 40.00
SSAB Andrew Benintendi 30.00 80.00
SSAJ Aaron Judge 40.00 100.00
SSAM Adalberto Mejia 2.50 6.00
SSAR Alex Reyes 3.00 8.00
SSBR Brooks Robinson 10.00 25.00
SSBS Braden Shipley 2.50 6.00
SSCF Carson Fulmer 2.50 6.00
SSCK Carson Kelly 3.00 8.00
SSCP Chad Pinder 2.50 6.00
SSDD David Dahl 3.00 8.00
SSDM Don Mattingly 20.00 50.00
SSDP David Price 3.00 8.00
SSDP David Paulino 3.00 8.00
SSDS Dansby Swanson 6.00 15.00
SSEG Erik Gonzalez 2.50 6.00
SSGC Gavin Cecchini 2.50 6.00
SSHR Hunter Renfroe 3.00 8.00
SSJA Jorge Alfaro 3.00 8.00
SSJA Jose Abreu 5.00 12.00
SSJB Josh Bell 5.00 12.00
SSJC Jharel Cotton 2.50 6.00
SSJD Jose De Leon 2.50 6.00
SSJH Jeff Hoffman 2.50 6.00
SSJJ Jacoby Jones 3.00 8.00
SSJM Joe Musgrove 8.00 20.00
SSJR Jose Rondon 2.50 6.00
SSJT Josh Tomlin 5.00 12.00
SSJT Jake Thompson 2.50 6.00
SSLW Luke Weaver 3.00 8.00
SSMM Manny Margot 2.50 6.00
SSMO Matt Olson 6.00 15.00
SSMS Mike Schmidt 20.00 50.00
SSNC Nelson Cruz 4.00 10.00
SSNM Nomar Mazara 2.50 6.00
SSOA Orlando Arcia 4.00 10.00
SSRH Ryon Healy 3.00 8.00
SSRL Reynaldo Lopez
SSRQ Roman Quinn
SSRR Rio Ruiz 4.00 10.00
SSRT Raimel Tapia 3.00 8.00
SSSS Stephen Strasburg 12.00 30.00
SSTG Tom Glavine 8.00 20.00
SSTG Tyler Glasnow 8.00 20.00
SSTH Teoscar Hernandez
SSTM Trey Mancini 5.00 12.00
SSVG Vladimir Guerrero 8.00 20.00
SSYM Yohander Mendez 2.50 6.00
SSYM Yoan Moncada 15.00 40.00

2017 Donruss Significant Signatures

*BLUE/49: .5X TO 1.2X BASIC
*BLUE/20-25: .6X TO 1.5X BASIC
*RED/20-25: .6X TO 1.5X BASIC
SIGBG Bob Gibson 10.00 25.00
SIGBM Bill Mazeroski 10.00 25.00
SIGCY Carl Yastrzemski 30.00 80.00
SIGDW Dave Winfield 10.00 25.00
SIGEM Eddie Murray 15.00 40.00
SIGJM Joe Morgan 10.00 25.00
SIGJM Juan Marichal 10.00 25.00
SIGKG Ken Griffey Jr. 50.00 120.00
SIGOC Orlando Cepeda 6.00 15.00
SIGOS Ozzie Smith 10.00 25.00
SIGPR Pete Rose 15.00 40.00
SIGRC Rod Carew 12.00 30.00
SIGRC Roger Clemens 20.00 50.00
SIGRH Rickey Henderson 25.00 60.00
SIGRJ Reggie Jackson 20.00 50.00
SIGRS Ryne Sandberg 15.00 40.00
SIGSC Steve Carlton 10.00 25.00
SIGTL Tommy Lasorda 20.00 50.00
SIGWM Willie McCovey 15.00 40.00

2017 Donruss Studio Signatures

*BLUE/49: .5X TO 1.2X BASIC
*RED/25: .5X TO 1.2X BASIC
STSDW David Wright 5.00 12.00
STSFL Francisco Lindor
STSJA Jake Arrieta 15.00 40.00
STSMS Max Scherzer 10.00 25.00

2017 Donruss Studio Signatures Purple

PRINT RUNS B/WN 7-25 COPIES PER
NO PRICING ON QTY 15 OR LESS
STSDP Dustin Pedroia/25 15.00 40.00

2017 Donruss The Prospects

*CYAN BACK: .75X TO 2X BASIC
*GRAY/199: 1X TO 2.5X BASIC
*GOLD PP/99: 1.5X TO 4X BASIC
*AQS TEST/49: 1.5X TO 4X BASIC
*PINK/25: 3X TO 8X BASIC
TP1 Brendan Rodgers .40 1.00
TP2 Austin Meadows .75 2.00
TP3 Victor Robles .75 2.00
TP4 Ozhaino Albies 1.25 3.00
TP5 Anderson Espinoza .30 .75
TP6 Clint Frazier .60 1.50
TP7 Rafael Devers .60 1.50
TP8 Gleyber Torres 5.00 12.00
TP9 Jorge Mateo .30 .75
TP10 Ian Happ .60 1.50
TP11 Eloy Jimenez 1.25 3.00
TP12 Bradley Zimmer .40 1.00
TP13 Corey Ray .40 1.00
TP14 Cody Bellinger 5.00 12.00
TP15 Francis Martes .30 .75

2017 Donruss The Rookies

RANDOM INSERTS IN PACKS
*CYAN BACK: .75X TO 2X BASIC
*GRAY/199: 1X TO 2.5X BASIC
*GOLD PP/99: 1.5X TO 4X BASIC
*AQS TEST/49: 1.5X TO 4X BASIC
*PINK/25: 3X TO 8X BASIC
TR1 Yoan Moncada 1.00 2.50
TR2 David Dahl .40 1.00
TR3 Dansby Swanson .75 2.00
TR4 Andrew Benintendi 1.00 2.50
TR5 Alex Reyes .40 1.00
TR6 Tyler Glasnow 1.25 3.00
TR7 Josh Bell .75 2.00
TR8 Aaron Judge 4.00 10.00
TR9 Jose De Leon .30 .75
TR10 Jeff Hoffman .30 .75
TR11 Hunter Renfroe .40 1.00
TR12 Carson Fulmer .30 .75
TR13 Alex Bregman 1.50 4.00
TR14 Orlando Arcia .50 1.25
TR15 Manny Margot .30 .75

2017 Donruss Whammy

W1 Mike Trout 60.00 150.00
W2 Ken Griffey Jr. 25.00 60.00
W3 Kris Bryant 15.00 40.00
W4 Bryce Harper 20.00 50.00

2018 Donruss

1 Anthony Rizzo DK .75 2.00
2 Yoan Moncada DK .60 1.50
3 Evan Longoria DK .50 1.25
4 Joey Votto DK .60 1.50
5 Corey Kluber DK .50 1.25
6 Adrian Beltre DK .60 1.50
7 Jose Bautista DK .50 1.25
8 Nolan Arenado DK 1.00 2.50
9 Miguel Cabrera DK .60 1.50
10 Bryce Harper DK 1.00 2.50
11 Jose Altuve DK .50 1.25
12 Eric Hosmer DK .50 1.25
13 Mike Trout DK 3.00 8.00
14 Clayton Kershaw DK 1.00 2.50
15 Justin Bour DK .40 1.00
16 Ryan Braun DK .50 1.25
17 Brian Dozier DK .50 1.25
18 Noah Syndergaard DK .50 1.25
19 Aaron Judge DK 1.50 4.00
20 Matt Olson DK .60 1.50
21 Odubel Herrera DK .50 1.25
22 Paul Goldschmidt DK .60 1.50
23 Freddie Freeman DK .75 2.00
24 Andrew McCutchen DK .60 1.50
25 Adam Jones DK .50 1.25
26 Wil Myers DK .50 1.25
27 Mookie Betts DK 1.25 3.00
28 Madison Bumgarner DK .50 1.25
29 Robinson Cano DK .50 1.25
30 Adam Wainwright DK .50 1.25
31 Miguel Andujar RR RC 1.50 4.00
32 Nick Williams RR RC .50 1.25
33 Clint Frazier RR RC .75 2.00
34 Paul Blackburn RR RC .40 1.00
35 Rafael Devers RR RC 1.25 3.00
36 Ozzie Albies RR RC 1.25 3.00
37 Amed Rosario RR RC .50 1.25
38 Rhys Hoskins RR RC 1.50 4.00
39 Ryan McMahon RR RC 1.00 2.50
40 Willie Calhoun RR RC .60 1.50
41 Walker Buehler RR RC 2.00 5.00
42 Victor Robles RR RC 1.00 2.50
43 Luiz Gohara RR RC .40 1.00
44 J.P. Crawford RR RC .40 1.00
45 Alex Verdugo RR RC .60 1.50
46 Tyler Mahle RR RC .50 1.25
47 Dominic Smith RR RC .50 1.25
48 Brandon Woodruff RR RC 1.25 3.00
49 Chris Flexen RR RC .40 1.00
50 Dustin Fowler RR RC .40 1.00
51 Paul Goldschmidt .25 .60
52 David Peralta .15 .40
53 Zack Greinke .25 .60
54 Jake Lamb .20 .50
55 Robbie Ray .15 .40
56 Freddie Freeman .30 .75
57 Ender Inciarte .15 .40
58 Anthony Rendon .25 .60
59 Eddie Mathews .25 .60
60 Jonathan Schoop .15 .40
61 Trey Mancini .20 .50
62 Adam Jones .20 .50
63 J.A. Happ .20 .50
64 Cal Ripken .75 2.00
65 Jim Palmer .20 .50
66 Justin Smoak .15 .40
67 Xander Bogaerts .25 .60
68 Dustin Pedroia .25 .60
69 Jackie Bradley Jr. .25 .60
70 Jean Segura .15 .40
71 Drew Pomeranz .15 .40
72 Brian Dozier .20 .50
73 Wade Boggs .20 .50
74 Duke Snider .20 .50
75 Jake Arrieta .20 .50
76 Javier Baez .30 .75
77 Cole Hamels .20 .50
78 Kyle Hendricks .25 .60
79 Miguel Sano .20 .50
80 Willson Contreras .25 .60
81 Logan Morrison .15 .40
82 Jon Lester .20 .50
83 Kyle Schwarber .25 .60
84 Ryne Sandberg .50 1.25
85 Avisail Garcia .20 .50
86 Jose Abreu .25 .60
87 Frank Thomas .25 .60
88 Luis Castillo .20 .50
89 Tom Seaver .20 .50
90 Zack Cozart .15 .40
91 Barry Larkin .20 .50
92 Joe Morgan .20 .50
93 Jay Bruce .20 .50
94 Sonny Gray .20 .50
95 Odubel Herrera .20 .50
96 James Paxton .20 .50
97 Carlos Carrasco .15 .40
98 Andrew Miller .20 .50
99 Michael Brantley .20 .50
100 Roberto Alomar .20 .50
101 Edwin Encarnacion .25 .60
102 Nelson Cruz .25 .60
103 Trevor Story .25 .60
104 Charlie Blackmon .25 .60
105 DJ LeMahieu .25 .60
106 Kyle Freeland .20 .50
107 Jonathan Gray .15 .40
108 Reggie Jackson .20 .50
109 Michael Fulmer .15 .40
110 Al Kaline .25 .60
111 Justin Verlander .25 .60
112 Dave Winfield .20 .50
113 Madison Bumgarner .20 .50
114 Manuel Margot .15 .40
115 Juan Marichal .20 .50
116 Wil Myers .20 .50
117 Lorenzo Cain .15 .40
118 Eric Hosmer .20 .50
119 Marcus Stroman .20 .50
120 George Brett .50 1.25
121 Ryon Healy .15 .40
122 Andrelton Simmons .15 .40
123 Rod Carew .20 .50
124 Aaron Altherr .15 .40
125 Justin Turner .25 .60
126 Khris Davis .25 .60
127 Yu Darvish .25 .60
128 Kenley Jansen .20 .50
129 Alex Wood .15 .40
130 Didi Gregorius .20 .50
131 Justin Bour .15 .40
132 Christian Yelich .30 .75
133 Dee Gordon .15 .40
134 Marcell Ozuna .25 .60
135 Ervin Santana .15 .40
136 Ryan Braun .20 .50
137 Travis Shaw .15 .40
138 Eric Thames .20 .50
139 Orlando Arcia .15 .40
140 Chris Sale .25 .60
141 Anthony Rizzo .30 .75
142 Kirby Puckett .25 .60
143 Giancarlo Stanton .25 .60
144 Noah Syndergaard .20 .50
145 Michael Conforto .20 .50
146 Jacob deGrom .50 1.25
147 Joey Votto .25 .60
148 Aaron Judge .60 1.50
149 Cody Bellinger .50 1.25
150 Gary Sanchez .25 .60
151 Luis Severino .20 .50
152 Jordan Montgomery .15 .40
153 Corey Kluber .20 .50
154 Clayton Kershaw .40 1.00
155 Mike Trout 1.25 3.00
156 Miguel Cabrera .25 .60
157 Francisco Lindor .25 .60
158 Corey Seager .25 .60
159 Andrew McCutchen .25 .60
160 Josh Bell .20 .50
161 Gerrit Cole .25 .60
162 Alex Bregman .25 .60
163 Carlos Correa .25 .60
164 Dallas Keuchel .20 .50
165 Tony Gwynn .25 .60
166 Jose Altuve .20 .50
167 Buster Posey .30 .75
168 George Springer .20 .50
169 Andrew Benintendi .25 .60
170 Kyle Seager .15 .40
171 Robinson Cano .20 .50
172 Nolan Arenado .40 1.00
173 Jose Ramirez .20 .50
174 Felix Hernandez .20 .50
175 Ken Griffey Jr. .50 1.25
176 Yadier Molina .30 .75
177 Matt Carpenter .25 .60
178 Carlos Martinez .20 .50
179 Evan Longoria .20 .50
180 Ian Happ .20 .50
181 Chris Archer .15 .40
182 Adrian Beltre .25 .60
183 Kris Bryant .30 .75
184 Joey Gallo .20 .50
185 Elvis Andrus .20 .50
186 Nomar Mazara .15 .40
187 Nolan Ryan .75 2.00
188 Josh Donaldson .20 .50
189 Manny Machado .25 .60
190 Salvador Perez .20 .50
191 Mookie Betts .50 1.25
192 Bryce Harper .40 1.00
193 Max Scherzer .25 .60
194 Daniel Murphy .20 .50
195 Chipper Jones .25 .60
196 Trea Turner .20 .50
197 Ryan Zimmerman .20 .50
198 Stephen Strasburg .25 .60
199 J.D. Martinez .25 .60
200 Mickey Mantle .75 2.00
201 A.Judge/C.Frazier .60 1.50
202 G.Maddux/T.Glavine .30 .75
203 Andre Dawson .20 .50
Gary Carter
204 A.Pujols/M.Trout 1.25 3.00
205 Eric Hosmer .20 .50
Lorenzo Cain
206 A.Pettitte/R.Clemens .30 .75
207 Gary Carter .20 .50
Dwight Gooden
208 M.Cabrera/N.Castellanos .25 .60
209 Harmon Killebrew .25 .60
Rod Carew
210 Nelson Cruz .30 .75
Yadier Molina
211 J.Altuve/C.Correa .25 .60
212 Manny Machado .25 .60
Byron Buxton
213 DJ LeMahieu .40 1.00
Nolan Arenado
214 O.Smith/R.Sandberg .50 1.25
215 Barry Larkin .20 .50
Gary Sheffield
216 Dave Concepcion .20 .50
Tony Perez
217 Correa/Lindor/Molina .30 .75
218 G.Springer/C.Correa .25 .60
219 G.Brett/W.Boggs .50 1.25
220 C.Kershaw/C.Seager .40 1.00
221 Ted Giannoulas RETRO .15 .40
222 Paul Goldschmidt RETRO .25 .60
223 Freddie Freeman RETRO .30 .75
224 Trey Mancini RETRO .20 .50
225 Anthony Rizzo RETRO .30 .75
226 Mookie Betts RETRO .50 1.25
227 Benintendi RETRO .25 .60
228 Kris Bryant RETRO .30 .75
229 Ian Happ RETRO .20 .50
230 Yoan Moncada RETRO .25 .60
231 Joey Votto RETRO .25 .60
232 Joe Morgan RETRO .20 .50
233 Corey Kluber RETRO .20 .50
234 Lindor RETRO .25 .60
235 Charlie Blackmon RETRO .25 .60
236 Nolan Arenado RETRO .40 1.00
237 Miguel Cabrera RETRO .25 .60
238 Justin Verlander RETRO .25 .60
239 Jose Altuve RETRO .20 .50
240 George Springer RETRO .20 .50
241 George Brett RETRO .50 1.25
242 Mike Trout RETRO 1.25 3.00
243 Cody Bellinger RETRO .50 1.25
244 Kershaw RETRO .40 1.00
245 Corey Seager RETRO .25 .60
246 Marcell Ozuna RETRO .25 .60
247 Ryan Braun RETRO .20 .50
248 Eric Thames RETRO .20 .50
249 Brian Dozier RETRO .20 .50
250 Harmon Killebrew RETRO .25 .60

251 Noah Syndergaard RETRO .20 .50
252 Mike Piazza RETRO .25 .60
253 Aaron Judge RETRO .60 1.50
254 Mickey Mantle RETRO .75 2.00
255 Matt Olson RETRO .25 .60
256 Nolan Ryan RETRO .75 2.00
257 Andrew McCutchen RETRO .25 .60
258 Tony Gwynn RETRO .25 .60
259 Madison Bumgarner RETRO .20 .50
260 Kyle Seager RETRO .15 .40
261 Robinson Cano RETRO .20 .50
262 Adam Wainwright RETRO .20 .50
263 Matt Carpenter RETRO .25 .60
264 Ozzie Smith RETRO .30 .75
265 Evan Longoria RETRO .20 .50
266 Adrian Beltre RETRO .25 .60
267 Cole Hamels RETRO .20 .50
268 Josh Donaldson RETRO .20 .50
269 Max Scherzer RETRO .25 .60
270 Bryce Harper RETRO .40 1.00
271 Christian Villanueva RR RC .40 1.00
272 Shohei Ohtani RR 3.00 8.00
273 Austin Hays RR RC .60 1.50
274 Chance Sisco RR RC .50 1.25
275 Harrison Bader RR RC .60 1.50
276 Francisco Mejia RR RC .50 1.25
277 Erick Fedde RR RC .40 1.00
278 J.D. Davis RR RC .50 1.25
279 Scott Kingery RR RC .60 1.50
280 Juan Soto RR RC 4.00 10.00
281A Ohtani RR RC Eng 10.00 25.00
281B Ohtani RR Jpnse 15.00 40.00
282A G.Torres RR RC 4.00 10.00
282B Torres RR Twttr 6.00 15.00
283A R.Acuna RR RC 12.00 30.00
283B Acuna RR Full name 20.00 50.00

2018 Donruss Blank Backs

*BLANK DK: .75X TO 2X BASIC
*BLANK RR: .75X TO 2X BASIC
*BLANK VET: 2X TO 5X BASIC
*BLANK RET: 2X TO 5X BASIC
RANDOM INSERTS IN PACKS

2018 Donruss Career Stat Line

*CAR DK p/r 284-540: .75X TO 2X BASIC
*CAR RR p/r 317-500: .75X TO 2X BASIC
*CAR p/r 251-500: 2X TO 5X BASIC
*CAR DK p/r 231: 1X TO 2.5X BASIC
*CAR p/r 230-236: 2.5X TO 6X BASIC
*CAR DK p/r 100-201: 1.2X TO 3X BASIC
*CAR RR p/r 133-150: 1.2X TO 3X BASIC
*CAR p/r 114-203: 3X TO 8X BASIC
*CAR p/r 57-89: 4X TO 10X BASIC
RANDOM INSERTS IN PACKS
PRINT RUNS B/WN 17-540 COPIES PER
NO PRICING ON QTY 17

2018 Donruss Father's Day Ribbon

*FATHER DK: 1.2X TO 3X BASIC
*FATHER RR: 1.2X TO 3X BASIC
*FATHER VET: 3X TO 8X BASIC
*FATHER RET: 3X TO 8X BASIC
RANDOM INSERTS IN PACKS
STATED PRINT RUN 49 SER.#'d SETS

2018 Donruss Game Day Stat Line

*GAME DAY p/r 25: 8X TO 20X BASIC
RANDOM INSERTS IN PACKS
PRINT RUNS B/WN 1-25 COPIES PER
NO PRICING ON QTY 19 OR LESS

2018 Donruss Gold Press Proof

*GOLD PP DK: 1.2X TO 3X BASIC
*GOLD PP RR: 1.2X TO 3X BASIC
*GOLD PP VET: 3X TO 8X BASIC
*GOLD PP RET: 3X TO 8X BASIC
RANDOM INSERTS IN PACKS
STATED PRINT RUN 99 SER.#'d SETS

2018 Donruss Holo Blue

*HOLO BLUE: 1.2X TO 3X BASIC
RANDOM INSERTS IN PACKS

2018 Donruss Holo Green

*HOLO GREEN: 1.2X TO 3X BASIC
RANDOM INSERTS IN PACKS

2018 Donruss Mother's Day Ribbon

*MOTHER DK: 1.5X TO 4X BASIC
*MOTHER RR: 1.5X TO 4X BASIC
*MOTHER VET: 4X TO 10X BASIC
*MOTHER RET: 4X TO 10X BASIC
RANDOM INSERTS IN PACKS
STATED PRINT RUN 25 SER.#'d SETS

2018 Donruss Season Stat Line

*SEA DK p/r 265-307: .75X TO 2X BASIC
*SEA RR p/r 250-500: .75X TO 2X BASIC
*SEA p/r 250-500: 2X TO 5X BASIC
*SEA DK p/r 231 : 1X TO 2.5X BASIC
*SEA p/r 226-249: 2.5X TO 6X BASIC
*SEA DK p/r 100-204: 1.2X TO 3X BASIC
*SEA RR p/r 126: 1.2X TO 3X BASIC
*SEA p/r 100-225: 3X TO 8X BASIC
*SEA DK p/r 82-96: 1.5X TO 4X BASIC
*SEA p/r 52-97: 4X TO 10X BASIC
*SEA RR p/r 43-48: 2X TO 5X BASIC
*SEA p/r 36-47: 5X TO 12X BASIC
*SEA DK p/r 28-33: 2.5X TO 6X BASIC
*SEA p/r 26-34: 6X TO 15X BASIC
*SEA DK p/r 23-24: 3X TO 8X BASIC
*SEA RR p/r 23: 3X TO 8X BASIC
*SEA p/r 20-25: 8X TO 20X BASIC
RANDOM INSERTS IN PACKS
PRINT RUNS B/WN 4-500 COPIES PER
NO PRICING ON QTY 14

2018 Donruss Teal Border

*TEAL DK: .75X TO 2X BASIC
*TEAL RR: .75X TO 2X BASIC
*TEAL VET: 2X TO 5X BASIC
*TEAL RET: 2X TO 5X BASIC
RANDOM INSERTS IN PACKS
STATED PRINT RUN 199 SER.#'d SETS

2018 Donruss Variations

RANDOM INSERTS IN PACKS
*BLANK: .75X TO 2X BASIC
*CAR p/r 276-500: .75X TO 2X BASIC
*CAR p/r 231: .1X TO 2.5X BASIC
*CAR p/r 100-211: 1.2X TO 3X BASIC
*SEA p/r 250-312:.75X TO 2X BASIC
*SEA p/r 228-243:.1X TO 2.5X BASIC
*SEA p/r 101-220:1.2X TO 3X BASIC
*SEA p/r 54-95: 1.5X TO 4X BASIC
*SEA p/r 29-33: 2.5X TO 6X BASIC
*SEA p/r 20-24: 3X TO 8X BASIC
*TEAL/199: .75X TO 2X BASIC
*GOLD PP/99: 1.2X TO 3X BASIC
*FATHER/49 : 1.2X TO 3X BASIC
*MOTHER/25: 1.5X TO 4X BASIC
59 Eddie Mathews .60 1.50
64 Cal Ripken 2.00 5.00
65 Jim Palmer .50 1.25
69 Jackie Bradley Jr. .60 1.50
86 Jose Abreu .60 1.50
87 Frank Thomas .60 1.50
92 Joe Morgan .50 1.25
100 Roberto Alomar .50 1.25
104 Charlie Blackmon .60 1.50
108 Reggie Jackson .50 1.25
110 Al Kaline .60 1.50
120 George Brett 1.25 3.00
123 Rod Carew .50 1.25
134 Marcell Ozuna .60 1.50
141 Anthony Rizzo .75 2.00
142 Kirby Puckett .60 1.50
143 Giancarlo Stanton .60 1.50
144 Noah Syndergaard .50 1.25
148A Aaron Judge 1.50 4.00
NY 12th Judicial District
148B Aaron Judge 1.50 4.00
ROY
149A Cody Bellinger 1.25 3.00
Unanimous ROY
149B Cody Bellinger 1.25 3.00
Running
150 Gary Sanchez .60 1.50
153 Corey Kluber .50 1.25
154 Clayton Kershaw 1.00 2.50
155 Mike Trout 3.00 8.00
157 Francisco Lindor .60 1.50
158 Corey Seager .60 1.50
159 Andrew McCutchen .60 1.50
162 Alex Bregman .60 1.50
163 Carlos Correa .60 1.50
165 Tony Gwynn .60 1.50
166 Jose Altuve .50 1.25
167A Buster Posey .75 2.00
Gerald Dempsey Posey
167B Buster Posey .75 2.00
Red Sleeves
169A Andrew Benintendi .60 1.50
Sepia photo
169B Andrew Benintendi .60 1.50
Benny Baseball
172 Nolan Arenado 1.00 2.50
173 Jose Ramirez .50 1.25
175 Ken Griffey Jr. 1.25 3.00
176 Yadier Molina .75 2.00
183A Kris Bryant .75 2.00
Sepia photo
KB
183B Kris Bryant .75 2.00
no sunglasses
187 Nolan Ryan 2.00 5.00
189 Manny Machado .60 1.50
191A Mookie Betts 1.25 3.00
Markus Lynn Betts
191B Mookie Betts 1.25 3.00
Black Sleeves
192 Bryce Harper 1.00 2.50
195 Chipper Jones .60 1.50
200 Mickey Mantle 2.00 5.00
225 Anthony Rizzo RETRO .75 2.00
227 Andrew Benintendi RETRO .60 1.50
228 Kris Bryant RETRO .75 2.00
230 Yoan Moncada RETRO .60 1.50
234 Francisco Lindor RETRO .60 1.50
242 Mike Trout RETRO 3.00 8.00
243 Cody Bellinger RETRO 1.25 3.00
253 Aaron Judge RETRO 1.50 4.00
254 Mickey Mantle RETRO 2.00 5.00
256 Nolan Ryan RETRO 2.00 5.00

2018 Donruss '84 Retro Materials

RANDOM INSERTS IN PACKS
*GOLD/99: .5X TO 1.2X BASIC
R84CS Corey Seager 3.00 8.00
R84MM Manuel Margot 2.00 5.00
R84AB Alex Bregman 3.00 8.00
R84JA Jose Abreu 3.00 8.00
R84LS Luis Severino 2.50 6.00
R84JB Javier Baez 4.00 10.00
R84JG Jacob deGrom 6.00 15.00
R84JR Jose Ramirez 2.50 6.00
R84SM Sean Manaea 2.00 5.00
R84DP Dustin Pedroia 3.00 8.00
R84EH Eric Hosmer 2.50 6.00
R84AB Aaron Blair 2.00 5.00
R84KW Kolten Wong 2.50 6.00
R84MM Manny Machado 3.00 8.00
R84JG Jonathan Gray 2.00 5.00
R84AB Andrew Benintendi 4.00 10.00
R84VR Victor Robles 4.00 10.00
R84JG Juan Gonzalez 2.00 5.00
R84AJ Aaron Judge 8.00 20.00
R84KK Kevin Kiermaier 2.50 6.00
R84AR Alex Reyes 2.50 6.00
R84AB Archie Bradley 2.00 5.00
R84AR Addison Russell 2.50 6.00
R84MS Miguel Sano 2.50 6.00
R84KS Kyle Schwarber 3.00 8.00

2018 Donruss '84 Retro Signatures

RANDOM INSERTS IN PACKS
1 Bob Gibson 12.00 30.00
2 Ozzie Smith 15.00 40.00
3 Rickey Henderson 20.00 50.00
4 Darrell Evans 10.00 25.00
5 Keith Hernandez 15.00 40.00
6 Robin Yount 20.00 50.00
7 Jose Ramirez 3.00 8.00
8 Luis Severino 20.00 50.00
9 Alex Bregman 15.00 40.00
10 Carlos Correa 20.00 50.00
11 Kyle Seager 4.00 10.00
12 Marcell Ozuna 4.00 10.00
13 Paul Goldschmidt 12.00 30.00
14 David Wright 10.00 25.00
15 Yadier Molina 30.00 80.00
16 Carlton Fisk 10.00 25.00
17 Aaron Judge 75.00 200.00
18 Cody Bellinger 50.00 120.00
19 Greg Bird 3.00 8.00
20 John Franco 4.00 10.00
21 Salvador Perez 10.00 25.00
22 Joe Carter 10.00 25.00
23 Steve Carlton
24 Nomar Mazara

2018 Donruss '84 Retro Signatures Blue

*BLUE/35-99: .5X TO 1.2X BASIC
*BLUE/25: .6X TO 1.5X BASIC
RANDOM INSERTS IN PACKS
PRINT RUNS B/WN 25-99 COPIES PER
25 Al Kaline/25 25.00 50.00

2018 Donruss '84 Retro Signatures Red

*RED/20-25: .6X TO 1.5X BASIC
RANDOM INSERTS IN PACKS
PRINT RUNS B/WN 20-25 COPIES PER
25 Al Kaline/20 25.00 50.00

2018 Donruss All Stars

RANDOM INSERTS IN PACKS
STATED PRINT RUN 999 SER.#'d SETS
*CRYSTAL: .5X TO 1.2X BASIC
*SILVER/349: .5X TO 1.2X BASIC
*BLUE/249: .6X TO 1.5X BASIC
*RED/149: .6X TO 1.5X BASIC
*GOLD/99: 1X TO 2.5X BASIC
*GREEN/25: 1.5X TO 4X BASIC
1 Aaron Judge 1.50 4.00
2 Carlos Correa .60 1.50
3 Mookie Betts 1.25 3.00
4 Francisco Lindor .60 1.50
5 Corey Kluber .50 1.25
6 Chris Sale .60 1.50
7 Nolan Arenado 1.00 2.50
8 Charlie Blackmon .60 1.50
9 Corey Seager .60 1.50
10 Max Scherzer .60 1.50
11 Clayton Kershaw 1.00 2.50
12 Mike Trout 3.00 8.00

2018 Donruss American Pride

RANDOM INSERTS IN PACKS
STATED PRINT RUN 999 SER.#'d SETS
*CRYSTAL: .5X TO 1.2X BASIC
*SILVER/349: .5X TO 1.2X BASIC
*BLUE/249: .6X TO 1.5X BASIC
*RED/149: .6X TO 1.5X BASIC
*GOLD/99: 1X TO 2.5X BASIC
*GREEN/25: 1.5X TO 4X BASIC
AP1 Seth Beer 1.50 4.00
AP2 Steven Gingery .50 1.25
AP3 Nick Madrigal 1.50 4.00
AP4 Jake McCarthy .60 1.50
AP5 Nick Meyer .50 1.25
AP6 Casey Mize 3.00 8.00
AP7 Konnor Pilkington .50 1.25
AP8 Dallas Woolfolk .40 1.00
AP9 Tyler Frank .40 1.00
AP10 Cadyn Grenier .50 1.25
AP11 Gianluca Dalatri .40 1.00
AP12 Braden Shewmake 1.25 3.00
AP13 Bryce Tucker .40 1.00
AP14 Andrew Vaughn 1.25 3.00
AP15 Steele Walker .50 1.25
AP16 Jeremy Eierman .40 1.00
AP17 Patrick Raby .50 1.25
AP18 Grant Koch .40 1.00
AP19 Travis Swaggerty 1.25 3.00
AP20 Tim Cate .60 1.50
AP21 Nick Sprengel .40 1.00
AP22 Johnny Aiello .40 1.00
AP23 Ryley Gilliam .50 1.25
AP24 Jon Olsen .40 1.00
AP25 Tyler Holton .50 1.25
AP26 Sean Wymer .40 1.00

2018 Donruss Diamond Collection Memorabilia

*GOLD/99: .5X TO 1.2X BASIC
DCCP Chad Pinder 2.00 5.00
DCJE Jerad Eickhoff 2.00 5.00
DCOA Orlando Arcia 2.00 5.00
DCBP Brett Phillips 2.00 5.00
DCJL Jose De Leon 2.00 5.00
DCRT Raimel Tapia 2.00 5.00
DCJG Jonathan Gray 2.00 5.00
DCTG Tyler Glasnow 3.00 8.00
DCAS Antonio Senzatela 2.00 5.00
DCJB Josh Bell 2.50 6.00
DCDM Deven Marrero 2.00 5.00
DCJJ Jacoby Jones 2.50 6.00
DCCS Corey Seager 3.00 8.00
DCJC Jharel Cotton 2.00 5.00
DCJH Jeff Hoffman 2.00 5.00
DCJP Jose Peraza 2.50 6.00
DCBS Braden Shipley 2.00 5.00
DCJC Jeimer Candelario 2.50 6.00
DCDS Dansby Swanson 3.00 8.00
DCAG Amir Garrett 2.00 5.00
DCCF Carson Fulmer 2.00 5.00
DCTT Tim Tebow 5.00 12.00
DCJT Jake Thompson 2.00 5.00
DCDL Dinelson Lamet 2.00 5.00
DCTH Teoscar Hernandez 3.00 8.00
DCCR Colin Rea 2.00 5.00
DCHR Hunter Renfroe 2.00 5.00
DCGM German Marquez 2.00 5.00
DCPB Peter O'Brien 2.00 5.00
DCJM Joe Musgrove 3.00 8.00
DCDD David Dahl 2.00 5.00
DCLW Luke Weaver 2.50 6.00
DCMK Max Kepler 2.50 6.00
DCRD Rafael Devers 4.00 10.00
DCGB Greg Bird 2.50 6.00
DCKM Ketel Marte 2.50 6.00
DCRL Reynaldo Lopez 2.50 6.00
DCCJ Carl Edwards Jr. 2.00 5.00

2018 Donruss Dominators

RANDOM INSERTS IN PACKS
STATED PRINT RUN 999 SER.#'d SETS
*CRYSTAL: .5X TO 1.2X BASIC
*SILVER/349: .5X TO 1.2X BASIC
*BLUE/249: .6X TO 1.5X BASIC
*RED/149: .6X TO 1.5X BASIC
*GOLD/99: 1X TO 2.5X BASIC
*GREEN/25: 1.5X TO 4X BASIC
1 Mookie Betts 1.25 3.00
2 Jose Altuve .50 1.25
3 Joey Votto .60 1.50
4 Max Scherzer .60 1.50
5 Justin Verlander .60 1.50
6 Corey Kluber .50 1.25
7 Nolan Arenado 1.00 2.50
8 Corey Seager .60 1.50
9 Shohei Ohtani 10.00 25.00
10 Mickey Mantle 2.00 5.00

2018 Donruss Elite Series

RANDOM INSERTS IN PACKS
STATED PRINT RUN 999 SER.#'d SETS
*CRYSTAL: .5X TO 1.2X BASIC
*SILVER/349: .5X TO 1.2X BASIC
*BLUE/249: .6X TO 1.5X BASIC
*RED/149: .6X TO 1.5X BASIC
*GOLD/99: 1X TO 2.5X BASIC
*GREEN/25: 1.5X TO 4X BASIC
ES1 Kris Bryant .75 2.00
ES2 Clayton Kershaw 1.00 2.50
ES3 Bryce Harper 1.00 2.50
ES4 Manny Machado .60 1.50
ES5 Carlos Correa .60 1.50
ES6 Trea Turner .50 1.25
ES7 Buster Posey .75 2.00
ES8 Mike Trout 3.00 8.00
ES9 Jose Ramirez .50 1.25
ES10 Paul Goldschmidt .60 1.50

2018 Donruss Foundations

RANDOM INSERTS IN PACKS
STATED PRINT RUN 999 SER.#'d SETS
*CRYSTAL: .5X TO 1.2X BASIC
*SILVER/349: .5X TO 1.2X BASIC
*BLUE/249: .6X TO 1.5X BASIC
*RED/149: .6X TO 1.5X BASIC
*GOLD/99: 1X TO 2.5X BASIC
*GREEN/25: 1.5X TO 4X BASIC
F1 Cody Bellinger 1.25 3.00
F2 Aaron Judge 1.50 4.00
F3 Manny Machado .60 1.50
F4 Mike Trout 3.00 8.00
F5 Mookie Betts 1.25 3.00
F6 Bryce Harper 1.00 2.50
F7 Shohei Ohtani 10.00 25.00
F8 Jose Ramirez .50 1.25
F9 Jose Altuve .50 1.25

2018 Donruss Long Ball Leaders

RANDOM INSERTS IN PACKS
STATED PRINT RUN 999 SER.#'d SETS
*CRYSTAL: .5X TO 1.2X BASIC
*SILVER/349: .5X TO 1.2X BASIC
*BLUE/249: .6X TO 1.5X BASIC
*RED/149: .6X TO 1.5X BASIC
*GOLD/99: 1X TO 2.5X BASIC
*GREEN/25: 1.5X TO 4X BASIC
LBL1 Giancarlo Stanton .60 1.50
LBL2 Aaron Judge 1.50 4.00
LBL3 J.D. Martinez .60 1.50
LBL4 Khris Davis .60 1.50
LBL5 Joey Gallo .50 1.25
LBL6 Cody Bellinger 1.25 3.00
LBL7 Nelson Cruz .60 1.50
LBL8 Logan Morrison .40 1.00
LBL9 Nolan Arenado 1.00 2.50
LBL10 Justin Smoak .40 1.00

2018 Donruss Mound Marvels

RANDOM INSERTS IN PACKS
STATED PRINT RUN 999 SER.#'d SETS
*CRYSTAL: .5X TO 1.2X BASIC
*SILVER/349: .5X TO 1.2X BASIC
*BLUE/249: .6X TO 1.5X BASIC
*RED/149: .6X TO 1.5X BASIC
*GOLD/99: 1X TO 2.5X BASIC
*GREEN/25: 1.5X TO 4X BASIC
1 Clayton Kershaw 1.00 2.50
2 Max Scherzer .60 1.50
3 Shohei Ohtani 10.00 25.00
4 Corey Kluber .50 1.25
5 Chris Sale .60 1.50
6 Justin Verlander .60 1.50

2018 Donruss Out of this World

RANDOM INSERTS IN PACKS
STATED PRINT RUN 999 SER.#'d SETS
*CRYSTAL: .5X TO 1.2X BASIC
*SILVER/349: .5X TO 1.2X BASIC
*BLUE/249: .6X TO 1.5X BASIC
*RED/149: .6X TO 1.5X BASIC
*GOLD/99: 1X TO 2.5X BASIC
*GREEN/25: 1.5X TO 4X BASIC
OW1 Aaron Judge 1.50 4.00
OW2 Jose Altuve .50 1.25
OW3 Mike Trout 3.00 8.00
OW4 Joey Gallo .50 1.25
OW5 Shohei Ohtani 10.00 25.00
OW6 Giancarlo Stanton .60 1.50
OW7 Mickey Mantle 2.00 5.00
OW8 J.D. Martinez .60 1.50
OW9 Cody Bellinger 1.25 3.00
OW10 Nolan Arenado 1.00 2.50
OW11 Marcell Ozuna .60 1.50
OW12 Paul Goldschmidt .60 1.50

2018 Donruss Passing the Torch Signatures

RANDOM INSERTS IN PACKS
*BLUE/49: .5X TO 1.2X BASIC
*BLUE/25: .6X TO 1.5X BASIC
*RED/25: .6X TO 1.5X BASIC
1 deGrom/Glavine 50.00 120.00
2 Gonzalez/Bellinger
3 Jackson/Judge 50.00 120.00
4 Brock/Henderson 25.00 60.00
5 Garciaparra/Bogaerts 20.00 50.00
6 Baez/Sandberg 25.00 60.00
7 Griffey Sr/Griffey Jr
9 Sanchez/Posada 40.00 100.00
10 Gonzalez/Mazara 12.00 30.00

2018 Donruss Private Signings

RANDOM INSERTS IN PACKS
STATED PRINT RUN 50 SER.#'d SETS
PSS01 Shohei Ohtani 300.00 600.00
Issued in '18 Donruss
PSS02 Shohei Ohtani 300.00 600.00
Issued in '18 Diamond Kings
PSS03 Shohei Ohtani 300.00 600.00
Issued in '18 Donruss
PSS04 Shohei Ohtani 300.00 600.00
Issued in '18 Diamond Kings

2018 Donruss Promising Pros Materials

RANDOM INSERTS IN PACKS
*GOLD/99: .5X TO 1.2X BASIC
*BLACK/25: .6X TO 1.5X BASIC
PPMJR Jose Rondon 2.00 5.00
PPMMW Mac Williamson 2.00 5.00
PPMDP David Paulino 2.00 5.00
PPMJL Jorge Lopez 2.00 5.00
PPMTT Trayce Thompson 2.50 6.00
PPMTD Tyler Duffey 2.00 5.00
PPMGY Gabriel Ynoa 2.00 5.00
PPMKT Kelby Tomlinson 2.00 5.00
PPMSO Shohei Ohtani 10.00 25.00
PPMCW Christian Walker 2.50 6.00
PPMFM Frankie Montas 2.00 5.00
PPMAF Adam Frazier 2.00 5.00
PPMDA Dariel Alvarez 2.00 5.00
PPMAD Alex Dickerson 2.00 5.00
PPMJL John Lamb 2.00 5.00
PPMPS Pedro Severino 2.00 5.00
PPMED Elias Diaz 2.00 5.00
PPMFM Francis Martes 2.00 5.00
PPMKW Kyle Waldrop 2.00 5.00
PPMBE Brian Ellington 2.00 5.00
PPMBJ Brian Johnson 2.00 5.00
PPMDR Daniel Robertson 2.00 5.00
PPMLJ Luke Jackson 2.00 5.00
PPMEG Erik Gonzalez 2.00 5.00
PPMAM Adalberto Mejia 2.00 5.00

2018 Donruss Promising Pros Materials Signatures

RANDOM INSERTS IN PACKS
*GOLD/25: .75X TO 2X BASIC
PPMSAF Adam Frazier 3.00 8.00
PPMSBJ Brian Johnson 3.00 8.00
PPMSDR Daniel Robertson 3.00 8.00
PPMSJM Joe Musgrove 5.00 12.00
PPMSMM Manuel Margot 3.00 8.00
PPMSSO Shohei Ohtani 200.00 400.00
PPMSBS Braden Shipley 3.00 8.00
PPMSPS Pedro Severino 3.00 8.00
PPMSTT Trayce Thompson 4.00 10.00
PPMSTD Tyler Duffey 3.00 8.00

2018 Donruss Rated Prospects Signatures

RANDOM INSERTS IN PACKS
STATED PRINT RUN 50 SER.#'d SETS
1 Shohei Ohtani 300.00 600.00
2 Shohei Ohtani 300.00 600.00

2018 Donruss Recollection Buyback Autographs

RANDOM INSERTS IN PACKS
PRINT RUNS B/WN 1-50 COPIES PER
NO PRICING ON QTY 18 OR LESS
TBA3 Adam Duvall/25 5.00 12.00
TBA11 Matt Carpenter/50 5.00 12.00
TBA12 Matt Carpenter/50 5.00 12.00
TBA21 Odubel Herrera/25 5.00 12.00
TBA22 Wil Myers/23 5.00 12.00
TBA23 Wil Myers/25 5.00 12.00

2018 Donruss Signature Series

RANDOM INSERTS IN PACKS
*BLUE/99: .5X TO 1.2X BASIC
*RED/25: .6X TO 1.5X BASIC
1 Anthony Banda 2.50 6.00
SSMF Max Fried 10.00 25.00
SSOA Ozzie Albies 10.00 25.00
5 Lucas Sims 2.50 6.00
6 Austin Hays 4.00 10.00
SSCS Chance Sisco 3.00 8.00
8 Anthony Santander 4.00 10.00
SSRD Rafael Devers 12.00 30.00
10 Victor Caratini 3.00 8.00
11 Nicky Delmonico 2.50 6.00
12 Tyler Mahle 3.00 8.00
13 Francisco Mejia 6.00 15.00
14 Greg Allen 2.50 6.00
15 Ryan McMahon 6.00 15.00
16 J.D. Davis 3.00 8.00
17 Cameron Gallagher 2.50 6.00
SSWB Walker Buehler 15.00 40.00
SSAV Alex Verdugo 6.00 15.00
20 Kyle Farmer 4.00 10.00
21 Brian Anderson 3.00 8.00
22 Dillon Peters 2.50 6.00
23 Brandon Woodruff 8.00 20.00
24 Mitch Garver 2.50 6.00
25 Zack Granite 4.00 10.00
26 Felix Jorge 2.50 6.00
27 Tomas Nido 4.00 10.00
28 Dominic Smith 3.00 8.00
29 Chris Flexen 2.50 6.00
SSAR Amed Rosario 6.00 15.00
SSCL Clint Frazier 5.00 12.00
SSMA Miguel Andujar 8.00 20.00
33 Tyler Wade 3.00 8.00
34 Dustin Fowler 2.50 6.00
35 Paul Blackburn 2.50 6.00
36 J.P. Crawford 2.50 6.00
37 Nick Williams 3.00 8.00
38 Rhys Hoskins 10.00 25.00
39 Thyago Vieira 2.50 6.00
40 Reyes Moronta 2.50 6.00
41 Jack Flaherty 10.00 25.00
42 Harrison Bader 4.00 10.00
43 Willie Calhoun 4.00 10.00
44 Richard Urena 2.50 6.00
45 Victor Robles 5.00 12.00
46 Erick Fedde 2.50 6.00
47 Andrew Stevenson 2.50 6.00
48 Jimmie Sherfy 2.50 6.00
49 Shohei Ohtani 150.00 300.00
50 Jose Abreu 5.00 12.00

2018 Donruss Significant Signatures

RANDOM INSERTS IN PACKS
*BLUE/49-99: .5X TO 1.2X BASIC
*BLUE/25: .6X TO 1.5X BASIC
*RED/25: .6X TO 1.5X BASIC
1 Wade Boggs 8.00 20.00
2 Ivan Rodriguez 8.00 20.00
3 Willie McGee 8.00 20.00
4 Fergie Jenkins 6.00 15.00
5 Tony La Russa 3.00 8.00
6 Jerry Koosman 6.00 15.00
7 Frank Thomas 25.00 60.00
8 Alan Trammell 10.00 25.00
9 Paul Molitor 8.00 20.00
10 Jeff Bagwell 10.00 25.00
11 George Brett 100.00 250.00
12 Cal Ripken
13 Gary Sheffield 4.00 10.00
14 Pete Rose 12.00 30.00
15 Dwight Gooden 10.00 25.00

2018 Donruss Signing Day Signatures

RANDOM INSERTS IN PACKS
STATED PRINT RUN 50 SER.#'d SETS
1 Shohei Ohtani 300.00 600.00

2018 Donruss The Famous San Diego Chicken Dual Material

RANDOM INSERTS IN PACKS
STATED PRINT RUN 84 SER.#'d SETS
1 Ted Giannoulas 20.00 50.00

2018 Donruss The Famous San Diego Chicken Dual Material Signatures

RANDOM INSERTS IN PACKS
STATED PRINT RUN 84 SER.#'d SETS
1 Ted Giannoulas 50.00 120.00

2018 Donruss Whammy

RANDOM INSERTS IN PACKS
1 Mickey Mantle 20.00 50.00
2 Shohei Ohtani 60.00 150.00
3 Rhys Hoskins 12.00 30.00
4 Aaron Judge 25.00 60.00
5 Cody Bellinger 8.00 20.00

2019 Donruss

1 Mookie Betts DK 1.25 3.00
2 Aaron Judge DK 1.50 4.00
3 Blake Snell DK .50 1.25
4 Justin Smoak DK .40 1.00
5 Adam Jones DK .50 1.25
6 Jose Ramirez DK .50 1.25
7 Jose Berrios DK .50 1.25
8 Nicholas Castellanos DK .60 1.50
9 Yoan Moncada DK .60 1.50
10 Whit Merrifield DK .60 1.50
11 Alex Bregman DK .60 1.50
12 Matt Chapman DK .60 1.50
13 Mitch Haniger DK .50 1.25
14 Shohei Ohtani DK 1.00 2.50
15 Jurickson Profar DK .50 1.25
16 Ronald Acuna Jr. DK 3.00 8.00
17 Max Scherzer DK .60 1.50
18 Aaron Nola DK .50 1.25
19 Jacob deGrom DK 1.25 3.00
20 J.T. Realmuto DK .60 1.50
21 Christian Yelich DK .75 2.00
22 Javier Baez DK .75 2.00
23 Matt Carpenter DK .60 1.50
24 Starling Marte DK .50 1.25
25 Eugenio Suarez DK .50 1.25
26 Max Muncy DK .50 1.25
27 Trevor Story DK .60 1.50
28 Paul Goldschmidt DK .60 1.50
29 Brandon Crawford DK .50 1.25
30 Hunter Renfroe DK .40 1.00
31 Cedric Mullins RR RC .75 2.00
32 Christin Stewart RR RC .50 1.25
33 Corbin Burnes RR RC 3.00 8.00
34 Dakota Hudson RR RC .50 1.25
35 Danny Jansen RR RC .40 1.00
36 David Fletcher RR RC 1.25 3.00
37 Dennis Santana RR RC .40 1.00
38 Garrett Hampson RR RC .60 1.50
39 Jake Bauers RR RC .60 1.50
40 Jeff McNeil RR RC 1.00 2.50
41 Jonathan Loaisiga RR RC .50 1.25
42 Justus Sheffield RR RC .60 1.50
43 Kyle Tucker RR RC 1.00 2.50
44 Kyle Wright RR RC .60 1.50
45 Luis Urias RR RC .60 1.50
46 Michael Kopech RR RC 1.25 3.00
47 Ramon Laureano RR RC .75 2.00
48 Ryan O'Hearn RR RC .40 1.00
49 Steven Duggar RR RC .50 1.25
50 Touki Toussaint RR RC .50 1.25
51 Chris Sale .25 .60
52 Stephen Strasburg .25 .60
53 Cody Bellinger .50 1.25
54 David Peralta .15 .40
55 Jose Ramirez .20 .50
56 Brandon Nimmo .20 .50
57 Kris Bryant .30 .75
58 Nicholas Castellanos .25 .60
59 Ryan Yarbrough .15 .40
60 Whit Merrifield .25 .60
61 Juan Soto .75 2.00
62 J.D. Martinez .25 .60
63 Michael Brantley .20 .50
64 José Abreu .25 .60
65 George Springer .20 .50
66 Sean Manaea .15 .40
67 Brandon Belt .20 .50
68 Francisco Lindor .25 .60
69 Jaime Barria .15 .40
70 Jose Altuve .20 .50
71 Adam Jones .20 .50
72 Chris Archer .15 .40
73 Wade Davis .15 .40
74 Andrelton Simmons .15 .40
75 A.J. Pollock .15 .40
76 Andrew Benintendi .25 .60
77 Blake Treinen .15 .40
78 Carlos Correa .25 .60
79 Odubel Herrera .20 .50
80 Adrian Beltre .25 .60
81 Yadier Molina .30 .75
82 Austin Meadows .25 .60
83 Joey Wendle .20 .50
84 Felix Hernandez .20 .50
85 Edwin Diaz .20 .50
86 Corey Kluber .20 .50
87 Ronald Acuna Jr. 1.25 3.00
88 Clayton Kershaw .40 1.00
89 Albert Pujols .30 .75
90 Miles Mikolas .25 .60
91 Josh Donaldson .20 .50
92 David Wright .20 .50
93 Francisco Mejia .20 .50
94 Jeremy Jeffress .15 .40
95 Justin Turner .25 .60
96 Mallex Smith .15 .40
97 Justin Smoak .15 .40
98 Kyle Schwarber .25 .60
99 Matt Olson .25 .60
100 Miguel Cabrera .25 .60
101 Mookie Betts .50 1.25
102 Trevor Williams .15 .40
103 Eddie Rosario .20 .50
104 Rhys Hoskins .30 .75
105 J.T. Realmuto .25 .60
106 Adalberto Mondesi .20 .50
107 Shane Bieber .25 .60
108 Jon Lester .20 .50
109 Nick Williams .15 .40
110 Luis Severino .20 .50
111 Franmil Reyes .15 .40
112 Joey Gallo .20 .50
113 Yoan Moncada .25 .60
114 Jose Urena .15 .40
115 Hunter Renfroe .15 .40
116 Max Scherzer .25 .60
117 Sean Newcomb .15 .40
118 Mike Minor .15 .40
119 Starling Marte .20 .50
120 Manny Machado .25 .60
121 Aaron Judge .60 1.50
122 Robinson Cano .20 .50
123 Jacob deGrom .50 1.25
124 Eugenio Suarez .20 .50
125 Nomar Mazara .15 .40
126 Kyle Freeland .20 .50
127 Miguel Sano .20 .50
128 Rafael Devers .30 .75
129 Miguel Andujar .25 .60
130 Nelson Cruz .25 .60
131 Charlie Blackmon .25 .60
132 Jose Berrios .20 .50
133 Walker Buehler .30 .75
134 Tyler O'Neill .20 .50
135 Mike Foltynewicz .25 .60
136 Noah Syndergaard .20 .50
137 Scooter Gennett .20 .50
138 David Bote .20 .50
139 Zack Greinke .25 .60
140 Kevin Pillar .15 .40
141 Trea Turner .20 .50
142 Carlos Rodon .25 .60
143 Willy Adames .15 .40
144 Jose Martinez .15 .40
145 Aaron Nola .20 .50
146 Mitch Haniger .20 .50
147 Freddy Peralta .25 .60
148 Joey Votto .25 .60
149 Ji-Man Choi .15 .40
150 Willie Calhoun .15 .40
151 Carlos Carrasco .15 .40
152 Paul Goldschmidt .25 .60
153 Trey Mancini .20 .50
154 Madison Bumgarner .20 .50
155 Amed Rosario .20 .50
156 Ozzie Albies .25 .60
157 Gleyber Torres .50 1.25
158 Wilson Ramos .15 .40
159 Brandon Crawford .20 .50
160 Andrew Heaney .15 .40
161 James Paxton .20 .50
162 Gerrit Cole .25 .60
163 Giancarlo Stanton .25 .60
164 Shohei Ohtani .40 1.00
165 Javier Baez .30 .75
166 Jesus Aguilar .20 .50
167 Jackie Bradley Jr. .25 .60
168 Hunter Pence .20 .50
169 Khris Davis .25 .60
170 Mike Trout 1.25 3.00
171 Matt Carpenter .25 .60
172 Justin Verlander .25 .60
173 Brian Anderson .15 .40
174 Victor Robles .30 .75
175 Freddie Freeman .30 .75
176 Jack Flaherty .25 .60
177 Nick Markakis .20 .50
178 Dereck Rodriguez .15 .40
179 Salvador Perez .20 .50
180 Anthony Rendon .25 .60
181 Blake Snell .20 .50
182 Alex Bregman .25 .60
183 Bryce Harper .40 1.00
184 Lorenzo Cain .15 .40
185 Trevor Story .25 .60
186 Mike Moustakas .20 .50
187 Anthony Rizzo .30 .75
188 Jameson Taillon .20 .50
189 Edwin Encarnacion .25 .60
190 Christian Yelich .30 .75
191 Michael Conforto .20 .50
192 Matt Chapman .25 .60
193 Teoscar Hernandez .25 .60
194 Eric Hosmer .20 .50
195 German Marquez .15 .40
196 Jeimer Candelario .15 .40
197 Xander Bogaerts .25 .60

198 Sandy Alcantara .15 .40
199 Harrison Bader .20 .50
200 Nolan Arenado .40 1.00
201 Trevor Richards RETRO RC .40 1.00
202 Hoby Milner RETRO RC .40 1.00
203 Pablo Lopez RETRO RC .40 1.00
204 Trevor Oaks RETRO .15 .40
205 Grayson Greiner RETRO .15 .40
206 Johan Camargo RETRO .15 .40
207 Fernando Romero RETRO .15 .40
208 Heath Fillmyer RETRO RC .40 1.00
209 Tanner Rainey RETRO RC .40 1.00
210 Albert Almora Jr. RETRO RC .50 1.25
211 Max Muncy RETRO .20 .50
212 Arodys Vizcaino RETRO .15 .40
213 Daniel Palka RETRO .15 .40
214 Patrick Corbin RETRO .20 .50
215 Justin Williams RETRO RC .40 1.00
216 Taylor Ward RETRO RC .40 1.00
217 Kevin Newman RETRO RC .60 1.50
218 Stephen Gonsalves RETRO RC .40 1.00
219 Sean Reid-Foley RETRO RC .40 1.00
220 Kevin Kramer RETRO RC .50 1.25
221 Jonathan Davis RETRO RC .50 1.25
222 Daniel Ponce de Leon RETRO RC .60 1.50
223 Josh James RETRO RC .60 1.50
224 Jacob Nix RETRO RC .50 1.25
225 Patrick Wisdom RETRO RC .40 1.00
226 Brad Keller RETRO RC .40 1.00
227 Ryan Borucki RETRO RC .40 1.00
228 Luis Ortiz RETRO RC .40 1.00
229 Jake Cave RETRO RC .50 1.25
230 Kolby Allard RETRO RC .60 1.50
231 Framber Valdez RETRO RC .40 1.00
232 Brandon Lowe RETRO RC .60 1.50
233 Cionel Perez RETRO RC .40 1.00
234 Myles Straw RETRO RC .60 1.50
235 Reese McGuire RETRO RC .60 1.50
236 Enyel De Los Santos RETRO RC .40 1.00
237 Chris Shaw RETRO .40 1.00
238 Bryse Wilson RETRO RC .50 1.25
239 Rowdy Tellez RETRO RC .60 1.50
240 Chance Adams RETRO RC .40 1.00
241 Willians Astudillo RETRO RC .40 1.00
242 Kyle Gibson RETRO .20 .50
243 Matt Boyd RETRO .15 .40
244 Luke Voit RETRO .40 1.00
245 Caleb Ferguson RETRO RC .50 1.25
246 Eric Haase RETRO RC .40 1.00
247 Brett Kennedy RETRO RC .40 1.00
248 Ryan Meisinger RETRO RC .40 1.00
249 Nick Martini RETRO RC .40 1.00
250 Julio Urias RETRO .25 .60
251 Domingo Ayala FOIL 15.00 40.00
252 Yusei Kikuchi RR RC .60 1.50
253 Chris Paddack RR RC .75 2.00
254 Fernando Tatis Jr. RR RC 6.00 15.00
255 Pete Alonso RR RC 3.00 8.00
256 Vladimir Guerrero Jr. RR RC 2.50 6.00
257 Eloy Jimenez RR RC 1.50 4.00
258 Jon Duplantier RR RC .40 1.00
259 Carter Kieboom RR RC .60 1.50
260 Nick Senzel RR RC 1.25 3.00
261 Michael Chavis RR RC .60 1.50
262 Nathaniel Lowe RR RC 2.00 5.00

2019 Donruss 150th Anniversary
*150TH DK: 1X TO 2.5X BASIC
*150TH RR: 1X TO 2.5X BASIC
*150TH VET: 2.5X TO 6X BASIC
*150TH RET: 2.5X TO 6X BASIC
RANDOM INSERTS IN PACKS
STATED PRINT RUN 150 SER.#'d SETS

2019 Donruss 42 Tribute
*42 DK: 1.2X TO 3X BASIC
*42 RR: 1.2X TO 3X BASIC
*42 VET: 3X TO 8X BASIC
*42 RET: 3X TO 8X BASIC
RANDOM INSERTS IN PACKS
STATED PRINT RUN 42 SER.#'d SETS

2019 Donruss Career Stat Line
*CAR DK p/r 154-500: .75X TO 2X BASIC
*CAR RR p/r 154-500: .75X TO 2X BASIC
*CAR p/r 154-500: 2X TO 5X BASIC
*CAR DK p/r 100-146: 1X TO 2.5X BASIC
*CAR RR p/r 100-146: 1X TO 2.5X BASIC
*CAR p/r 100-146: 2.5X TO 6X BASIC
*CAR DK p/r 26-96: 1.2X TO 3X BASIC
*CAR RR p/r 26-96: 1.2X TO 3X BASIC
*CAR p/r 26-96: 3X TO 8X BASIC
*CAR DK p/r 20-25: 2X TO 5X BASIC
*CAR RR p/r 20-25: 2X TO 5X BASIC
*CAR p/r 20-25: 5X TO 12X BASIC
RANDOM INSERTS IN PACKS
PRINT RUNS B/WN 10-500 COPIES PER
NO PRICING ON QTY 19 OR LESS

2019 Donruss Father's Day Ribbon
*FD DK: 1.2X TO 3X BASIC
*FD RR: 1.2X TO 3X BASIC
*FD VET: 3X TO 8X BASIC
*FD RET: 3X TO 8X BASIC
RANDOM INSERTS IN PACKS
STATED PRINT RUN 49 SER.#'d SETS

2019 Donruss Holo Back
*HOLO BK DK: 1.2X TO 3X BASIC
*HOLO BK RR: 1.2X TO 3X BASIC
*HOLO BK VET: 3X TO 8X BASIC
*HOLO BK RET: 3X TO 8X BASIC
RANDOM INSERTS IN PACKS
STATED PRINT RUN 99 SER.#'d SETS

2019 Donruss Holo Orange
*HOLO ORNG RR: .5X TO 1.2X BASIC
*HOLO ORNG VET: 1.2X TO 3X BASIC
*HOLO ORNG RET: 1.2X TO 3X BASIC
RANDOM INSERTS IN PACKS

2019 Donruss Holo Pink
*HOLO PINK RR: .5X TO 1.2X BASIC
*HOLO PINK VET: 1.2X TO 3X BASIC
*HOLO PINK RET: 1.2X TO 3X BASIC
RANDOM INSERTS IN PACKS

2019 Donruss Holo Purple
*HOLO PRPL RR: .5X TO 1.2X BASIC
*HOLO PRPL VET: 1.2X TO 3X BASIC
*HOLO PRPL RET: 1.2X TO 3X BASIC
RANDOM INSERTS IN PACKS

2019 Donruss Holo Red
*HOLO RED RR: .5X TO 1.2X BASIC
*HOLO RED VET: 1.2X TO 3X BASIC
*HOLO RED RET: 1.2X TO 3X BASIC
RANDOM INSERTS IN PACKS

2019 Donruss Independence Day
*IND DAY RR: .5X TO 1.2X BASIC
*IND DAY DK: .5X TO 1.2X BASIC
*IND DAY VET: 1.2X TO 3X BASIC
*IND DAY RET: 1.2X TO 3X BASIC
RANDOM INSERTS IN PACKS

2019 Donruss Mother's Day Ribbon
*MD DK: 2X TO 5X BASIC
*MD RR: 2X TO 5X BASIC
*MD VET: 5X TO 12X BASIC
*MD RET: 5X TO 12X BASIC
RANDOM INSERTS IN PACKS
STATED PRINT RUN 25 SER.#'d SETS

2019 Donruss Season Stat Line
*SEA DK p/r 154-500: .75X TO 2X BASIC
*SEA RR p/r 154-500: .75X TO 2X BASIC
*SEA p/r 154-500: 2X TO 5X BASIC
*SEA DK p/r 100-149: 1X TO 2.5X BASIC
*SEA RR p/r 100-149: 1X TO 2.5X BASIC
*SEA p/r 100-149: 2.5X TO 6X BASIC
*SEA DK p/r 26-99: 1.2X TO 3X BASIC
*SEA RR p/r 26-99: 1.2X TO 3X BASIC
*SEA p/r 26-99: 3X TO 8X BASIC
*SEA DK p/r 20-25: 2X TO 5X BASIC
*SEA RR p/r 20-25: 2X TO 5X BASIC
*SEA p/r 20-25: 5X TO 12X BASIC
RANDOM INSERTS IN PACKS
PRINT RUNS B/WN 4-500 COPIES PER
NO PRICING ON QTY 19 OR LESS

2019 Donruss Variations
RANDOM INSERTS IN PACKS
*ID VAR: .5X TO 1.2X BASIC
*CAR p/r 156-500: .75X TO 2X BASIC
*CAR p/r 107-144: 1X TO 2.5X BASIC
*CAR p/r 27-93: 1.2X TO 3X BASIC
*CAR p/r 22-25: 2X TO 5X BASIC
*SEA p/r 151-500: .75X TO 2X BASIC
*SEA p/r 101-147: 1X TO 2.5X BASIC
*SEA p/r 27-96: 1.2X TO 3X BASIC
*SEA p/r 20-24: 2X TO 5X BASIC
*150 VAR/150: 1X TO 2.5X BASIC
*HOLO BCK VAR/99: 1.2X TO 3X BASIC
*FD VAR/49: 1.2X TO 3X BASIC
*42 VAR/42: 1.2X TO 3X BASIC
*MD VAR/25: 2X TO 5X BASIC
51 Chris Sale .60 1.50
55 Jose Ramirez .50 1.25
57 Kris Bryant .75 2.00
61 Juan Soto 2.00 5.00
62 J.D. Martinez .60 1.50
68 Francisco Lindor .60 1.50
70 Jose Altuve .50 1.25
76 Andrew Benintendi .60 1.50
80 Adrian Beltre .60 1.50
81 Yadier Molina .75 2.00
82 Austin Meadows .60 1.50
86 Corey Kluber .50 1.25
87 Ronald Acuna Jr. 3.00 8.00
90 Miles Mikolas .60 1.50
101 Mookie Betts 1.25 3.00
104 Rhys Hoskins .75 2.00
105 J.T. Realmuto .60 1.50
121 Aaron Judge 1.50 4.00
123 Jacob deGrom 1.25 3.00
126 Kyle Freeland .50 1.25
128 Rafael Devers .75 2.00
129 Miguel Andujar .60 1.50
133 Walker Buehler .75 2.00
145 Aaron Nola .50 1.25
152 Paul Goldschmidt .60 1.50
156 Ozzie Albies .60 1.50
157 Gleyber Torres 1.25 3.00
164 Shohei Ohtani 1.00 2.50
165 Javier Baez .75 2.00
166 Jesus Aguilar .50 1.25
170 Mike Trout 3.00 8.00
172 Justin Verlander .60 1.50
179 Salvador Perez .50 1.25
181 Blake Snell .50 1.25
182 Alex Bregman .60 1.50
183 Bryce Harper 1.00 2.50
185 Trevor Story .60 1.50
187 Anthony Rizzo .75 2.00
190 Christian Yelich .75 2.00
192 Matt Chapman .60 1.50
201 Trevor Richards RETRO .40 1.00
207 Fernando Romero RETRO .40 1.00
211 Max Muncy RETRO .50 1.25
213 Daniel Palka RETRO .40 1.00
215 Justin Williams RETRO .40 1.00
218 Stephen Gonsalves RETRO .40 1.00
223 Josh James RETRO .60 1.50
232 Brandon Lowe RETRO .60 1.50
239 Rowdy Tellez RETRO .60 1.50
244 Luke Voit RETRO 1.00 2.50

2019 Donruss '85 Retro Materials
RANDOM INSERTS IN PACKS
*GOLD/25-99: .5X TO 1.2X BASIC
1 Justin Verlander 2.50 6.00
2 Andrew McCutchen 2.50 6.00
3 Marcell Ozuna 2.50 6.00
4 Daniel Murphy 2.00 5.00
5 Christian Yelich 3.00 8.00
6 Gerrit Cole 2.50 6.00
7 Giancarlo Stanton 2.50 6.00
8 Lorenzo Cain 1.50 4.00
9 Mike Moustakas 2.00 5.00
10 Stephen Piscotty 1.50 4.00
11 Manny Machado 2.50 6.00
12 Nick Markakis 2.00 5.00
13 Starlin Castro 1.50 4.00
14 Eric Hosmer 2.00 5.00
15 Dee Gordon 1.50 4.00
16 Adrian Beltre 2.50 6.00
17 Adrian Gonzalez 2.00 5.00
18 Ian Desmond 1.50 4.00
19 Didi Gregorius 2.00 5.00
20 Tommy Pham 1.50 4.00
21 Albert Pujols 3.00 8.00
22 Chris Sale 2.50 6.00
23 J.A. Happ 2.00 5.00
24 Cole Hamels 2.00 5.00
25 Miguel Cabrera 2.50 6.00

2019 Donruss '85 Retro Rated Rookies Signatures
RANDOM INSERTS IN PACKS
EXCHANGE DEADLINE 09/06/2020
85SYK Yusei Kikuchi 15.00 100.00

2019 Donruss '85 Retro Signatures
RANDOM INSERTS IN PACKS
EXCHANGE DEADLINE 09/06/2020
*BLUE/49-99: .5X TO 1.2X BASIC
*BLUE/25: .75X TO 2X BASIC
*RED/25: .75X TO 2X BASIC
1 Aaron Judge EXCH 50.00 120.00
2 Anthony Rizzo 10.00 25.00
3 Ichiro 125.00 300.00
4 Clint Frazier 3.00 8.00
5 David Ortiz 30.00 80.00
6 Eddie Murray 12.00 30.00
7 Gary Sanchez 12.00 30.00
8 Rhys Hoskins 10.00 25.00
9 Trea Turner 8.00 20.00
10 Ivan Rodriguez 10.00 25.00
11 Cody Bellinger 12.00 30.00
12 Yoan Moncada 6.00 15.00
14 Phil Niekro 3.00 8.00
15 Ozzie Smith 20.00 50.00
16 Pedro Martinez 12.00 30.00
17 Roger Clemens 12.00 30.00
18 Dwight Gooden 6.00 15.00
19 Willie McGee 6.00 15.00
20 Don Mattingly 25.00 60.00

2019 Donruss Action All-Stars
RANDOM INSERTS IN PACKS
STATED PRINT RUN 999 SER.#'d SETS
*BRONZE/349: .5X TO 1.2X BASIC
*DIAMOND: .5X TO 1.2X BASIC
*PINK: .6X TO 1.5X BASIC
*BLUE/249: .6X TO 1.5X BASIC
*RAPTURE: .6X TO 1.5X BASIC
*RED/149: .6X TO 1.5X BASIC
*VECTOR: .6X TO 1.5X BASIC
*GOLD/99: 1X TO 2.5X BASIC
*GREEN/25: 1.5X TO 4X BASIC
1 Jose Altuve .50 1.25
2 Aaron Judge 1.50 4.00
3 Mike Trout 3.00 8.00
4 Shohei Ohtani 1.00 2.50
5 Mookie Betts 1.25 3.00
6 Clayton Kershaw 1.00 2.50
7 Kris Bryant .75 2.00
8 Bryce Harper 1.00 2.50
9 Khris Davis .60 1.50
10 Manny Machado .60 1.50
11 Charlie Blackmon .60 1.50
12 Ronald Acuna Jr. 3.00 8.00
13 Christian Yelich .75 2.00
14 J.D. Martinez .60 1.50
15 Francisco Lindor .60 1.50

2019 Donruss American Pride
RANDOM INSERTS IN PACKS
STATED PRINT RUN 999 SER.#'d SETS
*BRONZE/349: .5X TO 1.2X BASIC
*DIAMOND: .5X TO 1.2X BASIC
*PINK: .6X TO 1.5X BASIC
*BLUE/249: .6X TO 1.5X BASIC
*RAPTURE: .6X TO 1.5X BASIC
*RED/149: .6X TO 1.5X BASIC
*VECTOR: .6X TO 1.5X BASIC
*GOLD/99: 1X TO 2.5X BASIC
*GREEN/25: 1.5X TO 4X BASIC
1 Daniel Cabrera 1.50 4.00
2 Will Wilson .60 1.50
3 Braden Shewmake 1.25 3.00
4 John Doxakis .50 1.25
5 Bryson Stott 1.25 3.00
6 Andrew Vaughn 1.25 3.00
7 Mason Feole .40 1.00
8 Shea Langeliers .75 2.00
9 Spencer Torkelson 5.00 12.00
10 Josh Jung 1.25 3.00
11 Bryant Packard .60 1.50
12 Jake Agnos .60 1.50
13 Andre Pallante .50 1.25
14 Dominic Fletcher .40 1.00
15 Adley Rutschman 2.50 6.00
16 Graeme Stinson .40 1.00
17 Matt Cronin .40 1.00
18 Max Meyer 1.25 3.00
19 Kenyon Yovan .40 1.00
20 Tanner Burns .60 1.50
21 Drew Parrish .40 1.00
22 Kyle Brnovich .40 1.00
23 Zack Hess .40 1.00
24 Zach Watson .60 1.50
25 Zack Thompson .60 1.50
26 Parker Caracci .40 1.00

2019 Donruss Bleachers Inc. Autographs
RANDOM INSERTS IN PACKS
EXCHANGE DEADLINE 09/06/2020
*BLUE/49-99: .5X TO 1.2X BASIC
*RED/25: .75X TO 2X BASIC
1 Shohei Ohtani 75.00 200.00
2 Aaron Judge 40.00 100.00
3 Mike Soroka 4.00 10.00
4 Harrison Bader 3.00 8.00
5 Nick Williams 2.50 6.00
6 Dustin Fowler 2.50 6.00
7 Brian Anderson 2.50 6.00
8 J.D. Davis 2.50 6.00
9 Luiz Gohara 2.50 6.00
10 Anthony Banda 2.50 6.00
11 Willy Adames 2.50 6.00
12 Erick Fedde 2.50 6.00
13 Mitch Garver 2.50 6.00
14 Rhys Hoskins 12.00 30.00
15 Billy McKinney 2.50 6.00

2019 Donruss Dominators
RANDOM INSERTS IN PACKS
STATED PRINT RUN 999 SER.#'d SETS
*BRONZE/349: .5X TO 1.2X BASIC
*DIAMOND: .5X TO 1.2X BASIC
*PINK: .6X TO 1.5X BASIC
*BLUE/249: .6X TO 1.5X BASIC
*RAPTURE: .6X TO 1.5X BASIC
*RED/149: .6X TO 1.5X BASIC
*VECTOR: .6X TO 1.5X BASIC
*GOLD/99: 1X TO 2.5X BASIC
*GREEN/25: 1.5X TO 4X BASIC
1 Mike Trout 3.00 8.00
2 J.D. Martinez .60 1.50
3 Jacob deGrom 1.25 3.00
4 Manny Machado .60 1.50
5 Trevor Story .60 1.50
6 Alex Bregman .60 1.50
7 Miguel Andujar .60 1.50
8 Jose Ramirez .50 1.25
9 Freddie Freeman .75 2.00
10 Blake Snell .50 1.25

2019 Donruss Elite Series
RANDOM INSERTS IN PACKS
STATED PRINT RUN 999 SER.#'d SETS
*BRONZE/349: .5X TO 1.2X BASIC
*DIAMOND: .5X TO 1.2X BASIC
*PINK: .6X TO 1.5X BASIC
*BLUE/249: .6X TO 1.5X BASIC
*RAPTURE: .6X TO 1.5X BASIC
*RED/149: .6X TO 1.5X BASIC
*VECTOR: .6X TO 1.5X BASIC
*GOLD/99: 1.2X TO 3X BASIC
*GREEN/25: 2X TO 5X BASIC
1 Ronald Acuna Jr. 5.00 12.00
2 Shohei Ohtani 1.50 4.00
3 Christian Yelich 1.25 3.00
4 Gleyber Torres 2.00 5.00
5 Juan Soto 3.00 8.00
6 Javier Baez 1.25 3.00
7 Mookie Betts 2.00 5.00
8 Nolan Arenado 1.50 4.00
9 Francisco Lindor 1.00 2.50
10 Mike Trout 5.00 12.00

2019 Donruss Franchise Features
RANDOM INSERTS IN PACKS
STATED PRINT RUN 999 SER.#'d SETS
*BRONZE/349: .5X TO 1.2X BASIC
*DIAMOND: .5X TO 1.2X BASIC
*PINK: .6X TO 1.5X BASIC
*BLUE/249: .6X TO 1.5X BASIC
*RAPTURE: .6X TO 1.5X BASIC
*RED/149: .6X TO 1.5X BASIC
*VECTOR: .6X TO 1.5X BASIC
*GOLD/99: 1X TO 2.5X BASIC
*GREEN/25: 1.5X TO 4X BASIC
1 Arenado/Guerrero Jr. 2.50 6.00
2 Lindor/Tatis Jr. 6.00 15.00
3 Ozuna/Jimenez 1.50 4.00
4 Bryant/Senzel 1.25 3.00
5 Carlos Correa
Royce Lewis .75 2.00
6 Forrest Whitley
Justin Verlander .60 1.50
7 Corey Seager
Brendan Rodgers .60 1.50
8 Bo Bichette
Trevor Story 1.25 3.00
9 Turner/Franco 8.00 20.00
10 Judge/Kiriloff 1.50 4.00
11 Corey Kluber
Mitch Keller .50 1.25
12 Max Scherzer
Brent Honeywell .60 1.50
13 Rizzo/McKay .75 2.00
14 Puk/Kershaw 1.00 2.50
15 Adell/Trout 3.00 8.00
16 Posey/Bart 1.25 3.00
17 Goldschmidt/Alonso 3.00 8.00
18 Charlie Blackmon
Leody Taveras .60 1.50
19 deGrom/Duplantier 1.25 3.00
20 Altuve/Madrigal 1.50 4.00
21 George Springer
Estevan Florial .60 1.50

2019 Donruss Highlights
RANDOM INSERTS IN PACKS
STATED PRINT RUN 999 SER.#'d SETS
*BRONZE/349: .5X TO 1.2X BASIC
*DIAMOND: .5X TO 1.2X BASIC
*PINK: .6X TO 1.5X BASIC
*BLUE/249: .6X TO 1.5X BASIC
*RAPTURE: .6X TO 1.5X BASIC
*RED/149: .6X TO 1.5X BASIC
*VECTOR: .6X TO 1.5X BASIC
*GOLD/99: 1X TO 2.5X BASIC
*GREEN/25: 1.5X TO 4X BASIC
1 Shohei Ohtani 1.00 2.50
2 Albert Pujols .75 2.00
3 Sean Manaea .40 1.00
4 James Paxton .50 1.25
5 Max Scherzer .60 1.50
6 George Springer .50 1.25
7 Christian Yelich .75 2.00
8 Juan Soto 2.00 5.00
9 Mookie Betts 1.25 3.00
10 Jose Ramirez .50 1.25
11 Brock Holt .40 1.00
12 Walker Buehler .75 2.00

2019 Donruss Majestic Materials
RANDOM INSERTS IN PACKS
*GOLD/30-99: .5X TO 1.2X BASIC
1 Aaron Judge 8.00 20.00
2 Ronald Acuna Jr. 5.00 12.00
3 Juan Soto 4.00 10.00
4 Gleyber Torres 3.00 8.00
5 Ozzie Albies 2.50 6.00
6 Rhys Hoskins 2.50 6.00
7 Shohei Ohtani 5.00 12.00
8 Harrison Bader 2.00 5.00
9 Walker Buehler 3.00 8.00
10 Ryan McMahon 2.50 6.00
11 Jordan Hicks 2.00 5.00
12 Rafael Devers 3.00 8.00
13 Ronald Guzman 1.50 4.00
14 Austin Hays 2.50 6.00
15 Clint Frazier 2.00 5.00
16 Miguel Andujar 2.50 6.00
17 Jose Altuve 2.00 5.00
18 Victor Robles 3.00 8.00
19 Willy Adames 1.50 4.00
20 David Bote 2.00 5.00
21 Mike Trout 10.00 25.00
22 Khris Davis 2.50 6.00
23 Nolan Arenado 4.00 10.00
24 Christian Yelich 3.00 8.00
25 Alex Bregman 2.50 6.00
26 Trevor Story 2.50 6.00
27 Mookie Betts 5.00 12.00
28 Javier Baez 3.00 8.00
29 Jose Ramirez 2.00 5.00
30 Matt Olson 2.50 6.00
31 Jacob deGrom 5.00 12.00
32 Blake Snell 2.00 5.00
33 Whit Merrifield 2.50 6.00
34 Joey Votto 2.50 6.00
35 Freddie Freeman 3.00 8.00
36 Nicholas Castellanos 2.50 6.00
37 Matt Chapman 2.50 6.00
38 Bryce Harper 4.00 10.00

2019 Donruss Nicknames
RANDOM INSERTS IN PACKS
STATED PRINT RUN 999 SER.#'d SETS
*BRONZE/349: .5X TO 1.2X BASIC
*DIAMOND: .5X TO 1.2X BASIC
*PINK: .6X TO 1.5X BASIC
*BLUE/249: .6X TO 1.5X BASIC
*RAPTURE: .6X TO 1.5X BASIC
*RED/149: .6X TO 1.5X BASIC
*VECTOR: .6X TO 1.5X BASIC
*GOLD/99: 1X TO 2.5X BASIC
*GREEN/25: 1.5X TO 4X BASIC
1 Aaron Judge 2.50 6.00
2 Paul Goldschmidt 1.00 2.50
3 Mike Trout 5.00 12.00
4 Javier Baez 1.25 3.00
5 Juan Soto 3.00 8.00
6 Shohei Ohtani 1.50 4.00

2019 Donruss Rated Prospect Material Signatures
RANDOM INSERTS IN PACKS
EXCHANGE DEADLINE 09/06/2020
*GOLD/99: .5X TO 1.2X BASIC
1 Vladimir Guerrero Jr. 30.00 80.00
2 Fernando Tatis Jr. 75.00 200.00
3 Eloy Jimenez 15.00 40.00
4 Brendan McKay 4.00 10.00
5 Yordan Alvarez 20.00 50.00
6 Wander Franco 40.00 100.00
7 Julio Pablo Martinez 2.50 6.00
8 Peter Alonso 40.00 100.00
9 Taylor Trammell 12.00 30.00
10 Ke'Bryan Hayes 6.00 15.00

2019 Donruss Rated Prospect Materials
RANDOM INSERTS IN PACKS
*GOLD/99: .5X TO 1.2X BASIC
1 Eloy Jimenez 4.00 10.00
2 Vladimir Guerrero Jr. 8.00 20.00
3 Nick Senzel 3.00 8.00
4 Fernando Tatis Jr. 8.00 20.00
5 Taylor Trammell 2.50 6.00
6 Brendan McKay 2.50 6.00
7 Carter Kieboom 2.50 6.00
8 Jesus Sanchez 2.50 6.00
9 A.J. Puk 2.50 6.00
10 Yordan Alvarez 10.00 25.00
11 Ke'Bryan Hayes 8.00 20.00
12 Leody Taveras 2.50 6.00
13 Peter Alonso 8.00 20.00
14 Franklin Perez 1.50 4.00
15 Dustin May 3.00 8.00
16 Luis Robert 10.00 25.00
17 Wander Franco 8.00 20.00
18 Kaito Yuki 2.50 6.00
19 Julio Pablo Martinez 1.50 4.00
20 Francisco Morales 2.00 5.00
21 Noelvi Marte 6.00 15.00
22 Marco Luciano 6.00 15.00
23 Estanli Castillo 1.50 4.00
24 Keston Hiura 3.00 8.00
25 Austin Riley 5.00 12.00

2019 Donruss Rated Rookies Signatures
RANDOM INSERTS IN PACKS
EXCHANGE DEADLINE 09/06/2020
1 Yusei Kikuchi EXCH 30.00 80.00

2019 Donruss Sensational Signatures
RANDOM INSERTS IN PACKS
EXCHANGE DEADLINE 09/06/2020
*BLUE/49: .5X TO 1.2X BASIC
*RED/25: .6X TO 1.5X BASIC
1 Domingo Ayala 10.00 25.00

2019 Donruss Signature Series
RANDOM INSERTS IN PACKS
EXCHANGE DEADLINE 09/06/2020
*BLUE/99: .5X TO 1.2X BASIC
*RED/25: .75X TO 2X BASIC
1 Bryse Wilson 3.00 8.00
2 Kolby Allard 4.00 10.00
3 Kyle Wright 4.00 10.00
4 Touki Toussaint 3.00 8.00
5 Cedric Mullins 8.00 20.00
6 Luis Ortiz 2.50 6.00
7 Michael Kopech 8.00 20.00
8 Brandon Lowe 6.00 15.00
9 Garrett Hampson 4.00 10.00
10 Christin Stewart 3.00 8.00
11 Cionel Perez 2.50 6.00
12 Framber Valdez 2.50 6.00
13 Josh James 6.00 15.00
14 Myles Straw 4.00 10.00
15 Kyle Tucker 6.00 15.00
16 Brad Keller 2.50 6.00
17 Ryan O'Hearn 2.50 6.00
18 David Fletcher 8.00 20.00
19 Taylor Ward 2.50 6.00
20 Dennis Santana 2.50 6.00
21 Corbin Burnes 8.00 20.00
22 Jake Cave 3.00 8.00
23 Stephen Gonsalves 2.50 6.00
24 Caleb Ferguson 3.00 8.00
25 Jeff McNeil 6.00 15.00
26 Chance Adams 2.50 6.00
27 Jonathan Loaisiga
28 Justus Sheffield 4.00 10.00
29 Ramon Laureano 6.00 15.00
30 Enyel De Los Santos 2.50 6.00
31 Kevin Kramer 3.00 8.00
32 Kevin Newman 4.00 10.00
33 Jacob Nix 3.00 8.00
34 Luis Urias 4.00 10.00
35 Chris Shaw 2.50 6.00
36 Steven Duggar 3.00 8.00
37 Dakota Hudson 3.00 8.00
38 Daniel Ponce de Leon 4.00 10.00
39 Patrick Wisdom 2.50 6.00
40 Jake Bauers 4.00 10.00
41 Danny Jansen 2.50 6.00
42 Jonathan Davis 3.00 8.00
43 Reese McGuire 4.00 10.00
44 Rowdy Tellez 4.00 10.00
45 Ryan Borucki 2.50 6.00
46 Sean Reid-Foley 2.50 6.00
47 Eloy Jimenez 15.00 40.00
48 Vladimir Guerrero Jr. 30.00 80.00
49 Fernando Tatis Jr. 50.00 120.00
50 Nick Senzel EXCH 8.00 20.00

2019 Donruss The Famous San Diego Chicken 6 Piece
RANDOM INSERTS IN PACKS
STATED PRINT RUN 85 SER.#'d SETS
1 Ted Giannoulas 25.00 60.00
2 Ted Giannoulas 25.00 60.00
3 Ted Giannoulas 25.00 60.00
4 Ted Giannoulas 25.00 60.00
5 Ted Giannoulas 25.00 60.00
6 Ted Giannoulas 25.00 60.00

2019 Donruss The Famous San Diego Chicken 6 Piece Signatures
RANDOM INSERTS IN PACKS
STATED PRINT RUN 85 SER.#'d SETS
EXCHANGE DEADLINE 09/09/2020
1 Ted Giannoulas 50.00 120.00
2 Ted Giannoulas 50.00 120.00
3 Ted Giannoulas 50.00 120.00
4 Ted Giannoulas 50.00 120.00
5 Ted Giannoulas 50.00 120.00
6 Ted Giannoulas 50.00 120.00

2019 Donruss Whammy
RANDOM INSERTS IN PACKS
1 Mookie Betts 15.00 40.00
2 Ronald Acuna Jr. 20.00 50.00
3 Vladimir Guerrero Jr. 25.00 60.00
4 Juan Soto 15.00 40.00
5 Javier Baez 10.00 25.00

2020 Donruss
1 Fernando Tatis Jr. DK 3.00 8.00
2 Buster Posey DK .75 2.00
3 Cody Bellinger DK 1.25 3.00
4 Eugenio Suarez DK .50 1.25
5 Christian Yelich DK .75 2.00
6 Brian Anderson DK .40 1.00
7 Pete Alonso DK 1.50 4.00
8 Ronald Acuna Jr. DK 2.50 6.00
9 Mike Trout DK 3.00 8.00
10 Marcus Semien DK .60 1.50
11 Miguel Cabrera DK .60 1.50
12 Lucas Giolito DK .50 1.25
13 Nelson Cruz DK .60 1.50
14 Vladimir Guerrero Jr. DK 1.00 2.50
15 Austin Meadows DK .60 1.50
16 Rafael Devers DK .75 2.00
17 Trey Mancini DK .60 1.50
18 Shane Bieber DK .60 1.50
19 Jorge Soler DK .60 1.50
20 Alex Bregman DK .60 1.50
21 Lance Lynn DK .40 1.00
22 Marco Gonzales DK .40 1.00
23 Juan Soto DK 2.00 5.00
24 Bryce Harper DK 1.00 2.50
25 Paul Goldschmidt DK .60 1.50
26 Javier Baez DK .75 2.00
27 Josh Bell DK .50 1.25
28 Ketel Marte DK .50 1.25
29 Nolan Arenado DK 1.00 2.50
30 Aaron Judge DK 1.50 4.00
31 Bryan Abreu RR RC .40 1.00
32 Dustin May RR RC 1.25 3.00
33 Mauricio Dubon RR RC .50 1.25
34 Jesus Luzardo RR RC .75 2.00
35 Jordan Yamamoto RR RC .40 1.00
36 Brendan McKay RR RC .60 1.50
37 Bo Bichette RR RC 3.00 8.00
38 Nico Hoerner RR RC 1.50 4.00
39 Aristides Aquino RR RC 1.00 2.50
40 Brock Burke RR RC .40 1.00
41 Justin Dunn RR RC .50 1.25
42 Sean Murphy RR RC .60 1.50
43 Trent Grisham RR RC 1.50 4.00
44 Gavin Lux RR RC 2.00 5.00
45 Yordan Alvarez RR RC 4.00 10.00
46 Sam Hilliard RR RC .60 1.50
47 Patrick Sandoval RR RC .60 1.50
48 Isan Diaz RR RC .60 1.50
49 A.J. Puk RR RC .60 1.50
50 Logan Webb RR RC .60 1.50
51 Randy Arozarena RR RC 3.00 8.00
52 Anthony Kay RR RC .40 1.00
53 Dylan Cease RR RC .60 1.50
54 Zac Gallen RR RC 1.00 2.50
55 Adrian Morejon RR RC .40 1.00
56 Kyle Lewis RR RC 2.50 6.00
57 Nick Solak RR RC 1.50 4.00
58 Brusdar Graterol RR RC .60 1.50
59 Tony Gonsolin RR RC 1.50 4.00
60 Matt Thaiss RR RC .50 1.25
61 Eduardo Rodriguez .15 .40
62 Walker Buehler .30 .75
63 Michael Conforto .20 .50
64 Ozzie Albies .25 .60
65 Eric Hosmer .20 .50
66 Charlie Blackmon .25 .60
67 Stephen Strasburg .25 .60
68 Nick Senzel .25 .60
69 Yadier Molina .30 .75
70 Jean Segura .20 .50
71 Jacob deGrom .50 1.25
72 Hunter Dozier .15 .40
73 Luis Severino .20 .50
74 Gary Sanchez .25 .60
75 Xander Bogaerts .25 .60
76 Lucas Giolito .20 .50
77 Mookie Betts .50 1.25
78 Ketel Marte .20 .50
79 Hyun-Jin Ryu .20 .50
80 Lorenzo Cain .15 .40
81 Corey Kluber .20 .50
82 Joey Votto .25 .60
83 Fernando Tatis Jr. 1.25 3.00
84 Cody Bellinger .50 1.25
85 Aroldis Chapman .25 .60
86 Robbie Ray .15 .40
87 Josh Donaldson .20 .50
88 Khris Davis .25 .60
89 Jeff McNeil .20 .50
90 Javier Baez .30 .75
91 Gleyber Torres .50 1.25
92 Marcus Semien .25 .60
93 Buster Posey .30 .75
94 Shohei Ohtani .40 1.00
95 Mike Minor .15 .40
96 German Marquez .25 .60
97 Yu Darvish .25 .60
98 Charlie Morton .25 .60
99 Max Muncy .20 .50
100 Mitch Haniger .20 .50
101 Johnny Cueto .20 .50
102 Vladimir Guerrero Jr. .40 1.00
103 Matt Olson .25 .60
104 Shane Bieber .25 .60
105 Jorge Polanco .20 .50
106 Corey Seager .25 .60
107 Jose Abreu .25 .60
108 Trea Turner .20 .50
109 Justin Turner .25 .60
110 Christian Yelich .30 .75
111 Aaron Judge .60 1.50
112 Alex Bregman .25 .60
113 Nelson Cruz .25 .60
114 Chris Sale .25 .60
115 Gerrit Cole .40 1.00
116 Michael Brantley .20 .50
117 Madison Bumgarner .20 .50
118 Clayton Kershaw .40 1.00
119 DJ LeMahieu .25 .60
120 Masahiro Tanaka .25 .60
121 Eloy Jimenez .50 1.25
122 Cavan Biggio .30 .75
123 Max Scherzer .25 .60
124 Eugenio Suarez .20 .50
125 Jordan Hicks .20 .50
126 Aaron Nola .20 .50
127 Paul Goldschmidt .25 .60
128 Luke Weaver .15 .40
129 Mike Trout 1.25 3.00
130 Nomar Mazara .15 .40
131 Hunter Renfroe .15 .40
132 Anthony Rizzo .30 .75
133 Josh Hader .20 .50
134 Marcell Ozuna .25 .60
135 Brandon Woodruff .25 .60
136 Luis Castillo .20 .50
137 Jonathan Villar .15 .40
138 David Fletcher .25 .60
139 Tim Anderson .25 .60
140 David Dahl .15 .40
141 Max Kepler .20 .50
142 Kyle Hendricks .25 .60
143 Max Fried .20 .50
144 Austin Meadows .25 .60
145 Yoan Moncada .25 .60
146 Josh Bell .20 .50
147 Nolan Arenado .40 1.00
148 Francisco Lindor .25 .60
149 Matt Chapman .25 .60
150 Willie Calhoun .15 .40
151 Tyler Glasnow .25 .60
152 Mike Soroka .25 .60
153 Kevin Newman .25 .60
154 Anthony Rendon .25 .60
155 Trevor Bauer .30 .75
156 Elvis Andrus .20 .50
157 Justin Verlander .25 .60
158 Jose Ramirez .20 .50
159 Jose Altuve .20 .50
160 Bryan Reynolds .20 .50
161 Eddie Rosario .20 .50
162 Juan Soto .75 2.00
163 Chris Paddack .25 .60
164 Rafael Devers .30 .75
165 Brian Anderson .15 .40
166 Trevor Story .25 .60
167 Jose Berrios .20 .50
168 Brandon Lowe .20 .50
169 Freddie Freeman .30 .75
170 Ronald Acuna Jr. 1.00 2.50
171 Starling Marte .20 .50
172 Adalberto Mondesi .20 .50
173 Noah Syndergaard .20 .50
174 Tommy Pham .15 .40
175 Blake Snell .20 .50
176 George Springer .20 .50
177 Trey Mancini .25 .60
178 Kyle Schwarber .25 .60
179 Ramon Laureano .20 .50
180 Kris Bryant .30 .75
181 Rhys Hoskins .30 .75
182 Marco Gonzales .15 .40
183 J.D. Martinez .25 .60

184 Keston Hiura .30 .75
185 Manny Machado .25 .60
186 Carlos Santana .20 .50
187 David Peralta .15 .40
188 Albert Pujols .30 .75
189 Brandon Crawford .20 .50
190 Yandy Diaz .20 .50
191 Sandy Alcantara .15 .40
192 Jack Flaherty .20 .50
193 Bryce Harper .40 1.00
194 Yusei Kikuchi .20 .50
195 Giancarlo Stanton .25 .60
196 Joey Gallo .25 .60
197 Willson Contreras .25 .60
198 Mitch Garver .15 .40
199 Christian Vazquez .20 .50
200 Luis Arraez .30 .75
201 Sonny Gray .20 .50
202 Jorge Soler .25 .60
203 Matt Carpenter .25 .60
204 Pete Alonso .60 1.50
205 Whit Merrifield .25 .60
206 John Means .25 .60
207 Eduardo Escobar .15 .40
208 Kirby Yates .15 .40
209 Mike Yastrzemski .40 1.00
210 Tommy Edman .25 .60
211 Barry Larkin RETRO .25 .60
212 Jose Canseco RETRO .20 .50
213 Andres Galarraga RETRO .20 .50
214 Kevin Mitchell RETRO .15 .40
215 Wade Boggs RETRO .20 .50
216 Don Mattingly RETRO .50 1.25
217 Kirby Puckett RETRO .25 .60
218 Tony Gwynn RETRO .25 .60
219 Rickey Henderson RETRO .25 .60
220 Roger Clemens RETRO .30 .75
221 Bert Blyleven RETRO .20 .50
222 Dwight Gooden RETRO .15 .40
223 Nolan Ryan RETRO .75 2.00
224 Cal Ripken RETRO .75 2.00
225 Alan Trammell RETRO .20 .50
226 Jim Rice RETRO .20 .50
227 Keith Hernandez RETRO .15 .40
228 Eddie Murray RETRO .20 .50
229 George Brett RETRO .50 1.25
230 Gary Carter RETRO .20 .50
231 Darryl Strawberry RETRO .15 .40
232 Dave Winfield RETRO .20 .50
233 Robin Yount RETRO .25 .60
234 Dale Murphy RETRO .25 .60
235 Paul Molitor RETRO .25 .60
236 Willi Castro RETRO RC .60 1.50
237 Andres Munoz RETRO RC .60 1.50
238 Jonathan Hernandez RETRO RC .40 1.00
239 Josh Rojas RETRO RC .40 1.00
240 Sheldon Neuse RETRO RC .50 1.25
241 Yonathan Daza RETRO RC .50 1.25
242 Bobby Bradley RETRO RC .40 1.00
243 Logan Allen RETRO RC .40 1.00
244 Joe Palumbo RETRO RC .40 1.00
245 Jaylin Davis RETRO RC .60 1.50
246 Jake Fraley RETRO RC .50 1.25
247 Zack Collins RETRO RC .50 1.25
248 Danny Mendick RETRO RC .50 1.25
249 Edwin Rios RETRO RC 1.00 2.50
250 Travis Demeritte RETRO RC .60 1.50
251 Lewis Thorpe RETRO RC .40 1.00
252 Donnie Walton RETRO RC 1.00 2.50
253 Tyrone Taylor RETRO RC .40 1.00
254 Aaron Civale RETRO RC .75 2.00
255 Domingo Leyba RETRO RC .50 1.25
256 Michael King RETRO RC .60 1.50
257 Abraham Toro RETRO RC .50 1.25
258 Adbert Alzolay RETRO RC .50 1.25
259 Yu Chang RETRO RC .60 1.50
260 Jake Rogers RETRO RC .40 1.00
261 Ted Giannoulas .15 .40
262 Domingo Ayala 2.00 5.00
263 Yoshitomo Tsutsugo RR RC 1.00 2.50
264 Luis Robert RR RC 3.00 8.00

2020 Donruss Look At This

*LOOK AT THIS DK: 2X TO 5X BASIC
*LOOK AT THIS RR: 2X TO 5X BASIC
*LOOK AT THIS: 5X TO 12X BASIC
RANDOM INSERTS IN PACKS
STATED PRINT RUN 25 SER.#'d SETS
37 Bo Bichette RR 25.00 60.00
38 Nico Hoerner RR 25.00 60.00
44 Gavin Lux RR 20.00 50.00
264 Luis Robert RR 100.00 250.00

2020 Donruss Presidential Collection

*PRES DK: 1.2X TO 3X BASIC
*PRES RR: 1.2X TO 3X BASIC
*PRES: 3X TO 8X BASIC
RANDOM INSERTS IN PACKS
STATED PRINT RUN 50 SER.#'d SETS
38 Nico Hoerner RR 15.00 40.00
264 Luis Robert RR 60.00 150.00

2020 Donruss American Pride

RANDOM INSERTS IN PACKS
STATED PRINT RUN 999 SER.#'d SETS
*SILVER/349: .5X TO 1.2X BASIC
*DIAMOND: .5X TO 1.2X BASIC
*PINK: .6X TO 1.5X BASIC
*BLUE/249: .6X TO 1.5X BASIC
*RAPTURE: .6X TO 1.5X BASIC
*RED/149: .6X TO 1.5X BASIC
*VECTOR: .6X TO 1.5X BASIC
*GOLD/99: 1X TO 2.5X BASIC
*GREEN/25: 1.5X TO 4X BASIC
1 A.Rutschman/P.Bailey 2.50 6.00
2 B.McKay/R.Detmers 1.00 2.50
3 C.Cowser/D.Dahl .50 1.25
4 A.Lacy/C.Kershaw 2.50 6.00
5 A.Martin/C.Jones 1.25 3.00
6 M.Chapman/M.Meyer 1.50 4.00
7 G.Mitchell/M.Trout 3.00 8.00
8 A.Bregman/S.Torkelson 4.00 10.00
9 C.Wilcox/M.Scherzer .60 1.50
10 A.Williams/B.Witt Jr. 2.50 6.00
11 L.Allen/W.Buehler .75 2.00
12 A.Abbott/M.Stroman .50 1.25
13 G.Cole/T.Brown 1.00 2.50
14 B.Carraway/J.Verlander .75 2.00
15 A.Vaughn/J.Foscue 1.50 4.00
16 A.Bohm/N.Loftin 2.50 6.00
17 D.Nikhazy/N.Song .50 1.25
18 K.Griffey Jr./T.Allen 1.25 3.00
19 A.Burleson/J.Gallo .60 1.50
20 C.Cavalli/F.Whitley .75 2.00
21 J.Flaherty/J.Criswell .60 1.50
22 N.Frasso/S.Strasburg .60 1.50
23 H.Kjerstad/J.Adell 3.00 8.00
24 K.Bryant/L.Waddell .75 2.00
25 A.Puk/C.McMahon .60 1.50
26 C.Opitz/Y.Grandal .60 1.50

2020 Donruss As Seen

RANDOM INSERTS IN PACKS
STATED PRINT RUN 999 SER.#'d SETS
*SILVER/349: .5X TO 1.2X BASIC
*DIAMOND: .5X TO 1.2X BASIC
*PINK: .6X TO 1.5X BASIC
*BLUE/249: .6X TO 1.5X BASIC
*RAPTURE: .6X TO 1.5X BASIC
*RED/149: .6X TO 1.5X BASIC
*VECTOR: .6X TO 1.5X BASIC
*GOLD/99: 1X TO 2.5X BASIC
*GREEN/25: 1.5X TO 4X BASIC
1 Fernando Tatis Jr. 3.00 8.00
2 Christian Yelich .75 2.00
3 Jose Altuve .50 1.25
4 Anthony Rizzo .75 2.00
5 Clayton Kershaw 1.00 2.50
6 Vladimir Guerrero Jr. 1.00 2.50

2020 Donruss Classics Autographs

RANDOM INSERTS IN PACKS
EXCHANGE DEADLINE 08/05/2021
*BLUE/99: .5X TO 1.2X BASIC
*BLUE/49-50: .6X TO 1.5X BASIC
*BLUE/25: .75X TO 2X BASIC
*GOLD/25: .75X TO 2X BASIC
1 Ken Griffey Jr. 125.00 300.00
2 Luis Arraez 6.00 15.00
3 Juan Soto 30.00 80.00
5 Kenny Lofton 8.00 20.00
6 Trevor Hoffman 8.00 20.00
7 Ryne Sandberg 10.00 25.00
8 Patrick Corbin 3.00 8.00
9 Adalberto Mondesi 3.00 8.00
10 Andres Galarraga 6.00 15.00
CAGC Gerrit Cole 15.00 40.00

2020 Donruss Classified Signatures

RANDOM INSERTS IN PACKS
EXCHANGE DEADLINE 08/05/2021
*BLUE/99: .5X TO 1.2X BASIC
*BLUE/49: .6X TO 1.5X BASIC
*GOLD/25: .75X TO 2X BASIC
1 Aaron Judge EXCH 40.00 100.00
2 Cody Bellinger 25.00 60.00
3 Josh Bell 6.00 15.00
4 Max Fried 8.00 20.00
5 Willy Adames 2.50 6.00
6 Hunter Dozier 2.50 6.00
7 Trea Turner 6.00 15.00
8 Fernando Tatis Jr. EXCH 50.00 120.00
9 Vladimir Guerrero Jr. 30.00 80.00
10 Eloy Jimenez 12.00 30.00

2020 Donruss Contenders

RANDOM INSERTS IN PACKS
STATED PRINT RUN 999 SER.#'d SETS
*BLUE/99: .6X TO 1.5X BASIC
*GOLD/25: 1X TO 2.5X BASIC
1 Rizzo/Ross/Baez/Brynt 1.25 3.00
2 Bregmn/Correa/Sprngr/Altve 1.00 2.50
3 Benini/Sale/Martnz/Betts 2.00 5.00
4 Rendn/Parra/Soto/Schrzr/Stras 3.00 8.00

2020 Donruss Contenders Blue

*BLUE/99: .6X TO 1.5X BASIC
RANDOM INSERTS IN PACKS
STATED PRINT RUN 99 SER.#'d SETS
1 Rizzo/Ross/Baez/Brynt 10.00 25.00
2 Bregmn/Correa/Sprngr/Altve 6.00 15.00
3 Benini/Sale/Martnz/Betts 4.00 10.00

2020 Donruss Contenders Gold

*GOLD/25: 1X TO 2.5X BASIC
RANDOM INSERTS IN PACKS
STATED PRINT RUN 25 SER.#'d SETS
1 Rizzo/Ross/Baez/Brynt 15.00 40.00
2 Bregmn/Correa/Sprngr/Altve 10.00 25.00
3 Benini/Sale/Martnz/Betts 6.00 15.00

2020 Donruss Divisions

RANDOM INSERTS IN PACKS
1 Jdge/Snel/Bets/Mncni/Vlad Jr 5.00 12.00
2 Jimnz/Lndor/Solr/Keplr/Miggy 6.00 15.00
3 Vogel/Gallo/Altve/Davis/Trout 10.00 25.00
4 Andrsn/Harpr/Soto/Alnso/Acuna Jr. 8.00 20.00
5 Yelch/Baez/Votto/Gldschmdt/Mrte 8.00 20.00
6 Belli/Longo/Tatis Jr/Mrte/Arendo 6.00 15.00

2020 Donruss Dominators

RANDOM INSERTS IN PACKS
STATED PRINT RUN 999 SER.#'d SETS
*SILVER/349: .5X TO 1.2X BASIC
*DIAMOND: .5X TO 1.2X BASIC
*PINK: .6X TO 1.5X BASIC
*BLUE/249: .6X TO 1.5X BASIC
*RAPTURE: .6X TO 1.5X BASIC
*RED/149: .6X TO 1.5X BASIC
*VECTOR: .6X TO 1.5X BASIC
*GOLD/99: 1X TO 2.5X BASIC
*GREEN/25: 1.5X TO 4X BASIC
1 Max Scherzer .60 1.50
2 Pete Alonso 1.50 4.00
3 Gerrit Cole 1.00 2.50
4 Aaron Judge 1.50 4.00
5 Rafael Devers .75 2.00
6 Hyun-Jin Ryu .50 1.25
7 Jorge Soler .60 1.50
8 Austin Meadows .60 1.50
9 Ketel Marte .50 1.25
10 Jacob deGrom 1.25 3.00
11 Jorge Polanco .50 1.25
12 Josh Bell .50 1.25
13 Marcus Semien .60 1.50

2020 Donruss Domingo Ayala Material Signatures

RANDOM INSERTS IN PACKS
1 Domingo Ayala 10.00 25.00

2020 Donruss Elite Series

RANDOM INSERTS IN PACKS
STATED PRINT RUN 999 SER.#'d SETS
*SILVER/349: .5X TO 1.2X BASIC
*DIAMOND: .5X TO 1.2X BASIC
*PINK: .6X TO 1.5X BASIC
*BLUE/249: .6X TO 1.5X BASIC
*RAPTURE: .6X TO 1.5X BASIC
*RED/149: .6X TO 1.5X BASIC
*VECTOR: .6X TO 1.5X BASIC
1 Christian Yelich 1.25 3.00
2 Javier Baez 1.25 3.00
3 Nolan Arenado 1.50 4.00
4 Cody Bellinger 2.00 5.00
5 Mike Trout 5.00 12.00
6 Alex Bregman 1.00 2.50
7 Justin Verlander 1.00 2.50
8 Ronald Acuna Jr. 4.00 10.00
9 Juan Soto 3.00 8.00
10 Mookie Betts 2.00 5.00
11 Matt Chapman 1.00 2.50
12 Paul Goldschmidt 1.00 2.50
13 Yoan Moncada 1.00 2.50

2020 Donruss Elite Series Gold

*GOLD/99: 1X TO 2.5X BASIC
RANDOM INSERTS IN PACKS
STATED PRINT RUN 99 SER.#'d SETS
9 Juan Soto 10.00 25.00

2020 Donruss Elite Series Green

*GREEN/25: 1.5X TO 4X BASIC
RANDOM INSERTS IN PACKS
STATED PRINT RUN 25 SER.#'d SETS
5 Mike Trout 50.00 120.00
9 Juan Soto 15.00 40.00

2020 Donruss Highlights

RANDOM INSERTS IN PACKS
STATED PRINT RUN 999 SER.#'d SETS
*SILVER/349: .5X TO 1.2X BASIC
*DIAMOND: .5X TO 1.2X BASIC
*PINK: .6X TO 1.5X BASIC
*BLUE/249: .6X TO 1.5X BASIC
*RAPTURE: .6X TO 1.5X BASIC
*RED/149: .6X TO 1.5X BASIC
*VECTOR: .6X TO 1.5X BASIC
*GOLD/99: 1X TO 2.5X BASIC
*GREEN/25: 1.5X TO 4X BASIC
1 Justin Verlander .60 1.50
2 Joey Gallo .60 1.50
3 Albert Pujols .75 2.00
4 Pete Alonso 2.00 5.00
5 Trevor Story .60 1.50
6 Shohei Ohtani 1.00 2.50
7 Bryce Harper 1.00 2.50
8 Aristides Aquino 3.00 8.00
9 Ronald Acuna Jr. 4.00 10.00
10 Mike Trout 5.00 12.00
11 Eugenio Suarez .50 1.25
12 Bo Bichette 4.00 10.00

2020 Donruss Materials

RANDOM INSERTS IN PACKS
*RED/99: .5X TO 1.2X BASIC
*GOLD/25: .6X TO 1.5X BASIC
1 Aaron Judge 10.00 25.00
2 Rafael Devers 3.00 8.00
3 Ivan Rodriguez 4.00 10.00
4 Rhys Hoskins 3.00 8.00
5 Joe Torre 2.00 5.00
6 Randy Johnson 5.00 12.00
7 Kolten Wong 2.00 5.00
8 Masahiro Tanaka 2.50 6.00
9 Keston Hiura 3.00 8.00
10 Ronald Acuna Jr. 10.00 25.00
11 Red Schoendienst 3.00 8.00
12 Nolan Arenado 3.00 8.00
13 Matt Olson 2.50 6.00
14 Alex Verdugo 2.00 5.00
15 Adalberto Mondesi 2.00 5.00
16 Eloy Jimenez 5.00 12.00
17 Noah Syndergaard 2.00 5.00
18 Brendan Rodgers 2.50 6.00
19 Dansby Swanson 2.50 6.00
20 Corey Seager 3.00 8.00
21 Clayton Kershaw 4.00 10.00
22 Justin Verlander 2.50 6.00
23 Mookie Betts 6.00 15.00
24 Brandon Nimmo 2.00 5.00
25 David Bote 2.00 5.00
26 Ken Griffey Jr. 6.00 15.00
27 Kris Bryant 3.00 8.00
28 Austin Riley 3.00 8.00
29 Pete Alonso 5.00 12.00
30 Rickey Henderson 8.00 20.00
31 Jack Flaherty 2.50 6.00
32 Addison Russell 2.00 5.00
33 Brandon Lowe 2.00 5.00
34 Vladimir Guerrero Jr. 4.00 10.00
35 Joey Votto 2.50 6.00
36 Alex Bregman 4.00 10.00
37 Hunter Renfroe 1.50 4.00
38 Max Fried 2.50 6.00
39 Michael Chavis 2.00 5.00
40 Tony Gwynn 4.00 10.00
41 Joe Morgan 2.00 5.00
42 Brandon Woodruff 2.50 6.00
43 Walker Buehler 3.00 8.00
44 Kyle Schwarber 2.50 6.00
45 Joc Pederson 2.00 5.00
46 Hunter Dozier 1.50 4.00
47 Juan Soto 8.00 20.00

2020 Donruss Now Playing

RANDOM INSERTS IN PACKS
STATED PRINT RUN 999 SER.#'d SETS
*SILVER/349: .5X TO 1.2X BASIC
*DIAMOND: .5X TO 1.2X BASIC
*PINK: .6X TO 1.5X BASIC
*BLUE/249: .6X TO 1.5X BASIC
*RAPTURE: .6X TO 1.5X BASIC
*RED/149: .6X TO 1.5X BASIC
*VECTOR: .6X TO 1.5X BASIC
*GOLD/99: 1X TO 2.5X BASIC
*GREEN/25: 1.5X TO 4X BASIC
1 Vladimir Guerrero Jr. 1.00 2.50
2 Fernando Tatis Jr. 4.00 10.00
3 Pete Alonso 3.00 8.00
4 Yordan Alvarez 4.00 10.00
5 Bo Bichette 6.00 15.00
6 Eloy Jimenez 1.25 3.00
7 Jesus Luzardo .75 2.00
8 Aristides Aquino 4.00 10.00
9 Gavin Lux 2.00 5.00
10 Brendan McKay .60 1.50
11 Keston Hiura .75 2.00
12 Austin Riley .75 2.00

2020 Donruss Rated Prospects Blue

*BLUE/249: .6X TO 1.5X BASIC
RANDOM INSERTS IN PACKS
STATED PRINT RUN 249 SER.#'d SETS
2 Bobby Witt Jr. 8.00 20.00

2020 Donruss Rated Prospects Diamond

*DIAMOND: .5X TO 1.2X BASIC
RANDOM INSERTS IN PACKS
2 Bobby Witt Jr. 6.00 15.00

2020 Donruss Rated Prospects Gold

*GOLD/99: 1X TO 2.5X BASIC
RANDOM INSERTS IN PACKS
STATED PRINT RUN 99 SER.#'d SETS
2 Bobby Witt Jr. 15.00 40.00

2020 Donruss Rated Prospects Green

*GREEN/25: 1.5X TO 4X BASIC
RANDOM INSERTS IN PACKS
STATED PRINT RUN 25 SER.#'d SETS
2 Bobby Witt Jr. 25.00 60.00

2020 Donruss Rated Prospects Pink Fireworks

*PINK: .6X TO 1.5X BASIC
RANDOM INSERTS IN PACKS
2 Bobby Witt Jr. 8.00 20.00

2020 Donruss Rated Prospects Rapture

*RAPTURE: .6X TO 1.5X BASIC
RANDOM INSERTS IN PACKS
2 Bobby Witt Jr. 8.00 20.00

2020 Donruss Rated Prospects Red

*RED/149: .6X TO 1.5X BASIC
RANDOM INSERTS IN PACKS
STATED PRINT RUN 149 SER.#'d SETS
2 Bobby Witt Jr. 8.00 20.00

2020 Donruss Rated Prospects Silver

*SILVER: .5X TO 1.2X BASIC
RANDOM INSERTS IN PACKS
STATED PRINT RUN 349 SER.#'d SETS
2 Bobby Witt Jr. 6.00 15.00

2020 Donruss Rated Prospects Vector

*VECTOR: .6X TO 1.5X BASIC
RANDOM INSERTS IN PACKS
2 Bobby Witt Jr. 8.00 20.00

2020 Donruss Retro '86 Materials

RANDOM INSERTS IN PACKS
*GOLD/25: .6X TO 1.5X BASIC
1 Trey Mancini 2.50 6.00
2 Jung-Ho Kang 1.50 4.00
3 Josh Bell 2.00 5.00
4 Gary Sanchez 2.50 6.00
5 Freddie Freeman 3.00 8.00
6 Duke Snider 2.00 5.00
7 Vladimir Guerrero Jr. 4.00 10.00
8 Fernando Tatis Jr. 6.00 15.00
9 John Smoltz 2.50 6.00
10 Kyle Seager 1.50 4.00
11 Albert Pujols 4.00 10.00
12 Edgar Martinez 4.00 10.00
13 Luis Arraez 3.00 8.00
14 Jackie Bradley Jr. 2.50 6.00
15 Carlton Fisk 3.00 8.00
16 Aaron Judge 10.00 25.00
17 Cal Ripken 6.00 15.00
18 Mariano Rivera 5.00 12.00
19 Mike Piazza 2.50 6.00
20 Julio Teheran 2.00 5.00
21 Chipper Jones 4.00 10.00
22 Jacob deGrom 5.00 12.00
23 Alex Gordon 2.00 5.00
24 Javier Baez 3.00 8.00
25 Darryl Strawberry 1.50 4.00
26 Larry Walker 3.00 8.00
27 Mark McGwire 6.00 15.00
28 Luis Severino 2.00 5.00
29 Pete Rose 8.00 20.00
30 Barry Larkin 2.00 5.00
31 David Wright 3.00 8.00
32 Gerrit Cole 4.00 10.00
33 Jeff McNeil 2.00 5.00
34 David Ortiz 2.50 6.00
35 Shin-Soo Choo 2.00 5.00
36 Alex Rodriguez 3.00 8.00
37 Nomar Mazara 1.50 4.00
38 Frank Thomas 4.00 10.00
39 George Brett 5.00 12.00
40 Shohei Ohtani 5.00 12.00
41 Miguel Cabrera 2.50 6.00
42 Giancarlo Stanton 2.50 6.00
43 Don Mattingly 5.00 12.00
44 Ozzie Albies 4.00 10.00
45 Felix Hernandez 4.00 10.00
46 Greg Maddux 6.00 15.00
47 Gleyber Torres 6.00 15.00
48 Johnny Bench 2.50 6.00
49 Salvador Perez 2.50 6.00
50 Mike Soroka 2.50 6.00

2020 Donruss Retro '86 Signatures

RANDOM INSERTS IN PACKS
EXCHANGE DEADLINE 08/05/2021
*PINK/199: .4X TO 1X BASIC
*PINK/99-100: .5X TO 1.2X BASIC
*PINK/49-50: .6X TO 1.5X BASIC
*PINK/25: .75X TO 2X BASIC
*RED/99: .5X TO 1.2X BASIC
*RED/49: .6X TO 1.5X BASIC
*RED/25: .75X TO 2X BASIC
*GOLD/25: .75X TO 2X BASIC
1 Brusdar Graterol 4.00 10.00
2 Michael King 4.00 10.00
3 Deivy Grullon 2.50 6.00
4 Jonathan Hernandez 2.50 6.00
5 Isan Diaz 4.00 10.00
6 Lewis Thorpe 2.50 6.00
7 Aaron Civale 5.00 12.00
8 Willi Castro 4.00 10.00
9 Logan Webb 4.00 10.00
10 Sam Hilliard 4.00 10.00
11 Bobby Bradley 2.50 6.00
12 Jesus Luzardo 5.00 12.00
13 Zack Collins 3.00 8.00
14 Joe Palumbo 2.50 6.00
15 Anthony Kay 2.50 6.00
16 Travis Demeritte 4.00 10.00
17 Zac Gallen 6.00 15.00
18 Yu Chang 4.00 10.00
19 Sean Murphy 4.00 10.00
20 Yordan Alvarez 25.00 60.00
21 Justin Dunn 3.00 8.00
22 Dylan Cease 4.00 10.00
23 Mauricio Dubon 3.00 8.00
24 Jake Fraley 3.00 8.00
25 Logan Allen 2.50 6.00
26 Bo Bichette 25.00 60.00
27 Dustin May 8.00 20.00
28 Trent Grisham 10.00 25.00
29 Adrian Morejon 2.50 6.00
30 Aristides Aquino 6.00 15.00
31 Kyle Lewis 20.00 50.00
32 Patrick Sandoval 4.00 10.00
33 Sheldon Neuse 3.00 8.00
34 Brendan McKay 4.00 10.00
35 Gavin Lux 12.00 30.00
36 Randy Arozarena 20.00 50.00
37 Nick Solak 5.00 12.00
38 Brock Burke 2.50 6.00
39 Abraham Toro 3.00 8.00
40 Bryan Abreu 2.50 6.00
41 Nico Hoerner 10.00 25.00
42 Tony Gonsolin 10.00 25.00
43 Andres Munoz 4.00 10.00
44 Jake Rogers 2.50 6.00
45 A.J. Puk 4.00 10.00
46 Matt Thaiss 3.00 8.00
47 Adbert Alzolay 3.00 8.00
48 Domingo Leyba 3.00 8.00
49 Jordan Yamamoto 2.50 6.00
50 Edwin Rios 6.00 15.00
51 Ronald Bolanos 2.50 6.00
52 Tyrone Taylor 2.50 6.00
53 Jaylin Davis 4.00 10.00
54 Michel Baez 2.50 6.00
55 Danny Mendick 3.00 8.00
56 Donnie Walton 6.00 15.00
57 Tres Barrera 4.00 10.00
58 Josh Rojas 2.50 6.00
59 T.J. Zeuch 2.50 6.00
60 Rico Garcia 4.00 10.00
61 Yonathan Daza 3.00 8.00
62 Austin Dean 2.50 6.00
63 Luis Robert 50.00 120.00
64 Jalen Beeks 2.50 6.00
65 Jo Adell 20.00 50.00
66 Michael Shawaryn 2.50 6.00
67 Andrew Knizner 2.50 6.00
68 Ji-Man Choi 2.50 6.00
69 Taylor Hearn 2.50 6.00
70 Hanser Alberto 2.50 6.00
71 Genesis Cabrera 4.00 10.00
72 Anthony Santander 2.50 6.00
73 German Marquez 4.00 10.00
74 Bobby Dalbec 10.00 25.00
75 Royce Lewis 10.00 25.00
76 Taylor Clarke 2.50 6.00
78 Ryan Helsley 3.00 8.00
79 Shed Long Jr. 3.00 8.00
80 Darwinzon Hernandez 2.50 6.00
81 Oscar Mercado 4.00 10.00
82 Bryan Reynolds 10.00 25.00
83 Roger Clemens
84 Peter Lambert 2.50 6.00
85 Griffin Canning 4.00 10.00
87 Nicky Lopez 2.50 6.00
88 Yu Darvish 10.00 25.00
89 Alec Bohm 30.00 80.00
90 J.D. Davis 5.00 12.00
91 Forrest Whitley 4.00 10.00
92 Cole Tucker 4.00 10.00
93 Hunter Dozier 2.50 6.00
94 Eric Hosmer 3.00 8.00
95 Roberto Alomar 10.00 25.00
96 Omar Vizquel 3.00 8.00
97 Trey Mancini 4.00 10.00
98 Kyle Schwarber 10.00 25.00
99 Jack Flaherty 10.00 25.00
100 Sixto Sanchez 20.00 50.00

2020 Donruss Retro '86 Signatures Gold

*GOLD/25: .75X TO 2X BASIC
RANDOM INSERTS IN PACKS
PRINT RUNS B/WN 4-25 COPIES PER
NO PRICING ON QTY 15 OR LESS
EXCHANGE DEADLINE 08/05/2021
63 Luis Robert/25 125.00 300.00
89 Alec Bohm/25 75.00 200.00

2020 Donruss Retro '86 Signatures Pink Fireworks

*PINK/199: .4X TO 1X BASIC
*PINK/99-100: .5X TO 1.2X BASIC
*PINK/49-50: .6X TO 1.5X BASIC
*PINK/25: .75X TO 2X BASIC
RANDOM INSERTS IN PACKS
PRINT RUNS B/WN 25-199 COPIES PER
EXCHANGE DEADLINE 08/05/2021
89 Alec Bohm/100 50.00 120.00

2020 Donruss Retro '86 Signatures Red

*RED/99: .5X TO 1.2X BASIC
*RED/49: .6X TO 1.5X BASIC
*RED/25: .75X TO 2X BASIC
RANDOM INSERTS IN PACKS
PRINT RUNS B/WN 10-99 COPIES PER
NO PRICING ON QTY 15 OR LESS
EXCHANGE DEADLINE 08/05/2021
88 Yu Darvish/25 25.00 60.00
89 Alec Bohm/99 50.00 120.00

2020 Donruss Signature Series Blue

*BLUE/99: .5X TO 1.2X BASIC
*BLUE/49: .6X TO 1.5X BASIC
RANDOM INSERTS IN PACKS
PRINT RUNS B/WN 49-99 COPIES PER
EXCHANGE DEADLINE 08/05/2021

2020 Donruss Signature Series Gold

*GOLD/25: .75X TO 2X BASIC
RANDOM INSERTS IN PACKS
STATED PRINT RUN 25 SER.#'d SETS
EXCHANGE DEADLINE 08/05/2021

2020 Donruss Sky High Signatures

RANDOM INSERTS IN PACKS
EXCHANGE DEADLINE 08/05/2021
*BLUE/99: .5X TO 1.2X BASIC
*BLUE/50: .6X TO 1.5X BASIC
*BLUE/25: .75X TO 2X BASIC
*GOLD/25: .75X TO 2X BASIC
SHSSO Shohei Ohtani 60.00 150.00
2 Ronald Acuna Jr. 40.00 100.00
3 J.P. Crawford 2.50 6.00
4 Paul DeJong 8.00 20.00
5 Cal Quantrill 2.50 6.00
6 David Dahl 5.00 12.00
7 Mitch Haniger 3.00 8.00
8 Charlie Blackmon 4.00 10.00
9 Michael Chavis 6.00 15.00
10 Bryan Reynolds 10.00 25.00

2020 Donruss The Rookies Green

*GREEN/25: 1.5X TO 4X BASIC
RANDOM INSERTS IN PACKS
STATED PRINT RUN 25 SER.#'d SETS
6 Bo Bichette 20.00 50.00
8 Gavin Lux 15.00 40.00

2020 Donruss Whammy

RANDOM INSERTS IN PACKS
1 Pete Alonso 20.00 50.00
2 Yordan Alvarez 25.00 60.00
3 Fernando Tatis Jr. 40.00 100.00
4 Alex Bregman 8.00 20.00
5 Albert Pujols 10.00 25.00

2021 Donruss

1 Brandon Lowe DK .50 1.25
2 Aaron Judge DK 1.50 4.00
3 Vladimir Guerrero Jr. DK 1.00 2.50
4 Anthony Santander DK .40 1.00
5 Rafael Devers DK .75 2.00
6 Nelson Cruz DK .60 1.50
7 Tim Anderson DK .60 1.50
8 Jose Ramirez DK .50 1.25
9 Whit Merrifield DK .60 1.50
10 Miguel Cabrera DK .60 1.50
11 Matt Chapman DK .60 1.50
12 Carlos Correa DK .60 1.50
13 Kyle Lewis DK 1.50 4.00
14 Mike Trout DK 3.00 8.00
15 Joey Gallo DK .60 1.50
16 Ronald Acuna Jr. DK 2.50 6.00
17 Starling Marte DK .50 1.25
18 Bryce Harper DK 1.00 2.50
19 Pete Alonso DK 1.50 4.00
20 Juan Soto DK 2.00 5.00
21 Anthony Rizzo DK .75 2.00
22 Jack Flaherty DK .60 1.50
23 Trevor Bauer DK .75 2.00
24 Christian Yelich DK .75 2.00
25 Josh Bell DK .50 1.25
26 Cody Bellinger DK 1.25 3.00
27 Fernando Tatis Jr. DK 3.00 8.00
28 Mike Yastrzemski DK 1.00 2.50
29 Nolan Arenado DK 1.00 2.50
30 Ketel Marte DK .50 1.25
31 Cristian Pache RR RC 4.00 10.00
32 Brailyn Marquez RR RC 1.00 2.50
33 Jo Adell RR RC 2.50 6.00
34 Sixto Sanchez RR RC 2.00 5.00
35 Alec Bohm RR RC 4.00 10.00
36 Joey Bart RR RC 2.50 6.00
37 Dylan Carlson RR RC 3.00 8.00
38 Nate Pearson RR RC 1.25 3.00
39 Casey Mize RR RC 3.00 8.00
40 Alex Kirilloff RR RC 1.50 4.00
41 Clarke Schmidt RR RC .60 1.50
42 Cristian Javier RR RC .75 2.00
43 Ke'Bryan Hayes RR RC 4.00 10.00
44 Sam Huff RR RC .75 2.00
45 Luis V. Garcia RR RC 2.00 5.00
46 Daulton Varsho RR RC 1.00 2.50
47 Ian Anderson RR RC 2.50 6.00
48 Bobby Dalbec RR RC 3.00 8.00
49 Nick Madrigal RR RC 3.00 8.00
50 Triston McKenzie RR RC 1.25 3.00
51 Brady Singer RR RC 2.00 5.00
52 Keibert Ruiz RR RC 1.25 3.00
53 Andres Gimenez RR RC 1.00 2.50
54 Deivi Garcia RR RC 3.00 8.00
55 Luis Patino RR RC 1.50 4.00
56 Leody Taveras RR RC 1.25 3.00
57 Tyler Stephenson RR RC 2.00 5.00
58 Jazz Chisholm RR RC 1.50 4.00
59 Ryan Mountcastle RR RC 4.00 10.00
60 Evan White RR RC 2.50 6.00
61 David Peterson RR RC .75 2.00
62 Jake Cronenworth RR RC 2.50 6.00
63 Corey Kluber .25 .60
64 Marcell Ozuna .30 .75
65 J.P. Crawford .20 .50
66 Dansby Swanson .30 .75
67 Mike Yastrzemski .50 1.25
68 Donovan Solano .30 .75
69 Joey Votto .25 .60
70 Albert Pujols .40 1.00
71 Fernando Tatis Jr. 1.50 4.00
72 Noah Syndergaard .25 .60
73 Alex Verdugo .25 .60
74 Sonny Gray .25 .60
75 Bryan Reynolds .25 .60
76 Carlos Correa .30 .75
77 Trevor Story .30 .75
78 Liam Hendriks .20 .50
79 Josh Donaldson .25 .60
80 Cavan Biggio .40 1.00
81 Justin Turner .30 .75
82 Keston Hiura .40 1.00
83 Kolten Wong .25 .60
84 Yu Darvish .30 .75
85 Whit Merrifield .30 .75
86 Isiah Kiner-Falefa .25 .60
87 Kyle Hendricks .30 .75
88 Gleyber Torres .60 1.50
89 Kevin Gausman .30 .75
90 Lucas Giolito .25 .60
91 Carlos Carrasco .20 .50
92 Jeimer Candelario .20 .50
93 Trea Turner .25 .60
94 Wilmer Flores .25 .60
95 Kyle Lewis .75 2.00
96 Freddie Freeman .40 1.00
97 Martin Perez .20 .50
98 Giancarlo Stanton .30 .75
99 Trent Grisham .40 1.00
100 Didi Gregorius .25 .60
101 Walker Buehler .40 1.00
102 Mike Soroka .30 .75
103 Charlie Blackmon .30 .75
104 Aaron Nola .25 .60
105 Clayton Kershaw .50 1.25
106 Jose Abreu .30 .75
107 Anthony Rendon .30 .75
108 Tyler Glasnow .30 .75
109 Corey Seager .30 .75
110 Kwang-Hyun Kim .25 .60
111 Chris Bassitt .20 .50
112 Rhys Hoskins .40 1.00
113 Ketel Marte .25 .60
114 Cody Bellinger .60 1.50
115 Zack Wheeler .25 .60
116 Brian Anderson .20 .50
117 Nick Ahmed .20 .50
118 Austin Meadows .30 .75
119 Kole Calhoun .20 .50
120 Nelson Cruz .30 .75
121 Framber Valdez .20 .50
122 Matt Olson .30 .75
123 Kyle Tucker .30 .75
124 Luis Castillo .25 .60
125 Randy Arozarena .75 2.00
126 Corbin Burnes .30 .75
127 DJ LeMahieu .30 .75
128 Xander Bogaerts .30 .75
129 John Means .30 .75
130 Javier Baez .40 1.00
131 Jose Ramirez .25 .60
132 Josh Bell .25 .60
133 Zac Gallen .25 .60
134 Josh Hader .25 .60
135 Ramon Laureano .25 .60
136 Byron Buxton .30 .75
137 Adam Wainwright .25 .60
138 Brad Hand .20 .50
139 Francisco Lindor .30 .75
140 Ian Happ .25 .60
141 Rafael Devers .40 1.00
142 Manny Machado .30 .75
143 Luis Robert 1.00 2.50
144 Pablo Lopez .20 .50
145 Salvador Perez .25 .60
146 Nolan Arenado .50 1.25
147 Marco Gonzales .20 .50
148 Eloy Jimenez .60 1.50
149 Sandy Alcantara .25 .60
150 Jacob deGrom .60 1.50
151 Michael Conforto .25 .60
152 J.T. Realmuto .30 .75
153 Jack Flaherty .30 .75
154 Starling Marte .25 .60
155 Brandon Lowe .25 .60
156 Brandon Belt .25 .60
157 Jeff McNeil .25 .60
158 Dustin May .30 .75
159 George Springer .25 .60
160 Patrick Corbin .25 .60
161 Kris Bryant .40 1.00
162 Blake Snell .25 .60
163 Anthony Rizzo .40 1.00
164 Jose Berrios .25 .60
165 Bo Bichette .75 2.00
166 Miguel Cabrera .30 .75
167 Hyun-Jin Ryu .25 .60
168 Matt Chapman .30 .75
169 Johnny Cueto .25 .60
170 Mike Trout 1.50 4.00
171 Renato Nunez .25 .60
172 Yadier Molina .40 1.00
173 Bryce Harper .50 1.25
174 Yordan Alvarez .75 2.00
175 Max Fried .30 .75
176 Kenta Maeda .25 .60
177 Mookie Betts .60 1.50
178 Tim Anderson .30 .75
179 Vladimir Guerrero Jr. .50 1.25
180 David Fletcher .30 .75
181 Pete Alonso .75 2.00
182 Aaron Judge .75 2.00
183 Shane Bieber .30 .75
184 Jesus Luzardo .30 .75
185 Brad Keller .20 .50
186 Mike Clevinger .25 .60
187 Dallas Keuchel .25 .60
188 Brandon Woodruff .30 .75

189 Joey Gallo .30 .75
190 Adalberto Mondesi .25 .60
191 Luke Voit .40 1.00
192 Ronald Acuna Jr. 1.25 3.00
193 Wil Myers .25 .60
194 Eugenio Suarez .25 .60
195 Juan Soto 1.00 2.50
196 Nicholas Castellanos .30 .75
197 Dominic Smith .20 .50
198 Lance Lynn .20 .50
199 Shohei Ohtani .50 1.25
200 Christian Yelich .40 1.00
201 Paul Goldschmidt .30 .75
202 Jose Altuve .25 .60
203 German Marquez .30 .75
204 Trevor Bauer .40 1.00
205 Dylan Bundy .25 .60
206 Max Scherzer .30 .75
207 Chris Paddack .30 .75
208 Antonio Senzatela .20 .50
209 Anthony Santander .20 .50
210 Miguel Rojas .20 .50
211 Dinelson Lamet .20 .50
212 Gerrit Cole .50 1.25
213 Bo Jackson RETRO .30 .75
214 Rafael Palmeiro RETRO .25 .60
215 Barry Larkin RETRO .25 .60
216 Jim Thome RETRO .25 .60
217 Vladimir Guerrero RETRO .25 .60
218 Randy Johnson RETRO .30 .75
219 Gary Carter RETRO .25 .60
220 Frank Thomas RETRO .30 .75
221 George Brett RETRO .60 1.50
222 Jeff Bagwell RETRO .25 .60
223 Lance Berkman RETRO .25 .60
224 Orel Hershiser RETRO .20 .50
225 Nolan Ryan RETRO 1.00 2.50
226 Dwight Gooden RETRO .20 .50
227 Larry Walker RETRO .25 .60
228 Babe Ruth RETRO .75 2.00
229 Craig Biggio RETRO .25 .60
230 Fergie Jenkins RETRO .25 .60
231 Ozzie Smith RETRO .40 1.00
232 Mike Piazza RETRO .30 .75
233 Reggie Jackson RETRO .25 .60
234 Cal Ripken RETRO 1.00 2.50
235 Ken Griffey Jr. RETRO .60 1.50
236 Roger Clemens RETRO .40 1.00
237 Pedro Martinez RETRO .25 .60
238 Wade Boggs RETRO .25 .60
239 Sammy Sosa RETRO .30 .75
240 Bartolo Colon RETRO .20 .50
241 Jason Giambi RETRO .20 .50
242 Troy Glaus RETRO .30 .75
243 Jonathan Papelbon RETRO .25 .60
244 Ichiro RETRO .40 1.00
245 Ryne Sandberg RETRO .60 1.50
246 Miguel Tejada RETRO .20 .50
247 Rickey Henderson RETRO .30 .75
248 Andy Pettitte RETRO .25 .60
249 Paul Konerko RETRO .25 .60
250 Rod Carew RETRO .25 .60
251 Steve Garvey RETRO .20 .50
252 David Ortiz RETRO .30 .75
253 Alex Rodriguez RETRO .40 1.00
254 John Smoltz RETRO .30 .75
255 Dale Murphy RETRO .30 .75
256 Keith Hernandez RETRO .20 .50
257 Paul Molitor RETRO .30 .75
258 Andre Dawson RETRO .25 .60
259 Jose Canseco RETRO .25 .60
260 Mariano Rivera RETRO .40 1.00
261 Greg Maddux RETRO .40 1.00
262 Mark McGwire RETRO .50 1.25
263 Ted Giannoulas .20 .50
264 Domingo Ayala 8.00 20.00

2021 Donruss Career Stat Line
*CAR DK p/r 151-500: .75X TO 2X BASIC
*CAR RR p/r 151-500: .75X TO 2X BASIC
*CAR VET p/r 151-500: 1.5X TO 4X BASIC
*CAR DK p/r 101-150: 1X TO 2.5X BASIC
*CAR RR p/r 101-150: 1X TO 2.5X BASIC
*CAR VET p/r 101-150: 2X TO 5X BASIC
*CAR DK p/r 29-100: 1.2X TO 3X BASIC
*CAR RR p/r 29-100: 1.2X TO 3X BASIC
*CAR VET p/r 29-100: 2.5X TO 6X BASIC
*CAR DK p/r 16-25: 2X TO 5X BASIC
*CAR RR p/r 16-25: 2X TO 5X BASIC
*CAR VET p/r 16-25: 4X TO 10X BASIC
RANDOM INSERTS IN PACKS
PRINT RUNS B/WN 3-500 COPIES PER
NO PRICING ON QTY 15 OR LESS
35 Alec Bohm RR/338 15.00 40.00
37 Dylan Carlson RR/16 40.00 100.00

2021 Donruss Holo Blue
*HOLO BLUE DK: .5X TO 1.2X BASIC DK
*HOLO BLUE RR: .5X TO 1.2X BASIC RR
*HOLO BLUE VET: 1X TO 2.5X BASIC VET
RANDOM INSERTS IN HOBBY PACKS
35 Alec Bohm RR 8.00 20.00

2021 Donruss Holo Orange
*HOLO ORNG DK: .5X TO 1.2X BASIC DK
*HOLO ORNG RR: .5X TO 1.2X BASIC RR
*HOLO ORNG VET: 1X TO 2.5X BASIC VET
RANDOM INSERTS IN HANGER PACKS
35 Alec Bohm RR 8.00 20.00

2021 Donruss Holo Pink
*HOLO PINK DK: .5X TO 1.2X BASIC DK
*HOLO PINK RR: .5X TO 1.2X BASIC RR
*HOLO PINK VET: 1X TO 2.5X BASIC VET
RANDOM INSERTS IN MEGA PACKS
35 Alec Bohm RR 8.00 20.00

2021 Donruss Holo Purple
*HOLO PRPL DK: .5X TO 1.2X BASIC DK
*HOLO PRPL RR: .5X TO 1.2X BASIC RR
*HOLO PRPL VET: 1X TO 2.5X BASIC VET
RANDOM INSERTS IN BLASTER PACKS
35 Alec Bohm RR 8.00 20.00

2021 Donruss Holo Red
*HOLO RED DK: .5X TO 1.2X BASIC DK
*HOLO RED RR: .5X TO 1.2X BASIC RR
*HOLO RED VET: 1X TO 2.5X BASIC VET
RANDOM INSERTS IN FAT PACKS
35 Alec Bohm RR 8.00 20.00

2021 Donruss Independence Day
*INDPNDCE DAY DK: .5X TO 1.2X BASIC DK
*INDPNDCE DAY RR: .5X TO 1.2X BASIC RR
*INDPNDCE DAY VET: 1X TO 2.5X BASIC VET
RANDOM INSERTS IN PACKS
35 Alec Bohm RR 8.00 20.00

2021 Donruss Liberty
*LIBERTY DK: .5X TO 1.2X BASIC DK
*LIBERTY RR: .5X TO 1.2X BASIC RR
*LIBERTY VET: 1X TO 2.5X BASIC VET
RANDOM INSERTS IN PACKS
35 Alec Bohm RR 8.00 20.00

2021 Donruss Mask Emoji
*EMOJI DK: 2X TO 5X BASIC
*EMOJI RR: 2X TO 5X BASIC
*EMOJI VET: 4X TO 10X BASIC
RANDOM INSERTS IN PACKS
STATED PRINT RUN 19 SER.#'d SETS
14 Mike Trout DK 20.00 50.00
27 Fernando Tatis Jr. DK 15.00 40.00
35 Alec Bohm RR 60.00 150.00
36 Joey Bart RR 25.00 60.00
37 Dylan Carlson RR 40.00 100.00
40 Alex Kirilloff RR 25.00 60.00

2021 Donruss On Fire
*FIRE DK: 1.2X TO 3X BASIC
*FIRE RR: 1.2X TO 3X BASIC
*FIRE VET: 2.5X TO 6X BASIC
RANDOM INSERTS IN PACKS
STATED PRINT RUN 75 SER.#'d SETS
14 Mike Trout DK 12.00 30.00
35 Alec Bohm RR 40.00 100.00
36 Joey Bart RR 15.00 40.00
37 Dylan Carlson RR 25.00 60.00
40 Alex Kirilloff RR 15.00 40.00

2021 Donruss One Hundred
*100 DK: 1.2X TO 3X BASIC
*100 RR: 1.2X TO 3X BASIC
*100 VET: 2.5X TO 6X BASIC
RANDOM INSERTS IN PACKS
STATED PRINT RUN 100 SER.#'d SETS
14 Mike Trout DK 12.00 30.00
27 Fernando Tatis Jr. DK 15.00 40.00
35 Alec Bohm RR 40.00 100.00
36 Joey Bart RR 15.00 40.00
37 Dylan Carlson RR 25.00 60.00
40 Alex Kirilloff RR 15.00 40.00

2021 Donruss Presidential Collection
*PRES.DK: 1.2X TO 3X BASIC
*PRES.RR: 1.2X TO 3X BASIC
*PRES.VET: 2.5X TO 6X BASIC
RANDOM INSERTS IN PACKS
STATED PRINT RUN 50 SER.#'d SETS
14 Mike Trout DK 12.00 30.00
27 Fernando Tatis Jr. DK 15.00 40.00
35 Alec Bohm RR 40.00 100.00
36 Joey Bart RR 15.00 40.00
37 Dylan Carlson RR 25.00 60.00
40 Alex Kirilloff RR 15.00 40.00

2021 Donruss Red
*RED DK: .6X TO 1.5X BASIC DK
*RED RR: .6X TO 1.5X BASIC DK
*RED VET: 1.2X TO 3X BASIC VET
RANDOM INSERTS IN PACKS
STATED PRINT RUN 2021 SER.#'d SETS
35 Alec Bohm RR 12.00 30.00

2021 Donruss Season Stat Line
*SEA DK p/r 151-400: .75X TO 2X BASIC
*SEA RR p/r 151-400: .75X TO 2X BASIC
*SEA VET p/r 151-400: 1.5X TO 4X BASIC
*SEA DK p/r 101-150: 1X TO 2.5X BASIC
*SEA RR p/r 101-150: 1X TO 2.5X BASIC
*SEA VET p/r 101-150: 2X TO 5X BASIC
*SEA DK p/r 26-100: 1.2X TO 3X BASIC
*SEA RR p/r 26-100: 1.2X TO 3X BASIC
*SEA VET p/r 26-100: 2.5X TO 6X BASIC
*SEA DK p/r 16-25: 2X TO 5X BASIC
*SEA RR p/r 16-25: 2X TO 5X BASIC
*SEA VET p/r 16-25: 4X TO 10X BASIC
RANDOM INSERTS IN PACKS
PRINT RUNS B/WN 1-400 COPIES PER
NO PRICING ON QTY 15 OR LESS
14 Mike Trout DK/56 12.00 30.00
27 Fernando Tatis Jr. DK/17 25.00 60.00
35 Alec Bohm RR/23 60.00 150.00

2021 Donruss Variations Career Stat Line
*VAR.CAR p/r 151-500: 1.5X TO 4X BASIC
*VAR.CAR p/r 101-150: 2X TO 5X BASIC
*VAR.CAR p/r 26-100: 2.5X TO 6X BASIC
*VAR.CAR p/r 16-25: 4X TO 10X BASIC
RANDOM INSERTS IN PACKS
PRINT RUNS B/WN 11-500 COPIES PER
NO PRICING ON QTY 15 OR LESS
143 Luis Robert/88 20.00 50.00

2021 Donruss Variations Mask Emoji
*VAR.EMOJI: 4X TO 10X BASIC
RANDOM INSERTS IN PACKS
STATED PRINT RUN 19 SER.#'d SETS
71 Fernando Tatis Jr. 25.00 60.00
143 Luis Robert 30.00 80.00
170 Mike Trout 20.00 50.00

2021 Donruss Variations On Fire
*VAR.FIRE: 2.5X TO 6X BASIC
RANDOM INSERTS IN PACKS
STATED PRINT RUN 75 SER.#'d SETS
71 Fernando Tatis Jr. 15.00 40.00
143 Luis Robert 20.00 50.00
170 Mike Trout 12.00 30.00

2021 Donruss Variations One Hundred
*VAR.100: 2.5X TO 6X BASIC
RANDOM INSERTS IN PACKS
STATED PRINT RUN 100 SER.#'d SETS
71 Fernando Tatis Jr. 15.00 40.00
143 Luis Robert 20.00 50.00
170 Mike Trout 12.00 30.00

2021 Donruss Variations Presidential Collection
*VAR.PRES.: 2.5X TO 6X BASIC
RANDOM INSERTS IN PACKS
STATED PRINT RUN 50 SER.#'d SETS
71 Fernando Tatis Jr. 15.00 40.00
143 Luis Robert 20.00 50.00
170 Mike Trout 12.00 30.00

2021 Donruss Variations Season Stat Line
*VAR.SEA p/r 151-400: 1.5X TO 4X BASIC
*VAR.SEA p/r 101-150: 2X TO 5X BASIC
*VAR.SEA p/r 26-100: 2.5X TO 6X BASIC
*VAR.SEA p/r 16-25: 4X TO 10X BASIC
RANDOM INSERTS IN PACKS
PRINT RUNS B/WN 10-400 COPIES PER
NO PRICING ON QTY 15 OR LESS
143 Luis Robert/33 20.00 50.00

2021 Donruss Classics Autographs
RANDOM INSERTS IN PACKS
EXCHANGE DEADLINE 9/3/2022
*BLUE/99: .5X TO 1.2X BASIC
*BLUE/25: .75X TO 2X BASIC
1 Dwight Gooden 10.00 25.00
2 Wade Boggs 20.00 50.00
3 Mike Piazza 50.00 120.00
4 Joe Maddon 40.00 100.00
5 Sammy Sosa 40.00 100.00
6 Bartolo Colon 5.00 12.00
7 Tony Oliva 10.00 25.00
8 Mike Schmidt 40.00 100.00
9 Don Sutton 12.00 30.00
10 Ozzie Smith 30.00 80.00

2021 Donruss Classified Signatures
RANDOM INSERTS IN PACKS
EXCHANGE DEADLINE 9/3/2022
*BLUE/99: .5X TO 1.2X BASIC
*BLUE/25: .75X TO 2X BASIC
*GOLD/25: .75X TO 2X BASIC
1 Renato Nunez 3.00 8.00
2 Ronald Acuna Jr. EXCH 50.00 120.00
3 Kyle Tucker 10.00 25.00
4 Cesar Hernandez 2.50 6.00
5 Michael Brantley 10.00 25.00
6 David Fletcher 4.00 10.00
7 Wilmer Flores 3.00 8.00
8 Vladimir Guerrero Jr. 20.00 50.00
9 Zach Davies 2.50 6.00
10 Dylan Bundy 5.00 12.00

2021 Donruss Dominators
RANDOM INSERTS IN PACKS
STATED PRINT RUN 999 SER.#'d SETS
*DIAMOND: .5X TO 1.2X BASIC
*PINK FWKS: .5X TO 1.2X BASIC
*RAPTURE: .5X TO 1.2X BASIC
*VECTOR: .5X TO 1.2X BASIC
*SILVER/349: .5X TO 1.2X BASIC
*BLUE/249: .6X TO 1.5X BASIC
*RED/149: .6X TO 1.5X BASIC
*GOLD/99: 1X TO 2.5X BASIC
*GREEN/25: 1.5X TO 4X BASIC
1 Yu Darvish .60 1.50
2 Jacob deGrom 1.25 3.00
3 Babe Ruth 6.00 15.00
4 Randy Arozarena 1.50 4.00
5 Carlos Correa .60 1.50
6 Manny Machado .60 1.50
7 Jose Ramirez .50 1.25
8 Charlie Blackmon .60 1.50
9 Lourdes Gurriel .50 1.25
10 Dallas Keuchel .50 1.25
11 Dominic Smith .40 1.00
12 Corey Seager .60 1.50
13 Xander Bogaerts .60 1.50

2021 Donruss Domingo Ayala Materials
RANDOM INSERTS IN PACKS
1 Domingo Ayala 8.00 20.00

2021 Donruss Elite Series
RANDOM INSERTS IN PACKS
STATED PRINT RUN 999 SER.#'d SETS
*DIAMOND: .5X TO 1.2X BASIC
*PINK FWKS: .5X TO 1.2X BASIC
*RAPTURE: .5X TO 1.2X BASIC
*VECTOR: .5X TO 1.2X BASIC
*SILVER/349: .5X TO 1.2X BASIC
*BLUE/249: .6X TO 1.5X BASIC
*RED/149: .6X TO 1.5X BASIC
*GOLD/99: 1.2X TO 3X BASIC
1 Juan Soto 3.00 8.00
2 Mike Trout 6.00 15.00
3 Babe Ruth 2.50 6.00
4 Ronald Acuna Jr. 4.00 10.00
5 Trevor Bauer 1.25 3.00
6 Zac Gallen .75 2.00
7 Luke Voit 1.25 3.00
8 Trea Turner .75 2.00
9 Trevor Story 1.00 2.50
10 Freddie Freeman 2.50 6.00
11 Gerrit Cole 1.50 4.00
12 Yadier Molina 3.00 8.00
13 Adalberto Mondesi .75 2.00

2021 Donruss Elite Series Green
*GREEN/25: 2X TO 5X BASIC
RANDOM INSERTS IN PACKS
STATED PRINT RUN 25 SER.#'d SETS
1 Juan Soto 25.00 60.00
2 Mike Trout 40.00 100.00
3 Babe Ruth 20.00 50.00

2021 Donruss Highlights
RANDOM INSERTS IN PACKS
STATED PRINT RUN 999 SER.#'d SETS
*DIAMOND: .5X TO 1.2X BASIC
*PINK FWKS: .5X TO 1.2X BASIC
*RAPTURE: .5X TO 1.2X BASIC
*VECTOR: .5X TO 1.2X BASIC
*SILVER/349: .5X TO 1.2X BASIC
*BLUE/249: .6X TO 1.5X BASIC
*RED/149: .6X TO 1.5X BASIC
1 Mookie Betts 2.50 6.00
2 Jose Abreu .60 1.50
3 Juan Soto 2.00 5.00
4 Lucas Giolito .50 1.25
5 DJ LeMahieu .60 1.50
6 Alex Kirilloff 1.50 4.00
7 Tim Anderson .60 1.50
8 Ronald Acuna Jr. 2.50 6.00
9 Will Smith .60 1.50
10 Josh Hader .50 1.25
11 Clayton Kershaw 1.00 2.50
12 Shane Bieber .60 1.50

2021 Donruss Highlights Gold
*GOLD/99: 1X TO 2.5X BASIC
RANDOM INSERTS IN PACKS
STATED PRINT RUN 99 SER.#'d SETS
3 Juan Soto 8.00 20.00
8 Ronald Acuna Jr. 8.00 20.00

2021 Donruss Highlights Green
*GREEN/25: 1.5X TO 4X BASIC
RANDOM INSERTS IN PACKS
STATED PRINT RUN 25 SER.#'d SETS
3 Juan Soto 12.00 30.00
8 Ronald Acuna Jr. 20.00 50.00

2021 Donruss Livestream
RANDOM INSERTS IN PACKS
STATED PRINT RUN 999 SER.#'d SETS
*DIAMOND: .5X TO 1.2X BASIC
*PINK FWKS: .5X TO 1.2X BASIC
*RAPTURE: .5X TO 1.2X BASIC
*VECTOR: .5X TO 1.2X BASIC
*SILVER/349: .5X TO 1.2X BASIC
*BLUE/249: .6X TO 1.5X BASIC
*RED/149: .6X TO 1.5X BASIC
*GOLD/99: 1X TO 2.5X BASIC
*GREEN/25: 1.5X TO 4X BASIC
1 Mike Trout 6.00 15.00
2 Luis Robert 5.00 12.00
3 Aaron Judge 1.50 4.00
4 Fernando Tatis Jr. 6.00 15.00
5 Ronald Acuna Jr. 2.50 6.00
6 Mookie Betts 1.25 3.00

2021 Donruss Rated Prospects
RANDOM INSERTS IN PACKS
STATED PRINT RUN 999 SER.#'d SETS
*DIAMOND: .5X TO 1.2X BASIC
*PINK FWKS: .5X TO 1.2X BASIC
*RAPTURE: .5X TO 1.2X BASIC
*VECTOR: .5X TO 1.2X BASIC
*SILVER/349: .5X TO 1.2X BASIC
*BLUE/249: .6X TO 1.5X BASIC
*RED/149: .6X TO 1.5X BASIC
*GOLD/99: 1X TO 2.5X BASIC
*GREEN/25: 1.5X TO 4X BASIC
1 Wander Franco 20.00 50.00
2 Yoelqui Cespedes 1.00 2.50
3 Yiddi Cappe .60 1.50
4 MacKenzie Gore .75 2.00
5 Riley Greene 1.50 4.00
6 Nick Gonzales 1.25 3.00
7 Max Meyer 1.00 2.50
8 Kristian Robinson 1.25 3.00
9 CJ Abrams 1.25 3.00
10 Zac Veen 1.25 3.00

2021 Donruss Retro '87 Materials
RANDOM INSERTS IN PACKS
1 Babe Ruth
2 Gavin Lux 5.00 12.00
3 Shohei Ohtani 5.00 12.00
4 Cristian Pache
5 Aroldis Chapman 2.50 6.00
6 Sammy Sosa 4.00 10.00
7 Cavan Biggio 3.00 8.00
8 Jo Adell 4.00 10.00
9 Leody Taveras 5.00 12.00
10 Felix Hernandez 2.00 5.00
11 Fernando Tatis Jr. 4.00 10.00
12 Aaron Judge 6.00 15.00
13 Vladimir Guerrero Jr. 4.00 10.00
14 Luis Robert 6.00 15.00
15 Nico Hoerner 4.00 10.00
16 Brendan McKay 2.00 5.00
17 Bo Jackson 2.50 6.00
18 Greg Maddux 6.00 15.00
19 Barry Larkin 2.00 5.00
20 Rafael Palmeiro 2.00 5.00
21 Mark McGwire 4.00 10.00
22 Mike Schmidt 4.00 10.00
23 Walker Buehler 3.00 8.00
24 Mookie Betts 5.00 12.00
25 Juan Soto 4.00 10.00
26 Jose Abreu 5.00 12.00
27 Mike Trout 10.00 25.00
28 Nelson Cruz 2.50 6.00
29 Teoscar Hernandez 2.50 6.00
30 Manny Machado 2.50 6.00
31 Corey Seager 2.50 6.00
32 Freddie Freeman 3.00 8.00
33 Tim Anderson 2.50 6.00
34 Jose Ramirez 2.00 5.00
35 Dansby Swanson 2.50 6.00
36 Bryce Harper 8.00 20.00
37 Brandon Lowe 2.00 5.00
38 Clayton Kershaw 4.00 10.00
39 Gleyber Torres 5.00 12.00
40 Yu Darvish 2.50 6.00
41 Gerrit Cole 4.00 10.00
42 Max Fried 2.50 6.00
43 Carlos Correa 2.50 6.00
44 Ramon Laureano 2.00 5.00
45 Sixto Sanchez 8.00 20.00
46 Yandy Diaz 2.00 5.00
47 Gio Urshela 2.50 6.00
48 Wil Myers 2.00 5.00
49 Tyler Glasnow 2.50 6.00
50 Dinelson Lamet 1.50 4.00
51 Josh Hader 2.00 5.00
52 Kenta Maeda 2.00 5.00
53 Rafael Devers 3.00 8.00
54 Jack Flaherty 2.50 6.00
55 Yoan Moncada 2.50 6.00
56 Mike Soroka 2.50 6.00
57 Yordan Alvarez 4.00 10.00
58 Eloy Jimenez 5.00 12.00
59 Austin Meadows 2.50 6.00
60 Bo Bichette 6.00 15.00
61 Chris Paddack 2.50 6.00
62 Keston Hiura 3.00 8.00
63 Victor Robles 3.00 8.00
64 Amed Rosario 2.00 5.00
65 Jordan Hicks 2.00 5.00
66 Nate Pearson 8.00 20.00
67 Casey Mize 4.00 10.00
68 Joey Bart 3.00 8.00
69 Alec Bohm
70 Nick Senzel 2.50 6.00
71 Kyle Tucker 2.50 6.00
72 Dustin May 2.50 6.00
73 Nomar Mazara 1.50 4.00
74 Christian Yelich 3.00 8.00
75 Paul Goldschmidt 2.50 6.00
76 Max Scherzer 2.50 6.00
77 Michael Conforto 2.00 5.00
78 Andre Dawson 2.00 5.00
79 Kirby Puckett 12.00 30.00
80 Roger Clemens 3.00 8.00
81 Ryne Sandberg 5.00 12.00
82 Ozzie Smith 3.00 8.00
83 Tony Gwynn
84 Keith Hernandez 1.50 4.00
85 Wade Boggs 8.00 20.00
86 Nolan Ryan 8.00 20.00
87 Don Mattingly 8.00 20.00
88 Ken Griffey Jr. 12.00 30.00
89 Cal Ripken 8.00 20.00
90 Javier Baez 3.00 8.00
91 Nolan Arenado 4.00 10.00
92 Alex Bregman 2.50 6.00
93 Marcus Semien 2.50 6.00
94 Alex Kirilloff 6.00 15.00
95 Ian Anderson 4.00 10.00
96 Ke'Bryan Hayes 15.00 40.00
97 Keibert Ruiz 5.00 12.00

2021 Donruss Retro '87 Materials Gold
*GOLD/16-25: .75X TO 2X BASIC
RANDOM INSERTS IN PACKS
PRINT RUNS B/WN 3-25 COPIES PER
NO PRICING ON QTY 15 OR LESS
EXCHANGE DEADLINE 9/3/2022
4 Cristian Pache/25 20.00 50.00
69 Alec Bohm/25 25.00 60.00

2021 Donruss Retro '87 Materials Red
*RED/34-99: .5X TO 1.2X BASIC
*RED/25: .75X TO 2X BASIC
RANDOM INSERTS IN PACKS
PRINT RUNS B/WN 5-99 COPIES PER
NO PRICING ON QTY 15 OR LESS
4 Cristian Pache/99 12.00 30.00
69 Alec Bohm/99 15.00 40.00

2021 Donruss Short and Sweet Signatures
RANDOM INSERTS IN PACKS
EXCHANGE DEADLINE 9/3/2022
1 Pete Alonso 30.00 80.00
2 Shohei Ohtani EXCH 125.00 300.00
3 Yoan Moncada 8.00 20.00
4 Aroldis Chapman
5 Adam Duvall 6.00 15.00
6 Wil Myers 5.00 12.00
7 Corey Seager 15.00 40.00
8 Salvador Perez 20.00 50.00
9 Victor Reyes 5.00 12.00
10 Wilmer Flores 3.00 8.00

2021 Donruss Short and Sweet Signatures Blue
*BLUE/99: .5X TO 1.2X BASIC
*BLUE/49: .6X TO 1.5X BASIC
*BLUE/25: .75X TO 2X BASIC
RANDOM INSERTS IN PACKS
PRINT RUNS B/WN 10-99 COPIES PER
NO PRICING ON QTY 15 OR LESS
EXCHANGE DEADLINE 9/3/2022
6 Wil Myers/99 8.00 20.00

2021 Donruss Short and Sweet Signatures Gold
*GOLD/25: .75X TO 2X BASIC
RANDOM INSERTS IN PACKS
PRINT RUNS B/WN 5-25 COPIES PER
NO PRICING ON QTY 15 OR LESS
EXCHANGE DEADLINE 9/3/2022
4 Aroldis Chapman/25 25.00 60.00
6 Wil Myers/25 15.00 40.00

2021 Donruss Signature Series
RANDOM INSERTS IN PACKS
EXCHANGE DEADLINE 9/3/2022
1 Casey Mize 15.00 40.00
2 Josh Fleming 2.50 6.00
3 Sherten Apostel 4.00 10.00
4 Evan White 4.00 10.00
5 Luis Gonzalez 2.50 6.00
6 Ryan Mountcastle 10.00 25.00
7 Luis Campusano 4.00 10.00
8 Clarke Schmidt 4.00 10.00
9 Zach McKinstry 40.00 100.00
10 Adonis Medina 4.00 10.00
11 Jake Cronenworth 10.00 25.00
12 Keegan Akin 2.50 6.00
13 Daulton Jefferies 2.50 6.00
14 Ryan Jeffers 5.00 12.00
15 Tanner Houck 4.00 10.00
16 Leody Taveras 3.00 8.00
17 Jo Adell EXCH 25.00 60.00
18 Sixto Sanchez
19 Monte Harrison 4.00 10.00
20 Nate Pearson 10.00 25.00
21 Braxton Garrett 2.50 6.00
22 Joey Bart 12.00 30.00
23 David Peterson 5.00 12.00
24 Bobby Dalbec 15.00 40.00
25 Alejandro Kirk 10.00 25.00
26 Triston McKenzie 8.00 20.00
27 Jazz Chisholm 10.00 25.00
28 Garrett Crochet 10.00 25.00
29 Rafael Marchan 3.00 8.00
30 Anderson Tejeda 6.00 15.00
31 Jared Oliva 6.00 15.00
32 Keibert Ruiz 10.00 25.00
33 Brady Singer 6.00 15.00
34 Dylan Carlson 20.00 50.00
35 Jorge Mateo 5.00 12.00
36 Trevor Rogers 6.00 15.00
37 Daulton Varsho 6.00 15.00
38 Nick Neidert 4.00 10.00
39 Deivi Garcia
41 Lewin Diaz 2.50 6.00
42 Ryan Weathers 8.00 20.00
43 Ke'Bryan Hayes 30.00 80.00
44 Jesus Sanchez 8.00 20.00
45 Alex Kirilloff 10.00 25.00
46 Alec Bohm 30.00 80.00
47 Cristian Javier 6.00 15.00
48 Nick Madrigal 12.00 30.00
49 Tarik Skubal 12.00 30.00
50 William Contreras 8.00 20.00

2021 Donruss Signature Series Blue
*BLUE/99: .5X TO 1.2X BASIC
RANDOM INSERTS IN PACKS
STATED PRINT RUN 99 SER.#'d SETS
EXCHANGE DEADLINE 9/3/2022
6 Ryan Mountcastle 25.00 60.00
18 Sixto Sanchez 12.00 30.00
33 Brady Singer 15.00 40.00
46 Alec Bohm 50.00 120.00

2021 Donruss Signature Series Gold
*GOLD/25: .75X TO 2X BASIC
RANDOM INSERTS IN PACKS
STATED PRINT RUN 25 SER.#'d SETS
EXCHANGE DEADLINE 9/3/2022
6 Ryan Mountcastle 40.00 100.00
17 Jo Adell EXCH 60.00 150.00
18 Sixto Sanchez 30.00 80.00
24 Bobby Dalbec 75.00 200.00
33 Brady Singer 25.00 60.00
34 Dylan Carlson 50.00 120.00
46 Alec Bohm 100.00 250.00

2021 Donruss The Famous San Diego Chicken Material Signatures
RANDOM INSERTS IN PACKS 4.00 10.00
STATED PRINT RUN 87 SER.#'d SETS 5.00 12.00
1 Ted Giannoulas 100.00 250.00

2021 Donruss The Famous San Diego Chicken Materials
RANDOM INSERTS IN PACKS
1 Ted Giannoulas 75.00 200.00

2021 Donruss The Rookies
RANDOM INSERTS IN PACKS
STATED PRINT RUN 999 SER.#'d SETS
*DIAMOND: .5X TO 1.2X BASIC
*PINK FWKS: .5X TO 1.2X BASIC
*RAPTURE: .5X TO 1.2X BASIC
*VECTOR: .5X TO 1.2X BASIC
*SILVER/349: .5X TO 1.2X BASIC
*BLUE/249: .6X TO 1.5X BASIC
*RED/149: .6X TO 1.5X BASIC
*GOLD/99: 1X TO 2.5X BASIC
*GREEN/25: 1.5X TO 4X BASIC
1 Joey Bart 1.25 3.00
2 Jo Adell 6.00 15.00
3 Dylan Carlson 5.00 12.00
4 Cristian Pache 6.00 15.00
5 Casey Mize 5.00 12.00
6 Nate Pearson 2.00 5.00
7 Alec Bohm 12.00 30.00
8 Sixto Sanchez 2.00 5.00

2021 Donruss Trending
RANDOM INSERTS IN PACKS
STATED PRINT RUN 999 SER.#'d SETS
*DIAMOND: .5X TO 1.2X BASIC
*PINK FWKS: .5X TO 1.2X BASIC
*RAPTURE: .5X TO 1.2X BASIC
*VECTOR: .5X TO 1.2X BASIC
*SILVER/349: .5X TO 1.2X BASIC
*BLUE/249: .6X TO 1.5X BASIC
*RED/149: .6X TO 1.5X BASIC
*GOLD/99: 1X TO 2.5X BASIC
*GREEN/25: 1.5X TO 4X BASIC
1 Gleyber Torres 1.25 3.00
2 Mike Soroka .60 1.50
3 Vladimir Guerrero Jr. 1.00 2.50
4 Ozzie Albies .60 1.50
5 Gavin Lux 1.25 3.00
6 Luis Arraez .75 2.00
7 Julio Urias .60 1.50
8 Jesus Luzardo .60 1.50
9 Luis Robert 5.00 12.00
10 Dustin May .60 1.50
11 Andres Munoz .40 1.00
12 Deivi Garcia 3.00 8.00

2021 Donruss Unleashed
RANDOM INSERTS IN PACKS
STATED PRINT RUN 999 SER.#'d SETS
*DIAMOND: .5X TO 1.2X BASIC
*PINK FWKS: .5X TO 1.2X BASIC
*RAPTURE: .5X TO 1.2X BASIC
*VECTOR: .5X TO 1.2X BASIC
*SILVER/349: .5X TO 1.2X BASIC
*BLUE/249: .6X TO 1.5X BASIC
*RED/149: .6X TO 1.5X BASIC
*GOLD/99: 1.2X TO 3X BASIC
*GREEN/25: 2X TO 5X BASIC
1 Yordan Alvarez 2.50 6.00
2 Mike Trout 10.00 25.00
3 Babe Ruth 6.00 15.00
4 Cody Bellinger 8.00 20.00
5 Ronald Acuna Jr. 8.00 20.00
6 Giancarlo Stanton 5.00 12.00
7 Pete Alonso 4.00 10.00
8 Aaron Judge 8.00 20.00
9 Mookie Betts 6.00 15.00
10 Jose Abreu 5.00 12.00
11 Marcell Ozuna 4.00 10.00
12 Nelson Cruz 3.00 8.00
13 Luis Robert 20.00 50.00
14 Juan Soto 15.00 40.00
15 Fernando Tatis Jr. 8.00 20.00
16 Ken Griffey Jr. 8.00 20.00
17 Kris Bryant 5.00 12.00
18 Sammy Sosa 5.00 12.00
19 Mark McGwire 5.00 12.00
20 Christian Yelich 8.00 20.00
21 Nolan Arenado 5.00 12.00
22 Bryce Harper 6.00 15.00
23 Alex Rodriguez 5.00 12.00
24 Bo Bichette 10.00 25.00
25 Rafael Devers 3.00 8.00
26 Frank Thomas 3.00 8.00

2021 Donruss Whammy
RANDOM INSERTS IN PACKS
1 Babe Ruth 75.00 200.00
2 Bo Bichette 50.00 120.00
3 Luis Robert 75.00 200.00
4 Jo Adell 50.00 120.00
5 Francisco Lindor 20.00 60.00
6 Joey Bart 50.00 120.00
7 Ryne Sandberg 30.00 80.00
8 George Brett 30.00 80.00
9 Wander Franco 50.00 120.00
10 Christian Yelich 30.00 80.00

2001 Donruss Baseball's Best Bronze
COMP.FACT.SET (330) 125.00 200.00
*STARS 1-150: 1.5X TO 4X BASIC CARDS
*ROOKIES 151-200: .2X TO .5X BASIC
*FAN CLUB 201-220: .4X TO 1X BASIC
ONE 330-CARD SET PER COUPON VIA MAIL
COUPON ODDS 1:720 '01 DONRUSS PACKS
STATED PRINT RUN 999 SERIAL #'d SETS
COUPON EXCHANGE DEADLINE 01/20/02
5 Derek Jeter 8.00 20.00
156 Albert Pujols RR 40.00 100.00
195 Ichiro Suzuki RR 10.00 25.00
205 Derek Jeter FC 8.00 20.00

2001 Donruss Baseball's Best Bronze Rookies
*BRONZE: .6X TO 1.5X BASIC ROOKIES
ONE SET PER BRONZE FACTORY SET
STATED PRINT RUN 999 SERIAL #'d SETS
COUPON EXCHANGE DEADLINE 01/20/02

2001 Donruss Baseball's Best Bronze Rookies Diamond Kings
*BRONZE DK's: .4X TO 1X BASIC DK's
ONE SET PER BRONZE FACTORY SET
STATED PRINT RUN 999 SERIAL #'d SETS
COUPON EXCHANGE DEADLINE 01/20/02
RDK3 Albert Pujols DK 40.00 100.00

2001 Donruss Baseball's Best Gold
COMP.FACT.SET (330) 350.00 600.00
*STARS 1-150: 6X TO 15X BASIC CARDS
*ROOKIES 151-200: .6X TO 1.5X BASIC
*FAN CLUB 201-220: 1.5X TO 4X BASIC
ONE 330-CARD SET PER COUPON VIA MAIL
STATED PRINT RUN 99 SERIAL #'d SETS.
COUPON EXCHANGE DEADLINE 01/20/02
5 Derek Jeter 20.00 50.00
156 Albert Pujols RR 75.00 200.00
195 Ichiro Suzuki RR 30.00 80.00
205 Derek Jeter FC 20.00 50.00

2001 Donruss Baseball's Best Gold Rookies
*GOLD: 2X TO 5X BASIC ROOKIES
ONE SET PER GOLD FACTORY SET
STATED PRINT RUN 99 SERIAL #'d SETS
COUPON EXCHANGE DEADLINE 01/20/02

2001 Donruss Baseball's Best Gold Rookies Diamond Kings
*GOLD DK'S: 1.25X TO 3X BASIC DK'S
ONE SET PER GOLD FACTORY SET
STATED PRINT RUN 99 SERIAL #'d SETS
RDK3 Albert Pujols DK 75.00 200.00

2001 Donruss Baseball's Best Silver
COMP.FACT.SET (330) 175.00 300.00
*STARS 1-150: 2.5X TO 6X BASIC CARDS
*ROOKIES 151-200: .3X TO .8X BASIC
*FAN CLUB 201-220: .6X TO 1.5X BASIC
ONE 330-CARD SET PER COUPON VIA MAIL
STATED PRINT RUN 499 SERIAL #'d SETS
COUPON EXCHANGE DEADLINE 01/20/02
5 Derek Jeter 12.50 30.00
205 Derek Jeter FC 12.50 30.00

2001 Donruss Baseball's Best Silver Rookies
*SILVER: 1X TO 2.5X BASIC ROOKIES
ONE SET PER SILVER FACTORY SET
STATED PRINT RUN 499 SERIAL #'d SETS
COUPON EXCHANGE DEADLINE 01/20/02

2001 Donruss Baseball's Best Silver Rookies Diamond Kings
*SILVER DK'S: .6X TO 1.5X BASIC DK'S
ONE SET PER SILVER FACTORY SET
STATED PRINT RUN 499 SERIAL #'d SETS

2002 Donruss Best of Fan Club
COMP.SET w/o SP's (200) 15.00 40.00
COMMON CARD (1-200) .20 .50
COMMON (201-260/U201-U225) 1.50 4.00
201-260/U201-U225 PRINT 1350 #'d SETS
COMMON CARD (261-300) 1.50 4.00
261-300 PRINT RUN 2025 SERIAL #'d SETS
201-300 RANDOM INSERTS IN HOBBY PACKS
201-300 DISPLAY CUMULATIVE PRINT RUN
201-300 ACTUAL PRINT RUN LISTED BELOW
PRINT RUNS PROVIDED BY DONRUSS
1 Alex Rodriguez .60 1.50

2 Pedro Martinez .30 .75
3 Vladimir Guerrero .50 1.25
4 Jim Edmonds .20 .50
5 Derek Jeter 1.25 3.00
6 Johnny Damon .30 .75
7 Rafael Furcal .20 .50
8 Cal Ripken 1.50 4.00
9 Brad Radke .20 .50
10 Bret Boone .20 .50
11 Pat Burrell .20 .50
12 Roy Oswalt .20 .50
13 Cliff Floyd .20 .50
14 Robin Ventura .20 .50
15 Frank Thomas .50 1.25
16 Mariano Rivera .50 1.25
17 Paul LoDuca .20 .50
18 Geoff Jenkins .20 .50
19 Tony Gwynn .60 1.50
20 Chipper Jones .50 1.25
21 Eric Chavez .20 .50
22 Kerry Wood .20 .50
23 Jorge Posada .30 .75
24 J.D. Drew .20 .50
25 Garret Anderson .20 .50
26 Javier Vazquez .20 .50
27 Kenny Lofton .20 .50
28 Mike Mussina .30 .75
29 Paul Konerko .20 .50
30 Bernie Williams .30 .75
31 Eric Milton .20 .50
32 Craig Wilson .20 .50
33 Paul O'Neill .30 .75
34 Dmitri Young .20 .50
35 Andres Galarraga .20 .50
36 Gary Sheffield .20 .50
37 Ben Grieve .20 .50
38 Scott Rolen .30 .75
39 Mark Grace .30 .75
40 Albert Pujols 1.00 2.50
41 Barry Zito .20 .50
42 Edgar Martinez .30 .75
43 Jarrod Washburn .20 .50
44 Juan Pierre .20 .50
45 Mark Buehrle .20 .50
46 Larry Walker .20 .50
47 Trot Nixon .20 .50
48 Wade Miller .20 .50
49 Robert Fick .20 .50
50 Sean Casey .20 .50
51 Joe Mays .20 .50
52 Brad Fullmer .20 .50
53 Chan Ho Park .20 .50
54 Carlos Delgado .20 .50
55 Phil Nevin .20 .50
56 Mike Cameron .20 .50
57 Raul Mondesi .20 .50
58 Roberto Alomar .30 .75
59 Ryan Klesko .20 .50
60 Andruw Jones .30 .75
61 Gabe Kapler .20 .50
62 Darin Erstad .20 .50
63 Cristian Guzman .20 .50
64 Kazuhiro Sasaki .20 .50
65 Doug Mientkiewicz .20 .50
66 Sammy Sosa .50 1.25
67 Mike Hampton .20 .50
68 Rickey Henderson .50 1.25
69 Mark Mulder .20 .50
70 Jeff Conine .20 .50
71 Freddy Garcia .20 .50
72 Ivan Rodriguez .30 .75
73 Terrence Long .20 .50
74 Adam Dunn .20 .50
75 Moises Alou .20 .50
76 Todd Helton .30 .75
77 Preston Wilson .20 .50
78 Roger Cedeno .20 .50
79 Tony Armas .20 .50
80 Manny Ramirez .30 .75
81 Jose Vidro .20 .50
82 Randy Johnson .50 1.25
83 Richie Sexson .20 .50
84 Troy Glaus .20 .50
85 Kevin Brown .20 .50
86 Woody Williams .20 .50
87 Adrian Beltre .20 .50
88 Brian Giles .20 .50
89 Jermaine Dye .20 .50
90 Craig Biggio .30 .75
91 Richard Hidalgo .20 .50
92 Magglio Ordonez .20 .50
93 Al Leiter .20 .50
94 Jeff Kent .20 .50
95 Curt Schilling .20 .50
96 Tim Hudson .20 .50
97 Fred McGriff UER .30 .75
120 HR for the Cubs in 2001
98 Barry Larkin .30 .75
99 Jim Thome .30 .75
100 Tom Glavine .30 .75
101 Alfonso Soriano .20 .50
102 Jamie Moyer .20 .50
103 Vinny Castilla .20 .50
104 Rich Aurilia .20 .50
105 Matt Morris .20 .50
106 Rafael Palmeiro .30 .75
107 Joe Crede .20 .50
108 Barry Bonds 1.25 3.00
109 Robert Person .20 .50
110 Nomar Garciaparra .75 2.00
111 Brandon Duckworth .20 .50
112 Russ Ortiz .20 .50
113 Jeff Weaver .20 .50
114 Carlos Beltran .20 .50
115 Ellis Burks .20 .50
116 Jeremy Giambi .20 .50
117 Carlos Lee .20 .50
118 Ken Griffey Jr. 1.00 2.50
119 Torii Hunter .20 .50
120 Andy Pettitte .30 .75
121 Jose Canseco .30 .75
122 Charles Johnson .20 .50
123 Nick Johnson .20 .50
124 Luis Gonzalez .20 .50
125 Rondell White .20 .50
126 Miguel Tejada .20 .50
127 Jose Cruz Jr. .20 .50
128 Brent Abernathy .20 .50
129 Scott Brosius .20 .50
130 Jon Lieber .20 .50
131 John Smoltz .30 .75
132 Mike Sweeney .20 .50
133 Shannon Stewart .20 .50
134 Derrek Lee .30 .75
135 Brian Jordan .20 .50
136 Rusty Greer .20 .50
137 Mike Piazza .75 2.00
138 Billy Wagner .20 .50
139 Shawn Green .20 .50
140 Orlando Cabrera .20 .50
141 Jeff Bagwell .30 .75
142 Aaron Sele .20 .50
143 Hideo Nomo .50 1.25
144 Marlon Anderson .20 .50
145 Todd Walker .20 .50
146 Bobby Higginson .20 .50
147 Ichiro Suzuki 1.00 2.50
148 Juan Uribe .20 .50
149 Jason Kendall .20 .50
150 Mark Quinn .20 .50
151 Ben Sheets .20 .50
152 Paul Abbott .20 .50
153 Aubrey Huff .20 .50
154 Greg Maddux .75 2.00
155 Darryl Kile .20 .50
156 John Burkett .20 .50
157 Juan Gonzalez .20 .50
158 Javy Lopez .20 .50
159 Aramis Ramirez .20 .50
160 Lance Berkman .20 .50
161 David Cone .20 .50
162 Edgar Renteria .20 .50
163 Roger Clemens 1.00 2.50
164 Frank Catalanotto .20 .50
165 Bartolo Colon .20 .50
166 Mark McGwire 1.25 3.00
167 Jay Gibbons .20 .50
168 Tony Clark .20 .50
169 Tsuyoshi Shinjo .20 .50
170 Brad Penny .20 .50
171 Marcus Giles .20 .50
172 Matt Williams .20 .50
173 Bud Smith .20 .50
174 Tino Martinez .30 .75
175 Ryan Dempster .20 .50
176 Jimmy Rollins .20 .50
177 Edgardo Alfonzo .20 .50
178 Jason Giambi .20 .50
179 Aaron Boone .20 .50
180 Ray Durham .20 .50
181 Mike Lowell .20 .50
182 Jose Ortiz .20 .50
183 Johnny Estrada .20 .50
184 Shane Reynolds .20 .50
185 Joe Kennedy .20 .50
186 Corey Patterson .20 .50
187 Jeromy Burnitz .20 .50
188 C.C. Sabathia .20 .50
189 Doug Davis .20 .50
190 Omar Vizquel .30 .75
191 John Olerud .20 .50
192 Dee Brown .20 .50
193 Kip Wells .20 .50
194 A.J. Burnett .20 .50
195 Josh Towers .20 .50
196 Jason Varitek .50 1.25
197 Jason Isringhausen .20 .50
198 Fernando Vina .20 .50
199 Ramon Ortiz .20 .50
200 Bobby Abreu .20 .50
201 Willie Harris/850 1.50 4.00
202 Angel Santos/1350 1.50 4.00
203 Corky Miller/850 1.50 4.00
204 Michael Rivera/1350 1.50 4.00
205 Justin Duchscherer/850 1.50 4.00
206 Rick Bauer/1350 1.50 4.00
207 Angel Berroa/1250 1.50 4.00
208 Juan Cruz/1175 1.50 4.00
209 Dewon Brazelton/1298 1.50 4.00
210 Mark Prior/925 2.00 5.00
211 Mark Teixeira/925 2.00 5.00
212 Geronimo Gil/1350 1.50 4.00
213 Casey Fossum/1250 1.50 4.00
214 Ken Harvey/1350 1.50 4.00
215 Michael Cuddyer/1298 1.50 4.00
216 Wilson Betemit/850 1.50 4.00
217 David Brous/850 1.50 4.00
218 Juan A. Pena/1162 1.50 4.00
219 Travis Hafner/975 1.50 4.00
220 Erick Almonte/1350 1.50 4.00
221 Morgan Ensberg/1298 1.50 4.00
222 Martin Vargas/850 1.50 4.00
223 Brandon Berger/850 1.50 4.00
224 Zach Day/850 1.50 4.00
225 Brad Voyles/850 1.50 4.00
226 Jeremy Affeldt/1100 1.50 4.00
227 Nick Neugebauer/1125 1.50 4.00
228 Tim Redding/850 1.50 4.00
229 Adam Johnson/925 1.50 4.00
230 Doug DeVore/1050 RC 1.50 4.00
231 Cody Ransom/850 1.50 4.00
232 Marlon Byrd/875 1.50 4.00
233 Delvin James/975 1.50 4.00
234 Eric Munson/1025 1.50 4.00
235 Dennis Tankersley/850 1.50 4.00
236 Josh Beckett/1325 1.50 4.00
237 Bill Hall/900 1.50 4.00
238 Kevin Olsen/1025 1.50 4.00
239 Francis Beltran/1350 RC 1.50 4.00
240 Antonio Perez/825 1.50 4.00
241 Orlando Hudson/825 1.50 4.00
242 Anderson Machado/1350 RC 1.50 4.00
243 Tom Shearn/1350 RC 1.50 4.00
244 Brian Mallette/1350 RC 1.50 4.00
245 Raul Chavez/1350 RC 1.50 4.00
246 Andy Pratt/1350 RC 1.50 4.00
247 Jorge De La Rosa/1350 RC 1.50 4.00
248 Jeff Deardorff/875 1.50 4.00
249 Ben Howard/1350 RC 1.50 4.00
250 Brandon Backe/1350 RC 2.00 5.00
251 Ed Rogers/950 1.50 4.00
252 Travis Hughes/1350 RC 1.50 4.00
253 Rodrigo Rosario/1350 RC 1.50 4.00
254 Alfredo Amezaga/1350 1.50 4.00
255 Jorge Padilla/1350 RC 1.50 4.00
256 Victor Martinez/1350 2.00 5.00
257 Steve Bechler/1350 RC 1.50 4.00
258 Chris Baker/1350 RC 1.50 4.00
259 Ryan Jamison/1350 1.50 4.00
260 Allan Simpson/875 RC 1.50 4.00
261 Alex Rodriguez FC/2000 2.50 6.00
262 Vladimir Guerrero FC/2000 2.00 5.00
263 Bud Smith FC/2002 1.50 4.00
264 Miguel Tejada FC/2025 1.50 4.00
265 Craig Biggio FC/2010 2.00 5.00
266 Luis Gonzalez FC/2010 1.50 4.00
267 Ivan Rodriguez FC/2025 2.00 5.00
268 C.C. Sabathia FC/2000 1.50 4.00
269 Jeff Bagwell FC/2010 2.00 5.00
270 Aramis Ramirez FC/2025 1.50 4.00
271 Bob Abreu FC/2025 1.50 4.00
272 Rich Aurilia FC/2000 1.50 4.00
273 Jason Giambi FC/2025 1.50 4.00
274 Rickey Henderson FC/2025 2.00 5.00
275 Wade Miller FC/2002 1.50 4.00
276 Andruw Jones FC/2025 2.00 5.00
277 Troy Glaus FC/2025 1.50 4.00
278 Roy Oswalt FC/1950 1.50 4.00
279 Tony Gwynn FC/2000 2.50 6.00
280 Adam Dunn FC/2000 1.50 4.00
281 Larry Walker FC/2025 1.50 4.00
282 Jose Canseco FC/2025 2.00 5.00
283 Todd Helton FC/2025 2.00 5.00
284 Lance Berkman FC/2010 1.50 4.00
285 Cal Ripken FC/2010 6.00 15.00
286 Albert Pujols FC/2000 4.00 10.00
287 Alfonso Soriano FC/2000 1.50 4.00
288 Mark Mulder FC/2025 1.50 4.00
289 Mike Hampton FC/2025 1.50 4.00
290 Andres Galarraga FC/2000 1.50 4.00
291 Barry Bonds FC/2025 5.00 12.00
292 Ben Sheets FC/2010 1.50 4.00
293 Ichiro Suzuki FC/2025 4.00 10.00
294 J.D. Drew FC/2000 1.50 4.00
295 Jose Ortiz FC/2025 1.50 4.00
296 Kerry Wood FC/2010 1.50 4.00
297 Mark McGwire FC/2025 5.00 12.00
298 Mike Sweeney FC/2025 1.50 4.00
299 Pat Burrell FC/2025 1.50 4.00
300 Tim Hudson FC/2000 1.50 4.00
U201 Kirk Saarloos RC 1.50 4.00
U202 Oliver Perez RC 2.00 5.00
U203 So Taguchi RC 2.00 5.00
U204 Runelvys Hernandez RC 1.50 4.00
U205 Freddy Sanchez RC 2.00 5.00
U206 Cliff Lee RC 5.00 12.00
U207 Kazuhisa Ishii RC 2.00 5.00
U208 Kevin Cash RC 1.50 4.00
U209 Trey Hodges RC 1.50 4.00
U210 Wilson Valdez RC 1.50 4.00
U211 Satoru Komiyama RC 1.50 4.00
U212 Luis Ugueto RC 1.50 4.00
U213 Joe Borchard 1.50 4.00
U214 Brian Tallet RC 1.50 4.00
U215 Jeriome Robertson RC 1.50 4.00
U216 Eric Junge RC 1.50 4.00
U217 Aaron Cook RC 1.50 4.00
U218 Jason Simontacchi RC 1.50 4.00
U219 Miguel Asencio RC 1.50 4.00
U220 Josh Bard RC 1.50 4.00
U221 Earl Snyder RC 1.50 4.00
U222 Felix Escalona RC 1.50 4.00
U223 Rene Reyes RC 1.50 4.00
U224 Chone Figgins RC 2.00 5.00
U225 Chris Snelling RC 1.50 4.00

2002 Donruss Best of Fan Club Autographs

200-300 DISPLAY CUMULATIVE PRINT RUN
200-300 PRINT RUN PROVIDED BY DONRUSS
SEE BECKETT.COM FOR UNLISTED PR.RUNS
NO PRICING ON QTY OF 25 OR LESS
SKIP-NUMBERED 76-CARD SET
201 Willie Harris/500 4.00 10.00
203 Corky Miller/500 4.00 10.00
205 Justin Duchscherer/500 4.00 10.00
207 Angel Berroa/100 6.00 15.00
208 Juan Cruz/175 4.00 10.00
209 Dewon Brazelton/52 8.00 20.00
210 Mark Prior/425 4.00 10.00
211 Mark Teixeira/425 10.00 25.00
213 Casey Fossum/100 6.00 15.00
215 Michael Cuddyer/52 8.00 20.00
216 Wilson Betemit/500 4.00 10.00
217 David Brous/500 4.00 10.00
218 Juan A. Pena/188 4.00 10.00
219 Travis Hafner/375 6.00 15.00
221 Morgan Ensberg/52 10.00 25.00
222 Martin Vargas/500 4.00 10.00
223 Brandon Berger/500 4.00 10.00
224 Zach Day/500 4.00 10.00
225 Brad Voyles/500 4.00 10.00
226 Jeremy Affeldt/250 4.00 10.00
227 Nick Neugebauer/225 4.00 10.00
228 Tim Redding/500 4.00 10.00
229 Adam Johnson/425 4.00 10.00
230 Doug DeVore/300 6.00 15.00
231 Cody Ransom/500 4.00 10.00
232 Marlon Byrd/475 4.00 10.00
233 Delvin James/375 4.00 10.00
234 Eric Munson/325 4.00 10.00
235 Dennis Tankersley/500 4.00 10.00
237 Bill Hall/450 6.00 15.00
238 Kevin Olsen/325 4.00 10.00
240 Antonio Perez/525 4.00 10.00
241 Orlando Hudson/525 4.00 10.00
248 Jeff Deardorff/475 4.00 10.00
251 Ed Rogers/400 4.00 10.00
255 Jorge Padilla/450 6.00 15.00
260 Allan Simpson/475 6.00 15.00
U201 Kirk Saarloos/100 4.00 10.00
U206 Cliff Lee/50 30.00 60.00
U208 Kevin Cash/50 6.00 15.00
U209 Trey Hodges/100 4.00 10.00
U210 Wilson Valdez/50 6.00 15.00
U212 Luis Ugueto/75 4.00 10.00
U213 Joe Borchard/50 8.00 20.00
U214 Brian Tallet/50 4.00 10.00
U220 Josh Bard/50 6.00 15.00
U221 Earl Snyder/100 4.00 10.00
U223 Rene Reyes/50 6.00 15.00
U224 Chone Figgins/100 10.00 25.00
U225 Chris Snelling/50 12.50 30.00

2002 Donruss Best of Fan Club Spotlight

*DC 1-200: 5X TO 12X BASIC CARDS
*DC 261-300: 1.25X TO 3X BASIC CARDS
*DC U201-U225: 1X TO 2.5X BASIC CARDS
STATED PRINT RUN 100 SERIAL #'d SETS

2002 Donruss Best of Fan Club Artists

COMPLETE SET (14) 50.00 100.00
RANDOM INSERTS IN PACKS
STATED PRINT RUN 300 SERIAL #'d SETS
A1 Pedro Martinez/285 2.50 6.00
A2 Curt Schilling/285 2.00 5.00
A3 Kevin Brown/275 2.00 5.00
A4 Tim Hudson/275 2.00 5.00
A5 Kerry Wood/285 2.00 5.00
A6 Barry Zito/200 2.00 5.00
A7 Hideo Nomo 10.00 25.00
A8 Randy Johnson/285 4.00 10.00
A9 Greg Maddux/285 6.00 15.00
A10 Roger Clemens/285 8.00 20.00
A11 Kazuhiro Sasaki 2.00 5.00
A12 Joe Mays 2.00 5.00
A13 Mark Mulder 2.00 5.00
A14 Javier Vazquez 2.00 5.00

2002 Donruss Best of Fan Club Artists Autographs

RANDOM INSERTS IN PACKS
CARDS DISPLAY CUMULATIVE PRINT RUN
ACTUAL PRINT RUNS LISTED BELOW
PRINT RUNS PROVIDED BY DONRUSS
NO PRICING ON QUANTITY OF 25 OR LESS
SKIP-NUMBERED 9-CARD SET
A6 Barry Zito/100 5.00 12.00

2002 Donruss Best of Fan Club Master Artists Jerseys

RANDOM INSERTS IN HOBBY PACKS
STATED PRINT RUN 150 SERIAL #'d SETS
ALL CARDS ARE GAME JERSEYS
A1 Pedro Martinez 10.00 25.00
A2 Curt Schilling 6.00 15.00
A3 Kevin Brown 6.00 15.00
A4 Tim Hudson 6.00 15.00
A5 Kerry Wood 6.00 15.00
A6 Barry Zito 6.00 15.00
A7 Hideo Nomo 30.00 60.00
A8 Randy Johnson 10.00 25.00
A9 Greg Maddux 10.00 25.00
A10 Roger Clemens 15.00 40.00
A11 Kazuhiro Sasaki 6.00 15.00
A12 Joe Mays 6.00 15.00
A13 Mark Mulder 6.00 15.00
A14 Javier Vazquez 6.00 15.00

2002 Donruss Best of Fan Club Craftsmen

COMPLETE SET (18) 15.00 40.00
RANDOM INSERTS IN PACKS
STATED PRINT RUN 300 SERIAL #'d SETS
CARDS DISPLAY CUMULATIVE PRINT RUN
ACTUAL PRINT RUNS LISTED BELOW
PRINT RUNS PROVIDED BY DONRUSS
C1 Ichiro Suzuki/300 3.00 8.00
C2 Todd Helton/285 1.50 4.00
C3 Manny Ramirez/285 1.50 4.00
C4 Luis Gonzalez/285 1.00 2.50
C5 Roberto Alomar/285 1.50 4.00
C6 Moises Alou/275 1.00 2.50
C7 Darin Erstad/275 1.00 2.50
C8 Mike Piazza/300 2.50 6.00
C9 Edgar Martinez/285 1.50 4.00
C10 Vladimir Guerrero/275 1.50 4.00
C11 Juan Gonzalez/285 1.00 2.50
C12 Nomar Garciaparra/285 1.50 4.00
C13 Tony Gwynn/285 2.50 6.00
C14 Jeff Bagwell/285 1.50 4.00
C15 Albert Pujols/275 5.00 12.00
C16 Larry Walker/300 1.50 4.00
C17 Paul LoDuca/200 1.00 2.50
C18 Lance Berkman/300 1.50 4.00

2002 Donruss Best of Fan Club Craftsmen Autographs

RANDOM INSERTS IN PACKS
CARDS DISPLAY CUMULATIVE PRINT RUNS
ACTUAL PRINT RUNS LISTED BELOW
PRINT RUNS PROVIDED BY DONRUSS
NO PRICING ON QUANTITY OF 25 OR LESS
SKIP-NUMBERED 14-CARD SET
C17 Paul LoDuca/100 10.00 25.00

2002 Donruss Best of Fan Club Master Craftsmen Bats

RANDOM INSERTS IN HOBBY PACKS
STATED PRINT RUN 150 SERIAL #'d SETS
ALL CARDS ARE GAME BAT UNLESS STATED
C1 Ichiro Suzuki Ball/51 50.00 100.00
C2 Todd Helton 10.00 25.00
C3 Manny Ramirez 10.00 25.00
C4 Luis Gonzalez 6.00 15.00
C5 Roberto Alomar 10.00 25.00
C6 Moises Alou 6.00 15.00
C7 Darin Erstad 6.00 15.00
C8 Mike Piazza 10.00 25.00
C9 Edgar Martinez 10.00 25.00
C10 Vladimir Guerrero 10.00 25.00
C11 Juan Gonzalez 6.00 15.00
C12 Nomar Garciaparra 15.00 40.00
C13 Tony Gwynn/175 12.50 30.00
C14 Jeff Bagwell 10.00 25.00
C15 Albert Pujols/175 6.00 15.00
C16 Larry Walker/175 6.00 15.00
C17 Paul LoDuca/175 6.00 15.00
C18 Lance Berkman 6.00 15.00

2002 Donruss Best of Fan Club Double Features

RANDOM INSERTS IN PACKS
STATED PRINT RUN 125 SERIAL #'d SETS
DF1 L.Walker 6.00 15.00
T.Helton
DF2 V.Guerrero 6.00 15.00
J.Vidro
DF3 J.Giambi 6.00 15.00
J.Giambi
DF4 M.Ramirez 12.50 30.00
N.Garciaparra
DF5 T.Glaus 6.00 15.00
D.Erstad
DF6 S.Green 6.00 15.00
P.LoDuca
DF7 J.Bagwell 6.00 15.00
C.Biggio
DF8 P.Martinez 10.00 25.00
H.Nomo
DF9 R.Johnson 6.00 15.00
C.Schilling
DF10 C.Jones 6.00 15.00
A.Jones

2002 Donruss Best of Fan Club Double Features Lumber

RANDOM INSERTS IN HOBBY PACKS
STATED PRINT RUN 50 SERIAL #'d SETS
DF1 L.Walker/T.Helton 15.00 40.00
DF2 V.Guerrero/J.Vidro 15.00 40.00
DF3 J.Giambi/J.Giambi 15.00 40.00
DF4 M.Ramirez/N.Garciaparra 40.00 80.00
DF5 T.Glaus/D.Erstad 15.00 40.00
DF6 S.Green/P.LoDuca 15.00 40.00
DF7 J.Bagwell/C.Biggio 15.00 40.00
DF8 P.Martinez/H.Nomo 40.00 80.00
DF9 Johnson/Schilling Glv 15.00 40.00
DF10 C.Jones/A.Jones 15.00 40.00

2002 Donruss Best of Fan Club Franchise Features

COMPLETE SET (40) 30.00 80.00
RANDOM INSERTS IN PACKS
STATED PRINT RUN 300 SERIAL #'d SETS
CARDS DISPLAY CUMULATIVE PRINT RUN
ACTUAL PRINT RUNS LISTED BELOW
PRINT RUNS PROVIDED BY DONRUSS
FF1 Cliff Floyd/300 1.00 2.50
FF2 Mike Piazza/300 2.50 6.00
FF3 Cal Ripken/275 8.00 20.00
FF4 Mike Sweeney/300 1.00 2.50
FF5 Curt Schilling/275 1.50 4.00
FF6 Aramis Ramirez/200 1.00 2.50
FF7 Vladimir Guerrero/275 1.50 4.00
FF8 Andruw Jones/300 1.00 2.50
FF9 Tim Hudson/250 1.50 4.00
FF10 Bernie Williams/275 1.50 4.00
FF11 Pedro Martinez/285 1.50 4.00
FF12 Roberto Alomar/285 1.50 4.00
FF13 Joe Mays/225 1.00 2.50
FF14 Jason Giambi/300 1.00 2.50
FF15 Kazuhiro Sasaki/300 1.00 2.50
FF16 Magglio Ordonez/300 1.50 4.00
FF17 Nomar Garciaparra/285 1.50 4.00
FF18 Juan Gonzalez/275 1.00 2.50
FF19 Carlos Beltran/200 1.00 2.50
FF20 Javier Vazquez/275 1.00 2.50
FF21 Miguel Tejada/300 1.50 4.00
FF22 Luis Gonzalez/285 1.00 2.50
FF23 Greg Maddux/285 4.00 10.00
FF24 Rafael Palmeiro/275 1.50 4.00
FF25 Freddy Garcia/200 1.00 2.50
FF26 Barry Zito/200 1.00 2.50
FF27 Paul LoDuca/200 1.00 2.50
FF28 Robert Fick/200 1.00 2.50
FF29 Roger Clemens/285 3.00 8.00
FF30 Eric Chavez/250 1.00 2.50
FF31 Ivan Rodriguez/285 1.50 4.00
FF32 Chipper Jones/300 2.50 6.00
FF33 Kerry Wood/285 1.00 2.50
FF34 Randy Johnson/285 2.50 6.00
FF35 Alex Rodriguez/285 3.00 8.00
FF36 Manny Ramirez/275 1.50 4.00
FF37 Mark Buehrle/200 1.50 4.00
FF38 Mark Mulder/300 1.00 2.50
FF39 Ichiro Suzuki/300 3.00 8.00
FF40 Troy Glaus/275 1.00 2.50

2002 Donruss Best of Fan Club Franchise Features Autographs

RANDOM INSERTS IN PACKS
CARDS DISPLAY CUMULATIVE PRINT RUN
ACTUAL PRINT RUNS LISTED BELOW
PRINT RUNS PROVIDED BY DONRUSS
NO PRICING ON QUANTITY OF 25 OR LESS
SKIP-NUMBERED 29-CARD SET
FF6 Aramis Ramirez/100 10.00 25.00
FF13 Joe Mays/75 10.00 25.00
FF19 Carlos Beltran/100 10.00 25.00
FF25 Freddy Garcia/100 10.00 25.00
FF26 Barry Zito/100 8.00 20.00
FF27 Paul LoDuca/100 10.00 25.00
FF28 Robert Fick/100 10.00 25.00
FF37 Mark Buehrle/100 12.50 30.00

2002 Donruss Best of Fan Club Franchise Features Materials

RANDOM INSERTS IN HOBBY PACKS
STATED PRINT RUN 150 SERIAL #'d SETS
FF1 Cliff Floyd Jsy 6.00 15.00
FF2 Mike Piazza Jsy 10.00 25.00
FF3 Cal Ripken Jsy 40.00 80.00
FF4 Mike Sweeney Jsy 6.00 15.00
FF5 Curt Schilling Jsy/175 6.00 15.00
FF6 Aramis Ramirez Jsy 6.00 15.00
FF7 Vladimir Guerrero Jsy 10.00 25.00
FF8 Andruw Jones Jsy/175 10.00 25.00
FF9 Tim Hudson Jsy 6.00 15.00
FF10 Bernie Williams Jsy 10.00 25.00
FF11 Pedro Martinez Jsy 10.00 25.00
FF12 Roberto Alomar Jsy 10.00 25.00
FF13 Joe Mays Jsy 6.00 15.00
FF14 Jason Giambi Jsy 6.00 15.00
FF15 Kazuhiro Sasaki Jsy 6.00 15.00
FF16 Magglio Ordonez Jsy 6.00 15.00
FF17 Nomar Garciaparra Jsy 15.00 40.00
FF18 Juan Gonzalez Jsy 6.00 15.00
FF19 Carlos Beltran Jsy 6.00 15.00
FF20 Javier Vazquez Jsy 6.00 15.00
FF21 Miguel Tejada Jsy 6.00 15.00
FF22 Luis Gonzalez Jsy 6.00 15.00
FF23 Greg Maddux Jsy/175 10.00 25.00
FF24 Rafael Palmeiro Jsy 10.00 25.00
FF25 Freddy Garcia Jsy 6.00 15.00
FF26 Barry Zito Jsy 6.00 15.00
FF27 Paul LoDuca Jsy 6.00 15.00
FF28 Robert Fick Jsy 6.00 15.00
FF29 Roger Clemens Jsy/175 20.00 50.00
FF30 Eric Chavez Bat 6.00 15.00
FF31 Ivan Rodriguez Jsy 10.00 25.00
FF32 Chipper Jones Jsy 10.00 25.00
FF33 Kerry Wood Jsy 6.00 15.00
FF34 Randy Johnson Jsy 10.00 25.00
FF35 Alex Rodriguez Jsy 15.00 40.00
FF36 Manny Ramirez Jsy 10.00 25.00
FF37 Mark Buehrle Jsy 6.00 15.00
FF38 Mark Mulder Jsy 6.00 15.00
FF39 Ichiro Suzuki Ball/51 50.00 100.00
FF40 Troy Glaus Jsy 6.00 15.00

2002 Donruss Best of Fan Club League Leaders

COMPLETE SET (45) 200.00 400.00
RANDOM INSERTS IN PACKS
STATED PRINT RUN 300 SERIAL #'d SETS
CARDS DISPLAY CUMULATIVE PRINT RUN
ACTUAL PRINT RUNS LISTED BELOW
LL1 Roger Clemens Wins/275* 8.00 20.00
LL2 Curt Schilling Wins/275* 2.00 5.00
LL3 Matt Morris Wins/300* 2.00 5.00
LL4 Randy Johnson Wins/285* 4.00 10.00
LL5 Mark Mulder Wins/200* 2.00 5.00
LL6 Curt Schilling ERA/275* 2.00 5.00
LL7 Mike Mussina ERA/275* 2.50 6.00
LL8 Joe Mays ERA/275* 2.00 5.00
LL9 Matt Morris ERA/300* 2.00 5.00
LL10 Tim Hudson ERA/250* 2.00 5.00
LL11 Mark Buehrle ERA/200* 2.00 5.00
LL12 Greg Maddux ERA/275* 6.00 15.00
LL13 Freddy Garcia ERA/200* 2.00 5.00
LL14 Randy Johnson ERA/275* 4.00 10.00
LL15 Curt Schilling K's/275* 2.00 5.00
LL16 Chan Ho Park K's/285* 2.00 5.00
LL17 Roger Clemens K's/285* 8.00 20.00
LL18 Mike Mussina K's/285* 2.50 6.00
LL19 Javier Vazquez K's/200* 2.00 5.00
LL20 Kerry Wood K's/270* 2.00 5.00
LL21 Randy Johnson K's/285* 4.00 10.00
LL22 Barry Zito K's/200* 2.00 5.00
LL23 Hideo Nomo K's/300* 10.00 25.00
LL24 Ichiro Suzuki Hits/300* 6.00 15.00
LL25 Todd Helton Hits/275* 2.50 6.00
LL26 Albert Pujols Hits/200* 6.00 15.00
LL27 Alex Rodriguez Hits/285* 5.00 12.00
LL28 Shannon Stewart Hits/200* 2.00 5.00
LL29 Luis Gonzalez Hits/285* 2.00 5.00
LL30 Alex Rodriguez HR/285* 5.00 12.00
LL31 Barry Bonds HR/300* 10.00 25.00
LL32 Sammy Sosa HR/300* 4.00 10.00
LL33 Luis Gonzalez HR/285* 2.00 5.00
LL34 Todd Helton HR/275* 2.50 6.00
LL35 Jim Thome HR/300* 2.50 6.00
LL36 Shawn Green HR/285* 2.00 5.00
LL37 Jeff Bagwell RBI/285* 2.50 6.00
LL38 Todd Helton RBI/285* 2.50 6.00
LL39 Luis Gonzalez RBI/285* 2.00 5.00
LL40 Lance Berkman RBI/300* 2.00 5.00
LL41 Juan Gonzalez RBI/275* 2.00 5.00
LL42 Larry Walker Avg/300* 2.00 5.00
LL43 Ichiro Suzuki Avg/300* 6.00 15.00
LL44 Lance Berkman 2B's/300* 2.00 5.00
LL45 Todd Helton 2B's/285* 2.50 6.00

2002 Donruss Best of Fan Club League Leaders Autographs

RANDOM INSERTS IN PACKS
CARDS DISPLAY CUMULATIVE PRINT RUN
ACTUAL PRINT RUN LISTED BELOW
NO PRICING ON QUANTITY OF 30 OR LESS
PRINT RUNS PROVIDED BY DONRUSS
SKIP-NUMBERED 34-CARD SET
LL5 Mark Mulder Wins/100 10.00 25.00
LL11 Mark Buehrle ERA/100 12.50 30.00
LL13 Freddy Garcia ERA/100 10.00 25.00
LL19 Javier Vazquez K's/100 10.00 25.00
LL26 Albert Pujols Hits/100 150.00 300.00
LL28 Shannon Stewart Hits/100 10.00 25.00

2002 Donruss Best of Fan Club League Leaders Materials

RANDOM INSERTS IN HOBBY PACKS
STATED PRINT RUNS LISTED BELOW
CARD NUMBERS 3 AND 9 DO NOT EXIST
LL1 R.Clemens Wins Jsy/175 8.00 20.00
LL2 C.Schilling Wins Jsy/150 4.00 10.00
LL4 R.Johnson Wins Jsy/175 6.00 15.00
LL5 M.Mulder Wins Jsy/175 2.50 6.00
LL6 C.Schilling ERA Shoe/150 4.00 10.00
LL7 M.Mussina ERA Shoe/50 4.00 10.00
LL8 J.Mays ERA Jsy/175 2.50 6.00
LL10 T.Hudson ERA Jsy/175 4.00 10.00
LL11 M.Buehrle ERA Jsy/175 4.00 10.00
LL12 G.Maddux ERA Jsy/175 10.00 25.00
LL13 F.Garcia ERA Jsy/175 2.50 6.00
LL14 R.Johnson ERA Jsy/175 6.00 15.00
LL15 C.Schilling K's Jsy/150 4.00 10.00
LL16 C.Park K's Jsy/175 4.00 10.00
LL17 R.Clemens K's Jsy/175 8.00 20.00
LL18 M.Mussina K's Shoe/50 4.00 10.00
LL19 J.Vazquez K's Jsy/175 2.50 6.00
LL20 K.Wood K's Jsy/175 2.50 6.00
LL21 R.Johnson K's Jsy/175 6.00 15.00
LL22 B.Zito K's Jsy/175 2.50 6.00
LL23 H.Nomo K's Jsy/175 6.00 15.00
LL24 I.Suzuki Hits Ball/51 8.00 20.00
LL25 T.Helton Hits Jsy/175 4.00 10.00
LL26 A.Pujols Hits Jsy/175 12.00 30.00
LL27 A.Rodriguez Hits Jsy/150 8.00 20.00
LL28 S.Stewart Hits Jsy/175 2.50 6.00
LL29 L.Gonzalez Hits Jsy/150 2.50 6.00
LL30 A.Rodriguez HR Jsy/150 8.00 20.00
LL31 B.Bonds HR Jsy/175 10.00 25.00
LL32 S.Sosa HR Jsy/150 6.00 15.00
LL33 L.Gonzalez HR Jsy/150 2.50 6.00
LL34 T.Helton HR Jsy/175 4.00 10.00
LL35 J.Thome HR Jsy/175 4.00 10.00
LL36 S.Green HR Jsy/175 2.50 6.00
LL37 J.Bagwell RBI Jsy/150 4.00 10.00
LL38 T.Helton RBI Jsy/175 4.00 10.00
LL39 L.Gonzalez RBI Jsy/150 2.50 6.00
LL40 L.Berkman RBI Jsy/175 4.00 10.00
LL41 J.Gonzalez RBI Jsy/150 2.50 6.00
LL42 L.Walker Avg Jsy/175 4.00 10.00
LL43 I.Suzuki Avg Ball/51 8.00 20.00
LL44 L.Berkman 2B's Jsy/175 4.00 10.00
LL45 T.Helton 2B's Jsy/175 4.00 10.00

2002 Donruss Best of Fan Club Pure Power

COMPLETE SET (18) 75.00 150.00
RANDOM INSERTS IN PACKS
STATED PRINT RUN 300 SERIAL #'d SETS
PP1 Sammy Sosa 4.00 10.00
PP2 Lance Berkman 2.00 5.00
PP3 Chipper Jones 4.00 10.00
PP4 Troy Glaus/275 2.00 5.00
PP5 Barry Bonds 10.00 25.00
PP6 Todd Helton/275 2.50 6.00
PP7 Manny Ramirez/285 2.50 6.00
PP8 Jason Giambi 2.00 5.00
PP9 Juan Gonzalez/285 2.00 5.00
PP10 Albert Pujols/275 6.00 15.00
PP11 Jim Thome 2.50 6.00
PP12 Mike Piazza 6.00 15.00
PP13 Frank Thomas/275 4.00 10.00
PP14 Richie Sexson/200 2.00 5.00
PP15 Jeff Bagwell/285 2.50 6.00
PP16 Rafael Palmeiro/275 2.50 6.00
PP17 Luis Gonzalez/285 2.00 5.00
PP18 Shawn Green 2.00 5.00

2002 Donruss Best of Fan Club Pure Power Autographs

RANDOM INSERTS IN PACKS
CARDS DISPLAY CUMULATIVE PRINT RUN
ACTUAL PRINT RUNS LISTED BELOW
PRINT RUNS PROVIDED BY DONRUSS
NO PRICING ON QUANTITY OF 25 OR LESS
SKIP-NUMBERED 10-CARD SET
PP14 Richie Sexson/100 10.00 25.00

2002 Donruss Best of Fan Club Pure Power Masters Game Bat

RANDOM INSERTS IN HOBBY PACKS
STATED PRINT RUN 150 SERIAL #'d SETS
PP1 Sammy Sosa 6.00 15.00
PP2 Lance Berkman 4.00 10.00
PP3 Chipper Jones 6.00 15.00
PP4 Troy Glaus 2.50 6.00
PP5 Barry Bonds 10.00 25.00
PP6 Todd Helton 4.00 10.00
PP7 Manny Ramirez 4.00 10.00
PP8 Jason Giambi 2.50 6.00
PP9 Juan Gonzalez 2.50 6.00
PP10 Albert Pujols 12.00 30.00
PP11 Jim Thome 4.00 10.00
PP12 Mike Piazza 6.00 15.00
PP13 Frank Thomas 6.00 15.00
PP14 Richie Sexson 2.50 6.00
PP15 Jeff Bagwell 4.00 10.00
PP16 Rafael Palmeiro 4.00 10.00
PP17 Luis Gonzalez 2.50 6.00
PP18 Shawn Green 2.50 6.00

2002 Donruss Best of Fan Club Records

COMPLETE SET (5) 40.00 80.00
RANDOM INSERTS IN PACKS
STATED PRINT RUN 300 SERIAL #'d SETS
R1 Barry Bonds HR 10.00 25.00
R2 Barry Bonds BB 10.00 25.00
R3 Barry Bonds SLUG 10.00 25.00
R4 Rickey Henderson Runs 6.00 15.00
R5 Rickey Henderson Hits 6.00 15.00

2002 Donruss Best of Fan Club Records Game Bat

RANDOM INSERTS IN HOBBY PACKS
STATED PRINT RUN 150 SERIAL #'d SETS
R1 Barry Bonds HR 20.00 50.00
R2 Barry Bonds BB 12.00 30.00
R3 Barry Bonds SLUG 20.00 50.00
R4 Rickey Henderson Runs 15.00 40.00
R5 Rickey Henderson Hits 15.00 40.00

2003 Donruss Champions Samples

*SAMPLES: 1.25X TO 3X BASIC

2003 Donruss Champions

COMP.LO SET (301) 20.00 50.00
COMP.UPDATE SET (8) 3.00 8.00
COMMON CARD (1-301) .12 .30
COMMON RC 1-301 .15 .40
COMMON RETIRED 1-301 .12 .30
COMMON CARD (302-309) .15 .40
302-309 ISSUED IN DLP R/T PACKS
1 Adam Kennedy .12 .30
2 Alfredo Amezaga .12 .30
3 Chone Figgins .12 .30
4 Darin Erstad .12 .30
5 David Eckstein .12 .30
6 Garret Anderson .12 .30
7 Jarrod Washburn .12 .30
8 Nolan Ryan Angels 1.00 2.50
9 Tim Salmon .12 .30
10 Troy Glaus .12 .30
11 Troy Percival .12 .30
12 Curt Schilling .20 .50
13 Junior Spivey .12 .30
14 Luis Gonzalez .12 .30
15 Mark Grace .20 .50
16 Randy Johnson .30 .75
17 Steve Finley .12 .30
18 Andruw Jones .12 .30
19 Chipper Jones .30 .75
20 Dale Murphy .30 .75
21 Gary Sheffield .12 .30
22 Greg Maddux .40 1.00
23 John Smoltz .30 .75

24 Andy Pratt .12 .30
25 Adam LaRoche .12 .30
26 Trey Hodges .12 .30
27 Warren Spahn .20 .50
28 Cal Ripken 1.00 2.50
29 Ed Rogers .12 .30
30 Brian Roberts .12 .30
31 Geronimo Gil .12 .30
32 Jay Gibbons .12 .30
33 Josh Towers .12 .30
34 Casey Fossum .12 .30
35 Cliff Floyd .12 .30
36 Derek Lowe .12 .30
37 Fred Lynn .12 .30
38 Freddy Sanchez .12 .30
39 Manny Ramirez .30 .75
40 Nomar Garciaparra .20 .50
41 Pedro Martinez .20 .50
42 Rickey Henderson .30 .75
43 Shea Hillenbrand .12 .30
44 Trot Nixon .12 .30
45 Bobby Hill .12 .30
46 Corey Patterson .12 .30
47 Fred McGriff .20 .50
48 Hee Seop Choi .12 .30
49 Juan Cruz .12 .30
50 Kerry Wood .12 .30
51 Mark Prior .20 .50
52 Moises Alou .12 .30
53 Nic Jackson .12 .30
54 Ryne Sandberg .60 1.50
55 Sammy Sosa .30 .75
56 Carlos Lee .12 .30
57 Corwin Malone .12 .30
58 Frank Thomas .30 .75
59 Joe Borchard .12 .30
60 Joe Crede .12 .30
61 Magglio Ordonez .20 .50
62 Mark Buehrle .20 .50
63 Paul Konerko .20 .50
64 Tim Hummel .12 .30
65 Jon Adkins .12 .30
66 Adam Dunn .20 .50
67 Austin Kearns .12 .30
68 Barry Larkin .20 .50
69 Jose Acevedo .12 .30
70 Corky Miller .12 .30
71 Eric Davis .12 .30
72 Ken Griffey Jr. .60 1.50
73 Sean Casey .12 .30
74 Wily Mo Pena .12 .30
75 Bob Feller .20 .50
76 Brian Tallet .12 .30
77 C.C. Sabathia .20 .50
78 Cliff Lee .75 2.00
79 Earl Snyder .12 .30
80 Ellis Burks .12 .30
81 Jeremy Guthrie .12 .30
82 Travis Hafner .12 .30
83 Luis Garcia .12 .30
84 Omar Vizquel .20 .50
85 Ricardo Rodriguez .12 .30
86 Ryan Church .12 .30
87 Victor Martinez .20 .50
88 Brandon Phillips .12 .30
89 Jack Cust .12 .30
90 Jason Jennings .12 .30
91 Jeff Baker .12 .30
92 Garrett Atkins .12 .30
93 Juan Uribe .12 .30
94 Larry Walker .20 .50
95 Rene Reyes .12 .30
96 Todd Helton .20 .50
97 Alan Trammell .20 .50
98 Fernando Rodney .12 .30
99 Carlos Pena .20 .50
100 Jack Morris .20 .50
101 Bobby Higginson .12 .30
102 Mike Maroth .12 .30
103 Robert Fick .12 .30
104 Jesus Medrano .12 .30
105 Josh Beckett .12 .30
106 Luis Castillo .12 .30
107 Mike Lowell .12 .30
108 Juan Pierre .12 .30
109 Josh Wilson .12 .30
110 Tim Redding .12 .30
111 Carlos Hernandez .12 .30
112 Craig Biggio .20 .50
113 Henri Stanley .12 .30
114 Jason Lane .12 .30
115 Jeff Bagwell .20 .50
116 John Buck .12 .30
117 Kirk Saarloos .12 .30
118 Lance Berkman .20 .50
119 Nolan Ryan Astros 1.00 2.50
120 Richard Hidalgo .12 .30
121 Rodrigo Rosario .12 .30
122 Roy Oswalt .20 .50
123 Tommy Whiteman .12 .30
124 Wade Miller .12 .30
125 Alexis Gomez .12 .30
126 Angel Berroa .12 .30
127 Brandon Berger .12 .30
128 Carlos Beltran .20 .50
129 George Brett .60 1.50
130 Jimmy Gobble .12 .30
131 Dee Brown .12 .30
132 Mike Sweeney .12 .30
133 Raul Ibanez .20 .50
134 Runelvys Hernandez .12 .30
135 Adrian Beltre .30 .75
136 Brian Jordan .12 .30
137 Cesar Izturis .12 .30
138 Victor Alvarez .12 .30
139 Hideo Nomo .30 .75
140 Joe Thurston .12 .30
141 Kazuhisa Ishii .12 .30
142 Kevin Brown .12 .30
143 Odalis Perez .12 .30
144 Paul Lo Duca .12 .30
145 Shawn Green .12 .30
146 Ben Sheets .12 .30
147 Bill Hall .12 .30
148 Nick Neugebauer .12 .30
149 Richie Sexson .12 .30
150 Robin Yount .30 .75
151 Shane Nance .12 .30
152 Takahito Nomura .12 .30
153 A.J. Pierzynski .12 .30
154 Joe Mays .12 .30
155 Kirby Puckett .30 .75
156 Adam Johnson .12 .30
157 Rob Bowen .12 .30
158 Torii Hunter .12 .30
159 Andres Galarraga .20 .50
160 Endy Chavez .12 .30
161 Javier Vazquez .12 .30
162 Jose Vidro .12 .30
163 Vladimir Guerrero .20 .50
164 Dwight Gooden .12 .30
165 Mike Piazza .30 .75
166 Roberto Alomar .20 .50
167 Tom Glavine .20 .50
168 Alfonso Soriano .20 .50
169 Bernie Williams .20 .50
170 Brandon Claussen .12 .30
171 Derek Jeter .75 2.00
172 Don Mattingly .60 1.50
173 Drew Henson .12 .30
174 Jason Giambi .12 .30
175 Joe Torre MG .20 .50
176 Jorge Posada .20 .50
177 Mike Mussina .20 .50
178 Nick Johnson .12 .30
179 Roger Clemens .40 1.00
180 Whitey Ford .20 .50
181 Adam Morrissey .12 .30
182 Barry Zito .20 .50
183 David Justice .12 .30
184 Eric Chavez .12 .30
185 Jermaine Dye .12 .30
186 Mark Mulder .12 .30
187 Miguel Tejada .20 .50
188 Reggie Jackson .20 .50
189 Terrence Long .12 .30
190 Tim Hudson .20 .50
191 Anderson Machado .12 .30
192 Bobby Abreu .12 .30
193 Brandon Duckworth .12 .30
194 Jim Thome .20 .50
195 Eric Junge .12 .30
196 Jeremy Giambi .12 .30
197 Johnny Estrada .12 .30
198 Jorge Padilla .12 .30
199 Marlon Byrd .12 .30
200 Mike Schmidt .50 1.25
201 Pat Burrell .12 .30
202 Steve Carlton .20 .50
203 Aramis Ramirez .12 .30
204 Brian Giles .12 .30
205 Carlos Rivera .12 .30
206 Craig Wilson .12 .30
207 Dave Williams .12 .30
208 Jack Wilson .12 .30
209 Jose Castillo .12 .30
210 Kip Wells .12 .30
211 Roberto Clemente .75 2.00
212 Walter Young .12 .30
213 Ben Howard .12 .30
214 Brian Lawrence .12 .30
215 Cliff Bartosh .12 .30
216 Dennis Tankersley .12 .30
217 Oliver Perez .12 .30
218 Phil Nevin .12 .30
219 Ryan Klesko .12 .30
220 Sean Burroughs .12 .30
221 Tony Gwynn .30 .75
222 Xavier Nady .12 .30
223 Mike Rivera .12 .30
224 Barry Bonds .50 1.25
225 Benito Santiago .12 .30
226 Jason Schmidt .12 .30
227 Jeff Kent .12 .30
228 Kenny Lofton .12 .30
229 Rich Aurilia .12 .30
230 Robb Nen .12 .30
231 Tsuyoshi Shinjo .12 .30
232 Bret Boone .12 .30
233 Chris Snelling .12 .30
234 Edgar Martinez .20 .50
235 Freddy Garcia .12 .30
236 Ichiro Suzuki .40 1.00
237 John Olerud .12 .30
238 Kazuhiro Sasaki .12 .30
239 Mike Cameron .12 .30
240 Rafael Soriano .12 .30
241 Albert Pujols .40 1.00
242 J.D. Drew .12 .30
243 Jim Edmonds .20 .50
244 Ozzie Smith .40 1.00
245 Scott Rolen .20 .50
246 So Taguchi .12 .30
247 Stan Musial .50 1.25
248 Antonio Perez .12 .30
249 Aubrey Huff .12 .30
250 Dewon Brazelton .12 .30
251 Delvin James .12 .30
252 Joe Kennedy .12 .30
253 Toby Hall .12 .30
254 Alex Rodriguez .40 1.00
255 Ben Kozlowski .12 .30
256 Gerald Laird .12 .30
257 Hank Blalock .12 .30
258 Ivan Rodriguez .20 .50
259 Juan Gonzalez .12 .30
260 Kevin Mench .12 .30
261 Mario Ramos .12 .30
262 Mark Teixeira .20 .50
263 Nolan Ryan Rangers 1.00 2.50
264 Rafael Palmeiro .20 .50
265 Alexis Rios .30 .75
266 Carlos Delgado .12 .30
267 Eric Hinske .12 .30
268 Josh Phelps .12 .30
269 Kevin Cash .12 .30
270 Orlando Hudson .12 .30
271 Roy Halladay .20 .50
272 Shannon Stewart .12 .30
273 Vernon Wells .12 .30
274 Vinny Chulk .12 .30
275 Jason Anderson .12 .30
276 Craig Brazell RC .15 .40
277 Termel Sledge RC .15 .40
278 Ryan Cameron RC .15 .40
279 Clint Barmes RC .40 1.00
280 Jhonny Peralta .12 .30
281 Todd Wellemeyer RC .15 .40
282 John Leicester RC .15 .40
283 Brandon Webb RC .50 1.25
284 Tim Olson RC .15 .40
285 Matt Kata RC .15 .40
286 Rob Hammock RC .15 .40
287 Pete LaForest RC .15 .40
288 Nook Logan RC .15 .40
289 Prentice Redman RC .15 .40
290 Joe Valentine RC .15 .40
291 Jose Contreras RC .40 1.00
292 Josh Stewart RC .15 .40
293 Mike Nicolas RC .15 .40
294 Marshall McDougall .12 .30
295 Travis Chapman .12 .30
296 Jose Morban .12 .30
297 Michael Hessman RC .15 .40
298 Buddy Hernandez RC .15 .40
299 Shane Victorino RC .50 1.25
300 Jason Dubois .12 .30
301 Hideki Matsui RC .75 2.00
302 Ryan Wagner RC .15 .40
303 Adam Loewen RC .15 .40
304 Chien-Ming Wang RC .60 1.50
305 Hong-Chih Kuo RC .75 2.00
306 Delmon Young RC 1.00 2.50
307 Dan Haren RC .75 2.00
308 Rickie Weeks RC .50 1.25
309 Ramon Nivar RC .15 .40

2003 Donruss Champions Autographs

1-300 RANDOM INSERTS IN PACKS
302-309 RANDOM IN DLP R/T PACKS
PRINT RUNS B/WN 4-500 COPIES PER
NO PRICING ON QTY OF 45 OR LESS
2 Alfredo Amezaga/325 4.00 10.00
3 Chone Figgins/375 6.00 15.00
13 Junior Spivey/45 6.00 15.00
24 Andy Pratt/475 4.00 10.00
25 Adam LaRoche/400 4.00 10.00
26 Trey Hodges/305 4.00 10.00
29 Ed Rogers/500 4.00 10.00
30 Brian Roberts/500 10.00 25.00
31 Geronimo Gil/150 4.00 10.00
32 Jay Gibbons/475 4.00 10.00
33 Josh Towers/500 4.00 10.00
34 Casey Fossum/160 4.00 10.00
35 Cliff Floyd/70 10.00 25.00
37 Fred Lynn/50 15.00 40.00
38 Freddy Sanchez/400 6.00 15.00
46 Corey Patterson/100 6.00 15.00
49 Juan Cruz/250 4.00 10.00
51 Mark Prior/50 12.50 30.00
53 Nic Jackson/100 6.00 15.00
57 Corwin Malone/400 4.00 10.00
59 Joe Borchard/215 4.00 10.00
64 Tim Hummel/400 4.00 10.00
65 Jon Adkins/400 4.00 10.00
66 Adam Dunn/100 15.00 40.00
67 Austin Kearns/50 6.00 15.00
69 Jose Acevedo/315 4.00 10.00
70 Corky Miller/295 4.00 10.00
71 Eric Davis/45 15.00 40.00
74 Wily Mo Pena/450 6.00 15.00
76 Brian Tallet/250 4.00 10.00
78 Cliff Lee/330 6.00 15.00
79 Earl Snyder/225 4.00 10.00
81 Jeremy Guthrie/400 6.00 15.00
83 Luis Garcia/395 4.00 10.00
86 Ryan Church/395 6.00 15.00
87 Victor Martinez/250 10.00 25.00
88 Brandon Phillips/375 6.00 15.00
89 Jack Cust/498 4.00 10.00
90 Jason Jennings/375 4.00 10.00
91 Jeff Baker/400 4.00 10.00
92 Garrett Atkins/400 4.00 10.00
95 Rene Reyes/350 4.00 10.00
98 Fernando Rodney/500 4.00 10.00
100 Jack Morris/50 15.00 40.00
102 Mike Maroth/400 4.00 10.00
104 Jesus Medrano/500 4.00 10.00
109 Josh Wilson/400 4.00 10.00
110 Tim Redding/375 4.00 10.00
111 Carlos Hernandez/250 4.00 10.00
113 Henri Stanley/390 4.00 10.00
114 Jason Lane/250 6.00 15.00
117 Kirk Saarloos/149 4.00 10.00
120 Richard Hidalgo/120 4.00 10.00
121 Rodrigo Rosario/500 4.00 10.00
122 Roy Oswalt/100 10.00 25.00
123 Tommy Whiteman/375 4.00 10.00
124 Wade Miller/125 4.00 10.00
126 Angel Berroa/400 4.00 10.00
127 Brandon Berger/325 4.00 10.00
130 Jimmy Gobble/400 4.00 10.00
131 Dee Brown/500 4.00 10.00
132 Mike Sweeney/45 10.00 25.00
134 Runelvys Hernandez/400 4.00 10.00
138 Victor Alvarez/308 4.00 10.00
144 Paul Lo Duca/45 10.00 25.00
146 Ben Sheets/50 10.00 25.00
147 Bill Hall/450 4.00 10.00
148 Nick Neugebauer/375 4.00 10.00
151 Shane Nance/150 4.00 10.00
152 Takahito Nomura/50 10.00 25.00
153 A.J. Pierzynski/250 6.00 15.00
156 Adam Johnson/500 4.00 10.00
157 Rob Bowen/375 4.00 10.00
158 Torii Hunter/45 6.00 15.00
160 Endy Chavez/280 4.00 10.00
161 Javier Vazquez/50 10.00 25.00
162 Jose Vidro/45 6.00 15.00
164 Dwight Gooden/45 15.00 40.00
170 Brandon Claussen/475 4.00 10.00
178 Nick Johnson/500 6.00 15.00
181 Adam Morrissey/395 4.00 10.00
185 Jermaine Dye/125 6.00 15.00
189 Terrence Long/250 4.00 10.00
191 Anderson Machado/500 4.00 10.00
193 Brandon Duckworth/100 6.00 15.00
195 Eric Junge/279 4.00 10.00
196 Jeremy Giambi/195 4.00 10.00
205 Carlos Rivera/400 4.00 10.00
206 Craig Wilson/245 4.00 10.00
207 Dave Williams/265 4.00 10.00
208 Jack Wilson/500 6.00 15.00
209 Jose Castillo/400 4.00 10.00
210 Kip Wells/500 4.00 10.00
212 Walter Young/400 4.00 10.00
213 Ben Howard/500 4.00 10.00
214 Brian Lawrence/500 4.00 10.00
215 Cliff Bartosh/400 4.00 10.00
222 Xavier Nady/250 4.00 10.00
223 Mike Rivera/90 6.00 15.00
233 Chris Snelling/200 4.00 10.00
240 Rafael Soriano/500 4.00 10.00
248 Antonio Perez/500 4.00 10.00
249 Aubrey Huff/475 6.00 15.00
250 Dewon Brazelton/50 6.00 15.00
251 Delvin James/400 4.00 10.00
252 Joe Kennedy/250 4.00 10.00
253 Toby Hall/500 4.00 10.00
255 Ben Kozlowski/400 4.00 10.00
256 Gerald Laird/450 4.00 10.00
257 Hank Blalock/50 10.00 25.00
260 Kevin Mench/475 6.00 15.00
261 Mario Ramos/475 4.00 10.00
262 Mark Teixeira/40 15.00 40.00
265 Alexis Rios/400 8.00 20.00
267 Eric Hinske/390 4.00 10.00
269 Kevin Cash/375 5.00 12.00
274 Vinny Chulk/100 6.00 15.00
275 Jason Anderson/493 10.00 25.00
277 Termel Sledge/500 4.00 10.00
278 Ryan Cameron/475 4.00 10.00
279 Clint Barmes/475 5.00 12.00
280 Jhonny Peralta/500 6.00 15.00
281 Todd Wellemeyer/477 4.00 10.00
282 John Leicester/480 4.00 10.00
283 Brandon Webb/500 6.00 15.00
284 Tim Olson/500 4.00 10.00
285 Matt Kata/487 4.00 10.00
286 Rob Hammock/486 4.00 10.00
287 Pete LaForest/500 4.00 10.00
288 Nook Logan/500 6.00 15.00
289 Prentice Redman/488 4.00 10.00
290 Joe Valentine/475 4.00 10.00
291 Jose Contreras/100 12.50 30.00
292 Josh Stewart/485 4.00 10.00
293 Mike Nicolas/500 4.00 10.00
295 Travis Chapman/100 6.00 15.00
296 Jose Morban/475 4.00 10.00
297 Michael Hessman/500 4.00 10.00
298 Buddy Hernandez/500 4.00 10.00
299 Shane Victorino/480 6.00 15.00
300 Jason Dubois/480 4.00 10.00
302 Ryan Wagner/100 4.00 10.00
303 Adam Loewen/100 10.00 25.00
304 Chien-Ming Wang/100 30.00 60.00
305 Hong-Chih Kuo/100 50.00 100.00
307 Dan Haren/100 6.00 15.00
309 Ramon Nivar/100 4.00 10.00

2003 Donruss Champions Metalized

*METALIZED ACTIVE 1-301: 4X TO 10X
*METALIZED RETIRED 1-301: 4X TO 10X
*METALIZED RC'S 1-301: 3X TO 8X
*METALIZED RC'S 302-309: 3X TO 8X
1-301 RANDOM INSERTS IN PACKS
302-309 RANDOM IN DLP R/T PACKS
STATED PRINT RUN 100 SERIAL #'d SETS

2003 Donruss Champions Call to the Hall

STATED PRINT RUN 2500 SERIAL #'d SETS
HOLO-FOIL PRINT RUN 25 #'d SETS
NO HOLO-FOIL PRICING DUE TO SCARCITY
*METALIZED: 1.2X TO 3X BASIC CALL
METALIZED PRINT RUN 100 #'d SETS
1 Nolan Ryan 3.00 8.00
2 Tom Seaver .60 1.50
3 Phil Rizzuto .60 1.50
4 Orlando Cepeda .60 1.50
5 Al Kaline .60 1.50
6 Hoyt Wilhelm .60 1.50
7 Luis Aparicio .60 1.50
8 Billy Williams .60 1.50
9 Jim Palmer .60 1.50
10 Mike Schmidt 1.50 4.00

2003 Donruss Champions Grand Champions

STATED ODDS 1:18 HOBBY, 1:23 RETAIL
HOLO-FOIL RANDOM INSERTS IN PACKS
HOLO-FOIL PRINT RUN 25 #'d SETS
NO HOLO-FOIL PRICING DUE TO SCARCITY
*METALIZED: 1.2X TO 3X BASIC GRAND
METALIZED PRINT RUN 100 SERIAL #'d SETS
1 Stan Musial 1.50 4.00
2 Bob Feller .60 1.50
3 Reggie Jackson .60 1.50
4 George Brett 2.00 5.00
5 Jim Palmer .60 1.50
6 Harmon Killebrew 1.00 2.50
7 Ernie Banks 1.00 2.50
8 Frank Robinson .60 1.50
9 Greg Maddux 1.25 3.00
10 Whitey Ford .60 1.50
11 Bob Gibson .60 1.50
12 Mike Schmidt 1.50 4.00
13 Nolan Ryan 3.00 8.00
14 Warren Spahn .60 1.50
15 Rod Carew .60 1.50
16 Hoyt Wilhelm .60 1.50
17 Duke Snider .60 1.50
18 Tom Seaver .60 1.50
19 Steve Carlton .60 1.50
20 Yogi Berra 1.00 2.50
21 Cal Ripken 3.00 8.00
22 Tony Gwynn 1.00 2.50
23 Wade Boggs .60 1.50
24 Rickey Henderson 1.00 2.50
25 Roger Clemens 1.25 3.00

2003 Donruss Champions Statistical Champs

STATED ODDS 1:10 HOBBY, ONE IN 23 RETAIL
1 Alex Rodriguez 1.25 3.00
2 Alfonso Soriano .60 1.50
3 Curt Schilling .60 1.50
4 Eddie Mathews 1.00 2.50
5 Fred Lynn .40 1.00
6 Harmon Killebrew 1.00 2.50
7 Hideo Nomo 1.00 2.50
8 Jim Thome .60 1.50
9 Kirby Puckett 1.00 2.50
10 Luis Gonzalez .40 1.00
11 Manny Ramirez 1.00 2.50
12 Jason Giambi .40 1.00
13 Mike Schmidt 1.50 4.00
14 Nomar Garciaparra .60 1.50
15 Lou Brock .60 1.50
16 Randy Johnson 1.00 2.50
17 Reggie Jackson .60 1.50
18 Rickey Henderson 1.00 2.50
19 Roberto Clemente 2.50 6.00
20 Barry Zito .60 1.50
21 Todd Helton .60 1.50
22 Tom Seaver .60 1.50
23 Tony Gwynn 1.00 2.50
24 Torii Hunter .40 1.00
25 Troy Glaus .40 1.00
26 Wade Boggs .60 1.50
27 Rod Carew .60 1.50
28 Juan Gonzalez .40 1.00
29 Sammy Sosa 1.00 2.50
30 Warren Spahn .60 1.50

2003 Donruss Champions Statistical Champs Materials

STATED PRINT RUNS LISTED BELOW
NO PRICING ON QTY OF 25 OR LESS
1 Alex Rodriguez Jsy/250 10.00 25.00
3 Curt Schilling Jsy/225 4.00 10.00
4 Eddie Mathews Jsy/200 10.00 25.00
5 Fred Lynn Jsy/50 15.00 40.00
6 Harmon Killebrew Jsy/250 10.00 25.00
7 Hideo Nomo Jsy/110 30.00 60.00
8 Jim Thome Jsy/250 6.00 15.00
9 Kirby Puckett Jsy/250 10.00 25.00
10 Luis Gonzalez Jsy/250 4.00 10.00
11 Manny Ramirez Jsy/155 6.00 15.00
12 Jason Giambi Jsy/250 4.00 10.00
13 Mike Schmidt Jsy/250 15.00 40.00
14 Nomar Garciaparra Jsy/99 15.00 40.00
15 Lou Brock Jsy/250 10.00 25.00
16 Randy Johnson Jsy/100 10.00 25.00
17 Reggie Jackson Jsy/200 10.00 25.00
18 Rickey Henderson Jsy/184 6.00 15.00
20 Barry Zito Jsy/100 6.00 15.00
21 Todd Helton Jsy/250 6.00 15.00
22 Tom Seaver Jsy/100 15.00 40.00
23 Tony Gwynn Jsy/250 10.00 25.00
24 Torii Hunter Jsy/50 6.00 15.00
25 Troy Glaus Jsy/125 6.00 15.00
26 Wade Boggs Jsy/250 10.00 25.00
27 Rod Carew Hat/150 10.00 25.00
28 Juan Gonzalez Jsy/250 4.00 10.00
29 Sammy Sosa Jsy/250 6.00 15.00
30 Warren Spahn Jsy/150 10.00 25.00

2003 Donruss Champions Team Colors

STATED ODDS 1:10 HOBBY, 1:23 RETAIL
1 Miguel Tejada .60 1.50
2 Mike Schmidt 1.50 4.00
3 George Brett 2.00 5.00
4 Magglio Ordonez .60 1.50
5 Ryne Sandberg 2.00 5.00
6 Adam Dunn .60 1.50
7 Mark Prior .60 1.50
8 Tony Gwynn 1.00 2.50
9 Troy Glaus .40 1.00
10 Stan Musial 1.50 4.00
11 Kirby Puckett 1.00 2.50
12 Don Mattingly 2.00 5.00
13 Bobby Abreu .40 1.00
14 Ichiro Suzuki 1.25 3.00
15 Cal Ripken 3.00 8.00
16 Chipper Jones 1.00 2.50
17 Carlos Beltran .60 1.50
18 Alfonso Soriano .60 1.50
19 Albert Pujols 1.25 3.00
20 Andruw Jones .40 1.00
21 Bernie Williams .60 1.50
22 Todd Helton .60 1.50
23 Roberto Clemente 2.50 6.00
24 Jim Thome .60 1.50
25 Carlos Delgado .40 1.00
26 Derek Jeter 2.50 6.00
27 Garret Anderson .40 1.00
28 Nomar Garciaparra .60 1.50
29 Torii Hunter .40 1.00
30 Vladimir Guerrero .60 1.50

2003 Donruss Champions Team Colors Materials

STATED PRINT RUNS LISTED BELOW
NO PRICING ON QTY OF 25 OR LESS
1 Miguel Tejada Jsy/50 6.00 15.00
2 Mike Schmidt Jsy/200 15.00 40.00
3 George Brett Jsy/200 10.00 25.00
4 Magglio Ordonez Jsy/100 4.00 10.00
5 Ryne Sandberg Jsy/200 10.00 25.00
6 Adam Dunn Jsy/44 6.00 15.00
7 Mark Prior Jsy/200 6.00 15.00
8 Tony Gwynn Jsy/200 8.00 20.00
9 Troy Glaus Jsy/200 3.00 8.00
10 Stan Musial Jsy/200 15.00 40.00
11 Kirby Puckett Jsy/200 6.00 15.00
12 Don Mattingly Jsy/200 15.00 40.00
13 Bobby Abreu Jsy/200 3.00 8.00
14 Ichiro Suzuki Base/200 10.00 25.00
15 Cal Ripken Jsy/200 30.00 60.00
16 Chipper Jones Jsy/200 4.00 10.00
17 Carlos Beltran Jsy/200 3.00 8.00
19 Albert Pujols Base/200 6.00 15.00
20 Andruw Jones Jsy/200 4.00 10.00
21 Bernie Williams Jsy/200 4.00 10.00
22 Todd Helton Jsy/200 4.00 10.00
23 Roberto Clemente Jsy/200 20.00 50.00
24 Jim Thome Jsy/200 4.00 10.00
25 Carlos Delgado Jsy/200 3.00 8.00
26 Derek Jeter Base/200 10.00 25.00
27 Garret Anderson Jsy/50 6.00 15.00
28 Nomar Garciaparra Jsy/200 10.00 25.00
29 Torii Hunter Jsy/200 3.00 8.00
30 Vladimir Guerrero Jsy/200 4.00 10.00

2003 Donruss Champions Total Game

STATED ODDS 1:9 HOBBY, 1:12 RETAIL
1 Vladimir Guerrero .60 1.50
2 Nomar Garciaparra .60 1.50
3 Magglio Ordonez .60 1.50
4 Garret Anderson .40 1.00
5 Derek Jeter 2.50 6.00
6 Jim Thome .60 1.50
7 Torii Hunter .40 1.00
8 Todd Helton .60 1.50
9 Andruw Jones .40 1.00
10 Alfonso Soriano .60 1.50
11 Luis Gonzalez .40 1.00
12 Manny Ramirez 1.00 2.50
13 Paul Konerko .60 1.50
14 Alex Rodriguez 1.25 3.00
15 Carlos Beltran .60 1.50
16 Bernie Williams .60 1.50
17 Barry Bonds 1.50 4.00
18 Miguel Tejada .60 1.50
19 Jason Giambi .40 1.00
20 Ichiro Suzuki 1.25 3.00
21 Ivan Rodriguez .60 1.50
22 Rafael Palmeiro .60 1.50
23 Carlos Delgado .40 1.00
24 Vernon Wells .40 1.00
25 Sammy Sosa 1.00 2.50
26 Chipper Jones 1.00 2.50
27 Adam Dunn .60 1.50
28 Larry Walker .60 1.50
29 Shawn Green .40 1.00
30 Richie Sexson .40 1.00
31 Jose Vidro .40 1.00
32 Mike Piazza 1.00 2.50
33 Roberto Alomar .60 1.50
34 Bobby Abreu .40 1.00
35 Pat Burrell .40 1.00
36 Brian Giles .40 1.00
37 Albert Pujols 1.25 3.00
38 Lance Berkman .60 1.50
39 Ryan Klesko .40 1.00
40 Jeff Kent .40 1.00

2003 Donruss Champions Total Game Materials

STATED PRINT RUNS LISTED BELOW
NO PRICING ON QTY OF 25 OR LESS
1 Vladimir Guerrero Jsy/200 6.00 15.00
2 Nomar Garciaparra Jsy/100 10.00 25.00
3 Magglio Ordonez Jsy/100 6.00 15.00
4 Garret Anderson Jsy/50 8.00 20.00
5 Derek Jeter Base/200 10.00 25.00
6 Jim Thome Jsy/200 6.00 15.00
7 Torii Hunter Jsy/200 4.00 10.00
8 Todd Helton Jsy/200 6.00 15.00
9 Andruw Jones Jsy/200 6.00 15.00
11 Luis Gonzalez Jsy/200 4.00 10.00
12 Manny Ramirez Jsy/200 6.00 15.00
13 Paul Konerko Jsy/200 4.00 10.00
14 Alex Rodriguez Jsy/200 10.00 25.00
15 Carlos Beltran Jsy/200 4.00 10.00
16 Bernie Williams Jsy/200 6.00 15.00
17 Barry Bonds Base/200 10.00 25.00
18 Miguel Tejada Jsy/50 8.00 20.00
19 Jason Giambi Base/200 4.00 10.00
20 Ichiro Suzuki Base/200 10.00 25.00
21 Ivan Rodriguez Jsy/100 10.00 25.00
22 Rafael Palmeiro Jsy/200 6.00 15.00
23 Carlos Delgado Jsy/200 4.00 10.00
24 Vernon Wells Jsy/200 4.00 10.00
25 Sammy Sosa Jsy/200 6.00 15.00
26 Chipper Jones Jsy/200 6.00 15.00
27 Adam Dunn Jsy/44 8.00 20.00
28 Larry Walker Jsy/200 4.00 10.00
29 Shawn Green Jsy/100 6.00 15.00
30 Richie Sexson Jsy/200 4.00 10.00
31 Jose Vidro Jsy/200 4.00 10.00
32 Mike Piazza Jsy/50 10.00 25.00
33 Roberto Alomar Jsy/100 10.00 25.00
34 Bobby Abreu Jsy/200 4.00 10.00
35 Pat Burrell Jsy/200 4.00 10.00
36 Brian Giles Jsy/200 4.00 10.00
37 Albert Pujols Base/200 6.00 15.00
38 Lance Berkman Jsy/50 8.00 20.00
39 Ryan Klesko Jsy/200 4.00 10.00
40 Jeff Kent Jsy/200 4.00 10.00

2003 Donruss Champions World Series Champs

STATED PRINT RUN 2002 SERIAL #'d SETS
HOLO-FOIL PRINT RUN 25 #'d SETS
NO HOLO-FOIL PRICING DUE TO SCARCITY
*METALIZED: 1.25X TO 3X BASIC WS
METALIZED PRINT RUN 100 #'d SETS
1 Troy Glaus .75 2.00
2 Jarrod Washburn .75 2.00
3 Darin Erstad .75 2.00
4 Troy Percival .75 2.00
5 David Eckstein .75 2.00
6 Francisco Rodriguez 1.25 3.00
7 Garret Anderson .75 2.00
8 John Lackey 1.25 3.00
9 Tim Salmon .75 2.00
10 Chone Figgins .75 2.00
11 Adam Kennedy .75 2.00
12 Scott Spiezio .75 2.00
13 Ben Molina .75 2.00
14 Brad Fullmer .75 2.00
15 Troy Glaus MVP .75 2.00

2003 Donruss Champions Atlantic City National

PRINT RUN 5 SERIAL #'d SETS

2005 Donruss Champions

COMPLETE SET (450) 40.00 80.00
COMMON CARD (1-450) .20 .50
COMMON RC (1-450) .20 .50
PRESS PLATES RANDOM IN PACKS
PLATE PRINT RUN 1 SET PER COLOR
BLACK-CYAN-MAGENTA-YELLOW ISSUED
NO PLATE PRICING DUE TO SCARCITY
1 Adam Dunn .30 .75
2 Albert Pujols .60 1.50
3 Albert Pujols .60 1.50
4 Ichiro Suzuki .60 1.50
5 Alex Rodriguez .60 1.50
6 Andruw Jones .20 .50
7 Carlos Beltran Royals .30 .75
8 Derrek Lee .20 .50
9 Hideki Matsui .75 2.00
10 Ichiro Suzuki .60 1.50
11 Ichiro Suzuki .60 1.50
12 Jeff Kent Giants .20 .50
13 Ken Griffey Jr. 1.00 2.50
14 Ken Griffey Jr. 1.00 2.50
15 Sammy Sosa .50 1.25
16 Sean Casey Reds .20 .50
17 Troy Glaus Angels .20 .50
18 Derek Jeter 1.25 3.00
19 Cal Ripken 1.50 4.00
20 Roberto Alomar Indians .30 .75
21 B.J. Surhoff .20 .50
22 Brian Jordan .20 .50
23 Corey Koskie .20 .50
24 Doug Davis .20 .50
25 Jason Varitek .50 1.25
26 Jim Edmonds .30 .75
27 Kevin Mench .20 .50
28 Roberto Alomar O's .30 .75
29 Tony Armas Jr. .20 .50
30 Ramon Ortiz .20 .50
31 Rodrigo Lopez .20 .50
32 Andres Galarraga Giants .30 .75
33 Brian Lawrence .20 .50
34 Jay Payton .20 .50
35 Ryan Ludwick .20 .50
36 Hee Seop Choi .20 .50
37 J.D. Drew Cards .20 .50
38 Raul Mondesi .20 .50
39 Brian Jordan .20 .50
40 Luis Matos .20 .50
41 Russell Branyan .20 .50
42 Tony Gwynn .60 1.50
43 Francisco Rodriguez .30 .75
44 Frank Robinson .30 .75
45 Jeff Bagwell .30 .75
46 Tony Gwynn .60 1.50
47 Tony Gwynn .60 1.50
48 Will Clark .30 .75
49 Antonio Perez .20 .50
50 Rickey Henderson Yanks .50 1.25
51 Brian Lawrence .20 .50
52 Carlos Beltran Mets .30 .75
53 Chris Snelling .20 .50
54 Darryl Strawberry Dgr .20 .50
55 Doug Mientkiewicz Mets .20 .50
56 Edgardo Alfonzo .20 .50
57 Eric Chavez .20 .50
58 Eric Davis .20 .50
59 Guillermo Quiroz .20 .50
60 J.D. Drew Braves .20 .50
61 J.D. Drew Dgr .20 .50
62 Walter Young .20 .50
63 John Kruk .20 .50
64 Jose Reyes .30 .75
65 Jose Vidro .20 .50
66 Josh Phelps .20 .50
67 Larry Walker Expos .30 .75
68 Lyle Overbay .20 .50
69 Manny Ramirez .50 1.25
70 Marlon Byrd Phils .20 .50
71 Matt Williams .30 .75
72 Melvin Mora .20 .50
73 Nook Logan .20 .50
74 Orlando Hudson .20 .50
75 Orlando Hudson .20 .50
76 Orlando Hudson .20 .50
77 Paul Konerko .30 .75
78 Raul Mondesi .20 .50
79 Reed Johnson .20 .50
80 Ryan Ludwick .20 .50
81 So Taguchi .20 .50
82 Toby Hall .20 .50
83 Todd Helton .30 .75
84 Tommy John Dgr .20 .50
85 Tony Clark .20 .50
86 Victor Martinez .20 .50
87 Vladimir Guerrero Angels .30 .75
88 Wade Boggs .30 .75
89 Roberto Clemente 1.25 3.00
90 Angel Berroa .20 .50
91 Termel Sledge .20 .50
92 Andres Galarraga Rockies .30 .75
93 Brooks Robinson .30 .75
94 Brooks Robinson .30 .75
95 Dennis Tankersley .20 .50
96 Don Mattingly 1.00 2.50
97 Ricardo Rodriguez Rgr .20 .50
98 Deivi Cruz Nats .20 .50
99 Deivi Cruz Giants .20 .50
100 Pete LaForest .20 .50
101 Roger Clemens Sox .60 1.50
102 Frankie Francisco .20 .50
103 Kevin Millwood Phils .20 .50
104 Tony Womack .20 .50
105 Jeff Bagwell .30 .75
106 Billy Martin .30 .75
107 J.T. Snow .20 .50
108 Juan Uribe .20 .50
109 Ryan Dempster .20 .50
110 Toby Hall .20 .50
111 Dennis Tankersley .20 .50
112 Freddy Garcia .20 .50
113 Garrett Atkins .20 .50
114 Troy Glaus Angels .20 .50

115 Gabe Kapler .20 .50
116 Jeff Kent Jays .20 .50
117 Rondell White .20 .50
118 C.C. Sabathia .30 .75
119 Javier Vazquez .20 .50
120 Mike Cameron .20 .50
121 Pat Burrell .20 .50
122 Lew Ford .20 .50
123 Brad Radke .20 .50
124 Preston Wilson .20 .50
125 Ray Durham .20 .50
126 Vernon Wells .20 .50
127 Bo Jackson Sox .50 1.25
128 Dmitri Young .20 .50
129 Doug Davis .20 .50
130 Brandon Duckworth .20 .50
131 Brandon Backe .20 .50
132 Juan Encarnacion Tigers .20 .50
133 Mike Maroth .20 .50
134 Sean Casey Indians .20 .50
135 Travis Hafner Rgr .20 .50
136 Wes Helms .20 .50
137 Randy Johnson M's .50 1.25
138 Larry Walker Cards .30 .75
139 Luis Gonzalez .20 .50
140 John Olerud M's .20 .50
141 Kazuhisa Ishii .20 .50
142 Mike Lowell .20 .50
143 Kevin Millwood Braves .20 .50
144 Chad Gaudin .20 .50
145 Bret Boone .20 .50
146 Cliff Floyd M's .20 .50
147 Dale Murphy .50 1.25
148 Rickey Henderson M's .50 1.25
149 Ricardo Rodriguez Indians .20 .50
150 Richard Hidalgo Astros .20 .50
151 Joe Kennedy Rockies .20 .50
152 Juan Pierre Rockies .20 .50
153 Juan Pierre M's .20 .50
154 Lance Berkman .30 .75
155 Joe Borchard .20 .50
156 Craig Monroe .20 .50
157 Abraham Nunez .20 .50
158 Willie Wilson .20 .50
159 Carlos Lee Brewers .20 .50
160 Carl Everett .20 .50
161 Frank White .20 .50
162 Craig Biggio .30 .75
163 Jason Varitek .50 1.25
164 Magglio Ordonez .30 .75
165 Carlos Delgado M's .20 .50
166 Casey Kotchman .20 .50
167 Kenny Lofton Braves .20 .50
168 Gil Hodges .30 .75
169 Rafael Furcal .20 .50
170 Ramon Vazquez .20 .50
171 Jeff Bagwell .30 .75
172 Jason Lane .20 .50
173 Nomar Garciaparra .30 .75
174 Willie Harris .20 .50
175 Adam Dunn .30 .75
176 Jose Cruz Jr. D'backs .20 .50
177 Robin Ventura Sox .20 .50
178 Al Oliver Rgr .20 .50
179 Wily Mo Pena .20 .50
180 Erubiel Durazo .20 .50
181 Joey Gathright .20 .50
182 Luis Castillo .20 .50
183 Mark Teixeira .30 .75
184 Delmon Young .50 1.25
185 Esteban Loaiza .20 .50
186 Bo Jackson Royals .50 1.25
187 Freddy Sanchez .20 .50
188 Jason Bay .20 .50
189 Rickey Henderson A's .50 1.25
190 Shawn Green D'backs .20 .50
191 Roger Cedeno Mets .20 .50
192 Hideki Matsui .75 2.00
193 Andruw Jones .20 .50
194 David Wright .40 1.00
195 Cesar Izturis Dgr .20 .50
196 Chipper Jones .50 1.25
197 Troy Glaus D'backs .20 .50
198 Cliff Floyd Mets .20 .50
199 Jason Jennings .20 .50
200 Mike Lowell .20 .50
201 Johnny Damon .30 .75
202 Aramis Ramirez Cubs .20 .50
203 John Smoltz .50 1.25
204 Alan Trammell .30 .75
205 Moises Alou Astros .20 .50
206 Randy Johnson Expos .50 1.25
207 Reggie Sanders .20 .50
208 Rickey Henderson Dgr .50 1.25
209 Runelvys Hernandez .20 .50
210 Ryan Klesko .20 .50
211 Casey Fossum .20 .50
212 Robert Fick Tigers .20 .50
213 Al Oliver Dgr .20 .50
214 Kazuo Matsui .20 .50
215 Pedro Martinez Dgr .30 .75
216 Roberto Alomar Sox .30 .75
217 Greg Maddux .60 1.50
218 Mark Ellis .20 .50
219 Shawn Green Dgr .20 .50
220 Shawn Green Jays .20 .50
221 Willie McCovey .30 .75
222 Rafael Furcal .20 .50
223 Richie Ashburn .30 .75
224 Edgar Martinez .30 .75
225 Carlos Delgado Jays .20 .50
226 David Justice Braves .20 .50
227 Jose Cruz .20 .50
228 Larry Walker Rockies .30 .75
229 Miguel Tejada .30 .75
230 Andres Galarraga Braves .30 .75
231 Trot Nixon .20 .50
232 Willie Mays Mets 1.00 2.50
233 Dennis Eckersley .30 .75
234 Michael Barrett .20 .50
235 Jose Cruz Jr. Jays .20 .50
236 Nolan Ryan Astros 1.50 4.00
237 Hal Newhouser .30 .75
238 Roger Clemens Yanks .60 1.50
239 Victor Martinez .30 .75
240 Sean Burroughs .20 .50
241 Andres Galarraga Rgr .30 .75
242 Cal Ripken 1.50 4.00
243 Doug Mientkiewicz Twins .20 .50
244 Hank Aaron 1.00 2.50
245 Vladimir Guerrero Expos .30 .75
246 Reggie Jackson .30 .75
247 Terrence Long .20 .50
248 Tommy Lasorda .30 .75
249 Bert Blyleven .30 .75
250 Ken Boyer .30 .75
251 Maury Wills .20 .50
252 Lou Brock .30 .75
253 Don Sutton .30 .75
254 Enos Slaughter .30 .75
255 Ernie Banks .50 1.25
256 Gaylord Perry .30 .75
257 Joe Carter Jays .20 .50
258 Keith Hernandez .20 .50
259 Orlando Cabrera .20 .50
260 Phil Niekro Braves .30 .75
261 Robin Ventura Yanks .20 .50
262 Rod Carew .30 .75
263 Rollie Fingers .30 .75
264 Sammy Sosa .50 1.25
265 Byung-Hyun Kim .20 .50
266 Zach Day .20 .50
267 Richie Ashburn .30 .75
268 Mike Piazza .50 1.25
269 Tommy John Yanks .20 .50
270 Craig Biggio .30 .75
271 Hideki Matsui .75 2.00
272 Cesar Izturis Jays .20 .50
273 Paul Molitor Brewers .50 1.25
274 Steve Carlton Phils .30 .75
275 Justin Morneau .30 .75
276 Albert Pujols .60 1.50
277 John Olerud Jays .20 .50
278 Austin Kearns .20 .50
279 Travis Hafner Indians .20 .50
280 Charles Johnson M's .20 .50
281 Craig Wilson .20 .50
282 Joe Carter Indians .20 .50
283 Josh Beckett .20 .50
284 Dale Murphy .50 1.25
285 Robert Fick Padres .20 .50
286 David Justice Yanks .20 .50
287 Kirby Puckett .50 1.25
288 Juan Encarnacion M's .20 .50
289 Moises Alou Giants .20 .50
290 Shannon Stewart Twins .20 .50
291 Alfonso Soriano Rgr .30 .75
292 Jacque Jones .20 .50
293 Pee Wee Reese .30 .75
294 Deion Sanders .30 .75
295 Richard Hidalgo Rgr .20 .50
296 Rocco Baldelli .20 .50
297 Bill Hall .20 .50
298 Mike Sweeney .20 .50
299 Paul Molitor Twins .50 1.25
300 Will Clark .30 .75
301 Torii Hunter .20 .50
302 Jim Thome .30 .75
303 Kevin Mench .20 .50
304 John Buck .20 .50
305 Joe Morgan .30 .75
306 Wilson Betemit .20 .50
307 Ivan Rodriguez .30 .75
308 Michael Young .20 .50
309 Moises Alou Cubs .20 .50
310 So Taguchi .20 .50
311 Rickey Henderson Padres .50 1.25
312 Kenny Lofton Indians .20 .50
313 Rickey Henderson Sox .50 1.25
314 Shannon Stewart Jays .20 .50
315 Fred Lynn .20 .50
316 Mark Prior .30 .75
317 Tony Perez .30 .75
318 Dontrelle Willis .20 .50
319 Xavier Nady .20 .50
320 Juan Uribe .20 .50
321 Chipper Jones .50 1.25
322 Joe Crede .20 .50
323 Kerry Wood .20 .50
324 Eric Hinske .20 .50
325 Carlos Lee Sox .20 .50
326 Joe Borchard .20 .50
327 Sean Casey Indians .20 .50
328 Joe Kennedy Rays .20 .50
329 Brandon Duckworth .20 .50
330 Willie Mays NY Giants 1.00 2.50
331 Andruw Jones .20 .50
332 Brandon Claussen .20 .50
333 Brandon Claussen .20 .50
334 Brian Giles .20 .50
335 Gary Sheffield .20 .50
336 Mark Grace .30 .75
337 Ryne Sandberg 1.00 2.50
338 Sammy Sosa .50 1.25
339 Steve Carlton Cards .30 .75
340 Vernon Wells .20 .50
341 Wade Miller .20 .50
342 Andre Dawson .30 .75
343 Darryl Strawberry Mets .20 .50
344 Nolan Ryan Angels 1.50 4.00
345 Curt Schilling .30 .75
346 Bo Jackson Royals .50 1.25
347 Darin Erstad .20 .50
348 Alfonso Soriano Yanks .30 .75
349 A.J. Burnett .20 .50
350 David Ortiz Sox .50 1.25
351 George Foster .20 .50
352 Rafael Palmeiro .30 .75
353 Alan Trammell .30 .75
354 Willie Mays SF Giants 1.00 2.50
355 Bernie Williams .30 .75
356 Phil Niekro Yanks .30 .75
357 Hank Blalock .20 .50
358 Miguel Cabrera .50 1.25
359 Carl Yastrzemski .60 1.50
360 Aramis Ramirez Pirates .20 .50
361 Frank Thomas .50 1.25
362 Tony Oliva .20 .50
363 Roger Clemens Astros .60 1.50
364 Adam Loewen .20 .50
365 Alex Cintron .20 .50
366 Alfredo Simon .20 .50
367 Angel Guzman .20 .50
368 Anthony Lerew .20 .50
369 Ben Hendrickson .20 .50
370 Brandon McCarthy RC .30 .75
371 Bubba Nelson .20 .50
372 Clint Nageotte .20 .50
373 Eddy Rodriguez .20 .50
374 Edwin Moreno .20 .50
375 J.J. Putz .20 .50
376 Jake Woods .20 .50
377 Jeff Suppan .20 .50
378 Jeremy Affeldt .20 .50
379 Jose Castillo .20 .50
380 Justin Leone .20 .50
381 Justin Verlander RC 4.00 10.00
382 Marlon Byrd Nats .20 .50
383 Mike Gosling .20 .50
384 Prince Fielder RC 1.00 2.50
385 Randy Wolf .20 .50
386 Raul Ibanez .30 .75
387 Raul Tablado RC .20 .50
388 Rick Dempsey .20 .50
389 Roberto Novoa .20 .50
390 Russ Ortiz .20 .50
391 Ryan Wing .20 .50
392 Scot Shields .20 .50
393 Steve Stone .20 .50
394 Tadahito Iguchi RC .30 .75
395 Todd Wellemeyer .20 .50
396 Travis Blackley .20 .50
397 Troy Percival .20 .50
398 Wilson Valdez .20 .50
399 Kevin Youkilis .20 .50
400 Jose Guillen .20 .50
401 Duke Snider .30 .75
402 Jeff Niemann RC .50 1.25
403 Johan Santana .30 .75
404 Nellie Fox .30 .75
405 Nellie Fox .30 .75
406 Marlon Byrd Nats .20 .50
407 Mike Piazza .50 1.25
408 Bobby Higginson .20 .50
409 Don Mattingly 1.00 2.50
410 Jayson Werth .30 .75
411 Al Kaline .50 1.25
412 Bobby Higginson .20 .50
413 Roger Cedeno Cards .20 .50
414 Roger Cedeno Mets .20 .50
415 Roger Cedeno Tigers .20 .50
416 Roger Cedeno Astros .20 .50
417 Roger Cedeno Dgr .20 .50
418 Magglio Ordonez .30 .75
419 Don Mattingly 1.00 2.50
420 Morgan Ensberg .20 .50
421 Charles Johnson Sox .20 .50
422 Albert Pujols .60 1.50
423 Dave Righetti .20 .50
424 Roy Halladay .30 .75
425 Tom Seaver .30 .75
426 Early Wynn .30 .75
427 Bob Gibson .30 .75
428 Doug Mientkiewicz Sox .20 .50
429 Jason Varitek .50 1.25
430 Tom Glavine .30 .75
431 Erik Bedard .20 .50
432 Pedro Martinez Sox .30 .75
433 David Ortiz Twins .50 1.25
434 Kazuhisa Ishii .20 .50
435 Trevor Hoffman .30 .75
436 Paul Molitor Twins .50 1.25
437 Derrek Lee .20 .50
438 Fergie Jenkins .30 .75
439 Tony Gwynn .60 1.50
440 Jeff Bagwell .30 .75
441 Steve Carlton Giants .30 .75
442 Adam Dunn .30 .75
443 Sean Casey Reds .20 .50
444 Geoff Jenkins .20 .50
445 Derek Jeter 1.25 3.00
446 J.T. Snow .20 .50
447 Kenny Lofton Giants .20 .50
448 Benito Santiago .20 .50
449 Tim Salmon .20 .50
450 Ichiro Suzuki .60 1.50

2005 Donruss Champions Impressions

*IMP: 1.25X TO 3X BASIC
*IMP: .75X TO 2X BASIC RC
STATED ODDS 1:3

2005 Donruss Champions Impressions Black

STATED PRINT RUN 5 SERIAL #'d SETS
NO PRICING DUE TO SCARCITY

2005 Donruss Champions Impressions Blue

*IMP BLUE: 2X TO 5X BASIC
*IMP BLUE: 1.25X TO 3X BASIC RC
RANDOM INSERTS IN PACKS
STATED PRINT RUN 100 SERIAL #'d SETS

2005 Donruss Champions Impressions Gold

*IMP GOLD: 2.5X TO 6X BASIC
*IMP GOLD: 1.5X TO 4X BASIC RC
RANDOM INSERTS IN PACKS
STATED PRINT RUN 50 SERIAL #'d SETS

2005 Donruss Champions Impressions Green

*IMP GREEN: 3X TO 8X BASIC
RANDOM INSERTS IN PACKS
STATED PRINT RUN 25 SERIAL #'d SETS
NO RC YR PRICING DUE TO SCARCITY

2005 Donruss Champions Impressions Orange

*IMP ORANGE: 2X TO 5X BASIC
*IMP ORANGE: 1.25X TO 3X BASIC RC
RANDOM INSERTS IN RETAIL PACKS
STATED PRINT RUN 75 SERIAL #'d SETS

2005 Donruss Champions Impressions Red

*IMP RED: 1.5X TO 4X BASIC
*IMP RED: 1X TO 2.5X BASIC RC
RANDOM INSERTS IN PACKS
STATED PRINT RUN 250 SERIAL #'d SETS

2005 Donruss Champions Impressions Autograph

STATED ODDS 1:46
ASTERISK PRINT RUNS B/WN 1-94 PER
TIER 1 PRINT RUNS B/WN 101-250 PER
TIER 2 PRINT RUNS B/WN 251-500 PER
TIER 3 PRINT RUNS B/WN 501-800 PER
TIER 4 PRINT RUNS B/WN 801-1200 PER
TIER 5 PRINT RUNS B/WN 1201-1500 PER
CARDS ARE NOT SERIAL-NUMBERED
PRINT RUN INFO PROVIDED BY DONRUSS
NO PRICING ON QTY OF 19 OR LESS
19 Cal Ripken/65 * 75.00 150.00
42 Tony Gwynn/65 * 15.00 40.00
44 Frank Robinson/59 * 12.50 30.00
46 Tony Gwynn/65 * 15.00 40.00
47 Tony Gwynn/61 * 15.00 40.00
206 Randy Johnson Expos/62 * 40.00 80.00
242 Cal Ripken/25 * 30.00 80.00
262 Rod Carew/37 * 12.50 30.00
279 Travis Hafner Indians/49 * 8.00 20.00
297 Bill Hall/52 * 5.00 12.00
322 Joe Crede/34 * 10.00 25.00
364 Adam Loewen T1 4.00 10.00
365 Alex Cintron T1 4.00 10.00
366 Alfredo Simon T2 4.00 10.00
367 Angel Guzman T2 4.00 10.00
369 Ben Hendrickson T3 4.00 10.00
371 Bubba Nelson T2 4.00 10.00
372 Clint Nageotte T2 4.00 10.00
373 Eddy Rodriguez/89 * 4.00 10.00
374 Edwin Moreno/55 * 5.00 12.00
375 J.J. Putz T3 4.00 10.00
376 Jake Woods T1 4.00 10.00
377 Jeff Suppan T4 4.00 10.00
378 Jeremy Affeldt T1 4.00 10.00
379 Jose Castillo T1 4.00 10.00
380 Justin Leone T2 4.00 10.00
382 Marlon Byrd Nats T1 4.00 10.00
383 Mike Gosling/93 * 4.00 10.00
385 Randy Wolf T1 4.00 10.00
386 Raul Ibanez T1 6.00 15.00
387 Raul Tablado/74 * 4.00 10.00
388 Rick Dempsey T4 8.00 20.00
389 Roberto Novoa T2 4.00 10.00
390 Russ Ortiz/49 * 5.00 12.00
391 Ryan Wing T1 4.00 10.00
392 Scot Shields T5 4.00 10.00
393 Steve Stone/65 * 8.00 20.00
395 Todd Wellemeyer/92 * 4.00 10.00
396 Travis Blackley/87 * 4.00 10.00
397 Troy Percival T1 6.00 15.00
398 Wilson Valdez T5 4.00 10.00
399 Kevin Youkilis T2 6.00 15.00
401 Duke Snider/30 * 15.00 40.00
402 Jeff Niemann/77 * 6.00 15.00
403 Johan Santana/29 * 15.00 40.00
423 Dave Righetti T1 6.00 15.00
425 Tom Seaver/28 * 20.00 50.00

2005 Donruss Champions Impressions Ball

*BALL p/r 75-100: .5X TO 1.2X MAT T1-T5
*BALL p/r 37-65: .6X TO 1.5X MAT T1-T5
*BALL p/r 25-31: .75X TO 2X MAT T1-T5
RANDOM INSERTS IN PACKS
PRINT RUNS B/WN 1-100 COPIES PER
NO PRICING ON QTY OF 24 OR LESS
192 Hideki Matsui/40 15.00 40.00
316 Mark Prior/31 5.00 12.00
348 Alfonso Soriano Yanks/75 2.50 6.00
352 Rafael Palmeiro/65 4.00 10.00
390 Russ Ortiz/50 3.00 8.00

2005 Donruss Champions Impressions Batting Glove

RANDOM INSERTS IN PACKS
PRINT RUNS B/WN 44-145 COPIES PER
306 Wilson Betemit/145 2.00 5.00
320 Juan Uribe/125 2.00 5.00
322 Joe Crede/89 2.50 6.00
325 Carlos Lee Sox/71 2.50 6.00
334 Brian Giles/44 3.00 8.00
419 Don Mattingly/125 6.00 15.00

2005 Donruss Champions Impressions Button

PRINT RUNS B/WN 1-16 COPIES PER
PRICING DUE TO SCARCITY

2005 Donruss Champions Impressions Fielding Glove

PRINT RUNS B/WN 26-250 COPIES PER
317 Tony Perez/49 4.00 10.00
319 Xavier Nady/97 2.50 6.00
321 Chipper Jones/26 15.00 40.00
328 Joe Kennedy Rays/130 2.00 5.00
331 Andruw Jones/82 3.00 8.00
332 Brandon Claussen/250 2.00 5.00
336 Mark Grace/186 3.00 8.00
337 Ryne Sandberg/64 10.00 25.00
339 Steve Carlton Cards/86 3.00 8.00
341 Wade Miller/117 2.00 5.00
420 Morgan Ensberg/87 2.50 6.00

2005 Donruss Champions Impressions Hat

RANDOM INSERTS IN PACKS
PRINT RUNS B/WN 1-250 COPIES PER
NO PRICING ON QTY OF 1
313 Rickey Henderson Sox/219 4.00 10.00
314 Shannon Stewart Jays/250 2.00 5.00
316 Mark Prior/250 2.50 6.00
329 Brandon Duckworth/157 2.00 5.00
332 Brandon Claussen/250 2.00 5.00
340 Vernon Wells/26 4.00 10.00

2005 Donruss Champions Impressions Material

STATED ODDS 1:8
ASTERISK PRINT RUNS B/WN 2-90 PER
TIER 1 PRINT RUNS B/WN 101-250 PER
TIER 2 PRINT RUNS B/WN 251-500 PER
TIER 3 PRINT RUNS B/WN 501-800 PER
TIER 4 PRINT RUNS B/WN 801-1200 PER
TIER 5 PRINT RUNS B/WN 1201-1500 PER
CARDS ARE NOT SERIAL-NUMBERED
PRINT RUN INFO PROVIDED BY DONRUSS
NO PRICING ON QTY OF 24 OR LESS
21 B.J. Surhoff Jsy T5 2.00 5.00
22 Brian Jordan Jsy T5 2.00 5.00
23 Corey Koskie Jsy T5 2.00 5.00
24 Doug Davis Jsy T5 2.00 5.00
25 Jason Varitek Jsy T5 3.00 8.00
26 Jim Edmonds Jsy/65 * 3.00 8.00
27 Kevin Mench Jsy T5 2.00 5.00
28 Roberto Alomar O's Jsy T5 2.50 6.00
29 Tony Armas Jr. Jsy T5 2.00 5.00
30 Ramon Ortiz Jsy T5 2.00 5.00
31 Rodrigo Lopez Jsy T5 2.00 5.00
32 A.Galarraga Giants Jsy T4 3.00 8.00
33 Brian Lawrence Jsy T5 2.00 5.00
34 Jay Payton Jsy T5 2.00 5.00
36 Hee Seop Choi Jsy T5 2.00 5.00
37 J.D. Drew Cards Jsy T4 2.00 5.00
38 Raul Mondesi Jsy T4 2.00 5.00
39 Brian Jordan Jsy T4 2.00 5.00
40 Luis Matos Jsy T5 2.00 5.00
41 Russell Branyan Jsy T4 2.00 5.00
42 Tony Gwynn Jsy T4 4.00 10.00
43 Francisco Rodriguez Jsy T4 2.00 5.00
44 Frank Robinson Jkt T5 2.50 6.00
45 Jeff Bagwell Pants T5 2.50 6.00
46 Tony Gwynn Pants T5 4.00 10.00
47 Tony Gwynn Pants T5 4.00 10.00
48 Will Clark Pants T5 3.00 8.00
50 R.Henderson Yanks Jkt T3 4.00 10.00
51 Brian Lawrence Bat T4 2.00 5.00
52 Carlos Beltran Mets Bat T5 2.00 5.00
53 Chris Snelling Bat T5 2.00 5.00
54 D.Strawberry Dgr Bat/50 * 4.00 10.00
55 D.Mientkiewicz Mets Bat T5 2.00 5.00
56 Edgardo Alfonzo Bat T5 2.00 5.00
57 Eric Chavez Bat T5 2.00 5.00
58 Eric Davis Bat T5 3.00 8.00
59 Guillermo Quiroz Bat T5 2.00 5.00
60 J.D. Drew Braves Bat T5 2.00 5.00
61 J.D. Drew Dgr Bat T5 2.00 5.00
62 Walter Young Bat T4 2.00 5.00
63 John Kruk Bat T5 2.50 6.00
64 Jose Reyes Bat T5 2.00 5.00
65 Jose Vidro Bat T5 2.00 5.00
66 Josh Phelps Bat T5 2.00 5.00
67 Larry Walker Expos Bat T5 2.00 5.00
68 Lyle Overbay Bat T5 2.00 5.00
69 Manny Ramirez Bat T1 2.50 6.00
70 Marlon Byrd Phils Bat T5 2.00 5.00
71 Matt Williams Bat T5 3.00 8.00
72 Melvin Mora Bat T5 2.00 5.00
73 Nook Logan Bat T5 2.00 5.00
74 Orlando Hudson Bat T5 2.00 5.00
75 Orlando Hudson Bat T5 2.00 5.00
76 Orlando Hudson Bat T5 2.00 5.00
77 Paul Konerko Bat T5 2.00 5.00
78 Raul Mondesi Bat T4 2.00 5.00
79 Reed Johnson Bat T5 2.00 5.00
81 So Taguchi Bat T4 2.00 5.00
82 Toby Hall Bat T5 2.00 5.00
83 Todd Helton Bat T2 2.50 6.00
84 Tommy John Dgr Bat T5 2.50 6.00
85 Tony Clark Bat T4 2.00 5.00
86 Victor Martinez Bat T5 2.00 5.00
87 V.Guerrero Angels Bat/51 * 5.00 12.00
88 Wade Boggs Bat T5 2.50 6.00
89 Roberto Clemente Bat T5 20.00 50.00
90 Angel Berroa Bat T5 2.00 5.00
91 Termel Sledge Bat T5 2.00 5.00
92 A.Galarraga Rockies Bat T4 3.00 8.00
93 Brooks Robinson Bat T5 3.00 8.00
94 Brooks Robinson Bat T4 3.00 8.00
95 Dennis Tankersley Bat T4 2.00 5.00
96 Don Mattingly Bat T4 5.00 12.00
97 R.Rodriguez Rgr Bat T4 2.00 5.00
98 Deivi Cruz Nats Bat T5 2.00 5.00
99 Deivi Cruz Giants Bat T3 2.00 5.00
100 Pete LaForest Bat T4 2.00 5.00
101 R.Clemens Sox Jsy T1 6.00 15.00
102 Frankie Francisco Jsy T4 2.00 5.00
103 Kevin Millwood Phils Jsy T4 2.00 5.00
104 Tony Womack Jsy T4 2.00 5.00
105 Jeff Bagwell Jsy T4 2.50 6.00
106 Billy Martin Jsy T3 4.00 10.00
107 J.T. Snow Jsy T3 2.00 5.00
108 Juan Uribe Jsy T4 2.00 5.00
109 Ryan Dempster Jsy T3 2.00 5.00
110 Toby Hall Jsy T4 2.00 5.00
111 Dennis Tankersley Jsy T3 2.00 5.00
112 Freddy Garcia Jsy T4 2.00 5.00
113 Garrett Atkins Jsy T4 2.00 5.00
114 Troy Glaus Angels Jsy T3 2.00 5.00
115 Gabe Kapler Jsy T4 2.00 5.00
116 Jeff Kent Jays Jsy T4 2.00 5.00
117 Rondell White Jsy T3 2.00 5.00
118 C.C. Sabathia Jsy T3 2.00 5.00
119 Javier Vazquez Jsy T4 2.00 5.00
120 Mike Cameron Jsy T3 2.00 5.00
121 Pat Burrell Jsy T3 2.00 5.00
122 Lew Ford Jsy T3 2.00 5.00
123 Brad Radke Jsy T3 2.00 5.00
124 Preston Wilson Jsy T3 2.00 5.00
125 Ray Durham Jsy T3 2.00 5.00
126 Vernon Wells Jsy T3 2.00 5.00
127 Bo Jackson Sox Jsy T3 4.00 10.00
128 Dmitri Young Jsy T3 2.00 5.00
129 Doug Davis Jsy T3 2.00 5.00
130 Brandon Duckworth Jsy T3 2.00 5.00
131 Brandon Backe Jsy T3 2.00 5.00
132 J.Encarn Tigers Jsy T3 2.00 5.00
133 Mike Maroth Jsy T3 2.00 5.00
134 Sean Casey Indians Jsy T4 2.00 5.00
135 Travis Hafner Rgr Jsy T3 2.00 5.00
136 Wes Helms Jsy T3 2.00 5.00
137 Randy Johnson M's Jsy T3 3.00 8.00
138 Larry Walker Cards Jsy T2 2.50 6.00
139 Luis Gonzalez Jsy T2 2.00 5.00
140 John Olerud M's Jsy T1 2.00 5.00
141 Kazuhisa Ishii Jsy T4 2.00 5.00
142 Mike Lowell Jsy T2 2.00 5.00
143 K.Millwood Braves Jsy T2 2.00 5.00
144 Chad Gaudin Jsy T2 2.00 5.00
145 Bret Boone Jsy T2 2.00 5.00
146 Cliff Floyd M's Jsy T2 2.00 5.00
147A Dale Murphy Jsy T3 3.00 8.00
147B Dale Murphy Bat 3.00 8.00
148 R.Henderson M's Pants T4 4.00 10.00
149 R.Rod Indians Pants T2 2.00 5.00
150 Richard Hidalgo Pants T3 2.00 5.00
151 J.Kennedy Rockies Bat T4 2.00 5.00
152 Juan Pierre Rockies Bat T4 2.00 5.00
153 Juan Pierre M's Bat T4 2.00 5.00
154 Lance Berkman Bat T4 2.00 5.00
155 Joe Borchard Bat T4 2.00 5.00
156 Craig Monroe Bat T4 2.00 5.00
157 Abraham Nunez Bat T1 2.00 5.00
158 Willie Wilson Bat T4 2.50 6.00
159 Carlos Lee Brewers Bat T3 2.00 5.00
160 Carl Everett Bat T4 2.00 5.00
161 Frank White Bat T4 2.50 6.00
162 Craig Biggio Bat T4 2.50 6.00
163 Jason Varitek Bat T4 3.00 8.00
164 Magglio Ordonez Bat T4 2.00 5.00
165 Carlos Delgado M's Bat T4 2.00 5.00
166 Casey Kotchman Bat T4 2.00 5.00
167 Kenny Lofton Braves Bat T4 2.50 6.00
168 Gil Hodges Bat T4 6.00 15.00
169 Rafael Furcal Bat T3 2.00 5.00
170 Ramon Vazquez Bat T3 2.00 5.00
171 Jeff Bagwell Bat T3 2.50 6.00
172 Jason Lane Bat T3 2.00 5.00
173 Nomar Garciaparra Bat T3 3.00 8.00
174 Willie Harris Bat T3 2.00 5.00
175 Adam Dunn Bat T3 2.00 5.00
176 J.Cruz Jr. D'backs Bat T3 2.00 5.00
177 Robin Ventura Sox Bat T3 2.50 6.00
178 Al Oliver Rgr Bat T3 2.50 6.00
179 Wily Mo Pena Bat T3 2.00 5.00
180 Erubiel Durazo Bat T3 2.00 5.00
181 Joey Gathright Bat T3 2.00 5.00
182 Luis Castillo Bat T3 2.00 5.00
183 Mark Teixeira Bat T3 2.50 6.00
184 Delmon Young Bat T3 2.00 5.00
185 Esteban Loaiza Bat T3 2.00 5.00
186 Bo Jackson Royals Bat T3 4.00 10.00
187 Freddy Sanchez Bat T3 2.00 5.00
188 Jason Bay Bat T3 2.00 5.00
189 R.Henderson A's Bat T3 4.00 10.00
190 S.Green D'backs Bat T2 2.00 5.00
191 Roger Cedeno Mets Bat T4 2.00 5.00
192 Hideki Matsui Bat T3 6.00 15.00
193 Andruw Jones Bat T3 2.50 6.00
194 David Wright Bat T3 4.00 10.00
195 Cesar Izturis Dgr Bat T2 2.00 5.00
196 Chipper Jones Bat T3 3.00 8.00
197 Troy Glaus D'backs Bat T3 2.00 5.00
198 Cliff Floyd Mets Bat T3 2.00 5.00
199 Jason Jennings Bat T2 2.00 5.00
200 Mike Lowell Bat T2 2.00 5.00
201 Johnny Damon Jsy T2 2.50 6.00
202 Aramis Ramirez Cubs Jsy T1 2.00 5.00
203 John Smoltz Jsy T2 2.50 6.00
204 Alan Trammell Jsy T2 2.50 6.00
205 Moises Alou Astros Jsy T2 2.00 5.00
206 R.Johnson Expos Jsy T2 3.00 8.00
207 Reggie Sanders Jsy T2 2.00 5.00
208 R.Henderson Dgr Jsy T2 4.00 10.00
209 Ru.Hernandez Jsy T2 2.00 5.00
210 Ryan Klesko Jsy T2 2.00 5.00
211 Casey Fossum Jsy T2 2.00 5.00
212 Robert Fick Tigers Jsy T2 2.00 5.00
213 Al Oliver Dgr Jsy T2 2.50 6.00
214 Kazuo Matsui Jsy T2 2.00 5.00
215 Pedro Martinez Dgr Jsy T2 2.50 6.00
216 Roberto Alomar Sox Jsy T1 2.50 6.00
217 Greg Maddux Jsy T1 4.00 10.00
218 Mark Ellis Jsy T2 2.00 5.00
219 Shawn Green Dgr Jsy T1 2.00 5.00
220 Shawn Green Jays Jsy T1 2.00 5.00
221 Willie McCovey Jsy T2 3.00 8.00
222 Rafael Furcal Jsy T1 2.00 5.00
223 Richie Ashburn Jsy T1 4.00 10.00
225 Carlos Delgado Jays Jsy T2 2.00 5.00
226 D.Justice Braves Jsy T2 3.00 8.00
227 Jose Cruz Jsy T2 2.50 6.00
228 L.Walker Rockies Jsy T1 2.00 5.00
229 Miguel Tejada Jsy T1 2.00 5.00
230 A.Galarraga Braves Jsy T1 3.00 8.00
231 Trot Nixon Jsy T1 2.00 5.00
232 Willie Mays Mets Jsy T2 10.00 25.00
233 Dennis Eckersley Jsy T1 2.50 6.00
234 Michael Barrett Jsy T1 2.00 5.00
235 Jose Cruz Jr. Jays Jsy T1 2.00 5.00
236 Nolan Ryan Astros Jsy T1 10.00 25.00
237 Hal Newhouser Jsy T1 2.50 6.00
238 R.Clemens Yanks Jsy T1 6.00 15.00
239 Victor Martinez Jsy/50 * 3.00 8.00
240 Sean Burroughs Jsy/90 * 2.50 6.00
241 A.Galarraga Rgr Jsy/84 * 4.00 10.00
242 Cal Ripken Jsy T1 15.00 40.00
243 D.Mient Twins Jsy/68 * 2.50 6.00
244 Hank Aaron Jsy/60 * 15.00 40.00
246 Reggie Jackson Jsy/35 * 6.00 15.00
247 Terrence Long Jsy/73 * 2.50 6.00
265 Byung-Hyun Kim Jsy T2 3.00 8.00
266 Zach Day Pants T2 2.00 5.00
267 Richie Ashburn Pants T2 4.00 10.00
268 Mike Piazza Pants T2 3.00 8.00
269 T.John Yanks Pants T1 2.50 6.00
270 Craig Biggio Pants T1 2.50 6.00
271 Hideki Matsui Pants T1 6.00 15.00
272 Cesar Izturis Jays Pants T1 2.00 5.00
273 P.Molitor Brewers Pants T1 2.50 6.00
274 S.Carlton Phils Pants/40 * 4.00 10.00
275 Justin Morneau Bat T2 2.00 5.00
276 Albert Pujols Bat T2 6.00 15.00
277 John Olerud Jays Bat T2 2.00 5.00
278 Austin Kearns Bat T2 2.00 5.00
279 T.Hafner Indians Bat T2 2.00 5.00
280 Charles Johnson M's Bat T2 2.00 5.00
281 Craig Wilson Bat T2 2.00 5.00
282 Joe Carter Indians Bat T2 3.00 8.00
283 Josh Beckett Bat T2 2.00 5.00
284 Dale Murphy Bat/42 * 5.00 12.00
285 Robert Fick Padres Bat T2 2.00 5.00
286 David Justice Yanks Bat T2 3.00 8.00
287 Kirby Puckett Bat T2 3.00 8.00
288 J.Encarnacion M's Bat T2 2.00 5.00
289 Moises Alou Giants Bat T2 2.00 5.00
290 S.Stewart Twins Bat T2 2.00 5.00
291 Alfonso Soriano Rgr Bat T2 2.00 5.00
292 Jacque Jones Bat T2 2.00 5.00
293 Pee Wee Reese Bat T2 3.00 8.00
294 Deion Sanders Bat/81 * 4.00 10.00
295 R.Hidalgo Rgr Bat T2 2.00 5.00
296 Rocco Baldelli Bat T2 2.00 5.00
297 Bill Hall Bat T2 2.00 5.00
298 Mike Sweeney Bat T1 2.00 5.00
299 Paul Molitor Twins Bat T2 2.50 6.00
300 Will Clark Bat T1 3.00 8.00
301 Torii Hunter Bat T1 2.00 5.00
305 Joe Morgan Bat/95 * 3.00 8.00
311 R.Henderson Padres Bat T1 4.00 10.00
315 Fred Lynn Bat/40 * 4.00 10.00
318 Dontrelle Willis Bat/51 * 3.00 8.00
342 Andre Dawson Bat/25 * 5.00 12.00
350 David Ortiz Sox Bat T1 2.50 6.00
351 George Foster Bat T1 2.50 6.00
353 Alan Trammell Bat T1 2.50 6.00
354 W.Mays SF Giants Bat T1 12.50 30.00
355 Bernie Williams Bat T1 2.50 6.00
356 Phil Niekro Yanks Bat T1 2.50 6.00
357 Hank Blalock Bat T1 2.00 5.00
358 Miguel Cabrera Bat T1 2.50 6.00
359 Carl Yastrzemski Bat/47 * 8.00 20.00
360 A.Ramirez Pirates Bat/57 * 3.00 8.00
361 Frank Thomas Bat T1 3.00 8.00
404 Nellie Fox Bat T5 6.00 15.00
405 Nellie Fox Bat T5 6.00 15.00
406 Marlon Byrd Nats Bat T5 2.00 5.00
407 Mike Piazza Bat T2 3.00 8.00
408 Bobby Higginson Bat T4 2.00 5.00
410 Jayson Werth Bat T5 2.00 5.00
411 Al Kaline Bat T4 4.00 10.00
412 Bobby Higginson Bat T3 2.00 5.00
413 R.Cedeno Cards Bat T4 2.00 5.00
414 R.Cedeno Mets Bat T4 2.00 5.00
415 R.Cedeno Tigers Bat T4 2.00 5.00
416 R.Cedeno Astros Bat T4 2.00 5.00
417 R.Cedeno Dgr Bat T4 2.00 5.00
418 Magglio Ordonez Bat T5 2.00 5.00
424 Roy Halladay Jsy/89 * 2.50 6.00
426 Early Wynn Jsy T1 3.00 8.00
427 Bob Gibson Jsy/36 * 5.00 12.00
428 D.Mientkiewicz Sox Jsy T5 2.00 5.00
429 Jason Varitek Jsy T2 3.00 8.00
430 Tom Glavine Jsy T1 2.50 6.00
431 Erik Bedard Jsy T2 2.00 5.00
432 Pedro Martinez Sox Jsy T2 2.50 6.00
433 David Ortiz Twins Jsy T3 2.50 6.00
434 Kazuhisa Ishii Jsy T2 2.00 5.00
435 Trevor Hoffman Jsy T2 2.00 5.00
436 Paul Molitor Twins Jsy T1 2.50 6.00
437 Derrek Lee Jsy T1 2.50 6.00
439 Tony Gwynn Pants T5 4.00 10.00
440 Jeff Bagwell Pants T4 2.50 6.00

2005 Donruss Champions Impressions Material Prime

*PRIME p/r 101-250: .6X TO 1.5X MAT T1-T5
*PRIMEp/r101-250: .5X TO 1.2X MATp/r68-95
*PRM.RETp/r101-250: .6XTO1.5X MAT T1-T5
*PRM.RETp/r101-250:.5XTO1.2XMATp/r68-95
*PRIME p/r 68-98: .75XTO 2X MAT T1-T5
*PRM.RET p/r 68-98: .75X TO 2X MAT T1-T5
*PRIME p/r 36-65: 1X TO 2.5X MAT T1-T5
*PRIME p/r 36-65: .75X TO 2X MAT p/r 68-95
*PRM.RET p/r 36-65: 1X TO 2.5X MAT T1-T5
*PRM.RETp/r36-65: .6X TO 1.5X MATp/r36-65
*PRIME p/r 25-34: 1.25X TO 3X MAT T1-T5
*PRIME p/r 25-34: 1X TO 2.5X MAT p/r 68-95
*PRM.RET p/r 25-34: 1.25X TO 3X MAT T1-T5
PRINT RUNS B/WN 1-250 COPIES PER
NO PRICING ON QTY OF 24 OR LESS
245 V.Guerrero Expos Jsy/250 5.00 12.00
248 Tommy Lasorda Jsy/186 15.00 40.00
249 Bert Blyleven Jsy/150 4.00 10.00
250 Ken Boyer Jsy/141 15.00 40.00
251 Maury Wills Jsy/37 6.00 15.00
252 Lou Brock Jsy/73 6.00 15.00
253 Don Sutton Jsy/108 4.00 10.00
254 Enos Slaughter Jsy/61 10.00 25.00
256 Gaylord Perry Jsy/127 4.00 10.00
257 Joe Carter Jays Jsy/153 5.00 12.00
258 Keith Hernandez Jsy/93 5.00 12.00
259 Orlando Cabrera Jsy/157 3.00 8.00
260 Phil Niekro Braves Jsy/82 5.00 12.00
261 R.Ventura Yanks Jsy/173 5.00 12.00
262 Rod Carew Jsy/86 6.00 15.00
263 Rollie Fingers Jsy/197 4.00 10.00
264 Sammy Sosa Jsy/250 5.00 12.00
438 Fergie Jenkins Pants/75 5.00 12.00
441 Steve Carlton Giants Jsy/54 6.00 15.00

2005 Donruss Champions Impressions MLB Logo Patch

PRINT RUNS B/WN 1-7 COPIES PER
PRICING DUE TO SCARCITY

2005 Donruss Champions Impressions Shoe

RANDOM INSERTS IN PACKS
PRINT RUNS B/WN 2-226 COPIES PER
NO PRICING ON QTY OF 15 OR LESS
310 So Taguchi/226 2.00 5.00
312 Kenny Lofton Indians/103 2.50 6.00
323 Kerry Wood/89 2.50 6.00
324 Eric Hinske/133 2.00 5.00
326 Joe Borchard/200 2.00 5.00
327 Sean Casey Indians/51 3.00 8.00
338 Sammy Sosa/75 4.00 10.00
421 Charles Johnson Sox/196 2.00 5.00

2005 Donruss Champions Impressions Combos

PRINT RUNS B/WN 1-210 COPIES PER
A/B VARIATION INFO ISSUED BY DONRUSS
NO PRICING ON QTY OF 19 OR LESS
302A Jim Thome Jsy-Jsy/105 3.00 8.00
302B Jim Thome Bat-Jsy/45 * 5.00 12.00
303 Kevin Mench Bat-Jsy/175 2.50 6.00
304 J.Buck Bat-Chest Prot/150 2.50 6.00
305 Joe Morgan Bat-Jsy/80 4.00 10.00
306A W.Betemit Bat-Hat/210 2.50 6.00
306B W.Betemit Hat-Shoe/65 * 4.00 10.00
307A I.Rod Bat-Chest Prot/175 3.00 8.00
307B I.Rod Chest Prot-Jsy/35 * 6.00 15.00
308A Michael Young Bat-Jsy/180 2.50 6.00
308B Michael Young Jsy-Jsy/50 * 4.00 10.00
310 So Taguchi Bat-Jsy/150 2.50 6.00
311 R.Henderson Hat-Pants/40 8.00 20.00

313 R.Henderson Bat-Jsy/85 6.00 12.00
315A Fred Lynn Bat-Jsy/60 5.00 12.00
316A Mark Prior Bat-Fld Glv/53 5.00 12.00
317 Tony Perez Bat-Jsy/62 5.00 12.00
319A X.Nady Btg Glv-Hat/50 4.00 10.00
320 Juan Uribe Bat-Shoe/59 4.00 10.00
322A J.Crede Hat-Shoe/190 2.50 6.00
322B J.Crede Bat-Btg Glv/40 * 4.00 10.00
323A K.Wood Hat-Jsy/33 5.00 12.00
324A Eric Hinske Jsy-Jsy/132 2.50 6.00
325A Carlos Lee Hat-Jsy/52 4.00 10.00
326A Joe Borchard Jsy-Jsy/57 4.00 10.00
332A B.Clauss Fld Glv-Shoe/165 2.50 6.00
334A Brian Giles Fld Glv-Jsy/90 3.00 8.00
342A A.Dawson Bat-Pants/165 3.00 8.00
342B A.Dawson Jsy-Pants/50 * 5.00 12.00
343 D.Strawberry Jsy-Pants/73 4.00 10.00
345 Curt Schilling Jsy-Jsy/89 4.00 10.00
350A David Ortiz Bat-Jsy/53 5.00 12.00
352 R.Palmeiro Bat-Jsy/201 3.00 8.00
355 B.Williams Bat-Jsy/43 5.00 12.00
357 Hank Blalock Bat-Jsy/47 4.00 10.00
359 C.Yastrzemski Bat-Jsy/73 12.50 30.00
362 Tony Oliva Bat-Jsy/93 4.00 10.00

2005 Donruss Champions Impressions Combos Prime

*PRM.RETp/r39-50: .6XTO1.5X COMp/r73-93
*PRM.RETp/r39-50: .5XTO1.2X COMp/r40-62
*PRIMEp/r25-33: 1X TO 2.5X COMp/r105-210
RANDOM INSERTS IN PACKS
PRINT RUNS B/WN 1-50 COPIES PER
NO PRICING ON QTY OF 24 OR LESS
301 Torii Hunter Hat-Bat/40 5.00 12.00
302 Jim Thome Jsy-Bat/40 6.00 15.00
306 W.Betemit Hat-Hat/25 6.00 15.00
309 Moises Alou Jsy-Bat/50 5.00 12.00
314 S.Stewart Jsy-Jsy/30 6.00 15.00
315 Fred Lynn Jsy-Jsy/39 6.00 15.00
318 D.Willis Jsy-Jsy/31 6.00 15.00
326 Joe Borchard Jsy-Jsy/50 5.00 12.00
328 Joe Kennedy Jsy-Jsy/50 5.00 12.00
335 G.Sheffield Jsy-Fld Glv/47 5.00 12.00
338 Sammy Sosa Jsy-Hat/49 8.00 20.00
340 Vernon Wells Jsy-Jsy/50 5.00 12.00
346 Bo Jackson Jsy-Jsy/50 10.00 25.00
347 Darin Erstad Jsy-Bat/33 6.00 15.00
349 A.J. Burnett Jsy-Jsy/39 5.00 12.00
351 G.Foster Jsy-Bat/50 6.00 15.00
360 A.Ramirez Jsy-Bat/50 5.00 12.00
363 R.Clemens Jsy-Jsy/26 15.00 40.00

2005 Donruss Champions Recollection Autographs

RANDOM INSERTS IN PACKS
PRINT RUNS B/WN 1-319 COPIES PER
NO PRICING ON QTY OF 23 OR LESS
AR2 Aramis Ramirez 02 DK/34 10.00 25.00
AR3 Aramis Ramirez 04 DK/33 10.00 25.00
BBR1 Brian Bruney 03 DK/151 4.00 10.00
BG3 Bobby Grich 87 D/68 4.00 10.00
BL1 Barry Larkin 03 DK/33 20.00 50.00
BM4 Bill Madlock 83 DK/35 10.00 25.00
BN1 Bubba Nelson 03 DK/147 4.00 10.00
BO1 Ben Oglivie 81 D/44 8.00 20.00
BO2 Ben Oglivie 82 D/81 6.00 15.00
BO3 Ben Oglivie 83 D/28 10.00 25.00
BO6 Ben Oglivie 86 D/62 8.00 20.00
BO7 Ben Oglivie 87 D/132 6.00 15.00
BW2 Brandon Webb 03 DK/51 8.00 20.00
CF2 Chone Figgins 03 DK/68 6.00 15.00
CLE2 Cliff Lee 03 DK/73 8.00 20.00
CS1 Chris Snelling 02 DK/47 5.00 12.00
DC1 David Cone 87 D/25 10.00 25.00
DC2 David Cone 89 DK/116 6.00 15.00
DH1 Dan Haren 03 DK/146 4.00 10.00
EA1 Erick Almonte 01 Eli ED/29 6.00 15.00
EC2 Eric Chavez 03 DK/33 10.00 25.00
EM3 Edgar Martinez 01 Eli/35 15.00 40.00
EM9 Edgar Martinez 03 DK/33 15.00 40.00
GG1 Geronimo Gil 01 Eli/40 5.00 12.00
GQ1 Guillermo Quiroz 03 DK/149 4.00 10.00
JD1 Jermaine Dye 00 D/25 10.00 25.00
JD2 Jermaine Dye 01 D/25 10.00 25.00
JD4 Jermaine Dye 03 DK/33 10.00 25.00
JGI1 Jay Gibbons 03 DK/27 6.00 15.00
JGU1 Jose Guillen 04 D/35 10.00 25.00
JG1 Jason Giambi 99 D/25 15.00 40.00
JG2 Jason Giambi 00 D/25 15.00 40.00
JG3 Jason Giambi 01 D/25 15.00 40.00
JJ2 Jacque Jones 03 DK/32 10.00 25.00
JK1 Jason Kubel 03 DK/151 4.00 10.00
JM6 Jack Morris 03 DK/74 6.00 15.00
JS1 Jae Weong Seo 04 DK/33 10.00 25.00
JV2 Jose Vidro 03 DK/71 6.00 15.00
MB1 Marlon Byrd 01 Eli ED/319 4.00 10.00
MB2 Marlon Byrd 03 D Sig Fld/25 6.00 15.00
MB3 Marlon Byrd 03 D Sig Hit/25 6.00 15.00
MB5 Marlon Byrd 04 DK/35 6.00 15.00
MLO1 Mike Lowell 03 DK/33 10.00 25.00
ML2 Mike Lieberthal 03 DK/27 10.00 25.00
MO4 M.Ordonez 03 Don DK/33 10.00 25.00
MO5 Magglio Ordonez 03 DK/33 10.00 25.00
PK1 Paul Konerko 04 DK/33 15.00 40.00
RD1 Rob Dibble 89 D/33 6.00 15.00
RD6 Rob Dibble 93 D/28 6.00 15.00
RHA1 Rich Harden 04 DK/33 10.00 25.00
RHO1 Ryan Howard 03 DK/150 60.00 120.00
RI1 Raul Ibanez 03 DK/72 8.00 20.00
RO1 Roy Oswalt 02 DK/73 6.00 15.00
RR1 R.Rodriguez 01 Eli ED/63 5.00 12.00
SB1 Sean Burroughs 03 DK/72 4.00 10.00
SS1 Shannon Stewart 02 DK/75 6.00 15.00
THU2 Torii Hunter 03 DK/72 6.00 15.00
TN1 Trot Nixon 04 DK/33 10.00 25.00
TW1 Todd Wellemeyer 03 DK/146 4.00 10.00
VW1 Vernon Wells 03 DK/33 10.00 25.00
VW2 Vernon Wells 03 PC/49 8.00 20.00
WM2 Wade Miller 03 DK/89 4.00 10.00

2001 Donruss Class of 2001 Samples

*STARS: 1.5X TO 4X BASIC CARDS
*GOLD: 1.5X TO 4X BASIC SAMPLES
GOLD: 10% OF THE TOTAL PRINT RUN

2001 Donruss Class of 2001

COMP.SET w/o SP's (100) 10.00 25.00
COMMON CARD (1-100) .15 .40
COMMON CARD (101-200) 1.50 4.00
101-200 PRINT RUN 1875 SERIAL #'d SETS
101-200 DISPLAY CUMULATIVE PRINT RUNS
101-200 ACTUAL PRINT RUNS LISTED BELOW
COMMON CARD (201-300) 2.50 6.00
201-300 PRINT RUN 625 SERIAL #'d SETS
201-300 DISPLAY CUMULATIVE PRINT RUNS
201-300 ACTUAL PRINT RUNS LISTED BELOW
101-300 RANDOM INSERTS IN PACKS
PRINT RUNS PROVIDED BY DONRUSS
1 Alex Rodriguez .50 1.25
2 Barry Bonds 1.00 2.50
3 Vladimir Guerrero .40 1.00
4 Jim Edmonds .15 .40
5 Derek Jeter 1.00 2.50
6 Jose Canseco .25 .60
7 Rafael Furcal .15 .40
8 Cal Ripken 1.25 3.00
9 Brad Radke .15 .40
10 Miguel Tejada .15 .40
11 Pat Burrell .15 .40
12 Ken Griffey Jr. .75 2.00
13 Cliff Floyd .15 .40
14 Luis Gonzalez .15 .40
15 Frank Thomas .40 1.00
16 Mike Sweeney .15 .40
17 Paul LoDuca .15 .40
18 Lance Berkman .15 .40
19 Tony Gwynn .50 1.25
20 Chipper Jones .40 1.00
21 Eric Chavez .15 .40
22 Kerry Wood .15 .40
23 Jorge Posada .25 .60
24 J.D. Drew .15 .40
25 Garret Anderson .15 .40
26 Mike Piazza .60 1.50
27 Kenny Lofton .15 .40
28 Mike Mussina .25 .60
29 Paul Konerko .15 .40
30 Bernie Williams .25 .60
31 Eric Milton .15 .40
32 Shawn Green .15 .40
33 Paul O'Neill .25 .60
34 Juan Gonzalez .15 .40
35 Andres Galarraga .15 .40
36 Gary Sheffield .15 .40
37 Ben Grieve .15 .40
38 Scott Rolen .25 .60
39 Mark Grace .25 .60
40 Hideo Nomo .40 1.00
41 Barry Zito .25 .60
42 Edgar Martinez .25 .60
43 Jarrod Washburn .15 .40
44 Greg Maddux .60 1.50
45 Mark Buehrle .25 .60
46 Larry Walker .15 .40
47 Trot Nixon .15 .40
48 Nomar Garciaparra .60 1.50
49 Robert Fick .15 .40
50 Sean Casey .15 .40
51 Joe Mays .15 .40
52 Roger Clemens .75 2.00
53 Chan Ho Park .15 .40
54 Carlos Delgado .15 .40
55 Phil Nevin .15 .40
56 Jason Giambi .15 .40
57 Raul Mondesi .15 .40
58 Roberto Alomar .25 .60
59 Ryan Klesko .15 .40
60 Andruw Jones .25 .60
61 Gabe Kapler .15 .40
62 Darin Erstad .15 .40
63 Cristian Guzman .15 .40
64 Kazuhiro Sasaki .15 .40
65 Doug Mientkiewicz .15 .40
66 Sammy Sosa .40 1.00
67 Mike Hampton .15 .40
68 Rickey Henderson .40 1.00
69 Mark Mulder .15 .40
70 Mark McGwire 1.00 2.50
71 Freddy Garcia .15 .40
72 Ivan Rodriguez .25 .60
73 Terrence Long .15 .40
74 Jeff Bagwell .25 .60
75 Moises Alou .15 .40
76 Todd Helton .25 .60
77 Preston Wilson .15 .40
78 Pedro Martinez .25 .60
79 Bobby Abreu .15 .40
80 Manny Ramirez Sox .25 .60
81 Jose Vidro .15 .40
82 Randy Johnson .40 1.00
83 Richie Sexson .15 .40
84 Troy Glaus .15 .40
85 Kevin Brown .15 .40
86 Carlos Lee .15 .40
87 Adrian Beltre .15 .40
88 Brian Giles .15 .40
89 Jermaine Dye .15 .40
90 Craig Biggio .25 .60
91 Richard Hidalgo .15 .40
92 Magglio Ordonez .15 .40
93 Aramis Ramirez .15 .40
94 Jeff Kent .15 .40
95 Curt Schilling .15 .40
96 Tim Hudson .15 .40
97 Fred McGriff .25 .60
98 Barry Larkin .25 .60
99 Jim Thome .25 .60
100 Tom Glavine .25 .60
101 Sean Douglass/1875 RC 1.50 4.00
102 Rob MacKowiak/1875 RC 2.50 6.00
103 Jeremy Fikac/1875 RC 1.50 4.00
104 Henry Mateo/1875 RC 1.50 4.00
105 Geronimo Gil/1875 RC 1.50 4.00
106 Ramon Vazquez/1875 RC 1.50 4.00
107 Pedro Santana/1875 RC 1.50 4.00
108 Ryan Jensen/1875 RC 1.50 4.00
109 Paul Phillips/1625 RC 1.50 4.00
110 Saul Rivera/1875 RC 1.50 4.00
111 Larry Bigbie/1875 1.50 4.00
112 Josh Phelps/1875 1.50 4.00
113 Justin Kaye/1875 RC 1.50 4.00
114 Kris Keller/1625 RC 1.50 4.00
115 Adam Bernero/1625 1.50 4.00
116 Victor Zambrano/1875 RC 2.50 6.00
117 Felipe Lopez/1875 1.50 4.00
118 Brian Roberts/1875 RC 4.00 10.00
119 Kurt Ainsworth/1875 1.50 4.00
120 George Perez/1625 RC 1.50 4.00
121 Wilson Guzman/1875 RC 1.50 4.00
122 Derrick Lewis/1875 RC 1.50 4.00
123 Nate Teut/1625 RC 1.50 4.00
124 Martin Vargas/1625 RC 1.50 4.00
125 Brandon Inge/1875 1.50 4.00
126 Travis Phelps/1875 RC 1.50 4.00
127 Les Walrond/1625 RC 1.50 4.00
128 Justin Atchley/1875 RC 1.50 4.00
129 Stubby Clapp/1875 RC 1.50 4.00
130 Bret Prinz/1875 RC 1.50 4.00
131 Bert Snow/1875 RC 1.50 4.00
132 Joe Crede/1625 2.50 6.00
133 Nick Punto/1875 RC 1.50 4.00
134 Carlos Hernandez/1875 1.50 4.00
135 Ken Vining/1875 RC 1.50 4.00
136 Luis Pineda/1875 RC 1.50 4.00
137 Winston Abreu/1625 RC 1.50 4.00
138 Matt Ginter/1625 1.50 4.00
139 Jason Smith/1875 RC 1.50 4.00
140 Gene Altman/1625 RC 1.50 4.00
141 Brian Rogers/1875 RC 1.50 4.00
142 Michael Cuddyer/1625 1.50 4.00
143 Mike Penney/1625 RC 1.50 4.00
144 Scott Podsednik/1875 RC 6.00 15.00
145 Esix Snead/1625 RC 1.50 4.00
146 Steve Watkins/1875 RC 1.50 4.00
147 Orlando Woodards/1625 RC 1.50 4.00
148 Jeff Deardorff/1775 RC 1.50 4.00
149 Eric Cyr/1875 RC 1.50 4.00
150 Blaine Neal/1625 RC 1.50 4.00
151 Ben Sheets/1875 2.50 6.00
152 Scott Stewart/1875 RC 1.50 4.00
153 Mike Koplove/1875 RC 1.50 4.00
154 Kyle Lohse/1875 RC 2.50 6.00
155 Fernando Rodney/1875 RC 1.50 4.00
156 Aubrey Huff/1625 1.50 4.00
157 Pablo Ozuna/1625 1.50 4.00
158 Bill Ortega/1625 RC 1.50 4.00
159 Toby Hall/1875 1.50 4.00
160 Kevin Olsen/1625 RC 1.50 4.00
161 Will Ohman/1625 RC 1.50 4.00
162 Nate Cornejo/1875 1.50 4.00
163 Jack Cust/1625 1.50 4.00
164 Juan Rivera/1875 1.50 4.00
165 Jerrod Riggan/1875 RC 1.50 4.00
166 Dustan Mohr/1875 RC 1.50 4.00
167 Doug Nickle/1875 RC 1.50 4.00
168 Craig Monroe/1625 RC 3.00 8.00
169 Jason Jennings/1625 1.50 4.00
170 Bart Miadich/1875 RC 1.50 4.00
171 Luis Rivas/1625 1.50 4.00
172 Tim Christman/1875 RC 1.50 4.00
173 Luke Hudson/1625 RC 1.50 4.00
174 Brett Jodie/1875 RC 1.50 4.00
175 Jorge Julio/1875 RC 1.50 4.00
176 David Espinosa/1625 1.50 4.00
177 Mike Maroth/1625 RC 2.50 6.00
178 Keith Ginter/1625 1.50 4.00
179 Juan Moreno/1875 RC 1.50 4.00
180 Brandon Knight/1875 RC 1.50 4.00
181 Steve Lomasney/1625 1.50 4.00
182 John Grabow/1625 RC 1.50 4.00
183 Steve Green/1875 RC 1.50 4.00
185 Bob File/1875 RC 1.50 4.00
186 Brent Abernathy/1625 1.50 4.00
187 Morgan Ensberg/1875 RC 4.00 10.00
188 Wily Mo Pena/1625 1.50 4.00
189 Ken Harvey/1875 1.50 4.00
190 Josh Pearce/1875 RC 1.50 4.00
191 Cesar Izturis/1625 1.50 4.00
192 Eric Hinske/1625 RC 2.50 6.00
193 Joe Beimel/1875 RC 1.50 4.00
194 Timo Perez/1775 1.50 4.00
195 Troy Mattes/1875 RC 1.50 4.00
196 Eric Valent/1625 1.50 4.00
197 Ed Rogers/1875 RC 1.50 4.00
198 Grant Balfour/1875 RC 1.50 4.00
199 Benito Baez/1875 RC 1.50 4.00
200 Vernon Wells/1875 1.50 4.00
201 Joe Kennedy PH/525* RC 4.00 10.00
202 Wilson Betemit PH/525* RC 4.00 10.00
203 Christian Parker PH/525* RC 2.50 6.00
204 Jay Gibbons PH/525* RC 4.00 10.00
205 Carlos Garcia PH/425* RC 2.50 6.00
206 Jack Wilson PH/525* RC 4.00 10.00
207 Johnny Estrada PH/425* RC 4.00 10.00
208 Wilkin Ruan PH/425* RC 2.50 6.00
209 Bran Duckworth PH/525* RC 2.50 6.00
210 Willie Harris PH/625 RC 2.50 6.00
211 Marlon Byrd PH/525* RC 2.50 6.00
212 C.C. Sabathia PH/600* 2.50 6.00
213 Den Tankersley PH/525* RC 2.50 6.00
214 Brandon Larson PH/425* RC 2.50 6.00
215 Alexis Gomez PH/425* RC 2.50 6.00
216 Bill Hall PH/525* RC 6.00 15.00
217 Antonio Perez PH/525* RC 4.00 10.00
218 Jeremy Affeldt PH/425* RC 2.50 6.00
219 Junior Spivey PH/625 RC 4.00 10.00
220 Casey Fossum PH/425* RC 2.50 6.00
221 Brandon Lyon PH/625 RC 2.50 6.00
222 Angel Santos PH/625 RC 2.50 6.00
223 Lance Davis PH/625 RC 2.50 6.00
224 Zach Day PH/425* RC 2.50 6.00
225 David Williams PH/425* RC 2.50 6.00
226 Cesar Crespo PH/625 RC 2.50 6.00
227 Jose Acevedo PH/425* RC 2.50 6.00
228 Travis Hafner PH/625 RC 8.00 20.00
229 Orlando Hudson PH/525* RC 4.00 10.00
230 Jose Mieses PH/425* RC 2.50 6.00
231 Ric Rodriguez PH/425* RC 2.50 6.00
232 Alfonso Soriano PH/525* 4.00 10.00
233 Jason Hart PH/525* 2.50 6.00
234 Endy Chavez PH/425* RC 2.50 6.00
235 Delvin James PH/525* RC 2.50 6.00
236 Ryan Drese PH/625 RC 4.00 10.00
237 Jeremy Owens PH/425* RC 2.50 6.00
238 Brad Voyles PH/425* RC 2.50 6.00
239 Nate Frese PH/425* RC 2.50 6.00
240 Josh Beckett PH/600* 4.00 10.00
241 Roy Oswalt PH/525* 4.00 10.00
242 Juan Uribe PH/475* RC 4.00 10.00
243 Cory Aldridge PH/425* RC 2.50 6.00
244 Adam Dunn PH/525* 4.00 10.00
245 Bud Smith PH/525* 2.50 6.00
246 Adr Hernandez PH/525* RC 2.50 6.00
247 Matt Guerrier PH/625 RC 2.50 6.00
248 Jimmy Rollins PH/625 2.50 6.00
249 Wilmy Caceres PH/425* RC 2.50 6.00
250 Jason Michaels PH/425* RC 2.50 6.00
251 Ichiro Suzuki PH/625 RC 12.00 30.00
252 John Buck PH/525* 6.00 15.00
252 Adam Johnson PH/625 2.50 6.00
253 Andres Torres PH/525* RC 2.50 6.00
254 Alfredo Amezaga PH/625 RC 2.50 6.00
255 Corky Miller PH/525* RC 2.50 6.00
256 Rafael Soriano PH/425* RC 2.50 6.00
257 Donaldo Mendez PH/425* RC 2.50 6.00
258 Victor Martinez PH/625 RC 15.00 40.00
259 Corey Patterson PH/525* 2.50 6.00
260 Horacio Ramirez PH/425* RC 4.00 10.00
261 Elpidio Guzman PH/425* RC 2.50 6.00
262 Juan Diaz PH/425* RC 2.50 6.00
263 Mike Rivera PH/625 RC 2.50 6.00
264 Brian Lawrence PH/425* RC 2.50 6.00
265 Josue Perez PH/425* RC 2.50 6.00
266 Jose Nunez PH/425* RC 2.50 6.00
267 Erik Bedard PH/625 RC 10.00 25.00
268 Albert Pujols PH/525* RC 60.00 150.00
269 Duaner Sanchez PH/425* RC 2.50 6.00
270 Cody Ransom PH/625 RC 2.50 6.00
271 Greg Miller PH/425* RC 2.50 6.00
272 Adam Pettyjohn PH/425* RC 2.50 6.00
273 Tsuyoshi Shinjo PH/625 RC 4.00 10.00
274 Claudio Vargas PH/425* RC 2.50 6.00
275 Just Duchscherer PH/625 RC 2.50 6.00
276 T.Spooneybarger PH/625 RC 2.50 6.00
277 Rick Bauer PH/625 RC 2.50 6.00
278 Josh Fogg PH/625 RC 2.50 6.00
279 Brian Reith PH/425* RC 2.50 6.00
280 Scott MacRae PH/625 RC 2.50 6.00
281 Ryan Ludwick PH/625 RC 6.00 15.00
282 Erick Almonte PH/625 RC 2.50 6.00
283 Josh Towers PH/525* RC 4.00 10.00
284 Juan A.Pena PH/625 RC 2.50 6.00
285 David Brous PH/425* RC 2.50 6.00
286 Erik Hiljus PH/625 RC 2.50 6.00
287 Nick Neugebauer PH/525* 2.50 6.00
288 Jackson Melian PH/625 RC 2.50 6.00
289 Billy Sylvester PH/425* RC 2.50 6.00
290 C Valderrama PH/425 RC 2.50 6.00
291 Jose Cueto PH/625 RC 2.50 6.00
292 Matt White PH/425* RC 2.50 6.00
293 Nick Maness PH/425* RC 2.50 6.00
294 Jason Lane PH/625 RC 2.50 6.00
295 Brandon Berger PH/625 RC 2.50 6.00
296 Angel Berroa PH/525* RC 4.00 10.00
297 Juan Cruz PH/525* RC 2.50 6.00
298 Dewon Brazelton PH/525* RC 2.50 6.00
299 Mark Prior PH/525* RC 5.00 12.00
300 Mark Teixeira PH/525* RC 10.00 25.00

2001 Donruss Class of 2001 First Class

*1ST CLASS 1-100: 6X TO 15X BASIC
1-100 PRINT RUN 100 SERIAL #'d SETS
CARDS DISPLAY CUMULATIVE PRINT RUNS
*1ST CLASS 101-200: .75X TO 2X BASIC
*1ST CLASS 201-300: .6X TO 1.5X BASIC
101-300 PRINT RUN 50 SERIAL #'d SETS
SKIP-NUMBERED 284-CARD SET
1 Alex Rodriguez SP/75 8.00 20.00
3 Vladimir Guerrero SP/75 6.00 15.00
14 Luis Gonzalez SP/75 2.50 6.00
15 Frank Thomas SP/75 6.00 15.00
18 Lance Berkman SP/75 2.50 6.00
20 Chipper Jones SP/75 6.00 15.00
22 Kerry Wood SP/75 2.50 6.00
24 J.D. Drew SP/75 2.50 6.00
27 Kenny Lofton SP/75 2.50 6.00
28 Mike Mussina SP/75 4.00 10.00
30 Bernie Williams SP/75 4.00 10.00
32 Shawn Green SP/85 2.50 6.00
34 Juan Gonzalez SP/75 2.50 6.00
35 Andres Galarraga SP/75 2.50 6.00
36 Gary Sheffield SP/75 2.50 6.00
38 Scott Rolen SP/75 4.00 10.00
44 Greg Maddux SP/75 10.00 25.00
48 Nomar Garciaparra SP/85 10.00 25.00
52 Roger Clemens SP/75 12.50 30.00
53 Chan Ho Park SP/85 2.50 6.00
58 Roberto Alomar SP/85 4.00 10.00
59 Ryan Klesko SP/50 2.50 6.00
62 Darin Erstad SP/75 2.50 6.00
72 Ivan Rodriguez SP/75 4.00 10.00
74 Jeff Bagwell SP/85 4.00 10.00
75 Moises Alou SP/75 2.50 6.00
76 Todd Helton SP/75 4.00 10.00
78 Pedro Martinez SP/85 4.00 10.00
80 Manny Ramirez Sox SP/85 4.00 10.00
82 Randy Johnson SP/85 6.00 15.00
85 Kevin Brown SP/75 2.50 6.00
88 Brian Giles SP/75 2.50 6.00
90 Craig Biggio SP/85 4.00 10.00
95 Curt Schilling SP/75 2.50 6.00
98 Barry Larkin SP/85 4.00 10.00
100 Tom Glavine SP/75 4.00 10.00
258 Victor Martinez PH 20.00 50.00

2001 Donruss Class of 2001 First Class Autographs

PRINT RUNS LISTED BELOW
CARDS DISPLAY CUMULATIVE PRINT RUNS
PRINT RUNS PROVIDED BY DONRUSS
NO PRICING ON QTY OF 25 OR LESS
SKIP-NUMBERED 53-CARD SET
10 Miguel Tejada/75 15.00 40.00
17 Paul LoDuca/100 10.00 25.00
21 Eric Chavez/100 10.00 25.00
41 Barry Zito/100 10.00 25.00
45 Mark Buehrle/100 20.00 50.00
49 Robert Fick/100 10.00 25.00
50 Sean Casey/100 10.00 25.00
51 Joe Mays/100 10.00 25.00
69 Mark Mulder/100 10.00 25.00
73 Terrence Long/100 10.00 25.00
81 Jose Vidro/100 10.00 25.00
83 Richie Sexson/100 10.00 25.00
84 Troy Glaus/100 10.00 25.00
89 Jermaine Dye/100 10.00 25.00
91 Richard Hidalgo/100 10.00 25.00
93 Aramis Ramirez/100 10.00 25.00
96 Tim Hudson/100 10.00 25.00

2001 Donruss Class of 2001 Rookie Autographs

STATED PRINT RUNS LISTED BELOW
CARDS DISPLAY CUMULATIVE PRINT RUNS
PRINT RUNS PROVIDED BY DONRUSS
SEE BECKETT.COM FOR UNLISTED PR.RUNS
SKIP-NUMBERED 109-CARD SET
NO PRICING ON QTY OF 25 OR LESS
109 Paul Phillips/250* 4.00 10.00
114 Kris Keller/250* 4.00 10.00
115 Adam Bernero/250* 4.00 10.00
120 George Perez/250 4.00 10.00
123 Nate Teut/250* 4.00 10.00
124 Martin Vargas/250* 4.00 10.00
127 Les Walrond/250* 4.00 10.00
132 Joe Crede/250* 10.00 25.00
137 Winston Abreu/250* 4.00 10.00
138 Matt Ginter/250* 4.00 10.00
140 Gene Altman/250* 4.00 10.00
142 Michael Cuddyer/250* 10.00 25.00
143 Mike Penney/250* 4.00 10.00
145 Esix Snead/250* 4.00 10.00
147 Orlando Woodards/250* 4.00 10.00
148 Jeff Deardorff/100* 6.00 15.00
150 Blaine Neal/250* 4.00 10.00
156 Aubrey Huff/250* 6.00 15.00
157 Pablo Ozuna/250* 4.00 10.00
158 Bill Ortega/250* 4.00 10.00
160 Kevin Olsen/250* 4.00 10.00
161 Will Ohman/250* 4.00 10.00
163 Jack Cust/250* 4.00 10.00
168 Craig Monroe/250* 12.50 30.00
169 Jason Jennings/250* 4.00 10.00
171 Luis Rivas/250* 4.00 10.00
173 Luke Hudson/250* 4.00 10.00
176 David Espinosa/250* 4.00 10.00
177 Mike Maroth/250* 6.00 15.00
178 Keith Ginter/250* 4.00 10.00
181 Steve Lomasney/250* 4.00 10.00
182 John Grabow/250* 4.00 10.00
184 Jason Karnuth/250* 4.00 10.00
186 Brent Abernathy/250* 4.00 10.00
188 Wily Mo Pena/250* 6.00 15.00
191 Cesar Izturis/250* 4.00 10.00
192 Eric Hinske/250* 6.00 15.00
194 Timo Perez/100* 6.00 15.00
196 Eric Valent/250* 4.00 10.00
201 Joe Kennedy PH/100* 6.00 15.00
202 Wilson Betemit PH/100* 10.00 25.00
203 Christian Parker PH/100* 6.00 15.00
204 Jay Gibbons PH/100* 6.00 15.00
205 Carlos Garcia PH/200* 4.00 10.00
206 Jack Wilson PH/100* 6.00 15.00
207 Johnny Estrada PH/200* 6.00 15.00
208 Wilkin Ruan PH/200* 4.00 10.00
209 Bran Duckworth PH/100* 6.00 15.00
211 Marlon Byrd PH/100* 6.00 15.00
213 Den Tankersley PH/100* 6.00 15.00
214 Brandon Larson PH/200* 4.00 10.00
215 Alexis Gomez PH/200* 4.00 10.00
216 Bill Hall PH/100* 30.00 60.00
217 Antonio Perez PH/100* 6.00 15.00
218 Jeremy Affeldt PH/200* 4.00 10.00
220 Casey Fossum PH/200* 4.00 10.00
224 Zach Day PH/200* 4.00 10.00
225 David Williams PH/200* 4.00 10.00
227 Jose Acevedo PH/200* 4.00 10.00
229 Orlando Hudson PH/100* 6.00 15.00
230 Jose Mieses PH/200* 4.00 10.00
231 Ric Rodriguez PH/200* 4.00 10.00
232 Alfonso Soriano PH/100* 6.00 15.00
233 Jason Hart PH/100* 6.00 15.00
234 Endy Chavez PH/200* 4.00 10.00
235 Delvin James PH/100* 6.00 15.00
237 Jeremy Owens PH/200* 4.00 10.00
238 Brad Voyles PH/200* 4.00 10.00
239 Nate Frese PH/200* 4.00 10.00
241 Roy Oswalt PH/100* 15.00 40.00
242 Juan Uribe PH/150* 6.00 15.00
243 Cory Aldridge PH/200* 4.00 10.00
244 Adam Dunn PH/100* 15.00 40.00
245 Bud Smith PH/100* 6.00 15.00
246 Adr Hernandez PH/100* 6.00 15.00
249 Wilmy Caceres PH/200* 4.00 10.00
250 Jason Michaels PH/200* 4.00 10.00
252 John Buck PH/100* 10.00 25.00
253 Andres Torres PH/100* 6.00 15.00
255 Corky Miller PH/100* 6.00 15.00
256 Rafael Soriano PH/100* 6.00 15.00
257 Donaldo Mendez PH/200* 4.00 10.00
259 Corey Patterson PH/100* 6.00 15.00
260 Horacio Ramirez PH/200* 6.00 15.00
261 Elpidio Guzman PH/200* 4.00 10.00
262 Juan Diaz PH/200* 4.00 10.00
264 Brian Lawrence PH/200* 4.00 10.00
265 Josue Perez PH/200* 4.00 10.00
266 Jose Nunez PH/200* 4.00 10.00
268 Albert Pujols PH/100* 300.00 800.00
269 Duaner Sanchez PH/200* 4.00 10.00
271 Greg Miller PH/200* 4.00 10.00
272 Adam Pettyjohn PH/200* 4.00 10.00
274 Claudio Vargas PH/200* 4.00 10.00
279 Brian Reith PH/200* 4.00 10.00
283 Josh Towers PH/100* 6.00 15.00
285 David Brous PH/200* 4.00 10.00
287 Nick Neugebauer PH/100* 6.00 15.00
289 Billy Sylvester PH/200* 4.00 10.00
290 Carlos Valderrama PH/200* 4.00 10.00
292 Matt White PH/200* 4.00 10.00
293 Nick Maness PH/200* 4.00 10.00
296 Angel Berroa PH/100* 6.00 15.00
297 Juan Cruz PH/100* 6.00 15.00
298 Dewon Brazelton PH/100* 6.00 15.00
299 Mark Prior PH/100* 6.00 15.00
300 Mark Teixeira PH/100* 60.00 120.00

2001 Donruss Class of 2001 Aces

COMPLETE SET (20) 50.00 100.00
STATED ODDS 1:30
A1 Roger Clemens 5.00 12.00
A2 Randy Johnson 2.50 6.00
A3 Freddy Garcia 2.00 5.00
A4 Greg Maddux 4.00 10.00
A5 Tim Hudson 2.00 5.00
A6 Curt Schilling 2.00 5.00
A7 Mark Buehrle 2.00 5.00
A8 Matt Morris 2.00 5.00
A9 Joe Mays 2.00 5.00
A10 Javier Vazquez 2.00 5.00
A11 Mark Mulder 2.00 5.00
A12 Wade Miller 2.00 5.00
A13 Barry Zito 2.00 5.00
A14 Pedro Martinez 2.00 5.00
A15 Al Leiter 2.00 5.00
A16 Chan Ho Park 2.00 5.00
A17 John Burkett 2.00 5.00
A18 C.C. Sabathia 2.00 5.00
A19 Jamie Moyer 2.00 5.00
A20 Mike Mussina 2.00 5.00

2001 Donruss Class of 2001 Diamond Aces

STATED PRINT RUNS LISTED BELOW
CARD NUMBER A8 DOES NOT EXIST
A1 Roger Clemens/200 15.00 40.00
A2 Randy Johnson/750 6.00 15.00
A3 Freddy Garcia/350 4.00 10.00
A4 Greg Maddux/750 10.00 25.00
A5 Tim Hudson/550 4.00 10.00
A6 Curt Schilling/525 4.00 10.00
A7 Mark Buehrle/750 6.00 15.00
A9 Joe Mays/750 4.00 10.00
A10 Javier Vazquez/500 4.00 10.00
A11 Mark Mulder/300 4.00 10.00
A12 Wade Miller/525 4.00 10.00
A13 Barry Zito/550 6.00 15.00
A14 Pedro Martinez/550 6.00 15.00
A15 Al Leiter/525 4.00 10.00
A16 Chan Ho Park/400 4.00 10.00
A17 John Burkett/700 4.00 10.00
A18 C.C. Sabathia/550 4.00 10.00
A19 Jamie Moyer/700 4.00 10.00

2001 Donruss Class of 2001 BobbleHead

ONE PER BOX
STATED PRINT RUN 2000 SERIAL #'d SETS
1 Ichiro Suzuki 20.00 50.00
2 Cal Ripken 15.00 40.00
3 Derek Jeter 12.50 30.00
4 Mark McGwire 15.00 40.00
5 Albert Pujols 25.00 60.00
6 Ken Griffey Jr. 10.00 25.00
7 Nomar Garciaparra 8.00 20.00
8 Mike Piazza 8.00 20.00
9 Alex Rodriguez 6.00 15.00
10 Manny Ramirez Sox 6.00 15.00
11 Tsuyoshi Shinjo 6.00 15.00
12 Hideo Nomo 6.00 15.00
13 Chipper Jones 6.00 15.00
14 Sammy Sosa 6.00 15.00
15 Roger Clemens 10.00 25.00
16 Tony Gwynn 6.00 15.00
17 Barry Bonds 12.50 30.00
18 Kazuhiro Sasaki 4.00 10.00
19 Pedro Martinez 6.00 15.00
20 Jeff Bagwell 6.00 15.00
21 Ichiro Suzuki ROY 15.00 40.00
22 Albert Pujols ROY 25.00 60.00

2001 Donruss Class of 2001 BobbleHead Cards

COMPLETE SET (22) 40.00 100.00
ONE PER BOX
STATED PRINT RUN 2000 SERIAL #'d SETS
1 Ichiro Suzuki 12.00 30.00
2 Cal Ripken 8.00 20.00
3 Derek Jeter 6.00 15.00
4 Mark McGwire 8.00 20.00
5 Albert Pujols 10.00 25.00
6 Ken Griffey Jr. 5.00 12.00
7 Nomar Garciaparra 4.00 10.00
8 Mike Piazza 4.00 10.00
9 Alex Rodriguez 3.00 8.00
10 Manny Ramirez Sox 3.00 8.00
11 Tsuyoshi Shinjo 3.00 8.00
12 Hideo Nomo 4.00 10.00
13 Chipper Jones 3.00 8.00
14 Sammy Sosa 3.00 8.00
15 Roger Clemens 5.00 12.00
16 Tony Gwynn 3.00 8.00
17 Barry Bonds 6.00 15.00
18 Kazuhiro Sasaki 2.00 5.00
19 Pedro Martinez 3.00 8.00
20 Jeff Bagwell 3.00 8.00
21 Ichiro Suzuki ROY 15.00 40.00
22 Albert Pujols ROY 15.00 40.00

2001 Donruss Class of 2001 Crusade

STATED PRINT RUN 300 SERIAL #'d SETS
CARDS DISPLAY CUMULATIVE PRINT RUNS
PRINT RUNS PROVIDED BY DONRUSS
SEE BECKETT.COM FOR UNLISTED PR.RUNS
C1 Roger Clemens/275 10.00 25.00
C2 Luis Gonzalez/275 3.00 8.00
C3 Troy Glaus/275 3.00 8.00
C4 Freddy Garcia/300 3.00 8.00
C5 Sean Casey/285 3.00 8.00
C6 Bobby Abreu/300 3.00 8.00
C7 Matt Morris/300 3.00 8.00
C8 Cal Ripken/275 15.00 40.00
C9 Miguel Tejada/285 3.00 8.00
C10 Vladimir Guerrero/275 5.00 12.00
C11 Mark Buehrle/100 3.00 8.00
C12 Mike Sweeney/300 3.00 8.00
C13 Ivan Rodriguez/275 3.00 8.00
C14 Jeff Bagwell/275 3.00 8.00
C15 Joe Mays/250 3.00 8.00
C16 Cliff Floyd/300 3.00 8.00
C17 Lance Berkman/300 3.00 8.00
C18 Aramis Ramirez/100 3.00 8.00
C19 Tony Gwynn/300 6.00 15.00
C20 Shannon Stewart/100 3.00 8.00
C21 Todd Helton/275 3.00 8.00
C22 Chipper Jones/275 5.00 12.00
C23 Javier Vazquez/100 3.00 8.00
C24 Shawn Green/275 3.00 8.00
C25 Barry Bonds/300 12.50 30.00
C26 Albert Pujols/250 60.00 120.00
C27 Wilson Betemit/100 3.00 8.00
C28 C.C. Sabathia/290 3.00 8.00
C29 Roy Oswalt/100 4.00 10.00
C30 Johnny Estrada/100 3.00 8.00
C31 Nick Johnson/100 3.00 8.00
C32 Aubrey Huff/100 3.00 8.00
C33 Corey Patterson/200 3.00 8.00
C34 Jay Gibbons/100 3.00 8.00
C35 Marcus Giles/100 3.00 8.00
C36 Juan Cruz/100 3.00 8.00
C37 Tsuyoshi Shinjo/300 3.00 8.00
C38 Ben Sheets/285 3.00 8.00
C39 Bud Smith/100 3.00 8.00
C40 Alex Escobar/100 3.00 8.00
C41 Joe Kennedy/100 3.00 8.00
C42 Alexis Gomez/100 3.00 8.00
C43 Jimmy Rollins/300 3.00 8.00
C44 Josh Towers/100 3.00 8.00
C45 Joe Crede/100 4.00 10.00
C46 Brandon Duckworth/100 3.00 8.00
C47 Ichiro Suzuki/300 30.00 80.00
C48 Jose Ortiz/100 3.00 8.00
C49 Casey Fossum/100 3.00 8.00
C50 Adam Dunn/200 3.00 8.00

2001 Donruss Class of 2001 Crusade Autographs

CARDS DISPLAY CUMULATIVE PRINT RUNS
PRINT RUNS PROVIDED BY DONRUSS
NO PRICING ON QTY OF 25 OR LESS
SEE BECKETT.COM FOR UNLISTED PR.RUNS
SKIP-NUMBERED 39-CARD SET
C11 Mark Buehrle/200 6.00 15.00
C18 Aramis Ramirez/200 6.00 15.00
C20 Shannon Stewart/200 6.00 15.00
C23 Javier Vazquez/200 6.00 15.00
C26 Albert Pujols/50 300.00 800.00
C27 Wilson Betemit/200 10.00 25.00
C29 Roy Oswalt/200 6.00 15.00
C30 Johnny Estrada/200 10.00 25.00
C31 Nick Johnson/200 6.00 15.00
C32 Aubrey Huff/200 6.00 15.00
C33 Corey Patterson/100 4.00 10.00
C34 Jay Gibbons/200 10.00 25.00
C35 Marcus Giles/200 6.00 15.00
C36 Juan Cruz/200 6.00 15.00
C39 Bud Smith/200 4.00 10.00
C40 Alex Escobar/200 4.00 10.00
C41 Joe Kennedy/200 10.00 25.00
C42 Alexis Gomez/200 4.00 10.00
C44 Josh Towers/200 10.00 25.00
C45 Joe Crede/200 10.00 25.00
C46 Brandon Duckworth/200 4.00 10.00
C48 Jose Ortiz/200 4.00 10.00
C49 Casey Fossum/200 6.00 15.00
C50 Adam Dunn/100 8.00 20.00

2001 Donruss Class of 2001 Dominators

COMPLETE SET (30) 75.00 150.00
STATED ODDS 1:20
DM1 Manny Ramirez Sox 2.00 5.00
DM2 Lance Berkman 2.00 5.00
DM3 Juan Gonzalez 2.00 5.00
DM4 Albert Pujols 10.00 25.00
DM5 Jason Giambi 2.00 5.00
DM6 Mike Sweeney 2.00 5.00
DM7 Rafael Palmeiro 2.00 5.00
DM8 Luis Gonzalez 2.00 5.00
DM9 Ichiro Suzuki 8.00 20.00
DM10 Cliff Floyd 2.00 5.00
DM11 Roberto Alomar 2.00 5.00
DM12 Paul LoDuca 2.00 5.00
DM13 Shannon Stewart 2.00 5.00
DM14 Barry Bonds 6.00 15.00
DM15 Larry Walker 2.00 5.00
DM16 Shawn Green 2.00 5.00
DM17 Moises Alou 2.00 5.00
DM18 Cal Ripken 8.00 20.00
DM19 Brian Giles 2.00 5.00
DM20 Magglio Ordonez 2.00 5.00
DM21 Jose Vidro 2.00 5.00
DM22 Edgar Martinez 2.00 5.00
DM23 Aramis Ramirez 2.00 5.00
DM24 Tony Gwynn 3.00 8.00
DM25 Richie Sexson 2.00 5.00
DM26 Todd Helton 2.00 5.00
DM27 Garret Anderson 2.00 5.00
DM28 Chipper Jones 2.50 6.00
DM29 Troy Glaus 2.00 5.00
DM30 Jeff Bagwell 2.00 5.00

2001 Donruss Class of 2001 Diamond Dominators

STATED PRINT RUNS LISTED BELOW
SEE BECKETT.COM FOR UNLISTED PR.RUNS
DM1 Manny Ramirez Sox Bat/725 6.00 15.00
DM2 Lance Berkman Bat/725 4.00 10.00
DM3 Juan Gonzalez Bat/500 4.00 10.00
DM4 Albert Pujols Bat/125 60.00 150.00
DM5 Jason Giambi Bat/250 4.00 10.00
DM6 Mike Sweeney Jsy/325 4.00 10.00
DM7 Rafael Palmeiro Bat/550 6.00 15.00
DM8 Luis Gonzalez Bat/725 4.00 10.00
DM9 Ichiro Suzuki Ball/50 50.00 120.00
DM10 Cliff Floyd Jsy/725 4.00 10.00
DM11 Roberto Alomar Bat/200 6.00 15.00
DM12 Paul LoDuca Jsy/600 4.00 10.00
DM13 Shannon Stewart Bat/725 4.00 10.00
DM14 Barry Bonds Bat/250 10.00 25.00
DM15 Larry Walker Bat/725 4.00 10.00
DM16 Shawn Green Bat/500 4.00 10.00
DM17 Moises Alou Bat/550 4.00 10.00

DM18 Cal Ripken Bat/250 15.00 40.00
DM19 Brian Giles Bat/725 4.00 10.00
DM20 Magglio Ordonez Bat/725 4.00 10.00
DM21 Jose Vidro Jsy/725 4.00 10.00
DM22 Edgar Martinez Jsy/200 6.00 15.00
DM23 Aramis Ramirez Bat/200 4.00 10.00
DM24 Tony Gwynn Bat/500 6.00 15.00
DM25 Richie Sexson Bat/725 4.00 10.00
DM26 Todd Helton Bat/725 6.00 15.00
DM27 Garret Anderson Bat/725 4.00 10.00
DM28 Chipper Jones Bat/725 6.00 15.00
DM29 Troy Glaus Jsy/200 4.00 10.00
DM30 Jeff Bagwell Jsy/325 6.00 15.00

2001 Donruss Class of 2001 Rewards

STATED ODDS 1:212
RW1 Jason Giambi MVP 4.00 10.00
RW2 Ichiro Suzuki MVP 15.00 40.00
RW3 Roger Clemens CY 12.50 30.00
RW4 Freddy Garcia CY 4.00 10.00
RW5 Ichiro Suzuki ROY 15.00 40.00
RW6 Albert Pujols ROY 25.00 50.00
RW7 Barry Bonds MVP 12.50 30.00
RW8 Albert Pujols MVP 25.00 50.00
RW9 Randy Johnson CY 6.00 15.00
RW10 Matt Morris CY 4.00 10.00

2001 Donruss Class of 2001 Final Rewards

STATED PRINT RUNS LISTED BELOW
CARD RW-10 DOES NOT EXIST
RW1 J.Giambi MVP Jsy/250 4.00 10.00
RW2 I.Suzuki MVP Ball/50 50.00 120.00
RW3 R.Clemens CY Jsy/200 8.00 20.00
RW4 F.Garcia CY Jsy/250 4.00 10.00
RW5 I.Suzuki ROY Ball/50 50.00 120.00
RW6 A.Pujols ROY Bat/125 60.00 150.00
RW7 B.Bonds MVP Jsy/200 10.00 25.00
RW8 A.Pujols MVP Bat/125 100.00 250.00
RW9 R.Johnson CY Jsy/250 6.00 15.00

2001 Donruss Class of 2001 Rookie Team

COMPLETE SET (15) 75.00 150.00
STATED ODDS 1:83
RT1 Jay Gibbons 3.00 8.00
RT2 Alfonso Soriano 3.00 8.00
RT3 Jimmy Rollins 2.00 5.00
RT4 Wilson Betemit 3.00 8.00
RT5 Albert Pujols 25.00 50.00
RT6 Johnny Estrada 3.00 8.00
RT7 Ichiro Suzuki 12.00 30.00
RT8 Tsuyoshi Shinjo 3.00 8.00
RT9 Adam Dunn 3.00 8.00
RT10 C.C. Sabathia 2.00 5.00
RT11 Ben Sheets 3.00 8.00
RT12 Roy Oswalt 3.00 8.00
RT13 Bud Smith 2.00 5.00
RT14 Josh Towers 3.00 8.00
RT15 Juan Cruz 2.00 5.00

2001 Donruss Class of 2001 Rookie Team Materials

STATED PRINT RUNS LISTED BELOW
RT1 Jay Gibbons Btg Glv/100 8.00 20.00
RT2 Alfonso Soriano Btg Glv/100 8.00 20.00
RT3 Jimmy Rollins Jsy/200 4.00 10.00
RT4 Wilson Betemit Hat/100 8.00 20.00
RT5 Albert Pujols Bat/100 75.00 200.00
RT6 Johnny Estrada Shoes/100 6.00 15.00
RT7 Ichiro Suzuki Ball/50 50.00 120.00
RT8 T.Shinjo Shoes/200 6.00 15.00
RT9 Adam Dunn Bat/200 6.00 15.00
RT10 C.C. Sabathia Jsy/200 4.00 10.00
RT11 Ben Sheets Bat/200 6.00 15.00
RT12 Roy Oswalt Btg Glv/50 10.00 25.00
RT13 Bud Smith Jsy/250 4.00 10.00
RT14 Josh Towers Pants/200 6.00 15.00
RT15 Juan Cruz Jsy/200 4.00 10.00

2001 Donruss Class of 2001 Yearbook

COMPLETE SET (25) 75.00 150.00
STATED ODDS 1:24
YB1 Barry Bonds 6.00 15.00
YB2 Mark Mulder 1.50 4.00
YB3 Luis Gonzalez 1.50 4.00
YB4 Lance Berkman 1.50 4.00
YB5 Matt Morris 1.50 4.00
YB6 Roy Oswalt 2.50 6.00
YB7 Todd Helton 1.50 4.00
YB8 Tsuyoshi Shinjo 1.50 4.00
YB9 C.C. Sabathia 1.50 4.00
YB10 Curt Schilling 1.50 4.00
YB11 Rickey Henderson 2.50 6.00
YB12 Jamie Moyer 1.50 4.00
YB13 Shawn Green 1.50 4.00
YB14 Randy Johnson 2.50 6.00
YB15 Jim Thome 1.50 4.00
YB16 Larry Walker 1.50 4.00
YB17 Jimmy Rollins 1.50 4.00
YB18 Kazuhiro Sasaki 1.50 4.00
YB19 Hideo Nomo 2.50 6.00
YB20 Roger Clemens 5.00 12.00
YB21 Bud Smith 1.50 4.00
YB22 Ichiro Suzuki 8.00 20.00
YB23 Albert Pujols 12.00 30.00
YB24 Cal Ripken 8.00 20.00
YB25 Tony Gwynn 3.00 8.00

2001 Donruss Class of 2001 Scrapbook

STATED PRINT RUNS LISTED BELOW
CARD SB-5 DOES NOT EXIST
SB1 Barry Bonds Pants/525 10.00 25.00
SB2 Mark Mulder/500 4.00 10.00
SB3 Luis Gonzalez/500 4.00 10.00
SB4 Lance Berkman/525 4.00 10.00
SB6 Roy Oswalt/150 6.00 15.00
SB7 Todd Helton/525 6.00 15.00
SB8 Tsuyoshi Shinjo/75 6.00 15.00
SB9 C.C. Sabathia/500 4.00 10.00
SB10 Curt Schilling/525 4.00 10.00
SB11 R.Henderson Bat/200 6.00 15.00
SB12 Jamie Moyer/500 4.00 10.00
SB13 Shawn Green/525 4.00 10.00
SB14 Randy Johnson/500 6.00 15.00
SB15 Jim Thome/400 6.00 15.00
SB16 Larry Walker/500 4.00 10.00
SB18 Kazuhiro Sasaki/500 4.00 10.00
SB19 Hideo Nomo/150 10.00 25.00
SB20 Roger Clemens/475 10.00 25.00
SB21 Bud Smith/525 4.00 10.00
SB22 Ichiro Suzuki Ball/75 40.00 100.00
SB23 Albert Pujols Bat/150 60.00 150.00
SB24 Cal Ripken/525 15.00 40.00
SB25 Tony Gwynn Pants/500 6.00 15.00

2001 Donruss Classics

COMP.SET w/o SP's (100) 10.00 25.00
COMMON CARD (1-100) .25 .60
COMMON CARD (101-150) 2.00 5.00
101-150 PRINT RUN 585 SERIAL #'d SETS
COMMON CARD (151-200) 1.50 4.00
151-200 PRINT RUN 1755 SERIAL #'d SETS
101-200 RANDOM INSERTS IN PACKS
162/185 NOT MEANT FOR PUBLIC RELEASE
1 Alex Rodriguez .75 2.00
2 Barry Bonds 1.50 4.00
3 Cal Ripken 2.00 5.00
4 Chipper Jones .60 1.50
5 Derek Jeter 1.50 4.00
6 Troy Glaus .25 .60
7 Frank Thomas .60 1.50
8 Greg Maddux 1.00 2.50
9 Ivan Rodriguez .40 1.00
10 Jeff Bagwell .40 1.00
11 Cliff Floyd .25 .60
12 Todd Helton .40 1.00
13 Ken Griffey Jr. 1.25 3.00
14 Manny Ramirez Sox .40 1.00
15 Mark McGwire 1.50 4.00
16 Mike Piazza 1.00 2.50
17 Nomar Garciaparra 1.00 2.50
18 Pedro Martinez .40 1.00
19 Randy Johnson .60 1.50
20 Rick Ankiel .25 .60
21 Rickey Henderson .60 1.50
22 Roger Clemens 1.25 3.00
23 Sammy Sosa .60 1.50
24 Tony Gwynn .75 2.00
25 Vladimir Guerrero .60 1.50
26 Kazuhiro Sasaki .25 .60
27 Roberto Alomar .40 1.00
28 Barry Zito .40 1.00
29 Pat Burrell .25 .60
30 Harold Baines .25 .60
31 Carlos Delgado .25 .60
32 J.D. Drew .25 .60
33 Jim Edmonds .25 .60
34 Darin Erstad .25 .60
35 Jason Giambi .25 .60
36 Tom Glavine .40 1.00
37 Juan Gonzalez .25 .60
38 Mark Grace .40 1.00
39 Shawn Green .25 .60
40 Tim Hudson .25 .60
41 Andruw Jones .40 1.00
42 Jeff Kent .25 .60
43 Barry Larkin .40 1.00
44 Rafael Furcal .25 .60
45 Mike Mussina .40 1.00
46 Hideo Nomo .60 1.50
47 Rafael Palmeiro .40 1.00
48 Scott Rolen .40 1.00
49 Gary Sheffield .25 .60
50 Bernie Williams .40 1.00
51 Bob Abreu .25 .60
52 Edgardo Alfonzo .25 .60
53 Edgar Martinez .40 1.00
54 Magglio Ordonez .25 .60
55 Kerry Wood .25 .60
56 Adrian Beltre .25 .60
57 Lance Berkman .25 .60
58 Kevin Brown .25 .60
59 Sean Casey .25 .60
60 Eric Chavez .25 .60
61 Bartolo Colon .25 .60
62 Johnny Damon .40 1.00
63 Jermaine Dye .25 .60
64 Juan Encarnacion .25 .60
65 Carl Everett .25 .60
66 Brian Giles .25 .60
67 Mike Hampton .25 .60
68 Richard Hidalgo .25 .60
69 Geoff Jenkins .25 .60
70 Jacque Jones .25 .60
71 Jason Kendall .25 .60
72 Ryan Klesko .25 .60
73 Chan Ho Park .25 .60
74 Richie Sexson .25 .60
75 Mike Sweeney .25 .60
76 Fernando Tatis .25 .60
77 Miguel Tejada .25 .60
78 Jose Vidro .25 .60
79 Larry Walker .25 .60
80 Preston Wilson .25 .60
81 Craig Biggio .40 1.00
82 Fred McGriff .40 1.00
83 Jim Thome .40 1.00
84 Garret Anderson .25 .60
85 Russell Branyan .25 .60
86 Tony Batista .25 .60
87 Terrence Long .25 .60
88 Brad Fullmer .25 .60
89 Rusty Greer .25 .60
90 Orlando Hernandez .25 .60
91 Gabe Kapler .25 .60
92 Paul Konerko .25 .60
93 Carlos Lee .25 .60
94 Kenny Lofton .25 .60
95 Raul Mondesi .25 .60
96 Jorge Posada .40 1.00
97 Tim Salmon .40 1.00
98 Greg Vaughn .25 .60
99 Mo Vaughn .25 .60
100 Omar Vizquel .40 1.00
101 Aubrey Huff SP 2.00 5.00
102 Jimmy Rollins SP 2.00 5.00
103 Cory Aldridge SP RC 2.00 5.00
104 Wilmy Caceres SP RC 2.00 5.00
105 Josh Beckett SP 3.00 8.00
106 Wilson Betemit SP RC 3.00 8.00
107 Timo Perez SP 2.00 5.00
108 Albert Pujols SP RC 60.00 150.00
109 Bud Smith SP RC 2.00 5.00
110 Jack Wilson SP RC 3.00 8.00
111 Alex Escobar SP 2.00 5.00
112 Johnny Estrada SP RC 3.00 8.00
113 Pedro Feliz SP 2.00 5.00
114 Nate Frese SP RC 2.00 5.00
115 Carlos Garcia SP RC 2.00 5.00
116 Brandon Larson SP RC 2.00 5.00
117 Alexis Gomez SP RC 2.00 5.00
118 Jason Hart SP 2.00 5.00
119 Adam Dunn SP 3.00 8.00
120 Marcus Giles SP 2.00 5.00
121 Christian Parker SP RC 2.00 5.00
122 Jackson Melian SP RC 2.00 5.00
123 Endy Chavez SP RC 2.00 5.00
124 Adrian Hernandez SP RC 2.00 5.00
125 Joe Kennedy SP RC 3.00 8.00
126 Jose Mieses SP RC 2.00 5.00
127 C.C. Sabathia SP 2.00 5.00
128 Eric Munson SP 2.00 5.00
129 Xavier Nady SP 2.00 5.00
130 Horacio Ramirez SP RC 3.00 8.00
131 Abraham Nunez SP 2.00 5.00
132 Jose Ortiz SP 2.00 5.00
133 Jeremy Owens SP RC 2.00 5.00
134 Claudio Vargas SP RC 2.00 5.00
135 Corey Patterson SP 2.00 5.00
136 Andres Torres SP RC 2.00 5.00
137 Ben Sheets SP 3.00 8.00
138 Joe Crede SP 3.00 8.00
139 Adam Pettyjohn SP RC 2.00 5.00
140 Elpidio Guzman SP RC 2.00 5.00
141 Jay Gibbons SP RC 3.00 8.00
142 Wilkin Ruan SP RC 2.00 5.00
143 Tsuyoshi Shinjo SP RC 3.00 8.00
144 Alfonso Soriano SP 3.00 8.00
145 Nick Johnson SP 2.00 5.00
146 Ichiro Suzuki SP RC 40.00 100.00
147 Juan Uribe SP RC 3.00 8.00
148 Jack Cust SP 2.00 5.00
149 Carlos Valderrama SP RC 2.00 5.00
150 Matt White SP RC 2.00 5.00
151 Hank Aaron LGD 4.00 10.00
152 Ernie Banks LGD 2.00 5.00
153 Johnny Bench LGD 2.00 5.00
154 George Brett LGD 4.00 10.00
155 Lou Brock LGD 2.00 5.00
156 Rod Carew LGD 2.00 5.00
157 Steve Carlton LGD 1.50 4.00
158 Bob Feller LGD 1.50 4.00
159 Bob Gibson LGD 2.00 5.00
160 Reggie Jackson LGD 2.00 5.00
161 Al Kaline LGD 2.00 5.00
163 Don Mattingly LGD 4.00 10.00
164 Willie Mays LGD 4.00 10.00
165 Willie McCovey LGD 1.50 4.00
166 Joe Morgan LGD 1.50 4.00
167 Stan Musial LGD 3.00 8.00
168 Jim Palmer LGD 1.50 4.00
169 Brooks Robinson LGD 2.00 5.00
170 Frank Robinson LGD 2.00 5.00
171 Nolan Ryan LGD 5.00 12.00
172 Mike Schmidt LGD 4.00 10.00
173 Tom Seaver LGD 2.00 5.00
174 Warren Spahn LGD 2.00 5.00
175 Robin Yount LGD 2.00 5.00
176 Wade Boggs LGD 2.00 5.00
177 Ty Cobb LGD 3.00 8.00
178 Lou Gehrig LGD 4.00 10.00
179 Luis Aparicio LGD 1.50 4.00
180 Babe Ruth LGD 6.00 15.00
181 Ryne Sandberg LGD 4.00 10.00
182 Yogi Berra LGD 2.00 5.00
183 Roberto Clemente LGD 5.00 12.00
184 Eddie Murray LGD 2.00 5.00
186 Duke Snider LGD 2.00 5.00
187 Orlando Cepeda LGD 1.50 4.00
188 Billy Williams LGD 1.50 4.00
189 Juan Marichal LGD 1.50 4.00
190 Harmon Killebrew LGD 2.00 5.00
191 Kirby Puckett LGD 2.00 5.00
192 Carlton Fisk LGD 2.00 5.00
193 Dave Winfield LGD 1.50 4.00
194 Whitey Ford LGD 2.00 5.00
195 Paul Molitor LGD 1.50 4.00
196 Tony Perez LGD 1.50 4.00
197 Ozzie Smith LGD 3.00 8.00
198 Ralph Kiner LGD 2.00 5.00
199 Fergie Jenkins LGD 1.50 4.00
200 Phil Rizzuto LGD 2.00 5.00

2001 Donruss Classics Significant Signatures

STATED ODDS 1:18
101 Aubrey Huff 3.00 8.00
103 Cory Aldridge 3.00 8.00
105 Josh Beckett SP 6.00 15.00
106 Wilson Betemit 10.00 25.00
107 Timo Perez 3.00 8.00
108 Albert Pujols 250.00 600.00
110 Jack Wilson 3.00 6.00
111 Alex Escobar 3.00 8.00
112 Johnny Estrada 3.00 8.00
113 Pedro Feliz 3.00 8.00
114 Nate Frese 3.00 8.00
115 Carlos Garcia 3.00 8.00
116 Brandon Larson 3.00 8.00
118 Jason Hart 3.00 8.00
119 Adam Dunn SP 5.00 12.00
120 Marcus Giles 3.00 8.00
121 Christian Parker 3.00 8.00
126 Jose Mieses 3.00 8.00
127 C.C. Sabathia SP 20.00 50.00
129 Xavier Nady 3.00 8.00
130 Horacio Ramirez 3.00 8.00
131 Abraham Nunez 3.00 8.00
132 Jose Ortiz 3.00 8.00
133 Jeremy Owens 3.00 8.00
134 Claudio Vargas 3.00 8.00
135 Corey Patterson SP 4.00 10.00
136 Andres Torres 3.00 8.00
137 Ben Sheets SP 10.00 25.00
138 Joe Crede 3.00 8.00
139 Adam Pettyjohn 3.00 8.00
140 Elpidio Guzman 3.00 8.00
141 Jay Gibbons 3.00 8.00
142 Wilkin Ruan 3.00 8.00
144 Alfonso Soriano SP 6.00 15.00
145 Nick Johnson SP 6.00 15.00
147 Juan Uribe 8.00 20.00
149 Carlos Valderrama 3.00 8.00
151 Hank Aaron SP 400.00 600.00
152 Ernie Banks 30.00 80.00
153 Johnny Bench SP 40.00 80.00
154 George Brett SP 75.00 150.00
155 Lou Brock 15.00 40.00
156 Rod Carew 15.00 40.00
157 Steve Carlton 12.50 30.00
158 Bob Feller 12.50 30.00
159 Bob Gibson 15.00 40.00
160 Reggie Jackson SP 50.00 100.00
161 Al Kaline 12.00 30.00
162A Nolan Ryan Astros SP 125.00 200.00
163 Don Mattingly 25.00 60.00
164 Willie Mays SP 125.00 300.00
165 Willie McCovey 8.00 20.00
166 Joe Morgan 15.00 40.00
167 Stan Musial SP 300.00 600.00
168 Jim Palmer 8.00 20.00
169 Brooks Robinson 15.00 40.00
170 Frank Robinson 12.50 30.00
171 Nolan Ryan Rangers SP 50.00 100.00
172 Mike Schmidt 25.00 60.00
173 Tom Seaver 30.00 80.00
174 Warren Spahn 20.00 50.00
175 Robin Yount SP 30.00 80.00
176 Wade Boggs SP 30.00 60.00
179 Luis Aparicio 8.00 20.00
181 Ryne Sandberg 20.00 50.00
182 Yogi Berra 25.00 60.00
184 Eddie Murray 20.00 50.00
185 Ron Santo 12.50 30.00
186 Duke Snider 20.00 50.00
187 Orlando Cepeda 8.00 20.00
188 Billy Williams 12.50 30.00
189 Juan Marichal 8.00 20.00
190 Harmon Killebrew 12.00 30.00
191 Kirby Puckett SP 150.00 300.00
192 Carlton Fisk 15.00 40.00
193 Dave Winfield SP 15.00 40.00
194 Whitey Ford 20.00 50.00
195 Paul Molitor SP 30.00 60.00
196 Tony Perez 8.00 20.00
197 Ozzie Smith SP 40.00 80.00
198 Ralph Kiner 10.00 25.00
199 Fergie Jenkins 12.50 30.00
200 Phil Rizzuto 20.00 50.00

2001 Donruss Classics Timeless Tributes

*TRIBUTE 1-100: 2.5X TO 6X BASIC
*TRIBUTE 101-150: .5X TO 1.2X BASIC
*TRIBUTE 151-200: 1.25X TO 3X BASIC
STATED PRINT RUN 100 SERIAL #'d SETS
162 AND 185 NOT INTENDED FOR RELEASE
PRICING UNAVAILABLE FOR 162 AND 185
108 Albert Pujols 100.00 250.00
146 Ichiro Suzuki 50.00 120.00

2001 Donruss Classics Benchmarks

STATED ODDS 1:18 HOBBY, 1:72 RETAIL
CARDS 11, 19 AND 24 WERE EXCHANGE
NO EXCH.PRICING DUE TO SCARCITY
BM1 Todd Helton 2.50 6.00
BM2 Roberto Clemente 10.00 25.00
BM3 Mark McGwire 6.00 15.00
BM4 Barry Bonds 6.00 15.00
BM5 Bob Gibson 2.50 6.00
BM6 Ken Griffey Jr. 8.00 20.00
BM7 Frank Robinson 2.50 6.00
BM8 Greg Maddux 6.00 15.00
BM9 Reggie Jackson 3.00 8.00
BM10 Sammy Sosa 2.50 6.00
BM11 Willie Stargell 50.00 100.00
BM12 Vladimir Guerrero 4.00 10.00
BM13 Johnny Bench 4.00 10.00
BM14 Tony Gwynn 4.00 10.00
BM15 Mike Schmidt 6.00 15.00
BM16 Ivan Rodriguez 2.50 6.00
BM17 Jeff Bagwell 2.50 6.00
BM18 Cal Ripken 12.00 30.00
BM20 Kirby Puckett 4.00 10.00
BM21 Frank Thomas 4.00 10.00
BM22 Joe Morgan 2.50 6.00
BM23 Mike Piazza 10.00 25.00
BM24 Hank Aaron 20.00 50.00
BM25 Andruw Jones 2.50 6.00

2001 Donruss Classics Combos

CARDS DISPLAY CUMULATIVE PRINT RUNS
PRINT RUNS B/WN 40-100 COPIES PER
1 Roberto Clemente/100 30.00 60.00
2 Willie Stargell/100 15.00 40.00
3 Babe Ruth/100 250.00 400.00
4 Lou Gehrig/100 125.00 250.00
5 Hank Aaron/100 40.00 80.00
6 Eddie Mathews/100 10.00 25.00
7 Johnny Bench/100 12.50 30.00
8 Joe Morgan/100 10.00 25.00
9 Robin Yount/100 10.00 25.00
10 Paul Molitor/100 10.00 25.00
11 Steve Carlton/85 10.00 25.00
12 Mike Schmidt/85 12.50 30.00
13 Stan Musial/100 12.50 30.00
14 Lou Brock/100 15.00 40.00
15 Yogi Berra/100 10.00 25.00
16 Phil Rizzuto/100 10.00 25.00
17 Ernie Banks/85 10.00 25.00
18 Billy Williams/85 10.00 25.00
19 Don Mattingly/100 12.50 30.00
20 Wade Boggs/100 15.00 40.00
21 Jackie Robinson/100 50.00 100.00
22 Duke Snider/100 30.00 60.00
23 Frank Robinson/85 15.00 40.00
24 Brooks Robinson/85 15.00 40.00
25 Orlando Cepeda/100 10.00 25.00
26 Willie McCovey/100 10.00 25.00
27 Ryne Sandberg/100 10.00 25.00
28 Andre Dawson/100 10.00 25.00
29 Harmon Killebrew/100 20.00 50.00
30 Rod Carew/100 15.00 40.00
31 R.Clemente/W.Stargell/50 75.00 150.00
32 B.Ruth/L.Gehrig/50 300.00 600.00
33 H.Aaron/E.Mathews/50 30.00 80.00
34 J.Bench/J.Morgan/50 20.00 50.00
35 R.Yount/P.Molitor/50 20.00 50.00
36 S.Carlton/M.Schmidt/40 25.00 60.00
37 S.Musial/L.Brock/50 20.00 50.00
38 Y.Berra/P.Rizzuto/50 75.00 150.00
39 E.Banks/B.Williams/40 20.00 50.00
40 D.Mattingly/W.Boggs/50 20.00 50.00
41 J.Robinson/D.Snider/50 50.00 100.00
42 B.Robinson/F.Robinson/40 20.00 50.00
43 O.Cepeda/W.McCovey/50 30.00 60.00
44 A.Dawson/R.Sandberg/50 30.00 60.00
45 H.Killebrew/R.Carew/50 30.00 60.00

2001 Donruss Classics Legendary Lumberjacks

STATED ODDS 1:18 HOBBY, 1:72 RETAIL
SP PRINT RUNS PROVIDED BY DONRUSS
SP'S ARE NOT SERIAL-NUMBERED
LL1 Hack Wilson SP/244 * 40.00 80.00
LL2 Chipper Jones 6.00 15.00
LL3 Rogers Hornsby SP/301 * 20.00 50.00
LL4 Nellie Fox SP/300 * 50.00 100.00
LL5 Ivan Rodriguez 4.00 10.00
LL6 Jimmie Foxx SP/300 * 20.00 50.00
LL7 Hank Aaron 12.00 30.00
LL8 Yogi Berra SP/400 * 6.00 15.00
LL9 Ernie Banks SP/300 * 10.00 25.00
LL10 George Brett 12.00 30.00
LL11 Ty Cobb SP/100 * 30.00 80.00
LL12 R.Clemente SP/100 * 100.00 200.00
LL13 Carlton Fisk 4.00 10.00
LL14 Reggie Jackson 5.00 12.00
LL15 Al Kaline 6.00 15.00
LL16 Harmon Killebrew 6.00 15.00
LL17 Ralph Kiner 4.00 10.00
LL18 Roger Maris SP/275 * 12.00 30.00
LL19 Eddie Mathews SP/400 * 6.00 15.00
LL20 Ted Williams SP/300 * 25.00 60.00
LL21 Willie McCovey 4.00 10.00
LL22 Eddie Murray 4.00 10.00
LL23 Joe Morgan SP/268 * 10.00 25.00
LL24 Frank Robinson 4.00 10.00
LL25 Tony Perez 4.00 10.00
LL26 Mike Schmidt 4.00 10.00
LL27 Ryne Sandberg 4.00 10.00
LL29 Willie Stargell SP/500 * 30.00 60.00
LL30 Billy Williams 4.00 10.00
LL31 Dave Winfield 4.00 10.00
LL32 Robin Yount 6.00 15.00
LL33 Barry Bonds 10.00 25.00
LL34 Stan Musial SP/300 * 10.00 25.00
LL36 Orlando Cepeda 4.00 10.00
LL37 Todd Helton 4.00 10.00
LL38 Frank Thomas 6.00 15.00
LL40 Cal Ripken SP/500 * 10.00 25.00
LL41 Rafael Palmeiro 4.00 10.00
LL43 Vladimir Guerrero 6.00 15.00
LL45 Tony Gwynn 6.00 15.00
LL46 Rod Carew 4.00 10.00
LL47 Lou Brock 4.00 10.00
LL48 Wade Boggs 4.00 10.00
LL49 Babe Ruth SP/60 * 100.00 250.00
LL50 Lou Gehrig SP/100 * 60.00 150.00

2001 Donruss Classics Stadium Stars

STATED ODDS 1:18 HOBBY, 1:72 RETAIL
SS1 Babe Ruth SP 20.00 50.00
SS2 Cal Ripken 8.00 20.00
SS3 Brooks Robinson 1.50 4.00
SS4 Tony Gwynn SP 6.00 15.00
SS5 Ty Cobb 8.00 20.00
SS6 Vladimir Guerrero SP 6.00 15.00
SS7 Lou Gehrig SP 12.00 30.00
SS8 Nomar Garciaparra 1.50 4.00
SS9 Sammy Sosa SP 4.00 10.00
SS10 Reggie Jackson SP 5.00 12.00
SS11 Alex Rodriguez 3.00 8.00
SS12 Derek Jeter 10.00 25.00
SS13 Willie McCovey SP 4.00 10.00
SS14 Mark McGwire 4.00 10.00
SS15 Chipper Jones 2.50 6.00
SS16 Honus Wagner 6.00 15.00
SS17 Ken Griffey Jr. 5.00 12.00
SS18 Frank Robinson 1.50 4.00
SS19 Barry Bonds SP 10.00 25.00
SS20 Yogi Berra SP 6.00 15.00
SS21 Mike Piazza SP 6.00 15.00
SS22 Roger Clemens 4.00 10.00
SS23 Duke Snider SP 4.00 10.00
SS24 Frank Thomas 2.50 6.00
SS25 Andruw Jones 1.50 4.00

2001 Donruss Classics Timeless Treasures

STATED ODDS 1:420 HOBBY, 1:1680 RETAIL
TT1 Mark McGwire Ball SP 125.00 200.00
TT2 Babe Ruth Seat 12.50 30.00
TT3 Harmon Killebrew Bat SP 12.50 30.00
TT4 Derek Jeter Base 12.50 30.00
TT5 Barry Bonds Ball SP 30.00 60.00

2002 Donruss Classics Samples

*SAMPLES: .75X TO 2X BASIC CARDS
*GOLD: 1.5X TO 4X BASIC SAMPLES

2002 Donruss Classics

COMP.SET w/o SP's (100) 10.00 25.00
COMMON CARD (1-100) .25 .60
COMMON (101-150/201-225) 1.50 4.00
COMMON CARD (151-200) 1.50 4.00
101-200 TWO PER 9-PACK MINI BOX
201-225 RANDOM IN DONRUSS ROOK.PACKS
101-225 PRINT RUN 1500 SERIAL #'d SETS
1 Alex Rodriguez .75 2.00
2 Barry Bonds 1.50 4.00
3 C.C. Sabathia .25 .60
4 Chipper Jones .60 1.50
5 Derek Jeter 1.50 4.00
6 Troy Glaus .25 .60
7 Frank Thomas .60 1.50
8 Greg Maddux 1.00 2.50
9 Ivan Rodriguez .40 1.00
10 Jeff Bagwell .40 1.00
11 Mark Buehrle .25 .60
12 Todd Helton .40 1.00
13 Ken Griffey Jr. 1.25 3.00
14 Manny Ramirez .40 1.00
15 Brad Penny .25 .60
16 Mike Piazza 1.00 2.50
17 Nomar Garciaparra 1.00 2.50
18 Pedro Martinez .40 1.00
19 Randy Johnson .60 1.50
20 Bud Smith .25 .60
21 Rickey Henderson .60 1.50
22 Roger Clemens 1.25 3.00
23 Sammy Sosa .60 1.50
24 Brandon Duckworth .25 .60
25 Vladimir Guerrero .60 1.50
26 Kazuhiro Sasaki .25 .60
27 Roberto Alomar .40 1.00
28 Barry Zito .25 .60
29 Rich Aurilia .25 .60
30 Ben Sheets .25 .60
31 Carlos Delgado .25 .60
32 J.D. Drew .25 .60
33 Jermaine Dye .25 .60
34 Darin Erstad .25 .60
35 Jason Giambi .25 .60
36 Tom Glavine .40 1.00
37 Juan Gonzalez .25 .60
38 Luis Gonzalez .25 .60
39 Shawn Green .25 .60
40 Tim Hudson .25 .60
41 Andruw Jones .40 1.00
42 Shannon Stewart .25 .60
43 Barry Larkin .40 1.00
44 Wade Miller .25 .60
45 Mike Mussina .40 1.00
46 Hideo Nomo .60 1.50
47 Rafael Palmeiro .40 1.00
48 Scott Rolen .40 1.00
49 Gary Sheffield .25 .60
50 Bernie Williams .40 1.00
51 Bob Abreu .25 .60
52 Javier Vazquez .25 .60
53 Edgar Martinez .40 1.00
54 Magglio Ordonez .25 .60
55 Kerry Wood .25 .60
56 Adrian Beltre .25 .60
57 Lance Berkman .25 .60
58 Kevin Brown .25 .60
59 Sean Casey .25 .60
60 Eric Chavez .25 .60
61 Robert Person .25 .60
62 Jeremy Giambi .25 .60
63 Freddy Garcia .25 .60
64 Alfonso Soriano .25 .60
65 Doug Davis .25 .60
66 Brian Giles .25 .60
67 Moises Alou .25 .60
68 Richard Hidalgo .25 .60
69 Paul LoDuca .25 .60
70 Aramis Ramirez .25 .60
71 Andres Galarraga .25 .60
72 Ryan Klesko .25 .60
73 Chan Ho Park .25 .60
74 Richie Sexson .25 .60
75 Mike Sweeney .25 .60
76 Aubrey Huff .25 .60
77 Miguel Tejada .25 .60
78 Jose Vidro .25 .60
79 Larry Walker .25 .60
80 Roy Oswalt .25 .60
81 Craig Biggio .40 1.00
82 Juan Pierre .25 .60
83 Jim Thome .40 1.00
84 Josh Towers .25 .60
85 Alex Escobar .25 .60
86 Cliff Floyd .25 .60
87 Terrence Long .25 .60
88 Curt Schilling .25 .60
89 Carlos Beltran .25 .60
90 Albert Pujols 1.25 3.00
91 Gabe Kapler .25 .60
92 Mark Mulder .25 .60
93 Carlos Lee .25 .60
94 Robert Fick .25 .60
95 Raul Mondesi .25 .60
96 Ichiro Suzuki 1.25 3.00
97 Adam Dunn .25 .60
98 Corey Patterson .25 .60
99 Tsuyoshi Shinjo .25 .60
100 Joe Mays .25 .60
101 Juan Cruz ROO 1.50 4.00
102 Marlon Byrd ROO 1.50 4.00
103 Luis Garcia ROO 1.50 4.00
104 Jorge Padilla ROO RC 1.50 4.00
105 Dennis Tankersley ROO 1.50 4.00
106 Josh Pearce ROO 1.50 4.00
107 Ramon Vazquez ROO 1.50 4.00
108 Chris Baker ROO RC 1.50 4.00
109 Eric Cyr ROO 1.50 4.00
110 Reed Johnson ROO RC 2.00 5.00
111 Ryan Jamison ROO 1.50 4.00
112 Antonio Perez ROO 1.50 4.00
113 Satoru Komiyama ROO RC 1.50 4.00
114 Austin Kearns ROO 1.50 4.00
115 Juan Pena ROO 1.50 4.00
116 Orlando Hudson ROO 1.50 4.00
117 Kazuhisa Ishii ROO RC 2.00 5.00
118 Erik Bedard ROO 1.50 4.00
119 Luis Ugueto ROO RC 1.50 4.00
120 Ben Howard ROO RC 1.50 4.00
121 Morgan Ensberg ROO 1.50 4.00
122 Doug Devore ROO RC 1.50 4.00
123 Josh Phelps ROO 1.50 4.00
124 Angel Berroa ROO 1.50 4.00
125 Ed Rogers ROO 1.50 4.00
126 Takahito Nomura ROO RC 1.50 4.00
127 John Ennis ROO RC 1.50 4.00
128 Bill Hall ROO 1.50 4.00
129 Dewon Brazelton ROO 1.50 4.00
130 Hank Blalock ROO 2.00 5.00
131 So Taguchi ROO RC 2.00 5.00
132 Jorge De La Rosa ROO RC 1.50 4.00
133 Matt Thornton ROO RC 1.50 4.00
134 Brandon Backe ROO RC 2.00 5.00
135 Jeff Deardorff ROO 1.50 4.00
136 Steve Smyth ROO 1.50 4.00
137 Anderson Machado ROO RC 1.50 4.00
138 John Buck ROO 1.50 4.00
139 Mark Prior ROO 2.00 5.00
140 Sean Burroughs ROO 1.50 4.00
141 Alex Herrera ROO 1.50 4.00
142 Francis Beltran ROO RC 1.50 4.00
143 Jason Romano ROO 1.50 4.00
144 Michael Cuddyer ROO 1.50 4.00
145 Steve Bechler ROO RC 1.50 4.00
146 Alfredo Amezaga ROO 1.50 4.00
147 Ryan Ludwick ROO 1.50 4.00
148 Martin Vargas ROO 1.50 4.00
149 Allan Simpson ROO RC 1.50 4.00
150 Mark Teixeira ROO 2.00 5.00
151 Dale Murphy LGD 2.00 5.00
152 Ernie Banks LGD 2.00 5.00
153 Johnny Bench LGD 2.00 5.00
154 George Brett LGD 3.00 8.00
155 Lou Brock LGD 2.00 5.00
156 Rod Carew LGD 2.00 5.00
157 Steve Carlton LGD 1.50 4.00
158 Joe Torre LGD 2.00 5.00
159 Dennis Eckersley LGD 1.50 4.00
160 Reggie Jackson LGD 2.00 5.00
161 Al Kaline LGD 2.00 5.00
162 Dave Parker LGD 1.50 4.00
163 Don Mattingly LGD 3.00 8.00
164 Tony Gwynn LGD 2.00 5.00
165 Willie McCovey LGD 1.50 4.00
166 Joe Morgan LGD 1.50 4.00
167 Stan Musial LGD 2.50 6.00
168 Jim Palmer LGD 1.50 4.00
169 Brooks Robinson LGD 2.00 5.00
170 Bo Jackson LGD 2.00 5.00
171 Nolan Ryan LGD 4.00 10.00
172 Mike Schmidt LGD 3.00 8.00
173 Tom Seaver LGD 2.00 5.00
174 Cal Ripken LGD 5.00 12.00
175 Robin Yount LGD 2.00 5.00
176 Wade Boggs LGD 2.00 5.00
177 Gary Carter LGD 1.50 4.00
178 Ron Santo LGD 2.00 5.00
179 Luis Aparicio LGD 1.50 4.00
180 Bobby Doerr LGD 2.00 5.00
181 Ryne Sandberg LGD 3.00 8.00
182 Yogi Berra LGD 2.00 5.00
183 Will Clark LGD 2.00 5.00
184 Eddie Murray LGD 2.00 5.00
185 Andre Dawson LGD 1.50 4.00
186 Duke Snider LGD 2.00 5.00
187 Orlando Cepeda LGD 1.50 4.00
188 Billy Williams LGD 1.50 4.00
189 Juan Marichal LGD 1.50 4.00
190 Harmon Killebrew LGD 2.00 5.00
191 Kirby Puckett LGD 2.00 5.00
192 Carlton Fisk LGD 2.00 5.00
193 Dave Winfield LGD 1.50 4.00
194 Alan Trammell LGD 1.50 4.00
195 Paul Molitor LGD 1.50 4.00
196 Tony Perez LGD 1.50 4.00
197 Ozzie Smith LGD 2.50 6.00
198 Ralph Kiner LGD 1.50 4.00
199 Fergie Jenkins LGD 1.50 4.00
200 Phil Rizzuto LGD 2.00 5.00
201 Oliver Perez ROO RC 2.00 5.00
202 Aaron Cook ROO RC 1.50 4.00
203 Eric Junge ROO RC 1.50 4.00
204 Freddy Sanchez ROO RC 2.00 5.00
205 Cliff Lee ROO RC 4.00 10.00
206 Runelvys Hernandez ROO RC 1.50 4.00
207 Chone Figgins ROO RC 2.00 5.00
208 Rodrigo Rosario ROO RC 1.50 4.00
209 Kevin Cash ROO RC 1.50 4.00
210 Josh Bard ROO RC 1.50 4.00
211 Felix Escalona ROO RC 1.50 4.00
212 Jeriome Robertson ROO RC 1.50 4.00
213 Jason Simontacchi ROO RC 1.50 4.00
214 Shane Nance ROO RC 1.50 4.00
215 Ben Kozlowski ROO RC 1.50 4.00
216 Brian Tallet ROO RC 1.50 4.00
217 Earl Snyder ROO RC 1.50 4.00
218 Andy Pratt ROO RC 1.50 4.00
219 Trey Hodges ROO RC 1.50 4.00
220 Kirk Saarloos ROO RC 1.50 4.00
221 Rene Reyes ROO RC 1.50 4.00
222 Joe Borchard ROO 1.50 4.00
223 Wilson Valdez ROO RC 1.50 4.00
224 Miguel Asencio ROO RC 1.50 4.00
225 Chris Snelling ROO RC 1.50 4.00

2002 Donruss Classics National

ISSUED AT '02 NATIONAL CONVENTION
STATED PRINT RUN 5 SERIAL #'d SETS
NO PRICING DUE TO SCARCITY

2002 Donruss Classics Significant Signatures

STATED PRINT RUNS LISTED BELOW
NO PRICING ON QTY OF 25 OR LESS
SKIP-NUMBERED 202-CARD SET
101 Juan Cruz ROO/400 4.00 10.00
102 Marlon Byrd ROO/500 4.00 10.00
103 Luis Garcia ROO/500 4.00 10.00
104 Jorge Padilla ROO/500 4.00 10.00
105 Dennis Tankersley ROO/250 6.00 15.00
106 Josh Pearce ROO/500 4.00 10.00
107 Ramon Vazquez ROO/500 4.00 10.00
108 Chris Baker ROO/500 4.00 10.00

109 Eric Cyr ROO/500 4.00 10.00
110 Reed Johnson ROO/500 6.00 15.00
111 Ryan Jamison ROO/500 4.00 10.00
112 Antonio Perez ROO/500 4.00 10.00
113 Satoru Komiyama ROO/50 15.00 40.00
114 Austin Kearns ROO/500 4.00 10.00
115 Juan Pena ROO/500 4.00 10.00
116 Orlando Hudson ROO/400 4.00 10.00
117 Kazuhisa Ishii ROO/50 15.00 40.00
118 Erik Bedard ROO/500 6.00 15.00
119 Luis Ugueto ROO/250 4.00 10.00
120 Ben Howard ROO/500 4.00 10.00
121 Morgan Ensberg ROO/500 6.00 15.00
122 Doug Devore ROO/500 4.00 10.00
123 Josh Phelps ROO/500 4.00 10.00
124 Angel Berroa ROO/500 4.00 10.00
125 Ed Rogers ROO/500 4.00 10.00
127 John Ennis ROO/500 4.00 10.00
128 Bill Hall ROO/400 6.00 15.00
129 Dewon Brazelton ROO/400 4.00 10.00
130 Hank Blalock ROO/100 6.00 15.00
131 So Taguchi ROO/150 12.50 30.00
132 Jorge De La Rosa ROO/500 4.00 10.00
133 Matt Thornton ROO/500 4.00 10.00
134 Brandon Backe ROO/500 6.00 15.00
135 Jeff Deardorff ROO/500 4.00 10.00
136 Steve Smyth ROO/400 4.00 10.00
137 Anderson Machado ROO/500 4.00 10.00
138 John Buck ROO/500 4.00 10.00
139 Mark Prior ROO/250 6.00 15.00
140 Sean Burroughs ROO/500 6.00 15.00
141 Alex Herrera ROO/500 4.00 10.00
142 Francis Beltran ROO/500 4.00 10.00
143 Jason Romano ROO/500 4.00 10.00
144 Michael Cuddyer ROO/400 4.00 10.00
145 Steve Bechler ROO/500 4.00 10.00
146 Alfredo Amezaga ROO/500 4.00 10.00
147 Ryan Ludwick ROO/500 6.00 15.00
148 Martin Vargas ROO/500 4.00 10.00
149 Allan Simpson ROO/500 4.00 10.00
150 Mark Teixeira ROO/200 10.00 25.00
155 Lou Brock LGD/100 10.00 25.00
157 Steve Carlton LGD/125 10.00 25.00
159 Dennis Eckersley LGD/500 6.00 15.00
161 Al Kaline LGD/125 12.00 30.00
162 Dave Parker LGD/500 6.00 15.00
163 Don Mattingly LGD/50 30.00 60.00
168 Jim Palmer LGD/125 10.00 25.00
169 Brooks Robinson LGD/125 15.00 40.00
177 Gary Carter LGD/150 10.00 25.00
178 Ron Santo LGD/500 8.00 20.00
179 Luis Aparicio LGD/400 8.00 20.00
180 Bobby Doerr LGD/500 6.00 15.00
185 Andre Dawson LGD/200 6.00 15.00
187 Orlando Cepeda LGD/125 6.00 15.00
188 Billy Williams LGD/200 8.00 20.00
189 Juan Marichal LGD/500 8.00 20.00
190 Harmon Killebrew LGD/100 10.00 25.00
194 Alan Trammell LGD/200 6.00 15.00
196 Tony Perez LGD/150 8.00 20.00
198 Ralph Kiner LGD/125 10.00 25.00
199 Fergie Jenkins LGD/200 8.00 20.00
200 Phil Rizzuto LGD/125 15.00 40.00
201 Oliver Perez ROO/50 30.00 60.00
203 Eric Junge ROO/50 6.00 15.00
205 Cliff Lee ROO/100 30.00 60.00
207 Chone Figgins ROO/100 10.00 25.00
208 Rodrigo Rosario ROO/250 4.00 10.00
209 Kevin Cash ROO/100 4.00 10.00
210 Josh Bard ROO/100 4.00 10.00
214 Shane Nance ROO/200 4.00 10.00
215 Ben Kozlowski ROO/200 4.00 10.00
216 Brian Tallet ROO/100 4.00 10.00
217 Earl Snyder ROO/100 4.00 10.00
218 Andy Pratt ROO/250 4.00 10.00
219 Trey Hodges ROO/250 4.00 10.00
220 Kirk Saarloos ROO/100 4.00 10.00
221 Rene Reyes ROO/50 6.00 15.00
222 Joe Borchard ROO/100 6.00 15.00
223 Wilson Valdez ROO/100 4.00 10.00
225 Chris Snelling ROO/100 8.00 20.00

2002 Donruss Classics Timeless Tributes

*TRIBUTE 1-100: 2.5X TO 6X BASIC
*TRIB.101-150/201-225: .6X TO 1.5X BASIC
*TRIB.151-200: 1.25X TO 3X BASIC
1-200 RANDOM INSERTS IN PACKS
STATED PRINT 100 SERIAL #'d SETS

2002 Donruss Classics Classic Singles

STATED PRINT RUNS LISTED BELOW
1 Cal Ripken Jsy/100 12.50 30.00
2 Eddie Murray Jsy/100 6.00 15.00
3 George Brett Jsy/100 10.00 25.00
4 Bo Jackson Jsy/100 6.00 15.00
5 Ted Williams Bat/50 20.00 50.00
6 Jimmie Foxx Sox Bat/50 20.00 50.00
7 Steve Carlton Jsy/50 6.00 15.00
8 Reg.Jackson Yanks Jsy/100 6.00 15.00
9 Mel Ott Jsy/50 40.00 80.00
10 Catfish Hunter Jsy/100 6.00 15.00
11 Nolan Ryan Jsy/100 20.00 50.00
12 Rickey Henderson Jsy/100 6.00 15.00
13 Robin Yount Jsy/100 6.00 15.00
14 Orlando Cepeda Jsy/100 4.00 10.00
15 Ty Cobb Bat/50 40.00 80.00
16 Babe Ruth Bat/50 125.00 250.00
17 Dave Parker Jsy/100 4.00 10.00
18 Willie Stargell Jsy/100 6.00 15.00
19 Ernie Banks Bat/100 6.00 15.00
20 Mike Schmidt Jsy/100 10.00 25.00
21 Duke Snider Jsy/50 10.00 25.00
22 Jackie Robinson Jsy/50 50.00 100.00
23 Rickey Henderson Bat/100 6.00 15.00
24 Dale Murphy Bat/100 6.00 15.00
25 Lou Gehrig Bat/50 125.00 200.00
26 Jimmie Foxx A's Bat/50 15.00 40.00
27 Reggie Jackson A's Jsy/100 6.00 15.00
28 Tony Gwynn Bat/100 10.00 25.00
29 Bobby Doerr Jsy/100 4.00 10.00
30 Joe Torre Jsy/100 6.00 15.00

2002 Donruss Classics Legendary Hats

RANDOM INSERTS IN PACKS
STATED PRINT RUN 50 SERIAL #'d SETS
1 Don Mattingly 60.00 120.00
2 George Brett 60.00 120.00
3 Wade Boggs 20.00 50.00
4 Reggie Jackson 20.00 50.00
5 Ryne Sandberg 20.00 50.00

2002 Donruss Classics Legendary Leather

STATED PRINT RUN 50 SERIAL #'d SETS
1 Don Mattingly Btg Glv 10.00 25.00
2 Wade Boggs Btg Glv 20.00 50.00
3 Tony Gwynn Fld Glv 50.00 100.00
4 Kirby Puckett Fld Glv 40.00 80.00
5 Mike Schmidt Fld Glv 15.00 40.00

2002 Donruss Classics Legendary Lumberjacks

STATED PRINT RUNS LISTED BELOW
1 Don Mattingly/500 10.00 25.00
2 George Brett/400 6.00 15.00
3 Stan Musial/100 20.00 50.00
4 Lou Gehrig/50 50.00 100.00
5 Mike Piazza/500 5.00 12.00
6 Mel Ott/50 25.00 60.00
7 Ted Williams/50 50.00 100.00
8 Bo Jackson/500 5.00 12.00
9 Kirby Puckett/500 5.00 12.00
10 Rafael Palmeiro/500 3.00 8.00
11 Andre Dawson/500 3.00 8.00
12 Ozzie Smith/500 6.00 15.00
13 Paul Molitor/500 5.00 12.00
14 Babe Ruth/50 125.00 250.00
15 Carlton Fisk/500 3.00 8.00
16 Rickey Henderson/500 5.00 12.00
17 Gary Carter/500 3.00 8.00
18 Cal Ripken/100 15.00 40.00
19 Eddie Mathews/100 5.00 12.00
20 Luis Aparicio/500 3.00 8.00
21 Al Kaline/100 5.00 12.00
22 Eddie Murray/500 3.00 8.00
23 Yogi Berra/100 5.00 12.00
24 Alex Rodriguez/500 6.00 15.00
25 Tony Gwynn/500 5.00 12.00
26 Roberto Clemente/100 25.00 100.00
27 Mike Schmidt/400 8.00 20.00
28 Reggie Jackson/500 3.00 8.00
29 Ryne Sandberg/500 10.00 25.00
30 Joe Morgan/400 3.00 8.00
31 Joe Torre/500 3.00 8.00
32 Gary Sheffield/500 2.00 5.00
33 Nomar Garciaparra/500 3.00 8.00
34 Jeff Bagwell/500 3.00 8.00
35 Manny Ramirez/500 3.00 8.00

2002 Donruss Classics Legendary Spikes

RANDOM INSERTS IN PACKS
STATED PRINT RUN 50 SERIAL #'d SETS
1 Don Mattingly 10.00 25.00
2 Eddie Murray 30.00 60.00
3 Paul Molitor 15.00 40.00
4 Harmon Killebrew 15.00 40.00
5 Mike Schmidt 20.00 50.00

2002 Donruss Classics New Millennium Classics

*MULTI-COLOR PATCH: 1.25X TO 3X BASIC
SEE BECKETT.COM FOR PRINT RUNS
1 Curt Schilling Jsy/500 3.00 8.00
2 Vladimir Guerrero Jsy/100 6.00 15.00
3 Jim Thome Jsy/500 4.00 10.00
4 Troy Glaus Jsy/400 3.00 8.00
5 Ivan Rodriguez Jsy/200 6.00 15.00
6 Todd Helton Jsy/400 4.00 10.00
7 Sean Casey Jsy/500 3.00 8.00
8 Scott Rolen Jsy/475 4.00 10.00
9 Ken Griffey Jr. Base/150 6.00 15.00
10 Hideo Nomo Jsy/100 10.00 25.00
11 Tom Glavine Jsy/350 4.00 10.00
12 Pedro Martinez Jsy/100 6.00 15.00
13 Cliff Floyd Jsy/500 3.00 8.00
14 Shawn Green Jsy/125 4.00 10.00
15 Rafael Palmeiro Jsy/250 4.00 10.00
16 Luis Gonzalez Jsy/100 4.00 10.00
17 Lance Berkman Jsy/100 4.00 10.00
18 Frank Thomas Jsy/500 8.00 20.00
19 Randy Johnson Jsy/400 4.00 10.00
20 Moises Alou Jsy/500 3.00 8.00
21 Chipper Jones Jsy/500 4.00 10.00
22 Larry Walker Jsy/300 3.00 8.00
23 Mike Sweeney Jsy/500 3.00 8.00
24 Juan Gonzalez Jsy/300 3.00 8.00
25 Roger Clemens Jsy/100 10.00 25.00
26 Albert Pujols Base/300 6.00 15.00
27 Magglio Ordonez Jsy/500 3.00 8.00
28 Alex Rodriguez Jsy/400 10.00 25.00
29 Jeff Bagwell Jsy/125 6.00 15.00
30 Kazuhiro Sasaki Jsy/500 3.00 8.00
31 Barry Larkin Jsy/300 4.00 10.00
32 Andruw Jones Jsy/350 4.00 10.00
33 Kerry Wood Jsy/200 4.00 10.00
34 Rickey Henderson Jsy/100 8.00 20.00
35 Greg Maddux Jsy/100 10.00 25.00
36 Brian Giles Jsy/400 3.00 8.00
37 Craig Biggio Jsy/100 6.00 15.00
38 Roberto Alomar Jsy/400 4.00 10.00
39 Mike Piazza Jsy/400 6.00 15.00
40 Bernie Williams Jsy/100 6.00 15.00
41 Ichiro Suzuki Ball/100 15.00 40.00
42 Kenny Lofton Jsy/450 3.00 8.00
43 Mark Mulder Jsy/500 3.00 8.00
44 Kazuhisa Ishii Jsy/100 6.00 15.00
45 Darin Erstad Jsy/500 3.00 8.00
46 Jose Vidro Jsy/500 3.00 8.00
47 Miguel Tejada Jsy/475 3.00 8.00
48 Roy Oswalt Jsy/500 3.00 8.00
49 So Taguchi Jsy/100 6.00 15.00
50 Barry Zito Jsy/500 3.00 8.00
51 Manny Ramirez Jsy/400 4.00 10.00
52 Nomar Garciaparra Jsy/100 6.00 15.00
53 C.C. Sabathia Jsy/500 3.00 8.00
54 Carlos Delgado Jsy/500 3.00 8.00
55 Gary Sheffield Jsy/500 3.00 8.00
56 J.D. Drew Jsy/500 3.00 8.00
57 Barry Bonds Ball/150 15.00 40.00
58 Derek Jeter Ball/150 10.00 25.00
59 Edgar Martinez Jsy/400 4.00 10.00
60 Sammy Sosa Ball/150 6.00 15.00

2002 Donruss Classics Timeless Treasures

RANDOM INSERTS IN PACKS
STATED PRINT RUNS LISTED BELOW
NO PRICING ON QUANTITIES OF 25 OR LESS
5 Ted Williams Crown Bat/42 30.00 60.00
6 Ted Williams Crown Bat/47 30.00 60.00
7 Ted Williams MVP Bat/46 30.00 60.00
8 Ted Williams MVP Bat/49 30.00 60.00
10 Cal Ripken Iron Man Jsy/98 20.00 50.00
11 Cal Ripken ROY Jsy/82 20.00 50.00
12 Cal Ripken MVP Jsy/83 20.00 50.00
13 Cal Ripken MVP Jsy/91 20.00 50.00

2003 Donruss Classics Samples

*SAMPLES: 1.5X TO 4X BASIC CARDS
ONE PER SEALED BBC MAGAZINE
*GOLD: 4X TO 10X BASIC SAMPLES

2003 Donruss Classics

COMP.LO SET w/o SP's (100) 10.00 25.00
COMMON CARD (1-100) .25 .60
COMMON CARD (101-150) .40 1.00
101-150 STATED ODDS 1:9
COMMON CARD (151-200) .40 1.00
151-200 STATED ODDS 1:9
101-200 PRINT RUN 1500 SERIAL #'d SETS
COMMON CARD (201-211) .60 1.50
201-211 PRINT RUN 1000 SERIAL #'d SETS
1 Troy Glaus .25 .60
2 Barry Bonds 1.00 2.50
3 Miguel Tejada .40 1.00
4 Randy Johnson .60 1.50
5 Eric Hinske .25 .60
6 Barry Zito .40 1.00
7 Jason Jennings .25 .60
8 Derek Jeter 1.50 4.00
9 Vladimir Guerrero .40 1.00
10 Corey Patterson .25 .60
11 Manny Ramirez .60 1.50
12 Edgar Martinez .40 1.00
13 Roy Oswalt .40 1.00
14 Andruw Jones .25 .60
15 Alex Rodriguez .75 2.00
16 Mark Mulder .25 .60
17 Kazuhisa Ishii .25 .60
18 Gary Sheffield .25 .60
19 Jay Gibbons .25 .60
20 Roberto Alomar .40 1.00
21 A.J. Pierzynski .25 .60
22 Eric Chavez .25 .60
23 Roger Clemens .75 2.00
24 C.C. Sabathia .40 1.00
25 Jose Vidro .25 .60
26 Shannon Stewart .25 .60
27 Mark Teixeira .40 1.00
28 Joe Thurston .25 .60
29 Josh Beckett .25 .60
30 Jeff Bagwell .40 1.00
31 Geronimo Gil .25 .60
32 Curt Schilling .40 1.00
33 Frank Thomas .60 1.50
34 Lance Berkman .40 1.00
35 Adam Dunn .40 1.00
36 Christian Parker .25 .60
37 Jim Thome .40 1.00
38 Shawn Green .25 .60
39 Drew Henson .25 .60
40 Chipper Jones .60 1.50
41 Kevin Mench .25 .60
42 Hideo Nomo .60 1.50
43 Andres Galarraga .40 1.00
44 Doug Davis .25 .60
45 Mark Prior .40 1.00
46 Sean Casey .25 .60
47 Magglio Ordonez .40 1.00
48 Tom Glavine .40 1.00
49 Marlon Byrd .25 .60
50 Albert Pujols .75 2.00
51 Mark Buehrle .40 1.00
52 Aramis Ramirez .25 .60
53 Pat Burrell .25 .60
54 Craig Biggio .40 1.00
55 Alfonso Soriano .40 1.00
56 Kerry Wood .25 .60
57 Wade Miller .25 .60
58 Hank Blalock .25 .60
59 Cliff Floyd .25 .60
60 Jason Giambi .25 .60
61 Carlos Beltran .40 1.00
62 Brian Roberts .25 .60
63 Paul Lo Duca .25 .60
64 Tim Redding .25 .60
65 Sammy Sosa .60 1.50
66 Joe Borchard .25 .60
67 Ryan Klesko .25 .60
68 Richie Sexson .25 .60
69 Carlos Lee .25 .60
70 Rickey Henderson .60 1.50
71 Brian Tallet .25 .60
72 Luis Gonzalez .25 .60
73 Satoru Komiyama .25 .60
74 Tim Hudson .40 1.00
75 Ken Griffey Jr. 1.25 3.00
76 Adam Johnson .25 .60
77 Bobby Abreu .25 .60
78 Adrian Beltre .60 1.50
79 Rafael Palmeiro .40 1.00
80 Ichiro Suzuki .75 2.00
81 Kenny Lofton .25 .60
82 Brian Giles .25 .60
83 Barry Larkin .40 1.00
84 Robert Fick .25 .60
85 Ben Sheets .25 .60
86 Scott Rolen .40 1.00
87 Nomar Garciaparra .40 1.00
88 Brandon Phillips .25 .60
89 Ben Kozlowski .25 .60
90 Bernie Williams .40 1.00
91 Pedro Martinez .40 1.00
92 Todd Helton .40 1.00
93 Jermaine Dye .25 .60
94 Carlos Delgado .25 .60
95 Mike Piazza .60 1.50
96 Junior Spivey .25 .60
97 Torii Hunter .25 .60
98 Mike Sweeney .25 .60
99 Ivan Rodriguez .40 1.00
100 Greg Maddux .75 2.00
101 Ernie Banks LGD 1.00 2.50
102 Steve Garvey LGD .40 1.00
103 George Brett LGD 2.00 5.00
104 Lou Brock LGD .60 1.50
105 Hoyt Wilhelm LGD .60 1.50
106 Steve Carlton LGD .60 1.50
107 Joe Torre LGD .60 1.50
108 Dennis Eckersley LGD .60 1.50
109 Reggie Jackson LGD .60 1.50
110 Al Kaline LGD .60 1.50
111 Harold Reynolds LGD .40 1.00
112 Don Mattingly LGD 2.00 5.00
113 Tony Gwynn LGD 1.00 2.50
114 Willie McCovey LGD .60 1.50
115 Joe Morgan LGD .60 1.50
116 Stan Musial LGD 1.50 4.00
117 Jim Palmer LGD .60 1.50
118 Brooks Robinson LGD .60 1.50
119 Don Sutton LGD .60 1.50
120 Nolan Ryan LGD 3.00 8.00
121 Mike Schmidt LGD 1.50 4.00
122 Tom Seaver LGD .60 1.50
123 Cal Ripken LGD 3.00 8.00
124 Robin Yount LGD 1.00 2.50
125 Bob Feller LGD .60 1.50
126 Joe Carter LGD .40 1.00
127 Jack Morris LGD .60 1.50
128 Luis Aparicio LGD .60 1.50
129 Bobby Doerr LGD .60 1.50
130 Dave Parker LGD .40 1.00
131 Yogi Berra LGD 1.00 2.50
132 Will Clark LGD .60 1.50
133 Fred Lynn LGD .40 1.00
134 Andre Dawson LGD .60 1.50
135 Duke Snider LGD .60 1.50
136 Orlando Cepeda LGD .60 1.50
137 Billy Williams LGD .60 1.50
138 Dale Murphy LGD 1.00 2.50
139 Harmon Killebrew LGD 1.00 2.50
140 Kirby Puckett LGD 1.00 2.50
141 Carlton Fisk LGD .60 1.50
142 Eric Davis LGD .40 1.00
143 Alan Trammell LGD .60 1.50
144 Paul Molitor LGD 1.00 2.50
145 Jose Canseco LGD .60 1.50
146 Ozzie Smith LGD 1.25 3.00
147 Ralph Kiner LGD .60 1.50
148 Dwight Gooden LGD .60 1.50
149 Phil Rizzuto LGD .60 1.50
150 Lenny Dykstra LGD .40 1.00
151 Adam LaRoche ROO .40 1.00
152 Tim Hummel ROO .40 1.00
153 Matt Kata ROO RC .40 1.00
154 Jeff Baker ROO .40 1.00
155 Josh Stewart ROO RC .40 1.00
156 Marshall McDougall ROO .40 1.00
157 Jhonny Peralta ROO .40 1.00
158 Mike Nicolas ROO RC .40 1.00
159 Jeremy Guthrie ROO .40 1.00
160 Craig Brazell ROO RC .40 1.00
161 Joe Valentine ROO RC .40 1.00
162 Buddy Hernandez ROO RC .40 1.00
163 Freddy Sanchez ROO .40 1.00
164 Shane Victorino ROO RC 1.25 3.00
165 Corwin Malone ROO .40 1.00
166 Jason Dubois ROO .40 1.00
167 Josh Wilson ROO .40 1.00
168 Tim Olson ROO RC .40 1.00
169 Cliff Bartosh ROO .40 1.00
170 Michael Hessman ROO RC .40 1.00
171 Ryan Church ROO .40 1.00
172 Garrett Atkins ROO .40 1.00
173 Jose Morban ROO .40 1.00
174 Ryan Cameron ROO RC .40 1.00
175 Todd Wellemeyer ROO RC .40 1.00
176 Travis Chapman ROO .40 1.00
177 Jason Anderson ROO .40 1.00
178 Adam Morrissey ROO .40 1.00
179 Jose Contreras ROO RC 1.00 2.50
180 Nic Jackson ROO .40 1.00
181 Rob Hammock ROO RC .40 1.00
182 Carlos Rivera ROO .40 1.00
183 Vinny Chulk ROO .40 1.00
184 Pete LaForest ROO RC .40 1.00
185 Jon Leicester ROO RC .40 1.00
186 Termel Sledge ROO RC .40 1.00
187 Jose Castillo ROO .40 1.00
188 Gerald Laird ROO .40 1.00
189 Nook Logan ROO RC .40 1.00
190 Clint Barmes ROO RC 1.00 2.50
191 Jesus Medrano ROO .40 1.00
192 Henri Stanley ROO .40 1.00
193 Hideki Matsui ROO RC 2.00 5.00
194 Walter Young ROO .40 1.00
195 Jon Adkins ROO .40 1.00
196 Tommy Whiteman ROO .40 1.00
197 Rob Bowen ROO .40 1.00
198 Brandon Webb ROO RC 1.25 3.00
199 Prentice Redman ROO RC .40 1.00
200 Jimmy Gobble ROO .40 1.00
201 J.Bonderman ROO RC 2.50 6.00
202 Adam Loewen ROO RC .60 1.50
203 Chien-Ming Wang ROO RC 2.50 6.00
204 Hong-Chih Kuo ROO RC 3.00 8.00
205 Ryan Wagner ROO RC .60 1.50
206 Dan Haren ROO RC 3.00 8.00
207 Dontrelle Willis ROO .60 1.50
208 Rickie Weeks ROO RC 2.00 5.00
209 Ramon Nivar ROO RC .60 1.50
210 Chad Gaudin ROO RC .60 1.50
211 Delmon Young ROO RC 4.00 10.00

2003 Donruss Classics Significant Signatures

ONE AUTO OR GAME-USED PER 9-PACK BOX
PRINT RUNS B/WN 5-500 COPIES PER
NO PRICING ON QTY OF 45 OR LESS
5 Eric Hinske/250 4.00 10.00
7 Jason Jennings/250 4.00 10.00
10 Corey Patterson/100 6.00 15.00
13 Roy Oswalt/100 10.00 25.00
16 Mark Mulder/100 6.00 15.00
19 Jay Gibbons/250 4.00 10.00
21 A.J. Pierzynski/75 10.00 25.00
25 Jose Vidro/75 6.00 15.00
27 Mark Teixeira/50 15.00 40.00
31 Geronimo Gil/50 6.00 15.00
35 Adam Dunn/100 15.00 40.00
36 Christian Parker/250 4.00 10.00
39 Drew Henson/100 6.00 15.00
41 Kevin Mench/250 6.00 15.00
45 Mark Prior/50 12.00 30.00
57 Wade Miller/200 4.00 10.00
58 Hank Blalock/50 10.00 25.00
62 Brian Roberts/250 10.00 25.00
63 Paul Lo Duca/100 10.00 25.00
64 Tim Redding/250 4.00 10.00
66 Joe Borchard/100 6.00 15.00
73 Satoru Komiyama/124 10.00 25.00
76 Adam Johnson/200 4.00 10.00
84 Robert Fick/50 6.00 15.00
88 Brandon Phillips/250 4.00 10.00
89 Ben Kozlowski/150 4.00 10.00
93 Jermaine Dye/100 10.00 25.00
96 Junior Spivey/100 6.00 15.00
97 Torii Hunter/50 10.00 25.00
102 Steve Garvey LGD/100 10.00 25.00
108 Dennis Eckersley LGD/50 15.00 40.00
111 Harold Reynolds LGD/50 15.00 40.00
119 Don Sutton LGD/100 10.00 25.00
120 Nolan Ryan LGD/50 50.00 120.00
123 Cal Ripken LGD/50 75.00 150.00
126 Joe Carter LGD/100 10.00 25.00
127 Jack Morris LGD/100 10.00 25.00
128 Luis Aparicio LGD/50 15.00 40.00
133 Fred Lynn LGD/50 15.00 40.00
134 Andre Dawson LGD/50 15.00 40.00
136 Orlando Cepeda LGD/100 10.00 25.00
137 Billy Williams LGD/100 10.00 25.00
142 Eric Davis LGD/50 15.00 40.00
143 Alan Trammell LGD/50 15.00 40.00
148 Dwight Gooden LGD/50 15.00 40.00
150 Lenny Dykstra LGD/50 10.00 25.00
151 Adam LaRoche ROO/250 4.00 10.00
152 Tim Hummel ROO/500 4.00 10.00
153 Matt Kata ROO/500 4.00 10.00
154 Jeff Baker ROO/500 4.00 10.00
155 Josh Stewart ROO/177 4.00 10.00
156 Marshall McDougall ROO/500 4.00 10.00
157 Jhonny Peralta ROO/500 6.00 15.00
158 Mike Nicolas ROO/500 4.00 10.00
159 Jeremy Guthrie ROO/500 4.00 10.00
160 Craig Brazell ROO/500 4.00 10.00
161 Joe Valentine ROO/172 4.00 10.00
162 Buddy Hernandez ROO/500 4.00 10.00
163 Freddy Sanchez ROO/500 6.00 15.00
164 Shane Victorino ROO/351 6.00 15.00
165 Corwin Malone ROO/500 4.00 10.00
166 Jason Dubois ROO/500 4.00 10.00
167 Josh Wilson ROO/500 4.00 10.00
168 Tim Olson ROO/500 4.00 10.00
169 Cliff Bartosh ROO/500 4.00 10.00
170 Michael Hessman ROO/427 4.00 10.00
171 Ryan Church ROO/500 6.00 15.00
172 Garrett Atkins ROO/500 4.00 10.00
173 Jose Morban ROO/500 4.00 10.00
174 Ryan Cameron ROO/500 4.00 10.00
175 Todd Wellemeyer ROO/500 4.00 10.00
176 Travis Chapman ROO/477 4.00 10.00
177 Jason Anderson ROO/500 6.00 15.00
178 Adam Morrissey ROO/500 4.00 10.00
179 Jose Contreras ROO/100 6.00 15.00
180 Nic Jackson ROO/500 4.00 10.00
181 Rob Hammock ROO/500 4.00 10.00
182 Carlos Rivera ROO/500 4.00 10.00
183 Vinny Chulk ROO/500 4.00 10.00
184 Pete LaForest ROO/177 4.00 10.00
185 John Leicester ROO/500 4.00 10.00
186 Termel Sledge ROO/500 4.00 10.00
187 Jose Castillo ROO/500 4.00 10.00
188 Gerald Laird ROO/500 4.00 10.00
189 Nook Logan ROO/427 6.00 15.00
190 Clint Barmes ROO/100 8.00 20.00
191 Jesus Medrano ROO/500 4.00 10.00
192 Henri Stanley ROO/500 4.00 10.00
194 Walter Young ROO/500 4.00 10.00
195 Jon Adkins ROO/500 4.00 10.00
196 Tommy Whiteman ROO/500 4.00 10.00
197 Rob Bowen ROO/500 4.00 10.00
198 Brandon Webb ROO/500 4.00 10.00
199 Prentice Redman ROO/127 4.00 10.00
200 Jimmy Gobble ROO/500 4.00 10.00
201 J.Bonderman ROO/100 15.00 40.00
202 Adam Loewen ROO/100 10.00 25.00
203 C.Wang ROO/50 60.00 120.00
205 Ryan Wagner ROO/100 4.00 10.00
206 Dan Haren ROO/100 12.00 30.00
209 Ramon Nivar ROO/100 4.00 10.00

2003 Donruss Classics Timeless Tributes

*TRIBUTE 1-100: 2.5X TO 6X BASIC
*TRIB.101-150: 1.5X TO 4X BASIC
*TRIBUTE 151-200: 1.5X TO 4X BASIC
*TRIBUTE 201-211: 1X TO 2.5X BASIC
STATED PRINT RUN 100 SERIAL #'d SETS

2003 Donruss Classics Classic Combos

RANDOM INSERTS IN PACKS
PRINT RUNS B/WN 25-50 COPIES PER
NO PRICING ON QTY OF 25 OR LESS
1 Ruth Jsy/Gehrig Jsy/50 400.00 600.00
2 Jackie Jsy/Reese Jsy/50 50.00 100.00
4 H.Wag Seat/R.Clem Jsy/50 90.00 150.00

2003 Donruss Classics Classic Singles

PRINT RUNS B/WN 25-100 COPIES PER
NO PRICING ON QTY OF 25 OR LESS
1 Babe Ruth Jsy/100 100.00 250.00
2 Lou Gehrig Jsy/80 75.00 150.00
3 Jackie Robinson Jsy/80 50.00 100.00
5 Bobby Doerr Jsy/100 8.00 20.00
6 Fred Lynn Jsy/100 8.00 20.00
7 Honus Wagner Seat/100 20.00 50.00
8 Roberto Clemente Jsy/80 60.00 120.00
9 Kirby Puckett Jsy/100 15.00 40.00
10 Torii Hunter Jsy/100 6.00 15.00
11 Sammy Sosa Jsy/100 10.00 25.00
12 Ryne Sandberg Jsy/100 30.00 60.00
13 Hideo Nomo Jsy/50 60.00 120.00
14 Kazuhisa Ishii Jsy/50 10.00 25.00
15 Mike Schmidt Jsy/100 30.00 60.00
16 Steve Carlton Jsy/100 8.00 20.00
17 Robin Yount Jsy/100 15.00 40.00
18 Paul Molitor Jsy/100 8.00 20.00
19 Mike Piazza Jsy/100 10.00 25.00
20 Duke Snider Jsy/50 15.00 40.00
21 Al Kaline Jsy/50 30.00 60.00
23 Don Mattingly Jsy/100 8.00 20.00
24 Jason Giambi Jsy/100 6.00 15.00
26 Ozzie Smith Jsy/100 15.00 40.00
27 Roger Clemens Jsy/100 12.00 30.00
28 Pedro Martinez Jsy/100 8.00 20.00
29 Thurman Munson Jsy/50 30.00 60.00

2003 Donruss Classics Dress Code

PRINT RUNS B/WN 50-500 COPIES PER
1 Roger Clemens Yanks Jsy/500 6.00 15.00
2 Miguel Tejada Triple/250 3.00 8.00
3 Vladimir Guerrero Jsy/425 3.00 8.00
4 Kazuhisa Ishii Jsy/250 2.00 5.00
5 Chipper Jones Jsy/425 5.00 12.00
6 Troy Glaus Jsy/425 2.00 5.00
7 Rafael Palmeiro Jsy/425 3.00 8.00
8 R.Henderson R.Sox Jsy/250 5.00 12.00
9 Pedro Martinez Jsy/425 3.00 8.00
10 Andruw Jones Jsy/425 2.00 5.00
11 Nomar Garciaparra Jsy/500 3.00 8.00
12 Carlos Delgado Jsy/500 2.00 5.00
13 R.Hend Padres Hat-Jsy/250 5.00 12.00
14 Kerry Wood Hat-Jsy/250 2.00 5.00
15 Lance Berkman Hat-Jsy/250 3.00 8.00
16 Tony Gwynn Quad/100 5.00 12.00
17 Mark Mulder Jsy/425 2.00 5.00
18 Jim Thome Jsy/500 3.00 8.00
19 Mike Piazza Jsy/500 5.00 12.00
20 Mike Mussina Jsy/500 3.00 8.00
21 Luis Gonzalez Jsy/500 2.00 5.00
22 Ryan Klesko Jsy/500 2.00 5.00
23 Richie Sexson Jsy/500 2.00 5.00
24 Curt Schilling Jsy/500 3.00 8.00
25 Alex Rodriguez Rgr Jsy/500 6.00 15.00
26 Bernie Williams Jsy/425 3.00 8.00
27 Cal Ripken Jsy/500 10.00 20.00
28 C.C. Sabathia Jsy/500 3.00 8.00
29 Mike Piazza Bat-Jsy/200 5.00 12.00
30 R.Hend Mets Hat-Jsy/250 5.00 12.00
31 Torii Hunter Jsy/425 2.00 5.00
32 Mark Teixeira Jsy/425 3.00 8.00
33 Dale Murphy Bat-Jsy/300 5.00 12.00
34 Todd Helton Jsy/425 3.00 8.00
35 Eric Chavez Jsy/425 2.00 5.00
36 Vernon Wells Jsy/425 2.00 5.00
37 Jeff Bagwell Hat-Jsy/250 3.00 8.00
38 Nick Johnson Jsy/425 2.00 5.00
39 Tim Hudson Hat-Jsy/250 3.00 8.00
40 Shawn Green Jsy/425 2.00 5.00
41 Mark Buehrle Jsy/500 3.00 8.00
42 Garret Anderson Jsy/100 2.00 5.00
43 Alex Rodriguez M's Jsy/500 6.00 15.00
44 Jason Giambi Jsy/500 2.00 5.00
45 Carlos Beltran Jsy/500 3.00 8.00
46 Adam Dunn Hat-Jsy/100 3.00 8.00
47 Jorge Posada Jsy/425 3.00 8.00
48 Roy Oswalt Hat-Jsy/200 3.00 8.00
49 Rich Aurilia Jsy/500 2.00 5.00
50 Jason Jennings Quad/250 2.00 5.00
51 Mark Prior Quad/250 3.00 8.00
52 Jim Edmonds Jsy/500 3.00 8.00
53 Fred McGriff Jsy/500 3.00 8.00
54 A.Soriano Jsy-Shoe/100 3.00 8.00
55 Jeff Kent Jsy/425 2.00 5.00
56 Hideo Nomo R.Sox Jsy/200 5.00 12.00
57 Manny Ramirez Jsy/425 5.00 12.00
58 Jose Canseco Bat-Jsy/350 3.00 8.00
59 Magglio Ordonez Jsy/500 3.00 8.00
60 Alan Trammell Bat-Jsy/250 3.00 8.00
61 Bobby Abreu Jsy/500 2.00 5.00
62 R.Henderson A's Hat-Jsy/200 5.00 12.00
63 Josh Beckett Jsy/500 2.00 5.00
64 Barry Larkin Jsy/500 3.00 8.00
65 Randy Johnson Jsy/200 5.00 12.00
66 Juan Gonzalez Jsy/500 2.00 5.00
67 Barry Zito Hat-Jsy/250 3.00 8.00
68 Roger Clemens R.Sox Jsy/500 6.00 15.00
69 R.Henderson M's Hat-Jsy/100 5.00 12.00
70 Hideo Nomo Mets Jsy/100 5.00 12.00
71 Paul Konerko Jsy/400 3.00 8.00
72 Pat Burrell Jsy/100 2.00 5.00
73 Frank Thomas Jsy-Pants/500 5.00 12.00
74 Sammy Sosa Jsy/500 5.00 12.00
75 Greg Maddux Btg Glv-Jsy/50 6.00 15.00

2003 Donruss Classics Legendary Hats

RANDOM INSERTS IN PACKS
STATED PRINT RUN 50 SERIAL #'d SETS
1 Roberto Clemente/50 50.00 100.00
2 Kirby Puckett 30.00 60.00
3 Mike Schmidt 60.00 120.00
4 Tony Gwynn 12.50 30.00
5 Rickey Henderson 12.00 30.00

2003 Donruss Classics Legendary Leather

RANDOM INSERTS IN PACKS
STATED PRINT RUN 25 SERIAL #'d SETS
NO PRICING DUE TO SCARCITY
1 Nolan Ryan Fld Glv/80 60.00 120.00

2003 Donruss Classics Legendary Lumberjacks

PRINT RUNS B/WN 11-400 COPIES PER
NO PRICING ON QTY OF 25 OR LESS
1 Babe Ruth/100 100.00 200.00
2 Lou Gehrig/80 75.00 150.00
3 George Brett/250 12.50 30.00
4 Duke Snider/250 10.00 25.00
6 Ryne Sandberg/400 12.50 30.00
7 Robin Yount/300 8.00 20.00
8 Harmon Killebrew/250 10.00 25.00
9 Al Kaline/250 10.00 25.00
10 Eddie Mathews/225 10.00 25.00
11 Brooks Robinson/400 8.00 20.00
13 Kirby Puckett/375 8.00 20.00
14 Jose Canseco/400 8.00 20.00
15 Nellie Fox/325 8.00 20.00
16 Don Mattingly/400 8.00 20.00
17 Joe Torre/250 6.00 15.00
18 Cal Ripken/250 10.00 25.00
19 Richie Ashburn/250 10.00 25.00
20 Mike Schmidt/250 12.50 30.00
21 Dale Murphy/250 10.00 25.00
22 Thurman Munson/400 8.00 20.00
23 Tony Gwynn/400 8.00 20.00
24 Orlando Cepeda/225 6.00 15.00
26 Paul Molitor/325 6.00 15.00
27 Ralph Kiner/200 6.00 15.00
28 Frank Robinson/225 10.00 25.00
29 Yogi Berra/50 30.00 60.00
30 Reggie Jackson/375 8.00 20.00
31 Rod Carew/325 8.00 20.00
32 Carlton Fisk/325 8.00 20.00
33 Rogers Hornsby/50 10.00 25.00
34 Mel Ott/125 15.00 40.00
35 Jimmie Foxx/50 40.00 80.00

2003 Donruss Classics Legendary Spikes

RANDOM INSERTS IN PACKS
STATED PRINT RUN 50 SERIAL #'d SETS
1 Kirby Puckett 30.00 60.00
2 Tony Gwynn 50.00 100.00
3 Don Mattingly 20.00 50.00
4 Frank Robinson 20.00 50.00
5 Gary Carter 15.00 40.00

2003 Donruss Classics Legends of the Fall

RANDOM INSERTS IN PACKS
STATED PRINT RUN 2500 SERIAL #'d SETS
1 Reggie Jackson .60 1.50
2 Duke Snider .60 1.50
3 Roberto Clemente 2.50 6.00
4 Mel Ott 1.00 2.50
5 Yogi Berra 1.00 2.50
6 Jackie Robinson 1.00 2.50
7 Enos Slaughter .60 1.50
8 Willie Stargell .60 1.50
9 Bobby Doerr .60 1.50
10 Thurman Munson 1.00 2.50

2003 Donruss Classics Legends of the Fall Fabrics

PRINT RUNS B/WN 15-100 COPIES PER
NO PRICING ON QTY OF 25 OR LESS
1 Reggie Jackson/100 10.00 25.00
3 Roberto Clemente/50 75.00 150.00
6 Jackie Robinson/50 20.00 50.00
8 Willie Stargell/100 10.00 25.00
9 Bobby Doerr/100 8.00 20.00

2003 Donruss Classics Membership

RANDOM INSERTS IN PACKS
STATED PRINT RUN 2500 SERIAL #'d SETS
1 Babe Ruth 2.50 6.00
2 Steve Carlton .60 1.50
3 Honus Wagner 1.00 2.50
4 Warren Spahn .60 1.50
5 Eddie Mathews 1.00 2.50
6 Nolan Ryan 3.00 8.00
7 Rogers Hornsby .60 1.50
8 Ernie Banks 1.00 2.50
9 Harmon Killebrew 1.00 2.50
10 Tom Seaver .60 1.50
11 Jimmie Foxx 1.00 2.50
12 Ty Cobb 1.50 4.00
13 Frank Robinson .60 1.50
14 Mel Ott 1.00 2.50
15 Lou Gehrig 2.00 5.00

2003 Donruss Classics Membership VIP Memorabilia

PRINT RUNS B/WN 14-81 COPIES PER
NO PRICING ON QTY OF 31 OR LESS
2 Steve Carlton Jsy/81 10.00 25.00
4 Warren Spahn Jsy/61 30.00 60.00
5 Eddie Mathews Bat/67 30.00 60.00
6 Nolan Ryan Jsy/80 50.00 100.00
8 Ernie Banks Jsy/70 30.00 60.00
9 Harmon Killebrew Jsy/71 30.00 60.00
10 Tom Seaver Jsy/81 15.00 40.00
11 Jimmie Foxx Bat/40 40.00 80.00
13 Frank Robinson Jsy/71 20.00 50.00
14 Mel Ott Jsy/45 15.00 40.00

2003 Donruss Classics Timeless Treasures

RANDOM INSERTS IN PACKS
PRINT RUNS B/WN 25-50 COPIES PER
NO PRICING ON QTY OF 25 OR LESS
1 Musial Jsy 10.00 25.00
Gwynn Jsy/50
3 Clemente Jsy 30.00 60.00
Vladdie Jsy/50
5 Mattingly Jsy 20.00 50.00
Giambi Jsy/50

2003 Donruss Classics Atlantic City National

PRINT RUN 5 SERIAL #'d SETS

2004 Donruss Classics

COMP.SET w/o SP's (153) 10.00 25.00
COMMON CARD (1-150) .25 .60
COMMON (151-175/206-210) .60 1.50
COMMON CARD (176-205) 1.25 3.00
151-210 STATED ODDS 2:9
151-210 PRINT RUN 1999 SERIAL #'d SETS
COMMON CARD (211-213) .40 1.00
211-213 APPROXIMATE ODDS 1:18
211-213 ODDS INFO PROVIDED BY DONRUSS
1 Albert Pujols .75 2.00
2 Derek Jeter 1.50 4.00
3 Hank Blalock .25 .60
4 Shannon Stewart .25 .60
5 Jason Giambi .25 .60
6 Carlos Lee .25 .60
7 Trot Nixon .25 .60
8 Bret Boone .25 .60
9 Mark Mulder .25 .60
10 Mariano Rivera .75 2.00
11 Scott Podsednik .25 .60
12 Jim Edmonds .40 1.00

13 Mike Lowell .25 .60
14 Robin Ventura .25 .60
15 Brian Giles .25 .60
16 Jose Vidro .25 .60
17 Manny Ramirez .60 1.50
18 Alex Rodriguez Rgr .75 2.00
19 Carlos Beltran .40 1.00
20 Hideki Matsui 1.00 2.50
21 Johan Santana .40 1.00
22 Richie Sexson .25 .60
23 Chipper Jones .60 1.50
24 Steve Finley .25 .60
25 Mark Prior .40 1.00
26 Alexis Rios .25 .60
27 Rafael Palmeiro .40 1.00
28 Jorge Posada .40 1.00
29 Barry Zito .40 1.00
30 Jamie Moyer .25 .60
31 Preston Wilson .25 .60
32 Miguel Cabrera .60 1.50
33 Pedro Martinez .40 1.00
34 Curt Schilling .40 1.00
35 Hee Seop Choi .25 .60
36 Dontrelle Willis .25 .60
37 Rafael Soriano .25 .60
38 Richard Fischer .25 .60
39 Brian Tallet .25 .60
40 Jose Castillo .25 .60
41 Wade Miller .25 .60
42 Jose Contreras .25 .60
43 Runelvys Hernandez .25 .60
44 Joe Borchard .25 .60
45 Kazuhisa Ishii .25 .60
46 Jose Reyes .40 1.00
47 Adam Dunn .40 1.00
48 Randy Johnson .60 1.50
49 Brandon Phillips .25 .60
50 Scott Rolen .40 1.00
51 Ken Griffey Jr. 1.25 3.00
52 Tom Glavine .40 1.00
53 Cliff Lee .40 1.00
54 Chien-Ming Wang 1.00 2.50
55 Roy Oswalt .40 1.00
56 Austin Kearns .25 .60
57 Jhonny Peralta .25 .60
58 Greg Maddux Braves .75 2.00
59 Mark Grace .40 1.00
60 Jae Weong Seo .25 .60
61 Nic Jackson .25 .60
62 Roger Clemens .75 2.00
63 Jimmy Gobble .25 .60
64 Travis Hafner .25 .60
65 Paul Konerko .40 1.00
66 Jerome Williams .25 .60
67 Ryan Klesko .25 .60
68 Alexis Gomez .25 .60
69 Omar Vizquel .40 1.00
70 Zach Day .25 .60
71 Rickey Henderson .60 1.50
72 Morgan Ensberg .25 .60
73 Josh Beckett .25 .60
74 Garrett Atkins .25 .60
75 Sean Casey .25 .60
76 Julio Franco .25 .60
77 Lyle Overbay .25 .60
78 Josh Phelps .25 .60
79 Juan Gonzalez .25 .60
80 Rich Harden .25 .60
81 Bernie Williams .40 1.00
82 Torii Hunter .25 .60
83 Angel Berroa .25 .60
84 Jody Gerut .25 .60
85 Roberto Alomar .40 1.00
86 Byung-Hyun Kim .25 .60
87 Jay Gibbons .25 .60
88 Chone Figgins .25 .60
89 Fred McGriff .25 .60
90 Rich Aurilia .25 .60
91 Xavier Nady .25 .60
92 Marlon Byrd .25 .60
93 Mike Piazza .60 1.50
94 Vladimir Guerrero .40 1.00
95 Shawn Green .25 .60
96 Jeff Kent .25 .60
97 Ivan Rodriguez .40 1.00
98 Jay Payton .25 .60
99 Barry Larkin .40 1.00
100 Mike Sweeney .25 .60
101 Adrian Beltre .60 1.50
102 Robby Hammock .25 .60
103 Orlando Hudson .25 .60
104 Mark Teixeira .40 1.00
105 Hong-Chih Kuo .25 .60
106 Eric Chavez .25 .60
107 Nick Johnson .25 .60
108 Jacque Jones .25 .60
109 Ken Harvey .25 .60
110 Aramis Ramirez .25 .60
111 Victor Martinez .40 1.00
112 Joe Crede .25 .60
113 Jason Varitek .60 1.50
114 Troy Glaus .25 .60
115 Billy Wagner .25 .60
116 Kerry Wood .25 .60
117 Hideo Nomo .60 1.50
118 Brandon Webb .25 .60
119 Craig Biggio .40 1.00
120 Orlando Cabrera .25 .60
121 Sammy Sosa .60 1.50
122 Bobby Abreu .25 .60
123 Andruw Jones .25 .60
124 Jeff Bagwell .40 1.00
125 Jim Thome .40 1.00
126 Javy Lopez .25 .60
127 Luis Castillo .25 .60
128 Todd Helton .40 1.00
129 Roy Halladay .40 1.00
130 Mike Mussina .40 1.00
131 Eric Byrnes .25 .60
132 Eric Hinske .25 .60
133 Nomar Garciaparra .40 1.00
134 Edgar Martinez .40 1.00
135 Rocco Baldelli .25 .60
136 Miguel Tejada .40 1.00
137 Alfonso Soriano Yanks .40 1.00
138 Carlos Delgado .25 .60
139 Rafael Furcal .25 .60
140 Ichiro Suzuki .75 2.00
141 Aubrey Huff .25 .60
142 Garret Anderson .25 .60
143 Vernon Wells .25 .60
144 Magglio Ordonez .40 1.00
145 Brett Myers .25 .60
146 Luis Gonzalez .25 .60
147 Lance Berkman .40 1.00
148 Frank Thomas .60 1.50
149 Gary Sheffield .25 .60
150 Tim Hudson .40 1.00
151 Duke Snider LGD 1.00 2.50
152 Carl Yastrzemski LGD 1.50 4.00
153 Whitey Ford LGD 1.00 2.50
154 Cal Ripken LGD 5.00 12.00
155 Dwight Gooden LGD .60 1.50
156 Warren Spahn LGD 1.00 2.50
157 Bob Gibson LGD 1.00 2.50
158 Don Mattingly LGD 3.00 8.00
159 Jack Morris LGD 1.00 2.50
160 Jim Bunning LGD 1.00 2.50
161 Fergie Jenkins LGD 1.00 2.50
162 Brooks Robinson LGD 1.00 2.50
163 George Kell LGD 1.00 2.50
164 Darryl Strawberry LGD .60 1.50
165 Robin Roberts LGD 1.00 2.50
166 Monte Irvin LGD 1.00 2.50
167 Ernie Banks LGD 1.50 4.00
168 Wade Boggs LGD 1.00 2.50
169 Gaylord Perry LGD 1.00 2.50
170 Keith Hernandez LGD .60 1.50
171 Lou Brock LGD 1.00 2.50
172 Frank Robinson LGD 1.00 2.50
173 Nolan Ryan LGD 5.00 12.00
174 Stan Musial LGD 2.50 6.00
175 Eddie Murray LGD 1.00 2.50
176 Byron Gettis ROO 1.25 3.00
177 Merkin Valdez ROO RC 1.25 3.00
178 Rickie Weeks ROO 1.25 3.00
179 Akinori Otsuka ROO RC 1.25 3.00
180 Brian Bruney ROO 1.25 3.00
181 Freddy Guzman ROO RC 1.25 3.00
182 Brendan Harris ROO 1.25 3.00
183 John Gall ROO RC 1.25 3.00
184 Jason Kubel ROO 1.25 3.00
185 Delmon Young ROO 2.00 5.00
186 Ryan Howard ROO 2.50 6.00
187 Adam Loewen ROO 1.25 3.00
188 J.D. Durbin ROO 1.25 3.00
189 Dan Haren ROO 1.25 3.00
190 Dustin McGowan ROO 1.25 3.00
191 Chad Gaudin ROO 1.25 3.00
192 Preston Larrison ROO 1.25 3.00
193 Ramon Nivar ROO 1.25 3.00
194 Ronald Belisario ROO RC 1.25 3.00
195 Mike Gosling ROO RC 1.25 3.00
196 Kevin Youkilis ROO 1.25 3.00
197 Ryan Wagner ROO 1.25 3.00
198 Bubba Nelson ROO 1.25 3.00
199 Edwin Jackson ROO 1.25 3.00
200 Chris Burke ROO 1.25 3.00
201 Carlos Hines ROO RC 1.25 3.00
202 Greg Dobbs ROO RC 1.25 3.00
203 Jamie Brown ROO RC 1.25 3.00
204 Dave Crouthers ROO RC 1.25 3.00
205 Ian Snell ROO RC 1.25 3.00
206 Gary Carter LGD 1.00 2.50
207 Dale Murphy LGD 1.50 4.00
208 Ryne Sandberg LGD 3.00 8.00
209 Phil Niekro LGD 1.00 2.50
210 Don Sutton LGD 1.00 2.50
211 Alex Rodriguez Yanks SP 1.25 3.00
212 Alfonso Soriano Rgr SP .60 1.50
213 Greg Maddux Cubs SP 1.25 3.00

2004 Donruss Classics Significant Signatures Green

PRINT RUNS B/WN 1-100 COPIES PER
NO PRICING ON QTY OF 15 OR LESS
3 Hank Blalock/25 10.00 25.00
4 Shannon Stewart/50 8.00 20.00
7 Trot Nixon/25 10.00 25.00
13 Mike Lowell/25 10.00 25.00
14 Robin Ventura/25 10.00 25.00
19 Carlos Beltran/25 10.00 25.00
21 Johan Santana/50 4.00 10.00
24 Steve Finley/25 15.00 40.00
26 Alexis Rios/100 6.00 15.00
32 Miguel Cabrera/50 20.00 50.00
36 Dontrelle Willis/25 15.00 40.00
37 Rafael Soriano/100 6.00 15.00
38 Richard Fischer/100 4.00 10.00
39 Brian Tallet/100 4.00 10.00
40 Jose Castillo/100 4.00 10.00
41 Wade Miller/25 6.00 15.00
43 Runelvys Hernandez/20 6.00 15.00
44 Joe Borchard/50 5.00 12.00
47 Adam Dunn/25 15.00 40.00
49 Brandon Phillips/50 5.00 12.00
53 Cliff Lee/50 8.00 20.00
54 Chien-Ming Wang/50 50.00 100.00
57 Jhonny Peralta/100 6.00 15.00
60 Jae Weong Seo/50 8.00 20.00
61 Nic Jackson/100 4.00 10.00
63 Jimmy Gobble/45 5.00 12.00
64 Travis Hafner/50 8.00 20.00
66 Jerome Williams/50 5.00 12.00
68 Alexis Gomez/50 5.00 12.00
70 Zach Day/50 5.00 12.00
72 Morgan Ensberg/50 8.00 20.00
74 Garrett Atkins/99 4.00 10.00
77 Lyle Overbay/100 4.00 10.00
78 Josh Phelps/25 6.00 15.00
79 Juan Gonzalez/25 10.00 25.00
80 Rich Harden/50 8.00 20.00
84 Jody Gerut/50 5.00 12.00
87 Jay Gibbons/50 5.00 12.00
88 Chone Figgins/50 8.00 20.00
98 Jay Payton/50 5.00 12.00
99 Barry Larkin/25 20.00 50.00
102 Robby Hammock/50 5.00 12.00
103 Orlando Hudson/50 5.00 12.00
105 Hong-Chih Kuo/50 8.00 20.00
106 Eric Chavez/25 10.00 25.00
108 Jacque Jones/50 8.00 20.00
109 Ken Harvey/100 4.00 10.00
110 Aramis Ramirez/50 8.00 20.00
111 Victor Martinez/50 8.00 20.00
112 Joe Crede/50 8.00 20.00
113 Jason Varitek/25 20.00 50.00
118 Brandon Webb/25 6.00 15.00
121 Sammy Sosa/21 50.00 100.00
127 Luis Castillo/25 6.00 15.00
134 Edgar Martinez/25 20.00 50.00
145 Brett Myers/50 8.00 20.00
149 Gary Sheffield/25 20.00 50.00
151 Duke Snider LGD/25 20.00 50.00
153 Whitey Ford LGD/25 20.00 50.00
155 Dwight Gooden LGD/50 10.00 25.00
158 Don Mattingly LGD/25 20.00 50.00
159 Jack Morris LGD/50 6.00 15.00
160 Jim Bunning LGD/25 10.00 25.00
161 Fergie Jenkins LGD/50 10.00 25.00
163 George Kell LGD/50 15.00 40.00
164 Darryl Strawberry LGD/50 10.00 25.00
165 Robin Roberts LGD/25 12.50 30.00
166 Monte Irvin LGD/25 12.50 30.00
167 Ernie Banks LGD/25 30.00 60.00
168 Wade Boggs LGD/25 30.00 60.00
169 Gaylord Perry LGD/50 6.00 15.00
170 Keith Hernandez LGD/50 10.00 25.00
172 Frank Robinson LGD/25 20.00 50.00
173 Nolan Ryan LGD/25 75.00 150.00
174 Stan Musial LGD/25 30.00 80.00
175 Eddie Murray LGD/25 50.00 100.00
176 Byron Gettis ROO/100 4.00 10.00
177 Merkin Valdez ROO/100 4.00 10.00
178 Rickie Weeks ROO/25 10.00 25.00
180 Brian Bruney ROO/100 4.00 10.00
181 Freddy Guzman ROO/100 4.00 10.00
182 Brendan Harris ROO/100 4.00 10.00
183 John Gall ROO/100 4.00 10.00
184 Jason Kubel ROO/100 4.00 10.00
185 Delmon Young ROO/50 20.00 50.00
186 Ryan Howard ROO/100 6.00 15.00
187 Adam Loewen ROO/100 4.00 10.00
188 J.D. Durbin ROO/100 4.00 10.00
189 Dan Haren ROO/100 4.00 10.00
190 Dustin McGowan ROO/100 4.00 10.00
191 Chad Gaudin ROO/100 4.00 10.00
192 Preston Larrison ROO/100 4.00 10.00
193 Ramon Nivar ROO/100 4.00 10.00
195 Mike Gosling ROO/100 4.00 10.00
196 Kevin Youkilis ROO/100 6.00 15.00
197 Ryan Wagner ROO/100 4.00 10.00
198 Bubba Nelson ROO/100 4.00 10.00
199 Edwin Jackson ROO/100 6.00 15.00
200 Chris Burke ROO/100 6.00 15.00
201 Carlos Hines ROO/100 4.00 10.00
202 Greg Dobbs ROO/50 5.00 12.00
203 Jamie Brown ROO/100 4.00 10.00
205 Ian Snell ROO/100 6.00 15.00
206 Gary Carter LGD/50 10.00 25.00
207 Dale Murphy LGD/50 15.00 40.00
208 Ryne Sandberg LGD/50 40.00 80.00
209 Phil Niekro LGD/50 10.00 25.00
210 Don Sutton LGD/50 10.00 25.00

2004 Donruss Classics Significant Signatures Platinum

STATED PRINT RUN 1 SERIAL #'d SET
NO PRICING DUE TO SCARCITY

2004 Donruss Classics Significant Signatures Red

PRINT RUNS B/WN 1-250 COPIES PER
NO PRICING ON QTY OF 15 OR LESS
3 Hank Blalock/50 8.00 20.00
4 Shannon Stewart/100 6.00 15.00
6 Carlos Lee/25 10.00 25.00
7 Trot Nixon/50 8.00 20.00
9 Mark Mulder/25 10.00 25.00
12 Jim Edmonds/25 15.00 40.00
13 Mike Lowell/50 8.00 20.00
14 Robin Ventura/50 8.00 20.00
16 Jose Vidro/25 6.00 15.00
19 Carlos Beltran/25 10.00 25.00
21 Johan Santana/100 3.00 8.00
24 Steve Finley/100 10.00 25.00
26 Alexis Rios/250 6.00 15.00
27 Rafael Palmeiro/25 50.00 100.00
28 Jorge Posada/25 75.00 150.00
32 Miguel Cabrera/100 30.00 60.00
36 Dontrelle Willis/100 10.00 25.00
37 Rafael Soriano/250 4.00 10.00
38 Richard Fischer/250 4.00 10.00
39 Brian Tallet/250 4.00 10.00
40 Jose Castillo/250 4.00 10.00
41 Wade Miller/92 4.00 10.00
42 Jose Contreras/25 10.00 25.00
43 Runelvys Hernandez/50 5.00 12.00
44 Joe Borchard/250 4.00 10.00
47 Adam Dunn/25 15.00 40.00
49 Brandon Phillips/70 4.00 10.00
50 Scott Rolen/25 15.00 40.00
53 Cliff Lee/100 6.00 15.00
54 Chien-Ming Wang/250 15.00 40.00
55 Roy Oswalt/25 10.00 25.00
56 Austin Kearns/25 6.00 15.00
57 Jhonny Peralta/250 6.00 15.00
60 Jae Weong Seo/100 6.00 15.00
61 Nic Jackson/250 4.00 10.00
63 Jimmy Gobble/200 4.00 10.00
64 Travis Hafner/100 6.00 15.00
65 Paul Konerko/25 15.00 40.00
66 Jerome Williams/250 4.00 10.00
68 Alexis Gomez/100 4.00 10.00
70 Zach Day/100 4.00 10.00
72 Morgan Ensberg/100 6.00 15.00
74 Garrett Atkins/245 4.00 10.00
76 Julio Franco/25 10.00 25.00
77 Lyle Overbay/250 4.00 10.00
78 Josh Phelps/50 5.00 12.00
79 Juan Gonzalez/25 10.00 25.00
80 Rich Harden/150 6.00 15.00
82 Torii Hunter/25 10.00 25.00
84 Jody Gerut/100 4.00 10.00
87 Jay Gibbons/100 4.00 10.00
88 Chone Figgins/100 6.00 15.00
90 Rich Aurilia/25 6.00 15.00
92 Marlon Byrd/25 6.00 15.00
98 Jay Payton/100 4.00 10.00
99 Barry Larkin/25 20.00 50.00
102 Robby Hammock/150 4.00 10.00
103 Orlando Hudson/100 4.00 10.00
105 Hong-Chih Kuo/100 6.00 15.00
106 Eric Chavez/25 10.00 25.00
107 Nick Johnson/25 10.00 25.00
108 Jacque Jones/100 6.00 15.00
109 Ken Harvey/250 4.00 10.00
110 Aramis Ramirez/100 6.00 15.00
111 Victor Martinez/99 6.00 15.00
112 Joe Crede/250 6.00 15.00
113 Jason Varitek/50 20.00 50.00
114 Troy Glaus/25 6.00 15.00
118 Brandon Webb/50 5.00 12.00
119 Craig Biggio/25 15.00 40.00
120 Orlando Cabrera/50 8.00 20.00
121 Sammy Sosa/25 50.00 100.00
122 Bobby Abreu/25 10.00 25.00
123 Andruw Jones/25 8.00 20.00
124 Jeff Bagwell/25 50.00 100.00
127 Luis Castillo/50 5.00 12.00
131 Eric Byrnes/25 6.00 15.00
132 Eric Hinske/25 6.00 15.00
134 Edgar Martinez/50 20.00 50.00
135 Rocco Baldelli/25 10.00 25.00
143 Vernon Wells/25 10.00 25.00
144 Magglio Ordonez/25 15.00 40.00
145 Brett Myers/100 6.00 15.00
149 Gary Sheffield/50 15.00 40.00
150 Tim Hudson/25 15.00 40.00
151 Duke Snider LGD/50 15.00 40.00
153 Whitey Ford LGD/50 15.00 40.00
155 Dwight Gooden LGD/100 8.00 20.00
156 Warren Spahn LGD/25 30.00 60.00
158 Don Mattingly LGD/25 20.00 50.00
159 Jack Morris LGD/100 6.00 15.00
160 Jim Bunning LGD/100 6.00 15.00
161 Fergie Jenkins LGD/100 8.00 20.00
162 Brooks Robinson LGD/20 30.00 60.00
163 George Kell LGD/100 12.50 30.00
164 Darryl Strawberry LGD/100 8.00 20.00
165 Robin Roberts LGD/100 6.00 15.00
166 Monte Irvin LGD/100 8.00 20.00
167 Ernie Banks LGD/50 20.00 50.00
168 Wade Boggs LGD/50 20.00 50.00
169 Gaylord Perry LGD/100 6.00 15.00
170 Keith Hernandez LGD/100 8.00 20.00
171 Lou Brock LGD/25 40.00 80.00
172 Frank Robinson LGD/50 15.00 40.00
173 Nolan Ryan LGD/50 60.00 120.00
174 Stan Musial LGD/50 25.00 60.00
175 Eddie Murray LGD/50 40.00 80.00
176 Byron Gettis ROO/250 4.00 10.00
177 Merkin Valdez ROO/250 4.00 10.00
178 Rickie Weeks ROO/50 8.00 20.00
180 Brian Bruney ROO/250 4.00 10.00
181 Freddy Guzman ROO/250 4.00 10.00
182 Brendan Harris ROO/250 4.00 10.00
183 John Gall ROO/250 4.00 10.00
184 Jason Kubel ROO/250 4.00 10.00
185 Delmon Young ROO/100 20.00 50.00
186 Ryan Howard ROO/250 6.00 15.00
187 Adam Loewen ROO/250 4.00 10.00
188 J.D. Durbin ROO/250 4.00 10.00
189 Dan Haren ROO/250 4.00 10.00
190 Dustin McGowan ROO/250 4.00 10.00
191 Chad Gaudin ROO/250 4.00 10.00
192 Preston Larrison ROO/250 4.00 10.00
193 Ramon Nivar ROO/250 4.00 10.00
195 Mike Gosling ROO/250 4.00 10.00
196 Kevin Youkilis ROO/250 6.00 15.00
197 Ryan Wagner ROO/250 4.00 10.00
198 Bubba Nelson ROO/250 4.00 10.00
199 Edwin Jackson ROO/250 6.00 15.00
200 Chris Burke ROO/250 6.00 15.00
201 Carlos Hines ROO/250 4.00 10.00
202 Greg Dobbs ROO/100 4.00 10.00
203 Jamie Brown ROO/250 4.00 10.00
204 Dave Crouthers ROO/250 4.00 10.00
205 Ian Snell ROO/250 6.00 15.00
206 Gary Carter LGD/100 10.00 25.00
207 Dale Murphy LGD/50 15.00 40.00
208 Ryne Sandberg LGD/25 50.00 100.00
209 Phil Niekro LGD/100 10.00 25.00
210 Don Sutton LGD/100 8.00 20.00

2004 Donruss Classics Timeless Tributes Green

*GREEN 1-150: 3X TO 8X BASIC
*GREEN 151-175/206-210: 1.5X TO 4X BASIC
*GREEN 176-205: .75X TO 2X BASIC
*GREEN 211-213: 2X TO 5X BASIC
RANDOM INSERTS IN PACKS
STATED PRINT RUN 50 SERIAL #'d SETS

2004 Donruss Classics Timeless Tributes Red

*RED 1-150: 2.5X TO 6X BASIC
*RED 151-175/206-210: 1.25X TO 3X BASIC
*RED 176-205: .6X TO 1.5X BASIC
*RED 211-213: 1.5X TO 4X BASIC
RANDOM INSERTS IN PACKS
STATED PRINT RUN 100 SERIAL #'d SETS

2004 Donruss Classics Classic Combos Bat

RANDOM INSERTS IN PACKS
PRINT RUNS B/WN 25-50 COPIES PER
ALL CARDS FEATURE BAT-BAT COMBOS
1 B.Ruth/L.Gehrig/25 200.00 350.00
2 R.Campanella/P.Reese/50 15.00 40.00
3 T.Williams/C.Yastrzemski/25 50.00 100.00
4 R.Clemente/W.Stargell/25 75.00 150.00
5 E.Murray/C.Ripken/50 12.50 30.00
6 R.Maris/Y.Berra/25 20.00 50.00
10 N.Ryan/R.Carew/50 12.00 30.00
11 D.Mattingly/R.Hend/50 15.00 40.00
15 R.Yount/P.Molitor/50 15.00 40.00
16 M.Grace/S.Sosa/50 6.00 15.00
17 T.Williams/B.Doerr/25 75.00 150.00
18 R.Jackson/R.Carew/50 15.00 40.00

2004 Donruss Classics Classic Combos Jersey

PRINT RUNS B/WN 10-50 COPIES PER
NO PRICING ON QTY OF 10 OR LESS
PRIME PRINT RUN 1 SERIAL #'d SET
NO PRIME PRICING DUE TO SCARCITY
RANDOM INSERTS IN PACKS
ALL ARE JSY-JSY COMBOS UNLESS NOTED
2 R.Campy Pants/P.Reese/25 20.00 50.00
3 T.Williams/C.Yaz/15 175.00 300.00
4 R.Clemente/W.Stargell/25 75.00 150.00
5 E.Murray/C.Ripken/25 60.00 120.00
6 R.Maris/Y.Berra/25 50.00 100.00
8 W.Ford/Y.Berra/25 10.00 25.00
9 M.Marion/S.Musial/25 30.00 60.00
10 N.Ryan/R.Carew/25 30.00 60.00
11 D.Mattingly/R.Hend/50 15.00 40.00
12 J.Morris/A.Trammell/50 10.00 25.00
13 W.Ford/P.Rizzuto/25 20.00 50.00
14 M.Marion/R.Schoen/25 15.00 40.00
15 R.Yount/P.Molitor/50 15.00 40.00
16 M.Grace/S.Sosa/50 15.00 40.00
17 T.Williams/B.Doerr/15 150.00 250.00
18 R.Jackson/R.Carew/50 15.00 40.00

2004 Donruss Classics Classic Combos Quad

PRINT RUNS B/WN 5-25 COPIES PER
NO PRICING ON QTY OF 5 OR LESS
PRIME PRINT RUN 1 SERIAL #'d SET
NO PRIME PRICING DUE TO SCARCITY
2 R.Campy Pants/P.Reese/25 50.00 100.00
3 T.Williams/C.Yaz/15 250.00 400.00
4 R.Clemente/W.Stargell/25 175.00 300.00
5 E.Murray/C.Ripken/25 125.00 200.00
6 R.Maris/Y.Berra/15 150.00 250.00
10 N.Ryan/R.Carew/25 60.00 120.00
11 D.Mattingly/R.Hend/25 30.00 60.00
15 R.Yount/P.Molitor/25 50.00 100.00
16 M.Grace/S.Sosa/25 30.00 60.00
17 T.Williams/B.Doerr/15 75.00 150.00
18 R.Jackson/R.Carew/25 40.00 80.00

2004 Donruss Classics Classic Singles Bat

RANDOM INSERTS IN PACKS
PRINT RUNS B/WN 10-50 COPIES PER
NO PRICING ON QTY OF 10 OR LESS
1 Babe Ruth/15 250.00 400.00
3 Stan Musial/25 20.00 50.00
4 Ted Williams/25 60.00 120.00
5 Lou Gehrig/50 40.00 100.00
6 Eddie Murray/50 12.00 30.00
7 Roy Campanella/50 12.00 30.00
8 Robin Yount/50 12.00 30.00
9 Roberto Clemente/25 20.00 50.00
10 Don Mattingly/50 20.00 50.00
12 Carl Yastrzemski/50 15.00 40.00
13 Mark Grace/50 10.00 25.00
15 Rickey Henderson/50 12.00 30.00
16 Reggie Jackson/50 10.00 25.00
17 Pee Wee Reese/50 10.00 25.00
20 Roger Maris/25 12.00 30.00
21 Cal Ripken/50 40.00 80.00
23 Willie Stargell/50 10.00 25.00
24 Paul Molitor/50 6.00 15.00
26 Alan Trammell/50 6.00 15.00
27 Sammy Sosa/50 12.00 30.00
28 Bobby Doerr/50 6.00 15.00
29 Rod Carew/50 10.00 25.00
30 Yogi Berra/25 15.00 40.00
32 George Brett/50 20.00 50.00

2004 Donruss Classics Classic Singles Jersey

PRINT RUNS B/WN 10-100 COPIES PER
NO PRICING ON QTY FO 10 OR LESS
PRIME PRINT RUN 1 SERIAL #'d SET
NO PRIME PRICING DUE TO SCARCITY
RANDOM INSERTS IN PACKS
2 Nolan Ryan/50 20.00 50.00
3 Stan Musial/15 30.00 60.00
6 Eddie Murray/100 8.00 20.00
7 Roy Campanella Pants/50 12.50 30.00
8 Robin Yount/100 8.00 20.00
9 Roberto Clemente/25 60.00 120.00
10 Don Mattingly/100 15.00 40.00
11 Bob Gibson/15 15.00 40.00
12 Carl Yastrzemski/50 15.00 40.00
13 Mark Grace/25 12.50 30.00
14 Jack Morris/100 4.00 10.00
15 Rickey Henderson/25 15.00 40.00
16 Reggie Jackson/50 10.00 25.00
17 Pee Wee Reese/25 12.50 30.00
18 Marty Marion/100 4.00 10.00
19 Tommy John/100 4.00 10.00
20 Roger Maris/25 15.00 40.00
21 Cal Ripken/25 60.00 120.00
22 Red Schoendienst/25 8.00 20.00
23 Willie Stargell/100 6.00 15.00
24 Paul Molitor/100 4.00 10.00
25 Whitey Ford/50 10.00 25.00
26 Alan Trammell/100 4.00 10.00
27 Sammy Sosa/50 8.00 20.00
28 Bobby Doerr/50 6.00 15.00
29 Rod Carew/100 6.00 15.00
30 Yogi Berra/15 20.00 50.00
31 Phil Rizzuto/25 12.50 30.00
32 George Brett/25 30.00 60.00

2004 Donruss Classics Classic Singles Jersey-Bat

PRINT RUNS B/WN 5-25 COPIES PER
NO PRICING ON QTY OF 10 OR LESS
PRIME PRINT RUN 1 SERIAL #'d SET
NO PRIME PRICING DUE TO SCARCITY
ALL ARE JSY-BAT COMBOS UNLESS NOTED
2 Nolan Ryan/25 30.00 60.00
3 Stan Musial/15 40.00 80.00
6 Eddie Murray/25 20.00 50.00
7 Roy Campanella Pants/25 20.00 50.00
8 Robin Yount/25 20.00 50.00
9 Roberto Clemente/25 50.00 100.00
10 Don Mattingly/25 40.00 80.00
12 Carl Yastrzemski/25 30.00 60.00
13 Mark Grace/25 15.00 40.00
15 Rickey Henderson/25 20.00 50.00
16 Reggie Jackson/25 15.00 40.00
17 Pee Wee Reese/25 15.00 40.00
20 Roger Maris/15 60.00 120.00
21 Cal Ripken/25 50.00 100.00
23 Willie Stargell/25 15.00 40.00
24 Paul Molitor/25 10.00 25.00
26 Alan Trammell/25 10.00 25.00
27 Sammy Sosa/25 20.00 50.00
28 Bobby Doerr/25 10.00 25.00
29 Rod Carew/25 15.00 40.00
30 Yogi Berra/15 30.00 60.00
32 George Brett/25 40.00 80.00

2004 Donruss Classics Dress Code Bat

STATED PRINT RUN 50 SERIAL #'d SETS
S.STEWART PRINT 10 SERIAL #'d CARDS
*DC COMBO MTRL: .5X TO 1.2X BASIC
DC COMBO MTRL PRINT 50 SERIAL #'d SETS
DC COMBO MTRL STEWART 10 #'d CARDS
RANDOM INSERTS IN PACKS
NO S.STEWART PRICING DUE TO SCARCITY
1 Derek Jeter 15.00 40.00
2 Kerry Wood 4.00 10.00
3 Nomar Garciaparra 8.00 20.00
4 Jacque Jones 4.00 10.00
5 Mark Teixeira 6.00 15.00
6 Troy Glaus 4.00 10.00
7 Todd Helton 6.00 15.00
8 Miguel Tejada 4.00 10.00
9 Mike Piazza 8.00 20.00
11 Mike Sweeney 4.00 10.00
12 Albert Pujols 10.00 25.00
13 Rickey Henderson 6.00 15.00
14 Chipper Jones 6.00 15.00
15 Don Mattingly 20.00 50.00
16 Shawn Green 4.00 10.00
17 Mark Grace 6.00 15.00
18 Jason Giambi 4.00 10.00
19 Barry Zito 4.00 10.00
20 Sammy Sosa 6.00 15.00
22 Rafael Palmeiro 6.00 15.00
23 Frank Thomas 6.00 15.00
24 Manny Ramirez 6.00 15.00
25 Mike Mussina 6.00 15.00
26 Magglio Ordonez 4.00 10.00
27 Rocco Baldelli 4.00 10.00
28 Andruw Jones 6.00 15.00
29 Torii Hunter 4.00 10.00
30 Ivan Rodriguez 6.00 15.00
31 Jeff Bagwell 6.00 15.00
32 Mark Mulder 4.00 10.00
33 Trot Nixon 4.00 10.00
34 Cal Ripken 15.00 40.00
35 Dontrelle Willis 6.00 15.00
36 Hank Blalock 4.00 10.00
37 Brandon Webb 4.00 10.00
38 Miguel Cabrera 6.00 15.00
39 Hideo Nomo 6.00 15.00
41 Tim Hudson 4.00 10.00
42 Pedro Martinez 6.00 15.00
43 Hee Seop Choi 4.00 10.00
44 Randy Johnson 6.00 15.00
45 Tony Gwynn 10.00 25.00
46 Mark Prior 6.00 15.00
47 Eric Chavez 4.00 10.00
48 Alex Rodriguez 6.00 15.00
50 Alfonso Soriano 4.00 10.00

2004 Donruss Classics Dress Code Combos Signature

PRINT RUNS B/WN 1-25 COPIES PER
NO PRICING ON QTY OF 10 OR LESS
PRIME PRINT RUN 1 SERIAL #'d SET
NO PRIME PRICING DUE TO SCARCITY
RANDOM INSERTS IN PACKS
4 Jacque Jones Jsy/25 10.00 25.00
21 Jay Gibbons Jsy/25 10.00 25.00
32 Mark Mulder Jsy/25 10.00 25.00
33 Trot Nixon Jsy/25 10.00 25.00
35 Dontrelle Willis Jsy/25 15.00 40.00
38 Miguel Cabrera Jsy/25 20.00 50.00
40 Shannon Stewart Jsy/25 10.00 25.00
49 Johan Santana Jsy/25 15.00 40.00

2004 Donruss Classics Dress Code Jersey

STATED PRINT RUN 100 SERIAL #'d SETS
RIPKEN PRINT RUN 25 SERIAL #'d CARDS
*NUMBER: .4X TO 1X BASIC
*NUMBER RIPKEN: .15X TO .4X BASIC RIPKEN
NUMBER PRINT RUN 100 SERIAL #'d SETS
*PRIME: 1.5X TO 4X BASIC
*PRIME RIPKEN: .6X TO 1.2X BASIC RIPKEN
PRIME PRINT RUN 25 SERIAL #'d SETS
PRIME SORIANO PRINT 12 #'d CARDS
NO PRIME SORIANO PRICING AVAILABLE
1 Derek Jeter 12.00 30.00
2 Kerry Wood 2.00 5.00
3 Nomar Garciaparra 3.00 8.00
4 Jacque Jones 2.00 5.00
5 Mark Teixeira 3.00 8.00
6 Troy Glaus 2.00 5.00
7 Todd Helton 3.00 8.00
8 Miguel Tejada 3.00 8.00
9 Mike Piazza 5.00 12.00
11 Mike Sweeney 2.00 5.00
12 Albert Pujols 6.00 15.00
13 Rickey Henderson 5.00 12.00
14 Chipper Jones 5.00 12.00
15 Don Mattingly 15.00 40.00
16 Shawn Green 2.00 5.00
17 Mark Grace 3.00 8.00
18 Jason Giambi 2.00 5.00
19 Barry Zito 3.00 8.00
20 Sammy Sosa 5.00 12.00
21 Jay Gibbons 2.00 5.00
22 Rafael Palmeiro 3.00 8.00
23 Frank Thomas 5.00 12.00
24 Manny Ramirez 5.00 12.00
25 Mike Mussina 3.00 8.00
26 Magglio Ordonez 3.00 8.00
27 Rocco Baldelli 2.00 5.00
28 Andruw Jones 2.00 5.00
29 Torii Hunter 2.00 5.00
30 Ivan Rodriguez 3.00 8.00
31 Jeff Bagwell 3.00 8.00
32 Mark Mulder 2.00 5.00
33 Trot Nixon 2.00 5.00
34 Cal Ripken/25 40.00 100.00
35 Dontrelle Willis 2.00 5.00
36 Hank Blalock 2.00 5.00
37 Brandon Webb 2.00 5.00
38 Miguel Cabrera 5.00 12.00
39 Hideo Nomo 5.00 12.00
40 Shannon Stewart 2.00 5.00
41 Tim Hudson 3.00 8.00
42 Pedro Martinez 3.00 8.00
43 Hee Seop Choi 2.00 5.00
44 Randy Johnson 5.00 12.00
45 Tony Gwynn 5.00 12.00
46 Mark Prior 3.00 8.00
47 Eric Chavez 2.00 5.00
48 Alex Rodriguez 6.00 15.00
49 Johan Santana 3.00 8.00
50 Alfonso Soriano 3.00 8.00

2004 Donruss Classics Famous Foursomes

RANDOM INSERTS IN PACKS
STATED PRINT RUN 99 SERIAL #'d SETS
1 Campy 6.00 15.00
Reese
Jackie
Duke
2 Musial 10.00 25.00
Gibson
Schoen
Boyer

2004 Donruss Classics Famous Foursomes Jersey

STATED PRINT RUN 10 SERIAL #'d SETS
PRIME PRINT RUN 1 SERIAL #'d SET
NO PRIME PRICING DUE TO SCARCITY
RANDOM INSERTS IN PACKS
ALL ARE QUAD JSY CARDS UNLESS NOTED

2004 Donruss Classics Legendary Hats Material

RANDOM INSERTS IN PACKS
PRINT RUNS B/WN 5-25 COPIES PER
NO PRICING ON QTY OF 10 OR LESS
2 Mike Schmidt/25 40.00 80.00
6 George Brett/25 40.00 80.00
14 Cal Ripken/25 75.00 150.00
16 Kirby Puckett/25 20.00 50.00
20 Reggie Jackson Yanks/25 15.00 40.00
22 Ernie Banks/25 20.00 50.00
29 Dave Winfield/25 10.00 25.00
40 Wade Boggs/25 15.00 40.00
42 Rickey Henderson A's/25 20.00 50.00
49 Reggie Jackson Angels/25 15.00 40.00
51 Rafael Palmeiro/25 15.00 40.00
52 Sammy Sosa/25 20.00 50.00
55 Steve Carlton/25 10.00 25.00
56 Rod Carew Angels/25 15.00 40.00
60 R.Henderson Angels/25 20.00 50.00

2004 Donruss Classics Legendary Jackets Material

RANDOM INSERTS IN PACKS
STATED PRINT RUN 100 SERIAL #'d SETS
2 Mike Schmidt 12.50 30.00
8 Reggie Jackson A's 6.00 15.00
17 Don Mattingly 15.00 40.00
32 Gary Carter 4.00 10.00
54 Nolan Ryan 20.00 50.00
56 Rod Carew Angels 6.00 15.00

2004 Donruss Classics Legendary Jerseys Material

PRINT RUNS B/WN 5-50 COPIES PER
NO PRICING ON QTY OF 10 OR LESS
PRIME PRINT RUN 1 SERIAL #'d SET
NO PRIME PRICING DUE TO SCARCITY
1 Tony Gwynn/50 10.00 25.00
2 Mike Schmidt/25 30.00 60.00
3 Johnny Bench/50 10.00 25.00
6 George Brett/25 30.00 60.00
7 Carlton Fisk/50 10.00 25.00
8 Reggie Jackson A's/25 12.50 30.00
9 Joe Morgan/25 8.00 20.00
10 Bo Jackson/25 15.00 40.00
12 Andre Dawson/50 6.00 15.00
13 R.Henderson Yanks/25 15.00 40.00
14 Cal Ripken/25 60.00 120.00
15 Dale Murphy/25 12.50 30.00
16 Kirby Puckett/50 12.50 30.00
17 Don Mattingly/50 20.00 50.00
18 Brooks Robinson/50 10.00 25.00
19 Orlando Cepeda/50 6.00 15.00
20 Reggie Jackson Yanks/25 12.50 30.00
21 Roberto Clemente/25 30.00 60.00
23 Frank Robinson/50 6.00 15.00
24 Harmon Killebrew/50 12.50 30.00
25 Willie Stargell/50 10.00 25.00
26 Al Kaline/15 20.00 50.00
27 Carl Yastrzemski/50 15.00 40.00
29 Dave Winfield/50 6.00 15.00
30 Eddie Murray/50 12.50 30.00
31 Eddie Mathews/25 15.00 40.00
32 Gary Carter/50 6.00 15.00
33 Rod Carew Twins/25 12.50 30.00
36 Paul Molitor/50 6.00 15.00
37 Thurman Munson/15 20.00 50.00
39 Robin Yount/50 12.50 30.00
40 Wade Boggs/50 10.00 25.00
42 Rickey Henderson A's/25 20.00 50.00
44 Yogi Berra/15 25.00 60.00
46 Luis Aparicio/50 6.00 15.00
47 Phil Rizzuto/25 12.50 30.00
48 Roger Maris A's/25 15.00 40.00
49 Reggie Jackson Angels/50 10.00 25.00
51 Rafael Palmeiro/50 10.00 25.00
52 Sammy Sosa/50 12.50 30.00
53 Roger Clemens/50 12.50 30.00
54 Nolan Ryan/50 20.00 50.00
55 Steve Carlton/50 6.00 15.00
56 Rod Carew Angels/50 10.00 25.00
57 Whitey Ford/25 12.50 30.00

2004 Donruss Classics Legendary Jerseys Material Number

*NUMBER p/r 50: .4X TO 1X BASIC p/r 50
*NUMBER p/r 25: .5X TO 1.2X BASIC p/r 50
*NUMBER p/r 25: .4X TO 1X BASIC p/r 25
*NUMBER p/r 15: .5X TO 1.2X BASIC p/r 25
*NUMBER p/r 15: .4X TO 1X BASIC p/r 15
RANDOM INSERTS IN PACKS
PRINT RUNS B/WN 3-50 COPIES PER
NO PRICNG ON QTY OF 10 OR LESS
45 Roy Campanella Pants/25 15.00 40.00
58 Fergie Jenkins Pants/25 8.00 20.00

2004 Donruss Classics Legendary Leather Material

RANDOM INSERTS IN PACKS
PRINT RUNS B/WN 5-25 COPIES PER
NO PRICING ON QTY OF 10 OR LESS
16 Kirby Puckett Fld Glv/25 20.00 50.00
32 Gary Carter Fld Glv/25 10.00 25.00
51 Rafael Palmeiro Fld Glv/25 15.00 40.00
52 Sammy Sosa Btg Glv/25 20.00 50.00
55 Steve Carlton Fld Glv/25 10.00 25.00
58 Fergie Jenkins Fld Glv/25 10.00 25.00

2004 Donruss Classics Legendary Lumberjacks

STATED PRINT RUN 1000 SERIAL #'d SETS
*HATS: 1.5X TO 4X LUMBERJACKS
HATS PRINT RUN 50 SERIAL #'d SETS
*JACKETS: 1.5X TO 4X LUMBERJACKS
JACKET PRINT RUN 50 SERIAL #'d SETS
*JERSEYS: .6X TO 1.5X LUMBERJACKS
JERSEY PRINT RUN 500 SERIAL #'d SETS
*LEATHER: 1.2X TO 3X LUMBERJACKS
LEATHER PRINT RUN 100 SERIAL #'d SETS
*PANTS: 1.5X TO 4X LUMBERJACKS
PANTS PRINT RUN 50 SERIAL #'d SETS
*SPIKES: 1.25X TO 3X LUMBERJACKS
SPIKES PRINT RUN 100 SERIAL #'d SETS
1 Tony Gwynn 1.25 3.00
2 Mike Schmidt 2.00 5.00
3 Johnny Bench 1.25 3.00
4 Roger Maris Yanks 1.25 3.00
5 Ted Williams 2.50 6.00
6 George Brett 2.50 6.00
7 Carlton Fisk .75 2.00
8 Reggie Jackson A's .75 2.00
9 Joe Morgan .75 2.00
10 Bo Jackson 1.25 3.00
11 Stan Musial 2.00 5.00
12 Andre Dawson .75 2.00
13 Rickey Henderson Yanks 1.25 3.00
14 Cal Ripken 4.00 10.00
15 Dale Murphy 1.25 3.00
16 Kirby Puckett 1.25 3.00
17 Don Mattingly 2.50 6.00
18 Brooks Robinson .75 2.00
19 Orlando Cepeda .75 2.00
20 Reggie Jackson Yanks .75 2.00
21 Roberto Clemente 3.00 8.00
22 Ernie Banks 1.25 3.00
23 Frank Robinson .75 2.00
24 Harmon Killebrew 1.25 3.00
25 Willie Stargell .75 2.00
26 Al Kaline 1.25 3.00
27 Carl Yastrzemski 1.25 3.00
28 Duke Snider .75 2.00
29 Dave Winfield .75 2.00
30 Eddie Murray .75 2.00
31 Eddie Mathews 1.25 3.00
32 Gary Carter .75 2.00
33 Rod Carew Twins .75 2.00
34 Jimmie Foxx 1.25 3.00
35 Mel Ott 1.25 3.00
36 Paul Molitor 1.25 3.00
37 Thurman Munson 1.25 3.00
38 Rogers Hornsby .75 2.00
39 Robin Yount 1.25 3.00
40 Wade Boggs .75 2.00
41 Jackie Robinson 1.25 3.00
42 Rickey Henderson A's 1.25 3.00
43 Ty Cobb 2.00 5.00
44 Yogi Berra 1.25 3.00
45 Roy Campanella 1.25 3.00
46 Luis Aparicio .75 2.00
47 Phil Rizzuto .75 2.00
48 Roger Maris A's 1.25 3.00
49 Reggie Jackson Angels .75 2.00
50 Lou Gehrig 2.50 6.00
51 Rafael Palmeiro .75 2.00
52 Sammy Sosa 1.25 3.00
53 Roger Clemens 1.50 4.00
54 Nolan Ryan 4.00 10.00
55 Steve Carlton .75 2.00
56 Rod Carew Angels .75 2.00
57 Whitey Ford .75 2.00
58 Fergie Jenkins .75 2.00
59 Babe Ruth 3.00 8.00
60 R.Henderson Angels 1.25 3.00

2004 Donruss Classics Legendary Lumberjacks Material

RANDOM INSERTS IN PACKS
PRINT RUNS B/WN 10-100 COPIES PER
NO PRICING ON QTY OF 10 OR LESS
1 Tony Gwynn/100 8.00 20.00
2 Mike Schmidt/100 10.00 25.00
3 Johnny Bench/100 6.00 15.00
4 Roger Maris Yanks/25 30.00 60.00
5 Ted Williams/25 60.00 120.00
6 George Brett/100 10.00 25.00
7 Carlton Fisk/100 6.00 15.00
8 Reggie Jackson A's/100 6.00 15.00
9 Joe Morgan/100 4.00 10.00
10 Bo Jackson/100 8.00 20.00
11 Stan Musial/25 20.00 50.00
12 Andre Dawson/100 4.00 10.00
13 R.Henderson Yanks/100 8.00 20.00
14 Cal Ripken/100 20.00 50.00
15 Dale Murphy/100 6.00 15.00
16 Kirby Puckett/100 8.00 20.00
17 Don Mattingly/100 10.00 25.00
18 Brooks Robinson/100 6.00 15.00
19 Orlando Cepeda/100 4.00 10.00
20 Reggie Jackson Yanks/100 6.00 15.00
21 Roberto Clemente/25 50.00 100.00
22 Ernie Banks/100 8.00 20.00
23 Frank Robinson/100 4.00 10.00
24 Harmon Killebrew/100 8.00 20.00
25 Willie Stargell/100 6.00 15.00
26 Al Kaline/100 8.00 20.00
27 Carl Yastrzemski/100 12.50 30.00
29 Dave Winfield/100 4.00 10.00
30 Eddie Murray/100 8.00 20.00
31 Eddie Mathews/50 12.50 30.00
32 Gary Carter/100 4.00 10.00
33 Rod Carew Twins/100 6.00 15.00
35 Mel Ott/25 15.00 40.00
36 Paul Molitor/100 4.00 10.00
37 Thurman Munson/50 10.00 25.00
38 Rogers Hornsby/25 40.00 80.00
39 Robin Yount/100 8.00 20.00
40 Wade Boggs/100 6.00 15.00
42 Rickey Henderson A's/50 12.50 30.00
44 Yogi Berra/25 15.00 40.00
45 Roy Campanella/25 15.00 40.00
46 Luis Aparicio/100 4.00 10.00
48 Roger Maris A's/25 30.00 60.00
49 Reggie Jackson Angels/100 6.00 15.00
50 Lou Gehrig/25 125.00 200.00
51 Rafael Palmeiro/100 6.00 15.00
52 Sammy Sosa/100 8.00 20.00
56 Rod Carew Angels/100 6.00 15.00
60 R.Henderson Angels/100 8.00 20.00

2004 Donruss Classics Legendary Pants Material

RANDOM INSERTS IN PACKS
PRINT RUNS B/WN 3-50 COPIES PER
NO PRICING ON QTY OF 10 OR LESS
1 Tony Gwynn/25 15.00 40.00
12 Andre Dawson/25 8.00 20.00
24 Harmon Killebrew/50 12.50 30.00
26 Al Kaline/50 12.50 30.00
45 Roy Campanella/25 15.00 40.00
46 Luis Aparicio/50 6.00 15.00
47 Phil Rizzuto/50 10.00 25.00
48 Roger Maris A's/25 30.00 60.00
51 Rafael Palmeiro/25 12.50 30.00
56 Rod Carew Angels/50 10.00 25.00
57 Whitey Ford/25 12.50 30.00
58 Fergie Jenkins/25 8.00 20.00

2004 Donruss Classics Legendary Spikes Material

RANDOM INSERTS IN PACKS
PRINT RUNS B/WN 10-50 COPIES PER
NO PRICING ON QTY OF 10 OR LESS
13 R.Henderson Yanks/25 20.00 50.00
17 Don Mattingly/50 40.00 80.00
29 Dave Winfield/50 8.00 20.00
42 Rickey Henderson A's/25 20.00 50.00
51 Rafael Palmeiro/25 15.00 40.00
52 Sammy Sosa/50 15.00 40.00
60 R.Henderson Angels/25 20.00 50.00

2004 Donruss Classics Membership

RANDOM INSERTS IN PACKS
STATED PRINT RUN 2499 SERIAL #'d SETS
1 Stan Musial 1.50 4.00
2 Ted Williams 2.00 5.00
3 Early Wynn .60 1.50
4 Roberto Clemente 2.50 6.00
5 Al Kaline 1.00 2.50
6 Bob Gibson .60 1.50
7 Lou Brock .60 1.50
8 Carl Yastrzemski 1.00 2.50
9 Gaylord Perry .60 1.50
10 Fergie Jenkins .60 1.50
11 Steve Carlton .60 1.50
12 Reggie Jackson .60 1.50
13 Rod Carew .60 1.50
14 Bert Blyleven .60 1.50
15 Mike Schmidt 1.50 4.00
16 Nolan Ryan 3.00 8.00
17 Robin Yount 1.00 2.50
18 George Brett 2.00 5.00
19 Eddie Murray .60 1.50
20 Tony Gwynn 1.00 2.50
21 Cal Ripken 3.00 8.00
22 Randy Johnson 1.00 2.50
23 Sammy Sosa 1.00 2.50
24 Rafael Palmeiro .60 1.50
25 Roger Clemens 1.25 3.00

2004 Donruss Classics Membership VIP Bat

RANDOM INSERTS IN PACKS
PRINT RUNS B/WN 10-25 COPIES PER
NO PRICING ON QTY OF 10 OR LESS
1 Stan Musial/25 20.00 50.00
2 Ted Williams/25 60.00 120.00
4 Roberto Clemente/25 50.00 100.00
5 Al Kaline/25 15.00 40.00
7 Lou Brock/25 12.50 30.00
8 Carl Yastrzemski/25 20.00 50.00
11 Steve Carlton/25 8.00 20.00
12 Reggie Jackson/25 12.50 30.00
13 Rod Carew/25 12.50 30.00
15 Mike Schmidt/25 30.00 60.00
17 Robin Yount/25 15.00 40.00
19 Eddie Murray/25 15.00 40.00
20 Tony Gwynn/25 15.00 40.00
22 Randy Johnson/25 15.00 40.00
23 Sammy Sosa/25 15.00 40.00
24 Rafael Palmeiro/25 12.50 30.00
25 Roger Clemens/25 15.00 40.00

2004 Donruss Classics Membership VIP Combos Material

PRINT RUNS B/WN 9-25 COPIES PER
NO PRICING ON QTY OF 10 OR LESS
PRIME PRINT RUN 1 SERIAL #'d SET
NO PRIME PRICING DUE TO SCARCITY
RANDOM INSERTS IN PACKS
1 Stan Musial Bat-Jsy/15 40.00 80.00
4 Rob Clemente Bat-Jsy/25 125.00 200.00
5 Al Kaline Bat-Pants/25 20.00 50.00
8 Carl Yastrzemski Bat-Jsy/25 30.00 60.00
10 F.Jenkins Fld Glv-Pants/25 10.00 25.00
11 Steve Carlton Bat-Jsy/25 10.00 25.00
12 Reggie Jackson Bat-Jsy/25 15.00 40.00
13 Rod Carew Bat-Pants/25 15.00 40.00
15 Mike Schmidt Bat-Jsy/25 40.00 80.00
16 Nolan Ryan Bat-Jsy/25 30.00 60.00
17 Robin Yount Bat-Jsy/25 20.00 50.00
18 George Brett Bat-Jsy/25 40.00 80.00
19 Eddie Murray Bat-Jsy/25 20.00 50.00
20 Tony Gwynn Bat-Jsy/25 30.00 60.00
21 Cal Ripken Bat-Jsy/25 75.00 150.00
22 Randy Johnson Bat-Jsy/25 20.00 50.00
23 Sammy Sosa Bat-Jsy/25 20.00 50.00
24 Rafael Palmeiro Bat-Jsy/25 15.00 40.00
25 Roger Clemens Bat-Jsy/25 20.00 50.00

2004 Donruss Classics Membership VIP Combos Signature

PRINT RUNS B/WN 1-50 COPIES PER
NO PRICING ON QTY OF 5 OR LESS
PRIME PRINT RUN 1 SERIAL #'d SET
NO PRIME PRICING DUE TO SCARCITY
5 Al Kaline Pants/25 60.00 150.00
9 Gaylord Perry Jsy/50 10.00 25.00
10 Fergie Jenkins Pants/50 15.00 40.00
11 Steve Carlton Jsy/25 20.00 50.00
14 Bert Blyleven Jsy/50 10.00 25.00

2004 Donruss Classics Membership VIP Jersey

PRINT RUNS B/WN 9-25 COPIES PER
NO PRICING ON QTY OF 10 OR LESS
PRIME PRINT RUN 1 SERIAL #'d SET
NO PRIME PRICING DUE TO SCARCITY
RANDOM INSERTS IN PACKS
1 Stan Musial/15 30.00 60.00
4 Roberto Clemente/25 25.00 60.00
5 Al Kaline Pants/25 15.00 40.00
8 Carl Yastrzemski/25 20.00 50.00
9 Gaylord Perry/25 8.00 20.00
10 Fergie Jenkins Pants/25 8.00 20.00
11 Steve Carlton/25 8.00 20.00
12 Reggie Jackson/25 12.50 30.00
13 Rod Carew/25 12.50 30.00
14 Bert Blyleven/25 8.00 20.00
15 Mike Schmidt/25 30.00 60.00
16 Nolan Ryan/25 30.00 60.00
17 Robin Yount/25 15.00 40.00
18 George Brett/25 30.00 60.00
19 Eddie Murray/25 15.00 40.00
20 Tony Gwynn/25 15.00 40.00
21 Cal Ripken/25 15.00 40.00
22 Randy Johnson/25 15.00 40.00
23 Sammy Sosa/25 15.00 40.00
24 Rafael Palmeiro/25 12.50 30.00
25 Roger Clemens/25 15.00 40.00

2004 Donruss Classics Membership VIP Signatures

RANDOM INSERTS IN PACKS
PRINT RUNS B/WN 1-50 COPIES PER
NO PRICING ON QTY OF 5 OR LESS
5 Al Kaline/20 40.00 100.00
9 Gaylord Perry/50 6.00 15.00
10 Fergie Jenkins/50 10.00 25.00
11 Steve Carlton/20 12.50 30.00
14 Bert Blyleven/50 6.00 15.00

2004 Donruss Classics October Heroes

RANDOM INSERTS IN PACKS
STATED PRINT RUN 2499 SERIAL #'d SETS
1 Reggie Jackson 1.00 2.50
2 Bob Gibson 1.00 2.50
3 Carlton Fisk 1.00 2.50
4 Whitey Ford 1.00 2.50
5 George Brett 3.00 8.00
6 Roberto Clemente 4.00 10.00
7 Roy Campanella 1.50 4.00
8 Babe Ruth 4.00 10.00

2004 Donruss Classics October Heroes Bat

RANDOM INSERTS IN PACKS
PRINT RUNS B/WN 10-25 COPIES PER
NO PRICING 0ON QTY OF 10 OR LESS
1 Reggie Jackson/25 12.50 30.00
3 Carlton Fisk/25 12.50 30.00
6 Roberto Clemente/25 50.00 100.00
7 Roy Campanella/25 15.00 40.00

2004 Donruss Classics October Heroes Combos Material

PRINT RUNS B/WN 3-25 COPIES PER
NO PRICING ON QTY OF 5 OR LESS
PRIME PRINT RUN 1 SERIAL #'d SET
NO PRIME PRICING DUE TO SCARCITY
RANDOM INSERTS IN PACKS
1 Reggie Jackson Bat-Hat/25 15.00 40.00
3 Carlton Fisk Bat-Jsy/25 15.00 40.00
5 George Brett Bat-Jsy/25 20.00 50.00
7 R.Campanella Bat-Pants/25 20.00 50.00

2004 Donruss Classics October Heroes Combos Signature

PRINT RUNS B/WN 5-50 COPIES PER
NO PRICING ON QTY OF 5 OR LESS
PRIME PRINT RUN 1 SERIAL #'d SET
NO PRIME PRICING DUE TO SCARCITY
RANDOM INSERTS IN PACKS
4 Whitey Ford Jsy/50 30.00 60.00

2004 Donruss Classics October Heroes Fabric

PRINT RUNS B/WN 5-25 COPIES PER
NO PRICING ON QTY OF 5 OR LESS
PRIME PRINT RUN 1 SERIAL #'d SET
NO PRIME PRICING DUE TO SCARCITY
2 Bob Gibson Jsy/15 15.00 40.00
3 Carlton Fisk Jsy/25 12.50 30.00
4 Whitey Ford Jsy/25 12.50 30.00
5 George Brett Jsy/25 12.50 30.00
7 Roy Campanella Pants/25 15.00 40.00

2004 Donruss Classics October Heroes Signature

RANDOM INSERTS IN PACKS
PRINT RUNS B/WN 5-50 COPIES PER
NO PRICING ON QTY OF 5 OR LESS
4 Whitey Ford/50 15.00 40.00

2004 Donruss Classics Team Colors Bat

RANDOM INSERTS IN PACKS
PRINT RUNS B/WN 10-50 COPIES PER
NO PRICING ON QTY OF 10 OR LESS
2 Steve Garvey/50 6.00 15.00
3 Eric Davis/25 12.50 30.00
4 Al Oliver/50 4.00 10.00
6 Bobby Doerr/25 8.00 20.00
7 Paul Molitor/50 6.00 15.00
8 Dale Murphy/50 10.00 25.00
11 Jose Canseco/50 10.00 25.00
12 Jim Rice/50 6.00 15.00
13 Will Clark/50 20.00 50.00
14 Alan Trammell/50 6.00 15.00
16 Dwight Evans/50 10.00 25.00
18 Dave Parker Pirates/25 8.00 20.00
21 Andre Dawson Expos/50 6.00 15.00
22 Darryl Strawberry Dgr/50 6.00 15.00
23 George Foster/50 4.00 10.00
26 Bo Jackson/50 12.50 30.00
27 Cal Ripken/50 10.00 25.00
28 Deion Sanders/25 12.50 30.00
29 Don Mattingly/50 10.00 25.00
30 Mark Grace/50 10.00 25.00
31 Fred Lynn/50 4.00 10.00
33 Ernie Banks/25 15.00 40.00
34 Gary Carter/50 6.00 15.00
35 Roger Maris/25 30.00 60.00
36 Ron Santo/50 10.00 25.00
38 Tony Gwynn/50 10.00 25.00
40 Red Schoendienst/25 8.00 20.00
41 Steve Carlton/25 8.00 20.00
42 Wade Boggs/25 12.50 30.00
44 Luis Aparicio/25 8.00 20.00
46 Andre Dawson Cubs/25 8.00 20.00
48 Darryl Strawberry Mets/50 6.00 15.00
49 Dave Parker Reds/50 6.00 15.00

2004 Donruss Classics Team Colors Combos Material

STATED PRINT RUN 25 SERIAL #'d SETS
MARIS PRINT RUN 10 SERIAL #'d CARDS
NO MARIS PRICING DUE TO SCARCITY
PRIME PRINT RUN 1 SERIAL #'d SET
NO PRIME PRICING DUE TO SCARCITY
RANDOM INSERTS IN PACKS
2 Steve Garvey Bat-Jsy 10.00 25.00
3 Eric Davis Bat-Jsy 15.00 40.00
5 Nolan Ryan Bat-Jsy 30.00 60.00
6 Bobby Doerr Bat-Jsy 10.00 25.00
7 Paul Molitor Bat-Jsy 10.00 25.00
8 Dale Murphy Bat-Jsy 15.00 40.00
11 Jose Canseco Bat-Jsy 15.00 40.00
12 Jim Rice Bat-Jsy 10.00 25.00
13 Will Clark Bat-Jsy 40.00 80.00
14 Alan Trammell Bat-Jsy 10.00 25.00
16 Dwight Evans Bat-Jsy 15.00 40.00
18 Dave Parker Pirates Bat-Jsy 10.00 25.00
21 Andre Dawson Expos Bat-Jsy 10.00 25.00
22 Darryl Strawberry Dgr Bat-Jsy 10.00 25.00
23 George Foster Bat-Jsy 8.00 20.00
26 Bo Jackson Bat-Jsy 20.00 50.00
27 Cal Ripken Bat-Jsy 75.00 150.00
28 Deion Sanders Bat-Jsy 15.00 40.00
29 Don Mattingly Bat-Jsy 40.00 80.00
30 Mark Grace Bat-Jsy 15.00 40.00
33 Ernie Banks Bat-Jsy 20.00 50.00
34 Gary Carter Bat-Jacket 10.00 25.00
38 Tony Gwynn Bat-Jsy 30.00 60.00
40 Red Schoendienst Bat-Jsy 10.00 25.00
41 Steve Carlton Bat-Jsy 10.00 25.00
42 Wade Boggs Bat-Jsy 15.00 40.00
44 Luis Aparicio Bat-Jsy 10.00 25.00
46 Andre Dawson Cubs Bat-Jsy 10.00 25.00
48 D.Strawberry Mets Bat-Jsy 10.00 25.00
49 Dave Parker Reds Bat-Jsy 10.00 25.00

2004 Donruss Classics Team Colors Combos Signature

PRINT RUNS B/WN 2-100 COPIES PER
NO PRICING ON QTY OF 10 OR LESS
PRIME PRINT RUN 1 SERIAL #'d SET
NO PRIME PRICING DUE TO SCARCITY
RANDOM INSERTS IN PACKS
1 L.Dykstra Mets Fld Glv/100 10.00 25.00
2 Steve Garvey Jsy/100 10.00 25.00
3 Eric Davis Jsy/100 10.00 25.00
4 Al Oliver Bat/100 10.00 25.00
6 Bobby Doerr Jsy/100 10.00 25.00
9 Harold Baines Jsy/100 10.00 25.00
10 Dwight Gooden Jsy/100 10.00 25.00
12 Jim Rice Jsy/100 10.00 25.00
14 Alan Trammell Jsy/100 10.00 25.00
15 Lee Smith Jsy/100 10.00 25.00
16 Dwight Evans Jsy/100 10.00 25.00
17 Tony Oliva Jsy/100 10.00 25.00
18 Dave Parker Pirates Jsy/100 10.00 25.00
19 Jack Morris Jsy/100 10.00 25.00
20 Luis Tiant Jsy/100 10.00 25.00
21 Andre Dawson Expos Jsy/50 15.00 40.00
22 D.Strawberry Dgr Jsy/100 10.00 25.00
23 George Foster Jsy/100 10.00 25.00
24 Marty Marion Jsy/100 10.00 25.00
25 Dennis Eckersley Jsy/100 10.00 25.00
31 Fred Lynn Jsy/100 10.00 25.00
33 Ernie Banks Jsy/25 60.00 120.00
34 Gary Carter Jacket/50 15.00 40.00
36 Ron Santo Bat/25 20.00 50.00
37 Keith Hernandez Jsy/25 20.00 50.00
39 Jim Palmer Jsy/50 15.00 40.00
40 Red Schoendienst Jsy/100 10.00 25.00
41 Steve Carlton Jsy/50 15.00 40.00
43 Tommy John Jsy/100 10.00 25.00
44 Luis Aparicio Jsy/100 10.00 25.00
45 Bob Feller Jsy/100 10.00 25.00
46 Andre Dawson Cubs Jsy/50 15.00 40.00
47 Bert Blyleven Jsy/100 10.00 25.00
48 D.Strawberry Mets Jsy/100 10.00 25.00
49 Dave Parker Reds Jsy/100 10.00 25.00
50 L.Dykstra Phils Btg Glv/30 20.00 50.00

2004 Donruss Classics Team Colors Jersey

PRINT RUNS B/WN 10-100 COPIES PER
NO PRICING ON QTY OF 10 OR LESS
PRIME PRINT RUN 1 SERIAL #'d SET
NO PRIME PRICING DUE TO SCARCITY
RANDOM INSERTS IN PACKS
1 L.Dykstra Mets Fld Glv/25 8.00 20.00
2 Steve Garvey/100 4.00 10.00
3 Eric Davis/25 12.50 30.00
5 Nolan Ryan/50 10.00 25.00
6 Bobby Doerr/25 8.00 20.00
7 Paul Molitor/100 4.00 10.00
8 Dale Murphy/50 10.00 25.00
9 Harold Baines/100 6.00 15.00
10 Dwight Gooden/50 6.00 15.00
11 Jose Canseco/100 6.00 15.00
12 Jim Rice/100 4.00 10.00
13 Will Clark/50 20.00 50.00
14 Alan Trammell/100 4.00 10.00
15 Lee Smith/100 4.00 10.00
16 Dwight Evans/50 10.00 25.00
17 Tony Oliva/100 4.00 10.00
18 Dave Parker Pirates/25 8.00 20.00
19 Jack Morris/100 4.00 10.00
20 Luis Tiant/100 4.00 10.00
21 Andre Dawson Expos/100 4.00 10.00
22 Darryl Strawberry Dgr/100 4.00 10.00
23 George Foster/100 4.00 10.00
24 Marty Marion/50 6.00 15.00
25 Dennis Eckersley/100 4.00 10.00
26 Bo Jackson/50 12.50 30.00
27 Cal Ripken/100 15.00 40.00
28 Deion Sanders/50 10.00 25.00
29 Don Mattingly Jacket/100 15.00 40.00
30 Mark Grace/50 10.00 25.00
31 Fred Lynn/50 6.00 15.00
33 Ernie Banks/25 15.00 40.00
34 Gary Carter Jacket/100 4.00 10.00
37 Keith Hernandez/25 8.00 20.00
38 Tony Gwynn/50 10.00 25.00
39 Jim Palmer/25 8.00 20.00
40 Red Schoendienst/25 8.00 20.00
41 Steve Carlton/25 8.00 20.00
42 Wade Boggs/25 12.50 30.00
43 Tommy John/100 4.00 10.00
44 Luis Aparicio/25 8.00 20.00
46 Andre Dawson Cubs/25 8.00 20.00
47 Bert Blyleven/100 4.00 10.00
48 Darryl Strawberry Mets/100 4.00 10.00
49 Dave Parker Reds/100 4.00 10.00

2004 Donruss Classics Team Colors Signatures

RANDOM INSERTS IN PACKS
PRINT RUNS B/WN 1-50 COPIES PER
NO PRICING ON QTY OF 10 OR LESS
1 Len Dykstra Mets/50 10.00 25.00
2 Steve Garvey/50 10.00 25.00
3 Eric Davis/50 15.00 40.00
4 Al Oliver/50 6.00 15.00
6 Bobby Doerr/50 10.00 25.00
9 Harold Baines/50 6.00 15.00
10 Dwight Gooden/50 10.00 25.00
12 Jim Rice/50 10.00 25.00
14 Alan Trammell/50 12.50 30.00
15 Lee Smith/50 10.00 25.00
16 Dwight Evans/50 10.00 25.00
17 Tony Oliva/50 10.00 25.00
18 Dave Parker Pirates/50 10.00 25.00
19 Jack Morris/50 6.00 15.00
20 Luis Tiant/50 6.00 15.00
21 Andre Dawson Expos/25 12.50 30.00
22 Darryl Strawberry Dgr/50 10.00 25.00
23 George Foster/50 6.00 15.00
24 Marty Marion/50 10.00 25.00
25 Dennis Eckersley/50 15.00 40.00
31 Fred Lynn/50 6.00 15.00
34 Gary Carter/20 20.00 50.00
37 Keith Hernandez/25 12.50 30.00
39 Jim Palmer/20 12.50 30.00
40 Red Schoendienst/50 10.00 25.00
41 Steve Carlton/20 12.50 30.00
43 Tommy John/50 6.00 15.00
44 Luis Aparicio/50 10.00 25.00
45 Bob Feller/50 10.00 25.00
46 Andre Dawson Cubs/25 12.50 30.00
47 Bert Blyleven/50 10.00 25.00
48 Darryl Strawberry Mets/50 10.00 25.00
49 Dave Parker Reds/50 6.00 15.00
50 Len Dykstra Phils/50 10.00 25.00

2004 Donruss Classics Timeless Triples

RANDOM INSERTS IN PACKS
STATED PRINT RUN 500 SERIAL #'d SETS
1 T.Williams/Yaz/Fisk 4.00 10.00
2 Gehrig/Maris/Munson 4.00 10.00
3 Robinson/Robinson/Ripken 6.00 15.00
4 Clemens/Pettite/Oswalt 2.50 6.00
5 Madduz/Prior/Wood 2.50 6.00
6 Arod/Jeter/Sheffield 5.00 12.00

2004 Donruss Classics Timeless Triples Bat

RANDOM INSERTS IN PACKS
STATED PRINT RUN 25 SERIAL #'d SETS
1 T.Williams 150.00 250.00
Yaz
Fisk
2 Gehrig/Maris/Munson 175.00 300.00
3 Robinson/Robinson/Ripken 100.00 175.00

2004 Donruss Classics Timeless Triples Jersey

PRINT RUNS B/WN 10-25 COPIES PER
NO PRICING ON QTY OF 10 OR LESS
ALL ARE JSY SWATCHES UNLESS NOTED
GEHRIG IS PANTS SWATCH
PRIME PRINT RUN 1 SERIAL #'d SET
NO PRIME PRICING DUE TO SCARCITY
RANDOM INSERTS IN PACKS
3 Robinson/Robinson/Ripken/25 125.00 200.00

2005 Donruss Classics

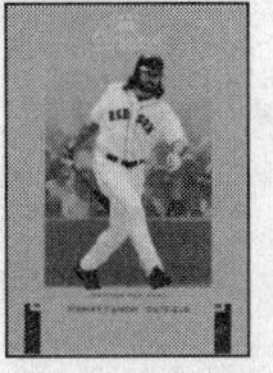

COMP.SET w/o SP's (200) 15.00 40.00
COMMON CARD (1-200) .25 .60
COM AU p/r 1200-1500 3.00 8.00
COM AU p/r 750-785 3.00 8.00
COM AU p/r 400 4.00 10.00
AU 201-225 OVERALL AU-GU ODDS 1:6
AU 201-225 PRINT RUN B/WN 400-1500 PER
COMMON CARD (226-250) .60 1.50
226-250 OVERALL INSERT ODDS 1:2
226-250 PRINT RUN 1000 SERIAL #'d SETS
DO NOT EXIST: 203/209/211-212
DO NOT EXIST: 214/216/220/222
1 Scott Rolen .40 1.00
2 Derek Jeter 1.50 4.00
3 Jose Vidro .25 .60
4 Johnny Damon .40 1.00
5 Nomar Garciaparra .40 1.00
6 Jose Guillen .25 .60
7 Trot Nixon .25 .60
8 Mark Loretta .25 .60
9 Jody Gerut .25 .60
10 Miguel Tejada .40 1.00
11 Barry Larkin .40 1.00
12 Jeff Kent .25 .60
13 Carl Crawford .40 1.00
14 Paul Konerko .40 1.00
15 Jim Edmonds .40 1.00
16 Garret Anderson .25 .60
17 Jay Gibbons .25 .60
18 Moises Alou .25 .60
19 Mike Lowell .25 .60
20 Mark Mulder .25 .60
21 Josh Beckett .25 .60
22 Tim Salmon .25 .60
23 Shannon Stewart .25 .60
24 Miguel Cabrera .60 1.50
25 Jim Thome .40 1.00
26 Kevin Youkilis .25 .60
27 Justin Morneau .40 1.00
28 Austin Kearns .25 .60
29 Cliff Lee .40 1.00
30 Ken Griffey Jr. 1.25 3.00
31 Mike Piazza .60 1.50
32 Roy Halladay .40 1.00
33 Larry Walker .40 1.00
34 David Ortiz .60 1.50
35 Dontrelle Willis .25 .60
36 Craig Wilson .25 .60
37 Jeff Suppan .25 .60
38 Curt Schilling .40 1.00
39 Larry Bigbie .25 .60
40 Rich Harden .25 .60
41 Victor Martinez .40 1.00
42 Jorge Posada .40 1.00
43 Joey Gathright .25 .60
44 Adam Dunn .40 1.00
45 Pedro Martinez .40 1.00
46 Dallas McPherson .25 .60
47 Tom Glavine .40 1.00
48 Torii Hunter .25 .60
49 Angel Berroa .25 .60
50 Mark Prior .40 1.00
51 Ichiro Suzuki .75 2.00
52 C.C. Sabathia .40 1.00
53 Bobby Abreu .25 .60
54 Shigetoshi Hasegawa .25 .60
55 Brandon Webb .40 1.00
56 Mark Buehrle .40 1.00
57 Johan Santana .40 1.00
58 Francisco Rodriguez .40 1.00
59 Roy Oswalt .40 1.00
60 Mike Sweeney .25 .60
61 Jake Peavy .25 .60
62 Akinori Otsuka .25 .60
63 Dioner Navarro .25 .60
64 Kazuhito Tadano .25 .60
65 Ryan Wagner .25 .60
66 Abe Alvarez .25 .60
67 Mark Teixeira .40 1.00
68 Jermaine Dye .25 .60
69 Todd Walker .25 .60
70 Octavio Dotel .25 .60
71 Frank Thomas .60 1.50
72 Javy Lopez .25 .60
73 Scott Podsednik .25 .60
74 B.J. Upton .40 1.00
75 Barry Zito .40 1.00
76 Raul Ibanez .40 1.00
77 Orlando Cabrera .25 .60
78 Sean Burroughs .25 .60
79 Esteban Loaiza .25 .60
80 Jason Schmidt .25 .60
81 Vinny Castilla .25 .60
82 Shingo Takatsu .25 .60
83 Juan Pierre .25 .60
84 David Dellucci .25 .60
85 Travis Blackley .25 .60
86 Brad Penny .25 .60
87 Nick Johnson .25 .60
88 Brian Roberts .25 .60
89 Kazuo Matsui .25 .60
90 Mike Lieberthal .25 .60
91 Craig Biggio .40 1.00
92 Sean Casey .25 .60
93 Andy Pettitte .40 1.00
94 Milton Bradley .25 .60
95 Rocco Baldelli .25 .60
96 Adrian Gonzalez .50 1.25
97 Chad Tracy .25 .60
98 Chad Cordero .25 .60
99 Albert Pujols .75 2.00
100 Jason Kubel .25 .60
101 Rafael Furcal .25 .60
102 Jack Wilson .25 .60
103 Eric Chavez .25 .60
104 Casey Kotchman .25 .60
105 Jeff Bagwell .40 1.00
106 Melvin Mora .25 .60
107 Bobby Crosby .25 .60
108 Preston Wilson .25 .60
109 Hank Blalock .25 .60
110 Vernon Wells .25 .60
111 Francisco Cordero .25 .60
112 Steve Finley .25 .60
113 Omar Vizquel .40 1.00
114 Eric Byrnes .25 .60
115 Tim Hudson .40 1.00
116 Aramis Ramirez .25 .60
117 Lance Berkman .40 1.00
118 Shea Hillenbrand .25 .60
119 Aubrey Huff .25 .60
120 Lew Ford .25 .60
121 Sammy Sosa .60 1.50
122 Marcus Giles .25 .60
123 Rickie Weeks .25 .60
124 Manny Ramirez .60 1.50
125 Jason Giambi .25 .60
126 Adam LaRoche .25 .60
127 Vladimir Guerrero .40 1.00
128 Ken Harvey .25 .60
129 Adrian Beltre .60 1.50
130 Magglio Ordonez .40 1.00
131 Greg Maddux .75 2.00
132 Russ Ortiz .25 .60
133 Jason Varitek .60 1.50
134 Kerry Wood .25 .60
135 Mike Mussina .40 1.00
136 Joe Nathan .25 .60
137 Troy Glaus .25 .60
138 Carlos Zambrano .40 1.00
139 Ben Sheets .25 .60
140 Jae Weong Seo .25 .60
141 Derrek Lee .25 .60
142 Carlos Beltran .40 1.00
143 John Lackey .40 1.00
144 Aaron Rowand .25 .60
145 Dewon Brazelton .25 .60
146 Jason Bay .25 .60
147 Alfonso Soriano .40 1.00
148 Travis Hafner .25 .60
149 Ryan Church .25 .60
150 Bret Boone .25 .60
151 Bernie Williams .40 1.00
152 Wade Miller .25 .60
153 Zack Greinke .75 2.00
154 Scott Kazmir .60 1.50
155 Hideki Matsui 1.00 2.50
156 Livan Hernandez .25 .60
157 Jose Capellan .25 .60
158 David Wright .50 1.25
159 Chone Figgins .25 .60
160 Jeremy Reed .25 .60
161 J.D. Drew .25 .60
162 Hideo Nomo .60 1.50
163 Merkin Valdez .25 .60
164 Shawn Green .25 .60
165 Alexis Rios .25 .60
166 Johnny Estrada .25 .60
167 Danny Graves .25 .60
168 Carlos Lee .25 .60
169 John Van Benschoten .25 .60
170 Randy Johnson .60 1.50
171 Randy Wolf .25 .60
172 Luis Gonzalez .25 .60
173 Chipper Jones .60 1.50
174 Delmon Young .60 1.50
175 Edwin Jackson .25 .60
176 Carlos Delgado .25 .60
177 Matt Clement .25 .60
178 Jacque Jones .25 .60
179 Gary Sheffield .25 .60
180 Laynce Nix .25 .60
181 Tom Gordon .25 .60
182 Jose Castillo .25 .60
183 Andruw Jones .25 .60
184 Brian Giles .25 .60
185 Paul Lo Duca .25 .60
186 Roger Clemens .75 2.00
187 Todd Helton .40 1.00
188 Keith Foulke .25 .60
189 Jeremy Bonderman .25 .60
190 Troy Percival .25 .60
191 Michael Young .25 .60
192 Carlos Guillen .25 .60
193 Rafael Palmeiro .40 1.00
194 Brett Myers .25 .60
195 Carl Pavano .25 .60
196 Alex Rodriguez .75 2.00
197 Lyle Overbay .25 .60
198 Ivan Rodriguez .40 1.00
199 Khalil Greene .25 .60
200 Edgar Renteria .25 .60
201 Justin Verlander AU/400 RC 40.00 100.00
202 Miguel Negron AU/1300 RC 30.00 8.00
204 Paul Reynoso AU/1200 RC 3.00 8.00
205 Colter Bean AU/1200 RC 4.00 10.00
206 Raul Tablado AU/1200 RC 3.00 8.00
207 M.McLemore AU/1500 RC 3.00 8.00
208 Russ Rohlicek AU/1200 RC 3.00 8.00
210 Chris Seddon AU/785 RC 3.00 8.00
213 Mike Morse AU/1200 RC 5.00 12.00
215 R.Messenger AU/1200 RC 3.00 8.00
217 Carlos Ruiz AU/1200 RC 3.00 8.00
218 Chris Roberson AU/1200 RC 3.00 8.00
219 Ryan Speier AU/1200 RC 3.00 8.00
223 Dave Gassner AU/1200 RC 3.00 8.00
224 Sean Tracey AU/1200 RC 3.00 8.00
225 C.Rogowski AU/1500 RC 4.00 10.00
226 Billy Williams LGD 1.00 2.50
227 Ralph Kiner LGD 1.00 2.50
228 Ozzie Smith LGD 2.00 5.00
229 Rod Carew LGD 1.00 2.50
230 Nolan Ryan LGD 5.00 12.00
231 Fergie Jenkins LGD 1.00 2.50
232 Paul Molitor LGD 1.50 4.00
233 Carlton Fisk LGD 1.00 2.50
234 Rollie Fingers LGD 1.00 2.50
235 Lou Brock LGD 1.00 2.50
236 Gaylord Perry LGD 1.00 2.50
237 Don Mattingly LGD 3.00 8.00
238 Maury Wills LGD .60 1.50
239 Luis Aparicio LGD 1.00 2.50
240 George Brett LGD 3.00 8.00
241 Mike Schmidt LGD 2.50 6.00
242 Joe Morgan LGD 1.00 2.50
243 Dennis Eckersley LGD 1.00 2.50
244 Reggie Jackson LGD 1.00 2.50
245 Bobby Doerr LGD 1.00 2.50
246 Bob Feller LGD 1.00 2.50
247 Cal Ripken LGD 5.00 12.00

248 Harmon Killebrew LGD 1.50 4.00
249 Frank Robinson LGD 1.00 2.50
250 Stan Musial LGD 2.50 6.00

2005 Donruss Classics Significant Signatures Gold

*GOLD p/r 100: .5X TO 1.2X SILV p/r 200
*GOLD p/r 50: .6X TO 1.5X SILV p/r 200
*GOLD p/r 50: .5X TO 1.2X SILV p/r 100
*GOLD p/r 25: .5X TO 1.2X SILV p/r 50
OVERALL AU-GU ODDS 1:6
PRINT RUNS B/WN 1-100 COPIES PER
NO PRICING ON QTY OF 10 OR LESS

2005 Donruss Classics Significant Signatures Platinum

OVERALL AU-GU ODDS 1:6
STATED PRINT RUN 1 SERIAL #'d SET
NO PRICING DUE TO SCARCITY

2005 Donruss Classics Significant Signatures Silver

OVERALL AU-GU ODDS 1:6
PRINT RUNS B/WN 1-200 COPIES PER
1-200/226-250 NO PRICING ON 10 OR LESS
201-225 NO PRICING ON QTY OF 25
17 Jay Gibbons/25 6.00 15.00
22 Tim Salmon/100 10.00 25.00
26 Kevin Youkilis/25 6.00 15.00
29 Cliff Lee/200 10.00 25.00
37 Jeff Suppan/200 6.00 15.00
39 Larry Bigbie/100 6.00 15.00
40 Rich Harden/100 6.00 15.00
41 Victor Martinez/25 10.00 25.00
43 Joey Gathright/100 4.00 10.00
61 Jake Peavy/25 15.00 40.00
63 Dioner Navarro/100 6.00 15.00
64 Kazuhito Tadano/100 10.00 25.00
65 Ryan Wagner/50 5.00 12.00
66 Abe Alvarez/100 6.00 15.00
68 Jermaine Dye/25 10.00 25.00
69 Todd Walker/25 6.00 15.00
70 Octavio Dotel/25 10.00 25.00
73 Scott Podsednik/25 15.00 40.00
77 Orlando Cabrera/25 10.00 25.00
79 Esteban Loaiza/50 8.00 20.00
84 David Dellucci/50 12.50 30.00
85 Travis Blackley/200 4.00 10.00
86 Brad Penny/25 6.00 15.00
88 Brian Roberts/100 6.00 15.00
90 Mike Lieberthal/25 10.00 25.00
94 Milton Bradley/100 6.00 15.00
96 Adrian Gonzalez/200 10.00 25.00
97 Chad Tracy/100 4.00 10.00
98 Chad Cordero/100 6.00 15.00
100 Jason Kubel/200 4.00 10.00
102 Jack Wilson/100 6.00 15.00
104 Casey Kotchman/100 6.00 15.00
106 Melvin Mora/100 6.00 15.00
107 Bobby Crosby/100 6.00 15.00
111 Francisco Cordero/50 8.00 20.00
114 Eric Byrnes/50 5.00 12.00
118 Shea Hillenbrand/25 10.00 25.00
119 Aubrey Huff/25 10.00 25.00
120 Lew Ford/25 6.00 15.00
126 Adam LaRoche/25 6.00 15.00
128 Ken Harvey/50 5.00 12.00
132 Russ Ortiz/25 6.00 15.00
136 Joe Nathan/100 4.00 10.00
138 Carlos Zambrano/25 15.00 40.00
143 John Lackey/200 6.00 15.00
145 Dewon Brazelton/200 4.00 10.00
146 Jason Bay/25 10.00 25.00
148 Travis Hafner/100 6.00 15.00
152 Wade Miller/50 5.00 12.00
154 Scott Kazmir/25 10.00 25.00
156 Livan Hernandez/25 10.00 25.00
158 David Wright/25 60.00 120.00
159 Chone Figgins/50 5.00 12.00
163 Merkin Valdez/200 4.00 10.00
165 Alexis Rios/50 8.00 20.00
166 Johnny Estrada/200 4.00 10.00
167 Danny Graves/50 5.00 12.00
168 Carlos Lee/25 10.00 25.00
171 Randy Wolf/25 10.00 25.00
175 Edwin Jackson/25 6.00 15.00
178 Jacque Jones/25 10.00 25.00
180 Laynce Nix/200 4.00 10.00
181 Tom Gordon/25 10.00 25.00
182 Jose Castillo/100 4.00 10.00
188 Keith Foulke/25 15.00 40.00
189 Jeremy Bonderman/50 8.00 20.00
190 Troy Percival/25 10.00 25.00
194 Brett Myers/50 8.00 20.00
197 Lyle Overbay/25 6.00 15.00
202 Miguel Negron/100 5.00 12.00
204 Paulino Reynoso/100 4.00 10.00
205 Colter Bean/100 5.00 12.00
206 Raul Tablado/100 4.00 10.00
207 Mark McLemore/100 4.00 10.00
208 Russ Rohlicek/100 4.00 10.00
210 Chris Seddon/100 4.00 10.00
213 Mike Morse/100 10.00 25.00
217 Carlos Ruiz/100 8.00 20.00
218 Chris Roberson/100 4.00 10.00
219 Ryan Speier/100 4.00 10.00
221 Ambiorix Burgos/100 4.00 10.00
223 Dave Gassner/100 4.00 10.00
224 Sean Tracey/100 4.00 10.00
225 Casey Rogowski/100 5.00 12.00
236 Gaylord Perry LGD/25 10.00 25.00
245 Bobby Doerr LGD/25 10.00 25.00
246 Bob Feller LGD/25 15.00 40.00

2005 Donruss Classics Timeless Tributes Gold

*GOLD 1-200: 3X TO 8X BASIC
*GOLD 226-250: 2X TO 5X BASIC
OVERALL INSERT ODDS 1:2
STATED PRINT RUN 50 SERIAL #'d SETS

2005 Donruss Classics Timeless Tributes Platinum

OVERALL INSERT ODDS 1:2
STATED PRINT RUN 1 SERIAL #'d SET
NO PRICING DUE TO SCARCITY

2005 Donruss Classics Timeless Tributes Silver

*SILV 1-200: 2X TO 5X BASIC
*SILV 201-225: .15X TO .4X AU p/r 1200-1500
*SILV 201-225: .15X TO .4X AU p/r 750-785
*SILV 201-225: .12X TO .3X AU p/r 400
*SILV 226-250: 1.2X TO 3X BASIC
OVERALL INSERT ODDS 1:2
STATED PRINT RUN 100 SERIAL #'d SETS

2005 Donruss Classics Classic Combos

STATED PRINT RUN 400 SERIAL #'d SETS
*GOLD: 1.5X TO 4X BASIC
GOLD PRINT RUN 25 SERIAL #'d SETS
PLATINUM PRINT RUN 1 SERIAL #'d SET
NO PLATINUM PRICING DUE TO SCARCITY
OVERALL INSERT ODDS 1:2
33 B.Ruth/T.Williams 6.00 15.00
34 R.Clemente/V.Guerrero 6.00 15.00
35 W.Mays/W.McCovey 5.00 12.00
36 Y.Berra/M.Piazza 2.50 6.00
37 S.Koufax/N.Ryan 8.00 20.00
38 H.Killebrew/M.Schmidt 4.00 10.00
39 W.Ford/R.Johnson 2.50 6.00
40 C.Ripken/G.Brett 8.00 20.00
41 H.Aaron/S.Musial 5.00 12.00
42 C.Yastrzemski/F.Robinson 3.00 8.00
43 B.Feller/R.Clemens 3.00 8.00
44 B.Gibson/T.Seaver 1.50 4.00
45 R.Maris/J.Thome 2.50 6.00
46 A.Pujols/D.Mattingly 5.00 12.00
47 D.Snider/S.Sosa 2.50 6.00
48 R.Henderson/B.Jackson 2.50 6.00
49 E.Banks/R.Jackson 2.50 6.00
50 B.Grimes/G.Maddux 3.00 8.00

2005 Donruss Classics Classic Combos Bat

OVERALL AU-GU ODDS 1:6
STATED PRINT RUN 5 SERIAL #'d SETS
NO PRICING DUE TO SCARCITY

2005 Donruss Classics Classic Combos Jersey

PRINT RUNS B/WN 5-50 COPIES PER
NO PRICING ON QTY OF 10 OR LESS
PRIME PRINT RUNS B/WN 1-5 COPIES PER
NO PRIME PRICING DUE TO SCARCITY
OVERALL AU-GU ODDS 1:6
38 H.Killebrew/M.Schmidt/50 15.00 40.00
39 W.Ford/R.Johnson/25 12.50 30.00
40 C.Ripken/G.Brett/50 40.00 80.00
45 R.Maris/J.Thome/25 30.00 80.00
46 A.Pujols/D.Mattingly/50 10.00 25.00
47 D.Snider/S.Sosa/25 12.50 30.00
48 R.Henderson/B.Jackson/50 10.00 25.00

2005 Donruss Classics Classic Combos Materials

*MTL p/r 25: .5X TO 1.2X JSY p/r 50
PRINT RUNS B/WN 1-25 COPIES PER
NO PRICING ON QTY OF 10 OR LESS
ALL ARE BAT-JSY COMBOS UNLESS NOTED
PRIME PRINT RUN 5 SERIAL #'d SETS
NO PRIME PRICING DUE TO SCARCITY
OVERALL AU-GU ODDS 1:6

2005 Donruss Classics Classic Combos Materials HR

*MTL HR p/r 25: .5X TO 1.2X JSY p/r 50
OVERALL AU-GU ODDS 1:6
PRINT RUNS B/WN 1-25 COPIES PER
ALL ARE BAT-JSY COMBOS UNLESS NOTED
NO PRICING ON QTY OF 10 OR LESS

2005 Donruss Classics Classic Combos Signature

OVERALL AU-GU ODDS 1:6
STATED PRINT RUN 1 SERIAL #'d SET
NO PRICING DUE TO SCARCITY

2005 Donruss Classics Classic Combos Signature Bat

OVERALL AU-GU ODDS 1:6
STATED PRINT RUN 1 SERIAL #'d SET
NO PRICING DUE TO SCARCITY

2005 Donruss Classics Classic Combos Signature Jersey

PRINT RUNS B/WN 1-5 COPIES PER
NO PRICING DUE TO SCARCITY
PRIME PRINT RUN 1 SERIAL #'d SET
NO PRIME PRICING DUE TO SCARCITY
OVERALL AU-GU ODDS 1:6

2005 Donruss Classics Classic Combos Signature Materials

STATED PRINT RUN 1 SERIAL #'d SET
ALL ARE BAT-JSY COMBOS UNLESS NOTED
HR PRINT RUN 1 SERIAL #'d SET
PRIME PRINT RUN 1 SERIAL #'d SET
OVERALL AU-GU ODDS 1:6
NO PRICING DUE TO SCARCITY

2005 Donruss Classics Classic Singles

STATED PRINT RUN 400 SERIAL #'d SETS
*GOLD: 1.5X TO 4X BASIC
GOLD PRINT RUN 25 SERIAL #'d SETS
PLATINUM PRINT RUN 1 SERIAL #'d SET
NO PLATINUM PRICING DUE TO SCARCITY
OVERALL INSERT ODDS 1:2
1 Hank Aaron 5.00 12.00
2 Tom Seaver 1.50 4.00
3 Harmon Killebrew 2.50 6.00
4 Paul Molitor 2.50 6.00
5 Brooks Robinson 1.50 4.00
6 Stan Musial 4.00 10.00
7 Bobby Doerr 1.50 4.00
8 Cal Ripken 8.00 20.00
9 Phil Niekro 1.50 4.00
10 Eddie Murray 1.50 4.00
11 Randy Johnson 2.50 6.00
12 Steve Carlton 1.50 4.00
13 Rickey Henderson 2.50 6.00
14 Ernie Banks 2.50 6.00
15 Curt Schilling 1.50 4.00
16 Whitey Ford 1.50 4.00
17 Al Kaline 2.50 6.00
18 Gary Carter 1.50 4.00
19 Robin Yount 2.50 6.00
20 Johnny Bench 2.50 6.00
21 Bob Feller 1.50 4.00
22 Jim Palmer 1.50 4.00
23 Don Mattingly 5.00 12.00
24 Willie Mays 5.00 12.00
25 Dave Righetti 1.00 2.50
26 Roger Clemens 3.00 8.00
27 Juan Marichal 1.50 4.00
28 Tony Gwynn 3.00 8.00
29 Nolan Ryan 8.00 20.00
30 Carlton Fisk 1.50 4.00
31 Greg Maddux 3.00 8.00
32 Sandy Koufax 5.00 12.00

2005 Donruss Classics Classic Singles Bat

*BAT p/r 50: .5X TO 1.2X JSY p/r 100
*BAT p/r 50: .4X TO 1X JSY p/r 50
*BAT p/r 50: .3X TO .8X JSY p/r 25
*BAT p/r 25: .6X TO 1.5X JSY p/r 100
*BAT p/r 25: .5X TO 1.2X JSY p/r 50
*BAT p/r 25: .4X TO 1X JSY p/r 25
OVERALL AU-GU ODDS 1:6
PRINT RUNS B/WN 25-50 COPIES PER
1 Hank Aaron/25 20.00 50.00
6 Stan Musial/25 12.50 30.00
17 Al Kaline/25 10.00 25.00
24 Willie Mays/25 20.00 50.00

2005 Donruss Classics Classic Singles Jersey

PRINT RUNS B/WN 10-100 COPIES PER
NO PRICING ON QTY OF 10
PRIME PRINT RUNS B/WN 1-5 COPIES PER
NO PRIME PRICING DUE TO SCARCITY
OVERALL AU-GU ODDS 1:6
2 Tom Seaver/25 8.00 20.00
3 Harmon Killebrew/25 10.00 25.00
4 Paul Molitor/50 4.00 10.00
5 Brooks Robinson/50 6.00 15.00
7 Bobby Doerr Pants/100 3.00 8.00
8 Cal Ripken/25 15.00 40.00
9 Phil Niekro/50 4.00 10.00
10 Eddie Murray/50 8.00 20.00
11 Randy Johnson/100 6.00 15.00
12 Steve Carlton/25 5.00 12.00
13 Rickey Henderson/100 8.00 20.00
14 Ernie Banks/25 10.00 25.00
15 Curt Schilling/100 5.00 12.00
16 Whitey Ford/25 8.00 20.00
18 Gary Carter/100 3.00 8.00
19 Robin Yount/50 8.00 20.00
20 Johnny Bench/50 8.00 20.00
21 Bob Feller Pants/25 8.00 20.00
22 Jim Palmer/100 3.00 8.00
23 Don Mattingly/100 10.00 25.00
25 Dave Righetti/50 4.00 10.00
26 Roger Clemens/25 10.00 25.00
27 Juan Marichal/50 4.00 10.00
28 Tony Gwynn/100 6.00 15.00
29 Nolan Ryan/50 10.00 25.00
30 Carlton Fisk/50 8.00 20.00
31 Greg Maddux/100 6.00 15.00
32 Sandy Koufax/25 75.00 150.00

2005 Donruss Classics Classic Singles Materials

*MTL p/r 25: .75X TO 2X JSY p/r 100
*MTL p/r 25: .6X TO 1.5X JSY p/r 50
*MTL p/r 25: .5X TO 1.2X JSY p/r 25
PRINT RUNS B/WN 10-25 COPIES PER
NO PRICING ON QTY OF 10
PRIME PRINT RUNS B/WN 1-5 COPIES PER
NO PRIME PRICING DUE TO SCARCITY
OVERALL AU-GU ODDS 1:6

2005 Donruss Classics Classic Singles Materials HR

*MTL HR p/r 25: .75X TO 2X JSY p/r 100
*MTL HR p/r 25: .6X TO 1.5X JSY p/r 50
*MTL HR p/r 25: .5X TO 1.2X JSY p/r 25
OVERALL AU-GU ODDS 1:6
PRINT RUNS B/WN 10-25 COPIES PER
NO PRICING ON QTY OF 10

2005 Donruss Classics Classic Singles Signature

OVERALL AU-GU ODDS 1:6
PRINT RUNS B/WN 1-5 COPIES PER
NO PRICING DUE TO SCARCITY

2005 Donruss Classics Classic Singles Signature Bat

OVERALL AU-GU ODDS 1:6
PRINT RUNS B/WN 1-10 COPIES PER
NO PRICING DUE TO SCARCITY

2005 Donruss Classics Classic Singles Signature Jersey

PRINT RUNS B/WN 1-5 COPIES PER
PRIME PRINT RUN 1 SERIAL #'d SET
OVERALL AU-GU ODDS 1:6
NO PRICING DUE TO SCARCITY

2005 Donruss Classics Classic Singles Signature Materials

PRINT RUNS B/WN 1-10 COPIES PER
PRIME PRINT RUNS B/WN 1-5 COPIES PER
OVERALL AU-GU ODDS 1:6
NO PRICING DUE TO SCARCITY

2005 Donruss Classics Classic Singles Signature Materials HR

OVERALL AU-GU ODDS 1:6
PRINT RUNS B/WN 1-10 COPIES PER
NO PRICING DUE TO SCARCITY

2005 Donruss Classics Dress Code Bat

*BAT p/r 100: .3X TO .8X MTL p/r 100
*BAT p/r 50: .3X TO .8X MTL p/r 50
OVERALL AU-GU ODDS 1:6
PRINT RUNS B/WN 50-100 COPIES PER
14 Mark Prior/50 5.00 12.00

2005 Donruss Classics Dress Code Jersey Number

*JSY NBR p/r 38-57: .4X TO 1X MTL p/r 100
*JSY NBR p/r 38-57: .3X TO .8X MTL p/r 50
*JSY NBR p/r 20-34: .5X TO 1.2X MTL p/r 100
*JSY NBR p/r 15-17: .6X TO 1.5X MTL p/r 100
*JSY NBR p/r 15-17: .5X TO 1.2X MTL p/r 50
OVERALL AU-GU ODDS 1:6
PRINT RUNS B/WN 5-57 COPIES PER
NO PRICING ON QTY OF 13 OR LESS
12 Johan Santana/57 5.00 12.00
13 Mark Mulder/20 4.00 10.00
14 Mark Prior/22 6.00 15.00
20 Randy Johnson Pants/51 6.00 15.00
21 Roger Clemens/23 10.00 25.00
24 Tim Hudson/15 5.00 12.00

2005 Donruss Classics Dress Code Jersey Prime

*PRIME: .75X TO 2X MTL p/r 100
*PRIME: .6X TO 1.5X MTL p/r 50
OVERALL AU-GU ODDS 1:6
STATED PRINT RUN 25 SERIAL #'d SETS
3 Carl Crawford 6.00 15.00
12 Johan Santana 10.00 25.00
13 Mark Mulder 6.00 15.00
14 Mark Prior 10.00 25.00
20 Randy Johnson 12.50 30.00
21 Roger Clemens 15.00 40.00
24 Tim Hudson 6.00 15.00

2005 Donruss Classics Dress Code Materials

PRINT RUNS B/WN 5-100 COPIES PER
NO PRICING ON QTY OF 5
PRIME PRINT RUN 5 SERIAL #'d SETS
NO PRIME PRICING DUE TO SCARCITY
OVERALL AU-GU ODDS 1:6
1 Albert Pujols Bat-Jsy/100 10.00 25.00
2 Bernie Williams Bat-Jsy/50 6.00 15.00
4 C.Beltran Bat-Bat 3.00 8.00
Jsy/100
5 Chipper Jones Bat-Jsy/100 6.00 15.00
6 Curt Schilling Bat-Jsy/50 6.00 15.00
7 David Ortiz Bat-Hat/100 5.00 12.00
8 Hank Blalock Bat-Jsy/100 3.00 8.00
9 Hideki Matsui Bat-Jsy/100 15.00 40.00
10 Jim Edmonds Bat-Jsy/100 3.00 8.00
11 Jim Thome Jsy-Jsy/100 5.00 12.00
15 Mark Teixeira Bat-Jsy/100 5.00 12.00
16 Miguel Cabrera Jsy-Jsy/100 5.00 12.00
17 Miguel Tejada Bat-Jsy/100 3.00 8.00
18 Mike Piazza Bat-Jsy/100 6.00 15.00
19 Pedro Martinez Bat-Jsy/100 5.00 12.00
22 Sammy Sosa Bat-Jsy/100 6.00 15.00
23 Scott Rolen Bat-Jsy/100 5.00 12.00
25 Todd Helton Jsy-Jsy/50 6.00 15.00
26 Torii Hunter Bat-Jsy/100 3.00 8.00
27 Travis Hafner Jsy-Shoes/50 4.00 10.00
28 Vernon Wells Jsy-Jsy/50 4.00 10.00
29 Victor Martinez Jsy-Jsy/50 4.00 10.00
30 V.Guerrero Bat-Jsy/100 6.00 15.00

2005 Donruss Classics Dress Code Signature Bat

*BAT p/r 25: .4X TO 1X JSY p/r 25
OVERALL AU-GU ODDS 1:6
PRINT RUNS B/WN 1-25 COPIES PER
NO PRICING ON QTY OF 5 OR LESS

2005 Donruss Classics Dress Code Signature Jersey

PRINT RUNS B/WN 5-25 COPIES PER
NO PRICING ON QTY OF 10 OR LESS
PRIME PRINT RUNS B/WN 1-5 COPIES PER
NO PRIME PRICING DUE TO SCARCITY
OVERALL AU-GU ODDS 1:6
7 David Ortiz/25 30.00 60.00
8 Hank Blalock/25 12.50 30.00
12 Johan Santana/25 12.50 30.00
16 Miguel Cabrera/25 12.00 30.00
26 Torii Hunter/25 12.50 30.00
27 Travis Hafner/25 12.50 30.00
28 Vernon Wells/25 12.50 30.00
29 Victor Martinez/25 12.50 30.00

2005 Donruss Classics Dress Code Signature Jersey Number

*NBR p/r 25: .4X TO 1X JSY p/r 25
OVERALL AU-GU ODDS 1:6
PRINT RUNS B/WN 1-25 COPIES PER
NO PRICING ON QTY-OF 10 OR LESS

2005 Donruss Classics Dress Code Signature Materials

PRINT RUNS B/WN 1-5 COPIES PER
PRIME PRINT RUNS B/WN 1-5 COPIES PER
OVERALL AU-GU ODDS 1:6
NO PRICING DUE TO SCARCITY

2005 Donruss Classics Home Run Heroes

STATED PRINT RUN 1000 SERIAL #'d SETS
*GOLD: 1.5X TO 4X BASIC
GOLD PRINT RUN 50 SERIAL #'d SETS
PLATINUM PRINT RUN 1 SERIAL #'d SET
NO PLATINUM PRICING DUE TO SCARCITY
OVERALL INSERT ODDS 1:2
1 Mike Schmidt 2.50 6.00
2 Ken Griffey Jr. 3.00 8.00
3 Babe Ruth 4.00 10.00
4 Duke Snider 1.00 2.50
5 Johnny Bench 1.50 4.00
6 Stan Musial 2.50 6.00
7 Willie McCovey 1.00 2.50
8 Willie Stargell 1.00 2.50
9 Ted Williams 3.00 8.00
10 Frank Thomas 1.50 4.00
11 Gary Sheffield .60 1.50
12 Jim Thome 1.00 2.50
13 Harmon Killebrew 1.50 4.00
14 Ernie Banks 1.50 4.00
15 George Foster .60 1.50
16 Albert Pujols 2.00 5.00
17 Tony Perez .60 1.50
18 Richie Sexson .60 1.50
19 Juan Gonzalez .60 1.50
20 Frank Robinson 1.00 2.50
21 Sammy Sosa 1.50 4.00
22 Jeff Bagwell 1.00 2.50
23 Mark Teixeira 1.00 2.50
24 Willie Mays 3.00 8.00
25 Rafael Palmeiro 1.00 2.50
26 Billy Williams 1.00 2.50
27 Vladimir Guerrero 1.00 2.50
28 Gary Carter 1.00 2.50
29 Fred McGriff 1.00 2.50
30 Orlando Cepeda 1.00 2.50
31 Dave Winfield 1.00 2.50
32 Shawn Green .60 1.50
33 Jose Canseco 1.00 2.50
34 Hideki Matsui 2.50 6.00
35 Roger Maris 1.50 4.00
36 Andre Dawson 1.00 2.50
37 Paul Konerko 1.00 2.50
38 Darryl Strawberry .60 1.50
39 Dave Parker .60 1.50
40 Adam Dunn 1.00 2.50
41 Ralph Kiner 1.00 2.50
42 Miguel Tejada 1.00 2.50
43 Dale Murphy 1.50 4.00
44 Hank Aaron 3.00 8.00
45 Mike Piazza 1.50 4.00
46 Reggie Jackson 1.00 2.50
47 Adrian Beltre 1.50 4.00
48 Cal Ripken 5.00 12.00
49 Manny Ramirez 1.50 4.00
50 Alex Rodriguez 2.00 5.00

2005 Donruss Classics Home Run Heroes Bat

*BAT p/r 36-66: .4X TO 1X JSY p/r 36-66
*BAT p/r 36-66: .3X TO .8X JSY p/r 25
*BAT p/r 23-34: .4X TO 1X JSY p/r 23-34
*BAT p/r 19: .4X TO 1X JSY p/r 19
OVERALL AU-GU ODDS 1:6
PRINT RUNS B/WN 4-66 COPIES PER
NO PRICING ON QTY OF 14 OR LESS
3 Babe Ruth/25 125.00 200.00
6 Stan Musial/39 10.00 25.00
17 Tony Perez/24 5.00 12.00
20 Frank Robinson/49 4.00 10.00

2005 Donruss Classics Home Run Heroes Jersey HR

PRINT RUNS B/WN 1-66 COPIES PER
NO PRICING ON QTY OF 14 OR LESS
PRIME PRINT RUN 1 SERIAL #'d SET
NO PRIME PRICING DUE TO SCARCITY
OVERALL AU-GU ODDS 1:6
1 Mike Schmidt/48 12.50 30.00
3 Babe Ruth/25 175.00 300.00
5 Johnny Bench/45 8.00 20.00
7 Willie McCovey/23 8.00 20.00
8 Willie Stargell/48 6.00 15.00
9 Ted Williams/43 30.00 60.00
10 Frank Thomas/43 6.00 15.00
11 Gary Sheffield/36 3.00 8.00
12 Jim Thome/47 5.00 12.00
13 Harmon Killebrew/49 8.00 20.00
14 Ernie Banks Pants/47 8.00 20.00
15 George Foster/25 5.00 12.00
16 Albert Pujols/46 15.00 40.00
18 Richie Sexson/45 3.00 8.00
19 Juan Gonzalez/47 3.00 8.00
21 Sammy Sosa/66 6.00 15.00
22 Jeff Bagwell/47 5.00 12.00
23 Mark Teixeira/38 5.00 12.00
24 Willie Mays/51 30.00 60.00
25 Rafael Palmeiro/47 5.00 12.00
26 Billy Williams/26 5.00 12.00
27 Vladimir Guerrero/44 6.00 15.00
28 Gary Carter/31 5.00 12.00
29 Fred McGriff/32 6.00 15.00
30 Orlando Cepeda Pants/46 4.00 10.00
31 Dave Winfield/34 5.00 12.00
32 Shawn Green/49 4.00 10.00
33 Jose Canseco/44 8.00 20.00
34 Hideki Matsui Pants/31 30.00 60.00
35 Roger Maris Pants/19 30.00 60.00
36 Andre Dawson/49 4.00 10.00
38 Darryl Strawberry/24 5.00 12.00
39 Dave Parker/34 5.00 12.00
40 Adam Dunn/46 3.00 8.00
42 Miguel Tejada/34 4.00 10.00
43 Dale Murphy/44 6.00 15.00
44 Hank Aaron/47 30.00 60.00
45 Mike Piazza/40 6.00 15.00
46 Reggie Jackson/39 6.00 15.00
47 Adrian Beltre/48 3.00 8.00
48 Cal Ripken/34 30.00 60.00
49 Manny Ramirez/43 5.00 12.00

2005 Donruss Classics Home Run Heroes Materials

*MTL p/r 36-66: .5X TO 1.2X JSY p/r 36-66
*MTL p/r 36-66: .4X TO 1X JSY p/r 25
*MTL p/r 23-34: .5X TO 1.2X JSY p/r 23-34
*MTL p/r 19: .5X TO 1.2X JSY p/r 19
PRINT RUNS B/WN 1-66 COPIES PER
NO PRICING ON QTY OF 14 OR LESS
PRIME PRINT RUN 1 SERIAL #'d SET
NO PRIME PRICING DUE TO SCARCITY
OVERALL AU-GU ODDS 1:6
3 Babe Ruth Bat-Jsy/25 250.00 400.00
17 Tony Perez Bat-Fld Glv/24 6.00 15.00

2005 Donruss Classics Home Run Heroes Signature

OVERALL AU-GU ODDS 1:6
PRINT RUNS B/WN 1-10 COPIES PER
NO PRICING DUE TO SCARCITY

2005 Donruss Classics Home Run Heroes Signature Materials

PRINT RUNS B/WN 1-10 COPIES PER
PRIME PRINT RUN 1 SERIAL #'d SET
OVERALL AU-GU ODDS 1:6
NO PRICING DUE TO SCARCITY

2005 Donruss Classics Legendary Lumberjacks Bat

OVERALL AU-GU ODDS 1:6
PRINT RUNS B/WN 1-50 COPIES PER
NO PRICING ON QTY OF 6 OR LESS
2 Babe Ruth/25 75.00 200.00
6 Brooks Robinson/50 6.00 15.00
7 Cal Ripken/50 10.00 25.00
8 Carlton Fisk/50 6.00 15.00
10 Don Mattingly/50 12.50 30.00
12 Eddie Murray/50 8.00 20.00
13 Ernie Banks/50 8.00 20.00
15 Frank Robinson/50 4.00 10.00
17 George Brett/50 12.50 30.00
19 Harmon Killebrew/50 8.00 20.00
21 Joe Morgan/50 4.00 10.00
22 Johnny Bench/50 8.00 20.00
24 Lou Brock/50 6.00 15.00
26 Mike Schmidt/50 12.50 30.00
28 Ozzie Smith/50 10.00 25.00
29 Paul Molitor/50 4.00 10.00
30 Pee Wee Reese/50 6.00 15.00
34 Reggie Jackson/50 6.00 15.00
35 Rickey Henderson/50 8.00 20.00
36 Roberto Clemente/50 40.00 80.00
37 Robin Yount/50 8.00 20.00
38 Rod Carew/50 6.00 15.00
39 Roger Maris/25 20.00 50.00
40 Stan Musial/25 12.50 30.00
42 Ted Williams/25 30.00 60.00
44 Tony Gwynn/50 8.00 20.00
46 Wade Boggs/50 6.00 15.00
49 Willie McCovey/50 6.00 15.00
50 Yogi Berra/25 10.00 25.00

2005 Donruss Classics Legendary Lumberjacks Jersey

*JSY p/r 50: .4X TO 1X BAT p/r 50
*JSY p/r 25: .5X TO 1.2X BAT p/r 50
OVERALL AU-GU ODDS 1:6
PRINT RUNS B/WN 1-50 COPIES PER
NO PRICING ON QTY OF 10 OR LESS
3 Billy Williams/25 5.00 12.00
25 Maury Wills/25 5.00 12.00

2005 Donruss Classics Legendary Lumberjacks Jersey HR

*JSY HR p/r 25: .5X TO 1.2X BAT p/r 50
OVERALL AU-GU ODDS 1:6
PRINT RUNS B/WN 1-25 COPIES PER
NO PRICING ON QTY OF 10 OR LESS
45 Tony Perez/25 5.00 12.00

2005 Donruss Classics Legendary Lumberjacks Materials

*MTL p/r 44-50: .5X TO 1.2X BAT p/r 50
OVERALL AU-GU ODDS 1:6
PRINT RUNS B/WN - COPIES PER
NO PRICING ON QTY OF 10 OR LESS
*MTL p/r 25: .6X TO 1.5X BAT p/r 50
2 Babe Ruth Bat-Jsy/25 250.00 400.00

2005 Donruss Classics Legendary Players

STATED PRINT RUN 800 SERIAL #'d SETS
*GOLD: 1.25X TO 3X BASIC
GOLD PRINT RUN 75 SERIAL #'d SETS
PLATINUM PRINT RUN 1 SERIAL #'d SET
NO PLATINUM PRICING DUE TO SCARCITY
*LUMBERJACK: .6X TO 1.5X BASIC
LUMBERJACK PRINT RUN 400 #'d SETS
OVERALL INSERT ODDS 1:2
1 Al Kaline 1.50 4.00
2 Babe Ruth 4.00 10.00
3 Billy Williams 1.00 2.50
4 Bob Feller 1.00 2.50
5 Bob Gibson 1.00 2.50
6 Brooks Robinson 1.00 2.50
7 Cal Ripken 5.00 12.00
8 Carlton Fisk 1.00 2.50
9 Dennis Eckersley 1.00 2.50
10 Don Mattingly 3.00 8.00
11 Duke Snider 1.00 2.50
12 Eddie Murray 1.00 2.50
13 Ernie Banks 1.50 4.00
14 Fergie Jenkins 1.00 2.50
15 Frank Robinson 1.00 2.50
16 Gaylord Perry 1.00 2.50
17 George Brett 3.00 8.00
18 George Kell 1.00 2.50
19 Harmon Killebrew 1.50 4.00
20 Jim Palmer 1.00 2.50
21 Joe Morgan 1.00 2.50
22 Johnny Bench 1.50 4.00
23 Juan Marichal 1.00 2.50
24 Lou Brock 1.00 2.50
25 Maury Wills .60 1.50
26 Mike Schmidt 2.50 6.00
27 Nolan Ryan 5.00 12.00
28 Ozzie Smith 2.00 5.00
29 Paul Molitor 1.50 4.00
30 Pee Wee Reese 1.00 2.50
31 Phil Niekro 1.00 2.50
32 Phil Rizzuto 1.00 2.50
33 Ralph Kiner 1.00 2.50
34 Reggie Jackson 1.00 2.50
35 Rickey Henderson 1.50 4.00
36 Roberto Clemente 4.00 10.00
37 Robin Yount 1.50 4.00
38 Rod Carew 1.00 2.50
39 Roger Maris 1.50 4.00
40 Stan Musial 2.50 6.00
41 Steve Carlton 1.00 2.50
42 Ted Williams 3.00 8.00
43 Tom Seaver 1.00 2.50
44 Tony Gwynn 2.00 5.00
45 Tony Perez 1.00 2.50
46 Wade Boggs 1.00 2.50
47 Warren Spahn 1.00 2.50
48 Whitey Ford 1.00 2.50
49 Willie McCovey 1.00 2.50
50 Yogi Berra 1.50 4.00

2005 Donruss Classics Legendary Players Hat

*HAT p/r 25: .4X TO 1X JSY NBR p/r 20-35
*HAT p/r 25: .3X TO .8X JSY NBR p/r 16-19
OVERALL AU-GU ODDS 1:6
PRINT RUNS B/WN 1-25 COPIES PER
NO PRICING ON QTY OF 10 OR LESS
13 Ernie Banks/25 10.00 25.00
17 George Brett/25 15.00 40.00
28 Ozzie Smith/25 12.50 30.00

2005 Donruss Classics Legendary Players Jacket

*JKT: .6X TO 1.5X JSY NBR p/r 72
*JKT: .5X TO 1.2X JSY NBR p/r 36-44
*JKT: .4X TO 1X JSY NBR p/r 20-34
OVERALL AU-GU ODDS 1:6
STATED PRINT RUN 25 SERIAL #'d SETS
7 Cal Ripken 40.00 80.00
34 Reggie Jackson 8.00 20.00
42 Ted Williams 40.00 80.00

2005 Donruss Classics Legendary Players Jersey Number

PRINT RUNS B/WN 1-72 COPIES PER
NO PRICING ON QTY OF 14 OR LESS
PRIME PRINT RUN 1 SERIAL #'d SET
NO PRIME PRICING DUE TO SCARCITY
OVERALL AU-GU ODDS 1:6
3 Billy Williams/26 5.00 12.00
8 Carlton Fisk/72 4.00 10.00
9 Dennis Eckersley/43 4.00 10.00
10 Don Mattingly/23 20.00 50.00
12 Eddie Murray/33 10.00 25.00
16 Gaylord Perry/36 4.00 10.00
20 Jim Palmer/22 5.00 12.00
23 Juan Marichal/27 5.00 12.00
24 Lou Brock/20 8.00 20.00
25 Maury Wills/30 5.00 12.00
26 Mike Schmidt/20 15.00 40.00
27 Nolan Ryan/34 20.00 50.00
31 Phil Niekro/35 5.00 12.00
35 Rickey Henderson/24 10.00 25.00
37 Robin Yount/19 12.50 30.00
38 Rod Carew/29 8.00 20.00
41 Steve Carlton/32 5.00 12.00
43 Tom Seaver/41 6.00 15.00
44 Tony Gwynn/19 12.50 30.00
45 Tony Perez/24 5.00 12.00
46 Wade Boggs/26 8.00 20.00
47 Warren Spahn/24 8.00 20.00
48 Whitey Ford/16 10.00 25.00
49 Willie McCovey/44 6.00 15.00

2005 Donruss Classics Legendary Players Leather

*LTR p/r 25: .6X TO 1.5X JSY p/r 20-34
*LTR p/r 25: .5X TO 1.2X JSY p/r 16-19
OVERALL AU-GU ODDS 1:6
PRINT RUNS B/WN 10-25 COPIES PER
NO PRICING ON QTY OF 10
14 Fergie Jenkins Fld Glv/25 8.00 20.00

2005 Donruss Classics Legendary Players Pants

*PNT p/r 24-25: .5X TO 1.2X JSY NUM p/r 36-44
*PNT p/r 24-25: .4X TO 1X JSY NUM p/r 20-34
*PNT p/r 24-25: .3X TO .8X JSY NUM p/r 16-19
OVERALL AU-GU ODDS 1:6
PRINT RUNS B/WN 1-25 COPIES PER
NO PRICING ON QTY OF 10 OR LESS
4 Bob Feller/19 10.00 25.00
7 Cal Ripken/25 40.00 80.00
11 Duke Snider/25 8.00 20.00
14 Fergie Jenkins/25 5.00 12.00
22 Johnny Bench/25 10.00 25.00
28 Ozzie Smith/25 12.50 30.00
29 Paul Molitor/25 5.00 12.00
39 Roger Maris/25 20.00 50.00

2005 Donruss Classics Legendary Players Spikes

*SPK p/r 25: .5X TO 1.2X JSY NUM p/r 16-19
OVERALL AU-GU ODDS 1:6
PRINT RUNS B/WN 1-25 COPIES PER
NO PRICING ON QTY OF 10 OR LESS
15 Frank Robinson/25 8.00 20.00

2005 Donruss Classics Legendary Players Signature

OVERALL AU-GU ODDS 1:6
PRINT RUNS B/WN 1-10 COPIES PER
NO PRICING DUE TO SCARCITY

2005 Donruss Classics Membership

STATED PRINT RUN 1000 SERIAL #'d SETS
*GOLD: 1.5X TO 4X BASIC
GOLD PRINT RUN 50 SERIAL #'d SETS
PLATINUM PRINT RUN 1 SERIAL #'d SET
NO PLATINUM PRICING DUE TO SCARCITY
OVERALL INSERT ODDS 1:2
1 Bobby Doerr 1.00 2.50
2 Tom Seaver 1.00 2.50
3 Cal Ripken 5.00 12.00
4 Paul Molitor 1.50 4.00
5 Brooks Robinson 1.00 2.50
6 Al Kaline 1.50 4.00
7 Steve Carlton 1.00 2.50
8 Carl Yastrzemski 2.00 5.00
9 Bob Feller 1.00 2.50
10 Fred Lynn .60 1.50
11 Luis Aparicio 1.00 2.50
12 Hank Aaron 3.00 8.00
13 Willie Mays 3.00 8.00
14 Bob Gibson 1.00 2.50
15 Joe Morgan 1.00 2.50
16 Whitey Ford 1.00 2.50
17 Don Sutton 1.00 2.50
18 Harmon Killebrew 1.50 4.00
19 Tony Gwynn 2.00 5.00
20 Lou Brock 1.00 2.50
21 Dennis Eckersley 1.00 2.50
22 Jim Palmer 1.00 2.50
23 Don Mattingly 3.00 8.00
24 Carlton Fisk 1.00 2.50
25 Gaylord Perry 1.00 2.50
26 Mike Schmidt 2.50 6.00
27 Nolan Ryan 5.00 12.00
28 Sandy Koufax 3.00 8.00
29 Rod Carew 1.00 2.50
30 Maury Wills .60 1.50

2005 Donruss Classics Membership VIP Bat

*BAT p/r 25: .5X TO 1.2X JSY p/r 50
*BAT p/r 25: .4X TO 1X JSY p/r 25
OVERALL AU-GU ODDS 1:6
STATED PRINT RUN 25 SERIAL #'d SETS
1 Bobby Doerr 5.00 12.00
2 Tom Seaver 8.00 20.00
3 Cal Ripken 30.00 60.00
4 Paul Molitor 5.00 12.00
5 Brooks Robinson 8.00 20.00
6 Al Kaline 10.00 25.00
8 Carl Yastrzemski 8.00 20.00

12 Hank Aaron 20.00 50.00
13 Willie Mays 20.00 50.00
18 Harmon Killebrew 10.00 25.00

2005 Donruss Classics Membership VIP Jersey

PRINT RUNS B/WN 5-50 COPIES PER
NO PRICING ON QTY OF 10 OR LESS
PRIME PRINT RUN 1 SERIAL #'d SET
NO PRIME PRICING DUE TO SCARCITY
OVERALL AU-GU ODDS 1:6
7 Steve Carlton/25 5.00 12.00
10 Fred Lynn/25 5.00 12.00
11 Luis Aparicio/25 5.00 12.00
15 Joe Morgan/25 5.00 12.00
17 Don Sutton/50 4.00 10.00
19 Tony Gwynn/50 8.00 20.00
20 Lou Brock/25 8.00 20.00
21 Dennis Eckersley/50 4.00 10.00
22 Jim Palmer/25 5.00 12.00
23 Don Mattingly/25 10.00 25.00
24 Carlton Fisk/25 8.00 20.00
25 Gaylord Perry/50 4.00 10.00
26 Mike Schmidt/50 12.00 30.00
27 Nolan Ryan/25 10.00 25.00
29 Rod Carew/50 6.00 15.00

2005 Donruss Classics Membership VIP Materials

*MTL p/r 25: .6X TO 1.5X JSY p/r 50
*MTL p/r 25: .5X TO 1.2X JSY p/r 25
PRINT RUNS B/WN 5-25 COPIES PER
NO PRICING ON QTY OF 10 OR LESS
PRIME PRINT RUN 1 SERIAL #'d SET
NO PRIME PRICING DUE TO SCARCITY
OVERALL AU-GU ODDS 1:6
1 Bobby Doerr Bat-Pants/25 6.00 15.00
2 Tom Seaver Bat-Jsy/25 10.00 25.00
3 Cal Ripken Bat-Jsy/25 30.00 60.00
4 Paul Molitor Bat-Jsy/25 6.00 15.00
5 Brooks Robinson Bat-Jsy/25 10.00 25.00
18 Harmon Killebrew Bat-Jsy/25 12.50 30.00

2005 Donruss Classics Membership VIP Materials HR

*MTL HR p/r 37-49: .5X TO 1.2X JSY p/r 50
*MTL HR p/r 37-49: .4X TO 1X JSY p/r 25
*MTL HR p/r 21-35: .5X TO 1.2X JSY p/r 25
*MTL HR p/r 17: .75X TO 2X JSY p/r 50
OVERALL AU-GU ODDS 1:6
PRINT RUNS B/WN 6-49 COPIES PER
NO PRICING ON QTY OF 14 OR LESS
1 Bobby Doerr Jsy-Pants/27 6.00 15.00
3 Cal Ripken Jsy-Pants/34 30.00 60.00
4 Paul Molitor Bat-Jsy/22 6.00 15.00
8 Carl Yastrzemski Bat-Jsy/44 15.00 40.00
12 Hank Aaron Bat-Jsy/47 40.00 80.00
18 Harmon Killebrew Bat-Jsy/49 10.00 25.00

2005 Donruss Classics Membership VIP Signature Materials

PRINT RUNS B/WN 1-25 COPIES PER
NO PRICING ON QTY OF 10 OR LESS
PRIME PRINT RUN 1 SERIAL #'d SET
NO PRIME PRICING DUE TO SCARCITY
OVERALL AU-GU ODDS 1:6
1 Bobby Doerr Bat-Pants/25 15.00 40.00
10 Fred Lynn Bat-Jsy/25 15.00 40.00
11 Luis Aparicio Bat-Jsy/25 15.00 40.00
20 Lou Brock Bat-Jsy/25 30.00 60.00

2005 Donruss Classics Membership VIP Signature Materials Awards

OVERALL AU-GU ODDS 1:6
PRINT RUNS B/WN 1-10 COPIES PER
NO PRICING DUE TO SCARCITY

2005 Donruss Classics Stars of Summer

STATED PRINT RUN 1000 SERIAL #'d SETS
*GOLD: 1.5X TO 4X BASIC
GOLD PRINT RUN 50 SERIAL #'d SETS
PLATINUM PRINT RUN 1 SERIAL #'d SET
NO PLATINUM PRICING DUE TO SCARCITY
OVERALL INSERT ODDS 1:2
1 Andre Dawson 1.00 2.50
2 Bert Blyleven 1.00 2.50
3 Bill Madlock .60 1.50
4 Dale Murphy 1.50 4.00
5 Darryl Strawberry .60 1.50
6 Dave Parker .60 1.50
7 Dave Righetti .60 1.50
8 Dwight Evans 1.00 2.50
9 Dwight Gooden .60 1.50
10 Fred Lynn .60 1.50
11 George Foster .60 1.50
12 Harold Baines 1.00 2.50
13 Jack Morris 1.00 2.50
14 Jim Rice 1.00 2.50
15 Keith Hernandez .60 1.50
16 Kirk Gibson .60 1.50
17 Luis Aparicio 1.00 2.50
18 Mark Grace 1.00 2.50
19 Marty Marion .60 1.50
20 Orel Hershiser .60 1.50
21 Ron Guidry .60 1.50
22 Ron Santo 1.00 2.50
23 Steve Garvey .60 1.50
24 Tony Oliva .60 1.50
25 Will Clark 1.00 2.50

2005 Donruss Classics Stars of Summer Material

OVERALL AU-GU ODDS 1:6
PRINT RUNS B/WN 100-250 COPIES PER
1 Andre Dawson Jsy/250 3.00 8.00
2 Bert Blyleven Jsy/150 3.00 8.00
3 Bill Madlock Bat/250 3.00 8.00
4 Dale Murphy Jsy/100 5.00 12.00
5 Darryl Strawberry Jsy/250 3.00 8.00
6 Dave Parker Jsy/100 3.00 8.00
7 Dave Righetti Jsy/150 3.00 8.00
8 Dwight Evans Bat/250 5.00 12.00
9 Dwight Gooden Bat/150 3.00 8.00
10 Fred Lynn Jsy/100 3.00 8.00
11 George Foster Bat/250 3.00 8.00
12 Harold Baines Jsy/250 3.00 8.00
13 Jack Morris Jsy/100 3.00 8.00
14 Jim Rice Pants/250 3.00 8.00
15 Keith Hernandez Bat/100 3.00 8.00
16 Kirk Gibson Jsy/250 3.00 8.00
17 Luis Aparicio Bat/250 3.00 8.00
18 Mark Grace Bat/250 5.00 12.00
22 Ron Santo Bat/150 5.00 12.00
23 Steve Garvey Jsy/250 3.00 8.00
24 Tony Oliva Jsy/250 3.00 8.00
25 Will Clark Bat/250 5.00 12.00

2005 Donruss Classics Stars of Summer Signature

*SIG p/r 50: .4X TO 1X MTL SIG p/r 100
*SIG p/r 50: .3X TO .8X MTL SIG p/r 50
*SIG p/r 50: .25X TO .6X MTL SIG p/r 25
*SIG p/r 25: .4X TO 1X MTL SIG p/r 50
*SIG p/r 25: .3X TO .8X MTL SIG p/r 25
OVERALL AU-GU ODDS 1:6
PRINT RUNS B/WN 10-100 COPIES PER
NO PRICING ON QTY OF 10
2 Bert Blyleven/50 12.50 30.00
5 Darryl Strawberry/100 6.00 15.00
19 Marty Marion/50 8.00 20.00
21 Ron Guidry/25 15.00 40.00

2005 Donruss Classics Stars of Summer Signature Material

OVERALL AU-GU ODDS 1:6
PRINT RUNS B/WN 25-100 COPIES PER
1 Andre Dawson Jsy/100 8.00 20.00
2 Bert Blyleven Jsy/50 10.00 25.00
3 Bill Madlock Bat/100 8.00 20.00
4 Dale Murphy Jsy/25 20.00 50.00
6 Dave Parker Jsy/50 10.00 25.00
7 Dave Righetti Jsy/50 10.00 25.00
8 Dwight Evans Jsy/50 15.00 40.00
9 Dwight Gooden Bat/25 12.50 30.00
10 Fred Lynn Jsy/100 8.00 20.00
11 George Foster Bat/50 10.00 25.00
12 Harold Baines Jsy/100 8.00 20.00
13 Jack Morris Jsy/100 8.00 20.00
14 Jim Rice Pants/50 10.00 25.00
15 Keith Hernandez Jsy/50 10.00 25.00
16 Kirk Gibson Jsy/25 12.50 30.00
17 Luis Aparicio Bat/50 10.00 25.00
18 Mark Grace Bat/25 20.00 50.00
22 Ron Santo Bat/50 20.00 50.00
23 Steve Garvey Jsy/50 10.00 25.00
24 Tony Oliva Jsy/50 10.00 25.00
25 Will Clark Bat/25 20.00 50.00

2005 Donruss Classics Team Colors

STATED PRINT RUN 800 SERIAL #'d SETS
*GOLD: 1.5X TO 4X BASIC
GOLD PRINT RUN 50 SERIAL #'d SETS
PLATINUM PRINT RUN 1 SERIAL #'d SET
NO PLATINUM PRICING DUE TO SCARCITY
OVERALL INSERT ODDS 1:2
1 Adam Dunn 1.00 2.50
2 Albert Pujols 2.00 5.00
3 Andruw Jones .60 1.50
4 Aramis Ramirez .60 1.50
5 Aubrey Huff .60 1.50
6 Bobby Abreu .60 1.50
7 Cal Ripken 5.00 12.00
8 Carlos Lee .60 1.50
9 Craig Biggio 1.00 2.50
10 Derrek Lee .60 1.50
11 Garret Anderson .60 1.50
12 Gary Carter 1.00 2.50
13 Geoff Jenkins .60 1.50
14 Greg Maddux 2.00 5.00
15 Hank Blalock .60 1.50
16 Hideki Matsui 2.50 6.00
17 Jake Peavy .60 1.50
18 Jim Edmonds 1.00 2.50
19 Jim Palmer 1.00 2.50
20 Jose Guillen .60 1.50
21 Jose Vidro .60 1.50
22 Juan Pierre .60 1.50
23 Lew Ford .60 1.50
24 Lyle Overbay .60 1.50
25 Manny Ramirez 1.50 4.00
26 Mark Loretta .60 1.50
27 Mark Teixeira 1.00 2.50
28 Melvin Mora .60 1.50
29 Michael Young .60 1.50
30 Miguel Cabrera 1.50 4.00
31 Mike Lowell .60 1.50
32 Mike Mussina 1.00 2.50
33 Milton Bradley .60 1.50
34 Randy Johnson 1.50 4.00
35 Roger Clemens 2.00 5.00
36 Sean Casey .60 1.50
37 Shawn Green .60 1.50
38 Steve Carlton 1.00 2.50
39 Todd Helton 1.00 2.50
40 Travis Hafner .60 1.50

2005 Donruss Classics Team Colors Bat

OVERALL AU-GU ODDS 1:6
STATED PRINT RUN 100 SERIAL #'d SETS
1 Adam Dunn 2.50 6.00
2 Albert Pujols 8.00 20.00
3 Andruw Jones 4.00 10.00
4 Aramis Ramirez 2.50 6.00
7 Cal Ripken 15.00 40.00
9 Craig Biggio 4.00 10.00
10 Derrek Lee 4.00 10.00
11 Garret Anderson 2.50 6.00
12 Gary Carter 2.50 6.00
15 Hank Blalock 2.50 6.00
16 Hideki Matsui 15.00 40.00
18 Jim Edmonds 2.50 6.00
21 Jose Vidro 2.50 6.00
22 Juan Pierre 2.50 6.00
23 Lew Ford 2.50 6.00
27 Mark Teixeira 4.00 10.00
28 Melvin Mora 2.50 6.00
29 Michael Young 2.50 6.00
30 Miguel Cabrera 4.00 10.00
31 Mike Lowell 2.50 6.00
36 Sean Casey 2.50 6.00
37 Shawn Green 2.50 6.00

2005 Donruss Classics Team Colors Jersey Prime

*JSY PRIME p/r 25: 1X TO 2.5X BAT p/r 100
OVERALL AU-GU ODDS 1:6
PRINT RUNS B/WN 5-25 COPIES PER
NO PRICING ON QTY OF 5
5 Aubrey Huff/25 5.00 12.00
6 Bobby Abreu/25 5.00 12.00
8 Carlos Lee/25 5.00 12.00
13 Geoff Jenkins/25 5.00 12.00
24 Lyle Overbay/25 5.00 12.00
32 Mike Mussina/25 8.00 20.00
34 Randy Johnson/25 10.00 25.00
35 Roger Clemens/25 15.00 40.00
38 Steve Carlton/25 5.00 12.00
39 Todd Helton/25 8.00 20.00
40 Travis Hafner/25 5.00 12.00

2005 Donruss Classics Team Colors Materials

*MTL p/r 100: .5X TO 1.2X BAT p/r 100
*MTL p/r 50: .6X TO 1.5X BAT p/r 100
PRINT RUNS B/WN 25-100 COPIES PER
PRIME PRINT RUN 5 SERIAL #'d SETS
NO PRIME PRICING DUE TO SCARCITY
OVERALL AU-GU ODDS 1:6
6 Bobby Abreu Jsy-Jsy/100 3.00 8.00
8 Carlos Lee Jsy-Jsy/100 3.00 8.00
13 Geoff Jenkins Jsy-Pants/100 3.00 8.00
19 Jim Palmer Jsy-Pants/25 5.00 12.00
25 Manny Ramirez Jsy-Jsy/100 3.00 8.00
39 Todd Helton Jsy-Jsy/50 6.00 15.00

2005 Donruss Classics Team Colors Signature

*SIG p/r 25: .3X TO .8X SIG JSY p/r 25
OVERALL AU-GU ODDS 1:6
PRINT RUNS B/WN 1-25 COPIES PER
NO PRICING ON QTY OF 10 OR LESS
17 Jake Peavy/25 10.00 25.00
20 Jose Guillen/25 10.00 25.00
26 Mark Loretta/25 6.00 15.00
33 Milton Bradley/25 10.00 25.00

2005 Donruss Classics Team Colors Signature Bat

*SIG BAT p/r 25: .4X TO 1X SIG JSY p/r 25
OVERALL AU-GU ODDS 1:6
PRINT RUNS B/WN 5-25 COPIES PER
NO PRICING ON QTY OF 10 OR LESS
10 Derrek Lee/25 20.00 50.00

2005 Donruss Classics Team Colors Signature Jersey

PRINT RUNS B/WN 1-25 COPIES PER
NO PRICING ON QTY OF 10 OR LESS
PRIME PRINT RUN 1 SERIAL #'d SET
NO PRIME PRICING DUE TO SCARCITY
OVERALL AU-GU ODDS 1:6
1 Adam Dunn/25 20.00 50.00
4 Aramis Ramirez/25 12.50 30.00
5 Aubrey Huff/25 12.50 30.00
8 Carlos Lee/25 12.50 30.00
11 Garret Anderson/25 8.00 20.00
12 Gary Carter/25 12.50 30.00
15 Hank Blalock/25 12.50 30.00
21 Jose Vidro/25 12.50 30.00
23 Lew Ford/25 8.00 20.00
24 Lyle Overbay/25 8.00 20.00
28 Melvin Mora/25 12.50 30.00
29 Michael Young/25 12.50 30.00
40 Travis Hafner/25 12.50 30.00

2005 Donruss Classics Team Colors Signature Materials

*SIG MTL p/r 25: .5X TO 1.2X SIG JSY p/r 25
PRINT RUNS B/WN 5-25 COPIES PER
NO PRICING ON QTY OF 10 OR LESS
PRIME PRINT RUN 1 SERIAL #'d SET
NO PRIME PRICING DUE TO SCARCITY
OVERALL AU-GU ODDS 1:6

1998 Donruss Collections Samples

COMPLETE SET (200) 600.00 1200.00
1 Paul Molitor 5.00 12.00
2 Juan Gonzalez 4.00 10.00
3 Darryl Kile .75 2.00
4 Randy Johnson 6.00 15.00
5 Tom Glavine 3.00 8.00
6 Pat Hentgen .75 2.00
7 David Justice 1.50 4.00
8 Kevin Brown 2.50 6.00
9 Mike Mussina 3.00 8.00
10 Ken Caminiti 1.50 4.00
11 Todd Hundley 1.50 4.00
12 Frank Thomas 5.00 12.00
13 Ray Lankford 1.50 4.00
14 Justin Thompson .75 2.00
15 Jason Dickson .75 2.00
16 Kenny Lofton 2.50 6.00
17 Ivan Rodriguez 5.00 12.00
18 Pedro Martinez 5.00 12.00
19 Brady Anderson 1.50 4.00
20 Barry Larkin 3.00 8.00
21 Chipper Jones 10.00 25.00
22 Tony Gwynn 8.00 20.00
23 Roger Clemens 8.00 20.00
24 Sandy Alomar Jr. 1.50 4.00
25 Tino Martinez 1.50 4.00
26 Jeff Bagwell 5.00 12.00
27 Shawn Estes .75 2.00
28 Ken Griffey Jr. 15.00 40.00
29 Javier Lopez 1.50 4.00
30 Denny Neagle .75 2.00
31 Mike Piazza 12.50 25.00
32 Andres Galarraga 3.00 8.00
33 Larry Walker 1.50 4.00
34 Alex Rodriguez 12.50 25.00
35 Greg Maddux 10.00 25.00
36 Albert Belle 1.50 4.00
37 Barry Bonds 8.00 20.00
38 Mo Vaughn .75 2.00
39 Kevin Appier 1.50 4.00
40 Wade Boggs 5.00 12.00
41 Garret Anderson 1.50 4.00
42 Jeffrey Hammonds .75 2.00
43 Marquis Grissom 1.50 4.00
44 Jim Edmonds 3.00 8.00
45 Brian Jordan 1.50 4.00
46 Raul Mondesi 1.50 4.00
47 John Valentin .75 2.00
48 Brad Radke 1.50 4.00
49 Ismael Valdes .75 2.00
50 Matt Stairs .75 2.00
51 Matt Williams 2.50 6.00
52 Reggie Jefferson .80 2.00
53 Alan Benes .75 2.00
54 Charles Johnson .75 2.00
55 Chuck Knoblauch 1.50 4.00
56 Edgar Martinez 2.50 6.00
57 Nomar Garciaparra 12.50 25.00
58 Craig Biggio 2.50 6.00
59 Bernie Williams 3.00 8.00
60 David Cone 2.50 6.00
61 Cal Ripken 16.00 40.00
62 Mark McGwire 16.00 30.00
63 Roberto Alomar 3.00 8.00
64 Fred McGriff 2.50 6.00
65 Eric Karros 1.50 4.00
66 Robin Ventura 1.50 4.00
67 Darin Erstad 3.00 8.00
68 Michael Tucker .75 2.00
69 Jim Thome 3.00 8.00
70 Mark Grace 3.00 8.00
71 Lou Collier .75 2.00
72 Karim Garcia 2.50 6.00
73 Alex Fernandez .75 2.00
74 J.T. Snow 1.50 4.00
75 Reggie Sanders 1.50 4.00
76 John Smoltz 1.50 4.00
77 Tim Salmon 2.50 6.00
78 Paul O'Neill 1.50 4.00
79 Vinny Castilla 1.50 4.00
80 Rafael Palmeiro 3.00 8.00
81 Jaret Wright .75 2.00
82 Jay Buhner 1.50 4.00
83 Brett Butler 1.50 4.00
84 Todd Greene .75 2.00
85 Scott Rolen 3.00 8.00
86 Sammy Sosa 8.00 20.00
87 Jason Giambi 4.00 10.00
88 Carlos Delgado 3.00 8.00
89 Deion Sanders 1.50 4.00
90 Wilton Guerrero .75 2.00
91 Andy Pettitte 1.50 4.00
92 Brian Giles 2.50 6.00
93 Dmitri Young 1.50 4.00
94 Ron Coomer .75 2.00
95 Mike Cameron 1.50 4.00
96 Edgardo Alfonzo 3.20 8.00
97 Jimmy Key .75 2.00
98 Ryan Klesko 1.50 4.00
99 Andy Benes .75 2.00
100 Derek Jeter 16.00 40.00
101 Jeff Fassero .75 2.00
102 Neifi Perez .75 2.00
103 Hideo Nomo 10.00 25.00
104 Andruw Jones 3.00 8.00
105 Todd Helton 5.00 12.00
106 Livan Hernandez .75 2.00
107 Brett Tomko .75 2.00
108 Shannon Stewart 1.50 4.00
109 Bartolo Colon 1.50 4.00
110 Matt Morris 2.50 6.00
111 Miguel Tejada 4.00 10.00
112 Pokey Reese .75 2.00
113 Fernando Tatis 1.50 4.00
114 Todd Dunwoody .75 2.00
115 Jose Cruz Jr. 1.50 4.00
116 Chan Ho Park 1.50 4.00
117 Kevin Young .75 2.00
118 Rickey Henderson 8.00 20.00
119 Hideki Irabu .75 2.00
120 Francisco Cordova .75 2.00
121 Al Martin .75 2.00
122 Tony Clark .75 2.00
123 Curt Schilling 4.00 10.00
124 Rusty Greer 1.50 4.00
125 Jose Canseco 5.00 12.00
126 Edgar Renteria 2.50 6.00
127 Todd Walker 1.50 4.00
128 Wally Joyner 1.50 4.00
129 Bill Mueller 2.50 6.00
130 Jose Guillen 2.50 6.00
131 Manny Ramirez 5.00 12.00
132 Bobby Higginson 1.50 4.00
133 Kevin Orie .75 2.00
134 Will Clark 6.00 15.00
135 Dave Nilsson .75 2.00
136 Jason Kendall 1.50 4.00
137 Ivan Cruz .75 2.00
138 Gary Sheffield 4.00 10.00
139 Bubba Trammell .75 2.00
140 Vladimir Guerrero 6.00 15.00
141 Dennis Reyes .75 2.00
142 Bobby Bonilla .75 2.00
143 Ruben Rivera .75 2.00
144 Ben Grieve 1.50 4.00
145 Moises Alou 1.50 4.00
146 Tony Womack .75 2.00
147 Eric Young .75 2.00
148 Paul Konerko 1.50 4.00
149 Dante Bichette 1.50 4.00
150 Joe Carter 1.50 4.00
151 Rondell White 1.50 4.00
152 Chris Holt .75 2.00
153 Shawn Green 3.00 8.00
154 Mark Grudzielanek .75 2.00
155 Jermaine Dye 1.50 4.00
156 Ken Griffey Jr. FC 8.00 20.00
157 Frank Thomas FC 3.00 8.00
158 Chipper Jones FC 3.00 8.00
159 Mike Piazza FC 6.00 15.00
160 Cal Ripken FC 8.00 20.00
161 Greg Maddux FC 4.00 10.00
162 Juan Gonzalez FC 1.50 4.00
163 Alex Rodriguez FC 5.00 12.00
164 Mark McGwire FC 6.00 15.00
165 Derek Jeter FC 8.00 20.00
166 Larry Walker CL 1.50 4.00
167 Tony Gwynn CL 4.00 10.00
168 Tino Martinez CL .75 2.00
169 Scott Rolen CL 2.50 6.00
170 Nomar Garciaparra CL 6.00 12.00
171 Mark Kotsay RR 1.50 4.00
172 Neifi Perez RR .75 2.00
173 Paul Konerko RR 1.50 4.00
174 Jose Cruz RR 1.50 4.00
175 Hideki Irabu RR .75 2.00
176 Mike Cameron RR 1.50 4.00
177 Jeff Suppan RR .75 2.00
178 Kevin Orie RR .75 2.00
179 Pokey Reese RR .75 2.00
180 Todd Dunwoody RR .75 2.00
181 Miguel Tejada RR 4.00 10.00
182 Jose Guillen RR 2.50 6.00
183 Bartolo Colon RR 3.00 8.00
184 Derrek Lee RR .75 2.00
185 Antone Williamson RR .75 2.00
186 Wilton Guerrero RR .75 2.00
187 Jaret Wright RR .75 2.00
188 Todd Helton RR 5.00 12.00
189 Shannon Stewart RR 1.50 4.00
190 Nomar Garciaparra RR 12.50 30.00
191 Brett Tomko RR .75 2.00
192 Fernando Tatis RR 1.50 4.00
193 Raul Ibanez RR 1.50 4.00
194 Dennis Reyes RR .75 2.00
195 Bobby Estalella RR .75 2.00
196 Lou Collier RR .75 2.00
197 Bubba Trammell RR .75 2.00
198 Ben Grieve RR 1.50 4.00
199 Ivan Cruz RR .75 2.00
200 Karim Garcia RR 2.50 6.00

1998 Donruss Collections Donruss

The Donruss Collections set was issued in one series totalling 200 cards and inserted at a rate of two cards per pack. The five-card packs retailed for $4.99 each. The set contains the subsets: Fan Club (156-165), Rated Rookie (176-205), and Checklists (166-170). The fronts feature color action photography surrounded by a background of blue and silver stars.

COMPLETE SET (200) 60.00 120.00
1 Paul Molitor .25 .60
2 Juan Gonzalez .25 .60
3 Darryl Kile .25 .60
4 Randy Johnson .60 1.50
5 Tom Glavine .40 1.00
6 Pat Hentgen .15 .40
7 David Justice .25 .60
8 Kevin Brown .40 1.00
9 Mike Mussina .40 1.00
10 Ken Caminiti .25 .60
11 Todd Hundley .15 .40
12 Frank Thomas .60 1.50
13 Ray Lankford .25 .60
14 Justin Thompson .15 .40
15 Jason Dickson .15 .40
16 Kenny Lofton .25 .60
17 Ivan Rodriguez .40 1.00
18 Pedro Martinez .40 1.00
19 Brady Anderson .25 .60
20 Barry Larkin .40 1.00
21 Chipper Jones .60 1.50
22 Tony Gwynn .75 2.00
23 Roger Clemens 1.25 3.00
24 Sandy Alomar Jr. .15 .40
25 Tino Martinez .40 1.00
26 Jeff Bagwell .40 1.00
27 Shawn Estes .15 .40
28 Ken Griffey Jr. 1.25 3.00
29 Javier Lopez .25 .60
30 Denny Neagle .15 .40
31 Mike Piazza 1.00 2.50
32 Andres Galarraga .25 .60
33 Larry Walker .25 .60
34 Alex Rodriguez 1.00 2.50
35 Greg Maddux 1.00 2.50
36 Albert Belle .25 .60
37 Barry Bonds 1.50 4.00
38 Mo Vaughn .25 .60
39 Kevin Appier .25 .60
40 Wade Boggs .40 1.00
41 Garret Anderson .25 .60
42 Jeffrey Hammonds .15 .40
43 Marquis Grissom .25 .60
44 Jim Edmonds .25 .60
45 Brian Jordan .25 .60
46 Raul Mondesi .25 .60
47 John Valentin .15 .40
48 Brad Radke .25 .60
49 Ismael Valdes .15 .40
50 Matt Stairs .15 .40
51 Matt Williams .25 .60
52 Reggie Jefferson .15 .40
53 Alan Benes .15 .40
54 Charles Johnson .25 .60
55 Chuck Knoblauch .25 .60
56 Edgar Martinez .40 1.00
57 Nomar Garciaparra 1.00 2.50
58 Craig Biggio .40 1.00
59 Bernie Williams .40 1.00
60 David Cone .25 .60
61 Cal Ripken 2.00 5.00
62 Mark McGwire 1.50 4.00
63 Roberto Alomar .40 1.00
64 Fred McGriff .40 1.00
65 Eric Karros .25 .60
66 Robin Ventura .25 .60
67 Darin Erstad .25 .60
68 Michael Tucker .15 .40
69 Jim Thome .40 1.00
70 Mark Grace .40 1.00
71 Lou Collier .15 .40
72 Karim Garcia .15 .40
73 Alex Fernandez .15 .40
74 J.T. Snow .25 .60
75 Reggie Sanders .25 .60
76 John Smoltz .40 1.00
77 Tim Salmon .40 1.00
78 Paul O'Neill .40 1.00
79 Vinny Castilla .25 .60
80 Rafael Palmeiro .40 1.00
81 Jaret Wright .15 .40
82 Jay Buhner .25 .60
83 Brett Butler .25 .60
84 Todd Greene .15 .40
85 Scott Rolen .40 1.00
86 Sammy Sosa .60 1.50
87 Jason Giambi .25 .60
88 Carlos Delgado .25 .60
89 Deion Sanders .40 1.00
90 Wilton Guerrero .15 .40
91 Andy Pettitte .40 1.00
92 Brian Giles .25 .60
93 Dmitri Young .25 .60
94 Ron Coomer .15 .40
95 Mike Cameron .15 .40
96 Edgardo Alfonzo .15 .40
97 Jimmy Key .25 .60
98 Ryan Klesko .25 .60
99 Andy Benes .15 .40
100 Derek Jeter 1.50 4.00
101 Jeff Fassero .15 .40
102 Neifi Perez .15 .40
103 Hideo Nomo .60 1.50
104 Andruw Jones .40 1.00
105 Todd Helton .40 1.00
106 Livan Hernandez .25 .60
107 Brett Tomko .15 .40
108 Shannon Stewart .25 .60
109 Bartolo Colon .25 .60
110 Matt Morris .25 .60
111 Miguel Tejada .60 1.50
112 Pokey Reese .15 .40
113 Fernando Tatis .15 .40
114 Todd Dunwoody .15 .40
115 Jose Cruz Jr. .15 .40
116 Chan Ho Park .25 .60
117 Kevin Young .25 .60
118 Rickey Henderson .60 1.50
119 Hideki Irabu .15 .40
120 Francisco Cordova .15 .40
121 Al Martin .15 .40
122 Tony Clark .15 .40
123 Curt Schilling .25 .60
124 Rusty Greer .25 .60
125 Jose Canseco .40 1.00
126 Edgar Renteria .25 .60
127 Todd Walker .15 .40
128 Wally Joyner .25 .60
129 Bill Mueller .25 .60
130 Jose Guillen .25 .60
131 Manny Ramirez .40 1.00
132 Bobby Higginson .25 .60
133 Kevin Orie .15 .40
134 Will Clark .40 1.00
135 Dave Nilsson .15 .40
136 Jason Kendall .25 .60
137 Ivan Cruz .15 .40
138 Gary Sheffield .25 .60
139 Bubba Trammell .15 .40
140 Vladimir Guerrero .60 1.50
141 Dennis Reyes .15 .40
142 Bobby Bonilla .25 .60
143 Ruben Rivera .15 .40
144 Ben Grieve .15 .40
145 Moises Alou .25 .60
146 Tony Womack .15 .40
147 Eric Young .15 .40
148 Paul Konerko .25 .60
149 Dante Bichette .25 .60
150 Joe Carter .25 .60
151 Rondell White .25 .60
152 Chris Holt .15 .40
153 Shawn Green .25 .60
154 Mark Grudzielanek .15 .40
155 Jermaine Dye .25 .60
156 Ken Griffey Jr. FC .75 2.00
157 Frank Thomas FC .40 1.00
158 Chipper Jones FC .40 1.00
159 Mike Piazza FC .60 1.50
160 Cal Ripken FC 1.00 2.50
161 Greg Maddux FC .60 1.50
162 Juan Gonzalez FC .15 .40
163 Alex Rodriguez FC .60 1.50
164 Mark McGwire FC .75 2.00
165 Derek Jeter FC .75 2.00
166 Larry Walker CL .15 .40
167 Tony Gwynn CL .40 1.00
168 Tino Martinez CL .25 .60
169 Scott Rolen CL .25 .60
170 Nomar Garciaparra CL .60 1.50
176 Mark Kotsay RR .25 .60
177 Neifi Perez RR .15 .40
178 Paul Konerko RR .25 .60
179 Jose Cruz Jr. RR .15 .40
180 Hideki Irabu RR .15 .40
181 Mike Cameron RR .15 .40
182 Jeff Suppan RR .15 .40
183 Kevin Orie RR .15 .40
184 Pokey Reese RR .15 .40
185 Todd Dunwoody RR .15 .40
186 Miguel Tejada RR .60 1.50
187 Jose Guillen RR .25 .60
188 Bartolo Colon RR .25 .60
189 Derrek Lee RR .40 1.00
190 Antone Williamson RR .15 .40
191 Wilton Guerrero RR .15 .40
192 Jaret Wright RR .15 .40
193 Todd Helton RR .40 1.00
194 Shannon Stewart RR .25 .60
195 Nomar Garciaparra RR 1.00 2.50
196 Brett Tomko RR .15 .40
197 Fernando Tatis RR .15 .40
198 Raul Ibanez RR .25 .60
199 Dennis Reyes RR .15 .40
200 Bobby Estalella RR .15 .40
201 Lou Collier RR .15 .40
202 Bubba Trammell RR .15 .40
203 Ben Grieve RR .15 .40
204 Ivan Cruz RR .15 .40
205 Karim Garcia RR .15 .40

1998 Donruss Prized Collections Donruss

COMPLETE SET (200) 600.00 1200.00
*STARS: 1.25X TO 3X BASIC CARDS
LESS THAN 560 SETS PRINTED

1998 Donruss Collections Elite

These cards were issued one card per Donruss Collection pack. These cards parallel the Donruss Elite set and have the same checklist and subsets as the regular Donruss cards.

401 Ken Griffey Jr. 2.00 5.00
402 Frank Thomas 1.00 2.50
403 Alex Rodriguez 1.50 4.00
404 Mike Piazza 1.50 4.00
405 Greg Maddux 1.50 4.00
406 Cal Ripken 3.00 8.00
407 Chipper Jones 1.00 2.50
408 Derek Jeter 2.50 6.00
409 Tony Gwynn 1.25 3.00
410 Andruw Jones .60 1.50
411 Juan Gonzalez .40 1.00
412 Jeff Bagwell .60 1.50
413 Mark McGwire 2.50 6.00
414 Roger Clemens 2.00 5.00
415 Albert Belle .40 1.00
416 Barry Bonds 2.50 6.00
417 Kenny Lofton .40 1.00
418 Ivan Rodriguez .60 1.50
419 Manny Ramirez .60 1.50
420 Jim Thome .60 1.50
421 Chuck Knoblauch .40 1.00
422 Paul Molitor .40 1.00
423 Barry Larkin .60 1.50
424 Andy Pettitte .60 1.50
425 John Smoltz .60 1.50
426 Randy Johnson 1.00 2.50
427 Bernie Williams .60 1.50
428 Larry Walker .40 1.00
429 Mo Vaughn .40 1.00
430 Bobby Higginson .40 1.00
431 Edgardo Alfonzo .40 1.00
432 Justin Thompson .25 .60
433 Jeff Suppan .25 .60
434 Roberto Alomar .60 1.50
435 Hideo Nomo 1.00 2.50
436 Rusty Greer .40 1.00
437 Tim Salmon .60 1.50
438 Jim Edmonds .60 1.50
439 Gary Sheffield .40 1.00
440 Ken Caminiti .40 1.00
441 Sammy Sosa 1.00 2.50
442 Tony Womack .25 .60
443 Matt Williams .40 1.00
444 Andres Galarraga .40 1.00
445 Garret Anderson .40 1.00
446 Rafael Palmeiro .60 1.50
447 Mike Mussina .60 1.50
448 Craig Biggio .60 1.50
449 Wade Boggs .60 1.50
450 Tom Glavine .60 1.50
451 Jason Giambi .40 1.00
452 Will Clark .60 1.50
453 David Justice .40 1.00
454 Sandy Alomar Jr. .25 .60
455 Edgar Martinez .60 1.50
456 Brady Anderson .40 1.00
457 Eric Young .25 .60
458 Ray Lankford .40 1.00
459 Kevin Brown .40 1.00
460 Raul Mondesi .40 1.00
461 Bobby Bonilla .40 1.00
462 Javier Lopez .40 1.00
463 Fred McGriff .60 1.50
464 Rondell White .40 1.00
465 Todd Hundley .25 .60
466 Mark Grace .60 1.50
467 Alan Benes .25 .60
468 Jeff Abbott .25 .60
469 Bob Abreu .40 1.00
470 Deion Sanders .60 1.50
471 Tino Martinez .60 1.50
472 Shannon Stewart .40 1.00
473 Homer Bush .25 .60
474 Carlos Delgado .40 1.00
475 Raul Ibanez .25 .60
476 Hideki Irabu .25 .60
477 Jose Cruz Jr. .25 .60
478 Tony Clark .25 .60
479 Wilton Guerrero .25 .60
480 Vladimir Guerrero 1.00 2.50
481 Scott Rolen .60 1.50
482 Nomar Garciaparra 1.50 4.00
483 Darin Erstad .40 1.00
484 Chan Ho Park .40 1.00
485 Mike Cameron .25 .60
486 Todd Walker .25 .60
487 Todd Dunwoody .25 .60
488 Neifi Perez .25 .60
489 Brett Tomko .25 .60
490 Jose Guillen .25 .60
491 Matt Morris .40 1.00
492 Bartolo Colon .40 1.00
493 Jaret Wright .25 .60
494 Shawn Estes .25 .60
495 Livan Hernandez .40 1.00
496 Bobby Estalella .25 .60
497 Ben Grieve .25 .60
498 Paul Konerko .40 1.00
499 David Ortiz 1.25 3.00
500 Todd Helton .60 1.50
501 Juan Encarnacion .25 .60
502 Bubba Trammell .25 .60
503 Miguel Tejada 1.00 2.50
504 Jacob Cruz .25 .60
505 Todd Greene .25 .60
506 Kevin Orie .25 .60
507 Mark Kotsay .40 1.00
508 Fernando Tatis .25 .60
509 Jay Payton .25 .60
510 Pokey Reese .25 .60
511 Derrek Lee .60 1.50
512 Richard Hidalgo .25 .60
513 Ricky Ledee .25 .60
514 Lou Collier .25 .60
515 Ruben Rivera .25 .60
516 Shawn Green .40 1.00
517 Moises Alou .40 1.00
518 Ken Griffey Jr. GEN 1.25 3.00
519 Frank Thomas GEN .60 1.50
520 Alex Rodriguez GEN 1.00 2.50
521 Mike Piazza GEN 1.00 2.50
522 Greg Maddux GEN 1.00 2.50
523 Cal Ripken GEN 1.50 4.00
524 Chipper Jones GEN .60 1.50
525 Derek Jeter GEN 1.25 3.00
526 Tony Gwynn GEN .60 1.50
527 Andruw Jones GEN .60 1.50

528 Juan Gonzalez GEN .25 .60
529 Jeff Bagwell GEN .40 1.00
530 Mark McGwire GEN 1.25 3.00
531 Roger Clemens GEN 1.00 2.50
532 Albert Belle GEN .25 .60
533 Barry Bonds GEN 1.00 2.50
534 Kenny Lofton GEN .25 .60
535 Ivan Rodriguez GEN .40 1.00
536 Manny Ramirez GEN .60 1.50
537 Jim Thome GEN .40 1.00
538 Chuck Knoblauch GEN .25 .60
539 Paul Molitor GEN .25 .60
540 Barry Larkin GEN .40 1.00
541 Mo Vaughn GEN .25 .60
542 Hideki Irabu GEN .25 .60
543 Jose Cruz Jr. GEN .25 .60
544 Tony Clark GEN .25 .60
545 Vladimir Guerrero GEN .60 1.50
546 Scott Rolen GEN .60 1.50
547 Nomar Garciaparra GEN 1.00 2.50
548 Nomar Garciaparra CL 1.00 2.50
549 Larry Walker CL .25 .60
550 Tino Martinez CL .40 1.00

1998 Donruss Prized Collections Elite

COMPLETE SET (150) 1000.00 2000.00
*STARS: 1.5X TO 4X BASIC CARDS
LESS THAN 220 SETS PRINTED

1998 Donruss Collections Leaf

The Donruss Collections Leaf set contains 200 cards and inserted at a rate of two cards per pack. The set contains the subsets: Curtain Calls (347-356), Gold Leaf Stars (357-376), Gold Leaf Rookies (377-396), and Checklists (397-399).

201 Rusty Greer .30 .75
202 Tino Martinez .50 1.25
203 Bobby Bonilla .30 .75
204 Jason Giambi .30 .75
205 Matt Morris .30 .75
206 Craig Counsell .20 .50
207 Reggie Jefferson .20 .50
208 Brian Rose .20 .50
209 Ruben Rivera .20 .50
210 Shawn Estes .20 .50
211 Tony Gwynn 1.00 2.50
212 Jeff Abbott .20 .50
213 Jose Cruz Jr. .20 .50
214 Francisco Cordova .20 .50
215 Ryan Klesko .30 .75
216 Tim Salmon .50 1.25
217 Brett Tomko .20 .50
218 Matt Williams .30 .75
219 Joe Carter .30 .75
220 Harold Baines .30 .75
221 Gary Sheffield .30 .75
222 Charles Johnson .30 .75
223 Aaron Boone .30 .75
224 Eddie Murray .75 2.00
225 Matt Stairs .20 .50
226 David Cone .30 .75
227 Jon Nunnally .20 .50
228 Chris Stynes .20 .50
229 Enrique Wilson .20 .50
230 Randy Johnson .75 2.00
231 Garret Anderson .30 .75
232 Manny Ramirez .50 1.25
233 Jeff Suppan .20 .50
234 Rickey Henderson .75 2.00
235 Scott Spiezio .20 .50
236 Rondell White .30 .75
237 Todd Greene .20 .50
238 Delino DeShields .20 .50
239 Kevin Brown .50 1.25
240 Chili Davis .30 .75
241 Jimmy Key .30 .75
242 Mike Mussina .50 1.25
243 Joe Randa .30 .75
244 Chan Ho Park .30 .75
245 Brad Radke .30 .75
246 Geronimo Berroa .20 .50
247 Wade Boggs .50 1.25
248 Kevin Appier .30 .75
249 Moises Alou .30 .75
250 David Justice .30 .75
251 Ivan Rodriguez .50 1.25
252 J.T. Snow .30 .75
253 Brian Giles .30 .75
254 Will Clark .50 1.25
255 Justin Thompson .20 .50
256 Javier Lopez .30 .75
257 Hideki Irabu .20 .50
258 Mark Grudzielanek .20 .50
259 Abraham Nunez .20 .50
260 Todd Hollandsworth .20 .50
261 Jay Bell .30 .75
262 Nomar Garciaparra 1.25 3.00
263 Vinny Castilla .30 .75
264 Lou Collier .20 .50
265 Kevin Orie .20 .50
266 John Valentin .20 .50
267 Robin Ventura .30 .75
268 Denny Neagle .20 .50
269 Tony Womack .20 .50
270 Dennis Reyes .20 .50
271 Wally Joyner .30 .75
272 Kevin Brown .50 1.25
273 Ray Durham .30 .75
274 Mike Cameron .20 .50
275 Dante Bichette .30 .75
276 Jose Guillen .30 .75
277 Carlos Delgado .30 .75
278 Paul Molitor .30 .75
279 Jason Kendall .30 .75
280 Mark Bellhorn .30 .75
281 Damian Jackson .20 .50
282 Bill Mueller .30 .75
283 Kevin Young .30 .75
284 Curt Schilling .30 .75
285 Jeffrey Hammonds .20 .50
286 Sandy Alomar Jr. .20 .50
287 Bartolo Colon .30 .75
288 Wilton Guerrero .20 .50
289 Bernie Williams .50 1.25
290 Deion Sanders .50 1.25
291 Mike Piazza 1.25 3.00
292 Butch Huskey .20 .50
293 Edgardo Alfonzo .20 .50
294 Alan Benes .20 .50
295 Craig Biggio .50 1.25
296 Mark Grace .50 1.25
297 Shawn Green .30 .75
298 Derrek Lee .50 1.25
299 Ken Griffey Jr. 1.50 4.00
300 Tim Raines .30 .75
301 Pokey Reese .20 .50
302 Lee Stevens .20 .50
303 Shannon Stewart .30 .75
304 John Smoltz .50 1.25
305 Frank Thomas .75 2.00
306 Jeff Fassero .20 .50
307 Jay Buhner .30 .75
308 Jose Canseco .50 1.25
309 Omar Vizquel .50 1.25
310 Travis Fryman .30 .75
311 Dave Nilsson .20 .50
312 John Olerud .30 .75
313 Larry Walker .30 .75
314 Jim Edmonds .30 .75
315 Bobby Higginson .30 .75
316 Todd Hundley .20 .50
317 Paul O'Neill .50 1.25
318 Bip Roberts .20 .50
319 Ismael Valdes .20 .50
320 Pedro Martinez .50 1.25
321 Jeff Cirillo .20 .50
322 Andy Benes .20 .50
323 Bobby Jones .20 .50
324 Brian Hunter .20 .50
325 Darryl Kile .30 .75
326 Pat Hentgen .20 .50
327 Marquis Grissom .30 .75
328 Eric Davis .30 .75
329 Chipper Jones .75 2.00
330 Edgar Martinez .50 1.25
331 Andy Pettitte .50 1.25
332 Cal Ripken 2.50 6.00
333 Scott Rolen .50 1.25
334 Ron Coomer .20 .50
335 Luis Castillo .20 .50
336 Fred McGriff .50 1.25
337 Neifi Perez .20 .50
338 Eric Karros .30 .75
339 Alex Fernandez .20 .50
340 Jason Dickson .20 .50
341 Lance Johnson .20 .50
342 Ray Lankford .30 .75
343 Sammy Sosa .75 2.00
344 Eric Young .20 .50
345 Bubba Trammell .20 .50
346 Todd Walker .20 .50
347 Mo Vaughn CC .20 .50
348 Jeff Bagwell CC .30 .75
349 Kenny Lofton CC .20 .50
350 Raul Mondesi CC .20 .50
351 Mike Piazza CC .75 2.00
352 Chipper Jones CC .50 1.25
353 Larry Walker CC .20 .50
354 Greg Maddux CC .75 2.00
355 Ken Griffey Jr. CC 1.00 2.50
356 Frank Thomas CC .50 1.25
357 Darin Erstad GLS .20 .50
358 Roberto Alomar GLS .30 .75
359 Albert Belle GLS .20 .50
360 Jim Thome GLS .30 .75
361 Tony Clark GLS .20 .50
362 Chuck Knoblauch GLS .20 .50
363 Derek Jeter GLS 1.00 2.50
364 Alex Rodriguez GLS .75 2.00
365 Tony Gwynn GLS .50 1.25
366 Roger Clemens GLS .75 2.00
367 Barry Larkin GLS .30 .75
368 Andres Galarraga GLS .20 .50
369 Vladimir Guerrero GLS .50 1.25
370 Mark McGwire GLS 1.00 2.50
371 Barry Bonds GLS .75 2.00
372 Juan Gonzalez GLS .20 .50
373 Andruw Jones GLS .30 .75
374 Paul Molitor GLS .20 .50
375 Hideo Nomo GLS .50 1.25
376 Cal Ripken GLS 1.25 3.00
377 Brad Fullmer GLR .20 .50
378 Jaret Wright GLR .20 .50
379 Bobby Estalella GLR .20 .50
380 Ben Grieve GLR .20 .50
381 Paul Konerko GLR .30 .75
382 David Ortiz GLR 1.00 2.50
383 Todd Helton GLR .50 1.25
384 Juan Encarnacion GLR .20 .50
385 Miguel Tejada GLR .75 2.00
386 Jacob Cruz GLR .20 .50
387 Mark Kotsay GLR .30 .75
388 Fernando Tatis GLR .20 .50
389 Ricky Ledee GLR .20 .50
390 Richard Hidalgo GLR .20 .50
391 Richie Sexson GLR .20 .50
392 Luis Ordaz GLR .20 .50
393 Eli Marrero GLR .20 .50
394 Livan Hernandez GLR .30 .75
395 Homer Bush GLR .20 .50
396 Raul Ibanez GLR .20 .50
397 Nomar Garciaparra CL .75 2.00
398 Scott Rolen CL .30 .75
399 Jose Cruz Jr. CL .20 .50
400 Al Martin .20 .50

1998 Donruss Prized Collections Leaf

COMPLETE SET (200) 500.00 1000.00
*STARS: 1.25X TO 3X BASIC CARDS
LESS THAN 400 SETS PRINTED

1998 Donruss Collections Preferred

These cards, which parallel the regular Donruss Preferred set were issued one every two packs. According to published reports, less than 1400 sets were produced. Again, the checklist matches the regular Donruss Preferred set.

551 Ken Griffey Jr. EX 6.00 15.00
552 Frank Thomas EX 3.00 8.00
553 Cal Ripken EX 10.00 25.00
554 Alex Rodriguez EX 5.00 12.00
555 Greg Maddux EX 5.00 12.00
556 Mike Piazza EX 5.00 12.00
557 Chipper Jones EX 3.00 8.00
558 Tony Gwynn FB 4.00 10.00
559 Derek Jeter FB 8.00 20.00
560 Jeff Bagwell EX 2.00 5.00
561 Juan Gonzalez EX 1.25 3.00
562 Nomar Garciaparra EX 5.00 12.00
563 Andruw Jones FB 2.00 5.00
564 Hideo Nomo FB 3.00 8.00
565 Roger Clemens FB 6.00 15.00
566 Mark McGwire FB 8.00 20.00
567 Scott Rolen FB 2.00 5.00
568 Vladimir Guerrero FB 3.00 8.00
569 Barry Bonds FB 8.00 20.00
570 Darin Erstad FB 1.25 3.00
571 Albert Belle FB 1.25 3.00
572 Kenny Lofton FB 1.25 3.00
573 Mo Vaughn FB 1.25 3.00
574 Tony Clark FB .75 2.00
575 Ivan Rodriguez FB 2.00 5.00
576 Larry Walker CB 1.25 3.00
577 Eddie Murray CB 3.00 8.00
578 Andy Pettitte CB 2.00 5.00
579 Roberto Alomar CB 2.00 5.00
580 Randy Johnson CB 3.00 8.00
581 Manny Ramirez CB 2.00 5.00
582 Paul Molitor FB 1.25 3.00
583 Mike Mussina CB 2.00 5.00
584 Jim Thome FB 2.00 5.00
585 Tino Martinez CB 2.00 5.00
586 Gary Sheffield CB 1.25 3.00
587 Chuck Knoblauch CB 1.25 3.00
588 Bernie Williams CB 2.00 5.00
589 Tim Salmon CB 2.00 5.00
590 Sammy Sosa CB 3.00 8.00
591 Wade Boggs GS 2.00 5.00
592 Will Clark GS 2.00 5.00
593 Andres Galarraga CB 1.25 3.00
594 Raul Mondesi CB 1.25 3.00
595 Rickey Henderson GS 3.00 8.00
596 Jose Canseco GS 2.00 5.00
597 Pedro Martinez GS 2.00 5.00
598 Jay Buhner GS 1.25 3.00
599 Ryan Klesko GS 1.25 3.00
600 Barry Larkin CB 2.00 5.00
601 Charles Johnson GS 1.25 3.00
602 Tom Glavine GS 2.00 5.00
603 Edgar Martinez CB 2.00 5.00
604 Fred McGriff GS 2.00 5.00
605 Moises Alou ME 1.25 3.00
606 Dante Bichette GS 1.25 3.00
607 Jim Edmonds CB 1.25 3.00
608 Mark Grace ME 2.00 5.00
609 Chan Ho Park ME 1.25 3.00
610 Justin Thompson ME .75 2.00
611 John Smoltz ME 2.00 5.00
612 Craig Biggio CB 2.00 5.00
613 Ken Caminiti ME 1.25 3.00
614 Deion Sanders ME 2.00 5.00
615 Carlos Delgado GS 1.25 3.00
616 David Justice CB 1.25 3.00
617 J.T. Snow GS 1.25 3.00
618 Jason Giambi CB 1.25 3.00
619 Garret Anderson ME 1.25 3.00
620 Rondell White ME 1.25 3.00
621 Matt Williams ME 1.25 3.00
622 Brady Anderson ME 1.25 3.00
623 Eric Karros GS 1.25 3.00
624 Javier Lopez GS 1.25 3.00
625 Pat Hentgen GS .75 2.00
626 Todd Hundley GS .75 2.00
627 Ray Lankford GS 1.25 3.00
628 Denny Neagle GS .75 2.00
629 Henry Rodriguez GS .75 2.00
630 Sandy Alomar Jr. ME 1.25 3.00
631 Rafael Palmeiro ME 2.00 5.00
632 Robin Ventura GS 1.25 3.00
633 John Olerud GS 1.25 3.00
634 Omar Vizquel GS 2.00 5.00
635 Joe Randa GS .75 2.00
636 Lance Johnson GS .75 2.00
637 Kevin Brown GS 2.00 5.00
638 Curt Schilling GS 1.25 3.00
639 Ismael Valdes GS .75 2.00
640 Francisco Cordova GS .75 2.00
641 David Cone GS 1.25 3.00
642 Paul O'Neill GS 2.00 5.00
643 Jimmy Key GS 1.25 3.00
644 Brad Radke GS 1.25 3.00
645 Kevin Appier GS 1.25 3.00
646 Al Martin GS .75 2.00
647 Rusty Greer ME 1.25 3.00
648 Reggie Jefferson GS .75 2.00
649 Ron Coomer GS .75 2.00
650 Vinny Castilla GS 1.25 3.00
651 Bobby Bonilla ME 1.25 3.00
652 Eric Young GS .75 2.00
653 Tony Womack GS .75 2.00
654 Jason Kendall GS 1.25 3.00
655 Jeff Suppan GS .75 2.00
656 Shawn Estes ME .75 2.00
657 Shawn Green GS 1.25 3.00
658 Edgardo Alfonzo ME .75 2.00
659 Alan Benes ME .75 2.00
660 Bobby Higginson GS 1.25 3.00
661 Mark Grudzielanek GS .75 2.00
662 Wilton Guerrero GS .75 2.00
663 Todd Greene ME .75 2.00
664 Pokey Reese GS .75 2.00
665 Jose Guillen CB 1.25 3.00
666 Neifi Perez ME .75 2.00
667 Luis Castillo GS .75 2.00
668 Edgar Renteria GS 1.25 3.00
669 Karim Garcia GS .75 2.00
670 Butch Huskey GS .75 2.00
671 Michael Tucker GS .75 2.00
672 Jason Dickson GS .75 2.00
673 Todd Walker ME .75 2.00
674 Brian Jordan GS 1.25 3.00
675 Joe Carter GS 1.25 3.00
676 Matt Morris ME 1.25 3.00
677 Brett Tomko ME .75 2.00
678 Mike Cameron CB .75 2.00
679 Russ Davis GS .75 2.00
680 Shannon Stewart ME 1.25 3.00
681 Kevin Orie GS .75 2.00
682 Scott Spiezio GS .75 2.00
683 Brian Giles GS 1.25 3.00
684 Raul Casanova GS .75 2.00
685 Jose Cruz Jr. CB .75 2.00
686 Hideki Irabu GS .75 2.00
687 Bubba Trammell GS .75 2.00
688 Richard Hidalgo CB .75 2.00
689 Paul Konerko CB 1.25 3.00
690 Todd Helton FB 2.00 5.00
691 Miguel Tejada CB 3.00 8.00
692 Fernando Tatis ME .75 2.00
693 Ben Grieve FB .75 2.00
694 Travis Lee FB .75 2.00
695 Mark Kotsay CB 1.25 3.00
696 Eli Marrero ME .75 2.00
697 David Ortiz CB 4.00 10.00
698 Juan Encarnacion ME .75 2.00
699 Jaret Wright ME .75 2.00
700 Livan Hernandez CB 1.25 3.00
701 Ruben Rivera GS .75 2.00
702 Brad Fullmer ME .75 2.00
703 Dennis Reyes GS .75 2.00
704 Enrique Wilson ME .75 2.00
705 Todd Dunwoody ME .75 2.00
706 Derrick Gibson ME .75 2.00
707 Aaron Boone ME 1.25 3.00
708 Ron Wright ME .75 2.00
709 Preston Wilson ME 1.25 3.00
710 Abraham Nunez GS .75 2.00
711 Shane Monahan GS .75 2.00
712 Carl Pavano GS 1.25 3.00
713 Derrek Lee GS 2.00 5.00
714 Jeff Abbott GS .75 2.00
715 Wes Helms ME .75 2.00
716 Brian Rose GS .75 2.00
717 Bobby Estalella GS .75 2.00
718 Ken Griffey Jr. PP GS 4.00 10.00
719 Frank Thomas PP GS 2.00 5.00
720 Cal Ripken PP GS 5.00 12.00
721 Alex Rodriguez PP GS 3.00 8.00
722 Greg Maddux PP GS 3.00 8.00
723 Mike Piazza PP GS 3.00 8.00
724 Chipper Jones PP GS 2.00 5.00
725 Tony Gwynn PP GS 2.00 5.00
726 Derek Jeter PP GS 4.00 10.00
727 Jeff Bagwell PP GS 1.25 3.00
728 Juan Gonzalez PP GS 1.25 3.00
729 Nomar Garciaparra PP GS 3.00 8.00
730 Andruw Jones PP GS 1.25 3.00
731 Hideo Nomo PP GS 2.00 5.00
732 Roger Clemens PP GS 3.00 8.00
733 Mark McGwire PP GS 4.00 10.00
734 Scott Rolen PP GS 2.00 5.00
735 Barry Bonds PP GS 3.00 8.00
736 Darin Erstad PP GS .75 2.00
737 Mo Vaughn PP GS .75 2.00
738 Ivan Rodriguez PP GS 2.00 5.00
739 Larry Walker PP ME 1.25 3.00
740 Andy Pettitte PP GS 1.25 3.00
741 Randy Johnson PP ME 2.00 5.00
742 Paul Molitor PP GS .75 2.00
743 Jim Thome PP GS 1.25 3.00
744 Tino Martinez PP ME 1.25 3.00
745 Gary Sheffield PP GS .75 2.00
746 Albert Belle PP GS .75 2.00
747 Jose Cruz Jr. PP GS .75 2.00
748 Todd Helton CL GS 1.25 3.00
749 Ben Grieve CL GS .75 2.00
750 Paul Konerko CL GS .75 2.00

1998 Donruss Prized Collections Preferred

*STARS: 1.25X TO 3X BASIC CARDS
LESS THAN 55 SETS PRINTED

1997 Donruss Elite

The 1997 Donruss Elite set was issued in one series totalling 150 cards. The product was distributed exclusively to hobby dealers around February, 1997. Each foil-wrapped pack contained eight cards and carried a suggested retail price of $3.49. Player selection was limited to the top stars (plus three player checklist cards) and card design is very similar to the Donruss Elite hockey set that was released one year earlier. Strangely enough, the backs only provide career statistics neglecting statistics from the previous season.

COMPLETE SET (150) 10.00 25.00
1 Juan Gonzalez .15 .40
2 Alex Rodriguez .60 1.50
3 Frank Thomas .40 1.00
4 Greg Maddux .60 1.50
5 Ken Griffey Jr. .75 2.00
6 Cal Ripken 1.25 3.00
7 Mike Piazza .60 1.50
8 Chipper Jones .40 1.00
9 Albert Belle .15 .40
10 Andruw Jones .25 .60
11 Vladimir Guerrero .40 1.00
12 Mo Vaughn .15 .40
13 Ivan Rodriguez .25 .60
14 Andy Pettitte .25 .60
15 Tony Gwynn .50 1.25
16 Barry Bonds 1.00 2.50
17 Jeff Bagwell .25 .60
18 Manny Ramirez .25 .60
19 Kenny Lofton .15 .40
20 Roberto Alomar .25 .60
21 Mark McGwire 1.00 2.50
22 Ryan Klesko .15 .40
23 Tim Salmon .25 .60
24 Derek Jeter 1.00 2.50
25 Eddie Murray .40 1.00
26 Jermaine Dye .15 .40
27 Ruben Rivera .15 .40
28 Jim Edmonds .15 .40
29 Mike Mussina .25 .60
30 Randy Johnson .40 1.00
31 Sammy Sosa .40 1.00
32 Hideo Nomo .40 1.00
33 Chuck Knoblauch .15 .40
34 Paul Molitor .15 .40
35 Rafael Palmeiro .25 .60
36 Brady Anderson .15 .40
37 Will Clark .25 .60
38 Craig Biggio .25 .60
39 Jason Giambi .15 .40
40 Roger Clemens .75 2.00
41 Jay Buhner .15 .40
42 Edgar Martinez .25 .60
43 Gary Sheffield .15 .40
44 Fred McGriff .25 .60
45 Bobby Bonilla .15 .40
46 Tom Glavine .25 .60
47 Wade Boggs .25 .60
48 Jeff Conine .15 .40
49 John Smoltz .25 .60
50 Jim Thome .25 .60
51 Billy Wagner .15 .40
52 Jose Canseco .25 .60
53 Javy Lopez .15 .40
54 Cecil Fielder .15 .40
55 Garret Anderson .15 .40
56 Alex Ochoa .15 .40
57 Scott Rolen .25 .60
58 Darin Erstad .15 .40
59 Rey Ordonez .15 .40
60 Dante Bichette .15 .40
61 Joe Carter .15 .40
62 Moises Alou .15 .40
63 Jason Isringhausen .15 .40
64 Karim Garcia .15 .40
65 Brian Jordan .15 .40
66 Ruben Sierra .15 .40
67 Todd Hollandsworth .15 .40
68 Paul Wilson .15 .40
69 Ernie Young .15 .40
70 Ryne Sandberg .60 1.50
71 Raul Mondesi .15 .40
72 George Arias .15 .40
73 Ray Durham .15 .40
74 Dean Palmer .15 .40
75 Shawn Green .15 .40
76 Eric Young .15 .40
77 Jason Kendall .15 .40
78 Greg Vaughn .15 .40
79 Terrell Wade .15 .40
80 Bill Pulsipher .15 .40
81 Bobby Higginson .15 .40
82 Mark Grudzielanek .15 .40
83 Ken Caminiti .15 .40
84 Todd Greene .15 .40
85 Carlos Delgado .15 .40
86 Mark Grace .25 .60
87 Rondell White .15 .40
88 Barry Larkin .25 .60
89 J.T. Snow .15 .40
90 Alex Gonzalez .15 .40
91 Raul Casanova .15 .40
92 Marc Newfield .15 .40
93 Jermaine Allensworth .15 .40
94 John Mabry .15 .40
95 Kirby Puckett .40 1.00
96 Travis Fryman .15 .40
97 Kevin Brown .15 .40
98 Andres Galarraga .15 .40
99 Marty Cordova .15 .40
100 Henry Rodriguez .15 .40
101 Sterling Hitchcock .15 .40
102 Trey Beamon .15 .40
103 Brett Butler .15 .40
104 Rickey Henderson .40 1.00
105 Tino Martinez .25 .60
106 Kevin Appier .15 .40
107 Brian Hunter .15 .40
108 Eric Karros .15 .40
109 Andre Dawson .15 .40
110 Darryl Strawberry .15 .40
111 James Baldwin .15 .40
112 Chad Mottola .15 .40
113 Dave Nilsson .15 .40
114 Carlos Baerga .15 .40
115 Chan Ho Park .15 .40
116 John Jaha .15 .40
117 Alan Benes .15 .40
118 Mariano Rivera .40 1.00
119 Ellis Burks .15 .40
120 Tony Clark .15 .40
121 Todd Walker .15 .40
122 Dwight Gooden .15 .40
123 Ugueth Urbina .15 .40
124 David Cone .15 .40
125 Ozzie Smith .60 1.50
126 Kimera Bartee .15 .40
127 Rusty Greer .15 .40
128 Pat Hentgen .15 .40
129 Charles Johnson .15 .40
130 Quinton McCracken .15 .40
131 Troy Percival .15 .40
132 Shane Reynolds .15 .40
133 Charles Nagy .15 .40
134 Tom Goodwin .15 .40
135 Ron Gant .15 .40
136 Dan Wilson .15 .40
137 Matt Williams .15 .40
138 LaTroy Hawkins .15 .40
139 Kevin Seitzer .15 .40
140 Michael Tucker .15 .40
141 Todd Hundley .15 .40
142 Alex Fernandez .15 .40
143 Marquis Grissom .15 .40
144 Steve Finley .15 .40
145 Curtis Pride .15 .40
146 Derek Bell .15 .40
147 Butch Huskey .15 .40
148 Dwight Gooden CL .15 .40
149 Al Leiter CL .15 .40
150 Hideo Nomo CL .15 .40

1997 Donruss Elite Gold Stars

*STARS: 4X TO 10X BASIC CARDS
RANDOM INSERTS IN PACKS
CONDITION SENSITIVE SET

1997 Donruss Elite Leather and Lumber

STATED PRINT RUN 500 SERIAL #'d SETS
1 Ken Griffey Jr. 10.00 25.00
2 Alex Rodriguez 6.00 15.00
3 Frank Thomas 5.00 12.00
4 Chipper Jones 5.00 12.00
5 Ivan Rodriguez 3.00 8.00
6 Cal Ripken 15.00 40.00
7 Barry Bonds 8.00 20.00
8 Chuck Knoblauch 2.00 5.00
9 Manny Ramirez 3.00 8.00
10 Mark McGwire 8.00 20.00

1997 Donruss Elite Passing the Torch

COMPLETE SET (12) 40.00 80.00
1 Cal Ripken 10.00 25.00
2 Alex Rodriguez 5.00 12.00
3 C.Ripken 10.00 25.00
A.Rodriguez
4 Kirby Puckett 3.00 8.00
5 Andruw Jones 2.00 5.00
6 K.Puckett 2.50 6.00
A.Jones
7 Cecil Fielder 1.25 3.00
8 Frank Thomas 3.00 8.00
9 F.Thomas 2.50 6.00
C.Fielder
10 Ozzie Smith 4.00 10.00
11 Derek Jeter 6.00 15.00
12 D.Jeter 6.00 15.00
O.Smith

1997 Donruss Elite Passing the Torch Autographs

RANDOM INSERTS IN PACKS
STATED PRINT RUN 150 SERIAL #'d SETS
1 Cal Ripken 75.00 150.00
2 Alex Rodriguez 125.00 250.00
3 C.Ripken/A.Rodriguez 250.00 400.00
4 Kirby Puckett 100.00 200.00
5 Andruw Jones 10.00 25.00
6 K.Puckett/A.Jones 150.00 300.00
7 Cecil Fielder 20.00 50.00
8 Frank Thomas 50.00 100.00
9 F.Thomas/C.Fielder 60.00 120.00
10 Ozzie Smith 75.00 150.00
11 Derek Jeter 200.00 400.00
12 D.Jeter/O.Smith 200.00 350.00

1997 Donruss Elite Turn of the Century

COMPLETE SET (20) 15.00 40.00
STATED PRINT RUN 3000 SERIAL #'d SETS
*DIE CUTS: 2X TO 5X BASIC TURN CENT.
DC STATED PRINT RUN 500 SERIAL #'d SETS
RANDOM INSERTS IN PACKS
1 Alex Rodriguez 2.00 5.00
2 Andruw Jones .60 1.50
3 Chipper Jones 1.50 4.00
4 Todd Walker .60 1.50
5 Scott Rolen 1.00 2.50
6 Trey Beamon .60 1.50
7 Derek Jeter 4.00 10.00
8 Darin Erstad .60 1.50
9 Tony Clark .60 1.50
10 Todd Greene .60 1.50
11 Jason Giambi .60 1.50
12 Justin Thompson .60 1.50
13 Ernie Young .60 1.50
14 Jason Kendall .60 1.50
15 Alex Ochoa .60 1.50
16 Brooks Kieschnick .60 1.50
17 Bobby Higginson .60 1.50
18 Ruben Rivera .60 1.50
19 Chan Ho Park .60 1.50
20 Chad Mottola .60 1.50
P5 S.Rolen Promo 1.00 2.50
P7 Derek Jeter PROMO 4.00 10.00
P20 Chad Mottola PROMO .60 1.50

1998 Donruss Elite

The 1998 Donruss Elite set was issued in one series totalling 150 cards and distributed in five-card packs with a suggested retail price of $3.99. The fronts feature color player action photos. The backs carry player information. The set contains the topical subset: Generations (118-147). A special embossed Frank Thomas autograph card (parallel to basic issue card number two, except, of course, for Thomas' signature) was available to lucky collectors who pulled a Back to the Future Frank Thomas/David Ortiz card serial numbered between 1 and 100 and redeemed it to Donruss/Leaf.

COMPLETE SET (150) 10.00 25.00
THOMAS AU AVAIL VIA MAIL EXCHANGE
1 Ken Griffey Jr. .60 1.50
2 Frank Thomas .30 .75
3 Alex Rodriguez .50 1.25
4 Mike Piazza .50 1.25
5 Greg Maddux .50 1.25
6 Cal Ripken 1.00 2.50
7 Chipper Jones .30 .75
8 Derek Jeter .75 2.00
9 Tony Gwynn .40 1.00
10 Andruw Jones .20 .50
11 Juan Gonzalez .10 .30
12 Jeff Bagwell .20 .50
13 Mark McGwire .75 2.00
14 Roger Clemens .60 1.50
15 Albert Belle .10 .30
16 Barry Bonds .75 2.00
17 Kenny Lofton .10 .30
18 Ivan Rodriguez .20 .50
19 Manny Ramirez .20 .50
20 Jim Thome .20 .50
21 Chuck Knoblauch .10 .30
22 Paul Molitor .10 .30
23 Barry Larkin .20 .50
24 Andy Pettitte .20 .50
25 John Smoltz .20 .50
26 Randy Johnson .30 .75
27 Bernie Williams .20 .50
28 Larry Walker .10 .30
29 Mo Vaughn .10 .30
30 Bobby Higginson .10 .30
31 Edgardo Alfonzo .10 .30
32 Justin Thompson .10 .30
33 Jeff Suppan .10 .30
34 Roberto Alomar .20 .50
35 Hideo Nomo .30 .75
36 Rusty Greer .10 .30
37 Tim Salmon .20 .50
38 Jim Edmonds .10 .30
39 Gary Sheffield .10 .30
40 Ken Caminiti .10 .30
41 Sammy Sosa .30 .75
42 Tony Womack .10 .30
43 Matt Williams .10 .30
44 Andres Galarraga .10 .30
45 Garret Anderson .10 .30
46 Rafael Palmeiro .20 .50
47 Mike Mussina .20 .50
48 Craig Biggio .20 .50
49 Wade Boggs .20 .50
50 Tom Glavine .20 .50
51 Jason Giambi .10 .30
52 Will Clark .20 .50
53 David Justice .10 .30
54 Sandy Alomar Jr. .10 .30
55 Edgar Martinez .20 .50
56 Brady Anderson .10 .30
57 Eric Young .10 .30
58 Ray Lankford .10 .30
59 Kevin Brown .20 .50
60 Raul Mondesi .10 .30
61 Bobby Bonilla .10 .30
62 Javier Lopez .10 .30
63 Fred McGriff .20 .50
64 Rondell White .10 .30
65 Todd Hundley .10 .30
66 Mark Grace .20 .50
67 Alan Benes .10 .30
68 Jeff Abbott .10 .30
69 Bob Abreu .10 .30
70 Deion Sanders .20 .50
71 Tino Martinez .20 .50
72 Shannon Stewart .10 .30
73 Homer Bush .10 .30
74 Carlos Delgado .10 .30
75 Raul Ibanez .10 .30
76 Hideki Irabu .10 .30
77 Jose Cruz Jr. .10 .30
78 Tony Clark .10 .30
79 Wilton Guerrero .10 .30
80 Vladimir Guerrero .30 .75
81 Scott Rolen .20 .50
82 Nomar Garciaparra .50 1.25
83 Darin Erstad .10 .30
84 Chan Ho Park .10 .30
85 Mike Cameron .10 .30
86 Todd Walker .10 .30
87 Todd Dunwoody .10 .30
88 Neifi Perez .10 .30
89 Brett Tomko .10 .30
90 Jose Guillen .10 .30
91 Matt Morris .10 .30
92 Bartolo Colon .10 .30
93 Jaret Wright .10 .30
94 Shawn Estes .10 .30
95 Livan Hernandez .10 .30
96 Bobby Estalella .10 .30
97 Ben Grieve .10 .30
98 Paul Konerko .10 .30
99 David Ortiz .40 1.00
100 Todd Helton .20 .50
101 Juan Encarnacion .10 .30
102 Bubba Trammell .10 .30
103 Miguel Tejada .30 .75
104 Jacob Cruz .10 .30
105 Todd Greene .10 .30
106 Kevin Orie .10 .30
107 Mark Kotsay .10 .30
108 Fernando Tatis .10 .30
109 Jay Payton .10 .30
110 Pokey Reese .10 .30
111 Derrek Lee .20 .50
112 Richard Hidalgo .10 .30
113 Ricky Ledee UER .10 .30
114 Lou Collier .10 .30
115 Ruben Rivera .10 .30
116 Shawn Green .10 .30
117 Moises Alou .10 .30
118 Ken Griffey Jr. GEN .40 1.00
119 Frank Thomas GEN .20 .50
120 Alex Rodriguez GEN .30 .75
121 Mike Piazza GEN .30 .75
122 Greg Maddux GEN .30 .75
123 Cal Ripken GEN .50 1.25
124 Chipper Jones GEN .20 .50
125 Derek Jeter GEN .40 1.00
126 Tony Gwynn GEN .20 .50
127 Andruw Jones GEN .10 .30
128 Juan Gonzalez GEN .10 .30
129 Jeff Bagwell GEN .10 .30
130 Mark McGwire GEN .40 1.00
131 Roger Clemens GEN .30 .75
132 Albert Belle GEN .10 .30
133 Barry Bonds GEN .40 1.00
134 Kenny Lofton GEN .10 .30
135 Ivan Rodriguez GEN .10 .30
136 Manny Ramirez GEN .20 .50
137 Jim Thome GEN .10 .30
138 Chuck Knoblauch GEN .10 .30
139 Paul Molitor GEN .10 .30
140 Barry Larkin GEN .10 .30
141 Mo Vaughn GEN .10 .30
142 Hideki Irabu GEN .10 .30

143 Jose Cruz Jr. GEN .10 .30
144 Tony Clark GEN .10 .30
145 Vladimir Guerrero GEN .20 .50
146 Scott Rolen GEN .10 .30
147 Nomar Garciaparra GEN .30 .75
148 Nomar Garciaparra CL .30 .75
149 Larry Walker CL .10 .30
150 Tino Martinez CL .10 .30
AU2 F.Thomas AUTO/100 40.00 80.00

1998 Donruss Elite Aspirations

*ASPIRATION: 3X TO 8X BASIC CARDS
RANDOM INSERTS IN PACKS
STATED PRINT RUN 750 SETS

1998 Donruss Elite Status

COMPLETE SET (150) 4000.00 8000.00
*STATUS: 10X TO 25X BASIC
RANDOM INSERTS IN PACKS
STATED PRINT RUN 100 SERIAL #'d SETS
8 Derek Jeter 30.00 80.00

1998 Donruss Elite Back to the Future

COMPLETE SET (8) 60.00 120.00
STATED PRINT RUN 1400 SERIAL #'d SETS
1 C.Ripken 6.00 15.00
P.Konerko
2 J.Bagwell 1.25 3.00
T.Helton
3 E.Mathews 2.00 5.00
C.Jones
4 J.Gonzalez .75 2.00
B.Grieve
5 H.Aaron 3.00 8.00
J.Cruz Jr.
6 F.Thomas 2.50 6.00
D.Ortiz
7 N.Ryan 8.00 20.00
G.Maddux
8 A.Rodriguez 3.00 8.00
N.Garciaparra

1998 Donruss Elite Back to the Future Autographs

RANDOM INSERTS IN PACKS
STATED PRINT RUN 100 SERIAL #'d SETS
AU CARD NUMBER 6 DOES NOT EXIST
CARD 1A SIGNED BY KONERKO ONLY
CARD 1B SIGNED BY RIPKEN ONLY
ALL OTHERS SIGNED BY BOTH PLAYERS
COMP.SET INCLUDES CARDS 1A AND 1B
1A Paul Konerko AU/100 15.00 40.00
1B Cal Ripken AU/200 75.00 150.00
2 J.Bagwell/T.Helton 75.00 150.00
3 E.Mathews/C.Jones 300.00 500.00
4 J.Gonzalez/B.Grieve 50.00 120.00
5 H.Aaron/J.Cruz Jr. 150.00 250.00
7 N.Ryan/G.Maddux 800.00 1200.00
8 A.Rodriguez/N.Garciaparra 200.00 400.00

1998 Donruss Elite Craftsmen

COMPLETE SET (30) 30.00 60.00
STATED PRINT RUN 3500 SERIAL #'d SETS
*MASTER: 2.5X TO 6X BASIC CRAFTSMEN
MASTER PRINT RUN 100 SERIAL #'d SETS
RANDOM INSERTS IN PACKS
1 Ken Griffey Jr. 2.00 5.00
2 Frank Thomas 1.00 2.50
3 Alex Rodriguez 1.25 3.00
4 Cal Ripken 3.00 8.00
5 Greg Maddux 1.25 3.00
6 Mike Piazza 1.00 2.50
7 Chipper Jones 1.00 2.50
8 Derek Jeter 2.50 6.00
9 Tony Gwynn 1.00 2.50
10 Nomar Garciaparra .60 1.50
11 Scott Rolen .60 1.50
12 Jose Cruz Jr. .40 1.00
13 Tony Clark .40 1.00
14 Vladimir Guerrero .60 1.50
15 Todd Helton .60 1.50
16 Ben Grieve .40 1.00
17 Andruw Jones .40 1.00
18 Jeff Bagwell .60 1.50
19 Mark McGwire 1.50 4.00
20 Juan Gonzalez .40 1.00
21 Roger Clemens 1.25 3.00
22 Albert Belle .40 1.00
23 Barry Bonds 1.50 4.00
24 Kenny Lofton .40 1.00
25 Ivan Rodriguez .60 1.50
26 Paul Molitor 1.00 2.50
27 Barry Larkin .60 1.50
28 Mo Vaughn .40 1.00
29 Larry Walker .60 1.50
30 Tino Martinez .40 1.00

1998 Donruss Elite Prime Numbers Samples

COMPLETE SET (36) 175.00 350.00
1A Ken Griffey Jr. 2 6.00 15.00
1B Ken Griffey Jr. 9 6.00 15.00
1C Ken Griffey Jr. 4 6.00 15.00
2A Frank Thomas 4 2.50 6.00
2B Frank Thomas 5 2.50 6.00
2C Frank Thomas 6 2.50 6.00
3A Mark McGwire 3 6.00 15.00
3B Mark McGwire 8 6.00 15.00
3C Mark McGwire 7 6.00 15.00
4A Cal Ripken 5 8.00 20.00
4B Cal Ripken 1 8.00 20.00
4C Cal Ripken 7 8.00 20.00
5A Mike Piazza 5 6.00 15.00
5B Mike Piazza 7 6.00 15.00
5C Mike Piazza 6 6.00 15.00
6A Chipper Jones 4 4.00 10.00
6B Chipper Jones 8 4.00 10.00
6C Chipper Jones 9 4.00 10.00
7A Tony Gwynn 3 4.00 10.00
7B Tony Gwynn 7 4.00 10.00
7C Tony Gwynn 2 4.00 10.00
8A Barry Bonds 3 4.00 10.00
8B Barry Bonds 7 4.00 10.00
8C Barry Bonds 4 4.00 10.00
9A Jeff Bagwell 4 2.50 6.00
9B Jeff Bagwell 2 2.50 6.00
9C Jeff Bagwell 5 2.50 6.00
10A Juan Gonzalez 5 2.00 5.00
10B Juan Gonzalez 8 2.00 5.00
10C Juan Gonzalez 9 2.00 5.00
11A Alex Rodriguez 5 6.00 15.00
11B Alex Rodriguez 3 6.00 15.00
11C Alex Rodriguez 4 6.00 15.00
12A Kenny Lofton 3 1.50 4.00
12B Kenny Lofton 5 1.50 4.00
12C Kenny Lofton 4 1.50 4.00

1998 Donruss Elite Prime Numbers

RANDOM INSERTS IN PACKS
PRINT RUNS B/WN 17-670 COPIES PER
1A Ken Griffey Jr. 2 (94) 25.00 60.00
1B Ken Griffey Jr. 9/204 6.00 15.00
1C Ken Griffey Jr. 4/290 6.00 15.00
2A Frank Thomas 4/56 12.00 30.00
2B Frank Thomas 5/406 3.00 8.00
2C Frank Thomas 6/450 3.00 8.00
3A Mark McGwire 3/87 20.00 50.00
3B Mark McGwire 8/307 5.00 12.00
3C Mark McGwire 7/380 5.00 12.00
4A Cal Ripken 5/17 50.00 125.00
4B Cal Ripken 1/507 10.00 25.00
4C Cal Ripken 7/510 10.00 25.00
5A Mike Piazza 5/76 12.00 30.00
5B Mike Piazza 7/506 3.00 8.00
5C Mike Piazza 6/570 3.00 8.00
6A Chipper Jones 4/89 12.00 30.00
6B Chipper Jones 8/409 3.00 8.00
6C Chipper Jones 9/480 3.00 8.00
7A Tony Gwynn 3/72 12.00 30.00
7B Tony Gwynn 7/302 3.00 8.00
7C Tony Gwynn 2/370 3.00 8.00
8A Barry Bonds 3/74 20.00 50.00
8B Barry Bonds 7/304 5.00 12.00
8C Barry Bonds 4/370 5.00 12.00
9A Jeff Bagwell 4/25 10.00 25.00
9B Jeff Bagwell 2/405 2.00 5.00
9C Jeff Bagwell 5/420 2.00 5.00
10A Juan Gonzalez 5/89 5.00 12.00
10B Juan Gonzalez 8/509 1.25 3.00
10C Juan Gonzalez 9/580 1.25 3.00
11A Alex Rodriguez 5/34 20.00 50.00
11B Alex Rodriguez 3/504 4.00 10.00
11C Alex Rodriguez 4/530 4.00 10.00
12A Kenny Lofton 3/54 5.00 12.00
12B Kenny Lofton 5/304 1.25 3.00
12C Kenny Lofton 4 (350) 1.25 3.00

1998 Donruss Elite Prime Numbers Die Cuts

RANDOM INSERTS IN PACKS
PRINT RUNS IN PARENTHESIS BELOW
1A Ken Griffey Jr. 2/200 12.50 30.00
1B Ken Griffey Jr. 9/90 75.00 150.00
1C Ken Griffey Jr. 4/4
2A Frank Thomas 4/400 4.00 10.00
2B Frank Thomas 5/50 15.00 40.00
2C Frank Thomas 6/6
3A Mark McGwire 3/300 15.00 40.00
3B Mark McGwire 8/80 40.00 100.00
3C Mark McGwire 7/7
4A Cal Ripken 5/500 12.50 30.00
4B Cal Ripken 1/10
4C Cal Ripken 7/7
5A Mike Piazza 5/500 6.00 15.00
5B Mike Piazza 7/70 20.00 50.00
5C Mike Piazza 6/6
6A Chipper Jones 4/400 4.00 10.00
6B Chipper Jones 8/80 12.50 30.00
7A Tony Gwynn 3/300 6.00 15.00
7B Tony Gwynn 7/70 15.00 40.00
7C Tony Gwynn 2/2
8A Barry Bonds 3/300 12.50 30.00
8B Barry Bonds 7/70 30.00 80.00
8C Barry Bonds 4/4
9A Jeff Bagwell 4/400 2.50 6.00
9B Jeff Bagwell 2/20 30.00 80.00
9C Jeff Bagwell 5/5
10A Juan Gonzalez 5/500 2.00 5.00
10B Juan Gonzalez 8/80 6.00 15.00
10C Juan Gonzalez 9/9
11A Alex Rodriguez 5/500 6.00 15.00
11B Alex Rodriguez 3/30 40.00 100.00
11C Alex Rodriguez 4/4
12A Kenny Lofton 3/300 2.00 5.00
12B Kenny Lofton 5/50 8.00 20.00
12C Kenny Lofton 4/4

2001 Donruss Elite

COMP.SET w/o SP's (150) 10.00 25.00
COMMON CARD (1-150) .10 .30
COMMON CARD (151-200) 3.00 8.00
151-200 RANDOM INSERTS IN PACKS
151-200 PRINT RUN 900 SERIAL #'d SETS
151-200 1st 100 #'d COPIES ARE TC DIE CUTS
COMMON CARD (201-250) 4.00 10.00
201-250 COUPON STATED ODDS 1:14
201-250 ARE SERIAL #'d OF 1000 ON FRONT
201-250 ACTUAL PRINT RUNS LISTED BELOW
201-250 PR.RUNS PROVIDED BY DONRUSS
201-250 COUPON EXCH.DEADLINE 01/20/02
EACH COUPON WAS $5.99 TO REDEEM
ED ROGERS AU RANDOM IN ELITE FB PACKS
1 Alex Rodriguez .40 1.00
2 Barry Bonds .75 2.00
3 Cal Ripken 1.00 2.50
4 Chipper Jones .30 .75
5 Derek Jeter .75 2.00
6 Troy Glaus .10 .30
7 Frank Thomas .30 .75
8 Greg Maddux .50 1.25
9 Ivan Rodriguez .20 .50
10 Jeff Bagwell .20 .50
11 Jose Canseco .20 .50
12 Todd Helton .20 .50
13 Ken Griffey Jr. .60 1.50
14 Manny Ramirez Sox .20 .50
15 Mark McGwire .75 2.00
16 Mike Piazza .50 1.25
17 Nomar Garciaparra .50 1.25
18 Pedro Martinez .20 .50
19 Randy Johnson .30 .75
20 Rick Ankiel .10 .30
21 Rickey Henderson .30 .75
22 Roger Clemens .60 1.50
23 Sammy Sosa .30 .75
24 Tony Gwynn .40 1.00
25 Vladimir Guerrero .30 .75
26 Eric Davis .10 .30
27 Roberto Alomar .20 .50
28 Mark Mulder .10 .30
29 Pat Burrell .10 .30
30 Harold Baines .10 .30
31 Carlos Delgado .10 .30
32 J.D. Drew .10 .30
33 Jim Edmonds .10 .30
34 Darin Erstad .10 .30
35 Jason Giambi .10 .30
36 Tom Glavine .20 .50
37 Juan Gonzalez .10 .30
38 Mark Grace .20 .50
39 Shawn Green .10 .30
40 Tim Hudson .10 .30
41 Andruw Jones .20 .50
42 David Justice .10 .30
43 Jeff Kent .10 .30
44 Barry Larkin .20 .50
45 Pokey Reese .10 .30
46 Mike Mussina .20 .50
47 Hideo Nomo .30 .75
48 Rafael Palmeiro .20 .50
49 Adam Piatt .10 .30
50 Scott Rolen .20 .50
51 Gary Sheffield .10 .30
52 Bernie Williams .20 .50
53 Bob Abreu .10 .30
54 Edgardo Alfonzo .10 .30
55 Jermaine Clark RC .30 .75
56 Albert Belle .10 .30
57 Craig Biggio .20 .50
58 Andres Galarraga .10 .30
59 Edgar Martinez .20 .50
60 Fred McGriff .20 .50
61 Magglio Ordonez .10 .30
62 Jim Thome .20 .50
63 Matt Williams .10 .30
64 Kerry Wood .10 .30
65 Moises Alou .10 .30
66 Brady Anderson .10 .30
67 Garret Anderson .10 .30
68 Tony Armas Jr. .10 .30
69 Tony Batista .10 .30
70 Jose Cruz Jr. .10 .30
71 Carlos Beltran .10 .30
72 Adrian Beltre .10 .30
73 Kris Benson .10 .30
74 Lance Berkman .10 .30
75 Kevin Brown .10 .30
76 Jay Buhner .10 .30
77 Jeromy Burnitz .10 .30
78 Ken Caminiti .10 .30
79 Sean Casey .10 .30
80 Luis Castillo .10 .30
81 Eric Chavez .10 .30
82 Jeff Cirillo .10 .30
83 Bartolo Colon .10 .30
84 David Cone .10 .30
85 Freddy Garcia .10 .30
86 Johnny Damon .20 .50
87 Ray Durham .10 .30
88 Jermaine Dye .10 .30
89 Juan Encarnacion .10 .30
90 Terrence Long .10 .30
91 Carl Everett .10 .30
92 Steve Finley .10 .30
93 Cliff Floyd .10 .30
94 Brad Fullmer .10 .30
95 Brian Giles .10 .30
96 Luis Gonzalez .10 .30
97 Rusty Greer .10 .30
98 Jeffrey Hammonds .10 .30
99 Mike Hampton .10 .30
100 Orlando Hernandez .10 .30
101 Richard Hidalgo .10 .30
102 Geoff Jenkins .10 .30
103 Jacque Jones .10 .30
104 Brian Jordan .10 .30
105 Gabe Kapler .10 .30
106 Eric Karros .10 .30
107 Jason Kendall .10 .30
108 Adam Kennedy .10 .30
109 Byung-Hyun Kim .10 .30
110 Ryan Klesko .10 .30
111 Chuck Knoblauch .10 .30
112 Paul Konerko .10 .30
113 Carlos Lee .10 .30
114 Kenny Lofton .10 .30
115 Javy Lopez .10 .30
116 Tino Martinez .20 .50
117 Ruben Mateo .10 .30
118 Kevin Millwood .10 .30
119 Ben Molina .10 .30
120 Raul Mondesi .10 .30
121 Trot Nixon .10 .30
122 John Olerud .10 .30
123 Paul O'Neill .20 .50
124 Chan Ho Park .10 .30
125 Andy Pettitte .20 .50
126 Jorge Posada .20 .50
127 Mark Quinn .10 .30
128 Aramis Ramirez .10 .30
129 Mariano Rivera .30 .75
130 Tim Salmon .20 .50
131 Curt Schilling .10 .30
132 Richie Sexson .10 .30
133 John Smoltz .20 .50
134 J.T. Snow .10 .30
135 Jay Payton .10 .30
136 Shannon Stewart .10 .30
137 B.J. Surhoff .10 .30
138 Mike Sweeney .10 .30
139 Fernando Tatis .10 .30
140 Miguel Tejada .10 .30
141 Jason Varitek .30 .75
142 Greg Vaughn .10 .30
143 Mo Vaughn .10 .30
144 Robin Ventura .10 .30
145 Jose Vidro .10 .30
146 Omar Vizquel .20 .50
147 Larry Walker .10 .30
148 David Wells .10 .30
149 Rondell White .10 .30
150 Preston Wilson .10 .30
151 Brent Abernathy SP 3.00 8.00
152 Cory Aldridge SP RC 3.00 8.00
153 Gene Altman SP RC 3.00 8.00
154 Josh Beckett SP 4.00 10.00
155 Wilson Betemit SP RC 4.00 10.00
156 Albert Pujols SP RC 100.00 250.00
157 Joe Crede SP 4.00 10.00
158 Jack Cust SP 3.00 8.00
159 Ben Sheets SP 4.00 10.00
160 Alex Escobar SP 3.00 8.00
161 Adrian Hernandez SP RC 3.00 8.00
162 Pedro Feliz SP 3.00 8.00
163 Nate Frese SP RC 3.00 8.00
164 Carlos Garcia SP RC 3.00 8.00
165 Marcus Giles SP 3.00 8.00
166 Alexis Gomez SP RC 3.00 8.00
167 Jason Hart SP 3.00 8.00
168 Aubrey Huff SP 3.00 8.00
169 Cesar Izturis SP 3.00 8.00
170 Nick Johnson SP 3.00 8.00
171 Jack Wilson SP RC 4.00 10.00
172 Brian Lawrence SP RC 3.00 8.00
173 Christian Parker SP RC 3.00 8.00
174 Nick Maness SP RC 3.00 8.00
175 Jose Mieses SP RC 3.00 8.00
176 Greg Miller SP RC 3.00 8.00
177 Eric Munson SP 3.00 8.00
178 Xavier Nady SP 3.00 8.00
179 Blaine Neal SP RC 3.00 8.00
180 Abraham Nunez SP 3.00 8.00
181 Jose Ortiz SP 3.00 8.00
182 Jeremy Owens SP RC 3.00 8.00
183 Jay Gibbons SP RC 4.00 10.00
184 Corey Patterson SP 3.00 8.00
185 Carlos Pena SP 3.00 8.00
186 C.C. Sabathia SP 3.00 8.00
187 Timo Perez SP 3.00 8.00
188 Adam Pettyjohn SP RC 3.00 8.00
189 Donaldo Mendez SP RC 3.00 8.00
190 Jackson Melian SP RC 3.00 8.00
191 Wilkin Ruan SP RC 3.00 8.00
192 Duaner Sanchez SP RC 3.00 8.00
193 Alfonso Soriano SP 4.00 10.00
194 Rafael Soriano SP RC 3.00 8.00
195 Ichiro Suzuki SP RC 40.00 100.00
196 Billy Sylvester SP RC 3.00 8.00
197 Juan Uribe SP RC 4.00 10.00
198 Tsuyoshi Shinjo SP RC 4.00 10.00
199 Carlos Valderrama SP RC 3.00 8.00
200 Matt White SP RC 3.00 8.00
201 Adam Dunn/468 6.00 15.00
202 Joe Kennedy/465 XRC 6.00 15.00
203 Mike Rivera/427 XRC 4.00 10.00
204 Erick Almonte/401 XRC 4.00 10.00
205 Bran Duckworth/444 XRC 4.00 10.00
206 Victor Martinez/410 XRC 8.00 20.00
207 Rick Bauer/390 XRC 4.00 10.00
208 Jeff Deardorff/396 XRC 4.00 10.00
209 Antonio Perez/448 XRC 6.00 15.00
210 Bill Hall/404 XRC 15.00 40.00
211 Dennis Tankersley/425 XRC 4.00 10.00
212 Jeremy Affeldt/386 XRC 4.00 10.00
213 Junior Spivey/377 XRC 6.00 15.00
214 Casey Fossum/393 XRC 4.00 10.00
215 Brandon Lyon/402 XRC 4.00 10.00
216 Angel Santos/408 XRC 4.00 10.00
217 Cody Ransom/404 XRC 4.00 10.00
218 Jason Lane/424 XRC 6.00 15.00
219 David Williams/408 XRC 4.00 10.00
220 Alex Herrera/405 XRC 4.00 10.00
221 Ryan Drese/378 XRC 6.00 15.00
222 Travis Hafner/419 XRC 8.00 20.00
223 Bud Smith/468 XRC 4.00 10.00
224 Johnny Estrada/415 XRC 6.00 15.00
225 Ricardo Rodriguez/428 XRC 4.00 10.00
226 Brandon Berger/428 XRC 4.00 10.00
227 Claudio Vargas/395 XRC 4.00 10.00
228 Luis Garcia/438 XRC 4.00 10.00
229 Marlon Byrd/452 XRC 4.00 10.00
230 Hee Seop Choi/479 XRC 6.00 15.00
231 Corky Miller/431 XRC 4.00 10.00
232 Justin Duchscherer/423 XRC 4.00 10.00
233 Tim Spooneybarger/423 XRC 4.00 10.00
234 Roy Oswalt/427 6.00 15.00
235 Willie Harris/418 XRC 4.00 10.00
236 Josh Towers/437 XRC 6.00 15.00
237 Juan A.Pena/400 XRC 4.00 10.00
238 Alfredo Amezaga/420 XRC 4.00 10.00
239 Geronimo Gil/396 XRC 4.00 10.00
240 Juan Cruz/489 XRC 4.00 10.00
241 Ed Rogers/429 XRC 4.00 10.00
242 Joe Thurston/420 XRC 4.00 10.00
243 Orlando Hudson/450 XRC 6.00 15.00
244 John Buck/416 XRC 8.00 20.00
245 Martin Vargas/400 XRC 4.00 10.00
246 David Brous/399 XRC 4.00 10.00
247 Dewon Brazelton/471 XRC 4.00 10.00
248 Mark Prior/556 XRC 15.00 40.00
249 Angel Berroa/420 XRC 6.00 15.00
250 Mark Teixeira/543 XRC 10.00 25.00

2001 Donruss Elite Aspirations

*1-150 PRINT RUN b/wn 81-100: 4X TO 10X
*1-150 PRINT RUN b/wn 66-80: 5X TO 12X
*1-150 PRINT RUN b/wn 51-65: 5X TO 12X
*1-150 PRINT RUN b/wn 36-50: 6X TO 15X
*1-150 PRINT RUN b/wn 26-35: 8X TO 20X
COMMON (151-200) p/r 81-100 1.50 4.00
MINOR 151-200 p/r 81-100 2.50 6.00
UNLISTED 151-200 p/r 81-100 6.00 15.00
MINOR 151-200 p/r 66-80 3.00 8.00
SEMISTARS 151-200 p/r 66-80 5.00 12.00
UNLISTED 151-200 p/r 66-80 8.00 20.00
MINOR 151-200 p/r 51-65 4.00 10.00
UNLISTED 151-200 p/r 51-65 10.00 25.00
COMMON (151-200) p/r 36-50 3.00 8.00
MINOR 151-200 p/r 36-50 5.00 12.00
SEMISTARS 151-200 p/r 36-50 8.00 20.00
UNLISTED 151-200 p/r 36-50 12.50 30.00
COMMON (151-200) p/r 26-35 4.00 10.00
MINOR 151-200 p/r 26-35 6.00 15.00
UNLISTED 151-200 p/r 26-35 15.00 40.00
UNLISTED 151-200 p/r 21-25 20.00 50.00
MINOR 151-200 p/r 16-20 10.00 25.00
SEE BECKETT.COM FOR PRINT RUNS
PRINTS b/wn 1-15 TOO SCARCE TO PRICE
RC'S OF 25 OR LESS TOO SCARCE TO PRICE
195 Ichiro Suzuki/49 150.00 400.00

2001 Donruss Elite Status

*1-150 PRINT RUN b/wn 81-100: 4X TO 10X
*1-150 PRINT RUN b/wn 66-80: 5X TO 12X
*1-150 PRINT RUN b/wn 51-65: 5X TO 12X
*1-150 PRINT RUN b/wn 36-50: 6X TO 15X
*1-150 PRINT RUN b/wn 26-35: 8X TO 20X
*1-150 PRINT RUN b/wn 21-25: 10X TO 25X
*1-150 PRINT RUN b/wn 16-20: 12.5X TO 30X
MINOR 151-200 p/r 81-100 2.50 6.00
COMMON (151-200) p/r 66-80 2.00 5.00
MINOR 151-200 p/r 66-80 3.00 8.00
UNLISTED 151-200 p/r 66-80 8.00 20.00
COMMON (151-200) p/r 51-65 2.50 6.00
MINOR 151-200 p/r 51-65 4.00 10.00
SEMISTARS 151-200 p/r 51-65 6.00 15.00
UNLISTED 151-200 p/r 51-65 10.00 25.00
MINOR 151-200 p/r 36-50 5.00 12.00
SEMISTARS 151-200 p/r 36-50 8.00 20.00
MINOR 151-200 p/r 21-25 8.00 20.00
UNLISTED 151-200 p/r 21-25 20.00 50.00
MINOR 151-200 p/r 16-20 10.00 25.00
SEMISTARS 151-200 p/r 16-20 15.00 40.00
UNLISTED 151-200 p/r 16-20 25.00 60.00
SEE BECKETT.COM FOR PRINT RUNS
PRINTS b/wn 1-15 TOO SCARCE TO PRICE
156 Albert Pujols/68 300.00 800.00
195 Ichiro Suzuki/51 200.00 500.00

2001 Donruss Elite Extra Edition Autographs

AVAILABLE VIA MAIL EXCHANGE
STATED PRINT RUN 100 SERIAL #'d SETS
234 Roy Oswalt 6.00 15.00
238 Alfredo Amezaga 6.00 15.00
241 Ed Rogers 6.00 15.00

2001 Donruss Elite Turn of the Century Autographs

STATED PRINT RUN 100 SERIAL #'d SETS
CARDS DISPLAY CUMULATIVE PRINT RUN
CARDS 195 AND 198 DO NOT EXIST
151 Brent Abernathy 6.00 15.00
152 Cory Aldridge 4.00 10.00
153 Gene Altman 4.00 10.00
154 Josh Beckett 40.00 80.00
155 Wilson Betemit 20.00 50.00
156 Albert Pujols 600.00 1500.00
157 Joe Crede 15.00 40.00
158 Jack Cust 6.00 15.00
159 Ben Sheets 15.00 40.00
160 Alex Escobar 6.00 15.00
161 Adrian Hernandez 4.00 10.00
162 Pedro Feliz 6.00 15.00
163 Nate Frese 6.00 15.00
164 Carlos Garcia 4.00 10.00
165 Marcus Giles 10.00 25.00
166 Alexis Gomez 4.00 10.00
167 Jason Hart 6.00 15.00
168 Aubrey Huff 10.00 25.00
169 Cesar Izturis 6.00 15.00
170 Nick Johnson 10.00 25.00
171 Jack Wilson 10.00 25.00
172 Brian Lawrence 6.00 15.00
173 Christian Parker 4.00 10.00
174 Nick Maness 6.00 15.00
175 Jose Mieses 6.00 15.00
176 Greg Miller 4.00 10.00
177 Eric Munson 6.00 15.00
178 Xavier Nady 15.00 40.00
179 Blaine Neal 4.00 10.00
180 Abraham Nunez 6.00 15.00
181 Jose Ortiz 6.00 15.00
182 Jeremy Owens 6.00 15.00
183 Jay Gibbons 10.00 25.00
184 Corey Patterson 6.00 15.00
185 Carlos Pena 6.00 15.00
186 C.C. Sabathia 10.00 25.00
187 Timo Perez 6.00 15.00
188 Adam Pettyjohn 4.00 10.00
189 Donaldo Mendez 4.00 10.00
190 Jackson Melian 4.00 10.00
191 Wilkin Ruan 6.00 15.00
192 Duaner Sanchez 4.00 10.00
193 Alfonso Soriano 6.00 15.00
194 Rafael Soriano 6.00 15.00
196 Billy Sylvester 4.00 10.00
197 Juan Uribe 10.00 25.00
199 Carlos Valderrama 4.00 10.00
200 Matt White 6.00 15.00

2001 Donruss Elite Back 2 Back Jacks

SINGLES PRINT RUN 100 SERIAL #'d SETS
DOUBLES PRINT RUN 50 SERIAL #'d SETS
SP PRINT RUNS LISTED BELOW
BB1 Ernie Banks SP/75 10.00 25.00
BB2 Ryne Sandberg SP/75 20.00 50.00
BB3 Babe Ruth 100.00 200.00
BB4 Lou Gehrig 75.00 150.00
BB5 Eddie Mathews 10.00 25.00
BB6 Troy Glaus SP/50 10.00 25.00
BB7 Don Mattingly SP/50 30.00 60.00
BB8 Todd Helton 10.00 25.00
BB9 Wade Boggs 10.00 25.00
BB10 Tony Gwynn 10.00 25.00
BB11 Robin Yount 6.00 15.00
BB12 Paul Molitor SP/50 10.00 25.00
BB13 Mike Schmidt SP/50 20.00 50.00
BB14 Scott Rolen SP/75 10.00 25.00
BB15 Reggie Jackson 10.00 25.00
BB16 Dave Winfield 6.00 15.00
BB17 Johnny Bench SP/50 15.00 40.00
BB18 Joe Morgan 6.00 15.00
BB19 Brooks Robinson SP/50 15.00 40.00
BB20 Cal Ripken 20.00 50.00
BB21 Ty Cobb 25.00 60.00
BB22 Al Kaline SP/50 15.00 40.00
BB23 Frank Robinson SP/50 15.00 40.00
BB24 Frank Thomas 10.00 25.00
BB25 Roberto Clemente 15.00 40.00
BB26 Vladimir Guerrero SP/50 15.00 40.00
BB27 Harmon Killebrew SP/50 15.00 40.00
BB28 Kirby Puckett 15.00 40.00
BB29 Yogi Berra SP/75 15.00 40.00
BB30 Phil Rizzuto SP/75 15.00 40.00
BB31 Banks/Sandberg 50.00 100.00
BB32 Ruth/Gehrig 150.00 250.00
BB33 Mathews/Glaus 30.00 60.00
BB34 Mattingly/Helton 50.00 100.00
BB35 Boggs/Gwynn 15.00 40.00
BB36 Yount/Molitor 30.00 60.00
BB37 Schmidt/Rolen 50.00 100.00
BB38 R.Jackson/Winfield 15.00 40.00
BB39 Bench/Morgan 30.00 60.00
BB40 B.Robinson/Ripken 60.00 120.00
BB41 Cobb/Kaline 100.00 200.00
BB42 F.Robinson/Thomas 30.00 60.00
BB43 Clemente/Guerrero 60.00 120.00
BB44 Killebrew/Puckett 50.00 100.00

2001 Donruss Elite Back 2 Back Jacks Autograph

STATED PRINT RUNS LISTED BELOW
NO PRICING ON QTY OF 25 OR LESS
BB6 Troy Glaus/50 10.00 25.00
BB7 Don Mattingly/50 30.00 60.00
BB12 Paul Molitor/50 30.00 60.00
BB13 Mike Schmidt/50 40.00 80.00
BB17 Johnny Bench/50 60.00 120.00
BB19 Brooks Robinson/50 15.00 40.00
BB22 Al Kaline/50 60.00 150.00
BB23 Frank Robinson/50 15.00 40.00
BB26 Vladimir Guerrero/50 60.00 120.00
BB27 Harmon Killebrew/50 75.00 150.00

2001 Donruss Elite Passing the Torch

SINGLES PRINT RUN 1000 SERIAL #'d SETS
DOUBLES PRINT RUN 500 SERIAL #'d SETS
PT1 Stan Musial 3.00 8.00
PT2 Tony Gwynn 2.00 5.00
PT3 Willie Mays 4.00 10.00
PT4 Barry Bonds 3.00 8.00
PT5 Mike Schmidt 3.00 8.00
PT6 Scott Rolen 1.25 3.00
PT7 Cal Ripken 6.00 15.00
PT8 Alex Rodriguez 2.50 6.00
PT9 Hank Aaron 4.00 10.00
PT10 Andruw Jones 1.25 3.00
PT11 Nolan Ryan 6.00 15.00
PT12 Pedro Martinez 1.25 3.00
PT13 Wade Boggs 1.25 3.00
PT14 Nomar Garciaparra 1.25 3.00
PT15 Don Mattingly 4.00 10.00
PT16 Todd Helton 1.25 3.00
PT17 S.Musial 3.00 8.00
T.Gwynn
PT18 W.Mays 4.00 10.00
B.Bonds
PT19 M.Schmidt 3.00 8.00
S.Rolen
PT20 C.Ripken 6.00 15.00
A.Rodriguez
PT21 H.Aaron 4.00 10.00
A.Jones
PT22 N.Ryan 6.00 15.00
P.Martinez
PT23 W.Boggs 1.25 3.00
N.Garciaparra
PT24 D.Mattingly 4.00 10.00
T.Helton

2001 Donruss Elite Passing the Torch Autographs

SINGLES PRINT RUN 100 SERIAL #'d SETS
DOUBLES PRINT RUN 50 SERIAL #'d SETS
PT1 Stan Musial 60.00 120.00
PT2 Tony Gwynn 40.00 80.00
PT3 Willie Mays 200.00 400.00
PT4 Barry Bonds 125.00 250.00
PT5 Mike Schmidt 30.00 80.00
PT6 Scott Rolen 30.00 60.00
PT7 Cal Ripken 125.00 200.00
PT8 Alex Rodriguez 100.00 175.00
PT9 Hank Aaron 175.00 300.00
PT10 Andruw Jones 20.00 50.00
PT11 Nolan Ryan 75.00 150.00
PT12 Pedro Martinez 75.00 150.00
PT13 Wade Boggs 30.00 60.00
PT14 Nomar Garciaparra 20.00 50.00
PT15 Don Mattingly 60.00 120.00
PT16 Todd Helton 20.00 50.00
PT17 S.Musial/T.Gwynn 250.00 500.00
PT18 W.Mays/B.Bonds 900.00 1200.00
PT19 M.Schmidt/S.Rolen 125.00 200.00
PT20 C.Ripken/A.Rodriguez 500.00 800.00
PT21 H.Aaron/A.Jones 250.00 400.00
PT22 N.Ryan/P.Martinez 250.00 400.00
PT22FBA N.Ryan/R.Clemens FB 250.00 500.00
PT22FBB Roger Clemens
Nolan Ryan FB
PT23FB W.Boggs/N.G'parra FB 150.00 300.00
PT24FB D.Mattingly/T.Helton FB 60.00 120.00

2001 Donruss Elite Primary Colors Red

COMPLETE SET (40) 200.00 400.00
STATED PRINT RUN 975 SERIAL #'d SETS
*BLUE: .6X TO 1.5X BASIC RED
BLUE PRINT RUN 200 SERIAL #'d SETS
*BLUE DIE CUT: 1.25X TO 3X BASIC RED
BLUE DC PRINT RUN 50 SERIAL #'d SETS
*RED DIE CUT: 2X TO 5X BASIC RED
RED DC PRINT RUN 25 SERIAL #'d SETS
*YELLOW: 2X TO 5X BASIC RED
YELLOW PRINT RUN 25 SERIAL #'d SETS
*YELLOW DIE CUT: 1X TO 2.5X BASIC RED
YELLOW DC PRINT RUN 75 SERIAL #'d SETS
PC1 Alex Rodriguez 5.00 12.00
PC2 Barry Bonds 8.00 20.00
PC3 Cal Ripken 12.50 30.00
PC4 Chipper Jones 4.00 10.00
PC5 Derek Jeter 4.00 10.00
PC6 Troy Glaus 2.00 5.00
PC7 Frank Thomas 4.00 10.00
PC8 Greg Maddux 6.00 15.00
PC9 Ivan Rodriguez 2.50 6.00
PC10 Jeff Bagwell 2.50 6.00
PC11 Todd Helton 2.50 6.00
PC12 Ken Griffey Jr. 8.00 20.00
PC13 Manny Ramirez Sox 2.50 6.00
PC14 Mark McGwire 10.00 25.00
PC15 Mike Piazza 6.00 15.00
PC16 Nomar Garciaparra 6.00 15.00
PC17 Pedro Martinez 2.50 6.00
PC18 Randy Johnson 4.00 10.00
PC19 Rick Ankiel 2.00 5.00
PC20 Roger Clemens 8.00 20.00
PC21 Sammy Sosa 4.00 10.00
PC22 Tony Gwynn 5.00 12.00
PC23 Vladimir Guerrero 4.00 10.00
PC24 Carlos Delgado 2.00 5.00
PC25 Jason Giambi 2.00 5.00
PC26 Andruw Jones 2.50 6.00
PC27 Bernie Williams 2.50 6.00
PC28 Roberto Alomar 2.50 6.00
PC29 Shawn Green 2.00 5.00
PC30 Barry Larkin 2.50 6.00
PC31 Scott Rolen 2.50 6.00
PC32 Gary Sheffield 2.00 5.00
PC33 Rafael Palmeiro 2.50 6.00
PC34 Albert Belle 2.00 5.00
PC35 Magglio Ordonez 2.00 5.00
PC36 Jim Thome 2.50 6.00
PC37 Jim Edmonds 2.00 5.00
PC38 Darin Erstad 2.00 5.00
PC39 Kris Benson 2.00 5.00
PC40 Sean Casey 2.00 5.00

2001 Donruss Elite Prime Numbers

RANDOM INSERTS IN PACKS
STATED PRINT RUNS LISTED BELOW
PN1A Alex Rodriguez/300 6.00 15.00
PN1B Alex Rodriguez/50 15.00 40.00
PN2A Ken Griffey Jr./400 10.00 25.00
PN2B Ken Griffey Jr./30 25.00 60.00
PN3A Mark McGwire/500 8.00 20.00
PN3B Mark McGwire/50 20.00 50.00
PN4A Cal Ripken/400 15.00 40.00
PN5A Derek Jeter/300 12.00 30.00
PN5B Derek Jeter/20 30.00 80.00
PN6A Mike Piazza/300 5.00 12.00
PN6B Mike Piazza/60 12.00 30.00
PN7A Nomar Garciaparra/300 3.00 8.00
PN7B Nomar Garciaparra/70 8.00 20.00
PN8A Sammy Sosa/300 3.00 8.00
PN8B Sammy Sosa/80 8.00 20.00
PN9A Vladimir Guerrero/300 5.00 12.00
PN9B Vladimir Guerrero/40 12.00 30.00
PN10A Tony Gwynn/300 5.00 12.00
PN10B Tony Gwynn/90 12.00 30.00

2001 Donruss Elite Prime Numbers Die Cuts

PN1A Alex Rodriguez/58 15.00 40.00
PN1B Alex Rodriguez/308 6.00 15.00
PN1C Alex Rodriguez/350 6.00 15.00
PN2A Ken Griffey Jr./38 40.00 100.00
PN2B Ken Griffey Jr./408 15.00 40.00
PN2C Ken Griffey Jr./430 15.00 40.00
PN3A Mark McGwire/54 20.00 50.00
PN3B Mark McGwire/504 8.00 20.00
PN3C Mark McGwire/550 8.00 20.00
PN4B Cal Ripken/407 15.00 40.00
PN4C Cal Ripken/410 15.00 40.00
PN5A Derek Jeter/22 30.00 80.00
PN5B Derek Jeter/302 12.00 30.00
PN5C Derek Jeter/320 12.00 30.00
PN6A Mike Piazza/62 12.00 30.00
PN6B Mike Piazza/302 5.00 12.00
PN6C Mike Piazza/360 5.00 12.00
PN7A Nomar Garciaparra/72 8.00 20.00
PN7B Nomar Garciaparra/302 3.00 8.00
PN7C Nomar Garciaparra/370 3.00 8.00
PN8A Sammy Sosa/86 8.00 20.00
PN8B Sammy Sosa/306 3.00 8.00
PN8C Sammy Sosa/380 3.00 8.00
PN9A Vladimir Guerrero/45 12.00 30.00
PN9B Vladimir Guerrero/305 5.00 12.00
PN9C Vladimir Guerrero/340 5.00 12.00
PN10A Tony Gwynn/94 12.00 30.00
PN10B Tony Gwynn/304 5.00 12.00
PN10C Tony Gwynn/390 5.00 12.00

2001 Donruss Elite Throwback Threads

SINGLES PRINT RUN 100 SERIAL #'d SETS
DOUBLES PRINT RUN 50 SERIAL #'d SETS
SP PRINT RUNS LISTED BELOW
NO PRICING ON QTY OF 25 OR LESS
TT1 Stan Musial SP/75 30.00 60.00
TT2 Tony Gwynn SP/75 15.00 40.00
TT3 Willie McCovey 6.00 15.00
TT4 Barry Bonds 20.00 50.00
TT5 Babe Ruth 175.00 300.00
TT6 Lou Gehrig 75.00 150.00
TT7 Mike Schmidt SP/75 20.00 50.00
TT8 Scott Rolen 10.00 25.00
TT9 Harmon Killebrew SP/75 15.00 40.00
TT10 Kirby Puckett 10.00 25.00
TT11 Al Kaline SP/75 15.00 40.00
TT12 Eddie Mathews 10.00 25.00
TT13 Hank Aaron SP/75 40.00 80.00
TT14 Andruw Jones SP/50 15.00 40.00
TT15 Lou Brock 10.00 25.00
TT16 Ozzie Smith 10.00 25.00
TT18 Ryne Sandberg 20.00 50.00
TT19 Roberto Clemente 50.00 100.00
TT20 Vladimir Guerrero SP/50 15.00 40.00
TT21 Frank Robinson SP/50 15.00 40.00
TT22 Frank Thomas SP/50 15.00 40.00
TT23 Brooks Robinson SP/50 15.00 40.00
TT24 Cal Ripken 10.00 25.00
TT25 Roger Clemens 10.00 25.00
TT26 Pedro Martinez 10.00 25.00
TT27 Reggie Jackson 10.00 25.00
TT28 Dave Winfield 6.00 15.00
TT29 Don Mattingly SP/50 30.00 60.00

TT30 Todd Helton 10.00 25.00
TT32 McCovey/Bonds 50.00 100.00
TT33 B.Ruth/L.Gehrig 350.00 600.00
TT35 Killebrew/Puckett 40.00 80.00
TT36 Kaline/Mathews 50.00 100.00
TT37 Aaron/A.Jones 20.00 50.00
TT38 Brock/O.Smith 15.00 40.00
TT40 Clemente/Guerrero 30.00 60.00
TT41 F.Robinson/Thomas 30.00 60.00
TT42 B.Robinson/Ripken 50.00 100.00
TT43 Clemens/Pedro 40.00 80.00
TT44 R.Jackson/Winfield 12.00 30.00
TT45 Mattingly/Helton 40.00 80.00

2001 Donruss Elite Throwback Threads Autographs

PRINT RUNS LISTED BELOW
NO PRICING ON QTY OF 25 OR LESS
TT14 Andruw Jones/50 6.00 15.00
TT20 Vladimir Guerrero/50 50.00 100.00
TT21 Frank Robinson/50 FB 40.00 80.00
TT22 Frank Thomas/50 FB 75.00 150.00
TT23 Brooks Robinson/50 40.00 80.00
TT29 Don Mattingly/50 75.00 150.00

2001 Donruss Elite Title Waves

COMPLETE SET (30) 50.00 120.00
*HOLO: 1.5X TO 4X BASIC WAVES
HOLO-FOIL PRINT RUN 100 SERIAL #'d SETS
TW1 Tony Gwynn/1994 2.00 5.00
TW2 Todd Helton/2000 1.25 3.00
TW3 Nomar Garciaparra/2000 1.25 3.00
TW4 Frank Thomas/1997 2.00 5.00
TW5 Alex Rodriguez/1996 2.50 6.00
TW6 Jeff Bagwell/1994 1.25 3.00
TW7 Mark McGwire/1998 3.00 8.00
TW8 Sammy Sosa/2000 1.25 3.00
TW9 Ken Griffey Jr./1997 4.00 10.00
TW10 Albert Belle/1995 .75 2.00
TW11 Barry Bonds/1993 3.00 8.00
TW12 Jose Canseco/1991 1.25 3.00
TW13 Manny Ramirez Sox/1999 2.00 5.00
TW14 Sammy Sosa/1998 1.25 3.00
TW15 Andres Galarraga/1996 1.25 3.00
TW16 Todd Helton/2000 1.25 3.00
TW17 Ken Griffey Jr./1997 4.00 10.00
TW18 Jeff Bagwell/1994 1.25 3.00
TW19 Mike Piazza/1995 2.00 5.00
TW20 Alex Rodriguez/1995 2.50 6.00
TW21 Jason Giambi/2000 .75 2.00
TW22 Ivan Rodriguez/1999 1.25 3.00
TW23 Greg Maddux/1997 3.00 8.00
TW24 Pedro Martinez/1994 1.25 3.00
TW25 Derek Jeter/2000 5.00 12.00
TW26 Bernie Williams/1998 1.25 3.00
TW27 Roger Clemens/1999 3.00 8.00
TW28 Chipper Jones/1995 2.00 5.00
TW29 Mark McGwire/1990 3.00 8.00
TW30 Cal Ripken/1983 6.00 15.00

2002 Donruss Elite Samples

*SAMPLES: 1.5X TO 4X BASIC CARDS
ONE PER SEALED BBCM 207
*GOLD: 4X TO 10X BASIC SAMPLES
GOLD 10% OF PRESS RUN

2002 Donruss Elite

COMP.LO SET w/o SP's (100) 8.00 20.00
COMMON CARD (1-100) .10 .30
COMMON CARD (101-150) .75 2.00
101-150 STATED ODDS 1:10
COMMON CARD (151-200) 2.00 5.00
151-200 RANDOM INSERTS IN PACKS
151-200 STATED PRINT RUN 1500
151-200 1st 150 #'d COPIES ARE TC DIE CUTS
COMMON CARD (201-275) 2.00 5.00
201-275 RANDOM IN DONRUSS ROOK.PACKS
201-275 STATED PRINT RUN 1000
201-275 1st 100 #'D COPIES ARE TC DIE CUT
CARDS 256/263/267-271 DO NOT EXIST
1 Vladimir Guerrero .30 .75
2 Bernie Williams .20 .50
3 Ichiro Suzuki .60 1.50
4 Roger Clemens .60 1.50
5 Greg Maddux .50 1.25
6 Fred McGriff .20 .50
7 Jermaine Dye .10 .30
8 Ken Griffey Jr. .60 1.50
9 Todd Helton .20 .50
10 Torii Hunter .10 .30
11 Pat Burrell .10 .30
12 Chipper Jones .30 .75
13 Ivan Rodriguez .20 .50
14 Roy Oswalt .10 .30
15 Shannon Stewart .10 .30
16 Magglio Ordonez .10 .30
17 Lance Berkman .10 .30
18 Mark Mulder .10 .30
19 Al Leiter .10 .30
20 Sammy Sosa .30 .75
21 Scott Rolen .20 .50
22 Aramis Ramirez .10 .30
23 Alfonso Soriano .10 .30
24 Phil Nevin .10 .30
25 Barry Bonds .75 2.00
26 Joe Mays .10 .30
27 Jeff Kent .10 .30
28 Mark Quinn .10 .30
29 Adrian Beltre .10 .30
30 Freddy Garcia .10 .30
31 Pedro Martinez .20 .50
32 Darryl Kile .10 .30
33 Mike Cameron .10 .30
34 Frank Catalanotto .10 .30
35 Jose Vidro .10 .30
36 Jim Thome .20 .50
37 Javy Lopez .10 .30
38 Paul Konerko .10 .30
39 Jeff Bagwell .20 .50
40 Curt Schilling .10 .30
41 Miguel Tejada .10 .30
42 Jim Edmonds .10 .30
43 Ellis Burks .10 .30
44 Mark Grace .20 .50
45 Robb Nen .10 .30
46 Jeff Conine .10 .30
47 Derek Jeter .75 2.00
48 Mike Lowell .10 .30
49 Javier Vazquez .10 .30
50 Manny Ramirez .20 .50
51 Bartolo Colon .10 .30
52 Carlos Beltran .10 .30
53 Tim Hudson .10 .30
54 Rafael Palmeiro .20 .50
55 Jimmy Rollins .10 .30
56 Andruw Jones .20 .50
57 Orlando Cabrera .10 .30
58 Dean Palmer .10 .30
59 Bret Boone .10 .30
60 Carlos Febles .10 .30
61 Ben Grieve .10 .30
62 Richie Sexson .10 .30
63 Alex Rodriguez .40 1.00
64 Juan Pierre .10 .30
65 Bobby Higginson .10 .30
66 Barry Zito .10 .30
67 Raul Mondesi .10 .30
68 Albert Pujols .60 1.50
69 Omar Vizquel .20 .50
70 Bobby Abreu .10 .30
71 Corey Koskie .10 .30
72 Tom Glavine .20 .50
73 Paul LoDuca .10 .30
74 Terrence Long .10 .30
75 Matt Morris .10 .30
76 Andy Pettitte .20 .50
77 Rich Aurilia .10 .30
78 Todd Walker .10 .30
79 John Olerud .10 .30
80 Mike Sweeney .10 .30
81 Ray Durham .10 .30
82 Fernando Vina .10 .30
83 Nomar Garciaparra .50 1.25
84 Mariano Rivera .30 .75
85 Mike Piazza .50 1.25
86 Mark Buehrle .10 .30
87 Adam Dunn .10 .30
88 Luis Gonzalez .10 .30
89 Richard Hidalgo .10 .30
90 Brad Radke .10 .30
91 Russ Ortiz .10 .30
92 Brian Giles .10 .30
93 Billy Wagner .10 .30
94 Cliff Floyd .10 .30
95 Eric Milton .10 .30
96 Bud Smith .10 .30
97 Wade Miller .10 .30
98 Jon Lieber .10 .30
99 Derrek Lee .20 .50
100 Jose Cruz Jr. .10 .30
101 Dmitri Young STAR .75 2.00
102 Mo Vaughn STAR .75 2.00
103 Tino Martinez STAR 1.25 3.00
104 Larry Walker STAR .75 2.00
105 Chuck Knoblauch STAR .75 2.00
106 Troy Glaus STAR .75 2.00
107 Jason Giambi STAR .75 2.00
108 Travis Fryman STAR .75 2.00
109 Josh Beckett STAR .75 2.00
110 Edgar Martinez STAR 1.25 3.00
111 Tim Salmon STAR 1.25 3.00
112 C.C. Sabathia STAR .75 2.00
113 Randy Johnson STAR 2.00 5.00
114 Juan Gonzalez STAR .75 2.00
115 Carlos Delgado STAR .75 2.00
116 Hideo Nomo STAR 2.00 5.00
117 Kerry Wood STAR .75 2.00
118 Brian Jordan STAR .75 2.00
119 Carlos Pena STAR .75 2.00
120 Roger Cedeno STAR .75 2.00
121 Chan Ho Park STAR .75 2.00
122 Rafael Furcal STAR .75 2.00
123 Frank Thomas STAR 2.00 5.00
124 Mike Mussina STAR 1.25 3.00
125 Rickey Henderson STAR 2.00 5.00
126 Sean Casey STAR .75 2.00
127 Barry Larkin STAR 1.25 3.00
128 Kazuhiro Sasaki STAR .75 2.00
129 Moises Alou STAR .75 2.00
130 Jeff Cirillo STAR .75 2.00
131 Jason Kendall STAR .75 2.00
132 Gary Sheffield STAR .75 2.00
133 Ryan Klesko STAR .75 2.00
134 Kevin Brown STAR .75 2.00
135 Darin Erstad STAR .75 2.00
136 Roberto Alomar STAR 1.25 3.00
137 Brad Fullmer STAR .75 2.00
138 Eric Chavez STAR .75 2.00
139 Ben Sheets STAR .75 2.00
140 Trot Nixon STAR .75 2.00
141 Garret Anderson STAR .75 2.00
142 Shawn Green STAR .75 2.00
143 Troy Percival STAR .75 2.00
144 Craig Biggio STAR 1.25 3.00
145 Jorge Posada STAR 1.25 3.00
146 J.D. Drew STAR .75 2.00
147 Johnny Damon STAR 1.25 3.00
148 Jeromy Burnitz STAR .75 2.00
149 Robin Ventura STAR .75 2.00
150 Aaron Sele STAR .75 2.00
151 Cam Esslinger/1350* RC 2.00 5.00
152 Ben Howard/1350* RC 2.00 5.00
153 Brandon Backe/1350* RC 3.00 8.00
154 Jorge De La Rosa/1350* RC 2.00 5.00
155 Austin Kearns/1350* 2.00 5.00
156 Carlos Zambrano/1350* 2.00 5.00
157 Kyle Kane/1350* RC 2.00 5.00
158 So Taguchi/1350* RC 3.00 8.00
159 Brian Mallette/1350* RC 2.00 5.00
160 Brett Jodie/1350* 2.00 5.00
161 Elio Serrano/1350* RC 2.00 5.00
162 Joe Thurston/1350* 2.00 5.00
163 Kevin Olsen/1350* 2.00 5.00
164 Rodrigo Rosario/1350* RC 2.00 5.00
165 Matt Guerrier/1350* 2.00 5.00
166 Anderson Machado/1350* RC 2.00 5.00
167 Bert Snow/1350* 2.00 5.00
168 Franklyn German/1350* RC 2.00 5.00
169 Brandon Claussen/1350* 2.00 5.00
170 Jason Romano/1350* 2.00 5.00
171 Jorge Padilla/1350* RC 2.00 5.00
172 Jose Cueto/1350* 2.00 5.00
173 Allan Simpson/1350* RC 2.00 5.00
174 Doug Devore/1350* RC 2.00 5.00
175 Justin Duchscherer/1350* 2.00 5.00
176 Josh Pearce/1350* 2.00 5.00
177 Steve Bechler/1350* RC 2.00 5.00
178 Josh Phelps/1350* 2.00 5.00
179 Juan Diaz/1350* 2.00 5.00
180 Victor Alvarez/1350* RC 2.00 5.00
181 Ramon Vazquez/1350* 2.00 5.00
182 Mike Rivera/1350* 2.00 5.00
183 Kazuhisa Ishii/1350* RC 3.00 8.00
184 Henry Mateo/1350* 2.00 5.00
185 Travis Hughes/1350* RC 2.00 5.00
186 Zach Day/1350* 2.00 5.00
187 Brad Voyles/1350* 2.00 5.00
188 Sean Douglass/1350* 2.00 5.00
189 Nick Neugebauer/1350* 2.00 5.00
190 Tom Shearn/1350* RC 2.00 5.00
191 Eric Cyr/1350* 2.00 5.00
192 Adam Johnson/1350* 2.00 5.00
193 Michael Cuddyer/1350* 2.00 5.00
194 Erik Bedard/1350* 2.00 5.00
195 Mark Ellis/1350* 2.00 5.00
196 Carlos Hernandez/1350* 2.00 5.00
197 Deivis Santos/1350* 2.00 5.00
198 Morgan Ensberg/1350* 2.00 5.00
199 Ryan Jamison/1350* 2.00 5.00
200 Cody Ransom/1350* 2.00 5.00
201 Chris Snelling/900* RC 2.00 5.00
202 Satoru Komiyama/900* RC 2.00 5.00
203 Jason Simontacchi/925* RC 2.00 5.00
204 Tim Kalita/900* RC 2.00 5.00
205 Runelvys Hernandez/900* RC 2.00 5.00
206 Kirk Saarloos/900* RC 2.00 5.00
207 Aaron Cook/900* RC 2.00 5.00
208 Luis Ugueto/900* RC 2.00 5.00
209 Gustavo Chacin/900* RC 3.00 8.00
210 Francis Beltran/900* RC 2.00 5.00
211 Takahito Nomura/900* RC 2.00 5.00
212 Oliver Perez/900* RC 4.00 10.00
213 Miguel Asencio/900* RC 2.00 5.00
214 Rene Reyes/900* RC 2.00 5.00
215 Jeff Baker/900* RC 3.00 8.00
216 Jon Adkins/900* RC 2.00 5.00
217 Carlos Rivera/900* RC 2.00 5.00
218 Corey Thurman/900* RC 2.00 5.00
219 Earl Snyder/900* RC 2.00 5.00
220 Felix Escalona/900* RC 2.00 5.00
221 Jeremy Guthrie/900* RC 2.50 6.00
222 Josh Hancock/900* RC 2.00 5.00
223 Ben Kozlowski/900* RC 2.00 5.00
224 Eric Good/900* RC 2.00 5.00
225 Eric Junge/900* RC 2.00 5.00
226 Andy Pratt/900* RC 2.00 5.00
227 Matt Thornton/900* RC 2.00 5.00
228 Jorge Sosa/900* RC 3.00 8.00
229 Mike Smith/900* RC 2.00 5.00
230 Mitch Wylie/900* RC 2.00 5.00
231 John Ennis/900* RC 2.00 5.00
232 Reed Johnson/900* RC 3.00 8.00
233 Joe Borchard/900* 2.00 5.00
234 Ron Calloway/900* RC 2.00 5.00
235 Brian Tallet/900* RC 2.00 5.00
236 Chris Baker/900* RC 2.00 5.00
237 Cliff Lee/900* RC 6.00 15.00
238 Matt Childers/900* RC 2.00 5.00
239 Freddy Sanchez/900* RC 4.00 10.00
240 Chone Figgins/900* RC 3.00 8.00
241 Kevin Cash/900* RC 2.00 5.00
242 Josh Bard/900* RC 2.00 5.00
243 Jeriome Robertson/900* RC 2.00 5.00
244 Jeremy Hill/900* RC 2.00 5.00
245 Shane Nance/900* RC 2.00 5.00
246 Wes Obermueller/900* RC 2.00 5.00
247 Trey Hodges/900* RC 2.00 5.00
248 Eric Eckenstahler/900* RC 2.00 5.00
249 Jim Rushford/900* RC 2.00 5.00
250 Jose Castillo/900* RC 6.00 15.00
251 Garrett Atkins/900* RC 6.00 15.00
252 Alexis Rios/900* RC 6.00 15.00
253 Ryan Church/900* RC 3.00 8.00
254 Jimmy Gobble/900* RC 2.00 5.00
255 Corwin Malone/900* RC 2.00 5.00
257 Nic Jackson/900* RC 2.00 5.00
258 Tommy Whiteman/900* RC 2.00 5.00
259 Mario Ramos/900* RC 2.00 5.00
260 Rob Bowen/900* RC 2.00 5.00
261 Josh Wilson/900* RC 2.00 5.00
262 Tim Hummel/900* RC 2.00 5.00
264 Gerald Laird/900* RC 3.00 8.00
265 Vinny Chulk/900* RC 2.00 5.00
266 Jesus Medrano/900* RC 2.00 5.00
272 Adam LaRoche/900* RC 6.00 15.00
273 Adam Morrissey/900* RC 2.00 5.00
274 Henri Stanley/900* RC 2.00 5.00
275 Walter Young/900* RC 2.00 5.00

2002 Donruss Elite Aspirations

*1-100 PRINT RUN b/wn 26-35 8X TO 20X
*1-100 PRINT RUN b/wn 36-50 6X TO 15X
*1-100 PRINT RUN b/wn 51-65 5X TO 12X
*1-100 PRINT RUN b/wn 66-80 5X TO 12X
*101-150 PRINT RUN b/wn 26-35 1.25X TO 3X
*101-150 PRINT RUN b/wn 36-50 1X TO 2.5X
*101-150 PRINT RUN b/wn 51-65 .75X TO 2X
UNLISTED 151-200 p/r 81-99 6.00 15.00
COMMON (151-200) p/r 66-80 3.00 8.00
SEMIS 151-200 p/r 66-80 5.00 12.00
UNLISTED 151-200 p/r 66-80 8.00 20.00
COMMON (151-200) p/r 51-65 4.00 10.00
SEMIS 151-200 p/r 51-65 6.00 15.00
UNLISTED 151-200 p/r 51-65 10.00 25.00
COMMON (151-200) p/r 36-50 5.00 12.00
SEMIS 151-200 p/r 36-50 5.00 20.00
UNLISTED 151-200 p/r 36-50 12.50 30.00
COMMON (151-200) p/r 26-35 6.00 15.00
SEMIS 151-200 p/r 26-35 10.00 25.00
UNLISTED 151-200 p/r 26-35 15.00 40.00
SEE BECKETT.COM FOR PRINT RUNS
NO PRICING ON QUANTITIES OF 25 OR LESS

2002 Donruss Elite Status

*1-100 PRINT RUN b/wn 36-50 6X TO 15X
*1-100 PRINT RUN b/wn 51-65 5X TO 12X
*1-100 PRINT RUN b/wn 66-80 5X TO 12X
*1-100 PRINT RUN b/wn 81-98 4X TO 10X
*101-150 PRINT RUN b/wn 36-50 1X TO 2.5X
*101-150 PRINT RUN b/wn 51-65 .75X TO 2X
*101-150 PRINT RUN b/wn 66-80 .75X TO 2X
*101-150 PRINT RUN b/wn 81-99 .6X TO 1.5X
COMMON (151-200) p/r 81-99 2.50 6.00
SEMIS 151-200 p/r 81-99 4.00 10.00
UNLISTED 151-200 p/r 81-99 6.00 15.00
COMMON (151-200) p/r 66-80 3.00 8.00
SEMIS 151-200 p/r 66-80 5.00 12.00
UNLISTED 151-200 p/r 66-80 8.00 20.00
COMMON (151-200) p/r 51-65 4.00 10.00
SEMIS 151-200 p/r 51-65 6.00 15.00
UNLISTED 151-200 p/r 51-65 10.00 25.00
COMMON (151-200) p/r 36-50 5.00 12.00
SEMIS 151-200 p/r 36-50 8.00 20.00
UNLISTED 151-200 p/r 36-50 12.50 30.00
COMMON (151-200) p/r 26-35 6.00 15.00
SEMIS 151-200 p/r 26-35 10.00 25.00
UNLISTED 151-200 p/r 26-35 15.00 40.00
SEE BECKETT.COM FOR PRINT RUNS
NO PRICING ON QUANTITIES OF 25 OR LESS

2002 Donruss Elite Turn of the Century

*TOC p/r 100-150: .6X TO 1.5X BASIC
*TOC p/r 50-75: .75X TO 2X BASIC
151-200 RANDOM INSERTS IN ELITE PACKS
201-275 RANDOM IN DON.ROOKIES UPDATE
CARDS DISPLAY CUMULATIVE PRINT RUNS
SEE BECKETT.COM FOR PRINT RUNS
PRINT RUNS B/WN 25-150 COPIES PER
151-200 DIE CUTS ARE 1ST 150 #'d OF 1500
201-275 DIE CUTS ARE 1ST 100 #'d OF 1000
SKIP-NUMBERED 72-CARD SET
NO PRICING ON QTY OF 25 OR LESS
252 Alexis Rios/100* 15.00 40.00

2002 Donruss Elite Turn of the Century Autographs

151-200 RANDOM INSERTS IN ELITE PACKS
201-275 RANDOM IN DONRUSS ROOK.PACKS
CARDS DISPLAY CUMULATIVE PRINT RUNS
ACTUAL PRINT RUNS LISTED BELOW
PRINT RUNS PROVIDED BY DONRUSS
151-200 DC ARE 1st 150 #'d CARDS OF 1500
201-275 DC ARE 1st 100 #'d CARDS OF 1000
94-CARD SKIP-NUMBERED SET
NO PRICING ON QTY OF 25 OR LESS
151 Cam Esslinger/150* 6.00 15.00
152 Ben Howard/150* 6.00 15.00
153 Brandon Backe/150* 10.00 25.00
154 Jorge De La Rosa/100* 6.00 15.00
155 Austin Kearns/150* 6.00 15.00
156 Carlos Zambrano/100* 12.00 25.00
157 Kyle Kane/100* 6.00 15.00
158 So Taguchi/125* 10.00 25.00
159 Brian Mallette/100* 6.00 15.00
160 Brett Jodie/100* 6.00 15.00
161 Elio Serrano/150* 6.00 15.00
162 Joe Thurston/150* 6.00 15.00
163 Kevin Olsen/150* 6.00 15.00
164 Rodrigo Rosario/150* 6.00 15.00
165 Matt Guerrier/100* 6.00 15.00
166 Anderson Machado/150* 6.00 15.00
167 Bert Snow/150* 6.00 15.00
168 Franklyn German/100* 6.00 15.00
169 Brandon Claussen/100* 6.00 15.00
170 Jason Romano/150* 6.00 15.00
171 Jorge Padilla/100* 6.00 15.00
172 Jose Cueto/100* 6.00 15.00
173 Allan Simpson/150* 6.00 15.00
174 Doug Devore/150* 6.00 15.00
175 Justin Duchscherer/150* 12.50 30.00
176 Josh Pearce/100* 6.00 15.00
177 Steve Bechler/100* 6.00 15.00
178 Josh Phelps/100* 6.00 15.00
179 Juan Diaz/150* 6.00 15.00
180 Victor Alvarez/100* 6.00 15.00
181 Ramon Vazquez/150* 6.00 15.00
182 Michael Rivera/100* 6.00 15.00
184 Henry Mateo/100* 6.00 15.00
185 Travis Hughes/150* 6.00 15.00
186 Zach Day/100* 6.00 15.00
187 Brad Voyles/150* 6.00 15.00
188 Sean Douglass/150* 6.00 15.00
189 Nick Neugebauer/50* 10.00 25.00
190 Tom Shearn/150* 6.00 15.00
191 Eric Cyr/150* 6.00 15.00
193 Michael Cuddyer/100* 6.00 15.00
194 Erik Bedard/150* 6.00 15.00
195 Mark Ellis/125* 6.00 15.00
197 Deivis Santos/150* 6.00 15.00
198 Morgan Ensberg/100* 6.00 15.00
199 Ryan Jamison/150* 6.00 15.00
201 Chris Snelling/50* 15.00 40.00
206 Kirk Saarloos/50* 10.00 25.00
215 Jeff Baker/100* 15.00 40.00
216 Jon Adkins/100* 6.00 15.00
217 Carlos Rivera/100* 6.00 15.00
221 Jeremy Guthrie/100* 10.00 25.00
223 Ben Kozlowski/100* 6.00 15.00
224 Eric Good/100* 6.00 15.00
240 Chone Figgins/100* 15.00 40.00
241 Kevin Cash/100* 6.00 15.00
247 Trey Hodges/100* 6.00 15.00
251 Garrett Atkins/100* 20.00 50.00
253 Ryan Church/100* 15.00 40.00
254 Jimmy Gobble/100* 6.00 15.00
255 Corwin Malone/100* 6.00 15.00
258 Tommy Whiteman/100* 6.00 15.00
259 Mario Ramos/100* 6.00 15.00
260 Rob Bowen/100* 6.00 15.00
261 Josh Wilson/100* 6.00 15.00
262 Tim Hummel/100* 6.00 15.00
264 Gerald Laird/100* 10.00 25.00
266 Jesus Medrano/100* 6.00 15.00
272 Adam LaRoche/100* 10.00 25.00
273 Adam Morrissey/100* 6.00 15.00
274 Henri Stanley/100* 6.00 15.00

2002 Donruss Elite All-Star Salutes

COMPLETE SET (25) 25.00 60.00
STATED PRINT RUNS LISTED BELOW
*CENTURY: 1.25X TO 3X BASIC AS SALUTE
CENTURY PRINT RUN 100 SERIAL #'d SETS
1 Ichiro Suzuki/2001 2.00 5.00
2 Tony Gwynn/2001 1.50 4.00
3 Magglio Ordonez/2001 1.00 2.50
4 Cal Ripken/2001 5.00 12.00
5 Roger Clemens/1998 2.00 5.00
6 Kazuhiro Sasaki/2001 .60 1.50
7 Freddy Garcia/2001 .60 1.50
8 Luis Gonzalez/2001 .60 1.50
9 Lance Berkman/2001 1.00 2.50
10 Derek Jeter/2000 4.00 10.00
11 Chipper Jones/2000 1.50 4.00
12 Randy Johnson/2000 1.50 4.00
13 Andruw Jones/2000 .60 1.50
14 Pedro Martinez/1999 1.00 2.50
15 Jim Thome/1999 1.00 2.50
16 Rafael Palmeiro/1999 1.00 2.50
17 Barry Larkin/1999 1.00 2.50
18 Ivan Rodriguez/1998 1.00 2.50
19 Omar Vizquel/1998 1.00 2.50
20 Edgar Martinez/1997 1.00 2.50
21 Larry Walker/1997 1.00 2.50
22 Javy Lopez/1997 .60 1.50
23 Mariano Rivera/1997 1.50 4.00
24 Frank Thomas/1995 1.50 4.00
25 Greg Maddux/1994 2.50 6.00

2002 Donruss Elite Back 2 Back Jacks

DUAL PRINT RUN 75 SERIAL #'d SETS
SINGLE PRINT RUN 150 SERIAL #'d SETS
1 I.Rodriguez/A.Rodriguez 6.00 15.00
2 K.Puckett/D.Winfield 25.00 60.00
3 T.Williams/N.Garciaparra 15.00 40.00
4 J.Bagwell/C.Biggio 20.00 50.00
5 E.Murray/C.Ripken 15.00 40.00
6 A.Jones/C.Jones 20.00 50.00
7 R.Clemente/W.Stargell 25.00 60.00
8 L.Gehrig/D.Mattingly 100.00 200.00
9 L.Walker/T.Helton 20.00 50.00
10 M.Ramirez/T.Nixon 15.00 40.00
11 Ivan Rodriguez 10.00 25.00
12 Alex Rodriguez 10.00 25.00
13 Kirby Puckett 15.00 40.00
14 Dave Winfield 10.00 25.00
15 Ted Williams 15.00 40.00
16 Nomar Garciaparra 10.00 25.00
17 Jeff Bagwell 10.00 25.00
18 Craig Biggio 10.00 25.00
19 Eddie Murray 15.00 40.00
20 Cal Ripken 20.00 50.00
21 Andruw Jones 10.00 25.00
22 Chipper Jones 10.00 25.00
23 Roberto Clemente 15.00 40.00
24 Willie Stargell 10.00 25.00
25 Lou Gehrig 75.00 150.00
26 Don Mattingly 15.00 40.00
27 Larry Walker 6.00 15.00
28 Todd Helton 10.00 25.00
29 Manny Ramirez 10.00 25.00
30 Trot Nixon 6.00 15.00

2002 Donruss Elite Back to the Future

COMPLETE SET (23) 60.00 120.00
DUAL PRINT RUN 500 SERIAL #'d SETS
SINGLE PRINT RUN 1000 SERIAL #'d SETS
CARDS 6 AND 20 DO NOT EXIST
1 S.Rolen 2.50 6.00
M.Byrd
2 J.Crede 1.50 4.00
F.Thomas
3 L.Berkman 2.50 6.00
J.Bagwell
4 M.Giles 2.50 6.00
C.Jones
5 S.Green 2.00 5.00
P.LoDuca
7 K.Wood 2.00 5.00
J.Cruz
8 V.Guerrero 2.50 6.00
O.Cabrera
9 Scott Rolen 1.50 4.00
10 Marlon Byrd 1.50 4.00
11 Frank Thomas 2.00 5.00
12 Joe Crede 1.50 4.00
13 Jeff Bagwell 1.50 4.00
14 Lance Berkman 1.50 4.00
15 Chipper Jones 2.00 5.00
16 Marcus Giles 1.50 4.00
17 Shawn Green 1.50 4.00
18 Paul LoDuca 1.50 4.00
19 Jim Edmonds 1.50 4.00
21 Kerry Wood 1.50 4.00
22 Juan Cruz 1.50 4.00
23 Vladimir Guerrero 2.00 5.00
24 Orlando Cabrera 1.50 4.00

2002 Donruss Elite Back to the Future Threads

DUAL PRINT RUN 50 SERIAL #'d SETS
SINGLE PRINT RUN 100 SERIAL #'d SETS
ALL CARDS FEATURE JERSEY UNLESS NOTED
ONLY TAGUCHI WILL SIGN CARD #6
1 S.Rolen/M.Byrd 15.00 40.00
2 F.Thomas/J.Crede Hat 6.00 15.00
3 J.Bagwell/L.Berkman 15.00 40.00
4 C.Jones/M.Giles 15.00 40.00
5 S.Green/P.LoDuca 10.00 25.00
6 Taguchi AU/Edmonds 20.00 50.00
7 K.Wood/J.Cruz 10.00 25.00
8 V.Guerrero/O.Cabrera 15.00 40.00
9 Scott Rolen 10.00 25.00
10 Marlon Byrd 6.00 15.00
11 Frank Thomas 15.00 40.00
12 Joe Crede Shoes 6.00 15.00
13 Jeff Bagwell 10.00 25.00
14 Lance Berkman 6.00 15.00
15 Chipper Jones 15.00 40.00
16 Marcus Giles 6.00 15.00
17 Shawn Green 6.00 15.00
18 Paul LoDuca 6.00 15.00
19 Jim Edmonds 6.00 15.00
20 So Taguchi AU 12.50 30.00
21 Kerry Wood 6.00 15.00
22 Juan Cruz 6.00 15.00
23 Vladimir Guerrero 15.00 40.00
24 Orlando Cabrera 6.00 15.00

2002 Donruss Elite Career Best

PRINT RUN B/WN 8-1379 COPIES PER
NO PRICING ON QUANTITIES OF 25 OR LESS
1 Albert Pujols OPS/1013 5.00 12.00
2 Alex Rodriguez HR/52 6.00 15.00
3 Alex Rodriguez RBI/135 5.00 12.00
4 Andruw Jones RBI/104 1.50 4.00
5 Barry Bonds HR/73 8.00 20.00
6 Barry Bonds OPS/1379 4.00 10.00
7 Barry Bonds BB/177 6.00 15.00
8 C.C. Sabathia K/171 2.50 6.00
9 Carlos Beltran OPS/876 1.00 2.50
10 Chipper Jones BA/330 3.00 8.00
11 Derek Jeter SB/900 6.00 15.00
12 Eric Chavez RBI/114 1.50 4.00
13 Frank Catalanotto BA/330 1.25 3.00
14 Ichiro Suzuki OPS/838 3.00 8.00
15 Ichiro Suzuki RUN/127 5.00 12.00
17 J.D. Drew HR/27 2.50 6.00
18 J.D. Drew OPS/1027 1.00 2.50
19 Jason Giambi SLG/660 1.00 2.50
20 Jim Thome HR/49 3.00 8.00
21 Jim Thome SLG/624 1.50 4.00
22 Jorge Posada RBI/95 3.00 8.00
23 Jose Cruz Jr. SLG/856 1.00 2.50
24 Kazuhiro Sasaki SV/45 2.00 5.00
25 Kerry Wood ERA/336 2.00 5.00
26 Lance Berkman OPS/1050 1.50 4.00
27 Magglio Ordonez OB/382 2.00 5.00
28 Mark Mulder ERA/345 1.25 3.00
29 Pat Burrell HR/27 2.50 6.00
30 Pat Burrell SLG/469 1.25 3.00
31 Randy Johnson K/372 3.00 8.00
33 Richie Sexson SLG/547 1.00 2.50
34 Roberto Alomar OPS/956 1.50 4.00
35 Sammy Sosa RBI/160 4.00 10.00
36 Sammy Sosa OPS/1174 2.50 6.00
37 Shawn Green RBI/125 1.50 4.00
39 Trot Nixon HIT/150 1.50 4.00
40 Troy Glaus RBI/108 1.50 4.00

2002 Donruss Elite Passing the Torch

COMPLETE SET (24) 125.00 250.00
DUAL PRINT RUN 500 SERIAL #'d SETS
SINGLE PRINT RUN 1000 SERIAL #'d SETS
1 F.Jenkins 3.00 8.00
M.Prior
2 N.Ryan 12.50 30.00
R.Oswalt
3 O.Smith 6.00 15.00
J.Drew
4 G.Brett 10.00 25.00
C.Beltran
5 K.Puckett 4.00 10.00
M.Cuddyer
6 J.Bench 4.00 10.00
A.Dunn
7 D.Snider 4.00 10.00
P.LoDuca
8 T.Gwynn 6.00 15.00
X.Nady
9 Fergie Jenkins 2.00 5.00
10 Mark Prior 2.00 5.00
11 Nolan Ryan 8.00 20.00
12 Roy Oswalt 2.00 5.00
13 Ozzie Smith 5.00 12.00
14 J.D. Drew 2.00 5.00
15 George Brett 8.00 20.00
16 Carlos Beltran 2.00 5.00
17 Kirby Puckett 3.00 8.00
18 Michael Cuddyer 2.00 5.00
19 Johnny Bench 3.00 8.00
20 Adam Dunn 2.00 5.00
21 Duke Snider 2.00 5.00
22 Paul LoDuca 2.00 5.00
23 Tony Gwynn 4.00 10.00
24 Xavier Nady 2.00 5.00

2002 Donruss Elite Passing the Torch Autographs

STATED PRINT RUNS LISTED BELOW
NO PRICING ON QUANTITIES OF 25 OR LESS
1 F.Jenkins/M.Prior/50 10.00 25.00
2 N.Ryan/R.Oswalt/50 50.00 100.00
3 O.Smith/J.Drew/50 60.00 120.00
5 K.Puckett/M.Cuddyer/50 60.00 120.00
6 J.Bench/A.Dunn/50 20.00 50.00
7 D.Snider/P.LoDuca/50 50.00 100.00
8 T.Gwynn/X.Nady/50 50.00 100.00
9 Fergie Jenkins/50 10.00 25.00
10 Mark Prior/100 10.00 25.00
11 Nolan Ryan/100 60.00 120.00
12 Roy Oswalt/100 10.00 25.00
14 J.D. Drew/100 10.00 25.00
16 Carlos Beltran/100 10.00 25.00
18 Michael Cuddyer/100 10.00 25.00
19 Johnny Bench/100 30.00 60.00
20 Adam Dunn/50 10.00 25.00
21 Duke Snider/100 12.00 30.00
22 Paul LoDuca/100 10.00 25.00
23 Tony Gwynn/100 30.00 60.00
24 Xavier Nady/100 10.00 25.00

2002 Donruss Elite Recollection Autographs

RANDOM INSERTS IN PACKS
SEE BECKETT.COM FOR PRINT RUNS
NO PRICING ON QTY OF 25 OR LESS
2 Alfredo Amezaga 01/50 8.00 20.00
14 Orlando Hudson 01/50 8.00 20.00
19 Antonio Perez 01/50 8.00 20.00
21 Mike Rivera 01/50 8.00 20.00
23 Claudio Vargas 01/50 8.00 20.00
24 Martin Vargas 01/50 8.00 20.00

2002 Donruss Elite Throwback Threads

DUAL PRINT RUN 50 SERIAL #'d SETS
SINGLE PRINT RUN 100 SERIAL #'d SETS
CARD 28 DOES NOT EXIST
1 T.Williams/M.Ramirez 50.00 100.00
2 C.Fisk/M.Piazza 15.00 40.00
3 B.Jackson/G.Brett 40.00 80.00
4 C.Schilling/R.Johnson 20.00 50.00
5 D.Mattingly/L.Gehrig 150.00 250.00
6 B.Williams/D.Winfield 20.00 50.00
7 R.Henderson/R.Henderson 12.00 30.00
8 R.Yount/P.Molitor 20.00 50.00
9 S.Musial/J.Drew 40.00 80.00
10 A.Dawson/R.Sandberg 30.00 60.00
11 B.Ruth/R.Jackson 250.00 400.00
12 B.Robinson/C.Ripken 20.00 50.00
13 T.Williams/N.Garciaparra 20.00 50.00
14 J.Robinson/S.Green 20.00 50.00
15 C.Ripken/T.Gwynn 30.00 60.00
16 Ted Williams 25.00 60.00
17 Manny Ramirez 10.00 25.00
18 Carlton Fisk Red Sox 15.00 40.00
19 Mike Piazza 10.00 25.00
20 Bo Jackson 15.00 40.00
21 George Brett 15.00 40.00
22 Curt Schilling 6.00 15.00
23 Randy Johnson 10.00 25.00
24 Don Mattingly 15.00 40.00
25 Lou Gehrig 75.00 200.00
26 Bernie Williams 10.00 25.00
27 Dave Winfield 10.00 25.00
29 Rickey Henderson Mariners 10.00 25.00
30 Robin Yount 15.00 40.00
31 Paul Molitor 10.00 25.00
32 Stan Musial 30.00 60.00
33 J.D. Drew 6.00 15.00
34 Andre Dawson 10.00 25.00
35 Ryne Sandberg 20.00 50.00
36 Babe Ruth 200.00 400.00
37 Reggie Jackson 15.00 40.00
38 Brooks Robinson 15.00 40.00
39 Cal Ripken Running 12.50 30.00
41 Jackie Robinson 20.00 50.00
42 Shawn Green 6.00 15.00
43 Pedro Martinez Grey 10.00 25.00
44 Nolan Ryan Astros 10.00 25.00
45 Kazuhiro Sasaki 6.00 15.00
46 Tony Gwynn 15.00 40.00
47 Carlton Fisk White Sox 15.00 40.00
48 Cal Ripken Batting 20.00 50.00
49 Rod Carew Angels 15.00 40.00
50 Nolan Ryan Rangers 30.00 60.00
51 Alex Rodriguez 10.00 25.00
52 Greg Maddux 10.00 25.00
53 Pedro Martinez White 10.00 25.00
54 Rickey Henderson Padres 10.00 25.00
55 Rod Carew Twins 15.00 40.00
56 Roberto Clemente 20.00 50.00
57 Hideo Nomo 10.00 25.00
58 Rickey Henderson Mets 10.00 25.00
59 Dave Parker 10.00 25.00
60 Eddie Mathews 15.00 40.00
61 Eddie Murray 15.00 40.00
62 Nolan Ryan Angels 30.00 60.00
63 Tom Seaver 15.00 40.00
64 Roger Clemens 15.00 40.00
65 Rickey Henderson A's 10.00 25.00

2002 Donruss Elite Throwback Threads Autographs

RANDOM INSERTS IN PACKS
CARDS DISPLAY CUMULATIVE PRINT RUNS
SEE BECKETT.COM FOR PRINT RUNS
PRINT RUNS PROVIDED BY DONRUSS
SKIP-NUMBERED 29-CARD SET
NO PRICING ON QTY OF 25 OR LESS
28 Rickey Henderson/100 30.00 80.00

2003 Donruss Elite

COMP.SET w/o SP's (180) 8.00 20.00
COMMON CARD (1-180) .12 .30
COMMON CARD (181-200) .75 2.00
181-200 RANDOM INSERTS IN PACKS
181-200 PRINT RUN 1750 SERIAL #'d SETS
1 Darin Erstad .12 .30
2 David Eckstein .12 .30
3 Garret Anderson .12 .30
4 Jarrod Washburn .12 .30
5 Tim Salmon .12 .30
6 Troy Glaus .12 .30
7 Marty Cordova .12 .30
8 Melvin Mora .12 .30
9 Rodrigo Lopez .12 .30
10 Tony Batista .12 .30
11 Derek Lowe .12 .30
12 Johnny Damon .20 .50
13 Manny Ramirez .30 .75
14 Nomar Garciaparra .20 .50
15 Pedro Martinez .20 .50
16 Shea Hillenbrand .12 .30
17 Carlos Lee .12 .30
18 Joe Crede .12 .30
19 Frank Thomas .30 .75
20 Magglio Ordonez .20 .50
21 Mark Buehrle .20 .50
22 Paul Konerko .20 .50
23 C.C. Sabathia .20 .50
24 Ellis Burks .12 .30
25 Omar Vizquel .20 .50
26 Brian Tallet .12 .30
27 Bobby Higginson .12 .30
28 Carlos Pena .20 .50
29 Mark Redman .12 .30
30 Steve Sparks .12 .30
31 Carlos Beltran .20 .50
32 Joe Randa .12 .30
33 Mike Sweeney .12 .30
34 Raul Ibanez .20 .50
35 Runelvys Hernandez .12 .30
36 Brad Radke .12 .30

37 Corey Koskie .12 .30
38 Cristian Guzman .12 .30
39 David Ortiz .30 .75
40 Doug Mientkiewicz .12 .30
41 Jacque Jones .12 .30
42 Torii Hunter .12 .30
43 Alfonso Soriano .20 .50
44 Andy Pettitte .20 .50
45 Bernie Williams .20 .50
46 David Wells .12 .30
47 Derek Jeter .75 2.00
48 Jason Giambi .12 .30
49 Jeff Weaver .12 .30
50 Jorge Posada .20 .50
51 Mike Mussina .20 .50
52 Roger Clemens .40 1.00
53 Barry Zito .20 .50
54 Eric Chavez .12 .30
55 Jermaine Dye .12 .30
56 Mark Mulder .12 .30
57 Miguel Tejada .20 .50
58 Tim Hudson .20 .50
59 Bret Boone .12 .30
60 Chris Snelling .12 .30
61 Edgar Martinez .20 .50
62 Freddy Garcia .12 .30
63 Ichiro Suzuki .40 1.00
64 Jamie Moyer .12 .30
65 John Olerud .12 .30
66 Kazuhiro Sasaki .12 .30
67 Aubrey Huff .12 .30
68 Joe Kennedy .12 .30
69 Paul Wilson .12 .30
70 Alex Rodriguez .40 1.00
71 Chan Ho Park .20 .50
72 Hank Blalock .12 .30
73 Juan Gonzalez .12 .30
74 Kevin Mench .12 .30
75 Rafael Palmeiro .20 .50
76 Carlos Delgado .12 .30
77 Eric Hinske .12 .30
78 Josh Phelps .12 .30
79 Roy Halladay .20 .50
80 Shannon Stewart .12 .30
81 Vernon Wells .12 .30
82 Curt Schilling .20 .50
83 Junior Spivey .12 .30
84 Luis Gonzalez .12 .30
85 Mark Grace .20 .50
86 Randy Johnson .30 .75
87 Steve Finley .12 .30
88 Andruw Jones .12 .30
89 Chipper Jones .30 .75
90 Gary Sheffield .12 .30
91 Greg Maddux .40 1.00
92 John Smoltz .30 .75
93 Corey Patterson .12 .30
94 Kerry Wood .12 .30
95 Mark Prior .20 .50
96 Moises Alou .12 .30
97 Sammy Sosa .30 .75
98 Adam Dunn .20 .50
99 Austin Kearns .12 .30
100 Barry Larkin .20 .50
101 Ken Griffey Jr. .60 1.50
102 Sean Casey .12 .30
103 Jason Jennings .12 .30
104 Jay Payton .12 .30
105 Larry Walker .20 .50
106 Todd Helton .20 .50
107 A.J. Burnett .12 .30
108 Josh Beckett .12 .30
109 Juan Encarnacion .12 .30
110 Mike Lowell .12 .30
111 Craig Biggio .20 .50
112 Daryle Ward .12 .30
113 Jeff Bagwell .20 .50
114 Lance Berkman .20 .50
115 Roy Oswalt .20 .50
116 Jason Lane .12 .30
117 Adrian Beltre .30 .75
118 Hideo Nomo .30 .75
119 Kazuhisa Ishii .12 .30
120 Kevin Brown .12 .30
121 Odalis Perez .12 .30
122 Paul Lo Duca .12 .30
123 Shawn Green .12 .30
124 Ben Sheets .12 .30
125 Jeffrey Hammonds .12 .30
126 Jose Hernandez .12 .30
127 Richie Sexson .12 .30
128 Bartolo Colon .12 .30
129 Brad Wilkerson .12 .30
130 Javier Vazquez .12 .30
131 Jose Vidro .12 .30
132 Michael Barrett .12 .30
133 Vladimir Guerrero .20 .50
134 Al Leiter .12 .30
135 Mike Piazza .30 .75
136 Mo Vaughn .12 .30
137 Pedro Astacio .12 .30
138 Roberto Alomar .20 .50
139 Pat Burrell .12 .30
140 Vicente Padilla .12 .30
141 Jimmy Rollins .20 .50
142 Bobby Abreu .12 .30
143 Marlon Byrd .12 .30
144 Brian Giles .12 .30
145 Jason Kendall .12 .30
146 Aramis Ramirez .12 .30
147 Josh Fogg .12 .30
148 Ryan Klesko .12 .30
149 Phil Nevin .12 .30
150 Sean Burroughs .12 .30
151 Mark Kotsay .12 .30
152 Barry Bonds .50 1.25
153 Damian Moss .12 .30
154 Jason Schmidt .12 .30
155 Benito Santiago .12 .30
156 Rich Aurilia .12 .30
157 Scott Rolen .20 .50
158 J.D. Drew .12 .30
159 Jim Edmonds .20 .50
160 Matt Morris .12 .30
161 Tino Martinez .12 .30
162 Albert Pujols .40 1.00
163 Russ Ortiz .12 .30
164 Rey Ordonez .12 .30
165 Paul Byrd .12 .30
166 Kenny Lofton .12 .30
167 Kenny Rogers .12 .30
168 Rickey Henderson .30 .75
169 Fred McGriff .20 .50
170 Charles Johnson .12 .30
171 Mike Hampton .12 .30
172 Jim Thome .20 .50
173 Travis Hafner .12 .30
174 Ivan Rodriguez .20 .50
175 Ray Durham .12 .30
176 Jeremy Giambi .12 .30
177 Jeff Kent .12 .30
178 Cliff Floyd .12 .30
179 Kevin Millwood .12 .30
180 Tom Glavine .20 .50
181 Hideki Matsui ROO RC 4.00 10.00
182 Jose Contreras ROO RC 2.00 5.00
183 Termel Sledge ROO RC .75 2.00
184 Lew Ford ROO RC .75 2.00
185 Jhonny Peralta ROO .75 2.00
186 Alexis Rios ROO .75 2.00
187 Jeff Baker ROO .75 2.00
188 Jeremy Guthrie ROO .75 2.00
189 Jose Castillo ROO .75 2.00
190 Garrett Atkins ROO .75 2.00
191 Jeremy Bonderman ROO RC 3.00 8.00
192 Adam LaRoche ROO .75 2.00
193 Vinny Chulk ROO .75 2.00
194 Walter Young ROO .75 2.00
195 Jimmy Gobble ROO .75 2.00
196 Prentice Redman ROO RC .75 2.00
197 Jason Anderson ROO .75 2.00
198 Nic Jackson ROO .75 2.00
199 Travis Chapman ROO .75 2.00
200 Shane Victorino ROO RC 2.50 6.00

2003 Donruss Elite Aspirations

*1-180 PRINT RUN b/wn 36-50 6X TO 15X
*1-180 PRINT RUN b/wn 51-65: 5X TO 12X
*1-180 PRINT RUN b/wn 66-80 5X TO 12X
*1-180 PRINT RUN b/wn 81-99 4X TO 10X
COMMON (181-200) p/r 81-99 1.50 4.00
SEMIS 181-200 p/r 81-99 2.50 6.00
UNLISTED 181-200 p/r 81-99 4.00 10.00
COMMON (181-200) p/r 51-65 2.50 6.00
SEMIS 181-200 p/r 51-65 4.00 10.00
UNLISTED 181-200 p/r 51-65 6.00 15.00
COMMON (181-200) p/r 36-50 2.50 6.00
SEMIS 181-200 p/r 36-50 4.00 10.00
UNLISTED 181-200 p/r 36-50 6.00 15.00
COMMON (181-200) p/r 26-35 3.00 8.00
SEMIS 181-200 p/r 26-35 5.00 12.00
UNLISTED 181-200 p/r 26-35 8.00 20.00
SEE BECKETT.COM FOR PRINT RUNS
NO PRICING ON QTY OF 25 OR LESS

2003 Donruss Elite Aspirations Gold

STATED PRINT RUN 1 SERIAL #'d SET
NO PRICING DUE TO SCARCITY

2003 Donruss Elite Atlantic City National

PRINT RUN 5 SERIAL #'d SETS

2003 Donruss Elite Status

*1-180 PRINT RUN b/wn 26-35: 8X TO 20X
*1-180 PRINT RUN b/wn 36-50: 6X TO 15X
*1-180 PRINT RUN b/wn 51-65: 5X TO 12X
*1-180 PRINT RUN b/wn 66-80: 5X TO 12X
*1-180 PRINT RUN b/wn 81-99: 4X TO 10X
COMMON (181-200) p/r 66-80 2.00 5.00
SEMIS 181-200 p/r 66-80 3.00 8.00
UNLISTED 181-200 p/r 66-80 5.00 12.00
COMMON (181-200) p/r 51-65 2.50 6.00
SEMIS 181-200 p/r 51-65 4.00 10.00
UNLISTED 181-200 p/r 51-65 6.00 15.00
COMMON (181-200) p/r 36-50 2.50 6.00
SEMIS 181-200 p/r 36-50 4.00 10.00
UNLISTED 181-200 p/r 36-50 6.00 15.00
SEE BECKETT.COM FOR PRINT RUNS
NO PRICING ON QTY OF 25 OR LESS

2003 Donruss Elite Status Gold

STATED PRINT RUN 24 SERIAL #'d SETS
NO PRICING DUE TO SCARCITY

2003 Donruss Elite Turn of the Century Autographs

STATED PRINT RUN 50 SERIAL #'d SETS
182 Jose Contreras ROO 15.00 40.00
183 Termel Sledge ROO 6.00 15.00
184 Lew Ford ROO 10.00 25.00
185 Jhonny Peralta ROO 15.00 40.00
186 Alexis Rios ROO 6.00 15.00
187 Jeff Baker ROO 6.00 15.00
188 Jeremy Guthrie ROO 6.00 15.00
189 Jose Castillo ROO 6.00 15.00
190 Garrett Atkins ROO 6.00 15.00
191 Jeremy Bonderman ROO 40.00 80.00
192 Adam LaRoche ROO 6.00 15.00
193 Vinny Chulk ROO 6.00 15.00
194 Walter Young ROO 6.00 15.00
195 Jimmy Gobble ROO 6.00 15.00
196 Prentice Redman ROO 6.00 15.00
197 Jason Anderson ROO 6.00 15.00
198 Nic Jackson ROO 6.00 15.00
199 Travis Chapman ROO 6.00 15.00
200 Shane Victorino ROO 40.00 80.00

2003 Donruss Elite All-Time Career Best

STATED ODDS 1:9
*PARALLEL 1-25 p/r 211-239: 1X TO 2.5X
*PARALLEL 1-25 p/r 105-140: 1.25X TO 3X
*PARALLEL 1-25 p/r 53-60: 2X TO 5X
*PARALLEL 1-25 p/r 39-49: 2.5X TO 6X
*PARALLEL 1-25 p/r 29-31: 3X TO 8X
*PARALLEL 26-50 p/r 393: .6X TO 1.5X
*PARALLEL 26-50 p/r 130-137: 1X TO 2.5X
*PARALLEL 26-50 p/r 55-66: 1.5X TO 4X
*PARALLEL 26-50 p/r 37-49: 2X TO 5X
*PARALLEL 26-50 p/r 35: 2.5X TO 6X
PARALLEL PRINTS B/WN 1-393 COPIES PER
NO PARALLEL PRICING ON QTY OF 25 OR LESS
1 Babe Ruth 2.50 6.00
2 Ty Cobb 1.50 4.00
3 Jackie Robinson 1.00 2.50
4 Lou Gehrig 2.00 5.00
5 Thurman Munson 1.00 2.50
6 Nolan Ryan 3.00 8.00
7 Mike Schmidt 1.50 4.00
8 Don Mattingly 2.00 5.00
9 Yogi Berra 1.00 2.50
10 Rod Carew .60 1.50
11 Reggie Jackson .60 1.50
12 Al Kaline .60 1.50
13 Harmon Killebrew 1.00 2.50
14 Eddie Mathews 1.00 2.50
15 Stan Musial 1.50 4.00
16 Jim Palmer .60 1.50
17 Phil Rizzuto .60 1.50
18 Brooks Robinson .60 1.50
19 Tom Seaver .60 1.50
20 Robin Yount 1.00 2.50
21 Carlton Fisk .60 1.50
22 Dale Murphy 1.00 2.50
23 Cal Ripken 3.00 8.00
24 Tony Gwynn 1.00 2.50
25 Andre Dawson .60 1.50
26 Derek Jeter 2.50 6.00
27 Ken Griffey Jr. 2.00 5.00
28 Albert Pujols 1.25 3.00
29 Sammy Sosa 1.00 2.50
30 Jason Giambi .40 1.00
31 Randy Johnson 1.00 2.50
32 Greg Maddux 1.25 3.00
33 Rickey Henderson 1.00 2.50
34 Pedro Martinez .60 1.50
35 Jeff Bagwell .60 1.50
36 Alex Rodriguez 1.25 3.00
37 Vladimir Guerrero .60 1.50
38 Chipper Jones 1.00 2.50
39 Shawn Green .40 1.00
40 Tom Glavine .60 1.50
41 Curt Schilling .60 1.50
42 Todd Helton .60 1.50
43 Roger Clemens 1.25 3.00
44 Lance Berkman .60 1.50
45 Nomar Garciaparra .60 1.50

2003 Donruss Elite All-Time Career Best Materials

*MULTI-COLOR PATCH: 1.5X TO 4X HI COL
PRINT RUNS B/WN 25-400 COPIES PER
NO PRICING ON QTY OF 25 OR LESS
3 Jackie Robinson Jkt/50 15.00 40.00
4 Lou Gehrig Bat/100 50.00 100.00
5 Thurman Munson Bat/200 10.00 25.00
6 Nolan Ryan Jkt/400 12.50 30.00
7 Mike Schmidt Jkt/400 8.00 20.00
8 Don Mattingly Hat/250 15.00 40.00
9 Yogi Berra Bat/100 12.50 30.00
10 Rod Carew Bat/400 6.00 15.00
11 Reggie Jackson Bat/400 6.00 15.00
12 Al Kaline Bat/400 8.00 20.00
13 Harmon Killebrew Pants/400 8.00 20.00
14 Eddie Mathews Bat/200 10.00 25.00
15 Stan Musial Bat/100 10.00 25.00
16 Jim Palmer Jsy/200 8.00 20.00
17 Phil Rizzuto Bat/400 6.00 15.00
18 Brooks Robinson Bat/400 4.00 10.00
19 Tom Seaver Jsy/400 6.00 15.00
20 Robin Yount Bat/400 8.00 20.00
21 Carlton Fisk Bat/400 6.00 15.00
22 Dale Murphy Bat/400 6.00 15.00
23 Cal Ripken Bat/400 10.00 25.00
24 Tony Gwynn Pants/400 6.00 15.00
25 Andre Dawson Bat/400 4.00 10.00
26 Derek Jeter Base/400 10.00 25.00
27 Ken Griffey Jr. Base/400 6.00 15.00
28 Albert Pujols Base/400 6.00 15.00
29 Sammy Sosa Bat/400 4.00 10.00
30 Jason Giambi Bat/400 3.00 8.00
31 Randy Johnson Jsy/400 4.00 10.00
32 Greg Maddux Jsy/400 4.00 10.00
33 Rickey Henderson Bat/400 6.00 15.00
34 Pedro Martinez Jsy/400 4.00 10.00
35 Jeff Bagwell Pants/400 4.00 10.00
36 Alex Rodriguez Bat/400 6.00 15.00
37 Vladimir Guerrero Bat/400 4.00 10.00
38 Chipper Jones Bat/400 4.00 10.00
39 Shawn Green Bat/400 3.00 8.00
40 Tom Glavine Jsy/400 4.00 10.00
41 Curt Schilling Jsy/400 3.00 8.00
42 Todd Helton Bat/400 4.00 10.00
43 Roger Clemens Jsy/400 8.00 20.00
44 Lance Berkman Bat/400 3.00 8.00
45 Nomar Garciaparra Bat/400 6.00 15.00

2003 Donruss Elite All-Time Career Best Materials Parallel

PRINT RUNS B/WN 1-393 COPIES PER
NO PRICING ON QTY OF 25 OR LESS
1 Babe Ruth Bat/60 75.00 150.00
4 Lou Gehrig Bat/49 75.00 150.00
5 Thurman Munson Bat/105 15.00 40.00
7 Mike Schmidt Jkt/48 15.00 40.00
8 Don Mattingly Hat/53 40.00 80.00
9 Yogi Berra Bat/30 30.00 60.00
10 Rod Carew Bat/239 6.00 15.00
11 Reggie Jackson Bat/39 15.00 40.00
12 Al Kaline Bat/29 30.00 60.00
13 Harmon Killebrew Pants/140 10.00 25.00
14 Eddie Mathews Bat/31 30.00 60.00
15 Stan Musial Bat/39 20.00 50.00
18 Brooks Robinson Bat/118 6.00 15.00
20 Robin Yount Bat/49 20.00 50.00
21 Carlton Fisk Bat/107 10.00 25.00
22 Dale Murphy Bat/44 15.00 40.00
23 Cal Ripken Bat/211 12.00 30.00
24 Tony Gwynn Pants/220 8.00 20.00
25 Andre Dawson Bat/49 10.00 25.00
27 Ken Griffey Jr. Base/56 15.00 40.00
28 Albert Pujols Base/37 20.00 50.00
29 Sammy Sosa Bat/66 10.00 25.00
30 Jason Giambi Bat/137 4.00 10.00
33 Rickey Henderson Bat/130 6.00 15.00
35 Jeff Bagwell Pants/47 10.00 25.00
36 Alex Rodriguez Bat/393 6.00 15.00
37 Vladimir Guerrero Bat/44 15.00 40.00
38 Chipper Jones Bat/45 15.00 40.00
39 Shawn Green Bat/49 6.00 15.00
41 Curt Schilling Jsy/35 6.00 15.00
42 Todd Helton Bat/59 10.00 25.00
44 Lance Berkman Bat/55 6.00 15.00
45 Nomar Garciaparra Bat/35 40.00 80.00

2003 Donruss Elite Back to Back Jacks

1-25 PRINT RUN 250 SERIAL #'d SETS
26-35 PRINT RUN 125 SERIAL #'d SETS
36-40 PRINT RUN 100 SERIAL #'d SETS
41-45 PRINT RUN 75 SERIAL #'d SETS
46-50 PRINT RUN 50 SERIAL #'d SETS
1 Adam Dunn 3.00 8.00
2 Alex Rodriguez 6.00 15.00
3 Alfonso Soriano 3.00 8.00
4 Andruw Jones 4.00 10.00
5 Chipper Jones 4.00 10.00
6 Jason Giambi 3.00 8.00
7 Jeff Bagwell 4.00 10.00
8 Jim Thome 4.00 10.00
9 Juan Gonzalez 3.00 8.00
10 Lance Berkman 3.00 8.00
11 Magglio Ordonez 3.00 8.00
12 Manny Ramirez 4.00 10.00
13 Miguel Tejada 3.00 8.00
14 Mike Piazza 6.00 15.00
15 Nomar Garciaparra 6.00 15.00
16 Rafael Palmeiro 4.00 10.00
17 Rickey Henderson 4.00 10.00
18 Sammy Sosa 4.00 10.00
19 Scott Rolen 4.00 10.00
20 Shawn Green 3.00 8.00
21 Todd Helton 4.00 10.00
22 Vladimir Guerrero 4.00 10.00
23 Ivan Rodriguez 4.00 10.00
24 Eric Chavez 3.00 8.00
25 Larry Walker 3.00 8.00
26 G.Anderson/T.Glaus 8.00 20.00
27 A.Dunn/A.Kearns 8.00 20.00
28 A.Rodriguez/R.Palmeiro 12.50 30.00
29 M.Tejada/E.Chavez 8.00 20.00
30 M.Ordonez/F.Thomas 10.00 25.00
31 L.Berkman/J.Bagwell 8.00 20.00
32 N.Garciaparra/M.Ramirez 15.00 40.00
33 V.Guerrero/J.Vidro 10.00 25.00
34 M.Piazza/R.Alomar 10.00 25.00
35 T.Helton/L.Walker 8.00 20.00
36 Babe Ruth 100.00 250.00
37 Cal Ripken 12.50 30.00
38 Don Mattingly 20.00 50.00
39 Kirby Puckett 15.00 40.00
40 Roberto Clemente 30.00 60.00
41 A.Soriano/P.Rizzuto 8.00 20.00
42 S.Sosa/A.Dawson 10.00 25.00
43 O.Smith/S.Rolen 8.00 20.00
44 D.Mattingly/J.Giambi 12.00 30.00
45 R.Henderson/T.Cobb 50.00 100.00
46 J.Morgan/J.Bench 30.00 60.00
47 C.Ripken/B.Robinson 75.00 150.00
48 G.Brett/B.Jackson 50.00 100.00
49 B.Ruth/L.Gehrig 250.00 400.00
50 Y.Berra/T.Munson 30.00 60.00

2003 Donruss Elite Back to the Future

1-10 PRINT RUN 1000 SERIAL #'d SETS
11-15 PRINT RUN 500 SERIAL #'d SETS
1 Kerry Wood .40 1.00
2 Mark Prior .60 1.50
3 Magglio Ordonez .60 1.50
4 Joe Borchard .40 1.00
5 Lance Berkman .60 1.50
6 Jason Lane .40 1.00
7 Rafael Palmeiro .60 1.50
8 Mark Teixeira .60 1.50
9 Carlos Delgado .40 1.00
10 Josh Phelps .40 1.00
11 K.Wood .75 2.00
M.Prior
12 M.Ordonez .75 2.00
J.Borchard
13 L.Berkman .75 2.00
J.Lane
14 R.Palmeiro .75 2.00
M.Teixeira
15 C.Delgado .50 1.25
J.Phelps

2003 Donruss Elite Back to the Future Threads

*MULTI-COLOR PATCH: .75X TO 2X HI COL
1-10 PRINT RUN 250 SERIAL #'d SETS
11-15 PRINT RUN 125 SERIAL #'d SETS
1 Kerry Wood 3.00 8.00
2 Mark Prior 4.00 10.00
3 Magglio Ordonez 3.00 8.00
4 Joe Borchard 3.00 8.00
5 Lance Berkman 3.00 8.00
6 Jason Lane 3.00 8.00
7 Rafael Palmeiro 4.00 10.00
8 Mark Teixeira 4.00 10.00
9 Carlos Delgado 3.00 8.00
10 Josh Phelps 3.00 8.00
11 K.Wood/M.Prior 6.00 15.00
12 M.Ordonez/J.Borchard 6.00 15.00
13 L.Berkman/J.Lane 6.00 15.00
14 R.Palmeiro/M.Teixeira 6.00 15.00
15 C.Delgado/J.Phelps 6.00 15.00

2003 Donruss Elite Career Bests

PRINT RUNS B/WN 4-417 COPIES PER
NO PRICING ON QTY OF 25 OR LESS
3 Garret Anderson 2B/56 2.50 6.00
4 Andruw Jones BB/83 2.50 6.00
6 Magglio Ordonez HR/38 5.00 12.00
7 Magglio Ordonez RBI/135 2.50 6.00
8 Adam Dunn HR/26 6.00 15.00
10 Lance Berkman HR/42 5.00 12.00
11 Lance Berkman RBI/128 2.50 6.00
12 Shawn Green OBP/385 1.25 3.00
13 Alfonso Soriano HR/39 5.00 12.00
14 Alfonso Soriano AVG/300 2.00 5.00
15 Jason Giambi RUN/120 1.50 4.00
16 Derek Jeter SB/32 25.00 60.00
17 Vladimir Guerrero SB/40 5.00 12.00
18 Vladimir Guerrero OBP/417 2.00 5.00
20 Miguel Tejada HR/34 6.00 15.00
21 Barry Bonds BB/198 6.00 15.00
22 Barry Bonds AVG/370 5.00 12.00
23 Ichiro Suzuki OBP/388 4.00 10.00
24 Alex Rodriguez HR/57 8.00 20.00
25 Alex Rodriguez RBI/142 5.00 12.00

2003 Donruss Elite Career Bests Materials

SHOE MINOR STARS 4.00 10.00
SHOE SEMISTARS 6.00 15.00
SHOE UNLISTED STARS 6.00 15.00
STATED PRINT RUN 500 SERIAL #'d SETS
1 Randy Johnson WIN Jsy 4.00 10.00
2 Curt Schilling WIN Jsy 3.00 8.00
3 Garret Anderson 2B Bat 3.00 8.00
4 Andruw Jones BB Bat 4.00 10.00
5 Kerry Wood CG Shoe 4.00 10.00
6 Magglio Ordonez HR Bat 3.00 8.00
7 Magglio Ordonez RBI Bat 3.00 8.00
8 Adam Dunn HR Bat 3.00 8.00
9 Roy Oswalt WIN Jsy 3.00 8.00
10 Lance Berkman HR Bat 3.00 8.00
11 Lance Berkman RBI Bat 3.00 8.00
12 Shawn Green OBP Bat 3.00 8.00
13 Alfonso Soriano HR Bat 3.00 8.00
14 Alfonso Soriano AVG Bat 3.00 8.00
15 Jason Giambi RUN Bat 3.00 8.00
16 Derek Jeter SB Base 8.00 20.00
17 Vladimir Guerrero SB Bat 4.00 10.00
18 Vladimir Guerrero OBP Bat 4.00 10.00
19 Barry Zito WIN Jsy 3.00 8.00
20 Miguel Tejada HR Bat 3.00 8.00
21 Barry Bonds BB Base 8.00 20.00
22 Barry Bonds AVG Base 8.00 20.00
23 Ichiro Suzuki OBP Base 6.00 15.00
24 Alex Rodriguez HR Jsy 6.00 15.00
25 Alex Rodriguez RBI Jsy 6.00 15.00

2003 Donruss Elite Career Bests Materials Autographs

PRINT RUNS B/WN 5-250 COPIES PER
NO PRICING ON QTY OF 25 OR LESS
3 Garret Anderson 2B Bat/75 20.00 50.00
8 Adam Dunn HR Bat/100 5.00 12.00
9 Roy Oswalt WIN Jsy/250 8.00 20.00
17 Vlad Guerrero SB Bat/50 12.50 30.00
18 Vlad Guerrero OBP Bat/50 50.00 100.00
19 Barry Zito WIN Jsy/75 30.00 60.00

2003 Donruss Elite Highlights

RANDOM INSERTS IN PACKS
STATED PRINT RUN 500 SERIAL #'d SETS
1 Sammy Sosa 500 HR 1.50 4.00
2 Rafael Palmeiro 500 HR 1.00 2.50
3 Hideki Matsui Debut 3.00 8.00
4 Jose Contreras Debut 1.50 4.00
5 Kevin Millwood No-Hit .60 1.50

2003 Donruss Elite Highlights Autographs

STATED PRINT RUN 50 SERIAL #'d SETS
2 Rafael Palmeiro 500 HR 10.00 25.00
4 Jose Contreras Debut 15.00 40.00

2003 Donruss Elite Passing the Torch

1-10 PRINT RUN 1000 SERIAL #'d SETS
11-15 PRINT RUN 500 SERIAL #'d SETS
1 Stan Musial 1.50 4.00
2 Jim Edmonds .60 1.50
3 Dale Murphy 1.00 2.50
4 Andruw Jones .40 1.00
5 Roger Clemens 1.25 3.00
6 Mark Prior .60 1.50
7 Tom Seaver .60 1.50
8 Tom Glavine .60 1.50
9 Mike Schmidt 1.50 4.00
10 Pat Burrell .40 1.00
11 S.Musial 2.00 5.00
J.Edmonds
12 D.Murphy 1.25 3.00
A.Jones
13 R.Clemens 1.50 4.00
M.Prior
14 T.Seaver .75 2.00
T.Glavine
15 M.Schmidt 2.00 5.00
P.Burrell

2003 Donruss Elite Passing the Torch Autographs

1-10 PRINT RUN 50 SERIAL #'d SETS
11-15 PRINT RUN 25 SERIAL #'d SETS
NO 11-15 PRICING DUE TO SCARCITY
1 Stan Musial 40.00 80.00
2 Jim Edmonds 40.00 80.00
3 Dale Murphy 40.00 80.00
4 Andruw Jones 10.00 25.00
5 Roger Clemens 100.00 200.00
6 Mark Prior 20.00 50.00
7 Tom Seaver 40.00 100.00
8 Tom Glavine 40.00 80.00
9 Mike Schmidt 20.00 50.00
10 Pat Burrell 20.00 50.00

2003 Donruss Elite Recollection Autographs

PRINT RUNS B/WN 1-100 COPIES PER
NO PRICING ON QTY OF 25 OR LESS
1 Jeremy Affeldt 01/75 4.00 10.00
2 Erick Almonte 01/75 4.00 10.00
4 Adrian Beltre 02/36 12.00 30.00
7 Brandon Berger 01/83 4.00 10.00
8 Angel Berroa 01/28 10.00 25.00
13 Jeff Deardorff 01/53 4.00 10.00
14 Ryan Drese 01/100 6.00 15.00
21 Luis Garcia 01/28 6.00 15.00
22 Geronimo Gil 01/75 4.00 10.00
28 Travis Hafner 01 Black/52 10.00 25.00
30 Bill Hall 01/27 10.00 25.00
35 Gerald Laird 02/46 6.00 15.00
36 Jason Lane 01/27 10.00 25.00
44 Victor Martinez 01/52 60.00 120.00
46 Roy Oswalt 01 Black/61 6.00 15.00
51 Ricardo Rodriguez 01/75 4.00 10.00
55 Bud Smith 01/50 6.00 15.00
56 Bud Smith 02/28 6.00 15.00
58 Junior Spivey 01/45 6.00 15.00
59 Tim Spooneybarger 01/100 4.00 10.00
61 Shannon Stewart 02/35 10.00 25.00
64 Claudio Vargas 01/51 4.00 10.00

2003 Donruss Elite Throwback Threads

1-45 PRINT RUN 250 SERIAL #'d SETS
46-75 PRINT RUN 125 SERIAL #'d SETS
76-90 PRINT RUN 100 SERIAL #'d SETS
91-95 PRINT RUN 75 SERIAL #'d SETS
96-100 PRINT RUN RUN 50 SERIAL #'d SETS
*MULTI-COLOR PATCH: .75X TO 2X HI COL
1 Randy Johnson D'backs 4.00 10.00
2 Randy Johnson M's 4.00 10.00
3 Roger Clemens Yanks 5.00 12.00
4 Roger Clemens Red Sox 5.00 12.00
5 Manny Ramirez 4.00 10.00
6 Greg Maddux 5.00 12.00
7 Jason Giambi Yanks 1.50 4.00
8 Jason Giambi A's 1.50 4.00
9 Alex Rodriguez Rgr 5.00 12.00
10 Alex Rodriguez M's 5.00 12.00
11 Miguel Tejada 2.50 6.00
12 Alfonso Soriano 2.50 6.00
13 Nomar Garciaparra 2.50 6.00
14 Pedro Martinez Red Sox 2.50 6.00
15 Pedro Martinez Expos 2.50 6.00
16 Andruw Jones 1.50 4.00
17 Chipper Jones 4.00 10.00
18 Barry Zito 2.50 6.00
19 Mark Mulder 1.50 4.00
20 Lance Berkman 2.50 6.00
21 Magglio Ordonez 2.50 6.00
22 Mike Piazza Mets 4.00 10.00
23 Mike Piazza Dodgers 4.00 10.00
24 Rickey Henderson Padres 4.00 10.00
25 Rickey Henderson Mets 4.00 10.00
26 Rickey Henderson M's 4.00 10.00
27 Sammy Sosa 4.00 10.00
28 Shawn Green 1.50 4.00
29 Troy Glaus 1.50 4.00
30 Vladimir Guerrero 2.50 6.00
31 Adam Dunn 2.50 6.00
32 Jeff Bagwell 2.50 6.00
33 Curt Schilling 2.50 6.00
34 Hideo Nomo Dodgers 4.00 10.00
35 Hideo Nomo Red Sox 4.00 10.00
36 Hideo Nomo Mets 4.00 10.00
37 Kerry Wood 1.50 4.00
38 Mark Prior 2.50 6.00
39 Roberto Alomar 2.50 6.00
40 Todd Helton 2.50 6.00
41 Jim Thome 2.50 6.00
42 Rafael Palmeiro 2.50 6.00
43 Juan Gonzalez 1.50 4.00
44 Vernon Wells 1.50 4.00
45 Torii Hunter 1.50 4.00
46 R.Johnson D'backs-M's 6.00 15.00
47 R.Clemens Yanks-Sox 8.00 20.00
48 J.Giambi Yanks-A's 2.50 6.00
49 A.Rodriguez Rangers/M's 8.00 20.00
50 P.Martinez Red Sox-Expos 4.00 10.00
51 M.Piazza Mets-Dodgers 6.00 15.00
52 R.Henderson A's-M's 6.00 15.00
53 R.Henderson Padres-Mets 6.00 15.00
54 R.Henderson Angels-Padres 6.00 15.00
55 H.Nomo Dodgers-Sox 6.00 15.00
56 R.Johnson D'backs-Expos 6.00 15.00
57 R.Johnson/C.Schilling 6.00 15.00
58 A.Soriano/J.Giambi 4.00 10.00
59 B.Zito/M.Mulder 4.00 10.00
60 A.Jones/C.Jones 6.00 15.00
61 G.Maddux/T.Glavine 8.00 20.00
62 L.Berkman/J.Bagwell 4.00 10.00
63 R.Clemens/M.Prior 8.00 20.00
64 A.Rodriguez/R.Palmeiro 8.00 20.00
65 J.Thome/R.Alomar 4.00 10.00
66 M.Piazza/R.Alomar 6.00 15.00
67 S.Sosa/M.Grace 6.00 15.00
68 T.Helton/L.Walker 4.00 10.00
69 A.Dunn/A.Kearns 4.00 10.00
70 A.Rodriguez/I.Rodriguez 8.00 20.00
71 B.Abreu/M.Byrd 2.50 6.00
72 M.Tejada/E.Chavez 4.00 10.00
73 G.Maddux/J.Smoltz 8.00 20.00
74 K.Wood/M.Prior 4.00 10.00
75 B.Zito/T.Hudson 4.00 10.00
76 Babe Ruth 150.00 300.00
77 Ty Cobb 50.00 120.00
78 Jackie Robinson 50.00 100.00
79 Lou Gehrig 100.00 200.00
80 Thurman Munson 20.00 50.00
81 Nolan Ryan Astros 12.00 30.00
82 Don Mattingly 15.00 40.00
83 Mike Schmidt 15.00 40.00
84 Reggie Jackson 10.00 25.00
85 George Brett 15.00 40.00
86 Cal Ripken 30.00 60.00
87 Tony Gwynn 10.00 25.00
88 Yogi Berra 10.00 25.00
89 Stan Musial 12.50 30.00
90 Jim Palmer 8.00 20.00
91 T.Munson/J.Posada 15.00 40.00
92 D.Murphy/C.Jones 20.00 50.00
93 D.Mattingly/J.Giambi 40.00 80.00
94 A.Dawson/S.Sosa 15.00 40.00
95 N.Ryan/M.Prior 15.00 40.00
96 B.Ruth/L.Gehrig 300.00 500.00
97 T.Seaver/J.Morgan 30.00 60.00
98 H.Killebrew/R.Carew 30.00 60.00
99 N.Ryan Rangers-Angels 40.00 80.00
100 R.Jackson Yanks-A's 30.00 60.00

2003 Donruss Elite Throwback Threads Autographs

RANDOM INSERTS IN PACKS
PRINT RUNS B/WN 5-75 COPIES PER
30 Vladimir Guerrero/50 10.00 25.00
31 Adam Dunn/50 10.00 25.00
37 Kerry Wood/50 15.00 40.00
38 Mark Prior/75 30.00 60.00
39 Roberto Alomar/50 50.00 100.00

2003 Donruss Elite Throwback Threads Prime

1-45 PRINT RUN 25 SERIAL #'d SETS
46-75 PRINT RUN 15 SERIAL #'d SETS
76-95 PRINT RUN 10 SERIAL #'d SETS
96-100 PRINT RUN 5 SERIAL #'d SETS

2003 Donruss Elite Extra Edition

RANDOM INSERTS IN DLP R/T PACKS
STATED PRINT RUN 900 SERIAL #'d SETS
CARDS 42/51/54/56 DO NOT EXIST
1 Adam Loewen RC .50 1.25
2 Brandon Webb RC 1.50 4.00
3 Chien-Ming Wang RC 2.00 5.00
4 Hong-Chih Kuo RC 2.50 6.00
5 Clint Barmes RC 1.25 3.00
6 Guillermo Quiroz RC .50 1.25
7 Edgar Gonzalez RC .50 1.25
8 Todd Wellemeyer RC .50 1.25
9 Alfredo Gonzalez RC .50 1.25
10 Craig Brazell RC .50 1.25
11 Tim Olson RC .50 1.25
12 Rich Fischer RC .50 1.25
13 Daniel Cabrera RC .75 2.00
14 Francisco Rosario RC .50 1.25
15 Francisco Cruceta RC .50 1.25
16 Alejandro Machado RC .50 1.25
17 Andrew Brown RC .50 1.25
18 Rob Hammock RC .50 1.25
19 Arnie Munoz RC .50 1.25
20 Felix Sanchez RC .50 1.25
21 Nook Logan RC .50 1.25
22 Cory Stewart RC .50 1.25
23 Michel Hernandez RC .50 1.25
24 Rett Johnson RC .50 1.25
25 Josh Hall RC .50 1.25
26 Doug Waechter RC .50 1.25
27 Matt Kata RC .50 1.25
28 Dan Haren RC 2.50 6.00
29 Dontrelle Willis .50 1.25
30 Ramon Nivar RC .50 1.25
31 Chad Gaudin RC .50 1.25
32 Rickie Weeks RC 1.50 4.00
33 Ryan Wagner RC .50 1.25
34 Kevin Correia RC .50 1.25
35 Bo Hart RC .50 1.25
36 Oscar Villarreal RC .50 1.25
37 Josh Willingham RC 1.50 4.00
38 Jeff Duncan RC .50 1.25
39 David DeJesus RC 1.25 3.00
40 Dustin McGowan RC .50 1.25
41 Preston Larrison RC .50 1.25
43 Kevin Youkilis RC 3.00 8.00
44 Bubba Nelson RC .50 1.25
45 Chris Burke RC .50 1.25
46 J.D. Durbin RC .50 1.25
47 Ryan Howard RC 4.00 10.00
48 Jason Kubel RC 1.50 4.00
49 Brendan Harris RC .50 1.25
50 Brian Bruney RC .50 1.25
52 Byron Gettis RC .50 1.25
53 Edwin Jackson RC .75 2.00
55 Daniel Garcia RC .50 1.25
57 Chad Cordero RC .50 1.25
58 Delmon Young RC 3.00 8.00

2003 Donruss Elite Extra Edition Aspirations

*ASP P/R b/wn 51-65: .75X TO 2X
*ASP RC's P/R b/wn 81-120: .6X TO 1.5X
*ASP RC's P/R b/wn 66-80: .75X TO 2X
*ASP RC's P/R b/wn 51-65: .75X TO 2X
*ASP RC's P/R b/wn 36-50: 1X TO 2.5X
*ASP RC's P/R b/wn 26-35: 1.25X TO 3X
PRINT RUNS B/WN 24-98 COPIES PER
NO PRICING ON QTY OF 25 OR LESS
CARDS 42/51/54/56 DO NOT EXIST

2003 Donruss Elite Extra Edition Aspirations Gold

STATED PRINT RUN 1 SERIAL #'d SET
NO PRICING DUE TO SCARCITY
CARDS 42/51/54/56 DO NOT EXIST

2003 Donruss Elite Extra Edition Status

*STATUS P/R b/wn 26-35: 1.25X TO 3X
*STATUS RC's P/R b/wn 66-80: .75X TO 2X
*STATUS RC's P/R b/wn 51-65: .75X TO 2X
*STATUS RC's P/R b/wn 36-50: 1X TO 2.5X
*STATUS RC's P/R b/wn 26-35: 1.25X TO 3X
PRINT RUNS B/WN 2-76 COPIES PER
NO PRICING ON QTY OF 25 OR LESS
CARDS 42/51/54/56 DO NOT EXIST

2003 Donruss Elite Extra Edition Status Gold

STATED PRINT RUN 24 SERIAL #'d SETS
NO PRICING DUE TO SCARCITY
CARDS 42/51/54/56 DO NOT EXIST

2003 Donruss Elite Extra Edition Turn of the Century

*TOC P/R b/wn 66-80: .75X TO 2X
*TOC RC's P/R b/wn 66-80: .75X TO 2X
PRINT RUNS B/WN 75-100 COPIES PER

2003 Donruss Elite Extra Edition Turn of the Century Autographs

RANDOM INSERTS IN DLP R/T PACKS
STATED PRINT RUN 100 SERIAL #'d SETS
CARDS 29/32/34 PRINT RUN 25 #'d SETS
NO PRICING ON QTY OF 25 OR LESS
1 Adam Loewen 10.00 25.00
2 Brandon Webb 40.00 80.00
3 Chien-Ming Wang 75.00 150.00
4 Hong-Chih Kuo 100.00 200.00
5 Clint Barmes 4.00 10.00
6 Guillermo Quiroz 4.00 10.00
7 Edgar Gonzalez 4.00 10.00
8 Todd Wellemeyer 4.00 10.00
9 Alfredo Gonzalez 4.00 10.00
10 Craig Brazell 4.00 10.00
11 Tim Olson 4.00 10.00

12 Rich Fischer 4.00 10.00
13 Daniel Cabrera 15.00 40.00
14 Francisco Rosario 4.00 10.00
15 Francisco Cruceta 4.00 10.00
16 Alejandro Machado 4.00 10.00
17 Andrew Brown 6.00 15.00
18 Rob Hammock 4.00 10.00
19 Arnie Munoz 4.00 10.00
20 Felix Sanchez 4.00 10.00
21 Nook Logan 6.00 15.00
22 Cory Stewart 4.00 10.00
23 Michel Hernandez 4.00 10.00
24 Rett Johnson 4.00 10.00
25 Josh Hall 4.00 10.00
26 Doug Waechter 6.00 15.00
27 Matt Kata 4.00 10.00
28 Dan Haren 20.00 50.00
30 Ramon Nivar 4.00 10.00
31 Chad Gaudin 4.00 10.00
33 Ryan Wagner 4.00 10.00
35 Bo Hart 4.00 10.00
36 Oscar Villarreal 6.00 15.00
37 Josh Willingham 15.00 40.00
38 Jeff Duncan 4.00 10.00
40 Dustin McGowan 6.00 15.00
41 Preston Larrison 4.00 10.00
43 Kevin Youkilis 15.00 40.00
44 Bubba Nelson 4.00 10.00
45 Chris Burke 15.00 40.00
46 J.D. Durbin 4.00 10.00
47 Ryan Howard 175.00 350.00
48 Jason Kubel 15.00 40.00
49 Brendan Harris 6.00 15.00
50 Brian Bruney 6.00 15.00
52 Byron Gettis 4.00 10.00
53 Edwin Jackson 8.00 20.00
55 Daniel Garcia 4.00 10.00
58 Delmon Young 8.00 20.00

2004 Donruss Elite

COMP.SET w/o SP's (150) 10.00 25.00
COMMON CARD 1-150 .12 .30
COMMON AUTO (151-180) 3.00 8.00
151-180 RANDOM INSERTS IN PACKS
151-180 PRINT RUN B/WN 750-1000 #'d PER
COMMON CARD (181-200) .40 1.00
181-200 RANDOM INSERTS IN PACKS
181-200 PRINT RUN 1000 SERIAL #'d SETS
CARD NUMBER 169 DOES NOT EXIST
1 Troy Glaus .12 .30
2 Darin Erstad .12 .30
3 Garret Anderson .12 .30
4 Tim Salmon .12 .30
5 Bartolo Colon .12 .30
6 Jose Guillen .12 .30
7 Miguel Tejada .20 .50
8 Adam Loewen .12 .30
9 Jay Gibbons .12 .30
10 Melvin Mora .12 .30
11 Javy Lopez .12 .30
12 Pedro Martinez .20 .50
13 Curt Schilling .20 .50
14 David Ortiz .30 .75
15 Keith Foulke .12 .30
16 Nomar Garciaparra .20 .50
17 Magglio Ordonez .20 .50
18 Frank Thomas .30 .75
19 Carlos Lee .12 .30
20 Paul Konerko .20 .50
21 Mark Buehrle .20 .50
22 Jody Gerut .12 .30
23 Victor Martinez .20 .50
24 C.C. Sabathia .20 .50
25 Ellis Burks .12 .30
26 Bobby Higginson .12 .30
27 Jeremy Bonderman .12 .30
28 Fernando Vina .12 .30
29 Carlos Pena .20 .50
30 Dmitri Young .12 .30
31 Carlos Beltran .20 .50
32 Benito Santiago .12 .30
33 Mike Sweeney .12 .30
34 Angel Berroa .12 .30
35 Runelvys Hernandez .12 .30
36 Johan Santana .20 .50
37 Doug Mientkiewicz .12 .30
38 Shannon Stewart .12 .30
39 Torii Hunter .12 .30
40 Derek Jeter .75 2.00
41 Jason Giambi .12 .30
42 Bernie Williams .20 .50
43 Alfonso Soriano .20 .50
44 Gary Sheffield .12 .30
45 Mike Mussina .20 .50
46 Jorge Posada .20 .50
47 Hideki Matsui .50 1.25
48 Kevin Brown .12 .30
49 Javier Vazquez .12 .30
50 Mariano Rivera .40 1.00
51 Eric Chavez .12 .30
52 Tim Hudson .20 .50
53 Mark Mulder .12 .30
54 Barry Zito .20 .50
55 Ichiro Suzuki .40 1.00
56 Edgar Martinez .20 .50
57 Bret Boone .12 .30
58 John Olerud .12 .30
59 Scott Spiezio .12 .30
60 Aubrey Huff .12 .30
61 Rocco Baldelli .12 .30
62 Jose Cruz Jr. .12 .30
63 Delmon Young .20 .50
64 Mark Teixeira .20 .50
65 Hank Blalock .12 .30
66 Michael Young .12 .30
67 Alex Rodriguez .40 1.00
68 Carlos Delgado .12 .30
69 Eric Hinske .12 .30
70 Roy Halladay .20 .50
71 Vernon Wells .12 .30
72 Randy Johnson .30 .75
73 Richie Sexson .12 .30
74 Brandon Webb .12 .30
75 Luis Gonzalez .12 .30
76 Steve Finley .12 .30
77 Chipper Jones .30 .75
78 Andruw Jones .12 .30
79 Marcus Giles .12 .30
80 Rafael Furcal .12 .30
81 J.D. Drew .12 .30
82 Sammy Sosa .30 .75
83 Kerry Wood .12 .30
84 Mark Prior .20 .50
85 Derrek Lee .12 .30
86 Moises Alou .12 .30
87 Corey Patterson .12 .30
88 Ken Griffey Jr. .60 1.50
89 Austin Kearns .12 .30
90 Adam Dunn .20 .50
91 Barry Larkin .20 .50
92 Todd Helton .20 .50
93 Larry Walker .20 .50
94 Preston Wilson .12 .30
95 Charles Johnson .12 .30
96 Luis Castillo .12 .30
97 Josh Beckett .12 .30
98 Mike Lowell .12 .30
99 Miguel Cabrera .30 .75
100 Juan Pierre .12 .30
101 Dontrelle Willis .12 .30
102 Andy Pettitte .20 .50
103 Wade Miller .12 .30
104 Jeff Bagwell .20 .50
105 Craig Biggio .20 .50
106 Lance Berkman .20 .50
107 Jeff Kent .12 .30
108 Roy Oswalt .20 .50
109 Hideo Nomo .30 .75
110 Adrian Beltre .30 .75
111 Paul Lo Duca .12 .30
112 Shawn Green .12 .30
113 Fred McGriff .12 .30
114 Eric Gagne .12 .30
115 Geoff Jenkins .12 .30
116 Rickie Weeks .12 .30
117 Scott Podsednik .12 .30
118 Nick Johnson .12 .30
119 Orlando Cabrera .12 .30
120 Jose Vidro .12 .30
121 Kazuo Matsui RC .20 .50
122 Tom Glavine .20 .50
123 Al Leiter .12 .30
124 Mike Piazza .30 .75
125 Jose Reyes .20 .50
126 Mike Cameron .12 .30
127 Pat Burrell .12 .30
128 Jim Thome .20 .50
129 Mike Lieberthal .12 .30
130 Bobby Abreu .12 .30
131 Kip Wells .12 .30
132 Jack Wilson .12 .30
133 Pokey Reese .12 .30
134 Brian Giles .12 .30
135 Sean Burroughs .12 .30
136 Ryan Klesko .12 .30
137 Trevor Hoffman .20 .50
138 Jason Schmidt .12 .30
139 J.T. Snow .12 .30
140 A.J. Pierzynski .12 .30
141 Ray Durham .12 .30
142 Jim Edmonds .20 .50
143 Albert Pujols .40 1.00
144 Edgar Renteria .12 .30
145 Scott Rolen .20 .50
146 Matt Morris .12 .30
147 Ivan Rodriguez .20 .50
148 Vladimir Guerrero .20 .50
149 Greg Maddux .40 1.00
150 Kevin Millwood .12 .30
151 Hector Gimenez AU/750 RC 3.00 8.00
152 Willy Taveras AU/750 RC 3.00 8.00
153 Ruddy Yan AU/750 3.00 8.00
154 Graham Koonce AU/750 3.00 8.00
155 Jose Capellan AU/750 RC 3.00 8.00
156 Onil Joseph AU/750 RC 3.00 8.00
157 John Gall AU/1000 RC 3.00 8.00
158 Carlos Hines AU/750 RC 3.00 8.00
159 Jerry Gil AU/750 RC 3.00 8.00
160 Mike Gosling AU/750 RC 3.00 8.00
161 Jason Frasor AU/750 RC 3.00 8.00
162 Justin Knoedler AU/750 RC 3.00 8.00
163 Merkin Valdez AU/500 RC 3.00 8.00
164 Angel Chavez AU/1000 RC 3.00 8.00
165 Ivan Ochoa AU/750 RC 3.00 8.00
166 Greg Dobbs AU/750 RC 3.00 8.00
167 Ronald Belisario AU/750 RC 3.00 8.00
168 Aarom Baldiris AU/750 RC 3.00 8.00
170 Dave Crouthers AU/750 RC 3.00 8.00
171 Freddy Guzman AU/750 RC 3.00 8.00
172 Akinori Otsuka AU/250 RC 6.00 15.00
173 Ian Snell AU/750 RC 6.00 15.00
174 Nick Regilio AU/1000 RC 3.00 8.00
175 Jamie Brown AU/750 RC 3.00 8.00
176 Jerome Gamble AU/750 RC 3.00 8.00
177 Roberto Novoa AU/1000 RC 3.00 8.00
178 Sean Henn AU/1000 RC 3.00 8.00
179 Ramon Ramirez AU/1000 RC 3.00 8.00
180 Jason Bartlett AU/1000 RC 4.00 10.00
181 Bob Gibson RET .60 1.50
182 Cal Ripken RET 3.00 8.00
183 Carl Yastrzemski RET 1.00 2.50
184 Dale Murphy RET 1.00 2.50
185 Don Mattingly RET 2.00 5.00
186 Eddie Murray RET .60 1.50
187 George Brett RET 2.00 5.00
188 Jackie Robinson RET 1.00 2.50
189 Jim Palmer RET .60 1.50
190 Lou Gehrig RET 2.00 5.00
191 Mike Schmidt RET 1.50 4.00
192 Ozzie Smith RET 1.25 3.00
193 Nolan Ryan RET 3.00 8.00
194 Reggie Jackson RET .60 1.50
195 Roberto Clemente RET 2.50 6.00
196 Robin Yount RET 1.00 2.50
197 Stan Musial RET 1.50 4.00
198 Ted Williams RET 2.00 5.00
199 Tony Gwynn RET 1.00 2.50
200 Ty Cobb RET 1.50 4.00

2004 Donruss Elite Aspirations

*1-150 PRINT RUN b/wn 81-99: 4X TO 10X
*1-150 PRINT RUN b/wn 66-80: 5X TO 12X
*1-150 PRINT RUN b/wn 51-65: 5X TO 12X
*1-150 PRINT RUN b/wn 36-50: 6X TO 15X
*1-150 PRINT RUN b/wn 26-35: 8X TO 20X
*1-150 PRINT RUN b/wn 16-25: 10X TO 25X
COMMON CARD (151-180) 2.50 6.00
SEMISTARS 151-180 4.00 10.00
UNLISTED STARS 151-180 6.00 15.00
*181-200 P/R b/wn 81-99: 1.25X TO 3X
*181-200 P/R b/wn 66-80: 1.5X TO 4X
*181-200 P/R b/wn 51-65: 1.5X TO 4X
RANDOM INSERTS IN PACKS
PRINT RUNS B/WN 19-99 COPIES PER
1-150/181-200 NO PRICING ON 15 OR LESS
151-180 NO PRICING ON 25 OR LESS
121 Kazuo Matsui/75
151 Hector Gimenez ROO/30 2.50 6.00
152 Willy Taveras ROO/99 6.00 15.00
153 Ruddy Yan ROO/38 2.50 6.00
154 Graham Koonce ROO/82 2.50 6.00
155 Jose Capellan ROO/29 2.50 6.00
156 Onil Joseph ROO/24 2.50 6.00
157 John Gall ROO/19 2.50 6.00
158 Carlos Hines ROO/31 2.50 6.00
159 Jerry Gil ROO/38 2.50 6.00
160 Mike Gosling ROO/56 2.50 6.00
161 Jason Frasor ROO/22 2.50 6.00
162 Justin Knoedler ROO/40 2.50 6.00
163 Merkin Valdez ROO/39 2.50 6.00
164 Angel Chavez ROO/41 2.50 6.00
165 Ivan Ochoa ROO/26 2.50 6.00
166 Greg Dobbs ROO/40 2.50 6.00
167 Ronald Belisario ROO/29 2.50 6.00
168 Aarom Baldiris ROO/35 2.50 6.00
169 Kazuo Matsui ROO/75 4.00 10.00
170 Dave Crouthers ROO/30 2.50 6.00
171 Freddy Guzman ROO/35 2.50 6.00
172 Akinori Otsuka ROO/84 2.50 6.00
173 Ian Snell ROO/51 2.50 6.00
174 Nick Regilio ROO/36 2.50 6.00
175 Jamie Brown ROO/48 2.50 6.00
176 Jerome Gamble ROO/38 2.50 6.00
177 Roberto Novoa ROO/49 2.50 6.00
178 Sean Henn ROO/37 2.50 6.00
179 Ramon Ramirez ROO/34 2.50 6.00
180 Jason Bartlett ROO/20 8.00 20.00

2004 Donruss Elite Status

*1-150 PRINT RUN b/wn 66-80: 5X TO 12X
*1-150 PRINT RUN b/wn 51-65: 5X TO 12X
*1-150 PRINT RUN b/wn 36-50: 6X TO 15X
*1-150 PRINT RUN b/wn 26-35: 8X TO 20X
*1-150 PRINT RUN b/wn 16-25: 10X TO 25X
COMMON CARD (151-180) 2.50 6.00
SEMISTARS 151-180 4.00 10.00
UNLISTED STARS 151-180 6.00 15.00
*181-200 P/R b/wn 36-50: 2X TO 5X
*181-200 P/R b/wn 26-35: 2.5X TO 6X
*181-200 P/R b/wn 16-25: 3X TO 8X
RANDOM INSERTS IN PACKS
PRINT RUNS B/WN 1-81 COPIES PER
1-120/122-50/181-200 NO PRICE 15 OR LESS
121/151-180 NO PRICING ON 25 OR LESS
151 Hector Gimenez ROO/70 2.50 6.00
152 Willy Taveras ROO/1
153 Ruddy Yan ROO/62 2.50 6.00
154 Graham Koonce ROO/18 2.50 6.00
155 Jose Capellan ROO/71 2.50 6.00
156 Onil Joseph ROO/76 2.50 6.00
157 John Gall ROO/81 2.50 6.00
158 Carlos Hines ROO/69 2.50 6.00
159 Jerry Gil ROO/62 2.50 6.00
160 Mike Gosling ROO/44 2.50 6.00
161 Jason Frasor ROO/78 2.50 6.00
162 Justin Knoedler ROO/60 2.50 6.00
163 Merkin Valdez ROO/61 2.50 6.00
164 Angel Chavez ROO/59 2.50 6.00
165 Ivan Ochoa ROO/74 2.50 6.00
166 Greg Dobbs ROO/60 2.50 6.00
167 Ronald Belisario ROO/71 2.50 6.00
168 Aarom Baldiris ROO/65 2.50 6.00
169 Kazuo Matsui ROO/25 4.00 10.00
170 Dave Crouthers ROO/70 2.50 6.00
171 Freddy Guzman ROO/65 2.50 6.00
172 Akinori Otsuka ROO/16 2.50 6.00
173 Ian Snell ROO/49 2.50 6.00
174 Nick Regilio ROO/64 2.50 6.00
175 Jamie Brown ROO/52 2.50 6.00
176 Jerome Gamble ROO/62 2.50 6.00
177 Roberto Novoa ROO/51 2.50 6.00
178 Sean Henn ROO/63 2.50 6.00
179 Ramon Ramirez ROO/66 2.50 6.00
180 Jason Bartlett ROO/80 8.00 20.00

2004 Donruss Elite Status Gold

*GOLD 1-120/122-150: 10X TO 25X BASIC
*GOLD 181-200: 3X TO 8X BASIC
RANDOM INSERTS IN PACKS
STATED PRINT RUN 24 SERIAL #'d SETS
121/151-180 NO PRICING DUE TO SCARCITY

2004 Donruss Elite Turn of the Century

*TOC 1-120/122-150: 1.5X TO 4X BASIC
*TOC 121: 1.25X TO 3X BASIC
1-150 PRINT RUN 750 SERIAL #'d SETS
*TOC 181-200: .75X TO 2X BASIC
181-200 PRINT RUN 250 SERIAL #'d SETS
RANDOM INSERTS IN PACKS
CARDS 151-180 DO NOT EXIST

2004 Donruss Elite Back 2 Back Jacks

RANDOM INSERTS IN PACKS
SINGLE PRINT RUNS B/WN 25-125 PER
DUAL PRINT RUNS B/WN 25-50 PER
1 Albert Pujols/125 6.00 15.00
2 Alex Rodriguez Rgr/125 4.00 10.00
3 Alfonso Soriano/125 3.00 8.00
4 Andruw Jones/125 4.00 10.00
5 Chipper Jones/125 4.00 10.00
6 Derek Jeter/125 8.00 20.00
7 Frank Thomas/125 4.00 10.00
8 Miguel Cabrera/125 4.00 10.00
9 Jason Giambi/125 3.00 8.00
10 Jim Thome/125 4.00 10.00
11 Mike Piazza/125 4.00 10.00
12 Nomar Garciaparra/25 10.00 25.00
13 Sammy Sosa/125 4.00 10.00
14 Shawn Green/125 3.00 8.00
15 Vladimir Guerrero/125 4.00 10.00
16 A.Jones/C.Jones/50 10.00 25.00
17 A.Soriano/D.Jeter/50 15.00 40.00
18 J.Bagwell/L.Berkman/50 10.00 25.00
19 A.Rodriguez/R.Palmeiro/50 10.00 25.00
20 A.Dunn/A.Kearns/25 8.00 20.00
21 Al Kaline/100 6.00 15.00
22 Babe Ruth/50 75.00 150.00
23 Cal Ripken/100 10.00 25.00
24 Dale Murphy/100 6.00 15.00
25 Don Mattingly/100 6.00 15.00
26 George Brett/100 6.00 15.00
27 Lou Gehrig/100 40.00 80.00
28 Mike Schmidt/100 6.00 15.00
29 Roberto Clemente/100 15.00 40.00
30 Roy Campanella/100 6.00 15.00
31 B.Ruth/R.Maris/25 150.00 250.00
32 H.Killebrew/K.Puckett/50 15.00 40.00
33 P.Molitor/R.Yount/50 10.00 25.00
34 R.Jackson/R.Jackson/50 10.00 25.00
35 L.Gehrig/T.Cobb/50 125.00 200.00
36 D.Mattingly/J.Giambi/50 12.50 30.00
37 T.Williams/Nomar/50 15.00 40.00
38 A.Dawson/S.Sosa/50 10.00 25.00
39 D.Murphy/C.Jones/50 10.00 25.00
40 S.Musial/J.Edmonds/50 12.50 30.00

2004 Donruss Elite Back 2 Back Jacks Combos

*COMBO 1-15: .75X TO 2X B2B p/r 125
*COMBO 1-15: .4X TO 1X B2B p/r 25
*COMBO 16-20: .6X TO 1.5X B2B p/r 50
*COMBO 16-20: .5X TO 1.2X B2B p/r 25
*COMBO 21-30 p/r 50:.6X TO 1.5X BTBp/r100
*COMBO 21-30 p/r 25: 1X TO 2.5X BTB p/r 100
*COMBO 21-30 p/r 25: .6X TO 1.5X BTB p/r 50
*COMBO 31-40 p/r 25: .6X TO 1.5X B2B p/r 50
RANDOM INSERTS IN PACKS
SINGLE PRINT RUNS B/WN 25-50 PER
DUAL PRINT RUNS B/WN 10-25 PER
NO PRICING ON QTY OF 10 OR LESS
12 N.Garciaparra Bat-Jsy/50 10.00 25.00
22 Babe Ruth Bat-Jsy/25 250.00 400.00
27 Lou Gehrig Bat-Jsy/25 100.00 200.00
32 H.Killebrew/K.Puckett/25 50.00 100.00
35 L.Gehrig/T.Cobb/25 150.00 300.00
37 T.Williams/Nomar/25 30.00 60.00

2004 Donruss Elite Back to the Future

COMMON CARD (1-6) .60 1.50
SEMISTARS 1-6 1.00 2.50
UNLISTED STARS 1-6 1.50 4.00
1-6 PRINT RUN 500 SERIAL #'d SETS
COMMON CARD (6-9) .75 2.00
SEMISTARS 6-9 1.25 3.00
UNLISTED STARS 6-9 2.00 5.00
6-9 PRINT RUN 250 SERIAL #'d SETS
*BLACK 1-6: 1X TO 2.5X BASIC
*BLACK 7-9: 1.25X TO 3X BASIC
BLACK 1-6 PRINT RUN 50 SERIAL #'d SETS
BLACK 7-9 PRINT RUN 25 SERIAL #'d SETS
*GOLD 1-6: .6X TO 1.5X BASIC
*GOLD 7-9: .75X TO 2X BASIC
GOLD 1-6 PRINT RUN 100 SERIAL #'d SETS
GOLD 7-9 PRINT RUN 50 SERIAL #'d SETS
*RED 1-6: .5X TO 1.2X BASIC
*RED 7-9: .5X TO 1.2X BASIC
RED 1-6 PRINT RUN 250 SERIAL #'d SETS
RED 7-9 PRINT RUN 125 SERIAL #'d SETS
RANDOM INSERTS IN PACKS
1 Tim Hudson 1.00 2.50
2 Rich Harden .60 1.50
3 Alex Rodriguez Rgr 2.00 5.00
4 Hank Blalock .60 1.50
5 Sammy Sosa 1.50 4.00
6 Hee Seop Choi .60 1.50
7 T.Hudson R.Harden 1.25 3.00
8 A.Rodriguez H.Blalock 2.50 6.00
9 S.Sosa H.Choi 2.00 5.00

2004 Donruss Elite Back to the Future Bats

1-6 PRINT RUN 200 SERIAL #'d SETS
8-9 PRINT RUN 100 SERIAL #'d SETS
RANDOM INSERTS IN PACKS
1 Tim Hudson 2.50 6.00
3 Alex Rodriguez Rgr 4.00 10.00
4 Hank Blalock 2.50 6.00
5 Sammy Sosa 3.00 8.00
6 Hee Seop Choi 2.50 6.00
8 A.Rodriguez/H.Blalock 6.00 15.00
9 S.Sosa/H.Choi 5.00 12.00

2004 Donruss Elite Back to the Future Jerseys

1-6 PRINT RUN 200 SERIAL #'d SETS
7-9 PRINT RUN 100 SERIAL #'d SETS
*PRIME: 1.25X TO 3X BASIC
PRIME 1-6 PRINT RUN 50 SERIAL #'d SETS
PRIME 7-9 PRINT RUN 25 SERIAL #'d SETS
1 Tim Hudson 2.50 6.00
2 Rich Harden 2.50 6.00
3 Alex Rodriguez Rgr 4.00 10.00
4 Hank Blalock 2.50 6.00
5 Sammy Sosa 3.00 8.00
6 Hee Seop Choi 2.50 6.00
7 T.Hudson/R.Harden 4.00 10.00
8 A.Rodriguez/H.Blalock 6.00 15.00
9 S.Sosa/H.Choi 5.00 12.00

2004 Donruss Elite Career Best

STATED PRINT RUN 1000 SERIAL #'d SETS
*BLACK: 1.25X TO 3X BASIC
BLACK PRINT RUN 100 SERIAL #'d SETS
*GOLD p/r 220-390: 1X TO 2.5X BASIC
*GOLD p/r 130-193: 1X TO 2.5X BASIC
*GOLD p/r 113-116: 1.25X TO 3X BASIC
*GOLD p/r 40-57: 2X TO 5X BASIC
*GOLD p/r 23-33: 3X TO 8X BASIC
*GOLD p/r 18-20: 4X TO 10X BASIC
GOLD PRINT RUNS B/WN 14-393 PER
NO GOLD PRICING ON QTY OF 14 OR LESS
RANDOM INSERTS IN PACKS
1 Albert Pujols 1.25 3.00
2 Alex Rodriguez Rgr 1.25 3.00
3 Alfonso Soriano .60 1.50
4 Andruw Jones .40 1.00
5 Barry Zito .60 1.50
6 Cal Ripken 3.00 8.00
7 Chipper Jones 1.00 2.50
8 Curt Schilling .60 1.50
9 Derek Jeter 2.50 6.00
10 Don Mattingly 2.00 5.00
11 Dontrelle Willis .40 1.00
12 Doc Gooden .40 1.00
13 Eddie Murray .60 1.50
14 Frank Thomas 1.00 2.50
15 Gary Sheffield .40 1.00
16 George Brett 2.00 5.00
17 Greg Maddux 1.25 3.00
18 Hideo Nomo 1.00 2.50
19 Ichiro Suzuki 1.25 3.00
20 Ivan Rodriguez .60 1.50
21 Jason Giambi .40 1.00
22 Jeff Bagwell .60 1.50
23 Jim Thome .60 1.50
24 Kerry Wood .40 1.00
25 Lance Berkman .60 1.50
26 Magglio Ordonez .60 1.50
27 Mark Prior .60 1.50
28 Mike Piazza 1.00 2.50
29 Mike Schmidt 1.50 4.00
30 Nomar Garciaparra .60 1.50
31 Pedro Martinez .60 1.50
32 Randy Johnson 1.00 2.50
33 Roger Clemens 1.25 3.00
34 Sammy Sosa 1.00 2.50
35 Tony Gwynn 1.00 2.50

2004 Donruss Elite Career Best Bats

PRINT RUNS B/WN 100-200 COPIES PER
*COMBO p/r 50: 1X TO 2.5X BASIC p/r 200
*COMBO p/r 50: .75X TO 2X BASIC p/r 100
*COMBO p/r 25: 1.25X TO 3X BASIC p/r 200
COMBO PRINT RUNS B/WN 25-50 PER
RANDOM INSERTS IN PACKS
1 Albert Pujols/200 6.00 15.00
2 Alex Rodriguez Rgr/200 4.00 10.00
3 Alfonso Soriano/200 2.50 6.00
4 Andruw Jones/200 3.00 8.00
5 Barry Zito/200 2.50 6.00
6 Cal Ripken/200 15.00 40.00
7 Chipper Jones/200 3.00 8.00
8 Curt Schilling/200 2.50 6.00
9 Derek Jeter/200 6.00 15.00
10 Don Mattingly/200 6.00 15.00
11 Dontrelle Willis/100 4.00 10.00
12 Doc Gooden/200 3.00 8.00
13 Eddie Murray/200 4.00 10.00
14 Frank Thomas/200 3.00 8.00
15 Gary Sheffield/200 2.50 6.00
16 George Brett/200 6.00 15.00
17 Greg Maddux/100 5.00 12.00
18 Hideo Nomo/100 4.00 10.00
20 Ivan Rodriguez/200 3.00 8.00
21 Jason Giambi/200 2.50 6.00
22 Jeff Bagwell/200 3.00 8.00
23 Jim Thome/200 3.00 8.00
24 Kerry Wood/100 3.00 8.00
25 Lance Berkman/200 2.50 6.00
26 Magglio Ordonez/200 2.50 6.00
27 Mark Prior/100 4.00 10.00
28 Mike Piazza/200 4.00 10.00
29 Mike Schmidt/200 6.00 15.00
30 Nomar Garciaparra/200 4.00 10.00
31 Pedro Martinez/200 3.00 8.00
32 Randy Johnson/200 3.00 8.00
33 Roger Clemens/200 6.00 15.00
34 Sammy Sosa/200 3.00 8.00
35 Tony Gwynn/200 6.00 15.00

2004 Donruss Elite Career Best Jerseys

PRINT RUNS B/WN 50-200 COPIES PER
*PRIME p/r 50: 1.25X TO 3X BASIC p/r 200
*PRIME p/r 25: 1.5X TO 4X BASIC p/r 200
*PRIME p/r 25: 1X TO 2.5X BASIC p/r 100
*PRIME p/r 25: 1X TO 2.5X BASIC p/r 50
PRIME PRINT RUNS B/WN 25-50 COPIES PER
1 Albert Pujols/200 6.00 15.00
2 Alex Rodriguez/200 4.00 10.00
3 Alfonso Soriano/200 2.50 6.00
4 Andruw Jones/200 3.00 8.00
5 Barry Zito/200 2.50 6.00
6 Cal Ripken/50 30.00 60.00
7 Chipper Jones/200 3.00 8.00
8 Curt Schilling/200 2.50 6.00
9 Derek Jeter/200 8.00 20.00
10 Don Mattingly/50 12.50 30.00
11 Dontrelle Willis/200 3.00 8.00
12 Doc Gooden/200 3.00 8.00
13 Eddie Murray/200 4.00 10.00
14 Frank Thomas/200 3.00 8.00
15 Gary Sheffield/200 2.50 6.00
16 George Brett/50 12.50 30.00
17 Greg Maddux/200 4.00 10.00
18 Hideo Nomo/200 4.00 10.00
20 Ivan Rodriguez/200 3.00 8.00
21 Jason Giambi/200 2.50 6.00
22 Jeff Bagwell/200 3.00 8.00
23 Jim Thome/200 3.00 8.00
24 Kerry Wood/200 2.50 6.00
25 Lance Berkman/200 2.50 6.00
26 Magglio Ordonez/200 2.50 6.00
27 Mark Prior/200 3.00 8.00
28 Mike Piazza/200 4.00 10.00
29 Mike Schmidt/100 10.00 25.00
30 Nomar Garciaparra/200 4.00 10.00
31 Pedro Martinez/200 3.00 8.00
32 Randy Johnson/200 3.00 8.00
33 Roger Clemens/200 6.00 15.00
34 Sammy Sosa/200 3.00 8.00
35 Tony Gwynn/50 10.00 25.00

2004 Donruss Elite Fans of the Game

RANDOM INSERTS IN PACKS
201 James Gandolfini 2.00 5.00
202 Freddy Adu 1.25 3.00
203 Summer Sanders .75 2.00
204 Janet Evans .75 2.00
205 Brandi Chastain 1.25 3.00

2004 Donruss Elite Fans of the Game Autographs

RANDOM INSERTS IN PACKS
SP PRINT RUNS PROVIDED BY DONRUSS
SP'S ARE NOT SERIAL-NUMBERED
201 James Gandolfini 60.00 150.00
202 Freddy Adu 10.00 25.00
203 Summer Sanders SP/250 10.00 25.00
204 Janet Evans SP/250 10.00 25.00
205 Brandi Chastain SP/250 10.00 25.00

2004 Donruss Elite Passing the Torch

1-30 PRINT RUN 1000 SERIAL #'d SETS
31-45 PRINT RUN 500 SERIAL #'d SETS
*BLACK 1-30: .75X TO 2X BASIC
*BLACK 31-45: 1X TO 2.5X BASIC
BLACK 1-30 PRINT RUN 100 #'d SETS
BLACK 31-45 PRINT RUN 50 #'d SETS
*BLUE 1-30: .6X TO 1.5X BASIC
*BLUE 31-45: .6X TO 1.5X BASIC
BLUE 1-30 PRINT RUN 250 #'d SETS
BLUE 31-45 PRINT RUN 125 #'d SETS
*GOLD 1-30: 1.25X TO 3X BASIC
*GOLD 31-45: 1.5X TO 4X BASIC
GOLD 1-30 PRINT RUN 50 #'d SETS
GOLD 31-45 PRINT RUN 25 #'d SETS
*GREEN 1-30: .5X TO 1.2X BASIC
*GREEN 31-45: .5X TO 1.2X BASIC
GREEN 1-30 PRINT RUN 500 #'d SETS
GREEN 31-45 PRINT RUN 250 #'d SETS
1 Whitey Ford .75 2.00
2 Andy Pettitte .75 2.00
3 Willie McCovey .75 2.00
4 Will Clark .75 2.00
5 Stan Musial 2.00 5.00
6 Albert Pujols 1.50 4.00
7 Andre Dawson .75 2.00
8 Vladimir Guerrero .75 2.00
9 Dale Murphy 1.25 3.00
10 Chipper Jones 1.25 3.00
11 Joe Morgan .75 2.00
12 Barry Larkin .75 2.00
13 Catfish Hunter .75 2.00
14 Tim Hudson .75 2.00
15 Jim Rice .75 2.00
16 Manny Ramirez 1.25 3.00
17 Greg Maddux 1.50 4.00
18 Mark Prior .75 2.00
19 Don Mattingly 2.50 6.00
20 Jason Giambi .50 1.25
21 Roy Campanella 1.25 3.00
22 Mike Piazza 1.25 3.00
23 Ozzie Smith 1.50 4.00
24 Scott Rolen .75 2.00
25 Roger Clemens 1.50 4.00
26 Mike Mussina .75 2.00
27 Babe Ruth 3.00 8.00
28 Roger Maris 1.25 3.00
29 Nolan Ryan 4.00 10.00
30 Roy Oswalt .75 2.00
31 W.Ford A.Pettitte 1.00 2.50
32 W.McCovey W.Clark 1.00 2.50
33 S.Musial A.Pujols 2.50 6.00
34 A.Dawson V.Guerrero 1.00 2.50
35 D.Murphy C.Jones 1.50 4.00
36 J.Morgan B.Larkin 1.00 2.50
37 C.Hunter T.Hudson 1.00 2.50
38 J.Rice M.Ramirez 1.50 4.00
39 G.Maddux M.Prior 2.00 5.00
40 D.Mattingly J.Giambi 3.00 8.00
41 R.Campanella M.Piazza 1.50 4.00
42 O.Smith S.Rolen 2.00 5.00
43 R.Clemens M.Mussina 2.00 5.00
44 B.Ruth R.Maris 4.00 10.00
45 N.Ryan R.Oswalt 5.00 12.00

2004 Donruss Elite Passing the Torch Autographs

RANDOM INSERTS IN PACKS
SINGLE PRINT RUNS B/WN 5-50 PER
DUAL PRINT RUNS B/WN 1-5 COPIES PER
NO PRICING ON QTY OF 10 OR LESS
4 Will Clark/15 75.00 200.00
7 Andre Dawson/50 8.00 20.00
9 Dale Murphy/50 10.00 25.00
11 Joe Morgan/15 15.00 40.00
14 Tim Hudson/15 30.00 60.00
15 Jim Rice/50 8.00 20.00
18 Mark Prior/15 20.00 50.00
24 Scott Rolen/15 30.00 60.00
30 Roy Oswalt/50 8.00 20.00

2004 Donruss Elite Passing the Torch Bats

1-30 PRINT RUNS B/WN 25-200 COPIES PER
31-45 PRINT RUNS B/WN 25-50 COPIES PER
2 Andy Pettitte/200 3.00 8.00
3 Willie McCovey/100 4.00 10.00
4 Will Clark/100 6.00 15.00
5 Stan Musial/100 6.00 15.00
6 Albert Pujols/200 6.00 15.00
7 Andre Dawson/100 4.00 10.00
8 Vladimir Guerrero/200 3.00 8.00
9 Dale Murphy/100 6.00 15.00
10 Chipper Jones/200 3.00 8.00
11 Joe Morgan/200 3.00 8.00
12 Barry Larkin/200 3.00 8.00
14 Tim Hudson/200 2.50 6.00
15 Jim Rice/200 3.00 8.00
16 Manny Ramirez/200 3.00 8.00
17 Greg Maddux/200 4.00 10.00
18 Mark Prior/200 3.00 8.00
19 Don Mattingly/100 8.00 20.00
20 Jason Giambi/200 2.50 6.00
21 Roy Campanella/50 12.50 30.00
22 Mike Piazza/200 4.00 10.00
23 Ozzie Smith/200 6.00 15.00
24 Scott Rolen/200 3.00 8.00
25 Roger Clemens/200 6.00 15.00
26 Mike Mussina/200 3.00 8.00
27 Babe Ruth/25 100.00 200.00
28 Roger Maris/50 20.00 50.00
29 Nolan Ryan/100 10.00 25.00
30 Roy Oswalt/200 2.50 6.00
32 W.McCovey/W.Clark/50 10.00 25.00
33 S.Musial/A.Pujols/50 20.00 50.00
34 A.Dawson/V.Guerrero/50 6.00 15.00
35 D.Murphy/C.Jones/50 6.00 15.00
36 J.Morgan/B.Larkin/50 6.00 15.00
38 J.Rice/M.Ramirez/50 6.00 15.00
39 G.Maddux/M.Prior/50 10.00 25.00
40 D.Mattingly/J.Giambi/50 6.00 15.00
41 R.Campanella/M.Piazza/25 15.00 40.00
42 O.Smith/S.Rolen/50 8.00 20.00
43 R.Clemens/M.Mussina/50 8.00 20.00
44 B.Ruth/R.Maris/25 125.00 250.00
45 N.Ryan/R.Oswalt/50 15.00 40.00

2004 Donruss Elite Passing the Torch Jerseys

1-30 PRINT RUNS B/WN 25-200 COPIES PER
31-45 PRINT RUNS B/WN 25-50 COPIES PER
1 Whitey Ford/100 6.00 15.00
2 Andy Pettitte/200 3.00 8.00
3 Willie McCovey/100 4.00 10.00
4 Will Clark/100 12.50 30.00
5 Stan Musial/100 12.50 30.00
6 Albert Pujols/200 6.00 15.00
7 Andre Dawson/200 3.00 8.00
8 Vladimir Guerrero/200 3.00 8.00
9 Dale Murphy/100 6.00 15.00
10 Chipper Jones/200 3.00 8.00
11 Joe Morgan/100 4.00 10.00
12 Barry Larkin/200 3.00 8.00
13 Catfish Hunter/100 6.00 15.00
14 Tim Hudson/200 2.50 6.00
15 Jim Rice/200 3.00 8.00
16 Manny Ramirez/200 3.00 8.00
18 Mark Prior/200 3.00 8.00
19 Don Mattingly/100 10.00 25.00
20 Jason Giambi/200 2.50 6.00
21 Roy Campanella/50 12.50 30.00
22 Mike Piazza/200 4.00 10.00
23 Ozzie Smith/100 8.00 20.00
24 Scott Rolen/200 3.00 8.00
25 Roger Clemens/200 6.00 15.00
26 Mike Mussina/200 3.00 8.00
27 Babe Ruth/25 250.00 400.00
28 Roger Maris/50 15.00 40.00
29 Nolan Ryan/100 12.50 30.00
30 Roy Oswalt/200 2.50 6.00
31 W.Ford/A.Pettitte/50 10.00 25.00
32 W.McCovey/W.Clark/50 10.00 25.00
33 S.Musial/A.Pujols/50 20.00 50.00
34 A.Dawson/V.Guerrero/50 10.00 25.00
35 D.Murphy/C.Jones/50 10.00 25.00
36 J.Morgan/B.Larkin/50 10.00 25.00
37 C.Hunter/T.Hudson/50 10.00 25.00
38 J.Rice/M.Ramirez/50 10.00 25.00
40 D.Mattingly/J.Giambi/50 15.00 40.00
41 R.Campanella/M.Piazza/25 20.00 50.00
42 O.Smith/S.Rolen/50 12.50 30.00
43 R.Clemens/M.Mussina/50 12.50 30.00
45 N.Ryan/R.Oswalt/50 20.00 50.00

2004 Donruss Elite Recollection Autographs

RANDOM INSERTS IN PACKS
PRINT RUNS B/WN 1-95 COPIES PER
NO PRICING ON QTY OF 14 OR LESS
1 Jeremy Affeldt 01/25 8.00 20.00
2 Erick Almonte 01/26 6.00 15.00
4 Jeff Baker 02/25 15.00 40.00
5 Brandon Berger 01/25 6.00 15.00
6 Marlon Byrd 01/24 8.00 20.00
8 Ryan Drese 02/45 6.00 15.00
9 Brandon Duckworth 01/16 6.00 15.00
10 Casey Fossum 01/23 8.00 20.00
11 Geronimo Gil 01/25 6.00 15.00
13 Jeremy Guthrie 02/25 8.00 20.00
14 Nic Jackson 02/95 4.00 10.00
21 Ricardo Rodriguez 01/25 6.00 15.00
23 Bud Smith 01/25 6.00 15.00
25 Junior Spivey 01/20 8.00 20.00
26 Tim Spooneybarger 01/25 6.00 15.00
28 Martin Vargas 01/37 4.00 10.00

2004 Donruss Elite Team

STATED PRINT RUN 1500 SERIAL #'d SETS
*BLACK: 1X TO 2.5X BASIC
BLACK PRINT RUN 150 SERIAL #'d SETS
*GOLD: .75X TO 2X BASIC
GOLD PRINT RUN 250 SERIAL #'d SETS
RANDOM INSERTS IN PACKS
1 Ripken Murray Palmer 3.00 8.00
2 Jeter Clemens Bernie Pett 2.50 6.00
3 Bench Perez Foster Conc 1.00 2.50

4 Beckett .60 1.50
Willis
I.Rod
5 Randy 1.00 2.50
Schill
L.Gonz
Grace
6 Jeter 2.50 6.00
Boggs
Strawberry
7 Chip 1.25 3.00
Glav
Maddux
Klesko
8 Gooden .60 1.50
Carter
Strawberry
9 Jackie 1.00 2.50
Campy
Snider
10 Rizzuto 1.00 2.50
Berra
Ford
11 Musial 1.50 4.00
Sch
Marion
Slaugh

2004 Donruss Elite Team Bats

RANDOM INSERTS IN PACKS
STATED PRINT RUN 100 SERIAL #'d SETS
2 Jeter/Clemens/Bernie/Pett 15.00 40.00
3 Bench/Perez/Foster/Conc 20.00 50.00
4 Beckett/Willis/I.Rod 6.00 15.00
5 Randy/Schill/L.Gonz/Grace 10.00 25.00
6 Jeter/Boggs/Strawberry 12.50 30.00
7 Chip/Glav/Maddux/Klesko 12.50 30.00
8 Gooden/Carter/Strawberry 6.00 15.00

2004 Donruss Elite Team Jerseys

RANDOM INSERTS IN PACKS
STATED PRINT RUN 100 SERIAL #'d SETS
JACKIE/CAMPY/SNIDER PRINT 50 #'d CARDS
ROY CAMPANELLA SWATCH IS PANTS
1 Ripken/Murray/Palmer 15.00 40.00
2 Jeter/Clemens/Bernie/Pett 15.00 40.00
4 Beckett/Willis/I.Rod 6.00 15.00
5 Randy/Schill/L.Gonz/Grace 10.00 25.00
6 Jeter/Boggs/Strawberry 12.50 30.00
7 Chip/Glav/Maddux/Klesko 12.50 30.00
9 Jackie/Campy/Snider/50 40.00 80.00
10 Rizzuto/Berra/Ford 15.00 40.00
11 Musial/Sch/Marion/Slaugh 30.00 60.00

2004 Donruss Elite Throwback Threads

1-20 PRINT RUN 150 SERIAL #'d SETS
21-30 PRINT RUN 75 SERIAL #'d SETS
RUTH 31 PRINT RUN 50 #'d CARDS
32-50 PRINT RUN 100 SERIAL #'d SETS
RUTH/GEHRIG 51 PRINT 25 #'d CARDS
52-60 PRINT RUN 50 SERIAL #'d SETS
*PRIME 1-20: 1.5X TO 4X BASIC 1-20
*PRIME 21-30: 1X TO 2.5X BASIC 21-30
*PRIME 31-50: 1.25X TO 3X BASIC 31-50
PRIME SINGLE PRINTS B/WN 10-25 PER
PRIME DUAL PRINTS B/WN 5-15 PER
NO PRIME PRICING ON QTY OF 10 OR LESS
CARD NUMBER 3 DOES NOT EXIST
1 Albert Pujols/150 6.00 15.00
2 Alex Rodriguez Rgr/150 4.00 10.00
4 Chipper Jones/150 3.00 8.00
5 Derek Jeter/150 6.00 15.00
6 Greg Maddux/150 4.00 10.00
7 Hideo Nomo/150 4.00 10.00
8 Miguel Cabrera/150 3.00 8.00
9 Ivan Rodriguez/150 3.00 8.00
10 Jason Giambi/150 2.50 6.00
11 Jeff Bagwell/150 3.00 8.00
12 Lance Berkman/150 2.50 6.00
13 Mark Prior/150 3.00 8.00
14 Mike Piazza/150 4.00 10.00
15 Nomar Garciaparra/150 4.00 10.00
16 Pedro Martinez/150 3.00 8.00
17 Randy Johnson/150 3.00 8.00
18 Sammy Sosa/150 3.00 8.00
19 Shawn Green/150 2.50 6.00
20 Vladimir Guerrero/150 3.00 8.00
21 A.Dunn/A.Kearns/75 6.00 15.00
22 B.Zito/M.Mulder/75 6.00 15.00
23 C.Schilling/C.Schilling/75 6.00 15.00
24 D.Jeter/J.Giambi/75 8.00 20.00
25 D.Willis/J.Beckett/75 8.00 20.00
26 F.Thomas/M.Ordonez/75 8.00 20.00
27 J.Thome/J.Thome/75 8.00 20.00
28 K.Wood/M.Prior/75 6.00 15.00
29 H.Blalock/M.Teixeira/75 8.00 20.00
30 A.Pujols/S.Rolen/75 15.00 40.00
31 Babe Ruth/50 200.00 300.00
32 Cal Ripken/100 12.00 30.00
33 Carl Yastrzemski/100 10.00 25.00
34 Deion Sanders/100 6.00 15.00
35 Don Mattingly/100 10.00 25.00
36 George Brett/100 10.00 25.00
37 Jim Palmer/100 4.00 10.00
38 Kirby Puckett/100 12.50 30.00
39 Lou Gehrig/100 100.00 200.00
40 Mark Grace/100 6.00 15.00
41 Mike Schmidt/100 10.00 25.00
42 Nolan Ryan/100 12.50 30.00
43 Ozzie Smith/100 8.00 20.00
44 Reggie Jackson/100 6.00 15.00
45 Rickey Henderson/100 6.00 15.00
46 Roberto Clemente/100 30.00 60.00
47 Roger Clemens/100 8.00 20.00
48 Roger Maris/100 20.00 50.00
49 Roy Campanella Pants/100 10.00 25.00
50 Tony Gwynn/100 8.00 20.00
51 B.Ruth/L.Gehrig/25 200.00 400.00
52 C.Ripken/E.Murray/50 30.00 60.00
53 T.Williams/Yaz/50 50.00 100.00
54 A.Dawson/G.Carter/50 8.00 20.00
55 R.Jackson/R.Carew/50 10.00 25.00
56 D.Jeter/P.Rizzuto/50 20.00 50.00
57 N.Ryan/R.Oswalt/50 12.50 30.00
58 R.Clemens/M.Mussina/50 12.50 30.00
59 A.Pujols/S.Musial/50 20.00 50.00
60 Nomar/T.Williams/50 40.00 80.00

2004 Donruss Elite Throwback Threads Autographs

STATED PRINT RUN 25 SERIAL #'d SETS
PRIME PRINT RUNS B/WN 5-10 COPIES PER
NO PRIME PRICING DUE TO SCARCITY
9 Ivan Rodriguez/25 40.00 80.00
13 Mark Prior/25 10.00 25.00
18 Sammy Sosa/25 50.00 100.00
35 Don Mattingly/25 75.00 150.00
37 Jim Palmer/25 10.00 25.00

2004 Donruss Elite Extra Edition

COMP.SET w/o SP's (150) 10.00 25.00
COMMON CARD (1-150) .12 .30
COMMON CARD (206-215) .40 1.00
206-215 RANDOM INSERTS IN PACKS
206-215 PRINT RUN 1000 SERIAL #'d SETS
COMMON NO AU (234-254) .75 2.00
NO AU MINORS 234-254 .75 2.00
NO AU SEMIS 234-254 1.25 3.00
NO AU UNLISTED 234-254 2.00 5.00
NO AU 234-254 RANDOM IN PACKS
NO AU 234-254 PRINT RUN 1000 #'d SETS
COMMON AU p/r 803-1195 3.00 8.00
COMMON AU p/r 522-799 3.00 8.00
COMMON AU p/r 350-493 4.00 10.00
COMMON AU p/r 260 5.00 12.00
216-355 OVERALL AU-GU ODDS 1:4
216-355 PRINT RUNS B/WN 260-1617 PER
DO NOT EXIST: 151-205/232/236-238/240
DO NOT EXIST: 241/245/248-249/251/255
DO NOT EXIST: 274/339
1 Troy Glaus .12 .30
2 John Lackey .20 .50
3 Garret Anderson .12 .30
4 Francisco Rodriguez .20 .50
5 Casey Kotchman .12 .30
6 Jose Guillen .12 .30
7 Miguel Tejada .20 .50
8 Rafael Palmeiro .20 .50
9 Jay Gibbons .12 .30
10 Melvin Mora .12 .30
11 Javy Lopez .12 .30
12 Pedro Martinez .20 .50
13 Curt Schilling .20 .50
14 David Ortiz .30 .75
15 Manny Ramirez .30 .75
16 Nomar Garciaparra .20 .50
17 Magglio Ordonez .20 .50
18 Frank Thomas .30 .75
19 Esteban Loaiza .12 .30
20 Paul Konerko .20 .50
21 Mark Buehrle .20 .50
22 Jody Gerut .12 .30
23 Victor Martinez .20 .50
24 C.C. Sabathia .20 .50
25 Travis Hafner .12 .30
26 Cliff Lee .20 .50
27 Jeremy Bonderman .12 .30
28 Dallas McPherson .12 .30
29 Jermaine Dye .12 .30
30 Carlos Guillen .12 .30
31 Carlos Beltran .20 .50
32 Ken Harvey .12 .30
33 Mike Sweeney .12 .30
34 Angel Berroa .12 .30
35 Joe Nathan .12 .30
36 Johan Santana .20 .50
37 Jacque Jones .12 .30
38 Shannon Stewart .12 .30
39 Torii Hunter .12 .30
40 Derek Jeter .75 2.00
41 Jason Giambi .12 .30
42 Danny Graves .12 .30
43 Alfonso Soriano .20 .50
44 Gary Sheffield .12 .30
45 Mike Mussina .20 .50
46 Jorge Posada .20 .50
47 Hideki Matsui .50 1.25
48 Francisco Cordero .12 .30
49 Javier Vazquez .12 .30
50 Mariano Rivera .40 1.00
51 Eric Chavez .12 .30
52 Tim Hudson .20 .50
53 Mark Mulder .12 .30
54 Barry Zito .20 .50
55 Ichiro Suzuki .40 1.00
56 Edgar Martinez .20 .50
57 Bret Boone .12 .30
58 Lew Ford .12 .30
59 B.J. Upton .20 .50
60 Aubrey Huff .12 .30
61 Rocco Baldelli .12 .30
62 Carl Crawford .20 .50
63 Delmon Young .20 .50
64 Mark Teixeira .20 .50
65 Hank Blalock .12 .30
66 Michael Young .12 .30
67 Alex Rodriguez .40 1.00
68 Carlos Delgado .12 .30
69 Milton Bradley .12 .30
70 Roy Halladay .20 .50
71 Vernon Wells .12 .30
72 Randy Johnson .30 .75
73 Bobby Crosby .12 .30
74 Lyle Overbay .12 .30
75 Luis Gonzalez .12 .30
76 Steve Finley .12 .30
77 Chipper Jones .30 .75
78 Andruw Jones .12 .30
79 Marcus Giles .12 .30
80 Rafael Furcal .12 .30
81 J.D. Drew .12 .30
82 Sammy Sosa .30 .75
83 Kerry Wood .12 .30
84 Mark Prior .20 .50
85 Derrek Lee .12 .30
86 Moises Alou .12 .30
87 Carlos Zambrano .20 .50
88 Ken Griffey Jr. .60 1.50
89 Austin Kearns .12 .30
90 Adam Dunn .20 .50
91 Barry Larkin .20 .50
92 Todd Helton .20 .50
93 Larry Walker Cards .20 .50
94 Preston Wilson .12 .30
95 Sean Casey .12 .30
96 Luis Castillo .12 .30
97 Josh Beckett .12 .30
98 Mike Lowell .12 .30
99 Miguel Cabrera .30 .75
100 Brad Penny .12 .30
101 Dontrelle Willis .12 .30
102 Andy Pettitte .20 .50
103 Wade Miller .12 .30
104 Jeff Bagwell .20 .50
105 Craig Biggio .20 .50
106 Lance Berkman .20 .50
107 Jeff Kent .12 .30
108 Roy Oswalt .20 .50
109 Hideo Nomo .30 .75
110 Adrian Beltre .30 .75
111 Paul Lo Duca .12 .30
112 Shawn Green .12 .30
113 Roger Clemens .40 1.00
114 Eric Gagne .12 .30
115 Danny Kolb .12 .30
116 Rickie Weeks .12 .30
117 Scott Podsednik .12 .30
118 Livan Hernandez .12 .30
119 Orlando Cabrera .12 .30
120 Jose Vidro .12 .30
121 David Wright .25 .60
122 Tom Glavine .20 .50
123 Al Leiter .12 .30
124 Mike Piazza .30 .75
125 Jose Reyes .20 .50
126 Richard Hidalgo .12 .30
127 Eric Milton .12 .30
128 Jim Thome .20 .50
129 Mike Lieberthal .12 .30
130 Bobby Abreu .12 .30
131 Kip Wells .12 .30
132 Jack Wilson .12 .30
133 Jason Bay .20 .50
134 Brian Giles .12 .30
135 Sean Burroughs .12 .30
136 Khalil Greene .20 .50
137 Jake Peavy .12 .30
138 Jason Schmidt .12 .30
139 J.T. Snow .12 .30
140 Craig Wilson .12 .30
141 Chase Utley .20 .50
142 Jim Edmonds .20 .50
143 Albert Pujols .40 1.00
144 Edgar Renteria .12 .30
145 Scott Rolen .20 .50
146 Matt Morris .12 .30
147 Ivan Rodriguez .20 .50
148 Vladimir Guerrero .20 .50
149 Greg Maddux .40 1.00
150 Ben Sheets .12 .30
206 Will Clark RET .60 1.50
207 Nolan Ryan RET 3.00 8.00
208 Bob Feller RET .60 1.50
209 Red Schoendienst RET .60 1.50
210 Brooks Robinson RET .60 1.50
211 Al Kaline RET 1.00 2.50
212 Ozzie Smith RET 1.25 3.00
213 Maury Wills RET .40 1.00
214 Steve Carlton RET .60 1.50
215 Duke Snider RET .60 1.50
216 Scott Lewis AU/603 RC 8.00 20.00
217 Josh Johnson AU/597 RC 4.00 10.00
218 Jeff Fiorentino AU/597 RC 5.00 12.00
219 Grant Hansen AU/599 RC 3.00 8.00
220 Yov Gallardo AU/803 RC 4.00 10.00
221 Eddie Prasch AU/603 RC 4.00 10.00
222 Danny Hill AU/603 RC 3.00 8.00
223 Chuck Lofgren AU/803 RC 6.00 15.00
224 Blake Johnson AU/811 RC 4.00 10.00
225 Cory Dunlap AU/599 RC 6.00 15.00
226 Carlos Vasquez AU/869 RC 3.00 8.00
227 Jesse Crain AU/1000 RC 3.00 8.00
228 Yhency Brazoban AU/1000 3.00 8.00
229 Abe Alvarez AU/1000 RC 4.00 10.00
230 Scott Kazmir AU/350 RC 15.00 40.00
231 J.A. Happ AU/1195 RC 3.00 8.00
233 Mark Jecmen AU/1047 RC 3.00 8.00
234 Kameron Loe/1000 RC .75 2.00
235 Ervin Santana/1000 RC 2.00 5.00
239 Josh Karp/1000 RC .75 2.00
242 Alberto Callaspo/1000 RC 2.00 5.00
243 Jesse Hoover AU/1191 RC 4.00 10.00
246 Just Hoyman AU/1124 RC 4.00 10.00
247 Juan Cedeno/1000 RC .75 2.00
250 Jake Dittler/1000 RC .75 2.00
252 Ben Zobrist AU/1178 RC 8.00 20.00
253 Jeff Salazar/1000 RC .75 2.00
254 Fausto Carmona/1000 RC 1.25 3.00
256 Jor Vasquez AU/1000 RC 3.00 8.00
257 Raf Gonzalez AU/603 RC 3.00 8.00
258 Andrew Dobies AU/601 RC 3.00 8.00
259 Colby Miller AU/997 RC 3.00 8.00
260 K.C. Herren AU/735 RC 3.00 8.00
261 Ryan Meaux AU/546 RC 3.00 8.00
262 Dust Pedroia AU/1114 RC 30.00 80.00
263 Fern Nieve AU/1000 RC 3.00 8.00
264 Mar Gomez AU/1000 RC 15.00 30.00
265 Eric Campbell AU/260 RC 70.00 120.00
266 Billy Killian AU/703 RC 4.00 10.00
267 Mike Rouse AU/999 RC 3.00 8.00
268 Kyle Bono AU/1203 RC 3.00 8.00
269 M.Einertson AU/1047 RC 6.00 15.00
270 Scott Proctor AU/1000 RC 3.00 8.00
271 Tim Bittner AU/1000 RC 3.00 8.00
272 Christian Garcia AU/799 RC 4.00 10.00
273 Yadier Molina AU/1000 RC 300.00 800.00
275 C.Thomas AU/907 RC 3.00 8.00
276 Trav Blackley AU/1000 RC 3.00 8.00
277 F.Francisco AU/1000 RC 3.00 8.00
278 Dion Navarro AU/1000 RC 3.00 8.00
279 Joey Gathright AU/1000 RC 3.00 8.00
280 Kaz Tadano AU/1000 RC 4.00 10.00
281 Matt Bush AU/1100 RC 3.00 8.00
282 David Haehnel AU/865 RC 4.00 10.00
283 Tommy Hottovy AU/825 RC 4.00 10.00
284 Chris Carter AU/973 RC 6.00 15.00
285 Mark Rogers AU/578 RC 8.00 20.00
286 Jeremy Sowers AU/537 RC 15.00 30.00
287 Homer Bailey AU/1571 RC 6.00 15.00
288 Mike Butia AU/825 RC 3.00 8.00
289 Chris Nelson AU/465 RC 5.00 12.00
290 T.Diamond AU/1055 RC 6.00 15.00
291 Neil Walker AU/1343 RC 4.00 10.00
292 Sean Gamble AU/1229 RC 3.00 8.00
293 Bill Bray AU/1073 RC 3.00 8.00
294 Reid Brignac AU/522 RC 8.00 20.00
295 R.Klosterman AU/865 RC 3.00 8.00
296 David Purcey AU/1485 RC 3.00 8.00
297 Scott Elbert AU/1617 RC 8.00 20.00
298 Josh Fields AU/961 RC 15.00 30.00
299 Chris Lambert AU/954 RC 4.00 10.00
300 Trevor Plouffe AU/1329 RC 3.00 8.00
301 Greg Golson AU/1334 RC 4.00 10.00
302 Josh Baker AU/525 RC 3.00 8.00
303 Philip Hughes AU/1485 RC 6.00 15.00
304 Matt Macri AU/979 RC 4.00 10.00
305 Kyle Waldrop AU/823 RC 6.00 15.00
306 Rich Robnett AU/1575 RC 4.00 10.00
307 T.Tankersley AU/1073 RC 4.00 10.00
308 Blake DeWitt AU/1562 RC 4.00 10.00
309 Daryl Jones AU/575 RC 12.50 30.00
310 Eric Hurley AU/1021 RC 10.00 25.00
311 J.P. Howell AU/1453 RC 4.00 10.00
312 Zach Jackson AU/1069 RC 3.00 8.00
313 Justin Orenduff AU/473 RC 12.50 30.00
314 Tyler Lumsden AU/473 RC 4.00 10.00
315 Matt Fox AU/473 RC 4.00 10.00
316 Danny Putnam AU/473 RC 4.00 10.00
317 Jon Poterson AU/464 RC 6.00 10.00
318 Gio Gonzalez AU/473 RC 5.00 12.00
319 Jay Rainville AU/823 RC 10.00 25.00
320 Huston Street AU/709 RC 6.00 15.00
321 Jeff Marquez AU/493 RC 4.00 10.00
322 Eric Beattie AU/930 RC 4.00 10.00
323 B.Szymanski AU/1327 RC 4.00 10.00
324 Seth Smith AU/1065 RC 3.00 8.00
325 Rob Johnson AU/790 RC 4.00 10.00
326 Wes Whisler AU/473 RC 4.00 10.00
327 Billy Buckner AU/673 RC 4.00 10.00
328 Jon Zeringue AU/473 RC 3.00 8.00
329 Curtis Thigpen AU/673 RC 12.50 30.00
330 Donny Lucy AU/573 RC 3.00 8.00
331 Mike Ferris AU/558 RC 4.00 10.00
332 Anthony Swarzak AU/370 RC 3.00 8.00
333 Jason Jaramillo AU/573 RC 4.00 10.00
334 Hunter Pence AU/672 RC 8.00 20.00
335 Mike Rozier AU/628 RC 4.00 10.00
336 Kurt Suzuki AU/473 RC 6.00 15.00
337 Jason Vargas AU/621 RC 6.00 15.00
338 Brian Bixler AU/665 RC 10.00 25.00
340 Dexter Fowler AU/623 RC 6.00 15.00
341 Mark Trumbo AU/1321 RC 5.00 12.00
342 Jeff Frazier AU/423 RC 4.00 10.00
343 Steve Register AU/673 RC 3.00 8.00
344 M.Schlact AU/477 RC 4.00 10.00
345 Garrett Mock AU/471 RC 4.00 10.00
346 Eric Haberer AU/473 RC 4.00 10.00
347 M.Tuiasosopo AU/473 RC 10.00 25.00
348 Jason Windsor AU/473 RC 4.00 10.00
349 Grant Johnson AU/815 RC 4.00 10.00
350 J.C. Holt AU/673 RC 4.00 10.00
351 Joe Bauserman AU/472 RC 4.00 10.00
352 Jamar Walton AU/481 RC 4.00 10.00
353 Eric Patterson AU/1571 RC 6.00 15.00
354 Tyler Johnson AU/775 RC 6.00 15.00
355 Nick Adenhart AU/653 RC 6.00 15.00

2004 Donruss Elite Extra Edition Aspirations

*1-150 p/r 81-99: 4X TO 10X
*1-150 p/r 51-80: 5X TO 12X
*1-150 p/r 36-50: 6X TO 15X
*1-150 p/r 26-35: 8X TO 20X
*1-150 p/r 16-25: 10X TO 25X
*206-215 p/r 81-99: 1.25X TO 3X
*206-215 p/r 51-80: 1.5X TO 4X
*216-355 p/r 51-80: .6X TO 1.5X NO AU
*216-355 p/r 36-50: .75X TO 2X NO AU
*216-355p/r81-99: .3X TO .8X AUp/r803-1617
*216-355p/r81-99: .25X TO .6X AUp/r522-799
*216-355p/r81-99: .2X TO .5X AU p/r 350-493
*216-355p/r51-80: .4X TO 1X AU p/r 803-1617
*216-355p/r51-80: .3X TO .8X AU p/r 522-799
*216-355p/r51-80: .25X TO .6X AUp/r350-493
*216-355 p/r 51-80: .15X TO .4X AU p/r 260
*216-355p/r36-50:.5X TO 1.2X AUp/r803-1617
*216-355 p/r 36-50: .4X TO 1X AU p/r 522-799
*216-355p/r36-50: .3X TO .8X AU p/r 350-493
*216-355 p/r 26-35: .4X TO 1X AU p/r 350-493
PRINT RUNS B/WN 4-99 COPIES PER
NO PRICING ON QTY OF 13 OR LESS

2004 Donruss Elite Extra Edition Aspirations Gold

*ASP.GOLD 1-150: 10X TO 25X
*ASP.GOLD 206-215: 3X TO 8X
RANDOM INSERTS IN PACKS
STATED PRINT RUN 25 SERIAL #'d SETS
216-355 NO PRICING DUE TO SCARCITY

2004 Donruss Elite Extra Edition Status

*1-150 p/r 51-80: 5X TO 12X
*1-150 p/r 36-50: 6X TO 15X
*1-150 p/r 26-35: 8X TO 20X
*1-150 p/r 16-25: 10X TO 25X
*206-215 p/r 26-35: 2.5X TO 6X
*206-215 p/r 16-25: 3X TO 8X
*216-355 p/r 36-50: .75X TO 2X NO AU
*216-355p/r81-96: .3X TO .8X AUp/r803-1617
*216-355p/r51-80: .4X TO 1X AU p/r 803-1617
*216-355p/r51-80: .3X TO .8X AU p/r 522-799
*216-355p/r51-80: .25X TO .6X AUp/r350-493
*216-355p/r36-50:.5X TO 1.2X AUp/r803-1617
*216-355 p/r 36-50: .4X TO 1X AU p/r 522-799
*216-355p/r36-50: .3X TO .8X AU p/r 350-493
*216-355p/r26-35:.6X TO 1.5X AUp/r803-1617
*216-355p/r26-35: .5X TO 1.2X AUp/r 522-799
*216-355 p/r 26-35: .4X TO 1X AU p/r 350-493
*216-355 p/r 26-35: .25X TO .6X AU p/r 260
PRINT RUNS B/WN 1-96 COPIES PER
1-215 NO PRICING ON QTY OF 15 OR LESS
216-355 NO PRICING ON QTY 25 OR LESS

2004 Donruss Elite Extra Edition Status Gold

STATED PRINT RUN 10 SERIAL #'d SETS
NO PRICING DUE TO SCARCITY

2004 Donruss Elite Extra Edition Turn of the Century

*1-150: 2.5X TO 6X BASIC
1-150 PRINT RUN 250 SERIAL #'d SETS
*206-215: 1.25X TO 3X BASIC
*216-355: .5X TO 1.2X NO AU p/r 1000
206-355 PRINT RUN 100 SERIAL #'d SETS
RANDOM INSERTS IN PACKS

2004 Donruss Elite Extra Edition Signature

*216-355 p/r 50: 1X TO 2.5X AU p/r 803-1617
OVERALL AU-GU ODDS 1:4
PRINT RUNS B/WN 1-50 #'d COPIES PER
NO PRICING ON QTY OF 10 OR LESS
132 Jack Wilson/25 12.50 30.00
133 Jason Bay/25 12.50 30.00
234 Kameron Loe ROO/50 10.00 25.00
235 Ervin Santana ROO/50 8.00 20.00
239 Josh Karp ROO/50 8.00 20.00
247 Juan Cedeno ROO/50 8.00 20.00
253 Jeff Salazar ROO/50 10.00 25.00
254 Fausto Carmona ROO/50 40.00 80.00

2004 Donruss Elite Extra Edition Signature Aspirations

*216-355 p/r 100: .6X TO 1.5X p/r 803-1617
*216-355 p/r 100: .6X TO 1.5X p/r 522-799
*216-355 p/r 100: .5X TO 1.2X p/r 350-493
*216-355 p/r 49-50: 1.25X TO 3X p/r 803-1617
*216-355 p/r 49-50: 1X TO 2.5X p/r 522-799
*216-355 p/r 49-50: .75X TO 2X p/r 350-493
OVERALL AU-GU ODDS 1:4
PRINT RUNS B/WN 1-100 COPIES PER
NO PRICING ON QTY OF 10 OR LESS
220 Yovani Gallardo ROO/50 40.00 80.00
273 Yadier Molina ROO/50 600.00 1500.00
278 Dioner Navarro ROO/50 6.00 15.00
287 Homer Bailey DP/100 10.00 25.00
303 Philip Hughes DP/100 12.50 30.00
318 Gio Gonzalez DP/100 10.00 25.00
334 Hunter Pence DP/50 12.00 30.00
340 Dexter Fowler DP/50 20.00 50.00
341 Mark Trumbo DP/50 8.00 20.00
347 Matt Tuiasosopo DP/100 20.00 40.00
355 Nick Adenhart DP/100 12.50 30.00

2004 Donruss Elite Extra Edition Signature Aspirations Gold

OVERALL AU-GU ODDS 1:4
PRINT RUNS B/WN 1-25 COPIES PER
NO PRICING DUE TO SCARCITY

2004 Donruss Elite Extra Edition Signature Status

*216-355 p/r 50: 1.25X TO 3X p/r 803-1617
*216-355 p/r 50: 1X TO 2.5X p/r 522-799
*216-355 p/r 50: .75X TO 2X p/r 350-493
*216-355 p/r 50: .5X TO 1.2X p/r 260
OVERALL AU-GU ODDS 1:4
PRINT RUNS B/WN 1-50 COPIES PER
NO PRICING ON QTY OF 25 OR LESS
289 Chris Nelson DP/50 8.00 20.00
303 Philip Hughes DP/50 50.00 100.00
308 Blake DeWitt DP/50 15.00 40.00
318 Gio Gonzalez DP/50 12.50 30.00
334 Hunter Pence DP/50 12.00 30.00
340 Dexter Fowler DP/50 20.00 50.00
341 Mark Trumbo DP/50 8.00 20.00
347 Matt Tuiasosopo DP/50 30.00 60.00
355 Nick Adenhart DP/50 15.00 40.00

2004 Donruss Elite Extra Edition Signature Status Gold

OVERALL AU-GU ODDS 1:4
PRINT RUNS B/WN 1-10 COPIES PER
NO PRICING DUE TO SCARCITY

2004 Donruss Elite Extra Edition Signature Turn of the Century

*216-355p/r150-250: .6X TO 1.5X p/r803-1617
*216-355p/r150-250: .5X TO 1.2X p/r 522-799
*216-355p/r150-250: .4X TO 1X p/r 350-493
*216-355 p/r 100: .75X TO 2X p/r 803-1617
*216-355 p/r 100: .6X TO 1.5X p/r 522-799
*216-355 p/r 100: .5X TO 1.2X p/r 350-493
*216-355 p/r 50: .75X TO 2X p/r 350-493
OVERALL AU-GU ODDS 1:4
PRINT RUNS B/WN 1-250 COPIES PER
NO PRICING ON QTY OF 25 OR LESS
220 Yovani Gallardo ROO/100 12.50 30.00
252 Ben Zobrist DP/150 15.00 40.00
273 Yadier Molina ROO/100 500.00 1200.00
274 Justin Leone ROO/100 6.00 15.00
281 Matt Bush DP/250 8.00 20.00
285 Mark Rogers DP/100 12.50 30.00
287 Homer Bailey DP/250 6.00 15.00
303 Philip Hughes DP/250 20.00 50.00
308 Blake DeWitt DP/250 10.00 25.00
310 Eric Hurley DP/250 12.50 30.00
318 Gio Gonzalez DP/250 6.00 15.00
334 Hunter Pence DP/200 10.00 25.00
340 Dexter Fowler DP/250 12.50 30.00
341 Mark Trumbo DP/250 6.00 15.00
347 Matt Tuiasosopo DP/250 6.00 15.00
355 Nick Adenhart DP/100 12.50 30.00

2004 Donruss Elite Extra Edition Back to Back Picks Signature

OVERALL AU-GU ODDS 1:4
1-10 PRINT RUNS B/WN 10-50 COPIES PER
11-20 PRINT RUNS B/WN 100-250 PER
NO PRICING ON QTY OF 10 OR LESS
1 D.Young/R.Weeks/25 8.00 20.00
3 A.Dunn/A.Kearns/25 30.00 60.00
5 M.Young/V.Wells/25 30.00 60.00
6 B.Roberts/L.Bigbie/50 6.00 15.00
7 R.Cey/S.Garvey/50 20.00 50.00
8 B.Madlock/D.Parker/50 40.00 80.00
9 D.Lee/Torii/Nixon/50 30.00 60.00
11 Nelson/Bush/Brignac/250 25.00 60.00
12 Szym/Golson/Frazier/250 15.00 40.00
13 Trumbo/Aden/T.Johns/100 20.00 50.00
14 Carter/Putnam/Jecmen/100 15.00 40.00
15 Killian/D.Jones/Bush/100 15.00 40.00
16 DeWitt/Orenduff/Elbert/250 12.50 30.00
17 R'ville/Waldrop/Plouffe/250 8.00 20.00
18 Marquez/Poter/Hughes/100 30.00 60.00
19 Gio/Lumsden/Whisler/100 12.50 30.00
20 Thigpen/Purcey/Z.Jack/100 12.50 30.00

2004 Donruss Elite Extra Edition Career Best All-Stars

RANDOM INSERTS IN PACKS
STATED PRINT RUN 500 SERIAL #'d SETS
1 Randy Johnson 1.50 4.00
2 David Ortiz 1.50 4.00
3 Edgar Renteria .60 1.50
4 Victor Martinez 1.00 2.50
5 Albert Pujols 2.00 5.00
6 Hideki Matsui 2.50 6.00
7 Mariano Rivera 2.00 5.00
8 Carlos Zambrano 1.00 2.50
9 Hank Blalock .60 1.50
10 Michael Young .60 1.50
11 Mike Piazza 1.50 4.00
12 Alfonso Soriano 1.00 2.50
13 Carl Crawford 1.00 2.50
14 Scott Rolen 1.00 2.50
15 Vladimir Guerrero 1.00 2.50
16 Lance Berkman 1.00 2.50
17 Todd Helton 1.00 2.50
18 Curt Schilling 1.00 2.50
19 Francisco Cordero .60 1.50
20 Mark Mulder .60 1.50
21 Sammy Sosa 1.50 4.00
22 Roger Clemens 2.00 5.00
23 Miguel Cabrera 1.50 4.00
24 Manny Ramirez 1.50 4.00
25 Jim Thome 1.00 2.50

2004 Donruss Elite Extra Edition Career Best All-Stars Jersey

STATED PRINT RUN 50 SERIAL #'d SETS
*PRIME p/r 25: .75X TO 2X BASIC
PRIME PRINT RUN B/WN 5-25 COPIES PER
NO PRIME PRICING ON QTY OF 5
OVERALL AU-GU ODDS 1:4
1 Randy Johnson 6.00 15.00
2 David Ortiz 6.00 15.00
3 Edgar Renteria 4.00 10.00
4 Victor Martinez 4.00 10.00
5 Albert Pujols 10.00 25.00
6 Hideki Matsui 12.50 30.00
7 Mariano Rivera 6.00 15.00
8 Carlos Zambrano 4.00 10.00
9 Hank Blalock 4.00 10.00
10 Michael Young 4.00 10.00
11 Mike Piazza 8.00 20.00
12 Alfonso Soriano 4.00 10.00
13 Carl Crawford 4.00 10.00
14 Scott Rolen 6.00 15.00
15 Vladimir Guerrero 6.00 15.00
16 Lance Berkman 4.00 10.00
17 Todd Helton 6.00 15.00
18 Curt Schilling 6.00 15.00
19 Francisco Cordero 4.00 10.00
20 Mark Mulder 4.00 10.00
21 Sammy Sosa 6.00 15.00
22 Roger Clemens 8.00 20.00
23 Miguel Cabrera 6.00 15.00
24 Manny Ramirez 6.00 15.00
25 Jim Thome 6.00 15.00

2004 Donruss Elite Extra Edition Career Best All-Stars Signature Jersey Gold

PRINT RUNS B/WN 1-25 COPIES PER
NO PRICING ON QTY OF 10 OR LESS
SIG BLACK PRINT RUN B/WN 1-5 PER
NO SIG BLACK PRICING DUE TO SCARCITY
SIG GOLD PRINT RUN B/WN 1-10 PER
NO SIG GOLD PRICING DUE TO SCARCITY
SIG JSY PRIME PRINT RUN B/WN 1-10 PER
NO SIG JSY PRIME PRICING AVAILABLE
OVERALL AU-GU ODDS 1:4
2 David Ortiz/25 40.00 80.00
3 Edgar Renteria/25 15.00 40.00
4 Victor Martinez/25 10.00 25.00
8 Carlos Zambrano/25 15.00 40.00
10 Michael Young/25 15.00 40.00
13 Carl Crawford/25 15.00 40.00
19 Francisco Cordero/25 10.00 25.00

2004 Donruss Elite Extra Edition Draft Class

RANDOM INSERTS IN PACKS
STATED PRINT RUN 500 SERIAL #'d SETS
1 J.Bench 5.00 12.00
N.Ryan
2 B.Blyleven 1.00 2.50
D.Evans
3 J.Rice 1.00 2.50
K.Hernandez
4 D.Eckersley 1.00 2.50
G.Carter
5 F.Lynn 1.50 4.00
R.Yount
6 A.Dawson 1.00 2.50
L.Smith
7 A.Trammell 1.00 2.50
J.Morris
8 H.Baines 1.50 4.00
P.Molitor
9 C.Ripken 5.00 12.00
K.Gibson
10 D.Mattingly 3.00 8.00
O.Hershiser
11 D.Strawberry .60 1.50
E.Davis
12 D.Gooden 1.00 2.50
J.Canseco
13 R.Palmeiro 1.50 4.00
R.Johnson
14 C.Schilling 1.00 2.50
G.Sheffield
15 M.Piazza 1.50 4.00
R.Ventura
16 F.Thomas 1.50 4.00
J.Bagwell
17 C.Jones 1.50 4.00
M.Mussina
18 G.Anderson 1.00 2.50
J.Posada
19 S.Rolen 1.00 2.50
T.Hunter
20 K.Wood 1.00 2.50
T.Helton
21 E.Chavez 1.00 2.50
R.Oswalt
22 J.Estrada .60 1.50
V.Wells
23 L.Berkman 1.00 2.50
T.Hudson
24 M.Buehrle 1.00 2.50
M.Mulder
25 C.Sabathia 1.00 2.50
S.Burroughs
26 A.Pujols 2.00 5.00
B.Zito
27 R.Harden .60 1.50
R.Baldelli
28 B.Crosby 1.00 2.50
M.Teixeira
29 C.Kotchman 1.00 2.50
M.Prior
30 D.Brazelton .60 1.50
J.Bonderman
31 J.Holt .60 1.50
J.Zeringue
32 K.Bono .60 1.50
M.Fox
33 D.Fowler 2.00 5.00
M.Rozier
34 H.Street 1.00 2.50
J.Howell
35 G.Johnson 1.00 2.50
M.Macri
36 E.Beattie .60 1.50
J.Frazier
37 J.Windsor 1.00 2.50
K.Suzuki
38 J.Fields 1.50 4.00
M.Tuiasosopo
39 J.Bauserman .60 1.50
K.Herren
40 C.Lambert .60 1.50
E.Haberer

2004 Donruss Elite Extra Edition Draft Class Signature

OVERALL AU-GU ODDS 1:4
1-30 PRINT RUNS B/WN 5-50 COPIES PER
31-40 PRINT RUNS B/WN 100-250 PER
NO PRICING ON QTY OF 10 OR LESS
2 B.Blyleven/D.Evans/50 10.00 25.00
3 J.Rice/K.Hernandez/50 15.00 40.00
4 D.Eckersley/G.Carter/25 30.00 60.00
6 A.Dawson/L.Smith/50 15.00 40.00
7 A.Trammell/J.Morris/50 15.00 40.00
8 H.Baines/P.Molitor/25 20.00 50.00
11 D.Strawberry/E.Davis/50 20.00 50.00
12 D.Gooden/J.Canseco/25 50.00 100.00
21 E.Chavez/R.Oswalt/25 20.00 50.00
22 J.Estrada/V.Wells/25 20.00 50.00
25 C.Sabathia/S.Burroughs/50 10.00 25.00
28 B.Crosby/M.Teixeira/25 30.00 60.00
29 C.Kotchman/M.Prior/25 20.00 50.00
30 D.Brazelton/J.Bonder/50 15.00 40.00
31 J.Holt/J.Zeringue/100 10.00 25.00
32 K.Bono/M.Fox/100 8.00 20.00
33 D.Fowler/M.Rozier/250 10.00 20.00
34 H.Street/J.Howell/100 10.00 25.00
35 G.Johnson/M.Macri/100 8.00 20.00
36 E.Beattie/J.Frazier/100 8.00 20.00
37 J.Windsor/K.Suzuki/100 10.00 25.00
38 J.Fields/M.Tuiasosopo/100 20.00 50.00
39 J.Bauserman/K.Herren/100 8.00 20.00
40 C.Lambert/E.Haberer/100 8.00 20.00

2004 Donruss Elite Extra Edition Passing the Torch

RANDOM INSERTS IN PACKS
STATED PRINT RUN 500 SERIAL #'d SETS
1 D.Eckersley 1.00 2.50
H.Street
2 M.Bush 1.50 4.00
T.Gwynn
3 H.Bailey 1.00 2.50
T.Seaver
4 B.Feller 1.00 2.50
J.Sowers
5 J.Fields 1.00 2.50
R.Ventura
6 N.Ryan 5.00 12.00
T.Diamond
7 E.Patterson 3.00 8.00
R.Sandberg
8 R.Robnett 1.50 4.00
R.Henderson
9 M.Ferris 2.50 6.00
S.Musial
10 B.Doerr 4.00 10.00
D.Pedroia

2004 Donruss Elite Extra Edition Passing the Torch Autograph Gold

PRINT RUNS B/WN 5-25 COPIES PER
BLACK PRINT RUNS B/WN 5-10 PER
OVERALL AU-GU ODDS 1:4
NO PRICING DUE TO SCARCITY

2004 Donruss Elite Extra Edition Round Numbers

RANDOM INSERTS IN PACKS
STATED PRINT RUN 500 SERIAL #'d SETS
1 Ozzie Smith 2.00 5.00
2 Derek Jeter 4.00 10.00
3 Alex Rodriguez 2.00 5.00
4 Paul Molitor 1.50 4.00
5 George Brett 3.00 8.00
6 Delmon Young 1.00 2.50
7 Dontrelle Willis .60 1.50
8 Gary Carter 1.00 2.50
9 Reggie Jackson 1.00 2.50
10 Andre Dawson 1.00 2.50
11 Neil Walker 1.00 2.50
12 Laynce Nix .60 1.50
13 Matt Bush 1.00 2.50
14 Lyle Overbay .60 1.50

15 Carlos Beltran 1.00 2.50
16 Todd Helton 1.00 2.50
17 Mark Grace 1.00 2.50
18 Fred Lynn .60 1.50
19 Robin Yount 1.50 4.00
20 Mike Schmidt 2.50 6.00
21 Roger Clemens 2.00 5.00
22 Will Clark 1.00 2.50
23 Don Mattingly 3.00 8.00
24 Blake DeWitt 1.00 2.50
25 Rafael Palmeiro 1.00 2.50
26 Wade Boggs 1.00 2.50
27 Mark Rogers 1.00 2.50
28 Billy Buckner .60 1.50
29 Jeff Baker .60 1.50
30 Nolan Ryan 5.00 12.00
31 Mike Piazza 1.50 4.00
32 Alexis Rios .60 1.50
33 Eddie Murray 1.00 2.50
34 Jose Canseco 1.00 2.50
35 Mike Mussina 1.00 2.50
36 Eric Beattie .60 1.50
37 Keith Hernandez .60 1.50
38 Michael Young .60 1.50
39 Dwight Evans .60 1.50
40 Scott Elbert .60 1.50
41 Adrian Gonzalez 1.25 3.00
42 Johnny Bench 1.50 4.00
43 Dennis Eckersley 1.00 2.50
44 Dale Murphy 1.50 4.00
45 Ryne Sandberg 3.00 8.00
46 David Wright 1.25 3.00
47 Hank Blalock .60 1.50
48 Orel Hershiser .60 1.50
49 Sean Casey .60 1.50
50 Albert Pujols 2.00 5.00

2004 Donruss Elite Extra Edition Round Numbers Signature

OVERALL AU-GU ODDS 1:4
PRINT RUNS B/WN 5-250 COPIES PER
NO PRICING ON QTY OF 10 OR LESS
1 Ozzie Smith/25 20.00 50.00
4 Paul Molitor/25 10.00 25.00
6 Delmon Young/50 12.50 30.00
7 Dontrelle Willis/25 15.00 40.00
8 Gary Carter/50 15.00 40.00
10 Andre Dawson/50 8.00 20.00
11 Neil Walker/250 6.00 15.00
12 Laynce Nix/50 5.00 12.00
13 Matt Bush/100 8.00 20.00
14 Lyle Overbay/50 5.00 12.00
15 Carlos Beltran/25 10.00 25.00
17 Mark Grace/25 15.00 40.00
18 Fred Lynn/50 5.00 12.00
20 Mike Schmidt/25 50.00 100.00
22 Will Clark/20 15.00 40.00
23 Don Mattingly/25 50.00 100.00
24 Blake DeWitt/250 6.00 15.00
27 Mark Rogers/100 12.50 30.00
28 Billy Buckner/100 6.00 15.00
32 Alexis Rios/50 8.00 20.00
34 Jose Canseco/25 20.00 50.00
36 Eric Beattie/100 6.00 15.00
37 Keith Hernandez/50 8.00 20.00
38 Michael Young/50 8.00 20.00
39 Dwight Evans/50 12.50 30.00
40 Scott Elbert/250 6.00 15.00
41 Adrian Gonzalez/50 10.00 25.00
43 Dennis Eckersley/50 12.50 30.00
44 Dale Murphy/50 12.50 30.00
46 David Wright/25 50.00 100.00
47 Hank Blalock/25 8.00 20.00
49 Sean Casey/25 8.00 20.00

2004 Donruss Elite Extra Edition Throwback Threads

OVERALL AU-GU ODDS 1:4
1 Roger Maris 30.00 60.00
2 Ted Williams 40.00 80.00
3 Cal Ripken 15.00 40.00
4 Duke Snider 10.00 25.00
5 George Brett 15.00 40.00

2004 Donruss Elite Extra Edition Throwback Threads Autograph

OVERALL AU-GU ODDS 1:4
PRINT RUNS B/WN 5-10 COPIES PER
NO PRICING DUE TO SCARCITY

2004 Donruss Elite Ripken World Series

COMPLETE SET
RWS1 Babe Ruth
Cal Ripken
RWS2 Cal Ripken
Billy Ripken

2005 Donruss Elite

COMP.SET w/o SP's (150) 10.00 25.00
COMMON CARD (1-150) .10 .30
COMMON CARD (151-170) .40 1.00
151-170 RANDOM INSERTS IN PACKS
151-170 PRINT RUN 1250 SERIAL #'d SETS
COMMON CARD (188-189) .60 1.50
COMMON AUTO p/r 1000+ 3.00 8.00
COMMON AUTO p/r 500-671 3.00 8.00
171-200: OVERALL AU-GU ODDS 3 PER BOX
171-200 PRINT RUNS B/WN 500-1500 PER
CARD 185 DOES NOT EXIST
1 Bartolo Colon .12 .30
2 Casey Kotchman .12 .30
3 Chone Figgins .12 .30
4 Darin Erstad .12 .30
5 Garret Anderson .12 .30
6 Jose Guillen .12 .30
7 Vladimir Guerrero .20 .50
8 Luis Gonzalez .12 .30
9 Randy Johnson .30 .75
10 Troy Glaus .12 .30
11 Andruw Jones .12 .30
12 Chipper Jones .30 .75
13 J.D. Drew .12 .30
14 John Smoltz .30 .75
15 Johnny Estrada .12 .30
16 Marcus Giles .12 .30
17 Rafael Furcal .12 .30
18 Javy Lopez .12 .30
19 Jay Gibbons .12 .30
20 Melvin Mora .12 .30
21 Miguel Tejada .20 .50
22 Rafael Palmeiro .20 .50
23 Sidney Ponson .12 .30
24 Curt Schilling .20 .50
25 David Ortiz .30 .75
26 Derek Lowe .12 .30
27 Jason Varitek .30 .75
28 Johnny Damon .20 .50
29 Manny Ramirez .30 .75
30 Pedro Martinez .20 .50
31 Aramis Ramirez .12 .30
32 Carlos Zambrano .20 .50
33 Corey Patterson .12 .30
34 Derrek Lee .12 .30
35 Greg Maddux .40 1.00
36 Kerry Wood .12 .30
37 Mark Prior .20 .50
38 Moises Alou .12 .30
39 Nomar Garciaparra .20 .50
40 Sammy Sosa .30 .75
41 Carlos Lee .12 .30
42 Frank Thomas .30 .75
43 Jermaine Dye .12 .30
44 Magglio Ordonez .20 .50
45 Mark Buehrle .20 .50
46 Paul Konerko .20 .50
47 Adam Dunn .20 .50
48 Austin Kearns .12 .30
49 Barry Larkin .20 .50
50 Ken Griffey Jr. .60 1.50
51 Sean Casey .12 .30
52 C.C. Sabathia .20 .50
53 Cliff Lee .20 .50
54 Travis Hafner .12 .30
55 Victor Martinez .20 .50
56 Jeromy Burnitz .12 .30
57 Preston Wilson .12 .30
58 Todd Helton .20 .50
59 Brandon Inge .12 .30
60 Ivan Rodriguez .20 .50
61 Jeremy Bonderman .12 .30
62 Troy Percival .12 .30
63 Dontrelle Willis .12 .30
64 Josh Beckett .12 .30
65 Juan Pierre .12 .30
66 Miguel Cabrera .30 .75
67 Mike Lowell .12 .30
68 Paul Lo Duca .12 .30
69 Andy Pettitte .20 .50
70 Brad Ausmus .12 .30
71 Carlos Beltran .20 .50
72 Craig Biggio .20 .50
73 Jeff Bagwell .20 .50
74 Lance Berkman .20 .50
75 Roger Clemens .40 1.00
76 Roy Oswalt .20 .50
77 Juan Gonzalez .12 .30
78 Mike Sweeney .12 .30
79 Zack Greinke .40 1.00
80 Adrian Beltre .30 .75
81 Hideo Nomo .30 .75
82 Jeff Kent .12 .30
83 Milton Bradley .12 .30
84 Shawn Green .12 .30
85 Steve Finley .12 .30
86 Ben Sheets .12 .30
87 Lyle Overbay .12 .30
88 Scott Podsednik .12 .30
89 Lew Ford .12 .30
90 Shannon Stewart .12 .30
91 Torii Hunter .12 .30
92 David Wright .25 .60
93 Jose Reyes .20 .50
94 Kazuo Matsui .12 .30
95 Mike Piazza .30 .75
96 Tom Glavine .20 .50
97 Alex Rodriguez .40 1.00
98 Bernie Williams .20 .50
99 Derek Jeter .75 2.00
100 Gary Sheffield .12 .30
101 Hideki Matsui .50 1.25
102 Jason Giambi .12 .30
103 Kevin Brown .12 .30
104 Mike Mussina .20 .50
105 Barry Zito .20 .50
106 Bobby Crosby .12 .30
107 Eric Chavez .12 .30
108 Jason Kendall .12 .30
109 Mark Mulder .12 .30
110 Bobby Abreu .12 .30
111 Jim Thome .20 .50
112 Kevin Millwood .12 .30
113 Pat Burrell .12 .30
114 Craig Wilson .12 .30
115 Jack Wilson .12 .30
116 Jason Bay .12 .30
117 Brian Giles .12 .30
118 Khalil Greene .12 .30
119 Mark Loretta .12 .30
120 Ryan Klesko .12 .30
121 Sean Burroughs .12 .30
122 Edgardo Alfonzo .12 .30
123 J.T. Snow .12 .30
124 Jason Schmidt .12 .30
125 Omar Vizquel .20 .50
126 Ichiro Suzuki .40 1.00
127 Jamie Moyer .12 .30
128 Bret Boone .12 .30
129 Richie Sexson .12 .30
130 Albert Pujols .40 1.00
131 Edgar Renteria .12 .30
132 Jeff Suppan .12 .30
133 Jim Edmonds .20 .50
134 Larry Walker .20 .50
135 Scott Rolen .20 .50
136 Aubrey Huff .12 .30
137 B.J. Upton .20 .50
138 Carl Crawford .20 .50
139 Rocco Baldelli .12 .30
140 Alfonso Soriano .20 .50
141 Hank Blalock .12 .30
142 Kenny Rogers .12 .30
143 Laynce Nix .12 .30
144 Mark Teixeira .20 .50
145 Michael Young .12 .30
146 Carlos Delgado .12 .30
147 Eric Hinske .12 .30
148 Roy Halladay .20 .50
149 Vernon Wells .12 .30
150 Jose Vidro .12 .30
151 Bob Gibson RET .60 1.50
152 Brooks Robinson RET .60 1.50
153 Cal Ripken RET 3.00 8.00
154 Carl Yastrzemski RET 1.25 3.00
155 Don Mattingly RET 2.00 5.00
156 Eddie Murray RET .60 1.50
157 Ernie Banks RET 1.00 2.50
158 Frank Robinson RET .60 1.50
159 George Brett RET 2.00 5.00
160 Harmon Killebrew RET 1.00 2.50
161 Johnny Bench RET 1.00 2.50
162 Mike Schmidt RET 1.50 4.00
163 Nolan Ryan RET 3.00 8.00
164 Paul Molitor RET 1.00 2.50
165 Stan Musial RET 1.50 4.00
166 Steve Carlton RET .60 1.50
167 Tony Gwynn RET 1.25 3.00
168 Warren Spahn RET .60 1.50
169 Willie Mays RET 2.00 5.00
170 Willie McCovey RET .60 1.50
171 Miguel Negron AU/1500 RC 4.00 10.00
172 Mike Morse AU/1000 RC 6.00 15.00
173 W.Balentien AU/1500 RC 4.00 10.00
174 A.Concepcion AU/651 RC 3.00 8.00
175 Ubaldo Jimenez AU/500 RC 10.00 25.00
176 Justin Verlander AU/500 RC 60.00 150.00
177 Ryan Speier AU/1000 RC 3.00 8.00
178 Geovany Soto AU/500 RC 30.00 60.00
179 M.McLemore AU/1200 RC 3.00 8.00
180 Ambiorix Burgos AU/599 RC 3.00 8.00
181 C.Roberson AU/1000 RC 3.00 8.00
182 Colter Bean AU/625 RC 4.00 10.00
183 Erick Threets AU/500 RC 3.00 8.00
184 Carlos Ruiz AU/1000 RC 5.00 12.00
186 J.Gothreaux AU/1500 RC 3.00 8.00
187 L.Hernandez AU/1000 RC 3.00 8.00
188 Agustin Montero/1000 RC .40 1.00
189 Paulino Reynoso/1000 RC .40 1.00
190 Garrett Jones AU/500 RC 10.00 25.00
191 S.Thompson AU/500 RC 3.00 8.00
192 Matt Lindstrom AU/1500 RC 3.00 8.00
193 Nate McLouth AU/500 RC 8.00 20.00
194 Luke Scott AU/671 RC 10.00 25.00
195 John Hattig AU/1500 RC 3.00 8.00
196 Jason Hammel AU/1500 RC 6.00 15.00
197 Danny Rueckel AU/671 RC 3.00 8.00
198 Justin Wechsler AU/500 RC 3.00 8.00
199 Chris Resop AU/500 RC 4.00 10.00
200 Jeff Miller AU/500 RC 3.00 8.00

2005 Donruss Elite Aspirations

*1-150 p/r 81-99: 5X TO 12X
*1-150 p/r 51-80: 5X TO 12X
*1-150 p/r 36-50: 5X TO 12X
*1-150 p/r 16-25: 10X TO 25X
*151-170 p/r 51-80: 1.25X TO 3X
RANDOM INSERTS IN PACKS
PRINT RUNS B/WN 15-99 COPIES PER
NO PRICING ON QTY OF 15
171 Miguel Negron/81 2.50 6.00
172 Mike Morse/63 5.00 12.00
173 Wladimir Balentien/62 2.50 6.00
174 Ambiorix Concepcion/40 1.50 4.00
175 Ubaldo Jimenez/59 4.00 10.00
176 Justin Verlander/41 30.00 80.00
177 Ryan Speier/77 1.50 4.00
178 Geovany Soto/47 8.00 20.00
179 Mark McLemore/38 1.50 4.00
180 Ambiorix Burgos/50 1.50 4.00
181 Chris Roberson/80 1.50 4.00
182 Colter Bean/29 1.50 4.00
183 Erick Threets/19 1.50 4.00
184 Carlos Ruiz/78 2.50 6.00
186 Jared Gothreaux/40 1.50 4.00
187 Luis Hernandez/25 1.50 4.00
190 Garrett Jones/50 2.50 6.00
191 Sean Thompson/27 1.50 4.00
192 Matt Lindstrom/33 1.50 4.00
193 Nate McLouth/36 2.50 6.00
194 Luke Scott/70 4.00 10.00
195 John Hattig/75 1.50 4.00
196 Jason Hammel/27 4.00 10.00
197 Danny Rueckel/40 1.50 4.00
198 Justin Wechsler/36 1.50 4.00
199 Chris Resop/28 1.50 4.00
200 Jeff Miller/38 1.50 4.00

2005 Donruss Elite Status

*1-150 p/r 51-80: 6X TO 15X
*1-150 p/r 36-50: 6X TO 15X
*1-150 p/r 26-35: 6X TO 15X
*1-150 p/r 16-25: 6X TO 15X
*151-170 p/r 36-50: 2X TO 5X
*151-170 p/r 26-35: 2X TO 5X
*151-170 p/r 16-25: 2X TO 5X
*171-200 p/r 51-80: .3X TO .8X AU 1000+
*171-200 p/r 36-50: .4X TO 1X AU 1000+
COMMON (171-200) 1.50 4.00
SEMISTARS 2.50 6.00
UNLISTED STARS 4.00 10.00
*188-189 p/r 51-80: .75X TO 2X BASIC
*188-189 p/r 36-50: .75X TO 2X BASIC
RANDOM INSERTS IN PACKS
PRINT RUNS B/WN 1-81 COPIES PER
NO PRICING ON QTY OF 15 OR LESS
171 Miguel Negron/19 2.50 6.00
172 Mike Morse/37 5.00 12.00
173 Wladimir Balentien/38 2.50 6.00
174 Ambiorix Concepcion/60 1.50 4.00
175 Ubaldo Jimenez/41 4.00 10.00
176 Justin Verlander/59 30.00 80.00
177 Ryan Speier/23 1.50 4.00
178 Geovany Soto/53 8.00 20.00
179 Mark McLemore/62 1.50 4.00
180 Ambiorix Burgos/50 1.50 4.00
181 Chris Roberson/20 1.50 4.00
182 Colter Bean/71 1.50 4.00
183 Erick Threets/81 1.50 4.00
184 Carlos Ruiz/22 2.50 6.00
186 Jared Gothreaux/60 1.50 4.00
187 Luis Hernandez/75 1.50 4.00
188 Agustin Montero/50 1.25 3.00
189 Paulino Reynoso/61 1.25 3.00
190 Garrett Jones/50 2.50 6.00
191 Sean Thompson/73 1.50 4.00
192 Matt Lindstrom/67 1.50 4.00
193 Nate McLouth/64 2.50 6.00
194 Luke Scott/30 4.00 10.00
195 John Hattig/25 1.50 4.00
196 Jason Hammel/73 4.00 10.00
197 Danny Rueckel/60 1.50 4.00
198 Justin Wechsler/64 1.50 4.00
199 Chris Resop/72 1.50 4.00
200 Jeff Miller/62 1.50 4.00

2005 Donruss Elite Status Gold

*GOLD 1-150: 15X TO 40X BASIC
*GOLD 151-170: 4X TO 10X BASIC
RANDOM INSERTS IN PACKS
STATED PRINT RUN 24 SERIAL #'d SETS
171-200 NO PRICING DUE TO SCARCITY

2005 Donruss Elite Turn of the Century

*TOC 1-150: 1.5X TO 4X BASIC
1-150 PRINT RUN 750 SERIAL #'d SETS
*TOC 151-170: .6X TO 1.5X BASIC
151-170 PRINT RUN 250 SERIAL #'d SETS
COMMON CARD (171-200) .60 1.50
SEMIS 171-200 1.00 2.50
UNLISTED 171-200 1.50 4.00
*TOC 171-200: .15X TO .4X AU 1000+
*TOC 171-200: .15X TO .4X AU 500-671
*TOC 188-189: .4X TO 1X BASIC 1000
171-200 PRINT RUN 500 SERIAL #'d SETS
RANDOM INSERTS IN PACKS
175 Ubaldo Jimenez 6.00 15.00

2005 Donruss Elite Back 2 Back Jacks

1-30 PRINT RUNS B/WN 25-200 COPIES PER
31-36 PRINT RUN 50 SERIAL #'d SETS
OVERALL AU-GU ODDS THREE PER BOX
1 Adam Dunn/200 2.50 6.00
3 Albert Pujols/100 6.00 15.00
4 Babe Ruth/50 50.00 100.00
5 Cal Ripken/100 12.50 30.00
6 David Ortiz/200 3.00 8.00
7 Eddie Murray/150 4.00 10.00
8 Ernie Banks/50 6.00 15.00
9 Frank Robinson/50 4.00 10.00
10 Gary Sheffield/200 2.50 6.00
11 George Foster/125 3.00 8.00
12 Don Mattingly/100 6.00 15.00
13 Hideki Matsui/25 12.50 30.00
14 Jason Giambi/50 4.00 10.00
16 Jim Rice/125 3.00 8.00
17 Jim Thome/200 3.00 8.00
18 Johnny Bench/125 5.00 12.00
19 Lance Berkman/200 2.50 6.00
20 Manny Ramirez/200 3.00 8.00
21 Mike Piazza/200 3.00 8.00
22 Mike Schmidt/125 6.00 15.00
23 Rafael Palmeiro/200 3.00 8.00
24 Reggie Jackson/125 4.00 10.00
25 Sammy Sosa/100 4.00 10.00
26 Scott Rolen/200 3.00 8.00
27 Stan Musial/125 6.00 15.00
28 Willie Mays/50 10.00 25.00
29 Kirk Gibson/125 3.00 8.00
30 Will Clark/125 4.00 10.00
31 W.Mays/S.Sosa/50 10.00 25.00
32 E.Murray/M.Piazza/50 6.00 15.00
33 M.Schmidt/J.Thome/50 10.00 25.00
34 R.Palmeiro/K.Gibson/50 6.00 15.00
35 J.Rice/M.Ramirez/50 6.00 15.00
36 A.Beltre/W.Clark/50 6.00 15.00
37 R.Jackson/D.Ortiz/50 6.00 15.00
38 J.Bench/A.Dunn/50 8.00 20.00

2005 Donruss Elite Back 2 Back Jacks Combos

*1-30 p/r 100: .6X TO 1.5X B2B p/r 200
*1-30 p/r 100: .5X TO 1.2X B2B p/r 100
*1-30 p/r 50: .75X TO 2X B2B p/r 150-200
*1-30 p/r 50: .6X TO 1.5X B2B p/r 100-125
*1-30 p/r 50: .5X TO 1.2X B2B p/r 50
*1-30 p/r 25: .5X TO 1.2X B2B p/r 25
1-30 PRINT RUNS B/WN 25-100 COPIES PER
*31-36 p/r 50: .5X TO 1.2X B2B p/r 50
*31-36 p/r 25: .6X TO 1.5X B2B p/r 50
31-36 PRINT RUNS B/WN 10-50 COPIES PER
31-36 ARE ALL DUAL BAT-JSY COMBOS
OVERALL AU-GU ODDS THREE PER BOX
2 Adrian Beltre Bat-Jsy/100 4.00 10.00
4 Babe Ruth Bat-Pants/25 175.00 350.00
15 Jim Edmonds Bat-Jsy/100 4.00 10.00
40 C.Ripken/A.Pujols/25 60.00 120.00

2005 Donruss Elite Career Best

STATED PRINT RUN 1500 SERIAL #'d SETS
*BLACK: 1X TO 2.5X BASIC
BLACK PRINT RUN 150 SERIAL #'d SETS
*BLUE: .75X TO 2X BASIC
BLUE PRINT RUN 250 SERIAL #'d SETS
*GOLD: .6X TO 1.5X BASIC
GOLD PRINT RUN 500 SERIAL #'d SETS
1 Adam Dunn .60 1.50
2 Adrian Beltre 1.00 2.50
3 Albert Pujols 1.25 3.00
4 Andruw Jones .40 1.00
5 Ben Sheets .40 1.00
6 Bo Jackson 1.00 2.50
7 Brooks Robinson .60 1.50
8 Cal Ripken 3.00 8.00
9 Dale Murphy 1.00 2.50
10 Don Mattingly 2.00 5.00
11 Eddie Murray .60 1.50
12 George Brett 2.00 5.00
13 Hank Blalock .40 1.00
14 Ichiro Suzuki 1.25 3.00
15 Jim Thome .60 1.50
16 Kerry Wood .40 1.00
17 Lance Berkman .60 1.50
18 Mark Prior .60 1.50
19 Mark Teixeira .60 1.50
20 Mike Schmidt 1.50 4.00
21 Pedro Martinez .60 1.50
22 Randy Johnson 1.00 2.50
23 Rickey Henderson 1.00 2.50
24 Sammy Sosa 1.00 2.50
25 Tony Gwynn 1.25 3.00

2005 Donruss Elite Career Best Bats

*BAT p/r 150-250: .4X TO 1X JSY p/r 150-250
*BAT p/r 150-250: .3X TO .8X JSY p/r 100
*BAT p/r 150-250: .25X TO .6X JSY p/r 50
*BAT p/r 100: .5X TO 1.2X JSY p/r 150-250
*BAT p/r 100: .4X TO 1X JSY p/r 100
OVERALL AU-GU ODDS THREE PER BOX
PRINT RUNS B/WN 50-250 COPIES PER

2005 Donruss Elite Career Best Jerseys

OVERALL AU-GU ODDS THREE PER BOX
PRINT RUNS B/WN 50-250 COPIES PER
1 Adam Dunn/250 2.50 6.00
2 Adrian Beltre/250 2.50 6.00
3 Albert Pujols/250 6.00 15.00
4 Andruw Jones/250 3.00 8.00
5 Ben Sheets/250 2.50 6.00
6 Bo Jackson/250 4.00 10.00
7 Brooks Robinson/50 5.00 12.00
8 Cal Ripken/150 10.00 25.00
9 Dale Murphy/100 4.00 10.00
10 Don Mattingly/150 5.00 12.00
11 Eddie Murray/100 5.00 12.00
12 George Brett/100 6.00 15.00
13 Hank Blalock/250 2.50 6.00
15 Jim Thome/250 3.00 8.00
16 Kerry Wood/250 2.50 6.00
17 Lance Berkman/250 2.50 6.00
18 Mark Prior/250 3.00 8.00
19 Mark Teixeira/250 3.00 8.00
20 Mike Schmidt/100 6.00 15.00
21 Pedro Martinez/250 3.00 8.00
22 Randy Johnson/100 4.00 10.00
23 Rickey Henderson/50 6.00 15.00
24 Sammy Sosa/250 3.00 8.00
25 Tony Gwynn/250 4.00 10.00

2005 Donruss Elite Career Best Combos

*COMBO p/r 150: .5X TO 1.2X JSY p/r 150-250
*COMBO p/r 125: .6X TO 1.5X JSY p/r 150-250
*COMBO p/r 25: 1X TO 2.5X JSY p/r 150-250
*COMBO p/r 25: .75X TO 2X JSY p/r 100
*COMBO p/r 25: .6X TO 1.5X JSY p/r 50
OVERALL AU-GU ODDS THREE PER BOX
PRINT RUNS B/WN 25-150 COPIES PER

2005 Donruss Elite Face 2 Face

STATED PRINT RUN 1500 SERIAL #'d SETS
*BLACK: .6X TO 1.5X BASIC
BLACK PRINT RUN 500 SERIAL #'d SETS
*GOLD: 1X TO 2.5X BASIC
GOLD PRINT RUN 150 SERIAL #'d SETS
*RED: .5X TO 1.2X BASIC
RED PRINT RUN 750 SERIAL #'d SETS
RANDOM INSERTS IN PACKS
1 R.Clemens 1.25 3.00
S.Rolen
2 G.Maddux 1.25 3.00
J.Bagwell
3 M.Prior 1.00 2.50
M.Piazza
4 M.Mussina .60 1.50
I.Rodriguez
5 J.Beckett 1.00 2.50
S.Sosa
6 R.Oswalt 1.00 2.50
M.Cabrera
7 R.Clemens 1.25 3.00
A.Pujols
8 P.Martinez .60 1.50
V.Guerrero
9 R.Johnson 1.00 2.50
J.Edmonds
10 C.Schilling 2.50 6.00
D.Jeter
11 K.Wood .60 1.50
L.Berkman
12 T.Hudson .60 1.50
G.Anderson
13 P.Martinez .60 1.50
G.Sheffield
14 B.Zito .60 1.50
M.Ordonez
15 K.Wood .40 1.00
S.Green
16 M.Mussina .60 1.50
M.Tejada
17 R.Johnson 1.25 3.00
A.Pujols
18 N.Ryan 3.00 8.00
G.Brett
19 T.Seaver 1.50 4.00
M.Schmidt
20 J.Palmer 1.00 2.50
H.Killebrew

2005 Donruss Elite Face 2 Face Bats

*BAT p/r 150: .4X TO 1X JSY p/r 200
*BAT p/r 150: .3X TO .8X JSY p/r 75
*BAT p/r 150: .25X TO .6X JSY p/r 50
*BAT p/r 100: .5X TO 1.2X JSY p/r 200
*BAT p/r 100: .25X TO .6X JSY p/r 25
*BAT p/r 50: .6X TO 1.5X JSY p/r 200
*BAT p/r 50: .5X TO 1.2X JSY p/r 75
*BAT p/r 25: .75X TO 2X JSY p/r 200
OVERALL AU-GU ODDS THREE PER BOX
PRINT RUNS B/WN 25-150 COPIES PER
9 R.Johnson/J.Edmonds/50 6.00 15.00

2005 Donruss Elite Face 2 Face Jerseys

OVERALL AU-GU ODDS THREE PER BOX
PRINT RUNS B/WN 25-200 COPIES PER
1 R.Clemens/S.Rolen/200 4.00 10.00
2 G.Maddux/J.Bagwell/75 5.00 12.00
3 M.Prior/M.Piazza/200 6.00 15.00
4 M.Mussina/I.Rodriguez/200 4.00 10.00
5 J.Beckett/S.Sosa/200 4.00 10.00
6 R.Oswalt/M.Cabrera/200 4.00 10.00
7 R.Clemens/A.Pujols/200 10.00 25.00
8 P.Martinez/V.Guerrero/75 5.00 12.00
11 K.Wood/L.Berkman/200 3.00 8.00
12 T.Hudson/G.Anderson/75 4.00 10.00
13 P.Martinez/G.Sheffield/75 5.00 12.00
14 B.Zito/M.Ordonez/200 3.00 8.00
15 K.Wood/S.Green/200 3.00 8.00
16 M.Mussina/M.Tejada/200 4.00 10.00
17 R.Johnson/A.Pujols/75 10.00 25.00
18 N.Ryan/G.Brett/25 30.00 60.00
19 T.Seaver/M.Schmidt/50 10.00 25.00
20 J.Palmer/H.Killebrew/25 10.00 25.00

2005 Donruss Elite Face 2 Face Combos

*COMBO p/r 250: .4X TO 1X JSY p/r 200
*COMBO p/r 75-100: .5X TO 1.2X JSY p/r 200
*COMBO p/r 75-100: .4X TO 1X JSY p/r 75
*COMBO p/r 50: .4X TO 1X JSY p/r 50
*COMBO p/r 25: .4X TO 1X JSY p/r 25
OVERALL AU-GU ODDS THREE PER BOX
PRINT RUNS B/WN 25-250 COPIES PER

2005 Donruss Elite Passing the Torch

1-30 PRINT RUN 1000 SERIAL #'d SETS
31-45 PRINT RUN 500 SERIAL #'d SETS
*BLACK 1-30: 1.25X TO 3X BASIC
*BLACK 31-45: 1.5X TO 4X BASIC
BLACK 1-30 PRINT RUN 50 #'d SETS
BLACK 31-45 PRINT RUN 25 #'d SETS
*GOLD 1-30: .75X TO 2X BASIC
*GOLD 31-45: 1X TO 2.5X BASIC
GOLD 1-30 PRINT RUN 100 #'d SETS
GOLD 31-45 PRINT RUN 50 #'d SETS
*GREEN 1-30: .6X TO 1.5X BASIC
*GREEN 31-45: .6X TO 1.5X BASIC
GREEN 1-30 PRINT RUN 250 #'d SETS
GREEN 31-45 PRINT RUN 125 #'d SETS
*RED 1-30: .5X TO 1.2X BASIC
*RED 31-45: .5X TO 1.2X BASIC
RED 1-30 PRINT RUN 500 #'d SETS
RED 31-45 PRINT RUN 250 #'d SETS
1 Adrian Beltre 1.00 2.50
2 Albert Pujols 1.25 3.00
3 Alex Rodriguez 1.25 3.00
4 Andruw Jones .40 1.00
5 Babe Ruth 2.50 6.00
6 Ben Sheets .40 1.00
7 Brooks Robinson .60 1.50
8 Cal Ripken 3.00 8.00
9 Carl Yastrzemski 1.25 3.00
10 Dale Murphy 1.00 2.50
11 David Ortiz 1.00 2.50
12 Derek Jeter 2.50 6.00
13 Don Mattingly 2.00 5.00
14 George Brett 2.00 5.00
15 Greg Maddux 1.25 3.00
16 Hank Blalock .40 1.00
17 Jeff Bagwell .60 1.50
18 Johnny Bench 1.00 2.50
19 Magglio Ordonez .60 1.50
20 Mark Prior .60 1.50
21 Mark Teixeira .60 1.50
22 Miguel Cabrera 1.00 2.50
23 Mike Schmidt 1.50 4.00
24 Nolan Ryan 3.00 8.00
25 Pedro Martinez .60 1.50
26 Sammy Sosa 1.00 2.50
27 Scott Rolen .60 1.50
28 Tom Seaver .60 1.50
29 Vladimir Guerrero .60 1.50
30 Willie Mays 2.00 5.00
31 C.Fisk 1.25 3.00
M.Ordonez
32 N.Ryan 6.00 15.00
B.Sheets
33 B.Ruth 5.00 12.00
A.Rodriguez
34 C.Ripken 6.00 15.00
B.Upton
35 W.Mays 4.00 10.00
A.Jones
36 G.Brett 4.00 10.00
H.Blalock
37 G.Maddux 2.50 6.00
W.Ford
38 H.Killebrew 2.00 5.00
A.Beltre
39 T.Seaver 1.25 3.00
M.Prior
40 D.Mattingly 4.00 10.00
M.Teixeira
41 S.Musial 3.00 8.00
C.Beltran
42 D.Murphy 2.00 5.00
L.Berkman
43 W.McCovey 1.25 3.00
J.Bagwell
44 A.Dawson 2.00 5.00
M.Cabrera
45 B.Robinson 1.25 3.00
S.Rolen

2005 Donruss Elite Passing the Torch Autographs

1-30 SINGLE PRINT RUNS B/WN 5-100 PER
31-45 DUAL PRINT RUNS B/WN 5-25 PER
NO PRICING ON QTY OF 10 OR LESS
1 Adrian Beltre/75 10.00 25.00
6 Ben Sheets/75 6.00 15.00
7 Brooks Robinson/100 8.00 20.00
10 Dale Murphy/100 10.00 25.00
13 Don Mattingly/50 20.00 50.00
16 Hank Blalock/25 10.00 25.00
18 Johnny Bench/25 20.00 50.00
19 Magglio Ordonez/75 6.00 15.00
20 Mark Prior/25 12.50 30.00
21 Mark Teixeira/75 10.00 25.00
22 Miguel Cabrera/75 20.00 50.00
23 Mike Schmidt/25 30.00 60.00
27 Scott Rolen/25 10.00 25.00
28 Tom Seaver/25 25.00 60.00
31 C.Fisk/M.Ordonez/25 30.00 60.00
32 N.Ryan/B.Sheets/25 125.00 200.00
44 A.Dawson/M.Cabrera/25 40.00 80.00
45 B.Robinson/S.Rolen/25 40.00 80.00

2005 Donruss Elite Passing the Torch Bats

*1-30 p/r 150-250: .4X TO 1X JSY p/r 150-250
*1-30 p/r 150-250: .25X TO .6X JSY p/r 50
*1-30 p/r 150-250: .2X TO .5X JSY p/r 25
*1-30 p/r 50: .6X TO 1.5X JSY p/r 150-250
*1-30 p/r 50: .4X TO 1X JSY p/r 50
*1-30 p/r 50: .3X TO .8X JSY p/r 25
1-30 PRINT RUNS B/WN 25-250 PER
*31-45 p/r 150-250: .4X TO 1X JSY p/r 150
*31-45 p/r 150-250: .3X TO .8X JSY p/r 100
*31-45 p/r 150-250: .25X TO .6X JSY p/r 50
*31-45 p/r 150-250: .2X TO .5X JSY p/r 25
*31-45 p/r 50: .6X TO 1.5X JSY p/r 150
*31-45 p/r 50: .4X TO 1X JSY p/r 50
*31-45 p/r 25: .5X TO 1.2X JSY p/r 50
*31-45 p/r 25: .4X TO 1X JSY p/r 25
31-45 PRINT RUNS B/WN 25-250 PER
OVERALL AU-GU ODDS THREE PER BOX
5 Babe Ruth/25 125.00 200.00

2005 Donruss Elite Passing the Torch Jerseys

31-45 PRINT RUNS B/WN 25-150 PER
OVERALL AU-GU ODDS THREE PER BOX
1 Adrian Beltre/250 2.50 6.00
2 Albert Pujols/250 6.00 15.00
4 Andruw Jones/250 3.00 8.00
5 Babe Ruth Pants/25 150.00 250.00
6 Ben Sheets/250 2.50 6.00
7 Brooks Robinson/25 6.00 15.00
8 Cal Ripken/250 10.00 25.00
9 Carl Yastrzemski Pants/50 6.00 15.00
10 Dale Murphy/250 3.00 8.00
11 David Ortiz/250 3.00 8.00
13 Don Mattingly/150 5.00 12.00
14 George Brett/50 8.00 20.00
15 Greg Maddux/250 4.00 10.00
16 Hank Blalock/250 2.50 6.00
17 Jeff Bagwell/250 3.00 8.00
18 Johnny Bench Pants/150 4.00 10.00
19 Magglio Ordonez/250 2.50 6.00
20 Mark Prior/250 3.00 8.00
21 Mark Teixeira/250 3.00 8.00
22 Miguel Cabrera/250 3.00 8.00
23 Mike Schmidt/150 5.00 12.00
24 Nolan Ryan/50 10.00 25.00
25 Pedro Martinez/250 3.00 8.00
26 Sammy Sosa/250 3.00 8.00
27 Scott Rolen/250 3.00 8.00
28 Tom Seaver/50 5.00 12.00
29 Vladimir Guerrero/250 3.00 8.00
30 Willie Mays/25 30.00 60.00
31 C.Fisk/M.Ordonez/50 5.00 12.00
32 N.Ryan/B.Sheets/50 15.00 40.00
34 C.Ripken/B.Upton/50 10.00 25.00
35 W.Mays/A.Jones/50 30.00 60.00
36 G.Brett/H.Blalock/50 10.00 25.00
37 G.Maddux/W.Ford/25 15.00 40.00
38 H.Killebrew/A.Beltre/50 8.00 20.00
39 T.Seaver/M.Prior/25 8.00 20.00
40 D.Mattingly/M.Teixeira/100 8.00 20.00
41 S.Musial Pants/C.Beltran/25 12.50 30.00
42 D.Murphy/L.Berkman/150 4.00 10.00
43 W.McCovey/J.Bagwell/50 6.00 15.00
44 A.Dawson/M.Cabrera/150 4.00 10.00
45 B.Robinson/S.Rolen/25 8.00 20.00

2005 Donruss Elite Teams

STATED PRINT RUN 1500 SERIAL #'d SETS
*BLACK: .75X TO 2X BASIC
BLACK PRINT RUN 250 SERIAL #'d SETS
*BLUE: .4X TO 1X BASIC
BLUE PRINT RUN 1000 SERIAL #'d SETS
*GOLD: 1.25X TO 3X BASIC
GOLD PRINT RUN 100 SERIAL #'d SETS
*GREEN: .5X TO 1.2X BASIC
GREEN PRINT RUN 750 SERIAL #'d SETS
*RED: .6X TO 1.5X BASIC
RED PRINT RUN 500 SERIAL #'d SETS
1 Manny 1.25 3.00
Pedro
Ortiz
2 Pujols 1.50 4.00
Rolen
Edmonds
3 Clem 1.50 4.00
Bag
Berk
Bigg
4 M.Cab 1.25 3.00
Beckett
Lowell
5 Wood 1.50 4.00
Prior
Sos
Madd
6 Beltre 1.25 3.00
Green
Nomo
Ishii
7 Ripken 4.00 10.00
Murray
Palmer
8 Brett 2.50 6.00
Bo
F.White
9 Clem 1.50 4.00
Muss
Sor
Bernie
10 Glav 1.50 4.00
Madd
Kles
Just

2005 Donruss Elite Teams Bats
*BAT p/r 100: .5X TO 1.2X JSY p/r 150
*BAT p/r 100: .3X TO .8X JSY p/r 50
*BAT p/r 50: .6X TO 1.5X JSY p/r 150
*BAT p/r 50: .4X TO 1X JSY p/r 50
OVERALL AU-GU ODDS THREE PER BOX
PRINT RUNS B/WN 50-100 COPIES PER
8 Brett/Bo/F.White/100 12.50 30.00

2005 Donruss Elite Teams Jerseys
OVERALL AU-GU ODDS THREE PER BOX
PRINT RUNS B/WN 50-150 COPIES PER
1 Manny/Pedro/Ortiz/150 6.00 15.00
2 Pujols/Rolen/Edmonds/150 12.50 30.00
3 Clem/Bag/Berk/Bigg/150 10.00 25.00
4 M.Cab/Beckett/Lowell/50 6.00 15.00
5 Wood/Prior/Sos/Madd/150 12.50 30.00
6 Beltre/Green/Nomo/Ishii/50 10.00 25.00
7 Ripken/Murray/Palmer/100 20.00 50.00
9 Clem/Muss/Sor/Bernie/100 10.00 25.00
10 Glav/Madd/Kles/Just/100 15.00 40.00

2005 Donruss Elite Throwback Threads
1-40 PRINT RUNS B/WN 10-200 PER
1-40 NO PRICING ON QTY OF 10
41-60 PRINT RUNS B/WN 5-150 PER
41-60 NO PRICING ON QTY OF 5
OVERALL AU-GU ODDS THREE PER BOX
1 Albert Pujols/200 6.00 15.00
2 Babe Ruth Pants/25 150.00 250.00
3 Bert Blyleven/200 2.50 6.00
4 Bobby Doerr Pants/200 2.50 6.00
5 Brooks Robinson/25 6.00 15.00
6 Cal Ripken/150 10.00 25.00
7 Carl Yastrzemski Pants/150 5.00 12.00
8 Dale Murphy/150 3.00 8.00
9 Dennis Eckersley/50 4.00 10.00
10 Don Mattingly/200 5.00 12.00
11 Don Sutton/100 3.00 8.00
12 Duke Snider Pants/25 6.00 15.00
13 Early Wynn/50 4.00 10.00
14 Eddie Murray/100 5.00 12.00
15 George Brett/25 10.00 25.00
16 Greg Maddux/150 4.00 10.00
17 Harmon Killebrew/100 5.00 12.00
18 Hoyt Wilhelm/150 2.50 6.00
19 Jim Edmonds/200 2.50 6.00
20 Jim Palmer/25 5.00 12.00
21 Lou Boudreau/50 4.00 10.00
22 Lou Brock/100 4.00 10.00
23 Miguel Cabrera/200 3.00 8.00
24 Mike Mussina/150 3.00 8.00
25 Mike Piazza/150 3.00 8.00
26 Mike Schmidt/150 5.00 12.00
27 Nolan Ryan/50 10.00 25.00
28 Phil Niekro/100 3.00 8.00
29 Randy Johnson/150 3.00 8.00
30 Rickey Henderson/150 4.00 10.00
31 Sammy Sosa/150 3.00 8.00
32 Scott Rolen/200 3.00 8.00
34 Steve Carlton/100 3.00 8.00
35 Ted Williams/25 50.00 100.00
36 Tommy John/150 2.50 6.00
37 Vladimir Guerrero/200 3.00 8.00
38 Whitey Ford/25 6.00 15.00
39 Willie Mays/50 20.00 50.00
40 Willie McCovey/150 3.00 8.00
42 W.Ford/R.Clemens/25 15.00 40.00
44 T.Williams/T.Gwynn/25 60.00 120.00
45 W.Mays Pants/M.Cabr/25 30.00 60.00
46 L.Brock/R.Henderson/100 5.00 12.00
47 B.Robinson/G.Brett/25 30.00 60.00
48 W.McCovey/D.Ortiz/25 8.00 20.00
49 B.Jackson/D.Sanders/150 4.00 10.00
50 N.Ryan/C.Schilling/100 12.50 30.00
51 D.Sutton/G.Maddux/100 6.00 15.00
52 H.Killebrew/R.Palmeiro/100 5.00 12.00
53 D.Murphy/D.Evans/150 4.00 10.00
54 S.Carlton/R.Johnson/25 10.00 25.00
55 C.Yaz/V.Guerrero/50 8.00 20.00
56 E.Murray/M.Piazza/100 5.00 12.00
57 J.Bench/I.Rodriguez/50 6.00 15.00
58 J.Palmer/T.Hudson/50 5.00 12.00
59 C.Ripken/H.Blalock/50 20.00 50.00
60 J.Rice/M.Ramirez/100 5.00 12.00

2005 Donruss Elite Throwback Threads Prime
*1-40 p/r 25: 1.5X TO 4X TT p/r 150-200
*1-40 p/r 25: 1.25X TO 3X TT p/r 100
*1-40 p/r 25: 1X TO 2.5X TT p/r 50
*1-40 p/r 25: .75X TO 2X TT p/r 25
1-40 PRINT RUNS B/WN 5-25 COPIES PER
*41-60 p/r 25: 2X TO 5X TT p/r 150-200
*41-60 p/r 25: 1.5X TO 4X TT p/r 100
*41-60 p/r 25: 1.25X TO 3X TT p/r 50
*41-60 p/r 25: 1X TO 2.5X TT p/r 25
41-60 PRINT RUNS B/WN 1-25 COPIES PER
OVERALL AU-GU ODDS THREE PER BOX
NO PRICDING ON QTY OF 10 OR LESS
59 C.Ripken/H.Blalock/25 60.00 120.00

2005 Donruss Elite Throwback Threads Autographs
PRINT RUNS B/WN 5-100 COPIES PER
NO PRICING ON QTY OF 10 OR LESS
PRIME PRINT RUNS B/WN 1-10 PER
NO PRIME PRICING DUE TO SCARCITY
OVERALL AU-GU ODDS THREE PER BOX
3 Bert Blyleven/100 8.00 20.00
4 Bobby Doerr Pants/100 8.00 20.00
5 Brooks Robinson/50 15.00 40.00
8 Dale Murphy/100 12.50 30.00
9 Dennis Eckersley/75 10.00 25.00
10 Don Mattingly/25 40.00 80.00
11 Don Sutton/50 10.00 25.00
17 Harmon Killebrew/75 20.00 50.00
20 Jim Palmer/75 8.00 20.00
22 Lou Brock Jkt/75 12.00 30.00
23 Miguel Cabrera/75 15.00 40.00
40 Willie McCovey/25 20.00 50.00

2010 Donruss Elite National Convention
ANNOUNCED PRINT RUN 499 SETS
49 Cito Culver 4.00 10.00
50 Bryan Holaday 3.00 8.00
51 Cole Leonida 3.00 8.00
52 Chris Sale 6.00 15.00

2010 Donruss Elite National Convention Aspirations
*ASPIRATIONS: .8X TO 2X BASIC CARDS
ANNOUNCED PRINT RUN 50

2010 Donruss Elite National Convention Status
*STATUS: .8X TO 2X BASIC CARDS
ANNOUNCED PRINT RUN 25

2007 Donruss Elite Extra Edition
COMPLETE SET (142)
COMP.SET w/o AU's (92) 8.00 20.00
COMMON CARD (1-92) .20 .50
COMMON AU (92-142) 4.00 10.00
OVERALL AUTO/MEM ODDS 1:5
AU PRINT RUNS B/WN 374-999 COPIES PER
EXCHANGE DEADLINE 07/01/2009
1 Andrew Brackman .30 .75
2 Austin Gallagher .20 .50
3 Brett Cecil .20 .50
4 Darwin Barney .50 1.25
5 David Price 2.00 5.00
6 J. P. Arencibia .40 1.00
7 Josh Donaldson 1.25 3.00
8 Brandon Hicks .20 .50
9 Brian Rike .20 .50
10 Bryan Morris .20 .50
11 Cale Iorg .20 .50
12 Casey Weathers .20 .50
13 Corey Kluber .50 1.25
14 Daniel Moskos .20 .50
15 Danny Payne .20 .50
16 David Kopp .20 .50
17 Dellin Betances .75 2.00
18 Derrick Robinson .20 .50
19 Drew Stubbs .20 .50
20 Eric Eiland .20 .50
21 Francisco Pena .20 .50
22 Greg Reynolds .20 .50
23 Jeff Samardzija 1.25 3.00
24 Jess Todd .20 .50
25 John Tolisano .20 .50
26 Jordan Zimmerman UER 1.00 2.50
27 Julian Sampson .20 .50
28 Luke Hochevar .50 1.25
29 Mat Latos .75 2.00
30 Matt Mangini .20 .50
31 Matt Spencer .30 .75
32 Matthew Sweeney .50 1.25
33 Max Scherzer .75 2.00
34 Mitch Canham .20 .50
35 Nick Schmidt .20 .50
36 Paul Kelly .20 .50
37 Ryan Pope .30 .75
38 Sam Runion .20 .50
39 Steven Souza .60 1.50
40 Travis Mattair .20 .50
41 Trystan Magnuson .20 .50
42 Will Middlebrooks .30 .75
43 Zack Cozart .60 1.50
44 James Adkins .20 .50
45 Cory Luebke .20 .50
46 Aaron Poreda .20 .50
47 Clayton Mortensen .20 .50
48 Bradley Suttle .30 .75
49 Tony Butler .30 .75
50 Zach Britton 1.25 3.00
51 Scott Cousins .20 .50
52 Wendell Fairley .50 1.25
53 Eric Sogard .20 .50
54 Jonathan Lucroy .30 .75
55 Lars Davis .20 .50
77 Jennie Finch .50 1.25
91 Charlie Culberson .60 1.50
92 Jacob Smolinski .20 .50
93 Blake Beaven AU/719 5.00 12.00
94 Brad Chalk AU/613 4.00 10.00
95 Brett Anderson AU/549 5.00 12.00
96 Chris Withrow AU/700 4.00 10.00
97 Clay Fuller AU/674 4.00 10.00
98 Damon Sublett AU/674 8.00 20.00
99 Devin Mesoraco AU/674 6.00 15.00
100 Drew Cumberland AU/744 4.00 10.00
101 Jack McGeary AU/674 6.00 15.00
102 Jake Arrieta AU/949 30.00 80.00
103 James Simmons AU/624 4.00 10.00
104 Jarrod Parker AU/499 10.00 25.00
105 Jason Dominguez AU/744 4.00 10.00
106 Jason Heyward AU/750 12.00 30.00
107 Joe Savery AU/750 5.00 12.00
108 Jon Gilmore AU/819 3.00 8.00
109 Jordan Walden AU/794 5.00 12.00
110 Josh Smoker AU/719 5.00 12.00
111 Josh Vitters AU/769 6.00 15.00
112 Julio Borbon AU/594 8.00 20.00
113 Justin Jackson AU/850 4.00 10.00
114 Kellen Kulbacki AU/549 5.00 12.00
115 Kevin Ahrens AU/794 8.00 20.00
116 Kyle Lotzkar AU/611 4.00 10.00
117 Madison Bumgarner AU/794 25.00 60.00
118 Matt Dominguez AU/769 4.00 10.00
119 Matt LaPorta AU/594 5.00 12.00
120 Matt Wieters AU/799 8.00 20.00
121 Michael Burgess AU/672 4.00 10.00
122 Michael Main AU/794 5.00 12.00
123 Mike Moustakas AU/999 8.00 20.00
124 Nathan Vineyard AU/700 5.00 12.00
125 Neil Ramirez AU/774 6.00 15.00
126 Nick Hagadone AU/544 4.00 10.00
127 Pete Kozma AU/719 5.00 12.00
128 Phillippe Aumont AU/674 5.00 12.00
129 Preston Mattingly AU/519 8.00 20.00
130 Joba Chamberlain AU/250 8.00 20.00
131 Ross Detwiler AU/650 5.00 12.00
132 Tim Alderson AU/719 8.00 20.00
133 Todd Frazier AU/774 15.00 40.00
134 Wes Roemer AU/694 5.00 12.00
135 Ben Revere AU/700 5.00 12.00
136 Chris Davis AU/374 12.00 30.00
138 Bryan Anderson AU/474 4.00 10.00
141 Austin Jackson AU/794 10.00 25.00
142 Beau Mills AU/624 8.00 20.00
149 Tommy Hunter AU/474 8.00 20.00

2007 Donruss Elite Extra Edition Aspirations
*ASP 1-92: 3X TO 8X BASIC
OVERALL INSERT ODDS 1:4
STATED PRINT RUN 100 SER.#'d SETS
5 David Price 30.00 60.00
23 Jeff Samardzija 8.00 20.00
33 Max Scherzer 8.00 20.00
92 Jacob Smolinski 1.50 4.00
93 Blake Beaven 1.50 4.00
94 Brad Chalk 1.50 4.00
95 Brett Anderson 2.50 6.00
96 Chris Withrow 1.50 4.00
97 Clay Fuller 1.50 4.00
98 Damon Sublett 2.50 6.00
99 Devin Mesoraco 2.00 5.00
100 Drew Cumberland 1.50 4.00
101 Jack McGeary 2.00 5.00
102 Jake Arrieta 6.00 15.00
103 James Simmons 1.50 4.00
104 Jarrod Parker 8.00 20.00
105 Jason Dominguez 1.50 4.00
106 Jason Heyward 50.00 100.00
107 Joe Savery 2.00 5.00
108 Jon Gilmore 2.00 5.00
109 Jordan Walden 2.50 6.00
110 Josh Smoker 2.50 6.00
111 Josh Vitters 5.00 12.00
112 Julio Borbon 2.00 5.00
113 Justin Jackson 1.50 4.00
114 Kellen Kulbacki 2.00 5.00
115 Kevin Ahrens 2.00 5.00
116 Kyle Lotzkar 1.50 4.00
117 Madison Bumgarner 12.00 30.00
118 Matt Dominguez 6.00 15.00
119 Matt LaPorta 8.00 20.00
120 Matt Wieters 6.00 15.00
121 Michael Burgess 6.00 15.00
122 Michael Main 2.00 5.00
123 Mike Moustakas 6.00 15.00
124 Nathan Vineyard 2.00 5.00
125 Neil Ramirez 1.50 4.00
126 Nick Hagadone 2.50 6.00
127 Pete Kozma 1.50 4.00
128 Phillippe Aumont 5.00 12.00
129 Preston Mattingly 4.00 10.00
131 Ross Detwiler 2.50 6.00
132 Tim Alderson 2.50 6.00
133 Todd Frazier 2.00 5.00
134 Wes Roemer 1.50 4.00
135 Ben Revere 2.50 6.00
141 Austin Jackson 4.00 10.00
142 Beau Mills 4.00 10.00
149 Tommy Hunter

2007 Donruss Elite Extra Edition Signature Aspirations
OVERALL AU/MEM ODDS 1:5
PRINT RUNS B/WN 5-100 COPIES PER
NO PRICING ON QTY 25 OR LESS
EXCHANGE DEADLINE 07/01/2007
1 Andrew Brackman/100 10.00 25.00
2 Austin Gallagher/100 12.50 30.00
3 Brett Cecil /100 6.00 15.00
4 Danny Worth/100 6.00 15.00
5 David Price/100 50.00 100.00
6 J. P. Arencibia/100 8.00 20.00
7 Josh Donaldson/100 20.00 50.00
8 Brandon Hicks/100 4.00 10.00
9 Brian Rike/100 4.00 10.00
10 Bryan Morris/100 4.00 10.00
11 Cale Iorg/100 12.50 30.00
12 Casey Weathers/100 6.00 15.00
13 Corey Kluber/100 40.00 100.00
14 Daniel Moskos/100 4.00 10.00
15 Danny Payne/50 6.00 15.00
16 David Kopp/36 6.00 15.00
17 Dellin Betances/50 8.00 20.00
18 Derrick Robinson/100 4.00 10.00
19 Drew Stubbs/100 15.00 40.00
20 Eric Eiland/100 6.00 15.00
21 Francisco Pena/100 8.00 20.00
22 Greg Reynolds/100 4.00 10.00
23 Jeff Samardzija/15
24 Jess Todd/50 12.50 30.00
25 John Tolisano/100 10.00 25.00
26 Jordan Zimmerman/75 12.50 30.00
27 Julian Sampson/50 4.00 10.00
28 Luke Hochevar/25
29 Mat Latos/34 50.00 100.00
30 Matt Mangini/80 10.00 25.00
31 Matt Spencer/30 6.00 15.00
32 Matthew Sweeney/100 EXCH 8.00 20.00
34 Mitch Canham/25
35 Nick Schmidt/25
36 Paul Kelly/100 4.00 10.00
37 Ryan Pope/100 12.50 30.00
38 Sam Runion/50 6.00 15.00
39 Steven Souza/100 10.00 25.00
40 Travis Mattair/50 6.00 15.00
41 Trystan Magnuson/50 4.00 10.00
42 Will Middlebrooks/25
43 Zack Cozart/25
44 James Adkins/100 10.00 25.00
45 Cory Luebke/100 4.00 10.00
46 Aaron Poreda/100 6.00 15.00
47 Clayton Mortensen/100 6.00 15.00
48 Bradley Suttle/100 12.50 30.00
49 Tony Butler/100 4.00 10.00
50 Zach Britton/100 15.00 40.00
51 Scott Cousins /50 6.00 15.00
52 Wendell Fairley/100 12.50 30.00
53 Eric Sogard/100 4.00 10.00
54 Jonathan Lucroy/100 20.00 50.00
55 Lars Davis/100 4.00 10.00
56 Tony Thomas/100 4.00 10.00
59 Nick Noonan/100 EXCH 4.00 10.00
60 Henry Sosa/100 EXCH 4.00 10.00
73 Corey Brown/5 EXCH
77 Jennie Finch/50 15.00 40.00
91 Charlie Culberson/100 15.00 40.00
92 Jacob Smolinski/100 8.00 20.00
93 Blake Beaven/100 6.00 15.00
94 Brad Chalk/100 4.00 10.00
95 Brett Anderson/100 5.00 12.00
96 Chris Withrow/100 6.00 15.00
97 Clay Fuller/100 6.00 15.00
98 Damon Sublett/50 6.00 15.00
99 Devin Mesoraco/100 10.00 25.00
100 Drew Cumberland/100 5.00 12.00
101 Jack McGeary/100 6.00 15.00
102 Jake Arrieta/100 50.00 120.00
103 James Simmons/50 EXCH 4.00 10.00
104 Jarrod Parker/50 20.00 50.00
105 Jason Dominguez/100 5.00 12.00
106 Jason Heyward/100 75.00 150.00
107 Joe Savery/100 5.00 12.00
108 Jon Gilmore/100 6.00 15.00
109 Jordan Walden/50 8.00 20.00
110 Josh Smoker/100 5.00 12.00
111 Josh Vitters/100 15.00 40.00
112 Julio Borbon/100 10.00 25.00
113 Justin Jackson/50 10.00 25.00
114 Kellen Kulbacki/100 8.00 20.00
115 Kevin Ahrens/50 15.00 40.00
116 Kyle Lotzkar/100 12.50 30.00
117 Madison Bumgarner/50 75.00 150.00
118 Matt Dominguez/50 10.00 25.00
119 Matt LaPorta/100 10.00 25.00
120 Matt Wieters/50 30.00 60.00
121 Michael Burgess/50 30.00 60.00
122 Michael Main/50 12.50 30.00
123 Mike Moustakas/100 12.00 30.00
124 Nathan Vineyard/100 5.00 12.00
125 Neil Ramirez/100 4.00 10.00
126 Nick Hagadone/50 12.50 30.00
127 Pete Kozma/100 6.00 15.00
128 Phillippe Aumont/100 12.50 30.00
129 Preston Mattingly/50 30.00 60.00
131 Ross Detwiler/100 4.00 10.00
132 Tim Alderson/100 15.00 40.00
133 Todd Frazier/100 25.00 60.00
134 Wes Roemer/100 6.00 15.00
135 Ben Revere/100 5.00 12.00
138 Bryan Anderson/50 EXCH 4.00 10.00
141 Austin Jackson/50 10.00 25.00
142 Beau Mills/50 EXCH 6.00 15.00
144 Chris Davis/50 25.00 60.00
149 Tommy Hunter/50

2007 Donruss Elite Extra Edition Signature Status
OVERALL AU/MEM ODDS 1:5
PRINT RUNS B/WN 1-50 COPIES PER
NO PRICING ON QTY 25 OR LESS
EXCHANGE DEADLINE 07/01/2007
1 Andrew Brackman/50 15.00 40.00
2 Austin Gallagher/50 20.00 50.00
3 Brett Cecil /50 20.00 50.00
4 Danny Worth/50 EXCH 8.00 20.00
5 David Price/50 60.00 120.00
6 J. P. Arencibia/50 30.00 60.00
7 Josh Donaldson/50 25.00 60.00
8 Brandon Hicks/50 6.00 15.00
9 Brian Rike/50 6.00 15.00
10 Bryan Morris/50 6.00 15.00
11 Cale Iorg/50 12.50 30.00
12 Casey Weathers/50 10.00 25.00
13 Corey Kluber/50 50.00 120.00
14 Daniel Moskos/50 6.00 15.00
15 Danny Payne/25
16 David Kopp/25
17 Dellin Betances/25
18 Derrick Robinson/50 6.00 15.00
19 Drew Stubbs/50 8.00 20.00
20 Eric Eiland/50 10.00 25.00
21 Francisco Pena/50 12.50 30.00
22 Greg Reynolds/50 6.00 15.00
23 Jeff Samardzija/10
24 Jess Todd/25
25 John Tolisano/50 15.00 40.00
26 Jordan Zimmerman/25
27 Julian Sampson/25
28 Luke Hochevar/10
29 Mat Latos/25
30 Matt Mangini/50 15.00 40.00
31 Matt Spencer/15
32 Matthew Sweeney/50 EXCH 12.50 30.00
33 Max Scherzer/12
34 Mitch Canham/10
35 Nick Schmidt/10
36 Paul Kelly/50 6.00 15.00
37 Ryan Pope/50 20.00 50.00
38 Sam Runion/25
39 Steven Souza/50 12.00 30.00
40 Travis Mattair/25
41 Trystan Magnuson/25
42 Will Middlebrooks/10
43 Zack Cozart/10
44 James Adkins/50 15.00 40.00
45 Cory Luebke/50 6.00 15.00
46 Aaron Poreda/50 10.00 25.00
47 Clayton Mortensen/50 10.00 25.00
48 Bradley Suttle/50 20.00 50.00
49 Tony Butler/50 6.00 15.00
50 Zach Britton/50 10.00 25.00
51 Scott Cousins /19
52 Wendell Fairley/50 20.00 50.00
53 Eric Sogard/50 6.00 15.00
54 Jonathan Lucroy/50 20.00 50.00
55 Lars Davis/50 6.00 15.00
56 Tony Thomas/50 EXCH 6.00 15.00
59 Nick Noonan/50 6.00 15.00
60 Henry Sosa/50 EXCH 6.00 15.00
73 Corey Brown/1 EXCH
77 Jennie Finch/25
91 Charlie Culberson/50 8.00 20.00
92 Jacob Smolinski/50 12.50 30.00
93 Blake Beaven/50 10.00 25.00
94 Brad Chalk/50 6.00 15.00
95 Brett Anderson/50 10.00 25.00
96 Chris Withrow/50 10.00 25.00
97 Clay Fuller/50 10.00 25.00
98 Damon Sublett/25
99 Devin Mesoraco/50 15.00 40.00
100 Drew Cumberland/50 8.00 20.00
101 Jack McGeary/50 10.00 25.00
102 Jake Arrieta/50 60.00 150.00
103 James Simmons/25 EXCH
104 Jarrod Parker/25
105 Jason Dominguez/50 8.00 20.00
106 Jason Heyward/50 60.00 120.00
107 Joe Savery/50 8.00 20.00
108 Jon Gilmore/50 10.00 25.00
109 Jordan Walden/25
110 Josh Smoker/50 50.00 100.00
111 Josh Vitters/50 12.50 30.00
112 Julio Borbon/50 12.50 30.00
113 Justin Jackson/25
114 Kellen Kulbacki/50 12.50 30.00
115 Kevin Ahrens/25
116 Kyle Lotzkar/50 10.00 25.00
117 Madison Bumgarner/25
118 Matt Dominguez/25
119 Matt LaPorta/50 15.00 40.00
120 Matt Wieters/25
121 Michael Burgess/25
122 Michael Main/25
123 Mike Moustakas/50 20.00 50.00
124 Nathan Vineyard/50 8.00 20.00
125 Neil Ramirez/50 12.50 30.00
126 Nick Hagadone/25
127 Pete Kozma/50 10.00 25.00
128 Phillippe Aumont/50 20.00 50.00
129 Preston Mattingly/25
131 Ross Detwiler/50 10.00 25.00
132 Tim Alderson/50 30.00 60.00
133 Todd Frazier/50 30.00 80.00
134 Wes Roemer/50 10.00 25.00
135 Ben Revere/50 8.00 20.00
138 Bryan Anderson/25 EXCH
141 Austin Jackson/25
142 Beau Mills/25 EXCH
144 Chris Davis/25
149 Tommy Hunter/25

2007 Donruss Elite Extra Edition Signature Turn of the Century
OVERALL AU/MEM ODDS 1:5
PRINT RUNS B/WN 10-500 COPIES PER
NO PRICING ON QTY 25 OR LESS
EXCHANGE DEADLINE 07/01/2007
1 Andrew Brackman/500 8.00 20.00
2 Austin Gallagher/500 10.00 25.00
3 Brett Cecil /500 8.00 20.00
4 Danny Worth/500 6.00 15.00
5 David Price/500 20.00 50.00
6 J. P. Arencibia/500 8.00 20.00
7 Josh Donaldson/500 20.00 50.00
8 Brandon Hicks/419 5.00 12.00
9 Brian Rike/500 5.00 12.00
10 Bryan Morris/500 4.00 10.00
11 Cale Iorg/397 6.00 15.00
12 Casey Weathers/500 5.00 12.00
13 Corey Kluber/419 20.00 50.00
14 Daniel Moskos/500 4.00 10.00
15 Danny Payne/394 4.00 10.00
16 David Kopp/449 4.00 10.00
17 Dellin Betances/494 6.00 15.00
18 Derrick Robinson/500 4.00 10.00
19 Drew Stubbs/494 4.00 10.00
20 Eric Eiland/419 6.00 15.00
21 Francisco Pena/396 6.00 15.00
22 Greg Reynolds/500 4.00 10.00
23 Jeff Samardzija/219 10.00 25.00
24 Jess Todd/394 12.50 30.00
25 John Tolisano/419 6.00 15.00
26 Jordan Zimmerman/469 6.00 15.00
27 Julian Sampson/494 4.00 10.00
28 Luke Hochevar/158 12.50 30.00
29 Mat Latos/499 6.00 15.00
30 Matt Mangini/500 5.00 12.00
31 Matt Spencer/500 4.00 10.00
32 Matthew Sweeney/500 6.00 15.00
33 Max Scherzer/250 60.00 150.00
34 Mitch Canham/209 5.00 12.00
35 Nick Schmidt/409 4.00 10.00
36 Paul Kelly/500 4.00 10.00
37 Ryan Pope/500 6.00 15.00
38 Sam Runion/494 5.00 12.00
39 Steven Souza/500 8.00 20.00
40 Travis Mattair/494 6.00 15.00
41 Trystan Magnuson/246 4.00 10.00
42 Will Middlebrooks/409 4.00 10.00
43 Zack Cozart/409 6.00 15.00
44 James Adkins/500 4.00 10.00
45 Cory Luebke/469 4.00 10.00
46 Aaron Poreda/500 5.00 12.00
47 Clayton Mortensen/500 4.00 10.00
48 Bradley Suttle/500 5.00 12.00
49 Tony Butler/419 4.00 10.00
50 Zach Britton/437 8.00 20.00
51 Scott Cousins /500 5.00 12.00
52 Wendell Fairley/500 10.00 25.00
53 Eric Sogard/500 5.00 12.00
54 Jonathan Lucroy/500 15.00 40.00
55 Lars Davis/500 4.00 10.00
56 Tony Thomas/300 4.00 10.00
59 Nick Noonan/300 EXCH 4.00 10.00
60 Henry Sosa/300 5.00 12.00
73 Corey Brown/10 EXCH
77 Jennie Finch/119 12.00 30.00
91 Charlie Culberson/500 10.00 25.00
92 Jacob Smolinski/500 6.00 15.00
93 Blake Beaven/100 6.00 15.00
94 Brad Chalk/100 5.00 12.00
95 Brett Anderson/145 5.00 12.00
96 Chris Withrow/168 5.00 12.00
97 Clay Fuller/145 5.00 12.00
98 Damon Sublett/220 10.00 25.00
99 Devin Mesoraco/145 5.00 12.00
100 Drew Cumberland/125 5.00 12.00
101 Jack McGeary/145 6.00 15.00
102 Jake Arrieta/145 50.00 120.00
103 James Simmons/100 EXCH 5.00 12.00
104 Jarrod Parker/55 20.00 50.00
105 Jason Dominguez/100 5.00 12.00
106 Jason Heyward/169 12.00 30.00
107 Joe Savery/119 6.00 15.00
108 Jon Gilmore/100 6.00 15.00
109 Jordan Walden/100 10.00 25.00
110 Josh Smoker/200 15.00 40.00
111 Josh Vitters/150 8.00 20.00
112 Julio Borbon/100 10.00 25.00
113 Justin Jackson/100 6.00 15.00
114 Kellen Kulbacki/145 5.00 12.00
115 Kevin Ahrens/100 10.00 25.00
116 Kyle Lotzkar/100 6.00 15.00
117 Madison Bumgarner/100 60.00 120.00
118 Matt Dominguez/100 10.00 25.00
119 Matt LaPorta/100 10.00 25.00
120 Matt Wieters/100 10.00 25.00
121 Michael Burgess/100 15.00 40.00
122 Michael Main/100 6.00 15.00
123 Mike Moustakas/345 10.00 25.00
124 Nathan Vineyard/119 6.00 15.00
125 Neil Ramirez/145 6.00 15.00
126 Nick Hagadone/100 6.00 15.00
127 Pete Kozma/100 5.00 12.00
128 Phillippe Aumont/120 5.00 12.00
129 Preston Mattingly/100 15.00 40.00
131 Ross Detwiler/119 10.00 25.00
132 Tim Alderson/100 15.00 40.00
133 Todd Frazier/145 8.00 20.00
134 Wes Roemer/100 5.00 12.00
135 Ben Revere/119 5.00 12.00
138 Bryan Anderson/100 EXCH 4.00 10.00
139 Marc Gasol EXCH 4.00 10.00
141 Austin Jackson/100 10.00 25.00
142 Beau Mills/100 EXCH 12.00 30.00
144 Chris Davis/100 20.00 50.00
149 Tommy Hunter 12.00 30.00

2007 Donruss Elite Extra Edition Status
*STATUS 1-92: 4X TO 10X BASIC
OVERALL INSERT ODDS 1:4
STATED PRINT RUN 50 SER.#'d SETS
92 Jacob Smolinski 2.00 5.00
93 Blake Beaven 2.00 5.00
94 Brad Chalk 2.00 5.00
95 Brett Anderson 3.00 8.00
96 Chris Withrow 2.00 5.00
97 Clay Fuller 2.00 5.00
98 Damon Sublett 3.00 8.00
99 Devin Mesoraco 2.50 6.00
100 Drew Cumberland 2.00 5.00
101 Jack McGeary 2.50 6.00
102 Jake Arrieta 8.00 20.00
103 James Simmons 2.00 5.00
104 Jarrod Parker 10.00 25.00
105 Jason Dominguez 2.00 5.00
106 Jason Heyward 60.00 120.00
107 Joe Savery 2.00 5.00
108 Jon Gilmore 2.00 5.00
109 Jordan Walden 3.00 8.00
110 Josh Smoker 3.00 8.00
111 Josh Vitters 6.00 15.00
112 Julio Borbon 2.50 6.00
113 Justin Jackson 2.00 5.00
114 Kellen Kulbacki 2.50 6.00
115 Kevin Ahrens 2.00 5.00
116 Kyle Lotzkar 2.00 5.00
117 Madison Bumgarner 15.00 40.00
118 Matt Dominguez 8.00 20.00
119 Matt LaPorta 10.00 25.00
120 Matt Wieters 6.00 15.00
121 Michael Burgess 8.00 20.00
122 Michael Main 2.50 6.00
123 Mike Moustakas 8.00 20.00
124 Nathan Vineyard 2.50 6.00
125 Neil Ramirez 2.00 5.00
126 Nick Hagadone 3.00 8.00
127 Pete Kozma 2.00 5.00
128 Phillippe Aumont 6.00 15.00
129 Preston Mattingly 5.00 12.00
131 Ross Detwiler 3.00 8.00
132 Tim Alderson 3.00 8.00
133 Todd Frazier 2.50 6.00
134 Wes Roemer 2.00 5.00
135 Ben Revere 3.00 8.00
141 Austin Jackson 12.50 30.00
142 Beau Mills 5.00 12.00

2007 Donruss Elite Extra Edition College Ties
STATED PRINT RUN 1500 SER.#'d SETS
*GOLD: .6X TO 1.5X BASIC
GOLD PRINT RUN 500 SER.#'d SETS
*RED: 1X TO 2.5X BASIC
RED PRINT RUN 100 SER.#'d SETS
OVERALL INSERT ODDS 1:4
1 D.Moskos/D.Kopp .75 2.00
2 N.Schmidt/J.Todd .75 2.00
3 J.Arencibia/J.Borbon .75 2.00
4 D.Price/C.Weathers 1.50 4.00
5 T.Green/M.LaPorta 1.25 3.00
6 J.Finch/A.Beard 1.50 4.00
7 J.Boeheim/D.Nichols .75 2.00
8 D.Payne/M.Wieters 1.50 4.00
9 D.Barney/M.Canham .75 2.00
10 L.Hochevar/J.Adkins .75 2.00
11 D.Cook/C.Luebke .75 2.00
12 D.Strawberry/B.Cecil .75 2.00

2007 Donruss Elite Extra Edition College Ties Autographs
OVERALL AUTO/MEM ODDS 1:5
PRINT RUNS B/WN 50-100 COPIES PER
EXCHANGE DEADLINE 07/01/2009
1 D.Moskos/D.Kopp 6.00 15.00
2 N.Schmidt/J.Todd 6.00 15.00
3 J.Arencibia/J.Borbon 10.00 25.00
4 D.Price/C.Weathers 8.00 20.00
5 T.Green/M.LaPorta 10.00 25.00
6 J.Finch/A.Beard 60.00 120.00
7 J.Boeheim/D.Nichols EXCH 6.00 15.00
8 D.Payne/M.Wieters 60.00 120.00
9 D.Barney/M.Canham EXCH 6.00 15.00
10 L.Hochevar/J.Adkins 6.00 15.00
11 D.Cook/C.Luebke 10.00 25.00
12 D.Strawberry/B.Cecil EXCH 6.00 15.00

2007 Donruss Elite Extra Edition College Ties Jerseys
OVERALL AUTO/MEM ODDS 1:5
PRINT RUNS B/WN 50-500 COPIES PER
1 D.Moskos/D.Kopp/75 4.00 10.00
6 J.Finch/A.Beard/50 6.00 15.00
9 D.Barney/M.Canham/500 3.00 8.00

2007 Donruss Elite Extra Edition College Ties Jerseys Prime
OVERALL AU/MEM ODDS 1:5
PRINT RUNS B/WN 5-50 COPIES PER
NO PRICING ON QTY 25 OR LESS
1 Daniel Moskos/David Kopp/5
6 Jennie Finch/Amanda Beard/25
9 Darwin Barney/Mitch Canham/50 4.00 10.00

2007 Donruss Elite Extra Edition Collegiate Patches
OVERALL AUTO/MEM ODDS 1:5
PRINT RUNS B/WN 25-250 COPIES PER
NO PRICING ON QTY 25 OR LESS
10 Jennie Finch/249 12.50 30.00
19 Josh Donaldson/250 20.00 50.00
25 Drew Stubbs/250 6.00 15.00
26 Andrew Brackman/250 6.00 15.00
27 Casey Weathers/250 10.00 25.00
28 Daniel Moskos/250 6.00 15.00
29 David Price/250 6.00 15.00
30 Greg Reynolds/250 6.00 15.00
31 J. P. Arencibia/249 6.00 15.00
32 Jeff Samardzija/150 12.50 30.00
33 Julio Borbon/250 6.00 15.00
34 Luke Hochevar/100 12.50 30.00
35 Matt LaPorta/250 6.00 15.00
36 Matt Mangini/250 6.00 15.00
37 Matt Wieters/250 12.50 30.00
38 Max Scherzer/182 30.00 80.00
39 Mitch Canham/250 6.00 15.00
40 Nick Schmidt/250 6.00 15.00
41 James Adkins/250 6.00 15.00
42 Tony Thomas/250 8.00 20.00
45 Tommy Hunter/250 8.00 20.00
52 Cale Iorg/250 6.00 15.00
54 Nick Hagadone/250 6.00 15.00
55 Trystan Magnuson/248 6.00 15.00
64 Matt Spencer/249 6.00 15.00
65 Corey Brown/250 EXCH 6.00 15.00
67 Connie Mack III/100 6.00 15.00

2007 Donruss Elite Extra Edition School Colors
OVERALL INSERT ODDS 1:4
STATED PRINT RUN 1500 SER.#'d SETS
1 David Price 2.00 5.00
2 Daniel Moskos .75 2.00
3 Greg Reynolds .75 2.00
4 Matt LaPorta 1.25 3.00
5 Matt Wieters 3.00 8.00
6 Luke Hochevar .75 2.00
7 Max Scherzer 2.00 5.00
26 Nick Schmidt .75 2.00
29 Beau Mills .75 2.00
30 James Simmons .75 2.00
31 Joe Savery .75 2.00
32 Ross Detwiler .75 2.00
33 J. P. Arencibia .75 2.00
34 Drew Stubbs .75 2.00

2007 Donruss Elite Extra Edition School Colors Autographs
OVERALL AUTO/MEM ODDS 1:5
PRINT RUNS B/WN 10-50 COPIES PER
NO PRICING ON QTY 25 OR LESS
EXCHANGE DEADLINE 07/01/2009
1 David Price/50 40.00 100.00
2 Daniel Moskos/50 6.00 15.00
3 Greg Reynolds/50 6.00 15.00
4 Matt LaPorta/50 6.00 15.00
5 Matt Wieters/50 12.50 30.00
6 Luke Hochevar/50 10.00 25.00
7 Max Scherzer/50 60.00 150.00
26 Nick Schmidt/50 6.00 15.00
29 Beau Mills/50 10.00 25.00
30 James Simmons/50 EXCH 6.00 15.00
31 Joe Savery/50 6.00 15.00
32 Ross Detwiler/50 10.00 25.00
33 J. P. Arencibia/50 30.00 60.00
34 Drew Stubbs/50 10.00 25.00
35 Josh Vitters/50 12.50 30.00

2007 Donruss Elite Extra Edition Throwback Threads
OVERALL AUTO/MEM ODDS 1:5
PRINT RUNS B/WN 44-500 COPIES PER
3 Drew Stubbs/500 3.00 8.00
4 Drew Cumberland/500 3.00 8.00
6 Mat Latos/500 6.00 15.00
7 Brett Cecil /500 3.00 8.00
9 Brett Anderson/500 3.00 8.00
10 Casey Weathers/75 4.00 10.00
11 Daniel Moskos/500 3.00 8.00
12 Darwin Barney/500 6.00 15.00
13 Kellen Kulbacki/500 3.00 8.00
14 Matt Dominguez/500 3.00 8.00
15 Matt Mangini/500 3.00 8.00
16 Mitch Canham/500 3.00 8.00
18 Will Middlebrooks/500 3.00 8.00
23 Nick Schmidt/500 3.00 8.00
24 Zack Cozart/500 3.00 8.00

2007 Donruss Elite Extra Edition Throwback Threads Prime
*PRIME: .75X TO 2X BASIC
OVERALL AUTO/MEM ODDS 1:5
PRINT RUNS B/WN 3-50 COPIES PER
NO PRICING ON QTY 25 OR LESS
10 Casey Weathers/3

2007 Donruss Elite Extra Edition Throwback Threads Autographs
OVERALL AUTO/MEM ODDS 1:5
PRINT RUNS B/WN 50-100 COPIES PER
EXCHANGE DEADLINE 07/01/2009
3 Drew Stubbs/100 8.00 20.00
4 Drew Cumberland/100 6.00 15.00
6 Mat Latos/100 20.00 50.00
9 Brett Anderson/100 6.00 15.00
10 Casey Weathers/100 10.00 25.00
11 Daniel Moskos/100 6.00 15.00
12 Josh Vitters/100 10.00 25.00
13 Kellen Kulbacki/100 6.00 15.00
14 Matt Dominguez/100 6.00 15.00
15 Matt Mangini/100 10.00 25.00
16 Mitch Canham/100 6.00 15.00
18 Will Middlebrooks/100 6.00 15.00
23 Nick Schmidt/100 6.00 15.00
24 Zack Cozart/100 6.00 15.00

2008 Donruss Elite Extra Edition

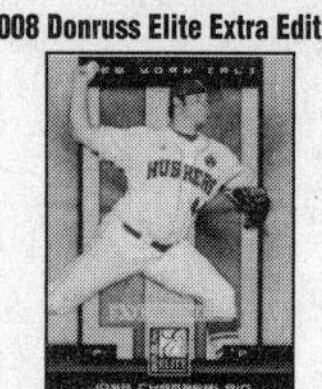

COMP.SET w/o AU's (100) 10.00 25.00
COMMON CARD (1-100) .20 .50
COMMON AU (101-200) 3.00 8.00
RANDOM INSERTS IN PACKS
PRINT RUNS B/WN 99-1495
EXCH DEADLINE 5/26/2010
1 Aaron Cunningham .20 .50
2 Aaron Pribanic .20 .50
3 Aaron Shafer .20 .50
4 Adam Mills .20 .50
5 Adam Moore .20 .50
6 Beamer Weems .20 .50
7 Beau Mills .20 .50
8 Blake Tekotte .30 .75
9 Bobby Lanigan .20 .50
10 Brad Hand .30 .75
11 Brandon Crawford .50 1.25
12 Brandon Waring .30 .75
13 Brent Morel .30 .75
14 Brett Jacobson .20 .50
15 Caleb Gindl .20 .50
16 Carlos Peguero .30 .75
17 Charlie Blackmon 1.50 4.00
18 Charlie Furbush .20 .50
19 Chris Davis .40 1.00
20 Chris Valaika .20 .50
21 Clark Murphy .30 .75
22 Clayton Cook .30 .75
23 Cody Adams .30 .75
24 Cody Satterwhite .30 .75
25 Cole St. Clair .20 .50
26 Corey Young .20 .50
27 Curtis Petersen .20 .50
28 Danny Rams .30 .75
29 Dennis Raben .30 .75
30 Derek Norris .30 .75
31 Tyson Brummett .20 .50
32 Dusty Coleman .20 .50
33 Edgar Olmos .20 .50
34 Engel Beltre .60 1.50
35 Eric Beaulac .20 .50
36 Geison Aguasviva .20 .50
37 Gerardo Parra .20 .50
38 Graham Hicks .30 .75
39 Greg Halman .30 .75
40 Hector Gomez .50 1.25
41 J.D. Alfaro .20 .50
42 Jack Egbert .30 .75
43 James Darnell .30 .75
44 Jay Austin .20 .50
45 Jeremy Beckham .30 .75
46 Jeremy Farrell .20 .50
47 Jeremy Hamilton .20 .50
48 Jericho Jones .20 .50
49 Jesse Darcy .20 .50
50 Jeudy Valdez .30 .75
51 Jharmidy De Jesus .20 .50
52 Joba Chamberlain .20 .50
53 Johnny Giavotella .60 1.50
54 Jon Mark Owings .30 .75
55 Jordan Meaker .30 .75
56 Jose Duran .30 .75
57 Josh Harrison .30 .75
58 Josh Lindblom .30 .75
59 Josh Reddick .60 1.50
60 Juan Carlos Sulbaran .20 .50
61 Justin Bristow .20 .50
62 Kenny Gilbert .20 .50
63 Kirk Nieuwenhuis .20 .50
64 Kyle Hudson .20 .50
65 Kyle Russell .20 .50
66 Kyle Weiland .50 1.25
67 L. J. Hoes .20 .50
68 Mark Cohoon .30 .75
69 Mark Sobolewski .50 1.25
70 Mat Gamel .50 1.25
71 Matt Harrison .30 .75
72 Max Ramirez .20 .50
73 Tony Delmonico .30 .75
74 Mike Stanton 2.50 6.00
75 Mitch Abeita .20 .50
76 Neftali Feliz .60 1.50
77 Neftali Soto .30 .75
78 Niko Vasquez .50 1.25
79 Omar Aguilar .30 .75
80 Petey Paramore .30 .75
81 Ray Kruml .20 .50
82 Rolando Gomez .30 .75
83 Ryan Chaffee .30 .75
84 Ryan Pressly .30 .75
85 Sam Freeman .50 1.25
86 Sawyer Carroll .30 .75
87 Scott Green .20 .50
88 Sean Ratliff .20 .50
89 Shane Peterson .30 .75
90 T.J. Steele .30 .75
91 Tim Federowicz .30 .75
92 Tyler Chatwood .30 .75
93 Tyler Cline .20 .50
94 Tyler Ladendorf .30 .75
95 Tyler Yockey .20 .50
96 Wilmer Flores .75 2.00
97 Wilson Ramos .60 1.50
98 Zach McAllister .30 .75
99 Zachary Stewart .20 .50
100 Zeke Spruill .50 1.25
101 Adrian Nieto AU/521 4.00 10.00
102 Alan Horne AU/349 6.00 15.00
103 Andrew Cashner AU/685 6.00 15.00
104 Anthony Hewitt AU/920 6.00 15.00
105 Brad Holt AU/432 5.00 12.00
106 Bryan Petersen AU/319 3.00 8.00
107 Bryan Price AU/572 4.00 10.00
108 Bud Norris AU/1095 3.00 8.00
109 Carlos Gutierrez AU/202 5.00 12.00
110 Chase D'Arnaud AU/1218 4.00 10.00
111 Chris Johnson AU/99 15.00 40.00
112 Christian Friedrich AU/402 8.00 20.00
113 Christian Marrero AU/662 4.00 10.00
114 Clayton Conner AU/819 3.00 8.00
115 Cole Rohrbough AU/719 4.00 10.00
116 Collin DeLome AU/819 3.00 8.00
117 Daniel Cortes AU/680 3.00 8.00
118 Daniel Schlereth AU/570 3.00 8.00
119 Denny Almonte AU/821 3.00 8.00
120 Allan Dykstra AU/1069 4.00 10.00
121 Dominic Brown AU/996 10.00 25.00
122 Evan Fredrickson AU/922 3.00 8.00
123 Gordon Beckham AU/710 5.00 12.00
124 Greg Veloz AU/819 3.00 8.00
125 Ike Davis AU/995 6.00 15.00
126 Isaac Galloway AU/1099 3.00 8.00
127 Jacob Jefferies AU/819 3.00 8.00
128 Michael Kohn AU/199 3.00 8.00
129 Jared Goedert AU/819 3.00 8.00
130 Jason Knapp AU/999 4.00 10.00
131 Jhoulys Chacin AU/821 4.00 10.00
132 Jordy Mercer AU/483 3.00 8.00
133 Jorge Bucardo AU/819 4.00 10.00
134 Jose Ceda AU/1470 3.00 8.00
135 Jose Martinez AU/868 3.00 8.00
136 Josh Roenicke AU/829 3.00 8.00
137 Juan Francisco AU/1495 5.00 12.00
138 Justin Parker AU/719 3.00 8.00
139 Kyle Ginley AU/819 3.00 8.00
140 Lance Lynn AU/570 3.00 8.00
141 Logan Forsythe AU/162 8.00 20.00
142 Logan Morrison AU/360 4.00 10.00
143 Logan Schafer AU/793 3.00 8.00
144 Lorenzo Cain AU/817 10.00 25.00
145 Lucas Duda AU/124 8.00 20.00
146 Matt Mitchell AU/719 3.00 8.00
147 Danny Espinosa AU/443 6.00 15.00
148 Michael Taylor AU/720 6.00 15.00
149 Michel Inoa AU/1199 6.00 15.00
150 Mike Montgomery AU/922 6.00 15.00
151 Cord Phelps AU/693 5.00 12.00
152 Pablo Sandoval AU/819 4.00 10.00
153 Quincy Latimore AU/819 3.00 8.00
154 R. J. Seidel AU/819 3.00 8.00
155 Rayner Contreras AU/1349 3.00 8.00
156 Rick Porcello AU/1299 4.00 10.00
157 Robert Hernandez AU/859 3.00 8.00
158 Ryan Kalish AU/1129 5.00 12.00
159 Ryan Perry AU/745 4.00 10.00
160 Shelby Ford AU/819 3.00 8.00
161 Shooter Hunt AU/397 8.00 20.00
162 Tyler Kolodny AU/819 4.00 10.00
163 Tyler Sample AU/619 4.00 10.00
164 Tyson Ross AU/999 3.00 8.00
166 Waldis Joaquin AU/819 3.00 8.00
167 Wellington Castillo AU/1319 3.00 8.00
168 Wilin Rosario AU/1099 6.00 15.00
169 Xavier Avery AU/199 10.00 25.00
170 Zach Collier AU/217 10.00 25.00
171 Zach Putnam AU/444 3.00 8.00
172 Anthony Gose AU/519 6.00 15.00
173 Roger Kieschnick AU/569 8.00 20.00
174 Andrew Liebel AU/219 5.00 12.00
175 Tim Murphy AU/244 4.00 10.00
176 Vance Worley AU/219 6.00 15.00
177 Buster Posey AU/934 25.00 60.00
178 Kenn Kasparek AU/694 3.00 8.00
179 J.P. Ramirez AU/719 5.00 12.00
180 Evan Bigley AU/819 3.00 8.00
181 Trey Haley AU/719 3.00 8.00
182 Robbie Grossman AU/719 3.00 8.00
183 Jordan Danks AU/254 12.50 30.00
184 Brett Hunter AU/269 4.00 10.00
185 Rafael Rodriguez AU/999 5.00 12.00
186 Yeicok Calderon AU/819 6.00 15.00
187 Gustavo Pierre AU/719 4.00 10.00
188 Will Smith AU/719 3.00 8.00
189 Daniel Thomas AU/719 3.00 8.00
190 Carson Blair AU/719 3.00 8.00
191 Chris Hicks AU/719 4.00 10.00
192 Rashun Dixon AU/199 5.00 12.00
193 Marcus Lemon AU/199 5.00 12.00
194 Kyle Nicholson AU/719 6.00 15.00
195 Mike Cisco AU/719 3.00 8.00
196 Jarek Cunningham AU/719 3.00 8.00
197 Cat Osterman AU/719 4.00 10.00
198 Derrick Rose AU/99 15.00 40.00
199 Michael Beasley AU/99 4.00 10.00
200 O.J. Mayo AU/99 4.00 10.00

2008 Donruss Elite Extra Edition Aspirations

*ASP 1-100: 2.5X TO 6X BASIC
RANDOM INSERTS IN PACKS
STATED PRINT RUN 150 SER.#'d SETS
101 Adrian Nieto 1.25 3.00
102 Alan Horne 1.25 3.00
103 Andrew Cashner 3.00 8.00
104 Anthony Hewitt 1.25 3.00
105 Brad Holt 1.25 3.00
106 Bryan Petersen 1.25 3.00
107 Bryan Price 1.25 3.00
108 Bud Norris 1.25 3.00
109 Carlos Gutierrez 3.00 8.00
110 Chase D'Arnaud 1.25 3.00
111 Chris Johnson 2.00 5.00
112 Christian Friedrich 3.00 8.00
113 Christian Marrero 2.00 5.00
114 Clayton Conner 1.25 3.00
115 Cole Rohrbough 1.25 3.00
116 Collin DeLome 2.00 5.00
117 Daniel Cortes 3.00 8.00
118 Daniel Schlereth 1.25 3.00
119 Denny Almonte 2.00 5.00
120 Allan Dykstra 1.25 3.00
121 Dominic Brown 5.00 12.00
122 Evan Fredrickson 1.25 3.00
123 Gordon Beckham 3.00 8.00
124 Greg Veloz 1.25 3.00
125 Ike Davis 2.50 6.00
126 Isaac Galloway 2.00 5.00
127 Jacob Jefferies 1.25 3.00
128 Michael Kohn 1.25 3.00
129 Jared Goedert 1.25 3.00
130 Jason Knapp 1.25 3.00
131 Jhoulys Chacin 6.00 15.00
132 Jordy Mercer 1.25 3.00
133 Jorge Bucardo 1.25 3.00
134 Jose Ceda 1.25 3.00
135 Jose Martinez 1.25 3.00
136 Josh Roenicke 1.25 3.00
137 Juan Francisco 6.00 15.00
138 Justin Parker 1.25 3.00
139 Kyle Ginley 1.25 3.00
140 Lance Lynn 3.00 8.00
141 Logan Forsythe 1.25 3.00
142 Logan Morrison 5.00 12.00
143 Logan Schafer 1.25 3.00
144 Lorenzo Cain 5.00 12.00
145 Lucas Duda 4.00 10.00
146 Matt Mitchell 1.25 3.00
147 Danny Espinosa 2.00 5.00
148 Michael Taylor 3.00 8.00
149 Michel Inoa 3.00 8.00
150 Mike Montgomery 2.00 5.00
151 Cord Phelps 1.25 3.00
152 Pablo Sandoval 5.00 12.00
153 Quincy Latimore 1.25 3.00
154 R. J. Seidel 1.25 3.00
155 Rayner Contreras 1.25 3.00
156 Rick Porcello 3.00 8.00
157 Robert Hernandez 1.25 3.00
158 Ryan Kalish 3.00 8.00
159 Ryan Perry 2.00 5.00
160 Shelby Ford 2.00 5.00
161 Shooter Hunt 1.25 3.00
162 Tyler Kolodny 3.00 8.00
163 Tyler Sample 1.25 3.00
164 Tyson Ross 2.00 5.00
166 Waldis Joaquin 1.25 3.00
167 Wellington Castillo 1.25 3.00
168 Wilin Rosario 2.00 5.00
169 Xavier Avery 3.00 8.00
170 Zach Collier 2.00 5.00
171 Zach Putnam 1.25 3.00
172 Anthony Gose 2.00 5.00
173 Roger Kieschnick 2.00 5.00
174 Andrew Liebel 1.25 3.00
175 Tim Murphy 1.25 3.00
176 Vance Worley 6.00 15.00
177 Buster Posey 4.00 10.00
178 Kenn Kasparek 3.00 8.00
179 J.P. Ramirez 1.25 3.00
180 Evan Bigley 1.25 3.00
181 Trey Haley 1.25 3.00
182 Robbie Grossman 2.00 5.00
183 Jordan Danks 3.00 8.00
184 Brett Hunter 1.25 3.00
185 Rafael Rodriguez 1.25 3.00
186 Yeicok Calderon 1.25 3.00
187 Gustavo Pierre 1.25 3.00
188 Will Smith
189 Daniel Thomas 1.25 3.00
190 Carson Blair 1.25 3.00
191 Chris Hicks 1.25 3.00
192 Rashun Dixon 1.25 3.00
193 Marcus Lemon 1.25 3.00
194 Kyle Nicholson 1.25 3.00
195 Mike Cisco 1.25 3.00
196 Jarek Cunningham 1.25 3.00
197 Cat Osterman 6.00 15.00
198 Derrick Rose 6.00 15.00
199 Michael Beasley 1.25 3.00
200 O.J. Mayo 3.00 8.00

2008 Donruss Elite Extra Edition Status

*STATUS 1-100: 4X TO 10X BASIC
*STATUS 101-200: .6X TO 1.5X ASP
RANDOM INSERTS IN PACKS
STATED PRINT RUN 50 SER.#'d SETS
101 Adrian Nieto 2.00 5.00
102 Alan Horne 2.00 5.00
103 Andrew Cashner 5.00 12.00
104 Anthony Hewitt 2.00 5.00
105 Brad Holt 2.00 5.00
106 Bryan Petersen 2.00 5.00
107 Bryan Price 2.00 5.00
108 Bud Norris 2.00 5.00
109 Carlos Gutierrez 5.00 12.00
110 Chase D'Arnaud 2.00 5.00
111 Chris Johnson 3.00 8.00
112 Christian Friedrich 5.00 12.00
113 Christian Marrero 3.00 8.00
114 Clayton Conner 2.00 5.00
115 Cole Rohrbough 2.00 5.00
116 Collin DeLome 3.00 8.00
117 Daniel Cortes 5.00 12.00
118 Daniel Schlereth 2.00 5.00
119 Denny Almonte 3.00 8.00
120 Allan Dykstra 2.00 5.00
121 Dominic Brown 8.00 20.00
122 Evan Fredrickson 2.00 5.00
123 Gordon Beckham 5.00 12.00
124 Greg Veloz 2.00 5.00
125 Ike Davis 4.00 10.00
126 Isaac Galloway 3.00 8.00
127 Jacob Jefferies 2.00 5.00
128 Michael Kohn 2.00 5.00
129 Jared Goedert 2.00 5.00
130 Jason Knapp 2.00 5.00
131 Jhoulys Chacin 10.00 25.00
132 Jordy Mercer 2.00 5.00
133 Jorge Bucardo 2.00 5.00
134 Jose Ceda 2.00 5.00
135 Jose Martinez 2.00 5.00
136 Josh Roenicke 2.00 5.00
137 Juan Francisco 4.00 10.00
138 Justin Parker 2.00 5.00
139 Kyle Ginley 2.00 5.00
140 Lance Lynn 5.00 12.00
141 Logan Forsythe 2.00 5.00
142 Logan Morrison 8.00 20.00
143 Logan Schafer 2.00 5.00
144 Lorenzo Cain 8.00 20.00
145 Lucas Duda 6.00 15.00
146 Matt Mitchell 2.00 5.00
147 Danny Espinosa 3.00 8.00
148 Michael Taylor 5.00 12.00
149 Michel Inoa 5.00 12.00
150 Mike Montgomery 3.00 8.00
151 Cord Phelps 2.00 5.00
152 Pablo Sandoval 8.00 20.00
153 Quincy Latimore 2.00 5.00
154 R. J. Seidel 2.00 5.00
155 Rayner Contreras 2.00 5.00
156 Rick Porcello 5.00 12.00
157 Robert Hernandez 2.00 5.00
158 Ryan Kalish 5.00 12.00
159 Ryan Perry 3.00 8.00
160 Shelby Ford 3.00 8.00
161 Shooter Hunt 2.00 5.00
162 Tyler Kolodny 5.00 12.00
163 Tyler Sample 2.00 5.00
164 Tyson Ross 3.00 8.00
166 Waldis Joaquin 2.00 5.00
167 Wellington Castillo 2.00 5.00
168 Wilin Rosario 3.00 8.00
169 Xavier Avery 5.00 12.00
170 Zach Collier 3.00 8.00
171 Zach Putnam 2.00 5.00
172 Anthony Gose 3.00 8.00
173 Roger Kieschnick 3.00 8.00
174 Andrew Liebel 2.00 5.00
175 Tim Murphy 2.00 5.00
176 Vance Worley 10.00 25.00
177 Buster Posey 25.00 60.00
178 Kenn Kasparek 5.00 12.00
179 J.P. Ramirez 2.00 5.00
180 Evan Bigley 2.00 5.00
181 Trey Haley 2.00 5.00
182 Robbie Grossman 3.00 8.00
183 Jordan Danks 5.00 12.00
184 Brett Hunter 2.00 5.00
185 Rafael Rodriguez 2.00 5.00
186 Yeicok Calderon 2.00 5.00
187 Gustavo Pierre 2.00 5.00
188 Will Smith
189 Daniel Thomas 2.00 5.00
190 Carson Blair 2.00 5.00
191 Chris Hicks 2.00 5.00
192 Rashun Dixon 2.00 5.00
193 Marcus Lemon 2.00 5.00
194 Kyle Nicholson 2.00 5.00
195 Mike Cisco 2.00 5.00
196 Jarek Cunningham 2.00 5.00
197 Cat Osterman 8.00 20.00
198 Derrick Rose 8.00 20.00
199 Michael Beasley 1.50 4.00
200 O.J. Mayo 6.00 15.00

2008 Donruss Elite Extra Edition Signature Aspirations

OVERALL AUTO/MEM ODDS 1:5
PRINT RUN B/WN 5-100 COPIES PER
NO PRICING ON QTY 25 OR LESS
EXCH DEADLINE 5/26/2010
1 Aaron Cunningham/50 6.00 15.00
2 Aaron Pribanic/100 5.00 12.00
3 Aaron Shafer/100 4.00 10.00
4 Adam Mills/100 4.00 10.00
5 Adam Moore/100 8.00 20.00
6 Beamer Weems/100 4.00 10.00
7 Beau Mills/50 6.00 15.00
9 Bobby Lanigan/100 4.00 10.00
10 Brad Hand/50 20.00 50.00
11 Brandon Crawford/50 15.00 40.00
12 Brandon Waring/100 5.00 12.00
13 Brent Morel/100 6.00 15.00
14 Brett Jacobson/100 5.00 12.00
15 Caleb Gindl/100 8.00 20.00
16 Carlos Peguero/100 12.50 30.00
17 Charlie Blackmon/50 20.00 50.00
18 Charlie Furbush/100 5.00 12.00
19 Chris Davis/100 20.00 50.00
20 Chris Valaika/100 4.00 10.00
21 Clark Murphy/50 4.00 10.00
22 Clayton Cook/100 4.00 10.00
23 Cody Adams/50 4.00 10.00
24 Cody Satterwhite/50 10.00 25.00
25 Cole St. Clair/100 5.00 12.00
26 Corey Young/100 4.00 10.00
27 Curtis Petersen/100 4.00 10.00
28 Danny Rams/100 5.00 12.00
29 Dennis Raben/50 8.00 20.00
30 Derek Norris/50 15.00 40.00
31 Tyson Brummett/100 4.00 10.00
32 Dusty Coleman/50 5.00 12.00
33 Edgar Olmos/100 4.00 10.00
35 Eric Beaulac/100 4.00 10.00
36 Geison Aguasviva/100 4.00 10.00
37 Gerardo Parra/100 6.00 15.00
38 Graham Hicks/100 4.00 10.00
39 Greg Halman/100 12.00 30.00
40 Hector Gomez/100 5.00 12.00
41 J.D. Alfaro/100 4.00 10.00
42 Jack Egbert/100 4.00 10.00
43 James Darnell/50 6.00 15.00
44 Jay Austin/50 5.00 12.00
45 Jeremy Beckham/100 EXCH 6.00 15.00
46 Jeremy Farrell/100 4.00 10.00
47 Jeremy Hamilton/100 4.00 10.00
48 Jericho Jones/100 8.00 20.00
49 Jesse Darcy/100 5.00 12.00
50 Jeudy Valdez/100 4.00 10.00
51 Jharmidy De Jesus/50 12.50 30.00
53 Johnny Giavotella/100 10.00 25.00
54 Jon Mark Owings/100 5.00 12.00
55 Jordan Meaker/100 4.00 10.00
56 Jose Duran/100 12.50 30.00
57 Josh Harrison/100 8.00 20.00
58 Josh Lindblom/50 4.00 10.00
59 Josh Reddick/100 6.00 15.00
60 Juan Carlos Sulbaran/100 5.00 12.00
61 Justin Bristow/100 4.00 10.00
62 Kenny Gilbert/100 4.00 10.00
63 Kirk Nieuwenhuis/100 5.00 12.00
64 Kyle Hudson/50 5.00 12.00
65 Kyle Russell/50 5.00 12.00
66 Kyle Weiland/50 5.00 12.00
67 L. J. Hoes/50 5.00 12.00
68 Mark Cohoon/100 5.00 12.00
69 Mark Sobolewski/100 15.00 40.00
70 Mat Gamel/50 12.50 30.00
71 Matt Harrison/100 10.00 25.00
72 Max Ramirez/100 8.00 20.00
73 Tony Delmonico/50 6.00 15.00
75 Mitch Abeita/100 4.00 10.00
76 Neftali-Feliz/50 20.00 50.00
77 Neftali Soto/50 10.00 25.00
78 Niko Vasquez/50 6.00 15.00
79 Omar Aguilar/100 4.00 10.00
80 Petey Paramore/100 4.00 10.00
81 Ray Kruml/100 5.00 12.00
82 Rolando Gomez/50 4.00 10.00
83 Ryan Chaffee/100 5.00 12.00
84 Ryan Pressly/100 4.00 10.00
85 Sam Freeman/100 8.00 20.00
86 Sawyer Carroll/100 4.00 10.00
87 Scott Green/100 6.00 15.00
88 Sean Ratliff/100 8.00 20.00
89 Shane Peterson/50 8.00 20.00
90 T.J. Steele/50 8.00 20.00
91 Tim Federowicz/100 6.00 15.00
92 Tyler Chatwood/50 4.00 10.00
93 Tyler Cline/100 4.00 10.00
94 Tyler Ladendorf/50 5.00 12.00
95 Tyler Yockey/100 6.00 15.00
96 Wilmer Flores/50 12.00 30.00
97 Wilson Ramos/100 12.50 30.00
98 Zach McAllister/100 6.00 15.00
99 Zachary Stewart/100 4.00 10.00
100 Zeke Spruill/50 EXCH 12.50 30.00
102 Alan Horne/100 10.00 25.00
106 Bryan Petersen/50 4.00 10.00
108 Bud Norris/50 4.00 10.00
113 Christian Marrero/50 5.00 12.00
114 Clayton Conner/50 4.00 10.00
116 Collin DeLome/50 5.00 12.00
119 Denny Almonte/50 4.00 10.00
121 Dominic Brown/50 75.00 150.00
124 Greg Veloz/50 4.00 10.00
127 Jacob Jefferies/50 4.00 10.00
129 Jared Goedert/50 4.00 10.00
130 Jason Knapp/50 15.00 40.00
131 Jhoulys Chacin/50 10.00 25.00
132 Jordy Mercer/75 4.00 10.00
133 Jorge Bucardo/50 5.00 12.00
134 Jose Ceda/100 5.00 12.00
135 Jose Martinez/75 4.00 10.00
136 Josh Roenicke/50 4.00 10.00
137 Juan Francisco/100 EXCH 10.00 25.00
139 Kyle Ginley/50 4.00 10.00
143 Logan Schafer/50 8.00 20.00
144 Lorenzo Cain/50 20.00 50.00
148 Michael Taylor/50 5.00 12.00
152 Pablo Sandoval/50 50.00 120.00
153 Quincy Latimore/50 4.00 10.00
154 R. J. Seidel/50 4.00 10.00
155 Rayner Contreras/100 4.00 10.00
157 Robert Hernandez/50 4.00 10.00
158 Ryan Kalish/50 20.00 50.00
160 Shelby Ford/50 4.00 10.00
162 Tyler Kolodny/50 10.00 25.00
166 Waldis Joaquin/50 4.00 10.00
167 Wellington Castillo/50 4.00 10.00
173 Roger Kieschnick/50 5.00 12.00
180 Evan Bigley/50 6.00 15.00
186 Yeicok Calderon/50 12.50 30.00
200 O.J. Mayo/25 6.00 15.00

2008 Donruss Elite Extra Edition Signature Status

OVERALL AUTO/MEM ODDS 1:5
PRINT RUN B/WN 5-50 COPIES PER
NO PRICING ON QTY 25 OR LESS
EXCH DEADLINE 5/26/2010
2 Aaron Pribanic/50 6.00 15.00
3 Aaron Shafer/50 4.00 10.00
4 Adam Mills/50 4.00 10.00
5 Adam Moore/50 8.00 20.00
6 Beamer Weems/50 4.00 10.00
9 Bobby Lanigan/50 4.00 10.00
12 Brandon Waring/50 5.00 12.00
13 Brent Morel/50 8.00 20.00
14 Brett Jacobson/50 5.00 12.00
15 Caleb Gindl/50 8.00 20.00
16 Carlos Peguero/50 12.50 30.00
18 Charlie Furbush/50 5.00 12.00
19 Chris Davis/50 25.00 60.00
20 Chris Valaika/50 4.00 10.00
22 Clayton Cook/50 4.00 10.00
25 Cole St. Clair/50 5.00 12.00
26 Corey Young/50 4.00 10.00
27 Curtis Petersen/50 4.00 10.00
28 Danny Rams/50 5.00 12.00
31 Tyson Brummett/50 5.00 12.00
33 Edgar Olmos/50 4.00 10.00
35 Eric Beaulac/50 4.00 10.00
36 Geison Aguasviva/50 4.00 10.00
37 Gerardo Parra/50 5.00 12.00
38 Graham Hicks/50 4.00 10.00
39 Greg Halman/50 15.00 40.00
40 Hector Gomez/50 5.00 12.00
41 J.D. Alfaro/50 4.00 10.00
42 Jack Egbert/50 4.00 10.00
45 Jeremy Beckham/50 EXCH 6.00 15.00
46 Jeremy Farrell/50 4.00 10.00
47 Jeremy Hamilton/50 4.00 10.00
48 Jericho Jones/50 8.00 20.00
49 Jesse Darcy/50 5.00 12.00
50 Jeudy Valdez/50 4.00 10.00
53 Johnny Giavotella/50 12.50 30.00
54 Jon Mark Owings/50 5.00 12.00
55 Jordan Meaker/50 4.00 10.00
56 Jose Duran/50 12.50 30.00
57 Josh Harrison/50 10.00 25.00
59 Josh Reddick/50 20.00 50.00
60 Juan Carlos Sulbaran/50 5.00 12.00
61 Justin Bristow/50 4.00 10.00
62 Kenny Gilbert/50 4.00 10.00
63 Kirk Nieuwenhuis/50 12.50 30.00
68 Mark Cohoon/50 5.00 12.00
69 Mark Sobolewski/50 15.00 40.00
71 Matt Harrison/50 12.50 30.00
72 Max Ramirez/50 8.00 20.00
75 Mitch Abeita/50 4.00 10.00
79 Omar Aguilar/50 4.00 10.00
80 Petey Paramore/50 4.00 10.00
81 Ray Kruml/50 5.00 12.00
83 Ryan Chaffee/50 5.00 12.00
84 Ryan Pressly/50 4.00 10.00
85 Sam Freeman/50 5.00 12.00
86 Sawyer Carroll/50 4.00 10.00
87 Scott Green/50 6.00 15.00
88 Sean Ratliff/50 8.00 20.00
91 Tim Federowicz/50 6.00 15.00
93 Tyler Cline/50 4.00 10.00
95 Tyler Yockey/50 6.00 15.00
97 Wilson Ramos/50 15.00 40.00
98 Zach McAllister/50 6.00 15.00
99 Zachary Stewart/50 5.00 12.00
132 Jordy Mercer/40 5.00 12.00
134 Jose Ceda/50 5.00 12.00
135 Jose Martinez/50 4.00 10.00

2008 Donruss Elite Extra Edition Signature Turn of the Century

OVERALL AUTO/MEM ODDS 1:5
PRINT RUNS B/WN 8-999 COPIES PER
EXCH DEADLINE 5/26/2010
1 Aaron Cunningham/150 5.00 12.00
2 Aaron Pribanic/269 4.00 10.00
3 Aaron Shafer/117 4.00 10.00
4 Adam Mills/841 3.00 8.00
5 Adam Moore/844 4.00 10.00
6 Beamer Weems/844 3.00 8.00
7 Beau Mills/64 6.00 15.00
8 Blake Tekotte/194 4.00 10.00
9 Bobby Lanigan/594 3.00 8.00
10 Brad Hand/447 4.00 10.00
11 Brandon Crawford/718 6.00 15.00
12 Brandon Waring/369 4.00 10.00
13 Brent Morel/269 4.00 10.00
14 Brett Jacobson/488 4.00 10.00
15 Caleb Gindl/245 3.00 8.00
16 Carlos Peguero/344 4.00 10.00
17 Charlie Blackmon/122 25.00 60.00
18 Charlie Furbush/469 3.00 8.00
19 Chris Davis/399 10.00 25.00
20 Chris Valaika/309 3.00 8.00
21 Clark Murphy/644 3.00 8.00
22 Clayton Cook/844 3.00 8.00
23 Cody Adams/447 3.00 8.00
24 Cody Satterwhite/322 6.00 15.00
25 Cole St. Clair/342 4.00 10.00
26 Corey Young/594 3.00 8.00
27 Curtis Petersen/199 3.00 8.00
28 Danny Rams/594 3.00 8.00
29 Dennis Raben/172 6.00 15.00
30 Derek Norris/744 4.00 10.00
31 Tyson Brummett/919 3.00 8.00
32 Dusty Coleman/719 3.00 8.00
33 Edgar Olmos/594 3.00 8.00
35 Eric Beaulac/594 3.00 8.00
36 Geison Aguasviva/368 3.00 8.00
37 Gerardo Parra/421 5.00 12.00
38 Graham Hicks/594 3.00 8.00
39 Greg Halman/429 5.00 12.00
40 Hector Gomez/320 4.00 10.00
41 J.D. Alfaro/790 3.00 8.00
42 Jack Egbert/844 3.00 8.00
43 James Darnell/89 5.00 12.00
44 Jay Austin/207 4.00 10.00
45 Jeremy Beckham/199 5.00 12.00
46 Jeremy Farrell/844 3.00 8.00
47 Jeremy Hamilton/844 3.00 8.00
48 Jericho Jones/844 6.00 15.00
49 Jesse Darcy/594 3.00 8.00
50 Jeudy Valdez/374 3.00 8.00
51 Jharmidy De Jesus/269 10.00 25.00
52 Joba Chamberlain/39 10.00 25.00
53 Johnny Giavotella/844 6.00 15.00
54 Jon Mark Owings/844 4.00 10.00
55 Jordan Meaker/844 3.00 8.00
56 Jose Duran/262 10.00 25.00
57 Josh Harrison/844 5.00 12.00
58 Josh Lindblom/131 3.00 8.00
59 Josh Reddick/320 6.00 15.00
60 Juan Carlos Sulbaran/844 4.00 10.00
61 Justin Bristow/594 3.00 8.00
62 Kenny Gilbert/842 3.00 8.00
63 Kirk Nieuwenhuis/844 4.00 10.00
64 Kyle Hudson/419 4.00 10.00
65 Kyle Russell/594 4.00 10.00
66 Kyle Weiland/394 4.00 10.00
67 L. J. Hoes/494 5.00 12.00
68 Mark Cohoon/844 3.00 8.00
69 Mark Sobolewski/269 12.50 30.00
70 Mat Gamel/145 8.00 20.00
71 Matt Harrison/244 6.00 15.00
72 Max Ramirez/604 5.00 12.00
73 Tony Delmonico/744 5.00 12.00
74 Mike Stanton/100 100.00 250.00
75 Mitch Abeita/769 3.00 8.00
76 Neftali Feliz/999 8.00 20.00
77 Neftali Soto/645 5.00 12.00
78 Niko Vasquez/494 5.00 12.00
79 Omar Aguilar/594 4.00 10.00
80 Petey Paramore/519 3.00 8.00
81 Ray Kruml/844 4.00 10.00
82 Rolando Gomez/544 3.00 8.00
83 Ryan Chaffee/594 4.00 10.00
84 Ryan Pressly/844 5.00 12.00
85 Sam Freeman/819 3.00 8.00
86 Sawyer Carroll/544 3.00 8.00
87 Scott Green/294 3.00 8.00
88 Sean Ratliff/544 3.00 8.00
89 Shane Peterson/132 6.00 15.00
90 T.J. Steele/122 6.00 15.00
91 Tim Federowicz/844 4.00 10.00
92 Tyler Chatwood/257 5.00 12.00
93 Tyler Cline/594 3.00 8.00
94 Tyler Ladendorf/227 4.00 10.00
95 Tyler Yockey/844 3.00 8.00
96 Wilmer Flores/99 12.00 30.00
97 Wilson Ramos/745 3.00 8.00
98 Zach McAllister/844 3.00 8.00
99 Zachary Stewart/294 4.00 10.00
100 Zeke Spruill/99 EXCH 10.00 25.00
101 Adrian Nieto/50 10.00 25.00
102 Alan Horne/125 10.00 25.00
103 Andrew Cashner/50 8.00 20.00
104 Anthony Hewitt/50 8.00 20.00
105 Brad Holt/50 10.00 25.00
106 Bryan Petersen/100 4.00 10.00
107 Bryan Price/50 4.00 10.00
108 Bud Norris/100 4.00 10.00
109 Carlos Gutierrez/50 6.00 15.00
110 Chase D'Arnaud/50 5.00 12.00
111 Chris Johnson/50 12.50 30.00
112 Christian Friedrich/50 12.50 30.00
113 Christian Marrero/100 5.00 12.00
114 Clayton Conner/100 4.00 10.00
115 Cole Rohrbough/50 10.00 25.00
116 Collin DeLome/100 5.00 12.00
117 Daniel Cortes/50 8.00 20.00
118 Daniel Schlereth/50 4.00 10.00
119 Denny Almonte/100 4.00 10.00
120 Allan Dykstra/50 12.50 30.00
121 Dominic Brown/100 50.00 100.00
122 Evan Fredrickson/50 4.00 10.00
123 Gordon Beckham/50 12.50 30.00
124 Greg Veloz/100 4.00 10.00
125 Ike Davis/50 10.00 25.00
126 Isaac Galloway/50 10.00 25.00
127 Jacob Jefferies/100 4.00 10.00
128 Michael Kohn/40 4.00 10.00
129 Jared Goedert/100 4.00 10.00
130 Jason Knapp/125 10.00 25.00
131 Jhoulys Chacin/50 10.00 25.00
132 Jordy Mercer/50 5.00 12.00
133 Jorge Bucardo/100 5.00 12.00
134 Jose Ceda/250 4.00 10.00
135 Jose Martinez/100 4.00 10.00
136 Josh Roenicke/100 4.00 10.00
137 Juan Francisco/250 10.00 25.00
138 Justin Parker/50 5.00 12.00
139 Kyle Ginley/100 4.00 10.00
140 Lance Lynn/50 20.00 50.00
142 Logan Morrison/50 10.00 25.00
143 Logan Schafer/125 6.00 15.00
144 Lorenzo Cain/100 15.00 40.00
146 Matt Mitchell/50 4.00 10.00
147 Danny Espinosa/50 15.00 40.00
148 Michael Taylor/100 20.00 50.00
149 Michel Inoa/50 12.50 30.00
150 Mike Montgomery/50 20.00 50.00
151 Cord Phelps/50 6.00 15.00
152 Pablo Sandoval/100 20.00 50.00
153 Quincy Latimore/100 4.00 10.00
154 R. J. Seidel/100 4.00 10.00
155 Rayner Contreras/250 4.00 10.00
156 Rick Porcello/50 12.00 30.00
157 Robert Hernandez/100 4.00 10.00
158 Ryan Kalish/100 5.00 12.00
159 Ryan Perry/50 8.00 20.00
160 Shelby Ford/100 4.00 10.00
161 Shooter Hunt/50 15.00 40.00
162 Tyler Kolodny/100 10.00 25.00
163 Tyler Sample/50 5.00 12.00
164 Tyson Ross/50 4.00 10.00
166 Waldis Joaquin/100 4.00 10.00
167 Wellington Castillo/100 4.00 10.00
168 Wilin Rosario/50 10.00 25.00
169 Xavier Avery/50 3.00 8.00
170 Zach Collier/50 12.50 30.00
171 Zach Putnam/50 5.00 12.00
172 Anthony Gose/50 30.00 60.00
173 Roger Kieschnick/50 10.00 25.00
174 Andrew Liebel/50 6.00 15.00
175 Tim Murphy/50 5.00 12.00
176 Vance Worley/50 40.00 80.00
177 Buster Posey/50 125.00 250.00
178 Kenn Kasparek/50 4.00 10.00
179 J.P. Ramirez/50 4.00 10.00
180 Evan Bigley/100 6.00 15.00
181 Trey Haley/50 6.00 15.00
182 Robbie Grossman/50 6.00 15.00
183 Jordan Danks/40 EXCH 20.00 50.00
184 Brett Hunter/50 5.00 12.00
185 Rafael Rodriguez/50 20.00 50.00
186 Yeicok Calderon/100 12.50 30.00
187 Gustavo Pierre/50 6.00 15.00
188 Will Smith/50 4.00 10.00
189 Daniel Thomas/50 4.00 10.00
190 Carson Blair/50 8.00 20.00
191 Chris Hicks/50 8.00 20.00
193 Marcus Lemon/40 6.00 15.00
194 Kyle Nicholson/50 10.00 25.00
195 Mike Cisco/50 4.00 10.00
196 Jarek Cunningham/50 4.00 10.00
197 Cat Osterman/50 20.00 50.00
198 Derrick Rose/25 25.00 60.00
199 Michael Beasley/25 6.00 15.00
200 O.J. Mayo/25 6.00 15.00

2008 Donruss Elite Extra Edition College Ties Green

STATED PRINT RUN 1500 SER.#'d SETS
*GOLD: .75X TO 2X BASIC
OVERALL INSERT ODDS 1:2
GOLD PRINT RUN 100 SER.#'d SETS
*RED: 1.2X TO 3X BASIC
OVERALL INSERT ODDS 1:2
RED PRINT RUN 50 SER.#'d SETS
1 Cord Phelps/Sean Ratliff .75 2.00
2 Ryan Perry/T.J. Steele 1.25 3.00
3 Mitch Abeita/Aaron Pribanic .75 2.00
4 Ryan Perry/Daniel Schlereth 1.25 3.00
5 Daniel Schlereth/T.J. Steele 1.25 3.00
6 Matt Mangini/Jordy Mercer .75 2.00
7 Blake Tekotte/Mark Sobolewski 1.25 3.00
8 Nick Schmidt/Logan Forsythe .75 2.00
9 Wieters/Blackmon 4.00 10.00
10 M.Abeita/J.Chamberlain .50 1.25
11 Andrew Cashner/Andrew Walker 2.00 5.00
12 Sawyer Carroll/Scott Green .75 2.00
13 Taylor Teagarden/Kyle Russell .75 2.00
14 Carlos Gutierrez/Dennis Raben 2.00 5.00
15 Lance Lynn/Cody Satterwhite 1.25 3.00
16 Jordan Danks/Cat Osterman 1.25 3.00
17 Dusty Coleman/Aaron Shafer .75 2.00
18 J.Chamberlain/A.Pribanic .50 1.25
19 Bryan Price/Cole St. Clair .75 2.00
20 Cat Osterman/Kenn Kasparek 1.25 3.00
21 Jose Duran/Brandon Hicks .75 2.00
22 Roger Kieschnick/Zachary Stewart .75 2.00
23 Shane Peterson/Danny Espinosa 1.25 3.00
24 David Price/Brett Jacobson 1.00 2.50
25 Joe Savery/Bryan Price .50 1.25
26 Paramore/Davis 1.00 2.50
27 Brent Morel/Logan Schafer 1.25 3.00
28 Dennis Raben/Mark Sobolewski 1.25 3.00
29 Andrew Liebel/Shane Peterson 1.25 3.00
30 B.Posey/T.Thomas 2.00 5.00
31 Joe Savery/Cole St. Clair .50 1.25
32 Cat Osterman/Bradley Suttle .75 2.00

33 Dennis Raben/Blake Tekotte 1.25 3.00
34 Carlos Gutierrez/Mark Sobolewski 1.25 3.00
35 Carlos Gutierrez/Blake Tekotte 2.00 5.00

2008 Donruss Elite Extra Edition College Ties Autographs
OVERALL AUTO/MEM ODDS 1:5
PRINT RUNS B/N 20-44 COPIES PER
NO PRICING ON QTY 25 OR LESS
EXCH DEADLINE 5/26/2010
24 David Price/Brett Jacobson/44 10.00 25.00

2008 Donruss Elite Extra Edition College Ties Jerseys
OVERALL AU/MEM ODDS 1:5
PRINT RUNS B/WN 100-500 COPIES PER
6 Matt Mangini/Jordy Mercer/500 3.00 8.00
8 Nick Schmidt/Logan Forsythe/500 3.00 8.00
11 Andrew Cashner/Andrew Walker/500 3.00 8.00
15 Lance Lynn/Cody Satterwhite/500 3.00 8.00
16 J.Danks/C.Osterman/100 5.00 12.00
20 C.Osterman/K.Kasparek/100 6.00 15.00
21 Jose Duran/Brandon Hicks/100 4.00 10.00
30 B.Posey/T.Thomas/500 10.00 25.00

2008 Donruss Elite Extra Edition College Ties Jerseys Prime
OVERALL AU/MEM ODDS 1:5
STATED PRINT RUN 25 SER.#'d SETS
NO PRICING DUE TO SCARCITY

2008 Donruss Elite Extra Edition Collegiate Patches Autographs
OVERALL AUTO/MEM ODDS 1:5
PRINT RUNS B/WN 20-255 COPIES PER
NO PRICING ON QTY 25 OR LESS
EXCH DEADLINE 5/26/2010
1 Ryan Patterson/250 4.00 10.00
2 Mark Melancon/250 8.00 20.00
3 Buster Posey/250 20.00 50.00
4 O.J. Mayo/50 10.00 25.00
5 Gordon Beckham/250 10.00 25.00
6 Josh Roenicke/250 4.00 10.00
7 Michael Beasley/100 8.00 20.00
8 Jack Egbert/249 4.00 10.00
11 Tyson Brummett/250 4.00 10.00
12 Ike Davis/250 6.00 15.00
13 Andrew Cashner/250 5.00 12.00
14 Charlie Furbush/250 6.00 15.00
15 Ryan Perry/248 4.00 10.00
16 Sean Doolittle/250 4.00 10.00
17 Alan Horne/250 8.00 20.00
18 Daniel Schlereth/250 4.00 10.00
19 Carlos Gutierrez/249 8.00 20.00
20 Shooter Hunt/250 10.00 25.00
21 Cat Osterman/250 10.00 25.00
22 Lance Lynn/249 10.00 25.00
23 Byron Wiley/248 4.00 10.00
24 Brad Mills/249 4.00 10.00
25 Bryan Price/249 4.00 10.00
26 Logan Forsythe/249 4.00 10.00
27 Brian Duensing/50 6.00 15.00
28 Tyson Ross/255 5.00 12.00
29 Shane Peterson/250 6.00 15.00
30 Josh Lindblom/249 6.00 15.00
31 Aaron Shafer/250 4.00 10.00
32 Dennis Raben/250 4.00 10.00
33 Cody Satterwhite/250 4.00 10.00
34 James Darnell/250 6.00 15.00
35 Charlie Blackmon/240 15.00 40.00
36 Blake Wood/250 4.00 10.00
37 Jordan Danks/250 6.00 15.00
38 Jordy Mercer/247 5.00 12.00
39 Roger Kieschnick/250 5.00 12.00
40 Zachary Stewart/250 4.00 10.00
41 Daniel McCutchen/250 4.00 10.00
42 Brent Morel/250 4.00 10.00
43 Kyle Hudson/249 5.00 12.00
44 Tim Murphy/250 4.00 10.00
45 Petey Paramore/250 4.00 10.00
46 Kyle Russell/250 5.00 12.00
47 Logan Schafer/250 4.00 10.00
48 Andrew Liebel/248 6.00 15.00
49 Aaron Pribanic/250 4.00 10.00
50 Scott Green/250 6.00 15.00
51 Blake Tekotte/248 5.00 12.00
52 Vance Worley/250 8.00 20.00
53 Taylor Teagarden/250 5.00 12.00
54 Cord Phelps/250 4.00 10.00
55 Kyle Weiland/250 6.00 15.00
56 Allan Dykstra/250 5.00 12.00
57 Danny Espinosa/250 12.50 30.00
59 Zach Putnam/244 4.00 10.00
60 Mark Sobolewski/250 10.00 25.00
61 Regis Philbin/50 20.00 50.00
62 Randy Couture/50 30.00 60.00
63 Jose Duran/250 4.00 10.00
64 Lucas Duda/249 6.00 15.00

2008 Donruss Elite Extra Edition School Colors
OVERALL INSERT ODDS 1:2
STATED PRINT RUN 1500 SER.#'d SET
1 T.J. Steele 1.25 3.00
2 Brett Jacobson .50 1.25
3 Buster Posey 3.00 8.00
4 O.J. Mayo 1.25 3.00
5 Gordon Beckham 1.50 4.00
6 Sean Ratliff .75 2.00
7 Michael Beasley 1.25 3.00
8 Jose Duran .75 2.00
9 Derrick Rose 2.50 6.00
10 Joba Chamberlain .75 2.00
11 Sam Freeman 1.25 3.00
12 Ike Davis 1.50 4.00
13 Andrew Cashner 2.00 5.00
14 Chase D'Arnaud .75 2.00
15 Ryan Perry 1.25 3.00
16 Blake Tekotte 1.25 3.00
17 Cole St. Clair .75 2.00
18 Daniel Schlereth .75 2.00
19 Carlos Gutierrez 1.25 3.00
20 Shooter Hunt .75 2.00
21 Zach Putnam .75 2.00
22 Lance Lynn 1.25 3.00
23 Mitch Abeita .75 2.00
24 Jordan Danks 1.25 3.00
25 Bryan Price .75 2.00
26 Logan Forsythe .75 2.00
27 Brandon Crawford 2.00 5.00
28 Tyson Ross .75 2.00
29 Shane Peterson 1.25 3.00
30 Josh Lindblom .75 2.00
31 Aaron Shafer .75 2.00
32 Dennis Raben 1.25 3.00
33 Cody Satterwhite .75 2.00
34 James Darnell 1.25 3.00
35 Charlie Blackmon 6.00 15.00
36 Sawyer Carroll .75 2.00
37 Cat Osterman 2.00 5.00
38 Jordy Mercer .75 2.00
39 Roger Kieschnick .75 2.00
40 Zachary Stewart .75 2.00
41 Kyle Weiland 2.00 5.00
42 Brent Morel 1.25 3.00
43 Lucas Duda 1.50 4.00
44 Tim Murphy .75 2.00
45 Petey Paramore .75 2.00
46 Kyle Russell .75 2.00
47 Logan Schafer .75 2.00
48 Andrew Liebel .75 2.00
49 Aaron Pribanic .75 2.00
50 Scott Green .75 2.00

2008 Donruss Elite Extra Edition School Colors Autographs
OVERALL AUTO/MEM ODDS 1:5
PRINT RUNS B/WN 25-50 COPIES PER
NO PRICING ON QTY 25 OR LESS
EXCH DEADLINE 5/26/2010
3 Buster Posey/50 60.00 120.00
4 O.J. Mayo/25 6.00 15.00
5 Gordon Beckham/50 12.50 30.00
7 Michael Beasley/25 6.00 15.00
8 Jose Duran/50 4.00 10.00
9 Derrick Rose/25 25.00 60.00
12 Ike Davis/50 10.00 25.00
13 Andrew Cashner/50 10.00 25.00
14 Chase D'Arnaud/50 5.00 12.00
15 Ryan Perry/50 4.00 10.00
16 Blake Tekotte/50 4.00 10.00
18 Daniel Schlereth/50 4.00 10.00
22 Lance Lynn/50 6.00 15.00
25 Bryan Price/50 5.00 12.00
31 Aaron Shafer/50 4.00 10.00
32 Dennis Raben/50 10.00 25.00
33 Cody Satterwhite/50 8.00 20.00
35 Charlie Blackmon/50 20.00 50.00
42 Brent Morel/50 10.00 25.00
46 Kyle Russell/50 8.00 20.00
47 Logan Schafer/50 4.00 10.00

2008 Donruss Elite Extra Edition School Colors Materials
OVERALL AU/MEM ODDS 1:5
STATED PRINT RUN 100 SER.#'d SETS
3 Buster Posey 6.00 15.00
4 O.J. Mayo 4.00 10.00
5 Gordon Beckham 4.00 10.00
7 Michael Beasley 4.00 10.00
8 Jose Duran 4.00 10.00
9 Derrick Rose 6.00 15.00
13 Andrew Cashner 4.00 10.00
33 Cody Satterwhite 6.00 15.00
37 Cat Osterman 8.00 20.00

2008 Donruss Elite Extra Edition Throwback Threads
OVERALL AU/MEM ODDS 1:5
PRINT RUNS B/WN 15-500 COPIES PER
NO PRICING ON QTY 25 OR LESS
1 Rick Porcello/500 6.00 15.00
2 Gordon Beckham/500 4.00 10.00
3 Andrew Cashner/500 4.00 10.00
6 Cody Satterwhite/500 6.00 15.00
9 Jose Duran/500 3.00 8.00
10 Derrick Rose/500 4.00 10.00
11 Michael Beasley/500 3.00 8.00
12 O.J. Mayo/400 3.00 8.00
13 Buster Posey/250 12.50 30.00
20 Cat Osterman/100 6.00 15.00
24 Tim Alderson/500 3.00 8.00
25 Michael Burgess/500 3.00 8.00

2008 Donruss Elite Extra Edition Throwback Threads Prime
OVERALL AU/MEM ODDS 1:5
PRINT RUNS B/WN 1-50 COPIES PER
NO PRICING ON QTY 10 OR LESS
24 Tim Alderson/50 6.00 15.00
25 Michael Burgess/50 6.00 15.00

2008 Donruss Elite Extra Edition Throwback Threads Autographs
OVERALL AUTO/MEM ODDS 1:5
PRINT RUNS B/WN 4-100 COPIES PER
NO PRICING ON QTY 25 OR LESS
EXCH DEADLINE 5/26/2010
1 Rick Porcello/100 15.00 40.00
2 Gordon Beckham/100 10.00 25.00
3 Andrew Cashner/100 10.00 25.00
5 Xavier Avery/35 20.00 50.00
9 Jose Duran/100 10.00 25.00
10 Derrick Rose/25 40.00 100.00
11 Michael Beasley/25 12.00 30.00
12 O.J. Mayo/25 6.00 15.00
13 Buster Posey/100 50.00 100.00
20 Cat Osterman/50 10.00 25.00
24 Tim Alderson/40 10.00 25.00

2008 Donruss Elite Extra Edition Throwback Threads Autographs Prime
OVERALL AUTO/MEM ODDS 1:5
PRINT RUNS B/WN 1-25 COPIES PER
NO PRICING DUE TO SCARCITY
EXCH DEADLINE 5/26/2010

2009 Donruss Elite Extra Edition
COMP.SET w/o AU's (50) 6.00 15.00
COMMON CARD (1-50) .20 .50
COMMON AU (51-150) 3.00 8.00
AU SEMIS 4.00 10.00
AU UNLISTED 5.00 12.00
OVERALL AUTO ODDS 1:5 HOBBY
AU PRINT RUNS B/WN 99-999 COPIES PER
EXCHANGE DEADLINE 7/20/2011
1 Bobby Borchering .30 .75
2 Blake Smith .20 .50
3 Drew Storen .30 .75
4 J.R. Murphy .20 .50
5 Zack Wheeler .60 1.50
6 Nolan Arenado 2.50 6.00
7 Matt Bashore .20 .50
8 Josh Phegley .30 .75
9 Jacob Turner .75 2.00
10 Mike Leake .60 1.50
11 Kelly Dugan .20 .50
12 Bill Bullock .20 .50
13 Shelby Miller .60 1.50
14 Alex Wilson .20 .50
15 Ben Paulsen .20 .50
16 Max Stassi .30 .75
17 A.J. Pollock .50 1.25
18 Aaron Miller .20 .50
19 Brooks Pounders .30 .75
20 Shaver Hansen .20 .50
21 Tyler Skaggs .50 1.25
22 Jiovanni Mier .30 .75
23 Everett Williams .20 .50
24 Rich Poythress .20 .50
25 Chad Jenkins .20 .50
26 Rey Fuentes .20 .50
27 Ryan Jackson .20 .50
28 Eric Arnett .30 .75
29 Chris Owings .20 .50
30 Garrett Gould .20 .50
31 Tyler Matzek .30 .75
32 Donnie Joseph .30 .75
33 Brandon Belt .50 1.25
34 Jon Gaston .20 .50
35 Tracye Thompson .50 1.25
36 Marc Krauss .20 .50
37 Kyrell Hudson .30 .75
38 Ben Tootle .20 .50
39 Jake Marisnick .30 .75
40 Aaron Baker .20 .50
41 Kent Matthes .20 .50
42 Andrew Oliver .20 .50
43 Cameron Garfield .20 .50
44 Adam Warren .20 .50
45 Dustin Dickerson .30 .75
46 James Jones .20 .50
47 Brooks Raley .20 .50
48 Jenrry Mejia .30 .75
49 Brock Holt .30 .75
50 Wes Hatton .20 .50
51 Dustin Ackley AU/899 3.00 8.00
52 D.Tate AU/999 6.00 15.00
53 T.Sanchez AU/435 8.00 20.00
54 Matt Hobgood AU/681 5.00 12.00
55 Alex White AU/599 5.00 12.00
56 Jared Mitchell AU/370 6.00 15.00
57 Mike Trout AU/495 1000.00 2500.00
58 Brett Jackson AU/534 12.50 30.00
59 Mike Minor AU/570 3.00 8.00
60 S.Heathcott AU/754 3.00 8.00
61 T.Mendonca AU/569 4.00 10.00
62 Wil Myers AU/799 8.00 20.00
63 J.Kipnis AU/319 6.00 15.00
64 Robert Stock AU/569 3.00 8.00
65 Tim Wheeler AU/794 5.00 12.00
66 M.Givens AU/794 5.00 12.00
67 Grant Green AU/444 3.00 8.00
68 D.LeMahieu AU/645 30.00 80.00
69 Rex Brothers AU/699 3.00 8.00
70 Thomas Joseph AU/99 20.00 50.00
71 Wade Gaynor AU/730 3.00 8.00
72 Ryan Wheeler AU/690 6.00 15.00
73 K.Heckathorn AU/599 4.00 10.00
74 C.James AU/99 15.00 40.00
75 Victor Black AU/694 4.00 10.00
76 T.Glaesmann AU/494 4.00 10.00
77 Tyler Kehrer AU/99 15.00 40.00
78 Steve Baron AU/700 3.00 8.00
79 M.Davidson AU/599 6.00 15.00
80 Jeff Kobernus AU/570 5.00 12.00
81 Kentrail Davis AU/655 4.00 10.00
82 Kyle Gibson AU/645 4.00 10.00
83 G.Richards AU/470 4.00 10.00
84 B.Boxberger AU/550 4.00 10.00
85 Evan Chambers AU/695 3.00 8.00
86 Telvin Nash AU/725 3.00 8.00
87 Austin Kirk AU/599 3.00 8.00
88 M.Cooper AU/99 10.00 25.00
89 Jason Christian AU/730 3.00 8.00
90 R.Grichuk AU/770 4.00 10.00
91 Nick Franklin AU/724 5.00 12.00
92 Eric Smith AU/99 12.50 30.00
93 J.Hazelbaker AU/640 3.00 8.00
94 Zach Dotson AU/699 3.00 8.00
95 Josh Fellhauer AU/494 4.00 10.00
96 Jeff Malm AU/650 4.00 10.00
97 Caleb Cotham AU/549 5.00 12.00
98 Trevor Holder AU/649 3.00 8.00
99 Joe Kelly AU/690 4.00 10.00
100 Robbie Shields AU/749 3.00 8.00
101 Kyle Bellamy AU/695 3.00 8.00
102 Braxton Lane AU/710 3.00 8.00
103 Justin Marks AU/99 3.00 8.00
104 Ryan Goins AU/599 3.00 8.00
105 Chase Anderson AU/619 3.00 8.00
106 Kyle Seager AU/744 4.00 10.00
107 C.Cain AU/99 20.00 50.00
108 D.Renfroe AU/695 6.00 15.00
109 Travis Banwart AU/645 3.00 8.00
110 Joe Testa AU/699 3.00 8.00
111 Brandon Jacobs AU/725 5.00 12.00
112 Brett Brach AU/699 3.00 8.00
113 Brad Brach AU/695 3.00 8.00
114 Keon Broxton AU/675 3.00 8.00
115 Nathan Karns AU/734 4.00 10.00
116 Kendal Volz AU/695 3.00 8.00
117 Charles Ruiz AU/594 3.00 8.00
118 Mike Spina AU/580 4.00 10.00
119 Jamie Johnson AU/619 3.00 8.00
120 B.Mitchell AU/699 4.00 10.00
121 Chad Bell AU/744 3.00 8.00
122 Dan Taylor AU/650 3.00 8.00
123 K.Davis AU/150 25.00 60.00
124 Ashur Tolliver AU/99 30.00 60.00
125 Cody Rogers AU/690 4.00 10.00
126 Trent Stevenson AU/744 3.00 8.00
127 Dean Weaver AU/599 3.00 8.00
128 Matt Helm AU/790 5.00 12.00
129 Andrew Doyle AU/640 3.00 8.00
130 Matt Graham AU/690 3.00 8.00
131 Kevan Hess AU/719 3.00 8.00
132 Luke Bailey AU/475 3.00 8.00
133 Steve Matz AU/790 6.00 15.00
134 Tanner Bushue AU/652 4.00 10.00
135 Neil Medchill AU/710 6.00 15.00
136 Edward Paredes AU/725 3.00 8.00
137 A.J. Jimenez AU/695 3.00 8.00
138 Grant Desme AU/744 5.00 12.00
139 Von Rosenberg AU/770 4.00 10.00
140 Daniel Fields AU/749 6.00 15.00
141 Graham Stoneburner AU/719 3.00 8.00
142 David Holmberg AU/710 3.00 8.00
143 C.Dominguez AU/719 4.00 10.00
144 Luke Murton AU/750 4.00 10.00
145 Danny Rosenbaum AU/695 6.00 15.00
146 T.Townsend AU/99 6.00 15.00
147 Louis Coleman AU/597 3.00 8.00
148 Patrick Schuster AU/695 3.00 8.00
149 Jeff Hunt AU/99 15.00 40.00
150 A.Chapman AU/695 12.00 30.00

2009 Donruss Elite Extra Edition Aspirations
*ASP 1-50: 2.5X TO 6X BASIC
RANDOM INSERTS IN PACKS
STATED PRINT RUN 150 SER.#'d SETS
51 Dustin Ackley 2.00 5.00
52 Donavan Tate 2.00 5.00
53 Tony Sanchez 3.00 8.00
54 Matt Hobgood 3.00 8.00
55 Alex White 3.00 8.00
56 Jared Mitchell 2.00 5.00
57 Mike Trout 75.00 150.00
58 Brett Jackson 4.00 10.00
59 Mike Minor 2.00 5.00
60 Slade Heathcott 4.00 10.00
61 Tom Mendonca 1.25 3.00
62 Wil Myers 3.00 8.00
63 Jason Kipnis 5.00 12.00
64 Robert Stock 2.00 5.00
65 Tim Wheeler 2.00 5.00
66 Mychal Givens 2.00 5.00
67 Grant Green 1.25 3.00
68 D.J. LeMahieu 8.00 20.00
69 Rex Brothers 2.00 5.00
70 Thomas Joseph 4.00 10.00
71 Wade Gaynor 1.25 3.00
72 Ryan Wheeler 2.00 5.00
73 Kyle Heckathorn 2.00 5.00
74 Chad James 2.00 5.00
75 Victor Black 2.00 5.00
76 Todd Glaesmann 1.25 3.00
77 Tyler Kehrer 2.00 5.00
78 Steve Baron 2.00 5.00
79 Matt Davidson 4.00 10.00
80 Jeff Kobernus 2.00 5.00
81 Kentrail Davis 2.00 5.00
82 Kyle Gibson 3.00 8.00
83 Garrett Richards 3.00 8.00
84 Brad Boxberger 2.00 5.00
85 Evan Chambers 1.25 3.00
86 Telvin Nash 4.00 10.00
87 Austin Kirk 1.25 3.00
88 Marquise Cooper 2.00 5.00
89 Jason Christian 1.25 3.00
90 Randal Grichuk 3.00 8.00
91 Nick Franklin 3.00 8.00
92 Eric Smith 1.25 3.00
93 Jeremy Hazelbaker 3.00 8.00
94 Zach Dotson 1.25 3.00
95 Josh Fellhauer 1.25 3.00
96 Jeff Malm 1.25 3.00
97 Caleb Cotham 2.00 5.00
98 Trevor Holder 1.25 3.00
99 Joe Kelly 1.25 3.00
100 Robbie Shields 1.25 3.00
101 Kyle Bellamy 1.25 3.00
102 Braxton Lane 1.25 3.00
103 Justin Marks 1.25 3.00
104 Ryan Goins 2.00 5.00
105 Chase Anderson 1.25 3.00
106 Kyle Seager 3.00 8.00
107 Colton Cain 2.00 5.00
108 David Renfroe 1.25 3.00
109 Travis Banwart 1.25 3.00
110 Joe Testa 1.25 3.00
111 Brandon Jacobs 2.00 5.00
112 Brett Brach 1.25 3.00
113 Brad Brach 1.25 3.00
114 Keon Broxton 1.25 3.00
115 Nathan Karns 1.25 3.00
116 Kendal Volz 2.00 5.00
117 Charles Ruiz 1.25 3.00
118 Mike Spina 1.25 3.00
119 Jamie Johnson 1.25 3.00
120 Bryan Mitchell 1.25 3.00
121 Chad Bell 3.00 8.00
122 Dan Taylor 1.25 3.00
123 Khris Davis 6.00 15.00
124 Ashur Tolliver 2.00 5.00
125 Cody Rogers 1.25 3.00
126 Trent Stevenson 1.25 3.00
127 Dean Weaver 1.25 3.00
128 Matt Helm 2.00 5.00
129 Andrew Doyle 1.25 3.00
130 Matt Graham 1.25 3.00
131 Kevan Hess 1.25 3.00
132 Luke Bailey 1.25 3.00
133 Steve Matz 2.50 6.00
134 Tanner Bushue 1.25 3.00
135 Neil Medchill 1.25 3.00
136 Edward Paredes 1.25 3.00
137 A.J. Jimenez 1.25 3.00
138 Grant Desme 1.25 3.00
139 Zack Von Rosenberg 1.25 3.00
140 Daniel Fields 1.25 3.00
141 Graham Stoneburner 1.25 3.00
142 David Holmberg 3.00 8.00
143 Chris Dominguez 1.25 3.00
144 Luke Murton 1.25 3.00
145 Danny Rosenbaum 2.00 5.00
146 Tyler Townsend 2.00 5.00
147 Louis Coleman 1.25 3.00
148 Patrick Schuster 1.25 3.00
149 Jeff Hunt 3.00 8.00
150 Aroldis Chapman 6.00 15.00

2009 Donruss Elite Extra Edition Status
*STATUS 1-50: 4X TO 10X BASIC
*STATUS 51-150: .6X TO 1.5X ASP
RANDOM INSERTS IN PACKS
STATED PRINT RUN 100 SER.#'d SETS
57 Mike Trout 150.00 250.00

2009 Donruss Elite Extra Edition Status Gold
*STAT.GOLD 1-50: 5X TO 12X BASIC
*STAT.GOLD 51-150: .75X TO 2X ASP
RANDOM INSERTS IN PACKS
STATED PRINT RUN 50 SER.#'d SETS
57 Mike Trout 200.00 400.00

2009 Donruss Elite Extra Edition Signature Aspirations
OVERALL AUTO ODDS 1:4 HOBBY
STATED PRINT RUN 100 SER.#'d SETS
EXCHANGE DEADLINE 7/20/2011
1 Bobby Borchering 4.00 10.00
2 Blake Smith 4.00 10.00
3 Drew Storen 6.00 15.00
4 J.R. Murphy 10.00 25.00
5 Zack Wheeler 25.00 60.00
6 Nolan Arenado 75.00 200.00
7 Matt Bashore 4.00 10.00
8 Josh Phegley 4.00 10.00
9 Jacob Turner 12.00 30.00
10 Mike Leake 8.00 20.00
11 Kelly Dugan 4.00 10.00
12 Bill Bullock 4.00 10.00
13 Shelby Miller 4.00 10.00
14 Alex Wilson 4.00 10.00
15 Ben Paulsen 4.00 10.00
16 Max Stassi 8.00 20.00
17 A.J. Pollock 6.00 15.00
18 Aaron Miller 6.00 15.00
19 Brooks Pounders 4.00 10.00
20 Shaver Hansen 3.00 8.00
21 Tyler Skaggs 8.00 20.00
22 Jiovanni Mier 6.00 15.00
23 Everett Williams 8.00 20.00
25 Chad Jenkins 6.00 15.00
27 Ryan Jackson 8.00 20.00
28 Eric Arnett 3.00 8.00
29 Chris Owings 12.00 30.00
30 Garrett Gould 8.00 20.00
32 Donnie Joseph 3.00 8.00
33 Brandon Belt 15.00 40.00
34 Jon Gaston 5.00 12.00
35 Tracye Thompson 15.00 40.00
36 Marc Krauss 3.00 8.00
38 Ben Tootle 3.00 8.00
39 Jake Marisnick 10.00 25.00
40 Aaron Baker 4.00 10.00
41 Kent Matthes 4.00 10.00
42 Andrew Oliver 5.00 12.00
43 Cameron Garfield 5.00 12.00
44 Adam Warren 8.00 20.00
45 Dustin Dickerson 4.00 10.00
47 Brooks Raley 4.00 10.00
48 Jenrry Mejia 6.00 15.00
49 Brock Holt 5.00 12.00
50 Wes Hatton 4.00 10.00
51 Dustin Ackley 5.00 12.00
52 Donavan Tate 3.00 8.00
53 Tony Sanchez 12.50 30.00
54 Matt Hobgood 8.00 20.00
55 Alex White 5.00 12.00
56 Jared Mitchell 3.00 8.00
57 Mike Trout 800.00 1500.00
58 Brett Jackson 6.00 15.00
59 Mike Minor 8.00 20.00
60 Slade Heathcott 8.00 20.00
61 Tom Mendonca 8.00 20.00
62 Wil Myers 12.00 30.00
63 Jason Kipnis 12.00 30.00
64 Robert Stock 10.00 25.00
65 Tim Wheeler 5.00 12.00
66 Mychal Givens 12.50 30.00
67 Grant Green 5.00 12.00
68 D.J. LeMahieu 40.00 100.00
69 Rex Brothers 5.00 12.00
71 Wade Gaynor 5.00 12.00
72 Ryan Wheeler 6.00 15.00
73 Kyle Heckathorn 5.00 12.00
75 Victor Black 4.00 10.00
76 Todd Glaesmann 5.00 12.00
78 Steve Baron 3.00 8.00
79 Matt Davidson 15.00 40.00
80 Jeff Kobernus 5.00 12.00
81 Kentrail Davis 10.00 25.00
82 Kyle Gibson 6.00 15.00
83 Garrett Richards 12.50 30.00
84 Brad Boxberger 10.00 25.00
85 Evan Chambers 3.00 8.00
86 Telvin Nash 8.00 20.00
87 Austin Kirk 4.00 10.00
89 Jason Christian 3.00 8.00
90 Randal Grichuk 25.00 60.00
91 Nick Franklin 8.00 20.00
93 Jeremy Hazelbaker 12.00 30.00
94 Zach Dotson 4.00 10.00
95 Josh Fellhauer 4.00 10.00
96 Jeff Malm 8.00 20.00
97 Caleb Cotham 10.00 25.00
98 Trevor Holder 6.00 15.00
99 Joe Kelly 12.50 30.00
100 Robbie Shields 3.00 8.00
101 Kyle Bellamy 4.00 10.00
102 Braxton Lane 5.00 12.00
104 Ryan Goins 5.00 12.00
105 Chase Anderson 6.00 15.00
106 Kyle Seager 12.00 30.00
108 David Renfroe 15.00 40.00
109 Travis Banwart 3.00 8.00
110 Joe Testa 6.00 15.00
111 Brandon Jacobs 8.00 20.00
112 Brett Brach 3.00 8.00
113 Brad Brach 3.00 8.00
114 Keon Broxton 5.00 12.00
115 Nathan Karns 4.00 10.00
116 Kendal Volz 5.00 12.00
117 Charles Ruiz 3.00 8.00
118 Mike Spina 8.00 20.00
119 Jamie Johnson 4.00 10.00
120 Bryan Mitchell 4.00 10.00
121 Chad Bell 3.00 8.00
122 Dan Taylor 3.00 8.00
125 Cody Rogers 6.00 15.00
126 Trent Stevenson 5.00 12.00
127 Dean Weaver 4.00 10.00
128 Matt Helm 10.00 25.00
129 Andrew Doyle 3.00 8.00
130 Matt Graham 4.00 10.00
131 Kevan Hess 4.00 10.00
132 Luke Bailey 5.00 12.00
133 Steve Matz 10.00 25.00
134 Tanner Bushue 6.00 15.00
135 Neil Medchill 10.00 25.00
136 Edward Paredes 4.00 10.00
137 A.J. Jimenez 6.00 15.00
138 Grant Desme 5.00 12.00
139 Zack Von Rosenberg 6.00 15.00
140 Daniel Fields 8.00 20.00
141 Graham Stoneburner 5.00 12.00
142 David Holmberg 8.00 20.00
143 Chris Dominguez 12.50 30.00
144 Luke Murton 8.00 20.00
145 Danny Rosenbaum 3.00 8.00
147 Louis Coleman 4.00 10.00
148 Patrick Schuster 4.00 10.00
150 Aroldis Chapman 15.00 40.00

2009 Donruss Elite Extra Edition Signature Status
OVERALL AUTO ODDS 1:4 HOBBY
STATED PRINT RUN 50 SER.#'d SETS
EXCHANGE DEADLINE 7/20/2011
1 Bobby Borchering 5.00 12.00
3 Drew Storen 6.00 15.00
4 J.R. Murphy 12.50 30.00
5 Zack Wheeler 30.00 80.00
6 Nolan Arenado 100.00 250.00
7 Matt Bashore 5.00 12.00
8 Josh Phegley 5.00 12.00
9 Jacob Turner 15.00 40.00
10 Mike Leake 15.00 40.00
11 Kelly Dugan 5.00 12.00
12 Bill Bullock 5.00 12.00
13 Shelby Miller 5.00 12.00
14 Alex Wilson 5.00 12.00
15 Ben Paulsen 5.00 12.00
16 Max Stassi 10.00 25.00
17 A.J. Pollock 8.00 20.00
18 Aaron Miller 15.00 40.00
19 Brooks Pounders 6.00 15.00
20 Shaver Hansen 3.00 8.00
21 Tyler Skaggs 10.00 25.00
22 Jiovanni Mier 12.50 30.00
23 Everett Williams 12.50 30.00
25 Chad Jenkins 10.00 25.00
27 Ryan Jackson 5.00 12.00
28 Eric Arnett 4.00 10.00
29 Chris Owings 12.00 30.00
30 Garrett Gould 6.00 15.00
32 Donnie Joseph 4.00 10.00
33 Brandon Belt 100.00 200.00
34 Jon Gaston 15.00 40.00
35 Tracye Thompson 20.00 50.00
36 Marc Krauss 4.00 10.00
38 Ben Tootle 3.00 8.00
39 Jake Marisnick 12.00 30.00
40 Aaron Baker 3.00 8.00
41 Kent Matthes 3.00 8.00
42 Andrew Oliver 8.00 20.00
43 Cameron Garfield 10.00 25.00
44 Adam Warren 8.00 20.00
45 Dustin Dickerson 4.00 10.00
47 Brooks Raley 5.00 12.00
48 Jenrry Mejia 6.00 15.00
49 Brock Holt 6.00 15.00
50 Wes Hatton 5.00 12.00
51 Dustin Ackley 6.00 15.00
52 Donavan Tate 4.00 10.00
53 Tony Sanchez 12.50 30.00
54 Matt Hobgood 15.00 40.00
55 Alex White 12.50 30.00
56 Jared Mitchell 3.00 8.00
57 Mike Trout 1000.00 2000.00
58 Brett Jackson 6.00 15.00
59 Mike Minor 12.50 30.00
60 Slade Heathcott 10.00 25.00
61 Tom Mendonca 5.00 12.00
62 Wil Myers 15.00 40.00
63 Jason Kipnis 15.00 40.00
64 Robert Stock 12.00 30.00
65 Tim Wheeler 6.00 15.00
66 Mychal Givens 15.00 40.00
67 Grant Green 6.00 15.00
68 D.J. LeMahieu 50.00 120.00
69 Rex Brothers 6.00 15.00
71 Wade Gaynor 6.00 15.00
72 Ryan Wheeler 10.00 25.00
73 Kyle Heckathorn 8.00 20.00
75 Victor Black 10.00 25.00
76 Todd Glaesmann 8.00 20.00
78 Steve Baron 5.00 12.00
79 Matt Davidson 25.00 60.00
80 Jeff Kobernus 4.00 10.00
81 Kentrail Davis 30.00 60.00
82 Kyle Gibson 20.00 50.00
83 Garrett Richards 20.00 50.00
84 Brad Boxberger 15.00 40.00
85 Evan Chambers 4.00 10.00
86 Telvin Nash 10.00 25.00
87 Austin Kirk 4.00 10.00
89 Jason Christian 4.00 10.00
90 Randal Grichuk 30.00 80.00
91 Nick Franklin 6.00 15.00
93 Jeremy Hazelbaker 15.00 40.00
94 Zach Dotson 6.00 15.00
95 Josh Fellhauer 8.00 20.00
96 Jeff Malm 15.00 40.00
97 Caleb Cotham 10.00 25.00
98 Trevor Holder 3.00 8.00
99 Joe Kelly 6.00 15.00
100 Robbie Shields 5.00 12.00
101 Kyle Bellamy 3.00 8.00
102 Braxton Lane 10.00 25.00
104 Ryan Goins 4.00 10.00
105 Chase Anderson 6.00 15.00
106 Kyle Seager 15.00 40.00
108 David Renfroe 30.00 60.00
109 Travis Banwart 3.00 8.00
110 Joe Testa 5.00 12.00
111 Brandon Jacobs 10.00 25.00
112 Brett Brach 10.00 25.00
113 Brad Brach 3.00 8.00
114 Keon Broxton 10.00 25.00
115 Nathan Karns 4.00 10.00
116 Kendal Volz 8.00 20.00
117 Charles Ruiz 3.00 8.00
118 Mike Spina 6.00 15.00
119 Jamie Johnson 4.00 10.00
120 Bryan Mitchell 6.00 15.00
121 Chad Bell 5.00 12.00
122 Dan Taylor 12.00 30.00
125 Cody Rogers 10.00 25.00
127 Dean Weaver 4.00 10.00
128 Matt Helm 6.00 15.00
129 Andrew Doyle 3.00 8.00
130 Matt Graham 4.00 10.00
131 Kevan Hess 6.00 15.00
132 Luke Bailey 6.00 15.00
133 Steve Matz 12.00 30.00
134 Tanner Bushue 12.00 30.00
135 Neil Medchill 15.00 40.00
136 Edward Paredes 4.00 10.00
137 A.J. Jimenez 4.00 10.00
138 Grant Desme 8.00 20.00
139 Zack Von Rosenberg 10.00 25.00
140 Daniel Fields 15.00 40.00
141 Graham Stoneburner 10.00 25.00
142 David Holmberg 10.00 25.00
143 Chris Dominguez 30.00 60.00
144 Luke Murton 10.00 25.00
145 Danny Rosenbaum 4.00 10.00
147 Louis Coleman 6.00 15.00
148 Patrick Schuster 8.00 20.00
150 Aroldis Chapman 25.00 60.00

2009 Donruss Elite Extra Edition Signature Turn of the Century
OVERALL AUTO ODDS 1:5 HOBBY
AU PRINT RUNS B/WN 10-844 COPIES PER
EXCHANGE DEADLINE 7/20/2011
1 B.Borchering AU/799 3.00 8.00
2 Blake Smith AU/794 3.00 8.00
3 Drew Storen AU/519 6.00 15.00
4 J.R. Murphy AU/840 6.00 15.00
5 Z.Wheeler AU/744 3.00 8.00
6 Nolan Arenado AU/844 50.00 120.00
7 Matt Bashore AU/655 3.00 8.00
8 Josh Phegley AU/613 3.00 8.00
9 Jacob Turner AU/799 6.00 15.00
10 Mike Leake AU/356 5.00 12.00
11 Kelly Dugan AU/799 3.00 8.00
12 Bill Bullock AU/640 3.00 8.00
13 Shelby Miller AU/690 3.00 8.00
14 Alex Wilson AU/710 3.00 8.00
15 Ben Paulsen AU/599 3.00 8.00
16 Max Stassi AU/810 5.00 12.00
17 A.J. Pollock AU/499 4.00 10.00
18 Aaron Miller AU/650 4.00 10.00
19 Brooks Pounders AU/844 3.00 8.00
20 Shaver Hansen AU/425 3.00 8.00
21 Tyler Skaggs AU/620 6.00 15.00
22 Jiovanni Mier AU/825 4.00 10.00
23 E.Williams AU/799 4.00 10.00
24 R.Poythress AU/150 10.00 25.00
25 Chad Jenkins AU/785 3.00 8.00
26 R.Fuentes AU/99 EXCH 15.00 40.00
27 Ryan Jackson AU/558 5.00 12.00
28 Eric Arnett AU/669 3.00 8.00
29 Chris Owings AU/799 6.00 15.00
30 Garrett Gould AU/799 3.00 8.00
31 T.Matzek AU/125 EXCH 15.00 40.00
32 Donnie Joseph AU/699 3.00 8.00
33 Brandon Belt AU/610 4.00 10.00
34 Jon Gaston AU/725 3.00 8.00
35 Tracye Thompson AU/699 6.00 15.00
36 Marc Krauss AU/619 3.00 8.00
37 K.Hudson AU/99 EXCH 20.00 50.00
38 Ben Tootle AU/825 3.00 8.00
39 Jake Marisnick AU/799 6.00 15.00
40 Aaron Baker AU/359 3.00 8.00
41 Kent Matthes AU/619 3.00 8.00
42 Andrew Oliver AU/710 3.00 8.00
43 Cameron Garfield AU/844 3.00 8.00
44 Adam Warren AU/675 4.00 10.00
45 Dustin Dickerson AU/650 3.00 8.00
46 James Jones AU/99 5.00 12.00
47 Brooks Raley AU/494 3.00 8.00
48 Jenrry Mejia AU/844 4.00 10.00
49 Brock Holt AU/619 4.00 10.00
50 Wes Hatton AU/790 3.00 8.00
51 Dustin Ackley AU/75 6.00 15.00
52 D.Tate AU/225 8.00 20.00
53 Tony Sanchez AU/50 20.00 50.00
54 M.Hobgood AU/75 8.00 20.00
55 Alex White AU/70 6.00 15.00
56 Jared Mitchell AU/60 10.00 25.00
57 Mike Trout AU/149 600.00 1000.00
58 Brett Jackson AU/49 6.00 15.00
60 S.Heathcott AU/40 30.00 60.00
61 Tom Mendonca AU/50 10.00 25.00
62 Wil Myers AU/50 15.00 40.00
64 Robert Stock AU/50 15.00 40.00
66 M.Givens AU/299 5.00 12.00
69 Rex Brothers AU/100 5.00 12.00
71 Wade Gaynor AU/110 3.00 8.00
72 R.Wheeler AU/150 6.00 15.00
73 K.Heckathorn AU/50 6.00 15.00
75 Victor Black AU/100 6.00 15.00

76 T.Glaesmann AU/50 4.00 10.00
78 Steve Baron AU/125 4.00 10.00
79 M.Davidson AU/125 12.50 30.00
80 Jeff Kobernus AU/99 5.00 12.00
81 Kentrail Davis AU/50 20.00 50.00
82 Kyle Gibson AU/99 10.00 25.00
83 G.Richards AU/99 12.00 30.00
84 B.Boxberger AU/110 5.00 12.00
85 Evan Chambers AU/149 3.00 8.00
86 Telvin Nash AU/100 8.00 20.00
87 Austin Kirk AU/199 4.00 10.00
89 Jason Christian AU/111 3.00 8.00
90 Randal Grichuk AU/50 30.00 80.00
91 N.Franklin AU/120 15.00 40.00
93 J.Hazelbaker AU/204 12.00 30.00
94 Zach Dotson AU/100 3.00 8.00
95 J.Fellhauer AU/125 4.00 10.00
96 Jeff Malm AU/149 10.00 25.00
97 Caleb Cotham AU/50 10.00 25.00
98 Trevor Holder AU/100 3.00 8.00
99 Joe Kelly AU/99 4.00 10.00
100 Robbie Shields AU/99 3.00 8.00
101 Kyle Bellamy AU/149 3.00 8.00
102 Braxton Lane AU/125 3.00 8.00
104 Ryan Goins AU/150 5.00 12.00
106 Kyle Seager AU/100 8.00 20.00
108 David Renfroe AU/149 8.00 20.00
109 Travis Banwart AU/199 3.00 8.00
110 Joe Testa AU/125 4.00 10.00
111 B.Jacobs AU/100 5.00 12.00
112 Brett Brach AU/75 3.00 8.00
113 Brad Brach AU/100 3.00 8.00
114 Keon Broxton AU/114 4.00 10.00
115 Nathan Karns AU/110 3.00 8.00
116 Kendal Volz AU/99 12.00 30.00
117 Charles Ruiz AU/125 3.00 8.00
118 Mike Spina AU/115 3.00 8.00
119 Jamie Johnson AU/100 4.00 10.00
120 Bryan Mitchell AU/125 4.00 10.00
121 Chad Bell AU/100 3.00 8.00
122 Dan Taylor AU/175 3.00 8.00
125 Cody Rogers AU/150 4.00 10.00
126 Trent Stevenson AU/100 3.00 8.00
127 Dean Weaver AU/199 3.00 8.00
128 Matt Helm AU/50 6.00 15.00
129 Andrew Doyle AU/155 3.00 8.00
130 Matt Graham AU/150 4.00 10.00
131 Kevan Hess AU/125 3.00 8.00
132 Luke Bailey AU/100 5.00 12.00
133 Steve Matz AU/50 12.00 30.00
134 T.Bushue AU/190 4.00 10.00
135 Neil Medchill AU/125 10.00 25.00
136 Edward Paredes AU/110 3.00 8.00
137 A.J. Jimenez AU/149 8.00 20.00
138 G.Desme AU/100 6.00 15.00
139 Von Rosenberg AU/50 8.00 20.00
140 Daniel Fields AU/90 15.00 40.00
141 G.Stoneburner AU/125 4.00 10.00
142 David Holmberg AU/110 8.00 20.00
143 C.Dominguez AU/125 8.00 20.00
144 Luke Murton AU/90 6.00 15.00
145 Danny Rosenbaum AU/149 6.00 15.00
147 L.Coleman AU/199 4.00 10.00
148 P.Schuster AU/149 4.00 10.00
150 A.Chapman AU/149 25.00 60.00

2009 Donruss Elite Extra Edition Back to Back Materials

RANDOM INSERTS IN PACKS
PRINT RUNS B/WN 35-250 COPIES PER
1 I.Davis/R.Jackson 5.00 12.00
2 J.Kipnis/R.Jackson 4.00 10.00
3 R.Grossman/Q.Latimore 3.00 8.00
4 B.Posey/W.Clark 15.00 40.00

2009 Donruss Elite Extra Edition Back to the Future Signatures

OVERALL AUTO ODDS 1:5 HOBBY
PRINT RUNS B/WN 1-99 COPIES PER
NO PRICING ON QTY 25 OR LESS
1 Allan Dykstra/99 3.00 8.00
2 Alan Horne/99 3.00 8.00
3 Jim Palmer/49 3.00 8.00
4 Andrew Cashner/99 4.00 10.00
5 Andrew Lambo/99 5.00 12.00
6 Anthony Hewitt/99 4.00 10.00
8 Brandon Crawford/99 8.00 20.00
9 Brett Hunter/99 3.00 8.00
10 Bryan Price/99 3.00 8.00
11 Buster Posey/99 15.00 40.00
12 Chase D'Arnaud/99 3.00 8.00
14 Christian Friedrich/99 6.00 15.00
16 Dwight Gooden/99 4.00 10.00
18 Evan Frederickson/99 4.00 10.00
19 Mark Fidrych/49 8.00 20.00
20 George Brett/30 40.00 80.00
22 Ike Davis/99 15.00 40.00
23 Jason Knapp/99 3.00 8.00
26 Logan Schafer/99 3.00 8.00
27 Michael Ynoa/99 4.00 10.00
28 Mike Cisco/50 3.00 8.00
32 Pete Rose/99 15.00 40.00
33 Rafael Rodriguez/99 3.00 8.00
35 Robin Yount/49 15.00 40.00
37 Steve Garvey/50 15.00 40.00
39 Zach McAllister/99 4.00 10.00
40 Zeke Spruill/99 3.00 8.00

2009 Donruss Elite Extra Edition College Ties Green

COMPLETE SET (10) 8.00 20.00
RANDOM INSERTS IN PACKS
*GOLD: .6X TO 1.5X BASIC
GOLD RANDOMLY INSERTED
GOLD PRINT RUN 100 SER.#'d SETS
RED RANDOMLY INSERTED
RED PRINT RUN 25 SER.#'d SETS
NO RED PRICING AVAILABLE
1 D.Ackley/A.White 1.00 2.50
2 M.Leake/J.Kipnis 1.25 3.00
3 Mike Minor/Caleb Cotham .60 1.50
4 J.Kipnis/I.Davis 1.25 3.00
5 Brad Boxberger/Robert Stock .60 1.50
6 Garrett Richards/Jamie Johnson 1.00 2.50
7 Chase Anderson/Aaron Baker .40 1.00
8 Shaver Hansen/Dustin Dickerson .60 1.50
9 Kendal Volz/Aaron Miller .60 1.50
10 Brooks Raley/Jose Duran .60 1.50
11 Robert Stock/Grant Green .60 1.50
12 Chad Jenkins/Kyle Heckathorn .60 1.50
13 Eric Arnett/Josh Phegley .60 1.50
14 Matt Bashore/Josh Phegley .60 1.50
15 Jared Mitchell/D.J. LeMahieu 2.50 6.00
16 Victor Black/Ryan Goins .60 1.50
17 B.Jackson/J.Kobernus 1.25 3.00
18 B.Jackson/B.Smith 1.25 3.00
19 Trevor Holder/Rich Poythress .40 1.00
20 J.Danks/B.Belt 1.00 2.50

2009 Donruss Elite Extra Edition College Ties Autographs

OVERALL AUTO ODDS 1:5 HOBBY
PRINT RUNS B/WN 4-50 COPIES PER
NO PRICING ON QTY 25 OR LESS
EXCHANGE DEADLINE 7/20/2011
1 Ackley/White/50 20.00 50.00
2 Leake/Kipnis/50 EXCH 8.00 20.00
3 Minor/Cotham/50 5.00 12.00
4 Kipnis/Davis/50 10.00 25.00
5 Boxberger/Stock/50 8.00 20.00
7 Chase Anderson/Aaron Baker/50 5.00 12.00
8 Shaver Hansen/Dustin Dickerson/50 5.00 12.00
9 Kendal Volz/Aaron Miller/50 5.00 12.00
11 Stock/Green/50 8.00 20.00
12 Jenkins/Heckathorn/50 6.00 15.00
13 Arnett/Phegley/50 10.00 25.00
14 Bashore/Phegley/50 8.00 20.00
16 V.Black/RGoins/50 6.00 15.00
17 Jackson/Kobernus/50 6.00 15.00
18 B.Jackson/B.Smith/50 10.00 25.00
19 Holder/Poythress/50 8.00 20.00

2009 Donruss Elite Extra Edition College Ties Jerseys

RANDOM INSERTS IN PACKS
STATED PRINT RUN 250 SER.#'d SETS
7 Chase Anderson/Aaron Baker 3.00 8.00
10 Brooks Raley/Jose Duran 3.00 8.00

2009 Donruss Elite Extra Edition Collegiate Patches Autographs

OVERALL AUTO ODDS 1:5 HOBBY
PRINT RUNS B/WN 104-125 COPIES PER
EXCHANGE DEADLINE 7/20/2011
1 Dustin Ackley/118 5.00 12.00
2 Tony Sanchez/125 10.00 25.00
3 Mike Minor/125 8.00 20.00
4 Mike Leake/125 6.00 15.00
5 Drew Storen/125 8.00 20.00
6 Grant Green/125 8.00 20.00
7 Alex White/124 12.50 30.00
8 A.J. Pollock/123 12.00 30.00
9 Jared Mitchell/125 10.00 25.00
10 Eric Arnett/125 6.00 15.00
11 Brett Jackson/125 6.00 15.00
12 Aaron Miller/117 5.00 12.00
13 Josh Phegley/125 5.00 12.00
14 Kentrail Davis/125 8.00 20.00
15 Garrett Richards/104 12.00 30.00
16 Brad Boxberger/125 8.00 20.00
17 Matt Bashore/124 5.00 12.00
18 Jeff Kobernus/125 6.00 15.00
19 Rich Poythress/124 15.00 40.00
20 Blake Smith/125 4.00 10.00
21 Andrew Oliver/125 6.00 15.00
22 Tom Mendonca/125 5.00 12.00
23 Jason Kipnis/125 10.00 25.00
24 Marc Krauss/120 8.00 20.00
25 Robert Stock/125 8.00 20.00
26 Bill Bullock/125 5.00 12.00
27 Alex Wilson/125 4.00 10.00
28 D.J. LeMahieu/125 20.00 50.00
29 Trevor Holder/125 4.00 10.00
30 Donnie Joseph/125 4.00 10.00
31 Ben Paulsen/125 5.00 12.00
32 Kent Matthes/125 5.00 12.00
33 Adam Warren/125 8.00 20.00
34 Brandon Belt/125 15.00 40.00
35 Ryan Jackson/125 6.00 15.00
36 Caleb Cotham/125 10.00 25.00
37 Shaver Hansen/124 6.00 15.00
38 Josh Fellhauer/125 4.00 10.00
39 Jamie Johnson/125 4.00 10.00
40 Khris Davis/125 EXCH 30.00 80.00
41 Dustin Dickerson/125 4.00 10.00
42 Brock Holt/125 15.00 40.00
43 Charles Ruiz/125 4.00 10.00
44 Aaron Baker/125 3.00 8.00
45 Mike Spina/125 5.00 12.00
46 Jim Abbott/125 10.00 25.00
47 Fred Lynn/125 6.00 15.00
48 John Olerud/125 EXCH 10.00 25.00
49 Robin Ventura/125 5.00 12.00

2009 Donruss Elite Extra Edition Elite Series

RANDOM INSERTS IN PACKS
1 Dustin Ackley .75 2.00
2 Donavan Tate .75 2.00
3 Mike Leake 1.50 4.00
4 Tony Sanchez 1.25 3.00
5 Al Kaline 1.25 3.00
6 Mike Minor .75 2.00
7 A.J. Pollock 1.25 3.00
8 Nolan Ryan 4.00 10.00
9 Will Clark .75 2.00
10 Albert Pujols 1.50 4.00

2009 Donruss Elite Extra Edition Elite Series Autographs

OVERALL AUTO ODDS 1:5 HOBBY
PRINT RUNS B/WN 20-199 COPIES PER
NO PRICING ON QTY 20 OR LESS
1 Dustin Ackley/100 5.00 12.00
2 Donavan Tate/199 10.00 25.00
3 Mike Leake/100 6.00 15.00
4 Tony Sanchez/100 6.00 15.00
5 Al Kaline/100 20.00 50.00
6 Mike Minor/40 10.00 25.00
7 A.J. Pollock/100 8.00 20.00
8 Nolan Ryan/50 50.00 100.00
9 Will Clark/52 15.00 40.00

2009 Donruss Elite Extra Edition Passing the Torch Autographs

OVERALL AUTO ODDS 1:5 HOBBY
PRINT RUNS B/WN 5-100 COPIES PER
NO PRICING ON QTY 25 OR LESS
1 Posey/Sanchez/100 30.00 60.00

2009 Donruss Elite Extra Edition Private Signings

OVERALL AUTO ODDS 1:5 HOBBY
PRINT RUNS B/WN 5-250 COPIES PER
NO PRICING ON QTY 25 OR LESS
EXCHANGE DEADLINE 7/20/2011
3 Bobby Borchering/50 12.50 30.00
6 Donavan Tate/245 6.00 20.00
7 Drew Storen/100 6.00 15.00
8 Dustin Ackley/250 5.00 12.00
10 Grant Green/50 6.00 15.00
11 Jacob Turner/100 12.00 30.00
13 Kyle Gibson/50 10.00 25.00
15 Matt Hobgood/100 20.00 50.00
16 Mike Leake/50 10.00 25.00
18 Mike Minor/50 6.00 15.00
20 Slade Heathcott/50 20.00 50.00
23 Tony Sanchez/50 15.00 40.00
24 Tyler Matzek/100 6.00 15.00
25 Zack Wheeler/100 6.00 15.00

2009 Donruss Elite Extra Edition School Colors

COMPLETE SET (20) 8.00 20.00
RANDOM INSERTS IN PACKS
1 Dustin Ackley .60 1.50
2 Grant Green .40 1.00
3 Mike Leake 1.25 3.00
4 Drew Storen .60 1.50
5 Jared Mitchell .60 1.50
6 Ryan Jackson .40 1.00
7 Tom Mendonca .40 1.00
8 Josh Phegley .60 1.50
9 A.J. Pollock 1.00 2.50
10 Tony Sanchez 1.00 2.50
11 Marc Krauss .40 1.00
12 Garrett Richards 1.00 2.50
13 Shaver Hansen .40 1.00
14 Josh Fellhauer .40 1.00
15 Brandon Belt 1.00 2.50
16 Bill Bullock .40 1.00
17 Mike Minor .60 1.50
18 Kent Matthes .40 1.00
19 Ben Paulsen .40 1.00
20 Aaron Baker .40 1.00

2009 Donruss Elite Extra Edition School Colors Autographs

OVERALL AUTO ODDS 1:5 HOBBY
PRINT RUNS B/WN 20-100 COPIES PER
NO PRICING ON QTY 20 OR LESS
1 Dustin Ackley/100 5.00 12.00
2 Grant Green/100 5.00 12.00
3 Mike Leake/100 20.00 50.00
4 Drew Storen/100 6.00 15.00
5 Jared Mitchell/100 12.00 30.00
6 Ryan Jackson/100 4.00 10.00
7 Tom Mendonca/100 6.00 15.00
9 A.J. Pollock/100 8.00 20.00
10 Tony Sanchez/100 8.00 20.00
11 Marc Krauss/100 4.00 10.00
12 Garrett Richards/100 12.00 30.00
13 Shaver Hansen/100 3.00 8.00
14 Josh Fellhauer/100 3.00 8.00
15 Brandon Belt/100 6.00 15.00
16 Bill Bullock/100 3.00 8.00
18 Kent Matthes/100 6.00 15.00
19 Ben Paulsen/100 3.00 8.00
20 Aaron Baker/100 3.00 8.00

2009 Donruss Elite Extra Edition School Colors Materials

RANDOM INSERTS IN PACKS
STATED PRINT RUN 250 SER.#'d SETS
5 Jared Mitchell 3.00 8.00
13 Shaver Hansen 3.00 8.00
16 Bill Bullock 3.00 8.00
17 Mike Minor 3.00 8.00
20 Aaron Baker 3.00 8.00

2009 Donruss Elite Extra Edition Throwback Threads

RANDOM INSERTS IN PACKS
PRINT RUNS B/WN 50-250 COPIES PER
TTMT Mike Trout/250 150.00 400.00
2 Shelby Miller/250 6.00 15.00
3 Mike Minor/250 3.00 8.00
4 Jason Kipnis/250 4.00 10.00
5 Bill Bullock/250 3.00 8.00
6 Jared Mitchell/250 3.00 8.00
9 Kyle Russell/250 3.00 8.00
10 Jose Duran/250 3.00 8.00
11 Buster Posey/149 4.00 10.00
14 Pete Rose/250 10.00 25.00
16 Robbie Grossman/250 3.00 8.00
17 Shaver Hansen/250 3.00 8.00
18 Tim Wheeler/250 3.00 8.00
19 Josh Vitters/50 4.00 10.00
20 Todd Glaesmann/250 3.00 8.00
21 Mike Cisco/250 3.00 8.00
22 Aaron Baker/250 3.00 8.00
23 Chase Anderson/250 3.00 8.00
24 Brooks Raley/250 3.00 8.00

2009 Donruss Elite Extra Edition Throwback Threads Autographs

OVERALL AUTO ODDS 1:5 HOBBY
PRINT RUNS B/WN 5-250 COPIES PER
NO PRICING ON QTY 25 OR LESS
EXCHANGE DEADLINE 7/20/2011
1 Mike Trout/100 500.00 800.00
2 Shelby Miller/100 12.00 30.00
3 Mike Minor/53 12.50 30.00
4 Jason Kipnis/100 15.00 40.00
5 Bill Bullock/199 4.00 10.00
6 Jared Mitchell/149 10.00 25.00
14 Pete Rose/149 20.00 50.00
20 Todd Glaesmann/250 4.00 10.00
21 Mike Cisco/250 4.00 10.00
23 Chase Anderson/100 4.00 10.00
24 Brooks Raley/250 4.00 10.00

2009 Donruss Elite Extra Edition Throwback Threads Autographs Prime

*PRIME: .6X TO 1.5X BASIC
OVERALL AUTO ODDS 1:5 HOBBY
PRINT RUNS B/WN 1-50 COPIES PER
NO PRICING ON QTY 25 OR LESS

2010 Donruss Elite Extra Edition

COMP.SET w/o AU's (100) 10.00 25.00
COMMON CARD (1-100) .20 .50
COMMON AUTO (101-200) 3.00 8.00
AU SEMIS 4.00 10.00
AU UNLISTED 5.00 12.00
OVERALL AUTO ODDS 6 PER BOX
AUTO PRINT RUNS B/WN 99-825 COPIES PER
EXCHANGE DEADLINE 4/6/2012
1 Bryce Brentz .50 1.25
2 Drew Vettleson .30 .75
3 Mike Olt .60 1.50
4 Tyrell Jenkins .60 1.50
5 Delino DeShields Jr. .30 .75
6 Asher Wojciechowski .50 1.25
7 Bobby Doran .20 .50
8 Hunter Morris .20 .50
9 J.R. Bradley .20 .50
10 Nick Castellanos 1.00 2.50
11 Chad Bettis .20 .50
12 Drew Robinson .50 1.25
13 Aaron Sanchez .75 2.00
14 Brandon Workman .20 .50
15 Matt Moore 1.50 4.00
16 Cole Leonida .20 .50
17 Seth Rosin .30 .75
18 Josh Rutledge 1.25 3.00
19 Vincent Velasquez .75 2.00
20 Matt den Dekker .30 .75
21 Rett Varner .20 .50
22 Reggie Golden .20 .50
23 Derek Dietrich .50 1.25
24 Robbie Aviles .20 .50
25 DeAngelo Mack .30 .75
26 Alex Wimmers .30 .75
28 Mike Antonio .20 .50
29 Andy Wilkins .20 .50
30 Cody Buckel .50 1.25
31 Kevin Munson .20 .50
32 Chris Hawkins .20 .50
33 Drew Smyly .30 .75
34 Gary Sanchez 2.00 5.00
35 Dan Klein .20 .50
36 Yordy Cabrera .30 .75
37 Ralston Cash .20 .50
38 Jonathan Galvez .20 .50
39 Sam Dyson .20 .50
40 Rob Segedin .20 .50
41 Jimmy Nelson .20 .50
42 Daniel Tillman .20 .50
43 Raoul Torrez .20 .50
44 Sammy Solis .50 1.25
45 Austin Wates .20 .50
46 Matt Harvey 1.25 3.00
47 Connor Narron .30 .75
48 Bryan Morgado .30 .75
49 Chris Hernandez .20 .50
50 Hayden Simpson .30 .75
51 Brooks Hall .30 .75
52 Devin Lohman .20 .50
53 Pat Dean .20 .50
54 Gary Brown 1.00 2.50
55 Stetson Allie .30 .75
56 Griffin Murphy .30 .75
57 Jake Thompson .20 .50
58 Cody Wheeler .20 .50
59 Niko Goodrum .60 1.50
60 Rob Brantly .20 .50
61 Austin Ross .20 .50
62 Kevin Rath .20 .50
63 A.J. Cole .30 .75
64 Scott Lawson .30 .75
65 Logan Bawcom .20 .50
66 Connor Powers .20 .50
67 Mike Nesseth .30 .75
68 Jose Vinicio .30 .75
69 Ryan Casteel .20 .50
70 Rick Hague .20 .50
71 Kyle Blair .20 .50
72 Jordan Swagerty .50 1.25
73 Jake Anderson .20 .50
74 Brian Garman .20 .50
75 Mark Canha .50 1.25
76 Perci Garner .30 .75
77 Edinson Rincon .20 .50
78 Jonathan Jones .20 .50
79 Ross Wilson .20 .50
80 Mel Rojas Jr. .20 .50
81 Luke Jackson .30 .75
82 Cole Nelson .20 .50
83 David Filak .20 .50
84 Kyle Bellows .20 .50
85 Sam Tuivailala .30 .75
86 Cole Cook .20 .50
87 Jesse Hahn .20 .50
88 A.J. Griffin .20 .50
89 Max Walla .20 .50
90 Jurickson Profar .50 1.25
91 Zach Cates .20 .50
92 Ronald Torreyes .60 1.50
93 Marcus Littlewood .30 .75
94 Parker Bridwell .50 1.25
95 Tyler Austin .50 1.25
96 Rob Rasmussen .20 .50
97 Seth Blair .30 .75
98 Tyler Holt .20 .50
99 Micah Gibbs .30 .75
100 Pamela Anderson .50 1.25
101 Michael Choice AU/470 6.00 15.00
102 C.Colon AU/432 6.00 15.00
103 Chris Sale AU/655 30.00 80.00
104 Jake Skole AU/675 5.00 12.00
105 Mike Foltynewicz AU/653 6.00 15.00
106 Kolbrin Vitek AU/542 4.00 10.00
107 Kellin Deglan AU/640 3.00 8.00
108 Jesse Biddle AU/800 6.00 15.00
109 Justin O'Conner AU/794 4.00 10.00
110 Cito Culver AU/589 3.00 8.00
111 Mike Kvasnicka AU/530 3.00 8.00
112 Matt Lipka AU/722 5.00 12.00
113 N.Syndergaard AU/809 10.00 25.00
114 Ryan LaMarre AU/564 3.00 8.00
115 Josh Sale AU/536 6.00 15.00
116 Zack Cox AU/478 6.00 15.00
117 Bryan Holaday AU/500 3.00 8.00
118 Todd Cunningham AU/699 4.00 10.00
119 Jarrett Parker AU/580 4.00 10.00
120 Leon Landry AU/550 4.00 10.00
121 Cam Bedrosian AU/652 4.00 10.00
122 Ryan Bolden AU/799 3.00 8.00
123 Cameron Rupp AU/498 5.00 12.00
124 Jedd Gyorko AU/675 4.00 10.00
125 Matt Curry AU/209 3.00 8.00
126 Drew Pomeranz AU/527 8.00 20.00
127 Yasmani Grandal AU/395 4.00 10.00
128 Deck McGuire AU/441 10.00 25.00
129 Chevez Clarke AU/799 5.00 12.00
130 Jameson Taillon AU/699 6.00 15.00
131 Kaleb Cowart AU/750 4.00 10.00
132 Manny Machado AU/425 40.00 100.00
133 Tony Thompson AU/199 4.00 10.00
134 Dee Gordon AU/310 5.00 12.00
135 Chance Ruffin AU/550 3.00 8.00
136 J.Realmuto AU/99 50.00 120.00
137 Kevin Chapman AU/694 3.00 8.00
138 Kyle Roller AU/810 3.00 8.00
139 Stephen Pryor AU/819 5.00 12.00
140 Jonathan Singleton AU/699 4.00 10.00
141 Drew Cisco AU/399 4.00 10.00
142 Blake Forsythe AU/401 4.00 10.00
143 Kellen Sweeney AU/819 3.00 8.00
144 Brett Eibner AU/545 5.00 12.00
145 Martin Perez AU/494 10.00 25.00
146 Jean Segura AU/811 8.00 20.00
147 Christian Yelich AU/815 40.00 100.00
148 Robby Rowland AU/799 3.00 8.00
149 Trent Mummey AU/694 3.00 8.00
150 Zach Lee AU/650 6.00 15.00
151 Jason Mitchell AU/600 3.00 8.00
152 Nick Longmire AU/819 4.00 10.00
153 Robbie Erlin AU/699 3.00 8.00
154 Addison Reed AU/601 4.00 10.00
155 Austin Reed AU/499 4.00 10.00
156 Tyler Thornburg AU/819 5.00 12.00
157 Ty Linton AU/99 5.00 12.00
158 Chris Balcom-Miller AU/819 3.00 8.00
159 Wes Mugarian AU/799 3.00 8.00
161 Justin Grimm AU/99 8.00 20.00
162 Alex Lavisky AU/499 4.00 10.00
163 Taijuan Walker AU/819 6.00 15.00
164 Arodys Vizcaino AU/770 4.00 10.00
165 Brody Colvin AU/819 6.00 15.00
166 Christian Carmichael AU/815 3.00 8.00
167 Josh Spence AU/699 3.00 8.00
168 Joc Pederson AU/799 10.00 25.00
169 Justin Nicolino AU/399 8.00 20.00
170 Nick Tepesch AU/550 4.00 10.00
171 Joe Gardner AU/819 3.00 8.00
172 Taylor Morton AU/815 4.00 10.00
173 Jason Martinson AU/815 3.00 8.00
174 Matt Miller AU/585 3.00 8.00
175 Justin Bloxom AU/790 3.00 8.00
176 Matt Suschak AU/780 3.00 8.00
177 Zach Neal AU/750 3.00 8.00
178 Ben Gamel AU/801 5.00 12.00
179 Jimmy Reyes AU/810 3.00 8.00
180 Matt Price AU/699 3.00 8.00
181 Aaron Shipman AU/701 3.00 8.00
182 Hector Noesi AU/819 6.00 15.00
183 Peter Tago AU/649 3.00 8.00
184 Kyle Knudson AU/825 3.00 8.00
185 M.Kirkland AU/99 5.00 12.00
186 Mickey Wiswall AU/499 3.00 8.00
187 Steve Geltz AU/599 3.00 8.00
188 Shawn Tolleson AU/815 3.00 8.00
189 Greg Holle AU/810 3.00 8.00
190 Erik Goeddel AU/810 3.00 8.00
191 Paul Goldschmidt AU/820 25.00 60.00
192 L.Washington AU/199 6.00 15.00
193 Trey McNutt AU/249 8.00 20.00
194 Henry Rodriguez AU/620 5.00 12.00
195 Adrian Sanchez AU/620 4.00 10.00
196 Daniel Bibona AU/420 3.00 8.00
197 Chad Lewis AU/799 3.00 8.00
198 Brodie Greene AU/625 3.00 8.00
199 Carter Jurica AU/685 3.00 8.00
200 A.Ranaudo AU/150 12.50 30.00

2010 Donruss Elite Extra Edition Aspirations

*ASP 1-100: 2X TO 5X BASIC
RANDOM INSERTS IN PACKS
STATED PRINT RUN 200 SER.#'d SETS
100 Pamela Anderson 8.00 20.00
101 Michael Choice 1.50 4.00
102 Christian Colon 1.50 4.00
103 Chris Sale 15.00 40.00
104 Jake Skole 1.50 4.00
105 Mike Foltynewicz 2.50 6.00
106 Kolbrin Vitek 2.50 6.00
107 Kellin Deglan 1.00 2.50
108 Jesse Biddle 1.50 4.00
109 Justin O'Conner 1.00 2.50
110 Cito Culver 1.50 4.00
111 Mike Kvasnicka 1.50 4.00
112 Matt Lipka 4.00 10.00
113 Noah Syndergaard 4.00 10.00
114 Ryan LaMarre 1.50 4.00
115 Josh Sale 3.00 8.00
116 Zack Cox 3.00 8.00
117 Bryan Holaday
118 Todd Cunningham 1.50 4.00
119 Jarrett Parker 3.00 8.00
120 Leon Landry 2.50 6.00
121 Cam Bedrosian 1.50 4.00
122 Ryan Bolden 1.00 2.50
123 Cameron Rupp 1.50 4.00
124 Jedd Gyorko 1.50 4.00
125 Matt Curry 1.50 4.00
126 Drew Pomeranz 2.50 6.00
127 Yasmani Grandal 1.50 4.00
128 Deck McGuire 1.50 4.00
129 Chevez Clarke 1.50 4.00
130 Jameson Taillon 1.50 4.00
131 Kaleb Cowart 1.50 4.00
132 Manny Machado 30.00 80.00
133 Tony Thompson 1.00 2.50
134 Dee Gordon 2.00 5.00
135 Chance Ruffin 1.00 2.50
136 J.T. Realmuto 12.00 30.00
137 Kevin Chapman 1.00 2.50
138 Kyle Roller 1.50 4.00
139 Stephen Pryor 1.00 2.50
140 Jonathan Singleton 2.50 6.00
141 Drew Cisco 1.50 4.00
142 Blake Forsythe 1.00 2.50
143 Kellen Sweeney 1.50 4.00
144 Brett Eibner 2.50 6.00
145 Martin Perez 2.50 6.00
146 Jean Segura 5.00 12.00
147 Christian Yelich 12.00 30.00
148 Robby Rowland 1.00 2.50
149 Trent Mummey 1.00 2.50
150 Zach Lee 2.50 6.00
151 Jason Mitchell 1.00 2.50
152 Nick Longmire 1.50 4.00
153 Robbie Erlin 2.50 6.00
154 Addison Reed 2.50 6.00
155 Austin Reed 1.00 2.50
156 Tyler Thornburg 2.50 6.00
157 Ty Linton 1.00 2.50
158 Chris Balcom-Miller 1.50 4.00
159 Wes Mugarian 1.00 2.50
160 Tony Wolters 1.50 4.00
161 Justin Grimm 1.50 4.00
162 Alex Lavisky 1.50 4.00
163 Taijuan Walker 2.50 6.00
164 Arodys Vizcaino 2.50 6.00
165 Brody Colvin 1.50 4.00
166 Christian Carmichael 1.50 4.00
167 Josh Spence 1.00 2.50
168 Joc Pederson 4.00 10.00
169 Justin Nicolino 1.50 4.00
170 Nick Tepesch 6.00 15.00
171 Joe Gardner 1.00 2.50
172 Taylor Morton 2.50 6.00
173 Jason Martinson 1.00 2.50
174 Matt Miller 1.00 2.50
175 Justin Bloxom 1.00 2.50
176 Matt Suschak 1.00 2.50
177 Zach Neal 1.00 2.50
178 Ben Gamel 1.50 4.00
179 Jimmy Reyes 1.00 2.50
180 Matt Price 1.00 2.50
181 Aaron Shipman 1.50 4.00
182 Hector Noesi 1.50 4.00
183 Peter Tago 1.50 4.00
184 Kyle Knudson 1.00 2.50
185 Matt Kirkland 1.00 2.50
186 Mickey Wiswall 1.00 2.50
187 Steve Geltz 1.00 2.50
188 Shawn Tolleson 1.00 2.50
189 Greg Holle 1.50 4.00
190 Erik Goeddel 1.50 4.00
191 Paul Goldschmidt 10.00 25.00
192 LeVon Washington 1.50 4.00
193 Trey McNutt 1.00 2.50
194 Henry Rodriguez 1.00 2.50
195 Adrian Sanchez 1.00 2.50
196 Daniel Bibona 1.50 4.00
197 Chad Lewis 1.50 4.00
198 Brodie Greene 1.00 2.50
199 Carter Jurica 1.00 2.50
200 Anthony Ranaudo 3.00 8.00

2010 Donruss Elite Extra Edition Status

*STATUS 1-100: 2.5X TO 6X BASIC
RANDOM INSERTS IN PACKS
STATED PRINT RUN 100 SER.#'d SETS
100 Pamela Anderson 10.00 25.00
101 Michael Choice 2.00 5.00
102 Christian Colon 2.00 5.00
103 Chris Sale 20.00 50.00
104 Jake Skole 2.00 5.00
105 Mike Foltynewicz 3.00 8.00
106 Kolbrin Vitek 3.00 8.00
107 Kellin Deglan 1.25 3.00
108 Jesse Biddle 2.00 5.00
109 Justin O'Conner 1.25 3.00
110 Cito Culver 2.00 5.00
111 Mike Kvasnicka 2.00 5.00
112 Matt Lipka 5.00 12.00
113 Noah Syndergaard 5.00 12.00
114 Ryan LaMarre 2.00 5.00
115 Josh Sale 4.00 10.00
116 Zack Cox 4.00 10.00
117 Bryan Holaday
118 Todd Cunningham 2.00 5.00
119 Jarrett Parker 4.00 10.00
120 Leon Landry 3.00 8.00
121 Cam Bedrosian 2.00 5.00
122 Ryan Bolden 1.25 3.00
123 Cameron Rupp 2.00 5.00
124 Jedd Gyorko 2.00 5.00
125 Matt Curry 2.00 5.00
126 Drew Pomeranz 3.00 8.00
127 Yasmani Grandal 2.00 5.00
128 Deck McGuire 2.00 5.00
129 Chevez Clarke 2.00 5.00
130 Jameson Taillon 2.00 5.00
131 Kaleb Cowart 2.00 5.00
132 Manny Machado 40.00 100.00
133 Tony Thompson 1.25 3.00
134 Dee Gordon 2.50 6.00
135 Chance Ruffin 1.25 3.00
136 J.T. Realmuto 15.00 40.00
137 Kevin Chapman 1.25 3.00
138 Kyle Roller 2.00 5.00
139 Stephen Pryor 1.25 3.00
140 Jonathan Singleton 3.00 8.00
141 Drew Cisco 2.00 5.00
142 Blake Forsythe 1.25 3.00
143 Kellen Sweeney 2.00 5.00
144 Brett Eibner 3.00 8.00
145 Martin Perez 3.00 8.00
146 Jean Segura 6.00 15.00
147 Christian Yelich 15.00 40.00
148 Robby Rowland 1.25 3.00
149 Trent Mummey 1.25 3.00
150 Zach Lee 3.00 8.00
151 Jason Mitchell 1.25 3.00
152 Nick Longmire 2.00 5.00
153 Robbie Erlin 3.00 8.00
154 Addison Reed 3.00 8.00
155 Austin Reed 1.25 3.00
156 Tyler Thornburg 3.00 8.00
157 Ty Linton 1.25 3.00
158 Chris Balcom-Miller 2.00 5.00
159 Wes Mugarian 1.25 3.00
160 Tony Wolters 2.00 5.00
161 Justin Grimm 2.00 5.00
162 Alex Lavisky 2.00 5.00
163 Taijuan Walker 3.00 8.00
164 Arodys Vizcaino 3.00 8.00
165 Brody Colvin 2.00 5.00
166 Christian Carmichael 2.00 5.00
167 Josh Spence 1.25 3.00
168 Joc Pederson 5.00 12.00
169 Justin Nicolino 2.00 5.00
170 Nick Tepesch 8.00 20.00
171 Joe Gardner 1.25 3.00
172 Taylor Morton 3.00 8.00
173 Jason Martinson 1.25 3.00
174 Matt Miller 1.25 3.00
175 Justin Bloxom 1.25 3.00
176 Matt Suschak 1.25 3.00
177 Zach Neal 1.25 3.00
178 Ben Gamel 2.00 5.00
179 Jimmy Reyes 1.25 3.00
180 Matt Price 1.25 3.00
181 Aaron Shipman 2.00 5.00
182 Hector Noesi 2.00 5.00
183 Peter Tago 2.00 5.00
184 Kyle Knudson 1.25 3.00
185 Matt Kirkland 1.25 3.00
186 Mickey Wiswall 1.25 3.00
187 Steve Geltz 1.25 3.00
188 Shawn Tolleson 1.25 3.00
189 Greg Holle 2.00 5.00
190 Erik Goeddel 2.00 5.00
191 Paul Goldschmidt 12.00 30.00
192 LeVon Washington 2.00 5.00
193 Trey McNutt 1.25 3.00
194 Henry Rodriguez 1.25 3.00
195 Adrian Sanchez 1.25 3.00
196 Daniel Bibona 2.00 5.00
197 Chad Lewis 2.00 5.00
198 Brodie Greene 1.25 3.00
199 Carter Jurica 1.25 3.00
200 Anthony Ranaudo 4.00 10.00

2010 Donruss Elite Extra Edition Signature Aspirations

OVERALL AUTO ODDS SIX PER BOX
STATED PRINT RUN 100 SER.#'d SETS
EXCHANGE DEADLINE 4/6/2012
1 Bryce Brentz 15.00 40.00
2 Drew Vettleson 10.00 25.00
3 Mike Olt 8.00 20.00
4 Tyrell Jenkins 6.00 15.00
5 Delino DeShields Jr. 8.00 20.00
6 Asher Wojciechowski 8.00 20.00
7 Bobby Doran 3.00 8.00
8 Hunter Morris 6.00 15.00
9 J.R. Bradley 4.00 10.00
10 Nick Castellanos 10.00 25.00
11 Chad Bettis 5.00 12.00
12 Drew Robinson 5.00 12.00
13 Aaron Sanchez 10.00 25.00
14 Brandon Workman 8.00 20.00
15 Matt Moore 6.00 15.00
16 Cole Leonida 5.00 12.00
17 Seth Rosin 3.00 8.00
18 Josh Rutledge 3.00 8.00
19 Vincent Velasquez 12.00 30.00
20 Matt den Dekker 8.00 20.00
21 Rett Varner 3.00 8.00
22 Reggie Golden 3.00 8.00
23 Derek Dietrich 40.00 100.00
24 Robbie Aviles 6.00 15.00
25 DeAngelo Mack 10.00 25.00
26 Alex Wimmers 6.00 15.00
28 Mike Antonio 5.00 12.00
29 Andy Wilkins 5.00 12.00
30 Cody Buckel 4.00 10.00
31 Kevin Munson 4.00 10.00
32 Chris Hawkins 10.00 25.00
33 Drew Smyly 12.50 30.00
34 Gary Sanchez 60.00 150.00
35 Dan Klein 3.00 8.00
36 Yordy Cabrera 8.00 20.00
37 Ralston Cash 4.00 10.00
38 Jonathan Galvez 3.00 8.00
39 Sam Dyson 4.00 10.00
40 Rob Segedin 5.00 12.00
41 Jimmy Nelson 8.00 20.00
42 Daniel Tillman 4.00 10.00
43 Raoul Torrez 3.00 8.00
44 Sammy Solis 4.00 10.00
45 Austin Wates 5.00 12.00
46 Matt Harvey 75.00 150.00
47 Connor Narron 4.00 10.00
48 Bryan Morgado 4.00 10.00
49 Chris Hernandez 4.00 10.00
50 Hayden Simpson 10.00 25.00
51 Brooks Hall 8.00 20.00
52 Devin Lohman 4.00 10.00
53 Pat Dean 10.00 25.00
54 Gary Brown 15.00 40.00
55 Stetson Allie 8.00 20.00
56 Griffin Murphy 8.00 20.00
57 Jake Thompson 4.00 10.00
58 Cody Wheeler 3.00 8.00
59 Niko Goodrum 10.00 25.00
60 Rob Brantly 5.00 12.00
61 Austin Ross 4.00 10.00

62 Kevin Rath 3.00 8.00
63 A.J. Cole 3.00 8.00
64 Scott Lawson 3.00 8.00
65 Logan Bawcom 3.00 8.00
66 Connor Powers 3.00 8.00
67 Mike Nesseth 3.00 8.00
68 Jose Vinicio 6.00 15.00
69 Ryan Casteel 4.00 10.00
70 Rick Hague 4.00 10.00
71 Kyle Blair 4.00 10.00
72 Swagerty UER Magic AU 15.00 40.00
73 Jake Anderson 5.00 12.00
74 Brian Garman 3.00 8.00
75 Mark Canha 5.00 12.00
76 Perci Garner 4.00 10.00
77 Edinson Rincon 4.00 10.00
78 Jonathan Jones 5.00 12.00
79 Ross Wilson 3.00 8.00
80 Mel Rojas Jr. 5.00 12.00
81 Luke Jackson 3.00 8.00
82 Cole Nelson 4.00 10.00
83 David Filak 4.00 10.00
84 Kyle Bellows 4.00 10.00
85 Sam Tuivailala 4.00 10.00
86 Cole Cook 4.00 10.00
87 Jesse Hahn 3.00 8.00
88 A.J. Griffin 10.00 25.00
89 Max Walla 8.00 20.00
90 Jurickson Profar 12.00 30.00
91 Zach Cates 4.00 10.00
92 Ronald Torreyes 12.00 30.00
93 Marcus Littlewood 6.00 15.00
94 Parker Bridwell 10.00 25.00
95 Tyler Austin 5.00 12.00
96 Rob Rasmussen 4.00 10.00
97 Seth Blair 5.00 12.00
98 Tyler Holt 6.00 15.00
99 Micah Gibbs 6.00 15.00
101 Michael Choice 6.00 15.00
102 Christian Colon 4.00 10.00
103 Chris Sale 40.00 100.00
104 Jake Skole 5.00 12.00
105 Mike Foltynewicz 12.00 30.00
106 Kolbrin Vitek 6.00 15.00
107 Kellin Deglan 3.00 8.00
108 Jesse Biddle 3.00 8.00
109 Justin O'Conner 5.00 12.00
110 Cito Culver 3.00 8.00
111 Mike Kvasnicka 5.00 12.00
112 Matt Lipka 3.00 8.00
113 Noah Syndergaard 15.00 40.00
114 Ryan LaMarre 6.00 15.00
115 Josh Sale 15.00 40.00
116 Zack Cox 6.00 15.00
117 Bryan Holaday 5.00 12.00
118 Todd Cunningham 6.00 15.00
119 Jarrett Parker 6.00 15.00
120 Leon Landry 6.00 15.00
121 Cam Bedrosian 6.00 15.00
122 Ryan Bolden 5.00 12.00
123 Cameron Rupp 6.00 15.00
124 Jedd Gyorko 20.00 50.00
125 Matt Curry 10.00 25.00
126 Drew Pomeranz 15.00 40.00
127 Yasmani Grandal 6.00 15.00
128 Deck McGuire 8.00 20.00
129 Chevez Clarke 5.00 12.00
130 Jameson Taillon 15.00 40.00
131 Kaleb Cowart 12.50 30.00
132 Manny Machado 75.00 200.00
133 Tony Thompson 4.00 10.00
134 Dee Gordon 12.00 30.00
135 Chance Ruffin 4.00 10.00
136 J.T. Realmuto 50.00 120.00
137 Kevin Chapman 4.00 10.00
138 Kyle Roller 6.00 15.00
139 Stephen Pryor 10.00 25.00
140 Jonathan Singleton 12.00 30.00
141 Drew Cisco 6.00 15.00
142 Blake Forsythe 4.00 10.00
143 Kellen Sweeney 10.00 25.00
144 Brett Eibner 8.00 20.00
145 Martin Perez 12.00 30.00
146 Jean Segura 12.00 30.00
147 Christian Yelich 40.00 100.00
148 Robby Rowland 4.00 10.00
149 Trent Mummey 4.00 10.00
150 Zach Lee 6.00 15.00
151 Jason Mitchell 3.00 8.00
152 Nick Longmire 6.00 15.00
153 Robbie Erlin 5.00 12.00
154 Addison Reed 6.00 15.00
155 Austin Reed 3.00 8.00
156 Tyler Thornburg 3.00 8.00
157 Ty Linton 5.00 12.00
158 Chris Balcom-Miller 5.00 12.00
159 Wes Mugarian 3.00 8.00
160 Tony Wolters 4.00 10.00
161 Justin Grimm 5.00 12.00
162 Alex Lavisky 6.00 15.00
163 Taijuan Walker 12.00 30.00
164 Arodys Vizcaino 6.00 15.00
165 Brody Colvin 6.00 15.00
166 Christian Carmichael 4.00 10.00
167 Josh Spence 5.00 12.00
168 Joc Pederson 12.00 30.00
169 Justin Nicolino 3.00 8.00
170 Nick Tepesch 8.00 20.00
171 Joe Gardner 4.00 10.00
172 Taylor Morton 8.00 20.00
173 Jason Martinson 3.00 8.00
174 Matt Miller 6.00 15.00
175 Justin Bloxom 4.00 10.00
176 Matt Suschak 3.00 8.00
177 Zach Neal 4.00 10.00
178 Ben Gamel 8.00 20.00
179 Jimmy Reyes 3.00 8.00
180 Matt Price 3.00 8.00
181 Aaron Shipman 5.00 12.00
182 Hector Noesi 10.00 25.00
183 Peter Tago 5.00 12.00
184 Kyle Knudson 4.00 10.00
185 Matt Kirkland 3.00 8.00
186 Mickey Wiswall 3.00 8.00
187 Steve Geltz 3.00 8.00
188 Shawn Tolleson 4.00 10.00
189 Greg Holle 5.00 12.00
190 Erik Goeddel 4.00 10.00
191 Paul Goldschmidt 40.00 100.00
192 LeVon Washington 6.00 15.00
193 Trey McNutt 4.00 10.00
194 Henry Rodriguez 5.00 12.00
195 Adrian Sanchez 4.00 10.00
196 Daniel Bibona 3.00 8.00
197 Chad Lewis 5.00 12.00
198 Brodie Greene 4.00 10.00
200 Anthony Ranaudo 10.00 25.00

2010 Donruss Elite Extra Edition Signature Status

OVERALL AUTO ODDS SIX PER BOX
STATED PRINT RUN 50 SER.#'d SETS
EXCHANGE DEADLINE 4/6/2012
1 Bryce Brentz 15.00 40.00
2 Drew Vettleson 20.00 50.00
3 Mike Olt 10.00 25.00
4 Tyrell Jenkins 8.00 20.00
5 Delino DeShields Jr. 10.00 25.00
6 Asher Wojciechowski 5.00 12.00
7 Bobby Doran 4.00 10.00
8 Hunter Morris 8.00 20.00
9 J.R. Bradley 5.00 12.00
10 Nick Castellanos 12.00 30.00
11 Chad Bettis 10.00 25.00
12 Drew Robinson 6.00 15.00
13 Aaron Sanchez 12.00 30.00
14 Brandon Workman 5.00 12.00
15 Matt Moore 8.00 20.00
16 Cole Leonida 6.00 15.00
17 Seth Rosin 4.00 10.00
18 Josh Rutledge 8.00 20.00
19 Vincent Velasquez 15.00 40.00
20 Matt den Dekker 10.00 25.00
21 Rett Varner 4.00 10.00
22 Reggie Golden 4.00 10.00
23 Derek Dietrich 50.00 120.00
24 Robbie Aviles 8.00 20.00
25 DeAngelo Mack 6.00 15.00
26 Alex Wimmers 5.00 12.00
28 Mike Antonio 6.00 15.00
29 Andy Wilkins 6.00 15.00
30 Cody Buckel 15.00 40.00
31 Kevin Munson 5.00 12.00
32 Chris Hawkins 12.00 30.00
33 Drew Smyly 4.00 10.00
34 Gary Sanchez 100.00 250.00
35 Dan Klein 4.00 10.00
36 Yordy Cabrera 10.00 25.00
37 Ralston Cash 5.00 12.00
38 Jonathan Galvez 10.00 25.00
39 Sam Dyson 5.00 12.00
40 Rob Segedin 10.00 25.00
41 Jimmy Nelson 4.00 10.00
42 Daniel Tillman 8.00 20.00
43 Raoul Torrez 4.00 10.00
44 Sammy Solis 5.00 12.00
45 Austin Wates 10.00 25.00
46 Matt Harvey 100.00 200.00
47 Connor Narron 5.00 12.00
48 Bryan Morgado 5.00 12.00
49 Chris Hernandez 10.00 25.00
50 Hayden Simpson 12.00 30.00
51 Brooks Hall 6.00 15.00
52 Devin Lohman 8.00 20.00
53 Pat Dean 6.00 15.00
54 Gary Brown 20.00 50.00
55 Stetson Allie 5.00 12.00
56 Griffin Murphy 10.00 25.00
57 Jake Thompson 5.00 12.00
58 Cody Wheeler 4.00 10.00
59 Niko Goodrum 12.00 30.00
60 Rob Brantly 5.00 12.00
61 Austin Ross 5.00 12.00
62 Kevin Rath 4.00 10.00
63 A.J. Cole 10.00 25.00
64 Scott Lawson 6.00 15.00
65 Logan Bawcom 4.00 10.00
66 Connor Powers 4.00 10.00
67 Mike Nesseth 4.00 10.00
68 Jose Vinicio 6.00 15.00
69 Ryan Casteel 5.00 12.00
70 Rick Hague 5.00 12.00
71 Kyle Blair 5.00 12.00
72 Swagerty UER Magic AU 12.00 30.00
73 Jake Anderson 6.00 15.00
74 Brian Garman 4.00 10.00
75 Mark Canha 6.00 15.00
76 Perci Garner 5.00 12.00
77 Edinson Rincon 10.00 25.00
78 Jonathan Jones 6.00 15.00
79 Ross Wilson 4.00 10.00
80 Mel Rojas Jr. 6.00 15.00
81 Luke Jackson 10.00 25.00
82 Cole Nelson 5.00 12.00
83 David Filak 5.00 12.00
84 Kyle Bellows 5.00 12.00
85 Sam Tuivailala 5.00 12.00
86 Cole Cook 5.00 12.00
87 Jesse Hahn 4.00 10.00
88 A.J. Griffin 6.00 15.00
89 Max Walla 15.00 40.00
90 Jurickson Profar 15.00 40.00
91 Zach Cates 6.00 15.00
92 Ronald Torreyes 15.00 40.00
93 Marcus Littlewood 8.00 20.00
94 Parker Bridwell 12.00 30.00
95 Tyler Austin 6.00 15.00
96 Rob Rasmussen 5.00 12.00
97 Seth Blair 10.00 25.00
98 Tyler Holt 4.00 10.00
99 Micah Gibbs 8.00 20.00
101 Michael Choice 30.00 60.00
102 Christian Colon 12.00 30.00
103 Chris Sale 50.00 120.00
104 Jake Skole 10.00 25.00
105 Mike Foltynewicz 15.00 40.00
106 Kolbrin Vitek 5.00 12.00
107 Kellin Deglan 4.00 10.00
108 Jesse Biddle 20.00 50.00
109 Justin O'Conner 10.00 25.00
110 Cito Culver 4.00 10.00
111 Mike Kvasnicka 6.00 15.00
112 Matt Lipka 4.00 10.00
113 Noah Syndergaard 25.00 60.00
114 Ryan LaMarre 5.00 12.00
115 Josh Sale 20.00 50.00
116 Zack Cox 15.00 40.00
117 Bryan Holaday 6.00 15.00
118 Todd Cunningham 8.00 20.00
119 Jarrett Parker 8.00 20.00
120 Leon Landry 8.00 20.00
121 Cam Bedrosian EXCH 8.00 20.00
122 Ryan Bolden 6.00 15.00
123 Cameron Rupp 8.00 20.00
124 Jedd Gyorko 15.00 40.00
125 Matt Curry 5.00 12.00
126 Drew Pomeranz 10.00 25.00
127 Yasmani Grandal 8.00 20.00
128 Deck McGuire 5.00 12.00
129 Chevez Clarke 12.00 30.00
130 Jameson Taillon 20.00 50.00
131 Kaleb Cowart 15.00 40.00
132 Manny Machado 100.00 250.00
133 Tony Thompson 5.00 12.00
134 Dee Gordon 20.00 50.00
135 Chance Ruffin 5.00 12.00
136 J.T. Realmuto 60.00 150.00
137 Kevin Chapman 5.00 12.00
138 Kyle Roller 10.00 25.00
139 Stephen Pryor 8.00 20.00
140 Jonathan Singleton 20.00 50.00
141 Drew Cisco 8.00 20.00
142 Blake Forsythe 8.00 20.00
143 Kellen Sweeney 12.00 30.00
144 Brett Eibner 5.00 12.00
145 Martin Perez 15.00 40.00
146 Jean Segura 15.00 40.00
147 Christian Yelich 50.00 120.00
148 Robby Rowland 5.00 12.00
149 Trent Mummey 5.00 12.00
150 Zach Lee 8.00 20.00
151 Jason Mitchell 4.00 10.00
152 Nick Longmire 8.00 20.00
153 Robbie Erlin 5.00 12.00
154 Addison Reed 15.00 40.00
155 Austin Reed 4.00 10.00
156 Tyler Thornburg 4.00 10.00
157 Ty Linton 10.00 25.00
158 Chris Balcom-Miller 10.00 25.00
159 Wes Mugarian 4.00 10.00
160 Tony Wolters 5.00 12.00
161 Justin Grimm 5.00 12.00
162 Alex Lavisky 8.00 20.00
163 Taijuan Walker 20.00 50.00
164 Arodys Vizcaino 5.00 12.00
165 Brody Colvin 20.00 50.00
166 Christian Carmichael 5.00 12.00
167 Josh Spence 6.00 15.00
168 Joc Pederson 15.00 40.00
169 Justin Nicolino 4.00 10.00
170 Nick Tepesch 15.00 40.00
171 Joe Gardner 6.00 15.00
172 Taylor Morton 10.00 25.00
173 Jason Martinson 4.00 10.00
174 Matt Miller 4.00 10.00
175 Justin Bloxom 5.00 12.00
176 Matt Suschak 4.00 10.00
177 Zach Neal 5.00 12.00
178 Ben Gamel 10.00 25.00
179 Jimmy Reyes 4.00 10.00
180 Matt Price 4.00 10.00
181 Aaron Shipman 6.00 15.00
182 Hector Noesi 12.00 30.00
183 Peter Tago 6.00 15.00
184 Kyle Knudson 5.00 12.00
185 Matt Kirkland 6.00 15.00
186 Mickey Wiswall 4.00 10.00
187 Steve Geltz 4.00 10.00
188 Shawn Tolleson 5.00 12.00
189 Greg Holle 6.00 15.00
190 Erik Goeddel 4.00 10.00
191 Paul Goldschmidt 50.00 120.00
192 LeVon Washington 8.00 20.00
193 Trey McNutt 5.00 12.00
194 Henry Rodriguez 6.00 15.00
195 Adrian Sanchez 5.00 12.00
196 Daniel Bibona 4.00 10.00
197 Chad Lewis 6.00 15.00
198 Brodie Greene 5.00 12.00
200 Anthony Ranaudo 15.00 40.00

2010 Donruss Elite Extra Edition Back to the Future Signatures

OVERALL AUTO ODDS 6 PER BOX
PRINT RUNS B/WN 5-249 COPIES PER
EXCHANGE DEADLINE 4/6/2012
1 Pedro Baez/249 3.00 8.00
2 Colton Cain/249 3.00 8.00
3 Tyler Townsend/249 3.00 8.00
4 James Jones/249 8.00 20.00
5 Ashur Tolliver/249 4.00 10.00
6 Jeff Hunt/95 3.00 8.00
7 Aaron Baker/235 3.00 8.00
8 Tyler Matzek/150 8.00 20.00
9 Reymond Fuentes/249 3.00 8.00
10 Thomas Joseph/249 8.00 20.00
11 Chad James/244 3.00 8.00
12 Khris Davis/249 20.00 50.00
13 Eric Smith/249 3.00 8.00
14 Tyler Kehrer/249 3.00 8.00
17 Bob Gibson/50 12.50 30.00
19 Don Sutton/49 4.00 10.00
20 Frank Howard/30 12.50 30.00

2010 Donruss Elite Extra Edition College Ties

COMPLETE SET (10) 10.00 25.00
RANDOM INSERTS IN PACKS
1 Z.Cox/B.Eibner 1.25 3.00
2 Brandon Workman/Chance Ruffin .40 1.00
3 Matt Curry/Bryan Holaday .60 1.50
4 Micah Gibbs/Leon Landry 1.00 2.50
5 C.Colon/G.Brown 2.00 5.00
6 M.Choice/R.Varner .60 1.50
7 D.McGuire/D.Dietrich 1.00 2.50
8 Ryan LaMarre/Matt Miller .60 1.50
9 Dan Klein/Rob Rasmussen .40 1.00
10 Chad Bettis/Bobby Doran .40 1.00

2010 Donruss Elite Extra Edition College Ties Autographs

OVERALL AUTO ODDS 6 PER BOX
STATED PRINT RUN 50 SER.#'d SETS
EXCHANGE DEADLINE 4/6/2012
1 Z.Cox/B.Eibner 6.00 15.00
2 B.Workman/C.Ruffin 8.00 20.00
3 M.Curry/B.Holaday 8.00 20.00
5 Colon/Brown 8.00 20.00
6 M.Choice/R.Varner 6.00 15.00
7 D.McGuire/D.Dietrich 12.00 30.00
8 Ryan LaMarre/Matt Miller 6.00 15.00
9 Dan Klein/Rob Rasmussen 6.00 15.00
10 C.Bettis/B.Doran 12.50 30.00

2010 Donruss Elite Extra Edition Collegiate Patches Autographs

OVERALL AUTO ODDS 6 PER BOX
PRINT RUNS B/WN 49-150 COPIES PER
EXCHANGE DEADLINE 4/6/2012
ANW Andy Wilkins/125 5.00 12.00
AR A.Ranaudo/125 8.00 20.00
AUW Austin Wates/125 6.00 15.00
AW Alex Wimmers/125 10.00 25.00
BD Bobby Doran/125 5.00 12.00
BE Brett Eibner/125 10.00 25.00
BF Blake Forsythe/125 10.00 25.00
BG Brodie Greene/125 5.00 12.00
BH Bryan Holaday/125 8.00 20.00
BJS B.Surhoff/125 6.00 15.00
BMC Ben McDonald/125 10.00 25.00
BW B.Workman/125 5.00 12.00
CAR Cameron Rupp/124 5.00 12.00
CB Chad Bettis/125 4.00 10.00
CH Chris Hernandez/125 4.00 10.00
CJ Carter Jurica/125 4.00 10.00
CL Cole Leonida/140 4.00 10.00
CR Chance Ruffin/125 5.00 12.00
DD Derek Dietrich/125 10.00 25.00
DK Dan Klein/125 4.00 10.00
DL Devin Lohman/125 4.00 10.00
DM Deck McGuire/125 8.00 20.00
DP Drew Pomeranz/125 4.00 10.00
GB Gary Brown/49 50.00 100.00
HM Hunter Morris/150 8.00 20.00
JG Jedd Gyorko/125 10.00 25.00
JN Jimmy Nelson/125 4.00 8.00
JOS Swagerty/125 UER Magic AU 30.00 60.00
JP Jarrett Parker/125 10.00 25.00
JS Josh Spence/125 6.00 15.00
JT Jake Thompson/125 4.00 10.00
JUG Justin Grimm/125 6.00 15.00
KB Kyle Blair/125 4.00 10.00
KC Kevin Chapman/125 8.00 20.00
KG Kirk Gibson/125 12.50 30.00
LL Leon Landry/125 10.00 25.00
MC Matt Curry/125 4.00 10.00
MD Matt den Dekker/125 6.00 15.00
MG Micah Gibbs/125 5.00 12.00
MH Matt Harvey/125 40.00 80.00
MK Mike Kvasnicka/125 6.00 15.00
MN Mike Nesseth/125 4.00 10.00
MO Mike Olt/125 10.00 25.00
PD Pat Dean/125 5.00 12.00
PI P.Incaviglia/125 EXCH 5.00 12.00
RH Rick Hague/125 4.00 10.00
RL Ryan LaMarre/125 5.00 12.00
RR Rob Rasmussen/125 5.00 12.00
SB Seth Blair/125 4.00 10.00
SD Sam Dyson/125 4.00 10.00
SS Sammy Solis/125 5.00 12.00
TH Tyler Holt/125 5.00 12.00
TM Trent Mummey/125 6.00 15.00
YG Y.Grandal/125 15.00 40.00
ZC Zack Cox/125 12.50 30.00

2010 Donruss Elite Extra Edition Draft Hits Autographs

OVERALL AUTO ODDS 6 PER BOX
PRINT RUNS B/WN 5-299 COPIES PER
1 R.Monday/99 EXCH 4.00 10.00
2 Dale Murphy/99 8.00 20.00
7 Alan Trammell/40 10.00 25.00
8 B.Surhoff/299 4.00 10.00
9 Jack Morris/150 3.00 8.00
12 R.Ventura/99 8.00 20.00
14 P.Incaviglia/99 4.00 10.00
15 Ben McDonald/299 3.00 8.00
16 Ron Blomberg/299 3.00 8.00
17 Jeff Bagwell/35 EXCH 20.00 50.00
18 Jay Buhner/99 3.00 8.00
19 Tino Martinez/99 6.00 15.00

2010 Donruss Elite Extra Edition Elite Series

COMPLETE SET (20) 15.00 40.00
RANDOM INSERTS IN PACKS
1 Kaleb Cowart .60 1.50
2 Christian Colon .60 1.50
3 Brandon Workman .40 1.00
4 Michael Choice .60 1.50
5 Delino DeShields Jr. .60 1.50
6 Jarrett Parker 1.25 3.00
7 Kolbrin Vitek 1.00 2.50
8 Manny Machado 12.00 30.00
9 Dave Winfield .60 1.50
10 Yasmani Grandal .60 1.50
11 Chance Ruffin .40 1.00
12 Cito Culver .60 1.50
13 Zach Lee 1.00 2.50
14 Zack Cox 1.25 3.00
15 Drew Pomeranz 1.00 2.50
16 Josh Sale 1.25 3.00
17 Matt Harvey 2.50 6.00
18 Mike Olt 1.25 3.00
19 Jameson Taillon .60 1.50
20 Nick Castellanos 2.00 5.00

2010 Donruss Elite Extra Edition Elite Series Autographs

OVERALL AUTO ODDS 6 PER BOX
PRINT RUNS B/WN 19-100 COPIES PER
3 B.Workman/95 6.00 15.00
4 Michael Choice/100 10.00 25.00
5 D.DeShields Jr./75 10.00 25.00
6 Jarrett Parker/100 12.00 30.00
7 Kolbrin Vitek/100 8.00 20.00
10 Y.Grandal/100 8.00 20.00
13 Zach Lee/50 8.00 20.00
14 Zack Cox/49 40.00 80.00
15 Drew Pomeranz/49 12.50 30.00
18 Mike Olt/100 10.00 25.00
19 Jameson Taillon/49 12.00 30.00
20 Nick Castellanos/50 20.00 50.00

2010 Donruss Elite Extra Edition Franchise Futures Signatures

OVERALL AUTO ODDS 6 PER BOX
PRINT RUNS B/WN 49-150 COPIES PER
EXCHANGE DEADLINE 4/6/2012
1 Bryce Brentz/719 4.00 10.00
2 Drew Vettleson/690 3.00 8.00
3 Mike Olt/399 8.00 20.00
4 Tyrell Jenkins/599 4.00 10.00
5 D.DeShields Jr./499 3.00 8.00
6 A.Wojciechowski/675 5.00 12.00
7 Bobby Doran/644 4.00 10.00
8 Hunter Morris/619 6.00 15.00
9 J.R. Bradley/625 3.00 8.00
10 N.Castellanos/699 6.00 15.00
11 Chad Bettis/635 3.00 8.00
12 Drew Robinson/550 5.00 12.00
13 Aaron Sanchez/499 6.00 15.00
14 B.Workman/450 5.00 12.00
15 Matt Moore/819 5.00 12.00
16 Cole Leonida/669 3.00 8.00
17 Seth Rosin/710 3.00 8.00
18 Josh Rutledge/595 6.00 15.00
19 Vincent Velasquez/799 8.00 20.00
20 Matt den Dekker/694 3.00 8.00
21 Rett Varner/650 3.00 8.00
22 Reggie Golden/819 5.00 12.00
23 Derek Dietrich/490 20.00 50.00
24 Robbie Aviles/810 3.00 8.00
25 DeAngelo Mack/819 3.00 8.00
26 A.Wimmers/199 5.00 12.00
28 Mike Antonio/99 10.00 25.00
29 Andy Wilkins/494 3.00 8.00
30 Cody Buckel/816 6.00 15.00
31 Kevin Munson/819 3.00 8.00
32 Chris Hawkins/99 10.00 25.00
33 Drew Smyly/799 4.00 10.00
34 Gary Sanchez/669 40.00 100.00
35 Dan Klein/599 4.00 10.00
36 Yordy Cabrera/818 4.00 10.00
37 Ralston Cash/819 3.00 8.00
38 Jonathan Galvez/810 3.00 8.00
39 Sam Dyson/199 3.00 8.00
40 Rob Segedin/816 4.00 10.00
41 Jimmy Nelson/640 3.00 8.00
42 Daniel Tillman/816 3.00 8.00
43 Raoul Torrez/325 3.00 8.00
44 Sammy Solis/699 3.00 8.00
45 Austin Wates/99 12.50 30.00
46 Matt Harvey/149 50.00 100.00
47 Connor Narron/835 3.00 8.00
48 Bryan Morgado/601 4.00 10.00
49 Chris Hernandez/690 3.00 8.00
50 Hayden Simpson/599 5.00 12.00
51 Brooks Hall/819 4.00 10.00
52 Devin Lohman/694 3.00 8.00
53 Pat Dean/525 4.00 10.00
54 G.Brown/199 5.00 12.00
55 Stetson Allie/599 6.00 15.00
56 Griffin Murphy/775 3.00 8.00
57 Jake Thompson/699 3.00 8.00
58 Cody Wheeler/815 3.00 8.00
59 Niko Goodrum/819 8.00 20.00
60 Rob Brantly/819 4.00 10.00
61 Austin Ross/819 3.00 8.00
62 Kevin Rath/820 3.00 8.00
63 A.J. Cole/819 3.00 8.00
64 Scott Lawson/694 3.00 8.00
65 Logan Bawcom/790 3.00 8.00
66 Connor Powers/811 3.00 8.00
67 Mike Nesseth/590 3.00 8.00
68 Jose Vinicio/99 5.00 12.00
69 Ryan Casteel/817 3.00 8.00
70 Rick Hague/490 3.00 8.00
71 Kyle Blair/749 4.00 10.00
72 Swagerty/450 UER Magic AU 12.00 30.00
73 Jake Anderson/810 4.00 10.00
74 Brian Garman/810 3.00 8.00
75 Mark Canha/799 3.00 8.00
76 Perci Garner/799 3.00 8.00
77 Edinson Rincon/819 3.00 8.00
78 Jonathan Jones/694 3.00 8.00
79 Ross Wilson/815 3.00 8.00
80 Mel Rojas Jr./819 4.00 10.00
81 Luke Jackson/99 6.00 15.00
82 Cole Nelson/819 3.00 8.00
83 David Filak/817 3.00 8.00
84 Kyle Bellows/819 3.00 8.00
85 Sam Tuivailala/820 3.00 8.00
86 Cole Cook/840 3.00 8.00
87 Jesse Hahn/99 12.00 30.00
88 A.J. Griffin/99 12.00 30.00
89 Max Walla/819 3.00 8.00
90 Jurickson Profar/390 5.00 12.00
91 Zach Cates/816 3.00 8.00
92 Ronald Torreyes/599 10.00 25.00
93 M.Littlewood/825 4.00 10.00
94 Parker Bridwell/99 12.00 30.00
95 Tyler Austin/811 3.00 8.00
96 Rob Rasmussen/658 3.00 8.00
97 Seth Blair/99 4.00 10.00
98 Tyler Holt/694 4.00 10.00
99 Micah Gibbs/390 4.00 10.00
100 Pamela Anderson/35 125.00 250.00

2010 Donruss Elite Extra Edition Private Signings

OVERALL AUTO ODDS 6 PER BOX
PRINT RUNS B/WN 8-149 COPIES PER
1 Andy Wilkins/149 10.00 25.00
2 Bryan Holaday/50 10.00 25.00
3 Michael Choice/99 6.00 15.00
4 Cameron Rupp/50 8.00 20.00
5 Josh Sale/125 5.00 12.00
10 Kaleb Cowart/49 40.00 80.00
12 Jake Skole/125 5.00 12.00
13 Dee Gordon/100 5.00 12.00
14 Martin Perez/125 10.00 25.00
15 Hayden Simpson/125 6.00 15.00
16 Brandon Workman/99 5.00 12.00
18 Kolbrin Vitek/100 6.00 15.00
19 Rett Varner/99 3.00 8.00
20 Matt Lipka/100 8.00 20.00
21 Chris Sale/125 12.00 30.00
22 Cam Bedrosian/149 6.00 15.00
23 Cito Culver/149 12.50 30.00
24 Tyrell Jenkins/125 6.00 15.00
25 Mike Olt/125 4.00 10.00
26 Bryce Brentz/100 8.00 20.00
27 Wojciechowski/125 8.00 20.00
28 Zack Cox/99 10.00 25.00
29 Drew Vettleson/149 3.00 8.00
30 Gary Sanchez/149 50.00 120.00
31 Brett Eibner/99 8.00 20.00
32 J.R. Bradley/149 5.00 12.00
33 Micah Gibbs/99 8.00 20.00
34 Kellin Deglan/149 3.00 8.00
36 Matt Curry/100 6.00 15.00
37 Drew Pomeranz/100 3.00 8.00
38 Mike Foltynewicz/149 10.00 25.00
39 Aaron Sanchez/125 10.00 25.00
40 Zach Lee/110 6.00 15.00

2010 Donruss Elite Extra Edition School Colors

COMPLETE SET (20) 10.00 25.00
RANDOM INSERTS IN PACKS
1 Jordan Swagerty 1.00 2.50
2 Christian Colon .60 1.50
3 Michael Choice .60 1.50
4 Zack Cox 1.25 3.00
5 Yasmani Grandal .60 1.50
6 Kolbrin Vitek 1.00 2.50
7 Ryan LaMarre .60 1.50
8 Drew Pomeranz 1.00 2.50
9 Jarrett Parker 1.25 3.00
10 Blake Forsythe .40 1.00
11 Josh Rutledge 2.50 6.00
12 Sam Dyson .40 1.00
13 Hunter Morris .40 1.00
14 Deck McGuire .60 1.50
15 Mike Kvasnicka .60 1.50
16 Cameron Rupp .60 1.50
17 Todd Cunningham .60 1.50
18 Micah Gibbs .60 1.50
19 Alex Wimmers .60 1.50
20 Derek Dietrich 1.00 2.50

2010 Donruss Elite Extra Edition School Colors Autographs

OVERALL AUTO ODDS 6 PER BOX
PRINT RUNS B/WN 19-299 COPIES PER
1 Swagerty/149 UER Magic AU 10.00 25.00
2 Christian Colon/49 10.00 25.00
3 Michael Choice/99 10.00 25.00
5 Yasmani Grandal/99 6.00 15.00
6 Kolbrin Vitek/68 10.00 25.00
7 Ryan LaMarre/90 5.00 12.00
10 Blake Forsythe/49 6.00 15.00
11 Josh Rutledge/99 8.00 20.00
12 Sam Dyson/49 5.00 12.00
13 Hunter Morris/50 6.00 15.00
14 Deck McGuire/49 8.00 20.00
15 Mike Kvasnicka/165 4.00 10.00
16 Cameron Rupp/70 5.00 12.00
17 Todd Cunningham/82 3.00 8.00
18 Micah Gibbs/149 8.00 20.00
19 Alex Wimmers/49 5.00 12.00
20 Derek Dietrich/199 10.00 25.00

2011 Donruss Elite Extra Edition

COMPLETE SET (25) 5.00 12.00
COMMON CARD .20 .50
1 Josh Hamilton .30 .75
2 Adrian Gonzalez .40 1.00
3 Clayton Kershaw .75 2.00
4 Albert Pujols .60 1.50
5 Chris Perez .20 .50
6 Jeremy Hellickson RC .50 1.25
7 Curtis Granderson .40 1.00
8 Justin Upton .30 .75
9 Jordan Walden RC .20 .50
10 Brian McCann .30 .75
11 Starlin Castro .30 .75
12 Ichiro Suzuki .60 1.50
13 Trevor Cahill .20 .50
14 Justin Verlander .50 1.25
15 Danny Espinosa RC .20 .50
16 Andrew McCutchen .50 1.25
17 Dustin Pedroia .50 1.25
18 Adam Jones .30 .75
19 Ben Revere RC .30 .75
20 David Freese .20 .50
21 Michael Pineda RC .50 1.25
22 Heath Bell .20 .50
23 Andy Dirks RC .50 1.25
24 Troy Tulowitzki .50 1.25
25 Jay Bruce .30 .75

2011 Donruss Elite Extra Edition Aspirations

*ASPIRATIONS: 2X TO 5X BASIC
STATED PRINT RUN 200 SER.#'d SETS

2011 Donruss Elite Extra Edition Status

*STATUS: 2.5X TO 6X BASIC
STATED PRINT RUN 100 SER.#'d SETS

2011 Donruss Elite Extra Edition Back to the Future Signatures

OVERALL SIX AUTOS PER HOBBY BOX
PRINT RUNS B/WN 49-720 COPIES PER
EXCHANGE DEADLINE 06/28/2013
2 J.T. Realmuto 20.00 50.00
3 Jordan Swagerty 5.00 12.00
5 Austin Wates 5.00 12.00
6 Kyle Blair 6.00 15.00
7 A.J. Griffin 5.00 12.00
8 Jurickson Profar 5.00 12.00
10 Nick Castellanos 15.00 40.00
11 Chris Hawkins 6.00 15.00
12 Justin Nicolino 6.00 15.00
16 Jose Vinicio 3.00 8.00
19 Manny Machado 20.00 50.00
20 Stetson Allie 6.00 15.00
21 Drew Robinson 5.00 12.00
25 Jonathan Singleton 4.00 10.00

2011 Donruss Elite Extra Edition Best Compared To

RANDOM INSERTS IN PACKS
STATED PRINT RUN 499 SER.#'d SETS
1 Lincecum/Bauer 5.00 12.00
2 Bundy/Beckett 1.50 4.00
3 Cron/Trumbo 1.50 4.00
4 Starling/Hamilton .75 2.00
5 Spangenberg/Pedroia 1.25 3.00
6 Rendon/Zimmerman 5.00 12.00
7 Cole/Strasburg 5.00 12.00
8 Roy Oswalt/Sonny Gray 1.25 3.00
9 H.Ramirez/J.Baez 6.00 15.00
10 Colby Rasmus/Kes Carter .75 2.00
11 Granden Goetzman/Jayson Werth .75 2.00
12 T.Story/T.Tulowitzki 8.00 20.00

2011 Donruss Elite Extra Edition Building Blocks Dual

COMPLETE SET (15) 8.00 20.00
STATED ODDS 1:10 HOBBY
1 B.Starling/J.Bell 2.50 6.00
2 Brandon Drury 1.00 2.50
Kyle Kubitza
3 G.Cole/T.Bauer 4.00 10.00
4 Abel Baker .40 1.00
Pratt Maynard
5 Tyler Collins .40 1.00
Tyler Gibson
6 Logan Verrett .75 2.00
Phillip Evans
7 Nick Ramirez .60 1.50
Sean Halton
8 Jake Lowery .40 1.00
Jake Sisco
9 Jace Peterson .40 1.00
Lee Orr
10 Brandon Parrent .40 1.00
Nick Fleece
11 Jeff Ames .40 1.00
Steven Ames
12 Aaron Westlake .40 1.00
Dean Green
13 Chris Wallace .40 1.00
Michael Goodnight
14 Bryan Brickhouse 1.00 2.50
Cameron Gallagher
15 Cole Green .40 1.00
Kyle McMyne

2011 Donruss Elite Extra Edition Building Blocks Dual Signatures

PRINT RUNS B/WN 10-49 COPIES PER
NO PRICING ON QTY 20 OR LESS
EXCHANGE DEADLINE 06/28/2013
2 B.Drury/K.Kubitza 4.00 10.00
4 A.Baker/P.Maynard 8.00 20.00
5 T.Collins/T.Gibson 8.00 20.00
6 L.Verrett/P.Evans 6.00 15.00
7 N.Ramirez/S.Halton 10.00 25.00
8 J.Lowery/J.Sisco 12.50 30.00
9 J.Peterson/L.Orr 5.00 12.00
10 B.Parrent/N.Fleece 5.00 12.00
11 J.Ames/S.Ames 5.00 12.00
12 A.Westlake/D.Green 6.00 15.00
13 Chris Wallace 4.00 10.00
Michael Goodnight
14 B.Brickhouse/C.Gallagher 6.00 15.00
15 C.Green/K.McMyne 10.00 25.00

2011 Donruss Elite Extra Edition Building Blocks Quad

COMPLETE SET (10) 8.00 20.00
STATED ODDS 1:10 HOBBY
1 Aaron Westlake/Corey Williams
Grayson Garvin/Sonny Gray 1.00 2.50
2 Lin/Hag/Baez/Mich 5.00 12.00
3 Brian Flynn/James McCann
Jason King/Jason Krizan 1.00 2.50
4 Erik Johnson/Keenyn Walker
Kyle McMillen/Scott Snodgress .40 1.00
5 Granden Goetzman/Johnny Eierman
Kes Carter/Mikie Mahtook 1.00 2.50
6 Andrew Susac/Blake Swihart
Jake Lowery/John Hicks .60 1.50
7 Holtz/Bundy/Cole/Bauer 4.00 10.00
8 Rend/Martin/Esposito/Dean 4.00 10.00
9 Nmm/String/Smith/Bell 2.50 6.00
10 Austin Hedges/Jace Peterson
Joe Ross/Michael Kelly 1.00 2.50

2011 Donruss Elite Extra Edition Building Blocks Trio

COMPLETE SET (15) 8.00 20.00
STATED ODDS 1:10 HOBBY
1 Rendon/Goodwin/Purke 4.00 10.00
2 Bradley/Bundy/Fulmer 1.25 3.00
3 Dan Vogelbach/Dillon Maples
Matt Szczur 1.25 3.00
4 Hsr/Spingr/Hmbln 2.50 6.00
5 Cole Green/James Allen
Robert Stephenson .75 2.00
6 Snell/Ames/Guerrieri 1.50 4.00
7 Alex Hassan/Kendrick Perkins
Williams Jerez .40 1.00
8 Hultzen/Bradley/Anderson 2.00 5.00
9 Norris/Musgrove/Comer 2.00 5.00
10 Larry Greene/Mitch Walding
Roman Quinn 1.00 2.50

2011 Donruss Elite Extra Edition Elite Series

STATED ODDS 1:10 HOBBY
1 Jackie Bradley Jr. 1.50 4.00
2 Josh Bell 2.50 6.00
3 Angelo Songco .60 1.50
4 Brad Miller .40 1.00
5 Tyler Goeddel .40 1.00
6 Matt Purke 1.00 2.50
7 Blake Swihart .60 1.50
8 Roman Quinn 1.00 2.50
9 Jordan Cote 1.00 2.50
10 Anthony Rendon 4.00 10.00
11 Zeke DeVoss .60 1.50
12 Tyler Collins .40 1.00
13 Logan Verrett .75 2.00
14 Charlie Tilson 1.00 2.50
15 Brandon Nimmo 2.00 5.00

16 Taylor Jungmann .60 1.50
17 Joe Panik 1.00 2.50
18 Gerrit Cole 4.00 10.00
19 Abel Baker .40 1.00
20 Tyler Gibson .40 1.00

2011 Donruss Elite Extra Edition Elite Series Signatures

OVERALL SIX AUTOS PER HOBBY BOX
PRINT RUNS B/WN 25-228 COPIES PER
EXCHANGE DEADLINE 06/28/2013

1 Jackie Bradley Jr. 8.00 20.00
2 Josh Bell 15.00 40.00
3 Angelo Songco 6.00 15.00
5 Tyler Goeddel 4.00 10.00
6 Matt Purke 6.00 15.00
7 Blake Swihart 6.00 15.00
8 Roman Quinn 4.00 10.00
9 Jordan Cote 8.00 20.00
10 Anthony Rendon 15.00 40.00
11 Zeke DeVoss 6.00 15.00
12 Tyler Collins 6.00 15.00
13 Logan Verrett 8.00 20.00
14 Charlie Tilson 8.00 20.00
15 Brandon Nimmo 10.00 25.00
16 Taylor Jungmann 8.00 20.00
17 Joe Panik 12.00 30.00
18 Gerrit Cole 20.00 50.00
19 Abel Baker 8.00 20.00
20 Tyler Gibson 4.00 10.00

2011 Donruss Elite Extra Edition Franchise Futures Signatures

OVERALL SIX AUTOS PER HOBBY BOX
PRINT RUNS B/WN 137-1264 COPIES PER
EXCHANGE DEADLINE 06/28/2013

1 Tyler Goeddel 4.00 10.00
2 Dante Bichette Jr. 10.00 25.00
3 James Harris 5.00 12.00
4 Cory Mazzoni 5.00 12.00
5 Abel Baker 4.00 10.00
6 Alex Dickerson 5.00 12.00
7 Justin Bour 8.00 20.00
8 Tyler Anderson 4.00 10.00
9 Jeff Ames 4.00 10.00
10 Cristhian Adames 3.00 8.00
11 Jason Krizan 3.00 8.00
12 Michael Kelly 6.00 15.00
13 Kyle McMillen 3.00 8.00
14 Charlie Tilson 6.00 15.00
15 Brad Miller 4.00 10.00
16 Blake Snell 10.00 25.00
17 Daniel Norris 5.00 12.00
18 Williams Jerez 8.00 20.00
19 Erik Johnson 3.00 8.00
20 Gabriel Rosa 8.00 20.00
21 Adam Morgan 3.00 8.00
22 Aaron Westlake 4.00 10.00
23 Brandon Loy 3.00 8.00
24 Zach Good 3.00 8.00
25 Angelo Songco 5.00 12.00
26 Jordan Akins 4.00 10.00
27 Josh Osich 5.00 12.00
28 Austin Hedges 8.00 20.00
29 Jake Sisco 3.00 8.00
30 B.A. Vollmuth 3.00 8.00
31 Austin Wood 3.00 8.00
32 Dan Vogelbach 3.00 8.00
33 Carl Thomore 3.00 8.00
34 Blake Swihart 5.00 12.00
35 James Allen 4.00 10.00
36 Carlos Sanchez 3.00 8.00
37 Michael Goodnight 3.00 8.00
38 James McCann 6.00 15.00
39 Will Lamb 4.00 10.00
40 Taylor Featherston 4.00 10.00
41 Nick Ramirez 4.00 10.00
42 Johnny Eierman 4.00 10.00
43 Logan Verrett 12.00 30.00
44 Neftali Rosario 5.00 12.00
45 Kevin Comer 3.00 8.00
46 Kendrick Perkins 4.00 10.00
47 Tyler Grimes 5.00 12.00
48 Kyle Winkler 3.00 8.00
49 John Hicks 3.00 8.00
50 Taylor Guerrieri 5.00 12.00
51 Dillon Maples 4.00 10.00
52 Harold Martinez 4.00 10.00
53 Grayson Garvin 3.00 8.00
54 Zeke DeVoss 3.00 8.00
55 Mitch Walding 4.00 10.00
56 Clay Holmes 4.00 10.00
57 Hudson Boyd 4.00 10.00
58 Granden Goetzman 4.00 10.00
59 Bryan Brickhouse 3.00 8.00
60 Shane Opitz 4.00 10.00
61 Nick Fleece 3.00 8.00
62 Barret Loux 4.00 10.00
63 Jake Lowery 6.00 15.00
64 Madison Boer 5.00 12.00
65 Tony Zych 3.00 8.00
66 Sean Halton 3.00 8.00
67 Cavan Cohoes 4.00 10.00
68 Dean Green 6.00 15.00
69 Miles Hamblin 3.00 8.00
70 J.R. Graham 5.00 12.00
71 Tom Robson 3.00 8.00
72 Riccio Torrez 3.00 8.00
73 Adam Conley 3.00 8.00
74 Pratt Maynard 6.00 15.00
75 Jordan Cote 6.00 15.00
76 Kyle Gaedele 3.00 8.00
77 Christian Lopes 4.00 10.00
78 Travis Shaw 3.00 8.00
79 Parker Markel 3.00 8.00
80 Chad Comer 3.00 8.00
81 Adrian Houser 5.00 12.00
82 Corey Williams 3.00 8.00
83 Brian Flynn 3.00 8.00
84 Phillip Evans 3.00 8.00
85 Lee Orr 3.00 8.00
86 Brandon Parrent 3.00 8.00
87 Roman Quinn 5.00 12.00
88 Jake Floethe 3.00 8.00
89 Andrew Susac 6.00 15.00
90 Navery Moore 4.00 10.00
91 Chris Schwinden 4.00 10.00
92 Cole Green 4.00 10.00
93 Chris Wallace 3.00 8.00
94 Steven Ames 3.00 8.00
95 James Baldwin 4.00 10.00
96 Forrest Snow 3.00 8.00
97 Bobby Crocker 5.00 12.00
98 Dwight Smith Jr. 5.00 12.00
99 Greg Bird 15.00 40.00
100 Bryson Myles 4.00 10.00
151 Anthony Meo 4.00 10.00
152 Shawon Dunston Jr. 4.00 10.00
153 Rookie Davis 4.00 10.00
154 Rob Scahill 3.00 8.00
155 Chris Heston 6.00 15.00
156 Adam Jorgenson 3.00 8.00
157 Elliot Soto 3.00 8.00
158 Tyler Cloyd 5.00 12.00
159 Pierre LePage 3.00 8.00
160 Brett Jacobson 3.00 8.00
161 Casey Lawrence 3.00 8.00
162 Joe O'Gara 3.00 8.00
163 Mariekson Gregorius 30.00 80.00
164 Dan Osterbrock 3.00 8.00
165 Jared Hoying 3.00 8.00
166 Alan DeRatt 3.00 8.00
167 Charlie Leesman 5.00 12.00
168 Adam Davis 3.00 8.00
169 Danry Vasquez 6.00 15.00
170 Jon Griffin 4.00 10.00
171 Hernan Perez/810 4.00 10.00
172 Jeremy Cruz 3.00 8.00
173 Jose Osuna 4.00 10.00
174 Red Patterson 3.00 8.00
175 Jamaine Cotton 3.00 8.00
176 Pedro Villarreal 3.00 8.00
177 Justin Boudreaux 3.00 8.00
178 Chris Hanna 3.00 8.00
179 Mike Walker 4.00 10.00
180 David Herbek 3.00 8.00
181 Zack MacPhee 3.00 8.00
182 Ryan Tatusko 3.00 8.00
183 Dan Meadows 3.00 8.00
184 Albert Cartwright 4.00 10.00
185 Brandon Drury 5.00 12.00
186 Eddie Rosario 8.00 20.00
187 Jake Dunning 4.00 10.00
188 Miles Head 5.00 12.00
189 Duanel Jones 4.00 10.00
190 Rob Lyerly 4.00 10.00

2011 Donruss Elite Extra Edition Prospects

OVERALL SIX AUTOS PER HOBBY BOX
PRINT RUNS B/WN 334-865 COPIES PER
EXCHANGE DEADLINE 06/28/2013

1 Tyler Goeddel .20 .50
2 Dante Bichette Jr. .30 .75
3 James Harris .20 .50
4 Cory Mazzoni .20 .50
5 Abel Baker .20 .50
6 Alex Dickerson .30 .75
7 Justin Bour .50 1.25
8 Tyler Anderson .20 .50
9 Jeff Ames .20 .50
10 Cristhian Adames .20 .50
11 Jason Krizan .20 .50
12 Michael Kelly .20 .50
13 Kyle McMillen .20 .50
14 Charlie Tilson .50 1.25
15 Brad Miller .20 .50
16 Blake Snell .75 2.00
17 Daniel Norris .60 1.50
18 Williams Jerez .20 .50
19 Erik Johnson .20 .50
20 Gabriel Rosa .20 .50
21 Adam Morgan .30 .75
22 Aaron Westlake .20 .50
23 Brandon Loy .20 .50
24 Zach Good .20 .50
25 Angelo Songco .30 .75
26 Jordan Akins .20 .50
27 Josh Osich .30 .75
28 Austin Hedges .20 .50
29 Jake Sisco .20 .50
30 B.A. Vollmuth .20 .50
31 Austin Wood .20 .50
32 Dan Vogelbach .60 1.50
33 Carl Thomore .20 .50
34 Blake Swihart .30 .75
35 James Allen .20 .50
36 Carlos Sanchez .20 .50
37 Michael Goodnight .20 .50
38 James McCann .50 1.25
39 Will Lamb .20 .50
40 Taylor Featherston .20 .50
41 Nick Ramirez .30 .75
42 Johnny Eierman .20 .50
43 Logan Verrett .40 1.00
44 Neftali Rosario .20 .50
45 Kevin Comer .30 .75
46 Kendrick Perkins .20 .50
47 Tyler Grimes .20 .50
48 Kyle Winkler .20 .50
49 John Hicks .30 .75
50 Taylor Guerrieri .20 .50
51 Dillon Maples .20 .50
52 Harold Martinez .30 .75
53 Grayson Garvin .30 .75
54 Zeke DeVoss .30 .75
55 Mitch Walding .20 .50
56 Clay Holmes .20 .50
57 Hudson Boyd .20 .50
58 Granden Goetzman .20 .50
59 Bryan Brickhouse .50 1.25
60 Shane Opitz .30 .75
61 Nick Fleece .20 .50
62 Barret Loux .20 .50
63 Jake Lowery .20 .50
64 Madison Boer .20 .50
65 Tony Zych .20 .50
66 Sean Halton .20 .50
67 Cavan Cohoes .20 .50
68 Dean Green .20 .50
69 Miles Hamblin .20 .50
70 J.R. Graham .20 .50
71 Tom Robson .30 .75
72 Riccio Torrez .20 .50
73 Adam Conley .20 .50
74 Pratt Maynard .20 .50
75 Jordan Cote .50 1.25
76 Kyle Gaedele .20 .50
77 Christian Lopes .50 1.25
78 Travis Shaw .50 1.25
79 Parker Markel .20 .50
80 Chad Comer .20 .50
81 Adrian Houser .30 .75
82 Corey Williams .20 .50
83 Brian Flynn .20 .50
84 Phillip Evans .20 .50
85 Lee Orr .20 .50
86 Brandon Parrent .20 .50
87 Roman Quinn .50 1.25
88 Jake Floethe .20 .50
89 Andrew Susac .30 .75
90 Navery Moore .60 1.50
91 Chris Schwinden .20 .50
92 Cole Green .20 .50
93 Chris Wallace .30 .75
94 Steven Ames .20 .50
95 James Baldwin .20 .50
96 Forrest Snow .30 .75
97 Bobby Crocker .20 .50
98 Dwight Smith Jr. .20 .50
99 Greg Bird .40 1.00
100 Bryson Myles .30 .75
151 Anthony Meo .20 .50
152 Shawon Dunston Jr. .20 .50
153 Rookie Davis .50 1.25
154 Rob Scahill .20 .50
155 Chris Heston .30 .75
156 Adam Jorgenson .20 .50
157 Elliot Soto .20 .50
158 Tyler Cloyd .30 .75
159 Pierre LePage .20 .50
160 Brett Jacobson .20 .50
161 Casey Lawrence .30 .75
162 Joe O'Gara .30 .75
163 Mariekson Gregorius 5.00 12.00
164 Dan Osterbrock .20 .50
165 Jared Hoying .30 .75
166 Alan DeRatt .20 .50
167 Charlie Leesman .20 .50
168 Adam Davis .20 .50
169 Danry Vasquez .20 .50
170 Jon Griffin .20 .50
171 Hernan Perez .30 .75
172 Jeremy Cruz .20 .50
173 Jose Osuna .20 .50
174 Red Patterson .20 .50
175 Jamaine Cotton .20 .50
176 Pedro Villarreal .20 .50
177 Justin Boudreaux .20 .50
178 Chris Hanna .20 .50
179 Mike Walker .30 .75
180 David Herbek .20 .50
181 Zack MacPhee .30 .75
182 Ryan Tatusko .30 .75
183 Dan Meadows .20 .50
184 Albert Cartwright .30 .75
185 Brandon Drury .50 1.25
186 Eddie Rosario .60 1.50
187 Jake Dunning .20 .50
188 Miles Head .30 .75
189 Duanel Jones .20 .50
190 Rob Lyerly .20 .50
P1 Trevor Bauer AU/405 15.00 40.00
P2 Anthony Rendon AU/653 10.00 25.00
P3 Gerrit Cole AU/515 30.00 80.00
P4 Dylan Bundy AU/435 6.00 15.00
P5 C.J. Cron AU/465 6.00 15.00
P6 Tyler Collins AU/665 4.00 10.00
P7 C.Spangenberg AU/465 3.00 8.00
P8 Archie Bradley AU/464 4.00 10.00
P9 Jason Esposito AU/559 5.00 12.00
P10 Bubba Starling AU 6.00 15.00
P11 Joe Panik AU/572 3.00 8.00
P12 Kolten Wong AU/365 6.00 15.00
P13 Levi Michael AU/465 5.00 12.00
P14 Sonny Gray AU/364 6.00 15.00
P15 Javier Baez AU/565 25.00 60.00
P16 Danny Hultzen AU/642 6.00 15.00
P17 Alex Hassan AU/763 4.00 10.00
P18 Jace Peterson AU/665 3.00 8.00
P19 Jason King AU/862 3.00 8.00
P20 Kyle Kubitza AU/865 3.00 8.00
P21 Matt Szczur AU/783 5.00 12.00
P22 Sean Gilmartin AU/366 5.00 12.00
P23 Kevin Matthews AU/565 4.00 10.00
P24 Brandon Nimmo AU/565 3.00 8.00
P25 Jed Bradley AU/565 5.00 12.00
P26 C.Gallagher AU/760 4.00 10.00
P27 Mikie Mahtook AU/365 5.00 12.00
P28 Jacob Anderson AU/615 4.00 10.00
P29 Michael Fulmer AU/564 6.00 15.00
P30 Jackie Bradley Jr. AU/692 8.00 20.00
P31 T.Jungmann AU/465 3.00 8.00
P32 Matt Dean AU/855 4.00 10.00
P33 Joe Ross AU/365 6.00 15.00
P34 Jake Hager AU/665 4.00 10.00
P35 Josh Bell AU/692 15.00 40.00
P36 George Springer AU/537 10.00 25.00
P37 Chris Reed AU/500 3.00 8.00
P38 Brian Goodwin AU/750 3.00 8.00
P39 Francisco Lindor AU/557 30.00 80.00
P40 Tyler Gibson AU/665 4.00 10.00
P41 Robert Stephenson AU/334 6.00 15.00
P42 Brandon Martin AU/646 5.00 12.00
P43 Matt Purke AU/465 5.00 12.00
P44 Leonys Martin AU/746 4.00 10.00
P45 Keenyn Walker AU/665 3.00 8.00
P46 Kyle Parker AU/622 5.00 12.00
P47 Travis Harrison AU/664 3.00 8.00
P48 Matt Barnes AU/564 3.00 8.00
P49 Trevor Story AU/464 10.00 25.00
P50 Kyle Crick AU/614 5.00 12.00

2011 Donruss Elite Extra Edition Prospects Aspirations

*ASPIRATIONS: 2X TO 5X BASIC
COMMON CARD (P1-P50) 1.00 2.50
STATED PRINT RUN 200 SER.#'d SETS

74 Pratt Maynard 8.00 20.00
P1 Trevor Bauer 10.00 25.00
P2 Anthony Rendon 10.00 25.00
P3 Gerrit Cole 2.50 6.00
P4 Dylan Bundy 3.00 8.00
P5 C.J. Cron 5.00 12.00
P6 Tyler Collins 1.00 2.50
P7 Cory Spangenberg 1.50 4.00
P8 Archie Bradley 3.00 8.00
P9 Jason Esposito 2.50 6.00
P10 Bubba Starling 3.00 8.00
P11 Joe Panik 4.00 10.00
P12 Kolten Wong 1.50 4.00
P13 Levi Michael 1.50 4.00
P14 Sonny Gray 3.00 8.00
P15 Javier Baez 15.00 40.00
P16 Danny Hultzen 5.00 12.00
P17 Alex Hassan 1.00 2.50
P18 Jace Peterson 1.00 2.50
P19 Jason King 1.00 2.50
P20 Kyle Kubitza 1.00 2.50
P21 Matt Szczur 2.50 6.00
P22 Sean Gilmartin 1.00 2.50
P23 Kevin Matthews 1.00 2.50
P24 Brandon Nimmo 2.00 5.00
P25 Jed Bradley 1.50 4.00
P26 Cameron Gallagher 2.50 6.00
P27 Mikie Mahtook 2.50 6.00
P28 Jacob Anderson 3.00 8.00
P29 Michael Fulmer 2.50 6.00
P30 Jackie Bradley Jr. 4.00 10.00
P31 Taylor Jungmann 1.50 4.00
P32 Matt Dean 1.50 4.00
P33 Joe Ross 2.50 6.00
P34 Jake Hager 1.00 2.50
P35 Josh Bell 6.00 15.00
P36 George Springer 6.00 15.00
P37 Chris Reed 1.50 4.00
P38 Brian Goodwin 2.50 6.00
P39 Francisco Lindor 12.00 30.00
P40 Tyler Gibson 1.00 2.50
P41 Robert Stephenson 2.00 5.00
P42 Brandon Martin 1.50 4.00
P43 Matt Purke 2.50 6.00
P44 Leonys Martin 1.50 4.00
P45 Keenyn Walker 1.00 2.50
P46 Kyle Parker 1.50 4.00
P47 Travis Harrison 1.50 4.00
P48 Matt Barnes 1.50 4.00
P49 Trevor Story 15.00 40.00
P50 Kyle Crick 2.50 6.00

2011 Donruss Elite Extra Edition Prospects Status

*STATUS: 2.5X TO 6X BASIC
STATED PRINT RUN 100 SER.#'d SETS

74 Pratt Maynard 10.00 25.00
P1 Trevor Bauer 12.00 30.00
P2 Anthony Rendon 12.00 30.00
P3 Gerrit Cole 3.00 8.00
P4 Dylan Bundy 4.00 10.00
P5 C.J. Cron 6.00 15.00
P6 Tyler Collins 1.25 3.00
P7 Cory Spangenberg 2.00 5.00
P8 Archie Bradley 4.00 10.00
P9 Jason Esposito 3.00 8.00
P11 Joe Panik 5.00 12.00
P12 Kolten Wong 2.00 5.00
P13 Levi Michael 2.00 5.00
P14 Sonny Gray 4.00 10.00
P15 Javier Baez 15.00 40.00
P16 Danny Hultzen 6.00 15.00
P17 Alex Hassan 1.25 3.00
P18 Jace Peterson 1.25 3.00
P19 Jason King 1.25 3.00
P20 Kyle Kubitza 1.25 3.00
P21 Matt Szczur 3.00 8.00
P22 Sean Gilmartin 1.25 3.00
P23 Kevin Matthews 1.25 3.00
P24 Brandon Nimmo 3.00 6.00
P25 Jed Bradley 2.00 5.00
P26 Cameron Gallagher 3.00 8.00
P27 Mikie Mahtook 3.00 8.00
P28 Jacob Anderson 4.00 10.00
P29 Michael Fulmer 3.00 8.00
P30 Jackie Bradley Jr. 5.00 12.00
P31 Taylor Jungmann 2.00 5.00
P32 Matt Dean 2.00 5.00
P33 Joe Ross 3.00 8.00
P34 Jake Hager 1.25 3.00
P35 Josh Bell 8.00 20.00
P36 George Springer 8.00 20.00
P37 Chris Reed 2.00 5.00
P38 Brian Goodwin 3.00 8.00
P39 Francisco Lindor 15.00 40.00
P40 Tyler Gibson 1.25 3.00
P41 Robert Stephenson 2.50 6.00
P42 Brandon Martin 2.00 5.00
P43 Matt Purke 3.00 8.00
P44 Leonys Martin 2.00 5.00
P45 Keenyn Walker 1.25 3.00
P46 Kyle Parker 2.00 5.00
P47 Travis Harrison 2.00 5.00
P48 Matt Barnes 2.00 5.00
P49 Trevor Story 20.00 50.00
P50 Kyle Crick 3.00 8.00

2011 Donruss Elite Extra Edition Prospects Signature Aspirations

OVERALL SIX AUTOS PER HOBBY BOX
STATED PRINT RUN 100 SER.#'d SETS
EXCHANGE DEADLINE 06/28/2013

1 Tyler Goeddel 4.00 10.00
2 Dante Bichette Jr. 15.00 40.00
3 James Harris 5.00 12.00
4 Cory Mazzoni 10.00 25.00
5 Abel Baker 4.00 10.00
6 Alex Dickerson 8.00 20.00
7 Justin Bour 8.00 20.00
8 Tyler Anderson 10.00 25.00
9 Jeff Ames 4.00 10.00
10 Cristhian Adames 3.00 8.00
11 Jason Krizan 5.00 12.00
12 Michael Kelly 10.00 25.00
13 Kyle McMillen 3.00 8.00
14 Charlie Tilson 6.00 15.00
15 Brad Miller 5.00 12.00
16 Blake Snell 8.00 20.00
17 Daniel Norris 6.00 15.00
18 Williams Jerez 6.00 15.00
19 Erik Johnson 4.00 10.00
20 Gabriel Rosa 6.00 15.00
21 Adam Morgan 12.50 30.00
22 Aaron Westlake 6.00 15.00
23 Brandon Loy 4.00 10.00
24 Zach Good 3.00 8.00
25 Angelo Songco 8.00 20.00
26 Jordan Akins 5.00 12.00
27 Josh Osich 6.00 15.00
28 Austin Hedges 8.00 20.00
29 Jake Sisco 5.00 12.00
30 B.A. Vollmuth 8.00 20.00
31 Austin Wood 3.00 8.00
32 Dan Vogelbach 5.00 12.00
33 Carl Thomore 5.00 12.00
34 Blake Swihart 6.00 15.00
35 James Allen 3.00 8.00
36 Carlos Sanchez 3.00 8.00
37 Michael Goodnight 4.00 10.00
38 James McCann 8.00 20.00
39 Will Lamb 5.00 12.00
40 Taylor Featherston 3.00 8.00
41 Nick Ramirez 4.00 10.00
42 Johnny Eierman 8.00 20.00
43 Logan Verrett 5.00 12.00
44 Neftali Rosario 5.00 12.00
45 Kevin Comer 5.00 12.00
46 Kendrick Perkins 4.00 10.00
47 Tyler Grimes 3.00 8.00
48 Kyle Winkler 3.00 8.00
50 Taylor Guerrieri 5.00 12.00
51 Dillon Maples 6.00 15.00
52 Harold Martinez 3.00 8.00
53 Grayson Garvin 6.00 15.00
54 Zeke DeVoss 4.00 10.00
55 Mitch Walding 5.00 12.00
56 Clay Holmes 4.00 10.00
57 Hudson Boyd 5.00 12.00
58 Granden Goetzman 5.00 12.00
59 Bryan Brickhouse 4.00 10.00
60 Shane Opitz 4.00 10.00
61 Nick Fleece 4.00 10.00
62 Barret Loux 6.00 15.00
63 Jake Lowery 5.00 12.00
64 Madison Boer 4.00 10.00
65 Tony Zych 3.00 8.00
66 Sean Halton 5.00 12.00
67 Cavan Cohoes 6.00 15.00
68 Dean Green 4.00 10.00
69 Miles Hamblin 4.00 10.00
70 J.R. Graham 8.00 20.00
71 Tom Robson 5.00 12.00
72 Riccio Torrez 3.00 8.00
73 Adam Conley 3.00 8.00
74 Pratt Maynard 6.00 15.00
75 Jordan Cote 6.00 15.00
76 Kyle Gaedele 3.00 8.00
77 Christian Lopes 5.00 12.00
78 Travis Shaw 15.00 40.00
79 Parker Markel 3.00 8.00
80 Chad Comer 3.00 8.00
81 Adrian Houser 8.00 20.00
82 Corey Williams 5.00 12.00
84 Phillip Evans 4.00 10.00
85 Lee Orr 3.00 8.00
87 Roman Quinn 6.00 15.00
88 Jake Floethe 4.00 10.00
89 Andrew Susac 10.00 25.00
90 Navery Moore 5.00 12.00
91 Chris Schwinden 5.00 12.00
92 Cole Green 4.00 10.00
93 Chris Wallace 5.00 12.00
94 Steven Ames 5.00 12.00
95 James Baldwin 6.00 15.00
96 Forrest Snow 5.00 12.00
97 Bobby Crocker 5.00 12.00
98 Dwight Smith Jr. 8.00 20.00
99 Greg Bird 60.00 150.00
100 Bryson Myles 4.00 10.00
151 Anthony Meo 4.00 10.00
152 Shawon Dunston Jr. 6.00 15.00
153 Rookie Davis 30.00 60.00
154 Rob Scahill 3.00 8.00
155 Chris Heston 12.00 30.00
156 Adam Jorgenson 4.00 10.00
157 Elliot Soto 3.00 8.00
158 Tyler Cloyd 12.00 30.00
159 Pierre LePage 4.00 10.00
160 Brett Jacobson 3.00 8.00
161 Casey Lawrence 4.00 10.00
162 Joe O'Gara 5.00 12.00
163 Marlekson Gregorius 50.00 120.00
164 Dan Osterbrock 4.00 10.00
165 Jared Hoying 4.00 10.00
166 Alan DeRatt 3.00 8.00
167 Charlie Leesman 3.00 8.00
168 Adam Davis 3.00 8.00
169 Danry Vasquez 4.00 10.00
170 Jon Griffin 8.00 20.00
171 Hernan Perez 5.00 12.00
173 Jose Osuna 10.00 25.00
174 Red Patterson 4.00 10.00
175 Jamaine Cotton 4.00 10.00
176 Pedro Villarreal 5.00 12.00
177 Justin Boudreaux 4.00 10.00
180 David Herbek 3.00 8.00
181 Zack MacPhee 3.00 8.00
182 Ryan Tatusko 5.00 12.00
183 Dan Meadows 3.00 8.00
184 Albert Cartwright 4.00 10.00
185 Brandon Drury 8.00 20.00
186 Eddie Rosario 6.00 15.00
187 Jake Dunning 5.00 12.00
188 Miles Head 10.00 25.00
189 Duanel Jones 4.00 10.00
190 Rob Lyerly 4.00 10.00
P1 Trevor Bauer 20.00 50.00
P2 Anthony Rendon 10.00 25.00
P3 Gerrit Cole 50.00 120.00
P4 Dylan Bundy 30.00 60.00
P5 C.J. Cron 4.00 10.00
P6 Tyler Collins 4.00 10.00
P7 Cory Spangenberg 8.00 20.00
P8 Archie Bradley 5.00 12.00
P9 Jason Esposito 8.00 20.00
P10 Bubba Starling 12.50 30.00
P11 Joe Panik 6.00 15.00
P12 Kolten Wong 10.00 25.00
P13 Levi Michael 6.00 15.00
P14 Sonny Gray 5.00 12.00
P15 Javier Baez 40.00 100.00
P16 Danny Hultzen 30.00 60.00
P17 Alex Hassan 8.00 20.00
P18 Jace Peterson 3.00 8.00
P19 Jason King 4.00 10.00
P20 Kyle Kubitza 4.00 10.00
P21 Matt Szczur 6.00 15.00
P22 Sean Gilmartin 6.00 15.00
P23 Kevin Matthews 4.00 10.00
P24 Brandon Nimmo 4.00 10.00
P25 Jed Bradley 5.00 12.00
P26 Cameron Gallagher 5.00 12.00
P27 Mikie Mahtook 6.00 15.00
P28 Jacob Anderson 10.00 25.00
P29 Michael Fulmer 12.00 30.00
P30 Jackie Bradley Jr. 8.00 20.00
P31 Taylor Jungmann 6.00 15.00
P32 Matt Dean 8.00 20.00
P33 Joe Ross 8.00 20.00
P34 Jake Hager 3.00 8.00
P35 Josh Bell 15.00 40.00
P36 George Springer 25.00 60.00
P37 Chris Reed 10.00 25.00
P38 Brian Goodwin 4.00 10.00
P39 Francisco Lindor 40.00 100.00
P40 Tyler Gibson 6.00 15.00
P41 Robert Stephenson 10.00 25.00
P42 Brandon Martin 3.00 8.00
P43 Matt Purke 12.50 30.00
P44 Leonys Martin 4.00 10.00
P45 Keenyn Walker 4.00 10.00
P46 Kyle Parker 3.00 8.00
P47 Travis Harrison 6.00 15.00
P48 Matt Barnes 4.00 10.00
P49 Trevor Story 15.00 40.00
P50 Kyle Crick 4.00 10.00

2011 Donruss Elite Extra Edition Prospects Signature Status

OVERALL SIX AUTOS PER HOBBY BOX
STATED PRINT RUN 50 SER.#'d SETS
EXCHANGE DEADLINE 06/28/2013

1 Tyler Goeddel 6.00 15.00
2 Dante Bichette Jr. 60.00 120.00
3 James Harris 6.00 15.00
4 Cory Mazzoni 4.00 10.00
5 Abel Baker 5.00 12.00
6 Alex Dickerson 15.00 40.00
7 Justin Bour 10.00 25.00
8 Tyler Anderson 5.00 12.00
9 Jeff Ames 6.00 15.00
10 Cristhian Adames 6.00 15.00
11 Jason Krizan 5.00 12.00
12 Michael Kelly 5.00 12.00
13 Kyle McMillen 4.00 10.00
14 Charlie Tilson 10.00 25.00
15 Brad Miller 8.00 20.00
16 Blake Snell 10.00 25.00
17 Daniel Norris 15.00 40.00
18 Williams Jerez 5.00 12.00
19 Erik Johnson 6.00 15.00
20 Gabriel Rosa 10.00 25.00
21 Adam Morgan 6.00 15.00
22 Aaron Westlake 10.00 25.00
23 Brandon Loy 6.00 15.00
24 Zach Good 4.00 10.00
25 Angelo Songco 10.00 25.00
26 Jordan Akins 6.00 15.00
27 Josh Osich 6.00 15.00
28 Austin Hedges 8.00 20.00
29 Jake Sisco 5.00 12.00
30 B.A. Vollmuth 8.00 20.00
31 Austin Wood 4.00 10.00
32 Dan Vogelbach 6.00 15.00
33 Carl Thomore 8.00 20.00
34 Blake Swihart 10.00 25.00
35 James Allen 4.00 10.00
36 Carlos Sanchez 5.00 12.00
37 Michael Goodnight 5.00 12.00
38 James McCann 10.00 25.00
39 Will Lamb 6.00 15.00
40 Taylor Featherston 4.00 10.00
41 Nick Ramirez 6.00 15.00
42 Johnny Eierman 8.00 20.00
43 Logan Verrett 8.00 20.00
44 Neftali Rosario 5.00 12.00
45 Kevin Comer 8.00 20.00
46 Kendrick Perkins 4.00 10.00
47 Tyler Grimes 4.00 10.00
48 Kyle Winkler 4.00 10.00
50 Taylor Guerrieri 12.50 30.00
51 Dillon Maples 10.00 25.00
52 Harold Martinez 5.00 12.00
53 Grayson Garvin 10.00 25.00
54 Zeke DeVoss 6.00 15.00
55 Mitch Walding 8.00 20.00
56 Clay Holmes 5.00 12.00
57 Hudson Boyd 6.00 15.00
58 Granden Goetzman 8.00 20.00
59 Bryan Brickhouse 6.00 15.00
60 Shane Opitz 5.00 12.00
61 Nick Fleece 5.00 12.00
62 Barret Loux 6.00 15.00
63 Jake Lowery 5.00 12.00
64 Madison Boer 6.00 15.00
65 Tony Zych 4.00 10.00
66 Sean Halton 6.00 15.00
67 Cavan Cohoes 8.00 20.00
68 Dean Green 6.00 15.00
69 Miles Hamblin 5.00 12.00
70 J.R. Graham 10.00 25.00
71 Tom Robson 8.00 20.00
72 Riccio Torrez 4.00 10.00
73 Adam Conley 4.00 10.00
74 Pratt Maynard 6.00 15.00
75 Jordan Cote 12.50 30.00
76 Kyle Gaedele 6.00 15.00
77 Christian Lopes 10.00 25.00
78 Travis Shaw 20.00 50.00
79 Parker Markel 4.00 10.00
80 Chad Comer 5.00 12.00
81 Adrian Houser 8.00 20.00
82 Corey Williams 10.00 25.00
83 Brian Flynn 6.00 15.00
84 Phillip Evans 6.00 15.00
85 Lee Orr 4.00 10.00
87 Roman Quinn 6.00 15.00
88 Jake Floethe 8.00 20.00
89 Andrew Susac 10.00 25.00
90 Navery Moore 5.00 12.00
91 Chris Schwinden 6.00 15.00
92 Cole Green 8.00 20.00
93 Chris Wallace 5.00 12.00
94 Steven Ames 5.00 12.00
95 James Baldwin 5.00 12.00
96 Forrest Snow 8.00 20.00
97 Bobby Crocker 10.00 25.00
98 Dwight Smith Jr. 10.00 25.00
99 Greg Bird 75.00 200.00
100 Bryson Myles 8.00 20.00
151 Anthony Meo 5.00 12.00
152 Shawon Dunston Jr. 5.00 12.00
153 Rookie Davis 10.00 25.00
154 Rob Scahill 4.00 8.00
155 Chris Heston 12.00 30.00
156 Adam Jorgenson 4.00 10.00
157 Elliot Soto 5.00 12.00
158 Tyler Cloyd 20.00 50.00
159 Pierre LePage 8.00 20.00
160 Brett Jacobson 4.00 10.00
161 Casey Lawrence 8.00 20.00
162 Joe O'Gara 6.00 15.00
163 Marlekson Gregorius 60.00 15.00
164 Dan Osterbrock 4.00 10.00
165 Jared Hoying 8.00 20.00
166 Alan DeRatt 4.00 10.00
167 Charlie Leesman 4.00 10.00
168 Adam Davis 4.00 10.00
169 Danry Vasquez 8.00 20.00
170 Jon Griffin 8.00 20.00
171 Hernan Perez 6.00 15.00
172 Jeremy Cruz 4.00 10.00
173 Jose Osuna 12.00 30.00
174 Red Patterson 4.00 10.00
175 Jamaine Cotton 5.00 12.00
176 Pedro Villarreal 6.00 15.00
177 Justin Boudreaux 5.00 12.00
180 David Herbek 4.00 10.00
181 Zack MacPhee 4.00 10.00
182 Ryan Tatusko 5.00 12.00
183 Dan Meadows 5.00 12.00
184 Albert Cartwright 4.00 10.00
185 Brandon Drury 12.50 30.00
186 Eddie Rosario 10.00 25.00
187 Jake Dunning 5.00 12.00
188 Miles Head 10.00 25.00
189 Duanel Jones 5.00 12.00
190 Rob Lyerly 5.00 12.00
P1 Trevor Bauer 25.00 60.00
P2 Anthony Rendon 12.00 30.00
P3 Gerrit Cole 60.00 150.00
P4 Dylan Bundy 20.00 50.00
P5 C.J. Cron 5.00 12.00
P6 Tyler Collins 5.00 12.00
P7 Cory Spangenberg 8.00 20.00
P8 Archie Bradley 20.00 50.00
P9 Jason Esposito 4.00 10.00
P10 Bubba Starling 20.00 50.00
P11 Joe Panik 15.00 40.00
P12 Kolten Wong 12.00 30.00
P13 Levi Michael 8.00 20.00
P14 Sonny Gray 15.00 40.00
P15 Javier Baez 50.00 120.00
P16 Danny Hultzen 12.00 30.00
P17 Alex Hassan 6.00 15.00
P18 Jace Peterson 8.00 20.00
P19 Jason King 5.00 12.00
P20 Kyle Kubitza 8.00 20.00
P21 Matt Szczur 8.00 20.00
P22 Sean Gilmartin 8.00 20.00
P23 Kevin Matthews 8.00 20.00
P24 Brandon Nimmo 6.00 15.00
P25 Jed Bradley 6.00 15.00
P26 Cameron Gallagher 6.00 15.00
P27 Mikie Mahtook 20.00 50.00
P28 Jacob Anderson 20.00 50.00
P29 Michael Fulmer 15.00 40.00
P30 Jackie Bradley Jr. 10.00 25.00
P31 Taylor Jungmann 12.50 30.00
P32 Matt Dean 10.00 25.00
P33 Joe Ross 10.00 25.00
P34 Jake Hager 5.00 12.00
P35 Josh Bell 20.00 50.00
P36 George Springer 30.00 80.00
P37 Chris Reed 15.00 40.00
P38 Brian Goodwin 5.00 12.00
P39 Francisco Lindor 50.00 120.00
P40 Tyler Gibson 15.00 40.00
P41 Robert Stephenson 12.50 30.00
P42 Brandon Martin 5.00 12.00
P43 Matt Purke 15.00 40.00
P44 Leonys Martin 20.00 50.00
P45 Keenyn Walker 4.00 10.00
P46 Kyle Parker 4.00 10.00
P47 Travis Harrison 8.00 20.00
P48 Matt Barnes 30.00 60.00
P49 Trevor Story 20.00 50.00
P50 Kyle Crick 5.00 12.00

2011 Donruss Elite Extra Edition Two Sport Stars

RANDOM INSERTS IN PACKS
STATED PRINT RUN 499 SER.#'d SETS

1 Kyle Parker .75 2.00
2 Jace Peterson .50 1.25
3 Archie Bradley 1.50 4.00
4 Zach Lee .75 2.00
5 Sonny Gray 1.25 3.00

6 Bubba Starling .75 2.00
7 Matt Szczur 1.25 3.00
8 Shane Opitz .75 2.00

2011 Donruss Elite Extra Edition Yearbook

STATED ODDS 1:10 HOBBY
1 Matt Purke 1.00 2.50
2 Christian Lopes 1.00 2.50
3 Andrew Susac .60 1.50
4 Dante Bichette Jr. .60 1.50
5 Brian Goodwin 1.00 2.50
6 Greg Bird .75 2.00
7 Ty Linton .40 1.00
8 Zach Cone .60 1.50
9 Anthony Meo .40 1.00
10 Sean Gilmartin .40 1.00
11 Phillip Evans .40 1.00
12 Justin O'Conner .40 1.00
13 Tony Wolters .40 1.00
14 Nick Castellanos 2.00 5.00
15 Dan Vogelbach 1.25 3.00
16 Williams Jerez .40 1.00
17 Matt Skole .60 1.50
18 Jackie Bradley Jr. 1.50 4.00
19 Tyler Goeddel .40 1.00
20 Angelo Songco .60 1.50

2011 Donruss Elite Extra Edition Yearbook Signatures

PRINT RUNS B/WN 25-899 COPIES PER
OVERALL SIX AUTOS PER HOBBY BOX
NO PRICING ON QTY 25 OR LESS
EXCHANGE DEADLINE 06/28/2013
2 Christian Lopes 4.00 10.00
3 Andrew Susac 5.00 12.00
4 Dante Bichette Jr. 5.00 12.00
5 Brian Goodwin 6.00 15.00
6 Greg Bird 20.00 50.00
7 Ty Linton 4.00 10.00
8 Zach Cone 4.00 10.00
9 Anthony Meo 3.00 8.00
10 Sean Gilmartin 6.00 15.00
14 Nick Castellanos 8.00 20.00
15 Dan Vogelbach 10.00 25.00
16 Williams Jerez 6.00 15.00
17 Matt Skole 5.00 12.00
18 Jackie Bradley Jr. 40.00 100.00
19 Tyler Goeddel 3.00 8.00
20 Angelo Songco 4.00 10.00

2012 Elite Extra Edition

COMP.SET w/o AU's (100) 12.50 30.00
COMMON CARD (1-100) .20 .50
COMMON SP (1-100) 5.00 12.00
COMMON AU (101-200) 3.00 8.00
AU SEMIS 4.00 10.00
AU UNLISTED 5.00 12.00
AU PRINT RUNS B/WN 299-799 COPIES
EXCHANGE DEADLINE 07/16/2014
1A Addison Russell .50 1.25
Batting
1B Addison Russell 15.00 40.00
Fielding SP
2A Albert Almora .75 2.00
Facing left
2B Albert Almora 15.00 40.00
Facing right SP
3A Andrew Heaney .40 1.00
Light jersey
3B Andrew Heaney 5.00 12.00
Dark jersey SP
4A Michael Wacha .60 1.50
White jersey
4B Michael Wacha 15.00 40.00
Blue jersey SP
5 Marcus Stroman .50 1.25
6 Pat Light .20 .50
7 Keon Barnum .30 .75
8 Mitch Gueller .30 .75
9A Max White .30 .75
Facing left
9B Max White 5.00 12.00
Facing right SP
10A Carson Kelly .50 1.25
Hand up
10B Carson Kelly 8.00 20.00
Hands down SP
11 Nick Travieso .40 1.00
12 Chris Stratton .30 .75
13 Tyrone Taylor .20 .50
14A Brian Johnson .30 .75
No ball
14B Brian Johnson 5.00 12.00
Ball visible SP
15A Luke Bard .30 .75
Facing forward
16 Matt Smoral .30 .75
17 Jesmuel Valentin .40 1.00
18 Patrick Wisdom .30 .75
19 Eddie Butler .30 .75
20 Dane Phillips .20 .50
21 Robert Refsnyder .50 1.25
22 Nolan Fontana .20 .50
23 Tyler Gonzales .20 .50
24 Joe DeCarlo .30 .75
25A Sam Selman .40 1.00
Glove visible
25B Sam Selman 5.00 12.00
No glove SP
26 Dylan Cozens .50 1.25
27 Duane Underwood .20 .50
28 Chris Beck .20 .50
29 Martin Agosta .30 .75
30 Alex Wood .20 .50
31 Adam Walker .20 .50
32 Avery Romero .30 .75
33 Ryan McNeil .20 .50
34 Matt Koch .20 .50
35 Austin Schotts .30 .75
36 Edwin Diaz .60 1.50
37 Kieran Lovegrove .20 .50
38 Brett Mooneyham .20 .50
39 Andrew Toles .20 .50
40 Jake Barrett .20 .50
41 Zach Quintana .20 .50
42 Nathan Mikolas .30 .75
43 Tyler Pike .20 .50
44 Zach Green .20 .50
45 Zack Jones .20 .50
46 Patrick Kivlehan .20 .50
47 Branden Kaupe .30 .75
48 Alex Mejia .20 .50
49 Ty Buttrey .30 .75
50 Charles Taylor .20 .50
51 Drew VerHagen .20 .50
52 Tyler Wagner .20 .50
53 Chris Serritella .20 .50
54 Corey Black .30 .75
55A Royce Bolinger .20 .50
Facing left
55B Royce Bolinger 8.00 20.00
Facing right SP
56 Adrian Sampson .20 .50
57 Nick Basto .20 .50
58 Dylan Baker .30 .75
59 Spencer Kieboom .20 .50
60 Ty Blach .20 .50
61 Cory Jones .20 .50
62 Ronnie Freeman .30 .75
63 Lex Rutledge .30 .75
64 Colin Rodgers .30 .75
65 Kolby Copeland .30 .75
66 Zach Lovvorn .20 .50
67 Eric Stamets .30 .75
68 Damion Carroll .20 .50
69 Felipe Perez .20 .50
70 Mason Melotakis .20 .50
71 Rowan Wick .30 .75
72 Jairo Beras .30 .75
73 Dario Pizzano .30 .75
74 Logan Taylor .20 .50
75 Nick Kingham .30 .75
76 Omar Luis Rodriguez .20 .50
77 Rio Ruiz .20 .50
78 Trey Lang .20 .50
79 Alex Muren .30 .75
80 D'Vone McClure .30 .75
81 Matt Price .20 .50
82 Alexis Rivera .30 .75
83 Aaron West .30 .75
84 Slade Smith .20 .50
85 Matt Juengel .20 .50
86 Kaleb Merck .20 .50
87 Anthony Melchionda .20 .50
88 J.O. Berrios 2.50 6.00
89 J.T. Chargois .30 .75
90 Fernando Perez .20 .50
91 Tom Murphy .30 .75
92 Bryan De La Rosa .30 .75
93 Angel Ortega .20 .50
94 Seth Maness .20 .50
95 Will Clinard .20 .50
96 Scott Oberg .20 .50
97 Jacob Wilson .30 .75
98 Anthony Banda .30 .75
99 Josh Conway .20 .50
100 Andrew Lockett .20 .50
101 Carlos Correa AU/470 60.00 150.00
102 Byron Buxton AU/599 20.00 50.00
103 Mike Zunino AU/677 4.00 10.00
104 Kevin Gausman AU/399 5.00 12.00
105 Kyle Zimmer AU/690 5.00 12.00
106 Max Fried AU/545 10.00 25.00
107 David Dahl AU/509 5.00 12.00
108 Gavin Cecchini AU/299 4.00 10.00
109 Courtney Hawkins AU/499 4.00 10.00
110 Tyler Naquin AU/612 8.00 20.00
111 Lucas Giolito AU/722 10.00 25.00
112 D.J. Davis AU/390 3.00 8.00
113 Corey Seager AU/330 40.00 100.00
114 Victor Roache AU/748 5.00 12.00
115 Deven Marrero AU/430 3.00 8.00
116 Lucas Sims AU/699 3.00 8.00
117 Stryker Trahan AU/597 4.00 10.00
118 Lewis Brinson AU/789 8.00 20.00
119 Kevin Plawecki AU/744 4.00 10.00
120 Richie Shaffer AU/722 3.00 8.00
121 Barrett Barnes AU/621 3.00 8.00
122 Shane Watson AU/799 3.00 8.00
123 Matt Olson AU/782 8.00 20.00
124 Lance McCullers AU/412 5.00 12.00
125 Mitch Haniger AU/750 5.00 12.00
126 Stephen Piscotty AU/680 5.00 12.00
127 Ty Hensley AU/790 3.00 8.00
128 Jesse Winker AU/494 15.00 40.00
129 Walker Weickel AU/597 3.00 8.00
130 James Ramsey AU/631 3.00 8.00
131 Joey Gallo AU/498 8.00 20.00
132 Mitch Nay AU/799 3.00 8.00
133 Alex Yarbrough AU/782 3.00 8.00
134 Preston Beck AU/782 3.00 8.00
135 Nick Goody AU/574 3.00 8.00
136 Daniel Robertson AU/589 3.00 8.00
137 Jake Thompson AU/740 3.00 8.00
138 Austin Nola AU/798 3.00 8.00
139 Tony Renda AU/598 3.00 8.00
140 Austin Aune AU/699 3.00 8.00
141 Tanner Rahier AU/612 3.00 8.00
142 Josh Elander AU/593 3.00 8.00
143 Tim Lopes AU/799 3.00 8.00
144 Ross Stripling AU/760 3.00 8.00
145 Bruce Maxwell AU/641 3.00 8.00
146 Mallex Smith AU/711 3.00 8.00
147 Collin Wiles AU/622 3.00 8.00
148 Pierce Johnson AU/799 3.00 8.00
149 Damien Magnifico AU/711 3.00 8.00
150 Travis Jankowski AU/641 3.00 8.00
151 Jeff Gelalich AU/497 3.00 8.00
152 Paul Blackburn AU/594 3.00 8.00
153 Steve Bean AU/397 3.00 8.00
154 Spencer Edwards AU/793 3.00 8.00
155 Branden Kline AU/588 3.00 8.00
156 Jeremy Baltz AU/799 3.00 8.00
157 Max White AU/510 3.00 8.00
158 Chase DeJong AU/799 3.00 8.00
159 Jamie Jarmon AU/580 3.00 8.00
160 Mitch Brown AU/610 3.00 8.00
161 Jamie Callahan AU/766 3.00 8.00
162 Joe Munoz AU/498 3.00 8.00
163 Peter O'Brien AU/360 3.00 8.00
164 Matt Koch AU/795 3.00 8.00
165 Patrick Cantwell AU/699 3.00 8.00
166 Blake Brown AU/651 3.00 8.00
167 Max Muncy AU/782 12.00 30.00
168 Justin Chigbogu AU/797 3.00 8.00
169 Alex Mejia AU/799 3.00 8.00
170 Jeff McVaney AU/710 3.00 8.00
171 Michael Earley AU/772 3.00 8.00
172 Steve Okert AU/780 3.00 8.00
173 Dan Langfield AU/799 3.00 8.00
174 Austin Maddox AU/352 3.00 8.00
175 Kenny Diekroeger AU/793 3.00 8.00
176 Brandon Brennan AU/749 3.00 8.00
177 Zach Isler AU/797 3.00 8.00
178 Stefen Romero AU/677 5.00 12.00
179 Mac Williamson AU/533 3.00 8.00
180 Seth Willoughby AU/749 3.00 8.00
181 Tyler Wagner AU/478 3.00 8.00
182 Jake Lamb AU/596 3.00 8.00
183 Preston Tucker AU/781 8.00 20.00
184 Josh Turley AU/799 3.00 8.00
185 Logan Vick AU/776 3.00 8.00
186 R.J. Alvarez AU/690 3.00 8.00
187 Clint Coulter AU/528 10.00 25.00
188 Joe Rogers AU/675 3.00 8.00
189 Evan Marzilli AU/791 3.00 8.00
190 Carlos Escobar AU/752 3.00 8.00
191 Wyatt Mathisen AU/739 8.00 20.00
192 Matt Reynolds AU/562 3.00 8.00
193 Nick Williams AU/490 4.00 10.00
194 Brady Rodgers AU/490 3.00 8.00
195 Tim Cooney AU/792 3.00 8.00
196 Brett Vertigan AU/554 4.00 10.00
197 Hoby Milner AU/799 3.00 8.00
198 Luke Maile AU/690 3.00 8.00
199 Darin Ruf AU/562 3.00 8.00
200 Adrian Marin AU/685 3.00 8.00

2012 Elite Extra Edition Aspirations

*ASPIRATIONS: 1.5X TO 4X BASIC
STATED PRINT RUN 200 SER.#'d SETS
101 Carlos Correa 10.00 25.00
102 Byron Buxton 6.00 15.00
103 Mike Zunino 2.00 5.00
104 Kevin Gausman 4.00 10.00
105 Kyle Zimmer 1.50 4.00
106 Max Fried 5.00 12.00
107 David Dahl 6.00 15.00
108 Gavin Cecchini 1.50 4.00
109 Courtney Hawkins 1.25 3.00
110 Tyler Naquin 2.00 5.00
111 Lucas Giolito 4.00 10.00
112 D.J. Davis 1.50 4.00
113 Corey Seager 5.00 12.00
114 Victor Roache 2.50 6.00
115 Deven Marrero 1.25 3.00
116 Lucas Sims 1.50 4.00
117 Stryker Trahan 1.25 3.00
118 Lewis Brinson 4.00 10.00
119 Kevin Plawecki 1.50 4.00
120 Richie Shaffer 1.50 4.00
121 Barrett Barnes 1.50 4.00
122 Shane Watson 1.50 4.00
123 Matt Olson 6.00 15.00
124 Lance McCullers 1.50 4.00
125 Mitch Haniger 3.00 8.00
126 Stephen Piscotty 2.50 6.00
127 Ty Hensley 1.50 4.00
128 Jesse Winker 5.00 12.00
129 Walker Weickel .75 2.00
130 James Ramsey 1.25 3.00
131 Joey Gallo 4.00 10.00
132 Mitch Nay .75 2.00
133 Alex Yarbrough .75 2.00
134 Preston Beck .75 2.00
135 Nick Goody 1.25 3.00
136 Daniel Robertson .75 2.00
137 Jake Thompson 1.25 3.00
138 Austin Nola .75 2.00
139 Tony Renda .75 2.00
140 Austin Aune 1.50 4.00
141 Tanner Rahier .75 2.00
142 Josh Elander .75 2.00
143 Tim Lopes .75 2.00
144 Ross Stripling .75 2.00
145 Bruce Maxwell 1.25 3.00
146 Mallex Smith .75 2.00
147 Collin Wiles .75 2.00
148 Pierce Johnson 1.50 4.00
149 Damien Magnifico .75 2.00
150 Travis Jankowski 1.50 4.00
151 Jeff Gelalich .75 2.00
152 Paul Blackburn 1.25 3.00
153 Steve Bean 1.50 4.00
154 Spencer Edwards 1.25 3.00
155 Branden Kline 1.25 3.00
156 Jeremy Baltz .75 2.00
157 Max White 1.25 3.00
158 Chase DeJong 1.50 4.00
159 Jamie Jarmon 1.25 3.00
160 Mitch Brown 1.25 3.00
161 Jamie Callahan .75 2.00
162 Joe Munoz .75 2.00
163 Peter O'Brien 2.00 5.00
164 Matt Koch .75 2.00
165 Patrick Cantwell .75 2.00
166 Blake Brown .75 2.00
167 Max Muncy 6.00 15.00
168 Justin Chigbogu 1.25 3.00
169 Alex Mejia .75 2.00
170 Jeff McVaney .75 2.00
171 Michael Earley 1.25 3.00
172 Steve Okert .75 2.00
173 Dan Langfield .75 2.00
174 Austin Maddox 1.25 3.00
175 Kenny Diekroeger 1.25 3.00
176 Brandon Brennan 1.25 3.00
177 Zach Isler 1.25 3.00
178 Stefen Romero 1.25 3.00
179 Mac Williamson 4.00 10.00
180 Seth Willoughby .75 2.00
181 Tyler Wagner .75 2.00
182 Jake Lamb 2.00 5.00
183 Preston Tucker 2.00 5.00
184 Josh Turley 1.25 3.00
185 Logan Vick .75 2.00
186 R.J. Alvarez 1.25 3.00
187 Clint Coulter 1.25 3.00
188 Joe Rogers .75 2.00
189 Evan Marzilli .75 2.00
190 Carlos Escobar .75 2.00
191 Wyatt Mathisen 1.25 3.00
192 Matt Reynolds 1.25 3.00
193 Nick Williams 1.25 3.00
194 Brady Rodgers .75 2.00
195 Tim Cooney .75 2.00
196 Brett Vertigan .75 2.00
197 Hoby Milner 1.25 3.00
198 Luke Maile .75 2.00
199 Darin Ruf 8.00 20.00
200 Adrian Marin 1.25 3.00

2012 Elite Extra Edition Back to the Future Signatures

PRINT RUNS B/WN 46-699 COPIES PER
EXCHANGE DEADLINE 07/16/2014
1 Dillon Maples/396 3.00 8.00
2 Hudson Boyd/73 3.00 8.00
3 Alex Dickerson/99 6.00 15.00
4 Christian Lopes/58 4.00 10.00
5 Barret Loux/599 3.00 8.00
6 Jordan Cote/51 8.00 20.00
7 Greg Bird/249 15.00 40.00
8 Elliot Soto/649 3.00 8.00
9 Austin Hedges/210 4.00 10.00
10 Rob Scahill/599 3.00 8.00
11 Travis Shaw/46 15.00 40.00
12 Daniel Norris/290 4.00 10.00
13 Justin Bour/499 3.00 8.00
14 Rob Lyerly/512 3.00 8.00
15 James McCann/61 8.00 20.00
16 Logan Verrett/48 6.00 15.00
17 Nick Ramirez/47 3.00 8.00
18 Eddie Rosario/699 4.00 10.00
19 Tommy Shirley/699 3.00 8.00
20 Didi Gregorius/621 12.00 30.00

2012 Elite Extra Edition Building Blocks Dual

1 Alex Wood/Lucas Sims .75 2.00
2 M.Wacha/T.Naquin 1.25 3.00
3 L.Giolito/M.Fried 2.50 6.00
4 Spencer Edwards/Steve Bean .75 2.00
5 D.J. Davis/Marcus Stroman 1.00 2.50
6 Alex Mejia/Robert Refsnyder 1.00 2.50
7 C.Correa/J.Berrios 5.00 12.00
8 B.Johnson/M.Zunino 1.00 2.50
9 Martin Agosta/Patrick Wisdom .60 1.50
10 Courtney Hawkins/Wyatt Mathisen .60 1.50
11 Aaron West/Jake Lamb 1.00 2.50
12 Brady Rodgers/Deven Marrero .60 1.50
13 Patrick Cantwell/Travis Jankowski .75 2.00
14 Evan Marzilli/Matt Price .40 1.00
15 B.Buxton/C.Correa 5.00 12.00
16 Richie Shaffer/Spencer Kieboom .75 2.00
17 James Ramsey/Preston Tucker 1.00 2.50
18 Damien Magnifico/Steve Okert .40 1.00
19 M.Zunino/S.Trahan 1.00 2.50
20 D.Cozens/M.Nay 1.00 2.50

2012 Elite Extra Edition Building Blocks Dual Signatures

PRINT RUNS B/WN 5-49 COPIES PER
NO PRICING ON QTY 25 OR LESS
EXCHANGE DEADLINE 07/16/2014
4 Spencer Edwards/Steve Bean/49 5.00 12.00
6 Alex Mejia/Robert Refsnyder/49 10.00 25.00
9 Martin Agosta/Patrick Wisdom/49 5.00 12.00
11 A.West/J.Lamb/49 8.00 20.00
13 Patrick Cantwell/Travis Jankowski/49 5.00 12.00
14 E.Marzilli/M.Price/49 6.00 15.00
18 D.Magnifico/S.Okert/49 8.00 20.00

2012 Elite Extra Edition Building Blocks Trio

1 Turley/Vick/Muncy 3.00 8.00
2 Wacha/Stripling/Naquin 1.25 3.00
3 Yrbrgh/Muncy/Beck 3.00 8.00
4 Johnson/Zunino/Fontana 1.00 2.50
5 Drew VerHagen/Sam Selman
Will Clinard .75 2.00
6 Correa/Berrios/Valentin 5.00 12.00
7 Jake Thompson/Spencer Edwards
Steve Bean .75 2.00
8 Andrew Heaney/Damien Magnifico
Steve Okert .75 2.00
9 Austin Aune/Nathan Mikolas
Peter O'Brien 1.00 2.50
10 Mnyhm/Psctty/Dkrgr 1.25 3.00

2012 Elite Extra Edition Diamond Kings

20 Jeff Gelalich .40 1.00
DK1 Darin Ruf 4.00 10.00
DK2 Mike Zunino 1.00 2.50
DK3 Carlos Correa 5.00 12.00
DK4 Corey Seager 2.50 6.00
DK5 Kevin Gausman 2.00 5.00
DK6 Andrew Heaney .75 2.00
DK7 David Dahl 2.00 5.00
DK8 Albert Almora 1.50 4.00
DK9 Stefen Romero .60 1.50
DK10 Lance McCullers .60 1.50
DK11 Joey Gallo 2.00 5.00
DK12 Byron Buxton 3.00 8.00
DK13 Kyle Zimmer .75 2.00
DK14 Chris Stratton .60 1.50
DK15 Gavin Cecchini .75 2.00
DK16 Marcus Stroman 1.00 2.50
DK17 Omar Luis Rodriguez .40 1.00
DK18 Tyler Naquin 1.00 2.50
DK19 Courtney Hawkins .60 1.50

2012 Elite Extra Edition Elite Series

1 Albert Almora 1.50 4.00
2 Andrew Heaney .75 2.00
3 Joey Gallo 2.00 5.00
4 Lance McCullers .60 1.50
5 David Dahl 2.00 5.00
6 Carlos Correa 5.00 12.00
7 Deven Marrero .60 1.50
8 Byron Buxton 3.00 8.00
9 Corey Seager 2.50 6.00
10 Jake Thompson .40 1.00
11 Travis Jankowski .75 2.00
12 Kevin Gausman 2.00 5.00
13 Jesse Winker 2.50 6.00
14 Lucas Giolito 2.00 5.00
15 Courtney Hawkins .60 1.50
16 Victor Roache 1.25 3.00
17 Mike Zunino 1.00 2.50
18 Matt Reynolds .60 1.50
19 Kyle Zimmer .75 2.00
20 Nolan Fontana .40 1.00

2012 Elite Extra Edition Elite Series Signatures

PRINT RUNS B/WN 25-199 COPIES PER
EXCHANGE DEADLINE 07/16/2014
1 Albert Almora/49 10.00 25.00
2 Andrew Heaney/125 5.00 12.00
3 Joey Gallo/199 12.00 30.00
4 Lance McCullers/99 8.00 20.00
5 David Dahl/125 6.00 15.00
6 Carlos Correa/49 60.00 150.00
7 Deven Marrero/99 6.00 15.00
8 Byron Buxton/49 60.00 120.00
9 Corey Seager/150 40.00 100.00
10 Jake Thompson/199 3.00 8.00
11 Travis Jankowski/50 4.00 10.00
12 Kevin Gausman/50 12.50 30.00
13 Jesse Winker/125 15.00 40.00
14 Lucas Giolito/149 12.00 30.00
15 Courtney Hawkins/50 10.00 25.00
16 Victor Roache/99 10.00 25.00
17 Mike Zunino/39 50.00 100.00
18 Matt Reynolds/199 4.00 10.00
19 Kyle Zimmer/25 20.00 50.00
20 Nolan Fontana/119 4.00 10.00

2012 Elite Extra Edition First Overall Pick Jersey

STATED PRINT RUN 999 SER.#'d SETS
1 Carlos Correa 6.00 15.00

2012 Elite Extra Edition Franchise Futures Signatures

PRINT RUNS B/WN 117-799 COPIES PER
EXCHANGE DEADLINE 07/16/2014
1 Addison Russell/250 6.00 15.00
2 Albert Almora/210 4.00 10.00
3 Andrew Heaney/175 3.00 8.00
4 Michael Wacha/210 4.00 10.00
5 Marcus Stroman/195 5.00 12.00
6 Pat Light/149 3.00 8.00
7 Keon Barnum/225 3.00 8.00
8 Mitch Gueller/220 4.00 10.00
9 Max White/229 3.00 8.00
10 Carson Kelly/205 4.00 10.00
11 Nick Travieso/125 6.00 15.00
12 Chris Stratton/120 10.00 25.00
13 Tyrone Taylor/192 8.00 20.00
14 Brian Johnson/212 3.00 8.00
15 Luke Bard/117 3.00 8.00
16 Matt Smoral/222 3.00 8.00
17 Jesmuel Valentin/180 8.00 20.00
18 Patrick Wisdom AU/161
19 Eddie Butler/160 3.00 8.00
20 Dane Phillips/189 3.00 8.00
21 Robert Refsnyder/799 5.00 12.00
22 Nolan Fontana/210 3.00 8.00
23 Tyler Gonzales/151 6.00 15.00
24 Joe DeCarlo/190 3.00 8.00
25 Sam Selman/200 3.00 8.00
26 Dylan Cozens/199 12.00 30.00
27 Duane Underwood/152 8.00 20.00
28 Chris Beck/145 3.00 8.00
29 Martin Agosta/200 4.00 10.00
30 Alex Wood/200 8.00 20.00
31 Adam Walker/225 8.00 20.00
32 Avery Romero/275 3.00 8.00
33 Ryan McNeil/239 3.00 8.00
34 Matt Koch/300 3.00 8.00
35 Austin Schotts/499 5.00 12.00
36 Edwin Diaz AU/355 10.00 25.00
37 Kieran Lovegrove/249 3.00 8.00
38 Brett Mooneyham/350 3.00 8.00
39 Andrew Toles/317 3.00 8.00
40 Jake Barrett/319 3.00 8.00
41 Zach Quintana/381 3.00 8.00
42 Nathan Mikolas/355 5.00 12.00
43 Tyler Pike/799 3.00 8.00
44 Zach Green/419 6.00 15.00
45 Zack Jones/376 3.00 8.00
46 Patrick Kivlehan/352 3.00 8.00
47 Branden Kaupe/347 4.00 10.00
48 Alex Mejia/397 3.00 8.00
49 Ty Buttrey/499 3.00 8.00
50 Charles Taylor/492 3.00 8.00
51 Drew VerHagen/699 3.00 8.00
52 Tyler Wagner/461 3.00 8.00
53 Chris Serritella/312 3.00 8.00
54 Corey Black/283 3.00 8.00
55 Royce Bolinger/697 3.00 8.00
56 Adrian Sampson/180 3.00 8.00
57 Nick Basto/290 3.00 8.00
58 Dylan Baker AU/788 3.00 8.00
59 Spencer Kieboom/475 3.00 8.00
60 Ty Blach/560 3.00 8.00
61 Cory Jones/781 3.00 8.00
62 Ronnie Freeman/290 4.00 10.00
63 Lex Rutledge/471 3.00 8.00
64 Colin Rodgers/399 3.00 8.00
65 Kolby Copeland/433 3.00 8.00
66 Zach Lovvorn/592 3.00 8.00
67 Eric Stamets/590 3.00 8.00
68 Damion Carroll/649 3.00 8.00
69 Felipe Perez/799 3.00 8.00
70 Mason Melotakis/575 3.00 8.00
71 Rowan Wick/442 3.00 8.00
72 Jairo Beras/490 3.00 8.00
73 Dario Pizzano AU/490 4.00 10.00
74 Logan Taylor/712 3.00 8.00
75 Nick Kingham/599 3.00 8.00
76 Omar Luis Rodriguez/499 6.00 15.00
77 Rio Ruiz/590 3.00 8.00
78 Trey Lang/451 3.00 8.00
79 Alex Muren/788 3.00 8.00
80 D'Vone McClure AU/496 3.00 8.00
81 Matt Price/790 3.00 8.00
82 Alexis Rivera/797 3.00 8.00
83 Aaron West AU/788 3.00 8.00
84 Slade Smith AU/799 3.00 8.00
85 Matt Juengel AU/799 3.00 8.00
86 Kaleb Merck/799 3.00 8.00
87 Anthony Melchionda/791 3.00 8.00
88 J.O. Berrios/175 12.00 30.00
89 J.T. Chargois/175 4.00 10.00
90 Fernando Perez AU/692 3.00 8.00
91 Tom Murphy/371 3.00 8.00
92 Bryan De La Rosa/779 3.00 8.00
93 Angel Ortega/699 3.00 8.00
94 Seth Maness/722 3.00 8.00
95 Will Clinard/790 3.00 8.00
96 Scott Oberg/799 3.00 8.00
97 Jacob Wilson AU/749 3.00 8.00
98 Anthony Banda/500 3.00 8.00
99 Josh Conway/280 3.00 8.00
100 Andrew Lockett/299 3.00 8.00

2012 Elite Extra Edition Signature Aspirations

STATED PRINT RUN 100 SER.#'d SETS
EXCHANGE DEADLINE 07/16/2014
1 Addison Russell 20.00 50.00
2 Albert Almora 4.00 10.00
3 Andrew Heaney 4.00 10.00
4 Michael Wacha 4.00 10.00
5 Marcus Stroman 8.00 20.00
6 Pat Light 5.00 12.00
7 Keon Barnum 5.00 12.00
8 Mitch Gueller 6.00 15.00
9 Max White 3.00 8.00
10 Carson Kelly 6.00 15.00
11 Nick Travieso 4.00 10.00
12 Chris Stratton 4.00 10.00
13 Tyrone Taylor 5.00 12.00
14 Brian Johnson 4.00 10.00
15 Luke Bard 3.00 8.00
16 Matt Smoral 6.00 15.00
17 Jesmuel Valentin 8.00 20.00
18 Patrick Wisdom 4.00 10.00
19 Eddie Butler 3.00 8.00
20 Dane Phillips 3.00 8.00
21 Robert Refsnyder 25.00 60.00
22 Nolan Fontana 3.00 8.00
23 Tyler Gonzales 4.00 10.00
24 Joe DeCarlo 3.00 8.00
25 Sam Selman 4.00 10.00
26 Dylan Cozens 15.00 40.00
27 Duane Underwood 4.00 10.00
28 Chris Beck 4.00 10.00
29 Martin Agosta 6.00 15.00
30 Alex Wood 10.00 25.00
31 Adam Walker 5.00 12.00
32 Avery Romero 3.00 8.00
33 Ryan McNeil 5.00 12.00
34 Matt Koch 3.00 8.00
35 Austin Schotts 10.00 25.00
36 Edwin Diaz 12.00 30.00
37 Kieran Lovegrove 4.00 10.00
38 Brett Mooneyham 4.00 10.00
39 Andrew Toles 4.00 10.00
40 Jake Barrett 4.00 10.00
41 Zach Quintana 3.00 8.00
42 Nathan Mikolas 8.00 20.00
43 Tyler Pike 5.00 12.00
44 Zach Green 3.00 8.00
45 Zack Jones 3.00 8.00
46 Patrick Kivlehan 3.00 8.00
47 Branden Kaupe 5.00 12.00
48 Alex Mejia 3.00 8.00
49 Ty Buttrey 4.00 10.00
50 Charles Taylor 3.00 8.00
51 Drew VerHagen 3.00 8.00
52 Tyler Wagner 3.00 8.00
53 Chris Serritella 4.00 10.00
54 Corey Black 5.00 12.00
55 Royce Bolinger 3.00 8.00
56 Adrian Sampson 4.00 10.00
57 Nick Basto 3.00 8.00
58 Dylan Baker 6.00 15.00
60 Ty Blach 3.00 8.00
61 Cory Jones 3.00 8.00
62 Ronnie Freeman 3.00 8.00
63 Lex Rutledge 3.00 8.00
64 Colin Rodgers 5.00 12.00
65 Kolby Copeland 4.00 10.00
66 Zach Lovvorn 3.00 8.00
67 Eric Stamets 3.00 8.00
68 Damion Carroll 3.00 8.00
69 Felipe Perez 3.00 8.00
70 Mason Melotakis 3.00 8.00
71 Rowan Wick 3.00 8.00
72 Jairo Beras 5.00 12.00
73 Dario Pizzano 8.00 20.00
74 Logan Taylor 3.00 8.00
75 Nick Kingham 4.00 10.00
76 Omar Luis Rodriguez 10.00 25.00
77 Rio Ruiz 3.00 8.00
78 Trey Lang 3.00 8.00
79 Alex Muren 3.00 8.00
80 D'Vone McClure 10.00 25.00
81 Matt Price 3.00 8.00
82 Alexis Rivera 6.00 15.00
83 Aaron West 10.00 25.00
85 Matt Juengel 3.00 8.00
86 Kaleb Merck 3.00 8.00
87 Anthony Melchionda 3.00 8.00
88 J.O. Berrios 12.00 30.00
89 J.T. Chargois 3.00 8.00
90 Fernando Perez 5.00 12.00
91 Tom Murphy 3.00 8.00
92 Bryan De La Rosa 3.00 8.00
93 Angel Ortega 3.00 8.00
94 Seth Maness 4.00 10.00
95 Will Clinard 3.00 8.00
96 Scott Oberg 3.00 8.00
97 Jacob Wilson 4.00 10.00
98 Anthony Banda 3.00 8.00
100 Andrew Lockett 3.00 8.00
101 Carlos Correa 60.00 150.00
102 Byron Buxton 25.00 60.00
103 Mike Zunino 30.00 60.00
104 Kevin Gausman 4.00 10.00
105 Kyle Zimmer 8.00 20.00
106 Max Fried 12.00 30.00
107 David Dahl 15.00 40.00
108 Gavin Cecchini 5.00 12.00
109 Courtney Hawkins 6.00 15.00
110 Tyler Naquin 10.00 25.00
111 Lucas Giolito 15.00 40.00
112 D.J. Davis 8.00 20.00
113 Corey Seager 50.00 120.00
114 Victor Roache 6.00 15.00
115 Deven Marrero 5.00 12.00
116 Lucas Sims 8.00 20.00
117 Stryker Trahan 6.00 15.00
118 Lewis Brinson 10.00 25.00
119 Kevin Plawecki 5.00 12.00
120 Richie Shaffer 6.00 15.00
121 Barrett Barnes 5.00 12.00
122 Shane Watson 4.00 10.00
123 Matt Olson 12.00 30.00
124 Lance McCullers 8.00 20.00
125 Mitch Haniger 10.00 25.00
126 Stephen Piscotty 10.00 25.00
128 Jesse Winker 15.00 40.00
129 Walker Weickel 5.00 12.00
130 James Ramsey 5.00 12.00
131 Joey Gallo 12.00 30.00
132 Mitch Nay 3.00 8.00
133 Alex Yarbrough 5.00 12.00
134 Preston Beck 3.00 8.00
135 Nick Goody 4.00 10.00
136 Daniel Robertson 4.00 10.00
137 Jake Thompson 4.00 10.00
138 Austin Nola 3.00 8.00
140 Austin Aune 5.00 12.00
142 Josh Elander 3.00 8.00
144 Ross Stripling 10.00 25.00
145 Bruce Maxwell 3.00 8.00
146 Mallex Smith 3.00 8.00
147 Collin Wiles 4.00 10.00
148 Pierce Johnson 6.00 15.00
149 Damien Magnifico 4.00 10.00
151 Jeff Gelalich 3.00 8.00
152 Paul Blackburn 4.00 10.00
153 Steve Bean 4.00 10.00
154 Spencer Edwards 4.00 10.00
155 Branden Kline 5.00 12.00
156 Jeremy Baltz 3.00 8.00
157 Max White 3.00 8.00
158 Chase DeJong 4.00 10.00
159 Jamie Jarmon 4.00 10.00
160 Mitch Brown 4.00 10.00
161 Jamie Callahan 3.00 8.00
162 Joe Munoz 4.00 10.00
163 Peter O'Brien 6.00 15.00
164 Matt Koch 3.00 8.00
165 Patrick Cantwell 3.00 8.00
166 Blake Brown 4.00 10.00
167 Max Muncy 12.00 30.00
168 Justin Chigbogu 5.00 12.00
169 Alex Mejia 3.00 8.00
170 Jeff McVaney 3.00 8.00
171 Michael Earley 3.00 8.00
172 Steve Okert 3.00 8.00
173 Dan Langfield 4.00 10.00
174 Austin Maddox 4.00 10.00
175 Kenny Diekroeger 3.00 8.00
176 Brandon Brennan 3.00 8.00
177 Zach Isler 3.00 8.00
178 Stefen Romero 5.00 12.00
179 Mac Williamson 4.00 10.00
180 Seth Willoughby 3.00 8.00
181 Tyler Wagner 3.00 8.00
182 Jake Lamb 8.00 20.00
183 Preston Tucker 10.00 25.00
184 Josh Turley 5.00 12.00
185 Logan Vick 3.00 8.00
186 R.J. Alvarez 5.00 12.00
187 Clint Coulter 15.00 40.00
189 Evan Marzilli 3.00 8.00
190 Carlos Escobar 3.00 8.00
191 Wyatt Mathisen 5.00 12.00
192 Matt Reynolds 4.00 10.00
193 Nick Williams 6.00 15.00
194 Brady Rodgers 5.00 12.00
195 Tim Cooney 3.00 8.00
196 Brett Vertigan 3.00 8.00
197 Hoby Milner 6.00 15.00
198 Luke Maile 3.00 8.00
199 Darin Ruf 40.00 80.00
200 Adrian Marin 4.00 10.00

2012 Elite Extra Edition Signature Status Blue

STATED PRINT RUN 50 SER.#'d SETS
EXCHANGE DEADLINE 07/16/2014
1 Addison Russell 20.00 50.00
2 Albert Almora 5.00 12.00
3 Andrew Heaney 10.00 25.00
4 Michael Wacha 5.00 12.00
5 Marcus Stroman 10.00 25.00
7 Keon Barnum 10.00 25.00
8 Mitch Gueller 8.00 20.00
9 Max White 4.00 10.00
11 Nick Travieso 8.00 20.00
12 Chris Stratton 20.00 50.00
13 Tyrone Taylor 8.00 20.00
14 Brian Johnson 8.00 20.00
16 Matt Smoral 10.00 25.00
17 Jesmuel Valentin 12.50 30.00
18 Patrick Wisdom 8.00 20.00
19 Eddie Butler 6.00 15.00
20 Dane Phillips 3.00 8.00
21 Robert Refsnyder 30.00 80.00
22 Nolan Fontana 5.00 12.00
23 Tyler Gonzales 10.00 25.00
24 Joe DeCarlo 4.00 10.00
25 Sam Selman 10.00 25.00
26 Dylan Cozens 20.00 50.00
27 Duane Underwood 6.00 15.00
28 Chris Beck 3.00 8.00
30 Alex Wood 12.00 30.00
31 Adam Walker 15.00 40.00
32 Avery Romero 5.00 12.00
33 Ryan McNeil 5.00 12.00
34 Matt Koch 4.00 10.00
35 Austin Schotts 20.00 50.00
36 Edwin Diaz 15.00 40.00
37 Kieran Lovegrove 5.00 12.00
38 Brett Mooneyham 5.00 12.00
39 Andrew Toles 5.00 12.00
40 Jake Barrett 4.00 10.00
41 Zach Quintana 8.00 20.00
42 Nathan Mikolas 6.00 15.00
43 Tyler Pike 6.00 15.00
44 Zach Green 6.00 15.00
46 Patrick Kivlehan 4.00 10.00

47 Branden Kaupe 5.00 12.00
49 Ty Buttrey 4.00 10.00
50 Charles Taylor 3.00 8.00
51 Drew VerHagen 5.00 12.00
52 Tyler Wagner 4.00 10.00
53 Chris Serritella 6.00 15.00
54 Corey Black 8.00 20.00
55 Royce Bolinger 3.00 8.00
56 Adrian Sampson 5.00 12.00
57 Nick Basto 3.00 8.00
58 Dylan Baker 6.00 15.00
59 Spencer Kieboom 3.00 8.00
60 Ty Blach 3.00 8.00
61 Cory Jones 3.00 8.00
62 Ronnie Freeman 3.00 8.00
63 Lex Rutledge 4.00 10.00
65 Kolby Copeland 4.00 10.00
66 Zach Lovvorn 3.00 8.00
67 Eric Stamets 3.00 8.00
68 Damion Carroll 3.00 8.00
69 Felipe Perez 5.00 12.00
70 Mason Melotakis 3.00 8.00
71 Rowan Wick 5.00 12.00
72 Jairo Beras 12.50 30.00
73 Dario Pizzano 12.50 30.00
74 Logan Taylor 6.00 15.00
76 Omar Luis Rodriguez 10.00 25.00
77 Rio Ruiz 5.00 12.00
78 Trey Lang 5.00 12.00
80 D'Vone McClure 15.00 40.00
81 Matt Price 5.00 12.00
82 Alexis Rivera 10.00 25.00
84 Slade Smith 6.00 15.00
85 Matt Juengel 3.00 8.00
86 Kaleb Merck 3.00 8.00
87 Anthony Melchionda 4.00 10.00
88 J.O. Berrios 15.00 40.00
89 J.T. Chargois 5.00 12.00
90 Fernando Perez 6.00 15.00
91 Tom Murphy 6.00 15.00
92 Bryan De La Rosa 6.00 15.00
93 Angel Ortega 4.00 10.00
94 Seth Maness 8.00 20.00
95 Will Clinard 3.00 8.00
96 Scott Oberg 3.00 8.00
99 Josh Conway 6.00 15.00
100 Andrew Lockett 4.00 10.00
101 Carlos Correa 75.00 200.00
102 Byron Buxton 30.00 80.00
103 Mike Zunino 12.50 30.00
104 Kevin Gausman 6.00 15.00
105 Kyle Zimmer 12.50 30.00
106 Max Fried 15.00 40.00
107 David Dahl 20.00 50.00
108 Gavin Cecchini 6.00 15.00
109 Courtney Hawkins 10.00 25.00
110 Tyler Naquin 12.00 30.00
111 Lucas Giolito 20.00 50.00
112 D.J. Davis 8.00 20.00
113 Corey Seager 60.00 150.00
115 Deven Marrero 8.00 20.00
116 Lucas Sims 12.50 30.00
117 Stryker Trahan 12.50 30.00
118 Lewis Brinson 12.50 30.00
119 Kevin Plawecki 5.00 12.00
120 Richie Shaffer 12.50 30.00
121 Barrett Barnes 6.00 15.00
122 Shane Watson 5.00 12.00
123 Matt Olson 15.00 40.00
124 Lance McCullers 20.00 50.00
125 Mitch Haniger 12.00 30.00
126 Stephen Piscotty 12.00 30.00
128 Jesse Winker 20.00 50.00
129 Walker Weickel 5.00 12.00
130 James Ramsey 5.00 12.00
131 Joey Gallo 15.00 40.00
132 Mitch Nay 6.00 15.00
133 Alex Yarbrough 6.00 15.00
134 Preston Beck 3.00 8.00
135 Nick Goody 4.00 10.00
136 Daniel Robertson 8.00 20.00
137 Jake Thompson 5.00 12.00
138 Austin Nola 3.00 8.00
139 Tony Renda 4.00 10.00
140 Austin Aune 10.00 25.00
141 Tanner Rahier 4.00 10.00
142 Josh Elander 4.00
144 Ross Stripling 12.00 30.00
146 Mallex Smith 4.00 10.00
147 Collin Wiles 4.00 10.00
148 Pierce Johnson 5.00 12.00
149 Damien Magnifico 6.00 15.00
151 Jeff Gelalich 4.00 10.00
152 Paul Blackburn 4.00 10.00
153 Steve Bean 5.00 12.00
154 Spencer Edwards 5.00 12.00
155 Branden Kline 5.00 12.00
157 Max White 4.00 10.00
158 Chase DeJong 10.00 25.00
159 Jamie Jarmon 10.00 25.00
160 Mitch Brown 5.00 12.00
161 Jamie Callahan 3.00 8.00
162 Joe Munoz 4.00 10.00
163 Peter O'Brien 8.00 20.00
164 Matt Koch 4.00 10.00
165 Patrick Cantwell 3.00 8.00
166 Blake Brown 4.00 10.00
167 Max Muncy 15.00 40.00
168 Justin Chigbogu 5.00 12.00
169 Alex Mejia 4.00 10.00
170 Jeff McVaney 3.00 8.00
171 Michael Earley 4.00 10.00
173 Dan Langfield 4.00 10.00
174 Austin Maddox 5.00 12.00
175 Kenny Diekroeger 4.00 10.00
176 Brandon Brennan 3.00 8.00
177 Zach Isler 8.00 20.00
178 Stefen Romero 20.00 50.00
179 Mac Williamson 12.00 30.00
180 Seth Willoughby 3.00 8.00
181 Tyler Wagner 3.00 8.00
183 Preston Tucker 12.00 30.00
184 Josh Turley 5.00 12.00
185 Logan Vick 4.00 10.00
186 R.J. Alvarez 6.00 15.00
187 Clint Coulter 4.00 10.00
188 Joe Rogers 3.00 8.00
189 Evan Marzilli 3.00 8.00
190 Carlos Escobar 3.00 8.00
191 Wyatt Mathisen 6.00 15.00
192 Matt Reynolds 6.00 15.00
193 Nick Williams 10.00 25.00
194 Brady Rodgers 8.00 20.00
196 Brett Vertigan 3.00 8.00
197 Hoby Milner 8.00 20.00
198 Luke Maile 3.00 8.00
199 Darin Ruf 12.00 30.00
200 Adrian Marin 5.00 12.00

2012 Elite Extra Edition Status

*STATUS: 2.5X TO 6X BASIC
STATED PRINT RUN 100 SER.#'d SETS
101 Carlos Correa 15.00 40.00
102 Byron Buxton 10.00 25.00
103 Mike Zunino 3.00 8.00
104 Kevin Gausman 6.00 15.00
105 Kyle Zimmer 2.50 6.00
106 Max Fried 8.00 20.00
107 David Dahl 6.00 15.00
108 Gavin Cecchini 2.50 6.00
109 Courtney Hawkins 2.00 5.00
110 Tyler Naquin 3.00 8.00
111 Lucas Giolito 6.00 15.00
112 D.J. Davis 2.50 6.00
113 Corey Seager 8.00 20.00
114 Victor Roache 4.00 10.00
115 Deven Marrero 2.00 5.00
116 Lucas Sims 2.50 6.00
117 Stryker Trahan 2.00 5.00
118 Lewis Brinson 6.00 15.00
119 Kevin Plawecki 2.50 6.00
120 Richie Shaffer 2.50 6.00
121 Barrett Barnes 2.50 6.00
122 Shane Watson 2.50 6.00
123 Matt Olson 10.00 25.00
124 Lance McCullers 2.00 5.00
125 Mitch Haniger 5.00 12.00
126 Stephen Piscotty 4.00 10.00
127 Ty Hensley 2.50 6.00
128 Jesse Winker 8.00 20.00
129 Walker Weickel 1.25 3.00
130 James Ramsey 2.00 5.00
131 Joey Gallo 6.00 15.00
132 Mitch Nay 1.25 3.00
133 Alex Yarbrough 2.00 5.00
134 Preston Beck 1.25 3.00
135 Nick Goody 2.00 5.00
136 Daniel Robertson 1.25 3.00
137 Jake Thompson 1.25 3.00
138 Austin Nola 1.25 3.00
139 Tony Renda 1.25 3.00
140 Austin Aune 2.50 6.00
141 Tanner Rahier 2.00 5.00
142 Josh Elander 1.25 3.00
143 Tim Lopes 1.25 3.00
144 Ross Stripling 1.25 3.00
145 Bruce Maxwell 2.00 5.00
147 Collin Wiles 1.25 3.00
148 Pierce Johnson 2.50 6.00
149 Damien Magnifico 1.25 3.00
150 Travis Jankowski 2.50 6.00
151 Jeff Gelalich 1.25 3.00
152 Paul Blackburn 2.00 5.00
153 Steve Bean 2.50 6.00
154 Spencer Edwards 2.00 5.00
155 Branden Kline 2.00 5.00
156 Jeremy Baltz 1.25 3.00
157 Max White 2.00 5.00
158 Chase DeJong 2.50 6.00
159 Jamie Jarmon 2.00 5.00
160 Mitch Brown 2.00 5.00
161 Jamie Callahan 1.25 3.00
162 Joe Munoz 1.25 3.00
163 Peter O'Brien 3.00 8.00
164 Matt Koch 1.25 3.00
165 Patrick Cantwell 1.25 3.00
166 Blake Brown 1.25 3.00
167 Max Muncy 10.00 25.00
168 Justin Chigbogu 2.00 5.00
169 Alex Mejia 1.25 3.00
170 Jeff McVaney 1.25 3.00
171 Michael Earley 2.00 5.00
172 Steve Okert 1.25 3.00
173 Dan Langfield 1.25 3.00
174 Austin Maddox 2.00 5.00
175 Kenny Diekroeger 1.25 3.00
176 Brandon Brennan 2.00 5.00
177 Zach Isler 2.00 5.00
178 Stefen Romero 2.00 5.00
179 Mac Williamson 4.00 10.00
180 Seth Willoughby 1.25 3.00
181 Tyler Wagner 1.25 3.00
182 Jake Lamb 3.00 8.00
183 Preston Tucker 3.00 8.00
184 Josh Turley 2.00 5.00
185 Logan Vick 1.25 3.00
186 R.J. Alvarez 2.00 5.00
187 Clint Coulter 2.00 5.00
188 Joe Rogers 1.25 3.00
189 Evan Marzilli 1.25 3.00
190 Carlos Escobar 1.25 3.00
191 Wyatt Mathisen 2.00 5.00
192 Matt Reynolds 2.00 5.00
193 Nick Williams 2.00 5.00
194 Brady Rodgers 1.25 3.00
195 Tim Cooney 1.25 3.00
196 Brett Vertigan 1.25 3.00
197 Hoby Milner 2.00 5.00
198 Luke Maile 1.25 3.00
199 Darin Ruf 12.00 30.00
200 Adrian Marin 2.00 5.00

2012 Elite Extra Edition Team Panini

1 A.Russell/C.Correa 10.00 25.00
2 K.Plawecki/M.Zunino 2.00 5.00
3 A.Almora/B.Buxton 6.00 15.00
4 C.Seager/D.Marrero 5.00 12.00
5 C.Hawkins/D.Dahl 4.00 10.00
6 R.Shaffer/S.Piscotty 2.50 6.00
7 Kevin Gausman/Kyle Zimmer 4.00 10.00
8 J.Ramsey/J.Gallo 6.00 15.00
9 Jesse Winker/Nick Williams 5.00 12.00
10 D.J. Davis/Nolan Fontana 1.50 4.00
11 Andrew Heaney/Brian Johnson 1.50 4.00
12 Chris Stratton/Marcus Stroman 2.00 5.00
13 Barrett Barnes/Lewis Brinson 4.00 10.00
14 L.Giolito/T.Hensley 4.00 10.00
15 Gavin Cecchini/Daniel Robertson 1.50 4.00

2012 Elite Extra Edition USA Baseball 15U Game Jersey Signatures

STATED PRINT RUN 99 SER.#'d SETS
EXCHANGE DEADLINE 07/16/2014
1 John Aiello 5.00 12.00
2 Nick Anderson 4.00 10.00
3 Luken Baker 4.00 10.00
4 Solomon Bates 3.00 8.00
5 Chris Betts 5.00 12.00
6 Danny Casals 6.00 15.00
7 Chris Cullen 12.50 30.00
8 Kyle Dean 8.00 20.00
9 Bailey Falter 5.00 12.00
10 Isaak Gutierrez 3.00 8.00
11 Nico Hoerner 15.00 40.00
12 Parker Kelly 6.00 15.00
13 Nick Madrigal 12.00 30.00
15 Jio Orozco 3.00 8.00
16 Kyle Robeniol 5.00 12.00
17 Blake Rutherford 8.00 20.00
18 Cole Sands 6.00 15.00
19 Kyle Tucker 10.00 25.00
20 Coby Weaver 4.00 10.00

2012 Elite Extra Edition USA Baseball 15U Signatures

STATED PRINT RUN 125 SER.#'d SETS
EXCHANGE DEADLINE 07/16/2014
1 John Aiello 4.00 10.00
2 Nick Anderson 3.00 8.00
3 Luken Baker 4.00 10.00
4 Solomon Bates 3.00 8.00
5 Chris Betts 8.00 20.00
6 Danny Casals 3.00 8.00
7 Chris Cullen 5.00 12.00
8 Kyle Dean 3.00 8.00
9 Bailey Falter 3.00 8.00
10 Isaak Gutierrez 4.00 10.00
11 Nico Hoerner 10.00 25.00
12 Parker Kelly 4.00 10.00
13 Nick Madrigal 15.00 40.00
15 Jio Orozco 4.00 10.00
16 Kyle Robeniol 3.00 8.00
17 Blake Rutherford 10.00 25.00
18 Cole Sands 3.00 8.00
19 Kyle Tucker 12.00 30.00
20 Coby Weaver 4.00 10.00

2012 Elite Extra Edition USA Baseball 18U Game Jersey Signatures

STATED PRINT RUN 249 SER.#'d SETS
EXCHANGE DEADLINE 07/16/2014
1 Willie Abreu 5.00 12.00
2 Christian Arroyo 3.00 8.00
3 Cavan Biggio 8.00 20.00
4 Ryan Boldt 6.00 15.00
5 Bryson Brigman 3.00 8.00
6 Kevin Davis 3.00 8.00
7 Stephen Gonsalves 6.00 15.00
8 Connor Heady 4.00 10.00
9 John Kilichowski 3.00 8.00
10 Ian Clarkin 6.00 15.00
11 Jeremy Martinez 5.00 12.00
12 Reese McGuire 10.00 25.00
13 Dom Nunez 3.00 8.00
14 Chris Okey 3.00 8.00
15 Ryan Olson 4.00 10.00
16 Carson Sands 4.00 10.00
17 Dominic Taccolini 3.00 8.00
18 Keegan Thompson 3.00 8.00
19 Garrett Williams 4.00 10.00

2012 Elite Extra Edition USA Baseball 18U Signatures

STATED PRINT RUN 299 SER.#'d SETS
EXCHANGE DEADLINE 07/16/2014
1 Willie Abreu 3.00 8.00
2 Christian Arroyo 3.00 8.00
3 Cavan Biggio 10.00 25.00
4 Ryan Boldt 5.00 12.00
5 Bryson Brigman 6.00 15.00
6 Kevin Davis 3.00 8.00
7 Stephen Gonsalves 5.00 12.00
8 Connor Heady 3.00 8.00
9 John Kilichowski 3.00 8.00
10 Ian Clarkin 6.00 15.00
11 Jeremy Martinez 6.00 15.00
12 Reese McGuire 6.00 15.00
13 Dom Nunez 3.00 8.00
14 Chris Okey 3.00 8.00
15 Ryan Olson 3.00 8.00
16 Carson Sands 3.00 8.00
17 Dominic Taccolini 4.00 10.00
18 Keegan Thompson 4.00 10.00
19 Garrett Williams 4.00 10.00

2012 Elite Extra Edition Yearbook

1 Tyler Naquin 1.00 2.50
2 Nick Travieso .75 2.00
3 Addison Russell 1.00 2.50
4 Joey Gallo 2.00 5.00
5 Max Fried 2.50 6.00
6 Matt Olson 3.00 8.00
7 Jake Thompson .40 1.00
8 David Dahl 2.00 5.00
9 Preston Beck .40 1.00
10 Carlos Correa 5.00 12.00
11 Albert Almora 1.50 4.00
12 Gavin Cecchini .75 2.00
13 Deven Marrero .60 1.50
14 Lucas Giolito 2.00 5.00
15 Mike Zunino 1.00 2.50
16 Jesse Winker 2.50 6.00
17 Clint Coulter .60 1.50
18 Kyle Zimmer .75 2.00
19 Corey Seager 2.50 6.00
20 Byron Buxton 3.00 8.00

2013 Elite Extra Edition

AU PRINT RUNS B/WN 74-899 COPIES
EXCHANGE DEADLINE 07/09/2014
1A Colin Moran .25 .60
1B Colin Moran VAR
2A Trey Ball .30 .75
Green cap
2B Ball Grn Wht Cap SP
3A Hunter Renfroe .30 .75
Red jersey
3B Renfroe Pinstripes SP
4A Braden Shipley .20 .50
Red jersey
4B Shipley Wht jsy SP
5A Chris Anderson .25 .60
Ball visible
5B Anderson No ball SP
6A Marco Gonzales .30 .75
6B Marco Gonzales VAR
7A Ryan Walker .20 .50
7B Ryan Walker VAR
8A Phillip Ervin .20 .50
Red jersey
8B Ervin Dark jsy SP
9A Ryne Stanek .40 1.00
9B Ryne Stanek VAR
10A Sean Manaea .20 .50
Leg up
10B Manaea Hands together SP
11 Josh Hart .20 .50
12 Michael Lorenzen .25 .60
13 Andrew Thurman .25 .60
14 Trevor Williams .20 .50
15 Cody Reed .20 .50
16 Johnny Field .20 .50
17 Justin Williams .25 .60
18 Blake Taylor .20 .50
19 Chance Sisco .40 1.00
20 Tyler Danish .40 1.00
21 Victor Caratini .60 1.50
22 Marten Gasparini .20 .50
23 Jake Sweaney .20 .50
24 Alex Balog .20 .50
25 Tucker Neuhaus .20 .50
26 Dace Kime .20 .50
27 Ivan Wilson .20 .50
28 Carter Hope .25 .60
29 Barrett Astin .20 .50
30 Daniel Palka .20 .50
31 Keynan Middleton .20 .50
32 Carlos Salazar .20 .50
33 Mason Smith .20 .50
34 Cody Dickson .20 .50
35 Stephen Gonsalves .20 .50
36 K.J. Woods .20 .50
37 Jonah Heim .20 .50
38 Kean Wong .20 .50
39 Jared King .25 .60
40 Josh Uhen .20 .50
41 Cory Thompson .20 .50
42 Ryan Aper .20 .50
43 Cal Drummond .20 .50
44 Brian Navarreto .20 .50
45 Konner Wade .20 .50
46 Jake Bauers .30 .75
47 Tyler Horan .20 .50
48 Scott Brattvet .20 .50
49 David Napoli .20 .50
50 Mitch Garver .25 .60
51 D.J. Snelten .20 .50
52 Brad Goldberg .20 .50
53 Carlos Asuaje .20 .50
54 Erik Schoenrock .20 .50
55 Garrett Smith .20 .50
56 Domingo Tapia .20 .50
57 Bruce Kern .20 .50
58 Trae Arbet .20 .50
59 Amed Rosario .30 .75
60 Andy Burns .20 .50
61 Miguel Almonte .20 .50
62 Anthony DeSclafani .20 .50
63 Cameron Perkins .20 .50
64 Chris Taylor .30 .75
65 Dixon Machado .20 .50
66 Matt Duffy .30 .75
67 Joel Payamps .20 .50
68 Taylor Garrison .20 .50
69 Corey Black .25 .60
70 Junior Arias .20 .50
71 Gleyber Torres 3.00 8.00
72 Chad Rogers .20 .50
73 D.J. Baxendale .20 .50
74 Jason Coats .20 .50
75 Daniel Winkler .20 .50
76 Devon Travis .30 .75
77 Yoel Mecias .20 .50
78 Francisco Sosa .20 .50
79 Ronny Carvajal .20 .50
80 Eugenio Suarez .40 1.00
81 Akeel Morris .20 .50
82 Mike O'Neill .20 .50
83 Randy Rosario .20 .50
84 Orlando Castro .20 .50
85 Jesus Solorzano .20 .50
86 Rainy Lara .20 .50
87 Sam Moll .25 .60
88 Tyler Wade .30 .75
89 Roberto Osuna .20 .50
90 Rock Shoulders .20 .50
91 Jeremy Rathjen .20 .50
92 Luis Mateo .25 .60
93 Jose Abreu 1.50 4.00
94 Jordan Patterson .20 .50
95 Adrian De Horta .20 .50
96 David Garner .20 .50
97 Trey Michalczewski .20 .50
98 Drew Dosch .20 .50
99 Ryan Garvey .20 .50
100 Dereck Rodriguez .60 1.50
101 Mark Appel AU/320 4.00 10.00
102 Kris Bryant AU/324 40.00 100.00
103 Jonathan Gray AU/329 8.00 20.00
104 Kohl Stewart AU/275 6.00 15.00
105 Clint Frazier AU/324 8.00 20.00
106 Hunter Dozier AU/325 3.00 8.00
107 Austin Meadows AU/322 10.00 25.00
108 Dominic Smith AU/275 4.00 10.00
109 D.J. Peterson AU/299 6.00 15.00
110 Reese McGuire AU/324 8.00 20.00
111 J.P. Crawford AU/411 10.00 25.00
112 Tim Anderson AU/374 10.00 25.00
113 Jonathon Crawford AU/374 3.00 8.00
114 Nick Ciuffo AU/373 4.00 10.00
115 Hunter Harvey AU/499 3.00 8.00
116 Alex Gonzalez AU/420 10.00 25.00
117 Billy McKinney AU/322 4.00 10.00
118 Rob Kaminsky AU/364 3.00 8.00
119 Eric Jagielo AU/314 3.00 8.00
120 Travis Demeritte AU/599 4.00 10.00
121 Jason Hursh AU/227 4.00 10.00
122 Aaron Judge AU/599 60.00 150.00
123 Ian Clarkin AU/370 4.00 10.00
124 Aaron Blair AU/274 3.00 8.00
125 Corey Knebel AU/699 3.00 8.00
126 Rob Zastryzny AU/690 3.00 8.00
127 Ryan McMahon AU/899 6.00 15.00
128 Ryan Eades AU/674 3.00 8.00
129 Teddy Stankiewicz AU/674 3.00 8.00
130 Andrew Church AU/899 3.00 8.00
131 Austin Wilson AU/174 5.00 12.00
132 Dustin Peterson AU/599 3.00 8.00
133 Andrew Knapp AU/173 3.00 8.00
134 Devin Williams AU/655 6.00 15.00
135 Tom Windle AU/671 3.00 8.00
136 Oscar Mercado AU/799 4.00 10.00
137 Kevin Ziomek AU/669 3.00 8.00
138 Hunter Green AU/899 EXCH 3.00 8.00
139 Riley Unroe AU/590 3.00 8.00
140 Akeem Bostick AU/674 3.00 8.00
141 Dillon Overton AU/672 3.00 8.00
142 Ryder Jones AU/580 3.00 8.00
143 Gosuke Katoh AU/314 4.00 10.00
144 Kevin Franklin AU/799 3.00 8.00
145 Chad Pinder AU/671 3.00 8.00
146 Colby Suggs AU/674 3.00 8.00
147 Jacob Hannemann AU/669 3.00 8.00
148 Jonathan Denney AU/172 5.00 12.00
149 Patrick Murphy AU/670 3.00 8.00
150 Stuart Turner AU/674 3.00 8.00
151 Jacob May AU/899 3.00 8.00
152 Jacoby Jones AU/673 4.00 10.00
153 Brandon Dixon AU/672 4.00 10.00
154 Michael O'Neill AU/349 4.00 10.00
155 Drew Ward AU/371 4.00 10.00
156 Chris Kohler AU/672 3.00 8.00
157 Tyler Skulina AU/670 3.00 8.00
158 Cody Bellinger AU/673 100.00 250.00
159 Mason Katz AU/667 3.00 8.00
160 Brian Ragira AU/274 5.00 12.00
161 Tony Kemp AU/899 EXCH 3.00 8.00
162 Trey Masek AU/673 3.00 8.00
163 Aaron Slegers AU/662 3.00 8.00
164 Joe Jackson AU/664 EXCH 3.00 8.00
165 Dan Slania AU/670 5.00 12.00
166 Luke Farrell AU/673 3.00 8.00
167 Jacob Nottingham AU/899 3.00 8.00
168 Brandon Diaz AU/663 3.00 8.00
169 Kyle Farmer AU/670 3.00 8.00
170 Michael Ratterree AU/670 3.00 8.00
171 Kasey Coffman AU/668 3.00 8.00
172 Tyler Webb AU/673 3.00 8.00
173 Kendall Coleman AU/672 3.00 8.00
174 Chase Jensen AU/655 3.00 8.00
175 Mikey Reynolds AU/672 3.00 8.00
176 Ben Verlander AU/370 5.00 12.00
177 Austin Kubitza AU/600 3.00 8.00
178 Chris Garia AU/772 3.00 8.00
179 Alen Hanson AU/550 3.00 8.00
180 Micah Johnson AU/232 4.00 10.00
181 Anthony Garcia AU/272 4.00 10.00
182 Cameron Flynn AU/899 3.00 8.00
183 Gregory Polanco AU/667 8.00 20.00
184 Maikel Franco AU/299 5.00 12.00
185 Rosell Herrera AU/174 EXCH 12.00 30.00
186 Mike Yastrzemski AU/740 10.00 25.00
187 Cory Vaughn AU/74 5.00 12.00
188 Jayce Boyd AU/299 4.00 10.00
189 Matt Andriese AU/771 3.00 8.00
190 Luis Torrens AU/470 EXCH 3.00 8.00
191 Jorge Alfaro AU/74 8.00 20.00
192 Tim Atherton AU/765 3.00 8.00
193 Zach Borenstein AU/749 EXCH 3.00 8.00
194 Hunter Lockwood AU/773 3.00 8.00
195 Terry McClure AU/769 3.00 8.00
196 Cody Stubbs AU/322 3.00 8.00
197 Kyle Crockett AU/774 3.00 8.00
198 Kent Emanuel AU/670 3.00 8.00
199 Tanner Norton AU/760 3.00 8.00
200 Amaurys Minier AU/674 8.00 20.00

2013 Elite Extra Edition Aspirations

*ASPIRATIONS: 2.5X TO 6X BASIC
STATED PRINT RUN 200 SER.#'d SETS
101 Mark Appel 2.00 5.00
102 Kris Bryant 20.00 50.00
103 Jonathan Gray 1.50 4.00
104 Kohl Stewart 1.50 4.00
105 Clint Frazier 6.00 15.00
106 Hunter Dozier 1.25 3.00
107 Austin Meadows 3.00 8.00
108 Dominic Smith 2.00 5.00
109 D.J. Peterson 1.25 3.00
110 Reese McGuire 1.50 4.00
111 J.P. Crawford 2.00 5.00
112 Tim Anderson 5.00 12.00
113 Jonathon Crawford 1.25 3.00
114 Nick Ciuffo 1.25 3.00
115 Hunter Harvey 1.50 4.00
116 Alex Gonzalez 2.00 5.00
117 Billy McKinney 1.50 4.00
118 Rob Kaminsky 1.50 4.00
119 Eric Jagielo 1.50 4.00
120 Travis Demeritte 1.50 4.00
121 Jason Hursh 1.25 3.00
122 Aaron Judge 30.00 80.00
123 Ian Clarkin 1.25 3.00
124 Aaron Blair 1.25 3.00
125 Corey Knebel 1.25 3.00
126 Rob Zastryzny 2.00 5.00
127 Ryan McMahon 3.00 8.00
128 Ryan Eades 1.25 3.00
129 Teddy Stankiewicz 1.50 4.00
130 Andrew Church 1.25 3.00
131 Austin Wilson 1.50 4.00
132 Dustin Peterson 1.25 3.00
133 Andrew Knapp 1.25 3.00
134 Devin Williams 3.00 8.00
135 Tom Windle 1.25 3.00
136 Oscar Mercado 2.00 5.00
137 Kevin Ziomek 1.25 3.00
138 Hunter Green 1.25 3.00
139 Riley Unroe 1.25 3.00
140 Akeem Bostick .75 2.00
141 Dillon Overton 1.25 3.00
142 Ryder Jones 2.00 5.00
143 Gosuke Katoh 1.50 4.00
144 Kevin Franklin 1.25 3.00
145 Chad Pinder .75 2.00
146 Colby Suggs 1.50 4.00
147 Jacob Hannemann .75 2.00
148 Jonathan Denney 1.50 4.00
149 Patrick Murphy 1.25 3.00
150 Stuart Turner 1.25 3.00
151 Jacob May 1.25 3.00
152 Jacoby Jones 2.00 5.00
153 Brandon Dixon 1.50 4.00
154 Michael O'Neill 1.25 3.00
155 Drew Ward 1.50 4.00
156 Chris Kohler 1.50 4.00
157 Tyler Skulina .75 2.00
158 Cody Bellinger 20.00 50.00
159 Mason Katz 1.25 3.00
160 Brian Ragira 1.25 3.00
161 Tony Kemp .75 2.00
162 Trey Masek .75 2.00
163 Aaron Slegers 1.50 4.00
164 Joe Jackson .75 2.00
165 Dan Slania .75 2.00
166 Luke Farrell 1.25 3.00
167 Jacob Nottingham 1.25 3.00
168 Brandon Diaz 1.25 3.00
169 Kyle Farmer .75 2.00
170 Michael Ratterree .75 2.00
171 Kasey Coffman .75 2.00
172 Tyler Webb .75 2.00
173 Kendall Coleman 1.25 3.00
174 Chase Jensen .75 2.00
175 Mikey Reynolds .75 2.00
176 Ben Verlander 1.50 4.00
177 Austin Kubitza 1.25 3.00
178 Chris Garia .75 2.00
179 Alen Hanson 1.50 4.00
180 Micah Johnson 1.50 4.00
181 Anthony Garcia 2.00 5.00
182 Cameron Flynn 1.25 3.00
183 Gregory Polanco 2.50 6.00
184 Maikel Franco 2.00 5.00
185 Rosell Herrera 1.50 4.00
186 Mike Yastrzemski 4.00 10.00
187 Cory Vaughn 1.25 3.00
188 Jayce Boyd 1.25 3.00
189 Matt Andriese 1.50 4.00
190 Luis Torrens 1.25 3.00
191 Jorge Alfaro 2.50 6.00
192 Tim Atherton .75 2.00
193 Zach Borenstein 2.00 5.00
194 Hunter Lockwood .75 2.00
195 Terry McClure .75 2.00
196 Cody Stubbs 1.25 3.00
197 Kyle Crockett 1.25 3.00
198 Kent Emanuel .75 2.00
199 Tanner Norton .75 2.00
200 Amaurys Minier 1.25 3.00

2013 Elite Extra Edition Status

*STATUS: 3X TO 8X BASIC
STATED PRINT RUN 100 SER.#'d SETS
93 Jose Abreu 12.00 30.00
101 Mark Appel 2.50 6.00
102 Kris Bryant 15.00 40.00
103 Jonathan Gray 2.00 5.00
104 Kohl Stewart 2.00 5.00
105 Clint Frazier 8.00 20.00
106 Hunter Dozier 1.50 4.00
107 Austin Meadows 4.00 10.00
108 Dominic Smith 2.50 6.00
109 D.J. Peterson 1.50 4.00
110 Reese McGuire 2.00 5.00
111 J.P. Crawford 2.50 6.00
112 Tim Anderson 6.00 15.00
113 Jonathon Crawford 1.50 4.00
114 Nick Ciuffo 1.50 4.00
115 Hunter Harvey 2.00 5.00
116 Alex Gonzalez 2.50 6.00
117 Billy McKinney 2.00 5.00
118 Rob Kaminsky 2.00 5.00
119 Eric Jagielo 2.00 5.00
120 Travis Demeritte 2.00 5.00
121 Jason Hursh 1.50 4.00
122 Aaron Judge 40.00 100.00
123 Ian Clarkin 1.50 4.00
124 Aaron Blair 1.50 4.00
125 Corey Knebel 1.50 4.00
126 Rob Zastryzny 2.50 6.00
127 Ryan McMahon 4.00 10.00
128 Ryan Eades 1.50 4.00
129 Teddy Stankiewicz 2.00 5.00
130 Andrew Church 1.50 4.00
131 Austin Wilson 2.00 5.00
132 Dustin Peterson 1.50 4.00
133 Andrew Knapp 1.50 4.00
134 Devin Williams 4.00 10.00
135 Tom Windle 1.50 4.00
136 Oscar Mercado 2.50 6.00
137 Kevin Ziomek 1.50 4.00
138 Hunter Green 1.50 4.00
139 Riley Unroe 1.50 4.00
140 Akeem Bostick 1.00 2.50
141 Dillon Overton 1.50 4.00
142 Ryder Jones 2.50 6.00
143 Gosuke Katoh 2.00 5.00
144 Kevin Franklin 1.50 4.00
145 Chad Pinder 1.00 2.50
146 Colby Suggs 2.00 5.00
147 Jacob Hannemann 1.00 2.50
148 Jonathan Denney 2.00 5.00
149 Patrick Murphy 1.50 4.00
150 Stuart Turner 1.50 4.00
151 Jacob May 1.50 4.00
152 Jacoby Jones 2.50 6.00
153 Brandon Dixon 2.00 5.00
154 Michael O'Neill 1.50 4.00
155 Drew Ward 2.00 5.00
156 Chris Kohler 2.00 5.00
157 Tyler Skulina 1.00 2.50
158 Cody Bellinger 25.00 60.00
159 Mason Katz 1.50 4.00
160 Brian Ragira 1.50 4.00
161 Tony Kemp 1.00 2.50
162 Trey Masek 1.00 2.50
163 Aaron Slegers 2.00 5.00
164 Joe Jackson 1.00 2.50
165 Dan Slania 1.00 2.50
166 Luke Farrell 1.50 4.00
167 Jacob Nottingham 1.50 4.00
168 Brandon Diaz 1.50 4.00
169 Kyle Farmer 1.00 2.50
170 Michael Ratterree 1.00 2.50
171 Kasey Coffman 1.00 2.50
172 Tyler Webb 1.00 2.50
173 Kendall Coleman 1.50 4.00
174 Chase Jensen 1.00 2.50
175 Mikey Reynolds 1.00 2.50
176 Ben Verlander 2.00 5.00
177 Austin Kubitza 1.50 4.00
178 Chris Garia 1.00 2.50
179 Alen Hanson 2.00 5.00
180 Micah Johnson 2.00 5.00
181 Anthony Garcia 2.50 6.00
182 Cameron Flynn 1.50 4.00
183 Gregory Polanco 3.00 8.00
184 Maikel Franco 2.50 6.00
185 Rosell Herrera 2.00 5.00
186 Mike Yastrzemski 5.00 12.00
187 Cory Vaughn 1.50 4.00
188 Jayce Boyd 1.50 4.00
189 Matt Andriese 2.00 5.00
190 Luis Torrens 1.50 4.00
191 Jorge Alfaro 3.00 8.00
192 Tim Atherton 1.00 2.50
193 Zach Borenstein 2.50 6.00
194 Hunter Lockwood 1.00 2.50
195 Terry McClure 1.00 2.50
196 Cody Stubbs 1.50 4.00
197 Kyle Crockett 1.50 4.00
198 Kent Emanuel 1.00 2.50
199 Tanner Norton 1.00 2.50
200 Amaurys Minier 1.50 4.00

2013 Elite Extra Edition Status Emerald

*STATUS EMERALD: 6X TO 15X BASIC
STATED PRINT RUN 25 SER.#'d SETS
101 Mark Appel 5.00 12.00
102 Kris Bryant 30.00 80.00
103 Jonathan Gray 4.00 10.00
104 Kohl Stewart 4.00 10.00
105 Clint Frazier 15.00 40.00
106 Hunter Dozier 3.00 8.00
107 Austin Meadows 8.00 20.00
108 Dominic Smith 5.00 12.00
109 D.J. Peterson 3.00 8.00
110 Reese McGuire 4.00 10.00
111 J.P. Crawford 5.00 12.00
112 Tim Anderson 12.00 30.00
113 Jonathon Crawford 3.00 8.00
114 Nick Ciuffo 3.00 8.00
115 Hunter Harvey 4.00 10.00
116 Alex Gonzalez 5.00 12.00
117 Billy McKinney 4.00 10.00
118 Rob Kaminsky 4.00 10.00
119 Eric Jagielo 4.00 10.00
120 Travis Demeritte 4.00 10.00
121 Jason Hursh 3.00 8.00
122 Aaron Judge 75.00 200.00
123 Ian Clarkin 3.00 8.00
124 Aaron Blair 3.00 8.00
125 Corey Knebel 3.00 8.00
126 Rob Zastryzny 5.00 12.00
127 Ryan McMahon 8.00 20.00
128 Ryan Eades 3.00 8.00
129 Teddy Stankiewicz 4.00 10.00
130 Andrew Church 3.00 8.00
131 Austin Wilson 4.00 10.00
132 Dustin Peterson 3.00 8.00
133 Andrew Knapp 3.00 8.00
134 Devin Williams 8.00 20.00
135 Tom Windle 3.00 8.00
136 Oscar Mercado 5.00 12.00
137 Kevin Ziomek 3.00 8.00
138 Hunter Green 3.00 8.00
139 Riley Unroe 3.00 8.00
140 Akeem Bostick 2.00 5.00
141 Dillon Overton 3.00 8.00
142 Ryder Jones 5.00 12.00
143 Gosuke Katoh 4.00 10.00
144 Kevin Franklin 3.00 8.00
145 Chad Pinder 2.00 5.00
146 Colby Suggs 4.00 10.00
147 Jacob Hannemann 2.00 5.00
148 Jonathan Denney 4.00 10.00
149 Patrick Murphy 3.00 8.00
150 Stuart Turner 3.00 8.00
151 Jacob May 3.00 8.00
152 Jacoby Jones 5.00 12.00
153 Brandon Dixon 4.00 10.00
154 Michael O'Neill 3.00 8.00
155 Drew Ward 4.00 10.00
156 Chris Kohler 4.00 10.00
157 Tyler Skulina 2.00 5.00
158 Cody Bellinger 50.00 125.00
159 Mason Katz 3.00 8.00
160 Brian Ragira 3.00 8.00
161 Tony Kemp 2.00 5.00
162 Trey Masek 2.00 5.00
163 Aaron Slegers 4.00 10.00
164 Joe Jackson 2.00 5.00
165 Dan Slania 2.00 5.00
166 Luke Farrell 3.00 8.00
167 Jacob Nottingham 3.00 8.00
168 Brandon Diaz 3.00 8.00
169 Kyle Farmer 2.00 5.00
170 Michael Ratterree 2.00 5.00
171 Kasey Coffman 2.00 5.00
172 Tyler Webb 2.00 5.00
173 Kendall Coleman 3.00 8.00

174 Chase Jensen 2.00 5.00
175 Mikey Reynolds 2.00 5.00
176 Ben Verlander 4.00 10.00
177 Austin Kubitza 3.00 8.00
178 Chris Garia 2.00 5.00
179 Alen Hanson 4.00 10.00
180 Micah Johnson 4.00 10.00
181 Anthony Garcia 5.00 12.00
182 Cameron Flynn 3.00 8.00
183 Gregory Polanco 6.00 15.00
184 Maikel Franco 5.00 12.00
185 Rosell Herrera 4.00 10.00
186 Mike Yastrzemski 10.00 25.00
187 Cory Vaughn 3.00 8.00
188 Jayce Boyd 3.00 8.00
189 Matt Andriese 4.00 10.00
190 Luis Torrens 3.00 8.00
191 Jorge Alfaro 6.00 15.00
192 Tim Atherton 2.00 5.00
193 Zach Borenstein 5.00 12.00
194 Hunter Lockwood 2.00 5.00
195 Terry McClure 2.00 5.00
196 Cody Stubbs 3.00 8.00
197 Kyle Crockett 3.00 8.00
198 Kent Emanuel 2.00 5.00
199 Tanner Norton 2.00 5.00
200 Amaurys Minier 3.00 8.00

2013 Elite Extra Edition Back to the Future Signatures

PRINT RUNS B/WN 10-299 COPIES PER
NO PRICING ON QTY 10
EXCHANGE DEADLINE 07/09/2014
1 Nick Travieso/299 3.00 8.00
2 Courtney Hawkins/99 4.00 10.00
3 Keon Barnum/299 3.00 8.00
4 Josh Turley/299 3.00 8.00
5 Tom Murphy/299 3.00 8.00
6 Brian Johnson/150 3.00 8.00
7 Patrick Wisdom/199 3.00 8.00
8 Rio Ruiz/299 3.00 8.00
9 Dylan Cozens/99 4.00 10.00
10 Byron Buxton/25 50.00 100.00
11 J.O. Berrios/199 6.00 15.00
12 Jairo Beras/284 3.00 8.00
13 Stefen Romero/299 3.00 8.00
14 Wyatt Mathisen/99 3.00 8.00
15 Austin Nola/199 3.00 8.00
17 Drew VerHagen/99 5.00 12.00
18 Damion Carroll/99 3.00 8.00
19 Jeff McVaney/299 3.00 8.00
20 Charles Taylor/99 3.00 8.00

2013 Elite Extra Edition Bloodlines

COMPLETE SET (8) 4.00 10.00
1 C.Yaz/M.YaZ 1.25 3.00
2 D.Peterson/D.Peterson .50 1.25
3 M.O'Neill/P.O'Neill .60 1.50
4 D.Rodriguez/I.Rodriguez 1.50 4.00
5 R.Garvey/S.Garvey .50 1.25
6 B.Surhoff/C.Moran .60 1.50
7 B.Harvey/H.Harvey .60 1.50
8 J.May/L.May .50 1.25

2013 Elite Extra Edition Bloodlines Signatures

PRINT RUNS B/WN 5-25 COPIES PER
NO PRICING ON QTY 5
EXCHANGE DEADLINE 07/09/2014
2 D.Peterson/D.Peterson/25
3 M.O'Neill/P.O'Neill/25
4 D.Rodriguez/I.Rodriguez/25 50.00 120.00
5 R.Garvey/S.Garvey/25 40.00 100.00
6 B.Surhoff/C.Moran/25
7 Harvey/Harvey/25 EXCH 12.50 30.00
8 J.May/L.May/25 EXCH 5.00 12.00

2013 Elite Extra Edition Elite Series

1 Byron Buxton 1.25 3.00
2 Kris Bryant 6.00 15.00
3 Clint Frazier 1.25 3.00
4 Kohl Stewart .30 .75
5 Mark Appel .40 1.00
6 Colin Moran .30 .75
7 Trey Ball .40 1.00
8 Hunter Renfroe .40 1.00
9 Jonathan Gray .30 .75
10 D.J. Peterson .25 .60
11 Billy McKinney .30 .75
12 Hunter Dozier .25 .60
13 Miguel Sano .30 .75
14 Braden Shipley .25 .60
15 Phillip Ervin .25 .60
16 J.P. Crawford .40 1.00
17 Dominic Smith .40 1.00
18 Reese McGuire .30 .75
19 Hunter Harvey .30 .75
20 Maikel Franco .40 1.00

2013 Elite Extra Edition Elite Series Signatures

PRINT RUNS B/WN 25-199 COPIES PER
EXCHANGE DEADLINE 07/09/2014
1 Byron Buxton/199 10.00 25.00
2 Kris Bryant/25 100.00 250.00
3 Clint Frazier/50 30.00 60.00
4 Kohl Stewart/99 8.00 20.00
5 Mark Appel/50
6 Colin Moran/25 15.00 40.00
7 Trey Ball/99 12.50 30.00
8 Hunter Renfroe/49 4.00 10.00
9 Jonathan Gray/50 15.00 40.00
10 D.J. Peterson/50 10.00 25.00
11 Billy McKinney/50 12.50 30.00
12 Hunter Dozier/49 10.00 25.00
13 Miguel Sano/199 10.00 25.00
14 Braden Shipley/80 6.00 15.00
15 Phillip Ervin/80 10.00 25.00
16 J.P. Crawford/99 12.00 30.00
17 Dominic Smith/99 12.50 30.00
18 Reese McGuire/99 8.00 20.00
19 Hunter Harvey/149 6.00 15.00
20 Maikel Franco/99 8.00 20.00

2013 Elite Extra Edition Franchise Futures Signatures

PRINT RUNS B/WN 99-899 COPIES PER
EXCHANGE DEADLINE 07/09/2014
1 Colin Moran/250 3.00 8.00
2 Trey Ball/270 6.00 15.00
3 Hunter Renfroe/308 4.00 10.00
4 Braden Shipley/404 3.00 8.00
5 Chris Anderson/265 4.00 10.00
6 Marco Gonzales/298 4.00 10.00
7 Ryan Walker/699 3.00 8.00
8 Phillip Ervin/243 3.00 8.00
9 Ryne Stanek/530 4.00 10.00
10 Sean Manaea/565 3.00 8.00
11 Josh Hart/322 4.00 10.00
12 Michael Lorenzen/849 EXCH 3.00 8.00
13 Andrew Thurman/725 3.00 8.00
14 Trevor Williams/810 3.00 8.00
15 Cody Reed/672 3.00 8.00
16 Johnny Field/725 3.00 8.00
17 Justin Williams/672 3.00 8.00
18 Blake Taylor/672 3.00 8.00
19 Chance Sisco/672 4.00 10.00
20 Tyler Danish/670 EXCH 3.00 8.00
21 Victor Caratini/224 15.00 40.00
22 Marten Gasparini/652 3.00 8.00
23 Jake Sweaney/749 3.00 8.00
24 Alex Balog/661 3.00 8.00
25 Tucker Neuhaus/324 3.00 8.00
26 Dace Kime/669 3.00 8.00
27 Ivan Wilson/271 4.00 10.00
28 Carter Hope/672 3.00 8.00
29 Barrett Astin/899 3.00 8.00
30 Daniel Palka/549 3.00 8.00
31 Keynan Middleton/639 EXCH 3.00 8.00
32 Carlos Salazar/625 3.00 8.00
33 Mason Smith/668 3.00 8.00
34 Cody Dickson/672 3.00 8.00
35 Stephen Gonsalves/349 3.00 8.00
36 K.J. Woods/650 3.00 8.00
37 Jonah Heim/649 3.00 8.00
38 Kean Wong/625 3.00 8.00
39 Jared King/669 3.00 8.00
40 Josh Uhen/660 3.00 8.00
41 Cory Thompson/660 3.00 8.00
42 Ryan Aper/668 3.00 8.00
43 Cal Drummond/670 3.00 8.00
44 Brian Navarreto/710 3.00 8.00
45 Konner Wade/698 3.00 8.00
46 Jake Bauers/671 6.00 15.00
47 Tyler Horan/672 3.00 8.00
48 Scott Brattvet/671 3.00 8.00
49 David Napoli/671 3.00 8.00
50 Mitch Garver/655 3.00 8.00
51 D.J. Snelten/667 3.00 8.00
52 Brad Goldberg/672 3.00 8.00
53 Carlos Asuaje/672 3.00 8.00
54 Erik Schoenrock/662 3.00 8.00
55 Garrett Smith/801 3.00 8.00
56 Domingo Tapia/802 3.00 8.00
57 Bruce Kern/799 3.00 8.00
58 Trae Arbet/650 3.00 8.00
59 Amed Rosario/250 30.00 80.00
60 Andy Burns/399 3.00 8.00
61 Miguel Almonte/899 3.00 8.00
62 Anthony DeSclafani/603 3.00 8.00
63 Cameron Perkins/525 3.00 8.00
64 Chris Taylor/390 12.00 30.00
65 Dixon Machado/272 3.00 8.00
66 Matt Duffy/250 EXCH 12.00 30.00
67 Joel Payamps/749 3.00 8.00
68 Taylor Garrison/639 3.00 8.00
69 Corey Black/700 3.00 8.00
70 Junior Arias/671 3.00 8.00
71 Gleyber Torres/250 60.00 150.00
72 Chad Rogers/350 3.00 8.00
73 D.J. Baxendale/375 3.00 8.00
74 Jason Coats/499 3.00 8.00
75 Daniel Winkler/175 5.00 12.00
76 Devon Travis/115 10.00 25.00
77 Yoel Mecias/799 3.00 8.00
78 Francisco Sosa/250 EXCH 3.00 8.00
79 Ronny Carvajal/250 EXCH 3.00 8.00
80 Eugenio Suarez/299 12.00 30.00
81 Akeel Morris/720 3.00 8.00
82 Mike O'Neill/352 3.00 8.00
83 Randy Rosario/790 3.00 8.00
84 Orlando Castro/663 EXCH 3.00 8.00
85 Jesus Solorzano/199 EXCH 3.00 8.00
86 Rainy Lara/99 4.00 10.00
87 Sam Moll/699 3.00 8.00
88 Tyler Wade/699 4.00 10.00
89 Roberto Osuna/224 6.00 15.00
90 Rock Shoulders/267 5.00 12.00
91 Jeremy Rathjen/159 4.00 10.00
92 Luis Mateo/799 3.00 8.00
93 Jose Abreu/799 12.00 30.00
94 Jordan Patterson/670 3.00 8.00
95 Adrian De Horta/659 3.00 8.00
96 David Garner/670 3.00 8.00
97 Trey Michalczewski/312 3.00 8.00
98 Drew Dosch/665 3.00 8.00
99 Ryan Garvey/550 3.00 8.00
100 Dereck Rodriguez/200 25.00 60.00

2013 Elite Extra Edition Historic Picks

COMPLETE SET (10) 4.00 10.00
1 Craig Biggio .40 1.00
2 Shawn Green .30 .75
3 Ken Griffey Jr. 1.00 2.50
4 Roger Clemens .60 1.50
5 Chipper Jones .50 1.25
6 Joe Carter .30 .75
7 Johnny Damon .40 1.00
8 Jim Abbott .30 .75
9 Mike Piazza .50 1.25
10 Troy Glaus .30 .75

2013 Elite Extra Edition Historic Picks Signatures

PRINT RUNS B/WN 5-99 COPIES PER
NO PRICING ON QTY 10 OR LESS
EXCHANGE DEADLINE 07/09/2014
1 Craig Biggio/99 20.00 50.00
2 Shawn Green/99 3.00 8.00
6 Joe Carter/25 12.50 30.00
7 Johnny Damon/37 10.00 25.00
8 Jim Abbott/22 10.00 25.00

2013 Elite Extra Edition Panini High School All Stars

1 Clint Frazier 10.00 25.00
2 Josh Hart 2.00 5.00
3 Riley Unroe 2.00 5.00
4 Carlos Salazar 2.00 5.00
5 Trey Ball 3.00 8.00
6 Austin Meadows 5.00 12.00
7 Jake Bauers 3.00 8.00
8 Dustin Peterson 2.00 5.00
9 Jacob Nottingham 2.00 5.00
10 Kohl Stewart 2.50 6.00
11 Dominic Smith 3.00 8.00
12 Billy McKinney 2.50 6.00
13 Nick Ciuffo 2.00 5.00
14 Tyler Danish 4.00 10.00
15 Rob Kaminsky 2.50 6.00
16 Reese McGuire 2.50 6.00
17 J.P. Crawford 3.00 8.00
18 Hunter Harvey 2.50 6.00
19 Travis Demeritte 2.50 6.00
20 Ian Clarkin 2.00 5.00

2013 Elite Extra Edition Scouting 101

1 Austin Meadows .75 2.00
2 Nick Ciuffo .30 .75
3 Travis Demeritte .40 1.00
4 Eric Jagielo .40 1.00
5 Jake Bauers .50 1.25
6 Tim Anderson 1.25 3.00
7 Billy McKinney .40 1.00
8 Sean Manaea .30 .75
9 Ryne Stanek .60 1.50
10 Jonathon Crawford .30 .75
11 Riley Unroe .30 .75
12 Ian Clarkin .30 .75
13 Chris Anderson .40 1.00
14 Jonathan Denney .40 1.00
15 Jason Hursh .30 .75
16 Dominic Smith .50 1.25
17 Hunter Renfroe .50 1.25
18 Josh Hart .30 .75
19 Kris Bryant 2.00 5.00
20 Mark Appel .50 1.25

2013 Elite Extra Edition Signature Aspirations

STATED PRINT RUN 100 SER.#'d SETS
EXCHANGE DEADLINE 07/09/2014
1 Colin Moran 4.00 10.00
2 Trey Ball 10.00 25.00
3 Hunter Renfroe 12.00 30.00
4 Braden Shipley 3.00 8.00
5 Chris Anderson
6 Marco Gonzales 6.00 15.00
7 Ryan Walker 4.00 10.00
8 Phillip Ervin 8.00 20.00
9 Ryne Stanek 6.00 15.00
10 Sean Manaea 4.00 10.00
11 Josh Hart 4.00 10.00
12 Michael Lorenzen EXCH 4.00 10.00
13 Andrew Thurman 3.00 8.00
14 Trevor Williams 4.00 10.00
15 Cody Reed 12.50 30.00
16 Johnny Field 3.00 8.00
17 Justin Williams
18 Blake Taylor 3.00 8.00
19 Chance Sisco 4.00 10.00
20 Tyler Danish EXCH 4.00 10.00
21 Victor Caratini 15.00 40.00
22 Marten Gasparini 5.00 12.00
23 Jake Sweaney 3.00 8.00
24 Alex Balog 3.00 8.00
25 Tucker Neuhaus 3.00 8.00
26 Dace Kime 6.00 15.00
27 Ivan Wilson 4.00 10.00
28 Carter Hope 3.00 8.00
29 Barrett Astin 3.00 8.00
30 Daniel Palka 3.00 8.00
31 Keynan Middleton EXCH 5.00 12.00
32 Carlos Salazar 5.00 12.00
33 Mason Smith 3.00 8.00
34 Cody Dickson 3.00 8.00
35 Stephen Gonsalves 5.00 12.00
36 K.J. Woods 3.00 8.00
37 Jonah Heim 3.00 8.00
38 Kean Wong 3.00 8.00
39 Jared King 6.00 15.00
40 Josh Uhen 5.00 12.00
41 Cory Thompson 3.00 8.00
42 Ryan Aper 3.00 8.00
43 Cal Drummond
44 Brian Navarreto 3.00 8.00
45 Konner Wade
46 Jake Bauers 6.00 15.00
47 Tyler Horan 8.00 20.00
48 Scott Brattvet 3.00 8.00
49 David Napoli 3.00 8.00
50 Mitch Garver 3.00 8.00
51 D.J. Snelten 3.00 8.00
52 Brad Goldberg 5.00 12.00
53 Carlos Asuaje 3.00 8.00
54 Erik Schoenrock 3.00 8.00
55 Garrett Smith 3.00 8.00
56 Domingo Tapia 3.00 8.00
57 Bruce Kern
58 Trae Arbet 4.00 10.00
59 Amed Rosario 30.00 80.00
60 Andy Burns 3.00 8.00
61 Miguel Almonte 3.00 8.00
62 Anthony DeSclafani 3.00 8.00
63 Cameron Perkins 3.00 8.00
64 Chris Taylor 12.00 30.00
65 Dixon Machado 3.00 8.00
66 Matt Duffy EXCH 30.00 80.00
67 Joel Payamps 3.00 8.00
68 Taylor Garrison
69 Corey Black 3.00 8.00
70 Junior Arias 3.00 8.00
71 Gleyber Torres 60.00 150.00
72 Chad Rogers 3.00 8.00
73 D.J. Baxendale
74 Jason Coats 3.00 8.00
75 Daniel Winkler 5.00 12.00
76 Devon Travis 10.00 25.00
77 Yoel Mecias 4.00 10.00
78 Francisco Sosa EXCH 4.00 10.00
79 Ronny Carvajal EXCH 6.00 15.00
80 Eugenio Suarez 10.00 25.00
81 Akeel Morris 3.00 8.00
82 Mike O'Neill 4.00 10.00
83 Randy Rosario 3.00 8.00
84 Orlando Castro EXCH 3.00 8.00
85 Jesus Solorzano EXCH 4.00 10.00
86 Rainy Lara 15.00 40.00
87 Sam Moll 3.00 8.00
88 Tyler Wade 15.00 40.00
89 Roberto Osuna 5.00 12.00
90 Rock Shoulders
91 Jeremy Rathjen 4.00 10.00
92 Luis Mateo 3.00 8.00
93 Jose Abreu 15.00 40.00
94 Jordan Patterson 3.00 8.00
95 Adrian De Horta 3.00 8.00
96 David Garner 3.00 8.00
97 Trey Michalczewski 4.00 10.00
98 Drew Dosch
99 Ryan Garvey 5.00 12.00
100 Dereck Rodriguez 12.00 30.00
101 Mark Appel 6.00 15.00
102 Kris Bryant 50.00 120.00
103 Jonathan Gray 8.00 20.00
104 Kohl Stewart 6.00 15.00
105 Clint Frazier 15.00 40.00
106 Hunter Dozier 6.00 15.00
107 Austin Meadows 12.00 30.00
108 Dominic Smith 10.00 25.00
109 D.J. Peterson 10.00 25.00
110 Reese McGuire 8.00 20.00
111 J.P. Crawford 12.00 30.00
112 Tim Anderson 10.00 25.00
113 Jonathon Crawford 4.00 10.00
114 Nick Ciuffo 4.00 10.00
115 Hunter Harvey 3.00 8.00
116 Alex Gonzalez 10.00 25.00
117 Billy McKinney 8.00 20.00
118 Rob Kaminsky 4.00 10.00
119 Eric Jagielo 6.00 15.00
120 Travis Demeritte 4.00 10.00
121 Jason Hursh 6.00 15.00
122 Aaron Judge 75.00 200.00
123 Ian Clarkin 5.00 12.00
124 Aaron Blair 3.00 8.00
125 Corey Knebel 3.00 8.00
126 Rob Zastryzny 5.00 12.00
127 Ryan McMahon 10.00 25.00
128 Ryan Eades 3.00 8.00
129 Teddy Stankiewicz 6.00 15.00
130 Andrew Church 3.00 8.00
131 Austin Wilson 3.00 8.00
132 Dustin Peterson 5.00 12.00
133 Andrew Knapp 4.00 10.00
134 Devin Williams 8.00 20.00
135 Tom Windle 3.00 8.00
136 Oscar Mercado 4.00 10.00
137 Kevin Ziomek 3.00 8.00
138 Hunter Green EXCH 3.00 8.00
139 Riley Unroe 3.00 8.00
140 Akeem Bostick 5.00 12.00
141 Dillon Overton 4.00 10.00
142 Ryder Jones 6.00 15.00
143 Gosuke Katoh 5.00 12.00
144 Kevin Franklin 3.00 8.00
145 Chad Pinder 3.00 8.00
146 Colby Suggs 3.00 8.00
147 Jacob Hannemann 3.00 8.00
148 Jonathan Denney 5.00 12.00
149 Patrick Murphy 4.00 10.00
150 Stuart Turner 5.00 12.00
151 Jacob May 5.00 12.00
152 Jacoby Jones 5.00 12.00
153 Brandon Dixon 5.00 12.00
154 Michael O'Neill 4.00 10.00
155 Drew Ward 8.00 20.00
156 Chris Kohler 5.00 12.00
157 Tyler Skulina 3.00 8.00
158 Cody Bellinger 125.00 300.00
159 Mason Katz 3.00 8.00
160 Brian Ragira 5.00 12.00
161 Tony Kemp EXCH 6.00 15.00
162 Trey Masek 3.00 8.00
163 Aaron Slegers 20.00 50.00
164 Joe Jackson EXCH 4.00 10.00
165 Dan Slania 5.00 12.00
166 Luke Farrell 3.00 8.00
167 Jacob Nottingham 3.00 8.00
168 Brandon Diaz
169 Kyle Farmer 3.00 8.00
170 Michael Ratterree 4.00 10.00
171 Kasey Coffman 4.00 10.00
172 Tyler Webb 5.00 12.00
173 Kendall Coleman 3.00 8.00
174 Chase Jensen 3.00 8.00
175 Mikey Reynolds 4.00 10.00
176 Ben Verlander 6.00 15.00
177 Austin Kubitza 4.00 10.00
178 Chris Garia
179 Alen Hanson 3.00 8.00
180 Micah Johnson 4.00 10.00
181 Anthony Garcia 4.00 10.00
182 Cameron Flynn 3.00 8.00
183 Gregory Polanco 6.00 15.00
184 Maikel Franco 8.00 20.00
185 Rosell Herrera EXCH 12.00 30.00
186 Mike Yastrzemski 12.00 30.00
187 Cory Vaughn 5.00 12.00
188 Jayce Boyd 3.00 8.00
189 Matt Andriese 4.00 10.00
190 Luis Torrens EXCH 3.00 8.00
191 Jorge Alfaro 10.00 25.00
192 Tim Atherton 3.00 8.00
193 Zach Borenstein EXCH 10.00 25.00
194 Hunter Lockwood 3.00 8.00
195 Terry McClure 3.00 8.00
196 Cody Stubbs 3.00 8.00
197 Kyle Crockett 4.00 10.00
198 Kent Emanuel 3.00 8.00
199 Tanner Norton 3.00 8.00
200 Amaurys Minier 10.00 25.00

2013 Elite Extra Edition Signature Status Blue

STATED PRINT RUN 50 SER.#'d SETS
EXCHANGE DEADLINE 07/09/2014
1 Colin Moran 5.00 12.00
2 Trey Ball
3 Hunter Renfroe 15.00 40.00
4 Braden Shipley 4.00 10.00
5 Chris Anderson
6 Marco Gonzales 5.00 12.00
7 Ryan Walker
8 Phillip Ervin 12.50 30.00
9 Ryne Stanek 8.00 20.00
10 Sean Manaea 8.00 20.00
11 Josh Hart 5.00 12.00
12 Michael Lorenzen EXCH 5.00 12.00
13 Andrew Thurman 4.00 10.00
14 Trevor Williams 5.00 12.00
15 Cody Reed 15.00 40.00
16 Johnny Field
17 Justin Williams 4.00 10.00
18 Blake Taylor 4.00 10.00
19 Chance Sisco
20 Tyler Danish EXCH 5.00 12.00
21 Victor Caratini 20.00 50.00
22 Marten Gasparini 6.00 15.00
23 Jake Sweaney 4.00 10.00
24 Alex Balog
25 Tucker Neuhaus 4.00 10.00
26 Dace Kime 6.00 15.00
27 Ivan Wilson 5.00 12.00
28 Carter Hope 4.00 10.00
29 Barrett Astin 4.00 10.00
30 Daniel Palka 4.00 10.00
31 Keynan Middleton EXCH
32 Carlos Salazar 4.00 10.00
33 Mason Smith 4.00 10.00
34 Cody Dickson 4.00 10.00
35 Stephen Gonsalves 8.00 20.00
36 K.J. Woods 4.00 10.00
37 Jonah Heim
38 Kean Wong 4.00 10.00
39 Jared King 6.00 15.00
40 Josh Uhen 5.00 12.00
41 Cory Thompson 4.00 10.00
42 Ryan Aper
43 Cal Drummond 4.00 10.00
44 Brian Navarreto 4.00 10.00
45 Konner Wade
46 Jake Bauers 8.00 20.00
47 Tyler Horan 10.00 25.00
48 Scott Brattvet 4.00 10.00
49 David Napoli 4.00 10.00
50 Mitch Garver 4.00 10.00
51 D.J. Snelten 4.00 10.00
52 Brad Goldberg 4.00 10.00
53 Carlos Asuaje 4.00 10.00
54 Erik Schoenrock 4.00 10.00
55 Garrett Smith 4.00 10.00
56 Domingo Tapia
57 Bruce Kern 4.00 10.00
58 Trae Arbet 5.00 12.00
59 Amed Rosario 40.00 100.00
60 Andy Burns 4.00 10.00
61 Miguel Almonte 4.00 10.00
62 Anthony DeSclafani 4.00 10.00
63 Cameron Perkins 4.00 10.00
64 Chris Taylor 15.00 40.00
65 Dixon Machado 4.00 10.00
66 Matt Duffy EXCH 40.00 100.00
67 Joel Payamps
68 Taylor Garrison 4.00 10.00
69 Corey Black 4.00 10.00
70 Junior Arias 4.00 10.00
71 Gleyber Torres 150.00 300.00
72 Chad Rogers 4.00 10.00
73 D.J. Baxendale
74 Jason Coats
75 Daniel Winkler 6.00 15.00
76 Devon Travis 12.50 30.00
77 Yoel Mecias 5.00 12.00
78 Francisco Sosa EXCH 5.00 12.00
79 Ronny Carvajal EXCH 8.00 20.00
80 Eugenio Suarez 12.00 30.00
81 Akeel Morris 4.00 10.00
82 Mike O'Neill 5.00 12.00
83 Randy Rosario 4.00 10.00
84 Orlando Castro EXCH 4.00 10.00
85 Jesus Solorzano EXCH 5.00 12.00
86 Rainy Lara
87 Sam Moll 4.00 10.00
88 Tyler Wade 20.00 50.00
89 Roberto Osuna 6.00 15.00
90 Rock Shoulders 5.00 12.00
91 Jeremy Rathjen 4.00 10.00
92 Luis Mateo 4.00 10.00
93 Jose Abreu 20.00 50.00
94 Jordan Patterson 4.00 10.00
95 Adrian De Horta 6.00 15.00
96 David Garner 4.00 10.00
97 Trey Michalczewski
98 Drew Dosch
99 Ryan Garvey 4.00 10.00
100 Dereck Rodriguez 15.00 40.00
101 Mark Appel 8.00 20.00
102 Kris Bryant 75.00 200.00
103 Jonathan Gray 6.00 15.00
104 Kohl Stewart 8.00 20.00
105 Clint Frazier 50.00 120.00
106 Hunter Dozier 8.00 20.00
107 Austin Meadows 50.00 120.00
108 Dominic Smith 12.50 30.00
109 D.J. Peterson 12.50 30.00
110 Reese McGuire 10.00 25.00
111 J.P. Crawford 15.00 40.00
112 Tim Anderson 12.00 30.00
113 Jonathon Crawford 6.00 15.00
114 Nick Ciuffo 8.00 20.00
115 Hunter Harvey 5.00 12.00
116 Alex Gonzalez 12.00 30.00
117 Billy McKinney 15.00 40.00
118 Rob Kaminsky 6.00 15.00
119 Eric Jagielo 8.00 20.00
120 Travis Demeritte 5.00 12.00
121 Jason Hursh 6.00 15.00
122 Aaron Judge 150.00 400.00
123 Ian Clarkin
124 Aaron Blair 4.00 10.00
125 Corey Knebel 4.00 10.00
126 Rob Zastryzny 6.00 15.00
127 Ryan McMahon 15.00 40.00
128 Ryan Eades 4.00 10.00
129 Teddy Stankiewicz 5.00 12.00
130 Andrew Church 4.00 10.00
131 Austin Wilson 4.00 10.00
132 Dustin Peterson 6.00 15.00
133 Andrew Knapp 5.00 12.00
134 Devin Williams 10.00 25.00
135 Tom Windle 4.00 10.00
136 Oscar Mercado 5.00 12.00
137 Kevin Ziomek 4.00 10.00
138 Hunter Green EXCH 4.00 10.00
139 Riley Unroe 4.00 10.00
140 Akeem Bostick 6.00 15.00
141 Dillon Overton 4.00 10.00
142 Ryder Jones 4.00 10.00
143 Gosuke Katoh 5.00 12.00
144 Kevin Franklin 4.00 10.00
145 Chad Pinder 4.00 10.00
146 Colby Suggs 4.00 10.00
147 Jacob Hannemann 4.00 10.00
148 Jonathan Denney 6.00 15.00
149 Patrick Murphy 5.00 12.00
150 Stuart Turner 6.00 15.00
151 Jacob May
152 Jacoby Jones 6.00 15.00
153 Brandon Dixon 6.00 15.00
154 Michael O'Neill 5.00 12.00
155 Drew Ward 10.00 25.00
156 Chris Kohler 5.00 12.00
157 Tyler Skulina 4.00 10.00
158 Cody Bellinger 150.00 400.00
159 Mason Katz 4.00 10.00
160 Brian Ragira 4.00 10.00
161 Tony Kemp EXCH 5.00 12.00
162 Trey Masek 4.00 10.00
163 Aaron Slegers 25.00 60.00
164 Joe Jackson EXCH 5.00 12.00
165 Dan Slania
166 Luke Farrell 4.00 10.00
167 Jacob Nottingham
168 Brandon Diaz 5.00 12.00
169 Kyle Farmer 4.00 10.00
170 Michael Ratterree 5.00 12.00
171 Kasey Coffman 4.00 10.00
172 Tyler Webb
173 Kendall Coleman 4.00 10.00
174 Chase Jensen 4.00 10.00
175 Mikey Reynolds 5.00 12.00
176 Ben Verlander 8.00 20.00
177 Austin Kubitza 5.00 12.00
178 Chris Garia
179 Alen Hanson 4.00 10.00
180 Micah Johnson 5.00 12.00
181 Anthony Garcia 5.00 12.00
182 Cameron Flynn
183 Gregory Polanco 15.00 40.00
184 Maikel Franco 10.00 25.00
185 Rosell Herrera EXCH 20.00 50.00
186 Mike Yastrzemski 15.00 40.00
187 Cory Vaughn 6.00 15.00
188 Jayce Boyd 4.00 10.00
189 Matt Andriese 5.00 12.00
190 Luis Torrens EXCH
191 Jorge Alfaro 10.00 25.00
192 Tim Atherton
193 Zach Borenstein EXCH 8.00 20.00
194 Hunter Lockwood
195 Terry McClure 4.00 10.00
196 Cody Stubbs 4.00 10.00
197 Kyle Crockett 5.00 12.00
198 Kent Emanuel 4.00 10.00
199 Tanner Norton 4.00 10.00
200 Amaurys Minier

2013 Elite Extra Edition USA Baseball 15U Game Jerseys

1 Nick Allen 2.50 6.00
2 Jordan Butler 2.50 6.00
3 Daniel Cabrera 5.00 12.00
4 Sam Ferri 2.50 6.00
5 Isaak Gutierrez 2.50 6.00
6 Brandon Martorano 2.50 6.00
7 Mickey Moniak 4.00 10.00
8 Christian Moya 2.50 6.00
9 Manuel Perez 2.50 6.00
10 Todd Peterson 2.50 6.00
11 Logan Pouelsen 2.50 6.00
12 Nick Pratto 2.50 6.00
13 Ben Ramirez 2.50 6.00
14 DJ Roberts 2.50 6.00
15 Matthew Rudick 2.50 6.00
16 Blake Sabol 2.50 6.00
17 Chase Strumpf 2.50 6.00
18 Mason Thompson 2.50 6.00
19 Andrew Vaughn 4.00 10.00

2013 Elite Extra Edition USA Baseball 15U Game Jerseys Prime

*PRIME: .5X TO 1.2X BASIC
STATED PRINT RUN 49 SER.#'d SETS

2013 Elite Extra Edition USA Baseball 15U Signatures

PRINT RUNS B/WN 24-199 COPIES PER
EXCHANGE DEADLINE 07/09/2014
1 Nick Allen/199 3.00 8.00
2 Jordan Butler/199 3.00 8.00
3 Daniel Cabrera/188 6.00 15.00
4 Sam Ferri/161 3.00 8.00
5 Isaak Gutierrez/24 3.00 8.00
6 Brandon Martorano/199 3.00 8.00
7 Mickey Moniak/199 20.00 50.00
8 Christian Moya/197 3.00 8.00
9 Manuel Perez/199 3.00 8.00
10 Todd Peterson/189 3.00 8.00
11 Logan Pouelsen/199 3.00 8.00
12 Nick Pratto/199 3.00 8.00
13 Ben Ramirez/199 3.00 8.00
14 DJ Roberts/199 3.00 8.00
15 Matthew Rudick/199 3.00 8.00
16 Blake Sabol/199 3.00 8.00
17 Chase Strumpf/199 3.00 8.00
18 Mason Thompson/179 3.00 8.00
19 Andrew Vaughn/185 15.00 40.00

2013 Elite Extra Edition USA Baseball 18U Dual Game Jersey Signatures

PRINT RUNS B/WN 2-25 COPIES PER
NO PRICING ON QTY 3 OR LESS
EXCHANGE DEADLINE 07/09/2014
1 Brady Aiken/25 20.00 50.00
2 Bryson Brigman/25
3 Joe DeMers/25 4.00 10.00
4 Alex Destino/25 4.00 10.00
5 Jack Flaherty/25 6.00 15.00
6 Marvin Gorgas/25 4.00 10.00
7 Adam Haseley/25 5.00 12.00
8 Scott Hurst/25 4.00 10.00
9 Kel Johnson/25 10.00 25.00
10 Trace Loehr/25 4.00 10.00
11 Mac Marshall/25 5.00 12.00
13 Jacob Nix/25
14 Luis Ortiz/25 4.00 10.00
16 Michael Rivera/25 4.00 10.00
17 JJ Schwarz/25
18 Justus Sheffield/25 6.00 15.00
20 Cole Tucker/25

2013 Elite Extra Edition USA Baseball 18U Game Jerseys

1 Brady Aiken 6.00 15.00
2 Bryson Brigman 2.50 6.00
3 Joe DeMers 2.50 6.00
4 Alex Destino 2.50 6.00
5 Jack Flaherty 2.50 6.00
6 Marvin Gorgas 2.50 6.00
7 Adam Haseley 2.50 6.00
8 Scott Hurst 2.50 6.00
9 Kel Johnson 3.00 8.00
10 Trace Loehr 2.50 6.00
11 Mac Marshall 2.50 6.00
12 Keaton McKinney 2.50 6.00
13 Jacob Nix 2.50 6.00
14 Luis Ortiz 2.50 6.00
15 Jakson Reetz 6.00 15.00
16 Michael Rivera 2.50 6.00
17 JJ Schwarz 2.50 6.00
18 Justus Sheffield 2.50 6.00
19 Lane Thomas 2.50 6.00
20 Cole Tucker 2.50 6.00

2013 Elite Extra Edition USA Baseball 18U Game Jerseys Prime

*PRIME: .5X TO 1.2X BASIC
STATED PRINT RUN 49 SER.#'d SETS

2013 Elite Extra Edition USA Baseball 18U Signatures

PRINT RUNS B/WN 4-299 COPIES PER
NO PRICING ON QTY 5 OR LESS
EXCHANGE DEADLINE 07/09/2014
1 Brady Aiken/299 15.00 40.00
2 Bryson Brigman/299 3.00 8.00
3 Joe DeMers/299 3.00 8.00
4 Alex Destino/299 3.00 8.00
5 Jack Flaherty/299 4.00 10.00
6 Marvin Gorgas/299 3.00 8.00
7 Adam Haseley/299 3.00 8.00
8 Scott Hurst/299 3.00 8.00
9 Kel Johnson/299 4.00 10.00
10 Trace Loehr/299 3.00 8.00
11 Mac Marshall/299 3.00 8.00
13 Jacob Nix/299 3.00 8.00
14 Luis Ortiz/299 4.00 10.00
16 Michael Rivera/299 3.00 8.00
17 JJ Schwarz/299 3.00 8.00
18 Justus Sheffield/299 10.00 25.00
20 Cole Tucker/299 3.00 8.00

2014 Elite Extra Edition

COMP.SET w/o SP's (95) 12.00 30.00
SP's RANDOMLY INSERTED
NO SP PRICING DUE TO SCARCITY
1A Jose Pujols .20 .50
2A Jhoandro Alfaro .20 .50
3A Michael Kopech 1.25 3.00
4A Joey Pankake .20 .50
5A Forrest Wall .30 .75
6A Dermis Garcia .30 .75
7A James Norwood .20 .50
8A Luke Dykstra .40 1.00
9A Brandon Downes .25 .60
10A Chase Vallot .20 .50
11 Logan Moon .25 .60
12 Mark Payton .20 .50
13 Jonathan Holder .20 .50
14 Reed Reilly .20 .50
15 Deivi Grullon .20 .50
16 Ryan O'Hearn .40 1.00
17 Jordan Brink .25 .60
18 Derek Campbell .20 .50
19 Cole Lankford .20 .50
20 Javi Salas .20 .50
22 John Curtiss .20 .50
23 Gareth Morgan .20 .50
24 Casey Soltis .20 .50
25 Zach Thompson .20 .50
26 Jake Reed .20 .50
27 Dan Altavilla .20 .50
28 Lane Thomas .30 .75
29 Josh Prevost .20 .50
30 Jake Jewell .20 .50
31 Corey Ray .20 .50
32 Drew Van Orden .20 .50
33 Tejay Antone .20 .50
35 Jared Walker .20 .50
36 Lane Ratliff .20 .50
38 Trace Loehr .20 .50
39 Jake Peter .20 .50
40 Kevin McAvoy .20 .50
41 Austin Gomber .25 .60
42 Ross Kivett .20 .50
43 Grant Hockin .20 .50
44 Brett Graves .20 .50
45 Greg Mahle .20 .50
46 Chris Ellis .20 .50
47 Jeff Brigham .20 .50
48 Greg Allen .20 .50
49 A.J. Vanegas .20 .50

50 Marcus Wilson .20 .50
51 Kevin Padlo .20 .50
52 Danny Diekroeger .20 .50
53 Sam Coonrod .20 .50
54 Mac James .20 .50
55 Brian Anderson .20 .50
56 Jace Fry .20 .50
57 Mark Zagunis .20 .50
58 Cy Sneed .20 .50
59 Matt Railey .20 .50
60 Sam Hentges .20 .50
61 Eric Skoglund .20 .50
62 Brock Burke .20 .50
63 Grayson Greiner .20 .50
64 Jordan Luplow .20 .50
66 Jake Yacinich .20 .50
68 Richard Prigatano .20 .50
69 Brian Schales .20 .50
70 Dustin DeMuth .20 .50
71 Sam Clay .20 .50
72 Dillon Peters .20 .50
73 Skyler Ewing .25 .60
74 Gilbert Lara .20 .50
75 Michael Suchy .20 .50
76 Dalton Pompey .30 .75
77 Zech Lemond .20 .50
78 Troy Stokes .20 .50
79 Zac Curtis .20 .50
80 Austin Fisher .20 .50
81 Brandon Leibrandt .20 .50
82 Spencer Moran .20 .50
83 Jared Robinson .20 .50
84 Austin Coley .20 .50
85 Cody Reed .20 .50
86 Jose Trevino .20 .50
87 J.P. Feyereisen .20 .50
88 J.B. Kole .20 .50
89 Max Murphy .20 .50
90 Kevin Steen .20 .50
91 Keaton Steele .20 .50
92 Max George .20 .50
93 Andy Ferguson .20 .50
94 Dean Kiekhefer .20 .50
95 Carson Sands .20 .50
96 Justin Shafer .20 .50
97 Jorge Soler .40 1.00
98 Nelson Gomez .25 .60
99 Adrian Rondon .25 .60
100 Mike Strentz .20 .50

2014 Elite Extra Edition Inspirations

*INSPIRATIONS: 1.5X TO 4X BASIC
RANDOM INSERTS IN PACKS
STATED PRINT RUN 200 SER.#'d SETS

2014 Elite Extra Edition Status Blue

*BLUE: 2.5X TO 6X BASIC
RANDOM INSERTS IN PACKS
STATED PRINT RUN 150 SER.#'d SETS

2014 Elite Extra Edition Status Emerald

*EMERALD: 6X TO 15X BASIC
RANDOM INSERTS IN PACKS
STATED PRINT RUN 150 SER.#'d SETS

2014 Elite Extra Edition Status Purple

*PURPLE: 2X TO 5X BASIC
RANDOM INSERTS IN PACKS
STATED PRINT RUN 150 SER.#'d SETS

2014 Elite Extra Edition Signature Inspirations

*INSPRIATIONS: .5X TO 1.2X FUTURES
RANDOM INSERTS IN PACKS
STATED PRINT RUN 100 SER.#'d SETS
EXCHANGE DEADLINE 7/7/2016

2014 Elite Extra Edition Signature Status Blue

*BLUE: .6X TO 1.5X FUTURES
RANDOM INSERTS IN PACKS
STATED PRINT RUN 50 SER.#'d SETS
EXCHANGE DEADLINE 7/7/2016

2014 Elite Extra Edition Signature Status Emerald

*EMERALD: .75X TO 2X FUTURES
RANDOM INSERTS IN PACKS
STATED PRINT RUN 25 SER.#'d SETS
EXCHANGE DEADLINE 7/7/2016

2014 Elite Extra Edition Signature Status Purple

*PURPLE: .6X TO 1.5X FUTURES
RANDOM INSERTS IN PACKS
STATED PRINT RUN 75 SER.#'d SETS
EXCHANGE DEADLINE 7/7/2016

2014 Elite Extra Edition Back to the Future Signatures

RANDOM INSERTS IN PACKS
PRINT RUNS B/WN 10-99 COPIES PER
NO PRICING ON QTY 15 OR LESS
EXCHANGE DEADLINE 7/7/2016
4 Kyle Zimmer/49 3.00 8.00
8 Miguel Sano/25 12.00 30.00
16 Noah Syndergaard/99 10.00 25.00
19 Jorge Alfaro/49 4.00 10.00
20 Sean Manaea/49 8.00 20.00

2014 Elite Extra Edition Elite Expectations

RANDOM INSERTS IN PACKS
1 Adrian Rondon .60 1.50
2 Michael Chavis 2.50 6.00
3 Dalton Pompey .75 2.00
4 Tyler Kolek .50 1.25
5 Carlos Rodon 1.25 3.00
6 Alex Jackson .60 1.50
7 Kyle Schwarber 2.00 5.00
8 Kyle Freeland 1.00 2.50
9 Cole Tucker .50 1.25
10 Trea Turner 1.50 4.00
11 Erick Fedde .50 1.25
12 Bradley Zimmer .75 2.00
13 Michael Conforto 1.00 2.50
14 Jack Flaherty 3.00 8.00
15 Sean Newcomb .75 2.00
16 Aaron Nola 3.00 8.00
17 Max Pentecost .50 1.25
18 Jeff Hoffman .75 2.00
19 Kodi Medeiros .50 1.25
20 Rusney Castillo .60 1.50

2014 Elite Extra Edition Elite Expectations Signatures

RANDOM INSERTS IN PACKS
STATED PRINT RUN 25 SER.#'d SETS
EXCHANGE DEADLINE 7/7/2016
1 Adrian Rondon EXCH 12.00 30.00
2 Michael Chavis 40.00 100.00
4 Tyler Kolek 6.00 15.00
5 Carlos Rodon 25.00 60.00
8 Kyle Freeland 12.00 30.00
9 Cole Tucker 6.00 15.00
14 Jack Flaherty 12.00 30.00
17 Max Pentecost 6.00 15.00
18 Jeff Hoffman 10.00 25.00
19 Kodi Medeiros 6.00 15.00

2014 Elite Extra Edition Elite Series

COMPLETE SET (20)
RANDOM INSERTS IN PACKS
1 Alex Blandino .50 1.25
2 Derek Hill .50 1.25
3 Max Pentecost .50 1.25
4 Nick Howard .50 1.25
5 Luke Weaver 1.50 4.00
6 Derek Fisher .75 2.00
7 Aaron Nola 3.00 8.00
8 Trea Turner 1.50 4.00
9 Kodi Medeiros .50 1.25
10 Casey Gillaspie .75 2.00
11 Raisel Iglesias .60 1.50
12 Luis Ortiz .50 1.25
13 Grant Holmes .50 1.25
14 Michael Gettys .60 1.50
15 Joey Pankake .50 1.25
16 Austin Cousino .50 1.25
17 Jorge Soler 1.00 2.50
18 Luis Severino .75 2.00
19 J.D. Davis .75 2.00
20 Dylan Davis .60 1.50

2014 Elite Extra Edition Elite Series Signatures

RANDOM INSERTS IN PACKS
PRINT RUNS B/WN 4-149 COPIES PER
NO PRICING ON QTY 4 OR LESS
EXCHANGE DEADLINE 7/7/2016
1 Alex Blandino/49 3.00 8.00
2 Derek Hill/49 6.00 15.00
4 Nick Howard/49 8.00 20.00
8 Trea Turner/49 20.00 50.00
9 Kodi Medeiros/149 3.00 8.00
10 Casey Gillaspie/49 5.00 12.00
13 Grant Holmes/49 12.00 30.00
14 Michael Gettys/99 4.00 10.00
15 Joey Pankake/99 3.00 8.00
16 Austin Cousino/99 8.00 20.00
19 J.D. Davis/99 5.00 12.00
20 Dylan Davis/104 12.00 30.00

2014 Elite Extra Edition Franchise Futures Signatures

RANDOM INSERTS IN PACKS
PRINT RUNS B/WN 20-799 COPIES PER
EXCHANGE DEADLINE 7/7/2016
*EMERALD/25: .75X TO 2X BASIC
1 Jose Pujols/699 3.00 8.00
2 Jhoandro Alfaro/499 3.00 8.00
3 Michael Kopech/399 12.00 30.00
4 Joey Pankake/799 3.00 8.00
5 Forrest Wall/399 5.00 12.00
6 Dermis Garcia/634 5.00 12.00
7 James Norwood/799 3.00 8.00
9 Brandon Downes/799 4.00 10.00
10 Chase Vallot/399 3.00 8.00
11 Logan Moon/799 4.00 10.00
12 Mark Payton/799 3.00 8.00
13 Jonathan Holder/799 3.00 8.00
14 Reed Reilly/799 3.00 8.00
15 Deivi Grullon/799 3.00 8.00
16 Ryan O'Hearn/799 6.00 15.00
17 Jordan Brink/799 4.00 10.00
18 Derek Campbell/799 3.00 8.00
19 Cole Lankford/799 3.00 8.00
20 Javi Salas/799 3.00 8.00
23 Gareth Morgan/299 3.00 8.00
24 Casey Soltis/799 3.00 8.00
25 Zach Thompson/799 3.00 8.00
26 Jake Reed/799 3.00 8.00
27 Dan Altavilla/799 3.00 8.00
28 Lane Thomas/799 5.00 12.00
29 Josh Prevost/699 3.00 8.00
30 Jake Jewell/699 3.00 8.00
31 Corey Ray/699 3.00 8.00
32 Drew Van Orden/699 3.00 8.00
33 Tejay Antone/699 3.00 8.00
35 Jared Walker/799 3.00 8.00
36 Lane Ratliff/799 3.00 8.00
38 Trace Loehr/799 3.00 8.00
39 Jake Peter/799 3.00 8.00
40 Kevin McAvoy/799 3.00 8.00
41 Austin Gomber/799 4.00 10.00
42 Ross Kivett/799 3.00 8.00
43 Grant Hockin/499 3.00 8.00
44 Brett Graves/220 3.00 8.00
45 Greg Mahle/799 3.00 8.00
46 Chris Ellis/599 3.00 8.00
47 Jeff Brigham/799 3.00 8.00
48 Greg Allen/799 3.00 8.00
49 A.J. Vanegas/799 3.00 8.00
50 Marcus Wilson/499 5.00 12.00
51 Kevin Padlo/699 3.00 8.00
52 Danny Diekroeger/799 3.00 8.00
53 Sam Coonrod/699 3.00 8.00
54 Mac James/799 3.00 8.00
55 Brian Anderson/649 3.00 8.00
57 Mark Zagunis/799 6.00 15.00
58 Cy Sneed/799 3.00 8.00
59 Matt Railey/649 3.00 8.00
60 Sam Hentges/799 3.00 8.00
61 Eric Skoglund/649 3.00 8.00
62 Brock Burke/799 3.00 8.00
63 Grayson Greiner/599 3.00 8.00
64 Jordan Luplow/699 3.00 8.00
68 Richard Prigatano/799 3.00 8.00
69 Brian Schales/69 3.00 8.00
70 Dustin DeMuth/799 3.00 8.00
71 Sam Clay/799 3.00 8.00
72 Dillon Peters/699 3.00 8.00
73 Skyler Ewing/799 4.00 10.00
75 Michael Suchy/599 3.00 8.00
76 Dalton Pompey/524 5.00 12.00
77 Zech Lemond/699 3.00 8.00
79 Zac Curtis/799 3.00 8.00
80 Austin Fisher/799 3.00 8.00
81 Brandon Leibrandt/799 3.00 8.00
82 Spencer Moran/799 3.00 8.00
83 Jared Robinson/799 3.00 8.00
84 Austin Coley/799 3.00 8.00
86 Jose Trevino/699 3.00 8.00
87 J.P. Feyereisen/424 3.00 8.00
88 J.B. Kole/799 3.00 8.00
89 Max Murphy/799 3.00 8.00
90 Kevin Steen/799 3.00 8.00
91 Keaton Steele/799 3.00 8.00
92 Max George/799 3.00 8.00
93 Andy Ferguson/799 3.00 8.00
94 Dean Kiekhefer/799 3.00 8.00
95 Carson Sands/120 3.00 8.00
96 Justin Shafer/799 3.00 8.00
97 Jorge Soler/149 6.00 15.00
99 Adrian Rondon/499 10.00 25.00
100 Mike Strentz/799 3.00 8.00

2014 Elite Extra Edition Historic Picks

COMPLETE SET (10) 10.00 25.00
RANDOM INSERTS IN PACKS
1 Ken Griffey Jr. 3.00 8.00
2 Chipper Jones 1.50 4.00
3 Mike Piazza 1.50 4.00
4 Luis Gonzalez 1.00 2.50
5 Dusty Baker 1.00 2.50
6 Johnny Bench 1.50 4.00
7 Nolan Ryan 5.00 12.00
8 Mark Grace 1.25 3.00
9 Jorge Posada 1.25 3.00
10 Andy Pettitte 1.25 3.00

2014 Elite Extra Edition Passing the Torch Signatures

RANDOM INSERTS IN PACKS
STATED PRINT RUN 25 SER.#'d SETS
EXCHANGE DEADLINE 7/7/2016
6 G.Lara/M.Sano EXCH 20.00 50.00
8 N.Howard/R.Stephenson 15.00 40.00
9 J.Hoffman/M.Pentecost 25.00 60.00

2014 Elite Extra Edition Prospects Inspirations

RANDOM INSERTS IN PACKS
STATED PRINT RUN 200 SER.#'d SETS
*PURPLE/150: .5X TO 1.2X BASIC
*BLUE/100: .6X TO 1.5X BASIC
*EMERALD/25: 1.2X TO 3X BASIC
1 Braxton Davidson .75 2.00
2 Tyler Kolek .75 2.00
3 Carlos Rodon 2.00 5.00
4 Kyle Schwarber 3.00 8.00
5 Derek Fisher 1.25 3.00
6 Alex Jackson 1.00 2.50
7 Aaron Nola 5.00 12.00
8 Kyle Freeland 1.50 4.00
9 Jeff Hoffman 1.25 3.00
10 Michael Conforto 1.50 4.00
11 Max Pentecost .75 2.00
12 Kodi Medeiros .75 2.00
13 Trea Turner 2.50 6.00
14 Tyler Beede 1.25 3.00
15 Sean Newcomb 1.25 3.00
16 J.D. Davis 1.50 4.00
17 Brandon Finnegan .75 2.00
18 Erick Fedde .75 2.00
19 A.J. Reed 1.50 4.00
20 Casey Gillaspie 1.25 3.00
21 Bradley Zimmer 1.25 3.00
22 Grant Holmes .75 2.00
23 Derek Hill .75 2.00
24 Cole Tucker .75 2.00
25 Matt Chapman 5.00 12.00
26 Michael Chavis 4.00 10.00
27 Luke Weaver 2.50 6.00
28 Foster Griffin .75 2.00
29 Alex Blandino .75 2.00
30 Luis Ortiz .75 2.00
31 Michael Cederoth 1.00 2.50
32 Aramis Garcia .75 2.00
33 Joe Gatto .75 2.00
35 Jacob Lindgren 1.00 2.50
36 Scott Blewett .75 2.00
37 Austin Cousino .75 2.00
38 Taylor Sparks .75 2.00
39 Ti'Quan Forbes .75 2.00
40 Cameron Varga .75 2.00
41 Eudor Garcia .75 2.00
42 Alex Verdugo 1.50 4.00
43 Spencer Turnbull .75 2.00
44 Mitch Keller 1.25 3.00
45 John Richy .75 2.00
46 Aaron Brown .75 2.00
47 Sam Travis 1.00 2.50
48 Justin Twine .75 2.00
49 Chris Oliver .75 2.00
51 Raisel Iglesias 1.00 2.50
52 Nick Howard .75 2.00
53 Sam Howard .75 2.00
54 Dylan Davis 1.00 2.50
55 Wyatt Strahan .75 2.00
56 Daniel Mengden .75 2.00
57 Auston Bousfield .75 2.00
58 Logan Webb 1.25 3.00
59 Josh Ockimey 1.25 3.00
60 Adam Ravenelle 1.00 2.50
61 Shane Zeile .75 2.00
62 Jake Cosart 1.00 2.50
63 Michael Mader .75 2.00
64 Justin Steele .75 2.00
65 Jakson Reetz .75 2.00
66 Luis Severino 1.25 3.00
67 Rusney Castillo 1.00 2.50
68 Bobby Bradley 1.00 2.50
69 Jordan Montgomery 1.50 4.00
70 Dariel Alvarez .75 2.00
71 Taylor Gushue .75 2.00
72 Jordan Schwartz .75 2.00
73 Gilbert Lara .75 2.00
74 Justus Sheffield 1.50 4.00
75 Connor Joe .75 2.00
76 Spencer Adams 1.00 2.50
77 Nick Burdi .75 2.00
78 Matt Imhof .75 2.00
79 Mitch Watrous 1.00 2.50
80 Dylan Cease 2.00 5.00
81 Jake Stinnett .75 2.00
82 Jacob Gatewood .75 2.00
83 Monte Harrison 1.50 4.00
84 Nick Wells .75 2.00
85 Milton Ramos .75 2.00
86 Wes Rogers .75 2.00
87 Mason McCullough .75 2.00
88 Chris Diaz 1.00 2.50
89 Dalier Hinojosa .75 2.00
90 Josh Morgan .75 2.00
91 Michael Gettys 1.00 2.50
92 Ryan Castellani .75 2.00
93 Victor Arano .75 2.00
94 Trey Supak .75 2.00
95 Andrew Morales .75 2.00
96 Jack Flaherty 5.00 12.00
97 Daniel Gossett .75 2.00
98 Ronnie Williams .75 2.00
99 Isan Diaz 2.00 5.00
100 Sean Reid-Foley .75 2.00

2014 Elite Extra Edition Prospects Signatures

RANDOM INSERTS IN PACKS
PRINT RUNS B/WN 34-799 COPIES PER
EXCHANGE DEADLINE 7/7/2016
1 Braxton Davidson/499 3.00 8.00
2 Tyler Kolek/299 3.00 8.00
3 Carlos Rodon/299 10.00 25.00
4 Kyle Schwarber/299 25.00 60.00
5 Derek Fisher/499 5.00 12.00
6 Alex Jackson/299 4.00 10.00
7 Aaron Nola/399 5.00 12.00
8 Kyle Freeland/399 6.00 15.00
9 Jeff Hoffman/399 4.00 10.00
10 Michael Conforto/299 EXCH 12.00 30.00
11 Max Pentecost/399 3.00 8.00
12 Kodi Medeiros/399 3.00 8.00
13 Trea Turner/449 12.00 30.00
14 Tyler Beede/399 5.00 12.00
15 Sean Newcomb/399 5.00 12.00
16 J.D. Davis/799 5.00 12.00
17 Brandon Finnegan/399 3.00 8.00
18 Erick Fedde/399 3.00 8.00
19 A.J. Reed/599 6.00 15.00
20 Casey Gillaspie/399 5.00 12.00
21 Bradley Zimmer/399 3.00 8.00
22 Grant Holmes/199 8.00 20.00
23 Derek Hill/449 3.00 8.00
24 Cole Tucker/399 3.00 8.00
25 Matt Chapman/399 10.00 25.00
26 Michael Chavis/474 20.00 50.00
27 Luke Weaver/399 10.00 25.00
28 Foster Griffin/399 3.00 8.00
29 Alex Blandino/204 3.00 8.00
30 Luis Ortiz/399 3.00 8.00
31 Michael Cederoth/699 3.00 8.00
32 Aramis Garcia/499 3.00 8.00
33 Joe Gatto/599 3.00 8.00
35 Jacob Lindgren/499 3.00 8.00
36 Scott Blewett/349 3.00 8.00
37 Austin Cousino/599 3.00 8.00
38 Taylor Sparks/499 3.00 8.00
39 Ti'Quan Forbes/499 3.00 8.00
40 Cameron Varga/399 3.00 8.00
41 Eudor Garcia/799 3.00 8.00
42 Alex Verdugo/499 6.00 15.00
43 Spencer Turnbull/499 3.00 8.00
44 Mitch Keller/499 3.00 8.00
45 John Richy/799 3.00 8.00
46 Aaron Brown/599 3.00 8.00
47 Sam Travis/524 4.00 10.00
48 Justin Twine/399 3.00 8.00
49 Chris Oliver/799 3.00 8.00
51 Raisel Iglesias/399 8.00 20.00
52 Nick Howard/399 3.00 8.00
53 Sam Howard/799 3.00 8.00
54 Dylan Davis/799 4.00 10.00
55 Wyatt Strahan/599 3.00 8.00
56 Daniel Mengden/799 3.00 8.00
57 Auston Bousfield/699 3.00 8.00
58 Logan Webb/599 5.00 12.00
59 Josh Ockimey/799 5.00 12.00
60 Adam Ravenelle/599 4.00 10.00
61 Shane Zeile/599 3.00 8.00
62 Jake Cosart/799 3.00 8.00
63 Michael Mader/799 3.00 8.00
64 Justin Steele/799 3.00 8.00
65 Jakson Reetz/599 3.00 8.00
66 Luis Severino/399 10.00 25.00
67 Rusney Castillo/699 4.00 10.00
68 Bobby Bradley/799 4.00 10.00
69 Jordan Montgomery/699 3.00 8.00
70 Dariel Alvarez/499 3.00 8.00
71 Taylor Gushue/699 3.00 8.00
72 Jordan Schwartz/799 3.00 8.00
73 Gilbert Lara/34 EXCH 20.00 50.00
74 Justus Sheffield/449 6.00 15.00
75 Connor Joe/399 3.00 8.00
76 Spencer Adams/549 4.00 10.00
77 Nick Burdi/499 3.00 8.00
78 Matt Imhof/499 3.00 8.00
79 Mitch Watrous/799 4.00 10.00
80 Dylan Cease/799 8.00 20.00
81 Jake Stinnett/499 3.00 8.00
82 Jacob Gatewood/399 3.00 8.00
83 Monte Harrison/499 6.00 15.00
84 Nick Wells/599 3.00 8.00
85 Milton Ramos/799 3.00 8.00
86 Wes Rogers/699 3.00 8.00
87 Mason McCullough/699 3.00 8.00
88 Chris Diaz/699 4.00 10.00
89 Dalier Hinojosa/699 3.00 8.00
90 Josh Morgan/799 3.00 8.00
91 Michael Gettys/499 4.00 10.00
92 Ryan Castellani/499 3.00 8.00
93 Victor Arano/799 8.00 20.00
94 Trey Supak/499 3.00 8.00
95 Andrew Morales/499 3.00 8.00
96 Jack Flaherty/599 8.00 20.00
97 Daniel Gossett/499 3.00 8.00
98 Ronnie Williams/499 3.00 8.00
99 Isan Diaz/570 8.00 20.00
100 Sean Reid-Foley/499 3.00 8.00

2014 Elite Extra Edition Prospects Signatures Red Ink

*RED INK: .75X TO 2X BASIC
RANDOM INSERTS IN PACKS
STATED PRINT RUN 25 SER.#'d SETS
EXCHANGE DEADLINE 7/7/2016
73 Gilbert Lara EXCH 20.00 50.00

2014 Elite Extra Edition Prospects Signatures Inspirations

*INSPIRATIONS: .5X TO 1.2X BASIC
RANDOM INSERTS IN PACKS
STATED PRINT RUN 100 SER.#'d SETS
EXCHANGE DEADLINE 7/7/2016
73 Gilbert Lara EXCH 10.00 25.00

2014 Elite Extra Edition Prospects Signatures Status Blue

*BLUE: .6X TO 1.5X BASIC
RANDOM INSERTS IN PACKS
STATED PRINT RUN 50 SER.#'d SETS
EXCHANGE DEADLINE 7/7/2016
73 Gilbert Lara EXCH 15.00 40.00

2014 Elite Extra Edition Prospects Signatures Status Emerald

*EMERALD: .75X TO 2X BASIC
RANDOM INSERTS IN PACKS
STATED PRINT RUN 25 SER.#'d SETS
EXCHANGE DEADLINE 7/7/2016
73 Gilbert Lara EXCH 20.00 50.00

2014 Elite Extra Edition Prospects Signatures Status Purple

*PURPLE: .6X TO 1.5X BASIC
RANDOM INSERTS IN PACKS
STATED PRINT RUN 75 SER.#'d SETS
EXCHANGE DEADLINE 7/7/2016
73 Gilbert Lara EXCH 15.00 40.00

2014 Elite Extra Edition Throwback Threads

RANDOM INSERTS IN PACKS
STATED PRINT RUN 79 SER.#'d SETS
1 Jose Abreu 12.00 30.00

2014 Elite Extra Edition USA Baseball 15U Game Jerseys

RANDOM INSERTS IN PACKS
*PRIME/25: .5X TO 1.2X BASIC
1 Blake Paugh 2.50 6.00
2 Alejandro Toral 3.00 8.00
3 Hugh Fisher 2.50 6.00
4 Steven Williams 2.00 5.00
5 John Dearth 2.00 5.00
6 Doug Nikhazy 2.00 5.00
7 Raymond Gil 2.00 5.00
8 Noah Campbell 2.00 5.00
9 Mark Vientos 3.00 8.00
10 Justin Bullock 2.50 6.00
11 Christopher Austin Martin 4.00 10.00
12 Thomas Burbank 2.50 6.00
13 Ryan Vilade 4.00 10.00
14 Kristofer Armstrong 2.00 5.00
15 Royce Lewis 5.00 12.00
16 Devin Ortiz 2.00 5.00
17 Hunter Greene 6.00 15.00
18 Jacob Blas 2.00 5.00
19 Cordell Dunn Jr. 2.00 5.00
20 Brice Turang 6.00 15.00

2014 Elite Extra Edition USA Baseball 15U Signatures

RANDOM INSERTS IN PACKS
STATED PRINT RUN 199 SER.#'d SETS
EXCHANGE DEADLINE 7/7/2016
1 Blake Paugh 4.00 10.00
2 Alejandro Toral 5.00 12.00
3 Hugh Fisher 4.00 10.00
4 Steven Williams 3.00 8.00
5 John Dearth 3.00 8.00
6 Doug Nikhazy 3.00 8.00
7 Raymond Gil 3.00 8.00
8 Noah Campbell 3.00 8.00
9 Mark Vientos 5.00 12.00
10 Justin Bullock 4.00 10.00
11 Christopher Austin Martin 15.00 40.00
12 Thomas Burbank 4.00 10.00
13 Ryan Vilade 6.00 15.00
14 Kristofer Armstrong 3.00 8.00
15 Royce Lewis 15.00 40.00
16 Devin Ortiz 3.00 8.00
17 Hunter Greene 40.00 100.00
18 Jacob Blas 3.00 8.00
19 Cordell Dunn Jr. 3.00 8.00
20 Brice Turang 10.00 25.00

2014 Elite Extra Edition USA Baseball 18U Dual Game Jersey Signatures

RANDOM INSERTS IN PACKS
STATED PRINT RUN 25 SER.#'d SETS
EXCHANGE DEADLINE 7/7/2016
6 Peter Lambert 4.00 10.00
7 Lucas Herbert 4.00 10.00
19 Max Wotell 5.00 12.00

2014 Elite Extra Edition USA Baseball 18U Game Jerseys

RANDOM INSERTS IN PACKS
*PRIME/20-25: .5X TO 1.2X BASIC
1 L.T. Tolbert 2.00 5.00
2 Austin Smith 2.00 5.00
3 Blake Rutherford 4.00 10.00
4 Nick Madrigal 4.00 10.00
5 Xavier LeGrant 2.00 5.00
6 Peter Lambert 2.00 5.00
7 Lucas Herbert 2.00 5.00
8 Ke'Bryan Hayes 8.00 20.00
9 Mitchell Hansen 2.00 5.00
10 Gray Fenter 2.00 5.00
11 Joe DeMers 2.00 5.00
12 Trenton Clark 2.50 6.00
13 Daz Cameron 4.00 10.00
14 Kale Breaux 3.00 8.00
15 Austin Bergner 2.50 6.00
16 Luken Baker 3.00 8.00
17 Kolby Allard 4.00 10.00
18 Kyle Molnar 2.00 5.00
19 Max Wotell 2.50 6.00
20 Elih Marrero 2.00 5.00

2014 Elite Extra Edition USA Baseball 18U Signatures

RANDOM INSERTS IN PACKS
STATED PRINT RUN 199 SER.#'d SETS
EXCHANGE DEADLINE 7/7/2016
1 L.T. Tolbert 3.00 8.00
2 Austin Smith 3.00 8.00
3 Blake Rutherford 6.00 15.00
5 Xavier LeGrant 3.00 8.00
6 Peter Lambert 3.00 8.00
7 Lucas Herbert 3.00 8.00
8 Ke'Bryan Hayes 20.00 50.00
9 Mitchell Hansen 3.00 8.00
10 Gray Fenter 3.00 8.00
11 Joe DeMers 3.00 8.00
12 Trenton Clark 4.00 10.00
13 Daz Cameron 15.00 40.00
14 Kale Breaux 5.00 12.00
15 Austin Bergner 4.00 10.00
16 Luken Baker 5.00 12.00
17 Kolby Allard 6.00 15.00
18 Kyle Molnar 3.00 8.00
19 Max Wotell 4.00 10.00
20 Elih Marrero 3.00 8.00

2014 Elite Extra Edition Signature Status Dual

RANDOM INSERTS IN PACKS
PRINT RUNS B/WN 10-49 COPIES PER
NO PRICING ON QTY 15 OR LESS
EXCHANGE DEADLINE 7/7/2016
5 A.Reed/D.Fisher 20.00 50.00
7 G.Greiner/J.Montgomery 15.00 40.00
8 S.Travis/D.DeMuth 10.00 25.00

2015 Elite Extra Edition

COMPLETE SET (196) 60.00 150.00
1 Yoan Moncada 1.00 2.50
2 Dansby Swanson 1.25 3.00
3 Alex Bregman 1.00 2.50
4 Brendan Rodgers .75 2.00
5 Dillon Tate .25 .60
6 Kyle Tucker 1.50 4.00
7 Tyler Jay .20 .50
8 Andrew Benintendi 1.00 2.50
9 Carson Fulmer .20 .50
10 Ian Happ .75 2.00
11 Cornelius Randolph .20 .50
12 Tyler Stephenson .50 1.25
13 Josh Naylor .25 .60
14 Garrett Whitley .30 .75
15 Kolby Allard .20 .50
16 Trenton Clark .20 .50
17 James Kaprielian .20 .50
18 Yadier Alvarez .30 .75
19 Phil Bickford .20 .50
20 Kevin Newman .50 1.25
21 Richie Martin .20 .50
22 Ashe Russell .20 .50
23 Beau Burrows .20 .50
24 Nick Plummer .25 .60
25 Walker Buehler 1.25 3.00
26 DJ Stewart .25 .60
27 Taylor Ward .30 .75
28 Mike Nikorak .20 .50
29 Mike Soroka 1.25 3.00
30 Jon Harris .25 .60
31 Kyle Holder .25 .60
32 Chris Shaw .20 .50
33 Ke'Bryan Hayes 1.50 4.00
34 Nolan Watson .20 .50
35 Christin Stewart .25 .60
36 Lucius Fox .30 .75
37 Ryan Mountcastle 1.00 2.50
38 Daz Cameron .30 .75
39 Tyler Nevin .30 .75
40 Jake Woodford .20 .50
41 Nathan Kirby .25 .60
42 Austin Riley 2.50 6.00
43 Triston McKenzie .60 1.50
44 Alex Young .20 .50
45 Peter Lambert .20 .50
46 Eric Jenkins .20 .50
47 Thomas Eshelman .20 .50
48 Donnie Dewees .30 .75
49 Scott Kingery .30 .75
50 Antonio Santillan .25 .60
51 Brett Lilek .20 .50
52 Austin Smith .20 .50
53 Chris Betts .25 .60
54 Desmond Lindsay .30 .75
55 Lucas Herbert .20 .50
56 Cody Ponce .20 .50
57 Harrison Bader .30 .75
58 Jeff Degano .25 .60
59 Andrew Stevenson .20 .50
60 Juan Hillman .20 .50
61 Nick Neidert .20 .50
62 Andrew Suarez .25 .60
63 Kevin Kramer .20 .50
64 Mikey White .25 .60
65 Josh Staumont .20 .50
66 Tyler Alexander .20 .50
67 Bryce Denton .30 .75
68 Mitchell Hansen .20 .50
69 Wei-Chieh Huang .25 .60
70 Blake Perkins .20 .50
71 Jahmai Jones .25 .60
72 Brent Honeywell .30 .75
73 Austin Byler .20 .50
74 Mariano Rivera III .30 .75
75 Tyler White .25 .60
76 A.J. Minter .25 .60
77 Taylor Clarke .20 .50
78 Javier Medina .20 .50
79 Michael Matuella .25 .60
80 Riley Ferrell .20 .50
81 Travis Blankenhorn 1.00 2.50
82 Austin Rei .25 .60
83 Bryan Hudson .20 .50
84 Lucas Williams .20 .50
85 Blake Trahan .20 .50
86 Joe McCarthy .20 .50
87 Jacob Nix .20 .50
88 Brandon Lowe .30 .75
89 Max Wotell .20 .50
90 Yoan Lopez .20 .50
91 Skye Bolt .25 .60
92 Justin Maese .20 .50
93 Drew Finley .20 .50
94 Mark Mathias .25 .60
95 Braden Bishop .20 .50
96 Jalen Miller .20 .50
97 Casey Hughston .20 .50
98 Dakota Chalmers .20 .50
99 Anderson Miller .30 .75
100 Josh Hader .25 .60
101 Ketel Marte .40 1.00
102 Philip Pfeifer .20 .50
103 Garrett Cleavinger .25 .60
104 Rhett Wiseman .20 .50
105 Grayson Long .20 .50
106 Jordan Hicks .40 1.00
107 Breckin Williams .20 .50
108 Domingo Acevedo .30 .75
109 Jake Lemoine .20 .50
110 Anthony Hermelyn .20 .50
111 Trey Cabbage .20 .50
112 Tate Matheny .20 .50
113 Zack Erwin .20 .50
114 Max Schrock .20 .50
115 Kyle Martin .20 .50
116 Miles Gordon .25 .60
117 Cody Poteet .20 .50
118 Austin Allen .25 .60
119 Brandon Koch .20 .50
120 David Thompson .25 .60
121 Josh Graham .25 .60
122 Demi Orimoloye .25 .60
123 Carl Wise .25 .60
124 Jeff Hendrix .25 .60
125 Tyler Krieger .20 .50
126 Alex Robinson .20 .50
127 Thomas Szapucki .25 .60
128 Elias Diaz .20 .50
129 Ryan Ripken .25 .60
130 Jeison Guzman .25 .60
131 Raffy Ozuna .25 .60
132 Brian Gonzalez .20 .50
133 Max Povse .25 .60
134 Brent Jones .20 .50
135 Chad Sobotka .20 .50
136 Julio Urias .60 1.50
137 Domingo Leyba .20 .50
138 Jarlin Garcia .25 .60
139 Orlando Arcia .25 .60
140 Justin Garza .20 .50
141 Richard Urena .30 .75
142 Reydel Medina .20 .50
143 Aristides Aquino 10.00 25.00
144 Yairo Munoz .25 .60
145 Ozhaino Albies 2.00 5.00
146 Edmundo Sosa .25 .60
147 Daniel Carbonell .25 .60
148 Magneuris Sierra .30 .75
149 Julian Leon .20 .50
150 Jesus Lopez .20 .50
151 Manuel Margot .20 .50
152 Francisco Mejia .50 1.25
153 Jairo Labourt .20 .50
154 Marcos Molina .20 .50
155 Teoscar Hernandez .75 2.00
156 Reynaldo Lopez .25 .60
157 Austin Voth .20 .50
158 Correlle Prime .20 .50
159 Andrew Faulkner .20 .50
160 Brett Phillips .20 .50
161 John Curtiss .20 .50
162 Tanner Rainey .20 .50
163 Jorge Mateo .60 1.50
164 Omar Carrizales .25 .60
165 Jace Fry .20 .50
166 Javier Guerra .40 1.00
167 Mauricio Dubon .25 .60
168 Jhailyn Ortiz .40 1.00
169 Vladimir Guerrero Jr. 3.00 8.00
170 Jose Lopez .20 .50
171 Wander Javier .30 .75
172 Jharel Cotton .30 .75
173 Nash Walters .20 .50
174 Steven Brault .20 .50
175 Fernando Tatis Jr. 12.00 30.00
176 Preston Morrison .20 .50
177 Christian Pache .50 1.25
178 Drew Jackson .25 .60
179 Rookie Davis .20 .50
180 Gleyber Torres 3.00 8.00
181 Gregory Guerrero .30 .75
182 Leodys Taveras .75 2.00
183 Antenee Seymour .20 .50
184 Wilson Contreras 1.25 3.00
185 Micker Adolfo .25 .60
186 Cristian Olivo .30 .75
187 Derian Cruz .20 .50
188 Carlos Vargas .20 .50
189 Jonathan Arauz .25 .60
190 Antonio Senzatela .25 .60
191 Ryan Burr .20 .50
192 Victor Robles .75 2.00
193 Domingo German .30 .75
194 Rafael Devers 1.25 3.00
195 Franklin Reyes .20 .50
196 Franklin Barreto .25 .60

2015 Elite Extra Edition Aspirations Die Cut
*ASPIRATIONS: 1.2X TO 3X BASIC
RANDOM INSERTS IN PACKS
STATED PRINT RUN 200 SER.#'d SETS
75 Tyler White .75 2.00

2015 Elite Extra Edition Status Blue Die Cut
*STATUS BLUE: 2X TO 5X BASIC
RANDOM INSERTS IN PACKS
STATED PRINT RUN 100 SER.#'d SETS
75 Tyler White 1.25 3.00

2015 Elite Extra Edition Status Emerald Die Cut
*STATUS EMERALD: 3X TO 8X BASIC
RANDOM INSERTS IN PACKS
STATED PRINT RUN 25 SER.#'d SETS
75 Tyler White 2.00 5.00

2015 Elite Extra Edition Status Purple Die Cut
*STATUS PURPLE: 1.5X TO 4X BASIC
RANDOM INSERTS IN PACKS
STATED PRINT RUN 150 SER.#'d SETS
75 Tyler White 1.00 2.50

2015 Elite Extra Edition Back to the Future Signatures
RANDOM INSERTS IN PACKS
STATED ODDS B/WN 10-149 COPIES PER
NO PRICING ON QTY 15 OR LESS
1 Kyle Schwarber/25 75.00 200.00
2 Corey Seager/30 30.00 80.00
5 Robert Stephenson/49 4.00 10.00
7 Hunter Harvey/25 4.00 10.00
8 Justus Sheffield/49 8.00 20.00
9 Bobby Bradley/149 8.00 20.00
10 Trevor Story/49 15.00 40.00
11 Austin Cousino/99 4.00 10.00
12 Grant Holmes/49 5.00 12.00
14 Kyle Zimmer/25 4.00 10.00
15 Aaron Judge/25 60.00 150.00
16 Logan Moon/75 12.00 30.00
17 Casey Gillaspie/25 6.00 15.00
22 Jhoandro Alfaro/25 4.00 10.00
24 Jorge Alfaro/49 3.00 8.00
30 Nick Williams/25 12.00 30.00

2015 Elite Extra Edition Collegiate Legacy
RANDOM INSERTS IN PACKS
1 Dansby Swanson 1.50 4.00
2 Alex Bregman 1.25 3.00
3 Tyler Jay .25 .60
4 Andrew Benintendi 1.25 3.00
5 Carson Fulmer .25 .60
6 Ian Happ 1.00 2.50
7 James Kaprielian .25 .60
8 Kevin Newman .60 1.50
9 Richie Martin .25 .60
10 Walker Buehler 1.50 4.00
11 Taylor Ward .40 1.00
12 Aaron Nola .40 1.00
13 Tyler Naquin .40 1.00
14 Kyle Schwarber 1.00 2.50
15 Jeff Degano .30 .75
16 Robert Refsnyder .30 .75
17 Hunter Renfroe .40 1.00
18 DJ Stewart .30 .75
19 Christin Stewart .30 .75
20 A.J. Reed .30 .75

2015 Elite Extra Edition Collegiate Legacy Signatures
RANDOM INSERTS IN PACKS
PRINT RUNS BW/N 10-99 COPIES PER
NO PRICING ON QTY 15 OR LESS
10 Walker Buehler/49 12.00 30.00
17 Hunter Renfroe/25 6.00 15.00

2015 Elite Extra Edition Elite Status Dual Signatures
RANDOM INSERTS IN PACKS
PRINT RUNS BW/N 10-25 COPIES PER
NO PRICING ON QTY 10
11 Woodford/Plummer/25 10.00 25.00
12 Alvarez/Lopez/25 12.00 30.00
17 Bradley/Zimmer/25 12.00 30.00

2015 Elite Extra Edition Future Threads Silhoutte Signatures
RANDOM INSERTS IN PACKS
PRINT RUNS BW/N 21-149 COPIES PER
*PRIME: X TO X BASIC
1 Yoan Moncada/25 60.00 150.00
2 Kyle Schwarber/49 60.00 150.00
3 Manuel Margot/49 4.00 10.00
5 Aaron Judge/49 75.00 200.00
8 Luis Encarnacion/149 10.00 25.00
9 Jorge Alfaro/49 8.00 20.00
10 Michael Conforto/25 30.00 80.00
11 Lucas Giolito/49 10.00 25.00
12 Tyler Beede/49 15.00 40.00
13 Trea Turner/25 15.00 40.00
14 Richard Urena/99 8.00 20.00
15 Jairo Labourt/149 4.00 10.00
17 Teoscar Hernandez/99 15.00 40.00
18 Reynaldo Lopez/49 5.00 12.00
19 Lucas Sims/49 4.00 10.00
22 Tyler Glasnow/25 20.00 50.00
23 Edmundo Sosa/149 5.00 12.00
25 Raul Mondesi/49 6.00 15.00
29 Rafael Devers/125 25.00 60.00
30 Matt Olson/49 12.00 30.00
31 Nomar Mazara/49 12.00 30.00
35 Aaron Nola/49 6.00 15.00
36 Corey Seager/75 15.00 40.00
37 Miguel Sano/49 5.00 12.00
38 Robert Refsnyder/49 8.00 20.00
39 Blake Snell/49 8.00 20.00

2015 Elite Extra Edition Future Threads Silhoutte Signatures Prime
*PRIME: X TO X BASIC
RANDOM INSERTS IN PACKS
PRINT RUNS B/WN 6-25 COPIES PER
NO PRICING ON QTY 10 OR LESS

2015 Elite Extra Edition Hype
RANDOM INSERTS IN PACKS
1 Vladimir Guerrero Jr. 4.00 10.00
2 Corey Seager 1.25 3.00
3 Orlando Arcia .30 .75
4 Kyle Schwarber 1.00 2.50
5 Yadier Alvarez .40 1.00
6 Lucius Fox .40 1.00
7 Jhailyn Ortiz .50 1.25
8 Lucas Giolito .50 1.25
9 Nomar Mazara .40 1.00
10 Rafael Devers 1.50 4.00
11 Ozhaino Albies 2.50 6.00
12 Cornelius Randolph .25 .60
13 Manuel Margot .25 .60
14 Julio Urias .75 2.00
15 Luis Severino .30 .75
16 Yoan Lopez .25 .60
17 Daz Cameron .40 1.00
18 Gilbert Lara .30 .75
19 Wander Javier .40 1.00
20 Franklin Barreto .30 .75

2015 Elite Extra Edition Hype Signatures
RANDOM INSERTS IN PACKS
PRINT RUNS BW/N 10-149 COPIES PER
NO PRICING ON QTY 10 OR LESS
1 Vladimir Guerrero Jr./25 200.00 500.00
2 Corey Seager/30 25.00 60.00
5 Yadier Alvarez/49 20.00 50.00
6 Lucius Fox/25 40.00 100.00
9 Nomar Mazara/25 20.00 50.00
16 Yoan Lopez/149 4.00 10.00
17 Daz Cameron/40 10.00 25.00
19 Wander Javier/49 8.00 20.00

2015 Elite Extra Edition International Pride
RANDOM INSERTS IN PACKS
1 Yoan Moncada 1.25 3.00
2 Yoan Lopez .25 .60
3 Julio Urias .75 2.00
4 Domingo Leyba .25 .60
5 Jarlin Garcia .30 .75
6 Richard Urena .40 1.00
7 Mike Soroka 1.50 4.00
8 Yairo Munoz .30 .75
9 Yadier Alvarez .40 1.00
10 Edmundo Sosa .30 .75
11 Orlando Arcia .30 .75
12 Manuel Margot .25 .60
13 Teoscar Hernandez 1.00 2.50
14 Reynaldo Lopez .30 .75
15 Marcos Molina .25 .60
16 Ketel Marte .50 1.25
17 Magneuris Sierra .40 1.00
18 Daniel Carbonell .30 .75
19 Ozhaino Albies 2.50 6.00
20 Vladimir Guerrero Jr. 4.00 10.00
21 Jhailyn Ortiz .50 1.25
22 Lucius Fox .40 1.00
23 Jorge Alfaro .40 1.00
24 Wei-Chieh Huang .30 .75
25 Gilbert Lara .30 .75
26 Dariel Alvarez .25 .60
27 Franklin Barreto .30 .75
28 Carlos Vargas .25 .60
29 Gleyber Torres 4.00 10.00
30 Julian Leon .25 .60

2015 Elite Extra Edition International Pride Signatures
RANDOM INSERTS IN PACKS
STATED ODDS B/WN 10-149 COPIES PER
NO PRICING ON QTY 10
2 Yoan Lopez/99 4.00 10.00
4 Domingo Leyba/99 4.00 10.00
5 Jarlin Garcia/75 5.00 12.00
7 Mike Soroka/37 12.00 30.00
10 Edmundo Sosa/99 5.00 12.00
11 Orlando Arcia/49 5.00 12.00
13 Teoscar Hernandez/99 15.00 40.00
14 Reynaldo Lopez/25 5.00 12.00
16 Ketel Marte/149 8.00 20.00
17 Magneuris Sierra/149 6.00 15.00
18 Daniel Carbonell/99 5.00 12.00
19 Ozhaino Albies/99 40.00 100.00
22 Lucius Fox/49 6.00 15.00
23 Jorge Alfaro/99 6.00 15.00
24 Wei-Chieh Huang/99 8.00 20.00
25 Gilbert Lara/99 5.00 12.00
28 Carlos Vargas/49 4.00 10.00
29 Gleyber Torres/149 40.00 100.00
30 Julian Leon/25 4.00 10.00

2015 Elite Extra Edition Passing the Torch Signatures
RANDOM INSERTS IN PACKS
PRINT RUNS B/WN 10-20 COPIES PER
NO PRICING ON QTY 10

2015 Elite Extra Edition Prospect Autographs
RANDOM INSERTS IN PACKS
1 Yoan Moncada 20.00 60.00
2 Dansby Swanson 10.00 25.00
3 Alex Bregman 10.00 25.00
4 Brendan Rodgers 6.00 15.00
5 Dillon Tate 5.00 12.00
6 Kyle Tucker 10.00 25.00
7 Tyler Jay 8.00 20.00
8 Andrew Benintendi 20.00 50.00
9 Carson Fulmer 2.50 6.00
10 Ian Happ 12.00 30.00
11 Cornelius Randolph 12.00 30.00
12 Tyler Stephenson 6.00 15.00
14 Garrett Whitley 8.00 20.00
15 Kolby Allard 2.50 6.00
16 Trenton Clark 2.50 6.00
17 James Kaprielian 2.50 6.00
18 Yadier Alvarez 6.00 15.00
20 Kevin Newman 10.00 25.00
21 Richie Martin 2.50 6.00
23 Beau Burrows 2.50 6.00
24 Nick Plummer 3.00 8.00
25 Walker Buehler 20.00 50.00
26 DJ Stewart 3.00 8.00
27 Taylor Ward 4.00 10.00
28 Mike Nikorak 2.50 6.00
29 Mike Soroka 12.00 30.00
30 Jon Harris 3.00 8.00
31 Kyle Holder 3.00 8.00
33 Ke'Bryan Hayes 10.00 25.00
34 Nolan Watson 2.50 6.00
35 Christin Stewart 3.00 8.00
36 Lucius Fox 4.00 10.00
37 Ryan Mountcastle 10.00 25.00
38 Daz Cameron 12.00 30.00
39 Tyler Nevin 4.00 10.00
40 Jake Woodford 2.50 6.00
41 Nathan Kirby 3.00 8.00
42 Austin Riley 30.00 80.00
43 Triston McKenzie 10.00 25.00
44 Alex Young 2.50 6.00
45 Peter Lambert 2.50 6.00
46 Eric Jenkins 2.50 6.00
47 Thomas Eshelman 2.50 6.00
48 Donnie Dewees 4.00 10.00
49 Scott Kingery 4.00 10.00
51 Brett Lilek 2.50 6.00
52 Austin Smith 2.50 6.00
53 Chris Betts 3.00 8.00
54 Desmond Lindsay 4.00 10.00
55 Lucas Herbert 4.00 10.00
56 Cody Ponce 2.50 6.00
57 Harrison Bader 8.00 20.00
58 Jeff Degano 3.00 8.00
59 Andrew Stevenson 2.50 6.00
60 Juan Hillman 2.50 6.00
61 Nick Neidert 2.50 6.00
62 Andrew Suarez 3.00 8.00
63 Kevin Kramer 3.00 8.00
64 Mikey White 3.00 8.00
65 Josh Staumont 3.00 8.00
66 Tyler Alexander 2.50 6.00
67 Bryce Denton 4.00 10.00
68 Mitchell Hansen 2.50 6.00
69 Wei-Chieh Huang 3.00 8.00
70 Blake Perkins 2.50 6.00
71 Jahmai Jones 3.00 8.00
72 Brent Honeywell 4.00 10.00
73 Austin Byler 2.50 6.00
74 Mariano Rivera III 4.00 10.00
75 Tyler White 3.00 8.00
76 A.J. Minter 3.00 8.00
77 Taylor Clarke 2.50 6.00
78 Javier Medina 2.50 6.00
79 Michael Matuella 3.00 8.00
80 Riley Ferrell 2.50 6.00
81 Travis Blankenhorn 6.00 15.00
82 Austin Rei 3.00 8.00
83 Bryan Hudson 2.50 6.00
84 Lucas Williams 2.50 6.00
85 Blake Trahan 2.50 6.00
86 Joe McCarthy 2.50 6.00
87 Jacob Nix 2.50 6.00
88 Brandon Lowe 6.00 15.00
89 Max Wotell 2.50 6.00
90 Yoan Lopez 2.50 6.00
91 Skye Bolt 3.00 8.00
92 Justin Maese 2.50 6.00
93 Drew Finley 2.50 6.00
95 Braden Bishop 2.50 6.00
96 Jalen Miller 2.50 6.00
97 Casey Hughston 2.50 6.00
98 Dakota Chalmers 2.50 6.00
99 Anderson Miller 4.00 10.00
100 Josh Hader 3.00 8.00
101 Ketel Marte 5.00 12.00
102 Philip Pfeifer 2.50 6.00
103 Garrett Cleavinger 3.00 8.00
104 Rhett Wiseman 2.50 6.00
105 Grayson Long 2.50 6.00
106 Jordan Hicks 5.00 12.00
107 Breckin Williams 2.50 6.00
108 Domingo Acevedo 4.00 10.00
109 Jake Lemoine 2.50 6.00
110 Anthony Hermelyn 2.50 6.00
111 Trey Cabbage 2.50 6.00
112 Tate Matheny 2.50 6.00
113 Zack Erwin 2.50 6.00
114 Max Schrock 2.50 6.00
115 Kyle Martin 2.50 6.00
116 Miles Gordon 3.00 8.00
117 Cody Poteet 2.50 6.00
118 Austin Allen 3.00 8.00
119 Brandon Koch 2.50 6.00
120 David Thompson 3.00 8.00
121 Josh Graham 3.00 8.00
122 Demi Orimoloye 3.00 8.00
123 Carl Wise 3.00 8.00
124 Jeff Hendrix 3.00 8.00
125 Tyler Krieger 2.50 6.00
126 Alex Robinson 2.50 6.00
127 Thomas Szapucki 2.50 6.00
128 Elias Diaz 2.50 6.00
129 Ryan Ripken 3.00 8.00
130 Jeison Guzman 3.00 8.00
131 Raffy Ozuna 3.00 8.00
132 Brian Gonzalez 2.50 6.00
133 Max Povse 3.00 8.00
134 Brent Jones 2.50 6.00
135 Chad Sobotka 2.50 6.00
136 Julio Urias UER 8.00 20.00
137 Domingo Leyba 2.50 6.00
138 Jarlin Garcia 3.00 8.00
140 Justin Garza 2.50 6.00
142 Reydel Medina 2.50 6.00
143 Aristides Aquino 40.00 100.00
144 Yairo Munoz 3.00 8.00
145 Ozhaino Albies 25.00 60.00
146 Edmundo Sosa 3.00 8.00
147 Daniel Carbonell 3.00 8.00
148 Magneuris Sierra 3.00 8.00
149 Julian Leon 2.50 6.00
150 Jesus Lopez 2.50 6.00
151 Manuel Margot 2.50 6.00
152 Francisco Mejia 8.00 20.00
153 Jairo Labourt 2.50 6.00
154 Marcos Molina 2.50 6.00
155 Teoscar Hernandez 10.00 25.00
157 Austin Voth 2.50 6.00
158 Correlle Prime 2.50 6.00
159 Andrew Faulkner 2.50 6.00
160 Brett Phillips 2.50 6.00
161 John Curtiss 2.50 6.00
162 Tanner Rainey 2.50 6.00
163 Jorge Mateo 6.00 15.00
164 Omar Carrizales 3.00 8.00
165 Jace Fry 2.50 6.00
166 Javier Guerra 2.50 6.00
167 Mauricio Dubon 3.00 8.00
169 Vladimir Guerrero Jr. 75.00 200.00
170 Jose Lopez 2.50 6.00
171 Wander Javier 4.00 10.00
172 Jharel Cotton 4.00 10.00
174 Steven Brault 2.50 6.00
175 Tatis Jr. Sgnd in red 125.00 300.00
176 Preston Morrison 2.50 6.00
177 Christian Pache 8.00 20.00
178 Drew Jackson 3.00 8.00
179 Rookie Davis 2.50 6.00
180 Gleyber Torres 50.00 120.00
181 Gregory Guerrero 4.00 10.00
183 Anfernee Seymour 2.50 6.00
184 Willson Contreras 8.00 20.00
185 Micker Adolfo 3.00 8.00
187 Derian Cruz 6.00 15.00
188 Carlos Vargas 2.50 6.00
189 Jonathan Arauz 3.00 8.00
190 Antonio Senzatela 3.00 8.00
191 Ryan Burr 2.50 6.00
192 Victor Robles 8.00 20.00
193 Domingo German 12.00 30.00
194 Rafael Devers 15.00 40.00
195 Franklin Reyes 2.50 6.00
196 Franklin Barreto 3.00 8.00

2015 Elite Extra Edition Prospect Autographs Aspirations Die Cut
*ASPRTNS DC: .5X TO 1.2X BASIC
RANDOM INSERTS IN PACKS
PRINT RUNS B/WN 26-100 COPIES PER
1 Yoan Moncada/100 30.00 80.00
2 Dansby Swanson/100 12.00 30.00
3 Alex Bregman/100 12.00 30.00
4 Brendan Rodgers/100 8.00 20.00
5 Dillon Tate/100 6.00 15.00
6 Kyle Tucker/100 12.00 30.00
7 Tyler Jay/100 10.00 25.00
9 Carson Fulmer/100 3.00 8.00
10 Ian Happ/100 15.00 40.00
11 Cornelius Randolph/100 15.00 40.00
12 Tyler Stephenson/100 8.00 20.00
14 Garrett Whitley/100 10.00 25.00
15 Kolby Allard/100 3.00 8.00
16 Trenton Clark/100 3.00 8.00
17 James Kaprielian/100 3.00 8.00
18 Yadier Alvarez/100 8.00 20.00
20 Kevin Newman/100 12.00 30.00
21 Richie Martin/100 3.00 8.00
23 Beau Burrows/100 3.00 8.00
24 Nick Plummer/100 4.00 10.00
25 Walker Buehler/100 25.00 60.00
26 DJ Stewart/100 4.00 10.00
27 Taylor Ward/100 5.00 12.00
28 Mike Nikorak/100 3.00 8.00
29 Mike Soroka/100 15.00 40.00
30 Jon Harris/100 4.00 10.00
31 Kyle Holder/100 4.00 10.00
33 Ke'Bryan Hayes/98 12.00 30.00
34 Nolan Watson/100 3.00 8.00
35 Christin Stewart/100 4.00 10.00
36 Lucius Fox/100 5.00 12.00
37 Ryan Mountcastle/100 12.00 30.00
38 Daz Cameron/100 15.00 40.00
39 Tyler Nevin/100 5.00 12.00
40 Jake Woodford/100 3.00 8.00
41 Nathan Kirby/100 4.00 10.00
42 Austin Riley/100 40.00 100.00
44 Alex Young/100 3.00 8.00
45 Peter Lambert/100 3.00 8.00
46 Eric Jenkins/100 3.00 8.00
47 Thomas Eshelman/100 3.00 8.00
48 Donnie Dewees/100 5.00 12.00
49 Scott Kingery/100 5.00 12.00
51 Brett Lilek/100 3.00 8.00
52 Austin Smith/100 3.00 8.00
53 Chris Betts/100 4.00 10.00
54 Desmond Lindsay/100 5.00 12.00
55 Lucas Herbert/100 5.00 12.00
56 Cody Ponce/100 3.00 8.00
57 Harrison Bader/100 10.00 25.00
58 Jeff Degano/100 4.00 10.00
59 Andrew Stevenson/100 3.00 8.00
60 Juan Hillman/100 3.00 8.00
61 Nick Neidert/100 3.00 8.00
62 Andrew Suarez/100 4.00 10.00
63 Kevin Kramer/100 4.00 10.00
64 Mikey White/100 4.00 10.00
65 Josh Staumont/100 4.00 10.00
66 Tyler Alexander/100 3.00 8.00
67 Bryce Denton/26 5.00 12.00
68 Mitchell Hansen/100 3.00 8.00
69 Wei-Chieh Huang/100 4.00 10.00
70 Blake Perkins/100 3.00 8.00
71 Jahmai Jones/100 4.00 10.00
72 Brent Honeywell/100 5.00 12.00
73 Austin Byler/100 3.00 8.00
74 Mariano Rivera III/100 5.00 12.00
75 Tyler White/100 4.00 10.00
76 A.J. Minter/100 4.00 10.00
77 Taylor Clarke/100 3.00 8.00
78 Javier Medina/96 3.00 8.00
79 Michael Matuella/100 4.00 10.00
80 Riley Ferrell/100 3.00 8.00
81 Travis Blankenhorn/100 8.00 20.00
82 Austin Rei/100 4.00 10.00
83 Bryan Hudson/100 3.00 8.00
84 Lucas Williams/100 3.00 8.00
85 Blake Trahan/100 3.00 8.00
86 Joe McCarthy/100 3.00 8.00
87 Jacob Nix/100 3.00 8.00
88 Brandon Lowe/100 8.00 20.00
89 Max Wotell/100 3.00 8.00
90 Yoan Lopez/100 3.00 8.00
91 Skye Bolt/100 4.00 10.00
92 Justin Maese/100 3.00 8.00
93 Drew Finley/100 3.00 8.00
95 Braden Bishop/100 3.00 8.00
96 Jalen Miller/100 3.00 8.00
97 Casey Hughston/100 3.00 8.00
98 Dakota Chalmers/100 3.00 8.00
99 Anderson Miller/100 5.00 12.00
100 Josh Hader/100 4.00 10.00
101 Ketel Marte/100 6.00 15.00
102 Philip Pfeifer/100 3.00 8.00
103 Garrett Cleavinger/100 4.00 10.00
104 Rhett Wiseman/100 3.00 8.00
105 Grayson Long/100 3.00 8.00
107 Breckin Williams/100 3.00 8.00
108 Domingo Acevedo/100 5.00 12.00
109 Jake Lemoine/100 3.00 8.00
110 Anthony Hermelyn/100 3.00 8.00
111 Trey Cabbage/100 3.00 8.00
112 Tate Matheny/100 3.00 8.00
113 Zack Erwin/100 3.00 8.00
114 Max Schrock/100 3.00 8.00
115 Kyle Martin/100 3.00 8.00
116 Miles Gordon/100 4.00 10.00
117 Cody Poteet/100 3.00 8.00
118 Austin Allen/100 4.00 10.00
119 Brandon Koch/100 3.00 8.00
120 David Thompson/100 4.00 10.00
121 Josh Graham/100 4.00 10.00
122 Demi Orimoloye/100 4.00 10.00
123 Carl Wise/100 4.00 10.00
124 Jeff Hendrix/100 4.00 10.00
125 Tyler Krieger/100 3.00 8.00
126 Alex Robinson/100 3.00 8.00
127 Thomas Szapucki/100 3.00 8.00
128 Elias Diaz/100 3.00 8.00
129 Ryan Ripken/100 4.00 10.00
130 Jeison Guzman/100 4.00 10.00
131 Raffy Ozuna/100 4.00 10.00
132 Brian Gonzalez/100 3.00 8.00
133 Max Povse/100 4.00 10.00
134 Brent Jones/100 3.00 8.00
135 Chad Sobotka/100 3.00 8.00
136 Julio Urias/100 10.00 25.00
UER Wrong position
137 Domingo Leyba/100 3.00 8.00
138 Jarlin Garcia/100 4.00 10.00
140 Justin Garza/100 3.00 8.00
141 Richard Urena/34 5.00 12.00
142 Reydel Medina/100 3.00 8.00
143 Aristides Aquino/100 50.00 120.00
144 Yairo Munoz/100 4.00 10.00
145 Ozhaino Albies/100 30.00 80.00
146 Edmundo Sosa/100 4.00 10.00
147 Daniel Carbonell/100 4.00 10.00
148 Magneuris Sierra/100 4.00 10.00
149 Julian Leon/100 3.00 8.00
150 Jesus Lopez/100 3.00 8.00
151 Manuel Margot/100 3.00 8.00
152 Francisco Mejia/100 10.00 25.00
153 Jairo Labourt/100 3.00 8.00
154 Marcos Molina/100 3.00 8.00
155 Teoscar Hernandez/100 12.00 30.00
157 Austin Voth/100 3.00 8.00
158 Correlle Prime/100 3.00 8.00
159 Andrew Faulkner/100 3.00 8.00
160 Brett Phillips/100 3.00 8.00
161 John Curtiss/100 3.00 8.00
162 Tanner Rainey/100 3.00 8.00
163 Jorge Mateo/100 8.00 20.00
164 Omar Carrizales/100 4.00 10.00
165 Jace Fry/100 3.00 8.00
166 Javier Guerra/100 3.00 8.00
167 Mauricio Dubon/100 4.00 10.00
169 Vladimir Guerrero Jr./100 100.00 250.00
170 Jose Lopez/100 3.00 8.00
171 Wander Javier/100 5.00 12.00
172 Jharel Cotton/100 5.00 12.00
174 Steven Brault/100 3.00 8.00
175 Fernando Tatis Jr./100 150.00 400.00
176 Preston Morrison/100 3.00 8.00
177 Christian Pache/100 10.00 25.00
178 Drew Jackson/100 4.00 10.00
179 Rookie Davis/100 3.00 8.00
180 Gleyber Torres/100 60.00 150.00
181 Gregory Guerrero/100 5.00 12.00
183 Anfernee Seymour/100 3.00 8.00
184 Willson Contreras/100 10.00 25.00
185 Micker Adolfo/100 4.00 10.00
187 Derian Cruz/100 8.00 20.00
188 Carlos Vargas/100 3.00 8.00
189 Jonathan Arauz/100 4.00 10.00
190 Antonio Senzatela/100 4.00 10.00
191 Ryan Burr/100 3.00 8.00
192 Victor Robles/100 10.00 25.00
193 Domingo German/100 15.00 40.00
194 Rafael Devers/100 20.00 50.00
195 Franklin Reyes/100 3.00 8.00
196 Franklin Barreto/100 4.00 10.00

2015 Elite Extra Edition Prospect Autographs Red Ink
*RED INK: .75X TO 2X BASIC
RANDOM INSERTS IN PACKS
STATED PRINT RUN 25 SER.#'d SETS
141 Richard Urena/25 8.00 20.00

2015 Elite Extra Edition Prospect Autographs Status Blue Die Cut
*STAT BLUE DC: .6X TO 1.5X BASIC
RANDOM INSERTS IN PACKS
STATED PRINT RUN 50 SER.#'d SETS
141 Richard Urena/50 6.00 15.00

2015 Elite Extra Edition Prospect Autographs Status Emerald Die Cut
*STAT.EMRLD DC: .75X TO 2X BASIC
RANDOM INSERTS IN PACKS
PRINT RUNS B/WN 22-25 COPIES PER
141 Richard Urena/25 8.00 20.00

2015 Elite Extra Edition Prospect Autographs Status Purple Die Cut
*STAT PRPL DC: .5X TO 1.2X BASIC
RANDOM INSERTS IN PACKS
STATED PRINT RUN 75 SER.#'d SETS
141 Richard Urena 5.00 12.00

2015 Elite Extra Edition Prospect Status
RANDOM INSERTS IN PACKS
1 Aaron Judge 4.00 10.00
2 Corey Seager 1.25 3.00
3 Luis Severino .30 .75
4 Luke Weaver .40 1.00
5 Michael Kopech .75 2.00
6 Bobby Bradley .30 .75
7 Luis Ortiz .25 .60
8 Sean Reid-Foley .30 .75
9 Dillon Tate .30 .75
10 Willy Adames .40 1.00
11 Sean Newcomb .30 .75
12 Tyler Naquin .40 1.00
13 Kyle Schwarber 1.00 2.50
14 Lucas Giolito .50 1.25
15 Eudor Garcia .25 .60
16 Dariel Alvarez .25 .60
17 Yoan Moncada 1.25 3.00
18 Tyler Glasnow 1.00 2.50
19 Trea Turner .75 2.00
20 Orlando Arcia .30 .75
21 Nomar Mazara .40 1.00
22 Franklin Barreto .30 .75
23 Austin Meadows .60 1.50
24 Bradley Zimmer .40 1.00
25 Brett Phillips .25 .60
26 Raul Mondesi .40 1.00
27 Robert Stephenson .25 .60
28 Brent Honeywell .40 1.00
29 Julio Urias .75 2.00
30 Jorge Mateo .75 2.00

2015 Elite Extra Edition Prospect Status Signatures
RANDOM INSERTS IN PACKS
PRINT RUNS BW/N 10-149 COPIES PER
NO PRICING ON QTY 10
1 Aaron Judge/25 60.00 150.00
2 Corey Seager/30 25.00 60.00
4 Luke Weaver/25 6.00 15.00
6 Bobby Bradley/149 8.00 20.00
7 Luis Ortiz/25 4.00 10.00
8 Sean Reid-Foley/49 5.00 12.00
12 Tyler Naquin/49 6.00 15.00
13 Kyle Schwarber/25 30.00 80.00
16 Dariel Alvarez/49 4.00 10.00
18 Tyler Glasnow/25 25.00 60.00
19 Trea Turner/49 12.00 30.00
21 Nomar Mazara/49 15.00 40.00
26 Raul Mondesi/49 6.00 15.00
27 Robert Stephenson/49 4.00 10.00
28 Brent Honeywell/25 6.00 15.00
30 Jorge Mateo/49 8.00 20.00

2015 Elite Extra Edition USA Baseball 15U Jerseys
RANDOM INSERTS IN PACKS
*PRIME/25-49: .6X TO 1.5X BASIC
1 Brandon Walker 2.50 6.00
2 Luis Tuero 2.50 6.00
3 Lyon Richardson 4.00 10.00
4 Connor Ollio 2.50 6.00
5 Zachary Morgan 2.50 6.00
6 Chris McElvain 2.50 6.00
7 Justyn-Henry Malloy 2.50 6.00
8 Jeremiah Jackson 6.00 15.00
9 Jared Hart 2.50 6.00
10 Rohan Handa 2.50 6.00
11 Ryder Green 4.00 10.00
12 Jaden Fein 3.00 8.00
13 Jonathan Childress 2.50 6.00
14 Joseph Charles 2.50 6.00
15 Triston Casas 4.00 10.00
17 C.J. Brown 2.50 6.00
18 Gabe Briones 2.50 6.00
19 Colton Bowman 2.50 6.00
20 Branden Boissiere 2.50 6.00

2015 Elite Extra Edition USA Baseball 15U Signatures
RANDOM INSERTS IN PACKS
1 Brandon Walker 3.00 8.00
2 Luis Tuero 3.00 8.00
3 Lyon Richardson 5.00 12.00
4 Connor Ollio 3.00 8.00
5 Zachary Morgan 8.00 20.00
6 Chris McElvain 3.00 8.00
7 Justyn-Henry Malloy 6.00 15.00
8 Jeremiah Jackson 8.00 20.00
9 Jared Hart 3.00 8.00
10 Rohan Handa 3.00 8.00
11 Ryder Green 8.00 20.00
12 Jaden Fein 4.00 10.00
13 Jonathan Childress 3.00 8.00
14 Joseph Charles 3.00 8.00
15 Triston Casas 12.00 30.00
16 Kendrick Calilao 4.00 10.00
17 C.J. Brown 10.00 25.00
18 Gabe Briones 8.00 20.00
19 Colton Bowman 5.00 12.00
20 Branden Boissiere 3.00 8.00

2015 Elite Extra Edition USA Baseball 18U Dual Jerseys Signatures
RANDOM INSERTS IN PACKS
STATED PRINT RUN 50 SER.#'d SETS
1 Forrest Whitley 15.00 40.00
2 Cole Stobbe 5.00 12.00
3 Blake Rutherford 10.00 25.00
4 Ryan Rolison 10.00 25.00
5 Nicholas Quintana 10.00 25.00
6 Nicholas Pratto 5.00 12.00
7 Mickey Moniak 20.00 50.00
8 Morgan McCullough 5.00 12.00
9 Reggie Lawson 5.00 12.00
10 Cooper Johnson 5.00 12.00
11 Hunter Greene 15.00 40.00
12 Kevin Gowdy 8.00 20.00
13 Braxton Garrett 8.00 20.00
14 Hagen Danner 15.00 40.00
15 Jordan Butler 5.00 12.00
16 Austin Bergner 5.00 12.00
17 William Benson 10.00 25.00
19 Ian Anderson 6.00 15.00
20 Michael Amditis 5.00 12.00

2015 Elite Extra Edition USA Baseball 18U Jerseys
RANDOM INSERTS IN PACKS
*PRIME/25-49: .6X TO 1.5X BASIC
1 Forrest Whitley 5.00 12.00
2 Cole Stobbe 2.50 6.00
3 Blake Rutherford 5.00 12.00
4 Ryan Rolison 5.00 12.00
5 Nicholas Quintana 5.00 12.00
6 Nicholas Pratto 2.50 6.00
7 Mickey Moniak 6.00 15.00
8 Morgan McCullough 2.50 6.00
9 Reggie Lawson 2.50 6.00
10 Cooper Johnson 2.50 6.00
11 Hunter Greene 6.00 15.00
12 Kevin Gowdy 4.00 10.00
13 Braxton Garrett 4.00 10.00
14 Hagen Danner 5.00 12.00
15 Jordan Butler 2.50 6.00
16 Austin Bergner 2.50 6.00
17 William Benson 3.00 8.00
18 Daniel Bakst 2.50 6.00
19 Ian Anderson 8.00 20.00
20 Michael Amditis 2.50 6.00

2015 Elite Extra Edition USA Baseball 18U Signatures
RANDOM INSERTS IN PACKS
1 Forrest Whitley 15.00 40.00
2 Cole Stobbe 3.00 8.00
3 Blake Rutherford 10.00 25.00
4 Ryan Rolison 5.00 12.00
5 Nicholas Quintana 6.00 15.00
6 Nicholas Pratto 3.00 8.00
7 Mickey Moniak 20.00 50.00
8 Morgan McCullough 3.00 8.00
9 Reggie Lawson 3.00 8.00
10 Cooper Johnson 3.00 8.00
11 Hunter Greene 10.00 25.00
12 Kevin Gowdy 6.00 15.00
13 Braxton Garrett 5.00 12.00
14 Hagen Danner 15.00 40.00
15 Jordan Butler 3.00 8.00
16 Austin Bergner 3.00 8.00
17 William Benson 15.00 40.00
18 Daniel Bakst 6.00 15.00
19 Ian Anderson 6.00 15.00
20 Michael Amditis 3.00 8.00

2016 Elite Extra Edition
STATED PRINT RUN 999 SER.#'d SETS
1 Tyler O'Neill .50 1.25
2 Nick Senzel 5.00 12.00
3 Ian Anderson 2.00 5.00
4 Riley Pint .40 1.00
5 Corey Ray .50 1.25
6 A.J. Puk .60 1.50
7 Braxton Garrett .50 1.25
8 Cal Quantrill .40 1.00
9 Matt Manning .60 1.50
10 Nash Walters .40 1.00
11 Kyle Lewis 8.00 20.00
12 Jason Groome .75 2.00
13 Joshua Lowe .40 1.00
14 Will Benson .60 1.50
15 Alex Kirilloff 4.00 10.00
16 Matt Thaiss .40 1.00
17 Brandon Waddell .40 1.00
18 Bryson Brigman .40 1.00
19 Justin Dunn .40 1.00
20 Gavin Lux 2.50 6.00
21 T.J. Zeuch .50 1.25
22 Will Craig .40 1.00
23 Delvin Perez 1.25 3.00
24 Matt Strahm .60 1.50
25 Eric Lauer .50 1.25
26 Zack Burdi .50 1.25
27 Cody Sedlock .40 1.00
28 Carter Kieboom 2.50 6.00
29 Dane Dunning 1.25 3.00
30 Cole Ragans .50 1.25
31 Anthony Kay .40 1.00
32 Will Smith 1.00 2.50
33 Dylan Carlson 6.00 15.00
34 Dakota Hudson .60 1.50
35 Taylor Trammell 2.50 6.00
36 Jordan Sheffield .40 1.00
37 Daulton Jefferies .50 1.25
38 Robert Tyler .40 1.00
39 Anfernee Grier .50 1.25
40 Joey Wentz .60 1.50
41 Skylar Szynski .40 1.00
42 German Marquez .60 1.50
43 Chris Okey .40 1.00
44 Anderson Espinoza .50 1.25
45 Alex Reyes .50 1.25
46 Drew Harrington .40 1.00
48 Buddy Reed .50 1.25
49 Alec Hansen .50 1.25
50 Joe Rizzo .40 1.00
51 C.J. Chatham .50 1.25
52 Andrew Yerzy .40 1.00
53 Ryan Boldt .50 1.25
54 Andrew Yerzy .40 1.00
55 Nolan Jones .60 1.50
56 Ben Rortvedt .50 1.25
57 J.B. Woodman .60 1.50
58 Sheldon Neuse .50 1.25
59 Bryan Reynolds 1.25 3.00
60 Matt Thaiss .40 1.00
61 Ronnie Dawson .40 1.00
62 Nick Solak 1.50 4.00
63 Shawn Morimando
64 Peter Alonso 8.00 20.00
65 T.J. Zeuch .50 1.25
66 Bobby Dalbec 4.00 10.00
67 A.J. Puckett .50 1.25
68 Travis MacGregor .50 1.25
69 Cody Sedlock .40 1.00
70 Connor Jones .50 1.25
71 Willie Calhoun .60 1.50
72 Logan Ice .40 1.00
73 Jose Miranda .50 1.25
74 Braden Webb .40 1.00
75 Mario Feliciano .50 1.25
76 Jake Rogers 2.00 5.00
77 Luis Arraez 1.50 4.00

78 TJ Friedl .75 2.00
79 Raimel Tapia .50 1.25
80 Ryan Hendrix .40 1.00
81 Chris Paddack 1.00 2.50
82 Luis Urias .75 2.00
83 J.T. Riddle .40 1.00
84 Mitchell White .40 1.00
85 Jake Fraley .50 1.25
86 Cole Stobbe .40 1.00
87 Corbin Burnes 3.00 8.00
88 Andy Ibanez .60 1.50
89 Andrew Knapp .40 1.00
90 Payton Henry .40 1.00
91 Chris Rodriguez .40 1.00
92 Thomas Jones .40 1.00
93 Mason Thompson .40 1.00
94 Matthias Dietz .40 1.00
95 Nick Gordon .40 1.00
96 Shaun Anderson .50 1.25
97 Jon Duplantier .50 1.25
98 Austin Franklin .40 1.00
99 Tim Tebow 10.00 25.00
100 Bernardo Flores .40 1.00
101 Zack Trageton .50 1.25
102 Jesus Luzardo 2.50 6.00
103 Heath Quinn .75 2.00
104 Nolan Williams .40 1.00
105 Jace Vines .50 1.25
106 Nolan Martinez .50 1.25
107 Kole Enright .50 1.25
108 Matt Krook .40 1.00
109 Dustin May 2.00 5.00
110 Zach Jackson .40 1.00
111 Khalil Lee .60 1.50
112 Mitchell Kranson .40 1.00
113 Stephen Alemais .60 1.50
114 Zac Gallen .40 1.00
115 Hudson Potts .50 1.25
116 Josh Rogers .60 1.50
117 Andrew Velazquez .40 1.00
118 Clayton Blackburn .40 1.00
119 Francis Martes .40 1.00
120 David Martinelli .40 1.00
121 Adalberto Mejia .40 1.00
122 Tyler Eppler .40 1.00
123 Mike Gerber .40 1.00
124 Mark Mathias .40 1.00
125 Drew Smith .40 1.00
126 J.D. Busfield .40 1.00
127 Scott Heineman .40 1.00
128 Kyle Garlick .40 1.00
129 Eloy Jimenez 1.50 4.00
130 Nicholas Lopez .60 1.50
131 Stefan Crichton .50 1.25
132 Guillermo Heredia .60 1.50
133 Nick Longhi .40 1.00
134 Hoy Jun Park .50 1.25
135 Raudy Read .40 1.00
136 Kelvin Gutierrez .40 1.00
137 Hunter Wood .40 1.00
138 Trey Mancini 1.25 3.00
139 Austen Williams .40 1.00
141 Hunter Cole .40 1.00
142 Yandy Diaz .75 2.00
143 Lazaro Armenteros 1.00 2.50
144 Brandon Marsh 1.00 2.50
145 Jason Jester .40 1.00
146 Kade Scivicque .40 1.00
147 Forrest Whitley 1.50 4.00
148 Kevin Maitan .60 1.50
149 Blake Rutherford 1.50 4.00
150 Alex Speas .50 1.25
151 Nate Griep .40 1.00
152 Zack Collins .50 1.25
153 Kyle Muller .50 1.25
154 Jose Azocar .40 1.00
155 Yu-Cheng Chang 1.00 2.50
156 Albert Abreu .50 1.25
157 Jimmy Herget .40 1.00
158 Matt Gage .50 1.25
159 George Bryner Bell .40 1.00
160 Kyle Funkhouser .50 1.25
161 Connor Walsh .40 1.00
162 Jordan Balazovic .75 2.00
163 Eric Stout .40 1.00
164 Matt Cooper .40 1.00
165 Juan Soto 60.00 150.00
166 Miguelangel Sierra .75 2.00
167 Josh VanMeter .50 1.25
168 Max Kranick .60 1.50
169 Jake Newberry .40 1.00
170 Brody Koerner .40 1.00
171 Phil Maton .40 1.00
172 Braulio Ortiz .40 1.00
173 Reggie Lawson .40 1.00
174 Chih-Wei Hu .50 1.25
176 Willi Castro .40 1.00
177 Isaiah White .40 1.00
178 Nestor Cortes .40 1.00
179 Jeremy Martinez 1.00 2.50
180 Dietrich Enns .50 1.25
181 Rhys Hoskins 1.50 4.00
182 Junior Fernandez .60 1.50
183 Dawel Lugo .40 1.00
184 Steven Duggar .40 1.00

2016 Elite Extra Edition Aspirations Blue

*ASP BLUE: .75X TO 2X BASIC
STATED PRINT RUN 75 SER.#'d SETS

2016 Elite Extra Edition Aspirations Purple

*ASP PRPLE: .6X TO 1.5X BASIC
STATED PRINT RUN 200 SER.#'d SETS

2016 Elite Extra Edition Aspirations Tie Dye

*ASP.TIE DYE: 1.2X TO 3X BASIC
STATED PRINT RUN 25 SER.#'d SETS

2016 Elite Extra Edition Status Black Die Cut

*STAT.BLK DC: .75X TO 2X BASIC
STATED PRINT RUN 99 SER.#'d SETS

2016 Elite Extra Edition Status Emerald Die Cut

*STAT.EMRLD.DC: 1X TO 2.5X BASIC
STATED PRINT RUN 49 SER.#'d SETS

2016 Elite Extra Edition Status Red Die Cut

*STAT.RED DC: .75X TO 2X BASIC
STATED PRINT RUN 99 SER.#'d SETS

2016 Elite Extra Edition Autographs

RANDOM INSERTS IN PACKS
PRINTING PLATES RANDOMLY INSERTED
PLATE PRINT RUN 1 SET PER COLOR
NO PLATE PRICING DUE TO SCARCITY
1 Tyler O'Neill 3.00 8.00
2 Nick Senzel 8.00 20.00
3 Ian Anderson 15.00 40.00
4 Riley Pint 2.50 6.00
6 A.J. Puk 4.00 10.00
7 Braxton Garrett 3.00 8.00
8 Cal Quantrill 2.50 6.00
9 Matt Manning 4.00 10.00
10 Nash Walters 2.50 6.00
12 Jason Groome 5.00 12.00
13 Joshua Lowe 2.50 6.00
14 Will Benson 4.00 10.00
15 Alex Kirilloff 8.00 20.00
16 Matt Thaiss 3.00 8.00
17 Brandon Waddell 2.50 6.00
18 Bryson Brigman 2.50 6.00
19 Justin Dunn 2.50 6.00
21 T.J. Zeuch 3.00 8.00
22 Will Craig 2.50 6.00
24 Matt Strahm 4.00 10.00
25 Eric Lauer 3.00 8.00
26 Zack Burdi 3.00 8.00
27 Cody Sedlock 2.50 6.00
28 Carter Kieboom 12.00 30.00
29 Dane Dunning 5.00 12.00
30 Cole Ragans 3.00 8.00
31 Anthony Kay 2.50 6.00
32 Will Smith 6.00 15.00
33 Dylan Carlson 20.00 50.00
34 Dakota Hudson 4.00 10.00
35 Taylor Trammell 10.00 25.00
36 Jordan Sheffield 2.50 6.00
37 Daulton Jefferies 3.00 8.00
38 Robert Tyler 2.50 6.00
39 Anfernee Grier 3.00 8.00
40 Joey Wentz 4.00 10.00
41 Skylar Szynski 2.50 6.00
42 German Marquez 4.00 10.00
43 Chris Okey 2.50 6.00
44 Anderson Espinoza 3.00 8.00
45 Alex Reyes 6.00 15.00
46 Drew Harrington 2.50 6.00
48 Buddy Reed 3.00 8.00
49 Alec Hansen 5.00 12.00
50 Joe Rizzo 2.50 6.00
51 C.J. Chatham 3.00 8.00
52 Andrew Yerzy 2.50 6.00
53 Ryan Boldt 3.00 8.00
54 Andrew Yerzy 2.50 6.00
55 Nolan Jones 6.00 15.00
56 Ben Rortvedt 3.00 8.00
57 J.B. Woodman 4.00 10.00
59 Bryan Reynolds 5.00 12.00
60 Matt Thaiss 3.00 8.00
61 Ronnie Dawson 2.50 6.00
62 Nick Solak 10.00 25.00
63 Shawn Morimando
64 Peter Alonso 25.00 60.00
65 T.J. Zeuch 3.00 8.00
66 Bobby Dalbec 20.00 50.00
67 A.J. Puckett 3.00 8.00
68 Travis MacGregor 3.00 8.00
69 Cody Sedlock 2.50 6.00
70 Connor Jones 3.00 8.00
72 Logan Ice 2.50 6.00
73 Jose Miranda 3.00 8.00
74 Braden Webb 2.50 6.00
75 Mario Feliciano 3.00 8.00
76 Jake Rogers 8.00 20.00
77 Luis Arraez 6.00 15.00
78 TJ Friedl 5.00 12.00
79 Raimel Tapia 3.00 8.00
80 Ryan Hendrix 2.50 6.00
82 Luis Urias 8.00 20.00
83 J.T. Riddle 2.50 6.00
84 Mitchell White 2.50 6.00
85 Jake Fraley 3.00 8.00
86 Cole Stobbe 2.50 6.00
87 Corbin Burnes 20.00 50.00
88 Andy Ibanez 5.00 12.00
89 Andrew Knapp 2.50 6.00
90 Payton Henry 2.50 6.00
91 Chris Rodriguez 2.50 6.00
92 Thomas Jones 2.50 6.00
93 Mason Thompson 2.50 6.00
95 Nick Gordon 2.50 6.00
96 Shaun Anderson 3.00 8.00
97 Jon Duplantier 2.50 6.00
98 Austin Franklin 2.50 6.00
99 Tim Tebow 40.00 100.00
100 Bernardo Flores 2.50 6.00
101 Zack Trageton 3.00 8.00
102 Jesus Luzardo 6.00 15.00
103 Heath Quinn 3.00 8.00
104 Nolan Williams 2.50 6.00
105 Jace Vines 2.50 6.00
106 Nolan Martinez 3.00 8.00
107 Kole Enright 3.00 8.00
108 Matt Krook 4.00 10.00
109 Dustin May 10.00 25.00
110 Zach Jackson 2.50 6.00
111 Khalil Lee 4.00 10.00
112 Mitchell Kranson 2.50 6.00
113 Stephen Alemais 4.00 10.00
114 Zac Gallen 2.50 6.00
115 Hudson Potts 3.00 8.00
116 Josh Rogers 4.00 10.00
117 Andrew Velazquez 2.50 6.00
118 Clayton Blackburn 2.50 6.00
119 Francis Martes 2.50 6.00
120 David Martinelli 2.50 6.00
122 Tyler Eppler 2.50 6.00
123 Mike Gerber 2.50 6.00
124 Mark Mathias 2.50 6.00
125 Drew Smith 2.50 6.00
126 J.D. Busfield 2.50 6.00
127 Scott Heineman 2.50 6.00
128 Kyle Garlick 2.50 6.00
129 Eloy Jimenez 15.00 40.00
131 Stefan Crichton 3.00 8.00
133 Nick Longhi 2.50 6.00
134 Hoy Jun Park 3.00 8.00
135 Raudy Read 2.50 6.00
136 Kelvin Gutierrez 2.50 6.00
137 Hunter Wood 2.50 6.00
138 Trey Mancini 5.00 12.00
139 Austen Williams 2.50 6.00
141 Hunter Cole 2.50 6.00
143 Lazaro Armenteros 6.00 15.00
144 Brandon Marsh 6.00 15.00
145 Jason Jester 2.50 6.00
146 Kade Scivicque 2.50 6.00
147 Forrest Whitley 15.00 40.00
148 Kevin Maitan 4.00 10.00
150 Alex Speas 3.00 8.00
151 Nate Griep 2.50 6.00
152 Zack Collins 3.00 8.00
153 Kyle Muller 3.00 8.00
154 Jose Azocar 2.50 6.00
157 Jimmy Herget 2.50 6.00
158 Matt Gage 3.00 8.00
159 George Bryner Bell 2.50 6.00
161 Connor Walsh 2.50 6.00
163 Eric Stout 2.50 6.00
164 Matt Cooper 2.50 6.00
166 Miguelangel Sierra 5.00 12.00
167 Josh VanMeter 3.00 8.00
168 Max Kranick 4.00 10.00
169 Jake Newberry 2.50 6.00
170 Brody Koerner 2.50 6.00
171 Phil Maton 2.50 6.00
172 Braulio Ortiz 2.50 6.00
173 Reggie Lawson 2.50 6.00
174 Chih-Wei Hu 3.00 8.00
177 Isaiah White 2.50 6.00
178 Nestor Cortes 2.50 6.00
179 Jeremy Martinez 3.00 8.00
180 Dietrich Enns 3.00 8.00
181 Rhys Hoskins 8.00 20.00
182 Junior Fernandez 4.00 10.00
183 Dawel Lugo 2.50 6.00
184 Steven Duggar 2.50 6.00

2016 Elite Extra Edition Autographs Aspirations Blue

*ASP BLUE/50: .6X TO 1.5X BASIC
*ASP BLUE/25: .75X TO 2X BASIC
RANDOM INSERTS IN PACKS
PRINT RUNS B/WN 10-50 COPIES PER
NO PRICING ON QTY 15 OR LESS

2016 Elite Extra Edition Autographs Aspirations Purple

*ASP PRPLE/100: .6X TO 1.5X BASIC
*ASP PRPLE/25: .75X TO 2X BASIC
RANDOM INSERTS IN PACKS
PRINT RUNS B/WN 15-100 COPIES PER
NO PRICING ON QTY 15

2016 Elite Extra Edition Autographs Charcoal

*CHARCOAL/25: .75X TO 2X BASIC
RANDOM INSERTS IN PACKS
PRINT RUNS B/WN 10-25 COPIES PER
NO PRICING ON QTY 10

2016 Elite Extra Edition Autographs Status Emerald Die Cut

*STAT.EMRLD.DC/25: .75X TO 2X BASIC
RANDOM INSERTS IN PACKS
PRINT RUNS B/WN 5-25 COPIES PER
NO PRICING ON QTY 10 OR LESS

2016 Elite Extra Edition Autographs Status Red Die Cut

*STAT.RED DC/75: .6X TO 1.5X BASIC
*STAT.RED DC/25: .75X TO 2X BASIC
RANDOM INSERTS IN PACKS
PRINT RUNS B/WN 10-75 COPIES PER
NO PRICING ON QTY 15 OR LESS

2016 Elite Extra Edition College Ticket Autographs

RANDOM INSERTS IN PACKS
*CRACKED ICE/24: .6X TO 1.5X BASIC
PRINTING PLATES RANDOMLY INSERTED
PLATE PRINT RUN 1 SET PER COLOR
BLACK-CYAN-MAGENTA-YELLOW ISSUED
NO PLATE PRICING DUE TO SCARCITY
1 Nick Senzel 12.00 30.00
3 A.J. Puk 10.00 25.00
4 Cal Quantrill 2.50 6.00
5 Daulton Jefferies 3.00 8.00
6 Robert Tyler 2.50 6.00
7 Zack Collins 3.00 8.00
9 Will Craig 2.50 6.00
10 T.J. Zeuch 3.00 8.00
11 Eric Lauer 6.00 15.00
12 Zack Burdi 3.00 8.00
13 Cody Sedlock 2.50 6.00
14 Dakota Hudson 4.00 10.00
15 Rhys Hoskins 25.00 60.00
16 Jordan Sheffield 2.50 6.00
18 Logan Shore 5.00 12.00
19 Buddy Reed 10.00 25.00
20 Alec Hansen 3.00 8.00
21 Ryan Boldt 3.00 8.00
23 Bryan Reynolds 5.00 12.00
24 Nick Solak 10.00 25.00
25 Connor Jones 3.00 8.00
26 Logan Ice 2.50 6.00
27 Kade Scivicque 2.50 6.00
28 Justin Dunn 2.50 6.00
29 Will Smith
30 Jason Jester 2.50 6.00
31 Dietrich Enns 3.00 8.00
32 C.J. Chatham 6.00 15.00
33 Connor Walsh 2.50 6.00
34 J.B. Woodman 4.00 10.00
35 Ronnie Dawson 2.50 6.00
36 Pete Alonso 75.00 200.00

2016 Elite Extra Edition Dual Materials

RANDOM INSERTS IN PACKS
STATED PRINT RUN 299 SER.#'d SETS
*SILVER/149: .4X TO 1X BASIC
*HOLO GLD/99: .5X TO 1.2X BASIC
*HOLO SLVR/49: .5X TO 1.2X BASIC
*PURPLE/25: .6X TO 1.5X BASIC
1 Jake Fraley 3.00 8.00
2 Cole Stobbe 2.50 6.00
3 Braden Shipley 2.50 6.00
4 Drew Harrington 2.50 6.00
5 Aaron Knapp 2.50 6.00
6 Braden Webb 2.50 6.00
7 Chris Rodriguez 2.50 6.00
8 Thomas Jones 2.50 6.00
9 Mason Thompson 2.50 6.00
10 Hoy Jun Park 3.00 8.00
11 Bryson Brigman 2.50 6.00
12 Shaun Anderson 3.00 8.00
13 Jon Duplantier 2.50 6.00
14 Austin Franklin 2.50 6.00
15 Hunter Cole 2.50 6.00
16 Nick Longhi 2.50 6.00
17 Jordan Balazovic 5.00 12.00
18 Jesus Luzardo 6.00 15.00
19 Heath Quinn 4.00 10.00
20 Nolan Williams 2.50 6.00

2016 Elite Extra Edition Future Threads Silhouette Autographs

RANDOM INSERTS IN PACKS
PRINT RUNS B/WN 115-299 COPIES PER
12 J.T. Riddle/299 3.00 8.00
25 Jake Fraley/149 4.00 10.00
26 Cole Stobbe/299 3.00 8.00
28 Drew Harrington/199 3.00 8.00
29 Aaron Knapp/299 3.00 8.00
31 Chris Rodriguez/199 3.00 8.00
35 Bryson Brigman/299 3.00 8.00
39 Hunter Cole/149 3.00 8.00
48 Matt Krook/115 3.00 8.00
49 Dustin May/199 12.00 30.00

2016 Elite Extra Edition Future Threads Silhouette Autographs Purple

*PURPLE/25: .6X TO 1.5X SILVER
RANDOM INSERTS IN PACKS
PRINT RUNS B/WN 10-25 COPIES PER
NO PRICING ON QTY 15 OR LESS
2 Yoan Moncada/25 15.00 40.00
5 Alex Reyes/25 15.00 40.00
14 Clint Frazier/25 15.00 40.00
16 Josh Bell/25 20.00 50.00
20 Carson Fulmer/25 6.00 15.00
21 David Dahl/25 8.00 20.00
22 Matt Olson/25 15.00 40.00
45 Sean Newcomb/25 8.00 20.00

2016 Elite Extra Edition Future Threads Silhouette Autographs Red

*RED/49: .5X TO 1.2X SILVER
*RED/25: .6X TO 1.5X SILVER
RANDOM INSERTS IN PACKS
PRINT RUNS B/WN 15-49 COPIES PER
NO PRICING ON QTY 15
3 Dansby Swanson/25 25.00 60.00
4 Tyler Glasnow/25
5 Alex Reyes/49 12.00 30.00
7 Andrew Benintendi/49 75.00 200.00
14 Clint Frazier/49 12.00 30.00
17 Alex Bregman/25 30.00 80.00
18 Aaron Judge/49 75.00 200.00
20 Carson Fulmer/49 5.00 12.00
21 David Dahl/49 6.00 15.00
22 Matt Olson/49 12.00 30.00
45 Sean Newcomb/49 6.00 15.00

2016 Elite Extra Edition Future Threads Silhouette Autographs Silver

RANDOM INSERTS IN PACKS
STATED PRINT RUN 99 SER.#'d SETS
1 Orlando Arcia 5.00 12.00
6 Rafael Devers 15.00 40.00
8 Manuel Margot 4.00 10.00
9 Clayton Blackburn 4.00 10.00
10 Francis Martes 4.00 10.00
11 Adalberto Mejia 4.00 10.00
12 J.T. Riddle 4.00 10.00
13 Mike Gerber 4.00 10.00
15 Raimel Tapia 5.00 12.00
23 Matt Chapman 12.00 30.00
24 Brett Phillips 4.00 10.00
25 Jake Fraley 5.00 12.00
26 Cole Stobbe 4.00 10.00
28 Drew Harrington 4.00 10.00
29 Aaron Knapp 4.00 10.00
31 Chris Rodriguez 4.00 10.00
32 Thomas Jones 4.00 10.00
33 Mason Thompson 4.00 10.00
34 Hoy Jun Park 5.00 12.00
35 Bryson Brigman 4.00 10.00
36 Shaun Anderson 5.00 12.00
37 Jon Duplantier 4.00 10.00
38 Austin Franklin 4.00 10.00
39 Hunter Cole 4.00 10.00
40 Nick Longhi 4.00 10.00
41 Jordan Balazovic 8.00 20.00
42 Jesus Luzardo 10.00 25.00
43 Heath Quinn 6.00 15.00
44 Nolan Williams 4.00 10.00
46 Nolan Martinez 5.00 12.00
47 Kole Enright 4.00 10.00
48 Matt Krook 4.00 10.00
49 Dustin May 15.00 40.00
50 Zach Jackson 4.00 10.00
51 Khalil Lee 6.00 15.00
52 Mitchell Kranson 4.00 10.00
53 Stephen Alemais 6.00 15.00
55 Josh Rogers 6.00 15.00
56 Andrew Velazquez 4.00 10.00

2016 Elite Extra Edition Future Threads Silhouettes Duals

RANDOM INSERTS IN PACKS
PRINT RUNS B/WN 125-299 COPIES PER
1 Devers/Moncada/125 5.00 12.00
4 Chapman/Olson/299 5.00 12.00
6 Fulmer/Glasnow/199 10.00 25.00
7 Dahl/Tapia/299 3.00 8.00
8 Martes/Newcomb/299 3.00 8.00
10 Rogers/Martinez/299 4.00 10.00
11 Margot/Thompson/299 2.50 6.00
12 Mejia/Blackburn/299 2.50 6.00
14 Manuel Margot/299 2.50 6.00
15 Brett Phillips/299 2.50 6.00
16 Reyes/Glasnow/299 10.00 25.00
18 Frazier/Gerber/299 10.00 25.00

2016 Elite Extra Edition Future Threads Silhouettes Duals Holo Gold

*HOLO GOLD: .5X TO 1.2X BASIC
5 Benintendi/Frazier 8.00 20.00
9 Phillips/Arcia 4.00 10.00

2016 Elite Extra Edition Future Threads Silhouettes Duals Holo Silver

*HOLO SILVER/49: .5X TO 1.2X BASIC
*HOLO SILVER/25: .6X TO 1.5X BASIC
RANDOM INSERTS IN PACKS
PRINT RUNS B/WN 25-49 COPIES PER
2 Bregman/Swanson/49 10.00 25.00
3 Judge/Mateo/49 10.00 25.00
5 Benintendi/Frazier/49 8.00 20.00
9 Phillips/Arcia/49 4.00 10.00
13 Dansby Swanson/25 10.00 25.00
17 Bell/Glasnow/49 6.00 15.00
19 Moncada/Benintendi/49 12.00 30.00
20 Arcia/Mateo/49 4.00 10.00

2016 Elite Extra Edition Future Threads Silhouettes Duals Purple

*PURPLE: .6X TO 1.5X BASIC
RANDOM INSERTS IN PACKS
PRINT RUNS B/WN 10-25 COPIES PER
NO PRICING ON QTY 15 OR LESS
2 Bregman/Swanson/25 12.00 30.00
3 Judge/Mateo/25 12.00 30.00
5 Benintendi/Frazier/25 10.00 25.00
9 Phillips/Arcia/25 5.00 12.00
17 Bell/Glasnow/25 8.00 20.00
20 Arcia/Mateo/25 5.00 12.00

2016 Elite Extra Edition Future Threads Silhouettes Duals Silver

*HOLO SILVER/149: .4X TO 1X BASIC
*HOLO SILVER/75: .5X TO 1.2X BASIC
RANDOM INSERTS IN PACKS
PRINT RUNS B/WN 75-149 COPIES PER
5 Benintendi/Frazier/149 6.00 15.00
9 Phillips/Arcia/149 3.00 8.00

2016 Elite Extra Edition Quad Materials

RANDOM INSERTS IN PACKS
STATED PRINT RUN 299 SER.#'d SETS
7 Manuel Margot 2.50 6.00
8 Clayton Blackburn 2.50 6.00
11 Mike Gerber 2.50 6.00
12 Clint Frazier 5.00 12.00
13 Raimel Tapia 3.00 8.00
15 Aaron Judge 15.00 40.00
19 Matt Olson 5.00 12.00

2016 Elite Extra Edition Quad Materials Holo Gold

*HOLO GLD/149: .5X TO 1.2X BASIC
RANDOM INSERTS IN PACKS
PRINT RUNS B/WN 49-99 COPIES PER
1 Orlando Arcia/99 4.00 10.00
2 Yoan Moncada/99 6.00 15.00
3 Tyler Glasnow/99 12.00 30.00
4 Alex Reyes/99 4.00 10.00
5 Rafael Devers/75 3.00 8.00
9 Francis Martes/99 3.00 8.00
10 Adalberto Mejia/99 3.00 8.00
14 Alex Bregman/99 8.00 20.00
16 Jorge Mateo/99 3.00 8.00
17 Carson Fulmer/99 3.00 8.00
18 David Dahl/99 4.00 10.00
20 Brett Phillips/99 3.00 8.00

2016 Elite Extra Edition Quad Materials Holo Silver

*HOLO SILVER/49: .5X TO 1.2X BASIC
*HOLO SILVER/25: .6X TO 1.5X BASIC
RANDOM INSERTS IN PACKS
PRINT RUNS B/WN 25-49 COPIES PER
1 Orlando Arcia/49 4.00 10.00
2 Yoan Moncada/49 6.00 15.00
3 Tyler Glasnow/49 12.00 30.00
4 Alex Reyes/49 4.00 10.00
5 Rafael Devers/49 4.00 10.00
6 Andrew Benintendi/49 6.00 15.00
9 Francis Martes/49 3.00 8.00
10 Adalberto Mejia/49 3.00 8.00
14 Alex Bregman/49 8.00 20.00
16 Jorge Mateo/25 4.00 10.00
17 Carson Fulmer/49 3.00 8.00
18 David Dahl/49 4.00 10.00
20 Brett Phillips/49 3.00 8.00

2016 Elite Extra Edition Quad Materials Purple

*PURPLE: .6X TO 1.5X BASIC
NO PRICING ON QTY 15
RANDOM INSERTS IN PACKS
PRINT RUNS B/WN 15-25 COPIES PER
1 Orlando Arcia/25 5.00 12.00
2 Yoan Moncada/25 8.00 20.00
3 Tyler Glasnow/25 15.00 40.00
4 Alex Reyes/25 5.00 12.00
5 Rafael Devers/25 5.00 12.00
9 Francis Martes/25 4.00 10.00
10 Adalberto Mejia/25 4.00 10.00
14 Alex Bregman/25 10.00 25.00
17 Carson Fulmer/25 4.00 10.00
18 David Dahl/25 5.00 12.00
20 Brett Phillips/25 4.00 10.00

2016 Elite Extra Edition Quad Materials Silver

*SILVER/149: .4X TO 1X BASIC
*SILVER/75-99: .5X TO 1.2X BASIC
RANDOM INSERTS IN PACKS
PRINT RUNS B/WN 75-149 COPIES PER
1 Orlando Arcia/149 3.00 8.00
2 Yoan Moncada/149 5.00 12.00
3 Tyler Glasnow/149 10.00 25.00
4 Alex Reyes/149 3.00 8.00
5 Rafael Devers/99 4.00 10.00
9 Francis Martes/149 2.50 6.00
10 Adalberto Mejia/149 2.50 6.00
16 Jorge Mateo/75 3.00 8.00
18 David Dahl/149 3.00 8.00
20 Brett Phillips/149 2.50 6.00

2016 Elite Extra Edition Triple Materials

RANDOM INSERTS IN PACKS
STATED PRINT RUN 299 SER.#'d SETS
1 Sean Newcomb/299 3.00 8.00
2 Nolan Martinez/299 3.00 8.00
3 Kole Enright/299 3.00 8.00
4 Matt Krook/299 2.50 6.00
5 Dustin May/299 6.00 15.00
6 Zach Jackson/299 2.50 6.00
7 Khalil Lee/299 4.00 10.00
8 Mitchell Kranson/299 2.50 6.00
9 Stephen Alemais/299 4.00 10.00
11 Josh Rogers/299 4.00 10.00
12 Andrew Velazquez/299 2.50 6.00
14 J.T. Riddle/299 2.50 6.00
16 Matt Chapman/299 8.00 20.00
17 Dansby Swanson/149 6.00 15.00

2016 Elite Extra Edition Triple Materials Holo Gold

*HOLO GOLD: .5X TO 1.2X BASIC
RANDOM INSERTS IN PACKS
PRINT RUNS B/WN 65-99 COPIES PER
18 Yoan Moncada/99 5.00 12.00
19 Andrew Benintendi/99 6.00 15.00
20 Alex Bregman/99 6.00 15.00

2016 Elite Extra Edition Triple Materials Holo Silver

*HOLO SILVER: .5X TO 1.2X BASIC
RANDOM INSERTS IN PACKS
STATED PRINT RUN 49 SER.#'d SETS
18 Yoan Moncada 5.00 12.00
19 Andrew Benintendi 6.00 15.00
20 Alex Bregman 6.00 15.00

2016 Elite Extra Edition Triple Materials Purple

*PURPLE: .6X TO 1.5X BASIC
RANDOM INSERTS IN PACKS
PRINT RUNS B/WN 15-25 COPIES PER
NO PRICING ON QTY 15 OR LESS
18 Yoan Moncada/25 6.00 15.00
20 Alex Bregman/25 8.00 20.00

2016 Elite Extra Edition Triple Materials Silver

*SILVER/125-149: .4X TO 1X BASIC
*SILVER/99: .5X TO 1.2X BASIC
RANDOM INSERTS IN PACKS
PRINT RUNS B/WN 99-149 COPIES PER
18 Yoan Moncada/149 4.00 10.00
19 Andrew Benintendi/125 5.00 12.00
20 Alex Bregman/149 5.00 12.00

2016 Elite Extra Edition USA 15U and Collegiate National Team Quad Materials

RANDOM INSERTS IN PACKS
STATED PRINT RUN 199 SER.#'d SETS
*SILVER/99: .6X TO 1.5X BASIC
*PURPLE/25: .75X TO 2X BASIC
1 Olasin/Hairston/Dixon/Friedl 3.00 8.00
2 Skoug/Briones/Rivera/Young 4.00 10.00
3 Volpe/Cairo/Burger/Guthrie 4.00 10.00
4 Brgmn/Olsn/Whte/Hra 6.00 15.00
5 Bukauskas/McCaughan/Long/Jones 4.00 10.00
6 Faedo/Campbell/Johnson/Scott 4.00 10.00
7 McKay/Naranjo/Gorby/Peterson 5.00 12.00
8 Berkwich/Cate/Thomas/Jacob 3.00 8.00
9 Lange/Faltine/Houck/Martinez 3.00 8.00
10 Wright/Sims/Wohlgemuth/Otto 3.00 8.00
11 Doughty/Faltine/Faedo/Houck 4.00 10.00
12 Olasin/Briones/Harrison/Walls 3.00 8.00
13 Brgmn/Beer/Dxn/Kndll 6.00 15.00
14 Cairo/Harrison/Young/Hairston 4.00 10.00
15 Peterson/Campbell/Otto/Gorby 3.00 8.00
16 Young/Rivera/Berkwich/Friedl 4.00 10.00
17 Long/Wright/Thomas/Naranjo 3.00 8.00
18 Brigman/Walls/Briones/Hiura 5.00 12.00
19 Guthrie/Gorby/Burger/Jacob 3.00 8.00

2016 Elite Extra Edition USA Baseball 18U Ticket Autographs

RANDOM INSERTS IN PACKS
*CRACKED ICE/24: .6X TO 1.5X BASIC
PRINTING PLATES RANDOMLY INSERTED
PLATE PRINT RUN 1 SET PER COLOR
BLACK-CYAN-MAGENTA-YELLOW ISSUED
NO PLATE PRICING DUE TO SCARCITY
1 Nick Allen 3.00 8.00
2 Hans Crouse 4.00 10.00
3 Hagen Danner 6.00 15.00
4 Hunter Greene 12.00 30.00
5 Quentin Holmes 3.00 8.00
6 Royce Lewis 6.00 15.00
7 Nick Pratto 3.00 8.00
8 Shane Baz 4.00 10.00
9 Logan Allen 2.50 6.00
10 Jordan Butler 2.50 6.00
11 Brice Turang 10.00 25.00
12 Mike Siani 2.50 6.00
14 Blayne Enlow 4.00 10.00
15 Patrick Bailey 5.00 12.00
16 Ryan Vilade 5.00 12.00
17 CJ Van Eyk 2.50 6.00
18 Mitchell Stone 2.50 6.00
19 M.J. Melendez 10.00 25.00
20 Triston Casas 10.00 25.00

2016 Elite Extra Edition USA Baseball Ticket Autographs

RANDOM INSERTS IN PACKS
*CRACKED ICE/24: .6X TO 1.5X BASIC
PRINTING PLATES RANDOMLY INSERTED
PLATE PRINT RUN 1 SET PER COLOR
BLACK-CYAN-MAGENTA-YELLOW ISSUED
NO PLATE PRICING DUE TO SCARCITY
1 Darren McCaughan 2.50 6.00
2 Seth Beer 8.00 20.00
3 J.B. Bukauskas 10.00 25.00
4 Jake Burger 6.00 15.00
5 Tyler Johnson 2.50 6.00
6 Alex Faedo 3.00 8.00
7 TJ Friedl 5.00 12.00
8 Dalton Guthrie 3.00 8.00
10 KJ Harrison 5.00 12.00
11 Keston Hiura 20.00 50.00
12 Tanner Houck 12.00 30.00
13 Jeren Kendall 10.00 25.00
14 Alex Lange 4.00 10.00
15 Brendan McKay 6.00 15.00
16 Glenn Otto 2.50 6.00
17 David Peterson 5.00 12.00
18 Mike Rivera
19 Evan Skoug 3.00 8.00
20 Ricky Tyler Thomas 2.50 6.00
21 Taylor Walls 3.00 8.00
22 Tim Cate 3.00 8.00
23 Evan White 6.00 15.00
24 Kyle Wright 8.00 20.00
25 Nelson Berkwich 3.00 8.00
26 Coleman Brigman 2.50 6.00
27 Gabe Briones 2.50 6.00
28 Christian Cairo 4.00 10.00
29 Justin Campbell 3.00 8.00
30 Jasiah Dixon 4.00 10.00
31 Cade Doughty 3.00 8.00
32 Sammy Faltine 2.50 6.00
33 Nick Gorby 4.00 10.00
34 Tony Jacob 4.00 10.00
35 Jared Jones 2.50 6.00
36 Ethan Long 4.00 10.00
37 Zach Martinez 5.00 12.00
38 Joe Naranjo 3.00 8.00
39 Colton Olasin 2.50 6.00
40 Wesley Scott 8.00 20.00
41 Landon Sims 3.00 8.00
42 Anthony Volpe 15.00 40.00
43 Nate Wohlgemuth 2.50 6.00
44 Carter Young 6.00 15.00

2016 Elite Extra Edition USA Collegiate Silhouette Autographs

RANDOM INSERTS IN PACKS
STATED PRINT RUN 99 SER.#'d SETS
*SILVER/49: .5X TO 1.2X BASIC
*PURPLE/25: .6X TO 1.5X BASIC
1 Darren McCaughan 4.00 10.00
2 Seth Beer 10.00 25.00
3 J.B. Bukauskas 10.00 25.00
4 Jake Burger 6.00 15.00
5 Tyler Johnson 4.00 10.00
6 Alex Faedo 6.00 15.00
7 TJ Friedl 4.00 10.00
8 Dalton Guthrie 5.00 12.00
9 Devin Hairston 4.00 10.00
10 KJ Harrison 8.00 20.00
11 Keston Hiura 10.00 25.00
12 Tanner Houck 10.00 25.00
13 Jeren Kendall 8.00 20.00
14 Alex Lange 8.00 20.00
15 Brendan McKay 10.00 25.00
16 Glenn Otto 4.00 10.00
17 David Peterson 8.00 20.00
18 Mike Rivera
19 Evan Skoug 6.00 15.00
20 Ricky Tyler Thomas 4.00 10.00
21 Taylor Walls 5.00 12.00
22 Tim Cate 5.00 12.00
23 Evan White 8.00 20.00
24 Kyle Wright 15.00 40.00

2017 Elite Extra Edition

STATED PRINT RUN 999 SER.#'d SETS
1 Royce Lewis 2.00 5.00
3 MacKenzie Gore 2.00 5.00
4 Brendan McKay 1.00 2.50
5 Kyle Wright .75 2.00
6 Austin Beck 1.00 2.50
7 Pavin Smith .40 1.00
8 Adam Haseley .50 1.25
9 Keston Hiura 1.25 3.00
10 Jo Adell 3.00 8.00
11 Jake Burger .50 1.25
12 Shane Baz .40 1.00
13 Trevor Rogers .60 1.50
14 Nick Pratto .40 1.00
15 J.B. Bukauskas .40 1.00
16 Clarke Schmidt .40 1.00
17 Evan White .60 1.50
18 Alex Faedo .40 1.00
19 Heliot Ramos 2.50 6.00
20 David Peterson .50 1.25
21 DL Hall .30 .75
22 Logan Warmoth .40 1.00
23 Jeren Kendall .50 1.25
24 Tanner Houck 1.25 3.00
25 Seth Romero .25 .60
26 Bubba Thompson .40 1.00
27 Brendon Little .30 .75
28 Nate Pearson 1.50 4.00
29 Christopher Seise .40 1.00
30 Alex Lange .40 1.00
31 Ronald Acuna 10.00 25.00
32 Jeter Downs .50 1.25
33 Kevin Merrell .30 .75
34 Tristen Lutz .40 1.00
35 Brent Rooker .60 1.50
36 Brian Miller .30 .75
38 Stuart Fairchild .30 .75
39 Luis Campusano .30 .75
40 Michael Mercado .30 .75
41 Drew Waters 1.50 4.00

2016 Elite Extra Edition Aspirations Blue

43 Greg Deichmann .50 1.25
44 Drew Ellis .40 1.00
45 Spencer Howard .75 2.00
46 Tanner Scott .25 .60
47 Griffin Canning .40 1.00
48 Ryan Vilade .40 1.00
49 Gavin Sheets .40 1.00
50 Brett Netzer .30 .75
51 Joseph Dunand .50 1.25
52 M.J. Melendez .40 1.00
53 Joe Perez .30 .75
54 Matt Sauer .30 .75
55 Sam Carlson .30 .75
56 Corbin Martin .25 .60
57 Tomas Nido .25 .60
58 Jacob Gonzalez .75 2.00
59 Mark Vientos .40 1.00
60 Ryan Lillie .25 .60
61 Hagen Danner .30 .75
62 Morgan Cooper .30 .75
63 Evan Steele .30 .75
64 Quentin Holmes .30 .75
65 Wil Crowe .40 1.00
66 Hans Crouse .60 1.50
67 Michel Baez .40 1.00
68 Daulton Varsho .40 1.00
69 Blake Hunt .25 .60
70 Tommy Doyle .25 .60
71 Tyler Freeman .25 .60
72 Tyler Buffett .25 .60
73 Nathan Lukes .25 .60
74 Ernie Clement .30 .75
75 J.J. Matijevic .30 .75
76 Blayne Enlow .30 .75
77 Colton Hock .30 .75
78 Mason House .40 1.00
79 Aneury Tavarez .25 .60
80 Freddy Tarnok .30 .75
81 Tim Locastro .30 .75
82 Matt Tabor .25 .60
83 Connor Seabold .25 .60
84 KJ Harrison .40 1.00
85 Jacob Pearson .25 .60
86 Will Gaddis .25 .60
87 Nick Dini .25 .60
88 Dylan Busby .25 .60
89 Taylor Walls .25 .60
90 Charcer Burks .25 .60
91 Ronaldo Hernandez .40 1.00
92 Trevor Stephan .40 1.00
93 Brennon Lund .25 .60
94 Esteury Ruiz .40 1.00
95 Joey Morgan .30 .75
96 Seth Corry .25 .60
97 Quinn Brodey .25 .60
98 Mike Baumann .30 .75
100 Jaime Barria .30 .75
101 Trenton Kemp .40 1.00
102 JoJo Romero .60 1.50
103 Diego Castillo .40 1.00
104 Buddy Kennedy .40 1.00
105 Shed Long .25 .60
106 Daniel Tillo .40 1.00
107 Andres Gimenez .60 1.50
108 Brayan Hernandez .25 .60
109 Carlos Soto .25 .60
110 Ronald Bolanos .25 .60
111 Myles Straw .40 1.00
112 Edwin Lora .30 .75
113 Joan Baez .25 .60
114 Adrian Morejon .40 1.00
115 Adonis Medina .40 1.00
116 Johan Oviedo .30 .75
117 Luis Almanzar .25 .60
118 Chance Adams .30 .75
119 David Garcia .30 .75
120 Ronald Guzman .30 .75
121 Luis Alexander Basabe .40 1.00
122 Jesus Sanchez 1.25 3.00
123 Yasel Antuna 1.25 3.00
124 Estevan Florial 1.50 4.00
125 Luis Garcia .40 1.00
126 Jordan Holloway .25 .60
127 Abraham Gutierrez UER .40 1.00
Abrahan Gutierrez
128 Yefry Ramirez .25 .60
129 Dustin Fowler .30 .75
130 Joshua Palacios 1.50 4.00
131 Carlos Rincon .25 .60
132 Nicky Lopez .40 1.00
133 Jelfry Marte .40 1.00
134 Luis V. Garcia 2.00 5.00
135 Ronny Mauricio 1.25 3.00
136 Julio Rodriguez 2.50 6.00
137 Larry Ernesto .25 .60
138 Adrian Hernandez .25 .60
139 Ynmanol Marinez .30 .75
140 George Valera .50 1.25
141 Ronny Rojas .25 .60
142 Carlos Aguiar .30 .75
143 Luis Robert 5.00 12.00
144 Kyri Washington .60 1.50
145 Jose Miguel Fernandez .25 .60
146 Bryan Mata .30 .75
147 Daniel Flores .25 .60
148 Oneil Cruz .40 1.00
149 Bryan Garcia .25 .60
150 Jake Junis .40 1.00
151 Freddy Peralta .40 1.00
152 Michael Rucker .50 1.25
153 Seby Zavala .40 1.00
154 Zack Granite .75 2.00
155 Nelson Beltran .25 .60
156 Junior Paniagua .40 1.00
157 Omar Florentino .25 .60
158 Ricardo Balogh Aybar .25 .60
159 Ayendi Ortiz .25 .60
160 Noelvi Marte 1.25 3.00
161 Wilmin Candelario .40 1.00
162 Juan Jerez .30 .75
163 Julio Heureaux .40 1.00
164 Ilvin Fernandez .25 .60
165 Moises Ramirez .25 .60
166 Frankely Hurtado .25 .60
167 Orlando Chivilli .25 .60
168 Marco Luciano 1.25 3.00
169 Jeferson Geraldo .25 .60
170 Alberto Fabian .25 .60
171 Henry Morales .25 .60
172 Jeffrey Diaz .25 .60
173 Estanli Castillo .40 1.00
174 Lucas Erceg .25 .60
175 Yeison Lemos .40 1.00
176 Jose Hernandez .25 .60
177 Robert Puason 1.25 3.00
178 Jhon Diaz .40 1.00
179 Bayron Lora 1.25 3.00
180 Emmanuel Rodriguez .25 .60
181 Franyel Baez .25 .60
182 Algenis Vasquez .25 .60
183 Junio Tilien .40 1.00
184 Malfrin Sosa .25 .60
185 Isaac Paredes 1.25 3.00
186 Seuly Matias .50 1.25
187 Cole Brannen .40 1.00
188 Connor Wong .40 1.00
189 Gerson Moreno .25 .60
190 Pedro Vasquez .25 .60
191 Adrian Valerio .25 .60
192 Brendan Murphy .25 .60
193 Zach Kirtley .30 .75
194 Lincoln Henzman .25 .60
195 Dane Myers .40 1.00
196 Jonah Todd .40 1.00
197 Bryce Johnson .25 .60
198 Nick Allen .30 .75
199 Kevin Smith .25 .60
200 Jake Thompson .25 .60

2017 Elite Extra Edition Aspirations Blue

*ASP.BLUE: .75X TO 2X BASIC
RANDOM INSERTS IN PACKS
STATED PRINT RUN 75 SER.#'d SETS

2017 Elite Extra Edition Aspirations Orange

*ASP.ORANGE: .75X TO 2X BASIC
RANDOM INSERTS IN PACKS
STATED PRINT RUN 100 SER.#'d SETS

2017 Elite Extra Edition Aspirations Purple

*ASP PRPLE: .6X TO 1.5X BASIC
RANDOM INSERTS IN PACKS
STATED PRINT RUN 200 SER.#'d SETS

2017 Elite Extra Edition Aspirations Red

*ASP.RED: .6X TO 1.5X BASIC
RANDOM INSERTS IN PACKS
STATED PRINT RUN 150 SER.#'d SETS

2017 Elite Extra Edition Aspirations Tie Dye

*ASP.TIE DYE: 1.2X TO 3X BASIC
RANDOM INSERTS IN PACKS
STATED PRINT RUN 25 SER.#'d SETS

2017 Elite Extra Edition Status Die Cut Emerald

*STAT.EMRLD.DC: 1X TO 2.5X BASIC
RANDOM INSERTS IN PACKS
STATED PRINT RUN 49 SER.#'d SETS

2017 Elite Extra Edition Status Die Cut Red

*STAT.RED DC: .75X TO 2X BASIC
RANDOM INSERTS IN PACKS
STATED PRINT RUN 99 SER.#'d SETS

2017 Elite Extra Edition Autographs

RANDOM INSERTS IN PACKS
PRINTING PLATES RANDOMLY INSERTED
PLATE PRINT RUN 1 SET PER COLOR
BLACK-CYAN-MAGENTA-YELLOW ISSUED
NO PLATE PRICING DUE TO SCARCITY
EXCHANGE DEADLINE 6/6/2019
1 Royce Lewis 8.00 20.00
3 MacKenzie Gore 30.00 80.00
4 Brendan McKay 8.00 20.00
5 Kyle Wright 4.00 10.00
6 Austin Beck 5.00 12.00
7 Pavin Smith 4.00 10.00
8 Adam Haseley 5.00 12.00
9 Keston Hiura 8.00 20.00
10 Jo Adell 15.00 40.00
11 Jake Burger 5.00 12.00
12 Shane Baz 4.00 10.00
13 Trevor Rogers 6.00 15.00
14 Nick Pratto 8.00 20.00
15 J.B. Bukauskas 4.00 10.00
16 Clarke Schmidt 4.00 10.00
17 Evan White 6.00 15.00
18 Alex Faedo 4.00 10.00
19 Heliot Ramos 6.00 15.00
20 David Peterson 5.00 12.00
21 DL Hall 3.00 8.00
22 Logan Warmoth 8.00 20.00
23 Jeren Kendall 5.00 12.00
24 Tanner Houck 10.00 25.00
26 Bubba Thompson 4.00 10.00
27 Brendon Little 3.00 8.00
28 Nate Pearson 15.00 40.00
29 Christopher Seise 4.00 10.00
30 Alex Lange 4.00 10.00
31 Ronald Acuna 75.00 200.00
32 Jeter Downs 8.00 20.00
33 Kevin Merrell 3.00 8.00
34 Tristen Lutz 4.00 10.00
35 Brent Rooker 2.50 6.00
36 Brian Miller 3.00 8.00
38 Stuart Fairchild 3.00 8.00
39 Luis Campusano 3.00 8.00
40 Michael Mercado 3.00 8.00
41 Drew Waters 8.00 20.00
43 Greg Deichmann 5.00 12.00
44 Drew Ellis 4.00 10.00
45 Spencer Howard 8.00 20.00
46 Tanner Scott 2.50 6.00
47 Griffin Canning 4.00 10.00
48 Ryan Vilade 4.00 10.00
49 Gavin Sheets 4.00 10.00
50 Brett Netzer 3.00 8.00
51 Joseph Dunand 5.00 12.00
52 M.J. Melendez 4.00 10.00
53 Joe Perez 3.00 8.00
54 Matt Sauer 3.00 8.00
55 Sam Carlson 3.00 8.00
57 Tomas Nido 2.50 6.00
58 Jacob Gonzalez
59 Mark Vientos 4.00 10.00
60 Ryan Lillie 2.50 6.00
61 Hagen Danner 3.00 8.00
62 Morgan Cooper 3.00 8.00
63 Evan Steele 3.00 8.00
64 Quentin Holmes 3.00 8.00
65 Wil Crowe 4.00 10.00
68 Daulton Varsho 8.00 20.00
69 Blake Hunt 2.50 6.00
70 Tommy Doyle 2.50 6.00
71 Tyler Freeman 2.50 6.00
72 Tyler Buffett 2.50 6.00
73 Nathan Lukes 2.50 6.00
74 Ernie Clement 3.00 8.00
75 J.J. Matijevic 3.00 8.00
76 Blayne Enlow 3.00 8.00
77 Colton Hock 3.00 8.00
78 Mason House 4.00 10.00
79 Aneury Tavarez 2.50 6.00
80 Freddy Tarnok 3.00 8.00
81 Tim Locastro 3.00 8.00
82 Matt Tabor 2.50 6.00
83 Connor Seabold 2.50 6.00
84 KJ Harrison 4.00 10.00
85 Jacob Pearson 2.50 6.00
86 Will Gaddis 2.50 6.00
87 Nick Dini 2.50 6.00
88 Dylan Busby 2.50 6.00
89 Taylor Walls 2.50 6.00
90 Charcer Burks 2.50 6.00
92 Trevor Stephan 4.00 10.00
93 Brennon Lund 2.50 6.00
95 Joey Morgan 3.00 8.00
96 Seth Corry 2.50 6.00
97 Quinn Brodey 2.50 6.00
98 Mike Baumann 3.00 8.00
100 Jaime Barria 3.00 8.00
101 Trenton Kemp 4.00 10.00
102 JoJo Romero 4.00 10.00
103 Diego Castillo 4.00 10.00
104 Buddy Kennedy 4.00 10.00
105 Shed Long 2.50 6.00
106 Daniel Tillo 4.00 10.00
107 Andres Gimenez 6.00 15.00
110 Ronald Bolanos 2.50 6.00
111 Myles Straw 4.00 10.00
112 Edwin Lora 3.00 8.00
113 Joan Baez 2.50 6.00
114 Adrian Morejon 4.00 10.00
115 Adonis Medina 4.00 10.00
116 Johan Oviedo 3.00 8.00
117 Luis Almanzar 2.50 6.00
118 Chance Adams 6.00 15.00
119 David Garcia 3.00 8.00
120 Ronald Guzman 3.00 8.00
121 Luis Alexander Basabe 4.00 10.00
122 Jesus Sanchez 20.00 50.00
123 Yasel Antuna 12.00 30.00
124 Estevan Florial 15.00 40.00
125 Luis Garcia 4.00 10.00
126 Jordan Holloway 2.50 6.00
127 Abraham Gutierrez UER 4.00 10.00
Abrahan Gutierrez
128 Yefry Ramirez 2.50 6.00
129 Dustin Fowler 3.00 8.00
131 Carlos Rincon 2.50 6.00
132 Nicky Lopez 3.00 8.00
133 Jelfry Marte 4.00 10.00
134 Luis V. Garcia 6.00 15.00
135 Ronny Mauricio 8.00 20.00
136 Julio Rodriguez 15.00 40.00
137 Larry Ernesto 2.50 6.00
138 Adrian Hernandez 2.50 6.00
139 Ynmanol Marinez 3.00 8.00
140 George Valera 5.00 12.00
141 Ronny Rojas 2.50 6.00
142 Carlos Aguiar 3.00 8.00
143 Luis Robert 100.00 250.00
144 Kyri Washington 6.00 15.00
145 Jose Miguel Fernandez 2.50 6.00
146 Bryan Mata 3.00 8.00
147 Daniel Flores 2.50 6.00
148 Oneil Cruz 4.00 10.00
149 Bryan Garcia 2.50 6.00
150 Jake Junis 4.00 10.00
151 Freddy Peralta 4.00 10.00
152 Michael Rucker 5.00 12.00
153 Seby Zavala 4.00 10.00
154 Zack Granite 8.00 20.00
155 Nelson Beltran 2.50 6.00
156 Junior Paniagua 4.00 10.00
157 Omar Florentino 2.50 6.00
158 Ricardo Balogh Aybar 2.50 6.00
159 Ayendi Ortiz 2.50 6.00
160 Noelvi Marte 5.00 12.00
161 Wilmin Candelario 4.00 10.00
162 Juan Jerez 3.00 8.00
163 Julio Heureaux 4.00 10.00
164 Ilvin Fernandez 2.50 6.00
165 Moises Ramirez 2.50 6.00
166 Frankely Hurtado 2.50 6.00
167 Orlando Chivilli 2.50 6.00
168 Marco Luciano 15.00 40.00
169 Jeferson Geraldo 2.50 6.00
170 Alberto Fabian 2.50 6.00
171 Henry Morales 2.50 6.00
172 Jeffrey Diaz 2.50 6.00
173 Estanli Castillo 4.00 10.00
175 Yeison Lemos 4.00 10.00
176 Jose Hernandez 2.50 6.00
177 Robert Puason 8.00 20.00
178 Jhon Diaz 4.00 10.00
179 Bayron Lora 25.00 60.00
180 Emmanuel Rodriguez 2.50 6.00
181 Franyel Baez 2.50 6.00
182 Algenis Vasquez 2.50 6.00
183 Junio Tilien 4.00 10.00
185 Isaac Paredes 12.00 30.00
186 Seuly Matias 4.00 10.00
187 Cole Brannen 4.00 10.00
188 Connor Wong 4.00 10.00
189 Gerson Moreno 2.50 6.00
190 Pedro Vasquez 2.50 6.00
191 Adrian Valerio 2.50 6.00
192 Brendan Murphy 2.50 6.00
193 Zach Kirtley 3.00 8.00
194 Lincoln Henzman 2.50 6.00
195 Dane Myers 4.00 10.00
196 Jonah Todd 4.00 10.00
197 Bryce Johnson 2.50 6.00
198 Nick Allen 3.00 8.00
199 Kevin Smith 2.50 6.00
200 Jake Thompson 2.50 6.00

2017 Elite Extra Edition Autographs Aspirations Blue

*ASP BLUE/50: .6X TO 1.5X BASIC
*ASP BLUE/25: .75X TO 2X BASIC
RANDOM INSERTS IN PACKS
PRINT RUNS B/WN 10-50 COPIES PER
NO PRICING ON QTY 10 OR LESS
EXCHANGE DEADLINE 6/6/2019
130 Joshua Palacios/50 25.00 60.00

2017 Elite Extra Edition Autographs Aspirations Purple

*ASP PRPLE/100: .5X TO 1.2X BASIC
*ASP PRPLE/50: .6X TO 1.5X BASIC
*ASP PRPLE/25: .75X TO 2X BASIC
RANDOM INSERTS IN PACKS
PRINT RUNS B/WN 25-100 COPIES PER
EXCHANGE DEADLINE 6/6/2019
130 Joshua Palacios/100 20.00 50.00

2017 Elite Extra Edition Autographs Emerald

*EMERALD: .75X TO 2X BASIC
RANDOM INSERTS IN PACKS
STATED PRINT RUN 25 SER.#'d SETS
EXCHANGE DEADLINE 6/6/2019
130 Joshua Palacios 30.00 80.00

2017 Elite Extra Edition Autographs Status Die Cut Emerald

*STAT.EMRLD.DC/25: .75X TO 2X BASIC
RANDOM INSERTS IN PACKS
PRINT RUNS B/WN 10-25 COPIES PER
NO PRICING ON QTY 10
EXCHANGE DEADLINE 6/6/2019
130 Joshua Palacios/25 30.00 80.00

2017 Elite Extra Edition Autographs Status Die Cut Red

*STAT.RED DC/75: .5X TO 1.2X BASIC
*STAT.RED DC/25-35: .75X TO 2X BASIC
RANDOM INSERTS IN PACKS
PRINT RUNS B/WN 25-75 COPIES PER
EXCHANGE DEADLINE 6/6/2019
130 Joshua Palacios/75 20.00 50.00

2017 Elite Extra Edition Dual Materials

RANDOM INSERTS IN PACKS
PRINT RUNS B/WN 299-399 COPIES PER
1 Tyler O'Neill/349 2.00 5.00
2 Kevin Maitan/349 3.00 8.00
3 Ronald Acuna/299 10.00 25.00
4 Gleyber Torres/299 4.00 10.00
5 Michael Kopech/299 5.00 12.00
6 Luis Robert/299 6.00 15.00
7 Willy Adames/399 2.00 5.00
8 Victor Robles/399 4.00 10.00
10 Dominic Smith/299 1.50 4.00
11 Lucius Fox/299 1.50 4.00
12 Dustin Peterson/399
13 Austin Voth/399 1.50 4.00
14 Zack Collins/299 2.00 5.00
15 Luis Almanzar/399 1.50 4.00
16 Jomar Reyes/299 1.50 4.00
18 Nick Senzel/299 3.00 8.00
19 David Garcia/399 2.00 5.00
20 Dillon Peters/299 1.50 4.00

2017 Elite Extra Edition Dual Materials Holo Gold

*HOLO GOLD: .5X TO 1.2X BASIC
RANDOM INSERTS IN PACKS
STATED PRINT RUN 99 SER.#'d SETS
9 Nick Gordon 2.00 5.00

2017 Elite Extra Edition Dual Materials Holo Silver

*HOLO SILVER: .5X TO 1.2X BASIC
RANDOM INSERTS IN PACKS
STATED PRINT RUN 49 SER.#'d SETS
9 Nick Gordon 2.00 5.00

2017 Elite Extra Edition Dual Materials Purple

*PURPLE: .6X TO 1.5X BASIC
RANDOM INSERTS IN PACKS
PRINT RUNS B/WN 10-25 COPIES PER
NO PRICING ON QTY 10
9 Nick Gordon/25 2.50 6.00

2017 Elite Extra Edition Dual Materials Silver

*SILVER: .4X TO 1X BASIC
RANDOM INSERTS IN PACKS
STATED PRINT RUN 149 SER.#'d SETS
9 Nick Gordon 1.50 4.00

2017 Elite Extra Edition Future Threads Dual Silhouettes

RANDOM INSERTS IN PACKS
PRINT RUNS B/WN 299-399 COPIES PER
7 Peters/Garcia/295 1.50 4.00
9 Locastro/Alvarez/299 2.50 6.00
11 Sedlock/Scott/139 1.50 4.00
13 O'Neil/Robles/299 3.00 8.00
17 Bader/Oviedo/150 3.00 8.00
18 Garcia/Guzman/162 2.00 5.00
20 Adams/Torres/221 6.00 15.00

2017 Elite Extra Edition Future Threads Dual Silhouettes Holo Gold

*HOLO GOLD/65-99: .5X TO 1.2X BASIC
*HOLO GOLD/25: .6X TO 1.5X BASIC
RANDOM INSERTS IN PACKS
PRINT RUNS B/WN 25-49 COPIES PER
12 Maitan/Acuna/97 8.00 20.00
14 Fox/Adames/94 2.50 6.00
15 Honeywell/Kopech/99 6.00 15.00

2017 Elite Extra Edition Future Threads Dual Silhouettes Holo Silver

*HOLO SILVER/35-49: .5X TO 1.2X BASIC
*HOLO SILVER/25: .6X TO 1.5X BASIC
RANDOM INSERTS IN PACKS
PRINT RUNS B/WN 23-49 COPIES PER
10 Robert/Kopech/49 8.00 20.00
16 Smith/Gordon/23 2.50 6.00

2017 Elite Extra Edition Future Threads Dual Silhouettes Purple

*PURPLE/25: .6X TO 1.5X BASIC
RANDOM INSERTS IN PACKS
PRINT RUNS B/WN 5-25 COPIES PER
NO PRICING ON QTY 10 OR LESS

2017 Elite Extra Edition Future Threads Dual Silhouettes Silver

*SILVER: .4X TO 1X BASIC
RANDOM INSERTS IN PACKS
PRINT RUNS B/WN 99-149 COPIES PER
1 Hernandez/Aguiar/125 2.00 5.00
2 Marte/Garcia/149 3.00 8.00
3 Mauricio/Rojas/99 4.00 10.00
4 Fernandez/Marinez/149 2.00 5.00
5 Rodriguez/Ernesto/113 6.00 15.00
6 Tavarez/Mars/132 3.00 8.00
8 Rodgers/Torres/149 5.00 12.00
19 Gillaspie/Hoskins/136 4.00 10.00

2017 Elite Extra Edition Future Threads Silhouette Autographs

RANDOM INSERTS IN PACKS
PRINT RUNS B/WN 59-99 COPIES PER
EXCHANGE DEADLINE 6/6/2019
1 Tyler O'Neill/99 4.00 10.00
3 Victor Robles/99 10.00 25.00
5 Willy Adames/99 4.00 10.00
6 Brent Honeywell/99 4.00 10.00
7 Luis Robert/99 100.00 250.00
10 Dominic Smith/99 3.00 8.00
11 Danny Mars/99 8.00 20.00
12 Ronny Rojas/99 3.00 8.00
13 Jomar Reyes/99 3.00 8.00
14 Ronald Acuna/99 60.00 150.00
16 Carlos Aguiar/99 4.00 10.00
17 Abraham Gutierrez/99 UER 5.00 12.00
Abrahan Gutierrez
18 Aneury Tavarez/99 3.00 8.00
19 Casey Gillaspie/99 3.00 8.00
20 Cody Sedlock/59 3.00 8.00
21 Dillon Peters/99 3.00 8.00
23 Tomas Nido/99 3.00 8.00
24 Luis V. Garcia/99 5.00 12.00
25 Luis Ortiz/99 3.00 8.00
27 A.J. Minter/99 4.00 10.00
28 Dustin Fowler/99 5.00 12.00
29 Austin Voth/99 3.00 8.00
30 Chance Adams/99 8.00 20.00
31 David Garcia/99 4.00 10.00
32 Dustin Peterson/99 3.00 8.00
33 Harrison Bader/99 5.00 12.00
34 Jarlin Garcia/99 3.00 8.00
35 Johan Oviedo/99 4.00 10.00
36 Jose Miguel Fernandez/99 3.00 8.00
37 Luis Almanzar/99 3.00 8.00
38 Rhys Hoskins/99 15.00 40.00
39 Ronald Guzman/99 4.00 10.00
40 Tanner Scott/99 3.00 8.00
41 Yasel Antuna/99 5.00 12.00
42 Jelfry Marte/99 5.00 12.00
43 Luis Garcia/99 5.00 12.00
44 Ronny Mauricio/99 6.00 15.00
45 Julio Rodriguez/99 25.00 60.00
46 Larry Ernesto/99 3.00 8.00
47 Adrian Hernandez/99 3.00 8.00
48 Ynmanol Marinez/99 4.00 10.00
51 Jaime Barria/99 4.00 10.00
52 Marco Luciano/99 12.00 30.00
53 Bayron Lora/99 25.00 60.00
54 Merandy Gonzalez/99 5.00 12.00
55 Nick Dini/99 3.00 8.00
56 Nathan Lukes/99 3.00 8.00
58 Tim Locastro/99 4.00 10.00

2017 Elite Extra Edition Future Threads Silhouette Autographs Red

*RED: .5X TO 1.2X BASIC
RANDOM INSERTS IN PACKS
PRINT RUNS B/WN 25-35 COPIES PER
EXCHANGE DEADLINE 6/6/2019
2 Gleyber Torres/35 60.00 150.00
4 Michael Kopech/35 12.00 30.00
9 Nick Gordon/35 4.00 10.00
15 Lucius Fox/35 4.00 10.00
22 Zack Collins/35 5.00 12.00
26 Yadier Alvarez/35 6.00 15.00
49 Brendan Rodgers/35 8.00 20.00
50 Ian Anderson/35 20.00 50.00

2017 Elite Extra Edition Future Threads Silhouette Autographs Silver

*SILVER: .5X TO 1.2X BASIC
RANDOM INSERTS IN PACKS
STATED PRINT RUN 49 SER.#'d SETS
EXCHANGE DEADLINE 6/6/2019
2 Gleyber Torres 60.00 150.00
4 Michael Kopech 12.00 30.00
8 Kevin Maitan 6.00 15.00
9 Nick Gordon 4.00 10.00
15 Lucius Fox 4.00 10.00
22 Zack Collins 5.00 12.00
26 Yadier Alvarez 6.00 15.00
49 Brendan Rodgers 8.00 20.00
50 Ian Anderson 20.00 50.00

2017 Elite Extra Edition Future Threads Silhouettes

RANDOM INSERTS IN PACKS
PRINT RUNS B/WN 99-399 COPIES PER
1 Tyler O'Neill/299 2.00 5.00
3 Victor Robles/399 4.00 10.00
4 Michael Kopech/149 5.00 12.00
5 Willy Adames/399 2.00 5.00
6 Brent Honeywell/399 2.00 5.00
8 Kevin Maitan/299 3.00 8.00
10 Dominic Smith/99 2.00 5.00
11 Danny Mars/149 3.00 8.00
12 Jomar Reyes/299 1.50 4.00
15 Zack Collins/299 2.00 5.00
17 Rhys Hoskins/125 5.00 12.00
18 Robert Puason/299 3.00 8.00
19 Yasel Antuna/318 3.00 8.00
20 Tom De Blok/399 1.50 4.00

2017 Elite Extra Edition Future Threads Silhouettes Holo Gold

*HOLO GOLD: .5X TO 1.2X p/r 125-399
*HOLO GOLD: .4X TO 1X p/r 99
RANDOM INSERTS IN PACKS
PRINT RUNS B/WN 49-99 COPIES PER
2 Gleyber Torres/99 5.00 12.00
7 Luis Robert/99 10.00 25.00
13 Ronald Acuna/99 8.00 20.00
14 Lucius Fox/49 2.00 5.00
16 Nick Senzel/49 4.00 10.00

2017 Elite Extra Edition Future Threads Silhouettes Holo Silver

*HOLO SILVER: .5X TO 1.2X p/r 125-399
*HOLO SILVER: .4X TO 1X p/r 99
RANDOM INSERTS IN PACKS
PRINT RUNS B/WN 25-49 COPIES PER
2 Gleyber Torres/49 5.00 12.00
7 Luis Robert/49 10.00 25.00
13 Ronald Acuna/49 8.00 20.00
14 Lucius Fox/25 2.50 6.00
16 Nick Senzel/25 5.00 12.00

2017 Elite Extra Edition Future Threads Silhouettes Purple

*PURPLE/25: .6X TO 1.5X p/r 125-399
RANDOM INSERTS IN PACKS
PRINT RUNS B/WN 10-25 COPIES PER
NO PRICING ON QTY 15 OR LESS

2017 Elite Extra Edition Future Threads Silhouettes Silver

*SILVER/149: .4X TO 1X BASIC
*SILVER/99: .5X TO 1.2X BASIC
RANDOM INSERTS IN PACKS
STATED PRINT RUN 149 SER.#'d SETS
2 Gleyber Torres/149 4.00 10.00
7 Luis Robert/149 10.00 25.00
13 Ronald Acuna/149 6.00 15.00
16 Nick Senzel/99 4.00 10.00

2017 Elite Extra Edition Jumbo Materials

RANDOM INSERTS IN PACKS
PRINT RUNS B/WN 99-299 COPIES PER
1 Tyler O'Neill/299 2.00 5.00
2 Gleyber Torres/175 4.00 10.00
3 Victor Robles/299 4.00 10.00
5 Willy Adames/299 2.00 5.00
6 Brent Honeywell/299 2.00 5.00
7 Luis Robert/149 10.00 25.00
8 Kevin Maitan/299 3.00 8.00
9 Nick Gordon/199 1.50 4.00
10 Dominic Smith/99 2.00 5.00
11 Danny Mars/199 3.00 8.00
13 J.P. Crawford/299 1.50 4.00
15 Richard Urena/299 2.50 6.00

2017 Elite Extra Edition Jumbo Materials Purple

*PURPLE/20-25: .6X TO 1.5X p/r 149-299
RANDOM INSERTS IN PACKS
PRINT RUNS B/WN 10-25 COPIES PER
NO PRICING ON QTY 15 OR LESS
4 Michael Kopech/20 8.00 20.00
12 Jomar Reyes/25 2.50 6.00
16 Ronald Acuna/25 12.00 30.00

2017 Elite Extra Edition Jumbo Materials Red

*RED/49: .5X TO 1.2X p/r 149-299
*RED/25: .6X TO 1.5X p/r 149-299
*RED/25: .5X TO 1.2X p/r 99
RANDOM INSERTS IN PACKS
PRINT RUNS B/WN 25-49 COPIES PER
4 Michael Kopech/49 6.00 15.00
12 Jomar Reyes/49 2.00 5.00
14 Nick Senzel/25 5.00 12.00
16 Ronald Acuna/49 10.00 25.00

2017 Elite Extra Edition Jumbo Materials Silver

*SILVER: .5X TO 1.2X p/r 149-299
*SILVER: .4X TO 1X p/r 99
RANDOM INSERTS IN PACKS
PRINT RUNS B/WN 49-99 COPIES PER
4 Michael Kopech/99 6.00 15.00
14 Nick Senzel/75 4.00 10.00
16 Ronald Acuna/99 10.00 25.00

2017 Elite Extra Edition Quad Materials

RANDOM INSERTS IN PACKS
PRINT RUNS B/WN 199-399 COPIES PER
1 Tyler O'Neill/299 2.00 5.00
2 Kevin Maitan/199 3.00 8.00
4 Gleyber Torres/299 4.00 10.00
5 Michael Kopech/299 5.00 12.00
6 Luis Robert/299 5.00 12.00
7 Willy Adames/399 2.00 5.00
8 Victor Robles/399 4.00 10.00
12 Casey Gillaspie/399 1.50 4.00
13 Cody Sedlock/299 1.50 4.00
14 Johan Oviedo/299 2.00 5.00
15 Harrison Bader/299 3.00 8.00
16 Ronald Guzman/299 2.00 5.00
17 Tanner Scott/399 1.50 4.00
19 Dustin Fowler/299 3.00 8.00
20 Jose Miguel Fernandez/399 1.50 4.00

2017 Elite Extra Edition Quad Materials Holo Gold

*HOLO GOLD: .5X TO 1.2X BASIC
RANDOM INSERTS IN PACKS
PRINT RUNS B/WN 49-99 COPIES PER
3 Ronald Acuna/49 8.00 20.00
10 Dominic Smith/49 2.00 5.00
11 Lucius Fox/49 2.00 5.00
18 Nick Senzel/99 4.00 10.00

2017 Elite Extra Edition Quad Materials Holo Silver

*HOLO SILVER/49: .5X TO 1.2X BASIC
*HOLO SILVER/25: .6X TO 1.5X BASIC
RANDOM INSERTS IN PACKS
PRINT RUNS B/WN 25-49 COPIES PER
3 Ronald Acuna/25 10.00 25.00
9 Nick Gordon/49 2.00 5.00
10 Dominic Smith/25 2.50 6.00
11 Lucius Fox/25 2.50 6.00
18 Nick Senzel/49 4.00 10.00

2017 Elite Extra Edition Quad Materials Purple

*PURPLE: .6X TO 1.5X BASIC
RANDOM INSERTS IN PACKS
PRINT RUNS B/WN 10-25 COPIES PER
NO PRICING ON QTY 10
9 Nick Gordon/25 2.50 6.00

2017 Elite Extra Edition Quad Materials Silver

*SILVER/149: .4X TO 1X BASIC
*SILVER/99: .5X TO 1.2X BASIC
RANDOM INSERTS IN PACKS
PRINT RUNS B/WN 99-149 COPIES PER
11 Lucius Fox/99 2.00 5.00
18 Nick Senzel/125 3.00 8.00

2017 Elite Extra Edition Triple Materials

RANDOM INSERTS IN PACKS
PRINT RUNS B/WN 99-399 COPIES PER
1 Tyler O'Neill/299 2.00 5.00
2 Kevin Maitan/299 3.00 8.00
4 Gleyber Torres/299 4.00 10.00
5 Michael Kopech/299 5.00 12.00
6 Luis Robert/299 5.00 12.00
7 Willy Adames/399 2.00 5.00
8 Victor Robles/399 4.00 10.00
10 Dominic Smith/99 2.00 5.00
11 Lucius Fox/299 1.50 4.00
12 A.J. Minter/399 2.00 5.00
13 Jarlin Garcia/349 1.50 4.00
14 Luis Ortiz/399 1.50 4.00
15 Rhys Hoskins/299 5.00 12.00
16 Yadier Alvarez/399 2.50 6.00
17 Yasel Antuna/325 3.00 8.00
18 Nick Senzel/299 3.00 8.00
19 Danny Mars/299 3.00 8.00
20 Chance Adams/299 3.00 8.00

2017 Elite Extra Edition Triple Materials Holo Gold

*HOLO GOLD: .5X TO 1.2X p/r 299-399
*HOLO GOLD: .4X TO 1X p/r 99
RANDOM INSERTS IN PACKS
PRINT RUNS B/WN 49-99 COPIES PER
3 Ronald Acuna/49 8.00 20.00
9 Nick Gordon/99 2.00 5.00

2017 Elite Extra Edition Triple Materials Holo Silver

*HOLO SILVER/49: .5X TO 1.2X p/r 299-399
*HOLO SILVER/25: .5X TO 1.2X p/r 99
RANDOM INSERTS IN PACKS
PRINT RUNS B/WN 25-49 COPIES PER
3 Ronald Acuna/25 10.00 25.00
9 Nick Gordon/49 2.00 5.00

2017 Elite Extra Edition Triple Materials Purple

*PURPLE/25: .6X TO 1.5X p/r 299-399
RANDOM INSERTS IN PACKS
PRINT RUNS B/WN 25-49 COPIES PER
NO PRICING ON QTY 10
9 Nick Gordon/25 2.50 6.00

2017 Elite Extra Edition Triple Materials Silver

*SILVER/125-149: .4X TO 1X p/r 299-399
RANDOM INSERTS IN PACKS
PRINT RUNS B/WN 99-149 COPIES PER
3 Ronald Acuna/99 8.00 20.00
9 Nick Gordon/125 1.50 4.00

2017 Elite Extra Edition USA Collegiate Silhouette Autographs

RANDOM INSERTS IN PACKS
STATED PRINT RUN 99 SER.#'d SETS
EXCHANGE DEADLINE 6/6/2019
*SILVER/49: .5X TO 1.2X BASIC
*PURPLE/25: .6X TO 1.5X BASIC
1 Seth Beer 10.00 25.00
2 Steven Gingery 6.00 15.00
3 Nick Madrigal 8.00 20.00
4 Jake McCarthy 5.00 12.00
5 Nick Meyer 5.00 12.00
6 Casey Mize 12.00 30.00
7 Konnor Pilkington 5.00 12.00
8 Dallas Woolfolk 4.00 10.00
9 Tyler Frank 5.00 12.00
10 Cadyn Grenier 5.00 12.00
11 Gianluca Dalatri 4.00 10.00
12 Braden Shewmake 12.00 30.00
13 Bryce Tucker 4.00 10.00
14 Andrew Vaughn 10.00 25.00
15 Steele Walker 5.00 12.00
16 Jeremy Eierman 6.00 15.00
17 Patrick Raby 6.00 15.00
18 Grant Koch 4.00 10.00
19 Travis Swaggerty 6.00 15.00
20 Tim Cate 5.00 12.00
21 Nick Sprengel 4.00 10.00
22 Johnny Aiello 5.00 12.00
23 Ryley Gilliam 4.00 10.00
24 Jon Olsen 8.00 20.00
25 Tyler Holton 4.00 10.00
26 Sean Wymer 4.00 10.00

2018 Elite Extra Edition

STATED PRINT RUN 999 SER.#'d SETS
1 Casey Mize 2.00 5.00
2 Joey Bart 2.50 6.00
3 Alec Bohm 1.50 4.00
4 Nick Madrigal 1.00 2.50
5 Jonathan India 1.50 4.00
6 Jarred Kelenic 2.50 6.00
7 Ryan Weathers .30 .75
8 Franklin Perez .30 .75
9 Travis Swaggerty .75 2.00
10 Grayson Rodriguez .50 1.25
11 Jordan Groshans .75 2.00
12 Connor Scott .30 .75
13 Logan Gilbert .40 1.00
14 Cole Winn .40 1.00
15 Matthew Liberatore .30 .75
16 Jordyn Adams 1.00 2.50
17 Brady Singer 1.25 3.00
18 Nolan Gorman 1.50 4.00
19 Trevor Larnach 1.50 4.00
20 Brice Turang .75 2.00
21 Ryan Rolison .50 1.25
22 Anthony Seigler .60 1.50
23 Nico Hoerner 1.25 3.00
24 Diego Cartaya 1.50 4.00
25 Triston Casas 3.00 8.00
26 Mason Denaburg .30 .75
27 Seth Beer 1.00 2.50
28 Bo Naylor .30 .75
29 Taylor Hearn .25 .60
30 Shane McClanahan .40 1.00
31 Nick Schnell .25 .60
32 Jackson Kowar .75 2.00
33 Daniel Lynch .30 .75
34 Ethan Hankins .30 .75
35 Richard Palacios .25 .60
36 Cadyn Grenier .30 .75
37 Xavier Edwards .75 2.00
38 Jake McCarthy .40 1.00
39 Kris Bubic .40 1.00
40 Lenny Torres Jr. .30 .75
41 Grant Lavigne 1.25 3.00
42 Griffin Roberts .25 .60
43 Parker Meadows .50 1.25
44 Sean Hjelle .30 .75
45 Steele Walker .30 .75
46 Lyon Richardson .40 1.00
47 Simeon Woods-Richardson .30 .75
48 Greyson Jenista .40 1.00
49 Jameson Hannah .40 1.00
50 Braxton Ashcraft .30 .75
51 Griffin Conine .50 1.25
52 Osiris Johnson .30 .75
53 Josh Stowers .60 1.50
54 Owen White .40 1.00
55 Tyler Frank .25 .60
56 Jeremiah Jackson .40 1.00
57 Jonathan Bowlan .25 .60
58 Ryan Jeffers .50 1.25
59 Joe Gray .40 1.00
60 Josh Breaux .30 .75
61 Brennen Davis 2.00 5.00
62 Alek Thomas 1.00 2.50
63 Nick Decker .50 1.25
64 Tim Cate .40 1.00
65 Jayson Schroeder .25 .60
66 Nick Sandlin .25 .60
67 Wander Franco 5.00 12.00
68 Will Banfield .30 .75
69 Jeremy Eierman .25 .60
70 Tanner Dodson .30 .75
71 Josiah Gray .40 1.00
72 Micah Bello .40 1.00
73 Grant Little .25 .60
74 Luken Baker .40 1.00
75 Mitchell Kilkenny .25 .60
76 Cole Roederer .75 2.00
77 Blaine Knight .30 .75
78 Kody Clemens .40 1.00
79 Jake Wong .25 .60
80 Konnor Pilkington .30 .75
81 Tristan Pompey .25 .60
82 Carlos Cortes .30 .75
83 Owen Miller .25 .60
84 Cal Raleigh .25 .60
85 Connor Kaiser .25 .60
86 Kevin Sanchez .25 .60
87 Adbert Alzolay .30 .75
88 Akil Baddoo 5.00 12.00
89 Jose Siri .25 .60
90 Nick Margevicius .25 .60
91 Jeisson Rosario .40 1.00
92 Sandro Fabian .25 .60
93 Aramis Ademan .30 .75
94 Miguel Aparicio .25 .60
95 James Nelson .25 .60
96 Bo Bichette 1.00 2.50
97 D.J. Wilson .25 .60
98 Samir Duenez .25 .60
99 Sixto Sanchez .75 2.00
100 Samad Taylor .25 .60
101 Lency Delgado .50 1.25
102 Austin Listi .25 .60
103 Yunior Severino .30 .75
104 Jayce Easley .25 .60
105 Ford Proctor .30 .75
106 Kyle Isbel .60 1.50
107 Mateo Gil .25 .60
108 Terrin Vavra .50 1.25
109 Jimmy Herron .25 .60
110 Reid Schaller .25 .60
111 Victor Victor Mesa 1.00 2.50
112 Orelvis Martinez .50 1.25
113 Noelvi Marte 1.25 3.00
114 Marco Luciano 1.25 3.00
115 Jose de la Cruz .40 1.00
116 Junior Sanquintin .30 .75
117 Kevin Alcantara .40 1.00
118 Francisco Morales .30 .75
119 Omar Florentino .30 .75
120 Sergio Campana .25 .60
121 Landon Leach .30 .75
122 Jose Suarez .25 .60
123 Luis Escobar .25 .60
124 Yordan Alvarez 5.00 12.00
125 Keibert Ruiz 1.25 3.00
126 DJ Peters .60 1.50
127 Francisco Alvarez .50 1.25
128 Julio Pablo Martinez .40 1.00
129 Jose Garcia 1.00 2.50
130 Alexander Canario .25 .60
131 Freudis Nova .50 1.25
132 Daniel Brito .25 .60
133 Genesis Cabrera .40 1.00
134 Erling Moreno .50 1.25
135 Jose Mujica .25 .60
136 Wadye Ynfante .25 .60
137 Dean Kremer .30 .75
138 Jonathan Ornelas .60 1.50
139 Tony Gonsolin 1.00 2.50
140 Ryder Green .30 .75
141 Jackson Goddard .25 .60
142 Durbin Feltman .40 1.00
143 Jeremy Pena .50 1.25
144 John Rooney .30 .75
145 Everson Pereira .40 1.00
146 Jhoan Urena .25 .60
147 Sandy Baez .25 .60
148 Henry Henry .25 .60
149 Taylor Widener .25 .60
150 Trent Deveaux .30 .75
151 Elehuris Montero .50 1.25
152 Miguel Amaya .40 1.00
153 Richard Gallardo .50 1.25
154 Gabriel Rodriguez .50 1.25
155 Luis Oviedo .25 .60
156 Brewer Hicklen .40 1.00
157 Peter Solomon .25 .60
158 Chad Spanberger .40 1.00
159 Andres Munoz .40 1.00
160 Misael Urbina .75 2.00
161 Luis Medina .40 1.00
162 Osiel Rodriguez .40 1.00
163 Roberto Ramos .40 1.00
164 Tristan Beck .30 .75
165 DaShawn Keirsey Jr. .40 1.00
166 Eric Cole .30 .75
167 Steven Jennings .25 .60
168 Jose Cosma .25 .60
169 Luis De La Cruz .25 .60
170 Gregory Duran .25 .60
171 Luis Encarnacion .25 .60
172 Jose Pena .25 .60
173 Lizandro Rodriguez .30 .75
174 Leonel Sanchez .25 .60
175 Luis Gil .30 .75
176 Yonaldi Soto .25 .60
177 Ariel Almonte .25 .60
178 Jonathan Bautista .25 .60
179 Saul Bautista .25 .60
180 Luis Castillo .25 .60
181 Armando Cruz .25 .60
182 Danny De Andrande .25 .60
183 Manny De La Rosa .25 .60
184 Yamal Encarnacion .25 .60
185 Willy Fana .25 .60
186 Yamal Flores .25 .60
187 Jayson Jimenez .25 .60
188 Fraidel Liriano .25 .60
189 Robelin Lopez .25 .60
190 Yendel Mateo .25 .60
191 Keiderson Pavon .25 .60
192 Victor Quezada .25 .60
193 Luis Ravelo .25 .60
194 Elias Reynoso .25 .60
195 Cristian Santana .60 1.50
196 Dervy Ventura .25 .60
197 Kaito Yuki .40 1.00
198 Jake Irvin .25 .60
199 Blaze Alexander .50 1.25
200 Zach Haake .25 .60

2018 Elite Extra Edition Aspirations Blue

*ASP.BLUE: .75X TO 2X BASIC
RANDOM INSERTS IN PACKS
STATED PRINT RUN 75 SER.#'d SETS

2018 Elite Extra Edition Aspirations Orange

*ASP ORANGE: .6X TO 1.5X BASIC
RANDOM INSERTS IN PACKS
STATED PRINT RUN 100 SER.#'d SETS

2018 Elite Extra Edition Aspirations Red

*ASP RED: .6X TO 1.5X BASIC
RANDOM INSERTS IN PACKS
STATED PRINT RUN 150 SER.#'d SETS

2018 Elite Extra Edition Aspirations Tie Dye

*ASP.TIE DYE: 1.2X TO 3X BASIC
RANDOM INSERTS IN PACKS
STATED PRINT RUN 25 SER.#'d SETS

2018 Elite Extra Edition Pink

*PINK: .6X TO 1.5X BASIC
RANDOM INSERTS IN PACKS

2018 Elite Extra Edition Status Die Cut Emerald

*STAT.EMRLD.DC: 1X TO 2.5X BASIC
RANDOM INSERTS IN PACKS
STATED PRINT RUN 49 SER.#'d SETS

2018 Elite Extra Edition Status Die Cut Red

*STAT.RED DC: .75X TO 2X BASIC
RANDOM INSERTS IN PACKS
STATED PRINT RUN 99 SER.#'d SETS

2018 Elite Extra Edition Autographs

RANDOM INSERTS IN PACKS
EXCHANGE DEADLINE 6/12/2020
*BLUE/50: .5X TO 1.2X BASIC
*BLUE/25: .6X TO 1.5X BASIC
*PURPLE/50-100: .5X TO 1.2X BASIC
*PURPLE/25: .6X TO 1.5X BASIC
*EMERALD/25: .6X TO 1.5X BASIC
*DC EMERALD/25: .6X TO 1.5X BASIC
*DC RED/50-75: .5X TO 1.2X BASIC
*DC RED/25: .6X TO 1.5X BASIC
1 Casey Mize 12.00 30.00
2 Joey Bart 40.00 100.00
3 Alec Bohm 12.00 30.00
4 Nick Madrigal 8.00 20.00
5 Jonathan India 20.00 50.00
6 Jarred Kelenic 20.00 50.00
8 Franklin Perez 3.00 8.00
9 Travis Swaggerty 5.00 12.00
10 Grayson Rodriguez 5.00 12.00
11 Jordan Groshans 12.00 30.00
13 Logan Gilbert 4.00 10.00
14 Cole Winn 4.00 10.00
15 Matthew Liberatore 3.00 8.00
16 Jordyn Adams 8.00 20.00
17 Brady Singer 8.00 20.00
18 Nolan Gorman 12.00 30.00
19 Trevor Larnach 6.00 15.00
20 Brice Turang 4.00 10.00
21 Ryan Rolison 3.00 8.00
22 Anthony Seigler 4.00 10.00
23 Nico Hoerner 10.00 25.00
24 Diego Cartaya 30.00 80.00
25 Triston Casas 6.00 15.00
26 Mason Denaburg 3.00 8.00
27 Seth Beer 6.00 15.00
28 Bo Naylor 3.00 8.00
29 Taylor Hearn 2.50 6.00
30 Shane McClanahan 4.00 10.00
31 Nick Schnell 2.50 6.00
32 Jackson Kowar 5.00 12.00
33 Daniel Lynch 3.00 8.00
34 Ethan Hankins 3.00 8.00
35 Richard Palacios 2.50 6.00
36 Cadyn Grenier 3.00 8.00
37 Xavier Edwards 8.00 20.00
38 Jake McCarthy 4.00 10.00
39 Kris Bubic 4.00 10.00
40 Lenny Torres Jr. 3.00 8.00
41 Grant Lavigne 5.00 12.00
42 Griffin Roberts 2.50 6.00
43 Parker Meadows 4.00 10.00
44 Sean Hjelle 3.00 8.00
45 Steele Walker 3.00 8.00
46 Lyon Richardson 4.00 10.00
47 Simeon Woods-Richardson 3.00 8.00
48 Greyson Jenista 3.00 8.00
49 Jameson Hannah 2.50 6.00
50 Braxton Ashcraft 3.00 8.00
51 Griffin Conine 3.00 8.00
52 Osiris Johnson 3.00 8.00
53 Josh Stowers 4.00 10.00
54 Owen White 4.00 10.00
55 Tyler Frank 2.50 6.00
56 Jeremiah Jackson 4.00 10.00
57 Jonathan Bowlan 2.50 6.00
58 Ryan Jeffers 3.00 8.00
59 Joe Gray 4.00 10.00
60 Josh Breaux 3.00 8.00
61 Brennen Davis 15.00 40.00
62 Alek Thomas 4.00 10.00
63 Nick Decker 3.00 8.00
64 Tim Cate 4.00 10.00
65 Jayson Schroeder 2.50 6.00
66 Nick Sandlin 2.50 6.00
67 Wander Franco 40.00 100.00
68 Will Banfield 3.00 8.00
69 Jeremy Eierman 3.00 8.00
70 Tanner Dodson 3.00 8.00
71 Josiah Gray 4.00 10.00
72 Micah Bello 4.00 10.00
74 Luken Baker 4.00 10.00
75 Mitchell Kilkenny 2.50 6.00
76 Cole Roederer 4.00 10.00
77 Blaine Knight 3.00 8.00
78 Kody Clemens 5.00 12.00
79 Jake Wong 2.50 6.00
80 Konnor Pilkington 3.00 8.00
81 Tristan Pompey 2.50 6.00
82 Carlos Cortes 3.00 8.00
83 Owen Miller 2.50 6.00
84 Cal Raleigh 2.50 6.00
85 Connor Kaiser 2.50 6.00
86 Kevin Sanchez 2.50 6.00
87 Adbert Alzolay 3.00 8.00
88 Akil Baddoo 10.00 25.00
90 Nick Margevicius 2.50 6.00
91 Jeisson Rosario 4.00 10.00
92 Sandro Fabian 4.00 10.00
93 Aramis Ademan 2.50 6.00
94 Miguel Aparicio 2.50 6.00
95 James Nelson 2.50 6.00
96 Bo Bichette 20.00 50.00
97 D.J. Wilson 2.50 6.00
98 Samir Duenez 2.50 6.00
99 Sixto Sanchez 10.00 25.00
100 Samad Taylor 2.50 6.00
101 Lency Delgado 2.50 6.00
102 Austin Listi 2.50 6.00
103 Yunior Severino 3.00 8.00
104 Jayce Easley 2.50 6.00
105 Ford Proctor 3.00 8.00
107 Mateo Gil 2.50 6.00
108 Terrin Vavra 3.00 8.00
109 Jimmy Herron 2.50 6.00
110 Reid Schaller 2.50 6.00
111 Victor Victor Mesa 30.00 80.00
112 Orelvis Martinez 6.00 15.00
113 Noelvi Marte 5.00 12.00
114 Marco Luciano 10.00 25.00
115 Jose de la Cruz 4.00 10.00
116 Junior Sanquintin 3.00 8.00
117 Kevin Alcantara 6.00 15.00
118 Francisco Morales 3.00 8.00
119 Omar Florentino 3.00 8.00
120 Sergio Campana 2.50 6.00
121 Landon Leach 3.00 8.00
122 Jose Suarez 2.50 6.00
123 Luis Escobar 2.50 6.00
124 Yordan Alvarez 25.00 60.00
125 Keibert Ruiz 6.00 15.00
126 DJ Peters 4.00 10.00
128 Julio Pablo Martinez 10.00 25.00
129 Jose Garcia 10.00 25.00
130 Alexander Canario 2.50 6.00
131 Freudis Nova 8.00 20.00
132 Daniel Brito 2.50 6.00
133 Genesis Cabrera 4.00 10.00
134 Erling Moreno 10.00 25.00
135 Jose Mujica 2.50 6.00
136 Wadye Ynfante 2.50 6.00
137 Dean Kremer 3.00 8.00
138 Jonathan Ornelas 5.00 12.00
139 Tony Gonsolin 10.00 25.00
140 Ryder Green 2.50 6.00
141 Jackson Goddard 2.50 6.00
142 Durbin Feltman 4.00 10.00
143 Jeremy Pena 5.00 12.00
144 John Rooney 3.00 8.00
145 Everson Pereira 6.00 15.00
146 Jhoan Urena 2.50 6.00
147 Sandy Baez 2.50 6.00
148 Henry Henry 2.50 6.00
149 Taylor Widener 2.50 6.00
150 Trent Deveaux 3.00 8.00
151 Elehuris Montero 5.00 12.00
152 Miguel Amaya 12.00 30.00
153 Richard Gallardo 5.00 12.00
155 Luis Oviedo 2.50 6.00
156 Brewer Hicklen 4.00 10.00
157 Peter Solomon 2.50 6.00
158 Chad Spanberger 4.00 10.00
159 Andres Munoz 5.00 12.00
161 Luis Medina 4.00 10.00
162 Osiel Rodriguez 6.00 15.00
163 Roberto Ramos 4.00 10.00
164 Tristan Beck 3.00 8.00
165 DaShawn Keirsey Jr. 4.00 10.00
166 Eric Cole 5.00 12.00
167 Steven Jennings 2.50 6.00
168 Jose Cosma 2.50 6.00
169 Luis De La Cruz 2.50 6.00
170 Gregory Duran 2.50 6.00
171 Luis Encarnacion 2.50 6.00
172 Jose Pena 2.50 6.00
173 Lizandro Rodriguez 3.00 8.00
174 Leonel Sanchez 2.50 6.00
175 Luis Gil 3.00 8.00
176 Yonaldi Soto 2.50 6.00
177 Ariel Almonte 2.50 6.00
178 Jonathan Bautista 2.50 6.00
179 Saul Bautista 2.50 6.00
180 Luis Castillo 2.50 6.00
181 Armando Cruz 2.50 6.00
182 Danny De Andrande 2.50 6.00
183 Manny De La Rosa 2.50 6.00
184 Yamal Encarnacion 2.50 6.00
185 Willy Fana 2.50 6.00
187 Jayson Jimenez 2.50 6.00
188 Fraidel Liriano 2.50 6.00
189 Robelin Lopez 2.50 6.00
190 Yendel Mateo 2.50 6.00
191 Keiderson Pavon 2.50 6.00
192 Victor Quezada 2.50 6.00
193 Luis Ravelo 2.50 6.00
194 Elias Reynoso 2.50 6.00
195 Cristian Santana 5.00 12.00
196 Dervy Ventura 2.50 6.00
197 Kaito Yuki 4.00 10.00
198 Jake Irvin 2.50 6.00
199 Blaze Alexander 5.00 12.00
200 Zach Haake 2.50 6.00

2018 Elite Extra Edition Contenders College Tickets

RANDOM INSERTS IN PACKS
*HOLO: .5X TO 1.2X BASIC
1 Casey Mize 2.00 5.00
2 Blaine Knight .30 .75
3 Tristan Pompey .25 .60
4 Cal Raleigh .25 .60
5 Ford Proctor .30 .75
6 Konnor Pilkington .30 .75
7 Kyle Isbel .60 1.50
8 Terrin Vavra .50 1.25
9 Jimmy Herron .25 .60
10 Jackson Goddard .25 .60
11 Durbin Feltman .40 1.00
12 Reid Schaller .25 .60
13 Jake Irvin .25 .60
14 Kody Clemens .40 1.00
15 Nick Madrigal 1.00 2.50
16 Logan Gilbert .40 1.00
17 Brady Singer 1.25 3.00
18 Trevor Larnach 1.50 4.00
19 Nico Hoerner 1.25 3.00
20 Seth Beer 1.00 2.50
21 Cadyn Grenier .30 .75
22 Jake McCarthy .40 1.00
23 Luken Baker .40 1.00
24 Travis Swaggerty .75 2.00
25 Jeremy Eierman .25 .60
26 Ryan Rolison .50 1.25
27 Tim Cate .40 1.00
28 Steele Walker .30 .75
29 Tyler Frank .25 .60
30 Shane McClanahan .40 1.00
31 Casey Mize 2.00 5.00
32 Nick Madrigal 1.00 2.50
33 Seth Beer 1.00 2.50
34 Griffin Roberts .25 .60

2018 Elite Extra Edition Contenders College Tickets Signatures

RANDOM INSERTS IN PACKS
PRINT RUNS B/WN 5-99 COPIES PER
NO PRICING ON QTY 5
EXCHANGE DEADLINE 6/12/2020
*HOLO/25: .5X TO 1.2X p/r 40-99
1 Casey Mize/40 15.00 40.00
2 Blaine Knight/99 4.00 10.00
3 Tristan Pompey/99 3.00 8.00
4 Cal Raleigh/99 3.00 8.00
5 Ford Proctor/99 4.00 10.00
6 Konnor Pilkington/99 4.00 10.00
8 Terrin Vavra/99 4.00 10.00
9 Jimmy Herron/99 3.00 8.00
10 Jackson Goddard/99 3.00 8.00
11 Durbin Feltman/99 5.00 12.00
12 Reid Schaller/99 3.00 8.00
13 Jake Irvin/99 3.00 8.00
15 Nick Madrigal/25 12.00 30.00
20 Seth Beer/99 6.00 15.00
21 Cadyn Grenier/99 4.00 10.00
22 Jake McCarthy/99 5.00 12.00
23 Luken Baker/99 5.00 12.00
24 Travis Swaggerty/25 8.00 20.00
25 Jeremy Eierman/99 4.00 10.00
26 Ryan Rolison/99 4.00 10.00
27 Tim Cate/99 5.00 12.00
28 Steele Walker/99 4.00 10.00
29 Tyler Frank/99 3.00 8.00
31 Casey Mize/43 15.00 40.00
32 Nick Madrigal/25 12.00 30.00
33 Seth Beer/99 6.00 15.00
34 Griffin Roberts/99 3.00 8.00

2018 Elite Extra Edition Contenders USA Collegiate Tickets

RANDOM INSERTS IN PACKS
*HOLO: .5X TO 1.2X BASIC
1 Daniel Cabrera 1.00 2.50
2 Will Wilson .40 1.00
3 Braden Shewmake .75 2.00
4 John Doxakis .25 .60
5 Bryson Stott .75 2.00
6 Andrew Vaughn .75 2.00
7 Mason Feole .40 1.00
8 Shea Langeliers .50 1.25
9 Spencer Torkelson 1.50 4.00
10 Josh Jung .75 2.00
11 Bryant Packard .50 1.25
12 Jake Agnos .40 1.00
13 Andre Pallante .25 .60
14 Dominic Fletcher .30 .75
15 Adley Rutschman 1.50 4.00
16 Graeme Stinson .30 .75
17 Matt Cronin .25 .60
18 Max Meyer 1.00 2.50
19 Kenyon Yovan .30 .75
20 Tanner Burns .40 1.00
21 Drew Parrish .25 .60
22 Kyle Brnovich .25 .60
23 Zack Hess .30 .75
24 Zach Watson .25 .60
25 Zack Thompson .50 1.25
26 Parker Caracci .25 .60

2018 Elite Extra Edition Contenders USA Collegiate Tickets Signatures

RANDOM INSERTS IN PACKS
STATED PRINT RUN 99 SER.#'d SETS
EXCHANGE DEADLINE 6/12/2020
*RED/100: .4X TO 1X BASIC
*HOLO/25: .5X TO 1.2X BASIC
1 Daniel Cabrera 12.00 30.00
2 Will Wilson 5.00 12.00
3 Braden Shewmake 10.00 25.00
4 John Doxakis 3.00 8.00
5 Bryson Stott 10.00 25.00
6 Andrew Vaughn 12.00 30.00
7 Mason Feole 5.00 12.00
8 Shea Langeliers 12.00 30.00
9 Spencer Torkelson 50.00 120.00
10 Josh Jung 10.00 25.00
11 Bryant Packard 12.00 30.00
12 Jake Agnos 10.00 25.00
13 Andre Pallante 3.00 8.00
14 Dominic Fletcher 8.00 20.00
15 Adley Rutschman 100.00 250.00
16 Graeme Stinson 4.00 10.00
17 Matt Cronin 3.00 8.00
18 Max Meyer 12.00 30.00
19 Kenyon Yovan 4.00 10.00
20 Tanner Burns 5.00 12.00
21 Drew Parrish 3.00 8.00
22 Kyle Brnovich 3.00 8.00
23 Zack Hess 4.00 10.00
24 Zach Watson 3.00 8.00
25 Zack Thompson 6.00 15.00
26 Parker Caracci 3.00 8.00

2018 Elite Extra Edition Dual Materials

RANDOM INSERTS IN PACKS
PRINT RUNS B/WN 175-399 COPIES PER
1 Genesis Cabrera/199 2.50 6.00
2 Nick Senzel/199 4.00 10.00
3 Brendan Rodgers/399 2.00 5.00
4 Franklin Perez/199 2.00 5.00
5 Forrest Whitley/199 2.50 6.00
6 Kevin Maitan/399 2.00 5.00
7 Braxton Garrett/199 1.50 4.00
8 Corey Ray/199 2.00 5.00
10 Chris Shaw/199 1.50 4.00
11 Tyler Kolek/199 2.00 5.00
12 Bobby Bradley/199 2.00 5.00
13 Diego Infante/199 1.50 4.00
16 Luis Almanzar/199 1.50 4.00
17 Bo Bichette/399 3.00 8.00
18 Akil Baddoo/175 4.00 10.00
19 Cal Quantrill/399 1.50 4.00
20 Taylor Trammell/399 2.50 6.00

2018 Elite Extra Edition Dual Materials Gold

*GOLD: .4X TO 1X BASIC
RANDOM INSERTS IN PACKS
STATED PRINT RUN 99 SER.#'d SETS
14 Joshua Palacios 6.00 15.00
15 Kyle Lewis 3.00 8.00

2018 Elite Extra Edition Dual Materials Purple

*PURPLE: .6X TO 1.5X BASIC
RANDOM INSERTS IN PACKS
STATED PRINT RUN 25 SER.#'d SETS
14 Joshua Palacios 10.00 25.00
15 Kyle Lewis 5.00 12.00

2018 Elite Extra Edition Dual Materials Red

*RED: .4X TO 1X BASIC
RANDOM INSERTS IN PACKS
STATED PRINT RUN 49 SER.#'d SETS
14 Joshua Palacios 6.00 15.00
15 Kyle Lewis 3.00 8.00

2018 Elite Extra Edition Dual Materials Silver

*SILVER: .4X TO 1X BASIC
RANDOM INSERTS IN PACKS
STATED PRINT RUN 149 SER.#'d SETS
14 Joshua Palacios 6.00 15.00
15 Kyle Lewis 3.00 8.00

2018 Elite Extra Edition Dual Silhouettes

RANDOM INSERTS IN PACKS
STATED PRINT RUN 199 SER.#'d SETS
*GOLD/99: .4X TO 1X BASIC
*RED/49: .4X TO 1X BASIC
*SILVER/149: .4X TO 1X BASIC
*PURPLE/25: .6X TO 1.5X BASIC
1 Michael Chavis 2.50 6.00
2 Luis Robert 5.00 12.00
3 Eloy Jimenez 5.00 12.00
4 Yordan Alvarez 6.00 15.00
5 Brandon Marsh 2.50 6.00
6 DJ Peters 4.00 10.00
7 Nick Gordon 1.50 4.00
8 Justus Sheffield 2.00 5.00
9 Estevan Florial 6.00 15.00
10 Mitch Keller 2.00 5.00

2018 Elite Extra Edition Future Threads Silhouette Autographs

RANDOM INSERTS IN PACKS
PRINT RUNS B/WN 144-299 COPIES PER
EXCHANGE DEADLINE 6/12/2020
FTSAFT Fernando Tatis Jr./299 100.00 250.00
12 Jahmai Jones/268 3.00 8.00
14 Josh Staumont/299 3.00 8.00
15 Lucas Erceg/299 3.00 8.00
16 Estanli Castillo/299 3.00 8.00
18 Francisco Morales/299 4.00 10.00
22 Nathan Lukes/253 3.00 8.00
23 JoJo Romero/299 4.00 10.00
24 Yanio Perez/299 3.00 8.00
26 Kevin Sanchez/299 3.00 8.00
28 Akil Baddoo/199 20.00 50.00
29 Jose Siri/199 3.00 8.00
30 Nick Margevicius/286 3.00 8.00
31 Luis Escobar/299 3.00 8.00
32 Miguel Aparicio/144 3.00 8.00
34 James Nelson/144 3.00 8.00
35 DJ Peters/199 4.00 10.00
36 Samir Duenez/299 3.00 8.00
40 Daniel Brito/299 3.00 8.00
44 D.J. Wilson/299 3.00 8.00

2018 Elite Extra Edition Future Threads Silhouette Autographs Gold

*GOLD: .4X TO 1X BASIC
RANDOM INSERTS IN PACKS
STATED PRINT RUN 99 SER.#'d SETS
EXCHANGE DEADLINE 6/12/2020
4 Carter Kieboom 10.00 25.00
8 Estevan Florial 20.00 50.00
9 Kevin Newman 5.00 12.00
10 Leody Taveras 5.00 12.00
11 Jose de la Cruz 5.00 12.00
33 Yordan Alvarez 50.00 120.00

2018 Elite Extra Edition Future Threads Silhouette Autographs Purple

*PURPLE/25: .5X TO 1.2X BASIC
RANDOM INSERTS IN PACKS
PRINT RUNS B/WN 15-25 COPIES PER
NO PRICING ON QTY 15
EXCHANGE DEADLINE 6/12/2020
2 Ke'Bryan Hayes/25 15.00 40.00
5 Orelvis Martinez/25 15.00 40.00
6 Noelvi Marte/25 8.00 20.00
7 Marco Luciano/25 30.00 80.00
8 Estevan Florial/25 30.00 80.00
9 Kevin Newman/25 8.00 20.00
10 Leody Taveras/25 8.00 20.00
11 Jose de la Cruz/25 8.00 20.00
13 Austin Riley/25 50.00 120.00
17 Kevin Alcantara/25 20.00 50.00
19 Chris Shaw/25 5.00 12.00
20 Mitch Keller/25 10.00 25.00
21 Taylor Trammell/25 15.00 40.00
25 Peter Alonso/25 75.00 200.00
27 Omar Florentino/25 8.00 20.00
37 Julio Pablo Martinez/25 25.00 60.00
38 Jose Garcia/25 20.00 50.00
39 Freudis Nova/25 10.00 25.00
41 Sergio Campana/25 5.00 12.00
42 Wander Franco/25 125.00 300.00
43 Bo Bichette/25 20.00 50.00

2018 Elite Extra Edition Future Threads Silhouette Autographs Red

*RED/49: .4X TO 1X BASIC
*RED/25: .5X TO 1.2X BASIC
RANDOM INSERTS IN PACKS
PRINT RUNS B/WN 25-49 COPIES PER
EXCHANGE DEADLINE 6/12/2020
3 Shane Baz/25 6.00 15.00
6 Noelvi Marte/49 6.00 15.00
7 Marco Luciano/49 25.00 60.00
8 Estevan Florial/49 25.00 60.00
9 Kevin Newman/49 6.00 15.00
10 Leody Taveras/49 6.00 15.00
11 Jose de la Cruz/49 6.00 15.00
17 Kevin Alcantara/49 15.00 40.00
19 Chris Shaw/49 4.00 10.00
20 Mitch Keller/49 8.00 20.00
21 Taylor Trammell/49 12.00 30.00
25 Peter Alonso/49 25.00 60.00
27 Omar Florentino/49 6.00 15.00
38 Jose Garcia/49 15.00 40.00
39 Freudis Nova/49 8.00 20.00
41 Sergio Campana/49 4.00 10.00
42 Wander Franco/49 100.00 250.00

2018 Elite Extra Edition OptiChrome

RANDOM INSERTS IN PACKS
*HOLO: .5X TO 1.2X BASIC
1 Casey Mize 2.00 5.00
2 Joey Bart 2.50 6.00
3 Alec Bohm 1.50 4.00
4 Nick Madrigal 1.00 2.50
5 Jonathan India 1.50 4.00
6 Jarred Kelenic 2.50 6.00
7 Ryan Weathers .30 .75
8 Franklin Perez .30 .75
9 Travis Swaggerty .75 2.00
10 Grayson Rodriguez .50 1.25
12 Connor Scott .30 .75
15 Matthew Liberatore .30 .75
20 Brice Turang .75 2.00
22 Anthony Seigler .60 1.50
24 Diego Cartaya 1.50 4.00
25 Triston Casas 3.00 8.00
26 Mason Denaburg .30 .75
34 Ethan Hankins .30 .75
36 Cadyn Grenier .30 .75
38 Jake McCarthy .40 1.00
56 Jeremiah Jackson .40 1.00
62 Alek Thomas 1.00 2.50
68 Will Banfield .30 .75
78 Kody Clemens .40 1.00
86 Kevin Sanchez .25 .60
87 Adbert Alzolay .30 .75
88 Akil Baddoo 5.00 12.00
89 Jose Siri .25 .60
90 Nick Margevicius .25 .60
91 Jeisson Rosario .40 1.00
92 Sandro Fabian .25 .60
94 Miguel Aparicio .25 .60
95 James Nelson .25 .60
96 Bo Bichette 1.00 2.50
99 Sixto Sanchez .75 2.00
100 Samad Taylor .25 .60
107 Mateo Gil .25 .60
111 Victor Victor Mesa 1.00 2.50
112 Casey Mize 2.00 5.00
113 Bo Bichette 1.00 2.50

2018 Elite Extra Edition OptiChrome Signatures

RANDOM INSERTS IN PACKS
PRINT RUNS B/WN 5-99 COPIES PER
NO PRICING ON QTY 10 OR LESS
EXCHANGE DEADLINE 6/12/2020
*HOLO/25: .5X TO 1.2X p/r 49-99
4 Nick Madrigal/99 10.00 25.00
5 Jonathan India/25 30.00 80.00
6 Jarred Kelenic/99 30.00 80.00
7 Ryan Weathers/99 4.00 10.00
15 Matthew Liberatore/99 4.00 10.00
20 Brice Turang/99 5.00 12.00
22 Anthony Seigler/99 5.00 12.00
25 Triston Casas/99 5.00 12.00
26 Mason Denaburg/99 4.00 10.00
34 Ethan Hankins/99 4.00 10.00
36 Cadyn Grenier/99 4.00 10.00
38 Jake McCarthy/52 5.00 12.00
56 Jeremiah Jackson/79 5.00 12.00
62 Alek Thomas/99 6.00 15.00
68 Will Banfield/99 4.00 10.00
78 Kody Clemens/99 6.00 15.00
86 Kevin Sanchez/49 3.00 8.00
91 Jeisson Rosario/49 5.00 12.00
92 Sandro Fabian/49 5.00 12.00
100 Samad Taylor/76 3.00 8.00
107 Mateo Gil/99 3.00 8.00

2018 Elite Extra Edition Prospect Materials

RANDOM INSERTS IN PACKS
STATED PRINT RUN 199 SER.#'d SETS
1 Austin Riley 3.00 8.00
2 Jose Siri 1.50 4.00
3 Taylor Trammell 2.50 6.00
4 Josh Staumont 1.50 4.00
5 Samir Duenez 1.50 4.00
6 Jahmai Jones 1.50 4.00
7 Brayan Hernandez 1.50 4.00
8 James Nelson 1.50 4.00
9 Lucas Erceg 1.50 4.00
11 Kevin Newman 2.50 6.00
13 Cal Quantrill 1.50 4.00
14 Bryan Reynolds 2.50 6.00
15 Heliot Ramos 2.50 6.00
16 Jesus Sanchez 2.50 6.00
18 Miguel Aparicio 1.50 4.00
19 Carter Kieboom 2.50 6.00
20 Fernando Tatis Jr. 15.00 40.00

2018 Elite Extra Edition Prospect Materials Gold

*GOLD: .4X TO 1X BASIC
RANDOM INSERTS IN PACKS
STATED PRINT RUN 99 SER.#'d SETS
10 JoJo Romero 2.00 5.00
12 Luis Escobar 1.50 4.00
17 Wei-Chieh Huang 2.50 6.00

2018 Elite Extra Edition Prospect Materials Purple

*PURPLE: .6X TO 1.5X BASIC
RANDOM INSERTS IN PACKS
STATED PRINT RUN 25 SER.#'d SETS
10 JoJo Romero 3.00 8.00
12 Luis Escobar 2.50 6.00
17 Wei-Chieh Huang 4.00 10.00

2018 Elite Extra Edition Prospect Materials Red

*RED: .4X TO 1X BASIC
RANDOM INSERTS IN PACKS
STATED PRINT RUN 49 SER.#'d SETS
10 JoJo Romero 2.00 5.00
17 Wei-Chieh Huang 2.50 6.00

2018 Elite Extra Edition Prospect Materials Silver

*SILVER: .4X TO 1X BASIC
RANDOM INSERTS IN PACKS
STATED PRINT RUN 149 SER.#'d SETS
10 JoJo Romero 2.00 5.00
12 Luis Escobar 1.50 4.00

2018 Elite Extra Edition Quad Materials

RANDOM INSERTS IN PACKS
PRINT RUNS B/WN 199-399 COPIES PER
1 Jon Duplantier/399 1.50 4.00
2 D.J. Wilson/399 1.50 4.00
3 Akil Baddoo/199 4.00 10.00
4 Luis Ortiz/249 1.50 4.00
5 Brayan Hernandez/399 1.50 4.00
6 DJ Peters/399 4.00 10.00
8 Ke'Bryan Hayes/399 8.00 20.00

9 Shane Baz/399 2.00 5.00
11 Cal Quantrill/399 1.50 4.00
13 Aneury Tavarez/399 1.50 4.00
14 Max Pentecost/399 1.50 4.00
16 Thairo Estrada/299 2.50 6.00
18 Yusniel Diaz/399 5.00 12.00
19 Erling Moreno/399 3.00 8.00
20 Freudis Nova/399 5.00 12.00

2018 Elite Extra Edition Quad Materials Gold
*GOLD: .4X TO 1X BASIC
RANDOM INSERTS IN PACKS
PRINT RUNS B/WN 75-99 COPIES PER
7 Jose Siri/99 1.50 4.00
15 Nathan Lukes/99 1.50 4.00
17 Yanio Perez/99 1.50 4.00

2018 Elite Extra Edition Quad Materials Purple
*PURPLE: .6X TO 1.5X BASIC
RANDOM INSERTS IN PACKS
STATED PRINT RUN 25 SER.#'d SETS
7 Jose Siri 2.50 6.00
10 Jomar Reyes 10.00 25.00
12 Julio Pablo Martinez 8.00 20.00
15 Nathan Lukes 2.50 6.00
17 Yanio Perez 2.50 6.00

2018 Elite Extra Edition Quad Materials Red
*RED: .4X TO 1X BASIC
RANDOM INSERTS IN PACKS
STATED PRINT RUN 49 SER.#'d SETS
15 Nathan Lukes 1.50 4.00
17 Yanio Perez 1.50 4.00

2018 Elite Extra Edition Quad Materials Silver
*SILVER: .4X TO 1X BASIC
RANDOM INSERTS IN PACKS
PRINT RUNS B/WN 99-149 COPIES PER
7 Jose Siri/125 1.50 4.00
15 Nathan Lukes/149 1.50 4.00
17 Yanio Perez/149 1.50 4.00

2018 Elite Extra Edition Triple Materials
RANDOM INSERTS IN PACKS
STATED PRINT RUN 399 SER.#'d SETS
1 Wander Franco 6.00 15.00
2 Justus Sheffield 2.00 5.00
3 Franklin Perez 2.00 5.00
5 James Nelson 1.50 4.00
7 Austin Riley 3.00 8.00
8 Chris Shaw 1.50 4.00
9 Heliot Ramos 2.50 6.00
10 Jahmai Jones 1.50 4.00
11 Miguel Aparicio 1.50 4.00
13 JoJo Romero 2.00 5.00
14 Jesus Sanchez 2.50 6.00
15 Carter Kieboom 2.50 6.00
16 Sean Murphy 2.50 6.00
17 Josh Staumont 1.50 4.00
18 Lucas Erceg 1.50 4.00
20 Luis Escobar 1.50 4.00

2018 Elite Extra Edition Triple Materials Gold
*GOLD: .4X TO 1X BASIC
RANDOM INSERTS IN PACKS
STATED PRINT RUN 99 SER.#'d SETS
4 Yordan Alvarez 3.00 8.00
6 Brandon Marsh 2.50 6.00
12 Kevin Newman 2.50 6.00
19 Nick Margevicius 1.50 4.00

2018 Elite Extra Edition Triple Materials Purple
*PURPLE: .6X TO 1.5X BASIC
RANDOM INSERTS IN PACKS
STATED PRINT RUN 25 SER.#'d SETS
4 Yordan Alvarez 5.00 12.00
6 Brandon Marsh 4.00 10.00
12 Kevin Newman 4.00 10.00
19 Nick Margevicius 2.50 6.00

2018 Elite Extra Edition Triple Materials Red
*RED: .4X TO 1X BASIC
RANDOM INSERTS IN PACKS
STATED PRINT RUN 49 SER.#'d SETS
4 Yordan Alvarez 3.00 8.00
6 Brandon Marsh 2.50 6.00
12 Kevin Newman 2.50 6.00
19 Nick Margevicius 1.50 4.00

2018 Elite Extra Edition Triple Materials Silver
*SILVER: .4X TO 1X BASIC
RANDOM INSERTS IN PACKS
STATED PRINT RUN 149 SER.#'d SETS
4 Yordan Alvarez 3.00 8.00
6 Brandon Marsh 2.50 6.00
12 Kevin Newman 2.50 6.00
19 Nick Margevicius 1.50 4.00

2018 Elite Extra Edition USA Baseball 15U Signatures
RANDOM INSERTS IN PACKS
STATED PRINT RUN 99 SER.#'d SETS
EXCHANGE DEADLINE 6/12/2020
*RED/100: .4X TO 1X BASIC
*BLUE/25: .5X TO 1.2X BASIC
1 Ryan Spikes 3.00 8.00
2 Davis Diaz 3.00 8.00
4 Tyree Reed 3.00 8.00
5 Rheego McIntosh 3.00 8.00
6 Karson Bowen 8.00 20.00
7 Justin Colon 4.00 10.00
8 Gage Ziehl 3.00 8.00
9 Cale Lansville 3.00 8.00
10 Ryan Clifford 6.00 15.00
11 Samuel Dutton 3.00 8.00
12 Joseph Brown 3.00 8.00
13 Cody Schrier 3.00 8.00
14 Charlie Saum 3.00 8.00
15 Luke Leto 10.00 25.00
16 Andrew Painter 4.00 10.00
17 Brady House 4.00 10.00
18 Josh Hartle 4.00 10.00
19 Christian Little 3.00 8.00
20 Thomas DiLandri 4.00 10.00

2018 Elite Extra Edition USA Baseball 18U Signatures
RANDOM INSERTS IN PACKS
STATED PRINT RUN 99 SER.#'d SETS
EXCHANGE DEADLINE 6/12/2020
*RED/100: .4X TO 1X BASIC
*BLUE/25: .5X TO 1.2X BASIC
1 CJ Abrams 12.00 30.00
6 Tyler Callihan 4.00 10.00
7 Corbin Carroll 8.00 20.00
9 Riley Cornelio 3.00 8.00
10 Pete Crow-Armstrong 6.00 15.00
13 Sammy Faltine 4.00 10.00
15 Riley Greene 12.00 30.00
17 Ryan Hawks 4.00 10.00
23 Jared Kelley 3.00 8.00
24 Jack Leiter 4.00 10.00
25 Brennan Malone 5.00 12.00
26 Jacob Meador 3.00 8.00
33 Max Rajcic 3.00 8.00
36 Avery Short 4.00 10.00
39 Anthony Volpe 12.00 30.00
42 Bobby Witt Jr. 50.00 120.00
45 Dylan Crews 8.00 20.00
46 Yohandy Morales 4.00 10.00
48 Drew Romo 8.00 20.00
49 Timmy Manning 5.00 12.00

2018 Elite Extra Edition USA Collegiate Silhouette Autographs
RANDOM INSERTS IN PACKS
STATED PRINT RUN 99 SER.#'d SETS
EXCHANGE DEADLINE 6/12/2020
*GOLD/49: .5X TO 1.2X BASIC
*RED/25: .6X TO 1.5X BASIC
1 Daniel Cabrera 12.00 30.00
2 Will Wilson 5.00 12.00
3 Braden Shewmake 10.00 25.00
4 John Doxakis 3.00 8.00
5 Bryson Stott 10.00 25.00
6 Andrew Vaughn 15.00 40.00
7 Mason Feole 5.00 12.00
8 Shea Langeliers 12.00 30.00
9 Spencer Torkelson 50.00 120.00
10 Josh Jung 10.00 25.00
11 Bryant Packard 8.00 20.00
12 Jake Agnos 8.00 20.00
13 Andre Pallante 3.00 8.00
14 Dominic Fletcher 4.00 10.00
15 Adley Rutschman 60.00 150.00
16 Graeme Stinson 4.00 10.00
17 Matt Cronin 3.00 8.00
18 Max Meyer 12.00 30.00
19 Kenyon Yovan 4.00 10.00
20 Tanner Burns 5.00 12.00
21 Drew Parrish 3.00 8.00
22 Kyle Brnovich 3.00 8.00
23 Zack Hess 4.00 10.00
24 Zach Watson 3.00 8.00
25 Zack Thompson 6.00 15.00
26 Parker Caracci 3.00 8.00

2018 Elite Extra Edition USA Materials
RANDOM INSERTS IN PACKS
PRINT RUNS B/WN 225-399 COPIES PER
29 Alex Faedo/399 2.50 6.00
30 A.J. Puk/225 2.50 6.00
32 Corey Ray/399 2.00 5.00

2018 Elite Extra Edition USA Materials Gold
*GOLD: .4X TO 1X BASIC
RANDOM INSERTS IN PACKS
STATED PRINT RUN 99 SER.#'d SETS
1 Casey Mize/99 6.00 15.00
3 Jarred Kelenic/99 5.00 12.00
4 Ryan Weathers/99 2.00 5.00
5 Travis Swaggerty/99 4.00 10.00
6 Connor Scott/99 2.00 5.00
7 Matthew Liberatore/99 2.00 5.00
8 Nolan Gorman/99 6.00 15.00
9 Brice Turang/99 3.00 8.00
10 Ryan Rolison/99 3.00 8.00
11 Anthony Seigler/99 3.00 8.00
12 Nico Hoerner/99 4.00 10.00
13 Triston Casas/99 4.00 10.00
15 Seth Beer/99 8.00 20.00
17 Ethan Hankins/99 2.00 5.00
18 Cadyn Grenier/99 2.00 5.00
19 Jake McCarthy/99 2.50 6.00
20 Steele Walker/99 2.00 5.00
21 Tyler Frank/99 1.50 4.00
22 Jeremiah Jackson/99 3.00 8.00
23 Alek Thomas/99 3.00 8.00
24 Tim Cate/99 2.50 6.00
25 Will Banfield/99 2.00 5.00
26 Jeremy Eierman/99 1.50 4.00
27 Luken Baker/99 3.00 8.00
28 Brendan McKay/99 2.50 6.00
31 Shane Baz/99 2.00 5.00
33 Royce Lewis/99 6.00 15.00
35 Bryan Reynolds/99 2.50 6.00
36 Forrest Whitley/99 2.50 6.00
37 Braxton Garrett/99 1.50 4.00
38 Keston Hiura/99 3.00 8.00
39 Zack Collins/99 2.00 5.00
40 Evan White/99 4.00 10.00

2018 Elite Extra Edition USA Materials Purple
*PURPLE: .6X TO 1.5X BASIC
RANDOM INSERTS IN PACKS
STATED PRINT RUN 25 SER.#'d SETS
1 Casey Mize/25 10.00 25.00
2 Nick Madrigal/25 8.00 20.00
3 Jarred Kelenic/25 8.00 20.00
4 Ryan Weathers/25 3.00 8.00
5 Travis Swaggerty/25 6.00 15.00
6 Connor Scott/25 3.00 8.00
7 Matthew Liberatore/25 3.00 8.00
8 Nolan Gorman/25 10.00 25.00
10 Ryan Rolison/25 5.00 12.00
11 Anthony Seigler/25 5.00 12.00
12 Nico Hoerner/25 6.00 15.00
13 Triston Casas/25 6.00 15.00
15 Seth Beer/25 12.00 30.00
17 Ethan Hankins/25 3.00 8.00
19 Jake McCarthy/25 4.00 10.00
20 Steele Walker/25 3.00 8.00
21 Tyler Frank/25 2.50 6.00
22 Jeremiah Jackson/25 5.00 12.00
24 Tim Cate/25 4.00 10.00
25 Will Banfield/25 3.00 8.00
26 Jeremy Eierman/25 2.50 6.00
28 Brendan McKay/25 4.00 10.00
31 Shane Baz/25 3.00 8.00
33 Royce Lewis/25 10.00 25.00
34 Kyle Wright/25 5.00 12.00
38 Keston Hiura/25 5.00 12.00
40 Evan White/25 6.00 15.00

2018 Elite Extra Edition USA Materials Red
*RED: .4X TO 1X BASIC
RANDOM INSERTS IN PACKS
STATED PRINT RUN 49 SER.#'d SETS
1 Casey Mize/49 6.00 15.00
2 Nick Madrigal/49 5.00 12.00
3 Jarred Kelenic/49 5.00 12.00
4 Ryan Weathers/49 2.00 5.00
5 Travis Swaggerty/49 4.00 10.00
6 Connor Scott/49 2.00 5.00
7 Matthew Liberatore/49 2.00 5.00
8 Nolan Gorman/49 6.00 15.00
9 Brice Turang/49 3.00 8.00
10 Ryan Rolison/49 3.00 8.00
11 Anthony Seigler/49 3.00 8.00
12 Nico Hoerner/49 4.00 10.00
13 Triston Casas/49 4.00 10.00
15 Seth Beer/49 8.00 20.00
17 Ethan Hankins/49 2.00 5.00
18 Cadyn Grenier/49 2.00 5.00
19 Jake McCarthy/49 2.50 6.00
20 Steele Walker/49 2.00 5.00
21 Tyler Frank/49 1.50 4.00
22 Jeremiah Jackson/49 3.00 8.00
23 Alek Thomas/49 3.00 8.00
24 Tim Cate/49 2.50 6.00
25 Will Banfield/49 2.00 5.00
26 Jeremy Eierman/49 1.50 4.00
27 Luken Baker/49 3.00 8.00
28 Brendan McKay/49 2.50 6.00
31 Shane Baz/49 2.00 5.00
33 Royce Lewis/49 6.00 15.00
34 Kyle Wright/49 2.50 6.00
35 Bryan Reynolds/49 2.50 6.00
36 Forrest Whitley/49 2.50 6.00
37 Braxton Garrett/49 1.50 4.00
38 Keston Hiura/49 3.00 8.00
39 Zack Collins/49 2.00 5.00
40 Evan White/49 4.00 10.00

2018 Elite Extra Edition USA Materials Silver
*SILVER: .4X TO 1X BASIC
RANDOM INSERTS IN PACKS
PRINT RUNS B/WN 99-149 COPIES PER
1 Casey Mize/149 6.00 15.00
3 Jarred Kelenic/149 5.00 12.00
5 Travis Swaggerty/149 4.00 10.00
27 Luken Baker/149 3.00 8.00
28 Brendan McKay/149 2.50 6.00
36 Forrest Whitley/149 2.50 6.00
37 Braxton Garrett/149 1.50 4.00

2019 Elite Extra Edition
STATED PRINT RUN 999 SER.#'d SETS
1 Adley Rutschman 4.00 10.00
2 Bobby Witt Jr. 5.00 12.00
3 Andrew Vaughn .75 2.00
4 JJ Bleday 1.25 3.00
5 Riley Greene 1.50 4.00
6 CJ Abrams 1.25 3.00
7 Nick Lodolo .50 1.25
8 Josh Jung .75 2.00
9 Shea Langeliers .50 1.25
10 Hunter Bishop .75 2.00
11 Alek Manoah .50 1.25
12 Brett Baty .50 1.25
13 Keoni Cavaco .60 1.50
14 Bryson Stott .75 2.00
15 Will Wilson .40 1.00
16 Corbin Carroll .40 1.00
17 Jackson Rutledge .50 1.25
18 Quinn Priester .30 .75
19 Zack Thompson .40 1.00
20 George Kirby .40 1.00
21 Braden Shewmake .75 2.00
22 Greg Jones .30 .75
23 Michael Toglia .40 1.00
24 Daniel Espino .30 .75
25 Kody Hoese .75 2.00
26 Blake Walston .40 1.00
27 Ryan Jensen .40 1.00
28 Ethan Small .30 .75
29 Logan Davidson .25 .60
30 Anthony Volpe 1.00 2.50
31 Michael Busch .75 2.00
32 Korey Lee .50 1.25
33 Brennan Malone .25 .60
34 Drey Jameson .25 .60
35 Kameron Misner .60 1.50
36 J.J. Goss .30 .75
37 Sammy Siani .30 .75
38 T.J. Sikkema .40 1.00
39 Matt Wallner .50 1.25
40 Seth Johnson .25 .60
41 Davis Wendzel .40 1.00
42 Gunnar Henderson .50 1.25
43 Cameron Cannon .50 1.25
44 Brady McConnell .40 1.00
45 Matthew Thompson .30 .75
46 Nasim Nunez .25 .60
47 Nick Quintana .50 1.25
48 Joshua Mears .50 1.25
49 Rece Hinds .30 .75
50 Ryan Garcia .25 .60
51 Logan Wyatt .40 1.00
52 Kendall Williams .40 1.00
53 Josh Wolf .30 .75
54 Matt Canterino .30 .75
55 Will Holland .40 1.00
56 Glenallen Hill Jr. .40 1.00
57 Matt Gorski .40 1.00
58 Trejyn Fletcher .40 1.00
59 Brandon Williamson .40 1.00
60 Beau Philip .40 1.00
61 John Doxakis .30 .75
62 Aaron Schunk .50 1.25
63 Yordys Valdes .50 1.25
64 Chase Strumpf .50 1.25
65 Antoine Kelly .50 1.25
66 Tyler Baum .30 .75
67 Josh Smith .50 1.25
68 Jacob Sanford .50 1.25
69 Matthew Lugo .40 1.00
70 Alec Marsh .30 .75
71 Kyle Stowers .40 1.00
72 Jared Triolo .40 1.00
73 Logan Driscoll .40 1.00
74 Tommy Henry .30 .75
75 Dominic Fletcher .25 .60
76 Isaiah Campbell .50 1.25
77 Karl Kauffmann .25 .60
78 Jimmy Lewis .25 .60
79 Zach Watson .40 1.00
80 Tyler Callihan .30 .75
81 Matthew Allan .50 1.25
82 Jack Kochanowicz .30 .75
83 Dasan Brown .60 1.50
84 Ryan Pepiot .25 .60
85 Tristin English .25 .60
86 Erik Miller .60 1.50
87 Matt Cronin .25 .60
88 Graeme Stinson .25 .60
89 Brandon Lewis .40 1.00
90 Kyle McCann .30 .75
91 Logan O'Hoppe .25 .60
92 D'Shawn Knowles .30 .75
93 Miguel Vargas 1.25 3.00
94 Sheryven Newton .40 1.00
95 Deivi Garcia 2.50 6.00
96 Brailyn Marquez .60 1.50
97 Brayan Rocchio 1.00 2.50
98 Shane Sasaki .25 .60
99 Randy Arozarena 8.00 20.00
100 Jarren Duran 1.50 4.00
114 Sherten Apostel .60 1.50
115 Noah Song .75 2.00
116 Andrew Dalquist .25 .60
117 Miguel Hiraldo .75 2.00
118 Jasseel De La Cruz .25 .60
119 Abraham Toro .40 1.00
120 Ismael Mena .40 1.00
121 Devin Mann 1.25 3.00
122 Austin Shenton .25 .60
123 Evan Fitterer .60 1.50
124 Antonio Cabello .50 1.25
125 Jhoan Duran .40 1.00
126 Kyren Paris .25 .60
127 Moises Gomez .40 1.00
128 Jose Devers .40 1.00
129 Carlos Rodriguez .25 .60
130 Jhon Torres .25 .60
131 Randy Florentino .25 .60
132 Ryne Nelson .30 .75
133 Livan Soto .30 .75
134 Gabriel Maciel .25 .60
135 Ronny Brito .25 .60
136 Yeison Coca .25 .60
137 Lenyn Sosa .25 .60
138 Oswaldo Cabrera .25 .60
139 Ivan Herrera .40 1.00
140 Michael Grove .25 .60
141 Aaron Hernandez .25 .60
142 CJ Alexander .75 2.00
143 Mason Englert .25 .60
144 Brenden Spillane .25 .60
145 Hogan Harris .25 .60
146 Tucker Davidson .25 .60
147 Michael Massey .30 .75
148 Jasson Dominguez 20.00 50.00
149 Spencer Steer .25 .60
150 Tyler Dyson .25 .60
151 Cody Bolton .40 1.00
152 Osleivis Basabe .25 .60
153 Eddy Diaz .25 .60
154 Michael Harris .25 .60
155 Ryan Zeferjahn .30 .75
156 Liover Peguero .40 1.00
157 Aaron Ashby .25 .60
158 Alvaro Seijas .30 .75
159 Canaan Smith .40 1.00
160 Jose Soriano
161 Sandy Gaston .25 .60
162 Gabriel Moreno .40 1.00
163 Gilberto Jimenez 1.50 4.00
164 Joe Ryan .40 1.00
165 Joey Cantillo .50 1.25
166 Jose Salas .40 1.00
167 David Parkinson .25 .60
168 Luis Matos .40 1.00
169 Luisangel Acuna .75 2.00
170 Tarik Skubal 1.25 3.00
171 Thad Ward .25 .60
172 Jose Rodriguez .25 .60
173 Drew Rom .25 .60
174 Israel Pineda .40 1.00
175 Wilderd Patino .25 .60
176 Trevor McDonald .25 .60
177 Avery Short .25 .60
178 Trey Harris .30 .75
179 Luis Toribio .25 .60
180 Nathan Patterson .25 .60
181 Leo Crawford .25 .60
182 Alejandro Kirk 1.00 2.50
183 Justin Dean .30 .75
184 Cristian Batista .25 .60
185 Jefferson De La Cruz .25 .60
186 Cristofer Espinola .25 .60
187 Wilton Lara .25 .60
188 Fidel Montero .40 1.00
189 Aneudis Mordan .25 .60
190 Joel Peguero .25 .60
191 John Peguero .25 .60
192 Bryan Pena .25 .60
193 Salvador Ramirez .25 .60
194 Rhaybel Roso .25 .60
195 Jay Vargas .25 .60
196 Wesley Zapata .25 .60
197 Josefrailin Alcantara .60 1.50
198 Rodolfo Caraballo .25 .60
199 Elizual Chalas .25 .60
200 Elian Cortorreal .25 .60
201 Randy De Jesus .25 .60
202 Aneudi Escanio .25 .60
203 Xaviel Guillen .30 .75
204 Yanki Jean .25 .60
205 Maximo Maria .25 .60
206 Juan Martinez .25 .60
207 Yasser Mercedes .25 .60
208 Jeral Perez .30 .75
209 Jhonny Severino .25 .60
210 Ivan Sosa .30 .75
211 Miguel Tamares .25 .60
212 Braylin Tavera .25 .60
213 Sebastian Castro .25 .60

2019 Elite Extra Edition Aspirations Blue
*ASP.BLUE: .75X TO 2X BASIC
RANDOM INSERTS IN PACKS
STATED PRINT RUN 75 SER.#'d SETS

2019 Elite Extra Edition Aspirations Orange
*ASP ORANGE: .6X TO 1.5X BASIC
RANDOM INSERTS IN PACKS
STATED PRINT RUN 100 SER.#'d SETS

2019 Elite Extra Edition Aspirations Purple
*ASP PURPLE: .5X TO 1.2X BASIC
RANDOM INSERTS IN PACKS
STATED PRINT RUN 250 SER.#'d SETS

2019 Elite Extra Edition Aspirations Red
*ASP RED: .6X TO 1.5X BASIC
RANDOM INSERTS IN PACKS
STATED PRINT RUN 150 SER.#'d SETS

2019 Elite Extra Edition Aspirations Tie Dye
*ASP.TIE DYE: 1.2X TO 3X BASIC
RANDOM INSERTS IN PACKS
STATED PRINT RUN 25 SER.#'d SETS

2019 Elite Extra Edition Pink
*PINK: .6X TO 1.5X BASIC
RANDOM INSERTS IN PACKS

2019 Elite Extra Edition Status Die Cut Blue
*STAT.BLUE DC: .75X TO 2X BASIC
RANDOM INSERTS IN PACKS
STATED PRINT RUN 75 SER.#'d SETS

2019 Elite Extra Edition Status Die Cut Emerald
*STAT.EMRLD.DC: 1X TO 2.5X BASIC
RANDOM INSERTS IN PACKS
STATED PRINT RUN 49 SER.#'d SETS

2019 Elite Extra Edition Status Die Cut Purple
*STAT.PURPLE DC: .6X TO 1.5X BASIC
RANDOM INSERTS IN PACKS
STATED PRINT RUN 125 SER.#'d SETS

2019 Elite Extra Edition Status Die Cut Red
*STAT.RED DC: .75X TO 2X BASIC
RANDOM INSERTS IN PACKS
STATED PRINT RUN 99 SER.#'d SETS

2019 Elite Extra Edition Status Die Cut Tie Dye
*STAT.TIE DYE DC: 1.2X TO 3X BASIC
RANDOM INSERTS IN PACKS
STATED PRINT RUN 25 SER.#'d SETS

2019 Elite Extra Edition Autographs
1 Adley Rutschman 30.00 80.00
2 Bobby Witt Jr. 20.00 50.00
3 Andrew Vaughn 10.00 25.00
4 JJ Bleday 12.00 30.00
5 Riley Greene 15.00 40.00
6 CJ Abrams 10.00 25.00
7 Nick Lodolo 5.00 12.00
8 Josh Jung 10.00 25.00
9 Shea Langeliers 5.00 12.00
10 Hunter Bishop 8.00 20.00
11 Alek Manoah 6.00 15.00
12 Brett Baty
13 Keoni Cavaco 6.00 15.00
14 Bryson Stott 8.00 20.00
15 Will Wilson 6.00 15.00
16 Corbin Carroll 6.00 15.00
17 Jackson Rutledge 5.00 12.00
18 Quinn Priester 3.00 8.00
19 Zack Thompson 5.00 12.00
20 George Kirby 4.00 10.00
21 Braden Shewmake 5.00 12.00
22 Greg Jones 5.00 12.00
23 Michael Toglia 4.00 10.00
24 Daniel Espino 3.00 8.00
25 Kody Hoese 5.00 12.00
26 Blake Walston 4.00 10.00
27 Ryan Jensen 4.00 10.00
28 Ethan Small 3.00 8.00
29 Logan Davidson 2.50 6.00
30 Anthony Volpe 6.00 15.00
32 Korey Lee 5.00 12.00
34 Drey Jameson 2.50 6.00
35 Kameron Misner 5.00 12.00
36 J.J. Goss 3.00 8.00
37 Sammy Siani 3.00 8.00
38 T.J. Sikkema 4.00 10.00
39 Matt Wallner 5.00 12.00
40 Seth Johnson 2.50 6.00
41 Davis Wendzel 4.00 10.00
42 Gunnar Henderson 5.00 12.00
43 Cameron Cannon 5.00 12.00
44 Brady McConnell 4.00 10.00
45 Matthew Thompson 3.00 8.00
46 Nasim Nunez 2.50 6.00
47 Nick Quintana 5.00 12.00
48 Joshua Mears 3.00 8.00
49 Rece Hinds 3.00 8.00
50 Ryan Garcia 2.50 6.00
51 Logan Wyatt 4.00 10.00
52 Kendall Williams 4.00 10.00
53 Josh Wolf 3.00 8.00
54 Matt Canterino 3.00 8.00
55 Will Holland 4.00 10.00
56 Glenallen Hill Jr. 4.00 10.00
57 Matt Gorski 4.00 10.00
58 Trejyn Fletcher 4.00 10.00
59 Brandon Williamson 4.00 10.00
60 Beau Philip 4.00 10.00
62 Aaron Schunk 5.00 12.00
63 Yordys Valdes 5.00 12.00
64 Chase Strumpf 5.00 12.00
65 Antoine Kelly 5.00 12.00
66 Tyler Baum 3.00 8.00
67 Josh Smith 5.00 12.00
68 Jacob Sanford 5.00 12.00
69 Matthew Lugo 4.00 10.00
70 Alec Marsh 3.00 8.00
71 Kyle Stowers 4.00 10.00
72 Jared Triolo 4.00 10.00
73 Logan Driscoll 4.00 10.00
74 Tommy Henry 3.00 8.00
75 Dominic Fletcher 2.50 6.00
76 Isaiah Campbell 5.00 12.00
77 Karl Kauffmann 2.50 6.00
78 Jimmy Lewis 2.50 6.00
79 Zach Watson 4.00 10.00
80 Tyler Callihan 3.00 8.00
81 Matthew Allan 5.00 12.00
82 Jack Kochanowicz 3.00 8.00
83 Dasan Brown 6.00 15.00
84 Ryan Pepiot 2.50 6.00
85 Tristin English 2.50 6.00
87 Matt Cronin 2.50 6.00
88 Graeme Stinson 2.50 6.00
89 Brandon Lewis 4.00 10.00
90 Kyle McCann 3.00 8.00
91 Logan O'Hoppe 2.50 6.00
93 Miguel Vargas 10.00 25.00
94 Sheryven Newton 4.00 10.00
95 Deivi Garcia 20.00 50.00
96 Brailyn Marquez 6.00 15.00
97 Brayan Rocchio 10.00 25.00
98 Shane Sasaki 2.50 6.00
99 Randy Arozarena 50.00 120.00
100 Jarren Duran 8.00 20.00
114 Sherten Apostel 6.00 15.00
115 Noah Song 8.00 20.00
116 Andrew Dalquist 2.50 6.00
117 Miguel Hiraldo 8.00 20.00
118 Jasseel De La Cruz 2.50 6.00
119 Abraham Toro 4.00 10.00
121 Devin Mann 4.00 10.00
124 Antonio Cabello 5.00 12.00
125 Jhoan Duran 4.00 10.00
126 Kyren Paris 2.50 6.00
127 Moises Gomez 4.00 10.00
129 Carlos Rodriguez 2.50 6.00
130 Jhon Torres 2.50 6.00
131 Randy Florentino 2.50 6.00
133 Livan Soto 3.00 8.00
134 Gabriel Maciel 2.50 6.00
136 Yeison Coca 2.50 6.00
137 Lenyn Sosa 2.50 6.00
138 Oswaldo Cabrera 2.50 6.00
139 Ivan Herrera 4.00 10.00
140 Michael Grove 2.50 6.00
141 Aaron Hernandez 2.50 6.00
142 CJ Alexander 8.00 20.00
143 Mason Englert 2.50 6.00
144 Brenden Spillane 2.50 6.00
145 Hogan Harris 2.50 6.00
146 Tucker Davidson 2.50 6.00
147 Michael Massey 3.00 8.00
148 Jasson Dominguez 100.00 250.00
149 Spencer Steer 2.50 6.00
150 Tyler Dyson 2.50 6.00
151 Cody Bolton 4.00 10.00
152 Osleivis Basabe 2.50 6.00
154 Michael Harris 2.50 6.00
155 Ryan Zeferjahn 3.00 8.00
156 Liover Peguero 8.00 20.00
157 Aaron Ashby 2.50 6.00
158 Alvaro Seijas 3.00 8.00
159 Canaan Smith 4.00 10.00
160 Jose Soriano 4.00 10.00
161 Sandy Gaston 2.50 6.00
162 Gabriel Moreno 8.00 20.00
163 Gilberto Jimenez 12.00 30.00
164 Joe Ryan 4.00 10.00
165 Joey Cantillo 5.00 12.00
166 Jose Salas 4.00 10.00
167 David Parkinson 2.50 6.00
168 Luis Matos 4.00 10.00
169 Luisangel Acuna 8.00 20.00
170 Tarik Skubal 12.00 30.00
171 Thad Ward 2.50 6.00
172 Jose Rodriguez 2.50 6.00
173 Drew Rom 2.50 6.00
174 Israel Pineda 4.00 10.00
175 Wilderd Patino 2.50 6.00
176 Trevor McDonald 2.50 6.00
177 Avery Short 2.50 6.00
178 Trey Harris 3.00 8.00
179 Luis Toribio 2.50 6.00
180 Nathan Patterson 2.50 6.00
181 Leo Crawford 2.50 6.00
182 Alejandro Kirk 6.00 15.00
183 Justin Dean 3.00 8.00
184 Cristian Batista 2.50 6.00
185 Jefferson De La Cruz 2.50 6.00
186 Cristofer Espinola 2.50 6.00
187 Wilton Lara 2.50 6.00
188 Fidel Montero 4.00 10.00
189 Aneudis Mordan 2.50 6.00
190 Joel Peguero 2.50 6.00
191 John Peguero 2.50 6.00
192 Bryan Pena 2.50 6.00
193 Salvador Ramirez 2.50 6.00
194 Rhaybel Roso 2.50 6.00
195 Jay Vargas 2.50 6.00
196 Wesley Zapata 2.50 6.00
198 Rodolfo Caraballo 2.50 6.00
199 Elizual Chalas 2.50 6.00
200 Elian Cortorreal 2.50 6.00
201 Randy De Jesus 2.50 6.00
202 Aneudi Escanio 2.50 6.00
203 Xaviel Guillen 3.00 8.00
204 Yanki Jean 2.50 6.00
205 Maximo Maria 2.50 6.00
206 Juan Martinez 2.50 6.00
207 Yasser Mercedes 2.50 6.00
208 Jeral Perez 3.00 8.00
209 Jhonny Severino 2.50 6.00
210 Ivan Sosa 3.00 8.00
211 Miguel Tamares 2.50 6.00
212 Braylin Tavera 2.50 6.00
213 Sebastian Castro 2.50 6.00

2019 Elite Extra Edition Autographs Aspirations Blue
148 Jasson Dominguez/25 300.00 800.00

2019 Elite Extra Edition Autographs Emerald
148 Jasson Dominguez/25 300.00 800.00

2019 Elite Extra Edition Autographs Status Die Cut Emerald
148 Jasson Dominguez/25 300.00 800.00

2019 Elite Extra Edition Base OptiChrome
RANDOM INSERTS IN PACKS
*HOLO: .5X TO 1.2X BASIC
1 Adley Rutschman 1.50 4.00
2 Bobby Witt Jr. 1.50 4.00
3 Andrew Vaughn .75 2.00
4 JJ Bleday 1.25 3.00
5 Riley Greene 1.50 4.00
6 CJ Abrams 1.25 3.00
7 Nick Lodolo .50 1.25
8 Josh Jung .75 2.00
9 Shea Langeliers .50 1.25
10 Hunter Bishop .75 2.00
11 Alek Manoah .50 1.25
14 Bryson Stott .75 2.00
15 Will Wilson .40 1.00
16 Corbin Carroll .40 1.00
22 Greg Jones .30 .75
24 Daniel Espino .30 .75
25 Kody Hoese .75 2.00
29 Logan Davidson .25 .60
30 Anthony Volpe 1.00 2.50
33 Brennan Malone .25 .60
35 Kameron Misner .60 1.50
49 Rece Hinds .30 .75
51 Logan Wyatt .40 1.00
80 Tyler Callihan .30 .75
81 Matthew Allan .50 1.25
84 Ryan Pepiot .25 .60
85 Tristin English .25 .60
86 Erik Miller .60 1.50
87 Matt Cronin .25 .60
88 Graeme Stinson .25 .60
89 Brandon Lewis .40 1.00
90 Kyle McCann .30 .75
91 Logan O'Hoppe .25 .60
93 Miguel Vargas 1.25 3.00
94 Sheryven Newton .40 1.00
96 Brailyn Marquez .60 1.50
97 Brayan Rocchio 1.00 2.50
99 Randy Arozarena 2.50 6.00
100 Jarren Duran 1.50 4.00
148 Jasson Dominguez 25.00 60.00

2019 Elite Extra Edition Base OptiChrome Signatures
1 Adley Rutschman 25.00 60.00
2 Bobby Witt Jr. 15.00 40.00
3 Andrew Vaughn 8.00 20.00
4 JJ Bleday 12.00 30.00
5 Riley Greene 15.00 40.00
6 CJ Abrams 12.00 30.00
7 Nick Lodolo 5.00 12.00
8 Josh Jung 8.00 20.00
9 Shea Langeliers 5.00 12.00
10 Hunter Bishop 8.00 20.00
11 Alek Manoah 5.00 12.00
14 Bryson Stott 8.00 20.00
15 Will Wilson 4.00 10.00
16 Corbin Carroll 4.00 10.00
22 Greg Jones 3.00 8.00
24 Daniel Espino 3.00 8.00
25 Kody Hoese 8.00 20.00
29 Logan Davidson 2.50 6.00
30 Anthony Volpe 10.00 25.00
33 Brennan Malone 2.50 6.00
35 Kameron Misner 6.00 15.00
49 Rece Hinds 3.00 8.00
51 Logan Wyatt 4.00 10.00
80 Tyler Callihan 3.00 8.00
81 Matthew Allan 5.00 12.00
84 Ryan Pepiot 2.50 6.00
86 Erik Miller 6.00 15.00
87 Matt Cronin 2.50 6.00
88 Graeme Stinson 2.50 6.00
89 Brandon Lewis 4.00 10.00
90 Kyle McCann 3.00 8.00
91 Logan O'Hoppe 2.50 6.00
93 Miguel Vargas 12.00 30.00
94 Sheryven Newton 4.00 10.00
96 Brailyn Marquez 6.00 15.00
97 Brayan Rocchio 10.00 25.00
99 Randy Arozarena 25.00 60.00
100 Jarren Duran 20.00 50.00
148 Jasson Dominguez 100.00 250.00

2019 Elite Extra Edition College Tickets
RANDOM INSERTS IN PACKS
*HOLO: .5X TO 1.2X BASIC
1 Adley Rutschman 1.50 4.00
2 Andrew Vaughn .75 2.00
3 JJ Bleday 1.25 3.00
4 Nick Lodolo .50 1.25
5 Josh Jung .75 2.00
6 Shea Langeliers .50 1.25
7 Hunter Bishop .75 2.00
8 Alek Manoah .50 1.25
9 Bryson Stott .75 2.00
10 Will Wilson .40 1.00

11 Zack Thompson .40 1.00
12 Michael Massey .30 .75
13 Braden Shewmake .75 2.00
14 Noah Song .75 2.00
15 Michael Toglia .40 1.00
16 Kody Hoese .75 2.00
17 Ryan Jensen .40 1.00
18 Ethan Small .30 .75
19 Logan Davidson .25 .60
20 Michael Busch .75 2.00
21 Korey Lee .50 1.25
22 Drey Jameson .25 .60
23 Kameron Misner .60 1.50
24 T.J. Sikkema .40 1.00
25 Matt Wallner .50 1.25
26 Tyler Dyson .25 .60
27 Davis Wendzel .40 1.00
28 Cameron Cannon .50 1.25
29 Brady McConnell .40 1.00
30 Nick Quintana .50 1.25
31 Ryan Garcia .25 .60
32 Logan Wyatt .40 1.00
33 Matt Canterino .30 .75

2019 Elite Extra Edition College Tickets Signatures

1 Adley Rutschman 25.00 60.00
2 Andrew Vaughn 8.00 20.00
3 JJ Bleday 12.00 30.00
4 Nick Lodolo 5.00 12.00
5 Josh Jung 8.00 20.00
6 Shea Langeliers 5.00 12.00
7 Hunter Bishop 8.00 20.00
8 Alek Manoah 5.00 12.00
9 Bryson Stott 8.00 20.00
10 Will Wilson 4.00 10.00
11 Zack Thompson 4.00 10.00
12 Michael Massey 3.00 8.00
13 Braden Shewmake 8.00 20.00
14 Noah Song 8.00 20.00
15 Michael Toglia 4.00 10.00
16 Kody Hoese 8.00 20.00
17 Ryan Jensen 4.00 10.00
18 Ethan Small 3.00 8.00
19 Logan Davidson 2.50 6.00
20 Michael Busch 8.00 20.00
21 Korey Lee 5.00 12.00
22 Drey Jameson 2.50 6.00
23 Kameron Misner 6.00 15.00
24 T.J. Sikkema 4.00 10.00
25 Matt Wallner 5.00 12.00
26 Tyler Dyson 2.50 6.00
27 Davis Wendzel 4.00 10.00
28 Cameron Cannon 5.00 12.00
29 Brady McConnell 4.00 10.00
30 Nick Quintana 5.00 12.00
31 Ryan Garcia 2.50 6.00
32 Logan Wyatt 4.00 10.00
33 Matt Canterino 3.00 8.00

2019 Elite Extra Edition Dominican Prospect League Jumbo Materials Red

1 Robert Puason
2 Bayron Lora
3 Emmanuel Rodriguez
4 Dauris Lorenzo
5 Alexander Ramirez
6 Jose Pastrano
7 Christian Cardozo
8 Jhon Diaz
9 Adael Amador
10 Rikelvin Castro

2019 Elite Extra Edition Dominican Prospect League Signatures

RANDOM INSERTS IN PACKS
101 Robert Puason 8.00 20.00
102 Bayron Lora 10.00 25.00
103 Emmanuel Rodriguez 4.00 10.00
104 Alexander Ramirez
105 Jhon Diaz 5.00 12.00
106 Adael Amador 3.00 8.00
107 Malfrin Sosa 3.00 8.00
108 Dauris Lorenzo 3.00 8.00
109 Jose Pastrano 3.00 8.00
110 Brailin Minier 4.00 10.00
111 Rikelvin Castro 3.00 8.00
112 Junior Tilien 3.00 8.00
113 Christian Cardozo 3.00 8.00

2019 Elite Extra Edition Dual Prospect Materials Black

3 Antonio Santillan/399 1.50 4.00
4 Royce Lewis/399 3.00 8.00
10 Gabriel Arias/299 2.50 6.00
11 Evan White/399 4.00 10.00
13 Khalil Lee/249 1.50 4.00
14 Victor Victor Mesa/399 3.00 8.00
15 Sixto Sanchez/399 5.00 12.00
17 Vidal Brujan/399 4.00 10.00
18 Brent Rooker/399 2.00 5.00
19 Lazaro Armenteros/399 2.00 5.00
20 Leody Taveras/399 2.50 6.00

2019 Elite Extra Edition First Round Materials Black

1 Adley Rutschman/399 10.00 25.00
3 Andrew Vaughn/399 5.00 12.00
5 Riley Greene/399 10.00 25.00
6 CJ Abrams/399 8.00 20.00
7 Josh Jung/262 5.00 12.00

2019 Elite Extra Edition Future Threads Signatures Black

1 Victor Mesa Jr./299 6.00 15.00
2 Brent Rooker/249 4.00 10.00
3 Bryson Brigman/299 3.00 8.00
4 Eli White/299 5.00 12.00
5 Jordan Yamamoto/299 3.00 8.00
6 Sean Murphy/199 4.00 10.00
7 Brailyn Marquez/240 8.00 20.00
8 Kyle Lewis/99 10.00 25.00
9 Victor Victor Mesa/299 6.00 15.00
10 Deivi Garcia/199 10.00 25.00
11 Andres Gimenez/99 8.00 20.00
12 Bobby Dalbec/199 20.00 50.00
13 Dane Dunning/199 6.00 15.00
14 Domingo Acevedo/199 3.00 8.00
15 Gabriel Arias/199 5.00 12.00
16 Gavin Lux/199 20.00 50.00
17 Hudson Potts/199 3.00 8.00
18 Jonathan Hernandez/299 3.00 8.00
19 Keibert Ruiz/199 15.00 40.00
20 Kevin Smith/299 3.00 8.00
21 Luis V. Garcia/199 12.00 30.00
23 Nick Neidert/299 3.00 8.00
24 Ryan Mountcastle/299 15.00 40.00
26 Taylor Widener/199 3.00 8.00
27 Trent Grisham/249 6.00 15.00
28 Vidal Brujan/199 8.00 20.00
29 Brandon Marsh/199 5.00 12.00
30 Jarren Duran/299
31 Ben Braymer/199 3.00 8.00
33 Ryan McKenna/199 3.00 8.00
34 George Valera/199 6.00 15.00
36 Monte Harrison/249 5.00 12.00
39 Michael King/195 5.00 12.00
40 Evan White/149 8.00 20.00
41 Jesus Sanchez/125 5.00 12.00
42 Jasson Dominguez/74 150.00 400.00
44 Luis Garcia/249 12.00 30.00

2019 Elite Extra Edition Future Threads Signatures Purple

42 Jasson Dominguez/25 300.00 600.00

2019 Elite Extra Edition Hidden Gems Autographs Black

1 Bobby Bradley 4.00 10.00
2 Trevor McDonald 2.50 6.00
3 Avery Short 2.50 6.00
4 Osleivis Basabe 2.50 6.00
5 Carlos Rodriguez 2.50 6.00
6 Randy Florentino 2.50 6.00
7 Livan Soto 3.00 8.00
8 Gabriel Maciel 2.50 6.00
10 Yeison Coca 2.50 6.00
11 Lenyn Sosa 2.50 6.00
12 Oswaldo Cabrera 2.50 6.00
13 Ivan Herrera 4.00 10.00
14 Cody Bolton 4.00 10.00
15 Sam Hentges 2.50 6.00
16 Yu Chang 3.00 8.00
17 Bo Bichette 15.00 40.00
18 Mauricio Dubon 6.00 15.00
19 Logan O'Hoppe 2.50 6.00
20 Brayan Rocchio 10.00 25.00
21 Miguel Vargas 10.00 25.00
22 Yordan Alvarez 40.00 100.00
23 Canaan Smith 4.00 10.00
24 Aristides Aquino 10.00 25.00
25 Logan Webb 4.00 10.00
26 Brock Burke 2.50 6.00
27 A.J. Puk 4.00 10.00
28 Thad Ward 2.50 6.00
29 Willi Castro 2.50 6.00
30 Brendan McKay 4.00 10.00

2019 Elite Extra Edition Prospect Materials Black

1 Evan White 4.00 10.00
2 Victor Victor Mesa 3.00 8.00
3 Brent Rooker 2.00 5.00
4 Eli White 2.50 6.00
5 Sixto Sanchez 5.00 12.00
6 Royce Lewis 3.00 8.00
7 Tucker Davidson 1.50 4.00
8 Michael King 2.50 6.00
10 Antonio Santillan 1.50 4.00
12 Dane Dunning 5.00 12.00
13 Gabriel Arias 2.50 6.00
15 Taylor Trammell 2.50 6.00
16 Jonathan Hernandez 1.50 4.00
17 Keibert Ruiz 8.00 20.00
18 Kevin Smith 1.50 4.00
19 Nick Neidert 1.50 4.00
20 Taylor Widener 1.50 4.00
21 Trent Grisham 5.00 12.00
22 Vidal Brujan 4.00 10.00
23 Wander Franco 12.00 30.00
24 Khalil Lee 1.50 4.00
27 Luis Garcia 6.00 15.00
28 Braxton Garrett 1.50 4.00
29 Monte Harrison 2.50 6.00
30 Triston McKenzie 3.00 8.00

2019 Elite Extra Edition Triple Prospect Materials Black

1 Leody Taveras/399 2.50 6.00
2 Vidal Brujan/399 4.00 10.00
4 Ryan McKenna/399 1.50 4.00
5 Bobby Dalbec/399 10.00 25.00
6 Gabriel Arias/199 2.50 6.00
9 Royce Lewis/399 3.00 8.00

2019 Elite Extra Edition Triple Silhouettes Black

1 Wander Franco/399 12.00 30.00
2 Victor Mesa Jr./399 3.00 8.00
4 Kyle Lewis/399 3.00 8.00
5 Jo Adell/399 6.00 15.00
8 Sixto Sanchez/399 5.00 12.00
9 Ryan Mountcastle/399 8.00 20.00
10 Matt Manning/149 2.50 6.00
11 Forrest Whitley/399 2.50 6.00
12 Leody Taveras/399 2.50 6.00
13 Yusniel Diaz/363 2.50 6.00
15 Andres Gimenez/399 4.00 10.00
17 Sean Murphy/199 2.00 5.00
18 JoJo Romero/299 1.50 4.00
19 Royce Lewis/399 3.00 8.00

2019 Elite Extra Edition USA Baseball 15U Signatures Red

1 Brandon Barriera 2.50 6.00
2 Karson Bowen 2.50 6.00
3 Joseph Brown 2.50 6.00
4 Drew Burress 2.50 6.00
5 Spencer Butt 2.50 6.00
6 Kai Caranto 2.50 6.00
7 Duke Ekstrom 2.50 6.00
8 Termarr Johnson 5.00 12.00
9 Dylan Lina 3.00 8.00
10 Matthew Matthijs 4.00 10.00
11 Ethan McElvain 2.50 6.00
12 Steven Milam 2.50 6.00
13 Aidan Miller 2.50 6.00
14 Brandon Olivera 2.50 6.00
15 Benjamin Reiland 5.00 12.00
16 Louis Rodriguez 2.50 6.00
17 Mikey Romero 2.50 6.00
18 Logan Saloman 2.50 6.00
19 Nolan Schubart 2.50 6.00
20 Colton Wombles 5.00 12.00

2019 Elite Extra Edition USA Baseball 18U Signatures Red

1 Mick Abel 4.00 10.00
2 Drew Bowser 2.50 6.00
3 Jack Bulger 2.50 6.00
4 Pete Crow-Armstrong 5.00 12.00
5 Lucas Gordon 2.50 6.00
6 Hunter Haas 3.00 8.00
7 Colby Halter 2.50 6.00
8 Kyle Harrison 6.00 15.00
9 Robert Hassell 6.00 15.00
10 Rawley Hector 2.50 6.00
11 Austin Hendrick 10.00 25.00
12 Ben Hernandez 2.50 6.00
13 Nolan McLean 2.50 6.00
14 Max Rajcic 2.50 6.00
15 Drew Romo 6.00 15.00
16 Alejandro Rosario 5.00 12.00
17 Jason Savacool 4.00 10.00
18 Tyler Soderstrom 5.00 12.00
19 Milan Tolentino 3.00 8.00

2019 Elite Extra Edition USA Collegiate Material Signatures Black

1 Andrew Abbott 3.00 8.00
2 Logan Allen 3.00 8.00
3 Tanner Allen 3.00 8.00
4 Patrick Bailey 6.00 15.00
5 Tyler Brown 5.00 12.00
6 Alec Burleson 5.00 12.00
7 Burl Carraway 6.00 15.00
8 Cade Cavalli 6.00 15.00
9 Colton Cowser 4.00 10.00
10 Jeff Criswell 5.00 12.00
11 Reid Detmers 6.00 15.00
12 Justin Foscue 8.00 20.00
13 Nick Frasso 3.00 8.00
14 Heston Kjerstad 20.00 50.00
15 Asa Lacy 25.00 60.00
16 Nick Loftin 3.00 8.00
17 Austin Martin 20.00 50.00
18 Chris McMahon 3.00 8.00
19 Max Meyer 10.00 25.00
20 Doug Nikhazy 3.00 8.00
21 Casey Opitz 5.00 12.00
22 Spencer Torkelson 50.00 120.00
23 Luke Waddell 3.00 8.00
24 Cole Wilcox 4.00 10.00
25 Alika Williams 5.00 12.00
26 Lucas Dunn 3.00 8.00

2019 Elite Extra Edition USA Collegiate Tickets

RANDOM INSERTS IN PACKS
*HOLO: .5X TO 1.2X BASIC
1 Andrew Abbott .25 .60
2 Logan Allen .25 .60
3 Tanner Allen .25 .60
4 Patrick Bailey .75 2.00
5 Tyler Brown .40 1.00
6 Alec Burleson .40 1.00
7 Burl Carraway .50 1.25
8 Cade Cavalli .50 1.25
9 Colton Cowser .30 .75
10 Jeff Criswell .40 1.00
11 Reid Detmers .75 2.00
12 Justin Foscue 1.00 2.50
13 Nick Frasso .25 .60
14 Heston Kjerstad 1.00 2.50
15 Asa Lacy 1.25 3.00
16 Nick Loftin .25 .60
17 Austin Martin .75 2.00
18 Chris McMahon .25 .60
19 Max Meyer .75 2.00
20 Doug Nikhazy .25 .60
21 Casey Opitz .40 1.00
22 Spencer Torkelson 3.00 8.00
23 Luke Waddell .25 .60
24 Cole Wilcox .30 .75
25 Alika Williams .40 1.00
26 Lucas Dunn .25 .60
27 Garrett Mitchell 1.50 4.00

2019 Elite Extra Edition USA Collegiate Tickets Signatures

1 Andrew Abbott
2 Logan Allen
3 Tanner Allen
4 Patrick Bailey
5 Tyler Brown
6 Alec Burleson
7 Burl Carraway
8 Cade Cavalli
9 Colton Cowser
10 Jeff Criswell
11 Reid Detmers
12 Justin Foscue
13 Nick Frasso
14 Heston Kjerstad
15 Asa Lacy
16 Nick Loftin
17 Austin Martin
18 Chris McMahon
19 Max Meyer
20 Doug Nikhazy
21 Casey Opitz
22 Spencer Torkelson
23 Luke Waddell
24 Cole Wilcox
25 Alika Williams
26 Lucas Dunn
27 Garrett Mitchell

2019 Elite Extra Edition USA Materials Black

1 Adley Rutschman/199 10.00 25.00
2 Bobby Witt Jr./452 10.00 25.00
3 Andrew Vaughn/499 5.00 12.00
4 Riley Greene/499 10.00 25.00
5 CJ Abrams/499 8.00 20.00
6 Josh Jung/399 5.00 12.00
8 Bryson Stott/289 5.00 12.00
9 Will Wilson/499 2.50 6.00
10 Corbin Carroll/199 2.50 6.00
11 Zack Thompson/199 2.50 6.00
12 Braden Shewmake/499 5.00 12.00
13 Anthony Volpe/499 6.00 15.00
14 Brennan Malone/299 1.50 4.00
15 Bryson Brigman/499 1.50 4.00
16 Tyler Callihan/180 2.00 5.00
17 Matthew Thompson/499 2.00 5.00
18 Logan Allen/499 1.50 4.00
22 John Doxakis/499 2.00 5.00
23 Seth Beer/499 4.00 10.00
24 Nick Quintana/275 3.00 8.00
26 Jarred Kelenic/499 6.00 15.00
27 Matt Cronin/399 1.50 4.00
28 Graeme Stinson/231 1.50 4.00
29 Evan White/499 4.00 10.00
30 Triston Casas/499 6.00 15.00

2020 Elite Extra Edition

STATED PRINT RUN 999 SER.#'d SETS
1 Spencer Torkelson 5.00 12.00
2 Heston Kjerstad 3.00 8.00
3 Max Meyer 1.00 2.50
4 Asa Lacy 2.00 5.00
5 Austin Martin .75 2.00
6 Emerson Hancock 1.00 2.50
7 Nick Gonzales 2.00 5.00
8 Robert Hassell 2.50 6.00
9 Zac Veen 2.50 6.00
10 Reid Detmers .60 1.50
11 Garrett Crochet .60 1.50
12 Austin Hendrick 4.00 10.00
13 Patrick Bailey .75 2.00
14 Justin Foscue 1.00 2.50
15 Mick Abel .40 1.00
16 Ed Howard 3.00 8.00
17 Nick Yorke 1.25 3.00
18 Bryce Jarvis .30 .75
19 Pete Crow-Armstrong .75 2.00
20 Garrett Mitchell 2.00 5.00
21 Jordan Walker .75 2.00
22 Cade Cavalli .50 1.25
23 Carson Tucker .75 2.00
24 Nick Bitsko .75 2.00
25 Jared Shuster .50 1.25
26 Tyler Soderstrom 1.00 2.50
27 Aaron Sabato .50 1.25
28 Austin Wells 1.00 2.50
29 Bobby Miller 1.00 2.50
31 Carmen Mlodzinski .30 .75
32 Nick Loftin .40 1.00
33 Slade Cecconi .30 .75
34 Justin Lange .25 .60
35 Drew Romo .60 1.50
36 Tanner Burns .40 1.00
37 Alika Williams .30 .75
38 Dillon Dingler .75 2.00
39 Hudson Haskin 1.00 2.50
40 Dax Fulton .40 1.00
41 Ben Hernandez .40 1.00
42 CJ Van Eyk .40 1.00
43 Zach DeLoach 1.00 2.50
44 Jared Jones .40 1.00
45 Owen Caissie .50 1.25
46 Gage Workman 1.50 4.00
47 Jared Kelley .25 .60
48 Jesse Franklin 1.00 2.50
49 Casey Schmitt .60 1.50
50 Evan Carter 2.00 5.00
51 Trevor Hauver .40 1.00
53 Freddy Zamora .40 1.00
54 Masyn Winn 1.00 2.50
55 Cole Henry .30 .75
56 Logan T. Allen .25 .60
57 Ian Seymour .25 .60
58 Jeff Criswell .30 .75
59 Alerick Soularie .30 .75
60 Landon Knack .60 1.50
61 Kyle Nicolas .40 1.00
62 Daniel Cabrera 1.00 2.50
63 Markevian Hence .25 .60
64 Connor Phillips .40 1.00
65 Jackson Miller .60 1.50
66 Clayton Beeter .60 1.50
67 Nick Swiney .50 1.25
68 Jimmy Glowenke .50 1.25
69 Isaiah Greene 1.00 2.50
70 Alec Burleson .40 1.00
71 Sammy Infante 1.00 2.50
72 Alex Santos .75 2.00
73 Trei Cruz 1.00 2.50
74 Anthony Servideo .30 .75
75 Zach McCambley .25 .60
76 Tyler Gentry .50 1.25
77 Trent Palmer .30 .75
78 Kaden Polcovich .40 1.00
79 Nick Garcia .40 1.00
81 Sam Weatherly .25 .60
82 David Calabrese .50 1.25
83 Petey Halpin .60 1.50
84 Bryce Bonnin .40 1.00
86 Tekoah Roby .25 .60
87 Casey Martin .75 2.00
88 Jordan Nwogu 1.00 2.50
89 Tyler Keenan .40 1.00
90 Liam Norris .25 .60
91 Anthony Walters .30 .75
92 Zavier Warren .25 .60
93 Levi Prater .30 .75
94 Roberto Campos 2.50 6.00
95 Holden Powell .30 .75
96 Malcom Nunez .50 1.25
97 Norge Vera .30 .75
98 Jake Vogel .30 .75
99 Yiddi Cappe .50 1.25
100 Oscar Colas .75 2.00
101 Zion Bannister .30 .75
102 Ji-Hwan Bae .40 1.00
103 Hunter Barnhart .25 .60
104 Christian Roa .30 .75
105 Michael Guldberg .30 .75
106 Burl Carraway .50 1.25
107 Hunter Greene .40 1.00
108 Tyler Brown .40 1.00
109 Cody Thomas .40 1.00
110 Adisyn Coffey .25 .60
111 Jake Eder .25 .60
112 Nick Frasso .25 .60
113 Juan Then .25 .60
114 Packy Naughton .25 .60
115 Jack Hartman .25 .60
116 Levi Thomas .25 .60
117 Case Williams .30 .75
118 Werner Blakely .30 .75
119 Kade Mechals .25 .60
120 Mac Wainwright .30 .75
121 R.J. Dabovich .25 .60
122 Dylan MacLean .40 1.00
123 Aaron Bracho .25 .60
124 Luke Little .40 1.00
125 Jeremy Wu-Yelland .40 1.00
126 A.J. Vukovich .50 1.25
127 Matthew Dyer .40 1.00
128 Joey Wiemer .40 1.00
129 Ian Bedell .30 .75
130 Brady Lindsly .40 1.00
131 Milan Tolentino .40 1.00
132 Tanner Murray .30 .75
133 Spencer Strider .40 1.00
134 Dane Acker .40 1.00
135 Marco Raya .50 1.25
136 Beck Way .25 .60
137 Carson Taylor .40 1.00
138 Zach Daniels .40 1.00
139 Colten Keith 1.50 6.00
140 Carter Baumler .40 1.00
141 Kyle Hurt .25 .60
142 Will Klein .30 .75
143 Zach Britton .30 .75
144 Taylor Dollard .25 .60
145 Logan Hofmann .25 .60
146 Kristian Robinson .75 2.00
147 Jack Blomgren .40 1.00
148 Adam Seminaris .30 .75
149 Bailey Horn .30 .75
150 Joe Boyle .40 1.00
151 Maximo Acosta .60 1.50
152 Vidal Brujan 2.00 5.00
153 Baron Radcliff .30 .75
154 Keithron Moss .25 .60
155 Shane Drohan .30 .75
156 Brandon Pfaadt .25 .60
157 Eric Orze .25 .60
158 Hayden Cantrelle .25 .60
159 LJ Jones IV .40 1.00
160 Mitchell Parker .25 .60
161 Mason Hickman .30 .75
162 Jeff Hakanson .25 .60
163 Alexander Ovalles .25 .60
164 Stevie Emanuels .25 .60
165 Kala'i Rosario .30 .75
166 Gavin Stone .50 1.25
167 Shay Whitcomb .30 .75
168 Yoelqui Cespedes 1.00 2.50
169 Kale Emshoff .25 .60
170 Nivaldo Rodriguez .50 1.25
171 Drew Rasmussen .40 1.00
172 Felix Cotes .25 .60
173 Jose Dejesus .25 .60
174 Fraymi De Leon .25 .60
175 Henry Ramos .25 .60
176 Jose Rodriguez .30 .75
177 Jimmy Troncoso .25 .60
178 Yoendry Vargas .25 .60
179 Yofry Solano .25 .60
180 Kelvin Hidalgo .25 .60
181 Felnin Celesten .25 .60
182 Yoelin Cespedes .50 1.25
183 Jelson Coca .25 .60
184 Camilo Diaz .25 .60
185 Welbin Francisca .25 .60
186 Rainer Vargas .25 .60
187 Daniel Rojas .30 .75
188 Elvin Gonzalez .25 .60
189 Jodainy Henriquez .25 .60
190 Fabian Lopez .30 .75
191 Yerlin Luis .25 .60
192 Brian Martinez .25 .60
193 Juan Bito .25 .60
194 Emil Valencia .25 .60
195 Eddie Perez .25 .60
196 German Ramirez .25 .60
197 Elvis Rojas .25 .60
198 Juan Sanchez .25 .60
199 Angel Trinidad .30 .75
200 Lenny Carela .25 .60

2020 Elite Extra Edition 203rd Decade Die Cut

*203: .6X TO 1.5X BASIC
RANDOM INSERTS IN PACKS
STATED PRINT RUN 999 SER.#'d SETS

2020 Elite Extra Edition Aspirations Die Cut

*ASP.CUT/26-49: 1X TO 2.5X BASIC
*ASP.CUT/19-25: 1.2X TO 3X BASIC
RANDOM INSERTS IN PACKS
PRINT RUNS B/WN 19-49 COPIES PER

2020 Elite Extra Edition Aspirations Die Cut Gold

*ASP.CUT GOLD: 1.2X TO 3X BASIC
RANDOM INSERTS IN PACKS
STATED PRINT RUN 24 SER.#'d SETS

2020 Elite Extra Edition Aspirations Orange

*ORNG ASP: .6X TO 1.5X BASIC
RANDOM INSERTS IN PACKS
STATED PRINT RUN 149 SER.#'d SETS

2020 Elite Extra Edition Pink

*PINK: .6X TO 1.5X BASIC
RANDOM INSERTS IN PACKS

2020 Elite Extra Edition Status Blue

*STAT.BLUE: .6X TO 1.5X BASIC
RANDOM INSERTS IN PACKS
STATED PRINT RUN 249 SER.#'d SETS

2020 Elite Extra Edition Status Die Cut

RANDOM INSERTS IN PACKS
PRINT RUNS B/WN 1-31 COPIES PER
NO PRICING ON QTY 18 OR LESS

2020 Elite Extra Edition Status Purple

*STAT.PRPL: .6X TO 1.5X BASIC
RANDOM INSERTS IN PACKS
STATED PRINT RUN 249 SER.#'d SETS

2020 Elite Extra Edition Turn of the Century

*TURN: .6X TO 1.5X BASIC
RANDOM INSERTS IN PACKS
STATED PRINT RUN 196 SER.#'d SETS

2020 Elite Extra Edition All-Time First Round Materials

RANDOM INSERTS IN PACKS
*ORANGE/99-199: .5X TO 1.2X BASIC
*ORANGE/49: .6X TO 1.5X BASIC
*RED: .6X TO 1.5X BASIC
1 Chipper Jones 4.00 10.00
2 Paul Konerko 3.00 8.00
3 CC Sabathia 5.00 12.00
4 Mark McGwire 4.00 10.00
5 Barry Larkin 2.00 5.00
6 Rafael Palmeiro 4.00 10.00
7 Robin Yount 2.50 6.00
8 Reggie Jackson 8.00 20.00
9 Alex Rodriguez 5.00 12.00
10 Craig Biggio 2.00 5.00
11 Ken Griffey Jr. 10.00 25.00
12 Frank Thomas 2.50 6.00
13 Roger Clemens 3.00 8.00

2020 Elite Extra Edition Dominican Prospect League Material Signatures

RANDOM INSERTS IN PACKS
PRINT RUNS B/WN 135-199 COPIES PER
EXCHANGE DEADLINE 7/6/22
*ORANGE: .4X TO 1X BASIC
*RED: .4X TO 1X BASIC
*PURPLE: .6X TO 1.5X BASIC
1 Lenny Carela/199 3.00 8.00
2 Felix Cotes/199 3.00 8.00
3 Jose Dejesus/149 3.00 8.00
4 Fraymi De Leon/199 3.00 8.00
5 Henry Ramos/149 3.00 8.00
6 Jose Rodriguez/145 4.00 10.00
7 Kelvin Hidalgo/135 3.00 8.00
8 Yoendry Vargas/149 3.00 8.00
9 Yofry Solano/195 3.00 8.00
10 Emil Valencia/149 3.00 8.00
11 Felnin Celesten/149 3.00 8.00
12 Yoelin Cespedes/185 10.00 25.00
13 Jelson Coca/199 3.00 8.00
14 Camilo Diaz/149 3.00 8.00
15 Welbin Francisca/199 3.00 8.00
16 Daniel Rojas/199 4.00 10.00
17 Juan Bito/149 3.00 8.00
18 Elvin Gonzalez/149 3.00 8.00
19 Jodainy Henriquez/149 3.00 8.00
20 Fabian Lopez/199 4.00 10.00
21 Yerlin Luis/149 3.00 8.00
22 Brian Martinez/149 3.00 8.00
23 Rainer Vargas/190 3.00 8.00
24 Jimmy Troncoso/149 3.00 8.00
25 Eddie Perez/149 3.00 8.00
26 German Ramirez/149 3.00 8.00
27 Elvis Rojas/149 3.00 8.00
28 Juan Sanchez/199 3.00 8.00
29 Angel Trinidad/149 4.00 10.00

2020 Elite Extra Edition Dominican Prospect League Materials

RANDOM INSERTS IN PACKS
*ORANGE: .5X TO 1.2X BASIC
*RED: .6X TO 1.5X BASIC
1 Teudy Cortoreal 1.50 4.00
2 Jonathan Peguero 1.50 4.00
3 Cristian Santana 1.50 4.00
4 German Ramirez 1.50 4.00
5 Shalin Polanco 1.50 4.00
6 Danny De Andrande 1.50 4.00
7 Lenny Carela 1.50 4.00
8 Daniel Rojas 2.00 5.00
9 Victor Acosta 1.50 4.00
10 Jodainy Henriquez 1.50 4.00
11 Willy Fanas 1.50 4.00
12 Ambioris Tavarez 1.50 4.00
13 Manuel Pena 1.50 4.00
14 Fran Alduey 1.50 4.00
15 Elias Reynoso 2.00 5.00
16 Angel Trinidad 2.00 5.00
17 Brayan Rijo 1.50 4.00
18 Hendry Mendez 1.50 4.00
19 Gabriel Terrero 1.50 4.00
20 Yofry Solano 1.50 4.00
21 Victor Quezada 1.50 4.00
22 Jefry Rivera 1.50 4.00
23 Rayner Doncon 1.50 4.00
24 Keiderson Pavon 1.50 4.00
25 Jimmy Troncoso 1.50 4.00

2020 Elite Extra Edition Dominican Prospect League Signatures

RANDOM INSERTS IN PACKS
EXCHANGE DEADLINE 7/6/22
1 Teudy Cortoreal 2.50 6.00
2 Jonathan Peguero 2.50 6.00
3 Cristian Santana 6.00 15.00
4 Keiderson Pavon 5.00 12.00
6 Danny De Andrande 5.00 12.00
7 Rayner Doncon 2.50 6.00
8 Jefry Rivera 2.50 6.00
9 Victor Acosta 5.00 12.00
10 Victor Quezada 2.50 6.00
11 Willy Fanas 2.50 6.00
12 Ambioris Tavarez 10.00 25.00
13 Manuel Pena 5.00 12.00
14 Fran Alduey 5.00 12.00
15 Elias Reynoso 3.00 8.00
16 Gabriel Terrero 2.50 6.00
17 Brayan Rijo 8.00 20.00

2020 Elite Extra Edition First Round Materials

RANDOM INSERTS IN PACKS
*ORANGE/199: .5X TO 1.2X BASIC
*ORANGE/44: .6X TO 1.5X BASIC
*RED: .6X TO 1.5X BASIC
1 Spencer Torkelson 10.00 25.00
2 Heston Kjerstad 6.00 15.00
3 Max Meyer 6.00 15.00
5 Austin Martin 5.00 12.00
6 Emerson Hancock 6.00 15.00
7 Nick Gonzales 5.00 12.00
8 Robert Hassell 6.00 15.00
9 Zac Veen 6.00 15.00
10 Reid Detmers 4.00 10.00

2020 Elite Extra Edition Future Threads Signatures

RANDOM INSERTS IN PACKS
PRINT RUNS B/WN 49-299 COPIES PER
EXCHANGE DEADLINE 7/6/22
1 Adonis Medina/299 5.00 12.00
2 Daniel Lynch/299 6.00 15.00
3 Jarren Duran/299 12.00 30.00
4 Kris Bubic/299 5.00 12.00
6 Nick Neidert/199 3.00 8.00
7 Spencer Howard/49 15.00 40.00
9 Tarik Skubal/99 12.00 30.00
10 Trevor Rogers/99 10.00 25.00
11 Tristen Lutz/299 4.00 10.00
12 Nate Pearson/99 12.00 30.00
13 Triston McKenzie/99 10.00 25.00
14 Bryson Stott/189 5.00 12.00
15 Colton Welker/99 4.00 10.00
16 Shane Baz/99 4.00 10.00
17 Matt Manning/99 5.00 12.00
19 Daulton Varsho/293 5.00 12.00
20 Erick Pena/149 8.00 20.00
21 Freudis Nova/149 3.00 8.00
22 Miguel Amaya/299 6.00 12.00
23 Brice Turang/299 3.00 8.00
25 Bobby Dalbec/99 25.00 60.00
26 Brady Singer/99 12.00 30.00
27 Corbin Carroll/99 6.00 15.00
28 Andres Gimenez/99 10.00 25.00
29 Cristian Pache/99 15.00 40.00
30 Drew Waters/99 20.00 50.00
34 Dylan Carlson/99 15.00 40.00
37 Bobby Witt Jr./99 25.00 60.00
38 Ryan Mountcastle/299 10.00 25.00
39 Casey Mize/99 12.00 30.00
40 Luis V. Garcia/99 15.00 40.00

2020 Elite Extra Edition Future Threads Signatures Orange

*ORANGE/149: .4X TO 1X p/r 149-299
*ORANGE/75-99: .5X TO 1.2X p/r 149-299
*ORANGE/75-99: .4X TO 1X p/r 49-99
RANDOM INSERTS IN PACKS
PRINT RUNS B/WN 75-149 COPIES PER
EXCHANGE DEADLINE 7/6/22
7 Spencer Howard/149 12.00 30.00
25 Bobby Dalbec/75 15.00 40.00

2020 Elite Extra Edition Future Threads Signatures Purple

*PURPLE: .6X TO 1.5X p/r 149-299
*PURPLE: .5X TO 1.2X p/r 49-99
RANDOM INSERTS IN PACKS
STATED PRINT RUN 25 SER.#'d SETS
EXCHANGE DEADLINE 7/6/22
7 Spencer Howard 20.00 50.00
25 Bobby Dalbec 20.00 50.00
31 Brett Baty 15.00 40.00
34 Dylan Carlson 25.00 60.00
37 Bobby Witt Jr. 40.00 100.00

2020 Elite Extra Edition Future Threads Signatures Red

*RED: .5X TO 1.2X p/r 149-299
*RED: .4X TO 1X p/r 49-99
RANDOM INSERTS IN PACKS
PRINT RUNS B/WN 49-99 COPIES PER
EXCHANGE DEADLINE 7/6/22
7 Spencer Howard/99 15.00 40.00
25 Bobby Dalbec/49 15.00 40.00
34 Dylan Carlson/49 20.00 50.00

2020 Elite Extra Edition Hidden Gems Autographs

RANDOM INSERTS IN PACKS
EXCHANGE DEADLINE 7/6/22
1 Ji-Hwan Bae 4.00 10.00
2 Oscar Colas 12.00 30.00
3 Jordan Mikel 2.50 6.00
4 Kale Emshoff 2.50 6.00
5 JJ Bleday 8.00 20.00
6 Thomas Girard 2.50 6.00
7 Jojanse Torres 3.00 8.00
8 Nivaldo Rodriguez 5.00 12.00
9 Kramer Robertson 2.50 6.00
10 Clay Aguilar 4.00 10.00
11 Brett Auerbach 4.00 10.00
12 Jeremy Arocho 2.50 6.00
13 Ripken Reyes 2.50 6.00
14 Jackson Coutts 3.00 8.00
15 Daniel Alvarez 2.50 6.00
16 Junior Martina 2.50 6.00
17 Santiago Florez 3.00 8.00
18 Jack Patterson 5.00 12.00
19 A.J. Block 2.50 6.00
20 Jamari Baylor 3.00 8.00
21 Jonathan Hughes 2.50 6.00
22 Grant McCray 4.00 10.00
23 Jake Agnos 2.50 6.00
24 Jacob Wallace 3.00 8.00
25 Victor Vodnik 2.50 6.00
26 Justin Lavey 3.00 8.00
27 Matt Scheffler 2.50 6.00
29 Helcris Olivarez 3.00 8.00
30 Hyun-il Choi 4.00 10.00
31 Gilberto Celestino 2.50 6.00
32 Vaughn Grissom 4.00 10.00
33 Josh Fleming 3.00 8.00
34 Jackson Cluff 5.00 12.00
35 CJ Abrams 12.00 30.00
36 Jordan DiValerio 2.50 6.00
37 Bradlee Beesley 4.00 10.00
38 Brayan Buelvas 3.00 8.00
39 Keithron Moss 2.50 6.00
40 Gus Steiger 2.50 6.00
41 Dylan File 3.00 8.00
42 Joan Adon 2.50 6.00

43 Hobie Harris 3.00 8.00
44 Eduard Bazardo 2.50 6.00
45 William Holmes 3.00 8.00
46 Jose Rojas 2.50 6.00
47 Kyle Hart 2.50 6.00
48 Willie MacIver 2.50 6.00
49 Estevan Florial 4.00 10.00
50 Isaac Paredes 8.00 20.00
51 Jarred Kelenic 20.00 50.00
52 Triston Casas 8.00 20.00
53 Matthew Liberatore 3.00 8.00
54 Mike Baumann 3.00 8.00
55 Josh Jung 5.00 12.00
56 Heliot Ramos 5.00 12.00
57 Hunter Greene 10.00 25.00
58 MacKenzie Gore 15.00 40.00
59 Riley Greene 8.00 20.00

2020 Elite Extra Edition Hidden Gems Autographs Red White Blue

*RWB: .6X TO 1.5X BASIC
RANDOM INSERTS IN PACKS
PRINT RUNS B/WN 15-25 COPIES PER
NO PRICING ON QTY 15
EXCHANGE DEADLINE 7/6/22
2 Oscar Colas/25 50.00 120.00
35 CJ Abrams/25 50.00 120.00

2020 Elite Extra Edition OptiChrome

RANDOM INSERTS IN PACKS
*HOLO: .5X TO 1.2X BASIC
1 Spencer Torkelson 4.00 10.00
2 Heston Kjerstad 2.00 5.00
4 Asa Lacy 1.50 4.00
6 Emerson Hancock 1.00 2.50
8 Robert Hassell 2.00 5.00
9 Zac Veen 1.25 3.00
10 Reid Detmers .60 1.50
12 Austin Hendrick 2.50 6.00
14 Justin Foscue 1.00 2.50
15 Mick Abel .40 1.00
16 Ed Howard 2.00 5.00
17 Nick Yorke 1.25 3.00
19 Pete Crow-Armstrong .75 2.00
21 Jordan Walker .75 2.00
23 Carson Tucker .75 2.00
24 Nick Bitsko .75 2.00
26 Tyler Soderstrom 1.00 2.50
32 Nick Loftin .40 1.00
34 Justin Lange .25 .60
35 Drew Romo .60 1.50
40 Dax Fulton .40 1.00
41 Ben Hernandez .40 1.00
44 Jared Jones .40 1.00
45 Owen Caissie .50 1.25
47 Jared Kelley .25 .60
50 Evan Carter .60 1.50
54 Masyn Winn 1.00 2.50
63 Markevian Hence .25 .60
67 Nick Swiney .50 1.25
69 Isaiah Greene 1.00 2.50
70 Alec Burleson .40 1.00
71 Sammy Infante 1.00 2.50
72 Alex Santos .75 2.00
74 Anthony Servideo .30 .75
76 Tyler Gentry .50 1.25
79 Nick Garcia .40 1.00
81 Sam Weatherly .25 .60
82 David Calabrese .50 1.25
83 Petey Halpin .60 1.50
89 Tyler Keenan .40 1.00
94 Roberto Campos 1.25 3.00
98 Jake Vogel .30 .75
99 Yiddi Cappe .50 1.25
100 Oscar Colas .75 2.00
101 Zion Bannister .30 .75
111 Jake Eder .25 .60
112 Nick Frasso .25 .60
118 Werner Blakely .30 .75
120 Mac Wainwright .30 .75
168 Yoelqui Cespedes 1.00 2.50

2020 Elite Extra Edition OptiChrome College Tickets

RANDOM INSERTS IN PACKS
*HOLO: .5X TO 1.2X BASIC
1 Spencer Torkelson 4.00 10.00
2 Max Meyer 1.00 2.50
3 Austin Martin .75 2.00
4 Nick Gonzales 1.25 3.00
5 Garrett Crochet .60 1.50
6 Patrick Bailey .75 2.00
7 Bryce Jarvis .30 .75
8 Garrett Mitchell 2.00 5.00
9 Cade Cavalli .50 1.25
10 Jared Shuster .50 1.25
11 Aaron Sabato .50 1.25
12 Austin Wells 1.00 2.50
13 Bobby Miller 1.00 2.50
14 Jordan Westburg .60 1.50
15 Carmen Mlodzinski .30 .75
16 Slade Cecconi .30 .75
17 Tanner Burns .40 1.00
18 Alika Williams .30 .75
19 Dillon Dingler .75 2.00
20 Hudson Haskin 1.00 2.50
21 CJ Van Eyk .40 1.00
22 Zach DeLoach 1.00 2.50
23 Christian Roa .30 .75
24 Casey Schmitt .60 1.50
25 Burl Carraway .50 1.25
26 A.J. Block .25 .60
27 Freddy Zamora .40 1.00
28 Cole Henry .30 .75
29 Alerick Soularie .30 .75
30 Rylan Bannon .30 .75
31 Kyle Nicolas .40 1.00
32 Daniel Cabrera 1.00 2.50
33 Clayton Beeter .60 1.50
34 Jimmy Glowenke .50 1.25
35 Trei Cruz 1.00 2.50
36 Ryne Nelson .30 .75
37 Trent Palmer .30 .75
38 Kaden Polcovich .40 1.00
39 Casey Martin .75 2.00
40 Anthony Walters .30 .75
41 Zavier Warren .25 .60
42 Michael Guldberg .30 .75
43 Gage Workman 1.00 2.50
44 Tyler Keenan .40 1.00
45 Tanner Houck .60 1.50
46 Jeremy Wu-Yelland .40 1.00
47 Michael Toglia .25 .60
48 Zach Britton .30 .75
49 Baron Radcliff .30 .75
50 Mason Hickman .30 .75

2020 Elite Extra Edition OptiChrome College Tickets Signatures

RANDOM INSERTS IN PACKS
EXCHANGE DEADLINE 7/6/22
*HOLO: .5X TO 1.2X BASIC
1 Spencer Torkelson 40.00 100.00
2 Max Meyer 5.00 12.00
3 Austin Martin 15.00 40.00
4 Nick Gonzales 12.00 30.00
5 Garrett Crochet 15.00 40.00
6 Patrick Bailey 5.00 12.00
7 Bryce Jarvis 3.00 8.00
8 Garrett Mitchell 10.00 25.00
9 Cade Cavalli 3.00 8.00
10 Jared Shuster 5.00 12.00
11 Aaron Sabato 5.00 12.00
12 Austin Wells 6.00 15.00
13 Bobby Miller 8.00 20.00
14 Jordan Westburg 4.00 10.00
15 Carmen Mlodzinski 3.00 8.00
16 Slade Cecconi 3.00 8.00
17 Tanner Burns 4.00 10.00
18 Alika Williams 3.00 8.00
19 Dillon Dingler 8.00 20.00
20 Hudson Haskin 10.00 25.00
21 CJ Van Eyk 4.00 10.00
22 Zach DeLoach 5.00 12.00
23 Christian Roa 3.00 8.00
24 Casey Schmitt 4.00 10.00
25 Burl Carraway 3.00 8.00
26 A.J. Block 2.50 6.00
27 Freddy Zamora 4.00 10.00
28 Cole Henry 3.00 8.00
29 Alerick Soularie 3.00 8.00
30 Rylan Bannon 3.00 8.00
31 Kyle Nicolas 4.00 10.00
32 Daniel Cabrera 5.00 12.00
33 Clayton Beeter 4.00 10.00
34 Jimmy Glowenke 3.00 8.00
35 Trei Cruz 3.00 8.00
36 Ryne Nelson 3.00 8.00
37 Trent Palmer 3.00 8.00
38 Kaden Polcovich 4.00 10.00
40 Anthony Walters 3.00 8.00
41 Zavier Warren 2.50 6.00
42 Michael Guldberg 3.00 8.00
43 Gage Workman 5.00 12.00
44 Tyler Keenan 4.00 10.00
45 Tanner Houck 5.00 12.00
46 Jeremy Wu-Yelland 4.00 10.00
47 Michael Toglia 2.50 6.00
48 Zach Britton 3.00 8.00
49 Baron Radcliff 3.00 8.00
50 Mason Hickman 3.00 8.00

2020 Elite Extra Edition OptiChrome Signatures

RANDOM INSERTS IN PACKS
EXCHANGE DEADLINE 7/6/22
*HOLO: .5X TO 1.2X BASIC
1 Spencer Torkelson 40.00 100.00
2 Heston Kjerstad 15.00 40.00
4 Asa Lacy 8.00 20.00
6 Emerson Hancock 6.00 15.00
8 Robert Hassell 10.00 25.00
9 Zac Veen 10.00 25.00
10 Reid Detmers 5.00 12.00
12 Austin Hendrick 12.00 30.00
14 Justin Foscue 3.00 8.00
15 Mick Abel 4.00 10.00
16 Ed Howard 12.00 30.00
17 Nick Yorke 6.00 15.00
19 Pete Crow-Armstrong 8.00 20.00
21 Jordan Walker 8.00 20.00
23 Carson Tucker 3.00 8.00
24 Nick Bitsko 4.00 10.00
26 Tyler Soderstrom 6.00 15.00
32 Nick Loftin 4.00 10.00
34 Justin Lange 2.50 6.00
35 Drew Romo 4.00 10.00
40 Dax Fulton 4.00 10.00
41 Ben Hernandez 4.00 10.00
44 Jared Jones 4.00 10.00
45 Owen Caissie 4.00 10.00
47 Jared Kelley 2.50 6.00
50 Evan Carter 4.00 10.00
54 Masyn Winn 5.00 12.00
63 Markevian Hence 2.50 6.00
67 Nick Swiney 5.00 12.00
69 Isaiah Greene 5.00 12.00
70 Alec Burleson 4.00 10.00
71 Sammy Infante 3.00 8.00
72 Alex Santos 3.00 8.00
74 Anthony Servideo 3.00 8.00
76 Tyler Gentry 5.00 12.00
79 Nick Garcia 4.00 10.00
81 Sam Weatherly 2.50 6.00
82 David Calabrese 3.00 8.00
83 Petey Halpin 4.00 10.00
89 Tyler Keenan 4.00 10.00
94 Roberto Campos 10.00 25.00
98 Jake Vogel 3.00 8.00
99 Yiddi Cappe 5.00 12.00
100 Oscar Colas 12.00 30.00
101 Zion Bannister 3.00 8.00
111 Jake Eder 2.50 6.00
112 Nick Frasso 2.50 6.00
118 Werner Blakely 3.00 8.00
168 Yoelqui Cespedes 30.00 80.00

2020 Elite Extra Edition Prime Numbers A

*PRIME A: .6X TO 1.5X BASIC
RANDOM INSERTS IN PACKS
PRINT RUNS B/WN 130-242 COPIES PER

2020 Elite Extra Edition Prime Numbers A Die Cut

*PRIME A CUT/50-98: .8X TO 2X
*PRIME A CUT/26-49: 1X TO 2.5X
*PRIME A CUT/18-25: 1.2X TO 3X
RANDOM INSERTS IN PACKS
PRINT RUNS B/WN 2-98 COPIES PER
NO PRICING ON QTY 15 OR LESS

2020 Elite Extra Edition Prime Numbers B

*PRIME B: .8X TO 2X BASIC
RANDOM INSERTS IN PACKS
PRINT RUNS B/WN 51-68 COPIES PER

2020 Elite Extra Edition Prime Numbers B Die Cut

RANDOM INSERTS IN PACKS
PRINT RUNS B/WN 51-68 COPIES PER

2020 Elite Extra Edition Prospect Materials

RANDOM INSERTS IN PACKS
*ORANGE: .5X TO 1.2X BASIC
*RED: .6X TO 1.5X BASIC
1 Dylan Carlson 6.00 15.00
2 Nate Pearson 5.00 12.00
3 Luis V. Garcia 6.00 15.00
4 Adley Rutschman 5.00 12.00
5 Casey Mize 5.00 12.00
6 Taylor Trammell 2.50 6.00
7 Josh Jung 4.00 10.00
8 Shea Langeliers 3.00 8.00
9 Sixto Sanchez 5.00 12.00
10 Julio Rodriguez 8.00 20.00
11 Jonathan India 10.00 25.00
12 Riley Greene 6.00 15.00
13 Bobby Witt Jr. 8.00 20.00
14 Nick Madrigal 6.00 15.00
15 Alec Bohm 5.00 12.00
16 Jo Adell 6.00 15.00
17 Joey Bart 5.00 12.00
18 Royce Lewis 4.00 10.00
19 Jasson Dominguez 12.00 30.00
20 Evan White 4.00 10.00
21 Andres Gimenez 4.00 10.00
22 JJ Bleday 5.00 12.00
23 Brady Singer 8.00 20.00
24 Daniel Lynch 1.50 4.00
25 Daulton Varsho 2.50 6.00
26 Estevan Florial 2.50 6.00
27 Forrest Whitley 2.50 6.00
28 Ke'Bryan Hayes 5.00 12.00
29 Leody Taveras 2.50 6.00
30 Luis Rodriguez 4.00 10.00
31 Wander Franco 6.00 15.00

2020 Elite Extra Edition Pulse

RANDOM INSERTS IN PACKS
1 Spencer Torkelson 40.00 100.00
2 Heston Kjerstad 12.00 30.00
3 Austin Martin 15.00 40.00
4 Nick Gonzales 8.00 20.00
5 Max Meyer 6.00 15.00
6 Asa Lacy 10.00 25.00
7 Oscar Colas 15.00 40.00
8 Wander Franco 15.00 40.00
9 Jasson Dominguez 40.00 100.00
10 Adley Rutschman 15.00 40.00
11 Yiddi Cappe 5.00 12.00
12 Julio Rodriguez 20.00 50.00
13 Bobby Witt Jr. 12.00 30.00
14 Yoelqui Cespedes 12.00 30.00
15 Triston Casas 4.00 10.00
16 Jo Adell 10.00 25.00
17 Garrett Mitchell 12.00 30.00
18 CJ Abrams 5.00 12.00
19 Nolan Gorman 10.00 25.00
20 Norge Vera 2.00 5.00

2020 Elite Extra Edition Signatures

RANDOM INSERTS IN PACKS
EXCHANGE DEADLINE 7/6/22
*NEW DECADE: .4X TO 1X BASIC
*PRIME A: .5X TO 1.2X BASIC
1 Spencer Torkelson 40.00 100.00
2 Heston Kjerstad 15.00 40.00
3 Max Meyer 5.00 12.00
4 Asa Lacy 8.00 20.00
5 Austin Martin 15.00 40.00
6 Emerson Hancock 10.00 25.00
7 Nick Gonzales 12.00 30.00
8 Robert Hassell 10.00 25.00
9 Zac Veen 10.00 25.00
10 Reid Detmers 5.00 12.00
11 Garrett Crochet 10.00 25.00
12 Austin Hendrick 12.00 30.00
13 Patrick Bailey 5.00 12.00
14 Justin Foscue 3.00 8.00
15 Mick Abel 4.00 10.00
16 Ed Howard 12.00 30.00
17 Nick Yorke 6.00 15.00
18 Bryce Jarvis 3.00 8.00
19 Pete Crow-Armstrong 8.00 20.00
20 Garrett Mitchell EXCH 10.00 25.00
21 Jordan Walker 8.00 20.00
22 Cade Cavalli 3.00 8.00
23 Carson Tucker 3.00 8.00
24 Nick Bitsko 4.00 10.00
25 Jared Shuster 5.00 12.00
26 Tyler Soderstrom 6.00 15.00
27 Aaron Sabato 6.00 15.00
28 Austin Wells 6.00 15.00
29 Bobby Miller 8.00 20.00
31 Carmen Mlodzinski 3.00 8.00
32 Nick Loftin 4.00 10.00
33 Slade Cecconi 3.00 8.00
34 Justin Lange 2.50 6.00
35 Drew Romo 4.00 10.00
36 Tanner Burns 4.00 10.00
37 Alika Williams 3.00 8.00
38 Dillon Dingler 8.00 20.00
39 Hudson Haskin 10.00 25.00
40 Dax Fulton 4.00 10.00
41 Ben Hernandez 4.00 10.00
42 CJ Van Eyk 4.00 10.00
43 Zach DeLoach 5.00 12.00
44 Jared Jones 4.00 10.00
45 Owen Caissie 4.00 10.00
46 Gage Workman 5.00 12.00
47 Jared Kelley 5.00 12.00
48 Jesse Franklin 4.00 10.00
49 Casey Schmitt 4.00 10.00
50 Evan Carter 4.00 10.00
51 Trevor Hauver 4.00 10.00
53 Freddy Zamora 4.00 10.00
54 Masyn Winn 5.00 12.00
55 Cole Henry 3.00 8.00
56 Logan T. Allen 2.50 6.00
57 Ian Seymour 2.50 6.00
58 Jeff Criswell 3.00 8.00
59 Alerick Soularie 3.00 8.00
60 Landon Knack 3.00 8.00
61 Kyle Nicolas 4.00 10.00
62 Daniel Cabrera 5.00 12.00
63 Markevian Hence 2.50 6.00
64 Connor Phillips 4.00 10.00
65 Jackson Miller 3.00 8.00
66 Clayton Beeter 4.00 10.00
67 Nick Swiney 5.00 12.00
68 Jimmy Glowenke 3.00 8.00
69 Isaiah Greene 5.00 12.00
70 Alec Burleson 4.00 10.00
71 Sammy Infante 3.00 8.00
72 Alex Santos 3.00 8.00
73 Trei Cruz 3.00 8.00
74 Anthony Servideo 5.00 12.00
75 Zach McCambley 2.50 6.00
76 Tyler Gentry 5.00 12.00
77 Trent Palmer 3.00 8.00
78 Kaden Polcovich 4.00 10.00
79 Nick Garcia 4.00 10.00
81 Sam Weatherly 2.50 6.00
82 David Calabrese 3.00 8.00
83 Petey Halpin 4.00 10.00
84 Bryce Bonnin 4.00 10.00
86 Tekoah Roby 8.00 20.00
87 Casey Martin 5.00 12.00
88 Jordan Nwogu 6.00 15.00
89 Tyler Keenan 4.00 10.00
90 Liam Norris 2.50 6.00
91 Anthony Walters 3.00 8.00
92 Zavier Warren 2.50 6.00
93 Levi Prater 3.00 8.00
94 Roberto Campos 10.00 25.00
95 Holden Powell 3.00 8.00
96 Malcom Nunez 5.00 12.00
97 Norge Vera 3.00 8.00
98 Jake Vogel 3.00 8.00
99 Yiddi Cappe 5.00 12.00
100 Oscar Colas 12.00 30.00
101 Zion Bannister 3.00 8.00
102 Ji-Hwan Bae 4.00 10.00
103 Hunter Barnhart 2.50 6.00
104 Christian Roa 3.00 8.00
105 Michael Guldberg 3.00 8.00
106 Burl Carraway 3.00 8.00
107 Hunter Greene 4.00 10.00
108 Tyler Brown 4.00 10.00
109 Cody Thomas 4.00 10.00
110 Adisyn Coffey 2.50 6.00
111 Jake Eder 2.50 6.00
112 Nick Frasso 2.50 6.00
113 Juan Then 2.50 6.00
114 Packy Naughton 2.50 6.00
115 Jack Hartman 2.50 6.00
116 Levi Thomas 2.50 6.00
117 Case Williams 3.00 8.00
118 Werner Blakely 3.00 8.00
119 Kade Mechals 2.50 6.00
121 R.J. Dabovich 2.50 6.00
122 Dylan MacLean 4.00 10.00
123 Aaron Bracho 2.50 6.00
124 Luke Little 4.00 10.00
125 Jeremy Wu-Yelland 4.00 10.00
126 A.J. Vukovich 5.00 12.00
127 Matthew Dyer 4.00 10.00
128 Joey Wiemer 4.00 10.00
129 Ian Bedell 3.00 8.00
130 Brady Lindsly 4.00 10.00
131 Milan Tolentino 4.00 10.00
132 Tanner Murray 3.00 8.00
133 Spencer Strider 4.00 10.00
134 Dane Acker 4.00 10.00
135 Marco Raya 5.00 12.00
136 Beck Way 2.50 6.00
137 Carson Taylor 4.00 10.00
138 Zach Daniels 4.00 10.00
139 Colten Keith 3.00 8.00
140 Carter Baumler 4.00 10.00
141 Kyle Hurt 5.00 12.00
142 Will Klein 3.00 8.00
143 Zach Britton 3.00 8.00
144 Taylor Dollard 2.50 6.00
145 Logan Hofmann 2.50 6.00
146 Kristian Robinson 8.00 20.00
147 Jack Blomgren 4.00 10.00
148 Adam Seminaris 3.00 8.00
149 Bailey Horn 3.00 8.00
150 Joe Boyle 4.00 10.00
152 Vidal Brujan 10.00 25.00
153 Baron Radcliff 3.00 8.00
154 Keithron Moss 2.50 6.00
155 Shane Drohan 3.00 8.00
156 Brandon Pfaadt 2.50 6.00
157 Eric Orze 2.50 6.00
158 Hayden Cantrelle 2.50 6.00
159 LJ Jones IV 4.00 10.00
160 Mitchell Parker 2.50 6.00
161 Mason Hickman 3.00 8.00
162 Jeff Hakanson 5.00 12.00
164 Stevie Emanuels 2.50 6.00
165 Kala'i Rosario 3.00 8.00
166 Gavin Stone 5.00 12.00
167 Shay Whitcomb 3.00 8.00
168 Yoelqui Cespedes 30.00 80.00
169 Kale Emshoff 2.50 6.00
170 Nivaldo Rodriguez 5.00 12.00
171 Drew Rasmussen 4.00 10.00
172 Felix Cotes 2.50 6.00
173 Jose Dejesus 2.50 6.00
174 Fraymi De Leon 2.50 6.00
175 Henry Ramos 2.50 6.00
176 Jose Rodriguez 3.00 8.00
177 Jimmy Troncoso 2.50 6.00
178 Yoendry Vargas 2.50 6.00
179 Yofry Solano 2.50 6.00
180 Kelvin Hidalgo 2.50 6.00
181 Felnin Celesten 2.50 6.00
182 Yoelin Cespedes 8.00 20.00
183 Jelson Coca 2.50 6.00
184 Camilo Diaz 2.50 6.00
185 Welbin Francisca 2.50 6.00
186 Rainer Vargas 2.50 6.00
187 Daniel Rojas 3.00 8.00
188 Elvin Gonzalez 2.50 6.00
189 Jodainy Henriquez 2.50 6.00
190 Fabian Lopez 3.00 8.00
191 Yerlin Luis 2.50 6.00
192 Brian Martinez 2.50 6.00
193 Juan Bito 2.50 6.00
194 Emil Valencia 2.50 6.00
195 Eddie Perez 2.50 6.00
196 German Ramirez 2.50 6.00
197 Elvis Rojas 2.50 6.00
198 Juan Sanchez 2.50 6.00
199 Angel Trinidad 3.00 8.00
200 Lenny Carela 2.50 6.00

2020 Elite Extra Edition Signatures Aspirations Die Cut

*ASP.CUT: .6X TO 1.5X BASIC
RANDOM INSERTS IN PACKS
PRINT RUNS B/WN 19-49 COPIES PER
EXCHANGE DEADLINE 7/6/22
1 Spencer Torkelson/24 100.00 250.00
5 Austin Martin/27 40.00 100.00
11 Garrett Crochet/29 20.00 50.00
100 Oscar Colas/33 25.00 60.00

2020 Elite Extra Edition Signatures Aspirations Die Cut Gold

*ASP.CUT GOLD: .6X TO 1.5X BASIC
RANDOM INSERTS IN PACKS
STATED PRINT RUN 24 SER.#'d SETS
EXCHANGE DEADLINE 7/6/22
1 Spencer Torkelson 100.00 250.00
4 Asa Lacy 20.00 50.00
5 Austin Martin 50.00 120.00
11 Garrett Crochet 20.00 501.00
94 Roberto Campos/24 40.00 100.00
100 Oscar Colas 40.00 100.00

2020 Elite Extra Edition Signatures Prime Numbers A Die Cut

*PRIME A CUT: .6X TO 1.5X BASIC
RANDOM INSERTS IN PACKS
PRINT RUNS B/WN 2-98 COPIES PER
NO PRICING ON QTY 15 OR LESS
EXCHANGE DEADLINE 7/6/22
1 Spencer Torkelson/20 100.00 250.00
5 Austin Martin/85 30.00 80.00

2020 Elite Extra Edition Signatures Prime Numbers B

*PRIME B: .6X TO 1.5X BASIC
RANDOM INSERTS IN PACKS
PRINT RUNS B/WN 51-68 COPIES PER
EXCHANGE DEADLINE 7/6/22
1 Spencer Torkelson/61 75.00 200.00
5 Austin Martin/60 30.00 80.00
11 Garrett Crochet/66 20.00 50.00
100 Oscar Colas/61 25.00 60.00

2020 Elite Extra Edition Signatures Prime Numbers B Die Cut

*PRIME B CUT: .6X TO 1.5X BASIC
RANDOM INSERTS IN PACKS
PRINT RUNS B/WN 32-49 COPIES PER
EXCHANGE DEADLINE 7/6/22
1 Spencer Torkelson/39 75.00 200.00
5 Austin Martin/40 40.00 100.00
11 Garrett Crochet/34 20.00 50.00
100 Oscar Colas/39 25.00 60.00

2020 Elite Extra Edition Signatures Status Die Cut

*STATUS CUT: .6X TO 1.5X BASIC
RANDOM INSERTS IN PACKS
PRINT RUNS B/WN 1-31 COPIES PER
NO PRICING ON QTY 19 OR LESS
EXCHANGE DEADLINE 7/6/22
1 Spencer Torkelson/26 75.00 200.00
5 Austin Martin/23 50.00 120.00
11 Garrett Crochet/21 20.00 50.00

2020 Elite Extra Edition USA Materials

RANDOM INSERTS IN PACKS
*ORANGE/59-199: .5X TO 1.2X BASIC
*RED/22-49: .6X TO 1.5X BASIC
2 Alec Bohm 4.00 10.00
3 Alec Burleson 2.50 6.00
4 Alika Williams 2.00 5.00
5 Andrew Vaughn 8.00 20.00
6 Asa Lacy 4.00 10.00
7 Austin Hendrick 4.00 10.00
8 Austin Martin 5.00 12.00
9 Austin Wells 6.00 15.00
10 Ben Hernandez 2.50 6.00
11 Bobby Dalbec 10.00 25.00
12 Brennan Malone 1.50 4.00
13 Burl Carraway 3.00 8.00
14 Cade Cavalli 3.00 8.00
16 Chris McMahon 2.50 6.00
17 CJ Van Eyk 2.50 6.00
18 Cole Henry 2.00 5.00
19 Cole Wilcox 2.00 5.00
20 Daniel Cabrera 6.00 15.00
21 Drew Romo 4.00 10.00
22 Gage Workman 6.00 15.00
23 Garrett Mitchell 6.00 15.00
24 Graeme Stinson 1.50 4.00
25 Hans Crouse 1.50 4.00
26 Heston Kjerstad 12.00 30.00
27 Jared Jones 2.50 6.00
28 Jared Kelley 1.50 4.00
29 Jarred Kelenic 10.00 25.00
30 Jeff Criswell 2.00 5.00
31 Jo Adell 6.00 15.00
32 John Doxakis 2.50 6.00
33 Justin Foscue 6.00 15.00
34 Logan T. Allen 1.50 4.00
35 Matthew Allan 3.00 8.00
36 Max Meyer 6.00 15.00
37 Mick Abel 2.50 6.00
38 Milan Tolentino 2.50 6.00
39 Nick Loftin 2.50 6.00
40 Nick Madrigal 6.00 15.00
41 Nick Yorke 6.00 15.00
42 Noah Song 2.00 5.00
43 Patrick Bailey 5.00 12.00
44 Pete Crow-Armstrong 5.00 12.00
45 Petey Halpin 4.00 10.00
46 Reid Detmers 4.00 10.00
47 Robert Hassell 6.00 15.00
48 Spencer Torkelson 10.00 25.00
49 Tanner Burns 2.50 6.00
50 Tanner Houck 4.00 10.00
51 Triston Casas 3.00 8.00
52 Tyler Soderstrom 3.00 8.00

2003 Donruss Estrellas

COMPLETE SET 12.50 30.00
1 Jose Contreras RC .25 .60
2 Darin Erstad .10 .25
3 Francisco Rodriguez .15 .40
4 Troy Glaus .10 .25
5 Curt Schilling .15 .40
6 Luis Gonzalez .10 .25
7 Randy Johnson .25 .60
8 Andruw Jones .10 .25
9 Chipper Jones .25 .60
10 Greg Maddux .30 .75
11 Rodrigo Lopez .10 .25
12 Manny Ramirez .25 .60
13 Rickey Henderson .25 .60
14 Nomar Garciaparra .15 .40
15 Pedro Martinez .15 .40
16 Mark Prior .15 .40
17 Kerry Wood .10 .25
18 Sammy Sosa .25 .60
19 Bartolo Colon .10 .25
20 Magglio Ordonez .15 .40
21 Carlos Lee .10 .25
22 Ken Griffey Jr. .50 1.25
23 Barry Larkin .15 .40
24 Adam Dunn .15 .40
25 Jeremy Guthrie .10 .25
26 C.C. Sabathia .15 .40
27 Omar Vizquel .15 .40
28 Jeff Baker .10 .25
29 Larry Walker .15 .40
30 Jason Jennings .10 .25
31 Todd Helton .15 .40
32 Josh Beckett .10 .25
33 Ivan Rodriguez .15 .40
34 Jeff Kent .10 .25
35 Craig Biggio .15 .40
36 Richard Hidalgo .10 .25
37 Jeff Bagwell .15 .40
38 Lance Berkman .15 .40
39 Carlos Beltran .15 .40
40 Mike Sweeney .10 .25
41 Hideo Nomo .25 .60
42 Kazuhisa Ishii .10 .25
43 Fred McGriff .15 .40
44 Odalis Perez .10 .25
45 Shawn Green .10 .25
46 Adrian Beltre .25 .60
47 Ben Sheets .10 .25
48 Richie Sexson .10 .25
49 Torii Hunter .10 .25
50 Joe Mays .10 .25
51 Cristian Guzman .10 .25
52 Jose Vidro .10 .25
53 Javier Vazquez .10 .25
54 Vladimir Guerrero .15 .40
55 Cliff Floyd .10 .25
56 Mike Piazza .25 .60
57 Tom Glavine .15 .40
58 Roberto Alomar .15 .40
59 Hideki Matsui .50 1.25
60 Bernie Williams .15 .40
61 Derek Jeter .60 1.50
62 Alfonso Soriano .15 .40
63 Jason Giambi .10 .25
64 Jorge Posada .15 .40
65 Mariano Rivera .30 .75
66 Mike Mussina .15 .40
67 Roger Clemens .30 .75
68 Barry Zito .15 .40
69 Eric Chavez .10 .25
70 Mark Mulder .10 .25
71 Miguel Tejada .15 .40
72 Tim Hudson .15 .40
73 Jim Thome .15 .40
74 Vicente Padilla .10 .25
75 Bobby Abreu .10 .25
76 Jimmy Rollins .15 .40
77 Pat Burrell .10 .25
78 Jose Castillo .10 .25
79 Brian Giles .10 .25
80 Sean Burroughs .10 .25
81 Phil Nevin .10 .25
82 Ryan Klesko .10 .25
83 Barry Bonds .40 1.00
84 Benito Santiago .10 .25
85 Rich Aurilia .10 .25
86 Bret Boone .10 .25
87 Edgar Martinez .15 .40
88 Freddy Garcia .10 .25
89 Ichiro Suzuki .30 .75
90 Scott Rolen .15 .40
91 J.D. Drew .10 .25
92 Jim Edmonds .15 .40
93 Albert Pujols .30 .75
94 Tino Martinez .10 .25
95 Matt Morris .10 .25
96 Alex Rodriguez .30 .75
97 Juan Gonzalez .10 .25
98 Rafael Palmeiro .15 .40
99 Eric Hinske .10 .25
100 Carlos Delgado .10 .25

2003 Donruss Estrellas Estrellas

COMPLETE SET 6.00 15.00
1 Albert Pujols .60 1.50
2 Alex Rodriguez .60 1.50
3 Cal Ripken Jr 1.50 4.00
4 Derek Jeter 1.25 3.00
5 Miguel Tejada .30 .75

2003 Donruss Estrellas Leyendas Del Pasado

COMPLETE SET 8.00 20.00
1 Cal Ripken Jr 1.50 4.00
2 Don Mattingly 1.00 2.50
3 George Brett 1.00 2.50
4 Juan Marichal .30 .75
5 Luis Aparicio .30 .75
6 Roberto Clemente 1.25 3.00
7 Orlando Cepeda .30 .75
8 Rod Carew .30 .75
9 Tony Gwynn .50 1.25
10 Tony Perez .30 .75

2003 Donruss Estrellas Nacion de Origen

COMPLETE SET 8.00 20.00
1 Francisco Rodriguez .15 .40
2 Andruw Jones .10 .25
3 Sammy Sosa .25 .60
4 Magglio Ordonez .15 .40
5 Carlos Lee .10 .25
6 Roberto Clemente .60 1.50
7 Alfonso Soriano .15 .40
8 Jose Contreras .25 .60
9 Tony Batista .10 .25
10 Hideki Matsui .50 1.25
11 Vicente Padilla .10 .25
12 Ichiro Suzuki .30 .75
13 Edgar Renteria .10 .25
14 Rafael Palmeiro .15 .40
15 Ivan Rodriguez .15 .40

2003 Donruss Estrellas Poder De Cuadrangular

COMPLETE SET 8.00 20.00
1 Jason Giambi .10 .25
2 Jim Thome .15 .40
3 Rafael Palmeiro .15 .40
4 Alfonso Soriano .15 .40
5 Eric Chavez .10 .25
6 Troy Glaus .10 .25
7 Adam Dunn .15 .40
8 Albert Pujols .30 .75
9 Barry Bonds .40 1.00
10 Hideki Matsui .50 1.25
11 Frank Thomas .25 .60
12 Manny Ramirez .25 .60
13 Sammy Sosa .25 .60
14 Alex Rodriguez .30 .75
15 Miguel Tejada .15 .40

2003 Donruss Estrellas Posters de su Jugador

COMPLETE SET 6.00 15.00
1 Adam Dunn .15 .40
2 Albert Pujols .30 .75
3 Albert Pujols .30 .75
4 Alex Rodriguez .30 .75
5 Alex Rodriguez .30 .75
6 Alfonso Soriano .15 .40
7 Alfonso Soriano .15 .40
8 Barry Bonds .40 1.00
9 Derek Jeter .60 1.50
10 Derek Jeter .60 1.50
11 Francisco Rodriguez .15 .40
12 Hideki Matsui .50 1.25
13 Ichiro Suzuki .30 .75
14 Jason Giambi .10 .25
15 Jose Contreras .25 .60
16 Jose Contreras .25 .60
17 Sammy Sosa .25 .60
18 Sammy Sosa .25 .60
19 Miguel Tejada .15 .40
20 Mike Piazza .25 .60
21 Nomar Garciaparra .15 .40
22 Pedro Martinez .15 .40
23 Pedro Martinez .15 .40
24 Roberto Clemente .60 1.50
25 Vladimir Guerrero .15 .40

2003 Donruss Estrellas Precision De Lanzamiento

COMPLETE SET 4.00 10.00
1 Jose Contreras 1.00 2.50
2 Randy Johnson 1.00 2.50
3 Francisco Rodriguez .60 1.50
4 Nolan Ryan 3.00 8.00
5 Pedro Martinez .60 1.50

2004 Donruss Estrellas

COMMON CARD .25 .60
1 Adam Dunn .40 1.00
2 Adrian Beltre .60 1.50
3 Albert Pujols .75 2.00
4 Alex Rodriguez .75 2.00
5 Alfonso Soriano .40 1.00
6 Andruw Jones .25 .60
7 Barry Larkin .40 1.00
8 Barry Zito .40 1.00
9 Bartolo Colon .25 .60
10 Ben Sheets .25 .60
11 Benito Santiago .25 .60
12 Bernie Williams .40 1.00
13 Bobby Abreu .25 .60
14 Bret Boone .25 .60
15 Brian Giles .25 .60
16 C.C. Sabathia .40 1.00
17 Carlos Beltran .40 1.00
18 Carlos Delgado .25 .60
19 Carlos Lee .25 .60
20 Chipper Jones .60 1.50

21 Cliff Floyd .25 .60
22 Craig Biggio .40 1.00
23 Cristian Guzman .25 .60
24 Curt Schilling .40 1.00
25 Darin Erstad .25 .60
26 Derek Jeter 1.50 4.00
27 Edgar Martinez .40 1.00
28 Eric Chavez .25 .60
29 Eric Hinske .25 .60
30 Francisco Rodriguez .40 1.00
31 Fred McGriff .25 .60
32 Freddy Garcia .25 .60
33 Greg Maddux .75 2.00
34 Hideki Matsui 1.00 2.50
35 Hideo Nomo .60 1.50
36 Ichiro Suzuki .75 2.00
37 Ivan Rodriguez .40 1.00
38 J.D. Drew .25 .60
39 Jason Giambi .25 .60
40 Jason Jennings .25 .60
41 Javier Vazquez .25 .60
42 Jeff Bagwell .40 1.00
43 Jeff Baker .25 .60
44 Jeff Kent .25 .60
45 Jeremy Guthrie .25 .60
46 Jim Edmonds .40 1.00
47 Jim Thome .40 1.00
48 Jimmy Rollins .40 1.00
49 Joe Mays .25 .60
50 Jorge Posada .40 1.00
51 Jose Castillo .25 .60
52 Jose Contreras .25 .60
53 Jose Vidro .25 .60
54 Josh Beckett .25 .60
55 Juan Gonzalez .25 .60
56 Kazuhisa Ishii .25 .60
57 Kazuo Matsui .40 1.00
58 Ken Griffey Jr. 1.25 3.00
59 Kerry Wood .25 .60
60 Lance Berkman .40 1.00
61 Larry Walker .40 1.00
62 Luis Gonzalez .25 .60
63 Magglio Ordonez .40 1.00
64 Manny Ramirez .60 1.50
65 Mariano Rivera .75 2.00
66 Mark Mulder .25 .60
67 Mark Prior .40 1.00
68 Matt Morris .25 .60
69 Miguel Tejada .40 1.00
70 Mike Mussina .40 1.00
71 Mike Piazza .60 1.50
72 Mike Sweeney .25 .60
73 Nomar Garciaparra .40 1.00
74 Odalis Perez .25 .60
75 Omar Vizquel .40 1.00
76 Pat Burrell .25 .60
77 Pedro Martinez .40 1.00
78 Phil Nevin .25 .60
79 Rafael Palmeiro .40 1.00
80 Randy Johnson .60 1.50
81 Rich Aurilia .25 .60
82 Richard Hidalgo .25 .60
83 Richie Sexson .25 .60
84 Rickey Henderson .60 1.50
85 Roberto Alomar .40 1.00
86 Rodrigo Lopez .25 .60
87 Roger Clemens .75 2.00
88 Ryan Klesko .25 .60
89 Sammy Sosa .60 1.50
90 Scott Rolen .40 1.00
91 Sean Burroughs .25 .60
92 Shawn Green .25 .60
93 Tim Hudson .40 1.00
94 Tino Martinez .40 1.00
95 Todd Helton .40 1.00
96 Tom Glavine .40 1.00
97 Torii Hunter .25 .60
98 Troy Glaus .25 .60
99 Vicente Padilla .25 .60
100 Vladimir Guerrero .40 1.00

2004 Donruss Estrellas Estrellas

COMPLETE SET 4.00 10.00
1 Cal Ripken Jr. 1.50 4.00
2 Miguel Tejada .30 .75
3 Alex Rodriguez .60 1.50
4 Derek Jeter 1.25 3.00
5 Albert Pujols .60 1.50

2004 Donruss Estrellas Leyendas del Pasado

COMPLETE SET 3.00 8.00
1 Cal Ripken Jr. 1.50 4.00
2 Luis Aparicio .30 .75
3 Tony Perez .30 .75
4 George Brett 1.00 2.50
5 Rod Carew .30 .75
6 Don Mattingly 1.00 2.50
7 Roberto Clemente 1.25 3.00
8 Tony Gwynn .50 1.25
9 Juan Marichal .30 .75
10 Orlando Cepeda .30 .75

2004 Donruss Estrellas Nacion de Origen

COMPLETE SET 3.00 8.00
1 Alfonso Soriano .30 .75
2 Andruw Jones .20 .50
3 Carlos Lee .20 .50
4 Edgar Renteria .20 .50
5 Francisco Rodriguez .30 .75
6 Hideki Matsui .75 2.00
7 Ichiro Suzuki .60 1.50
8 Ivan Rodriguez .30 .75
9 Jose Contreras .20 .50
10 Magglio Ordonez .30 .75
11 Rafael Palmeiro .30 .75
12 Roberto Clemente 1.25 3.00
13 Sammy Sosa .50 1.25
14 Tony Batista .20 .50
15 Vicente Padilla .20 .50

2004 Donruss Estrellas Poder de Cuadrangular

COMPLETE SET 3.00 8.00
1 Adam Dunn .30 .75
2 Albert Pujols .60 1.50
3 Alex Rodriguez .60 1.50
4 Alfonso Soriano .30 .75
5 Carlos Delgado .20 .50
6 Eric Chavez .20 .50
7 Frank Thomas .50 1.25
8 Hideki Matsui .75 2.00
9 Jason Giambi .20 .50
10 Jim Thome .30 .75
11 Manny Ramirez .50 1.25
12 Miguel Tejada .30 .75
13 Rafael Palmeiro .30 .75
14 Sammy Sosa .50 1.25
15 Troy Glaus .20 .50

2004 Donruss Estrellas Precision de Lanzameinto

COMPLETE SET 2.00 5.00
1 Francisco Rodriguez .30 .75
2 Jose Contreras .20 .50
3 Nolan Ryan 1.50 4.00
4 Pedro Martinez .30 .75
5 Randy Johnson .50 1.25

2002 Donruss Fan Club

COMP.SET w/o SP's (240) 15.00 40.00
COMMON (1-200/261-300) .10 .30
COMMON (201-260/U201-U225) .75 2.00
201-260 ODDS 1:4 FAN CLUB
U201-U225 ODDS 1:4 DONR.ROOK.RETAIL
1 Alex Rodriguez .40 1.00
2 Pedro Martinez .20 .50
3 Vladimir Guerrero .30 .75
4 Jim Edmonds .10 .30
5 Derek Jeter .75 2.00
6 Johnny Damon .20 .50
7 Rafael Furcal .10 .30
8 Cal Ripken 1.00 2.50
9 Brad Radke .10 .30
10 Bret Boone .10 .30
11 Pat Burrell .10 .30
12 Roy Oswalt .10 .30
13 Cliff Floyd .10 .30
14 Robin Ventura .10 .30
15 Frank Thomas .30 .75
16 Mariano Rivera .30 .75
17 Paul LoDuca .10 .30
18 Geoff Jenkins .10 .30
19 Tony Gwynn .40 1.00
20 Chipper Jones .30 .75
21 Eric Chavez .10 .30
22 Kerry Wood .10 .30
23 Jorge Posada .20 .50
24 J.D. Drew .10 .30
25 Garret Anderson .10 .30
26 Javier Vazquez .10 .30
27 Kenny Lofton .10 .30
28 Mike Mussina .20 .50
29 Paul Konerko .10 .30
30 Bernie Williams .20 .50
31 Eric Milton .10 .30
32 Craig Wilson .10 .30
33 Paul O'Neill .20 .50
34 Dmitri Young .10 .30
35 Andres Galarraga .10 .30
36 Gary Sheffield .10 .30
37 Ben Grieve .10 .30
38 Scott Rolen .20 .50
39 Mark Grace .20 .50
40 Albert Pujols .60 1.50
41 Barry Zito .10 .30
42 Edgar Martinez .20 .50
43 Jarrod Washburn .10 .30
44 Juan Pierre .10 .30
45 Mark Buehrle .10 .30
46 Larry Walker .10 .30
47 Trot Nixon .10 .30
48 Wade Miller .10 .30
49 Robert Fick .10 .30
50 Sean Casey .10 .30
51 Joe Mays .10 .30
52 Brad Fullmer .10 .30
53 Chan Ho Park .10 .30
54 Carlos Delgado .10 .30
55 Phil Nevin .10 .30
56 Mike Cameron .10 .30
57 Raul Mondesi .10 .30
58 Roberto Alomar .20 .50
59 Ryan Klesko .10 .30
60 Andruw Jones .20 .50
61 Gabe Kapler .10 .30
62 Darin Erstad .10 .30
63 Cristian Guzman .10 .30
64 Kazuhiro Sasaki .10 .30
65 Doug Mientkiewicz .10 .30
66 Sammy Sosa .30 .75
67 Mike Hampton .10 .30
68 Rickey Henderson .30 .75
69 Mark Mulder .10 .30
70 Jeff Conine .10 .30
71 Freddy Garcia .10 .30
72 Ivan Rodriguez .20 .50
73 Terrence Long .10 .30
74 Adam Dunn .10 .30
75 Moises Alou .10 .30
76 Todd Helton .20 .50
77 Preston Wilson .10 .30
78 Roger Cedeno .10 .30
79 Tony Armas Jr. .10 .30
80 Manny Ramirez .20 .50
81 Jose Vidro .10 .30
82 Randy Johnson .30 .75
83 Richie Sexson .10 .30
84 Troy Glaus .10 .30
85 Kevin Brown .10 .30
86 Woody Williams .10 .30
87 Adrian Beltre .10 .30
88 Brian Giles .10 .30
89 Jermaine Dye .10 .30
90 Craig Biggio .20 .50
91 Richard Hidalgo .10 .30
92 Magglio Ordonez .10 .30
93 Al Leiter .10 .30
94 Jeff Kent .10 .30
95 Curt Schilling .10 .30
96 Tim Hudson .10 .30
97 Fred McGriff .20 .50
98 Barry Larkin .20 .50
99 Jim Thome .20 .50
100 Tom Glavine .20 .50
101 Alfonso Soriano .10 .30
102 Jamie Moyer .10 .30
103 Vinny Castilla .10 .30
104 Rich Aurilia .10 .30
105 Matt Morris .10 .30
106 Rafael Palmeiro .20 .50
107 Joe Crede .10 .30
108 Barry Bonds .75 2.00
109 Robert Person .10 .30
110 Nomar Garciaparra .50 1.25
111 Brandon Duckworth .10 .30
112 Russ Ortiz .10 .30
113 Jeff Weaver .10 .30
114 Carlos Beltran .10 .30
115 Ellis Burks .10 .30
116 Jeremy Giambi .10 .30
117 Carlos Lee .10 .30
118 Ken Griffey Jr. .60 1.50
119 Torii Hunter .10 .30
120 Andy Pettitte .20 .50
121 Jose Canseco .20 .50
122 Charles Johnson .10 .30
123 Nick Johnson .10 .30
124 Luis Gonzalez .10 .30
125 Rondell White .10 .30
126 Miguel Tejada .10 .30
127 Jose Cruz Jr. .10 .30
128 Brent Abernathy .10 .30
129 Scott Brosius .10 .30
130 Jon Lieber .10 .30
131 John Smoltz .20 .50
132 Mike Sweeney .10 .30
133 Shannon Stewart .10 .30
134 Derrek Lee .20 .50
135 Brian Jordan .10 .30
136 Rusty Greer .10 .30
137 Mike Piazza .50 1.25
138 Billy Wagner .10 .30
139 Shawn Green .10 .30
140 Orlando Cabrera .10 .30
141 Jeff Bagwell .20 .50
142 Aaron Sele .10 .30
143 Hideo Nomo .30 .75
144 Marlon Anderson .10 .30
145 Todd Walker .10 .30
146 Bobby Higginson .10 .30
147 Ichiro Suzuki .60 1.50
148 Juan Uribe .10 .30
149 Jason Kendall .10 .30
150 Mark Quinn .10 .30
151 Ben Sheets .10 .30
152 Paul Abbott .10 .30
153 Aubrey Huff .10 .30
154 Greg Maddux .50 1.25
155 Darryl Kile .10 .30
156 John Burkett .10 .30
157 Juan Gonzalez .10 .30
158 Javy Lopez .10 .30
159 Aramis Ramirez .10 .30
160 Lance Berkman .10 .30
161 David Cone .10 .30
162 Edgar Renteria .10 .30
163 Roger Clemens .60 1.50
164 Frank Catalanotto .10 .30
165 Bartolo Colon .10 .30
166 Mark McGwire .75 2.00
167 Jay Gibbons .10 .30
168 Tony Clark .10 .30
169 Tsuyoshi Shinjo .10 .30
170 Brad Penny .10 .30
171 Marcus Giles .10 .30
172 Matt Williams .10 .30
173 Bud Smith .10 .30
174 Tino Martinez .20 .50
175 Ryan Dempster .10 .30
176 Jimmy Rollins .10 .30
177 Edgardo Alfonzo .10 .30
178 Jason Giambi .10 .30
179 Aaron Boone .10 .30
180 Ray Durham .10 .30
181 Mike Lowell .10 .30
182 Jose Ortiz .10 .30
183 Johnny Estrada .10 .30
184 Shane Reynolds .10 .30
185 Joe Kennedy .10 .30
186 Corey Patterson .10 .30
187 Jeromy Burnitz .10 .30
188 C.C. Sabathia .10 .30
189 Doug Davis .10 .30
190 Omar Vizquel .20 .50
191 John Olerud .10 .30
192 Dee Brown .10 .30
193 Kip Wells .10 .30
194 A.J. Burnett .10 .30
195 Josh Towers .10 .30
196 Jason Varitek .30 .75
197 Jason Isringhausen .10 .30
198 Fernando Vina .10 .30
199 Ramon Ortiz .10 .30
200 Bobby Abreu .10 .30
201 Willie Harris .75 2.00
202 Angel Santos .75 2.00
203 Corky Miller .75 2.00
204 Michael Rivera .75 2.00
205 Justin Duchscherer .75 2.00
206 Rick Bauer .75 2.00
207 Angel Berroa .75 2.00
208 Juan Cruz .75 2.00
209 Dewon Brazelton .75 2.00
210 Mark Prior 1.25 3.00
211 Mark Teixeira 1.25 3.00
212 Geronimo Gil .75 2.00
213 Casey Fossum .75 2.00
214 Ken Harvey .75 2.00
215 Michael Cuddyer .75 2.00
216 Wilson Betemit .75 2.00
217 David Brous .75 2.00
218 Juan A. Pena .75 2.00
219 Travis Hafner .75 2.00
220 Erick Almonte .75 2.00
221 Morgan Ensberg .75 2.00
222 Martin Vargas .75 2.00
223 Brandon Berger .75 2.00
224 Zach Day .75 2.00
225 Brad Voyles .75 2.00
226 Jeremy Affeldt .75 2.00
227 Nick Neugebauer .75 2.00
228 Tim Redding .75 2.00
229 Adam Johnson .75 2.00
230 Doug DeVore RC .75 2.00
231 Cody Ransom .75 2.00
232 Marlon Byrd .75 2.00
233 Delvin James .75 2.00
234 Eric Munson .75 2.00
235 Dennis Tankersley .75 2.00
236 Josh Beckett .75 2.00
237 Bill Hall .75 2.00
238 Kevin Olsen .75 2.00
239 Francis Beltran RC .75 2.00
240 Antonio Perez .75 2.00
241 Orlando Hudson .75 2.00
242 Anderson Machado RC .75 2.00
243 Tom Shearn RC .75 2.00
244 Brian Mallette RC .75 2.00
245 Raul Chavez RC .75 2.00
246 Andy Pratt RC .75 2.00
247 Jorge De La Rosa RC .75 2.00
248 Jeff Deardorff .75 2.00
249 Ben Howard RC .75 2.00
250 Brandon Backe RC 1.25 3.00
251 Ed Rogers .75 2.00
252 Travis Hughes RC .75 2.00
253 Rodrigo Rosario RC .75 2.00
254 Alfredo Amezaga .75 2.00
255 Jorge Padilla RC .75 2.00
256 Victor Martinez 1.25 3.00
257 Steve Bechler RC .75 2.00
258 Chris Baker RC .75 2.00
259 Ryan Jamison .75 2.00
260 Allan Simpson RC .75 2.00
261 Alex Rodriguez FC .40 1.00
262 Vladimir Guerrero FC .30 .75
263 Bud Smith FC .10 .30
264 Miguel Tejada FC .10 .30
265 Craig Biggio FC .20 .50
266 Luis Gonzalez FC .10 .30
267 Ivan Rodriguez FC .20 .50
268 C.C. Sabathia FC .10 .30
269 Jeff Bagwell FC .20 .50
270 Aramis Ramirez FC .10 .30
271 Bob Abreu FC .10 .30
272 Rich Aurilia FC .10 .30
273 Jason Giambi FC .10 .30
274 Rickey Henderson FC .30 .75
275 Wade Miller FC .10 .30
276 Andruw Jones FC .20 .50
277 Troy Glaus FC .10 .30
278 Roy Oswalt FC .10 .30
279 Tony Gwynn FC .40 1.00
280 Adam Dunn FC .10 .30
281 Larry Walker FC .10 .30
282 Jose Canseco FC .20 .50
283 Todd Helton FC .20 .50
284 Lance Berkman FC .10 .30
285 Cal Ripken FC 1.00 2.50
286 Albert Pujols FC .60 1.50
287 Alfonso Soriano FC .10 .30
288 Mark Mulder FC .10 .30
289 Mike Hampton FC .10 .30
290 Andres Galarraga FC .10 .30
291 Barry Bonds FC .75 2.00
292 Ben Sheets FC .10 .30
293 Ichiro Suzuki FC .60 1.50
294 J.D. Drew FC .10 .30
295 Jose Ortiz FC .10 .30
296 Kerry Wood FC .10 .30
297 Mark McGwire FC .75 2.00
298 Mike Sweeney FC .10 .30
299 Pat Burrell FC .10 .30
300 Tim Hudson FC .10 .30
U201 Kirk Saarloos RC .75 2.00
U202 Oliver Perez RC 1.50 4.00
U203 So Taguchi RC 1.25 3.00
U204 Runelvys Hernandez RC .75 2.00
U205 Freddy Sanchez RC 1.50 4.00
U206 Cliff Lee RC 2.00 5.00
U207 Kazuhisa Ishii RC 1.25 3.00
U208 Kevin Cash RC .75 2.00
U209 Trey Hodges RC .75 2.00
U210 Wilson Valdez RC .75 2.00
U211 Satoru Komiyama RC .75 2.00
U212 Luis Ugueto RC .75 2.00
U213 Joe Borchard .75 2.00
U214 Brian Tallet RC .75 2.00
U215 Jeriome Robertson RC .75 2.00
U216 Eric Junge RC .75 2.00
U217 Aaron Cook RC .75 2.00
U218 Jason Simontacchi RC .75 2.00
U219 Miguel Asencio RC .75 2.00
U220 Josh Bard RC .75 2.00
U221 Earl Snyder RC .75 2.00
U222 Felix Escalona RC .75 2.00
U223 Rene Reyes RC .75 2.00
U224 Chone Figgins RC 1.25 3.00
U225 Chris Snelling RC 1.00 2.50

2002 Donruss Fan Club Autographs

201-260 RANDOM INSERTS IN RETAIL PACKS
STATED PRINT RUNS LISTED BELOW
CARDS ARE NOT SERIAL-NUMBERED
PRINT RUNS PROVIDED BY DONRUSS
SKIP-NUMBERED 53-CARD SET
NO PRICING DUE TO LACK OF INFO
U206 Cliff Lee/50 20.00 50.00

2002 Donruss Fan Club Credits

*STARS 1-200/261-300: 8X TO 20X BASIC
*PROSPECTS 201-260: 1.5X TO 4X BASIC
1-300 RANDOM IN FAN CLUB RETAIL PACKS
U201-U225 RANDOM IN DON.ROOK.PACKS
STATED PRINT RUN 100 SERIAL #'d SETS

2002 Donruss Fan Club Die-Cuts

*DIE CUTS 1-200: 1.5X TO 4X BASIC
STATED ODDS 1:4 RETAIL

2002 Donruss Fan Club Artists

COMPLETE SET (14) 50.00 100.00
*ARTISTS: .4X TO 1X HOBBY INSERTS
STATED ODDS 1:172 RETAIL

2002 Donruss Fan Club Craftsmen

COMPLETE SET (18) 75.00 150.00
*CRAFTSMEN: .4X TO 1X HOBBY INSERTS
STATED ODDS 1:134 RETAIL

2002 Donruss Fan Club Double Features

COMPLETE SET (10) 100.00 200.00
*DOUB.FEAT: .4X TO 1X HOBBY INSERTS
STATED ODDS 1:240 RETAIL

2002 Donruss Fan Club Franchise Features

COMPLETE SET (40) 150.00 300.00
*FRAN.FEAT: .4X TO 1X HOBBY INSERTS
STATED ODDS 1:60 RETAIL

2002 Donruss Fan Club League Leaders

COMPLETE SET (45) 200.00 400.00
*LEADERS: .4X TO 1X HOBBY INSERTS
STATED ODDS 1:54 RETAIL

2002 Donruss Fan Club Pure Power

COMPLETE SET (18) 75.00 150.00
*POWER: .4X TO 1X HOBBY INSERTS
STATED ODDS 1:134 RETAIL

2002 Donruss Fan Club Records

COMPLETE SET (5) 40.00 80.00
*RECORDS: .4X TO 1X HOBBY INSERTS
RANDOM INSERTS IN PACKS

2005 Donruss Greats

COMPLETE SET (150) 12.50 30.00
COMMON CARD (1-100) .25 .60
COMMON CARD (101-150) .25 .60
COMMON RC (101-150) .25 .60
1 Al Kaline .60 1.50
2 Alan Trammell .40 1.00
3 Andre Dawson .40 1.00
4 Barry Larkin .40 1.00
5 Bert Blyleven .40 1.00
6 Billy Williams .40 1.00
7 Bo Jackson .60 1.50
8 Bob Feller .40 1.00
9 Bobby Doerr .40 1.00
10 Brooks Robinson .40 1.00
11 Cal Ripken 2.00 5.00
12 Dale Murphy .60 1.50
13 Darryl Strawberry .25 .60
14 Dave Parker .25 .60
15 Dave Stewart .25 .60
16 David Cone .25 .60
17 Dennis Eckersley .40 1.00
18 Don Larsen .25 .60
19 Don Mattingly 1.25 3.00
20 Don Sutton .40 1.00
21 Duke Snider .40 1.00
22 Dwight Evans .40 1.00
23 Dwight Gooden .25 .60
24 Earl Weaver .40 1.00
25 Fergie Jenkins .40 1.00
26 Frank Robinson .40 1.00
27 Fred Lynn .25 .60
28 Gary Carter .40 1.00
29 Gaylord Perry .40 1.00
30 George Brett 1.25 3.00
31 George Foster .25 .60
32 George Kell .40 1.00
33 Harmon Killebrew .60 1.50
34 Harold Baines .40 1.00
35 Harold Reynolds .25 .60
36 Jack Morris .40 1.00
37 Jim Abbott .25 .60
38 Jim Bunning .40 1.00
39 Jim Palmer .40 1.00
40 Jim Rice .40 1.00
41 Jim Leyritz .25 .60
42 Joe Morgan Swing .40 1.00
43 John Kruk .25 .60
44 Johnny Bench .60 1.50
45 Johnny Podres .25 .60
46 Jose Canseco .40 1.00
47 Juan Marichal .40 1.00
48 Keith Hernandez .25 .60
49 Kent Hrbek .25 .60
50 Kirby Puckett .60 1.50
51 Lee Smith .25 .60
52 Lenny Dykstra .25 .60
53 Luis Aparicio .40 1.00
54 Luis Tiant .25 .60
55 Mark Grace .40 1.00
56 Marty Marion .25 .60
57 Matt Williams .40 1.00
58 Maury Wills .25 .60
59 Mike Schmidt 1.00 2.50
60 Minnie Minoso .25 .60
61 Nolan Ryan 2.00 5.00
62 Ozzie Smith .75 2.00
63 Paul Molitor .60 1.50
64 Phil Rizzuto .40 1.00
65 Ralph Kiner .40 1.00
66 Randy Jones .25 .60
67 Red Schoendienst .40 1.00
68 Rich Gossage .40 1.00
69 Rob Dibble .25 .60
70 Robin Roberts .40 1.00
71 Rod Carew .40 1.00
72 Rollie Fingers .40 1.00
73 Ron Guidry .25 .60
74 Ron Santo .40 1.00
75 Ryne Sandberg 1.25 3.00
76 Stan Musial 1.00 2.50
77 Steve Carlton .40 1.00
78 Steve Garvey .25 .60
79 Steve Stone .25 .60
80 Terry Pendleton .25 .60
81 Terry Steinbach .25 .60
82 Tom Seaver .40 1.00
83 Tommy John .25 .60
84 Tony Gwynn .75 2.00
85 Tony Oliva .25 .60
86 Whitey Ford .40 1.00
87 Will Clark .40 1.00
88 Willie Mays 1.25 3.00
89 Willie McCovey .40 1.00
90 Roberto Clemente 1.50 4.00
91 Roger Maris .60 1.50
92 Bob Gibson .40 1.00
93 Carl Yastrzemski .75 2.00
94 Catfish Hunter .40 1.00
95 Warren Spahn .40 1.00
96 Reggie Jackson .40 1.00
97 Lou Brock .40 1.00
98 Joe Morgan Stand .40 1.00
99 Carlton Fisk .40 1.00
100 Eddie Murray .40 1.00
101 Roger Clemens Astros .75 2.00
102 Greg Maddux Cubs .75 2.00
103 Derek Jeter 1.50 4.00
104 Albert Pujols .75 2.00
105 Ken Griffey Jr. Reds 1.25 3.00
106 Alex Rodriguez Yanks .75 2.00
107 Mike Piazza .60 1.50
108 Manny Ramirez .60 1.50
109 Sammy Sosa .60 1.50
110 Rafael Palmeiro .40 1.00
111 Randy Johnson Yanks .60 1.50
112 Vladimir Guerrero Angels .40 1.00
113 Ichiro Suzuki .75 2.00
114 David Ortiz .60 1.50
115 Miguel Cabrera .60 1.50
116 Frank Thomas .60 1.50
117 Pedro Martinez Mets .40 1.00
118 Chipper Jones .60 1.50
119 Todd Helton .40 1.00
120 Alfonso Soriano .40 1.00
121 Ivan Rodriguez .40 1.00
122 Carlos Delgado .25 .60
123 Carlos Beltran .40 1.00
124 Jeff Kent .25 .60
125 Curt Schilling .40 1.00
126 Derrek Lee .25 .60
127 Jason Bay .25 .60
128 Mark Teixeira .40 1.00
129 Craig Biggio .40 1.00
130 Miguel Tejada .40 1.00
131 Johan Santana .40 1.00
132 Jim Thome .40 1.00
133 Tim Hudson .40 1.00
134 Barry Zito .40 1.00
135 Mark Mulder .25 .60
136 Hideki Matsui 1.00 2.50
137 John Smoltz .60 1.50
138 Mark Prior .40 1.00
139 Andruw Jones .25 .60
140 Adam Dunn .40 1.00
141 Prince Fielder RC 1.25 3.00
142 Tadahito Iguchi RC .40 1.00
143 Randy Johnson D'backs .60 1.50
144 Pedro Martinez Sox .40 1.00
145 Alex Rodriguez M's .75 2.00
146 Roger Clemens Yanks .75 2.00
147 Vladimir Guerrero Expos .40 1.00
148 Greg Maddux Braves .75 2.00
149 Ken Griffey Jr. M's 1.25 3.00
150 Roger Clemens Sox .75 2.00

2005 Donruss Greats Gold HoloFoil

*GOLD 1-100: 2.5X TO 6X BASIC
*GOLD 101-150: 2.5X TO 6X BASIC
*GOLD 101-150: 2X TO 5X BASIC RC
ONE GOLD OR PLAT PER 15-PACK BOX
GOLD PRINT RUN 100 SERIAL #'d SETS

2005 Donruss Greats Platinum HoloFoil

*PLAT 1-100: 3X TO 8X BASIC
*PLAT 101-150: 3X TO 8X BASIC
*PLAT 101-150: 2.5X TO 6X BASIC RC
ONE PLAT OR GOLD PER 15-PACK BOX
PLAT PRINT RUN 50 SERIAL #'d SETS

2005 Donruss Greats Silver HoloFoil

*SILVER 1-100: .75X TO 2X BASIC
*SILVER 101-150: .75X TO 2X BASIC
*SILVER 101-150: .75X TO 2X BASIC RC
STATED ODDS 1:3

2005 Donruss Greats Signature Gold HoloFoil

OVERALL AU ODDS 2 PER 15-PACK BOX
TIER 1 QTY B/WN 1-50 COPIES PER
TIER 2 QTY B/WN 51-100 COPIES PER
TIER 3 QTY B/WN 101-250 COPIES PER
TIER 4 QTY B/WN 251-800 COPIES PER
TIER 5 QTY B/WN 801-1200 COPIES PER
TIER 6 QTY B/WN 1201-2000 COPIES PER
CARDS ARE NOT SERIAL-NUMBERED
PRINT RUN INFO PROVIDED BY DONRUSS
1 Al Kaline T2 12.00 30.00
2 Alan Trammell T3 6.00 15.00
3 Andre Dawson T5 6.00 15.00
4 Barry Larkin T2/55 * 20.00 50.00
5 Bert Blyleven T4 6.00 12.00
6 Billy Williams T2/55 * 8.00 20.00
7 Bo Jackson T1/35 * 25.00 60.00
8 Bob Feller T6 4.00 10.00
9 Bobby Doerr T5 8.00 20.00
10 Brooks Robinson T2 12.00 30.00
11 Cal Ripken T3 40.00 80.00
12 Dale Murphy T3 10.00 25.00
13 Darryl Strawberry T6 6.00 15.00
14 Dave Parker T3 6.00 15.00
15 Dave Stewart T4 4.00 10.00
16 David Cone T2 8.00 20.00
17 Dennis Eckersley T2 6.00 15.00
18 Don Larsen T4 6.00 15.00
19 Don Mattingly T1/45 * 40.00 80.00
20 Don Sutton T3 6.00 15.00
21 Duke Snider T2/55 * 15.00 40.00
22 Dwight Evans T3 6.00 15.00
23 Dwight Gooden T4 4.00 10.00
24 Earl Weaver T4 8.00 20.00
25 Fergie Jenkins T3 4.00 10.00
26 Frank Robinson T2 8.00 20.00
27 Fred Lynn T4 5.00 12.00
28 Gary Carter T2/55 * 12.00 30.00
29 Gaylord Perry T3 6.00 15.00
30 George Brett T1/35 * 40.00 80.00
31 George Foster T5 5.00 12.00
32 George Kell T6 6.00 15.00
33 Harmon Killebrew T2/55 * 15.00 40.00
34 Harold Baines T4 4.00 10.00
35 Harold Reynolds T4 4.00 10.00
36 Jack Morris T5 6.00 15.00
37 Jim Abbott T4 4.00 10.00
38 Jim Bunning T2 12.00 30.00
39 Jim Palmer T3 8.00 20.00
40 Jim Rice T2 8.00 20.00
41 Jim Leyritz T3 * 4.00 10.00
42 Joe Morgan Swing T1/35 * 12.00 30.00
43 John Kruk T2 8.00 20.00
44 Johnny Bench T1/35 * 20.00 50.00
45 Johnny Podres T6 6.00 15.00
46 Jose Canseco T1/45 * 20.00 50.00
47 Juan Marichal T2 8.00 20.00
48 Keith Hernandez T5 6.00 15.00
49 Kent Hrbek T5 6.00 15.00
50 Kirby Puckett T1/35 * 100.00 200.00
51 Lee Smith T5 10.00 25.00
52 Lenny Dykstra T4 4.00 10.00
53 Luis Aparicio T3 6.00 15.00
54 Luis Tiant T3 4.00 10.00
55 Mark Grace T1/45 * 10.00 25.00
56 Marty Marion T4 6.00 15.00
57 Matt Williams T5 4.00 10.00
58 Maury Wills T4 6.00 15.00
59 Mike Schmidt T1/35 * 30.00 60.00
60 Minnie Minoso T5 8.00 20.00
61 Nolan Ryan T2/75 * 40.00 80.00
62 Ozzie Smith T2/55 * 15.00 40.00
63 Paul Molitor T2/55 * 8.00 20.00
64 Phil Rizzuto T2/55 * 12.00 30.00
65 Ralph Kiner T5 4.00 10.00
66 Randy Jones T4 4.00 10.00
67 Red Schoendienst T3 6.00 15.00
68 Rich Gossage T3 6.00 15.00
69 Rob Dibble T4 4.00 10.00
70 Robin Roberts T2 10.00 25.00
71 Rod Carew T2/55 * 12.00 30.00
72 Rollie Fingers T3 6.00 15.00
73 Ron Guidry T3 4.00 10.00
74 Ron Santo T3 15.00 40.00
75 Ryne Sandberg T1/35 * 15.00 40.00
76 Stan Musial T1/35 * 30.00 60.00
77 Steve Carlton T2 8.00 20.00
78 Steve Garvey T3 6.00 15.00
79 Steve Stone T5 6.00 15.00
81 Terry Steinbach T3 4.00 10.00
82 Tom Seaver T1/35 * 12.00 30.00
83 Tommy John T6 4.00 10.00
84 Tony Gwynn T1/45 * 20.00 50.00
85 Tony Oliva T5 10.00 25.00
86 Whitey Ford T1/35 * 20.00 50.00
87 Will Clark T2/55 * 15.00 40.00
88 Willie Mays T2 100.00 200.00
89 Willie McCovey T1/45 * 15.00 40.00

2005 Donruss Greats Signature Platinum HoloFoil

*PLAT: .75X TO 2X GOLD T5-T6
*PLAT: .75X TO 2X GOLD T4
*PLAT: .6X TO 1.5X GOLD T3
OVERALL AU ODDS 2 PER 15-PACK BOX
TIER 1 QTY B/WN 1-50 COPIES PER
CARDS ARE NOT SERIAL-NUMBERED
PRINT RUN INFO PROVIDED BY DONRUSS
NO PRICING ON QTY OF 10 OR LESS
SEE BECKETT.COM FOR ALL PRINT RUNS

2005 Donruss Greats Dodger Blues Brooklyn Material

TIER 1 QTY B/WN 1-50 COPIES PER
TIER 4 QTY B/WN 251-800 COPIES PER
PRIME T1 QTY B/WN 1-50 COPIES PER
NO PRIME PRICING DUE TO SCARCITY
OVERALL GU ODDS 1:5
CARDS ARE NOT SERIAL-NUMBERED
PRINT RUN INFO PROVIDED BY DONRUSS
1 Sandy Koufax Jsy T1/43 * 75.00 150.00
2 Duke Snider Pants T1/27 * 15.00 40.00
3 Burleigh Grimes Pants T4 15.00 40.00
4 Tommy Lasorda Jsy T4 4.00 10.00

2005 Donruss Greats Dodger Blues Brooklyn Material Prime

OVERALL GAME-USED ODDS 1:5
TIER 1 QTY B/WN 1-50 COPIES PER
CARDS ARE NOT SERIAL-NUMBERED
PRINT RUN INFO PROVIDED BY DONRUSS
NO PRICING DUE TO SCARCITY

2005 Donruss Greats Dodger Blues Brooklyn Signature Material

TIER 1 QTY B/WN 1-50 COPIES PER
NO PRICING ON QTY OF 10
PRIME T1 QTY B/WN 1-50 COPIES PER
NO PRIME PRICING DUE TO SCARCITY
OVERALL AU ODDS 2 PER 15-PACK BOX
CARDS ARE NOT SERIAL-NUMBERED
PRINT RUN INFO PROVIDED BY DONRUSS

2005 Donruss Greats Dodger Blues Brooklyn Signature Material Prime

OVERALL AU ODDS 2 PER 15-PACK BOX
TIER 1 QTY B/WN 1-50 COPIES PER
CARDS ARE NOT SERIAL-NUMBERED
PRINT RUN INFO PROVIDED BY DONRUSS
NO PRICING DUE TO SCARCITY

2005 Donruss Greats Dodger Blues LA Material

TIER 1 QTY B/WN 1-50 COPIES PER
TIER 2 QTY B/WN 51-100 COPIES PER
TIER 3 QTY B/WN 101-250 COPIES PER
TIER 5 QTY B/WN 801-1200 COPIES PER
PRIME T1 QTY B/WN 1-50 COPIES PER
NO PRIME PRICING DUE TO SCARCITY

OVERALL GU ODDS 1:5
CARDS ARE NOT SERIAL-NUMBERED
PRINT RUN INFO PROVIDED BY DONRUSS
1 Sandy Koufax Jsy T1/43 * 20.00 50.00
2 Duke Snider Pants T2/55 * 12.50 30.00
4 Tommy Lasorda Jsy T5 4.00 10.00
5 Orel Hershiser Jsy T3 8.00 20.00
6 Don Sutton Jsy T3 8.00 20.00

2005 Donruss Greats Dodger Blues LA Material Prime

OVERALL GAME-USED ODDS 1:5
TIER 1 QTY B/WN 1-50 COPIES PER
CARDS ARE NOT SERIAL-NUMBERED
PRINT RUN INFO PROVIDED BY DONRUSS
NO PRICING DUE TO SCARCITY

2005 Donruss Greats Dodger Blues LA Signature Material

TIER 1 QTY B/WN 1-50 COPIES PER
NO PRICING ON QTY OF 10
PRIME T1 QTY B/WN 1-50 COPIES PER
NO PRIME PRICING DUE TO SCARCITY
OVERALL AU ODDS 2 PER 15-PACK BOX
CARDS ARE NOT SERIAL-NUMBERED
PRINT RUN INFO PROVIDED BY DONRUSS

2005 Donruss Greats Dodger Blues LA Signature Material Prime

OVERALL AU ODDS 2 PER 15-PACK BOX
TIER 1 QTY B/WN 1-50 COPIES PER
CARDS ARE NOT SERIAL-NUMBERED
PRINT RUN INFO PROVIDED BY DONRUSS
NO PRICING DUE TO SCARCITY

2005 Donruss Greats Hall of Fame Souvenirs

OVERALL INSERT ODDS 2 PER 15-PACK BOX
1 Willie Mays Giants 2.50 6.00
2 Hank Aaron Mil 2.50 6.00
3 Hank Aaron Atl 2.50 6.00
4 Willie Mays Mets 2.50 6.00
5 Nolan Ryan 4.00 10.00
6 R.Clemente Kneeling 3.00 8.00
7 Nellie Fox .75 2.00
8 Pee Wee Reese .75 2.00
9 Babe Ruth 3.00 8.00
10 Bobby Doerr .75 2.00
11 Brooks Robinson .75 2.00
12 Carlton Fisk .75 2.00
13 Eddie Murray .75 2.00
14 Ernie Banks 1.25 3.00
15 Frank Robinson .75 2.00
16 Gary Carter .75 2.00
17 Hack Wilson .75 2.00
18 Harmon Killebrew 1.25 3.00
19 Joe Morgan .75 2.00
20 Kirby Puckett 1.25 3.00
21 Lou Brock .75 2.00
22 Orlando Cepeda .75 2.00
23 Red Schoendienst .75 2.00
24 Richie Ashburn .75 2.00
25 Stan Musial 2.00 5.00
26 R.Clemente Standing 3.00 8.00
27 Wade Boggs Sox .75 2.00
28 Wade Boggs Yanks .75 2.00

2005 Donruss Greats Hall of Fame Souvenirs Material Bat

OVERALL GU ODDS 1:5
TIER 1 QTY B/WN 1-50 COPIES PER
TIER 3 QTY B/WN 101-250 COPIES PER
TIER 4 QTY B/WN 251-800 COPIES PER
TIER 5 QTY B/WN 801-1200 COPIES PER
TIER 6 QTY B/WN 1201-2000 COPIES PER
CARDS ARE NOT SERIAL-NUMBERED
PRINT RUN INFO PROVIDED BY DONRUSS
1 Willie Mays Giants T3 10.00 25.00
2 Hank Aaron Mil T3 10.00 25.00
3 Hank Aaron Atl T3 10.00 25.00
4 Willie Mays Mets T3 10.00 25.00
5 Nolan Ryan T1/30 * 10.00 25.00
6 R.Clemente Kneeling T6 15.00 40.00
7 Nellie Fox T5 4.00 10.00
8 Pee Wee Reese T4 4.00 10.00
9 Babe Ruth T4 75.00 150.00
11 Brooks Robinson T5 3.00 8.00
12 Carlton Fisk T5 3.00 8.00
13 Eddie Murray T5 4.00 10.00
14 Ernie Banks T5 5.00 12.00
15 Frank Robinson T4 2.50 6.00
16 Gary Carter T5 6.00 15.00
17 Hack Wilson T4 12.00 30.00
18 Harmon Killebrew T4 4.00 10.00
19 Joe Morgan T5 2.50 6.00
20 Kirby Puckett T5 4.00 10.00
21 Lou Brock T6 3.00 8.00
22 Orlando Cepeda T5 2.50 6.00
23 Red Schoendienst T4 3.00 8.00
24 Richie Ashburn T5 4.00 10.00
25 Stan Musial T4 8.00 20.00
26 R.Clemente Standing T6 12.00 30.00
27 Wade Boggs Sox T6 3.00 8.00
28 Wade Boggs Yanks T6 3.00 8.00

2005 Donruss Greats Hall of Fame Souvenirs Material Combo

OVERALL GU ODDS 1:5
TIER 1 QTY B/WN 1-50 COPIES PER
TIER 3 QTY B/WN 101-250 COPIES PER
TIER 4 QTY B/WN 251-800 COPIES PER
CARDS ARE NOT SERIAL-NUMBERED
PRINT RUN INFO PROVIDED BY DONRUSS
NO PRICING ON QTY OF 24 OR LESS
1 W.Mays Giants B-J T1/25 * 20.00 50.00
2 H.Aaron Mil Bat-Jsy T1/25 * 20.00 50.00
3 H.Aaron Atl Bat-Jsy T1/25 * 20.00 50.00
4 W.Mays Mets B-J T1/25 * 20.00 50.00
5 N.Ryan Bat-Jsy T1/25 * 15.00 40.00
8 P.Reese Bat-Jsy T1/38 * 12.50 30.00
9 B.Ruth Bat-Pants T1/50 * 200.00 300.00
10 B.Doerr Bat-Pants T4 4.00 10.00
11 B.Rob Bat-Hat T1/29 * 10.00 25.00
12 C.Fisk Bat-Jsy T4 5.00 12.00
13 E.Murray Bat-Jsy T4 6.00 15.00
14 E.Banks Bat-Jsy T3 10.00 25.00
16 G.Carter Bat-Pants T4 4.00 10.00
18 H.Killebrew Bat-Jsy T4 6.00 15.00
24 R.Ashburn Bat-Pants T4 6.00 15.00
25 S.Musial Bat-Pants T3 12.50 30.00
26 R.Clem Stand Bat-Hat T3 40.00 80.00
27 W.Boggs Sox Bat-Jsy T3 6.00 15.00

2005 Donruss Greats Hall of Fame Souvenirs Material Jersey

OVERALL GU ODDS 1:5
TIER 1 QTY B/WN 1-50 COPIES PER
TIER 3 QTY B/WN 101-250 COPIES PER
TIER 4 QTY B/WN 251-800 COPIES PER
CARDS ARE NOT SERIAL-NUMBERED
PRINT RUN INFO PROVIDED BY DONRUSS
NO PRICING ON QTY OF 22
1 Willie Mays Giants T1/25 * 15.00 40.00
2 Hank Aaron Mil T1/25 * 15.00 40.00
3 Hank Aaron Atl T1/25 * 15.00 40.00
4 Willie Mays Mets T1/25 * 15.00 40.00
5 Nolan Ryan T1/25 * 10.00 25.00
9 Babe Ruth Pants T1/25 * 150.00 250.00
10 Bobby Doerr Pants T3 3.00 8.00
12 Carlton Fisk Jkt T4 3.00 8.00
24 Richie Ashburn Pants T3 5.00 12.00
25 Stan Musial T1/50 * 12.50 30.00
27 Wade Boggs Sox T4 3.00 8.00

2005 Donruss Greats Hall of Fame Souvenirs Signature

OVERALL AU ODDS 2 PER 15-PACK BOX
TIER 1 QTY B/WN 1-50 COPIES PER
CARDS ARE NOT SERIAL-NUMBERED
PRINT RUN INFO PROVIDED BY DONRUSS
NO PRICING DUE TO SCARCITY

2005 Donruss Greats Hall of Fame Souvenirs Signature Material Bat

OVERALL AU ODDS 2 PER 15-PACK BOX
TIER 1 QTY B/WN 1-50 COPIES PER
TIER 2 QTY B/WN 51-100 COPIES PER
TIER 3 QTY B/WN 101-250 COPIES PER
CARDS ARE NOT SERIAL-NUMBERED
PRINT RUN INFO PROVIDED BY DONRUSS
NO PRICING ON QTY OF 22 OR LESS
10 Bobby Doerr T2 8.00 20.00
11 Brooks Robinson T2 12.00 30.00
12 Carlton Fisk T2 12.00 30.00
15 Frank Robinson T2 20.00 50.00
16 Gary Carter T2 12.00 30.00
18 Harmon Killebrew T2 15.00 40.00
19 Joe Morgan T2 8.00 20.00
20 Kirby Puckett T2/52 * 75.00 150.00
21 Lou Brock T2 12.00 30.00
22 Orlando Cepeda T2 12.00 30.00
23 Red Schoendienst T3 10.00 25.00
25 Stan Musial T2/50 * 30.00 80.00

2005 Donruss Greats Hall of Fame Souvenirs Signature Material Combo

OVERALL AU ODDS 2 PER 15-PACK BOX
TIER 1 QTY B/WN 1-50 COPIES PER
TIER 2 QTY B/WN 51-100 COPIES PER
TIER 3 QTY B/WN 101-250 COPIES PER
CARDS ARE NOT SERIAL-NUMBERED
PRINT RUN INFO PROVIDED BY DONRUSS
NO PRICING ON QTY OF 10 OR LESS
10 B.Doerr Bat-Pants T3 8.00 20.00
11 B.Robinson Bat-Hat T2 15.00 40.00
12 C.Fisk Bat-Hat T1/50 * 20.00 50.00
15 F.Rob Bat-Shoes T1/39 * 12.50 30.00
16 G.Carter Bat-Jsy T3 10.00 25.00
18 H.Killebrew Bat-Jsy T3 30.00 60.00
19 J.Morgan Bat-Jsy T1/23 * 12.50 30.00
20 K.Puckett Bat-Jsy T1/45 * 125.00 250.00
22 O.Cepeda Bat-Pants T2 10.00 25.00
25 S.Musial Bat-Jsy T2 30.00 80.00
27 W.Boggs Sox B-J T1/50 * 15.00 40.00
28 W.Boggs Yanks B-H T1/31 * 15.00 40.00

2005 Donruss Greats Hall of Fame Souvenirs Signature Material Jersey

OVERALL AU ODDS 2 PER 15-PACK BOX
TIER 1 QTY B/WN 1-50 COPIES PER
TIER 2 QTY B/WN 51-100 COPIES PER
TIER 3 QTY B/WN 101-250 COPIES PER
CARDS ARE NOT SERIAL-NUMBERED
PRINT RUN INFO PROVIDED BY DONRUSS
NO PRICING ON QTY OF 16 OR LESS
10 Bobby Doerr Pants T3 6.00 15.00
12 Carlton Fisk Jkt T2 12.50 30.00
15 Frank Robinson T1/27 * 10.00 25.00
16 Gary Carter T2/63 * 12.50 30.00
18 Harmon Killebrew T2 30.00 60.00
22 O.Cepeda Pants T2/68 * 8.00 20.00
23 Red Schoendienst Hat T3 12.50 30.00
25 Stan Musial T2 25.00 60.00
27 Wade Boggs Sox T1/50 * 15.00 40.00

2005 Donruss Greats Redbirds Material

OVERALL GU ODDS 1:5
TIER 2 QTY B/WN 51-100 COPIES PER
TIER 3 QTY B/WN 101-250 COPIES PER
TIER 4 QTY B/WN 251-800 COPIES PER
CARDS ARE NOT SERIAL-NUMBERED
PRINT RUN INFO PROVIDED BY DONRUSS
1 S.Musial w 15.00 40.00
Glove Jsy T2
2 Ozzie Smith Jkt T4 8.00 20.00
3 Enos Slaughter Jsy T4 8.00 20.00
4 Frankie Frisch Jkt T3 10.00 25.00
5 Lou Brock Jsy T2 15.00 40.00
6 Bob Gibson Jsy T2 15.00 40.00
7 Ken Boyer Jsy T3 10.00 25.00
8 Lee Smith Jsy T4 3.00 8.00
9 Albert Pujols Jsy T2 15.00 40.00
10 S.Musial w 15.00 40.00
Bat Pants T2

2005 Donruss Greats Redbirds Material Prime

*PRIME T1 p/r 25: .75X TO 2X BAT T3
OVERALL GAME-USED ODDS 1:5
TIER 1 QTY B/WN 1-50 COPIES PER
CARDS ARE NOT SERIAL-NUMBERED
PRINT RUN INFO PROVIDED BY DONRUSS
NO PRICING ON QTY OF 5 OR LESS
7 Ken Boyer Jsy T1/25 * 15.00 40.00

2005 Donruss Greats Redbirds Signature Material

TIER 1 QTY B/WN 1-50 COPIES PER
NO PRICING ON QTY OF 10 OR LESS
PRIME T1 QTY B/WN 1-50 COPIES PER
NO PRIME PRICING DUE TO SCARCITY
OVERALL AU ODDS 2 PER 15-PACK BOX
CARDS ARE NOT SERIAL-NUMBERED
PRINT RUN INFO PROVIDED BY DONRUSS
8 Lee Smith Jsy T1/50 * 10.00 25.00

2005 Donruss Greats Redbirds Signature Material Prime

OVERALL AU ODDS 2 PER 15-PACK BOX
TIER 1 QTY B/WN 1-50 COPIES PER
CARDS ARE NOT SERIAL-NUMBERED
PRINT RUN INFO PROVIDED BY DONRUSS
NO PRICING DUE TO SCARCITY

2005 Donruss Greats Souvenirs

OVERALL INSERT ODDS 2 PER 15-PACK BOX
1 Jim Thorpe 2.00 5.00
2 Joe Carter .50 1.25
3 Will Clark .75 2.00
4 Cal Ripken 4.00 10.00
5 Dwight Evans .75 2.00
6 George Foster .50 1.25
7 Steve Garvey .50 1.25
8 Don Mattingly 2.50 6.00
9 Deion Sanders .75 2.00
10 Ron Santo .75 2.00
11 Alan Trammell .75 2.00
12 Robin Ventura .50 1.25
13 Matt Williams .75 2.00

2005 Donruss Greats Souvenirs Material Bat

OVERALL GU ODDS 1:5
TIER 5 QTY B/WN 801-1200 COPIES PER
CARDS ARE NOT SERIAL-NUMBERED
PRINT RUN INFO PROVIDED BY DONRUSS
2 Joe Carter T5 2.50 6.00
3 Will Clark T5 3.00 8.00
5 Dwight Evans T5 3.00 8.00
6 George Foster T5 2.50 6.00
7 Steve Garvey T5 2.50 6.00
8 Don Mattingly T5 6.00 15.00
9 Deion Sanders T5 3.00 8.00
10 Ron Santo T5 3.00 8.00
11 Alan Trammell T5 2.50 6.00
12 Robin Ventura T5 2.50 6.00
13 Matt Williams T5 3.00 8.00

2005 Donruss Greats Souvenirs Material Combo

OVERALL GU ODDS 1:5
TIER 1 QTY B/WN 1-50 COPIES PER
TIER 2 QTY B/WN 51-100 COPIES PER
CARDS ARE NOT SERIAL-NUMBERED
PRINT RUN INFO PROVIDED BY DONRUSS
2 Joe Carter Bat-Jsy T1/50 * 5.00 12.00
3 Will Clark Bat-Jsy T2 5.00 12.00
9 Deion Sanders Bat-Jsy T2 5.00 12.00
11 Alan Trammell Bat-Jsy T2 4.00 10.00
13 Matt Williams Bat-Jsy T2 5.00 12.00

2005 Donruss Greats Souvenirs Material Jersey

OVERALL GU ODDS 1:5
TIER 1 QTY B/WN 1-50 COPIES PER
TIER 2 QTY B/WN 51-100 COPIES PER
TIER 3 QTY B/WN 101-250 COPIES PER
TIER 4 QTY B/WN 251-800 COPIES PER
TIER 5 QTY B/WN 801-1200 COPIES PER
CARDS ARE NOT SERIAL-NUMBERED
PRINT RUN INFO PROVIDED BY DONRUSS
NO PRICING ON QTY OF 7 OR LESS
1 Jim Thorpe T4 25.00 60.00
3 Will Clark T2 5.00 12.00
4 Cal Ripken T4 10.00 25.00
9 Deion Sanders T5 3.00 8.00
11 Alan Trammell T2/68 * 4.00 10.00
12 Robin Ventura T1/48 * 5.00 12.00
13 Matt Williams T3 4.00 10.00

2005 Donruss Greats Souvenirs Signature

OVERALL AU ODDS 2 PER 15-PACK BOX
TIER 1 QTY B/WN 1-50 COPIES PER
TIER 2 QTY B/WN 51-100 COPIES PER
CARDS ARE NOT SERIAL-NUMBERED
PRINT RUN INFO PROVIDED BY DONRUSS
NO PRICING ON QTY OF 10
3 Will Clark T2 12.50 30.00
5 Dwight Evans T1/25 * 10.00 25.00
7 Steve Garvey T2 8.00 20.00
10 Ron Santo T2 12.50 30.00
11 Alan Trammell T2 8.00 20.00

2005 Donruss Greats Souvenirs Signature Material Bat

OVERALL AU ODDS 2 PER 15-PACK BOX
TIER 2 QTY B/WN 51-100 COPIES PER
CARDS ARE NOT SERIAL-NUMBERED
PRINT RUN INFO PROVIDED BY DONRUSS
3 Will Clark T2 15.00 40.00
5 Dwight Evans T2 8.00 20.00
7 Steve Garvey T2 8.00 20.00
10 Ron Santo T2 20.00 50.00
11 Alan Trammell T2 12.50 30.00
12 Robin Ventura T2 8.00 20.00

2005 Donruss Greats Souvenirs Signature Material Combo

OVERALL AU ODDS 2 PER 15-PACK BOX
TIER 1 QTY B/WN 1-50 COPIES PER
TIER 2 QTY B/WN 51-100 COPIES PER
TIER 3 QTY B/WN 101-250 COPIES PER
CARDS ARE NOT SERIAL-NUMBERED
PRINT RUN INFO PROVIDED BY DONRUSS
NO PRICING ON QTY OF 10 OR LESS
3 Will Clark Bat-Jsy T2 15.00 40.00
7 Steve Garvey Bat-Jsy T2 10.00 25.00
11 Alan Trammell Bat-Jsy T2 10.00 25.00

2005 Donruss Greats Souvenirs Signature Material Jersey

OVERALL AU ODDS 2 PER 15-PACK BOX
TIER 1 QTY B/WN 1-50 COPIES PER
TIER 2 QTY B/WN 51-100 COPIES PER
TIER 3 QTY B/WN 101-250 COPIES PER
CARDS ARE NOT SERIAL-NUMBERED
PRINT RUN INFO PROVIDED BY DONRUSS
NO PRICING ON QTY OF 5 OR LESS
3 Will Clark T3 10.00 25.00
5 Dwight Evans T1/42 * 10.00 25.00
7 Steve Garvey T3 6.00 15.00
11 Alan Trammell T2 8.00 20.00

2005 Donruss Greats Sox Nation Material

TIER 2 QTY B/WN 51-100 COPIES PER
TIER 3 QTY B/WN 101-250 COPIES PER
TIER 4 QTY B/WN 251-800 COPIES PER
TIER 5 QTY B/WN 801-1200 COPIES PER
PRIME T1 QTY B/WN 1-50 COPIES PER
NO PRIME PRICING DUE TO SCARCITY
OVERALL GU ODDS 1:5
CARDS ARE NOT SERIAL-NUMBERED
PRINT RUN INFO PROVIDED BY DONRUSS
1 Ted Williams Jsy T3 20.00 80.00
2 Bobby Doerr Pants T3 8.00 20.00
3 Roger Clemens Jsy T2/55 * 20.00 50.00
4 Carl Yastrzemski Pants T4 10.00 25.00
5 Carl Yastrzemski Jsy T3 12.50 30.00
6 Jim Rice Left Pants T3 6.00 15.00
7 Jim Rice Right Jsy T3 6.00 15.00
8 J.Cronin Standing Pants T5 4.00 10.00
9 Joe Cronin Left Jsy T5 4.00 10.00
10 Carlton Fisk Jsy T2/55 * 15.00 40.00
11 Fred Lynn Jsy T3 6.00 15.00
12 W.Boggs Away Jsy T3 6.00 15.00
13 W.Boggs Home Jsy T2/55 * 15.00 40.00

2005 Donruss Greats Sox Nation Material Prime

OVERALL GAME-USED ODDS 1:5
TIER 1 QTY B/WN 1-50 COPIES PER
CARDS ARE NOT SERIAL-NUMBERED
PRINT RUN INFO PROVIDED BY DONRUSS
NO PRICING DUE TO SCARCITY

2005 Donruss Greats Sox Nation Signature Material

TIER 1 QTY B/WN 1-50 COPIES PER
NO PRICING ON QTY OF 5
PRIME T1 QTY B/WN 1-50 COPIES PER
NO PRIME PRICING DUE TO SCARCITY
OVERALL AU ODDS 2 PER 15-PACK BOX
CARDS ARE NOT SERIAL-NUMBERED
PRINT RUN INFO PROVIDED BY DONRUSS
2 Bobby Doerr Pants T1/50 * 10.00 25.00
6 Jim Rice Left Pants T1/50 * 10.00 25.00
7 Jim Rice Right Jsy T1/50 * 10.00 25.00
11 Fred Lynn Jsy T1/50 * 10.00 25.00

2005 Donruss Greats Sox Nation Signature Material Prime

OVERALL AU ODDS 2 PER 15-PACK BOX
TIER 1 QTY B/WN 1-50 COPIES PER
CARDS ARE NOT SERIAL-NUMBERED
PRINT RUN INFO PROVIDED BY DONRUSS
NO PRICING DUE TO SCARCITY

2005 Donruss Greats Yankee Clippings Material

OVERALL GU ODDS 1:5
TIER 1 QTY B/WN 1-50 COPIES PER
TIER 2 QTY B/WN 51-100 COPIES PER
TIER 3 QTY B/WN 100-250 COPIES PER
TIER 4 QTY B/WN 250-800 COPIES PER
TIER 5 QTY B/WN 801-1200 COPIES PER
TIER 6 QTY B/WN 1201-2000 COPIES PER
CARDS ARE NOT SERIAL-NUMBERED
PRINT RUN INFO PROVIDED BY DONRUSS
2 Babe Ruth Look Up Jsy T2 250.00 400.00
3 B.Martin Fielding Pants T3 10.00 25.00
4 B.Martin Kneeling Jsy T3 10.00 25.00
5 Bobby Murcer Pants T5 6.00 15.00
6 Bucky Dent Pants T5 4.00 10.00
7 C.Hunter w 4.00 10.00
Glove Pants T4
8 C.Hunter w 4.00 10.00
o Glove Jsy T5
9 Darryl Strawberry Jsy T2 10.00 25.00
10 Dave Righetti Jsy T5 4.00 10.00
11 Dave Winfield Pants T6 4.00 10.00
12 D.Sanders w 6.00 15.00
Helmet Jsy T5
13 D.Sand w 6.00 15.00
o Helmet Pants T4
14 Don Mattingly Jsy T2 15.00 40.00
15 Elston Howard Pants T5 6.00 15.00
16 Graig Nettles Pants T5 4.00 10.00
17 Roger Clemens Jsy T1/43 * 50.00 100.00
18 Luis Tiant Pants T4 4.00 10.00
19 Mickey Rivers Pants T5 4.00 10.00
20 Phil Rizzuto Jsy T4 6.00 15.00
21 Reggie Jackson Pants T3 10.00 25.00
22 Rickey Henderson Pants T5 6.00 15.00
23 R.Maris w/Bat Jsy T2 20.00 50.00
24 R.Maris w/o Bat Pants T2 20.00 50.00
25 Ron Guidry Pants T4 6.00 15.00
26 Sparky Lyle Pants T5 4.00 10.00
27 Phil Niekro Jsy T1/49 * 15.00 40.00
28 Tommy John Jsy T2 10.00 25.00
29 Whitey Ford Jsy T2 10.00 25.00
30 Yogi Berra Pants T2 12.00 30.00

2005 Donruss Greats Yankee Clippings Material Prime

OVERALL GAME-USED ODDS 1:5
TIER 1 QTY B/WN 1-50 COPIES PER
CARDS ARE NOT SERIAL-NUMBERED
PRINT RUN INFO PROVIDED BY DONRUSS
NO PRICING ON QTY OF 8 OR LESS
27 Phil Niekro Jsy T1/33 * 20.00 50.00

2005 Donruss Greats Yankee Clippings Signature Material

TIER 1 QTY B/WN 1-50 COPIES PER
NO PRICING ON QTY OF 10 OR LESS
PRIME T1 QTY B/WN 1-50 COPIES PER
NO PRIME PRICING DUE TO SCARCITY
OVERALL AU ODDS 2 PER 15-PACK BOX
CARDS ARE NOT SERIAL-NUMBERED
PRINT RUN INFO PROVIDED BY DONRUSS
9 D.Strawberry Jsy T1/25 * 20.00 50.00
18 Luis Tiant Pants T1/50 * 15.00 40.00
20 Phil Rizzuto Jsy T1/25 * 30.00 60.00
25 Ron Guidry Pants T1/25 * 30.00 60.00
28 Tommy John Jsy T1/25 * 15.00 40.00

2005 Donruss Greats Yankee Clippings Signature Material Prime

OVERALL AU ODDS 2 PER 15-PACK BOX
TIER 1 QTY B/WN 1-50 COPIES PER
CARDS ARE NOT SERIAL-NUMBERED
PRINT RUN INFO PROVIDED BY DONRUSS
NO PRICING DUE TO SCARCITY

1997 Donruss Limited

The 1997 Donruss Limited set was issued in one series totalling 200 cards and distributed in five-card packs with a suggested retail price of $4.99. The set is divided into four unique subsets: Counterparts, Double Team, Star Factor and Unlimited Potential/Talent. The Counterparts subset features 100 double-sided cards with full-bleed photos of two star players who play the same position. The Double Team subset displays color action photos of two star teammates back-to-back on 40 double-sided cards. The Star Factor subset highlights 40 superstars with a different photo of the same player on each side of the card plus unique player statistics. The Unlimited Potential/Talent subset features double-front cards with color photo matchups of a veteran and a rookie. Less than 1100 of each Star Factor card was produced. Judging from case breakdowns provided to us from dealers in the field, the odds appear to be as follows: Double Team 1:6, Star Factor 1:24 and Unlimited Potential/Talent 1:36.

COMP.COUNTER SET (100) 10.00 25.00
COMMON COUNTERPART .10 .30
COMMON DOUBLE TEAM .75 2.00
DOUBLE TEAM STATED ODDS 1:6
COMMON STAR FACTOR 1.50 4.00
STAR FACTOR STATED ODDS 1:24
LESS THAN 1100 OF EACH STAR FACT.MADE
COMMON UNLIMITED 1.25 3.00
UNLIMITED POTENTIAL STATED ODDS 1:36
1 K.Griffey Jr. .60 1.50
R.White C
2 G.Maddux .50 1.25
D.Cone C
3 G.Sheffield .75 2.00
M.Alou D
4 Frank Thomas S 2.50 6.00
5 C.Ripken 1.00 2.50
K.Orie C
6 V.Guerrero 5.00 12.00
B.Bonds U
7 E.Murray .30 .75
R.Jefferson C
8 M.Ramirez 1.25 3.00
M.Grissom D
9 Mike Piazza S 4.00 10.00
10 B.Larkin .20 .50
R.Ordonez C
11 J.Bagwell .30 .75
E.Karros C
12 C.Knoblauch .10 .30
R.Durham C
13 A.Rodriguez .50 1.25
E.Renteria C
14 M.Williams .10 .30
V.Castilla C
15 T.Hollandsworth .20 .50
B.Johnson C
16 J.Smoltz .20 .50
P.Martinez C
17 J.Canseco .20 .50
C.Davis C
18 J.Cruz Jr. 4.00 10.00
K.Griffey Jr. U
19 Ken Griffey Jr. S 5.00 12.00
20 P.Molitor .10 .30
J.Olerud C
21 R.Alomar .20 .50
L.Castillo C
22 D.Jeter .60 1.50
L.Collier C
23 C.Jones .30 .75
R.Ventura C
24 G.Sheffield .10 .30
R.Gant C
25 R.Martinez .10 .30
B.Jones C
26 M.Piazza 2.00 5.00
R.Mondesi D
27 J.Bagwell 2.00 5.00
D.Erstad U
28 Ivan Rodriguez S 2.50 6.00
29 J.T.Snow .10 .30
K.Young C
30 R.Sandberg .50 1.25
J.Franco C
31 T.Fryman .10 .30
C.Snopek C
32 W.Boggs .20 .50
R.Davis C
33 B.Kieschnick .10 .30
M.Cordova C
34 A.Pettitte .20 .50
D.Neagle C
35 P.Molitor .75 2.00
M.Lawton D
36 S.Rolen 6.00 15.00
C.Ripken U
37 Cal Ripken S 8.00 20.00
38 J.Thome .20 .50
D.Nilsson C
39 T.Womack RC .10 .30
C.Baerga C
40 N.Garciaparra .50 1.25
M.Grudz. C
41 T.Greene .10 .30
C.Widger C
42 D.Sanders .20 .50
B.Gilkey C
43 H.Nomo .30 .75
C.Nagy C
44 I.Rodriguez 1.25 3.00
R.Greer D
45 T.Walker 2.00 5.00
C.Jones U
46 Greg Maddux S 4.00 10.00
47 M.Vaughn .10 .30
C.Fielder C
48 C.Biggio .20 .50
S.Spiezio C
49 P.Reese .10 .30
J.Blauser C
50 K.Caminiti .10 .30
J.Randa C
51 A.Belle .10 .30
S.Green C
52 R.Johnson .30 .75
J.Dickson C
53 H.Nomo 1.25 3.00
C.Park D
54 S.Spiezio 1.25 3.00
C.Knoblauch U
55 Chipper Jones S 2.50 6.00
56 T.Martinez .20 .50
R.McGuire C
57 E.Young .10 .30
W.Guerrero C
58 R.Coomer .10 .30
D.Hollins C
59 S.Sosa .30 .75
A.Echevarria C
60 D.Reyes RC .10 .30
J.Key C
61 B.Larkin 1.25 3.00
D.Sanders D
62 W.Guerrero 2.00 5.00
R.Alomar U
63 Albert Belle S 1.50 4.00
64 M.McGwire .75 2.00
A.Galarraga C
65 E.Martinez .20 .50
T.Walker C
66 S.Finley .10 .30
R.Becker C
67 T.Glavine .20 .50
A.Ashby C
68 S.Sosa 1.25 3.00
R.Sandberg D
69 N.Garciaparra 3.00 8.00
A.Rod. U
70 Jeff Bagwell S 2.50 6.00
71 D.Erstad .20 .50
M.Grace C
72 S.Rolen .20 .50
E.Alfonzo C
73 K.Lofton .10 .30
L.Johnson C
74 J.Hamilton .10 .30
B.Tomko C
75 E.Murray 1.25 3.00
T.Salmon D
76 D.Young 1.25 3.00
M.Vaughn U
77 Juan Gonzalez S 1.50 4.00
78 F.Thomas .30 .75
T.Clark C
79 S.Stewart .10 .30
B.Roberts C
80 S.Estes .10 .30
A.Fernandez C
81 J.Smoltz 1.25 3.00
J.Lopez D
82 T.Greene 3.00 8.00
M.Piazza U
83 Derek Jeter S 6.00 15.00
84 D.Young .10 .30
A.Williamson C
85 R.Henderson .30 .75
D.Hamilton C
86 B.Wagner .10 .30
D.Eckersley C
87 L.Walker .75 2.00
E.Young D
88 M.Kotsay RC 2.00 5.00
J.Gonz. U
89 Barry Bonds S 6.00 15.00
90 W.Clark .20 .50
J.Conine C
91 T.Gwynn .40 1.00
B.Butler C
92 J.Wetteland .10 .30
R.Beck C
93 B.Williams 1.25 3.00
T.Martinez D
94 A.Jones 2.00 5.00
K.Lofton U
95 Mo Vaughn S 1.50 4.00
96 J.Carter .20 .50
D.Lee C
97 J.Mabry .10 .30
F.P.Santangelo C
98 E.Loaiza .10 .30
W.Alvarez C
99 M.Williams .75 2.00
D.Justice D
100 D.Lee 2.00 5.00
F.Thomas U
101 Mark McGwire S 6.00 15.00
102 F.McGriff .20 .50
P.Sorrento C
103 J.Allensworth .20 .50
B.Williams C
104 I.Valdes .10 .30
C.Holt C
105 F.McGriff 1.25 3.00
R.Klesko D
106 T.Clark 5.00 12.00
M.McGwire U
107 Tony Gwynn S 3.00 8.00
108 J.Hammonds .10 .30
E.Burks C
109 S.Reynolds .10 .30
A.Benes C
110 R.Clemens 2.50 6.00
C.Delgado D
111 K.Garcia 1.25 3.00
A.Belle U
112 Paul Molitor S 1.50 4.00
113 T.Beamon .10 .30
E.Owens C
114 C.Schilling .10 .30
D.Kile C
115 T.Glavine 1.25 3.00
M.Tucker D
116 P.Reese 5.00 12.00
D.Jeter U
117 Manny Ramirez S 2.50 6.00
118 J.Gonzalez .10 .30
B.Brown C
119 J.Guzman .10 .30
F.Cordova C
120 R.Johnson 1.25 3.00
E.Martinez D
121 H.Irabu 3.00 8.00
G.Maddux U
122 Alex Rodriguez S 4.00 10.00
123 B.Bonds .75 2.00
Q.McCracken C
124 R.Clemens .60 1.50
A.Benes C
125 W.Boggs 1.25 3.00
P.O'Neill D
126 M.Cameron 1.25 3.00
L.Walker U
127 Gary Sheffield S 1.50 4.00
128 A.Jones .20 .50
R.Mondesi C
129 B.Anderson .10 .30
T.Wade C
130 B.Anderson 1.25 3.00
R.Palmeiro D
131 N.Perez 2.00 5.00
B.Larkin U
132 Ken Caminiti S 1.50 4.00
133 L.Walker .10 .30
R.Greer C
134 M.Rivera .30 .75
M.Wohlers C
135 H.Irabu RC 1.25 3.00
A.Pettitte D
136 J.Guillen 2.50 6.00
T.Gwynn U
137 Hideo Nomo S 2.50 6.00
138 V.Guerrero .30 .75
J.Edmonds C
139 J.Thompson .10 .30
D.Gooden C
140 A.Galarraga .75 2.00
D.Bichette D
141 Kenny Lofton S 1.50 4.00
142 T.Salmon .20 .50
M.Ramirez C
143 K.Brown .10 .30
M.Morris C
144 C.Biggio 1.25 3.00
B.Abreu D
145 Roberto Alomar S 2.50 6.00
146 J.Guillen .10 .30
B.Jordan C
147 B.Colon .10 .30
K.Appier C
148 R.Lankford .75 2.00
B.Jordan D
149 Chuck Knoblauch S 1.50 4.00
150 H.Rodriguez .10 .30
R.Lankford C
151 J.Wright RC .10 .30
B.McDon. C
152 B.Bonilla .75 2.00
K.Brown D
153 Barry Larkin S 2.50 6.00
154 D.Justice .10 .30
R.Sanders C
155 M.Mussina .20 .50
K.Hill C
156 M.Grace 1.25 3.00
B.Kieschnick D
157 Jim Thome S 2.50 6.00
158 M.Tucker .10 .30
C.Goodwin C
159 J.Suppan .10 .30
J.Fassero C
160 M.Mussina 1.25 3.00
J.Hammonds D
161 John Smoltz S 2.50 6.00
162 M.Alou .10 .30
E.Davis C
163 S.Alomar Jr. .10 .30
D.Wilson C
164 R.White .75 2.00
H.Rodriguez D
165 Roger Clemens S 5.00 12.00
166 B.Anderson .10 .30
A.Martin C
167 J.Kendall .10 .30
C.Johnson C
168 J.Giambi 1.25 3.00
J.Canseco D
169 Larry Walker S 1.50 4.00
170 J.Buhner .10 .30
G.Berroa C
171 I.Rodriguez .20 .50
M.Sweeney C
172 K.Appier .75 2.00
J.Rosado D
173 Bernie Williams S 2.50 6.00
174 B.Giles RC .60 1.50
T.Dunw C
175 J.Lopez .10 .30
S.Hatteberg C
176 J.Jaha .75 2.00
J.Cirillo D
177 Andy Pettitte S 2.50 6.00
178 D.Bichette .10 .30
B.Huskey C
179 R.Casanova .10 .30
T.Hundley C
180 J.Edmonds .75 2.00
G.Anderson D
181 Deion Sanders S 2.50 6.00
182 R.Klesko .20 .50
P.O'Neill C
183 J.Carter .75 2.00
P.Hentgen D
184 Brady Anderson S 1.50 4.00
185 C.Delgado .10 .30
W.Joyner C
186 J.Dye 1.25 3.00
J.Damon D
187 Randy Johnson S 2.50 6.00

188 T.Hundley .75 2.00
C.Baerga D
189 Tom Glavine S 2.50 6.00
190 D.Mashore .75 2.00
J.McDonald D
191 Wade Boggs S 2.50 6.00
192 A.Martin .75 2.00
J.Kendall D
193 Matt Williams S 1.50 4.00
194 W.Clark 1.25 3.00
D.Palmer D
195 Sammy Sosa S 2.50 6.00
196 J.Cruz Jr. RC .75 2.00
J.Buhner D
197 Eddie Murray S 2.50 6.00
198 D.Erstad .75 2.00
J.Dickson D
199 Fred McGriff S 2.50 6.00
200 B.Trammell RC .75 2.00
B.Higg. D
S4 Frank Thomas Sample .75

1997 Donruss Limited Exposure
*COUNTER.STARS: 2.5X TO 6X BASIC CARDS
*COUNTER.ROOKIES: .75X TO 2X BASIC
*DOUBLE TEAM: 1.5X TO 4X BASIC CARDS
*UNLIMITED: 1.25X TO 3X BASIC CARDS
RANDOM INSERTS IN PACKS
LESS THAN 40 OF EACH STAR FACTOR MADE
NON-GLOSS: RANDOM ERRORS IN PACKS
NO EXCHANGE AVAIL.ON NON-GLOSS CARDS

1997 Donruss Limited Exposure Non-Glossy
*NON-GLOSSY: .1X TO .25X BASIC CARDS
*ROOKIES: .4X TO 1X BASIC CARDS
RANDOM ERRORS INSERTED IN PACKS

1997 Donruss Limited Fabric of the Game
1000 OF EACH MAJOR LG.MATERIAL
750 OF EACH STAR MATERIAL
500 OF EACH SUPERSTAR MATERIAL
250 OF EACH HOF MATERIAL
100 OF EACH LEGENDARY MATERIAL
RANDOM INSERTS IN PACKS
1 Cal Ripken HF 30.00 80.00
2 Tony Gwynn SS 15.00 40.00
3 Ivan Rodriguez S 4.00 10.00
4 Rickey Henderson L 15.00 40.00
5 Ken Griffey Jr. SS 20.00 50.00
6 Chipper Jones ML 5.00 12.00
7 Sammy Sosa S 6.00 15.00
8 Wade Boggs HF 6.00 15.00
9 Manny Ramirez ML 3.00 8.00
10 Barry Bonds HF 25.00 60.00
11 Mike Piazza S 12.50 30.00
12 Rondell White ML 2.00 5.00
13 Albert Belle S 2.50 6.00
14 Tony Clark ML 1.25 3.00
15 Edgar Martinez SS 5.00 12.00
16 Deion Sanders S 4.00 10.00
17 Juan Gonzalez SS 3.00 8.00
18 Nomar Garciaparra ML 8.00 20.00
19 Rafael Palmeiro SS 5.00 12.00
20 Dave Justice S 2.50 6.00
21 Bob Abreu ML 3.00 8.00
22 Paul Molitor L 10.00 25.00
23 Vladimir Guerrero ML 5.00 12.00
24 Chuck Knoblauch SS 3.00 8.00
25 Tony Gwynn HF 12.50 30.00
26 Darin Erstad ML 2.00 5.00
27 Mark McGwire HF 12.50 30.00
28 Larry Walker S 2.50 6.00
29 Gary Sheffield S 2.50 6.00
30 Jose Cruz Jr. ML 2.00 5.00
31 Kenny Lofton HF 4.00 10.00
32 Andres Galarraga SS 3.00 8.00
33 Raul Mondesi ML 2.00 5.00
34 Eddie Murray L 15.00 40.00
35 Tino Martinez ML 3.00 8.00
36 Todd Walker ML 1.25 3.00
37 Frank Thomas SS 8.00 20.00
38 Ken Caminiti S 2.50 6.00
39 Pokey Reese ML 1.25 3.00
40 Barry Bonds HF 25.00 60.00
41 Barry Larkin SS 5.00 12.00
42 Bernie Williams S 4.00 10.00
43 Cal Ripken HF 15.00 40.00
44 Bobby Bonilla SS 3.00 8.00
45 Ken Griffey Jr. S 15.00 40.00
46 Tim Salmon S 4.00 10.00
47 Ryne Sandberg HF 25.00 60.00
48 Rusty Greer ML 2.00 5.00
49 Matt Williams SS 3.00 8.00
50 Eric Young S 1.50 4.00
51 Andruw Jones ML 3.00 8.00
52 Jeff Bagwell S 4.00 10.00
53 Wilton Guerrero ML 1.25 3.00
54 Fred McGriff HF 6.00 15.00
55 Jose Guillen ML 2.00 5.00
56 Brady Anderson SS 3.00 8.00
57 Mo Vaughn S 2.50 6.00
58 Craig Biggio SS 5.00 12.00
59 Dmitri Young ML 2.00 5.00
60 Frank Thomas S 6.00 15.00
61 Derek Jeter ML 10.00 25.00
62 Albert Belle SS 3.00 8.00
63 Scott Rolen ML 3.00 8.00
64 Roberto Alomar HF 6.00 15.00
65 Jeff Bagwell S 4.00 10.00
66 Mark Grace SS 5.00 12.00
67 Gary Sheffield S 2.50 6.00
68 Joe Carter HF 4.00 10.00
69 Jim Thome ML 3.00 8.00

1998 Donruss Limited Exposure Sample
S Frank Thomas S 1.25 3.00

2011 Donruss Limited Cuts 1
PRINT RUNS B/WN 1-49 COPIES PER
NO PRICING ON QTY 19 OR LESS
2 Al Barlick/49 8.00 20.00
3 Al Lopez/49 12.50 30.00
7 Amos Strunk/49 20.00 50.00
16 Ben Chapman/20 20.00 50.00
19 Bill Dickey/28 20.00 50.00
24 Bill Terry/49 15.00 40.00
27 Billy Herman/49 10.00 25.00
32 Bob Feller/49 12.50 30.00
34 Bob Lemon/49 10.00 25.00
41 Buck Leonard/49 15.00 40.00
47 Burleigh Grimes/35 30.00 60.00
51 Carl Hubbell/49 20.00 50.00
53 Catfish Hunter/49 15.00 40.00
57 Charlie Gehringer/49 15.00 40.00
68 Cool Papa Bell/49 60.00 120.00
94 Duke Snider/49 12.50 30.00
97 Earl Averill/49 15.00 40.00
105 Edd Roush/49 20.00 50.00
114 Enos Slaughter/49 12.50 30.00
133 Gene Woodling/49 12.50 30.00
136 George Kell/49 15.00 40.00
137 George L. Kelly/48 15.00 40.00
139 George Selkirk/31 15.00 40.00
145 Gil McDougald/49 10.00 25.00
152 Gus Suhr/49 10.00 25.00
159 Hank Sauer/49 8.00 20.00
173 Hoyt Wilhelm/49 10.00 25.00
176 Jack Haley/33 40.00 80.00
179 Jesse Haines/49 30.00 60.00
186 Jocko Conlan/33 12.50 30.00
193 Joe McCarthy/49 20.00 50.00
196 Joe Sewell/49 10.00 25.00
200 Johnny Mize/49 15.00 40.00
202 Johnny Sain/25 10.00 25.00
214 Larry Doyle/49 15.00 40.00
216 Larry Kopf/25 12.50 30.00
218 Lefty Gomez/49 20.00 50.00
223 Leon Day/20 40.00 80.00
225 Lloyd Waner/49 20.00 50.00
227 Lou Boudreau/49 10.00 25.00
230 Luke Appling/49 12.50 30.00
235 Marv Breuer/49 6.00 15.00
236 Max Carey/49 20.00 50.00
240 Mickey Vernon/25 6.00 15.00
244 Monty Stratton/34 10.00 25.00
248 Ossie Bluege/49 10.00 25.00
255 Pete Runnels/22 8.00 20.00
259 Preacher Roe/49 12.50 30.00
260 Ralph Houk/49 10.00 25.00
271 Rick Ferrell/49 10.00 25.00
273 Rip Repulski/35 10.00 25.00
280 Roger Peckinpaugh/49 15.00 40.00
297 Smoky Burgess/25 10.00 25.00
300 Sparky Anderson/25 12.50 30.00
302 Stanley Coveleski/49 20.00 50.00
303 Stan Hack/26 15.00 40.00
306 Taylor Douthit/27 15.00 40.00
309 Ted Lyons/49 15.00 40.00
312 Tom Tresh/23 20.00 50.00
319 Travis Jackson/49 20.00 50.00
325 Vic Raschi/48 15.00 40.00
326 Vic Wertz/31 10.00 25.00
328 Waite Hoyt/49 20.00 50.00
331 Walter Alston/24 40.00 80.00
336 Warren Spahn/49 20.00 50.00
342 William Wambsganss/38 20.00 50.00
343 Willie Kamm/49 10.00 25.00
344 Willie Stargell/33 20.00 50.00
345 Willis Hudlin/32 15.00 40.00

2011 Donruss Limited Cuts 2
PRINT RUNS B/WN 1-49 COPIES PER
NO PRICING ON QTY 19 OR LESS
2 Al Barlick/25 8.00 20.00
3 Al Lopez/49 12.50 30.00
19 Bill Dickey/25 20.00 50.00
22 Bill Rigney/49 6.00 15.00
24 Bill Terry/49 12.50 30.00
27 Billy Herman/49 10.00 25.00
32 Bob Feller/49 12.50 30.00
34 Bob Lemon/49 10.00 25.00
35 Bob Meusel/25 30.00 60.00
36 Bob O'Farrell/31 10.00 25.00
41 Buck Leonard/49 15.00 40.00
51 Carl Hubbell/49 20.00 50.00
53 Catfish Hunter/49 15.00 40.00
57 Charlie Gehringer/49 15.00 40.00
68 Cool Papa Bell/49 60.00 120.00
88 Dolph Camilli/26 15.00 40.00
94 Duke Snider/49 12.50 30.00
97 Earl Averill/41 15.00 40.00
105 Edd Roush/49 20.00 50.00
108 Eddie Mathews/26 20.00 50.00
114 Enos Slaughter/49 12.50 30.00
117 Ernie Shore/25 20.00 50.00
122 Frankie Crosetti/49 6.00 15.00
133 Gene Woodling/49 12.50 30.00
136 George Kell/49 15.00 40.00
137 George L. Kelly/49 15.00 40.00
138 George Pipgras/25 15.00 40.00
139 George Selkirk/49 10.00 25.00
152 Gus Suhr/49 10.00 25.00
159 Hank Sauer/49 8.00 20.00
173 Hoyt Wilhelm/49 10.00 25.00
179 Jesse Haines/49 30.00 60.00
186 Jocko Conlan/25 12.50 30.00
193 Joe McCarthy/49 20.00 50.00
196 Joe Sewell/49 10.00 25.00
200 Johnny Mize/49 15.00 40.00
202 Johnny Sain/25 10.00 25.00
214 Larry Doyle/49 15.00 40.00
218 Lefty Gomez/49 20.00 50.00
225 Lloyd Waner/49 20.00 50.00
227 Lou Boudreau/49 12.50 30.00
230 Luke Appling/49 12.50 30.00
236 Max Carey/49 20.00 50.00
240 Mickey Vernon/25 6.00 15.00
248 Ossie Bluege/49 10.00 25.00
256 Phil Rizzuto/32 20.00 50.00
260 Ralph Houk/49 10.00 25.00
272 Riggs Stephenson/25 12.50 30.00
274 Rip Sewell/24 12.50 30.00
280 Roger Peckinpaugh/49 15.00 40.00
297 Smoky Burgess/21 10.00 25.00
300 Sparky Anderson/21 12.50 30.00
302 Stanley Coveleski/49 20.00 50.00
303 Stan Hack/25 15.00 40.00
306 Taylor Douthit/25 15.00 40.00
309 Ted Lyons/49 15.00 40.00
319 Travis Jackson/39 20.00 50.00
326 Vic Wertz/49 10.00 25.00
328 Waite Hoyt/49 20.00 50.00
336 Warren Spahn/45 20.00 50.00
343 Willie Kamm/49 10.00 25.00
345 Willis Hudlin/28 15.00 40.00

2011 Donruss Limited Cuts 3
PRINT RUNS B/WN 1-49 COPIES PER
NO PRICING ON QTY 19 OR LESS
2 Al Barlick/42 8.00 20.00
3 Al Lopez/49 12.50 30.00
19 Bill Dickey/25 20.00 50.00
22 Bill Rigney/29 20.00 50.00
24 Bill Terry/49 12.50 30.00
27 Billy Herman/49 10.00 25.00
32 Bob Feller/49 12.50 30.00
34 Bob Lemon/49 10.00 25.00
36 Bob O'Farrell/21 15.00 40.00
41 Buck Leonard/49 15.00 40.00
53 Catfish Hunter/49 15.00 40.00
57 Charlie Gehringer/49 15.00 40.00
68 Cool Papa Bell/49 60.00 120.00
97 Earl Averill/25 15.00 40.00
105 Edd Roush/49 20.00 50.00
108 Eddie Mathews/20 20.00 50.00
114 Enos Slaughter/49 12.50 30.00
117 Ernie Shore/25 20.00 50.00
118 Ewell Blackwell/21 12.50 30.00
122 Frankie Crosetti/20 6.00 15.00
136 George Kell/49 15.00 40.00
139 George Selkirk/33 15.00 40.00
145 Gil McDougald/49 10.00 25.00
152 Gus Suhr/24 10.00 25.00
154 Hal Newhouser/27 15.00 40.00
159 Hank Sauer/25 8.00 20.00
173 Hoyt Wilhelm/34 12.50 30.00
179 Jesse Haines/49 30.00 60.00
193 Joe McCarthy/25 30.00 60.00
196 Joe Sewell/49 10.00 25.00
200 Johnny Mize/49 15.00 40.00
202 Johnny Sain/25 10.00 25.00
204 Judy Johnson/32 20.00 50.00
214 Larry Doyle/32 15.00 40.00
223 Leon Day/23 40.00 80.00
225 Lloyd Waner/49 20.00 50.00
227 Lou Boudreau/49 12.50 30.00
230 Luke Appling/49 12.50 30.00
236 Max Carey/49 20.00 50.00
248 Ossie Bluege/46 10.00 25.00
259 Preacher Roe/49 12.50 30.00
260 Ralph Houk/49 10.00 25.00
270 Richie Ashburn/26 40.00 80.00
271 Rick Ferrell/49 10.00 25.00
272 Riggs Stephenson/25 12.50 30.00
280 Roger Peckinpaugh/27 15.00 40.00
302 Stanley Coveleski/49 20.00 50.00
306 Taylor Douthit/25 15.00 40.00
309 Ted Lyons/49 15.00 40.00
328 Waite Hoyt/49 20.00 50.00
331 Walter Alston/30 40.00 80.00
343 Willie Kamm/49 10.00 25.00

2011 Donruss Limited Cuts 4
PRINT RUNS B/WN 1-49 COPIES PER
NO PRICING ON QTY 19 OR LESS
3 Al Lopez/49 12.50 30.00
6 Allie Reynolds/21 20.00 50.00
27 Billy Herman/49 10.00 25.00
32 Bob Feller/49 12.50 30.00
36 Bob O'Farrell/35 8.00 20.00
41 Buck Leonard/46 15.00 40.00
51 Carl Hubbell/49 20.00 50.00
53 Catfish Hunter/29 20.00 50.00
57 Charlie Gehringer/47 15.00 40.00
68 Cool Papa Bell/49 60.00 120.00
82 Dick Williams/23 12.50 30.00
91 Don Drysdale/21 30.00 60.00
94 Duke Snider/41 12.50 30.00
105 Edd Roush/49 20.00 50.00
133 Gene Woodling/21 8.00 20.00
136 George Kell/49 15.00 40.00
137 George L. Kelly/49 15.00 40.00
152 Gus Suhr/23 10.00 25.00
154 Hal Newhouser/26 15.00 40.00
155 Hal Trosky/23 15.00 40.00
186 Jocko Conlan/25 12.50 30.00
193 Joe McCarthy/24 30.00 60.00
196 Joe Sewell/49 10.00 25.00
200 Johnny Mize/49 15.00 40.00
203 Johnny Vander Meer/25 8.00 20.00
214 Larry Doyle/28 15.00 40.00
218 Lefty Gomez/25 30.00 60.00
225 Lloyd Waner/49 20.00 50.00
227 Lou Boudreau/49 12.50 30.00
230 Luke Appling/44 12.50 30.00
236 Max Carey/49 20.00 50.00
244 Monty Stratton/23 10.00 25.00
248 Ossie Bluege/38 10.00 25.00
260 Ralph Houk/49 10.00 25.00
271 Rick Ferrell/35 10.00 25.00
274 Rip Sewell/21 12.50 30.00
277 Robin Roberts/39 20.00 50.00
280 Roger Peckinpaugh/37 15.00 40.00
302 Stanley Coveleski/49 20.00 50.00
328 Waite Hoyt/27 20.00 50.00
343 Willie Kamm/49 10.00 25.00

2016 Donruss Optic
COMP.SET w/o SPs (165) 30.00 80.00
1 Zack Greinke DK .60 1.50
2 Nick Markakis DK .50 1.25
3 Manny Machado DK .75 2.00
4 David Price DK .50 1.25
5 Jason Heyward DK .50 1.25
6 Chris Sale DK .60 1.50
7 Brandon Phillips DK .40 1.00
8 Michael Brantley DK .50 1.25
9 Carlos Gonzalez DK .50 1.25
10 Miguel Cabrera DK .60 1.50
11 Jose Altuve DK .60 1.50
12 Eric Hosmer DK .50 1.25
13 Albert Pujols DK .75 2.00
14 Joc Pederson DK .50 1.25
15 Jose Fernandez DK .60 1.50
16 Jonathan Lucroy DK .50 1.25
17 Brian Dozier DK .50 1.25
18 Jacob deGrom DK 1.25 3.00
19 Alex Rodriguez DK .75 2.00
20 Billy Burns DK .40 1.00
21 Odubel Herrera DK .50 1.25
22 Andrew McCutchen DK .60 1.50
23 Matt Kemp DK .50 1.25
24 Buster Posey DK .75 2.00
25 Nelson Cruz DK .60 1.50
26 Yadier Molina DK .75 2.00
27 Evan Longoria DK .50 1.25
28 Prince Fielder DK .50 1.25
29 Josh Donaldson DK .50 1.25
30 Bryce Harper DK 1.00 2.50
31 Kyle Schwarber RR RC 1.25 3.00
32 Corey Seager RR RC 4.00 10.00
33 Trea Turner RR RC 1.25 3.00
34 Rob Refsnyder RR RC .50 1.25
35 Miguel Sano RR RC .60 1.50
36 Stephen Piscotty RR RC .60 1.50
37 Aaron Nola RR RC .75 2.00
38 Michael Conforto RR RC .50 1.25
39 Ketel Marte RR RC .75 2.00
40 Luis Severino RR RC .50 1.25
41 Greg Bird RR RC .50 1.25
42 Hector Olivera RR RC .50 1.25
43 Jose Peraza RR RC .50 1.25
44 Henry Owens RR RC .50 1.25
45 Richie Shaffer RR RC .40 1.00
46 Byung-ho Park RR RC .60 1.50
47 Tyler Naquin RR RC .60 1.50
48 Jonathan Gray RR RC .40 1.00
49 Peter O'Brien RR RC .40 1.00
50 Aledmys Diaz RR RC .60 1.50
51 Tyler White RR RC .40 1.00
52 Nomar Mazara RR RC .60 1.50
53 Trevor Story RR RC 2.00 5.00
54 Max Kepler RR RC .60 1.50
55 Ross Stripling RR RC .40 1.00
56 Tom Murphy RR RC .40 1.00
57 Travis Jankowski RR RC .40 1.00
58 Socrates Brito RR RC .40 1.00
59 Kenta Maeda RR RC .75 2.00
60 Tyler Duffey RR RC .40 1.00
61 Jeremy Hazelbaker RR RC .50 1.25
62 Brandon Drury RR RC .60 1.50
63 Jerad Eickhoff RR RC .60 1.50
64 Jorge Lopez RR RC .40 1.00
65 Zach Davies RR RC .50 1.25
66 Chris Sale .40 1.00
67 Adrian Gonzalez .30 .75
68 Ian Kinsler .30 .75
69 Justin Upton .30 .75
70 Todd Frazier .25 .60
71 Corey Kluber .30 .75
72 Carlos Gonzalez .30 .75
73 Yadier Molina .50 1.25
74A Kris Bryant .50 1.25
74B K.Bryant SP ROY 2.00 5.00
75 Evan Gattis .25 .60
76 Dallas Keuchel .30 .75
77 Lorenzo Cain .25 .60
78 Starling Marte .30 .75
79 Yoenis Cespedes .40 1.00
80 Odubel Herrera .30 .75
81 Paul Goldschmidt .40 1.00
82 Ichiro Suzuki .50 1.25
83 Yasmany Tomas .25 .60
84 Alcides Escobar .30 .75
85 Evan Longoria .30 .75
86 Aroldis Chapman .40 1.00
87 James Shields .25 .60
88 Yasiel Puig .40 1.00
89 Mike Trout 4.00 10.00
90 Kole Calhoun .25 .60
91 Brian McCann .30 .75
92 Yu Darvish .40 1.00
93 Eddie Rosario .30 .75
94 Jason Heyward .30 .75
95 Jake Arrieta .30 .75
96 Freddie Freeman .50 1.25
97 Max Scherzer .40 1.00
98 Jorge Soler .40 1.00
99 Gerrit Cole .40 1.00
100 Alex Rodriguez .50 1.25
101 Addison Russell .40 1.00
102 Adam Wainwright .30 .75
103 Billy Hamilton .30 .75
104 Chris Davis .25 .60
105 Joey Votto .40 1.00
106 Nelson Cruz .40 1.00
107 Nolan Arenado .60 1.50
108 Johnny Cueto .30 .75
109 Matt Kemp .30 .75
110 Brandon Crawford .30 .75
111 Steven Matz .25 .60
112 Jose Fernandez .40 1.00
113 Jason Kipnis .30 .75
114A Jose Bautista .30 .75
114B Btsta SP Joey Bats 1.25 3.00
115 Matt Carpenter .40 1.00
116 David Wright .30 .75
117A Bryce Harper .60 1.50
117B B.Harper SP MVP 2.50 6.00
118 Jacob deGrom .75 2.00
119 Sonny Gray .30 .75
120 David Price .30 .75
121 Adam Jones .30 .75
122 Prince Fielder .30 .75
123 Giancarlo Stanton .40 1.00
124 Zack Greinke .40 1.00
125 Troy Tulowitzki .40 1.00
126 David Ortiz .40 1.00
127 Andrew McCutchen .40 1.00
128 Joc Pederson .30 .75
129 Billy Burns .25 .60
130 Adrian Beltre .40 1.00
131 Edwin Encarnacion .40 1.00
132 Miguel Cabrera .40 1.00
133 Francisco Lindor .40 1.00
134 Charlie Blackmon .40 1.00
135 Ryan Braun .30 .75
136 Robinson Cano .30 .75
137 Stephen Strasburg .40 1.00
138 Eric Hosmer .30 .75
139A Carlos Correa .40 1.00
139B C.Correa SP ROY 1.50 4.00
140 Maikel Franco .30 .75
141 Albert Pujols .50 1.25
142 Manny Machado .40 1.00
143 Jeff Samardzija .25 .60
144 Dee Gordon .25 .60
145 Xander Bogaerts .40 1.00
146 Chris Archer .25 .60
147 Salvador Perez .30 .75
148 Andrelton Simmons .25 .60
149 Anthony Rizzo .50 1.25
150 Madison Bumgarner .30 .75
151 Jonathan Lucroy .30 .75
152 Adam Eaton .25 .60
153 Matt Holliday .40 1.00
154 Jose Altuve .30 .75
155 Buster Posey .50 1.25
156 Cole Hamels .30 .75
157 Mookie Betts .75 2.00
158 Felix Hernandez .30 .75
159 Brian Dozier .30 .75
160 A.J. Pollock .25 .60
161A Josh Donaldson .30 .75
161B J.Donaldson SP MVP 1.25 3.00
162 Clayton Kershaw .60 1.50
163 Jose Abreu .40 1.00
164 Noah Syndergaard .30 .75
165 The Famous San Diego Chicken .25 .60
Ted Giannoulas
166 Mac Williamson RR AU RC 2.50 6.00
167 Trayce Thompson RR AU RC 4.00 10.00
168 Zack Godley RR AU RC 2.50 6.00
169 John Lamb RR AU RC 2.50 6.00
170 Brian Ellington RR AU RC 2.50 6.00
171 Colin Rea RR AU RC 2.50 6.00
172 Frankie Montas RR AU RC 3.00 8.00
173 Alex Dickerson RR AU RC 2.50 6.00
174 Kaleb Cowart RR AU RC 2.50 6.00
175 Pedro Severino RR AU RC 2.50 6.00

2016 Donruss Optic Aqua
*AQUA DK: .75X TO 2X BASIC DK
*AQUA RR: .75X TO 2X BASIC RR
*AQUA VET: 1.2X TO 3X BASIC VET
*AQUA AU: .5X TO 1.2X BASIC AU
RANDOM INSERTS IN PACKS
STATED PRINT RUN 299 SER.#'d SETS
AU PRINT RUNS B/WN 4-125 COPIES PER
NO PRICING ON QTY 4
EXCHANGE DEADLINE 1/20/2018
50 Aledmys Diaz RR 10.00 25.00
89 Mike Trout 15.00 40.00

2016 Donruss Optic Black
*BLACK DK: 2X TO 5X BASIC DK
*BLACK RR: 2X TO 5X BASIC RR
*BLACK VET: 3X TO 8X BASIC VET
*BLACK AU: .75X TO 2X BASIC AU
RANDOM INSERTS IN PACKS
STATED PRINT RUN 25 SER.#'d SETS
EXCHANGE DEADLINE 1/20/2018
50 Aledmys Diaz RR 60.00 150.00
89 Mike Trout 60.00 150.00

2016 Donruss Optic Blue
*BLUE DK: 1X TO 2.5X BASIC DK
*BLUE RR: 1X TO 2.5X BASIC RR
*BLUE VET: 1.5X TO 4X BASIC VET
*BLUE SP: .4X TO 1X BASIC SP
*BLUE AU: .6X TO 1.5X BASIC AU
RANDOM INSERTS IN PACKS
STATED PRINT RUN 149 SER.#'d SETS
AU PRINT RUN 75 SER.#'d SETS
EXCHANGE DEADLINE 1/20/2018
50 Aledmys Diaz RR 20.00 50.00
89 Mike Trout 20.00 50.00

2016 Donruss Optic Carolina Blue
*CAR.BLU DK: 1.5X TO 4X BASIC DK
*CAR.BLU RR: 1.5X TO 4X BASIC RR
*CAR.BLU VET: 2.5X TO 6X BASIC VET
*CAR.BLU AU: .75X TO 2X BASIC AU
RANDOM INSERTS IN PACKS
STATED PRINT RUN 50 SER.#'d SETS
AU PRINT RUN 35 SER.#'d SETS
EXCHANGE DEADLINE 1/20/2018
50 Aledmys Diaz RR 50.00 120.00
89 Mike Trout 50.00 120.00

2016 Donruss Optic Holo
*HOLO DK: .5X TO 1.2X BASIC DK
*HOLO RR: .5X TO 1.2X BASIC RR
*HOLO VET: .75X TO 2X BASIC VET
*HOLO AU: .5X TO 1.2X BASIC AU
RANDOM INSERTS IN PACKS
AU PRINT RUNS B/WN 5-150 COPIES PER
NO PRICING ON QTY 5
EXCHANGE DEADLINE 1/20/2018
89 Mike Trout 25.00 60.00

2016 Donruss Optic Orange
*ORANGE DK: .6X TO 1.5X BASIC DK
*ORANGE RR: 1X TO 2.5X BASIC RR
*ORANGE VET: 1.5X TO 4X BASIC VET
*ORANGE AU: .6X TO 1.5X BASIC AU
RANDOM INSERTS IN PACKS
STATED PRINT RUN 199 SER.#'d SETS
AU PRINT RUNS B/WN 5-75 COPIES PER
NO PRICING ON QTY 5
EXCHANGE DEADLINE 1/20/2018
50 Aledmys Diaz RR 20.00 50.00
89 Mike Trout 20.00 50.00

2016 Donruss Optic Pink
*PINK DK: .6X TO 1.5X BASIC DK
*PINK RR: .6X TO 1.5X BASIC RR
*PINK VET: 1X TO 2.5X BASIC VET
RANDOM INSERTS IN PACKS

2016 Donruss Optic Purple
*PURPLE DK: .6X TO 1.5X BASIC DK
*PURPLE RR: .6X TO 1.5X BASIC RR
*PURPLE VET: 1X TO 2.5X BASIC VET
INSERTED IN RETAIL PACKS

2016 Donruss Optic Red
*RED DK: 1.2X TO 3X BASIC DK
*RED RR: 1.2X TO 3X BASIC RR
*RED VET: 2X TO 5X BASIC VET
*RED SP: .5X TO 1.2X BASIC SP
*RED AU: .6X TO 1.5X BASIC AU
RANDOM INSERTS IN PACKS
STATED PRINT RUN 99 SER.#'d SETS
AU PRINT RUN 50 SER.#'d SETS
EXCHANGE DEADLINE 1/20/2018
50 Aledmys Diaz RR 30.00 80.00
89 Mike Trout 25.00 60.00

2016 Donruss Optic Autographs
RANDOM INSERTS IN PACKS
*BLUE/50: .5X TO 1.2X BASIC
*BLUE/25: .6X TO 1.5X BASIC
*RED/25: .6X TO 1.5X BASIC
EXCHANGE DEADLINE 1/20/2018
OAAR Anthony Rizzo 15.00 40.00
OABH Billy Hamilton 4.00 10.00
OABJ Brian Johnson 2.50 6.00
OACK Clayton Kershaw 25.00 60.00
OACM Carlos Martinez 3.00 8.00
OADO David Ortiz
OADP David Price 8.00 20.00
OADW David Wright 6.00 15.00
OAED Elias Diaz 2.50 6.00
OAEG Evan Gattis 2.50 6.00
OAEL Evan Longoria 8.00 20.00
OAGC Gerrit Cole 10.00 25.00
OAGP Gregory Polanco 3.00 8.00
OAJA Jose Abreu 8.00 20.00
OAJB Jose Bautista 10.00 25.00
OAJD Josh Donaldson 10.00 25.00
OAJL Jorge Lopez 2.50 6.00
OAKM Ketel Marte 4.00 10.00
OAMA Matt Adams 2.50 6.00
OAMB Mookie Betts 50.00 120.00
OARS Richie Shaffer 2.50 6.00
OASM Starling Marte 3.00 8.00
OATJ Travis Jankowski 2.50 6.00
OATS Trevor Story 8.00 20.00
OATT Trea Turner 10.00 25.00

2016 Donruss Optic Back to the Future
RANDOM INSERTS IN PACKS
*BLUE/149: 1X TO 2.5X BASIC
*RED/99: 1.2X TO 3X BASIC
BF1 Adrian Beltre .60 1.50
BF2 Miguel Cabrera .60 1.50
BF3 Jason Heyward .50 1.25
BF4 Yoenis Cespedes .60 1.50
BF5 Chris Davis .40 1.00
BF6 Josh Donaldson .50 1.25
BF7 Albert Pujols .75 2.00
BF8 Jake Arrieta .50 1.25
BF9 Zack Greinke .60 1.50
BF10 David Price .50 1.25
BF11 Prince Fielder .50 1.25
BF12 Josh Hamilton .50 1.25
BF13 Anthony Rizzo .75 2.00
BF14 Max Scherzer .60 1.50
BF15 David Ortiz .60 1.50

2016 Donruss Optic Back to the Future Signatures
RANDOM INSERTS IN PACKS
*BLUE/50: .5X TO 1.2X BASIC
*BLUE/25: .6X TO 1.5X BASIC
*RED/25: .6X TO 1.5X BASIC
EXCHANGE DEADLINE 1/20/2018
BTFAG Adrian Gonzalez 3.00 8.00
BTFBB Bill Buckner 3.00 8.00
BTFDM Don Mattingly 25.00 60.00
BTFDO David Ortiz 15.00 40.00
BTFDP David Price 6.00 15.00
BTFFT Frank Thomas 20.00 50.00
BTFJD Josh Donaldson 10.00 25.00
BTFJU Justin Upton 3.00 8.00
BTFKG Ken Griffey Jr. 50.00 120.00
BTFKM Kris Medlen 4.00 10.00
BTFLG Luke Gregerson 2.50 6.00
BTFMG Mark Grace 6.00 15.00
BTFMS Max Scherzer 10.00 25.00
BTFNS Nick Swisher 6.00 15.00
BTFOV Omar Vizquel 5.00 12.00
BTFPF Prince Fielder
BTFRA Roberto Alomar 10.00 25.00
BTFRH Rickey Henderson 20.00 50.00
BTFRS Ryne Sandberg 15.00 40.00
BTFTF Todd Frazier 2.50 6.00
BTFTG Ted Giannoulas 25.00 60.00
BTFTT Troy Tulowitzki 8.00 20.00
BTFTW Tim Wakefield 15.00 40.00
BTFYC Yoenis Cespedes

2016 Donruss Optic Illusion
RANDOM INSERTS IN PACKS
*BLUE/149: 1X TO 2.5X BASIC
*RED/99: 1.2X TO 3X BASIC
1 Mike Trout 3.00 8.00
2 Bryce Harper 1.00 2.50
3 David Ortiz .60 1.50
4 Jose Bautista .50 1.25
5 Jose Abreu .60 1.50
6 Miguel Cabrera .60 1.50
7 Carlos Correa .60 1.50
8 Robinson Cano .50 1.25
9 Kris Bryant .75 2.00
10 Giancarlo Stanton .60 1.50
11 Andrew McCutchen .60 1.50
12 Chris Davis .40 1.00
13 Jason Heyward .50 1.25
14 Justin Upton .50 1.25
15 Clayton Kershaw 1.00 2.50
16 Jacob deGrom 1.25 3.00
17 Matt Harvey .50 1.25
18 Johnny Cueto .50 1.25
19 Noah Syndergaard .50 1.25
20 David Price .50 1.25

2016 Donruss Optic Masters of the Game
RANDOM INSERTS IN PACKS
*BLUE/149: 1X TO 2.5X BASIC
*RED/99: 1.2X TO 3X BASIC
1 Rickey Henderson .60 1.50
2 Roger Clemens .75 2.00
3 Juan Gonzalez .40 1.00
4 Frank Thomas .60 1.50
5 Steve Carlton .50 1.25
6 Mariano Rivera .75 2.00
7 Mark McGwire 1.00 2.50
8 Randy Johnson .60 1.50
9 Ken Griffey Jr. 1.25 3.00
10 Cal Ripken 2.00 5.00
11 Ryne Sandberg 1.25 3.00
12 Mike Piazza .60 1.50
13 Edgar Martinez .50 1.25
14 Pete Rose 1.25 3.00
15 Johnny Bench .60 1.50

2016 Donruss Optic Power Alley
RANDOM INSERTS IN PACKS
*BLUE/149: 1X TO 2.5X BASIC
*RED/99: 1.2X TO 3X BASIC
1 Bryce Harper 1.00 2.50
2 Mike Trout 3.00 8.00
3 Josh Donaldson .50 1.25
4 Carlos Correa .60 1.50
5 Miguel Sano .60 1.50
6 Giancarlo Stanton .60 1.50
7 Madison Bumgarner .50 1.25
8 Kyle Schwarber 1.25 3.00
9 Eric Hosmer .50 1.25
10 Jose Bautista .50 1.25
11 Kris Bryant .75 2.00
12 Albert Pujols .75 2.00
13 Paul Goldschmidt .60 1.50
14 David Ortiz .60 1.50
15 Yoenis Cespedes .60 1.50

2016 Donruss Optic Rated Rookies Signatures
RANDOM INSERTS IN PACKS
*AQUA/50-125: .5X TO 1.2X BASIC
*BLACK/25: .6X TO 1.5X BASIC
*BLUE/75: .5X TO 1.2X BASIC
*BLUE/25-35: .6X TO 1.5X BASIC
*CAR.BLUE/35: .6X TO 1.5X BASIC
*HOLO/75-150: .5X TO 1.2X BASIC
*ORANGE/50-99: .5X TO 1.2X BASIC
*ORANGE/35: .6X TO 1.5X BASIC
*RED/50: .5X TO 1.2X BASIC
*RED/25: .6X TO 1.5X BASIC
EXCHANGE DEADLINE 1/20/2018
1 Aaron Nola 5.00 12.00
2 Brandon Drury 4.00 10.00
3 Brian Johnson 2.50 6.00
4 Byung-ho Park 3.00 8.00
5 Carl Edwards Jr. 3.00 8.00
6 Corey Seager 60.00 150.00
7 Dariel Alvarez 2.50 6.00
8 Elias Diaz 2.50 6.00
9 Greg Bird 3.00 8.00
10 Henry Owens
11 Jerad Eickhoff 4.00 10.00
12 Jonathan Gray
13 Jorge Lopez
14 Jose Peraza 3.00 8.00
15 Kelby Tomlinson 2.50 6.00
17 Ketel Marte 5.00 12.00
18 Kyle Schwarber 8.00 20.00
19 Kyle Waldrop 3.00 8.00
20 Luis Severino 3.00 8.00
21 Luke Jackson
22 Max Kepler 5.00 12.00
23 Michael Conforto 15.00 40.00
24 Michael Reed 2.50 6.00
25 Miguel Sano 8.00 20.00
26 Peter O'Brien
27 Raul Mondesi 5.00 12.00
28 Richie Shaffer 2.50 6.00
29 Rob Refsnyder 5.00 12.00
30 Socrates Brito 2.50 6.00
31 Stephen Piscotty 4.00 10.00
32 Tom Murphy 2.50 6.00
33 Travis Jankowski 2.50 6.00
34 Trea Turner 8.00 20.00
35 Tyler Duffey 2.50 6.00
36 Zach Davies 6.00 15.00
37 A.J. Reed 6.00 15.00

2016 Donruss Optic Significant Signatures
RANDOM INSERTS IN PACKS
*BLUE/50: .5X TO 1.2X BASIC
*BLUE/25: .6X TO 1.5X BASIC
*RED/25: .6X TO 1.5X BASIC
EXCHANGE DEADLINE 1/20/2018
1 Don Newcombe
2 Al Kaline 20.00 50.00
3 Jim Palmer 5.00 10.00
4 Steve Carlton 8.00 20.00
5 Gaylord Perry 4.00 10.00
6 Andres Galarraga 5.00 12.00
7 Fergie Jenkins 6.00 15.00
8 Alan Trammell 20.00 50.00
9 Andre Dawson
10 Andy Pettitte 12.00 30.00
11 Bernie Williams 10.00 25.00
12 Bert Blyleven 5.00 12.00
13 Bob Gibson 10.00 25.00
14 Phil Niekro 12.00 30.00
15 Edgar Martinez 8.00 20.00
16 Paul Molitor 6.00 15.00
17 Fred Lynn 4.00 10.00
18 Rollie Fingers
19 Jim Rice 6.00 15.00
20 Frank Thomas 20.00 50.00
21 Rocky Colavito 25.00 60.00
22 Todd Helton 12.00 30.00
23 Will Clark 30.00 80.00
24 Carlton Fisk
25 Billy Williams

2016 Donruss Optic Studio Signatures
RANDOM INSERTS IN PACKS
*BLUE/50: .5X TO 1.2X BASIC
*BLUE/25: .6X TO 1.5X BASIC
*RED/25: .6X TO 1.5X BASIC
EXCHANGE DEADLINE 1/20/2018
1 Kris Bryant 50.00 120.00
2 Michael Taylor 2.50 6.00
3 Miguel Sano 4.00 10.00
4 Corey Seager 8.00 20.00
5 Kyle Schwarber 10.00 25.00
6 Carl Edwards Jr. 3.00 8.00
7 Lucas Giolito 4.00 10.00
8 Charlie Blackmon 4.00 10.00
9 Evan Gattis 2.50 6.00
10 Evan Longoria 5.00 12.00
11 George Springer 3.00 8.00
12 Joe Mauer
13 Maikel Franco 3.00 8.00
14 Addison Russell 10.00 25.00

15 Vladimir Guerrero Jr. 125.00 300.00
16 Zack Wheeler 3.00 8.00
17 A.J. Reed 2.50 6.00
18 Anthony Ranaudo 2.50 6.00
19 Carlos Martinez 3.00 8.00
20 Didi Gregorius 3.00 8.00
21 Eddie Rosario 3.00 8.00
22 Jose Berrios 4.00 10.00
23 Josh Harrison 2.50 6.00
24 Kaleb Cowart 2.50 6.00
25 Orlando Arcia 3.00 8.00

2016 Donruss Optic The Prospects

RANDOM INSERTS IN PACKS
*BLUE/149: 1X TO 2.5X BASIC
*RED/99: 1.2X TO 3X BASIC
1 Lucas Giolito .60 1.50
2 Julio Urias 1.25 3.00
3 Yoan Moncada 1.00 2.50
4 Tyler Glasnow 1.50 4.00
5 Brendan Rodgers .60 1.50
6 Dansby Swanson 1.50 4.00
7 Orlando Arcia .50 1.25
8 Rafael Devers 1.25 3.00
9 Vladimir Guerrero Jr. 6.00 15.00
10 A.J. Reed .40 1.00
11 Andrew Benintendi 1.25 3.00
12 Bradley Zimmer .60 1.50
13 Alex Reyes .50 1.25
14 Clint Frazier 1.50 4.00
15 Josh Bell .75 2.00

2016 Donruss Optic The Rookies

RANDOM INSERTS IN PACKS
*BLUE/149: 1X TO 2.5X BASIC
*RED/99: 1.2X TO 3X BASIC
1 Kyle Schwarber 1.25 3.00
2 Corey Seager 4.00 10.00
3 Trea Turner 1.25 3.00
4 Rob Refsnyder .50 1.25
5 Miguel Sano .60 1.50
6 Stephen Piscotty .60 1.50
7 Aaron Nola .75 2.00
8 Michael Conforto .50 1.25
9 Ketel Marte .75 2.00
10 Luis Severino .50 1.25
11 Greg Bird .50 1.25
12 Hector Olivera .50 1.25
13 Jose Peraza .50 1.25
14 Henry Owens .50 1.25
15 Richie Shaffer .40 1.00

2017 Donruss Optic

COMP.SET w/o SPs (165) 30.00 80.00
EXCHANGE DEADLINE 1/19/2019
SPs RANDOMLY INSERTED
1 Paul Goldschmidt DK .50 1.25
2 Freddie Freeman DK .60 1.50
3 Mark Trumbo DK .30 .75
4 Chris Sale DK .50 1.25
5 Anthony Rizzo DK .60 1.50
6 Lucas Giolito DK .40 1.00
7 Mickey Mantle DK 1.50 4.00
8 Corey Kluber DK .40 1.00
9 Nolan Arenado DK .75 2.00
10 Justin Verlander DK .50 1.25
11 Carlos Correa DK .50 1.25
12 Salvador Perez DK .40 1.00
13 Mike Trout DK 2.50 6.00
14 Corey Seager DK .50 1.25
15 Christian Yelich DK .60 1.50
16 Jonathan Villar DK .30 .75
17 Miguel Sano DK .40 1.00
18 Noah Syndergaard DK .40 1.00
19 Joey Votto DK .50 1.25
20 Khris Davis DK .50 1.25
21 Maikel Franco DK .40 1.00
22 Gregory Polanco DK .40 1.00
23 Wil Myers DK .40 1.00
24 Madison Bumgarner DK .40 1.00
25 Robinson Cano DK .40 1.00
26 Dexter Fowler DK .40 1.00
27 Kevin Kiermaier DK .40 1.00
28 Rougned Odor DK .40 1.00
29 Troy Tulowitzki DK .50 1.25
30 Daniel Murphy DK .40 1.00
31 Yoan Moncada RR RC 1.00 2.50
32 David Dahl RR RC .40 1.00
33 Dansby Swanson RR RC .75 2.00
34 Andrew Benintendi RR RC 1.00 2.50
35 Alex Reyes RR RC .40 1.00
36 Tyler Glasnow RR RC 1.25 3.00
37 Josh Bell RR RC .75 2.00
38 Aaron Judge RR RC 4.00 10.00
39 Jose De Leon RR RC .30 .75
40 Ian Happ RR RC .60 1.50
41 Hunter Renfroe RR RC .40 1.00
42 Carson Fulmer RR RC .30 .75
43 Alex Bregman RR RC 1.50 4.00
44 Orlando Arcia RR RC .50 1.25
45 Manuel Margot RR RC .30 .75
46 Joe Musgrove RR RC 1.00 2.50
47 David Paulino RR RC .40 1.00
48 Reynaldo Lopez RR RC .30 .75
49 Jake Thompson RR RC .30 .75
50 Braden Shipley RR RC .30 .75
51 Jorge Alfaro RR RC .40 1.00
52 Luke Weaver RR RC .40 1.00
53 Raimel Tapia RR RC .40 1.00
54 Adalberto Mejia RR RC .30 .75
55 Gavin Cecchini RR RC .30 .75
56 Renato Nunez RR RC .60 1.50
57 Jacoby Jones RR RC .40 1.00
58 Magneuris Sierra RR RC .30 .75
59 Trey Mancini RR RC .60 1.50
60 Ryon Healy RR RC .40 1.00
61 Jordan Montgomery RR RC .50 1.25
62 Teoscar Hernandez RR RC 1.25 3.00
63 Christian Arroyo RR RC .50 1.25
64 Mitch Haniger RR RC .50 1.25
65 Cody Bellinger RR RC 8.00 20.00
66 Paul Goldschmidt .30 .75
67 Yasmany Tomas .20 .50
68 Zack Greinke .30 .75
69 Freddie Freeman .40 1.00
70 Matt Kemp .25 .60
71 Nick Markakis .25 .60
72 Adam Jones .25 .60
73 Manny Machado .30 .75
74 Chris Sale .30 .75
75 Dustin Pedroia .30 .75
76 Jackie Bradley Jr. .30 .75
77 Mookie Betts .60 1.50
78 Rick Porcello .25 .60
79 Xander Bogaerts .30 .75
80 Addison Russell .30 .75
81A Anthony Rizzo .40 1.00
81B Rizzo SP Rizz .40 1.00
82 Javier Baez .40 1.00
83A Kris Bryant .40 1.00
83B Bryant SP MVP .40 1.00
84 Kyle Hendricks .30 .75
85 Kyle Schwarber .30 .75
86 Jose Abreu .30 .75
87 Todd Frazier .20 .50
88 Joey Votto .30 .75
89 Corey Kluber .25 .60
90 Francisco Lindor .30 .75
91 Tyler Naquin .30 .75
92 Andrew Miller .25 .60
93 Charlie Blackmon .30 .75
94 Nolan Arenado .50 1.25
95 Trevor Story .30 .75
96 Carlos Gonzalez .25 .60
97 Justin Verlander .30 .75
98 Michael Fulmer .20 .50
99 Miguel Cabrera .30 .75
100 Carlos Correa .30 .75
101 George Springer .25 .60
102 Jose Altuve .25 .60
103 Eric Hosmer .25 .60
104 Kendrys Morales .20 .50
105 Salvador Perez .25 .60
106 Albert Pujols .40 1.00
107A Mike Trout 1.50 4.00
107B Trout SP MVP 5.00 12.00
108 Clayton Kershaw .50 1.25
109A Corey Seager .30 .75
109B Seager SP ROY .30 .75
110 Kenta Maeda .25 .60
111 Christian Yelich .40 1.00
112 Dee Gordon .20 .50
113 Giancarlo Stanton .30 .75
114 Chris Carter .20 .50
115 Ryan Braun .25 .60
116 Brian Dozier .30 .75
117 Miguel Sano .25 .60
118 Jacob deGrom .60 1.50
119 Jay Bruce .25 .60
120 Noah Syndergaard .25 .60
121 Yoenis Cespedes .30 .75
122 Gary Sanchez .30 .75
123 Masahiro Tanaka .25 .60
124 Khris Davis .30 .75
125 Marcus Semien .30 .75
126 Freddy Galvis .20 .50
127 Maikel Franco .25 .60
128 Andrew McCutchen .30 .75
129 Gregory Polanco .25 .60
130 Starling Marte .25 .60
131 Alex Dickerson .20 .50
132 Wil Myers .25 .60
133 Brandon Belt .25 .60
134 Buster Posey .40 1.00
135 Madison Bumgarner .25 .60
136 Felix Hernandez .25 .60
137 Robinson Cano .25 .60
138 Matt Carpenter .30 .75
139 Stephen Piscotty .25 .60
140 Yadier Molina .40 1.00
141 Dexter Fowler .25 .60
142 Brad Miller .25 .60
143 Evan Longoria .25 .60
144 Kevin Kiermaier .25 .60
145 Adrian Beltre .30 .75
146 Nomar Mazara .20 .50
147 Rougned Odor .25 .60
148 Yu Darvish .30 .75
149 Jose Bautista .25 .60
150 Josh Donaldson .25 .60
151 Troy Tulowitzki .30 .75
152 Bryce Harper .50 1.25
153 Daniel Murphy .25 .60
154 Trea Turner .25 .60
155 Edwin Encarnacion .30 .75
156 Cal Ripken 1.00 2.50
157 Duke Snider .25 .60
158 Frank Thomas .30 .75
159 Ken Griffey Jr. .60 1.50
160 Kirby Puckett .30 .75
161 Nolan Ryan 1.00 2.50
162 Pete Rose .60 1.50
163 Ryne Sandberg .60 1.50
164 Tony Gwynn .30 .75
165A Mickey Mantle 1.00 2.50
165B Mantle SP The Mick 3.00 8.00
166 Roman Quinn RR AU 2.50 6.00
167 Matt Olson RR AU 6.00 15.00
168 Rio Ruiz RR AU 2.50 6.00
169 Chad Pinder RR AU 2.50 6.00
170 Teoscar Hernandez RR AU 10.00 25.00
171 Erik Gonzalez RR AU 2.50 6.00
172 German Marquez RR AU 4.00 10.00
173 Jharel Cotton RR AU 2.50 6.00
174 Carson Kelly RR AU 3.00 8.00
175 Jose Rondon RR AU 2.50 6.00

2017 Donruss Optic Aqua

*AQUA DK: .75X TO 2X BASIC DK
*AQUA RR: .75X TO 2X BASIC RR
*AQUA VET: 1.2X TO 3X BASIC VET
*AQUA AU: .5X TO 1.2X BASIC AU
RANDOM INSERTS IN PACKS
STATED PRINT RUN 299 SER.#'d SETS
AU PRINT RUN 125 SER.#'d SETS
EXCHANGE DEADLINE 1/19/2019

2017 Donruss Optic Black

*BLACK DK: 2.5X TO 6X BASIC DK
*BLACK RR: 2.5X TO 6X BASIC RR
*BLACK VET: 4X TO 10X BASIC VET
*BLACK AU: 1X TO 2.5X BASIC AU
RANDOM INSERTS IN PACKS
STATED PRINT RUN 25 SER.#'d SETS
EXCHANGE DEADLINE 1/19/2019

2017 Donruss Optic Blue

*BLUE DK: 1.2X TO 3X BASIC DK
*BLUE RR: 1.2X TO 3X BASIC RR
*BLUE VET: 2X TO 5X BASIC VET
*BLUE SP: .6X TO 1.5X BASIC SP
*BLUE AU: .6X TO 1.5X BASIC AU
RANDOM INSERTS IN PACKS
STATED PRINT RUN 149 SER.#'d SETS
AU PRINT RUN 75 SER.#'d SETS
EXCHANGE DEADLINE 1/19/2019

2017 Donruss Optic Carolina Blue

*CAR.BLU DK: 2X TO 5X BASIC DK
*CAR.BLU RR: 2X TO 5X BASIC RR
*CAR.BLU VET: 3X TO 8X BASIC VET
*CAR.BLU AU: .75X TO 2X BASIC AU
RANDOM INSERTS IN PACKS
STATED PRINT RUN 50 SER.#'d SETS
AU PRINT RUN 35 SER.#'d SETS
EXCHANGE DEADLINE 1/19/2019

2017 Donruss Optic Holo

*HOLO DK: .5X TO 1.2X BASIC DK
*HOLO RR: .5X TO 1.2X BASIC RR
*HOLO VET: .75X TO 2.5X BASIC VET
*HOLO AU: .5X TO 1.2X BASIC AU
RANDOM INSERTS IN PACKS
AU PRINT RUN 150 SER.#'d SETS
EXCHANGE DEADLINE 1/19/2019

2017 Donruss Optic Orange

*ORANGE DK: 1.2X TO 3X BASIC DK
*ORANGE RR: 1.2X TO 3X BASIC RR
*ORANGE VET: 2X TO 5X BASIC VET
*ORANGE SP: .6X TO 1.5X BASIC SP
*ORANGE AU: .6X TO 1.5X BASIC AU
RANDOM INSERTS IN PACKS
STATED PRINT RUN 199 SER.#'d SETS
AU PRINT RUN 99 SER.#'d SETS
EXCHANGE DEADLINE 1/19/2019

2017 Donruss Optic Pink

*PINK DK: .75X TO 2X BASIC DK
*PINK RR: .75X TO 2X BASIC RR
*PINK VET: 1.2X TO 3X BASIC VET
RANDOM INSERTS IN PACKS

2017 Donruss Optic Purple

*PURPLE DK: .75X TO 2X BASIC DK
*PURPLE RR: .75X TO 2X BASIC RR
*PURPLE VET: 1.2X TO 3X BASIC VET
INSERTED IN RETAIL PACKS

2017 Donruss Optic Red

*RED DK: 1.5X TO 4X BASIC DK
*RED RR: 1.5X TO 4X BASIC RR
*RED VET: 2.5X TO 6X BASIC VET
*RED SP: .75X TO 2X BASIC SP
*RED AU: .6X TO 1.5X BASIC AU
RANDOM INSERTS IN PACKS
STATED PRINT RUN 99 SER.#'d SETS
AU PRINT RUN 50 SER.#'d SETS
EXCHANGE DEADLINE 1/19/2019
38 Aaron Judge RR/99 30.00 80.00

2017 Donruss Optic All Stars

RANDOM INSERTS IN PACKS
*BLUE/149: 1X TO 2.5X BASIC
*RED/99: 1.2X TO 3X BASIC
AS1 Addison Russell .60 1.50
AS2 Bryce Harper 1.00 2.50
AS3 Chris Sale .60 1.50
AS4 Eric Hosmer .50 1.25
AS5 Johnny Cueto .50 1.25
AS6 Jose Altuve .50 1.25
AS7 Kris Bryant .75 2.00
AS8 Manny Machado .60 1.50
AS9 Marcell Ozuna .60 1.50
AS10 Mike Trout 3.00 8.00
AS11 Mookie Betts 1.25 3.00
AS12 Yoenis Cespedes .60 1.50
AS13 Salvador Perez .50 1.25
AS14 Corey Kluber .50 1.25
AS15 Aledmys Diaz .50 1.25

2017 Donruss Optic Autographs

RANDOM INSERTS IN PACKS
EXCHANGE DEADLINE 1/19/2019
OAAT Alan Trammell 6.00 15.00
OACB Cody Bellinger 40.00 100.00
OAER Eddie Rosario 3.00 8.00
OAFF Freddie Freeman 20.00 50.00
OAIH Ian Happ 6.00 15.00
OAIN Ivan Nova 3.00 8.00
OAJL Jorge Lopez 2.50 6.00
OAJM James McCann 3.00 8.00
OAKH Keith Hernandez 8.00 20.00
OAKP Kevin Pillar 2.50 6.00
OALT Leodys Taveras 10.00 25.00
OAMC Matt Carpenter 5.00 12.00
OAMF Mike Foltynewicz 2.50 6.00
OANA Norichika Aoki 4.00 10.00
OAPO Paulo Orlando 2.50 6.00
OAWM Willie McGee 5.00 12.00

2017 Donruss Optic Autographs Blue

*BLUE/50: .6X TO 1.5X BASIC
*BLUE/25: .75X TO 2X BASIC
RANDOM INSERTS IN PACKS
PRINT RUNS BW/N 10-50 COPIES PER
NO PRICING ON QTY 15 OR LESS
EXCHANGE DEADLINE 1/19/2019
OAAN Aaron Nola/50 12.00 30.00

2017 Donruss Optic Autographs Red

*RED/25: .75X TO 2X BASIC
RANDOM INSERTS IN PACKS
PRINT RUNS BW/N 7-25 COPIES PER
NO PRICING ON QTY 15 OR LESS
EXCHANGE DEADLINE 1/19/2019
OAAN Aaron Nola/25 15.00 40.00

2017 Donruss Optic Back to the Future Signatures

RANDOM INSERTS IN PACKS
EXCHANGE DEADLINE 1/19/2019
*RED/25: .75X TO 2X BASIC
1 Josh Donaldson 10.00 25.00
2 Max Scherzer 15.00 40.00
4 Michael Kopech 8.00 20.00
6 Jose De Leon 2.50 6.00
8 Lucas Giolito 3.00 8.00
10 Jorge Alfaro 3.00 8.00
12 Cole Hamels
13 Nelson Cruz 4.00 10.00
15 Willie McGee 5.00 12.00
17 Trea Turner 6.00 15.00
20 Khris Davis 4.00 10.00
23 John Lamb 2.50 6.00
24 Peter O'Brien 2.50 6.00
25 Jean Segura

2017 Donruss Optic Back to the Future Signatures Blue

*BLUE/50: .6X TO 1.5X BASIC
*BLUE/25: .75X TO 2X BASIC
RANDOM INSERTS IN PACKS
PRINT RUNS BW/N 10-50 COPIES PER
NO PRICING ON QTY 15 OR LESS
EXCHANGE DEADLINE 1/19/2019
18 Justin Turner/25 12.00 20.00

2017 Donruss Optic Dominators

RANDOM INSERTS IN PACKS
*BLUE/149: 1X TO 2.5X BASIC
*RED/99: 1.2X TO 3X BASIC
D1 Kris Bryant .75 2.00
D2 Mike Trout 3.00 8.00
D3 Corey Seager .60 1.50
D4 Mookie Betts 1.25 3.00
D5 Jose Altuve .50 1.25
D6 Joey Votto .60 1.50
D7 Brian Dozier .60 1.50
D8 Rick Porcello .50 1.25
D9 Corey Kluber .50 1.25
D10 Miguel Cabrera .60 1.50
D11 Robinson Cano .50 1.25
D12 Khris Davis .60 1.50
D13 Kyle Hendricks .60 1.50
D14 Max Scherzer .60 1.50
D15 Nolan Arenado 1.00 2.50

2017 Donruss Optic Masters of the Game

RANDOM INSERTS IN PACKS
*BLUE/149: 1X TO 2.5X BASIC
*RED/99: 1.2X TO 3X BASIC
MG1 Cal Ripken 2.00 5.00
MG2 Fernando Valenzuela .40 1.00
MG3 George Brett 1.25 3.00
MG4 Lou Brock .50 1.25
MG5 Mike Mussina .50 1.25
MG6 Mike Piazza .60 1.50
MG7 Mickey Mantle 2.00 5.00
MG8 Pedro Martinez .50 1.25
MG9 Reggie Jackson .50 1.25
MG10 Rod Carew .50 1.25
MG11 Don Mattingly 1.25 3.00
MG12 Ken Griffey Jr. 1.25 3.00
MG13 Todd Helton .50 1.25
MG14 Ryne Sandberg 1.25 3.00
MG15 Greg Maddux .75 2.00

2017 Donruss Optic Rated Rookies Signatures

RANDOM INSERTS IN PACKS
EXCHANGE DEADLINE 1/19/2019
*AQUA/75-125: .5X TO 1.2X BASIC
*BLACK/25: .75X TO 2X BASIC
2017 Donruss Optic Autographs Blue
2017 Donruss Optic Autographs Blue
*CAR.BLU/35: .6X TO 1.5X BASIC
*CAR.BLU/20-25: .75X TO 2X BASIC
*HOLO/99-150: .5X TO 1.2X BASIC
*ORANGE/75-99: .5X TO 1.2X BASIC
*RED/35-50: .6X TO 1.5X BASIC
*RED/25: .75X TO 2X BASIC
RRSAB Alex Bregman 12.00 30.00
RRSAJ Aaron Judge 75.00 200.00
RRSAM Adalberto Mejia 2.50 6.00
RRSAR Alex Reyes 3.00 8.00
RRSAX Andrew Benintendi 10.00 25.00
RRSBR Brendan Rodgers
RRSBS Braden Shipley 2.50 6.00
RRSCF Carson Fulmer 2.50 6.00
RRSCL Clint Frazier 12.00 30.00
RRSDD David Dahl 3.00 8.00
RRSDP David Paulino 3.00 8.00
RRSDS Dansby Swanson 15.00 40.00
RRSGC Gavin Cecchini 2.50 6.00
RRSHR Hunter Renfroe 3.00 8.00
RRSJA Jorge Alfaro 3.00 8.00
RRSJB Josh Bell 6.00 15.00
RRSJDL Jose De Leon 2.50 6.00
RRSJH Jeff Hoffman 2.50 6.00
RRSJJ Jacoby Jones 3.00 8.00
RRSJM Joe Musgrove 8.00 20.00
RRSJT Jake Thompson 2.50 6.00
RRSLB Lewis Brinson 5.00 12.00
RRSLW Luke Weaver 3.00 8.00
RRSMM Manuel Margot 2.50 6.00
RRSOA Orlando Arcia EXCH 5.00 12.00
RRSRH Ryon Healy 4.00 10.00
RRSRL Reynaldo Lopez 2.50 6.00
RRSRN Renato Nunez 5.00 12.00
RRSRT Raimel Tapia 3.00 8.00
RRSTG Tyler Glasnow 10.00 25.00
RRSTM Trey Mancini 5.00 12.00
RRSYM Yoan Moncada 30.00 80.00
RRSYO Yohander Mendez 2.50 6.00

2017 Donruss Optic Significant Signatures

RANDOM INSERTS IN PACKS
EXCHANGE DEADLINE 1/19/2019
*BLUE/50: .6X TO 1.5X BASIC
*RED/25: .75X TO 2X BASIC
21 Al Oliver 4.00 10.00
23 Pat Gillick 4.00 10.00

2017 Donruss Optic Studio Signatures

RANDOM INSERTS IN PACKS
EXCHANGE DEADLINE 1/19/2019
*RED/25: .75X TO 2X BASIC
6 Giannoulas SD Chicken 5.00 12.00
8 Matt Szczur 3.00 8.00
10 Tyler Naquin 4.00 10.00
11 Dilson Herrera 3.00 8.00
14 Willson Contreras 8.00 20.00
17 Michael Reed 2.50 6.00
21 Cory Spangenberg 2.50 6.00
22 Trevor May 2.50 6.00
23 Greg Bird 3.00 8.00
24 Jameson Taillon 4.00 10.00
25 Tim Anderson 4.00 10.00

2017 Donruss Optic Studio Signatures Blue

*BLUE/50: .6X TO 1.5X BASIC
*BLUE/25: .75X TO 2X BASIC
RANDOM INSERTS IN PACKS
PRINT RUNS BW/N 10-50 COPIES PER
NO PRICING ON QTY 10
EXCHANGE DEADLINE 1/19/2019
9 Andres Galarraga/25 6.00 15.00
16 Corey Seager/25 20.00 50.00

2017 Donruss Optic The Elite Series

RANDOM INSERTS IN PACKS
*BLUE/149: 1X TO 2.5X BASIC
*RED/99: 1.2X TO 3X BASIC
ES1 Kris Bryant .75 2.00
ES2 Clayton Kershaw 1.00 2.50
ES3 Bryce Harper 1.00 2.50
ES4 Manny Machado .60 1.50
ES5 Anthony Rizzo .75 2.00
ES6 Adrian Beltre .60 1.50
ES7 Mickey Mantle 2.00 5.00
ES8 Chris Sale .60 1.50
ES9 Gary Sanchez .60 1.50
ES10 Trevor Story .60 1.50
ES11 Trea Turner .50 1.25
ES12 Kenta Maeda .50 1.25
ES13 Buster Posey .75 2.00
ES14 Mike Trout 3.00 8.00
ES15 Francisco Lindor .60 1.50
ES16 Kyle Schwarber .60 1.50
ES17 Dustin Pedroia .60 1.50
ES18 Corey Kluber .50 1.25
ES19 Yoenis Cespedes .60 1.50
ES20 Madison Bumgarner .50 1.25

2017 Donruss Optic The Prospects

RANDOM INSERTS IN PACKS
*BLUE/149: .6X TO 1.5X BASIC
*RED/99: .75X TO 2X BASIC
TP1 Brendan Rodgers .40 1.00
TP2 Austin Meadows .75 2.00
TP3 Victor Robles .75 2.00
TP4 Ozhaino Albies 1.25 3.00
TP5 Anderson Espinoza .30 .75
TP6 Clint Frazier .60 1.50
TP7 Rafael Devers .60 1.50
TP8 Gleyber Torres 5.00 12.00
TP9 Jorge Mateo .30 .75
TP10 Vladimir Guerrero Jr. 4.00 10.00
TP11 Eloy Jimenez 1.25 3.00
TP12 Bradley Zimmer .40 1.00
TP13 Corey Ray .40 1.00
TP14 Amed Rosario .50 1.25
TP15 Francis Martes .30 .75

2017 Donruss Optic The Rookies

RANDOM INSERTS IN PACKS
*BLUE/149: 1X TO 2.5X BASIC
*RED/99: 1.2X TO 3X BASIC
TR1 Yoan Moncada 1.00 2.50
TR2 David Dahl .40 1.00
TR3 Dansby Swanson .75 2.00
TR4 Andrew Benintendi 1.00 2.50
TR5 Alex Reyes .40 1.00
TR6 Tyler Glasnow 1.25 3.00
TR7 Josh Bell .75 2.00
TR8 Aaron Judge 4.00 10.00
TR9 Jose De Leon .30 .75
TR10 Ian Happ .60 1.50
TR11 Hunter Renfroe .40 1.00
TR12 Carson Fulmer .30 .75
TR13 Alex Bregman 1.50 4.00
TR14 Orlando Arcia .50 1.25
TR15 Cody Bellinger 5.00 12.00

2018 Donruss Optic

COMPLETE SET (185) 20.00 50.00
1 Anthony Rizzo DK .60 1.50
2 Yoan Moncada DK .50 1.25
3 Chris Archer DK .30 .75
4 Joey Votto DK .50 1.25
5 Corey Kluber DK .40 1.00
6 Adrian Beltre DK .50 1.25
7 Jose Bautista DK .40 1.00
8 Nolan Arenado DK .75 2.00
9 Miguel Cabrera DK .50 1.25
10 Bryce Harper DK .75 2.00
11 Jose Altuve DK .40 1.00
12 Eric Hosmer DK .40 1.00
13 Mike Trout DK 2.50 6.00
14 Clayton Kershaw DK .75 2.00
15 Justin Bour DK .30 .75
16 Ryan Braun DK .40 1.00
17 Brian Dozier DK .40 1.00
18 Noah Syndergaard DK .40 1.00
19 Aaron Judge DK 1.25 3.00
20 Matt Olson DK .50 1.25
21 Odubel Herrera DK .40 1.00
22 Paul Goldschmidt DK .50 1.25
23 Freddie Freeman DK .60 1.50
24 Andrew McCutchen DK .50 1.25
25 Adam Jones DK .40 1.00
26 Salvador Perez DK .40 1.00
27 Mookie Betts DK 1.00 2.50
28 Josh Bell DK .40 1.00
29 Robinson Cano DK .40 1.00
30 Adam Wainwright DK .40 1.00
31 Miguel Andujar RR RC 1.25 3.00
32 Nick Williams RR RC .40 1.00
33 Clint Frazier RR RC .60 1.50
34 Paul Blackburn RR RC .30 .75
35 Rafael Devers RR RC 1.00 2.50
36 Ozzie Albies RR RC 1.00 2.50
37 Amed Rosario RR RC .40 1.00
38 Rhys Hoskins RR RC 1.25 3.00
39 Ryan McMahon RR RC .75 2.00
40 Willie Calhoun RR RC .50 1.25
41 Walker Buehler RR RC 1.50 4.00
42 Victor Robles RR RC .75 2.00
43 Luiz Gohara RR RC .30 .75
44 J.P. Crawford RR RC .30 .75
45 Alex Verdugo RR RC .50 1.25
46 Scott Kingery RR RC .50 1.25
47 Dominic Smith RR RC .40 1.00
48 Yoshihisa Hirano RR RC .50 1.25
49 Ronald Guzman RR RC .30 .75
50 Dustin Fowler RR RC .30 .75
51 Chance Sisco RR RC .40 1.00
52 Tyler Wade RR RC .40 1.00
53 Thyago Vieira RR RC .30 .75
54 Harrison Bader RR RC .50 1.25
55 Jack Flaherty RR RC 1.25 3.00
56 Shohei Ohtani RR RC 4.00 10.00
57 Tyler O'Neill RR RC .50 1.25
58 Austin Hays RR RC .50 1.25
59 Nicky Delmonico RR RC .30 .75
60 Greg Allen RR RC .30 .75
61 Mitch Garver RR RC .30 .75
62 Zack Granite RR RC .30 .75
63 Ronald Acuna Jr. RR RC 15.00 40.00
64 Cameron Gallagher RR RC .30 .75
65 Gleyber Torres RR RC 3.00 8.00
66 Paul Goldschmidt .30 .75
67 Zack Greinke .30 .75
68 Freddie Freeman .40 1.00
69 Eddie Mathews .30 .75
70 Adam Jones .25 .60
71 Cal Ripken 1.00 2.50
72 Dustin Pedroia .30 .75
73 Jean Segura .20 .50
74 Brian Dozier .25 .60
75 Javier Baez .40 1.00
76 Kyle Hendricks .30 .75
77 Miguel Sano .25 .60
78 Kyle Schwarber .30 .75
79 Ryne Sandberg .60 1.50
80 Jose Abreu .30 .75
81 Frank Thomas .30 .75
82 Zack Cozart .20 .50
83 Barry Larkin .25 .60
84 Joe Morgan .25 .60
85 Odubel Herrera .25 .60
86 Andrew Miller .25 .60
87 Edwin Encarnacion .30 .75
88 Trevor Story .30 .75
89 Charlie Blackmon .30 .75
90 Jonathan Gray .20 .50
91 Reggie Jackson .25 .60
92 Michael Fulmer .20 .50
93 Justin Verlander .30 .75
94 Madison Bumgarner .25 .60
95 Manuel Margot .20 .50
96 Marcus Stroman .25 .60
97 George Brett .60 1.50
98 Justin Turner .30 .75
99 Yu Darvish .30 .75
100 Kenley Jansen .25 .60
101 Christian Yelich .40 1.00
102 Dee Gordon .20 .50
103 Marcell Ozuna .30 .75
104 Ryan Braun .25 .60
105 Orlando Arcia .20 .50
106 Chris Sale .30 .75
107 Anthony Rizzo .40 1.00
108 Kirby Puckett .30 .75
109 Giancarlo Stanton .30 .75
110 Noah Syndergaard .25 .60
111 Michael Conforto .25 .60
112 Jacob deGrom .60 1.50
113 Joey Votto .30 .75
114 Aaron Judge .75 2.00
115 Cody Bellinger .60 1.50
116 Gary Sanchez .30 .75
117 Luis Severino .25 .60
118 Jordan Montgomery .20 .50
119 Corey Kluber .25 .60
120 Clayton Kershaw .50 1.25
121 Mike Trout 1.50 4.00
122 Miguel Cabrera .30 .75
123 Francisco Lindor .30 .75
124 Corey Seager .30 .75
125 Andrew McCutchen .30 .75
126 Josh Bell .25 .60
127 Gerrit Cole .30 .75
128 Alex Bregman .30 .75
129 Carlos Correa .30 .75
130 Dallas Keuchel .25 .60
131 Tony Gwynn .30 .75
132 Jose Altuve .25 .60
133 Buster Posey .40 1.00
134 George Springer .25 .60
135 Andrew Benintendi .30 .75
136 Kyle Seager .20 .50
137 Robinson Cano .25 .60
138 Nolan Arenado .50 1.25
139 Jose Ramirez .25 .60
140 Felix Hernandez .25 .60
141 Ken Griffey Jr. .60 1.50
142 Yadier Molina .40 1.00
143 Matt Carpenter .30 .75
144 Carlos Martinez .25 .60
145 Evan Longoria .25 .60
146 Ian Happ .25 .60
147 Chris Archer .20 .50
148 Adrian Beltre .30 .75
149 Kris Bryant .40 1.00
150 Joey Gallo .25 .60
151 Nomar Mazara .20 .50
152 Nolan Ryan 1.00 2.50
153 Josh Donaldson .25 .60
154 Manny Machado .30 .75
155 Salvador Perez .25 .60
156 Mookie Betts .60 1.50
157 Bryce Harper .50 1.25
158 Max Scherzer .30 .75
159 Daniel Murphy .25 .60
160 Chipper Jones .30 .75
161 Trea Turner .25 .60
162 Ryan Zimmerman .25 .60
163 Stephen Strasburg .30 .75
164 J.D. Martinez .30 .75
165 Mickey Mantle 1.00 2.50
166 Joey Votto AS .30 .75
167 Gary Sanchez AS .30 .75
168 Lance McCullers AS .20 .50
169 Jose Ramirez AS .25 .60
170 Carlos Correa AS .30 .75
171 Aaron Judge AS .75 2.00
172 Cody Bellinger AS .60 1.50
173 Bryce Harper AS .50 1.25
174 Yadier Molina AS .40 1.00
175 Nolan Arenado AS .50 1.25
177 Erick Fedde RR RC .20 .50
178 Caleb Smith RR RC .20 .50
179 Francisco Mejia RR RC .25 .60
180 Shohei Ohtani RR 5.00 12.00
181 Juan Soto RR RC 5.00 12.00
182 Kyle Farmer RR RC .20 .50
183 Willy Adames RR RC .25 .60
184 Anthony Santander RR RC .20 .50
185 Brian Anderson RR RC .25 .60
186 Richard Urena RR RC .20 .50

2018 Donruss Optic Aqua

*AQUA DK: .75X TO 2X BASIC DK
*AQUA RR: .75X TO 2X BASIC RR
*AQUA VET: 1.2X TO 3X BASIC VET
RANDOM INSERTS IN PACKS
STATED PRINT RUN 299 SER.#'d SETS
63 Ronald Acuna Jr. RR 50.00 120.00

2018 Donruss Optic Black

*BLACK DK: 1.5X TO 4X BASIC DK
*BLACK RR: 1.5X TO 4X BASIC RR
*BLACK VET: 2.5X TO 6X BASIC VET
RANDOM INSERTS IN PACKS
STATED PRINT RUN 25 SER.#'d SETS
13 Mike Trout DK 10.00 25.00
63 Ronald Acuna Jr. RR 200.00 500.00
71 Cal Ripken 15.00 40.00
97 George Brett 10.00 25.00
108 Kirby Puckett 25.00 60.00
121 Mike Trout 10.00 25.00
131 Tony Gwynn 8.00 20.00
141 Ken Griffey Jr. 15.00 40.00
152 Nolan Ryan 15.00 40.00

2018 Donruss Optic Blue

*BLUE DK: .75X TO 2X BASIC DK
*BLUE RR: .75X TO 2X BASIC RR
*BLUE VET: 1.2X TO 3X BASIC VET
RANDOM INSERTS IN PACKS
STATED PRINT RUN 149 SER.#'d SETS
63 Ronald Acuna Jr. RR 50.00 120.00

2018 Donruss Optic Bronze

*BRONZE DK: .5X TO 1.2X BASIC DK
*BRONZE RR: .5X TO 1.2X BASIC RR
*BRONZE VET: .75X TO 2.5X BASIC VET
RANDOM INSERTS IN PACKS

2018 Donruss Optic Carolina Blue

*CAR.BLU DK: 1X TO 2.5X BASIC DK
*CAR.BLU RR: 1X TO 2.5X BASIC RR
*CAR.BLU VET: 1.5X TO 4X BASIC VET
RANDOM INSERTS IN PACKS
STATED PRINT RUN 50 SER.#'d SETS
63 Ronald Acuna Jr. RR 125.00 300.00
71 Cal Ripken 10.00 25.00
97 George Brett 6.00 15.00
108 Kirby Puckett 10.00 25.00
131 Tony Gwynn 5.00 12.00
152 Nolan Ryan 10.00 25.00

2018 Donruss Optic Holo

*HOLO DK: .5X TO 1.2X BASIC DK
*HOLO RR: .5X TO 1.2X BASIC RR
*HOLO VET: .75X TO 2.5X BASIC VET
RANDOM INSERTS IN PACKS

2018 Donruss Optic Orange

*ORANGE DK: .75X TO 2X BASIC DK
*ORANGE RR: .75X TO 2X BASIC RR
*ORANGE VET: 1.2X TO 3X BASIC VET
RANDOM INSERTS IN PACKS
STATED PRINT RUN 199 SER.#'d SETS
63 Ronald Acuna Jr. RR 50.00 120.00

2018 Donruss Optic Pink

*PINK DK: .5X TO 1.2X BASIC DK
*PINK RR: .5X TO 1.2X BASIC RR
*PINK VET: .75X TO 2X BASIC VET
RANDOM INSERTS IN PACKS

2018 Donruss Optic Purple

*PURPLE DK: .5X TO 1.2X BASIC DK
*PURPLE RR: .5X TO 1.2X BASIC RR
*PURPLE VET: .75X TO 2X BASIC VET
INSERTED IN RETAIL PACKS

2018 Donruss Optic Red

*RED DK: 1X TO 2.5X BASIC DK
*RED RR: 1X TO 2.5X BASIC RR
*RED VET: 1.5X TO 4X BASIC VET
RANDOM INSERTS IN PACKS
STATED PRINT RUN 99 SER.#'d SETS
63 Ronald Acuna Jr. RR 125.00 300.00
108 Kirby Puckett 10.00 25.00

2018 Donruss Optic Red and Yellow

*RED YEL DK: .5X TO 1.2X BASIC DK
*RED YEL RR: .5X TO 1.2X BASIC RR
*RED YEL VET: .75X TO 2X BASIC VET
RANDOM INSERTS IN PACKS

2018 Donruss Optic Shock

*SHOCK DK: .5X TO 1.2X BASIC DK
*SHOCK RR: .5X TO 1.2X BASIC RR
*SHOCK VET: .75X TO 2.5X BASIC VET
RANDOM INSERTS IN PACKS

2018 Donruss Optic Variations

RANDOM INSERTS IN PACKS
31 Miguel Andujar RR 1.25 3.00
32 Nick Williams RR .40 1.00
33 Clint Frazier RR .60 1.50
35 Rafael Devers RR 1.00 2.50
36 Ozzie Albies RR 1.00 2.50
37 Amed Rosario RR .40 1.00
38 Rhys Hoskins RR 1.25 3.00
39 Ryan McMahon RR .75 2.00
40 Willie Calhoun RR .50 1.25
41 Walker Buehler RR 1.50 4.00
42 Victor Robles RR .75 2.00
51 Chance Sisco RR .40 1.00

56 Shohei Ohtani RR 4.00 10.00
65 Gleyber Torres RR 3.00 8.00
109 Giancarlo Stanton .30 .75
114 Aaron Judge .75 2.00
115 Cody Bellinger .60 1.50
121 Mike Trout 1.50 4.00
122 Miguel Cabrera .30 .75
123 Francisco Lindor .30 .75
125 Andrew McCutchen .30 .75
135 Andrew Benintendi .30 .75
148 Adrian Beltre .30 .75
165 Mickey Mantle 1.00 2.50
176 Shohei Ohtani RR 4.00 10.00

2018 Donruss Optic Variations Aqua

*AQUA RR: .75X TO 2X BASIC RR
*AQUA VET: 1.2X TO 3X BASIC VET
RANDOM INSERTS IN PACKS
STATED PRINT RUN 299 SER.#'d SETS

2018 Donruss Optic Variations Black

*BLACK RR: 1.5X TO 4X BASIC RR
*BLACK VET: 2.5X TO 6X BASIC VET
RANDOM INSERTS IN PACKS
STATED PRINT RUN 25 SER.#'d SETS
121 Mike Trout 10.00 25.00

2018 Donruss Optic Variations Blue

*BLUE RR: .75X TO 2X BASIC RR
*BLUE VET: 1.2X TO 3X BASIC VET
RANDOM INSERTS IN PACKS
STATED PRINT RUN 149 SER.#'d SETS

2018 Donruss Optic Variations Bronze

*BRONZE RR: .5X TO 1.2X BASIC RR
*BRONZE VET: .75X TO 2.5X BASIC VET
RANDOM INSERTS IN PACKS

2018 Donruss Optic Variations Carolina Blue

*CAR.BLU RR: 1X TO 2.5X BASIC RR
*CAR.BLU VET: 1.5X TO 4X BASIC VET
RANDOM INSERTS IN PACKS
STATED PRINT RUN 50 SER.#'d SETS

2018 Donruss Optic Variations Holo

*HOLO RR: .5X TO 1.2X BASIC RR
*HOLO VET: .75X TO 2.5X BASIC VET
RANDOM INSERTS IN PACKS

2018 Donruss Optic Variations Orange

*ORANGE RR: .75X TO 2X BASIC RR
*ORANGE VET: 1.2X TO 3X BASIC VET
RANDOM INSERTS IN PACKS
STATED PRINT RUN 199 SER.#'d SETS

2018 Donruss Optic Variations Pink

*PINK RR: .5X TO 1.2X BASIC RR
*PINK VET: .75X TO 2X BASIC VET
RANDOM INSERTS IN PACKS

2018 Donruss Optic Variations Purple

*PURPLE RR: .5X TO 1.2X BASIC RR
*PURPLE VET: .75X TO 2X BASIC VET

2018 Donruss Optic Variations Red

*RED RR: 1X TO 2.5X BASIC RR
*RED VET: 1.5X TO 4X BASIC VET
RANDOM INSERTS IN PACKS
STATED PRINT RUN 99 SER.#'d SETS

2018 Donruss Optic Variations Red and Yellow

*RED YEL RR: .5X TO 1.2X BASIC RR
*RED YEL VET: .75X TO 2X BASIC VET
RANDOM INSERTS IN PACKS

2018 Donruss Optic Variations Shock

*SHOCK RR: .5X TO 1.2X BASIC RR
*SHOCK VET: .75X TO 2X BASIC VET
RANDOM INSERTS IN PACKS

2018 Donruss Optic Autographs

RANDOM INSERTS IN PACKS
EXCHANGE DEADLINE 01/18/2020
*BLUE/50: .6X TO 1.5X BASIC
*BLUE/20-25: .75X TO 2X BASIC
*RED/25: .75X TO 2X BASIC
1 Darryl Strawberry 5.00 12.00
2 David Cone
3 David Price 3.00 8.00
4 David Wells 6.00 15.00
5 Eric Hosmer 3.00 8.00
6 Fernando Valenzuela
7 Francisco Lindor 12.00 30.00
8 Gary Sanchez 10.00 25.00
9 George Springer 5.00 12.00
10 Graig Nettles 2.50 6.00
11 Hunter Pence 3.00 8.00
12 Jameson Taillon
13 Jim Bunning 5.00 12.00
14 Joey Votto
15 Jonathan Lucroy 3.00 8.00
16 Jose Abreu
17 Kyle Seager 2.50 6.00
18 Lorenzo Cain 6.00 15.00
19 Luke Weaver 3.00 8.00
20 Maikel Franco 3.00 8.00
21 Matt Carpenter 6.00 15.00
22 Max Scherzer
23 Ozzie Smith 12.00 30.00
24 Ron Guidry 5.00 12.00
25 Roy Oswalt 3.00 8.00
26 Ryan Braun 5.00 12.00
27 Shelby Miller
28 Willie McGee 5.00 12.00
29 Andres Gimenez 6.00 15.00
30 Aneury Tavarez 2.50 6.00
31 Austin Voth 2.50 6.00
32 Jesus Sanchez 4.00 10.00
33 Bobby Bradley 3.00 8.00
34 Brett Phillips 2.50 6.00
35 Bruce Maxwell 2.50 6.00
36 Casey Gillaspie
37 Christopher Seise 2.50 6.00
38 Dan Vogelbach 2.50 6.00
39 Derek Law 2.50 6.00
40 Diego Castillo 2.50 6.00
41 Leody Taveras 4.00 10.00
42 Dustin Peterson
43 Josh Hader 3.00 8.00
44 Michael Chavis 10.00 25.00
45 Nick Gordon 2.50 6.00
46 Kyle Lewis 20.00 50.00
47 Johan Oviedo 2.50 6.00
48 Tyler O'Neill 8.00 20.00
49 Kyle Tucker 6.00 15.00
50 Randal Grichuk 2.50 6.00

2018 Donruss Optic Long Ball Leaders

RANDOM INSERTS IN PACKS
*BLUE/149: .6X TO 1.5X BASIC
*RED/99: .75X TO 2X BASIC
1 Giancarlo Stanton .50 1.25
2 Aaron Judge 1.25 3.00
3 J.D. Martinez .50 1.25
4 Khris Davis .50 1.25
5 Joey Gallo .40 1.00
6 Cody Bellinger 1.00 2.50
7 Nelson Cruz .50 1.25
8 Logan Morrison .30 .75
9 Nolan Arenado .75 2.00
10 Justin Smoak .30 .75

2018 Donruss Optic Looking Back

RANDOM INSERTS IN PACKS
*BLUE/149: 1X TO 2.5X BASIC
*RED/99: 1.2X TO 3X BASIC
1 Griffey Jr/Griffey Sr. 1.00 2.50
2 Robinson/Machado .50 1.25
3 Judge/Jackson 1.25 3.00
4 Ichiro/Rose 1.00 2.50
5 Baez/Sandberg 1.00 2.50
6 Kershaw/Ryan 1.50 4.00
7 Biggio/Altuve .40 1.00
8 Thomas/Abreu .50 1.25
9 C.Sale/R.Clemens .60 1.50
10 Lindor/Vizquel .50 1.25

2018 Donruss Optic Mound Marvels

RANDOM INSERTS IN PACKS
*BLUE/149: .75X TO 2X BASIC
*RED/99: 1X TO 2.5X BASIC
1 Clayton Kershaw .75 2.00
2 Max Scherzer .50 1.25
3 Shohei Ohtani 8.00 20.00
4 Corey Kluber .40 1.00
5 Chris Sale .50 1.25
6 Justin Verlander .50 1.25
7 Noah Syndergaard .40 1.00
8 Nolan Ryan 1.50 4.00

2018 Donruss Optic Out of This World

RANDOM INSERTS IN PACKS
*BLUE/149: 1X TO 2.5X BASIC
*RED/99: 1.2X TO 3X BASIC
1 Aaron Judge 1.25 3.00
2 Jose Altuve .40 1.00
3 Mike Trout 2.50 6.00
4 Joey Gallo .40 1.00
5 Shohei Ohtani 8.00 20.00
6 Giancarlo Stanton .50 1.25
7 Mickey Mantle 1.50 4.00
8 J.D. Martinez .50 1.25
9 Cody Bellinger 1.00 2.50
10 Nolan Arenado .75 2.00
11 Marcell Ozuna .50 1.25
12 Paul Goldschmidt .50 1.25
13 Ken Griffey Jr. 1.00 2.50
14 Joey Votto .50 1.25
15 Nelson Cruz .50 1.25

2018 Donruss Optic Premiere Rookies

RANDOM INSERTS IN PACKS
*BLUE/149: 1X TO 2.5X BASIC
1 Rafael Devers 1.00 2.50
2 Clint Frazier .60 1.50
3 Victor Robles .75 2.00
4 Shohei Ohtani 8.00 20.00
5 Ozzie Albies 1.00 2.50
6 Francisco Mejia .40 1.00
7 Amed Rosario .40 1.00
8 Rhys Hoskins 1.25 3.00
9 Ryan McMahon .75 2.00
10 Miguel Andujar 1.25 3.00

2018 Donruss Optic Premiere Rookies Red

*RED: 1.2X TO 3X BASIC
RANDOM INSERTS IN PACKS
STATED PRINT RUN 99 SER.#'d SETS
4 Shohei Ohtani 20.00 50.00

2018 Donruss Optic Rated Prospects

RANDOM INSERTS IN PACKS
*BLUE/149: 1X TO 2.5X BASIC
*RED/99: 1.2X TO 3X BASIC
1 Vladimir Guerrero Jr. 3.00 8.00
2 Fernando Tatis Jr. 3.00 8.00
3 Eloy Jimenez 1.25 3.00
4 Bo Bichette 1.25 3.00
5 Nick Senzel 1.00 2.50
6 Brendan Rodgers .40 1.00
7 Kyle Tucker .75 2.00
8 Leody Taveras .50 1.25

2018 Donruss Optic Rated Prospects Signatures

RANDOM INSERTS IN PACKS
EXCHANGE DEADLINE 01/18/2020
*AQUA/75-100: .5X TO 1.2X BASIC
*BLACK/25: .75X TO 2X BASIC
*BLUE/75: .5X TO 1.2X BASIC
*BLUE/50: .6X TO 1.5X BASIC
*BRONZE: .4X TO 1X BASIC
*CAR.BLUE/35: .6X TO 1.5X BASIC
*CAR.BLUE/20-25: .75X TO 2X BASIC
*HOLO: .4X TO 1X BASIC
*ORANGE/ 60-99: .5X TO 1.2X BASIC
*RED/35-50: .6X TO 1.5X BASIC
1 Gleyber Torres 30.00 80.00
2 Vladimir Guerrero Jr. 60.00 150.00
3 Eloy Jimenez 15.00 40.00
4 Ronald Acuna Jr. 75.00 200.00
5 Rafael Devers 10.00 25.00
6 Kyle Tucker 6.00 15.00
7 Nick Senzel EXCH 15.00 40.00
8 Michael Kopech 6.00 15.00
9 Brent Honeywell 4.00 10.00
10 Luis Robert 30.00 80.00
11 Justus Sheffield 8.00 20.00
12 Kevin Maitan 3.00 8.00
13 Yadier Alvarez 3.00 8.00
14 Franklin Perez 5.00 12.00
15 Willy Adames 3.00 8.00

2018 Donruss Optic Rated Rookies '84 Retro

RANDOM INSERTS IN PACKS
*BLUE/149: 1X TO 2.5X BASIC
*RED/99: 1.2X TO 3X BASIC
1 Shohei Ohtani 8.00 20.00
2 Clint Frazier .60 1.50
3 Rafael Devers 1.00 2.50
4 Walker Buehler 1.50 4.00
5 Ozzie Albies 1.00 2.50
6 Francisco Mejia .40 1.00
7 Ryan McMahon .75 2.00
8 Rhys Hoskins 1.25 3.00
9 Victor Robles .75 2.00
10 Amed Rosario .40 1.00
11 Willie Calhoun .50 1.25
12 Nick Williams .40 1.00
13 Dominic Smith .40 1.00
14 J.P. Crawford .30 .75
15 Dustin Fowler .30 .75

2018 Donruss Optic Rated Rookies '84 Retro Signatures

RANDOM INSERTS IN PACKS
EXCHANGE DEADLINE 01/18/2020
*AQUA/60-125: .5X TO 1.2X BASIC
*AQUA/35: .6X TO 1.5X BASIC
*BLACK/25: .75X TO 2X BASIC
*BLUE/60-75: .5X TO 1.2X BASIC
*BLUE/35-50: .6X TO 1.5X BASIC
*BLUE/25: .75X TO 2X BASIC
*BRONZE: .4X TO 1X BASIC
*CAR.BLUE/35: .6X TO 1.5X BASIC
*CAR.BLUE/20-25: .75X TO 2X BASIC
*HOLO: .4X TO 1X BASIC
*ORANGE/ 60-99: .5X TO 1.2X BASIC
*ORANGE/30-49: .6X TO 1.5X BASIC
*RED/35-50: .6X TO 1.5X BASIC
*RED/25: .75X TO 2X BASIC
1 Ozzie Albies 12.00 30.00
2 Austin Hays 4.00 10.00
3 Chance Sisco 3.00 8.00
4 Rafael Devers 10.00 25.00
5 Victor Caratini 3.00 8.00
6 Nicky Delmonico 2.50 6.00
7 Francisco Mejia 3.00 8.00
8 Cameron Gallagher 2.50 6.00
9 Walker Buehler 12.00 30.00
10 Alex Verdugo 4.00 10.00
11 Kyle Farmer 2.50 6.00
12 Zack Granite 2.50 6.00
13 Tomas Nido 2.50 6.00
14 Ryan McMahon 6.00 15.00
15 Amed Rosario 3.00 8.00
16 Clint Frazier 5.00 12.00
17 Miguel Andujar 15.00 40.00
18 Tyler Wade 3.00 8.00
19 J.P. Crawford EXCH 2.50 6.00
20 Nick Williams 3.00 8.00
21 Rhys Hoskins 15.00 40.00
22 Shohei Ohtani 150.00 300.00
23 Willie Calhoun 4.00 10.00
24 Victor Robles 6.00 15.00
25 Erick Fedde 2.50 6.00

2018 Donruss Optic Rated Rookies Signatures

RANDOM INSERTS IN PACKS
EXCHANGE DEADLINE 01/18/2020
*AQUA/75-125: .5X TO 1.2X BASIC
*AQUA/35: .6X TO 1.5X BASIC
*BLACK/25: .75X TO 2X BASIC
*BLUE/60-75: .5X TO 1.2X BASIC
*BLUE/50: .6X TO 1.5X BASIC
*BLUE/20: .75X TO 2X BASIC
*BRONZE: .4X TO 1X BASIC
*CAR.BLUE/35: .6X TO 1.5X BASIC
*CAR.BLUE/25: .75X TO 2X BASIC
*HOLO: .4X TO 1X BASIC
*ORANGE/ 60-99: .5X TO 1.2X BASIC
*ORANGE/25: .75X TO 2X BASIC
*RED/35-50: .6X TO 1.5X BASIC
RRSAB Anthony Banda 2.50 6.00
RRSAH Austin Hays 10.00 25.00
RRSAR Amed Rosario 3.00 8.00
RRSAS Andrew Stevenson 2.50 6.00
RRSAV Alex Verdugo 4.00 10.00
RRSAY Anthony Santander 2.50 6.00
RRSBA Brian Anderson 3.00 8.00
RRSBW Brandon Woodruff 8.00 20.00
RRSCF Chris Flexen 2.50 6.00
RRSCG Cameron Gallagher 2.50 6.00
RRSCL Clint Frazier 5.00 12.00
RRSCS Chance Sisco 3.00 8.00
RRSDF Dustin Fowler 2.50 6.00
RRSDP Dillon Peters 2.50 6.00
RRSEF Erick Fedde 2.50 6.00
RRSFJ Felix Jorge 2.50 6.00
RRSFM Francisco Mejia 3.00 8.00
RRSGA Greg Allen 2.50 6.00
RRSHB Harrison Bader 4.00 10.00
RRSJC J.P. Crawford EXCH 2.50 6.00
RRSJD J.D. Davis 3.00 8.00
RRSJF Jack Flaherty 10.00 25.00
RRSJS Jimmie Sherfy 2.50 6.00
RRSKF Kyle Farmer 2.50 6.00
RRSLG Luiz Gohara 2.50 6.00
RRSLS Lucas Sims 2.50 6.00
RRSMA Miguel Andujar 10.00 25.00
RRSMF Max Fried 10.00 25.00
RRSMG Mitch Garver 2.50 6.00
RRSND Nicky Delmonico 2.50 6.00
RRSNW Nick Williams 3.00 8.00
RRSOA Ozzie Albies 8.00 20.00
RRSPB Paul Blackburn 2.50 6.00
RRSRA Ronald Acuna 75.00 200.00
RRSRD Rafael Devers 10.00 25.00
RRSRH Rhys Hoskins 10.00 25.00
RRSRM Reyes Moronta 2.50 6.00
RRSRU Richard Urena 2.50 6.00
RRSRY Ryan McMahon 6.00 15.00
RRSSO Shohei Ohtani 75.00 200.00
RRSTM Tyler Mahle 3.00 8.00
RRSTN Tomas Nido 2.50 6.00
RRSTV Thyago Vieira 2.50 6.00
RRSTW Tyler Wade 3.00 8.00
RRSVC Victor Caratini 3.00 8.00
RRSVG Vladimir Guerrero Jr 30.00 80.00
Issued in '19 Donruss Optic
RRSVR Victor Robles 10.00 25.00
RRSWB Walker Buehler 15.00 40.00
RRSWC Willie Calhoun 4.00 10.00
RRSZG Zack Granite 2.50 6.00

2018 Donruss Optic '84 Retro Signatures

RANDOM INSERTS IN PACKS
EXCHANGE DEADLINE 01/18/2020
*BRONZE: .4X TO 1X BASIC
*HOLO: .4X TO 1X BASIC
1 Ken Griffey Jr. 100.00 250.00
2 Jose Altuve EXCH 20.00 50.00
3 Anthony Rizzo
4 Cal Ripken
5 Cody Bellinger EXCH 15.00 40.00
6 Aaron Judge 60.00 150.00
7 Mark McGwire

2018 Donruss Optic Signature Series

RANDOM INSERTS IN PACKS
EXCHANGE DEADLINE 01/18/2020
*BLUE/50: .6X TO 1.5X BASIC
*BLUE/20-25: .75X TO 2X BASIC
*RED/25: .75X TO 2X BASIC
1 Albert Almora Jr. 3.00 8.00
2 Alex Gordon 5.00 12.00
3 Brian Dozier 3.00 8.00
4 Carlos Correa 10.00 25.00
5 Chris Davis
7 Corey Kluber 6.00 15.00
8 Josh Donaldson 3.00 8.00
9 Juan Marichal
10 Justin Turner 8.00 20.00
11 Kyle Schwarber 6.00 15.00
12 Starling Marte 3.00 8.00
13 Yoan Moncada
14 Ryan Mountcastle 12.00 30.00
15 Jacoby Jones 3.00 8.00
16 Adrian Valerio 2.50 6.00
17 Albert Abreu 2.50 6.00
18 Brendan McKay 4.00 10.00
19 Brendan Rodgers 8.00 20.00
20 Keith Hernandez 5.00 12.00
21 Jarrett Parker 2.50 6.00
22 Guillermo Heredia 12.00 30.00
23 Willy Adames 3.00 8.00
24 Mitch Keller 3.00 8.00
25 Kyle Wright 4.00 10.00

2018 Donruss Optic Significant Signatures

RANDOM INSERTS IN PACKS
EXCHANGE DEADLINE 01/18/2020
*BLUE/50: .6X TO 1.5X BASIC
*BLUE/20: .75X TO 2X BASIC
*RED/25: .75X TO 2X BASIC
1 Adrian Beltre 12.00 30.00
2 Alan Trammell 8.00 20.00
4 Andre Dawson 5.00 12.00
5 Andruw Jones 4.00 10.00
6 Barry Larkin
7 Bernie Williams 8.00 20.00
8 Bill Mazeroski 8.00 20.00
10 Bob Gibson 10.00 25.00
11 Brooks Robinson 6.00 15.00
12 Curt Schilling 8.00 20.00
13 Dave Winfield
14 Eddie Murray 20.00 50.00
15 Fergie Jenkins 3.00 8.00
16 Paul Molitor 6.00 15.00
17 Phil Niekro 4.00 10.00
18 Rickey Henderson 20.00 50.00
19 Rollie Fingers 6.00 15.00
20 Roy Halladay 20.00 50.00
21 Steve Garvey 15.00 40.00
22 Todd Helton 8.00 20.00
23 Wade Boggs 6.00 15.00
24 Whitey Ford 25.00 60.00
25 Whitey Herzog 8.00 20.00

2018 Donruss Optic Standouts

RANDOM INSERTS IN PACKS
*BLUE/149: .6X TO 1.5X BASIC
*RED/99: .75X TO 2X BASIC
1 Giancarlo Stanton .50 1.25
2 Aaron Judge 1.25 3.00

2018 Donruss Optic Year in Review

RANDOM INSERTS IN PACKS
*BLUE/149: .6X TO 1.5X BASIC
*RED/99: .75X TO 2X BASIC
1 Aaron Judge 1.25 3.00
2 Giancarlo Stanton .50 1.25
3 Cody Bellinger 1.00 2.50
4 Jose Altuve .40 1.00
5 Albert Pujols .60 1.50
6 Miguel Cabrera .50 1.25
7 Aaron Judge 1.25 3.00
8 Adrian Beltre .50 1.25
9 Rhys Hoskins 1.25 3.00
10 Cody Bellinger 1.00 2.50
11 Chris Sale .50 1.25
12 Jose Ramirez .40 1.00

2019 Donruss Optic

1 Mookie Betts DK 1.00 2.50
2 Aaron Judge DK 1.25 3.00
3 Blake Snell DK .40 1.00
4 Justin Smoak DK .30 .75
5 Trey Mancini DK .40 1.00
6 Jose Ramirez DK .40 1.00
7 Jose Berrios DK .40 1.00
8 Nicholas Castellanos DK .50 1.25
9 Yoan Moncada DK .50 1.25
10 Whit Merrifield DK .50 1.25
11 Alex Bregman DK .50 1.25
12 Matt Chapman DK .50 1.25
13 Mitch Haniger DK .40 1.00
14 Shohei Ohtani DK .75 2.00
15 Joey Gallo DK .40 1.00
16 Ronald Acuna Jr. DK 2.50 6.00
17 Max Scherzer DK .50 1.25
18 Aaron Nola DK .40 1.00
19 Jacob deGrom DK 1.00 2.50
20 Jose Urena DK .30 .75
21 Christian Yelich DK .60 1.50
22 Javier Baez DK .60 1.50
23 Matt Carpenter DK .50 1.25
24 Starling Marte DK .40 1.00
25 Eugenio Suarez DK .40 1.00
26 Max Muncy DK .40 1.00
27 Trevor Story DK .50 1.25
28 David Peralta DK .30 .75
29 Brandon Crawford DK .40 1.00
30 Manny Machado DK .50 1.25
31 Cedric Mullins RR RC .60 1.50
32 Christin Stewart RR RC .40 1.00
33 Corbin Burnes RR RC 2.50 6.00
34 Dakota Hudson RR RC .40 1.00
35 Danny Jansen RR RC .30 .75
36 David Fletcher RR RC 1.00 2.50
37 Dennis Santana RR RC .30 .75
38 Garrett Hampson RR RC .50 1.25
39 Jake Bauers RR RC .50 1.25
40 Jeff McNeil RR RC .75 2.00
41 Jonathan Loaisiga RR RC .40 1.00
42 Justus Sheffield RR RC .50 1.25
43 Kyle Tucker RR RC .75 2.00
44 Kyle Wright RR RC .50 1.25
45 Luis Urias RR RC .50 1.25
46 Michael Kopech RR RC 1.00 2.50
47 Ramon Laureano RR RC .60 1.50
48 Ryan O'Hearn RR RC .30 .75
49 Steven Duggar RR RC .40 1.00
50 Touki Toussaint RR RC .40 1.00
51 Chris Shaw RR RC .30 .75
52 Rowdy Tellez RR RC .50 1.25
53 Brandon Lowe RR RC .50 1.25
54 Taylor Hearn RR RC .30 .75
55 Reese McGuire RR RC .50 1.25
56 Taylor Ward RR RC .30 .75
57 Jake Cave RR RC .40 1.00
58 Ty France RR RC 1.00 2.50
59 Myles Straw RR RC .50 1.25
60 Brad Keller RR RC .30 .75
61 Bryse Wilson RR RC .40 1.00
62 Caleb Ferguson RR RC .40 1.00
63 Chance Adams RR RC .30 .75
64 Vladimir Guerrero Jr. RR RC 2.00 5.00
65 Daniel Ponce de Leon RR RC .50 1.25
66 Enyel De Los Santos RR RC .30 .75
67 Framber Valdez RR RC .30 .75
68 Jacob Nix RR RC .40 1.00
69 Josh James RR RC .50 1.25
70 Kolby Allard RR RC .50 1.25
71 Luis Ortiz RR RC .30 .75
72 Ryan Borucki RR RC .30 .75
73 Sean Reid-Foley RR RC .30 .75
74 Stephen Gonsalves RR RC .30 .75
75 Kevin Kramer RR RC .40 1.00
76 Kevin Newman RR RC .50 1.25
77 Yusei Kikuchi RR RC .50 1.25
78 Michael Perez RR RC .30 .75
79 Williams Astudillo RR RC .30 .75
80 Trevor Richards RR RC .30 .75
81 Michael Chavis RR RC .50 1.25
82 Pete Alonso RR RC 4.00 10.00
83 Eloy Jimenez RR RC 1.25 3.00
84 Fernando Tatis Jr. RR RC 20.00 50.00
85 Jon Duplantier RR RC .30 .75
86 Darwinzon Hernandez RR RC .30 .75
87 Cole Tucker RR RC .50 1.25
88 Chris Paddack RR RC .60 1.50
89 Nick Senzel RR RC 1.00 2.50
90 Griffin Canning RR RC .50 1.25
91 Cal Quantrill RR RC .30 .75
92 Carter Kieboom RR RC .50 1.25
93 Keston Hiura RR RC 1.00 2.50
94 Corbin Martin RR RC .50 1.25
95 Austin Riley RR RC 1.50 4.00
96 Brendan Rodgers RR RC .50 1.25
97 Bryce Harper AS .75 2.00
98 Aaron Judge AS .75 2.00
99 Mookie Betts AS .60 1.50
100 Mike Trout AS 1.50 4.00
101 Mookie Betts .60 1.50
102 Chris Sale .30 .75
103 Eddie Rosario .25 .60
104 Rhys Hoskins .40 1.00
105 J.T. Realmuto .30 .75
106 Cody Bellinger .60 1.50
107 Jose Ramirez .25 .60
108 Jon Lester .25 .60
109 Kris Bryant .40 1.00
110 Luis Severino .25 .60
111 Whit Merrifield .30 .75
112 Joey Gallo .25 .60
113 Juan Soto 1.00 2.50
114 Jose Urena .20 .50
115 J.D. Martinez .30 .75
116 Max Scherzer .30 .75
117 Sean Newcomb .20 .50
118 Francisco Lindor .30 .75
119 Starling Marte .25 .60
120 Manny Machado .30 .75
121 Aaron Judge .75 2.00
122 Robinson Cano .25 .60
123 Jacob deGrom .60 1.50
124 Eugenio Suarez .25 .60
125 Nomar Mazara .20 .50
126 Kyle Freeland .20 .50
127 Miguel Sano .25 .60
128 Rafael Devers .40 1.00
129 Miguel Andujar .30 .75
130 Nelson Cruz .30 .75
131 Charlie Blackmon .30 .75
132 Jose Berrios .25 .60
133 Walker Buehler .40 1.00
134 Tyler O'Neill .25 .60
135 Mike Foltynewicz .30 .75
136 Noah Syndergaard .25 .60
137 Scooter Gennett .25 .60
138 David Bote .25 .60
139 Zack Greinke .30 .75
140 Andrew Benintendi .30 .75
141 Trea Turner .25 .60
142 Carlos Rodon .30 .75
143 Carlos Correa .30 .75
144 Jose Martinez .20 .50
145 Aaron Nola .25 .60
146 Mitch Haniger .25 .60
147 Yadier Molina .40 1.00
148 Joey Votto .30 .75
149 Felix Hernandez .25 .60
150 Willie Calhoun .20 .50
151 Carlos Carrasco .20 .50
152 Paul Goldschmidt .30 .75
153 Trey Mancini .25 .60
154 Madison Bumgarner .25 .60
155 Amed Rosario .25 .60
156 Ozzie Albies .30 .75
157 Gleyber Torres .60 1.50
158 Wilson Ramos .20 .50
159 Brandon Crawford .25 .60
160 Andrew Heaney .20 .50
161 James Paxton .25 .60
162 Gerrit Cole .30 .75
163 Giancarlo Stanton .30 .75
164 Shohei Ohtani .50 1.25
165 Javier Baez .40 1.00
166 Jesus Aguilar .25 .60
167 Jackie Bradley Jr. .30 .75
168 Corey Kluber .25 .60
169 Khris Davis .30 .75
170 Mike Trout 1.50 4.00
171 Matt Carpenter .30 .75
172 Justin Verlander .30 .75
173 Brian Anderson .20 .50
174 Victor Robles .40 1.00
175 Freddie Freeman .40 1.00
176 Jack Flaherty .30 .75
177 Ronald Acuna Jr. 1.50 4.00
178 Clayton Kershaw .50 1.25
179 Salvador Perez .25 .60
180 Anthony Rendon .30 .75
181 Blake Snell .25 .60
182 Alex Bregman .30 .75
183 Bryce Harper .50 1.25
184 Lorenzo Cain .20 .50
185 Trevor Story .30 .75
186 Mike Moustakas .25 .60
187 Anthony Rizzo .40 1.00
188 Jameson Taillon .25 .60
189 Edwin Encarnacion .30 .75
190 Christian Yelich .40 1.00
191 Michael Conforto .25 .60
192 Matt Chapman .30 .75
193 Albert Pujols .40 1.00
194 Eric Hosmer .25 .60
195 German Marquez .20 .50
196 Jeimer Candelario .20 .50
197 Xander Bogaerts .30 .75
198 Miguel Cabrera .30 .75
199 Harrison Bader .25 .60
200 Nolan Arenado .50 1.25

2019 Donruss Optic Black

*BLACK DK: 1.5X TO 4X BASIC DK
*BLACK RR: 1.5X TO 4X BASIC RR
*BLACK VET: 2.5X TO 6X BASIC VET
RANDOM INSERTS IN PACKS
STATED PRINT RUN 25 SER.#'d SETS
40 Jeff McNeil RR 10.00 25.00
64 Vladimir Guerrero Jr. RR 25.00 60.00
82 Pete Alonso RR 20.00 50.00
83 Eloy Jimenez RR 10.00 25.00

2019 Donruss Optic Blue

*BLUE DK: 1X TO 2.5X BASIC DK
*BLUE RR: 1X TO 2.5X BASIC RR
*BLUE VET: 1.5X TO 4X BASIC VET
RANDOM INSERTS IN PACKS
STATED PRINT RUN 75 SER.#'d SETS
64 Vladimir Guerrero Jr. RR 12.00 30.00
82 Pete Alonso RR 12.00 30.00
83 Eloy Jimenez RR 6.00 15.00

2019 Donruss Optic Blue Pandora

*BLUE PAN. DK: 1X TO 2.5X BASIC DK
*BLUE PAN. RR: 1X TO 2.5X BASIC RR
*BLUE PAN. VET: 1.5X TO 4X BASIC VET
RANDOM INSERTS IN PACKS
STATED PRINT RUN 99 SER.#'d SETS
64 Vladimir Guerrero Jr. RR 12.00 30.00
82 Pete Alonso RR 12.00 30.00
83 Eloy Jimenez RR 6.00 15.00

2019 Donruss Optic Carolina Blue

*CAR.BLU DK: 1.2X TO 3X BASIC DK
*CAR.BLU RR: 1.2X TO 3X BASIC RR
*CAR.BLU VET: 2X TO 5X BASIC VET
RANDOM INSERTS IN PACKS
STATED PRINT RUN 50 SER.#'d SETS
40 Jeff McNeil RR 8.00 20.00
64 Vladimir Guerrero Jr. RR 20.00 50.00
82 Pete Alonso RR 15.00 40.00
83 Eloy Jimenez RR 8.00 20.00

2019 Donruss Optic Carolina Blue and White

*CAR.BLU.WHT DK: .5X TO 1.2X BASIC DK
*CAR.BLU.WHT RR: .5X TO 1.2X BASIC RR
*CAR.BLU.WHT VET: .75X TO 2.5X BASIC VET
RANDOM INSERTS IN PACKS
64 Vladimir Guerrero Jr. RR 6.00 15.00
82 Pete Alonso RR 8.00 20.00
83 Eloy Jimenez RR 3.00 8.00

2019 Donruss Optic Holo

*HOLO DK: .5X TO 1.2X BASIC DK
*HOLO RR: .5X TO 1.2X BASIC RR
*HOLO VET: .75X TO 2.5X BASIC VET
RANDOM INSERTS IN PACKS
64 Vladimir Guerrero Jr. RR 6.00 15.00
82 Pete Alonso RR 8.00 20.00
83 Eloy Jimenez RR 3.00 8.00

2019 Donruss Optic Lime Green

*LIME GRN DK: .5X TO 1.2X BASIC DK
*LIME GRN RR: .5X TO 1.2X BASIC RR
*LIME GRN VET: .75X TO 2.5X BASIC VET
RANDOM INSERTS IN PACKS
64 Vladimir Guerrero Jr. RR 6.00 15.00
82 Pete Alonso RR 8.00 20.00
83 Eloy Jimenez RR 3.00 8.00

2019 Donruss Optic Orange

*ORANGE DK: 1X TO 2.5X BASIC DK
*ORANGE RR: 1X TO 2.5X BASIC RR
*ORANGE VET: 1.5X TO 4X BASIC VET
RANDOM INSERTS IN PACKS
STATED PRINT RUN 99 SER.#'d SETS
64 Vladimir Guerrero Jr. RR 12.00 30.00
82 Pete Alonso RR 12.00 30.00
83 Eloy Jimenez RR 6.00 15.00

2019 Donruss Optic Pandora

*PANDORA DK: 1X TO 2.5X BASIC DK
*PANDORA RR: 1X TO 2.5X BASIC RR
*PANDORA VET: 1.5X TO 4X BASIC VET
RANDOM INSERTS IN PACKS
STATED PRINT RUN 99 SER.#'d SETS
64 Vladimir Guerrero Jr. RR 12.00 30.00
82 Pete Alonso RR 12.00 30.00
83 Eloy Jimenez RR 6.00 15.00

2019 Donruss Optic Pink

*PINK DK: .5X TO 1.2X BASIC DK
*PINK RR: .5X TO 1.2X BASIC RR
*PINK VET: .75X TO 2.5X BASIC VET
RANDOM INSERTS IN PACKS
64 Vladimir Guerrero Jr. RR 6.00 15.00
82 Pete Alonso RR 8.00 20.00
83 Eloy Jimenez RR 3.00 8.00

2019 Donruss Optic Pink Velocity

*PINK VEL. DK: .75X TO 2X BASIC DK
*PINK VEL. RR: .75X TO 2X BASIC RR
*PINK VEL. VET: 1.2X TO 3X BASIC VET
RANDOM INSERTS IN PACKS
STATED PRINT RUN 199 SER.#'d SETS
64 Vladimir Guerrero Jr. RR 10.00 25.00
82 Pete Alonso RR 10.00 25.00
83 Eloy Jimenez RR 5.00 12.00

2019 Donruss Optic Purple Pandora

*PRPL PAN. DK: 1X TO 2.5X BASIC DK
*PRPL PAN. RR: 1X TO 2.5X BASIC RR
*PRPL PAN. VET: 1.5X TO 4X BASIC VET
RANDOM INSERTS IN PACKS
STATED PRINT RUN 99 SER.#'d SETS
64 Vladimir Guerrero Jr. RR 12.00 30.00
82 Pete Alonso RR 12.00 30.00
83 Eloy Jimenez RR 6.00 15.00

2019 Donruss Optic Purple Stars

*PRPL STRS DK: .75X TO 2X BASIC DK
*PRPL STRS RR: .75X TO 2X BASIC RR
*PRPL STRS VET: 1.2X TO 3X BASIC VET
RANDOM INSERTS IN PACKS
STATED PRINT RUN 125 SER.#'d SETS
64 Vladimir Guerrero Jr. RR 10.00 25.00
82 Pete Alonso RR 10.00 25.00
83 Eloy Jimenez RR 5.00 12.00

2019 Donruss Optic Red

*RED DK: 1X TO 2.5X BASIC DK
*RED RR: 1X TO 2.5X BASIC RR
*RED VET: 1.5X TO 4X BASIC VET
RANDOM INSERTS IN PACKS
STATED PRINT RUN 60 SER.#'d SETS
64 Vladimir Guerrero Jr. RR 12.00 30.00
82 Pete Alonso RR 12.00 30.00
83 Eloy Jimenez RR 6.00 15.00

2019 Donruss Optic Red Pandora

*RED PAN. DK: 1X TO 2.5X BASIC DK
*RED PAN. RR: 1X TO 2.5X BASIC RR
*RED PAN. VET: 1.5X TO 4X BASIC VET
RANDOM INSERTS IN PACKS
STATED PRINT RUN 99 SER.#'d SETS
64 Vladimir Guerrero Jr. RR 12.00 30.00
82 Pete Alonso RR 12.00 30.00
83 Eloy Jimenez RR 6.00 15.00

2019 Donruss Optic Red Wave

*RED WAVE DK: .5X TO 1.2X BASIC DK
*RED WAVE RR: .5X TO 1.2X BASIC RR
*RED WAVE VET: .75X TO 2.5X BASIC VET
RANDOM INSERTS IN PACKS
64 Vladimir Guerrero Jr. RR 6.00 15.00
82 Pete Alonso RR 8.00 20.00
83 Eloy Jimenez RR 3.00 8.00

2019 Donruss Optic Red White and Blue 150th Anniversary

*RWB 150th DK: .75X TO 2X BASIC DK
*RWB 150th RR: .75X TO 2X BASIC RR
*RWB 150th VET: 1.2X TO 3X BASIC VET
RANDOM INSERTS IN PACKS
STATED PRINT RUN 150 SER.#'d SETS
64 Vladimir Guerrero Jr. RR 10.00 25.00
82 Pete Alonso RR 10.00 25.00
83 Eloy Jimenez RR 5.00 12.00

2019 Donruss Optic Teal Velocity

*TEAL VEL. DK: 1.2X TO 3X BASIC DK
*TEAL VEL. RR: 1.2X TO 3X BASIC RR
*TEAL VEL. VET: 2X TO 5X BASIC VET
RANDOM INSERTS IN PACKS
STATED PRINT RUN 35 SER.#'d SETS
40 Jeff McNeil RR 8.00 20.00
64 Vladimir Guerrero Jr. RR 20.00 50.00
82 Pete Alonso RR 15.00 40.00
83 Eloy Jimenez RR 8.00 20.00

2019 Donruss Optic '85 Retro Signatures

RANDOM INSERTS IN PACKS
EXCHANGE DEADLINE 01/17/2021

*HOLO p/r 75-99: .5X TO 1.2X BASIC
*HOLO/49: .6X TO 1.5X BASIC
*HOLO p/r 20-25: .75X TO 2X BASIC
*BLUE p/r 35-50: .6X TO 1.5X BASIC
*BLUE/25: .75X TO 2X BASIC
*RED/25: .75X TO 2X BASIC
2 Chris Sabo 2.50 6.00
3 Ted Simmons 15.00 40.00
5 Keith Hernandez 2.50 6.00
6 Ken Griffey Sr. 2.50 6.00
7 Darryl Strawberry 2.50 6.00
8 Dave Stewart 2.50 6.00
10 Ozzie Guillen 2.50 6.00
11 Pete Rose 10.00 25.00
12 Jose Canseco 3.00 8.00
14 Omar Vizquel 3.00 8.00
16 Dave Concepcion 2.50 6.00
17 Joe Carter 2.50 6.00
18 Jim Rice 3.00 8.00
19 Darrell Evans 2.50 6.00
20 Lou Whitaker 2.50 6.00

2019 Donruss Optic Action All-Stars

RANDOM INSERTS IN PACKS
*HOLO: 1X TO 2.5X BASIC
1 Jose Altuve .30 .75
2 Aaron Judge 1.00 2.50
3 Mike Trout 2.00 5.00
4 Shohei Ohtani .60 1.50
5 Mookie Betts .75 2.00
6 Clayton Kershaw .60 1.50
7 Kris Bryant .50 1.25
8 Bryce Harper .60 1.50
9 Khris Davis .40 1.00
10 Manny Machado .40 1.00
11 Charlie Blackmon .40 1.00
12 Ronald Acuna Jr. 2.00 5.00
13 Christian Yelich .50 1.25
14 J.D. Martinez .40 1.00
15 Francisco Lindor .40 1.00

2019 Donruss Optic Autographs

RANDOM INSERTS IN PACKS
EXCHANGE DEADLINE 01/17/2021
*HOLO/99: .5X TO 1.2X BASIC
*HOLO/25: .75X TO 2X BASIC
*BLUE/50: .6X TO 1.5X BASIC
*RED/25: .75X TO 2X BASIC
1 Stephen Piscotty 2.50 6.00
2 Salvador Perez 3.00 8.00
3 Ronald Acuna Jr. 40.00 100.00
4 Nolan Arenado 20.00 50.00
5 Francisco Lindor 10.00 25.00
6 Franklin Barreto 2.50 6.00
8 Aaron Nola 3.00 8.00
9 Brandon Belt 3.00 8.00
10 Cody Bellinger 25.00 60.00
12 Franmil Reyes 2.50 6.00
13 Jason Kipnis 3.00 8.00
14 Mitch Haniger 3.00 8.00
15 Paul Goldschmidt 4.00 10.00
16 Trea Turner 3.00 8.00
17 Xander Bogaerts 4.00 10.00
18 Yoshihisa Hirano 2.50 6.00
19 Pete Alonso 20.00 50.00
20 Jose Abreu 4.00 10.00

2019 Donruss Optic Highlights

RANDOM INSERTS IN PACKS
*HOLO: 1X TO 2.5X BASIC
1 Shohei Ohtani .60 1.50
2 Albert Pujols .50 1.25
3 Sean Manaea .25 .60
4 James Paxton .30 .75
5 Max Scherzer .40 1.00
6 George Springer .30 .75
7 Christian Yelich .50 1.25
8 Juan Soto 1.25 3.00
9 Mookie Betts .75 2.00
10 Jose Ramirez .30 .75

2019 Donruss Optic Illusions

RANDOM INSERTS IN PACKS
*HOLO: 1X TO 2.5X BASIC
1 Mike Trout 2.00 5.00
2 Paul Goldschmidt .40 1.00
3 Trea Turner .30 .75
4 Christian Yelich .50 1.25
5 Trevor Story .40 1.00
6 Ronald Acuna Jr. 2.00 5.00
7 Javier Baez .50 1.25
8 Juan Soto 1.25 3.00
9 Carlos Correa .40 1.00
10 Aaron Judge 1.00 2.50
11 Kris Bryant .50 1.25
12 Corey Seager .40 1.00

2019 Donruss Optic MVP

RANDOM INSERTS IN PACKS
*HOLO: 1X TO 2.5X BASIC
1 Mookie Betts .75 2.00
2 Christian Yelich .50 1.25
3 Giancarlo Stanton .40 1.00
4 Jose Altuve .30 .75
5 Kris Bryant .50 1.25
6 Mike Trout 2.50 6.00
7 Bryce Harper .60 1.50
8 Miguel Cabrera .40 1.00
9 Ichiro .50 1.25
10 Albert Pujols .50 1.25
11 Clayton Kershaw .60 1.50
12 Josh Donaldson .30 .75
13 Buster Posey .50 1.25
14 Joey Votto .40 1.00
15 Dustin Pedroia .40 1.00

2019 Donruss Optic MVP Signatures

RANDOM INSERTS IN PACKS
EXCHANGE DEADLINE 01/17/2021
*HOLO: .4X TO 1X BASIC
*PINK VEL.: .4X TO 1X BASIC
*BLUE p/r 17-33: .75X TO 2X BASIC
*LGHT BLUE p/r 17-33: .75X TO 2X BASIC
*ORANGE p/r 17-33: .75X TO 2X BASIC
*PURPLE p/r 17-33: .75X TO 2X BASIC
*RED p/r 17-33: .75X TO 2X BASIC
*TEAL VEL. p/r 17-33: .75X TO 2X BASIC
*BLK CRK ICE p/r 17-25: .75X TO 2X BASIC
MVPAM Andrew McCutchen 25.00 60.00
MVPAP Albert Pujols 40.00 100.00
MVPAR Alex Rodriguez
MVPBL Barry Larkin 12.00 30.00
MVPBR Brooks Robinson 12.00 30.00
MVPDE Dennis Eckersley 6.00 15.00
MVPDM Dale Murphy 15.00 40.00
MVPFT Frank Thomas 30.00 80.00
MVPGB George Brett 40.00 100.00
MVPIR Ivan Rodriguez 12.00 30.00
MVPJC Jose Canseco 8.00 20.00
MVPJG Jason Giambi 4.00 10.00
MVPJM Joe Morgan 10.00 25.00
MVPJR Ken Griffey Jr. 75.00 200.00
MVPJV Joey Votto 12.00 30.00
MVPKH Keith Hernandez 2.50 6.00
MVPKM Kevin Mitchell 2.50 6.00
MVPPR Pete Rose 12.00 30.00
MVPRC Rod Carew 10.00 25.00
MVPRH Rickey Henderson 20.00 50.00
MVPRS Ryne Sandberg 8.00 20.00
MVPSG Steve Garvey 10.00 25.00
MVPWM Willie McGee 2.50 6.00

2019 Donruss Optic Mythical

RANDOM INSERTS IN PACKS
*HOLO: 1X TO 2.5X BASIC
1 Mike Trout 2.00 5.00
2 Aaron Judge 1.00 2.50
3 Mookie Betts .75 2.00
4 Kris Bryant .50 1.25
5 Bryce Harper .60 1.50
6 Jose Altuve .30 .75
7 Nolan Arenado .60 1.50
8 Shohei Ohtani .60 1.50

2019 Donruss Optic Peak Performers

RANDOM INSERTS IN PACKS
*HOLO: 1X TO 2.5X BASIC
1 Shohei Ohtani .60 1.50
2 Christian Yelich .50 1.25
3 Mookie Betts .75 2.00
4 Blake Snell .30 .75
5 Jacob deGrom .75 2.00
6 Ronald Acuna Jr. 2.00 5.00
7 Edwin Diaz .30 .75
8 Josh Hader .30 .75
9 J.D. Martinez .40 1.00
10 Khris Davis .40 1.00
11 Aaron Nola .30 .75
12 Mike Trout 2.00 5.00
13 Max Scherzer .40 1.00
14 Vladimir Guerrero Jr. 1.50 4.00
15 Fernando Tatis Jr. 4.00 10.00
16 Nolan Arenado .60 1.50

2019 Donruss Optic Rated Prospects

RANDOM INSERTS IN PACKS
*HOLO: 1X TO 2.5X BASIC
1 Royce Lewis .50 1.25
2 Jo Adell 1.00 2.50
3 Alec Bohm 1.50 4.00
4 Victor Victor Mesa .50 1.25
5 Casey Mize .60 1.50
6 Estevan Florial .40 1.00
7 Wander Franco 5.00 12.00
8 Cavan Biggio 1.25 3.00
9 Everson Pereira .40 1.00
10 Nico Hoerner .75 2.00

2019 Donruss Optic Rated Prospects Signatures

RANDOM INSERTS IN PACKS
EXCHANGE DEADLINE 01/17/2021
*HOLO: .4X TO 1X BASIC
*PINK VEL.: .4X TO 1X BASIC
*PURPLE/125: .5X TO 1.2X BASIC
*PURPLE/60: .6X TO 1.5X BASIC
*ORANGE/99: .6X TO 1.5X BASIC
*ORANGE/49: .75X TO 2X BASIC
*BLUE/75: .6X TO 1.5X BASIC
*BLUE/35: .75X TO 2X BASIC
*BLACK/50: .75X TO 2X BASIC
*RED/50: .75X TO 2X BASIC
*RED/25: 1X TO 2.5X BASIC
1 Fernando Tatis Jr. 60.00 150.00
2 Wander Franco 60.00 150.00
3 Victor Victor Mesa 5.00 12.00
4 Taylor Trammell 15.00 40.00
5 Alex Kirilloff 6.00 15.00
RPSKH Keston Hiura 12.00 30.00
8 Jon Duplantier 2.50 6.00
9 Dylan Cease 4.00 10.00
10 Yordan Alvarez 20.00 50.00
11 Jo Adell 25.00 60.00
12 Triston McKenzie 6.00 15.00
13 Brendan Rodgers 4.00 10.00
14 Forrest Whitley 4.00 10.00
15 Austin Riley 6.00 15.00

2019 Donruss Optic Rated Prospects Signatures Black Cracked Ice

*BLK CRK ICE/25: 1X TO 2.5X BASIC
RANDOM INSERTS IN PACKS
PRINT RUNS B/WN 15-25 COPIES PER
NO PRICING DUE TO SCARCITY
EXCHANGE DEADLINE 01/17/2021
10 Yordan Alvarez/25 75.00 200.00

2019 Donruss Optic Rated Prospects Signatures Light Blue

*LGHT BLUE/35: .75X TO 2X BASIC
*LGHT BLUE/20: 1X TO 1.5X BASIC
RANDOM INSERTS IN PACKS
PRINT RUNS B/WN 5-35 COPIES PER
NO PRICING DUE TO SCARCITY
EXCHANGE DEADLINE 01/17/2021

2019 Donruss Optic Rated Prospects Signatures Teal Velocity

*TEAL VEL./35: .75X TO 2X BASIC
*TEAL VEL./20: 1X TO 2.5X BASIC
RANDOM INSERTS IN PACKS
PRINT RUNS B/WN 20-35 COPIES PER
EXCHANGE DEADLINE 01/17/2021

2019 Donruss Optic Rated Rookies '85 Retro Signatures

RANDOM INSERTS IN PACKS
EXCHANGE DEADLINE 01/17/2021
*HOLO/99: .5X TO 1.2X BASIC
*BLUE/50: .6X TO 1.5X BASIC
*BLUE/25: .75X TO 2X BASIC
*RED/25: .75X TO 2X BASIC
1 Yusei Kikuchi 8.00 20.00
2 Michael Kopech 8.00 20.00
3 Kyle Tucker 6.00 15.00
4 Corbin Burnes 8.00 20.00
5 Justus Sheffield 4.00 10.00
6 Ryan O'Hearn 2.50 6.00
7 Christin Stewart 3.00 8.00
8 Touki Toussaint 3.00 8.00
9 Luis Urias 4.00 10.00
10 Ramon Laureano 6.00 15.00
11 Jeff McNeil 6.00 15.00
12 Josh James 4.00 10.00
13 Stephen Gonsalves 2.50 6.00
14 Danny Jansen 2.50 6.00
15 Brandon Lowe 6.00 15.00
17 Myles Straw 4.00 10.00
18 Brad Keller 2.50 6.00
19 Chris Shaw 2.50 6.00
20 Chance Adams 2.50 6.00

2019 Donruss Optic Rated Rookies Signatures

RANDOM INSERTS IN PACKS
EXCHANGE DEADLINE 01/17/2021
*HOLO: .4X TO 1X BASIC
*PINK VEL.: .4X TO 1X BASIC
*PURPLE/125: .5X TO 1.2X BASIC
*PURPLE/60: .6X TO 1.5X BASIC
1 Brad Keller 2.50 6.00
2 Bryse Wilson 3.00 8.00
3 Cedric Mullins 8.00 20.00
4 Chance Adams 2.50 6.00
5 Chris Shaw 2.50 6.00
6 Christin Stewart 3.00 8.00
7 Cionel Perez 2.50 6.00
8 Corbin Burnes 8.00 20.00
9 Dakota Hudson 3.00 8.00
10 Daniel Ponce de Leon 4.00 10.00
11 Danny Jansen 2.50 6.00
12 David Fletcher 8.00 20.00
13 Dennis Santana 2.50 6.00
14 Enyel De Los Santos 2.50 6.00
15 Framber Valdez 2.50 6.00
16 Brandon Lowe 6.00 15.00
17 Garrett Hampson 4.00 10.00
18 Jacob Nix 3.00 8.00
19 Jake Bauers 4.00 10.00
20 Jake Cave 3.00 8.00
21 Jeff McNeil 8.00 20.00
22 Jonathan Davis 3.00 8.00
23 Jonathan Loaisiga 3.00 8.00
24 Josh James 4.00 10.00
25 Justus Sheffield 4.00 10.00
26 Kevin Kramer 3.00 8.00
27 Kevin Newman 4.00 10.00
28 Kolby Allard 4.00 10.00
RRSKT Kyle Tucker 12.00 30.00
RRSKW Kyle Wright 4.00 10.00
31 Luis Ortiz 2.50 6.00
32 Luis Urias 4.00 10.00
33 Michael Kopech 6.00 15.00
34 Myles Straw 4.00 10.00
35 Patrick Wisdom 2.50 6.00
36 Ramon Laureano 5.00 12.00
37 Reese McGuire 4.00 10.00
38 Rowdy Tellez 4.00 10.00
39 Ryan Borucki 2.50 6.00
40 Ryan O'Hearn 2.50 6.00
41 Sean Reid-Foley 2.50 6.00
42 Stephen Gonsalves 2.50 6.00
43 Steven Duggar 3.00 8.00
44 Taylor Ward 2.50 6.00
45 Touki Toussaint 3.00 8.00
46 Caleb Ferguson 3.00 8.00
47 Vladimir Guerrero Jr. 50.00 120.00
48 Fernando Tatis Jr. 75.00 200.00
49 Eloy Jimenez 30.00 80.00
50 Nick Senzel 15.00 40.00

2019 Donruss Optic Rated Rookies Signatures Black

*BLACK: .75X TO 2X BASIC
RANDOM INSERTS IN PACKS
STATED PRINT RUN 50 SER.#'d SETS
EXCHANGE DEADLINE 01/17/2021

2019 Donruss Optic Rated Rookies Signatures Blue

*BLUE/75: .6X TO 1.5X BASIC
*BLUE/35: .75X TO 2X BASIC
RANDOM INSERTS IN PACKS
PRINT RUNS B/WN 35-75 COPIES PER
EXCHANGE DEADLINE 01/17/2021

2019 Donruss Optic Rated Rookies Signatures Light Blue

*LGHT BLUE/35: .75X TO 2X BASIC
*LGHT BLUE/20: 1X TO 2.5X BASIC
RANDOM INSERTS IN PACKS
PRINT RUNS B/WN 20-35 COPIES PER
EXCHANGE DEADLINE 01/17/2021

2019 Donruss Optic Rated Rookies Signatures Orange

*ORANGE/99: .6X TO 1.5X BASIC
*ORANGE/49: .75X TO 2X BASIC
RANDOM INSERTS IN PACKS
PRINT RUNS B/WN 49-99 COPIES PER
EXCHANGE DEADLINE 01/17/2021

2019 Donruss Optic Rated Rookies Signatures Red

*RED/50: .75X TO 2X BASIC
*RED/25: 1X TO 2.5X BASIC
RANDOM INSERTS IN PACKS
PRINT RUNS B/WN 25-50 COPIES PER
EXCHANGE DEADLINE 01/17/2021

2019 Donruss Optic Rated Rookies Signatures Teal Velocity

*TEAL VEL./35: .75X TO 2X BASIC
*TEAL VEL./20: 1X TO 2.5X BASIC
RANDOM INSERTS IN PACKS
PRINT RUNS B/WN 20-35 COPIES PER
EXCHANGE DEADLINE 01/17/2021

2019 Donruss Optic Signature Series

RANDOM INSERTS IN PACKS
EXCHANGE DEADLINE 01/17/2021
*HOLO/99: .5X TO 1.2X BASIC
*HOLO/49: .6X TO 1.5X BASIC
*HOLO/25: .75X TO 2X BASIC
*BLUE/50: .6X TO 1.5X BASIC
*BLUE/25: .75X TO 2X BASIC
*RED/25: .75X TO 2X BASIC
1 Adbert Alzolay 2.50 6.00
2 Corey Ray 2.50 6.00
3 Sean Murphy 3.00 8.00
4 Yusniel Diaz 4.00 10.00
7 Ian Desmond 2.50 6.00
8 Shane Bieber 12.00 30.00
9 Wil Myers 3.00 8.00
10 Odubel Herrera 3.00 8.00
11 Kyle Schwarber 4.00 10.00
12 Josh Donaldson 3.00 8.00
13 Eric Thames 2.50 6.00
14 Carson Kelly 2.50 6.00
15 Matt Olson 4.00 10.00
17 Trevor Story 8.00 20.00
18 Chris Paddack 5.00 12.00
19 Victor Robles 5.00 12.00

2019 Donruss Optic Significant Signatures

RANDOM INSERTS IN PACKS
EXCHANGE DEADLINE 01/17/2021
*HOLO/99: .5X TO 1.2X BASIC
*HOLO/25: .75X TO 2X BASIC
1 Craig Biggio 8.00 20.00
2 Luis Tiant 2.50 6.00
3 Bobby Richardson 2.50 6.00
5 David Ross 2.50 6.00
6 Gary Sheffield 2.50 6.00
7 Larry Walker 3.00 8.00
10 Charles Johnson 2.50 6.00
11 Dontrelle Willis 2.50 6.00
14 Roberto Alomar 3.00 8.00
15 Don Sutton 3.00 8.00
16 Juan Gonzalez 6.00 15.00
18 Tim Wakefield 3.00 8.00
19 Bob Horner 2.50 6.00

2019 Donruss Optic Significant Signatures Blue

*BLUE p/r 35-50: .6X TO 1.5X BASIC
RANDOM INSERTS IN PACKS
PRINT RUNS B/WN 10-50 COPIES PER
NO PRICING ON QTY 15 OR LESS
EXCHANGE DEADLINE 01/17/2021
3 Bobby Richardson/35 12.00 30.00

2019 Donruss Optic Significant Signatures Red

*RED/25: .75X TO 2X BASIC
RANDOM INSERTS IN PACKS
PRINT RUNS B/WN 7-25 COPIES PER
NO PRICING ON QTY 15 OR LESS
EXCHANGE DEADLINE 01/17/2021
3 Bobby Richardson/25 15.00 40.00

2019 Donruss Optic The Rookies

RANDOM INSERTS IN PACKS
*HOLO: 1X TO 2.5X BASIC
1 Yusei Kikuchi .40 1.00
2 Kyle Tucker .60 1.50
3 Michael Kopech .75 2.00
4 Christin Stewart .30 .75
5 Justus Sheffield .40 1.00
6 Corbin Burnes 2.00 5.00
7 Jonathan Loaisiga .30 .75
8 Josh James .40 1.00
9 Touki Toussaint .30 .75
10 Danny Jansen .25 .60
11 Vladimir Guerrero Jr. 1.50 4.00
12 Eloy Jimenez 1.00 2.50
13 Fernando Tatis Jr. 4.00 10.00
14 Pete Alonso 2.00 5.00

2019 Donruss Optic We The People

*WTP DK: 1X TO 2.5X BASIC DK
*WTP RR: 1X TO 2.5X BASIC RR
*WTP VET: 1.5X TO 4X BASIC VET
RANDOM INSERTS IN PACKS
STATED PRINT RUN 76 SER.#'d SETS
64 Vladimir Guerrero Jr. RR 12.00 30.00
82 Pete Alonso RR 12.00 30.00
83 Eloy Jimenez RR 6.00 15.00

2020 Donruss Optic

1 Fernando Tatis Jr. DK 2.50 6.00
2 Buster Posey DK .60 1.50
3 Cody Bellinger DK 1.00 2.50
4 Eugenio Suarez DK .40 1.00
5 Christian Yelich DK .60 1.50
6 Brian Anderson DK .30 .75
7 Pete Alonso DK 1.25 3.00
8 Ronald Acuna Jr. DK 2.00 5.00
9 Mike Trout DK 2.50 6.00
10 Marcus Semien DK .50 1.25
11 Miguel Cabrera DK .50 1.25
12 Lucas Giolito DK .40 1.00
13 Nelson Cruz DK .50 1.25
14 Vladimir Guerrero Jr. DK .75 2.00
15 Austin Meadows DK .50 1.25
16 Rafael Devers DK .60 1.50
17 Trey Mancini DK .50 1.25
18 Shane Bieber DK .50 1.25
19 Jorge Soler DK .50 1.25
20 Alex Bregman DK .50 1.25
21 Lance Lynn DK .30 .75
22 Marco Gonzales DK .30 .75
23 Juan Soto DK 1.50 4.00
24 Bryce Harper DK .75 2.00
25 Paul Goldschmidt DK .50 1.25
26 Javier Baez DK .60 1.50
27 Josh Bell DK .40 1.00
28 Ketel Marte DK .40 1.00
29 Nolan Arenado DK .75 2.00
30 Aaron Judge DK 1.25 3.00
31 Bryan Abreu RR RC .30 .75
32 Dustin May RR RC 1.00 2.50
33 Mauricio Dubon RR RC .40 1.00
34 Jesus Luzardo RR RC .60 1.50
35 Jordan Yamamoto RR RC .30 .75
36 Brendan McKay RR RC .50 1.25
37 Bo Bichette RR RC 3.00 8.00
38 Nico Hoerner RR RC 1.25 3.00
39 Aristides Aquino RR RC 4.00 10.00
40 Brock Burke RR RC .30 .75
41 Justin Dunn RR RC .40 1.00
42 Sean Murphy RR RC .50 1.25
43 Trent Grisham RR RC 1.25 3.00
44 Gavin Lux RR RC 1.50 4.00
45 Yordan Alvarez RR RC 2.00 5.00
46 Sam Hilliard RR RC .50 1.25
47 Patrick Sandoval RR RC .50 1.25
48 Isan Diaz RR RC .50 1.25
49 A.J. Puk RR RC .50 1.25
50 Logan Webb RR RC .50 1.25
51 Randy Arozarena RR RC 5.00 12.00
52 Anthony Kay RR RC .30 .75
53 Dylan Cease RR RC .50 1.25
54 Zac Gallen RR RC .75 2.00
55 Adrian Morejon RR RC .30 .75
56 Kyle Lewis RR RC 3.00 8.00
57 Nick Solak RR RC 1.25 3.00
58 Brusdar Graterol RR RC .50 1.25
59 Tony Gonsolin RR RC 1.25 3.00
60 Matt Thaiss RR RC .40 1.00
61 Yoshitomo Tsutsugo RR RC .75 2.00
62 Luis Robert RR RC 5.00 12.00
63 Bobby Bradley RR RC .30 .75
64 Edwin Rios RR RC .75 2.00
65 Travis Demeritte RR RC .50 1.25
66 Domingo Leyba RR RC .40 1.00
67 Josh Rojas RR RC .30 .75
68 Abraham Toro RR RC .40 1.00
69 Sheldon Neuse RR RC .40 1.00
70 Donnie Walton RR RC .75 2.00
71 Zack Collins RR RC .40 1.00
72 Jake Rogers RR RC .30 .75
73 Deivy Grullon RR RC .30 .75
74 Tres Barrera RR RC .60 1.50
75 Logan Allen RR RC .30 .75
76 Lewis Thorpe RR RC .30 .75
77 Yonathan Daza RR RC .40 1.00
78 Tyrone Taylor RR RC .30 .75
79 Jaylin Davis RR RC .50 1.25
80 Jake Fraley RR RC .40 1.00
81 Michael King RR RC .50 1.25
82 Andres Munoz RR RC .50 1.25
83 Michel Baez RR RC .30 .75
84 Ronald Bolanos RR RC .30 .75
85 Joe Palumbo RR RC .30 .75
86 T.J. Zeuch RR RC .30 .75
87 Adbert Alzolay RR RC .40 1.00
88 Aaron Civale RR RC .60 1.50
89 Rico Garcia RR RC .50 1.25
90 Jonathan Hernandez RR RC .30 .75
91 Danny Mendick RR RC .40 1.00
92 Willi Castro RR RC .50 1.25
93 Yu Chang RR RC .50 1.25
94 Kwang-Hyun Kim RR RC .60 1.50
95 Shun Yamaguchi RR RC .40 1.00
96 Shogo Akiyama RR RC .50 1.25
97 Walker Buehler .40 1.00
98 Ozzie Albies .30 .75
99 Charlie Blackmon .30 .75
100 Stephen Strasburg .30 .75
101 Nick Senzel .30 .75
102 Yadier Molina .40 1.00
103 Jacob deGrom .60 1.50
104 Luis Severino .25 .60
105 Mookie Betts .60 1.50
106 Ketel Marte .25 .60
107 Hyun-Jin Ryu .25 .60
108 Lorenzo Cain .20 .50
109 Corey Kluber .25 .60
110 Joey Votto .30 .75
111 Fernando Tatis Jr. 1.50 4.00
112 Cody Bellinger .60 1.50
113 Josh Donaldson .25 .60
114 Jeff McNeil .25 .60
115 Javier Baez .40 1.00
116 Gleyber Torres .60 1.50
117 Marcus Semien .30 .75
118 Shohei Ohtani .50 1.25
119 Buster Posey .40 1.00
120 Charlie Morton .30 .75
121 Mitch Haniger .25 .60
122 Johnny Cueto .25 .60
123 Vladimir Guerrero Jr. .50 1.25
124 Matt Olson .30 .75
125 Shane Bieber .30 .75
126 Jorge Polanco .25 .60
127 Jose Abreu .30 .75
128 Trea Turner .25 .60
129 Christian Yelich .40 1.00
130 Aaron Judge .75 2.00
131 Alex Bregman .30 .75
132 Chris Sale .30 .75
133 Gerrit Cole .50 1.25
134 Madison Bumgarner .25 .60
135 Clayton Kershaw .50 1.25
136 Eloy Jimenez .60 1.50
137 Cavan Biggio .40 1.00
138 Max Scherzer .30 .75
139 Eugenio Suarez .25 .60
140 Aaron Nola .25 .60
141 Paul Goldschmidt .30 .75
142 Mike Trout 1.50 4.00
143 Anthony Rizzo .40 1.00
144 Jonathan Villar .20 .50
145 Kyle Hendricks .30 .75
146 Austin Meadows .30 .75
147 Yoan Moncada .30 .75
148 Josh Bell .25 .60
149 Nolan Arenado .50 1.25
150 Francisco Lindor .30 .75
151 Matt Chapman .30 .75
152 Willie Calhoun .20 .50
153 Mike Soroka .30 .75
154 Kevin Newman .30 .75
155 Anthony Rendon .30 .75
156 Elvis Andrus .25 .60
157 Justin Verlander .30 .75
158 Jose Ramirez .25 .60
159 Jose Altuve .25 .60
160 Bryan Reynolds .25 .60
161 Juan Soto 1.00 2.50
162 Chris Paddack .30 .75
163 Rafael Devers .40 1.00
164 Brian Anderson .20 .50
165 Trevor Story .30 .75
166 Jose Berrios .25 .60
167 Brandon Lowe .25 .60
168 Freddie Freeman .40 1.00
169 Ronald Acuna Jr. 1.25 3.00
170 Starling Marte .25 .60
171 Adalberto Mondesi .25 .60
172 Blake Snell .25 .60
173 Trey Mancini .30 .75
174 Ramon Laureano .25 .60
175 Kris Bryant .40 1.00
176 Rhys Hoskins .40 1.00
177 Marco Gonzales .20 .50
178 J.D. Martinez .30 .75
179 Keston Hiura .40 1.00
180 Manny Machado .30 .75
181 Sandy Alcantara .20 .50
182 Jack Flaherty .30 .75
183 Bryce Harper .50 1.25
184 Joey Gallo .30 .75
185 Jorge Soler .30 .75
186 Matt Carpenter .30 .75
187 Pete Alonso .75 2.00
188 Whit Merrifield .30 .75
189 John Means .30 .75
190 Luis Arraez .40 1.00
191 Tommy Edman .30 .75
192 Max Muncy .25 .60
193 Albert Pujols .40 1.00
194 George Springer .25 .60
195 Tim Anderson .30 .75
196 Masahiro Tanaka .30 .75
197 Mike Trout AS 1.50 4.00
198 Christian Yelich AS .40 1.00
199 Ronald Acuna Jr. AS 1.25 3.00
200 Javier Baez AS .40 1.00

2020 Donruss Optic Black

*BLACK DK: 1.5X TO 4X BASIC DK
*BLACK RR: 1.5X TO 4X BASIC DK
*BLACK VET: 2.5X TO 6X BASIC VET
RANDOM INSERTS IN PACKS
STATED PRINT RUN 25 SER.#'d SETS
32 Dustin May RR 10.00 25.00
33 Mauricio Dubon RR 6.00 15.00
37 Bo Bichette RR 40.00 100.00
38 Nico Hoerner RR 12.00 30.00
44 Gavin Lux RR 10.00 25.00
45 Yordan Alvarez RR 20.00 50.00
56 Kyle Lewis RR 40.00 100.00
62 Luis Robert RR 125.00 300.00
96 Shogo Akiyama RR 15.00 40.00

2020 Donruss Optic Black Stars

*BLK STARS .75X TO 2X BASIC DK
*BLK STARS RR: .75X TO 2X BASIC RR
*BLK STARS VET: 1.2X TO 3X BASIC VET
RANDOM INSERTS IN PACKS
STATED PRINT RUN 125 SER.#'d SETS
32 Dustin May RR 5.00 12.00
33 Mauricio Dubon RR 3.00 8.00
37 Bo Bichette RR 12.00 30.00
38 Nico Hoerner RR 5.00 12.00
44 Gavin Lux RR 6.00 15.00
45 Yordan Alvarez RR 10.00 25.00
56 Kyle Lewis RR 20.00 50.00
62 Luis Robert RR 60.00 150.00
96 Shogo Akiyama RR 6.00 15.00

2020 Donruss Optic Blue

*BLUE DK: 1X TO 2.5X BASIC DK
*BLUE RR: 1X TO 2.5X BASIC DK
*BLUE VET: 1.5X TO 4X BASIC VET
RANDOM INSERTS IN PACKS
STATED PRINT RUN 75 SER.#'d SETS
32 Dustin May RR 6.00 15.00
33 Mauricio Dubon RR 4.00 10.00
37 Bo Bichette RR 25.00 60.00
38 Nico Hoerner RR 8.00 20.00
44 Gavin Lux RR 8.00 20.00
45 Yordan Alvarez RR 12.00 30.00
56 Kyle Lewis RR 25.00 60.00
62 Luis Robert RR 75.00 200.00
96 Shogo Akiyama RR 10.00 25.00

2020 Donruss Optic Carolina Blue

*CAR.BLUE DK: 1.2X TO 3X BASIC DK
*CAR.BLUE RR: 1.2X TO 3X BASIC DK
*CAR.BLUE VET: 2X TO 5X BASIC VET
RANDOM INSERTS IN PACKS
STATED PRINT RUN 50 SER.#'d SETS
32 Dustin May RR 8.00 20.00
33 Mauricio Dubon RR 5.00 12.00
37 Bo Bichette RR 30.00 80.00
38 Nico Hoerner RR 10.00 25.00
44 Gavin Lux RR 10.00 25.00
45 Yordan Alvarez RR 15.00 40.00
56 Kyle Lewis RR 30.00 80.00
62 Luis Robert RR 100.00 250.00
96 Shogo Akiyama RR 12.00 30.00

2020 Donruss Optic Carolina Blue and White

*CBW DK: .5X TO 1.2X BASIC DK
*CBW RR: .5X TO 1.2X BASIC RR
*CBW VET: .8X TO 2X BASIC VET
RANDOM INSERTS IN PACKS
32 Dustin May RR 3.00 8.00
33 Mauricio Dubon RR 2.00 5.00
37 Bo Bichette RR 8.00 20.00
44 Gavin Lux RR 4.00 10.00
45 Yordan Alvarez RR 6.00 15.00
56 Kyle Lewis RR 8.00 20.00
62 Luis Robert RR 15.00 40.00
96 Shogo Akiyama RR 4.00 10.00

2020 Donruss Optic Freedom

*FREEDOM DK: 1.2X TO 3X BASIC DK
*FREEDOM RR: 1.2X TO 3X BASIC DK
*FREEDOM VET: 2X TO 5X BASIC VET
RANDOM INSERTS IN PACKS
STATED PRINT RUN 45 SER.#'d SETS
32 Dustin May RR 8.00 20.00
33 Mauricio Dubon RR 5.00 12.00
37 Bo Bichette RR 30.00 80.00
38 Nico Hoerner RR 10.00 25.00
44 Gavin Lux RR 10.00 25.00
45 Yordan Alvarez RR 15.00 40.00
56 Kyle Lewis RR 30.00 80.00
62 Luis Robert RR 100.00 250.00
96 Shogo Akiyama RR 12.00 30.00

2020 Donruss Optic Green Dragon

*GRN DRGN DK: 1X TO 2.5X BASIC DK
*GRN DRGN RR: 1X TO 2.5X BASIC DK
*GRN DRGN VET: 1.5X TO 4X BASIC VET
RANDOM INSERTS IN PACKS
STATED PRINT RUN 84 SER.#'d SETS
32 Dustin May RR 6.00 15.00
33 Mauricio Dubon RR 4.00 10.00
37 Bo Bichette RR 25.00 60.00
38 Nico Hoerner RR 8.00 20.00
44 Gavin Lux RR 8.00 20.00
45 Yordan Alvarez RR 12.00 30.00
56 Kyle Lewis RR 25.00 60.00
62 Luis Robert RR 75.00 200.00
96 Shogo Akiyama RR 10.00 25.00

2020 Donruss Optic Holo

*HOLO DK: .5X TO 1.2X BASIC DK
*HOLO RR: .5X TO 1.2X BASIC RR
*HOLO VET: .8X TO 2X BASIC VET
RANDOM INSERTS IN PACKS
32 Dustin May RR 3.00 8.00
33 Mauricio Dubon RR 2.00 5.00
37 Bo Bichette RR 8.00 20.00
44 Gavin Lux RR 4.00 10.00
45 Yordan Alvarez RR 6.00 15.00
56 Kyle Lewis RR 8.00 20.00
62 Luis Robert RR 15.00 40.00
96 Shogo Akiyama RR 4.00 10.00

2020 Donruss Optic Liberty

*LIBERTY DK: 1.2X TO 3X BASIC DK
*LIBERTY RR: 1.2X TO 3X BASIC DK
*LIBERTY VET: 2X TO 5X BASIC VET
RANDOM INSERTS IN PACKS
STATED PRINT RUN 45 SER.#'d SETS
32 Dustin May RR 8.00 20.00
33 Mauricio Dubon RR 5.00 12.00
37 Bo Bichette RR 30.00 80.00
38 Nico Hoerner RR 10.00 25.00
44 Gavin Lux RR 10.00 25.00
45 Yordan Alvarez RR 15.00 40.00
56 Kyle Lewis RR 30.00 80.00
62 Luis Robert RR 100.00 250.00
96 Shogo Akiyama RR 12.00 30.00

2020 Donruss Optic Lime Green

*LIME GRN DK: .5X TO 1.2X BASIC DK
*LIME GRN RR: .5X TO 1.2X BASIC RR
*LIME GRN VET: .8X TO 2X BASIC VET
RANDOM INSERTS IN PACKS
32 Dustin May RR 3.00 8.00
33 Mauricio Dubon RR 2.00 5.00
37 Bo Bichette RR 8.00 20.00
44 Gavin Lux RR 4.00 10.00
45 Yordan Alvarez RR 6.00 15.00
56 Kyle Lewis RR 8.00 20.00
62 Luis Robert RR 15.00 40.00
96 Shogo Akiyama RR 4.00 10.00

2020 Donruss Optic Orange

*ORANGE DK: 1X TO 2.5X BASIC DK
*ORANGE RR: 1X TO 2.5X BASIC DK
*ORANGE VET: 1.5X TO 4X BASIC VET
RANDOM INSERTS IN PACKS
STATED PRINT RUN 100 SER.#'d SETS
32 Dustin May RR 6.00 15.00
33 Mauricio Dubon RR 4.00 10.00
37 Bo Bichette RR 25.00 60.00
38 Nico Hoerner RR 8.00 20.00
44 Gavin Lux RR 8.00 20.00
45 Yordan Alvarez RR 12.00 30.00
56 Kyle Lewis RR 25.00 60.00
62 Luis Robert RR 75.00 200.00
96 Shogo Akiyama RR 10.00 25.00

2020 Donruss Optic Pink

*PINK DK: .5X TO 1.2X BASIC DK
*PINK RR: .5X TO 1.2X BASIC RR
*PINK VET: .8X TO 2X BASIC VET
RANDOM INSERTS IN PACKS
32 Dustin May RR 3.00 8.00
33 Mauricio Dubon RR 2.00 5.00
37 Bo Bichette RR 8.00 20.00
44 Gavin Lux RR 4.00 10.00
45 Yordan Alvarez RR 6.00 15.00
56 Kyle Lewis RR 8.00 20.00
62 Luis Robert RR 15.00 40.00
96 Shogo Akiyama RR 4.00 10.00

2020 Donruss Optic Pink Velocity

*PINK VEL. DK: .75X TO 2X BASIC DK
*PINK VEL. RR: .75X TO 2X BASIC RR
*PINK VEL. VET: 1.2X TO 3X BASIC VET
RANDOM INSERTS IN PACKS
STATED PRINT RUN 199 SER.#'d SETS
32 Dustin May RR 5.00 12.00
33 Mauricio Dubon RR 3.00 8.00
37 Bo Bichette RR 12.00 30.00
38 Nico Hoerner RR 5.00 12.00
44 Gavin Lux RR 6.00 15.00
45 Yordan Alvarez RR 10.00 25.00
56 Kyle Lewis RR 12.00 30.00
62 Luis Robert RR 60.00 150.00
96 Shogo Akiyama RR 6.00 15.00

2020 Donruss Optic Red

*RED DK: 1X TO 2.5X BASIC DK
*RED RR: 1X TO 2.5X BASIC DK
*RED VET: 1.5X TO 4X BASIC VET
RANDOM INSERTS IN PACKS
STATED PRINT RUN 60 SER.#'d SETS
32 Dustin May RR 6.00 15.00
33 Mauricio Dubon RR 4.00 10.00
37 Bo Bichette RR 25.00 60.00
38 Nico Hoerner RR 8.00 20.00
44 Gavin Lux RR 8.00 20.00
45 Yordan Alvarez RR 12.00 30.00

56 Kyle Lewis RR 25.00 60.00
62 Luis Robert RR 75.00 200.00
96 Shogo Akiyama RR 10.00 25.00

2020 Donruss Optic Red Dragon

*RED DRGN DK: 1X TO 2.5X BASIC DK
*RED DRGN RR: 1X TO 2.5X BASIC DK
*RED DRGN VET: 1.5X TO 4X BASIC VET
RANDOM INSERTS IN PACKS
STATED PRINT RUN 88 SER.#'d SETS
32 Dustin May RR 6.00 15.00
33 Mauricio Dubon RR 4.00 10.00
37 Bo Bichette RR 25.00 60.00
38 Nico Hoerner RR 8.00 20.00
44 Gavin Lux RR 8.00 20.00
45 Yordan Alvarez RR 12.00 30.00
56 Kyle Lewis RR 25.00 60.00
62 Luis Robert RR 75.00 200.00
96 Shogo Akiyama RR 10.00 25.00

2020 Donruss Optic Red Wave

*RED WAVE DK: .5X TO 1.2X BASIC DK
*RED WAVE RR: .5X TO 1.2X BASIC RR
*RED WAVE VET: .8X TO 2X BASIC VET
RANDOM INSERTS IN PACKS
32 Dustin May RR 3.00 8.00
33 Mauricio Dubon RR 2.00 5.00
37 Bo Bichette RR 8.00 20.00
44 Gavin Lux RR 4.00 10.00
45 Yordan Alvarez RR 6.00 15.00
56 Kyle Lewis RR 8.00 20.00
62 Luis Robert RR 15.00 40.00
96 Shogo Akiyama RR 4.00 10.00

2020 Donruss Optic Red White and Blue

*RWB DK: .75X TO 2X BASIC DK
*RWB RR: .75X TO 2X BASIC RR
*RWB VET: 1.2X TO 3X BASIC VET
RANDOM INSERTS IN PACKS
STATED PRINT RUN 150 SER.#'d SETS
32 Dustin May RR 5.00 12.00
33 Mauricio Dubon RR 3.00 8.00
37 Bo Bichette RR 12.00 30.00
38 Nico Hoerner RR 5.00 12.00
44 Gavin Lux RR 6.00 15.00
45 Yordan Alvarez RR 10.00 25.00
56 Kyle Lewis RR 12.00 30.00
62 Luis Robert RR 60.00 150.00
96 Shogo Akiyama RR 6.00 15.00

2020 Donruss Optic Spirit of 76

*76 DK: 1X TO 2.5X BASIC DK
*76 RR: 1X TO 2.5X BASIC RR
*76 VET: 1.5X TO 4X BASIC VET
RANDOM INSERTS IN PACKS
STATED PRINT RUN 76 SER.#'d SETS
32 Dustin May RR 6.00 15.00
33 Mauricio Dubon RR 4.00 10.00
37 Bo Bichette RR 25.00 60.00
38 Nico Hoerner RR 8.00 20.00
44 Gavin Lux RR 8.00 20.00
45 Yordan Alvarez RR 12.00 30.00
56 Kyle Lewis RR 25.00 60.00
62 Luis Robert RR 75.00 200.00
96 Shogo Akiyama RR 10.00 25.00

2020 Donruss Optic Stars and Stripes

RANDOM INSERTS IN PACKS
1 Aaron Judge 15.00 40.00
2 Mike Trout 60.00 150.00
3 Yordan Alvarez 40.00 100.00
4 Javier Baez 15.00 40.00
5 Ken Griffey Jr. 40.00 100.00
6 Shohei Ohtani 10.00 25.00
7 Clayton Kershaw 15.00 40.00
8 Juan Soto 15.00 40.00
9 Francisco Lindor 10.00 25.00
10 Bryce Harper 12.00 30.00

2020 Donruss Optic Teal Velocity

*TEAL VEL. DK: 1.2X TO 3X BASIC DK
*TEAL VEL. RR: 1.2X TO 3X BASIC DK
*TEAL VEL. VET: 2X TO 5X BASIC VET
RANDOM INSERTS IN PACKS
STATED PRINT RUN 35 SER.#'d SETS
32 Dustin May RR 8.00 20.00
33 Mauricio Dubon RR 5.00 12.00
37 Bo Bichette RR 30.00 80.00
38 Nico Hoerner RR 10.00 25.00
44 Gavin Lux RR 10.00 25.00
45 Yordan Alvarez RR 15.00 40.00
56 Kyle Lewis RR 30.00 80.00
62 Luis Robert RR 100.00 250.00
96 Shogo Akiyama RR 12.00 30.00

2020 Donruss Optic Autographs

RANDOM INSERTS IN PACKS
EXCHANGE DEADLINE 01/22/2022
1 Robel Garcia 2.50 6.00
2 Kris Bubic 4.00 10.00
3 Nolan Gorman 5.00 12.00
5 Matt Manning 3.00 8.00
6 Triston Casas 6.00 15.00
7 MacKenzie Gore 5.00 12.00
8 Drew Waters 8.00 20.00
9 Trevor Rogers 6.00 15.00
10 JJ Bleday 8.00 20.00
11 Shane Baz 2.50 6.00
12 Bobby Dalbec 15.00 40.00
13 Adonis Medina 4.00 10.00
14 Erick Fedde 2.50 6.00
15 Bryan Mata 2.50 6.00
16 Luis Rodriguez 15.00 40.00
17 Alex Faedo 3.00 8.00
18 Yoshitomo Tsutsugo 6.00 15.00
19 Luis Robert EXCH 75.00 200.00
21 Andy Pettitte 3.00 8.00
22 Austin Meadows 4.00 10.00
23 Kevin Newman 4.00 10.00
24 Sean Murphy 6.00 15.00
25 Richard Urena 2.50 6.00
26 J.D. Davis 2.50 6.00
27 Jonathan Loaisiga 3.00 8.00
28 Michael Chavis 5.00 12.00
29 Dillon Peters 2.50 6.00
30 Nick Martini 2.50 6.00
31 Ryan Mountcastle 12.00 30.00
32 Josh James 2.50 6.00
33 Richie Martin 2.50 6.00
34 Reynaldo Lopez 3.00 8.00
35 Cesar Hernandez 5.00 12.00
36 Josh Donaldson 10.00 25.00
37 Reese McGuire 3.00 8.00
39 Shed Long Jr. 3.00 8.00
40 Corey Ray 2.50 6.00

2020 Donruss Optic Autographs Holo

*HOLO: .5X TO 1.2X BASIC
RANDOM INSERTS IN PACKS
EXCHANGE DEADLINE 01/22/2022
28 Michael Chavis 8.00 20.00

2020 Donruss Optic Fireworks Signatures

RANDOM INSERTS IN PACKS
EXCHANGE DEADLINE 01/22/2022
1 Nolan Jones 4.00 10.00
2 Brice Turang 2.50 6.00
3 Luisangel Acuna 25.00 60.00
5 Johan Rojas 5.00 12.00
6 Corbin Carroll 4.00 10.00
8 Kristian Robinson 8.00 20.00
9 Luis Matos 20.00 50.00
10 Josh Jung 10.00 25.00
11 Riley Greene 12.00 30.00
13 Julio Rodriguez 15.00 40.00
14 Luis V. Garcia 10.00 25.00
16 Shogo Akiyama 8.00 20.00
17 Yoshitomo Tsutsugo 6.00 15.00
18 Alex Bregman EXCH 10.00 25.00
19 Tommy Edman 4.00 10.00
20 Evan White 6.00 15.00
21 Dylan Carlson 15.00 40.00
24 Shohei Ohtani EXCH 40.00 100.00
25 Yoan Moncada 15.00 40.00
26 Yordan Alvarez EXCH 25.00 60.00
27 Aristides Aquino 10.00 25.00
28 Adrian Beltre 10.00 25.00
29 Troy Glaus 6.00 15.00
30 Eugenio Suarez 5.00 12.00
33 Frank Thomas EXCH 20.00 50.00
34 Eloy Jimenez EXCH 20.00 50.00
36 Bobby Bradley 2.50 6.00
37 Kyle Lewis 25.00 60.00
38 Christin Stewart 2.50 6.00
39 Ty France 20.00 50.00
40 Nathaniel Lowe 6.00 15.00

2020 Donruss Optic Fireworks Signatures Holo

*HOLO: .5X TO 1.2X BASIC
RANDOM INSERTS IN PACKS
EXCHANGE DEADLINE 01/22/2022
21 Dylan Carlson 25.00 60.00
25 Yoan Moncada 25.00 60.00
26 Yordan Alvarez EXCH 40.00 100.00
37 Kyle Lewis 40.00 100.00

2020 Donruss Optic Highlights Signatures

RANDOM INSERTS IN PACKS
EXCHANGE DEADLINE 01/22/2022
1 Aaron Judge
2 Jose Abreu EXCH 4.00 10.00
3 Austin Riley 5.00 12.00
4 Juan Soto
5 Jose Altuve
6 Blake Snell 3.00 8.00
7 Ronald Acuna Jr. 40.00 100.00
8 Justin Turner 4.00 10.00
9 Pete Alonso 30.00 80.00
10 Vladimir Guerrero Jr. 20.00 50.00
11 Rafael Devers 10.00 25.00
12 Matt Chapman 4.00 10.00
13 Paul DeJong 4.00 10.00
14 Clayton Kershaw
15 Ozzie Albies
16 Josh Hader 3.00 8.00
17 Anthony Rizzo 15.00 40.00
18 Fernando Tatis Jr.
19 Rhys Hoskins 12.00 30.00

2020 Donruss Optic Highlights Signatures Black

*BLACK/20-35: .8X TO 2X BASIC
RANDOM INSERTS IN PACKS
PRINT RUNS B/WN 3-35 COPIES PER
NO PRICING QTY 15 OR LESS
EXCHANGE DEADLINE 01/22/2022
8 Justin Turner/20 15.00 40.00

2020 Donruss Optic Highlights Signatures Black Cracked Ice

*BLK CRKD ICE/20-25: .8X TO 2X BASIC
RANDOM INSERTS IN PACKS
PRINT RUNS B/WN 3-25 COPIES PER
NO PRICING QTY 15 OR LESS
EXCHANGE DEADLINE 01/22/2022
8 Justin Turner/25 15.00 40.00
15 Ozzie Albies/25 15.00 40.00

2020 Donruss Optic Highlights Signatures Blue

*BLUE/50: .6X TO 1.5X BASIC
*BLUE/20-35: .8X TO 2X BASIC
RANDOM INSERTS IN PACKS
PRINT RUNS B/WN 3-50 COPIES PER
NO PRICING QTY 15 OR LESS
EXCHANGE DEADLINE 01/22/2022
8 Justin Turner/20 15.00 40.00
15 Ozzie Albies/50 12.00 30.00

2020 Donruss Optic Highlights Signatures Carolina Blue

*CAR.BLUE/20-35: .8X TO 2X BASIC
RANDOM INSERTS IN PACKS
PRINT RUNS B/WN 3-35 COPIES PER
EXCHANGE DEADLINE 01/22/2022
8 Justin Turner/20 15.00 40.00

2020 Donruss Optic Highlights Signatures Holo

*HOLO: .5X TO 1.2X BASIC
RANDOM INSERTS IN PACKS
EXCHANGE DEADLINE 01/22/2022
8 Justin Turner 8.00 20.00
15 Ozzie Albies

2020 Donruss Optic Highlights Signatures Orange

*ORANGE/50: .6X TO 1.5X BASIC
*ORANGE/20: .8X TO 2X BASIC
RANDOM INSERTS IN PACKS
PRINT RUNS B/WN 3-50 COPIES PER
NO PRICING QTY 15 OR LESS
EXCHANGE DEADLINE 01/22/2022
8 Justin Turner/20 15.00 40.00
15 Ozzie Albies/50 12.00 30.00

2020 Donruss Optic Highlights Signatures Pink Velocity

*PINK VEL.: .5X TO 1.2X BASIC
RANDOM INSERTS IN PACKS
EXCHANGE DEADLINE 01/22/2022
8 Justin Turner 8.00 20.00
14 Clayton Kershaw 40.00 100.00
15 Ozzie Albies 10.00 25.00

2020 Donruss Optic Highlights Signatures Purple

*PURPLE/50: .6X TO 1.5X BASIC
*PURPLE/20: .8X TO 2X BASIC
RANDOM INSERTS IN PACKS
PRINT RUNS B/WN 3-50 COPIES PER
NO PRICING QTY 15 OR LESS
EXCHANGE DEADLINE 01/22/2022
8 Justin Turner/20 15.00 40.00
15 Ozzie Albies/50 12.00 30.00

2020 Donruss Optic Highlights Signatures Red

*RED/50: .6X TO 1.5X BASIC
*RED/20-35: .8X TO 2X BASIC
RANDOM INSERTS IN PACKS
PRINT RUNS B/WN 3-50 COPIES PER
NO PRICING QTY 15 OR LESS
EXCHANGE DEADLINE 01/22/2022
8 Justin Turner/20 15.00 40.00
15 Ozzie Albies/50 12.00 30.00

2020 Donruss Optic Highlights Signatures Teal Velocity

*TEAL VEL./20-35: .8X TO 2X BASIC
RANDOM INSERTS IN PACKS
PRINT RUNS B/WN 3-35 COPIES PER
NO PRICING QTY 15 OR LESS
EXCHANGE DEADLINE 01/22/2022
8 Justin Turner/35 15.00 40.00
15 Ozzie Albies/35 15.00 40.00

2020 Donruss Optic Illusions

RANDOM INSERTS IN PACKS
1 Jacob deGrom .75 2.00
2 Paul Goldschmidt .40 1.00
3 Buster Posey .50 1.25
4 Isan Diaz .40 1.00
5 Whit Merrifield .40 1.00
6 Yordan Alvarez 2.50 6.00
7 Mookie Betts .75 2.00
8 Eloy Jimenez .75 2.00
9 Corey Kluber .30 .75
10 Joey Votto .40 1.00
11 Josh Bell .30 .75
12 Austin Meadows .40 1.00
13 Shohei Ohtani .60 1.50
14 Trevor Story .40 1.00
15 Keston Hiura .50 1.25

2020 Donruss Optic Illusions Holo

*HOLO: 1X TO 2.5X BASIC
RANDOM INSERTS IN PACKS
15 Keston Hiura 2.00 5.00

2020 Donruss Optic Mythical

RANDOM INSERTS IN PACKS
*HOLO: 1X TO 2.5X BASIC
1 Luis Robert 5.00 12.00
2 Manny Machado .40 1.00
3 Francisco Lindor .40 1.00
4 Mike Trout 2.00 5.00
5 Cody Bellinger .75 2.00
6 Fernando Tatis Jr. 2.00 5.00
7 Wander Franco 2.50 6.00
8 Vladimir Guerrero Jr. .60 1.50
9 Javier Baez .50 1.25
10 Ronald Acuna Jr. 1.50 4.00
11 Alex Bregman .40 1.00
12 Aristides Aquino .60 1.50
13 Juan Soto 1.25 3.00
14 Aaron Judge 1.00 2.50
15 Pete Alonso 1.00 2.50

2020 Donruss Optic Pandora

*PANDORA DK: 1X TO 2.5X BASIC DK
*PANDORA RR: 1X TO 2.5X BASIC DK
*PANDORA VET: 1.5X TO 4X BASIC VET
RANDOM INSERTS IN PACKS
STATED PRINT RUN 99 SER.#'d SETS
32 Dustin May RR 6.00 15.00
33 Mauricio Dubon RR 4.00 10.00
37 Bo Bichette RR 25.00 60.00
38 Nico Hoerner RR 8.00 20.00
44 Gavin Lux RR 8.00 20.00
45 Yordan Alvarez RR 15.00 40.00
56 Kyle Lewis RR 25.00 60.00
62 Luis Robert RR 75.00 200.00
96 Shogo Akiyama RR 10.00 25.00

2020 Donruss Optic Pandora Blue

*PAND.BLUE DK: 1X TO 2.5X BASIC DK
*PAND.BLUE RR: 1X TO 2.5X BASIC DK
*PAND.BLUE VET: 1.5X TO 4X BASIC VET
RANDOM INSERTS IN PACKS
STATED PRINT RUN 99 SER.#'d SETS
32 Dustin May RR 6.00 15.00
33 Mauricio Dubon RR 4.00 10.00
37 Bo Bichette RR 25.00 60.00
38 Nico Hoerner RR 8.00 20.00
44 Gavin Lux RR 8.00 20.00
45 Yordan Alvarez RR 15.00 40.00
56 Kyle Lewis RR 25.00 60.00
62 Luis Robert RR 75.00 200.00
96 Shogo Akiyama RR 10.00 25.00

2020 Donruss Optic Pandora Purple

*PAND.PURP. DK: 1X TO 2.5X BASIC DK
*PAND.PURP.RR: 1X TO 2.5X BASIC DK
*PAND.PURP.VET: 1.5X TO 4X BASIC VET
RANDOM INSERTS IN PACKS
STATED PRINT RUN 99 SER.#'d SETS
32 Dustin May RR 6.00 15.00
33 Mauricio Dubon RR 4.00 10.00
37 Bo Bichette RR 25.00 60.00
38 Nico Hoerner RR 8.00 20.00
44 Gavin Lux RR 8.00 20.00
45 Yordan Alvarez RR 15.00 40.00
56 Kyle Lewis RR 25.00 60.00
62 Luis Robert RR 75.00 200.00
96 Shogo Akiyama RR 10.00 25.00

2020 Donruss Optic Pandora Red

*PAND.RED DK: 1X TO 2.5X BASIC DK
*PAND.RED RR: 1X TO 2.5X BASIC DK
*PAND.RED VET: 1.5X TO 4X BASIC VET
RANDOM INSERTS IN PACKS
STATED PRINT RUN 79 SER.#'d SETS
32 Dustin May RR 6.00 15.00
33 Mauricio Dubon RR 4.00 10.00
37 Bo Bichette RR 25.00 60.00
38 Nico Hoerner RR 8.00 20.00
44 Gavin Lux RR 8.00 20.00
45 Yordan Alvarez RR 15.00 40.00
56 Kyle Lewis RR 25.00 60.00
62 Luis Robert RR 75.00 200.00
96 Shogo Akiyama RR 10.00 25.00

2020 Donruss Optic Rated Prospects

RANDOM INSERTS IN PACKS
1 Wander Franco 5.00 12.00
2 Bobby Witt Jr. 1.50 4.00
3 Jo Adell 2.50 6.00
4 Casey Mize .75 2.00
5 Royce Lewis .60 1.50
6 Nate Pearson .75 2.00
7 Cristian Pache 2.00 5.00
8 Alex Kirilloff .50 1.25
9 Forrest Whitley .40 1.00
10 Dylan Carlson 1.00 2.50
11 Jasson Dominguez 12.00 30.00
12 Tristen Lutz .30 .75
13 Adley Rutschman 3.00 8.00
14 MacKenzie Gore .50 1.25
15 Jarred Kelenic 6.00 15.00
16 Joey Bart .75 2.00
17 CJ Abrams .75 2.00
18 Andrew Vaughn 1.00 2.50
19 Ryan Mountcastle 1.25 3.00
20 Nick Madrigal 1.00 2.50

2020 Donruss Optic Rated Prospects Holo

*HOLO: 1X TO 2.5X BASIC
RANDOM INSERTS IN PACKS
1 Wander Franco 15.00 40.00
4 Casey Mize 5.00 12.00
14 MacKenzie Gore 4.00 10.00
16 Joey Bart 4.00 10.00
17 CJ Abrams 3.00 8.00
20 Nick Madrigal 3.00 8.00

2020 Donruss Optic Rated Prospects Signatures

RANDOM INSERTS IN PACKS
EXCHANGE DEADLINE 01/22/2022
1 Wander Franco 40.00 100.00
2 Luis Robert
3 Forrest Whitley 4.00 10.00
4 Royce Lewis
5 Bobby Witt Jr.
6 Jo Adell 20.00 50.00
7 Alec Bohm 15.00 40.00
8 Alex Kirilloff 5.00 12.00
9 Dylan Carlson 15.00 40.00
10 Joey Bart 20.00 50.00
11 Jonathan India 30.00 80.00
12 Victor Mesa Jr. 10.00 25.00
13 JJ Bleday 6.00 15.00
14 Deivi Garcia 12.00 30.00
15 Jasson Dominguez 100.00 250.00
16 Miguel Amaya 2.50 6.00
17 Oneil Cruz 3.00 8.00
18 Andres Gimenez 20.00 50.00
19 Nick Neidert 2.50 6.00
20 Ronaldo Hernandez 2.50 6.00

2020 Donruss Optic Rated Prospects Signatures Black

*BLACK/50: .6X TO 1.5X BASIC
*BLACK/20-35: .8X TO 2X BASIC
RANDOM INSERTS IN PACKS
PRINT RUNS B/WN 15-50 COPIES PER
NO PRICING QTY 15 OR LESS
EXCHANGE DEADLINE 01/22/2022
1 Wander Franco/50 150.00 400.00
3 Forrest Whitley/35 8.00 20.00
5 Bobby Witt Jr./35 250.00 600.00
7 Alec Bohm/50 40.00 100.00
8 Alex Kirilloff/50 25.00 60.00
9 Dylan Carlson/50 30.00 80.00
15 Jasson Dominguez/50 400.00 1000.00
17 Oneil Cruz/50 12.00 30.00

2020 Donruss Optic Rated Prospects Signatures Black Cracked Ice

*BLK CRKD ICE: .8X TO 2X BASIC
RANDOM INSERTS IN PACKS
STATED PRINT RUN 25 SER.#'d SETS
EXCHANGE DEADLINE 01/22/2022
1 Wander Franco 200.00 500.00
2 Luis Robert 200.00 500.00
3 Forrest Whitley 8.00 20.00
5 Bobby Witt Jr. 250.00 600.00
7 Alec Bohm 50.00 120.00
8 Alex Kirilloff 30.00 80.00
9 Dylan Carlson 40.00 100.00
15 Jasson Dominguez 500.00 1200.00
17 Oneil Cruz 15.00 40.00

2020 Donruss Optic Rated Prospects Signatures Blue

*BLUE/50-75: .6X TO 1.5X BASIC
*BLUE/20: .8X TO 2X BASIC
RANDOM INSERTS IN PACKS
PRINT RUNS B/WN 20-75 COPIES PER
EXCHANGE DEADLINE 01/22/2022
1 Wander Franco/75 125.00 300.00
2 Luis Robert/20 200.00 500.00
3 Forrest Whitley/50 6.00 15.00
5 Bobby Witt Jr./50 200.00 500.00
7 Alec Bohm/50 40.00 100.00
8 Alex Kirilloff/50 25.00 60.00
9 Dylan Carlson/50 30.00 80.00
15 Jasson Dominguez/50 400.00 1000.00
17 Oneil Cruz/50 12.00 30.00

2020 Donruss Optic Rated Prospects Signatures Blue Mojo

*BLUE MOJO/49-99: .6X TO 1.5X BASIC
RANDOM INSERTS IN PACKS
PRINT RUNS B/WN 49-99 COPIES PER
EXCHANGE DEADLINE 01/22/2022
1 Wander Franco/99 125.00 300.00
2 Luis Robert/99 150.00 400.00
3 Forrest Whitley/99 6.00 15.00
5 Bobby Witt Jr./99 200.00 500.00
7 Alec Bohm/49 40.00 100.00
8 Alex Kirilloff/99 25.00 60.00
9 Dylan Carlson/99 30.00 80.00
15 Jasson Dominguez/49 400.00 1000.00
17 Oneil Cruz/99 12.00 30.00

2020 Donruss Optic Rated Prospects Signatures Carolina Blue

*CAR.BLUE/20-35: .8X TO 2X BASIC
RANDOM INSERTS IN PACKS
PRINT RUNS B/WN 15-35 COPIES PER
NO PRICING QTY 15 OR LESS
EXCHANGE DEADLINE 01/22/2022
1 Wander Franco/35 200.00 500.00
3 Forrest Whitley/35 8.00 20.00
5 Bobby Witt Jr./35 250.00 600.00
7 Alec Bohm/35 50.00 120.00
8 Alex Kirilloff/35 30.00 80.00
9 Dylan Carlson/35 40.00 100.00
15 Jasson Dominguez/35 500.00 1200.00
17 Oneil Cruz/35 15.00 40.00

2020 Donruss Optic Rated Prospects Signatures Green Mojo

*GRN MOJO/49-99: .6X TO 1.5X BASIC
RANDOM INSERTS IN PACKS
PRINT RUNS B/WN 49-99 COPIES PER
EXCHANGE DEADLINE 01/22/2022
1 Wander Franco/99 125.00 300.00
2 Luis Robert/99 150.00 400.00
3 Forrest Whitley/99 6.00 15.00
5 Bobby Witt Jr./99 200.00 500.00
7 Alec Bohm/49 40.00 100.00
8 Alex Kirilloff/99 25.00 60.00
9 Dylan Carlson/99 30.00 80.00
15 Jasson Dominguez/49 400.00 1000.00
17 Oneil Cruz/99 12.00 30.00

2020 Donruss Optic Rated Prospects Signatures Holo

*HOLO: .5X TO 1.2X BASIC
RANDOM INSERTS IN PACKS
EXCHANGE DEADLINE 01/22/2022
1 Wander Franco 60.00 150.00
2 Luis Robert 100.00 250.00
5 Bobby Witt Jr. 125.00 300.00
9 Dylan Carlson 25.00 60.00
15 Jasson Dominguez 150.00 400.00

2020 Donruss Optic Rated Prospects Signatures Orange

*ORANGE/50-75: .6X TO 1.5X BASIC
*ORANGE/20: .8X TO 2X BASIC
RANDOM INSERTS IN PACKS
PRINT RUNS B/WN 20-75 COPIES PER
EXCHANGE DEADLINE 01/22/2022
1 Wander Franco/75 125.00 300.00
2 Luis Robert/20 200.00 500.00
3 Forrest Whitley/50 6.00 15.00
5 Bobby Witt Jr./50 200.00 500.00
8 Alex Kirilloff/75 25.00 60.00
9 Dylan Carlson/75 30.00 80.00
15 Jasson Dominguez/75 200.00 500.00
17 Oneil Cruz/75 12.00 30.00

2020 Donruss Optic Rated Prospects Signatures Pink Velocity

*PINK VEL.: .5X TO 1.2X BASIC
RANDOM INSERTS IN PACKS
EXCHANGE DEADLINE 01/22/2022
1 Wander Franco 100.00 250.00
2 Luis Robert 100.00 250.00
5 Bobby Witt Jr. 125.00 300.00
9 Dylan Carlson 25.00 60.00
15 Jasson Dominguez 200.00 500.00

2020 Donruss Optic Rated Prospects Signatures Purple

*PURPLE/50-99: .6X TO 1.5X BASIC
*PURPLE/20: .8X TO 2X BASIC
RANDOM INSERTS IN PACKS
PRINT RUNS B/WN 20-99 COPIES PER
EXCHANGE DEADLINE 01/22/2022
1 Wander Franco/99 125.00 300.00
2 Luis Robert/20 200.00 500.00
3 Forrest Whitley/50 6.00 15.00
5 Bobby Witt Jr./50 200.00 500.00
8 Alex Kirilloff/75 25.00 60.00
9 Dylan Carlson/75 30.00 80.00
15 Jasson Dominguez/75 200.00 500.00
17 Oneil Cruz/75 12.00 30.00

2020 Donruss Optic Rated Prospects Signatures Red

*RED/50: .6X TO 1.5X BASIC
*RED/20-35: .8X TO 2X BASIC
RANDOM INSERTS IN PACKS
PRINT RUNS B/WN 15-50 COPIES PER
NO PRICING QTY 15 OR LESS
EXCHANGE DEADLINE 01/22/2022
1 Wander Franco/50 150.00 400.00
3 Forrest Whitley/50 6.00 15.00
5 Bobby Witt Jr./50 200.00 500.00
7 Alec Bohm/50 40.00 100.00
8 Alex Kirilloff/50 25.00 60.00
9 Dylan Carlson/50 30.00 80.00
15 Jasson Dominguez/50 400.00 1000.00
17 Oneil Cruz/50 12.00 30.00

2020 Donruss Optic Rated Prospects Signatures Red Mojo

*RED MOJO/49-99: .6X TO 1.5X BASIC
RANDOM INSERTS IN PACKS
PRINT RUNS B/WN 49-99 COPIES PER
EXCHANGE DEADLINE 01/22/2022
1 Wander Franco/99 125.00 300.00
2 Luis Robert/99 150.00 400.00
3 Forrest Whitley/99 6.00 15.00
5 Bobby Witt Jr./99 200.00 500.00
7 Alec Bohm/49 40.00 100.00
8 Alex Kirilloff/99 25.00 60.00
9 Dylan Carlson/99 30.00 80.00
15 Jasson Dominguez/49 400.00 1000.00
17 Oneil Cruz/99 12.00 30.00

2020 Donruss Optic Rated Prospects Signatures Teal Velocity

*TEAL VEL./30-35: .8X TO 2X BASIC
RANDOM INSERTS IN PACKS
PRINT RUNS B/WN 15-35 COPIES PER
NO PRICING QTY 15 OR LESS
EXCHANGE DEADLINE 01/22/2022
1 Wander Franco/35 200.00 500.00
3 Forrest Whitley/30 8.00 20.00
5 Bobby Witt Jr./30 250.00 600.00
7 Alec Bohm/35 50.00 120.00
8 Alex Kirilloff/35 30.00 80.00
9 Dylan Carlson/35 40.00 100.00
15 Jasson Dominguez/35 500.00 1200.00
17 Oneil Cruz/35 15.00 40.00

2020 Donruss Optic Rated Prospects Signatures White Mojo

*WHT MOJO/49-99: .6X TO 1.5X BASIC
RANDOM INSERTS IN PACKS
PRINT RUNS B/WN 49-99 COPIES PER
EXCHANGE DEADLINE 01/22/2022
1 Wander Franco/99 125.00 300.00
2 Luis Robert/99 150.00 400.00
3 Forrest Whitley/99 6.00 15.00
5 Bobby Witt Jr./99 200.00 500.00
7 Alec Bohm/49 40.00 100.00
8 Alex Kirilloff/99 25.00 60.00
9 Dylan Carlson/99 30.00 80.00
15 Jasson Dominguez/49 400.00 1000.00
17 Oneil Cruz/99 12.00 30.00

2020 Donruss Optic Rated Rookies Signatures

RANDOM INSERTS IN PACKS
EXCHANGE DEADLINE 01/22/2022
1 Aristides Aquino 8.00 20.00
2 Brock Burke 2.50 6.00
3 Jesus Luzardo 8.00 20.00
4 Aaron Civale 5.00 12.00
5 Jake Rogers 2.50 6.00
6 Brendan McKay 6.00 15.00
7 Nick Solak 5.00 12.00
8 Matt Thaiss 3.00 8.00
9 Zack Collins 4.00 10.00
10 Dylan Cease 4.00 10.00
11 Kyle Lewis 40.00 100.00
12 Justin Dunn 3.00 8.00
14 Sheldon Neuse 3.00 8.00
15 Adbert Alzolay 3.00 8.00
16 Isan Diaz 8.00 20.00
17 Bobby Bradley 2.50 6.00
18 Zac Gallen 6.00 15.00
19 Nico Hoerner 10.00 25.00
20 Dustin May 8.00 20.00
21 Bo Bichette 50.00 120.00
22 Logan Webb 4.00 10.00
23 Willi Castro 8.00 20.00
24 Jonathan Hernandez 2.50 6.00
25 Jake Fraley 3.00 8.00
26 A.J. Puk 6.00 15.00
27 Mauricio Dubon 3.00 8.00
28 Logan Allen 2.50 6.00
29 Gavin Lux 25.00 60.00
30 Jordan Yamamoto 6.00 15.00
31 Domingo Leyba 3.00 8.00
32 Anthony Kay 2.50 6.00
33 Yu Chang 4.00 10.00
34 Adrian Morejon 2.50 6.00
35 Tony Gonsolin 6.00 15.00
36 Bryan Abreu 2.50 6.00
37 Sam Hilliard 4.00 10.00
38 Brusdar Graterol 4.00 10.00
39 Edwin Rios 6.00 15.00
40 Lewis Thorpe 2.50 6.00
41 Rico Garcia 4.00 10.00
42 Jaylin Davis 4.00 10.00
43 Patrick Sandoval 4.00 10.00
44 Abraham Toro 3.00 8.00
45 Michael King 4.00 10.00
46 Deivy Grullon 2.50 6.00
47 Donnie Walton 6.00 15.00
48 Tyrone Taylor 2.50 6.00
49 Ronald Bolanos 2.50 6.00
50 T.J. Zeuch 2.50 6.00
51 Randy Arozarena 40.00 100.00
52 Andres Munoz 4.00 10.00
53 Sean Murphy 4.00 10.00
54 Travis Demeritte 4.00 10.00
55 Yordan Alvarez 30.00 80.00
56 Tres Barrera 5.00 12.00
57 Danny Mendick 3.00 8.00
58 Josh Rojas 2.50 6.00
59 Michel Baez 2.50 6.00
60 Joe Palumbo 2.50 6.00
61 Yonathan Daza 3.00 8.00

2020 Donruss Optic Rated Rookies Signatures Black

*BLACK/50: .6X TO 1.5X BASIC
*BLACK/35: .8X TO 2X BASIC
RANDOM INSERTS IN PACKS
PRINT RUNS B/WN 35-50 COPIES PER
EXCHANGE DEADLINE 01/22/2022
1 Aristides Aquino/50 15.00 40.00
13 Trent Grisham/50 20.00 50.00
21 Bo Bichette/50 100.00 250.00
33 Yu Chang/50 10.00 25.00
53 Sean Murphy/50 10.00 25.00

2020 Donruss Optic Rated Rookies Signatures Black Cracked Ice

*BLK CRKD ICE: .8X TO 2X BASIC
RANDOM INSERTS IN PACKS
STATED PRINT RUN 25 SER.#'d SETS
EXCHANGE DEADLINE 01/22/2022
1 Aristides Aquino 20.00 50.00
13 Trent Grisham 25.00 60.00
21 Bo Bichette 125.00 300.00
33 Yu Chang 12.00 30.00
53 Sean Murphy 12.00 30.00

2020 Donruss Optic Rated Rookies Signatures Blue

*BLUE/50-75: .6X TO 1.5X BASIC
RANDOM INSERTS IN PACKS
PRINT RUNS B/WN 50-75 COPIES PER
EXCHANGE DEADLINE 01/22/2022
1 Aristides Aquino/75 15.00 40.00
13 Trent Grisham/75 20.00 50.00
33 Yu Chang/75 10.00 25.00
53 Sean Murphy/75 10.00 25.00

2020 Donruss Optic Rated Rookies Signatures Blue Mojo

*BLUE MOJO/49-99: .6X TO 1.5X BASIC
RANDOM INSERTS IN PACKS
PRINT RUNS B/WN 49-99 COPIES PER
EXCHANGE DEADLINE 01/22/2022
1 Aristides Aquino/99 15.00 40.00
13 Trent Grisham/99 20.00 50.00
33 Yu Chang/99 10.00 25.00
53 Sean Murphy/99 10.00 25.00

2020 Donruss Optic Rated Rookies Signatures Carolina Blue

*CAR.BLUE/35: .8X TO 2X BASIC
RANDOM INSERTS IN PACKS
STATED PRINT RUN 35 SER.#'d SETS
EXCHANGE DEADLINE 01/22/2022
1 Aristides Aquino 20.00 50.00
21 Bo Bichette 125.00 300.00
33 Yu Chang 12.00 30.00
53 Sean Murphy 12.00 30.00

2020 Donruss Optic Rated Rookies Signatures Green Mojo

*GRN MOJO/49-99: .6X TO 1.5X BASIC
RANDOM INSERTS IN PACKS
PRINT RUNS B/WN 49-99 COPIES PER
EXCHANGE DEADLINE 01/22/2022
1 Aristides Aquino/99 15.00 40.00
13 Trent Grisham/99 20.00 50.00
33 Yu Chang/99 10.00 25.00
53 Sean Murphy/99 10.00 25.00

2020 Donruss Optic Rated Rookies Signatures Holo

*HOLO: .5X TO 1.2X BASIC
RANDOM INSERTS IN PACKS
EXCHANGE DEADLINE 01/22/2022
13 Trent Grisham 15.00 40.00
33 Yu Chang 8.00 20.00
53 Sean Murphy 8.00 20.00

2020 Donruss Optic Rated Rookies Signatures Orange

*ORANGE/50-99: .6X TO 1.5X BASIC
RANDOM INSERTS IN PACKS
PRINT RUNS B/WN 50-99 COPIES PER
EXCHANGE DEADLINE 01/22/2022
1 Aristides Aquino/99 15.00 40.00
33 Yu Chang/99 10.00 25.00
53 Sean Murphy/99 10.00 25.00

2020 Donruss Optic Rated Rookies Signatures Pink Velocity

*PINK VEL.: .5X TO 1.2X BASIC
RANDOM INSERTS IN PACKS
EXCHANGE DEADLINE 01/22/2022
33 Yu Chang 8.00 20.00
53 Sean Murphy 8.00 20.00

2020 Donruss Optic Rated Rookies Signatures Purple

*PURPLE/75-125: .6X TO 1.5X BASIC
RANDOM INSERTS IN PACKS
PRINT RUNS B/WN 75-125 COPIES PER
EXCHANGE DEADLINE 01/22/2022
1 Aristides Aquino/125 15.00 40.00
13 Trent Grisham/125 20.00 50.00
33 Yu Chang/125 10.00 25.00
53 Sean Murphy/125 10.00 25.00

2020 Donruss Optic Rated Rookies Signatures Red

*RED/50: .6X TO 1.5X BASIC
*RED/35: .8X TO 2X BASIC
RANDOM INSERTS IN PACKS
PRINT RUNS B/WN 35-50 COPIES PER
EXCHANGE DEADLINE 01/22/2022
1 Aristides Aquino/50 15.00 40.00
21 Bo Bichette/50 100.00 250.00
33 Yu Chang/50 10.00 25.00
53 Sean Murphy/50 10.00 25.00

2020 Donruss Optic Rated Rookies Signatures Red Mojo

*RED MOJO/49-99: .6X TO 1.5X BASIC
RANDOM INSERTS IN PACKS
PRINT RUNS B/WN 49-99 COPIES PER
EXCHANGE DEADLINE 01/22/2022
1 Aristides Aquino/99 15.00 40.00
13 Trent Grisham/99 20.00 50.00
33 Yu Chang/99 10.00 25.00
53 Sean Murphy/99 10.00 25.00

2020 Donruss Optic Rated Rookies Signatures Teal Velocity

*TEAL VEL./30-35: .8X TO 2X BASIC
RANDOM INSERTS IN PACKS
PRINT RUNS B/WN 30-35 COPIES PER
EXCHANGE DEADLINE 01/22/2022
1 Aristides Aquino/35 20.00 50.00
13 Trent Grisham/35 25.00 60.00
21 Bo Bichette/35 125.00 300.00

33 Yu Chang/35 12.00 30.00
53 Sean Murphy/35 12.00 30.00

2020 Donruss Optic Rated Rookies Signatures White Mojo

*WHT MOJO/49-99: .6X TO 1.5X BASIC
RANDOM INSERTS IN PACKS
PRINT RUNS B/WN 49-99 COPIES PER
EXCHANGE DEADLINE 01/22/2022
1 Aristides Aquino/99 15.00 40.00
13 Trent Grisham/99 20.00 50.00
33 Yu Chang/99 10.00 25.00
53 Sean Murphy/99 10.00 25.00

2020 Donruss Optic Retro '86

RANDOM INSERTS IN PACKS
*HOLO: 1X TO 2.5X BASIC
1 Cal Ripken 1.25 3.00
2 Kirby Puckett .40 1.00
3 George Brett .75 2.00
4 Rickey Henderson .40 1.00
5 Jose Canseco .30 .75
6 Nolan Ryan 1.25 3.00
7 Alan Trammell .30 .75
8 Tony Gwynn .40 1.00
9 Darryl Strawberry .25 .60
10 Paul Molitor .40 1.00
11 Roger Clemens .50 1.25
12 Wade Boggs .30 .75
13 Barry Larkin .30 .75
14 Andres Galarraga .30 .75
15 Kevin Mitchell .25 .60
16 Don Mattingly .75 2.00
17 Bert Blyleven .30 .75
18 Jim Rice .30 .75
19 Keith Hernandez .25 .60
20 Eddie Murray .30 .75
21 Gary Carter .30 .75
22 Dave Winfield .30 .75
23 Dale Murphy .40 1.00
24 Robin Yount .40 1.00
25 Dwight Gooden .25 .60

2020 Donruss Optic Retro '86 Signatures

RANDOM INSERTS IN PACKS
EXCHANGE DEADLINE 01/22/2022
*PANDORA/25: .8X TO 2X BASIC
*PAN.BLUE/25: .8X TO 2X BASIC
*PAN.PURP./25: .8X TO 2X BASIC
*PAN.RED/25: .8X TO 2X BASIC
1 Noelvi Marte 10.00 25.00
2 Daulton Varsho 4.00 10.00
3 Freudis Nova 2.50 6.00
4 Miguel Vargas 6.00 15.00
5 Matthew Liberatore 3.00 8.00
6 Alek Thomas 3.00 8.00
7 Deivi Garcia 12.00 30.00
8 Luis Robert EXCH 100.00 250.00
9 Nick Madrigal 12.00 30.00
10 Hunter Greene 10.00 25.00
11 Evan White 8.00 20.00
12 Cristian Pache EXCH 12.00 30.00
13 Triston McKenzie 8.00 20.00
14 CJ Abrams 8.00 20.00
15 Shun Yamaguchi 3.00 8.00
16 CC Sabathia
17 Stephen Piscotty 6.00 15.00
18 Fernando Tatis Jr. 50.00 120.00
19 Randy Johnson EXCH
20 Cody Bellinger EXCH 40.00 100.00
21 Andrew McCutchen 25.00 60.00
22 Alex Rodriguez EXCH
24 Chipper Jones
25 Anthony Rizzo EXCH
26 Joey Votto 15.00 40.00
27 Jose Altuve 12.00 30.00
28 Vladimir Guerrero 15.00 40.00
29 Wade Boggs 12.00 30.00
30 Juan Marichal 8.00 20.00
31 Don Mattingly 30.00 80.00
32 Jose Abreu EXCH 5.00 12.00
33 Dustin Pedroia 10.00 25.00
34 Corey Seager EXCH
35 Nomar Mazara 2.50 6.00
36 Dakota Hudson 3.00 8.00
37 Aaron Sanchez 3.00 8.00
38 Mike Zunino 2.50 6.00
39 Raimel Tapia 2.50 6.00
41 Ryan O'Hearn 2.50 6.00
42 Jake Cave 3.00 8.00
43 Austin Dean 2.50 6.00
44 Taylor Clarke 2.50 6.00
45 Domingo German 3.00 8.00
46 Yu Chang 4.00 10.00

2020 Donruss Optic Retro '86 Signatures Holo

*HOLO: .5X TO 1.2X BASIC
RANDOM INSERTS IN PACKS
EXCHANGE DEADLINE 01/22/2022
24 Chipper Jones 40.00 100.00
34 Corey Seager EXCH 10.00 25.00

2020 Donruss Optic Signature Series

RANDOM INSERTS IN PACKS
EXCHANGE DEADLINE 01/22/2022
3 Jarren Duran 10.00 25.00
4 Tyler Freeman 3.00 8.00
5 Tarik Skubal 10.00 25.00
6 Vidal Brujan 8.00 20.00
7 Logan Gilbert 3.00 8.00
8 Ke'Bryan Hayes 12.00 30.00
9 Jesus Sanchez 4.00 10.00
10 Jarred Kelenic 25.00 60.00
11 Taylor Trammell 5.00 12.00
12 Ryan Mountcastle 12.00 30.00
13 Victor Victor Mesa 4.00 10.00
14 Heliot Ramos 4.00 10.00
15 Kwang-Hyun Kim 10.00 25.00
16 Alex Bregman EXCH 10.00 25.00
17 CC Sabathia 12.00 30.00
18 Adam Haseley 3.00 8.00
19 Tanner Rainey 2.50 6.00
20 Joe Ryan 3.00 8.00
21 Luis Ortiz 2.50 6.00
22 Jose Suarez 2.50 6.00
23 Mauricio Dubon 3.00 8.00
24 Edmundo Sosa 3.00 8.00
25 Monte Harrison 4.00 10.00
26 Brent Honeywell 3.00 8.00
27 Jonathan Davis 3.00 8.00
28 Eric Haase 2.50 6.00
29 Brian Anderson 2.50 6.00
30 Dylan Cease 4.00 10.00
31 Thomas Pannone 4.00 10.00
32 Duane Underwood 2.50 6.00
33 Cole Tucker 4.00 10.00
34 Clint Frazier 8.00 20.00
35 Brandon Lowe 6.00 15.00
36 Jose Berrios 3.00 8.00
37 Xander Bogaerts EXCH
38 Wil Myers 3.00 8.00
39 Jonathan Lucroy 3.00 8.00
40 Cole Hamels 3.00 8.00
41 Adam Plutko 2.50 6.00
42 Josh Naylor 2.50 6.00
43 Yandy Diaz 3.00 8.00
44 Michael Taylor 2.50 6.00
45 Corbin Burnes 8.00 20.00
46 Gleyber Torres EXCH
47 Mitch Moreland 2.50 6.00
48 Rickey Henderson 25.00 60.00
49 Aaron Judge 50.00 120.00
50 Vladimir Guerrero Jr. 20.00 50.00

2020 Donruss Optic Signature Series Holo

*HOLO: .5X TO 1.2X BASIC
RANDOM INSERTS IN PACKS
EXCHANGE DEADLINE 01/22/2022
46 Gleyber Torres EXCH 30.00 80.00

2020 Donruss Optic Signature Series Pandora

*PANDORA/20-35: .8X TO 2X BASIC
RANDOM INSERTS IN PACKS
PRINT RUNS B/WN 5-35 COPIES PER
NO PRICING QTY 15 OR LESS
EXCHANGE DEADLINE 01/22/2022
15 Kwang-Hyun Kim/25 25.00 60.00

2020 Donruss Optic Signature Series Pandora Blue

*PAN.BLUE/20-35: .8X TO 2X BASIC
RANDOM INSERTS IN PACKS
PRINT RUNS B/WN 5-35 COPIES PER
NO PRICING QTY 15 OR LESS
EXCHANGE DEADLINE 01/22/2022
15 Kwang-Hyun Kim/25 25.00 60.00

2020 Donruss Optic Signature Series Pandora Purple

*PAN.PURP./20-35: .8X TO 2X BASIC
RANDOM INSERTS IN PACKS
PRINT RUNS B/WN 5-35 COPIES PER
NO PRICING QTY 15 OR LESS
EXCHANGE DEADLINE 01/22/2022
15 Kwang-Hyun Kim/25 25.00 60.00

2020 Donruss Optic Signature Series Pandora Red

*PAN.RED/20-35: .8X TO 2X BASIC
RANDOM INSERTS IN PACKS
PRINT RUNS B/WN 5-35 COPIES PER
NO PRICING QTY 15 OR LESS
EXCHANGE DEADLINE 01/22/2022
15 Kwang-Hyun Kim/25 25.00 60.00

2020 Donruss Optic Stained Glass

RANDOM INSERTS IN PACKS
1 Nolan Arenado .60 1.50
2 Christian Yelich .50 1.25
3 Trey Mancini .40 1.00
4 Miguel Cabrera .40 1.00
5 Ketel Marte .30 .75
6 Gavin Lux 4.00 10.00
7 Rafael Devers .50 1.25
8 Evan White .60 1.50
9 Bo Bichette 5.00 12.00
10 Matt Chapman .40 1.00
11 Gleyber Torres .75 2.00
12 Bryce Harper .60 1.50
13 Josh Donaldson .30 .75
14 Yoshitomo Tsutsugo .60 1.50
15 Kris Bryant .50 1.25

2020 Donruss Optic Stained Glass Holo

*HOLO: 1X TO 2.5X BASIC
RANDOM INSERTS IN PACKS
1 Nolan Arenado 5.00 12.00

2020 Donruss Optic The Rookies

RANDOM INSERTS IN PACKS
1 Yordan Alvarez 3.00 8.00
2 Dylan Cease .40 1.00
3 Dustin May .75 2.00
4 Aristides Aquino .60 1.50
5 A.J. Puk .40 1.00
6 Bo Bichette 4.00 10.00
7 Brendan McKay .40 1.00
8 Gavin Lux 1.25 3.00
9 Luis Robert 5.00 12.00
10 Yoshitomo Tsutsugo .60 1.50

2020 Donruss Optic The Rookies Holo

*HOLO: 1X TO 2.5X BASIC
RANDOM INSERTS IN PACKS
3 Dustin May 3.00 8.00
5 A.J. Puk 3.00 8.00
8 Gavin Lux 5.00 12.00

2002 Donruss Originals Samples

*SAMPLES: 1.5X TO 4X BASIC
ONE PER SEALED BBCM 212
*GOLD:1.5X TO 4X BASIC SAMPLES
GOLD: 10% OF TOTAL PRINT RUN

2002 Donruss Originals

COMP.LOW SET (400) 100.00 200.00
COMP.UPDATE SET (25) 10.00 25.00
COMMON CARD (1-400) .15 .40
COMMON SP .40 1.00
SP APPX 20% TOUGHER THAN BASE CARD
COMMON CARD (401-425) .30 .75
401-425 ODDS 1:3 HOBBY, 1:4 RETAIL
401-425 DIST.IN DONRUSS ROOKIES PACKS
COMP.WILLIAMS PUZZLE (63) 15.00 40.00
PUZZLE PIECES RANDOM IN PACKS
1 So Taguchi 82 RR RC .20 .50
2 Allan Simpson 82 RR RC .15 .40
3 Brian Mallette 82 RR RC .15 .40
4 Ben Howard 82 RR RC .15 .40
5 Kazuhisa Ishii 82 RR RC .20 .50
6 Francis Beltran 82 RR RC .15 .40
7 Jorge Padilla 82 RR RC .15 .40
8 Brandon Puffer 82 RR RC .15 .40
9 Oliver Perez 82 RR RC .60 1.50
10 Kirk Saarloos 82 RR RC .15 .40
11 Travis Driskill 82 RR RC .15 .40
12 Jeremy Lambert 82 RR RC .15 .40
13 John Foster 82 RR RC .15 .40
14 Steve Kent 82 RR RC .15 .40
15 Shawn Sedlacek 82 RR RC .15 .40
16 Alex Rodriguez 82 .50 1.50
17 Lance Berkman 82 .15 .40
18 Kevin Brown 82 .15 .40
19 Garret Anderson 82 .15 .40
20 Bobby Abreu 82 .15 .40
21 Richard Hidalgo 82 .15 .40
22 Matt Morris 82 .15 .40
23 Manny Ramirez 82 SP .60 1.50
24 Derek Jeter 82 1.00 2.50
25 Kerry Wood 82 .15 .40
26 Mark Grace 82 .25 .60
27 Edgar Martinez 82 .25 .60
28 Nomar Garciaparra 82 .60 1.50
29 Roberto Alomar 82 SP .60 1.50
30 Jason Giambi 82 .15 .40
31 Juan Gonzalez 82 SP .40 1.00
32 Albert Pujols 82 .75 2.00
33 Juan Cruz 82 .15 .40
34 Troy Glaus 82 .15 .40
35 Greg Maddux 82 .60 1.50
36 Adam Dunn 82 SP .40 1.00
37 J.D. Drew 82 .15 .40
38 Tsuyoshi Shinjo 82 .15 .40
39 Vladimir Guerrero 82 .40 1.00
40 Barry Bonds 82 1.00 2.50
41 Carlos Delgado 82 .15 .40
42 Ken Griffey Jr. 82 .75 2.00
43 Carlos Pena 82 .15 .40
44 Jeff Kent 82 .15 .40
45 Roger Clemens 82 SP 1.50 4.00
46 Frank Thomas 82 .40 1.00
47 Larry Walker 82 .15 .40
48 Pedro Martinez 82 .25 .60
49 Moises Alou 82 .15 .40
50 Andruw Jones 82 SP .60 1.50
51 Luis Gonzalez 82 .15 .40
52 Adrian Beltre 82 .15 .40
53 Bobby Hill 82 .15 .40
54 Roy Oswalt 82 .15 .40
55 Tim Hudson 82 .15 .40
56 Trot Nixon 82 .15 .40
57 Jeff Bagwell 82 .25 .60
58 Bernie Williams 82 .25 .60
59 Magglio Ordonez 82 SP .40 1.00
60 Bartolo Colon 82 .15 .40
61 Shawn Green 82 .15 .40
62 Mark Buehrle 82 .15 .40
63 Sean Casey 82 .15 .40
64 Rickey Henderson 82 .40 1.00
65 Aramis Ramirez 82 SP .40 1.00
66 Ichiro Suzuki 82 .75 2.00
67 Cliff Floyd 82 .15 .40
68 Darin Erstad 82 .15 .40
69 Paul LoDuca 82 .15 .40
70 Ivan Rodriguez 82 .25 .60
71 Mo Vaughn 82 .15 .40
72 Todd Helton 82 SP .60 1.50
73 Raul Mondesi 82 .15 .40
74 Sammy Sosa 82 .40 1.00
75 Cristian Guzman 82 .15 .40
76 Jimmy Rollins 82 .15 .40
77 Hideo Nomo 82 .40 1.00
78 C.C. Sabathia 82 .15 .40
79 Wade Miller 82 .15 .40
80 Drew Henson 82 SP .40 1.00
81 Chipper Jones 82 .40 1.00
82 Miguel Tejada 82 .15 .40
83 Freddy Garcia 82 .15 .40
84 Richie Sexson 82 .15 .40
85 Robin Ventura 82 .15 .40
86 Jose Vidro 82 .15 .40
87 Rich Aurilla 82 .15 .40
88 Scott Rolen 82 .25 .60
89 Carlos Beltran 82 .15 .40
90 Austin Kearns 82 SP .40 1.00
91 Kazuhiro Sasaki 82 .15 .40
92 Carlos Hernandez 82 .15 .40
93 Randy Johnson 82 .40 1.00
94 Jim Thome 82 .25 .60
95 Curt Schilling 82 .15 .40
96 Alfonso Soriano 82 SP .40 1.00
97 Barry Larkin 82 .25 .60
98 Rafael Palmeiro 82 .25 .60
99 Tom Glavine 82 .25 .60
100 Barry Zito 82 .15 .40
101 Craig Biggio 82 .25 .60
102 Mike Piazza 82 .60 1.50
103 Ben Sheets 82 .15 .40
104 Mark Mulder 82 .15 .40
105 Mike Mussina 82 .25 .60
106 Jim Edmonds 82 .15 .40
107 Paul Konerko 82 .15 .40
108 Pat Burrell 82 .15 .40
109 Chan Ho Park 82 .15 .40
110 Mike Sweeney 82 .15 .40
111 Phil Nevin 82 .15 .40
112 Brian Giles 82 .15 .40
113 Eric Chavez 82 SP .40 1.00
114 Corey Patterson 82 .15 .40
115 Gary Sheffield 82 .15 .40
116 Kazuhisa Ishii 84 RR RC .20 .50
117 Kyle Kane 84 RR RC .15 .40
118 Eric Junge 84 RR RC .15 .40
119 Luis Ugueto 84 RR RC .15 .40
120 Cam Esslinger 84 RR RC .15 .40
121 Earl Snyder 84 RR RC .15 .40
122 Oliver Perez 84 RR RC .60 1.50
123 Victor Alvarez 84 RR RC .15 .40
124 Tom Shearn 84 RR RC .15 .40
125 Corey Thurman 84 RR RC .15 .40
126 Satoru Komiyama 84 RR RC .15 .40
127 Hansel Izquierdo 84 RR RC .15 .40
128 Elio Serrano 84 RR RC .15 .40
129 Mike Crudale 84 RR RC .15 .40
130 Chris Snelling 84 RR RC .25 .60
131 Nomar Garciaparra 84 .60 1.50
132 Roger Clemens 84 .75 2.00
133 Hank Blalock 84 .25 .60
134 Eric Chavez 84 .15 .40
135 Corey Patterson 84 .15 .40
136 Richie Sexson 84 .15 .40
137 Freddy Garcia 84 .15 .40
138 Miguel Tejada 84 .15 .40
139 Alex Rodriguez 84 SP 1.00 2.50
140 Adrian Beltre 84 .15 .40
141 Bobby Abreu 84 .15 .40
142 Bret Boone 84 .15 .40
143 Tim Hudson 84 .15 .40
144 Roy Oswalt 84 .15 .40
145 Derek Jeter 84 1.00 2.50
146 Rich Aurilla 84 .15 .40
147 Mark Grace 84 .25 .60
148 Kerry Wood 84 SP .40 1.00
149 Geronimo Gil 84 .15 .40
150 Mark Buehrle 84 .15 .40
151 Jim Edmonds 84 .15 .40
152 Ichiro Suzuki 84 .75 2.00
153 Juan Gonzalez 84 .15 .40
154 Darin Erstad 84 .15 .40
155 Barry Bonds 84 SP 2.00 5.00
156 Greg Maddux 84 .60 1.50
157 Adam Dunn 84 .15 .40
158 Todd Helton 84 .25 .60
159 Roberto Alomar 84 .25 .60
160 Sammy Sosa 84 .40 1.00
161 Sean Burroughs 84 .15 .40
162 Albert Pujols 84 .75 2.00
163 Carlos Delgado 84 .15 .40
164 Frank Thomas 84 .40 1.00
165 Ken Griffey Jr. 84 .75 2.00
166 Jason Giambi 84 SP .40 1.00
167 Chipper Jones 84 .40 1.00
168 Ivan Rodriguez 84 .25 .60
169 Pedro Martinez 84 SP .60 1.50
170 Gary Sheffield 84 .15 .40
171 Andruw Jones 84 .25 .60
172 Luis Gonzalez 84 SP .40 1.00
173 Raul Mondesi 84 .15 .40
174 Jose Vidro 84 .15 .40
175 Garret Anderson 84 SP .40 1.00
176 Scott Rolen 84 .25 .60
177 Kazuhiro Sasaki 84 .15 .40
178 Jeff Bagwell 84 .25 .60
179 Manny Ramirez 84 .25 .60
180 Jim Thome 84 .25 .60
181 Ben Sheets 84 .15 .40
182 Randy Johnson 84 .40 1.00
183 Lance Berkman 84 .15 .40
184 Shawn Green 84 .15 .40
185 Rickey Henderson 84 SP .75 2.00
186 Edgar Martinez 84 .25 .60
187 Barry Larkin 84 .25 .60
188 Bernie Williams 84 .25 .60
189 Luis Aparicio 84 .15 .40
190 Troy Glaus 84 SP .40 1.00
191 Mike Mussina 84 .25 .60
192 Pee Wee Reese 84 .25 .60
193 Craig Biggio 84 .25 .60
194 Vladimir Guerrero 84 .40 1.00
195 J.D. Drew 84 .15 .40
196 Jeff Kent 84 .15 .40
197 Dewon Brazelton 84 .15 .40
198 Tsuyoshi Shinjo 84 SP .40 1.00
199 Sean Casey 84 .15 .40
200 Hideo Nomo 84 .40 1.00
201 C.C. Sabathia 84 .15 .40
202 Larry Walker 84 .15 .40
203 Mark Teixeira 84 .40 1.00
204 Mike Sweeney 84 SP .40 1.00
205 Moises Alou 84 .15 .40
206 Mark Prior 84 .25 .60
207 Javier Vazquez 84 .15 .40
208 Phil Nevin 84 SP .40 1.00
209 Harmon Killebrew 84 .40 1.00
210 Brian Giles 84 .15 .40
211 Carlos Beltran 84 .15 .40
212 Don Drysdale 84 .25 .60
213 Matt Morris 84 .15 .40
214 Trot Nixon 84 .15 .40
215 Magglio Ordonez 84 .15 .40
216 Curt Schilling 84 SP .40 1.00
217 Mark Mulder 84 .15 .40
218 Alfonso Soriano 84 .15 .40
219 Rafael Palmeiro 84 SP .60 1.50
220 Tom Glavine 84 .25 .60
221 Barry Zito 84 .15 .40
222 Mike Piazza 84 .60 1.50
223 Bartolo Colon 84 .15 .40
224 Cliff Floyd 84 .15 .40
225 Paul LoDuca 84 SP .40 1.00
226 Cristian Guzman 84 .15 .40
227 Mo Vaughn 84 .15 .40
228 Aramis Ramirez 84 .15 .40
229 Pat Burrell 84 .15 .40
230 Chan Ho Park 84 .15 .40
231 Satoru Komiyama 86 RR RC .15 .40
232 Brandon Backe 86 RR RC .20 .50
233 Anderson Machado 86 RR RC .15 .40
234 Doug Devore 86 RR RC .15 .40
235 Steve Bechler 86 RR RC .15 .40
236 John Ennis 86 RR RC .15 .40
237 Rodrigo Rosario 86 RR RC .15 .40
238 Jorge Sosa 86 RR RC .20 .50
239 Ken Huckaby 86 RR RC .15 .40
240 Mike Moriarty 86 RR RC .15 .40
241 Kirk Saarloos 86 RR RC .15 .40
242 Kevin Frederick 86 RR RC .15 .40
243 Aaron Guiel 86 RR RC .15 .40
244 Jose Rodriguez 86 RR RC .15 .40
245 So Taguchi 86 RR RC .20 .50
246 Albert Pujols 86 .75 2.00
247 Derek Jeter 86 1.00 2.50
248 Brian Giles 86 .15 .40
249 Mike Cameron 86 .15 .40
250 Josh Beckett 86 .15 .40
251 Ken Griffey Jr. 86 SP 1.50 4.00
252 Aramis Ramirez 86 .15 .40
253 Miguel Tejada 86 .15 .40
254 Carlos Delgado 86 .15 .40
255 Pedro Martinez 86 .25 .60
256 Raul Mondesi 86 .15 .40
257 Roger Clemens 86 .75 2.00
258 Gary Sheffield 86 .15 .40
259 Jose Vidro 86 SP .40 1.00
260 Alex Rodriguez 86 .50 1.50
261 Larry Walker 86 .15 .40
262 Mark Mulder 86 .15 .40
263 Scott Rolen 86 .25 .60
264 Tim Hudson 86 .15 .40
265 Manny Ramirez 86 .25 .60
266 Rich Aurilla 86 .15 .40
267 Roy Oswalt 86 .15 .40
268 Mark Grace 86 .25 .60
269 Lance Berkman 86 SP .40 1.00
270 Nomar Garciaparra 86 SP 1.25 3.00
271 Barry Bonds 86 1.00 2.50
272 Ryan Klesko 86 .15 .40
273 Ichiro Suzuki 86 .75 2.00
274 Shawn Green 86 .15 .40
275 Darin Erstad 86 .15 .40
276 Bernie Williams 86 .25 .60
277 Greg Maddux 86 SP 1.25 3.00
278 Eric Hinske 86 .15 .40
279 Randy Johnson 86 .40 1.00
280 Todd Helton 86 .25 .60
281 Sammy Sosa 86 SP .75 2.00
282 Nick Johnson 86 .15 .40
283 Jose Cruz Jr. 86 .15 .40
284 Frank Thomas 86 .40 1.00
285 Tsuyoshi Shinjo 86 .15 .40
286 Troy Glaus 86 .15 .40
287 Jason Giambi 86 .15 .40
288 Chipper Jones 86 SP .75 2.00
289 Roberto Alomar 86 .25 .60
290 Bobby Hill 86 .15 .40
291 Garret Anderson 86 .15 .40
292 Andruw Jones 86 .25 .60
293 Luis Gonzalez 86 .15 .40
294 Mike Mussina 86 .25 .60
295 Ivan Rodriguez 86 SP .60 1.50
296 Barry Larkin 86 .25 .60
297 Kazuhiro Sasaki 86 .15 .40
298 Alfonso Soriano 86 .15 .40
299 Jeff Bagwell 86 SP .60 1.50
300 Bobby Abreu 86 .15 .40
301 Ben Sheets 86 .15 .40
302 Curt Schilling 86 .15 .40
303 Jim Thome 86 .25 .60
304 Kerry Wood 86 .15 .40
305 Mark Buehrle 86 SP .40 1.00
306 Rickey Henderson 86 .40 1.00
307 Rafael Palmeiro 86 .25 .60
308 Jim Edmonds 86 .15 .40
309 Mike Piazza 86 .60 1.50
310 Edgar Martinez 86 .25 .60
311 Tom Glavine 86 .25 .60
312 Adrian Beltre 86 .15 .40
313 Adam Dunn 86 .15 .40
314 Craig Biggio 86 .25 .60
315 Vladimir Guerrero 86 SP .75 2.00
316 Bret Boone 86 .15 .40
317 Hideo Nomo 86 SP .75 2.00
318 Jeff Kent 86 .15 .40
319 Juan Gonzalez 86 .15 .40
320 Sean Casey 86 .15 .40
321 C.C. Sabathia 86 .15 .40
322 J.D. Drew 86 .15 .40
323 Torii Hunter 86 SP .40 1.00
324 Chan Ho Park 86 .15 .40
325 Mike Sweeney 86 .15 .40
326 Javier Vazquez 86 .15 .40
327 Jorge Posada 86 .25 .60
328 Barry Zito 86 .15 .40
329 Willie McCovey 86 .15 .40
330 Kevin Brown 86 .15 .40
331 Mo Vaughn 86 .15 .40
332 Carlos Beltran 86 .15 .40
333 Bobby Doerr 86 .15 .40
334 Matt Morris 86 .15 .40
335 Trot Nixon 86 SP .40 1.00
336 Magglio Ordonez 86 .15 .40
337 Paul LoDuca 86 .15 .40
338 Phil Nevin 86 .15 .40
339 Eric Chavez 86 .15 .40
340 Corey Patterson 86 .15 .40
341 Richie Sexson 86 .15 .40
342 Pat Burrell 86 SP .40 1.00
343 Freddy Garcia 86 .15 .40
344 Bartolo Colon 86 .15 .40
345 Cliff Floyd 86 .15 .40
346 Deivis Santos 88 RR .15 .40
347 Felix Escalona 88 RR RC .15 .40
348 Miguel Asencio 88 RR RC .15 .40
349 Takahito Nomura 88 RR RC .15 .40
350 Jorge Padilla 88 RR RC .15 .40
351 Torii Hunter 88 .15 .40
352 Ichiro Suzuki 88 .75 2.00
353 Jay Gibbons 88 .15 .40
354 Alfonso Soriano 88 .15 .40
355 Mark Buehrle 88 .15 .40
356 Shawn Green 88 SP .40 1.00
357 Barry Larkin 88 .25 .60
358 Josh Fogg 88 .15 .40
359 Shannon Stewart 88 .15 .40
360 Andruw Jones 88 .25 .60
361 Juan Gonzalez 88 .15 .40
362 Ken Griffey Jr. 88 .75 2.00
363 Tim Hudson 88 .15 .40
364 Roy Oswalt 88 SP .40 1.00
365 Carlos Delgado 88 .15 .40
366 Albert Pujols 88 SP 1.50 4.00
367 Willie Stargell 88 .25 .60
368 Roger Clemens 88 .75 2.00
369 Luis Gonzalez 88 .15 .40
370 Barry Zito 88 .15 .40
371 Alex Rodriguez 88 .50 1.50
372 Troy Glaus 88 .15 .40
373 Vladimir Guerrero 88 .40 1.00
374 Jeff Bagwell 88 .25 .60
375 Randy Johnson 88 .40 1.00
376 Manny Ramirez 88 .25 .60
377 Derek Jeter 88 SP 2.00 5.00
378 C.C. Sabathia 88 .15 .40
379 Rickey Henderson 88 .40 1.00
380 J.D. Drew 88 SP .40 1.00
381 Nomar Garciaparra 88 .60 1.50
382 Darin Erstad 88 .15 .40
383 Ben Sheets 88 .15 .40
384 Frank Thomas 88 .40 1.00
385 Barry Bonds 88 1.00 2.50
386 Pedro Martinez 88 .25 .60
387 Mark Mulder 88 .15 .40
388 Greg Maddux 88 .60 1.50
389 Todd Helton 88 .25 .60
390 Lance Berkman 88 .15 .40
391 Sammy Sosa 88 .40 1.00
392 Mike Piazza 88 SP 1.25 3.00
393 Chipper Jones 88 .40 1.00
394 Adam Dunn 88 .15 .40
395 Jason Giambi 88 .15 .40
396 Eric Chavez 88 .15 .40
397 Bobby Abreu 88 .15 .40
398 Aramis Ramirez 88 .15 .40
399 Paul LoDuca 88 .15 .40
400 Miguel Tejada 88 .15 .40
401 Runelvys Hernandez 82 RC .30 .75
402 Wilson Valdez 82 RC .30 .75
403 Brian Tallet 82 RC .30 .75
404 Chone Figgins 82 RC .75 2.00
405 Jeriome Robertson 82 RC .30 .75
406 Shane Nance 84 RC .30 .75
407 Aaron Cook 84 RC .30 .75
408 Trey Hodges 84 RC .30 .75
409 Matt Childers 84 RC .30 .75
410 Mitch Wylie 84 RC .30 .75
411 Rene Reyes 84 RC .30 .75
412 Mike Smith 84 RC .30 .75
413 Jason Simontacchi 84 RC .15 .40
414 Luis Martinez 84 RC .30 .75
415 Kevin Cash 84 RC .30 .75
416 Todd Donovan 86 RC .30 .75
417 Scotty Layfield 86 RC .30 .75
418 Joe Borchard 86 .30 .75
419 Adrian Burnside 86 RC .30 .75
420 Ben Kozlowski 86 RC .30 .75
421 Clay Condrey 88 RC .30 .75
422 Cliff Lee 88 RC 1.00 2.50
423 Josh Bard 88 RC .30 .75
424 Freddy Sanchez 88 RC .75 2.00
425 Ron Calloway 88 RC .30 .75

2002 Donruss Originals Aqueous

*AQUEOUS: 3X TO 8X BASIC
*AQUEOUS: 1.5X TO 4X BASIC SP's
*AQUEOUS: 1.25X TO 3X BASIC RC's
RANDOM INSERTS IN PACKS

2002 Donruss Originals All-Stars

STATED ODDS 1:30 HOBBY, 1:120 RETAIL
1 George Brett 5.00 12.00
2 Rickey Henderson 2.00 5.00
3 Mike Schmidt 5.00 12.00
4 Vladimir Guerrero 2.00 5.00
5 Tony Gwynn 3.00 8.00
6 Curt Schilling 2.00 5.00
7 Don Mattingly 5.00 12.00
8 Roberto Alomar 2.00 5.00
9 Cal Ripken 8.00 20.00
10 Carlton Fisk 2.00 5.00
11 Roger Clemens 4.00 10.00
12 Jeff Bagwell 2.00 5.00
13 Kirby Puckett 2.00 5.00
14 Nolan Ryan 6.00 15.00
15 Ryne Sandberg 5.00 12.00
16 Ivan Rodriguez 2.00 5.00
17 Sammy Sosa 2.00 5.00
18 Greg Maddux 3.00 8.00
19 Alex Rodriguez 2.50 6.00
20 Todd Helton 2.00 5.00
21 Randy Johnson 2.00 5.00
22 Troy Glaus 2.00 5.00
23 Ichiro Suzuki 4.00 10.00
24 Barry Bonds 5.00 12.00
25 Derek Jeter 5.00 12.00

2002 Donruss Originals Box Bottoms

COMPLETE SET (4) .75 2.00
ONE SET PER BOX BOTTOM
NNO Kazuhisa Ishii 82 .20 .50
NNO Nomar Garciaparra 84 .20 .50
NNO Roger Clemens 86 .20 .50
NNO Mike Piazza 88 .20 .50

2002 Donruss Originals Champions

RANDOM INSERTS IN PACKS
STATED PRINT RUN 800 SERIAL #'d SETS
1 Nolan Ryan 8.00 20.00
2 George Brett 6.00 15.00
3 Edgar Martinez 3.00 8.00
4 Mike Schmidt 6.00 15.00
5 Randy Johnson 3.00 8.00
6 Tony Gwynn 4.00 10.00
7 John Smoltz 3.00 8.00
8 Roger Clemens 6.00 15.00
9 Mel Ott 3.00 8.00
10 Todd Helton 3.00 8.00
11 Bernie Williams 3.00 8.00
12 Troy Glaus 3.00 8.00
13 Steve Carlton 3.00 8.00
14 Ryne Sandberg 6.00 15.00
15 Ted Williams 5.00 12.00
16 Alex Rodriguez M's 4.00 10.00
17 Lou Boudreau 3.00 8.00
18 Luis Gonzalez 3.00 8.00
19 Rickey Henderson 3.00 8.00
20 Jose Canseco 3.00 8.00
21 Stan Musial 4.00 10.00
22 Randy Johnson 3.00 8.00
23 Don Mattingly 6.00 15.00
24 Nomar Garciaparra 5.00 12.00
25 Wade Boggs 3.00 8.00

2002 Donruss Originals Champions Materials

RANDOM INSERTS IN PACKS
STATED PRINT RUNS LISTED BELOW
ALL CARDS FEATURE JERSEY SWATCHES
1 Nolan Ryan/78 12.50 30.00
2 George Brett/80 15.00 40.00
3 Edgar Martinez/92 10.00 25.00
4 Mike Schmidt/80 15.00 40.00
5 Randy Johnson/94 10.00 25.00
6 Tony Gwynn/84 10.00 25.00
7 John Smoltz/96 10.00 25.00
8 Roger Clemens/88 10.00 25.00
10 Todd Helton/100 10.00 25.00
11 Bernie Williams/98 10.00 25.00
12 Troy Glaus/100 6.00 15.00
13 Steve Carlton/80 6.00 15.00
14 Ryne Sandberg/90 10.00 25.00
16 Alex Rodriguez M's/96 10.00 25.00
17 Lou Boudreau/44 10.00 25.00
18 Luis Gonzalez/99 6.00 15.00
19 Rickey Henderson/82 10.00 25.00
20 Jose Canseco/100 10.00 25.00
22 Randy Johnson/88 10.00 25.00
23 Don Mattingly/84 15.00 40.00
24 Nomar Garciaparra/100 10.00 25.00
25 Wade Boggs/88 10.00 25.00

2002 Donruss Originals Gamers

STATED PRINT RUNS LISTED BELOW
ALL CARDS FEATURE JERSEY SWATCHES
1 Alfonso Soriano/400 4.00 10.00
2 Shawn Green/500 4.00 10.00
3 Curt Schilling/250 6.00 15.00
4 Hideo Nomo Red Sox/100 4.00 10.00
5 Toby Hall/500 4.00 10.00
6 Andruw Jones/500 6.00 15.00
7 Cliff Floyd/500 4.00 10.00
8 Mark Ellis/500 4.00 10.00
9 Gabe Kapler/500 4.00 10.00
10 Andres Galarraga/500 4.00 10.00
11 Freddy Garcia/500 4.00 10.00
12 Tsuyoshi Shinjo/200 6.00 15.00
13 Robin Ventura/500 4.00 10.00
14 Paul LoDuca/500 4.00 10.00
15 Manny Ramirez/500 6.00 15.00
16 Garret Anderson/250 6.00 15.00
17 Joe Kennedy/500 4.00 10.00
18 Roger Clemens/500 8.00 20.00
19 Gary Sheffield/500 4.00 10.00
20 Vernon Wells/500 4.00 10.00
22 Hideo Nomo Dodgers/100 4.00 10.00
23 Tim Hudson/500 4.00 10.00
24 Larry Bigbie/500 4.00 10.00
25 Larry Walker/500 4.00 10.00
27 John Olerud/500 4.00 10.00
28 Chipper Jones/500 6.00 15.00
29 Tony Gwynn/500 6.00 15.00
30 Juan Gonzalez/500 4.00 10.00
31 Jacque Jones/500 4.00 10.00
32 Frank Thomas/500 6.00 15.00
33 Luis Gonzalez/500 4.00 10.00
34 Geoff Jenkins/500 4.00 10.00
35 J.D. Drew/500 4.00 10.00
36 Edgardo Alfonzo/500 4.00 10.00
37 Todd Helton/500 6.00 15.00
38 Brad Penny/500 4.00 10.00
39 Robert Fick/500 4.00 10.00
40 Will Clark/500 6.00 15.00
41 Tony Armas Jr./500 4.00 10.00
42 Nick Johnson/400 4.00 10.00
43 Ben Grieve/500 4.00 10.00
44 Vladimir Guerrero/500 6.00 15.00
45 Jason Jennings/500 4.00 10.00
46 Carlos Lee/500 4.00 10.00
47 Carlos Delgado/500 4.00 10.00
48 Chan Ho Park/500 4.00 10.00
49 Juan Diaz/500 4.00 10.00
50 Alex Rodriguez M's/400 6.00 15.00

2002 Donruss Originals Hit List

RANDOM INSERTS IN PACKS
STATED PRINT RUN 1500 SERIAL #'d SETS
1 Ichiro Suzuki 1.25 3.00
2 Shawn Green .40 1.00
3 Alex Rodriguez 1.25 3.00
4 Nomar Garciaparra .60 1.50
5 Derek Jeter 2.50 6.00
6 Barry Bonds 1.50 4.00
7 Mike Piazza 1.00 2.50
8 Albert Pujols 2.00 5.00
9 Chipper Jones 1.00 2.50
10 Sammy Sosa 1.00 2.50
11 Rickey Henderson 1.00 2.50
12 Frank Thomas 1.00 2.50
13 Jeff Bagwell .60 1.50
14 Vladimir Guerrero .60 1.50
15 Todd Helton .60 1.50

16 Adam Dunn .60 1.50
17 Rafael Palmeiro .60 1.50
18 Manny Ramirez .60 1.50
19 Lance Berkman .60 1.50
20 Jason Giambi A's .40 1.00

2002 Donruss Originals Hit List Total Bases

1 Ichiro Suzuki Base/316 5.00 12.00
2 Shawn Green Bat/370 1.50 4.00
3 Alex Rodriguez Rgr Bat/393 5.00 12.00
4 Nomar Garciaparra Bat/365 2.50 6.00
5 Derek Jeter Base/346 10.00 25.00
6 Barry Bonds Base/411 6.00 15.00
7 Mike Piazza Dodgers Bat/355 4.00 10.00
8 Albert Pujols Base/360 8.00 20.00
9 Chipper Jones Bat/359 4.00 10.00
10 Sammy Sosa Base/425 4.00 10.00
11 Rickey Henderson Bat/285 4.00 10.00
12 Frank Thomas Bat/364 4.00 10.00
13 Jeff Bagwell Bat/363 2.50 6.00
14 Vladimir Guerrero Bat/379 2.50 6.00
15 Todd Helton Bat/405 2.50 6.00
16 Adam Dunn Bat/141 2.50 6.00
17 Rafael Palmeiro Bat/356 2.50 6.00
18 Manny Ramirez Bat/346 2.50 6.00
19 Lance Berkman Bat/358 2.50 6.00
20 Jason Giambi A's Base/343 1.50 4.00

2002 Donruss Originals Making History

RANDOM INSERTS IN PACKS
STATED PRINT RUN 800 SERIAL #'d SETS
1 Rafael Palmeiro .60 1.50
2 Roger Clemens 1.25 3.00
3 Greg Maddux 1.50 4.00
4 Randy Johnson 1.00 2.50
5 Barry Bonds 1.50 4.00
6 Mike Piazza 1.00 2.50
7 Roberto Alomar .60 1.50
8 Rickey Henderson 1.00 2.50
9 Sammy Sosa 1.00 2.50
10 Tom Glavine .60 1.50

2002 Donruss Originals Making History Materials

RANDOM INSERTS IN PACKS
STATED PRINT RUN 100 SERIAL #'d SETS
1 Rafael Palmeiro Jsy 10.00 25.00
2 Roger Clemens Jsy 15.00 40.00
3 Greg Maddux Jsy 10.00 25.00
4 Randy Johnson Jsy 10.00 25.00
5 Barry Bonds Base 10.00 25.00
6 Mike Piazza Jsy 10.00 25.00
7 Roberto Alomar Jsy 10.00 25.00
8 Rickey Henderson Jsy 10.00 25.00
9 Sammy Sosa Base 10.00 25.00
10 Tom Glavine Jsy 10.00 25.00

2002 Donruss Originals Mound Marvels

COMPLETE SET (15) 12.00 30.00
STATED ODDS 1:40 HOBBY, 1:72 RETAIL
1 Roger Clemens 8/20/01 2.50 6.00
2 Matt Morris .75 2.00
3 Pedro Martinez 1.25 3.00
4 Randy Johnson 2.00 5.00
5 Wade Miller .75 2.00
6 Tim Hudson 1.25 3.00
7 Mike Mussina 1.25 3.00
8 C.C. Sabathia 1.25 3.00
9 Kazuhiro Sasaki .75 2.00
10 Curt Schilling 1.25 3.00
11 Hideo Nomo 2.00 5.00
12 Roger Clemens 10/30/01 2.50 6.00
13 Mark Buehrle 1.25 3.00
14 Barry Zito .75 2.00
15 Roy Oswalt 1.25 3.00

2002 Donruss Originals Mound Marvels High Heat

RANDOM INSERTS IN PACKS
STATED PRINT RUN 100 SERIAL #'d SETS
ALL CARDS FEATURE GAME-USED BALL
1 Roger Clemens 8/20/01 20.00 50.00
2 Matt Morris 8.00 20.00
3 Pedro Martinez 10.00 25.00
4 Randy Johnson 10.00 25.00
5 Wade Miller 8.00 20.00
6 Tim Hudson 8.00 20.00
7 Mike Mussina 10.00 25.00
8 C.C. Sabathia 8.00 20.00
9 Kazuhiro Sasaki 8.00 20.00
10 Curt Schilling 8.00 20.00
11 Hideo Nomo 12.00 30.00
12 Roger Clemens 10/30/01 20.00 50.00
13 Mark Buehrle 8.00 20.00
14 Barry Zito 8.00 20.00
15 Roy Oswalt 8.00 20.00

2002 Donruss Originals Nifty Fifty Bats

RANDOM INSERTS IN PACKS
STATED PRINT RUN 50 SERIAL #'d SETS
1 Alex Rodriguez Rangers 15.00 40.00
2 Kerry Wood 8.00 20.00
3 Ivan Rodriguez 10.00 25.00
4 Geronimo Gil 5.00 12.00
5 Vladimir Guerrero 10.00 25.00
6 Corky Miller 5.00 12.00
7 Todd Helton 10.00 25.00
8 Rickey Henderson Padres 10.00 25.00
9 Andruw Jones 10.00 25.00
10 Barry Bonds Ball 30.00 60.00
11 Tom Glavine 10.00 25.00
12 Mark Teixeira 10.00 25.00
13 Mike Piazza Mets 8.00 20.00
14 Austin Kearns 5.00 12.00
15 Rickey Henderson M's 10.00 25.00
16 Derek Jeter Ball 20.00 50.00
17 Barry Larkin 10.00 25.00
18 Jeff Bagwell 10.00 25.00
19 Bernie Williams 10.00 25.00
20 Frank Thomas 10.00 25.00
21 Lance Berkman 8.00 20.00
22 Marlon Byrd 5.00 12.00
23 Randy Johnson 10.00 25.00
24 Ichiro Suzuki Ball 30.00 60.00
25 Darin Erstad 8.00 20.00
26 Jason Lane 8.00 20.00
27 Roberto Alomar 10.00 25.00
28 Ken Griffey Jr. Ball 15.00 40.00
29 Tsuyoshi Shinjo 8.00 20.00
30 Pedro Martinez 10.00 25.00
31 Rickey Henderson Mets 10.00 25.00
32 Albert Pujols Ball 20.00 50.00
33 Nomar Garciaparra 15.00 40.00
34 Troy Glaus 8.00 20.00
35 Chipper Jones 10.00 25.00
36 Adam Dunn 8.00 20.00
37 Jason Giambi Ball 8.00 20.00
38 Greg Maddux 8.00 20.00
39 Mike Piazza Dodgers 15.00 40.00
40 So Taguchi 10.00 25.00
41 Manny Ramirez 10.00 25.00
42 Scott Rolen 10.00 25.00
43 Sammy Sosa Ball 10.00 25.00
44 Shawn Green 8.00 20.00
45 Rickey Henderson Red Sox 10.00 25.00
46 Alex Rodriguez M's 15.00 40.00
47 Hideo Nomo Red Sox 15.00 40.00
48 Kazuhisa Ishii 10.00 25.00
49 Luis Gonzalez 8.00 20.00
50 Jim Thome 10.00 25.00

2002 Donruss Originals Nifty Fifty Combos

RANDOM INSERTS IN PACKS
STATED PRINT RUN 50 SERIAL #'d SETS
ALL ARE BAT-JSY CARDS UNLESS STATED
1 Alex Rodriguez Rangers 8.00 20.00
2 Kerry Wood 12.50 30.00
3 Ivan Rodriguez 15.00 40.00
4 Geronimo Gil 8.00 20.00
5 Vladimir Guerrero 15.00 40.00
6 Corky Miller 8.00 20.00
7 Todd Helton 15.00 40.00
8 Rickey Henderson Padres 15.00 40.00
9 Andruw Jones 15.00 40.00
10 Barry Bonds Base/Ball 40.00 80.00
11 Tom Glavine 15.00 40.00
12 Mark Teixeira 15.00 40.00
13 Mike Piazza Mets 20.00 50.00
14 Austin Kearns 8.00 20.00
15 Rickey Henderson M's 15.00 40.00
16 Derek Jeter Base/Ball 30.00 60.00
17 Barry Larkin 15.00 40.00
18 Jeff Bagwell 15.00 40.00
19 Bernie Williams 15.00 40.00
20 Frank Thomas 15.00 40.00
21 Lance Berkman 12.50 30.00
22 Marlon Byrd 8.00 20.00
23 Randy Johnson 15.00 40.00
24 Ichiro Suzuki Base/Ball 20.00 50.00
25 Darin Erstad 12.50 30.00
26 Jason Lane 12.50 30.00
27 Roberto Alomar 15.00 40.00
28 Ken Griffey Jr. Base/Ball 20.00 50.00
29 Tsuyoshi Shinjo 12.50 30.00
30 Pedro Martinez 15.00 40.00
31 Rickey Henderson Mets 15.00 40.00
32 Albert Pujols Base/Ball 30.00 60.00
33 Nomar Garciaparra 20.00 50.00
34 Troy Glaus 12.50 30.00
35 Chipper Jones 15.00 40.00
36 Adam Dunn 12.50 30.00
37 Jason Giambi Base/Ball 12.50 30.00
38 Greg Maddux 20.00 50.00
39 Mike Piazza Dodgers 10.00 25.00
40 So Taguchi 15.00 40.00
41 Manny Ramirez 15.00 40.00
42 Scott Rolen 15.00 40.00
43 Sammy Sosa Base/Ball 15.00 40.00
44 Shawn Green 12.50 30.00
45 Rickey Henderson Red Sox 15.00 40.00
46 Alex Rodriguez M's 20.00 50.00
47 Hideo Nomo Red Sox 20.00 50.00
48 Kazuhisa Ishii 15.00 40.00
49 Luis Gonzalez 12.50 30.00
50 Jim Thome 15.00 40.00

2002 Donruss Originals Nifty Fifty Jerseys

RANDOM INSERTS IN PACKS
STATED PRINT RUN 50 SERIAL #'d SETS
2 Kerry Wood 8.00 20.00
3 Ivan Rodriguez 10.00 25.00
4 Geronimo Gil 5.00 12.00
5 Vladimir Guerrero 10.00 25.00
6 Corky Miller 5.00 12.00
7 Todd Helton 10.00 25.00
8 Rickey Henderson Padres 10.00 25.00
9 Andruw Jones 10.00 25.00
11 Tom Glavine 10.00 25.00
12 Mark Teixeira 10.00 25.00
13 Mike Piazza Mets 15.00 40.00
14 Austin Kearns 5.00 12.00
15 Rickey Henderson M's 10.00 25.00
16 Derek Jeter Base 20.00 50.00
17 Barry Larkin 10.00 25.00
18 Jeff Bagwell 10.00 25.00
19 Bernie Williams 10.00 25.00
20 Frank Thomas 10.00 25.00
21 Lance Berkman 8.00 20.00
22 Marlon Byrd 5.00 12.00
23 Randy Johnson 10.00 25.00
24 Ichiro Suzuki Base 30.00 60.00
25 Darin Erstad 8.00 20.00
26 Jason Lane 8.00 20.00
27 Roberto Alomar 10.00 25.00
28 Ken Griffey Jr. Base 15.00 40.00
29 Tsuyoshi Shinjo 8.00 20.00
30 Pedro Martinez 10.00 25.00
31 Rickey Henderson Mets 10.00 25.00
32 Albert Pujols Base 20.00 50.00
33 Nomar Garciaparra 15.00 40.00
34 Troy Glaus 8.00 20.00
35 Chipper Jones 10.00 25.00
36 Adam Dunn 8.00 20.00
37 Jason Giambi Base 8.00 20.00
38 Greg Maddux 15.00 40.00
39 Mike Piazza Dodgers 15.00 40.00
40 So Taguchi 10.00 25.00
41 Manny Ramirez 10.00 25.00
42 Scott Rolen 10.00 25.00
43 Sammy Sosa Base 10.00 25.00
44 Shawn Green 8.00 20.00
45 Rickey Henderson Red Sox 10.00 25.00
46 Alex Rodriguez M's 15.00 40.00
47 Hideo Nomo Red Sox 15.00 40.00
48 Kazuhisa Ishii 10.00 25.00
49 Luis Gonzalez 8.00 20.00
50 Jim Thome 10.00 25.00

2002 Donruss Originals On The Record

RANDOM INSERTS IN PACKS
STATED PRINT RUN 800 SERIAL #'d SETS
1 Ty Cobb HR 9 1.50 4.00
2 Jimmie Foxx 1.00 2.50
3 Lou Gehrig 2.00 5.00
4 Dale Murphy 1.00 2.50
5 Steve Carlton .60 1.50
6 Randy Johnson 1.00 2.50
7 Greg Maddux 1.50 4.00
8 Roger Clemens 1.25 3.00
9 Yogi Berra 1.00 2.50
10 Don Mattingly 2.00 5.00
11 Rickey Henderson 1.00 2.50
12 Stan Musial 1.50 4.00
13 Jackie Robinson 1.00 2.50
14 Roberto Clemente 2.50 6.00
15 Mike Schmidt 1.50 4.00

2002 Donruss Originals On The Record Materials

RANDOM INSERTS IN PACKS
STATED PRINT RUNS LISTED BELOW
NO PRICING ON QTY OF 50 OR LESS
4 Dale Murphy Jsy/83 6.00 15.00
5 Steve Carlton Jsy/72 6.00 15.00
6 Randy Johnson Jsy/100 6.00 15.00
7 Greg Maddux Jsy/93 8.00 20.00
8 Roger Clemens Jsy/87 10.00 25.00
9 Yogi Berra Jsy/51 6.00 15.00
10 Don Mattingly Jsy/85 15.00 40.00
11 Rickey Henderson Jsy/90 6.00 15.00
12 Stan Musial Jsy/43 10.00 25.00
14 Roberto Clemente Jsy/66 50.00 100.00
15 Mike Schmidt Jsy/80 15.00 40.00

2002 Donruss Originals Power Alley

STATED PRINT RUN 1500 SERIAL #'d SETS
*DIE CUTS: 1.25X TO 3X BASIC ALLEY
DIE CUT PRINT RUN 100 SERIAL #'d SETS
1 Barry Bonds 4.00 10.00
2 Sammy Sosa 1.50 4.00
3 Lance Berkman 1.50 4.00
4 Luis Gonzalez 1.50 4.00
5 Alex Rodriguez 2.00 5.00
6 Troy Glaus 1.50 4.00
7 Vladimir Guerrero 1.50 4.00
8 Jason Giambi 1.50 4.00
9 Mike Piazza 2.50 6.00
10 Todd Helton 1.50 4.00
11 Mike Schmidt 3.00 8.00
12 Don Mattingly 3.00 8.00
13 Andre Dawson 1.50 4.00
14 Reggie Jackson 1.50 4.00
15 Dale Murphy 4.00 10.00

2002 Donruss Originals Signature Marks

STATED PRINT RUNS LISTED BELOW
1 Kazuhisa Ishii/50 10.00 25.00
2 Eric Hinske/200 6.00 15.00
3 Cesar Izturis/200 4.00 10.00
4 Roy Oswalt/100 6.00 15.00
5 Jack Cust/200 4.00 10.00
6 Nick Johnson/200 6.00 15.00
7 Jason Hart/200 4.00 10.00
8 Mark Prior/100 6.00 15.00
9 Luis Garcia/200 4.00 10.00
10 Jay Gibbons/200 4.00 10.00
11 Corky Miller/200 4.00 10.00
12 Antonio Perez/100 4.00 10.00
13 Andres Torres/200 8.00 20.00
14 Brandon Claussen/200 4.00 10.00
15 Ed Rogers/200 4.00 10.00
16 Jorge Padilla/200 4.00 10.00
17 Francis Beltran/200 4.00 10.00
18 Kip Wells/200 4.00 10.00
19 Ryan Ludwick/200 20.00 50.00
21 Juan Diaz/200 4.00 10.00
22 Marcus Giles/200 6.00 15.00
23 Joe Kennedy/200 4.00 10.00
24 Wade Miller/100 4.00 10.00
25 Corey Patterson/100 4.00 10.00
26 Angel Berroa/200 4.00 10.00
27 Ricardo Rodriguez/200 4.00 10.00
28 Toby Hall/200 4.00 10.00
29 Carlos Pena/50 6.00 15.00
30 Jason Jennings/200 4.00 10.00
31 Rafael Soriano/200 4.00 10.00
32 Marlon Byrd/100 4.00 10.00
33 Rodrigo Rosario/200 4.00 10.00
35 Brent Abernathy/200 4.00 10.00
36 Bill Hall/200 6.00 15.00
38 Josh Pearce/200 4.00 10.00
39 Brian Lawrence/200 4.00 10.00
40 Tim Redding/200 4.00 10.00
42 Jeremy Giambi/200 4.00 10.00
43 Victor Martinez/200 15.00 40.00
44 Hank Blalock/50 10.00 25.00
46 Geronimo Gil/200 4.00 10.00
47 So Taguchi/50 15.00 40.00
48 Austin Kearns/200 4.00 10.00
49 Alfonso Soriano/50 6.00 15.00

2002 Donruss Originals Ted Williams Puzzle

COMMON PUZZLE PIECE .20 .50
RANDOM INSERTS IN PACKS
NNO Piece 1/Piece 2/Piece 3 .20 .50
NNO Piece 4/Piece 5/Piece 6 .20 .50
NNO Piece 7/Piece 8/Piece 9 .20 .50
NNO Piece 10/Piece 11/Piece 12 .20 .50
NNO Piece 13/Piece 14/Piece 15 .20 .50
NNO Piece 16/Piece 17/Piece 18 .20 .50
NNO Piece 19/Piece 20/Piece 21 .20 .50
NNO Piece 22/Piece 23/Piece 24 .20 .50
NNO Piece 25/Piece 26/Piece 27 .20 .50
NNO Piece 28/Piece 29/Piece 30 .20 .50
NNO Piece 31/Piece 32/Piece 33 .20 .50
NNO Piece 34/Piece 35/Piece 36 .20 .50
NNO Piece 37/Piece 38/Piece 39 .20 .50
NNO Piece 40/Piece 41/Piece 42 .20 .50
NNO Piece 43/Piece 44/Piece 45 .20 .50
NNO Piece 46/Piece 47/Piece 48 .20 .50
NNO Piece 49/Piece 50/Piece 51 .20 .50
NNO Piece 52/Piece 53/Piece 54 .20 .50
NNO Piece 55/Piece 56/Piece 57 .20 .50
NNO Piece 58/Piece 59/Piece 60 .20 .50
NNO Piece 61/Piece 62/Piece 63 .20 .50

2002 Donruss Originals What If 1978

WHAT IF STATED ODDS 1:12 HOB, 1:24 RET
1 Paul Molitor RR 3.00 8.00
2 Alan Trammell RR 2.00 5.00
3 Ozzie Smith RR 6.00 15.00
4 George Brett 6.00 15.00
5 Johnny Bench 4.00 10.00
6 Rod Carew 3.00 8.00
7 Carlton Fisk 3.00 8.00
8 Reggie Jackson 3.00 8.00
9 Dale Murphy 6.00 15.00
10 Joe Morgan 2.00 5.00
11 Eddie Murray 8.00 20.00
12 Jim Palmer 2.00 5.00
13 Tom Seaver 3.00 8.00
14 Willie Stargell 3.00 8.00
15 Dave Winfield 2.00 5.00
16 Dave Parker 2.00 5.00
17 Mike Schmidt 6.00 15.00
18 Eddie Mathews 4.00 10.00
19 Lou Brock 3.00 8.00
20 Willie McCovey 2.00 5.00
21 Andre Dawson 2.00 5.00
22 Dennis Eckersley 2.00 5.00
23 Robin Yount 4.00 10.00
24 Nolan Ryan 6.00 15.00
25 Steve Carlton 2.00 5.00
26 Paul Molitor 3.00 8.00
27 Ozzie Smith 4.00 10.00

2002 Donruss Originals What If 1980

WHAT IF STATED ODDS 1:12 HOB, 1:24 RET
1 Rickey Henderson RR 4.00 10.00
2 Johnny Bench 4.00 10.00
3 George Brett 6.00 15.00
4 Steve Carlton 2.00 5.00
5 Rod Carew 3.00 8.00
6 Gary Carter 2.00 5.00
7 Carlton Fisk 3.00 8.00
8 Reggie Jackson 3.00 8.00
9 Dave Parker 2.00 5.00
10 Dale Murphy 6.00 15.00
11 Paul Molitor 2.00 5.00
12 Mike Schmidt 6.00 15.00
13 Alan Trammell 2.00 5.00
14 Dave Winfield 2.00 5.00
15 Robin Yount 4.00 10.00
16 Joe Morgan 2.00 5.00
17 Jim Palmer 2.00 5.00
18 Nolan Ryan 6.00 15.00
19 Tom Seaver 3.00 8.00
20 Ozzie Smith 4.00 10.00
21 Willie McCovey 2.00 5.00
22 Andre Dawson 2.00 5.00
23 Eddie Murray 4.00 10.00
24 Al Kaline 4.00 10.00
25 Duke Snider 3.00 8.00

2002 Donruss Originals What If Rookies

WHAT IF STATED ODDS 1:12 HOB, 1:24 RET
1 Wade Boggs 82 RR 1.50 4.00
2 Ryne Sandberg 82 RR 5.00 12.00
3 Cal Ripken 82 RR 8.00 20.00
4 Tony Gwynn 82 2.50 6.00
5 Don Mattingly 82 5.00 12.00
6 Wade Boggs 82 1.50 4.00
7 Roger Clemens 84 RR 3.00 8.00
8 Kirby Puckett 84 RR 2.50 6.00
9 Eric Davis 84 RR 1.00 2.50
10 Dwight Gooden 84 RR 1.00 2.50
11 Eric Davis 84
12 Roger Clemens 84 3.00 8.00
13 Kirby Puckett 84 2.50 6.00
14 Dwight Gooden 84 1.00 2.50
15 Barry Bonds 86 RR 4.00 10.00
16 Will Clark 86 1.50 4.00
17 Barry Larkin 86 1.50 4.00
18 Greg Maddux 86 4.00 10.00
19 Rafael Palmeiro 86 1.50 4.00
20 Craig Biggio 88 1.50 4.00
21 Gary Sheffield 88 1.00 2.50
22 Randy Johnson 88 2.50 6.00
23 Curt Schilling 88 1.50 4.00

2002 Donruss Playoff ALCS Program

ALCS1 Cal Ripken Jr. Diamond Kings 4.00 10.00
ALCS2 Nomar Garciaparra Diamond Kings .75 2.00
ALCS3 Roger Clemens Diamond Kings 1.50 4.00
ALCS4 Alex Rodriguez Diamond Kings 1.50 4.00
ALCS5 Troy Glaus Diamond Kings .50 1.25
ALCS6 Miguel Tejada Diamond Kings .75 2.00
ALCS7 Alfonso Soriano Diamond Kings .75 2.00
ALCS8 Ted Williams Diamond Kings 2.50 6.00
ALCS9 Manny Ramirez Donruss Originals .75 2.00
ALCS10 Nolan Ryan Donruss Originals 4.00 10.00
ALCS11 Roger Clemens Donruss Originals 1.50 4.00
ALCS12 Alex Rodriguez Donruss Originals 1.50 4.00
ALCS13 Paul Konerko Donruss Originals .50 1.25
ALCS14 Don Mattingly Donruss Originals 2.50 6.00
ALCS15 Miguel Tejada Donruss Originals .75 2.00
ALCS16 TBD
ALCS17 Jim Thome Playoff Piece of the Game .75 2.00
ALCS18 Garret Anderson Playoff Piece of the Game .50 1.25
ALCS19 Alfonso Soriano Playoff Piece of the Game .75 2.00
ALCS20 Nomar Garciaparra Playoff Piece of the Game .75 2.00
ALCS21 Eric Chavez Playoff Piece of the Game .50 1.25
ALCS22 Magglio Ordonez Playoff Piece of the Game .75 2.00
ALCS23 Roger Clemens Playoff Piece of the Game 1.50 4.00
ALCS24 Torii Hunter Playoff Piece of the Game .50 1.25
ALCS25 Eric Hinske Studio .50 1.25
ALCS26 Edgar Martinez Studio .75 2.00
ALCS27 Pedro Martinez Studio .75 2.00
ALCS28 Roger Clemens Studio 1.50 4.00
ALCS29 Alex Rodriguez Studio 1.50 4.00
ALCS30 George Brett Studio 2.50 6.00
ALCS31 Dewon Brazelton Studio .50 1.25
ALCS32 Barry Zito Studio .50 1.25

2002 Donruss Playoff NLCS Program

NLCS1 Randy Johnson Diamond Kings 1.25 3.00
NLCS2 Josh Beckett Diamond Kings .50 1.25
NLCS3 Mike Piazza Diamond Kings 1.25 3.00
NLCS4 Greg Maddux Diamond Kings 2.00 5.00
NLCS5 Lance Berkman Diamond Kings .75 2.00
NLCS6 Mark Prior Diamond Kings .75 2.00
NLCS7 Adam Dunn Diamond Kings .75 2.00
NLCS8 Tony Gwynn Diamond Kings 1.25 3.00
NLCS9 Jeff Bagwell Playoff Piece of the Game .75 2.00
NLCS10 Shawn Green Playoff Piece of the Game .50 1.25
NLCS11 Vladimir Guerrero Playoff Piece of the Game .75 2.00
NLCS12 TBD
NLCS13 Luis Gonzalez Playoff Piece of the Game .50 1.25
NLCS14 Todd Helton Playoff Piece of the Game .75 2.00
NLCS15 Richie Sexson Playoff Piece of the Game .50 1.25
NLCS16 Chipper Jones Playoff Piece of the Game 1.25 3.00
NLCS17 J.D. Drew Studio .50 1.25
NLCS18 Randy Johnson Studio 1.25 3.00
NLCS19 Mike Piazza Studio 1.25 3.00
NLCS20 Ozzie Smith Studio 1.50 4.00
NLCS21 Jeff Kent Studio .50 1.25
NLCS22 Roy Oswalt Studio .75 2.00
NLCS23 Pat Burrell Studio .50 1.25
NLCS24 Todd Helton Studio .75 2.00
NLCS25 Mike Schmidt Donruss Originals 2.00 5.00
NLCS26 Andruw Jones Donruss Originals .50 1.25
NLCS27 Lance Berkman Donruss Originals .75 2.00
NLCS28 Vladimir Guerrero Donruss Originals .75 2.00
NLCS29 Roberto Clemente Donruss Originals 3.00 8.00
NLCS30 Austin Kearns Donruss Originals .50 1.25
NLCS31 Curt Schilling Donruss Originals .75 2.00
NLCS32 Kazuhisa Ishii Donruss Originals .75 2.00

1997 Donruss Preferred

The 1997 Donruss Preferred set was issued in one series totalling 200 cards and distributed in five-card packs with a suggested retail of $4.99. The set features color player photos on an all-foil, micro-etched card stock. The set is divided into 100 bronze (5:1 insert odds), 60 silver (1:3), 30 gold (1:12), and 10 platinum (1:48) cards. Notable Rookie Cards include Brian Giles (silver).

COMP.BRONZE SET (100) 10.00 25.00
SILVER STATED ODDS 1:3
GOLD STATED ODDS 1:12
PLATINUM STATED ODDS 1:48
1 Frank Thomas P 6.00 15.00
2 Ken Griffey Jr. P 10.00 25.00
3 Cecil Fielder B .15 .40
4 Chuck Knoblauch G 1.50 4.00
5 Garret Anderson B .15 .40
6 Greg Maddux P 8.00 20.00
7 Matt Williams S .75 2.00
8 Marquis Grissom S .75 2.00
9 Jason Isringhausen B .15 .40
10 Larry Walker S .75 2.00
11 Charles Nagy B .15 .40
12 Dan Wilson B .15 .40
13 Albert Belle G 1.50 4.00
14 Javier Lopez B .15 .40
15 David Cone B .15 .40
16 Bernard Gilkey B .15 .40
17 Andres Galarraga S .75 2.00
18 Bill Pulsipher B .15 .40
19 Alex Fernandez B .15 .40
20 Andy Pettitte S 1.25 3.00
21 Mark Grudzielanek B .15 .40
22 Juan Gonzalez P 6.00 15.00
23 Reggie Sanders B .15 .40
24 Kenny Lofton G 1.50 4.00
25 Andy Ashby B .15 .40
26 John Wetteland B .15 .40
27 Bobby Bonilla B .15 .40
28 Hideo Nomo G 4.00 10.00
29 Joe Carter B .15 .40
30 Jose Canseco B .25 .60
31 Ellis Burks B .15 .40
32 Edgar Martinez S 1.25 3.00
33 Chan Ho Park B .15 .40
34 Dave Justice B .15 .40
35 Carlos Delgado B .15 .40
36 Jeff Cirillo S .75 2.00
37 Charles Johnson B .15 .40
38 Manny Ramirez G 2.50 6.00
39 Greg Vaughn B .15 .40
40 Henry Rodriguez B .15 .40
41 Darryl Strawberry B .15 .40
42 Jim Thome G 2.50 6.00
43 Ryan Klesko S .75 2.00
44 Ruben Sierra B .15 .40
45 Brian Jordan G 1.50 4.00
46 Tony Gwynn P 6.00 15.00
47 Rafael Palmeiro G 2.50 6.00
48 Dante Bichette S .75 2.00
49 Ivan Rodriguez G 2.50 6.00
50 Mark McGwire G 10.00 25.00
51 Tim Salmon S 1.25 3.00
52 Roger Clemens B .75 2.00
53 Matt Lawton B .15 .40
54 Wade Boggs S 1.25 3.00
55 Travis Fryman B .15 .40
56 Bobby Higginson S .75 2.00
57 John Jaha S .75 2.00
58 Rondell White S .75 2.00
59 Tom Glavine S 1.25 3.00
60 Eddie Murray S 2.00 5.00
61 Vinny Castilla B .15 .40
62 Todd Hundley B .15 .40
63 Jay Buhner S .75 2.00
64 Paul O'Neill B .25 .60
65 Steve Finley B .15 .40
66 Kevin Appier B .15 .40
67 Ray Durham B .15 .40
68 Dave Nilsson B .15 .40
69 Jeff Bagwell G 2.50 6.00
70 Al Martin S .75 2.00
71 Paul Molitor G 1.50 4.00
72 Kevin Brown S .75 2.00
73 Ron Gant B .15 .40
74 Dwight Gooden B .15 .40
75 Quinton McCracken B .15 .40
76 Rusty Greer S .75 2.00
77 Juan Guzman B .15 .40
78 Fred McGriff S 1.25 3.00
79 Tino Martinez B .25 .60
80 Ray Lankford B .15 .40
81 Ken Caminiti G 1.50 4.00
82 James Baldwin B .15 .40
83 Jermaine Dye G 1.50 4.00
84 Mark Grace S 1.25 3.00
85 Pat Hentgen S .75 2.00
86 Jason Giambi S .75 2.00
87 Brian Hunter B .15 .40
88 Andy Benes B .15 .40
89 Jose Rosado B .15 .40
90 Shawn Green B .15 .40
91 Jason Kendall B .15 .40
92 Alex Rodriguez P 8.00 20.00
93 Chipper Jones P 6.00 15.00
94 Barry Bonds G 10.00 25.00
95 Brady Anderson G 1.50 4.00
96 Ryne Sandberg S 3.00 8.00
97 Lance Johnson B .15 .40
98 Cal Ripken P 10.00 25.00
99 Craig Biggio S 2.50 6.00
100 Dean Palmer B .15 .40
101 Gary Sheffield G 1.50 4.00
102 Johnny Damon B .25 .60
103 Mo Vaughn G 1.50 4.00
104 Randy Johnson S 2.00 5.00
105 Raul Mondesi S .75 2.00
106 Roberto Alomar G 2.50 6.00
107 Mike Piazza P 8.00 20.00
108 Rey Ordonez B .15 .40
109 Barry Larkin G 2.50 6.00
110 Tony Clark S .75 2.00
111 Bernie Williams S 1.25 3.00
112 John Smoltz G 2.50 6.00
113 Moises Alou B .15 .40
114 Will Clark B .25 .60
115 Sammy Sosa G 4.00 10.00
116 Jim Edmonds S .75 2.00
117 Jeff Conine B .15 .40
118 Joey Hamilton B .15 .40
119 Todd Hollandsworth B .15 .40
120 Troy Percival B .15 .40
121 Paul Wilson B .15 .40
122 Ken Hill B .15 .40
123 Mariano Rivera S 2.00 5.00
124 Eric Karros B .15 .40
125 Derek Jeter G 10.00 25.00
126 Eric Young S .15 .40
127 John Mabry B .15 .40
128 Gregg Jefferies B .15 .40
129 Ismael Valdes S .75 2.00
130 Marty Cordova B .15 .40
131 Omar Vizquel B .25 .60
132 Mike Mussina S 1.25 3.00
133 Darin Erstad B .15 .40
134 Edgar Renteria S .75 2.00
135 Billy Wagner B .15 .40
136 Alex Ochoa B .15 .40
137 Luis Castillo B .15 .40
138 Rocky Coppinger B .15 .40
139 Mike Sweeney B .15 .40
140 Michael Tucker B .15 .40
141 Chris Snopek B .15 .40
142 Dmitri Young S .75 2.00
143 Andruw Jones P 6.00 15.00
144 Mike Cameron S .75 2.00
145 Brant Brown B .15 .40
146 Todd Walker G 1.50 4.00
147 Nomar Garciaparra G 6.00 15.00
148 Glendon Rusch B .15 .40
149 Karim Garcia S .75 2.00
150 Bubba Trammell S RC .75 2.00
151 Todd Greene B .15 .40
152 Wilton Guerrero G 1.50 4.00
153 Scott Spiezio B .15 .40
154 Brooks Kieschnick B .15 .40
155 Vladimir Guerrero G 4.00 10.00
156 Brian Giles S RC 3.00 8.00
157 Pokey Reese B .15 .40
158 Jason Dickson G 1.50 4.00
159 Kevin Orie S 1.50 4.00
160 Scott Rolen G 2.50 6.00
161 Bartolo Colon S .75 2.00
162 Shannon Stewart G 1.50 4.00
163 Wendell Magee B .15 .40
164 Jose Guillen S .75 2.00
165 Bob Abreu S 1.25 3.00
166 Deivi Cruz B RC .15 .40
167 Alex Rodriguez NT B .60 1.50
168 Frank Thomas NT B .40 1.00
169 Cal Ripken NT B 1.25 3.00
170 Chipper Jones NT B .40 1.00
171 Mike Piazza NT B .60 1.50
172 Tony Gwynn NT S 2.50 6.00
173 Juan Gonzalez NT B .15 .40
174 Kenny Lofton NT S .75 2.00
175 Ken Griffey Jr. NT B .75 2.00
176 Mark McGwire NT B 1.00 2.50
177 Jeff Bagwell NT B .25 .60
178 Paul Molitor NT S .75 2.00
179 Andruw Jones NT B .25 .60
180 Manny Ramirez NT S 1.25 3.00
181 Ken Caminiti NT S .75 2.00
182 Barry Bonds NT B 1.00 2.50
183 Mo Vaughn NT B .15 .40
184 Derek Jeter NT B 1.00 2.50
185 Barry Larkin NT S 1.25 3.00
186 Ivan Rodriguez NT B .25 .60
187 Albert Belle NT S .75 2.00
188 John Smoltz NT S 1.25 3.00
189 Chuck Knoblauch NT S .75 2.00
190 Brian Jordan NT S .75 2.00
191 Gary Sheffield NT S .75 2.00
192 Jim Thome NT S 1.25 3.00
193 Brady Anderson NT S .75 2.00
194 Hideo Nomo NT S 2.00 5.00
195 Sammy Sosa NT S 2.00 5.00
196 Greg Maddux NT B .60 1.50
197 Vladimir Guerrero CL B .40 1.00
198 Scott Rolen CL B .15 .40
199 Todd Walker CL B (133-200) .15 .40
200 Nomar Garciaparra CL B .50 1.25

1997 Donruss Preferred Cut to the Chase

*BRONZE STARS: 3X TO 8X BASIC
*SILVER STARS: 1.5X TO 4X BASIC
*SILVER ROOKIES: .6X TO 1.5X BASIC
*GOLD STARS: 1X TO 2.5X BASIC
*PLAT.STARS: 1X TO 2.5X BASIC
RANDOM INSERTS IN PACKS

1997 Donruss Preferred Precious Metals

RANDOM INSERTS IN PACKS
STATED PRINT RUN 100 SETS
ONE GRAM OF PRECIOUS METAL PER CARD
1 Frank Thomas P 100.00 200.00
2 Ken Griffey Jr. P 75.00 200.00
3 Greg Maddux P 75.00 150.00
4 Albert Belle G 30.00 60.00
5 Juan Gonzalez P 30.00 60.00
6 Kenny Lofton G 30.00 60.00
7 Tony Gwynn P 60.00 120.00
8 Ivan Rodriguez G 40.00 80.00
9 Mark McGwire G 60.00 120.00
10 Matt Williams S 30.00 60.00
11 Wade Boggs S 40.00 80.00
12 Eddie Murray S 40.00 80.00
13 Jeff Bagwell G 40.00 80.00
14 Ken Caminiti G 30.00 60.00
15 Alex Rodriguez P 75.00 150.00
16 Chipper Jones P 40.00 80.00
17 Barry Bonds G 75.00 150.00
18 Cal Ripken P 100.00 200.00
19 Mo Vaughn G 30.00 60.00
20 Mike Piazza P 100.00 200.00
21 Derek Jeter G 125.00 250.00
22 Bernie Williams S 40.00 80.00
23 Andruw Jones P 40.00 80.00
24 Vladimir Guerrero G 50.00 100.00
25 Jose Guillen S 30.00 60.00

1997 Donruss Preferred Staremasters Samples

COMPLETE SET (20) 15.00 40.00
1 Alex Rodriguez 1.25 3.00
2 Frank Thomas .50 1.25
3 Chipper Jones 1.00 2.50
4 Cal Ripken 2.00 5.00
5 Mike Piazza 1.50 4.00
6 Juan Gonzalez .40 1.00
7 Derek Jeter 2.00 5.00
8 Jeff Bagwell .50 1.25
9 Ken Griffey Jr. 1.50 4.00
10 Tony Gwynn 1.00 2.50
11 Barry Bonds 1.00 2.50
12 Albert Belle .20 .50
13 Greg Maddux 1.00 2.50
14 Mark McGwire 1.50 4.00
15 Ken Caminiti .20 .50
16 Hideo Nomo .40 1.00
17 Gary Sheffield .50 1.25
18 Andruw Jones .60 1.50
19 Mo Vaughn .20 .50
20 Ivan Rodriguez .50 1.25

1997 Donruss Preferred Staremasters

RANDOM INSERTS IN PACKS
STATED PRINT RUN 1500 SERIAL #'d SETS
1 Alex Rodriguez 3.00 8.00
2 Frank Thomas 2.50 6.00
3 Chipper Jones 2.50 6.00
4 Cal Ripken 8.00 20.00
5 Mike Piazza 2.50 6.00
6 Juan Gonzalez 1.00 2.50
7 Derek Jeter 6.00 15.00
8 Jeff Bagwell 1.50 4.00
9 Ken Griffey Jr. 5.00 12.00
10 Tony Gwynn 2.50 6.00
11 Barry Bonds 4.00 10.00
12 Albert Belle 1.00 2.50
13 Greg Maddux 4.00 10.00
14 Mark McGwire 4.00 10.00
15 Ken Caminiti 1.00 2.50
16 Hideo Nomo 1.50 4.00
17 Gary Sheffield 1.00 2.50
18 Andruw Jones 1.00 2.50
19 Mo Vaughn 1.00 2.50
20 Ivan Rodriguez 1.50 4.00

1997 Donruss Preferred Tin Packs

COMPLETE SET (25) 8.00 20.00
DISTRIBUTED AS COLLECTIBLE PACKAGE
*GOLD PACKS: 4X TO 10X BASIC PACKS
ONE GOLD PACK PER BOX
GOLD PACKS: 1200 SERIAL #'d SETS
*BLUE BOXES: 3X TO 8X BASIC PACKS
BLUE BOXES: 1200 SERIAL #'d SETS
*GOLD BOXES: 8X TO 20X BASIC PACKS
GOLD BOXES: 299 SERIAL #'d SETS
PRICES BELOW REFER TO OPENED PACKS
1 Jeff Bagwell .10 .30
2 Albert Belle .08 .25
3 Barry Bonds .60 1.50
4 Roger Clemens .50 1.25
5 Juan Gonzalez .08 .25
6 Ken Griffey Jr. .50 1.25
7 Tony Gwynn .30 .75
8 Derek Jeter .60 1.50
9 Andruw Jones .10 .30
10 Chipper Jones .20 .50
11 Kenny Lofton .08 .25
12 Greg Maddux .40 1.00
13 Mark McGwire .60 1.50
14 Hideo Nomo .20 .50
15 Mike Piazza .40 1.00
16 Manny Ramirez .10 .30
17 Cal Ripken .75 2.00
18 Alex Rodriguez .40 1.00
19 Ivan Rodriguez .10 .30
20 Ryne Sandberg .40 1.00
21 Gary Sheffield .08 .25
22 John Smoltz .10 .30
23 Sammy Sosa .20 .50
24 Frank Thomas .20 .50
25 Mo Vaughn .08 .25
NNO Frank Thomas SAMPLE 1.00 2.50

1997 Donruss Preferred X-Ponential Power

COMPLETE SET (20) 15.00 40.00
RANDOM INSERTS IN PACKS
STATED PRINT RUN 3000 SERIAL #'d SETS
1A Manny Ramirez 1.00 2.50
1B Jim Thome 1.00 2.50
2A Paul Molitor 1.50 4.00
2B Chuck Knoblauch .60 1.50
3A Ivan Rodriguez 1.00 2.50
3B Juan Gonzalez .60 1.50
4A Albert Belle .60 1.50
4B Frank Thomas 1.50 4.00
5A Roberto Alomar 1.00 2.50
5B Cal Ripken 5.00 12.00
6A Tim Salmon .60 1.50
6B Jim Edmonds .60 1.50
7A Ken Griffey Jr. 3.00 8.00
7B Alex Rodriguez 2.00 5.00
8A Chipper Jones 1.50 4.00
8B Andruw Jones .60 1.50
9A Mike Piazza 1.50 4.00
9B Raul Mondesi .60 1.50
10A Tony Gwynn 1.50 4.00
10B Ken Caminiti .60 1.50

1997 Donruss Preferred Tins Fanfest

COMPLETE SET (25) 15.00 40.00
1 Jeff Bagwell .50 1.25
2 Albert Belle .20 .50
3 Barry Bonds 1.00 2.50
4 Roger Clemens 1.00 2.50
5 Juan Gonzalez .50 1.25
6 Ken Griffey Jr. 1.50 4.00
7 Tony Gwynn 1.00 2.50
8 Derek Jeter 2.00 5.00
9 Andruw Jones .60 1.50
10 Chipper Jones 1.00 2.50
11 Kenny Lofton .30 .75
12 Greg Maddux 1.25 3.00
13 Mark McGwire 1.50 4.00
14 Hideo Nomo .50 1.25
15 Mike Piazza 1.25 3.00
16 Manny Ramirez .50 1.25
17 Cal Ripken 2.00 5.00
18 Alex Rodriguez 1.25 3.00
19 Ivan Rodriguez .50 1.25
20 Ryne Sandberg .60 1.50
21 Gary Sheffield .40 1.00
22 John Smoltz .20 .50
23 Sammy Sosa 1.00 2.50
24 Frank Thomas .50 1.25
25 Mo Vaughn .20 .50

1998 Donruss Preferred

The Donruss Preferred set was issued in one series totalling 200 cards and distributed in five-card packs with a suggested retail price of $4.99. The fronts feature color player photos on micro-etched backgrounds with specially micro-etched borders unique to each color. The set is fractured into varying levels of scarcity as follows: 10 Executive Suite cards with an insertion rate of 1:65, 20 Field Box cards inserted 1:23, 30 Club Level cards inserted 1:12, 40 Mezzanine cards inserted 1:6, and 100 Grand Stand cards inserted four or five per pack.

COMP.GRAND STAND (100) 10.00 25.00
COMMON GRAND STAND .10 .30
COMP.MEZZANINE (40) 25.00 60.00
COMMON MEZZANINE .75 2.00
MEZZANINE STATED ODDS 1:6
COMP.CLUB LEVEL (30) 40.00 100.00
COMMON CLUB LEVEL 1.25 3.00
CLUB LEVEL STATED ODDS 1:12
COMP.FIELD BOX (20) 60.00 150.00
COMMON FIELD BOX 1.50 4.00
FIELD BOX STATED ODDS 1:23
COMP.EXEC.SUITE (10) 60.00 150.00
COMMON EXEC.SUITE 4.00 10.00
EXECUTIVE SUITE STATED ODDS 1:65
1 Ken Griffey Jr. EX 8.00 20.00
2 Frank Thomas EX 4.00 10.00
3 Cal Ripken EX 12.50 30.00
4 Alex Rodriguez EX 6.00 15.00
5 Greg Maddux EX 6.00 15.00
6 Mike Piazza EX 6.00 15.00
7 Chipper Jones EX 4.00 10.00
8 Tony Gwynn FB 5.00 12.00
9 Derek Jeter FB 10.00 25.00
10 Jeff Bagwell EX 4.00 10.00
11 Juan Gonzalez EX 4.00 10.00
12 Nomar Garciaparra EX 6.00 15.00
13 Andruw Jones FB 2.50 6.00
14 Hideo Nomo FB 4.00 10.00
15 Roger Clemens FB 8.00 20.00
16 Mark McGwire FB 10.00 25.00
17 Scott Rolen FB 2.50 6.00
18 Vladimir Guerrero FB 4.00 10.00
19 Barry Bonds FB 10.00 25.00
20 Darin Erstad FB 1.50 4.00
21 Albert Belle FB 1.50 4.00
22 Kenny Lofton FB 1.50 4.00
23 Mo Vaughn FB 1.50 4.00
24 Tony Clark FB 1.50 4.00
25 Ivan Rodriguez FB 2.50 6.00
26 Larry Walker CB 1.25 3.00
27 Eddie Murray CB 3.00 8.00
28 Andy Pettitte CB 2.00 5.00
29 Roberto Alomar CB 2.00 5.00
30 Randy Johnson CB 3.00 8.00
31 Manny Ramirez CB 2.00 5.00
32 Paul Molitor FB 1.50 4.00
33 Mike Mussina CB 2.00 5.00
34 Jim Thome FB 2.50 6.00
35 Tino Martinez CB 2.00 5.00
36 Gary Sheffield CB 1.25 3.00
37 Chuck Knoblauch CB 1.25 3.00
38 Bernie Williams CB 2.00 5.00
39 Tim Salmon CB 2.00 5.00
40 Sammy Sosa CB 3.00 8.00
41 Wade Boggs ME 1.25 3.00
42 Will Clark GS .20 .50
43 Andres Galarraga CB 1.25 3.00
44 Raul Mondesi CB 1.25 3.00
45 Rickey Henderson GS .30 .75
46 Jose Canseco GS .20 .50
47 Pedro Martinez GS .20 .50
48 Jay Buhner GS .10 .30
49 Ryan Klesko GS .10 .30
50 Barry Larkin CB 2.00 5.00
51 Charles Johnson GS .10 .30
52 Tom Glavine GS .20 .50
53 Edgar Martinez CB 2.00 5.00
54 Fred McGriff GS .20 .50
55 Moises Alou ME .75 2.00
56 Dante Bichette GS .10 .30
57 Jim Edmonds CB 1.25 3.00
58 Mark Grace ME 1.25 3.00
59 Chan Ho Park ME .75 2.00
60 Justin Thompson ME .75 2.00
61 John Smoltz ME 1.25 3.00
62 Craig Biggio CB 2.00 5.00
63 Ken Caminiti ME .75 2.00
64 Deion Sanders ME 1.25 3.00
65 Carlos Delgado GS .10 .30
66 David Justice CB 1.25 3.00
67 J.T. Snow GS .10 .30
68 Jason Giambi CB 1.25 3.00
69 Garret Anderson ME .75 2.00
70 Rondell White ME .75 2.00
71 Matt Williams ME .75 2.00
72 Brady Anderson ME .75 2.00
73 Eric Karros GS .10 .30
74 Javier Lopez GS .10 .30
75 Pat Hentgen GS .10 .30
76 Todd Hundley GS .10 .30
77 Ray Lankford GS .10 .30
78 Denny Neagle GS .10 .30
79 Henry Rodriguez GS .10 .30
80 Sandy Alomar Jr. ME .75 2.00
81 Rafael Palmeiro ME 1.25 3.00
82 Robin Ventura GS .10 .30
83 John Olerud GS .10 .30
84 Omar Vizquel GS .20 .50
85 Joe Randa GS .10 .30
86 Lance Johnson GS .10 .30
87 Kevin Brown GS .20 .50
88 Curt Schilling GS .10 .30
89 Ismael Valdes GS .10 .30
90 Francisco Cordova GS .10 .30
91 David Cone GS .10 .30
92 Paul O'Neill GS .20 .50
93 Jimmy Key GS .10 .30
94 Brad Radke GS .10 .30
95 Kevin Appier GS .10 .30
96 Al Martin GS .10 .30
97 Rusty Greer ME .75 2.00
98 Reggie Jefferson GS .10 .30
99 Ron Coomer GS .10 .30
100 Vinny Castilla GS .10 .30
101 Bobby Bonilla ME .75 2.00
102 Eric Young GS .10 .30
103 Tony Womack GS .10 .30
104 Jason Kendall GS .10 .30
105 Jeff Suppan GS .10 .30
106 Shawn Estes ME .75 2.00
107 Shawn Green GS .10 .30
108 Edgardo Alfonzo ME .75 2.00
109 Alan Benes ME .75 2.00
110 Bobby Higginson GS .10 .30
111 Mark Grudzielanek GS .10 .30
112 Wilton Guerrero GS .10 .30
113 Todd Greene ME .75 2.00
114 Pokey Reese GS .10 .30
115 Jose Guillen CB 1.25 3.00
116 Neifi Perez ME .75 2.00
117 Luis Castillo GS .10 .30
118 Edgar Renteria GS .10 .30
119 Karim Garcia GS .10 .30
120 Butch Huskey GS .10 .30
121 Michael Tucker GS .10 .30
122 Jason Dickson GS .10 .30
123 Todd Walker ME .75 2.00
124 Brian Jordan GS .10 .30
125 Joe Carter GS .10 .30
126 Matt Morris ME .75 2.00
127 Brett Tomko ME .75 2.00
128 Mike Cameron CB 1.25 3.00
129 Russ Davis GS .10 .30
130 Shannon Stewart ME .75 2.00
131 Kevin Orie GS .10 .30
132 Scott Spiezio GS .10 .30
133 Brian Giles GS .10 .30
134 Raul Casanova GS .10 .30
135 Jose Cruz Jr. CB 1.25 3.00
136 Hideki Irabu GS .10 .30
137 Bubba Trammell GS .10 .30
138 Richard Hidalgo CB 1.25 3.00
139 Paul Konerko CB 1.25 3.00
140 Todd Helton FB 2.50 6.00
141 Miguel Tejada CB 3.00 8.00
142 Fernando Tatis ME .75 2.00
143 Ben Grieve FB 1.50 4.00
144 Travis Lee FB 1.50 4.00
145 Mark Kotsay CB 1.25 3.00
146 Eli Marrero ME .75 2.00
147 David Ortiz CB 4.00 10.00
148 Juan Encarnacion ME .75 2.00
149 Jaret Wright ME .75 2.00
150 Livan Hernandez CB 1.25 3.00
151 Ruben Rivera GS .10 .30
152 Brad Fullmer ME .75 2.00
153 Dennis Reyes GS .10 .30
154 Enrique Wilson ME .75 2.00
155 Todd Dunwoody ME .75 2.00
156 Derrick Gibson ME .75 2.00
157 Aaron Boone ME .75 2.00
158 Ron Wright ME .75 2.00
159 Preston Wilson ME .75 2.00
160 Abraham Nunez GS .10 .30
161 Shane Monahan GS .10 .30
162 Carl Pavano GS .10 .30
163 Derrek Lee GS .20 .50
164 Jeff Abbott GS .10 .30
165 Wes Helms ME .75 2.00
166 Brian Rose GS .10 .30
167 Bobby Estalella GS .10 .30
168 Ken Griffey Jr. PP GS .60 1.50
169 Frank Thomas PP GS .30 .75
170 Cal Ripken PP GS 1.00 2.50
171 Alex Rodriguez PP GS .50 1.25
172 Greg Maddux PP GS .50 1.25
173 Mike Piazza PP GS .50 1.25
174 Chipper Jones PP GS .30 .75
175 Tony Gwynn PP GS .20 .50
176 Derek Jeter PP GS .75 2.00
177 Jeff Bagwell PP GS .20 .50
178 Juan Gonzalez PP GS .10 .30
179 Nomar Garciaparra PP GS .50 1.25
180 Andruw Jones PP GS .20 .50
181 Hideo Nomo PP GS .30 .75
182 Roger Clemens PP GS .60 1.50
183 Mark McGwire PP GS .75 2.00
184 Scott Rolen PP GS .20 .50
185 Barry Bonds PP GS .75 2.00
186 Darin Erstad PP GS .10 .30
187 Mo Vaughn PP GS .10 .30
188 Ivan Rodriguez PP GS .20 .50
189 Larry Walker PP ME .75 2.00
190 Andy Pettitte PP GS .20 .50
191 Randy Johnson PP ME 2.00 5.00
192 Paul Molitor PP GS .10 .30
193 Jim Thome PP GS .20 .50
194 Tino Martinez PP ME 1.25 3.00
195 Gary Sheffield PP GS .10 .30
196 Albert Belle PP GS .10 .30
197 Jose Cruz Jr. PP GS .10 .30
198 Todd Helton CL GS .10 .30
199 Ben Grieve CL GS .10 .30
200 Paul Konerko CL GS .10 .30

1998 Donruss Preferred Seating

COMPLETE SET (200) 1000.00 1800.00
COMP.GRAND STAND (100) 150.00 300.00
*GS STARS: 4X TO 10X BASIC CARDS
*MEZZ.STARS: .75X TO 2X BASIC CARDS
*CLUB LEV.STARS: .75X TO 2X BASIC CARDS
*FIELD BOX STARS: .75X TO 2X BASIC CARDS
*EXEC.STARS: .75X TO 2X BASIC CARDS
RANDOM INSERTS IN PACKS

1998 Donruss Preferred Great X-Pectations Samples

COMPLETE SET (26) 100.00 200.00
1 Jeff Bagwell 2.50 6.00
Travis Lee
2 Jose Cruz Jr. 10.00 25.00
Ken Griffey Jr.
3 Larry Walker .75 2.00
Ben Grieve
4 FrankThomas 4.00 10.00
Todd Helton
5 Jim Thome 1.00 2.50
Paul Konerko
6 Alex Rodriguez 6.00 15.00
Miguel Tejada
7 Greg Maddux 5.00 12.00
Livan Hernandez
8 Roger Clemens 4.00 10.00
Jaret Wright
9 Albert Belle 1.00 2.50
Juan Encarnacion
10 Mo Vaughn 1.00 2.50
David Ortiz
11 Manny Ramirez 2.50 6.00
Mark Kotsay
12 T.Salmon .75 2.00
B.Fullmer UER
13 Cal Ripken 8.00 20.00
Fernando Tatis
14 Hideo Nomo 4.00 10.00
Hideki Irabu
15 Mike Piazza 6.00 15.00
Todd Greene
16 Gary Sheffield 2.00 5.00
Ricardo Hidalgo
17 Paul Molitor 2.50 6.00
Darin Erstad
18 Ivan Rodriguez 2.50 6.00
Eli Marrero
19 Ken Caminiti .75 2.00
Todd Walker
20 Tony Gwynn 4.00 10.00
Jose Guillen
21 Derek Jeter 8.00 20.00
Nomar Garciaparra
22 Chipper Jones 5.00 12.00
Scott Rolen
23 Juan Gonzalez 2.00 5.00
Andruw Jones
24 Barry Bonds 3.00 8.00
Vladimir Guerrero
25 Mark McGwire 8.00 20.00
Tony Clark
26 Bernie Williams 2.00 5.00
Mike Cameron

1998 Donruss Preferred Great X-Pectations

COMPLETE SET (26) 30.00 80.00
STATED PRINT RUN 2700 SERIAL #'d SETS
*DIE CUTS: .75X TO 2X BASIC X-PECTATION
DIE CUT PRINT RUN 300 SERIAL #'d SETS
RANDOM INSERTS IN PACKS
1 J.Bagwell 1.00 2.50
T.Lee
2 J.Cruz Jr. 3.00 8.00
K.Griffey Jr.
3 L.Walker 1.00 2.50
B.Grieve
4 F.Thomas 1.50 4.00
T.Helton
5 J.Thome 1.00 2.50
P.Konerko
6 A.Rodriguez 2.00 5.00
M.Tejada
7 G.Maddux 2.00 5.00
L.Hernandez
8 R.Clemens 2.00 5.00
J.Wright
9 A.Belle .60 1.50
J.Encarnacion
10 M.Vaughn 2.00 5.00
D.Ortiz
11 M.Ramirez 1.50 4.00
M.Kotsay
12 T.Salmon .60 1.50
B.Fullmer UER
13 C.Ripken 5.00 12.00
F.Tatis
14 H.Nomo 1.50 4.00
H.Irabu
15 M.Piazza 1.50 4.00
T.Greene
16 G.Sheffield .60 1.50
R.Hidalgo
17 P.Molitor 1.50 4.00
D.Erstad
18 I.Rodriguez 1.00 2.50
E.Marrero
19 K.Caminiti .60 1.50
T.Walker
20 T.Gwynn 1.50 4.00
J.Guillen
21 D.Jeter 4.00 10.00
N.Garciaparra
22 C.Jones 1.50 4.00
S.Rolen
23 J.Gonzalez .60 1.50
A.Jones
24 B.Bonds 2.50 6.00
V.Guerrero
25 M.McGwire 2.50 6.00
T.Clark
26 B.Williams 1.00 2.50
M.Cameron

1998 Donruss Preferred Precious Metals

RANDOM INSERTS IN PACKS
STATED PRINT RUN 50 SETS
1 Ken Griffey Jr. 40.00 100.00
2 Frank Thomas 100.00 200.00
3 Cal Ripken 75.00 150.00
4 Alex Rodriguez 40.00 80.00
5 Greg Maddux P 40.00 80.00
6 Mike Piazza 40.00 80.00
7 Chipper Jones 20.00 50.00
8 Tony Gwynn 30.00 60.00
9 Derek Jeter 100.00 200.00
10 Jeff Bagwell 15.00 40.00
11 Juan Gonzalez 25.00 50.00
12 Nomar Garciaparra 40.00 80.00
13 Andruw Jones 15.00 40.00
14 Hideo Nomo 20.00 50.00
15 Roger Clemens G 50.00 100.00
16 Mark McGwire 75.00 150.00
17 Scott Rolen 15.00 40.00
18 Barry Bonds 60.00 120.00
19 Darin Erstad 12.00 30.00
20 Kenny Lofton G 25.00 50.00
21 Mo Vaughn 12.00 30.00
22 Ivan Rodriguez 15.00 40.00
23 Randy Johnson 20.00 50.00
24 Paul Molitor G 30.00 60.00
25 Jose Cruz Jr. 12.00 30.00
26 Paul Konerko 12.00 30.00
27 Todd Helton 15.00 40.00
28 Ben Grieve 12.00 30.00
29 Travis Lee 12.00 30.00
30 Mark Kotsay 12.00 30.00

1998 Donruss Preferred Tin Packs

COMP.GREEN SET (24) 6.00 15.00
ISSUED AS COLLECTIBLE PACKAGING
*GOLD PACKS: 8X TO 20X BASIC PACK
GOLD PACKS: RANDOM INSERTS IN BOXES
GOLD PACK PRINT RUN 199 SERIAL #'d SETS
*SILVER PACKS: 3X TO 8X BASIC PACK
SILVER PACK RANDOM INSERTS IN BOXES
SILVER PACK PR.RUN 999 SERIAL #'d SETS
*GREEN BOXES: 3X TO 8X BASIC PACK
GREEN BOX PRINT RUN 999 SERIAL #'d SETS
*GOLD BOXES: 8X TO 20X BASIC PACK
GOLD BOX PRINT RUN 199 SERIAL #'d SETS
PRICES BELOW ARE FOR OPEN GREEN PACKS
1 Todd Helton .15 .40
2 Ben Grieve .08 .25
3 Cal Ripken .75 2.00
4 Alex Rodriguez .40 1.00
5 Greg Maddux .40 1.00
6 Mike Piazza .40 1.00
7 Chipper Jones .25 .60
8 Travis Lee .08 .25
9 Derek Jeter .60 1.50
10 Jeff Bagwell .15 .40
11 Juan Gonzalez .08 .25
12 Mark McGwire .60 1.50
13 Hideo Nomo .25 .60
14 Roger Clemens .50 1.25
15 Andruw Jones .15 .40
16 Paul Molitor .08 .25
17 Vladimir Guerrero .25 .60
18 Jose Cruz Jr. .08 .25
19 Nomar Garciaparra PH .40 1.00
20 Scott Rolen PH .15 .40
21 Ken Griffey Jr. PH .50 1.25
22 Larry Walker PH .08 .25
23 Frank Thomas PH .25 .60
24 Tony Gwynn PH .30 .75

1998 Donruss Preferred Tin Packs Double-Wide

COMPLETE SET (12) 10.00 25.00
AVAILABLE ONLY IN RETAIL OUTLETS
PRICES BELOW REFER TO OPENED PACKS
1 T.Helton .30 .75
B.Grieve
2 C.Ripken 1.25 3.00
A.Rodriguez
3 G.Maddux .50 1.25
M.Piazza
4 C.Jones .40 1.00
T.Lee
5 D.Jeter 1.00 2.50
J.Bagwell
6 J.Gonzalez 1.00 2.50
M.McGwire
7 H.Nomo .75 2.00
R.Clemens
8 A.Jones .30 .75
P.Molitor
9 V.Guerrero .40 1.00
J.Cruz Jr.
10 N.Garciaparra .60 1.50
S.Rolen PH
11 K.Griffey Jr. .75 2.00
L.Walker PH
12 T.Gwynn .50 1.25
F.Thomas PH

1998 Donruss Preferred Title Waves

RANDOM INSERTS IN PACKS
PRINT RUN BASED ON TITLE YEAR
1 Nomar Garciaparra/1997 1.50 4.00
2 Scott Rolen/1997 1.50 4.00
3 Roger Clemens/1997 3.00 8.00
4 Gary Sheffield/1997 1.00 2.50
5 Jeff Bagwell/1997 1.50 4.00
6 Cal Ripken/1997 8.00 20.00
7 Frank Thomas/1997 2.50 6.00
8 Ken Griffey Jr./1997 5.00 12.00
9 Larry Walker/1997 1.50 4.00
10 Derek Jeter/1996 6.00 15.00
11 Juan Gonzalez/1996 1.00 2.50
12 Bernie Williams/1996 1.50 4.00
13 Andruw Jones/1996 1.00 2.50
14 Andy Pettitte/1996 1.50 4.00
15 Ivan Rodriguez/1996 1.50 4.00
16 Alex Rodriguez/1996 3.00 8.00
17 Mark McGwire/1996 4.00 10.00
18 Andres Galarraga/1996 1.50 4.00
19 Hideo Nomo/1995 2.50 6.00
20 Mo Vaughn/1995 1.00 2.50
21 Randy Johnson/1995 2.50 6.00
22 Chipper Jones/1995 2.50 6.00
23 Greg Maddux/1995 3.00 8.00
24 Manny Ramirez/1995 2.50 6.00
25 Tony Gwynn/1995 2.50 6.00
26 Albert Belle/1995 1.00 2.50
27 Kenny Lofton/1995 1.00 2.50
28 Mike Piazza/1993 2.50 6.00
29 Paul Molitor/1993 2.50 6.00
30 Barry Bonds/1993 4.00 10.00

1997 Donruss Signature

Distributed in five-card packs with one authentic autographed card per pack, this 100-card set was issued in two series. However, these regular cards were issued with both series and one could make sets from either series. These packs carried a suggested retail price of $14.99. The fronts feature color player photos with player information on the backs. The only Rookie Cards of note in this set are Jose Cruz Jr. and Mark Kotsay.

COMPLETE SET (100) 20.00 50.00
1 Mark McGwire 1.25 3.00
2 Kenny Lofton .20 .50
3 Tony Gwynn .60 1.50
4 Tony Clark .20 .50
5 Tim Salmon .30 .75
6 Ken Griffey Jr. 1.00 2.50
7 Mike Piazza .75 2.00
8 Greg Maddux .75 2.00
9 Roberto Alomar .30 .75
10 Andres Galarraga .20 .50
11 Roger Clemens 1.00 2.50
12 Bernie Williams .30 .75
13 Rondell White .20 .50
14 Kevin Appier .20 .50
15 Ray Lankford .20 .50
16 Frank Thomas .50 1.25
17 Will Clark .30 .75
18 Chipper Jones .50 1.25
19 Jeff Bagwell .30 .75
20 Manny Ramirez .30 .75
21 Ryne Sandberg .75 2.00
22 Paul Molitor .20 .50
23 Gary Sheffield .20 .50
24 Jim Edmonds .20 .50
25 Barry Larkin .30 .75
26 Rafael Palmeiro .30 .75
27 Alan Benes .20 .50
28 Dave Justice .20 .50
29 Randy Johnson .50 1.25
30 Barry Bonds 1.25 3.00
31 Mo Vaughn .20 .50
32 Michael Tucker .20 .50
33 Larry Walker .20 .50
34 Tino Martinez .30 .75
35 Jose Guillen .20 .50
36 Carlos Delgado .20 .50
37 Jason Dickson .20 .50
38 Tom Glavine .30 .75
39 Raul Mondesi .20 .50
40 Jose Cruz Jr. RC .20 .50
41 Johnny Damon .30 .75
42 Mark Grace .30 .75
43 Juan Gonzalez .20 .50
44 Vladimir Guerrero .50 1.25
45 Kevin Brown .20 .50
46 Justin Thompson .20 .50
47 Eric Young .20 .50
48 Ron Coomer .20 .50
49 Mark Kotsay RC .50 1.25
50 Scott Rolen .30 .75
51 Derek Jeter 1.25 3.00
52 Jim Thome .30 .75
53 Fred McGriff .30 .75
54 Albert Belle .20 .50
55 Garret Anderson .20 .50
56 Wilton Guerrero .20 .50
57 Jose Canseco .30 .75
58 Cal Ripken 1.50 4.00
59 Sammy Sosa .50 1.25
60 Dmitri Young .20 .50
61 Alex Rodriguez .75 2.00
62 Javier Lopez .20 .50
63 Sandy Alomar Jr. .20 .50
64 Joe Carter .20 .50
65 Dante Bichette .20 .50
66 Al Martin .20 .50
67 Darin Erstad .20 .50
68 Pokey Reese .20 .50
69 Brady Anderson .20 .50
70 Andruw Jones .30 .75
71 Ivan Rodriguez .30 .75
72 Nomar Garciaparra .75 2.00
73 Moises Alou .20 .50
74 Andy Pettitte .30 .75
75 Jay Buhner .20 .50
76 Craig Biggio .30 .75
77 Wade Boggs .30 .75
78 Shawn Estes .20 .50
79 Neifi Perez .20 .50
80 Rusty Greer .20 .50
81 Pedro Martinez .30 .75
82 Mike Mussina .30 .75
83 Jason Giambi .20 .50
84 Hideo Nomo .50 1.25
85 Todd Hundley .20 .50
86 Deion Sanders .30 .75
87 Mike Cameron .20 .50
88 Bobby Bonilla .20 .50
89 Todd Greene .20 .50
90 Kevin Orie .20 .50
91 Ken Caminiti .20 .50
92 Chuck Knoblauch .20 .50
93 Matt Morris .20 .50
94 Matt Williams .20 .50
95 Pat Hentgen .20 .50
96 John Smoltz .30 .75
97 Edgar Martinez .30 .75
98 Jason Kendall .20 .50
99 Ken Griffey Jr. CL .60 1.50
100 Frank Thomas CL .30 .75

1997 Donruss Signature Platinum Press Proofs

*STARS: 5X TO 12X BASIC CARDS
*ROOKIES: 2X TO 5X BASIC CARDS
RANDOM INSERTS IN PACKS
STATED PRINT RUN 150 SETS

1997 Donruss Signature Autographs

ONE AUTOGRAPH PER PACK
STATED PRINT RUNS LISTED BELOW
ASTERISK CARDS ARE IN SERIES A AND B
NNO CARDS LISTED IN ALPH.ORDER
1 Jeff Abbott/3900 2.00 5.00
2 Bob Abreu/3900 4.00 10.00
3 Edgardo Alfonzo/3900 2.00 5.00
4 Roberto Alomar/150 * 12.00 30.00
5 Sandy Alomar Jr./1400 6.00 15.00
6 Moises Alou/900 6.00 15.00
7 Garret Anderson/3900 4.00 10.00
8 Andy Ashby/3900 2.00 5.00
9 Trey Beamon/3900 2.00 5.00
10 Alan Benes/3900 2.00 5.00
11 Geronimo Berroa/3900 2.00 5.00
12 Wade Boggs/150 * 60.00 150.00
13 Kevin Brown C/3900 2.00 5.00
14 Brett Butler/1400 6.00 15.00
15 Mike Cameron/3900 4.00 10.00
16 Giovanni Carrara/2900 2.00 5.00
17 Luis Castillo/3900 4.00 10.00
18 Tony Clark/3900 2.00 5.00
19 Will Clark/1400 10.00 25.00
20 Lou Collier/3900 2.00 5.00
21 Bartolo Colon/3900 6.00 15.00
22 Ron Coomer/3900 2.00 5.00
23 Marty Cordova/3900 2.00 5.00
24 Jacob Cruz/3900 * 2.00 5.00
25 Jose Cruz Jr./900 * 3.00 8.00
26 Russ Davis/3900 2.00 5.00
27 Jason Dickson/3900 2.00 5.00
28 Todd Dunwoody/3900 2.00 5.00
29 Jermaine Dye/3900 4.00 10.00
30 Jim Edmonds/3900 5.00 12.00
31 Darin Erstad/900 * 3.00 8.00
32 Bobby Estalella/3900 2.00 5.00
33 Shawn Estes/3900 2.00 5.00
34 Jeff Fassero/3900 2.00 5.00
35 Andres Galarraga/900 8.00 20.00
36 Karim Garcia/3900 2.00 5.00
37 Derrick Gibson/3900 2.00 5.00
38 Brian Giles/3900 2.00 5.00
39 Tom Glavine/150 30.00 80.00
40 Rick Gorecki/900 3.00 8.00
41 Shawn Green/1900 4.00 10.00
42 Todd Greene/3900 2.00 5.00
43 Rusty Greer/3900 4.00 10.00
44 Ben Grieve/3900 2.00 5.00
45 Mark Grudzielanek/3900 2.00 5.00
46 Vladimir Guerrero/1900 * 12.00 30.00
47 Wilton Guerrero/2150 -2.00 5.00
48 Jose Guillen/2900 4.00 10.00
49 Jeffrey Hammonds/2150 2.00 5.00
50 Todd Helton/1400 10.00 25.00
51 Todd Hollandsworth/2900 2.00 5.00
52 Trenidad Hubbard/900 3.00 8.00
53 Todd Hundley/1400 6.00 15.00
54 Bobby Jones/3900 2.00 5.00
55 Brian Jordan/1400 6.00 15.00
56 David Justice/900 6.00 15.00
57 Eric Karros/650 6.00 15.00
58 Jason Kendall/3900 4.00 10.00
59 Jimmy Key/3900 4.00 10.00
60 Brooks Kieschnick/3900 2.00 5.00
61 Ryan Klesko/225 5.00 12.00
62 Paul Konerko/3900 6.00 15.00
63 Mark Kotsay/2400 6.00 15.00
64 Ray Lankford/3900 4.00 10.00
65 Barry Larkin/150 * 25.00 60.00
66 Derrek Lee/3900 4.00 10.00
67 Esteban Loaiza/3900 2.00 5.00
68 Javier Lopez/1400 8.00 20.00
69 Edgar Martinez/150 * 10.00 25.00
70 Pedro Martinez/900 50.00 120.00
71 Rafael Medina/3900 2.00 5.00
72 Raul Mondesi/650 6.00 15.00
73 Matt Morris/3900 4.00 10.00
74 Paul O'Neill/900 8.00 20.00
75 Kevin Orie/3900 2.00 5.00
76 David Ortiz/3900 100.00 250.00
77 Rafael Palmeiro/900 6.00 15.00
78 Jay Payton/3900 2.00 5.00
79 Neifi Perez/3900 2.00 5.00
80 Manny Ramirez/900 12.00 30.00
81 Joe Randa/3900 4.00 10.00
82 Pokey Reese/3900 4.00 10.00
83 Edgar Renteria SP 4.00 10.00
84 Dennis Reyes/3900 2.00 5.00
85 Henry Rodriguez/3900 2.00 5.00
86 Scott Rolen/1900 * 4.00 10.00
87 Kirk Rueter/2900 2.00 5.00
88 Ryne Sandberg/400 30.00 60.00
89 Dwight Smith/2900 2.00 5.00
90 J.T. Snow/900 4.00 10.00
91 Scott Spiezio/3900 2.00 5.00
92 Shannon Stewart/2900 4.00 10.00
93 Jeff Suppan/1900 4.00 10.00
94 Mike Sweeney/3900 2.00 5.00
95 Miguel Tejada/3900 4.00 10.00
96 Justin Thompson/2400 2.00 5.00
97 Brett Tomko/3900 2.00 5.00
98 Bubba Trammell/3900 2.00 5.00
99 Michael Tucker/3900 4.00 10.00
100 Javier Valentin/3900 2.00 5.00
101 Mo Vaughn/150 * 4.00 10.00
102 Robin Ventura/1400 6.00 15.00
103 Terrell Wade/3900 2.00 5.00
104 Billy Wagner/3900 4.00 10.00
105 Larry Walker/900 8.00 20.00
106 Todd Walker/2400 2.00 5.00
107 Rondell White/3900 2.00 5.00
108 Kevin Wickander/900 2.00 5.00
109 Chris Widger/3900 2.00 5.00
110 Matt Williams/150 * 6.00 15.00
111 Antone Williamson/3900 2.00 5.00
112 Dan Wilson/3900 3.00 8.00
113 Tony Womack/3900 3.00 8.00
114 Jaret Wright/3900 3.00 8.00
115 Dmitri Young/3900 4.00 10.00
116 Eric Young/3900 2.00 5.00
117 Kevin Young/3900 2.00 5.00
NNO Frank Thomas Fascimile .75 2.00

1997 Donruss Signature Autographs Century

RANDOM INSERTS IN PACKS
STATED PRINT RUN 100 SERIAL #'d SETS
ASTERISK CARDS ARE IN SERIES A AND B
NNO CARDS LISTED IN ALPH.ORDER
1 Jeff Abbott 6.00 15.00
2 Bob Abreu 15.00 40.00
3 Edgardo Alfonzo 10.00 25.00
4 Roberto Alomar * 40.00 100.00
5 Sandy Alomar Jr. 20.00 50.00
6 Moises Alou 20.00 50.00
7 Garret Anderson 20.00 50.00
8 Andy Ashby 6.00 15.00
9 Jeff Bagwell 75.00 150.00
10 Trey Beamon 6.00 15.00
11 Albert Belle 20.00 50.00
12 Alan Benes 6.00 15.00
13 Geronimo Berroa 6.00 15.00
14 Wade Boggs * 60.00 150.00

15 Barry Bonds 200.00 400.00
16 Bobby Bonilla * 20.00 50.00
17 Kevin Brown 10.00 25.00
18 Kevin Brown C 6.00 15.00
19 Jay Buhner 20.00 50.00
20 Brett Butler 6.00 15.00
21 Mike Cameron 6.00 15.00
22 Giovanni Carrara 6.00 15.00
23 Luis Castillo 6.00 15.00
24 Tony Clark 6.00 15.00
25 Will Clark 40.00 80.00
26 Roger Clemens * 175.00 300.00
27 Lou Collier 6.00 15.00
28 Bartolo Colon 20.00 50.00
29 Ron Coomer 6.00 15.00
30 Marty Cordova 6.00 15.00
31 Jacob Cruz * 6.00 15.00
32 Jose Cruz Jr. * 6.00 15.00
33 Russ Davis 6.00 15.00
34 Jason Dickson 6.00 15.00
35 Todd Dunwoody 6.00 15.00
36 Jermaine Dye 20.00 50.00
37 Jim Edmonds 60.00 120.00
38 Darin Erstad * 20.00 50.00
39 Bobby Estalella 6.00 15.00
40 Shawn Estes 6.00 15.00
41 Jeff Fassero 6.00 15.00
42 Andres Galarraga 20.00 50.00
43 Karim Garcia 6.00 15.00
44 N.Garciaparra SP/62 * 125.00 200.00
45 Derrick Gibson 6.00 15.00
46 Brian Giles 6.00 15.00
47 Tom Glavine 75.00 200.00
48 Juan Gonzalez 6.00 15.00
49 Rick Gorecki 6.00 15.00
50 Shawn Green 12.00 30.00
51 Todd Greene 6.00 15.00
52 Rusty Greer 20.00 50.00
53 Ben Grieve 6.00 15.00
54 Mark Grudzielanek 20.00 50.00
55 Vladimir Guerrero * 75.00 200.00
56 Wilton Guerrero 6.00 15.00
57 Jose Guillen 6.00 15.00
58 Tony Gwynn * 30.00 80.00
59 Jeffrey Hammonds 6.00 15.00
60 Todd Helton 40.00 80.00
61 Todd Hollandsworth 6.00 15.00
62 Trenidad Hubbard 6.00 15.00
63 Todd Hundley 6.00 15.00
64 Derek Jeter * 400.00 800.00
65 Andruw Jones * 50.00 100.00
66 Bobby Jones 6.00 15.00
67 Chipper Jones * 200.00 300.00
68 Brian Jordan 20.00 50.00
69 David Justice 30.00 80.00
70 Eric Karros 20.00 50.00
71 Jason Kendall 6.00 15.00
72 Jimmy Key 10.00 25.00
73 Brooks Kieschnick 6.00 15.00
74 Ryan Klesko 20.00 50.00
75 Chuck Knoblauch * 10.00 25.00
76 Paul Konerko 40.00 80.00
77 Mark Kotsay 20.00 50.00
78 Ray Lankford 8.00 20.00
79 Barry Larkin * 30.00 80.00
80 Derrek Lee 8.00 20.00
81 Esteban Loaiza 6.00 15.00
82 Javier Lopez 20.00 50.00
83 Greg Maddux * 200.00 400.00
84 Edgar Martinez * 50.00 100.00
85 Pedro Martinez 125.00 300.00
86 Tino Martinez * 50.00 100.00
87 Rafael Medina 6.00 15.00
88 Raul Mondesi 20.00 50.00
89 Matt Morris 6.00 15.00
90 Eddie Murray * 60.00 120.00
91 Mike Mussina 40.00 100.00
92 Paul O'Neill 20.00 50.00
93 Kevin Orie 6.00 15.00
94 David Ortiz 150.00 400.00
95 Rafael Palmeiro 8.00 20.00
96 Jay Payton 6.00 15.00
97 Neifi Perez 6.00 15.00
98 Andy Pettitte * 25.00 60.00
99 Manny Ramirez 30.00 80.00
100 Joe Randa 20.00 50.00
101 Pokey Reese 6.00 15.00
102 Edgar Renteria 12.00 30.00
103 Dennis Reyes 6.00 15.00
104 Cal Ripken 150.00 300.00
105 Alex Rodriguez 150.00 400.00
106 Henry Rodriguez 6.00 15.00
107 Ivan Rodriguez 50.00 100.00
108 Scott Rolen * 12.00 30.00
109 Kirk Rueter 6.00 15.00
110 Ryne Sandberg 75.00 200.00
111 Gary Sheffield * 25.00 60.00
112 Dwight Smith 6.00 15.00
113 J.T. Snow 20.00 50.00
114 Scott Spiezio 6.00 15.00
115 Shannon Stewart 6.00 15.00
116 Jeff Suppan 6.00 15.00
117 Mike Sweeney 10.00 25.00
118 Miguel Tejada 10.00 25.00
119 Frank Thomas 50.00 100.00
120 Jim Thome 75.00 200.00
121 Justin Thompson 6.00 15.00
122 Brett Tomko 6.00 15.00
123 Bubba Trammell 6.00 15.00
124 Michael Tucker 6.00 15.00
125 Javier Valentin 6.00 15.00
126 Mo Vaughn * 20.00 50.00
127 Robin Ventura 10.00 25.00
128 Terrell Wade 6.00 15.00
129 Billy Wagner 50.00 100.00
130 Larry Walker 25.00 60.00
131 Todd Walker 6.00 15.00
132 Rondell White 20.00 50.00
133 Kevin Wickander 6.00 15.00
134 Chris Widger 6.00 15.00
135 Bernie Williams 60.00 120.00
136 Matt Williams * 40.00 80.00
137 Antone Williamson 6.00 15.00
138 Dan Wilson 6.00 15.00
139 Tony Womack 6.00 15.00
140 Jaret Wright 6.00 15.00
141 Dmitri Young 6.00 15.00
142 Eric Young 6.00 15.00
143 Kevin Young 6.00 15.00

1997 Donruss Signature Autographs Millennium

RANDOM INSERTS IN PACKS
1000 OF EACH CARD UNLESS NOTED BELOW
ASTERISK CARDS ARE IN SERIES A AND B
NNO CARDS LISTED IN ALPH.ORDER
1 Jeff Abbott 3.00 8.00
2 Bob Abreu 4.00 10.00
3 Edgardo Alfonzo 3.00 8.00
4 Roberto Alomar * 15.00 40.00
5 Sandy Alomar Jr. 6.00 15.00
6 Moises Alou 6.00 15.00
7 Garret Anderson 6.00 15.00
8 Andy Ashby 3.00 8.00
9 Jeff Bagwell/400 30.00 60.00
10 Trey Beamon 3.00 8.00
11 Albert Belle/400 10.00 25.00
12 Alan Benes 3.00 8.00
13 Geronimo Berroa 3.00 8.00
14 Wade Boggs * 20.00 50.00
15 Barry Bonds/400 50.00 120.00
16 Bobby Bonilla/900 * 6.00 15.00
17 Kevin Brown/900 6.00 15.00
18 Kevin Brown C 3.00 8.00
19 Jay Buhner/900 10.00 25.00
20 Brett Butler 6.00 15.00
21 Mike Cameron 6.00 15.00
22 Giovanni Carrara 3.00 8.00
23 Luis Castillo 6.00 15.00
24 Tony Clark 3.00 8.00
25 Will Clark 6.00 15.00
26 Roger Clemens/400 * 30.00 60.00
27 Lou Collier 3.00 8.00
28 Bartolo Colon 6.00 15.00
29 Ron Coomer 3.00 8.00
30 Marty Cordova 3.00 8.00
31 Jacob Cruz 3.00 8.00
32 Jose Cruz Jr. * 4.00 10.00
33 Russ Davis 3.00 8.00
34 Jason Dickson 3.00 8.00
35 Todd Dunwoody 3.00 8.00
36 Jermaine Dye 6.00 15.00
37 Jim Edmonds 6.00 15.00
38 Darin Erstad * 3.00 8.00
39 Bobby Estalella 3.00 8.00
40 Shawn Estes 3.00 8.00
41 Jeff Fassero 3.00 8.00
42 Andres Galarraga 6.00 15.00
43 Karim Garcia 3.00 8.00
44 Nomar Garciaparra/650 * 15.00 40.00
45 Derrick Gibson 3.00 8.00
46 Brian Giles 3.00 8.00
47 Tom Glavine 10.00 25.00
48 Juan Gonzalez/900 10.00 25.00
49 Rick Gorecki 3.00 8.00
50 Shawn Green 6.00 15.00
51 Todd Greene 3.00 8.00
52 Rusty Greer 6.00 15.00
53 Ben Grieve 3.00 8.00
54 Mark Grudzielanek 6.00 15.00
55 Vladimir Guerrero * 10.00 25.00
56 Wilton Guerrero 3.00 8.00
57 Jose Guillen 6.00 15.00
58 Tony Gwynn/900 * 30.00 80.00
59 Jeffrey Hammonds 3.00 8.00
60 Todd Helton 6.00 15.00
61 Todd Hundley 3.00 8.00
62 Todd Hollandsworth 3.00 8.00
63 Trenidad Hubbard 3.00 8.00
64 Derek Jeter/400 * 150.00 400.00
65 Andruw Jones/900 * 10.00 25.00
66 Bobby Jones 3.00 8.00
67 Chipper Jones/900 * 40.00 80.00
68 Brian Jordan 6.00 15.00
69 David Justice 6.00 15.00
70 Eric Karros 6.00 15.00
71 Jason Kendall 6.00 15.00
72 Jimmy Key 6.00 15.00
73 Brooks Kieschnick 3.00 8.00
74 Ryan Klesko 3.00 8.00
75 Chuck Knoblauch/900 * 4.00 10.00
76 Paul Konerko 8.00 20.00
77 Mark Kotsay 8.00 20.00
78 Ray Lankford 6.00 15.00
79 Barry Larkin * 20.00 50.00
80 Derrek Lee 10.00 25.00
81 Esteban Loaiza 3.00 8.00
82 Javier Lopez 6.00 15.00
83 Greg Maddux/400 * 60.00 120.00
84 Edgar Martinez * 8.00 20.00
85 Pedro Martinez 50.00 120.00
86 Tino Martinez/900 * 15.00 40.00
87 Rafael Medina 3.00 8.00
88 Raul Mondesi 6.00 15.00
89 Matt Morris 3.00 8.00
90 Eddie Murray/900 * 20.00 50.00
91 Mike Mussina/900 20.00 50.00
92 Paul O'Neill 6.00 15.00
93 Kevin Orie 3.00 8.00
94 David Ortiz 125.00 300.00
95 Rafael Palmeiro 4.00 10.00
96 Jay Payton 3.00 8.00
97 Neifi Perez 3.00 8.00
98 Andy Pettitte/900 * 15.00 40.00
99 Manny Ramirez 10.00 25.00
100 Joe Randa 6.00 15.00
101 Pokey Reese 6.00 15.00
102 Edgar Renteria SP 6.00 15.00
103 Dennis Reyes 3.00 8.00
104 Cal Ripken/400 75.00 150.00
105 Alex Rodriguez/400 50.00 120.00
106 Henry Rodriguez 3.00 8.00
107 Ivan Rodriguez/900 10.00 25.00
108 Scott Rolen * 4.00 10.00
109 Kirk Rueter 3.00 8.00
110 Ryne Sandberg 30.00 80.00
111 Gary Sheffield/400 * 10.00 25.00
112 Dwight Smith 4.00 10.00
113 J.T. Snow 6.00 15.00
114 Scott Spiezio 3.00 8.00
115 Shannon Stewart 6.00 15.00
116 Jeff Suppan 6.00 15.00
117 Mike Sweeney 3.00 8.00
118 Miguel Tejada 4.00 10.00
119 Frank Thomas/400 30.00 60.00
120 Jim Thome/900 25.00 60.00
121 Justin Thompson 3.00 8.00
122 Brett Tomko 3.00 8.00
123 Bubba Trammell 4.00 10.00
124 Michael Tucker 6.00 15.00
125 Javier Valentin 3.00 8.00
126 Mo Vaughn * 6.00 15.00
127 Robin Ventura 6.00 15.00
128 Terrell Wade 3.00 8.00
129 Billy Wagner 4.00 10.00
130 Larry Walker 6.00 15.00
131 Todd Walker 3.00 8.00
132 Rondell White 6.00 15.00
133 Kevin Wickander 3.00 8.00
134 Chris Widger 3.00 8.00
135 Bernie Williams/400 60.00 120.00
136 Matt Williams * 6.00 15.00
137 Antone Williamson 3.00 8.00
138 Dan Wilson 3.00 8.00
139 Tony Womack 4.00 10.00
140 Jaret Wright 4.00 10.00
141 Dmitri Young 6.00 15.00
142 Eric Young 3.00 8.00
143 Kevin Young 3.00 8.00

1997 Donruss Signature Notable Nicknames

RANDOM INSERTS IN PACKS
STATED PRINT RUN 200 SERIAL #'d SETS
NNO CARDS LISTED IN ALPH.ORDER
1 Ernie Banks 75.00 150.00
2 Tony Clark 20.00 50.00
3 Roger Clemens 125.00 250.00
4 Reggie Jackson 100.00 200.00
5 Randy Johnson 200.00 500.00
6 Stan Musial 175.00 350.00
7 Ivan Rodriguez 100.00 200.00
9 Frank Thomas 100.00 200.00
10 Mo Vaughn 20.00 50.00
11 Billy Wagner 75.00 150.00

1997 Donruss Signature Significant Signatures

RANDOM INSERTS IN PACKS
STATED PRINT RUN 2000 SERIAL #'d SETS
NNO CARDS LISTED IN ALPH.ORDER
COMPLETE SET CONTAINS CARD 11A
1 Ernie Banks 40.00 100.00
2 Johnny Bench 15.00 40.00
3 Yogi Berra 20.00 50.00
4 George Brett 30.00 60.00
5 Lou Brock 10.00 25.00
6 Rod Carew 12.50 30.00
7 Steve Carlton 10.00 25.00
8 Larry Doby 20.00 50.00
9 Carlton Fisk 10.00 25.00
10 Bob Gibson 10.00 25.00
11 Reggie Jackson 20.00 50.00
11A R.Jackson Silver Ink 100.00 200.00
12 Al Kaline 12.00 30.00
13 Harmon Killebrew 20.00 50.00
14 Don Mattingly 20.00 50.00
15 Stan Musial 40.00 80.00
16 Jim Palmer 12.00 30.00
17 Brooks Robinson 10.00 25.00
18 Frank Robinson 10.00 25.00
19 Mike Schmidt 12.00 30.00
20 Tom Seaver 15.00 40.00
21 Duke Snider 12.00 30.00
22 Carl Yastrzemski 15.00 40.00

1998 Donruss Signature

The 140-card 1998 Donruss Signature set was distributed in five-card packs with one authentic autographed card per pack and a suggested retail price of $14.99. The fronts feature color action player photos in white borders. The backs carry player information and career statistics. Due to Pinnacle's bankruptcy, these cards were later released by Playoff. This set was released in very late December, 1998. Notable Rookie Cards in this set include J.D. Drew, Troy Glaus, Orlando Hernandez, Gabe Kapler, Kevin Millwood and Magglio Ordonez.

COMPLETE SET (140) 20.00 50.00
1 David Justice .15 .40
2 Derek Jeter 1.00 2.50
3 Nomar Garciaparra .60 1.50
4 Ryan Klesko .15 .40
5 Jeff Bagwell .25 .60
6 Dante Bichette .15 .40
7 Ivan Rodriguez .25 .60
8 Albert Belle .15 .40
9 Cal Ripken 1.25 3.00
10 Craig Biggio .25 .60
11 Barry Larkin .25 .60
12 Jose Guillen .15 .40
13 Will Clark .25 .60
14 J.T. Snow .15 .40
15 Chuck Knoblauch .15 .40
16 Todd Walker .15 .40
17 Scott Rolen .25 .60
18 Rickey Henderson .40 1.00
19 Juan Gonzalez .15 .40
20 Justin Thompson .15 .40
21 Roger Clemens .75 2.00
22 Ray Lankford .15 .40
23 Jose Cruz Jr. .15 .40
24 Ken Griffey Jr. .75 2.00
25 Andruw Jones .25 .60
26 Darin Erstad .15 .40
27 Jim Thome .25 .60
28 Wade Boggs .25 .60
29 Ken Caminiti .15 .40
30 Todd Hundley .15 .40
31 Mike Piazza .60 1.50
32 Sammy Sosa .40 1.00
33 Larry Walker .15 .40
34 Matt Williams .15 .40
35 Frank Thomas .40 1.00
36 Gary Sheffield .15 .40
37 Alex Rodriguez .60 1.50
38 Hideo Nomo .40 1.00
39 Kenny Lofton .15 .40
40 John Smoltz .25 .60
41 Mo Vaughn .15 .40
42 Edgar Martinez .25 .60
43 Paul Molitor .15 .40
44 Rafael Palmeiro .25 .60
45 Barry Bonds 1.00 2.50
46 Vladimir Guerrero .40 1.00
47 Carlos Delgado .15 .40
48 Bobby Higginson .15 .40
49 Greg Maddux .60 1.50
50 Jim Edmonds .15 .40
51 Randy Johnson .40 1.00
52 Mark McGwire 1.00 2.50
53 Rondell White .15 .40
54 Raul Mondesi .15 .40
55 Manny Ramirez .25 .60
56 Pedro Martinez .25 .60
57 Tim Salmon .25 .60
58 Moises Alou .15 .40
59 Fred McGriff .25 .60
60 Garret Anderson .15 .40
61 Sandy Alomar Jr. .15 .40
62 Chan Ho Park .15 .40
63 Mark Kotsay .15 .40
64 Mike Mussina .25 .60
65 Tom Glavine .25 .60
66 Tony Clark .15 .40
67 Mark Grace .25 .60
68 Tony Gwynn .50 1.25
69 Tino Martinez .25 .60
70 Kevin Brown .25 .60
71 Todd Greene .15 .40
72 Andy Pettitte .25 .60
73 Livan Hernandez .15 .40
74 Curt Schilling .15 .40
75 Andres Galarraga .15 .40
76 Rusty Greer .15 .40
77 Jay Buhner .15 .40
78 Bobby Bonilla .15 .40
79 Chipper Jones .40 1.00
80 Eric Young .15 .40
81 Jason Giambi .15 .40
82 Javy Lopez .15 .40
83 Roberto Alomar .25 .60
84 Bernie Williams .25 .60
85 A.J. Hinch .15 .40
86 Kerry Wood .20 .50
87 Juan Encarnacion .15 .40
88 Brad Fullmer .15 .40
89 Ben Grieve .15 .40
90 Magglio Ordonez RC 2.00 5.00
91 Todd Helton .25 .60
92 Richard Hidalgo .15 .40
93 Paul Konerko .15 .40
94 Aramis Ramirez .15 .40
95 Ricky Ledee .15 .40
96 Derrek Lee .25 .60
97 Travis Lee .15 .40
98 Matt Anderson RC .15 .40
99 Jaret Wright .15 .40
100 David Ortiz .50 1.25
101 Carl Pavano .15 .40
102 Orlando Hernandez RC .75 2.00
103 Fernando Tatis .15 .40
104 Miguel Tejada .40 1.00
105 Rolando Arrojo RC .25 .60
106 Kevin Millwood RC .60 1.50
107 Ken Griffey Jr. CL .50 1.25
108 Frank Thomas CL .25 .60
109 Cal Ripken CL .60 1.50
110 Greg Maddux CL .40 1.00
111 John Olerud .15 .40
112 David Cone .15 .40
113 Vinny Castilla .15 .40
114 Jason Kendall .15 .40
115 Brian Jordan .15 .40
116 Hideki Irabu .15 .40
117 Bartolo Colon .15 .40
118 Greg Vaughn .15 .40
119 David Segui .15 .40
120 Bruce Chen .15 .40
121 Julio Ramirez RC .15 .40
122 Troy Glaus RC 1.50 4.00
123 Jeremy Giambi RC .25 .60
124 Ryan Minor RC .15 .40
125 Richie Sexson .15 .40
126 Dermal Brown .15 .40
127 Adrian Beltre .15 .40
128 Eric Chavez .15 .40
129 J.D. Drew RC 1.25 3.00
130 Gabe Kapler RC .40 1.00
131 Masato Yoshii RC .25 .60
132 Mike Lowell RC 1.00 2.50
133 Jim Parque RC .25 .60
134 Roy Halladay .75 2.00
135 Carlos Lee RC 1.25 3.00
136 Jin Ho Cho RC .15 .40
137 Michael Barrett .15 .40
138 Fernando Seguignol RC .15 .40
139 Odalis Perez RC .60 1.50
140 Mark McGwire CL .50 1.25

1998 Donruss Signature Proofs

COMPLETE SET (140) 2000.00 4000.00
*STARS: 6X TO 15X BASIC CARDS
*RC's: 2X TO 5X BASIC CARDS
RANDOM INSERTS IN PACKS
STATED PRINT RUN 150 SETS

1998 Donruss Signature Autographs

ONE AUTOGRAPH PER PACK
CARDS LISTED IN ALPHABETICAL ORDER
NO PRICING ON QTY OF 25 OR LESS
1 Roberto Alomar/150* 20.00 50.00
2 Sandy Alomar Jr./700* 6.00 15.00
3 Moises Alou/900* 6.00 15.00
4 Gabe Alvarez/2900* 2.00 5.00
5 Wilson Alvarez/1600* 2.00 5.00
6 Jay Bell/1500* 2.00 5.00
7 Adrian Beltre/1900* 25.00 60.00
8 Andy Benes/2600* 2.00 5.00
9 Aaron Boone/3400* 6.00 15.00
10 Russell Branyan/1650* 3.00 8.00
11 Orlando Cabrera/3100* 6.00 15.00
12 Mike Cameron/1150* 2.00 5.00
13 Joe Carter/400* 6.00 15.00
14 Sean Casey/2275* 6.00 15.00
15 Bruce Chen/150* 6.00 15.00
16 Tony Clark/2275* 2.00 5.00
17 Will Clark/1400* 6.00 15.00
18 Matt Clement/1400* 6.00 15.00
19 Pat Cline/1400* 2.00 5.00
20 Ken Cloude/3400* 2.00 5.00
21 Michael Coleman/2800* 2.00 5.00
22 David Cone/25*
23 Jeff Conine/1400* 6.00 15.00
24 Jacob Cruz/3200* 2.00 5.00
25 Russ Davis/3500* 2.00 5.00
26 Jason Dickson/1400* 2.00 5.00
27 Todd Dunwoody/3500* 2.00 5.00
28 Juan Encarnacion/3400* 6.00 15.00
29 Darin Erstad/700* 6.00 15.00
30 Bobby Estalella/3400* 2.00 5.00
31 Jeff Fassero/3400* 2.00 5.00
32 John Franco/1800* 6.00 15.00
33 Brad Fullmer/3100* 2.00 5.00
34 Jason Giambi/3100* 4.00 10.00
35 Derrick Gibson/1200* 2.00 5.00
36 Todd Greene/1400* 2.00 5.00
37 Ben Grieve/1400* 2.00 5.00
38 Mark Grudzielanek/3200* 2.00 5.00
39 Vladimir Guerrero/2100* 15.00 40.00
40 Wilton Guerrero/1900* 2.00 5.00
41 Jose Guillen/2400* 2.00 5.00
42 Todd Helton/1300* 6.00 15.00
43 Richard Hidalgo/3400* 2.00 5.00
44 A.J. Hinch/2900* 2.00 5.00
45 Butch Huskey/1900* 2.00 5.00
46 Raul Ibanez/3300* 4.00 10.00
47 Damian Jackson/900* 2.00 5.00
48 Geoff Jenkins/3100* 6.00 15.00
49 Eric Karros/650* 6.00 15.00
50 Ryan Klesko/400* 2.00 5.00
51 Mark Kotsay/3600* 6.00 15.00
52 Ricky Ledee/2200* 2.00 5.00
53 Derrek Lee/3400* 4.00 10.00
54 Travis Lee/150* 6.00 15.00
55 Javier Lopez/650* 6.00 15.00
56 Mike Lowell/3500* 6.00 15.00
57 Greg Maddux/12*
58 Eli Marrero/3400* 2.00 5.00
59 Al Martin/1300* 2.00 5.00
60 Rafael Medina/1400* 2.00 5.00
61 Scott Morgan/900* 3.00 8.00
62 Abraham Nunez/3500* 2.00 5.00
63 Paul O'Neill/1000* 10.00 25.00
64 Luis Ordaz/2700* 2.00 5.00
65 Magglio Ordonez/3200* 6.00 15.00
66 Kevin Orie/1350* 2.00 5.00
67 David Ortiz/3400* 15.00 40.00
68 Rafael Palmeiro/1000* 6.00 15.00
69 Carl Pavano/2600* 6.00 15.00
70 Neifi Perez/3300* 2.00 5.00
71 Dante Powell/3050* 2.00 5.00
72 Aramis Ramirez/2800* 4.00 10.00
73 Mariano Rivera/900* 60.00 150.00
74 Felix Rodriguez/1400* 2.00 5.00
75 Henry Rodriguez/3400* 2.00 5.00
76 Scott Rolen/1900* 6.00 15.00
77 Brian Rose/1400* 2.00 5.00
78 Curt Schilling/900* 12.50 30.00
79 Richie Sexson/3500* 6.00 15.00
80 Randall Simon/3500* 2.00 5.00
81 J.T. Snow/400* 6.00 15.00
82 Jeff Suppan/1400* 6.00 15.00
83 Fernando Tatis/3900* 2.00 5.00
84 Miguel Tejada/3800* 5.00 12.00
85 Brett Tomko/3400* 2.00 5.00
86 Bubba Trammell/3900* 10.00 25.00
87 Ismael Valdes/1900* 2.00 5.00
88 Robin Ventura/1400* 6.00 15.00
89 Billy Wagner/900* 4.00 10.00
90 Todd Walker/1900* 2.00 5.00
91 Daryle Ward/400* 3.00 8.00
92 Rondell White/3400* 4.00 10.00
93 Antone Williamson/3350* 2.00 5.00
94 Dan Wilson/2400* 2.00 5.00
95 Enrique Wilson/3400* 2.00 5.00
96 Preston Wilson/2100* 2.00 5.00
97 Tony Womack/3500* 2.00 5.00
98 Kerry Wood/3400* 6.00 15.00
NNO Travis Lee Sample .40 1.00

1998 Donruss Signature Autographs Century

RANDOM INSERTS IN PACKS
100 OF EACH CARD UNLESS NOTED BELOW
NNO CARDS LISTED IN ALPH.ORDER
1 Roberto Alomar 20.00 50.00
2 Sandy Alomar Jr. 12.50 30.00
3 Moises Alou 20.00 50.00
4 Gabe Alvarez 12.50 30.00
5 Wilson Alvarez 12.50 30.00
6 Brady Anderson 20.00 50.00
7 Jay Bell 20.00 50.00
8 Albert Belle 20.00 50.00
9 Adrian Beltre 200.00 400.00
10 Andy Benes 12.50 30.00
11 Wade Boggs 50.00 100.00
12 Barry Bonds 200.00 400.00
13 Aaron Boone 12.50 30.00
14 Russell Branyan 12.50 30.00
15 Jay Buhner 20.00 50.00
16 Ellis Burks 20.00 50.00
17 Orlando Cabrera 20.00 50.00
18 Mike Cameron 20.00 50.00
19 Ken Caminiti 20.00 50.00
20 Joe Carter 20.00 50.00
21 Sean Casey 20.00 50.00
22 Bruce Chen 12.50 30.00
23 Tony Clark 12.50 30.00
24 Will Clark 40.00 80.00
25 Roger Clemens 125.00 250.00
26 Matt Clement 20.00 50.00
27 Pat Cline 12.50 30.00
28 Ken Cloude 12.50 30.00
29 Michael Coleman 12.50 30.00
30 David Cone 40.00 80.00
31 Jeff Conine 20.00 50.00
32 Jacob Cruz 12.50 30.00
33 Jose Cruz Jr. 12.50 30.00
34 Russ Davis 12.50 30.00
35 Jason Dickson 12.50 30.00
36 Todd Dunwoody 12.50 30.00
37 Scott Elarton 12.50 30.00
38 Darin Erstad 12.50 30.00
39 Bobby Estalella 12.50 30.00
40 Jeff Fassero 12.50 30.00
41 John Franco 12.50 30.00
42 Brad Fullmer 12.50 30.00
43 Andres Galarraga 20.00 50.00
44 Nomar Garciaparra 60.00 120.00
45 Jason Giambi 20.00 50.00
46 Derrick Gibson 12.50 30.00
47 Tom Glavine 50.00 100.00
48 Juan Gonzalez 20.00 50.00
49 Todd Greene 12.50 30.00
50 Ben Grieve 12.50 30.00
51 Mark Grudzielanek 12.50 30.00
52 Vladimir Guerrero 75.00 200.00
53 Wilton Guerrero 12.50 30.00
54 Jose Guillen 20.00 50.00
55 Tony Gwynn 60.00 120.00
56 Todd Helton 25.00 60.00
57 Richard Hidalgo 12.50 30.00
58 A.J. Hinch 12.50 30.00
59 Butch Huskey 12.50 30.00
60 Raul Ibanez 15.00 40.00
61 Damian Jackson 12.50 30.00
62 Geoff Jenkins 20.00 50.00
63 Derek Jeter 300.00 500.00
64 Randy Johnson 150.00 250.00
65 Chipper Jones 250.00 350.00
66 Eric Karros/50 20.00 50.00
67 Ryan Klesko 20.00 50.00
68 Chuck Knoblauch 20.00 50.00
69 Mark Kotsay 12.50 30.00
70 Ricky Ledee 12.50 30.00
71 Derrek Lee 40.00 80.00
72 Travis Lee 12.50 30.00
73 Javier Lopez 12.50 30.00
74 Mike Lowell 50.00 100.00
75 Greg Maddux 100.00 250.00
76 Eli Marrero 12.50 30.00
77 Al Martin 12.50 30.00
78 Rafael Medina 12.50 30.00
79 Paul Molitor 20.00 50.00
80 Scott Morgan 12.50 30.00
81 Mike Mussina 20.00 50.00
82 Abraham Nunez 12.50 30.00
83 Paul O'Neill 20.00 50.00
84 Luis Ordaz 12.50 30.00
85 Magglio Ordonez 12.50 30.00
86 Kevin Orie 12.50 30.00
87 David Ortiz 60.00 150.00
88 Rafael Palmeiro 60.00 120.00
89 Carl Pavano 20.00 50.00
90 Neifi Perez 12.50 30.00
91 Andy Pettitte 30.00 80.00
92 Aramis Ramirez 25.00 60.00
93 Cal Ripken 200.00 350.00
94 Mariano Rivera 300.00 500.00
95 Alex Rodriguez 100.00 250.00
96 Felix Rodriguez 12.50 30.00
97 Henry Rodriguez 12.50 30.00
98 Ivan Rodriguez 20.00 50.00
99 Scott Rolen 20.00 50.00
100 Brian Rose 12.50 30.00
101 Curt Schilling 30.00 60.00
102 Richie Sexson 20.00 50.00
103 Randall Simon 12.50 30.00
104 J.T. Snow 20.00 50.00
105 Darryl Strawberry 50.00 120.00
106 Jeff Suppan 20.00 50.00
107 Fernando Tatis 12.50 30.00
108 Brett Tomko 12.50 30.00
109 Bubba Trammell 12.50 30.00
110 Ismael Valdes 12.50 30.00
111 Robin Ventura 20.00 50.00
112 Billy Wagner 40.00 80.00
113 Todd Walker 12.50 30.00
114 Daryle Ward 20.00 50.00
115 Rondell White 12.00 30.00
116 Matt Williams/80 20.00 50.00
117 Antone Williamson 12.00 30.00
118 Dan Wilson 12.00 30.00
119 Enrique Wilson 12.00 30.00
120 Preston Wilson 20.00 50.00
121 Tony Womack 12.00 30.00
122 Kerry Wood 20.00 50.00

1998 Donruss Signature Autographs Millennium

RANDOM INSERTS IN PACKS
1000 OF EACH CARD UNLESS NOTED BELOW
NNO CARDS LISTED IN ALPH.ORDER
1 Roberto Alomar 6.00 15.00
2 Sandy Alomar Jr. 6.00 15.00
3 Moises Alou 6.00 15.00
4 Gabe Alvarez 3.00 8.00
5 Wilson Alvarez 3.00 8.00
6 Brady Anderson/800* 6.00 15.00
7 Jay Bell 6.00 15.00
8 Albert Belle/400* 10.00 25.00
9 Adrian Beltre 50.00 120.00
10 Andy Benes 3.00 8.00
11 Wade Boggs/900* 10.00 25.00
12 Barry Bonds/400* 75.00 200.00
13 Aaron Boone 6.00 15.00
14 Russell Branyan 3.00 8.00
15 Jay Buhner/400* 8.00 20.00
16 Ellis Burks/900* 4.00 10.00
17 Orlando Cabrera 6.00 15.00
18 Mike Cameron 6.00 15.00
19 Ken Caminiti/900* 6.00 15.00
20 Joe Carter 6.00 15.00
21 Sean Casey 6.00 15.00
22 Bruce Chen 3.00 8.00
23 Tony Clark 3.00 8.00
24 Will Clark 6.00 15.00
25 Roger Clemens/400* 30.00 60.00
26 Matt Clement/900* 6.00 15.00
27 Pat Cline 3.00 8.00
28 Ken Cloude 3.00 8.00
29 Michael Coleman 3.00 8.00
30 David Cone 10.00 25.00
31 Jeff Conine 6.00 15.00
32 Jacob Cruz 3.00 8.00
33 Jose Cruz Jr./850* 3.00 8.00
34 Russ Davis/950* 8.00 20.00
35 Jason Dickson/950* 3.00 8.00
36 Todd Dunwoody 3.00 8.00
37 Scott Elarton/900* 3.00 8.00
38 Juan Encarnacion 6.00 15.00
39 Darin Erstad 6.00 15.00
40 Bobby Estalella 3.00 8.00
41 Jeff Fassero 3.00 8.00
42 John Franco/950* 6.00 15.00
43 Brad Fullmer 3.00 8.00
44 Andres Galarraga/900* 6.00 15.00
45 Nomar Garciaparra/400* 15.00 40.00
46 Jason Giambi 4.00 10.00
47 Derrick Gibson 3.00 8.00
48 Tom Glavine/700* 15.00 40.00
49 Juan Gonzalez 15.00 40.00
50 Todd Greene 3.00 8.00
51 Ben Grieve 3.00 8.00
52 Mark Grudzielanek 3.00 8.00
53 Vladimir Guerrero 15.00 40.00
54 Wilton Guerrero 3.00 8.00
55 Jose Guillen 6.00 15.00
56 Tony Gwynn/900* 25.00 60.00
57 Todd Helton 8.00 20.00
58 Richard Hidalgo 3.00 8.00
59 A.J. Hinch 3.00 8.00
60 Butch Huskey 3.00 8.00
61 Raul Ibanez 4.00 10.00
62 Damian Jackson 3.00 8.00
63 Geoff Jenkins 6.00 15.00
64 Derek Jeter/400* 200.00 400.00
65 Randy Johnson/800* 40.00 80.00
66 Chipper Jones/900* 30.00 60.00
67 Eric Karros 6.00 15.00
68 Ryan Klesko 6.00 15.00
69 Chuck Knoblauch/900* 6.00 15.00
70 Mark Kotsay 6.00 15.00
71 Ricky Ledee 3.00 8.00
72 Derrek Lee 10.00 25.00
73 Travis Lee 3.00 8.00
74 Javier Lopez/800* 6.00 15.00
75 Mike Lowell 12.50 30.00
76 Greg Maddux/400* 60.00 120.00
77 Eli Marrero 3.00 8.00
78 Al Martin/950* 3.00 8.00
79 Rafael Medina/850* 3.00 8.00
80 Paul Molitor/900* 10.00 25.00
81 Scott Morgan 3.00 8.00
82 Mike Mussina/900* 10.00 25.00
83 Abraham Nunez 3.00 8.00
84 Paul O'Neill/900* 10.00 25.00
85 Luis Ordaz 3.00 8.00
86 Magglio Ordonez 5.00 12.00
87 Kevin Orie 3.00 8.00
88 David Ortiz 30.00 80.00
89 Rafael Palmeiro/900* 10.00 25.00
90 Carl Pavano 6.00 15.00
91 Neifi Perez 3.00 8.00
92 Andy Pettitte/900* 20.00 50.00
93 Dante Powell/950* 3.00 8.00
94 Aramis Ramirez 4.00 10.00
95 Cal Ripken/375* 50.00 120.00
96 Mariano Rivera 60.00 150.00
97 Alex Rodriguez/350* 30.00 80.00
98 Felix Rodriguez 3.00 8.00
99 Henry Rodriguez 3.00 8.00
100 Ivan Rodriguez 12.00 30.00
101 Scott Rolen 6.00 15.00
102 Brian Rose 3.00 8.00
103 Curt Schilling 10.00 25.00
104 Richie Sexson 6.00 15.00
105 Randall Simon 3.00 8.00
106 J.T. Snow 6.00 15.00
107 Darryl Strawberry/900* 15.00 40.00
108 Jeff Suppan 3.00 8.00
109 Fernando Tatis 6.00 15.00
110 Miguel Tejada 8.00 20.00
111 Brett Tomko 3.00 8.00
112 Bubba Trammell 3.00 8.00
113 Ismael Valdes 3.00 8.00
114 Robin Ventura 6.00 15.00
115 Billy Wagner/900* 6.00 15.00
116 Todd Walker 6.00 15.00
117 Daryle Ward 3.00 8.00
118 Rondell White 4.00 10.00
119 Matt Williams/820* 6.00 15.00
120 Antone Williamson 3.00 8.00
121 Dan Wilson 3.00 8.00
122 Enrique Wilson 3.00 8.00
123 Preston Wilson/400* 15.00 40.00
124 Tony Womack 3.00 8.00
125 Kerry Wood 6.00 15.00

1998 Donruss Signature Significant Signatures

RANDOM INSERTS IN PACKS
PRINT RUNS B/WN 1000-2000 COPIES PER
KOUFAX NOT MEANT FOR PUBLIC RELEASE
OZZIE NOT MEANT FOR PUBLIC RELEASE
RYAN NOT MEANT FOR PUBLIC RELEASE
CARD NUMBER 8 DOES NOT EXIST
EXCHANGE DEADLINE 12/31/99
1 Ernie Banks/2000 25.00 60.00
2 Yogi Berra/2000 40.00 100.00
3 George Brett/2000 30.00 80.00
4 Catfish Hunter/2000 12.00 30.00
5 Al Kaline/2000 15.00 40.00
6 Harmon Killebrew/2000 12.00 30.00
7 Ralph Kiner/2000 12.00 30.00
9 Eddie Mathews/2000 20.00 50.00
10 Don Mattingly/2000 20.00 50.00
11 Willie McCovey/2000 20.00 50.00
12 Stan Musial/2000 40.00 80.00
13 Phil Rizzuto/1000 15.00 40.00
14 Nolan Ryan No Auto 6.00 15.00
15 Ozzie Smith No Auto 2.00 5.00
16 Duke Snider/2000 12.00 30.00
17 Don Sutton/2000 10.00 25.00

18 Billy Williams/2000 10.00 25.00
18A Billy Williams No Auto 2.00 5.00
SP Nolan Ryan/1000 50.00 100.00
NNO S.Koufax Brooklyn/2000 100.00 250.00
NNO Ozzie Smith/2000 12.00 30.00

1998 Donruss Signature Significant Signatures Refractors

AVAILABLE VIA MAIL EXCHANGE
STATED PRINT RUN 2000 SERIAL #'d SETS
R1 Nolan Ryan 60.00 150.00
R2 Ozzie Smith 12.00 30.00
R3 Sandy Koufax LA 100.00 250.00

2001 Donruss Signature

COMP.SET w/o SP'S (110) 20.00 50.00
COMMON CARD (1-110) .40 1.00
COMMON AU (111-165) 4.00 10.00
COMMON AU RC (111-165) 4.00 10.00
COMMON NO AU (111-165) 3.00 8.00
NO AU SEMIS 111-165 4.00 10.00
111-165 RANDOM INSERTS IN GIFT BOXES
111-165 AU PRINT RUN 330 SERIAL #'d SETS
COMMON CARD (166-311) 2.00 5.00
COMMON RC (166-311) 2.00 5.00
166-311 STATED ODDS TWO PER GIFT BOX
166-311 PRINT RUN 800 SERIAL #'d SETS
1 Alex Rodriguez 1.25 3.00
2 Barry Bonds 2.50 6.00
3 Cal Ripken 3.00 8.00
4 Chipper Jones 1.00 2.50
5 Derek Jeter 2.50 6.00
6 Troy Glaus .40 1.00
7 Frank Thomas 1.00 2.50
8 Greg Maddux 1.50 4.00
9 Ivan Rodriguez .60 1.50
10 Jeff Bagwell .60 1.50
11 John Olerud .40 1.00
12 Todd Helton .60 1.50
13 Ken Griffey Jr. 2.00 5.00
14 Manny Ramirez Sox .60 1.50
15 Mark McGwire 2.50 6.00
16 Mike Piazza 1.50 4.00
17 Nomar Garciaparra 1.50 4.00
18 Moises Alou .40 1.00
19 Aramis Ramirez .40 1.00
20 Curt Schilling .40 1.00
21 Pat Burrell .40 1.00
22 Doug Mientkiewicz .40 1.00
23 Carlos Delgado .40 1.00
24 J.D. Drew .40 1.00
25 Cliff Floyd .40 1.00
26 Freddy Garcia .40 1.00
27 Roberto Alomar .60 1.50
28 Barry Zito .60 1.50
29 Juan Encarnacion .40 1.00
30 Paul Konerko .40 1.00
31 Mark Mulder .40 1.00
32 Andy Pettitte .60 1.50
33 Jim Edmonds .40 1.00
34 Darin Erstad .40 1.00
35 Jason Giambi .40 1.00
36 Tom Glavine .60 1.50
37 Juan Gonzalez .40 1.00
38 Fred McGriff .60 1.50
39 Shawn Green .40 1.00
40 Tim Hudson .40 1.00
41 Andruw Jones .60 1.50
42 Jeff Kent .40 1.00
43 Barry Larkin .60 1.50
44 Brad Radke .40 1.00
45 Mike Mussina .60 1.50
46 Hideo Nomo 1.00 2.50
47 Rafael Palmeiro .60 1.50
48 Scott Rolen .60 1.50
49 Gary Sheffield .40 1.00
50 Bernie Williams .60 1.50
51 Bob Abreu .40 1.00
52 Edgardo Alfonzo .40 1.00
53 Edgar Martinez .60 1.50
54 Magglio Ordonez .40 1.00
55 Kerry Wood .40 1.00
56 Adrian Beltre .40 1.00
57 Lance Berkman .40 1.00
58 Kevin Brown 1.00 2.50
59 Sean Casey .40 1.00
60 Eric Chavez .40 1.00
61 Bartolo Colon .40 1.00
62 Sammy Sosa 1.00 2.50
63 Jermaine Dye .40 1.00
64 Tony Gwynn 1.25 3.00
65 Carl Everett .40 1.00
66 Brian Giles .40 1.00
67 Mike Hampton .40 1.00
68 Richard Hidalgo .40 1.00
69 Geoff Jenkins .40 1.00
70 Tony Clark .40 1.00
71 Roger Clemens 2.00 5.00
72 Ryan Klesko .40 1.00
73 Chan Ho Park .40 1.00
74 Richie Sexson .40 1.00
75 Mike Sweeney .40 1.00
76 Kazuhiro Sasaki .40 1.00
77 Miguel Tejada .40 1.00
78 Jose Vidro .40 1.00
79 Larry Walker .40 1.00
80 Preston Wilson .40 1.00
81 Craig Biggio .60 1.50
82 Andres Galarraga .40 1.00
83 Jim Thome .60 1.50
84 Vladimir Guerrero 1.00 2.50
85 Rafael Furcal .40 1.00
86 Cristian Guzman .40 1.00
87 Terrence Long .40 1.00
88 Bret Boone .40 1.00
89 Wade Miller .40 1.00
90 Eric Milton .40 1.00
91 Gabe Kapler .40 1.00
92 Johnny Damon .60 1.50
93 Carlos Lee .40 1.00
94 Kenny Lofton .40 1.00
95 Raul Mondesi .40 1.00
96 Jorge Posada .60 1.50
97 Mark Grace .60 1.50
98 Robert Fick .40 1.00
99 Joe Mays .40 1.00
100 Aaron Sele .40 1.00
101 Ben Grieve .40 1.00
102 Luis Gonzalez .40 1.00
103 Ray Durham .40 1.00
104 Mark Quinn .40 1.00
105 Jose Canseco .60 1.50
106 David Justice .40 1.00
107 Pedro Martinez .60 1.50
108 Randy Johnson 1.00 2.50
109 Phil Nevin .40 1.00
110 Rickey Henderson 1.00 2.50
111 Alex Escobar AU 4.00 10.00
112 Johnny Estrada AU RC 6.00 15.00
113 Pedro Feliz AU 4.00 10.00
114 Nate Frese AU RC 4.00 10.00
115 Ricardo Rodriguez AU RC 4.00 10.00
116 Brandon Larson AU RC 4.00 10.00
117 Alexis Gomez AU RC 4.00 10.00
118 Jason Hart AU 4.00 10.00
119 C.C. Sabathia AU 10.00 25.00
120 Endy Chavez AU RC 4.00 10.00
121 Christian Parker AU RC 4.00 10.00
122 Jackson Melian RC 3.00 8.00
123 Joe Kennedy AU RC 6.00 15.00
124 Adrian Hernandez AU RC 4.00 10.00
125 Cesar Izturis AU 4.00 10.00
126 Jose Mieses AU RC 4.00 10.00
127 Roy Oswalt AU 10.00 25.00
128 Eric Munson AU 4.00 10.00
129 Xavier Nady AU 6.00 15.00
130 Horacio Ramirez AU RC 6.00 15.00
131 Abraham Nunez AU 4.00 10.00
132 Jose Ortiz AU 4.00 10.00
133 Jeremy Owens AU RC 4.00 10.00
134 Claudio Vargas AU RC 4.00 10.00
135 Corey Patterson AU 4.00 10.00
136 Carlos Pena 3.00 8.00
137 Bud Smith AU RC 4.00 10.00
138 Adam Dunn AU 10.00 25.00
139 Adam Pettyjohn AU RC 4.00 10.00
140 Elpidio Guzman AU RC 4.00 10.00
141 Jay Gibbons AU RC 6.00 15.00
142 Wilkin Ruan AU RC 4.00 10.00
143 Tsuyoshi Shinjo RC 4.00 10.00
144 Alfonso Soriano AU 4.00 10.00
145 Marcus Giles AU 6.00 15.00
146 Ichiro Suzuki RC 40.00 100.00
147 Juan Uribe AU RC 10.00 25.00
148 David Williams AU RC 4.00 10.00
149 Carlos Valderrama AU RC 4.00 10.00
150 Matt White AU RC 4.00 10.00
151 Albert Pujols AU RC 300.00 800.00
152 Donaldo Mendez AU RC 4.00 10.00
153 Cory Aldridge AU RC 4.00 10.00
154 Brandon Duckworth AU RC 4.00 10.00
155 Josh Beckett AU 6.00 15.00
156 Wilson Betemit AU RC 10.00 25.00
157 Ben Sheets AU 10.00 25.00
158 Andres Torres AU RC 10.00 25.00
159 Aubrey Huff AU 6.00 15.00
160 Jack Wilson AU RC 6.00 15.00
161 Rafael Soriano AU RC 4.00 10.00
162 Nick Johnson AU 6.00 15.00
163 Carlos Garcia AU RC 4.00 10.00
164 Josh Towers AU RC 6.00 15.00
165 Jason Michaels AU RC 4.00 10.00
166 Ryan Drese RC 3.00 8.00
167 Dewon Brazelton RC 2.00 5.00
168 Kevin Olsen RC 2.00 5.00
169 Benito Baez RC 2.00 5.00
170 Mark Prior RC 10.00 25.00
171 Wilmy Caceres RC 2.00 5.00
172 Mark Teixeira RC 6.00 15.00
173 Willie Harris RC 2.00 5.00
174 Mike Koplove RC 2.00 5.00
175 Brandon Knight RC 2.00 5.00
176 John Grabow RC 2.00 5.00
177 Jeremy Affeldt RC 2.00 5.00
178 Brandon Inge 2.00 5.00
179 Casey Fossum RC 2.00 5.00
180 Scott Stewart RC 2.00 5.00
181 Luke Hudson RC 2.00 5.00
182 Ken Vining RC 2.00 5.00
183 Toby Hall 2.00 5.00
184 Eric Knott RC 2.00 5.00
185 Kris Foster RC 2.00 5.00
186 David Brous RC 2.00 5.00
187 Roy Smith RC 2.00 5.00
188 Grant Balfour RC 2.00 5.00
189 Jeremy Fikac RC 2.00 5.00
190 Morgan Ensberg RC 3.00 8.00
191 Ryan Freel RC 3.00 8.00
192 Ryan Jensen RC 2.00 5.00
193 Lance Davis RC 2.00 5.00
194 Delvin James RC 2.00 5.00
195 Timo Perez 2.00 5.00
196 Michael Cuddyer 2.00 5.00
197 Bob File RC 2.00 5.00
198 Martin Vargas RC 2.00 5.00
199 Kris Keller RC 2.00 5.00
200 Tim Spooneybarger RC 2.00 5.00
201 Adam Everett 2.00 5.00
202 Josh Fogg RC 2.00 5.00
203 Kip Wells 2.00 5.00
204 Rick Bauer RC 2.00 5.00
205 Brent Abernathy 2.00 5.00
206 Erick Almonte RC 2.00 5.00
207 Pedro Santana RC 2.00 5.00
208 Ken Harvey 2.00 5.00
209 Jerrod Riggan RC 2.00 5.00
210 Nick Punto RC 2.00 5.00
211 Steve Green RC 2.00 5.00
212 Nick Neugebauer 2.00 5.00
213 Chris George 2.00 5.00
214 Mike Penney RC 2.00 5.00
215 Bret Prinz RC 2.00 5.00
216 Tim Christman RC 2.00 5.00
217 Sean Douglass RC 2.00 5.00
218 Brett Jodie RC 2.00 5.00
219 Juan Diaz RC 2.00 5.00
220 Carlos Hernandez 2.00 5.00
221 Alex Cintron 2.00 5.00
222 Juan Cruz RC 2.00 5.00
223 Larry Bigbie 2.00 5.00
224 Junior Spivey RC 3.00 8.00
225 Luis Rivas 2.00 5.00
226 Brandon Lyon RC 2.00 5.00
227 Tony Cogan RC 2.00 5.00
228 Justin Duchscherer RC 2.00 5.00
229 Tike Redman 2.00 5.00
230 Jimmy Rollins 2.00 5.00
231 Scott Podsednik RC 6.00 15.00
232 Jose Acevedo RC 2.00 5.00
233 Luis Pineda RC 2.00 5.00
234 Josh Phelps 2.00 5.00
235 Paul Phillips RC 2.00 5.00
236 Brian Roberts RC 3.00 8.00
237 Orlando Woodards RC 2.00 5.00
238 Bart Miadich RC 2.00 5.00
239 Les Walrond RC 2.00 5.00
240 Brad Voyles RC 2.00 5.00
241 Joe Crede 3.00 8.00
242 Juan Moreno RC 2.00 5.00
243 Matt Ginter 2.00 5.00
244 Brian Rogers RC 2.00 5.00
245 Pablo Ozuna 2.00 5.00
246 Geronimo Gil RC 2.00 5.00
247 Mike Maroth RC 3.00 8.00
248 Josue Perez RC 2.00 5.00
249 Dee Brown 2.00 5.00
250 Victor Zambrano RC 3.00 8.00
251 Nick Maness RC 2.00 5.00
252 Kyle Lohse RC 3.00 8.00
253 Greg Miller RC 2.00 5.00
254 Henry Mateo RC 2.00 5.00
255 Duaner Sanchez RC 2.00 5.00
256 Rob MacKowiak RC 3.00 8.00
257 Steve Lomasney 2.00 5.00
258 Angel Santos RC 2.00 5.00
259 Winston Abreu RC 2.00 5.00
260 Brandon Berger RC 2.00 5.00
261 Tomas De La Rosa 2.00 5.00
262 Ramon Vazquez RC 2.00 5.00
263 Mickey Callaway RC 2.00 5.00
264 Corky Miller RC 2.00 5.00
265 Keith Ginter 2.00 5.00
266 Cody Ransom RC 2.00 5.00
267 Doug Nickle RC 2.00 5.00
268 Derrick Lewis RC 2.00 5.00
269 Eric Hinske RC 3.00 8.00
270 Travis Phelps RC 2.00 5.00
271 Eric Valent 2.00 5.00
272 Michael Rivera RC 2.00 5.00
273 Esix Snead RC 2.00 5.00
274 Troy Mattes RC 2.00 5.00
275 Jermaine Clark RC 2.00 5.00
276 Nate Cornejo 2.00 5.00
277 George Perez RC 2.00 5.00
278 Juan Rivera 2.00 5.00
279 Justin Atchley RC 2.00 5.00
280 Adam Johnson 2.00 5.00
281 Gene Altman RC 2.00 5.00
282 Jason Jennings 2.00 5.00
283 Scott MacRae RC 2.00 5.00
284 Craig Monroe RC 3.00 8.00
285 Bert Snow RC 2.00 5.00
286 Stubby Clapp RC 2.00 5.00
287 Jack Cust 2.00 5.00
288 Will Ohman RC 2.00 5.00
289 Wily Mo Pena 2.00 5.00
290 Joe Beimel RC 2.00 5.00
291 Jason Karnuth RC 2.00 5.00
292 Bill Ortega RC 2.00 5.00
293 Nate Teut RC 2.00 5.00
294 Erik Hiljus RC 2.00 5.00
295 Jason Smith RC 2.00 5.00
296 Juan A.Pena RC 2.00 5.00
297 David Espinosa 2.00 5.00
298 Tim Redding 2.00 5.00
299 Brian Lawrence RC 2.00 5.00
300 Briah Reith RC 2.00 5.00
301 Chad Durbin 2.00 5.00
302 Kurt Ainsworth 2.00 5.00
303 Blaine Neal RC 2.00 5.00
304 Jorge Julio RC 2.00 5.00
305 Adam Bernero 2.00 5.00
306 Travis Hafner RC 3.00 8.00
307 Dustan Mohr RC 2.00 5.00
308 Cesar Crespo RC 2.00 5.00
309 Billy Sylvester RC 2.00 5.00
310 Zach Day RC 2.00 5.00
311 Angel Berroa RC 3.00 8.00

2001 Donruss Signature Proofs

*PROOFS 1-110: 1.5X TO 4X BASIC
1-110 PRINT RUN 175 SERIAL #'d SETS
111-311 PRINT RUN 25 SERIAL #'d SETS
111-311 NO PRICING DUE TO SCARCITY

2001 Donruss Signature Award Winning Signatures

STATED PRINT RUNS LISTED BELOW
1 Jeff Bagwell/94 12.00 30.00
2 Carlos Beltran/99 6.00 15.00
3 Johnny Bench/68 50.00 100.00
4 Yogi Berra/55 30.00 80.00
5 Craig Biggio/97 20.00 50.00
6 Barry Bonds/93 60.00 120.00
7 Rod Carew/77 6.00 15.00
8 Orlando Cepeda/67 12.50 30.00
9 Andre Dawson/77 6.00 15.00
10 Dennis Eckersley CY/92 12.50 30.00
11 Dennis Eckersley MVP/92 10.00 25.00
12 Whitey Ford/61 30.00 60.00
13 Jason Giambi/100 6.00 15.00
14 Bob Gibson/68 20.00 50.00
15 Juan Gonzalez/96 10.00 25.00
16 Orel Hershiser/88 6.00 15.00
17 Al Kaline/67 15.00 40.00
18 Fred Lynn/75 MVP 6.00 15.00
19 Fred Lynn/75 ROY 6.00 15.00
20 Jim Palmer/76 6.00 15.00
21 Cal Ripken/83 75.00 150.00
22 Phil Rizzuto/50 20.00 50.00
23 Brooks Robinson/64 10.00 25.00
24 Scott Rolen/97 10.00 25.00
25 Ryne Sandberg/84 60.00 120.00
26 Warren Spahn/57 30.00 60.00
27 Frank Thomas/94 20.00 50.00
28 Billy Williams/61 10.00 25.00
29 Kerry Wood/98 8.00 20.00
30 Robin Yount/89 40.00 80.00

2001 Donruss Signature Award Winning Signatures Masters Series

SOME CARDS UNPRICED DUE TO SCARCITY
2 Carlos Beltran 8.00 20.00
5 Craig Biggio 20.00 50.00
8 Orlando Cepeda 8.00 20.00
9 Andre Dawson 8.00 20.00
10 Dennis Eckersley CY 8.00 20.00
11 Dennis Eckersley MVP 8.00 20.00
12 Whitey Ford 40.00 80.00
14 Bob Gibson 15.00 40.00
16 Orel Hershiser 50.00 100.00
17 Al Kaline 40.00 100.00
18 Fred Lynn MVP 8.00 20.00
19 Fred Lynn ROY 8.00 20.00
20 Jim Palmer 8.00 20.00
22 Phil Rizzuto 15.00 40.00
23 Brooks Robinson 15.00 40.00
24 Scott Rolen 15.00 40.00
26 Warren Spahn 12.50 30.00
28 Billy Williams 8.00 20.00
29 Kerry Wood 8.00 20.00

2001 Donruss Signature Century Marks

STATED PRINT RUNS LISTED BELOW
1 Brent Abernathy/184 4.00 10.00
2 Roberto Alomar/102 15.00 40.00
3 Rick Ankiel/119 10.00 25.00
4 Lance Berkman/121 10.00 25.00
5 Mark Buehrle/224 10.00 25.00
6 Wilmy Caceres/194 4.00 10.00
7 Eric Chavez/170 6.00 15.00
8 Joe Crede/154 10.00 25.00
9 Jack Cust/178 4.00 10.00
10 Brandon Duckworth/183 4.00 10.00
11 David Espinosa/199 4.00 10.00
12 Johnny Estrada/198 6.00 15.00
13 Pedro Feliz/180 4.00 10.00
14 Robert Fick/232 4.00 10.00
15 Cliff Floyd/146 6.00 15.00
16 Casey Fossum/100 4.00 10.00
17 Jay Gibbons/175 6.00 15.00
18 Keith Ginter/163 4.00 10.00
19 Troy Glaus/144 10.00 25.00
20 Luis Gonzalez/101 6.00 15.00
21 Vladimir Guerrero/187 6.00 15.00
22 Richard Hidalgo/173 4.00 10.00
23 Tim Hudson/145 10.00 25.00
24 Adam Johnson/130 4.00 10.00
25 Gabe Kapler/150 6.00 15.00
26 Joe Kennedy/219 6.00 15.00
27 Ryan Klesko/176 6.00 15.00
28 Carlos Lee/179 6.00 15.00
29 Terrence Long/180 4.00 10.00
30 Edgar Martinez/110 15.00 40.00
31 Joe Mays/209 4.00 10.00
32 Greg Miller/194 4.00 10.00
33 Wade Miller/180 4.00 10.00
34 Mark Mulder/203 6.00 15.00
35 Xavier Nady/180 6.00 15.00
36 Magglio Ordonez/104 6.00 15.00
37 Jose Ortiz/187 4.00 10.00
38 Roy Oswalt/192 6.00 15.00
39 Wily Mo Pena/203 6.00 15.00
40 Brad Penny/198 4.00 10.00
41 Aramis Ramirez/241 6.00 15.00
42 Luis Rivas/163 4.00 10.00
43 Alex Rodriguez/110 50.00 120.00
44 Scott Rolen/106 10.00 25.00
45 Mike Sweeney/99 6.00 15.00
46 Eric Valent/163 4.00 10.00
47 Kip Wells/223 4.00 10.00
48 Kerry Wood/109 10.00 25.00

2001 Donruss Signature Century Marks Masters Series

SOME CARDS UNPRICED DUE TO SCARCITY
1 Brent Abernathy 4.00 10.00
2 Roberto Alomar 20.00 50.00
3 Rick Ankiel 10.00 25.00
4 Lance Berkman 10.00 25.00
5 Mark Buehrle 6.00 15.00
6 Wilmy Caceres 4.00 10.00
7 Eric Chavez 6.00 15.00
8 Joe Crede 10.00 25.00
9 Jack Cust 4.00 10.00
10 Brandon Duckworth 4.00 10.00
11 David Espinosa 4.00 10.00
12 Johnny Estrada 6.00 15.00
13 Pedro Feliz 4.00 10.00
14 Robert Fick 4.00 10.00
15 Cliff Floyd 6.00 15.00
16 Casey Fossum 4.00 10.00
17 Jay Gibbons 6.00 15.00
18 Keith Ginter 4.00 10.00
19 Troy Glaus 15.00 40.00
22 Richard Hidalgo 4.00 10.00
23 Tim Hudson 6.00 15.00
24 Adam Johnson 4.00 10.00
25 Gabe Kapler 6.00 15.00
26 Joe Kennedy 6.00 15.00
27 Ryan Klesko 6.00 15.00
28 Carlos Lee 6.00 15.00
29 Terrence Long 4.00 10.00
30 Edgar Martinez 6.00 15.00
31 Joe Mays 4.00 10.00
32 Greg Miller 4.00 10.00
33 Wade Miller 4.00 10.00
34 Mark Mulder 6.00 15.00
35 Xavier Nady 6.00 15.00
36 Magglio Ordonez 6.00 15.00
37 Jose Ortiz 4.00 10.00
38 Roy Oswalt 6.00 15.00
39 Wily Mo Pena 6.00 15.00
40 Brad Penny 4.00 10.00
41 Aramis Ramirez 6.00 15.00
42 Luis Rivas 4.00 10.00
45 Mike Sweeney 6.00 15.00
46 Eric Valent 4.00 10.00
47 Kip Wells 4.00 10.00

2001 Donruss Signature Milestone Marks

STATED PRINT RUNS LISTED BELOW
NO PRICING ON QTY OF 40 OR LESS
1 Ernie Banks/285 25.00 60.00
2 Yogi Berra/120 30.00 80.00
3 Wade Boggs/98 60.00 120.00
4 Barry Bonds/55 60.00 150.00
7 Lou Brock/83 12.50 30.00
8 Rod Carew/110 12.00 30.00
9 Steve Carlton/75 8.00 20.00
10 Gary Carter/213 10.00 25.00
11 Bobby Doerr/192 8.00 20.00
12 Bob Feller/202 10.00 25.00
13 Whitey Ford/186 40.00 100.00
14 Steve Garvey/175 15.00 40.00
15 Tony Gwynn/99 30.00 60.00
16 Fergie Jenkins/149 8.00 20.00
17 Al Kaline/149 30.00 80.00
18 Harmon Killebrew/127 15.00 40.00
19 Ralph Kiner/105 8.00 20.00
21 Paul Molitor/96 12.00 30.00
22 Eddie Murray 3000 Hits/46 75.00 150.00
24 Stan Musial/109 40.00 80.00
25 Phil Niekro/300 8.00 20.00
26 Tony Perez/146 8.00 20.00
28 Frank Robinson/136 12.00 30.00
31 Enos Slaughter/117 12.00 30.00
32 Warren Spahn/300 12.00 30.00
33 Alan Trammell/154 12.00 30.00
34 Hoyt Wilhelm/227 8.00 20.00

2001 Donruss Signature Milestone Marks Masters Series

SOME CARDS UNPRICED DUE TO SCARCITY
7 Lou Brock 12.00 30.00
8 Rod Carew 12.00 30.00
9 Steve Carlton 12.00 20.00
10 Gary Carter 20.00 50.00
11 Bobby Doerr 12.00 20.00
12 Bob Feller 12.00 20.00
13 Whitey Ford 50.00 120.00
14 Steve Garvey 12.00 20.00
15 Tony Gwynn 12.00 30.00
16 Fergie Jenkins 12.00 20.00
17 Al Kaline 50.00 120.00
18 Harmon Killebrew 50.00 100.00
19 Ralph Kiner 12.00 20.00
21 Paul Molitor 40.00 80.00
25 Phil Niekro 12.00 20.00
26 Tony Perez 12.00 20.00
28 Frank Robinson 12.00 30.00
31 Enos Slaughter 12.00 30.00
33 Alan Trammell 12.00 20.00
34 Hoyt Wilhelm 12.00 30.00

2001 Donruss Signature Notable Nicknames

STATED PRINT RUN 100 SERIAL #'d SETS
1 Ernie Banks 60.00 120.00
2 Orlando Cepeda 30.00 60.00
3 Will Clark 50.00 100.00
4 Roger Clemens SP/50 300.00 500.00
5 Andre Dawson 30.00 60.00
6 Bob Feller 40.00 80.00
7 Carlton Fisk 50.00 100.00
8 Andres Galarraga 50.00 100.00
9 Luis Gonzalez 8.00 20.00
10 Reggie Jackson 60.00 120.00
11 Harmon Killebrew 75.00 150.00
12 Stan Musial 175.00 350.00
13 Brooks Robinson 50.00 100.00
14 Nolan Ryan 250.00 400.00
15 Ryne Sandberg 125.00 200.00
16 Enos Slaughter 20.00 50.00
17 Duke Snider 20.00 50.00
18 Frank Thomas 60.00 120.00

2001 Donruss Signature Notable Nicknames Masters Series

SOME CARDS UNPRICED DUE TO SCARCITY
1 Ernie Banks 75.00 150.00
2 Orlando Cepeda 40.00 80.00
3 Will Clark 60.00 120.00
5 Andre Dawson 20.00 50.00
6 Bob Feller 40.00 80.00
7 Carlton Fisk 60.00 120.00
8 Andres Galarraga 20.00 50.00
9 Luis Gonzalez 20.00 50.00
11 Harmon Killebrew 50.00 100.00
13 Brooks Robinson 60.00 120.00
14 Nolan Ryan 300.00 500.00
15 Ryne Sandberg 175.00 300.00
16 Enos Slaughter 20.00 50.00
18 Frank Thomas 125.00 250.00

2001 Donruss Signature Stats

STATED PRINT RUNS LISTED BELOW
NO PRICING ON QTY OF 40 OR LESS
1 Roberto Alomar/120 15.00 40.00
2 Moises Alou/124 6.00 15.00
3 Luis Aparicio/313 6.00 15.00
4 Lance Berkman/297 6.00 15.00
5 Wade Boggs/51 30.00 60.00
6 Lou Brock/118 10.00 25.00
8 Joe Carter/121 6.00 15.00
9 Sean Casey/103 6.00 15.00
10 Darin Erstad/100 6.00 15.00
12 Cliff Floyd/45 6.00 15.00
13 Whitey Ford/72 30.00 60.00
14 Andres Galarraga/150 6.00 15.00
15 Bob Gibson/112 10.00 25.00
16 Brian Giles/123 6.00 15.00
17 Troy Glaus/102 10.00 25.00
18 Luis Gonzalez/114 6.00 15.00
19 Vladimir Guerrero/131 6.00 15.00
21 Richard Hidalgo/314 4.00 10.00
25 Al Kaline/128 12.00 30.00
26 Gabe Kapler/302 6.00 15.00
27 Ralph Kiner/54 15.00 40.00
29 Carlos Lee/261 6.00 15.00
30 Kenny Lofton/210 10.00 25.00
31 Edgar Martinez/145 10.00 25.00
32 Joe Mays/115 4.00 10.00
33 Paul Molitor/41 30.00 60.00
34 Mark Mulder/88 10.00 25.00
36 Magglio Ordonez/126 6.00 15.00
37 Rafael Palmeiro/47 30.00 60.00
41 Manny Ramirez/45 40.00 80.00
42 Alex Rodriguez/132 60.00 120.00
43 Ivan Rodriguez/113 15.00 40.00
46 Shannon Stewart/319 6.00 15.00
47 Mike Sweeney/144 6.00 15.00
48 Miguel Tejada/115 10.00 25.00
49 Joe Torre/230 15.00 40.00
50 Javier Vazquez/405 6.00 15.00
51 Jose Vidro/330 4.00 10.00
52 Hoyt Wilhelm/243 10.00 25.00

2001 Donruss Signature Stats Masters Series

SOME CARDS UNPRICED DUE TO SCARCITY
1 Roberto Alomar 30.00 60.00
2 Moises Alou 6.00 15.00
3 Luis Aparicio 6.00 15.00
4 Lance Berkman 10.00 25.00
6 Lou Brock 40.00 80.00
7 Gary Carter 10.00 25.00
8 Joe Carter 6.00 15.00
9 Sean Casey 6.00 15.00
10 Darin Erstad 30.00 60.00
11 Bob Feller 6.00 15.00
12 Cliff Floyd 6.00 15.00
13 Whitey Ford 40.00 80.00
14 Andres Galarraga 30.00 60.00
15 Bob Gibson 20.00 50.00
16 Brian Giles 6.00 15.00
17 Troy Glaus 12.50 30.00
21 Richard Hidalgo 4.00 10.00
22 Bo Jackson 40.00 80.00
23 Fergie Jenkins 6.00 15.00
25 Al Kaline 40.00 100.00
26 Gabe Kapler 6.00 15.00
27 Ralph Kiner 10.00 25.00
28 Ryan Klesko 6.00 15.00
29 Carlos Lee 6.00 15.00
30 Kenny Lofton 10.00 25.00
31 Edgar Martinez 20.00 50.00
32 Joe Mays 4.00 10.00
34 Mark Mulder 6.00 15.00
35 Phil Niekro 6.00 15.00
36 Magglio Ordonez 6.00 15.00
38 Jim Palmer 15.00 40.00
39 Chan Ho Park 125.00 200.00
44 Curt Schilling 30.00 60.00
46 Shannon Stewart 6.00 15.00
47 Mike Sweeney 6.00 15.00
48 Miguel Tejada 6.00 15.00
49 Joe Torre 15.00 40.00
50 Javier Vazquez 6.00 15.00
51 Jose Vidro 4.00 10.00

2001 Donruss Signature Team Trademarks

STATED PRINT RUNS LISTED BELOW
NO PRICING ON QTY OF 40 OR LESS
2 Rick Ankiel/179 10.00 25.00
3 Ernie Banks/180 30.00 80.00
5 Yogi Berra/124 30.00 80.00
6 Wade Boggs/89 60.00 120.00
7 Barry Bonds/77 100.00 175.00
9 Steve Carlton/174 6.00 15.00
10 Sean Casey/123 6.00 15.00
11 Orlando Cepeda/100 10.00 25.00
14 Andre Dawson/176 6.00 15.00
15 Bobby Doerr/193 6.00 15.00
16 Whitey Ford/94 20.00 50.00
17 Steve Garvey/182 6.00 15.00
18 Bob Gibson/98 15.00 40.00
19 Juan Gonzalez/70 20.00 50.00
20 Shawn Green/109 10.00 25.00
21 Orel Hershiser/210 12.00 30.00
22 Reggie Jackson/73 40.00 80.00
23 Fergie Jenkins/213 6.00 15.00
24 Chipper Jones/74 40.00 80.00
26 Don Mattingly/72 75.00 150.00
27 Willie Mays/197 100.00 200.00
28 Willie McCovey/26 40.00 80.00
29 Joe Morgan/33 20.00 50.00
30 Eddie Murray/45 20.00 50.00
31 Stan Musial/65 50.00 100.00
32 Mike Mussina Orioles/85 40.00 80.00
33 Mike Mussina Yankees/95 20.00 50.00
34 Phil Niekro/187 6.00 15.00
35 Rafael Palmeiro/99 20.00 50.00
36 Jim Palmer/142 6.00 15.00
37 Tony Perez/73 6.00 15.00
38 Manny Ramirez Sox/57 60.00 120.00
39 Cal Ripken/47 150.00 300.00
40 Phil Rizzuto/98 30.00 80.00
41 Brooks Robinson/146 10.00 25.00
42 Frank Robinson Orioles/118 12.50 30.00
43 Frank Robinson Reds/116 10.00 25.00
44 Alex Rodriguez/100 30.00 80.00
45 Ivan Rodriguez/62 20.00 50.00
47 Nolan Ryan/153 75.00 150.00
48 Ryne Sandberg/52 75.00 150.00
49 Curt Schilling/63 15.00 40.00
50 Mike Schmidt/107 20.00 50.00
52 Gary Sheffield/194 10.00 25.00
53 Enos Slaughter/215 10.00 25.00
54 Duke Snider/47 40.00 80.00
55 Warren Spahn/140 15.00 40.00
56 Joe Torre/90 30.00 60.00
57 Billy Williams/194 10.00 25.00
58 Kerry Wood/52 6.00 15.00

2001 Donruss Signature Team Trademarks Masters Series

SOME CARDS UNPRICED DUE TO SCARCITY
9 Steve Carlton 6.00 15.00
11 Orlando Cepeda 6.00 15.00
14 Andre Dawson 6.00 15.00
15 Bobby Doerr 6.00 15.00
17 Nomar Garciaparra 60.00 120.00
18 Steve Garvey 6.00 15.00
19 Bob Gibson 30.00 60.00
22 Orel Hershiser 40.00 80.00
24 Fergie Jenkins 6.00 15.00
27 Don Mattingly 75.00 150.00
35 Phil Niekro 6.00 15.00
37 Jim Palmer 12.50 30.00
38 Tony Perez 6.00 15.00
41 Phil Rizzuto 30.00 80.00
42 Brooks Robinson 20.00 50.00
43 Frank Robinson Orioles 40.00 80.00
48 Nolan Ryan 75.00 150.00
50 Curt Schilling 15.00 40.00
52 Tom Seaver 30.00 80.00
53 Gary Sheffield 6.00 15.00
54 Enos Slaughter 8.00 20.00
56 Warren Spahn 20.00 50.00
58 Billy Williams 6.00 15.00

2001-02 Donruss Signature Hawaii

112-306 NO PRICING DUE TO SCARCITY
ONE BOX PER MEET INDUSTRY ATTENDEE
1 Alex Rodriguez 8.00 20.00
2 Barry Bonds 10.00 25.00
3 Cal Ripken 12.50 30.00
4 Chipper Jones 5.00 12.00
5 Derek Jeter 12.50 30.00
6 Troy Glaus 2.50 6.00
7 Frank Thomas 2.50 6.00
8 Greg Maddux 8.00 20.00
9 Ivan Rodriguez 2.50 6.00
10 Jeff Bagwell 2.50 6.00
11 John Olerud 1.50 4.00
12 Todd Helton 2.50 6.00
13 Ken Griffey Jr. 8.00 20.00
14 Manny Ramirez 2.50 6.00
15 Mark McGwire 10.00 25.00
16 Mike Piazza 6.00 15.00
17 Nomar Garciaparra 8.00 20.00
18 Moises Alou 1.50 4.00
19 Aramis Ramirez 1.50 4.00
20 Curt Schilling 2.50 6.00
21 Pat Burrell 2.50 6.00
22 Doug Mientkiewicz 1.50 4.00
23 Carlos Delgado 1.50 4.00
24 J.D. Drew 1.50 4.00
25 Cliff Floyd 1.50 4.00
26 Freddy Garcia 1.50 4.00
27 Roberto Alomar 4.00 10.00
28 Barry Zito 4.00 10.00
29 Juan Encarnacion 1.50 4.00
30 Paul Konerko 1.50 4.00
31 Mark Mulder 1.50 4.00
32 Andy Pettitte 2.50 6.00
33 Jim Edmonds 1.50 4.00
34 Darin Erstad 2.50 6.00
35 Jason Giambi 4.00 10.00
36 Tom Glavine 4.00 10.00
37 Juan Gonzalez 4.00 10.00
38 Fred McGriff 2.50 6.00
39 Shawn Green 2.50 6.00
40 Tim Hudson 1.50 4.00
41 Andruw Jones 2.50 6.00
42 Jeff Kent 1.50 4.00
43 Barry Larkin 4.00 10.00
44 Brad Radke 1.50 4.00
45 Mike Mussina 4.00 10.00
46 Hideo Nomo 4.00 10.00
47 Rafael Palmeiro 2.50 6.00
48 Scott Rolen 2.50 6.00
49 Gary Sheffield 1.50 4.00
50 Bernie Williams 2.50 6.00
51 Bob Abreu 1.50 4.00
52 Edgardo Alfonzo 1.50 4.00
53 Edgar Martinez 2.50 6.00
54 Magglio Ordonez 1.50 4.00
55 Kerry Wood 2.50 6.00
56 Adrian Beltre 1.50 4.00
57 Lance Berkman 2.50 6.00
58 Kevin Brown 4.00 10.00
59 Sean Casey 1.50 4.00
60 Eric Chavez 1.50 4.00
61 Bartolo Colon 1.50 4.00
62 Sammy Sosa 6.00 15.00
63 Jermaine Dye 1.50 4.00
64 Tony Gwynn 6.00 15.00
65 Carl Everett 1.50 4.00
66 Brian Giles 1.50 4.00
67 Mike Hampton 1.50 4.00
68 Richard Hidalgo 1.50 4.00
69 Geoff Jenkins 1.50 4.00
70 Tony Clark 1.50 4.00
71 Roger Clemens 8.00 20.00
72 Ryan Klesko 1.50 4.00
73 Chan Ho Park 1.50 4.00
74 Richie Sexson 1.50 4.00
75 Mike Sweeney 1.50 4.00
76 Kazuhiro Sasaki 2.50 6.00
77 Miguel Tejada 1.50 4.00
78 Jose Vidro 1.50 4.00
79 Larry Walker 2.50 6.00
80 Preston Wilson 1.50 4.00
81 Craig Biggio 2.50 6.00
82 Andres Galarraga 1.50 4.00
83 Jim Thome 4.00 10.00
84 Vladimir Guerrero 4.00 10.00
85 Rafael Furcal 1.50 4.00
86 Cristian Guzman 1.50 4.00
87 Terrence Long 1.50 4.00
88 Bret Boone 1.50 4.00
89 Wade Miller 1.50 4.00
90 Eric Milton 1.50 4.00
91 Gabe Kapler 1.50 4.00
92 Johnny Damon 1.50 4.00
93 Carlos Lee 1.50 4.00
94 Kenny Lofton 1.50 4.00
95 Raul Mondesi 1.50 4.00
96 Jorge Posada 2.50 6.00
97 Mark Grace 4.00 10.00
98 Robert Fick 1.50 4.00
99 Joe Mays 1.50 4.00
100 Aaron Sele 1.50 4.00
101 Ben Grieve 1.50 4.00
102 Luis Gonzalez 1.50 4.00
103 Ray Durham 1.50 4.00
104 Mark Quinn 1.50 4.00
105 Jose Canseco 4.00 10.00
106 David Justice 1.50 4.00

107 Pedro Martinez 4.00 10.00
108 Randy Johnson 6.00 15.00
109 Phil Nevin 1.50 4.00
110 Rickey Henderson 6.00 15.00

2003 Donruss Signature

COMMON CARD (1-100) .40 1.00
COMMON CARD (101-150) .40 1.00
101-150 ARE NOT SHORTPRINTS
1 Garret Anderson .40 1.00
2 Tim Salmon .40 1.00
3 Troy Glaus .40 1.00
4 Curt Schilling .60 1.50
5 Luis Gonzalez .40 1.00
6 Mark Grace .60 1.50
7 Matt Williams .40 1.00
8 Randy Johnson 1.00 2.50
9 Andruw Jones .40 1.00
10 Chipper Jones 1.00 2.50
11 Gary Sheffield .40 1.00
12 Greg Maddux 1.25 3.00
13 Johnny Damon .60 1.50
14 Manny Ramirez 1.00 2.50
15 Nomar Garciaparra .60 1.50
16 Pedro Martinez .60 1.50
17 Corey Patterson .40 1.00
18 Kerry Wood .40 1.00
19 Mark Prior .60 1.50
20 Sammy Sosa 1.00 2.50
21 Bartolo Colon .40 1.00
22 Frank Thomas 1.00 2.50
23 Magglio Ordonez .60 1.50
24 Paul Konerko .60 1.50
25 Adam Dunn .60 1.50
26 Austin Kearns .40 1.00
27 Barry Larkin .60 1.50
28 Ken Griffey Jr. 2.00 5.00
29 C.C. Sabathia .60 1.50
30 Omar Vizquel .60 1.50
31 Larry Walker .60 1.50
32 Todd Helton .60 1.50
33 Ivan Rodriguez .60 1.50
34 Josh Beckett .40 1.00
35 Craig Biggio .60 1.50
36 Jeff Bagwell .60 1.50
37 Jeff Kent .40 1.00
38 Lance Berkman .60 1.50
39 Richard Hidalgo .40 1.00
40 Roy Oswalt .60 1.50
41 Carlos Beltran .60 1.50
42 Mike Sweeney .40 1.00
43 Runelvys Hernandez .40 1.00
44 Hideo Nomo 1.00 2.50
45 Kazuhisa Ishii .40 1.00
46 Paul Lo Duca .40 1.00
47 Shawn Green .40 1.00
48 Ben Sheets .40 1.00
49 Richie Sexson .40 1.00
50 A.J. Pierzynski .40 1.00
51 Torii Hunter .40 1.00
52 Javier Vazquez .40 1.00
53 Jose Vidro .40 1.00
54 Vladimir Guerrero .60 1.50
55 Cliff Floyd .40 1.00
56 David Cone .40 1.00
57 Mike Piazza 1.00 2.50
58 Roberto Alomar .60 1.50
59 Tom Glavine .60 1.50
60 Alfonso Soriano .60 1.50
61 Derek Jeter 2.50 6.00
62 Drew Henson .40 1.00
63 Jason Giambi .40 1.00
64 Mike Mussina .60 1.50
65 Nick Johnson .40 1.00
66 Roger Clemens 1.25 3.00
67 Barry Zito .60 1.50
68 Eric Chavez .40 1.00
69 Mark Mulder .40 1.00
70 Miguel Tejada .60 1.50
71 Tim Hudson .60 1.50
72 Bobby Abreu .40 1.00
73 Jim Thome .60 1.50
74 Kevin Millwood .40 1.00
75 Pat Burrell .40 1.00
76 Brian Giles .40 1.00
77 Jason Kendall .40 1.00
78 Kenny Lofton .40 1.00
79 Phil Nevin .40 1.00
80 Ryan Klesko .40 1.00
81 Andres Galarraga .60 1.50
82 Barry Bonds 1.50 4.00
83 Rich Aurilia .40 1.00
84 Edgar Martinez .60 1.50
85 Freddy Garcia .40 1.00
86 Ichiro Suzuki 1.25 3.00
87 Albert Pujols 1.25 3.00
88 Jim Edmonds .60 1.50
89 Scott Rolen .60 1.50
90 So Taguchi .40 1.00
91 Rocco Baldelli .40 1.00
92 Alex Rodriguez 1.25 3.00
93 Hank Blalock .40 1.00
94 Juan Gonzalez .40 1.00
95 Mark Teixeira .60 1.50
96 Rafael Palmeiro .60 1.50
97 Carlos Delgado .40 1.00
98 Eric Hinske .40 1.00
99 Roy Halladay .60 1.50
100 Vernon Wells .40 1.00
101 Hideki Matsui ROO RC 2.00 5.00
102 Jose Contreras ROO RC 1.00 2.50
103 Jeremy Bonderman ROO RC 1.50 4.00
104 Bernie Castro ROO RC .40 1.00
105 Alfredo Gonzalez ROO RC .40 1.00
106 Arnie Munoz ROO RC .40 1.00
107 Andrew Brown ROO RC .40 1.00
108 Josh Hall ROO RC .40 1.00
109 Josh Stewart ROO RC .40 1.00
110 Clint Barmes ROO RC 1.00 2.50
111 Brandon Webb ROO RC 1.25 3.00
112 Chien-Ming Wang ROO RC 1.50 4.00
113 Edgar Gonzalez ROO RC .40 1.00
114 Alejandro Machado ROO RC .40 1.00
115 Jeremy Griffiths ROO RC .40 1.00
116 Craig Brazell ROO RC .40 1.00
117 Shane Bazzell ROO RC .40 1.00
118 Fernando Cabrera ROO RC .40 1.00
119 Termel Sledge ROO RC .40 1.00
120 Rob Hammock ROO RC .40 1.00
121 Francisco Rosario ROO RC .40 1.00
122 Francisco Cruceta ROO RC .40 1.00
123 Rett Johnson ROO RC .40 1.00
124 Guillermo Quiroz ROO RC .40 1.00
125 Hong-Chih Kuo ROO RC 2.00 5.00
126 Ian Ferguson ROO RC .40 1.00
127 Tim Olson ROO RC .40 1.00
128 Todd Wellemeyer ROO RC .40 1.00
129 Rich Fischer ROO RC .40 1.00
130 Phil Seibel ROO RC .40 1.00
131 Joe Valentine ROO RC .40 1.00
132 Matt Kata ROO RC .40 1.00
133 Michael Hessman ROO RC .40 1.00
134 Michel Hernandez ROO RC .40 1.00
135 Doug Waechter ROO RC .40 1.00
136 Prentice Redman ROO RC .40 1.00
137 Nook Logan ROO RC .40 1.00
138 Oscar Villarreal ROO RC .40 1.00
139 Pete LaForest ROO RC .40 1.00
140 Matt Bruback ROO RC .40 1.00
141 Dontrelle Willis ROO .40 1.00
142 Greg Aquino ROO RC .40 1.00
143 Lew Ford ROO RC .40 1.00
144 Jeff Duncan ROO RC .40 1.00
145 Dan Haren ROO RC 2.00 5.00
146 Miguel Ojeda ROO RC .40 1.00
147 Rosman Garcia ROO RC .40 1.00
148 Felix Sanchez ROO RC .40 1.00
149 Jon Leicester ROO RC .40 1.00
150 Roger Deago ROO RC .40 1.00

2003 Donruss Signature Century Proofs

*CENTURY 1-100: 2X TO 5X BASIC
*CENTURY 101-150: 2X TO 5X BASIC
RANDOM INSERTS IN PACKS
STATED PRINT RUN 100 SERIAL #'d SETS

2003 Donruss Signature Decade Proofs

STATED PRINT RUN 10 SERIAL #'d SETS
NO PRICING DUE TO SCARCITY

2003 Donruss Signature Autographs

1-102 RANDOM INSERTS IN PACKS
1-102 SP PRINTS PROVIDED BY DONRUSS
1-102 SP'S ARE NOT SERIAL-NUMBERED
151-153 RANDOM IN DLP R/T PACKS
151-153 PRINT RUN 200 SERIAL #'d SETS
NO PRICING ON QTY OF 28 OR LESS
1 Garret Anderson 6.00 15.00
6 Mark Grace SP/141 15.00 40.00
7 Matt Williams 3.00 8.00
8 Randy Johnson SP/50 40.00 80.00
10 Chipper Jones SP/50 40.00 80.00
14 Manny Ramirez SP/50 20.00 50.00
27 Barry Larkin SP/159 20.00 50.00
33 Ivan Rodriguez SP/50 8.00 20.00
38 Lance Berkman SP/75 10.00 25.00
39 Richard Hidalgo 4.00 10.00
40 Roy Oswalt SP/150 10.00 25.00
42 Mike Sweeney 6.00 15.00
50 A.J. Pierzynski 6.00 15.00
51 Torii Hunter 6.00 15.00
53 Jose Vidro 6.00 15.00
54 Vladimir Guerrero 6.00 15.00
55 Cliff Floyd 6.00 15.00
56 David Cone SP/35 10.00 25.00
58 Roberto Alomar SP/50 15.00 40.00
65 Nick Johnson 6.00 15.00
67 Barry Zito SP/150 6.00 15.00
68 Eric Chavez 6.00 15.00
69 Mark Mulder SP/50 10.00 25.00
72 Bobby Abreu 6.00 15.00
78 Kenny Lofton SP/229 6.00 15.00
80 Ryan Klesko SP/150 6.00 15.00
81 Andres Galarraga 6.00 15.00
83 Rich Aurilia SP/122 4.00 10.00
84 Edgar Martinez 6.00 15.00
89 Scott Rolen SP/200 12.50 30.00
90 So Taguchi SP/220 8.00 20.00
95 Mark Teixeira SP/150 10.00 25.00
100 Vernon Wells 6.00 15.00
102 Jose Contreras ROO 8.00 20.00
141 D.Willis ROO SP/150 8.00 20.00
151 Delmon Young ROO 10.00 25.00
152 Rickie Weeks ROO 6.00 15.00
153 Edwin Jackson ROO 4.00 10.00

2003 Donruss Signature Autographs Century

1-102 RANDOM INSERTS IN PACKS
151-154 RANDOM IN DLP R/T PACKS
1-102 PRINT RUN 100 SERIAL #'d SETS
151-154 PRINT RUN 21 SERIAL #'d SETS
NO PRICING ON QTY OF 25 OR LESS
CARD 154 IS NOT SIGNED
1 Garret Anderson 10.00 25.00
7 Matt Williams 4.00 10.00
27 Barry Larkin 20.00 50.00
39 Richard Hidalgo 6.00 15.00
42 Mike Sweeney 10.00 25.00
50 A.J. Pierzynski 6.00 15.00
51 Torii Hunter 10.00 25.00
53 Jose Vidro 6.00 15.00
54 Vladimir Guerrero 8.00 20.00
55 Cliff Floyd 10.00 25.00
62 Drew Henson 6.00 15.00
65 Nick Johnson 10.00 25.00
69 Mark Mulder 10.00 25.00
72 Bobby Abreu 10.00 25.00
78 Kenny Lofton 6.00 15.00
81 Andres Galarraga 10.00 25.00
84 Edgar Martinez 8.00 20.00
89 Scott Rolen 8.00 20.00
90 So Taguchi 10.00 25.00
100 Vernon Wells 10.00 25.00
102 Jose Contreras ROO 12.50 30.00

2003 Donruss Signature Autographs Decade

STATED PRINT RUN 10 SERIAL #'d SETS
NO PRICING DUE TO SCARCITY
CARD 154 IS NOT SIGNED

2003 Donruss Signature Autographs Notations

PRINT RUNS B/WN 1-250 COPIES PER
NO PRICING ON QTY OF 30 OR LESS
1A Garret Anderson #16/75 10.00 25.00
1B Garret Anderson 7-27-94/45 12.50 30.00
1C Garret Anderson WSC 02/75 10.00 25.00
7A Matt Williams #9/250 6.00 15.00
7B Matt Williams 01 WS/50 10.00 25.00
45 Kazuhisa Ishii #17/35 12.50 30.00
50 A.J. Pierzynski 02 AS/200 4.00 10.00
53A Jose Vidro #3/40 8.00 20.00
62C Drew Henson DH #7/73 6.00 15.00
68A Eric Chavez #3/50 8.00 20.00
78 Kenny Lofton #7/150 6.00 15.00
80 Ryan Klesko #30/75 10.00 25.00
83 Rich Aurilia #35/61 8.00 20.00
84A Edgar Martinez #11/250 10.00 25.00
84B E.Martinez BT 92-95/60 20.00 50.00
100 Vernon Wells #10/75 10.00 25.00

2003 Donruss Signature Autographs Notations Century

RANDOM INSERTS IN PACKS
STATED PRINT RUN 100 SERIAL #'d SETS
1A Garret Anderson #16 10.00 25.00
1B Garret Anderson 7-27-94 10.00 25.00
7A Matt Williams #9 15.00 40.00
7B Matt Williams 01 WS 15.00 40.00
50 A.J. Pierzynski 02 AS 6.00 15.00
68A Eric Chavez #3 6.00 15.00
78 Kenny Lofton #7 15.00 40.00
84A Edgar Martinez #11 10.00 25.00

2003 Donruss Signature Autographs Notations Decade

STATED PRINT RUN 10 SERIAL #'d SETS
NO PRICING DUE TO SCARCITY

2003 Donruss Signature Cuts

PRINT RUNS B/WN 7-127 COPIES PER
NO PRICING ON QTY OF 25 OR FEWER
8 Randy Johnson/40 40.00 80.00
33 Ivan Rodriguez/122 10.00 25.00
54 Vladimir Guerrero/34 10.00 25.00
58 Roberto Alomar/100 6.00 15.00
64 Mike Mussina/82 10.00 25.00
73 Jim Thome/127 15.00 40.00
80 Ryan Klesko/35 12.50 30.00
81 Andres Galarraga/51 8.00 20.00
89 Scott Rolen/36 10.00 25.00

2003 Donruss Signature Cuts Decade

STATED PRINT RUN 10 SERIAL #'d SETS
NO PRICING DUE TO SCARCITY

2003 Donruss Signature INKredible Thre

RANDOM INSERTS IN PACKS
STATED PRINT RUN 50 SERIAL #'d SETS
1 Zito/Mulder/Hudson 150.00 250.00
2 Maddux/Chipper/Andruw 125.00 250.00
3 Wood/Prior/Banks 30.00 60.00
4 Puckett/Killebrew/Torii 200.00 400.00
5 Guerrero/Vidro/Vazquez 30.00 60.00

2003 Donruss Signature Legends of Summer

STATED PRINT RUN 250 SERIAL #'d SETS
*CENTURY: .6X TO 1.5X BASIC
CENTURY PRINT RUN 100 SERIAL #'d SETS
DECADE PRINT RUN 10 SERIAL #'d SETS
NO DECADE PRICING DUE TO SCARCITY
1 Al Kaline 1.25 3.00
2 Alan Trammell 1.25 3.00
3 Andre Dawson 1.25 3.00
4 Babe Ruth 5.00 12.00
5 Billy Williams 1.25 3.00
6 Bo Jackson 2.00 5.00
7 Bob Feller 1.25 3.00
8 Bobby Doerr 1.25 3.00
9 Brooks Robinson 1.25 3.00
10 Dale Murphy 2.00 5.00
11 Dennis Eckersley 1.25 3.00
12 Don Mattingly 4.00 10.00
13 Duke Snider 1.25 3.00
14 Eric Davis .75 2.00
15 Frank Robinson 1.25 3.00
16 Fred Lynn .75 2.00
17 Gary Carter 1.25 3.00
18 Harmon Killebrew 2.00 5.00
19 Jack Morris 1.25 3.00
20 Jim Palmer 1.25 3.00
21 Jim Abbott .75 2.00
22 Joe Morgan 1.25 3.00
23 Joe Torre 1.25 3.00
24 Johnny Bench 2.00 5.00
25 Jose Canseco 1.25 3.00
26 Kirby Puckett 2.00 5.00
27 Lenny Dykstra .75 2.00
28 Lou Brock 1.25 3.00
29 Ralph Kiner 1.25 3.00
30 Mike Schmidt 3.00 8.00
31 Nolan Ryan Rgr 6.00 15.00
32 Nolan Ryan Angels 6.00 15.00
33 Orel Hershiser .75 2.00
34 Phil Rizzuto 1.25 3.00
35 Orlando Cepeda 1.25 3.00
36 Ryne Sandberg 4.00 10.00
37 Stan Musial 3.00 8.00
38 Steve Garvey .75 2.00
39 Tony Perez 1.25 3.00
40 Ty Cobb 3.00 8.00

2003 Donruss Signature Legends of Summer Autographs

STATED ODDS 1:4
SP PRINT RUNS PROVIDED BY DONRUSS
SP'S ARE NOT SERIAL-NUMBERED
1 Al Kaline 12.00 30.00
2 Alan Trammell 6.00 15.00
3 Andre Dawson 8.00 20.00
5 Billy Williams 6.00 15.00
6 Bo Jackson SP/100 25.00 60.00
7 Bob Feller 10.00 25.00
8 Bobby Doerr 6.00 15.00
9 Brooks Robinson 10.00 25.00
10 Dale Murphy SP/75 15.00 40.00
11 Dennis Eckersley 6.00 15.00
12 Don Mattingly SP/50 50.00 100.00
13 Duke Snider SP/225 10.00 25.00
14 Eric Davis 6.00 15.00
15 Frank Robinson 10.00 25.00
16 Fred Lynn 6.00 15.00
17 Gary Carter 12.00 30.00
18 Harmon Killebrew SP/171 12.00 30.00
19 Jack Morris 6.00 15.00
20 Jim Palmer 6.00 15.00
21 Jim Abbott 6.00 15.00
22 Joe Morgan SP/125 10.00 25.00
23 Joe Torre 15.00 40.00
24 Johnny Bench SP/75 15.00 40.00
25 Jose Canseco SP/75 15.00 40.00
26 Kirby Puckett SP/75 50.00 100.00
27 Lenny Dykstra 6.00 15.00
28 Lou Brock 12.00 30.00
29 Ralph Kiner 6.00 15.00
30 Mike Schmidt SP/75 30.00 80.00
31 Nolan Ryan Rgr SP/75 50.00 100.00
33 Orel Hershiser 12.00 30.00
34 Phil Rizzuto 15.00 40.00
35 Orlando Cepeda 6.00 15.00
36 Ryne Sandberg SP/75 50.00 120.00
37 Stan Musial SP/200 30.00 80.00
38 Steve Garvey 10.00 25.00
39 Tony Perez 6.00 15.00

2003 Donruss Signature Legends of Summer Autographs Century

RANDOM INSERTS IN PACKS
STATED PRINT RUN 100 SERIAL #'d SETS
1 Al Kaline 20.00 50.00
2 Alan Trammell 6.00 15.00
3 Andre Dawson 10.00 25.00
5 Billy Williams 10.00 25.00
6 Bo Jackson 30.00 60.00
7 Bob Feller 12.00 30.00
8 Bobby Doerr 10.00 25.00
9 Brooks Robinson 15.00 40.00
11 Dennis Eckersley 10.00 25.00
12 Don Mattingly 15.00 40.00
14 Eric Davis 10.00 25.00
15 Frank Robinson 10.00 25.00
16 Fred Lynn 10.00 25.00
17 Gary Carter 20.00 50.00
19 Jack Morris 10.00 25.00
20 Jim Palmer 10.00 25.00
21 Jim Abbott 10.00 25.00
23 Joe Torre 15.00 40.00
27 Lenny Dykstra 6.00 15.00
28 Lou Brock 12.00 30.00
29 Ralph Kiner 12.00 30.00
33 Orel Hershiser 15.00 40.00
34 Phil Rizzuto 15.00 40.00
35 Orlando Cepeda 10.00 25.00
36 Ryne Sandberg 40.00 100.00
37 Stan Musial 50.00 100.00
38 Steve Garvey 15.00 40.00
39 Tony Perez 10.00 25.00

2003 Donruss Signature Legends of Summer Autographs Notations

PRINT RUNS B/WN 1-250 COPIES PER
NO PRICING ON QTY OF 25 OR LESS
1A Al Kaline #6/200 20.00 50.00
1B Al Kaline HOF '80/200 15.00 40.00
1C Al Kaline Mr. Tiger/200 15.00 40.00
2 A.Trammell 84 WS MVP/250 6.00 15.00
3A Andre Dawson #8/165 6.00 15.00
3B Andre Dawson 87 MVP/250 6.00 15.00
5B Billy Williams 61 ROY/250 6.00 15.00
5C Billy Williams 87 HOF/150 6.00 15.00
7A Bob Feller #19/250 6.00 15.00
7B Bob Feller HOF 62/250 6.00 15.00
8A Bobby Doerr #1/250 8.00 20.00
8B Bobby Doerr HOF 86/250 6.00 15.00
8C Bobby Doerr MVP 44/250 6.00 15.00
9A B.Robinson 64 MVP/150 15.00 40.00
9B B.Robinson 70 WS MVP/50 20.00 50.00
10A Dale Murphy MVP 82/50 20.00 50.00
10B Dale Murphy MVP 83/50 20.00 50.00
11A D.Eckersley 92 CY/250 6.00 15.00
11B D.Eckersley 92 CY-MVP/250 6.00 15.00
11C D.Eckersley 92 MVP/250 6.00 15.00
14A Eric Davis #44/250 10.00 25.00
14B Eric Davis 87 AS/150 10.00 25.00
14C Eric Davis 90 WS/200 10.00 25.00
16A Fred Lynn 75 MVP-ROY/240 6.00 15.00
16B Fred Lynn 75-83 AS/250 6.00 15.00
18A H.Killebrew #3/75 20.00 50.00
18B H.Killebrew 69 MVP/50 30.00 60.00
18C H.Killebrew 573 HR/50 30.00 60.00
18D H.Killebrew HOF 84/125 20.00 50.00
19A J.Morris 91 WS MVP/250 6.00 15.00
19B Jack Morris 92 WS/250 6.00 15.00
20A Jim Palmer 73 CY/190 6.00 15.00
20B Jim Palmer 75 CY/140 6.00 15.00
20C Jim Palmer 76 CY/50 12.50 30.00
21A Jim Abbott 4-8-89/200 8.00 20.00
21B Jim Abbott 9-4-93/100 10.00 25.00
21C Jim Abbott 6-15-99/75 10.00 25.00
21D Jim Abbott U of Mich/50 12.50 30.00
27 Lenny Dykstra 86 WS/226 6.00 15.00
28B Lou Brock HOF 85/50 20.00 50.00
29A Ralph Kiner #4/150 8.00 20.00
29C Ralph Kiner HOF/200 10.00 25.00
29D Ralph Kiner HOF 75/100 10.00 25.00
35A O.Cepeda Baby Bull/75 10.00 25.00
35B O.Cepeda MVP 67/40 10.00 25.00
35C O.Cepeda 58 ROY/40 10.00 25.00
35D O.Cepeda 67 WS/40 10.00 25.00
35E O.Cepeda 68 WS/40 10.00 25.00
38A Steve Garvey #6/150 6.00 15.00
38C Steve Garvey 78 AS MVP/50 12.50 30.00
38D Steve Garvey 81 WS/75 10.00 25.00
39A Tony Perez #24/250 10.00 25.00
39B Tony Perez HOF 02/175 10.00 25.00
39C Tony Perez WS 75/125 6.00 15.00
39D Tony Perez WS 76/75 6.00 15.00

2003 Donruss Signature Legends of Summer Autographs Notations Century

RANDOM INSERTS IN PACKS
STATED PRINT RUN 100 SERIAL #'d SETS
1A Al Kaline #6 20.00 50.00
1B Al Kaline HOF 80 20.00 50.00
1C Al Kaline Mr. Tiger 20.00 50.00
2 Alan Trammell 84 WS MVP 10.00 25.00
3A Andre Dawson #8 10.00 25.00
3B Andre Dawson 87 MVP 10.00 25.00
5A Billy Williams #26 10.00 25.00
5B Billy Williams 61 ROY 10.00 25.00
5C Billy Williams 87 HOF 10.00 25.00
7A Bob Feller #19 10.00 25.00
7B Bob Feller HOF 62 10.00 25.00
7C Bob Feller Triple Crown 10.00 25.00
8A Bobby Doerr #1 10.00 25.00
8B Bobby Doerr HOF 86 10.00 25.00
8C Bobby Doerr MVP 44 10.00 25.00
11A Dennis Eckersley 92 CY 12.50 30.00
11B D.Eckersley 92 CY-MVP 12.50 30.00
11C Dennis Eckersley 92 MVP 12.50 30.00
14A Eric Davis #44 10.00 25.00
14B Eric Davis 87 AS 10.00 25.00
14C Eric Davis 90 WS 10.00 25.00
16A Fred Lynn 75 MVP-ROY 10.00 25.00
16B Fred Lynn 75-83 AS 10.00 25.00
19A Jack Morris 91 WS MVP 10.00 25.00
19B Jack Morris 92 WS 10.00 25.00
20A Jim Palmer 73 CY 10.00 25.00
20B Jim Palmer 75 CY 10.00 25.00
20C Jim Palmer 76 CY 10.00 25.00
21A Jim Abbott 4-8-89 25.00 60.00
21B Jim Abbott 9-4-93 20.00 50.00
21C Jim Abbott 6-15-99 20.00 50.00
21D Jim Abbott U of Mich 20.00 50.00
21E Jim Abbott Yanks 20.00 50.00
27 Lenny Dykstra 86 WS 10.00 25.00
29A Ralph Kiner #4 12.50 30.00
29B Ralph Kiner 48-53 AS 10.00 25.00
29C Ralph Kiner HOF 10.00 25.00
29D Ralph Kiner HOF 75 10.00 25.00
38A Steve Garvey #6 10.00 25.00
38B Steve Garvey 74 MVP 10.00 25.00
38C Steve Garvey 78 AS MVP 10.00 25.00
38D Steve Garvey 81 WS 10.00 25.00
39A Tony Perez #24 10.00 25.00
39B Tony Perez HOF 02 10.00 25.00
39C Tony Perez WS 75 10.00 25.00
39D Tony Perez WS 76 10.00 25.00

2003 Donruss Signature Notable Nicknames

STATED PRINT RUN 750 SERIAL #'d SETS
*CENTURY: .6X TO 1.5X BASIC
CENTURY PRINT RUN 100 SERIAL #'d SETS
DECADE PRINT RUN 10 SERIAL #'d SETS
NO DECADE PRICING DUE TO SCARCITY
1 Andre Dawson 1.25 3.00
2 Torii Hunter .75 2.00
3 Brooks Robinson 1.25 3.00
4 Carlton Fisk 1.25 3.00
5 Mike Mussina 1.25 3.00
6 Don Mattingly 4.00 10.00
7 Duke Snider 1.25 3.00
8 Eric Davis .75 2.00
9 Frank Thomas 2.00 5.00
10 Randy Johnson 2.00 5.00
11 Lenny Dykstra .75 2.00
12 Ivan Rodriguez 1.25 3.00
13 Nolan Ryan 6.00 15.00
14 Phil Rizzuto 1.25 3.00
15 Reggie Jackson 1.25 3.00
16 Roger Clemens 2.50 6.00
17 Ryne Sandberg 4.00 10.00
18 Stan Musial 3.00 8.00
19 Luis Gonzalez .75 2.00
20 Will Clark 1.25 3.00

2003 Donruss Signature Notable Nicknames Century

*CENTURY: .6X TO 1.5X BASIC
RANDOM INSERTS IN PACKS
STATED PRINT RUN 100 SERIAL #'d SETS

2003 Donruss Signature Notable Nicknames Autographs

PRINT RUN 100 #'d SETS UNLESS NOTED
NO PRICING ON QTY OF 25 OR LESS
1 Andre Dawson 12.50 30.00
2 Torii Hunter 20.00 50.00
3 Brooks Robinson 15.00 40.00
4 Carlton Fisk 20.00 50.00
5 Mike Mussina 40.00 80.00
6 Don Mattingly 75.00 150.00
7 Duke Snider 40.00 80.00
8 Eric Davis/40 20.00 50.00
9 Frank Thomas 50.00 100.00
10 Randy Johnson 60.00 120.00
11 Lenny Dykstra 12.50 30.00
12 Ivan Rodriguez/75 40.00 80.00
14 Phil Rizzuto 40.00 80.00
15 Reggie Jackson 40.00 80.00
16 Roger Clemens 40.00 100.00
17 Ryne Sandberg 30.00 60.00
18 Stan Musial 60.00 120.00
19 Luis Gonzalez 20.00 50.00
20 Will Clark 20.00 50.00

2003 Donruss Signature Player Collection Autographs

PRINT RUNS B/WN 4-482 COPIES PER
NO PRICING ON QTY OF 25 OR LESS
1 Roberto Alomar/75 15.00 40.00
2 Adrian Beltre/104 10.00 25.00
3 Lance Berkman/50 5.00 12.00
6 Joe Borchard/53 8.00 20.00
9 J.D. Drew/52 12.50 30.00
10 Jim Edmonds/52 20.00 50.00
12 Todd Helton/50 8.00 20.00
13 Jason Jennings/49 8.00 20.00
16 Chipper Jones/51 30.00 60.00
18 Paul Lo Duca/227 6.00 15.00
19 Magglio Ordonez/102 10.00 25.00
22 Mark Prior/27 6.00 15.00
26 Ivan Rodriguez/52 20.00 50.00
27 Richie Sexson/50 12.50 30.00
29B Matt Williams/483 6.00 15.00

2003 Donruss Signature Team Trademarks

STATED PRINT RUN 500 SERIAL #'d SETS
*CENTURY: .6X TO 1.5X BASIC
CENTURY PRINT RUN 100 SERIAL #'d SETS
DECADE PRINT RUN 10 SERIAL #'d SETS
NO DECADE PRICING DUE TO SCARCITY
1 Adam Dunn 1.25 3.00
2 Andre Dawson 1.25 3.00
3 Babe Ruth 5.00 12.00
4 Barry Bonds 3.00 8.00
5 Brooks Robinson 1.25 3.00
6 Cal Ripken 6.00 15.00
7 Derek Jeter 5.00 12.00
8 Don Mattingly 4.00 10.00
9 Frank Robinson 1.25 3.00
10 Fred Lynn .75 2.00
11 Gary Carter 1.25 3.00
12 George Brett 4.00 10.00
13 Greg Maddux 2.50 6.00
14 Ichiro Suzuki 2.50 6.00
15 Jim Palmer 1.25 3.00
16 Jose Contreras 2.00 5.00
17 Kerry Wood .75 2.00
18 Lou Gehrig 4.00 10.00
19 Magglio Ordonez 1.25 3.00
20 Mark Grace 1.25 3.00
21 Mike Schmidt 3.00 8.00
22 Nolan Ryan Rgr 6.00 15.00
23 Nolan Ryan Astros 6.00 15.00
24 Reggie Jackson 1.25 3.00
25 Rickey Henderson 2.00 5.00
26 Roberto Clemente 5.00 12.00
27 Roger Clemens Sox 2.50 6.00
28 Roger Clemens Yanks 2.50 6.00
29 Ryne Sandberg 4.00 10.00
30 Sammy Sosa 2.00 5.00
31 Stan Musial 3.00 8.00
32 Steve Carlton 1.25 3.00
33 Tim Hudson 1.25 3.00
34 Tom Glavine 1.25 3.00
35 Tom Seaver 1.25 3.00
36 Tony Gwynn 2.00 5.00
37 Torii Hunter .75 2.00
38 Ty Cobb 3.00 8.00
39 Vladimir Guerrero 1.25 3.00
40 Will Clark 1.25 3.00

2003 Donruss Signature Team Trademarks Autographs

PRINT RUNS B/WN 25-250 COPIES PER
NO PRICING ON QTY OF 25 OR LESS
1 Adam Dunn/50 20.00 50.00
2 Andre Dawson/250 6.00 15.00
5 Brooks Robinson/250 10.00 25.00
6 Cal Ripken/50 40.00 100.00
8 Don Mattingly/75 20.00 50.00
10 Fred Lynn/250 6.00 15.00
11 Gary Carter/250 10.00 25.00
12 George Brett/50 30.00 60.00
13 Greg Maddux/50 60.00 120.00
16 Jose Contreras/250 8.00 20.00
17 Kerry Wood/50 20.00 50.00
19 Magglio Ordonez/75 10.00 25.00
23 Nolan Ryan Astros/50 75.00 150.00
24 Reggie Jackson/75 15.00 40.00
25 Rickey Henderson/50 50.00 100.00
27 Roger Clemens Sox/50 20.00 50.00
28 Roger Clemens Yanks/50 20.00 50.00
29 Ryne Sandberg/100 30.00 80.00
31 Stan Musial/200 40.00 80.00
32 Steve Carlton/150 6.00 15.00
33 Tim Hudson/100 15.00 40.00
34 Tom Glavine/50 20.00 50.00
35 Tom Seaver/50 25.00 60.00
36 Tony Gwynn/50 20.00 50.00
37 Torii Hunter/250 6.00 15.00
39 Vladimir Guerrero/250 10.00 25.00
40 Will Clark/125 15.00 40.00

2003 Donruss Signature Team Trademarks Autographs Century

STATED PRINT RUN 100 SERIAL #'d SETS
1 Andre Dawson 10.00 25.00
5 Brooks Robinson 10.00 25.00
9 Frank Robinson 10.00 25.00
10 Fred Lynn 10.00 25.00
11 Gary Carter 12.00 30.00
15 Jim Palmer 10.00 25.00
16 Jose Contreras 12.50 30.00
20 Mark Grace 15.00 40.00
29 Ryne Sandberg 25.00 60.00
31 Stan Musial 40.00 80.00
32 Steve Carlton 10.00 25.00
34 Tom Glavine 15.00 40.00
37 Torii Hunter 10.00 25.00
39 Vladimir Guerrero 10.00 25.00

2003 Donruss Signature Team Trademarks Autographs Notations

PRINT RUNS B/WN 5-250 COPIES PER
NO PRICING ON QTY OF 25 OR LESS
2A Andre Dawson #10/250 6.00 15.00
2B Andre Dawson ROY 77/150 6.00 15.00
5A B.Robinson 64 MVP/75 20.00 50.00
5B B.Robinson 70 WS MVP/125 15.00 40.00
10A Fred Lynn 75-83 AS/50 12.50 30.00
15A Jim Palmer 73 CY/32 12.50 30.00
15B Jim Palmer 75 CY/128 10.00 25.00
15C Jim Palmer 76 CY/150 6.00 15.00
29A Ryne Sandberg #23/40 30.00 60.00
29C Ryne Sandberg 84 MVP/55 30.00 60.00
32A Steve Carlton 72 CY/50 8.00 20.00
32B Steve Carlton 77 CY/50 8.00 20.00
32C Steve Carlton 80 CY/50 8.00 20.00
32D Steve Carlton 82 CY/50 8.00 20.00
33B Tim Hudson Huddy/50 20.00 50.00
40A Will Clark 89 MVP/52 30.00 60.00
40B Will Clark 89 WS/52 30.00 60.00

2003 Donruss Signature Team Trademarks Autographs Notations Century

RANDOM INSERTS IN PACKS
STATED PRINT RUN 100 SERIAL #'d SETS
2A Andre Dawson #10 6.00 15.00
2B Andre Dawson ROY 77 6.00 15.00
10A Fred Lynn 75-83 AS 6.00 15.00
10B Fred Lynn 75 MVP-ROY 6.00 15.00
15A Jim Palmer 73 CY 6.00 15.00
15B Jim Palmer 75 CY 6.00 15.00
15C Jim Palmer 76 CY 6.00 15.00

2005 Donruss Signature

COMMON CARD (1-150) .60 1.50
COMMON RC (1-150) .60 1.50
COM.DUAL AU T3-T6 4.00 10.00
151-156 DUAL AU STATED ODDS 1:14
COMMON TRI AU T4 6.00 15.00
COMMON TRI AU T2 8.00 20.00
157-158 TRIPLE AU STATED ODDS 1:51
COMMON QUAD AU T2 10.00 25.00
159 QUAD AU STATED ODDS 1:626
151-159 TIER 1 QTY B/WN 1-50 PER
151-159 TIER 2 QTY B/WN 51-100 PER
151-159 TIER 3 QTY B/WN 101-250 PER
151-159 TIER 4 QTY B/WN 251-800 PER
151-159 TIER 6 QTY B/WN 1201-2000 PER
151-159 ARE NOT SERIAL-NUMBERED
151-159 QTY INFO PROVIDED BY DONRUSS
155-156 NOT PRICED DUE TO SCARCITY
1 Scot Shields .60 1.50
2 Tim Salmon .60 1.50
3 Chone Figgins .60 1.50
4 Dallas McPherson .60 1.50
5 John Lackey 1.00 2.50
6 Ervin Santana .60 1.50
7 Casey Kotchman .60 1.50
8 Steve Finley .60 1.50
9 Brandon Webb 1.00 2.50
10 Chad Tracy .60 1.50
11 Russ Ortiz .60 1.50
12 Alex Cintron .60 1.50
13 Marcus Giles .60 1.50
14 Ichiro Suzuki 2.00 5.00
15 Tadahito Iguchi RC 1.00 2.50
16 Chipper Jones 1.50 4.00
17 Cal Ripken 5.00 12.00
18 Rick Dempsey .60 1.50
19 Adam Loewen .60 1.50
20 Eric Byrnes .60 1.50
21 Luis Matos .60 1.50
22 Miguel Tejada 1.00 2.50
23 Brooks Robinson 1.00 2.50
24 Kevin Youkilis .60 1.50
25 Keith Foulke .60 1.50
26 Trot Nixon .60 1.50
27 Edgar Renteria .60 1.50
28 Luis Tiant .60 1.50
29 Todd Walker .60 1.50
30 Mark Grace 1.00 2.50
31 Steve Stone .60 1.50
32 Ron Santo 1.00 2.50
33 Michael Wuertz .60 1.50
34 Russ Rohlicek RC .60 1.50
35 Ryne Sandberg 3.00 8.00
36 Andre Dawson 1.00 2.50
37 Aramis Ramirez .60 1.50
38 Derrek Lee .60 1.50
39 Paulino Reynoso RC .60 1.50
40 Jose Contreras .60 1.50
41 Freddy Garcia .60 1.50
42 Mark Buehrle 1.00 2.50
43 Bubba Nelson .60 1.50
44 Eric Davis .60 1.50
45 Adam Dunn 1.00 2.50
46 Travis Hafner .60 1.50
47 Larry Bigbie .60 1.50
48 Todd Helton 1.00 2.50
49 Chris Shelton .60 1.50
50 Willie Mays 3.00 8.00
51 Craig Monroe .60 1.50
52 Ivan Rodriguez 1.00 2.50
53 Miguel Cabrera 1.50 4.00
54 Chris Resop RC .60 1.50
55 Paul Lo Duca .60 1.50
56 Luke Scott RC 1.50 4.00
57 Brandon Backe .60 1.50
58 Mark McLemore RC .60 1.50
59 Devon Lowery RC .60 1.50
60 Jeremy Affeldt .60 1.50
61 Duke Snider 1.00 2.50
62 Johnny Podres .60 1.50
63 Rickie Weeks .60 1.50
64 Ben Sheets .60 1.50
65 Carlos Lee .60 1.50
66 Lew Ford .60 1.50
67 Travis Bowyer RC .60 1.50
68 Garrett Jones RC 1.00 2.50
69 Joe Nathan .60 1.50
70 Kent Hrbek .60 1.50
71 J.D. Durbin .60 1.50
72 Shannon Stewart .60 1.50
73 Torii Hunter .60 1.50
74 Kirby Puckett 1.50 4.00
75 Danny Graves .60 1.50
76 Jae Weong Seo .60 1.50
77 Matt Lindstrom RC .60 1.50
78 Dwight Gooden .60 1.50
79 Carlos Beltran 1.00 2.50
80 Mike Piazza 1.50 4.00
81 Tom Gordon .60 1.50
82 Adam LaRoche .60 1.50
83 Dave Righetti .60 1.50
84 Joe Pepitone .60 1.50
85 Gary Sheffield .60 1.50
86 Jim Leyritz .60 1.50
87 Rich Gossage 1.00 2.50
88 Don Larsen .60 1.50
89 Bernie Williams 1.00 2.50
90 Jorge Posada 1.00 2.50
91 Octavio Dotel .60 1.50
92 Rollie Fingers 1.00 2.50
93 Dennis Eckersley 1.00 2.50

94 Rich Harden .60 1.50
95 Art Howe .60 1.50
96 Jose Canseco 1.00 2.50
97 Barry Zito 1.00 2.50
98 Eric Chavez .60 1.50
99 Rickey Henderson 1.50 4.00
100 Chris Roberson RC .60 1.50
101 Eude Brito RC .60 1.50
102 Randy Wolf .60 1.50
103 Mike Lieberthal .60 1.50
104 John Kruk .60 1.50
105 Lenny Dykstra .60 1.50
106 Carlos Ruiz RC 1.00 2.50
107 Bobby Abreu .60 1.50
108 Bill Madlock .60 1.50
109 Mike Johnston .60 1.50
110 Ian Snell .60 1.50
111 Freddy Sanchez .60 1.50
112 Jose Castillo .60 1.50
113 Jeff Miller RC .60 1.50
114 John Candelaria .60 1.50
115 Jason Bay .60 1.50
116 Mark Loretta .60 1.50
117 Sean Thompson RC .60 1.50
118 Akinori Otsuka .60 1.50
119 Omar Vizquel 1.00 2.50
120 Will Clark 1.00 2.50
121 Clint Nageotte .60 1.50
122 J.J. Putz .60 1.50
123 Raul Ibanez 1.00 2.50
124 Wladimir Balentien RC 1.00 2.50
125 Jamie Moyer .60 1.50
126 Adrian Beltre 1.50 4.00
127 Richie Sexson .60 1.50
128 Edgar Martinez 1.00 2.50
129 Jeff Suppan .60 1.50
130 Marty Marion .60 1.50
131 Keith Hernandez .60 1.50
132 Ozzie Smith 2.00 5.00
133 Mark Mulder .60 1.50
134 Lee Smith .60 1.50
135 Jim Edmonds 1.00 2.50
136 Nomar Garciaparra 1.00 2.50
137 Delmon Young 1.50 4.00
138 Jason Hammel RC 1.50 4.00
139 Agustin Montero RC .60 1.50
140 Francisco Cordero .60 1.50
141 Michael Young .60 1.50
142 Al Oliver .60 1.50
143 David Dellucci .60 1.50
144 Nolan Ryan 5.00 12.00
145 Rafael Palmeiro 1.00 2.50
146 Alexis Rios .60 1.50
147 Jose Guillen .60 1.50
148 Danny Rueckel RC .60 1.50
149 Jose Vidro .60 1.50
150 Preston Wilson .60 1.50
151 R.Weeks/P.Fielder RC T3 6.00 15.00
152 H.Penn RC/A.Loewen T4 8.00 20.00
153 A.Otsuka/K.Yabu RC T4 20.00 50.00
154 B.McCar/A.Sanch RC T6 5.00 12.00
157 Niem/Verlan/Humb RC T4 20.00 50.00
158 Bal/Con/Neg RC T2/77 * 12.50 30.00
159 Ver/NiemPena/Jim RC T2/74 * 100.00 200.00

2005 Donruss Signature Century Proofs Gold

*GOLD: 1.5X TO 4X BASIC
RANDOM INSERTS IN PACKS
STATED PRINT RUN 25 SERIAL #'d SETS
NO RC PRICING DUE TO SCARCITY

2005 Donruss Signature Century Proofs Silver

*SILVER: 1X TO 2.5X BASIC
*SILVER: 1X TO 2.5X BASIC RC
RANDOM INSERTS IN PACKS
STATED PRINT RUN 75 SERIAL #'d SETS

2005 Donruss Signature Autograph Gold MS

*GOLD p/r 25-50: .6X TO 1.5X SILV T5-T6
*GOLD p/r 25-50: .6X TO 1.5X SILV T4
*GOLD p/r 25-50: .6X TO 1.5X SILV T3
*GOLD p/r 25-50: .5X TO 1.2X SILV T2
*GOLD p/r 25-50: 1X TO 1X SILV T1
RANDOM INSERTS IN PACKS
PRINT RUNS B/WN 3-50 COPIES PER
NO PRICING ON QTY OF 21 OR LESS
NO RC YR PRICING ON QTY OF 25 OR LESS
17 Cal Ripken/50 30.00 80.00
21 Luis Matos/50 6.00 15.00
49 Chris Shelton/43 12.50 30.00
88 Don Larsen/25 10.00 25.00
93 Dennis Eckersley/50 10.00 25.00
110 Ian Snell/34 6.00 15.00
142 Al Oliver/25 10.00 25.00
143 David Dellucci/25 10.00 25.00

2005 Donruss Signature Autograph Platinum MS

*PLAT p/r 25: .6X TO 1.5X SILV T5-T6
*PLAT p/r 25: .6X TO 1.5X SILV T4
*PLAT p/r 25: .6X TO 1.5X SILV T3
*PLAT p/r 25: .5X TO 1.2X SILV T2
*PLAT p/r 25: .4X TO 1X SILV T1
RANDOM INSERTS IN PACKS
PRINT RUNS B/WN 1-25 COPIES PER
NO PRICING ON QTY OF 22 OR LESS
NO RC YR PRICING DUE TO SCARCITY
17 Cal Ripken/25 75.00 150.00

2005 Donruss Signature Autograph Silver

STATED ODDS 1:2
TIER 1 QTY B/WN 1-50 COPIES PER
TIER 2 QTY B/WN 51-100 COPIES PER
TIER 3 QTY B/WN 101-250 COPIES PER
TIER 4 QTY B/WN 251-800 COPIES PER
TIER 5 QTY B/WN 801-1200 COPIES PER
TIER 6 QTY B/WN 1201-2000 COPIES PER
CARDS ARE NOT SERIAL-NUMBERED
PRINT RUN INFO PROVIDED BY DONRUSS
NO PRICING ON QTY OF 21 OR LESS
1 Scot Shields T6 4.00 10.00
2 Tim Salmon T4 6.00 15.00
3 Chone Figgins T3 6.00 15.00
4 Dallas McPherson T3 4.00 10.00
5 John Lackey T3 6.00 15.00
6 Ervin Santana T1/25 * 10.00 25.00
9 Brandon Webb T5 4.00 10.00
10 Chad Tracy T4 4.00 10.00
11 Russ Ortiz T4 4.00 10.00
12 Alex Cintron T4 4.00 10.00
17 Cal Ripken T5 20.00 50.00
18 Rick Dempsey T6 6.00 15.00
19 Adam Loewen T5 4.00 10.00
20 Eric Byrnes T4 4.00 10.00
24 Kevin Youkilis T6 6.00 15.00
25 Keith Foulke T5 6.00 15.00
26 Trot Nixon T4 6.00 15.00
27 Edgar Renteria T4 6.00 15.00
28 Luis Tiant T3 6.00 15.00
29 Todd Walker T5 4.00 10.00
30 Mark Grace T4 6.00 15.00
31 Steve Stone T3 6.00 15.00
32 Ron Santo T3 6.00 15.00
33 Michael Wuertz T3 4.00 10.00
34 Russ Rohlicek T2/60 * 5.00 12.00
35 Ryne Sandberg T4 20.00 50.00
39 Paulino Reynoso T2/86 * 5.00 12.00
43 Bubba Nelson T3 4.00 10.00
47 Larry Bigbie T2/92 * 8.00 20.00
53 Miguel Cabrera T4 10.00 25.00
54 Chris Resop T4 3.00 8.00
56 Luke Scott T3 8.00 20.00
58 Mark McLemore T1/43 * 6.00 15.00
59 Devon Lowery T4 3.00 8.00
61 Duke Snider T4 10.00 25.00
62 Johnny Podres T2/99 * 8.00 20.00
63 Rickie Weeks T4 6.00 15.00
64 Ben Sheets T4 6.00 15.00
66 Lew Ford T5 4.00 10.00
67 Travis Bowyer T5 3.00 8.00
68 Garrett Jones T4 5.00 12.00
69 Joe Nathan T4 6.00 15.00
70 Kent Hrbek T4 6.00 15.00
71 J.D. Durbin T1/39 * 6.00 15.00
75 Danny Graves T5 4.00 10.00
76 Jae Weong Seo T4 6.00 15.00
77 Matt Lindstrom T4 3.00 8.00
79 Carlos Beltran T1/37 * 10.00 25.00
81 Tom Gordon T5 4.00 10.00
82 Adam LaRoche T2/53 * 8.00 20.00
83 Dave Righetti T4 6.00 15.00
84 Joe Pepitone T3 6.00 15.00
85 Gary Sheffield T3 10.00 25.00
86 Jim Leyritz T2/93 * 8.00 20.00
87 Rich Gossage T2/65 * 15.00 40.00
91 Octavio Dotel T4 4.00 10.00
92 Rollie Fingers T4 6.00 15.00
94 Rich Harden T3 6.00 15.00
97 Barry Zito T1/26 * 10.00 25.00
100 Chris Roberson T4 3.00 8.00
101 Eude Brito T4 3.00 8.00
102 Randy Wolf T4 4.00 10.00
103 Mike Lieberthal T4 6.00 15.00
104 John Kruk T3 6.00 15.00
109 Mike Johnston T3 4.00 10.00
113 Jeff Miller T1/49 * 6.00 15.00
114 John Candelaria T1/43 * 10.00 25.00
116 Mark Loretta T5 4.00 10.00
117 Sean Thompson T3 4.00 10.00
118 Akinori Otsuka T2/52 * 8.00 20.00
119 Omar Vizquel T2/100 * 12.50 30.00
121 Clint Nageotte T5 4.00 10.00
122 J.J. Putz T6 6.00 15.00
123 Raul Ibanez T6 4.00 10.00
124 Wladimir Balentien T4 5.00 12.00
125 Jamie Moyer T4 6.00 15.00
129 Jeff Suppan T6 4.00 10.00
130 Marty Marion T5 8.00 20.00
131 Keith Hernandez T4 6.00 15.00
132 Ozzie Smith T2/94 * 20.00 50.00
133 Mark Mulder T3 6.00 15.00
137 Delmon Young T2/99 * 12.50 30.00
138 Jason Hammel T2/57 * 5.00 12.00
139 Agustin Montero T3 4.00 10.00
140 Francisco Cordero T3 4.00 10.00
144 Nolan Ryan T2/62 * 30.00 80.00
146 Alexis Rios T3 6.00 15.00
147 Jose Guillen T6 4.00 10.00
148 Danny Rueckel T4 3.00 8.00

2005 Donruss Signature Autograph Silver Notation

*NT T4: .5X TO 1.2X SILV T5-T6
*NT T3: .5X TO 1.2X SILV T5-T6
*NT T2: .6X TO 1.5X SILV T4
*NT T1 p/r 25-41: .75X TO 2X SILV T4
RANDOM INSERTS IN PACKS
TIER 1 QTY B/WN 1-50 COPIES PER
TIER 2 QTY B/WN 51-100 COPIES PER
TIER 3 QTY B/WN 101-250 COPIES PER
TIER 4 QTY B/WN 251-800 COPIES PER
CARDS ARE NOT SERIAL-NUMBERED
PRINT RUN INFO PROVIDED BY DONRUSS
NO PRICING ON QTY OF 24 OR LESS
17 Cal Ripken T1/25 * 75.00 150.00
105 Lenny Dykstra T1/41 * 12.50 30.00

2005 Donruss Signature Autograph Material Bat Gold

*BAT p/r 25-50: .6X TO 1.5X SILV T5-T6
*BAT p/r 25-50: .6X TO 1.5X SILV T3
*BAT p/r 25-50: .5X TO 1.2X SILV T2
RANDOM INSERTS IN PACKS
PRINT RUNS B/WN 1-50 COPIES PER
NO PRICING ON QTY OF 15 OR LESS
7 Casey Kotchman/25 10.00 25.00
24 Kevin Youkilis/25 6.00 15.00
65 Carlos Lee/25 10.00 25.00
108 Bill Madlock/50 10.00 25.00
111 Freddy Sanchez/42 6.00 15.00

2005 Donruss Signature Autograph Material Bat Platinum

*BAT p/r 25: .6X TO 1.5X SILV T3
*BAT p/r 25: .5X TO 1.2X SILV T2
RANDOM INSERTS IN PACKS
PRINT RUNS B/WN 1-25 COPIES PER
NO PRICING ON QTY OF 21 OR LESS
108 Bill Madlock/25 10.00 25.00
111 Freddy Sanchez/25 6.00 15.00

2005 Donruss Signature Autograph Material Bat Silver

*BAT T1 p/r 50: .6X TO 1.5X SILV T3
RANDOM INSERTS IN PACKS
TIER 1 QTY B/WN 1-50 COPIES PER
TIER 3 QTY B/WN 101-250 COPIES PER
CARDS ARE NOT SERIAL-NUMBERED
PRINT RUN INFO PROVIDED BY DONRUSS
NO PRICING ON QTY OF 22 OR LESS
108 Bill Madlock T3 6.00 15.00
119 Omar Vizquel T3 5.00 12.00

2005 Donruss Signature Autograph Material Button Platinum

PRINT RUNS B/WN 1-6 COPIES PER
NO PRICING DUE TO SCARCITY

2005 Donruss Signature Autograph Material Jersey Silver

*JSY T3: .4X TO 1X SILV T4 10.00 25.00
*JSY T2: .5X TO 1.2X SILV T4
*JSY T1 p/r 36-50: .6X TO 1.5X SILV T5-T6
TIER 1 QTY B/WN 1-50 COPIES PER
TIER 2 QTY B/WN 51-100 COPIES PER
TIER 3 QTY B/WN 101-250 COPIES PER
CARDS ARE NOT SERIAL-NUMBERED
PRINT RUN INFO PROVIDED BY DONRUSS
NO PRICING ON QTY OF 22 OR LESS
21 Luis Matos T3 4.00 10.00
30 Mark Grace T3 20.00 50.00
60 Jeremy Affeldt Pants T1/36 * 6.00 15.00
93 Dennis Eckersley T1/50 * 10.00 25.00

2005 Donruss Signature Autograph Material Jersey Number Platinum

*JSY NP p/r 25: .6X TO 1.5X SILV T5-T6
*JSY NP p/r 25: .6X TO 1.5X SILV T4
RANDOM INSERTS IN PACKS
PRINT RUNS B/WN 1-25 COPIES PER
NO PRICING ON QTY OF 14 OR LESS
21 Luis Matos/25 6.00 15.00
57 Brandon Backe/25 6.00 15.00
93 Dennis Eckersley/25 10.00 25.00

2005 Donruss Signature Autograph Material Jersey Position Gold

*JSY JP p/r 25-50: .6X TO 1.5X SILV T5-T6
*JSY JP p/r 25-50: .6X TO 1.5X SILV T4
RANDOM INSERTS IN PACKS
PRINT RUNS B/WN 1-50 COPIES PER
NO PRICING ON QTY OF 10 OR LESS
21 Luis Matos/50 6.00 15.00
57 Brandon Backe/50 6.00 15.00
93 Dennis Eckersley/50 10.00 25.00

2005 Donruss Signature Autograph Material Combo Gold

*COMBO p/r 25-46: .75X TO 2X SILV T4
RANDOM INSERTS IN PACKS
PRINT RUNS B/WN 1-46 COPIES PER
NO PRICING ON QTY OF 10 OR LESS
17 C.Ripken Bat-Pants/46 75.00 150.00

2005 Donruss Signature Autograph Material Combo Platinum

RANDOM INSERTS IN PACKS
PRINT RUNS B/WN 1-25 COPIES PER
NO PRICING ON QTY OF 10 OR LESS
44 Eric Davis Bat-Jsy/25 40.00 80.00
50 Willie Mays Bat-Jsy/25 75.00 200.00
78 D.Gooden Bat-Jsy/25 12.50 30.00

2005 Donruss Signature Autograph Material Combo Silver

*COMBO p/r 50: .75X TO 2X SILV T4
RANDOM INSERTS IN PACKS
TIER 1 QTY B/WN 1-50 COPIES PER
TIER 2 QTY B/WN 51-100 COPIES PER
CARDS ARE NOT SERIAL-NUMBERED
PRINT RUN INFO PROVIDED BY DONRUSS
NO PRICING ON QTY OF 22 OR LESS
17 C.Rip Bat-Pants T2/100 * 60.00 120.00

2005 Donruss Signature Club Autograph Barrel

RANDOM INSERTS IN PACKS
PRINT RUNS B/WN 1-4 COPIES PER
CARDS ARE NOT SERIAL-NUMBERED
PRINT RUN INFO PROVIDED BY DONRUSS
NO PRICING DUE TO SCARCITY

2005 Donruss Signature Club Autograph Bat

STATED ODDS 1:20
TIER 1 QTY B/WN 1-50 COPIES PER
TIER 2 QTY B/WN 51-100 COPIES PER
TIER 3 QTY B/WN 101-250 COPIES PER
TIER 4 QTY B/WN 251-800 COPIES PER
CARDS ARE NOT SERIAL-NUMBERED
PRINT RUN INFO PROVIDED BY DONRUSS
NO PRICING ON QTY OF 2
1 Paul O'Neill T1/32 * 15.00 40.00
2 Alan Trammell T2/70 * 8.00 20.00
3 Barry Larkin T3 20.00 50.00
4 Carlton Fisk T1/34 * 15.00 40.00
5 Dale Murphy T2/100 * 15.00 40.00
6 Frank Thomas T3 20.00 50.00
7 Magglio Ordonez T4 6.00 15.00
8 Mark Teixeira T2/100 * 12.00 30.00
10 Omar Vizquel T4 10.00 25.00
11 Steve Garvey T4 6.00 15.00

2005 Donruss Signature Hall of Fame

STATED ODDS 1:3
1 Al Kaline 2.00 5.00
2 Billy Williams 1.25 3.00
3 Bobby Doerr 1.25 3.00
4 Gaylord Perry 1.25 3.00
5 George Brett 4.00 10.00
6 Hank Aaron 4.00 10.00
7 Mike Schmidt 3.00 8.00
8 Nolan Ryan 6.00 15.00
9 Robin Roberts 1.25 3.00
10 Phil Niekro 1.25 3.00
11 Phil Rizzuto 1.25 3.00
12 Ralph Kiner 1.25 3.00
13 Rod Carew 1.25 3.00
14 Ryne Sandberg 4.00 10.00
15 Stan Musial 3.00 8.00
16 Steve Carlton 1.25 3.00
17 Tom Seaver 1.25 3.00
18 Willie McCovey 1.25 3.00
19 Willie Mays 4.00 10.00
20 Duke Snider 1.25 3.00
21 Rollie Fingers 1.25 3.00
22 Monte Irvin 1.25 3.00
23 Ozzie Smith 2.50 6.00
24 Johnny Bench 2.00 5.00
25 Luis Aparicio 1.25 3.00
26 Whitey Ford 1.25 3.00
27 Orlando Cepeda 1.25 3.00
28 Jim Bunning 1.25 3.00
29 Earl Weaver 1.25 3.00
30 Frank Robinson 1.25 3.00
31 Babe Ruth Yanks 5.00 12.00
32 Yogi Berra 2.00 5.00
33 Wade Boggs 1.25 3.00
34 Ted Williams 4.00 10.00
35 Roberto Clemente 5.00 12.00
36 Nellie Fox 1.25 3.00
37 Joe Morgan 1.25 3.00
38 Harmon Killebrew 2.00 5.00
39 Carlton Fisk 1.25 3.00
40 Babe Ruth Sox 5.00 12.00

2005 Donruss Signature Hall of Fame Material Bat

*BAT T3: .4X TO 1X JSY T4
*BAT T3: .4X TO 1X JSY T3
STATED ODDS 1:20
TIER 2 QTY B/WN 51-100 COPIES PER
TIER 3 QTY B/WN 101-250 COPIES PER
TIER 4 QTY B/WN 251-800 COPIES PER
TIER 5 QTY B/WN 801-1200 COPIES PER
CARDS ARE NOT SERIAL-NUMBERED
PRINT RUN INFO PROVIDED BY DONRUSS
31 Babe Ruth Yanks T3 90.00 150.00
33 Wade Boggs T4 4.00 10.00
35 Roberto Clemente T5 15.00 40.00

2005 Donruss Signature Hall of Fame Material Jersey

STATED ODDS 1:21
TIER 1 QTY B/WN 1-50 COPIES PER
TIER 2 QTY B/WN 51-100 COPIES PER
TIER 3 QTY B/WN 101-250 COPIES PER
TIER 4 QTY B/WN 251-800 COPIES PER
CARDS ARE NOT SERIAL-NUMBERED
PRINT RUN INFO PROVIDED BY DONRUSS
NO PRICING ON QTY OF 17 OR LESS
2 Billy Williams T1/25 * 5.00 12.00
3 Bobby Doerr T2/100 * 4.00 10.00
4 Gaylord Perry T3 3.00 8.00
6 Hank Aaron T3 10.00 25.00
8 Nolan Ryan T1/30 * 20.00 50.00
10 Phil Niekro T3 3.00 8.00
11 Phil Rizzuto T3 4.00 10.00
13 Rod Carew T3 4.00 10.00
15 Stan Musial T2/66 * 12.50 30.00
16 Steve Carlton Pants T3 3.00 8.00
19 Willie Mays Pants T4 12.50 30.00
21 Rollie Fingers T1/33 * 5.00 12.00
23 Ozzie Smith T1/47 * 8.00 20.00
24 J.Bench Pants T2/51 * 6.00 15.00
34 Ted Williams Jkt T4 15.00 40.00

2005 Donruss Signature Hall of Fame Material Combo

*COMBO T3: .6X TO 1.5X JSY T4
*COMBO T3: .6X TO 1.5X JSY T3
STATED ODDS 1:49
TIER 2 QTY B/WN 51-100 COPIES PER
TIER 3 QTY B/WN 101-250 COPIES PER
CARDS ARE NOT SERIAL-NUMBERED
PRINT RUN INFO PROVIDED BY DONRUSS
31 B.Ruth Yanks B-J T2/79 * 200.00 300.00

2005 Donruss Signature Hall of Fame Autograph

STATED ODDS 1:16
TIER 1 QTY B/WN 1-50 COPIES PER
TIER 2 QTY B/WN 51-100 COPIES PER
TIER 3 QTY B/WN 101-250 COPIES PER
TIER 4 QTY B/WN 251-800 COPIES PER
CARDS ARE NOT SERIAL-NUMBERED
PRINT RUN INFO PROVIDED BY DONRUSS
NO PRICING ON QTY OF 22 OR LESS
1 Al Kaline T2/82 * 20.00 50.00
2 Billy Williams T1/42 * 6.00 15.00
3 Bobby Doerr T1/25 * 10.00 25.00
4 Gaylord Perry T3 6.00 15.00
8 Nolan Ryan T1/25 * 60.00 120.00
9 Robin Roberts T4 8.00 20.00
11 Phil Rizzuto T3 12.50 30.00
14 Ryne Sandberg T2/55 * 30.00 60.00
15 Stan Musial T2/56 * 40.00 80.00
18 Willie McCovey T3 12.50 30.00
20 Duke Snider T4 10.00 25.00
21 Rollie Fingers T4 6.00 15.00
22 Monte Irvin T4 10.00 25.00
23 Ozzie Smith T4 15.00 40.00
24 Johnny Bench T3 20.00 50.00
27 Orlando Cepeda T1/30 * 10.00 25.00
28 Jim Bunning T1/25 * 6.00 15.00

2005 Donruss Signature Hall of Fame Autograph MS

*AUTO MS p/r 25: .6X TO 1.5X AUTO T4
*AUTO MS p/r 25: .6X TO 1.5X AUTO T3
*AUTO MS p/r 25: .5X TO 1.2X AUTO T2
*AUTO MS p/r 25: .4X TO 1X AUTO T1
RANDOM INSERTS IN PACKS
PRINT RUNS B/WN 1-25 COPIES PER
NO PRICING ON QTY OF 23 OR LESS
26 Whitey Ford/25 20.00 50.00
29 Earl Weaver/25 10.00 25.00

2005 Donruss Signature Hall of Fame Autograph Material Bat

STATED ODDS 1:63
TIER 1 QTY B/WN 1-50 COPIES PER
TIER 2 QTY B/WN 51-100 COPIES PER
CARDS ARE NOT SERIAL-NUMBERED
PRINT RUN INFO PROVIDED BY DONRUSS
NO PRICING ON QTY OF 10 OR LESS
12 Ralph Kiner T2/97 * 12.50 30.00
25 Luis Aparicio T2/100 * 8.00 20.00
33 Wade Boggs T2/56 * 12.50 30.00

2005 Donruss Signature Hall of Fame Autograph Material Jersey

*AU JSY T2: .5X TO 1.2X AU T4
*AU JSY T2: .5X TO 1.2X AU T3
*AU JSY T1: .6X TO 1.5X AU T3
*AU JSY T1: .5X TO 1.2X AU T2
*AU JSY T1: .4X TO 1X AU T1
TIER 1 QTY B/WN 1-50 COPIES PER
TIER 2 QTY B/WN 51-100 COPIES PER
CARDS ARE NOT SERIAL-NUMBERED
PRINT RUN INFO PROVIDED BY DONRUSS
NO PRICING ON QTY OF 20 OR LESS
6 Hank Aaron T1/25 * 125.00 200.00
16 Steve Carlton Pants T1/25 * 10.00 25.00
17 Tom Seaver T1/25 * 20.00 50.00
26 Whitey Ford T1/33 * 15.00 40.00

2005 Donruss Signature Hall of Fame Autograph Material Combo

*AU COM T2: .6X TO 1.5X AU T3
*AU COM T2: .5X TO 1.2X AU T2
*AU COM T1: .75X TO 2X AU T3
TIER 1 QTY B/WN 1-50 COPIES PER
TIER 2 QTY B/WN 51-100 COPIES PER
CARDS ARE NOT SERIAL-NUMBERED
PRINT RUN INFO PROVIDED BY DONRUSS
NO PRICING ON QTY OF 20 OR LESS
6 Hank Aaron Bat-Jsy T1/50 * 125.00 200.00
16 S.Carlton Bat-Pants T1/50 * 12.50 30.00
17 T.Seaver Jsy-Pants T1/50 * 25.00 60.00

2005 Donruss Signature HOF Combos Autograph

STATED ODDS 1:41
TIER 1 QTY B/WN 1-50 COPIES PER
TIER 2 QTY B/WN 51-100 COPIES PER
TIER 3 QTY B/WN 101-250 COPIES PER
CARDS ARE NOT SERIAL-NUMBERED
PRINT RUN INFO PROVIDED BY DONRUSS
NO PRICING ON QTY OF 10
41 H.Kill/R.Carew T1/25 * 60.00 120.00
42 R.Sand/Boggs T2/100 * 40.00 80.00
43 N.Ryan/G.Brett T1/36 * 75.00 150.00
44 S.Carlt/P.Rizz T2/100 * 30.00 60.00
45 T.Seav/R.Fing T2/100 * 25.00 60.00
46 J.Palmer/J.Morg T1/25 * 20.00 50.00
47 B.Doerr/W.McC T2/51 * 30.00 60.00
48 L.Aparicio/H.Kill T1/25 * 20.00 50.00
49 A.Kaline/D.Snid T1/25 * 40.00 100.00
50 J.Palmer/F.Rob T1/25 * 20.00 50.00
51 B.Doerr/C.Fisk T1/25 * 30.00 60.00
52 J.Bench/J.Morg T1/25 * 40.00 80.00
53 D.Snider/D.Sutt T2/100 * 20.00 50.00
54 W.Ford/P.Rizz T2/57 * 30.00 60.00
55 J.Bench/C.Fisk T1/25 * 40.00 80.00
57 W.Ford/S.Carlt T1/25 * 30.00 60.00
58 J.Palm/T.Seav T1/32 * 30.00 80.00
59 R.Jack/R.Fing T1/49 * 40.00 80.00
60 D.Snider/S.Musial T3 50.00 100.00

2005 Donruss Signature HOF Trios Autograph

STATED ODDS 1:80
TIER 1 QTY B/WN 1-50 COPIES PER
TIER 2 QTY B/WN 51-100 COPIES PER
CARDS ARE NOT SERIAL-NUMBERED
PRINT RUN INFO PROVIDED BY DONRUSS
NO PRICING ON QTY OF 15
61 B.Will/Jenk/Sand T2/100 * 60.00 120.00
64 Doerr/Morg/Sand T2/63 * 50.00 100.00
65 Apar/Rizz/Ozzie T1/50 * 50.00 100.00
67 F.Rob/Reg/Kiner T1/25 * 50.00 100.00
68 Perry/Jenk/Gibson T1/50 * 40.00 80.00
69 Oz/Musial/Gibs T2/100 * 100.00 200.00

2005 Donruss Signature HOF Quads Autograph

STATED ODDS 1:147
TIER 1 QTY B/WN 1-50 COPIES PER
TIER 2 QTY B/WN 51-100 COPIES PER
CARDS ARE NOT SERIAL-NUMBERED
PRINT RUN INFO PROVIDED BY DONRUSS
NO PRICING ON QTY OF 15
71 Per/Mar/Irv/McC T2/85 * 40.00 80.00
74 Brock/Irv/Kin/Will T1/41 * 30.00 60.00
75 Gib/Jen/Per/Seav T1/50 * 60.00 150.00
76 Ryan/Car/Sea/Sut T1/50 * 100.00 250.00

2005 Donruss Signature HOF Six Autograph

STATED ODDS 1:579
TIER 1 QTY B/WN 1-50 COPIES PER
CARDS ARE NOT SERIAL-NUMBERED
PRINT RUN INFO PROVIDED BY DONRUSS
NO PRICING ON QTY OF 5 OR LESS

2005 Donruss Signature INKcredible Combos

STATED ODDS 1:7
TIER 1 QTY B/WN 1-50 COPIES PER
TIER 2 QTY B/WN 51-100 COPIES PER
TIER 3 QTY B/WN 101-250 COPIES PER
TIER 4 QTY B/WN 251-800 COPIES PER
CARDS ARE NOT SERIAL-NUMBERED
PRINT RUN INFO PROVIDED BY DONRUSS
NO PRICING ON QTY OF 21 OR LESS
1 T.Percival/F.Rod T3 6.00 15.00
2 S.Shields/F.Rod T3 8.00 20.00
3 S.Shields/T.Percival T4 6.00 15.00
6 R.Weeks/P.Moli T1/28 * 12.50 30.00
7 O.Smith/M.Mar T2/100 * 30.00 60.00
8 J.Suppan/M.Mulder T4 6.00 15.00
9 R.Cey/R.Santo T1/25 * 30.00 60.00
11 S.Garvey/D.Sut T2/100 * 15.00 40.00
12 C.Ripken/B.Ripken T4 50.00 100.00
13 J.Palm/R.Demp T2/100 * 50.00 100.00
15 M.Loretta/S.Burr T4 4.00 10.00
17 B.Myers/R.Wolf T3 5.00 12.00
19 J.Morn/K.Hrbek T1/36 * 12.50 30.00
20 F.Thomas/P.Kon T1/50 * 50.00 100.00
21 L.Aparicio/M.Minoso T4 10.00 25.00
22 C.Rip/T.Gwynn T2/100 * 75.00 150.00
24 J.Guillen/T.Salmon T4 6.00 15.00
25 K.Youkilis/D.McPh T4 6.00 15.00
26 E.Loaiza/J.Guillen T4 6.00 15.00
31 L.Ford/J.Kubel T3 5.00 12.00
32 D.Graves/M.Lind T3 5.00 12.00
33 T.Salmon/G.Ander T3 12.50 30.00
34 C.Nageotte/J.Putz T4 4.00 10.00

2005 Donruss Signature INKcredible Trios

STATED ODDS 1:23
TIER 1 QTY B/WN 1-50 COPIES PER
TIER 2 QTY B/WN 51-100 COPIES PER
TIER 3 QTY B/WN 101-250 COPIES PER
TIER 4 QTY B/WN 251-800 COPIES PER
CARDS ARE NOT SERIAL-NUMBERED
PRINT RUN INFO PROVIDED BY DONRUSS
NO PRICING ON QTY OF 16 OR LESS
35 Shields/Perc/K-Rod T3 6.00 15.00
36 Zito/Muld/Hud T1/37 * 60.00 120.00
38 Hallad/Wells/Rios T1/39 * 20.00 50.00
40 Snid/Pod/Wills T2/100 * 30.00 60.00
42 K.Hern/Dyk/Oros T2/80 * 20.00 50.00
43 Loaiza/Guillen/Byrd T4 15.00 40.00
44 Rip/Palm/Demp T2/80 * 75.00 150.00
45 Myers/Wolf/Lieb T3 15.00 40.00
46 Jacq/Ford/Kubel T2/91 * 15.00 40.00
47 R.Jones/Oz/Fing T1/36 * 50.00 100.00
48 Guidry/Goose/Tiant T3 20.00 50.00
49 Guidry/Goose/Righ T3 20.00 50.00
50 Ozzie/Rip/Tram T2/99 * 125.00 200.00
51 Boggs/Sand/Gwy T2/95 * 75.00 150.00
52 Weav/Rip/F.Rob T1/38 * 75.00 150.00
53 Kill/Carew/Hrbek T1/28 * 75.00 150.00
54 Minoso/Apar/Fisk T1/25 * 40.00 80.00

2005 Donruss Signature INKcredible Quads

STATED ODDS 1:105
TIER 1 QTY B/WN 1-50 COPIES PER
TIER 2 QTY B/WN 51-100 COPIES PER
TIER 3 QTY B/WN 101-250 COPIES PER
CARDS ARE NOT SERIAL-NUMBERED
PRINT RUN INFO PROVIDED BY DONRUSS
NO PRICING ON QTY OF 11 OR LESS
60 Guil/Loiaz/Byrd/Spiv T3 8.00 20.00
61 Byrd/Guil/Livan/Loiaz T3 30.00 60.00
63 Eva/Rice/Tia/Fisk T2/73 * 60.00 120.00
65 Nomo/Has/Tag/Ots T1/45 * 200.00 350.00

2005 Donruss Signature INKcredible Six

STATED ODDS 1:188
TIER 1 QTY B/WN 1-50 COPIES PER
TIER 2 QTY B/WN 51-100 COPIES PER
TIER 3 QTY B/WN 101-250 COPIES PER
CARDS ARE NOT SERIAL-NUMBERED
PRINT RUN INFO PROVIDED BY DONRUSS
NO PRICING ON QTY OF 1
67 St.Louis Cardinals T3 30.00 80.00
68 Washington Nat'ls T2/70 * 50.00 100.00

2005 Donruss Signature K-Force

STATED ODDS 1:7
1 Nolan Ryan 6.00 15.00
2 Steve Carlton 1.25 3.00
3 Roger Clemens 2.50 6.00
4 Randy Johnson 2.00 5.00
5 Tom Seaver 1.25 3.00
6 Don Sutton 1.25 3.00
7 Gaylord Perry 1.25 3.00
8 Fergie Jenkins 1.25 3.00
9 Bob Gibson 1.25 3.00
10 Greg Maddux 2.50 6.00
11 David Cone .75 2.00
12 Bob Feller 1.25 3.00
13 Johan Santana 1.25 3.00
14 Roy Halladay 1.25 3.00
15 Juan Marichal 1.25 3.00

2005 Donruss Signature K-Force Autograph

RANDOM INSERTS IN PACKS
TIER 1 QTY B/WN 1-50 COPIES PER
TIER 2 QTY B/WN 51-100 COPIES PER
TIER 3 QTY B/WN 101-250 COPIES PER
CARDS ARE NOT SERIAL-NUMBERED
PRINT RUN INFO PROVIDED BY DONRUSS
NO PRICING ON QTY OF 20 OR LESS
1 Nolan Ryan T3 40.00 80.00
2 Steve Carlton T1/33 * 10.00 25.00
6 Don Sutton T3 6.00 15.00
7 Gaylord Perry T2/75 * 8.00 20.00
8 Fergie Jenkins T2/55 * 8.00 20.00
10 Greg Maddux T1/25 * 50.00 100.00
11 David Cone T3 6.00 15.00
12 Bob Feller T1/39 * 10.00 25.00
13 Johan Santana T2/55 * 12.50 30.00
15 Juan Marichal T3 10.00 25.00

2005 Donruss Signature K-Force Autograph MS

*AU MS p/r 25: .6X TO 1.5X AU T3
*AU MS p/r 25: .5X TO 1.2X AU T2
*AU MS p/r 25: .4X TO 1X AU T1
RANDOM INSERTS IN PACKS
PRINT RUNS B/WN 1-25 COPIES PER
NO PRICING ON QTY OF 20 OR LESS

2005 Donruss Signature K-Force Autograph Material

*AU MAT T3: .4X TO 1X AU T3
*AU MAT T3: .25X TO .6X AU T1
*AU MAT T2: .5X TO 1.2X AU T3
*AU MAT T1: .5X TO 1.2X AU T2
*AU MAT T1: .4X TO 1X AU T1
STATED ODDS 1:54
TIER 1 QTY B/WN 1-50 COPIES PER
TIER 2 QTY B/WN 51-100 COPIES PER
TIER 3 QTY B/WN 101-250 COPIES PER
CARDS ARE NOT SERIAL-NUMBERED
PRINT RUN INFO PROVIDED BY DONRUSS
NO PRICING ON QTY OF 7 OR LESS
9 Bob Gibson Jsy T1/41 * 20.00 50.00

2005 Donruss Signature Milestone Marks

STATED ODDS 1:10
CARD 8 DOES NOT EXIST
1 Duke Snider 1.25 3.00
2 Nolan Ryan 6.00 15.00
3 Gaylord Perry 1.25 3.00
4 Johnny Bench 2.00 5.00
5 Willie McCovey 1.25 3.00
6 Stan Musial 3.00 8.00
7 Randy Johnson 2.00 5.00
9 Gary Carter 1.25 3.00
10 Tony Gwynn 2.50 6.00

2005 Donruss Signature Milestone Marks Autograph

STATED ODDS 1:41
TIER 1 QTY B/WN 1-50 COPIES PER
TIER 3 QTY B/WN 101-250 COPIES PER
CARDS ARE NOT SERIAL-NUMBERED
PRINT RUN INFO PROVIDED BY DONRUSS
NO PRICING ON QTY OF 6 OR LESS
2 Nolan Ryan T3 20.00 50.00
3 Gaylord Perry T3 15.00 40.00
4 Johnny Bench T3 15.00 40.00
5 Willie McCovey T1/44 * 25.00 60.00
6 Stan Musial T3 40.00 80.00

2005 Donruss Signature Milestone Marks Autograph MS

*AU MS: .6X TO 1.5X AU T3
*AU MS: .4X TO 1X AU T1
RANDOM INSERTS IN PACKS
PRINT RUNS B/WN 20-25 COPIES PER
NO PRICING ON QTY OF 20
3 Gaylord Perry/25 10.00 25.00
10 Tony Gwynn/25 20.00 50.00

2005 Donruss Signature Milestone Marks Autograph Material Bat

*AU BAT T1 p/r 25: .6X TO 1.5X AU T3
STATED ODDS 1:1524
TIER 1 QTY B/WN 1-50 COPIES PER
CARDS ARE NOT SERIAL-NUMBERED
PRINT RUN INFO PROVIDED BY DONRUSS
NO PRICING ON QTY OF 5

2005 Donruss Signature Milestone Marks Autograph Material Jersey

*AU JSY T3: .4X TO 1X AU T3
*AU JSY T2: .3X TO .8X AU T1
STATED ODDS 1:134
TIER 1 QTY B/WN 1-50 COPIES PER
TIER 2 QTY B/WN 51-100 COPIES PER
TIER 3 QTY B/WN 101-250 COPIES PER
CARDS ARE NOT SERIAL-NUMBERED
PRINT RUN INFO PROVIDED BY DONRUSS
NO PRICING ON QTY OF 21
10 Tony Gwynn T2/75 * 20.00 50.00

2005 Donruss Signature Milestone Marks Autograph Material Combo

STATED ODDS 1:210
TIER 1 QTY B/WN 1-50 COPIES PER
TIER 3 QTY B/WN 101-250 COPIES PER
CARDS ARE NOT SERIAL-NUMBERED
PRINT RUN INFO PROVIDED BY DONRUSS
NO PRICING ON QTY OF 17 OR LESS
7 R.John Fld Glv-Jsy T1/25 * 40.00 80.00
10 T.Gwynn Jsy-Pants T3 15.00 40.00

2005 Donruss Signature Notable Nicknames 01

STATED PRINT RUN 100 SERIAL #'d SETS
NON #'d MASTER SERIES CARDS ISSUED
NO MAST.SER.PRICING DUE TO SCARCITY
RANDOM INSERTS IN PACKS
I-ROD AUTO IS NOT NOTATED
OZZIE AUTO IS NOT NOTATED
GM Greg Maddux Bulldog 250.00 400.00
IR Ivan Rodriguez Pudge 20.00 50.00
PR Phil Rizzuto Scooter 30.00 60.00

2005 Donruss Signature Recollection Autographs

STATED ODDS 1:116
NO PRICING DUE TO SCARCITY

2005 Donruss Signature Stamps Material Centennial

PRINT RUNS B/WN 40-100 COPIES PER
*PRO BALL: .4X TO 1X CENTENNIAL
PRO BALL PRINT RUNS B/WN 40-100 PER
RANDOM INSERTS IN PACKS
2 Cal Ripken Pants/50 10.00 25.00
5 Harmon Killebrew Bat/70 6.00 15.00
8 Adrian Beltre Shoes/100 4.00 10.00
10 Cal Ripken Pants/50 10.00 25.00
11 Jim Thorpe Jsy/68 90.00 150.00
12 Willie Mays Jsy/100 20.00 50.00
13 Roger Maris Pants/100 30.00 60.00

2005 Donruss Signature Stamps Autograph Centennial

PRINT RUNS B/WN 3-81 COPIES PER
*PRO BALL: .4X TO 1X CENTENNIAL
PRO BALL PRINT RUNS B/WN 3-81 PER
RANDOM INSERTS IN PACKS
NO PRICING ON QTY OF 17 OR LESS
2 Cal Ripken/50 75.00 150.00
4 Duke Snider/81 12.50 30.00
6 Orlando Cepeda/48 10.00 25.00
7 Don Larsen/50 10.00 25.00
10 Cal Ripken/50 75.00 150.00

2005 Donruss Signature Stamps Autograph Material Centennial

PRINT RUNS B/WN 2-50 COPIES PER
*PRO BALL: .4X TO 1X CENTENNIAL
PRO BALL PRINT RUNS B/WN 1-50 PER
RANDOM INSERTS IN PACKS
NO PRICING ON QTY OF 20 OR LESS

2 Cal Ripken Pants/50 75.00 150.00
5 Harmon Killebrew Bat/33 20.00 50.00
10 Cal Ripken Pants/50 40.00 80.00

2005 Donruss Signature Stamps Centennial Autograph

RANDOM INSERTS IN PACKS
PRINT RUNS B/WN 1-2 COPIES PER
NO PRICING DUE TO SCARCITY

2005 Donruss Signature Stars Autograph

STATED ODDS 1:47
TIER 1 QTY B/WN 1-50 COPIES PER
TIER 2 QTY B/WN 51-100 COPIES PER
TIER 3 QTY B/WN 101-250 COPIES PER
CARDS ARE NOT SERIAL-NUMBERED
PRINT RUN INFO PROVIDED BY DONRUSS
1 Mark Teixeira T1/42 * 6.00 15.00
2 Scott Rolen T3 10.00 25.00
3 Roy Oswalt T2/85 * 5.00 12.00
5 Morgan Ensberg T3 6.00 15.00
6 Mark Grace T2/86 * 6.00 15.00
7 Gary Sheffield T2/82 * 10.00 25.00
8 Sean Casey T3 6.00 15.00
10 Ryno Sandborg T3 20.00 50.00

2005 Donruss Signature Stars Autograph MS

*AU MS p/r 25: .6X TO 1.5X AU T3
*AU MS p/r 25: .5X TO 1.2X AU T2
*AU MS p/r 25: .4X TO 1X AU T1
RANDOM INSERTS IN PACKS
PRINT RUNS B/WN 1-25 COPIES PER
NO PRICING ON QTY OF 5 OR LESS
14 Barry Larkin/25 40.00 80.00

2005 Donruss Signature Stars Autograph Material Bat

*AU BAT T3: .3X TO .8X AU T2
*AU BAT T2: .3X TO .8X AU T1
STATED ODDS 1:35
TIER 1 QTY B/WN 1-50 COPIES PER
TIER 2 QTY B/WN 51-100 COPIES PER
TIER 3 QTY B/WN 101-250 COPIES PER
CARDS ARE NOT SERIAL-NUMBERED
PRINT RUN INFO PROVIDED BY DONRUSS
NO PRICING ON QTY OF 9
4 Hideo Nomo T1/36 * 175.00 300.00
11 Stan Musial T1/38 * 40.00 80.00
12 Joe Torre T1/44 * 15.00 40.00
13 Wade Boggs T1/40 * 15.00 40.00
14 Barry Larkin T3 15.00 40.00
15 Dale Murphy T2/100 * 12.50 30.00

2005 Donruss Signature Stars Autograph Material Jersey

*AU JSY T3: .4X TO 1X AU T3
*AU JSY T2: .5X TO 1.2X AU T3
*AU JSY T1: .5X TO 1.2X AU T2
STATED ODDS 1:64
TIER 1 QTY B/WN 1-50 COPIES PER
TIER 2 QTY B/WN 51-100 COPIES PER
TIER 3 QTY B/WN 101-250 COPIES PER
CARDS ARE NOT SERIAL-NUMBERED
PRINT RUN INFO PROVIDED BY DONRUSS
NO PRICING ON QTY OF 19 OR LESS
4 Hideo Nomo Pants T1/50 * 175.00 300.00
11 Stan Musial T1/44 * 40.00 80.00
12 Joe Torre T1/50 * 15.00 40.00
15 Dale Murphy T3 10.00 25.00

2005 Donruss Signature Stats Autograph

STATED ODDS 1:102
TIER 1 QTY B/WN 1-50 COPIES PER
TIER 3 QTY B/WN 101-250 COPIES PER
CARDS ARE NOT SERIAL-NUMBERED
PRINT RUN INFO PROVIDED BY DONRUSS
NO PRICING ON QTY OF 16 OR LESS
4 Alfonso Soriano T3 6.00 15.00
9 Miguel Cabrera T3 15.00 40.00
10 Mark Teixeira T1/41 * 6.00 15.00

2005 Donruss Signature Stats Autograph MS

*AU MS p/r 25: .6X TO 1.5X AU T3
*AU MS p/r 25: .4X TO 1X AU T1
RANDOM INSERTS IN PACKS
PRINT RUNS B/WN 1-25 COPIES PER
NO PRICING ON QTY OF 15 OR LESS
1 Tony Gwynn/25 20.00 50.00
2 Johan Santana/25 15.00 40.00
3 Orel Hershiser/25 10.00 25.00
5 Don Mattingly/25 40.00 80.00
8 Victor Martinez/25 10.00 25.00

2005 Donruss Signature Stats Autograph Material Bat

*AU BAT T4: .3X TO .8X AU T3
*AU BAT T3: .25X TO .6X AU T1
RANDOM INSERTS IN PACKS
TIER 1 QTY B/WN 1-50 COPIES PER
TIER 3 QTY B/WN 101-250 COPIES PER
TIER 4 QTY B/WN 251-800 COPIES PER
CARDS ARE NOT SERIAL-NUMBERED
PRINT RUN INFO PROVIDED BY DONRUSS
NO PRICING ON QTY OF 15
5 Don Mattingly T1/25 * 40.00 80.00

2005 Donruss Signature Stats Autograph Material Jersey

STATED ODDS 1:238
TIER 1 QTY B/WN 1-50 COPIES PER
TIER 2 QTY B/WN 51-100 COPIES PER
CARDS ARE NOT SERIAL-NUMBERED
PRINT RUN INFO PROVIDED BY DONRUSS
NO PRICING ON QTY OF 17 OR LESS
1 Tony Gwynn T1/25 * 30.00 80.00
2 Johan Santana T2/100 * 6.00 15.00
3 Orel Hershiser T1/25 * 10.00 25.00
8 Victor Martinez T1/25 * 10.00 25.00

2005 Donruss Signature Stats Autograph Material Combo

*AU COM T1: .75X TO 2X AU T3
STATED ODDS 1:186
TIER 1 QTY B/WN 1-50 COPIES PER
TIER 3 QTY B/WN 101-250 COPIES PER
CARDS ARE NOT SERIAL-NUMBERED
PRINT RUN INFO PROVIDED BY DONRUSS
NO PRICING ON QTY OF 14 OR LESS
1 T.Gwynn Jsy-Pants T3 15.00 40.00

2008 Donruss Sports Legends

COMPLETE SET (144) 40.00 100.00
1 Ted Williams 1.25 3.00
5 Willie Mays 1.25 3.00
10 Hank Aaron 1.25 3.00
15 Nolan Ryan 1.25 3.00
20 Stan Musial .75 2.00
30 Satchel Paige .60 1.50
35 Don Mattingly 1.25 3.00
40 Bob Gibson .50 1.25
45 Roberto Clemente 1.25 3.00
50 Joe Jackson 1.25 3.00
60 Yogi Berra .60 1.50
63 Pete Rose 1.25 3.00
65 Bob Feller .50 1.25
70 Brooks Robinson .50 1.25
75 Cal Ripken Jr. 2.00 5.00
80 Carl Yastrzemski .75 2.00
85 Carlton Fisk .50 1.25
90 Duke Snider .50 1.25
95 Eddie Murray .60 1.50
100 Frank Robinson .40 1.00
105 Jim Palmer .40 1.00
110 Johnny Bench .60 1.50
115 Juan Marichal .50 1.25
120 Mike Schmidt 1.00 2.50
122 Whitey Ford .50 1.25
125 Paul Molitor .60 1.50
128 Tony Gwynn .60 1.50
130 Reggie Jackson .60 1.50
135 Ryne Sandberg 1.00 2.50
140 Nolan Ryan 1.25 3.00
143 Willie McCovey .50 1.25
145 Al Kaline .60 1.50
150 Pete Rose 1.25 3.00

2008 Donruss Sports Legends Mirror Blue

*BLUE/100: 2X TO 5X BASIC CARDS
STATED PRINT RUN 100 SER.#'d SETS

2008 Donruss Sports Legends Mirror Gold

*GOLD/25: 3X TO 8X BASIC CARDS
STATED PRINT RUN 25 SER.#'d SETS

2008 Donruss Sports Legends Mirror Red

*RED/250: 1.5X TO 4X BASIC CARDS
STATED PRINT RUN 250 SER.#'d SETS

2008 Donruss Sports Legends Champions

SILVER PRINT RUN 1000 SER.#'d SETS
*GOLD/100: .6X TO 1.5X SILVER/1000
GOLD PRINT RUN 100 SER.#'d SETS
3 Whitey Ford 1.25 3.00
6 Bob Gibson 1.25 3.00
9 Pete Rose 3.00 8.00
11 Reggie Jackson 1.50 4.00
14 Don Larsen 1.00 2.50

2008 Donruss Sports Legends Champions Materials

STATED PRINT RUN 10-250
3 Whitey Ford Jsy/10
6 Bob Gibson Jsy/10
9 Pete Rose Jsy/25
11 Reggie Jackson Jsy/150 5.00 12.00

2008 Donruss Sports Legends Champions Signatures

STATED PRINT RUN 1-100
SERIAL #'d UNDER 25 NOT PRICED
3 Whitey Ford/25 25.00 50.00
6 Bob Gibson/25 12.00 30.00
9 Pete Rose/25 60.00 120.00

2008 Donruss Sports Legends College Heroes

SILVER PRINT RUN 1000 SER.#'d SETS
*GOLD/100: .6X TO 1.5X SILVER/1000
GOLD PRINT RUN 100 SER.#'d SETS
5 Gordon Beckham 2.00 5.00
8 Buster Posey 2.50 6.00

2008 Donruss Sports Legends College Heroes Materials

STATED PRINT RUN 50-250
5 Gordon Beckham Jsy/50 5.00 12.00
8 Buster Posey Jsy/50 5.00 12.00

2008 Donruss Sports Legends College Heroes Signatures

STATED PRINT RUN 25-100
5 Gordon Beckham/100 6.00 15.00
8 Buster Posey/50 12.50 30.00

2008 Donruss Sports Legends Collegiate Legends Patch Autographs

STATED PRINT RUN 25-250
1 Tom Seaver/50 30.00 80.00
2 Reggie Jackson/51 30.00 60.00
3 Robin Roberts/48

2008 Donruss Sports Legends Legends of the Game Combos

STATED PRINT RUN 25-100
UNPRICED PRIME PRINT RUN 1-10
2 P.Rose Jsy/J.Jackson Bat 50.00 100.00
5 D.Fouts Jsy/T.Gwynn Jsy 12.00 30.00
6 T.Williams Jsy/L.Bird Jsy/25 30.00 60.00
7 N.Ryan Jsy/T.Aikman Jsy 20.00 50.00
9 H.Aaron Bat/D.Wilkins Jsy 8.00 20.00
11 Ryan Jsy/Campbell Jsy 12.00 30.00
12 Mays Jsy/Montana Jsy/50 30.00 60.00
15 Ripken Jr. Bat/Berry Jsy 25.00 50.00

2008 Donruss Sports Legends Materials Mirror Blue

*MIRROR BLUE: .5X TO 1.2X MIRROR RED
MIRROR BLUE PRINT RUN 5-250
SERIAL #'d UNDER 15 NOT PRICED
30 Satchel Paige/25 15.00 40.00
35 Don Mattingly Jsy/25 12.00 30.00
50 Joe Jackson/25 60.00 120.00
85 Carlton Fisk Jsy/50 6.00 15.00
95 Eddie Murray/25 8.00 20.00
122 Whitey Ford/25 8.00 20.00
143 Willie McCovey/25 8.00 20.00

2008 Donruss Sports Legends Materials Mirror Gold

*GOLD/25: .8X TO 2X MIRROR RED
GOLD PRINT RUN 1-25 SER.#'d SETS
SERIAL #'d UNDER 20 NOT PRICED
5 Willie Mays/10
30 Satchel Paige/10
35 Don Mattingly/10
40 Bob Gibson/10
60 Yogi Berra/10
70 Brooks Robinson/25 8.00 20.00
80 Carl Yastrzemski/10
85 Carlton Fisk/25 10.00 25.00
95 Eddie Murray/10
105 Jim Palmer/10
110 Johnny Bench/10
115 Juan Marichal/10
122 Whitey Ford/10
135 Ryne Sandberg/10
143 Willie McCovey/10

2008 Donruss Sports Legends Materials Mirror Red

MIRROR RED PRINT RUN 10-500
SERIAL #'d UNDER 25 NOT PRICED
*GOLD/25: .8X TO 2X MIRROR RED
UNPRICED MIRROR EMERALD PRINT RUN 1-5
UNPRICED MIRROR BLACK PRINT RUN 1
1 Ted Williams Bat/100 12.00 30.00
10 Hank Aaron Bat/100 10.00 25.00
15 Nolan Ryan Jsy/250 8.00 20.00
45 Roberto Clemente Bat/250 10.00 25.00
50 Joe Jackson Bat/50 40.00 80.00
63 Pete Rose Jsy/250 12.00 30.00
75 Cal Ripken Jr. Jsy/100 12.00 30.00
100 Frank Robinson Jsy/100 3.00 8.00
120 Mike Schmidt Bat/250 6.00 15.00
125 Paul Molitor Jsy/50 5.00 12.00
128 Tony Gwynn Jsy/500 4.00 10.00
130 Reggie Jackson Bat/250 5.00 12.00
140 Nolan Ryan Jsy/100 8.00 20.00
150 Pete Rose Jsy/250 12.00 30.00

2008 Donruss Sports Legends Museum Collection

SILVER PRINT RUN 1000 SER.#'d SETS
*GOLD/100: .6X TO 1.5X SILVER/1000
GOLD PRINT RUN 100 SER.#'d SETS
1 Hank Aaron 3.00 8.00
5 Joe Jackson 3.00 8.00
7 Don Drysdale 1.25 3.00
11 Ted Williams 3.00 8.00
12 Cal Ripken Jr. 5.00 12.00
13 Satchel Paige 1.50 4.00
17 Willie Mays 3.00 8.00
21 Casey Stengel 1.25 3.00
22 Eddie Mathews 1.50 4.00
25 Pete Rose 3.00 8.00

2008 Donruss Sports Legends Museum Collection Materials

STATED PRINT RUN 25-250
*PRIME/25: .6X TO 1.5X BASIC MATERIAL
PRIME PRINT RUN 1-25
SERIAL #'d UNDER 25 NOT PRICED
1 Hank Aaron/100 10.00 25.00
5 Joe Jackson/100 40.00 80.00
7 Don Drysdale/50 5.00 12.00
11 Ted Williams/250 15.00 40.00
12 Cal Ripken Jr./100 15.00 40.00
13 Satchel Paige/50 15.00 40.00
17 Willie Mays/25 12.00 30.00
21 Casey Stengel/100 4.00 10.00
22 Eddie Mathews/25 8.00 20.00
25 Pete Rose/250 12.00 30.00

2008 Donruss Sports Legends Museum Collection Signatures

STATED PRINT RUN 1-250
SERIAL #'d UNDER 25 NOT PRICED
1 Hank Aaron/10
12 Cal Ripken Jr./8
17 Willie Mays/25 90.00 150.00
25 Pete Rose/25 40.00 80.00

2008 Donruss Sports Legends Museum Collection Signatures Materials

STATED PRINT RUN 1-50
SERIAL #'d UNDER 25 NOT PRICED

2008 Donruss Sports Legends Museum Curator Collection Materials

STATED PRINT RUN 10-100
*PRIME/25: .6X TO 1.5X BASIC MATERIAL
PRIME PRINT RUN 1-25
SERIAL #'d UNDER 25 NOT PRICED
1 Hank Aaron/10
5 Joe Jackson/50 125.00 250.00
7 Don Drysdale/25 6.00 15.00
11 Ted Williams/25 25.00 60.00
12 Cal Ripken Jr./25 25.00 60.00
13 Satchel Paige/25 20.00 50.00
17 Willie Mays/10
21 Casey Stengel/25 6.00 15.00
22 Eddie Mathews/100 5.00 12.00
25 Pete Rose/100 15.00 40.00

2008 Donruss Sports Legends Museum Curator Collection Signatures Materials

STATED PRINT RUN 1-25
SERIAL #'d UNDER 25 NOT PRICED

2008 Donruss Sports Legends Signature Connection Combos

STATED PRINT RUN 25-100
2 Ripken/Riggins/25 150.00 250.00
3 D.Fouts/T.Gwynn/25 60.00 100.00
4 N.Ryan/T.Aikman/25 100.00 175.00
7 B.Feller/J.Brown/25 60.00 120.00

2008 Donruss Sports Legends Signature Connection Triples

STATED PRINT RUN 25-250
3 Wdrd/Hyns/Gbsn/50 30.00 60.00

2008 Donruss Sports Legends Signatures Mirror Blue

MIRROR BLUE PRINT RUN 2-250
SERIAL #'d UNDER 10 NOT PRICED
UNPRICED MIRROR EMERALD PRINT RUN 1-5
UNPRICED MIRROR BLACK PRINT RUN 1
5 Willie Mays/25 90.00 150.00
10 Hank Aaron/25 125.00 200.00
15 Nolan Ryan/25 40.00 80.00
20 Stan Musial/25 30.00 60.00
35 Don Mattingly/25 30.00 60.00
40 Bob Gibson/25 12.00 30.00
60 Yogi Berra/25 30.00 80.00
63 Pete Rose/50 60.00 120.00
65 Bob Feller/50 12.00 30.00
70 Brooks Robinson/25 15.00 40.00
75 Cal Ripken Jr./25 60.00 120.00
80 Carl Yastrzemski/25 15.00 40.00
85 Carlton Fisk/25 15.00 40.00
90 Duke Snider/25 15.00 40.00
95 Eddie Murray/25 15.00 40.00
100 Frank Robinson/25 15.00 40.00
105 Jim Palmer/25 10.00 25.00
110 Johnny Bench/25 40.00 80.00
115 Juan Marichal/25 15.00 40.00
120 Mike Schmidt/25 15.00 40.00
122 Whitey Ford/25 25.00 60.00
125 Paul Molitor/25 10.00 25.00
128 Tony Gwynn/25 15.00 40.00
130 Reggie Jackson/25 15.00 40.00
135 Ryne Sandberg/25 30.00 60.00
140 Nolan Ryan/25 40.00 80.00
143 Willie McCovey/25 25.00 50.00
145 Al Kaline/50 20.00 50.00
150 Pete Rose/50 75.00 125.00

2008 Donruss Sports Legends Signatures Mirror Gold

MIRROR GOLD PRINT RUN 4-25
SERIAL #'d UNDER 10 NOT PRICED
5 Willie Mays/10 100.00 175.00
10 Hank Aaron/10 175.00 300.00
15 Nolan Ryan/10 50.00 100.00
20 Stan Musial/10 30.00 80.00
35 Don Mattingly/10 30.00 80.00
40 Bob Gibson/10 15.00 40.00
60 Yogi Berra/10 40.00 100.00
63 Pete Rose/25 75.00 135.00
65 Bob Feller/25 15.00 40.00
70 Brooks Robinson/10 20.00 50.00
75 Cal Ripken Jr./10 125.00 200.00
80 Carl Yastrzemski/10 20.00 50.00
85 Carlton Fisk/10 20.00 50.00
90 Duke Snider/10 20.00 50.00
95 Eddie Murray/10 20.00 50.00
100 Frank Robinson/10 20.00 50.00
105 Jim Palmer/10 12.00 30.00
110 Johnny Bench/10 50.00 100.00
115 Juan Marichal/10 20.00 50.00
120 Mike Schmidt/10 20.00 50.00
122 Whitey Ford/10 30.00 80.00
125 Paul Molitor/10 12.00 30.00
128 Tony Gwynn/10 20.00 50.00
130 Reggie Jackson/10 20.00 50.00
135 Ryne Sandberg/10 30.00 80.00
140 Nolan Ryan/10 50.00 100.00
143 Willie McCovey/10 25.00 60.00
145 Al Kaline/25 25.00 50.00
150 Pete Rose/25 75.00 135.00

2008 Donruss Sports Legends Signatures Mirror Red

*MIRROR RED: .3X TO .8X MIRROR BLUE
MIRROR RED PRINT RUN 25-1370
40 Bob Gibson/55 10.00 25.00
65 Bob Feller/100 10.00 25.00
100 Frank Robinson/25 15.00 40.00
122 Whitey Ford/50 20.00 50.00
125 Paul Molitor/50 8.00 20.00
145 Al Kaline/100 15.00 40.00

2002 Donruss Super Estrellas

COMP.SET w/o SP's (100) 15.00 40.00
COMMON CARD (1-100) .15 .40
COMMON CARD (101-150) .75 2.00
101-150 STATED ODDS 1:4
1 Darin Erstad .15 .40
2 Tim Salmon .25 .60
3 Troy Glaus .15 .40
4 Curt Schilling .15 .40
5 Luis Gonzalez .15 .40
6 Mark Grace .25 .60
7 Randy Johnson .40 1.00
8 Andruw Jones .25 .60
9 Chipper Jones .40 1.00
10 Greg Maddux .60 1.50
11 Javy Lopez .15 .40
12 Tom Glavine .25 .60
13 Manny Ramirez .25 .60
14 Nomar Garciaparra .60 1.50
15 Pedro Martinez .25 .60
16 Trot Nixon .15 .40
17 Fred McGriff .25 .60
18 Sammy Sosa .40 1.00
19 Kerry Wood .15 .40
20 Moises Alou .15 .40
21 Frank Thomas .40 1.00
22 Magglio Ordonez .15 .40
23 Adam Dunn .15 .40
24 Barry Larkin .25 .60
25 Juan Encarnacion .15 .40
26 Ken Griffey Jr. .75 2.00
27 Sean Casey .15 .40
28 C.C. Sabathia .15 .40
29 Jim Thome .25 .60
30 Omar Vizquel .25 .60
31 Larry Walker .15 .40
32 Mike Hampton .15 .40
33 Todd Helton .25 .60
34 Bobby Higginson .15 .40
35 Charles Johnson .15 .40
36 Craig Biggio .25 .60
37 Jeff Bagwell .25 .60
38 Lance Berkman .15 .40
39 Carlos Beltran .15 .40
40 Mike Sweeney .15 .40
41 Adrian Beltre .15 .40
42 Gary Sheffield .15 .40
43 Hideo Nomo .40 1.00
44 Kevin Brown .15 .40
45 Shawn Green .15 .40
46 Ben Sheets .15 .40
47 Richie Sexson .15 .40
48 Brad Radke .15 .40
49 Javier Vazquez .15 .40
50 Jose Vidro .15 .40
51 Vladimir Guerrero .40 1.00
52 Mike Piazza .60 1.50
53 Roberto Alomar .25 .60
54 Alfonso Soriano .15 .40
55 Bernie Williams .25 .60
56 Derek Jeter 1.00 2.50
57 Jason Giambi .15 .40
58 Jorge Posada .25 .60
59 Mariano Rivera .40 1.00
60 Mike Mussina .25 .60
61 Orlando Hernandez .15 .40
62 Roger Clemens .75 2.00
63 Barry Zito .15 .40
64 Eric Chavez .15 .40
65 Jermaine Dye .15 .40
66 Mark Mulder .15 .40
67 Miguel Tejada .15 .40
68 Tim Hudson .15 .40
69 Bobby Abreu .15 .40
70 Pat Burrell .15 .40
71 Scott Rolen .25 .60
72 Brian Giles .15 .40
73 Jason Kendall .15 .40
74 Phil Nevin .15 .40
75 Rickey Henderson .40 1.00
76 Ryan Klesko .15 .40
77 Andres Galarraga .15 .40
78 Barry Bonds 1.00 2.50
79 Tsuyoshi Shinjo .15 .40
80 Jeff Kent .15 .40
81 Bret Boone .15 .40
82 Edgar Martinez .25 .60
83 Freddy Garcia .15 .40
84 Ichiro Suzuki .75 2.00
85 Kazuhiro Sasaki .15 .40
86 John Olerud .15 .40
87 Albert Pujols .75 2.00
88 Bud Smith .15 .40
89 J.D. Drew .15 .40
90 Jim Edmonds .15 .40
91 Matt Morris .15 .40
92 Greg Vaughn .15 .40
93 Alex Rodriguez .50 1.50
94 Chan Ho Park .15 .40
95 Ivan Rodriguez .25 .60
96 Juan Gonzalez .15 .40
97 Rafael Palmeiro .25 .60
98 Carlos Delgado .15 .40
99 Raul Mondesi .15 .40
100 Shannon Stewart .15 .40
101 Marlon Byrd NV .75 2.00
102 Alex Herrera NV .75 2.00
103 Brandon Backe NV RC 1.00 2.50
104 Jorge De La Rosa NV RC .75 2.00
105 Corky Miller NV .75 2.00
106 Dennis Tankersley NV .75 2.00
107 Kyle Kane NV RC .75 2.00
108 Justin Duchscherer NV .75 2.00
109 Brian Mallette NV RC .75 2.00
110 Eric Hinske NV .75 2.00
111 Jason Lane NV .75 2.00
112 Hee Seop Choi NV .75 2.00
113 Juan Cruz NV .75 2.00
114 Rodrigo Rosario NV RC .75 2.00
115 Matt Guerrier NV .75 2.00
116 Anderson Machado NV RC .75 2.00
117 Geronimo Gil NV .75 2.00
118 Dewon Brazelton NV .75 2.00
119 Mark Prior NV 1.25 3.00
120 Bill Hall NV .75 2.00
121 Jorge Padilla NV RC .75 2.00
122 Josh Pearce NV .75 2.00
123 Allan Simpson NV RC .75 2.00
124 Doug Devore NV RC .75 2.00
125 Luis Garcia NV .75 2.00
126 Angel Berroa NV .75 2.00
127 Steve Bechler NV RC .75 2.00
128 Antonio Perez NV .75 2.00
129 Mark Teixeira NV 1.25 3.00
130 Mark Ellis NV .75 2.00
131 Michael Cuddyer NV .75 2.00
132 Mike Rivera NV .75 2.00
133 Raul Chavez NV RC .75 2.00
134 Juan Pena NV .75 2.00
135 Austin Kearns NV .75 2.00
136 Ryan Ludwick NV .75 2.00
137 Eddie Rogers NV .75 2.00
138 Wilson Betemit NV .75 2.00
139 Nick Neugebauer NV .75 2.00
140 Tom Shearn NV RC .75 2.00
141 Eric Cyr NV .75 2.00
142 Victor Martinez NV 1.25 3.00
143 Brandon Berger NV .75 2.00
144 Erik Bedard NV .75 2.00
145 Franklyn German NV RC .75 2.00
146 Joe Thurston NV .75 2.00
147 John Buck NV .75 2.00
148 Jeff Deardorff NV .75 2.00
149 Ryan Jamison NV .75 2.00
150 Alfredo Amezaga NV .75 2.00

2002 Donruss Super Estrellas Estrellas

COMPLETE SET (5) 4.00 10.00
STATED ODDS 1:12
1 Alex Rodriguez 1.00 2.50
2 Ivan Rodriguez .60 1.50
3 Vladimir Guerrero .75 2.00
4 Sammy Sosa .75 2.00
5 Nomar Garciaparra 1.25 3.00

2002 Donruss Super Estrellas Nacion De Origen

COMPLETE SET (20) 10.00 25.00
STATED ODDS 1:4
1 Livan Hernandez .60 1.50
2 Albert Pujols 1.50 4.00
3 Ivan Rodriguez .60 1.50
4 Mariano Rivera .75 2.00
5 Richard Hidalgo .60 1.50
6 Eric Chavez .60 1.50
7 Vinny Castilla .60 1.50
8 Geronimo Gil .60 1.50
9 Elmer Dessens .60 1.50
10 Ismael Valdes .60 1.50
11 Edgar Renteria .60 1.50
12 Rafael Palmeiro .60 1.50
13 Luis Gonzalez .60 1.50
14 Orlando Hernandez .60 1.50
15 Vladimir Guerrero .75 2.00
16 Manny Ramirez .60 1.50
17 Sammy Sosa .75 2.00
18 Vicente Padilla .60 1.50
19 Roberto Alomar .60 1.50
20 Bernie Williams .60 1.50

2002 Donruss Super Estrellas Poder De Cuadrangular

COMPLETE SET (15) 10.00 25.00
STATED ODDS 1:6
1 Sammy Sosa 1.00 2.50
2 Juan Gonzalez .75 2.00
3 Carlos Delgado .75 2.00
4 Todd Helton .75 2.00
5 Alex Rodriguez 1.25 3.00
6 Troy Glaus .75 2.00
7 Manny Ramirez .75 2.00
8 Vladimir Guerrero 1.00 2.50
9 Jim Thome .75 2.00
10 Luis Gonzalez .75 2.00
11 Shawn Green .75 2.00
12 Barry Bonds 2.50 6.00
13 Larry Walker .75 2.00
14 Jeff Bagwell .75 2.00
15 Rafael Palmeiro .75 2.00

2002 Donruss Super Estrellas Posters De Jugadores

COMPLETE SET (25) 8.00 20.00
ONE PER PACK
1 Roberto Alomar .20 .50
2 Jeff Bagwell .20 .50
3 Barry Bonds 1.00 2.50
4 Roger Clemens .75 2.00
5 Carlos Delgado .20 .50
6 Nomar Garciaparra .60 1.50
7 Jason Giambi .20 .50
8 Juan Gonzalez .20 .50
9 Ken Griffey Jr. .75 2.00
10 Vladimir Guerrero .20 .50
11 Tony Gwynn .50 1.25
12 Derek Jeter 1.00 2.50
13 Randy Johnson .20 .50
14 Chipper Jones .20 .50
15 Greg Maddux .60 1.50
16 Pedro Martinez .20 .50
17 Mike Piazza .60 1.50
18 Albert Pujols .75 2.00
19 Manny Ramirez .20 .50
20 Cal Ripken 1.25 3.00
21 Alex Rodriguez .50 1.50
22 Ivan Rodriguez .20 .50
23 Sammy Sosa .20 .50
24 Ichiro Suzuki .75 2.00
25 Frank Thomas .20 .50

2002 Donruss Super Estrellas Precision De Lanzamiento

COMPLETE SET (5) 4.00 10.00
STATED ODDS 1:12
1 Pedro Martinez .60 1.50
2 Greg Maddux 1.25 3.00
3 Randy Johnson .75 2.00
4 Roger Clemens 1.50 4.00
5 Curt Schilling .60 1.50

2003 Donruss Team Heroes Samples

*SAMPLES: 1.5X TO 4X BASIC CARDS

2003 Donruss Team Heroes Samples Gold

*GOLD SAMPLES: 4X TO 10X BASIC CARDS

2003 Donruss Team Heroes

COMP.LO SET (540) 20.00 50.00
COMP.UPDATE SET (8) 3.00 8.00
COMMON CARD (1-540) .12 .30
COMMON RETIRED 1-540 .12 .30
COMMON CARD (541-548) .12 .30
541-548 ISSUED IN DLP R/T PACKS
1 Adam Kennedy .12 .30
2 Steve Green .12 .30
3 Rod Carew Angels .20 .50
4 Alfredo Amezaga .12 .30
5 Reggie Jackson Angels .20 .50
6 Jarrod Washburn .12 .30
7 Nolan Ryan Angels 1.00 2.50
8 Tim Salmon .12 .30
9 Garret Anderson .12 .30
10 Darin Erstad .12 .30
11 Elpidio Guzman .12 .30
12 David Eckstein .12 .30
13 Troy Percival .12 .30
14 Troy Glaus .12 .30
15 Doug Devore .12 .30
16 Tony Womack .12 .30
17 Matt Williams .12 .30
18 Junior Spivey .12 .30
19 Mark Grace .20 .50
20 Curt Schilling .20 .50
21 Erubiel Durazo .12 .30
22 Craig Counsell .12 .30
23 Byung-Hyun Kim .12 .30
24 Randy Johnson D'backs .30 .75
25 Luis Gonzalez .12 .30
26 John Smoltz .30 .75
27 Tim Spooneybarger .12 .30
28 Dale Murphy .30 .75
29 Warren Spahn .20 .50
30 Jason Marquis .12 .30
31 Kevin Millwood .12 .30
32 Javy Lopez .12 .30
33 Vinny Castilla .12 .30
34 Julio Franco .12 .30
35 Trey Hodges .12 .30
36 Chipper Jones .30 .75
37 Gary Sheffield .12 .30
38 Billy Sylvester .12 .30
39 Tom Glavine .20 .50
40 Rafael Furcal .12 .30
41 Cory Aldridge .12 .30
42 Greg Maddux Braves .40 1.00
43 John Ennis .12 .30
44 Wes Helms .12 .30
45 Horacio Ramirez .12 .30
46 Derrick Lewis .12 .30
47 Marcus Giles .12 .30
48 Eddie Mathews .30 .75
49 Wilson Betemit .12 .30
50 Andruw Jones .12 .30
51 Josh Towers .12 .30
52 Ed Rogers .12 .30
53 Kris Foster .12 .30
54 Brooks Robinson .20 .50
55 Cal Ripken 1.00 2.50
56 Brian Roberts .12 .30
57 Luis Rivera .12 .30
58 Rodrigo Lopez .12 .30
59 Geronimo Gil .12 .30
60 Erik Bedard .12 .30
61 Jim Palmer .20 .50
62 Jay Gibbons .12 .30
63 Travis Driskill .12 .30
64 Larry Bigbie .12 .30
65 Eddie Murray .20 .50
66 Hoyt Wilhelm .20 .50
67 Bobby Doerr .20 .50
68 Pedro Martinez .20 .50
69 Roger Clemens Red Sox .40 1.00
70 Nomar Garciaparra .20 .50
71 Trot Nixon .12 .30
72 Dennis Eckersley Red Sox .20 .50
73 John Burkett .12 .30
74 Tim Wakefield .20 .50
75 Wade Boggs Red Sox .20 .50
76 Cliff Floyd .12 .30
77 Casey Fossum .12 .30
78 Johnny Damon .20 .50
79 Fred Lynn .12 .30
80 Rickey Henderson Red Sox .30 .75
81 Juan Diaz .12 .30
82 Manny Ramirez .30 .75
83 Carlton Fisk Red Sox .20 .50
84 Jorge De La Rosa .12 .30
85 Shea Hillenbrand .12 .30
86 Derek Lowe .12 .30
87 Jason Varitek .30 .75
88 Carlos Baerga .12 .30
89 Freddy Sanchez .12 .30
90 Ugueth Urbina .12 .30
91 Rey Sanchez .12 .30
92 Josh Hancock .12 .30
93 Tony Clark .12 .30
94 Dustin Hermanson .12 .30
95 Ryne Sandberg .60 1.50
96 Fred McGriff .20 .50
97 Alex Gonzalez .12 .30
98 Mark Bellhorn .12 .30
99 Fergie Jenkins .20 .50
100 Jon Lieber .12 .30
101 Francis Beltran .12 .30
102 Greg Maddux Cubs .40 1.00
103 Nate Frese .12 .30
104 Andre Dawson Cubs .20 .50
105 Carlos Zambrano .20 .50
106 Steve Smyth .12 .30
107 Ernie Banks .30 .75
108 Will Ohman .12 .30
109 Kerry Wood .12 .30
110 Bobby Hill .12 .30
111 Moises Alou .12 .30
112 Hee Seop Choi .12 .30
113 Corey Patterson .12 .30
114 Sammy Sosa .30 .75
115 Mark Prior .20 .50
116 Juan Cruz .12 .30
117 Ron Santo .20 .50
118 Billy Williams .20 .50
119 Antonio Alfonseca .12 .30
120 Matt Clement .12 .30
121 Carlton Fisk White Sox .20 .50
122 Joe Crede .12 .30
123 Magglio Ordonez .20 .50
124 Frank Thomas .30 .75
125 Joe Borchard .12 .30
126 Royce Clayton .12 .30
127 Luis Aparicio .20 .50
128 Willie Harris .12 .30
129 Kyle Kane .12 .30
130 Paul Konerko .20 .50
131 Matt Ginter .12 .30
132 Carlos Lee .12 .30
133 Mark Buehrle .20 .50
134 Adam Dunn .20 .50
135 Eric Davis .12 .30
136 Johnny Bench .30 .75
137 Joe Morgan .20 .50
138 Austin Kearns .12 .30
139 Barry Larkin .20 .50
140 Ken Griffey Jr. Reds .60 1.50
141 Luis Pineda .12 .30
142 Corky Miller .12 .30
143 Brandon Larson .12 .30
144 Wily Mo Pena .12 .30
145 Lance Davis .12 .30
146 Tom Seaver Reds .20 .50
147 Luke Hudson .12 .30
148 Sean Casey .12 .30
149 Tony Perez .20 .50
150 Todd Walker .12 .30
151 Aaron Boone .12 .30

152 Jose Rijo .12 .30
153 Ryan Dempster .12 .30
154 Danny Graves .12 .30
155 Matt Lawton .12 .30
156 Cliff Lee .75 2.00
157 Ryan Drese .12 .30
158 Danys Baez .12 .30
159 Einar Diaz .12 .30
160 Milton Bradley .12 .30
161 Earl Snyder .12 .30
162 Ellis Burks .12 .30
163 Lou Boudreau .20 .50
164 Bob Feller .20 .50
165 Ricardo Rodriguez .12 .30
166 Victor Martinez .20 .50
167 Alex Herrera .12 .30
168 Omar Vizquel .20 .50
169 David Elder .12 .30
170 C.C. Sabathia .20 .50
171 Alex Escobar .12 .30
172 Brian Tallet .12 .30
173 Jim Thome .20 .50
174 Rene Reyes .12 .30
175 Juan Uribe .12 .30
176 Jason Romano .12 .30
177 Juan Pierre .12 .30
178 Jason Jennings .12 .30
179 Jose Ortiz .12 .30
180 Larry Walker .20 .50
181 Cam Esslinger .12 .30
182 Todd Helton .20 .50
183 Aaron Cook .12 .30
184 Jack Cust .12 .30
185 Jack Morris Tigers .20 .50
186 Mike Rivera .12 .30
187 Bobby Higginson .12 .30
188 Fernando Rodney .12 .30
189 Al Kaline .20 .50
190 Carlos Pena .20 .50
191 Alan Trammell .20 .50
192 Mike Maroth .12 .30
193 Adam Pettyjohn .12 .30
194 David Espinosa .12 .30
195 Adam Bernero .12 .30
196 Franklyn German .12 .30
197 Robert Fick .12 .30
198 Andres Torres .12 .30
199 Luis Castillo .12 .30
200 Preston Wilson .12 .30
201 Pablo Ozuna .12 .30
202 Brad Penny .12 .30
203 Josh Beckett .12 .30
204 Charles Johnson .12 .30
205 Wilson Valdez .12 .30
206 A.J. Burnett .12 .30
207 Abraham Nunez .12 .30
208 Mike Lowell .12 .30
209 Jose Cueto .12 .30
210 Jeriome Robertson .12 .30
211 Jeff Bagwell .20 .50
212 Kirk Saarloos .12 .30
213 Craig Biggio .20 .50
214 Rodrigo Rosario .12 .30
215 Roy Oswalt .20 .50
216 John Buck .12 .30
217 Tim Redding .12 .30
218 Morgan Ensberg .12 .30
219 Richard Hidalgo .12 .30
220 Wade Miller .12 .30
221 Lance Berkman .20 .50
222 Raul Chavez .12 .30
223 Carlos Hernandez .12 .30
224 Greg Miller .12 .30
225 Tom Shearn .12 .30
226 Jason Lane .12 .30
227 Nolan Ryan Astros 1.00 2.50
228 Billy Wagner .12 .30
229 Octavio Dotel .12 .30
230 Shane Reynolds .12 .30
231 Julio Lugo .12 .30
232 Daryle Ward .12 .30
233 Mike Sweeney .12 .30
234 Angel Berroa .12 .30
235 George Brett .60 1.50
236 Brad Voyles .12 .30
237 Brandon Berger .12 .30
238 Chad Durbin .12 .30
239 Alexis Gomez .12 .30
240 Jeremy Affeldt .12 .30
241 Bo Jackson .30 .75
242 Dee Brown .12 .30
243 Tony Cogan .12 .30
244 Carlos Beltran .20 .50
245 Joe Randa .12 .30
246 Pee Wee Reese .20 .50
247 Andy Ashby .12 .30
248 Cesar Izturis .12 .30
249 Duke Snider .20 .50
250 Mark Grudzielanek .12 .30
251 Chin-Feng Chen .12 .30
252 Brian Jordan .12 .30
253 Steve Garvey .12 .30
254 Odalis Perez .12 .30
255 Hideo Nomo .30 .75
256 Kevin Brown .12 .30
257 Eric Karros .12 .30
258 Joe Thurston .12 .30
259 Carlos Garcia .12 .30
260 Shawn Green .12 .30
261 Paul Lo Duca .12 .30
262 Kazuhisa Ishii .12 .30
263 Victor Alvarez .12 .30
264 Eric Gagne .12 .30
265 Don Sutton .20 .50
266 Orel Hershiser .12 .30
267 Dave Roberts .20 .50
268 Adrian Beltre .30 .75
269 Don Drysdale .20 .50
270 Jackie Robinson .30 .75
271 Tyler Houston .12 .30
272 Omar Daal .12 .30
273 Marquis Grissom .12 .30
274 Paul Quantrill .12 .30
275 Paul Molitor .30 .75
276 Jose Hernandez .12 .30
277 Takahito Nomura .12 .30
278 Nick Neugebauer .12 .30
279 Jose Mieses .12 .30
280 Richie Sexson .12 .30
281 Matt Childers .12 .30
282 Bill Hall .12 .30
283 Ben Sheets .12 .30
284 Brian Mallette .12 .30
285 Geoff Jenkins .12 .30
286 Robin Yount .30 .75
287 Jeff Deardorff .12 .30
288 Luis Rivas .12 .30
289 Harmon Killebrew .30 .75
290 Michael Cuddyer .12 .30
291 Torii Hunter .12 .30
292 Kevin Frederick .12 .30
293 Adam Johnson .12 .30
294 Jack Morris Twins .20 .50
295 Rod Carew Twins .20 .50
296 Kirby Puckett .30 .75
297 Joe Mays .12 .30
298 Jacque Jones .12 .30
299 Cristian Guzman .12 .30
300 Kyle Lohse .12 .30
301 Eric Milton .12 .30
302 Brad Radke .12 .30
303 Doug Mientkiewicz .12 .30
304 Corey Koskie .12 .30
305 Jose Vidro .12 .30
306 Claudio Vargas .12 .30
307 Gary Carter Expos .20 .50
308 Andre Dawson Expos .20 .50
309 Henry Mateo .12 .30
310 Andres Galarraga .20 .50
311 Zach Day .12 .30
312 Bartolo Colon .12 .30
313 Endy Chavez .12 .30
314 Javier Vazquez .12 .30
315 Michael Barrett .12 .30
316 Vladimir Guerrero .20 .50
317 Orlando Cabrera .12 .30
318 Al Leiter .12 .30
319 Timo Perez .12 .30
320 Rey Ordonez .12 .30
321 Gary Carter .20 .50
322 Armando Benitez .12 .30
323 Dwight Gooden .12 .30
324 Pedro Astacio .12 .30
325 Roberto Alomar .20 .50
326 Edgardo Alfonzo .12 .30
327 Nolan Ryan Mets 1.00 2.50
328 Mo Vaughn .12 .30
329 Ryan Jamison .12 .30
330 Satoru Komiyama .12 .30
331 Mike Piazza .30 .75
332 Tom Seaver Mets .20 .50
333 Jorge Posada .20 .50
334 Derek Jeter .75 2.00
335 Babe Ruth .75 2.00
336 Lou Gehrig .60 1.50
337 Andy Pettitte .20 .50
338 Mariano Rivera .40 1.00
339 Robin Ventura .12 .30
340 Yogi Berra .30 .75
341 Phil Rizzuto .20 .50
342 Bernie Williams .20 .50
343 Alfonso Soriano .20 .50
344 Drew Henson .12 .30
345 Erick Almonte .12 .30
346 Rondell White .12 .30
347 Christian Parker .12 .30
348 Joe Torre Yankees .20 .50
349 Nick Johnson .12 .30
350 Raul Mondesi .12 .30
351 Brandon Claussen .12 .30
352 Reggie Jackson Yankees .20 .50
353 Roger Clemens Yankees .40 1.00
354 Don Mattingly .60 1.50
355 Jason Giambi .12 .30
356 Adrian Hernandez .12 .30
357 Jeff Weaver .12 .30
358 Mike Mussina .20 .50
359 Brett Jodie .12 .30
360 David Wells .12 .30
361 Enos Slaughter Yankees .20 .50
362 Whitey Ford .20 .50
363 Eric Chavez .12 .30
364 Miguel Tejada .20 .50
365 Barry Zito .20 .50
366 Bert Snow .12 .30
367 Rickey Henderson A's .30 .75
368 Juan Pena .12 .30
369 Terrence Long .12 .30
370 Dennis Eckersley A's .20 .50
371 Mark Ellis .12 .30
372 Tim Hudson .20 .50
373 Jose Canseco .20 .50
374 Reggie Jackson A's .20 .50
375 Mark Mulder .12 .30
376 David Justice .12 .30
377 Jermaine Dye .12 .30
378 Brett Myers .12 .30
379 Lenny Dykstra .12 .30
380 Vicente Padilla .12 .30
381 Bobby Abreu .12 .30
382 Pat Burrell .12 .30
383 Jorge Padilla .12 .30
384 Jeremy Giambi .12 .30
385 Mike Lieberthal .12 .30
386 Anderson Machado .12 .30
387 Marlon Byrd .12 .30
388 Bud Smith .12 .30
389 Eric Valent .12 .30
390 Elio Serrano .12 .30
391 Jimmy Rollins .20 .50
392 Brandon Duckworth .12 .30
393 Robin Roberts .20 .50
394 Marlon Anderson .12 .30
395 Robert Person .12 .30
396 Johnny Estrada .12 .30
397 Mike Schmidt .50 1.25
398 Eric Junge .12 .30
399 Jason Michaels .12 .30
400 Steve Carlton .20 .50
401 Placido Polanco .12 .30
402 John Grabow .12 .30
403 Tomas De La Rosa .12 .30
404 Tike Redman .12 .30
405 Willie Stargell .20 .50
406 Dave Williams .12 .30
407 John Candelaria .12 .30
408 Jack Wilson .12 .30
409 Matt Guerrier .12 .30
410 Jason Kendall .12 .30
411 Josh Fogg .12 .30
412 Aramis Ramirez .12 .30
413 Dave Parker .12 .30
414 Roberto Clemente .75 2.00
415 Kip Wells .12 .30
416 Brian Giles .12 .30
417 Honus Wagner .30 .75
418 Ramon Vazquez .12 .30
419 Oliver Perez .12 .30
420 Ryan Klesko .12 .30
421 Brian Lawrence .12 .30
422 Ben Howard .12 .30
423 Ozzie Smith Padres .40 1.00
424 Dennis Tankersley .12 .30
425 Tony Gwynn .30 .75
426 Sean Burroughs .12 .30
427 Xavier Nady .12 .30
428 Phil Nevin .12 .30
429 Trevor Hoffman .20 .50
430 Jake Peavy .12 .30
431 Cody Ransom .12 .30
432 Kenny Lofton .12 .30
433 Mel Ott .30 .75
434 Tsuyoshi Shinjo .12 .30
435 Deivis Santos .12 .30
436 Rich Aurilia .12 .30
437 Will Clark Giants .20 .50
438 Pedro Feliz .12 .30
439 J.T. Snow .12 .30
440 Robb Nen .12 .30
441 Carlos Valderrama .12 .30
442 Willie McCovey .20 .50
443 Jeff Kent .12 .30
444 Orlando Cepeda .20 .50
445 Barry Bonds .50 1.25
446 Alex Rodriguez M's .40 1.00
447 Allan Simpson .12 .30
448 Antonio Perez .12 .30
449 Edgar Martinez .20 .50
450 Freddy Garcia .12 .30
451 Chris Snelling .12 .30
452 Matt Thornton .12 .30
453 Kazuhiro Sasaki .12 .30
454 Harold Reynolds .12 .30
455 Randy Johnson M's .30 .75
456 Bret Boone .12 .30
457 Rafael Soriano .12 .30
458 Luis Ugueto .12 .30
459 Ken Griffey Jr. M's .60 1.50
460 Ichiro Suzuki .40 1.00
461 Jamie Moyer .12 .30
462 Joel Pineiro .12 .30
463 Jeff Cirillo .12 .30
464 John Olerud .12 .30
465 Mike Cameron .12 .30
466 Ruben Sierra .12 .30
467 Mark McLemore .12 .30
468 Carlos Guillen .12 .30
469 Dan Wilson .12 .30
470 Shigetoshi Hasegawa .12 .30
471 Ben Davis .12 .30
472 Ozzie Smith Cards .40 1.00
473 Matt Morris .12 .30
474 Edgar Renteria .12 .30
475 Les Walrond .12 .30
476 Albert Pujols .40 1.00
477 Stan Musial .50 1.25
478 J.D. Drew .12 .30
479 Josh Pearce .12 .30
480 Enos Slaughter Cards .20 .50
481 Jason Simontacchi .12 .30
482 Jeremy Lambert .12 .30
483 Tino Martinez .12 .30
484 Rogers Hornsby .20 .50
485 Rick Ankiel .12 .30
486 Jim Edmonds .20 .50
487 Scott Rolen .20 .50
488 Kevin Joseph .12 .30
489 Fernando Vina .12 .30
490 Jason Isringhausen .20 .50
491 Lou Brock .20 .50
492 Joe Torre Cards .20 .50
493 Bob Gibson .30 .75
494 Chuck Finley .12 .30
495 So Taguchi .12 .30
496 Ben Grieve .12 .30
497 Toby Hall .12 .30
498 Brent Abernathy .12 .30
499 Brandon Backe .20 .50
500 Felix Escalona .12 .30
501 Matt White .12 .30
502 Randy Winn .12 .30
503 Carl Crawford .20 .50
504 Dewon Brazelton .12 .30
505 Joe Kennedy .12 .30
506 Wade Boggs D-Rays .20 .50
507 Aubrey Huff .12 .30
508 Alex Rodriguez Rangers .40 1.00
509 Ivan Rodriguez .20 .50
510 Will Clark Rangers .20 .50
511 Hank Blalock .12 .30
512 Travis Hughes .12 .30
513 Travis Hafner .12 .30
514 Ryan Ludwick .12 .30
515 Doug Davis .12 .30
516 Juan Gonzalez .12 .30
517 Jason Hart .12 .30
518 Mark Teixeira .20 .50
519 Nolan Ryan Rangers 1.00 2.50
520 Rafael Palmeiro .20 .50
521 Kevin Mench .12 .30
522 Chan Ho Park .20 .50
523 Kenny Rogers .12 .30
524 Rusty Greer .12 .30
525 Michael Young .12 .30
526 Carlos Delgado .12 .30
527 Vernon Wells .12 .30
528 Orlando Hudson .12 .30
529 Shannon Stewart .12 .30
530 Joe Carter .12 .30
531 Chris Baker .12 .30
532 Eric Hinske .12 .30
533 Corey Thurman .12 .30
534 Josh Phelps .12 .30
535 Reed Johnson .12 .30
536 Brian Bowles .12 .30
537 Roy Halladay .20 .50
538 Jose Cruz Jr. .12 .30
539 Kelvim Escobar .12 .30
540 Chris Carpenter .20 .50
541 Rickie Weeks RC .40 1.00
542 Hideki Matsui RC .60 1.50
543 Ramon Nivar RC .12 .30
544 Adam Loewen RC .12 .30
545 Brandon Webb RC .40 1.00
546 Dan Haren RC .60 1.50
547 Delmon Young RC .75 2.00
548 Ryan Wagner RC .12 .30

2003 Donruss Team Heroes Autographs

1-540 RANDOM INSERTS IN PACKS
541-548 RANDOM IN DLP R/T PACKS
PRINT RUNS B/WN 5-250 COPIES PER
PRINT RUNS ABOVE 100 ARE NOT SERIAL #'d
NO PRICING ON QTY OF 25 OR LESS

4 Alfredo Amezaga/250 4.00 10.00
11 Elpidio Guzman/100 6.00 15.00
15 Doug Devore/122 6.00 15.00
35 Trey Hodges/250 4.00 10.00
38 Billy Sylvester/250 4.00 10.00
41 Cory Aldridge/250 4.00 10.00
45 Horacio Ramirez/200 4.00 10.00
46 Derrick Lewis/250 4.00 10.00
47 Marcus Giles/200 6.00 15.00
49 Wilson Betemit/75 6.00 15.00
51 Josh Towers/110 6.00 15.00
52 Ed Rogers/250 4.00 10.00
53 Kris Foster/250 4.00 10.00
56 Brian Roberts/250 10.00 25.00
59 Geronimo Gil/60 6.00 15.00
60 Erik Bedard/250 4.00 10.00
62 Jay Gibbons/181 4.00 10.00
64 Larry Bigbie/100 10.00 25.00
77 Casey Fossum/250 4.00 10.00
79 Fred Lynn/50 10.00 25.00
81 Juan Diaz/250 4.00 10.00
84 Jorge De La Rosa/250 4.00 10.00
99 Fergie Jenkins/50 10.00 25.00
101 Francis Beltran/250 4.00 10.00
103 Nate Frese/250 4.00 10.00
105 Carlos Zambrano/150 10.00 25.00
108 Will Ohman/50 6.00 15.00
110 Bobby Hill/150 4.00 10.00
115 Mark Prior/50 12.50 30.00
116 Juan Cruz/50 6.00 15.00
122 Joe Crede/50 6.00 15.00
125 Joe Borchard/250 4.00 10.00
127 Luis Aparicio/50 10.00 25.00
128 Willie Harris/129 6.00 15.00
129 Kyle Kane/100 6.00 15.00
131 Matt Ginter/250 4.00 10.00
132 Carlos Lee/50 10.00 25.00
133 Mark Buehrle/50 6.00 15.00
135 Eric Davis/75 10.00 25.00
138 Austin Kearns/71 6.00 15.00
142 Corky Miller/250 4.00 10.00
143 Brandon Larson/143 4.00 10.00
144 Wily Mo Pena/250 6.00 15.00
147 Luke Hudson/50 6.00 15.00
149 Tony Perez/50 10.00 25.00
156 Cliff Lee/250 6.00 15.00
161 Earl Snyder/250 4.00 10.00
165 Ricardo Rodriguez/250 4.00 10.00
166 Victor Martinez/200 6.00 15.00
167 Alex Herrera/250 4.00 10.00
171 Alex Escobar/125 6.00 15.00
172 Brian Tallet/250 4.00 10.00
174 Rene Reyes/250 4.00 10.00
176 Jason Romano/50 6.00 15.00
177 Juan Pierre/66 10.00 25.00
178 Jason Jennings/250 4.00 10.00
179 Jose Ortiz/250 4.00 10.00
181 Cam Esslinger/250 4.00 10.00
184 Jack Cust/250 4.00 10.00
185 Jack Morris Tigers/50 10.00 25.00
186 Mike Rivera/250 4.00 10.00
188 Fernando Rodney/250 4.00 10.00
190 Carlos Pena/96 6.00 15.00
192 Mike Maroth/250 4.00 10.00
193 Adam Pettyjohn/250 4.00 10.00
194 David Espinosa/250 4.00 10.00
195 Adam Bernero/250 4.00 10.00
196 Franklyn German/250 4.00 10.00
197 Robert Fick/50 6.00 15.00
198 Andres Torres/250 4.00 10.00
201 Pablo Ozuna/250 4.00 10.00
205 Wilson Valdez/250 4.00 10.00
207 Abraham Nunez/250 4.00 10.00
212 Kirk Saarloos/250 4.00 10.00
214 Rodrigo Rosario/250 4.00 10.00
215 Roy Oswalt/50 10.00 25.00
217 Tim Redding/250 4.00 10.00
218 Morgan Ensberg/250 6.00 15.00
219 Richard Hidalgo/100 6.00 15.00
220 Wade Miller/200 4.00 10.00
222 Raul Chavez/125 10.00 25.00
223 Carlos Hernandez/250 4.00 10.00
224 Greg Miller/90 6.00 15.00
226 Jason Lane/250 6.00 15.00
234 Angel Berroa/200 4.00 10.00
236 Brad Voyles/200 4.00 10.00
237 Brandon Berger/250 4.00 10.00
238 Chad Durbin/250 4.00 10.00
239 Alexis Gomez/165 4.00 10.00
240 Jeremy Affeldt/250 4.00 10.00
242 Dee Brown/50 6.00 15.00
243 Tony Cogan/250 4.00 10.00
248 Cesar Izturis/250 4.00 10.00
253 Steve Garvey/75 15.00 40.00
258 Joe Thurston/108 6.00 15.00
259 Carlos Garcia/100 6.00 15.00
261 Paul Lo Duca/50 10.00 25.00
263 Victor Alvarez/250 4.00 10.00
265 Don Sutton/50 10.00 25.00
277 Takahito Nomura/100 10.00 25.00
279 Jose Mieses/50 6.00 15.00
281 Matt Childers/50 6.00 15.00
283 Ben Sheets/100 10.00 25.00
284 Brian Mallette/250 4.00 10.00
287 Jeff Deardorff/100 6.00 15.00
288 Luis Rivas/200 4.00 10.00
290 Michael Cuddyer/250 4.00 10.00
291 Torii Hunter/100 10.00 25.00
294 Jack Morris Twins/50 10.00 25.00
305 Jose Vidro/50 6.00 15.00
306 Claudio Vargas/150 4.00 10.00
309 Henry Mateo/250 4.00 10.00
311 Zach Day/250 4.00 10.00
313 Endy Chavez/250 4.00 10.00
314 Javier Vazquez/50 6.00 15.00
344 Drew Henson/50 6.00 15.00
345 Erick Almonte/250 4.00 10.00
347 Christian Parker/200 4.00 10.00
351 Brandon Claussen/250 4.00 10.00
356 Adrian Hernandez/200 4.00 10.00
359 Brett Jodie/250 4.00 10.00
366 Bert Snow/250 4.00 10.00
368 Juan Pena/250 4.00 10.00
371 Mark Ellis/150 4.00 10.00
379 Lenny Dykstra/75 10.00 25.00
383 Jorge Padilla/250 4.00 10.00
384 Jeremy Giambi/100 6.00 15.00
386 Anderson Machado/250 4.00 10.00
387 Marlon Byrd/200 4.00 10.00
388 Bud Smith/125 6.00 15.00
389 Eric Valent/100 6.00 15.00
390 Elio Serrano/250 4.00 10.00
392 Brandon Duckworth/100 6.00 15.00
395 Robert Person/100 6.00 15.00
396 Johnny Estrada/209 4.00 10.00
398 Eric Junge/250 4.00 10.00
399 Jason Michaels/221 4.00 10.00
402 John Grabow/250 4.00 10.00
406 Dave Williams/250 4.00 10.00
407 John Candelaria/100 10.00 25.00
408 Jack Wilson/250 6.00 15.00
409 Matt Guerrier/200 4.00 10.00
412 Aramis Ramirez/50 6.00 15.00
413 Dave Parker/50 10.00 25.00
415 Kip Wells/250 4.00 10.00
418 Ramon Vazquez/200 4.00 10.00
419 Oliver Perez/150 6.00 15.00
421 Brian Lawrence/250 4.00 10.00
422 Ben Howard/250 6.00 15.00
427 Xavier Nady/50 6.00 15.00
431 Cody Ransom/100 6.00 15.00
435 Deivis Santos/100 6.00 15.00
438 Pedro Feliz/50 6.00 15.00
441 Carlos Valderrama/250 4.00 10.00
447 Allan Simpson/250 4.00 10:00
448 Antonio Perez/250 6.00 15.00
451 Chris Snelling/100 6.00 15.00
452 Matt Thornton/200 4.00 10.00
454 Harold Reynolds/100 10.00 25.00
457 Rafael Soriano/250 4.00 10.00
458 Luis Ugueto/50 6.00 15.00
475 Les Walrond/50 6.00 15.00
479 Josh Pearce/200 4.00 10.00
497 Toby Hall/200 4.00 10.00
498 Brent Abernathy/250 4.00 10.00
499 Brandon Backe/250 4.00 10.00
500 Felix Escalona/50 6.00 15.00
504 Dewon Brazelton/100 6.00 15.00
505 Joe Kennedy/200 4.00 10.00
507 Aubrey Huff/100 10.00 25.00
512 Travis Hughes/200 4.00 10.00
514 Ryan Ludwick/250 8.00 20.00
515 Doug Davis/250 4.00 10.00
517 Jason Hart/123 6.00 15.00
518 Mark Teixeira/50 15.00 40.00
521 Kevin Mench/250 6.00 15.00
528 Orlando Hudson/120 6.00 15.00
531 Chris Baker/200 4.00 10.00
532 Eric Hinske/250 4.00 10.00
533 Corey Thurman/250 4.00 10.00
534 Josh Phelps/150 4.00 10.00
535 Reed Johnson/250 4.00 10.00
536 Brian Bowles/250 4.00 10.00
543 Ramon Nivar/100 4.00 10.00
544 Adam Loewen/100 10.00 25.00
545 Brandon Webb/100 12.50 30.00
546 Dan Haren/100 10.00 25.00
548 Ryan Wagner/100 4.00 10.00

2003 Donruss Team Heroes Glossy

* ACTIVE PLAYERS: 1.25X TO 3X BASIC
*RETIRED PLAYERS: 1.25X TO 3X BASIC
ONE PER PACK

2003 Donruss Team Heroes Stat Line

*ACTIVE P/R b/wn 201-250: 2.5X TO 6X
*ACTIVE P/R b/wn 151-200: 3X TO 8X
*ACTIVE P/R b/wn 121-150: 3X TO 8X
*ACTIVE P/R b/wn 81-120: 4X TO 10X
*ACTIVE P/R b/wn 66-80: 5X TO 12X
*ACTIVE P/R b/wn 51-65: 5X TO 12X
*ACTIVE P/R b/wn 36-50: 6X TO 15X
*ACTIVE P/R b/wn 26-35: 8X TO 20X
*RETIRED P/R b/wn 201-250: 2.5X TO 6X
*RETIRED P/R b/wn 151-200: 3X TO 8X
*RETIRED P/R b/wn 121-150: 3X TO 8X
*RETIRED P/R b/wn 81-120: 4X TO 10X
*RETIRED P/R b/wn 66-80: 5X TO 12X
*RETIRED P/R b/wn 51-65: 5X TO 12X
*RETIRED P/R b/wn 36-50: 6X TO 15X
*RC's P/R b/wn 36-50: 6X TO 15X
*RC's P/R b/wn 26-35: 8X TO 20X
1-540 RANDOM INSERTS IN PACKS
541-548 RANDOM IN DLP R/T PACKS
PRINT RUNS B/WN 1-215 COPIES PER
NO ACTIVE PRICING ON QTY OF 25 OR LESS
NO RETIRED PRICING ON QTY OF 36 OR LESS
NO ROOKIE PRICING ON QTY OF 25 OR LESS

1 Adam Kennedy/148 1.00 2.50
3 Rod Carew Angels/58 3.00 8.00
5 Reggie Jackson Angels/39 3.00 8.00
6 Jarrod Washburn/139 1.00 2.50
7 Nolan Ryan Angels/61 12.00 30.00
8 Tim Salmon/138 1.00 2.50
9 Garret Anderson/123 1.00 2.50
10 Darin Erstad/177 1.00 2.50
11 Elpidio Guzman/112 1.25 3.00
12 David Eckstein/178 1.00 2.50
13 Troy Percival/68 1.50 4.00
14 Troy Glaus/111 1.25 3.00
15 Doug Devore/114 1.25 3.00
16 Tony Womack/160 1.00 2.50
17 Matt Williams/56 1.50 4.00
18 Junior Spivey/162 1.00 2.50
19 Mark Grace/75 2.50 6.00
21 Erubiel Durazo/58 1.50 4.00
22 Craig Counsell/123 1.00 2.50
23 Byung-Hyun Kim/92 1.25 3.00
25 Luis Gonzalez/151 1.00 2.50
26 John Smoltz/65 3.00 8.00
27 Tim Spooneybarger/51 1.50 4.00
28 Dale Murphy/39 5.00 12.00
29 Warren Spahn/63 2.50 6.00
30 Jason Marquis/84 1.25 3.00
31 Kevin Millwood/178 1.00 2.50
32 Javy Lopez/81 1.25 3.00
33 Vinny Castilla/126 1.00 2.50
34 Julio Franco/96 1.25 3.00
36 Chipper Jones/100 3.00 8.00
37 Gary Sheffield/84 1.25 3.00
38 Billy Sylvester/53 1.50 4.00
39 Tom Glavine/127 1.50 4.00
40 Rafael Furcal/175 1.00 2.50
42 Greg Maddux Braves/118 4.00 10.00
44 Wes Helms/51 1.50 4.00
45 Horacio Ramirez/69 1.50 4.00
46 Derrick Lewis/61 1.50 4.00
47 Marcus Giles/49 2.00 5.00
48 Eddie Mathews/47 5.00 12.00
49 Wilson Betemit/69 1.25 3.00
50 Andruw Jones/148 1.00 2.50
55 Cal Ripken/44 15.00 40.00
56 Brian Roberts/29 2.50 6.00
58 Rodrigo Lopez/136 1.00 2.50
59 Geronimo Gil/98 1.25 3.00
62 Jay Gibbons/121 1.00 2.50
63 Travis Driskill/78 1.50 4.00
65 Eddie Murray/124 1.50 4.00
66 Hoyt Wilhelm/143 1.50 4.00
67 Bobby Doerr/27 4.00 10.00
71 Trot Nixon/136 1.00 2.50
73 John Burkett/124 1.00 2.50
74 Tim Wakefield/134 1.50 4.00
76 Cliff Floyd/150 1.00 2.50
77 Casey Fossum/101 1.25 3.00
78 Johnny Damon/178 1.50 4.00
82 Manny Ramirez/107 3.00 8.00
84 Jorge De La Rosa/110 1.25 3.00
85 Shea Hillenbrand/186 1.00 2.50
87 Jason Varitek/124 2.50 6.00
88 Carlos Baerga/52 1.50 4.00
90 Ugueth Urbina/71 1.50 4.00
91 Rey Sanchez/102 1.25 3.00
93 Tony Clark/57 1.50 4.00
95 Ryne Sandberg/123 5.00 12.00
96 Fred McGriff/143 1.50 4.00
97 Alex Gonzalez/127 1.00 2.50
98 Mark Bellhorn/115 1.25 3.00
100 Jon Lieber/87 1.25 3.00
104 Andre Dawson Cubs/49 3.00 8.00
105 Carlos Zambrano/93 2.00 5.00
107 Ernie Banks/143 2.50 6.00
111 Moises Alou/133 1.00 2.50
113 Corey Patterson/150 1.00 2.50
114 Sammy Sosa/49 5.00 12.00
116 Juan Cruz/81 1.25 3.00
118 Billy Williams/137 1.50 4.00
119 Antonio Alfonseca/61 1.50 4.00
120 Matt Clement/215 .75 2.00
121 Carlton Fisk White Sox/107 2.00 5.00
122 Joe Crede/57 1.50 4.00
123 Maggio Ordonez/38 3.00 8.00
124 Frank Thomas/132 2.50 6.00
126 Royce Clayton/86 1.25 3.00
127 Luis Aparicio/92 2.00 5.00
130 Paul Konerko/173 1.50 4.00
131 Matt Ginter/37 2.00 5.00
132 Carlos Lee/130 1.00 2.50
134 Adam Dunn/26 4.00 10.00
135 Eric Davis/27 2.50 6.00
136 Johnny Bench/40 5.00 12.00
139 Barry Larkin/124 1.50 4.00
140 Ken Griffey Jr. Reds/52 8.00 20.00
141 Luis Pineda/31 2.50 6.00
142 Corky Miller/29 2.50 6.00
145 Lance Davis/78 1.50 4.00
146 Tom Seaver Reds/61 2.50 6.00
148 Sean Casey/111 1.25 3.00
149 Tony Perez/79 2.50 6.00
150 Todd Walker/183 1.00 2.50
151 Aaron Boone/146 1.00 2.50
152 Jose Rijo/38 2.00 5.00
153 Ryan Dempster/151 1.00 2.50
154 Danny Graves/58 1.50 4.00
155 Matt Lawton/98 1.25 3.00
157 Ryan Drese/102 1.25 3.00
158 Danys Baez/130 1.00 2.50
159 Einar Diaz/66 1.50 4.00
160 Milton Bradley/81 1.25 3.00
162 Ellis Burks/156 1.00 2.50
163 Lou Boudreau/46 3.00 8.00
164 Bob Feller/27 4.00 10.00
168 Omar Vizquel/160 1.50 4.00
170 C.C. Sabathia/149 1.50 4.00
173 Jim Thome/52 2.50 6.00
174 Rene Reyes/133 1.00 2.50
175 Juan Uribe/136 1.00 2.50
177 Juan Pierre/170 1.00 2.50
179 Jose Ortiz/48 2.00 5.00
180 Larry Walker/26 4.00 10.00
181 Cam Esslinger/29 2.50 6.00
182 Todd Helton/30 4.00 10.00
186 Mike Rivera/30 2.50 6.00
187 Bobby Higginson/125 1.00 2.50
189 Al Kaline/137 1.50 4.00
190 Carlos Pena/96 2.00 5.00
191 Alan Trammell/55 2.50 6.00
192 Mike Maroth/58 1.50 4.00
193 Adam Pettyjohn/40 2.00 5.00
194 David Espinosa/155 1.25 3.00
195 Adam Bernero/69 1.50 4.00
197 Robert Fick/150 1.00 2.50
199 Luis Castillo/185 1.00 2.50
200 Preston Wilson/124 1.00 2.50
202 Brad Penny/93 1.25 3.00
204 Charles Johnson/53 1.50 4.00
205 Wilson Valdez/98 1.25 3.00
206 A.J. Burnett/203 .75 2.00
208 Mike Lowell/165 1.00 2.50
209 Jose Cueto/47 2.00 5.00
211 Jeff Bagwell/31 4.00 10.00
212 Kirk Saarloos/54 1.50 4.00
214 Rodrigo Rosario/94 1.25 3.00
216 John Buck/116 1.25 3.00
217 Tim Redding/63 1.50 4.00
218 Morgan Ensberg/32 2.50 6.00
219 Richard Hidalgo/91 1.25 3.00
220 Wade Miller/144 1.00 2.50
221 Lance Berkman/42 3.00 8.00
223 Carlos Hernandez/93 1.25 3.00
224 Greg Miller/51 1.50 4.00
225 Tom Shearn/80 1.50 4.00
227 Nolan Ryan Astros/38 15.00 40.00
228 Billy Wagner/88 1.25 3.00
229 Octavio Dotel/118 1.25 3.00
230 Shane Reynolds/47 2.00 5.00
231 Julio Lugo/84 1.25 3.00
232 Daryle Ward/125 1.00 2.50
233 Mike Sweeney/160 1.00 2.50
235 George Brett/45 10.00 25.00
236 Brad Voyles/26 2.50 6.00
237 Brandon Berger/27 2.50 6.00
240 Jeremy Affeldt/67 1.50 4.00
241 Bo Jackson/32 6.00 15.00
243 Tony Cogan/62 1.50 4.00
244 Carlos Beltran/174 1.50 4.00
245 Joe Randa/155 1.00 2.50
246 Pee Wee Reese/33 4.00 10.00
247 Andy Ashby/107 1.25 3.00
248 Cesar Izturis/102 1.25 3.00
249 Duke Snider/136 1.50 4.00
250 Mark Grudzielanek/145 1.00 2.50
252 Brian Jordan/134 1.00 2.50
253 Steve Garvey/115 1.25 3.00
254 Odalis Perez/155 1.00 2.50
256 Kevin Brown/58 1.50 4.00
257 Eric Karros/142 1.00 2.50
260 Shawn Green/42 2.00 5.00
261 Paul Lo Duca/163 1.00 2.50
264 Eric Gagne/114 1.25 3.00
266 Orel Hershiser/59 1.50 4.00
267 Dave Roberts/157 2.00 5.00
268 Adrian Beltre/151 2.50 6.00
269 Don Drysdale/29 2.50 6.00
270 Jackie Robinson/39 5.00 12.00
271 Tyler Houston/90 1.25 3.00
272 Omar Daal/105 1.25 3.00
273 Marquis Grissom/95 1.25 3.00
274 Paul Quantrill/53 1.50 4.00
275 Paul Molitor/114 3.00 8.00
276 Jose Hernandez/151 1.00 2.50
278 Nick Neugebauer/47 2.00 5.00
279 Jose Mieses/55 1.50 4.00
280 Richie Sexson/102 1.25 3.00
283 Ben Sheets/170 1.00 2.50
285 Geoff Jenkins/59 1.50 4.00
286 Robin Yount/29 6.00 15.00
287 Jeff Deardorff/108 1.25 3.00
288 Luis Rivas/81 1.25 3.00
289 Harmon Killebrew/44 5.00 12.00
290 Michael Cuddyer/29 2.50 6.00
291 Torii Hunter/29 2.50 6.00
293 Adam Johnson/112 1.25 3.00
295 Rod Carew Twins/128 1.50 4.00
296 Kirby Puckett/31 6.00 15.00
297 Joe Mays/38 2.00 5.00
298 Jacque Jones/173 1.00 2.50
299 Cristian Guzman/170 1.00 2.50
300 Kyle Lohse/124 1.00 2.50
301 Eric Milton/121 1.00 2.50
302 Brad Radke/62 1.50 4.00
303 Doug Mientkiewicz/122 1.00 2.50
304 Corey Koskie/131 1.00 2.50
306 Claudio Vargas/95 1.25 3.00
307 Gary Carter Expos/105 2.00 5.00
308 Andre Dawson Expos/107 2.00 5.00
310 Andres Galarraga/76 2.50 6.00
312 Bartolo Colon/149 1.00 2.50
313 Endy Chavez/37 2.00 5.00
314 Javier Vazquez/179 1.00 2.50
315 Michael Barrett/99 1.25 3.00
316 Vladimir Guerrero/39 3.00 8.00
317 Orlando Cabrera/148 1.00 2.50
318 Al Leiter/172 1.00 2.50
319 Timo Perez/131 1.00 2.50
320 Rey Ordonez/117 2.00 5.00
322 Armando Benitez/79 1.50 4.00
324 Pedro Astacio/152 1.00 2.50
326 Edgardo Alfonzo/151 1.00 2.50
327 Nolan Ryan Mets/92 10.00 25.00
328 Mo Vaughn/126 1.00 2.50
329 Ryan Jamison/90 1.25 3.00
330 Satoru Komiyama/33 2.50 6.00
331 Mike Piazza/33 6.00 15.00
335 Babe Ruth/60 10.00 25.00
337 Andy Pettitte/97 2.00 5.00
338 Mariano Rivera/45 6.00 15.00
339 Robin Ventura/115 1.25 3.00
340 Yogi Berra/30 6.00 15.00
341 Phil Rizzuto/36 4.00 10.00
343 Alfonso Soriano/39 3.00 8.00
345 Erick Almonte/97 1.25 3.00
346 Rondell White/109 1.25 3.00

348 Joe Torre Yankees/103 2.00 5.00
350 Raul Mondesi/65 1.50 4.00
351 Brandon Claussen/73 1.50 4.00
354 Don Mattingly/53 8.00 20.00
355 Jason Giambi/41 2.00 5.00
357 Jeff Weaver/132 1.00 2.50
360 David Wells/137 1.00 2.50
361 Enos Slaughter Yankees/148 1.50 4.00
363 Eric Chavez/161 1.00 2.50
364 Miguel Tejada/34 4.00 10.00
366 Bert Snow/54 1.50 4.00
367 Rickey Henderson A's/108 3.00 8.00
368 Juan Pena/34 2.50 6.00
369 Terrence Long/141 1.00 2.50
370 Dennis Eckersley A's/33 4.00 10.00
371 Mark Ellis/94 1.25 3.00
373 Jose Canseco/100 2.00 5.00
374 Reggie Jackson A's/117 2.00 5.00
376 David Justice/106 1.25 3.00
377 Jermaine Dye/123 1.00 2.50
378 Brett Myers/34 2.50 6.00
380 Vicente Padilla/128 1.00 2.50
382 Pat Burrell/37 2.00 5.00
383 Jorge Padilla/124 1.00 2.50
384 Jeremy Giambi/81 1.25 3.00
385 Mike Lieberthal/133 1.00 2.50
386 Anderson Machado/113 1.25 3.00
390 Elio Serrano/45 2.00 5.00
391 Jimmy Rollins/156 1.50 4.00
392 Brandon Duckworth 167 1.00 2.50
393 Robin Roberts/28 4.00 10.00
394 Marlon Anderson 139 1.00 2.50
395 Robert Person/61 1.50 4.00
397 Mike Schmidt/30 10.00 25.00
399 Jason Michaels/28 2.50 6.00
401 Placido Polanco/158 1.00 2.50
402 John Grabow/97 1.25 3.00
403 Tomas De La Rosa/78 1.50 4.00
404 Tike Redman/84 1.25 3.00
405 Willie Stargell/48 3.00 8.00
406 Dave Williams/33 2.50 6.00
407 John Candelaria/177 1.00 2.50
408 Jack Wilson/133 1.00 2.50
409 Matt Guerrier/130 1.00 2.50
410 Jason Kendall/154 1.00 2.50
411 Josh Fogg/113 1.25 3.00
412 Aramis Ramirez/122 1.00 2.50
413 Dave Parker/125 1.00 2.50
414 Roberto Clemente/29 15.00 40.00
415 Kip Wells/134 1.00 2.50
416 Brian Giles/148 1.00 2.50
417 Honus Wagner/61 4.00 10.00
418 Ramon Vazquez/116 1.25 3.00
419 Oliver Perez/94 1.25 3.00
420 Ryan Klesko/162 1.00 2.50
421 Brian Lawrence/149 1.00 2.50
423 Ozzie Smith Padres/40 6.00 15.00
424 Dennis Tankersley/39 2.00 5.00
425 Tony Gwynn/49 5.00 12.00
426 Sean Burroughs/52 1.50 4.00
427 Xavier Nady/136 1.00 2.50
428 Phil Nevin/116 1.25 3.00
429 Trevor Hoffman/69 2.50 6.00
430 Jake Peavy/90 1.25 3.00
432 Kenny Lofton/139 1.00 2.50
433 Mel Ott/151 2.50 6.00
434 Tsuyoshi Shinjo/86 1.25 3.00
435 Deivis Santos/152 1.00 2.50
436 Rich Aurilia/138 1.00 2.50
437 Will Clark Giants/116 2.00 5.00
438 Pedro Feliz/37 2.00 5.00
439 J.T. Snow/104 1.25 3.00
440 Robb Nen/81 1.25 3.00
441 Carlos Valderrama/127 1.00 2.50
442 Willie McCovey/126 1.50 4.00
443 Jeff Kent/37 2.00 5.00
444 Orlando Cepeda/96 2.00 5.00
445 Barry Bonds/46 8.00 20.00
446 Alex Rodriguez M's/46 6.00 15.00
447 Allan Simpson/99 1.25 3.00
448 Antonio Perez/62 1.50 4.00
449 Edgar Martinez/91 2.00 5.00
450 Freddy Garcia/181 1.00 2.50
452 Matt Thornton/44 2.00 5.00
453 Kazuhiro Sasaki/73 1.50 4.00
454 Harold Reynolds/60 1.50 4.00
455 Randy Johnson M's/53 4.00 10.00
456 Bret Boone/169 1.00 2.50
457 Rafael Soriano/32 2.50 6.00
459 Ken Griffey Jr. M's/56 8.00 20.00
460 Ichiro Suzuki/51 5.00 12.00
461 Jamie Moyer/147 1.00 2.50
462 Joel Pineiro/136 1.00 2.50
463 Jeff Cirillo/121 1.00 2.50
464 John Olerud/166 1.00 2.50
465 Mike Cameron/130 1.00 2.50
466 Ruben Sierra/113 1.25 3.00
467 Mark McLemore/91 1.25 3.00
468 Carlos Guillen/124 1.00 2.50
469 Dan Wilson /106 1.25 3.00
470 Shigetoshi Hasegawa/39 2.00 5.00
471 Ben Davis/59 1.50 4.00
472 Ozzie Smith Cards/57 5.00 12.00
473 Matt Morris/171 1.00 2.50
474 Edgar Renteria/166 1.00 2.50
475 Les Walrond/142 1.00 2.50
476 Albert Pujols/34 8.00 20.00
477 Stan Musial/31 10.00 25.00
478 J.D. Drew/107 1.25 3.00
480 Enos Slaughter Cards/130 1.50 4.00
481 Jason Simontacchi/72 1.50 4.00
483 Tino Martinez/134 1.00 2.50
484 Rogers Hornsby/42 3.00 8.00
485 Rick Ankiel/27 2.50 6.00
486 Jim Edmonds/148 1.50 4.00
489 Fernando Vina/168 1.00 2.50
490 Jason Isringhausen/68 1.50 4.00
491 Lou Brock/52 2.50 6.00
492 Joe Torre Cards/100 2.00 5.00
494 Chuck Finley/174 1.00 2.50
496 Ben Grieve/121 1.00 2.50
497 Toby Hall/85 1.25 3.00
498 Brent Abernathy/112 1.25 3.00
500 Felix Escalona/34 2.50 6.00
501 Matt White/58 1.50 4.00
502 Randy Winn/181 1.00 2.50
503 Carl Crawford/67 2.50 6.00
505 Joe Kennedy/109 1.25 3.00
506 Wade Boggs D-Rays/60 2.50 6.00
507 Aubrey Huff/142 1.00 2.50
508 Alex Rodriguez Rangers/57 5.00 12.00
510 Will Clark Rangers/102 2.00 5.00
511 Hank Blalock/31 2.50 6.00
512 Travis Hughes/137 1.00 2.50
515 Doug Davis/28 2.50 6.00
516 Juan Gonzalez/78 1.50 4.00
518 Mark Teixeira/69 2.50 6.00
519 Nolan Ryan Rangers/51 12.00 30.00
520 Rafael Palmeiro/43 3.00 8.00
521 Kevin Mench/95 1.25 3.00
523 Kenny Rogers/107 1.25 3.00
524 Rusty Greer/59 1.50 4.00
525 Michael Young/150 1.00 2.50
526 Carlos Delgado/33 2.50 6.00
527 Vernon Wells/167 1.00 2.50
528 Orlando Hudson/53 1.50 4.00
529 Shannon Stewart/175 1.00 2.50
530 Joe Carter/121 1.00 2.50
531 Chris Baker/42 2.00 5.00
533 Corey Thurman/56 1.50 4.00
534 Josh Phelps/82 1.25 3.00
535 Reed Johnson/46 2.00 5.00
537 Roy Halladay/168 1.50 4.00
538 Jose Cruz Jr./114 1.25 3.00
539 Kelvim Escobar/85 1.25 3.00
540 Chris Carpenter/45 3.00 8.00
541 Rickie Weeks/27 8.00 20.00
542 Hideki Matsui/50 10.00 25.00
543 Ramon Nivar/39 2.00 5.00

2003 Donruss Team Heroes Timeline Threads

STATED PRINT RUNS LISTED BELOW
1 Bobby Doerr/39 12.50 30.00
2 Phil Rizzuto/47 20.00 50.00
3 Yogi Berra/47 30.00 60.00
4 Pee Wee Reese/58 12.50 30.00
6 Al Kaline/64 20.00 50.00
7 Orlando Cepeda/65 10.00 25.00
8 Eddie Mathews/66 20.00 50.00
9 Lou Brock/66 12.50 30.00
10 Juan Marichal/67 10.00 25.00
11 Ernie Banks/68 10.00 25.00
12 Willie Stargell/68 12.50 30.00
13 Jim Palmer/69 10.00 25.00
14 Luis Aparicio/69 10.00 25.00
15 Tom Seaver/69 12.50 30.00
16 Harmon Killebrew/71 25.00 60.00
17 Joe Morgan/74 10.00 25.00
18 Brooks Robinson/76 12.50 30.00
19 Mike Schmidt/81 20.00 50.00
20 Willie McCovey/77 10.00 25.00
21 Robin Yount/78 20.00 50.00
22 Reggie Jackson/79 12.50 30.00
23 Rod Carew/85 20.00 50.00
24 Nolan Ryan/91 30.00 60.00
25 Tony Gwynn/98 12.50 30.00
26 Alex Rodriguez/100 15.00 40.00
27 Carlos Delgado/101 8.00 20.00
28 Lance Berkman/102 8.00 20.00
29 Randy Johnson/100 12.50 30.00
30 Josh Beckett/101 8.00 20.00
31 Eric Davis/89 10.00 25.00
32 Todd Helton/100 10.00 25.00
33 Jose Canseco/89 12.50 30.00
34 Mike Piazza/101 15.00 40.00
35 Fred Lynn/75 10.00 25.00
36 Mike Sweeney/101 8.00 20.00
37 Miguel Tejada/101 8.00 20.00
38 Curt Schilling/101 8.00 20.00
39 Dale Murphy/87 12.50 30.00
40 Jim Thome/101 10.00 25.00
41 Adam Dunn/102 8.00 20.00
42 Nomar Garciaparra/100 15.00 40.00
43 Vladimir Guerrero/100 12.50 30.00
44 Alfonso Soriano/102 8.00 20.00
45 Wade Boggs/90 12.50 30.00
46 Randy Johnson/89 12.50 30.00
47 Hal Newhouser/55 10.00 25.00
48 Chipper Jones/93 12.50 30.00
49 Andruw Jones/96 10.00 25.00
50 Frank Thomas/94 12.50 30.00

2004 Donruss Team Heroes

COMPLETE SET (465) 50.00 100.00
COMMON ACTIVE (1-440) .15 .40
COMMON RC (1-440) .15 .40
COMMON RETIRED (1-440) .15 .40
COMMON SP (441-465) .40 1.00
441-465 APPX. 2X TOUGHER THAN 1-440
441-465 DIST.INFO PROVIDED BY DONRUSS
1 Troy Glaus .15 .40
2 Garret Anderson .15 .40
3 John Lackey .25 .60
4 Jarrod Washburn .15 .40
5 Bengie Molina .15 .40
6 Adam Kennedy .15 .40
7 Francisco Rodriguez .25 .60
8 Darin Erstad .15 .40
9 Ramon Ortiz .15 .40
10 Chone Figgins .15 .40
11 Rich Fischer .15 .40
12 David Eckstein .15 .40
13 Troy Percival .15 .40
14 Tim Salmon .15 .40
15 Nolan Ryan Angels 1.25 3.00
16 Luis Gonzalez .15 .40
17 Matt Kata .15 .40
18 Randy Johnson .40 1.00
19 Oscar Villarreal .15 .40
20 Tim Olson .15 .40
21 Rob Hammock .15 .40
22 Alex Cintron .15 .40
23 Brian Bruney .15 .40
24 Brandon Webb .15 .40
25 Greg Aquino .15 .40
26 Shea Hillenbrand .15 .40
27 Steve Finley .15 .40
28 Rod Barajas .15 .40
29 Mike Hampton .15 .40
30 Adam LaRoche .15 .40
31 Russ Ortiz .15 .40
32 Chipper Jones .40 1.00
33 John Smoltz .40 1.00
34 Andruw Jones .15 .40
35 Bubba Nelson .15 .40
36 Johnny Estrada .15 .40
37 Marcus Giles .15 .40
38 Rafael Furcal .15 .40
39 Horacio Ramirez .15 .40
40 Dale Murphy .40 1.00
41 Gaylord Perry Braves .25 .60
42 Mark DeRosa .15 .40
43 Adam Loewen .15 .40
44 Jerry Hairston Jr. .15 .40
45 Jose Morban .15 .40
46 Daniel Cabrera .15 .40
47 Jay Gibbons .15 .40
48 Larry Bigbie .15 .40
49 Luis Matos .15 .40
50 Rodrigo Lopez .15 .40
51 Melvin Mora .15 .40
52 Cal Ripken 1.25 3.00
53 Geronimo Gil .15 .40
54 Tony Batista .15 .40
55 Jason Johnson .15 .40
56 Jason Varitek .40 1.00
57 Bill Mueller .15 .40
58 Todd Walker .15 .40
59 Trot Nixon .15 .40
60 Tim Wakefield .25 .60
61 Kevin Youkilis .15 .40
62 David Ortiz .40 1.00
63 Johnny Damon .25 .60
64 Derek Lowe .15 .40
65 Pedro Martinez .25 .60
66 Carl Yastrzemski .40 1.00
67 Bobby Doerr .25 .60
68 Matt Clement .15 .40
69 Sammy Sosa .40 1.00
70 Randall Simon .15 .40
71 Nate Frese .15 .40
72 Carlos Zambrano .25 .60
73 Moises Alou .15 .40
74 Mark Prior .25 .60
75 Jason DuBois .15 .40
76 Nic Jackson .15 .40
77 Corey Patterson .15 .40
78 John Webb .15 .40
79 Kerry Wood .15 .40
80 Aramis Ramirez .15 .40
81 Brendan Harris .15 .40
82 Kenny Lofton .15 .40
83 Alex Gonzalez .15 .40
84 Gary Matthews Sr. .15 .40
85 Mark Grace .25 .60
86 Mark Grudzielanek .15 .40
87 Joe Borowski .15 .40
88 Joe Crede .15 .40
89 Mark Buehrle .25 .60
90 Paul Konerko .25 .60
91 Maggio Ordonez .25 .60
92 Corwin Malone .15 .40
93 Frank.Thomas .40 1.00
94 Jose Valentin .15 .40
95 Miguel Olivo .15 .40
96 Esteban Loaiza .15 .40
97 Carlos Lee .15 .40
98 Harold Baines .25 .60
99 Jason LaRue .15 .40
100 Sean Casey .15 .40
101 Adam Dunn .25 .60
102 Josh Hall .15 .40
103 Danny Graves .15 .40
104 Barry Larkin .25 .60
105 Ken Griffey Jr. .75 2.00
106 Brandon Claussen .15 .40
107 Austin Kearns .15 .40
108 D'Angelo Jimenez .15 .40
109 Ryan Wagner .15 .40
110 Tim Hummel .15 .40
111 Johnny Bench .40 1.00
112 Eric Davis .15 .40
113 Jose Rijo .15 .40
114 Travis Hafner .15 .40
115 Jody Gerut .15 .40
116 Fernando Cabrera .15 .40
117 Jhonny Peralta .15 .40
118 Ryan Church .15 .40
119 Francisco Cruceta .15 .40
120 Omar Vizquel .25 .60
121 Jason Davis .15 .40
122 Jeremy Guthrie .15 .40
123 C.C. Sabathia .25 .60
124 Milton Bradley .15 .40
125 Cliff Lee .25 .60
126 Victor Martinez .25 .60
127 Bob Feller .25 .60
128 Casey Blake .15 .40
129 Josh Bard .15 .40
130 Billy Traber .15 .40
131 Coco Crisp .15 .40
132 Larry Walker .25 .60
133 Jason Jennings .15 .40
134 Garrett Atkins .15 .40
135 Rene Reyes .15 .40
136 Chin-Hui Tsao .15 .40
137 Preston Wilson .15 .40
138 Jeff Baker .15 .40
139 Charles Johnson .15 .40
140 Shawn Chacon .15 .40
141 Todd Helton .25 .60
142 Jay Payton .15 .40
143 Omar Infante .15 .40
144 Bobby Higginson .15 .40
145 Dmitri Young .15 .40
146 Jorge Cordova .15 .40
147 Jeremy Bonderman .15 .40
148 Brandon Inge .15 .40
149 Franklyn German .15 .40
150 Nook Logan .15 .40
151 Alex Sanchez .15 .40
152 Craig Monroe .15 .40
153 Preston Larrison .15 .40
154 Carlos Pena .25 .60
155 Alan Trammell .25 .60
156 Jack Morris .25 .60
157 Eric Munson .15 .40
158 Mike Maroth .15 .40
159 Josh Beckett .15 .40
160 Josh Willingham .25 .60
161 Mike Lowell .15 .40
162 Luis Castillo .15 .40
163 Wilson Valdez .15 .40
164 Miguel Cabrera .40 1.00
165 Alex Gonzalez .15 .40
166 Carl Pavano .15 .40
167 Dontrelle Willis .15 .40
168 Juan Pierre .15 .40
169 Juan Encarnacion .15 .40
170 Brad Penny .15 .40
171 Ivan Rodriguez Marlins .25 .60
172 Josh Wilson .15 .40
173 Jeff Conine .15 .40
174 Mark Redman .15 .40
175 A.J. Burnett .15 .40
176 Jeff Bagwell .25 .60
177 Octavio Dotel .15 .40
178 Craig Biggio .25 .60
179 John Buck .15 .40
180 Rodrigo Rosario .15 .40
181 Tommy Whiteman .15 .40
182 Kirk Saarloos .15 .40
183 Jason Lane .15 .40
184 Wade Miller .15 .40
185 Lance Berkman .25 .60
186 Roy Oswalt .25 .60
187 Tim Redding .15 .40
188 Jeff Kent .15 .40
189 Chris Burke .15 .40
190 Morgan Ensberg .15 .40
191 Nolan Ryan Astros 1.25 3.00
192 Geoff Blum .15 .40
193 Jeremy Affeldt .15 .40
194 Mike Sweeney .15 .40
195 Angel Berroa .15 .40
196 Jimmy Gobble .15 .40
197 Ken Harvey .15 .40
198 Carlos Beltran .25 .60
199 Alexis Gomez .15 .40
200 Byron Gettis .15 .40
201 Mike MacDougal .15 .40
202 David DeJesus .15 .40
203 Runelvys Hernandez .15 .40
204 George Brett .75 2.00
205 Amos Otis .15 .40
206 Joe Randa .15 .40
207 Aaron Guiel .15 .40
208 Eric Gagne .15 .40
209 Shawn Green .15 .40
210 Kevin Brown .15 .40
211 Cesar Izturis .15 .40
212 Kazuhisa Ishii .15 .40
213 Joe Thurston .15 .40
214 Odalis Perez .15 .40
215 Rickey Henderson .40 1.00
216 Hideo Nomo .40 1.00
217 Hong-Chi Kuo .15 .40
218 Edwin Jackson .15 .40
219 Paul Lo Duca .15 .40
220 Adrian Beltre .40 1.00
221 Duke Snider .25 .60
222 Steve Garvey .15 .40
223 Rickie Weeks .15 .40
224 Bill Hall .15 .40
225 Doug Davis .15 .40
226 Geoff Jenkins .15 .40
227 Matt Childers .15 .40
228 Dan Kolb .15 .40
229 Scott Podsednik .15 .40
230 Pedro Liriano .15 .40
231 Ben Sheets .15 .40
232 Robin Yount .40 1.00
233 Gorman Thomas .15 .40
234 Ben Oglivie .15 .40
235 Matt LeCroy .15 .40
236 Cristian Guzman .15 .40
237 Lew Ford .15 .40
238 J.C. Romero .15 .40
239 Rob Bowen .15 .40
240 Corey Koskie .15 .40
241 Jacque Jones .15 .40
242 Brad Radke .15 .40
243 Shannon Stewart .15 .40
244 J.D. Durbin .15 .40
245 Doug Mientkiewicz .15 .40
246 Jason Kubel .15 .40
247 Torii Hunter .15 .40
248 Johan Santana .25 .60
249 Kirby Puckett .40 1.00
250 Luis Rivas .15 .40
251 Orlando Cabrera .15 .40
252 Tony Armas Jr. .15 .40
253 Brad Wilkerson .15 .40
254 Endy Chavez .15 .40
255 Jose Vidro .15 .40
256 Zach Day .15 .40
257 Livan Hernandez .15 .40
258 Termel Sledge .15 .40
259 Michael Barrett .15 .40
260 Gary Carter .25 .60
261 Andre Dawson .25 .60
262 Craig Brazell .15 .40
263 Mike Piazza .40 1.00
264 Jeff Duncan .15 .40
265 Jason Anderson .15 .40
266 Tom Glavine .25 .60
267 Danny Garcia .15 .40
268 Ty Wigginton .15 .40
269 Al Leiter .15 .40
270 Jeremy Griffiths .15 .40
271 Jose Reyes .25 .60
272 Prentice Redman .15 .40
273 Cliff Floyd .15 .40
274 Jae Seo .15 .40
275 Nolan Ryan Mets 1.25 3.00
276 Keith Hernandez .15 .40
277 Jason Phillips .15 .40
278 Kazuo Matsui RC .25 .60
279 Jose Contreras .15 .40
280 Aaron Boone .15 .40
281 Mike Mussina .25 .60
282 Jason Giambi .15 .40
283 Hideki Matsui .60 1.50
284 Derek Jeter 1.00 2.50
285 Mariano Rivera .50 1.25
286 Chien-Ming Wang .60 1.50
287 Bernie Williams .25 .60
288 Alfonso Soriano Yanks .25 .60
289 Jorge Posada .25 .60
290 Michel Hernandez .15 .40
291 Erik Almonte .15 .40
292 Don Mattingly .75 2.00
293 Roger Clemens Yanks .50 1.25
294 Gaylord Perry Rgr .25 .60
295 Tommy John .15 .40
296 Tim Hudson .25 .60
297 Rich Harden .15 .40
298 Eric Chavez .15 .40
299 Adam Morrissey .15 .40
300 Mark Mulder .15 .40
301 Eric Byrnes .15 .40
302 Jermaine Dye .15 .40
303 Barry Zito .25 .60
304 Erubiel Durazo .15 .40
305 Mark Ellis .15 .40
306 Bobby Crosby .15 .40
307 Shane Bazzell .15 .40
308 Mario Ramos .15 .40
309 Jose Canseco .25 .60
310 Placido Polanco .15 .40
311 Jimmy Rollins .25 .60
312 Jim Thome .25 .60
313 Brett Myers .15 .40
314 Jason Michaels .15 .40
315 Vicente Padilla .15 .40
316 Bobby Abreu .15 .40
317 Ryan Howard .30 .75
318 Chase Utley .25 .60
319 Pat Burrell .15 .40
320 Randy Wolf .15 .40
321 Franklin Perez .15 .40
322 Marlon Byrd .15 .40
323 Kevin Millwood .15 .40
324 Mike Lieberthal .15 .40
325 Anderson Machado .15 .40
326 Travis Chapman .15 .40
327 Steve Carlton .25 .60
328 Greg Luzinski .15 .40
329 David Bell .15 .40
330 Craig Wilson .15 .40
331 Kris Benson .15 .40
332 Jose Castillo .15 .40
333 Josh Fogg .15 .40
334 Jason Kendall .15 .40
335 Walter Young .15 .40
336 Oliver Perez .15 .40
337 Jason Bay .25 .60
338 Duaner Sanchez .15 .40
339 Jack Wilson .15 .40
340 Carlos Rivera .15 .40
341 Kip Wells .15 .40
342 Freddy Sanchez .15 .40
343 Roberto Clemente 1.00 2.50
344 Al Oliver .15 .40
345 Phil Nevin .15 .40
346 Trevor Hoffman .25 .60
347 Ryan Klesko .15 .40
348 Khalil Greene .25 .60
349 Freddy Guzman RC .15 .40
350 Brian Giles .15 .40
351 Brian Lawrence .15 .40
352 Sean Burroughs .15 .40
353 Ben Howard .15 .40
354 Xavier Nady .15 .40
355 Mark Loretta .15 .40
356 Ramon Vazquez .15 .40
357 Tony Gwynn .40 1.00
358 Adam Eaton .15 .40
359 Merkin Valdez RC .15 .40
360 Kevin Correia .15 .40
361 Edgardo Alfonzo .15 .40
362 Mike Cameron .15 .40
363 Ray Durham .15 .40
364 Jesse Foppert .15 .40
365 Robb Nen .15 .40
366 Marquis Grissom .15 .40
367 Jerome Williams .15 .40
368 Jason Schmidt .15 .40
369 Will Clark .25 .60
370 Bret Boone .15 .40
371 Freddy Garcia .15 .40
372 Dan Wilson .15 .40
373 Rhett Johnson .15 .40
374 Kazuhiro Sasaki .15 .40
375 Ichiro Suzuki .50 1.25
376 Edgar Martinez .25 .60
377 Jamie Moyer .15 .40
378 Joel Pineiro .15 .40
379 Carlos Guillen .15 .40
380 Randy Winn .15 .40
381 J.J. Putz .15 .40
382 John Olerud .15 .40
383 Matt Thornton .15 .40
384 Rafael Soriano .15 .40
385 Gil Meche .15 .40
386 Albert Pujols .50 1.25
387 Woody Williams .15 .40
388 Dan Haren .15 .40
389 Matt Morris .15 .40
390 Jim Edmonds .25 .60
391 Edgar Renteria .15 .40
392 Scott Rolen .25 .60
393 J.D. Drew .15 .40
394 Bo Hart .15 .40
395 Stan Musial .60 1.50
396 Red Schoendienst .25 .60
397 Terry Pendleton .15 .40
398 Mike Matheny .15 .40
399 Dewon Brazelton .15 .40
400 Chad Gaudin .15 .40
401 Aubrey Huff .15 .40
402 Victor Zambrano .15 .40
403 Antonio Perez .15 .40
404 Carl Crawford .25 .60
405 Joe Kennedy .15 .40
406 Pete LaForest .15 .40
407 Delmon Young .25 .60
408 Rocco Baldelli .15 .40
409 Doug Waechter .15 .40
410 Brian Stokes .15 .40
411 Edwin Almonte .15 .40
412 Toby Hall .15 .40
413 Lance Carter .15 .40
414 Greg Maddux Braves .50 1.25
415 Hank Blalock .15 .40
416 Colby Lewis .15 .40
417 Mark Teixeira .25 .60
418 Gerald Laird .15 .40
419 Ricardo Rodriguez .15 .40
420 Ben Kozlowski .15 .40
421 Kevin Mench .15 .40
422 Michael Young .15 .40
423 Ramon Nivar .15 .40
424 Laynce Nix .15 .40
425 Nolan Ryan Rgr 1.25 3.00
426 Einar Diaz .15 .40
427 Carlos Delgado .15 .40
428 Eric Hinske .15 .40
429 Dustin McGowan .15 .40
430 Frank Catalanotto .15 .40
431 Kevin Cash .15 .40
432 Roy Halladay .25 .60
433 Orlando Hudson .15 .40
434 Francisco Rosario .15 .40
435 Guillermo Quiroz .15 .40
436 Vernon Wells .15 .40
437 Josh Phelps .15 .40
438 Alexis Rios .15 .40
439 Reed Johnson .15 .40
440 Chris Woodward .15 .40
441 Bartolo Colon SP .40 1.00
442 Richie Sexson SP .40 1.00
443 Greg Maddux Cubs SP 1.25 3.00
444 Javy Lopez SP .40 1.00
445 Gary Sheffield SP .40 1.00
446 Curt Schilling SP .60 1.50
447 Nomar Garciaparra SP .60 1.50
448 Manny Ramirez SP 1.00 2.50
449 Derrek Lee SP .40 1.00
450 Roberto Alomar SP .60 1.50
451 Ivan Rodriguez Tigers SP .60 1.50
452 Junior Spivey SP .40 1.00
453 Alfonso Soriano Rgr SP .60 1.50
454 Vladimir Guerrero SP .60 1.50
455 Nick Johnson SP .40 1.00
456 Javier Vazquez SP .40 1.00
457 Andy Pettitte SP .60 1.50
458 Miguel Tejada SP .60 1.50
459 Rich Aurilia SP .40 1.00
460 A.J. Pierzynski SP .40 1.00
461 Raul Ibanez SP .60 1.50
462 Roger Clemens Astros SP 1.25 3.00
463 Juan Gonzalez SP .40 1.00
464 Rafael Palmeiro SP .60 1.50
465 Alex Rodriguez Yanks SP 1.25 3.00

2004 Donruss Team Heroes Autographs

STATED ODDS 1:24
#'d CARD PRINTS B/WN 1-86 COPIES PER
NO PRICING ON QTY OF 48 OR LESS
10 Chone Figgins 6.00 15.00
11 Rich Fischer 3.00 8.00
17 Matt Kata 3.00 8.00
19 Oscar Villarreal 3.00 8.00
20 Tim Olson 3.00 8.00
21 Rob Hammock/57 4.00 10.00
23 Brian Bruney 3.00 8.00
25 Greg Aquino 3.00 8.00
35 Bubba Nelson 3.00 8.00
45 Jose Morban 3.00 8.00
46 Daniel Cabrera 3.00 8.00
61 Kevin Youkilis/50 4.00 10.00
71 Nate Frese 3.00 8.00
75 Jason DuBois 3.00 8.00
76 Nic Jackson 3.00 8.00
78 John Webb 3.00 8.00
81 Brendan Harris 3.00 8.00
84 Gary Matthews Sr. 6.00 15.00
92 Corwin Malone 3.00 8.00
106 Brandon Claussen 3.00 8.00
110 Tim Hummel 3.00 8.00
116 Fernando Cabrera 3.00 8.00
117 Jhonny Peralta 4.00 10.00
118 Ryan Church 4.00 10.00
119 Francisco Cruceta/75 4.00 10.00
146 Jorge Cordova 3.00 8.00
149 Franklyn German 3.00 8.00
150 Nook Logan 3.00 8.00
153 Preston Larrison 3.00 8.00
160 Josh Willingham 3.00 8.00
163 Wilson Valdez 3.00 8.00
172 Josh Wilson 3.00 8.00
180 Rodrigo Rosario 3.00 8.00
181 Tommy Whiteman 3.00 8.00
189 Chris Burke 4.00 10.00
197 Ken Harvey 3.00 8.00
200 Byron Gettis 3.00 8.00
205 Amos Otis 6.00 15.00
211 Cesar Izturis 3.00 8.00
225 Doug Davis 3.00 8.00
227 Matt Childers 3.00 8.00
230 Pedro Liriano 3.00 8.00
233 Gorman Thomas 6.00 15.00
234 Ben Oglivie/86 8.00 20.00
237 Lew Ford 3.00 8.00
238 J.C. Romero 3.00 8.00
239 Rob Bowen 3.00 8.00
246 Jason Kubel/50 4.00 10.00
258 Terrmel Sledge 3.00 8.00
262 Craig Brazell 3.00 8.00
264 Jeff Duncan 3.00 8.00
265 Jason Anderson 3.00 8.00
267 Danny Garcia 3.00 8.00
270 Jeremy Griffiths 3.00 8.00
272 Prentice Redman 3.00 8.00
291 Erik Almonte/66 4.00 10.00
307 Shane Bazzell 3.00 8.00
308 Mario Ramos 3.00 8.00
321 Franklin Perez 3.00 8.00
325 Anderson Machado/50 4.00 10.00
326 Travis Chapman 3.00 8.00
328 Greg Luzinski 6.00 15.00
331 Kris Benson 4.00 10.00
335 Walter Young/67 4.00 10.00
338 Duaner Sanchez 3.00 8.00
353 Ben Howard 3.00 8.00
359 Merkin Valdez/50 6.00 15.00
360 Kevin Correia 3.00 8.00
373 Rhett Johnson/76 4.00 10.00
381 J.J. Putz 3.00 8.00
383 Matt Thornton/50 4.00 10.00
384 Rafael Soriano 3.00 8.00
406 Pete LaForest 3.00 8.00
410 Brian Stokes 3.00 8.00
411 Edwin Almonte 3.00 8.00
419 Ricardo Rodriguez 3.00 8.00
420 Ben Kozlowski 3.00 8.00
431 Kevin Cash 3.00 8.00

2004 Donruss Team Heroes Showdown Bronze

*BRONZE 1-440: 2.5X TO 6X BASIC
*BRONZE 1-440: 2X TO 5X BASIC RC
*BRONZE 441-465: 1X TO 2.5X BASIC SP
RANDOM INSERTS IN PACKS
STATED PRINT RUN 150 SERIAL #'d SETS

2004 Donruss Team Heroes Showdown Silver

*SILVER 1-440: 4X TO 10X BASIC
*SILVER 1-440: 3X TO 8X BASIC RC
*SILVER 441-465: 1.5X TO 4X BASIC SP
RANDOM INSERTS IN PACKS
STATED PRINT RUN 50 SERIAL #'d SETS

2005 Donruss Team Heroes

COMPLETE SET (440) 50.00 100.00
COMMON CARD (1-440) .15 .40
COMMON RC .15 .40
COMMON RETIRED .15 .40
1 Adam Kennedy .15 .40
2 Bartolo Colon .15 .40
3 Bengie Molina .15 .40
4 Casey Kotchman .15 .40
5 Chone Figgins .15 .40
6 Dallas McPherson .15 .40
7 Darin Erstad .15 .40
8 David Eckstein .15 .40
9 Francisco Rodriguez .25 .60
10 Garret Anderson .15 .40
11 Jarrod Washburn .15 .40
12 John Lackey .25 .60
13 Jose Guillen .15 .40
14 Robb Quinlan .15 .40
15 Tim Bittner .15 .40
16 Tim Salmon .15 .40
17 Vladimir Guerrero .25 .60
18 Alex Cintron .15 .40
19 Craig Counsell .15 .40
20 Brandon Webb .25 .60
21 Chad Tracy .15 .40
22 Doug Devore .15 .40
23 Luis Gonzalez .15 .40
24 Mark Grace .25 .60
25 Randy Johnson .40 1.00
26 Scott Hairston .15 .40
27 Shea Hillenbrand .15 .40
28 Tim Olson .15 .40
29 Adam LaRoche .15 .40
30 Andruw Jones .15 .40
31 Charles Thomas .15 .40
32 Chipper Jones .40 1.00
33 Dale Murphy .40 1.00
34 John Smoltz .40 1.00
35 Johnny Estrada .15 .40
36 Jose Capellan .15 .40
37 Marcus Giles .15 .40
38 Nick Green .15 .40
39 Phil Niekro .25 .60
40 Rafael Furcal .15 .40
41 Brian Roberts .15 .40
42 Cal Ripken 1.25 3.00
43 Javy Lopez .15 .40
44 Jay Gibbons .15 .40
45 Larry Bigbie .15 .40
46 Luis Matos .15 .40
47 Melvin Mora .15 .40
48 Miguel Tejada .25 .60
49 Rafael Palmeiro .25 .60
50 Rodrigo Lopez .15 .40
51 Sidney Ponson .15 .40
52 Abe Alvarez .15 .40
53 Bill Mueller .15 .40
54 Curt Schilling .25 .60
55 David Ortiz .40 1.00
56 Doug Mientkiewicz .15 .40
57 Dwight Evans .25 .60
58 Fred Lynn .15 .40
59 Jim Rice .25 .60
60 Johnny Damon .25 .60
61 Keith Foulke .15 .40
62 Kevin Youkilis .15 .40
63 Manny Ramirez .40 1.00
64 Tim Wakefield .25 .60
65 Trot Nixon .15 .40
66 Angel Guzman .15 .40
67 Aramis Ramirez .15 .40
68 Carlos Zambrano .25 .60
69 Corey Patterson .15 .40
70 Derrek Lee .15 .40
71 Greg Maddux .50 1.25
72 Kerry Wood .15 .40
73 Lee Smith .15 .40
74 Mark Prior .25 .60
75 Sammy Sosa .40 1.00
76 Aaron Rowand .15 .40
77 Carlos Lee .15 .40
78 Frank Thomas .40 1.00
79 Freddy Garcia .15 .40
80 Harold Baines .25 .60
81 Jose Contreras .15 .40

82 Juan Uribe .15 .40
83 Mark Buehrle .25 .60
84 Paul Konerko .25 .60
85 Shingo Takatsu .15 .40
86 Adam Dunn .25 .60
87 Austin Kearns .15 .40
88 Danny Graves .15 .40
89 Eric Davis .15 .40
90 Jacob Cruz .15 .40
91 Jason LaRue .15 .40
92 Ken Griffey Jr. .75 2.00
93 Ryan Wagner .15 .40
94 Sean Casey .15 .40
95 Casey Blake .15 .40
96 C.C. Sabathia .25 .60
97 Cliff Lee .25 .60
98 Grady Sizemore .25 .60
99 Jake Westbrook .15 .40
100 Jody Gerut .15 .40
101 Kazuhito Tadano .15 .40
102 Matt Lawton .15 .40
103 Travis Hafner .15 .40
104 Victor Martinez .25 .60
105 Charles Johnson .15 .40
106 Clint Barmes .15 .40
107 Garrett Atkins .15 .40
108 Jason Jennings .15 .40
109 Jeff Francis .15 .40
110 Joe Kennedy .15 .40
111 Matt Holliday .40 1.00
112 Preston Wilson .15 .40
113 Todd Helton .25 .60
114 Alan Trammell .25 .60
115 Bobby Higginson .15 .40
116 Brandon Inge .15 .40
117 Carlos Guillen .15 .40
118 Carlos Pena .25 .60
119 Craig Monroe .15 .40
120 Dmitri Young .15 .40
121 Eric Munson .15 .40
122 Ivan Rodriguez .25 .60
123 Jeremy Bonderman .15 .40
124 Roberto Novoa .15 .40
125 A.J. Burnett .15 .40
126 Alex Gonzalez .15 .40
127 Dontrelle Willis .15 .40
128 Guillermo Mota .15 .40
129 Josh Beckett .15 .40
130 Juan Pierre .15 .40
131 Luis Castillo .15 .40
132 Miguel Cabrera .40 1.00
133 Paul Lo Duca .15 .40
134 Adam Everett .15 .40
135 Andy Pettitte .25 .60
136 Brad Ausmus .15 .40
137 Chris Burke .15 .40
138 Craig Biggio .25 .60
139 Jeff Bagwell .25 .60
140 Lance Berkman .25 .60
141 Morgan Ensberg .15 .40
142 Nolan Ryan Astros 1.25 3.00
143 Roger Clemens .50 1.25
144 Roy Oswalt .25 .60
145 Tim Redding .15 .40
146 Wade Miller .15 .40
147 Andres Blanco .15 .40
148 Angel Berroa .15 .40
149 Benito Santiago .15 .40
150 Byron Gettis
151 George Brett .75 2.00
152 Jeremy Affeldt .15 .40
153 Ken Harvey .15 .40
154 Mike MacDougal .15 .40
155 Mike Sweeney .15 .40
156 Shawn Camp .15 .40
157 Zack Greinke .50 1.25
158 Brad Penny .15 .40
159 Cesar Izturis .15 .40
160 Edwin Jackson .15 .40
161 Eric Gagne .15 .40
162 Jerry Hairston .15 .40
163 Jeff Weaver .15 .40
164 Kazuhisa Ishii .15 .40
165 Milton Bradley .15 .40
166 Orel Hershiser .15 .40
167 Shawn Green .15 .40
168 Steve Garvey .15 .40
169 Tommy John .15 .40
170 Yhency Brazoban .15 .40
171 Ben Sheets .15 .40
172 Bill Hall .15 .40
173 Danny Kolb .15 .40
174 Lyle Overbay .15 .40
175 Paul Molitor .40 1.00
176 Robin Yount .40 1.00
177 Rollie Fingers .25 .60
178 Rickie Weeks .15 .40
179 Scott Podsednik .15 .40
180 Jack Morris .25 .60
181 Jacque Jones .15 .40
182 Jason Kubel .15 .40
183 Joe Mauer .30 .75
184 Joe Nathan .15 .40
185 Johan Santana .25 .60
186 Justin Morneau .25 .60
187 Lew Ford .15 .40
188 Matthew LeCroy .15 .40
189 Rod Carew .25 .60
190 Shannon Stewart .15 .40
191 Torii Hunter .15 .40
192 Aarom Baldiris .15 .40
193 Cliff Floyd .15 .40
194 Darryl Strawberry .15 .40
195 Dwight Gooden .15 .40
196 David Wright .30 .75
197 Victor Zambrano .15 .40
198 Jose Reyes .25 .60
199 Kazuo Matsui .15 .40
200 Keith Hernandez .15 .40
201 Mike Piazza .40 1.00
202 Tom Glavine .25 .60
203 Vance Wilson .15 .40
204 Tom Seaver .25 .60
205 Alex Rodriguez .50 1.25
206 Bernie Williams .25 .60
207 Chien-Ming Wang .60 1.50
208 Derek Jeter 1.00 2.50
209 Dioner Navarro .15 .40
210 Don Mattingly .75 2.00
211 Gary Sheffield .15 .40
212 Hideki Matsui .60 1.50
213 Jason Giambi .15 .40
214 Javier Vazquez .15 .40
215 Jim Leyritz .15 .40
216 Jorge Posada .25 .60
217 Kevin Brown .15 .40
218 Mariano Rivera .50 1.25
219 Mike Mussina .25 .60
220 Scott Proctor .15 .40
221 Tom Gordon .15 .40
222 Barry Zito .25 .60
223 Bobby Crosby .15 .40
224 Dave Stewart .15 .40
225 Dennis Eckersley .25 .60
226 Eric Byrnes .15 .40
227 Eric Chavez .15 .40
228 Erubiel Durazo .15 .40
229 Mark Kotsay .15 .40
230 Mark Mulder .15 .40
231 Octavio Dotel .15 .40
232 Rich Harden .15 .40
233 Tim Hudson .25 .60
234 Billy Wagner .15 .40
235 Bobby Abreu .15 .40
236 Brett Myers .15 .40
237 Chase Utley .25 .60
238 Jim Thome .25 .60
239 Jimmy Rollins .25 .60
240 Lenny Dykstra .15 .40
241 Marlon Byrd .15 .40
242 Mike Lieberthal .15 .40
243 Mike Schmidt .60 1.50
244 Pat Burrell .15 .40
245 Randy Wolf .15 .40
246 Ryan Howard .30 .75
247 Steve Carlton .25 .60
248 Bert Blyleven .25 .60
249 Bill Madlock .15 .40
250 Dave Parker .15 .40
251 Craig Wilson .15 .40
252 Jack Wilson .15 .40
253 Jason Bay .15 .40
254 Jason Kendall .15 .40
255 Jose Castillo .15 .40
256 Kip Wells .15 .40
257 Akinori Otsuka .15 .40
258 Brian Giles .15 .40
259 Brian Lawrence .15 .40
260 Freddy Guzman .15 .40
261 Gaylord Perry .25 .60
262 Jake Peavy .15 .40
263 Jay Payton .15 .40
264 Khalil Greene .15 .40
265 Mark Loretta .15 .40
266 Phil Nevin .15 .40
267 Ryan Klesko .15 .40
268 Sean Burroughs .15 .40
269 Tony Gwynn .50 1.25
270 Trevor Hoffman .25 .60
271 A.J. Pierzynski .15 .40
272 Dustan Mohr .15 .40
273 Edgardo Alfonzo .15 .40
274 Jason Schmidt .15 .40
275 Jerome Williams .15 .40
276 Matt Williams .25 .60
277 Merkin Valdez .15 .40
278 Todd Linden .15 .40
279 Will Clark .25 .60
280 Bret Boone .15 .40
281 Bucky Jacobsen .15 .40
282 Clint Nageotte .15 .40
283 Ichiro Suzuki .50 1.25
284 J.J. Putz .15 .40
285 Jamie Moyer .15 .40
286 Bobby Madritsch .15 .40
287 Mike Morse RC .50 1.25
288 Joel Pineiro .15 .40
289 Shigetoshi Hasegawa .15 .40
290 Travis Blackley .15 .40
291 Albert Pujols .50 1.25
292 Dan Haren .15 .40
293 Jason Isringhausen .15 .40
294 Jason Marquis .15 .40
295 Jeff Suppan .15 .40
296 Jim Edmonds .25 .60
297 Larry Walker .25 .60
298 Reggie Sanders .15 .40
299 Scott Rolen .25 .60
300 Yadier Molina 1.50 4.00
301 Aubrey Huff .15 .40
302 B.J. Upton .25 .60
303 Carl Crawford .25 .60
304 Chad Gaudin .15 .40
305 Delmon Young .40 1.00
306 Dewon Brazelton .15 .40
307 Joey Gathright .15 .40
308 Jose Cruz Jr. .15 .40
309 Rocco Baldelli .15 .40
310 Wade Boggs .25 .60
311 Adrian Gonzalez .30 .75
312 Alfonso Soriano .25 .60
313 Francisco Cordero .15 .40
314 Frankie Francisco .15 .40
315 Hank Blalock .15 .40
316 Kenny Rogers .15 .40
317 Laynce Nix .15 .40
318 Mark Teixeira .25 .60
319 Michael Young .15 .40
320 Alexis Rios .15 .40
321 Dave Bush .15 .40
322 Eric Hinske .15 .40
323 Frank Catalanotto .15 .40
324 Gabe Gross .15 .40
325 Guillermo Quiroz .15 .40
326 Rickey Henderson .40 1.00
327 Orlando Hudson .15 .40
328 Roy Halladay .25 .60
329 Ted Lilly .15 .40
330 Vernon Wells .15 .40
331 Alberto Callaspo .15 .40
332 Jeff Mathis .25 .60
333 Ervin Santana .15 .40
334 Troy Percival .15 .40
335 Troy Glaus .15 .40
336 Greg Aquino .15 .40
337 Tony Pena RC .15 .40
338 Luis Terrero .15 .40
339 J.D. Drew .15 .40
340 Jon Lieber .15 .40
341 Russ Ortiz .15 .40
342 Daniel Cabrera .15 .40
343 Kenny Lofton .15 .40
344 Val Majewski .15 .40
345 Orlando Cabrera .15 .40
346 Hanley Ramirez .25 .60
347 Jason Varitek .40 1.00
348 Pedro Martinez .25 .60
349 Derek Lowe .15 .40
350 Juan Cedeno .15 .40
351 Todd Walker .15 .40
352 Matt Clement .15 .40
353 Moises Alou .15 .40
354 Nomar Garciaparra .25 .60
355 Michael Barrett .15 .40
356 Todd Hollandsworth .15 .40
357 Jose Valentin .15 .40
358 Magglio Ordonez .25 .60
359 Pedro Lopez RC .15 .40
360 Barry Larkin .25 .60
361 Jaret Wright .15 .40
362 Elizardo Ramirez .15 .40
363 Omar Vizquel .25 .60
364 Fausto Carmona .15 .40
365 Jake Dittler .15 .40
366 Jeff Salazar .15 .40
367 Jeromy Burnitz .15 .40
368 Jayson Nix .15 .40
369 Ubaldo Jimenez RC .40 1.00
370 Vinny Castilla .15 .40
371 Justin Verlander RC 3.00 8.00
372 Armando Benitez .15 .40
373 Carl Pavano .15 .40
374 Chris Aguila .15 .40
375 Logan Kensing .15 .40
376 Mike Lowell .15 .40
377 Yorman Bazardo RC .15 .40
378 Willy Taveras .15 .40
379 Jeff Kent .15 .40
380 Carlos Beltran .25 .60
381 Kevin Millwood .15 .40
382 Juan Gonzalez .15 .40
383 Steve Finley .15 .40
384 Hideo Nomo .40 1.00
385 Adrian Beltre .40 1.00
386 Dave Krynzel .15 .40
387 Richie Sexson .15 .40
388 Jesse Crain .15 .40
389 Brad Radke .15 .40
390 Jason Lane .15 .40
391 Corey Koskie .15 .40
392 Cristian Guzman .15 .40
393 Brad Wilkerson .15 .40
394 Brendan Harris .15 .40
395 Chad Cordero .15 .40
396 Endy Chavez .15 .40
397 Jose Vidro .15 .40
398 Josh Karp .15 .40
399 Livan Hernandez .15 .40
400 Nick Johnson .15 .40
401 Ryan Church .15 .40
402 Terrmel Sledge .15 .40
403 Phil Humber RC .40 1.00
404 Ambiorix Concepcion RC .15 .40
405 Al Leiter .15 .40
406 Richard Hidalgo .15 .40
407 Kris Benson .15 .40
408 Mike Cameron .15 .40
409 Victor Diaz .15 .40
410 Tony Womack .15 .40
411 Ferdin Tejeda .15 .40
412 Nick Swisher .25 .60
413 Jairo Garcia .15 .40
414 Jermaine Dye .15 .40
415 Joe Blanton .15 .40
416 Eric Milton .15 .40
417 Gavin Floyd .15 .40
418 John Van Benschoten .15 .40
419 Matt Peterson .15 .40
420 David Wells .15 .40
421 J.T. Snow .15 .40
422 Willie Mays .75 2.00
423 Jeremy Reed .15 .40
424 Jose Lopez .15 .40
425 Raul Ibanez .25 .60
426 Wladimir Balentien RC .25 .60
427 Matt Morris .15 .40
428 Mike Matheny .15 .40
429 Edgar Renteria .15 .40
430 Woody Williams .15 .40
431 Jeff Niemann RC .40 1.00
432 Scott Kazmir .40 1.00
433 Tino Martinez .25 .60
434 Chris Young .25 .60
435 David Dellucci .15 .40
436 Kameron Loe .15 .40
437 Nolan Ryan Rgr 1.25 3.00
438 John-Ford Griffin .15 .40
439 Carlos Delgado .15 .40
440 Russ Adams .15 .40

2005 Donruss Team Heroes Showdown Blue

*BLUE: 2X TO 5X BASIC
*BLUE: 1.5X TO 4X BASIC RC'S
RANDOM INSERTS IN PACKS

2005 Donruss Team Heroes Showdown Bronze

*BRONZE: 3X TO 8X BASIC
*BRONZE: 2.5X TO 6X BASIC RC'S
RANDOM INSERTS IN PACKS
STATED PRINT RUN 100 SERIAL #'d SETS

2005 Donruss Team Heroes Showdown Red

*RED: 1.25X TO 3X BASIC
*RED: 1X TO 2.5X BASIC RC'S
RANDOM INSERTS IN PACKS

2005 Donruss Team Heroes Showdown Silver

*SILVER: 4X TO 10X BASIC
*SILVER: 3X TO 8X BASIC RC'S
RANDOM INSERTS IN PACKS
STATED PRINT RUN 50 SERIAL #'d SETS

2005 Donruss Team Heroes Autographs

RANDOM INSERTS IN PACKS
SP INFO PROVIDED BY DONRUSS
SP'S ARE NOT SERIAL-NUMBERED
SOME SP'S TOO SCARCE TO PRICE
4 Casey Kotchman SP 6.00 15.00
14 Robb Quinlan 4.00 10.00
15 Tim Bittner 4.00 10.00
18 Alex Cintron SP 6.00 15.00
22 Doug Devore 4.00 10.00
28 Tim Olson 4.00 10.00
38 Nick Green 4.00 10.00
44 Jay Gibbons SP 6.00 15.00
66 Angel Guzman 4.00 10.00
90 Jacob Cruz 4.00 10.00
97 Cliff Lee SP 6.00 15.00
101 Kazuhito Tadano 6.00 15.00
104 Victor Martinez SP 10.00 25.00
110 Joe Kennedy 4.00 10.00
116 Brandon Inge 4.00 10.00
119 Craig Monroe 4.00 10.00
124 Roberto Novoa 4.00 10.00
150 Byron Gettis SP 6.00 15.00
152 Jeremy Affeldt 4.00 10.00
156 Shawn Camp 4.00 10.00
170 Yhency Brazoban 4.00 10.00
172 Bill Hall SP 6.00 15.00
182 Jason Kubel SP 6.00 15.00
192 Aarom Baldiris SP 6.00 15.00
203 Vance Wilson 4.00 10.00
220 Scott Proctor 4.00 10.00
277 Merkin Valdez 4.00 10.00
278 Todd Linden SP 6.00 15.00
281 Bucky Jacobsen 4.00 10.00
282 Clint Nageotte 4.00 10.00
290 Travis Blackley 4.00 10.00
292 Dan Haren SP 6.00 15.00
295 Jeff Suppan 6.00 15.00
306 Dewon Brazelton 4.00 10.00
307 Joey Gathright SP 6.00 15.00
311 Adrian Gonzalez 10.00 25.00
314 Frankie Francisco 4.00 10.00
317 Laynce Nix 4.00 10.00
333 Ervin Santana 4.00 10.00
337 Tony Pena 4.00 10.00
346 Hanley Ramirez 6.00 51.00
350 Juan Cedeno 4.00 10.00
359 Pedro Lopez 4.00 10.00
364 Fausto Carmona 8.00 20.00
365 Jake Dittler 4.00 10.00
366 Jeff Salazar 4.00 10.00
368 Jayson Nix 4.00 10.00
377 Yorman Bazardo 4.00 10.00
398 Josh Karp 4.00 10.00
411 Ferdin Tejeda 4.00 10.00
419 Matt Peterson 4.00 10.00
435 David Dellucci SP 10.00 25.00
436 Kameron Loe 4.00 10.00

2005 Donruss Team Heroes Movie Gallery

RANDOM INSERT IN '05 D/P PRODUCTS
1 Cal Ripken .30 .75

1997 Donruss Team Sets

This 165-card set features color action player photos from eleven Major League teams printed on specially treated card stock with team color matching foil stamping. The set was distributed in five-card packs with a suggested retail price of $1.99. The Indians and Angels packs were sold exclusively at the respective ballparks during their home games. Due to manufacturing problems, Russ Davis (supposed to be #144) and Bernie Williams (supposed to be #131) were never printed, thus the set is complete at 163 cards.

COMP.ANGELS (1-15) .75 2.00
COMP.BRAVES (16-30) 2.00 5.00
COMP.ORIOLES (31-45) 1.25 3.00
COMP.RED SOX (46-60) 1.25 3.00
COMP.W.SOX (61-75) 2.00 3.00
COMP.INDIANS (76-90) 2.00 5.00
COMP.ROCKIES (91-105) 1.25 2.50
COMP.LA (106-120) 2.00 3.00
COMP.NYY (121-135) 2.00 5.00
COMP.SEATTLE (136-150) 2.00 5.00
COMP.CARDS (151-165) .75 2.00
CARD NUMBERS 131 AND 144 DO NOT EXIST
ANGELS/INDIANS DIST.THROUGH TEAM
1 Jim Edmonds .08 .25
2 Tim Salmon .15 .40
3 Tony Phillips .05 .15
4 Garret Anderson .08 .25
5 Troy Percival .08 .25
6 Mark Langston .05 .15
7 Chuck Finley .08 .25
8 Eddie Murray .25 .60
9 Jim Leyritz .05 .15
10 Darin Erstad .08 .25
11 Jason Dickson .05 .15
12 Allen Watson .05 .15
13 Shigetoshi Hasegawa .15 .40
14 Dave Hollins .05 .15
15 Gary DiSarcina .05 .15
16 Greg Maddux .50 1.25
17 Denny Neagle .05 .15
18 Chipper Jones .25 .60
19 Tom Glavine .15 .40
20 John Smoltz .15 .40
21 Ryan Klesko .08 .25
22 Fred McGriff .15 .40
23 Michael Tucker .05 .15
24 Kenny Lofton .08 .25
25 Javier Lopez .08 .25
26 Mark Wohlers .05 .15
27 Jeff Blauser .05 .15
28 Andruw Jones .15 .40
29 Tony Graffanino .05 .15
30 Terrell Wade .05 .15
31 Brady Anderson .08 .25
32 Roberto Alomar .15 .40
33 Rafael Palmeiro .15 .40
34 Mike Mussina .15 .40
35 Cal Ripken 1.00 2.50
36 Rocky Coppinger .05 .15
37 Randy Myers .08 .25
38 B.J. Surhoff .08 .25
39 Eric Davis .08 .25
40 Armando Benitez .05 .15
41 Jeffrey Hammonds .05 .15
42 Jimmy Key .08 .25
43 Chris Hoiles .05 .15
44 Mike Bordick .08 .25
45 Pete Incaviglia .05 .15
46 Mike Stanley .05 .15
47 Reggie Jefferson .05 .15
48 Mo Vaughn .08 .25
49 John Valentin .05 .15
50 Tim Naehring .05 .15
51 Jeff Suppan .05 .15
52 Tim Wakefield .08 .25
53 Jeff Frye .05 .15
54 Darren Bragg .05 .15
55 Steve Avery .05 .15
56 Shane Mack .05 .15
57 Aaron Sele .05 .15
58 Troy O'Leary .05 .15
59 Rudy Pemberton .05 .15
60 Nomar Garciaparra .50 1.25
61 Robin Ventura .08 .25
62 Wilson Alvarez .05 .15
63 Roberto Hernandez .05 .15
64 Frank Thomas .25 .60
65 Ray Durham .08 .25
66 James Baldwin .05 .15
67 Harold Baines .08 .25
68 Doug Drabek .05 .15
69 Mike Cameron .05 .15
70 Albert Belle .08 .25
71 Jaime Navarro .05 .15
72 Chris Snopek .05 .15
73 Lyle Mouton .05 .15
74 Dave Martinez .05 .15
75 Ozzie Guillen .08 .25
76 Manny Ramirez .15 .40
77 Jack McDowell .05 .15
78 Jim Thome .15 .40
79 Jose Mesa .05 .15
80 Brian Giles .40 1.00
81 Omar Vizquel .15 .40
82 Charles Nagy .05 .15
83 Orel Hershiser .08 .25
84 Matt Williams .08 .25
85 Marquis Grissom .08 .25
86 David Justice .08 .25
87 Sandy Alomar Jr. .05 .15
88 Kevin Seitzer .05 .15
89 Julio Franco .08 .25
90 Bartolo Colon .08 .25
91 Andres Galarraga .08 .25
92 Larry Walker .08 .25
93 Vinny Castilla .08 .25
94 Dante Bichette .08 .25
95 Jamey Wright .05 .15
96 Ellis Burks .08 .25
97 Eric Young .05 .15
98 Neifi Perez .05 .15
99 Quinton McCracken .05 .15
100 Bruce Ruffin .05 .15
101 Walt Weiss .05 .15
102 Roger Bailey .05 .15
103 Jeff Reed .05 .15
104 Bill Swift .05 .15
105 Kirt Manwaring .05 .15
106 Raul Mondesi .08 .25
107 Hideo Nomo .25 .60
108 Roger Cedeno .05 .15
109 Ismael Valdes .05 .15
110 Todd Hollandsworth .05 .15
111 Mike Piazza .50 1.25
112 Brett Butler .08 .25
113 Chan Ho Park .08 .25
114 Ramon Martinez .05 .15
115 Eric Karros .08 .25
116 Wilton Guerrero .05 .15
117 Todd Zeile .08 .25
118 Karim Garcia .05 .15
119 Greg Gagne .05 .15
120 Darren Dreifort .05 .15
121 Wade Boggs .15 .40
122 Paul O'Neill .15 .40
123 Derek Jeter .75 2.00
124 Tino Martinez .15 .40
125 David Cone .08 .25
126 Andy Pettitte .15 .40
127 Charlie Hayes .05 .15
128 Mariano Rivera .25 .60
129 Dwight Gooden .08 .25
130 Cecil Fielder .08 .25
132 Darryl Strawberry .08 .25
133 Joe Girardi .05 .15
134 David Wells .08 .25
135 Hideki Irabu .08 .25
136 Ken Griffey Jr. .60 1.50
137 Alex Rodriguez .50 1.25
138 Jay Buhner .08 .25
139 Randy Johnson .25 .60
140 Paul Sorrento .05 .15
141 Edgar Martinez .15 .40
142 Joey Cora .05 .15
143 Bob Wells .05 .15
145 Jamie Moyer .08 .25
146 Jeff Fassero .05 .15
147 Dan Wilson .05 .15
148 Jose Cruz Jr. .08 .25
149 Scott Sanders .05 .15
150 Rich Amaral .05 .15
151 Brian Jordan .08 .25
152 Andy Benes .05 .15
153 Ray Lankford .08 .25
154 John Mabry .05 .15
155 Tom Pagnozzi .05 .15
156 Ron Gant .08 .25
157 Alan Benes .05 .15
158 Dennis Eckersley .08 .25
159 Royce Clayton .05 .15
160 Todd Stottlemyre .05 .15
161 Gary Gaetti .08 .25
162 Willie McGee .08 .25
163 Delino DeShields .05 .15
164 Dmitri Young .08 .25
165 Matt Morris .08 .25

1997 Donruss Team Sets Pennant Edition

*STARS: 8X TO 20X BASIC CARDS
*ROOKIES: 4X TO 10X BASIC CARDS
RANDOM INSERTS IN PACKS

1997 Donruss Team Sets MVP's

STATED ODDS 1:36
STATED PRINT RUN 1000 SERIAL #'d SETS
1 Ivan Rodriguez 1.00 2.50
2 Mike Piazza 1.50 4.00
3 Frank Thomas 1.50 4.00
4 Jeff Bagwell 1.00 2.50
5 Chuck Knoblauch .60 1.50
6 Eric Young .60 1.50
7 Alex Rodriguez 2.00 5.00
8 Barry Larkin 1.00 2.50
9 Cal Ripken 5.00 12.00
10 Chipper Jones 1.50 4.00
11 Albert Belle .60 1.50
12 Barry Bonds 2.50 6.00
13 Ken Griffey Jr. 10.00 25.00
14 Kenny Lofton .60 1.50
15 Juan Gonzalez .60 1.50
16 Larry Walker 1.00 2.50
17 Roger Clemens 2.00 5.00
18 Greg Maddux 2.50 6.00

2008 Donruss Threads

COMP.SET w/o AU's (100) 10.00 25.00
COMMON CARD (1-50) .15 .40
COMMON CARD (51-100) .30 .75
COMMON AUTO (101-184) 3.00 8.00
AUTOS RANDOMLY INSERTED
AU PRINT RUN B/WN 99-199 COPIES
EXCHANGE DEADLINE 4/22/2010
1 Hank Aaron .75 2.00
2 Dale Murphy .25 .60
3 Brooks Robinson .25 .60
4 Cal Ripken Jr. 1.50 4.00
5 Eddie Murray .40 1.00
6 Carl Yastrzemski .60 1.50
7 Carlton Fisk .25 .60
8 Wade Boggs .25 .60
9 Joe Jackson 1.25 3.00
10 Johnny Pesky .15 .40
11 Jim Rice .15 .40
12 Fred Lynn .15 .40
13 Duke Snider .25 .60
14 Carl Erskine .15 .40
15 Ernie Banks .40 1.00
16 Ryne Sandberg .75 2.00
17 Don Sutton .15 .40
18 Luis Aparicio .15 .40
19 Tom Seaver .25 .60
20 Tony Perez .25 .60
21 Pete Rose 1.25 3.00
22 Bob Feller .25 .60
23 Al Kaline .40 1.00
24 Mark Fidrych .15 .40
25 Kirk Gibson .15 .40
26 Alan Trammell .15 .40
27 George Brett .75 2.00
28 Steve Garvey .15 .40
29 Robin Yount .40 1.00
30 Harmon Killebrew .40 1.00
31 Paul Molitor .40 1.00
32 Gary Carter .25 .60
34 Don Larsen .15 .40
35 Don Mattingly .75 2.00
36 Reggie Jackson .40 1.00
37 Tim Raines .15 .40
38 Mike Schmidt .60 1.50
39 Steve Carlton .25 .60
40 Tony Gwynn .40 1.00
41 Juan Marichal .25 .60
42 Willie Mays .75 2.00
43 Willie McCovey .25 .60
44 Will Clark .25 .60
45 Bob Gibson .25 .60
46 Dennis Eckersley .15 .40
47 Red Schoendienst .15 .40
48 Stan Musial .60 1.50
49 Nolan Ryan 1.00 2.50
50 Frank Howard .15 .40
51 Austin Romine .50 1.25
52 Chris Carter .50 1.25
53 Jordan Schafer .60 1.50
54 Michael Burgess .50 1.25
55 John Raynor .30 .75
56 Lars Anderson .25 .60
57 Josh Reddick .30 .75
58 Luis Esposito .30 .75
59 Aneury Rodriguez .75 2.00
60 Nick Weglarz .30 .75
61 Hector Gomez .30 .75
62 Jon Still .30 .75
63 Brandon Hamilton .50 1.25
64 Bud Norris .30 .75
65 Danny Duffy .50 1.25
66 Jovan Rosa .50 1.25
67 Sean O'Sullivan .30 .75
68 Edilio Colina .30 .75
69 Ryan Patterson .30 .75
70 Brent Brewer .30 .75
71 David Bromberg .30 .75
72 Bryan Petersen .50 1.25
73 Lucas Duda .50 1.25
74 Ruben Tejada .30 .75
75 Andrew Lambo .40 1.00
76 Jeff Corsaletti .30 .75
77 Alexis Oliveras .30 .75
78 Fernando Garcia .30 .75
79 Jairo Heredia .30 .75
80 Jesus Montero .75 2.00
81 Jose Tabata .30 .75
82 Carlos Gonzalez .50 1.25
83 Patrick Ryan .30 .75
84 Sean Doolittle .30 .75
85 Carlos Carrasco .50 1.25
86 Luis Cruz .50 1.25
87 Yefri Carvajal .30 .75
88 Stolmy Pimentel .30 .75
89 Wilber Bucardo .30 .75
90 Angel Villalona .75 2.00
91 Madison Bumgarner 1.00 2.50
92 Danny Carroll .30 .75
93 Juan Ramirez .30 .75
94 Lou Marson .30 .75
95 Josh Vitters .50 1.25
96 Desmond Jennings .50 1.25
97 Abraham Almonte .30 .75
98 Mat Gamel .50 1.25
99 Andrew LeFave .30 .75
100 Elvis Andrus .50 1.25
101 Emilio Bonifacio AU/1874 5.00 12.00
102 Wilin Rosario AU/999 4.00 10.00
103 Carlos Peguero AU/465 5.00 12.00
104 Tyler Flowers AU/999 5.00 12.00
105 Tyler Henson AU/999 4.00 10.00
106 Nevin Griffith AU/999 3.00 8.00
107 Caleb Gindl AU/465 5.00 12.00
108 Jose Ceda AU/999 3.00 8.00
109 Brandon Waring AU/465 6.00 15.00
110 Neftali Soto AU/500 8.00 20.00
111 Ryan Miller AU/999 3.00 8.00
112 Jack Egbert AU/999 3.00 8.00
113 Juan Silverio AU/999 5.00 12.00
114 Jhoulys Chacin AU/1999 6.00 15.00
115 Charlie Furbush AU/465 5.00 12.00
116 Hector Correa AU/999 3.00 8.00
117 Brad James AU/1999 3.00 8.00
119 Keaton Hayenga AU/999 4.00 10.00
120 Brent Fisher AU/1058 3.00 8.00
121 Juan Francisco AU/999 8.00 20.00
122 Andrew Romine AU/875 3.00 8.00
123 Mason Tobin AU/999 3.00 8.00
124 Anel De Los Santos AU/999 3.00 8.00
125 A.Walker AU/99 EXCH 6.00 15.00
126 Alfredo Silverio AU/999 3.00 8.00
127 Mario Martinez AU/1375 5.00 12.00
128 Taylor Green AU/999 6.00 15.00
129 D.J. Jones AU/399 4.00 10.00
130 Wilson Ramos AU/999 5.00 12.00
131 Trevor Reckling AU/875 4.00 10.00
132 Engel Beltre AU/465 8.00 20.00
133 Scott Moviel AU/1000 4.00 10.00
134 Josh Tomlin AU/875 6.00 15.00
135 Dominic Brown AU/999 10.00 25.00
136 Neftali Feliz AU/465 5.00 12.00
137 Brian Friday AU/1249 3.00 8.00
138 Drew Miller AU/1999 3.00 8.00
139 Steve Garrison AU/1999 3.00 8.00
140 Mike McBryde AU/950 3.00 8.00
141 Brian Duensing AU/575 3.00 8.00
142 Greg Halman AU/465 4.00 10.00
143 Jharmidy De Jesus AU/465 8.00 20.00
144 Mike Stanton AU/465 60.00 150.00
145 W.Flores AU/99 10.00 25.00
146 Heath Rollins AU/999 3.00 8.00
147 Alex Cobb AU/999 8.00 20.00
148 Omar Poveda AU/999 3.00 8.00
149 Yohermyn Chavez AU/999 6.00 15.00
150 Gerardo Parra AU/999 4.00 10.00
151 Clayton Conner AU/240 4.00 10.00
152 Tyler Kolodny AU/280 6.00 15.00
153 Ryan Kalish AU/240 4.00 10.00
154 Rick Porcello AU/240 12.00 30.00
155 Shane Peterson AU/240 5.00 12.00
156 Tyler Ladendorf AU/269 4.00 10.00
157 Josh Lindblom AU/240 5.00 12.00
158 Tyler Chatwood AU/240 5.00 12.00
159 Logan Morrison AU/240 10.00 25.00
160 Collin DeLome AU/240 6.00 15.00
161 Daniel Cortes AU/240 6.00 15.00
162 C.Johnson AU/280 EXCH 15.00 40.00
163 Matt Mitchell AU/240 5.00 12.00
164 Denny Almonte AU/280 6.00 15.00
165 Greg Veloz AU/250 8.00 20.00
166 R. J. Seidel AU/240 5.00 12.00
167 Xavier Avery AU/250 8.00 20.00
168 Quincy Latimore AU/240 6.00 15.00
169 A.Shafer AU/280 5.00 12.00
170 Rayner Contreras AU/270 5.00 12.00
171 Waldis Joaquin AU/280 5.00 12.00
172 Jorge Bucardo AU/280 5.00 12.00
173 James Darnell AU/280 8.00 20.00
174 Logan Forsythe AU/239 6.00 15.00
175 Kyle Ginley AU/240 5.00 12.00
176 Ike Davis AU/250 12.50 30.00
177 Max Ramirez AU/244 6.00 15.00
178 Chris Davis AU/250 20.00 50.00
180 Jay Austin AU/240 5.00 12.00
181 Brad Holt AU/240 4.00 10.00
182 Carlos Gutierrez AU/270 6.00 15.00
183 C.Friedrich AU/270 6.00 15.00
184 Zach Collier AU/280 10.00 25.00
186 Robert Hernandez AU/269 6.00 15.00
187 Christian Marrero AU/280 6.00 15.00

2008 Donruss Threads Century Proof Gold

*GOLD 1-50: 3X TO 8X BASIC
*GOLD 51-100: 3X TO 8X BASIC
*GOLD 101-150: 1.2X TO 3X GREEN
RANDOM INSERTS IN PACKS
STATED PRINT RUN 50 SER.#'d SETS
144 Mike Stanton 30.00 60.00

2008 Donruss Threads Century Proof Green

*GRN 1-50: 1X TO 2.5X BASIC
*GRN 51-100: 1X TO 2.5X BASIC
RANDOM INSERTS IN PACKS
STATED PRINT RUN 250 SER.#'d SETS
101 Emilio Bonifacio 1.50 4.00

102 Wilin Rosario 1.00 2.50
103 Carlos Peguero .75 2.00
104 Tyler Flowers 2.00 5.00
105 Tyler Henson 1.00 2.50
106 Nevin Griffith .75 2.00
107 Caleb Gindl .75 2.00
108 Jose Ceda .75 2.00
109 Brandon Waring 2.00 5.00
110 Neftali Soto 2.00 5.00
111 Ryan Miller .75 2.00
112 Jack Egbert .75 2.00
113 Juan Silverio 1.25 3.00
114 Jhoulys Chacin 2.50 6.00
115 Charlie Furbush 1.00 2.50
116 Hector Correa .75 2.00
117 Brad James .75 2.00
119 Keaton Hayenga 1.00 2.50
120 Brent Fisher .75 2.00
121 Juan Francisco 1.25 3.00
122 Andrew Romine .75 2.00
123 Mason Tobin .75 2.00
124 Anel De Los Santos .75 2.00
125 Andrew Walker .75 2.00
126 Alfredo Silverio .75 2.00
127 Mario Martinez 1.50 4.00
128 Taylor Green 1.00 2.50
129 D.J. Jones 1.00 2.50
130 Wilson Ramos 1.00 2.50
131 Trevor Reckling 1.00 2.50
132 Engel Beltre 1.00 2.50
133 Scott Moviel 1.00 2.50
134 Josh Tomlin .75 2.00
135 Dominic Brown 1.50 4.00
136 Neftali Feliz 3.00 8.00
137 Brian Friday .75 2.00
138 Drew Miller .75 2.00
139 Steve Garrison .75 2.00
140 Mike McBryde .75 2.00
141 Brian Duensing .75 2.00
142 Greg Halman 2.00 5.00
143 Jharmidy De Jesus 2.00 5.00
144 Mike Stanton 12.50 30.00
145 Wilmer Flores 3.00 8.00
146 Heath Rollins .75 2.00
147 Alex Cobb .75 2.00
148 Omar Poveda .75 2.00
149 Yohermyn Chavez 1.00 2.50
150 Gerardo Parra .75 2.00

2008 Donruss Threads Century Proof Silver

*SILVER 1-50: 1.5X TO 4X BASIC
*SILVER 51-100: 1.5X TO 4X BASIC
*SILVER 101-150: .6X TO 1.5X GREEN
RANDOM INSERTS IN PACKS
STATED PRINT RUN 100 SER.#'d SETS
144 Mike Stanton 15.00 40.00

2008 Donruss Threads Baseball Americana

RANDOM INSERTS IN PACKS
STATED PRINT RUN 500 SER.#'d SETS
3 Don Mattingly 2.50 6.00
4 Eddie Murray 1.25 3.00
5 Ryne Sandberg 2.00 5.00
6 Pete Rose 4.00 10.00
7 Cal Ripken Jr. 4.00 10.00
8 Ernie Banks 2.00 5.00
9 George Brett 2.50 6.00
10 Mike Schmidt 2.00 5.00
11 Johnny Bench 1.50 4.00
12 Carlton Fisk 1.50 4.00
13 Tony Gwynn 1.50 4.00
14 Hank Aaron 2.00 5.00
15 Willie Mays 2.00 5.00
16 Joe Jackson 4.00 10.00
17 Ted Williams 2.00 5.00
18 Stan Musial 2.00 5.00
19 Nolan Ryan 3.00 8.00
20 Bob Feller 1.50 4.00
41 Bob Gibson 1.50 4.00
42 Dennis Eckersley 1.50 4.00
43 Carl Yastrzemski 1.50 4.00
44 Don Drysdale 1.50 4.00
45 Satchel Paige 2.00 5.00
46 Casey Stengel 1.50 4.00
47 Eddie Mathews 1.50 4.00
48 Early Wynn 1.50 4.00

2008 Donruss Threads Baseball Americana Materials

RANDOM INSERTS IN PACKS
PRINT RUNS B/WN 1-500 PER
NO PRICING ON QTY 25 OR LESS
1 Bud Abbott/500 6.00 15.00
2 Lou Costello/250 8.00 20.00
3 Don Mattingly/100 10.00 25.00
4 Eddie Murray/150 5.00 12.00
6 Pete Rose/250 10.00 25.00
7 Cal Ripken Jr./100 12.50 30.00
9 George Brett/75 6.00 15.00
10 Mike Schmidt/100 6.00 15.00
11 Johnny Bench/50 12.50 30.00
12 Carlton Fisk/75 4.00 10.00
13 Tony Gwynn/250 3.00 8.00
17 Ted Williams/100 12.00 30.00
19 Nolan Ryan/100 10.00 25.00
41 Bob Gibson/100 3.00 8.00
42 Dennis Eckersley/100 4.00 10.00
43 Carl Yastrzemski/100 3.00 8.00
44 Don Drysdale/100 5.00 12.00
45 Satchel Paige/100 15.00 40.00
46 Casey Stengel/500 6.00 15.00
47 Eddie Mathews/100 8.00 20.00
48 Early Wynn/100 4.00 10.00

2008 Donruss Threads Baseball Americana Materials Position

RANDOM INSERTS IN PACKS
PRINT RUNS B/WN 1-250 PER
NO PRICING ON QTY 25 OR LESS
1 Bud Abbott/200 6.00 15.00
2 Lou Costello/100 8.00 20.00
3 Don Mattingly/50 8.00 20.00
4 Eddie Murray/50 6.00 15.00
6 Pete Rose/100 20.00 50.00
9 George Brett/75 6.00 15.00
10 Mike Schmidt/100 6.00 15.00
12 Carlton Fisk/75 4.00 10.00
13 Tony Gwynn/100 4.00 10.00
17 Ted Williams/50 30.00 60.00
19 Nolan Ryan/50 12.50 30.00
41 Bob Gibson/100 3.00 8.00
42 Dennis Eckersley/100 4.00 10.00
43 Carl Yastrzemski/100 3.00 8.00
44 Don Drysdale/100 5.00 12.00
45 Satchel Paige/100 15.00 40.00
46 Casey Stengel/250 6.00 15.00
47 Eddie Mathews/100 8.00 20.00
48 Early Wynn/100 4.00 10.00

2008 Donruss Threads Baseball Americana Signatures Materials

RANDOM INSERTS IN PACKS
PRINT RUNS B/WN 3-100 COPIES
NO PRICING ON QTY 25 OR LESS
6 Pete Rose/50 100.00 200.00
11 Johnny Bench/50 30.00 60.00
12 Carlton Fisk/50 10.00 25.00
13 Tony Gwynn/50 15.00 40.00
41 Bob Gibson/50 12.50 30.00

2008 Donruss Threads Bats

RANDOM INSERTS IN PACKS
PRINT RUNS B/WN 1-500 PER
NO PRICING ON QTY 20 OR LESS
1 Hank Aaron/500 10.00 25.00
9 Joe Jackson/100 100.00 200.00
35 Don Mattingly/250 5.00 12.00
36 Reggie Jackson/500 4.00 10.00
38 Mike Schmidt/500 5.00 12.00
42 Willie Mays/50 10.00 25.00
52 Chris Carter/500 3.00 8.00
53 Jordan Schafer/500 3.00 8.00
54 Michael Burgess/500 3.00 8.00
70 Brent Brewer/500 3.00 8.00
81 Jose Tabata/500 3.00 8.00
84 Sean Doolittle/500 3.00 8.00
92 Danny Carroll/500 3.00 8.00
96 Desmond Jennings/500 4.00 10.00
128 Taylor Green/500 3.00 8.00
142 Greg Halman/500 3.00 8.00
143 Jharmidy De Jesus/500 3.00 8.00

2008 Donruss Threads Century Collection Materials

RANDOM INSERTS IN PACKS
PRINT RUNS B/WN 10-100 PER
NO MAYS PRICING AVAILABLE
1 Cal Ripken Jr./100 12.50 30.00
2 Ryne Sandberg/75 8.00 20.00
3 Pete Rose/100 20.00 50.00
4 Fred Lynn/100 3.00 8.00
5 Tom Seaver/100 3.00 8.00
6 George Brett/50 10.00 25.00
7 Don Mattingly/75 6.00 15.00
8 Mike Schmidt/100 6.00 15.00
9 Tony Gwynn/100 4.00 10.00
11 Nolan Ryan/100 8.00 20.00
12 Dale Murphy/100 6.00 15.00
13 Pete Rose/100 20.00 50.00
15 Dave Winfield/100 3.00 8.00
16 Paul Molitor/100 3.00 8.00
17 Barry Larkin/100 4.00 10.00
18 Kirk Gibson/100 5.00 12.00
19 Pete Rose/100 20.00 50.00
20 Steve Garvey/100 5.00 12.00
21 Wade Boggs/100 3.00 8.00
22 Ted Williams/100 20.00 50.00
23 Steve Carlton/100 3.00 8.00
24 Robin Yount/100 4.00 10.00
25 Luis Aparicio/100 3.00 8.00
26 Jim Rice/100 3.00 8.00
27 Jim Palmer/100 3.00 8.00
28 Harmon Killebrew/100 5.00 12.00
29 Gaylord Perry/100 3.00 8.00
30 Gary Carter/100 4.00 10.00
31 Eddie Murray/50 4.00 10.00
32 Don Drysdale/100 4.00 10.00
33 Satchel Paige/100 15.00 40.00
34 Casey Stengel/100 6.00 15.00
35 Eddie Mathews/100 8.00 20.00
36 Dennis Eckersley/100 3.00 8.00
37 Carlton Fisk/100 4.00 10.00
38 Carl Yastrzemski/100 4.00 10.00
39 Early Wynn/100 4.00 10.00
40 Lefty Grove/50 75.00 150.00

2008 Donruss Threads Century Legends

RANDOM INSERTS IN PACKS
*CENTURY PROOF: .75X TO 2X BASIC
CENTRUY RANDOMLY INSERTED
CENTURY PRINT RUN 100 SER.#'d SETS
1 Stan Musial 2.00 5.00
2 Willie Mays 2.00 5.00
3 Hank Aaron 2.00 5.00
4 Ted Williams 2.00 5.00
5 Whitey Ford .75 2.00
6 Bob Gibson .75 2.00
7 Joe Jackson 3.00 8.00
8 Duke Snider 1.25 3.00
9 Ernie Banks 1.25 3.00
10 Bob Feller .75 2.00
11 Nolan Ryan 2.50 6.00
12 Mike Schmidt 1.50 4.00
13 Carl Yastrzemski 1.25 3.00
14 Pete Rose 3.00 8.00
15 Harmon Killebrew 1.25 3.00

2008 Donruss Threads Century Legends Materials

RANDOM INSERTS IN PACKS
PRINT RUNS B/WN 1-100 COPIES
NO PRICING ON QTY 25 OR LESS
4 Ted Williams/50 20.00 50.00
6 Bob Gibson/50 5.00 12.00
11 Nolan Ryan/100 6.00 15.00
12 Mike Schmidt/100 6.00 15.00
13 Carl Yastrzemski/100 5.00 12.00
14 Pete Rose/100 20.00 50.00
15 Harmon Killebrew/100 5.00 12.00

2008 Donruss Threads Century Stars Materials

RANDOM INSERTS IN PACKS
PRINT RUNS B/WN 50-100 PER
1 Carlton Fisk/100 4.00 10.00
2 Harmon Killebrew/100 3.00 8.00
3 Ryne Sandberg/50 15.00 40.00
4 Cal Ripken Jr./100 15.00 40.00
5 Mike Schmidt/100 6.00 15.00
6 Tony Gwynn/100 3.00 8.00
7 Pete Rose/100 20.00 50.00
9 Dale Murphy/100 3.00 8.00
10 Steve Carlton/100 3.00 8.00
11 Bob Gibson/100 3.00 8.00
12 Nolan Ryan/100 8.00 20.00
13 Robin Yount/100 3.00 8.00
14 Paul Molitor/100 3.00 8.00
15 Kirk Gibson/50 3.00 8.00

2008 Donruss Threads College Greats

RANDOM INSERTS IN PACKS
1 Tom Seaver 1.50 4.00
2 Reggie Jackson 1.50 4.00
3 Frank Howard 1.00 2.50
4 Dave Winfield 1.00 2.50
5 Paul Molitor 1.00 2.50
6 Barry Larkin 1.00 2.50
7 Kirk Gibson 1.00 2.50
8 Robin Roberts 1.00 2.50
9 Will Clark 1.50 4.00
10 Bob Gibson 1.50 4.00
11 Steve Garvey 1.00 2.50
12 Fred Lynn 1.00 2.50

2008 Donruss Threads College Greats Signatures

RANDOM INSERTS IN PACKS
PRINT RUNS B/WN 5-50 COPIES PER
NO PRICING ON QTY 25 OR LESS
3 Frank Howard/50 10.00 25.00
6 Barry Larkin/50 40.00 80.00
8 Robin Roberts/40 10.00 25.00
10 Bob Gibson/50 12.50 30.00
12 Fred Lynn/50 10.00 25.00

2008 Donruss Threads College Greats Signatures Combos

RANDOM INSERTS IN PACKS
STATED PRINT RUN 25 SER.#'d SETS
NO PRICING DUE TO SCARCITY

2008 Donruss Threads Diamond Kings

RANDOM INSERTS IN PACKS
*GOLD: .6X TO 1.5X BASIC
GOLD RANDOMLY INSERTED
GOLD PRINT RUN 100 SER.#'d SETS
FRM.BLK.RANDOMLY INSERTED
FRM.BLK.PRINT RUN 10 SER.#'d SETS
NO FRM.BLK PRINCING AVAILABLE
*FRM.BLUE: .75X TO 2X BASIC
FRM.BLUE RANDOMLY INSERTS
FRM.BLUE PRINT RUN 50 SER.#'d SETS
FRM.GRN.RANDOMLY INSERTED
FRM.GRN.PRINT RUN 25 SER.#'d SETS
NO FRM.GRN PRINCING AVAILABLE
*FRM.RED: .6X TO 1.5X BASIC
FRM.RED RANDOMLY INSERTS
FRM.RED PRINT RUN 100 SER.#'d SETS
PLAT.RANDOMLY INSERTED
PLAT.PRINT RUN 25 SER.#'d SETS
NO PLAT.PRINCING AVAILABLE
*SILVER: .5X TO 1.2X BASIC
SILVER RANDOMLY INSERTS
SILVER PRINT RUN 250 SER.#'d SETS
1 Jordan Schafer 1.00 2.50
2 Nolan Reimold 1.00 2.50
3 Matt McBride 1.00 2.50
4 Lars Anderson .60 1.50
5 Blake Wood 1.00 2.50
6 Josh Vitters 1.00 2.50
7 Chris Valaika 1.00 2.50
8 Mark Melancon 1.00 2.50
9 Drew Stubbs 1.00 2.50
10 Rick Porcello 2.50 6.00
11 Anthony Rizzo 2.50 6.00
12 Jon Jay 1.00 2.50
13 Clay Fuller 1.00 2.50
14 Damon Sublett 1.00 2.50
15 Brett Anderson 1.00 2.50
16 Matt Spencer 1.00 2.50
17 Drew Cumberland 1.00 2.50
18 Tim Alderson 1.00 2.50
19 Madison Bumgarner 1.00 2.50
20 Jess Todd 1.00 2.50
21 Michael Hollimon 1.00 2.50
22 Taylor Teagarden 1.00 2.50
23 Daniel McCutchen 1.00 2.50
24 Trystan Magnuson 1.00 2.50
25 Michael Burgess 1.00 2.50
26 Hank Aaron 2.50 6.00
27 Cal Ripken Jr. 3.00 8.00
28 Jim Palmer 1.00 2.50
29 Bobby Doerr 1.00 2.50
30 Duke Snider 1.25 3.00
31 Rod Carew 1.00 2.50
32 Ernie Banks 1.50 4.00
33 Ryne Sandberg 2.50 6.00
34 Billy Williams 1.00 2.50
35 Fergie Jenkins 1.00 2.50
36 Pete Rose 3.00 8.00
37 George Kell 1.00 2.50
38 George Brett 2.50 6.00
39 Reggie Jackson 1.25 3.00
40 Don Mattingly 2.50 6.00
41 Phil Niekro 1.00 2.50
42 Whitey Ford 1.25 3.00
43 Yogi Berra 1.50 4.00
44 Mike Schmidt 2.00 5.00
45 Tony Gwynn 1.50 4.00
46 Willie Mays 2.50 6.00
47 Gaylord Perry 1.00 2.50
48 Stan Musial 2.00 5.00
49 Lou Brock 1.25 3.00
50 Nolan Ryan 2.50 6.00
51 Joe Jackson 3.00 8.00
52 Gordon Beckham 2.50 6.00
56 Pete Rose 3.00 8.00
57 Rick Porcello 2.50 6.00
58 Nolan Ryan 2.50 6.00

2008 Donruss Threads Diamond Kings Materials

RANDOM INSERTS IN PACKS
PRINT RUNS B/WN 1-250 PER
NO PRICING ON QTY 25 OR LESS
1 Jordan Schafer/250 5.00 12.00
6 Josh Vitters/250 3.00 8.00
8 Mark Melancon/125 3.00 8.00
9 Drew Stubbs/250 3.00 8.00
10 Rick Porcello/250 5.00 12.00
13 Clay Fuller/250 3.00 8.00
14 Damon Sublett/250 5.00 12.00
15 Brett Anderson/250 3.00 8.00
16 Matt Spencer/250 3.00 8.00
17 Drew Cumberland/250 3.00 8.00
18 Tim Alderson/250 3.00 8.00
19 Madison Bumgarner/125 10.00 25.00
20 Jess Todd/250 3.00 8.00
24 Trystan Magnuson/250 3.00 8.00
25 Michael Burgess/250 3.00 8.00
27 Cal Ripken Jr./200 12.50 30.00
28 Jim Palmer/50 5.00 12.00
33 Ryne Sandberg/50 12.50 30.00
36 Pete Rose/250 20.00 50.00
38 George Brett/75 8.00 20.00
40 Don Mattingly/150 10.00 25.00
44 Mike Schmidt/75 8.00 20.00
45 Tony Gwynn/250 5.00 12.00
46 Willie Mays/50 20.00 50.00
49 Lou Brock/100 6.00 15.00
50 Nolan Ryan/50 12.50 30.00
56 Pete Rose/100 20.00 50.00
57 Rick Porcello/100 5.00 12.00
58 Nolan Ryan/50 12.50 30.00

2008 Donruss Threads Diamond Kings Signatures

RANDOM INSERTS IN PACKS
PRINT RUNS B/WN 5-500 COPIES PER
NO PRICING ON QTY 25 OR LESS
1 Jordan Schafer/199 10.00 25.00
2 Nolan Reimold/500 5.00 12.00
3 Matt McBride /500 4.00 10.00
4 Lars Anderson/474 8.00 20.00
5 Blake Wood/500 4.00 10.00
7 Chris Valaika/500 5.00 12.00
8 Mark Melancon/238 6.00 15.00
9 Drew Stubbs/465 6.00 15.00
10 Rick Porcello/300 6.00 15.00
11 Anthony Rizzo/500 30.00 80.00
15 Brett Anderson/315 4.00 10.00
18 Tim Alderson/215 5.00 12.00
19 Madison Bumgarner/223 30.00 80.00
21 Michael Hollimon/500 4.00 10.00
22 Taylor Teagarden/475 4.00 10.00
23 Daniel McCutchen/500 4.00 10.00
24 Trystan Magnuson/215 4.00 10.00
25 Michael Burgess/182 5.00 12.00
28 Jim Palmer/100 6.00 15.00
29 Bobby Doerr/250 6.00 15.00
30 Duke Snider/50 10.00 25.00
35 Fergie Jenkins/100 8.00 20.00
36 Pete Rose/50 20.00 50.00
41 Phil Niekro/50 10.00 25.00
42 Whitey Ford/100 10.00 25.00
47 Gaylord Perry/150 8.00 20.00
49 Lou Brock/50 12.00 30.00

2008 Donruss Threads Diamond Kings Signatures Materials

RANDOM INSERTS IN PACKS
PRINT RUNS B/WN 5-100 COPIES PER
NO PRICING ON MOST DUE TO SCARICTY
10 Rick Porcello/25 40.00 80.00
36 Pete Rose/25 125.00 250.00
49 Lou Brock/100 12.50 30.00
56 Pete Rose/25 40.00 80.00
57 Rick Porcello/25 15.00 40.00

2008 Donruss Threads Dynasty

RANDOM INSERTS IN PACKS
*CENTURY PROOF: .75X TO 2X BASIC
CENTRUY RANDOMLY INSERTED
CENTURY PRINT RUN 100 SER.#'d SETS
1 Ripken/Palmer/Murray 2.50 6.00
2 Bench/Rose/Morgan 3.00 8.00
3 Marichal/Mays/McCovey 2.00 5.00

2008 Donruss Threads Dynasty Materials

RANDOM INSERTS IN PACKS
PRINT RUN B/WN 50-100 COPIES PER
1 Ripken/Palmer/Murray/50 12.50 30.00
2 Bench/Rose/Morgan/100 40.00 80.00

2008 Donruss Threads Generations

RANDOM INSERTS IN PACKS
*CENTURY PROOF: .75X TO 2X BASIC
CENTRUY RANDOMLY INSERTED
CENTURY PRINT RUN 100 SER.#'d SETS
1 H.Aaron/D.Murphy 2.50 6.00
2 E.Murray/C.Ripken Jr. 3.00 8.00
3 E.Banks/R.Sandberg 3.00 8.00
4 W.Mays/W.McCovey 2.50 6.00
5 R.Carew/P.Molitor 2.00 5.00

2008 Donruss Threads Generations Materials

RANDOM INSERTS IN PACKS
PRINT RUNS B/WN 10-100 COPIES PER
NO PRICING ON QTY 15 OR LESS
2 E.Murray/C.Ripken Jr./100 15.00 40.00

2008 Donruss Threads Jerseys

RANDOM INSERTS IN PACKS
PRINT RUNS B/WN 5-500 PER
NO PRICING ON QTY 25 OR LESS
2 Dale Murphy/350 5.00 12.00
3 Brooks Robinson/250 5.00 12.00
4 Cal Ripken Jr./350 6.00 15.00
5 Eddie Murray/250 3.00 8.00
6 Carl Yastrzemski/400 3.00 8.00
7 Carlton Fisk/150 3.00 8.00
8 Wade Boggs/500 3.00 8.00
11 Jim Rice/350 3.00 8.00
12 Fred Lynn/350 3.00 8.00
16 Ryne Sandberg/150 5.00 12.00
18 Luis Aparicio/200 3.00 8.00
19 Tom Seaver/350 3.00 8.00
21 Pete Rose/100 10.00 25.00
25 Kirk Gibson/250 3.00 8.00
26 Alan Trammell/250 3.00 8.00
27 George Brett/250 5.00 12.00
28 Steve Garvey/150 4.00 10.00
29 Robin Yount/500 4.00 10.00
30 Harmon Killebrew/150 5.00 12.00
31 Paul Molitor/300 3.00 8.00
32 Gary Carter/450 3.00 8.00
35 Don Mattingly/150 6.00 15.00
36 Reggie Jackson/350 3.00 8.00
38 Mike Schmidt/350 4.00 10.00
39 Steve Carlton/250 4.00 10.00
40 Tony Gwynn/500 3.00 8.00
43 Willie McCovey/500 3.00 8.00
44 Will Clark/500 3.00 8.00
45 Bob Gibson/100 4.00 10.00
46 Dennis Eckersley/250 3.00 8.00
47 Red Schoendienst/300 4.00 10.00
49 Nolan Ryan/250 8.00 20.00
54 Michael Burgess/500 3.00 8.00
55 John Raynor/50 4.00 10.00
58 Luis Exposito/100 4.00 10.00
91 Madison Bumgarner/100 5.00 12.00
95 Josh Vitters/500 3.00 8.00
104 Tyler Flowers/95 4.00 10.00
105 Tyler Henson/50 3.00 8.00
146 Heath Rollins/90 3.00 8.00
147 Alex Cobb/95 3.00 8.00

2008 Donruss Threads Signatures Gold

RANDOM INSERTS IN PACKS
PRINT RUNS B/WN 10-999 COPIES PER
NO PRICING ON QTY 25 OR LESS
3 Brooks Robinson/50 10.00 25.00
4 Cal Ripken Jr./50 25.00 60.00
6 Carl Yastrzemski/50 20.00 50.00
7 Carlton Fisk/50 12.50 30.00
10 Johnny Pesky/100 12.50 30.00
11 Jim Rice/100 6.00 15.00
12 Fred Lynn/50 5.00 12.00
13 Duke Snider/50 12.50 30.00
14 Carl Erskine/75 5.00 12.00
16 Ryne Sandberg/50 20.00 50.00
17 Don Sutton/100 5.00 12.00
18 Luis Aparicio/50 5.00 12.00
19 Tom Seaver/50 20.00 50.00
21 Pete Rose/75 90.00 150.00
22 Bob Feller/100 12.50 30.00
23 Al Kaline/50 15.00 40.00
24 Mark Fidrych/100 20.00 50.00
26 Alan Trammell/75 5.00 12.00
28 Steve Garvey/45 10.00 25.00
29 Robin Yount/50 20.00 50.00
31 Paul Molitor/50 6.00 15.00
32 Gary Carter/50 8.00 20.00
34 Don Larsen/50 8.00 20.00
35 Don Mattingly/50 12.50 30.00
36 Reggie Jackson/50 12.50 30.00
38 Mike Schmidt/50 20.00 50.00
39 Steve Carlton/50 10.00 25.00
40 Tony Gwynn/50 15.00 40.00
41 Juan Marichal/50 10.00 25.00
42 Willie Mays/50 75.00 150.00
43 Willie McCovey/50 15.00 40.00
45 Bob Gibson/50 8.00 20.00
46 Dennis Eckersley/50 6.00 15.00
47 Red Schoendienst/100 8.00 20.00
48 Stan Musial/50 12.00 30.00
49 Nolan Ryan/50 40.00 80.00
50 Frank Howard/75 6.00 15.00
51 Austin Romine/725 6.00 15.00
52 Chris Carter/499 12.00 30.00
53 Jordan Schafer/275 15.00 40.00
55 John Raynor/575 4.00 10.00
56 Lars Anderson/499 5.00 12.00
57 Josh Reddick/499 6.00 15.00
58 Luis Exposito/971 4.00 10.00
59 Aneury Rodriguez/975 4.00 10.00
60 Nick Weglarz/999 4.00 10.00
61 Hector Gomez/499 5.00 12.00
62 Jon Still/725 4.00 10.00
63 Brandon Hamilton/972 4.00 10.00
64 Bud Norris/499 4.00 10.00
65 Danny Duffy/499 10.00 25.00
66 Jovan Rosa/973 4.00 10.00
67 Sean O'Sullivan/499 4.00 10.00
68 Edilio Colina/975 4.00 10.00
69 Ryan Patterson/775 4.00 10.00
70 Brent Brewer/470 5.00 12.00
71 David Bromberg/999 4.00 10.00
72 Bryan Petersen/475 4.00 10.00
73 Lucas Duda/250 12.00 30.00
74 Ruben Tejada/999 5.00 12.00
76 Jeff Corsaletti/975 4.00 10.00
77 Alexis Oliveras/975 4.00 10.00
78 Fernando Garcia/975 4.00 10.00
79 Jairo Heredia/999 4.00 10.00
80 Jesus Montero/975 10.00 25.00
81 Jose Tabata/975 10.00 25.00
82 Carlos Gonzalez/975 8.00 20.00
83 Patrick Ryan/499 4.00 10.00
84 Sean Doolittle/249 10.00 25.00
85 Carlos Carrasco/999 4.00 10.00
86 Luis Cruz/975 4.00 10.00
87 Yefri Carvajal/999 4.00 10.00
88 Stolmy Pimentel/975 4.00 10.00
89 Wilber Bucardo/420 4.00 10.00
91 Madison Bumgarner/250 20.00 50.00
92 Danny Carroll/999 4.00 10.00
93 Juan Ramirez/999 4.00 10.00
94 Lou Marson/725 5.00 12.00
96 Desmond Jennings/749 8.00 20.00
97 Abraham Almonte/975 4.00 10.00
99 Andrew LeFave/975 4.00 10.00
100 Elvis Andrus/749 6.00 15.00
101 Emilio Bonifacio/100 6.00 15.00
102 Wilin Rosario/100 5.00 12.00
104 Tyler Flowers/100 20.00 50.00
105 Tyler Henson/100 4.00 10.00
106 Nevin Griffith/100 4.00 10.00
108 Jose Ceda/100 4.00 10.00
110 Neftali Soto/100 20.00 50.00
111 Ryan Miller/100 4.00 10.00
112 Jack Egbert/100 6.00 15.00
113 Juan Silverio/100 6.00 15.00
114 Jhoulys Chacin/100 10.00 25.00
116 Hector Correa/100 4.00 10.00
117 Brad James/100 4.00 10.00
119 Keaton Hayenga/100 4.00 10.00
120 Brent Fisher/100 4.00 10.00
121 Juan Francisco/100 8.00 20.00
122 Andrew Romine/100 4.00 10.00
123 Mason Tobin/100 4.00 10.00
124 Anel De Los Santos/100 4.00 10.00
126 Alfredo Silverio/100 4.00 10.00
127 Mario Martinez/100 5.00 12.00
128 Taylor Green/100 5.00 12.00
129 D.J. Jones/100 4.00 10.00
130 Wilson Ramos/100 10.00 25.00
131 Trevor Reckling/100 8.00 20.00
133 Scott Moviel/100 4.00 10.00
134 Josh Tomlin/100 8.00 20.00
135 Dominic Brown/100 30.00 60.00
137 Brian Friday/100 4.00 10.00
138 Drew Miller/100 4.00 10.00
139 Steve Garrison/100 4.00 10.00
140 Mike McBryde/100 4.00 10.00
141 Brian Duensing/100 4.00 10.00
146 Heath Rollins/100 4.00 10.00
147 Alex Cobb/100 6.00 15.00
148 Omar Poveda/100 4.00 10.00
149 Yohermyn Chavez/100 5.00 12.00
150 Gerardo Parra/100 10.00 25.00

2004 Donruss Timelines

COMPLETE SET (50) 20.00 50.00
1 Adam Dunn .60 1.50
2 Albert Pujols 1.25 3.00
3 Alex Rodriguez 1.25 3.00
4 Alfonso Soriano .60 1.50
5 Andruw Jones .40 1.00
6 Austin Kearns .40 1.00
7 Miguel Cabrera 1.00 2.50
8 Barry Zito .60 1.50
9 Carlos Beltran .60 1.50
10 Carlos Delgado .40 1.00
11 Chipper Jones 1.00 2.50
12 Curt Schilling .60 1.50
13 Derek Jeter 2.50 6.00
14 Frank Thomas 1.00 2.50
15 Garret Anderson .40 1.00
16 Gary Sheffield .40 1.00
17 Greg Maddux 1.25 3.00
18 Hank Blalock .40 1.00
19 Hideki Matsui 1.50 4.00
20 Hideo Nomo 1.00 2.50
21 Ichiro Suzuki 1.25 3.00
22 Ivan Rodriguez .60 1.50
23 Jason Giambi .40 1.00
24 Jeff Bagwell .60 1.50
25 Jim Thome .60 1.50
26 Juan Gonzalez .40 1.00
27 Ken Griffey Jr. 2.00 5.00
28 Kevin Brown .40 1.00
29 Kerry Wood .40 1.00
30 Lance Berkman .60 1.50
31 Magglio Ordonez .60 1.50
32 Manny Ramirez 1.00 2.50
33 Mark Prior .60 1.50
34 Mike Mussina .60 1.50
35 Mike Piazza 1.00 2.50
36 Nomar Garciaparra .60 1.50
37 Pedro Martinez .60 1.50
38 Rafael Palmeiro .60 1.50
39 Randy Johnson 1.00 2.50
40 Richie Sexson .40 1.00
41 Roger Clemens 1.25 3.00
42 Roy Halladay .60 1.50
43 Sammy Sosa 1.00 2.50
44 Scott Rolen .60 1.50
45 Shawn Green .40 1.00
46 Tim Hudson .60 1.50
47 Todd Helton .60 1.50
48 Torii Hunter .40 1.00
49 Vernon Wells .40 1.00
50 Vladimir Guerrero .60 1.50

2004 Donruss Timelines Gold

*GOLD: 2.5X TO 6X BASIC
RANDOM INSERTS IN PACKS
STATED PRINT RUN 25 SERIAL #'d SETS

2004 Donruss Timelines Silver

*SILVER: 1X TO 2.5X BASIC
RANDOM INSERTS IN PACKS
STATED PRINT RUN 100 SERIAL #'d SETS

2004 Donruss Timelines Autograph Gold

STATED PRINT RUN 25 SERIAL #'d SETS
PLATINUM PRINT RUN 1 SERIAL #'d SET
NO PLATINUM PRICING DUE TO SCARCITY
RANDOM INSERTS IN PACKS
1 Adam Dunn 15.00 40.00
7 Miguel Cabrera 20.00 50.00
9 Carlos Beltran 10.00 25.00
15 Garret Anderson 10.00 25.00
18 Hank Blalock 10.00 25.00
22 Ivan Rodriguez 20.00 50.00
26 Juan Gonzalez 10.00 25.00
31 Magglio Ordonez 15.00 40.00
33 Mark Prior 12.50 30.00
44 Scott Rolen 10.00 25.00
48 Torii Hunter 10.00 25.00
49 Vernon Wells 10.00 25.00
50 Vladimir Guerrero 20.00 50.00

2004 Donruss Timelines Material

STATED ODDS 1:2
*COMBO: 1X TO 2.5X BASIC
*COMBO: .5X TO 1.2X BASIC SP
COMBO PRINT RUN 125 SERIAL #'d SETS
COMBOS FEATURE BAT-JSY SWATCHES
*PRIME: 1X TO 2.5X BASIC
PRIME PRINT RUN 125 SERIAL #'d SETS
PRIME M.CABRERA PRINT 10 #'d CARDS
NO PRIME M.CABRERA PRICING AVAIL.
1 Adam Dunn Jsy 3.00 8.00
2 Albert Pujols Jsy 6.00 15.00
3 Alex Rodriguez Jsy 6.00 15.00
4 Alfonso Soriano Jsy 3.00 8.00
5 Andruw Jones Jsy 4.00 10.00
7 Miguel Cabrera Jsy SP 8.00 20.00
10 Carlos Delgado Jsy 3.00 8.00
11 Chipper Jones Jsy 4.00 10.00
14 Frank Thomas Jsy 4.00 10.00
17 Greg Maddux Jsy 4.00 10.00
20 Hideo Nomo Jsy 6.00 15.00
22 Ivan Rodriguez Bat 4.00 10.00
23 Jason Giambi Bat 3.00 8.00
24 Jeff Bagwell Bat 4.00 10.00
25 Jim Thome Jsy 4.00 10.00
26 Juan Gonzalez Bat 3.00 8.00
30 Lance Berkman Jsy 3.00 8.00
33 Mark Prior Jsy 4.00 10.00
35 Mike Piazza Jsy 4.00 10.00
36 Nomar Garciaparra Jsy 6.00 15.00
37 Pedro Martinez Jsy 4.00 10.00
39 Randy Johnson Jsy 4.00 10.00
41 Roger Clemens Jsy 4.00 10.00
43 Sammy Sosa Jsy 4.00 10.00
45 Shawn Green Jsy 3.00 8.00
47 Todd Helton Jsy 4.00 10.00
49 Vernon Wells Jsy 3.00 8.00

2004 Donruss Timelines Material Autograph

PRINT RUNS B/WN 1-50 COPIES PER
NO PRICING ON QTY OF 5 OR LESS
PRIME PRINT RUN 1 SERIAL #'d SET
NO PRIME PRICING DUE TO SCARCITY
RANDOM INSERTS IN PACKS
7 Miguel Cabrera Bat/25 40.00 80.00
22 Ivan Rodriguez Bat/25 60.00 120.00
33 Mark Prior Jsy/50 20.00 50.00
49 Vernon Wells Jsy/50 15.00 40.00

2004 Donruss Timelines Boys of Summer

STATED PRINT RUN 250 SERIAL #'d SETS
*GOLD: 2X TO 5X BASIC
GOLD PRINT RUN 25 SERIAL #'d SETS
PLATINUM 1 SERIAL #'d SET
NO PLATINUM PRICING DUE TO SCARCITY
*SILVER: .6X TO 1.5X BASIC
SILVER PRINT RUN 100 SERIAL #'d SETS
RANDOM INSERTS IN PACKS
1 Alan Trammell 1.25 3.00
2 Marty Marion .75 2.00
3 Andre Dawson 1.25 3.00
4 Bo Jackson 2.00 5.00
5 Cal Ripken 6.00 15.00
6 Steve Garvey .75 2.00
7 Dale Murphy 2.00 5.00
8 Darren Daulton .75 2.00
9 Darryl Strawberry .75 2.00
10 Dave Parker .75 2.00
11 Doc Gooden .75 2.00
12 Don Mattingly 4.00 10.00
13 Eric Davis .75 2.00
14 Dwight Evans .75 2.00
15 Fred Lynn .75 2.00
16 Graig Nettles .75 2.00
17 Jay Buhner .75 2.00
18 Jim Rice 1.25 3.00
19 Jose Canseco 1.25 3.00
20 Keith Hernandez .75 2.00
21 Rickey Henderson 2.00 5.00
22 Jack Morris 1.25 3.00
23 Tony Gwynn 2.00 5.00
24 Vida Blue .75 2.00
25 Will Clark 1.25 3.00

2004 Donruss Timelines Boys of Summer Autograph

PLATINUM PRINT RUN 1 SERIAL #'d SET
NO PLATINUM PRICING DUE TO SCARCITY
RANDOM INSERTS IN PACKS
2 Marty Marion 6.00 15.00
3 Andre Dawson 8.00 20.00
6 Steve Garvey 6.00 15.00
8 Darren Daulton 8.00 20.00
9 Darryl Strawberry 6.00 15.00
10 Dave Parker 6.00 15.00
11 Doc Gooden 6.00 15.00
13 Eric Davis 6.00 15.00
15 Fred Lynn 6.00 15.00
16 Graig Nettles 6.00 15.00
17 Jay Buhner 6.00 15.00
20 Keith Hernandez 6.00 15.00
22 Jack Morris 6.00 15.00
24 Vida Blue 6.00 15.00

2004 Donruss Timelines Boys of Summer Autograph Gold

*GOLD: 1X TO 2.5X BASIC BOYS AUTO
RANDOM INSERTS IN PACKS
STATED PRINT RUN 25 SERIAL #'d SETS
1 Alan Trammell 12.50 30.00
12 Don Mattingly 40.00 80.00
14 Dwight Evans 20.00 50.00
18 Jim Rice 12.50 30.00
25 Will Clark 60.00 120.00

2004 Donruss Timelines Boys of Summer Autograph Silver

*SILVER: .6X TO 1.5X BASIC BOYS AUTO
RANDOM INSERTS IN PACKS
STATED PRINT RUN 100 SERIAL #'d SETS
12 Don Mattingly 20.00 50.00

2004 Donruss Timelines Boys of Summer Material

*COMBO: 1X TO 2.5X BASIC
COMBO PRINT RUN 100 SERIAL #'d SETS
MOST COMBOS ARE BAT-JSY SWATCHES
*PRIME: 1X TO 2.5X BASIC
PRIME PRINT RUN 100 SERIAL #'d SETS
RANDOM INSERTS IN PACKS

3 Andre Dawson Jsy 3.00 8.00
4 Bo Jackson Jsy 6.00 15.00
5 Cal Ripken Jsy 10.00 25.00
7 Dale Murphy Bat 4.00 10.00
9 Darryl Strawberry Jsy 3.00 8.00
11 Doc Gooden Jsy 3.00 8.00
12 Don Mattingly Jacket 8.00 20.00
19 Jose Canseco Bat 4.00 10.00
21 Rickey Henderson Jsy 6.00 15.00
22 Jack Morris Jsy 3.00 8.00
23 Tony Gwynn Jsy 6.00 15.00
25 Will Clark Jsy 4.00 10.00

2004 Donruss Timelines Boys of Summer Material Autograph

PRINT RUNS B/WN 5-150 COPIES PER
NO PRICING ON QTY OF 10 OR LESS
PRIME PRINT RUN 1 SERIAL #'d SET
NO PRIME PRICING DUE TO SCARCITY
RANDOM INSERTS IN PACKS
3 Andre Dawson Jsy/50 12.50 30.00
9 Darryl Strawberry Jsy/150 8.00 20.00
11 Doc Gooden Jsy/100 10.00 25.00
12 Don Mattingly Jacket/25 75.00 150.00
22 Jack Morris Jsy/150 8.00 20.00

2004 Donruss Timelines Call to the Hall

STATED PRINT RUN 250 SERIAL #'d SETS
*GOLD: 2X TO 5X BASIC
GOLD PRINT RUN 25 SERIAL #'d SETS
PLATINUM PRINT RUN 1 SERIAL #'d SET
NO PLATINUM PRICING DUE TO SCARCITY
*SILVER: .6X TO 1.5X BASIC
SILVER PRINT RUN 100 SERIAL #'d SETS
RANDOM INSERTS IN PACKS
1 Babe Ruth 5.00 12.00
2 Billy Williams 1.25 3.00
3 Bob Feller 1.25 3.00
4 Bobby Doerr 1.25 3.00
5 Carlton Fisk 1.25 3.00
6 Gary Carter 1.25 3.00
7 George Brett 4.00 10.00
8 Carl Yastrzemski 2.00 5.00
9 Harmon Killebrew 2.00 5.00
10 Jim Palmer 1.25 3.00
11 Joe Morgan 1.25 3.00
12 Johnny Bench 2.00 5.00
13 Kirby Puckett 2.00 5.00
14 Gaylord Perry 1.25 3.00
15 Mike Schmidt 3.00 8.00
16 Nolan Ryan 6.00 15.00
17 Ozzie Smith 2.50 6.00
18 Phil Rizzuto 1.25 3.00
19 Reggie Jackson 1.25 3.00
20 Roberto Clemente 5.00 12.00
21 Robin Yount 2.00 5.00
22 Rod Carew 1.25 3.00
23 Rollie Fingers 1.25 3.00
24 Steve Carlton 1.25 3.00
25 Tom Seaver 1.25 3.00

2004 Donruss Timelines Call to the Hall Autograph

PLATINUM PRINT RUN 1 SERIAL #'d SET
NO PLATINUM PRICING DUE TO SCARCITY
3 Bob Feller 8.00 20.00
4 Bobby Doerr 6.00 15.00
14 Gaylord Perry 6.00 15.00
23 Rollie Fingers 6.00 15.00

2004 Donruss Timelines Call to the Hall Autograph Gold

*GOLD: 1X TO 2.5X BASIC CALL AUTO
RANDOM INSERTS IN PACKS
STATED PRINT RUN 25 SERIAL #'d SETS
2 Billy Williams 15.00 40.00
6 Gary Carter 15.00 40.00
10 Jim Palmer 15.00 40.00
18 Phil Rizzuto 30.00 60.00
24 Steve Carlton 10.00 25.00

2004 Donruss Timelines Call to the Hall Autograph Silver

*SILVER: .6X TO 1.5X BASIC CALL AUTO
RANDOM INSERTS IN PACKS
STATED PRINT RUN 100 SERIAL #'d SETS
3 Bob Feller 12.50 30.00

2004 Donruss Timelines Call to the Hall Material

CLEMENTE PRINT RUN 100 #'d CARDS
B.RUTH PRINT RUN 50 #'d CARDS
ALL OTHER CARDS ARE NOT SERIAL #'d
*COMBO: 1X TO 2.5X BASIC
COMBO PRINT RUN 125 SERIAL #'d SETS
MOST COMBOS ARE BAT-JSY SWATCHES
RANDOM INSERTS IN PACKS
1 Babe Ruth Jsy/50 250.00 400.00
4 Bobby Doerr Bat 3.00 8.00
6 Gary Carter Jacket 3.00 8.00
7 George Brett Bat 8.00 20.00
8 Carl Yastrzemski Bat 8.00 20.00
13 Kirby Puckett Bat 6.00 15.00
15 Mike Schmidt Bat 8.00 20.00
16 Nolan Ryan Jsy 8.00 20.00
17 Ozzie Smith Bat 6.00 15.00
19 Reggie Jackson Bat 4.00 10.00
20 Roberto Clemente Bat/100 10.00 25.00

2004 Donruss Timelines Call to the Hall Material Autograph

RANDOM INSERTS IN PACKS
PRINT RUNS B/WN 5-100 COPIES PER
NO PRICING ON QTY OF 5 OR LESS
4 Bobby Doerr Bat/100 12.50 30.00
6 Gary Carter Jacket/25 20.00 50.00
19 Reggie Jackson Bat/25 40.00 80.00

2004 Donruss Timelines Recollection Autographs

STATED ODDS 1:2
PRINT RUNS B/WN 1-225 COPIES PER
NO PRICING ON QTY OF 15 OR LESS
1 Sandy Alomar Jr. 89/25 6.00 15.00
6 San Alomar Jr. 91 AS Black/32 6.00 15.00
12 Sandy Alomar Jr. 92 Black/20 6.00 15.00
21 Sandy Alomar Jr. 97/16 10.00 25.00
23 Sandy Alomar Jr. 98 Black/18 10.00 25.00
28 Wally Backman 83/38 5.00 12.00
29 Wally Backman 85/97 4.00 10.00
30 Wally Backman 86/67 5.00 12.00
31 Wally Backman 87/38 5.00 12.00
32 Wally Backman 88/190 4.00 10.00
33 Wally Backman 89/30 6.00 15.00
36 Wally Backman 90/74 5.00 12.00
37 Wally Backman 91/79 5.00 12.00
38 Wally Backman 92/59 5.00 12.00
47 H.Baines 83 Blue/20 10.00 25.00
48 H.Baines 84 Black/20 10.00 25.00
54 H.Baines 86 DK Black/32 10.00 25.00
56 H.Baines 87 Blue/59 8.00 20.00
59 H.Baines 88 Blue/26 10.00 25.00
62 H.Baines 89 Black/33 10.00 25.00
63 H.Baines 89 Blue/39 8.00 20.00
65 H.Baines 90 Blue/28 10.00 25.00
66 H.Baines 90 AS/19 15.00 40.00
69 H.Baines 92 Blue/17 15.00 40.00
77 Dusty Baker 81/36 8.00 20.00
78 Dusty Baker 82/20 10.00 25.00
79 Dusty Baker 83/36 8.00 20.00
80 Dusty Baker 84/37 8.00 20.00
81 Dusty Baker 85/30 10.00 25.00
82 Dusty Baker 86/35 10.00 25.00
83 Jesse Barfield 83/42 10.00 25.00
84 Jesse Barfield 84/63 5.00 12.00
85 Jesse Barfield 85/88 4.00 10.00
86 Jesse Barfield 86/41 5.00 12.00
87 Jesse Barfield 87/61 5.00 12.00
88 Jesse Barfield 88/42 5.00 12.00
90 Jesse Barfield 89/41 5.00 12.00
91 Jesse Barfield 90/42 5.00 12.00
93 Jesse Barfield 91 Blue/27 6.00 15.00
95 Jesse Barfield 92 Blue/28 6.00 15.00
96 Don Baylor 81 Black/30 8.00 20.00
97 Don Baylor 81 Blue/47 6.00 15.00
98 Don Baylor 82 Black/27 8.00 20.00
99 Don Baylor 82 Blue/56 6.00 15.00
100 Don Baylor 83 Black/23 8.00 20.00
101 Don Baylor 83 Blue/23 8.00 20.00
104 Don Baylor 85 Black/20 8.00 20.00
106 Don Baylor 86 Black/42 6.00 15.00
107 Don Baylor 86 Blue/28 8.00 20.00
108 Don Baylor 87 Black/28 8.00 20.00
109 Don Baylor 87 Blue/37 6.00 15.00
113 Carlos Beltran 01/56 8.00 20.00
114 Carlos Beltran 02/34 10.00 25.00
123 Kris Benson 01/104 6.00 15.00
130 Vida Blue 82/26 6.00 15.00
131 Vida Blue 82 DK/16 10.00 25.00
132 Vida Blue 83/26 6.00 15.00
133 Vida Blue 83 MVP/20 6.00 15.00
134 Vida Blue 86/51 5.00 12.00
135 Vida Blue 87/28 6.00 15.00
143 Bert Blyleven 84 Blue/23 6.00 15.00
144 Bert Blyleven 85 Black/52 5.00 12.00
147 Bert Blyleven 85 DK Blue/40 5.00 12.00
150 Bert Blyleven 87 Black/32 10.00 25.00
153 Bert Blyleven 88 Blue/101 4.00 10.00
156 Bert Blyleven 89 Black/39 5.00 12.00
159 Bert Blyleven 90 Black/57 5.00 12.00
161 Bert Blyleven 91 Black/52 5.00 12.00
200 Bill Buckner 81/25 12.00 30.00
201 Bill Buckner 82/25 12.00 30.00
202 Bill Buckner 83/25 12.00 30.00
203 Bill Buckner 83 DK/33 12.00 30.00
204 Bill Buckner 84/25 12.00 30.00
205 Bill Buckner 85 Black/21 12.00 30.00
207 Bill Buckner 86/25 12.00 30.00
208 Bill Buckner 87/25 12.00 30.00
209 Bill Buckner 88 Black/24 12.00 30.00
212 Bill Buckner 90 Blue/23 12.00 30.00
219 Jay Buhner 92/19 10.00 25.00
220 Jay Buhner 93/20 10.00 25.00
221 Jay Buhner 94/16 10.00 25.00
224 Jay Buhner 97/19 15.00 40.00
225 Jay Buhner 98/18 15.00 40.00
228 Marlon Byrd 02/28 6.00 15.00
231 Jose Canseco 87 DK/16 20.00 50.00
232 Jose Canseco 88/18 20.00 50.00
235 Jose Canseco 89 40-40/17 20.00 50.00
242 Jose Canseco 93/18 20.00 50.00
260 Steve Carlton 81/29 12.50 30.00
261 Steve Carlton 81 CY/30 12.50 30.00
262 Steve Carlton 82/30 12.50 30.00
263 Steve Carlton 83/57 12.50 30.00
264 Steve Carlton 83 DK/25 12.50 30.00
266 Steve Carlton 85/48 12.50 30.00
270 Gary Carter 81/27 10.00 25.00
271 Gary Carter 82/36 8.00 20.00
272 Gary Carter 82 DK/16 15.00 40.00
273 Gary Carter 83/42 15.00 40.00
275 Gary Carter 85/19 15.00 40.00
276 Gary Carter 86/61 15.00 40.00
277 Gary Carter 87/75 15.00 40.00
278 Gary Carter 88/47 15.00 40.00
280 Gary Carter 89 Black/16 15.00 40.00
285 Gary Carter 91/26 10.00 25.00
290 Gary Carter 93 CL/19 15.00 40.00
291 Jack Clark 84 DK/17 15.00 40.00
292 Jack Clark 88 DK/67 8.00 20.00
329 Jose Cruz Sr. 81/39 6.00 15.00
330 Jose Cruz Sr. 82/50 6.00 15.00
331 Jose Cruz Sr. 83/50 6.00 15.00
332 Jose Cruz Sr. 84/50 6.00 15.00
333 Jose Cruz Sr. 85/49 6.00 15.00
334 Jose Cruz Sr. 86/50 6.00 15.00
335 Jose Cruz Sr. 87/57 6.00 15.00
336 Darren Daulton 86/24 12.00 30.00
337 Darren Daulton 87 Black/32 15.00 40.00
338 Darren Daulton 87 Blue/68 10.00 25.00
339 Darren Daulton 88 Black/21 15.00 40.00
340 Darren Daulton 88 Blue/18 15.00 40.00
341 Darren Daulton 89 Black/30 12.00 30.00
342 Darren Daulton 89 Blue/104 8.00 20.00
348 Darren Daulton 93 Blue/23 12.00 30.00
357 Eric Davis 87/62 8.00 20.00
359 E.Davis 87 DK COR Blue/39 8.00 20.00
362 Eric Davis 88/80 15.00 40.00
365 Eric Davis 88 MVP/36 10.00 25.00
366 Eric Davis 89/71 10.00 25.00
367 Eric Davis 90/42 10.00 25.00
368 Eric Davis 90 AS/41 10.00 25.00
369 Eric Davis 91/66 10.00 25.00
370 Eric Davis 91 BC/102 10.00 25.00
371 Eric Davis 92/49 10.00 25.00
372 Eric Davis 93/20 10.00 25.00
373 Eric Davis 94/44 10.00 25.00
374 Eric Davis 97 #190/40 10.00 25.00
375 Eric Davis 97 #292/30 10.00 25.00
376 Eric Davis 99 Retro/95 10.00 25.00
377 Eric Davis 01/122 10.00 25.00
379 Andre Dawson 81/25 10.00 25.00
382 Andre Dawson 83 Black/20 12.50 30.00
384 Andre Dawson 84 Black/33 10.00 25.00
386 Andre Dawson 85 Black/17 15.00 40.00
388 Andre Dawson 86 Black/29 10.00 25.00
390 A.Dawson 86 DK Black/34 10.00 25.00
391 A.Dawson 86 DK Blue/19 15.00 40.00
392 Andre Dawson 87 Black/19 15.00 40.00
393 Andre Dawson 87 Blue/18 15.00 40.00
396 Andre Dawson 88 Black/20 12.50 30.00
400 A.Dawson 88 DK Black/35 12.50 30.00
401 A.Dawson 88 DK Blue/30 12.50 30.00
402 Andre Dawson 88 MVP/19 15.00 40.00
403 Andre Dawson 89 Black/20 12.50 30.00
406 A.Dawson 89 MVP Black/20 12.50 30.00
408 Andre Dawson 90 Black/18 15.00 40.00
410 Andre Dawson 91/20 12.50 30.00
411 A.Dawson 91 AS Black/20 12.50 30.00
413 Andre Dawson 92 Blue/30 10.00 25.00
416 Andre Dawson 93/19 15.00 40.00
420 Andre Dawson 97/18 15.00 40.00
421 Lenny Dykstra 86/17 15.00 40.00
422 Lenny Dykstra 87/80 8.00 20.00
423 Lenny Dykstra 88/88 6.00 15.00
425 Lenny Dykstra 89/71 8.00 20.00
427 Lenny Dykstra 90/51 8.00 20.00
428 Lenny Dykstra 91/43 8.00 20.00
429 Lenny Dykstra 91 AS/37 8.00 20.00
431 Lenny Dykstra 91 MVP/21 10.00 25.00
433 Lenny Dykstra 92/64 8.00 20.00
434 Lenny Dykstra 93/32 10.00 25.00
435 Lenny Dykstra 94/21 10.00 25.00
436 Lenny Dykstra 95/25 10.00 25.00
444 Jim Edmonds 99 Retro/25 10.00 25.00
445 Jim Edmonds 00 Retro/25 10.00 25.00
446 Jim Edmonds 01/25 10.00 25.00
448 Dwight Evans 81/36 12.50 30.00
449 Dwight Evans 82/16 20.00 50.00
451 Dwight Evans 83/42 12.50 30.00
452 Dwight Evans 84/16 20.00 50.00
453 Dwight Evans 85/29 15.00 40.00
454 Dwight Evans 86/28 15.00 40.00
455 Dwight Evans 87/25 15.00 40.00
457 Dwight Evans 88/25 15.00 40.00
459 Dwight Evans 88 DK/30 15.00 40.00
460 Dwight Evans 89/16 20.00 50.00
465 Sid Fernandez 87/30 10.00 25.00
466 Sid Fernandez 88/56 8.00 20.00
467 Sid Fernandez 89/26 10.00 25.00
474 Rollie Fingers 81/56 8.00 20.00
475 Rollie Fingers 82/42 8.00 20.00
476 Rollie Fingers 83/62 8.00 20.00
477 Rollie Fingers 83 DK/24 10.00 25.00
478 Rollie Fingers 85/34 10.00 25.00
479 Rollie Fingers 86/43 8.00 20.00
485 John Franco 85/37 5.00 12.00
486 John Franco 86/41 5.00 12.00
487 John Franco 87/112 4.00 10.00
488 John Franco 88/225 4.00 10.00
490 John Franco 89/83 10.00 25.00
491 John Franco 90/50 10.00 25.00
492 John Franco 90 DK/57 10.00 25.00
493 John Franco 91/72 10.00 25.00
494 John Franco 92/66 10.00 25.00
495 John Franco 93/64 10.00 25.00
496 John Franco 94/21 12.50 30.00
497 John Franco 95/19 12.50 30.00
498 John Franco 96/25 12.50 30.00
501 Julio Franco 85/30 12.50 30.00
502 Julio Franco 86/46 10.00 25.00
503 Julio Franco 87/59 10.00 25.00
504 Julio Franco 88/122 8.00 20.00
506 Julio Franco 88 DK/75 8.00 20.00
507 Julio Franco 89/48 10.00 25.00
508 Julio Franco 90/46 10.00 25.00
509 Julio Franco 90 AS/26 12.50 30.00
511 Julio Franco 91/62 10.00 25.00
512 Julio Franco 92/38 10.00 25.00
513 Julio Franco 93/33 12.50 30.00
515 Julio Franco 95/21 12.50 30.00
517 Freddy Garcia 01/50 8.00 20.00
520 Freddy Garcia 02/27 10.00 25.00
521 Freddy Garcia 03/25 10.00 25.00
522 Jay Gibbons 01 DR/50 5.00 12.00
524 Jay Gibbons 03/24 6.00 15.00
527 D.Gooden 85/31 15.00 40.00
529 D.Gooden 86 DK/28 10.00 25.00
531 D.Gooden 87 Blue/99 10.00 25.00
532 D.Gooden 88 Black/27 10.00 25.00
533 D.Gooden 88 Blue/121 10.00 25.00
535 D.Gooden 89 Black/48 10.00 25.00
536 D.Gooden 89 Blue/49 10.00 25.00
539 D.Gooden 90 Blue/87 10.00 25.00
541 D.Gooden 91 Blue/71 10.00 25.00
542 D.Gooden 92 Black/23 10.00 25.00
547 D.Gooden 94 Blue/20 10.00 25.00
548 D.Gooden 97 Black/16 15.00 40.00
558 Bobby Grich 81/88 4.00 10.00
559 Bobby Grich 82/88 4.00 10.00
560 Bobby Grich 83/70 5.00 12.00
561 Bobby Grich 84/73 5.00 12.00
562 Bobby Grich 85/84 4.00 10.00
563 Bobby Grich 86/67 5.00 12.00
564 Bobby Grich 87/90 4.00 10.00
601 Keith Hernandez 81/19 15.00 40.00
602 Keith Hernandez 82/36 8.00 20.00
603 Keith Hernandez 83/39 8.00 20.00
604 Keith Hernandez 83 DK/25 10.00 25.00
605 Keith Hernandez 84/36 8.00 20.00
606 Keith Hernandez 85/80 8.00 20.00
607 Keith Hernandez 86/66 8.00 20.00
608 Keith Hernandez 87/123 6.00 15.00
609 Keith Hernandez 88 Black/91 6.00 15.00
610 Keith Hernandez 88 Blue/74 8.00 20.00
612 Keith Hernandez 89/76 8.00 20.00
617 Keith Hernandez 90/87 6.00 15.00
618 Eric Hinske 03/20 6.00 15.00
620 Charlie Hough 82/60 5.00 12.00
621 Charlie Hough 83/56 5.00 12.00
622 Charlie Hough 84/79 5.00 12.00
623 Charlie Hough 85/69 5.00 12.00
624 Charlie Hough 86/58 5.00 12.00
625 Charlie Hough 87/150 4.00 10.00
626 Charlie Hough 87 DK/81 4.00 10.00
627 Charlie Hough 88/184 4.00 10.00
629 Charlie Hough 89/51 5.00 12.00
630 Charlie Hough 90/45 5.00 12.00
631 Charlie Hough 91/88 4.00 10.00
632 Charlie Hough 92/55 5.00 12.00
633 Charlie Hough 94/19 10.00 25.00
634 Art Howe 81/43 6.00 15.00
635 Art Howe 82 Black/37 6.00 15.00
636 Art Howe 82 Blue/57 6.00 15.00
637 Art Howe 83 Black/20 8.00 20.00
638 Art Howe 83 Blue/54 6.00 15.00
641 Tim Hudson 03/39 12.50 30.00
647 Fergie Jenkins 81/21 10.00 25.00
648 Fergie Jenkins 82/57 8.00 20.00
649 Fergie Jenkins 83/29 10.00 25.00
650 Fergie Jenkins 84/45 8.00 20.00
654 Tommy John 82 Blue/23 6.00 15.00
657 Tommy John 83 Blue/35 6.00 15.00
659 Tommy John 84 Blue/31 6.00 15.00
660 Tommy John 85 Black/19 10.00 25.00
661 Tommy John 85 Blue/25 6.00 15.00
662 Tommy John 88 Black/66 5.00 12.00
663 Tommy John 88 Blue/25 6.00 15.00
664 Tommy John 88 DK Blue/50 5.00 12.00
665 Howard Johnson 83/28 6.00 15.00
666 Howard Johnson 85/29 6.00 15.00
667 Howard Johnson 86/24 6.00 15.00
669 Howard Johnson 87 Blue/24 6.00 15.00
671 Howard Johnson 88/25 6.00 15.00
672 Howard Johnson 89/25 6.00 15.00
673 Howard Johnson 90/25 6.00 15.00
674 Howard Johnson 90 AS/28 6.00 15.00
675 Howard Johnson 90 MVP/24 6.00 15.00
676 Howard Johnson 91/25 6.00 15.00
677 Howard Johnson 92 Black/26 6.00 15.00
679 Howard Johnson 93/17 10.00 25.00
680 Howard Johnson 94/24 6.00 15.00
681 Nick Johnson 99 Retro/53 8.00 20.00
684 Nick Johnson 01/55 8.00 20.00
704 Dave Justice 90/24 15.00 40.00
710 Dave Justice 94/16 20.00 50.00
723 Dave Justice 01/25 15.00 40.00
725 Austin Kearns 03 Black/48 5.00 12.00
728 Jimmy Key 86/54 8.00 20.00
729 Jimmy Key 87/92 6.00 15.00
731 Jimmy Key 88/74 8.00 20.00
732 Jimmy Key 89/64 8.00 20.00
733 Jimmy Key 90/42 8.00 20.00
734 Jimmy Key 91/20 10.00 25.00
735 Jimmy Key 92/38 8.00 20.00
736 Jimmy Key 93/23 10.00 25.00
737 Jimmy Key 94/19 15.00 40.00
739 Jimmy Key 95/17 15.00 40.00
740 Jimmy Key 96/31 10.00 25.00
741 Jimmy Key 97/16 15.00 40.00
743 Carney Lansford 81 Black/87 4.00 10.00
745 Carney Lansford 82 Black/36 5.00 12.00
746 Carney Lansford 82 Blue/23 6.00 15.00
748 Carney Lansford 83 Blue/29 6.00 15.00
751 Carney Lansford 85/21 6.00 15.00
752 Carney Lansford 86/54 5.00 12.00
753 Carney Lansford 87/76 5.00 12.00
756 Carney Lansford 88 Blue/66 5.00 12.00
757 Carney Lansford 89/17 10.00 25.00
759 Carney Lansford 91/19 10.00 25.00
761 Carlos Lee 01/110 6.00 15.00
766 Greg Luzinski 81 Blue/72 8.00 20.00
767 Greg Luzinski 82/67 8.00 20.00
768 Greg Luzinski 83/52 8.00 20.00
769 Greg Luzinski 84/43 8.00 20.00
770 Greg Luzinski 85/44 8.00 20.00
771 Fred Lynn 81 Black/43 8.00 20.00
772 Fred Lynn 81 Blue/23 10.00 25.00
773 Fred Lynn 82 Black/17 15.00 40.00
774 Fred Lynn 82 Blue/37 8.00 20.00
776 Fred Lynn 83 Blue/42 8.00 20.00
777 Fred Lynn 84 Blue/25 10.00 25.00
779 Fred Lynn 84 DK/21 10.00 25.00
781 Fred Lynn 85 Blue/28 10.00 25.00
782 Fred Lynn 86 Black/43 8.00 20.00
784 Fred Lynn 87 Black/38 8.00 20.00
785 Fred Lynn 87 Blue/25 10.00 25.00
786 Fred Lynn 87 DK/82 6.00 15.00
787 Fred Lynn 88 Black/30 10.00 25.00
791 Fred Lynn 89 Blue/50 8.00 20.00
792 Fred Lynn 91/18 15.00 40.00
812 Edgar Martinez 89/39 20.00 50.00
820 E.Martinez 99 Retro/42 20.00 50.00
821 E.Martinez 00 Retro/43 20.00 50.00
822 Edgar Martinez 01/58 20.00 50.00
823 Edgar Martinez 02/25 20.00 50.00
834 Gary Matthews Sr. 82/76 5.00 12.00
835 Gary Matthews Sr. 83/52 5.00 12.00
836 G.Matthews Sr. 84 Black/49 5.00 12.00
838 Gary Matthews Sr. 85/45 6.00 15.00
839 Gary Matthews Sr. 86/54 6.00 15.00
856 Jack McDowell 88/213 6.00 15.00
857 Jack McDowell 89/114 6.00 15.00
858 Jack McDowell 91/19 12.50 30.00
859 Jack McDowell 92/26 12.50 30.00
864 Jack McDowell 96/17 15.00 40.00
922 Jack Morris 81/31 10.00 25.00
923 Jack Morris 82/56 8.00 20.00
924 Jack Morris 83/48 8.00 20.00
926 Jack Morris 84/36 8.00 20.00
927 Jack Morris 85/42 8.00 20.00
928 Jack Morris 86/45 8.00 20.00
929 Jack Morris 87/123 6.00 15.00
930 Jack Morris 87 DK/106 6.00 15.00
931 Jack Morris 88/139 6.00 15.00
934 Jack Morris 89/107 6.00 15.00
935 Jack Morris 90/71 8.00 20.00
936 Jack Morris 91/34 10.00 25.00
937 Jack Morris 92/59 8.00 20.00
938 Jack Morris 92 AS/40 8.00 20.00
939 Jack Morris 93/78 8.00 20.00
940 Jamie Moyer 87/50 8.00 20.00
941 Jamie Moyer 88/24 10.00 25.00
943 Jamie Moyer 89/44 8.00 20.00
944 Jamie Moyer 90/35 10.00 25.00
945 Jamie Moyer 94/19 15.00 40.00
946 Jamie Moyer 95/29 10.00 25.00
947 Jamie Moyer 96/16 15.00 40.00
949 Jamie Moyer 03/21 10.00 25.00
950 Dale Murphy 81 Black/21 15.00 40.00
954 Dale Murphy 83 Blue/24 15.00 40.00
964 Dale Murphy 87 Blue/37 15.00 40.00
966 Dale Murphy 87 DK Blue/64 15.00 40.00
968 Dale Murphy 88 Blue/40 15.00 40.00
975 Dale Murphy 89 Blue/40 15.00 40.00
980 Dale Murphy 92 Black/17 20.00 50.00
1015 Graig Nettles 82 Blue/27 10.00 25.00
1017 Graig Nettles 83 Blue/48 8.00 20.00
1018 Graig Nettles 84 Black/37 8.00 20.00
1020 Graig Nettles 85 Black/23 10.00 25.00
1022 Graig Nettles 86 Black/41 8.00 20.00
1033 Trot Nixon 01/110 6.00 15.00
1034 Trot Nixon 02/27 10.00 25.00
1035 Trot Nixon 03/25 10.00 25.00
1036 Al Oliver 81/65 5.00 12.00
1037 Al Oliver 82/60 5.00 12.00
1038 Al Oliver 83/49 5.00 12.00
1039 Al Oliver 84 Black/61 5.00 12.00
1041 Al Oliver 84 DK/29 6.00 15.00
1042 Al Oliver 85/55 5.00 12.00
1043 Al Oliver 86/58 5.00 12.00
1044 Paul O'Neill 86/21 15.00 40.00
1053 Paul O'Neill 01/29 15.00 40.00
1054 Paul O'Neill 02/29 15.00 40.00
1055 M.Ordonez 99 Retro/25 6.00 15.00
1056 M.Ordonez 00 Retro/25 6.00 15.00
1057 Magglio Ordonez 01/25 6.00 15.00
1058 Magglio Ordonez 02/25 6.00 15.00
1060 Jesse Orosco 85 DK Blue/25 6.00 15.00
1061 Roy Oswalt 01 DR/30 10.00 25.00
1064 Roy Oswalt 03/31 10.00 25.00
1065 Amos Otis 81/43 8.00 20.00
1066 Amos Otis 82/52 8.00 20.00
1067 Amos Otis 83/41 8.00 20.00
1068 Rafael Palmeiro 87/35 50.00 100.00
1078 J.Palmer 81 #473 Black/16 15.00 40.00
1079 J.Palmer 81 #473 Blue/19 15.00 40.00
1080 Jim Palmer 82/49 8.00 20.00
1083 Jim Palmer 84/17 15.00 40.00
1085 Dave Parker 82/31 10.00 25.00
1086 Dave Parker 83/39 8.00 20.00
1087 Dave Parker 84 Black/21 10.00 25.00
1088 Dave Parker 84 Blue/15 15.00 40.00
1090 Dave Parker 85 Blue/19 15.00 40.00
1092 Dave Parker 86 Blue/23 10.00 25.00
1093 Dave Parker 87 Black/66 8.00 20.00
1095 Dave Parker 88/85 6.00 15.00
1096 Dave Parker 89/21 10.00 25.00
1098 Dave Parker 90 Blue/18 15.00 40.00
1100 Dave Parker 91 MVP/20 20.00 50.00
1101 Tony Pena 82/61 20.00 50.00
1102 Tony Pena 83/51 20.00 50.00
1103 Tony Pena 84/45 20.00 50.00
1104 Tony Pena 85/22 30.00 80.00
1105 Tony Pena 86/29 30.00 80.00
1106 Tony Pena 87/69 20.00 50.00
1107 Tony Pena 88/46 20.00 50.00
1109 Tony Pena 89/36 20.00 50.00
1110 Tony Pena 90/16 30.00 80.00
1111 Tony Pena 91/17 30.00 80.00
1112 Tony Pena 92/30 20.00 50.00
1113 Tony Pena 93/43 20.00 50.00
1119 Terry Pendleton 85 ERR/16 20.00 50.00
1120 Terry Pendleton 86/48 10.00 25.00
1121 Terry Pendleton 87/53 10.00 25.00
1122 Terry Pendleton 88/58 10.00 25.00
1124 Terry Pendleton 89/54 10.00 25.00
1125 Terry Pendleton 90/60 10.00 25.00
1127 Terry Pendleton 91 Blue/36 10.00 25.00
1128 Terry Pendleton 92/18 10.00 25.00
1130 Terry Pendleton 93/43 10.00 25.00
1133 Terry Pendleton 96/17 20.00 50.00
1134 Terry Pendleton 97/21 12.50 30.00
1135 Gaylord Perry 81/91 6.00 15.00
1136 Gaylord Perry 82/79 8.00 20.00
1137 Gaylord Perry 83/55 8.00 20.00
1138 Jorge Posada 01/109 40.00 80.00
1143 Kirby Puckett 87/21 50.00 100.00
1144 Harold Reynolds 86/32 10.00 25.00
1145 Harold Reynolds 87/65 8.00 20.00
1146 Harold Reynolds 88/65 8.00 20.00
1147 Harold Reynolds 89/22 10.00 25.00
1152 Harold Reynolds 92/26 10.00 25.00
1153 Harold Reynolds 93/16 15.00 40.00
1156 Jim Rice 82 Black/23 10.00 25.00
1158 Jim Rice 83/25 10.00 25.00
1159 Jim Rice 84/20 10.00 25.00
1160 Jim Rice 85/17 15.00 40.00
1161 Jim Rice 85 DK Black/23 10.00 25.00
1163 Jim Rice 86/28 10.00 25.00
1165 Jim Rice 87 Blue/18 15.00 40.00
1166 Jim Rice 88/25 10.00 25.00
1192 M.Rivera 01 Black/27 50.00 100.00
1193 M.Rivera 01 Blue/23 50.00 100.00
1194 Frank Robinson 82/47 12.50 30.00
1195 Frank Robinson 83/36 12.50 30.00
1211 Ivan Rodriguez 93/28 12.50 30.00
1215 Ivan Rodriguez 96/16 60.00 120.00
1244 Nolan Ryan 90/25 100.00 200.00
1253 Curt Schilling 89/67 20.00 50.00
1254 Richie Sexson 99 Retro/30 10.00 25.00
1255 Richie Sexson 01/30 10.00 25.00
1256 Richie Sexson 02/29 10.00 25.00
1257 Gary Sheffield 89/19 50.00 100.00
1268 Ruben Sierra 87 Black/121 6.00 15.00
1269 Ruben Sierra 87 Blue/101 6.00 15.00
1270 Ruben Sierra 88 Black/18 15.00 40.00
1276 R.Sierra 89 MVP Black/26 10.00 25.00
1288 Duke Snider 84/26 15.00 40.00
1289 J.T. Snow 93 Black/34 6.00 15.00
1295 J.T. Snow 96 Blue/19 10.00 25.00
1297 J.T. Snow 97 #42 Blue/21 6.00 15.00
1300 J.T. Snow 98 Black/19 10.00 25.00
1304 J.T. Snow 01 Black/81 4.00 10.00
1305 J.T. Snow 01 Blue/19 10.00 25.00
1321 Junior Spivey 03/20 6.00 15.00
1322 Terry Steinbach 87/22 6.00 15.00
1326 Terry Steinbach 89/34 6.00 15.00
1327 Terry Steinbach 90/30 6.00 15.00
1341 Shannon Stewart 01/108 6.00 15.00
1342 Shannon Stewart 02/36 8.00 20.00
1343 Shannon Stewart 03/36 8.00 20.00
1348 Dave Stieb 84/30 10.00 25.00
1349 Dave Stieb 85/19 15.00 40.00
1350 Dave Stieb 86/23 10.00 25.00
1351 Dave Stieb 87/99 6.00 15.00
1352 Dave Stieb 88/51 8.00 20.00
1354 Dave Stieb 89/36 8.00 20.00
1356 Dave Stieb 90/29 10.00 25.00
1358 Dave Stieb 91 DK/17 15.00 40.00
1363 Darryl Strawberry 85/30 10.00 25.00
1366 Darryl Strawberry 87/83 6.00 15.00
1367 Darryl Strawberry 87 DK/81 6.00 15.00
1370 Darryl Strawberry 88/71 20.00 50.00
1373 D.Strawberry 88 MVP/38 8.00 20.00
1374 Darryl Strawberry 89/67 8.00 20.00
1376 D.Strawberry 89 MVP/63 8.00 20.00
1377 Darryl Strawberry 90/84 6.00 15.00
1378 Darryl Strawberry 91/33 10.00 25.00
1381 D.Strawberry 91 MVP/33 10.00 25.00
1382 Darryl Strawberry 92/23 10.00 25.00
1384 Darryl Strawberry 93/41 8.00 20.00
1386 Darryl Strawberry 95/22 10.00 25.00
1388 Darryl Strawberry 97/36 8.00 20.00
1393 B.J. Surhoff 87/108 6.00 15.00
1395 B.J. Surhoff 88/69 8.00 20.00
1397 B.J. Surhoff 89/44 8.00 20.00
1400 B.J. Surhoff 92/21 10.00 25.00
1404 B.J. Surhoff 01/92 6.00 15.00
1423 G.Thomas 82 Black/35 5.00 12.00
1424 Gorman Thomas 82 Blue/30 6.00 15.00
1425 G.Thomas 83 Black/28 6.00 15.00
1426 Gorman Thomas 83 Blue/34 6.00 15.00
1427 G.Thomas 84 Black/33 6.00 15.00
1428 Gorman Thomas 84 Blue/37 5.00 12.00
1429 G.Thomas 86 Black/27 6.00 15.00
1430 Gorman Thomas 86 Blue/31 6.00 15.00
1432 Robby Thompson 87/36 10.00 25.00
1434 R.Thompson 88 Black/77 10.00 25.00
1435 R.Thompson 88 Blue/62 10.00 25.00
1436 Robby Thompson 89/57 10.00 25.00
1437 Robby Thompson 90/65 10.00 25.00
1438 Robby Thompson 91/46 10.00 25.00
1439 Robby Thompson 92/25 12.50 30.00
1440 Robby Thompson 93/17 12.50 30.00
1441 Robby Thompson 94/20 12.50 30.00
1443 Robby Thompson 96/21 12.50 30.00
1444 Robby Thompson 97/27 12.50 30.00
1446 Luis Tiant 83/27 6.00 15.00
1450 A.Trammell 82 DK COR/21 10.00 25.00
1452 Alan Trammell 83 Black/21 10.00 25.00
1457 Alan Trammell 87 Black/38 8.00 20.00
1460 Alan Trammell 88/89 6.00 15.00
1462 Alan Trammell 88 DK/77 8.00 20.00
1463 Alan Trammell 88 MVP/18 15.00 40.00
1466 A.Tram 89 MVP Black/20 10.00 25.00
1472 Alan Trammell 93/16 15.00 40.00
1477 Jason Varitek 01/110 10.00 25.00
1480 Robin Ventura 91/17 15.00 40.00
1481 Robin Ventura 92/18 15.00 40.00
1486 Robin Ventura 01/34 10.00 25.00
1487 Robin Ventura 02/34 10.00 25.00
1489 Frank White 82/24 6.00 15.00
1490 Frank White 83/25 6.00 15.00
1495 Frank White 88/47 5.00 12.00
1497 Frank White 89/23 6.00 15.00
1501 Matt Williams 88/78 10.00 25.00
1502 Matt Williams 89/38 12.50 30.00
1507 Matt Williams 92/19 20.00 50.00
1508 Matt Williams 93/24 15.00 40.00
1510 Matt Williams 95/21 15.00 40.00
1516 M.Williams 99 Retro/50 12.50 30.00
1517 Matt Williams 01/35 15.00 40.00
1518 Matt Williams 02/28 15.00 40.00
1520 Mookie Wilson 82/39 8.00 20.00
1521 Mookie Wilson 83/24 10.00 25.00
1522 Mookie Wilson 84/26 10.00 25.00
1523 Mookie Wilson 85/50 8.00 20.00
1524 Mookie Wilson 86/40 8.00 20.00
1525 Mookie Wilson 87/35 10.00 25.00
1528 Mookie Wilson 89/28 10.00 25.00
1529 Mookie Wilson 90/20 10.00 25.00
1530 Mookie Wilson 91/25 10.00 25.00
1575 Barry Zito 03/25 15.00 40.00

1997 Donruss VxP 1.0

The 1997 Donruss VxP 1.0 set was issued in one series totalling 50 cards. The cards were distributed 10 to a pack with one CD trading card and feature a small player action photo with a head shot. When tilted slightly, the card changes to another photo of the same player beside a disc photo.

COMPLETE SET (50) 10.00 25.00
1 Darin Erstad .20 .50
2 Jim Thome .15 .40
3 Alex Rodriguez .50 1.25
4 Greg Maddux .50 1.25
5 Scott Rolen .15 .40
6 Roberto Alomar .15 .40
7 Tony Clark .02 .10
8 Randy Johnson .20 .50
9 Sammy Sosa .30 .75
10 Jose Guillen .08 .25
11 Cal Ripken .75 2.00
12 Paul Molitor .15 .40
13 Jose Cruz Jr. .20 .50
14 Barry Larkin .15 .40
15 Ken Caminiti .05 .15
16 Rafael Palmeiro .08 .25
17 Chuck Knoblauch .05 .15
18 Juan Gonzalez .15 .40
19 Larry Walker .05 .15
20 Tony Gwynn .40 1.00
21 Brady Anderson .05 .15
22 Derek Jeter .75 2.00
23 Rusty Greer .05 .15
24 Gary Sheffield .20 .50
25 Barry Bonds .40 1.00
26 Mo Vaughn .02 .10
27 Tino Martinez .05 .15
28 Ivan Rodriguez .20 .50
29 Jeff Bagwell .20 .50
30 Tim Salmon .15 .40
31 Nomar Garciaparra .40 1.00
32 Bernie Williams .15 .40
33 Kenny Lofton .08 .25
34 Mike Piazza .50 1.25
35 Jim Edmonds .15 .40
36 Frank Thomas .20 .50
37 Andy Pettitte .08 .25
38 Andruw Jones .40 1.00
39 Raul Mondesi .02 .10
40 John Smoltz .05 .15
41 Albert Belle .02 .10
42 Mark McGwire .50 1.25
43 Chipper Jones .40 1.00
44 Hideo Nomo .15 .40
45 David Justice .15 .40
46 Manny Ramirez .20 .50
47 Ken Griffey Jr. .60 1.50
48 Roger Clemens .40 1.00
49 Vladimir Guerrero .40 1.00
50 Ryne Sandberg .20 .50

1997 Donruss VxP 1.0 CD Roms

COMPLETE SET (6) 12.50 30.00
STATED ODDS 1:1
1 Ken Griffey Jr. 2.50 6.00
2 Greg Maddux 2.00 5.00
3 Mike Piazza 2.00 5.00
4 Cal Ripken 2.00 5.00
5 Alex Rodriguez 2.00 5.00
6 Frank Thomas 2.00 5.00

2004 Donruss World Series

COMP.SET w/o SP's (175) 15.00 40.00
COMP.SOX CHAMPS (25) 12.00 20.00
COMMON ACTIVE (1-175) .15 .40
COMMON RC (1-175) .15 .40
COMMON RETIRED (1-175) .15 .40
COM.(176-200) p/r 703-1000 3.00 8.00
COM.(176-200) p/r 487-568 3.00 8.00
176-200: OVERALL AU-GU ODDS 5 PER BOX
176-200 PRINT RUNS B/WN 487-1000 PER
COMMON (201-224/WS1) .40 1.00
201-224/WS1 ISSUED IN SOX CHAMPS SET
1 Bartolo Colon .15 .40
2 Darin Erstad .15 .40
3 Garret Anderson .15 .40
4 Tim Salmon .15 .40
5 Troy Glaus .15 .40
6 Vladimir Guerrero .25 .60
7 Brandon Webb .15 .40
8 Luis Gonzalez .15 .40
9 Randy Johnson .40 1.00
10 Roberto Alomar .25 .60
11 Shea Hillenbrand .15 .40
12 Steve Finley .15 .40
13 Andruw Jones .15 .40
14 Chipper Jones .40 1.00
15 J.D. Drew .15 .40
16 Marcus Giles .15 .40
17 Rafael Furcal .15 .40
18 Javy Lopez .15 .40
19 Jay Gibbons .15 .40
20 Luis Matos .15 .40
21 Melvin Mora .15 .40
22 Miguel Tejada .25 .60
23 Rafael Palmeiro .25 .60
24 Curt Schilling .25 .60
25 Dwight Evans .15 .40
26 Fred Lynn .15 .40
27 Jason Varitek .40 1.00
28 Jim Rice .25 .60
29 Johnny Damon .25 .60
30 Luis Tiant .15 .40
31 Manny Ramirez .40 1.00
32 Nomar Garciaparra .25 .60
33 Pedro Martinez .25 .60
34 Trot Nixon .15 .40
35 Aramis Ramirez .15 .40
36 Corey Patterson .15 .40
37 Derrek Lee .15 .40
38 Greg Maddux .50 1.25
39 Kerry Wood .15 .40
40 Mark Prior .25 .60
41 Moises Alou .15 .40
42 Sammy Sosa .40 1.00
43 Carlos Lee .15 .40
44 Frank Thomas .40 1.00
45 Luis Aparicio .25 .60
46 Magglio Ordonez .25 .60
47 Mark Buehrle .25 .60
48 Paul Konerko .25 .60
49 Adam Dunn .25 .60
50 Austin Kearns .15 .40
51 Barry Larkin .25 .60
52 Dave Concepcion .15 .40
53 George Foster .15 .40
54 Joe Morgan .25 .60
55 Sean Casey .15 .40
56 Tony Perez .25 .60
57 C.C. Sabathia .25 .60
58 Jody Gerut .15 .40
59 Omar Vizquel .25 .60
60 Victor Martinez .25 .60
61 Charles Johnson .15 .40
62 Jeromy Burnitz .15 .40
63 Larry Walker .25 .60

2004 Donruss World Series

64 Preston Wilson .15 .40
65 Todd Helton .25 .60
66 Alan Trammell .25 .60
67 Dmitri Young .15 .40
68 Ivan Rodriguez .25 .60
69 Jeremy Bonderman .15 .40
70 A.J. Burnett .15 .40
71 Brad Penny .15 .40
72 Dontrelle Willis .15 .40
73 Josh Beckett .15 .40
74 Juan Pierre .15 .40
75 Luis Castillo .15 .40
76 Miguel Cabrera .40 1.00
77 Mike Lowell .15 .40
78 Andy Pettitte .25 .60
79 Craig Biggio .25 .60
80 Jeff Bagwell .25 .60
81 Jeff Kent .15 .40
82 Lance Berkman .25 .60
83 Roger Clemens .50 1.25
84 Roy Oswalt .25 .60
85 Wade Miller .15 .40
86 Angel Berroa .15 .40
87 Carlos Beltran .25 .60
88 Juan Gonzalez .15 .40
89 Ken Harvey .15 .40
90 Mike Sweeney .15 .40
91 Adrian Beltre .40 1.00
92 Hideo Nomo .40 1.00
93 Kazuhisa Ishii .15 .40
94 Milton Bradley .15 .40
95 Orel Hershiser .15 .40
96 Paul Lo Duca .15 .40
97 Shawn Green .15 .40
98 Ben Sheets .15 .40
99 Geoff Jenkins .15 .40
100 Junior Spivey .15 .40
101 Rickie Weeks .15 .40
102 Scott Podsednik .15 .40
103 Jack Morris .25 .60
104 Jacque Jones .15 .40
105 Johan Santana .25 .60
106 Shannon Stewart .15 .40
107 Torii Hunter .15 .40
108 Jose Vidro .15 .40
109 Orlando Cabrera Sox .15 .40
110 Al Leiter .15 .40
111 Darryl Strawberry .15 .40
112 Dwight Gooden .15 .40
113 Jose Reyes .25 .60
114 Kazuo Matsui RC .25 .60
115 Keith Hernandez .15 .40
116 Lenny Dykstra .15 .40
117 Mike Piazza .40 1.00
118 Tom Glavine .25 .60
119 Alex Rodriguez .50 1.25
120 Bernie Williams .25 .60
121 Derek Jeter 1.00 2.50
122 Gary Sheffield .15 .40
123 Jason Giambi .15 .40
124 Javier Vazquez .15 .40
125 Jorge Posada .25 .60
126 Kenny Lofton .15 .40
127 Kevin Brown .15 .40
128 Mariano Rivera .50 1.25
129 Mike Mussina .25 .60
130 Barry Zito .25 .60
131 Eric Chavez .15 .40
132 Jermaine Dye .15 .40
133 Mark Mulder .15 .40
134 Rich Harden .15 .40
135 Tim Hudson .25 .60
136 Brett Myers .15 .40
137 Jim Thome .25 .60
138 Kevin Millwood .15 .40
139 Marlon Byrd .15 .40
140 Mike Lieberthal .15 .40
141 Pat Burrell .15 .40
142 Steve Carlton .25 .60
143 Dave Parker .15 .40
144 Jason Kendall .15 .40
145 Brian Giles .15 .40
146 Jay Payton .15 .40
147 Ryan Klesko .15 .40
148 J.T. Snow .15 .40
149 Jason Schmidt .15 .40
150 Bret Boone .15 .40
151 Edgar Martinez .25 .60
152 Jamie Moyer .15 .40
153 Rich Aurilia .15 .40
154 Shigetoshi Hasegawa .15 .40
155 Albert Pujols .50 1.25
156 Dan Haren .15 .40
157 Edgar Renteria .15 .40
158 Fernando Vina .15 .40
159 Jim Edmonds .25 .60
160 Matt Morris .15 .40
161 Scott Rolen .25 .60
162 Aubrey Huff .15 .40
163 Carl Crawford .25 .60
164 Dewon Brazelton .15 .40
165 Fred McGriff .15 .40
166 Rocco Baldelli .15 .40
167 Alfonso Soriano .25 .60
168 Hank Blalock .15 .40
169 Kenny Rogers .15 .40
170 Mark Teixeira .25 .60
171 Michael Young .15 .40
172 Carlos Delgado .15 .40
173 Eric Hinske .15 .40
174 Roy Halladay .25 .60
175 Vernon Wells .15 .40
176 Ivan Ochoa AU/487 RC 3.00 8.00
177 Jason Bartlett AU/1000 RC 4.00 10.00
178 J.Labandeira AU/703 RC 3.00 8.00
179 Phil Stockman AU/1000 RC 3.00 8.00
180 Ronny Cedeno AU/715 RC 6.00 15.00
181 Shawn Camp AU/1000 RC 3.00 8.00
182 Ruddy Yan AU/1000 3.00 8.00
183 Roberto Novoa AU/568 RC 3.00 8.00
184 Just Knoedler AU/1000 RC 3.00 8.00
185 Jesse Harper AU/1000 RC 3.00 8.00
186 Jas Szuminski AU/1000 RC 3.00 8.00
187 Jamie Brown AU/800 RC 3.00 8.00
188 Ed Rodriguez AU/1000 RC 4.00 10.00
189 Dennis Sarfate AU/1000 RC 3.00 8.00
190 Ryan Meaux AU/1000 RC 3.00 8.00
191 Ch.Thomas AU/1000 RC 4.00 10.00
192 F.Francisco AU/1000 RC 3.00 8.00
193 Orl Rodriguez AU/500 RC 3.00 8.00
194 Joey Gathright AU/1000 RC 4.00 10.00
195 Renyel Pinto AU/1000 RC 3.00 8.00
196 Justin Leone AU/1000 RC 4.00 10.00
197 Tim Bausher AU/834 RC 3.00 8.00
198 Trav Blackley AU/1000 RC 3.00 8.00
199 Yadier Molina AU/500 RC 150.00 400.00
200 Brad Halsey AU/500 RC 4.00 10.00
201 Curt Schilling WSC .60 1.50
202 Pedro Martinez WSC .60 1.50
203 Derek Lowe WSC .40 1.00
204 Tim Wakefield WSC .60 1.50
205 Bronson Arroyo WSC .40 1.00
206 Mike Timlin WSC .40 1.00
207 Curtis Leskanic WSC .40 1.00
208 Mike Myers WSC .40 1.00
209 Alan Embree WSC .40 1.00
210 Keith Foulke WSC .40 1.00
211 Jason Varitek WSC 1.00 2.50
212 Doug Mirabelli WSC .40 1.00
213 Doug Mientkiewicz WSC .40 1.00
214 Mark Bellhorn WSC .40 1.00
215 Pokey Reese WSC .40 1.00
216 Orlando Cabrera WSC .40 1.00
217 Bill Mueller WSC .40 1.00
218 Kevin Youkilis WSC .40 1.00
219 Manny Ramirez WSC 1.00 2.50
220 Johnny Damon WSC .60 1.50
221 Dave Roberts WSC .60 1.50
222 Trot Nixon WSC .40 1.00
223 Gabe Kapler WSC .40 1.00
224 David Ortiz WSC 1.00 2.50
WS1 Pedro 1.00 2.50
Schilling
Ortiz

2004 Donruss World Series HoloFoil 100

*HOLO 1-175: 3X TO 8X BASIC
*HOLO 1-175: 2.5X TO 6X BASIC RC's
*HOLO 176-200: .2X TO .5X BAS.p/r 703-1000 1.25 3.00
SEMISTARS 2.00 5.00
UNLISTED STARS 3.00 8.00
RANDOM INSERTS IN PACKS
STATED PRINT RUN 100 SERIAL #'d SETS

2004 Donruss World Series HoloFoil 50

*HOLO 1-175: 5X TO 12X BASIC
*HOLO 1-175: 4X TO 10X BASIC RC's
*HOLO 176-200: .3X TO .8X BAS.p/r 703-1000 2.00 5.00
SEMISTARS 3.00 8.00
UNLISTED STARS 5.00 12.00
RANDOM INSERTS IN PACKS
STATED PRINT RUN 50 SERIAL #'d SETS

2004 Donruss World Series HoloFoil 25

*HOLO 1-175: 5X TO 12X BASIC
RANDOM INSERTS IN PACKS
STATED PRINT RUN 25 SERIAL #'d SETS
NO RC YR PRICING DUE TO SCARCITY

2004 Donruss World Series Material Bat

*BAT: .5X TO 1.2X AL/NL p/r 250
*BAT: .4X TO 1X AL/NL p/r 100
OVERALL AU-GU ODDS FIVE PER BOX
STATED PRINT RUN 100 SERIAL #'d SETS
10 Roberto Alomar 3.00 8.00
15 J.D. Drew 2.00 5.00
18 Javy Lopez 2.00 5.00
27 Jason Varitek 4.00 10.00
29 Johnny Damon 3.00 8.00
32 Nomar Garciaparra 5.00 12.00
34 Trot Nixon 2.00 5.00
37 Derrek Lee 3.00 8.00
41 Moises Alou 2.00 5.00
45 Luis Aparicio 3.00 8.00
46 Magglio Ordonez 2.00 5.00
51 Barry Larkin 3.00 8.00
53 George Foster 3.00 8.00
54 Joe Morgan 3.00 8.00
55 Sean Casey 2.00 5.00
56 Tony Perez 3.00 8.00
61 Charles Johnson 2.00 5.00
66 Alan Trammell 3.00 8.00
68 Ivan Rodriguez 3.00 8.00
74 Juan Pierre 2.00 5.00
75 Luis Castillo 2.00 5.00
78 Andy Pettitte 3.00 8.00
83 Roger Clemens 5.00 12.00
84 Roy Oswalt 2.00 5.00
87 Carlos Beltran 2.00 5.00
88 Juan Gonzalez 2.00 5.00
89 Ken Harvey 2.00 5.00
107 Torii Hunter 2.00 5.00
108 Jose Vidro 2.00 5.00
109 Orlando Cabrera Sox 2.00 5.00
112 Dwight Gooden 3.00 8.00
113 Jose Reyes 2.00 5.00
114 Kazuo Matsui 4.00 10.00
115 Keith Hernandez 3.00 8.00
116 Lenny Dykstra 3.00 8.00
122 Gary Sheffield 2.00 5.00
125 Jorge Posada 6.00 15.00
126 Kenny Lofton 2.00 5.00
127 Kevin Brown 2.00 5.00
132 Jermaine Dye 2.00 5.00
145 Brian Giles 2.00 5.00
151 Edgar Martinez 3.00 8.00
153 Rich Aurilia 2.00 5.00
157 Edgar Renteria 2.00 5.00
167 Alfonso Soriano 2.00 5.00
170 Mark Teixeira 3.00 8.00
171 Michael Young 2.00 5.00
172 Carlos Delgado 2.00 5.00

2004 Donruss World Series Material Fabric AL/NL

OVERALL AU-GU ODDS FIVE PER BOX
STATED PRINT RUN 250 SERIAL #'d SETS
9/23/38/95/142-143/155 P/R 100 #'d PER
2 Darin Erstad Jsy 2.00 5.00
3 Garret Anderson Jsy 2.00 5.00
4 Tim Salmon Jsy 3.00 8.00
5 Troy Glaus Jsy 2.00 5.00
6 Vladimir Guerrero Jsy 3.00 8.00
7 Brandon Webb Pants 2.00 5.00
8 Luis Gonzalez Jsy 2.00 5.00
9 Randy Johnson Pants/100 4.00 10.00
12 Steve Finley Jsy 2.00 5.00
13 Andruw Jones Jsy 3.00 8.00
14 Chipper Jones Jsy 3.00 8.00
16 Marcus Giles Jsy 2.00 5.00
17 Rafael Furcal Jsy 2.00 5.00
19 Jay Gibbons Jsy 2.00 5.00
20 Luis Matos Jsy 2.00 5.00
21 Melvin Mora Jsy 2.00 5.00
22 Miguel Tejada Jsy 2.00 5.00
23 Rafael Palmeiro Jsy/100 3.00 8.00
25 Dwight Evans Jsy 4.00 10.00
26 Fred Lynn Jsy 3.00 8.00
28 Jim Rice Jsy 3.00 8.00
31 Manny Ramirez Jsy 3.00 8.00
33 Pedro Martinez Jsy 3.00 8.00
35 Aramis Ramirez Jsy 2.00 5.00
38 Greg Maddux Jsy/100 5.00 12.00
39 Kerry Wood Pants 2.00 5.00
40 Mark Prior Jsy 3.00 8.00
42 Sammy Sosa Jsy 3.00 8.00
43 Carlos Lee Jsy 2.00 5.00
44 Frank Thomas Jsy 3.00 8.00
47 Mark Buehrle Jsy 2.00 5.00
48 Paul Konerko Jsy 2.00 5.00
49 Adam Dunn Jsy 2.00 5.00
50 Austin Kearns Jsy 2.00 5.00
52 Dave Concepcion Jsy 3.00 8.00
57 C.C. Sabathia Jsy 2.00 5.00
58 Jody Gerut Jsy 2.00 5.00
59 Omar Vizquel Jsy 3.00 8.00
60 Victor Martinez Jsy 2.00 5.00
63 Larry Walker Jsy 2.00 5.00
64 Preston Wilson Jsy 2.00 5.00
65 Todd Helton Jsy 3.00 8.00
70 A.J. Burnett Jsy 2.00 5.00
71 Brad Penny Jsy 2.00 5.00
72 Dontrelle Willis Jsy 2.00 5.00
73 Josh Beckett Jsy 2.00 5.00
76 Miguel Cabrera Jsy 3.00 8.00
77 Mike Lowell Jsy 2.00 5.00
79 Craig Biggio Jsy 3.00 8.00
80 Jeff Bagwell Pants 3.00 8.00
81 Jeff Kent Jsy 2.00 5.00
82 Lance Berkman Jsy 2.00 5.00
86 Angel Berroa Pants 2.00 5.00
90 Mike Sweeney Jsy 2.00 5.00
91 Adrian Beltre Jsy 2.00 5.00
92 Hideo Nomo Jsy 3.00 8.00
93 Kazuhisa Ishii Jsy 2.00 5.00
95 Orel Hershiser Jsy/100 3.00 8.00
96 Paul Lo Duca Jsy 2.00 5.00
97 Shawn Green Jsy 2.00 5.00
98 Ben Sheets Pants 2.00 5.00
99 Geoff Jenkins Jsy 2.00 5.00
104 Jacque Jones Jsy 2.00 5.00
105 Johan Santana Jsy 3.00 8.00
106 Shannon Stewart Jsy 2.00 5.00
110 Al Leiter Jsy 2.00 5.00
111 Darryl Strawberry Jsy 2.00 5.00
117 Mike Piazza Jsy 4.00 10.00
118 Tom Glavine Jsy 3.00 8.00
120 Bernie Williams Jsy 3.00 8.00
123 Jason Giambi Jsy 2.00 5.00
128 Mariano Rivera Jsy 3.00 8.00
129 Mike Mussina Jsy 3.00 8.00
130 Barry Zito Jsy 2.00 5.00
131 Eric Chavez Jsy 2.00 5.00
133 Mark Mulder Jsy 2.00 5.00
135 Tim Hudson Jsy 2.00 5.00
136 Brett Myers Jsy 2.00 5.00
137 Jim Thome Jsy 3.00 8.00
138 Kevin Millwood Jsy 2.00 5.00
139 Marlon Byrd Jsy 2.00 5.00
141 Pat Burrell Jsy 2.00 5.00
142 Steve Carlton Jsy/100 3.00 8.00
143 Dave Parker Jsy/100 3.00 8.00
147 Ryan Klesko Jsy 2.00 5.00
152 Jamie Moyer Jsy 2.00 5.00
155 Albert Pujols Jsy/100 8.00 20.00
156 Dan Haren Jsy 2.00 5.00
159 Jim Edmonds Jsy 2.00 5.00
161 Scott Rolen Jsy 3.00 8.00
162 Aubrey Huff Jsy 2.00 5.00
163 Carl Crawford Jsy 2.00 5.00
164 Dewon Brazelton Jsy 2.00 5.00
165 Fred McGriff Jsy 3.00 8.00
166 Rocco Baldelli Jsy 2.00 5.00
168 Hank Blalock Jsy 2.00 5.00
174 Roy Halladay Jsy 2.00 5.00
175 Vernon Wells Jsy 2.00 5.00

2004 Donruss World Series Material Fabric Number

*NBR p/r 75: .5X TO 1.2X AL/NL p/r 250
*NBR p/r 36-65: .75X TO 2X AL/NL p/r 250
*NBR p/r 36-65: .5X TO 1.5X AL/NL p/r 100
*NBR p/r 20-35: 1.25X TO 3X AL/NL p/r 250
*NBR p/r 20-35: 1X TO 2.5X AL/NL p/r 100
*NBR p/r 15-19: 1.5X TO 4X AL/NL p/r 250
*NBR p/r 15-19: 1.25X TO 3X AL/NL p/r 100
OVERALL AU-GU ODDS FIVE PER BOX
PRINT RUNS B/WN 1-75 #'d COPIES PER
NO PRICING ON QTY OF 14 OR LESS
30 Luis Tiant Jsy/23 6.00 15.00
46 Magglio Ordonez Jsy/30 5.00 12.00
53 George Foster Jsy/15 8.00 20.00
98 Ben Sheets Pants/15 6.00 15.00
107 Torii Hunter Jsy/48 3.00 8.00
125 Jorge Posada Jsy/20 8.00 20.00

2004 Donruss World Series Signature

1-175 AU-GU ODDS FIVE PER BOX
1-175 PRINT RUNS B/WN 5-25 COPIES PER
1-175 NO PRICING ON QTY OF 10 OR LESS
201-222 ODDS 1:5 SOX CHAMPS SETS
201-222 ARE NOT SERIAL-NUMBERED
201-222 SP INFO PROVIDED BY DONRUSS
201-222 NO PRICING DUE TO SCARCITY
3 Garret Anderson/25 10.00 25.00
7 Brandon Webb/25 6.00 15.00
11 Shea Hillenbrand/25 10.00 25.00
12 Steve Finley/25 10.00 25.00
16 Marcus Giles/25 10.00 25.00
17 Rafael Furcal/25 10.00 25.00
19 Jay Gibbons/25 6.00 15.00
20 Luis Matos/25 6.00 15.00
21 Melvin Mora/25 10.00 25.00
25 Dwight Evans/25 15.00 40.00
26 Fred Lynn/25 10.00 25.00
28 Jim Rice/25 10.00 25.00
30 Luis Tiant/25 10.00 25.00
34 Trot Nixon/25 10.00 25.00
35 Aramis Ramirez/25 10.00 25.00
37 Derrek Lee/25 15.00 40.00
40 Mark Prior/25 12.50 30.00
43 Carlos Lee/25 10.00 25.00
45 Luis Aparicio/25 10.00 25.00
46 Magglio Ordonez/25 10.00 25.00
47 Mark Buehrle/25 20.00 50.00
49 Adam Dunn/25 10.00 25.00
50 Austin Kearns/25 6.00 15.00
52 Dave Concepcion/25 10.00 25.00
53 George Foster/25 10.00 25.00
56 Tony Perez/25 15.00 40.00
57 C.C. Sabathia/25 10.00 25.00
58 Jody Gerut/25 6.00 15.00
60 Victor Martinez/25 10.00 25.00
64 Preston Wilson/25 10.00 25.00
66 Alan Trammell/25 10.00 25.00
69 Jeremy Bonderman/25 10.00 25.00
71 Brad Penny/25 6.00 15.00
76 Miguel Cabrera/25 25.00 60.00
84 Roy Oswalt/25 10.00 25.00
85 Wade Miller/25 6.00 15.00
86 Angel Berroa/25 6.00 15.00
87 Carlos Beltran/25 10.00 25.00
89 Ken Harvey/25 6.00 15.00
94 Milton Bradley/25 10.00 25.00
96 Paul Lo Duca/25 10.00 25.00
101 Rickie Weeks/25 10.00 25.00
102 Scott Podsednik/25 15.00 40.00
103 Jack Morris/25 10.00 25.00
104 Jacque Jones/25 10.00 25.00
105 Johan Santana/25 15.00 40.00
106 Shannon Stewart/25 10.00 25.00
107 Torii Hunter/25 10.00 25.00
108 Jose Vidro/25 6.00 15.00
109 Orlando Cabrera Sox/25 15.00 40.00
111 Darryl Strawberry/25 10.00 25.00
112 Dwight Gooden/25 10.00 25.00
115 Keith Hernandez/25 10.00 25.00
116 Lenny Dykstra/25 10.00 25.00
132 Jermaine Dye/25 10.00 25.00
133 Mark Mulder/25 10.00 25.00
134 Rich Harden/25 10.00 25.00
139 Marlon Byrd/25 6.00 15.00
142 Steve Carlton/25 10.00 25.00
143 Dave Parker/25 10.00 25.00
146 Jay Payton/25 6.00 15.00
148 J.T. Snow/25 10.00 25.00
154 Shigetoshi Hasegawa/25 20.00 50.00
156 Dan Haren/25 6.00 15.00
162 Aubrey Huff/25 10.00 25.00
163 Carl Crawford/25 10.00 25.00
164 Dewon Brazelton/25 6.00 15.00
168 Hank Blalock/25 10.00 25.00
170 Mark Teixeira/25 15.00 40.00
171 Michael Young/25 10.00 25.00

2004 Donruss World Series Blue

COMPLETE SET (100) 30.00 80.00
ONE PER PACK
1 Josh Beckett .40 1.00
2 Miguel Cabrera 1.00 2.50
3 Derrek Lee .40 1.00
4 Mike Lowell .40 1.00
5 Brad Penny .40 1.00
6 Ivan Rodriguez .60 1.50
7 Dontrelle Willis .40 1.00
8 Luis Castillo .40 1.00
9 Garret Anderson .40 1.00
10 Troy Glaus .40 1.00
11 John Lackey .60 1.50
12 Chone Figgins .40 1.00
13 Tim Salmon .40 1.00
14 Darin Erstad .40 1.00
15 Troy Percival .40 1.00
16 Steve Finley .40 1.00
17 Mark Grace .60 1.50
18 Randy Johnson 1.00 2.50
19 Curt Schilling D'backs .60 1.50
20 Luis Gonzalez .40 1.00
21 Andy Pettitte .60 1.50
22 Bernie Williams .60 1.50
23 Jorge Posada .60 1.50
24 Mariano Rivera 1.25 3.00
25 Roger Clemens 1.25 3.00
26 Jose Canseco Yanks .60 1.50
27 David Justice .40 1.00
28 Paul O'Neill Yanks .60 1.50
29 Darryl Strawberry Yanks .40 1.00
30 David Wells .40 1.00
31 Wade Boggs .60 1.50
32 Charles Johnson .40 1.00
33 Cliff Floyd .40 1.00
34 Moises Alou .40 1.00
35 Edgar Renteria .40 1.00
36 Chipper Jones 1.00 2.50
37 Tom Glavine .60 1.50
38 John Smoltz 1.00 2.50
39 Greg Maddux 1.25 3.00
40 Ryan Klesko .40 1.00
41 Javy Lopez .40 1.00
42 Fred McGriff .60 1.50
43 Roberto Alomar .60 1.50
44 Joe Carter .40 1.00
45 Rickey Henderson Jays 1.00 2.50
46 Paul Molitor 1.00 2.50
47 Jack Morris Jays .60 1.50
48 Jack Morris Twins .60 1.50
49 Kirby Puckett 1.00 2.50
50 Eric Davis .40 1.00
51 Barry Larkin .60 1.50
52 Paul O'Neill Reds .60 1.50
53 Dennis Eckersley .60 1.50
54 Jose Canseco A's .60 1.50
55 Rickey Henderson A's 1.00 2.50
56 Dave Parker A's .40 1.00
57 Orel Hershiser .40 1.00
58 Kirk Gibson Dodgers .40 1.00
59 Bert Blyleven Twins .60 1.50
60 Dwight Gooden .40 1.00
61 Gary Carter .60 1.50
62 Lenny Dykstra .40 1.00
63 Keith Hernandez Mets .40 1.00
64 Darryl Strawberry Mets .40 1.00
65 George Brett 2.00 5.00
66 Kirk Gibson Tigers .40 1.00
67 Alan Trammell .60 1.50
68 Jim Palmer .60 1.50
69 Eddie Murray .60 1.50
70 Cal Ripken 3.00 8.00
71 Keith Hernandez Cards .40 1.00
72 Ozzie Smith 1.25 3.00
73 Steve Garvey .40 1.00
74 Steve Carlton .60 1.50
75 Mike Schmidt 1.50 4.00
76 John Candelaria .40 1.00
77 Bert Blyleven Pirates .60 1.50
78 Dave Parker Pirates .40 1.00
79 Willie Stargell 79 .60 1.50
80 Reggie Jackson Yanks .60 1.50
81 Johnny Bench 1.00 2.50
82 Dave Concepcion .40 1.00
83 George Foster .40 1.00
84 Joe Morgan .60 1.50
85 Tony Perez .60 1.50
86 Rollie Fingers .60 1.50
87 Catfish Hunter .60 1.50
88 Reggie Jackson A's .60 1.50
89 Al Oliver .40 1.00
90 Roberto Clemente 2.50 6.00
91 Willie Stargell 71 .60 1.50
92 Brooks Robinson .60 1.50
93 Frank Robinson .60 1.50
94 Nolan Ryan 3.00 8.00
95 Tom Seaver .60 1.50
96 Al Kaline 1.00 2.50
97 Bob Gibson .60 1.50
98 Lou Brock .60 1.50
99 Orlando Cepeda .60 1.50
100 Duke Snider .60 1.50

2004 Donruss World Series Blue HoloFoil 100

*HOLO: 1.5X TO 4X BLUE
RANDOM INSERTS IN PACKS
STATED PRINT RUN 100 SERIAL #'d SETS

2004 Donruss World Series Blue HoloFoil 50

*HOLO: 2.5X TO 6X BLUE
RANDOM INSERTS IN PACKS
STATED PRINT RUN 50 SERIAL #'d SETS

2004 Donruss World Series Blue HoloFoil 25

*HOLO: 4X TO 10X BLUE
RANDOM INSERTS IN PACKS
STATED PRINT RUN 25 SERIAL #'d SETS

2004 Donruss World Series Blue Material Bat

*BAT: .6X TO 1.5X BLUE WS p/r 67-103
OVERALL AU-GU ODDS FIVE PER BOX
STATED PRINT RUN 50 SERIAL #'d SETS
8 Luis Castillo 3.00 8.00
17 Mark Grace 6.00 15.00
23 Jorge Posada 5.00 12.00
27 David Justice 4.00 10.00
28 Paul O'Neill Yanks 6.00 15.00
34 Moises Alou 3.00 8.00
35 Edgar Renteria 3.00 8.00
42 Fred McGriff 5.00 12.00
43 Roberto Alomar 5.00 12.00
44 Joe Carter 4.00 10.00
45 Rickey Henderson Jays 8.00 20.00
46 Paul Molitor 4.00 10.00
49 Kirby Puckett 8.00 20.00
50 Eric Davis 4.00 10.00
52 Paul O'Neill Reds 6.00 15.00
56 Dave Parker A's 4.00 10.00
58 Kirk Gibson Dodgers 4.00 10.00
62 Lenny Dykstra 4.00 10.00
63 Keith Hernandez Mets 4.00 10.00
66 Kirk Gibson Tigers 4.00 10.00
67 Alan Trammell 4.00 10.00
72 Ozzie Smith 10.00 25.00
73 Steve Garvey 4.00 10.00
84 Joe Morgan 4.00 10.00
85 Tony Perez 4.00 10.00
89 Al Oliver 4.00 10.00
90 Roberto Clemente 25.00 60.00
92 Brooks Robinson 6.00 15.00
93 Frank Robinson 4.00 10.00
96 Al Kaline 8.00 20.00
99 Orlando Cepeda 4.00 10.00

2004 Donruss World Series Blue Material Fabric AL/NL

*AL/NL p/r 100: .4X TO 1X WS p/r 67-103
*AL/NL p/r 50: .6X TO 1.5X WS p/r 67-103
*AL/NL p/r 50: .4X TO 1X WS p/r 55
OVERALL AU-GU ODDS FIVE PER BOX
PRINT RUNS B/WN 5-100 COPIES PER
NO PRICING ON QTY OF 10 OR LESS

2004 Donruss World Series Blue Material Fabric WS

OVERALL AU-GU ODDS FIVE PER BOX
PRINT RUNS B/WN 55-103 COPIES PER
1 Josh Beckett Jsy/103 2.00 5.00
2 Miguel Cabrera Jsy/103 3.00 8.00
3 Derrek Lee Jsy/103 3.00 8.00
4 Mike Lowell Jsy/103 2.00 5.00
5 Brad Penny Jsy/103 2.00 5.00
6 Ivan Rodriguez Jsy/103 3.00 8.00
7 Dontrelle Willis Jsy/103 3.00 8.00
9 Garret Anderson Jsy/102 2.00 5.00
10 Troy Glaus Jsy/102 2.00 5.00
13 Tim Salmon Jsy/102 3.00 8.00
14 Darin Erstad Jsy/102 2.00 5.00
15 Troy Percival Jsy/102 2.00 5.00
16 Steve Finley Jsy/101 2.00 5.00
18 Randy Johnson Pants/101 4.00 10.00
19 C.Schill D'backs Jsy/101 2.00 5.00
20 Luis Gonzalez Jsy/101 2.00 5.00
21 Andy Pettitte Jsy/100 3.00 8.00
22 Bernie Williams Jsy/100 3.00 8.00
24 Mariano Rivera Jsy/100 4.00 10.00
25 Roger Clemens Jsy/100 5.00 12.00
29 D.Strawberry Yanks Jsy/99 3.00 8.00
30 David Wells Jsy/99 2.00 5.00
31 Wade Boggs Jsy/96 5.00 12.00
32 Charles Johnson Jsy/97 2.00 5.00
33 Cliff Floyd Jsy/97 2.00 5.00
36 Chipper Jones Jsy/95 4.00 10.00
37 Tom Glavine Jsy/95 3.00 8.00
39 Greg Maddux Jsy/95 5.00 12.00
40 Ryan Klesko Jsy/95 2.00 5.00
41 Javy Lopez Jsy/95 2.00 5.00
51 Barry Larkin Jsy/90 3.00 8.00
54 Jose Canseco A's Jsy/89 5.00 12.00
55 R.Henderson A's Jsy/89 6.00 15.00
57 Orel Hershiser Jsy/88 5.00 12.00
59 Bert Blyleven Twins Jsy/87 3.00 8.00
60 Dwight Gooden Jsy/86 3.00 8.00
61 Gary Carter Jkt/86 3.00 8.00
64 D.Strawberry Mets Jsy/86 3.00 8.00
65 George Brett Jsy/85 8.00 20.00
68 Jim Palmer Pants/83 3.00 8.00
69 Eddie Murray Jsy/83 6.00 15.00
70 Cal Ripken Jsy/83 20.00 50.00
71 K.Hernandez Cards Jsy/82 3.00 8.00
74 Steve Carlton Jsy/80 3.00 8.00
75 Mike Schmidt Jkt/80 8.00 20.00
78 Dave Parker Pirates Jsy/79 3.00 8.00
79 Willie Stargell 79 Jsy/79 5.00 12.00
80 R.Jackson Yanks Jsy/78 5.00 12.00
81 Johnny Bench Jsy/75 6.00 15.00
82 Dave Concepcion Jsy/75 3.00 8.00
83 George Foster Jsy/75 3.00 8.00
86 Rollie Fingers Jsy/74 3.00 8.00
87 Catfish Hunter Jsy/74 5.00 12.00
88 Reggie Jackson A's Jkt/73 5.00 12.00
91 Willie Stargell 71 Jsy/71 5.00 12.00
98 Lou Brock Jkt/67 5.00 12.00
100 Duke Snider Pants/55 6.00 15.00

2004 Donruss World Series Blue Signature

OVERALL AU-GU ODDS FIVE PER BOX
PRINT RUNS B/WN 5-50 COPIES PER
NO PRICING ON QTY OF 10 OR LESS
2 Miguel Cabrera/25 20.00 50.00
3 Derrek Lee/25 15.00 40.00
5 Brad Penny/25 6.00 15.00
9 Garret Anderson/25 10.00 25.00
11 John Lackey/50 5.00 12.00
12 Chone Figgins/25 6.00 15.00
16 Steve Finley/25 10.00 25.00
29 Darryl Strawberry Yanks/25 10.00 25.00
42 Fred McGriff/25 20.00 50.00
47 Jack Morris Jays/25 10.00 25.00
48 Jack Morris Twins/25 10.00 25.00
50 Eric Davis/25 10.00 25.00
53 Dennis Eckersley/25 6.00 15.00
56 Dave Parker A's/25 10.00 25.00
59 Bert Blyleven Twins/25 10.00 25.00
60 Dwight Gooden/25 10.00 25.00
62 Lenny Dykstra/25 10.00 25.00
63 Keith Hernandez Mets/25 10.00 25.00
64 Darryl Strawberry Mets/25 10.00 25.00
67 Alan Trammell/25 10.00 25.00
68 Jim Palmer/25 10.00 25.00
71 Keith Hernandez Cards/25 10.00 25.00
76 John Candelaria/25 10.00 25.00
77 Bert Blyleven Pirates/25 10.00 25.00
78 Dave Parker Pirates/25 10.00 25.00
82 Dave Concepcion/25 10.00 25.00
83 George Foster/25 10.00 25.00
85 Tony Perez/25 15.00 40.00
86 Rollie Fingers/25 10.00 25.00
89 Al Oliver/25 10.00 25.00

2004 Donruss World Series Face Off

COMMON RETIRED .60 1.50
STATED PRINT RUN 500 SERIAL #'d SETS
*HOLO: 2X TO 5X BASIC
HOLOFOIL PRINT RUN 25 SERIAL #'d SETS
1 R.Clemens 2.00 5.00
M.Piazza
2 M.Mussina 1.00 2.50
I.Rodriguez
3 M.Grace 1.00 2.50
J.Posada
4 G.Maddux 2.00 5.00
J.Thome
5 R.Henderson 1.50 4.00
C.Schilling
6 K.Puckett 1.50 4.00
T.Glavine
7 D.Eckersley 1.00 2.50
W.Clark
8 B.Williams 1.50 4.00
R.Johnson
9 C.Ripken 5.00 12.00
S.Carlton
10 T.Seaver 1.00 2.50
R.Jackson
11 M.Schmidt 3.00 8.00
G.Brett
12 W.Boggs 1.00 2.50
K.Hernandez
13 D.Gooden .60 1.50
D.Evans
14 J.Bench 1.50 4.00
C.Hunter
15 J.Palmer 1.00 2.50
D.Parker
16 B.Gibson 1.50 4.00
A.Kaline
17 C.Yastrzemski 1.50 4.00
L.Brock
18 D.Snider 1.00 2.50
W.Ford
19 C.Fisk 1.00 2.50
T.Perez
20 R.Clemente 4.00 10.00
F.Robinson

2004 Donruss World Series Face Off Material

OVERALL AU-GU ODDS FIVE PER BOX
PRINT RUNS B/WN 10-100 COPIES PER
NO PRICING ON QTY OF 10 OR LESS
1 Clemens Jsy/Piaz Jsy/100 10.00 25.00
2 Mussina Jsy/I.Rod Jsy/100 6.00 15.00
4 Maddux Jsy/Thome Jsy/25 15.00 40.00
5 Rickey Jsy/Schil Jsy/100 10.00 25.00
6 Puckett Jsy/Glav Jsy/100 10.00 25.00
8 Bern Jsy/Randy Pants/100 8.00 20.00
9 Ripken Jsy/Carlton Jsy/50 20.00 50.00
11 Schmidt Jkt/Brett Jsy/50 20.00 50.00
13 Gooden Jsy/Evans Jsy/50 12.50 30.00
15 Palmer Jsy/Parker Jsy/50 6.00 15.00
17 Yaz Jsy/Brock Jkt/50 10.00 25.00
18 Snider Pants/Ford Jsy/50 10.00 25.00
19 Fisk Jsy/Perez Fld Glv/50 10.00 25.00

2004 Donruss World Series Fans of the Game

STATED ODDS 1:24
1 Val Kilmer 1.25 3.00
2 Stan Lee 1.25 3.00
3 Apolo Anton Ohno 4.00 10.00
4 Gene Shalit .75 2.00
5 Leeann Tweeden 1.25 3.00

2004 Donruss World Series Fans of the Game Autographs

RANDOM INSERTS IN PACKS
SP PRINT RUNS PROVIDED BY DONRUSS
SP'S ARE NOT SERIAL-NUMBERED
1 Val Kilmer 15.00 40.00
2 Stan Lee 60.00 120.00
3 Apolo Anton Ohno SP/300 50.00 100.00
4 Gene Shalit 6.00 15.00
5 Leeann Tweeden 8.00 20.00

2004 Donruss World Series Legends of the Fall

STATED PRINT RUN 500 SERIAL #'d SETS
*HOLO: 2X TO 5X BASIC
HOLOFOIL PRINT RUN 25 SERIAL #'d SETS
RANDOM INSERTS IN PACKS
1 Bob Gibson 1.00 2.50
2 Brooks Robinson 1.00 2.50
3 Cal Ripken 5.00 12.00
4 Carl Yastrzemski 1.50 4.00
5 Carlton Fisk 1.00 2.50
6 Derek Jeter 4.00 10.00
7 Duke Snider 1.00 2.50
8 Eddie Murray 1.00 2.50
9 Frank Robinson 1.00 2.50
10 Gary Carter 1.00 2.50
11 George Brett 3.00 8.00
12 Jim Palmer 1.00 2.50
13 Johnny Bench 1.50 4.00
14 Mariano Rivera 2.00 5.00
15 Mike Schmidt 2.50 6.00
16 Phil Rizzuto 1.00 2.50
17 Red Schoendienst 1.00 2.50
18 Reggie Jackson 1.00 2.50
19 Rickey Henderson 1.50 4.00
20 Whitey Ford 1.00 2.50

2004 Donruss World Series Legends of the Fall Material

OVERALL AU-GU ODDS FIVE PER BOX
PRINT RUNS B/WN 25-100 COPIES PER
1 Bob Gibson Jsy/50 6.00 15.00
2 Brooks Robinson Bat/100 5.00 12.00
3 Cal Ripken Jkt/100 15.00 40.00
4 Carl Yastrzemski Bat/50 10.00 25.00
5 Carlton Fisk Bat/100 6.00 15.00
7 Duke Snider Pants/50 6.00 15.00
8 Eddie Murray Jsy/50 8.00 20.00
9 Frank Robinson Bat/100 3.00 8.00
10 Gary Carter Jkt/100 3.00 8.00
11 George Brett Bat/50 12.50 30.00
12 Jim Palmer Pants/25 6.00 15.00
13 Johnny Bench Bat/100 6.00 15.00
14 Mariano Rivera Jsy/100 6.00 15.00
15 Mike Schmidt Jkt/50 12.50 30.00
16 Phil Rizzuto Pants/50 10.00 25.00
17 Red Schoendienst Bat/100 3.00 8.00
18 Reggie Jackson Bat/100 5.00 12.00
19 Rickey Henderson Bat/100 6.00 15.00

2004 Donruss World Series Legends of the Fall Signature

*SIG p/r 50: .4X TO 1X SIG MTL p/r 100
*SIG p/r 25: .4X TO 1X SIG MTL p/r 50
*SIG p/r 25: .3X TO .8X SIG MTL p/r 25
OVERALL AU-GU ODDS FIVE PER BOX
PRINT RUNS B/WN 5-50 COPIES PER
NO PRICING ON QTY OF 10 OR LESS

2004 Donruss World Series Legends of the Fall Signature Material

OVERALL AU-GU ODDS FIVE PER BOX
PRINT RUNS B/WN 5-100 COPIES PER
NO PRICING ON QTY OF 10 OR LESS
1 Bob Gibson Jsy/25 20.00 50.00
2 Brooks Robinson Bat/50 15.00 40.00
7 Duke Snider Pants/50 15.00 40.00
9 Frank Robinson Bat/50 15.00 40.00

10 Gary Carter Jkt/50 10.00 25.00
12 Jim Palmer Pants/25 12.50 30.00
13 Johnny Bench Bat/25 40.00 80.00
16 Phil Rizzuto Pants/50 15.00 40.00
17 Red Schoendienst Bat/100 12.50 30.00

2004 Donruss World Series MVP

STATED PRINT RUN 1000 SERIAL #'d SETS
*HOLO: 1.5X TO 4X BASIC
HOLOFOIL PRINT RUN 50 SERIAL #'d SETS
RANDOM INSERTS IN PACKS
1 Whitey Ford .75 2.00
2 Bob Gibson .75 2.00
3 Frank Robinson .75 2.00
4 Brooks Robinson .75 2.00
5 Roberto Clemente 3.00 8.00
6 Reggie Jackson .75 2.00
7 Rollie Fingers .75 2.00
8 Johnny Bench 1.25 3.00
9 Reggie Jackson .75 2.00
10 Mike Schmidt 2.00 5.00
11 Alan Trammell .75 2.00
12 Orel Hershiser .50 1.25
13 Jack Morris .75 2.00
14 Paul Molitor 1.25 3.00
15 Tom Glavine .75 2.00

2004 Donruss World Series MVP Material

OVERALL AU-GU ODDS FIVE PER BOX
PRINT RUNS B/WN 10-100 COPIES PER
NO PRICING ON QTY OF 10 OR LESS
1 Whitey Ford Jsy/50 6.00 15.00
2 Bob Gibson Jsy/50 6.00 15.00
3 Frank Robinson Jsy/25 6.00 15.00
6 Reggie Jackson Jkt/100 5.00 12.00
7 Rollie Fingers Jsy/100 3.00 8.00
9 Reggie Jackson Jsy/25 10.00 25.00
10 Mike Schmidt Jsy/50 12.50 30.00
12 Orel Hershiser Jsy/100 3.00 8.00
15 Tom Glavine Jsy/100 5.00 12.00

2004 Donruss World Series MVP Signature

OVERALL AU-GU ODDS FIVE PER BOX
PRINT RUNS B/WN 5-25 COPIES PER
NO PRICING ON QTY OF 10 OR LESS
11 Alan Trammell/25 10.00 25.00
13 Jack Morris/25 10.00 25.00

2004 Donruss World Series MVP Signature Material

OVERALL AU-GU ODDS FIVE PER BOX
PRINT RUNS B/WN 5-100 COPIES PER
NO PRICING ON QTY OF 10 OR LESS
2 Bob Gibson Jsy/50 15.00 40.00
3 Frank Robinson Shoe/50 15.00 40.00
7 Rollie Fingers Jsy/100 12.50 30.00
12 Orel Hershiser Jsy/25 12.50 30.00

2004 Donruss World Series October Heroes

STATED PRINT RUN 500 SERIAL #'d SETS
*HOLO: 2X TO 5X BASIC
HOLOFOIL PRINT RUN 25 SERIAL #'d SETS
1 Alan Trammell 1.00 2.50
2 Andy Pettitte 1.00 2.50
3 Catfish Hunter 1.00 2.50
4 Chipper Jones 1.50 4.00
5 Dave Concepcion .60 1.50
6 David Wells .60 1.50
7 Jack Morris 1.00 2.50
8 Joe Morgan 1.00 2.50
9 Josh Beckett .60 1.50
10 Kirby Puckett 1.50 4.00
11 Kirk Gibson .60 1.50
12 Marty Marion .60 1.50
13 Miguel Cabrera 1.50 4.00
14 Paul Molitor 1.50 4.00
15 Paul O'Neill 1.00 2.50
16 Randy Johnson 1.50 4.00
17 Roger Clemens 2.00 5.00
18 Steve Carlton 1.00 2.50
19 Steve Garvey .60 1.50
20 Wade Boggs 1.00 2.50

2004 Donruss World Series October Heroes Material

OVERALL AU-GU ODDS FIVE PER BOX
PRINT RUNS B/WN 25-100 COPIES PER
1 Alan Trammell Jsy/25 6.00 15.00
2 Andy Pettitte Jsy/25 3.00 8.00
3 Catfish Hunter Jsy/25 10.00 25.00
4 Chipper Jones Jsy/100 4.00 10.00
5 Dave Concepcion Jsy/100 3.00 8.00
6 David Wells Jsy/25 5.00 12.00
9 Josh Beckett Jsy/100 2.00 5.00
10 Kirby Puckett Jsy/50 12.50 30.00
12 Marty Marion Jsy/25 6.00 15.00
13 Miguel Cabrera Jsy/100 3.00 8.00
16 Randy Johnson Pants/50 6.00 15.00
17 Roger Clemens Jsy/100 5.00 12.00
18 Steve Carlton Jsy/100 3.00 8.00
19 Steve Garvey Jsy/100 3.00 8.00
20 Wade Boggs Jsy/100 5.00 12.00

2004 Donruss World Series October Heroes Signature

*SIG p/r 25: .5X TO 1.2X SIG MTL p/r 100
*SIG p/r 25: .4X TO 1X SIG MTL p/r 50
OVERALL AU-GU ODDS FIVE PER BOX
PRINT RUNS B/WN 1-25 COPIES PER
NO PRICING ON QTY OF 10 OR LESS
7 Jack Morris/25 10.00 25.00

2004 Donruss World Series October Heroes Signature Material

OVERALL AU-GU ODDS FIVE PER BOX
PRINT RUNS B/WN 5-100 COPIES PER
NO PRICING ON QTY OF 10 OR LESS
1 Alan Trammell Jsy/100 8.00 20.00
5 Dave Concepcion Jsy/100 12.50 30.00
12 Marty Marion Jsy/100 8.00 20.00
13 Miguel Cabrera Jsy/100 20.00 50.00
18 Steve Carlton Jsy/50 10.00 25.00
19 Steve Garvey Jsy/100 8.00 20.00

2004 Donruss World Series October Legends

STATED PRINT RUN 500 SERIAL #'d SETS
*HOLO: 2X TO 5X BASIC
HOLOFOIL PRINT RUN 25 SERIAL #'d SETS
RANDOM INSERTS IN PACKS
1 Bob Gibson 1.00 2.50
2 Cal Ripken 5.00 12.00
3 Carl Yastrzemski 1.50 4.00
4 Carlton Fisk 1.00 2.50
5 Duke Snider 1.00 2.50
6 Eddie Murray 1.00 2.50
7 Frank Robinson 1.00 2.50
8 George Brett 3.00 8.00
9 Joe Morgan 1.00 2.50
10 Johnny Bench 1.50 4.00
11 Lou Brock 1.00 2.50
12 Mike Schmidt 2.50 6.00
13 Paul Molitor 1.50 4.00
14 Phil Rizzuto 1.00 2.50
15 Reggie Jackson 1.00 2.50
16 Robin Yount 1.50 4.00
17 Stan Musial 2.50 6.00
18 Steve Carlton 1.00 2.50
19 Whitey Ford 1.00 2.50
20 Willie McCovey 1.00 2.50

2004 Donruss World Series October Legends Material

OVERALL AU-GU ODDS FIVE PER BOX
PRINT RUNS B/WN 10-100 COPIES PER
NO PRICING ON QTY OF 10 OR LESS
1 Bob Gibson Jsy/50 6.00 15.00
2 Cal Ripken Jsy/50 30.00 60.00
3 Carl Yastrzemski Jsy/50 10.00 25.00
4 Carlton Fisk Jsy/100 5.00 12.00
5 Duke Snider Jsy/25 10.00 25.00
6 Eddie Murray Jsy/100 6.00 15.00
7 Frank Robinson Jsy/50 4.00 10.00
8 George Brett Jsy/50 12.50 30.00
10 Johnny Bench Jsy/50 8.00 20.00
11 Lou Brock Jkt/100 5.00 12.00
12 Mike Schmidt Jkt/100 8.00 20.00
14 Phil Rizzuto Pants/25 10.00 25.00
15 Reggie Jackson Jkt/100 8.00 20.00
16 Robin Yount Jsy/100 6.00 15.00
18 Steve Carlton Jsy/100 3.00 8.00
19 Whitey Ford Pants/25 10.00 25.00
20 Willie McCovey Jsy/25 10.00 25.00

2004 Donruss World Series October Legends Signature

*SIG p/r 25: .5X TO 1.2X SIG MTL p/r 100
*SIG p/r 25: .4X TO 1X SIG MTL p/r 50
OVERALL AU-GU ODDS FIVE PER BOX
PRINT RUNS B/WN 5-25 COPIES PER
NO PRICING ON QTY OF 10 OR LESS

2004 Donruss World Series October Legends Signature Material

OVERALL AU-GU ODDS FIVE PER BOX
PRINT RUNS B/WN 5-100 COPIES PER
NO PRICING ON QTY OF 10 OR LESS
1 Bob Gibson Jsy/50 15.00 40.00
4 Carlton Fisk Jsy/15 30.00 60.00
5 Duke Snider Jsy/50 15.00 40.00
7 Frank Robinson Jsy/50 15.00 40.00
11 Lou Brock Jsy/100 15.00 40.00
13 Paul Molitor Jsy/25 12.50 30.00
14 Phil Rizzuto Pants/50 15.00 40.00
16 Robin Yount Jsy/25 40.00 80.00
17 Stan Musial Jsy/25 50.00 100.00
18 Steve Carlton Jsy/100 8.00 20.00
19 Whitey Ford Pants/25 20.00 50.00
20 Willie McCovey Jsy/25 20.00 50.00

2004 Donruss World Series Playoff All-Stars

STATED PRINT RUN 500 SERIAL #'d SETS
*HOLO: 2X TO 5X BASIC
HOLOFOIL PRINT RUN 25 SERIAL #'d SETS
1 Mark Prior 1.00 2.50
2 Sammy Sosa 1.50 4.00
3 Steve Finley .60 1.50
4 David Ortiz 1.50 4.00
5 Mike Piazza 1.50 4.00
6 Edgar Martinez 1.00 2.50
7 Roy Oswalt 1.00 2.50
8 Johan Santana 1.00 2.50
9 Jacque Jones .60 1.50
10 Will Clark 1.00 2.50
11 Albert Pujols 2.00 5.00
12 Andre Dawson 1.00 2.50
13 Nolan Ryan 5.00 12.00
14 Fred Lynn .60 1.50
15 Jim Rice 1.00 2.50
16 Dwight Evans .60 1.50
17 Harmon Killebrew 1.50 4.00
18 Maury Wills .60 1.50
19 Mark Mulder .60 1.50
20 Frank Thomas 1.50 4.00

2004 Donruss World Series Playoff All-Stars Material 1

OVERALL AU-GU ODDS FIVE PER BOX
PRINT RUNS B/WN 50-100 COPIES PER
1 Mark Prior Jsy/100 3.00 8.00
2 Sammy Sosa Jsy/100 4.00 10.00
3 Steve Finley Jsy/100 2.00 5.00
4 David Ortiz Jsy/100 6.00 15.00
5 Mike Piazza Jsy/100 5.00 12.00
6 Edgar Martinez Jsy/50 5.00 12.00
7 Roy Oswalt Jsy/100 2.00 5.00
8 Johan Santana Jsy/100 3.00 8.00
9 Jacque Jones Jsy/100 2.00 5.00
10 Will Clark Bat/100 5.00 12.00
11 Albert Pujols Jsy/100 8.00 20.00
12 Andre Dawson Jsy/100 3.00 8.00
13 Nolan Ryan Jsy/100 8.00 20.00
14 Fred Lynn Jsy/50 4.00 10.00
15 Jim Rice Jsy/50 4.00 10.00
16 Dwight Evans Jsy/50 6.00 15.00
17 Harmon Killebrew Jsy/50 8.00 20.00
19 Mark Mulder Jsy/50 3.00 8.00
20 Frank Thomas Jsy/100 4.00 10.00

2004 Donruss World Series Playoff All-Stars Material 2

*MTL2 p/r 100: .6X TO 1.5X MTL1 p/r 100
*MTL2 p/r 100: .4X TO 1X MTL1 p/r 50
*MTL2 p/r 50: 1X TO 2.5X MTL1 p/r 100
*MTL2 p/r 50: .6X TO 1.5X MTL1 p/r 50
OVERALL AU-GU ODDS FIVE PER BOX
PRINT RUNS B/WN 50-100 COPIES PER

2004 Donruss World Series Playoff All-Stars Material 3

*MTL3 p/r 100: .75X TO 2X MTL1 p/r 100
*MTL3 p/r 100: .6X TO 1.5X MTL1 p/r 50
*MTL3 p/r 50: 1.25X TO 3X MTL1 p/r 100
*MTL3 p/r 50: .75X TO 2X MTL1 p/r 50
*MTL3 p/r 25: 1.25X TO 3X MTL1 p/r 50
OVERALL AU-GU ODDS FIVE PER BOX
PRINT RUNS B/WN 25-100 COPIES PER

2004 Donruss World Series Playoff All-Stars Signature

*SIG p/r 25: .5X TO 1.2X SIG MTL p/r 100
*SIG p/r 25: .4X TO 1X SIG MTL p/r 50
*SIG p/r 25: .3X TO .8X SIG MTL p/r 25
OVERALL AU-GU ODDS FIVE PER BOX
PRINT RUNS B/WN 5-25 COPIES PER
NO PRICING ON QTY OF 10 OR LESS
1 Mark Prior/25 12.50 30.00
13 Nolan Ryan/25 60.00 120.00
18 Maury Wills/25 10.00 25.00

2004 Donruss World Series Playoff All-Stars Signature Material 1

OVERALL AU-GU ODDS FIVE PER BOX
PRINT RUNS B/WN 5-100 COPIES PER
NO PRICING ON QTY OF 10 OR LESS
3 Steve Finley Jsy/100 8.00 20.00
4 David Ortiz Jsy/100 20.00 50.00
6 Edgar Martinez Jsy/50 15.00 40.00
7 Roy Oswalt Jsy/100 8.00 20.00
8 Johan Santana Jsy/100 15.00 40.00
9 Jacque Jones Jsy/100 8.00 20.00
10 Will Clark Bat/25 20.00 50.00
12 Andre Dawson Jsy/100 8.00 20.00
14 Fred Lynn Jsy/25 12.50 30.00
15 Jim Rice Jsy/25 12.50 30.00
16 Dwight Evans Jsy/50 20.00 50.00
19 Mark Mulder Jsy/25 12.50 30.00
20 Frank Thomas Jsy/25 30.00 60.00

2004 Donruss World Series Playoff All-Stars Signature Material 2

*SM2 p/r 100: .5X TO 1.2X SM1 p/r 100
*SM2 p/r 50: .6X TO 1.5X SM1 p/r 100
*SM2 p/r 50: .5X TO 1.2X SM1 p/r 50
*SM2 p/r 50: .4X TO 1X SM1 p/r 25
*SM2 p/r 25: .6X TO 1.5X SM1 p/r 50
*SM2 p/r 25: .5X TO 1.2X SM1 p/r 25
OVERALL AU-GU ODDS FIVE PER BOX
PRINT RUNS B/WN 5-100 COPIES PER
NO PRICING ON QTY OF 10 OR LESS
17 H.Killebrew Bat-Jsy/25 50.00 100.00

2004 Donruss World Series Playoff All-Stars Signature Material 3

*SM3 p/r 100: .6X TO 1.5X SM1 p/r 100
*SM3 p/r 100: .5X TO 1.2X SM1 p/r 50
*SM3 p/r 100: .4X TO 1X SM1 p/r 25
*SM3 p/r 50: .6X TO 1.5X SM1 p/r 50
*SM3 p/r 50: .5X TO 1.2X SM1 p/r 25
OVERALL AU-GU ODDS FIVE PER BOX
PRINT RUNS B/WN 5-100 COPIES PER
NO PRICING ON QTY OF 10 OR LESS

2004 Donruss World Series Records

STATED PRINT RUN 1000 SERIAL #'d SETS
*HOLO: 1.5X TO 4X BASIC
HOLOFOIL PRINT RUN 50 SERIAL #'d SETS
RANDOM INSERTS IN PACKS
1 Lou Brock 1.00 2.50
2 Yogi Berra 1.50 4.00
3 Reggie Jackson 1.00 2.50
4 Bob Gibson 1.00 2.50
5 Whitey Ford 1.00 2.50

2004 Donruss World Series Records Material

OVERALL AU-GU ODDS FIVE PER BOX
PRINT RUNS B/WN 10-100 COPIES PER
NO PRICING ON QTY OF 10 OR LESS
1 Lou Brock Bat/100 5.00 12.00
2 Yogi Berra Bat/50 8.00 20.00
3 Reggie Jackson Bat/100 5.00 12.00
5 Whitey Ford Pants/25 10.00 25.00

2004 Donruss World Series Records Signature

*SIG p/r 25: .5X TO 1.2X SIG MTL p/r 100
OVERALL AU-GU ODDS FIVE PER BOX
PRINT RUNS B/WN 10-25 COPIES PER
NO PRICING ON QTY OF 10 OR LESS

2004 Donruss World Series Records Signature Material

OVERALL AU-GU ODDS FIVE PER BOX
PRINT RUNS B/WN 10-100 COPIES PER
NO PRICING ON QTY OF 10 OR LESS
1 Lou Brock Bat/100 12.50 30.00
3 Reggie Jackson Bat/20 20.00 50.00

2004 Donruss World Series Signature Trio

OVERALL AU-GU ODDS FIVE PER BOX
PRINT RUNS B/WN 5-25 COPIES PER
NO PRICING ON QTY OF 10 OR LESS
2 Lee/Penny/Lowell/25 20.00 50.00
3 Lackey/Figgins/Garret/25 20.00 50.00
8 Alomar/Molitor/Morris/25 60.00 120.00
9 E.Davis/Larkin/O'Neill/25 75.00 150.00
10 Eck/Canseco/Parker/25 60.00 120.00
11 K.Hern/Gooden/G.Car/25 30.00 80.00
12 Straw/Dykstra/Foster/25 20.00 50.00
13 Trammell/Gibson/Morris/25 60.00 120.00
15 Blyleven/Candy/Parker/25 20.00 50.00

2004 Donruss World Series Souvenirs Playoff

OVERALL AU-GU ODDS FIVE PER BOX
STATED PRINT RUN 100 SERIAL #'d SETS
1 Chipper Jones Ball 6.00 15.00
2 Randy Johnson Ball 6.00 15.00
3 Albert Pujols Ball 10.00 25.00
4 Jason Schmidt Ball 4.00 10.00
5 Gary Sheffield Ball 4.00 10.00
6 Miguel Tejada Ball 4.00 10.00
7 J.D. Drew Ball 4.00 10.00
8 John Smoltz Ball 6.00 15.00
9 Eric Milton Ball 4.00 10.00
10 Mark Grace Ball 6.00 15.00
11 Tim Hudson Ball 4.00 10.00
12 Jeff Bagwell Ball 6.00 15.00
13 Jim Edmonds Ball 4.00 10.00
14 Sammy Sosa Ball 6.00 15.00
15 Albert Pujols Ball 10.00 25.00

2004 Donruss World Series Souvenirs WS

OVERALL AU-GU ODDS FIVE PER BOX
STATED PRINT RUN 100 SERIAL #'d SETS
1 Jason Schmidt Ball 4.00 10.00
2 Troy Glaus Base 4.00 10.00
3 Reggie Sanders Base 4.00 10.00
4 Tim Salmon Base 6.00 15.00
5 Garret Anderson Base 4.00 10.00
6 Francisco Rodriguez Base 4.00 10.00
7 Rich Aurilia Ball 4.00 10.00
8 Jeff Kent Ball 4.00 10.00
9 Darin Erstad Base 4.00 10.00
10 Troy Glaus Base 4.00 10.00
11 Jeff Kent Ball 4.00 10.00
12 Scott Spiezio Base 4.00 10.00
13 Troy Percival Base 4.00 10.00
14 Garret Anderson Base 4.00 10.00
15 Darin Erstad Base 4.00 10.00

2004 Donruss World Series Triple Threads

OVERALL AU-GU ODDS FIVE PER BOX
PRINT RUNS B/WN 50-100 PER
B = BAT, J = JSY, P = PANTS
1 Beck J/Cab J/Lowell B/100 8.00 20.00
2 Cast B/I.Rod J/Willis J/100 8.00 20.00
3 And B/Glaus J/Salm J/100 10.00 25.00
4 Schil J/Grac B/Randy P/50 12.50 30.00
5 Posa B/Bern J/Clem J/50 12.50 30.00
6 Pett J/Boggs J/Rivera J/50 12.50 30.00
7 C.Joh B/Floyd J/Alou B/100 5.00 12.00
8 Chip J/Glav J/Madd J/100 15.00 40.00
9 Carl J/Hend B/Wells J/100 10.00 25.00
10 Dav B/Lark B/O'Neill B/100 10.00 25.00
11 Good B/Cart J/Straw J/100 10.00 25.00
12 White B/Wils B/Brett J/100 15.00 40.00
13 Palm J/Murr J/Ripk Jkt/50 15.00 40.00
14 Starg J/Park J/Madl B/100 10.00 25.00
15 Bench B/Mor B/Per B/100 15.00 40.00
16 Conc J/Fost J/Bench B/50 20.00 50.00
17 Oli B/R.Clem B/Starg J/50 50.00 100.00
18 Pal J/F.Rob J/B.Rob B/50 12.50 30.00
19 Gibs J/Brock B/Cep B/50 12.50 30.00
20 Musial B/Sch B/Mari J/50 20.00 50.00

1953-55 Dormand

One of the most attractive and popular postcards ever issued are the full color postcards of Louis Dormand, which were issued as premiums by the Mason Candy Company. The cards are numbered on the reverse in the line which seperates the address portion from the message portion of the postcards. Two variations of the McDougald, Collins and Sain exist. Rizzuto and Mantle also exist in a 6" by 9" postcard, and a 9" by 12" postcard also exists. The Hodges card used to be considered quite scarce; however, recent major auction house "warehouse" finds of these cards have significantly increased the supply of these cards to the secondary market..

COMPLETE SET 1500.00 3000.00
COMMON POSTCARD 10.00 20.00
COMMON SP 200.00 400.00
101 Phil Rizzuto 25.00 50.00
101A Phil Rizzuto 25.00 50.00
Straight Sig at top
101B Phil Rizzuto 25.00 50.00
Straight Sig at top; smaller
101C Phil Rizzuto 25.00 50.00
Signature at an angle
101D Phil Rizzuto 60.00 120.00
Jumbo 6 by 9
102 Yogi Berra 40.00 80.00
103 Ed Lopat 12.50 25.00
104A Hank Bauer 20.00 40.00
Large Sig
104B Hank Bauer 20.00 40.00
Smaller Signature
105A Joe Collins 10.00 20.00
Patch on Sleeve
Signature on Top
105B Joe Collins 20.00 40.00
Patch on Sleeve
Signature at Bottom
105C Joe Collins 20.00 40.00
No Patch on Sleeve
Signature at top
105D Joe Collins 20.00 40.00
No Patch on Sleeve
Signature on Bott
106 Ralph Houk 12.50 25.00
107 Bill Miller 10.00 20.00
108 Ray Scarborough 10.00 20.00
109 Allie Reynolds 12.50 25.00
110 Gil McDougald 12.50 25.00
Large Signature
110A Gil McDougald 20.00 40.00
Small Signature Variation
111 Mickey Mantle 60.00 120.00
Batting Left
111A Mickey Mantle 100.00 200.00
Bat on Shoulder
111B Mickey Mantle 150.00 300.00
Jumbo 6 by 9
111C Mickey Mantle 150.00 300.00
Jumbo 9 by 12
112 Johnny Mize 40.00 80.00
113A Casey Stengel MG 40.00 80.00
Signature on Top
113B Casey Stengel 40.00 80.00
Signature on Bottom
114A Bobby Shantz 10.00 20.00
Signature on Top
114B Bobby Shantz 10.00 20.00
Signature at an angle
115 Whitey Ford 40.00 80.00
116 Johnny Sain 12.50 25.00
Pitching
116A Johnny Sain 50.00 100.00
Winding Up
117 Jim McDonald 10.00 20.00
118 Gene Woodling 12.50 25.00
119 Charlie Silvera 10.00 20.00
120 Don Bollweg 10.00 20.00
121 Billy Pierce 12.50 25.00
122 Chico Carrasquel 12.50 25.00
123 Willie Miranda 12.50 25.00
124 Carl Erskine 25.00 50.00
125 Roy Campanella 75.00 150.00
126 Jerry Coleman 12.50 25.00
127 Pee Wee Reese 40.00 80.00
128 Carl Furillo 20.00 40.00
129 Gil Hodges 200.00 400.00
130 Billy Martin 25.00 50.00
132 Irv Noren 10.00 20.00
133 Enos Slaughter 40.00 80.00
134 Tom Gorman 10.00 20.00
135 Eddie Robinson 10.00 20.00
136 Frank Crosetti CO 25.00 50.00
138 Jim Konstanty 50.00 100.00
139 Elston Howard 60.00 120.00
140 Bill Skowron 20.00 40.00

1986 Dorman's Cheese

This 20-card set was issued in panels of two cards. The individual cards measure approximately 1 1/2" by 2" whereas the panels measure 3" by 2". Team logos have been removed from the photos as these cards were not licensed by Major League Baseball (team owners). The backs contain a minimum of information.

COMPLETE PANEL SET 8.00 20.00
COMPLETE SET 4.00 10.00
COMMON PAIR .10 .25
1 George Brett 1.00 2.50
2 Jack Morris .20 .50
3 Gary Carter 1.25
4 Cal Ripken 2.00 5.00
5 Dwight Gooden .30 .75
6 Kent Hrbek .08 .25
7 Rickey Henderson .60 1.50
8 Mike Schmidt .60 1.50
9 Keith Hernandez .20 .50
10 Dale Murphy .40 1.00
11 Reggie Jackson .60 1.50
12 Eddie Murray .60 1.50
13 Don Mattingly 1.25 3.00
14 Ryne Sandberg 1.00 2.50
15 Willie McGee .20 .50
16 Robin Yount .50 1.25
17 Rick Sutcliffe .08 .25
18 Wade Boggs .50 1.25
19 Dave Winfield .50 1.25
20 Jim Rice .20 .50

1941 Double Play

The cards in this 75-card set measure approximately 2 1/2" by 3 1/8" was a blank-backed issue distributed by Gum Products. It consists of 75 numbered cards (two consecutive numbers per card), each depicting two players in sepia tone photographs. Cards 81-100 contain action poses, and the last 50 numbers of the set are slightly harder to find. Cards that have been cut in half to form "singles" have a greatly reduced value. These cards have a value from five to ten percent of the uncut strips and are very difficult to sell. The player on the left has an odd number and the other player has an even number. We are using only the odd numbers to identify these panels. Each penny pack contained two cards and they were issued 100 packs to a box.

COMPLETE SET (150) 2000.00 5000.00
COMMON PAIRS (1-100) 15.00 40.00
COMMON PAIRS (101-150) 20.00 50.00
WRAPPER (1-CENT) 400.00 500.00
1 L.French/V.Page XRC 50.00 100.00
3 B.Herman/S.Hack 40.00 80.00
5 L.Frey/J.VanderMeer XRC 30.00 60.00
7 P.Derringer/B.Walters 30.00 60.00
9 F.McCormick/B.Werber 15.00 40.00
11 J.Ripple/E.Lombardi 40.00 80.00
13 A.Kampouris/W.Wyatt 15.00 40.00
15 M.Owen/P.Waner 40.00 80.00
17 C.Lavagetto/P.Reiser XRC 20.00 50.00
19 J.Wasdell XRC/D.Camilli 20.00 50.00
21 D.Walker/J.Medwick 40.00 80.00
23 P.Reese XRC/K.Higbe XRC 150.00 300.00
25 H.Danning/C.Melton 15.00 40.00
27 H.Gumbert/B.Whitehead 15.00 40.00
29 J.Orengo XRC/J.Moore 15.00 40.00
31 M.Ott/N.Young 75.00 150.00
33 L.Handley/A.Vaughan 40.00 80.00
35 B.Klinger/S.Brown XRC 15.00 40.00
37 T.Moore XRC/G.Mancuso 20.00 50.00
39 J.Mize XRC/E.Slaughter XRC 125.00 250.00
41 J.Cooney/S.Sisti XRC 15.00 40.00
43 M.West/C.Rowell XRC 15.00 40.00
45 D.Litwhiler XRC/M.May 15.00 40.00
47 F.Hayes/A.Brancato XRC 15.00 40.00
49 B.Johnson/B.Nagel XRC 20.00 50.00
51 B.Newsom/H.Greenberg 75.00 150.00
53 B.McCosky/C.Gehringer 60.00 120.00
55 P.Higgins/D.Bartell 20.00 50.00
57 T.Williams/J.Tabor 400.00 800.00
59 J.Cronin/J.Foxx 150.00 300.00
61 L.Gomez/P.Rizzuto XRC 200.00 400.00
63 J.DiMaggio/C.Keller 300.00 600.00
65 R.Rolfe/B.Dickey 75.00 150.00
67 J.Gordon XRC/R.Ruffing 75.00 150.00
69 M.Tresh XRC/L.Appling 50.00 100.00
71 M.Solters/J.Rigney XRC 15.00 40.00
73 B.Meyer/B.Chapman 20.00 50.00
75 C.Travis/G.Case 20.00 50.00
77 J.Krakauskas/B.Feller 100.00 200.00
79 K.Keltner XRC/H.Trosky 20.00 50.00
81 T.Williams/J.Cronin 250.00 500.00
83 J.Gordon XRC/C.Keller 30.00 60.00
85 H.Greenberg/R.Ruffing 150.00 300.00
87 H.Trosky/G.Case 20.00 50.00
89 M.Ott/B.Whitehead 75.00 150.00
91 H.Danning/H.Gumbert 15.00 40.00
93 N.Young/C.Melton 15.00 40.00
95 J.Ripple/B.Walters 20.00 50.00
97 S.Hack/B.Klinger 20.00 50.00
99 J.Mize XRC/D.Litwhiler XRC 60.00 120.00
101 D.Dallessandro XRC/A.Galan 20.00 50.00
103 B.Lee/P.Cavarretta 30.00 60.00
105 L.Grove/B.Doerr 125.00 250.00
107 F.Pytlak/D.DiMaggio XRC 50.00 100.00
109 J.Priddy XRC/J.Murphy 30.00 60.00
111 T.Henrich/M.Russo XRC 40.00 80.00
113 F.Crosetti/J.Sturm XRC 40.00 80.00
115 I.Goodman/M.McCormick XRC 20.00 50.00
117 E.Joost/E.Koy XRC 20.00 50.00
119 L.Waner/H.Majeski XRC 50.00 100.00
121 B.Hassett/E.Moore 20.00 50.00
123 N.Etten XRC/J.Rizzo 20.00 50.00
125 S.Chapman/W.Moses 20.00 50.00
127 J.Babich/D.Siebert 20.00 50.00
129 N.Potter XRC/B.McCoy XRC 20.00 50.00
131 C.Camp XRC/L.Boud.XRC 60.00 120.00
133 R.Hemsley/M.Harder 30.00 60.00
135 G.Walker/J.Heving 20.00 50.00
137 J.Rucker/A.Adams XRC 20.00 50.00
139 M.Arnovich/C.Hubbell 75.00 150.00
141 L.Riggs/L.Durocher 60.00 120.00
143 F.Fitzsimmons/J.Vosmik 20.00 50.00
145 F.Crespi XRC/J.Brown 20.00 50.00
147 D.Heffner/H.Clift XRC 20.00 50.00
149 D.Garms/E.Fletcher 30.00 60.00

1978 Dover Publications Baseball Greats

COMPLETE SET (32) 25.00 60.00
1 Grover Cleveland Alexander 1.00 2.50
2 Chief Bender 1.00 2.50
3 Roger Bresnahan 1.00 2.50
4 Joe Bush .75 2.00
5 Frank Chance 1.00 2.50
6 Ty Cobb 2.00 5.00
7 Eddie Collins 1.00 2.50
8 Stan Coveleski 1.00 2.50
9 Sam Crawford 1.00 2.50
10 Frankie Frisch 1.00 2.50
11 Goose Goslin 1.00 2.50
12 Harry Heilman 1.00 2.50
13 Rogers Hornsby 1.00 2.50
14 Joe Jackson 1.50 4.00
15 Hugh Jennings 1.00 2.50
16 Walter Johnson 1.25 3.00
17 Sam Jones .75 2.00
18 Rabbit Maranville 1.00 2.50
19 Rube Marquard 1.00 2.50
20 Christy Mathewson 1.25 3.00
21 John McGraw 1.00 2.50
22 Herb Pennock 1.00 2.50
23 Eddie Plank 1.00 2.50
24 Edd Roush 1.00 2.50
25 Babe Ruth 3.00 8.00
26 George Sisler 1.00 2.50
27 Tris Speaker 1.00 2.50
28 Casey Stengel 1.00 2.50
29 Joe Tinker 1.00 2.50
30 Pie Traynor 1.00 2.50
31 Dazzy Vance 1.00 2.50
32 Cy Young 1.25 3.00

1950 Drake's Cookies

The cards in this 36-card set measure approximately 2 1/2" by 2 1/2". The 1950 Drake's Cookies set contains numbered black and white cards. The players are pictured inside a simulated television screen and the caption "TV Baseball Series" appears on the cards. The players selected for this set show a heavy representation of players from New York teams. The catalog designation for this set is D358.

COMPLETE SET (36) 2500.00 5000.00
1 Preacher Roe 60.00 120.00
2 Clint Hartung 50.00 100.00
3 Earl Torgeson 50.00 100.00
4 Lou Brissie 50.00 100.00
5 Duke Snider 300.00 600.00
6 Roy Campanella 300.00 600.00
7 Sheldon Jones 50.00 100.00
8 Whitey Lockman 50.00 100.00
9 Bobby Thomson 60.00 120.00
10 Dick Sisler 50.00 100.00
11 Gil Hodges 125.00 250.00
12 Eddie Waitkus 50.00 100.00
13 Bobby Doerr 100.00 200.00
14 Warren Spahn 250.00 500.00
15 Buddy Kerr 50.00 100.00
16 Sid Gordon 50.00 100.00
17 Willard Marshall 50.00 100.00
18 Carl Furillo 60.00 120.00
19 Pee Wee Reese 250.00 500.00
20 Alvin Dark 60.00 120.00
21 Del Ennis 60.00 120.00
22 Ed Stanky 60.00 120.00
23 Tom Henrich 75.00 150.00
24 Yogi Berra 250.00 500.00
25 Phil Rizzuto 125.00 250.00
26 Jerry Coleman 60.00 120.00
27 Joe Page 60.00 120.00
28 Allie Reynolds 60.00 120.00
29 Ray Scarborough 50.00 100.00
30 Birdie Tebbetts 50.00 100.00
31 Maurice McDermott 50.00 100.00
32 Johnny Pesky 60.00 120.00
33 Dom DiMaggio 75.00 150.00
34 Vern Stephens 60.00 120.00
35 Bob Elliott 60.00 120.00
36 Enos Slaughter 125.00 250.00

1981 Drake's

The cards in this 33-card set measure 2 1/2" by 3 1/2". The 1981 Drake's Bakeries set contains National and American League stars. Produced in conjunction with Topps and released to the public in Drake's Cakes, this set features red frames for American League players and blue frames for National League players. A Drake's Cakes logo with the words "Big Hitters" appears on the lower front of each card. The backs are quite similar to the 1981 Topps backs but contain the Drake's logo, a different card number, and a short paragraph entitled "What Makes a Big Hitter" at the top of the card.

COMPLETE SET (33) 2.50 6.00
1 Carl Yastrzemski .20 .50
2 Rod Carew .20 .50
3 Pete Rose .30 .75
4 Dave Parker .02 .10
5 George Brett .75 2.00
6 Eddie Murray .50 1.25
7 Mike Schmidt .40 1.00
8 Jim Rice .05 .15
9 Fred Lynn .02 .10
10 Reggie Jackson .20 .50
11 Steve Garvey .07 .20
12 Ken Singleton .01 .05
13 Bill Buckner .02 .10
14 Dave Winfield .30 .75
15 Jack Clark .02 .10
16 Cecil Cooper .02 .10
17 Bob Horner .01 .05
18 George Foster .02 .10
19 Dave Kingman .02 .10
20 Cesar Cedeno .02 .10
21 Joe Charboneau .07 .20
22 George Hendrick .01 .05
23 Gary Carter .20 .50
24 Al Oliver .02 .10
25 Bruce Bochte .01 .05
26 Jerry Mumphrey .01 .05
27 Steve Kemp .01 .05
28 Bob Watson .04 .10
29 John Castino .01 .05
30 Tony Armas .01 .05
31 John Mayberry .01 .05
32 Carlton Fisk .20 .50
33 Lee Mazzilli .02 .10

1982 Drake's

The cards in this 33-card set measure 2 1/2" by 3 1/2". The 1982 Drake's Big Hitters series cards each has the title "2nd Annual Collectors' Edition" in a ribbon design at the top of the picture area. Each color player photo has "photo mount" designs in the corners, red for the AL and green for the NL. The reverses are green and blue, the same as the regular 1982 Topps format, and the photos are larger than those of the previous year. Of the 33 hitters featured, 19 represent the National League. There are 21 returnees from the 1981 set and only one photo, that of Kennedy, is the same as that appearing in the regular Topps issue. The Drake's logo appears centered in the bottom border on the obverse. This set's card numbering is essentially in alphabetical order by the player's name.

COMPLETE SET (33) 2.50 6.00
1 Tony Armas .01 .05
2 Buddy Bell .02 .10
3 Johnny Bench .20 .50
4 George Brett .60 1.50
5 Bill Buckner .02 .10
6 Rod Carew .10 .30
7 Gary Carter .15 .40
8 Jack Clark .02 .10
9 Cecil Cooper .02 .10
10 Jose Cruz .02 .10
11 Dwight Evans .05 .15
12 Carlton Fisk .15 .40
13 George Foster .02 .10
14 Steve Garvey .07 .20
15 Kirk Gibson .07 .20
16 Mike Hargrove .02 .10
17 George Hendrick .01 .05
18 Bob Horner .01 .05
19 Reggie Jackson .15 .40
20 Terry Kennedy .01 .05
21 Dave Kingman .02 .10
22 Greg Luzinski .02 .10
23 Bill Madlock .01 .05
24 John Mayberry .01 .05
25 Eddie Murray .30 .75
26 Graig Nettles .02 .10
27 Jim Rice .02 .10
28 Pete Rose .30 .75
29 Mike Schmidt .30 .75
30 Ken Singleton .01 .05
31 Dave Winfield .20 .50
32 Butch Wynegar .01 .05
33 Richie Zisk .01 .05

1983 Drake's

The cards in this 33-card series measure 2 1/2" by 3 1/2". For the third year in a row, Drake's Cakes, in conjunction with Topps, issued a set entitled Big Hitters. The fronts appear very similar to those of the previous two years with slight variations on the framelines and player identification sections. The backs are the same as the Topps backs of this year except for the card number and the Drake's logo. This set's card numbering is essentially in alphabetical order by the player's name.

COMPLETE SET (33) 2.50 6.00
1 Don Baylor .02 .10
2 Bill Buckner .02 .10
3 Rod Carew .15 .40
4 Gary Carter .15 .40
5 Jack Clark .02 .10
6 Cecil Cooper .01 .05
7 Dwight Evans .05 .15
8 George Foster .02 .10
9 Pedro Guerrero .01 .05
10 George Hendrick .01 .05
11 Bob Horner .01 .05
12 Reggie Jackson .20 .50
13 Steve Kemp .01 .05
14 Dave Kingman .02 .10
15 Bill Madlock .01 .05
16 Gary Matthews .01 .05
17 Hal McRae .01 .05
18 Dale Murphy .15 .40
19 Eddie Murray .30 .75
20 Ben Oglivie .01 .05
21 Al Oliver .02 .10
22 Jim Rice .02 .10
23 Cal Ripken 1.25 3.00

24 Pete Rose .20 .50
25 Mike Schmidt .20 .50
26 Ken Singleton .01 .05
27 Gorman Thomas .01 .05
28 Jason Thompson .01 .05
29 Mookie Wilson .02 .10
30 Willie Wilson .01 .05
31 Dave Winfield .20 .50
32 Carl Yastrzemski .20 .50
33 Robin Yount .15 .40

1984 Drake's

The cards in this 33-card set measure 2 1/2" by 3 1/2". The Fourth Annual Collectors Edition of baseball cards produced by Drake's Cakes in conjunction with Topps continued this now annual set entitled Big Hitters. As in previous years, the front contains a frameline in which the title of the set, the Drake's logo, and the player's name, his team, and position appear. The cards all feature the player in a batting action pose. While the cards fronts are different from the Topps fronts of this year, the backs differ only in the card number and the use of the Drake's logo instead of the Topps logo. This set's card numbering is essentially in alphabetical order by the player's name.

COMPLETE SET (33) 2.50 6.00
1 Don Baylor .02 .10
2 Wade Boggs .40 1.00
3 George Brett .50 1.25
4 Bill Buckner .02 .10
5 Rod Carew .10 .30
6 Gary Carter .15 .40
7 Ron Cey .02 .10
8 Cecil Cooper .02 .10
9 Andre Dawson .07 .20
10 Steve Garvey .02 .10
11 Pedro Guerrero .01 .05
12 George Hendrick .01 .05
13 Keith Hernandez .02 .10
14 Bob Horner .01 .05
15 Reggie Jackson .15 .40
16 Steve Kemp .01 .05
17 Ron Kittle .01 .05
18 Greg Luzinski .02 .10
19 Fred Lynn .02 .10
20 Bill Madlock .02 .10
21 Gary Matthews .01 .05
22 Dale Murphy .10 .30
23 Eddie Murray .30 .75
24 Al Oliver .02 .10
25 Jim Rice .02 .10
26 Cal Ripken 1.25 3.00
27 Pete Rose .20 .50
28 Mike Schmidt .20 .50
29 Darryl Strawberry .07 .20
30 Alan Trammell .07 .20
31 Mookie Wilson .01 .05
32 Dave Winfield .20 .50
33 Robin Yount .15 .40

1985 Drake's

The cards in this 44-card set measure 2 1/2" by 3 1/2". The Fifth Annual Collectors Edition of baseball cards produced by Drake's Cakes in conjunction with Topps continued this apparently annual set with a new twist, for the first time, 11 pitchers were included. The "Big Hitters" are numbered 1-33 and the pitchers are numbered 34-44; each subgroup is ordered alphabetically. The cards are numbered in the upper right corner of the backs of the cards. The complete set could be obtained directly from the company by sending 2.95 with four proofs of purchase.

COMPLETE FACT. SET (44) 3.00 8.00
COMPLETE SET (44) 3.00 8.00
COMMON PLAYER (1-33) .02 .05
COMMON PLAYER (34-44) .04 .10
1 Tony Armas .01 .05
2 Harold Baines .05 .15
3 Don Baylor .02 .10
4 George Brett .40 1.00
5 Gary Carter .15 .40
6 Ron Cey .02 .10
7 Jose Cruz .02 .10
8 Alvin Davis .01 .05
9 Chili Davis .02 .10
10 Dwight Evans .02 .10
11 Steve Garvey .02 .10
12 Kirk Gibson .05 .15
13 Pedro Guerrero .01 .05
14 Tony Gwynn .75 2.00
15 Keith Hernandez .02 .10
16 Kent Hrbek .02 .10
17 Reggie Jackson .20 .50
18 Gary Matthews .01 .05
19 Don Mattingly .60 1.50
20 Dale Murphy .07 .20
21 Eddie Murray .20 .50
22 Dave Parker .02 .10
23 Lance Parrish .02 .10
24 Tim Raines .02 .10
25 Jim Rice .02 .10
26 Cal Ripken 1.00 2.50
27 Juan Samuel .01 .05
28 Ryne Sandberg .40 1.00
29 Mike Schmidt .20 .50
30 Darryl Strawberry .02 .10
31 Alan Trammell .05 .15
32 Dave Winfield .20 .50
33 Robin Yount .20 .50
34 Mike Boddicker .02 .10
35 Steve Carlton .20 .50
36 Dwight Gooden .08 .25
37 Willie Hernandez .02 .10
38 Mark Langston .05 .15
39 Dan Quisenberry .02 .10
40 Dave Righetti .02 .10
41 Tom Seaver .20 .50
42 Bob Stanley .02 .10
43 Rick Sutcliffe .02 .10
44 Bruce Sutter .05 .15

1986 Drake's

This set of 37 cards was distributed as back panels of various Drake's snack products. Each individual card measures 2 1/2" by 3 1/2". Each specially marked package features two, three, or four cards on the back. The set is easily recognized by the Drake's logo and "6th Annual Collector's Edition" at the top of the obverse. Cards are numbered on the front and the back. Cards below are coded based on the product upon which they appeared, for example, Apple Pies (AP), Cherry Pies (CP), Chocolate Donut Delites (CDD), Coffee Cake Jr. (CCJ), Creme Shortcakes (CS), Devil Dogs (DD), Fudge Brownies (FUD), Funny Bones (FB), Peanut Butter Squares (PBS), Powdered Sugar Donut Delites (PSDD), Ring Ding Jr. (RDJ), Sunny Doodles (SD), Swiss Rolls (SR), Yankee Doodles (YD), and Yodels (Y). The last nine cards are pitchers. Complete panels would be valued approximately 50 percent higher than the individual card prices listed below.

COMPLETE SET (37) 12.50 30.00
1 Gary Carter Y .60 1.50
2 Dwight Evans Y .20 .50
3 Reggie Jackson SR 1.25 3.00
4 Dave Parker SR .20 .50
5 Rickey Henderson FB 1.50 4.00
6 Pedro Guerrero FB .20 .50
7 Don Mattingly YD 3.00 8.00
8 Mike Marshall YD .08 .25
9 Keith Moreland YD .08 .25
10 Keith Hernandez CS .20 .50
11 Cal Ripken CS 6.00 15.00
12 Dale Murphy RDJ .40 1.00
13 Jim Rice RDJ .20 .50
14 George Brett CCJ 3.00 8.00
15 Tim Raines CCJ .20 .50
16 Darryl Strawberry DD .20 .50
17 Bill Buckner DD .20 .50
18 Dave Winfield AP 1.00 2.50
19 Ryne Sandberg AP 2.50 6.00
20 Steve Balboni AP .08 .25
21 Tommy Herr AP .08 .25
22 Pete Rose CP 1.25 3.00
23 Willie McGee CP .40 1.00
24 Harold Baines CP .30 .75
25 Eddie Murray CP 1.25 3.00
26 Mike Schmidt SD FUD 1.50 4.00
27 Wade Boggs SD FUD 2.00 5.00
28 Kirk Gibson SD FUD .20 .50
29 Bret Saberhagen PBS .20 .50
30 John Tudor PBS .08 .25
31 Orel Hershiser PBS .20 .50
32 Ron Guidry CDD .20 .50
33 Nolan Ryan CDD 6.00 15.00
34 Dave Stieb CDD .08 .25
35 Dwight Gooden SDD .20 .50
36 Fern.Valenzuela SDD .20 .50
37 Tom Browning SDD .08 .25

1987 Drake's

This 33-card set features 25 top hitters and eight top pitchers. Cards were printed in groups of two, three, or four on the backs of Drake's bakery products. Individual cards measure 2 1/2" by 3 1/2" and tout the 7th annual edition. Card backs feature year-by-year season statistics. The cards are numbered such that the pitchers are listed numerically last, e.g., top hitters 1-25 and pitchers 26-33). Complete panels would be valued approximately 50 percent higher than the individual card prices listed below.

COMPLETE SET (33) 12.00 30.00
1 Darryl Strawberry .20 .50
2 Wally Joyner .30 .75
3 Von Hayes .08 .25
4 Jose Canseco 1.50 4.00
5 Dave Winfield 1.25 3.00
6 Cal Ripken 6.00 15.00
7 Keith Moreland .08 .25
8 Don Mattingly 3.00 8.00
9 Willie McGee .20 .50
10 Keith Hernandez .20 .50
11 Tony Gwynn 3.00 8.00
12 Rickey Henderson 2.00 5.00
13 Dale Murphy .40 1.00
14 George Brett 3.00 8.00
15 Jim Rice .20 .50
16 Wade Boggs 1.50 4.00
17 Kevin Bass .08 .25
18 Dave Parker .20 .50
19 Kirby Puckett 1.25 3.00
20 Gary Carter .20 .50
21 Ryne Sandberg 1.25 3.00
22 Harold Baines .30 .75
23 Mike Schmidt 1.25 3.00
24 Eddie Murray 1.25 3.00
25 Steve Sax .08 .25
26 Dwight Gooden .20 .50
27 Jack Morris .20 .50
28 Ron Darling .08 .25
29 Fernando Valenzuela .20 .50
30 John Tudor .08 .25
31 Roger Clemens 6.00 10.00
32 Nolan Ryan 6.00 15.00
33 Mike Scott .08 .25

1988 Drake's

This 33-card set features 27 top hitters and six top pitchers. Cards were printed in groups of two, three, or four on the backs of Drake's bakery products. Individual cards measure approximately 2 1/2" by 3 1/2" and tout the 8th annual edition. Card backs feature year-by-year season statistics. The cards are numbered such that the pitchers are listed numerically last, e.g., top hitters 1-27 and pitchers 28-33). The product affiliations are as follows, 1-2 Ring Dings, 3-4 Devil Dogs, 5-6 Coffee Cakes, 7-9 Yankee Doodles, 10-11 Funny Bones, 12-14 Fudge Brownies, 15-18 Cherry Pies, 19-21 Sunny Doodles, 22-24 Powdered Sugar Donuts, 25-27 Chocolate Donuts, 28-29 Yodels, and 30-33 Apple Pies. Complete panels would be valued approximately 50 percent higher than the individual card prices listed below.

COMPLETE SET (33) 10.00 25.00
1 Don Mattingly 4.00 10.00
2 Tim Raines .20 .50
3 Darryl Strawberry .20 .50
4 Wade Boggs 2.00 5.00
5 Keith Hernandez .20 .50
6 Mark McGwire 5.00 12.00
7 Rickey Henderson 3.00 8.00
8 Mike Schmidt 1.50 4.00
9 Dwight Evans .20 .50
10 Gary Carter 1.25 3.00
11 Paul Molitor 2.00 5.00
12 Dave Winfield 1.50 4.00
13 Alan Trammell .30 .75
14 Tony Gwynn 4.00 10.00
15 Dale Murphy .40 1.00
16 Andre Dawson .40 1.00
17 Von Hayes .08 .25
18 Willie Randolph .20 .50
19 Kirby Puckett 1.25 3.00
20 Juan Samuel .08 .25
21 Eddie Murray 1.50 4.00
22 George Bell .08 .25
23 Larry Sheets .08 .25
24 Eric Davis .20 .50
25 Cal Ripken 8.00 20.00
26 Pedro Guerrero .08 .25
27 Will Clark 3.00 8.00
28 Dwight Gooden .20 .50
29 Frank Viola .08 .25
30 Roger Clemens 6.00 10.00
31 Rick Sutcliffe .08 .25
32 Jack Morris .20 .50
33 John Tudor .08 .25

1894 Duke Cabinets N142

These four cabinets were produced by W.H. Duke. These color cabinets measure approximately 6" X 9 1/2" and a portrait takes up almost the entire card. The player is identified on the bottom.

COMPLETE SET (4) 20000.00 40000.00
1 George Davis 5000.00 10000.00
2 Ed Delahanty 6000.00 12000.00
3 Billy Nash 2500.00 5000.00
4 Wilbert Robinson 7500.00 15000.00

2002 J.D. Drew

1 J.D. Drew .40 1.00

1893 Duke Talk of the Diamond N135

The 25 cards in Duke's Talk of the Diamond set feature a humorous situation placed alongside a baseball design. Since the reverse lists the manufacturer as a branch of the American Tobacco Company, it is thought that this set was issued about 1893. A list of the 25 titles appears on the back of each card. Most of the baseball designs are similar to those appearing in the Buchner Gold Coin set (N284).

COMPLETE SET (25) 1250.00 2500.00
COMMON CARD (1-25) 30.00 80.00

1987 DuPont

This 8 1/2" by 11" large size cards features Hall of Famers. The front is a posed shot from near the end of his career and the back features information about various DuPont products. It is possible there might be more players so any additions are appreciated.

COMPLETE SET (2) 4.00 10.00
1 Harmon Killebrew 4.00 10.00
2 Willie Mays 6.00 15.00

1993 Duracell Power Players I

This 24-card standard-size set was divided into six packs with four cards and one Duracell Official Order Form in each pack. One pack was free with a purchase of Duracell Saver Pack or could be ordered with proof of purchase of several other Duracell products.

COMPLETE SET (24) 1.25 3.00
1 Roger Clemens .20 .50
2 Frank Thomas .10 .30
3 Andre Dawson .05 .15
4 Orel Hershiser .02 .10
5 Kirby Puckett .10 .30
6 Edgar Martinez .05 .15
7 Craig Biggio .05 .15
8 Terry Pendleton .01 .05
9 Mark McGwire .20 .50
10 Dave Stewart .02 .10
11 Ozzie Smith .20 .50
12 Doug Drabek .01 .05
13 Dwight Gooden .02 .10
14 Tony Gwynn .20 .50
15 Carlos Baerga .01 .05
16 Robin Yount .08 .25
17 Barry Bonds .20 .50
18 Bip Roberts .01 .05
19 Don Mattingly .20 .50
20 Nolan Ryan .40 1.00
21 Tom Glavine .07 .20
22 Will Clark .07 .20
23 Cecil Fielder .02 .10
24 Dave Winfield .08 .25

1993 Duracell Power Players II

This 24-card standard-size set was divided into six packs with four cards and one Duracell Official Order Form in each pack. One pack was free with a purchase of a Duracell Saver Pack or could be ordered with proof of purchase of several other Duracell products.

COMPLETE SET (24) 1.25 3.00
1 Cal Ripken .40 1.00
2 Melido Perez .01 .05
3 John Kruk .02 .10
4 Charlie Hayes .01 .05
5 George Brett .20 .50
6 Ruben Sierra .02 .10
7 Deion Sanders .05 .15
8 Andy Van Slyke .01 .05
9 Fred McGriff .05 .15
10 Benito Santiago .01 .05
11 Charles Nagy .01 .05
12 Greg Maddux .25 .60
13 Ryne Sandberg .20 .50
14 Dennis Martinez .02 .10
15 Ken Griffey Jr. .30 .75
16 Jim Abbott .02 .10
17 Barry Larkin .07 .20
18 Gary Sheffield .07 .20
19 Jose Canseco .10 .30
20 Jack McDowell .01 .05
21 Darryl Strawberry .02 .10
22 Delino DeShields .01 .05
23 Dennis Eckersley .08 .25
24 Paul Molitor .20 .50

1914 E and S Publishing

These ornate styled postcards produced by the E and S Pub. Co. of Chicago in 1914 are extremely rare. This bluetone cards have a closeup head and shoulders caracture of the player surrounded by cartoon vignettes of his career done by an obviously gifted cartoonist, possibly from one of the Chicago newspapers. The art is signed T.S. Several additions were made in the past couple years; there are probably others as well; any further additions to this checklist are greatly appreciated.

COMPLETE SET 6000.00 12000.00
1 Joe Benz 500.00 1000.00
2 Ty Cobb 1500.00 3000.00
3 Miller Huggins 1000.00 2000.00
4 Joe Jackson 1250.00 2500.00
5 James Lavender 500.00 1000.00
6 Christy Mathewson 1000.00 2000.00
7 Frank Schulte 500.00 1000.00
8 Jim Scott 500.00 1000.00
9 Art Wilson 500.00 1000.00

1911 Close Candy E94

The cards in this 30-card set measure 1 1/2" by 2 3/4". The E94 format, like that of E93, consists of tinted, black and white photos on solid color backgrounds (seven colors seen; each player seen in more than one color). Issued in 1911, cards from this set may be found with advertising overstamps covering the gray print checklist on the back (begins with Moore). Some blank backs have been found, and the set is identical to M131. Listed pricing for these cards in raw condition references "VG" condition.

COMPLETE SET (30) 50000.00 100000.00
1 Jimmy Austin 200.00 350.00
2 Johnny Bates 200.00 350.00
3 Bob Bescher 200.00 350.00
4 Bobby Byrne 200.00 350.00
5 Frank Chance 500.00 800.00
6 Eddie Cicotte 500.00 800.00
7 Ty Cobb 2500.00 4000.00
8 Sam Crawford 500.00 800.00
9 Harry Davis 200.00 350.00
10 Art Devlin 200.00 350.00
11 Josh Devore 200.00 350.00
12 Mickey Doolan 200.00 350.00
13 Patsy Dougherty 200.00 350.00
14 Johnny Evers 500.00 800.00
15 Eddie Grant 200.00 350.00
16 Hugh Jennings 350.00 600.00
17 Red Kleinow 200.00 350.00
18 Napoleon Lajoie 500.00 800.00
19 Joe Lake 200.00 350.00
20 Tommy Leach 200.00 350.00
21 Hans Lobert 200.00 350.00
22 Harry Lord 200.00 350.00
23 Sherry Magee 300.00 500.00
24 John McGraw 350.00 600.00
25 Earl Moore 200.00 350.00
26 Red Murray 200.00 350.00
27 Tris Speaker 900.00 1500.00
28 Terry Turner 200.00 350.00
29 Honus Wagner 1800.00 3000.00
30 Cy Young 1200.00 2000.00

1909 E92-2 Croft's Candy

The cards in this 50-card set measure 1 1/2" by 2 3/4". Additional advertising backs can also be found for Croft's Candy, Dockman and Son's and Nadja - but pricing for these cards can be found in their own listings. The set contains poses identical to those in E101, E102, and E105. Of note, these cards were printed with the advertising on back done in black, blue and red ink variations. The black ink are most common and our pricing refernces these cards. Blue ink backs are considerably tougher and generally trade for two to three times the listed values. Red ink backs are extremely rare - so much so that establishing consistent values for them remains to this day a nearly impossible task. Finally, our listed prices for raw cards reference VgEx condition given the majority of cards found in this set are typically off-grade. Cards are unnumbered and checklisted alphabetically by each player's last name.

1 Jack Barry 125.00 200.00
2 Harry Bemis 125.00 200.00
3 Chief Bender Striped Cap 350.00 600.00
4 Chief Bender White Cap 350.00 600.00
5 Bill Bergen 125.00 200.00
6 Bob Bescher 125.00 200.00
7 Al Bridwell 125.00 200.00
8 Doc Casey 125.00 200.00
9 Frank Chance 350.00 600.00
10 Hal Chase 175.00 300.00
11 Ty Cobb 3500.00 6000.00
12 Eddie Collins 350.00 600.00
13 Sam Crawford 350.00 600.00
14 Harry Davis 125.00 200.00
15 Art Devlin 125.00 200.00
16 Bill Donovan 125.00 200.00
17 Red Dooin 125.00 200.00
18 Mickey Doolan 125.00 200.00
19 Patsy Dougherty 125.00 200.00
20 Larry Doyle Batting 125.00 200.00
21 Larry Doyle Throwing 125.00 200.00
22 Johnny Evers 350.00 600.00
23 George Gibson 125.00 200.00
24 Topsy Hartsel 125.00 200.00
25 Fred Jacklitsch 125.00 200.00
26 Hugh Jennings 125.00 200.00
27 Red Kleinow 125.00 200.00
28 Otto Knabe 125.00 200.00
29 John Knight 125.00 200.00
30 Nap Lajoie 500.00 800.00
31 Hans Lobert 125.00 200.00
32 Sherry Magee 125.00 200.00
33 Christy Mathewson UER 1200.00 2000.00
34 John McGraw 350.00 600.00
35 Larry McLean 125.00 200.00
36 Dots Miller Batting 125.00 200.00
37 Dots Miller Fielding 125.00 200.00
38 Danny Murphy 125.00 200.00
39 Bill O'Hara 125.00 200.00
40 Germany Schaefer 125.00 200.00
41 Admiral Schlei 125.00 200.00
42 Boss Smith (Schmidt) 125.00 200.00
43 Dave Shean 125.00 200.00
44 Johnny Seigle (Siegle) 125.00 200.00
45 Frank Smith 125.00 200.00
46 Joe Tinker 350.00 600.00
47 Honus Wagner Batting 2500.00 4000.00
48 Honus Wagner Throwing 1800.00 3000.00
49 Cy Young 900.00 1500.00
50 Heinie Zimmerman 125.00 200.00

1909 E92-3 Croft's Cocoa

The cards in this 50-card set measure 1 1/2" by 2 3/4". Additional advertising backs can also be found for Croft's Candy, Dockman and Son's and Nadja - but pricing for these cards can be found in their own listings. The set contains poses identical to those in E101, E102, and E105. Book prices reference VgEx condition given the majority of cards found in this set are typically off-grade. Cards are unnumbered and checklisted alphabetically by each player's last name.

1 Jack Barry 125.00 200.00
2 Harry Bemis 125.00 200.00
3 Chief Bender Striped Cap 350.00 600.00
4 Chief Bender White Cap 350.00 600.00
5 Bill Bergen 125.00 200.00
6 Bob Bescher 125.00 200.00
7 Al Bridwell 125.00 200.00
8 Doc Casey 125.00 200.00
9 Frank Chance 350.00 600.00
10 Hal Chase 175.00 300.00
11 Ty Cobb 3500.00 6000.00
12 Eddie Collins 350.00 600.00
13 Sam Crawford 350.00 600.00
14 Harry Davis 125.00 200.00
15 Art Devlin 125.00 200.00
16 Bill Donovan 125.00 200.00
17 Red Dooin 125.00 200.00
18 Mickey Doolan 125.00 200.00
19 Patsy Dougherty 125.00 200.00
20 Larry Doyle Batting 125.00 200.00
21 Larry Doyle Throwing 125.00 200.00
22 Johnny Evers 350.00 600.00
23 George Gibson 125.00 200.00
24 Topsy Hartsel 125.00 200.00
25 Fred Jacklitsch 125.00 200.00
26 Hugh Jennings 350.00 600.00
27 Red Kleinow 125.00 200.00
28 Otto Knabe 125.00 200.00
29 Jack Knight 125.00 200.00
30 Nap Lajoie 500.00 800.00
31 Hans Lobert 125.00 200.00
32 Sherry Magee 125.00 200.00
33 Christy Mathewson UER Matthewson 1200.00 2000.00
34 John McGraw 350.00 600.00
35 Larry McLean 125.00 200.00
36 Dots Miller Batting 125.00 200.00
37 Dots Miller Fielding 125.00 200.00
38 Danny Murphy 125.00 200.00
39 Bill O'Hara 125.00 200.00
40 Germany Schaefer 125.00 200.00
41 Admiral Schlei 125.00 200.00
42 Boss Smith (Schmidt) 125.00 200.00
43 Dave Shean 125.00 200.00
44 Johnny Seigle (Siegle) 125.00 200.00
45 Frank Smith 125.00 200.00
46 Joe Tinker 350.00 600.00
47 Honus Wagner Batting 2500.00 4000.00
48 Honus Wagner Throwing 1800.00 3000.00
49 Cy Young Cleveland 900.00 1500.00
50 Heinie Zimmerman 125.00 200.00

1909 E92-4 Nadja Caramel

The cards in this 62-card set measure 1 1/2" by 2 3/4". Additional advertising backs can also be found for Croft's Candy, Croft's Cocoa and Dockman and Son's - but pricing for these cards can be found in their own listings. Of note, the Nadja backed set contains a group of St. Louis players unavailable in the other E92 variations. The set contains poses identical to those in E101, E102, and E105. Book prices reference VgEx condition given the majority of cards found in this set are typically off-grade. Cards are unnumbered and checklisted alphabetically by each player's last name.

1 Bill Bailey 125.00 200.00
2 Jack Barry 125.00 200.00
3 Harry Bemis 125.00 200.00
4 Chief Bender Striped Cap 350.00 600.00
5 Chief Bender White Cap 350.00 600.00
6 Bill Bergen 125.00 200.00
7 Bob Bescher 125.00 200.00
8 Roger Bresnahan 350.00 600.00
9 Al Bridwell 125.00 200.00
10 Doc Casey 125.00 200.00
11 Frank Chance 350.00 600.00
12 Hal Chase 175.00 300.00
13 Ty Cobb 3500.00 6000.00
14 Eddie Collins 350.00 600.00
15 Sam Crawford 350.00 600.00
16 Harry Davis 125.00 200.00
17 Art Devlin 125.00 200.00
18 Bill Donovan 125.00 200.00
19 Red Dooin 125.00 200.00
20 Mickey Doolan 125.00 200.00
21 Patsy Dougherty 125.00 200.00
22 Larry Doyle Batting 125.00 200.00
23 Larry Doyle Throwing 125.00 200.00
24 Rube Ellis 125.00 200.00
25 Johnny Evers 350.00 600.00
26 George Gibson 125.00 200.00
27 Topsy Hartsel 125.00 200.00
28 Roy Hartzell Batting 125.00 200.00
29 Roy Hartzell Fielding 125.00 200.00
30 Harry Howell Follow Through 125.00 200.00
31 Harry Howell Ready to Pitch 125.00 200.00
32 Fred Jacklitsch 125.00 200.00
33 Hugh Jennings 350.00 600.00
34 Red Kleinow 125.00 200.00
35 Otto Knabe 125.00 200.00
36 Jack Knight 125.00 200.00
37 Nap Lajoie 500.00 800.00
38 Hans Lobert 125.00 200.00
39 Sherry Magee 125.00 200.00
40 Christy Mathewson UER 1200.00 2000.00
41 John McGraw 350.00 600.00
42 Larry McLean 125.00 200.00
43 Dots Miller Batting 125.00 200.00
44 Dots Miller Fielding 125.00 200.00
45 Danny Murphy 125.00 200.00
46 Rebel Oakes 125.00 200.00
47 Bill O'Hara 125.00 200.00
48 Ed Phelps 125.00 200.00
49 Germany Schaefer 125.00 200.00
50 Admiral Schlei 125.00 200.00
51 Boss Smith (Schmidt) 125.00 200.00
52 Dave Shean 125.00 200.00
53 Johnny Seigle (Siegle) 125.00 200.00
54 Frank Smith 125.00 200.00
55 George Stone Blue Background 125.00 200.00
56 George Stone Green Background 125.00 200.00
57 Joe Tinker 350.00 600.00
58 Honus Wagner Batting 2500.00 4000.00
59 Honus Wagner Throwing 1800.00 3000.00
60 Bobby Wallace 250.00 400.00
61 Cy Young 900.00 1500.00
62 Heinie Zimmerman 125.00 200.00

1910 E98 Set of 30

The cards in this 30-card set measure 1 1/2" by 2 3/4". E98 is an anonymous set with more similarities to Standard Caramel issues than to Briggs. Most players are found with four different background colors and the brown print checklist (starts with "1. Christy Mathewson") has been alphabetized below. The set was issued in 1910. Listed prices for raw cards references "VgEx" condition.

COMPLETE SET (30) 60000.00 120000.00
1 Chief Bender 500.00 800.00
2 Roger Bresnahan 500.00 800.00
3 Al Bridwell 300.00 500.00
4 Miner Brown 500.00 800.00
5 Frank Chance 500.00 800.00
6 Hal Chase 300.00 500.00
7 Fred Clarke 500.00 800.00
8 Ty Cobb 3000.00 5000.00
9 Eddie Collins 500.00 800.00
10 Jack Coombs 300.00 500.00
11 Bill Dahlen 300.00 500.00
12 Harry Davis 300.00 500.00
13 Red Dooin 300.00 500.00
14 Johnny Evers 500.00 800.00
15 Russ Ford 300.00 500.00
16 Hugh Jennings 500.00 800.00
17 Johnny Kling 300.00 500.00
18 Nap Lajoie 700.00 1200.00
19 Connie Mack 900.00 1500.00
20 Christy Mathewson 1800.00 3000.00
21 John McGraw 500.00 800.00
22 Larry McLean 300.00 500.00
23 Chief Meyers 300.00 500.00
24 George Mullin 300.00 500.00
25 Fred Tenney 300.00 500.00
26 Joe Tinker 500.00 800.00
27 Hippo Vaughn 300.00 500.00
28 Honus Wagner 2500.00 4000.00
29 Ed Walsh 500.00 800.00
30 Cy Young UER 1800.00 3000.00

1910 E101 Set of 50

The cards in this 50-card set measure 1 1/2" by 2 3/4". The "Prominent Members of National and American Leagues" portrayed in E101 are identical to the line drawings of E92 and E105. The set was distributed about 1910. The set issuer is not mentioned anywhere on the cards. The complete set price includes all variation cards listed in the checklist below.

COMPLETE SET (50) 6000.00 12000.00
1 Jack Barry 300.00 600.00
2 Harry Bemis 300.00 600.00
3A Chief Bender/white cap) 600.00 1200.00
3B Chief Bender/(striped cap) 600.00 1200.00
4 Bill Bergen 300.00 600.00
5 Bob Bescher 300.00 600.00
6 Al Bridwell 300.00 600.00
7 Doc Casey 300.00 600.00
8 Frank Chance 600.00 1200.00
9 Hal Chase 500.00 800.00
10 Ty Cobb 6000.00 12000.00
11 Eddie Collins 1000.00 2000.00
12 Sam Crawford 600.00 1200.00
13 Harry Davis 300.00 600.00
14 Art Devlin 300.00 600.00
15 Bill Donovan 300.00 600.00
16 Red Dooin 300.00 600.00
17 Mickey Doolan 300.00 600.00
18 Patsy Dougherty 300.00 600.00
19A Larry Doyle/(batting) 400.00 800.00
19B Larry Doyle/(throwing) 400.00 800.00
20 Johnny Evers 600.00 1200.00
21 George Gibson 300.00 600.00
22 Topsy Hartsel 300.00 600.00
23 Fred Jacklitsch 300.00 600.00
24 Hugh Jennings 600.00 1200.00
25 Red Kleinow 300.00 600.00
26 Otto Knabe 300.00 600.00
27 John Knight 300.00 600.00
28 Nap Lajoie 1000.00 2000.00
29 Hans Lobert 300.00 600.00
30 Sherry Magee 400.00 800.00
31 Christy Mathewson 2000.00 4000.00
32 John McGraw 1000.00 2000.00
33 Larry McLean 300.00 600.00
34A J.B. Miller/(batting) 300.00 600.00
34B J.B. Miller/(fielding) 300.00 600.00
35 Danny Murphy 300.00 600.00
36 Bill O'Hara 300.00 600.00
37 Germany Schaefer 400.00 800.00
38 Admiral Schlei 300.00 600.00
39 Boss Schmidt 300.00 600.00
40 Johnny Seigle/(sic& Siegle) 300.00 600.00
41 Dave Shean 300.00 600.00
42 Frank Smith 300.00 600.00
43 Joe Tinker 600.00 1200.00
44A Honus Wagner/(batting) 2000.00 4000.00
44B Honus Wagner/(throwing) 2000.00 4000.00
45 Cy Young 1000.00 2000.00
46 Heine Zimmerman 300.00 600.00

1910 E102 Set of 25

The cards in this 29-card set measure 1 1/2" by 2 3/4". The player poses in E102 are identical to those in E92. The reverse of each card carries an angled checklist (Begins with "COBB, Detroit") printed in black. Smith is not listed, and two poses exist for Doyle, Miller and Wagner. The set was issued circa 1910. The complete set price includes all variation cards listed in the checklist below.

COMPLETE SET (29) 25000.00 50000.00
1 Chief Bender 750.00 1500.00
2 Bob Bescher 400.00 800.00
3 Hal Chase 600.00 1200.00
4 Ty Cobb 7500.00 15000.00
5 Eddie Collins 750.00 1500.00
6 Sam Crawford 750.00 1500.00
7 Bill Donovan 400.00 800.00
8 Red Dooin 400.00 800.00
9 Patsy Dougherty 400.00 800.00
10A Larry Doyle Batting 500.00 1000.00
10B Larry Doyle Throwing 500.00 1000.00
11 Johnny Evers 750.00 1500.00
12 Red Kleinow 400.00 800.00
13 Otto Knabe 400.00 800.00
14 Nap Lajoie 1500.00 3000.00
15 Hans Lobert 400.00 800.00
16 Sherry Magee 500.00 1000.00
17 Christy Mathewson 2500.00 5000.00
18A Dots Miller Batting 500.00 1000.00
18B Dots Miller Fielding 2000.00 4000.00
19 Danny Murphy 400.00 800.00
20 Germany Schaefer 500.00 1000.00
21 Boss Schmidt 400.00 800.00
22 Boss Smith (Schmidt) 400.00 800.00
23 Dave Shean 400.00 800.00
24 Joe Tinker 750.00 1500.00
25A Honus Wagner Batting 2500.00 5000.00
25B Honus Wagner Throwing 2500.00 5000.00
26 Heinie Zimmerman 400.00 800.00

1922 E120 American Caramel Series of 240

The cards in this 240-card set measure 2" by 3 1/2". The 1922 E120 set was issued by American Caramels and contains unnumbered cards which are numbered here alphabetically within team for convenience. The order of teams is alphabetically within league: Boston AL (1-15), Chicago AL (16-30), Cleveland (31-45), Detroit (46-60), New York AL (61-75), Philadelphia AL (76-90), St. Louis AL (91-105), Washington (106-120), Boston NL (121-135), Brooklyn (136-150), Chicago NL (151-165), Cincinnati (166-180), New York NL (181-195), Philadelphia NL (196-210), Pittsburgh (211-225) and St. Louis NL (226-240). This set is one of the most popular of the E card sets.

COMPLETE SET (240) 6000.00 12000.00
1 George H. Burns 100.00 200.00
2 Shano Collins 100.00 200.00
3 Joe Dugan 125.00 250.00
4 Joe Harris 100.00 200.00
5 Bennie Karr 100.00 200.00
6 Nemo Leibold 100.00 200.00
7 Michael Menosky 100.00 200.00
8 Elmer Myers 100.00 200.00
9 Herb Pennock 200.00 400.00
10 Clarke Pittenger 100.00 200.00
11 Derrill Pratt 100.00 200.00
12 John Quinn 125.00 250.00
13 Muddy Ruel 100.00 200.00
14 Elmer Smith 100.00 200.00
15 Al Walters 100.00 200.00
16 Eddie Collins 300.00 600.00
17 Elmer Cox 100.00 200.00
18 Urban Faber 200.00 400.00
19 Bib Falk 100.00 200.00
20 Clarence Hodge 100.00 200.00
21 Harry Hooper 200.00 400.00
22 Ernie Johnson 100.00 200.00
23 Horace Leverette 100.00 200.00
24 Harvey McClellan 100.00 200.00
25 Johnny Mostil 100.00 200.00
26 Charles Robertson 100.00 200.00
27 Ray Schalk 200.00 400.00
28 Earl Sheely 100.00 200.00
29 Amos Strunk 100.00 200.00
30 Clarence Yaryan 100.00 200.00
31 Jim Bagby 100.00 200.00
32 Stan Coveleskie 200.00 400.00
33 Harry Gardner 100.00 200.00
34 Jack Graney 100.00 200.00
35 Charles Jamieson 100.00 200.00
36 John Mails 100.00 200.00
37 Stuffy McInnis 125.00 250.00
38 Leslie Nunamaker 100.00 200.00
39 Steve O'Neill 125.00 250.00
40 Joe Sewell 200.00 400.00
41 Allen Sothoron 100.00 200.00
42 Tris Speaker 500.00 1000.00
43 George Uhle 100.00 200.00
44 Bill Wambsganss 125.00 250.00
45 Joe Wood 150.00 300.00
46 John Bassler 100.00 200.00
47 Lu Blue 100.00 200.00
48 Ty Cobb 1500.00 3000.00
49 Bert Cole 100.00 200.00
50 George Cutshaw 100.00 200.00
51 George Dauss 100.00 200.00
52 Howard Ehmke 125.00 250.00
53 Ira Flagstead 100.00 200.00
54 Harry Heilman 200.00 400.00
55 Sylvester Johnson 100.00 200.00
56 Bob Jones 100.00 200.00
57 Herman Pillette 100.00 200.00
58 Emory Rigney 100.00 200.00
59 Bob Veach 100.00 200.00
60 Charles Woodall 100.00 200.00
61 Frank Baker 200.00 400.00
62 Joe Bush 125.00 250.00
63 Al DeVormer 100.00 200.00
64 Waite Hoyt 200.00 400.00
65 Sam Jones 125.00 250.00
66 Carl Mays 125.00 250.00
67 Michael McNally 100.00 200.00
68 Bob Meusel 150.00 300.00
69 Elmer Miller 100.00 200.00
70 Wally Pipp 125.00 250.00

71 Babe Ruth 2000.00 4000.00
72 Wallie Schang 100.00 200.00
73 Everett Scott 125.00 250.00
74 Bob Shawkey 125.00 250.00
75 Aaron Ward 100.00 200.00
76 Frank Calloway 100.00 200.00
77 Jimmy Dykes 150.00 300.00
78 Alfred Fuhrman 100.00 200.00
79 Chick Galloway 100.00 200.00
80 Bryan Harris 100.00 200.00
81 Robert Hasty 100.00 200.00
82 Joe Hauser 100.00 200.00
83 W.F. (Doc) Johnston 100.00 200.00
84 Bing Miller 100.00 200.00
85 Roy Moore 100.00 200.00
86 Roleine Naylor 100.00 200.00
87 Cy Perkins 100.00 200.00
88 Ed Rommel 125.00 250.00
89 Clarence Walker (Tillie) 100.00 200.00
90 Frank Welch 100.00 200.00
91 William Bayne 100.00 200.00
92 Pat Collins 100.00 200.00
93 David Danforth 100.00 200.00
94 Frank Davis 100.00 200.00
95 Francis Ellerbe 100.00 200.00
96 Walter Gerber 100.00 200.00
97 Will Jacobson 100.00 200.00
98 Marty McManus 100.00 200.00
99 Hank Severeid 100.00 200.00
100 Urban Shocker 125.00 250.00
101 Charles Shorten 100.00 200.00
102 George Sisler 300.00 600.00
103 John Tobin 100.00 200.00
104 Elam Van Gilder 100.00 200.00
105 Ken Williams 125.00 250.00
106 Henry Courtney 100.00 200.00
107 Edward Gharrity 100.00 200.00
108 Goose Goslin 200.00 400.00
109 Bucky Harris 200.00 400.00
110 Walter Johnson 600.00 1200.00
111 Joe Judge 100.00 200.00
112 Clyde Milan 125.00 250.00
113 George Mogridge 100.00 200.00
114 Roger Peckinpaugh 125.00 250.00
115 Tom Phillips 100.00 200.00
116 Val Picinich 100.00 200.00
117 Sam Rice 200.00 400.00
118 Howard Shanks 100.00 200.00
119 Earl Smith Wash 100.00 200.00
120 Tom Zachary 100.00 200.00
121 Walter Barbare 100.00 200.00
122 Norman Boeckel 100.00 200.00
123 Walton Cruise 100.00 200.00
124 Dana Fillingim 100.00 200.00
125 Horace Ford 100.00 200.00
126 Hank Gowdy 125.00 250.00
127 Walter Holke 100.00 200.00
128 Larry Kopf 100.00 200.00
129 Rube Marquard 200.00 400.00
130 Hugh McQuillan 100.00 200.00
131 Joe Oeschger 100.00 200.00
132 George O'Neil 100.00 200.00
133 Roy Powell 100.00 200.00
134 Billy Southworth 125.00 250.00
135 John Watson 100.00 200.00
136 Leon Cadore 100.00 200.00
137 Samuel Crane 100.00 200.00
138 Hank DeBerry 100.00 200.00
139 Tom Griffith 100.00 200.00
140 Burleigh Grimes 200.00 400.00
141 Bernard Hungling 100.00 200.00
142 Jimmy Johnston 100.00 200.00
143 Al Mamaux 100.00 200.00
144 Clarence Mitchell 100.00 200.00
145 Hy Myers 100.00 200.00
146 Ivan Olson 100.00 200.00
147 Dutch Reuther 125.00 250.00
148 Ray Schmandt 100.00 200.00
149 Sherrod Smith 100.00 200.00
150 Zach Wheat 200.00 400.00
151 Victor Aldridge 100.00 200.00
152 Grover C. Alexander 300.00 600.00
153 Tyrus Barber 100.00 200.00
154 Marty Callaghan 100.00 200.00
155 Virgil Cheeves 100.00 200.00
156 Max Flack 100.00 200.00
157 Oscar Grimes 100.00 200.00
158 Gabby Hartnett 200.00 400.00
159 Charles Hollocher 100.00 200.00
160 Percy Jones 100.00 200.00
161 Johnny Kelleher 100.00 200.00
162 Martin Krug 100.00 200.00
163 Hack Miller 100.00 200.00
164 Bob O'Farrell 125.00 250.00
165 Arnold Statz 100.00 200.00
166 Sammy Bohne 100.00 200.00
167 George J. Burns 100.00 200.00
168 James Caveney 100.00 200.00
169 Jake Daubert 125.00 250.00
170 Pete Donohue 100.00 200.00
171 Pat Duncan 100.00 200.00
172 John Gillespie 100.00 200.00
173 Gene Hargrave (Bubbles) 100.00 200.00
174 Dolph Luque 125.00 250.00
175 Cliff Markle 100.00 200.00
176 Greasy Neale 125.00 250.00
177 Ralph Pinelli 125.00 250.00
178 Eppa Rixey 200.00 400.00
179 Ed Roush 200.00 400.00
180 Ivy Wingo 100.00 200.00
181 Dave Bancroft 200.00 400.00
182 Jesse Barnes 100.00 200.00
183 Bill Cunningham 100.00 200.00
184 Phil Douglas 100.00 200.00
185 Frankie Frisch 300.00 600.00
186 Heine Groh 125.00 250.00
187 George Kelly 200.00 400.00
188 Emil Meusel 125.00 250.00
189 Art Nehf 100.00 200.00
190 John Rawlings 100.00 200.00
191 Ralph Shinners 100.00 200.00
192 Earl Smith New York 100.00 200.00
193 Frank Snyder 100.00 200.00
194 Fred Toney 100.00 200.00
195 Ross Youngs (Pep) 200.00 400.00
196 Walter Betts 100.00 200.00
197 Art Fletcher 100.00 200.00
198 Walter Henline 100.00 200.00
199 Wilbur Hubbell 125.00 250.00
200 Lee King 100.00 200.00
201 Roy Leslie 100.00 200.00
202 Henry Meadows 100.00 200.00
203 Frank Parkinson 100.00 200.00
204 Jack Peters 100.00 200.00
205 Joseph Rapp 100.00 200.00
206 James Ring 100.00 200.00
207 Colonel Snover 100.00 200.00
208 Curtis Walker 100.00 200.00
209 Cy Williams 125.00 250.00
210 Russel Wrightstone 100.00 200.00
211 Babe Adams 150.00 300.00
212 Clyde Barnhart 100.00 200.00
213 Carlson Bigbee 100.00 200.00
214 Max Carey 200.00 400.00
215 Wilbur Cooper 100.00 200.00
216 Charles Glazner 100.00 200.00
217 Johnny Gooch 100.00 200.00
218 Charlie Grimm 125.00 250.00
219 Earl Hamilton 100.00 200.00
220 Rabbit Maranville 200.00 400.00
221 John L. Mokan 100.00 200.00
222 John Morrison 100.00 200.00
223 Walter Schmidt 100.00 200.00
224 James Tierney 100.00 200.00
225 Pie Traynor 250.00 500.00
226 Edward Ainsmith 100.00 200.00
227 Vern Clemons 100.00 200.00
228 William Doak 100.00 200.00
229 John Fournier 100.00 200.00
230 Jesse Haines 200.00 400.00
231 Cliff Heathcoate 100.00 200.00
232 Rogers Hornsby 500.00 1000.00
233 John Lavan 100.00 200.00
234 Austin McHenry 100.00 200.00
235 Will Pertice 100.00 200.00
236 Joe Schultz 100.00 200.00
237 William Sherdel 100.00 200.00
238 Jack Smith 100.00 200.00
239 Milton Stock 100.00 200.00
240 George Torporcer 100.00 200.00

1922 E121 American Caramel Series of 120

The cards in this set measure 2" by 3 1/2". Many of the photos which appear in the "Series of 80" are duplicated in the so-called "Series of 120". As noted above, the variations in titling and photos have run the known number of cards past the original statement of length and collectors should expect to encounter additions to both E121 lists in the future. The cards have been alphabetized and numbered in the checklist below. The complete set price includes all variation cards listed in the checklist below.

COMPLETE SET (136) 25000.00 50000.00
1 Babe Adams 100.00 200.00
2 Grover C. Alexander 300.00 600.00
3 Jim Bagby 75.00 150.00
4 Dave Bancroft 150.00 300.00
5 Turner Barber 75.00 150.00
6A Carlson Bigbee 75.00 150.00
6B Carlson L. Bigbee 75.00 150.00
6C Corson L. Bigbee 75.00 150.00
6D L. Bigbee 75.00 150.00
7 Joe Bush 100.00 200.00
8 Max Carey 150.00 300.00
9 Cecil Causey 75.00 150.00
10A Ty Cobb Batting 1500.00 3000.00
10B Ty Cobb Throwing 1500.00 3000.00
11 Eddie Collins 200.00 400.00
12 Wilbur Cooper 75.00 150.00
13 Stan Coveleskie 150.00 300.00
14 Dave Danforth 75.00 150.00
15 Jake Daubert 100.00 200.00
16 George Dauss 75.00 150.00
17 Dixie Davis 75.00 150.00
18 Al DeVormer 75.00 150.00
19 William Doak 75.00 150.00
20 Phil Douglas 75.00 150.00
21 Urban Faber 150.00 300.00
22 Bib Falk 75.00 150.00
23 Chick Fewster 75.00 150.00
24 Max Flack 75.00 150.00
25 Ira Flagstead 75.00 150.00
26 Frankie Frisch 250.00 500.00
27 Larry Gardner 75.00 150.00
28 Alexander Gaston 75.00 150.00
29 Edward Gharrity 75.00 150.00
30 George Gibson 75.00 150.00
31 Whitey Glazner 75.00 150.00
32 Kid Gleason MG 100.00 200.00
33 Hank Gowdy 100.00 200.00
34 John Graney 75.00 150.00
35 Tom Griffith 75.00 150.00
36 Charlie Grimm 100.00 200.00
37 Heinie Groh 100.00 200.00
38 Jesse Haines 150.00 300.00
39 Harry Harper 75.00 150.00
40A Harry Heilman 150.00 300.00
40B Harry Heilmann 150.00 300.00
41 Clarence Hodge 75.00 150.00
42A Walter Holke Portrait 75.00 150.00
42B Walter Holke Throwing 75.00 150.00
43 Charles Hollocher 75.00 150.00
44 Harry Hooper 150.00 300.00
45 Rogers Hornsby 300.00 600.00
46 Waite Hoyt 150.00 300.00
47 Miller Huggins MG 150.00 300.00
48 Walter Johnson 250.00 500.00
49 Joe Judge 75.00 150.00
50 George Kelly 150.00 300.00
51 Dick Kerr 100.00 200.00
52 Pete Kilduff 75.00 150.00
53A Bill Killifer w/Bat 75.00 150.00
53B Bill Killifer Throwing 75.00 150.00
54 John Lavan 75.00 150.00
55 Walter Mails 75.00 150.00
56 Rabbit Maranville 150.00 300.00
57 Elwood Martin 75.00 150.00
58 Carl Mays 100.00 200.00
59 John McGraw MG 250.00 500.00
60 Jack McInnis 100.00 200.00
61 M.J. McNally 75.00 150.00
62 Emil Meusel 75.00 150.00
63 Bob Meusel 125.00 250.00
64 Clyde Milan 100.00 200.00
65 Elmer Miller 75.00 150.00
66 Otto Miller 75.00 150.00
67 Johnny Mostil 75.00 150.00
68 Eddie Mulligan 75.00 150.00
69A Hy Myers 75.00 150.00
69B Hy Myers 75.00 150.00
70 Greasy Neale 125.00 250.00
71 Art Nehf 75.00 150.00
72 Leslie Nunamaker 75.00 150.00
73 Joe Oeschger 75.00 150.00
74 Charley O'Leary 75.00 150.00
75 Steve O'Neill 100.00 200.00
76 Del Pratt 75.00 150.00
77 John Rawlings 75.00 150.00
78 Sam Rice 150.00 300.00
79A Eppa J. Rixey 150.00 300.00
79B Eppa Rixey 150.00 300.00
80 Wilbert Robinson MG 150.00 300.00
81 Tom Rogers 75.00 150.00
82A Ed Rommel 100.00 200.00
82B Ed Rounnel 100.00 200.00
83 Ed Roush 150.00 300.00
84 Muddy Ruel 75.00 150.00
85 Walter Ruether 100.00 200.00
86A Babe Ruth Montage 2500.00 5000.00
86B 'Babe' Ruth Montage 3000.00 6000.00
86C Babe Ruth Holding Bird 2500.00 5000.00
86D 'Babe' Ruth Holding Bird 3000.00 6000.00
86E Babe Ruth Holding Ball 2500.00 5000.00
87 Bill Ryan 75.00 150.00
88A Ray Schalk Catching 150.00 300.00
88B Ray Schalk Bunting 150.00 300.00
89 Wally Schang 75.00 150.00
90 Ferd Schupp 75.00 150.00
91 Everett Scott 100.00 200.00
92 Joe Sewell 150.00 300.00
93 Bob Shawkey 100.00 200.00
94 Pat Shea 75.00 150.00
95 Earl Sheely 75.00 150.00
96 Urban Shocker 100.00 200.00
97A George Sisler Batting 250.00 500.00
97B George Sisler Throwing 250.00 500.00
98 Earl Smith 75.00 150.00
99 Elmer Smith 75.00 150.00
100 Frank Snyder 75.00 150.00
101 Billy Southworth 100.00 200.00
102A Tris Speaker Large Proj 300.00 600.00
102B Tris Speaker Small Proj 300.00 600.00
103A Milton Stock 75.00 150.00
103B Milton J. Stock 75.00 150.00
104 Amos Strunk 75.00 150.00
105 Zeb Terry 75.00 150.00
106 Fred Toney 75.00 150.00
107 George Torporcer 75.00 150.00
108 Bob Veach 75.00 150.00
109 Oscar Vitt 75.00 150.00
110 Curtis Walker 75.00 150.00
111 Bill Wambsganss 100.00 200.00
112 Aaron Ward 75.00 150.00
113 Zach Wheat 150.00 300.00
114A George Whitted Brooklyn 75.00 150.00
114B George Whitted Pittsburgh 75.00 150.00
115 Fred Williams 100.00 200.00
116 Ivy Wingo 75.00 150.00
117 Ross Youngs (Young) 150.00 300.00

1921 E121 American Caramel Series of 80

The cards in this set measure 2" by 3 1/2". The E121 sets contain many errors, misspellings and minor variations in titles and photos, which accounts for the difficulty in collecting the entire set. Many photos were taken from E135 and a fine screen is apparent on the cards. The American Caramel Co. marketed this black and white issue about 1922. Many localized advertising reverses have been found, and these cards more properly belong to the W classification than to E121. The cards have been alphabetized and numbered in the checklist below. The complete set price includes all variation cards listed in the checklist below.

COMPLETE SET (134) 75000.00 15000.00
1A G.C. Alexander Arms Above 300.00 600.00
1B Grover Alexander Right Arm 250.00 500.00
2 Jim Bagby 75.00 150.00
3A J. Franklin Baker 150.00 300.00
3B Frank Baker 150.00 300.00
4A Dave Bancroft Batting 150.00 300.00
4B Dave Bancroft Fielding 150.00 300.00
5 Ping Bodie 75.00 150.00
6 George H. Burns 75.00 150.00
7 George J. Burns 75.00 150.00
8 Owen Bush 75.00 150.00
9A Max Carey Batting 150.00 300.00
9B Max Carey Hands at Hips 150.00 300.00
10 Cecil Causey 75.00 150.00
11A Ty Cobb Look Ahead 1500.00 3000.00
11B Ty Cobb Look Right Manager 1500.00 3000.00
11C Ty Cobb Look Right Mgr. 1500.00 3000.00
12 Eddie Collins 200.00 400.00
13 Rip Collins 75.00 150.00
14 Jake Daubert 100.00 200.00
15 George Dauss 75.00 150.00
16A Charles Deal Dark Uni 75.00 150.00
16B Charles Deal Light Uni 75.00 150.00
17 William Doak 75.00 150.00
18 Bill Donovan 75.00 150.00
19 Phil Douglas 75.00 150.00
20A Johnny Evers Manager 150.00 300.00
20B Johnny Evers Mgr. 150.00 300.00
21A Urban Faber Dark Uni 150.00 300.00
21B Urban Faber White Uni 150.00 300.00
22 Wilson Fewster 75.00 150.00
23 Eddie Foster 75.00 150.00
24 Frankie Frisch 200.00 400.00
25 Larry Gardner 75.00 150.00
26 Alexander Gaston 75.00 150.00
27 Kid Gleason MG 100.00 200.00
28 Mike Gonzalez 75.00 150.00
29 Hank Gowdy 100.00 200.00
30 John Graney 75.00 150.00
31 Tom Griffith 75.00 150.00
32 Heinie Groh 100.00 200.00
33 Harry Harper 75.00 150.00
34 Harry Heilmann 150.00 300.00
35A Walter Holke Portrait 75.00 150.00
35B Walter Holke Throwing 75.00 150.00
36 Charles Hollacher 75.00 150.00
37 Harry Hooper 150.00 300.00
38 Rogers Hornsby 300.00 600.00
39 Waite Hoyt 150.00 300.00
40 Miller Huggins MG 150.00 300.00
41 Baby Doll Jacobson 75.00 150.00
42 Hugh Jennings MG 150.00 300.00
43A Walter Johnson Throwing 750.00 1500.00
43B Walter Johnson Hands at Chest 750.00 1500.00
44 James Johnston 75.00 150.00
45 Joe Judge 75.00 150.00
46 George Kelly 150.00 300.00
47 Dick Kerr 100.00 200.00
48 Pete Kilduff 75.00 150.00
49A Bill Killefer 75.00 150.00
49B Bill Killifer 75.00 150.00
50 John Lavan 75.00 150.00
51 Nemo Leibold 75.00 150.00
52 Duffy Lewis 75.00 150.00
53 Al Mamaux 75.00 150.00
54 Rabbit Maranville 150.00 300.00
55A Carl Mays UER May 100.00 200.00
55B Carl Mays COR Mays 100.00 200.00
56 John McGraw MG 250.00 500.00
57 Snuffy McInnis 100.00 200.00
58 M.J. McNally 75.00 150.00
59 Emil Muesel 75.00 150.00
60 Bob Meusel 125.00 250.00
61 Clyde Milan 100.00 200.00
62 Elmer Miller 75.00 150.00
63 Otto Miller 75.00 150.00
64 Guy Morton 75.00 150.00
65 Eddie Murphy 75.00 150.00
66 Hy Myers 75.00 150.00
67 Art Nehf 75.00 150.00
68 Steve O'Neill 75.00 150.00
69A Roger Peckinbaugh UER 100.00 200.00
69B Roger Peckinpaugh COR 100.00 200.00
70 Jeff Pfeffer Brooklyn 75.00 150.00
71 Jeff Pfeffer Stl 75.00 150.00
72 Wally Pipp 100.00 200.00
73 Jack Quinn 75.00 150.00
74 John Rawlings 75.00 150.00
75 Sam Rice 150.00 300.00
76 Eppa Rixey 150.00 300.00
77 Wilburt Robinson MG 150.00 300.00
78 Tom Rogers 75.00 150.00
79 Robert Roth 75.00 150.00
80 Bill Ryan 75.00 150.00
81 Ed Roush 150.00 300.00
82A Babe Ruth 2000.00 4000.00
82B 'Babe' Ruth 2500.00 5000.00
82C George Ruth 2000.00 4000.00
83A Slim Sallee Glove 75.00 150.00
83B Slim Sallee No Glove 75.00 150.00
84 Ray Schalk 150.00 300.00
85 Walter Schang 75.00 150.00
86A Ferd Schupp UER 75.00 150.00
86B Fred Schupp COR 75.00 150.00
87 Everett Scott 75.00 150.00
88 Hank Severeid 75.00 150.00
89 Bob Shawkey 100.00 200.00
90A Pat Shea 75.00 150.00
90B Pat Shea 75.00 150.00
91A George Sisler Batting 250.00 500.00
91B George Sisler Throwing 250.00 500.00
92 Earl Smith 75.00 150.00
93 Frank Snyder 75.00 150.00
94A Tris Speaker Manager Large 300.00 600.00
94B Tris Speaker Manager Small 300.00 600.00
94C Tris Speaker Mgr. 300.00 600.00
95 Milton Stock 75.00 150.00
96 Amos Strunk 75.00 150.00
97 Zeb Terry 75.00 150.00
98 Chester Thomas 75.00 150.00
99A Fred Toney Trees 75.00 150.00
99B Fred Toney No Trees 75.00 150.00
100 George Tyler 75.00 150.00
101A Jim Vaughn Dark Hat 75.00 150.00
101B Jim Vaughn White Hat 75.00 150.00
102A Bob Veach Glove in Air 75.00 150.00
102B Bob Veach Arms Crossed 75.00 150.00
103 Oscar Vitt 75.00 150.00
104 Bill Wambsganss 100.00 200.00
105 Aaron Ward 75.00 150.00
106 Zach Wheat 150.00 300.00
107 George Whitted 75.00 150.00
108 Fred Williams 100.00 200.00
109 Ivy Wingo 75.00 150.00
110 Joe Wood 125.00 250.00
111 Pep Young 75.00 150.00

1910 Orange Borders

This unusual card set features black-and-white pictures surrounded by a thin orange border and measures approximately 1 5/8" by 2 5/8". These orange bordered cards apparently were part of a box of candy. Only 24 cards are checklisted below, but the box indicates that there are 144 in the whole set. Any known additions to the checklist would be welcomed.

COMPLETE SET 2000.00 4000.00
1 National League Champions, 1909/Pirates 150.00 300.00
2 American League Champions, 1909/Tigers 150.00 300.00
3 Bill Bergen 150.00 300.00
4 Bill Carrigan 150.00 300.00
5 Hal Chase 250.00 500.00
6 Fred Clark UER/(misspelled Clarke) 300.00 600.00
7 Ty Cobb 3000.00 6000.00
8 Sam Crawford 300.00 600.00
9 Lou Criger 150.00 300.00
10 Mickey Doolan 150.00 300.00
11 George Gibson 150.00 300.00
12 Frank LaPorte 150.00 300.00
13 Nap Lajoie 750.00 1500.00
14 Harry Lord 150.00 300.00
15 Christy Mathewson 750.00 1500.00
16 John McGraw 300.00 600.00
17 Dots Miller 150.00 300.00
18 George Mullin 200.00 400.00
19 Eddie Plank 300.00 600.00
20 Tris Speaker 600.00 1200.00
21 Jake Stahl 150.00 300.00
22 Heinie Wagner 150.00 300.00
23 Honus Wagner 1000.00 2000.00
24 Jack Warhop 150.00 300.00

1995 Eagle Ballpark Legends

Upper Deck produced this nine-card standard-size set as part of a promotion for Eagle Ballpark Style Peanuts. The set could be obtained by sending in a cash register receipt as evidence for the purchase of two cans Eagle Ballpark Style Peanuts (11 oz. or larger) and $1.00 to cover shipping and handling. The fronts freature full-bleed sepia-toned player photos. The sponsor logo appears in the upper left corner, the Upper Deck logo in the lower left, and the player's name across the bottom. The backs present player profile and career highlights. Some card sets contained randomly inserted autographed Harmon Killebrew cards.

COMPLETE SET (9) 4.00 10.00
1 Nolan Ryan 2.00 5.00
2 Reggie Jackson .75 2.00
3 Tom Seaver .75 2.00
4 Harmon Killebrew .30 .75
5 Ted Williams 1.50 4.00
6 Whitey Ford .75 2.00
7 Al Kaline .60 1.50
8 Willie Stargell .30 .75
9 Bob Gibson .30 .75
S4 Harmon Killebrew AU 15.00 40.00

1889 Edgerton R. Williams Game

The cards measure 2 7/16" by 3 1/2" and have green tinted backs and was issued as part of a parlor game. Each card features two players on the front -- therefore 38 players in total are featured in the set. Only the cards with Baseball players are included in this checklist.

COMPLETE SET (19) 4000.00 8000.00
1 Cap Anson / Buck Ewing 600.00 1200.00
2 Dan Brouthers / Arlie Latham 500.00 1000.00
3 Charlie Buffington / Bob Carruthers 300.00 600.00
4 Fred Carroll / Hick Carpenter 300.00 600.00
5 Roger Connor / Charles Comiskey 600.00 1200.00
6 Pop Corkhill / Jim Fogarty 300.00 600.00
7 John Clarkson / Tim Keefe 600.00 1200.00
8 Jerry Denny / Mike Tiernan 300.00 600.00
9 Dave Foutz / King Kelly 500.00 1000.00
10 Pud Galvin / Dave Orr 500.00 1000.00
11 Jack Glasscock / Tommy Tucker 400.00 800.00
12 Mike Griffin / Ed McKean 300.00 600.00
13 Dummy Hoy / John Reilly 400.00 800.00
14 Arthur Irwin / Ned Williamson 300.00 600.00
15 Silver King / John Tener 300.00 600.00
16 Al Myers / Cub Stricker 300.00 600.00
17 Fred Pfeffer / Jimmy Wolf 300.00 600.00
18 Toad Ramsey / Gus Weyhing 300.00 600.00
19 Mickey Ward / Curt Welch 300.00 600.00
20 Game Card 100.00 200.00

1994 El Sid Pogs

Titled "Limited Edition El Sid." Blank-backed white milk cap-types. Foil on fronts; measure about 1 5/8" in diameter. No other ID markings.

COMPLETE SET (5) .40 1.00
COMMON CARD (1-5) .10 .25

1990 Elite Senior League

The 1990 Elite Senior Pro League Set was a 126-card standard-size set issued after the conclusion of the first Senior League season. The card stock was essentially the same type of card stock used by Upper Deck. The set featured full-color fronts and had complete Senior League stats on the back. It has been reported that there were 5,000 cases of these cards produced. Prior to the debut of the set, Elite also passed out (to prospective dealers) two promo cards for the set, Earl Weaver (numbered 120 rather than 91) and Mike Easler (numbered 1 rather than 19).

COMPLETE SET (126) 2.00 5.00
1 Curt Flood COMM .08 .25
2 Bob Tolan .01 .05
3 Dick Bosman .01 .05
4 Ivan DeJesus .01 .05
5 Dock Ellis .02 .10
6 Roy Howell .01 .05
7 Lamar Johnson .01 .05
8 Steve Kemp .01 .05
9 Ken Landreaux .01 .05
10 Randy Lerch .01 .05
11 Jon Matlack .01 .05
12 Gary Rajsich .01 .05
13 Lenny Randle .01 .05
14 Elias Sosa .01 .05
15 Ozzie Virgil .01 .05
16 Milt Wilcox .01 .05
17 Steve Henderson 3X .01 .05
18 Ray Burris .01 .05
19 Mike Easler .01 .05
20 Juan Eichelberger .01 .05
21 Rollie Fingers .20 .50
22 Toby Harrah .01 .05
23 Randy Johnson .01 .05
24 Dave Kingman .08 .25
25 Lee Lacy .01 .05
26 Tito Landrum .01 .05
27 Paul Mirabella .01 .05
28 Mickey Rivers .02 .10
29 Rodney Scott .01 .05
30 Tim Stoddard .01 .05
31 Ron Washington .01 .05
32 Jerry White .01 .05
33 Dick Williams MG .02 .10
34 Clete Boyer MG .01 .05
35 Steve Dillard .01 .05
36 Garth Iorg .01 .05
37 Bruce Kison .01 .05
38 Wayne Krenchicki .01 .05
39 Ron LeFlore .02 .10
40 Tippy Martinez .01 .05
41 Omar Moreno .01 .05
42 Jim Morrison .01 .05
43 Graig Nettles .05 .15
44 Jim Nettles .01 .05
45 Wayne Nordhagen .01 .05
46 Al Oliver .05 .15
47 Jerry Royster .01 .05
48 Sammy Stewart .01 .05
49 Randy Bass .01 .05
50 Vida Blue .05 .15
51 Bruce Bochy .01 .05
52 Doug Corbett .01 .05
53 Jose Cruz .02 .10
54 Jamie Easterly .01 .05
55 Pete Falcone .01 .05
56 Bob Galasso .01 .05
57 Johnny Grubb .01 .05
58 Bake McBride .01 .05
59 Dyar Miller .02 .05
60 Tom Paciorek .01 .05
61 Ken Reitz .01 .05
62 U.L. Washington .01 .05
63 Alan Ashby .01 .05
64 Pat Dobson .01 .05
65 Doug Bird .01 .05
66 Marty Castillo .01 .05
67 Dan Driessen .01 .05
68 Wayne Garland .01 .05
69 Tim Ireland .01 .05
70 Ron Jackson .01 .05
71 Bobby Jones .01 .05
72 Dennis Leonard .01 .05
73 Rick Manning .01 .05
74 Amos Otis .02 .10
75 Pat Putnam .01 .05
76 Eric Rasmussen .01 .05
77 Paul Blair .01 .05
78 Bert Campaneris .02 .10
79 Cesar Cedeno .02 .10
80 Ed Figueroa .01 .05
81 Ross Grimsley .01 .05
82 George Hendrick .01 .05
83 Cliff Johnson .01 .05
84 Mike Kekich .01 .05
85 Rafael Landestoy .01 .05
86 Larry Milbourne .01 .05
87 Bobby Molinaro .01 .05
88 Sid Monge .01 .05
89 Rennie Stennett .01 .05
90 Derrell Thomas .01 .05
91 Earl Weaver MG .20 .50
92 Gary Allenson .01 .05
93 Pedro Borbon .01 .05
94 Al Bumbry .01 .05
95 Bill Campbell .01 .05
96 Bernie Carbo .01 .05
97 Fergie Jenkins .20 .50
98 Pete LaCock .01 .05
99 Bill Lee .02 .10
100 Tommy McMillan .01 .05
101 Joe Pittman .01 .05
102 Gene Richards .01 .05
103 Leon Roberts .01 .05
104 Tony Scott .01 .05
105 Doug Simunic .01 .05
106 Rick Wise .01 .05
107 Willie Aikens .01 .05
108 Juan Beniquez .01 .05
109 Bobby Bonds .05 .15
110 Sergio Ferrer .01 .05
111 Chuck Ficks .01 .05
112 George Foster .05 .15
113 Dave Hilton .01 .05
114 Al Holland .01 .05
115 Clint Hurdle .02 .10
116 Bill Madlock .05 .15
117 Steve Ontiveros .01 .05
118 Roy Thomas .01 .05
119 Luis Tiant .05 .15
120 Walt Williams .01 .05
121 Vida Blue .05 .15
122 Bobby Bonds .08 .25
123 Rollie Fingers .20 .50
124 George Foster .05 .15
125 Fergie Jenkins .20 .50
126 Dave Kingman .08 .25

2014 Elite

ISSUED IN 2014 DONRUSS SERIES PACKS
1 Paul Goldschmidt .50 1.25
2 Mark Trumbo .30 .75
3 Freddie Freeman .60 1.50
4 Justin Upton .40 1.00
5 Chris Davis .30 .75
6 Manny Machado .50 1.25
7 Adam Jones .40 1.00
8 Dustin Pedroia .50 1.25
9 David Ortiz .50 1.25
10 Chris Sale .50 1.25
11 Joey Votto .50 1.25
12 Aroldis Chapman .50 1.25
13 Yan Gomes .30 .75
14 Jason Kipnis .40 1.00
15 Troy Tulowitzki .50 1.25
16 Carlos Gonzalez .40 1.00
17 Miguel Cabrera .50 1.25
18 Justin Verlander .50 1.25
19 Max Scherzer .50 1.25
20 Eric Hosmer .40 1.00
21 Albert Pujols .60 1.50
22 Mike Trout 2.50 6.00
23 Adrian Gonzalez .40 1.00
24 Hanley Ramirez .40 1.00
25 Yasiel Puig .50 1.25
26 Clayton Kershaw .75 2.00
27 Giancarlo Stanton .50 1.25
28 Jose Fernandez .50 1.25
29 Ryan Braun .40 1.00
30 Carlos Gomez .30 .75
31 David Wright .40 1.00
32 Derek Jeter 1.25 3.00
33 Carlos Beltran .40 1.00
34 Ichiro .75 2.00
35 Josh Donaldson .40 1.00
36 Domonic Brown .40 1.00
37 Cliff Lee .40 1.00
38 Andrew McCutchen .50 1.25
39 Starling Marte .40 1.00
40 Gerrit Cole .50 1.25
41 Yadier Molina .60 1.50
42 Buster Posey .60 1.50
43 Brandon Belt .40 1.00
44 Pablo Sandoval .40 1.00
45 Madison Bumgarner .40 1.00
46 Robinson Cano .40 1.00
47 Felix Hernandez .40 1.00
48 Evan Longoria .40 1.00
49 Wil Myers .30 .75
50 Chris Archer .30 .75
51 Prince Fielder .40 1.00
52 Adrian Beltre .50 1.25
53 Yu Darvish .50 1.25
54 Edwin Encarnacion .50 1.25
55 Jose Bautista .40 1.00
56 Bryce Harper .75 2.00
57 Stephen Strasburg .50 1.25
58 Gerardo Parra .30 .75
59 Jason Heyward .40 1.00
60 Chris Tillman .30 .75
61 Anthony Rizzo .60 1.50
62 Starlin Castro .30 .75
63 Jay Bruce .40 1.00
64 Jose Altuve .40 1.00
65 Alex Gordon .40 1.00
66 Josh Hamilton .40 1.00
67 Hyun-Jin Ryu .40 1.00
68 Koji Uehara .30 .75
69 Joe Mauer .40 1.00
70 Matt Harvey .40 1.00
71 Yoenis Cespedes .50 1.25
72 Sonny Gray .40 1.00
73 Adam Wainwright .40 1.00
74 Chase Headley .30 .75
75 Chris Owings RC .40 1.00
76 Jonathan Schoop RC .40 1.00
77 Xander Bogaerts RC 1.25 3.00
78 Jose Abreu RC 3.00 8.00
79 Marcus Semien RC 2.00 5.00
80 Erik Johnson RC .40 1.00
81 Billy Hamilton RC .50 1.25
82 Nick Castellanos RC 1.25 3.00
83 Yordano Ventura RC .50 1.25
84 Travis d'Arnaud RC .50 1.25
85 Yangervis Solarte RC .40 1.00
86 Masahiro Tanaka RC 1.25 3.00
87 Kolten Wong RC .50 1.25
88 Abraham Almonte RC .40 1.00
89 James Paxton RC .60 1.50
90 Alex Guerrero RC .50 1.25
91 Nick Martinez RC .40 1.00
92 Jake Marisnick RC .40 1.00
93 J.R. Murphy RC .40 1.00
94 Matt Davidson RC .50 1.25
95 Wei-Chung Wang RC .40 1.00
96 Michael Choice RC .40 1.00
97 Taijuan Walker RC .40 1.00
98 Jimmy Nelson RC .40 1.00
99 Christian Bethancourt RC .40 1.00
100 George Springer RC 1.50 4.00

2014 Elite Status

*STATUS RC p/r 15-19: 5X TO 12X BASIC
*STATUS p/r 50-99: 3X TO 8X BASIC
*STATUS RC p/r 50-99: 2.5X TO 6X BASIC
*STATUS p/r 26-49: 4X TO 10X BASIC
*STATUS RC p/r 26-49: 3X TO 8X BASIC
*STATUS p/r 20-24: 5X TO 12X BASIC
*STATUS RC p/r 20-24: 4X TO 10X BASIC
*STATUS p/r 15-19: 6X TO 15X BASIC
RANDOM INSERTS IN PACKS
PRINT RUNS B/WN 2-99 COPIES PER
NO PRICING ON QTY 13 OR LESS
78 Jose Abreu/79 12.00 30.00

2014 Elite Status Gold

*STATUS GOLD: 3X TO 8X BASIC
*STATUS GOLD RC: 2.5X TO 6X BASIC RC
RANDOM INSERTS IN PACKS
STATED PRINT RUN 49 SER.#'d SETS
21 Albert Pujols 10.00 25.00
25 Yasiel Puig 12.00 30.00
78 Jose Abreu 20.00 50.00

2014 Elite Status Red

*STATUS RED: 6X TO 15X BASIC
*STATUS RED RC: 5X TO 12X BASIC RC
RANDOM INSERTS IN PACKS
STATED PRINT RUN 25 SER.#'d SETS
32 Derek Jeter 30.00 60.00
78 Jose Abreu 30.00 60.00

2014 Elite Face 2 Face

STATED PRINT RUN 999 SER.#'d SETS
1 J.Abreu/M.Tanaka 6.00 15.00
2 M.Trout/Y.Darvish 8.00 20.00
3 Harper/Bumgarner 2.50 6.00
4 J.Fernandez/Y.Puig 1.50 4.00
5 D.Jeter/F.Hernandez 4.00 10.00
6 McCutchen/Kershaw 2.50 6.00
7 C.Sale/M.Cabrera 1.50 4.00
8 H.Ryu/P.Goldschmidt 1.50 4.00
9 M.Scherzer/X.Bogaerts 3.00 8.00
10 S.Strasburg/Y.Molina 2.00 5.00
11 J.Cueto/T.Tulowitzki 1.50 4.00
12 C.Lee/G.Stanton 1.50 4.00
13 J.Verlander/P.Fielder 1.50 4.00
14 C.Archer/R.Cano 1.25 3.00
15 W.Myers/Y.Ventura 1.25 3.00

2014 Elite Inspirations

*STATUS RC p/r 15-19: 5X TO 12X BASIC
*STATUS p/r 50-99: 3X TO 8X BASIC
*STATUS RC p/r 50-99: 2.5X TO 6X BASIC
*STATUS p/r 26-49: 4X TO 10X BASIC
*STATUS RC p/r 26-49: 3X TO 8X BASIC
*STATUS p/r 20-24: 5X TO 12X BASIC
*STATUS RC p/r 20-24: 4X TO 10X BASIC
*STATUS p/r 15-19: 6X TO 15X BASIC
RANDOM INSERTS IN PACKS

PRINT RUNS B/WN 1-98 COPIES PER
NO RYU PRICING AVAILABLE
22 Mike Trout/73 10.00 25.00
32 Derek Jeter/98 10.00 25.00
78 Jose Abreu/21 15.00 40.00
86 Masahiro Tanaka/82 12.00 30.00

2014 Elite Passing the Torch Autographs

RANDOM INSERTS IN PACKS
PRINT RUNS B/WN 15-25 COPIES PER
NO PRICING ON QTY 15
EXCHANGE DEADLINE 8/26/2015
1 J.Abreu/P.Konerko/25 150.00 250.00
2 N.Garciaparra/X.Bogaerts/25 30.00 80.00
6 E.Longoria/W.Myers/25 12.00 30.00
7 F.McGriff/F.Freeman/25 20.00 50.00
8 Helton/Tulowitzki/25 30.00 60.00
9 Ripken Jr./Machado/25 100.00 250.00
10 B.Posey/S.Strasburg/25 30.00 60.00

2014 Elite Series Inserts

STATED PRINT RUN 999 SER.#'d SETS
1 Andrew McCutchen 2.00 5.00
2 Bryce Harper 3.00 8.00
3 Buster Posey 2.50 6.00
4 Chris Sale 2.00 5.00
5 Derek Jeter 5.00 12.00
6 Jose Abreu 6.00 15.00
7 Jose Fernandez 2.00 5.00
8 Masahiro Tanaka 6.00 15.00
9 Mike Trout 10.00 25.00
10 Miguel Cabrera 2.00 5.00
11 Nick Castellanos 4.00 10.00
12 Paul Goldschmidt 2.00 5.00
13 Xander Bogaerts 4.00 10.00
14 Yasiel Puig 2.00 5.00
15 Yu Darvish 2.00 5.00

2014 Elite Signature Status Gold

RANDOM INSERTS IN PACKS
PRINT RUNS B/WN 5-25 COPIES PER
NO PRICING ON QTY 10 OR LESS
EXCHANGE DEADLINE 8/26/2015
4 Andrew McCutchen/25 20.00 50.00
6 Anthony Rizzo/25 12.00 30.00
7 Brandon Phillips/25 12.00 30.00
8 Buster Posey/25 40.00 80.00
9 Carlos Gomez/25 12.00 30.00
13 Clayton Kershaw/25 50.00 100.00
14 David Ortiz/25 15.00 40.00
15 David Price/25 15.00 40.00
16 David Wright/25 30.00 60.00
19 Eric Hosmer/25 12.00 30.00
23 Gerrit Cole/25 8.00 20.00
27 Joe Mauer/25 40.00 80.00
28 Jose Bautista/25 12.00 30.00
30 Josh Donaldson/25 8.00 20.00
31 Josh Hamilton/25 15.00 40.00
33 Manny Machado/25 15.00 40.00
37 Paul Konerko/25 20.00 50.00
38 Robinson Cano/25 30.00 60.00
39 Ryan Braun/25 12.00 30.00
41 Starling Marte/25 6.00 15.00
42 Stephen Strasburg/25 30.00 60.00
43 Troy Tulowitzki/25 8.00 20.00
46 Xander Bogaerts/49 20.00 50.00
47 Nick Castellanos/49 12.00 30.00
48 Taijuan Walker/49 4.00 10.00
49 Jimmy Nelson/49 4.00 10.00
50 Jose Abreu/49 75.00 150.00
51 Christian Bethancourt/49 4.00 10.00
52 Yordano Ventura/49 8.00 20.00
53 Billy Hamilton/49 12.00 30.00
54 Erik Johnson/49 4.00 10.00
56 George Springer/49 12.00 30.00
57 Chris Owings/49 4.00 10.00
58 Jake Marisnick/49 4.00 10.00
59 Kolten Wong/49 12.00 30.00
60 Michael Choice/49 4.00 10.00
61 James Paxton/49 10.00 25.00
62 Enny Romero/49 4.00 10.00
64 Matt Davidson/49 10.00 25.00
65 Marcus Semien/49 20.00 50.00
67 Chad Bettis/49 4.00 10.00
69 Ethan Martin/49 4.00 10.00
70 Brian Flynn/49 4.00 10.00
71 David Holmberg/49 4.00 10.00
72 Heath Hembree/49 8.00 20.00
73 David Hale/49 8.00 20.00
75 Tim Beckham/49 6.00 15.00
76 Jose Ramirez/49 15.00 40.00
77 Max Stassi/49 8.00 20.00
78 Nick Martinez/49 4.00 10.00
79 Josmil Pinto/49 4.00 10.00
80 Stolmy Pimentel/49 4.00 10.00
81 Cameron Rupp/49 4.00 10.00
82 Abraham Almonte/49 4.00 10.00
83 Kevin Chapman/49 4.00 10.00
84 Ehire Adrianza/49 4.00 10.00
85 Reymond Fuentes/49 4.00 10.00
86 Kevin Pillar/49 4.00 10.00
87 Andrew Lambo/49 4.00 10.00
89 Matt den Dekker/49 8.00 20.00
90 Juan Centeno/49 4.00 10.00
91 Wilfredo Tovar/49 4.00 10.00
92 Ryan Goins/49 5.00 12.00
94 Oscar Taveras/49 12.00 30.00
95 Matt Shoemaker/49 6.00 15.00
96 Yangervis Solarte/49 4.00 10.00
98 Jon Singleton/49 5.00 12.00
100 Tanner Roark/49 15.00 40.00

2014 Elite Signature Status Red

RANDOM INSERTS IN PACKS
PRINT RUNS B/WN 5-25 COPIES PER
NO PRICING ON QTY 10 OR LESS
EXCHANGE DEADLINE 8/26/2015
46 Xander Bogaerts/25 25.00 60.00
48 Taijuan Walker/25 8.00 20.00
50 Jose Abreu/25 150.00 250.00
51 Christian Bethancourt/25 5.00 12.00
52 Yordano Ventura/25 10.00 25.00
53 Billy Hamilton/25 12.00 30.00
57 Chris Owings/25 5.00 12.00
59 Kolten Wong/25 12.00 30.00
61 James Paxton/25 10.00 25.00
62 Enny Romero/25 5.00 12.00
64 Matt Davidson/25 6.00 15.00
65 Marcus Semien/25 25.00 60.00
67 Chad Bettis/25 5.00 12.00
69 Ethan Martin/25 5.00 12.00
70 Brian Flynn/25 5.00 12.00
72 Heath Hembree/25 10.00 25.00
73 David Hale/25 5.00 12.00
75 Tim Beckham/25 8.00 20.00
76 Jose Ramirez/25 20.00 50.00
77 Max Stassi/25 5.00 12.00
81 Cameron Rupp/25 5.00 12.00
82 Abraham Almonte/25 5.00 12.00
83 Kevin Chapman/25 5.00 12.00
84 Ehire Adrianza/25 5.00 12.00
85 Reymond Fuentes/25 5.00 12.00
86 Kevin Pillar/25 5.00 12.00
87 Andrew Lambo/25 5.00 12.00
88 Tommy Medica/25 5.00 12.00
89 Matt den Dekker/25 12.00 30.00
90 Juan Centeno/25 5.00 12.00
91 Wilfredo Tovar/25 5.00 12.00
94 Oscar Taveras/25 12.00 30.00
95 Matt Shoemaker/25 8.00 20.00
96 Yangervis Solarte/25 5.00 12.00
98 Jon Singleton/25 6.00 15.00
99 C.J. Cron/25 8.00 20.00
100 Tanner Roark/25 30.00 60.00

2014 Elite Turn of the Century

*TOC: 1.5X TO 4X BASIC
*TOC RC: 1.2X TO 3X BASIC RC
RANDOM INSERTS IN PACKS
STATED PRINT RUN 199 SER.#'d SETS
22 Mike Trout 20.00 50.00
32 Derek Jeter 10.00 25.00
78 Jose Abreu 10.00 25.00

2014 Elite Turn of the Century Autographs

RANDOM INSERTS IN PACKS
EXCHANGE DEADLINE 8/26/2015
2 Adrian Beltre 8.00 20.00
3 Adrian Gonzalez 10.00 25.00
6 Anthony Rizzo 8.00 20.00
7 Brandon Phillips 3.00 8.00
8 Buster Posey 25.00 60.00
9 Carlos Gomez 3.00 8.00
11 Chris Davis 10.00 25.00
12 Chris Sale 6.00 15.00
13 Clayton Kershaw 30.00 60.00
14 David Ortiz 15.00 40.00
15 David Price 12.00 30.00
16 David Wright 12.00 30.00
17 Dustin Pedroia 12.00 30.00
18 Edwin Encarnacion 8.00 20.00
19 Eric Hosmer 8.00 20.00
20 Evan Longoria 8.00 20.00
22 Freddie Freeman 8.00 20.00
23 Gerrit Cole 3.00 8.00
25 Jason Kipnis 4.00 10.00
26 Jay Bruce 8.00 20.00
27 Joe Mauer 12.00 30.00
28 Jose Bautista 8.00 20.00
30 Josh Donaldson 8.00 20.00
31 Josh Hamilton 12.00 30.00
32 Justin Upton 15.00 40.00
33 Manny Machado 12.00 30.00
34 Max Scherzer 20.00 50.00
36 Mike Trout 100.00 200.00
37 Paul Konerko 8.00 20.00
38 Robinson Cano 10.00 25.00
39 Ryan Braun 6.00 15.00
40 Shelby Miller 4.00 10.00
41 Starling Marte 4.00 10.00
42 Stephen Strasburg 20.00 50.00
43 Troy Tulowitzki 8.00 20.00
44 Wil Myers 3.00 8.00
45 Yoenis Cespedes 5.00 12.00
46 Xander Bogaerts 12.00 30.00
47 Nick Castellanos 10.00 25.00
48 Taijuan Walker 3.00 8.00
49 Jimmy Nelson 3.00 8.00
50 Jose Abreu 6.00 15.00
51 Christian Bethancourt 3.00 8.00
52 Yordano Ventura 3.00 8.00
54 Erik Johnson 3.00 8.00
56 George Springer 10.00 25.00
57 Chris Owings 3.00 8.00
58 Jake Marisnick 3.00 8.00
59 Kolten Wong 4.00 10.00
60 Michael Choice 3.00 8.00
61 James Paxton 5.00 12.00
62 Enny Romero 3.00 8.00
63 J.R. Murphy 3.00 8.00
64 Matt Davidson 4.00 10.00
65 Marcus Semien 15.00 40.00
67 Chad Bettis 3.00 8.00
69 Ethan Martin 3.00 8.00
70 Brian Flynn 3.00 8.00
71 David Holmberg 3.00 8.00
72 Heath Hembree 6.00 15.00
73 David Hale 3.00 8.00
75 Tim Beckham 5.00 12.00
76 Jose Ramirez 15.00 40.00
77 Max Stassi 3.00 8.00
78 Nick Martinez 3.00 8.00
79 Josmil Pinto 3.00 8.00
80 Stolmy Pimentel 3.00 8.00
81 Cameron Rupp 3.00 8.00
82 Abraham Almonte 3.00 8.00
83 Kevin Chapman 3.00 8.00
84 Ehire Adrianza 3.00 8.00
85 Reymond Fuentes 3.00 8.00
86 Kevin Pillar 3.00 8.00
87 Andrew Lambo 3.00 8.00
88 Tommy Medica 3.00 8.00
89 Matt den Dekker 4.00 10.00
90 Juan Centeno 3.00 8.00
91 Wilfredo Tovar 3.00 8.00
92 Ryan Goins 4.00 10.00
94 Oscar Taveras 4.00 10.00
95 Matt Shoemaker 5.00 12.00
96 Yangervis Solarte 3.00 8.00
99 C.J. Cron 3.00 8.00
100 Tanner Roark 3.00 8.00

2015 Elite

COMPLETE SET (200) 20.00 50.00
1 Christian Walker RC .40 1.00
2 Rusney Castillo RC .25 .60
3 Yasmany Tomas RC .25 .60
4 Matt Barnes RC .20 .50
5 Brandon Finnegan RC .20 .50
6 Daniel Norris RC .20 .50
7 Kendall Graveman RC .20 .50
8 Yorman Rodriguez RC .20 .50
9 Gary Brown RC .20 .50
10 R.J. Alvarez RC .20 .50
11 Dalton Pompey RC .25 .60
12 Maikel Franco RC .25 .60
13 James McCann RC .30 .75
14 Lane Adams RC .20 .50
15 Joc Pederson RC .75 2.00
16 Steven Moya RC .25 .60
17 Cory Spangenberg RC .20 .50
18 Andy Wilkins RC .20 .50
19 Terrance Gore RC .20 .50
20 Ryan Rua RC .20 .50
21 Dilson Herrera RC .25 .60
22 Edwin Escobar RC .20 .50
23 Jorge Soler RC .30 .75
24 Matt Szczur RC .25 .60
25 Buck Farmer RC .20 .50
26 Michael Taylor RC .20 .50
27 Rymer Liriano RC .20 .50
28 Trevor May RC .20 .50
29 Jake Lamb RC .30 .75
30 Javier Baez RC 1.50 4.00
31 Mike Foltynewicz RC .20 .50
32 Matt Clark RC .20 .50
33 Anthony Ranaudo RC .20 .50
34 Mike Trout 1.25 3.00
35 Clayton Kershaw .40 1.00
36 Giancarlo Stanton .25 .60
37 Jose Abreu .25 .60
38 Jacob deGrom .50 1.25
39 Masahiro Tanaka .20 .50
40 Albert Pujols .30 .75
41 Miguel Cabrera .25 .60
42 Robinson Cano .20 .50
43 Ichiro .30 .75
44 Evan Longoria .20 .50
45 Yu Darvish .25 .60
46 Bryce Harper .40 1.00
47 Yasiel Puig .25 .60
48 Buster Posey .30 .75
49 Madison Bumgarner .20 .50
50 Paul Goldschmidt .25 .60
51 Adam Jones .20 .50
52 Joe Mauer .20 .50
53 Jose Bautista .20 .50
54 Nelson Cruz .25 .60
55 Yadier Molina .30 .75
56 David Ortiz .25 .60
57 Troy Tulowitzki .25 .60
58 Salvador Perez .20 .50
59 Jonathan Lucroy .20 .50
60 Jose Altuve .20 .50
61 Johnny Cueto .20 .50
62 Joey Votto .25 .60
63 Adrian Beltre .25 .60
64 Victor Martinez .20 .50
65 Matt Carpenter .25 .60
66 Anthony Rizzo .30 .75
67 Jon Lester .20 .50
68 Dee Gordon .15 .40
69 Felix Hernandez .20 .50
70 Chris Sale .25 .60
71 Adam Wainwright .20 .50
72 Jordan Zimmermann .20 .50
73 Henderson Alvarez .15 .40
74 Kyle Seager .15 .40
75 Julio Teheran .20 .50
76 Archie Bradley .15 .40
77 Eric Hosmer .20 .50
78 David Price .20 .50
79 Max Scherzer .25 .60
80 Adrian Gonzalez .20 .50
81 Zack Greinke .25 .60
82 Corey Kluber .20 .50
83 Anthony Rendon .25 .60
84 Dallas Keuchel .20 .50
85 Garrett Richards .20 .50
86 Jered Weaver .20 .50
87 Justin Verlander .25 .60
88 Matt Wieters .25 .60
89 Chase Utley .20 .50
90 Ryan Howard .20 .50
91 Jason Heyward .20 .50
92 Carlos Gomez .15 .40
93 Josh Donaldson .20 .50
94 Edwin Encarnacion .25 .60
95 Ian Desmond .15 .40
96 Brandon Moss .15 .40
97 Ian Kinsler .20 .50
98 Prince Fielder .20 .50
99 Ryan Braun .20 .50
100 Yoenis Cespedes .20 .50
101 Freddie Freeman .30 .75
102 Charlie Blackmon .25 .60
103 Josh Harrison .15 .40
104 Hunter Pence .20 .50
105 Mark Buehrle .20 .50
106 Alex Gordon .20 .50
107 Starlin Castro .15 .40
108 Torii Hunter .15 .40
109 Glen Perkins .15 .40
110 Tim Hudson .20 .50
111 Matt Shoemaker .20 .50
112 Kolten Wong .20 .50
113 Xander Bogaerts .25 .60
114 Mookie Betts .50 1.25
115 Wei-Chung Wang .15 .40
116 Wei-Yin Chen .15 .40
117 George Springer .20 .50
118 Joe Panik .20 .50
119 Gregory Polanco .20 .50
120 David Wright .20 .50
121 Nick Castellanos .25 .60
122 Addison Russell RC .60 1.50
123 Kevin Kiermaier .20 .50
124 Randal Grichuk .15 .40
125 Billy Hamilton .20 .50
126 Taijuan Walker .15 .40
127 C.J. Cron .15 .40
128 Aaron Sanchez .20 .50
129 Alex Guerrero .20 .50
130 Yordano Ventura .20 .50
131 Carlos Gonzalez .20 .50
132 Craig Kimbrel .20 .50
133 Greg Holland .15 .40
134 Jung-Ho Kang RC .20 .50
135 Hisashi Iwakuma .20 .50
136 Matt Harvey .20 .50
137 James Shields .15 .40
138 Stephen Strasburg .25 .60
139 Phil Hughes .15 .40
140 Trevor Rosenthal .20 .50
141 CC Sabathia .20 .50
142 Jose Reyes .20 .50
143 Matt Kemp .20 .50
144 Wil Myers .20 .50
145 Justin Upton .20 .50
146 Michael Brantley .20 .50
147 Adam LaRoche .15 .40
148 Wade Davis .15 .40
149 Ben Revere .15 .40
150 Carlos Santana .20 .50
151 Pedro Alvarez .15 .40
152 Todd Frazier .15 .40
153 Tim Lincecum .20 .50
154 Chris Davis .15 .40
155 Pablo Sandoval .20 .50
156 Dustin Pedroia .25 .60
157 Aroldis Chapman .25 .60
158 Brandon Phillips .15 .40
159 Nick Swisher .20 .50
160 Jimmy Rollins .20 .50
161 Jose Fernandez .25 .60
162 Kennys Vargas .15 .40
163 Carlos Beltran .20 .50
164 Alex Rodriguez .30 .75
165 Jacoby Ellsbury .20 .50
166 Cliff Lee .20 .50
167 Andrew McCutchen .25 .60
168 Neil Walker .15 .40
169 Starling Marte .20 .50
170 Carlos Rodon RC .50 1.25
171 Alex Cobb .15 .40
172 Shin-Soo Choo .20 .50
173 Andrelton Simmons .15 .40
174 Chris Johnson .15 .40
175 Nolan Arenado .40 1.00
176 Justin Verlander .25 .60
177 Buster Posey .30 .75
178 David Price .20 .50
179 Tim Lincecum .20 .50
180 Chase Utley .20 .50
181 Pedro Alvarez .15 .40
182 Matt Harvey .20 .50
183 Dustin Pedroia .25 .60
184 Josh Donaldson .20 .50
185 Alex Gordon .20 .50
186 Chris Sale .25 .60
187 Kyle Seager .15 .40
188 Kris Bryant RC 2.00 5.00
189 Max Scherzer .25 .60
190 Stephen Strasburg .25 .60
191 Ken Griffey Jr. .50 1.25
192 Ken Griffey Jr. .50 1.25
193 Frank Thomas .25 .60
194 George Brett .50 1.25
195 Cal Ripken .75 2.00
196 Nolan Ryan .75 2.00
197 Nolan Ryan .75 2.00
198 Mariano Rivera .30 .75
199 Pete Rose .50 1.25
200 Pete Rose .50 1.25

2015 Elite Status

*STAT p/r 75-84: 4X TO 10X BASIC
*STAT p/r 75-84 RC: 3X TO 8X BASIC RC
*STAT p/r 50-68: 5X TO 12X BASIC
*STAT p/r 50-68 RC: 4X TO 10X BASIC RC
*STAT p/r 25-49: 6X TO 15X BASIC
*STAT p/r 25-49 RC: 5X TO 12X BASIC RC
*STAT p/r 16-24: 8X TO 20X BASIC
*STAT p/r 16-24 RC: 6X TO 15X BASIC RC
RANDOM INSERTS IN PACKS
PRINT RUNS B/WN 1-84 COPIES PER
NO PRICING ON QTY 15 OR LESS

2015 Elite Status Gold

*STATUS GOLD: 6X TO 15X BASIC VET
*STATUS GOLD RC: 5X TO 12X BASIC RC
RANDOM INSERTS IN PACKS
STATED PRINT RUN 49 SER.#'d SETS

2015 Elite 21st Century

*21ST: 3X TO 8X BASIC VET
*21ST RC: 2.5X TO 6X BASIC RC
RANDOM INSERTS IN PACKS
STATED PRINT RUN 199 SER.#'d SETS

2015 Elite 21st Century Red

*21ST RED: 8X TO 20X BASIC VET
*21ST RED RC: 6X TO 15X BASIC RC
RANDOM INSERTS IN PACKS
STATED PRINT RUN 21 SER.#'d SETS

2015 Elite 21st Century Signatures

RANDOM INSERTS IN PACKS
EXCHANGE DEADLINE 7/7/2016
1 Christian Walker 6.00 15.00
2 Rusney Castillo 4.00 10.00
3 Yasmany Tomas 4.00 10.00
4 Matt Barnes 3.00 8.00
5 Brandon Finnegan 3.00 8.00
6 Daniel Norris 3.00 8.00
7 Kendall Graveman 3.00 8.00
8 Yorman Rodriguez 3.00 8.00
9 Gary Brown 3.00 8.00
10 R.J. Alvarez 3.00 8.00
11 Dalton Pompey 4.00 10.00
12 Maikel Franco 4.00 10.00
13 James McCann 5.00 12.00
14 Lane Adams 3.00 8.00
15 Joc Pederson 5.00 12.00
16 Steven Moya 4.00 10.00
17 Cory Spangenberg 3.00 8.00
18 Andy Wilkins 3.00 8.00
19 Terrance Gore 3.00 8.00
20 Ryan Rua 3.00 8.00
21 Dilson Herrera 4.00 10.00
22 Edwin Escobar 3.00 8.00
23 Jorge Soler 8.00 20.00
24 Matt Szczur 4.00 10.00
25 Buck Farmer 3.00 8.00
26 Michael Taylor 3.00 8.00
27 Rymer Liriano 3.00 8.00
28 Trevor May 3.00 8.00
29 Jake Lamb 5.00 12.00
30 Javier Baez 25.00 60.00
31 Mike Foltynewicz 3.00 8.00
32 Kennys Vargas 3.00 8.00
33 Anthony Ranaudo 3.00 8.00
34 Matt Clark 3.00 8.00
35 Brandon Belt 4.00 10.00
37 Charlie Blackmon 5.00 12.00
38 Jung-Ho Kang 4.00 10.00
41 Jameson Taillon 4.00 10.00
42 Bucky Dent 3.00 8.00
43 Kevin Kiermaier 4.00 10.00
45 Andrew Susac 3.00 8.00
46 Hisashi Iwakuma 4.00 10.00
48 Jose Canseco 10.00 25.00
52 Raul Ibanez 4.00 10.00
53 Bill Buckner 4.00 10.00
58 Kris Bryant 30.00 80.00
59 Anthony Rizzo 15.00 40.00
60 Dallas Keuchel 8.00 20.00
62 Starling Marte 4.00 10.00
64 Corey Kluber 8.00 20.00
65 Alex Gordon 6.00 15.00
66 Freddie Freeman 6.00 15.00
67 Taijuan Walker 3.00 8.00
68 Kyle Seager 3.00 8.00
69 Chris Sale 5.00 12.00
70 Jose Abreu 12.00 30.00
71 Miguel Sano 6.00 15.00
72 Salvador Perez 6.00 15.00
75 Marcus Stroman 4.00 10.00
76 Gregory Polanco 4.00 10.00
78 Kyle Parker 3.00 8.00
79 Jesse Hahn 3.00 8.00
80 Danny Santana 3.00 8.00
81 Odrisamer Despaigne 3.00 8.00
84 Matt Shoemaker 4.00 10.00
85 Carlos Contreras 3.00 8.00
86 Domingo Santana 4.00 10.00
87 Carlos Sanchez 3.00 8.00
88 Steven Souza 4.00 10.00
89 Gregg Jeffries 4.00 10.00
90 Tommy La Stella 3.00 8.00
93 Pedro Alvarez 3.00 8.00
97 Edwin Encarnacion 5.00 12.00
99 Shelby Miller 4.00 10.00

2015 Elite 21st Century Signatures Red

*RED: .6X TO 1.5X BASIC
RANDOM INSERTS IN PACKS
PRINT RUNS B/WN 10-21 COPIES PER
NO PRICING ON QTY 15 OR LESS
EXCHANGE DEADLINE 7/7/2016
91 Mookie Betts/21 50.00 120.00

2015 Elite All Star Salutes

COMPLETE SET (25) 3.00 8.00
RANDOM INSERTS IN PACKS
*GOLD/25: 3X TO 8X BASIC
1 Mike Trout 2.50 6.00
2 Jose Abreu .50 1.25
3 Clayton Kershaw .75 2.00
4 Miguel Cabrera .50 1.25
5 Andrew McCutchen .50 1.25
6 Giancarlo Stanton .50 1.25
7 Yasiel Puig .50 1.25
8 Jose Bautista .40 1.00
9 Robinson Cano .40 1.00
10 Troy Tulowitzki .50 1.25
11 Yadier Molina .60 1.50
12 Felix Hernandez .40 1.00
13 Adam Wainwright .40 1.00
14 Madison Bumgarner .40 1.00
15 Adam Jones .40 1.00
16 Paul Goldschmidt .50 1.25
17 Aramis Ramirez .30 .75
18 Salvador Perez .40 1.00
19 Chase Utley .40 1.00
20 Carlos Gomez .30 .75
21 Nelson Cruz .50 1.25
22 Max Scherzer .50 1.25
23 Glen Perkins .30 .75
24 Jonathan Lucroy .40 1.00
25 Jose Altuve .40 1.00

2015 Elite Back 2 Back Jacks

RANDOM INSERTS IN PACKS
1 A.Gordon/E.Hosmer 3.00 8.00
2 B.Posey/H.Pence 10.00 25.00
3 G.Springer/J.Singleton 3.00 8.00
4 E.Encarnacion/J.Bautista 4.00 10.00
5 D.Ortiz/D.Pedroia 4.00 10.00
6 A.Gonzalez/F.Freeman 5.00 12.00
7 J.Upton/W.Myers 3.00 8.00
8 N.Cruz/R.Cano 4.00 10.00
9 E.Longoria/M.Cabrera 5.00 12.00
10 C.Ripken/G.Brett 15.00 40.00

2015 Elite Career Bests Materials

RANDOM INSERTS IN PACKS
PRINT RUNS B/WN 49-299 COPIES PER
1 Justin Verlander/199 3.00 8.00
2 Chris Davis/100 2.00 5.00
3 Miguel Cabrera/150 4.00 10.00
4 CC Sabathia/299 2.50 6.00
5 Prince Fielder/299 2.50 6.00
6 Madison Bumgarner/299 2.50 6.00
7 Albert Pujols/299 4.00 10.00
8 Alex Rodriguez/299 4.00 10.00
9 Clayton Kershaw/49 5.00 12.00
10 Mike Trout/299 15.00 40.00
11 Andrew McCutchen/125 6.00 15.00
12 David Ortiz/299 3.00 8.00
13 Alex Rodriguez/299 4.00 10.00
14 Jimmy Rollins/199 2.50 6.00
15 Adrian Beltre/99 3.00 8.00
16 Jose Reyes/299 2.50 6.00
17 Albert Pujols/299 4.00 10.00
18 Felix Hernandez/199 2.50 6.00
19 Jose Bautista/299 2.50 6.00
20 Jose Abreu/299 4.00 10.00
21 Carlos Beltran/299 2.50 6.00
22 Nolan Ryan/299 8.00 20.00
23 Rickey Henderson/299 3.00 8.00
24 Mark McGwire/299 5.00 12.00
25 Barry Bonds/299 4.00 10.00

2015 Elite Collegiate Elite

COMPLETE SET (15) 4.00 10.00
RANDOM INSERTS IN PACKS
1 Brandon Finnegan .30 .75
2 Roger Clemens .60 1.50
3 Reggie Jackson .40 1.00
4 Stephen Strasburg .50 1.25
5 Mark McGwire .75 2.00
6 Bo Jackson .50 1.25
7 Dustin Ackley .30 .75
8 Buster Posey .60 1.50
9 Chase Utley .40 1.00
10 Jacoby Ellsbury .40 1.00
11 Dustin Pedroia .50 1.25
12 David Price .40 1.00
13 Tim Lincecum .40 1.00
14 Huston Street .30 .75
15 Mark Teixeira .40 1.00

2015 Elite Collegiate Elite Gold

*GOLD: 3X TO 8X BASIC
RANDOM INSERTS IN PACKS
STATED PRINT RUN 25 SER.#'d SETS
5 Mark McGwire 15.00 40.00
6 Bo Jackson 20.00 50.00
8 Buster Posey 20.00 50.00
13 Tim Lincecum 20.00 50.00

2015 Elite Collegiate Legacy Signatures

RANDOM INSERTS IN PACKS
PRINT RUNS B/WN 1-75 COPIES PER
NO PRICING ON QTY 15 OR LESS
EXCHANGE DEADLINE 7/7/2016
1 Kyle Seager/75 10.00 25.00
3 Matt Shoemaker/75 10.00 25.00
7 Charlie Blackmon/75 5.00 12.00
10 Michael Conforto/25 60.00 150.00
16 Anthony Ranaudo/50 3.00 8.00
18 Kendall Graveman/75 3.00 8.00
20 Josh Harrison/75 6.00 15.00
21 Christian Walker/75 6.00 15.00
22 Dallas Keuchel/75 6.00 15.00
23 Jake Lamb/75 5.00 12.00

2015 Elite Collegiate Patches Autographs Gold

RANDOM INSERTS IN PACKS
PRINT RUNS B/WN 1-30 COPIES PER
NO PRICING ON QTY 10 OR LESS
EXCHANGE DEADLINE 7/7/2016
3 Andrew Heaney/30 15.00 40.00
6 Brandon Belt/30 25.00 60.00

2015 Elite Collegiate Patches Autographs Silver

RANDOM INSERTS IN PACKS
PRINT RUNS B/WN 5-50 COPIES PER
NO PRICING ON QTY 10 OR LESS
EXCHANGE DEADLINE 7/7/2016
2 Trea Turner/50 20.00 50.00
3 Andrew Heaney/30 15.00 40.00
6 Brandon Belt/30 25.00 60.00
9 Corey Knebel/30 6.00 15.00
12 Andy Wilkins/50 6.00 15.00
13 Matt Szczur/50 8.00 20.00
14 Jake Lamb/50 10.00 25.00
15 Robert Refsnyder/50 8.00 20.00
16 Devon Travis/50 6.00 15.00
18 Stephen Piscotty/50 8.00 20.00

2015 Elite Elite Series Materials

RANDOM INSERTS IN PACKS
PRINT RUNS B/WN 25-299 COPIES PER
1 Jose Abreu/299 4.00 10.00
2 Giancarlo Stanton/199 3.00 8.00
3 Clayton Kershaw/49 5.00 12.00
4 Mike Trout/99 12.00 30.00
5 Masahiro Tanaka/25 6.00 15.00
6 Victor Martinez/199 2.50 6.00
8 Ichiro/188 4.00 10.00
9 Felix Hernandez/99 2.50 6.00
10 Miguel Cabrera/199 4.00 10.00
11 Yu Darvish/299 3.00 8.00
12 Nelson Cruz/299 3.00 8.00
13 Chris Sale/99 3.00 8.00
14 Matt Kemp/199 2.50 6.00
15 Adrian Beltre/199 3.00 8.00
16 Joe Mauer/99 2.50 6.00
17 Yasiel Puig/199 4.00 10.00
18 Buster Posey/49 12.00 30.00
19 Albert Pujols/99 4.00 10.00
20 Madison Bumgarner/299 2.50 6.00
21 Ken Griffey Jr./49 10.00 25.00
22 Pete Rose/299 5.00 12.00
23 Rickey Henderson/299 3.00 8.00
24 Nolan Ryan/199 6.00 15.00
25 Kris Bryant/299 8.00 20.00

2015 Elite Future Threads

RANDOM INSERTS IN PACKS
*PRIME/25: 1X TO 2.5X BASIC
1 Byron Buxton 8.00 20.00
2 Kennys Vargas 1.50 4.00
3 Michael Taylor 1.50 4.00
4 Addison Russell 5.00 12.00
5 Yasmany Tomas 2.00 5.00
6 Javier Baez 12.00 30.00
7 Cory Spangenberg 1.50 4.00
8 Kris Bryant 6.00 15.00
9 Kyle Schwarber 6.00 15.00
10 Edwin Escobar 1.50 4.00
11 Dilson Herrera 2.00 5.00
12 Jorge Soler 2.50 6.00
13 Francisco Lindor 15.00 40.00
14 Brandon Finnegan 1.50 4.00
15 Corey Seager 5.00 12.00
16 Miguel Sano 2.00 5.00
17 Trea Turner 5.00 12.00
18 Jake Lamb 2.50 6.00
19 Robert Refsnyder 2.00 5.00
20 Maikel Franco 2.00 5.00
21 Kendall Graveman 1.50 4.00
22 Rusney Castillo 2.00 5.00
23 Tyler Glasnow 6.00 15.00
24 Luis Severino 2.00 5.00
25 Rymer Liriano 1.50 4.00
26 Steven Moya 2.00 5.00
27 Archie Bradley 1.50 4.00
28 Gary Brown 1.50 4.00
29 Trevor May 1.50 4.00
30 Yorman Rodriguez 1.50 4.00

2015 Elite Future Threads Signatures

RANDOM INSERTS IN PACKS
PRINT RUNS B/WN 49-299 COPIES PER
EXCHANGE DEADLINE 7/7/2016
*PRIME/25: .6X TO 1.5X BASIC
2 Jose Abreu/49 15.00 40.00
3 Jonathan Gray/299 4.00 10.00
4 Robert Stephenson/299 4.00 10.00
6 Javier Baez/99 12.00 30.00
8 Jonathan Schoop/299 4.00 10.00
9 Kevin Kiermaier/299 6.00 15.00
10 Yordano Ventura/99 8.00 20.00
11 Joe Panik/299 5.00 12.00
12 Jacob deGrom/49 20.00 50.00
13 Francisco Lindor/99 15.00 40.00
14 Nick Martinez/268 4.00 10.00
15 Addison Russell/299 8.00 20.00
16 Jameson Taillon/299 5.00 12.00
17 Byron Buxton/99 40.00 100.00
18 Archie Bradley/99 4.00 10.00
19 Jake Marisnick/299 4.00 10.00
20 Kris Bryant/49 75.00 150.00
21 Odrisamer Despaigne/299 4.00 10.00
22 Tyler Collins/299 4.00 10.00
23 Kyle Zimmer/299 6.00 15.00
24 Marcus Stroman/299 5.00 12.00
25 Randal Grichuk/299 4.00 10.00

2015 Elite Gold Stars

COMPLETE SET (25) 8.00 20.00
RANDOM INSERTS IN PACKS
*GOLD/25: 3X TO 8X BASIC
1 Masahiro Tanaka .40 1.00
2 Jacob deGrom 1.00 2.50
3 Jose Abreu .50 1.25
4 Clayton Kershaw .75 2.00
5 Mike Trout 2.50 6.00
6 Kris Bryant 3.00 8.00
7 Victor Martinez .40 1.00
8 Madison Bumgarner .40 1.00
9 Nelson Cruz .50 1.25
10 David Price .40 1.00
11 Kirby Puckett .50 1.25
12 George Brett 1.00 2.50
13 Cal Ripken 1.50 4.00
14 Nolan Ryan 1.50 4.00
15 Ken Griffey Jr. 1.00 2.50
16 Frank Thomas .50 1.25
17 Greg Maddux .60 1.50
18 Randy Johnson .50 1.25
19 Rickey Henderson .50 1.25
20 Pete Rose 1.00 2.50
21 Roger Clemens .60 1.50
22 Mark McGwire .75 2.00
23 Jose Canseco .40 1.00
24 Mariano Rivera .60 1.50
25 Don Mattingly 1.00 2.50

2015 Elite Hype

COMPLETE SET (15) 8.00 20.00
RANDOM INSERTS IN PACKS
*GOLD/25: 3X TO 8X BASIC
1 Bryce Harper .75 2.00
2 Kris Bryant 3.00 8.00
3 Byron Buxton 1.50 4.00
4 Francisco Lindor 2.50 6.00
5 Carlos Correa 1.50 4.00
6 Miguel Sano .40 1.00
7 Rusney Castillo .40 1.00
8 Yasmany Tomas .40 1.00
9 Javier Baez 2.50 6.00
10 Jorge Soler .50 1.25
11 Anthony Ranaudo .30 .75
12 Kyle Schwarber 1.25 3.00
13 Addison Russell 1.00 2.50
14 Carlos Rodon .75 2.00
15 Corey Seager 1.50 4.00

2015 Elite Inspirations

*ISP p/r 75-99: 4X TO 10X BASIC
*ISP p/r 75-99 RC: 3X TO 8X BASIC RC
*ISP p/r 50-74: 5X TO 12X BASIC
*ISP p/r 50-74 RC: 4X TO 10X BASIC RC
*ISP p/r 25-49: 6X TO 15X BASIC
*ISP p/r 25-49 RC: 5X TO 12X BASIC RC
*ISP p/r 16-21: 8X TO 20X BASIC
*ISP p/r 16-21 RC: 6X TO 15X BASIC RC
RANDOM INSERTS IN PACKS
PRINT RUNS B/WN 16-99 COPIES PER

2015 Elite Legends of the Fall

COMPLETE SET (10) 4.00 10.00
RANDOM INSERTS IN PACKS
*GOLD/25: 3X TO 8X BASIC
1 Chipper Jones .50 1.25
2 Mariano Rivera .60 1.50
3 Reggie Jackson .40 1.00
4 Tom Glavine .40 1.00
5 Andy Pettitte .40 1.00
6 Bob Gibson .40 1.00
7 Jim Palmer .40 1.00
8 Curt Schilling .40 1.00
9 David Justice .30 .75
10 Randy Johnson .50 1.25

2015 Elite Members Only Materials

RANDOM INSERTS IN PACKS
*PRIME/25: .75X TO 2X BASIC
1 Jedd Gyorko 2.00 5.00
2 Alex Rodriguez 4.00 10.00
3 Chase Whitley 2.00 5.00
4 Drew Smyly 2.00 5.00
5 George Springer 2.50 6.00
6 Tyler Collins 2.00 5.00
7 David Wright 2.50 6.00

8 Aramis Ramirez 2.00 5.00
9 Evan Longoria 2.50 6.00
10 Dallas Keuchel 2.50 6.00
11 Billy Butler 2.00 5.00
12 Ryan Braun 2.50 6.00
13 Jurickson Profar 2.50 6.00
14 David Hale 2.00 5.00
15 Dillon Gee 2.00 5.00
16 Matt den Dekker 2.00 5.00
17 Brian McCann 2.50 6.00
18 Christian Bethancourt 2.00 5.00
19 Jake Marisnick 2.00 5.00
20 Kendrys Morales 2.00 5.00
21 Mark Trumbo 2.00 5.00
22 Elvis Andrus 2.50 6.00
23 Yordano Ventura 2.50 6.00
24 Roenis Elias 2.00 5.00
25 Leonys Martin 2.00 5.00
26 Pablo Sandoval 2.50 6.00
27 Nelson Cruz 3.00 8.00
28 Arismendy Alcantara 2.00 5.00
29 Jon Singleton 2.50 6.00
33 Nick Swisher 2.50 6.00
34 Jameson Taillon 2.50 6.00
35 Brian Dozier 2.50 6.00
37 Josh Donaldson 2.50 6.00
38 Mark Teixeira 2.50 6.00
39 David Ortiz 3.00 8.00
42 Jose Bautista 2.50 6.00
43 Robinson Cano 2.50 6.00
44 Edwin Encarnacion 3.00 8.00
46 Mike Napoli 2.00 5.00
48 Wil Myers 2.50 6.00
49 Alexei Ramirez 2.50 6.00
50 Hanley Ramirez 2.50 6.00

2015 Elite Rookie Essentials Signatures

RANDOM INSERTS IN PACKS
STATED PRINT RUN 75 SER.#'d SETS
EXCHANGE DEADLINE 7/7/2016
1 Christian Walker 6.00 15.00
2 Rusney Castillo 4.00 10.00
3 Yasmany Tomas 4.00 10.00
4 Matt Barnes 3.00 8.00
5 Brandon Finnegan 3.00 8.00
6 Daniel Norris 3.00 8.00
7 Kendall Graveman 3.00 8.00
8 Yorman Rodriguez 3.00 8.00
9 Gary Brown 3.00 8.00
10 R.J. Alvarez 3.00 8.00
11 Dalton Pompey 4.00 10.00
12 Maikel Franco 6.00 15.00
13 James McCann 6.00 15.00
14 Lane Adams 3.00 8.00
15 Joc Pederson 8.00 20.00
16 Steven Moya 4.00 10.00
17 Cory Spangenberg 3.00 8.00
19 Terrance Gore 3.00 8.00
20 Ryan Rua 3.00 8.00
21 Dilson Herrera 4.00 10.00
22 Edwin Escobar 3.00 8.00
23 Jorge Soler 4.00 10.00
24 Matt Szczur 4.00 10.00
25 Buck Farmer 3.00 8.00
26 Michael Taylor 3.00 8.00
27 Rymer Liriano 3.00 8.00
28 Trevor May 3.00 8.00
29 Jake Lamb 5.00 12.00
30 Javier Baez 8.00 20.00
33 Anthony Ranaudo 3.00 8.00
34 Kris Bryant 60.00 150.00
35 Archie Bradley 3.00 8.00

2015 Elite Signature Status Purple

RANDOM INSERTS IN PACKS
PRINT RUNS B/WN 20-99 COPIES PER
EXCHANGE DEADLINE 7/7/2016
*GREEN/25-49: .5X TO 1.2X PURPLE
1 Christian Walker/99 6.00 15.00
2 Rusney Castillo/49 5.00 12.00
3 Yasmany Tomas/49 5.00 12.00
4 Matt Barnes/99 3.00 8.00
5 Brandon Finnegan/99 3.00 8.00
6 Daniel Norris/99 3.00 8.00
7 Kendall Graveman/99 3.00 8.00
8 Yorman Rodriguez/99 3.00 8.00
9 Gary Brown/99 3.00 8.00
10 R.J. Alvarez/99 3.00 8.00
11 Dalton Pompey/99 4.00 10.00
12 Maikel Franco/99 4.00 10.00
13 James McCann/99 5.00 12.00
14 Lane Adams/99 3.00 8.00
15 Joc Pederson/99 8.00 20.00
16 Steven Moya/99 4.00 10.00
17 Cory Spangenberg/99 3.00 8.00
18 Andy Wilkins/99 3.00 8.00
19 Terrance Gore/99 3.00 8.00
20 Ryan Rua/99 3.00 8.00
21 Dilson Herrera/99 4.00 10.00
22 Edwin Escobar/99 3.00 8.00
23 Jorge Soler/99 10.00 25.00
24 Matt Szczur/99 4.00 10.00
25 Buck Farmer/99 3.00 8.00
26 Michael Taylor/99 3.00 8.00
27 Rymer Liriano/99 3.00 8.00
28 Trevor May/99 3.00 8.00
29 Jake Lamb/99 5.00 12.00
30 Javier Baez/99 25.00 60.00
31 Mike Foltynewicz/99 3.00 8.00
32 Kennys Vargas/99 3.00 8.00
33 Anthony Ranaudo/99 3.00 8.00
34 Matt Clark/99 3.00 8.00
35 Brandon Belt/49 10.00 25.00
37 Charlie Blackmon/99 5.00 12.00
38 Jung-Ho Kang/99 25.00 60.00
41 Jameson Taillon/99 4.00 10.00
42 Bucky Dent/99 3.00 8.00
43 Kevin Kiermaier/99 8.00 20.00
45 Andrew Susac/49 4.00 10.00
46 Hisashi Iwakuma/49 5.00 12.00
48 Jose Canseco/99 10.00 25.00
52 Raul Ibanez/49 5.00 12.00
53 Bill Buckner/99 4.00 10.00
57 Josh Donaldson/20 10.00 25.00
58 Kris Bryant/49 60.00 150.00
60 Dallas Keuchel/99 4.00 10.00
62 Starling Marte/99 3.00 8.00
64 Corey Kluber/49 8.00 20.00
66 Freddie Freeman/25 10.00 25.00
67 Taijuan Walker/49 4.00 10.00
68 Kyle Seager/99 3.00 8.00
69 Chris Sale/49 10.00 25.00
71 Miguel Sano/99 8.00 20.00
72 Salvador Perez/49 8.00 20.00
75 Marcus Stroman/99 4.00 10.00
78 Kyle Parker/99 3.00 8.00
79 Jesse Hahn/99 3.00 8.00
80 Danny Santana/99 3.00 8.00
81 Odrisamer Despaigne/99 3.00 8.00
83 Tyler Collins/99 3.00 8.00
84 Matt Shoemaker/99 4.00 10.00
85 Carlos Contreras/99 3.00 8.00
86 Domingo Santana/99 4.00 10.00
87 Carlos Sanchez/99 3.00 8.00
88 Steven Souza/99 6.00 15.00
89 Gregg Jeffries/99 6.00 15.00
90 Tommy La Stella/99 3.00 8.00
95 Evan Longoria/20 10.00 25.00
96 Troy Tulowitzki/20 12.00 30.00
97 Edwin Encarnacion/20 8.00 20.00
98 Jose Altuve/20 30.00 80.00
99 Shelby Miller/49 5.00 12.00

2015 Elite Stature

COMPLETE SET (10) 4.00 10.00
RANDOM INSERTS IN PACKS
*GOLD/25: 3X TO 8X BASIC
1 Mike Trout 2.50 6.00
2 Clayton Kershaw .75 2.00
3 Madison Bumgarner .40 1.00
4 Buster Posey .60 1.50
5 David Wright .40 1.00
6 Yu Darvish .50 1.25
7 Giancarlo Stanton .50 1.25
8 Jose Abreu .50 1.25
9 Yasiel Puig .50 1.25
10 Miguel Cabrera .50 1.25

2015 Elite Team Signatures

RANDOM INSERTS IN PACKS
PRINT RUNS B/WN 1-25 COPIES PER
NO PRICING ON QTY 5 OR LESS
EXCHANGE DEADLINE 7/7/2016

2015 Elite Throwback Threads

RANDOM INSERTS IN PACKS
*PRIME/25: .75X TO 2X BASIC
1 Ken Griffey Jr. 10.00 25.00
2 Barry Bonds 4.00 10.00
3 Mark McGwire 5.00 12.00
4 Pete Rose 6.00 15.00
5 Mike Schmidt 5.00 12.00
6 Rickey Henderson 3.00 8.00
7 Vladimir Guerrero 2.50 6.00
8 Nolan Ryan 10.00 25.00
9 Cal Ripken Jr. 8.00 20.00
10 Greg Maddux 4.00 10.00

1995 Emotion

This 200-card standard-size set was produced by Fleer/SkyBox. The first-year brand has double-thick card stock with borderless fronts. Card fronts and backs are either horizontal or vertical. On the front of each player card is a theme such as Class (Cal Ripken) and Confident (Barry Bonds). The backs have two player photos, '94 stats and career numbers. The checklist is arranged alphabetically by team with AL preceding NL. Notable Rookie Cards include Hideo Nomo.

COMPLETE SET (200) 12.50 30.00
1 Brady Anderson .15 .40
2 Kevin Brown .15 .40
3 Curtis Goodwin .07 .20
4 Jeffrey Hammonds .07 .20
5 Ben McDonald .07 .20
6 Mike Mussina .25 .60
7 Rafael Palmeiro .25 .60
8 Cal Ripken 1.25 3.00
9 Jose Canseco .25 .60
10 Roger Clemens .75 2.00
11 Vaughn Eshelman .07 .20
12 Mike Greenwell .07 .20
13 Erik Hanson .07 .20
14 Tim Naehring .07 .20
15 Aaron Sele .07 .20
16 John Valentin .07 .20
17 Mo Vaughn .15 .40
18 Chili Davis .15 .40
19 Gary DiSarcina .07 .20
20 Chuck Finley .15 .40
21 Tim Salmon .25 .60
22 Lee Smith .15 .40
23 J.T. Snow .15 .40
24 Jim Abbott .25 .60
25 Jason Bere .07 .20
26 Ray Durham .15 .40
27 Ozzie Guillen .15 .40
28 Tim Raines .15 .40
29 Frank Thomas .40 1.00
30 Robin Ventura .15 .40
31 Carlos Baerga .07 .20
32 Albert Belle .15 .40
33 Orel Hershiser .15 .40
34 Kenny Lofton .15 .40
35 Dennis Martinez .15 .40
36 Eddie Murray .40 1.00
37 Manny Ramirez .25 .60
38 Julian Tavarez .07 .20
39 Jim Thome .25 .60
40 Dave Winfield .15 .40
41 Chad Curtis .07 .20
42 Cecil Fielder .15 .40
43 Travis Fryman .15 .40
44 Kirk Gibson .15 .40
45 Bobby Higginson RC .40 1.00
46 Alan Trammell .15 .40
47 Lou Whitaker .15 .40
48 Kevin Appier .15 .40
49 Gary Gaetti .15 .40
50 Jeff Montgomery .07 .20
51 Jon Nunnally .07 .20
52 Ricky Bones .07 .20
53 Cal Eldred .07 .20
54 Joe Oliver .07 .20
55 Kevin Seitzer .07 .20
56 Marty Cordova .07 .20
57 Chuck Knoblauch .15 .40
58 Kirby Puckett .40 1.00
59 Wade Boggs .25 .60
60 Derek Jeter 1.00 2.50
61 Jimmy Key .15 .40
62 Don Mattingly 1.00 2.50
63 Jack McDowell .07 .20
64 Paul O'Neill .25 .60
65 Andy Pettitte .25 .60
66 Ruben Rivera .07 .20
67 Mike Stanley .07 .20
68 John Wetteland .15 .40
69 Geronimo Berroa .07 .20
70 Dennis Eckersley .15 .40
71 Rickey Henderson .40 1.00
72 Mark McGwire 1.00 2.50
73 Steve Ontiveros .07 .20
74 Ruben Sierra .15 .40
75 Terry Steinbach .07 .20
76 Jay Buhner .15 .40
77 Ken Griffey Jr. .75 2.00
78 Randy Johnson .40 1.00
79 Edgar Martinez .25 .60
80 Tino Martinez .25 .60
81 Marc Newfield .07 .20
82 Alex Rodriguez 1.00 2.50
83 Will Clark .25 .60
84 Benji Gil .07 .20
85 Juan Gonzalez .15 .40
86 Rusty Greer .15 .40
87 Dean Palmer .15 .40
88 Ivan Rodriguez .25 .60
89 Kenny Rogers .15 .40
90 Roberto Alomar .25 .60
91 Joe Carter .15 .40
92 David Cone .15 .40
93 Alex Gonzalez .07 .20
94 Shawn Green .15 .40
95 Pat Hentgen .07 .20
96 Paul Molitor .15 .40
97 John Olerud .15 .40
98 Devon White .15 .40
99 Steve Avery .07 .20
100 Tom Glavine .25 .60
101 Marquis Grissom .15 .40
102 Chipper Jones .40 1.00
103 David Justice .15 .40
104 Ryan Klesko .15 .40
105 Javier Lopez .15 .40
106 Greg Maddux .60 1.50
107 Fred McGriff .25 .60
108 John Smoltz .25 .60
109 Shawon Dunston .07 .20
110 Mark Grace .25 .60
111 Brian McRae .07 .20
112 Randy Myers .07 .20
113 Sammy Sosa .40 1.00
114 Steve Trachsel .07 .20
115 Bret Boone .15 .40
116 Ron Gant .15 .40
117 Barry Larkin .25 .60
118 Deion Sanders .25 .60
119 Reggie Sanders .15 .40
120 Pete Schourek .07 .20
121 John Smiley .07 .20
122 Jason Bates .07 .20
123 Dante Bichette .15 .40
124 Vinny Castilla .15 .40
125 Andres Galarraga .15 .40
126 Larry Walker .15 .40
127 Greg Colbrunn .07 .20
128 Jeff Conine .15 .40
129 Andre Dawson .15 .40
130 Chris Hammond .07 .20
131 Charles Johnson .15 .40
132 Gary Sheffield .15 .40
133 Quilvio Veras .07 .20
134 Jeff Bagwell .25 .60
135 Derek Bell .07 .20
136 Craig Biggio .25 .60
137 Jim Dougherty RC .08 .25
138 John Hudek .07 .20
139 Orlando Miller .07 .20
140 Phil Plantier .07 .20
141 Eric Karros .15 .40
142 Ramon Martinez .07 .20
143 Raul Mondesi .15 .40
144 Hideo Nomo RC 1.00 2.50
145 Mike Piazza .60 1.50
146 Ismael Valdes .07 .20
147 Todd Worrell .07 .20
148 Moises Alou .15 .40
149 Yamil Benitez RC .08 .25
150 Wil Cordero .07 .20
151 Jeff Fassero .07 .20
152 Cliff Floyd .15 .40
153 Pedro Martinez .25 .60
154 Carlos Perez RC .20 .50
155 Tony Tarasco .07 .20
156 Rondell White .15 .40
157 Edgardo Alfonzo .07 .20
158 Bobby Bonilla .15 .40
159 Rico Brogna .07 .20
160 Bobby Jones .07 .20
161 Bill Pulsipher .07 .20
162 Bret Saberhagen .15 .40
163 Ricky Bottalico .07 .20
164 Darren Daulton .15 .40
165 Lenny Dykstra .15 .40
166 Charlie Hayes .07 .20
167 Dave Hollins .07 .20
168 Gregg Jefferies .07 .20
169 Michael Mimbs RC .08 .25
170 Curt Schilling .15 .40
171 Heathcliff Slocumb .07 .20
172 Jay Bell .15 .40
173 Micah Franklin RC .08 .25
174 Mark Johnson RC .20 .50
175 Jeff King .07 .20
176 Al Martin .07 .20
177 Dan Miceli .07 .20
178 Denny Neagle .15 .40
179 Bernard Gilkey .07 .20
180 Ken Hill .07 .20
181 Brian Jordan .15 .40
182 Ray Lankford .15 .40
183 Ozzie Smith .60 1.50
184 Andy Benes .07 .20
185 Ken Caminiti .15 .40
186 Steve Finley .15 .40
187 Tony Gwynn .50 1.25
188 Joey Hamilton .07 .20
189 Melvin Nieves .07 .20
190 Scott Sanders .07 .20
191 Rod Beck .07 .20
192 Barry Bonds 1.00 2.50
193 Royce Clayton .07 .20
194 Glenallen Hill .07 .20
195 Darren Lewis .07 .20
196 Mark Portugal .07 .20
197 Matt Williams .15 .40
198 Checklist .07 .20
199 Checklist .07 .20
200 Checklist .07 .20
P8 Cal Ripken Promo .75 2.00

1995 Emotion Masters

COMPLETE SET (10) 12.00 30.00
STATED ODDS 1:8
1 Barry Bonds 3.00 8.00
2 Juan Gonzalez .50 1.25
3 Ken Griffey Jr. 2.50 6.00
4 Tony Gwynn 1.50 4.00
5 Kenny Lofton .50 1.25
6 Greg Maddux 2.00 5.00
7 Raul Mondesi .50 1.25
8 Cal Ripken 4.00 10.00
9 Frank Thomas 1.25 3.00
10 Matt Williams .50 1.25

1995 Emotion N-Tense

COMPLETE SET (12) 12.00 30.00
STATED ODDS 1:37
1 Jeff Bagwell 1.25 3.00
2 Albert Belle .75 2.00
3 Barry Bonds 3.00 8.00
4 Cecil Fielder .75 2.00
5 Ron Gant .75 2.00
6 Ken Griffey Jr. 4.00 10.00
7 Mark McGwire 3.00 8.00
8 Mike Piazza 2.00 5.00
9 Manny Ramirez 1.25 3.00
10 Frank Thomas 2.00 5.00
11 Mo Vaughn .75 2.00
12 Matt Williams .75 2.00

1995 Emotion Ripken

COMPLETE SET (10) 15.00 40.00
COMMON CARD (1-10) 2.00 5.00
STATED ODDS 1:12
COMMON MAIL (11-15) 2.00 5.00
MAIL-IN CARDS DIST.VIA WRAPPER EXCH.

1995 Emotion Rookies

COMPLETE SET (10) 10.00 25.00
STATED ODDS 1:5
1 Edgardo Alfonzo .40 1.00
2 Jason Bates .40 1.00
3 Marty Cordova .40 1.00
4 Ray Durham .40 1.00
5 Alex Gonzalez .40 1.00
6 Shawn Green .40 1.00
7 Charles Johnson .40 1.00
8 Chipper Jones .75 2.00
9 Hideo Nomo 1.50 4.00
10 Alex Rodriguez 3.00 8.00

1996 Emotion-XL

The 1996 Emotion-XL set (produced by Fleer/SkyBox) was issued in one series totalling 300 standard-size cards. The seven-card packs retailed for $4.99 each. The fronts feature a color action player photo with either a blue, green or maroon frame and the player's name and team printed in a foil-stamped medallion. A descriptive term describing the player completes the front. The backs carry player information and statistics. The cards are grouped alphabetically by team with AL preceding NL. A Manny Ramirez promo card was distributed to dealers and hobby media to preview the set.

COMPLETE SET (300) 25.00 60.00
PRODUCED BY FLEER
1 Roberto Alomar .50 1.25
2 Brady Anderson .30 .75
3 Bobby Bonilla .30 .75
4 Jeffrey Hammonds .30 .75
5 Chris Hoiles .30 .75
6 Mike Mussina .50 1.25
7 Randy Myers .30 .75
8 Rafael Palmeiro .50 1.25
9 Cal Ripken 2.50 6.00
10 B.J. Surhoff .30 .75
11 Jose Canseco .50 1.25
12 Roger Clemens 1.50 4.00
13 Wil Cordero .30 .75
14 Mike Greenwell .30 .75
15 Dwayne Hosey .30 .75
16 Tim Naehring .30 .75
17 Troy O'Leary .30 .75
18 Mike Stanley .30 .75
19 John Valentin .30 .75
20 Mo Vaughn .30 .75
21 Jim Abbott .50 1.25
22 Garret Anderson .30 .75
23 George Arias .30 .75
24 Chili Davis .30 .75
25 Jim Edmonds .30 .75
26 Chuck Finley .30 .75
27 Todd Greene .30 .75
28 Mark Langston .30 .75
29 Troy Percival .30 .75
30 Tim Salmon .50 1.25
31 Lee Smith .30 .75
32 J.T. Snow .30 .75
33 Harold Baines .30 .75
34 Jason Bere .30 .75
35 Ray Durham .30 .75
36 Alex Fernandez .30 .75
37 Ozzie Guillen .30 .75
38 Darren Lewis .30 .75
39 Lyle Mouton .30 .75
40 Tony Phillips .30 .75
41 Danny Tartabull .30 .75
42 Frank Thomas .75 2.00
43 Robin Ventura .30 .75
44 Sandy Alomar Jr. .30 .75
45 Carlos Baerga .30 .75
46 Albert Belle .30 .75
47 Julio Franco .30 .75
48 Orel Hershiser .30 .75
49 Kenny Lofton .30 .75
50 Dennis Martinez .30 .75
51 Jack McDowell .30 .75
52 Jose Mesa .30 .75
53 Eddie Murray .75 2.00
54 Charles Nagy .30 .75
55 Manny Ramirez .50 1.25
56 Jim Thome .50 1.25
57 Omar Vizquel .50 1.25
58 Chad Curtis .30 .75
59 Cecil Fielder .30 .75
60 Travis Fryman .30 .75
61 Chris Gomez .30 .75
62 Felipe Lira .30 .75
63 Alan Trammell .30 .75
64 Kevin Appier .30 .75
65 Johnny Damon .50 1.25
66 Tom Goodwin .30 .75
67 Mark Gubicza .30 .75
68 Jeff Montgomery .30 .75
69 Jon Nunnally .30 .75
70 Bip Roberts .30 .75
71 Ricky Bones .30 .75
72 Chuck Carr .30 .75
73 John Jaha .30 .75
74 Ben McDonald .30 .75
75 Matt Mieske .30 .75
76 Dave Nilsson .30 .75
77 Kevin Seitzer .30 .75
78 Greg Vaughn .30 .75
79 Rick Aguilera .30 .75
80 Marty Cordova .30 .75
81 Roberto Kelly .30 .75
82 Chuck Knoblauch .30 .75
83 Pat Meares .30 .75
84 Paul Molitor .30 .75
85 Kirby Puckett .75 2.00
86 Brad Radke .30 .75
87 Wade Boggs .50 1.25
88 David Cone .30 .75
89 Dwight Gooden .30 .75
90 Derek Jeter 2.00 5.00
91 Tino Martinez .50 1.25
92 Paul O'Neill .50 1.25
93 Andy Pettitte .50 1.25
94 Tim Raines .30 .75
95 Ruben Rivera .30 .75
96 Kenny Rogers .30 .75
97 Ruben Sierra .30 .75
98 John Wetteland .30 .75
99 Bernie Williams .50 1.25
100 Allen Battle .30 .75
101 Geronimo Berroa .30 .75
102 Brent Gates .30 .75
103 Doug Johns .30 .75
104 Mark McGwire 2.00 5.00
105 Pedro Munoz .30 .75
106 Ariel Prieto .30 .75
107 Terry Steinbach .30 .75
108 Todd Van Poppel .30 .75
109 Chris Bosio .30 .75
110 Jay Buhner .30 .75
111 Joey Cora .30 .75
112 Russ Davis .30 .75
113 Ken Griffey Jr. 1.50 4.00
114 Sterling Hitchcock .30 .75
115 Randy Johnson .75 2.00
116 Edgar Martinez .50 1.25
117 Alex Rodriguez 1.50 4.00
118 Paul Sorrento .30 .75
119 Dan Wilson .30 .75
120 Will Clark .50 1.25
121 Juan Gonzalez .30 .75
122 Rusty Greer .30 .75
123 Kevin Gross .30 .75
124 Ken Hill .30 .75
125 Dean Palmer .30 .75
126 Roger Pavlik .30 .75
127 Ivan Rodriguez .50 1.25
128 Mickey Tettleton .30 .75
129 Joe Carter .30 .75
130 Carlos Delgado .30 .75
131 Alex Gonzalez .30 .75
132 Shawn Green .30 .75
133 Erik Hanson .30 .75
134 Pat Hentgen .30 .75
135 Otis Nixon .30 .75
136 John Olerud .30 .75
137 Ed Sprague .30 .75
138 Steve Avery .30 .75
139 Jermaine Dye .30 .75
140 Tom Glavine .50 1.25
141 Marquis Grissom .30 .75
142 Chipper Jones .75 2.00
143 David Justice .30 .75
144 Ryan Klesko .30 .75
145 Javier Lopez .30 .75
146 Greg Maddux 1.25 3.00
147 Fred McGriff .50 1.25
148 Jason Schmidt .50 1.25
149 John Smoltz .50 1.25
150 Mark Wohlers .30 .75
151 Jim Bullinger .30 .75
152 Frank Castillo .30 .75
153 Kevin Foster .30 .75
154 Luis Gonzalez .30 .75
155 Mark Grace .50 1.25
156 Brian McRae .30 .75
157 Jaime Navarro .30 .75
158 Rey Sanchez .30 .75
159 Ryne Sandberg 1.25 3.00
160 Sammy Sosa .75 2.00
161 Bret Boone .30 .75
162 Jeff Brantley .30 .75
163 Vince Coleman .30 .75
164 Steve Gibralter .30 .75
165 Barry Larkin .50 1.25
166 Hal Morris .30 .75
167 Mark Portugal .30 .75
168 Reggie Sanders .30 .75
169 Pete Schourek .30 .75
170 John Smiley .30 .75
171 Jason Bates .30 .75
172 Dante Bichette .30 .75
173 Ellis Burks .30 .75
174 Vinny Castilla .30 .75
175 Andres Galarraga .30 .75
176 Kevin Ritz .30 .75
177 Bill Swift .30 .75
178 Larry Walker .30 .75
179 Walt Weiss .30 .75
180 Eric Young .30 .75
181 Kurt Abbott .30 .75
182 Kevin Brown .30 .75
183 John Burkett .30 .75
184 Greg Colbrunn .30 .75
185 Jeff Conine .30 .75
186 Chris Hammond .30 .75
187 Charles Johnson .30 .75
188 Terry Pendleton .30 .75
189 Pat Rapp .30 .75
190 Gary Sheffield .30 .75
191 Quilvio Veras .30 .75
192 Devon White .30 .75
193 Jeff Bagwell .50 1.25
194 Derek Bell .30 .75
195 Sean Berry .30 .75
196 Craig Biggio .50 1.25
197 Doug Drabek .30 .75
198 Tony Eusebio .30 .75
199 Mike Hampton .30 .75
200 Brian L.Hunter .30 .75
201 Derrick May .30 .75
202 Orlando Miller .30 .75
203 Shane Reynolds .30 .75
204 Mike Blowers .30 .75
205 Tom Candiotti .30 .75
206 Delino DeShields .30 .75
207 Greg Gagne .30 .75
208 Karim Garcia .30 .75
209 Todd Hollandsworth .30 .75
210 Eric Karros .30 .75
211 Ramon Martinez .30 .75
212 Raul Mondesi .30 .75
213 Hideo Nomo .75 2.00
214 Chan Ho Park .30 .75
215 Mike Piazza 1.25 3.00
216 Ismael Valdes .30 .75
217 Todd Worrell .30 .75
218 Moises Alou .30 .75
219 Yamil Benitez .30 .75
220 Jeff Fassero .30 .75
221 Darrin Fletcher .30 .75
222 Cliff Floyd .30 .75
223 Pedro Martinez .50 1.25
224 Carlos Perez .30 .75
225 Mel Rojas .30 .75
226 David Segui .30 .75
227 Rondell White .30 .75
228 Rico Brogna .30 .75
229 Carl Everett .30 .75
230 John Franco .30 .75
231 Bernard Gilkey .30 .75
232 Todd Hundley .30 .75
233 Jason Isringhausen .30 .75
234 Lance Johnson .30 .75
235 Bobby Jones .30 .75
236 Jeff Kent .30 .75
237 Rey Ordonez .30 .75
238 Bill Pulsipher .30 .75
239 Jose Vizcaino .30 .75
240 Paul Wilson .30 .75
241 Ricky Bottalico .30 .75
242 Darren Daulton .30 .75
243 Lenny Dykstra .30 .75
244 Jim Eisenreich .30 .75
245 Sid Fernandez .30 .75
246 Gregg Jefferies .30 .75
247 Mickey Morandini .30 .75
248 Benito Santiago .30 .75
249 Curt Schilling .30 .75
250 Mark Whiten .30 .75
251 Todd Zeile .30 .75
252 Jay Bell .30 .75
253 Carlos Garcia .30 .75
254 Charlie Hayes .30 .75
255 Jason Kendall .30 .75
256 Jeff King .30 .75
257 Al Martin .30 .75
258 Orlando Merced .30 .75
259 Dan Miceli .30 .75
260 Denny Neagle .30 .75
261 Alan Benes .30 .75
262 Andy Benes .30 .75
263 Royce Clayton .30 .75
264 Dennis Eckersley .30 .75
265 Gary Gaetti .30 .75
266 Ron Gant .30 .75
267 Brian Jordan .30 .75
268 Ray Lankford .30 .75
269 John Mabry .30 .75
270 Tom Pagnozzi .30 .75
271 Ozzie Smith 1.25 3.00
272 Todd Stottlemyre .30 .75
273 Andy Ashby .30 .75
274 Brad Ausmus .30 .75
275 Ken Caminiti .30 .75
276 Steve Finley .30 .75
277 Tony Gwynn 1.00 2.50
278 Joey Hamilton .30 .75
279 Rickey Henderson .75 2.00
280 Trevor Hoffman .30 .75
281 Wally Joyner .30 .75
282 Jody Reed .30 .75
283 Bob Tewksbury .30 .75
284 Fernando Valenzuela .30 .75
285 Rod Beck .30 .75
286 Barry Bonds 2.00 5.00
287 Mark Carreon .30 .75
288 Shawon Dunston .30 .75
289 Osvaldo Fernandez RC .30 .75
290 Glenallen Hill .30 .75
291 Stan Javier .30 .75
292 Mark Leiter .30 .75
293 Kirt Manwaring .30 .75
294 Robby Thompson .30 .75
295 William VanLandingham .30 .75
296 Allen Watson .30 .75
297 Matt Williams .30 .75
298 Checklist .30 .75
299 Checklist .30 .75
300 Checklist .30 .75
P55 Manny Ramirez Promo .40 1.00

1996 Emotion-XL D-Fense

COMPLETE SET (10) 10.00 25.00
STATED ODDS 1:4
1 Roberto Alomar .60 1.50
2 Barry Bonds 2.50 6.00
3 Mark Grace .60 1.50
4 Ken Griffey Jr. 2.00 5.00
5 Kenny Lofton .40 1.00
6 Greg Maddux 1.50 4.00
7 Raul Mondesi .40 1.00
8 Cal Ripken 3.00 8.00
9 Ivan Rodriguez .60 1.50
10 Matt Williams .40 1.00

1996 Emotion-XL Legion of Boom

COMPLETE SET (12) 75.00 150.00
STATED ODDS 1:36 HOBBY
1 Albert Belle 2.00 5.00
2 Barry Bonds 12.50 30.00
3 Juan Gonzalez 2.00 5.00
4 Ken Griffey Jr. 10.00 25.00
5 Mark McGwire 12.50 30.00
6 Mike Piazza 8.00 20.00
7 Manny Ramirez 3.00 8.00
8 Tim Salmon 3.00 8.00
9 Sammy Sosa 5.00 12.00
10 Frank Thomas 5.00 12.00
11 Mo Vaughn 2.00 5.00
12 Matt Williams 2.00 5.00

1996 Emotion-XL N-Tense

COMPLETE SET (10) 25.00 60.00
STATED ODDS 1:12
1 Albert Belle .75 2.00
2 Barry Bonds 5.00 12.00
3 Jose Canseco 1.25 3.00
4 Ken Griffey Jr. 4.00 10.00
5 Tony Gwynn 2.50 6.00
6 Randy Johnson 2.00 5.00
7 Greg Maddux 3.00 8.00
8 Cal Ripken 6.00 15.00
9 Frank Thomas 2.00 5.00
10 Matt Williams .75 2.00

1996 Emotion-XL Rare Breed

COMPLETE SET (10) 60.00 120.00
STATED ODDS 1:100
1 Garret Anderson 4.00 10.00
2 Marty Cordova 3.00 8.00
3 Brian L.Hunter 3.00 8.00
4 Jason Isringhausen 4.00 10.00
5 Charles Johnson 4.00 10.00
6 Chipper Jones 10.00 25.00
7 Raul Mondesi 4.00 10.00
8 Hideo Nomo 10.00 25.00
9 Manny Ramirez 6.00 15.00
10 Rondell White 4.00 10.00

1967-73 Equitable Sports Hall of Fame

This set consists of copies of art work found over a number of years in many national magazines, especially "Sports Illustrated," honoring sports heroes that Equitable Life Assurance Society selected to be in its very own Sports Hall of Fame. The cards consists of charcoal-type drawings on white backgrounds by artists, George Loh and Robert Riger, and measure approximately 11" by 7 3/4". The unnumbered cards have been assigned numbers below using a sport prefix (BB- baseball, BK- basketball, FB- football, HK- hockey, OT-other).

COMPLETE SET (95) 250.00 500.00
BB1 Ernie Banks 4.00 8.00
BB2 Roy Campanella 4.00 8.00
BB3 Johnny Evers 3.00 6.00
BB4 Bob Feller 3.00 6.00
BB5 Lou Gehrig 7.50 15.00
BB6 Lefty Grove 3.00 6.00
BB7 Tom Henrich 1.25 2.50
BB8 Carl Hubbell 3.00 6.00
BB9 Al Kaline 3.00 6.00
BB10 Jerry Koosman 2.00 4.00
BB11 Mickey Mantle 7.50 15.00
BB12 Ed Mathews 3.00 6.00
BB13 Willie Mays 6.00 12.00
BB14 Stan Musial 5.00 10.00
BB15 PeeWee Reese 4.00 8.00
BB16 Allie Reynolds 1.25 2.50
BB17 Robin Roberts 3.00 6.00
BB18 Brooks Robinson 4.00 8.00
BB19 Red Ruffing 2.00 4.00
BB20 Babe Ruth 7.50 15.00
BB21 Warren Spahn 3.00 6.00

2001 eTopps

ISSUED EACH WEEK VIA ETOPPS WEBSITE
DISTRIBUTION STARTED SEPT. 2001
DISTRIBUTION ENDED DEC. 2001
SKIP-NUMBERED 75 CARD SET
PRINT RUNS B/WN 338-10000 COPIES PER
1 Nomar Garciaparra/1315 5.00 12.00
2 Chipper Jones/674 30.00 60.00
3 Jeff Bagwell/485 10.00 25.00
4 Randy Johnson/1499 10.00 25.00
7 Adam Dunn/4197 5.00 12.00
8 J.D. Drew/767 5.00 12.00
9 Larry Walker/420 12.50 30.00
10 Edgardo Alfonzo/338 20.00 50.00
11 Lance Berkman/595 30.00 60.00
12 Tony Gwynn/828 15.00 40.00
13 Andruw Jones/908 3.00 8.00
15 Troy Glaus/862 3.00 8.00
17 Sammy Sosa/2487 2.50 6.00
21 Darin Erstad/664 4.00 10.00
22 Barry Bonds/1567 10.00 25.00
27 Derek Jeter/1041 20.00 50.00
29 Curt Schilling/2125 2.50 6.00
30 Roberto Alomar/448 12.50 30.00
31 Luis Gonzalez/1104 2.00 5.00
32 Jimmy Rollins/1307 5.00 12.00
34 Joe Crede/1050 5.00 12.00
39 Sean Casey/537 6.00 15.00
46 Alex Rodriguez/2212 15.00 40.00
47 Tom Glavine/437 20.00 50.00
50 Jose Ortiz/738 2.00 5.00
51 Cal Ripken/2201 12.50 30.00
52 Bob Abreu/677 15.00 40.00
55 Alex Escobar/931 2.00 5.00
56 Ivan Rodriguez/698 10.00 25.00
59 Jeff Kent/452 8.00 20.00
62 Rick Ankiel/752 10.00 25.00
65 Craig Biggio/410 20.00 50.00
66 Carlos Delgado/398 5.00 12.00
68 Greg Maddux/1031 8.00 20.00
69 Kerry Wood/1056 3.00 8.00
71 Todd Helton/978 6.00 15.00
72 Mariano Rivera/824 12.50 30.00
73 Jason Kendall/672 4.00 10.00
75 Scott Rolen/498 12.50 30.00
76 Kazuhiro Sasaki/5000 1.50 4.00
77 Roy Oswalt/915 12.50 30.00
78 C.C. Sabathia/1974 4.00 10.00
83 Brian Giles/400 12.50 30.00
87 Rafael Furcal/646 4.00 10.00
88 Mike Mussina/793 5.00 12.00
89 Gary Sheffield/359 20.00 50.00
92 Mark McGwire/2908 5.00 12.00
94 Tsuyoshi Shinjo/3000 1.50 4.00
99 Jose Vidro/443 8.00 20.00
100 Ichiro Suzuki/10000 12.00 30.00
105 Manny Ramirez Sox/1074 10.00 25.00
109 Juan Gonzalez/558 4.00 10.00
112 Ken Griffey Jr./2398 8.00 20.00
114 Tim Hudson/663 6.00 15.00
115 Nick Johnson/1217 2.00 5.00
118 Jason Giambi/897 3.00 8.00
122 Rafael Palmeiro/464 12.50 30.00
124 Vladimir Guerrero/854 12.50 30.00
125 Vernon Wells/349 40.00 80.00
127 Roger Clemens/1462 8.00 20.00
128 Frank Thomas/834 8.00 20.00
129 Carlos Beltran/489 10.00 25.00
130 Pat Burrell/1253 6.00 15.00
131 Pedro Martinez/1038 6.00 15.00
132 Mike Piazza/1379 5.00 12.00
135 Luis Montanez/5000 1.50 4.00
140 Sean Burroughs/5000 1.50 4.00
141 Barry Zito/843 10.00 25.00
142 Bobby Bradley/5000 1.50 4.00
143 Albert Pujols/5000 20.00 50.00
144 Ben Sheets/1713 6.00 15.00
145 Alfonso Soriano/1699 6.00 15.00
146 Josh Hamilton 8.00 20.00
147 Eric Munson/5000 1.50 4.00
150 Mark Mulder/4335 1.50 4.00

2002 eTopps

DISTRIBUTION STARTED APRIL 2002
PRINT RUNS B/WN 1725-9477 COPIES PER
1 Ichiro Suzuki/9477 3.00 8.00
2 Jason Giambi/5142 1.50 4.00
3 Roberto Alomar/2711 2.00 5.00
4 Bret Boone/2000 4.00 10.00
5 Frank Catalanotto/2000 6.00 15.00
6 Alex Rodriguez/6393 2.50 6.00
7 Jim Thome/2927 2.00 5.00
8 Toby Hall/2000 1.50 4.00
9 Troy Glaus/4323 1.50 4.00
10 Derek Jeter/8000 3.00 8.00
11 Alfonso Soriano/5000 2.00 5.00
12 Eric Chavez/4334 1.50 4.00
13 Preston Wilson/2000 1.50 4.00
14 Bernie Williams/4436 2.00 5.00
15 Larry Walker/2546 1.50 4.00
16 Todd Helton/3430 2.00 5.00
17 Moises Alou/2856 1.50 4.00
18 Lance Berkman/5000 10.00 25.00
19 Chipper Jones/4734 2.00 5.00
20 Andruw Jones/4849 2.00 5.00
21 Barry Bonds/6658 4.00 10.00
22 Sammy Sosa/8000 2.00 5.00
23 Luis Gonzalez/2671 1.50 4.00
24 Shawn Green/4438 1.50 4.00
25 Jeff Bagwell/3359 2.00 5.00
26 Albert Pujols/5531 8.00 20.00
27 Rafael Palmeiro/2700 2.00 5.00
28 Jimmy Rollins/5000 1.50 4.00
29 Vladimir Guerrero/6000 2.00 5.00
30 Jeff Kent/3000 1.50 4.00
31 Ken Griffey Jr./4569 2.50 6.00
32 Magglio Ordonez/4000 1.50 4.00
33 Mike Piazza/4202 2.00 5.00
34 Pedro Martinez/6000 2.00 5.00
35 Mark Mulder/4000 1.50 4.00
36 Roger Clemens/4567 3.00 8.00
37 Freddy Garcia/4986 1.50 4.00
38 Tim Hudson/2000 1.50 4.00
39 Mike Mussina/3708 2.00 5.00
40 Joe Mays/3000 1.50 4.00
41 Barry Zito/3590 1.50 4.00
42 Jermaine Dye/2693 1.50 4.00
43 Mariano Rivera/3709 2.00 5.00
44 Randy Johnson/6211 2.00 5.00
45 Curt Schilling/5190 1.50 4.00
46 Greg Maddux/4008 2.00 5.00
47 Javier Vazquez/3000 1.50 4.00
48 Kerry Wood/3346 1.50 4.00
49 Wilson Betemit/2377 1.50 4.00
50 Adam Dunn/6000 1.50 4.00
51 Josh Beckett/5000 1.50 4.00
52 Paul LoDuca/3998 1.50 4.00
53 Ben Sheets/3842 1.50 4.00
54 Eric Valent/5000 1.50 4.00
55 Brian Giles/2000 1.50 4.00
56 Mo Vaughn/2772 1.50 4.00
57 C.C. Sabathia/2525 1.50 4.00
58 Nick Johnson/5000 1.50 4.00
59 Miguel Tejada/4000 1.50 4.00
60 Carlos Delgado/3604 1.50 4.00
61 Tsuyoshi Shinjo/3000 1.50 4.00
62 Juan Gonzalez/2361 1.50 4.00
63 Mike Sweeney/3173 1.50 4.00
64 Ivan Rodriguez/3000 2.00 5.00
65 Bud Smith/3000 1.50 4.00
66 Brandon Duckworth/2000 6.00 15.00
67 Xavier Nady/4000 1.50 4.00
68 D'Angelo Jimenez/1725 1.50 4.00
69 Roy Oswalt/3523 1.50 4.00
70 J.D. Drew/3195 1.50 4.00
71 Cliff Floyd/3725 1.50 4.00
72 Kevin Brown/3000 1.50 4.00
73 Gary Sheffield/3593 1.50 4.00
74 Aramis Ramirez/3000 1.50 4.00
75 Nomar Garciaparra/5090 2.00 5.00
76 Phil Nevin/2348 1.50 4.00
77 Juan Cruz/4000 1.50 4.00
78 Hideo Nomo/2857 2.00 5.00
79 Chris George/3000 1.50 4.00
80 Matt Morris/3000 1.50 4.00
81 Corey Patterson/4000 1.50 4.00
82 Joel Pineiro/4776 1.50 4.00
83 Mark Buehrle/3000 4.00 10.00
84 Shannon Stewart/1992 1.50 4.00
85 Kazuhiro Sasaki/4000 1.50 4.00
86 Carlos Pena/4000 1.50 4.00
87 Brad Penny/3000 1.50 4.00
88 Rich Aurilia/2795 1.50 4.00
89 Wade Miller/4000 1.50 4.00
90 Tim Raines Jr./5000 1.50 4.00
91 Kazuhisa Ishii/6000 2.00 5.00
92 Hank Blalock/5000 3.00 8.00
93 So Taguchi/5000 2.00 5.00
94 Mark Prior/5000 3.00 8.00
95 Rickey Henderson/4013 3.00 8.00
96 Austin Kearns/6000 1.50 4.00
97 Tom Glavine/3000 2.00 5.00
98 Manny Ramirez/4905 2.00 5.00
99 Shea Hillenbrand/4000 1.50 4.00
100 Junior Spivey/5000 1.50 4.00
101 Derek Lowe/4911 1.50 4.00
102 Torii Hunter/4000 1.50 4.00
103 Juan Rivera/4000 1.50 4.00
104 Eric Hinske/5000 1.50 4.00
105 Bobby Hill/3000 1.50 4.00
106 Rafael Soriano/4000 1.50 4.00
107 Jim Edmonds/3851 1.50 4.00

2003 eTopps

DISTRIBUTION STARTED APRIL 2003
PRINT RUNS B/WN 763-8000 COPIES PER
1 Troy Glaus/1454 4.00 8.00
2 Manny Ramirez/1970 2.00 5.00
3 Magglio Ordonez/1007 4.00 8.00
4 Jim Thome/3393 2.00 5.00
5 Torii Hunter/2027 1.50 4.00
6 Jason Giambi/2065 1.50 4.00
7 Tim Hudson/1690 1.50 4.00
8 Ichiro Suzuki/3465 4.00 8.00
9 Aubrey Huff/3234 1.50 4.00
10 Alex Rodriguez/2847 4.00 8.00
11 Francisco Rodriguez/3627 1.50 4.00
12 Joe Borchard/3000 1.50 4.00
13 Mark Teixeira/5000 5.00 10.00
14 Marlon Byrd/1822 1.50 4.00
15 Carlos Delgado/2500 1.50 4.00
16 Tom Glavine/2407 2.00 5.00
17 Curt Schilling/1333 1.50 4.00
18 Mark Prior/4000 2.00 5.00
19 Ken Griffey Jr./1238 4.00 10.00
20 Todd Helton/2315 2.00 5.00
21 Jeff Bagwell/1678 2.00 5.00
22 Shawn Green/1162 1.50 4.00
23 Vladimir Guerrero/2523 2.00 5.00
24 Roberto Alomar/1394 2.00 5.00
25 Brian Giles/1500 1.50 4.00
26 Barry Bonds/4000 5.00 10.00
27 Albert Pujols/3000 5.00 10.00
28 Nomar Garciaparra/2177 2.00 5.00
29 Alfonso Soriano/3500 1.50 4.00
30 Barry Zito/2500 1.50 4.00
31 Edgar Martinez/2732 5.00 10.00
32 Ivan Rodriguez/1436 2.00 5.00
33 Greg Maddux/2004 2.00 5.00
34 Sammy Sosa/1425 4.00 8.00
35 Austin Kearns/3000 1.50 4.00
36 Craig Biggio/1317 2.00 5.00
37 Mike Piazza/1355 2.00 5.00
38 Andruw Jones/1589 2.00 5.00
39 Jeff Kent/1685 1.50 4.00
40 Roy Oswalt/2108 1.50 4.00
41 Miguel Tejada/2630 1.50 4.00
42 Derek Jeter/3054 4.00 8.00
43 Pedro Martinez/1754 2.00 5.00
44 Jarrod Washburn/1196 1.50 4.00
45 Randy Johnson/1117 5.00 10.00
46 Bernie Williams/1750 2.00 5.00
47 Chipper Jones/1443 2.00 5.00
48 Gary Sheffield/1500 1.50 4.00
49 Larry Walker/1001 4.00 8.00
50 Lance Berkman/1107 1.50 4.00
51 Garret Anderson/2647 2.00 5.00
52 Jason Schmidt/1840 4.00 8.00
53 Rodrigo Lopez/1500 1.50 4.00
54 Oliver Perez/1996 4.00 8.00
55 Derek Lowe/1434 1.50 4.00
56 Vicente Padilla/995 5.00 10.00
57 Paul Konerko/1151 4.00 8.00
58 Bartolo Colon/2028 1.50 4.00
59 Omar Vizquel/3413 2.00 5.00
60 Adam Dunn/1812 1.50 4.00
61 Carlos Pena/1402 1.50 4.00
62 Richie Sexson/1380 2.00 5.00
63 Paul Byrd/2000 1.50 4.00
64 Eric Gagne/2929 1.50 4.00
65 Brad Radke/827 5.00 10.00
66 A.J. Burnett/1009 10.00 20.00
67 Brandon Phillips/4000 1.50 4.00
68 Mike Hampton/763 7.50 15.00
69 Tim Salmon/1548 2.00 5.00
70 Roger Clemens/3000 4.00 8.00
71 Jake Peavy/2500 5.00 10.00
72 Pat Burrell/1168 4.00 8.00
73 Ben Sheets/1500 7.50 15.00
74 Fred McGriff/1323 2.00 5.00
75 John Smoltz/3161 5.00 10.00
76 Josh Phelps/2500 1.50 4.00
77 John Olerud/1620 2.00 5.00
78 Eric Chavez/2054 1.50 4.00
79 Jeff Weaver/1877 1.50 4.00
80 Scott Rolen/2000 2.00 5.00
81 Carl Crawford/1518 4.00 8.00
82 Rafael Palmeiro/1500 2.00 5.00
83 Roy Halladay/2500 2.00 5.00
84 Josh Beckett/1130 5.00 10.00
85 Jorge Posada/2171 2.00 5.00
86 Mark Mulder/2000 1.50 4.00
87 Eric Milton/1758 1.50 4.00
88 Angel Berroa/1614 1.50 4.00
89 Jason Lane/1952 1.50 4.00
90 Kerry Wood/2000 1.50 4.00
91 Brad Wilkerson/2944 2.00 5.00
92 Orlando Hudson/2500 2.00 5.00
93 Mike Mussina/2000 2.00 5.00
94 Hee Seop Choi/3000 1.50 4.00
95 Chris Snelling/2879 1.50 4.00
96 Tomo Ohka/1975 1.50 4.00
97 Andy Pettitte/2367 2.00 5.00
98 Drew Henson/3000 2.00 5.00
99 Chin-Feng Chen/2500 1.50 4.00
100 Jason Jennings/1761 1.50 4.00
101 Hideki Matsui/8000 2.00 5.00
102 Jose Contreras/6000 1.50 4.00
103 Rocco Baldelli/5000 1.50 4.00
104 Jeremy Bonderman/3000 5.00 12.00
105 Jesse Foppert/3500 4.00 8.00
106 Randy Wolf/1874 1.50 4.00
107 Kevin Millwood/3000 1.50 4.00
108 Eric Byrnes/2500 1.50 4.00
109 Edgar Renteria/2015 1.50 4.00
110 Jose Reyes/5000 6.00 15.00
111 Dontrelle Willis/5000 5.00 10.00
112 Mike Lowell/2500 1.50 4.00
113 Jerome Williams/3000 2.00 5.00
114 Esteban Loaiza/2364 1.50 4.00
115 Gil Meche/2000 2.00 5.00
116 Ty Wigginton/2000 1.50 4.00
118 Brett Myers/2115 1.50 4.00
119 Miguel Cabrera/2610 10.00 25.00
120 Brandon Webb/3000 4.00 10.00
121 Aaron Heilman/1229 1.50 4.00
122 Rich Harden/5000 2.00 5.00
123 Morgan Ensberg/1329 2.00 5.00
70P Roger Clemens
CHICAGO PROMO
AS1 Ichiro Suzuki 2.50 6.00
Albert Pujols/3938
Top Vote Getters

2004 eTopps

ISSUED VIA ETOPPS WEBSITE
PRINT RUNS B/WN 1267-5000 COPIES PER
SKIP-NUMBERED SET
24/26/29/39/48/50 DO NOT EXIST
66-67/77/86/88/97-98 DO NOT EXIST
1 Andy Pettitte/1991 2.00 5.00
2 Jason Giambi/1565 2.00 5.00
3 Kevin Youkilis/2171 1.50 4.00
4 Casey Blake/1420 1.50 4.00
5 Ryan Ludwick/1321 1.50 4.00
6 Craig Wilson/1544 1.50 4.00
7 Curt Schilling/2216 2.00 5.00
8 Mark Prior/3750 2.00 5.00
9 Casey Kotchman/2006 2.00 5.00
10 Scott Podsednik/2500 2.00 5.00
11 Jose Guillen/1541 2.00 5.00
12 Clint Nageotte/1526 1.50 4.00
13 Melvin Mora/1432 2.00 5.00
14 Ivan Rodriguez/2104 2.00 5.00
15 Travis Hafner/2500 2.00 5.00
16 Mike Piazza/2500 2.00 5.00
17 Brian Giles/1267 2.00 5.00
18 Derek Jeter/2708 4.00 8.00
19 Edwin Jackson/3655 1.50 4.00
20 Chipper Jones/2158 2.00 5.00
21 Jody Gerut/1436 1.50 4.00
22 Carlos Lee/1562 2.00 5.00
23 Jason Schmidt/1659 2.00 5.00
25 Ichiro Suzuki/2228 5.00 10.00
27 Corey Patterson/2500 1.50 4.00
28 Rafael Furcal/1410 2.00 5.00
30 Kerry Wood/1824 2.00 5.00
31 Jim Thome/1908 2.00 5.00
32 Hideki Matsui/2500 2.00 5.00
33 Rocco Baldelli/2500 2.00 5.00
34 Jose Reyes/1739 2.00 5.00
35 Dontrelle Willis/3750 2.00 5.00
36 Miguel Cabrera/3750 2.00 5.00
37 Brandon Webb/2072 1.50 4.00
38 Rich Harden/1823 2.00 5.00
40 Vladimir Guerrero/1913 2.00 5.00
41 Hank Blalock/3303 2.00 5.00
42 Kazuo Matsui/5000 2.00 5.00
43 Joe Mauer/4888 5.00 10.00
44 Keith Foulke/1896 2.00 5.00
45 Josh Beckett/3178 2.00 5.00
46 Jamie Moyer/1573 2.00 5.00
47 Victor Martinez/2500 4.00 8.00
49 Derrek Lee/1920 5.00 10.00
51 Roger Clemens/3750 4.00 8.00
52 David Ortiz/1655 2.00 5.00
53 Jason Bay/2336 5.00 10.00
54 Erubiel Durazo/1577 1.50 4.00
55 Gary Sheffield/1639 2.00 5.00
56 Jeff Kent/2036 2.00 5.00
57 Ken Harvey/1621 1.50 4.00
58 Jason Varitek/2698 2.00 5.00
59 Jeromy Burnitz/2148 2.00 5.00
60 Nomar Garciaparra/2074 2.00 5.00
61 Javy Lopez/3204 2.00 5.00
62 Eric Gagne/2279 2.00 5.00
63 Khalil Greene/3456 4.00 8.00
64 Carlos Zambrano/3492 2.00 5.00
65 Lyle Overbay/2789 1.50 4.00
68 Laynce Nix/1760 1.50 4.00
69 Manny Ramirez/1909 2.00 5.00
70 Alfonso Soriano/1820 2.00 5.00
71 Mike Lieberthal/1479 2.00 5.00
72 Juan Pierre/2500 2.00 5.00
73 Frank Thomas/1835 2.00 5.00
74 Sean Casey/1851 2.00 5.00
75 Albert Pujols/3750 6.00 12.00
76 Bill Mueller/1977 2.00 5.00
78 Randy Johnson/2725 2.00 5.00
79 Carlos Beltran/2500 2.00 5.00
80 Pedro Martinez/1726 2.00 5.00
81 Lew Ford/1932 1.50 4.00
82 Javier Vazquez/1936 2.00 5.00
83 Kevin Brown/2635 2.00 5.00
84 Johnny Estrada/1590 1.50 4.00
85 Ken Griffey Jr./2396 4.00 10.00
87 Jorge Posada/2176 2.00 5.00
89 Bobby Crosby/3498 2.00 5.00
90 Sammy Sosa/3248 2.00 5.00
91 Shingo Takatsu/1678 2.00 5.00
92 Akinori Otsuka/1544 1.50 4.00
93 Michael Young/2004 2.00 5.00
94 Aaron Miles/1608 1.50 4.00
95 Miguel Tejada/1548 2.00 5.00
96 Chad Tracy/2534 1.50 4.00
99 Todd Helton/1998 2.00 5.00
100 Alex Rodriguez/5000 4.00 8.00
101 Bartolo Colon/1973 2.00 5.00
102 Philadelphia Phillies/2500 1.50 4.00
103 Seattle Mariners/2500 1.50 4.00
104 Atlanta Braves/2500 2.00 5.00
105 Chicago White Sox/2458 1.50 4.00
106 Pittsburgh Pirates/2500 1.50 4.00
107 St. Louis Cardinals/2500 2.00 5.00
108 Houston Astros/2500 1.50 4.00
109 Toronto Blue Jays/2500 1.50 4.00
110 Arizona Diamondbacks/1818 10.00 20.00
111 New York Mets/2570 1.50 4.00
112 Minnesota Twins/2500 1.50 4.00
113 Baltimore Orioles/2750 1.50 4.00
114 Cleveland Indians/2219 1.50 4.00
115 Boston Red Sox/3750 4.00 8.00
116 Tampa Bay Devil Rays/2191 1.50 4.00
117 Chicago Cubs/3750 2.00 5.00
118 Texas Rangers/2500 1.50 4.00
119 Cincinnati Reds/2500 1.50 4.00
120 Anaheim Angels/2500 2.00 5.00
121 Colorado Rockies/2500 1.50 4.00
122 Kansas City Royals/2120 1.50 4.00
123 Florida Marlins/2500 1.50 4.00
124 Oakland Athletics/2375 1.50 4.00
125 Los Angeles Dodgers/2155 2.00 5.00
126 Milwaukee Brewers/2500 1.50 4.00
127 San Francisco Giants/2500 2.00 5.00
128 Montreal Expos/2500 1.50 4.00
129 San Diego Padres/2500 1.50 4.00
130 New York Yankees/3750 2.00 5.00
131 Detroit Tigers/2750 1.50 4.00
132 Matt Holliday/2425 2.00 5.00
133 Zack Greinke/3750 2.00 5.00
51p Roger Clemens
CHICAGO PROMO

2005 eTopps

PRINT RUNS B/WN 680-2956 COPIES PER
1 Los Angeles Angels Of Anaheim/1018.75 2.00
2 Arizona Diamondbacks/1000 .75 2.00
3 Atlanta Braves/1275 .75 2.00
4 Baltimore Orioles/1189 .75 2.00
5 Boston Red Sox/2538 2.00 5.00
6 Chicago Cubs/1300 2.00 5.00
7 Chicago White Sox/1199 .75 2.00
8 Cincinnati Reds/770 1.00 2.50
9 Cleveland Indians/974 1.00 2.50
10 Colorado Rockies/736 1.00 2.50
11 Detroit Tigers/832 1.00 2.50
12 Florida Marlins/863 1.00 2.50
13 Houston Astros/1227 .75 2.00
14 Kansas City Royals/807 1.00 2.50
15 Los Angeles Dodgers/1000 2.00 5.00
16 Milwaukee Brewers/728 1.00 2.50
17 Minnesota Twins/888 1.00 2.50
18 New York Mets/1300 2.00 5.00
19 New York Yankees/2600 2.00 5.00
20 Oakland Athletics/739 1.00 2.50
21 Philadelphia Phillies/890 2.50 6.00
22 Pittsburgh Pirates/776 2.50 6.00
23 San Diego Padres/818 1.00 2.50
24 San Francisco Giants/1051 .75 2.00
25 Seattle Mariners/800 1.00 2.50
26 St. Louis Cardinals/1300 2.00 5.00
27 Tampa Bay Devil Rays/688 1.00 2.50
28 Texas Rangers/705 1.00 2.50
29 Toronto Blue Jays/701 1.00 2.50
30 Washington Nationals/1300 .75 2.00
31 Adrian Beltre/1298 2.00 5.00
33 Albert Pujols/2600 2.50 6.00
34 Alex Rodriguez/2259 2.50 6.00
35 Alexis Rios/1158 .75 2.00
36 Alfonso Soriano/793 1.50 4.00
40 Carlos Beltran/1630 1.25 3.00
41 Carl Crawford/820 1.50 4.00
43 Carlos Guillen/920 1.00 2.50
44 Chipper Jones/927 2.50 6.00
45 Carl Pavano/826 1.00 2.50
46 Curt Schilling/1288 1.25 3.00
47 Derek Jeter/2000 5.00 12.00
48 David Ortiz/981 2.50 6.00
49 David Wright/2956 1.50 4.00
50 David Wells/851 1.00 2.50
51 Eric Gagne/688 1.00 2.50
53 Gary Sheffield/857 1.00 2.50
54 Hank Blalock/814 1.00 2.50
55 Hideki Matsui/1200 3.00 8.00
56 Ichiro Suzuki/2223 2.50 6.00
57 Ivan Rodriguez/773 1.50 4.00
61 Johan Santana/2600 1.25 3.00
63 Jim Thome/750 1.50 4.00
64 Ken Griffey Jr./1200 4.00 10.00
67 Kerry Wood/756 1.00 2.50
68 Livan Hernandez/1200 .75 2.00
69 Miguel Cabrera/1200 2.00 5.00
71 Mark Prior/1337 1.25 3.00
72 Mike Piazza/1057 2.00 5.00
73 Manny Ramirez/1200 2.00 5.00
74 Miguel Tejada/944 1.50 4.00
75 Mark Teixeira/1037 1.25 3.00
77 Pedro Martinez/1163 1.25 3.00
80 Roger Clemens/1667 2.50 6.00
82 Randy Johnson/2196 2.00 5.00
85 Scott Rolen/1020 1.25 3.00
86 Sammy Sosa/1200 2.00 5.00
89 Todd Helton/785 1.50 4.00
91 Vladimir Guerrero/1036 1.25 3.00
95 Dallas McPherson/2350 .75 2.00
99 Andy Marte/2000 .75 2.00
115 Grady Sizemore/1200 1.25 3.00
133 David DeJesus/680 1.00 2.50
142 J.J. Hardy/1523 .75 2.00
149 Justin Morneau/1664 1.25 3.00
152 Chien-Ming Wang/1200 3.00 8.00
153 Dioner Navarro/939 1.00 2.50
156 Gavin Floyd/1485 .75 2.00
165 David Aardsma/889 1.00 2.50
172 B.J. Upton/1910 1.25 3.00
174 Scott Kazmir/1760 2.00 5.00
175 Adrian Gonzalez/938 2.00 5.00
181 Brendan Harris/977 1.00 2.50
185 Tim Hudson/859 1.50 4.00
186 Mark Mulder/860 1.00 2.50
188 Jeff Bagwell/823 1.50 4.00
189 Troy Glaus/824 1.00 2.50
191 Jim Edmonds/874 1.50 4.00
193 Johnny Damon/1415 1.25 3.00
195 Billy Wagner/939 1.00 2.50
196 Dmitri Young/778 1.00 2.50
198 David Eckstein/874 1.00 2.50
199 Tadahito Iguchi/1200 1.25 3.00
200 Jason Bartlett/913 1.00 2.50
202 Joe Blanton/1097 .75 2.00
203 Huston Street/1200 .75 2.00
204 Clint Barmes/2000 .75 2.00
207 Brian Roberts/1200 .75 2.00
208 Jon Garland/1200 .75 2.00
209 Robinson Cano/1200 2.50 6.00
210 Zach Duke/2000 .75 2.00
211 Brad Eldred/849 1.00 2.50
212 Jeff Francoeur/2000 2.00 5.00
213 Jon Papelbon/1500
214 Conor Jackson/1278 1.25 3.00
215 Dan Johnson/1000 .75 2.00
216 Prince Fielder/2000 4.00 10.00
217 Jeremy Hermida/1400 1.25 3.00
219 Melky Cabrera/1000 2.50 6.00
220 Ryan Howard/2000 1.50 4.00
221 Rickie Weeks/1675 .75 2.00
222 Felix Hernandez/2000 2.50 6.00

2006 eTopps

1 John Koronka
2 Chone Figgins
3 Melky Cabrera
4 Josh Johnson
5 Dan Uggla 15.00 40.00
6 Tim Hudson
7 Joel Zumaya
8 Russell Martin
9 David Ortiz
10 Lastings Milledge
11 Tadahito Iguchi
12 Casey Janssen
13 Ken Griffey Jr.
14 Nick Swisher
15 Victor Martinez
16 Miguel Cabrera
17 Dontrelle Willis
18 Roy Oswalt
19 Lance Berkman 10.00 25.00
20 Yusmeiro Petit
21 Joe Mauer
22 Pedro Martinez
23 David Wright
24 Alex Rodriguez
25 Derek Jeter
26 Hideki Matsui
27 Gary Sheffield
28 Chris Ray
29 Eric Chavez
30 Rich Harden
31 Huston Street
32 Ryan Howard 4.00 10.00
33 Jason Bay
34 Jake Peavy
35 Matt Kemp
36 Ichiro Suzuki
37 Kenji Johjima
38 Albert Pujols
39 Jorge Cantu
40 Mark Teixeira
41 Carlos Delgado
42 A.J. Burnett
43 Johnny Damon
44 Josh Beckett
45 Troy Glaus
46 Rafael Furcal
47 Alfonso Soriano
48 B.J. Ryan
49 Jim Thome
50 Billy Wagner
51 Joe Torre
52 Bobby Cox
53 Mike Scioscia
54 Tony LaRussa
55 Ozzie Guillen
56 Frank Robinson
57 Jason Botts
58 Dusty Baker
59 Jeremy Sowers
60 Bruce Bochy
61 Craig Hansen
62 Hong-Chih Kuo
63 Joey Devine
64 Hanley Ramirez 6.00 15.00
65 Adam Wainwright
66 Ryan Zimmerman
67 Francisco Liriano
68 Tom Gorzelanny
69 Nelson Cruz
70 Ryan Garko
71 Anthony Lerew
72 B.J. Upton
73 Josh Barfield
74 Anderson Hernandez
75 Brian Anderson
76 Brian Bannister
77 Curtis Granderson
78 Ian Kinsler 6.00 15.00
79 Jason Kubel
80 Scott Olsen
81 Jeremy Hermida
82 Jonathan Papelbon
83 Josh Willingham
84 Justin Verlander
85 Matt Cain
86 Mike Jacobs
87 Nick Markakis
88 Prince Fielder
89 Chase Utley 10.00 25.00
90 Chien-Ming Wang
91 Chris Carpenter
92 Chris Shelton
93 Frank Thomas
94 Grady Sizemore
95 Jeff Francoeur
96 Jose Reyes 8.00 20.00
97 Robinson Cano
98 Travis Hafner
99 Kendry Morales
100 Cole Hamels
101 Conor Jackson
102 Brian McCann
103 Alay Soler
104 Jason Hirsh
105 Anthony Reyes
106 Jered Weaver
107 Stephen Drew
108 Takashi Saito
109 Chad Billingsley
110 Jon Lester
111 Zach Miner
112 Reggie Abercrombie
113 Sean Marshall
114 Howie Kendrick
115 Mike Pelfrey
116 Andre Ethier
117 Mike Napoli
118 Matt Garza
119 Ricky Nolasco
120 Roger Clemens
121 Derrek Lee
122 Miguel Tejada
123 Vladimir Guerrero
124 Manny Ramirez
125 Chris Capuano
126 Nomar Garciaparra
127 Alex Rios
128 Bronson Arroyo
129 Carl Crawford
130 Justin Morneau
NNO Nolan Ryan NSCC PROMO

2006 eTopps Event Series National VIP Promos

KG Kirk Gibson 2.00 5.00
NR Nolan Ryan 2.50 6.00

2007 eTopps

1 Derek Jeter/1199
2 Troy Tulowitzki/999
3 Delmon Young/1199
4 Kevin Kouzmanoff/799
5 Alex Gordon/999
6 Alfonso Soriano/799
7 Daisuke Matsuzaka/1499 8.00 20.00
8 Akinori Iwamura/799
9 Elijah Dukes/899
10 Alex Rodriguez/899
11 Felix Hernandez/799
12 Travis Buck/799
13 David Ortiz/749
14 Hideki Okajima/749
15 John Danks/749 3.00 8.00
16 Josh Hamilton/1739 8.00 20.00
17 Philip Hughes/1200
18 Johan Santana/899
19 Kei Igawa/749
20 Felix Pie/899
21 Adam Lind/749
22 Rich Hill/749
23 Andruw Jones/749
24 Ichiro Suzuki/749
25 Jarrod Saltalamacchia/749
26 Tim Lincecum/799 10.00 25.00
27 John Maine/799
28 Chase Utley/749 5.00 12.00
29 Matt Holliday/749
30 Joe Smith/897
31 David Wright/899
32 Hunter Pence/799 6.00 15.00
33 Andrew Miller/749
34 Tyler Clippard/749
35 Barry Zito/749
36 Carlos Lee/699
37 Fred Lewis/749
38 Micah Owings/799
39 Ryan Braun/999 15.00 40.00
40 Magglio Ordonez/749
41 Carlos Gomez/749
42 Kevin Slowey/799
43 Albert Pujols/999 5.00 12.00
44 J.J. Hardy/749
45 Homer Bailey/899
46 Yunel Escobar/749
47 Chase Headley/749
48 Andy Laroche/1097
49 Tony Abreu/799
50 Mark Reynolds/799 3.00 8.00
51 Ryan Howard/999 4.00 10.00
52 Ken Griffey Jr./999
53 Yovani Gallardo/999
54 Nate Schierholtz/749
55 Mike Fontenot/749
56 Torii Hunter/729
57 Jacoby Ellsbury/749
58 Josh Fields/749
59 Billy Butler/799
60 Dustin Pedroia/499 12.50 30.00
61 C.C. Sabathia/799
62 Brandon Wood/799
63 Ben Francisco/749
64 Michael Bourn/699
65 Brandon Morrow/699
66 Shelley Duncan/499
67 Kurt Suzuki/749
68 Ryan Sweeney/749
69 Ryan Raburn/499
70 Justin Upton/899 12.50 30.00
71 Joba Chamberlain/999
72 Cameron Maybin/999 2.50 6.00
73 Alejandro De Aza/749

2008 eTopps

1 Clay Buchholz/1499 *
2 Johan Santana/899 *
3 Kosuke Fukudome/1199 * 8.00 20.00
4 J.R. Towles/999 *
5 Nick Blackburn/899 *
6 Johnny Cueto/1199 *
7 Blake Dewitt/799 *
8 Clete Thomas/799 *
9 Albert Pujols/999 * 5.00 12.00
10 Ken Griffey Jr./899 *
11 Jed Lowrie/999 *
12 Denard Span/749 * 4.00 10.00
13 Hanley Ramirez/749 * 5.00 12.00
14 Chase Utley/749 * 4.00 10.00
15 Ian Kennedy/2185 *
16 Justin Masterson/999 * 10.00 25.00
17 Brandon Webb/749 *
18 Chipper Jones/749 * 4.00 10.00
19 Hiroki Kuroda/799 *
20 Jeff Clement/799 * 4.00 10.00
21 Derek Jeter/999 *
22 Ryan Church/699 *
23 Max Scherzer/999 * 8.00 20.00
24 Joey Votto/799 * 10.00 25.00
25 David Wright/899 * 2.50 6.00
26 Edinson Volquez/699 * 10.00 25.00
27 Luke Hochevar/899 *
28 Matt Joyce/799 *
29 Alex Rodriguez/899 *
30 Evan Longoria/1499 * 10.00 25.00
31 Nate McLouth/699 *
32 Greg Smith/799 *
33 Geovany Soto/699 *
34 Jay Bruce/1499 * 8.00 20.00
35 John Bowker/799 *
36 Nick Evans/749 *
37 Jimmy Rollins/799 * 1.50 4.00
38 Carlos Quentin/699 *
39 Clayton Kershaw/999 * 12.00 30.00
40 Seth Smith/749 *
41 Joe Saunders/699 *
42 Tim Lincecum/749 * 6.00 15.00
43 Alexei Ramirez/749 * 5.00 12.00
44 Armando Galarraga/749 *
45 Cole Hamels/749 *
46 Carlos Gonzalez/499 * 8.00 20.00
47 Charlie Morton/749 *
48 Cliff Lee/699 *
49 Max Ramirez/749 *
50 Brandon Jones/499 *
51 Jair Jurrjens/699 *
52 Brett Gardner/699 *
53 Chris Davis/749 *
54 C.C. Sabathia/499 *
55 Chris Volstad/699 *
56 Steve Pearce/699 *
57 Jeff Samardzija/749 *
58 Taylor Teagarden/649 *
59 Clayton Richard/699 *
60 Manny Ramirez/699 *
61 Ivan Rodriguez/499 *
62 Jason Bay/699 *
63 Gio Gonzalez/699 *
64 Mark Teixeira/649 *
65 Cliff Pennington/649 *
66 Daniel Murphy/499 *
67 Greg Maddux/649 *
68 Adam Dunn/649 *
69 Daric Barton/649 *

2009 eTopps

COMMON CARD 3.00 8.00
PRINT RUNS B/WN 499-1499
1 Emilio Bonifacio/699 * 4.00 10.00
2 Jordan Schafer/749 * 3.00 8.00
3 Mark Teixeira/649 * 5.00 12.00
4 Colby Rasmus/999 * 8.00 20.00
5 Koji Uehara/749 * 3.00 8.00
6 C.C. Sabathia/649 * 5.00 12.00
7 Rick Porcello/999 * 6.00 15.00
8 Travis Snider/749 * 5.00 12.00
9 Jordan Zimmermann/999 * 4.00 10.00
10 Shin-soo Choo/749 * 4.00 10.00
11 David Wright/799 * 5.00 12.00
12 Dexter Fowler/999 * 4.00 10.00
13 Trevor Cahill/749 * 4.00 10.00
14 Zack Greinke/749 * 6.00 15.00
15 Kevin Youkilis/649 * 4.00 10.00
16 Matt Laporta/999 * 4.00 10.00
17 Evan Longoria/999 * 5.00 12.00
18 Michael Bowden/749 * 4.00 10.00
19 Derek Holland/749 * 4.00 10.00
20 Mat Gamel/999 * 4.00 10.00
21 Roy Halladay/699 * 8.00 20.00
22 Pablo Sandoval/599 * 5.00 12.00
23 Nolan Reimold/699 * 5.00 12.00
24 Gerardo Parra/749 * 4.00 10.00
25 Raul Ibanez/749 * 4.00 10.00
26 Matt Wieters/1499 * 4.00 10.00
27 Fernando Martinez/999 * 4.00 10.00
28 Tim Lincecum/749 * 8.00 20.00
29 Gordon Beckham/999 * 8.00 20.00
30 Tommy Hanson/999 * 10.00 25.00
31 Adrian Gonzalez/699 * 5.00 12.00
32 Antonio Bastardo/699 * 3.00 8.00
33 Francisco Cervelli/699 * 3.00 8.00

34 Andrew McCutchen/999 * 8.00 20.00
35 Albert Pujols/999 * 10.00 25.00
36 Ricky Romero/699 * 5.00 12.00
37 Derek Jeter/999 * 4.00 10.00
38 Ian Kinsler/749 * 4.00 10.00
39 Daniel Bard/749 * 4.00 10.00
40 Elvis Andrus/1011 * 5.00 12.00
41 Ryan Howard/999 * 4.00 10.00
42 David Price/1199 * 5.00 12.00
43 Jake Fox/699 * 4.00 10.00
44 Kyle Blanks/699 * 3.00 8.00
45 Nick Swisher/699 * 3.00 8.00
46 Casey McGehee/749 * 5.00 12.00
47 Andrew Bailey/699 * 4.00 10.00
48 Mark DeRosa/659 * 4.00 10.00
49 Brett Anderson/699 * 4.00 10.00
50 Joe Mauer/599 * 5.00 12.00
51 Prince Fielder/699 * 5.00 12.00
52 Dan Haren/699 * 5.00 12.00
53 Ichiro Suzuki/749 * 5.00 12.00
54 Mat Latos/749 * 5.00 12.00
55 Matt Holliday/499 * 6.00 15.00
56 Victor Martinez/499 * 6.00 15.00
57 Chris Tillman/699 * 5.00 12.00
58 Matt Cain/699 * 5.00 12.00

2010 eTopps

1 Ike Davis/999 * 6.00 15.00
2 Roy Halladay/799 * 10.00 25.00
3 Brian Matusz/799 * 4.00 10.00
4 Austin Jackson/999 * 6.00 15.00
5 Tyler Colvin/799 * 5.00 12.00
6 Tim Lincecum/799 * 10.00 25.00
7 Albert Pujols/999 * 8.00 20.00
8 Justin Smoak/799 * 5.00 12.00
9 Ubaldo Jimenez/749 * 15.00 40.00
10 Mike Leake/749 * 6.00 15.00
11 Wade Davis/799 * 4.00 10.00
12 Derek Jeter/999 * 8.00 20.00
13 Starlin Castro/1499 * 4.00 10.00
14 Jason Heyward/1499 * 12.00 30.00
15 Ichiro Suzuki/749 * 5.00 12.00
16 Brennan Boesch/749 * 8.00 20.00
17 Miguel Cabrera/749 * 5.00 12.00
18 Trevor Plouffe/749 * 6.00 15.00
19 Justin Morneau/749 * 5.00 12.00
20 Cliff Lee/749 * 4.00 10.00
21 Buster Posey/799 * 12.00 30.00
22 Andrew Cashner/749 * 4.00 10.00
23 Stephen Strasburg/1999 * 12.00 30.00
24 Mike Stanton/999 * 20.00 50.00
25 David Freese/749 * 4.00 10.00

2007 eTopps Allen and Ginter Milestones

1 Alex Rodriguez/999 * 8.00 20.00
2 Mark Buehrle/999 * 4.00 10.00
3 Tom Glavine/999 * 4.00 10.00
4 Craig Biggio/999 * 5.00 12.00
5 Sammy Sosa/999 * 3.00 8.00
6 Frank Thomas/999 * 3.00 8.00
7 Jim Thome/999 * 4.00 10.00
8 Justin Verlander/999 * 8.00 20.00
9 Pedro Martinez/999 * 5.00 8.00
10 Curtis Granderson/999 * 4.00 10.00
11 Prince Fielder/999 * 4.00 10.00

2007 eTopps Allen and Ginter Moments

2 Barry Bonds/1499 * 3.00 8.00

2008 eTopps Allen and Ginter Presidential Candidates

1 Hillary Clinton 5.00 12.00
2 Barack Obama 12.00 30.00
3 Mitt Romney 6.00 15.00
4 John McCain 4.00 10.00

2008 eTopps Allen and Ginter Yankee Tribute

1 Babe Ruth/1499 * 8.00 20.00
2 Lou Gehrig/1499 * 5.00 12.00
3 Jackie Robinson/1499 * 6.00 15.00
4 Don Larsen/1499 * 4.00 10.00
5 Johnny Unitas/1499 * 4.00 10.00
6 Roger Maris/1499 * 5.00 12.00
7 Mickey Mantle/1499 * 10.00 25.00
8 Reggie Jackson/1499 * 4.00 10.00
9 Aaron Boone/1499 * 3.00 8.00
10 Pope Benedict XVI/1499 * 5.00 12.00
11 Yankee Stadium/1499 * 10.00 25.00

2005 eTopps Autographs

AVAILABLE DIRECT VIA ETOPPS WEBSITE
PRINT RUNS B/WN 32-103 COPIES PER

2007 eTopps Cards That Never Were

1 Joe Dimaggio/1499 5.00 12.00
2 Nolan Ryan/999 6.00 15.00
3 Alex Rodriguez/999 6.00 15.00
4 Ted Williams/1499 6.00 15.00
5 Ryne Sandberg/999 4.00 10.00
6 Roger Clemens/999 5.00 12.00
7 Stan Musial/999 5.00 12.00
8 Whitey Ford/999 5.00 12.00
9 Don Mattingly/999 6.00 15.00
10 Wade Boggs/749 4.00 10.00

2002 eTopps Classic

AVAILABLE VIA ETOPPS.COM WEBSITE
STATED PRINT RUN 4000 SERIAL #'d SETS
1 Babe Ruth 5.00 12.00
2 Tom Seaver 3.00 8.00
3 Honus Wagner 3.00 8.00
4 Warren Spahn 3.00 8.00
5 Frank Robinson 2.50 6.00
6 Whitey Ford 2.50 6.00
7 Bob Gibson 3.00 8.00
8 Reggie Jackson 3.00 8.00
9 Joe Morgan 2.50 6.00
10 Harmon Killebrew 3.00 8.00
11 Eddie Mathews 2.50 6.00
12 Willie Mays 4.00 10.00
13 Brooks Robinson 3.00 8.00
14 Ty Cobb 3.00 8.00
15 Carl Yastrzemski 3.00 8.00
16 Jackie Robinson 3.00 8.00
17 Mike Schmidt 3.00 8.00
18 Nolan Ryan 4.00 10.00
19 Duke Snider 3.00 8.00
20 Stan Musial 3.00 8.00

2003 eTopps Classic

AVAILABLE VIA ETOPPS.COM WEBSITE
PRINT RUNS B/WN 778-3049 COPIES PER
21 Gary Carter/908 4.00 10.00
22 Eddie Murray/930 6.00 15.00
23 Luis Aparicio/778 4.00 10.00
24 Lou Brock/1135 4.00 10.00
25 George Brett/1128 5.00 12.00
26 Bob Feller/962 4.00 10.00
27 Carlton Fisk/890 4.00 10.00
28 Willie McCovey/915 4.00 10.00
29 Willie Stargell/843 5.00 12.00
30 Roberto Clemente/1664 10.00 25.00
31 Lou Gehrig/3049 4.00 10.00
32 Johnny Bench/1144 8.00 20.00
33 Walter Johnson/888 6.00 15.00
34 Christy Mathewson/868 4.00 10.00
35 Rogers Hornsby/826 5.00 12.00
36 Lefty Grove/885 4.00 10.00
37 Josh Gibson/1133 4.00 10.00
38 Mel Ott/917 4.00 10.00
39 Nap Lajoie/886 4.00 10.00
40 Yogi Berra/1281 4.00 10.00

2004 eTopps Classic

AVAILABLE VIA ETOPPS.COM WEBSITE
PRINT RUNS B/WN 768-1250 COPIES PER
41 Orlando Cepeda/806 4.00 10.00
42 Wade Boggs/908 4.00 10.00
43 Al Kaline/962 8.00 20.00
44 Jim Palmer/768 6.00 15.00
45 Ozzie Smith/1161 4.00 10.00
46 Rod Carew/908 4.00 10.00
47 Paul Molitor/850 4.00 10.00
48 Hank Aaron/1250 6.00 15.00
49 Robin Yount/1002 4.00 10.00
50 Hank Greenberg/769 5.00 12.00
51 Robin Roberts/807 4.00 10.00
52 Casey Stengel/898 4.00 10.00
53 Cy Young/1200 4.00 10.00
54 Thurman Munson/1250 5.00 12.00
55 Roy Campanella/984 4.00 10.00
56 Satchel Paige/1222 4.00 10.00
57 Tris Speaker/795 4.00 10.00
58 Jimmie Foxx/952 4.00 10.00
59 Dizzy Dean/967 4.00 10.00
60 Cool Papa Bell/988 4.00 10.00

2005 eTopps Classic

61 Roger Maris 6.00 15.00
62 Ryne Sandberg 4.00 10.00
63 Don Mattingly 5.00 12.00
64 Ernie Banks 3.00 8.00
65 Mark Fidrych 3.00 8.00

2006 eTopps Classic

67 Tony Gwynn 5.00 12.00
68 Steve Carlton 3.00 8.00
69 Bo Jackson 4.00 10.00
70 Mickey Mantle 4.00 10.00
71 Ted Williams 4.00 10.00

2005 eTopps Classic Events

CE1 Bobby Thomson 2.50 6.00
CE2 Don Larsen 3.00 8.00
CE3 Bill Mazeroski 3.00 8.00
CE4 Bucky Dent 3.00 8.00
CE5 George Brett 3.00 8.00
CE6 Dwight Gooden 4.00 10.00
CE7 Bob Gibson 4.00 10.00
CE8 1989 World Series 2.50 6.00
CE9 Kirk Gibson 3.00 8.00
CE10 Reggie Jackson 4.00 10.00
CE11 Carlton Fisk 3.00 8.00
CE12 Mookie Wilson 3.00 8.00
CE13 Yogi Berra 3.00 8.00
CE14 Cal Ripken 5.00 12.00
CE15 Denny Mclain 4.00 10.00
CE16 Josh Gibson 3.00 8.00
CE17 Barry Bonds 4.00 10.00
CE18 Joe Carter 4.00 10.00
CE19 Nolan Ryan 4.00 10.00
CE20 Rickey Henderson 4.00 10.00

2006 eTopps Classic Events

21 Mickey Mantle/1499 * 5.00 12.00

2002 eTopps Event Series

ES1 Mike Cameron/5000* 2.00 5.00
ES2 Shawn Green/5000* 2.00 5.00
ES4 Oakland A's/5000* 2.00 5.00
ES5 Greg Maddux/3851* 2.50 6.00

2003 eTopps Event Series

ES9 Rafael Palmeiro/1633* 2.50 6.00
ES10 Roger Clemens/3418* 2.50 6.00
ES11 Barry Bonds/2649* 2.50 6.00
ES13 Carlos Delgado/630* 2.50 6.00

2009 eTopps Event Series

NYY27 New York Yankees/999 * 3.00 8.00

2004 eTopps ECON Cleveland

1 Bob Lemon/978* 2.00 5.00

2004 eTopps Event Series Playoffs

ISSUED DIRECT VIA ETOPPS WEBSITE
PRINT RUNS B/WN 983-2565 COPIES PER
1 A.Rod/C.Schilling/1500 3.00 8.00
2 C.Beltran/A.Pujols/1298 2.50 6.00
3 H.Matsui/M.Rivera/1294 2.50 6.00
4 Carlos Beltran/1427 2.00 5.00
5 J.Kent/D.Ortiz/1126 2.50 6.00
6 Jim Edmonds/983 2.50 6.00
7 D.Lowe/J.Damon/2116 2.00 5.00
8 S.Rolen/A.Pujols/1119 2.50 6.00
9 M.Belhorn/C.Schilling/1173 2.50 6.00
10 Pedro Martinez/1250 2.50 6.00
11 Derek Lowe/2565 2.50 6.00
12 Manny Ramirez/1500 2.50 6.00

2007 eTopps National Convention Cards That Never Were

254 Stan Musial 54T 1.25 3.00
408 Joe DiMaggio 52T 1.50 4.00
409 Ted Williams 52T 1.50 4.00
610 Nolan Ryan 67T 2.50 6.00
133T Ryne Sandberg 83TT 1.50 4.00

2005 eTopps Season Events

1 NL Transactions/862 * 2.00 5.00
2 AL Transactions/977 * 2.00 5.00
3 Opening Day/1000 * 2.50 6.00
4 David Ortiz/1000 * 2.50 6.00
5 David Wright/1000 * 2.50 6.00
6 Alex Rodriguez/1000 * 3.00 8.00
7 Derrek Lee/1000 * 2.00 5.00
8 Alex Rodriguez/1000 * 2.50 6.00
9 Nationals Win 10 In A Row/678 * 2.50 6.00
10 Bobby Abreu/800 * 2.50 6.00
11 Miguel Tejada/642 * 2.50 6.00
12 Rafael Palmeiro/1000 * 2.50 6.00
13 Greg Maddux/1000 * 2.50 6.00
14 Houston Astros/650 * 2.50 6.00
15 Tony LaRussa/550 * 4.00 10.00
16 Jeremy Hermida/760 * 2.50 6.00
17 Houston Marathon/1000 * 2.50 6.00
18 Complete Series/840 * 2.50 6.00
19 Houston Astros/579 * 2.50 6.00
20 Chicago White Sox/1000 * 2.50 6.00
21 Jermaine Dye/746 * 2.50 6.00

2009-10 eTopps T206 Tribute

1 Ernie Banks/749 * 8.00 20.00
2 Jackie Robinson/749 * 8.00 20.00
3 Babe Ruth/749 * 10.00 25.00
4 Lou Gehrig/749 * 8.00 20.00
5 Cy Young/749 * 6.00 15.00
6 Stan Musial/749 * 8.00 20.00
7 Mickey Mantle/749 * 20.00 50.00
8 Cal Ripken/749 * 10.00 25.00
9 Honus Wagner/749 * 20.00 50.00
10 Nolan Ryan/749 * 10.00 25.00
11 Yogi Berra/749 * 5.00 12.00
12 Mike Schmidt/749 * 8.00 20.00
13 Albert Pujols/749 * 15.00 40.00
14 Ichiro Suzuki/749 * 8.00 20.00
15 Tom Seaver/749 * 8.00 20.00
16 Eddie Murray/749 * 6.00 15.00
17 Rogers Hornsby/749 * 5.00 12.00
18 Derek Jeter/999 * 8.00 20.00
19 Al Kaline/749 * 5.00 12.00
20 Bob Feller/749 * 5.00 12.00
21 Alex Rodriguez/999 * 5.00 12.00
22 Jimmie Foxx/749 * 5.00 12.00
23 Christy Mathewson/749 *
24 Ozzie Smith/749 *
25 Mordecai Brown/749 *
26 Andre Dawson/749 *
27 Carl Yastrzemski/749 *
28 Phil Rizzuto/749 *
29 Willie Keeler/749 *
30 Johnny Bench/749 *
31 Roger Maris/749 *
32 Kid Elberfeld/749 *
33 Rickey Henderson/749 *

2009 eTopps World Baseball Classic

1A Yu Darvish/999 * 8.00 20.00
1B Yu Darvish/699 * 8.00 20.00
2 David Wright/999 * 4.00 10.00
3 Jin Young Lee/749 * 2.50 6.00
4 Frederich Cepeda/749 * 2.50 6.00
5 Derek Jeter/999 * 4.00 10.00
6 Yulieski Gourriel/749 * 2.50 6.00
7 Gift Ngoepe/749 * 3.00 8.00
8 Norichika Aoki/749 * 3.00 8.00
9 Ichiro Suzuki/749 * 5.00 12.00
10 Dae Ho Lee/749 * 2.50 6.00
11 Hisashi Iwakuma/999 * 2.50 6.00
12 Tae Kyun Kim/749 * 2.50 6.00
13 Japan Patch/505 * 15.00 40.00

1949 Eureka Stamps

This set features National League players only. Apparently the promotion was not successful enough to warrant continuing on to do the American League, even though it was pre-announced in the back of the stamp album. Album is available to house the stamps. The album measures 7 1/2" by 9 1/4" whereas the individual stamps measure approximately 1 1/2" by 2". The stamps are numbered and are in full color. The album and stamp numbering is organized by teams (and alphabetically within teams), e.g., Boston Braves (3-27), Brooklyn Dodgers (28-51), Chicago Cubs (52-75), Cincinnati Reds (76-100), New York Giants (101-126), Philadelphia Phillies (127-151), Pittsburgh Pirates (152-176) and St. Louis Cardinals (177-200). At the bottom of the stamp the player's name is given in a narrow yellow strip.

COMPLETE SET (200) 250.00 500.00
1 Happy Chandler COMM 2.50 5.00
2 Ford Frick PRES 2.50 5.00
3 Johnny Antonelli 1.00 2.00
4 Red Barrett .75 1.50
5 Clint Conaster .75 1.50
6 Alvin Dark 1.50 3.00
7 Bob Elliott 1.00 2.00
8 Glenn Elliott .75 1.50
9 Elbie Fletcher .75 1.50
10 Bob Hall .75 1.50
11 Jeff Heath .75 1.50
12 Bobby Hogue .75 1.50
13 Tommy Holmes 1.00 2.00
14 Al Lakeman .75 1.50
15 Phil Masi .75 1.50
16 Nelson Potter .75 1.50
17 Pete Reiser 1.50 3.00
18 Rick Rickert .75 1.50
19 Connie Ryan .75 1.50
20 Jim Russell .75 1.50
21 Johnny Sain 1.50 3.00
22 Bill Salkeld .75 1.50
23 Sibby Sisti .75 1.50
24 Billy Southworth MG .75 1.50
25 Warren Spahn 7.50 15.00
26 Eddie Stanky 1.25 2.50
27 Bill Voiselle .75 1.50
28 Jack Banta .75 1.50
29 Rex Barney 1.00 2.00
30 Ralph Branca 1.50 3.00
31 Tommy Brown .75 1.50
32 Roy Campanella 10.00 20.00
33 Billy Cox 1.00 2.00
34 Bruce Edwards .75 1.50
35 Carl Furillo 2.50 5.00
36 Joe Hatten .75 1.50
37 Gene Hermanski .75 1.50
38 Gil Hodges 5.00 10.00
39 Johnny Jorgensen .75 1.50
40 Lefty Martin .75 1.50
41 Mike McCormick .75 1.50
42 Eddie Miksis .75 1.50
43 Paul Minner .75 1.50
44 Sam Narron .75 1.50
45 Don Newcombe 2.50 5.00
46 Jake Pitler CO .75 1.50
47 Pee Wee Reese 7.50 15.00
48 Jackie Robinson 15.00 30.00
49 Burt Shotton MG .75 1.50
50 Duke Snider 10.00 20.00
51 Dick Whitman .75 1.50
52 Smoky Burgess 1.00 2.00
53 Phil Cavarretta 1.00 2.00
54 Bob Chipman .75 1.50
55 Walt Dubiel .75 1.50
56 Hank Edwards .75 1.50
57 Frankie Gustine .75 1.50
58 Hal Jeffcoat .75 1.50
59 Emil Kush .75 1.50
60 Doyle Lade .75 1.50
61 Dutch Leonard .75 1.50
62 Peanuts Lowrey .75 1.50
63 Gene Mauch 1.25 2.50
64 Cal McLish .75 1.50
65 Rube Novotney .75 1.50
66 Andy Pafko 1.00 2.00
67 Bob Ramazzotti .75 1.50
68 Herman Reich .75 1.50
69 Bob Rush .75 1.50
70 Johnny Schmitz .75 1.50
71 Bob Scheffing .75 1.50
72 Roy Smalley 1.00 2.00
73 Emil Verban .75 1.50
74 Al Walker .75 1.50
75 Harry Walker 1.00 2.00
76 Bobby Adams .75 1.50
77 Ewell Blackwell 1.25 2.50
78 Jimmy Bloodworth .75 1.50
79 Walker Cooper .75 1.50
80 Tony Cuccinello .75 1.50
81 Jess Dobernick .75 1.50
82 Eddie Erautt .75 1.50
83 Frank Fanovich .75 1.50
84 Howie Fox .75 1.50
85 Grady Hatton .75 1.50
86 Homer Howell .75 1.50
87 Ted Kluszewski 2.50 5.00
88 Danny Litwhiler .75 1.50
89 Everett Lively .75 1.50
90 Lloyd Merriman .75 1.50
91 Phil Page .75 1.50
92 Kent Peterson .75 1.50
93 Ken Raffensberger .75 1.50
94 Luke Sewell CO 1.00 2.00
95 Virgil Stallcup .75 1.50
96 John Vander Meer 1.50 3.00
97 Bucky Walters MG 1.25 2.50
98 Herman Wehmeier .75 1.50
99 Johnny Wyrostek .75 1.50
100 Benny Zientara .75 1.50
101 Hank Behrman .75 1.50
102 Leo Durocher MG 2.50 5.00
103 Augie Galan .75 1.50
104 Sid Gordon .75 1.50
105 Bert Haas .75 1.50
106 Andy Hansen .75 1.50
107 Clint Hartung 1.00 2.00
108 Kirby Higbe .75 1.50
109 George Hausman .75 1.50
110 Larry Jansen 1.00 2.00
111 Sheldon Jones .75 1.50
112 Monte Kennedy .75 1.50
113 Buddy Kerr .75 1.50
114 Dave Koslo .75 1.50
115 Joe Lafata .75 1.50
116 Whitey Lockman 1.00 2.00
117 Jack Lohrke .75 1.50
118 Willard Marshall .75 1.50
119 Bill Milne .75 1.50
120 Johnny Mize 5.00 10.00
121 Don Mueller 1.25 2.50
122 Ray Mueller .75 1.50
123 Bill Rigney 1.00 2.00
124 Bobby Thomson 1.50 3.00
125 Sam Webb .75 1.50
126 Wes Westrum 1.00 2.00
127 Richie Ashburn 5.00 10.00
128 Bennie Bengough CO .75 1.50
129 Charlie Bicknell .75 1.50
130 Buddy Blattner .75 1.50
131 Hank Borowy .75 1.50
132 Ralph Caballero .75 1.50
133 Blix Donnelly .75 1.50
134 Del Ennis 1.00 2.00
135 Granville Hamner 1.00 2.00
136 Ken Heintzelman .75 1.50
137 Stan Hollmig .75 1.50
138 Willie Jones .75 1.50
139 Jim Konstanty 1.25 2.50
140 Stan Lopata .75 1.50
141 Jackie Mayo .75 1.50
142 Bill Nicholson 1.00 2.00
143 Robin Roberts 5.00 10.00
144 Schoolboy Rowe 1.25 2.50
145 Eddie Sawyer MG 1.00 2.00
146 Andy Seminick .75 1.50
147 Ken Silvestri .75 1.50
148 Curt Simmons 1.25 2.50
149 Dick Sisler 1.00 2.00
150 Ken Trinkle .75 1.50
151 Eddie Waitkus 1.00 2.00
152 Romanus Basgall .75 1.50
153 Eddie Bockman .75 1.50
154 Ernie Bonham .75 1.50
155 Hugh Casey 1.00 2.00
156 Pete Castiglione .75 1.50
157 Cliff Chambers .75 1.50
158 Murry Dickson .75 1.50
159 Ed Fitzgerald .75 1.50
160 Les Fleming .75 1.50
161 Hal Gregg .75 1.50
162 Goldie Holt .75 1.50
163 Johnny Hopp 1.00 2.00
164 Ralph Kiner 5.00 10.00
165 Vic Lombardi .75 1.50
166 Clyde McCullough .75 1.50
167 Bill Meyer MG 1.00 2.00
168 Danny Murtaugh 1.00 2.00
169 Barnacle Bill Posedel .75 1.50
170 Elmer Riddle .75 1.50
171 Stan Rojek .75 1.50
172 Rip Sewell 1.00 2.00
173 Eddie Stevens .75 1.50
174 Dixie Walker 1.00 2.00
175 Bill Werle .75 1.50
176 Wally Westlake .75 1.50
177 Bill Baker .75 1.50
178 Al Brazle .75 1.50
179 Harry Brecheen 1.00 2.00
180 Chuck Diering .75 1.50
181 Eddie Dyer MG 1.00 2.00
182 Joe Garagiola 5.00 10.00
183 Tom Glaviano .75 1.50
184 Jim Hearn .75 1.50
185 Ken Johnson .75 1.50
186 Nippy Jones .75 1.50
187 Ed Kazak .75 1.50
188 Lou Klein .75 1.50
189 Marty Marion 1.50 3.00
190 George Munger .75 1.50
191 Stan Musial 12.50 25.00
192 Spike Nelson .75 1.50
193 Howie Pollet .75 1.50
194 Bill Reeder .75 1.50
195 Del Rice .75 1.50
196 Ed Sauer .75 1.50
197 Red Schoendienst 4.00 8.00
198 Enos Slaughter 5.00 10.00
199 Ted Wilks .75 1.50
200 Ray Yochim .75 1.50
XX Album

1997 E-X2000

This 100-card set (produced by Fleer/SkyBox) was distributed in two-card foil packs with a suggested retail price of $3.99. An oversized Alex Rodriguez card shipped in its own holder was mailed to dealers who ordered E-X 2000 cases. They are numbered out of 3,000 and priced below. Also priced below is the redemption card for a baseball signed by Rodriguez. 100 of these cards were produced and the redemption deadline was May 1, 1998.

COMPLETE SET (100) 30.00 80.00
A.ROD BALL EXCH.RANDOM IN PACKS
A.ROD.BASEBALL EXCH: 05/01/98
1 Jim Edmonds .30 .75
2 Darin Erstad .30 .75
3 Eddie Murray .75 2.00
4 Roberto Alomar .50 1.25
5 Brady Anderson .30 .75
6 Mike Mussina .50 1.25
7 Rafael Palmeiro .50 1.25
8 Cal Ripken 2.50 6.00
9 Steve Avery .30 .75
10 Nomar Garciaparra 1.25 3.00
11 Mo Vaughn .30 .75
12 Albert Belle .30 .75
13 Mike Cameron .30 .75
14 Ray Durham .30 .75
15 Frank Thomas .75 2.00
16 Robin Ventura .30 .75
17 Manny Ramirez .50 1.25
18 Jim Thome .50 1.25
19 Matt Williams .30 .75
20 Tony Clark .30 .75
21 Travis Fryman .30 .75
22 Bob Higginson .30 .75
23 Kevin Appier .30 .75
24 Johnny Damon .50 1.25
25 Jermaine Dye .30 .75
26 Jeff Cirillo .30 .75
27 Ben McDonald .30 .75
28 Chuck Knoblauch .30 .75
29 Paul Molitor .30 .75
30 Todd Walker .30 .75
31 Wade Boggs .50 1.25
32 Cecil Fielder .30 .75
33 Derek Jeter 2.00 5.00
34 Andy Pettitte .50 1.25
35 Ruben Rivera .30 .75
36 Bernie Williams .50 1.25
37 Jose Canseco .50 1.25
38 Mark McGwire 2.00 5.00
39 Jay Buhner .30 .75
40 Ken Griffey Jr. 1.50 4.00
41 Randy Johnson .75 2.00
42 Edgar Martinez .50 1.25
43 Alex Rodriguez 1.25 3.00
44 Dan Wilson .30 .75
45 Will Clark .50 1.25
46 Juan Gonzalez .30 .75
47 Ivan Rodriguez .50 1.25
48 Joe Carter .30 .75
49 Roger Clemens 1.50 4.00
50 Juan Guzman .30 .75
51 Pat Hentgen .30 .75
52 Tom Glavine .50 1.25
53 Andruw Jones .50 1.25
54 Chipper Jones .75 2.00
55 Ryan Klesko .30 .75
56 Kenny Lofton .30 .75
57 Greg Maddux 1.25 3.00
58 Fred McGriff .50 1.25
59 John Smoltz .50 1.25
60 Mark Wohlers .30 .75
61 Mark Grace .50 1.25
62 Ryne Sandberg 1.25 3.00
63 Sammy Sosa .75 2.00
64 Barry Larkin .50 1.25
65 Deion Sanders .50 1.25
66 Reggie Sanders .30 .75
67 Dante Bichette .30 .75
68 Ellis Burks .30 .75
69 Andres Galarraga .30 .75
70 Moises Alou .30 .75
71 Kevin Brown .30 .75
72 Cliff Floyd .30 .75
73 Edgar Renteria .30 .75
74 Gary Sheffield .30 .75
75 Bob Abreu .50 1.25
76 Jeff Bagwell .50 1.25
77 Craig Biggio .50 1.25
78 Todd Hollandsworth .30 .75
79 Eric Karros .30 .75
80 Raul Mondesi .30 .75
81 Hideo Nomo .75 2.00
82 Mike Piazza 1.25 3.00
83 Vladimir Guerrero .75 2.00
84 Henry Rodriguez .30 .75
85 Todd Hundley .30 .75
86 Alex Ochoa .30 .75
87 Rey Ordonez .30 .75
88 Gregg Jefferies .30 .75
89 Scott Rolen .50 1.25
90 Jermaine Allensworth .30 .75
91 Jason Kendall .30 .75
92 Ken Caminiti .30 .75
93 Tony Gwynn 1.00 2.50
94 Rickey Henderson .75 2.00
95 Barry Bonds 2.00 5.00
96 J.T. Snow .30 .75
97 Dennis Eckersley .30 .75
98 Ron Gant .30 .75
99 Brian Jordan .30 .75
100 Ray Lankford .30 .75
101 Checklist (1-74) .30 .75
102 Checklist (75-102 inserts) .30 .75
P43 Alex Rodriguez Promo Strip .60 1.50
S43 Alex Rodriguez Sample/3000 4.00 10.00
NNO A.Rod AU Ball/100 6.00 15.00

1997 E-X2000 Credentials

*STARS: 3X TO 8X BASIC CARDS
RANDOM INSERTS IN PACKS
STATED PRINT RUN 299 SERIAL #'d SETS

1997 E-X2000 Essential Credentials

*STARS: 8X TO 20X BASIC CARDS
RANDOM INSERTS IN PACKS
STATED PRINT RUN 99 SERIAL #'d SETS

1997 E-X2000 A Cut Above

COMPLETE SET (10) 150.00 300.00
STATED ODDS 1:288
1 Frank Thomas 40.00 100.00
2 Ken Griffey Jr. 150.00 250.00
3 Alex Rodriguez 8.00 20.00
4 Albert Belle 2.50 6.00
5 Juan Gonzalez 2.50 6.00
6 Mark McGwire 10.00 25.00
7 Mo Vaughn 2.50 6.00
8 Manny Ramirez 4.00 10.00
9 Barry Bonds 10.00 25.00
10 Fred McGriff 4.00 10.00

1997 E-X2000 Emerald Autographs

ONE CARD VIA MAIL PER EXCH.CARD
*EXCH.CARDS: .1X TO .25X BASIC AUTO
EXCH.CARDS STATED ODDS 1:500 PACKS
2 Darin Erstad 6.00 15.00
30 Todd Walker 6.00 15.00
43 Alex Rodriguez 60.00 120.00
78 Todd Hollandsworth 6.00 15.00
86 Alex Ochoa 6.00 15.00
89 Scott Rolen 10.00 25.00

1997 E-X2000 Hall or Nothing

COMPLETE SET (20) 60.00 120.00
STATED ODDS 1:20
1 Frank Thomas 2.00 5.00
2 Ken Griffey Jr. 4.00 10.00
3 Eddie Murray 2.00 5.00
4 Cal Ripken 6.00 15.00
5 Ryne Sandberg 3.00 8.00
6 Wade Boggs 1.25 3.00
7 Roger Clemens 4.00 10.00
8 Tony Gwynn 2.50 6.00
9 Alex Rodriguez 3.00 8.00
10 Mark McGwire 5.00 12.00
11 Barry Bonds 5.00 12.00
12 Greg Maddux 3.00 8.00
13 Juan Gonzalez .75 2.00
14 Albert Belle .75 2.00
15 Mike Piazza 3.00 8.00
16 Jeff Bagwell 1.25 3.00
17 Dennis Eckersley .75 2.00
18 Mo Vaughn .75 2.00
19 Roberto Alomar 1.25 3.00
20 Kenny Lofton .75 2.00

1997 E-X2000 Star Date 2000

COMPLETE SET (15) 12.50 30.00
STATED ODDS 1:9
1 Alex Rodriguez 2.00 5.00
2 Andruw Jones .75 2.00
3 Andy Pettitte .75 2.00
4 Brooks Kieschnick .50 1.25
5 Chipper Jones 1.25 3.00
6 Darin Erstad .50 1.25
7 Derek Jeter 3.00 8.00
8 Jason Kendall .50 1.25
9 Jermaine Dye .50 1.25
10 Neifi Perez .50 1.25
11 Scott Rolen .75 2.00
12 Todd Hollandsworth .50 1.25
13 Todd Walker .50 1.25
14 Tony Clark .50 1.25
15 Vladimir Guerrero 1.25 3.00

1998 E-X2001 Rodriguez Hawaii XIII Promo

This card was distributed to industry leaders at the 13th Annual Hawaii Trade Show in late February, 1998. It previewed the upcoming 1998 E-X2001 baseball release. A small gold foil "Hawaii XIII" stamp with a palm tree on the left-hand side of the card front distinguishes the card. According to informed sources, Fleer/SkyBox produced approximately 200 of these cards.

NNO Alex Rodriguez 10.00 25.00

1998 E-X2001

The 1998 E-X2001 set (made by Fleer/SkyBox) was issued in one series totalling 100 cards and distributed exclusively to hobby outlets. Cards were issued in two-card packs carrying a $3.99 suggested retail price. The cards are stunningly attractive, featuring full color action shots printed on clear acetate stock with sparkling foil backgrounds. An unnumbered Kerry Wood exchange card was randomly seeded into 1 in every 50 packs (the same pull rate as any other basic issue card). Unlike the acetate stock basic cards, this Wood exchange card was printed on paper stock and could be redeemed until March 31st, 1999 for a real E-X2001 acetate stock Wood card (number 101). In addition, an Alex Rodriguez sample card was issued a few months prior to the product's release. This sample card was distributed to dealers and hobby media to preview the upcoming release. The card is identical to a standard Alex Rodriguex E-X2001 except for the text "PROMOTIONAL SAMPLE" printed diagonally across the card back. There are no key Rookie Cards in this set.

COMPLETE SET (100) 30.00 80.00
K.WOOD EXCHANGE STATED ODDS 1:50
K.WOOD EXCH.DEADLINE 3/31/99
COMP.SET EXCLUDES WOOD EXCHANGE
COMP.SET EXCLUDES REDEMPTION 101
1 Alex Rodriguez 1.25 3.00
2 Barry Bonds 2.00 5.00
3 Greg Maddux 1.25 3.00
4 Roger Clemens 1.50 4.00
5 Juan Gonzalez .30 .75
6 Chipper Jones .75 2.00
7 Derek Jeter 2.00 5.00
8 Frank Thomas .75 2.00
9 Cal Ripken 2.50 6.00
10 Ken Griffey Jr. 1.50 4.00
11 Mark McGwire 2.00 5.00
12 Hideo Nomo .75 2.00
13 Tony Gwynn 1.00 2.50
14 Ivan Rodriguez .50 1.25
15 Mike Piazza 1.25 3.00
16 Roberto Alomar .50 1.25
17 Jeff Bagwell .50 1.25
18 Andruw Jones .50 1.25
19 Albert Belle .30 .75
20 Mo Vaughn .30 .75
21 Kenny Lofton .30 .75
22 Gary Sheffield .30 .75
23 Tony Clark .20 .50
24 Mike Mussina .50 1.25
25 Barry Larkin .50 1.25
26 Moises Alou .30 .75
27 Brady Anderson .30 .75
28 Andy Pettitte .50 1.25
29 Sammy Sosa .75 2.00
30 Raul Mondesi .30 .75
31 Andres Galarraga .30 .75
32 Chuck Knoblauch .30 .75
33 Jim Thome .50 1.25
34 Craig Biggio .50 1.25
35 Jay Buhner .30 .75
36 Rafael Palmeiro .50 1.25
37 Curt Schilling .30 .75
38 Tino Martinez .50 1.25
39 Pedro Martinez .50 1.25
40 Jose Canseco .50 1.25
41 Jeff Cirillo .20 .50
42 Dean Palmer .30 .75
43 Tim Salmon .50 1.25
44 Jason Giambi .30 .75
45 Bobby Higginson .30 .75
46 Jim Edmonds .30 .75
47 David Justice .30 .75
48 John Olerud .30 .75
49 Ray Lankford .30 .75
50 Al Martin .20 .50
51 Mike Lieberthal .30 .75
52 Henry Rodriguez .20 .50
53 Edgar Renteria .30 .75
54 Eric Karros .30 .75
55 Marquis Grissom .30 .75
56 Wilson Alvarez .20 .50
57 Darryl Kile .30 .75
58 Jeff King .20 .50
59 Shawn Estes .20 .50
60 Tony Womack .20 .50
61 Willie Greene .20 .50
62 Ken Caminiti .30 .75
63 Vinny Castilla .30 .75
64 Mark Grace .50 1.25
65 Ryan Klesko .30 .75
66 Robin Ventura .30 .75
67 Todd Hundley .20 .50
68 Travis Fryman .30 .75
69 Edgar Martinez .50 1.25
70 Matt Williams .30 .75
71 Paul Molitor .30 .75
72 Kevin Brown .50 1.25
73 Randy Johnson .75 2.00
74 Bernie Williams .50 1.25
75 Manny Ramirez .50 1.25
76 Fred McGriff .50 1.25
77 Tom Glavine .50 1.25
78 Carlos Delgado .30 .75
79 Larry Walker .30 .75
80 Hideki Irabu .20 .50
81 Ryan McGuire .20 .50
82 Justin Thompson .20 .50
83 Kevin Orie .20 .50
84 Jon Nunnally .20 .50
85 Mark Kotsay .30 .75
86 Todd Walker .20 .50
87 Jason Dickson .20 .50
88 Fernando Tatis .20 .50
89 Karim Garcia .20 .50
90 Ricky Ledee .20 .50
91 Paul Konerko .30 .75

92 Jaret Wright .20 .50
93 Darin Erstad .30 .75
94 Livan Hernandez .30 .75
95 Nomar Garciaparra 1.25 3.00
96 Jose Cruz Jr. .20 .50
97 Scott Rolen .50 1.25
98 Ben Grieve .20 .50
99 Vladimir Guerrero .75 2.00
100 Travis Lee .20 .50
101 Kerry Wood 1.50 4.00
NNO Kerry Wood .75 2.00
NNO Alex Rodriguez Sample .60 1.50

1998 E-X2001 Essential Credentials Future

RANDOM INSERTS IN PACKS
PRINT RUNS IN PARENTHESES BELOW
CARDS 76-100 TOO SCARCE TO PRICE
1 Alex Rodriguez/100 25.00 60.00
2 Barry Bonds/99 40.00 100.00
3 Greg Maddux/98 40.00 100.00
4 Roger Clemens/97 30.00 80.00
5 Juan Gonzalez/96 10.00 25.00
6 Chipper Jones/95 15.00 40.00
7 Derek Jeter/94 300.00 500.00
8 Frank Thomas/93 15.00 40.00
9 Cal Ripken/92 50.00 120.00
10 Ken Griffey Jr./91 300.00 500.00
11 Mark McGwire/90 40.00 100.00
12 Hideo Nomo/89 15.00 40.00
13 Tony Gwynn/88 20.00 50.00
14 Ivan Rodriguez/87 10.00 25.00
15 Mike Piazza/86 25.00 60.00
16 Roberto Alomar/85 10.00 25.00
17 Jeff Bagwell/84 10.00 25.00
18 Andruw Jones/83 10.00 25.00
19 Albert Belle/82 10.00 25.00
20 Mo Vaughn/81 10.00 25.00
21 Kenny Lofton/80 10.00 25.00
22 Gary Sheffield/79 10.00 25.00
23 Tony Clark/78 6.00 15.00
24 Mike Mussina/77 10.00 25.00
25 Barry Larkin/76 10.00 25.00
26 Moises Alou/75 10.00 25.00
27 Brady Anderson/74 10.00 25.00
28 Andy Pettitte/73 10.00 25.00
29 Sammy Sosa/72 15.00 40.00
30 Raul Mondesi/71 10.00 25.00
31 Andres Galarraga/70 10.00 25.00
32 Chuck Knoblauch/69 8.00 20.00
33 Jim Thome/68 12.50 30.00
34 Craig Biggio/67 12.50 30.00
35 Jay Buhner/66 8.00 20.00
36 Rafael Palmeiro/65 12.50 30.00
37 Curt Schilling/64 8.00 20.00
38 Tino Martinez/63 12.50 30.00
39 Pedro Martinez/62 12.50 30.00
40 Jose Canseco/61 12.50 30.00
41 Jeff Cirillo/60 5.00 12.00
42 Dean Palmer/59 8.00 20.00
43 Tim Salmon/58 12.50 30.00
44 Jason Giambi/57 8.00 20.00
45 Bobby Higginson/56 8.00 20.00
46 Jim Edmonds/55 8.00 20.00
47 David Justice/54 8.00 20.00
48 John Olerud/53 8.00 20.00
49 Ray Lankford/52 8.00 20.00
50 Al Martin/51 5.00 12.00
51 Mike Lieberthal/50 10.00 25.00
52 Henry Rodriguez/49 6.00 15.00
53 Edgar Renteria/48 10.00 25.00
54 Eric Karros/47 10.00 25.00
55 Marquis Grissom/46 10.00 25.00
56 Wilson Alvarez/45 6.00 15.00
57 Darryl Kile/44 10.00 25.00
58 Jeff King/43 6.00 15.00
59 Shawn Estes/42 6.00 15.00
60 Tony Womack/41 6.00 15.00
61 Willie Greene/40 6.00 15.00
62 Ken Caminiti/39 10.00 25.00
63 Vinny Castilla/38 10.00 25.00
64 Mark Grace/37 15.00 40.00
65 Ryan Klesko/36 10.00 25.00
66 Robin Ventura/35 15.00 40.00
67 Todd Hundley/34 12.50 30.00
68 Travis Fryman/33 15.00 40.00
69 Edgar Martinez/32 20.00 50.00
70 Matt Williams/31 15.00 40.00
71 Paul Molitor/30 15.00 40.00
72 Kevin Brown/29 20.00 50.00
73 Randy Johnson/28 30.00 80.00
74 Bernie Williams/27 20.00 50.00
75 Manny Ramirez/26 20.00 50.00
76 Fred McGriff/25
77 Tom Glavine/24
78 Carlos Delgado/23
79 Larry Walker/22
80 Hideki Irabu/21
81 Ryan McGuire/20
82 Justin Thompson/19
83 Kevin Orie/18
84 Jon Nunnally/17
85 Mark Kotsay/16
86 Todd Walker/15
87 Jason Dickson/14
88 Fernando Tatis/13
89 Karim Garcia/12
90 Ricky Ledee/11
91 Paul Konerko/10
92 Jaret Wright/9
93 Darin Erstad/8
94 Livan Hernandez/7
95 Nomar Garciaparra/6
96 Jose Cruz Jr./5
97 Scott Rolen/4
98 Ben Grieve/3
99 Vladimir Guerrero/2
100 Travis Lee/1

1998 E-X2001 Essential Credentials Now

RANDOM INSERTS IN PACKS
PRINT RUNS IN PARENTHESES BELOW
CARDS 1-25 NOT PRICED DUE TO SCARCITY
1 Alex Rodriguez/1
2 Barry Bonds/2
3 Greg Maddux/3
4 Roger Clemens/4
5 Juan Gonzalez/5
6 Chipper Jones/6
7 Derek Jeter (7)
8 Frank Thomas/8
9 Cal Ripken/9
10 Ken Griffey Jr./10
11 Mark McGwire/11
12 Hideo Nomo/12
13 Tony Gwynn/13
14 Ivan Rodriguez/14
15 Mike Piazza/15
16 Roberto Alomar/16
17 Jeff Bagwell/17
18 Andruw Jones/18
19 Albert Belle/19
20 Mo Vaughn/20
21 Kenny Lofton/21
22 Gary Sheffield/22
23 Tony Clark/23
24 Mike Mussina/24
25 Barry Larkin/25
26 Moises Alou/26 30.00 80.00
27 Brady Anderson/27 30.00 80.00
28 Andy Pettitte/28 40.00 100.00
29 Sammy Sosa/29 40.00 100.00
30 Raul Mondesi/30 30.00 80.00
31 Andres Galarraga/31 30.00 80.00
32 Chuck Knoblauch/32 30.00 80.00
33 Jim Thome/33 40.00 100.00
34 Craig Biggio/34 40.00 100.00
35 Jay Buhner/35 30.00 80.00
36 Rafael Palmeiro/36 30.00 80.00
37 Curt Schilling/37 20.00 50.00
38 Tino Martinez/38 30.00 80.00
39 Pedro Martinez/39 30.00 80.00
40 Jose Canseco/40 30.00 80.00
41 Jeff Cirillo/41 12.00 30.00
42 Dean Palmer/42 20.00 50.00
43 Tim Salmon/43 30.00 80.00
44 Jason Giambi/44 20.00 50.00
45 Bobby Higginson/45 20.00 50.00
46 Jim Edmonds/46 20.00 50.00
47 David Justice/47 20.00 50.00
48 John Olerud/48 20.00 50.00
49 Ray Lankford/49 20.00 50.00
50 Al Martin/50 12.00 30.00
51 Mike Lieberthal/51 15.00 40.00
52 Henry Rodriguez/52 10.00 25.00
53 Edgar Renteria/53 15.00 40.00
54 Eric Karros/54 15.00 40.00
55 Marquis Grissom/55 15.00 40.00
56 Wilson Alvarez/56 10.00 25.00
57 Darryl Kile/57 15.00 40.00
58 Jeff King/58 10.00 25.00
59 Shawn Estes/59 10.00 25.00
60 Tony Womack/60 10.00 25.00
61 Willie Greene/61 10.00 25.00
62 Ken Caminiti/62 15.00 40.00
63 Vinny Castilla/63 15.00 40.00
64 Mark Grace/64 20.00 50.00
65 Ryan Klesko/65 15.00 40.00
66 Robin Ventura/66 15.00 40.00
67 Todd Hundley/67 10.00 25.00
68 Travis Fryman/68 15.00 40.00
69 Edgar Martinez/69 20.00 50.00
70 Matt Williams/70 15.00 40.00
71 Paul Molitor/71 12.00 30.00
72 Kevin Brown/72 20.00 50.00
73 Randy Johnson/73 30.00 80.00
74 Bernie Williams/74 20.00 50.00
75 Manny Ramirez/75 30.00 80.00
76 Fred McGriff/76 20.00 50.00
77 Tom Glavine/77 20.00 50.00
78 Carlos Delgado/78 12.00 30.00
79 Larry Walker/79 12.00 30.00
80 Hideki Irabu/80 8.00 20.00
81 Ryan McGuire/81 8.00 20.00
82 Justin Thompson/82 8.00 20.00
83 Kevin Orie/83 8.00 20.00
84 Jon Nunnally/84 8.00 20.00
85 Mark Kotsay/85 12.00 30.00
86 Todd Walker/86 8.00 20.00
87 Jason Dickson/87 8.00 20.00
88 Fernando Tatis/88 8.00 20.00
89 Karim Garcia/89 8.00 20.00
90 Ricky Ledee/90 8.00 20.00
91 Paul Konerko/91 12.00 30.00
92 Jaret Wright/92 8.00 20.00
93 Darin Erstad/93 12.00 30.00
94 Livan Hernandez/94 12.00 30.00
95 Nomar Garciaparra/95 50.00 120.00
96 Jose Cruz Jr./96 8.00 20.00
97 Scott Rolen/97 20.00 50.00
98 Ben Grieve/98 8.00 20.00
99 Vladimir Guerrero/99 30.00 80.00
100 Travis Lee/100 8.00 20.00

1998 E-X2001 Cheap Seat Treats

COMPLETE SET (20) 40.00 100.00
STATED ODDS 1:24
1 Frank Thomas 3.00 8.00
2 Ken Griffey Jr. 6.00 15.00
3 Mark McGwire 8.00 20.00
4 Tino Martinez 2.00 5.00
5 Larry Walker 1.25 3.00
6 Juan Gonzalez 1.25 3.00
7 Mike Piazza 5.00 12.00
8 Jeff Bagwell 2.00 5.00
9 Tony Clark .75 2.00
10 Albert Belle 1.25 3.00
11 Andres Galarraga 1.25 3.00
12 Jim Thome 2.00 5.00
13 Mo Vaughn 1.25 3.00
14 Barry Bonds 8.00 20.00
15 Vladimir Guerrero 3.00 8.00
16 Scott Rolen 2.00 5.00
17 Travis Lee .75 2.00
18 David Justice 1.25 3.00
19 Jose Cruz Jr. .75 2.00
20 Andruw Jones 2.00 5.00

1998 E-X2001 Destination Cooperstown

STATED ODDS 1:720
1 Alex Rodriguez 12.00 30.00
2 Frank Thomas 10.00 25.00
3 Cal Ripken 30.00 80.00
4 Roger Clemens 12.00 30.00
5 Greg Maddux 12.00 30.00
6 Chipper Jones 10.00 25.00
7 Ken Griffey Jr. 75.00 200.00
8 Mark McGwire 15.00 40.00
9 Tony Gwynn 10.00 25.00
10 Mike Piazza 10.00 25.00
11 Jeff Bagwell 6.00 15.00
12 Jose Cruz Jr. 4.00 10.00
13 Derek Jeter 50.00 100.00
14 Hideo Nomo 10.00 25.00
15 Ivan Rodriguez 6.00 15.00

1998 E-X2001 Signature 2001

COMPLETE SET (17) 125.00 250.00
STATED ODDS 1:60
1 Ricky Ledee 4.00 10.00
2 Derrick Gibson 4.00 10.00
3 Mark Kotsay 6.00 15.00
4 Kevin Millwood 10.00 25.00
5 Brad Fullmer 4.00 10.00
6 Todd Walker 6.00 15.00
7 Ben Grieve 4.00 10.00
8 Tony Clark 4.00 10.00
9 Jaret Wright 4.00 10.00
10 Randall Simon 4.00 10.00
11 Paul Konerko 6.00 15.00
12 Todd Helton 6.00 15.00
13 David Ortiz 15.00 40.00
14 Alex Gonzalez 4.00 10.00
15 Bobby Estalella 4.00 10.00
16 Alex Rodriguez SP 50.00 100.00
17 Mike Lowell 12.50 30.00

1998 E-X2001 Star Date 2001

COMPLETE SET (15) 6.00 15.00
STATED ODDS 1:12
1 Travis Lee .40 1.00
2 Jose Cruz Jr. .40 1.00
3 Paul Konerko .40 1.00
4 Bobby Estalella .40 1.00
5 Magglio Ordonez 1.25 3.00
6 Juan Encarnacion .40 1.00
7 Richard Hidalgo .40 1.00
8 Abraham Nunez .40 1.00
9 Sean Casey .40 1.00
10 Todd Helton .60 1.50
11 Brad Fullmer .40 1.00
12 Ben Grieve .40 1.00
13 Livan Hernandez .40 1.00
14 Jaret Wright .40 1.00
15 Todd Dunwoody .40 1.00

1999 E-X Century

This 120-card set features color action player photos silhouetted on extra thick transparent plastic card stock. Each pack contained three cards and carried a suggested retail price of $5.99. The set contains a 30-card Rookie short-printed subset (91-120) with an insertion rate of 1:2 packs. A promotional sample card featuring Ben Grieve was distributed to dealer accounts and hobby media shortly before the product's national release. This card can be easily identified by the "PROMOTIONAL SAMPLE" text running across the back. Notable Rookie Cards include Pat Burrell.

COMPLETE SET (120) 15.00 40.00
COMP.SET w/o SP's (90) 8.00 20.00
COMMON CARD (1-90) .20 .50
COMMON SP (91-120) .40 1.00
SP STATED ODDS 1:2
1 Scott Rolen .30 .75
2 Nomar Garciaparra .30 .75
3 Mike Piazza .50 1.25
4 Tony Gwynn .50 1.25
5 Sammy Sosa .50 1.25
6 Alex Rodriguez .60 1.50
7 Vladimir Guerrero .30 .75
8 Chipper Jones .50 1.25
9 Derek Jeter 1.25 3.00
10 Kerry Wood .20 .50
11 Juan Gonzalez .20 .50
12 Frank Thomas .50 1.25
13 Mo Vaughn .20 .50
14 Greg Maddux .60 1.50
15 Jeff Bagwell .30 .75
16 Mark McGwire .75 2.00
17 Ken Griffey Jr. 1.00 2.50
18 Roger Clemens .60 1.50
19 Cal Ripken 1.50 4.00
20 Travis Lee .20 .50
21 Todd Helton .30 .75
22 Darin Erstad .20 .50
23 Pedro Martinez .30 .75
24 Barry Bonds .75 2.00
25 Andruw Jones .20 .50
26 Larry Walker .30 .75
27 Albert Belle .20 .50
28 Ivan Rodriguez .30 .75
29 Magglio Ordonez .30 .75
30 Andres Galarraga .30 .75
31 Mike Mussina .30 .75
32 Randy Johnson .50 1.25
33 Tom Glavine .30 .75
34 Barry Larkin .30 .75
35 Jim Thome .30 .75
36 Gary Sheffield .20 .50
37 Bernie Williams .30 .75
38 Carlos Delgado .20 .50
39 Rafael Palmeiro .30 .75
40 Edgar Renteria .20 .50
41 Brad Fullmer .20 .50
42 David Wells .20 .50
43 Dante Bichette .20 .50
44 Jaret Wright .20 .50
45 Ricky Ledee .20 .50
46 Ray Lankford .20 .50
47 Mark Grace .30 .75
48 Jeff Cirillo .20 .50
49 Rondell White .20 .50
50 Jeromy Burnitz .20 .50
51 Sean Casey .20 .50
52 Rolando Arrojo .20 .50
53 Jason Giambi .20 .50
54 John Olerud .20 .50
55 Will Clark .30 .75
56 Raul Mondesi .20 .50
57 Scott Brosius .20 .50
58 Bartolo Colon .20 .50
59 Steve Finley .20 .50
60 Javy Lopez .20 .50
61 Tim Salmon .20 .50
62 Roberto Alomar .30 .75
63 Vinny Castilla .20 .50
64 Craig Biggio .30 .75
65 Jose Guillen .20 .50
66 Greg Vaughn .20 .50
67 Jose Canseco .30 .75
68 Shawn Green .20 .50
69 Curt Schilling .20 .50
70 Orlando Hernandez .20 .50
71 Jose Cruz Jr. .20 .50
72 Alex Gonzalez .20 .50
73 Tino Martinez .20 .50
74 Todd Hundley .20 .50
75 Brian Giles .20 .50
76 Cliff Floyd .20 .50
77 Paul O'Neill .30 .75
78 Ken Caminiti .20 .50
79 Ron Gant .20 .50
80 Juan Encarnacion .20 .50
81 Ben Grieve .20 .50
82 Brian Jordan .20 .50
83 Rickey Henderson .50 1.25
84 Tony Clark .20 .50
85 Shannon Stewart .20 .50
86 Robin Ventura .20 .50
87 Todd Walker .20 .50
88 Kevin Brown .20 .50
89 Moises Alou .20 .50
90 Manny Ramirez .50 1.25
91 Gabe Alvarez SP .40 1.00
92 Jeremy Giambi SP .40 1.00
93 Adrian Beltre SP 1.00 2.50
94 George Lombard SP .40 1.00
95 Ryan Minor SP .40 1.00
96 Kevin Witt SP .40 1.00
97 Scott Hunter SP RC .40 1.00
98 Carlos Guillen SP .40 1.00
99 Derrick Gibson SP .40 1.00
100 Trot Nixon SP .40 1.00
101 Troy Glaus SP .40 1.00
102 Armando Rios SP .40 1.00
103 Preston Wilson SP .40 1.00
104 Pat Burrell SP RC 1.50 4.00
105 J.D. Drew SP .40 1.00
106 Bruce Chen SP .40 1.00
107 Matt Clement SP .40 1.00
108 Carlos Beltran SP .60 1.50
109 Carlos Febles SP .40 1.00
110 Rob Fick SP .40 1.00
111 Russell Branyan SP .40 1.00
112 Roosevelt Brown SP RC .40 1.00
113 Corey Koskie SP .40 1.00
114 Mario Encarnacion SP RC .40 1.00
115 Peter Tucci SP .40 1.00
116 Eric Chavez SP .40 1.00
117 Gabe Kapler SP .40 1.00
118 Marlon Anderson SP .40 1.00
119 A.J. Burnett SP RC .60 1.50
120 Ryan Bradley SP .40 1.00
P81 Ben Grieve Sample .40 1.00

1999 E-X Century Essential Credentials Future

RANDOM INSERTS IN PACKS
PRINT RUNS IN PARENTHESES BELOW
FUTURE CARDS FEATURE GOLD FOIL FRONTS
96-120 NOT PRICED DUE TO SCARCITY
1 Scott Rolen/120 6.00 15.00
2 Nomar Garciaparra/119 6.00 15.00
3 Mike Piazza/118 10.00 25.00
4 Tony Gwynn/117 10.00 25.00
5 Sammy Sosa/116 10.00 25.00
6 Alex Rodriguez/115 12.00 30.00
7 Vladimir Guerrero/114 6.00 15.00
8 Chipper Jones/113 10.00 25.00
9 Derek Jeter/112 25.00 60.00
10 Kerry Wood/111 4.00 10.00
11 Juan Gonzalez/110 4.00 10.00
12 Frank Thomas/109 10.00 25.00
13 Mo Vaughn/108 4.00 10.00
14 Greg Maddux/107 12.00 30.00
15 Jeff Bagwell/106 6.00 15.00
16 Mark McGwire/105 15.00 40.00
17 Ken Griffey Jr./104 125.00 300.00
18 Roger Clemens/103 12.00 30.00
19 Cal Ripken/102 30.00 80.00
20 Travis Lee/101 4.00 10.00
21 Todd Helton/100 8.00 20.00
22 Darin Erstad/99 5.00 12.00
23 Pedro Martinez/98 8.00 20.00
24 Barry Bonds/97 20.00 50.00
25 Andruw Jones/96 5.00 12.00
26 Larry Walker/95 8.00 20.00
27 Albert Belle/94 5.00 12.00
28 Ivan Rodriguez/93 8.00 20.00
29 Magglio Ordonez/92 8.00 20.00
30 Andres Galarraga/91 8.00 20.00
31 Mike Mussina/90 8.00 20.00
32 Randy Johnson/89 12.00 30.00
33 Tom Glavine/88 8.00 20.00
34 Barry Larkin/87 8.00 20.00
35 Jim Thome/86 8.00 20.00
36 Gary Sheffield/85 5.00 12.00
37 Bernie Williams/84 8.00 20.00
38 Carlos Delgado/83 5.00 12.00
39 Rafael Palmeiro/82 8.00 20.00
40 Edgar Renteria/81 5.00 12.00
41 Brad Fullmer/80 5.00 12.00
42 David Wells/79 5.00 12.00
43 Dante Bichette/78 5.00 12.00
44 Jaret Wright/77 5.00 12.00
45 Ricky Ledee/76 5.00 12.00
46 Ray Lankford/75 5.00 12.00
47 Mark Grace/74 8.00 20.00
48 Jeff Cirillo/73 5.00 12.00
49 Rondell White/72 5.00 12.00
50 Jeromy Burnitz/71 5.00 12.00
51 Sean Casey/70 5.00 12.00
52 Rolando Arrojo/69 5.00 12.00
53 Jason Giambi/68 5.00 12.00
54 John Olerud/67 5.00 12.00
55 Will Clark/66 8.00 20.00
56 Raul Mondesi/65 5.00 12.00
57 Scott Brosius/64 5.00 12.00
58 Bartolo Colon/63 5.00 12.00
59 Steve Finley/62 5.00 12.00
60 Javy Lopez/61 5.00 12.00
61 Tim Salmon/60 5.00 12.00
62 Roberto Alomar/59 8.00 20.00
63 Vinny Castilla/58 5.00 12.00
64 Craig Biggio/57 8.00 20.00
65 Jose Guillen/56 5.00 12.00
66 Greg Vaughn/55 5.00 12.00
67 Jose Canseco/54 8.00 20.00
68 Shawn Green/53 5.00 12.00
69 Curt Schilling/52 5.00 12.00
70 Orlando Hernandez/51 5.00 12.00
71 Jose Cruz Jr./50 6.00 15.00
72 Alex Gonzalez/49 6.00 15.00
73 Tino Martinez/48 6.00 15.00
74 Todd Hundley/47 6.00 15.00
75 Brian Giles/46 6.00 15.00
76 Cliff Floyd/45 6.00 15.00
77 Paul O'Neill/44 10.00 25.00
78 Ken Caminiti/43 6.00 15.00
79 Ron Gant/42 6.00 15.00
80 Juan Encarnacion/41 6.00 15.00
81 Ben Grieve/40 6.00 15.00
82 Brian Jordan/39 6.00 15.00
83 Rickey Henderson/38 15.00 40.00
84 Tony Clark/37 6.00 15.00
85 Shannon Stewart/36 6.00 15.00
86 Robin Ventura/35 6.00 15.00
87 Todd Walker/34 6.00 15.00
88 Kevin Brown/33 6.00 15.00
89 Moises Alou/32 6.00 15.00
90 Manny Ramirez/31 15.00 40.00
91 Gabe Alvarez/30 6.00 15.00
92 Jeremy Giambi/29 6.00 15.00
93 Adrian Beltre/28 15.00 40.00
94 George Lombard/27 6.00 15.00
95 Ryan Minor/26 6.00 15.00

1999 E-X Century Essential Credentials Now

RANDOM INSERTS IN PACKS
PRINT RUNS IN PARENTHESES BELOW
NOW CARDS FEATURE SILVER FOIL FRONTS
1-25 NOT PRICED DUE TO SCARCITY
26 Larry Walker/26 10.00 25.00
27 Albert Belle/27 6.00 15.00
28 Ivan Rodriguez/28 10.00 25.00
29 Magglio Ordonez/29 10.00 25.00
30 Andres Galarraga/30 10.00 25.00
31 Mike Mussina/31 10.00 25.00
32 Randy Johnson/32 15.00 40.00
33 Tom Glavine/33 10.00 25.00
34 Barry Larkin/34 10.00 25.00
35 Jim Thome/35 10.00 25.00
36 Gary Sheffield/36 6.00 15.00
37 Bernie Williams/37 10.00 25.00
38 Carlos Delgado/38 6.00 15.00
39 Rafael Palmeiro/39 10.00 25.00
40 Edgar Renteria/40 6.00 15.00
41 Brad Fullmer/41 6.00 15.00
42 David Wells/42 6.00 15.00
43 Dante Bichette/43 6.00 15.00
44 Jaret Wright/44 6.00 15.00
45 Ricky Ledee/45 6.00 15.00
46 Ray Lankford/46 6.00 15.00
47 Mark Grace/47 10.00 25.00
48 Jeff Cirillo/48 6.00 15.00
49 Rondell White/49 6.00 15.00
50 Jeromy Burnitz/50 6.00 15.00
51 Sean Casey/51 6.00 15.00
52 Rolando Arrojo/52 5.00 12.00
53 Jason Giambi/53 5.00 12.00
54 John Olerud/54 5.00 12.00
55 Will Clark/55 8.00 20.00
56 Raul Mondesi/56 5.00 12.00
57 Scott Brosius/57 5.00 12.00
58 Bartolo Colon/58 5.00 12.00
59 Steve Finley/59 5.00 12.00
60 Javy Lopez/60 5.00 12.00
61 Tim Salmon/61 5.00 12.00
62 Roberto Alomar/62 8.00 20.00
63 Vinny Castilla/63 5.00 12.00
64 Craig Biggio/64 8.00 20.00
65 Jose Guillen/65 5.00 12.00
66 Greg Vaughn/66 5.00 12.00
67 Jose Canseco/67 8.00 20.00
68 Shawn Green/68 5.00 12.00
69 Curt Schilling/69 5.00 12.00
70 Orlando Hernandez/70 5.00 12.00
71 Jose Cruz Jr./71 5.00 12.00
72 Alex Gonzalez/72 5.00 12.00
73 Tino Martinez/73 5.00 12.00
74 Todd Hundley/74 5.00 12.00
75 Brian Giles/75 5.00 12.00
76 Cliff Floyd/76 5.00 12.00
77 Paul O'Neill/77 8.00 20.00
78 Ken Caminiti/78 5.00 12.00
79 Ron Gant/79 5.00 12.00
80 Juan Encarnacion/80 5.00 12.00
81 Ben Grieve/81 5.00 12.00
82 Brian Jordan/82 5.00 12.00
83 Rickey Henderson/83 12.00 30.00
84 Tony Clark/84 5.00 12.00
85 Shannon Stewart/85 5.00 12.00
86 Robin Ventura/86 5.00 12.00
87 Todd Walker/87 5.00 12.00
88 Kevin Brown/88 5.00 12.00
89 Moises Alou/89 5.00 12.00
90 Manny Ramirez/90 12.00 30.00
91 Gabe Alvarez/91 5.00 12.00
92 Jeremy Giambi/92 5.00 12.00
93 Adrian Beltre/93 12.00 30.00
94 George Lombard/94 5.00 12.00
95 Ryan Minor/95 5.00 12.00
96 Kevin Witt/96 5.00 12.00
97 Scott Hunter/97 5.00 12.00
98 Carlos Guillen/98 5.00 12.00
99 Derrick Gibson/99 5.00 12.00
100 Trot Nixon/100 5.00 12.00
101 Troy Glaus/101 4.00 10.00
102 Armando Rios/102 4.00 10.00
103 Preston Wilson/103 4.00 10.00
104 Pat Burrell/104 15.00 40.00
105 J.D. Drew/105 4.00 10.00
106 Bruce Chen/106 4.00 10.00
107 Matt Clement/107 4.00 10.00
108 Carlos Beltran/108 6.00 15.00
109 Carlos Febles/109 4.00 10.00
110 Rob Fick/110 4.00 10.00
111 Russell Branyan/111 4.00 10.00
112 Roosevelt Brown/112 4.00 10.00
113 Corey Koskie/113 4.00 10.00
114 Mario Encarnacion/114 4.00 10.00
115 Peter Tucci/115 4.00 10.00
116 Eric Chavez/116 4.00 10.00
117 Gabe Kapler/117 4.00 10.00
118 Marlon Anderson/118 4.00 10.00
119 A.J. Burnett/119 6.00 15.00
120 Ryan Bradley/120 4.00 10.00

1999 E-X Century Authen-Kicks

RANDOM INSERTS IN PACKS
PRINT RUNS B/WN 160-205 COPIES PER
B1/R1 AU PRINT RUN 8 #'d OF EACH
NO B1/R1 PRICING DUE TO SCARCITY
COMP.SET EXCLUDES B1 AND R1
1 J.D. Drew/160 10.00 25.00
2 Travis Lee/175 6.00 15.00
3 Kevin Millwood/165 10.00 25.00
4 Bruce Chen/205 6.00 15.00
5 Troy Glaus/205 15.00 40.00
6 Todd Helton/205 15.00 40.00
7 Ricky Ledee/180 6.00 15.00
8 Scott Rolen/205 15.00 40.00
9 Jeremy Giambi/205 6.00 15.00
B1 J.D. Drew Black AU/8
R1 J.D. Drew Red AU/8

1999 E-X Century E-X Quisite

COMPLETE SET (15) 5.00 12.00
STATED ODDS 1:18
1 Troy Glaus .40 1.00
2 J.D. Drew .40 1.00
3 Pat Burrell 1.50 4.00
4 Russell Branyan .40 1.00
5 Kerry Wood .40 1.00
6 Eric Chavez .40 1.00
7 Ben Grieve .40 1.00
8 Gabe Kapler .40 1.00
9 Adrian Beltre 1.00 2.50
10 Todd Helton .60 1.50
11 Roosevelt Brown .40 1.00
12 Marlon Anderson .40 1.00
13 Jeremy Giambi .40 1.00
14 Magglio Ordonez .60 1.50
15 Travis Lee .40 1.00

1999 E-X Century Favorites for Fenway '99

COMPLETE SET (20) 25.00 60.00
STATED ODDS 1:36
1 Mo Vaughn .60 1.50
2 Nomar Garciaparra 1.00 2.50
3 Frank Thomas 1.50 4.00
4 Ken Griffey Jr. 3.00 8.00
5 Roger Clemens 2.00 5.00
6 Alex Rodriguez 2.00 5.00
7 Derek Jeter 4.00 10.00
8 Juan Gonzalez .60 1.50
9 Cal Ripken 5.00 12.00
10 Ivan Rodriguez 1.00 2.50
11 J.D. Drew .60 1.50
12 Barry Bonds 2.50 6.00
13 Tony Gwynn 1.50 4.00
14 Vladimir Guerrero 1.00 2.50
15 Chipper Jones 1.50 4.00
16 Kerry Wood .60 1.50
17 Mike Piazza 1.50 4.00
18 Sammy Sosa 1.50 4.00
19 Scott Rolen 1.00 2.50
20 Mark McGwire 2.50 6.00

1999 E-X Century Milestones of the Century

RANDOM INSERTS IN PACKS
PRINT RUNS B/WN 17-400 COPIES PER
NO PRICING ON QTY OF 20 OR LESS
2 Mark McGwire/70 12.00 30.00
3 Sammy Sosa/66 8.00 20.00
4 Ken Griffey Jr./350 15.00 40.00
5 Roger Clemens/98 10.00 25.00
7 Alex Rodriguez/40 10.00 25.00
8 Barry Bonds/400 12.00 30.00
9 N.Y. Yankees/114 40.00 80.00
10 Travis Lee/98 3.00 8.00

2000 E-X

COMPLETE SET (90) 40.00 100.00
COMP.SET w/o SP's (60) 8.00 20.00
COMMON CARD (1-60) .15 .40
COMMON PROS (61-90) .75 2.00
61-90 PRINT RUN 3499 SERIAL #'d SUBSETS
1 Alex Rodriguez .50 1.25
2 Jeff Bagwell .25 .60
3 Mike Piazza .40 1.00
4 Tony Gwynn .40 1.00
5 Ken Griffey Jr. .75 2.00
6 Juan Gonzalez .15 .40
7 Vladimir Guerrero .25 .60
8 Cal Ripken 1.25 3.00
9 Mo Vaughn .15 .40
10 Chipper Jones .40 1.00
11 Derek Jeter 1.00 2.50
12 Nomar Garciaparra .25 .60
13 Mark McGwire .60 1.50
14 Sammy Sosa .40 1.00
15 Pedro Martinez .25 .60
16 Greg Maddux .50 1.25
17 Frank Thomas .40 1.00
18 Shawn Green .15 .40
19 Carlos Beltran .25 .60
20 Roger Clemens .50 1.25
21 Randy Johnson .40 1.00
22 Bernie Williams .25 .60
23 Carlos Delgado .15 .40
24 Manny Ramirez .40 1.00
25 Freddy Garcia .15 .40
26 Barry Bonds .60 1.50
27 Tim Hudson .25 .60
28 Larry Walker .25 .60
29 Raul Mondesi .15 .40
30 Ivan Rodriguez .25 .60
31 Magglio Ordonez .25 .60
32 Scott Rolen .25 .60
33 Mike Mussina .25 .60
34 J.D. Drew .15 .40
35 Tom Glavine .25 .60
36 Barry Larkin .25 .60
37 Jim Thome .25 .60
38 Erubiel Durazo .15 .40
39 Curt Schilling .25 .60
40 Orlando Hernandez .15 .40
41 Rafael Palmeiro .25 .60
42 Gabe Kapler .15 .40
43 Mark Grace .25 .60
44 Jeff Cirillo .15 .40
45 Jeromy Burnitz .15 .40
46 Sean Casey .15 .40
47 Kevin Millwood .15 .40
48 Vinny Castilla .15 .40
49 Jose Canseco .25 .60
50 Roberto Alomar .25 .60
51 Craig Biggio .25 .60
52 Preston Wilson .15 .40
53 Jeff Weaver .15 .40
54 Robin Ventura .15 .40
55 Ben Grieve .15 .40
56 Troy Glaus .15 .40
57 Jacque Jones .15 .40
58 Brian Giles .15 .40
59 Kevin Brown .15 .40
60 Todd Helton .25 .60
61 Ben Petrick PROS .75 2.00
62 Chad Hermansen PROS .75 2.00
63 Kevin Barker PROS .75 2.00
64 Matt LeCroy PROS .75 2.00
65 Brad Penny PROS .75 2.00
66 D.T. Cromer PROS .75 2.00
67 Steve Lomasney PROS .75 2.00
68 Cole Liniak PROS .75 2.00
69 B.J. Ryan PROS .75 2.00
70 Wilton Veras PROS .75 2.00
71 Aaron McNeal PROS RC .75 2.00
72 Nick Johnson PROS .75 2.00
73 Adam Piatt PROS .75 2.00
74 Adam Kennedy PROS .75 2.00
75 Cesar King PROS .75 2.00
76 Peter Bergeron PROS .75 2.00
77 Rob Bell PROS .75 2.00
78 Wily Pena PROS .75 2.00
79 Ruben Mateo PROS .75 2.00
80 Kip Wells PROS .75 2.00
81 Alex Escobar PROS .75 2.00
82 Danys Baez PROS RC .75 2.00
83 Travis Dawkins PROS .75 2.00
84 Mark Quinn PROS .75 2.00
85 Jimmy Anderson PROS .75 2.00
86 Rick Ankiel PROS 1.25 3.00
87 Alfonso Soriano PROS 2.00 5.00
88 Pat Burrell PROS .75 2.00
89 Eric Munson PROS .75 2.00
90 Josh Beckett PROS 1.50 4.00

2000 E-X Essential Credentials Future

CARDS 36-60 NOT PRICED DUE TO SCARCITY
CARDS 66-90 NOT PRICED DUE TO SCARCITY
1 Alex Rodriguez/60 20.00 50.00
2 Jeff Bagwell/59 10.00 25.00
3 Mike Piazza/58 15.00 40.00
4 Tony Gwynn/57 15.00 40.00
5 Ken Griffey Jr./56 30.00 80.00
6 Juan Gonzalez/55 6.00 15.00
7 Vladimir Guerrero/54 10.00 25.00
8 Cal Ripken/53 50.00 125.00
9 Mo Vaughn/52 6.00 15.00
10 Chipper Jones/51 15.00 40.00
11 Derek Jeter/50 40.00 100.00
12 Nomar Garciaparra/49 10.00 25.00
13 Mark McGwire/48 25.00 60.00
14 Sammy Sosa/47 15.00 40.00
15 Pedro Martinez/46 10.00 25.00
16 Greg Maddux/45 20.00 50.00
17 Frank Thomas/44 15.00 40.00
18 Shawn Green/43 6.00 15.00
19 Carlos Beltran/42 10.00 25.00
20 Roger Clemens/41 20.00 50.00
21 Randy Johnson/40 15.00 40.00
22 Bernie Williams/39 10.00 25.00
23 Carlos Delgado/38 6.00 15.00
24 Manny Ramirez/37 15.00 40.00
25 Freddy Garcia/36 6.00 15.00
26 Barry Bonds/35 30.00 80.00
27 Tim Hudson/34 12.00 30.00
28 Larry Walker/33 12.00 30.00
29 Raul Mondesi/32 8.00 20.00
30 Ivan Rodriguez/31 12.00 30.00
31 Magglio Ordonez/30 12.00 30.00
32 Scott Rolen/29 12.00 30.00
33 Mike Mussina/28 12.00 30.00
34 J.D. Drew/27 8.00 20.00
35 Tom Glavine/26 12.00 30.00
61 Ben Petrick/30 8.00 20.00
62 Chad Hermansen/29 8.00 20.00
63 Kevin Barker/28 8.00 20.00
64 Matt LeCroy/27 8.00 20.00
65 Brad Penny/26 8.00 20.00

2000 E-X Essential Credentials Now

CARDS 1-25 NOT PRICED DUE TO SCARCITY
CARDS 61-85 NOT PRICED DUE TO SCARCITY
26 Barry Bonds/26 30.00 80.00
27 Tim Hudson/27 12.00 30.00
28 Larry Walker/28 12.00 30.00
29 Raul Mondesi/29 8.00 20.00
30 Ivan Rodriguez/30 12.00 30.00

31 Magglio Ordonez/31 12.00 30.00
32 Scott Rolen/32 12.00 30.00
33 Mike Mussina/33 12.00 30.00
34 J.D. Drew/34 8.00 20.00
35 Tom Glavine/35 12.00 30.00
36 Barry Larkin/36 10.00 25.00
37 Jim Thome/37 10.00 25.00
38 Erubiel Durazo/38 6.00 15.00
39 Curt Schilling/39 10.00 25.00
40 Orlando Hernandez/40 6.00 15.00
41 Rafael Palmeiro/41 10.00 25.00
42 Gabe Kapler/42 6.00 15.00
43 Mark Grace/43 10.00 25.00
44 Jeff Cirillo/44 6.00 15.00
45 Jeromy Burnitz/45 6.00 15.00
46 Sean Casey/46 6.00 15.00
47 Kevin Millwood/47 6.00 15.00
48 Vinny Castilla/48 6.00 15.00
49 Jose Canseco/49 10.00 25.00
50 Roberto Alomar/50 10.00 25.00
51 Craig Biggio/51 10.00 25.00
52 Preston Wilson/52 6.00 15.00
53 Jeff Weaver/53 6.00 15.00
54 Robin Ventura/54 6.00 15.00
55 Ben Grieve/55 6.00 15.00
56 Troy Glaus/56 6.00 15.00
57 Jacque Jones/57 6.00 15.00
58 Brian Giles/58 6.00 15.00
59 Kevin Brown/59 6.00 15.00
60 Todd Helton/60 10.00 25.00
86 Rick Ankiel/26 12.00 30.00
87 Alfonso Soriano/27 20.00 50.00
88 Pat Burrell/28 8.00 20.00
89 Eric Munson/29 8.00 20.00
90 Josh Beckett/30 15.00 40.00

2000 E-X E-Xceptional Red

COMPLETE SET (15) 20.00 50.00
STATED PRINT RUN 1999 SERIAL #'d SETS
*BLUE: 2.5X TO 6X RED
BLUE PRINT RUN 250 SERIAL #'d SETS
*GREEN: .6X TO 1.5X RED
GREEN PRINT RUN 999 SERIAL #'d SETS
XC1 Ken Griffey Jr. 2.50 6.00
XC2 Derek Jeter 3.00 8.00
XC3 Nomar Garciaparra .75 2.00
XC4 Mark McGwire 2.00 5.00
XC5 Sammy Sosa 1.25 3.00
XC6 Mike Piazza 1.25 3.00
XC7 Alex Rodriguez 1.50 4.00
XC8 Cal Ripken 4.00 10.00
XC9 Chipper Jones 1.25 3.00
XC10 Pedro Martinez .75 2.00
XC11 Jeff Bagwell .75 2.00
XC12 Greg Maddux 1.50 4.00
XC13 Roger Clemens 1.50 4.00
XC14 Tony Gwynn 1.25 3.00
XC15 Frank Thomas 1.25 3.00

2000 E-X E-Xciting

COMPLETE SET (10) 8.00 20.00
STATED ODDS 1:24
XT1 Mark McGwire 1.50 4.00
XT2 Ken Griffey Jr. 2.00 5.00
XT3 Randy Johnson 1.00 2.50
XT4 Sammy Sosa 1.00 2.50
XT5 Manny Ramirez 1.00 2.50
XT6 Jose Canseco .60 1.50
XT7 Derek Jeter 2.50 6.00
XT8 Scott Rolen .60 1.50
XT9 Juan Gonzalez .40 1.00
XT10 Barry Bonds 1.50 4.00

2000 E-X E-Xplosive

COMPLETE SET (20) 15.00 40.00
STATED PRINT RUN 2499 SERIAL #'d SETS 1.50
4.00
XP1 Tony Gwynn 1.25 3.00
XP2 Alex Rodriguez 1.50 4.00
XP3 Pedro Martinez .75 2.00
XP4 Sammy Sosa 1.25 3.00
XP5 Cal Ripken 4.00 10.00
XP6 Adam Piatt .50 1.25
XP7 Pat Burrell .50 1.25
XP8 J.D. Drew .50 1.25
XP9 Mike Piazza 1.25 3.00
XP10 Shawn Green .50 1.25
XP11 Troy Glaus .50 1.25
XP12 Randy Johnson 1.25 3.00
XP13 Juan Gonzalez .50 1.25
XP14 Chipper Jones 1.25 3.00
XP15 Ivan Rodriguez .75 2.00
XP16 Nomar Garciaparra .75 2.00
XP17 Ken Griffey Jr. 2.50 6.00
XP18 Nick Johnson .50 1.25
XP19 Mark McGwire 2.00 5.00
XP20 Frank Thomas 1.25 3.00

2000 E-X Generation E-X

COMPLETE SET (15) 8.00 20.00
STATED ODDS 1:8
1 Rick Ankiel .60 1.50
2 Josh Beckett .75 2.00
3 Carlos Beltran .60 1.50
4 Pat Burrell .40 1.00
5 Freddy Garcia .40 1.00
6 Alex Rodriguez 1.25 3.00
7 Derek Jeter 2.50 6.00
8 Tim Hudson .60 1.50
9 Shawn Green .40 1.00
10 Eric Munson .40 1.00
11 Adam Piatt .40 1.00
12 Adam Kennedy .40 1.00
13 Nick Johnson .40 1.00
14 Alfonso Soriano 1.00 2.50
15 Nomar Garciaparra .60 1.50

2000 E-X Genuine Coverage

STATED ODDS 1:144
SKIP-NUMBERED 9-CARD SET
2 Derek Jeter 8.00 20.00
3 Alex Rodriguez 4.00 10.00
8 Cal Ripken 10.00 25.00
10 Chipper Jones 3.00 8.00
11 Edgar Martinez 2.00 5.00
25 Barry Bonds 5.00 12.00
35 Mike Mussina 2.00 5.00
43 Raul Mondesi 1.25 3.00
47 Tom Glavine 2.00 5.00
52 Tim Hudson 2.00 5.00
NNO Heath Murray 1.25 3.00

2001 E-X

COMP.SET w/o SP's (100) 10.00 25.00
COMMON CARD (1-100) .20 .50
COMMON CARD (101-130) 3.00 8.00
101-130 RANDOM INSERTS IN PACKS
PRINT RUNS REFER TO UNSIGNED COPIES
STATED PRINT RUNS LISTED BELOW
COMMON CARD (131-140) 3.00 8.00
131-140 DIST.IN FLEER PLAT.RC HOB/RET
131-140 PRINT RUN 499 SERIAL #'d SETS
1 Jason Kendall .20 .50
2 Derek Jeter 1.25 3.00
3 Greg Vaughn .20 .50
4 Eric Chavez .20 .50
5 Nomar Garciaparra .75 2.00
6 Roberto Alomar .30 .75
7 Barry Larkin .30 .75
8 Matt Lawton .20 .50
9 Larry Walker .20 .50
10 Chipper Jones .50 1.25
11 Scott Rolen .30 .75
12 Carlos Lee .20 .50
13 Adrian Beltre .20 .50
14 Ben Grieve .20 .50
15 Mike Sweeney .20 .50
16 John Olerud .20 .50
17 Gabe Kapler .20 .50
18 Brian Giles .20 .50
19 Luis Gonzalez .20 .50
20 Sammy Sosa .50 1.25
21 Roger Clemens 1.00 2.50
22 Vladimir Guerrero .50 1.25
23 Ken Griffey Jr. 1.00 2.50
24 Mark McGwire 1.25 3.00
25 Orlando Hernandez .20 .50
26 Shannon Stewart .20 .50
27 Fred McGriff .30 .75
28 Lance Berkman .20 .50
29 Carlos Delgado .20 .50
30 Mike Piazza .75 2.00
31 Juan Encarnacion .20 .50
32 David Justice .20 .50
33 Greg Maddux .75 2.00
34 Frank Thomas .50 1.25
35 Jason Giambi .20 .50
36 Ruben Mateo .20 .50
37 Todd Helton .30 .75
38 Jim Edmonds .20 .50
39 Steve Finley .20 .50
40 Tom Glavine .30 .75
41 Mo Vaughn .20 .50
42 Phil Nevin .20 .50
43 Richie Sexson .20 .50
44 Craig Biggio .30 .75
45 Kerry Wood .20 .50
46 Pat Burrell .20 .50
47 Edgar Martinez .30 .75
48 Jim Thome .30 .75
49 Jeff Bagwell .30 .75
50 Bernie Williams .30 .75
51 Andruw Jones .30 .75
52 Gary Sheffield .20 .50
53 Johnny Damon .30 .75
54 Rondell White .20 .50
55 J.D. Drew .20 .50
56 Tony Batista .20 .50
57 Paul Konerko .20 .50
58 Rafael Palmeiro .30 .75
59 Cal Ripken 1.50 4.00
60 Darin Erstad .20 .50
61 Ivan Rodriguez .30 .75
62 Barry Bonds 1.25 3.00
63 Edgardo Alfonzo .20 .50
64 Ellis Burks .20 .50
65 Mike Lieberthal .20 .50
66 Robin Ventura .20 .50
67 Richard Hidalgo .20 .50
68 Magglio Ordonez .20 .50
69 Kazuhiro Sasaki .20 .50
70 Miguel Tejada .20 .50
71 David Wells .20 .50
72 Troy Glaus .20 .50
73 Jose Vidro .20 .50
74 Shawn Green .20 .50
75 Barry Zito .30 .75
76 Jermaine Dye .20 .50
77 Geoff Jenkins .20 .50
78 Jeff Kent .20 .50
79 Al Leiter .20 .50
80 Deivi Cruz .20 .50
81 Eric Karros .20 .50
82 Albert Belle .20 .50
83 Pedro Martinez .30 .75
84 Raul Mondesi .20 .50
85 Preston Wilson .20 .50
86 Rafael Furcal .20 .50
87 Rick Ankiel .20 .50
88 Randy Johnson .50 1.25
89 Kevin Brown .20 .50
90 Sean Casey .20 .50
91 Mike Mussina .30 .75
92 Alex Rodriguez .60 1.50
93 Andres Galarraga .20 .50
94 Juan Gonzalez .20 .50
95 Manny Ramirez Sox .30 .75
96 Mark Grace .30 .75
97 Carl Everett .20 .50
98 Tony Gwynn .60 1.50
99 Mike Hampton .20 .50
100 Ken Caminiti .20 .50
101 Jason Hart/1749 3.00 8.00
102 Corey Patterson/1199 3.00 8.00
103 Timo Perez/1999 3.00 8.00
104 Marcus Giles/1999 3.00 8.00
105 Ichiro Suzuki/1999 RC 20.00 50.00
106 Aubrey Huff/1499 3.00 8.00
107 Joe Crede/1999 4.00 10.00
108 Larry Barnes/1499 3.00 8.00
109 Esix Snead/1999 RC 3.00 8.00
110 Kenny Kelly/2249 3.00 8.00
111 Justin Miller/2249 3.00 8.00
112 Jack Cust/1999 3.00 8.00
113 Xavier Nady/999 3.00 8.00
114 Eric Munson/1499 3.00 8.00
115 Elpidio Guzman/1749 RC 3.00 8.00
116 Juan Pierre/2189 3.00 8.00
117 Winston Abreu/1999 RC 3.00 8.00
118 Keith Ginter/1999 3.00 8.00
119 Jace Brewer/2699 3.00 8.00
120 Paxton Crawford/2249 3.00 8.00
121 Jason Tyner/2249 3.00 8.00
122 Tike Redman/1999 3.00 8.00
123 John Riedling/2499 3.00 8.00
124 Jose Ortiz/1499 3.00 8.00
125 Oswaldo Mairena/2499 3.00 8.00
126 Eric Byrnes/2249 3.00 8.00
127 Brian Cole/999 3.00 8.00
128 Adam Piatt/2249 3.00 8.00
129 Nate Rolison/2499 3.00 8.00
130 Keith McDonald/2249 3.00 8.00
131 Albert Pujols/499 RC 75.00 200.00
132 Bud Smith/499 RC 3.00 8.00
133 Tsuyoshi Shinjo/499 RC 5.00 12.00
134 Wilson Betemit/499 RC 5.00 12.00
135 Adrian Hernandez/499 RC 3.00 8.00
136 Jackson Melian/499 RC 3.00 8.00
137 Jay Gibbons/499 RC 5.00 12.00
138 Johnny Estrada/499 RC 5.00 12.00
139 Morgan Ensberg/499 RC 5.00 12.00
140 Drew Henson/499 RC 5.00 12.00
NNO Derek Jeter Base AU/500 75.00 150.00
MM2 Derek Jeter MM/1996 5.00 12.00
NNO Derek Jeter MM AU/96 60.00 120.00

2001 E-X Prospect Autographs

PRINT RUNS B/WN 250-1500 COPIES PER
PRINT RUNS REFER TO SIGNED COPIES
101 Jason Hart/250 4.00 10.00
102 Corey Patterson/800 4.00 10.00
103 Timo Perez/1000 4.00 10.00
104 Marcus Giles/500 6.00 15.00
106 Aubrey Huff/500 6.00 15.00
107 Joe Crede/500 10.00 25.00
108 Larry Barnes/500 4.00 10.00
109 Esix Snead/500 4.00 10.00
110 Kenny Kelly/250 4.00 10.00
111 Justin Miller/250 4.00 10.00
112 Jack Cust/1000 4.00 10.00
113 Xavier Nady/1000 4.00 10.00
114 Eric Munson/1500 4.00 10.00
115 Elpidio Guzman/250 4.00 10.00
116 Juan Pierre/810 6.00 15.00
117 Winston Abreu/250 4.00 10.00
118 Keith Ginter/500 4.00 10.00
119 Jace Brewer/300 4.00 10.00
120 Paxton Crawford/250 4.00 10.00
121 Jason Tyner/250 4.00 10.00
122 Tike Redman/250 4.00 10.00
123 John Riedling/500 4.00 10.00
124 Jose Ortiz/500 4.00 10.00
125 Oswaldo Mairena/500 4.00 10.00
126 Eric Byrnes/250 4.00 10.00
127 Brian Cole/2000 10.00 25.00
128 Adam Piatt/250 4.00 10.00
129 Nate Rolison/500 4.00 10.00
130 Keith McDonald/250 4.00 10.00

2001 E-X Essential Credentials

COMMON CARD (1-100) 2.00 5.00
*STARS 1-100: 5X TO 12X BASIC CARDS
1-100 PRINT RUN 299 SERIAL #'d SETS
COMMON CARD (101-130) 6.00 15.00
101-130 PRINT RUN 29 SERIAL #'d SUBSETS

2001 E-X Behind the Numbers Game Jersey

STATED ODDS 1:33
BH1 Johnny Bench 6.00 15.00
BH2 Wade Boggs 6.00 15.00
BH3 George Brett 10.00 25.00
BH4 Lou Brock 6.00 15.00
BH5 Rollie Fingers 4.00 10.00
BH6 Carlton Fisk 6.00 15.00
BH7 Reggie Jackson 6.00 15.00
BH8 Al Kaline 6.00 15.00
BH9 Willie Mays 30.00 60.00
BH10 Willie McCovey 4.00 10.00
BH11 Paul Molitor 4.00 10.00
BH12 Eddie Murray 6.00 15.00
BH13 Jim Palmer 4.00 10.00
BH14 Ozzie Smith 6.00 15.00
BH15 Nolan Ryan 6.00 15.00
BH16 Mike Schmidt 10.00 25.00
BH17 Tom Seaver 6.00 15.00
BH18 Dave Winfield 4.00 10.00
BH19 Ted Williams 50.00 100.00
BH20 Robin Yount 6.00 15.00
BH21 Brady Anderson 4.00 10.00
BH22 Rick Ankiel 4.00 10.00
BH23 Albert Belle 4.00 10.00
BH24 Adrian Beltre 4.00 10.00
BH25 Barry Bonds 15.00 40.00
BH26 Eric Chavez 4.00 10.00
BH27 J.D. Drew 4.00 10.00
BH28 Darin Erstad 4.00 10.00
BH29 Troy Glaus 4.00 10.00
BH30 Mark Grace 6.00 15.00
BH31 Ben Grieve 4.00 10.00
BH32 Tony Gwynn 8.00 20.00
BH33 Todd Helton 6.00 15.00
BH34 Derek Jeter 15.00 40.00
BH35 Jeff Kent 4.00 10.00
BH36 Jason Kendall 4.00 10.00
BH37 Greg Maddux 8.00 20.00
BH38 John Olerud 4.00 10.00
BH39 Cal Ripken 10.00 25.00
BH40 Chipper Jones 6.00 15.00
BH41 John Smoltz 6.00 15.00
BH42 Frank Thomas 6.00 15.00
BH43 Robin Ventura 4.00 10.00
BH44 Bernie Williams 6.00 15.00

2001 E-X Behind the Numbers Game Jersey Autograph

STATED PRINT RUNS LISTED BELOW
NO PRICING ON QTY OF 25 OR LESS
2 Rick Ankiel/66 15.00 40.00
3 Albert Belle/88 20.00 50.00
4 Adrian Beltre/29 25.00 60.00
6 Wade Boggs/26 50.00 100.00
13 Rollie Fingers/34 20.00 50.00
14 Carlton Fisk/27 50.00 100.00
20 Reggie Jackson/44 50.00 100.00
26 Greg Maddux/31 175.00 300.00
27 Willie McCovey/44 40.00 80.00
29 Eddie Murray/33 50.00 100.00
33 Nolan Ryan/34 175.00 300.00
35 Tom Seaver/41 50.00 120.00
37 John Smoltz/29 40.00 80.00
38 Frank Thomas/35 50.00 100.00
40 Bernie Williams/51 50.00 100.00
41 Dave Winfield/31 40.00 80.00

2001 E-X Extra Innings

COMPLETE SET (10) 50.00 100.00
STATED ODDS 1:20 RETAIL
XI1 Mark McGwire 5.00 12.00
XI2 Sammy Sosa 2.00 5.00
XI3 Chipper Jones 2.00 5.00
XI4 Mike Piazza 3.00 8.00
XI5 Cal Ripken 6.00 15.00
XI6 Ken Griffey Jr. 4.00 10.00
XI7 Alex Rodriguez 2.50 6.00
XI8 Vladimir Guerrero 2.00 5.00
XI9 Nomar Garciaparra 3.00 8.00
XI10 Derek Jeter 5.00 12.00

2001 E-X Wall of Fame

STATED ODDS 1:24
1 Jeff Bagwell 4.00 10.00
2 Barry Bonds 10.00 25.00
3 Pat Burrell 3.00 8.00
4 Roger Clemens 6.00 15.00
5 Nomar Garciaparra 6.00 15.00
6 Jason Giambi 3.00 8.00
7 Troy Glaus 3.00 8.00
8 Juan Gonzalez 3.00 8.00
9 Ken Griffey Jr. 6.00 15.00
10 Vladimir Guerrero 4.00 10.00
11 Tony Gwynn 6.00 15.00
12 Todd Helton 4.00 10.00
13 Geoff Jenkins 3.00 8.00
14 Derek Jeter 10.00 25.00
15 Andruw Jones 4.00 10.00
16 Chipper Jones 4.00 10.00
17 Jason Kendall 3.00 8.00
18 Greg Maddux 4.00 10.00
19 Pedro Martinez 4.00 10.00
20 Mark McGwire 15.00 40.00
21 Paul Molitor 3.00 8.00
22 Mike Piazza 4.00 10.00
23 Manny Ramirez Sox 4.00 10.00
24 Cal Ripken 10.00 25.00
25 Alex Rodriguez 6.00 15.00
26 Ivan Rodriguez 4.00 10.00
27 Scott Rolen 4.00 10.00
28 Sammy Sosa 4.00 10.00
29 Frank Thomas 4.00 10.00
30 Robin Yount 4.00 10.00

2002 E-X

COMP.SET w/o SP's (100) 10.00 25.00
COMMON CARD (1-100) .20 .50
COMMON CARD (101-120) 2.00 5.00
101-120 RANDOM INSERTS IN PACKS
101-120 PRINT RUN 2499-2999 #'d SETS
COMMON CARD (121-125) 2.00 5.00
121-125 RANDOM INSERTS IN PACKS
121-125 PRINT RUN 1999 SERIAL #'d SETS
COMMON CARD (126-140) 2.00 5.00
126-140 STATED ODDS 1:24 HOB/RET
CARD 133 DOES NOT EXIST
1 Alex Rodriguez .60 1.50
2 Albert Pujols 1.00 2.50
3 Ken Griffey Jr. 1.00 2.50
4 Vladimir Guerrero .50 1.25
5 Sammy Sosa .50 1.25
6 Ichiro Suzuki 1.00 2.50
7 Jorge Posada .30 .75
8 Matt Williams .20 .50
9 Adrian Beltre .20 .50
10 Pat Burrell .20 .50
11 Roger Cedeno .20 .50
12 Tony Clark .20 .50
13 Steve Finley .20 .50
14 Rafael Furcal .20 .50
15 Rickey Henderson .50 1.25
16 Richard Hidalgo .20 .50
17 Jason Kendall .20 .50
18 Tino Martinez .30 .75
19 Scott Rolen .30 .75
20 Shannon Stewart .20 .50
21 Jose Vidro .20 .50
22 Preston Wilson .20 .50
23 Raul Mondesi .20 .50
24 Lance Berkman .20 .50
25 Rick Ankiel .20 .50
26 Kevin Brown .20 .50
27 Jeromy Burnitz .20 .50
28 Jeff Cirillo .20 .50
29 Carl Everett .20 .50
30 Eric Chavez .20 .50
31 Freddy Garcia .20 .50
32 Mark Grace .30 .75
33 David Justice .20 .50
34 Fred McGriff .30 .75
35 Mike Mussina .30 .75
36 John Olerud .20 .50
37 Magglio Ordonez .20 .50
38 Curt Schilling .20 .50
39 Aaron Sele .20 .50
40 Robin Ventura .20 .50
41 Adam Dunn .20 .50
42 Jeff Bagwell .30 .75
43 Barry Bonds 1.25 3.00
44 Roger Clemens 1.00 2.50
45 Cliff Floyd .20 .50
46 Jason Giambi .20 .50
47 Juan Gonzalez .20 .50
48 Luis Gonzalez .20 .50
49 Cristian Guzman .20 .50
50 Todd Helton .30 .75
51 Derek Jeter 1.25 3.00
52 Rafael Palmeiro .30 .75
53 Mike Sweeney .20 .50
54 Ben Grieve .20 .50
55 Phil Nevin .20 .50
56 Mike Piazza .75 2.00
57 Moises Alou .20 .50
58 Ivan Rodriguez .30 .75
59 Manny Ramirez .30 .75
60 Brian Giles .20 .50
61 Jim Thome .30 .75
62 Larry Walker .20 .50
63 Bobby Abreu .20 .50
64 Troy Glaus .20 .50
65 Garret Anderson .20 .50
66 Roberto Alomar .30 .75
67 Bret Boone .20 .50
68 Marty Cordova .20 .50
69 Craig Biggio .30 .75
70 Omar Vizquel .30 .75
71 Jermaine Dye .20 .50
72 Darin Erstad .20 .50
73 Carlos Delgado .20 .50
74 Nomar Garciaparra .75 2.00
75 Greg Maddux .75 2.00
76 Tom Glavine .30 .75
77 Frank Thomas .50 1.25
78 Shawn Green .20 .50
79 Bobby Higginson .20 .50
80 Jeff Kent .20 .50
81 Chuck Knoblauch .20 .50
82 Paul Konerko .20 .50
83 Carlos Lee .20 .50
84 Jon Lieber .20 .50
85 Paul LoDuca .20 .50
86 Mike Lowell .20 .50
87 Edgar Martinez .30 .75
88 Doug Mientkiewicz .20 .50
89 Pedro Martinez .30 .75
90 Randy Johnson .50 1.25
91 Aramis Ramirez .20 .50
92 J.D. Drew .20 .50
93 Chris Richard .20 .50
94 Jimmy Rollins .20 .50
95 Ryan Klesko .20 .50
96 Gary Sheffield .20 .50
97 Chipper Jones .50 1.25
98 Greg Vaughn .20 .50
99 Mo Vaughn .20 .50
100 Bernie Williams .30 .75
101 John Foster NT/2999 RC 2.00 5.00
102 Jorge DeLaRosa NT/2999 RC 2.00 5.00
103 Edwin Almonte NT/2999 RC 2.00 5.00
104 Chris Booker NT/2999 RC 2.00 5.00
105 Victor Alvarez NT/2999 RC 2.00 5.00
106 Cliff Bartosh NT/2999 RC 2.00 5.00
107 Felix Escalona NT/2999 RC 2.00 5.00
108 Corey Thurman NT/2999 RC 2.00 5.00
109 Kazuhisa Ishii NT/2999 RC 3.00 8.00
110 Miguel Asencio NT/2999 RC 2.00 5.00
111 P.J. Bevis NT/2499 RC 2.00 5.00
112 Gustavo Chacin NT/2499 RC 3.00 8.00
113 Steve Kent NT/2499 RC 2.00 5.00
114 Takahito Nomura NT/2499 RC 2.00 5.00
115 Adam Walker NT/2499 RC 2.00 5.00
116 So Taguchi NT/2499 RC 3.00 8.00
117 Reed Johnson NT/2499 RC 3.00 8.00
118 Rod Rosario NT/2499 RC 2.00 5.00
119 Luis Martinez NT/2499 RC 2.00 5.00
120 Sat Komiyama NT/2499 RC 2.00 5.00
121 Sean Burroughs NT/1999 2.00 5.00
122 Hank Blalock NT/1999 3.00 8.00
123 Marlon Byrd NT/1999 2.00 5.00
124 Nick Johnson NT/1999 2.00 5.00
125 Mark Teixeira NT/1999 3.00 8.00
126 David Espinosa NT 2.00 5.00
127 Adrian Burnside NT RC 2.00 5.00
128 Mark Corey NT RC 2.00 5.00
129 Matt Thornton NT RC 2.00 5.00
130 Dane Sardinha NT 2.00 5.00
131 Juan Rivera NT 2.00 5.00
132 Austin Kearns NT 2.00 5.00
134 Ben Broussard NT 2.00 5.00
135 Orlando Hudson NT 2.00 5.00
136 Carlos Pena NT 2.00 5.00
137 Kenny Kelly NT 2.00 5.00
138 Bill Hall NT 2.00 5.00
139 Ron Chiavacci NT 2.00 5.00
140 Mark Prior NT 2.00 5.00

2002 E-X Essential Credentials Future

SEE BECKETT.COM FOR PRINT RUNS
NO PRICING ON QTY OF 25 OR LESS
CARDS 1-60 FEATURE GAME USED ITEMS
1 Alex Rodriguez Jsy/60 30.00 60.00
2 Albert Pujols Base/59 10.00 25.00
3 Ken Griffey Jr. Base/58 30.00 60.00
4 Vladimir Guerrero Base/57 15.00 40.00
5 Sammy Sosa Base/56 15.00 40.00
7 Jorge Posada Bat/54 12.50 30.00
8 Matt Williams Bat/53 10.00 25.00
9 Adrian Beltre Bat/52 10.00 25.00
10 Pat Burrell Bat/51 10.00 25.00
11 Roger Cedeno Bat/50 10.00 25.00
12 Tony Clark Bat/49 10.00 25.00
13 Steve Finley Bat/48 12.50 30.00
14 Rafael Furcal Bat/47 12.50 30.00
15 Rickey Henderson Bat/46 20.00 50.00
16 Richard Hidalgo Bat/45 10.00 25.00
17 Jason Kendall Bat/44 12.50 30.00
18 Tino Martinez Bat/43 10.00 25.00
19 Scott Rolen Bat/42 15.00 40.00
20 Shannon Stewart Bat/41 12.50 30.00
21 Jose Vidro Bat/40 10.00 25.00
22 Preston Wilson Bat/39 12.50 30.00
23 Raul Mondesi Bat/38 12.50 30.00
24 Lance Berkman Bat/37 12.50 30.00
25 Rick Ankiel Jsy/36 10.00 25.00
26 Kevin Brown Jsy/35 15.00 40.00
27 Jeromy Burnitz Bat/34 15.00 40.00
28 Jeff Cirillo Jsy/33 12.50 30.00
29 Carl Everett Jsy/32 15.00 40.00
30 Eric Chavez Bat/31 15.00 40.00
31 Freddy Garcia Jsy/30 15.00 40.00
32 Mark Grace Jsy/29 20.00 50.00
33 David Justice Jsy/28 15.00 40.00
34 Fred McGriff Jsy/27 20.00 50.00
61 Jim Thome/125 5.00 12.00
62 Larry Walker/124 3.00 8.00
63 Bobby Abreu/123 3.00 8.00
64 Troy Glaus/122 3.00 8.00
65 Garret Anderson/121 3.00 8.00
66 Roberto Alomar/120 5.00 12.00
67 Bret Boone/119 3.00 8.00
68 Marty Cordova/118 3.00 8.00
69 Craig Biggio/117 5.00 12.00
70 Omar Vizquel/116 5.00 12.00
71 Jermaine Dye/115 3.00 8.00
72 Darin Erstad/114 3.00 8.00
73 Carlos Delgado/113 3.00 8.00
74 Nomar Garciaparra/112 12.50 30.00
75 Greg Maddux/111 12.50 30.00
76 Tom Glavine/110 5.00 12.00
77 Frank Thomas/109 8.00 20.00
78 Shawn Green/108 3.00 8.00
79 Bobby Higginson/107 3.00 8.00
80 Jeff Kent/106 3.00 8.00
81 Chuck Knoblauch/105 3.00 8.00
82 Paul Konerko/104 3.00 8.00
83 Carlos Lee/103 3.00 8.00
84 Jon Lieber/102 3.00 8.00
85 Paul LoDuca/101 3.00 8.00
86 Mike Lowell/100 3.00 8.00
87 Edgar Martinez/99 5.00 12.00
88 Doug Mientkiewicz/98 3.00 8.00
89 Pedro Martinez/97 5.00 12.00
90 Randy Johnson/96 8.00 20.00
91 Aramis Ramirez/95 3.00 8.00
92 J.D. Drew/94 3.00 8.00
93 Chris Richard/93 3.00 8.00
94 Jimmy Rollins/92 3.00 8.00
95 Ryan Klesko/91 3.00 8.00
96 Gary Sheffield/90 3.00 8.00
97 Chipper Jones/89 8.00 20.00
98 Greg Vaughn/88 3.00 8.00
99 Mo Vaughn/87 3.00 8.00
100 Bernie Williams/86 5.00 12.00
101 John Foster NT/85 3.00 8.00
102 Jorge De La Rosa NT/84 3.00 8.00
103 Edwin Almonte NT/83 3.00 8.00
104 Chris Booker NT/82 3.00 8.00
105 Victor Alvarez NT/81 3.00 8.00
106 Cliff Bartosh NT/80 4.00 10.00
107 Felix Escalona NT/79 4.00 10.00
108 Corey Thurman NT/78 4.00 10.00
109 Kazuhisa Ishii NT/77 6.00 15.00
110 Miguel Asencio NT/76 4.00 10.00
111 P.J. Bevis NT/75 4.00 10.00
112 Gustavo Chacin NT/74 10.00 25.00
113 Steve Kent NT/73 4.00 10.00
114 Takahito Nomura NT/72 4.00 10.00
115 Adam Walker NT/71 4.00 10.00
116 So Taguchi NT/70 6.00 15.00
117 Reed Johnson NT/69 6.00 15.00
118 Rodrigo Rosario NT/68 4.00 10.00
119 Luis Martinez NT/67 4.00 10.00
120 Satoru Komiyama NT/66 4.00 10.00
121 Sean Burroughs NT/65 5.00 12.00
122 Hank Blalock NT/64 8.00 20.00
123 Marlon Byrd NT/63 5.00 12.00
124 Nick Johnson NT/62 5.00 12.00
125 Mark Teixeira NT/61 12.50 30.00

2002 E-X Essential Credentials Now

SEE BECKETT.COM FOR PRINT RUNS
NO PRICING ON QUANTITIES OF 25 OR LESS
CARDS 1-60 FEATURE GAME USED ITEMS
26 Kevin Brown Jsy/26 15.00 40.00
27 Jeromy Burnitz Bat/27 15.00 40.00
28 Jeff Cirillo Jsy/28 12.50 30.00
29 Carl Everett Jsy/29 15.00 40.00
30 Eric Chavez Bat/30 15.00 40.00
31 Freddy Garcia Jsy/31 15.00 40.00
32 Mark Grace Jsy/32 20.00 50.00
33 David Justice Jsy/33 15.00 40.00
34 Fred McGriff Jsy/34 20.00 50.00
36 John Olerud Jsy/36 12.50 30.00
37 Magglio Ordonez Jsy/37 12.50 30.00
38 Curt Schilling Jsy/38 12.50 30.00
39 Aaron Sele Jsy/39 10.00 25.00
40 Robin Ventura Jsy/40 12.50 30.00
41 Adam Dunn Bat/41 12.50 30.00
42 Jeff Bagwell Jsy/42 15.00 40.00
43 Barry Bonds Pants/43 30.00 60.00
44 Roger Clemens Bat/44 50.00 100.00
45 Cliff Floyd Bat/45 12.50 30.00
46 Jason Giambi Base/46 12.50 30.00
47 Juan Gonzalez Jsy/47 12.50 30.00
48 Luis Gonzalez Base/48 12.50 30.00
49 Cristian Guzman Bat/49 10.00 25.00
50 Todd Helton Base/50 15.00 40.00
51 Derek Jeter Bat/51 60.00 120.00
52 Rafael Palmeiro Bat/52 12.50 30.00
53 Mike Sweeney Bat/53 10.00 25.00
54 Ben Grieve Jsy/54 8.00 20.00
55 Phil Nevin Bat/55 10.00 25.00
56 Mike Piazza Base/56 30.00 60.00
57 Moises Alou Bat/57 10.00 25.00
58 Ivan Rodriguez Jsy/58 12.50 30.00
59 Manny Ramirez Base/59 12.50 30.00
60 Brian Giles Bat/60 10.00 25.00
61 Jim Thome/61 8.00 20.00
62 Larry Walker/62 5.00 12.00
63 Bobby Abreu/63 5.00 12.00
64 Troy Glaus/64 5.00 12.00
65 Garret Anderson/65 5.00 12.00
66 Roberto Alomar/66 6.00 15.00
67 Bret Boone/67 4.00 10.00
68 Marty Cordova/68 4.00 10.00
69 Craig Biggio/69 6.00 15.00
70 Omar Vizquel/70 6.00 15.00
71 Jermaine Dye/71 4.00 10.00
72 Darin Erstad/72 4.00 10.00
73 Carlos Delgado/73 4.00 10.00
74 Nomar Garciaparra/74 15.00 40.00
75 Greg Maddux/75 15.00 40.00
76 Tom Glavine/76 6.00 15.00
77 Frank Thomas/77 10.00 25.00
78 Shawn Green/78 4.00 10.00
79 Bobby Higginson/79 4.00 10.00
80 Jeff Kent/80 4.00 10.00
81 Chuck Knoblauch/81 3.00 8.00
82 Paul Konerko/82 3.00 8.00
83 Carlos Lee/83 3.00 8.00
84 Jon Lieber/84 3.00 8.00
85 Paul LoDuca/85 3.00 8.00
86 Mike Lowell/86 3.00 8.00
87 Edgar Martinez/87 5.00 12.00
88 Doug Mientkiewicz/88 3.00 8.00
89 Pedro Martinez/89 5.00 12.00
90 Randy Johnson/90 8.00 20.00
91 Aramis Ramirez/91 3.00 8.00
92 J.D. Drew/92 3.00 8.00
93 Chris Richard/93 3.00 8.00
94 Jimmy Rollins/94 3.00 8.00
95 Ryan Klesko/95 3.00 8.00
96 Gary Sheffield/96 3.00 8.00
97 Chipper Jones/97 8.00 20.00
98 Greg Vaughn/98 3.00 8.00
99 Mo Vaughn/99 3.00 8.00
100 Bernie Williams/100 5.00 12.00
101 John Foster NT/101 3.00 8.00
102 Jorge De La Rosa NT/102 3.00 8.00
103 Edwin Almonte NT/103 3.00 8.00
104 Chris Booker NT/104 3.00 8.00
105 Victor Alvarez NT/105 3.00 8.00
106 Cliff Bartosh NT/106 3.00 8.00
107 Felix Escalona NT/107 3.00 8.00
108 Corey Thurman NT/108 3.00 8.00
109 Kazuhisa Ishii NT/109 5.00 12.00
110 Miguel Asencio NT/110 3.00 8.00
111 P.J. Bevis NT/111 3.00 8.00
112 Gustavo Chacin NT/112 8.00 20.00
113 Steve Kent NT/113 3.00 8.00
114 Takahito Nomura NT/114 3.00 8.00
115 Adam Walker NT/115 3.00 8.00
116 So Taguchi NT/116 5.00 12.00
117 Reed Johnson NT/117 5.00 12.00
118 Rodrigo Rosario NT/118 3.00 8.00
119 Luis Martinez NT/119 3.00 8.00
120 Satoru Komiyama NT/120 3.00 8.00
121 Sean Burroughs NT/121 3.00 8.00
122 Hank Blalock NT/122 5.00 12.00
123 Marlon Byrd NT/123 3.00 8.00
124 Nick Johnson NT/124 3.00 8.00
125 Mark Teixeira NT/125 8.00 20.00

2002 E-X Behind the Numbers

COMPLETE SET (35) 50.00 120.00
STATED ODDS 1:8 HOBBY, 1:12 RETAIL
1 Ichiro Suzuki 3.00 8.00
2 Jason Giambi 1.00 2.50
3 Mike Piazza 2.50 6.00
4 Brian Giles 1.00 2.50
5 Barry Bonds 4.00 10.00
6 Pedro Martinez 1.00 2.50
7 Nomar Garciaparra 2.50 6.00
8 Randy Johnson 1.50 4.00
9 Craig Biggio 1.00 2.50
10 Manny Ramirez 1.00 2.50
11 Mike Mussina 1.00 2.50
12 Kerry Wood 1.00 2.50
13 Jim Edmonds 1.00 2.50
14 Ivan Rodriguez 1.00 2.50
15 Jeff Bagwell 1.00 2.50
16 Roger Clemens 3.00 8.00
17 Chipper Jones 1.50 4.00
18 Shawn Green 1.00 2.50
19 Albert Pujols 3.00 8.00
20 Andruw Jones 1.00 2.50
21 Luis Gonzalez 1.00 2.50
22 Todd Helton 1.00 2.50
23 Jorge Posada 1.00 2.50
24 Scott Rolen 1.00 2.50
25 Ben Sheets 1.00 2.50
26 Alfonso Soriano 1.00 2.50
27 Greg Maddux 2.50 6.00
28 Gary Sheffield 1.00 2.50
29 Barry Zito 1.00 2.50
30 Alex Rodriguez 2.00 5.00
31 Larry Walker 1.00 2.50
32 Derek Jeter 4.00 10.00
33 Ken Griffey Jr. 3.00 8.00
34 Vladimir Guerrero 1.50 4.00
35 Sammy Sosa 1.50 4.00

2002 E-X Behind the Numbers Game Jersey

STATED ODDS 1:24 HOBBY, 1:130 RETAIL
1 Jeff Bagwell 2.00 5.00
2 Craig Biggio Jsy 2.00 5.00
Pants
4 Roger Clemens 4.00 10.00
5 Jim Edmonds 2.00 5.00
6 Brian Giles 1.25 3.00
7 Luis Gonzalez 1.25 3.00
8 Shawn Green 1.25 3.00
9 Todd Helton 2.00 5.00
10 Derek Jeter SP 8.00 20.00
11 Randy Johnson SP 6.00 15.00
12 Andruw Jones 1.25 3.00
13 Chipper Jones 3.00 8.00
14 Greg Maddux 5.00 12.00
15 Pedro Martinez 2.00 5.00
16 Mike Mussina 2.00 5.00
17 Mike Piazza Pants 3.00 8.00
18 Jorge Posada 2.00 5.00
19 Manny Ramirez 2.00 5.00
20 Alex Rodriguez 4.00 10.00
21 Ivan Rodriguez 2.00 5.00
22 Scott Rolen 2.00 5.00
23 Alfonso Soriano SP 4.00 10.00
24 Barry Zito 1.25 3.00

2002 E-X Barry Bonds 4X MVP

COMMON CARD (1-4) 4.00 10.00
RANDOM INSERTS IN PACKS
STATED PRINT RUN 1990-2001 #'d CARDS

2002 E-X Game Essentials

*PATCH PREMIUM: 1.5X TO 3X LISTED PRICE
1 Carlos Beltran Jsy 4.00 10.00
4 Kevin Brown Pants 4.00 10.00
5 Jeromy Burnitz Jsy 4.00 10.00
6 Carlos Delgado Bat 4.00 10.00

8 Rickey Henderson Bat 6.00 15.00
9 Rickey Henderson Jsy 8.00 20.00
10 Drew Henson Bat 4.00 10.00
11 Drew Henson Cleat 4.00 10.00
12 Drew Henson Fld Glv 6.00 15.00
13 Derek Jeter Cleat 20.00 50.00
14 Jason Kendall Jsy 4.00 10.00
16 Barry Larkin Fld Glv 10.00 25.00
17 Javy Lopez Jsy 4.00 10.00
18 Raul Mondesi Btg Glv 6.00 15.00
19 Raul Mondesi Jsy 4.00 10.00
20 Rafael Palmeiro Bat 6.00 15.00
21 Rafael Palmeiro Pants 6.00 15.00
22 Adam Piatt Jsy 4.00 10.00
23 Brad Radke Jsy 4.00 10.00
24 Cal Ripken Jsy 12.00 30.00
25 Mariano Rivera Jsy 6.00 15.00
26 Alex Rodriguez Btg Glv 10.00 25.00
29 Kazuhiro Sasaki Jsy 4.00 10.00
31 Mo Vaughn Jsy 4.00 10.00
32 Robin Ventura Btg Glv 6.00 15.00
33 Robin Ventura Jsy 4.00 10.00
34 Jose Vidro Jsy 4.00 10.00
35 Matt Williams Jsy 4.00 10.00

2002 E-X HardWear

COMPLETE SET (10) 40.00 100.00
STATED ODDS 1:72 HOBBY, 1:216 RETAIL
1 Ivan Rodriguez 3.00 8.00
2 Mike Piazza 5.00 12.00
3 Derek Jeter 8.00 20.00
4 Barry Bonds 8.00 20.00
5 Todd Helton 3.00 8.00
6 Roberto Alomar 3.00 8.00
7 Albert Pujols 6.00 15.00
8 Ichiro Suzuki 6.00 15.00
9 Ken Griffey Jr. 6.00 15.00
10 Jason Giambi 3.00 8.00

2002 E-X Hit and Run

COMPLETE SET (30) 15.00 40.00
STATED ODDS 1:12 HOBBY, 1:72 RETAIL
1 Adam Dunn .60 1.50
2 Derek Jeter 2.50 6.00
3 Frank Thomas 1.00 2.50
4 Albert Pujols 2.00 5.00
5 J.D. Drew .40 1.00
6 Richard Hidalgo .40 1.00
7 John Olerud .40 1.00
8 Roberto Alomar .60 1.50
9 Pat Burrell .40 1.00
10 Darin Erstad .40 1.00
11 Mark Grace .60 1.50
12 Chipper Jones 1.00 2.50
13 Jose Vidro .40 1.00
14 Cliff Floyd .40 1.00
15 Mo Vaughn .40 1.00
16 Nomar Garciaparra .60 1.50
17 Ivan Rodriguez .60 1.50
18 Luis Gonzalez .40 1.00
19 Jason Giambi .40 1.00
20 Bernie Williams .60 1.50
21 Mike Piazza 1.00 2.50
22 Barry Bonds 1.50 4.00
23 Jose Ortiz .40 1.00
24 Magglio Ordonez .60 1.50
25 Troy Glaus .40 1.00
26 Alex Rodriguez 1.25 3.00
27 Ichiro Suzuki 1.25 3.00
28 Sammy Sosa 1.00 2.50
29 Ken Griffey Jr. 2.00 5.00
30 Vladimir Guerrero .60 1.50

2002 E-X Hit and Run Game Base

STATED ODDS 1:120 HOBBY, 1:360 RETAIL
1 J.D. Drew 1.50 4.00
2 Adam Dunn 2.50 6.00
3 Jason Giambi 1.50 4.00
4 Troy Glaus 1.50 4.00
5 Ken Griffey Jr. 8.00 20.00
6 Vladimir Guerrero 2.50 6.00
7 Albert Pujols 8.00 20.00
8 Sammy Sosa 4.00 10.00
9 Ichiro Suzuki 5.00 12.00
10 Bernie Williams 2.50 6.00

2002 E-X Hit and Run Game Bat

STATED ODDS 1:24 HOBBY, 1:130 RETAIL
1 Roberto Alomar 2.50 6.00
2 J.D. Drew 1.50 4.00
3 Darin Erstad 1.50 4.00
4 Cliff Floyd 1.50 4.00
5 Nomar Garciaparra 2.50 6.00
6 Luis Gonzalez 1.50 4.00
7 Richard Hidalgo 1.50 4.00
8 Derek Jeter 10.00 25.00
9 Chipper Jones 4.00 10.00
10 John Olerud 1.50 4.00
11 Magglio Ordonez 2.50 6.00
12 Jose Ortiz 1.50 4.00
13 Mike Piazza 4.00 10.00
14 Alex Rodriguez 5.00 12.00
15 Ivan Rodriguez 2.50 6.00
16 Frank Thomas 4.00 10.00
17 Mo Vaughn 1.50 4.00
18 Jose Vidro 1.50 4.00
19 Bernie Williams 2.50 6.00

2002 E-X Hit and Run Game Bat and Base

STATED ODDS 1:240 HOBBY, 1:720 RETAIL
1 Roberto Alomar 4.00 10.00
2 Barry Bonds SP 10.00 25.00
3 Nomar Garciaparra 4.00 10.00
4 Derek Jeter 15.00 40.00
5 Chipper Jones 6.00 15.00
6 Mike Piazza 6.00 15.00
7 Alex Rodriguez 8.00 20.00
8 Mo Vaughn 2.50 6.00

2002 E-X Derek Jeter 4X Champ

COMMON CARD (1-4) 4.00 10.00
RANDOM INSERTS IN PACKS
STATED PRINT RUN 1996-2000 #'d CARDS

2003 E-X

COMP.SET w/o SP's (72) 15.00 40.00
COMMON CARD (1-72) .20 .50
COMMON CARD (73-82) .75 2.00
COMMON CARD (83-86) .75 2.00
COMMON CARD (87-102) .75 2.00
73-102 RANDOM INSERTS IN PACKS
1 Troy Glaus .20 .50
2 Darin Erstad .20 .50
3 Garret Anderson .20 .50
4 Curt Schilling .30 .75
5 Randy Johnson .50 1.25
6 Luis Gonzalez .20 .50
7 Greg Maddux .60 1.50
8 Chipper Jones .50 1.25
9 Andruw Jones .20 .50
10 Melvin Mora .20 .50
11 Jay Gibbons .20 .50
12 Nomar Garciaparra .30 .75
13 Pedro Martinez .30 .75
14 Manny Ramirez .50 1.25
15 Sammy Sosa .50 1.25
16 Kerry Wood .20 .50
17 Magglio Ordonez .30 .75
18 Frank Thomas .50 1.25
19 Roberto Alomar .30 .75
20 Barry Larkin .30 .75
21 Adam Dunn .30 .75
22 Austin Kearns .20 .50
23 Omar Vizquel .30 .75
24 Larry Walker .30 .75
25 Todd Helton .30 .75
26 Preston Wilson .20 .50
27 Dmitri Young .20 .50
28 Ivan Rodriguez .30 .75
29 Mike Lowell .20 .50
30 Jeff Kent .20 .50
31 Jeff Bagwell .30 .75
32 Roy Oswalt .30 .75
33 Craig Biggio .30 .75
34 Mike Sweeney .20 .50
35 Carlos Beltran .30 .75
36 Shawn Green .20 .50
37 Kazuhisa Ishii .20 .50
38 Richie Sexson .20 .50
39 Torii Hunter .20 .50
40 Jacque Jones .20 .50
41 Jose Vidro .20 .50
42 Vladimir Guerrero .30 .75
43 Mike Piazza .50 1.25
44 Tom Glavine .30 .75
45 Roger Clemens .60 1.50
46 Jason Giambi .20 .50
47 Bernie Williams .30 .75
48 Alfonso Soriano .30 .75
49 Mike Mussina .30 .75
50 Barry Zito .30 .75
51 Miguel Tejada .30 .75
52 Eric Chavez .20 .50
53 Eric Byrnes .20 .50
54 Jim Thome .30 .75
55 Kevin Millwood .20 .50
56 Brian Giles .20 .50
57 Xavier Nady .20 .50
58 Barry Bonds .75 2.00
59 Bret Boone .20 .50
60 Edgar Martinez .30 .75
61 Kazuhiro Sasaki .20 .50
62 Edgar Renteria .20 .50
63 J.D. Drew .20 .50
64 Scott Rolen .30 .75
65 Jim Edmonds .30 .75
66 Aubrey Huff .20 .50
67 Alex Rodriguez .60 1.50
68 Juan Gonzalez .20 .50
69 Hank Blalock .20 .50
70 Mark Teixeira .30 .75
71 Carlos Delgado .20 .50
72 Vernon Wells .20 .50
73 Shea Hillenbrand SP .75 2.00
74 Gary Sheffield SP .75 2.00
75 Mark Prior SP 1.25 3.00
76 Ken Griffey Jr. SP 4.00 10.00
77 Lance Berkman SP 1.25 3.00
78 Hideo Nomo SP 2.00 5.00
79 Derek Jeter SP 5.00 12.00
80 Ichiro Suzuki SP 2.50 6.00
81 Albert Pujols SP 2.50 6.00
82 Rafael Palmeiro SP 1.25 3.00
83 Jose Reyes ROO SP 2.00 5.00
84 Rocco Baldelli ROO SP .75 2.00
85 Hee Seop Choi ROO SP .75 2.00
86 Dontrelle Willis ROO SP .75 2.00
87 Robb Hammock ROO SP RC .75 2.00
88 Brandon Webb ROO SP RC 2.50 6.00
89 Matt Kata ROO SP RC .75 2.00
90 T.Wellemeyer ROO SP RC .75 2.00
91 Fran Cruceta ROO SP RC .75 2.00
92 Clint Barmes ROO SP RC 2.00 5.00
93 Jer Bonderman ROO SP RC 3.00 8.00
94 David Matranga ROO SP RC .75 2.00
95 Ryan Wagner ROO SP RC .75 2.00
96 Jeremy Griffiths ROO SP RC .75 2.00
97 Hideki Matsui ROO SP RC 4.00 10.00
98 Jose Contreras ROO SP RC 2.00 5.00
99 C.Wang ROO SP RC 3.00 8.00
100 Bo Hart ROO SP RC .75 2.00
101 Danny Haren ROO SP RC 4.00 10.00
102 Rickie Weeks ROO SP RC 2.50 6.00

2003 E-X Essential Credentials Future

*EC FUTURE 1-22: 4X TO 10X BASIC
*EC FUTURE 23-52: 5X TO 12X BASIC
*EC FUTURE 53-67: 6X TO 15X BASIC
*EC FUTURE 68-72: 8X TO 20X BASIC
*EC FUTURE 73-77: 1.5X TO 4X BASIC
PRINT RUNS B/WN 1-102 COPIES PER
78-102 NOT PRICED DUE TO SCARCITY

2003 E-X Essential Credentials Now

*EC NOW 26-30: 10X TO 25X BASIC
*EC NOW 31-35: 8X TO 20X BASIC
*EC NOW 36-50: 6X TO 15X BASIC
*EC NOW 51-72: 5X TO 12X BASIC
*EC NOW 73-80: .75X TO 2X BASIC
*EC NOW 81-82: .6X TO 1.5X BASIC
*EC NOW 83-102: .75X TO 2X BASIC
*EC NOW 83-102: .75X TO 2X BASIC RC'S
PRINT RUNS B/WN 1-102 COPIES PER
1-25 NO PRICING DUE TO SCARCITY

2003 E-X Behind the Numbers

STATED ODDS 1:80
1 Derek Jeter 6.00 15.00
2 Alex Rodriguez 3.00 8.00
3 Randy Johnson 2.50 6.00
4 Chipper Jones 2.50 6.00
5 Jim Thome 1.50 4.00
6 Alfonso Soriano 1.50 4.00
7 Adam Dunn 1.50 4.00
8 Nomar Garciaparra 1.50 4.00
9 Roger Clemens 3.00 8.00
10 Gary Sheffield 1.00 2.50
11 Vladimir Guerrero 1.50 4.00
12 Greg Maddux 3.00 8.00
13 Sammy Sosa 2.50 6.00
14 Mike Piazza 2.50 6.00
15 Troy Glaus 1.00 2.50

2003 E-X Behind the Numbers Game Jersey 500

PRINT RUN 500 SERIAL #'d SETS
*BTN 199: .5X TO 1.2X BTN 500
BTN 199 PRINT RUN 199 #'d SETS
*BTN 99 MULTI-PATCH: 1.25X TO 3X BTN 500
*BTN 99 ONE COLOR: .75X TO 2X BTN 500
BTN 99 PRINT RUN 99 #'d SETS
BTN 99 ARE MOSTLY PATCH CARDS
AD Adam Dunn 2.00 5.00
AR Alex Rodriguez 5.00 12.00
AS Alfonso Soriano 2.00 5.00
BM Brett Myers 2.00 5.00
BZ Barry Zito 2.00 5.00
CJ Chipper Jones 3.00 8.00
DJ Derek Jeter 8.00 20.00
DW Dontrelle Willis 3.00 8.00
GM Greg Maddux 4.00 10.00
GS Gary Sheffield 2.00 5.00
HB Hank Blalock 2.00 5.00
JT Jim Thome 3.00 8.00
LB Lance Berkman 2.00 5.00
MB Marlon Byrd 2.00 5.00
MP Mike Piazza 4.00 10.00
NG Nomar Garciaparra 5.00 12.00
RA Roberto Alomar 3.00 8.00
RB Rocco Baldelli 2.00 5.00
RC Roger Clemens 5.00 12.00
RJ Randy Johnson 3.00 8.00
RP Rafael Palmeiro 3.00 8.00
SS Sammy Sosa 3.00 8.00
TG Troy Glaus 2.00 5.00
TGL Tom Glavine 3.00 8.00
VG Vladimir Guerrero 3.00 8.00

2003 E-X Behind the Numbers Game Jersey Autographs

RANDOM INSERTS IN PACKS
PRINT RUNS B/WN 5-35 COPIES PER
NO PRICING ON QTY OF 9 OR LESS
EXCHANGE DEADLINE INDEFINITE
DW Dontrelle Willis/35 10.00 25.00

2003 E-X Behind the Numbers Game Jersey Number

PRINT RUNS B/WN 2-75 COPIES PER
NO PRICING ON QTY OF 25 OR LESS
AD Adam Dunn/44 8.00 20.00
BM Brett Myers/39 6.00 15.00
BZ Barry Zito/75 4.00 10.00
DW Dontrelle Willis/35 10.00 25.00
GM Greg Maddux/31 10.00 25.00
MB Marlon Byrd/29 8.00 20.00
MP Mike Piazza/31 15.00 40.00
RJ Randy Johnson/51 6.00 15.00
TGL Tom Glavine/47 8.00 20.00
VG Vladimir Guerrero/27 10.00 25.00

2003 E-X Diamond Essentials Autographs

RANDOM INSERTS IN PACKS
PRINT RUNS B/WN 100-299 COPIES PER
EXCHANGE DEADLINE INDEFINITE
DW Dontrelle Willis/265 10.00 25.00
RB Rocco Baldelli/299 6.00 15.00
RW Ryan Wagner/199 6.00 15.00

2003 E-X Diamond Essentials Game Jersey 345

STATED PRINT RUN 345 SERIAL #'d SETS
*DE 245: .5X TO 1.2X DE 345
DE 245 PRINT RUN 245 #'d SETS
*DE 145: .6X TO 1.5X DE 345
DE 145 PRINT RUN 145 #'d SETS
*DE 55 MULTI-PATCH: 1.25X TO 3X DE 345
*DE 55 ONE COLOR: 1X TO 2.5X DE 345
DE 55 PRINT RUN 55 #'d SETS
DE 55 ARE MOSTLY PATCH CARDS
DE 5 PRINT RUN 5 #'d SETS
NO DE 5 PRICING DUE TO SCARCITY
CJ Chipper Jones 3.00 8.00
DJ Derek Jeter 8.00 20.00
JB Jeff Bagwell 3.00 8.00
JG Jason Giambi 2.00 5.00
JR Jose Reyes 2.00 5.00
MP Mike Piazza 5.00 12.00
MP Mark Prior 3.00 8.00
PM Pedro Martinez 3.00 8.00
RJ Randy Johnson 3.00 8.00
SS Sammy Sosa 3.00 8.00

2003 E-X Emerald Essentials Autographs

PRINT RUNS B/WN 29-299 COPIES PER
EXCHANGE DEADLINE INDEFINITE
BW Brandon Webb/299 8.00 20.00
HB Hank Blalock/299 4.00 10.00

2003 E-X Emerald Essentials Game Jersey 375

STATED PRINT RUN 375 SERIAL #'d SETS
*EE 250: .5X TO 1.2X EE 375
EE 250 PRINT RUN 250 #'d SETS
*EE 175: .6X TO 1.5X EE 375
EE 175 PRINT RUN 175 #'d SETS
*EE 60 SWATCH: 1X TO 2.5X EE 375
*EE 60 MULTI-PATCH: 1.25X TO 3X EE 375
EE 60 PRINT RUN 60 #'d SETS
ABOUT HALF OF EE 60'S ARE PATCH CARDS
EE 15 PRINT RUN 15 #'d SETS
NO EE 15 PRICING DUE TO SCARCITY
AD Adam Dunn 2.00 5.00
AK Austin Kearns 2.00 5.00
AR Alex Rodriguez 5.00 12.00
AS Alfonso Soriano 2.00 5.00
HN Hideo Nomo 6.00 15.00
KW Kerry Wood 2.00 5.00
MT Miguel Tejada 2.00 5.00
NG Nomar Garciaparra 5.00 12.00
RC Roger Clemens 5.00 12.00
TG Troy Glaus 2.00 5.00

2003 E-X X-tra Innings

STATED ODDS 1:32
1 Ichiro Suzuki 2.00 5.00
2 Albert Pujols 2.00 5.00
3 Barry Bonds 2.50 6.00
4 Jason Giambi .60 1.50
5 Pedro Martinez 1.00 2.50
6 Mark Prior 1.00 2.50
7 Derek Jeter 4.00 10.00
8 Curt Schilling 1.00 2.50
9 Jeff Bagwell 1.00 2.50
10 Alex Rodriguez 2.00 5.00

2004 E-X

COMMON CARD (1-40) .40 1.00
COMMON CARD (41-65) 1.00 2.50
41-65 OVERALL ODDS ONE PER PACK
41-65 PRINT RUN 350 SERIAL #'d SETS
41-65 1ST 150 #'d COPIES ARE DIE CUTS
SEE PARALLEL SET FOR DIE CUT PRICES
1 Vladimir Guerrero .60 1.50
2 Randy Johnson 1.00 2.50
3 Chipper Jones 1.00 2.50
4 Miguel Tejada .60 1.50
5 Pedro Martinez .60 1.50
6 Nomar Garciaparra .60 1.50
7 Sammy Sosa 1.00 2.50
8 Greg Maddux 1.25 3.00
9 Frank Thomas 1.00 2.50
10 Ken Griffey Jr. 2.00 5.00
11 Omar Vizquel .60 1.50
12 Todd Helton .60 1.50
13 Ivan Rodriguez .60 1.50
14 Miguel Cabrera 1.00 2.50
15 Dontrelle Willis .40 1.00
16 Jeff Bagwell .60 1.50
17 Roger Clemens 1.25 3.00
18 Carlos Beltran .60 1.50
19 Hideo Nomo 1.00 2.50
20 Scott Podsednik .40 1.00
21 Torii Hunter .40 1.00
22 Jose Vidro .40 1.00
23 Mike Piazza 1.00 2.50
24 Hideki Matsui 1.50 4.00
25 Alex Rodriguez 1.25 3.00
26 Derek Jeter 2.50 6.00
27 Tim Hudson .60 1.50
28 Jim Thome .60 1.50
29 Craig Wilson .40 1.00
30 Brian Giles .40 1.00
31 Jason Schmidt .40 1.00
32 Ichiro Suzuki 1.25 3.00
33 Scott Rolen .60 1.50
34 Albert Pujols 1.25 3.00
35 Rocco Baldelli .40 1.00
36 Alfonso Soriano .60 1.50
37 Carlos Delgado .40 1.00
38 Curt Schilling .60 1.50
39 Mark Prior .60 1.50
40 Josh Beckett .40 1.00
41 Merkin Valdez ROO RC 1.00 2.50
42 Akinori Otsuka ROO RC 1.00 2.50
43 Ian Snell ROO RC 1.00 2.50
44 Kaz Matsui ROO RC 1.50 4.00
45 Jason Bartlett ROO RC 3.00 8.00
46 Dennis Sarfate ROO RC 1.00 2.50
47 Sean Henn ROO RC 1.00 2.50
48 David Aardsma ROO RC 1.00 2.50
49 Casey Kotchman ROO 1.00 2.50
50 John Gall ROO RC 1.00 2.50
51 William Bergolla ROO RC 1.00 2.50
52 Angel Chavez ROO RC 1.00 2.50
53 Hector Gimenez ROO RC 1.00 2.50
54 Aaron Baldiris ROO RC 1.00 2.50
55 Justin Leone ROO RC 1.00 2.50
56 Onil Joseph ROO RC 1.00 2.50
57 Freddy Guzman ROO RC 1.00 2.50
58 Andres Blanco ROO RC 1.00 2.50
59 Greg Dobbs ROO RC 1.00 2.50
60 Joe Mauer ROO 2.00 5.00
61 Luis Gonzalez ROO RC 1.00 2.50
62 Chris Saenz ROO RC 1.00 2.50
63 Zack Greinke ROO 4.00 10.00
64 Jose Capellan ROO RC 1.00 2.50
65 Brad Halsey ROO RC 1.00 2.50

2004 E-X Die Cuts

*DIE CUTS 41-65: .5X TO 1.2X BASIC
41-65 OVERALL ODDS ONE PER PACK
STATED PRINT RUN 150 SERIAL #'d SETS
DIE CUTS ARE 1ST 150 SERIAL #'d COPIES

2004 E-X Essential Credentials Future

*FUTURE p/r 51-65: 1.5X TO 4X BASIC
*FUTURE p/r 36-50: 2X TO 5X BASIC
*FUTURE p/r 26-35: 2.5X TO 6X BASIC
OVERALL PARALLEL ODDS 1:3
PRINT RUNS B/WN 1-65 COPIES PER
NO PRICING ON QTY OF 25 OR LESS

2004 E-X Essential Credentials Now

*NOW p/r 51-65: .75X TO 2X BASIC
*NOW p/r 41-50: 1X TO 2.5X BASIC
*NOW p/r 36-40: 2X TO 5X BASIC
*NOW p/r 26-35: 2.5X TO 6X BASIC
*NOW p/r 16-25: 3X TO 8X BASIC
OVERALL PARALLEL ODDS 1:3
PRINT RUNS B/WN 1-65 COPIES PER
NO PRICING ON QTY OF 14 OR LESS

2004 E-X Check Mates

OVERALL AUTO ODDS ONE PER PACK
PRINT RUNS B/WN 1-25 COPIES PER
NO PRICING ON QTY OF 1 COPY PER
EXCHANGE DEADLINE INDEFINITE
APSM Albert Pujols 300.00 400.00
Stan Musial/25
EBRS E.Banks/R.Sandberg/25 125.00 200.00
EMRP E.Murray/R.Palmeiro/25 90.00 150.00
RJDM R.Jackson/D.Mattingly/25 150.00 250.00
WBTG W.Boggs/T.Gwynn/25 100.00 175.00

2004 E-X Classic ConnExions Game Used Double

STATED PRINT RUN 22 SERIAL #'d SETS
DOUBLE EMERALD PRINT RUN 1 #'d SET
NO DOUBLE EMERALD PRICING AVAILABLE
OVERALL GU ODDS ONE PER PACK
BRJF Ruth B/Foxx B 150.00 250.00
CRBR Ripken J/Brooks B 75.00 150.00
CRNR Ripken J/Ryan J 75.00 150.00
CRRY Ripken J/Yount J 25.00 60.00
DMRJ Mattingly J/Reggie J 40.00 80.00
DMTM Mattingly J/Munson J 50.00 100.00
DWCY Winfield J/Yaz J 20.00 50.00
EMCR Murray J/Ripken J 75.00 150.00
EMRJ Murray J/Reggie J 25.00 60.00
HKAK Killebrew P/Kaline P 30.00 60.00
HWHG H.Wilson B/G'berg B 50.00 100.00
JBCF Bench J/Fisk P 25.00 60.00
JCRH Canseco J/Rickey J 25.00 60.00
KPDM Puckett J/Mattingly J 40.00 80.00
LBRC Brock J/Carew J 15.00 40.00
MSEM Schmidt J/Mathews P 75.00 150.00
NRTS Ryan J/Seaver J 60.00 120.00
PMRY Molitor J/Yount J 25.00 60.00
RCRJ Carew J/Reggie J 15.00 40.00
RHLB Rickey J/Brock J 25.00 60.00
RMBR Maris B/Ruth B 175.00 300.00
TGRH Gwynn J/Rickey J 20.00 50.00
TWCY T.Williams B/Yaz B 125.00 200.00
WBCY Boggs B/Yastrzemski J 25.00 60.00
WBDM Boggs J/Mattingly J 25.00 60.00
WBTG Boggs B/Gwynn J 25.00 60.00
WMWS McCovey B/Stargell B 15.00 40.00
WSWF Spahn J/Ford P 25.00 60.00
YBRC Berra B/Campanella B 25.00 60.00

2004 E-X Clearly Authentics Black Patch

*3-COLOR PATCHES: ADD 20% PREMIUM
*4-COLOR PATCHES: ADD 50% PREMIUM
*5-COLOR PATCHES: ADD 100% PREMIUM
*JSY TAG PATCHES: ADD 100% PREMIUM
OVERALL GU ODDS ONE PER PACK
STATED PRINT RUN 75 SERIAL #'d SETS
AD Adam Dunn 6.00 15.00
AJ Andruw Jones 8.00 20.00
AP Albert Pujols 20.00 50.00
AR Alex Rodriguez 15.00 40.00
AS Alfonso Soriano 6.00 15.00
BG Brian Giles 6.00 15.00
BZ Barry Zito 6.00 15.00
CJ Chipper Jones 10.00 25.00
CR Cal Ripken 20.00 50.00
CS Curt Schilling 8.00 20.00
DM Don Mattingly 20.00 50.00
DW Dontrelle Willis 8.00 20.00
EG Eric Gagne 6.00 15.00
EM Eddie Murray 15.00 40.00
FT Frank Thomas 10.00 25.00
GM Greg Maddux 12.50 30.00
HB Hank Blalock 6.00 15.00
HM Hideki Matsui 12.50 30.00
HN Hideo Nomo 15.00 40.00
IR Ivan Rodriguez 8.00 20.00
JB Jeff Bagwell 8.00 20.00
JB2 Josh Beckett 6.00 15.00
JG2 Jason Giambi 6.00 15.00
JT Jim Thome 8.00 20.00
KM Kaz Matsui 10.00 25.00
KW Kerry Wood 6.00 15.00
LB Lance Berkman 6.00 15.00
MC Miguel Cabrera 8.00 20.00
MO Magglio Ordonez 6.00 15.00
MP Mark Prior 8.00 20.00
MP2 Mike Piazza 15.00 40.00
MR Manny Ramirez 8.00 20.00
MT Mark Teixeira 8.00 20.00
MT2 Miguel Tejada 6.00 15.00
OS Ozzie Smith 15.00 40.00
PB Pat Burrell 6.00 15.00
PM Paul Molitor 6.00 15.00
PR Pedro Martinez 8.00 20.00
RB Rocco Baldelli 6.00 15.00
RC Roger Clemens 15.00 40.00
RC2 Rod Carew 10.00 25.00
RH Rickey Henderson 10.00 25.00
RJ Randy Johnson 10.00 25.00
RP Rafael Palmeiro 8.00 20.00
RW Rickie Weeks 6.00 15.00
SG Shawn Green 6.00 15.00
SR Scott Rolen 8.00 20.00
SS Sammy Sosa 10.00 25.00
TG Troy Glaus 6.00 15.00
TG2 Tony Gwynn 15.00 40.00
TH Todd Helton 8.00 20.00
TH2 Torii Hunter 6.00 15.00
TH3 Tim Hudson 6.00 15.00
VG Vladimir Guerrero 10.00 25.00

2004 E-X Clearly Authentics Bronze Jersey-Patch

*BRONZE JSY-PATCH: .6X TO 1.5X BASIC
*3-COLOR PATCHES: ADD 20% PREMIUM
*4-COLOR PATCHES: ADD 50% PREMIUM
*5-COLOR PATCHES: ADD 100% PREMIUM
*JSY TAG PATCHES: ADD 100% PREMIUM
OVERALL GU ODDS ONE PER PACK
STATED PRINT RUN 35 SERIAL #'d SETS
CY Carl Yastrzemski 25.00 60.00
RJ2 Reggie Jackson 15.00 40.00

2004 E-X Clearly Authentics Pewter Bat-Patch

*PEWTER BAT-PATCH: .6X TO 1.5X BASIC
*3-COLOR PATCHES: ADD 20% PREMIUM
*4-COLOR PATCHES: ADD 50% PREMIUM
*5-COLOR PATCHES: ADD 100% PREMIUM
*JSY TAG PATCHES: ADD 100% PREMIUM
OVERALL GU ODDS ONE PER PACK
STATED PRINT RUN 44 SERIAL #'d SETS
CY Carl Yastrzemski 25.00 60.00
RJ2 Reggie Jackson 15.00 40.00

2004 E-X Clearly Authentics Tan Double Patch

*TAN DOUBLE PATCH: .75X TO 2X BASIC
*3-COLOR PATCHES: ADD 20% PREMIUM
*4-COLOR PATCHES: ADD 50% PREMIUM
*5-COLOR PATCHES: ADD 100% PREMIUM
*JSY TAG PATCHES: ADD 100% PREMIUM
OVERALL GU ODDS ONE PER PACK
STATED PRINT RUN 22 SERIAL #'d SETS
CY Carl Yastrzemski 30.00 80.00
RJ2 Reggie Jackson 20.00 50.00

2004 E-X Clearly Authentics Signature Black Jersey

*3-COLOR PATCHES: ADD 20% PREMIUM
*4-COLOR PATCHES: ADD 50% PREMIUM
*5-COLOR PATCHES: ADD 100% PREMIUM
*JSY TAG PATCHES: ADD 100% PREMIUM
OVERALL AUTO ODDS ONE PER PACK
PRINT RUNS B/WN 17-50 COPIES PER
EXCHANGE DEADLINE INDEFINITE
AP Albert Pujols/50 40.00 150.00
BW Bernie Williams/42 20.00 50.00
BZ Barry Zito/18 15.00 40.00
CJ Chipper Jones/50 40.00 100.00
DW Dontrelle Willis/50 15.00 40.00
FT Frank Thomas/50 30.00 80.00
GS Gary Sheffield/50 15.00 40.00
HB Hank Blalock/50 10.00 25.00
IR Ivan Rodriguez/50 20.00 50.00
JB Josh Beckett/50 8.00 20.00
JD J.D. Drew/50 10.00 25.00
KW Kerry Wood/34 20.00 50.00
MC Miguel Cabrera/50 25.00 60.00
MP1 Mike Piazza/37 60.00 150.00
MR1 Manny Ramirez/50 12.00 30.00
MR2 Mariano Rivera/50 60.00 150.00
PM Pedro Martinez/23 75.00 200.00
RC Roger Clemens/50 25.00 60.00
RJ Randy Johnson/17 25.00 60.00
RO Roy Oswalt/49 10.00 25.00
RP Rafael Palmeiro/43 10.00 25.00
TG Troy Glaus/50 6.00 15.00
TH Todd Helton/50 15.00 40.00
VG Vladimir Guerrero/50 12.00 30.00

2004 E-X Clearly Authentics Signature Emerald MLB Logo

OVERALL AUTO ODDS ONE PER PACK
STATED PRINT RUN 1 SERIAL #'d SET
NO PRICING DUE TO SCARCITY
EXCHANGE DEADLINE INDEFINITE

2004 E-X Clearly Authentics Signature Pewter Jersey

*PTR p/r 36-41: .4X TO 1X BLK p/r 50
*PTR p/r 20-27: .5X TO 1.2X BLK p/r 50
*3-COLOR PATCHES: ADD 20% PREMIUM
*4-COLOR PATCHES: ADD 50% PREMIUM
*5-COLOR PATCHES: ADD 100% PREMIUM
*JSY TAG PATCHES: ADD 100% PREMIUM
OVERALL AUTO ODDS ONE PER PACK
PRINT RUNS B/WN 7-41 COPIES PER
NO PRICING ON QTY OF 10 OR LESS

2004 E-X Clearly Authentics Signature Tan Patch

*TAN p/r 75: .4X TO 1X BLK p/r 18
*TAN p/r 42-51: .6X TO 1.5X BLK p/r 42-50
*TAN p/r 42-51: .4X TO 1X BLK p/r 23
*TAN p/r 42-51: .4X TO 1X BLK p/r 17
*TAN p/r 21-35: .6X TO 1.5X BLK p/r 37-50
*TAN p/r 21-35: .5X TO 1.2X BLK p/r 34
*TAN p/r 17: .75X TO 2X BLK p/r 50
*3-COLOR PATCHES: ADD 20% PREMIUM
*4-COLOR PATCHES: ADD 50% PREMIUM
*5-COLOR PATCHES: ADD 100% PREMIUM
*JSY TAG PATCHES: ADD 100% PREMIUM
OVERALL AUTO ODDS ONE PER PACK
PRINT RUNS B/WN 5-75 COPIES PER
NO PRICING ON QTY OF 11 OR LESS
EXCHANGE DEADLINE INDEFINITE
MP1 Mike Piazza/31 75.00 200.00
MR2 Mariano Rivera/42 75.00 200.00
RC Roger Clemens/22 60.00 150.00

2004 E-X ConnExions Dual Autograph

OVERALL AUTO ODDS ONE PER PACK
PRINT RUNS B/WN 25-50 COPIES PER
EXCHANGE DEADLINE INDEFINITE
ABCB A.Beltre/C.Beltran/25 20.00 50.00
BBMW B.Buckner/M.Wilson/50 30.00 80.00
BDMT B.Dent/M.Torrez/50 10.00 25.00
BGMG B.Giles/M.Giles/25 20.00 50.00
BZTH B.Zito/T.Hudson/25 40.00 80.00
CKJM C.Kotchman/J.Mauer/50 15.00 40.00
CLMO C.Lee/M.Ordonez/25 12.00 30.00
CWJW C.Wilson/J.Wilson/25 20.00 50.00
DWMC D.Willis/M.Cabrera/25 50.00 100.00
JDTN J.Damon/T.Nixon/25 50.00 100.00
JNPN J.Niekro/P.Niekro/50 20.00 50.00
KGDE K.Gibson/D.Eckersley/25 40.00 80.00
MTHB M.Teixeira/H.Blalock/25 40.00 80.00
MYKG M.Young/K.Greene/50 40.00 80.00
RWDY R.Weeks/D.Young/25 40.00 80.00
SPLO S.Podsednik/L.Overbay/25 40.00 80.00
SSTH S.Stewart/T.Hunter/25 20.00 50.00

2004 E-X Double Barrel

OVERALL GU ODDS ONE PER PACK
STATED PRINT RUN 1 SERIAL #'d SET
NO PRICING DUE TO SCARCITY

2004 E-X Signings of the Times Best Year

OVERALL AUTO ODDS ONE PER PACK
PRINT RUNS B/WN 48-94 COPIES PER
EXCHANGE DEADLINE INDEFINITE
BJ Bo Jackson Jsy/89 30.00 60.00
CY Carl Yastrzemski Bat/67 40.00 80.00
DM Don Mattingly Jsy/85 40.00 80.00
DS Duke Snider Bat/55 20.00 50.00
DS2 Deion Sanders Jsy/92 30.00 60.00
EB Ernie Banks Bat/58 40.00 80.00
EM Eddie Murray Jsy/83 40.00 80.00
GB George Brett Jsy/80 50.00 100.00
JB Johnny Bench Jsy/72 30.00 60.00
JC Jose Canseco Jsy/88 15.00 40.00
KP Kirby Puckett Bat/88 75.00 200.00
MS Mike Schmidt Jsy/80 50.00 100.00
NR Nolan Ryan Jsy/73 75.00 150.00
OS Ozzie Smith Jsy/87 20.00 50.00
RH Rickey Henderson Jsy/90 40.00 80.00
RJ Reggie Jackson Jsy/73 30.00 60.00
RS Ryne Sandberg Bat/90 20.00 50.00
SM Stan Musial Bat/48 50.00 100.00
TG Tony Gwynn Jsy/94 30.00 60.00
TS Tom Seaver Jsy/69 25.00 60.00
WB Wade Boggs Bat/87 15.00 40.00
WC Will Clark Jsy/91 8.00 20.00
YB Yogi Berra Bat/54 50.00 120.00

2004 E-X Signings of the Times Debut Year

*DEBUT p/r 66-89: .4X TO 1X BEST p/r 69-94
*DEBUT p/r 41-61: .4X TO 1X BEST p/r 48-58
OVERALL AUTO ODDS ONE PER PACK
PRINT RUNS B/WN 41-89 COPIES PER
EXCHANGE DEADLINE INDEFINITE
KP Kirby Puckett Bat/84 75.00 200.00
NR Nolan Ryan Jsy/66 40.00 80.00

2004 E-X Signings of the Times Emerald

OVERALL AUTO ODDS ONE PER PACK
STATED PRINT RUN 1 SERIAL #'d SET
NO PRICING DUE TO SCARCITY
EXCHANGE DEADLINE INDEFINITE

2004 E-X Signings of the Times HOF Year

*HOF p/r 69-99: .4X TO 1X BEST p/r 67-82
*HOF p/r 69-99: .6X TO .8X BEST p/r 48-58
OVERALL AUTO ODDS ONE PER PACK
PRINT RUNS B/WN 1-99 COPIES PER
NO PRICING ON QTY OF 3 OR LESS
EXCHANGE DEADLINE INDEFINITE
CY Carl Yastrzemski Bat/89 30.00 80.00
DS Duke Snider Bat/80 15.00 40.00
EB Ernie Banks Bat/77 25.00 60.00
GB George Brett Jsy/99 40.00 100.00
JB Johnny Bench Jsy/89 25.00 60.00
MS Mike Schmidt Jsy/95 40.00 100.00
NR Nolan Ryan Jsy/99 40.00 100.00
RJ Reggie Jackson Jsy/93 25.00 60.00
SM Stan Musial Bat/69 40.00 80.00
TS Tom Seaver Jsy/92 25.00 60.00
YB Yogi Berra Bat/72 50.00 120.00

2004 E-X Signings of the Times Pewter

*PTR p/r 36-60: .5X TO 1.2X BEST p/r 83-92
*PTR p/r 36-60: .4X TO 1X BEST p/r 48
*PTR p/r 21-33: .6X TO 1.5X BEST p/r 85-94
*PTR p/r 21-33: .5X TO 1.2X BEST p/r 54-58
OVERALL AUTO ODDS ONE PER PACK
PRINT RUNS B/WN 21-60 COPIES PER

1921-24 Exhibits

Although the Exhibit Supply Company issued 64 cards in 1921 and 128 cards in each of the following three years, the category of 1921-24 was created because of the large number of pictures found repeated in all four years. Each exhibit card measures 3 3/8" by 5 3/8". The cards of 1921 are characterized by ornate hand-lettered names while the cards of 1922-24 have players' names hand-written in a plainer style. Also for 1921 cards, the abbreviation used for the junior circuit is "Am.L." In contrast, cards of the 1922-24 period have the American League abbreviated "A.L." All the cards in the 1921-24 category are black and white and have blank backs; some have white borders measuring approximately 3/16" in width. There is some mislabeling of pictures, incorrect assignment of proper names and many misspellings. Some of the cards have a horizontal (HOR) orientation.

COMPLETE SET (193) 4000.00 8000.00
1 Chas. B. Adams 20.00 50.00
2 Grover C. Alexander 40.00 80.00
3 James Bagby 15.00 40.00
4 J. Frank Baker 40.00 80.00
5 David Bancroft 40.00 80.00
6 Walter Barbare 15.00 40.00
7 Turner Barber 15.00 40.00
8 Clyde Barnhart 15.00 40.00
9 John Bassler 15.00 40.00
10 Carlson L. Bigbee 15.00 40.00
11 Ray Blades 15.00 40.00
12 Sam Bohne 15.00 40.00
13 James Bottomley 40.00 80.00
14 Geo. Burns (Cinn) 15.00 40.00
portrait
15 Geo. J. Burns/(New York NL) 15.00 40.00
16 George Burns/(Boston AL) 15.00 40.00
17 George Burns/(Cleveland) 15.00 40.00
18 Joe Bush 20.00 50.00
19 Owen Bush 15.00 40.00
20 Leon Cadore 15.00 40.00
21 Max G. Carey 40.00 80.00
22 Jim Caveney 15.00 40.00
23 Dan Clark 15.00 40.00
24 Ty R. Cobb 400.00 800.00
25 Eddie T. Collins 40.00 80.00
26 John Collins 15.00 40.00
27 Wilbur Cooper 15.00 40.00
28 Stanley Coveleskie 40.00 80.00
sic, Coveleski
29 Walton E. Cruse 15.00 40.00
sic, Cruise
30 George Cutshaw 15.00 40.00
31 Dave Danforth 15.00 40.00
32 Jacob E. Daubert 20.00 50.00

33 George Dauss 15.00 40.00
34 Charles A. Deal 15.00 40.00
35 Bill Doak/(Brooklyn) 15.00 40.00
36 Bill Doak/(St. Louis NL) 15.00 40.00
37 Joe Dugan/(Boston AL) 20.00 50.00
38 Joe A. Dugan/(New York AL) 20.00 50.00
39 Joe A. Dugan/(Philadelphia AL) 20.00 50.00
40 Pat Duncan 15.00 40.00
41 James Dykes 20.00 50.00
42 Howard J. Ehmke/(Boston AL) 20.00 50.00
43 Howard Ehmke/(Detroit)/(with border) 20.00 50.00
44 Wm. Evans/(Umpire) 75.00 150.00
45 U.C. Red Faber 40.00 80.00
46 Bib Falk 15.00 40.00
47 Dana Fillingim 15.00 40.00
48 Ira Flagstead/(Boston AL) 15.00 40.00
49 A. Fletcher 15.00 40.00
50 J.F. Fournier/(Brooklyn) 15.00 40.00
51 J.F. Fournier/(St. Louis NL) 15.00 40.00
52 Howard Freigau 15.00 40.00
53 Frank F. Frisch 40.00 80.00
54 C.E. Galloway 15.00 40.00
55 W.L. Gardner/(Cleveland) 15.00 40.00
56 Joe Genewich 15.00 40.00
57 Wally Gerber 15.00 40.00
58 Mike Gonzales 15.00 40.00
59 H.M. Hank Gowdy/(Boston NL) 20.00 50.00
60 H.M. Hank Gowdy/(New York NL) 20.00 50.00
61 Burleigh A. Grimes 40.00 80.00
62 Ray Grimes 15.00 40.00
63 Charles Grimm 20.00 50.00
64 Heinie Groh 20.00 50.00
Cincinnati
65 Heinie Groh 20.00 50.00
New York NL
66 Jesse Haines 40.00 80.00
67 Chas. L. Hartnett 40.00 80.00
68 George Harper 15.00 40.00
69 Sam Harris 15.00 40.00
70 Slim Harris 15.00 40.00
71 Clifton Heathcote 15.00 40.00
72 Harry Heilmann 40.00 80.00
73 Andy High 15.00 40.00
74 George Hildebrand UMP 20.00 50.00
75 Walter L. Holke 15.00 40.00
Boston NL
76 Walter L. Holke 15.00 40.00
Philadelphia NL
77 Chas.J. Hollicher 15.00 40.00
sic, Hollocher
78 Rogers Hornsby 75.00 150.00
79 Wilbert Hubbell 15.00 40.00
80 Bill Jacobson 15.00 40.00
81 Charles D. Jamieson 15.00 40.00
82 E.R. Johnson 15.00 40.00
83 James H. Johnston 15.00 40.00
84 Walter P. Johnson 150.00 300.00
85 Sam P. Jones 15.00 40.00
86 Joe Judge 15.00 40.00
87 Willie Kamm 15.00 40.00
88 Tony Kaufman 15.00 40.00
89 George L. Kelly 40.00 80.00
90 Dick Kerr 20.00 50.00
91 William L. Killefer 15.00 40.00
92 Bill Klem UMP 75.00 150.00
93 Ed Konetchy 15.00 40.00
94 John Doc Lavan 15.00 40.00
95 Dudley Lee 15.00 40.00
96 Nemo Leibold 15.00 40.00
Boston AL
97 Nemo Leibold 15.00 40.00
Washington
with border
98 Adolph Luque 20.00 50.00
99 Walter Mails 15.00 40.00
100 Geo. Maisel 15.00 40.00
101 Walt. J. Maranville 40.00 80.00
102 W.C. (Wid) Matthews 15.00 40.00
103 Carl W. Mays 20.00 50.00
104 John McGraw 40.00 80.00
105 J. Stuffy McInnis 20.00 50.00
Boston AL
106 J. Stuffy McInnis 20.00 50.00
Boston NL
107 Lee Meadows 15.00 40.00
108 Clyde Milan 20.00 50.00
109 Ed (Bing) Miller 15.00 40.00
110 Hack Miller 15.00 40.00
111 George Moriarty UMP 20.00 50.00
112 Johnny Morrison 15.00 40.00
113 John A. Mostil 15.00 40.00
114 Robert Meusel 30.00 60.00
115 Harry Myers 15.00 40.00
116 Rollie C. Naylor 15.00 40.00
117 A. Earl Neale 20.00 50.00
118 Arthur Nehf 20.00 50.00
119 Joe Oeschger 15.00 40.00
120 Ivan M. Olson 15.00 40.00
121 Geo. O'Neil 15.00 40.00
122 S.F.Steve O'Neil 20.00 50.00
sic, O'Neill
123 J.F. O'Neill 15.00 40.00
124 Ernest Padgett 15.00 40.00
125 Roger Peckinpaugh 20.00 50.00
New York AL
with border
126 Peckinpaugh 20.00 50.00
Washington
127 Ralph Cy Perkins 15.00 40.00
128 Val Picinich 15.00 40.00
Boston AL
129 Val Picinich 15.00 40.00
Washington
130 Bill Piercy 15.00 40.00
light background
131 Bill Piercy 15.00 40.00
dark background
132 Herman Pillett 15.00 40.00
133 Wally Pipp 20.00 50.00
134 Raymond R. Powell 15.00 40.00
light background
135 Raymond R. Powell 15.00 40.00
dark background
136 Del Pratt 15.00 40.00
Detroit
137 Derrill Pratt 15.00 40.00
Boston AL
138 Joe Goldie Rapp 15.00 40.00
139 Walter Reuther 15.00 40.00
140 Edgar S. Rice 40.00 80.00
141 Cy Rigler UMP 20.00 50.00
142 E.E. Rigney 15.00 40.00
143 Jimmy Ring 15.00 40.00
144 Eppa Rixey 40.00 80.00
145 Chas. Robertson 15.00 40.00
146 Eddie Rommel 20.00 50.00
147 Muddy Ruel 15.00 40.00
148 Babe Ruth 400.00 800.00
149 Babe Ruth 800.00 1600.00
with border
150 J. H. Sand 15.00 40.00
151 Ray W. Schalk 40.00 80.00
152 Wallie Schang 20.00 50.00
153 Everett Scott 20.00 50.00
Boston AL
154 Everett Scott 20.00 50.00
New York AL
155 Harry Severeid 15.00 40.00
156 Joseph Sewell 40.00 80.00
157 H.S. Shanks 15.00 40.00
photo actually
Wally Schang
158 Earl Sheely 15.00 40.00
159 Urban Shocker 20.00 50.00
160 Al Simmons 40.00 80.00
161 George H. Sisler 40.00 80.00
162 Earl Smith 15.00 40.00
New York NL
with border
163 Earl Smith 15.00 40.00
New York NL/2/3 shot
164 Elmer Smith 15.00 40.00
Boston AL
165 Jack Smith 15.00 40.00
166 R.E. Smith 15.00 40.00
167 Sherrod Smith 15.00 40.00
Brooklyn
168 Sherrod Smith 15.00 40.00
Cleveland
169 Frank Snyder 15.00 40.00
170 Allan Sothoron 15.00 40.00
171 Tris Speaker 100.00 200.00
172 Arnold Statz 15.00 40.00
173 Casey Stengel 100.00 200.00
174 J.R. Stevenson 15.00 40.00
175 Milton Stock 15.00 40.00
176 James Tierney 15.00 40.00
Boston NL
177 James Tierney 15.00 40.00
Pittsburgh
178 John Tobin 15.00 40.00
179 George Toporcer 15.00 40.00
180 Robert Veach 15.00 40.00
181 Clar.(Tillie)Walker 15.00 40.00
182 Curtis Walker 15.00 40.00
183 Aaron Ward 15.00 40.00
184 Zack D. Wheat 40.00 80.00
185 Geo. B. Whitted 15.00 40.00
186 Cy Williams 15.00 40.00
187 Kenneth R. Williams 20.00 50.00
188 Ivy B. Wingo 15.00 40.00
189 Joe Wood 30.00 6.00
190 L. Woodall 15.00 40.00
191 Russell G.Wrightstone 15.00 40.00
192 Moses Yellowhorse 15.00 40.00
193 Ross Youngs 40.00 80.00

1925 Exhibits

The most dramatic change in the 1925 series from that of the preceding group was the printed legend which appeared for the first time in this printing. The subject's name, position, team and the line "(Made in U.S.A.)" appear on four separate lines in a bottom corner, enclosed in a small white box. The name of the player is printed in large capitals while the other lines are of a smaller type size. The cards are black and white, have plain backs and are unnumbered. Each exhibit card measures 3 3/8" by 5 3/8". There are 128 cards in the set and numerous misspellings exist. Note: the card marked "Robert Veach" does not picture that player, but is thought to contain a photo of Ernest Vache. A few of the cards are presented in a horizontal (HOR) format. Players are arranged below in alphabetical order by team: Boston NL 1-8, Brooklyn 9-16, Chicago 17-24, Cincinnati 25-32, New York 33-40, Philadelphia 41-48, Pittsburgh 49-56, St. Louis 57-64, Boston AL 65-72, Chicago 73-80, Cleveland 81-88, Detroit 89-96, New York 97-104, Philadelphia 105-112, St. Louis 113-120 and Washington 121-128. There is a very early card of Lou Gehrig in this set.

COMPLETE SET (128) 6000.00 12000.00
1 David Bancroft 60.00 120.00
2 Jesse Barnes 40.00 80.00
3 Lawrence Benton 40.00 80.00
4 Maurice Burrus 40.00 80.00
5 Joseph Genewich 40.00 80.00
6 Frank Gibson 40.00 80.00
7 David Harris 40.00 80.00
8 George O'Neil 40.00 80.00
9 John H. Deberry 40.00 80.00
10 Art Decatur 40.00 80.00
11 Jacques F. Fournier 40.00 80.00
12 Burleigh A. Grimes 60.00 120.00
13 James H. Johnson/sic& Johnston 40.00 80.00
14 Milton J. Stock 40.00 80.00
15 A.C. Dazzy Vance 60.00 120.00
16 Zack Wheat 75.00 150.00
17 Sparky Adams 40.00 80.00
18 Grover C. Alexander 100.00 200.00
19 John Brooks 40.00 80.00
20 Howard Freigau 40.00 80.00
21 Charles Grimm 50.00 100.00
22 Leo Hartnett 60.00 120.00
23 Walter Maranville 60.00 120.00
24 A.J. Weis 40.00 80.00
25 Raymond Bressler 40.00 80.00
26 Hugh M. Critz 40.00 80.00
27 Peter Donohue 40.00 80.00
28 Charles Dressen 50.00 100.00
29 John (Stuffy)/McInnes (McInnis) 50.00 100.00
30 Eppa Rixey 60.00 120.00
31 Ed. Roush 75.00 150.00
32 Ivy Wingo 40.00 80.00
33 Frank Frisch 100.00 200.00
34 Heine Groh 50.00 100.00
35 Travis C. Jackson 60.00 120.00
36 Emil Meusel 40.00 80.00
37 Arthur Nehf 50.00 100.00
38 Frank Snyder 40.00 80.00
39 Wm. H. Southworth 50.00 100.00
40 William Terry 100.00 200.00
41 George Harper 40.00 80.00
42 Nelson Hawks 40.00 80.00
43 Walter Henline 40.00 80.00
44 Walter Holke 40.00 80.00
45 Wilbur Hubbell 40.00 80.00
46 John Mokan 40.00 80.00
47 John Sand 40.00 80.00
48 Fred Williams 40.00 80.00
49 Carson Bigbee 40.00 80.00
50 Max Carey 60.00 120.00
51 Hazen Cuyler 60.00 120.00
52 George Grantham 40.00 80.00
53 Ray Kremer 40.00 80.00
54 Earl Smith 40.00 80.00
55 Harold Traynor 75.00 150.00
56 Glenn Wright 40.00 80.00
57 Lester Bell HOR 40.00 80.00
58 Raymond Blates 40.00 80.00
sic, Blades
59 James Bottomly 60.00 120.00
sic, Bottomley
60 Max Flack 40.00 80.00
61 Rogers Hornsby 125.00 250.00
62 Clarence Mueller 40.00 80.00
63 William Sherdell 40.00 80.00
64 George Toporcer 40.00 80.00
65 Howard Ehmke 50.00 100.00
66 Ira Flagstead 40.00 80.00
67 I.Valentine Picinich 40.00 80.00
68 John Quinn 50.00 100.00
69 Red Ruffing 75.00 150.00
70 Philip Todt 40.00 80.00
71 Robert Veach 40.00 80.00
72 William Wambsganss 40.00 80.00
73 Eddie Collins 75.00 150.00
74 Bib Falk 40.00 80.00
75 Harry Hooper 75.00 150.00
76 Willie Kamm 40.00 80.00
77 I.M. Davis 60.00 120.00
78 Ray Shalk (Schalk) 60.00 120.00
79 Earl Sheely 40.00 80.00
80 Hollis Thurston 40.00 80.00
81 Wilson Fewster 40.00 80.00
82 Charles Jamieson 40.00 80.00
83 Walter Lutzke 40.00 80.00
84 Glenn Myatt 40.00 80.00
85 Joseph Sewell 60.00 120.00
86 Sherrod Smith 40.00 80.00
87 Tristram Speaker 125.00 250.00
88 Homer Summa 40.00 80.00
89 John Bassler 40.00 80.00
90 Tyrus Cobb 350.00 700.00
91 George Dauss 40.00 80.00
92 Harry Heilmann 75.00 150.00
93 Frank O'Rourke 40.00 80.00
94 Emory Rigney 40.00 80.00
95 Al Wings(Wingo) HOR 40.00 80.00
96 Larry Woodall 40.00 80.00
97 Lou Gehrig 5000.00 7500.00
98 Robert W. Muesel 50.00 100.00
sic, Meusel
99 Walter C. Pipp 60.00 120.00
100 Babe Ruth 700.00 1400.00
101 Walter H. Shang 50.00 100.00
sic, Schang
102 J.R. Shawkey 50.00 100.00
103 Urban J. Shocker 50.00 100.00
104 Aaron Ward 40.00 80.00
105 Max Bishop 40.00 80.00
106 James J. Dykes 50.00 100.00
107 Samuel Gray 40.00 80.00
108 Samuel Hale 40.00 80.00
109 Edmund(Bind) Miller 40.00 80.00
sic& Bing
110 Ralph Perkins 40.00 80.00
111 Edwin Rommel 50.00 100.00
112 Frank Welch 40.00 80.00
113 Walter Gerber 40.00 80.00
114 William Jacobson 40.00 80.00
115 Martin McManus 40.00 80.00
116 Henry Severid 40.00 80.00
sic, Severeid
117 George Sissler 100.00 200.00
sic, Sisler
118 John Tobin 40.00 80.00
119 Kenneth Williams 60.00 120.00
120 Ernest Wingard 40.00 80.00
121 Oswald Bluege 40.00 80.00
122 Stanley Coveleski 60.00 120.00
123 Leon Goslin 75.00 150.00
124 Bucky Harris 60.00 120.00
125 Walter Johnson 200.00 400.00
126 Joseph Judge 50.00 100.00
127 Earl McNeely 40.00 80.00
128 Harold Ruel 40.00 80.00

1926 Exhibits

The year 1926 marked the last of the 128-card sets produced by Exhibit Supply. Of this number, 70 cards are identical to those issued in 1925 but are easily identified because of the new blue-gray color introduced in 1926. Another 21 cards use 1925 pictures but contain the line "Ex. Sup. Co., U.S.A."; these are marked with an asterisk in the checklist below. The 37 photos new to this set have an unboxed legend and carry the new company line. Bischoff is incorrectly placed with Boston, N.L. (should be A.L.); the picture of Galloway is reversed; the photos of Hunnefield and Thomas are wrongly exchanged. Each exhibit card measures 3 3/8" by 5 3/8". Players are in alphabetical order by team: Boston NL 1-8, Brooklyn 9-16, Chicago 17-24, Cincinnati 25-32, New York 33-40, Philadelphia 41-48, Pittsburgh 49-56, St. Louis 57-64, Boston AL 65-72, Chicago 73-80, Cleveland 81-88, Detroit 89-96, New York 97-104, Philadelphia 105-112, St. Louis 113-120 and Washington 121-128.

COMPLETE SET (128) 4500.00 9000.00
1 Lawrence Benton 30.00 60.00
2 Andrew High 30.00 60.00
3 Maurice Burrus 30.00 60.00
4 David Bancroft 50.00 100.00
5 Joseph Genewich 30.00 60.00
6 Bernie F. Neis 30.00 60.00
7 Edward Taylor 30.00 60.00
8 John Taylor 30.00 60.00
9 John Butler 30.00 60.00
10 Jacques F. Furnier/(sic, Fournier) * 30.00 60.00
11 Burleigh A.Grimes 50.00 100.00
12 Wilson Fewster 30.00 60.00
13 Douglas McWeeny 30.00 60.00
14 George O'Neil 30.00 60.00
15 Walter Maranville 50.00 100.00
16 Zach Wheat 60.00 120.00
17 Sparky Adams 30.00 60.00
18 J. Fred Blake 30.00 60.00
19 James E. Cooney 30.00 60.00
20 Howard Freigau 30.00 60.00
21 Charles Grimm 40.00 80.00
22 Leo Hartnett 50.00 100.00
23 C.E. Heathcote 30.00 60.00
24 Joseph M. Munson 30.00 60.00
25 Raymond Bressler 30.00 60.00
26 Hugh M. Critz 30.00 60.00
27 Peter Donohue 30.00 60.00
28 Charles Dressen 40.00 80.00
29 Walter C. Pipp 40.00 80.00
30 Eppa Rixey 50.00 100.00
31 Ed. Roush 60.00 120.00
32 Ivy Wingo 30.00 60.00
33 Edward S. Farrell 30.00 60.00
34 Frank Frisch 100.00 200.00
35 Frank Snyder 30.00 60.00
36 Fredrick Lindstrom/(sic, Frederick) * 60.00 120.00
37 Hugh A.McQuillan 30.00 60.00
38 Emil Musel/(sic, Meusel) 30.00 60.00
39 James J. Ring 30.00 60.00
40 William Terry 100.00 200.00
41 John M. Bentley 30.00 60.00
42 Bernard Friberg 30.00 60.00
43 George Harper 30.00 60.00
44 Walter Henline 30.00 60.00
45 Clarence Huber 30.00 60.00
46 John Makan/(sic, Mokan) 30.00 60.00
47 John Sand 30.00 60.00
48 Russell Wrigstone/(sic, Wrightstone) * 30.0060.00
49 Carson Bigbee 30.00 60.00
50 Max Carey 50.00 100.00
51 Hazen Cuyler 50.00 100.00
52 George Grantham 30.00 60.00
53 Ray Kremer 30.00 60.00
54 Earl Smith 30.00 60.00
55 Harold Traynor 75.00 150.00
56 Glen Wright 30.00 60.00
57 Lester Bell 30.00 60.00
58 Raymond Blates/(sic, Blades) 30.00 60.00
59 James Bottomly/(sic, Bottomley) 60.00 120.00
60 Rogers Hornsby 100.00 200.00
61 Clarence Mueller 30.00 60.00
62 Robert O'Farrell 30.00 60.00
63 William Sherdell 30.00 60.00
64 George Torporcer 30.00 60.00
65 Ira Flagstead 30.00 60.00
66 Fred Haney 40.00 80.00
67 Ramon Herrera 30.00 60.00
68 John Quinn 40.00 80.00
69 Emory Rigney 40.00 80.00
70 Red Ruffing 60.00 120.00
71 Philip Todt 30.00 60.00
72 Fred Wingfield 30.00 60.00
73 Ted Blankenship 30.00 60.00
74 Eddie Collins 60.00 120.00
75 Bib Falk 30.00 60.00
76 Wm. Hunnefield/(sic, Tommy Thomas) 30.0060.00
77 Willie Kamm 30.00 60.00
78 Ray Shalk (Schalk) 50.00 100.00
79 Earl Sheely 30.00 60.00
80 Hollis Thurston 30.00 60.00
81 Geo.H. Burns HOR 30.00 60.00
82 Walter Lutzke 30.00 60.00
83 Glenn Myatt 30.00 60.00
84 Joseph Sewell 50.00 100.00
85 Sherrod Smith 30.00 60.00
86 Tristram Speaker 125.00 250.00
87 Fred Spurgeon 30.00 60.00
88 Homer Summa 30.00 60.00
89 John Bassler 30.00 60.00
90 Lucerne Blue/(sic, Luzerne) 30.00 60.00
91 Tyrus Cobb 450.00 900.00
92 George Dauss 30.00 60.00
93 Harry Heilmann 60.00 120.00
94 Frank O'Rourke 30.00 60.00
95 Charles Gehringer/(batting) 100.00 200.00
96 John Warner 30.00 60.00
97 Patrick T.Collins 30.00 60.00
98 Earle Combs 60.00 120.00
99 Henry L. Gehrig 450.00 900.00
100 Tony Lazzeri 50.00 100.00
101 Robert W. Muesel/(sic, Meusel) 40.00 80.00
102 Babe Ruth 600.00 1200.00
103 J. R. Shawkey 40.00 80.00
104 Urban J. Shocker 40.00 80.00
105 Max Bishop 30.00 60.00
106 Joseph Galloway 30.00 60.00
107 James J. Dykes 40.00 80.00
108 Joseph Hauser 40.00 80.00
109 Edmund(Bind) Miller 30.00 60.00
sic, Bing
110 Ralph Perkins 30.00 60.00
111 Edwin Rommel 40.00 80.00
112 Wm. Wambsganss 30.00 60.00
113 Wm. Hargrave 30.00 60.00
114 William Jacobson 30.00 60.00
115 Martin McManus 30.00 60.00
116 Oscar Melillo 30.00 60.00
117 Walter Gerber 30.00 60.00
118 George Sissler 100.00 200.00
sic, Sisler
119 Kenneth Williams 40.00 80.00
120 Ernest Wingard 30.00 60.00
121 Oswald Bluege 40.00 80.00
122 Stanley Coveleski 50.00 100.00
123 Leon Goslin 50.00 100.00
124 Bucky Harris 50.00 100.00
125 Walter Johnson 175.00 350.00
126 Joseph Judge 30.00 60.00
127 Earl McNeely 30.00 60.00
128 Harold Ruel 30.00 60.00

1927 Exhibits

Two innovations characterize the 64-card set produced by Exhibit Supply Company for 1927. The first was a radical departure from the color scheme of previous sets marked by this year's light green hue. The second was the installation of the divided legend, whereby the player's name (all caps) and team were set in one corner, and the lines "Ex. Sup. Co., Chgo." and "Made in U.S.A." were set in the other. All the photos employed in this set were taken from the previous issues in 1925 and 1926, although 13 players appear with new teams. The usual misspellings and incorrect labeling of names and initials occurs throughout the set. Note: Genewich and Hunnefield have a different style of print, and Myatt is missing the right side of the legend. Each card measures 3 3/8" by 5 3/8". Players are listed in alphabetical order by team: Boston NL 1-4, Brooklyn 5-8, Chicago 9-12, Cincinnati 13-16, New York 17-20, Philadelphia 21-24, Pittsburgh 25-28, St. Louis 29-32, Boston AL 33-36, Chicago 37-40, Cleveland 41-44, Detroit 45-48, New York 49-52, Philadelphia 53-56, St. Louis 57-60, Washington 61-64.

COMPLETE SET (64) 3000.00 6000.00
1 David Bancroft 75.00 150.00
2 Joseph Genewich 40.00 80.00
3 Andrew High 40.00 80.00
4 J. Taylor 40.00 80.00
5 John Buttler (Butler) 40.00 80.00
6 Wilson Fewster 40.00 80.00
7 Burleigh A. Grimes 75.00 150.00
8 Walter Henline 40.00 80.00
9 Sparky Adams 40.00 80.00
10 Charles Grimm 50.00 100.00
11 Leo Hartnett 75.00 150.00
12 Clifton Heathcote 40.00 80.00
13 Raymond Bressler 40.00 80.00
14 Walter C. Pipp 60.00 120.00
15 Eppa Rixey 75.00 150.00
16 Ivy Wingo 40.00 80.00
17 John M. Bentley 40.00 80.00
18 George Harper 40.00 80.00
19 Rogers Hornsby 125.00 250.00
20 Fredrick Lindstrom 75.00 150.00
21 A.R. Decatur 40.00 80.00
22 John Stuffy McInnes/(sic, McInnis) 50.00 100.00
23 John Mokan 40.00 80.00
24 Russell Wrightstone 40.00 80.00
25 Hazen Cuyler 75.00 150.00
26 Ray Kremer 40.00 80.00
27 Earl Smith 40.00 80.00
28 Harold Traynor 75.00 150.00
29 Grover C. Alexander 100.00 200.00
30 James Bottomly/(sic, Bottomley) 100.00 200.00
31 Robert O'Farrell 40.00 80.00
32 Wm. H. Southworth 50.00 100.00
33 Ira Flagstead 40.00 80.00
34 Fred Haney 40.00 80.00
35 Philip Todt 40.00 80.00
36 Fred Wingfield 40.00 80.00
37 Fred Blankenship/(sic, Ted) 40.00 80.00
38 Wm. Hunnefield/(sic, Tommy Thomas) 40.0080.00
39 Willie Kamm 40.00 80.00
40 Ray Schalk 75.00 150.00
41 Geo. H. Burns HOR 40.00 80.00
42 Walter Lutzke 40.00 80.00
43 Glenn Myatt 40.00 80.00
44 Bernie Neis 40.00 80.00
45 John Bassler 40.00 80.00
46 George Daus/(sic, Dauss) 40.00 80.00
47 Charles Gehringer 100.00 200.00
48 Harry Heilman/(sic, Heilmann) 75.00 150.00
49 Henry L. Gehrig 450.00 900.00
50 Tony Lazzeri 75.00 150.00
51 Robert W. Muesel/(sic, Meusel) 40.00 80.00
52 Babe Ruth 700.00 1400.00
53 Tyrus Cobb 450.00 900.00
54 Eddie Collins 75.00 150.00
55 William Wambsganns 50.00 100.00
sic, Wambsganss
56 Zach Wheat 75.00 150.00
57 Wm. Hargrave 40.00 80.00
58 Kenneth Williams 50.00 100.00
59 George Sissler 100.00 200.00
sic, Sisler
60 Ernest Wingard 40.00 80.00
61 Leon Goslin 75.00 150.00
62 Walter Johnson 250.00 500.00
63 Harold Ruel 40.00 80.00
64 Tristam Speaker 125.00 250.00
sic, Tristram

1928 Exhibits

In contrast to the green color of the preceding year, the 64 Exhibit cards of 1928 are blue in color. Each card measures 3 3/8" by 5 3/8". They may be found with blank backs, or postcard backs containing a small premium offer clip-off in one corner. The use of the divided legend was continued, with the Roush card being unique in the set as it also cites his position. Of the 64 players in the set, 24 appear for the first time, while 12 of the holdovers show new poses. In addition, four players are shown with new team affiliations. The remaining 24 cards are identical to those issued in 1927 except for color. Once again, there is at least one mistaken identity and many misspellings and wrong names. A few of the cards are presented horizontally (HOR). Players are listed below in alphabetical order by team: Boston NL 1-4, Brooklyn 5-8, Chicago 9-12, Cincinnati 13-16, New York 17-20, Philadelphia 21-24, Pittsburgh 25-28, St. Louis 29-32, Boston AL 33-36, Chicago 37-40, Cleveland 41-44, Detroit 45-48, New York 49-52, Philadelphia 53-56, St. Louis 57-60 and Washington 61-64.

COMPLETE SET (64) 2500.00 5000.00
1 Edward Brown 40.00 80.00
2 Rogers Hornsby HOR 150.00 300.00
3 Robert Smith 40.00 80.00
4 John Taylor 40.00 80.00
5 David Bancroft 75.00 150.00
6 Max G. Carey 75.00 150.00
7 Charles R. Hargraves 40.00 80.00
8 Arthur Dazzy Vance 75.00 150.00
9 Woody English 40.00 80.00
10 Leo Hartnett 75.00 150.00
11 Charlie Root 40.00 80.00
12 L.R. (Hack) Wilson 75.00 150.00
13 Hugh M. Critz 40.00 80.00
14 Eugene Hargrave 40.00 80.00
15 Adolph Luque 50.00 100.00
16 William A. Zitzmann 40.00 80.00
17 Virgil Barnes 40.00 80.00
18 J. Francis Hogan 40.00 80.00
19 Fredrick Lindstrom 75.00 150.00
sic, Frederick
20 Edd. Roush, Outfield 75.00 150.00
21 Fred Leach 40.00 80.00
22 James Ring 40.00 80.00
23 Henry Sand HOR 40.00 80.00
24 Fred Williams 50.00 100.00
25 Ray Kremer 40.00 80.00
26 Earl Smith 40.00 80.00
27 Paul Waner 75.00 150.00
28 Glenn Wright 40.00 80.00
29 Grover C. Alexander 75.00 150.00
no emblem
30 Francis R. Blades 40.00 80.00
31 Frank Frisch 100.00 200.00
32 James Wilson 50.00 100.00
33 Ira Flagstead 40.00 80.00
34 Bryan Slim Harriss 40.00 80.00
35 Fred Hoffman 40.00 80.00
36 Philip Todt 40.00 80.00
37 Chalmer W. Cissell HOR 40.00 80.00
38 Bib Falk 40.00 80.00
39 Theodore Lyons 75.00 150.00
40 Harry McCurdy 40.00 80.00
41 Chas. Jamieson 40.00 80.00
42 Glenn Myatt 40.00 80.00
43 Joseph Sewell 75.00 150.00
44 Geo. Uhle 40.00 80.00
45 Robert Fothergill 40.00 80.00
46 Jack Tavener HOR 40.00 80.00
47 Earl G. Whitehill 40.00 80.00
48 Lawrence Woodall 40.00 80.00
49 Pat Collins 40.00 80.00
50 Lou Gehrig 450.00 900.00
51 Babe Ruth 700.00 1400.00
52 Urban J. Shocker 40.00 80.00
53 Gordon S. Cochrane 100.00 200.00
54 Howard Ehmke 50.00 100.00
55 Joseph Hauser 40.00 80.00
56 Al. Simmons 75.00 150.00
57 L.A. Blue 40.00 80.00
58 John Ogden 40.00 80.00
sic, Warren Ogden
59 Walter Shang 50.00 100.00
sic, Schang
60 Fred Schulte 40.00 80.00
61 Leon Goslin 75.00 150.00
62 Bucky Harris 75.00 150.00
63 Sam Jones 50.00 100.00
64 Harold Ruel 40.00 80.00

1929-30 Exhibits Four-in-One

The years 1929-30 marked the initial appearance of the Exhibit Company's famous "Four-In-One" design. Each of the 32 cards depict four players from one team, with a total of 128 players shown (eight from each of 16 major league teams). Each of these exhibit cards measures 3 3/8" by 5 3/8". The player's names and teams are located under each picture in dark blue or white print. All the reverses are post card style with the premium clip-off across one corner. There are 11 color combinations known for the fronts. The backs may be uncolored, red (black/red front) or yellow (blue/yellow front). The card labeled "Babe Herman" actually depicts Jesse Petty. The catalog designation is W463-1.

COMPLETE SET (32) 1200.00 2400.00
1 Pat Collins/Joe Dugan
Edward Farrel/(sic& Farre 40.00 80.00
2 Lance Richbourg/Fred Maguire
Robert Smith/Georg 25.00 50.00
3 Brooklyn Dodgers 30.00 60.00
D'Arcy Flowers
Arthur Dazzy Vance
Nick Cullop
Harvey Hendrick
4 Floyd C. Herman/David Bancroft
John H. Deberry/ 30.00 60.00
5A Leo Hartnett/C.E. Beck
L.R. (Hack) Wilson/Roger 75.00 150.00
5B Clyde Beck/Gabby Hartnett/Hack Wilson/Rogers Ho
6 Charlie Root/Kiki Cuyler
Woody English/Charlie 30.00 60.00
7 H.M. Critz/W.C. Walker
George L. Kelly/V.J. Pic 30.00 60.00
8 Pid Purdy/Pinky Pittenger
Red Lucas/Hod Ford 25.00 50.00
9 Larry Benton/Melvin Ott
William Terry/Andrew Re 40.00 80.00
10 J.F. Hogan/Travis C. Jackson
J.D. Welsh/Fred Li 40.00 80.00
11 Frank O'Doul/Bernard Friberg
Fresco Thompson/Do 25.00 50.00
12 Cy Williams/A.C. Whitney
Ray Benge/Lester L. S 25.00 50.00
13 Earl J. Adams/R. Bartell
Harold Traynor/Earl Sh 30.00 60.00
14 Lloyd Waner/Charles R.
Hargreaves/Ray Kremer/Pau 40.00 80.00
15 Grover C. Alexander/James
Wilson/Frank Frisch/J 50.00 100.00
16 Fred G. Haney/Chas. J.
Haley/Taylor Douthit/Cha 30.00 60.00
17 J.A. Heving/J. Rothrock
Red Ruffing/B.Reeves 30.00 60.00
18 Phil Todt/Hal Rhyne
Bill Regan/Doug Taitt 25.00 50.00
19 Chalmer W. Cissell
John W. Clancy/John L. Kerr/ 25.00 50.00
20 Alex Metzler/Alphonse
Thomas/Carl Reynolds/Mart 25.00 50.00
21 Lew Fonseca/Joe Sewell
Carl Lind/Jackie Tavener 30.00 60.00
22 K. Holloway/Bibb A. Falk
Luke Sewell/Earl Averi 30.00 60.00
23 Dale Alexander/G.F.
McManus/H.F. Rice/C. Gehrin 40.00 80.00
24 M.J. Shea/G.E. Uhle
Harry E. Heilman/(sic& Heil 30.00 60.00
25 Waite Hoyt/Anthony Lazzeri
Benny Bengough/Earle 50.00 100.00
26 New York Yankees 400.00 800.00
Mark Koenig
Babe Ruth
Leo Durocher
Henry L. Gehrig
27 Jimmy Foxx/Gordon S. Cochrane
Robert M. Grove/G 75.00 150.00
28 Homer Summa/James Dykes
Samuel Hale/Max Bishop 25.00 50.00
29 Heine Manush/W.H. Shang
(sic& Schang)/S. Gray/ 30.00 60.00
30 Oscar Melillo/F.O. Rourke
(sic& O'Rourke)/L.A. 25.00 50.00
31 Leon Goslin/Oswald Bluege
Harold Ruel/Joseph Ju 30.00 60.00
32 Sam Rice/Jack Hayes
Sam P. Jones/Buddy M. Myer 30.00 60.00

1931-32 Exhibits Four-in-One

The collector should refer to the checklists when trying to determine the year of issue of any "Four-In-One" set because the checklist (showing the players as they are, appear in groups of four) and the card color will ultimately provide the right clues. Some of the colors of the previous issue -- black on green, orange, red or yellow, and blue on white -- are repeated in this series, but the 1931-32 cards are distinguishable by the combinations of players which appear. Each card measures 3 3/8" by 5 3/8". The backs contain a description of attainable "Free Prizes" for coupons. The backs also contain the clip-off premium coupon. There are numerous misspellings, as usual, in the set. The catalog designation for this set is W463-2.

COMPLETE SET (32) 2000.00 4000.00
1 Walter Maranville/J.T. Zachary
Alfred Spohrer/R 60.00 120.00
2 Lance Richbourg/Fred Maguire
Earl Sheely/Walter 50.00 100.00
3 Brooklyn Dodgers 60.00 120.00
D'Arcy Flowers
Arthur Dazzy Vance
Frank O'Doul
Fresco Thompson
4 Floyd C. Herman/Glenn Wright
Jack Quinn/Del L. 50.00 100.00
5 Leo Hartnett/J.R. Stevenson
(sic& Stephenson)/L 125.00 250.00
6 Charlie Root/Hazen Cuyler
Woody English/Charlie 60.00 120.00
7 Les Durocher/(sic& Leo)
W.C. Walker/Harry Heilm 75.00 150.00
8 W. Roettger/Gooch/C.F. Lucas
H.E. Ford 50.00 100.00
9 J.F. Hogan/Travis C. Jackson
H.M. Critz/Fred Li 60.00 120.00
10 Robert O'Farrell/Melvin Ott
William Terry/Fred 100.00 200.00
11 Chuck Klein/Pinky Whitney
Ray Benge/Buzz Arlett 60.00 120.00
12 Harry McCurdy/Bernard
Friberg/Richard Bartell/D 50.00 100.00
13 Adam Comorosky/Gus Suhr
Harold Traynor/T.J. The 60.00 120.00
14 Lloyd Waner/George Grantham
Ray Kremer/Paul Wan 60.00 120.00
15 Earl J. Adams/James Wilson
Frank Frisch/James B 75.00 150.00
16 Bill Hallahan/Chas. J. Haley
Taylor Douthit/Cha 60.00 120.00
17 Chas. Berry/J. Rothrock
Robt. Reeves/R.R. (R.E. 50.00 100.00
18 Earl Webb/Hal Rhyne
Bill Sweeney/Danny MacFayde 50.00 100.00
19 Luke L. Appling/Ted Lyons
Chalmer W. Cissell/Wi 60.00 120.00
20 Smead Jolley/Lu Blue
Carl Reynolds/Henry Tate 50.00 100.00
21 Hunnefield/J. Goldman
Ed Morgan/Wes Ferrell 50.00 100.00
22 Lew Fonseca/Bibb Falk
Luke Sewell/Earl Averill 60.00 120.00
23 Dale Alexander/G.F. McManus
G.E. Uhle/C. Gehrin 60.00 120.00
24 Wallie Schang/Liz Funk
Mark Koenig/Waite Hoyt 60.00 120.00
25 W. Dickey/Anthony Lazzeri
Herb Pennock/Earl B. 150.00 300.00
26 Lyn Lary/Geo. H. Babe Ruth
James Reese/Henry L. 600.00 1200.00
27 John Boley/James Dykes
Bing. Miller/Al Simmons 60.00 120.00
28 Jimmy Foxx/Gordon S. Cochrane
Robert M. Grove/G 100.00 200.00
29 O. Melillo/F.O. Rourke
(sic& O'Rourke)/Leon Gos 60.00 120.00
30 W. Stewart/Richard Farrell
(sic& Ferrell)/S. Gr 60.00 120.00
31 Roy Spencer/Heine Manush
Joe Cronin/Fred Marber 60.00 120.00
32 Ossie Bluege/Joe Judge
Sam Rice/Buddy Myer 60.00 120.00

1933 Exhibits Four-in-One

The physical dimensions of the cardboard sheet used by the Exhibit Supply Company in printing their card sets over the years allows the following correlation to be made when one establishes that 32 of the standard-sized cards (3 3/8" by 5 3/8") are printed per sheet. Sets of 128 cards are equal to four sheets, 64 cards to two sheets, 32 cards to one sheet and 16 cards to one-half sheet. Whether it was economics, the Depression, or simplicity of operation, something caused the company to change their set totals in a descending order since 1922 in 1933. The first of a series of 16-card sets was released. The fronts of these cards are black green, orange, red or yellow; the backs are blank. The catalog designation for this set is W463-3.

COMPLETE SET (16) 1200.00 2400.00
1 Lance Richbourg 40.00 80.00
Fred Maguire
Earl Sheely
Walter
2 Vincent Lopez (Al) 60.00 120.00
Glenn Wright
Arthur Dazzy Van

3 Riggs Stephenson 40.00 80.00
Charlie Grimm
Woody English
Ch
4 Taylor Douthit 50.00 100.00
George Grantham
G. F. Lucas
Chas
5 Fred Fitzsimmons 50.00 100.00
H. M. Critz
Fred Lindstrom
Rob
6 Chuck Klein 50.00 100.00
Ray Benge
Richard Bartell
Donald Hu
7 Tom J. Thevenow 60.00 120.00
Paul Waner
Gus Suhr
Lloyd Waner
8 Earl J. Adams 60.00 120.00
Frank Frisch
Bill Halloran
Chas.
9 Danny MacFayden 40.00 80.00
Earl Webb
Hal Rhyne
Charlie Ber
10 Charles Berry 50.00 100.00
Bob Seeds
Lu Blue
Ted Lyons
11 Wes Ferrell 50.00 100.00
Luke Sewell
Ed Morgan
Earl Averill
12 Muddy' Ruel/G.E. Uhle/Jonathon Stone/C. Gehri
60.00 120.00
13 Babe Ruth 600.00 1200.00
Herb Pennock
Anthony Lazzer
14 Mickey Cochrane 125.00 250.00
Jimmy Foxx (Jimmie)
Al Simmons
Robert M.
15 Richard Farrell/(sic& Ferrell) 60.00 120.00
O. Melillo
Leon
16 Heinie Manush 50.00 100.00
Firpo Marberry
Joe Judge
Roy Spen

1934 Exhibits Four-in-One

The emergence of the bubble gum card producers in 1933-34 may have motivated Exhibit Supply to make a special effort to provide a "quality" set for 1934. The new 16-card series was printed in colors of blue, brown, olive green and violet -- all in softer tones than used in previous years. No less than 25 players appeared on cards for the first time, and another 16 were given entirely new poses. For the first time in the history of the Exhibit baseball series, there were no spelling errors. However, perfection is rarely attained in any endeavor, and the "bugaboo" of 1934 was the labeling of Al Lopez as Vincent Lopez (famous band leader and prognosticator). The cards have plain backs. Each card measures 3 3/8" by 5 3/8". ACC catalog designation for this set is W463-4.

COMPLETE SET (16) 900.00 1800.00
1 Bill Urbansky/Ed Brandt
Walter Berger/Frank Hog 25.00 50.00
2 Vincent Lopez (Al)/Glenn Wright
Sam Leslie/Leon 30.00 60.00
3 Chas. Klein/C.J. Grimm
Woody English/Lon Warnek 30.00 60.00
4 Botchi Lombardi/Tony Piet
Jimmy Bottomley/Chas. 50.00 100.00
5 Blondy Ryan/Bill Terry/Carl
Hubbell/Mel Ott 75.00 150.00
6 Jimmy Wilson/Wesley
Schulmerich/Richard Bartell# 25.00 50.00
7 T.J. Thevenow/Paul Waner
Pie Traynor/Lloyd Wane 50.00 100.00
8 Pepper Martin/Frank Frisch
Bill Hallahan/John R 40.00 80.00
9 Lefty Grove/Roy Johnson
Bill Cissell/Rick Ferre 50.00 100.00
10 Luke Appling/Al Simmons
Evar Swanson/George Ear 40.00 80.00
11 Wes Ferrell/Frank Pytlak
Willie Kamm/Earl Averi 30.00 60.00
12 Mickey Cochrane/Goose Goslin
Fred Marberry/C. G 75.00 150.00
13 Babe Ruth/Lefty Gomez
Lou Gehrig/B.Dickey 400.00 800.00
14 Mickey Cochrane/Jimmy
Foxx/Al Simmons/Robert M. 50.00 100.00
15 Irving Burns/O. Melillo
Irving Hadley/Rollie He 25.00 50.00
16 Heine Manush/Alvin Crowder
Joe Cronin/Joe Kuhel 40.00 80.00

1935 Exhibits Four-in-One W463-5

The year 1935 marked the return of the 16-card Exhibit series to a simple slate blue color. Babe Ruth appears with Boston, N.L., the last time his card would be made while he was playing, after being included in every Exhibit series since 1921. Of the 64 players pictured, 17 are shown for the first time, while 11 of the returnees are graced with new poses. The infamous "Vincent Lopez" card returns with this set, and the photo purportedly showing Tony Cuccinello is really that of George Puccinello. The cards have plain backs. The cards measure 3 3/8" by 5 3/8".

COMPLETE SET (16) 1200.00 2400.00
1 Babe Ruth/Frank Hogan
Walter Berger/Ed Brand 400.00 800.00
2 Van Mungo/Vincent Lopez (Al)
Dan Taylor/Tony Cu 30.00 60.00
3 Chas. Klein/C.J. Grimm
Lon Warneke/Gabby Hartne 40.00 80.00
4 Botchi Lombardi/Paul Derringer
Jimmy Bottomley/ 50.00 100.00
5 Hughie Critz/Bill Terry
Carl Hubbell/Mel Ott 75.00 150.00
6 Philadelphia Phillies 25.00 50.00
Jimmy Wilson
Phil Collins
John Blondy Ryan
George Watkins
7 Paul Waner/Pie Traynor
Guy Bush/Floyd Vaughan 50.00 100.00
8 St. Louis Cardinals 125.00 250.00
Pepper Martin
Frank Frisch
Jerome Dizzy Dean
Paul Dean
9 Lefty Grove/Billy Werber
Joe Cronin/Rick Ferrel 75.00 150.00
10 Al Simmons/Jimmy Dykes
Ted Lyons/Henry Bonura 40.00 80.00
11 Mel Harder/Hal Trosky
Willie Kamm/Earl Averill 30.00 60.00
12 Mickey Cochrane/Goose Goslin
Linwood Rowe/(sic& 50.00 100.00
13 Tony Lazzeri/Lefty Gomez
Lou Gehrig/Bill Dicke 300.00 600.00
14 Slug Mahaffey/Jimmy Foxx
George Cramer/Bob John 40.00 80.00
15 Irving Burns/Oscar Melillo
L.N. Newson/Rollie H 25.00 50.00
16 Buddy Meyer (Myer)/Earl Whitehill
H. Manush/Fre 30.00 60.00

1936 Exhibits Four-in-One W463-6

In 1936, the 16-card Exhibit set retained the "slate" or blue-gray color of the preceding year, but also added an olive green hue to the set. The cards are blank-backed, but for the first time since the "Four-In-One" design was introduced in 1929, a line reading "Ptd. in U.S.A." was placed in the bottom border on the obverse. The set contains 16 players making their debut in Exhibit cards, while nine holdovers have new poses. The photos of George Puccinelli was correctly identified and placed with Philadelphia, A.L. The cards measure 3 3/8" by 5 3/8".

COMPLETE SET (16) 750.00 1500.00
1 Bill Urbanski/Pinky Whitney
Walter Berger/Danny 25.00 50.00
2 Van Mungo/Stan Bordagaray
Fred Lindstrom/Dutch 30.00 60.00
3 Billy Herman/Augie Galan
Lon Warneke/Gabby Hart 40.00 80.00
4 Botchie Lombardi/Paul Derringer
Babe Herman/Ale 30.00 60.00
5 Gus. Mancuso/Bill Terry
Carl Hubbell/Mel Ott 75.00 150.00
6 Jimmy Wilson/Curt Davis
Dolph Camilli/Johnny Mo 25.00 50.00
7 Paul Waner/Pie Traynor
Guy Bush/Floyd Vaughan 40.00 80.00
8 St. Louis Cardinals 75.00 150.00
Joe Ducky Medwick
Frank Frisch
Jerome Dizzy Dean
Paul Dean
9 Lefty Grove/Jimmy Foxx
Joe Cronin/Rick Ferrell 75.00 150.00
10 Luke Appling/Jimmy Dykes
Ted Lyons/Henry Bonura 40.00 80.00
11 Mel Harder/Hal Trosky
Joe Vosmik/Earl Averill 30.00 60.00
12 Mickey Cochrane/Goose Goslin
Linwood Rowe/(sic& 75.00 150.00
13 Tony Lazzeri/Vernon Gomez
Lou Gehrig/Red Ruffin 300.00 600.00
14 Charles Berry/Puccinelli
Frank Higgins/Bob John 25.00 50.00
15 Harland Clift/Sammy West
Paul Andrews/Rollie He 25.00 50.00
16 Buddy Meyer (Myer)
Earl Whitehill/Ossie Bluege/ 25.00 50.00

1937 Exhibits Four-in-One

It would appear that Exhibit Supply was merely "flip-flopping" color schemes during the three year period 1935-37. In 1935, the cards were blue-gray; in 1936, the cards were either blue-gray or green; in 1937, the cards appear in green only. As with the previous set, the name and team of each player is printed in two or three lines under his picture, the "Ptd. in U.S.A." line appears in the bottom border (missing on some cards) and the backs are blank. The ACC catalog designation for this set is W463-7

COMPLETE SET (16) 1000.00 2000.00
1 Bill Urbanski/Alfonso Lopez
Walter Berger/Danny 40.00 80.00
2 Van Mungo/E. English
Johnny Moore/(Philadelphia 30.00 60.00
3 Billy Herman/Augie Galan
Bill Lee/Gabby Hartnet 40.00 80.00
4 Botchi Lombardi/Paul Derringer
Lew Riggs/Phil W 30.00 60.00
5 Gus Mancuso/Sam Leslie
Carl Hubbell/Mel Ott 60.00 120.00
6 Pinky Whitney/Wm. Walters
Dolph Camilli/Johnny 30.00 60.00
7 Paul Waner/Gus Suhr
Cy Blanton/Floyd Vaughan 40.00 80.00
8 St. Louis Cardinals 100.00 200.00
Joe Duck Medwick
Lon Warneke
Jerome Dizzy Dean
Stuart Martin
9 Lefty Grove/Jimmy Foxx
Joe Cronin/Dick Ferrell 150.00 300.00
10 Luke Appling/Jimmy Dykes
Vernon Kennedy/Henry B 30.00 60.00
11 Bob Feller/Hal Trosky
Frank Pytlak/Earl Averill 100.00 200.00
12 Mickey Cochrane/Goose Goslin
Linwood Rowe/C. Ge 60.00 120.00
13 Tony Lazzeri/Vernon Gomez
Lou Gehrig/Joe DiMagg 400.00 800.00
14 Billy Weber/(sic& Werber)
Harry Kelly/(sic& Kel 30.00 60.00
15 Harland Clift/Sammy West
Orval Hildebrand/Rolli 30.00 60.00
16 Buddy Meyer (Myer)/Jonathan Stone
Joe Kuhel/L.N 30.00 60.00

1938 Exhibits Four-in-One

The 1938 set of 16 cards demonstrated the fact that one consistent "quality" of Exhibit Supply sets is their inconsistency. For example, the card of Tony Cuccinello once again contains the photo of George Puccinelli, a mistake first made in 1935, corrected in 1936 and now made again in 1938. The set is also rife with name and spelling errors. Of the 64 players depicted, 12 are new arrivals and three are returnees with new poses. Another ten retained their 1937 photos but were designated new team affiliations. The cards have blank backs. The set was the last to employ the "Four-In-One" format. The catalog designation is W463-8. The cards measure 3 3/8" by 5 3/8".

COMPLETE SET (16) 1200.00 2400.00
1 Tony Cuccinello/(sic, Geo.Puccinelli) 40.00 80.00
Roy Johnson
Vince DiMaggio
Danny MacFayden
2 Van Mungo 40.00 80.00
Leo Durocher
Dolph Camilli
Gordon Phelps
3 Billy Herman 125.00 250.00
Augie Galan
Jerome Dizzy Dean
Gabby Hartnett
4 Dutch Lombardi 40.00 80.00
Paul Derringer
Lew Riggs
Ival Goodman
5 Hank Leiber 75.00 150.00
Jim Ripple
Carl Hubbell
Mel Ott
6 Pinky Whitney 40.00 80.00
Bucky Walters
Chuck Klein
Morris Arnovich
7 Paul Waner 50.00 100.00
Gus Suhr
Cy Blanton
Floyd Vaughan
8 Joe Ducky Medwick 50.00 100.00
Lon Warneke
John Mize
Stuart Martin
9 Lefty Grove 75.00 150.00
Jimmy Foxx (Jimmie)
Joe Cronin
Joe Vosmik
10 Luke Appling 50.00 100.00
Luke Sewell
Mike Kreevich
Ted Lyons
11 Bob Feller 75.00 150.00
Hal Trosky
Odell Hale
Earl Averill
12 Hank Greenberg 75.00 150.00
Rudy York
Tom Bridges
Charlie Gehringer
13 Bill Dickey 500.00 1000.00
Lefty Gomez
Lou Gehrig
Joe DiMaggio
14 Billy Weber 40.00 80.00
sic, Werber
Harry Kelly
sic, Kelley
Wallace Moses
Bob Johnson
15 Harland Clift 40.00 80.00
Sammy West
Beau Bell
Bobo Newsom
16 Buddy Meyer (Myer) 40.00 80.00
Jonathan Stone
Wes Ferrell
Rick Ferrell

1939-46 Exhibits Salutation

This collection of exhibit cards shares a common style: the "Personal Greeting" or "Salutation". The specific greeting varies from card to card -- "Yours truly, Best wishes, etc." -- as does the location of the exhibit identification (lower left, LL, or lower right, LR). Some players appear with different teams and there are occasional misspellings. Each card measures 3 3/8" by 5 3/8". The Bob Feller (Yours Truly), Andy Pafko (Yours Truly) and Ted Williams (Sincerely Yours) cards are relatively quite common as they were still being printed into the middle to late 1950s, i.e., basically until the end of their respective careers. The Jeff Heath small picture variation (26B) is differentiated by measuring the distance between the top of his cap and the top edge of the card; for the small picture variation that distance is approximately 5/8" whereas it is only 3/8" for 26A. There is some doubt about whether Camilli #6B exists. An Andy Pafko sincerely yours card is rumored to exist but has never been verified, while the 50B Pafko is a very tough card since it was printed only in 1960.

COMPLETE SET (84) 4000.00 8000.00
1A Luke Appling LL 15.00 25.00
Sincerely Yours
1B Luke Appling LR 9.00 15.00
Sincerely Yours
2 Earl Averill 500.00 800.00
Very Best Wishes
3 Charles Red Barrett 3.00 5.00
Yours Truly
4 Henry Hank Borowy 3.00 5.00
Sincerely Yours
5 Lou Boudreau 5.00 8.00
Sincerely
6A Adolf Camilli LL 15.00 25.00
Very Truly Yours
6B Adolf Camilli LR 120.00 200.00
Very Truly Yours
7 Phil Cavarretta 3.00 5.00
Cordially Yours
8 Harland Clift 12.00 20.00
Very Truly Yours
9 Tony Cuccinello 25.00 40.00
Very Best Wishes
10 Dizzy Dean 60.00 100.00
Sincerely
11 Paul Derringer 3.00 5.00
Yours Truly
12A Bill Dickey LL 30.00 50.00
Cordially Yours
12B Bill Dickey LR 30.00 50.00
Cordially Yours
13 Joe DiMaggio 70.00 120.00
Cordially
14 Bob Elliott 3.00 5.00
Truly Yours
15A Bob Feller 70.00 120.00
Best Wishes
portrait
15B Bob Feller 9.00 15.00
Yours Truly
pitching pose
16 Dave Ferriss 3.00 5.00
Best of Luck
17 Jimmy Foxx 120.00 200.00
Sincerely
(Jimmie)
18 Lou Gehrig 1200.00 2000.00
Sincerely
19 Charlie Gehringer 75.00 125.00
Yours Truly
20 Lefty Gomez 120.00 200.00
21A Joe Gordon 15.00 25.00
Cleveland
Sincerely
21B Joe Gordon 3.00 5.00
New York
Sincerely
22A Hank Greenberg 20.00 35.00
Truly Yours
22B Henry Greenberg 90.00 150.00
Very Truly Yours
23 Robert Grove 75.00 125.00
Cordially Yours
24 Gabby Hartnett 200.00 350.00
Cordially
25 Buddy Hassett 15.00 25.00
Yours Truly
26A Jeff Heath 15.00 25.00
Best Wishes
26B Jeff Heath 3.00 5.00
Small Picture
Best Wishes
27 Kirby Higbe 15.00 25.00
Sincerely
28A Tommy Holmes 120.00 200.00
Sincerely Yours
28B Tommy Holmes 3.00 5.00
Yours Truly
29 Carl Hubbell 60.00 100.00
Best Wishes
30 Bob Johnson 15.00 25.00
Yours Truly
31A Charles Keller LL 15.00 25.00
Best Wishes
31B Charles Keller LR 6.00 10.00
Best Wishes
32 Ken Keltner 30.00 50.00
Sincerly sic
33 Chuck Klein 180.00 300.00
Yours Truly
34 Mike Kreevich 150.00 250.00
Sincerely
35 Joe Kuhel 3.00 5.00
Truly Yours
36 Bill Lee 12.00 20.00
Cordially Yours
37A Ernie Lombardi 250.00 400.00
1/2 B Cordially
38B Ernie Lombardi 6.00 10.00
Cordially Yours
39 Marty Marion 6.00 10.00
Best Wishes
40 Merrill May 15.00 25.00
Best Wishes
41A Frank McCormick LL 15.00 25.00
Sincerely
41B Frank McCormick LR 3.00 5.00
Sincerely
42A George McQuinn LL 15.00 25.00
Yours Truly
42B George McQuinn LR 3.00 5.00
Yours Truly
43 Joe Medwick 20.00 35.00
Very Best Wishes
44A Johnny Mize LL 25.00 40.00
Yours Truly
44B Johnny Mize LR 9.00 15.00
Yours Truly
45 Hugh Mulcahy 15.00 25.00
Cordially
46 Hal Newhouser 9.00 15.00
Best Wishes
47 Louis Buck Newsom 15.00 25.00
Sincerely
48 Buck Newson sic 180.00 300.00
Very Best Wishes
49A Mel Ott LL 30.00 50.00
Sincerely Yours
49B Mel Ott LR 25.00 40.00
Sincerely Yours
50A Andy Pafko 3.00 5.00
Yours Truly
50B Andy Pafko 20.00 40.00
Yours Truly
plain cap
51 Claude Passeau 3.00 5.00
Sincerely
52A Howard Pollet LL 15.00 25.00
Best Wishes
52B Howard Pollet LR 3.00 5.00
Best Wishes
53A Pete Reiser LL 60.00 100.00
Truly Yours
53B Pete Reiser LR 5.00 8.00
Truly Yours
54 Johnny Rizzo 300.00 500.00
Sincerely Yours
55 Glenn Russell 180.00 300.00
Sincerely
56 George Stirnweiss 3.00 5.00
Yours Truly
57 Cecil Travis 9.00 15.00
Best Wishes
58 Paul Trout 3.00 5.00
Truly Yours
59 Johnny Vander Meer 30.00 50.00
Cordially Yours
60 Arky Vaughan 15.00 25.00
Best Wishes
61A Fred Dixie Walker 3.00 5.00
D on Hat
Yours Truly
61B Fred Dixie Walker 40.00 75.00
Cap blanked out
Yours Truly
62 Bucky Walters 3.00 5.00
Sincerely Yours
63 Lon Warneke 12.00 20.00
Very Truly Yours
64A Ted Williams Sincerely #9 Showing 200.00400.00
64B Ted Williams Sincerely Yours #9 Not Showing
45.00 80.00
65 Rudy York 3.00 5.00
Cordially

1947-66 Exhibits

This grouping encompasses a wide time span but displays a common design. The following players have been illegally reprinted in mass quantities on a thinner-than-original cardboard which is also characterized by a dark gray back: Aaron, Ford, Fox, Hodges, Elston Howard, Mantle, Mays, Musial, Newcombe, Reese, Spahn, and Ted Williams. Each card measures 3 3/8" by 5 3/8". In the checklist below SIG refers to signature and SCR refers to script name on card. The abbreviations POR (portrait), BAT (batting), and FIE (fielding) are also used below. There are many levels of scarcity within this "set," essentially based on which year(s) the player's card was printed. The Mickey Mantle portrait card, for example, was only printed in 1966, the last year of production. Those scarce cards which were only produced one or two years are noted parenthetically below by the last two digits of the year(s) of issue. Cards which seem to be especially difficult to obtain are the ones produced only in 1966 which are the aforementioned Mantle Portrait, Ford, Kranepool, Richardson, Skowron (White Sox), Ward and Yastrzemski. Some leading exhibit experts believe that the salutation and these cards should be checklisted together because of the long printing history of some of the salutations. Please note that the following cards have been reprinted: Hank Aaron, Whitey Ford (no glove, throwing), Nelson Fox, Gil Hodges (Brooklyn cap), Elston Howard, Willie May (Batting, New York), Stan Musial (three bats, kneeling), Don Newcombe (Brooklyn cap), Pee Wee Reese (ball not visable), Warren Spahn (Boston).

COMPLETE SET (321) 4000.00 8000.00
1 Hank Aaron 30.00 60.00
2A Joe Adcock SCR 3.00 8.00
2B Joe Adcock SIG 3.00 8.00
3 Max Alvis 66 30.00 60.00
4A Johnny Antonelli 3.00 8.00
Braves
4B Johnny Antonelli 3.00 8.00
Giants
5A Luis Aparicio POR 4.00 10.00
5B Luis Aparicio BAT 64 40.00 80.00
6 Luke Appling 4.00 10.00
7A Richie Ashburn 30.00 60.00
Phillies
7B Ritchie Ashburn 6.00 15.00
sic, Richie
7C Richie Ashburn 40.00 80.00
Cubs 61
8 Bob Aspromonte 64/66 3.00 8.00
9 Toby Atwell 3.00 8.00
10A Ed Bailey 61 6.00 15.00
Cincinnati cap
10B Ed Bailey no cap 3.00 8.00
11 Gene Baker 3.00 8.00
12A Ernie Banks SCR 20.00 50.00
12B Ernie Banks SIG 10.00 25.00
12C Ernie Banks POR 20.00 50.00
64/66
13 Steve Barber 64/66 3.00 8.00
14 Earl Battey 64/66 3.00 8.00
15 Matt Batts 4.00 10.00
16A Hank Bauer 3.00 8.00
New York cap
16B Hank Bauer 61 20.00 50.00
plain cap
17 Frank Baumholtz 3.00 8.00
18 Gene Bearden 3.00 8.00
19 Joe Beggs 47 12.50 30.00
20A Yogi Berra 6.00 15.00
20B Larry Yogi Berra 30.00 60.00
64/66
21 Steve Bilko 3.00 8.00
22A Ewell Blackwell 4.00 10.00
foot up
22B Ewell Blackwell POR 3.00 8.00
23A Don Blasingame 3.00 8.00
St. Louis cap
23B Don Blasingame 4.00 10.00
plain cap
24 Ken Boyer 64/66 12.50 30.00
25 Ralph Branca 3.00 8.00
26 Jackie Brandt 61 40.00 80.00
27 Harry Brecheen 3.00 8.00
28 Tom Brewer 61 30.00 60.00
29 Lou Brissie 3.00 8.00
30 Bill Bruton 3.00 8.00
31A Lew Burdette 3.00 8.00
side view
31B Lew Burdette 15.00 40.00
facing 64
32 Johnny Callison 64/66 4.00 10.00
33 Roy Campanella 30.00 60.00
34A Chico Carrasquel 3.00 8.00
White Sox
34B Chico Carrasquel 10.00 25.00
plain cap
35 George Case 47 12.50 30.00
36 Hugh Casey 6.00 15.00
37 Norm Cash 64/66 10.00 25.00
38A Orlando Cepeda POR 10.00 25.00
60/61
38B Orlando Cepeda BAT 10.00 25.00
64/66
39A Bob Cerv 60 3.00 8.00
A's uniform
39B Bob Cerv 61 30.00 60.00
plain uniform
40 Dean Chance 64/66 3.00 8.00
41 Spud Chandler 47 12.50 30.00
42 Tom Cheney 64/66 3.00 8.00
43 Bubba Church 3.00 8.00
44 Roberto Clemente 75.00 150.00
45A Rocky Colavito POR 75.00 150.00
61
45B Rocky Colavito BAT 15.00 40.00
64/66
46 Choo Choo Coleman 64 15.00 40.00
47 Gordy Coleman 66 30.00 60.00
48 Jerry Coleman 3.00 8.00
49 Mort Cooper 47 15.00 40.00
50 Walker Cooper 3.00 8.00
51 Roger Craig 64/66 6.00 15.00
52 Delmar Crandall 3.00 8.00
53A Joe Cunningham POR 4.00 10.00
64/66
53B Joe Cunningham BAT 40.00 80.00
61
54 Guy Curtwright 47 12.50 30.00
sic, Curtright
55 Bud Daley 61 30.00 60.00
56A Alvin Dark 6.00 15.00
Boston cap
56B Alvin Dark 3.00 8.00
New York cap
56C Alvin Dark Cubs 60 20.00 50.00
57 Murray Dickson 3.00 8.00
58 Bob Dillinger 6.00 15.00
59 Dom DiMaggio 6.00 15.00
60 Joe Dobson 3.00 8.00
61 Larry Doby 3.00 8.00
62 Bobby Doerr 6.00 15.00
63A Dick Donovan 3.00 8.00
Braves, plain cap
63B Dick Donovan 3.00 8.00
White Sox
64 Walter Dropo 3.00 8.00
65A Don Drysdale POR/60/61 30.00 60.00
65B Don Drysdale 64/66/POR 1/2 30.00 60.00
66 Luke Easter 3.00 8.00
67 Bruce Edwards 6.00 15.00
68 Del Ennis 3.00 8.00
69 Al Evans 3.00 8.00
70 Walter Evers 3.00 8.00
71A Ferris Fain FIE 6.00 15.00
71B Ferris Fain POR 3.00 8.00
72 Dick Farrell 64/66 3.00 8.00
73A Whitey Ford 6.00 15.00
no glove, throwing
73B Whitey Ford POR 66 175.00 350.00
73C Ed 'Whitey' Ford/(glove on
shoulder)/64/66 30.00 60.00
74 Dick Fowler 3.00 8.00
75 Nelson Fox 10.00 25.00
76 Tito Francona 64/66 3.00 8.00
77 Bob Friend 3.00 8.00
78 Carl Furillo 12.50 30.00
79 Augie Galan 12.50 30.00
80 Jim Gentile 64/66 3.00 8.00
81 Tony Gonzalez 64/66 3.00 8.00
82A Billy Goodman FIE 3.00 8.00
fielding
82B Billy Goodman BAT 12.50 30.00
60/61
83 Ted Greengrass 6.00 15.00
sic, Jim
84 Dick Groat 3.00 8.00
85 Steve Gromek 6.00 15.00
86 Johnny Groth 3.00 8.00
87 Orval Grove 47 12.50 30.00
88A Frank Gustine 3.00 8.00
Pirates
88B Frank GustineCubs 3.00 8.00
89 Berthold Haas 12.50 30.00
90 Grady Hatton 3.00 8.00
91 Jim Hegan 3.00 8.00
92 Tommy Henrich 3.00 8.00
93 Ray Herbert 66 30.00 60.00
94 Gene Hermanski 6.00 15.00
95 Whitey Herzog 60/61 6.00 15.00
96 Kirby Higbe 47 12.50 30.00
97 Chuck Hinton 64/66 3.00 8.00
98 Don Hoak 64 15.00 40.00
99A Gil Hodges 6.00 15.00
Brooklyn cap
99B Gil Hodges 12.50 30.00
Los Angeles cap
100 Johnny Hopp 47 12.50 30.00
101 Elston Howard 3.00 8.00
102 Frank Howard 64/66 10.00 25.00
103 Ken Hubbs 64 75.00 150.00
104 Tex Hughson 47 12.50 30.00
105 Fred Hutchinson 50 6.00 15.00
106 Monte Irvin 6.00 15.00
107 Joey Jay 64/66 3.00 8.00
108 Jackie Jensen 60 40.00 80.00
109 Sam Jethroe 4.00 10.00
110 Bill Johnson 50 4.00 10.00
111 Walter Judnich 47 12.50 30.00
112A Al Kaline SCR 12.50 30.00
kneeling
112B Al Kaline SIG POR 10.00 25.00
113 George Kell 6.00 15.00
114 Charley Keller 6.00 15.00
115 Alex Kellner 3.00 8.00
116 Kenn Keltner 12.50 30.00
sic, Ken
117A Harmon Killebrew 30.00 60.00
pinstripes, batting
60/61
117B Harmon Killibrew 40.00 80.00
sic, Killebrew
POR 66
117C Harmon Killebrew 15.00 40.00
throwing 64/66
118 Ellis Kinder 3.00 8.00
119 Ralph Kiner 6.00 15.00
120 Billy Klaus 60 30.00 60.00
121A Ted KluszewskiReds 12.50 30.00
121B Ted Kluszewski 12.50 30.00
Pirates
121C Ted Kluszewski 40.00 80.00
plain uniform 60/61
122 Don Kolloway 50 6.00 15.00
123 Jim Konstanty 4.00 10.00
124 Sandy Koufax 64/66 75.00 150.00
125 Ed Kranepool 66 150.00 300.00
126A Tony Kubek 3.00 8.00
dark background
126B Tony Kubek 3.00 8.00
light background
127A Harvey Kuenn 60 6.00 15.00
Detroit
127B Harvey Kuenn 61 30.00 60.00
plain uniform
127C Harvey Kuenn 6.00 15.00
San Francisco 64/66
128 Whitey Kurowski 50 12.50 30.00
129 Eddie Lake 47 12.50 30.00
130 Jim Landis 64/66 3.00 8.00
131 Don Larsen 3.00 8.00
132A Bob Lemon 4.00 10.00
left arm not shown
132B Bob Lemon 40.00 80.00
left arm extended
133 Buddy Lewis 47 12.50 30.00
134 Johnny Lindell 50 12.50 30.00
135 Phil Linz 66 30.00 60.00
136 Don Lock 66 30.00 60.00
137 Whitey Lockman 3.00 8.00
138 Johnny Logan 3.00 8.00
139A Dale Long Pirates 3.00 8.00
139B Dale Long Cubs 61 30.00 60.00
140 Ed Lopat 3.00 8.00
141A Harry Lowery 6.00 15.00
sic, Lowrey
141B Harry Lowrey 3.00 8.00
142 Sal Maglie 3.00 8.00
143 Art Mahaffey 64/66 3.00 8.00
144 Hank Majeski 3.00 8.00
145 Frank Malzone 3.00 8.00
146A Mickey Mantle/(batting to waist)
(white outline 100.00 200.00
146B Mickey Mantle/(batting to waist)
(no white outli 150.00 300.00
146C Mickey Mantle/(batting full) 64/66 100.00200.00
146D Mickey Mantle POR/66 400.00 800.00
147 Marty Marion 3.00 8.00
148 Roger Maris 64/66 40.00 80.00
149 Willard Marshall 3.00 8.00
150A Ed Matthews SCR 10.00 25.00
sic, Mathews
150B Eddie Mathews SIG 15.00 40.00
151 Ed Mayo 3.00 8.00
152A Willie Mays Batting 30.00 60.00
New York
152B Willie Mays 30.00 60.00
San Francisco
153A Bill Mazeroski POR 8.00 20.00
60/61
153B Bill Mazeroski BAT 8.00 20.00
64/66
154 Ken McBride 64/66 3.00 8.00
155A Barney McCaskey 15.00 40.00
sic, McCosky
155B Barney McCoskey/(sic, McCosky) 50.00 100.00
156 Lindy McDaniel 60/61 3.00 8.00
157 Gil McDougald 3.00 8.00
158 Albert Mele 30.00 60.00
159 Sam Mele 6.00 15.00
160A Minnie Minoso 3.00 8.00
White Sox
160B Minnie Minoso 6.00 15.00
Cleveland
161 Dale Mitchell 3.00 8.00
162 Wally Moon 3.00 8.00
163 Don Mueller 15.00 40.00
164A Stan Musial 30.00 60.00
three bats, kneeling
164B Stan Musial BAT 64 100.00 200.00
165 Charles Neal 64 15.00 40.00
166A Don Newcombe 6.00 15.00
shaking hands
166B Don Newcombe 3.00 8.00
Brooklyn cap
166C Don Newcombe 10.00 25.00
plain cap
167 Hal Newhouser 6.00 15.00
168 Ron Northey 47 15.00 40.00
169 Bill O'Dell 64/66 3.00 8.00
170 Joe Page 50 12.50 30.00
171 Satchel Paige 75.00 150.00
172 Milt Pappas 64/66 3.00 8.00
173 Camilo Pascual 64/66 3.00 8.00
174 Albie Pearson 66 30.00 60.00
175 Johnny Pesky 3.00 8.00
176 Gary Peters 66 30.00 60.00
177 Dave Philley 3.00 8.00
178 Billy Pierce 60/61 3.00 8.00
179 Jimmy Piersall 66 50.00 100.00
180 Vada Pinson 64/66 10.00 25.00
181 Bob Porterfield 3.00 8.00
182 Boog Powell 66 75.00 150.00
183 Vic Raschi 3.00 8.00
184A Harold Peewee Reese
(ball visible along/bottom 10.00 25.00
184B Harold Peewee Reese 10.00 25.00
ball not visible
185 Del Rice 3.00 8.00
186 Bobby Richardson 66 175.00 350.00
187A Phil Rizzuto 10.00 25.00
small photo
187B Phil Rizzuto 6.00 15.00
larger photo
188A Robin Roberts SIG 6.00 15.00
188B Robin Roberts SCR 8.00 20.00
189 Brooks Robinson 30.00 60.00
190 Eddie Robinson POR 3.00 8.00
191 Floyd Robinson 66 30.00 60.00
192 Frankie Robinson 30.00 60.00
64/66

193 Jackie Robinson 40.00 80.00
194 Preacher Roe 3.00 8.00
195 Bob Rogers 66 sic, Rodgers 30.00 60.00
196 Richard Rollins 66 30.00 60.00
197 Pete Runnels 64 15.00 40.00
198 John Sain 3.00 8.00
199 Ron Santo 64/66 12.50 30.00
200 Henry Sauer 3.00 8.00
201A Carl Sawatski Milwaukee cap 3.00 8.00
201B Carl Sawatski Philadelphia cap 3.00 8.00
201C Carl Sawatski 61 plain cap 15.00 40.00
202 Johnny Schmitz 4.00 10.00
203A Red Schoendeinst/(one foot shown&/catching)/(si 15.00 40.00
203B Red Schoendeinst/(both feet shown&/catching)/(s 30.00 60.00
203C Red Schoendinst BAT sic, Schoendienst 6.00 15.00
204A Herb Score Cleveland cap 6.00 15.00
204B Herb Score 61 plain cap 30.00 60.00
205 Andy Seminick 3.00 8.00
206 Rip Sewell 47 15.00 40.00
207 Norm Siebern 3.00 8.00
208A Roy Sievers 51 Browns 40.00 80.00
208B Roy Sievers Senators dark background 3.00 8.00
208C Roy Sievers Senators light background 3.00 8.00
208D Roy Sievers 61 plain uniform 30.00 60.00
209 Curt Simmons 3.00 8.00
210 Dick Sisler 3.00 8.00
211A Bill Skowron New York 3.00 8.00
211B Bill Moose Skowron White Sox 66 150.00 300.00
212 Enos Slaughter 6.00 15.00
213A Duke Snider Brooklyn 10.00 25.00
213B Duke Snider Los Angeles 15.00 40.00
214A Warren Spahn Boston 6.00 15.00
214B Warren Spahn Milwaukee 12.50 30.00
215 Stanley Spence 12.50 30.00
216A Ed Stanky plain uniform 3.00 8.00
216B Ed Stanky Giants 3.00 8.00
217A Vern Stephens Browns 3.00 8.00
217B Vern Stephens Red Sox 4.00 10.00
218 Ed Stewart 3.00 8.00
219 Snuffy Stirnweiss 15.00 40.00
220 George Birdie Tebbets 10.00 25.00
221A Frankie Thomas BAT Bob Skinner picture 59 30.00 60.00
221B Frank Thomas Cubs 60/61 30.00 60.00
222 Lee Thomas 64/66 3.00 8.00
223 Bobby Thomson 6.00 15.00
224A Earl Torgeson Braves 3.00 8.00
224B Earl Torgeson 60/61 plain uniform 3.00 8.00
225 Gus Triandos 60/61 6.00 15.00
226 Virgil Trucks 3.00 8.00
227 Johnny Vandermeer 47 40.00 80.00
228 Emil Verban 15.00 40.00
229A Mickey Vernon throwing 3.00 8.00
229B Mickey Vernon BAT 3.00 8.00
230 Bill Voiselle 47 15.00 40.00
231 Leon Wagner 64/66 3.00 8.00
232A Eddie Waitkus BAT Cub uniform 3.00 8.00
232B Eddie Waitkus BAT plain uniform 3.00 8.00
232C Eddie Waitkus POR Phillies uniform 30.00 60.00
233 Dick Wakefield 3.00 8.00
234 Harry Walker 40.00 80.00
235 Bucky Walters 6.00 15.00
236 Pete Ward 66 125.00 250.00
237 Herman Wehmeier 3.00 8.00
238A Vic Wertz Tigers 3.00 8.00
238B Vic WertzRed Sox 3.00 8.00
239 Wally Westlake 3.00 8.00
240 Wes Westrum 30.00 60.00
241 Billy Williams 64/66 30.00 60.00
242 Maurice Wills 64/66 12.50 30.00
243A Gene Woodling SCR 3.00 8.00
243B Gene Woodling SIG 3.00 8.00
244 Taffy Wright 47 12.50 30.00
245 Carl Yastrzemski 66 250.00 500.00
246 Al Zarilla 51 6.00 15.00
247A Gus Zernial SCR 3.00 8.00
247B Gus Zernial SIG 3.00 8.00
248 Braves Team 1948
249 Dodgers Team 1949
250 Dodgers Team 1952
251 Dodgers Team 1955
252 Dodgers Team 1956
253 Giants Team 1951
254 Giants Team 1954
255 Indians Team 1948
256 Indians Team 1954
257 Phillies Team 1950
258 Yankees Team 1949
259 Yankees Team 1950
260 Yankees Team 1951
261 Yankees Team 1952
262 Yankees Team 1955
263 Yankees Team 1956

1948 Exhibit Hall of Fame

This exhibit set, entitled "Baseball's Great Hall of Fame," consists of black and white photos on gray background. The pictures are framed on the sides by Greek columns and a short biography is printed at the bottom. The cards are blank backed. Twenty four of the cards were reissued in 1974 on extremely white stock. Each card measures 3 3/8" by 5 3/8".

COMPLETE SET (33) 300.00 600.00
1 G.C. Alexander 4.00 8.00
2 Roger Bresnahan 2.50 5.00
3 Frank Chance 3.00 6.00
4 Jack Chesbro 2.50 5.00
5 Fred Clarke 2.50 5.00
6 Ty Cobb 40.00 80.00
7 Mickey Cochrane 4.00 8.00
8 Eddie Collins 2.50 5.00
9 Hugh Duffy 2.50 5.00
10 Johnny Evers 3.00 6.00
11 Frankie Frisch 3.00 6.00
12 Lou Gehrig 40.00 80.00
13 Clark Griffith 2.50 5.00
14 Lefty Grove 4.00 8.00
15 Rogers Hornsby 5.00 10.00
16 Carl Hubbell 3.00 6.00
17 Hughie Jennings 2.50 5.00
18 Walter Johnson 7.50 15.00
19 Willie Keeler 2.50 5.00
20 Nap Lajoie 5.00 10.00
21 Connie Mack 4.00 8.00
22 Christy Mathewson 7.50 15.00
23 John McGraw 5.00 10.00
24 Eddie Plank 3.00 6.00
25A Babe Ruth/(swinging) 25.00 50.00
25B Babe Ruth/(bats in front)/ten bats pose 150.00 300.00
26 George Sisler 3.00 6.00
27 Tris Speaker 5.00 10.00
28 Joe Tinker 3.00 6.00
29 Rube Waddell 2.50 5.00
30 Honus Wagner 7.50 15.00
31 Ed Walsh 2.50 5.00
32 Cy Young 5.00 10.00

1948-56 Exhibits Team

The cards found listed in this classification were not a separate issue from the individual player cards of the same period but have been assembled together in the Price Guide for emphasis. Each of these 1948-1956 Exhibit team cards was issued to honor the champions of the National and American Leagues, except for 1953, when none were printed. Reprints of these popular cards are known to exist. Each card measures 3 3/8" by 5 3/8".

COMPLETE SET (16) 600.00 1200.00
1 1948 Boston Braves 30.00 60.00
2 1948 Cleveland Indians 30.00 60.00
3 1949 Brooklyn Dodgers 40.00 80.00
4 1949 New York Yankees 40.00 80.00
5 1950 Philadelphia Phillies 40.00 80.00
6 1950 New York Yankees 40.00 80.00
7 1951 New York Giants 40.00 80.00
8 1951 New York Yankees 30.00 60.00
9 1952 Brooklyn Dodgers 40.00 80.00
10 1952 New York Yankees 40.00 80.00
11 1954 New York Giants 40.00 80.00
12 1954 Cleveland Indians 40.00 80.00
13 1955 Brooklyn Dodgers 150.00 300.00
14 1955 New York Yankees 100.00 200.00
15 1956 Brooklyn Dodgers 200.00 400.00
16 1956 New York Yankees 100.00 200.00

1953 Exhibits Canadian

This numbered, blank-backed set depicts both major league players (reprinted from American Exhibit sets) and International League Montreal Royals. The cards (3 1/4" by 5 1/4") are slightly smaller than regular Exhibit issues and are printed on gray stock. Numbers 1-32 are found in green or wine-red color, while 33-64 are blue or reddish-brown. Cards 1-32 are numbered in a small& diamond-shaped white box at lower right; cards 33-64 have a large, hand-lettered number at upper right.

COMPLETE SET (64) 600.00 1200.00
COMMON PLAYER (1-32) 4.00 10.00
COMMON PLAYER (33-64) 2.00 5.00
1 Preacher Roe 5.00 12.00
2 Luke Easter 4.00 10.00
3 Gene Bearden 4.00 10.00
4 Chico Carrasquel 4.00 10.00
5 Vic Raschi 5.00 12.00
6 Monte Irvin 8.00 20.00
7 Hank Sauer 4.00 10.00
8 Ralph Branca 5.00 12.00
9 Eddie Stanky 4.00 10.00
10 Sam Jethroe 4.00 10.00
11 Larry Doby 8.00 20.00
12 Hal Newhouser 8.00 20.00
13 Gil Hodges 12.50 30.00
14 Harry Brecheen 4.00 10.00
15 Ed Lopat 6.00 15.00
16 Don Newcombe 6.00 15.00
17 Bob Feller 30.00 60.00
18 Tommy Holmes 4.00 10.00
19 Jackie Robinson 100.00 200.00
20 Roy Campanella 50.00 100.00
21 Pee Wee Reese 20.00 50.00
22 Ralph Kiner 8.00 20.00
23 Dom DiMaggio 6.00 15.00
24 Bobby Doerr 8.00 20.00
25 Phil Rizzuto 15.00 40.00
26 Bob Elliott 4.00 10.00
27 Tom Henrich 5.00 12.00
28 Joe DiMaggio 150.00 300.00
29 Harry Lowery 4.00 10.00
30 Ted Williams 100.00 200.00
31 Bob Lemon 10.00 25.00
32 Warren Spahn 12.50 30.00
33 Don Hoak 4.00 10.00
34 Bob Alexander 2.00 5.00
35 John Simmons 2.00 5.00
36 Steve Lembo 2.00 5.00
37 Norman Larker 5.00 12.00
38 Bob Ludwick 2.00 5.00
39 Walter Moryn 4.00 10.00
40 Charlie Thompson 4.00 10.00
41 Ed Roebuck 4.00 10.00
42 Rose 2.00 5.00
43 Edmundo Amoros 5.00 12.00
44 Bob Milliken 4.00 10.00
45 Art Fabbro 2.00 5.00
46 Forrest Jacobs 4.00 10.00
47 Carmen Mauro 2.00 5.00
48 Walter Fiala 2.00 5.00
49 Rocky Nelson 2.00 5.00
50 Tom Lasorda 40.00 80.00
51 Ronnie Lee 2.00 5.00
52 Hampton Coleman 2.00 5.00
53 Frank Marchio 2.00 5.00
54 William Samson 2.00 5.00
55 Gil Mills 2.00 5.00
56 Al Ronning 2.00 5.00
57 Stan Musial 50.00 100.00
58 Walker Cooper 4.00 10.00
59 Mickey Vernon 5.00 12.00
60 Del Ennis 5.00 12.00
61 Walter Alston MG 20.00 50.00
62 Dick Sisler 4.00 10.00
63 Billy Goodman 4.00 10.00
64 Alex Kellner 4.00 10.00

1960-61 Exhibits Wrigley HOF

This Exhibit issue was distributed at Wrigley Field in Chicago in the early sixties. The set consists entirely of Hall of Famers, many of whom are depicted in their younger days. The set is complete at 24 cards and is interesting in that the full name of each respective Hall of famer is given on the front of the card. Card backs feature a postcard back on gray card stock. Each card measures 3 3/8" by 5 3/8".

COMPLETE SET (24) 300.00 600.00
1 Grover Cleveland Alexander 8.00 20.00
2 Cap Anson 8.00 20.00
3 Frank Baker 5.00 12.00
4 Roger Bresnahan 5.00 12.00
5 Mordecai Brown 5.00 12.00
6 Frank Chance 6.00 15.00
7 Tyrus Cobb 40.00 80.00
8 Eddie Collins 6.00 15.00
9 Jimmy Collins 5.00 12.00
10 Johnnie Evers 5.00 12.00
11 Lou Gehrig 40.00 80.00
12 Clark Griffith 5.00 12.00
13 Walter Johnson 15.00 40.00
14 Tony Lazzeri 5.00 12.00
15 Rabbit Maranville 5.00 12.00
16 Christy Mathewson 15.00 40.00
17 John McGraw 8.00 20.00
18 Melvin Ott 10.00 25.00
19 Herb Pennock 5.00 12.00
20 Babe Ruth 75.00 150.00
21 Al Simmons 5.00 12.00
22 Tris Speaker 10.00 25.00
23 Joe Tinker 5.00 12.00
24 Honus Wagner 15.00 40.00

1962 Exhibit Stat Back

The 32-card sheet was a standard production feature of the Exhibit Supply Company, although, generally more than one sheet comprised a set. The 32-card set issued in 1962 thus amounted to one-half a normal printing, and is differentiated from other concurrent Exhibit issues by the inclusion of records, printed in black or red, on the reverse of each card. Each card measures 3 3/8" by 5 3/8". Backs printed in red ink are slightly more difficult to find but there is no difference in price.

COMPLETE SET (32) 400.00 800.00
1 Hank Aaron 40.00 80.00
2 Luis Aparicio 8.00 20.00
3 Ernie Banks 15.00 40.00
4 Yogi Berra 30.00 60.00
5 Ken Boyer 6.00 15.00
6 Lew Burdette 4.00 10.00
7 Norm Cash 6.00 15.00
8 Orlando Cepeda 8.00 20.00
9 Roberto Clemente 60.00 120.00
10 Rocky Colavito 15.00 40.00
11 Whitey Ford 15.00 40.00
12 Nellie Fox 8.00 20.00
13 Tito Francona 2.50 6.00
14 Jim Gentile 2.50 6.00
15 Dick Groat 2.50 6.00
16 Don Hoak 2.50 6.00
17 Al Kaline 15.00 40.00
18 Harmon Killebrew 12.50 30.00
19 Sandy Koufax 50.00 100.00
20 Jim Landis 2.50 6.00
21 Art Mahaffey 2.50 6.00
22 Frank Malzone 2.50 6.00
23 Mickey Mantle 150.00 300.00
24 Roger Maris 30.00 60.00
25 Eddie Mathews 15.00 40.00
26 Willie Mays 40.00 80.00
27 Wally Moon 2.50 6.00
28 Stan Musial 40.00 80.00
29 Milt Pappas 2.50 6.00
30 Vada Pinson 4.00 10.00
31 Norm Siebern 2.50 6.00
32 Warren Spahn 12.50 30.00

1963 Exhibit Stat Back

The 1963 Exhibit issue features 64 thick-stock cards with statistics printed in red on the backs. Each card measures 3 3/8" by 5 3/8". The set is quite similar to the set of the previous year -- but this set can be distinguished by the red print on the backs and the additional year of statistics.

COMPLETE SET (64) 400.00 800.00
1 Hank Aaron 15.00 40.00
2 Luis Aparicio 4.00 10.00
3 Bob Aspromonte 1.25 3.00
4 Ernie Banks 8.00 20.00
5 Steve Barber 1.25 3.00
6 Earl Battey 1.25 3.00
7 Yogi Berra 12.50 30.00
8 Ken Boyer 4.00 10.00
9 Lew Burdette 2.00 5.00
10 Johnny Callison 1.50 4.00
11 Norm Cash 4.00 10.00
12 Orlando Cepeda 4.00 10.00
13 Dean Chance 1.25 3.00
14 Tom Cheney 1.25 3.00
15 Roberto Clemente 30.00 60.00
16 Rocky Colavito 4.00 10.00
17 Choo Choo Coleman 2.00 5.00
18 Roger Craig 2.00 5.00
19 Joe Cunningham 1.50 4.00
20 Don Drysdale 6.00 15.00
21 Dick Farrell 1.25 3.00
22 Whitey Ford 8.00 20.00
23 Nellie Fox 4.00 10.00
24 Tito Francona 1.25 3.00
25 Jim Gentile 1.50 4.00
26 Tony Gonzales 1.25 3.00
27 Dick Groat 2.00 5.00
28 Ray Herbert 1.25 3.00
29 Chuck Hinton 1.25 3.00
30 Don Hoak 1.25 3.00
31 Frank Howard 2.50 6.00
32 Ken Hubbs 8.00 20.00
33 Joey Jay 1.25 3.00
34 Al Kaline 8.00 20.00
35 Harmon Killebrew 6.00 15.00
36 Sandy Koufax 20.00 50.00
37 Harvey Kuenn 2.00 5.00
38 Jim Landis 1.25 3.00
39 Art Mahaffey 1.25 3.00
40 Frank Malzone 1.50 4.00
41 Mickey Mantle 75.00 150.00
42 Roger Maris 15.00 40.00
43 Eddie Mathews 6.00 15.00
44 Willie Mays 15.00 40.00
45 Bill Mazeroski 4.00 10.00
46 Ken McBride 1.25 3.00
47 Wally Moon 1.50 4.00
48 Stan Musial 15.00 40.00
49 Charlie Neal 2.00 5.00
50 Billy O'Dell 1.25 3.00
51 Milt Pappas 1.25 3.00
52 Camilo Pascual 1.25 3.00
53 Jim Piersall 3.00 8.00
54 Vada Pinson 3.00 8.00
55 Brooks Robinson 10.00 25.00
56 Frank Robinson 8.00 20.00
57 Pete Runnels 1.25 3.00
58 Ron Santo 3.00 8.00
59 Norm Siebern 1.25 3.00
60 Warren Spahn 6.00 15.00
61 Lee Thomas 1.25 3.00
62 Leon Wagner 1.25 3.00
63 Billy Williams 6.00 15.00
64 Maury Wills 4.00 10.00

1969 Expos Fud's Photography

This blank-backed set was apparently issued by Bob Solon in the Chicago area. The black-and-white cards measure approximately 3 1/2" by 3" and feature Montreal Expos players of the 1969 season. The fronts carry action player photos with a white border. The player's name appears in a white bar in the lower right corner of the photo. The words "Compliments of" are printed in the upper border, while the words "Fud's Photography" appear in the lower border. The cards are unnumbered and checklisted below in alphabetical order.

COMPLETE SET (14) 8.00 20.00
1 Bob Bailey .50 1.25
2 John Bateman .50 1.25
3 Don Bosch .40 1.00
4 Jim Grant .60 1.50
5 Mack Jones .50 1.25
6 Coco Laboy .50 1.25
7 Dan McGinn .40 1.00
8 Cal McLish CO .40 1.00
9 Carl Morton .50 1.25
10 Manny Mota .75 2.00
11 Rusty Staub 2.00 5.00
12 Gary Sutherland .40 1.00
13 Mike Wegener .40 1.00
14 Floyd Wicker .40 1.00

1969 Expos Postcards

These postcards were issued during the Expos debut season. More cards should exist so all additions to this list is appreciated. These postcards are sequenced by uniform number.

COMPLETE SET 4.00 10.00
17 Howie Reed .40 1.00
18 Steve Renko .40 1.00
19 Jerry Robertson .40 1.00
20 Gary Waslewski .40 1.00
21 Kevin Collins .40 1.00
22 Ron Fairly .75 2.00
23 Jose Herrera .40 1.00
24 Ty Cline .40 1.00
25 Adolfo Phillips .40 1.00
26 Floyd Wicker .40 1.00
27 Gene Mauch MG .60 1.50
28 Peanuts Lowrey CO .40 1.00
29 Cal McLish CO .40 1.00
30 Bob Oldis CO .40 1.00
31 Jerry Zimmerman CO .40 1.00

1970 Expos Postcards

These 16 Montreal Expos postcards measure approximately 3 1/2" by 5 1/2" and feature borderless posed color player photos on their fronts. The player's facsimile autograph appears near the bottom. The backs carry the player's name and bilingual position in black ink at the upper left. The cards are numbered on the back.

COMPLETE SET (16) 8.00 20.00
1 Roy Face .75 2.00
2 Don Shaw .40 1.00
3 Dan McGinn .40 1.00
4 Bill Stoneman .60 1.50
5 Mike Wegener .40 1.00
6 Bob Bailey .60 1.50
7 Gary Sutherland .40 1.00
8 Coco Laboy .50 1.25
9 Bobby Wine UER/(Misspelled Boby on back) .50 1.25
10 Mack Jones .50 1.25
11 Rusty Staub 2.00 5.00
12 Don Bosch .40 1.00
13 Larry Jaster .60 1.50
14 John Bateman .50 1.25
15 John Boccabella .50 1.25
16 Ron Brand .40 1.00

1971 Expos La Pizza Royale

Featuring members of the Montreal Expos, this set, like the Fud's set, is thought to have been issued by Bob Solon in the Chicago area. Printed on thick cardboard paper, the cards measure approximately 2 1/2" by 5". The fronts typically feature blue-tinted player photos on a dark blue background; however the set was also issued in at least three other colors: green, gold, and red. The words "La Pizza Royale" are printed in white letters above the photo, while the player's name and position in French appear under the photo. The backs are blank. The cards are unnumbered and checklisted below in alphabetical order.

COMPLETE SET (14) 10.00 25.00
1 Bob Bailey 1.25 3.00
2 John Boccabella 1.00 2.50
3 Ron Fairly 1.25 3.00
4 Jim Gosger .75 2.00
5 Coco Laboy 1.00 2.50
6 Gene Mauch MG 1.25 3.00
7 Rich Nye .75 2.00
8 John O'Donoghue .75 2.00
9 Adolfo Phillips .75 2.00
10 Howie Reed .75 2.00
11 Marv Staehle .75 2.00
12 Rusty Staub 3.00 8.00
13 Gary Sutherland .75 2.00
14 Bobby Wine 1.00 2.50

1971 Expos Pro Stars

Printed in Canada by Pro Stars Publications, these 28 blank-backed postcards measure approximately 3 1/2" by 5 1/2" and feature white-bordered color player photos. The player's name appears as a facsimile autograph across the bottom of the photo. The postcards are unnumbered and checklisted below in alphabetical order.

COMPLETE SET (28) 20.00 50.00
1 Bob Bailey 1.25 3.00
2 John Bateman 1.00 2.50
3 John Boccabella 1.00 2.50
4 Ron Brand .75 2.00
5 Boots Day .75 2.00
6 Jim Fairey .75 2.00
7 Ron Fairly 1.25 3.00
8 Jim Gosger .75 2.00
9 Don Hahn .75 2.00
10 Ron Hunt 1.25 3.00
11 Mack Jones 1.00 2.50
12 Coco Laboy 1.00 2.50
13 Mike Marshall 1.50 4.00
14 Clyde Mashore .75 2.00
15 Gene Mauch MG 1.25 3.00
16 Dan McGinn .75 2.00
17 Carl Morton 1.00 2.50
18 John O'Donoghue .75 2.00
19 Adolfo Phillips .75 2.00
20 Claude Raymond 1.00 2.50
21 Howie Reed .75 2.00
22 Steve Renko .75 2.00
23 Rusty Staub 3.00 8.00
24 Bill Stoneman 1.25 3.00
25 John Strohmayer .75 2.00
26 Gary Sutherland .75 2.00
27 Mike Wegener .75 2.00
28 Bobby Wine 1.00 2.50

1972 Expos Matchbooks

These seven matchbooks, which measure 2 1/8" by 4 3/8" were issued by the Eddy Match Co. The fronts have a player photo while the backs have the home team schedule. Since these are unnumbered, we have sequenced them in alphabetical order.

COMPLETE SET 6.00 15.00
1 Boots Day .75 2.00
2 Ron Fairly 1.00 2.50
3 Ron Hunt .75 2.00
4 Steve Renko .75 2.00
5 Rusty Staub 1.50 4.00
6 Bobby Wine .75 2.00
7 Scoreboard .75 2.00
Honoring Ron Hunt's 50th Hit by Pitche

1973 Expos Matchbooks

These seven matchbooks, which measure 2 1/8" by 4 3/8" were issued by the Eddy Match Co. The fronts have a player photo while the backs have the home team schedule. Since these are unnumbered, we have sequenced them in alphabetical order.

COMPLETE SET 5.00 12.00
1 Tim Foli .75 2.00
2 Ron Hunt .75 2.00
3 Mike Jorgensen .75 2.00
4 Gene Mauch MG .75 2.00
5 Balor Moore .75 2.00
6 Ken Singleton .75 2.00
7 Bill Stoneman 1.00 2.50
No-hitter congratulations

1973 Expos Postcards

This set features borderless black-and-white player portraits measuring approximately 3 1/2" by 5 1/2". The backs carry the sentence, "Souvenir of the Montreal Expos Baseball Club," in both English and French.The cards are unnumbered and checklisted below in alphabetical order. There are probably many additions to this set so all help is appreciated.

COMPLETE SET 12.50 30.00
COMMON CARD (1-7) 1.50 4.00
1 Jimmy Bragan 1.50 4.00
2 Hal Breeden 1.50 4.00
3 Larry Doby CO 4.00 10.00
4 Ron Fairly 2.00 5.00
5 Mike Jorgensen 1.50 4.00
6 Steve Rogers 2.00 5.00
7 Mike Torrez 2.00 5.00

1974 Expos Weston

This ten-card set, featuring members of the Montreal Expos, measures approximately 3 1/2" by 5 1/2". The fronts have color player photos inside a thin white border with a facsimile autograph in black ink, and the player's name under the photo. The player's uniforms and caps have been airbrushed to remove the Expos insignia. The backs carry biography and statistics in English and French. The cards are unnumbered and checklisted below in alphabetical order. These cards were originally issued one to a package of Weston 39 cent baseball bats.

COMPLETE SET (10) 8.00 20.00
1 Bob Bailey 1.25 3.00
2 John Boccabella 1.00 2.50
3 Boots Day .75 2.00
4 Tim Foli 1.00 2.50
5 Ron Hunt 1.25 3.00
6 Mike Jorgensen 1.00 2.50
7 Ernie McAnally .75 2.00
8 Steve Renko .75 2.00
9 Ken Singleton 2.00 5.00
10 Bill Stoneman 1.50 4.00

1975 Expos Postcards

This 39-card set of the Montreal Expos features player photos on postcard-size cards. The cards are unnumbered and checklisted below in alphabetical order.

COMPLETE SET (39) 8.00 20.00
1 Bob Bailey .20 .50
2 Larry Biittner .20 .50
3 Dennis Blair .20 .50
4 Hal Breeden .20 .50
5 Dave Bristol CO .20 .50
6 Don Carrithers .20 .50
7 Gary Carter 2.00 5.00
8 Rich Coggins .20 .50
9 Nate Colbert .20 .50
10 Don DeMola .20 .50
11 Jim Dwyer .20 .50
12 Tim Foli .20 .50
13 Barry Foote .20 .50
14 Pepe Frias .20 .50
15 Woodie Fryman .20 .50
16 Walt Hriniak .20 .50
17 Mike Jorgensen .20 .50
18 Jim Lyttle .20 .50
19 Pete Mackanin .20 .50
20 Pepe Mangual .20 .50
21 Gene Mauch MG .20 .50
22 Cal McLish .20 .50
23 Dave McNally .30 .75
24 John Montague .20 .50
25 Jose Morales .20 .50
26 Dale Murray .20 .50
27 Larry Parrish .20 .50
28 Steve Renko .20 .50
29 Bombo Rivera .20 .50
30 Steve Rogers .20 .50
31 Pat Scanlon .20 .50
32 Fred Scherman .20 .50
33 Tony Scott .20 .50
34 Duke Snider CO .60 1.50
35 Don Stanhouse .20 .50
36 Chuck Taylor .20 .50
37 Dan Warthen .20 .50
38 Jerry White .20 .50
39 Jerry Zimmerman CO .20 .50

1976 Expos Matchbooks

These seven matchbooks, which measure 2 1/8" by 4 3/8" were issued by the Eddy Match Co. The fronts have a player photo while the backs have the home team schedule. Since these are unnumbered, we have sequenced them in alphabetical order.

COMPLETE SET 5.00 12.00
1 Barry Foote .75 2.00
2 Mike Jorgensen .75 2.00
3 Pete Mackanin .75 2.00
4 Dale Murray .75 2.00
5 Larry Parrish 1.00 2.50
6 Steve Rogers .75 2.00
7 Dan Warthen .75 2.00

1976 Expos Postcards

This 31-card set of the Montreal Expos features playerphotos on postcard-size cards. The cards are unnumbered and checklisted below in alphabetical order.

COMPLETE SET (31) 6.00 15.00
1 Billy Adair CO .20 .50
2 Larry Bearnarth CO .20 .50
3 Don Carrithers .20 .50
4 Gary Carter 1.50 4.00
5 Nate Colbert .20 .50
6 Jim Cox .20 .50
7 Larry Doby CO .60 1.50
8 Jim Dwyer .20 .50
9 Tim Foli .20 .50
10 Barry Foote .20 .50
11 Pepe Frias .20 .50
12 Woodie Fryman .20 .50
13 Wayne Granger .20 .50
14 Mike Jorgensen .20 .50
15 Clay Kirby .20 .50
16 Karl Kuehl MG .20 .50
17 Chip Lang .20 .50
18 Jim Lyttle .20 .50
19 Pepe Mangual .20 .50
20 Pete MacKanin .20 .50
21 Jose Morales .20 .50
22 Dale Murray .20 .50
23 Larry Parrish .60 1.50
24 Ron Piche CO .20 .50
25 Bombo Rivera .20 .50
26 Steve Rogers .40 1.00
27 Fred Scherman .20 .50
28 Don Stanhouse .20 .50
29 Ozzie Virgil CO .20 .50
30 Dan Warthen .20 .50
31 Jerry White .20 .50

1976 Expos Redpath

This set of 1976 Montreal Expos was issued by the Redpath Sugar company. The sheets measure approximately 3 1/4" by 10" and each sheet features four team members. The white fronts have a color head shot of the player on the right with the player's name and position printed above the photo in French and below the photo in English. To the left of the photo is brief biography and how they were acquired by Montreal Expos written in both French and English. The players are listed below in alphabetical order.

COMPLETE SET 10.00 25.00
1 Bill Adair CO .30 .75
2 Larry Bearnarth CO .30 .75
3 Don Carrithers .30 .75
4 Gary Carter 1.50 4.00
5 Larry Doby CO .75 2.00
6 Steve Dunning .30 .75
7 Jim Dwyer .30 .75
8 Tim Foli .30 .75
9 Barry Foote .30 .75
10 Pepe Frias .30 .75
11 Woodie Fryman .30 .75
12 Wayne Garrett .30 .75
13 Wayne Granger .30 .75
14 Mike Jorgensen .30 .75
15 Joe Kerrigan .30 .75
16 Clay Kirby .30 .75
17 Karl Kuehl MG .30 .75
18 Chip Lang .30 .75
19 Jim Lyttle .30 .75
20 Pete MacKanin .30 .75
21 Jose Mangual .30 .75
22 Jose Morales .30 .75
23 Dale Murray .30 .75
24 Larry Parrish .30 .75
25 Ron Piche CO .30 .75
26 Bombo Rivera .30 .75
27 Steve Rogers .60 1.50
28 Fred Scherman .30 .75
29 Don Stanhouse .30 .75
30 Chuck Taylor .30 .75
31 Andre Thornton .40 1.00
32 Del Unser .30 .75
33 Ellis Valentine .40 1.00
34 Ossie Virgil CO .60 1.50
35 Dan Warthen .30 .75
36 Jerry White .30 .75

1977 Expos Postcards

These 39 postcards feature all sorts of people in the Expos orginization. This was not just issued as one set, but these postcards were continually printed during the season to account for new additions.

COMPLETE SET 15.00 40.00
1 Santo Alcala .30 .75
2 Bill Atkinson .30 .75
3 Bill Atkinson Tree in background .30 .75
4 Stan Bahnsen .30 .75
5 Tim Blackwell .30 .75
6 Jim Brewer CO .30 .75
7 Jackie Brown CO .30 .75
8 Gary Carter 1.50 4.00
9 Dave Cash .30 .75
10 Warren Cromartie .60 1.50
11 Andre Dawson 2.00 5.00
12 Andre Dawson Wearing batting helmet 2.00 5.00
13 Barry Foote .30 .75
14 Pepe Frias .30 .75
15 Bill Gardner .30 .75
16 Wayne Garrett .30 .75
17 Gerald Hannahs .30 .75
18 Mike Jorgenson .30 .75
19 Joe Kerrigan .30 .75
20 Pete Mackanin .30 .75
21 Will McEnaney .30 .75
22 Sam Mejias .30 .75
23 Jose Morales .30 .75
24 Larry Parrish .40 1.00
25 Tony Perez .75 2.00
26 Steve Rogers .40 1.00
27 Dan Schatzeder .30 .75
28 Chris Speier .30 .75
29 Don Stanhouse .30 .75
30 Jeff Terpko .30 .75
31 Wayne Twitchell .30 .75
32 Del Unser .30 .75
33 Ellis Valentine .30 .75
34 Mickey Vernon .40 1.00
35 Ozzie Virgil CO .30 .75
36 Tom Walker .30 .75
37 Dan Warthen .30 .75
38 Jerry White .30 .75
39 Dick Williams MG .40 1.00

1978 Expos Postcards

This 15-card set features a borderless front with the player's name and team in a box near the bottom. The player's position is also printed on the front in both French and English. Backs are blank. cards are aphabetically checklisted below.

COMPLETE SET (15) 6.00 15.00
1 Stan Bahnsen .30 .75
2 Gary Carter 1.50 4.00
3 Andre Dawson 1.25 3.00
4 Hal Dues .30 .75
5 Ross Grimsley .30 .75
6 Fred Holdsworth .30 .75
7 Darold Knowles .30 .75
8 Rudy May .30 .75
9 Stan Papi .30 .75
10 Larry Parrish .40 1.00
11 Bob Reece .30 .75
12 Norm Sherry CO .30 .75
13 Dan Schatzeder .30 .75
14 Chris Speier .40 1.00
15 Wayne Twitchell .30 .75

1979 Expos Postcards

These postcards feature members from the Montreal Expos organization. These postcards are blankbacked and are borderless. The only identification is the player's name and billingual player information on the bottom.

COMPLETE SET (32) 10.00 25.00
1 Felipe Alou CO .60 1.50
2 Stan Bahnsen .30 .75
3 Tony Bernazard .30 .75
4 Jim Brewer CO .30 .75
5 Dave Cash .30 .75
6 Warren Cromartie .40 1.00

7 Andre Dawson 1.25 3.00
8 Duffy Dyer .30 .75
9 Woodie Fryman .30 .75
10 Mike Garman .30 .75
11 Ed Herrmann .30 .75
12 Tommy Hutton .30 .75
13 Bill Lee .40 1.00
With facial hair
14 Bill Lee .40 1.00
Clean-shaven
15 Ken Macha .60 1.50
16 Jim Mason .30 .75
17 Pat Mullin .30 .75
18 Dave Palmer .30 .75
19 Tony Perez .75 2.00
20 Vern Rapp CO .30 .75
21 Steve Rogers .40 1.00
22 Scott Sanderson .60 1.50
23 Rodney Scott .30 .75
number 3 on uniform
24 Rodney Scott .30 .75
number 19 on uniform
25 Norm Sherry CO .30 .75
26 Tony Solaita .30 .75
27 Elias Sosa .30 .75
28 Rusty Staub .75 2.00
29 Ellis Valentine .40 1.00
30 Ozzie Virgil CO .40 1.00
31 Jerry White .30 .75
32 Dick Williams MG .40 1.00

1980 Expos Postcards

These postcards feature members of the 1980 Montreal Expos. These postcards are similar to those issued in the three previous seasons but they have no positions on them. These are all new photos that have red and blue shoulder striping. These cards are unnumbered so we have sequenced them in alphabetical order.

COMPLETE SET (35) 6.00 15.00
1 Bill Almon .20 .50
2 Felipe Alou CO .40 1.00
3 Stan Bahnsen .20 .50
4 Tony Bernazard .20 .50
5 Gary Carter 1.00 2.50
6 Galen Cisco CO .20 .50
7 Warren Cromartie .30 .75
8 Andre Dawson .75 2.00
9 Woodie Fryman .20 .50
10 Ross Grimsley .20 .50
11 Bill Gullickson .30 .75
12 Tommy Hutton .20 .50
13 Charlie Lea .20 .50
14 Bill Lee .30 .75
15 Ron LeFlore .20 .50
16 Ken Macha .30 .75
17 Pat Mullin CO .20 .50
18 Dale Murray .20 .50
19 Fred Norman .20 .50
20 Rowland Office .20 .50
21 David Palmer .20 .50
22 Larry Parrish .20 .50
23 Bobby Ramos .20 .50
24 Vern Rapp CO .20 .50
25 Steve Rogers .20 .50
26 Scott Sanderson .20 .50
27 Rodney Scott .20 .50
28 Norm Sherry CO .20 .50
29 Elias Sosa .20 .50
30 Chris Speier .20 .50
31 John Tamargo .20 .50
32 Ellis Valentine .20 .50
33 Ozzie Virgil CO .20 .50
34 Jerry White .20 .50
35 Dick Williams MG .40 1.00

1981 Expos Postcards

These postcards feature members of the 1981 Montreal Expos. These cards are unnumbered and we have sequenced them in alphabetical order. Many of the poses of the 1980 players were repeated. We have included only new players or players with different photos from the year before. Very early issues of Tim Raines, Jeff Reardon and Tim Wallach are included in this set.

COMPLETE SET (16) 4.00 10.00
1 Steve Boros CO .20 .50
2 Ray Burris .20 .50
3 Charlie Lea .20 .50
4 Bill Lee .30 .75
5 Jerry Manuel .20 .50
6 Willie Montanez .20 .50
7 Ron McLain .20 .50
8 Mike Phillips .20 .50
9 Tim Raines 2.00 5.00
10 Bobby Ramos .20 .50
11 Steve Ratzer .20 .50
12 Jeff Reardon 1.00 2.50
13 Steve Rogers .20 .50
14 Scott Sanderson .20 .50
15 Chris Speier .20 .50
16 Tim Wallach .60 1.50

1982 Expos Hygrade Meats

The cards in this 24-card set measure approximately 2" by 3". This series depicting the Montreal Expos was distributed by the Hygrade company in Quebec Province, Canada. Single cello-packed cards are found in packages of Hygrade smoked sausages; each has a color photo of an Expo player, with his name and uniform number in a white panel at the base of the picture. The back, printed only in French, advertises a leatherette album designed to hold a complete set of cards. The card stock is actually thick paper rather than cardboard, and the edges are rounded. The cards are unnumbered and checklisted below in alphabetical order.

COMPLETE SET (24) 15.00 40.00
1 Tim Blackwell .40 1.00
2 Ray Burris .40 1.00
3 Gary Carter 5.00 12.00
4 Warren Cromartie .75 2.00
5 Andre Dawson 4.00 10.00
6 Jim Fanning MG .40 1.00
7 Terry Francona 1.00 2.50
8 Woodie Fryman .40 1.00
9 Bill Gullickson .75 2.00
10 Bob James .40 1.00
11 Charlie Lea .40 1.00
12 Brad Mills .40 1.00
13 John Milner .40 1.00
14 Dan Norman .40 1.00
15 Al Oliver 1.00 2.50
16 Tim Raines 4.00 10.00
17 Jeff Reardon 1.50 4.00
18 Steve Rogers .60 1.50
19 Scott Sanderson .40 1.00
20 Bryn Smith .40 1.00
21 Chris Speier .40 1.00
22 Frank Taveras .40 1.00
23 Tim Wallach 1.50 4.00
24 Jerry White .40 1.00
xx0 Leatherette Album 3.00 8.00

1982 Expos Postcards

These postcards feature members of the 1982 Montreal Expos. These postcards are in the same style as used over the previous five years. The cards are unnumbered and we have sequenced them in alphabetical order.

COMPLETE SET (43) 10.00 25.00
1 Tim Blackwell .20 .50
2 Steve Boros CO .20 .50
3 Ray Burris .20 .50
4 Gary Carter 2.00 5.00
5 Galen Cisco CO .20 .50
6 Warren Cromartie .30 .75
7 Warren Cromartie/(Close-up) .30 .75
8 Andre Dawson 1.50 4.00
9 Billy DeMars CO .20 .50
10 Jim Fanning MG .20 .50
11 Doug Flynn .20 .50
12 Terry Francona .60 1.50
13 Woodie Fryman .20 .50
14 Bob Gebhard CO .20 .50
15 Bill Gullickson .20 .50
16 Bob James .20 .50
17 Roy Johnson .20 .50
18 Wallace Johnson .20 .50
19 Charlie Lea .20 .50
20 Bill Lee .30 .75
21 Bryan Little .20 .50
22 Brad Mills .20 .50
23 John Milner .20 .50
24 Don Norman .20 .50
25 Al Oliver/(Portrait) .40 1.00
26 Al Oliver/(Bat on shoulder) .40 1.00
27 Al Oliver/(Bat on shoulder .40 1.00
under stadium roof)
28 Rowland Office .20 .50
29 David Palmer .20 .50
30 Mike Phillips .20 .50
31 Tim Raines 1.50 4.00
32 Vern Rapp CO .20 .50
33 Jeff Reardon .60 1.50
34 Steve Rogers .20 .50
35 Scott Sanderson .20 .50
36 Dan Schatzeder .20 .50
37 Rodney Scott .20 .50
38 Bryn Smith .20 .50
39 Chris Speier .20 .50
40 Tim Wallach 1.25 3.00
41 Jerry White .20 .50
42 Joel Youngblood .20 .50
43 Frank Taveras .20 .50

1982 Expos Zellers

Sponsored by Zellers Department Stores and subtitled "Baseball Pro Tips," the 60 standard-size cards comprising this set were originally distributed in 20 perforated three-card panels. The yellow-bordered fronts feature circular color player action shots circumscribed by red, white, and blue lines. The player's name appears in black lettering in the yellow margin below the photo. Below his name is a description in both English and French of the action depicted. The back carries the "Pro Tip" in English and French explaining the techniques used by the player pictured on the front. The cards are numbered on the front, and each card is marked "A," "B" or "C" next to its number, which denotes its location on the original three-card panel. Eleven players and one coach of the Montreal Expos are featured, each explaining a particular facet of baseball in the three card sequences which comprise a panel. Gary Carter (5), Cromartie (2), Dawson (3) and Francona (2) are pictured on multiple panels. The prices below are for intact three-card panels.

COMPLETE SET (60) 8.00 20.00
1A Gary Carter/(Catching position) .75 2.00
1B Gary Carter/(Catching position)
1C Gary Carter/(Catching position)
2A Steve Rogers/(Pitching stance) .30 .75
2B Steve Rogers/(Pitching stance)
2C Steve Rogers/(Pitching stance)
3A Tim Raines/(Sliding) .75 2.00
3B Tim Raines/(Sliding)
3C Tim Raines/(Sliding)
4A Andre Dawson/(Batting stance) .75 2.00
4B Andre Dawson/(Batting stance)
4C Andre Dawson/(Batting stance)
5A Terry Francona/(Contact hitting) .60 1.50
5B Terry Francona/(Contact hitting)
5C Terry Francona/(Contact hitting)
6A Gary Carter/(Fielding pop fouls) .40 1.00
6B Gary Carter/(Fielding pop fouls)
6C Gary Carter/(Fielding pop fouls)
7A Warren Cromartie/(Fielding at 1B) .30 .75
7B Warren Cromartie/(Fielding at 1B)
7C Warren Cromartie/(Fielding at 1B)
8A Chris Speier/(Fielding at SS) .30 .75
8B Chris Speier/(Fielding at SS)
8C Chris Speier/(Fielding at SS)
9A Billy DeMars CO/(Signals) .30 .75
9B Billy DeMars CO/(Signals)
9C Billy DeMars CO/(Signals)
10A Andre Dawson/(Batting) .75 2.00
10B Andre Dawson/(Batting)
10C Andre Dawson/(Batting)
11A Terry Francona/(Outfield throws) .60 1.50
11B Terry Francona/(Outfield throws)
11C Terry Francona/(Outfield throws)
12A Woodie Fryman/(Holding runner) .30 .75
12B Woodie Fryman/(Holding runner)
12C Woodie Fryman/(Holding runner)
13A Gary Carter/(Fielding low balls) .75 2.00
13B Gary Carter/(Fielding low balls)
13C Gary Carter/(Fielding low balls)
14A Andre Dawson/(Playing CF) .75 2.00
14B Andre Dawson/(Playing CF)
14C Andre Dawson/(Playing CF)
15A Bill Gullickson/(Slurve) .40 1.00
15B Bill Gullickson/(Slurve)
15C Bill Gullickson/(Slurve)
16A Gary Carter/(Catching stance) .75 2.00
16B Gary Carter/(Catching stance)
16C Gary Carter/(Catching stance)
17A Scott Sanderson/(Fielding as a P) .30 .75
17B Scott Sanderson/(Fielding as a P)
17C Scott Sanderson/(Fielding as a P)
18A Warren Cromartie .30 .75
(Handling bad throws)
18B Warren Cromartie/(Handling bad throws)
18C Warren Cromartie/(Handling bad throws)
19A Gary Carter/(Hitting stride) .75 2.00
19B Gary Carter/(Hitting stride)
19C Gary Carter/(Hitting stride)
20A Ray Burris/(Holding runner) .30 .75
20B Ray Burris/(Holding runner)
20C Ray Burris/(Holding runner)

1983 Expos Postcards

These 39 blank-backed Expos postcards measure approximately 3 1/2" by 5 1/2" and feature posed color player photos that are borderless, except at the bottom, where a white margin carries the player's name in black lettering. The cards are unnumbered and checklisted below in alphabetical order.

COMPLETE SET (39) 12.50 30.00
1 Tim Blackwell .40 1.00
2 Ray Burris .40 1.00
3 Gary Carter 2.00 5.00
4 Galen Cisco CO .40 1.00
5 Warren Cromartie .50 1.25
6 Terry Crowley .40 1.00
7 Andre Dawson 1.25 3.00
8 Billy DeMars CO .40 1.00
9 Doug Flynn .40 1.00
10 Terry Francona .50 1.25
11 Woodie Fryman .40 1.00
12 Bill Gullickson .50 1.25
13 Bob James .40 1.00
14 Joe Kerrigan CO .40 1.00
15 Charlie Lea .40 1.00
16 Randy Lerch .40 1.00
17 Bryan Little .40 1.00
18 Ron McClain TR .40 1.00
19 Brad Mills .40 1.00
20 Al Oliver .75 2.00
21 David Palmer .40 1.00
22 Mike Phillips .40 1.00
23 Tim Raines 1.25 3.00
24 Bobby Ramos .40 1.00
25 Vern Rapp CO .40 1.00
26 Jeff Reardon 1.00 2.50
27 Steve Rogers .60 1.50
28 Scott Sanderson .40 1.00
29 Dan Schatzeder .40 1.00
30 Bryn Smith .40 1.00
31 Chris Speier .40 1.00
32 Mike Vail .40 1.00
33 Bill Virdon MG .50 1.25
34 Tim Wallach .75 2.00
35 Chris Welsh .40 1.00
36 Jerry White .40 1.00
37 Tom Wieghaus .40 1.00
38 Jim Wohlford .40 1.00
39 Mel Wright CO .40 1.00

1983 Expos Stuart

These 30 standard-size cards feature players of the Montreal Expos. The fronts carry white-bordered color player photos. The player's name and uniform number, along with the Montreal Expos' and Stuart's logo, appear within the broad white margin at the bottom. The plain back carries the player's bilingual biography and career highlights and features red and blue print on off-white card stock.

COMPLETE SET (30) 6.00 15.00
1 Bill Virdon MG .20 .50
2 Woodie Fryman .08 .25
3 Vern Rapp CO .08 .25
4 Andre Dawson .75 2.00
5 Jeff Reardon .30 .75
6 Al Oliver .30 .75
7 Doug Flynn .08 .25
8 Gary Carter 1.00 2.50
9 Tim Raines .75 2.00
10 Steve Rogers .20 .50
11 Billy DeMars CO .08 .25
12 Tim Wallach .30 .75
13 Galen Cisco CO .08 .25
14 Terry Francona .20 .50
15 Bill Gullickson .08 .25
16 Ray Burris .08 .25
17 Scott Sanderson .08 .25
18 Warren Cromartie .08 .25
19 Jerry White .08 .25
20 Bobby Ramos .08 .25
21 Jim Wohlford .08 .25
22 Dan Schatzeder .08 .25
23 Charlie Lea .08 .25
24 Bryan Little UER(Misspelled Brian) .08 .25
25 Mel Wright CO .08 .25
26 Tim Blackwell .08 .25
27 Chris Speier .08 .25
28 Randy Lerch .08 .25
29 Bryn Smith .08 .25
30 Brad Mills .08 .25

1984 Expos Postcards

These 36 Expos postcards measure approximately 3 1/2" by 5 1/2" and feature borderless posed color player photos on their fronts. The backs carry the player's name and uniform number at the upper left. Some backs also carry the bilingual Expos' product license seal and trademarks on the left side. The rectangle for the stamp and the year of issue appear at the upper right. The postcards are unnumbered and checklisted below in alphabetical order.

COMPLETE SET (36) 15.00 40.00
1 Felipe Alou CO .75 2.00
2 Fred Breining .40 1.00
3 Gary Carter 2.50 6.00
4 Galen Cisco CO .40 1.00
5 Andre Dawson 2.00 5.00
6 Billy DeMars CO .40 1.00
7 Miguel Dilone .40 1.00
8 Doug Flynn .40 1.00
9 Terry Francona .60 1.50
10 Mike Fuentes .40 1.00
11 Bill Gullickson .40 1.00
12 Greg A. Harris .40 1.00
13 Bob James .40 1.00
14 Roy Johnson .40 1.00
15 Joe Kerrigan CO .40 1.00
16 Charlie Lea .40 1.00
17 Bryan Little .40 1.00
18 Gary Lucas .40 1.00
19 Andy McGaffigan .40 1.00
20 Russ Nixon CO .40 1.00
21 David Palmer .40 1.00
22 Tim Raines 2.00 5.00
23 Bobby Ramos .40 1.00
24 Jeff Reardon .75 2.00
25 Steve Rogers .40 1.00
26 Pete Rose 3.00 8.00
27 Angel Salazar .40 1.00
28 Dan Schatzeder .40 1.00
29 Bryn Smith .40 1.00
30 Chris Speier .40 1.00
31 Mike Stenhouse .40 1.00
32 Derrel Thomas .40 1.00
33 Mike Vail .40 1.00
34 Bill Virdon MG .60 1.50
35 Tim Wallach .75 2.00
36 Jim Wohlford .40 1.00

1984 Expos Stuart

These 40 standard-size cards feature players of the Montreal Expos. The fronts carry white-bordered color player photos framed by a red line. The player's name and uniform number, along with the Montreal Expos' and Stuart's logo, appear within the broad white margin at the bottom. The white back is also framed by a red line and carries the player's bilingual biography and career highlights. The cards are numbered on the back. The first series of 20 cards was distributed from mid-April through June; the second series was distributed in July and August. After the completion of the promotion, the remainder of the first series cards were released to a few card dealers for distribution to the hobby. This set is distinguished from the previous year by the red border around the picture on the obverse. An album was also available for holding the cards; the album is gray, white, blue, and red and contains two-pocket plastic pages.

COMPLETE SET (40) 8.00 20.00
COMMON CARD (1-20) .10 .25
COMMON CARD (21-40) .20 .50
1 Youppi (Mascot) .20 .50
2 Bill Virdon MG .20 .50
3 Billy DeMars CO .08 .25
4 Galen Cisco CO .08 .25
5 Russ Nixon CO .08 .25
6 Felipe Alou CO .30 .75
7 Dan Schatzeder .08 .25
8 Charlie Lea .08 .25
9 Roberto Ramos .08 .25
10 Bob James .08 .25
11 Andre Dawson .60 1.50
12 Gary Lucas .08 .25
13 Jeff Reardon .20 .50
14 Tim Wallach .30 .75
15 Gary Carter .75 2.00
16 Bill Gullickson .20 .50
17 Pete Rose 1.25 3.00
18 Terry Francona .20 .50
19 Steve Rogers .20 .50
20 Tim Raines .60 1.50
21 Bryn Smith .20 .50
22 Greg A. Harris .20 .50
23 David Palmer .20 .50
24 Jim Wohlford .20 .50
25 Miguel Dilone .20 .50
26 Mike Stenhouse .20 .50
27 Chris Speier .20 .50
28 Derrel Thomas .20 .50
29 Doug Flynn .20 .50
30 Bryan Little .20 .50
31 Angel Salazar .20 .50
32 Mike Fuentes .20 .50
33 Joe Kerrigan CO .20 .50
34 Andy McGaffigan .20 .50
35 Fred Breining .20 .50
36 Expo '83 All Stars .60 1.50
Gary Carter
Andre Dawson
Tim
37 Co-Players of the Year .60 1.50
Andre Dawson
Tim Raines
38 Coaching Staff .30 .75
Bill Virdon MG
Felipe Alou CO
Ga
39 Expos Team Photo .30 .75
40 Checklist Card .30 .75
xx0 Album 1.25 3.00

1985 Expos Postcards

These 26 Expos postcards measure approximately 3 1/2" by 5 1/2" and feature borderless posed color player photos on their fronts. The backs carry the player's name and uniform number at the upper left. The bilingual Expos' product license seal and trademarks appear on the left side. The rectangle for the stamp and the year of issue appear at the upper right. The postcards are unnumbered and checklisted below in alphabetical order.

COMPLETE SET (26) 5.00 12.00
1 Skeeter Barnes .20 .50
2 Larry Bearnarth CO .20 .50
3 Hubie Brooks .30 .75
4 Tim Burke .20 .50
5 Sal Butera .20 .50
6 Andre Dawson 1.00 2.50
7 Dan Driessen .20 .50
8 Mike Fitzgerald .20 .50
9 Ron Hansen CO .20 .50
10 Joe Hesketh .20 .50
11 Vance Law .20 .50
12 Mickey Mahler .20 .50
13 Al Newman .20 .50
14 Steve Nicosia .20 .50
15 Jack O'Connor UER .20 .50
(Misspelled O'Conner on back)
16 David Palmer .20 .50
17 Tim Raines 1.00 2.50
18 Rick Renick CO .20 .50
19 Bert Roberge .20 .50
20 Buck Rodgers MG .20 .50
21 Razor Shines .30 .75
22 Bryn Smith .20 .50
23 Randy St. Claire .20 .50
24 U.L. Washington .20 .50
25 Herm Winningham .20 .50
26 Youppi (Mascot) .30 .75

1986 Expos Greats TCMA

This 12-card standard-size set features some of the best Expos players from their first two decades. The fronts have player photos, their names and position. The backs have vital statistics as well as career statistics.

COMPLETE SET (12) 1.25 3.00
1 Ron Fairly .20 .50
2 Dave Cash .08 .25
3 Tim Foli .08 .25
4 Bob Bailey .08 .25
5 Ken Singleton .08 .25
6 Ellis Valentine .08 .25
7 Rusty Staub .30 .75
8 John Bateman .08 .25
9 Steve Rogers .20 .50
10 Woodie Fryman .08 .25
11 Mike Marshall .08 .25
12 Jim Fanning MG .08 .25

1986 Expos Postcards

These postcards are very similar to the 85 Expos Postcards. These postcards feature no name box or fascimile autograph. The Expos logo and the player name are printed in blue. The cards are unnumbered and sequenced in alphabetical order. Andres Galarraga is featured in his Rookie Card year.

COMPLETE SET (20) 3.00 8.00
1 Dann Bilardello .20 .50
2 Tim Burke .20 .50
3 Mike Fitzgerald .20 .50
4 Andres Galarraga 1.50 4.00
5 Joe Hesketh .20 .50
6 Wayne Krenchicki .20 .50
7 Ken Macha .30 .75
8 Andy McGaffigan .20 .50
9 Al Newman .20 .50
10 Tom Nieto .20 .50
11 Jeff Parrett .20 .50
12 George Riley .20 .50
13 Dan Schatzeder .20 .50
14 Bryn Smith .20 .50
15 Jason Thompson .20 .50
16 Jay Tibbs .30 .75
17 Tim Wallach .40 1.00
18 Mitch Webster .20 .50
19 Bobby Winkles CO .20 .50
20 Floyd Youmans .20 .50

1986 Expos Provigo Panels

These 28 cards are found in lightly perforated panels of three (two player cards and an advertising card). The panel of three measures approximately 7 1/2" by 3 3/8", whereas each individual card measures 2 1/2" by 3 3/8". The fronts feature white-bordered color player action shots. The player's name and uniform number, along with the Provigo name and logo, appear within a yellow stripe across the bottom of the photo. The red, white, and blue Montreal Expos' logo appears at the top of the front. It also appears at the top of the white back, followed below by bilingual player biography and career highlights. An album was available to hold the cards; however in order to use the album, the cards had to be separated into individuals. The cards are attractive and the backs feature blue and red printing on a white card stock.

COMPLETE SET (28) 3.00 8.00
1 Hubie Brooks .20 .50
2 Dann Bilardello .08 .25
3 Buck Rodgers MG .08 .25
4 Andy McGaffigan .08 .25
5 Mitch Webster .08 .25
6 Jim Wohlford .08 .25
7 Tim Raines .40 1.00
8 Jay Tibbs .08 .25
9 Andre Dawson .40 1.00
10 Andres Galarraga .75 2.00
11 Tim Wallach .30 .75
12 Dan Schatzeder .08 .25
13 Jeff Reardon .30 .75
14 Coaching Staff .08 .25
Joe Kerrigan
Bobby Winkles
Larry
15 Jason Thompson .08 .25
16 Bert Roberge .08 .25
17 Tim Burke .08 .25
18 Al Newman .08 .25
19 Bryn Smith .08 .25
20 Wayne Krenchicki .08 .25
21 Joe Hesketh .08 .25
22 Herm Winningham .08 .25
23 Vance Law .08 .25
24 Floyd Youmans .08 .25
25 Jeff Parrett .08 .25
26 Mike Fitzgerald .08 .25
27 Youppi (Mascot) .08 .25
28 Coaching Staff .08 .25
Rick Renick
Ron Hansen
Ken Macha

1986 Expos Provigo Posters

These 12 blank-backed posters measure approximately 9" by 14 3/4", with the bottom 2 1/2" being a perforated strip carrying various Provigo coupons. The posters feature posed color photos of the Montreal Expos. These photos are borderless, except at the bottom, where a team color-coded border carries the player's name and uniform number, the Provigo and Expos logos, and the poster's number. The player's facsimile autograph appears across the photo. The backs are red and white or blue and blank.

COMPLETE SET (12) 6.00 15.00
1 Tim Raines .75 2.00
2 Bryn Smith .40 1.00
3 Hubie Brooks .60 1.50
4 Buck Rodgers MG .40 1.00
5 Mitch Webster .40 1.00
6 Joe Hesketh .40 1.00
7 Mike Fitzgerald .40 1.00
8 Andy McGaffigan .40 1.00
9 Andre Dawson 1.00 2.50
10 Tim Wallach .75 2.00
11 Jeff Reardon .75 2.00
12 Vance Law .40 1.00

1987 Expos Postcards

These 37 Montreal Expos postcards measure approximately 3 1/2" by 5 1/2" and feature borderless posed color player photos on their fronts. The backs are blank, except for the Expos logo and the player's name and uniform number printed in blue ink at the upper left. Otherwise, the postcards are unnumbered and so are checklisted below in alphabetical order.

COMPLETE SET (37) 6.00 15.00
1 Larry Bearnarth CO .20 .50
2 Hubie Brooks .30 .75
3 Tim Burke .20 .50
4 Casey Candaele .20 .50
5 Dave Engle .20 .50
6 Mike Fitzgerald .20 .50
7 Tom Foley .20 .50
8 Andres Galarraga 1.00 2.50
9 Ron Hansen CO .20 .50
10 Neal Heaton .20 .50
11 Joe Hesketh .20 .50
12 Wallace Johnson .20 .50
13 Vance Law .20 .50
14 Bob McClure .20 .50
15 Andy McGaffigan .20 .50
16 Ken Macha .30 .75
17 Jackie Moore CO .20 .50
18 Reid Nichols .20 .50
19 Jeff Parrett .20 .50
20 Alonzo Powell .20 .50
21 Tim Raines .60 1.50
22 Jeff Reed .20 .50
23 Luis Rivera .20 .50
24 Buck Rodgers MG .20 .50
25 Dan Schatzeder .20 .50
26 Bob Sebra .20 .50
27 Bryn Smith .20 .50
28 Lary Sorensen .20 .50
29 Randy St. Claire .20 .50
30 John Stefero .20 .50
31 Jay Tibbs .20 .50
32 Tim Wallach .40 1.00
33 Mitch Webster .20 .50
34 Bobby Winkles CO .20 .50
35 Herman Winningham .20 .50
36 Floyd Youmans .20 .50
37 Youppi (Mascot) .30 .75

1988 Expos Postcards

These postcards feature members of the 1988 Montreal Expos. They are similar in format to the 1987 Expos postcards. These cards are unnumbered and we have sequenced them in alphabetical order.

COMPLETE SET (38) 5.00 12.00
1 Larry Bearnarth CO .20 .50
2 Hubie Brooks .30 .75
3 Tim Burke .20 .50
4 Casey Candaele .20 .50
5 Leonel Carrion CO .20 .50
6 John Dodson .20 .50
7 Dave Engle .20 .50
8 Mike Fitzgerald .20 .50
9 Tom Foley .20 .50
10 Andres Galarraga 1.00 2.50
11 Ron Hansen CO .20 .50
12 Neal Heaton .20 .50
13 Joe Hesketh .20 .50
14 Brian Holman .20 .50
15 Rex Hudler .30 .75
16 Wallace Johnson .20 .50
17 Tracy Jones .20 .50
18 Dave Martinez .20 .50
19 Dennis Martinez .40 1.00
20 Bob McClure .20 .50
21 Andy McGaffigan .20 .50
22 Jackie Moore CO .20 .50
23 Graig Nettles .40 1.00
24 Otis Nixon .20 .50
25 Jeff Parrett .20 .50
26 Pascual Perez .20 .50
27 Tim Raines .60 1.50
28 Jeff Reed .20 .50
29 Luis Rivera .20 .50
30 Buck Rodgers MG .20 .50
31 Nelson Santovenia .20 .50
32 Bryn Smith .20 .50
33 Tim Wallach .40 1.00
34 Mitch Webster .20 .50
35 Bobby Winkles CO .20 .50
36 Herm Winningham .20 .50
37 Floyd Youmans .20 .50
38 Youppi (Mascot) .20 .50

1989 Expos Postcards

These cards are very similar to the 1988 Expos Postcards. The cards are unnumbered and we have sequenced them in alphabetical order. Cy Young award winner Randy Johnson has a very early card in this set.

COMPLETE SET (29) 8.00 20.00
1 Mike Aldrete .20 .50
2 Larry Bearnarth CO .20 .50
3 Hubie Brooks .30 .75
4 Tim Burke .20 .50
5 Mike Fitzgerald .20 .50
6 Tom Foley .20 .50
7 Steve Frey .20 .50
8 Andres Galarraga .75 2.00
9 Damaso Garcia .20 .50
10 Brett Gideon .20 .50
11 Kevin Gross .20 .50
12 Ron Hansen CO .20 .50
13 Gene Harris .20 .50
14 Joe Hesketh .20 .50
15 Randy Johnson 8.00 20.00
16 Rafael Landestoy CO .20 .50
17 Mark Langston .30 .75
18 Ken Macha .30 .75
19 Dave Martinez .20 .50
20 Dennis Martinez .40 1.00
21 Andy McGaffigan .20 .50
22 Jackie Moore CO .20 .50
23 Spike Owen .20 .50
24 Tim Raines .60 1.50
25 Buck Rodgers MG .20 .50
26 Nelson Santovenia .20 .50
27 Bryn Smith .20 .50
28 Joe Sparks CO .20 .50
29 Tim Wallach .40 1.00

1990 Expos Postcards

These postcards feature members of the 1990 Montreal Expos. Players featured early in their career include Delino DeShields, Marquis Grissom and Larry Walker. These cards are unnumbered are we have checklisted them in alphabetical order.

COMPLETE SET (37) 10.00 25.00
1 Mike Aldrete .20 .50
2 Larry Bearnarth CO .20 .50
3 Dennis Boyd .20 .50
4 Tim Burke .20 .50
5 John Costello .20 .50
6 Delino DeShields .75 2.00
7 Mike Fitzgerald .20 .50
8 Tom Foley .20 .50
9 Steve Frey .20 .50
10 Andres Galarraga .60 1.50
11 Mark Gardner .20 .50
12 Brett Gideon .20 .50
13 Marquis Grissom .75 2.00
14 Kevin Gross .20 .50
15 Drew Hall .20 .50
16 Tommy Harper CO .20 .50
17 Rex Hudler .30 .75
18 Jeff Huson .20 .50
19 Wallace Johnson .20 .50
20 Rafael Landestoy CO .20 .50
21 Ken Macha .30 .75
22 Dave Martinez .20 .50
23 Dennis Martinez .40 1.00
24 Hal McRae CO .20 .50
25 Otis Nixon .20 .50
26 Junior Noboa .20 .50
27 Spike Owen .20 .50
28 Tim Raines .60 1.50
29 Buck Rodgers MG .20 .50
30 Tom Runnells CO .20 .50
31 Bill Sampen .20 .50
32 Nelson Santovenia .20 .50
33 Dave Schmidt .20 .50
34 Zane Smith .20 .50
35 Rich Thompson .20 .50
36 Larry Walker 1.50 4.00
37 Tim Wallach .40 1.00

1991 Expos Postcards

These postcards feature members of the 1991 Montreal Expos. They measure approximately 3 1/2" by 5 1/2" and feature borderless posed color player photos. The player's name appears in a lower corner. These cards are unnumbered and sequenced in alphabetical order.

COMPLETE SET (22) 4.00 10.00
1 Brian Barnes .20 .50
2 Eric Bullock .20 .50
3 Ivan Calderon .20 .50
4 Mike Fitzgerald .20 .50
5 Tom Foley .20 .50
6 Steve Frey .20 .50
7 Andres Galarraga .75 2.00
8 Mark Gardner .20 .50
9 Chris Haney .20 .50
10 Ron Hassey .20 .50
11 Barry Jones .20 .50
12 Rick Mahler .20 .50
13 Dave Martinez .20 .50
14 Dennis Martinez .40 1.00
15 Chris Nabholz .20 .50
16 Junior Noboa .20 .50
17 Gilberto Reyes .20 .50
18 Mel Rojas .30 .75
19 Tom Runnells MG .20 .50
20 Scott Ruskin .20 .50
21 Nelson Santovenia .20 .50
22 Larry Walker .75 2.00

1992 Expos Donruss Durivage

Featuring the Montreal Expos, the 26-card standard-size set was produced by Donruss for Durivage (a Canadian bread company). The fronts have posed color photos of the players without hats, framed by a gray inner border and a dark green outer border. The team logo, "Durivage" set name, and player information appear at the bottom of card front. In a horizontal format, the bilingual (English and French) backs carry biography and recent major league performance statistics, on a background of gray vertical stripes that fade to white as one moves down the card. The cards are numbered on the back, "No. X de/of 20." The complete set price does include all variations and the unnumbered checklist card.

COMPLETE SET (26) 20.00 50.00
1 Bret Barberie .40 1.00
2A Chris Haney 1.00 2.50
2B Brian Barnes 2.00 5.00
3A Bill Sampen .40 1.00
3B Phil Bradley 1.00 2.50
4 Ivan Calderon .60 1.50
5 Gary Carter 3.00 8.00
6 Delino DeShields 1.50 4.00

7 Jeff Fassero .75 2.00
8 Darrin Fletcher .60 1.50
9 Mark Gardner .40 1.00
10 Marquis Grissom 1.50 4.00
11 Ken Hill .40 1.00
12 Dennis Martinez 1.00 2.50
13 Chris Nabholz .40 1.00
14 Spike Owen .40 1.00
15A Tom Runnells MG .75 2.00
15B Felipe Alou MG 2.50 6.00
16A John Vander Wal 1.00 2.50
16B Matt Stairs 2.50 6.00
17A Bill Landrum .40 1.00
17B Dave Wainhouse 1.00 2.50
18 Larry Walker 1.25 3.00
19 Tim Wallach 1.25 3.00
20 John Wetteland 1.25 3.00
xx0 Album 2.00 5.00
NNO0 Checklist Card SP 2.00 5.00

1992 Expos Postcards

These postcards feature members of the 1992 Montreal Expos. They measure approximately 3 1/2" by 5 1/2" and feature borderless posed color player photos. The player's name appears in a lower corner. These postcards are unnumbered and checklisted below in alphabetical order.

COMPLETE SET (32) 8.00 20.00
1 Felipe Alou MG .40 1.00
2 Moises Alou .60 1.50
3 Pierre Arsenault ANN .30 .75
4 Bret Barberie .20 .50
5 Eric Bullock .20 .50
6 Gary Carter 1.50 4.00
7 Ivan Calderon .20 .50
8 Rick Cerone .20 .50
9 Archi Cianfrocco .20 .50
10 Delino DeShields .30 .75
11 Jeff Fassero .20 .50
12 Darrin Fletcher .20 .50
13 Tom Foley .20 .50
14 Mark Gardner .20 .50
15 Marquis Grissom .40 1.00
16 Chris Haney .20 .50
17 Tommy Harper CO .20 .50
18 Ken Hill .20 .50
19 Joe Kerrigan CO .20 .50
20 Bill Landrum .20 .50
21 Jerry Manuel CO .20 .50
22 Dennis Martinez .40 1.00
23 Chris Nabholz .20 .50
24 Spike Owen .20 .50
25 Mel Rojas .20 .50
26 Tom Runnells MG .20 .50
27 Bill Sampen .20 .50
28 John Vander Wal .30 .75
29 Larry Walker .75 2.00
30 Tim Wallach .40 1.00
31 Jay Ward CO .20 .50
32 John Wetteland .40 1.00

1993 Expos Donruss McDonald's

This 33-card set was produced by Donruss for McDonald's and commemorates the Montreal Expos' 25th year in baseball. The standard-size cards have fronts displaying full-bleed action pictures with the McDonald's logo at the top left. Across the bottom, the player's name and uniform number are printed on a blue stripe, with the silver-foil 25-year Expos' logo stamped to the left. The horizontal backs carry biography, statistics, and career summaries in both French and English on a beige background. The player's name and number appear near the top, printed in a dark blue stripe edged in red. The 25-year Expos' logo is displayed in the top left in red, white, and blue. The certified signed and numbered (out of 2,000) Felipe Alou card was reportedly inserted at a rate of one per case of 2,500 packs. The cards were distributed in four-card foil packs.

COMPLETE SET (33) 4.00 10.00
1 Moises Alou .20 .50
2 Andre Dawson .40 1.00
3 Delino DeShields .20 .50
4 Andres Galarraga .60 1.50
5 Marquis Grissom .08 .25
6 Tim Raines .40 1.00
7 Larry Walker .40 1.00
8 Tim Wallach .02 .10
9 Ken Hill .02 .10
10 Dennis Martinez .08 .25
11 Jeff Reardon .08 .25
12 Gary Carter .60 1.50
13 Dave Cash .02 .10
14 Warren Cromartie .08 .25
15 Mack Jones .02 .10
16 Al Oliver .20 .50
17 Larry Parrish .08 .25
18 Rodney Scott .02 .10
19 Ken Singleton .08 .25
20 Rusty Staub .20 .50
21 Ellis Valentine .02 .10
22 Woodie Fryman .02 .10
23 Charlie Lea .02 .10
24 Bill Lee .08 .25
25 Mike Marshall .08 .25
26 Claude Raymond .08 .25
27 Steve Renko .02 .10
28 Steve Rogers .08 .25
29 Bill Stoneman .08 .25
30 Gene Mauch MG .02 .10
31 Felipe Alou MG .08 .25
32 Buck Rodgers MG .02 .10
33 Checklist 1-32 .02 .10
AU0 Felipe Alou AU/2000 (Certified autograph) 20.00 50.00

1993 Expos Postcards Named

These postcards are similar to the 1992 Expos postcards. They are blank-backed and we have sequenced them in alphabetical order. All these postcards have a blue background except for Wil Cordero.

COMPLETE SET (22) 4.00 10.00
1 Felipe Alou MG .30 .75
2 Moises Alou .40 1.00
3 Brian Barnes .20 .50
4 Sean Berry .20 .50
5 Frank Bolick .20 .50
6 Kent Bottenfield .20 .50
7 Greg Colbrunn .20 .50
8 Wil Cordero .20 .50
9 Jeff Fassero .30 .75
10 Darrin Fletcher .20 .50
11 Lou Frazier .20 .50
12 Mark Gardner .20 .50
13 Tim Johnson CO .20 .50
14 Jimmy Jones .20 .50
15 Mike Lansing .30 .75
16 Tim McIntosh .20 .50
17 Chris Nabholz .20 .50
18 Luis Pujols CO .20 .50
19 Mel Rojas .20 .50
20 Jeff Shaw .30 .75
21 Tim Spehr .20 .50
22 Larry Walker .75 2.00

1993 Expos Postcards

These cards have no border or player name on the front. Backs contain the Expos' logo and card number. The cards are checklisted aphabetically below.

COMPLETE SET (7) 2.00 5.00
1 Moises Alou .40 1.00
2 Archi Cianfrocco .20 .50
3 Wil Cordero .20 .50
4 Delino DeShields .30 .75
5 Dennis Martinez .40 1.00
6 Mel Rojas .20 .50
7 Larry Walker .75 2.00

1996 Expos Bookmarks

This six-card set of the Montreal Expos measures approximately 2 1/2" by 6 1/4". One side features a color player portrait with personal statistics in English and a facsimile autograph. The other side displays the same color portrait with personal statistics in French and a facsimile autograph. The cards are unnumbered and checklisted below in alphabetical order.

COMPLETE SET (6) 1.00 2.50
1 Felipe Alou MG .40 1.00
2 Shane Andrews .08 .25
3 Mark Grudzielanek .30 .75
4 Tim Scott .08 .25
5 David Segui .08 .25
6 Dave Veres .08 .25

1996 Expos Discs

This 24-disc set consists of six 1 5/8" perforated discs on each of four larger discs with 6 3/8" diameters. The small discs carry color action player photos with the player name, jersey number and a faded team logo on the back. The center disc in each of the large discs is the team logo.

COMPLETE SET (24) 2.00 5.00
1 Felipe Alou MG .08 .25
2 Moises Alou/(Batting) .20 .50
3 Moises Alou/(Sliding into base) .20 .50
4 Shane Andrews .02 .10
5 Derek Aucoin .02 .10
6 Rheal Cormier .02 .10
7 Jeff Fassero .02 .10
8 Darrin Fletcher .02 .10
9 Mark Grudzielanek/(Batting) .08 .25
10 Mark Grudzielanek/(Fielding) .08 .25
11 Mike Lansing .02 .10
12 Pedro Martinez/(With glove at mouth) .60 1.50
13 Pedro Martinez/(Pitching) .60 1.50
14 Carlos Perez .02 .10
15 Henry Rodriguez .02 .10
16 Mel Rojas .02 .10
17 Tim Scott .02 .10
18 David Segui/(Ready to catch the ball) .02 .10
19 David Segui/(Catching the ball) .02 .10
20 Tim Spehr .02 .10
21 Dave Veres .02 .10
22 Rondell White/(Batting) .30 .75
23 Rondell White/(Running to base) .30 .75
24 Youppi(Mascot) .08 .25

1999 Expos Postcards

These 3 1/2" by 5 1/2" blank backed postcards feature members of the 1999 Montreal Expos. Some of the poses were repeats of previous years so the only way to know that those players were issued in 1999 is by having a complete set. The postcards feature a player photo with the players name and uniform number in the lower left handed corner. We have sequenced this set in alphabetical order and notated new poses for 1999 but putting the word "NEW" next to the players name.

COMPLETE SET 6.00 15.00
1 Felipe Alou MG .20 .50
2 Shane Andrews .08 .25
3 Pierre Arsenault ANN .20 .50
4 Bobby Ayala NEW .08 .25
5 Michael Barrett NEW .30 .75
6 Miguel Batista .08 .25
7 Orlando Cabrera .30 .75
8 Darron Cox NEW .08 .25
9 Bobby Cuellar CO .08 .25
10 Brad Fullmer .08 .25
11 Gene Glynn CO NEW .08 .25
12 Vladimir Guerrero 1.25 3.00
13 Wilton Guerrero .08 .25
14 Tommy Harper CO .08 .25
15 Bob Henley NEW .08 .25
16 Dustin Hermanson NEW .08 .25
17 Steve Kline NEW .08 .25
18 Pete Mackanin CO .08 .25
19 Manny Martinez NEW .08 .25
20 Ryan McGuire .08 .25
21 Orlando Merced NEW .08 .25
22 Mike Mordecai .08 .25
23 Guillermo Mota NEW .08 .25
24 James Mouton NEW .08 .25
25 Carl Pavano NEW .60 1.50
26 Luis Pujols CO .08 .25
27 J.D. Smart NEW .08 .25
28 Dan Smith NEW .08 .25
29 Anthony Telford .08 .25
30 Mike Thurman .08 .25
31 Ugueth Urbina .08 .25
32 Javier Vazquez .60 1.50
33 Jose Vidro .40 1.00
34 Rondell White .20 .50
35 Chris Widger .08 .25
36 Youppi Mascot .20 .50

2000 Expos Postcards

COMPLETE SET 8.00 20.00
1 Felipe Alou MG .30 .75
2 Tony Armas Jr. .30 .75
3 Brad Arnsberg CO .20 .50
4 Pierre Arseneault ANN .20 .50
5 Michael Barrett .30 .75
6 Peter Bergeron .20 .50
7 Geoff Blum .20 .50
8 Orlando Cabrera .40 1.00
9 Bobby Cuellar CO .20 .50
10 Vladimir Guerrero 1.00 2.50
11 Wilton Guerrero .20 .50
12 Dustin Hermansen .20 .50
13 Perry Hill CO .20 .50
14 Hideki Irabu .30 .75
15 Mike Johnson .20 .50
16 Terry Jones .20 .50
17 Steve Kline .20 .50
18 Felipe Lira .20 .50
19 Pete Mackanin CO .20 .50
20 Mike Mordecai .20 .50
21 Carl Pavano .75 2.00
22 Luis Pujols CO .20 .50
23 Pat Roessler CO .20 .50
24 Fernando Seguignol .20 .50
25 Lee Stevens .20 .50
26 Scott Strickland .20 .50
27 Anthony Telford .20 .50
28 Mike Thurman .20 .50
29 Ugueth Urbina .30 .75
30 Javier Vazquez .75 2.00
31 Jose Vidro .60 1.50
32 Lenny Webster .20 .50
33 Rondell White .30 .75
34 Chris Widger .20 .50
35 Youppi Mascot .20 .50

2001 Expos Team Issue

COMPLETE SET (35) 6.00 15.00
1 Felipe Alou MG .20 .50
2 Tony Armas .20 .50
3 Michael Barrett .30 .75
4 Peter Bergeron .20 .50
5 Matt Blank .10 .25
6 Geoff Blum .10 .25
7 Milton Bradley .30 .75
8 Orlando Cabrera .30 .75
9 Tomas De La Rosa .10 .25
10 Vladimir Guerrero .75 2.00
11 Hideki Irabu .20 .50
12 Mike Johnson .10 .25
13 Terry Jones .10 .25
14 Felipe Lira .10 .25
15 Graeme Lloyd .10 .25
16 Sandy Martinez .10 .25
17 Mike Mordecai .10 .25
18 Guillermo Mota .10 .25
19 Carl Pavano .60 1.50
20 Chris Peters .10 .25
21 Tim Raines .30 .75
22 Britt Reames .10 .25
23 Brian Schneider .10 .25
24 Fernando Seguignol .10 .25
25 Mark Smith .10 .25
26 Lee Stevens .10 .25
27 Scott Strickland .10 .25
28 Fernando Tatis .10 .25
29 Anthony Telford .10 .25
30 Mike Thurman .10 .25
31 Andy Tracy .10 .25
32 Ugueth Urbina .20 .50
33 Javier Vazquez .60 1.50
34 Jose Vidro .40 1.00
35 Youppi! .30 .75

2003 Expos Donruss

COMPLETE SET 10.00 25.00
1 Claude Raymond .10 .25
2 Javier Vazquez .60 1.50
3 John Boccabella .10 .25
4 Bill Stoneman .10 .25
5 Carl Morton .10 .25
6 Ron Fairly .10 .25
7 Bob Bailey .10 .25
8 Steve Renko .10 .25
9 Mike Marshall .20 .50
10 Ron Hunt .10 .25
11 Ken Singleton .20 .50
12 Pedro Martinez 1.00 2.50
13 Tim Foli .10 .25
14 Mike Jorgensen .10 .25
15 Steve Rogers .10 .25
16 Willie Davis .10 .25
17 Larry Parrish .10 .25
18 Jerry White .10 .25
19 Ellis Valentine .10 .25
20 Woodie Fryman .10 .25
21 Andre Dawson .40 1.00
22 Warren Cromartie .10 .25
23 Vladimir Guerrero .75 2.00
24 Tony Perez .60 1.50
25 Chris Speier .10 .25
26 Dan Schatzeder .10 .25
27 Ross Grimsley .10 .25
28 Scott Sanderson .10 .25
29 Tim Wallach .20 .50
30 Dave Cash .10 .25
31 Bill Gullickson .10 .25
32 Tim Raines .40 1.00
33 Rodney Scott .10 .25
34 Ron LeFlore .10 .25
35 Charlie Lea .10 .25
36 Bill Lee .10 .25
37 Jeff Reardon .10 .25
38 Bryn Smith .10 .25
39 Al Oliver .20 .50
40 Hubie Brooks .10 .25
41 Terry Francona .20 .50
42 Gary Carter .60 1.50
43 Spike Owen .10 .25
44 Tim Burke .10 .25
45 Andres Galarraga .40 1.00
46 Marquis Grissom .30 .75
47 Larry Walker .40 1.00
48 Moises Alou .20 .50
49 Dennis Martinez .20 .50
50 Denis Boucher .10 .25
51 Rondell White .20 .50
52 Mel Rojas .10 .25
53 Henry Rodriguez .10 .25
54 David Segui .10 .25
55 Ugueth Urbina .10 .25
56 Jose Vidro .40 1.00
57 Darrin Fletcher .10 .25
58 Orlando Cabrera .30 .75
59 John Wetteland .20 .50

2003 Expos Team Issue

COMPLETE SET 10.00 25.00
1 Manny Acta .20 .50
2 Hector Almonte .20 .50
3 Tony Armas Jr. .20 .50
4 Luis Ayala .20 .50
5 Michael Barrett .40 1.00
6 Rocky Biddle .20 .50
7 Orlando Cabrera .60 1.50
8 Ron Calloway .20 .50
9 Jamey Carroll .20 .50
10 Endy Chavez .20 .50
11 Wil Cordero .20 .50
12 Zach Day .20 .50
13 Tim Drew .20 .50
14 Joey Eischen .20 .50
15 Vladimir Guerrero 1.00 2.50
16 Edward Guzman .20 .50
17 Livan Hernandez .60 1.50
18 Orlando Hernandez .30 .75
19 Eric Knott .20 .50
20 Jeff Liefer .20 .50
21 Jose Macias .20 .50
22 Julio Manon .30 .75
23 Henry Mateo .20 .50
24 Tom McCraw CO .20 .50
25 Brad Mills CO .20 .50
26 Jerry Morales CO .20 .50
27 Bob Natal .20 .50
28 Tomo Ohka .30 .75
29 Claude Raymond ANN .20 .50
30 Britt Reames .20 .50
31 Frank Robinson MG .60 1.50
32 Fernando Tatis .20 .50
33 T.J. Tucker .20 .50
34 Brian Schneider .20 .50
35 Dan Smith .20 .50
36 Randy St. Claire CO .20 .50
37 Scott Stewart .20 .50
38 Claudio Vargas .20 .50
39 Javier Vazquez .75 2.00
40 Jose Vidro .60 1.50
41 Joe Vitiello .20 .50
42 Brad Wilkerson .60 1.50
43 Youppi Mascot .20 .50

2006 Exquisite Collection

COMMON AU RC (1-90) 6.00 15.00
ISSUED AS EXCH CARDS IN VARIOUS
2006 UPPER DECK PRODUCTS
1-90 PRINT RUN 55 SER.#'d SETS
91-100 PRINT RUN 10 SER.#'d SETS
1-90 FEATURE ROOKIE LOGOS
NO PRICING ON 91-100 DUE TO SCARCITY
2 Hansen/Carmona 12.00 30.00
3 Ethier/Kubel 8.00 20.00
4 Billingsley/Bonser 6.00 15.00
5 Sowers/Carmona 20.00 50.00
6 Willingham/Paulino 6.00 15.00
7 Saito/Ethier 10.00 25.00
8 Hamels/Shields 20.00 50.00
9 Denorfia/Quentin 6.00 15.00
10 Hammel/Shields 10.00 25.00
11 Uggla/Kinsler 10.00 25.00
12 Accardo/Cain 6.00 15.00
13 Sowers/Maholm 10.00 25.00
14 Hamels/Sowers 10.00 25.00
15 Liriano/Bonser 15.00 40.00
16 Verlander/Zumaya 30.00 80.00
17 Ramirez/Drew 12.00 30.00
18 Soler/Bannister 10.00 25.00
19 Gassner/Bonser 10.00 25.00
20 Pagan/Theroit 12.00 30.00
21 Uggla/Hermida 6.00 15.00
22 Carmona/Hamels 6.00 15.00
23 Saito/Kuo 10.00 25.00
24 Maholm/Marshall 8.00 20.00
26 Kendrick/Uggla 6.00 15.00
27 Johnson/Petit 10.00 25.00
29 Martin/Ethier 10.00 25.00
30 Liriano/Weaver 15.00 40.00
31 Hamels/Jackson 6.00 15.00
32 Papelbon/Hansen 20.00 50.00
34 Denorfia/Hermida 4.00 10.00
35 Willingham/Ross 6.00 15.00
36 Drew/Weaver 12.00 30.00
38 Dunn/Shields 8.00 20.00
39 Kendrick/Morales 10.00 25.00
40 Maholm/Capps 10.00 25.00
41 Kinsler/Kendrick 10.00 25.00
42 Cain/Soler 6.00 15.00
44 Verlander/Sowers 30.00 60.00
45 Kendrick/Weaver 10.00 25.00
46 Ramirez/Willingham 10.00 25.00
47 Ramirez/Hermida 12.00 30.00
48 Uggla/Willingham 6.00 15.00
49 Soler/Hamels 6.00 15.00
50 Kubel/Bonser 10.00 25.00
51 Jacobs/Morales 4.00 10.00
52 Saito/Papelbon 10.00 25.00
53 Papelbon/Verlander 50.00 100.00
54 Ethier/Billingsley 10.00 25.00
55 Hermida/Gwynn Jr. 8.00 20.00
56 Zimmerman/Drew 40.00 80.00
57 Gwynn Jr./Barfield 12.00 30.00
58 Hensley/Thompson 6.00 15.00
59 Verlander/Johnson 30.00 60.00
60 Verlander/Weaver 50.00 100.00
62 Gwynn Jr./Ethier 6.00 15.00
63 Drew/Quentin 20.00 50.00
64 Jackson/Quentin 20.00 50.00
65 Zimmerman/Harris 10.00 25.00
66 Saito/Martin 12.00 30.00
67 Jacobs/Willingham 12.00 30.00
68 Jacobs/Ramiez 15.00 40.00
71 Hansen/Hamels 10.00 25.00
72 Ramirez/Bynum 6.00 15.00
74 Nieve/Buchholz 6.00 15.00
75 Wainwright/Johnson 15.00 40.00
76 Willingham/Martin 6.00 15.00
77 Martin/Nieves 15.00 40.00
78 Johnson/Thompson 8.00 20.00
79 Jackson/Hendrickson 8.00 20.00
80 Papelbon/Zumaya 20.00 50.00
81 Hendrickson/Capellan 6.00 15.00
82 Devine/Ray 6.00 15.00
84 Shoppach/Martin 6.00 15.00
85 Soler/Johnson 6.00 15.00
86 Soler/Hansen 10.00 25.00
87 Hansen/Billingsley 8.00 20.00
88 Billingsley/Cain 10.00 25.00
89 Liriano/Hansen 6.00 15.00
90 Jackson/Jacobs 12.00 30.00

2006 Exquisite Collection Gold

*GOLD 1-90: .5X TO 1.2X BASIC
ISSUED AS EXCH CARDS IN VARIOUS
2006 UPPER DECK PRODUCTS
1-90 PRINT RUN 30 SER.#'d SETS
91-100 PRINT RUN 5 SER.#'d SETS
NO PRICING ON 91-100 DUE TO SCARCITY

2006 Exquisite Collection Platinum

ISSUED AS EXCH CARDS IN VARIOUS
2006 UPPER DECK PRODUCTS
STATED PRINT RUN 1 SER.#'d SET
NO PRICING DUE TO SCARCITY

2006 Exquisite Collection Cuts

ISSUED AS EXCH CARDS IN VARIOUS
2006 UPPER DECK PRODUCTS
PRINT RUNS B/WN 25-65 COPIES PER
AC Al Campanis/65 40.00 80.00
BD Bill Dickey/65 75.00 150.00
BG Burleigh Grimes/65 60.00 120.00
BH Billy Herman/65 20.00 50.00
CG Charlie Gehringer/65 30.00 60.00
CH Carl Hubbell/65 40.00 80.00
DC Dolph Camilli/65 20.00 50.00
EA Earl Averill/65 20.00 50.00
EM Eddie Mathews/65 75.00 150.00
ER Edd Roush/65 50.00 100.00
GE George Selkirk/65 20.00 50.00
GS George Sisler/65 200.00 300.00
HG Hank Greenberg/65 125.00 250.00
JC Joe Cronin/65 20.00 50.00
JM Johnny Mize/65 20.00 50.00
LA Luke Appling/65 20.00 50.00
LB Lou Boudreau/65 20.00 50.00
LG Lefty Gomez/65 40.00 80.00
MC Max Carey/65 20.00 50.00
SC Stan Coveleski/65 50.00 100.00
VW Vic Wertz/65 20.00 50.00
WG Warren Giles/65 60.00 120.00
WH Waite Hoyt/65 20.00 50.00
WS Warren Spahn/65 60.00 120.00

2006 Exquisite Collection Cuts Dual

ISSUED AS EXCH CARDS IN VARIOUS
2006 UPPER DECK PRODUCTS
STATED PRINT RUN 5 SER.#'d SETS
NO PRICING DUE TO SCARCITY

2006 Exquisite Collection Endorsed Emblems

ISSUED AS EXCH CARDS IN VARIOUS
2006 UPPER DECK PRODUCTS
STATED PRINT RUN 25 SER.#'d SETS
AD Adam Dunn 20.00 50.00
AJ Andruw Jones 30.00 60.00
AR Alex Rios 30.00 60.00
BJ B.J. Upton 20.00 50.00
BR Brian Roberts 30.00 60.00
BS Ben Sheets 30.00 60.00
CB Craig Biggio 60.00 120.00
CU Chase Utley 30.00 60.00
DL Derrek Lee 50.00 100.00
FL Francisco Liriano 10.00 25.00
HS Huston Street 20.00 50.00
JM Joe Mauer 75.00 150.00
JO Jonathan Papelbon 100.00 150.00
JP Jake Peavy 10.00 25.00
JS Jeremy Sowers 20.00 50.00
JT Jim Thome 60.00 120.00
JU Justin Morneau 30.00 60.00
JU2 Justin Morneau 30.00 60.00
JV Justin Verlander 30.00 60.00
JW Jered Weaver 30.00 60.00
KG Ken Griffey Jr. 125.00 250.00
KG2 Ken Griffey Jr. 125.00 250.00
KG3 Ken Griffey Jr. 125.00 250.00
KH Khalil Greene 10.00 25.00
MC Miguel Cabrera 60.00 120.00
MG Marcus Giles 20.00 50.00
MH Matt Holliday 10.00 25.00
MT Mark Teixeira 20.00 50.00
MY Michael Young 20.00 50.00
NS Nick Swisher 30.00 60.00
RW Rickie Weeks 30.00 60.00
SD Stephen Drew 60.00 120.00
SM John Smoltz 100.00 150.00
TH Travis Hafner 12.00 30.00
TR Trevor Hoffman 20.00 50.00

2006 Exquisite Collection Endorsements

ISSUED AS EXCH CARDS IN VARIOUS
2006 UPPER DECK PRODUCTS
STATED PRINT RUN 40 SER.#'d SETS
AS Alay Soler 15.00 40.00
BF Bob Feller 20.00 50.00
BJ B.J. Upton 10.00 25.00
BR Brooks Robinson 30.00 60.00
CC Chris Carpenter 30.00 60.00
CF Carlton Fisk 30.00 60.00
CH Cole Hamels 30.00 60.00
CJ Chipper Jones 60.00 120.00
CR Cal Ripken Jr. 40.00 80.00
DO David Ortiz 40.00 80.00
DW Dontrelle Willis 20.00 50.00
FH Felix Hernandez 50.00 100.00
FL Francisco Liriano 10.00 25.00
FR Frank Robinson 30.00 60.00
GP Gaylord Perry 15.00 40.00
HK Howie Kendrick 12.50 30.00
JB Johnny Bench 30.00 60.00
JM Joe Mauer 20.00 50.00
JO Jonathan Papelbon 15.00 40.00
JP Jake Peavy 10.00 25.00
JR Jose Reyes 10.00 25.00
JS Jeremy Sowers 10.00 25.00
JT Jim Thome 30.00 60.00
JV Justin Verlander 25.00 60.00
JW Jered Weaver 20.00 50.00
KG Ken Griffey Jr. 60.00 120.00
KG2 Ken Griffey Jr. 60.00 120.00
MC Miguel Cabrera 40.00 80.00
MT Mark Teixeira 30.00 60.00
NR Nolan Ryan 50.00 100.00
PM Paul Molitor 15.00 40.00
RC Roger Clemens 30.00 60.00
RJ Reggie Jackson 40.00 80.00
RO Roy Oswalt 10.00 25.00
RS Ryne Sandberg 40.00 80.00
RZ Ryan Zimmerman 30.00 60.00
SD Stephen Drew 20.00 50.00
SK Scott Kazmir 10.00 40.00
SM Stan Musial 50.00 100.00
TH Travis Hafner 30.00 60.00
TI Tadahito Iguchi 12.00 30.00
VG Vladimir Guerrero 40.00 80.00
VM Victor Martinez 10.00 25.00
WC Will Clark 15.00 40.00

2006 Exquisite Collection Ensemble Dual Patches

ISSUED AS EXCH CARDS IN VARIOUS
2006 UPPER DECK PRODUCTS
STATED PRINT RUN 25 SER.#'d SETS
NO PRICING DUE TO SCARCITY

2006 Exquisite Collection Ensemble Endorsements Dual

ISSUED AS EXCH CARDS IN VARIOUS
2006 UPPER DECK PRODUCTS
STATED PRINT RUN 20 SER.#'d SETS
NO PRICING DUE TO SCARCITY

2006 Exquisite Collection Ensemble Endorsements Triple

ISSUED AS EXCH CARDS IN VARIOUS
2006 UPPER DECK PRODUCTS
STATED PRINT RUN 15 SER.#'d SETS
NO PRICING DUE TO SCARCITY

2006 Exquisite Collection Ensemble Endorsements Quad

ISSUED AS EXCH CARDS IN VARIOUS
2006 UPPER DECK PRODUCTS
STATED PRINT RUN 10 SER.#'d SETS
NO PRICING DUE TO SCARCITY

2006 Exquisite Collection Ensemble Triple Patches

ISSUED AS EXCH CARDS IN VARIOUS
2006 UPPER DECK PRODUCTS
STATED PRINT RUN 15 SER.#'d SETS
NO PRICING DUE TO SCARCITY

2006 Exquisite Collection Ensemble Quad Patches

ISSUED AS EXCH CARDS IN VARIOUS
2006 UPPER DECK PRODUCTS
STATED PRINT RUN 10 SER.#'d SETS
NO PRICING DUE TO SCARCITY

2006 Exquisite Collection Legends Memorabilia

ISSUED AS EXCH CARDS IN VARIOUS
2006 UPPER DECK PRODUCTS
STATED PRINT RUN 15 SER.#'d SETS
PLAT.ISSUED AS EXCH CARDS IN VARIOUS
2006 UPPER DECK PRODUCTS
PLATINUM PRINT RUN 1 SER.#'d SET
NO PLATINUM PRICING DUE TO SCARCITY
AK Al Kaline 20.00 50.00
BD Bill Dickey 40.00 80.00
BD2 Bill Dickey 40.00 80.00
BM Bill Mazeroski 30.00 60.00
BM2 Bill Mazeroski 30.00 60.00
BR Babe Ruth 900.00 1200.00
BR2 Babe Ruth 900.00 1200.00
CF Carlton Fisk 20.00 50.00
CR Cal Ripken Jr. 30.00 60.00
CR2 Cal Ripken Jr. 30.00 60.00
CR3 Cal Ripken Jr. 30.00 60.00
DM Don Mattingly 60.00 120.00
FR Frank Robinson 20.00 50.00
JB Johnny Bench 20.00 50.00
JB2 Johnny Bench 20.00 50.00
JC Joe Cronin 20.00 50.00
JD Joe DiMaggio 75.00 150.00
JD2 Joe DiMaggio 75.00 150.00
JF Jimmie Foxx 200.00 300.00
JM Joe Morgan 20.00 50.00
LG Lou Gehrig 300.00 500.00
LG2 Lou Gehrig 300.00 500.00
MO Mel Ott 40.00 80.00
MS Mike Schmidt 20.00 50.00
NR Nolan Ryan 75.00 150.00
NR2 Nolan Ryan 75.00 150.00
OC Orlando Cepeda 20.00 50.00
RC Roberto Clemente 250.00 300.00
RC2 Roberto Clemente 250.00 300.00
RH Rogers Hornsby 75.00 150.00
RH2 Rogers Hornsby 75.00 150.00
RJ Reggie Jackson 40.00 80.00
RJ2 Reggie Jackson 40.00 80.00
RO Brooks Robinson 20.00 50.00
RS Ryne Sandberg 40.00 80.00
SM Stan Musial 40.00 80.00
TG Tony Gwynn 30.00 60.00
TG2 Tony Gwynn 30.00 60.00
TM Thurman Munson 75.00 150.00
TM2 Thurman Munson 75.00 150.00
TW Ted Williams 150.00 250.00
WB Wade Boggs 30.00 60.00

2006 Exquisite Collection Material Cuts

ISSUED AS EXCH CARDS IN VARIOUS
2006 UPPER DECK PRODUCTS
STATED PRINT RUN 2 SER.#'d SETS
NO PRICING DUE TO SCARCITY

2006 Exquisite Collection Maximum Patch

ISSUED AS EXCH CARDS IN VARIOUS
2006 UPPER DECK PRODUCTS
STATED PRINT RUN 25 SER.#'d SETS
PRICING FOR NON-LOGO PATCHES
AD Adam Dunn 40.00 80.00
AP Albert Pujols 150.00 250.00
AS Alfonso Soriano 40.00 80.00
CA Carl Crawford 40.00 80.00
CB Carlos Beltran 50.00 100.00
CC Chris Carpenter 75.00 150.00
CD Carlos Delgado 40.00 80.00
CJ Chipper Jones 75.00 150.00
CR Craig Biggio 50.00 100.00
CS Curt Schilling 40.00 80.00
DJ Derek Jeter 300.00 400.00
DO David Ortiz 40.00 80.00
FH Felix Hernandez 75.00 150.00
FL Francisco Liriano 40.00 80.00
FT Frank Thomas 75.00 150.00
JG Jason Giambi 40.00 80.00
JO Jonathan Papelbon 30.00 60.00
JP Jake Peavy 40.00 80.00
JT Jim Thome 40.00 80.00
JV Justin Verlander 40.00 80.00
JW Jered Weaver 40.00 80.00
KG Ken Griffey Jr. 50.00 100.00
MC Miguel Cabrera 40.00 80.00
MI Miguel Tejada 40.00 80.00
MT Mark Teixeira 40.00 80.00
PF Prince Fielder 40.00 80.00
PM Pedro Martinez 40.00 80.00
TG Troy Glaus 40.00 80.00
TH Todd Helton 40.00 80.00
VG Vladimir Guerrero 40.00 80.00
VM Victor Martinez 40.00 80.00

2006 Exquisite Collection Memorabilia

ISSUED AS EXCH CARDS IN VARIOUS
2006 UPPER DECK PRODUCTS
STATED PRINT RUN 45 SER.#'d SETS
MEM.1 ISSUED AS EXCH CARD IN VARIOUS
2006 UPPER DECK PRODUCTS
MEM.1 PRINT RUN 1 SER.#'d SET
NO MEM.1 PRICING DUE TO SCARCITY
*GOLD: .5X TO 1.2X BASIC
GOLD ISSUED AS EXCH CARD IN VARIOUS
2006 UPPER DECK PRODUCTS
GOLD PRINT RUN 25 SER.#'d SETS
PLAT.ISSUED AS EXCH CARD IN VARIOUS
2006 UPPER DECK PRODUCTS
PLAT.PRINT RUN 15 SER.#'d SETS
NO PLAT.PRICING DUE TO SCARCITY
AD Adam Dunn 6.00 15.00
AD2 Adam Dunn 6.00 15.00
AJ Andruw Jones 10.00 25.00
AJ2 Andruw Jones 10.00 25.00
AP Albert Pujols 15.00 40.00
AP2 Albert Pujols 15.00 40.00
AR Alex Rodriguez 10.00 25.00
AS Alfonso Soriano 6.00 15.00
AS2 Alfonso Soriano 6.00 15.00
BR Babe Ruth 200.00 400.00
BR2 Babe Ruth 200.00 400.00
BZ Barry Zito 10.00 25.00
BZ2 Barry Zito 10.00 25.00
CB Carlos Beltran 10.00 25.00
CB2 Carlos Beltran 10.00 25.00
CF Carlton Fisk 10.00 25.00
CF2 Carlton Fisk 10.00 25.00
CJ Chipper Jones 15.00 40.00
CJ2 Chipper Jones 15.00 40.00
CR Cal Ripken Jr. 10.00 25.00
CR2 Cal Ripken Jr. 10.00 25.00
CR3 Cal Ripken Jr. 10.00 25.00
CS Curt Schilling 6.00 15.00
CU Chase Utley 15.00 40.00
CU2 Chase Utley 15.00 40.00
CY Carl Yastrzemski 10.00 25.00
CY2 Carl Yastrzemski 10.00 25.00
DA Daisuke Matsuzaka 150.00 250.00
DJ Derek Jeter 30.00 60.00
DJ2 Derek Jeter 30.00 60.00
DL Derrek Lee 10.00 25.00
DM Don Mattingly 20.00 50.00
DO David Ortiz 10.00 25.00
DO2 David Ortiz 10.00 25.00
FL Francisco Liriano 10.00 25.00
FL2 Francisco Liriano 10.00 25.00
GM Greg Maddux 10.00 25.00
GM2 Greg Maddux 10.00 25.00
HO Ryan Howard 10.00 25.00
HO2 Ryan Howard 10.00 25.00
IS Ichiro Suzuki 200.00 250.00
JA Jason Bay 6.00 15.00
JA2 Jason Bay 6.00 15.00
JB Jeff Bagwell 10.00 25.00
JB2 Jeff Bagwell 10.00 25.00
JD Joe DiMaggio 40.00 80.00
JM Joe Mauer 10.00 25.00
JP Jake Peavy 6.00 15.00
JP2 Jake Peavy 6.00 15.00
JS Johan Santana 10.00 25.00
JS2 Johan Santana 10.00 25.00
JT Jim Thome 10.00 25.00
JT2 Jim Thome 10.00 25.00
JV Justin Verlander 10.00 25.00
JV2 Justin Verlander 10.00 25.00
JW Jered Weaver 6.00 15.00

JW2 Jered Weaver 6.00 15.00
KG Ken Griffey Jr. 15.00 40.00
KG2 Ken Griffey Jr. 15.00 40.00
KG3 Ken Griffey Jr. 15.00 40.00
KJ Kenji Johjima 15.00 40.00
KJ2 Kenji Johjima 15.00 40.00
MA Manny Ramirez 10.00 25.00
MA2 Manny Ramirez 10.00 25.00
MA3 Manny Ramirez 10.00 25.00
MC Miguel Cabrera 10.00 25.00
MC2 Miguel Cabrera 10.00 25.00
MI Miguel Tejada 6.00 15.00
MI2 Miguel Tejada 6.00 15.00
MR Mariano Rivera 15.00 40.00
MR2 Mariano Rivera 15.00 40.00
MS Mike Schmidt 10.00 25.00
MS2 Mike Schmidt 10.00 25.00
MT Mark Teixeira 6.00 15.00
NR Nolan Ryan 20.00 50.00
NR2 Nolan Ryan 20.00 50.00
PE Pedro Martinez 15.00 40.00
PF Prince Fielder 10.00 25.00
PF2 Prince Fielder 10.00 25.00
PM Paul Molitor 6.00 15.00
PM2 Paul Molitor 6.00 15.00
RC Roger Clemens 12.50 30.00
RC2 Roger Clemens 12.50 30.00
RC3 Roger Clemens 12.50 30.00
RE Reggie Jackson 15.00 40.00
RE2 Reggie Jackson 15.00 40.00
RH Roy Halladay 6.00 15.00
RH2 Roy Halladay 6.00 15.00
RJ Randy Johnson 10.00 25.00
RO Roy Oswalt 6.00 15.00
RO2 Roy Oswalt 6.00 15.00
RY Robin Yount 10.00 25.00
RY2 Robin Yount 10.00 25.00
SM Stan Musial 15.00 40.00
SM2 Stan Musial 15.00 40.00
TG Tony Gwynn 10.00 25.00
TH Travis Hafner 6.00 15.00
VG Vladimir Guerrero 10.00 25.00
VG2 Vladimir Guerrero 10.00 25.00
WB Wade Boggs 10.00 25.00

2006 Exquisite Collection Patch

ISSUED AS EXCH CARDS IN VARIOUS
2006 UPPER DECK PRODUCTS
STATED PRINT RUN 25 SER.#'d SETS
NO PRICING ON MOST DUE TO SCARCITY
PATCH 1 ISSUED AS EXCH IN VARIOUS
2006 UPPER DECK PRODUCTS
PATCH 1 PRINT RUN 1 SER.#'d SET
NO PATCH 1 PRICING DUE TO SCARCITY
*PATCH 10: .5X TO 1.2X BASIC
PATCH 10 ISSUED AS EXCH IN VARIOUS
2006 UPPER DECK PRODUCTS
PATCH 10 PRINT RUN 10 SER.#'d SETS
PRICING IS FOR NON-LOGO PATCHES
AD Adam Dunn 15.00 40.00
AD2 Adam Dunn 15.00 40.00
AJ Andruw Jones 20.00 50.00
AJ2 Andruw Jones 20.00 50.00
AP Albert Pujols 60.00 120.00
AP2 Albert Pujols 60.00 120.00
AS Alfonso Soriano 30.00 60.00
AS2 Alfonso Soriano 30.00 60.00
BZ Barry Zito 15.00 40.00
BZ2 Barry Zito 15.00 40.00
CB Carlos Beltran 30.00 60.00
CB2 Carlos Beltran 30.00 60.00
CF Carlton Fisk 20.00 50.00
CF2 Carlton Fisk 20.00 50.00
CJ Chipper Jones 50.00 100.00
CJ2 Chipper Jones 50.00 100.00
CR Cal Ripken Jr. 75.00 150.00
CR2 Cal Ripken Jr. 75.00 150.00
CR3 Cal Ripken Jr. 75.00 150.00
CS Curt Schilling 20.00 50.00
CU Chase Utley 30.00 60.00
CU2 Chase Utley 30.00 60.00
DJ Derek Jeter 100.00 200.00
DJ2 Derek Jeter 100.00 200.00
DL Derrek Lee 20.00 50.00
DM Don Mattingly 60.00 120.00
DO David Ortiz 30.00 60.00
DO2 David Ortiz 30.00 60.00
FL Francisco Liriano 20.00 50.00
FL2 Francisco Liriano 20.00 50.00
GM Greg Maddux 50.00 100.00
GM2 Greg Maddux 50.00 100.00
HO Ryan Howard 50.00 100.00
HO2 Ryan Howard 50.00 100.00
JA Jason Bay 20.00 50.00
JA2 Jason Bay 20.00 50.00
JM Joe Mauer 40.00 80.00
JP Jake Peavy 30.00 60.00
JP2 Jake Peavy 30.00 60.00
JS Johan Santana 30.00 60.00
JS2 Johan Santana 30.00 60.00
JT Jim Thome 20.00 50.00
JT2 Jim Thome 20.00 50.00
JV Justin Verlander 20.00 50.00
JV2 Justin Verlander 20.00 50.00
JW Jered Weaver 15.00 40.00
JW2 Jered Weaver 15.00 40.00
KG Ken Griffey Jr. 75.00 150.00
KG2 Ken Griffey Jr. 75.00 150.00
KG3 Ken Griffey Jr. 75.00 150.00
KJ Kenji Johjima 15.00 40.00
KJ2 Kenji Johjima 15.00 40.00
MA Manny Ramirez 30.00 60.00
MA2 Manny Ramirez 30.00 60.00
MA3 Manny Ramirez 30.00 60.00
MC Miguel Cabrera 30.00 60.00
MC2 Miguel Cabrera 30.00 60.00
MI Miguel Tejada 20.00 50.00
MI2 Miguel Tejada 20.00 50.00
MR Mariano Rivera 40.00 80.00
MR2 Mariano Rivera 40.00 80.00
MS Mike Schmidt 20.00 50.00
MS2 Mike Schmidt 20.00 50.00
MT Mark Teixeira 20.00 50.00
NR Nolan Ryan 30.00 60.00
NR2 Nolan Ryan 30.00 60.00
PE Pedro Martinez 20.00 50.00
PF Prince Fielder 30.00 60.00
PF2 Prince Fielder 30.00 60.00
RC Roger Clemens 40.00 80.00
RC2 Roger Clemens 40.00 80.00
RC3 Roger Clemens 40.00 80.00
RE Reggie Jackson 20.00 50.00
RE2 Reggie Jackson 20.00 50.00
RH Roy Halladay 30.00 60.00
RH2 Roy Halladay 30.00 60.00
RJ Randy Johnson 20.00 50.00
RO Roy Oswalt 20.00 50.00
RO2 Roy Oswalt 20.00 50.00
RY Robin Yount 40.00 80.00
RY2 Robin Yount 40.00 80.00
TG Tony Gwynn 50.00 100.00
TH Travis Hafner 20.00 50.00
VG Vladimir Guerrero 30.00 60.00
VG2 Vladimir Guerrero 30.00 60.00
WB Wade Boggs 20.00 50.00

2006 Exquisite Collection Signature Patch

ISSUED AS EXCH CARDS IN VARIOUS
2006 UPPER DECK PRODUCTS
STATED PRINT RUN 30 SER.#'d SETS
NO PRICING ON MANY DUE TO SCARCITY
AD Adam Dunn 10.00 25.00
AJ Andruw Jones 12.00 30.00
AR Alex Rios 30.00 60.00
BJ B.J. Upton 15.00 40.00
BR Brian Roberts 20.00 50.00
CB Craig Biggio 30.00 60.00
CC Chris Carpenter 40.00 80.00
CL Carlos Lee 20.00 50.00
CU Chase Utley 60.00 120.00
CZ Carlos Zambrano 20.00 50.00
DJ Derek Jeter 500.00 600.00
DL Derrek Lee 10.00 25.00
DO David Ortiz 40.00 80.00
FH Felix Hernandez 100.00 200.00
FL Francisco Liriano 8.00 20.00
JB Jason Bay 10.00 25.00
JM Joe Mauer 50.00 100.00
JP Jake Peavy 30.00 60.00
JR Jose Reyes 100.00 200.00
JS Jeremy Sowers 30.00 60.00
JT Jim Thome 30.00 60.00
JU Justin Morneau 15.00 40.00
JU2 Justin Morneau 15.00 40.00
JV Justin Verlander 60.00 120.00
JW Jered Weaver 12.50 30.00
KG Ken Griffey Jr. 100.00 175.00
KG2 Ken Griffey Jr. 100.00 175.00
KG3 Ken Griffey Jr. 100.00 175.00
KH Khalil Greene 60.00 120.00
MC Miguel Cabrera 50.00 100.00
MG Marcus Giles 10.00 25.00
MH Matt Holliday 12.50 30.00
MI Miguel Tejada 10.00 25.00
MT Mark Teixeira 50.00 100.00
MY Michael Young 20.00 50.00
NS Nick Swisher 12.50 30.00
RO Roy Oswalt 20.00 50.00
RW Rickie Weeks 10.00 25.00
SD Stephen Drew 40.00 80.00
SK Scott Kazmir 40.00 80.00
TH Travis Hafner 12.50 30.00
TI Tadahito Iguchi 30.00 60.00
VM Victor Martinez 10.00 25.00

2006 Exquisite Collection Signature Patch Dual

ISSUED AS EXCH CARDS IN VARIOUS
2006 UPPER DECK PRODUCTS
STATED PRINT RUN 1 SER.#'d SET
NO PRICING DUE TO SCARCITY

2006 Exquisite Collection Signature Patch Triple

ISSUED AS EXCH CARDS IN VARIOUS
2006 UPPER DECK PRODUCTS
STATED PRINT RUN 1 SER.#'d SET
NO PRICING DUE TO SCARCITY

2010 Exquisite Collection

STATED PRINT RUN 75 SER.#'d SETS
1 Derek Jeter
2 Mark Teixeira
3 Joba Chamberlain
4 Hideki Matsui
5 Alex Rodriguez
6 David Ortiz
7 Jason Varitek
8 Daisuke Matsuzaka
9 Jonathan Papelbon
10 Dustin Pedroia
11 Evan Longoria
12 Carl Crawford
13 David Price
14 Roy Halladay
15 Koji Uehara
16 Matt Wieters
17 Tommy Hanson
18 Chipper Jones
19 Hanley Ramirez
20 Ryan Howard
21 Raul Ibanez
22 Chase Utley
23 Cole Hamels
24 Jose Reyes
25 David Wright
26 Johan Santana
27 Ryan Zimmerman
28 Gordon Beckham
29 Mark Buehrle
30 Grady Sizemore
31 Zack Greinke
32 Miguel Cabrera
33 Justin Verlander
34 Joe Mauer
35 Justin Morneau
36 Ryan Braun
37 Prince Fielder
38 Derrek Lee
39 Alfonso Soriano
40 Hunter Pence
41 Lance Berkman
42 Albert Pujols
43 Yadier Molina
44 Matt Holliday
45 Chris Carpenter
46 Adam Wainwright
47 Joey Votto
48 Ichiro Suzuki
49 Felix Hernandez
50 Ken Griffey Jr.
51 Josh Hamilton
52 Ian Kinsler
53 Torii Hunter
54 Vladimir Guerrero
55 Clayton Kershaw
56 Manny Ramirez
57 Matt Kemp
58 James Loney
59 Adrian Gonzalez
60 Pablo Sandoval
61 Tim Lincecum
62 Todd Helton
63 Troy Tulowitzki
64 Justin Upton
65 Dan Haren
66 Johnny Bench
67 Kirk Gibson
68 Willie Randolph
69 Nolan Ryan
70 Cal Ripken Jr.
71 Joe DiMaggio
72 Pete Rose
73 Mike Schmidt
74 Ryne Sandberg
75 Roger Maris
76 Alan Trammell
77 Brooks Robinson
78 Jose Canseco
79 Harold Baines
80 Bob Feller
81 Don Mattingly
82 Steve Carlton
83 Willie Stargell
84 Ted Williams
85 Dennis Eckersley
87 Bo Jackson
88 Robin Yount
89 Ozzie Smith
90 Ron Santo
91 Tony Perez
92 Howard Johnson
93 Pete Rose
94 Bob Gibson
95 Greg Maddux
96 Carlton Fisk
97 Joe Torre
98 Roberto Clemente
99 Dave Concepcion
100 Rod Carew

2010 Exquisite Collection Combo Patch

STATED PRINT RUN 35 SER.#'d SETS
ECP1 Ryan Braun
Prince Fielder
ECP2 Chad Billingsley
Clayton Kershaw
ECP3 Ozzie Smith
ECP4 Carl Crawford
Evan Longoria
ECP5 Alex Rodriguez
Ken Griffey Jr.
ECP6 Cal Ripken Jr.
Albert Pujols
ECP7 Todd Helton
Miguel Cabrera
ECP8 Ron Santo
Ryne Sandberg
ECP9 Randy Johnson
Pedro Martinez
ECP10 Daisuke Matsuzaka
Chien-Ming Wang
ECP11 Justin Morneau
Joe Mauer
ECP12 Jonathan Papelbon
Mariano Rivera
ECP14 Pete Rose
Mike Schmidt
ECP15 Brooks Robinson
Cal Ripken Jr.
ECP16 Alfonso Soriano
Derrek Lee
ECP17 Jose Canseco
Dennis Eckersley
ECP18 Justin Upton
B.J. Upton
ECP19 Chase Utley
Cole Hamels
ECP20 Ken Griffey Jr.
Ichiro Suzuki
ECP21 Nolan Ryan
Randy Johnson
ECP22 Albert Pujols
Chris Carpenter
ECP24 M.Cabrera/J.Beckett
ECP25 Manny Ramirez
Pedro Martinez

2010 Exquisite Collection Patch

PRINT RUNS B/WN 15-50 COPIES PER
NO PRICING ON QTY 15
AG Adrian Gonzalez/50
AP Albert Pujols/50
AR Alex Rodriguez/50
AS Alfonso Soriano/50
BJ Bo Jackson/50
BR Brooks Robinson
CB Carlos Beltran/50
CC Carl Crawford/50
CJ Chipper Jones/50
CR Cal Ripken Jr./50
CU Chase Utley/50
CW Chien-Ming Wang/50
DC Dave Concepcion/50
DE Dennis Eckersley/25
DM Don Mattingly/50
DO David Ortiz/50
EL Evan Longoria/15
FH Felix Hernandez/50
GI Kirk Gibson/50
GM Greg Maddux/50
GS Grady Sizemore/50
IK Ian Kinsler/50
IS Ichiro Suzuki/50
JB Josh Beckett/50
JC Jose Canseco/50
JE Jacoby Ellsbury/50
JL James Loney/50
JM Justin Morneau/50
JP Jonathan Papelbon/50
JR Jose Reyes
JV Justin Verlander/50
KG Ken Griffey Jr./50
MA Joe Mauer/50
MC Miguel Cabrera/50
MR Mariano Rivera/50
MZ Daisuke Matsuzaka/25
NR Nolan Ryan/15
PF Prince Fielder/50
RB Ryan Braun/50
RC Roberto Clemente/25
RH Roy Halladay/50
RJ Randy Johnson/50
RZ Ryan Zimmerman/50
SC Steve Carlton/50
TL Tim Lincecum/50
TT Troy Tulowitzki/50
VA Jason Varitek/50
ZG Zack Greinke

2010 Exquisite Collection Trio Patch

STATED PRINT RUN 25 SER.#'d SETS
ETP1 Stan Musial
Albert Pujols
Ozzie Smith
ETP2 Brian McCann
Joe Mauer
Yadier Molina
ETP3 Carl Crawford
Grady Sizemore
Josh Hamilton
ETP4 Derrek Lee
Ron Santo
Ryne Sandberg
ETP5 Matt Kemp/Clayton Kershaw/James Loney
ETP6 Tim Lincecum
Felix Hernandez
Zack Greinke
ETP7 Paul Molitor
Cecil Cooper
Robin Yount
ETP8 Daisuke Matsuzaka
Ichiro Suzuki
Hideki Matsui
ETP9 Alex Rodriguez
David Ortiz
Vladimir Guerrero
ETP10 Nolan Ryan
Nolan Ryan
Nolan Ryan
ETP11 Nolan Ryan
Greg Maddux
Randy Johnson
ETP12 CC Sabathia
Manny Ramirez
Jim Thome
ETP13 Ian Kinsler
Michael Young
Josh Hamilton
ETP14 Chipper Jones
Hanley Ramirez
Ryan Braun
ETP15 Jose Canseco
Bo Jackson
Don Mattingly

2007 Exquisite Collection Rookie Signatures

COMMON CARD (1-100) 1.50 4.00
ONE BASE CARD PER PACK
1-100 PRINT RUN 99 SER.#'d SETS
COMMON AU RC (101-191) 4.00 10.00
OVERALL FIVE AUTOS PER PACK
AU RC SER.#'d B/WN 150-235 PER
COMMON JSY AU RC (101-191) 6.00 15.00
OVERALL FIVE AUTOS PER PACK
JSY AU RC SER.#'d B/WN 125-199 PER
EXCHANGE DEADLINE 12/28/2009
1 Ichiro Suzuki 5.00 12.00
2 Alex Rodriguez 5.00 12.00
3 David Wright 3.00 8.00
4 Ryan Howard 3.00 8.00
5 Ken Griffey Jr. 8.00 20.00
6 Derek Jeter 8.00 20.00
7 Vladimir Guerrero 2.50 6.00
8 Roger Clemens 4.00 10.00
9 Greg Maddux 5.00 12.00
10 Johan Santana 2.50 6.00
11 Nomar Garciaparra 2.50 6.00
12 Carlos Beltran 2.50 6.00
13 Carlos Delgado 1.50 4.00
14 Manny Ramirez 4.00 10.00
15 John Lackey 2.50 6.00
16 David Ortiz 4.00 10.00
17 Curt Schilling 2.50 6.00
18 Cal Ripken Jr. 10.00 25.00
19 Albert Pujols 4.00 10.00
20 Frank Thomas 4.00 10.00
21 Chris Carpenter 2.50 6.00
22 Prince Fielder 2.50 6.00
23 Justin Morneau 2.50 6.00
24 Joe Mauer 3.00 8.00
25 Torii Hunter 1.50 4.00
26 Jake Peavy 1.50 4.00
27 Roy Oswalt 2.50 6.00
28 Craig Biggio 2.50 6.00
29 Lance Berkman 2.50 6.00
30 Carlos Zambrano 2.50 6.00
31 Derrek Lee 1.50 4.00
32 Aramis Ramirez 1.50 4.00
33 Noah Lowry 1.50 4.00
34 Magglio Ordonez 2.50 6.00
35 Ivan Rodriguez 2.50 6.00
36 Johnny Damon 2.50 6.00
37 Justin Verlander 4.00 10.00
38 John Smoltz 4.00 10.00
39 Chipper Jones 4.00 10.00
40 Jeff Francoeur 4.00 10.00
41 Hanley Ramirez 2.50 6.00
42 Miguel Cabrera 4.00 10.00
43 Josh Beckett 1.50 4.00
44 Cole Hamels 3.00 8.00
45 Chase Utley 2.50 6.00
46 Grady Sizemore 2.50 6.00
47 Travis Hafner 1.50 4.00
48 Victor Martinez 2.50 6.00
49 Russell Martin 1.50 4.00
50 Jason Varitek 4.00 10.00
51 Hideki Matsui 4.00 10.00
52 Carl Crawford 2.50 6.00
53 Scott Kazmir 2.50 6.00
54 Miguel Tejada 2.50 6.00
55 Erik Bedard 1.50 4.00
56 Carlos Lee 1.50 4.00
57 Sammy Sosa 4.00 10.00
58 Mark Teixeira 2.50 6.00
59 Michael Young 1.50 4.00
60 Jim Thome 2.50 6.00
61 Paul Konerko 2.50 6.00
62 Jermaine Dye 1.50 4.00
63 Mark Teahen 1.50 4.00
64 Felix Hernandez 2.50 6.00
65 Andruw Jones 1.50 4.00
66 Pedro Martinez 2.50 6.00
67 Randy Johnson 4.00 10.00
68 Ryan Zimmerman 2.50 6.00
69 Matt Holliday 4.00 10.00
70 Todd Helton 2.50 6.00
71 Brian Bannister 1.50 4.00
72 Jeremy Bonderman 1.50 4.00
73 Adam Dunn 2.50 6.00
74 Aaron Harang 1.50 4.00
75 Jason Bay 2.50 6.00
76 Adam LaRoche 1.50 4.00
77 Freddy Sanchez 1.50 4.00
78 Dan Uggla 1.50 4.00
79 Joe Nathan 1.50 4.00
80 Brad Penny 1.50 4.00
81 Takashi Saito 1.50 4.00
82 Jimmy Rollins 2.50 6.00
83 Jose Reyes 2.50 6.00
84 Jered Weaver 2.50 6.00
85 Chien-Ming Wang 2.50 6.00
86 Jonathan Papelbon 4.00 10.00
87 Mariano Rivera 5.00 12.00
88 Eric Byrnes 1.50 4.00
89 Nick Markakis 3.00 8.00
90 Brian Roberts 1.50 4.00
91 Omar Vizquel 2.50 6.00
92 Vernon Wells 1.50 4.00
93 Dan Haren 1.50 4.00
94 Ben Sheets 1.50 4.00
95 B.J. Upton 1.50 4.00
96 Adrian Gonzalez 3.00 8.00
97 J.J. Hardy 1.50 4.00
98 Mike Piazza 4.00 10.00
99 Roy Halladay 2.50 6.00
100 Alfonso Soriano 2.50 6.00
101 Sean Henn AU/235 (RC) 4.00 10.00
102 Sean White AU/235 RC 4.00 10.00
103 Mike Schultz AU/234 RC 4.00 10.00
104 Michael Bourn AU/234 (RC) 5.00 12.00
105 Matt Chico AU/235 (RC) 4.00 10.00
106 Matt Lindstrom AU/235 (RC) 4.00 10.00
107 Connor Robertson AU/235 RC 4.00 10.00
108 Jay Marshall AU/235 RC 4.00 10.00
109 Jared Burton AU/235 RC 4.00 10.00
110 Juan Perez AU/235 RC 4.00 10.00
111 Scott Moore AU/235 (RC) 4.00 10.00
112 Brad Salmon AU/235 RC 4.00 10.00
113 Danny Putnam AU/235 (RC) 4.00 10.00
114 Kelvin Jimenez AU/235 RC 4.00 10.00
115 Dennis Dove AU/235 (RC) 4.00 10.00
116 Yoel Hernandez AU/234 RC 4.00 10.00
117 Devern Hansack AU/235 RC 4.00 10.00
118 Mike Rabelo AU/235 RC 4.00 10.00
119 Miguel Montero AU/235 (RC) 4.00 10.00
120 Kevin Cameron AU/235 RC 4.00 10.00
121 Joseph Bisenius AU/235 RC 4.00 10.00
122 Ryan Z. Braun AU/234 RC 4.00 10.00
123 Levale Speigner AU/235 RC 4.00 10.00
124 Lee Gardner AU/235 (RC) 4.00 10.00
125 Ryan Rowland-Smith AU/234 RC 4.00 10.00
126 Zack Segovia AU/235 (RC) 4.00 10.00
127 Rick Vanden Hurk AU/235 RC 4.00 10.00
128 Dallas Braden AU/235 RC 4.00 10.00
129 Rocky Cherry AU/234 RC 4.00 10.00
130 Andy Gonzalez AU/235 (RC) 4.00 10.00
131 Neal Musser AU/235 RC 4.00 10.00
132 Garrett Jones AU/235 (RC) 5.00 12.00
133 Ben Francisco AU/235 (RC) 4.00 10.00
134 Jon Coutlangus AU/235 (RC) 4.00 10.00
135 A.J. Murray AU/235 RC 4.00 10.00
136 Brett Carroll AU/235 RC 4.00 10.00
137 J.Danks AU/235 RC 8.00 20.00
138 Kyle Kendrick AU/235 RC 6.00 15.00
139 Joaquin Arias AU/235 (RC) 4.00 10.00
140 Matt Brown AU/235 (RC) 4.00 10.00
141 Kurt Suzuki AU/150 (RC) 10.00 25.00
142 Curtis Thigpen AU/150 (RC) 4.00 10.00
143 Jerry Owens AU/150 (RC) 4.00 10.00
144 Billy Butler AU/150 (RC) 8.00 20.00
145 Kei Igawa AU/150 RC 15.00 40.00
146 Mike Fontenot AU/150 (RC) 5.00 12.00
147 Brandon Wood AU/150 (RC) 10.00 25.00
148 Alexi Casilla AU/150 RC 4.00 10.00
149 Jeff Baker AU/150 (RC) 4.00 10.00
150 Brian Barden AU/150 RC 4.00 10.00
151 Chris Stewart AU/150 RC 4.00 10.00
152 Jon Knott AU/150 (RC) 4.00 10.00
153 Chase Wright AU/150 RC 6.00 15.00
154 Chase Headley AU/150 (RC) 6.00 15.00
155 Jesse Litsch Jsy AU/199 RC 6.00 15.00
156 Tyler Clippard AU/150 (RC) 4.00 10.00
157 Matt DeSalvo AU/150 (RC) 4.00 10.00
158 Kory Casto AU/150 (RC) 4.00 10.00
159 J.Saltalamac.Jsy AU/199 (RC) 4.00 10.00
160 Glen Perkins AU/150 (RC) 4.00 10.00
161 Ryan Braun Jsy AU/199 (RC) 12.00 30.00
162 Justin Upton Jsy AU/199 RC 8.00 20.00
163 T.Linc Jsy AU/199 RC 15.00 40.00
164 Fred Lewis AU/150 (RC) 6.00 15.00
165 Alex Gordon Jsy AU/199 RC 10.00 25.00
166 Akinori Iwamura Jsy AU/199 RC 6.00 15.00
167 Delmon Young Jsy AU/199 (RC) 6.00 15.00
168 Tulowitzki Jsy AU/199 (RC) 20.00 50.00
169 Matsuzaka Jsy AU/199 RC 30.00 60.00
170 J.Hamilton Jsy AU/199 (RC) 10.00 25.00
171 Kevin Kouzmanoff Jsy AU/199 (RC) 6.00 15.00
172 Pence Jsy AU/199 (RC) 8.00 20.00
173 Felix Pie Jsy AU/199 (RC) 6.00 15.00
174 Andrew Miller Jsy AU/199 RC 6.00 15.00
175 Gallardo Jsy AU/199 (RC) 6.00 15.00
176 Ryan Sweeney Jsy AU/199 (RC) 6.00 15.00
177 Josh Fields Jsy AU/199 (RC) 6.00 10.00
178 M.Reynolds Jsy AU/199 RC 6.00 15.00
180 Homer Bailey AU/150 (RC) 6.00 15.00
182 J.Chamb.AU/150 RC 8.00 20.00
184 Travis Metcalf Jsy AU/125 RC 8.00 20.00
185 Kevin Slowey Jsy AU/199 (RC) 6.00 15.00
186 Phil Hughes AU/150 (RC) 12.50 30.00
187 Micah Owings AU/150 (RC) 10.00 25.00
188 Joe Smith AU/150 RC 4.00 10.00
189 Joakim Soria Jsy AU/199 RC 6.00 15.00
190 Adam Lind Jsy AU/199 (RC) 8.00 20.00
191 Andy LaRoche Jsy AU/199 (RC) 8.00 20.00
192 B.Morrow Jsy AU/175 RC 12.50 30.00
193 Carlos Gomez Jsy AU/125 RC 6.00 15.00
194 Yunel Escobar AU/150 (RC) 6.00 15.00

2007 Exquisite Collection Rookie Signatures Gold

*1-100 GOLD: .6X TO 1.5X BASIC
ONE BASE OR BASE PARALLEL PER PACK
1-100 PRINT RUN 75 SER.#'d SETS
*101-191 AU GOLD: .6X TO 1.5X BASIC
OVERALL FIVE AUTOS PER PACK
101-191 AU SER.#'d B/WN 25-75 PER
NO PRICING ON QTY 25 OR LESS
*101-191 JSY AU GOLD: .6X TO 1.5X BASIC
101-191 JSY AU SER.#'d B/WN 50-99 PER
EXCHANGE DEADLINE 12/28/2009

2007 Exquisite Collection Rookie Signatures Gold Spectrum Patches

OVERALL FIVE AUTOS PER PACK
STATED PRINT RUN 1 SER.#'d SET
NO PRICING DUE TO SCARCITY
EXCHANGE DEADLINE 12/28/2009

2007 Exquisite Collection Rookie Signatures Silver Spectrum

ONE BASE OR BASE PARALLEL PER PACK
1-100 STATED PRINT RUN 1 SER.#'d SET
OVERALL AU ODDS FIVE PER PACK
101-191 AU PRINT RUN 1 SER.#'d SET
101-191 JSY AU PRINT RUN 25 SER.#'d SETS
NO PRICING DUE TO SCARCITY
EXCHANGE DEADLINE 12/28/2009

2007 Exquisite Collection Rookie Signatures All Rookie Team Autographs

OVERALL FIVE AUTOS PER PACK
STATED PRINT RUN 20 SER.#'d SETS
NO PRICING DUE TO SCARCITY
COPPER SPEC.PRINT RUN 1 SER.#'d SET
NO COPPER SPEC PRICING AVAILABLE
GOLD SPEC. PRINT RUN 5 SER.#'d SETS
NO GOLD SPEC PRICING AVAILABLE
SILVER INK PRINT RUN 1 SER.#'d SET
NO SILVER INK PRICING AVAILABLE
SILVER SPEC PRINT RUN 15 SER.#'d SETS
NO SILVER SPEC PRICING AVAILABLE
EXCHANGE DEADLINE 12/28/2009

2007 Exquisite Collection Rookie Signatures Cal Ripken Jr. All Rookie Team Autographs

OVERALL FIVE AUTOS PER PACK
STATED PRINT RUN 8 SER.#'d SETS
NO PRICING DUE TO SCARCITY
SILVER SPEC PRINT RUN 1 SER.#'d SET
NO SILVER SPEC PRICING AVAILABLE

2007 Exquisite Collection Rookie Signatures College Ties Autographs

OVERALL FIVE AUTOS PER PACK
PRINT RUNS B/WN 10-25 COPIES PER
NO PRICING DUE TO SCARCITY
GOLD PRINT RUN 2 SER.#'d SETS
NO GOLD PRICING AVAILABLE
SILVER SPEC PRINT RUN 1 SER.#'d SET
NO SILVER SPEC PRICING AVAILABLE
EXCHANGE DEADLINE 12/28/2009

2007 Exquisite Collection Rookie Signatures Common Ground Signatures

OVERALL FIVE AUTOS PER PACK
STATED PRINT RUN 25 SER.#'d SETS
NO PRICING DUE TO SCARCITY
GOLD PRINT RUN 2 SER.#'d SETS
NO GOLD PRICING AVAILABLE
SILVER SPEC PRINT RUN 1 SER.#'d SET
NO SILVER SPEC PRICING AVAILABLE
EXCHANGE DEADLINE 12/28/2009

2007 Exquisite Collection Rookie Signatures Common Numbers

OVERALL FIVE AUTOS PER PACK
PRINT RUNS B/WN 2-60 COPIES PER
NO PRICING ON QTY 25 OR LESS
GOLD SPEC. PRINT RUN 1 SER.#'d SET
NO GOLD SPEC PRICING AVAILABLE
SILVER SPEC PRINT RUN 2 SER.#'d SETS
NO SILVER SPEC PRICING AVAILABLE
EXCHANGE DEADLINE 12/28/2009
BB J.Bay/J.Bonderman/38 10.00 25.00
BC R.Z.Braun/M.Chico/47 6.00 15.00
CP M.Corpas/G.Perkins/60 6.00 15.00
FR J.Fields/M.Reynolds/27 8.00 20.00
GH Y.Gallardo/P.Humber/49 10.00 25.00
GS J.Garcia/K.Slowey/59 8.00 20.00
MS A.Miller/J.Soria/48 6.00 15.00
VG J.Vermilyea/S.Gallagher/36 6.00 15.00
VT J.Verlander/F.Thomas/35 75.00 150.00

2007 Exquisite Collection Rookie Signatures Derek Jeter All Rookie Team Autographs

OVERALL FIVE AUTOS PER PACK
STATED PRINT RUN 2 SER.#'d SETS
NO PRICING DUE TO SCARCITY
SILVER SPEC PRINT RUN 1 SER.#'d SET
NO SILVER SPEC PRICING AVAILABLE

2007 Exquisite Collection Rookie Signatures Draft Choice Autographs

OVERALL FIVE AUTOS PER PACK
STATED PRINT RUN 20 SER.#'d SETS
NO PRICING DUE TO SCARCITY
COPPER SPEC.PRINT RUN 1 SER.#'d SET
NO COPPER SPEC PRICING AVAILABLE
GOLD SPEC. PRINT RUN 5 SER.#'d SETS
NO GOLD SPEC PRICING AVAILABLE
SILVER INK PRINT RUN 15 SER.#'d SETS
NO SILVER INK PRICING AVAILABLE
SILVER SPEC PRINT RUN 15 SER.#'d SETS
NO SILVER SPEC PRICING AVAILABLE
EXCHANGE DEADLINE 12/28/2009

2007 Exquisite Collection Rookie Signatures Draft Duals Autographs

OVERALL FIVE AUTOS PER PACK
STATED PRINT RUN 25 SER.#'d SETS
NO PRICING DUE TO SCARCITY
GOLD PRINT RUN 2 SER.#'d SETS
NO GOLD PRICING AVAILABLE
SILVER SPEC PRINT RUN 1 SER.#'d SET
NO SILVER SPEC PRICING AVAILABLE
EXCHANGE DEADLINE 12/28/2009

2007 Exquisite Collection Rookie Signatures Dual Signatures

OVERALL FIVE AUTOS PER PACK
PRINT RUNS B/WN 10-35 COPIES PER
NO PRICING ON QTY 10 OR LESS
GOLD #'d B/WN 5-25 COPIES PER
NO GOLD PRICING AVAILABLE
SILVER SPEC. #'d B/WN 1-10 COPIES PER
NO SILVER SPEC PRICING AVAILABLE
EXCHANGE DEADLINE 12/28/2009
AC A.Miller/Maybin/35 30.00 60.00
AD Casilla/Kelly/35 6.00 15.00
AJ Harang/Keppinger/35 10.00 25.00
AM Arias/Metcalf/35 6.00 15.00
BB Braun/Braun/35 8.00 20.00
BC Burton/Coutlangus/35 6.00 15.00
BG Bay/Gorzelanny/35 6.00 15.00
BH Burres/R.Hernandez/35 6.00 15.00
BI Braun/Iwamura/35 30.00 60.00
BJ Hall/Estrada/35 6.00 15.00
BK Billingsley/Kuo/35 20.00 50.00
BL Bailey/Lincecum/35 20.00 50.00
BR Barden/M.Reynolds/35 10.00 25.00
BW Butler/Wood/35 6.00 15.00
CC Granderson/Maybin/35 30.00 60.00
CD Chico/DeSalvo/35 6.00 15.00
CH Chamberlain/Hughes/35 75.00 150.00
CJ Casilla/G.Jones/35 6.00 15.00
CK C.Jimenez/K.Jimenez/35 6.00 15.00
CY Crawford/D.Young/35 6.00 15.00
DH Durbin/Y.Hernandez/35 6.00 15.00
DM Slaten/Schultz/35 6.00 15.00
DO S.Drew/Owings/35 10.00 25.00
DW DeSalvo/C.Wright/35 6.00 15.00
FE Fontenot/Ellis/35 6.00 15.00
FL P.Fielder/C.Lee/35 30.00 60.00
GB Gordon/Braun/35 20.00 50.00
GC Gallagher/Cherry/35 6.00 15.00
GG J.Garcia/Gardner/35 6.00 15.00
GJ V.Guerrero/A.Jones/35 30.00 60.00
GK A.Gonzalez/Kotchman/35 10.00 25.00
GL J.Garcia/Lindstrom/35 6.00 15.00
GM Molina/Montero/35 12.50 30.00
GP C.Gomez/Pie/35 10.00 25.00
GV Gardner/Vanden Hurk/35 6.00 15.00
HA Bailey/Harang/35 15.00 40.00
HB Y.Hernandez/Bisenius/35 6.00 15.00
HC Henn/Clippard/35 6.00 15.00
HD Henn/DeSalvo/35 6.00 15.00
HE R.Hernandez/Estrada/35 6.00 15.00
HG Hamilton/Granderson/35 40.00 80.00
HH Hampson/Headley/35 6.00 15.00
HK Hughes/Kuo/35 12.50 30.00
HL Hughes/Lincecum/35 50.00 100.00
HM Hamels/A.Miller/35 20.00 50.00
HP Bailey/Hughes/35 6.00 15.00
IC Igawa/Clippard/35 6.00 15.00
IH Igawa/Hughes/35 20.00 50.00
JE K/Johnson/Escobar/35 12.50 30.00
JJ Shields/Salas/35 6.00 15.00
KB Kinsler/Blalock/35 10.00 25.00
KH Kouzmanoff/Headley/35 6.00 15.00
KK Kendrick/Kotchman/35 12.50 30.00
KW Kendrick/Wood/35 12.50 30.00
LA An.LaRoche/Abreu/35 10.00 25.00
LB F.Lewis/Bourn/35 6.00 15.00
LE Lackey/Escobar/35 10.00 25.00
LH Lester/Hansack/35 12.50 30.00
LO Lincecum/Oswalt/35 60.00 120.00
LP C.Lee/Pence/35 30.00 60.00
LS Litsch/Slowey/35 6.00 15.00
ME McCann/Escobar/35 12.50 30.00
MH Markakis/Hamilton/35 30.00 60.00
MM R.Martin/McCann/35 12.50 30.00
MO A.Miller/Owings/35 12.50 30.00
MS Maine/J.Smith/35 10.00 25.00
NT Swisher/Buck/35 12.50 30.00
OC Owings/Chico/35 12.50 30.00

PH Pence/Hamilton/35 30.00 60.00
PM Patterson/Markakis/35 12.50 30.00
PO Pie/Owens/35 6.00 15.00
RB Reynolds/Braun/35 20.00 50.00
RM Robertson/Marshall/35 6.00 15.00
RO Reynolds/Owings/35 6.00 15.00
RU H.Ramirez/Uggla/35 12.50 30.00
RZ A.Ramirez/Zambrano/35 6.00 15.00
SA Soria/Accardo/35 6.00 15.00
SB Soria/R.Z.Braun/35 6.00 15.00
SG J.Smith/C.Gomez/35 6.00 15.00
SM K.Suzuki/G.Molina/35 6.00 15.00
SO Sweeney/Owens/35 6.00 15.00
SR C.Stewart/Rabelo/35 6.00 15.00
SS J.Smith/Slowey/35 6.00 15.00
ST Henn/Clippard/35 6.00 15.00
TB Tulowitzki/Baker/35 10.00 25.00
TE Escobar/Theriot/35 10.00 25.00
TF Theriot/Fontenot/35 8.00 20.00
TJ Thigpen/G.Jones/35 6.00 15.00
TL Thigpen/Lind/35 6.00 15.00
TR Hafner/Garko/35 8.00 20.00
TT F.Thomas/Thome/35 60.00 150.00
TV Hafner/V.Martinez/35 8.00 20.00
VL Vanden Hurk/Lindstrom/35 6.00 15.00
VM Verlander/A.Miller/35 20.00 50.00
WI C.Wright/Igawa/35 15.00 40.00
YT Gallardo/T.Lincecum/35 12.00 30.00
ZB Zimmerman/Braun/35 15.00 40.00
ZG Zimmerman/Gordon/35 15.00 40.00

2007 Exquisite Collection Rookie Signatures Endorsements Signatures

OVERALL FIVE AUTOS PER PACK
STATED PRINT RUN 50 SER.#'d SETS
GOLD PRINT RUN 15 SER.#'d SETS
NO GOLD PRICING AVAILABLE
SILVER SPEC PRINT RUN 1 SER.#'d SET
NO SILVER SPEC PRICING AVAILABLE
EXCHANGE DEADLINE 12/28/2009
AC Alexi Casilla 4.00 10.00
AE Andre Ethier 15.00 40.00
AL Adam Lind 6.00 15.00
BH Brendan Harris 6.00 15.00
BO Jeremy Bonderman 10.00 25.00
CP Corey Patterson 4.00 10.00
DH Dan Haren 4.00 10.00
DL Derrek Lee 10.00 25.00
DM David Murphy 6.00 15.00
DU Dan Uggla 4.00 10.00
FL Fred Lewis 6.00 15.00
FP Felix Pie 6.00 15.00
GP Glen Perkins 4.00 10.00
HB Homer Bailey 4.00 10.00
HP Hunter Pence 10.00 25.00
HR Hanley Ramirez 10.00 25.00
JB Jason Bay 6.00 15.00
JF Josh Fields 4.00 10.00
JL Jon Lester 15.00 40.00
JP Jonathan Papelbon 10.00 25.00
JS James Shields 4.00 10.00
JV Justin Verlander 20.00 50.00
KI Kei Igawa 5.00 12.00
KS Kevin Slowey 6.00 15.00
LG Luis Gonzalez 3.00 8.00
MH Matt Holliday 15.00 40.00
MO Micah Owings 6.00 15.00
NS Nick Swisher 6.00 15.00
PF Prince Fielder 10.00 25.00
RB Ryan Braun 10.00 25.00
RM Russell Martin 10.00 25.00
RS Ryan Sweeney 4.00 10.00
RT Ryan Theriot 6.00 15.00
RZ Ryan Zimmerman 10.00 25.00
SM Joe Smith 6.00 15.00
TH Travis Hafner 10.00 25.00
TL Tim Lincecum 15.00 40.00
TT Troy Tulowitzki 10.00 25.00
VM Victor Martinez 10.00 25.00
YE Yunel Escobar 10.00 25.00

2007 Exquisite Collection Rookie Signatures Ensemble Quad Signatures

OVERALL FIVE AUTOS PER PACK
STATED PRINT RUN 15 SER.#'d SETS
NO PRICING DUE TO SCARCITY
GOLD SPEC. PRINT RUN 1 SER.#'d SET
NO GOLD SPEC PRICING AVAILABLE
SILVER SPEC PRINT RUN 4 SER.#'d SETS
NO SILVER SPEC PRICING AVAILABLE
EXCHANGE DEADLINE 12/28/2009

2007 Exquisite Collection Rookie Signatures Ensemble Triple Signatures

OVERALL FIVE AUTOS PER PACK
PRINT RUNS B/WN 10-35 COPIES PER
NO PRICING ON QTY 10 OR LESS
GOLD SPEC. PRINT RUN 3 SER.#'d SETS
NO GOLD SPEC PRICING AVAILABLE
SILVER SPEC PRINT RUN 1 SER.#'d SET
NO SILVER SPEC PRICING AVAILABLE
EXCHANGE DEADLINE 12/28/2009
BGL Braun/Gordon/LaRoc 10.00 25.00
BLG Bourn/F.Lewis/C.Gomez 12.00 30.00
BTY Braun/Tulo/Delmon 20.00 50.00
BWL Butler/Wood/Lind 30.00 60.00
CSP Joba/Soria/Perkins 20.00 50.00
FCE Fontenot/Casilla/Escobar 20.00 50.00
GFC Gallagher/Fontenot/Cherry 12.00 30.00
GIB Gordon/Iwamura/Braun 50.00 100.00
IGR Iwamura/Gordon/Reynolds 12.00 30.00
LHB Lincecum/Hughes/Bailey 40.00 80.00
LLT Lind/Litsch/Thigpen 12.00 30.00
MKI A.Miller/Kendrick/Igawa 12.00 30.00
PHY Pence/Hamilton/Delmon 25.00 60.00
SHG Soria/Hampson/Gallagher 12.00 30.00
SMA Saltala./D.Murphy/Arias 15.00 40.00
UBB J.Upton/Buck/Butler 60.00 120.00

2007 Exquisite Collection Rookie Signatures First Signs Autographs

OVERALL FIVE AUTOS PER PACK
STATED PRINT RUN 20 SER.#'d SETS
NO PRICING DUE TO SCARCITY
COPPER SPEC.PRINT RUN 1 SER.#'d SET
NO COPPER SPEC PRICING AVAILABLE
GOLD SPEC. PRINT RUN 5 SER.#'d SETS
NO GOLD SPEC PRICING AVAILABLE
SILVER INK PRINT RUN 1 SER.#'d SET
NO SILVER INK PRICING AVAILABLE
SILVER SPEC PRINT RUN 15 SER.#'d SETS
NO SILVER SPEC PRICING AVAILABLE
EXCHANGE DEADLINE 12/28/2009

2007 Exquisite Collection Rookie Signatures Futures Autographs

OVERALL FIVE AUTOS PER PACK
STATED PRINT RUN 20 SER.#'d SETS
NO PRICING DUE TO SCARCITY
GOLD SPEC. PRINT RUN 1 SER.#'d SET
NO GOLD SPEC PRICING AVAILABLE
SILVER SPEC PRINT RUN 5 SER.#'d SETS
NO SILVER SPEC PRICING AVAILABLE
EXCHANGE DEADLINE 12/28/2009

2007 Exquisite Collection Rookie Signatures Game Dated Debut Signatures

OVERALL FIVE AUTOS PER PACK
STATED PRINT RUN 20 SER.#'d SETS
NO PRICING DUE TO SCARCITY
GOLD PRINT RUN 5 SER.#'d SETS
NO GOLD SPEC PRICING AVAILABLE
SILVER INK PRINT RUN 1 SER.#'d SET
NO SILVER INK PRICING AVAILABLE
SILVER SPEC PRINT RUN 15 SER.#'d SETS
NO SILVER SPEC PRICING AVAILABLE
EXCHANGE DEADLINE 12/28/2009

2007 Exquisite Collection Rookie Signatures Imagery Autographs

OVERALL FIVE AUTOS PER PACK
STATED PRINT RUN 25 SER.#'d SETS
NO PRICING ON MOST DUE TO SCARCITY
EACH VERSION PRICED EQUALLY
GOLD PRINT RUN 10 SER.#'d SETS
NO GOLD PRICING AVAILABLE
SILVER INK PRINT RUN 1 SER.#'d SET
NO SILVER INK PRICING AVAILABLE
SILVER SPEC PRINT RUN 1 SER.#'d SET
NO SILVER SPEC PRICING AVAILABLE
EXCHANGE DEADLINE 12/28/2009
AG Alex Gordon 8.00 20.00
AG2 Alex Gordon 8.00 20.00
AL Adam Lind 10.00 25.00
AL2 Adam Lind 10.00 25.00
BO Michael Bourn 6.00 15.00
BO2 Michael Bourn 6.00 15.00
CG Carlos Gomez 12.50 30.00
CG2 Carlos Gomez 12.50 30.00
CG3 Carlos Gomez 12.50 30.00
DM David Murphy 10.00 25.00
DM2 David Murphy 10.00 25.00
FL Fred Lewis 6.00 15.00
FL2 Fred Lewis 6.00 15.00
FL3 Fred Lewis 6.00 15.00
FP Felix Pie 6.00 15.00
FP2 Felix Pie 6.00 15.00
JB Jason Bay 6.00 15.00
JB2 Jason Bay 6.00 15.00
JF Josh Fields 6.00 15.00
JF2 Josh Fields 6.00 15.00
JF3 Josh Fields 6.00 15.00
JH Josh Hamilton 15.00 40.00
JH2 Josh Hamilton 15.00 40.00
JW Josh Willingham 6.00 15.00
JW2 Josh Willingham 6.00 15.00
KE Kyle Kendrick 10.00 25.00
KE2 Kyle Kendrick 10.00 25.00
KK Kevin Kouzmanoff 6.00 15.00
KK2 Kevin Kouzmanoff 6.00 15.00
KK3 Kevin Kouzmanoff 6.00 15.00
KS Kevin Slowey 6.00 15.00
KS2 Kevin Slowey 6.00 15.00
MF Mike Fontenot 6.00 15.00
MF2 Mike Fontenot 6.00 15.00
MF3 Mike Fontenot 6.00 15.00
MH Matt Holliday 10.00 25.00
MH2 Matt Holliday 10.00 25.00
MO Micah Owings 10.00 25.00
MO2 Micah Owings 10.00 25.00
MR Mark Reynolds 10.00 25.00
MR2 Mark Reynolds 10.00 25.00
RB Ryan Braun 20.00 50.00
RB2 Ryan Braun 20.00 50.00
RM Russell Martin 8.00 20.00
RM2 Russell Martin 8.00 20.00
RS Ryan Sweeney 6.00 15.00
RS2 Ryan Sweeney 6.00 15.00
RZ Ryan Zimmerman 20.00 50.00
RZ2 Ryan Zimmerman 20.00 50.00
SM Joe Smith 6.00 15.00
SM2 Joe Smith 6.00 15.00
TB Travis Buck 6.00 15.00
TB2 Travis Buck 6.00 15.00
TH Travis Hafner 6.00 15.00
TH2 Travis Hafner 6.00 15.00
VM Victor Martinez 6.00 15.00
VM2 Victor Martinez 6.00 15.00
VM3 Victor Martinez 6.00 15.00
YE Yunel Escobar 12.50 30.00
YE2 Yunel Escobar 12.50 30.00

2007 Exquisite Collection Rookie Signatures Ken Griffey Jr. All Rookie Team Autographs

OVERALL FIVE AUTOS PER PACK
STATED PRINT RUN 3 SER.#'d SETS
NO PRICING DUE TO SCARCITY
SILVER SPEC PRINT RUN 1 SER.#'d SET
NO SILVER SPEC PRICING AVAILABLE

2007 Exquisite Collection Rookie Signatures Phenoms Autographs

OVERALL FIVE AUTOS PER PACK
STATED PRINT RUN 20 SER.#'d SETS
NO PRICING DUE TO SCARCITY
GOLD PRINT RUN 15 SER.#'d SETS
NO GOLD PRICING AVAILABLE
SILVER INK PRINT RUN 1 SER.#'d SET
NO SILVER INK PRICING AVAILABLE
SILVER SPEC PRINT RUN 15 SER.#'d SETS
NO SILVER SPEC PRICING AVAILABLE
EXCHANGE DEADLINE 12/28/2009

2007 Exquisite Collection Rookie Signatures Reflections Autographs

OVERALL FIVE AUTOS PER PACK
PRINT RUNS B/WN 10-40 COPIES PER
NO PRICING QTY OF 20 OR LESS
GOLD #'d B/WN 5-20 COPIES PER
NO GOLD PRICING AVAILABLE
SILVER INK #'d B/WN 5-20 COPIES PER
NO SILVER INK PRICING AVAILABLE
SILVER SPEC #'d B/WN 1-10 COPIES PER
NO SILVER SPEC PRICING AVAILABLE
AB Gordon/Butler/40 12.00 30.00
AC Arias/Casilla/40 6.00 15.00
AH Harang/Bailey/40 20.00 50.00
AJ A.Miller/Sowers/40 10.00 25.00
BA M.Brown/Abreu/40 6.00 15.00
BB Bannister/Bonser/40 6.00 15.00
BD Bannister/Danks/40 12.50 30.00
BG Braun/Gordon/40 12.50 30.00
BH J.Barfield/Hafner/40 10.00 25.00
BJ Salmon/Burton/40 10.00 25.00
BL Bourn/F.Lewis/40 10.00 25.00
BS Bisenius/Segovia/40 6.00 15.00
BT Bannister/Teahen/40 10.00 25.00
BV Bonderman/Verlander/40 10.00 25.00
BW M.Brown/Wood/40 10.00 25.00
CG Crawford/C.Gomez/40 10.00 25.00
CH T.Cameron/Hampson/40 6.00 15.00
CK C.Thigpen/Kurt Suzuki/40 10.00 25.00
CS Cherry/Soria/40 6.00 15.00
DC DeSalvo/Chico/40 6.00 15.00
DH Durbin/Y.Hernandez/40 6.00 15.00
DO Danks/Owings/40 6.00 15.00
DS Durbin/Segovia/40 10.00 25.00
EC Escobar/Casilla/40 6.00 15.00
EL Ethier/F.Lewis/40 20.00 50.00
EP Ellis/Putnam/40 10.00 25.00
FM Fields/Metcalf/40 6.00 15.00
FO P.Fielder/Ortiz/40 12.50 30.00
FY F.Hernandez/Gallardo/40 12.50 30.00
GA Perkins/Casilla/40 6.00 15.00
GB Guthrie/Burres/40 10.00 25.00
GC Gallagher/Cherry/40 6.00 15.00
GG Guthrie/Gorzelanny/40 6.00 15.00
GK Gordon/Kouz/40 10.00 25.00
GL Gardner/Lindstrom/40 6.00 15.00
GM Molina/Montero/40 6.00 15.00
GV J.Garcia/Vanden Hurk/40 6.00 15.00
HB Hughes/Bailey/40 10.00 25.00
HC Hampson/Coutlangus/40 6.00 15.00
HD Street/Braden/40 30.00 60.00
HG R.Hill/Gallagher/40 10.00 25.00
HH Hughes/Henn/40 20.00 50.00
HK Headley/Kouz/40 6.00 15.00
HM Hamels/A.Miller/40 20.00 50.00
HP Hamilton/Pence/40 20.00 50.00
HT Bailey/Lincecum/40 40.00 80.00
HW Hermida/Willingham/40 6.00 15.00
IM Igawa/A.Miller/40 6.00 15.00
JC Shields/Billingsley/40 10.00 25.00
JD Jimenez/Dove/40 6.00 15.00
JE K.Johnson/Escobar/40 12.50 30.00
JJ Fields/Owens/40 10.00 25.00
JK Saltala/K.Suzuki/40 10.00 25.00
JL R.Johnson/Lind/40 6.00 15.00
JM Danks/Chico/40 6.00 15.00
KC Jimenez/Jimenez/40 10.00 25.00
KG K.Suzuki/Molina/40 6.00 15.00
LA An.LaRoche/Abreu/40 10.00 25.00
LB Lind/Baker/40 6.00 15.00
LH Lester/Hamels/40 20.00 50.00
LL Litsch/Lind/40 10.00 25.00
LO F.Lewis/Owens/40 6.00 15.00
MA Ellis/Casilla/40 6.00 15.00
MB J.Marshall/Braden/40 6.00 15.00
MG Markakis/Guthrie/40 12.50 30.00
MJ Holliday/Bay/40 20.00 50.00
MK Markakis/Knott/40 10.00 25.00
MM R.Martin/McCann/40 12.50 30.00
MR J.Marshall/C.Robertson/40 10.00 25.00
MS R.Martin/K.Suzuki/40 12.50 30.00
NR Musser/R.Z.Braun/40 10.00 25.00
OB Owings/Bailey/40 6.00 15.00
PB Putnam/Buck/40 6.00 15.00
PC Perkins/Chico/40 6.00 15.00
PD Perkins/DeSalvo/40 6.00 15.00
PG Pie/C.Gomez/40 12.50 30.00
PO Pie/Owens/40 6.00 15.00
RB M.Reynolds/Braun/40 10.00 25.00
RC Braun/Headley/40 15.00 40.00
RM Rabelo/Molina/40 6.00 15.00
RR R. Z.Braun/Braun/40 20.00 50.00
SB Soria/R.Z.Braun/40 6.00 15.00
SG Sheets/Gallardo/40 20.00 50.00
SH J.Smith/Hampson/40 10.00 25.00
SM Saltala/D.Murphy/40 10.00 25.00
SP Slowey/Perkins/40 10.00 25.00
SR K.Suzuki/Riggans/40 6.00 15.00
SS J.Smith/Slowey/40 6.00 15.00
ST Henn/Clippard/40 6.00 15.00
TJ C.Thigpen/G.Jones/40 6.00 15.00
TR C.Thigpen/Riggans/40 6.00 15.00
TS Teahen/Sanchez/40 6.00 15.00
VG Vanden Hurk/Gardner/40 6.00 15.00
WD C.Wright/Danks/40 6.00 15.00
WH Willingham/Hall/40 10.00 25.00
ZY Segovia/Y.Hernandez/40 6.00 15.00

2007 Exquisite Collection Rookie Signatures Retro Rookie Duals Autographs

OVERALL FIVE AUTOS PER PACK
PRINT RUNS B/WN 3-15 COPIES PER
NO PRICING DUE TO SCARCITY
GOLD PRINT RUN 2 SER.#'d SETS
NO GOLD PRICING AVAILABLE
SILVER SPEC PRINT RUN 1 SER.#'d SET
NO SILVER SPEC PRICING AVAILABLE
EXCHANGE DEADLINE 12/28/2009

2007 Exquisite Collection Rookie Signatures Rookie Biography Autographs

OVERALL FIVE AUTOS PER PACK
STATED PRINT RUN 20 SER.#'d SETS
NO PRICING DUE TO SCARCITY
BLUE.SPEC PRINT RUN 1 SER.#'d SET
NO BLUE SPEC PRICING AVAILABLE
GOLD PRINT RUN 15 SER.#'d SETS
NO GOLD PRICING AVAILABLE
GOLD SPEC. PRINT RUN 1 SER.#'d SET
NO GOLD SPEC PRICING AVAILABLE
SILVER INK PRINT RUN 1 SER.#'d SET
NO SILVER INK PRICING AVAILABLE
SILVER SPEC PRINT RUN 10 SER.#'d SETS
NO SILVER SPEC PRICING AVAILABLE
EXCHANGE DEADLINE 12/28/2009

2007 Exquisite Collection Rookie Signatures Rookie Heroes Autographs

OVERALL FIVE AUTOS PER PACK
STATED PRINT RUN 25 SER.#'d SETS
EACH VERSION PRICED EQUALLY
*GOLD: .6X TO 1.5X BASIC
GOLD PRINT RUN 15 SER.#'d SETS
GOLD SPEC. PRINT RUN 1 SER.#'d SET
NO GOLD SPEC PRICING AVAILABLE
SILVER INK PRINT RUN 1 SER.#'d SET
NO SILVER INK PRICING AVAILABLE
*SILVER SPEC: .75X TO 2X BASIC
SILVER SPEC PRINT RUN 10 SER.#'d SETS
EXCHANGE DEADLINE 12/28/2009
AI1 Akinori Iwamura 10.00 25.00
AI2 Akinori Iwamura 10.00 25.00
AI3 Akinori Iwamura 10.00 25.00
AI4 Akinori Iwamura 10.00 25.00
AI5 Akinori Iwamura 10.00 25.00
AM1 Andrew Miller 6.00 15.00
AM2 Andrew Miller 6.00 15.00
AM3 Andrew Miller 6.00 15.00
AM4 Andrew Miller 6.00 15.00
AM5 Andrew Miller 6.00 15.00
BB1 Billy Butler 10.00 25.00
BB2 Billy Butler 10.00 25.00
BB3 Billy Butler 10.00 25.00
BB4 Billy Butler 10.00 25.00
BB5 Billy Butler 10.00 25.00
CG1 Carlos Gomez 6.00 15.00
CG2 Carlos Gomez 6.00 15.00
CG3 Carlos Gomez 6.00 15.00
CG4 Carlos Gomez 6.00 15.00
CG5 Carlos Gomez 6.00 15.00
FL1 Fred Lewis 6.00 15.00
FL2 Fred Lewis 6.00 15.00
FL3 Fred Lewis 6.00 15.00
FL4 Fred Lewis 6.00 15.00
FL5 Fred Lewis 6.00 15.00
FP1 Felix Pie 6.00 15.00
FP2 Felix Pie 6.00 15.00
FP3 Felix Pie 6.00 15.00
FP4 Felix Pie 6.00 15.00
FP5 Felix Pie 6.00 15.00
HB1 Homer Bailey 6.00 15.00
HB2 Homer Bailey 6.00 15.00
HB3 Homer Bailey 6.00 15.00
HB4 Homer Bailey 6.00 15.00
HB5 Homer Bailey 6.00 15.00
HP1 Hunter Pence 12.50 30.00
HP2 Hunter Pence 12.50 30.00
HP3 Hunter Pence 12.50 30.00
HP4 Hunter Pence 12.50 30.00
HP5 Hunter Pence 12.50 30.00
JD1 John Danks 6.00 15.00
JD2 John Danks 6.00 15.00
JD3 John Danks 6.00 15.00
JD4 John Danks 6.00 15.00
JD5 John Danks 6.00 15.00
JS1 Jarrod Saltalamacchia 6.00 15.00
JS2 Jarrod Saltalamacchia 6.00 15.00
JS3 Jarrod Saltalamacchia 6.00 15.00
JS4 Jarrod Saltalamacchia 6.00 15.00
JS5 Jarrod Saltalamacchia 6.00 15.00
KE1 Kyle Kendrick 6.00 15.00
KE2 Kyle Kendrick 6.00 15.00
KE3 Kyle Kendrick 6.00 15.00
KE4 Kyle Kendrick 6.00 15.00
KE5 Kyle Kendrick 6.00 15.00
KK1 Kevin Kouzmanoff 6.00 15.00
KK2 Kevin Kouzmanoff 6.00 15.00
KK3 Kevin Kouzmanoff 6.00 15.00
KK4 Kevin Kouzmanoff 6.00 15.00
KK5 Kevin Kouzmanoff 6.00 15.00
KS1 Kevin Slowey 6.00 15.00
KS2 Kevin Slowey 6.00 15.00
KS3 Kevin Slowey 6.00 15.00
KS4 Kevin Slowey 6.00 15.00
KS5 Kevin Slowey 6.00 15.00
MR1 Mark Reynolds 8.00 20.00
MR2 Mark Reynolds 8.00 20.00
MR3 Mark Reynolds 8.00 20.00
MR4 Mark Reynolds 8.00 20.00
MR5 Mark Reynolds 8.00 20.00
RB1 Ryan Braun 12.50 30.00
RB2 Ryan Braun 12.50 30.00
RB3 Ryan Braun 12.50 30.00
RB4 Ryan Braun 12.50 30.00
RB5 Ryan Braun 12.50 30.00
SO1 Joakim Soria 6.00 15.00
SO2 Joakim Soria 6.00 15.00
SO3 Joakim Soria 6.00 15.00
SO4 Joakim Soria 6.00 15.00
SO5 Joakim Soria 6.00 15.00
TB1 Travis Buck 6.00 15.00
TB2 Travis Buck 6.00 15.00
TB3 Travis Buck 6.00 15.00
TB4 Travis Buck 6.00 15.00
TB5 Travis Buck 6.00 15.00
TL1 Tim Lincecum 75.00 150.00
TL2 Tim Lincecum 75.00 150.00
TL3 Tim Lincecum 75.00 150.00
TL4 Tim Lincecum 75.00 150.00
TL5 Tim Lincecum 75.00 150.00
TT1 Troy Tulowitzki 15.00 40.00
TT2 Troy Tulowitzki 10.00 25.00
TT3 Troy Tulowitzki 10.00 25.00
TT4 Troy Tulowitzki 10.00 25.00
TT5 Troy Tulowitzki 10.00 25.00
YE1 Yunel Escobar 6.00 15.00
YE2 Yunel Escobar 6.00 15.00
YE3 Yunel Escobar 6.00 15.00
YE4 Yunel Escobar 6.00 15.00
YE5 Yunel Escobar 6.00 15.00

2007 Exquisite Collection Rookie Signatures Signature Materials

OVERALL FIVE AUTOS PER PACK
PRINT RUNS B/WN 25-85 COPIES PER
NO PRICING ON QTY 25 OR LESS
*GOLD: .5X TO 1.2X BASIC
GOLD SER.#'d B/WN 15-50 COPIES PER
NO PRICING ON QTY 15 OR LESS
GOLD SPEC. PRINT RUN 1 SER.#'d SET
NO GOLD SPEC PRICING AVAILABLE
SILVER SPEC #'d B/WN 10-25 COPIES PER
NO SILVER SPEC PRICING AVAILABLE
EXCHANGE DEADLINE 12/28/2009
AD Adam Dunn/85 5.00 12.00
AG Adrian Gonzalez/85 6.00 15.00
AH Aaron Harang/85 5.00 12.00
AR Aramis Ramirez/85 6.00 15.00
BA Bronson Arroyo/85 5.00 12.00
BH Bill Hall/85 6.00 15.00
BL Joe Blanton/85 5.00 12.00
BO Jeremy Bonderman/85 10.00 25.00
BR Brian Roberts/85 6.00 15.00
BS Ben Sheets/85 5.00 12.00
BU B.J. Upton/85 8.00 20.00
CC Carl Crawford/85 6.00 15.00
CH Cole Hamels/85 15.00 40.00
CL Carlos Lee/85 5.00 12.00
CR Cal Ripken Jr./85 30.00 80.00
CZ Carlos Zambrano/85 10.00 25.00
DH Dan Haren/85 6.00 15.00
DL Derrek Lee/85 6.00 15.00
DU Dan Uggla/85 5.00 12.00
DW Dontrelle Willis/85 5.00 12.00
FH Felix Hernandez/85 15.00 40.00
FT Frank Thomas/85 30.00 60.00
HA Travis Hafner/85 6.00 15.00
HK Howie Kendrick/85 5.00 12.00
HR Hanley Ramirez/85 8.00 20.00
HS Huston Street/85 5.00 12.00
IK Ian Kinsler/85 10.00 25.00
JB Jason Bay/85 5.00 12.00
JM John Maine/85 6.00 15.00
JO Josh Barfield/85 5.00 12.00
JP Jonathan Papelbon/85 8.00 20.00
JV Justin Verlander/85 20.00 50.00
JW Josh Willingham/85 5.00 12.00
LS Luke Scott/85 5.00 12.00
MC Matt Cain/85 10.00 25.00
MO Justin Morneau/85 10.00 25.00
MT Mark Teixeira/85 20.00 50.00
NM Nick Markakis/85 10.00 25.00
NS Nick Swisher/85 6.00 15.00
PF Prince Fielder/85 12.50 30.00
RH Rich Harden/85 8.00 20.00
RM Russell Martin/85 5.00 12.00
RW Rickie Weeks/85 6.00 15.00
RZ Ryan Zimmerman/85 8.00 20.00
SD Stephen Drew/85 10.00 25.00
TH Torii Hunter/85 6.00 15.00
VM Victor Martinez/85 6.00 15.00

2007 Exquisite Collection Rookie Signatures The Future Autographs

OVERALL FIVE AUTOS PER PACK
STATED PRINT RUN 20 SER.#'d SETS
NO PRICING DUE TO SCARCITY
GOLD PRINT RUN 15 SER.#'d SETS
NO GOLD PRICING AVAILABLE
SILVER INK PRINT RUN 1 SER.#'d SET
NO SILVER INK PRICING AVAILABLE
SILVER SPEC PRINT RUN 1 SER.#'d SET
NO SILVER SPEC PRICING AVAILABLE
EXCHANGE DEADLINE 12/28/2009

2007 Exquisite Collection Rookie Signatures The Next Generation Signatures

OVERALL FIVE AUTOS PER PACK
STATED PRINT RUN 20 SER.#'d SETS
NO PRICING DUE TO SCARCITY
GOLD PRINT RUN 15 SER.#'d SETS
NO GOLD PRICING AVAILABLE
SILVER INK PRINT RUN 1 SER.#'d SET
NO SILVER INK PRICING AVAILABLE
SILVER SPEC PRINT RUN 1 SER.#'d SET
NO SILVER SPEC PRICING AVAILABLE
EXCHANGE DEADLINE 12/28/2009

2020 Exquisite Collection '03-04 Rookie Tribute Patch Autograph

RANDOM INSERTS IN PACKS
STATED PRINT RUN 99 SER.#'d SETS
03TCM Casey Mize 60.00 150.00
03TJD Jasson Dominguez 500.00 1200.00
03TWF Wander Franco EXCH 300.00 800.00

2020 Exquisite Collection '09-10 Rookie Tribute Autograph

RANDOM INSERTS IN PACKS
STATED PRINT RUN 99 SER.#'d SETS
09TCM Casey Mize 40.00 100.00
09TJD Jasson Dominguez 300.00 800.00
09TWF Wander Franco EXCH 200.00 500.00

1960 El Roy Face Motel

This one-card set was actually a business card advertising the motel in Penn Run, Pennsylvania, which was owned by El Roy Face of the Pittsburgh Pirates. The front features a black-and-white autographed photo of the player. The back displays the motel information. The card measures approximately 2 1/8" by 3 1/2".

1 Roy Face 6.00 15.00

1922 Fan T231

Little is known about this set. Only two cards, Carson Bigbie (in a photocopy) and Frank Baker have ever been discovered. The card has a sepia toned photo on the front and the back has batting information from the previous few seasons. Also on the back was a entry form for a contest, meaning these cards were probably sent back to the factory.

1 Carson Bigbee
61 Frank Baker 2000.00

1906 Fan Craze AL WG2

These cards were distributed as part of a baseball game produced in 1906. The cards each measure approximately 2 1/2" by 3 1/2" and have rounded corners. The card fronts show a black and white cameo photo of the player, his name, his team and the game outcome associated with that particular card. The card backs are all the same, each showing "Art Series" and "Fan Craze" in dark blue and white. This set features only players from the American League. Since the cards are unnumbered, they are listed below in alphabetical order. These sets were available, on a league basis, in retail catalogs of the period for 48 cents postpaid.

COMPLETE SET (51) 3000.00 6000.00
1 Nick Altrock 50.00 100.00
2 Jim Barrett 50.00 100.00
3 Harry Bay 50.00 100.00
4 Chief Bender 200.00 400.00
5 Bill Bernhardt 50.00 100.00
6 Bill Bradley 50.00 100.00
7 Jack Chesbro 200.00 400.00
8 Jimmy Collins 200.00 400.00
9 Sam Crawford 225.00 450.00
10 Lou Criger 50.00 100.00
11 Lave Cross 50.00 100.00
12 Monty Cross 50.00 100.00
13 Harry Davis 50.00 100.00
14 Bill Dineen 50.00 100.00
15 Pat Donovan 50.00 100.00
16 Pat Dougherty 50.00 100.00
17 Norman Elberfeld 50.00 100.00
18 Hobe Ferris 50.00 100.00
19 Elmer Flick 150.00 300.00
20 Buck Freeman 50.00 100.00
21 Fred Glade 50.00 100.00
22 Clark Griffith 150.00 300.00
23 Charles Hickman 50.00 100.00
24 William Holmes 50.00 100.00
25 Harry Howell 50.00 100.00
26 Frank Isbell 50.00 100.00
27 Albert Jacobson 50.00 100.00
28 Ban Johnson PRES 225.00 450.00
29 Fielder Jones 50.00 100.00
30 Adrian Joss 225.00 450.00
31 Willie Keeler 200.00 400.00
32 Nap Lajoie 225.00 450.00
33 Connie Mack MG 225.00 450.00
34 Jimmy McAleer 50.00 100.00
35 Jim McGuire 50.00 100.00
36 Earl Moore 50.00 100.00
37 George Mullen 75.00 150.00
38 Billy Owen 50.00 100.00
39 Fred Parent 50.00 100.00
40 Case Patten 50.00 100.00
41 Eddie Plank 225.00 450.00
42 Ossie Schreckengost 50.00 100.00
43 Jake Stahl 50.00 100.00
44 Fred Stone 50.00 100.00
45 William Sudhoff 50.00 100.00
46 Roy Turner 50.00 100.00
47 Rube Waddell 150.00 300.00
48 Bob Wallace 100.00 200.00
49 G. Harris White 50.00 100.00
50 George Winter 50.00 100.00
51 Cy Young 600.00 1200.00

1906 Fan Craze NL WG3

These cards were distributed as part of a baseball game produced in 1906. The game cost 50 cents upon issuance in 1906. The cards each measure approximately 2 1/2" by 3 1/2" and have rounded corners. The card fronts show a black and white cameo photo of the player, his name, his team, and the game outcome associated with that particular card. The card backs are all the same, each showing "Art Series" and "Fan Craze" in dark blue and white. This set features only players from the National League. Since the cards are unnumbered, they are arranged in alphabetical order in our checklist.

COMPLETE SET (54) 3000.00 6000.00
1 Red Ames 50.00 100.00
2 Ginger Beaumont 50.00 100.00
3 Jake Beckley 200.00 400.00
4 Billy Bergen 50.00 100.00
5 Roger Bresnahan 200.00 400.00
6 George Brown 50.00 100.00
7 Mordacai Brown 200.00 400.00
8 Doc Casey 50.00 100.00
9 Frank Chance 200.00 400.00
10 Fred Clarke 150.00 300.00
11 Tommy Corcoran 50.00 100.00
12 Bill Dahlen 60.00 120.00
13 Mike Donlin 50.00 100.00
14 Charley Dooin 50.00 100.00
15 Mickey Doolin 50.00 100.00
16 Hugh Duffy 150.00 300.00
17 John E. Dunleavy 50.00 100.00
18 Bob Ewing 50.00 100.00
19 Chick Fraser 50.00 100.00
20 Ned Hanlon MG 150.00 300.00
21 Del Howard 50.00 100.00
22 Miller Huggins 150.00 300.00
23 Joe Kelley 150.00 300.00
24 John Kling 50.00 100.00
25 Tommy Leach 50.00 100.00
26 Harry Lumley 50.00 100.00
27 Carl Lundgren 50.00 100.00
28 Bill Maloney 50.00 100.00
29 Dan McGann 50.00 100.00
30 Joe McGinnity 150.00 300.00
31 John McGraw MG 150.00 300.00
32 Harry McIntire 50.00 100.00
33 Kid Nichols 100.00 200.00
34 Mike O'Neil 50.00 100.00
35 Orval Overall 50.00 100.00
36 Frank Pfeffer 50.00 100.00
37 Deacon Philippe 50.00 100.00
38 Charley Pittinger 50.00 100.00
39 Harry C. Pulliam PRES 50.00 100.00
40 Ed Reulbach 50.00 100.00
41 Claude Ritchey 50.00 100.00
42 Cy Seymour 50.00 100.00
43 Jim Sheckard 50.00 100.00
44 Jack Taylor 50.00 100.00
45 Luther (Dummy) Taylor 50.00 100.00
46 Fred Tenney 50.00 100.00
47 Harry Theilman 50.00 100.00
48 Roy Thomas 50.00 100.00
49 Honus Wagner 1000.00 2000.00
50 Jake Weimer 50.00 100.00
51 Bob Wicker 50.00 100.00
52 Vic Willis 150.00 300.00
53 Lew Wiltsie 50.00 100.00
54 Irving Young 50.00 100.00

1994 FanFest Clemente

This standard-size redemption set was reportedly the brainchild of MLB's Ray Schulte, who obtained the cooperation of the five major baseball card manufacturers to each produce 15,000 special Roberto Clemente cards for the '94 All-Star FanFest in Pittsburgh, July 8-12. Each card was redeemable only at each manufacturer's booth for five wrappers of any '94 baseball product from that company. The undistributed cards were reportedly destroyed. It has been estimated that less than 10,000 of each card were distributed. All the cards are numbered on the back as "X of 5."

COMPLETE SET (5) 30.00 80.00
COMMON CARD (1-5) 6.00 15.00
4 Roberto Clemente/1954 Topps Archives 8.00 20.00

1995 FanFest Ryan

Five MLB licensors produced one card each as part of a wrapper redemption program featuring Nolan Ryan for All-Star FanFest in Dallas in July. Pinnacle, Ultra, and Upper Deck cards sport the design of the licensor's regular issue, while Donruss produced a special design and Topps modified Ryan's 1968 rookie card (shared with Jerry Koosman) to feature only Ryan. Again, Ray Schulte, promoter of the Pinnacle All-Star Fan Fest shows, was involved in the creation of this set. The cards are numbered on the back "X of 5."

COMPLETE SET (5) 15.00 40.00
COMMON CARD (1-5) 4.00 10.00
1 Nolan Ryan/1995 Upper Deck 5.00 12.00
4 Nolan Ryan/1995 Ultra 5.00 12.00

1996 FanFest Carlton

These five standard-size cards marked the third straight year that a set of one player's cards were issued in conjunction with the annual All-Star Fan Fest. MLB's Ray Schulte, who originated the idea of these cards was again instrumental in arranging for the companies to issue these cards as part of a wrapper redemption program.

COMPLETE SET (5) 10.00 25.00
COMMON CARD (1-5) 2.00 5.00
3 Steve Carlton Pinnacle 2.50 6.00
4 Steve Carlton/1965 Topps 2.50 6.00

1997 FanFest Jackie Robinson

These five cards marked the fourth straight year that a set of one player's cards were issued in conjunction with the annual All-Star Fan Fest. MLB's Ray Schulte, who originated the idea of these cards was again instrumental in arranging for the companies to issue these cards as part of a wrapper redemption program. Fleer/SkyBox also issued a Ultra Larry Doby card as part of the Fan Fest celebration. This card is priced below but not considered part of the Robinson set.

COMPLETE SET (5) 10.00 25.00
COMMON CARD (1-5) 2.00 5.00
6 Larry Doby Fleer Ultra 2.00 5.00

1998 FanFest Brock

These five cards marked the fifth straight year that a set of one player's cards were issued in conjunction with the annual All-Star FanFest. This five-card set features Lou Brock's cards including a reprint of his Topps 1962 Rookie card. The cards were issued as part of a wrapper redemption program.

COMPLETE SET (5) 8.00 20.00
COMMON CARD (1-5) 2.00 5.00
1 Lou Brock/1962 Topps 2.50 6.00

1999 FanFest Yastrzemski

This four-card standard-size set was issued as a wrapper redemption at the Baseball All-Star Fanfest held in Boston in July, 1999. Each major manufacturer issued a card of Carl Yastrzemski, who played more than 20 seasons for the Boston Red Sox. Only four cards were issued in 1999 due to Pinnacle's bankruptcy and subsequent leaving of the card producing business.

COMPLETE SET (4) 8.00 20.00
COMMON CARD (1-4) 2.00 5.00
1 Carl Yastrzemski/1960 Topps 2.50 6.00

2000 FanFest Aaron

COMPLETE SET (4) 7.50 15.00
COMMON CARD (1-4) 1.60 4.00

2000 FanFest Aaron Mastercard

1 Hank Aaron 2.00 5.00

2002 FanFest

COMPLETE SET (8) 6.00 15.00
1 Derek Jeter 2.00 5.00
Fleer
2 Ichiro Suzuki 2.00 5.00
Upper Deck
3 Sammy Sosa 1.00 2.50
Finest
3A Sammy Sosa REF 6.00 15.00
Finest
4 Barry Bonds 1.00 2.50
Studio
5 Robin Yount .40 1.00
Studio
6 Geoff Jenkins .20 .50
Finest
7 Ben Sheets .20 .50
Upper Deck
8 Richie Sexson .20 .50
Fleer

2002 FanFest Memorabilia

COMPLETE SET (4) 20.00 50.00
1 Barry Bonds 4.00 10.00
Studio
2 Derek Jeter 8.00 20.00
Fleer
3 Sammy Sosa 4.00 10.00
Topps
4 Ichiro Suzuki 8.00 20.00
Upper Deck

2003 Fanfest All-Star

COMPLETE SET 20.00 40.00
COMMON CARD .40 1.00
COMMON MEMORABILIA CARD 4.00 8.00
1 Hideki Matsui Base 5.00 10.00
Upper Deck
2 Barry Bonds Base 5.00 10.00
Topps
3 Derek Jeter Base 5.00 10.00
(Fleer Authentix
4 Sammy Sosa Base 4.00 8.00
Studio Masterstrokes
5 Frank Thomas 1.00 2.50
Upper Deck
6 Bartolo Colon .60 1.50
Topps
7 Paul Konerko .60 1.50
Fleer Authentix
8 Magglio Ordonez .75 2.00
Studio

2005 FanFest All-Star

COMPLETE SET (9)
COMMON JERSEY (1-3)
COMMON DUAL CARD
1 Ivan Rodriguez JSY 8.00 20.00
2 Jeremy Bonderman JSY 5.00 12.00
3 Dmitri Young JSY 4.00 10.00
4 Derek Jeter 2.00 5.00
5 Alex Rodriguez 1.50 4.00
6 Albert Pujols 2.00 5.00
7 Al Kaline 1.25 3.00
Ivan Rodriguez
8 Ivan Rodriguez 1.25 3.00
Al Kaline
9 Al Kaline 1.25 3.00
Ivan Rodriguez

2009 Fathead Tradeables

1 Dustin Pedroia 1.50 4.00
2 Albert Pujols 2.00 5.00
3 Chase Utley 1.00 2.50
4 Evan Longoria 1.00 2.50
5 David Wright 1.25 3.00
6 Derek Jeter 4.00 10.00
7 Alfonso Soriano 1.00 2.50
8 Justin Morneau 1.00 2.50
9 Ryan Braun 1.00 2.50
10 Cliff Lee 1.00 2.50
11 Tim Lincecum 1.00 2.50
12 Ervin Santana .60 1.50
13 Ronnie Belliard .60 1.50
14 Michael Young .60 1.50
15 Andre Ethier 1.00 2.50
16 Adrian Beltre 1.50 4.00
17 Jair Jurrjens .60 1.50
18 Aubrey Huff .60 1.50
19 Edinson Volquez .60 1.50
20 Jack Cust .60 1.50
21 Josh Johnson 1.00 2.50
22 Chris Young .60 1.50
23 Alex Rios .60 1.50
24 Troy Tulowitzki 1.50 4.00
25 Ryan Doumit .60 1.50
26 Alex Gordon 1.00 2.50
27 Curtis Granderson 1.25 3.00
28 Dan Haren .60 1.50
29 Daisuke Matsuzaka 1.00 2.50
30 Brad Ziegler .60 1.50
31 Brad Lidge .60 1.50
32 Mark Buehrle 1.00 2.50
33 Miguel Tejada 1.00 2.50
34 Bengie Molina .60 1.50
35 Andy Pettitte 1.00 2.50
36 Victor Martinez 1.00 2.50
37 Yadier Molina 2.00 5.00
38 Carlos Zambrano 1.00 2.50
39 Joba Chamberlain .60 1.50
40 Roy Halladay 1.00 2.50
41 Todd Helton 1.00 2.50
42 Russell Martin .60 1.50
43 Scott Kazmir .60 1.50
44 Jason Bay 1.00 2.50
45 Chad Billingsley 1.00 2.50
46 Joe Nathan .60 1.50
47 Melvin Mora .60 1.50
48 Johan Santana 1.00 2.50
49 Mike Lowell .60 1.50
50 Carlos Delgado .60 1.50
51 Justin Upton 1.00 2.50
52 Geovany Soto 1.00 2.50
53 Lance Berkman 1.00 2.50
54 Yuniesky Betancourt .60 1.50
55 Jermaine Dye .60 1.50
56 Jose Guillen .60 1.50
57 James Shields .60 1.50
58 Felix Hernandez 1.00 2.50
59 Kyle Lohse .60 1.50
60 Ricky Nolasco .60 1.50
61 John Lackey 1.00 2.50
62 Jacoby Ellsbury 1.25 3.00
63 Travis Hafner .60 1.50
64 Magglio Ordonez 1.00 2.50
65 Paul Konerko 1.00 2.50
66 Brian Wilson 1.50 4.00
67 Hunter Pence 1.00 2.50
68 Derrek Lee .60 1.50
69 Brandon Webb 1.00 2.50
70 Manny Ramirez 1.50 4.00
71 Hanley Ramirez 1.00 2.50
72 Corey Hart .60 1.50
73 Torii Hunter .60 1.50
74 Josh Hamilton 1.00 2.50
75 Carl Crawford 1.00 2.50
76 Brian McCann 1.00 2.50
77 Troy Glaus .60 1.50
78 Cristian Guzman .60 1.50
79 Brandon Phillips .60 1.50
80 Brad Hawpe .60 1.50
81 Justin Verlander 1.50 4.00
82 Carlos Marmol 1.00 2.50
83 Joe Saunders .60 1.50
84 Kevin Youkilis .60 1.50
85 Delmon Young 1.00 2.50
86 Alex Rodriguez 2.00 5.00
87 Roy Oswalt 1.00 2.50
88 Mike Cameron .60 1.50
89 Kosuke Fukudome 1.00 2.50
90 Aaron Rowand .60 1.50
91 Dan Uggla .60 1.50
92 Mariano Rivera 2.00 5.00
93 Vladimir Guerrero 1.00 2.50
94 J.D. Drew .60 1.50
95 Placido Polanco .60 1.50
96 Robinson Cano 1.00 2.50
97 J.J. Hardy .60 1.50
98 Jonathan Papelbon 1.00 2.50
99 James Loney .60 1.50
100 Adrian Gonzalez 1.25 3.00
101 Nate McLouth .60 1.50
102 Garrett Atkins .60 1.50
103 Ryan Zimmerman 1.00 2.50
104 Jim Thome 1.00 2.50
105 Carlos Lee .60 1.50
106 Josh Beckett .60 1.50
107 Jay Bruce 1.00 2.50
108 Ichiro Suzuki 2.00 5.00
109 Ryan Dempster .60 1.50
110 Hideki Matsui 1.50 4.00
111 Jayson Werth 1.00 2.50
112 Rafael Furcal .60 1.50
113 Vernon Wells .60 1.50
114 Ryan Howard 1.25 3.00
115 Chris Young .60 1.50
116 Grady Sizemore 1.00 2.50
117 Brian Roberts .60 1.50
118 Ian Kinsler 1.00 2.50
119 Carlos Pena 1.00 2.50
120 Jon Lester 1.00 2.50
121 David DeJesus .60 1.50
122 Miguel Cabrera 1.50 4.00
123 Freddy Sanchez .60 1.50
124 Carlos Beltran 1.00 2.50
125 Joe Mauer 1.25 3.00
126 Carlos Quentin .60 1.50
127 Jason Varitek 1.50 4.00
128 Jose Reyes 1.00 2.50
129 Jimmy Rollins 1.00 2.50
130 Chris Davis 1.00 2.50
131 Jake Peavy .60 1.50
132 Cole Hamels 1.25 3.00
133 Fausto Carmona .60 1.50
134 David Ortiz 1.50 4.00
135 Francisco Liriano .60 1.50
136 Prince Fielder 1.00 2.50
137 Johnny Damon 1.00 2.50
138 Stephen Drew .60 1.50
139 Adam LaRoche .60 1.50
140 Nick Markakis 1.25 3.00
141 A.J. Pierzynski .60 1.50
142 Jeremy Guthrie .60 1.50
143 Jorge Posada 1.00 2.50
144 Ryan Ludwick 1.00 2.50
145 Aramis Ramirez .60 1.50
146 Chien-Ming Wang 1.00 2.50
147 Shane Victorino 1.00 2.50
148 Justin Duchscherer .60 1.50
149 Chipper Jones 1.50 4.00
150 B.J. Upton 1.00 2.50

2009 Fat Head Tradeables Logos

L1 Arizona Diamondbacks .60 1.50
L2 Atlanta Braves .60 1.50
L3 Baltimore Orioles .60 1.50
L4 Boston Red Sox 1.50 4.00
L5 Chicago Cubs .60 1.50
L6 Chicago White Sox .60 1.50
L7 Cincinnati Reds .60 1.50
L8 Cleveland Indians .60 1.50
L9 Colorado Rockies .60 1.50
L10 Detroit Tigers .60 1.50
L11 Florida Marlins .60 1.50
L12 Houston Astros .60 1.50
L13 Kansas City Royals .60 1.50
L14 Los Angeles Dodgers .60 1.50
L15 Los Angeles Angels .60 1.50
L16 Milwaukee Brewers .60 1.50
L17 Minnesota Twins .60 1.50
L18 New York Mets .60 1.50
L19 New York Yankees 1.50 4.00
L20 Oakland Athletics .60 1.50
L21 Philadelphia Phillies .60 1.50
L22 Pittsburgh Pirates .60 1.50
L23 San Diego Padres .60 1.50
L24 San Francisco Giants .60 1.50
L25 Seattle Mariners .60 1.50
L26 St. Louis Cardinals .60 1.50
L27 Tampa Bay Rays .60 1.50
L28 Texas Rangers .60 1.50
L29 Toronto Blue Jays .60 1.50
L30 Washington Nationals .60 1.50

2010 Fathead Tradeables

1 Derek Jeter 4.00 10.00
2 Chase Utley 1.00 2.50
3 Albert Pujols 2.00 5.00
4 Joe Mauer 1.25 3.00
5 Tim Lincecum 1.00 2.50
6 Zack Greinke 1.50 4.00
7 Shin-Soo Choo 1.00 2.50
8 Ryan Braun 1.00 2.50
9 Jimmy Rollins 1.00 2.50
10 Ichiro Suzuki 2.00 5.00
11 Brian Roberts .60 1.50
12 Josh Hamilton 1.00 2.50
13 C.C. Sabathia 1.00 2.50
14 David Ortiz 1.50 4.00
15 Mark Buehrle 1.00 2.50
16 Rick Porcello 1.00 2.50
17 Johan Santana 1.00 2.50
18 Adam Dunn 1.00 2.50
19 Felix Hernandez 1.00 2.50
20 Nate McLouth .60 1.50
21 James Loney .60 1.50
22 Pablo Sandoval 1.00 2.50
23 Chris Coghlan .60 1.50
24 Andrew Bailey .60 1.50
25 Hanley Ramirez 1.00 2.50
26 Justin Verlander 1.50 4.00
27 Matt Holliday 1.50 4.00
28 Aramis Ramirez .60 1.50
29 Adam Lind 1.00 2.50
30 Torii Hunter .60 1.50
31 Ryan Theriot .60 1.50
32 Curtis Granderson 1.25 3.00
33 Mark Teixeira 1.00 2.50
34 Heath Bell .60 1.50
35 Bobby Abreu .60 1.50
36 Carlos Lee .60 1.50
37 Colby Rasmus 1.00 2.50
38 Jayson Werth 1.00 2.50
39 Justin Morneau 1.00 2.50
40 Kurt Suzuki .60 1.50
41 Michael Young .60 1.50
42 Nick Markakis 1.25 3.00
43 Prince Fielder 1.00 2.50
44 Ryan Zimmerman 1.00 2.50
45 Jacoby Ellsbury 1.25 3.00
46 Dustin Pedroia 1.50 4.00
47 Chipper Jones 1.50 4.00
48 Francisco Rodriguez 1.00 2.50
49 Troy Tulowitzki 1.50 4.00
50 Jose Reyes 1.00 2.50
51 David Wright 1.25 3.00
52 Chris Carpenter 1.00 2.50
53 A.J. Pierzynski .60 1.50
54 Alfonso Soriano 1.00 2.50
55 Kendry Morales .60 1.50
56 Miguel Cabrera 1.50 4.00
57 Paul Konerko 1.00 2.50
58 Carlos Zambrano 1.00 2.50
59 Andrew McCutchen 1.50 4.00
60 Adam Wainwright 1.00 2.50
61 Aaron Hill .60 1.50
62 Joey Votto 1.50 4.00
63 Lance Berkman 1.00 2.50
64 Nelson Cruz 1.50 4.00
65 Shane Victorino 1.00 2.50
66 Kevin Youkilis .60 1.50
67 Jered Weaver 1.00 2.50
68 Yadier Molina 2.00 5.00
69 Evan Longoria 1.00 2.50
70 Dan Haren .60 1.50
71 Carl Crawford 1.00 2.50
72 Carlos Beltran 1.00 2.50
73 Grady Sizemore 1.00 2.50
74 Ian Kinsler 1.00 2.50
75 Jake Peavy .60 1.50
76 Matt Kemp 1.25 3.00
77 Matt Cain 1.00 2.50
78 Raul Ibanez 1.00 2.50
79 Michael Cuddyer .60 1.50
80 Derrek Lee .60 1.50
81 Carlos Pena 1.00 2.50
82 Chad Billingsley 1.00 2.50
83 Jason Bartlett .60 1.50
84 Josh Johnson 1.00 2.50
85 Justin Upton 1.00 2.50
86 Jonathan Papelbon 1.00 2.50
87 Mark Reynolds .60 1.50
88 Manny Ramirez 1.50 4.00
89 Mariano Rivera 2.00 5.00
90 Ryan Howard 1.25 3.00
91 Adam Jones 1.00 2.50
92 Adrian Gonzalez 1.25 3.00
93 Josh Beckett .60 1.50
94 Andre Ethier 1.00 2.50
95 Brian McCann 1.00 2.50
96 Alex Rodriguez 2.00 5.00
97 Brandon Phillips .60 1.50
98 Andy LaRoche .60 1.50
99 Billy Butler .60 1.50
100 Todd Helton 1.00 2.50

2011 Fathead Tradeables

1 Buster Posey 2.00 5.00
2 Josh Hamilton 1.00 2.50
3 Roy Halladay 1.00 2.50
4 Felix Hernandez 1.00 2.50
5 Joey Votto 1.50 4.00
6 David Wright 1.25 3.00
7 Brian Wilson 1.50 4.00
8 Joe Mauer 1.25 3.00
9 Kevin Youkilis .60 1.50
10 C.C. Sabathia 1.00 2.50
11 Jason Heyward 1.25 3.00
12 Paul Konerko 1.00 2.50
13 Prince Fielder 1.00 2.50
14 Ubaldo Jimenez .60 1.50
15 Joakim Soria .60 1.50
16 Alex Rodriguez 2.00 5.00
17 Brandon Phillips .60 1.50
18 Johan Santana 1.00 2.50
19 Garrett Jones .60 1.50
20 Jon Lester 1.00 2.50
21 Albert Pujols 2.00 5.00
22 Matt Kemp 1.25 3.00
23 Jose Bautista 1.00 2.50
24 Jimmy Rollins 1.00 2.50
25 Jason Kubel .60 1.50
26 Neftali Feliz .60 1.50
27 Jose Reyes 1.00 2.50
28 David Price 1.25 3.00
29 Stephen Strasburg 1.50 4.00
30 Torii Hunter .60 1.50
31 Kevin Kouzmanoff .60 1.50
32 Matt Cain 1.00 2.50
33 Chase Utley 1.00 2.50
34 Alfonso Soriano 1.00 2.50
35 Elvis Andrus 1.00 2.50
36 Mark Teixeira 1.00 2.50
37 Ike Davis .60 1.50
38 Matt Holliday 1.50 4.00
39 Justin Morneau 1.00 2.50
40 Shane Victorino 1.00 2.50
41 Carlos Santana 1.50 4.00
42 Justin Verlander 1.50 4.00
43 Nelson Cruz 1.50 4.00
44 Carlos Lee .60 1.50
45 Clayton Kershaw 2.50 6.00
46 Adam Wainwright 1.00 2.50
47 Tim Lincecum 1.00 2.50
48 Troy Tulowitzki 1.50 4.00
49 Scott Rolen 1.00 2.50
50 Corey Hart .60 1.50
51 Carlos Gonzalez 1.00 2.50
52 Hanley Ramirez 1.00 2.50
53 Mariano Rivera 2.00 5.00
54 Mat Latos 1.00 2.50
55 Shin-Soo Choo 1.00 2.50
56 Miguel Cabrera 1.50 4.00
57 Derek Jeter 4.00 10.00
58 Josh Johnson 1.00 2.50
59 Cliff Lee 1.00 2.50
60 Brian McCann 1.00 2.50
61 Andrew Bailey .60 1.50
62 Starlin Castro 1.00 2.50
63 Evan Longoria 1.00 2.50
64 Dustin Pedroia 1.50 4.00
65 Hunter Pence 1.00 2.50
66 Andrew McCutchen 1.50 4.00
67 Michael Young .60 1.50
68 Chris Young .60 1.50
69 Austin Jackson .60 1.50
70 Nick Markakis 1.25 3.00
71 Ichiro Suzuki 2.00 5.00
72 Colby Rasmus 1.00 2.50
73 Ervin Santana .60 1.50
74 Mark Buehrle 1.00 2.50
75 Chipper Jones 1.50 4.00
76 Billy Butler .60 1.50
77 Andre Ethier 1.00 2.50
78 Aubrey Huff .60 1.50
79 Michael Bourn .60 1.50
80 Chris Carpenter 1.00 2.50
81 Martin Prado .60 1.50
82 Gordon Beckham .60 1.50
83 Marlon Byrd .60 1.50
84 Robinson Cano 1.00 2.50
85 Adam Jones 1.00 2.50
86 Justin Upton 1.00 2.50
87 Jered Weaver 1.00 2.50
88 Bobby Abreu .60 1.50
89 Ryan Howard 1.25 3.00
90 Jay Bruce 1.00 2.50
91 Clay Buchholz .60 1.50
92 Ryan Zimmerman 1.00 2.50
93 Jonathan Broxton .60 1.50
94 Nick Swisher 1.00 2.50
95 Denard Span .60 1.50
96 Ryan Braun 1.00 2.50
97 Ian Kinsler 1.00 2.50
98 Aramis Ramirez .60 1.50
99 David Ortiz 1.50 4.00
100 Heath Bell .60 1.50

1939 Father and Son Shoes

These black and white blank-backed cards, which measure approximately 3" by 4" feature members of both Philadelphia area baseball teams. The fronts have a posed action shot with the player's name, position and team on the bottom. Since these cards are unnumbered, we have sequenced them in alphabetical order.

COMPLETE SET 750.00 1500.00
1 Moe Arnovich 50.00 100.00
2 Earl Brucker 50.00 100.00
3 George Caster 50.00 100.00
4 Sam Chapman 60.00 120.00
5 Spud Davis 50.00 100.00
6 Joe Gantenbein 50.00 100.00
7 Bob Johnson 60.00 120.00
8 Chuck Klein 100.00 200.00
9 Herschel Martin 50.00 100.00
10 Pinky May 50.00 100.00
11 Wally Moses 60.00 120.00
12 Emmitt Mueller 50.00 100.00
13 Hugh Mulcahy 50.00 100.00
14 Skeeter Newsome 50.00 100.00
15 Claude Passeau 60.00 120.00
16 George Scharein 50.00 100.00
17 Dick Siebert 50.00 100.00

1910-13 Fatima Cigarettes Premiums

These 12 1/2" by 19" black and white blank-backed photos were issued by Fatima as a premium promotion. The player's photo takes up most of the card with a brief biography and advertisement for Fatima on the bottom. There may be additions to this checklist so any additional information is appreciated.

COMPLETE SET 3000.00 6000.00
15 Christy Mathewson 750.00 1500.00
22 Ty Cobb 1500.00 3000.00
31 Pittsburgh Pirates/1913 250.00 500.00
51 Walter Johnson 1000.00 2000.00

1913 Fatima Teams T200

The cards in this 16-card set measure approximately 2 5/8" by 5 13/16". The 1913 Fatima Cigarettes issue contains unnumbered glossy surface team cards. Both St. Louis team cards are considered difficult to obtain. A large 13" by 21" unnumbered, heavy cardboard parallel premium issue is also known to exist and is quite scarce. These unnumbered team cards are ordered below by team alphabetical order within league. Listed pricing references raw "VgEx" condition.

COMPLETE SET (16) 7500.00 15000.00
1 Boston Americans 300.00 500.00
2 Chicago Americans 300.00 500.00
3 Cleveland Americans 600.00 1000.00
4 Detroit Americans 700.00 1200.00
5 New York Americans 700.00 1200.00
6 Philadelphia Americans 175.00 300.00
7 St. Louis Americans 600.00 1000.00
8 Washington Americans 300.00 500.00
9 Boston Nationals 1500.00 2500.00
10 Brooklyn Nationals 300.00 500.00
11 Chicago Nationals 250.00 400.00
12 Cincinnati Nationals 175.00 300.00
13 New York Nationals 350.00 600.00
14 Philadelphia Nationals 175.00 300.00
15 Pittsburgh Nationals 300.00 500.00
16 St. Louis Nationals 300.00 500.00

1913 Fatima Teams Premiums T200

These premiums, which measure approximately 13" by 21" parallel the regular Fatima set. There is no pricing due to scarcity.

1914 Fatima Players T222

The cards in this 52-card set measure approximately 2 1/2" by 4 1/2" and are unnumbered. The cards are quite fragile on thin, brittle paper stock. The set was produced in 1914 by Liggett and Myers Tobacco Co. The players in the set have been alphabetized and numbered for reference in the checklist below.

COMPLETE SET (52) 25000.00 50000.00
1 Grover C. Alexander 750.00 1500.00
2 Jimmy Archer 400.00 800.00
3 James Austin 500.00 1000.00
4 Jack Barry 400.00 800.00
5 George Baumgardner 400.00 800.00
6 Rube Benton 400.00 800.00
7 Roger Bresnahan 750.00 1500.00
8 Mordecai Brown 750.00 1500.00
9 George J. Burns 400.00 800.00
10 Joe Bush 400.00 800.00
11 George Chalmers 400.00 800.00
12 Frank Chance 1250.00 2500.00
13 Albert Demaree 400.00 800.00
14 Arthur Fletcher 400.00 800.00
15 Earl Hamilton 400.00 800.00
16 John Henry 500.00 1000.00
17 Byron Houck 400.00 800.00
18 Miller Huggins 750.00 1500.00
19 Hugh Jennings MG 750.00 1500.00
20 Walter Johnson 5000.00 10000.00
21 Ray Keating 400.00 800.00
22 John Lapp 400.00 800.00
23 Thomas Leach 400.00 800.00
24 Nemo Leibold 400.00 800.00
25 John Frank Lelivelt 400.00 800.00
26 Hans Lobert 500.00 1000.00
27 Lee Magee 400.00 800.00
28 Sherry Magee 600.00 1200.00
29 Fritz Maisel 400.00 800.00
30 Rube Marquard 750.00 1500.00
31 George McBride 400.00 800.00
32 Stuffy McInnis 400.00 800.00
33 Larry McLean 400.00 800.00
34 Raymond Morgan 400.00 800.00
35 Eddie Murphy 400.00 800.00
36 Red Murray 400.00 800.00
37 Rube Oldring 500.00 1000.00
38 William J. Orr 400.00 800.00
39 Hub Perdue 500.00 1000.00
40 Arthur Phelan 400.00 800.00
41 Ed Reulbach 600.00 1200.00
42 Vic Saier 400.00 800.00
43 Slim Sallee 400.00 800.00
44 Wally Schang 500.00 1000.00
45 Frank Schulte 500.00 1000.00
46 Jimmy Smith 400.00 800.00
47 Amos Strunk 400.00 800.00
48 Bill Sweeney 400.00 800.00
49 Lefty Tyler 500.00 1000.00
50 Oscar Vitt 400.00 800.00
51 Ivy Wingo 400.00 800.00
52 Heinie Zimmerman 400.00 800.00

1993 Fax Pax World of Sport

COMPLETE SET (40) 6.00 15.00
1 Roger Clemens .75 2.00
2 Ken Griffey Jr. 1.50 4.00
3 John Olerud .20 .50
4 Nolan Ryan 1.25 3.00

1982 FBI Discs

These discs were issued in Canada. These blank-backed circular white cutouts from the perforated bottoms of boxes of various FBI Foods' Bantam drinks measure approximately 2 7/8" in diameter and display black-and-white player head shots. Two players were featured on each box bottom. The player's name appears to the left of his photo; his team's name appears to the right. The cards are unnumbered and checklisted below in alphabetical order.

COMPLETE SET (32) 600.00 1200.00
*COMPLETE BOXES: 2X COMBINED PRICES
1 Don Baylor 8.00 20.00
2 Vida Blue 8.00 20.00
3 George Brett 50.00 120.00
4 Rod Carew 40.00 80.00
5 Steve Carlton 40.00 80.00
6 Gary Carter 40.00 80.00
7 Warren Cromartie 4.00 10.00
8 Andre Dawson 30.00 60.00
9 Rollie Fingers 15.00 40.00
10 Steve Garvey 20.00 50.00
11 Rich Gossage 12.50 30.00
12 Alfredo Griffin 4.00 10.00
13 Bill Gullickson 4.00 10.00
14 Steve Henderson 4.00 10.00
15 Keith Hernandez 8.00 20.00
16 Larry Hisle 4.00 10.00
17 John Mayberry 4.00 10.00
18 Al Oliver 8.00 20.00
19 Dave Parker 8.00 20.00
20 Tim Raines 15.00 40.00
21 Jim Rice 8.00 20.00
22 Steve Rogers 4.00 10.00
23 Pete Rose 40.00 100.00
24 Nolan Ryan 100.00 250.00
25 Mike Schmidt 40.00 100.00
26 Tom Seaver 40.00 80.00
27 Ken Singleton 4.00 10.00
28 Dave Stieb 4.00 10.00
29 Bruce Sutter 8.00 20.00
30 Garry Templeton 4.00 10.00
31 Ellis Valentine 4.00 10.00
32 Dave Winfield 40.00 80.00

1993 FCA 50

This 50-card standard-size set was sponsored by Fellowship of Christian Athletes. The color player photos on the fronts are accented on three sides by a thin pink stripe; the card face itself shades from blue to white as one moves toward the bottom. The FCA logo, featuring a cross with two olive branches, is superimposed in the upper left corner, while the player's name is printed beneath the picture and his sport in the pink stripe on the left. On a blue background, the backs carry a close-up photo, biography, and the player's testimony.

COMPLETE SET (50) 10.00 20.00
18 Brian Harper BB .30 .75
20 Ed Hearn BB .20 .50
27 Jerry Kindall BB .20 .50
35 Greg Olson C BB .20 .50
47 Bill Wegman BB .20 .50

1996-98 Fiesta Chips

These chips, issued over a two year period, featured various baseball players and themes. Since they are unnumbered, we have sequenced them alphabetically within groups which are arranged by date of issue

COMPLETE SET 40.00 100.00
1 Ray Boone 2.00 5.00
Sports Edition
2 Mickey McDermott 2.00 5.00
Sports Edition
3 Duke Snider 6.00 15.00
Sports Edition
4 Ted Radcliffe 4.00 10.00
Negro League 3/97
5 Nap Gulley 2.50 6.00
Negro League 3/97
6 Marlon Duckett 2.50 6.00
Negro League 6/97
7 Tommy Henrich/6/97 4.00 10.00
8 Sam Jethroe 2.50 6.00
Negro League 6/97
9 Buck O'Neil 4.00 10.00
Negro League 9/97
10 Walt Dropo 2.00 5.00
ROY 1950 12/97
11 Lefty Mathis 2.00 5.00
Negro League 12/97
12 Ed Kranepool/1969 Mets 6/98 2.50 6.00
13 Amos Otis/1969 Mets 6/98 2.50 6.00
14 Ron Swoboda/1969 Mets 6/98 2.50 6.00
15 Pete Coscarat 2.00 5.00
Brooklyn Dodgers/9/98
16 Al Gionfriddo 2.00 5.00
Brooklyn Dodgers/9/98
17 Norm Sherry 2.00 5.00
Brooklyn Dodgers/9/98

1984 Fifth National Convention

These eight standard-size cards were given away at the 1984 5th Annual National held at the Aspen Hotel in Parsippany, N.J. August 9-12. Cards 1-5 below feature posed black-and-white player photos with white outer borders and brown inner borders. The player's name appears in white lettering within the brown margin below the photo. Cards 6-8 feature posed color player photos framed by a purple line and with green outer borders. Purple stars appear in the photos' upper corners. The player's name appears in white lettering in the bottom green margin. All the white backs carry the logo for the Fifth Annual National. All the players pictured were supposed to sign free autographs at the show. The cards are unnumbered and checklisted below in alphabetical order within each design type.

COMPLETE SET (8) 1.00 2.50
1 Tom Gorman UMP .08 .25
2 Bud Harrelson .20 .50
3 Gene Hermanski .08 .25
4 Ed Lopat .08 .25
5 Bobby Thomson .30 .75
6 Joe Collins .08 .25
7 Larry Doby .60 1.50
8 Willard Marshall .08 .25

1984 Fifth National Convention Tickets

This 18-card set of 5th Annual National Convention Tickets measures approximately 2" by 5 1/2" and features black-and-white head photos of 1954 baseball players on an orange background. The player's name and team are printed in black below the photo. The convention was held in Parsippany, New Jersey, on August 9 through August 12 at the Aspen Hotel. The backs are blank. The tickets are checklisted below in alphabetical order. The Dusty Rhodes ticket was available as a comp ticket only as none were available for sale.

COMPLETE SET (18) 12.50 30.00
1 Hank Bauer .40 1.00
2 Yogi Berra 1.00 2.50
3 Alvin Dark .30 .75
4 Carl Erskine .40 1.00
5 Carl Furillo .40 1.00
6 Whitey Ford 1.00 2.50
7 Bob Grim .20 .50
8 Gil Hodges 1.00 2.50
9 Whitey Lockman .30 .75
10 Sal Maglie .20 .50
Johnny Antonelli
11 Mickey Mantle 4.00 10.00
12 Willie Mays 2.00 5.00
13 Pee Wee Reese 1.00 2.50
14 Allie Reynolds .40 1.00
15 Dusty Rhodes .60 1.50
16 Jackie Robinson 2.00 5.00
17 Duke Snider 1.50 4.00
18 Hoyt Wilhelm .60 1.50

1984 Fifth National Convention Uncut Sheet

This nine-card uncut sheet features players who would be signing at the 5th National Sports Card Convention. The players on the sheet are featured in black and white photos and the back is blank.

1 Uncut Sheet 2.00 5.00
Bill Hands
Sal Yvars
Eddie Lopat
H

1993 Finest Promos

*REFRACTORS: 20X to 40X VALUE
88 Roberto Alomar 3.00 8.00
98 Don Mattingly AS 6.00 15.00
107 Nolan Ryan 12.50 30.00

1993 Finest

This 199-card standard-size single series set is widely recognized as one of the most important issues of the 1990's. The Finest brand was Topps first attempt at the super-premium card market. Production was announced at 4,000 cases and cards were distributed exclusively through hobby dealers in the fall of 1993. This was the first time in the history of the hobby that a major manufacturer publicly released production figures. Cards were issued in seven-card foil fin-wrapped packs that carried a suggested retail price of $3.99. The product was a smashing success upon release with pack prices immediately soaring well above suggested retail prices. The popularity of the product has continued to grow throughout the years as it's place in hobby lore is now well solidified. The cards have silver-blue metallic finishes on their fronts and feature color player action photos. The set's title appears at the top, and the player's name is shown at the bottom. J.T. Snow is the only Rookie Card of note in this set.

COMPLETE SET (199) 40.00 100.00
1 David Justice 1.00 2.50
2 Lou Whitaker 1.00 2.50
3 Bryan Harvey .60 1.50
4 Carlos Garcia .60 1.50
5 Sid Fernandez .60 1.50
6 Brett Butler 1.00 2.50
7 Scott Cooper .60 1.50
8 B.J. Surhoff 1.00 2.50
9 Steve Finley 1.00 2.50
10 Curt Schilling 1.00 2.50
11 Jeff Bagwell 1.50 4.00
12 Alex Cole .60 1.50
13 John Olerud 1.00 2.50
14 John Smiley .60 1.50
15 Bip Roberts .60 1.50
16 Albert Belle 1.00 2.50
17 Duane Ward .60 1.50
18 Alan Trammell 1.00 2.50
19 Andy Benes .60 1.50
20 Reggie Sanders 1.00 2.50
21 Todd Zeile .60 1.50
22 Rick Aguilera .60 1.50
23 Dave Hollins .60 1.50
24 Jose Rijo .60 1.50
25 Matt Williams 1.00 2.50
26 Sandy Alomar Jr. .60 1.50
27 Alex Fernandez .60 1.50
28 Ozzie Smith 4.00 10.00
29 Ramon Martinez .60 1.50
30 Bernie Williams 1.50 4.00
31 Gary Sheffield 1.00 2.50
32 Eric Karros 1.00 2.50
33 Frank Viola 1.00 2.50
34 Kevin Young 1.00 2.50
35 Ken Hill .60 1.50
36 Tony Fernandez .60 1.50
37 Tim Wakefield 2.50 6.00
38 John Kruk 1.00 2.50
39 Chris Sabo .60 1.50
40 Marquis Grissom 1.00 2.50
41 Glenn Davis .60 1.50
42 Jeff Montgomery .60 1.50
43 Kenny Lofton 1.00 2.50
44 John Burkett .60 1.50
45 Darryl Hamilton .60 1.50
46 Jim Abbott 1.50 4.00
47 Ivan Rodriguez 1.50 4.00
48 Eric Young .60 1.50
49 Mitch Williams .60 1.50
50 Harold Reynolds 1.00 2.50
51 Brian Harper .60 1.50
52 Rafael Palmeiro 1.50 4.00
53 Bret Saberhagen 1.00 2.50
54 Jeff Conine 1.00 2.50
55 Ivan Calderon .60 1.50
56 Juan Guzman .60 1.50
57 Carlos Baerga .60 1.50
58 Charles Nagy .60 1.50
59 Wally Joyner 1.00 2.50
60 Charlie Hayes .60 1.50
61 Shane Mack .60 1.50
62 Pete Harnisch .60 1.50
63 George Brett 6.00 15.00
64 Lance Johnson .60 1.50
65 Ben McDonald .60 1.50
66 Bobby Bonilla 1.00 2.50
67 Terry Steinbach .60 1.50
68 Ron Gant 1.00 2.50
69 Doug Jones .60 1.50
70 Paul Molitor 1.00 2.50
71 Brady Anderson 1.00 2.50
72 Chuck Finley 1.00 2.50
73 Mark Grace 1.50 4.00
74 Mike Devereaux .60 1.50
75 Tony Phillips .60 1.50
76 Chuck Knoblauch 1.00 2.50
77 Tony Gwynn 3.00 8.00
78 Kevin Appier 1.00 2.50
79 Sammy Sosa 2.50 6.00
80 Mickey Tettleton .60 1.50
81 Felix Jose .60 1.50
82 Mark Langston .60 1.50
83 Gregg Jefferies .60 1.50
84 Andre Dawson AS 1.50 4.00
85 Greg Maddux AS 4.00 10.00
86 Rickey Henderson AS 2.50 6.00
87 Tom Glavine AS 1.50 4.00
88 Roberto Alomar AS 1.50 4.00
89 Darryl Strawberry AS 1.00 2.50
90 Wade Boggs AS 1.50 4.00

91 Bo Jackson AS 2.50 6.00
92 Mark McGwire AS 6.00 15.00
93 Robin Ventura AS 1.00 2.50
94 Joe Carter AS 1.00 2.50
95 Lee Smith AS 1.00 2.50
96 Cal Ripken AS 8.00 20.00
97 Larry Walker AS 1.00 2.50
98 Don Mattingly AS 6.00 15.00
99 Jose Canseco AS 1.50 4.00
100 Dennis Eckersley AS 1.00 2.50
101 Terry Pendleton AS 1.00 2.50
102 Frank Thomas AS 2.50 6.00
103 Barry Bonds AS 6.00 15.00
104 Roger Clemens AS 5.00 12.00
105 Ryne Sandberg AS 4.00 10.00
106 Fred McGriff AS 1.50 4.00
107 Nolan Ryan AS 10.00 25.00
108 Will Clark AS 1.50 4.00
109 Pat Listach AS .60 1.50
110 Ken Griffey Jr. AS 5.00 12.00
111 Cecil Fielder AS 1.00 2.50
112 Kirby Puckett AS 2.50 6.00
113 Dwight Gooden AS 1.00 2.50
114 Barry Larkin AS 1.50 4.00
115 David Cone AS 1.00 2.50
116 Juan Gonzalez AS 1.00 2.50
117 Kent Hrbek 1.00 2.50
118 Tim Wallach .60 1.50
119 Craig Biggio 1.50 4.00
120 Roberto Kelly .60 1.50
121 Gregg Olson .60 1.50
122 Eddie Murray UER 2.50 6.00
122 career strikeouts should be 1224
123 Wil Cordero .60 1.50
124 Jay Buhner 1.00 2.50
125 Carlton Fisk 1.50 4.00
126 Eric Davis 1.00 2.50
127 Doug Drabek .60 1.50
128 Ozzie Guillen 1.00 2.50
129 John Wetteland 1.00 2.50
130 Andres Galarraga 1.00 2.50
131 Ken Caminiti 1.00 2.50
132 Tom Candiotti .60 1.50
133 Pat Borders .60 1.50
134 Kevin Brown 1.00 2.50
135 Travis Fryman 1.00 2.50
136 Kevin Mitchell .60 1.50
137 Greg Swindell .60 1.50
138 Benito Santiago 1.00 2.50
139 Reggie Jefferson .60 1.50
140 Chris Bosio .60 1.50
141 Deion Sanders 1.50 4.00
142 Scott Erickson .60 1.50
143 Howard Johnson .60 1.50
144 Orestes Destrade .60 1.50
145 Jose Guzman .60 1.50
146 Chad Curtis .60 1.50
147 Cal Eldred .60 1.50
148 Willie Greene .60 1.50
149 Tommy Greene .60 1.50
150 Erik Hanson .60 1.50
151 Bob Welch .60 1.50
152 John Jaha .60 1.50
153 Harold Baines 1.00 2.50
154 Randy Johnson 2.50 6.00
155 Al Martin .60 1.50
156 J.T.Snow RC 1.50 4.00
157 Mike Mussina 1.50 4.00
158 Ruben Sierra 1.00 2.50
159 Dean Palmer 1.00 2.50
160 Steve Avery .60 1.50
161 Julio Franco 1.00 2.50
162 Dave Winfield 1.00 2.50
163 Tim Salmon 1.50 4.00
164 Tom Henke .60 1.50
165 Mo Vaughn 1.00 2.50
166 John Smoltz 1.50 4.00
167 Danny Tartabull .60 1.50
168 Delino DeShields .60 1.50
169 Charlie Hough 1.00 2.50
170 Paul O'Neill 1.50 4.00
171 Darren Daulton 1.00 2.50
172 Jack McDowell .60 1.50
173 Junior Felix .60 1.50
174 Jimmy Key 1.00 2.50
175 George Bell .60 1.50
176 Mike Stanton .60 1.50
177 Len Dykstra 1.00 2.50
178 Norm Charlton .60 1.50
179 Eric Anthony .60 1.50
180 Rob Dibble 1.00 2.50
181 Otis Nixon .60 1.50
182 Randy Myers .60 1.50
183 Tim Raines 1.00 2.50
184 Orel Hershiser 1.00 2.50
185 Andy Van Slyke 1.50 4.00
186 Mike Lansing RC 1.00 2.50
187 Ray Lankford 1.00 2.50
188 Mike Morgan .60 1.50
189 Moises Alou 1.00 2.50
190 Edgar Martinez 1.50 4.00
191 John Franco 1.00 2.50
192 Robin Yount 4.00 10.00
193 Bob Tewksbury .60 1.50
194 Jay Bell 1.00 2.50
195 Luis Gonzalez 1.00 2.50
196 Dave Fleming .60 1.50
197 Mike Greenwell .60 1.50
198 David Nied .60 1.50
199 Mike Piazza 6.00 15.00

1993 Finest Refractors

STATED ODDS 1:18
SP CL: 3/10/12/25/34/38-41/47/70/79-81/84
SP CL: 116/123/134/155/159/173/182/193
ASTERISK CARDS: PERCEIVED SCARCITY
28 Ozzie Smith 40.00 80.00
41 Glenn Davis* 60.00 120.00
47 Ivan Rodriguez * 75.00 150.00
63 George Brett 125.00 200.00
77 Tony Gwynn 60.00 120.00
79 Sammy Sosa * 30.00 60.00
81 Felix Jose* 40.00 80.00
85 Greg Maddux AS 100.00 200.00
88 Roberto Alomar AS 40.00 80.00
91 Bo Jackson AS 50.00 100.00
92 Mark McGwire AS 75.00 150.00
96 Cal Ripken AS 200.00 400.00
98 Don Mattingly AS 125.00 250.00
99 Jose Canseco AS ! 40.00 80.00
102 Frank Thomas AS 150.00 300.00
103 Barry Bonds AS 125.00 250.00
104 Roger Clemens AS 125.00 200.00
105 Ryne Sandberg AS 75.00 150.00
107 Nolan Ryan AS ! 300.00 500.00
108 Will Clark AS ! 40.00 80.00
110 Ken Griffey Jr. AS ! 250.00 600.00
112 Kirby Puckett AS 60.00 120.00
114 Barry Larkin AS 40.00 80.00
116 Juan Gonzalez AS * 150.00 250.00
122 Eddie Murray 60.00 120.00
144 Orestes Destrade 75.00 150.00
154 Randy Johnson 75.00 150.00
157 Mike Mussina 40.00 80.00
192 Robin Yount 60.00 120.00
199 Mike Piazza 100.00 200.00

1993 Finest Jumbos

*STARS: 1X TO 2.5X BASIC CARDS
ONE CARD PER SEALED BOX

1994 Finest Pre-Production

COMPLETE SET (40) 30.00 60.00
TOPPS SER.2 ODDS 1:36H/R,1:15J,1:28 CEL
THREE PER REGULAR TOPPS FACTORY SET
NUMBERS CORRESPOND TO BASIC SET
22P Deion Sanders 5.00 12.00
23P Jose Offerman 2.00 5.00
26P Alex Fernandez 2.00 5.00
31P Steve Finley 3.00 8.00
35P Andres Galarraga 3.00 8.00
43P Reggie Sanders 3.00 8.00
47P Dave Hollins 2.00 5.00
52P David Cone 3.00 8.00
59P Dante Bichette 3.00 8.00
61P Orlando Merced 2.00 5.00
62P Brian McRae 2.00 5.00
66P Mike Mussina 5.00 12.00
76P Mike Stanley 2.00 5.00
78P Mark McGwire 20.00 50.00
79P Pat Listach 2.00 5.00
82P Dwight Gooden 3.00 8.00
84P Phil Plantier 2.00 5.00
90P Jeff Russell 2.00 5.00
92P Gregg Jefferies 2.00 5.00
93P Jose Guzman 2.00 5.00
100P John Smoltz 5.00 12.00
102P Jim Thome 5.00 12.00
121P Moises Alou 3.00 8.00
125P Devon White 3.00 8.00
126P Ivan Rodriguez 5.00 12.00
130P Dave Magadan 2.00 5.00
136P Ozzie Smith 12.50 30.00
141P Chris Hoiles 2.00 5.00
149P Jim Abbott 5.00 12.00
151P Bill Swift 2.00 5.00
154P Edgar Martinez 5.00 12.00
157P J.T. Snow 3.00 8.00
159P Alan Trammell 3.00 8.00
163P Roberto Kelly 2.00 5.00
166P Scott Erickson 2.00 5.00
168P Scott Cooper 2.00 5.00
169P Rod Beck 2.00 5.00
177P Dean Palmer 3.00 8.00
182P Todd Van Poppel 2.00 5.00
185P Paul Sorrento 2.00 5.00

1994 Finest

The 1994 Topps Finest baseball set consists of two series of 220 cards each, for a total of 440 standard-size cards. Each series includes 40 special design Finest cards: 20 top 1993 rookies (1-20), 20 top 1994 rookies (421-440) and 40 top veterans (201-240). It's believed that these subset cards are in slightly shorter supply than the basic issue cards, but the manufacturer has never confirmed this. These glossy and metallic cards have a color photo on front with green and gold borders. A color photo on back is accompanied by statistics and a "Finest Moment" note. Some series 2 packs contained either one or two series 1 cards. The only notable Rookie Card is Chan Ho Park.

COMPLETE SET (440) 30.00 80.00
COMPLETE SERIES 1 (220) 15.00 40.00
COMPLETE SERIES 2 (220) 15.00 40.00
SOME SER.2 PACKS HAVE 1 OR 2 SER.1 CARDS
1 Mike Piazza FIN 2.50 6.00
2 Kevin Stocker FIN .30 .75
3 Greg McMichael FIN .30 .75
4 Jeff Conine FIN .50 1.25
5 Rene Arocha FIN .30 .75
6 Aaron Sele FIN .30 .75
7 Brent Gates FIN .30 .75
8 Chuck Carr FIN .30 .75
9 Kirk Rueter FIN .30 .75
10 Mike Lansing FIN .30 .75
11 Al Martin FIN .30 .75
12 Jason Bere FIN .30 .75
13 Troy Neel FIN .30 .75
14 Armando Reynoso FIN .30 .75
15 Jeromy Burnitz FIN .50 1.25
16 Rich Amaral FIN .30 .75
17 David McCarty FIN .30 .75
18 Tim Salmon FIN .75 2.00
19 Steve Cooke FIN .30 .75
20 Wil Cordero FIN .30 .75
21 Kevin Tapani .30 .75
22 Deion Sanders .75 2.00
23 Jose Offerman .30 .75
24 Mark Langston .30 .75
25 Ken Hill .30 .75
26 Alex Fernandez .30 .75
27 Jeff Blauser .30 .75
28 Royce Clayton .30 .75
29 Brad Ausmus .75 2.00
30 Ryan Bowen .30 .75
31 Steve Finley .50 1.25
32 Charlie Hayes .30 .75
33 Jeff Kent .75 2.00
34 Mike Henneman .30 .75
35 Andres Galarraga .50 1.25
36 Wayne Kirby .30 .75
37 Joe Oliver .30 .75
38 Terry Steinbach .30 .75
39 Ryan Thompson .30 .75
40 Luis Alicea .30 .75
41 Randy Velarde .30 .75
42 Bob Tewksbury .30 .75
43 Reggie Sanders .50 1.25
44 Brian Williams .30 .75
45 Joe Orsulak .30 .75
46 Jose Lind .30 .75
47 Dave Hollins .30 .75
48 Graeme Lloyd .30 .75
49 Jim Gott .30 .75
50 Andre Dawson .50 1.25
51 Steve Buechele .30 .75
52 David Cone .50 1.25
53 Ricky Gutierrez .30 .75
54 Lance Johnson .30 .75
55 Tino Martinez .75 2.00
56 Phil Hiatt .30 .75
57 Carlos Garcia .30 .75
58 Danny Darwin .30 .75
59 Dante Bichette .50 1.25
60 Scott Kamieniecki .30 .75
61 Orlando Merced .30 .75
62 Brian McRae .30 .75
63 Pat Kelly .30 .75
64 Tom Henke .30 .75
65 Jeff King .30 .75
66 Mike Mussina .75 2.00
67 Tim Pugh .30 .75
68 Robby Thompson .30 .75
69 Paul O'Neill .75 2.00
70 Hal Morris .30 .75
71 Ron Karkovice .30 .75
72 Joe Girardi .30 .75
73 Eduardo Perez .30 .75
74 Raul Mondesi .50 1.25
75 Mike Gallego .30 .75
76 Mike Stanley .30 .75
77 Kevin Roberson .30 .75
78 Mark McGwire 3.00 8.00
79 Pat Listach .30 .75
80 Eric Davis .50 1.25
81 Mike Bordick .30 .75
82 Dwight Gooden .50 1.25
83 Mike Moore .30 .75
84 Phil Plantier .30 .75
85 Darren Lewis .30 .75
86 Rick Wilkins .30 .75
87 Darryl Strawberry .50 1.25
88 Rob Dibble .50 1.25
89 Greg Vaughn .30 .75
90 Jeff Russell .30 .75
91 Mark Lewis .30 .75
92 Gregg Jefferies .30 .75
93 Jose Guzman .30 .75
94 Kenny Rogers .50 1.25
95 Mark Lemke .30 .75
96 Mike Morgan .30 .75
97 Andujar Cedeno .30 .75
98 Orel Hershiser .50 1.25
99 Greg Swindell .30 .75
100 John Smoltz .75 2.00
101 Pedro A.Martinez RC .30 .75
102 Jim Thome .75 2.00
103 David Segui .30 .75
104 Charles Nagy .30 .75
105 Shane Mack .30 .75
106 John Jaha .30 .75
107 Tom Candiotti .30 .75
108 David Wells .50 1.25
109 Bobby Jones .30 .75
110 Bob Hamelin .30 .75
111 Bernard Gilkey .30 .75
112 Chili Davis .50 1.25
113 Todd Stottlemyre .30 .75
114 Derek Bell .30 .75
115 Mark McLemore .30 .75
116 Mark Whiten .30 .75
117 Mike Devereaux .30 .75
118 Terry Pendleton .50 1.25
119 Pat Meares .30 .75
120 Pete Harnisch .30 .75
121 Moises Alou .50 1.25
122 Jay Buhner .50 1.25
123 Wes Chamberlain .30 .75
124 Mike Perez .30 .75
125 Devon White .50 1.25
126 Ivan Rodriguez .75 2.00
127 Don Slaught .30 .75
128 John Valentin .30 .75
129 Jaime Navarro .30 .75
130 Dave Magadan .30 .75
131 Brady Anderson .50 1.25
132 Juan Guzman .30 .75
133 John Wetteland .50 1.25
134 Dave Stewart .50 1.25
135 Scott Servais .30 .75
136 Ozzie Smith 2.00 5.00
137 Darrin Fletcher .30 .75
138 Jose Mesa .30 .75
139 Wilson Alvarez .30 .75
140 Pete Incaviglia .30 .75
141 Chris Hoiles .30 .75
142 Darryl Hamilton .30 .75
143 Chuck Finley .50 1.25
144 Archi Cianfrocco .30 .75
145 Bill Wegman .30 .75
146 Joey Cora .30 .75
147 Darrell Whitmore .30 .75
148 David Hulse .30 .75
149 Jim Abbott .75 2.00
150 Curt Schilling .50 1.25
151 Bill Swift .30 .75
152 Tommy Greene .30 .75
153 Roberto Mejia .30 .75
154 Edgar Martinez .75 2.00
155 Roger Pavlik .30 .75
156 Randy Tomlin .30 .75
157 J.T. Snow .50 1.25
158 Bob Welch .30 .75
159 Alan Trammell .50 1.25
160 Ed Sprague .30 .75
161 Ben McDonald .30 .75
162 Derrick May .30 .75
163 Roberto Kelly .30 .75
164 Bryan Harvey .30 .75
165 Ron Gant .50 1.25
166 Scott Erickson .30 .75
167 Anthony Young .30 .75
168 Scott Cooper .30 .75
169 Rod Beck .30 .75
170 John Franco .50 1.25
171 Gary DiSarcina .30 .75
172 Dave Fleming .30 .75
173 Wade Boggs .75 2.00
174 Kevin Appier .50 1.25
175 Jose Bautista .30 .75
176 Wally Joyner .50 1.25
177 Dean Palmer .50 1.25
178 Tony Phillips .30 .75
179 John Smiley .30 .75
180 Charlie Hough .50 1.25
181 Scott Fletcher .30 .75
182 Todd Van Poppel .30 .75
183 Mike Blowers .30 .75
184 Willie McGee .50 1.25
185 Paul Sorrento .30 .75
186 Eric Young .30 .75
187 Bret Barberie .30 .75
188 Manuel Lee .30 .75
189 Jeff Branson .30 .75
190 Jim Deshaies .30 .75
191 Ken Caminiti .50 1.25
192 Tim Raines .50 1.25
193 Joe Grahe .30 .75
194 Hipolito Pichardo .30 .75
195 Denny Neagle .50 1.25
196 Dave Staton .30 .75
197 Mike Benjamin .30 .75
198 Milt Thompson .30 .75
199 Bruce Ruffin .30 .75
200 Chris Hammond UER .30 .75
Back of card has Mariners; should be Marlins
201 Tony Gwynn FIN 1.50 4.00
202 Robin Ventura FIN .50 1.25
203 Frank Thomas FIN 1.25 3.00
204 Kirby Puckett FIN 1.25 3.00
205 Roberto Alomar FIN .75 2.00
206 Dennis Eckersley FIN .50 1.25
207 Joe Carter FIN .50 1.25
208 Albert Belle FIN .50 1.25
209 Greg Maddux FIN 2.00 5.00
210 Ryne Sandberg FIN 2.00 5.00
211 Juan Gonzalez FIN .50 1.25
212 Jeff Bagwell FIN .75 2.00
213 Randy Johnson FIN 1.25 3.00
214 Matt Williams FIN .50 1.25
215 Dave Winfield FIN .50 1.25
216 Larry Walker FIN .50 1.25
217 Roger Clemens FIN 2.50 6.00
218 Kenny Lofton FIN .50 1.25
219 Cecil Fielder FIN .50 1.25
220 Darren Daulton FIN .50 1.25
221 John Olerud FIN .50 1.25
222 Jose Canseco FIN .75 2.00
223 Rickey Henderson FIN 1.25 3.00
224 Fred McGriff FIN .75 2.00
225 Gary Sheffield FIN .50 1.25
226 Jack McDowell FIN .30 .75
227 Rafael Palmeiro FIN .75 2.00
228 Travis Fryman FIN .50 1.25
229 Marquis Grissom FIN .50 1.25
230 Barry Bonds FIN 3.00 8.00
231 Carlos Baerga FIN .30 .75
232 Ken Griffey Jr. FIN 2.50 6.00
233 David Justice FIN .50 1.25
234 Bobby Bonilla FIN .50 1.25
235 Cal Ripken FIN 4.00 10.00
236 Sammy Sosa FIN 1.25 3.00
237 Len Dykstra FIN .50 1.25
238 Will Clark FIN .75 2.00
239 Paul Molitor FIN .50 1.25
240 Barry Larkin FIN .75 2.00
241 Bo Jackson 1.25 3.00
242 Mitch Williams .30 .75
243 Ron Darling .30 .75
244 Darryl Kile .50 1.25
245 Geronimo Berroa .30 .75
246 Gregg Olson .30 .75
247 Brian Harper .30 .75
248 Rheal Cormier .30 .75
249 Rey Sanchez .30 .75
250 Jeff Fassero .30 .75
251 Sandy Alomar Jr. .30 .75
252 Chris Bosio .30 .75
253 Andy Stankiewicz .30 .75
254 Harold Baines .50 1.25
255 Andy Ashby .30 .75
256 Tyler Green .30 .75
257 Kevin Brown .50 1.25
258 Mo Vaughn .50 1.25
259 Mike Harkey .30 .75
260 Dave Henderson .30 .75
261 Kent Hrbek .50 1.25
262 Darrin Jackson .30 .75
263 Bob Wickman .30 .75
264 Spike Owen .30 .75
265 Todd Jones .30 .75
266 Pat Borders .30 .75
267 Tom Glavine .75 2.00
268 Dave Nilsson .30 .75
269 Rich Batchelor .30 .75
270 Delino DeShields .30 .75
271 Felix Fermin .30 .75
272 Orestes Destrade .30 .75
273 Mickey Morandini .30 .75
274 Otis Nixon .30 .75
275 Ellis Burks .50 1.25
276 Greg Gagne .30 .75
277 John Doherty .30 .75
278 Julio Franco .50 1.25
279 Bernie Williams .75 2.00
280 Rick Aguilera .30 .75
281 Mickey Tettleton .30 .75
282 David Nied .30 .75
283 Johnny Ruffin .30 .75
284 Dan Wilson .30 .75
285 Omar Vizquel .75 2.00
286 Willie Banks .30 .75
287 Erik Pappas .30 .75
288 Cal Eldred .30 .75
289 Bobby Witt .30 .75
290 Luis Gonzalez .50 1.25
291 Greg Pirkl .30 .75
292 Alex Cole .30 .75
293 Ricky Bones .30 .75
294 Denis Boucher .30 .75
295 John Burkett .30 .75
296 Steve Trachsel .30 .75
297 Ricky Jordan .30 .75
298 Mark Dewey .30 .75
299 Jimmy Key .50 1.25
300 Mike Macfarlane .30 .75
301 Tim Belcher .30 .75
302 Carlos Reyes .30 .75
303 Greg A. Harris .30 .75
304 Brian Anderson RC .50 1.25
305 Terry Mulholland .30 .75
306 Felix Jose .30 .75
307 Darren Holmes .30 .75
308 Jose Rijo .30 .75
309 Paul Wagner .30 .75
310 Bob Scanlan .30 .75
311 Mike Jackson .30 .75
312 Jose Vizcaino .30 .75
313 Rob Butler .30 .75
314 Kevin Seitzer .30 .75
315 Geronimo Pena .30 .75
316 Hector Carrasco .30 .75
317 Eddie Murray 1.25 3.00
318 Roger Salkeld .30 .75
319 Todd Hundley .30 .75
320 Danny Jackson .30 .75
321 Kevin Young .30 .75
322 Mike Greenwell .30 .75
323 Kevin Mitchell .30 .75
324 Chuck Knoblauch .50 1.25
325 Danny Tartabull .30 .75
326 Vince Coleman .30 .75
327 Marvin Freeman .30 .75
328 Andy Benes .30 .75
329 Mike Kelly .30 .75
330 Karl Rhodes .30 .75
331 Allen Watson .30 .75
332 Damion Easley .30 .75
333 Reggie Jefferson .30 .75
334 Kevin McReynolds .30 .75
335 Arthur Rhodes .30 .75
336 Brian Hunter .30 .75
337 Tom Browning .30 .75
338 Pedro Munoz .30 .75
339 Billy Ripken .30 .75
340 Gene Harris .30 .75
341 Fernando Vina .30 .75
342 Sean Berry .30 .75
343 Pedro Astacio .30 .75
344 B.J. Surhoff .50 1.25
345 Doug Drabek .30 .75
346 Jody Reed .30 .75
347 Ray Lankford .50 1.25
348 Steve Farr .30 .75
349 Eric Anthony .30 .75
350 Pete Smith .30 .75
351 Lee Smith .50 1.25
352 Mariano Duncan .30 .75
353 Doug Strange .30 .75
354 Tim Bogar .30 .75
355 Dave Weathers .30 .75
356 Eric Karros .50 1.25
357 Randy Myers .30 .75
358 Chad Curtis .30 .75
359 Steve Avery .30 .75
360 Brian Jordan .50 1.25
361 Tim Wallach .30 .75
362 Pedro Martinez 1.25 3.00
363 Bip Roberts .30 .75
364 Lou Whitaker .50 1.25
365 Luis Polonia .30 .75
366 Benito Santiago .50 1.25
367 Brett Butler .50 1.25
368 Shawon Dunston .30 .75
369 Kelly Stinnett RC .50 1.25
370 Chris Turner .30 .75
371 Ruben Sierra .50 1.25
372 Greg A. Harris .30 .75
373 Xavier Hernandez .30 .75
374 Howard Johnson .30 .75
375 Duane Ward .30 .75
376 Roberto Hernandez .30 .75
377 Scott Leius .30 .75
378 Dave Valle .30 .75
379 Sid Fernandez .30 .75
380 Doug Jones .30 .75
381 Zane Smith .30 .75
382 Craig Biggio .75 2.00
383 Rick White RC .30 .75
384 Tom Pagnozzi .30 .75
385 Chris James .30 .75
386 Bret Boone .50 1.25
387 Jeff Montgomery .30 .75
388 Chad Kreuter .30 .75
389 Greg Hibbard .30 .75
390 Mark Grace .75 2.00
391 Phil Leftwich RC .30 .75
392 Don Mattingly 3.00 8.00
393 Ozzie Guillen .50 1.25
394 Gary Gaetti .50 1.25
395 Erik Hanson .30 .75
396 Scott Brosius .50 1.25
397 Tom Gordon .30 .75
398 Bill Gullickson .30 .75
399 Matt Mieske .30 .75
400 Pat Hentgen .30 .75
401 Walt Weiss .30 .75
402 Greg Blosser .30 .75
403 Stan Javier .30 .75
404 Doug Henry .30 .75
405 Ramon Martinez .30 .75
406 Frank Viola .50 1.25
407 Mike Hampton .50 1.25
408 Andy Van Slyke .75 2.00
409 Bobby Ayala .30 .75
410 Todd Zeile .30 .75
411 Jay Bell .50 1.25
412 Dennis Martinez .50 1.25
413 Mark Portugal .30 .75
414 Bobby Munoz .30 .75
415 Kirt Manwaring .30 .75
416 John Kruk .50 1.25
417 Trevor Hoffman .75 2.00
418 Chris Sabo .30 .75
419 Bret Saberhagen .50 1.25
420 Chris Nabholz .30 .75
421 James Mouton FIN .30 .75
422 Tony Tarasco FIN .30 .75
423 Carlos Delgado FIN .75 2.00
424 Rondell White FIN .50 1.25
425 Javier Lopez FIN .50 1.25
426 Chan Ho Park FIN RC .75 2.00
427 Cliff Floyd FIN .50 1.25
428 Dave Staton FIN .30 .75
429 J.R. Phillips FIN .30 .75
430 Manny Ramirez FIN 1.25 3.00
431 Kurt Abbott FIN RC .30 .75
432 Melvin Nieves FIN .30 .75
433 Alex Gonzalez FIN .30 .75
434 Rick Helling FIN .30 .75
435 Danny Bautista FIN .30 .75
436 Matt Walbeck FIN .30 .75
437 Ryan Klesko FIN .50 1.25
438 Steve Karsay FIN .30 .75
439 Salomon Torres FIN .30 .75
440 Scott Ruffcorn FIN .30 .75

1994 Finest Refractors

COMPLETE SET (440) 2000.00 3000.00
*STARS: 2.5X TO 6X BASIC CARDS
*ROOKIES: 1.5X TO 4X BASIC CARDS
STATED ODDS 1:9
240 Barry Larkin FIN 15.00 40.00

1994 Finest Jumbos

COMPLETE SET (80) 175.00 350.00
*JUMBOS: 1.25X TO 3X BASIC CARDS
ONE JUMBO PER BOX

1994 Finest Superstar Samplers

1 Mike Piazza 6.00 15.00
18 Tim Salmon 1.25 3.00
35 Andres Galarraga 2.50 6.00
74 Raul Mondesi 1.25 3.00
92 Gregg Jefferies .75 2.00
201 Tony Gwynn 6.00 15.00
203 Frank Thomas 4.00 10.00
204 Kirby Puckett 4.00 10.00
205 Roberto Alomar 2.50 6.00
207 Joe Carter 1.25 3.00
208 Albert Belle 1.25 3.00
209 Greg Maddux 8.00 20.00
210 Ryne Sandberg 5.00 12.00
211 Juan Gonzalez 2.50 6.00
212 Jeff Bagwell 4.00 10.00
213 Randy Johnson 5.00 12.00
214 Matt Williams 2.00 5.00
216 Larry Walker 3.00 8.00
217 Roger Clemens 6.00 15.00
219 Cecil Fielder 1.25 3.00
220 Darren Daulton 1.25 3.00
221 John Olerud 1.25 3.00
222 Jose Canseco 4.00 10.00
224 Fred McGriff 2.00 5.00
225 Gary Sheffield 4.00 10.00
226 Jack McDowell .75 2.00
227 Rafael Palmeiro 3.00 8.00
229 Marquis Grissom 1.25 3.00
230 Barry Bonds 6.00 15.00
231 Carlos Baerga .75 2.00
232 Ken Griffey Jr. 8.00 20.00
233 David Justice 2.50 6.00
234 Bobby Bonilla 1.25 3.00
235 Cal Ripken 12.00 30.00
237 Len Dykstra .75 2.00
238 Will Clark 2.50 6.00
239 Paul Molitor 3.00 8.00
240 Barry Larkin 2.50 6.00
258 Mo Vaughn 1.25 3.00
267 Tom Glavine 3.00 8.00
390 Mark Grace 2.00 5.00
392 Don Mattingly 3.00 8.00
408 Andy Van Slyke .75 2.00
427 Cliff Floyd 2.00 5.00
430 Manny Ramirez 4.00 10.00

1995 Finest

Consisting of 330 standard-size cards, this set (produced by Topps) was issued in series of 220 and 110. A protective film, designed to keep the card from scratching and to maintain original gloss, covers the front. With the Finest logo at the top, a silver baseball diamond design surrounded by green (field) form the background to an action photo. Horizontally designed backs have a photo to the right with statistical information to the left. A Finest Moment, or career highlight, is also included. Rookie Cards in this set include Bobby Higginson and Hideo Nomo.

COMPLETE SET (330) 25.00 60.00
COMPLETE SERIES 1 (220) 20.00 50.00
COMPLETE SERIES 2 (110) 6.00 15.00
1 Raul Mondesi .40 1.00
2 Kurt Abbott .20 .50
3 Chris Gomez .20 .50
4 Manny Ramirez .60 1.50
5 Rondell White .40 1.00
6 William VanLandingham .20 .50
7 Jon Lieber .20 .50
8 Ryan Klesko .40 1.00
9 John Hudek .20 .50
10 Joey Hamilton .20 .50
11 Bob Hamelin .20 .50
12 Brian Anderson .20 .50
13 Mike Lieberthal .40 1.00
14 Rico Brogna .20 .50
15 Rusty Greer .40 1.00
16 Carlos Delgado .40 1.00
17 Jim Edmonds .60 1.50
18 Steve Trachsel .20 .50
19 Matt Walbeck .20 .50
20 Armando Benitez .20 .50
21 Steve Karsay .20 .50
22 Jose Oliva .20 .50
23 Cliff Floyd .40 1.00
24 Kevin Foster .20 .50
25 Javier Lopez .40 1.00
26 Jose Valentin .20 .50
27 James Mouton .20 .50
28 Hector Carrasco .20 .50
29 Orlando Miller .20 .50
30 Garret Anderson .40 1.00
31 Marvin Freeman .20 .50
32 Brett Butler .40 1.00
33 Roberto Kelly .20 .50
34 Rod Beck .20 .50
35 Jose Rijo .20 .50
36 Edgar Martinez .60 1.50
37 Jim Thome .60 1.50
38 Rick Wilkins .20 .50
39 Wally Joyner .40 1.00
40 Wil Cordero .20 .50
41 Tommy Greene .20 .50
42 Travis Fryman .40 1.00
43 Don Slaught .20 .50
44 Brady Anderson .40 1.00
45 Matt Williams .40 1.00
46 Rene Arocha .20 .50
47 Rickey Henderson 1.00 2.50
48 Mike Mussina .60 1.50
49 Greg McMichael .20 .50
50 Jody Reed .20 .50
51 Tino Martinez .60 1.50
52 Dave Clark .20 .50
53 John Valentin .20 .50
54 Bret Boone .40 1.00
55 Walt Weiss .20 .50
56 Kenny Lofton .40 1.00
57 Scott Leius .20 .50
58 Eric Karros .40 1.00
59 John Olerud .40 1.00
60 Chris Hoiles .20 .50
61 Sandy Alomar Jr. .20 .50
62 Tim Wallach .20 .50
63 Cal Eldred .20 .50
64 Tom Glavine .60 1.50
65 Mark Grace .60 1.50
66 Rey Sanchez .20 .50
67 Bobby Ayala .20 .50
68 Dante Bichette .40 1.00
69 Andres Galarraga .40 1.00
70 Chuck Carr .20 .50
71 Bobby Witt .20 .50
72 Steve Avery .20 .50
73 Bobby Jones .20 .50
74 Delino DeShields .20 .50
75 Kevin Tapani .20 .50
76 Randy Johnson 1.00 2.50
77 David Nied .20 .50
78 Pat Hentgen .20 .50
79 Tim Salmon .60 1.50
80 Todd Zeile .20 .50
81 John Wetteland .40 1.00
82 Albert Belle .40 1.00
83 Ben McDonald .20 .50
84 Bobby Munoz .20 .50
85 Bip Roberts .20 .50
86 Mo Vaughn .40 1.00
87 Chuck Finley .40 1.00
88 Chuck Knoblauch .40 1.00
89 Frank Thomas 1.00 2.50
90 Danny Tartabull .20 .50
91 Dean Palmer .40 1.00
92 Len Dykstra .40 1.00
93 J.R. Phillips .20 .50
94 Tom Candiotti .20 .50
95 Marquis Grissom .40 1.00
96 Barry Larkin .60 1.50
97 Bryan Harvey .20 .50
98 David Justice .40 1.00
99 David Cone .40 1.00
100 Wade Boggs .60 1.50
101 Jason Bere .20 .50
102 Hal Morris .20 .50
103 Fred McGriff .60 1.50
104 Bobby Bonilla .40 1.00
105 Jay Buhner .40 1.00
106 Allen Watson .20 .50
107 Mickey Tettleton .20 .50
108 Kevin Appier .40 1.00
109 Ivan Rodriguez .60 1.50
110 Carlos Garcia .20 .50
111 Andy Benes .20 .50
112 Eddie Murray 1.00 2.50
113 Mike Piazza 1.50 4.00
114 Greg Vaughn .20 .50
115 Paul Molitor .40 1.00
116 Terry Steinbach .20 .50
117 Jeff Bagwell .60 1.50
118 Ken Griffey Jr. 4.00 10.00
119 Gary Sheffield .40 1.00
120 Cal Ripken 3.00 8.00
121 Jeff Kent .40 1.00
122 Jay Bell .40 1.00
123 Will Clark .60 1.50
124 Cecil Fielder .40 1.00
125 Alex Fernandez .20 .50
126 Don Mattingly 2.50 6.00
127 Reggie Sanders .40 1.00
128 Moises Alou .40 1.00
129 Craig Biggio .60 1.50
130 Eddie Williams .20 .50
131 John Franco .40 1.00
132 John Kruk .40 1.00
133 Jeff King .20 .50
134 Royce Clayton .20 .50
135 Doug Drabek .20 .50
136 Ray Lankford .40 1.00
137 Roberto Alomar .60 1.50
138 Todd Hundley .20 .50
139 Alex Cole .20 .50
140 Shawon Dunston .20 .50
141 John Roper .20 .50

142 Mark Langston .20 .50
143 Tom Pagnozzi .20 .50
144 Wilson Alvarez .20 .50
145 Scott Cooper .20 .50
146 Kevin Mitchell .20 .50
147 Mark Whiten .20 .50
148 Jeff Conine .40 1.00
149 Chili Davis .40 1.00
150 Luis Gonzalez .40 1.00
151 Juan Guzman .20 .50
152 Mike Greenwell .20 .50
153 Mike Henneman .20 .50
154 Rick Aguilera .20 .50
155 Dennis Eckersley .40 1.00
156 Darrin Fletcher .20 .50
157 Darren Lewis .20 .50
158 Juan Gonzalez .40 1.00
159 Dave Hollins .20 .50
160 Jimmy Key .40 1.00
161 Roberto Hernandez .20 .50
162 Randy Myers .20 .50
163 Joe Carter .40 1.00
164 Darren Daulton .40 1.00
165 Mike Macfarlane .20 .50
166 Bret Saberhagen .40 1.00
167 Kirby Puckett 1.00 2.50
168 Lance Johnson .20 .50
169 Mark McGwire 2.50 6.00
170 Jose Canseco .60 1.50
171 Mike Stanley .20 .50
172 Lee Smith .40 1.00
173 Robin Ventura .40 1.00
174 Greg Gagne .20 .50
175 Brian McRae .20 .50
176 Mike Bordick .20 .50
177 Rafael Palmeiro .60 1.50
178 Kenny Rogers .40 1.00
179 Chad Curtis .20 .50
180 Devon White .40 1.00
181 Paul O'Neill .60 1.50
182 Ken Caminiti .40 1.00
183 Dave Nilsson .20 .50
184 Tim Naehring .20 .50
185 Roger Clemens 2.00 5.00
186 Otis Nixon .20 .50
187 Tim Raines .40 1.00
188 Denny Martinez .40 1.00
189 Pedro Martinez .60 1.50
190 Jim Abbott .60 1.50
191 Ryan Thompson .20 .50
192 Barry Bonds 2.50 6.00
193 Joe Girardi .20 .50
194 Steve Finley .40 1.00
195 John Jaha .20 .50
196 Tony Gwynn 1.25 3.00
197 Sammy Sosa 1.00 2.50
198 John Burkett .20 .50
199 Carlos Baerga .20 .50
200 Ramon Martinez .20 .50
201 Aaron Sele .20 .50
202 Eduardo Perez .20 .50
203 Alan Trammell .40 1.00
204 Orlando Merced .20 .50
205 Deion Sanders .60 1.50
206 Robb Nen .40 1.00
207 Jack McDowell .20 .50
208 Ruben Sierra .40 1.00
209 Bernie Williams .60 1.50
210 Kevin Seitzer .20 .50
211 Charles Nagy .20 .50
212 Tony Phillips .20 .50
213 Greg Maddux 1.50 4.00
214 Jeff Montgomery .20 .50
215 Larry Walker .40 1.00
216 Andy Van Slyke .60 1.50
217 Ozzie Smith 1.50 4.00
218 Geronimo Pena .20 .50
219 Gregg Jefferies .20 .50
220 Lou Whitaker .40 1.00
221 Chipper Jones 1.00 2.50
222 Benji Gil .20 .50
223 Tony Phillips .20 .50
224 Trevor Wilson .20 .50
225 Tony Tarasco .20 .50
226 Roberto Petagine .20 .50
227 Mike Macfarlane .20 .50
228 Hideo Nomo RC 4.00 10.00
229 Mark McLemore .20 .50
230 Ron Gant .40 1.00
231 Andujar Cedeno .20 .50
232 Michael Mimbs RC .20 .50
233 Jim Abbott .60 1.50
234 Ricky Bones .20 .50
235 Marty Cordova .20 .50
236 Mark Johnson RC .50 1.25
237 Marquis Grissom .40 1.00
238 Tom Henke .20 .50
239 Terry Pendleton .40 1.00
240 John Wetteland .40 1.00
241 Lee Smith .40 1.00
242 Jaime Navarro .20 .50
243 Luis Alicea .20 .50
244 Scott Cooper .20 .50
245 Gary Gaetti .40 1.00
246 Edgardo Alfonzo UER .20 .50
Incomplete career BA
247 Brad Clontz .20 .50
248 Dave Mlicki .20 .50
249 Dave Winfield .40 1.00
250 Mark Grudzielanek RC .75 2.00
251 Alex Gonzalez .20 .50
252 Kevin Brown .40 1.00
253 Esteban Loaiza .20 .50
254 Vaughn Eshelman .20 .50
255 Bill Swift .20 .50
256 Brian McRae .20 .50
257 Bob Higginson RC .75 2.00
258 Jack McDowell .20 .50
259 Scott Stahoviak .20 .50
260 Jon Nunnally .20 .50
261 Charlie Hayes .20 .50
262 Jacob Brumfield .20 .50
263 Chad Curtis .20 .50
264 Heathcliff Slocumb .20 .50
265 Mark Whiten .20 .50
266 Mickey Tettleton .20 .50
267 Jose Mesa .20 .50
268 Doug Jones .20 .50
269 Trevor Hoffman .40 1.00
270 Paul Sorrento .20 .50
271 Shane Andrews .20 .50
272 Brett Butler .40 1.00
273 Curtis Goodwin .20 .50
274 Larry Walker .40 1.00
275 Phil Plantier .20 .50
276 Ken Hill .20 .50
277 Vinny Castilla UER .40 1.00
Rockies spelled Rockie
278 Billy Ashley .20 .50
279 Derek Jeter 2.50 6.00
280 Bob Tewksbury .20 .50
281 Jose Offerman .20 .50
282 Glenallen Hill .20 .50
283 Tony Fernandez .20 .50
284 Mike Devereaux .20 .50
285 John Burkett .20 .50
286 Geronimo Berroa .20 .50
287 Quilvio Veras .20 .50
288 Jason Bates .20 .50
289 Lee Tinsley .20 .50
290 Derek Bell .20 .50
291 Jeff Fassero .20 .50
292 Ray Durham .40 1.00
293 Chad Ogea .20 .50
294 Bill Pulsipher .20 .50
295 Phil Nevin .40 1.00
296 Carlos Perez RC .50 1.25
297 Roberto Kelly .20 .50
298 Tim Wakefield .40 1.00
299 Jeff Manto .20 .50
300 Brian L.Hunter .20 .50
301 C.J. Nitkowski .20 .50
302 Dustin Hermanson .20 .50
303 John Mabry .20 .50
304 Orel Hershiser .40 1.00
305 Ron Villone .20 .50
306 Sean Bergman .20 .50
307 Tom Goodwin .20 .50
308 Al Reyes .20 .50
309 Todd Stottlemyre .20 .50
310 Rich Becker .20 .50
311 Joey Cora .20 .50
312 Ed Sprague .20 .50
313 John Smoltz UER .60 1.50
3rd line; from spelled as form
314 Frank Castillo .20 .50
315 Chris Hammond .20 .50
316 Ismael Valdes .20 .50
317 Pete Harnisch .20 .50
318 Bernard Gilkey .20 .50
319 John Kruk .40 1.00
320 Marc Newfield .20 .50
321 Brian Johnson .20 .50
322 Mark Portugal .20 .50
323 David Hulse .20 .50
324 Luis Ortiz UER .20 .50
Below spelled beloe
325 Mike Benjamin .20 .50
326 Brian Jordan .40 1.00
327 Shawn Green .40 1.00
328 Joe Oliver .20 .50
329 Felipe Lira .20 .50
330 Andre Dawson .40 1.00

1995 Finest Refractors

*STARS: 4X TO 10X BASIC CARDS
*ROOKIES: 3X TO 8X BASIC CARDS
STATED ODDS 1:12
118 Ken Griffey Jr. 75.00 200.00

1995 Finest Flame Throwers

COMPLETE SET (9) 15.00 40.00
SER.1 STATED ODDS 1:48
FT1 Jason Bere 1.25 3.00
FT2 Roger Clemens 12.50 30.00
FT3 Juan Guzman 1.25 3.00
FT4 John Hudek 1.25 3.00
FT5 Randy Johnson 6.00 15.00
FT6 Pedro Martinez 4.00 10.00
FT7 Jose Rijo 1.25 3.00
FT8 Bret Saberhagen 2.50 6.00
FT9 John Wetteland 2.50 6.00

1995 Finest Power Kings

COMPLETE SET (18) 75.00 150.00
SER.1 STATED ODDS 1:24
PK1 Bob Hamelin 1.00 2.50
PK2 Raul Mondesi 2.00 5.00
PK3 Ryan Klesko 2.00 5.00
PK4 Carlos Delgado 2.00 5.00
PK5 Manny Ramirez 3.00 8.00
PK6 Mike Piazza 8.00 20.00
PK7 Jeff Bagwell 3.00 8.00
PK8 Mo Vaughn 2.00 5.00
PK9 Frank Thomas 5.00 12.00
PK10 Ken Griffey Jr. 10.00 25.00
PK11 Albert Belle 2.00 5.00
PK12 Sammy Sosa 5.00 12.00
PK13 Dante Bichette 2.00 5.00
PK14 Gary Sheffield 2.00 5.00
PK15 Matt Williams 2.00 5.00
PK16 Fred McGriff 3.00 8.00
PK17 Barry Bonds 12.50 30.00
PK18 Cecil Fielder 2.00 5.00

1995 Finest Bronze

Available exclusively direct from Topps, this six-card set features 1994 league leaders. The fronts feature chromium metallized graphics, mounted on bronze and factory sealed in clear resin. The cards are numbered on the back "X of 6."

COMPLETE SET (6) 30.00 80.00
1 Matt Williams 3.00 8.00
2 Tony Gwynn 10.00 25.00
3 Jeff Bagwell 6.00 15.00
4 Ken Griffey Jr. 15.00 40.00
5 Paul O'Neill 2.00 5.00
6 Frank Thomas 6.00 15.00

1996 Finest

The 1996 Finest set (produced by Topps) was issued in two series of 191 cards and 168 cards respectively, for a total of 359 cards. The six-card foil packs originally retailed for $5.00 each. A protective film, designed to keep the card from scratching and to maintain original gloss, covers the front. This product provides collectors with the opportunity to complete a number of sets within sets, each with a different degree of insertion. Each card is numbered twice to indicate the set count and the theme count. Series 1 set covers four distinct themes: Finest Phenoms, Finest Intimidators, Finest Gamers and Finest Sterling. Within the first three themes, some players will be common (bronze trim), some uncommon (silver) and some rare (gold). Finest Sterling consists of star players included within one of the other three themes, but featured with a new design and different photography. The breakdown for the player selection of common, uncommon and rare cards is completely random. There are 110 common, 55 uncommon (1:4 packs) and 25 rare cards (1:24 packs). Series 2 covers four distict themes also with common, uncommon and rare cards seeded at the same ratio. The four themes are: Finest Franchises which features 36 team leaders and bonafide superstars, Finest Additions which features 47 players who have switched teams in '96, Finest Prodigies which features 45 best up-and-coming players, and Finest Sterling with 39 top stars. In addition to the cards' special borders, each card will also have either "common," "uncommon", or "rare" written within the numbering box on the card backs to let collectors know which type of card they hold.

COMP.BRONZE SER.1 (110) 10.00 25.00
COMP.BRONZE SER.2 (110) 10.00 25.00
COMMON BRONZE .20 .50
COMMON GOLD 2.00 5.00
COMMON G RC 2.00 5.00
GOLD STATED ODDS 1:24
COMMON SILVER 1.00 2.50
SILVER STATED ODDS 1:4
SETS SKIP-NUMBERED BY COLOR
B5 Roberto Hernandez B .20 .50
B8 Terry Pendleton B .20 .50
B12 Ken Caminiti B .20 .50
B15 Dan Miceli B .20 .50
B16 Chipper Jones B .50 1.25
B17 John Wetteland B .20 .50
B19 Tim Naehring B .20 .50
B21 Eddie Murray B .50 1.25
B23 Kevin Appier B .20 .50
B24 Ken Griffey Jr. B 1.00 2.50
B26 Brian McRae B .20 .50
B27 Pedro Martinez B .30 .75
B28 Brian Jordan B .20 .50
B29 Mike Fetters B .20 .50
B30 Carlos Delgado B .20 .50
B31 Shane Reynolds B .20 .50
B32 Terry Steinbach B .20 .50
B34 Mark Leiter B .20 .50
B36 David Segui B .20 .50
B40 Fred McGriff B .30 .75
B44 Glenallen Hill B .20 .50
B45 Brady Anderson B .20 .50
B47 Jim Thome B .30 .75
B48 Frank Thomas B .50 1.25
B49 Chuck Knoblauch B .20 .50
B50 Len Dykstra B .20 .50
B53 Tom Pagnozzi B .20 .50
B55 Ricky Bones B .20 .50
B56 David Justice B .20 .50
B57 Steve Avery B .20 .50
B58 Robby Thompson B .20 .50
B61 Tony Gwynn B .60 1.50
B63 Denny Neagle B .20 .50
B67 Robin Ventura B .20 .50
B70 Kevin Seitzer B .20 .50
B71 Ramon Martinez B .20 .50
B75 Brian L.Hunter B .20 .50
B76 Alan Benes B .20 .50
B80 Ozzie Guillen B .20 .50
B82 Benji Gil B .20 .50
B85 Todd Hundley B .20 .50
B87 Pat Hentgen B .20 .50
B89 Chuck Finley B .20 .50
B92 Derek Jeter B 1.25 3.00
B93 Paul O'Neill B .30 .75
B94 Darrin Fletcher B .20 .50
B96 Delino DeShields B .20 .50
B97 Tim Salmon B .30 .75
B98 John Olerud B .20 .50
B101 Tim Wakefield B .20 .50
B103 Dave Stevens B .20 .50
B104 Orlando Merced B .20 .50
B106 Jay Bell B .20 .50
B107 John Burkett B .20 .50
B108 Chris Hoiles B .20 .50
B110 Dave Nilsson B .20 .50
B111 Rod Beck B .20 .50
B113 Mike Piazza B .75 2.00
B114 Mark Langston B .20 .50
B116 Rico Brogna B .20 .50
B118 Tom Goodwin B .20 .50
B119 Bryan Rekar B .20 .50
B120 David Cone B .20 .50
B122 Andy Pettitte B .30 .75
B123 Chili Davis B .20 .50
B124 John Smoltz B .30 .75
B125 Heathcliff Slocumb B .20 .50
B126 Dante Bichette B .20 .50
B128 Alex Gonzalez B .20 .50
B129 Jeff Montgomery B .20 .50
B131 Denny Martinez B .20 .50
B132 Mel Rojas B .20 .50
B133 Derek Bell B .20 .50
B134 Trevor Hoffman B .20 .50
B136 Darren Daulton B .20 .50
B137 Pete Schourek B .20 .50
B138 Phil Nevin B .20 .50
B139 Andres Galarraga B .20 .50
B140 Chad Fonville B .20 .50
B144 J.T. Snow B .20 .50
B146 Barry Bonds B 1.25 3.00
B147 Orel Hershiser B .20 .50
B148 Quilvio Veras B .20 .50
B149 Will Clark B .30 .75
B150 Jose Rijo B .20 .50
B152 Travis Fryman B .20 .50
B154 Alex Fernandez B .20 .50
B155 Wade Boggs B .30 .75
B156 Troy Percival B .20 .50
B157 Moises Alou B .20 .50
B158 Javy Lopez B .20 .50
B159 Jason Giambi B .20 .50
B162 Mark McGwire B 1.25 3.00
B163 Eric Karros B .20 .50
B166 Mickey Tettleton B .20 .50
B167 Barry Larkin B .30 .75
B169 Ruben Sierra B .20 .50
B170 Bill Swift B .20 .50
B172 Chad Curtis B .20 .50
B173 Dean Palmer B .20 .50
B175 Bobby Bonilla B .20 .50
B176 Greg Colbrunn B .20 .50
B177 Jose Mesa B .20 .50
B178 Mike Greenwell B .20 .50
B181 Doug Drabek B .20 .50
B183 Wilson Alvarez B .20 .50
B184 Marty Cordova B .20 .50
B185 Hal Morris B .20 .50
B187 Carlos Garcia B .20 .50
B190 Marquis Grissom B .20 .50
B193 Will Clark B .30 .75
B194 Paul Molitor B .20 .50
B195 Kenny Rogers B .20 .50
B196 Reggie Sanders B .20 .50
B199 Raul Mondesi B .20 .50
B200 Lance Johnson B .20 .50
B201 Alvin Morman B .20 .50
B203 Jack McDowell B .20 .50
B204 Randy Myers B .20 .50
B205 Harold Baines B .20 .50
B206 Marty Cordova B .20 .50
B207 Rich Hunter B RC .20 .50
B208 Al Leiter B .20 .50
B209 Greg Gagne B .20 .50
B210 Ben McDonald B .20 .50
B212 Terry Adams B .20 .50
B213 Paul Sorrento B .20 .50
B214 Albert Belle B .20 .50
B215 Mike Blowers B .20 .50
B216 Jim Edmonds B .20 .50
B217 Felipe Crespo B .20 .50
B219 Shawon Dunston B .20 .50
B220 Jimmy Haynes B .20 .50
B221 Jose Canseco B .30 .75
B222 Eric Davis B .20 .50
B224 Tim Raines B .20 .50
B225 Tony Phillips B .20 .50
B226 Charlie Hayes B .20 .50
B227 Eric Owens B .20 .50
B228 Roberto Alomar B .30 .75
B233 Kenny Lofton B .20 .50
B236 Mark McGwire B 1.25 3.00
B237 Jay Buhner B .20 .50
B238 Craig Biggio B .30 .75
B240 Barry Bonds B 1.25 3.00
B244 Ron Gant B .20 .50
B245 Paul Wilson B .20 .50
B246 Todd Hollandsworth B .20 .50
B247 Todd Zeile B .20 .50
B248 David Justice B .20 .50
B250 Moises Alou B .20 .50
B251 Bob Wolcott B .20 .50
B252 David Wells B .20 .50
B253 Juan Gonzalez B .20 .50
B254 Andres Galarraga B .20 .50
B255 Dave Hollins B .20 .50
B257 Sammy Sosa B .50 1.25
B258 Ivan Rodriguez B .30 .75
B259 Bip Roberts B .20 .50
B260 Tino Martinez B .30 .75
B262 Mike Stanley B .20 .50
B264 Butch Huskey B .20 .50
B265 Jeff Conine B .20 .50
B267 Mark Grace B .30 .75
B268 Jason Schmidt B .30 .75
B269 Otis Nixon B .20 .50
B271 Kirby Puckett B .50 1.25
B273 Andy Benes B .20 .50
B275 Mike Piazza B .75 2.00
B276 Rey Ordonez B .20 .50
B278 Gary Gaetti B .20 .50
B280 Robin Ventura B .20 .50
B281 Cal Ripken B 1.50 4.00
B282 Carlos Baerga B .20 .50
B283 Roger Cedeno B .20 .50
B285 Terrell Wade B .20 .50
B286 Kevin Brown B .20 .50
B287 Rafael Palmeiro B .30 .75
B288 Mo Vaughn B .20 .50
B292 Bob Tewksbury B .20 .50
B297 T.J. Mathews B .20 .50
B298 Manny Ramirez B .30 .75
B299 Jeff Bagwell B .30 .75
B301 Wade Boggs B .30 .75
B303 Steve Gibralter B .20 .50
B304 B.J. Surhoff B .20 .50
B306 Royce Clayton B .20 .50
B307 Sal Fasano B .20 .50
B309 Gary Sheffield B .20 .50
B310 Ken Hill B .20 .50
B311 Joe Girardi B .20 .50
B312 Matt Lawton B RC .30 .75
B314 Julio Franco B .20 .50
B315 Joe Carter B .20 .50
B316 Brooks Kieschnick B .20 .50
B318 Heathcliff Slocumb B .20 .50
B319 Barry Larkin B .30 .75
B320 Tony Gwynn B .60 1.50
B322 Frank Thomas B .50 1.25
B323 Edgar Martinez B .30 .75
B325 Henry Rodriguez B .20 .50
B326 Marvin Benard B RC .20 .50
B329 Ugueth Urbina B .20 .50
B331 Roger Salkeld B .20 .50
B332 Edgar Renteria B .20 .50
B333 Ryan Klesko B .20 .50
B334 Ray Lankford B .20 .50
B336 Justin Thompson B .20 .50
B339 Mark Clark B .20 .50
B340 Ruben Rivera B .30 .75
B342 Matt Williams B .20 .50
B343 Francisco Cordova B RC .20 .50
B344 Cecil Fielder B .20 .50
B348 Mark Grudzielanek B .20 .50
B349 Ron Coomer B .20 .50
B351 Rich Aurilia B RC .20 .50
B352 Jose Herrera B .20 .50
B356 Tony Clark B .20 .50
B358 Dan Naulty B RC .20 .50
B359 Checklist B .20 .50
G4 Marty Cordova G 2.00 5.00
G6 Tony Gwynn G 6.00 15.00
G9 Albert Belle G 2.00 5.00
G18 Kirby Puckett G 5.00 12.00
G20 Karim Garcia G 2.00 5.00
G25 Cal Ripken G 15.00 40.00
G33 Hideo Nomo G 5.00 12.00
G39 Ryne Sandberg G 8.00 20.00
G42 Jeff Bagwell G 1.50 4.00
G51 Jason Isringhausen G 2.00 5.00
G64 Mo Vaughn G 2.00 5.00
G66 Dante Bichette G 2.00 5.00
G74 Mark McGwire G 12.50 30.00
G81 Kenny Lofton G 2.00 5.00
G83 Jim Edmonds G 2.00 5.00
G90 Mike Mussina G 3.00 8.00
G100 Jeff Conine G 2.00 5.00
G102 Johnny Damon G 2.00 5.00
G105 Barry Bonds G 12.50 30.00
G117 Jose Canseco G 3.00 8.00
G135 Ken Griffey Jr. G 10.00 25.00
G141 Chipper Jones G 5.00 12.00
G145 Greg Maddux G 8.00 20.00
G164 Jay Buhner G 2.00 5.00
G186 Frank Thomas G 5.00 12.00
G191 Checklist G 2.00 5.00
G192 Chipper Jones G 5.00 12.00
G197 Roberto Alomar G 3.00 8.00
G198 Dennis Eckersley G 2.00 5.00
G202 George Arias G 2.00 5.00
G232 Hideo Nomo G 5.00 12.00
G243 Chris Snopek G 2.00 5.00
G249 Tim Salmon G 3.00 8.00
G266 Matt Williams G 2.00 5.00
G270 Randy Johnson G 5.00 12.00
G279 Paul Molitor G 2.00 5.00
G290 Cecil Fielder G 2.00 5.00
G294 Livan Hernandez G RC 4.00 10.00
G300 Marty Janzen G RC 2.00 5.00
G308 Ron Gant G 2.00 5.00
G321 Ryan Klesko G 2.00 5.00
G324 Jermaine Dye G 2.00 5.00
G330 Jason Giambi G 2.00 5.00
G335 Edgar Martinez G 3.00 8.00
G338 Rey Ordonez G 2.00 5.00
G347 Sammy Sosa G 5.00 12.00
G354 Juan Gonzalez G 2.00 5.00
G355 Craig Biggio G 3.00 8.00
S1 G.Maddux S UER 4.00 10.00
S2 Bernie Williams S 1.50 4.00
S3 Ivan Rodriguez S 1.50 4.00
S7 Barry Larkin S 1.50 4.00
S10 Ray Lankford S 1.00 2.50
S11 Mike Piazza S 4.00 10.00
S13 Larry Walker S 1.00 2.50
S14 Matt Williams S 1.00 2.50
S22 Tim Salmon S 1.50 4.00
S35 Edgar Martinez S 1.50 4.00
S37 Gregg Jefferies S 1.00 2.50
S38 Bill Pulsipher S 1.00 2.50
S41 Shawn Green S 1.00 2.50
S43 Jim Abbott S 1.50 4.00
S46 Roger Clemens S 5.00 12.00
S52 Rondell White S 1.00 2.50
S54 Dennis Eckersley S 1.00 2.50
S59 Hideo Nomo S 2.50 6.00
S60 Gary Sheffield S 1.00 2.50
S62 Will Clark S 1.50 4.00
S65 Bret Boone S 1.00 2.50
S68 Rafael Palmeiro S 1.50 4.00
S69 Carlos Baerga S 1.00 2.50
S72 Tom Glavine S 1.50 4.00
S73 Garret Anderson S 1.00 2.50
S77 Randy Johnson S 2.50 6.00
S78 Jeff King S 1.00 2.50
S79 Kirby Puckett S 2.50 6.00
S84 Cecil Fielder S 1.00 2.50
S86 Reggie Sanders S 1.00 2.50
S88 Ryan Klesko S 1.00 2.50
S91 John Valentin S 1.00 2.50
S95 Manny Ramirez S 1.50 4.00
S99 Vinny Castilla S 1.00 2.50
S109 Carlos Perez S 1.00 2.50
S112 Craig Biggio S 1.50 4.00
S115 Juan Gonzalez S 1.00 2.50
S121 Ray Durham S 1.00 2.50
S127 C.J. Nitkowski S 1.00 2.50
S130 Raul Mondesi S 1.00 2.50
S142 Lee Smith S 1.00 2.50
S143 Joe Carter S 1.00 2.50
S151 Mo Vaughn S 1.00 2.50
S153 Frank Rodriguez S 1.00 2.50
S160 Steve Finley S 1.00 2.50
S161 Jeff Bagwell S 1.50 4.00
S165 Cal Ripken S 8.00 20.00
S168 Lyle Mouton S 1.00 2.50
S171 Sammy Sosa S 2.50 6.00
S174 John Franco S 1.00 2.50
S179 Greg Vaughn S 1.00 2.50
S180 Mark Wohlers S 1.00 2.50
S182 Paul O'Neill S 1.50 4.00
S188 Albert Belle S 1.00 2.50
S189 Mark Grace S 1.50 4.00
S211 Ernie Young S 1.00 2.50
S218 Fred McGriff S 1.50 4.00
S223 Kimera Bartee S 1.00 2.50
S229 Rickey Henderson S 2.50 6.00
S230 Sterling Hitchcock S 1.00 2.50
S231 Bernard Gilkey S 1.00 2.50
S234 Ryne Sandberg S 4.00 10.00
S235 Greg Maddux S 4.00 10.00
S239 Todd Stottlemyre S 1.00 2.50
S241 Jason Kendall S 1.00 2.50
S242 Paul O'Neill S 1.50 4.00
S256 Devon White S 1.00 2.50
S261 Chuck Knoblauch S 1.00 2.50
S263 Wally Joyner S 1.00 2.50
S272 Andy Fox S 1.00 2.50
S274 Sean Berry S 1.00 2.50
S277 Benito Santiago S 1.00 2.50
S284 Chad Mottola S 1.00 2.50
S289 Dante Bichette S 1.00 2.50
S291 Dwight Gooden S 1.00 2.50
S293 Kevin Mitchell S 1.00 2.50
S295 Russ Davis S 1.00 2.50
S296 Chan Ho Park S 1.00 2.50
S302 Larry Walker S 1.00 2.50
S305 Ken Griffey Jr. S 5.00 12.00
S313 Billy Wagner S 1.00 2.50
S317 Mike Grace S RC 1.00 2.50
S327 Kenny Lofton S 1.00 2.50
S328 Derek Bell S 1.00 2.50
S337 Gary Sheffield S 1.00 2.50
S341 Mark Grace S 1.50 4.00
S345 Andres Galarraga S 1.00 2.50
S346 Brady Anderson S 1.00 2.50
S350 Derek Jeter S 5.00 12.00
S353 Jay Buhner S 1.00 2.50
S357 Tino Martinez S 1.00 2.50

1996 Finest Refractors

*BRONZE: 4X TO 10X BASIC BRONZE
BRONZE STATED ODDS 1:12
*GOLD: .75X TO 2X BASIC GOLD
GOLD STATED ODDS 1:288
*SILVER: 1.25X TO 3X BASIC SILVER
SILVER STATED ODDS 1:48
B92 Derek Jeter B 40.00 80.00
S350 Derek Jeter S 40.00 80.00

1996 Finest Landmark

This four-card limited edition medallion set came with a Certificate of Authenticity and was produced by Topps. Only 2,000 sets were made. The fronts feature color action player photos on a gold ball and star metallic background. The backs carry player biographical and career information including batting records.

1 Greg Maddux 8.00 20.00
2 Albert Belle 2.00 5.00
3 Cal Ripken 15.00 40.00
4 Eddie Murray 3.00 8.00

1997 Finest Promos

COMPLETE SET (5) 3.00 8.00
1 Barry Bonds C .60 1.50
15 Derek Jeter C 1.25 3.00
30 Mark McGwire C 1.00 2.50
143 Hideo Nomo U .40 1.00
159 Jeff Bagwell R .60 1.50

1997 Finest

The 1997 Finest set (produced by Topps) was issued in two series of 175 cards each and was distributed in six-card packs with a suggested retail price of $5.00. The fronts feature a borderless action player photo while the backs carry player information with another player photo. Series one is divided into five distinct themes: Finest Hurlers (top pitchers), Finest Blue Chips (up-and-coming future stars), Finest Power (long-ball hitters), Finest Warriors (superstar players), and Finest Masters (hottest players). Series two is also divided into five distinct themes: Finest Power (power hitters and pitchers), Finest Masters (top players), Finest Blue Chips (top new players), Finest Competitors (hottest players), and Finest Acquisitions (latest trades and new signings). All five themes of each series have common cards (1-100 and 176-275) designated with bronze trim, uncommon (101-150 and 276-325) with silver trim and an insertion rate of one in four for both series, and rare (151-175 and 326-350) with gold trim and an insertion rate of one in 24 for both series. The cards are numbered on the backs within the whole set and within the theme set. Notable Rookie Cards include Brian Giles.

COMP.BRONZE SER.1 (100) 12.50 30.00
COMP.BRONZE SER.2 (100) 12.50 30.00
COM.BRON.(1-100/176-275) .20 .50
COMP.SILVER SER.1 (50)
COMP.SILVER SER.2 (50)
COM.SILV.(101-150/276-325) .75 2.00
SILVER STATED ODDS 1:4
COMP.GOLD SER.1 (25)
COMP.GOLD SER.2 (25)
COM.GOLD (151-175/326-350) 2.00 5.00
GOLD STATED ODDS 1:24
BICHETTE/JETER BOTH NUMBERED 155
BICHETTE UER SHOULD BE NUMBER 5
1 Barry Bonds B 1.25 3.00
2 Ryne Sandberg B .75 2.00
3 Brian Jordan B .20 .50
4 Rocky Coppinger B .20 .50
5 Dante Bichette B UER 155 .20 .50
6 Al Martin B .20 .50
7 Charles Nagy B .20 .50
8 Otis Nixon B .20 .50
9 Mark Johnson B .20 .50
10 Jeff Bagwell B .30 .75
11 Ken Hill B .20 .50
12 Willie Adams B .20 .50
13 Raul Mondesi B .20 .50
14 Reggie Sanders B .20 .50
15 Derek Jeter B 1.25 3.00
16 Jermaine Dye B .20 .50
17 Edgar Renteria B .20 .50
18 Travis Fryman B .20 .50
19 Roberto Hernandez B .20 .50
20 Sammy Sosa B .50 1.25
21 Garret Anderson B .20 .50
22 Rey Ordonez B .20 .50
23 Glenallen Hill B .20 .50
24 Dave Nilsson B .20 .50
25 Kevin Brown B .20 .50
26 Brian McRae B .20 .50
27 Joey Hamilton B .20 .50
28 Jamey Wright B .20 .50
29 Frank Thomas B .50 1.25
30 Mark McGwire B 1.25 3.00
31 Ramon Martinez B .20 .50
32 Jaime Bluma B .20 .50
33 Frank Rodriguez B .20 .50
34 Andy Benes B .20 .50
35 Jay Buhner B .20 .50
36 Justin Thompson B .20 .50
37 Darin Erstad B .20 .50
38 Gregg Jefferies B .20 .50
39 Jeff D'Amico B .20 .50
40 Pedro Martinez B .30 .75
41 Nomar Garciaparra B .75 2.00
42 Jose Valentin B .20 .50
43 Pat Hentgen B .20 .50
44 Will Clark B .30 .75
45 Bernie Williams B .30 .75
46 Luis Castillo B .20 .50
47 B.J. Surhoff B .20 .50
48 Greg Gagne B .20 .50
49 Pete Schourek B .20 .50
50 Mike Piazza B .75 2.00
51 Dwight Gooden B .20 .50
52 Javy Lopez B .20 .50
53 Chuck Finley B .20 .50
54 James Baldwin B .20 .50
55 Jack McDowell B .20 .50
56 Royce Clayton B .20 .50
57 Carlos Delgado B .20 .50
58 Neifi Perez B .20 .50
59 Eddie Taubensee B .20 .50
60 Rafael Palmeiro B .30 .75
61 Marty Cordova B .20 .50
62 Wade Boggs B .30 .75
63 Rickey Henderson B .50 1.25
64 Mike Hampton B .20 .50
65 Troy Percival B .20 .50
66 Barry Larkin B .30 .75
67 Jermaine Allensworth B .20 .50
68 Mark Clark B .20 .50
69 Mike Lansing B .20 .50
70 Mark Grudzielanek B .20 .50
71 Todd Stottlemyre B .20 .50
72 Juan Guzman B .20 .50
73 John Burkett B .20 .50
74 Wilson Alvarez B .20 .50
75 Ellis Burks B .20 .50
76 Bobby Higginson B .20 .50
77 Ricky Bottalico B .20 .50
78 Omar Vizquel B .30 .75
79 Paul Sorrento B .20 .50
80 Denny Neagle B .20 .50
81 Roger Pavlik B .20 .50
82 Mike Lieberthal B .20 .50
83 Devon White B .20 .50
84 John Olerud B .20 .50
85 Kevin Appier B .20 .50
86 Joe Girardi B .20 .50
87 Paul O'Neill B .30 .75
88 Mike Sweeney B .20 .50
89 John Smiley B .20 .50
90 Ivan Rodriguez B .30 .75
91 Randy Myers B .20 .50
92 Bip Roberts B .20 .50
93 Jose Mesa B .20 .50
94 Paul Wilson B .20 .50
95 Mike Mussina B .30 .75
96 Ben McDonald B .20 .50
97 John Mabry B .20 .50
98 Tom Goodwin B .20 .50
99 Edgar Martinez B .30 .75
100 Andruw Jones B .30 .75
101 Jose Canseco S 1.25 3.00
102 Billy Wagner S .75 2.00
103 Dante Bichette S .75 2.00
104 Curt Schilling S .75 2.00
105 Dean Palmer S .75 2.00
106 Larry Walker S .75 2.00
107 Bernie Williams S 1.25 3.00
108 Chipper Jones S 2.00 5.00
109 Gary Sheffield S .75 2.00
110 Randy Johnson S 2.00 5.00
111 Roberto Alomar S 1.25 3.00
112 Todd Walker S .75 2.00
113 Sandy Alomar Jr. S .75 2.00
114 John Jaha S .75 2.00
115 Ken Caminiti S .75 2.00
116 Ryan Klesko S .75 2.00
117 Mariano Rivera S 2.00 5.00
118 Jason Giambi S .75 2.00
119 Lance Johnson S .75 2.00
120 Robin Ventura S .75 2.00
121 Todd Hollandsworth S .75 2.00
122 Johnny Damon S 1.25 3.00
123 William VanLandingham S .75 2.00
124 Jason Kendall S .75 2.00
125 Vinny Castilla S .75 2.00
126 Harold Baines S .75 2.00
127 Joe Carter S .75 2.00
128 Craig Biggio S 1.25 3.00
129 Tony Clark S .75 2.00
130 Ron Gant S .75 2.00
131 David Segui S .75 2.00
132 Steve Trachsel S .75 2.00
133 Scott Rolen S 1.25 3.00
134 Mike Stanley S .75 2.00
135 Cal Ripken S 6.00 15.00
136 John Smoltz S 1.25 3.00
137 Bobby Jones S .75 2.00
138 Manny Ramirez S 1.25 3.00
139 Ken Griffey Jr. S 4.00 10.00
140 Chuck Knoblauch S .75 2.00
141 Mark Grace S 1.25 3.00
142 Chris Snopek S .75 2.00
143 Hideo Nomo S 1.25 3.00
144 Tim Salmon S 1.25 3.00
145 David Cone S .75 2.00
146 Eric Young S .75 2.00
147 Jeff Brantley S .75 2.00
148 Jim Thome S .75 2.00
149 Trevor Hoffman S .75 2.00
150 Juan Gonzalez S .75 2.00
151 Mike Piazza G 8.00 20.00
152 Ivan Rodriguez G 3.00 8.00
153 Mo Vaughn G 2.00 5.00
154 Brady Anderson G 2.00 5.00
155 Mark McGwire G 12.50 30.00
156 Rafael Palmeiro G 3.00 8.00

157 Barry Larkin G 3.00 8.00
158 Greg Maddux G 8.00 20.00
159 Jeff Bagwell G 3.00 8.00
160 Frank Thomas G 5.00 12.00
161 Ken Caminiti G 2.00 5.00
162 Andruw Jones G 3.00 8.00
163 Dennis Eckersley G 2.00 5.00
164 Jeff Conine G 2.00 5.00
165 Jim Edmonds G 2.00 5.00
166 Derek Jeter G 15.00 40.00
167 Vladimir Guerrero G 5.00 12.00
168 Sammy Sosa G 5.00 12.00
169 Tony Gwynn G 6.00 15.00
170 Andres Galarraga G 2.00 5.00
171 Todd Hundley G 2.00 5.00
172 Jay Buhner G UER 164 2.00 5.00
173 Paul Molitor G 2.00 5.00
174 Kenny Lofton G 2.00 5.00
175 Barry Bonds G 12.50 30.00
176 Gary Sheffield B .20 .50
177 Dmitri Young B .20 .50
178 Jay Bell B .20 .50
179 David Wells B .20 .50
180 Walt Weiss B .20 .50
181 Paul Molitor B .20 .50
182 Jose Guillen B .20 .50
183 Al Leiter B .20 .50
184 Mike Fetters B .20 .50
185 Mark Langston B .20 .50
186 Fred McGriff B .30 .75
187 Darrin Fletcher B .20 .50
188 Brant Brown B .20 .50
189 Geronimo Berroa B .20 .50
190 Jim Thome B .30 .75
191 Jose Vizcaino B .20 .50
192 Andy Ashby B .20 .50
193 Rusty Greer B .20 .50
194 Brian Hunter B .20 .50
195 Chris Hoiles B .20 .50
196 Orlando Merced B .20 .50
197 Brett Butler B .20 .50
198 Derek Bell B .20 .50
199 Bobby Bonilla B .20 .50
200 Alex Ochoa B .20 .50
201 Wally Joyner B .20 .50
202 Mo Vaughn B .20 .50
203 Doug Drabek B .20 .50
204 Tino Martinez B .30 .75
205 Roberto Alomar B .30 .75
206 Brian Giles B RC 1.25 3.00
207 Todd Worrell B .20 .50
208 Alan Benes B .20 .50
209 Jim Leyritz B .20 .50
210 Darryl Hamilton B .20 .50
211 Jimmy Key B .20 .50
212 Juan Gonzalez B .20 .50
213 Vinny Castilla B .20 .50
214 Chuck Knoblauch B .20 .50
215 Tony Phillips B .20 .50
216 Jeff Cirillo B .20 .50
217 Carlos Garcia B .20 .50
218 Brooks Kieschnick B .20 .50
219 Marquis Grissom B .20 .50
220 Dan Wilson B .20 .50
221 Greg Vaughn B .20 .50
222 John Wetteland B .20 .50
223 Andres Galarraga B .20 .50
224 Ozzie Guillen B .20 .50
225 Kevin Elster B .20 .50
226 Bernard Gilkey B .20 .50
227 Mike Macfarlane B .20 .50
228 Heathcliff Slocumb B .20 .50
229 Wendell Magee Jr. B .20 .50
230 Carlos Baerga B .20 .50
231 Kevin Seitzer B .20 .50
232 Henry Rodriguez B .20 .50
233 Roger Clemens B 1.00 2.50
234 Mark Wohlers B .20 .50
235 Eddie Murray B .50 1.25
236 Todd Zeile B .20 .50
237 J.T. Snow B .20 .50
238 Ken Griffey Jr. B 1.00 2.50
239 Sterling Hitchcock B .20 .50
240 Albert Belle B .20 .50
241 Terry Steinbach B .20 .50
242 Robb Nen B .20 .50
243 Mark McLemore B .20 .50
244 Jeff King B .20 .50
245 Tony Clark B .20 .50
246 Tim Salmon B .30 .75
247 Benito Santiago B .20 .50
248 Robin Ventura B .20 .50
249 Bubba Trammell B RC .20 .50
250 Chili Davis B .20 .50
251 John Valentin B .20 .50
252 Cal Ripken B 1.50 4.00
253 Matt Williams B .20 .50
254 Jeff Kent B .20 .50
255 Eric Karros B .20 .50
256 Ray Lankford B .20 .50
257 Ed Sprague B .20 .50
258 Shane Reynolds B .20 .50
259 Jaime Navarro B .20 .50
260 Eric Davis B .20 .50
261 Orel Hershiser B .20 .50
262 Mark Grace B .30 .75
263 Rod Beck B .20 .50
264 Ismael Valdes B .20 .50
265 Manny Ramirez B .30 .75
266 Ken Caminiti B .20 .50
267 Tim Naehring B .20 .50
268 Jose Rosado B .20 .50
269 Greg Colbrunn B .20 .50
270 Dean Palmer B .20 .50
271 David Justice B .20 .50
272 Scott Spiezio B .20 .50
273 Chipper Jones B .50 1.25
274 Mel Rojas B .20 .50
275 Bartolo Colon B .20 .50
276 Darin Erstad S .75 2.00
277 Sammy Sosa S 2.00 5.00
278 Rafael Palmeiro S 1.25 3.00
279 Frank Thomas S 2.00 5.00
280 Ruben Rivera S .75 2.00
281 Hal Morris S .75 2.00
282 Jay Buhner S .75 2.00
283 Kenny Lofton S .75 2.00
284 Jose Canseco S 1.25 3.00
285 Alex Fernandez S .75 2.00
286 Todd Helton S 2.00 5.00
287 Andy Pettitte S 1.25 3.00
288 John Franco S .75 2.00
289 Ivan Rodriguez S 1.25 3.00
290 Ellis Burks S .75 2.00
291 Julio Franco S .75 2.00
292 Mike Piazza S 3.00 8.00
293 Brian Jordan S .75 2.00
294 Greg Maddux S 3.00 8.00
295 Bob Abreu S 1.25 3.00
296 Rondell White S .75 2.00
297 Moises Alou S .75 2.00
298 Tony Gwynn S 2.50 6.00
299 Deion Sanders S 1.25 3.00
300 Jeff Montgomery S .75 2.00
301 Ray Durham S .75 2.00
302 John Wasdin S .75 2.00
303 Ryne Sandberg S 3.00 8.00
304 Delino DeShields S .75 2.00
305 Mark McGwire S 5.00 12.00
306 Andruw Jones S 1.25 3.00
307 Kevin Orie S .75 2.00
308 Matt Williams S .75 2.00
309 Karim Garcia S .75 2.00
310 Derek Jeter S 5.00 12.00
311 Mo Vaughn S .75 2.00
312 Brady Anderson S .75 2.00
313 Barry Bonds S 5.00 12.00
314 Steve Finley S .75 2.00
315 Vladimir Guerrero S 2.00 5.00
316 Matt Morris S .75 2.00
317 Tom Glavine S 1.25 3.00
318 Jeff Bagwell S 1.25 3.00
319 Albert Belle S .75 2.00
320 Hideki Irabu S RC .75 2.00
321 Andres Galarraga S .75 2.00
322 Cecil Fielder S .75 2.00
323 Barry Larkin S 1.25 3.00
324 Todd Hundley S .75 2.00
325 Fred McGriff S 1.25 3.00
326 Gary Sheffield G 2.00 5.00
327 Craig Biggio G 3.00 8.00
328 Raul Mondesi G 2.00 5.00
329 Edgar Martinez G 3.00 8.00
330 Chipper Jones G 5.00 12.00
331 Bernie Williams G 3.00 8.00
332 Juan Gonzalez G 2.00 5.00
333 Ron Gant G 2.00 5.00
334 Cal Ripken G 15.00 40.00
335 Larry Walker G 2.00 5.00
336 Matt Williams G 2.00 5.00
337 Jose Cruz Jr. G RC 2.00 5.00
338 Joe Carter G 2.00 5.00
339 Wilton Guerrero G 2.00 5.00
340 Cecil Fielder G 2.00 5.00
341 Todd Walker G 2.00 5.00
342 Ken Griffey Jr. G 10.00 25.00
343 Ryan Klesko G 2.00 5.00
344 Roger Clemens G 10.00 25.00
345 Hideo Nomo G 5.00 12.00
346 Dante Bichette G 2.00 5.00
347 Albert Belle G 2.00 5.00
348 Randy Johnson G 5.00 12.00
349 Manny Ramirez G 3.00 8.00
350 John Smoltz G 3.00 8.00

1997 Finest Embossed

*SILV.STARS: .60X TO 1.5X BASIC CARD
*SILVER ROOKIES: .5X TO 1.25X BASIC
SILVER STATED ODDS 1:16
ALL SILVER CARDS ARE NON DIE CUT
*GOLD STARS: .75X TO 2X BASIC CARD
*GOLD ROOKIES: .5X TO 1.2X BASIC CARD
GOLD STATED ODDS 1:96
ALL GOLD CARDS ARE DIE CUT

1997 Finest Embossed Refractors

*SILVER STARS: 2.5X TO 6X BASIC CARDS
*SILVER ROOKIES: 2X TO 5X BASIC CARDS
SILVER STATED ODDS 1:192
ALL SILVER CARDS ARE NON DIE CUT
*SER.1 GOLD STARS: 8X TO 20X BASIC
*SER.2 GOLD STARS: 8X TO 20X BASIC
*SER.2 GOLD RC'S: 5X TO 12X BASIC
GOLD STATED ODDS 1:1152
ALL GOLD CARDS ARE DIE CUT

1997 Finest Refractors

*BRONZE STARS: 4X TO 10X BASIC CARD
*BRONZE RC'S: 1.25X TO 3X BASIC CARD
BRONZE STATED ODDS 1:12
*SILVER STARS: 1.25X TO 3X BASIC CARD
*SILVER ROOKIES: 1X TO 2.5X BASIC CARD
SILVER STATED ODDS 1:48
*GOLD STARS: 1.25X TO 3X BASIC CARD
*GOLD ROOKIES: .75X TO 2X BASIC CARD
GOLD STATED ODDS 1:288

1998 Finest Pre-Production

COMPLETE SET (5) 4.00 10.00
PP1 Nomar Garciaparra 1.00 2.50
PP2 Mark McGwire 1.00 2.50
PP3 Ivan Rodriguez .60 1.50
PP4 Ken Griffey Jr 1.25 3.00
PP5 Roger Clemens 1.00 2.50

1998 Finest

This 275-card set (produced by Topps) was distributed in first and second series six-card packs with a suggested retail price of $5. Series one contains cards 1-150 and series two contains cards 151-275. Each card features action color player photos printed on 26 pt. card stock with each position identified by a different card design. The backs carry player information and career statistics.

COMPLETE SET (275) 20.00 50.00
COMPLETE SERIES 1 (150) 10.00 25.00
COMPLETE SERIES 2 (125) 10.00 25.00
1 Larry Walker .15 .40
2 Andruw Jones .25 .60
3 Ramon Martinez .08 .25
4 Geronimo Berroa .08 .25
5 David Justice .15 .40
6 Rusty Greer .15 .40
7 Chad Ogea .08 .25
8 Tom Goodwin .08 .25
9 Tino Martinez .25 .60
10 Jose Guillen .15 .40
11 Jeffrey Hammonds .08 .25
12 Brian McRae .08 .25
13 Jeremi Gonzalez .08 .25
14 Craig Counsell .08 .25
15 Mike Piazza .60 1.50
16 Greg Maddux .60 1.50
17 Todd Greene .08 .25
18 Rondell White .15 .40
19 Kirk Rueter .08 .25
20 Tony Clark .08 .25
21 Brad Radke .15 .40
22 Jaret Wright .08 .25
23 Carlos Delgado .15 .40
24 Dustin Hermanson .08 .25
25 Gary Sheffield .15 .40
26 Jose Canseco .25 .60
27 Kevin Young .15 .40
28 David Wells .15 .40
29 Mariano Rivera .40 1.00
30 Reggie Sanders .15 .40
31 Mike Cameron .08 .25
32 Bobby Witt .08 .25
33 Kevin Orie .08 .25
34 Royce Clayton .08 .25
35 Edgar Martinez .25 .60
36 Neifi Perez .08 .25
37 Kevin Appier .15 .40
38 Darryl Hamilton .08 .25
39 Michael Tucker .08 .25
40 Roger Clemens .75 2.00
41 Carl Everett .15 .40
42 Mike Sweeney .15 .40
43 Pat Meares .08 .25
44 Brian Giles .15 .40
45 Matt Morris .15 .40
46 Jason Dickson .08 .25
47 Rich Loiselle RC .15 .40
48 Joe Girardi .15 .40
49 Steve Trachsel .08 .25
50 Ben Grieve .08 .25
51 Brian Johnson .08 .25
52 Hideki Irabu .08 .25
53 J.T. Snow .15 .40
54 Mike Hampton .15 .40
55 Dave Nilsson .08 .25
56 Alex Fernandez .08 .25
57 Brett Tomko .08 .25
58 Wally Joyner .15 .40
59 Kelvim Escobar .08 .25
60 Roberto Alomar .25 .60
61 Todd Jones .08 .25
62 Paul O'Neill .25 .60
63 Jamie Moyer .15 .40
64 Mark Wohlers .08 .25
65 Jose Cruz Jr. .08 .25
66 Troy Percival .15 .40
67 Rick Reed .08 .25
68 Will Clark .25 .60
69 Jamey Wright .08 .25
70 Mike Mussina .25 .60
71 David Cone .15 .40
72 Ryan Klesko .15 .40
73 Scott Hatteberg .08 .25
74 James Baldwin .08 .25
75 Tony Womack .08 .25
76 Carlos Perez .08 .25
77 Charles Nagy .08 .25
78 Jeromy Burnitz .15 .40
79 Shane Reynolds .08 .25
80 Cliff Floyd .15 .40
81 Jason Kendall .15 .40
82 Chad Curtis .08 .25
83 Matt Karchner .08 .25
84 Ricky Bottalico .08 .25
85 Sammy Sosa .40 1.00
86 Javy Lopez .15 .40
87 Jeff Kent .15 .40
88 Shawn Green .15 .40
89 Joey Cora .08 .25
90 Tony Gwynn .50 1.25
91 Bob Tewksbury .08 .25
92 Derek Jeter 1.00 2.50
93 Eric Davis .15 .40
94 Jeff Fassero .08 .25
95 Denny Neagle .08 .25
96 Ismael Valdes .08 .25
97 Tim Salmon .25 .60
98 Mark Grudzielanek .08 .25
99 Curt Schilling .15 .40
100 Ken Griffey Jr. .75 2.00
101 Edgardo Alfonzo .08 .25
102 Vinny Castilla .15 .40
103 Jose Rosado .08 .25
104 Scott Erickson .08 .25
105 Alan Benes .08 .25
106 Shannon Stewart .15 .40
107 Delino DeShields .08 .25
108 Mark Loretta .08 .25
109 Todd Hundley .08 .25
110 Chuck Knoblauch .15 .40
111 Todd Helton .25 .60
112 F.P. Santangelo .08 .25
113 Jeff Cirillo .08 .25
114 Omar Vizquel .25 .60
115 John Valentin .08 .25
116 Damion Easley .08 .25
117 Matt Lawton .08 .25
118 Jim Thome .25 .60
119 Sandy Alomar Jr. .08 .25
120 Albert Belle .15 .40
121 Chris Stynes .08 .25
122 Butch Huskey .08 .25
123 Shawn Estes .08 .25
124 Terry Adams .08 .25
125 Ivan Rodriguez .25 .60
126 Ron Gant .08 .25
127 John Mabry .08 .25
128 Jeff Shaw .08 .25
129 Jeff Montgomery .08 .25
130 Justin Thompson .08 .25
131 Livan Hernandez .15 .40
132 Ugueth Urbina .08 .25
133 Scott Servais .08 .25
134 Troy O'Leary .08 .25
135 Cal Ripken 1.25 3.00
136 Quilvio Veras .08 .25
137 Pedro Astacio .08 .25
138 Willie Greene .08 .25
139 Lance Johnson .08 .25
140 Nomar Garciaparra .60 1.50
141 Jose Offerman .08 .25
142 Scott Rolen .25 .60
143 Derek Bell .08 .25
144 Johnny Damon .25 .60
145 Mark McGwire 1.00 2.50
146 Chan Ho Park .15 .40
147 Edgar Renteria .15 .40
148 Eric Young .08 .25
149 Craig Biggio .25 .60
150 Checklist (1-150) .08 .25
151 Frank Thomas .40 1.00
152 John Wetteland .15 .40
153 Mike Lansing .08 .25
154 Pedro Martinez .25 .60
155 Rico Brogna .08 .25
156 Kevin Brown .25 .60
157 Alex Rodriguez .60 1.50
158 Wade Boggs .25 .60
159 Richard Hidalgo .08 .25
160 Mark Grace .25 .60
161 Jose Mesa .08 .25
162 John Olerud .15 .40
163 Tim Belcher .08 .25
164 Chuck Finley .15 .40
165 Brian Hunter .08 .25
166 Joe Carter .15 .40
167 Stan Javier .08 .25
168 Jay Bell .15 .40
169 Ray Lankford .15 .40
170 John Smoltz .25 .60
171 Ed Sprague .08 .25
172 Jason Giambi .15 .40
173 Todd Walker .08 .25
174 Paul Konerko .15 .40
175 Rey Ordonez .15 .40
176 Dante Bichette .15 .40
177 Bernie Williams .25 .60
178 Jon Nunnally .08 .25
179 Rafael Palmeiro .25 .60
180 Jay Buhner .15 .40
181 Devon White .15 .40
182 Jeff D'Amico .08 .25
183 Walt Weiss .15 .40
184 Scott Spiezio .08 .25
185 Moises Alou .15 .40
186 Carlos Baerga .08 .25
187 Todd Zeile .15 .40
188 Gregg Jefferies .08 .25
189 Mo Vaughn .15 .40
190 Terry Steinbach .08 .25
191 Ray Durham .15 .40
192 Robin Ventura .15 .40
193 Jeff Reed .08 .25
194 Ken Caminiti .15 .40
195 Eric Karros .15 .40
196 Wilson Alvarez .08 .25
197 Gary Gaetti .15 .40
198 Andres Galarraga .15 .40
199 Alex Gonzalez .08 .25
200 Garret Anderson .15 .40
201 Andy Benes .08 .25
202 Harold Baines .15 .40
203 Ron Coomer .08 .25
204 Dean Palmer .15 .40
205 Reggie Jefferson .08 .25
206 John Burkett .08 .25
207 Jermaine Allensworth .08 .25
208 Bernard Gilkey .08 .25
209 Jeff Bagwell .25 .60
210 Kenny Lofton .15 .40
211 Bobby Jones .08 .25
212 Bartolo Colon .15 .40
213 Jim Edmonds .15 .40
214 Pat Hentgen .08 .25
215 Matt Williams .15 .40
216 Bob Abreu .15 .40
217 Jorge Posada .25 .60
218 Marty Cordova .08 .25
219 Ken Hill .08 .25
220 Steve Finley .15 .40
221 Jeff King .08 .25
222 Quinton McCracken .08 .25
223 Matt Stairs .08 .25
224 Darin Erstad .15 .40
225 Fred McGriff .25 .60
226 Marquis Grissom .15 .40
227 Doug Glanville .08 .25
228 Tom Glavine .25 .60
229 John Franco .15 .40
230 Darren Bragg .08 .25
231 Barry Larkin .25 .60
232 Trevor Hoffman .15 .40
233 Brady Anderson .15 .40
234 Al Martin .08 .25
235 B.J. Surhoff .15 .40
236 Ellis Burks .15 .40
237 Randy Johnson .40 1.00
238 Mark Clark .08 .25
239 Tony Saunders .08 .25
240 Hideo Nomo .40 1.00
241 Brad Fullmer .08 .25
242 Chipper Jones .40 1.00
243 Jose Valentin .08 .25
244 Manny Ramirez .25 .60
245 Derrek Lee .25 .60
246 Jimmy Key .15 .40
247 Tim Naehring .08 .25
248 Bobby Higginson .15 .40
249 Charles Johnson .15 .40
250 Chili Davis .15 .40
251 Tom Gordon .08 .25
252 Mike Lieberthal .15 .40
253 Billy Wagner .15 .40
254 Juan Guzman .08 .25
255 Todd Stottlemyre .08 .25
256 Brian Jordan .15 .40
257 Barry Bonds 1.00 2.50
258 Dan Wilson .08 .25
259 Paul Molitor .15 .40
260 Juan Gonzalez .15 .40
261 Francisco Cordova .08 .25
262 Cecil Fielder .15 .40
263 Travis Lee .08 .25
264 Kevin Tapani .08 .25
265 Raul Mondesi .15 .40
266 Travis Fryman .15 .40
267 Armando Benitez .08 .25
268 Pokey Reese .08 .25
269 Rick Aguilera .08 .25
270 Andy Pettitte .25 .60
271 Jose Vizcaino .08 .25
272 Kerry Wood .20 .50
273 Vladimir Guerrero .40 1.00
274 John Smiley .08 .25
275 Checklist (151-275) .08 .25

1998 Finest No-Protectors

COMPLETE SET (275) 175.00 350.00
COMPLETE SERIES 1 (150) 100.00 200.00
COMPLETE SERIES 2 (125) 75.00 150.00
*STARS: 1.5X TO 4X BASIC CARDS
STATED ODDS 1:2, 1 PER HTA

1998 Finest Oversize

COMPLETE SERIES 1 (8) 50.00 120.00
COMPLETE SERIES 2 (8) 30.00 80.00
STATED ODDS 1:3 HOBBY/HTA BOXES
*REFRACTORS: .75X TO 2X BASIC OVERSIZE
REF.ODDS 1:6 HOBBY/HTA BOXES
A1 Mark McGwire 6.00 15.00
A2 Cal Ripken 8.00 20.00
A3 Nomar Garciaparra 4.00 10.00
A4 Mike Piazza 4.00 10.00
A5 Greg Maddux 4.00 10.00
A6 Jose Cruz Jr. .60 1.50
A7 Roger Clemens 5.00 12.00
A8 Ken Griffey Jr. 5.00 12.00
B1 Frank Thomas 2.50 6.00
B2 Bernie Williams 1.50 4.00
B3 Randy Johnson 2.50 6.00
B4 Chipper Jones 2.50 6.00
B5 Manny Ramirez 1.50 4.00
B6 Barry Bonds 6.00 15.00
B7 Juan Gonzalez 1.00 2.50
B8 Jeff Bagwell 1.50 4.00

1998 Finest Refractors

COMPLETE SET (275) 550.00 1100.00
*STARS: 5X TO 12X BASIC CARDS
STATED ODDS 1:12, 1:5 HTA
NO-PROTECTOR REF.ODDS 1:24, 1:10 HTA

1998 Finest Centurions

COMPLETE SET (20) 20.00 50.00
SER.1 ODDS 1:153 HOBBY, 1:71 HTA
STATED PRINT RUN 500 SERIAL #'d SETS
*REF: 2.5X TO 6X BASIC CENTURIONS
SER.1 REF.ODDS 1:1020 HOBBY, 1:471 HTA
REFRACTOR PR.RUN 75 SERIAL #'d SETS
BEWARE COUNTERFEITS
C1 Andruw Jones .75 2.00
C2 Vladimir Guerrero 1.25 3.00
C3 Nomar Garciaparra 1.25 3.00
C4 Scott Rolen 1.25 3.00
C5 Ken Griffey Jr. 25.00 60.00
C6 Jose Cruz Jr. .75 2.00
C7 Barry Bonds 3.00 8.00
C8 Mark McGwire 3.00 8.00
C9 Juan Gonzalez .75 2.00
C10 Jeff Bagwell 1.25 3.00
C11 Frank Thomas 2.00 5.00
C12 Paul Konerko .75 2.00
C13 Alex Rodriguez 2.50 6.00
C14 Mike Piazza 2.00 5.00
C15 Travis Lee .75 2.00
C16 Chipper Jones 2.00 5.00
C17 Larry Walker 1.25 3.00
C18 Mo Vaughn .75 2.00
C19 Livan Hernandez .75 2.00
C20 Jaret Wright .75 2.00

1998 Finest The Man

COMPLETE SET (20) 200.00 400.00
SER.2 STATED ODDS 1:119
STATED PRINT RUN 500 SERIAL #'d SETS
*REF: 1X TO 2.5X BASIC THE MAN
REF.SER.2 ODDS 1:793
REFRACTOR PR.RUN 75 SERIAL #'d SETS
TM1 Ken Griffey Jr. 30.00 80.00
TM2 Barry Bonds 15.00 40.00
TM3 Frank Thomas 12.00 30.00
TM4 Chipper Jones 12.00 30.00
TM5 Cal Ripken 20.00 50.00
TM6 Nomar Garciaparra 10.00 25.00
TM7 Mark McGwire 15.00 40.00
TM8 Mike Piazza 12.50 30.00
TM9 Derek Jeter 15.00 40.00
TM10 Alex Rodriguez 10.00 25.00
TM11 Jose Cruz Jr. 1.50 4.00
TM12 Larry Walker 2.50 6.00
TM13 Jeff Bagwell 4.00 10.00
TM14 Tony Gwynn 8.00 20.00
TM15 Travis Lee 1.50 4.00
TM16 Juan Gonzalez 2.50 6.00
TM17 Scott Rolen 4.00 10.00
TM18 Randy Johnson 6.00 15.00
TM19 Roger Clemens 12.50 30.00
TM20 Greg Maddux 10.00 25.00

1998 Finest Mystery Finest 1

SER.1 ODDS 1:36 HOBBY, 1:15 HTA
*REFRACTOR: 1X TO 2.5X BASIC MYSTERY
REF.SER.1 ODDS 1:144 HOBBY, 1:64 HTA
M1 F.Thomas / K.Griffey Jr. 8.00 20.00
M2 F.Thomas / M.Piazza 4.00 10.00
M3 F.Thomas / M.McGwire 10.00 25.00
M4 F.Thomas / F.Thomas 4.00 10.00
M5 K.Griffey Jr. / M.Piazza 8.00 20.00
M6 K.Griffey Jr. / M.McGwire 12.50 30.00
M7 K.Griffey Jr. / K.Griffey Jr. 8.00 20.00
M8 M.Piazza / M.McGwire 10.00 25.00
M9 M.Piazza / M.Piazza 8.00 20.00
M10 M.McGwire / M.McGwire 12.50 30.00
M11 N.Garciaparra / J.Cruz Jr. 6.00 15.00
M12 N.Garciaparra / D.Jeter 8.00 20.00
M13 N.Garciaparra / A.Jones 6.00 15.00
M14 N.Garciaparra / N.Garc 8.00 20.00
M15 J.Cruz Jr. / D.Jeter 10.00 25.00
M16 J.Cruz Jr. / A.Jones 2.50 6.00
M17 J.Cruz Jr. / J.Cruz Jr. 1.50 4.00
M18 D.Jeter / A.Jones 10.00 25.00
M19 D.Jeter / D.Jeter 12.50 30.00
M20 A.Jones / A.Jones 2.50 6.00
M21 C.Ripken / T.Gwynn 10.00 25.00
M22 C.Ripken / B.Bonds 12.50 30.00
M23 C.Ripken / G.Maddux 12.50 30.00
M24 C.Ripken / C.Ripken 15.00 40.00
M25 T.Gwynn / B.Bonds 12.50 30.00
M26 T.Gwynn / G.Maddux 6.00 15.00
M27 T.Gwynn / T.Gwynn 6.00 15.00
M28 B.Bonds / G.Maddux 12.50 30.00
M29 B.Bonds / B.Bonds 12.50 30.00
M30 G.Maddux / G.Maddux 8.00 20.00
M31 J.Gonzalez / L.Walker 1.50 4.00
M32 J.Gonzalez / A.Galarraga 1.50 4.00
M33 J.Gonzalez / C.Jones 4.00 10.00
M34 J.Gonzalez / J.Gonzalez 1.50 4.00
M35 L.Walker / A.Galarraga 1.50 4.00
M36 L.Walker / C.Jones 4.00 10.00
M37 L.Walker / L.Walker 1.50 4.00
M38 A.Galarraga / C.Jones 4.00 10.00
M39 A.Galarraga / A.Galarraga 1.50 4.00
M40 C.Jones / C.Jones 4.00 10.00
M41 G.Sheffield / S.Sosa 4.00 10.00
M42 G.Sheffield / J.Bagwell 2.50 6.00
M43 G.Sheffield / T.Martinez 2.50 6.00
M44 G.Sheffield / G.Sheffield 1.50 4.00
M45 S.Sosa / J.Bagwell 8.00 20.00
M46 S.Sosa / T.Martinez 4.00 10.00
M47 S.Sosa / S.Sosa 4.00 10.00
M48 J.Bagwell / T.Martinez 2.50 6.00
M49 J.Bagwell / J.Bagwell 2.50 6.00
M50 T.Martinez / T.Martinez 2.50 6.00

1998 Finest Mystery Finest 2

COMPLETE SET (40) 150.00 300.00
SER.2 STATED ODDS 1:36
*REFRACTOR: 1X TO 2.5X BASIC MYSTERY
REF.SER.2 ODDS 1:144
M1 N.Garciaparra / F.Thomas 4.00 10.00
M2 N.Garciaparra / A.Belle 4.00 10.00
M3 N.Garciaparra / S.Rolen 6.00 15.00
M4 F.Thomas / A.Belle 4.00 10.00
M5 F.Thomas / S.Rolen 4.00 10.00
M6 A.Belle / S.Rolen 2.50 6.00
M7 K.Griffey Jr. / J.Cruz Jr. 8.00 20.00
M8 K.Griffey Jr. / A.Rodriguez 8.00 20.00
M9 K.Griffey Jr. / R.Clemens 10.00 25.00
M10 J.Cruz Jr. / A.Rodriguez 6.00 15.00
M11 J.Cruz Jr. / R.Clemens 8.00 20.00
M12 A.Rodriguez / R.Clemens 6.00 15.00
M13 M.Piazza / B.Bonds 12.50 30.00
M14 M.Piazza / D.Jeter 10.00 25.00
M15 M.Piazza / B.Williams 6.00 15.00
M16 B.Bonds / D.Jeter 12.50 30.00
M17 B.Bonds / B.Williams 6.00 15.00
M18 D.Jeter / B.Williams 10.00 25.00
M19 M.McGwire / J.Bagwell 10.00 25.00
M20 M.McGwire / M.Vaughn 10.00 25.00
M21 M.McGwire / J.Thome 10.00 25.00
M22 J.Bagwell / M.Vaughn 2.50 6.00
M23 J.Bagwell / J.Thome 2.50 6.00
M24 M.Vaughn / J.Thome 2.50 6.00
M25 J.Gonzalez / T.Lee 1.50 4.00
M26 J.Gonzalez / B.Grieve 1.50 4.00
M27 J.Gonzalez / F.McGriff 2.50 6.00
M28 T.Lee / B.Grieve 1.50 4.00
M29 T.Lee / F.McGriff 2.50 6.00
M30 B.Grieve / F.McGriff 2.50 6.00
M31 A.Belle / A.Belle 1.50 4.00
M32 S.Rolen / S.Rolen 2.50 6.00
M33 A.Rodriguez / A.Rodriguez 8.00 20.00
M34 R.Clemens / R.Clemens 8.00 20.00
M35 B.Williams / B.Williams 2.50 6.00
M36 M.Vaughn / M.Vaughn 1.50 4.00
M37 J.Thome / J.Thome 2.50 6.00
M38 T.Lee / T.Lee 1.50 4.00
M39 F.McGriff / F.McGriff 2.50 6.00
M40 B.Grieve / B.Grieve 1.50 4.00

1998 Finest Mystery Finest Oversize

COMPLETE SET (3) 15.00 40.00
SER.2 STATED ODDS 1:6 HTA BOXES
*REFRACTOR: .75X TO 2X OVERSIZE
SER.2 REF.STATED ODDS 1:12 HTA BOXES
1 K.Griffey Jr. / A.Rodriguez 5.00 12.00
2 D.Jeter / B.Williams 6.00 15.00
3 M.McGwire / J.Bagwell 6.00 15.00

1998 Finest Power Zone

COMPLETE SET (20) 25.00 60.00
SER.1 STAT.ODDS 1:72 HOBBY, 1:32 HTA
P1 Ken Griffey Jr. 5.00 12.00
P2 Jeff Bagwell 1.50 4.00
P3 Jose Cruz Jr. 1.00 2.50
P4 Barry Bonds 4.00 10.00
P5 Mark McGwire 4.00 10.00
P6 Jim Thome 1.50 4.00
P7 Mo Vaughn 1.00 2.50
P8 Gary Sheffield 1.00 2.50
P9 Andres Galarraga 1.50 4.00
P10 Nomar Garciaparra 1.50 4.00
P11 Rafael Palmeiro 1.50 4.00
P12 Sammy Sosa 2.50 6.00
P13 Jay Buhner 1.00 2.50
P14 Tony Clark 1.00 2.50
P15 Mike Piazza 2.50 6.00
P16 Larry Walker 1.50 4.00
P17 Albert Belle 1.00 2.50
P18 Tino Martinez 1.00 2.50
P19 Juan Gonzalez 1.00 2.50
P20 Frank Thomas 2.50 6.00

1998 Finest Stadium Stars

COMPLETE SET (24) 40.00 100.00
JUMBOS: RANDOM IN SER.2 JUMBO BOXES
SS1 Ken Griffey Jr. 5.00 12.00
SS2 Alex Rodriguez 3.00 8.00
SS3 Mo Vaughn 1.00 2.50
SS4 Nomar Garciaparra 1.50 4.00
SS5 Frank Thomas 2.50 6.00
SS6 Albert Belle 1.00 2.50
SS7 Derek Jeter 6.00 15.00
SS8 Chipper Jones 2.50 6.00
SS9 Cal Ripken 8.00 20.00
SS10 Jim Thome 1.50 4.00
SS11 Mike Piazza 2.50 6.00
SS12 Juan Gonzalez 1.00 2.50
SS13 Jeff Bagwell 1.50 4.00
SS14 Sammy Sosa 2.50 6.00
SS15 Jose Cruz Jr. 1.00 2.50
SS16 Gary Sheffield 1.00 2.50
SS17 Larry Walker 1.50 4.00
SS18 Tony Gwynn 2.50 6.00
SS19 Mark McGwire 4.00 10.00
SS20 Barry Bonds 4.00 10.00
SS21 Tino Martinez 1.00 2.50
SS22 Manny Ramirez 2.50 6.00
SS23 Ken Caminiti 1.00 2.50
SS24 Andres Galarraga 1.50 4.00

1999 Finest Pre-Production

COMPLETE SET (6) 3.00 8.00
PP1 Darin Erstad .75 2.00
PP2 Javy Lopez .75 2.00
PP3 Vinny Castilla .40 1.00
PP4 Jim Thome .60 1.50

PP5 Tino Martinez .40 1.00
PP6 Mark Grace .75 2.00

1999 Finest

This 300-card set (produced by Topps) was distributed in first and second series six-card packs with a suggested retail price of $5. The fronts feature color action player photos printed on 27 pt. card stock using Chromium technology. The backs carry player information. The set includes the following subsets: Gems (101-120), Sensations (121-130) Rookies (131-150/277-299), Sterling (251-265) and Gamers (266-276). Card number 300 is a special Hank Aaron/Mark McGwire tribute. Cards numbered from 101 through 150 and 251 through 300 were short printed and seeded at a rate of one per hobby, one per retail and two per Home Team Advantage pack. Notable Rookie Cards include Pat Burrell, Sean Burroughs, Nick Johnson, Austin Kearns, Corey Patterson and Alfonso Soriano.

COMPLETE SET (300) 25.00 60.00
COMPLETE SERIES 1 (150) 15.00 40.00
COMPLETE SERIES 2 (150) 15.00 40.00
COMP.SER.1 w/o SP's (100) 6.00 15.00
COMP.SER.2 w/o SP's (100) 6.00 15.00
COMMON (1-100/151-250) .15 .40
COMMON (101-150/251-300) .20 .50
101-150/251-300 ODDS 1:1 H/R, 2:1 HTA
1 Darin Erstad .15 .40
2 Javy Lopez .15 .40
3 Vinny Castilla .15 .40
4 Jim Thome .25 .60
5 Tino Martinez .15 .40
6 Mark Grace .25 .60
7 Shawn Green .15 .40
8 Dustin Hermanson .15 .40
9 Kevin Young .15 .40
10 Tony Clark .15 .40
11 Scott Brosius .15 .40
12 Craig Biggio .25 .60
13 Brian McRae .15 .40
14 Chan Ho Park .25 .60
15 Manny Ramirez .40 1.00
16 Chipper Jones .40 1.00
17 Rico Brogna .15 .40
18 Quinton McCracken .15 .40
19 J.T. Snow .15 .40
20 Tony Gwynn .40 1.00
21 Juan Guzman .15 .40
22 John Valentin .15 .40
23 Rick Helling .15 .40
24 Sandy Alomar Jr. .15 .40
25 Frank Thomas .40 1.00
26 Jorge Posada .25 .60
27 Dmitri Young .15 .40
28 Rick Reed .15 .40
29 Kevin Tapani .15 .40
30 Troy Glaus .15 .40
31 Kenny Rogers .15 .40
32 Jeromy Burnitz .15 .40
33 Mark Grudzielanek .15 .40
34 Mike Mussina .25 .60
35 Scott Rolen .25 .60
36 Neifi Perez .15 .40
37 Brad Radke .15 .40
38 Darryl Strawberry .15 .40
39 Robb Nen .15 .40
40 Moises Alou .15 .40
41 Eric Young .15 .40
42 Livan Hernandez .15 .40
43 John Wetteland .15 .40
44 Matt Lawton .15 .40
45 Ben Grieve .15 .40
46 Fernando Tatis .15 .40
47 Travis Fryman .15 .40
48 David Segui .15 .40
49 Bob Abreu .15 .40
50 Nomar Garciaparra .25 .60
51 Paul O'Neill .25 .60
52 Jeff King .15 .40
53 Francisco Cordova .15 .40
54 John Olerud .15 .40
55 Vladimir Guerrero .25 .60
56 Fernando Vina .15 .40
57 Shane Reynolds .15 .40
58 Chuck Finley .15 .40
59 Rondell White .15 .40
60 Greg Vaughn .15 .40
61 Ryan Minor .15 .40
62 Tom Gordon .15 .40
63 Damion Easley .15 .40
64 Ray Durham .15 .40
65 Orlando Hernandez .15 .40
66 Bartolo Colon .15 .40
67 Jaret Wright .15 .40
68 Royce Clayton .15 .40
69 Tim Salmon .15 .40
70 Mark McGwire .60 1.50
71 Alex Gonzalez .15 .40
72 Tom Glavine .25 .60
73 David Justice .15 .40
74 Omar Vizquel .25 .60
75 Juan Gonzalez .15 .40
76 Bobby Higginson .15 .40
77 Todd Walker .15 .40
78 Dante Bichette .15 .40
79 Kevin Millwood .15 .40
80 Roger Clemens .50 1.25
81 Kerry Wood .15 .40
82 Cal Ripken 1.25 3.00
83 Jay Bell .15 .40
84 Barry Bonds .60 1.50
85 Alex Rodriguez .50 1.25
86 Doug Glanville .15 .40
87 Jason Kendall .15 .40
88 Sean Casey .15 .40
89 Aaron Sele .15 .40
90 Derek Jeter 1.00 2.50
91 Andy Ashby .15 .40
92 Rusty Greer .15 .40
93 Rod Beck .15 .40
94 Matt Williams .15 .40
95 Mike Piazza .40 1.00
96 Wally Joyner .15 .40
97 Barry Larkin .25 .60
98 Eric Milton .15 .40
99 Gary Sheffield .15 .40
100 Greg Maddux .50 1.25
101 Ken Griffey Jr. GEM 1.25 3.00
102 Frank Thomas GEM .60 1.50
103 Nomar Garciaparra GEM 1.00 2.50
104 Mark McGwire GEM 1.50 4.00
105 Alex Rodriguez GEM 1.00 2.50
106 Tony Gwynn GEM .75 2.00
107 Juan Gonzalez GEM .25 .60
108 Jeff Bagwell GEM .40 1.00
109 Sammy Sosa GEM .60 1.50
110 Vladimir Guerrero GEM .60 1.50
111 Roger Clemens GEM 1.25 3.00
112 Barry Bonds GEM 1.50 4.00
113 Darin Erstad GEM .25 .60
114 Mike Piazza GEM 1.00 2.50
115 Derek Jeter GEM 1.50 4.00
116 Chipper Jones GEM .60 1.50
117 Larry Walker GEM .25 .60
118 Scott Rolen GEM .40 1.00
119 Cal Ripken GEM 2.00 5.00
120 Greg Maddux GEM 1.00 2.50
121 Troy Glaus SENS .40 1.00
122 Ben Grieve SENS .20 .50
123 Ryan Minor SENS .20 .50
124 Kerry Wood SENS .25 .60
125 Travis Lee SENS .20 .50
126 Adrian Beltre SENS .25 .60
127 Brad Fullmer SENS .20 .50
128 Aramis Ramirez SENS .25 .60
129 Eric Chavez SENS .25 .60
130 Todd Helton SENS .40 1.00
131 Pat Burrell RC 1.25 3.00
132 Ryan Mills RC .20 .50
133 Austin Kearns RC 1.25 3.00
134 Josh McKinley RC .20 .50
135 Adam Everett RC .40 1.00
136 Marlon Anderson .20 .50
137 Bruce Chen .20 .50
138 Matt Clement .25 .60
139 Alex Gonzalez .20 .50
140 Roy Halladay .25 .60
141 Calvin Pickering .20 .50
142 Randy Wolf .20 .50
143 Ryan Anderson .20 .50
144 Ruben Mateo .20 .50
145 Alex Escobar RC .25 .60
146 Jeremy Giambi .20 .50
147 Lance Berkman .25 .60
148 Michael Barrett .20 .50
149 Preston Wilson .25 .60
150 Gabe Kapler .25 .60
151 Roger Clemens .75 2.00
152 Jay Buhner .15 .40
153 Brad Fullmer .15 .40
154 Ray Lankford .15 .40
155 Jim Edmonds .15 .40
156 Jason Giambi .15 .40
157 Bret Boone .15 .40
158 Jeff Cirillo .15 .40
159 Rickey Henderson .40 1.00
160 Edgar Martinez .25 .60
161 Ron Gant .15 .40
162 Mark Kotsay .15 .40
163 Trevor Hoffman .15 .40
164 Jason Schmidt .15 .40
165 Brett Tomko .15 .40
166 David Ortiz .40 1.00
167 Dean Palmer .15 .40
168 Hideki Irabu .15 .40
169 Mike Cameron .15 .40
170 Pedro Martinez .25 .60
171 Tom Goodwin .15 .40
172 Brian Hunter .15 .40
173 Al Leiter .15 .40
174 Charles Johnson .15 .40
175 Curt Schilling .15 .40
176 Robin Ventura .15 .40
177 Travis Lee .15 .40
178 Jeff Shaw .15 .40
179 Ugueth Urbina .15 .40
180 Roberto Alomar .25 .60
181 Cliff Floyd .15 .40
182 Adrian Beltre .15 .40
183 Tony Womack .15 .40
184 Brian Jordan .15 .40
185 Randy Johnson .40 1.00
186 Mickey Morandini .15 .40
187 Todd Hundley .15 .40
188 Jose Valentin .15 .40
189 Eric Davis .15 .40
190 Ken Caminiti .15 .40
191 David Wells .15 .40
192 Ryan Klesko .15 .40
193 Garret Anderson .15 .40
194 Eric Karros .15 .40
195 Ivan Rodriguez .25 .60
196 Aramis Ramirez .15 .40
197 Mike Lieberthal .15 .40
198 Will Clark .25 .60
199 Rey Ordonez .15 .40
200 Ken Griffey Jr. .75 2.00
201 Jose Guillen .15 .40
202 Scott Erickson .15 .40
203 Paul Konerko .15 .40
204 Johnny Damon .25 .60
205 Larry Walker .15 .40
206 Denny Neagle .15 .40
207 Jose Offerman .15 .40
208 Andy Pettitte .25 .60
209 Bobby Jones .15 .40
210 Kevin Brown .25 .60
211 John Smoltz .25 .60
212 Henry Rodriguez .15 .40
213 Tim Belcher .15 .40
214 Carlos Delgado .15 .40
215 Andruw Jones .25 .60
216 Andy Benes .15 .40
217 Fred McGriff .25 .60
218 Edgar Renteria .15 .40
219 Miguel Tejada .15 .40
220 Bernie Williams .25 .60
221 Justin Thompson .15 .40
222 Marty Cordova .15 .40
223 Delino DeShields .15 .40
224 Ellis Burks .15 .40
225 Kenny Lofton .15 .40
226 Steve Finley .15 .40
227 Eric Chavez .15 .40
228 Jose Cruz Jr. .15 .40
229 Marquis Grissom .15 .40
230 Jeff Bagwell .25 .60
231 Jose Canseco .25 .60
232 Edgardo Alfonzo .15 .40
233 Richie Sexson .15 .40
234 Jeff Kent .15 .40
235 Rafael Palmeiro .25 .60
236 David Cone .15 .40
237 Gregg Jefferies .15 .40
238 Mike Lansing .15 .40
239 Mariano Rivera .40 1.00
240 Albert Belle .15 .40
241 Chuck Knoblauch .15 .40
242 Derek Bell .15 .40
243 Pat Hentgen .15 .40
244 Andres Galarraga .15 .40
245 Mo Vaughn .15 .40
246 Wade Boggs .25 .60
247 Devon White .15 .40
248 Todd Helton .25 .60
249 Raul Mondesi .15 .40
250 Sammy Sosa .40 1.00
251 Nomar Garciaparra ST 1.00 2.50
252 Mark McGwire ST 1.50 4.00
253 Alex Rodriguez ST 1.00 2.50
254 Juan Gonzalez ST .25 .60
255 Vladimir Guerrero ST .60 1.50
256 Ken Griffey Jr. ST 1.25 3.00
257 Mike Piazza ST 1.00 2.50
258 Derek Jeter ST 1.50 4.00
259 Albert Belle ST .25 .60
260 Greg Vaughn ST .20 .50
261 Sammy Sosa ST .60 1.50
262 Greg Maddux ST 1.00 2.50
263 Frank Thomas ST .60 1.50
264 Mark Grace ST .40 1.00
265 Ivan Rodriguez ST .40 1.00
266 Roger Clemens GM 1.25 3.00
267 Mo Vaughn GM .25 .60
268 Jim Thome GM .40 1.00
269 Darin Erstad GM .25 .60
270 Chipper Jones GM .60 1.50
271 Larry Walker GM .25 .60
272 Cal Ripken GM 2.00 5.00
273 Scott Rolen GM .40 1.00
274 Randy Johnson GM .60 1.50
275 Tony Gwynn GM .75 2.00
276 Barry Bonds GM 1.50 4.00
277 Sean Burroughs RC .40 1.00
278 J.M. Gold RC .20 .50
279 Carlos Lee .25 .60
280 George Lombard .20 .50
281 Carlos Beltran .40 1.00
282 Fernando Seguignol .20 .50
283 Eric Chavez .25 .60
284 Carlos Pena RC .30 .75
285 Corey Patterson RC .60 1.50
286 Alfonso Soriano RC 3.00 8.00
287 Nick Johnson RC .60 1.50
288 Jorge Toca RC .25 .60
289 A.J. Burnett RC .60 1.50
290 Andy Brown RC .20 .50
291 Doug Mientkiewicz RC .40 1.00
292 Bobby Seay RC .20 .50
293 Chip Ambres RC .20 .50
294 C.C. Sabathia RC 1.50 4.00
295 Choo Freeman RC .25 .60
296 Eric Valent RC .25 .60
297 Matt Belisle RC .20 .50
298 Jason Tyner RC .20 .50
299 Masao Kida RC .25 .60
300 H.Aaron 1.25 3.00
M.McGwire

1999 Finest Gold Refractors

*STARS 1-100/151-250: 15X TO 40X BASIC
*STARS 101-150/251-300: 10X TO 25X BASIC
*ROOKIES: 6X TO 15X BASIC
SER.1 ODDS 1:82 HOB/RET, 1:38 HTA
SER.2 ODDS 1:57 HOB/RET, 1:26 HTA
STATED PRINT RUN 100 SERIAL #'d SETS

1999 Finest Refractors

*STARS 1-100/151-250: 3X TO 8X BASIC
*STARS 101-150/251-300: 2X TO 5X BASIC
*ROOKIES: 1.5X TO 4X BASIC
STATED ODDS 1:12 HOB/RET, 1:5 HTA

1999 Finest Aaron Award Contenders

COMPLETE SET (9) 10.00 25.00
HA1 SER.2 ODDS 1:216, 1:108 HTA
HA2 SER.2 ODDS 1:108, 1:54 HTA
HA3 SER.2 ODDS 1:72, 1:36 HTA
HA4 SER.2 ODDS 1:54, 1:27 HTA
HA5 SER.2 ODDS 1:43, 1:21 HTA
HA6 SER.2 ODDS 1:36, 1:18 HTA
HA7 SER.2 ODDS 1:31, 1:15 HTA
HA8 SER.2 ODDS 1:27, 1:13 HTA
HA9 SER.2 ODDS 1:24, 1:12 HTA
*REF: 5X TO 1.2X BASIC AARON
REF HA1 SER.2 ODDS 1:1728, 1:864 HTA
REF HA2 SER.2 ODDS 1:864, 1:432 HTA
REF HA3 SER.2 ODDS 1:576, 1:288 HTA
REF HA4 SER.2 ODDS 1:432, 1:216 HTA
REF HA5 SER.2 ODDS 1:344, 1:172 HTA
REF HA6 SER.2 ODDS 1:288, 1:144 HTA
REF HA7 SER.2 ODDS 1:248, 1:124 HTA
REF HA8 SER.2 ODDS 1:216, 1:108 HTA
REF HA9 SER.2 ODDS 1:192, 1:96 HTA
HA1 Juan Gonzalez .60 1.50
HA2 Vladimir Guerrero 1.00 2.50
HA3 Nomar Garciaparra 1.00 2.50
HA4 Albert Belle .60 1.50
HA5 Frank Thomas 1.50 4.00
HA6 Sammy Sosa 1.50 4.00
HA7 Alex Rodriguez 2.00 5.00
HA8 Ken Griffey Jr. 3.00 8.00
HA9 Mark McGwire 2.50 6.00

1999 Finest Complements

COMPLETE SET (7) 8.00 20.00
SER.2 STATED ODDS 1:56, 1:27 HTA
RIGHT/LEFT REF.VARIATIONS EQUAL VALUE
*DUAL REF: 1.2X TO 3X BASIC COMP.
DUAL REF.SER.2 ODDS 1:168, 1:81 HTA
C1 M.Piazza 1.00 2.50
I.Rodriguez
C2 Tony Gwynn 1.00 2.50
Wade Boggs
C3 Kerry Wood 1.25 3.00
Roger Clemens
C4 Juan Gonzalez 1.00 2.50
Sammy Sosa
C5 Derek Jeter 2.50 6.00
Nomar Garciaparra
C6 Mark McGwire 1.50 4.00
Frank Thomas
C7 Vladimir Guerrero .60 1.50
Andruw Jones

1999 Finest Double Feature

COMPLETE SET (7) 15.00 40.00
SER.2 STATED ODDS 1:56, 1:27 HTA
RIGHT/LEFT REF.VARIATIONS EQUAL VALUE
*DUAL REF: 1.25X TO 3X BASIC DOUB.FEAT.
*DUAL REF BURRELL: 1.25X TO 3X HI COL.
DUAL REF.SER.2 ODDS 1:168, 1:81 HTA
DF1 K.Griffey Jr. 3.00 8.00
A.Rodriguez
DF2 C.Jones 1.50 4.00
A.Jones
DF3 D.Erstad .60 1.50
M.Vaughn
DF4 C.Biggio 1.00 2.50
J.Bagwell
DF5 B.Grieve .60 1.50
E.Chavez
DF6 A.Belle 5.00 12.00
C.Ripken
DF7 S.Rolen 1.25 3.00
P.Burrell

1999 Finest Franchise Records

COMPLETE SET (10) 75.00 150.00
SER.2 STATED ODDS 1:129, 1:64 HTA
*REFRACTORS: .75X TO 2X BASIC FRAN.REC.
REF.SER.2 ODDS 1:378, 1:189 HTA
FR1 Frank Thomas 4.00 10.00
FR2 Ken Griffey Jr. 8.00 20.00
FR3 Mark McGwire 10.00 25.00
FR4 Juan Gonzalez 1.50 4.00
FR5 Nomar Garciaparra 6.00 15.00
FR6 Mike Piazza 6.00 15.00
FR7 Cal Ripken 12.50 30.00
FR8 Sammy Sosa 4.00 10.00
FR9 Barry Bonds 10.00 25.00
FR10 Tony Gwynn 5.00 12.00

1999 Finest Future's Finest

COMPLETE SET (10) 40.00 100.00
SER.2 STATED ODDS 1:171, 1:79 HTA
STATED PRINT RUN 500 SERIAL #'d SETS
FF1 Pat Burrell 6.00 15.00
FF2 Troy Glaus 4.00 10.00
FF3 Eric Chavez 4.00 10.00
FF4 Ryan Anderson 4.00 10.00
FF5 Ruben Mateo 4.00 10.00
FF6 Gabe Kapler 4.00 10.00
FF7 Alex Gonzalez 4.00 10.00
FF8 Michael Barrett 4.00 10.00
FF9 Adrian Beltre 4.00 10.00
FF10 Fernando Seguignol 4.00 10.00

1999 Finest Leading Indicators

COMPLETE SET (10) 20.00 50.00
SER.1 ODDS 1:24 HOB/RET, 1:11 HTA
L1 Mark McGwire 4.00 10.00
L2 Sammy Sosa 1.50 4.00
L3 Ken Griffey Jr. 3.00 8.00
L4 Greg Vaughn .60 1.50
L5 Albert Belle .60 1.50
L6 Juan Gonzalez .60 1.50
L7 Andres Galarraga .60 1.50
L8 Alex Rodriguez 2.50 6.00
L9 Barry Bonds 4.00 10.00
L10 Jeff Bagwell 1.00 2.50

1999 Finest Milestones

HIT SER.2 ODDS 1:29, 1:13 HTA
HIT PRINT RUN 3000 SERIAL #'d SUBSETS
HR SER.2 ODDS 1:171, 1:79 HTA
HR PRINT RUN 500 SERIAL #'d SUBSETS
RBI SER.2 ODDS 1:61, 1:28 HTA
RBI PRINT RUN 1400 SERIAL #'d SUBSETS
2B SER.2 ODDS 1:171, 1:79 HTA
2B PRINT RUN 500 SERIAL #'d SUBSETS
M1 Tony Gwynn HIT 1.50 4.00
M2 Cal Ripken HIT 5.00 12.00
M3 Wade Boggs HIT 1.00 2.50
M4 Ken Griffey Jr. HIT 3.00 8.00
M5 Frank Thomas HIT 1.50 4.00
M6 Barry Bonds HIT 2.50 6.00
M7 Travis Lee HIT .60 1.50
M8 Alex Rodriguez HIT 2.00 5.00
M9 Derek Jeter HIT 4.00 10.00
M10 Vladimir Guerrero HIT 1.00 2.50
M11 Mark McGwire HR 10.00 25.00
M12 Ken Griffey Jr. HR 12.00 30.00
M13 Vladimir Guerrero HR 4.00 10.00
M14 Alex Rodriguez HR 8.00 20.00
M15 Barry Bonds HR 10.00 25.00
M16 Sammy Sosa HR 6.00 15.00
M17 Albert Belle HR 2.50 6.00
M18 Frank Thomas HR 6.00 15.00
M19 Jose Canseco HR 4.00 10.00
M20 Mike Piazza HR 6.00 15.00
M21 Jeff Bagwell RBI 2.00 5.00
M22 Barry Bonds RBI 5.00 12.00
M23 Ken Griffey Jr. RBI 6.00 15.00
M24 Albert Belle RBI 1.25 3.00
M25 Juan Gonzalez RBI 1.25 3.00
M26 Vinny Castilla RBI 1.25 3.00
M27 Mark McGwire RBI 5.00 12.00
M28 Alex Rodriguez RBI 4.00 10.00
M29 Nomar Garciaparra RBI 2.00 5.00
M30 Frank Thomas RBI 3.00 8.00
M31 Barry Bonds 2B 10.00 25.00
M32 Albert Belle 2B 2.50 6.00
M33 Ben Grieve 2B 2.50 6.00
M34 Craig Biggio 2B 4.00 10.00
M35 Vladimir Guerrero 2B 4.00 10.00
M36 Nomar Garciaparra 2B 4.00 10.00
M37 Alex Rodriguez 2B 8.00 20.00
M38 Derek Jeter 2B 15.00 40.00
M39 Ken Griffey Jr. 2B 12.00 30.00
M40 Brad Fullmer 2B 2.50 6.00

1999 Finest Peel and Reveal Sparkle

COMPLETE SET (20) 60.00 120.00
SER.1 STATED ODDS 1:30 HOB/RET, 1:15 HTA
*HYPERPLAID: .6X TO 1.5X SPARKLE
HYPERPLAID SER.1 ODDS 1:60 H/R,1:30 HTA
*STADIUM STARS: 1.25X TO 3X SPARKLE
STAD.STAR SER.1 ODDS 1:120 H/R, 1:60 HTA
1 Kerry Wood .75 2.00
2 Mark McGwire 5.00 12.00
3 Sammy Sosa 2.00 5.00
4 Ken Griffey Jr. 4.00 10.00
5 Nomar Garciaparra 3.00 8.00
6 Greg Maddux 3.00 8.00
7 Derek Jeter 5.00 12.00
8 Andres Galarraga .75 2.00
9 Alex Rodriguez 3.00 8.00
10 Frank Thomas 2.00 5.00
11 Roger Clemens 4.00 10.00
12 Juan Gonzalez .75 2.00
13 Ben Grieve .75 2.00
14 Jeff Bagwell 1.25 3.00
15 Todd Helton 1.25 3.00
16 Chipper Jones 2.00 5.00
17 Barry Bonds 5.00 12.00
18 Travis Lee .75 2.00
19 Vladimir Guerrero 2.00 5.00
20 Pat Burrell 1.50 4.00

1999 Finest Prominent Figures

HR SER.1 ODDS 1:1749 HOB/RET, 1:807 HTA
HR PRINT RUN 70 SERIAL #'d SUBSETS
SLUGGING SER.1 ODDS 1:145 H/R, 1:67 HTA
SLG PRINT RUN 847 SERIAL #'d SUBSETS
BAT SER.1 ODDS 1:289 HOB/RET, 1:133 HTA
BAT PRINT RUN 424 SERIAL #'d SUBSETS
RBI SER.1 ODDS 1:644 HOB/RET, 1:297 HTA
RBI PRINT RUN 190 SERIAL #'d SUBSETS
TOT.BASES SER.1 ODDS 1:268 H/R, 1:124 HTA
TB PRINT RUN 457 SERIAL #'d SUBSETS
PF1 Mark McGwire HR 50.00 120.00
PF2 Sammy Sosa HR 30.00 80.00
PF3 Ken Griffey Jr. HR 60.00 150.00
PF4 Mike Piazza HR 30.00 80.00
PF5 Juan Gonzalez HR 12.00 30.00
PF6 Greg Vaughn HR 12.00 30.00
PF7 Alex Rodriguez HR 40.00 100.00
PF8 Manny Ramirez HR 30.00 80.00
PF9 Jeff Bagwell HR 20.00 50.00
PF10 Andres Galarraga HR 20.00 50.00
PF11 Mark McGwire SLG 10.00 25.00
PF12 Sammy Sosa SLG 6.00 15.00
PF13 Juan Gonzalez SLG 2.50 6.00
PF14 Ken Griffey Jr. SLG 12.00 30.00
PF15 Barry Bonds SLG 10.00 25.00
PF16 Greg Vaughn SLG 2.50 6.00
PF17 Larry Walker SLG 4.00 10.00
PF18 Andres Galarraga SLG 4.00 10.00
PF19 Jeff Bagwell SLG 4.00 10.00
PF20 Albert Belle SLG 2.50 6.00
PF21 Tony Gwynn BAT 8.00 20.00
PF22 Mike Piazza BAT 8.00 20.00
PF23 Larry Walker BAT 5.00 12.00
PF24 Alex Rodriguez BAT 10.00 25.00
PF25 John Olerud BAT 3.00 8.00
PF26 Frank Thomas BAT 8.00 20.00
PF27 Bernie Williams BAT 5.00 12.00
PF28 Chipper Jones BAT 8.00 20.00
PF29 Jim Thome BAT 5.00 12.00
PF30 Barry Bonds BAT 12.00 30.00
PF31 Juan Gonzalez RBI 5.00 12.00
PF32 Sammy Sosa RBI 12.00 30.00
PF33 Mark McGwire RBI 20.00 50.00
PF34 Albert Belle RBI 5.00 12.00
PF35 Ken Griffey Jr. RBI 25.00 60.00
PF36 Jeff Bagwell RBI 8.00 20.00
PF37 Chipper Jones RBI 12.00 30.00
PF38 Vinny Castilla RBI 5.00 12.00
PF39 Alex Rodriguez RBI 15.00 40.00
PF40 Andres Galarraga RBI 8.00 20.00
PF41 Sammy Sosa TB 8.00 20.00
PF42 Mark McGwire TB 12.00 30.00
PF43 Albert Belle TB 3.00 8.00
PF44 Ken Griffey Jr. TB 15.00 40.00
PF45 Jeff Bagwell TB 5.00 12.00
PF46 Juan Gonzalez TB 3.00 8.00
PF47 Barry Bonds TB 12.00 30.00
PF48 Vladimir Guerrero TB 5.00 12.00
PF49 Larry Walker TB 5.00 12.00
PF50 Alex Rodriguez TB 10.00 25.00

1999 Finest Split Screen Single Refractors

SER.1 STATED ODDS 1:28 HOB/RET, 1:14 HTA
RIGHT/LEFT REF.VARIATIONS EQUAL VALUE
*DUAL REF: .6X TO 1.5X BASIC SCREEN
DUAL REF.SER.1 ODDS 1:82 H/R, 1:42 HTA
SS1A McGwire REF/Sosa 1.50 4.00
SS1B McGwire/Sosa REF 1.50 4.00
SS2A Griffey REF/ARod 2.00 5.00
SS2B Griffey/ARod REF 2.00 5.00
SS3A Nomar REF/Jeter 2.50 6.00
SS3B Nomar/Jeter REF 2.50 6.00
SS4A Bonds REF/Belle 1.50 4.00
SS4B Bonds/Belle REF 1.50 4.00
SS5A Ripken REF/Gwynn 3.00 8.00
SS5B Ripken/Gwynn REF 3.00 8.00
SS6A Manny Ramirez REF 1.00 2.50
Juan Gonzalez
SS6B Manny Ramirez 1.00 2.50
Juan Gonzalez REF
SS7A Frank Thomas REF 1.00 2.50
Andres Galarraga
SS7B Frank Thomas 1.00 2.50
Andres Galarraga REF
SS8A Scott Rolen REF 1.00 2.50
Chipper Jones
SS8B Scott Rolen 1.00 2.50
Chipper Jones REF
SS9A Ivan Rodriguez REF 1.00 2.50
Mike Piazza
SS9B Ivan Rodriguez 1.00 2.50
Mike Piazza REF
SS10A Wood REF/Clemens 1.25 3.00
SS10B Wood/Clemens REF 1.25 3.00
SS11A Maddux REF/Glavine 1.25 3.00
SS11B Maddux/Glavine REF 1.25 3.00
SS12A Troy Glaus REF .40 1.00
Eric Chavez
SS12B Troy Glaus .40 1.00
Eric Chavez REF
SS13A Ben Grieve REF .60 1.50
Todd Helton
SS13B Ben Grieve .60 1.50
Todd Helton REF
SS14A Lee REF/Burrell 1.50 4.00
SS14B Lee/Burrell REF 1.50 4.00

1999 Finest Team Finest Blue

COMP.BLUE SET (20) 75.00 150.00
COMP.BLUE SER.2 (10) 30.00 80.00
BLUE SER.1 ODDS 1:82 HOB/RET, 1:38 HTA
BLUE SER.2 ODDS 1:57 HOB/RET, 1:26 HTA
BLUE PRINT RUN 1500 SERIAL #'d SETS
*BLUE REF: .75X TO 2X BASIC BLUE
BLUE REF.SER.1 ODDS 1:816 HOB, 1:377 HTA
BLUE REF.SER.2 ODDS 1:571 HOB, 1:263 HTA
BLUE REF.PRINT RUN 150 SERIAL #'d SETS
*RED: .5X TO 1.2X BASIC BLUE
RED SER.2 ODDS 1:18 HTA
RED SER.1 ODDS 1:25 HTA
RED PRINT RUN 500 SERIAL #'d SETS
*RED REF: 2.5X TO 6X BASIC BLUE
RED REF.SER.1 ODDS 1:254 HTA
RED REF.SER.2 ODDS 1:184 HTA
RED REF.PRINT RUN 50 SERIAL #'d SETS
*GOLD: .6X TO 1.5X BASIC BLUE
GOLD SER.1 ODDS 1:51 HTA
GOLD SER.2 ODDS 1:37 HTA
GOLD PRINT RUN 250 SERIAL #'d SETS
*GOLD REF: 4X TO 10X BASIC BLUE
GOLD REF.SER.1 ODDS 1:510 HTA
GOLD REF.SER.2 ODDS 1:369 HTA
GOLD REF.PRINT RUN 25 SERIAL #'d SETS
TF1 Greg Maddux 2.50 6.00
TF2 Mark McGwire 4.00 10.00
TF3 Sammy Sosa 1.50 4.00
TF4 Juan Gonzalez .75 2.00
TF5 Alex Rodriguez 2.50 6.00
TF6 Travis Lee .75 2.00
TF7 Roger Clemens 3.00 8.00
TF8 Darin Erstad .75 2.00
TF9 Todd Helton 1.00 2.50
TF10 Mike Piazza 2.50 6.00
TF11 Kerry Wood .75 2.00
TF12 Ken Griffey Jr. 3.00 8.00
TF13 Frank Thomas 1.50 4.00
TF14 Jeff Bagwell 1.00 2.50
TF15 Nomar Garciaparra 2.50 6.00
TF16 Derek Jeter 4.00 10.00
TF17 Chipper Jones 1.50 4.00
TF18 Barry Bonds 4.00 10.00
TF19 Tony Gwynn 2.00 5.00
TF20 Ben Grieve .75 2.00

2000 Finest Pre-Production

COMPLETE SET (5) 2.50 6.00
PP1 Brian Jordan .40 1.00
PP2 Bernie Williams .60 1.50
PP3 Pat Burrell .40 1.00
PP4 Corey Myers .40 1.00
PP5 Derek Jeter GEM 2.50 6.00

2000 Finest

COMP.SERIES 1 w/o SP's (100) 10.00 25.00
COMP.SERIES 2 w/o SP's (100) 10.00 25.00
COMMON (1-100/146-246) .15 .40
COMMON ROOKIE (101-120) .75 2.00
SER.1 ROOKIES ODDS 1:23 H/R, 1:6 HTA
SER.1 ROOKIES PRINT RUN 2000 #'d SETS
COMMON FEATURES (121-135) .40 1.00
FEATURES 121-135 ODDS 1:8 H/R, 1:3 HTA
COMM.GEM (136-145/277-286) .40 1.00
GEMS 136-145/277-268 1:24 H/R, 1:9 HTA
COMMON ROOKIE (247-266) .60 1.50
SER.2 ROOKIES ODDS 1:13 H/R, 1:5 HTA
SER.2 ROOKIES PRINT RUN 3000 #'d SETS
COMMON COUNTER (267-276) .40 1.00
COUNTER 267-276 ODDS 1:8 H/R 1:3 HTA
GRIFFEY 146 NOT INCL.IN 100-CARD SET
BOTH 146 GRIFFEY'S PRINTED EQUALLY
GRADED GEMS SER.1 ODDS 1:9344 HTA
GRADED GEMS SER.2 ODDS 1:8157 HTA
GRADED GEMS EXCH.DEADLINE 12/31/00
1 Nomar Garciaparra .25 .60
2 Chipper Jones .40 1.00
3 Erubiel Durazo .15 .40
4 Robin Ventura .15 .40
5 Garret Anderson .15 .40
6 Dean Palmer .15 .40
7 Mariano Rivera .50 1.25
8 Rusty Greer .15 .40
9 Jim Thome .25 .60
10 Jeff Bagwell .25 .60
11 Jason Giambi .15 .40
12 Jeromy Burnitz .15 .40
13 Mark Grace .25 .60
14 Russ Ortiz .15 .40
15 Kevin Brown .15 .40
16 Kevin Millwood .15 .40
17 Scott Williamson .15 .40
18 Orlando Hernandez .15 .40
19 Todd Walker .15 .40
20 Carlos Beltran .25 .60
21 Ruben Rivera .15 .40
22 Curt Schilling .25 .60
23 Brian Giles .15 .40
24 Eric Karros .15 .40
25 Preston Wilson .15 .40
26 Al Leiter .15 .40
27 Juan Encarnacion .15 .40
28 Tim Salmon .15 .40
29 B.J. Surhoff .15 .40
30 Bernie Williams .25 .60
31 Lee Stevens .15 .40
32 Pokey Reese .15 .40
33 Mike Sweeney .15 .40
34 Corey Koskie .15 .40
35 Roberto Alomar .25 .60
36 Tim Hudson .25 .60
37 Tom Glavine .25 .60
38 Jeff Kent .15 .40
39 Mike Lieberthal .15 .40
40 Barry Larkin .25 .60
41 Paul O'Neill .25 .60
42 Rico Brogna .15 .40
43 Brian Daubach .15 .40
44 Rich Aurilia .15 .40
45 Vladimir Guerrero .25 .60
46 Luis Castillo .15 .40
47 Bartolo Colon .15 .40
48 Kevin Appier .15 .40
49 Mo Vaughn .15 .40
50 Alex Rodriguez .50 1.25
51 Randy Johnson .40 1.00
52 Kris Benson .15 .40
53 Tony Clark .15 .40
54 Chad Allen .15 .40
55 Larry Walker .25 .60
56 Freddy Garcia .15 .40
57 Paul Konerko .15 .40
58 Edgardo Alfonzo .15 .40
59 Brady Anderson .15 .40
60 Derek Jeter 1.00 2.50
61 John Smoltz .40 1.00
62 Doug Glanville .15 .40
63 Shannon Stewart .15 .40
64 Greg Maddux .50 1.25
65 Mark McGwire .60 1.50
66 Gary Sheffield .15 .40
67 Kevin Young .15 .40
68 Tony Gwynn .40 1.00
69 Rey Ordonez .15 .40
70 Cal Ripken 1.25 3.00
71 Todd Helton .25 .60
72 Brian Jordan .15 .40
73 Jose Canseco .25 .60
74 Luis Gonzalez .15 .40
75 Barry Bonds .60 1.50
76 Jermaine Dye .15 .40
77 Jose Offerman .15 .40
78 Magglio Ordonez .25 .60
79 Fred Mcgriff .25 .60
80 Ivan Rodriguez .25 .60
81 Josh Hamilton .50 1.25
82 Vernon Wells .15 .40
83 Mark Mulder .15 .40
84 John Patterson .15 .40
85 Nick Johnson .15 .40
86 Pablo Ozuna .15 .40
87 A.J. Burnett .15 .40
88 Jack Cust .15 .40
89 Adam Piatt .15 .40
90 Rob Ryan .15 .40
91 Sean Burroughs .15 .40
92 D'Angelo Jimenez .15 .40
93 Chad Hermansen .15 .40
94 Robert Fick .15 .40
95 Ruben Mateo .15 .40
96 Alex Escobar .15 .40
97 Wily Pena .15 .40
98 Corey Patterson .15 .40
99 Eric Munson .15 .40
100 Pat Burrell .15 .40
101 Michael Tejera RC .75 2.00
102 Bobby Bradley RC .75 2.00
103 Larry Bigbie RC .75 2.00
104 B.J. Garbe RC .75 2.00
105 Josh Kalinowski RC .75 2.00
106 Brett Myers RC 2.50 6.00
107 Chris Mears RC .75 2.00
108 Aaron Rowand RC 4.00 10.00
109 Corey Myers RC .75 2.00
110 John Sneed RC .75 2.00
111 Ryan Christianson RC .75 2.00
112 Kyle Snyder .75 2.00
113 Mike Paradis .75 2.00
114 Chance Caple RC .75 2.00
115 Ben Christensen RC .75 2.00
116 Brad Baker RC .75 2.00
117 Rob Purvis RC .75 2.00
118 Rick Asadoorian RC .75 2.00
119 Ruben Salazar RC .75 2.00
120 Julio Zuleta RC .75 2.00
121 A.Rodriguez 2.00 5.00
K.Griffey Jr.
122 N.Garciaparra 2.50 6.00
D.Jeter
123 M.McGwire 1.50 4.00
S.Sosa
124 R.Johnson 1.00 2.50
P.Martinez
125 I.Rodriguez 1.00 2.50
M.Piazza
126 M.Ramirez 1.00 2.50
R.Alomar
127 C.Jones 1.00 2.50
A.Jones
128 C.Ripken 3.00 8.00
T.Gwynn
129 J.Bagwell .60 1.50
C.Biggio
130 B.Bonds 1.50 4.00
V.Guerrero
131 N.Johnson 1.00 2.50
A.Soriano
132 Josh Hamilton 1.25 3.00
133 C.Patterson .40 1.00
R.Mateo
134 L.Walker .60 1.50
T.Helton
135 R.Ordonez .40 1.00
E.Alfonzo
136 Derek Jeter GEM 2.50 6.00
137 Alex Rodriguez GEM 1.25 3.00

138 Chipper Jones GEM 1.00 2.50
139 Mike Piazza GEM 1.00 2.50
140 Mark McGwire GEM 1.50 4.00
141 Ivan Rodriguez GEM .60 1.50
142 Cal Ripken GEM 3.00 8.00
143 Vladimir Guerrero GEM .60 1.50
144 Randy Johnson GEM 1.00 2.50
145 Jeff Bagwell GEM .60 1.50
146 Ken Griffey Jr. ACTION .75 2.00
146A Ken Griffey Jr. PORT .75 2.00
147 Andruw Jones .15 .40
148 Kerry Wood .15 .40
149 Jim Edmonds .15 .40
150 Pedro Martinez .25 .60
151 Warren Morris .15 .40
152 Trevor Hoffman .25 .60
153 Ryan Klesko .15 .40
154 Andy Pettitte .25 .60
155 Frank Thomas .40 1.00
156 Damion Easley .15 .40
157 Cliff Floyd .15 .40
158 Ben Davis .15 .40
159 John Valentin .15 .40
160 Rafael Palmeiro .25 .60
161 Andy Ashby .15 .40
162 J.D. Drew .15 .40
163 Jay Bell .15 .40
164 Adam Kennedy .15 .40
165 Manny Ramirez .40 1.00
166 John Halama .15 .40
167 Octavio Dotel .15 .40
168 Darin Erstad .15 .40
169 Jose Lima .15 .40
170 Andres Galarraga .25 .60
171 Scott Rolen .25 .60
172 Delino DeShields .15 .40
173 J.T. Snow .15 .40
174 Tony Womack .15 .40
175 John Olerud .15 .40
176 Jason Kendall .15 .40
177 Carlos Lee .15 .40
178 Eric Milton .15 .40
179 Jeff Cirillo .15 .40
180 Gabe Kapler .15 .40
181 Greg Vaughn .15 .40
182 Denny Neagle .15 .40
183 Tino Martinez .15 .40
184 Doug Mientkiewicz .15 .40
185 Juan Gonzalez .15 .40
186 Ellis Burks .15 .40
187 Mike Hampton .15 .40
188 Royce Clayton .15 .40
189 Mike Mussina .25 .60
190 Carlos Delgado .15 .40
191 Ben Grieve .15 .40
192 Fernando Tatis .15 .40
193 Matt Williams .15 .40
194 Rondell White .15 .40
195 Shawn Green .15 .40
196 Hideki Irabu .15 .40
197 Troy Glaus .15 .40
198 Roger Cedeno .15 .40
199 Ray Lankford .15 .40
200 Sammy Sosa .40 1.00
201 Kenny Lofton .15 .40
202 Edgar Martinez .25 .60
203 Mark Kotsay .15 .40
204 David Wells .15 .40
205 Craig Biggio .25 .60
206 Ray Durham .15 .40
207 Troy O'Leary .15 .40
208 Rickey Henderson .40 1.00
209 Bob Abreu .15 .40
210 Neifi Perez .15 .40
211 Carlos Febles .15 .40
212 Chuck Knoblauch .15 .40
213 Moises Alou .15 .40
214 Omar Vizquel .25 .60
215 Vinny Castilla .15 .40
216 Javy Lopez .15 .40
217 Johnny Damon .25 .60
218 Roger Clemens .50 1.25
219 Miguel Tejada .25 .60
220 Carl Everett .15 .40
221 Matt Lawton .15 .40
222 Albert Belle .15 .40
223 Adrian Beltre .40 1.00
224 Dante Bichette .15 .40
225 Raul Mondesi .15 .40
226 Mike Piazza .40 1.00
227 Brad Penny .15 .40
228 Kip Wells .15 .40
229 Adam Everett .15 .40
230 Eddie Yarnall .15 .40
231 Matt LeCroy .15 .40
232 Jason Tyner .15 .40
233 Rick Ankiel .25 .60
234 Lance Berkman .25 .60
235 Rafael Furcal .25 .60
236 Dee Brown .15 .40
237 Gookie Dawkins .15 .40
238 Eric Valent .15 .40
239 Peter Bergeron .15 .40
240 Alfonso Soriano .40 1.00
241 Adam Dunn .25 .60
242 Jorge Toca .15 .40
243 Ryan Anderson .15 .40
244 Jason Dellaero .15 .40
245 Jason Grilli .15 .40
246 Milton Bradley .15 .40
247 Scott Downs RC .60 1.50
248 Keith Reed RC .60 1.50
249 Edgar Cruz RC .60 1.50
250 Wes Anderson RC .60 1.50
251 Lyle Overbay RC 1.00 2.50
252 Mike Lamb RC .60 1.50
253 Vince Faison RC .60 1.50
254 Chad Alexander .60 1.50
255 Chris Wakeland RC .60 1.50
256 Aaron McNeal RC .60 1.50
257 Tomo Ohka RC .60 1.50
258 Ty Howington RC .60 1.50
259 Javier Colina RC .60 1.50
260 Jason Jennings .60 1.50
261 Ramon Santiago RC .60 1.50
262 Johan Santana RC 6.00 15.00
263 Quincy Foster RC .60 1.50
264 Junior Brignac RC .60 1.50
265 Rico Washington RC .60 1.50
266 Scott Sobkowiak RC .60 1.50
267 P.Martinez .60 1.50
R.Ankiel
268 M.Ramirez 1.00 2.50
V.Guerrero
269 A.Burnett .40 1.00
M.Mulder
270 M.Piazza 1.00 2.50
E.Munson
271 Josh Hamilton 1.25 3.00
272 K.Griffey Jr. 2.00 5.00
S.Sosa
273 D.Jeter 2.50 6.00
A.Soriano
274 M.McGwire 1.50 4.00
P.Burrell
275 C.Jones 3.00 8.00
C.Ripken
276 N.Garciaparra 1.25 3.00
A.Rodriguez
277 Pedro Martinez GEM .60 1.50
278 Tony Gwynn GEM 1.00 2.50
279 Barry Bonds GEM 1.50 4.00
280 Juan Gonzalez GEM .40 1.00
281 Larry Walker GEM .60 1.50
282 Nomar Garciaparra GEM .60 1.50
283 Ken Griffey Jr. GEM 2.00 5.00
284 Manny Ramirez GEM 1.00 2.50
285 Shawn Green GEM .40 1.00
286 Sammy Sosa GEM 1.00 2.50

2000 Finest Gold Refractors

*STARS 1-100/146-246: 10X TO 25X BASIC
CARDS 1-100/146-246 1:240 H/R, 1:100 HTA
*ROOKIES 101-120: 2.5X TO 6X BASIC
*ROOKIES 247-266: 3X TO 8X BASIC
ROOKIES 101-120 ODDS 1:368 H/R, 1:187 HTA
ROOKIES 247-266 ODDS 1:448 H/R, 1:120 HTA
ROOKIES PRINT RUN 100 SERIAL #'d SETS
*FEATURES 121-135: 4X TO 10X BASIC
FEATURES ODDS 1:960 H/R, 1:400 HTA
*GEMS 136-145/277-286: 4X TO 10X BASIC
GEMS ODDS 1:2880 H/R, 1:1200 HTA
*COUNTER 267-276: 4X TO 10X BASIC
COUNTERPARTS ODDS 1:960 H/R 1:400 HTA
CARD 146 GRIFFEY REDS IS NOT AN SP
262 Johan Santana 60.00 120.00

2000 Finest Refractors

*STARS 1-100/146-246: 6X TO 15X BASIC
1-100/146-246 ODDS 1:24 H/R, 1:9 HTA
*ROOKIES 101-120: 2X TO 5X BASIC
SER.1 ROOKIES ODDS 1:93 H/R, 1:23 HTA
SER.1 ROOKIES PRINT RUN 500 #'d SETS
*FEATURES 121-135: 2.5X TO 6X BASIC
FEATURES ODDS 1:96 H/R, 1:40 HTA
*GEMS 136-145/277-286: 2.5X TO 6X BASIC
GEMS ODDS 1:288 H/R, 1:120 HTA
*ROOKIES 247-266: 2X TO 5X BASIC RC'S
SER.2 ROOKIES ODDS 1:49 H/R, 1:11 HTA
SER.2 ROOKIES PRINT RUN 1000 #'d SETS
*COUNTER 267-276: 2.5X TO 6X BASIC
COUNTERPARTS 1:96 H/R 1:40 HTA
CARD 146 GRIFFEY REDS IS NOT AN SP
262 Johan Santana 15.00 40.00

2000 Finest Gems Oversize

COMPLETE SET (20) 25.00 60.00
COMPLETE SERIES 1 (10) 12.50 30.00
COMPLETE SERIES 2 (10) 12.50 30.00
ONE PER HOBBY/RETAIL BOX CHIP-TOPPER
*REF: .4X TO 1X BASIC GEMS OVERSIZE
REFRACTORS ONE PER HTA CHIP-TOPPER
1 Derek Jeter 4.00 10.00
2 Alex Rodriguez 2.00 5.00
3 Chipper Jones 1.50 4.00
4 Mike Piazza 1.50 4.00
5 Mark McGwire 2.50 6.00
6 Ivan Rodriguez 1.00 2.50
7 Cal Ripken 5.00 12.00
8 Vladimir Guerrero 1.00 2.50
9 Randy Johnson 1.50 4.00
10 Jeff Bagwell 1.00 2.50
11 Nomar Garciaparra 1.00 2.50
12 Ken Griffey Jr. 3.00 8.00
13 Manny Ramirez 1.50 4.00
14 Shawn Green .60 1.50
15 Sammy Sosa 1.50 4.00
16 Pedro Martinez 1.00 2.50
17 Tony Gwynn 1.50 4.00
18 Barry Bonds 2.50 6.00
19 Juan Gonzalez .60 1.50
20 Larry Walker 1.00 2.50

2000 Finest Ballpark Bounties

COMPLETE SET (30) 40.00 100.00
COMPLETE SERIES 1 (15) 20.00 50.00
COMPLETE SERIES 2 (15) 20.00 50.00
STATED ODDS 1:24 HOB/RET, 1:12 HTA
BB1 Chipper Jones 2.00 5.00
BB2 Mike Piazza 2.00 5.00
BB3 Vladimir Guerrero 1.25 3.00
BB4 Sammy Sosa 2.00 5.00
BB5 Nomar Garciaparra 1.25 3.00
BB6 Manny Ramirez 2.00 5.00
BB7 Jeff Bagwell 1.25 3.00
BB8 Scott Rolen 1.25 3.00
BB9 Carlos Beltran 1.25 3.00
BB10 Pedro Martinez 1.25 3.00
BB11 Greg Maddux 2.50 6.00
BB12 Josh Hamilton 2.50 6.00
BB13 Adam Piatt .75 2.00
BB14 Pat Burrell .75 2.00
BB15 Alfonso Soriano 2.00 5.00
BB16 Alex Rodriguez 2.50 6.00
BB17 Derek Jeter 5.00 12.00
BB18 Cal Ripken 6.00 15.00
BB19 Larry Walker 1.25 3.00
BB20 Barry Bonds 3.00 8.00
BB21 Ken Griffey Jr. 4.00 10.00
BB22 Mark McGwire 3.00 8.00
BB23 Ivan Rodriguez 1.25 3.00
BB24 Andruw Jones .75 2.00
BB25 Todd Helton 1.25 3.00
BB26 Randy Johnson 2.00 5.00
BB27 Ruben Mateo .75 2.00
BB28 Corey Patterson .75 2.00
BB29 Sean Burroughs .75 2.00
BB30 Eric Munson .75 2.00

2000 Finest Dream Cast

COMPLETE SET (10) 40.00 100.00
SER.2 STATED ODDS 1:36 HOB/RET, 1:13 HTA
DC1 Mark McGwire 4.00 10.00
DC2 Roberto Alomar 1.50 4.00
DC3 Chipper Jones 2.50 6.00
DC4 Derek Jeter 6.00 15.00
DC5 Barry Bonds 4.00 10.00
DC6 Ken Griffey Jr. 5.00 12.00
DC7 Sammy Sosa 2.50 6.00
DC8 Mike Piazza 2.50 6.00
DC9 Pedro Martinez 1.50 4.00
DC10 Randy Johnson 2.50 6.00

2000 Finest For the Record

SER.1 STATED ODDS 1:71 H/R, 1:33 HTA
PRINT RUNS B/WN 302-410 COPIES PER
FR1A Derek Jeter/318 12.00 30.00
FR1B Derek Jeter/408 12.00 30.00
FR1C Derek Jeter/314 12.00 30.00
FR2A Mark McGwire/330 3.00 8.00
FR2B Mark McGwire/402 3.00 8.00
FR2C Mark McGwire/330 3.00 8.00
FR3A Ken Griffey Jr./331 4.00 10.00
FR3B Ken Griffey Jr./405 4.00 10.00
FR3C Ken Griffey Jr./327 4.00 10.00
FR4A Alex Rodriguez/331 2.50 6.00
FR4B Alex Rodriguez/405 2.50 6.00
FR4C Alex Rodriguez/327 2.50 6.00
FR5A Nomar Garciaparra/310 1.25 3.00
FR5B Nomar Garciaparra/390 1.25 3.00
FR5C Nomar Garciaparra/302 1.25 3.00
FR6A Cal Ripken/333 6.00 15.00
FR6B Cal Ripken/410 6.00 15.00
FR6C Cal Ripken/318 6.00 15.00
FR7A Sammy Sosa/355 2.00 5.00
FR7B Sammy Sosa/400 2.00 5.00
FR7C Sammy Sosa/353 2.00 5.00
FR8A Manny Ramirez/325 2.00 5.00
FR8B Manny Ramirez/410 2.00 5.00
FR8C Manny Ramirez/325 2.00 5.00
FR9A Mike Piazza/338 2.00 5.00
FR9B Mike Piazza/410 2.00 5.00
FR9C Mike Piazza/338 2.00 5.00
FR10A Chipper Jones/335 2.00 5.00
FR10B Chipper Jones/401 2.00 5.00
FR10C Chipper Jones/330 2.00 5.00

2000 Finest Going the Distance

COMPLETE SET (12) 12.50 30.00
SER.1 ODDS 1:24 HOB/RET, 1:12 HTA
GTD1 Tony Gwynn 1.00 2.50
GTD2 Alex Rodriguez 1.25 3.00
GTD3 Derek Jeter 2.50 6.00
GTD4 Chipper Jones 1.00 2.50
GTD5 Nomar Garciaparra .60 1.50
GTD6 Sammy Sosa 1.00 2.50
GTD7 Ken Griffey Jr. 2.00 5.00
GTD8 Vladimir Guerrero .60 1.50
GTD9 Mark McGwire 1.50 4.00
GTD10 Mike Piazza 1.00 2.50
GTD11 Manny Ramirez 1.00 2.50
GTD12 Cal Ripken 3.00 8.00

2000 Finest Moments

COMPLETE SET (4) 2.50 6.00
SER.2 STATED ODDS 1:9 H/R 1:4 HTA
*REFRACTORS: .75X TO 2X BASIC MOMENTS
SER.2 REF.ODDS 1:20 H/R 1:9 HTA
FM1 Chipper Jones 1.00 2.50
FM2 Ivan Rodriguez .60 1.50
FM3 Tony Gwynn 1.00 2.50
FM4 Wade Boggs .60 1.50

2000 Finest Moments Refractors Autograph

SER.2 STATED ODDS 1:425 H/R 1:196 HTA
FM1 Chipper Jones 40.00 100.00
FM2 Ivan Rodriguez 15.00 40.00
FM3 Tony Gwynn 30.00 80.00
FM4 Wade Boggs 20.00 50.00

2001 Finest

COMP.SET w/o SP's (100) 10.00 25.00
COMMON CARD (1-110) .15 .40
SP ODDS 1:32 HOBBY, 1:15 HTA
SP PRINT RUN 1999 SERIAL #'d SETS
COMMON PROSPECT (111-140) 4.00 10.00
111-140 ODDS 1:21 HOBBY, 1:10 HTA
111-140 PRINT RUN 999 SERIAL #'d SETS
1 Mike Piazza SP 3.00 8.00
2 Andruw Jones .25 .60
3 Jason Giambi .15 .40
4 Fred McGriff .25 .60
5 Vladimir Guerrero SP 3.00 8.00
6 Adrian Gonzalez 1.00 2.50
7 Pedro Martinez .25 .60
8 Mike Lieberthal .15 .40
9 Warren Morris .15 .40
10 Juan Gonzalez .15 .40
11 Jose Canseco .25 .60
12 Jose Valentin .15 .40
13 Jeff Cirillo .15 .40
14 Pokey Reese .15 .40
15 Scott Rolen .25 .60
16 Greg Maddux .60 1.50
17 Carlos Delgado .15 .40
18 Rick Ankiel .15 .40
19 Steve Finley .15 .40
20 Shawn Green .15 .40
21 Orlando Cabrera .15 .40
22 Roberto Alomar .25 .60
23 John Olerud .15 .40
24 Albert Belle .15 .40
25 Edgardo Alfonzo .15 .40
26 Rafael Palmeiro .25 .60
27 Mike Sweeney .15 .40
28 Bernie Williams .25 .60
29 Larry Walker .15 .40
30 Barry Bonds SP 5.00 12.00
31 Orlando Hernandez .15 .40
32 Randy Johnson .40 1.00
33 Shannon Stewart .15 .40
34 Mark Grace .25 .60
35 Alex Rodriguez SP 4.00 10.00
36 Tino Martinez .25 .60
37 Carlos Febles .15 .40
38 Al Leiter .15 .40
39 Omar Vizquel .25 .60
40 Chuck Knoblauch .15 .40
41 Tim Salmon .25 .60
42 Brian Jordan .15 .40
43 Edgar Renteria .15 .40
44 Preston Wilson .15 .40
45 Mariano Rivera .40 1.00
46 Gabe Kapler .15 .40
47 Jason Kendall .15 .40
48 Rickey Henderson .40 1.00
49 Luis Gonzalez .15 .40
50 Tom Glavine .25 .60
51 Jeromy Burnitz .15 .40
52 Garret Anderson .15 .40
53 Craig Biggio .25 .60
54 Vinny Castilla .15 .40
55 Jeff Kent .15 .40
56 Gary Sheffield .15 .40
57 Jorge Posada .25 .60
58 Sean Casey .15 .40
59 Johnny Damon .25 .60
60 Dean Palmer .15 .40
61 Todd Helton .25 .60
62 Barry Larkin .25 .60
63 Robin Ventura .15 .40
64 Kenny Lofton .15 .40
65 Sammy Sosa SP 2.00 5.00
66 Rafael Furcal .15 .40
67 Jay Bell .15 .40
68 J.T. Snow .15 .40
69 Jose Vidro .15 .40
70 Ivan Rodriguez .25 .60
71 Jermaine Dye .15 .40
72 Chipper Jones SP 3.00 8.00
73 Fernando Vina .15 .40
74 Ben Grieve .15 .40
75 Mark McGwire SP 5.00 12.00
76 Matt Williams .15 .40
77 Mark Grudzielanek .15 .40
78 Mike Hampton .15 .40
79 Brian Giles .15 .40
80 Tony Gwynn .50 1.25
81 Carlos Beltran .15 .40
82 Ray Durham .15 .40
83 Brad Radke .15 .40
84 David Justice .15 .40
85 Frank Thomas .40 1.00
86 Todd Zeile .15 .40
87 Pat Burrell .15 .40
88 Jim Thome .25 .60
89 Greg Vaughn .15 .40
90 Ken Griffey Jr. SP 6.00 15.00
91 Mike Mussina .25 .60
92 Magglio Ordonez .15 .40
93 Bob Abreu .15 .40
94 Alex Gonzalez .15 .40
95 Kevin Brown .15 .40
96 Jay Buhner .15 .40
97 Roger Clemens .75 2.00
98 Nomar Garciaparra SP 2.00 5.00
99 Derrek Lee .25 .60
100 Derek Jeter SP 8.00 20.00
101 Adrian Beltre .15 .40
102 Geoff Jenkins .15 .40
103 Javy Lopez .15 .40
104 Raul Mondesi .15 .40
105 Troy Glaus .15 .40
106 Jeff Bagwell .25 .60
107 Eric Karros .15 .40
108 Mo Vaughn .15 .40
109 Cal Ripken 1.25 3.00
110 Manny Ramirez Sox .25 .60
111 Scott Heard PROS 4.00 10.00
112 Luis Montanez PROS RC 4.00 10.00
113 Ben Diggins PROS 4.00 10.00
114 Shaun Boyd PROS RC 4.00 10.00
115 Sean Burnett PROS 4.00 10.00
116 Carmen Cali PROS RC 4.00 10.00
117 Derek Thompson PROS 4.00 10.00
118 David Parrish PROS RC 4.00 10.00
119 Dominic Rich PROS RC 4.00 10.00
120 Chad Petty PROS RC 4.00 10.00
121 Steve Smyth PROS RC 4.00 10.00
122 John Lackey PROS 4.00 10.00
123 Matt Galante PROS RC 4.00 10.00
124 Danny Borrell PROS RC 4.00 10.00
125 Bob Keppel PROS RC 4.00 10.00
126 Justin Wayne PROS RC 4.00 10.00
127 J.R. House PROS 4.00 10.00
128 Brian Sellier PROS RC 4.00 10.00
129 Dan Moylan PROS RC 4.00 10.00
130 Scott Pratt PROS RC 4.00 10.00
131 Victor Hall PROS RC 4.00 10.00
132 Joel Pineiro PROS 4.00 10.00
133 Josh Axelson PROS RC 4.00 10.00
134 Jose Reyes PROS RC 10.00 25.00
135 Greg Runser PROS RC 4.00 10.00
136 Bryan Hebson PROS RC 4.00 10.00
137 Sammy Serrano PROS RC 4.00 10.00
138 Kevin Joseph PROS RC 4.00 10.00
139 Juan Richardson PROS RC 4.00 10.00
140 Mark Fischer PROS RC 4.00 10.00

2001 Finest Refractors

*1-110 REF: 4X TO 10X BASIC 1-110
1-110 ODDS 1:13 HOBBY, 1:6 HTA
1-110 PRINT RUN 499 SERIAL #'d SETS
*SP REF: .5X TO 1.2X BASIC SP
SP STATED ODDS 1:159 HOBBY, 1:73 HTA
SP STATED PRINT RUN 399 SERIAL #'d SETS
*111-140 REF: .75X TO 2X BASIC 111-140
111-140 ODDS 1:88 HOBBY, 1:40 HTA
111-140 PRINT RUN 241 SERIAL #'d SETS

2001 Finest All-Stars

COMPLETE SET (10) 30.00 60.00
STATED ODDS 1:10 HOBBY, 1:5 HTA
*REF: 1X TO 2.5X BASIC ALL-STARS
REFRACTOR ODDS 1:40 HOBBY, 1:20 HTA
FAS1 Mark McGwire 4.00 10.00
FAS2 Derek Jeter 4.00 10.00
FAS3 Alex Rodriguez 2.00 5.00
FAS4 Chipper Jones 1.50 4.00
FAS5 Nomar Garciaparra 2.50 6.00
FAS6 Sammy Sosa 1.50 4.00
FAS7 Mike Piazza 2.50 6.00
FAS8 Barry Bonds 4.00 10.00
FAS9 Vladimir Guerrero 1.50 4.00
FAS10 Ken Griffey Jr. 3.00 8.00

2001 Finest Autographs

STATED ODDS 1:22 HOBBY, 1:10 HTA
FAAG Adrian Gonzalez 4.00 10.00
FAAH Adam Hyzdu 4.00 10.00
FAAK Adam Kennedy 6.00 15.00
FAAP Albert Pujols 200.00 500.00
FABD Ben Diggins 4.00 10.00
FABM Ben Molina 6.00 15.00
FABS Ben Sheets 10.00 25.00
FABZ Barry Zito 6.00 15.00
FABKC Brian Cole 10.00 25.00
FACD Chad Durham 4.00 10.00
FACP Carlos Pena 6.00 15.00
FADK Dave Krynzel 4.00 10.00
FADCP Corey Patterson 4.00 10.00
FAJC Joe Crede 10.00 25.00
FAJH Jason Hart 4.00 10.00
FAJM Justin Morneau 6.00 15.00
FAJO Jose Ortiz 4.00 10.00
FAJP Jay Payton 4.00 10.00
FAJHH Josh Hamilton 6.00 15.00
FAJRH J.R. House 4.00 10.00
FAKG Keith Ginter 4.00 10.00
FAKM Kevin Mench 6.00 15.00
FAMB Milton Bradley 6.00 15.00
FAMQ Mark Quinn 4.00 10.00
FAMR Mark Redman 4.00 10.00
FARF Rafael Furcal 6.00 15.00
FASB Sean Burnett 4.00 10.00
FATF Troy Farnsworth 4.00 10.00
FATL Terrence Long 4.00 10.00

2001 Finest Moments

COMPLETE SET (25) 60.00 120.00
STATED ODDS 1:12 HOBBY, 1:6 HTA
*REF: .75X TO 2X BASIC MOMENTS
REFRACTOR ODDS 1:40 HOBBY, 1:20 HTA
FM1 Pat Burrell 1.00 2.50
FM2 Adam Kennedy 1.00 2.50
FM3 Mike Lamb 1.00 2.50
FM4 Rafael Furcal 1.00 2.50
FM5 Terrence Long 1.00 2.50
FM6 Jay Payton 1.00 2.50
FM7 Mark Quinn 1.00 2.50
FM8 Ben Molina 1.00 2.50
FM9 Kazuhiro Sasaki 1.00 2.50
FM10 Mark Redman 1.00 2.50
FM11 Barry Bonds 6.00 15.00
FM12 Alex Rodriguez 3.00 8.00
FM13 Roger Clemens 5.00 12.00
FM14 Jim Edmonds 1.00 2.50
FM15 Jason Giambi 1.00 2.50
FM16 Todd Helton 1.50 4.00
FM17 Troy Glaus 1.00 2.50
FM18 Carlos Delgado 1.00 2.50
FM19 Darin Erstad 1.00 2.50
FM20 Cal Ripken 8.00 20.00
FM21 Paul Molitor 1.00 2.50
FM22 Robin Yount 2.50 6.00
FM23 George Brett 5.00 12.00
FM24 Dave Winfield 1.00 2.50
FM25 Eddie Murray 2.50 6.00

2001 Finest Moments Refractors Autograph

STATED ODDS 1:250 HOBBY, 1:115 HTA
FMABB Barry Bonds 90.00 150.00
FMACR Cal Ripken 40.00 100.00
FMADW Dave Winfield 20.00 50.00
FMAEM Eddie Murray 15.00 40.00
FMAGB George Brett 30.00 80.00
FMAJG Jason Giambi 10.00 25.00
FMAPM Paul Molitor 15.00 40.00
FMARY Robin Yount 25.00 60.00
FMATG Troy Glaus 10.00 25.00
FMATH Todd Helton 10.00 25.00

2001 Finest Origins

COMPLETE SET (15) 20.00 40.00
STATED ODDS 1:7 HOBBY, 1:4 HTA
*REF: 1X TO 2.5X BASIC ORIGINS
REFRACTOR ODDS 1:40 HOBBY, 1:20 HTA
FO1 Derek Jeter 5.00 12.00
FO2 Jason Kendall .75 2.00
FO3 Jose Vidro .75 2.00
FO4 Preston Wilson .75 2.00
FO5 Jim Edmonds .75 2.00
FO6 Vladimir Guerrero 2.00 5.00
FO7 Andruw Jones 1.25 3.00
FO8 Scott Rolen 1.25 3.00
FO9 Edgardo Alfonzo .75 2.00
FO10 Mike Sweeney .75 2.00
FO11 Alex Rodriguez 2.50 6.00
FO12 Jermaine Dye .75 2.00
FO13 Charles Johnson .75 2.00
FO14 Darren Dreifort .75 2.00
FO15 Neifi Perez .75 2.00

2002 Finest

COMP.SET w/o SP's (100) 10.00 25.00
COMMON CARD (1-100) .20 .50
COMMON CARD (101-110) 4.00 10.00
ONE AUTO OR RELIC PER 6-PACK MINI BOX
1 Mike Mussina .30 .75
2 Steve Sparks .20 .50
3 Randy Johnson .50 1.25
4 Orlando Cabrera .20 .50
5 Jeff Kent .20 .50
6 Carlos Delgado .20 .50
7 Ivan Rodriguez .30 .75
8 Jose Cruz .20 .50
9 Jason Giambi .20 .50
10 Brad Penny .20 .50
11 Moises Alou .20 .50
12 Mike Piazza .75 2.00
13 Ben Grieve .20 .50
14 Derek Jeter 1.25 3.00
15 Roy Oswalt .20 .50
16 Pat Burrell .20 .50
17 Preston Wilson .20 .50
18 Kevin Brown .20 .50
19 Barry Bonds 1.25 3.00
20 Phil Nevin .20 .50
21 Aramis Ramirez .20 .50
22 Carlos Beltran .20 .50
23 Chipper Jones .50 1.25
24 Curt Schilling .20 .50
25 Jorge Posada .30 .75
26 Alfonso Soriano .20 .50
27 Cliff Floyd .20 .50
28 Rafael Palmeiro .30 .75
29 Terrence Long .20 .50
30 Ken Griffey Jr. 1.00 2.50
31 Jason Kendall .20 .50
32 Jose Vidro .20 .50
33 Jermaine Dye .20 .50
34 Bobby Higginson .20 .50
35 Albert Pujols 1.00 2.50
36 Miguel Tejada .20 .50
37 Jim Edmonds .20 .50
38 Barry Zito .20 .50
39 Jimmy Rollins .20 .50
40 Rafael Furcal .20 .50
41 Omar Vizquel .30 .75
42 Kazuhiro Sasaki .20 .50
43 Brian Giles .20 .50
44 Darin Erstad .20 .50
45 Mariano Rivera .50 1.25
46 Troy Percival .20 .50
47 Mike Sweeney .20 .50
48 Vladimir Guerrero .50 1.25
49 Troy Glaus .20 .50
50 So Taguchi RC 1.00 2.50
51 Edgardo Alfonzo .20 .50
52 Roger Clemens 1.00 2.50
53 Eric Chavez .20 .50
54 Alex Rodriguez .60 1.50
55 Cristian Guzman .20 .50
56 Jeff Bagwell .30 .75
57 Bernie Williams .30 .75
58 Kerry Wood .20 .50
59 Ryan Klesko .20 .50
60 Ichiro Suzuki 1.00 2.50
61 Larry Walker .20 .50
62 Nomar Garciaparra .75 2.00
63 Craig Biggio .30 .75
64 J.D. Drew .20 .50
65 Juan Pierre .20 .50
66 Roberto Alomar .30 .75
67 Luis Gonzalez .20 .50
68 Bud Smith .20 .50
69 Magglio Ordonez .20 .50
70 Scott Rolen .30 .75
71 Tsuyoshi Shinjo .20 .50
72 Paul Konerko .20 .50
73 Garret Anderson .20 .50
74 Tim Hudson .20 .50
75 Adam Dunn .20 .50
76 Gary Sheffield .20 .50
77 Johnny Damon Sox .30 .75
78 Todd Helton .30 .75
79 Geoff Jenkins .20 .50
80 Shawn Green .20 .50
81 C.C. Sabathia .20 .50
82 Kazuhisa Ishii RC 1.00 2.50
83 Rich Aurilia .20 .50
84 Mike Hampton .20 .50
85 Ben Sheets .20 .50
86 Andruw Jones .30 .75
87 Richie Sexson .20 .50
88 Jim Thome .30 .75
89 Sammy Sosa .50 1.25
90 Greg Maddux .75 2.00
91 Pedro Martinez .30 .75
92 Jeromy Burnitz .20 .50
93 Raul Mondesi .20 .50
94 Bret Boone .20 .50
95 Jerry Hairston .20 .50
96 Mike Rivera .20 .50
97 Juan Cruz .20 .50
98 Morgan Ensberg .20 .50
99 Nathan Haynes .20 .50
100 Xavier Nady .20 .50
101 Nic Jackson FY AU RC 4.00 10.00
102 Mauricio Lara FY AU RC 4.00 10.00
103 Freddy Sanchez FY AU RC 4.00 10.00
104 Clint Nageotte FY AU RC 4.00 10.00
105 Beltran Perez FY AU RC 4.00 10.00
106 Garrett Gentry FY AU RC 4.00 10.00
107 Chad Qualls FY AU RC 4.00 10.00
108 Jason Bay FY AU RC 4.00 10.00
109 Michael Hill FY AU RC 4.00 10.00
110 Brian Tallet FY AU RC 4.00 10.00

2002 Finest Refractors

*REFRACTORS 1-100: 2.5X TO 6X BASIC
*REF.RC'S 1-100: 1.5X TO 4X BASIC
STATED ODDS 1:2 MINI BOXES
STATED PRINT RUN 499 SERIAL #'d SETS
101 Nic Jackson FY 2.00 5.00
102 Mauricio Lara FY 2.00 5.00
103 Freddy Sanchez FY 3.00 8.00
104 Clint Nageotte FY 3.00 8.00
105 Beltran Perez FY 2.00 5.00
106 Garett Gentry FY 2.00 5.00
107 Chad Qualls FY 3.00 8.00
108 Jason Bay FY 3.00 8.00
109 Michael Hill FY 2.00 5.00
110 Brian Tallet FY 2.00 5.00

2002 Finest X-Fractors

*XF 1-100: 3X TO 8X BASIC
*XF RC'S 1-100: 2X TO 5X BASIC
*XF 101-110: .5X TO 1.2X REFRACTOR
STATED ODDS 1:3 MINI BOXES
STATED PRINT RUN 299 SERIAL #'d SETS

2002 Finest X-Fractors Protectors

*XF PROT. 1-100: 6X TO 15X BASIC
*XF PROT.RC'S 1-100: 4X TO 10X BASIC
*XF PROT 101-110: .75X TO 2X REFRACTOR
STATED ODDS 1:7 MINI BOXES
STATED PRINT RUN 99 SERIAL #'d SETS

2002 Finest Bat Relics

STATED ODDS 1:12 MINI BOXES
FBRAJ Andruw Jones 6.00 15.00
FBRAP Albert Pujols 8.00 20.00
FBRAR Alex Rodriguez 6.00 15.00
FBRAS Alfonso Soriano 4.00 10.00
FBRBB Barry Bonds 10.00 25.00
FBRBO Bret Boone 4.00 10.00
FBRBW Bernie Williams 6.00 15.00
FBRCJ Chipper Jones 6.00 15.00
FBRIR Ivan Rodriguez 6.00 15.00
FBRLG Luis Gonzalez 4.00 10.00
FBRMP Mike Piazza 6.00 15.00
FBRNG Nomar Garciaparra 6.00 15.00
FBRTG Tony Gwynn 6.00 15.00
FBRTH Todd Helton 6.00 15.00
FBRTS Tsuyoshi Shinjo 4.00 10.00

2002 Finest Jersey Relics

STATED ODDS 1:4 MINI BOXES
FJRAJ Andruw Jones 6.00 15.00
FJRAR Alex Rodriguez 6.00 15.00
FJRBB Barry Bonds 10.00 25.00
FJRBO Bret Boone 4.00 10.00
FJRCD Carlos Delgado 4.00 10.00
FJRCJ Chipper Jones 6.00 15.00
FJRCS Curt Schilling 4.00 10.00
FJRFT Frank Thomas 6.00 15.00
FJRGM Greg Maddux 6.00 15.00
FJRHN Hideo Nomo 6.00 15.00
FJRIR Ivan Rodriguez 6.00 15.00
FJRJB Jeff Bagwell 6.00 15.00
FJRLG Luis Gonzalez 4.00 10.00
FJRLW Larry Walker 4.00 10.00
FJRMG Mark Grace 6.00 15.00
FJRMP Mike Piazza 6.00 15.00
FJRPM Pedro Martinez 6.00 15.00
FJRRA Roberto Alomar 6.00 15.00
FJRRH Rickey Henderson 6.00 15.00
FJRRP Rafael Palmeiro 6.00 15.00
FJRSG Shawn Green 4.00 10.00
FJRTG Tony Gwynn 6.00 15.00
FJRTH Todd Helton 6.00 15.00
FJRTS Tsuyoshi Shinjo 4.00 10.00

2002 Finest Moments Autographs

STATED ODDS 1:3 MINI BOXES
FMABG Bob Gibson 30.00 80.00
FMABR Bobby Richardson 6.00 15.00
FMABRO Brooks Robinson 12.00 30.00
FMABT Bobby Thomson 10.00 25.00
FMADL Don Larsen 10.00 25.00
FMADM Don Mattingly 25.00 60.00
FMAFJ Fergie Jenkins 6.00 15.00
FMAGG Goose Gossage 8.00 20.00
FMAGP Gaylord Perry 10.00 25.00
FMAJB Jim Bunning 8.00 20.00
FMAJS Johnny Sain 12.00 30.00
FMALA Luis Aparicio 10.00 25.00
FMAMS Mike Schmidt 25.00 60.00
FMARS Red Schoendienst 12.00 30.00
FMAYB Yogi Berra 30.00 80.00

2003 Finest

COMP.SET w/o SP's (100) 10.00 25.00
COMMON CARD (1-100) .20 .50
COMMON CARD (101-110) 6.00 15.00
COMMON RC (101-110) 4.00 10.00
101-110 STATED ODDS 1:4 MINI-BOXES
1993 FINEST BUYBACKS 1:333 MINI BOXES
1993 FINEST BUYBACKS ARE NOT STAMPED
1 Sammy Sosa .50 1.25
2 Paul Konerko .30 .75
3 Todd Helton .30 .75
4 Mike Lowell .20 .50
5 Lance Berkman .30 .75
6 Kazuhisa Ishii .20 .50
7 A.J. Pierzynski .20 .50
8 Jose Vidro .20 .50
9 Roberto Alomar .30 .75
10 Derek Jeter 1.25 3.00
11 Barry Zito .30 .75
12 Jimmy Rollins .30 .75
13 Brian Giles .20 .50
14 Ryan Klesko .20 .50
15 Rich Aurilia .20 .50
16 Jim Edmonds .30 .75
17 Aubrey Huff .20 .50
18 Ivan Rodriguez .30 .75
19 Eric Hinske .20 .50
20 Barry Bonds .75 2.00
21 Darin Erstad .20 .50
22 Curt Schilling .30 .75
23 Andruw Jones .20 .50
24 Jay Gibbons .20 .50
25 Nomar Garciaparra .30 .75
26 Kerry Wood .20 .50
27 Magglio Ordonez .30 .75
28 Austin Kearns .20 .50
29 Jason Jennings .20 .50
30 Jason Giambi .20 .50
31 Tim Hudson .30 .75
32 Edgar Martinez .30 .75
33 Carl Crawford .30 .75
34 Hee Seop Choi .20 .50
35 Vladimir Guerrero .30 .75
36 Jeff Kent .20 .50
37 John Smoltz .50 1.25
38 Frank Thomas .50 1.25
39 Cliff Floyd .20 .50
40 Mike Piazza .50 1.25
41 Mark Prior .30 .75
42 Tim Salmon .20 .50
43 Shawn Green .20 .50
44 Bernie Williams .30 .75
45 Jim Thome .30 .75
46 John Olerud .20 .50
47 Orlando Hudson .20 .50
48 Mark Teixeira .30 .75

49 Gary Sheffield .20 .50
50 Ichiro Suzuki .60 1.50
51 Tom Glavine .30 .75
52 Torii Hunter .20 .50
53 Craig Biggio .30 .75
54 Carlos Beltran .30 .75
55 Bartolo Colon .20 .50
56 Jorge Posada .30 .75
57 Pat Burrell .20 .50
58 Edgar Renteria .20 .50
59 Rafael Palmeiro .30 .75
60 Alfonso Soriano .30 .75
61 Brandon Phillips .20 .50
62 Luis Gonzalez .20 .50
63 Manny Ramirez .50 1.25
64 Garret Anderson .20 .50
65 Ken Griffey Jr. 1.00 2.50
66 A.J. Burnett .20 .50
67 Mike Sweeney .20 .50
68 Doug Mientkiewicz .20 .50
69 Eric Chavez .20 .50
70 Adam Dunn .30 .75
71 Shea Hillenbrand .20 .50
72 Troy Glaus .20 .50
73 Rodrigo Lopez .20 .50
74 Moises Alou .20 .50
75 Chipper Jones .50 1.25
76 Bobby Abreu .20 .50
77 Mark Mulder .20 .50
78 Kevin Brown .20 .50
79 Josh Beckett .20 .50
80 Larry Walker .30 .75
81 Randy Johnson .50 1.25
82 Greg Maddux .60 1.50
83 Johnny Damon .30 .75
84 Omar Vizquel .30 .75
85 Jeff Bagwell .30 .75
86 Carlos Pena .30 .75
87 Roy Oswalt .30 .75
88 Richie Sexson .20 .50
89 Roger Clemens .60 1.50
90 Miguel Tejada .30 .75
91 Vicente Padilla .20 .50
92 Phil Nevin .20 .50
93 Edgardo Alfonzo .20 .50
94 Bret Boone .20 .50
95 Albert Pujols .60 1.50
96 Carlos Delgado .20 .50
97 Jose Contreras RC .50 1.25
98 Scott Rolen .30 .75
99 Pedro Martinez .30 .75
100 Alex Rodriguez .60 1.50
101 Adam LaRoche AU 4.00 10.00
102 Andy Marte AU RC 4.00 10.00
103 Daryl Clark AU RC 4.00 10.00
104 J.D. Durbin AU RC 4.00 10.00
105 Craig Brazell AU RC 4.00 10.00
106 Brian Burgamy AU RC 4.00 10.00
107 Tyler Johnson AU RC 4.00 10.00
108 Joey Gomes AU RC 4.00 10.00
109 Bryan Bullington AU RC 4.00 10.00
110 Byron Gettis AU RC 4.00 10.00

2003 Finest Refractors

*REFRACTORS 1-100: 2X TO 5X BASIC
*REFRACTOR RC'S 1-100: 1.25X TO 3X BASIC
1-100 STATED ODDS ONE PER MINI-BOX
*REFRACTORS 101-110: .75X TO 2X BASIC
101-110 STATED ODDS 1:34 MINI-BOXES
101-110 STATED PRINT RUN 199 #'d SETS

2003 Finest X-Fractors

*X-FRACTORS 1-100: 6X TO 15X BASIC
*X-FRACTOR RC'S 1-100: 4X TO 10X BASIC
*X-FRACTORS 101-110: 1X TO 2.5X BASIC
STATED ODDS 1:7 MINI-BOXES
STATED PRINT RUN 99 SERIAL #'d SETS

2003 Finest Uncirculated Gold X-Fractors

*GOLD X-F 1-100: 5X TO 12X BASIC
*GOLD X-F RC'S 1-100: 3X TO 8X BASIC
*GOLD X-F 101-110: .75X TO 2X BASIC
ONE PER BASIC SEALED BOX
STATED PRINT RUN 199 SERIAL #'d SETS

2003 Finest Bat Relics

GROUP A STATED ODDS 1:104 MINI-BOXES
GROUP B STATED ODDS 1:32 MINI-BOXES
GROUP C STATED ODDS 1:29 MINI-BOXES
GROUP D STATED ODDS 1:42 MINI-BOXES
GROUP E STATED ODDS 1:40 MINI-BOXES
GROUP F STATED ODDS 1:23 MINI-BOXES
GROUP G STATED ODDS 1:18 MINI-BOXES
GROUP H STATED ODDS 1:24 MINI-BOXES
GROUP I STATED ODDS 1:12 MINI-BOXES
GROUP J STATED ODDS 1:22 MINI-BOXES
GROUP K STATED ODDS 1:21 MINI-BOXES
AD Adam Dunn H 2.00 5.00
AK Austin Kearns F 1.25 3.00
AP Albert Pujols I 4.00 10.00
AR Alex Rodriguez E 4.00 10.00
AS Alfonso Soriano H 2.00 5.00
BB Barry Bonds F 5.00 12.00
CJ Chipper Jones G 3.00 8.00
CR Cal Ripken B 10.00 25.00
DM Dale Murphy I 3.00 8.00
GM Greg Maddux F 4.00 10.00
IR Ivan Rodriguez G 2.00 5.00
JB Jeff Bagwell D 2.00 5.00
JT Jim Thome D 2.00 5.00
KP Kirby Puckett K 3.00 8.00
LB Lance Berkman C 2.00 5.00
MP Mike Piazza E 3.00 8.00
MR Manny Ramirez I 3.00 8.00
MS Mike Schmidt C 5.00 12.00
MT Miguel Tejada I 2.00 5.00
NG Nomar Garciaparra A 2.00 5.00
PM Paul Molitor C 3.00 8.00
RC Rod Carew K 2.00 5.00
RCL Roger Clemens J 4.00 10.00
RH Rickey Henderson B 3.00 8.00
RP Rafael Palmeiro J 2.00 5.00
TH Todd Helton B 2.00 5.00
WB Wade Boggs G 2.00 5.00

2003 Finest Moments Refractors Autographs

GROUP A STATED ODDS 1:113 MINI-BOXES
GROUP B STATED ODDS 1:5 MINI-BOXES
DL Don Larsen B 8.00 20.00
EB Ernie Banks A 40.00 100.00
GC Gary Carter B 6.00 15.00
GF George Foster B 6.00 15.00
GG Goose Gossage B 6.00 15.00
GP Gaylord Perry B 6.00 15.00
JP Jim Palmer B 6.00 15.00
JS Johnny Sain B 6.00 15.00
KH Keith Hernandez B 6.00 15.00
LB Lou Brock B 6.00 15.00
OC Orlando Cepeda B 6.00 15.00
PB Paul Blair B 6.00 15.00
WMA Willie Mays A 200.00 400.00

2003 Finest Uniform Relics

GROUP A STATED ODDS 1:28 MINI-BOXES
GROUP B STATED ODDS 1:11 MINI-BOXES
GROUP C STATED ODDS 1:11 MINI-BOXES
GROUP D STATED ODDS 1:10 MINI-BOXES
GROUP E STATED ODDS 1:19 MINI-BOXES
GROUP F STATED ODDS 1:12 MINI-BOXES
GROUP G STATED ODDS 1:34 MINI-BOXES
GROUP H STATED ODDS 1:17 MINI-BOXES
AD Adam Dunn B 2.50 6.00
AJ Andruw Jones H 1.50 4.00
AP Albert Pujols D 5.00 12.00
AR Alex Rodriguez F 5.00 12.00
AS Alfonso Soriano A 2.50 6.00
BB Barry Bonds D 6.00 15.00
CJ Chipper Jones B 4.00 10.00
CS Curt Schilling B 2.50 6.00
EC Eric Chavez B 1.50 4.00
GM Greg Maddux C 5.00 12.00
LG Luis Gonzalez D 1.50 4.00
LW Larry Walker C 2.50 6.00
MM Mark Mulder C 1.50 4.00
MP Mike Piazza C 4.00 10.00
MR Manny Ramirez E 4.00 10.00
MSW Mike Sweeney F 1.50 4.00
RJ Randy Johnson H 4.00 10.00
RO Roy Oswalt G 2.50 6.00
RP Rafael Palmeiro E 2.50 6.00
SS Sammy Sosa D 4.00 10.00
TH Todd Helton F 2.50 6.00
WM Willie Mays A 12.00 30.00

2004 Finest

COMP.SET w/o SP's (100) 10.00 25.00
COMMON CARD (1-100) .20 .50
COMMON CARD (101-110) 3.00 8.00
101-110 STATED ODDS 1:7 MINI-BOXES
COMMON CARD (111-122) 4.00 10.00
111-122 STATED ODDS 1:3 MINI-BOXES
EXCHANGE DEADLINE 04/30/06
CARD 112 EXCH UNABLE TO BE FULFILLED
04 WS HL B.THOMSON AU SENT INSTEAD
1 Juan Pierre .20 .50
2 Derek Jeter 1.25 3.00
3 Garret Anderson .20 .50
4 Javy Lopez .20 .50
5 Corey Patterson .20 .50
6 Todd Helton .30 .75
7 Roy Oswalt .30 .75
8 Shawn Green .20 .50
9 Vladimir Guerrero .30 .75
10 Jorge Posada .30 .75
11 Jason Kendall .20 .50
12 Scott Rolen .30 .75
13 Randy Johnson .50 1.25
14 Bill Mueller .20 .50
15 Magglio Ordonez .30 .75
16 Larry Walker .30 .75
17 Lance Berkman .30 .75
18 Richie Sexson .20 .50
19 Orlando Cabrera .20 .50
20 Alfonso Soriano .30 .75
21 Kevin Millwood .20 .50
22 Edgar Martinez .30 .75
23 Aubrey Huff .20 .50
24 Carlos Delgado .20 .50
25 Vernon Wells .20 .50
26 Mark Teixeira .30 .75
27 Troy Glaus .20 .50
28 Jeff Kent .20 .50
29 Hideo Nomo .50 1.25
30 Torii Hunter .20 .50
31 Hank Blalock .20 .50
32 Brandon Webb .20 .50
33 Tony Batista .20 .50
34 Bret Boone .20 .50
35 Ryan Klesko .20 .50
36 Barry Zito .30 .75
37 Edgar Renteria .20 .50
38 Geoff Jenkins .20 .50
39 Jeff Bagwell .30 .75
40 Dontrelle Willis .20 .50
41 Adam Dunn .30 .75
42 Mark Buehrle .30 .75
43 Esteban Loaiza .20 .50
44 Angel Berroa .20 .50
45 Ivan Rodriguez .30 .75
46 Jose Vidro .20 .50
47 Mark Mulder .20 .50
48 Roger Clemens .60 1.50
49 Jim Edmonds .30 .75
50 Eric Gagne .20 .50
51 Marcus Giles .20 .50
52 Curt Schilling .30 .75
53 Ken Griffey Jr. 1.00 2.50
54 Jason Schmidt .20 .50
55 Miguel Tejada .30 .75
56 Dmitri Young .20 .50
57 Mike Lowell .20 .50
58 Mike Sweeney .20 .50
59 Scott Podsednik .20 .50
60 Miguel Cabrera .50 1.25
61 Johan Santana .30 .75
62 Bernie Williams .30 .75
63 Eric Chavez .20 .50
64 Bobby Abreu .20 .50
65 Brian Giles .20 .50
66 Michael Young .20 .50
67 Paul Lo Duca .20 .50
68 Austin Kearns .20 .50
69 Jody Gerut .20 .50
70 Kerry Wood .20 .50
71 Luis Matos .20 .50
72 Greg Maddux .60 1.50
73 Alex Rodriguez Yanks .60 1.50
74 Mike Lieberthal .20 .50
75 Jim Thome .30 .75
76 Javier Vazquez .20 .50
77 Bartolo Colon .20 .50
78 Manny Ramirez .50 1.25
79 Jacque Jones .20 .50
80 Johnny Damon .30 .75
81 Carlos Beltran .30 .75
82 C.C. Sabathia .30 .75
83 Preston Wilson .20 .50
84 Luis Castillo .20 .50
85 Kevin Brown .20 .50
86 Shannon Stewart .20 .50
87 Cliff Floyd .20 .50
88 Mike Mussina .30 .75
89 Rafael Furcal .20 .50
90 Roy Halladay .30 .75
91 Frank Thomas .50 1.25
92 Melvin Mora .20 .50
93 Andruw Jones .20 .50
94 Luis Gonzalez .20 .50
95 David Ortiz .50 1.25
96 Gary Sheffield .20 .50
97 Tim Hudson .30 .75
98 Phil Nevin .20 .50
99 Ichiro Suzuki .60 1.50
100 Albert Pujols .60 1.50
101 Nomar Garciaparra SR Jsy 6.00 15.00
102 Sammy Sosa SR Jsy 4.00 10.00
103 Josh Beckett SR Jsy 3.00 8.00
104 Jason Giambi SR Jsy 3.00 8.00
105 Rocco Baldelli SR Jsy 3.00 8.00
106 Jose Reyes SR Jsy 3.00 8.00
107 Chipper Jones SR Jsy 4.00 10.00
108 Pedro Martinez SR Jsy 4.00 10.00
109 Mike Piazza SR Jsy 6.00 15.00
110 Mark Prior SR Jsy 4.00 10.00
111 Craig Ansman AU RC 4.00 10.00
113 David Murphy AU RC 5.00 12.00
114 Jason Hirsh AU RC 6.00 15.00
115 Matt Moses AU RC 4.00 10.00
116 Estee Harris AU RC 4.00 10.00
117 Logan Kensing AU RC 4.00 10.00
118 L.Milledge AU RC 3.00 8.00
119 Merkin Valdez AU RC 4.00 10.00
120 Travis Blackley AU RC 4.00 10.00
121 Vito Chiaravalloti AU RC 4.00 10.00
122 Dioner Navarro AU RC 4.00 10.00

2004 Finest Gold Refractors

*GOLD REF 1-100: 6X TO 15X BASIC
1-100 STATED ODDS 1:11
*GOLD REF 101-110: 1.25X TO 3X BASIC
101-110 STATED ODDS 1:102
*GOLD REF 111-122: 2X TO 4X BASIC
111-122 STATED ODDS 1:85
STATED PRINT RUN 50 SERIAL #'d SETS
CARD 112 EXCH UNABLE TO BE FULFILLED
EXCHANGE DEADLINE 04/30/06

2004 Finest Refractors

*REFRACTORS 1-100: 2X TO 5X BASIC
1-100 APPX.ODDS 3 IN EVERY 4 MINI-BOXES
*REFRACTORS 101-110: .5X TO 1.2X BASIC
101-110 STATED ODDS 1:26 MINI-BOXES
*REFRACTORS 111-122: .6X TO 1.5X BASIC
111-122 STATED ODDS 1:22 MINI-BOXES
EXCHANGE DEADLINE 04/30/06
CARD 112 EXCH UNABLE TO BE FULFILLED

2004 Finest Uncirculated Gold X-Fractors

*GOLD X-F 1-100: 4X TO 10X BASIC
*GOLD X-F 101-110: .75X TO 2X BASIC
*GOLD X-F 111-122: 1X TO 2.5X BASIC
ONE PER BASIC SEALED BOX
STATED PRINT RUN 139 SERIAL #'d SETS
EXCHANGE DEADLINE 04/30/06
CARD 112 EXCH UNABLE TO BE FULFILLED

2004 Finest Moments Autographs

GROUP A ODDS 1:86 MINI-BOXES
GROUP B ODDS 1:102 MINI-BOXES
GROUP C ODDS 1:5 MINI-BOXES
DS Duke Snider A 15.00 40.00
EK Ed Kranepool C 4.00 10.00
GS George Foster C 4.00 10.00
JA Jim Abbott A 20.00 50.00
JP Johnny Podres C 6.00 15.00
LD Lenny Dykstra C 4.00 10.00
OC Orlando Cepeda C 4.00 10.00
RY Robin Yount A 20.00 50.00
VB Vida Blue C 4.00 10.00
WM Willie Mays B 100.00 200.00

2004 Finest Relics

GROUP A ODDS 1:3 MINI-BOXES
GROUP B ODDS 1:4 MINI-BOXES
AB Angel Berroa Bat B 3.00 8.00
AD Adam Dunn Jsy A 3.00 8.00
AG Adrian Gonzalez Bat A 3.00 8.00
AJ Andruw Jones Bat A 4.00 10.00
AP Andy Pettitte Uni B 4.00 10.00
AP1 Albert Pujols Uni A 8.00 20.00
AP2 Albert Pujols Bat A 8.00 20.00
AR1 A.Rodriguez Rgr Jsy A 6.00 15.00
AR2 A.Rodriguez Yanks Jsy A 10.00 25.00
AS Alfonso Soriano Bat A 3.00 8.00
BM1 B.Myers Arm Down Jsy A 3.00 8.00
BM2 B.Myers Arm Up Jsy A 3.00 8.00
BW Bernie Williams Bat B 4.00 10.00
BZ Barry Zito Jsy A 3.00 8.00
CCS C.C. Sabathia Jsy A 3.00 8.00
CG Cristian Guzman Jsy A 3.00 8.00
CS Curt Schilling Jsy A 3.00 8.00
DE Darin Erstad Bat A 3.00 8.00
DL Derek Lowe Uni A 3.00 8.00
DW Dontrelle Willis Uni B 4.00 10.00
DY Delmon Young Bat B 4.00 10.00
EC Eric Chavez Uni B 3.00 8.00
FT Frank Thomas Jsy A 4.00 10.00
GM Greg Maddux Jsy A 6.00 15.00
GS Gary Sheffield Bat A 3.00 8.00
HB1 Hank Blalock Bat A 3.00 8.00
HB2 Hank Blalock Jsy B 3.00 8.00
IR1 I.Rodriguez Running Jsy A 4.00 10.00
IR2 I.Rodriguez w Glove Jsy A 4.00 10.00
IR3 Ivan Rodriguez Bat B 4.00 10.00
JB Jeff Bagwell Jsy A 4.00 10.00
JL Javy Lopez Jsy A 3.00 8.00
JP Juan Pierre Bat A 3.00 8.00
JPB1 Josh Beckett Jsy A 3.00 8.00
JR1 Jose Reyes White Jsy A 3.00 8.00
JR2 Jose Reyes Bat A 3.00 8.00
JR3 Jose Reyes Black Jsy B 3.00 8.00
JS John Smoltz Uni A 4.00 10.00
JT Jim Thome Jsy A 4.00 10.00
KI Kazuhisa Ishii Jsy A 3.00 8.00
KM Kevin Millwood Jsy A 3.00 8.00
KS Kazuhiro Sasaki Jsy A 3.00 8.00
KW1 Kerry Wood Jsy A 3.00 8.00
KW2 Kerry Wood Bat A 3.00 8.00
LB1 Lance Berkman Bat A 3.00 8.00
LB2 Lance Berkman Jsy A 3.00 8.00
LG Luis Gonzalez Jsy A 3.00 8.00
LW Larry Walker Jsy A 3.00 8.00
MB Marlon Byrd Jsy A 3.00 8.00
MC Miguel Cabrera Bat B 4.00 10.00
ML1 Mike Lowell Grey Jsy A 3.00 8.00
ML2 Mike Lowell Black Jsy B 3.00 8.00
MM Mark Mulder Uni B 3.00 8.00
MO1 Magglio Ordonez Jsy A 3.00 8.00
MO2 Magglio Ordonez Bat A 3.00 8.00
MP Mark Prior Bat A 4.00 10.00
MR Mariano Rivera Uni A 4.00 10.00
MT1 Miguel Tejada Bat A 3.00 8.00
MT2 Miguel Tejada Uni A 3.00 8.00
NG Nomar Garciaparra Bat A 6.00 15.00
PB Pat Burrell Jsy A 3.00 8.00
PW Preston Wilson Bat A 3.00 8.00
RB1 R.Baldelli Bat Down Jsy B 3.00 8.00
RB3 R.Baldelli Bat on Ball Jsy B 3.00 8.00
RH Rich Harden Uni B 3.00 8.00
RJ Randy Johnson Jsy A 4.00 10.00
RP1 Rafael Palmeiro Bat A 4.00 10.00
RP2 Rafael Palmeiro Uni A 4.00 10.00
RP3 Rafael Palmeiro Jsy B 4.00 10.00
SB Sean Burroughs Bat A 3.00 8.00
SG Shawn Green Jsy A 3.00 8.00
SR Scott Rolen Bat A 4.00 10.00
SS Sammy Sosa Bat A 4.00 10.00
TG Troy Glaus Bat A 3.00 8.00
TH Tim Hudson Uni B 3.00 8.00
TH1 Todd Helton Bat A 4.00 10.00
TH2 Todd Helton Jsy A 4.00 10.00
TKH1 Torii Hunter Bat A 3.00 8.00
TKH2 Torii Hunter Jsy B 3.00 8.00
VG Vladimir Guerrero Jsy B 4.00 10.00
VW Vernon Wells Jsy A 3.00 8.00

2005 Finest

COMP.SET w/o SP's (150) 40.00 80.00
COMMON CARD (1-140) .20 .50
COMMON CARD (157-166) .30 .75
AU p/r 970 ODDS 1:3 MINI BOXES
AU p/r 970 PRINT RUN 970 #'d SETS
AU p/r 375 ODDS 1:41 MINI BOXES
AU p/r 375 PRINT RUN 375 #'d SETS
OVERALL PLATE ODDS 1:51 MINI BOX
OVERALL AU PLATE ODDS 1:478 MINI BOX
PLATE PRINT RUN 1 SET PER COLOR
BLACK-CYAN-MAGENTA-YELLOW ISSUED
NO PLATE PRICING DUE TO SCARCITY
1 Alexis Rios .20 .50
2 Hank Blalock .20 .50
3 Bobby Abreu .20 .50
4 Curt Schilling .30 .75
5 Albert Pujols .60 1.50
6 Aaron Rowand .20 .50
7 B.J. Upton .30 .75
8 Andruw Jones .20 .50
9 Jeff Francis .20 .50
10 Sammy Sosa .50 1.25
11 Aramis Ramirez .20 .50
12 Carl Pavano .20 .50
13 Bartolo Colon .20 .50
14 Greg Maddux .60 1.50
15 Scott Kazmir .50 1.25
16 Melvin Mora .20 .50
17 Brandon Backe .20 .50
18 Bobby Crosby .20 .50
19 Carlos Lee .20 .50
20 Carl Crawford .30 .75
21 Brian Giles .20 .50
22 Jeff Bagwell .30 .75
23 J.D. Drew .20 .50
24 C.C. Sabathia .30 .75
25 Alfonso Soriano .30 .75
26 Chipper Jones .50 1.25
27 Austin Kearns .20 .50
28 Carlos Delgado .20 .50
29 Jack Wilson .20 .50
30 Dmitri Young .20 .50
31 Carlos Guillen .20 .50
32 Jim Thome .30 .75
33 Eric Chavez .20 .50
34 Jason Schmidt .20 .50
35 Brad Radke .20 .50
36 Frank Thomas .50 1.25
37 Darin Erstad .20 .50
38 Javier Vazquez .20 .50
39 Garret Anderson .20 .50
40 David Ortiz .50 1.25
41 Javy Lopez .20 .50
42 Geoff Jenkins .20 .50
43 Jose Vidro .20 .50
44 Aubrey Huff .20 .50
45 Bernie Williams .30 .75
46 Dontrelle Willis .20 .50
47 Jim Edmonds .30 .75
48 Ivan Rodriguez .30 .75
49 Gary Sheffield .20 .50
50 Alex Rodriguez .60 1.50
51 John Buck .20 .50
52 Andy Pettitte .30 .75
53 Ichiro Suzuki .60 1.50
54 Johnny Estrada .20 .50
55 Jake Peavy .20 .50
56 Carlos Zambrano .30 .75
57 Jose Reyes .30 .75
58 Bret Boone .20 .50
59 Jason Bay .20 .50
60 David Wright .40 1.00
61 Jeromy Burnitz .20 .50
62 Corey Patterson .20 .50
63 Juan Pierre .20 .50
64 Zack Greinke .60 1.50
65 Mike Lowell .20 .50
66 Ken Griffey Jr. 1.00 2.50
67 Marcus Giles .20 .50
68 Edgar Renteria .20 .50
69 Ken Harvey .20 .50
70 Pedro Martinez .30 .75
71 Johnny Damon .30 .75
72 Lyle Overbay .20 .50
73 Mike Maroth .20 .50
74 Jorge Posada .30 .75
75 Carlos Beltran .30 .75
76 Mark Buehrle .30 .75
77 Khalil Greene .20 .50
78 Josh Beckett .20 .50
79 Mark Loretta .20 .50
80 Rafael Palmeiro .30 .75
81 Justin Morneau .30 .75
82 Rocco Baldelli .20 .50
83 Ben Sheets .20 .50
84 Kerry Wood .20 .50
85 Miguel Tejada .30 .75
86 Magglio Ordonez .30 .75
87 Livan Hernandez .20 .50
88 Kazuo Matsui .20 .50
89 Manny Ramirez .50 1.25
90 Hideki Matsui .75 2.00
91 Jeff Kent .20 .50
92 Matt Lawton .20 .50
93 Richie Sexson .20 .50
94 Mike Mussina .30 .75
95 Adam Dunn .30 .75
96 Johan Santana .30 .75
97 Nomar Garciaparra .30 .75
98 Michael Young .20 .50
99 Victor Martinez .30 .75
100 Barry Bonds .75 2.00
101 Oliver Perez .20 .50
102 Randy Johnson .50 1.25
103 Mark Mulder .20 .50
104 Pat Burrell .20 .50
105 Mike Sweeney .20 .50
106 Mark Teixeira .30 .75
107 Paul Lo Duca .20 .50
108 Jon Lieber .20 .50
109 Mike Piazza .50 1.25
110 Roger Clemens .60 1.50
111 Rafael Furcal .20 .50
112 Troy Glaus .20 .50
113 Miguel Cabrera .50 1.25
114 Randy Wolf .20 .50
115 Lance Berkman .30 .75
116 Mark Prior .30 .75
117 Rich Harden .20 .50
118 Preston Wilson .20 .50
119 Roy Oswalt .30 .75
120 Luis Gonzalez .20 .50
121 Ronnie Belliard .20 .50
122 Sean Casey .20 .50
123 Barry Zito .30 .75
124 Larry Walker .30 .75
125 Derek Jeter 1.25 3.00
126 Tim Hudson .30 .75
127 Tom Glavine .30 .75
128 Scott Rolen .30 .75
129 Torii Hunter .20 .50
130 Paul Konerko .30 .75
131 Shawn Green .20 .50
132 Travis Hafner .20 .50
133 Vernon Wells .20 .50
134 Sidney Ponson .20 .50
135 Vladimir Guerrero .30 .75
136 Mark Kotsay .20 .50
137 Todd Helton .30 .75
138 Adrian Beltre .50 1.25
139 Wily Mo Pena .20 .50
140 Joe Mauer .40 1.00
141 Brian Stavisky AU/970 RC 4.00 10.00
142 Nate McLouth AU/970 RC 4.00 10.00
143 Glen Perkins AU/375 RC 4.00 10.00
144 Chip Cannon AU/970 RC 4.00 10.00
145 Shane Costa AU/970 RC 4.00 10.00
146 W.Swackhamer AU/970 RC 4.00 10.00
147 Kevin Melillo AU/970 RC 4.00 10.00
148 Billy Butler AU/970 RC 4.00 10.00
149 Landon Powell AU/970 RC 4.00 10.00
150 Scott Mathieson AU/970 RC 4.00 10.00
151 Chris Roberson AU/970 4.00 10.00
152 Chad Orvella AU/375 RC 4.00 10.00
153 Eric Nielsen AU/970 RC 4.00 10.00
154 Matt Campbell AU/970 RC 4.00 10.00
155 Mike Rogers AU/970 RC 4.00 10.00
156 Melky Cabrera AU/970 RC 6.00 15.00
157 Nolan Ryan RET 2.50 6.00
158 Bo Jackson RET .75 2.00
159 Wade Boggs RET .50 1.25
160 Andre Dawson RET .50 1.25
161 Dave Winfield RET .50 1.25
162 Reggie Jackson RET .50 1.25
163 David Justice RET .30 .75
164 Dale Murphy RET .75 2.00
165 Paul O'Neill RET .50 1.25
166 Tom Seaver RET .50 1.25

2005 Finest Refractors

*REF 1-140: 1.5X TO 4X BASIC
*REF 157-166: 1X TO 2.5X BASIC
1-140/157-166 ODDS ONE PER MINI BOX
COMMON AUTO (141-156) 4.00 10.00
*REF AU 141-156: .4X TO 1X p/r 970
*REF AU 141-156: .3X TO .8X p/r 375
AU 141-156 ODDS 1:5 MINI BOX
STATED PRINT RUN 399 SERIAL #'d SETS

2005 Finest Refractors Black

*REF BLACK 1-140: 4X TO 10X BASIC
*REF BLACK 157-166: 2.5X TO 6X BASIC
1-140/157-166 ODDS 1:2 MINI BOX
COMMON AUTO (141-156) 10.00 25.00
*REF BLK AU 141-156: .6X TO 1.5X p/r 970
*REF BLK AU 141-156: .5X TO 1.2X p/r 375
AU 141-156 ODDS 1:19 MINI BOX
STATED PRINT RUN 99 SERIAL #'d SETS

2005 Finest Refractors Blue

*REF BLUE 1-140: 1.5X TO 4X BASIC
*REF BLUE 157-166: 1X TO 2.5X BASIC
1-140/157-166 ODDS ONE PER MINI BOX
COMMON AUTO (141-156) 4.00 10.00
*REF BLUE AU 141-156: .4X TO 1X p/r 970
*REF BLUE AU 141-156: .3X TO .8X p/r 375
AU 141-156 ODDS 1:7 MINI BOX
STATED PRINT RUN 299 SERIAL #'d SETS

2005 Finest Refractors Gold

*REF GOLD 1-140: 5X TO 12X BASIC
*REF GOLD 157-166: 3X TO 8X BASIC
1-140/157-166 ODDS 1:5 MINI BOX
COMMON AUTO (141-156) 15.00 40.00
*REF GOLD AU 141-156: 1X TO 2.5X p/r 970
*REF GOLD AU 141-156: .75X TO 2X p/r 375
AU 141-156 ODDS 1:39 MINI BOX
STATED PRINT RUN 49 SERIAL #'d SETS
125 Derek Jeter 15.00 40.00

2005 Finest Refractors Green

*REF GREEN 1-140: 2X TO 5X BASIC
*REF GREEN 157-166: 1.25X TO 3X BASIC
1-140/157-166 ODDS ONE PER MINI BOX
COMMON AUTO (141-156) 5.00 12.00
*REF GRN AU 141-156: .4X TO 1X p/r 970
*REF GRN AU 141-156: .3X TO 8X p/r 375
AU 141-156 ODDS 1:10 MINI BOX
STATED PRINT RUN 199 SERIAL #'d SETS

2005 Finest Refractors White Framed

1-140/157-166 ODDS 1:202 MINI BOX
AU 141-165 ODDS 1:1914 MINI BOX
STATED PRINT RUN 1 SERIAL #'d SET
NO PRICING DUE TO SCARCITY

2005 Finest X-Fractors

*XF 1-140: 2X TO 5X BASIC
*XF 157-166: 1.25X TO 3X BASIC
1-140/157-166 ODDS ONE PER MINI BOX
COMMON AUTO (141-156) 4.00 10.00
*XF AU 141-156: .4X TO 1X p/r 970
*XF AU 141-156: .3X TO 8X p/r 375
AU 141-156 ODDS 1:8 MINI BOX
STATED PRINT RUN 250 SERIAL #'d SETS

2005 Finest X-Fractors Black

*XF BLACK 1-140: 8X TO 20X BASIC
*XF BLACK 157-166: 5X TO 12X BASIC
1-140/157-166 ODDS 1:8 MINI BOX
AU 141-156 ODDS 1:76 MINI BOX
STATED PRINT RUN 25 SERIAL #'d SETS
AU 141-156 NO PRICING DUE TO SCARCITY
157 Nolan Ryan RET 30.00 80.00

2005 Finest X-Fractors Blue

*XF BLUE 1-140: 2.5X TO 6X BASIC
*XF BLUE 157-166: 1.5X TO 4X BASIC
1-140/157-166 ODDS 1:2 MINI BOX
COMMON AUTO (141-156) 6.00 15.00
*XF BLUE AU 141-156: .5X TO 1.2X p/r 970
*XF BLUE AU 141-156: .4X TO 1X p/r 375
AU 141-156 ODDS 1:13 MINI BOX
STATED PRINT RUN 150 SERIAL #'d SETS

2005 Finest X-Fractors Gold

1-140/157-166 ODDS 1:20 MINI BOX
AU 141-156 ODDS 1:190 MINI BOX
STATED PRINT RUN 10 SERIAL #'d SETS
NO PRICING DUE TO SCARCITY

2005 Finest X-Fractors Green

*XF GREEN 1-140: 5X TO 12X BASIC
*XF GREEN 157-166: 3X TO 8X BASIC
1-140/157-166 ODDS 1:2 MINI BOX
COMMON AUTO (141-156) 12.50 30.00
*XF GRN AU 141-156: .75X TO 2X p/r 970
*XF GRN AU 141-156: .6X TO 1.5X p/r 375
AU 141-156 ODDS 1:38 MINI BOX
STATED PRINT RUN 50 SERIAL #'d SETS

2005 Finest A-Rod Moments

COMMON CARD (1-49) 3.00 8.00
ONE PER MASTER BOX
STATED PRINT RUN 190 SERIAL #'d SETS

2005 Finest A-Rod Moments Autographs

COMMON CARD (1-49) 90.00 180.00
APPROXIMATE ODDS 1:15 MASTER BOXES
STATED PRINT RUN 13 SERIAL #'d SETS

2005 Finest Autograph Refractors

GROUP A ODDS 1:435 MINI BOX
GROUP B ODDS 1:13 MINI BOX
GROUP C ODDS 1:32 MINI BOX
GROUP D ODDS 1:15 MINI BOX
GROUP A PRINT RUN 70 CARDS
GROUP A CARD IS NOT SERIAL-NUMBERED
GROUP A PRINT RUN PROVIDED BY TOPPS
OVERALL PLATE ODDS 1:513 MINI BOX
PLATE PRINT RUN 1 SET PER COLOR
BLACK-CYAN-MAGENTA-YELLOW ISSUED
NO PLATE PRICING DUE TO SCARCITY
SUPERFRACTOR ODDS 1:2051 MINI BOX
SUPERFRACTOR PRINT RUN 1 #'d SET
NO SUPERFRACTOR PRICING AVAILABLE
*X-FRACTOR: 1.25X TO 3X BASIC D
*X-FRACTOR: .75X TO 2X BASIC C
*X-FRACTOR: .6X TO 1.5X BASIC B
*X-FRACTOR: .6X TO 1.5X BASIC A
X-FRACTOR ODDS 1:81 MINI BOX
X-FRACTOR PRINT RUN 25 SERIAL #'d SETS
EXCHANGE DEADLINE 04/30/07
AS Alfonso Soriano B 6.00 15.00
BB Barry Bonds A/70 * 125.00 250.00
DO David Ortiz B 10.00 25.00
DW David Wright C 20.00 50.00
EC Eric Chavez B 6.00 15.00
EG Eric Gagne B 6.00 15.00
GS Gary Sheffield C 6.00 15.00
JB Jason Bay B 10.00 25.00
JE Johnny Estrada B 6.00 15.00
JS Johan Santana B 8.00 20.00
JST Jacob Stevens D 4.00 10.00
KM Kevin Millar B 15.00 40.00
MB Milton Bradley B 6.00 15.00
MR Mariano Rivera B 100.00 250.00

2005 Finest Moments Autograph Gold Refractors

STATED ODDS 1:305 MINI BOX
PEDRO PRINT RUN 50 SERIAL #'d CARDS
SCHILLING PRINT RUN 50 CARDS
SCHILLING IS NOT SERIAL-NUMBERED
SCHILLING QTY PROVIDED BY TOPPS
CS Curt Schilling/50 * 100.00 175.00
PM Pedro Martinez/50 60.00 120.00

2006 Finest

COMP.SET w/o AU's (140) 30.00 60.00
COMMON CARD (1-131) .20 .50
COMMON ROOKIE (132-140) .30 .75
COMMON AUTO (141-155) 4.00 10.00
141-155 AU ODDS 1:4 MINI BOX
141-155 AU PRINT RUN 963 SETS
141-155 AU's NOT SERIAL NUMBERED
PRINT RUN INFO PROVIDED BY TOPPS
1-140 PLATES RANDOM INSERTS IN PACKS
AU 141-155 PLATE ODDS 1:792 MINI BOX
PLATE PRINT RUN 1 SET PER COLOR
BLACK-CYAN-MAGENTA-YELLOW ISSUED
NO PLATE PRICING DUE TO SCARCITY
1 Vladimir Guerrero .30 .75
2 Troy Glaus .20 .50
3 Andruw Jones .20 .50
4 Miguel Tejada .30 .75
5 Manny Ramirez .50 1.25
6 Curt Schilling .30 .75
7 Mark Prior .30 .75
8 Kerry Wood .20 .50
9 Tadahito Iguchi .20 .50
10 Freddy Garcia .20 .50
11 Ryan Howard .40 1.00
12 Mark Buehrle .30 .75
13 Wily Mo Pena .20 .50
14 C.C. Sabathia .30 .75
15 Garret Anderson .20 .50
16 Shawn Green .20 .50
17 Rafael Furcal .20 .50
18 Jeff Francoeur .50 1.25
19 Ken Griffey Jr. 1.00 2.50
20 Derrek Lee .20 .50
21 Paul Konerko .30 .75
22 Rickie Weeks .20 .50
23 Magglio Ordonez .30 .75
24 Juan Pierre .20 .50
25 Felix Hernandez .30 .75
26 Roger Clemens .60 1.50
27 Zack Greinke .50 1.25
28 Johan Santana .30 .75
29 Jose Reyes .30 .75
30 Bobby Crosby .20 .50
31 Jason Schmidt .20 .50
32 Khalil Greene .20 .50
33 Richie Sexson .20 .50
34 Mark Mulder .20 .50
35 Mark Teixeira .30 .75
36 Nick Johnson .20 .50
37 Vernon Wells .20 .50
38 Scott Kazmir .30 .75
39 Jim Edmonds .30 .75
40 Adrian Beltre .50 1.25
41 Dan Johnson .20 .50
42 Carlos Lee .20 .50
43 Lance Berkman .30 .75
44 Josh Beckett .20 .50
45 Morgan Ensberg .20 .50
46 Garrett Atkins .20 .50
47 Chase Utley .30 .75
48 Joe Mauer .30 .75
49 Travis Hafner .20 .50
50 Alex Rodriguez .60 1.50
51 Austin Kearns .20 .50
52 Scott Podsednik .20 .50
53 Jose Contreras .20 .50
54 Greg Maddux .60 1.50
55 Hideki Matsui .50 1.25
56 Matt Clement .20 .50
57 Javy Lopez .20 .50
58 Tim Hudson .30 .75
59 Luis Gonzalez .20 .50
60 Bartolo Colon .20 .50
61 Marcus Giles .20 .50
62 Justin Morneau .30 .75
63 Nomar Garciaparra .30 .75
64 Robinson Cano .30 .75
65 Ervin Santana .20 .50
66 Brady Clark .20 .50
67 Edgar Renteria .20 .50
68 Jon Garland .20 .50
69 Felipe Lopez .20 .50
70 Ivan Rodriguez .30 .75
71 Dontrelle Willis .20 .50
72 Carlos Guillen .20 .50
73 J.D. Drew .20 .50
74 Rich Harden .20 .50
75 Albert Pujols .60 1.50
76 Livan Hernandez .20 .50
77 Roy Halladay .30 .75
78 Hank Blalock .20 .50
79 David Wright .40 1.00
80 Jimmy Rollins .30 .75
81 John Smoltz .50 1.25
82 Miguel Cabrera .50 1.25
83 David DeJesus .20 .50
83 Zach Duke .20 .50
84 Torii Hunter .20 .50
85 Adam Dunn .30 .75
86 Randy Johnson .50 1.25
87 Roy Oswalt .30 .75
88 Bobby Abreu .20 .50
89 Rocco Baldelli .20 .50
90 Ichiro Suzuki .60 1.50

91 Jorge Cantu .20 .50
92 Jack Wilson .20 .50
93 Jose Vidro .20 .50
94 Kevin Millwood .20 .50
95 David Ortiz .50 1.25
96 Victor Martinez .30 .75
97 Jeremy Bonderman .20 .50
98 Todd Helton .30 .75
99 Carlos Beltran .30 .75
100 Barry Bonds .75 2.00
101 Jeff Kent .20 .50
102 Mike Sweeney .20 .50
103 Ben Sheets .20 .50
104 Melvin Mora .20 .50
105 Gary Sheffield .20 .50
106 Craig Wilson .20 .50
107 Chris Carpenter .30 .75
108 Michael Young .20 .50
109 Gustavo Chacin .20 .50
110 Chipper Jones .50 1.25
111 Mark Loretta .20 .50
112 Andy Pettitte .30 .75
113 Carlos Delgado .20 .50
114 Pat Burrell .20 .50
115 Jason Bay .20 .50
116 Brian Roberts .20 .50
117 Joe Crede .20 .50
118 Jake Peavy .20 .50
119 Aubrey Huff .20 .50
120 Pedro Martinez .30 .75
121 Jorge Posada .30 .75
122 Barry Zito .30 .75
123 Scott Rolen .30 .75
124 Brett Myers .20 .50
125 Derek Jeter 1.25 3.00
126 Eric Chavez .20 .50
127 Carl Crawford .30 .75
128 Jim Thome .30 .75
129 Johnny Damon .30 .75
130 Alfonso Soriano .30 .75
131 Clint Barmes .20 .50
132 Dustin Nippert (RC) .30 .75
133 Hanley Ramirez (RC) .50 1.25
134 Matt Capps (RC) .30 .75
135 Miguel Perez (RC) .30 .75
136 Tom Gorzelanny (RC) .30 .75
137 Charlton Jimerson (RC) .30 .75
138 Bryan Bullington (RC) .30 .75
139 Kenji Johjima RC .75 2.00
140 Craig Hansen RC .75 2.00
141 Craig Breslow AU/963 RC * 4.00 10.00
142 A.Wainwright AU/963 (RC) * 6.00 15.00
143 Joey Devine AU/963 RC * 4.00 10.00
144 H.Kuo AU/963 (RC) * 20.00 50.00
145 Jason Botts AU/963 (RC) * 4.00 10.00
146 J.Johnson AU/963 (RC) * 6.00 15.00
147 J.Bergmann AU/963 RC * 4.00 10.00
148 Scott Olsen AU/963 (RC) * 4.00 10.00
149 D.Rasner AU/963 (RC) * 4.00 10.00
150 Dan Ortmeier AU/963 (RC) * 4.00 10.00
151 Chuck James AU/963 (RC) * 6.00 15.00
152 Ryan Garko AU/963 (RC) * 4.00 10.00
153 Nelson Cruz AU/963 (RC) * 12.00 30.00
154 A.Lerew AU/963 (RC) * 4.00 10.00
155 F.Liriano AU/963 (RC) * 4.00 10.00

2006 Finest Refractors

*REF 1-131: 1.5X TO 4X BASIC
*REF 132-140: 1.5X TO 4X BASIC
1-140 ODDS ONE PER MINI BOX
*REF AU 141-155: .4X TO 1X BASIC AU
AU 141-155 ODDS 1:8 MINI BOX
STATED PRINT RUN 399 SERIAL #'d SETS

2006 Finest Refractors Black

*REF BLACK 1-131: 4X TO 10X BASIC
*REF BLACK 132-140: 4X TO 10X BASIC
1-140 ODDS 1:4 MINI BOX
*REF BLK AU 141-155: .6X TO 1.5X BASIC AU
AU 141-155 ODDS 1:32 MINI BOX
STATED PRINT RUN 99 SERIAL #'d SETS

2006 Finest Refractors Blue

*REF BLUE 1-131: 1.5X TO 4X BASIC
*REF BLUE 132-140: 1.5X TO 4X BASIC
1-140 ODDS 1:2 MINI BOX
*REF BLUE AU 141-155: .4X TO 1X BASIC AU
AU 141-155 ODDS 1:11 MINI BOX
STATED PRINT RUN 299 SERIAL #'d SETS

2006 Finest Refractors Gold

*REF GOLD 1-131: 5X TO 12X BASIC
*REF GOLD 132-140: 5X TO 12X BASIC
1-140 ODDS 1:7 MINI BOX
*REF GOLD AU 141-155: 1X TO 2.5X BASIC AU
AU 141-155 ODDS 1:64 MINI BOX
STATED PRINT RUN 49 SERIAL #'d SETS

2006 Finest Refractors Green

*REF GREEN 1-131: 2X TO 5X BASIC
*REF GREEN 132-140: 2X TO 5X BASIC
1-140 ODDS 1:2 MINI BOX
*REF GRN AU 141-155: .4X TO 1X BASIC AU
AU 141-155 ODDS 1:16 MINI BOX
STATED PRINT RUN 199 SERIAL #'d SETS

2006 Finest Refractors White Framed

1-140 ODDS 1:340 MINI BOX
AU 141-155 ODDS 1:3342 MINI BOX
STATED PRINT RUN 1 SERIAL #'d SET
NO PRICING DUE TO SCARCITY

2006 Finest X-Fractors

*XF 1-131: 2X TO 5X BASIC
*XF 132-140: 2X TO 5X BASIC
1-140 ODDS 1:2 MINI BOX
*XF AU 141-155: .4X TO 1X BASIC AU
AU 141-155 ODDS 1:13 MINI BOX
STATED PRINT RUN 250 SERIAL #'d SETS

2006 Finest X-Fractors Black

*XF BLACK 1-131: 8X TO 20X BASIC
1-140 ODDS 1:14 MINI BOX
NO XF BLACK 132-140 PRICING
AU 141-155 ODDS 1:125 MINI BOX
STATED PRINT RUN 25 SERIAL #'d SETS
NO XF BLACK AU PRICING

2006 Finest X-Fractors Blue

*XF BLUE 1-131: 2.5X TO 6X BASIC
*XF BLUE 132-140: 2.5X TO 6X BASIC
1-140 ODDS 1:3 MINI BOX
*XF BLUE AU 141-155: .5X TO 1.2X BASIC AU
AU 141-155 ODDS 1:21 MINI BOX
STATED PRINT RUN 150 SERIAL #'d SETS

2006 Finest X-Fractors Green

*XF GREEN 1-131: 5X TO 12X BASIC
*XF GREEN 132-140: 5X TO 12X BASIC
1-140 ODDS 1:7 MINI BOX
*XF GREEN AU 141-155: .75X TO 2X BASIC AU
AU 141-155 ODDS 1:63 MINI BOX
STATED PRINT RUN 50 SERIAL #'d SETS

2006 Finest Autograph Refractors

GROUP A ODDS 1:22 MINI BOX
GROUP B ODDS 1:8 MINI BOX
GROUP C ODDS 1:214 MINI BOX
GROUP A PRINT RUN 720 CARDS
GROUP B PRINT RUN 470 CARDS
GROUP C PRINT RUN 220 CARDS
CARDS ARE NOT SERIAL NUMBERED
PRINT RUN INFO PROVIDED BY TOPPS
OVERALL PLATE ODDS 1:654 MINI BOX
PLATE PRINT RUN 1 SET PER COLOR
BLACK-CYAN-MAGENTA-YELLOW ISSUED
NO PLATE PRICING DUE TO SCARCITY
SUPERFRACTOR ODDS 1:2751 MINI BOX
SUPERFRACTOR PRINT RUN 1 #'d SET
NO SUPERFRACTOR PRICING AVAILABLE
*GROUP A-B XF: .75X TO 2X BASIC
*GROUP C XF: 1X TO 2X BASIC
X-FRACTOR ODDS 1:104 MINI BOX
X-FRACTOR PRINT RUN 25 SERIAL #'d SETS
X-F JOHJIMA PRICING NOT AVAILABLE
APPROX. 10 PERCENT OF D.LEE ARE EXCH
EXCHANGE DEADLINE 04/30/08
AJ Andruw Jones B/470 * 6.00 15.00
AR Alex Rodriguez C/220 * 40.00 100.00
CJ Chipper Jones B/470 * 60.00 150.00
CW Craig Wilson B/470 * 4.00 10.00
DL Derrek Lee A/720 * 4.00 10.00
DW David Wright B/470 * 6.00 15.00
DWI Dontrelle Willis B/470 * 6.00 15.00
EC Eric Chavez A/720 * 6.00 15.00
GS Gary Sheffield B/470 * 6.00 15.00
JB Jason Bay B/470 * 6.00 15.00
JG Jose Guillen B/470 * 4.00 10.00
KJ Kenji Johjima B/470 * 10.00 25.00
MC Miguel Cabrera B/470 * 15.00 40.00
MG Marcus Giles B/470 * 6.00 15.00
RC Robinson Cano B/470 * 10.00 25.00
RH Rich Harden B/470 * 6.00 15.00
RO Roy Oswalt B/470 * 6.00 15.00
VG Vladimir Guerrero A/720 * 10.00 25.00

2006 Finest Bonds Moments Refractors

COMMON CARD (M1-M25) 3.00 8.00
STATED ODDS 1:2 MASTER BOX
STATED PRINT RUN 425 SERIAL #'d SETS
*REF GOLD: .5X TO 1.25X BASIC
REF.GOLD STATED ODDS 1:4 MASTER BOX
REF.GOLD PRINT RUN 199 SERIAL #'d SETS

2006 Finest Mantle Moments

COMMON CARD (M1-M20) 2.50 6.00
STATED ODDS 1:3 MINI BOX
STATED PRINT RUN 850 SERIAL #'d SETS
PRINTING PLATES RANDOM IN PACKS
PLATE PRINT RUN 1 SET PER COLOR
BLACK-CYAN-MAGENTA-YELLOW ISSUED
NO PLATE PRICING DUE TO SCARCITY
*REF: .5X TO 1.25X BASIC
REF ODDS 1:6 MINI BOX
REF PRINT RUN 399 SERIAL #'d SETS
*REF BLACK: 1.25X TO 3X BASIC
REF BLACK ODDS 1:24 MINI BOX
REF BLACK PRINT RUN 99 SERIAL #'d SETS
*REF BLUE: .6X TO 1.5X BASIC
REF BLUE ODDS 1:8 MINI BOX
REF BLUE PRINT RUN 299 SERIAL #'d SETS
*REF GOLD: 2.5X TO 6X BASIC
REF GOLD ODDS 1:49 MINI BOX
REF GOLD PRINT RUN 49 SERIAL #'d SETS
*REF GREEN: .75X TO 2X BASIC
REF GREEN ODDS 1:12 MINI BOX
REF GREEN PRINT RUN 199 SERIAL #'d SETS
REF WHITE FRAME ODDS 1:2482 MINI BOX
REF WHITE FRAME PRINT RUN 1 #'d SET
NO REF WF PRICING DUE TO SCARCITY
SUPERFRACTORS ODDS 1:2482 MINI BOX
SUPERFRACTORS PRINT RUN 1 #'d SET
NO SF PRICING DUE TO SCARCITY
*X-FRAC: .6X TO 1.5X BASIC
X-FRAC ODDS 1:10 MINI BOX
X-FRAC PRINT RUN 250 SERIAL #'d SETS
*X-FRAC BLACK: 3X TO 8X BASIC
X-FRAC BLACK ODDS 1:95 MINI BOX
X-FRAC BLACK PRINT RUN 25 #'d SETS
*X-FRAC BLUE: .75X TO 2X BASIC
X-FRAC BLUE ODDS 1:16 MINI BOX
X-FRAC BLUE PRINT RUN 150 #'d SETS
*X-FRAC GOLD: 8X TO 20X BASIC
X-FRAC GOLD ODDS 1:238 MINI BOX
X-FRAC GOLD PRINT RUN 10 SERIAL #'d SETS
*X-FRAC GREEN: 2.5X TO 6X BASIC
X-FRAC GREEN ODDS 1:48 MINI BOX
X-FRAC GREEN PRINT RUN 50 #'d SETS
X-FRAC WF ODDS 1:2482 MINI BOX
X-FRAC WF PRINT RUN 1 SERIAL #'d SET
NO X-F WF PRICING DUE TO SCARCITY

2007 Finest

COMP.SET w/o AU's (150) 30.00 60.00
COMMON CARD (1-135) .15 .40
COMMON ROOKIE (136-150) .40 1.00
151-166 AU ODDS 1:3 MINI BOX
1-150 PLATE ODDS 1:96 MINI BOX
AU 151-166 PLATE ODDS 1:909 MINI BOX
PLATE PRINT RUN 1 SET PER COLOR
BLACK-CYAN-MAGENTA-YELLOW ISSUED
NO PLATE PRICING DUE TO SCARCITY
EXCHANGE DEADLINE 02/28/09
1 David Wright .30 .75
2 Jered Weaver .25 .60
3 Chipper Jones .40 1.00
4 Magglio Ordonez .25 .60
5 Ben Sheets .15 .40
6 Nick Johnson .15 .40
7 Melvin Mora .15 .40
8 Chien-Ming Wang .25 .60
9 Andre Ethier .25 .60
10 Carlos Beltran .25 .60
11 Ryan Zimmerman .25 .60
12 Troy Glaus .15 .40
13 Hanley Ramirez .25 .60
14 Mark Buehrle .25 .60
15 Dan Uggla .15 .40
16 Richie Sexson .15 .40
17 Scott Kazmir .25 .60
18 Garrett Atkins .15 .40
19 Matt Cain .25 .60
20 Jorge Posada .25 .60
21 Brett Myers .15 .40
22 Jeff Francoeur .40 1.00
23 Scott Rolen .25 .60
24 Derrek Lee .15 .40
25 Manny Ramirez .40 1.00
26 Johnny Damon .25 .60
27 Mark Teixeira .25 .60
28 Mark Prior .25 .60
29 Victor Martinez .25 .60
30 Greg Maddux .50 1.25
31 Prince Fielder .25 .60
32 Jeremy Bonderman .15 .40
33 Paul LoDuca .15 .40
34 Brandon Webb .25 .60
35 Robinson Cano .25 .60
36 Josh Beckett .15 .40
37 David DeJesus .15 .40
38 Kenny Rogers .15 .40
39 Jim Thome .25 .60
40 Brian McCann .15 .40
41 Lance Berkman .25 .60
42 Adam Dunn .25 .60
43 Rocco Baldelli .15 .40
44 Brian Roberts .25 .60
45 Vladimir Guerrero .25 .60
46 Dontrelle Willis .15 .40
47 Eric Chavez .15 .40
48 Carlos Zambrano .25 .60
49 Ivan Rodriguez .25 .60
50 Alex Rodriguez .50 1.25
51 Curt Schilling .25 .60
52 Carlos Delgado .15 .40
53 Matt Holliday .40 1.00
54 Mark Teahen .15 .40
55 Frank Thomas .40 1.00
56 Grady Sizemore .25 .60
57 Aramis Ramirez .15 .40
58 Rafael Furcal .15 .40
59 David Ortiz .40 1.00
60 Paul Konerko .25 .60
61 Barry Zito .25 .60
62 Travis Hafner .15 .40
63 Nick Swisher .25 .60
64 Johan Santana .25 .60
65 Miguel Tejada .25 .60
66 Carl Crawford .25 .60
67 Kenji Johjima .40 1.00
68 Derek Jeter 1.00 2.50
69 Francisco Liriano .15 .40
70 Ken Griffey Jr. .75 2.00
71 Pat Burrell .15 .40
72 Adrian Gonzalez .30 .75
73 Miguel Cabrera .40 1.00
74 Albert Pujols .50 1.25
75 Justin Verlander .40 1.00
76 Carlos Lee .15 .40
77 John Smoltz .40 1.00
78 Orlando Hudson .15 .40
79 Joe Mauer .30 .75
80 Freddy Sanchez .15 .40
81 Bobby Abreu .15 .40
82 Pedro Martinez .25 .60
83 Vernon Wells .15 .40
84 Justin Morneau .25 .60
85 Bill Hall .15 .40
86 Jason Schmidt .15 .40
87 Michael Young .15 .40
88 Tadahito Iguchi .15 .40
89 Kevin Millwood .15 .40
90 Randy Johnson .40 1.00
91 Roy Halladay .25 .60
92 Mike Lowell .15 .40
93 Jake Peavy .15 .40
94 Jason Varitek .40 1.00
95 Todd Helton .25 .60
96 Mark Loretta .15 .40
97 Gary Matthews Jr. .15 .40
98 Ryan Howard .30 .75
99 Jose Reyes .25 .60
100 Chris Carpenter .25 .60
101 Hideki Matsui .40 1.00
102 Brian Giles .15 .40
103 Torii Hunter .15 .40
104 Rich Harden .15 .40
105 Ichiro Suzuki .50 1.25
106 Chase Utley .25 .60
107 Nick Markakis .30 .75
108 Marcus Giles .15 .40
109 Gary Sheffield .15 .40
110 Jim Edmonds .25 .60
111 Brandon Phillips .15 .40
112 Roy Oswalt .25 .60
113 Jeff Kent .15 .40
114 Jason Bay .25 .60
115 Raul Ibanez .25 .60
116 Stephen Drew .15 .40
117 Hank Blalock .15 .40
118 Tom Glavine .25 .60
119 Andruw Jones .15 .40
120 Alfonso Soriano .25 .60
121 Mariano Rivera .50 1.25
122 Garret Anderson .15 .40
123 Erik Bedard UER .15 .40
124 Huston Street .15 .40
125 Austin Kearns .15 .40
126 Jermaine Dye .15 .40
127 C.C. Sabathia .25 .60
128 Joe Nathan .15 .40
129 Craig Monroe .15 .40
130 Aubrey Huff .15 .40
131 Billy Wagner .15 .40
132 Jorge Cantu .15 .40
133 Trevor Hoffman .25 .60
134 Ronnie Belliard .15 .40
135 B.J. Ryan .15 .40
136 Adam Lind (RC) .40 1.00
137 Hector Gimenez (RC) .40 1.00
138 Shawn Riggans UER (RC) .40 1.00
139 Joaquin Arias (RC) .40 1.00
140 Drew Anderson RC .40 1.00
141 Mike Rabelo RC .40 1.00
142 Chris Narveson (RC) .40 1.00
143 Ryan Feierabend (RC) .40 1.00
144 Vinny Rottino (RC) .40 1.00
145 Jon Knott (RC) .40 1.00
146 Oswaldo Navarro RC .40 1.00
147 Brian Stokes (RC) .40 1.00
148 Glen Perkins (RC) .40 1.00
149 Mitch Maier RC .40 1.00
150 Delmon Young (RC) .60 1.50
151 Andrew Miller AU RC 4.00 10.00
152 T.Tulowitzki AU (RC) 4.00 10.00
153 Philip Humber AU (RC) 4.00 10.00
154 K.Kouzmanoff AU (RC) 4.00 15.00
155 Michael Bourn AU (RC) 4.00 10.00
156 M.Montero AU (RC) 4.00 10.00
157 David Murphy AU (RC) 4.00 10.00
158 R.Sweeney AU (RC) 4.00 10.00
159 Jeff Baker AU (RC) 4.00 10.00
160 Jeff Salazar AU (RC) 4.00 10.00
161 J.Garcia AU RC 4.00 10.00
162 Josh Fields AU (RC) 4.00 10.00
163 Delwyn Young AU (RC) 4.00 10.00
164 Fred Lewis AU (RC) 4.00 10.00
165 Scott Moore AU (RC) 4.00 10.00
166 Chris Stewart AU RC 4.00 10.00

2007 Finest Refractors

*REF 1-135: .5X TO 1.2X BASIC
*REF 136-150: .5X TO 1.2X BASIC
1-150 ODDS TWO PER MINI BOX
*REF AU 151-166: .4X TO 1X BASIC AU
AU 151-166 ODDS 1:10 MINI BOX
AU 151-166 PRINT RUN 399 SER.#'d SETS
EXCHANGE DEADLINE 02/28/09

2007 Finest Refractors Black

*REF BLACK 1-135: 4X TO 10X BASIC
*REF BLACK 136-150: 2.5X TO 6X BASIC
1-150 ODDS 1:4 MINI BOX
*REF BLK AU 151-166: 1X TO 2.5X BASIC AU
AU 151-166 ODDS 1:37 MINI BOX
STATED PRINT RUN 99 SERIAL #'d SETS
EXCHANGE DEADLINE 02/28/09
159 Jeff Baker AU 5.00 12.00
160 Jeff Salazar AU 5.00 12.00
164 Fred Lewis AU 12.50 30.00

2007 Finest Refractors Blue

*REF BLUE 1-135: 1.5X TO 4X BASIC
*REF BLUE 136-150: 1X TO 2.5X BASIC
1-150 ODDS ONE PER MINI BOX
1-150 PRINT RUN 399 SER.#'d SETS
*REF BLUE AU 151-166: .5X TO 1.2X BASIC AU
AU 151-166 ODDS 1:13 MINI BOX
AU 151-166 PRINT RUN 299 SER.#'d SETS
EXCHANGE DEADLINE 02/28/09

2007 Finest Refractors Gold

*REF GOLD 1-135: 5X TO 12X BASIC
*REF GOLD 136-150: 4X TO 10X BASIC
1-150 ODDS 1:8 MINI BOX
1-150 PRINT RUN 50 SER.#'d SETS
*REF GOLD AU 151-166: 1.25X TO 3X BASIC AU
AU 151-166 ODDS 1:74 MINI BOX
AU 151-166 PRINT RUN 49 SER.#'d SETS
EXCHANGE DEADLINE 02/28/09
155 Michael Bourn AU 15.00 40.00
158 Ryan Sweeney AU 15.00 40.00
162 Josh Fields AU 15.00 40.00
164 Fred Lewis AU 15.00 40.00
165 Scott Moore AU 15.00 40.00

2007 Finest Refractors Green

*REF GREEN 1-135: 2X TO 5X BASIC
*REF GREEN 136-150: 1.25X TO 3X BASIC
1-150 ODDS 1:2 MINI BOX
*REF GRN AU 151-166: .6X TO 1.5X BASIC AU
AU 151-166 ODDS 1:19 MINI BOX
STATED PRINT RUN 199 SERIAL #'d SETS
EXCHANGE DEADLINE 02/28/09

2007 Finest X-Fractors

*XF 1-135: 8X TO 20X BASIC
1-150 ODDS 1:16 MINI BOX
AU 151-166 ODDS 1:144 MINI BOX
STATED PRINT RUN 25 SER.#'d SETS
NO ROOKIE PRICING AVAILABLE
EXCHANGE DEADLINE 02/28/09

2007 Finest Rookie Finest Moments

STATED ODDS 2 PER MINI BOX
PRINTING PLATE ODDS 1:289 MINI BOX
PLATE PRINT RUN 1 SET PER COLOR
BLACK-CYAN-MAGENTA-YELLOW ISSUED
NO PLATE PRICING DUE TO SCARCITY
*REF: .6X TO 1.5X BASIC
REFRACTOR ODDS 1 PER MINI BOX
*REF BLACK: 2.5X TO 6X BASIC
REF BLACK ODDS 1:12 MINI BOX
REF BLACK PRINT RUN 99 SER.#'d SETS
*REF BLUE: 1X TO 2.5X BASIC
REF BLUE ODDS 1:4 MINI BOX
REF BLUE PRINT RUN 299 SER.#'d SETS
*REF GOLD: 5X TO 12X BASIC
REF GOLD ODDS 1:23 MINI BOX
REF GOLD PRINT RUN 50 SER.#'d SETS
*REF GREEN: 1.25X TO 3X BASIC
REF GREEN ODDS 1:6 MINI BOX
REF GREEN PRINT RUN 199 SER.#'d SETS
SUPERFRACTOR ODDS 1:1156 MINI BOX
SUPERFRACTOR PRINT RUN 1 SER.#'d SET
NO SUPERFRACTOR PRICING AVAILABLE
*X-FRACTOR: 8X TO 20X BASIC
X-FRACTOR ODDS 1:46 MINI BOX
X-FRACTOR PRINT RUN 25 SER.#'d SETS
X-F WHITE ODDS 1:1156 MINI BOX
X-F WHITE PRINT RUN 1 SER.#'d SET
NO X-F WHITE PRICING AVAILABLE
AD Adam Dunn .40 1.00
AE Andre Ethier .40 1.00
AJ Andruw Jones .25 .60
AP Albert Pujols .75 2.00
AR Alex Rodriguez .75 2.00
AS Anibal Sanchez .25 .60
AW Adam Wainwright .40 1.00
CB Carlos Beltran .40 1.00
CC Carl Crawford .40 1.00
CH Cole Hamels .50 1.25
CJ Chipper Jones .60 1.50
CQ Carlos Quentin .25 .60
DJ Derek Jeter 1.50 4.00
DL Derrek Lee .25 .60
DO David Ortiz .60 1.50
DU Dan Uggla .25 .60
DW David Wright .50 1.25
FL Francisco Liriano .25 .60
HM Hideki Matsui .60 1.50
HR Hanley Ramirez .40 1.00
IK Ian Kinsler .40 1.00
IS Ichiro Suzuki .75 2.00
JB Jason Bay .40 1.00
JH Jason Hirsh .25 .60
JM Joe Mauer .50 1.25
JP Jonathan Papelbon .60 1.50
JR Jose Reyes .40 1.00
JS Jeremy Sowers .25 .60
JV Justin Verlander .60 1.50
JW Jered Weaver .40 1.00
KG Ken Griffey Jr. 1.25 3.00
KJ Kenji Johjima .60 1.50
MC Miguel Cabrera .60 1.50
MK Matt Kemp .50 1.25
MN Mike Napoli .25 .60
MP Mike Piazza .60 1.50
MR Manny Ramirez .60 1.50
MT Miguel Tejada .40 1.00
NC Nelson Cruz .60 1.50
NG Nomar Garciaparra .40 1.00
NM Nick Markakis .50 1.25
PF Prince Fielder .40 1.00
RH Ryan Howard .50 1.25
RM Russ Martin .25 .60
SD Stephen Drew .25 .60
VG Vladimir Guerrero .40 1.00
DWW Dontrelle Willis .25 .60
JBA Josh Barfield .25 .60
JST Brian Stokes .25 .60
MCA Melky Cabrera .25 .60

2007 Finest Rookie Finest Moments Autographs

STATED ODDS 1:5 MINI BOX
PRINTING PLATE ODDS 1:482 MINI BOX
PLATE PRINT RUN 1 SET PER COLOR
BLACK-CYAN-MAGENTA-YELLOW ISSUED
NO PLATE PRICING DUE TO SCARCITY
REFRACTOR ODDS 1:77 MINI BOX
REFRACTOR PRINT RUN 25 #'d SETS
NO REFRACTOR PRICING AVAILABLE
SUPERFRACTOR ODDS 1:1975 MINI BOX
NO SUPERFRACTOR PRICING AVAILABLE
SUPERFRACTOR PRINT RUN 1 #'d SET
AR Alex Rodriguez 30.00 80.00
AS Anibal Sanchez 3.00 8.00
AW Adam Wainwright 12.00 30.00
BP Brandon Phillips 5.00 12.00
BW Brad Wilkerson 3.00 8.00
CH Cole Hamels 6.00 15.00
CJ Chuck James 4.00 10.00
CQ Carlos Quentin 6.00 15.00
DO David Ortiz 20.00 50.00
DU Dan Uggla 3.00 8.00
DW David Wright 12.00 30.00
DWW Dontrelle Willis 6.00 15.00
DY Delmon Young 10.00 25.00
ES Ervin Santana 3.00 8.00
FC Fausto Carmona 5.00 12.00
HR Hanley Ramirez 5.00 12.00
JM Justin Morneau 3.00 8.00
JN Joe Nathan 3.00 8.00
JP Jonathan Papelbon 5.00 12.00
LM Lastings Milledge 6.00 15.00
MC Melky Cabrera 3.00 8.00
MN Mike Napoli 6.00 15.00
MTC Matt Cain 10.00 25.00
RC Robinson Cano 6.00 15.00
RH Rich Hill 4.00 12.00
RH Ryan Howard 10.00 25.00
RM Russ Martin 6.00 15.00
RZ Ryan Zimmerman 5.00 12.00
TH Travis Hafner 6.00 15.00
YP Yusmeiro Petit 3.00 8.00

2007 Finest Rookie Finest Moments Autographs Dual

STATED ODDS 1:32 MINI BOX
STATED PRINT RUN 74 SER.#'d SETS
REFRACTOR ODDS 1:93 MINI BOX
REFRACTOR PRINT RUN 25 #'d SETS
NO REFRACTOR PRICING AVAILABLE
REF GOLD ODDS 1:2387 MINI BOX
REF GOLD PRINT RUN 1 #'d SET
NO REF GOLD PRICING AVAILABLE
EXCHANGE DEADLINE 02/28/09
BM J.Bay/J.Morneau 8.00 20.00
CC E.Chavez/M.Cabrera 30.00 60.00
CK N.Cruz/M.Kemp 10.00 25.00
CR M.Cain/A.Reyes 15.00 40.00
CY R.Cano/M.Young 15.00 40.00
HJ R.Hill/J.Johnson 15.00 40.00
HM C.Hamels/B.Myers 20.00 50.00
HR T.Hafner/M.Ramirez 20.00 50.00
JH C.James/C.Hamels 8.00 20.00
MC L.Milledge/M.Cabrera 15.00 40.00
MG R.Martin/R.Garko 8.00 20.00
MK L.Milledge/M.Kemp 12.50 30.00
MN K.Morales/M.Napoli 8.00 20.00
MNA R.Martin/M.Napoli 10.00 25.00
OP R.Oswalt/M.Prior 8.00 20.00
PO Y.Petit/S.Olsen 8.00 20.00
PP J.Papelbon/D.Pedroia 20.00 50.00
RP M.Rivera/J.Posada 100.00 200.00
RU H.Ramirez/D.Uggla 10.00 25.00
UG D.Uggla/M.Giles 8.00 20.00
US D.Uggla/A.Sanchez 10.00 25.00
VE J.Verlander/H.Ramirez 20.00 50.00
WW C.Wang/B.Webb 25.00 60.00
ZC J.Zumaya/F.Carmona 8.00 20.00

2007 Finest Rookie Photo Variation

STATED ODDS 1:5 MINI BOX
STATED PRINT RUN 439 SER.#'d SETS
*REF: .75X TO 2X BASIC
REFRACTOR ODDS 1:13 MINI BOX
REFRACTOR PRINT RUN 149 #'d SETS
REF GOLD ODDS 1:1975 MINI BOX
REF GOLD PRINT RUN 1 SER.#'d SET
NO REF GOLD PRICING AVAILABLE
*X-FRACTOR: 2X TO 5X BASIC
X-FRACTOR ODDS 1:39 MINI BOX
X-FRACTOR PRINT RUN 50 SER.#'d SETS
136 A.Lind Bat Up .75 2.00
136 A.Lind Bat Out .75 2.00
137 H.Gimenez Posed .75 2.00
137 H.Gimenez Batting .75 2.00
138 S.Riggans w/Bat .75 2.00
138 S.Riggans w/Glove .75 2.00
139 J.Arias w/Bat .75 2.00
139 J.Arias Throw .75 2.00
140 D.Anderson Run Away .75 2.00
140 D.Anderson w/Glove .75 2.00
141 M.Rabelo Bat Shoulder .75 2.00
141 M.Rabelo Bat Up .75 2.00
142 C.Narveson Portrait .75 2.00
142 C.Narveson w/Glove .75 2.00
143 R.Feierabend Catch .75 2.00
143 R.Feierabend Pitch .75 2.00
144 V.Rottino Swing .75 2.00
144 V.Rottino Field .75 2.00
145 J.Knott Run .75 2.00
145 J.Knott w/Bat .75 2.00
146 O.Navarro Posed .75 2.00
146 O.Navarro Swing .75 2.00
147 B.Stokes Windup .75 2.00
147 B.Stokes Throw .75 2.00
148 G.Perkins Windup .75 2.00
148 G.Perkins w/Jacket .75 2.00
149 M.Maier In OF .75 2.00
149 M.Maier On Deck .75 2.00
150 D.Young Running 1.25 3.00
150 D.Young Portirat 1.25 3.00

2007 Finest Rookie Redemption

STATED ODDS 1:3 MINI BOX
REDEEMABLE FOR 07 RC LOGO PLAYER
EXCHANGE DEADLINE 12/30/07
1 Hideki Okajima 4.00 10.00
2 Elijah Dukes 1.25 3.00
3 Akinori Iwamura 2.00 5.00
4 Tim Lincecum 4.00 10.00
5 Daisuke Matsuzaka 3.00 8.00
6 Ryan Braun 4.00 10.00
7 D.Matsuzaka/H.Okajima 4.00 10.00
8 Justin Upton 2.50 6.00
9 Philip Hughes 2.00 5.00
10 Joba Chamberlain AU 6.00 15.00

2007 Finest Ryan Howard Finest Moments

COMMON CARD 1.50 4.00
STATED ODDS 2 PER HOWARD BOX LOADER
STATED PRINT RUN 459 SER.#'d SETS
*REF: .6X TO 1.5X BASIC
REFRACTOR ODDS 1:3 BOXES
REFRACTOR PRINT RUN 149 SER.#'d SETS
REF GOLD ODDS 1:329 BOXES
REF GOLD PRINT RUN 1 SER.#'d SET
NO REF GOLD PRICING AVAILABLE
*X-FRACTOR: .75X TO 2X BASIC
X-FRACTOR ODDS 1:7 BOXES
X-FRACTOR PRINT RUN 50 SER.#'d SETS

2008 Finest

COMP.SET w/o AUs (150) 40.00 80.00
COMMON CARD (1-125) .15 .40
COMMON RC (126-150) .75 2.00
COMMON AU RC (151-166) 4.00 10.00
151-166 AU ODDS 1:3 MINI BOX
1-150 PLATE ODDS 1:82 MINI BOX
AU 151-166 PLATE ODDS 1:775 MINI BOX
PLATE PRINT RUN 1 SET PER COLOR
BLACK-CYAN-MAGENTA-YELLOW ISSUED
NO PLATE PRICING DUE TO SCARCITY
1 Daisuke Matsuzaka .25 .60
2 Justin Upton .25 .60
3 Andruw Jones .15 .40
4 John Lackey .25 .60
5 Brandon Phillips .15 .40
6 Ryan Zimmerman .25 .60
7 Tim Lincecum .25 .60
8 Johnny Damon .25 .60
9 Garrett Atkins .15 .40
10 Magglio Ordonez .25 .60
11 Tom Gorzelanny .15 .40
12 Eric Chavez .15 .40
13 Troy Tulowitzki .40 1.00
14 Mike Lowell .15 .40
15 Brandon Webb .25 .60
16 Chipper Jones .40 1.00
17 Alex Gordon .25 .60
18 Ken Griffey Jr. .75 2.00
19 Roy Oswalt .25 .60
20 Miguel Cabrera .40 1.00
21 Chase Utley .25 .60
22 Scott Kazmir .25 .60
23 Kenji Johjima .15 .40
24 Frank Thomas .40 1.00
25 Ryan Braun .25 .60
26 Carlos Pena .25 .60
27 Robinson Cano .25 .60
28 Ben Sheets .15 .40
29 Russell Martin .15 .40
30 Joe Mauer .30 .75
31 Gary Sheffield .15 .40
32 Carlos Zambrano .25 .60
33 Jermaine Dye .15 .40
34 Dan Uggla .15 .40
35 Erik Bedard .15 .40
36 Tim Hudson .25 .60
37 David Ortiz .40 1.00
38 Tom Glavine .25 .60
39 Adrian Gonzalez .25 .60
40 Jorge Posada .25 .60
41 Noah Lowry .15 .40
42 Vernon Wells .15 .40
43 Johan Santana .25 .60
44 Dmitri Young .15 .40
45 Manny Ramirez .40 1.00
46 Jim Edmonds .25 .60
47 Roy Halladay .25 .60
48 Delmon Young .25 .60
49 Nick Swisher .25 .60
50 David Wright .25 .60
51 Paul Konerko .25 .60
52 Curt Schilling .25 .60
53 Torii Hunter .15 .40
54 Gary Matthews .15 .40
55 Derrek Lee .15 .40
56 John Smoltz .40 1.00
57 Adam Dunn .25 .60
58 C.C Sabathia .25 .60
59 Chris Young .15 .40
60 Jake Peavy .15 .40
61 Joba Chamberlain .25 .60
62 Jason Bay .25 .60
63 Chris Carpenter .25 .60
64 Jimmy Rollins .25 .60
65 Grady Sizemore .25 .60
66 Joe Blanton .15 .40
67 Justin Morneau .25 .60
68 Lance Berkman .25 .60
69 Jeff Francis .15 .40
70 Nick Markakis .30 .75
71 Orlando Cabrera .25 .60
72 Barry Zito .25 .60
73 Eric Byrnes .15 .40
74 Brian McCann .25 .60
75 Albert Pujols .50 1.25
76 Josh Beckett .15 .40
77 Jim Thome .25 .60
78 Fausto Carmona .15 .40
79 Brad Hawpe .15 .40
80 Prince Fielder .25 .60
81 Justin Verlander .40 1.00
82 Billy Butler .15 .40
83 J.J. Hardy .15 .40
84 Hideki Matsui .40 1.00
85 Matt Holliday .40 1.00
86 Bobby Crosby .15 .40
87 Orlando Hudson .15 .40
88 Ichiro Suzuki .50 1.25
89 Troy Glaus .15 .40
90 Hanley Ramirez .25 .60
91 Carlos Beltran .25 .60
92 Mark Buehrle .25 .60
93 Andy Pettitte .25 .60
94 Mark Teixeira .25 .60
95 Curtis Granderson .25 .60
96 Cole Hamels .30 .75
97 Jarrod Saltalamacchia .15 .40
98 Carl Crawford .25 .60
99 Dontrelle Willis .15 .40
100 Alex Rodriguez .50 1.25
101 Brad Penny .15 .40
102 Michael Young .15 .40
103 Greg Maddux .50 1.25
104 Brian Roberts .15 .40
105 Hunter Pence .15 .40
106 Aaron Harang .15 .40
107 Ivan Rodriguez .25 .60
108 Dan Haren .15 .40
109 Freddy Sanchez .15 .40
110 Alfonso Soriano .25 .60
111 Hank Blalock .15 .40
112 Chien- Ming Wang .25 .60
113 Carlos Delgado .15 .40
114 Aramis Ramirez .15 .40
115 Jose Reyes .25 .60
116 Victor Martinez .25 .60
117 Carlos Lee .15 .40
118 Jeff Kent .15 .40
119 Miguel Tejada .25 .60
120 Vladimir Guerrero .25 .60
121 Travis Hafner .15 .40
122 Todd Helton .25 .60
123 Chris Young .15 .40
124 Derek Jeter 1.00 2.50
125 Ryan Howard .25 .60
126 Alberto Gonzalez RC 1.25 3.00
127 Felipe Paulino RC 1.25 3.00
128 Donny Lucy (RC) .75 2.00
129 Nick Blackburn RC 1.25 3.00
130 Luke Hochevar RC 1.25 3.00
131 Bronson Sardinha (RC) .75 2.00
132 Heath Phillips RC 1.25 3.00
133 Bryan Bullington (RC) .75 2.00
134 Jeff Clement (RC) 1.25 3.00
135 Josh Banks (RC) .75 2.00
136 Emilio Bonifacio RC 2.00 5.00
137 Ryan Hanigan RC 1.25 3.00
138 Erick Threets (RC) .75 2.00
139 Seth Smith (RC) .75 2.00
140 Billy Buckner (RC) .75 2.00
141 Bill Murphy (RC) .75 2.00
142 Radhames Liz RC 1.25 3.00
143 Joey Votto (RC) 6.00 15.00
144 Mel Stocker RC .75 2.00
145 Dan Meyer (RC) .75 2.00
146 Rob Johnson (RC) .75 2.00
147 Josh Newman RC 1.25 3.00
148 Dan Giese (RC) .75 2.00
149 Luis Mendoza (RC) .75 2.00
150 Wladimir Balentien (RC) .75 2.00
151 B.Jones AU RC 4.00 10.00
152 Rich Thompson AU RC 4.00 10.00
153 C.Hu AU (RC) 4.00 10.00

154 Chris Seddon AU (RC) 4.00 10.00
155 S.Pearce AU RC 10.00 25.00
156 Lance Broadway AU (RC) 4.00 10.00
157 Nyjer Morgan AU (RC) 4.00 10.00
158 Jonathan Meloan AU RC 4.00 10.00
159 Josh Anderson AU (RC) 4.00 10.00
160 C.Buchholz AU (RC) 4.00 10.00
161 Joe Koshansky AU (RC) 4.00 10.00
162 Clint Sammons AU (RC) 4.00 10.00
163 Daric Barton AU (RC) 5.00 12.00
164 Ross Detwiler AU RC 5.00 12.00
165 Sam Fuld AU RC 6.00 15.00
166 Justin Ruggiano AU RC 4.00 10.00

2008 Finest Refractors

*REF VET: 1X TO 2.5X BASIC
*REF RC: .5X TO 1.2X BASIC RC
1-150 REF.RANDOMLY INSERTED
*REF AU: .4X TO 1X BASIC AU
151-166 ODDS 1:7 MINI PACKS
151-166 PRINT RUN 499 SER.#'d SETS

2008 Finest Refractors Black

*BLACK VET: 4X TO 10X BASIC
*BLACK RC: 1X TO 2.5X BASIC RC
1-150 ODDS 1:4 MINI BOXES
1-150 PRINT RUN 99 SER.#'d SETS
*REF AU: .6X TO 1.5X BASIC AU
151-166 ODDS 1:32 MINI PACKS
151-166 PRINT RUN 99 SER.#'d SETS
164 Ross Detwiler AU 10.00 25.00

2008 Finest Refractors Blue

*BLUE VET: 1.5X TO 4X BASIC
*BLUE RC: .6X TO 1.5X BASIC RC
1-150 ODDS 1:2 MINI BOXES
1-150 PRINT RUN 299 SER.#'d SETS
*REF AU: .5X TO 1.2X BASIC AU
151-166 ODDS 1:8 MINI PACKS
151-166 PRINT RUN 399 SER.#'d SETS

2008 Finest Refractors Gold

*GOLD VET: 6X TO 15X BASIC
*GOLD RC: 2X TO 5X BASIC RC
1-150 ODDS 1:7 MINI BOXES
1-150 PRINT RUN 50 SER.#'d SETS
*REF AU: 1X TO 2.5X BASIC AU
151-166 ODDS 1:64 MINI PACKS
151-166 PRINT RUN 50 SER.#'d SETS
24 Frank Thomas 20.00 50.00
88 Ichiro Suzuki 15.00 40.00
100 Alex Rodriguez 15.00 40.00
103 Greg Maddux 20.00 50.00
124 Derek Jeter 30.00 60.00
126 Alberto Gonzalez 10.00 25.00
129 Nick Blackburn 20.00 50.00
132 Heath Phillips 6.00 15.00
134 Jeff Clement 15.00 40.00
147 Josh Newman 6.00 15.00
148 Dan Giese 6.00 15.00
150 Wladimir Balentien 6.00 15.00
163 Daric Barton AU 15.00 40.00
164 Ross Detwiler AU 15.00 40.00

2008 Finest Refractors Green

*GREEN VET: 2X TO 5X BASIC
*GREEN RC: .75X TO 2X BASIC RC
1-150 ODDS 1:2 MINI BOXES
1-150 PRINT RUN 199 SER.#'d SETS
*REF AU: .5X TO 1.2X BASIC AU
151-166 ODDS 1:16 MINI PACKS
151-166 PRINT RUN 199 SER.#'d SETS

2008 Finest Refractors Red

1-150 ODDS 1:14 MINI BOXES
151-166 AU ODDS 1:128 MINI BOXES
STATED PRINT RUN 25 SER.#'d SETS
NO PRICING DUE TO SCARCITY

2008 Finest X-Fractors White Framed

1-150 ODDS 1:327 MINI BOXES
151-166 AU ODDS 1:2036 MINI BOXES
STATED PRINT RUN 1 SER.#'d SET
NO PRICING DUE TO SCARCITY

2008 Finest Finest Moments

*REF: .6X TO 1.5X BASIC
REF.RANDOMLY INSERTED
STATED ODDS XX PER MINI BOX
*BLACK REF: 1.5X TO 4X BASIC
BLACK ODDS 1:10 MINI BOXES
BLACK PRINT RUN 99 SER.#'d SETS
*BLUE REF: .75X TO 2X BASIC
BLUE ODDS 1:4 MINI BOXES
BLUE PRINT RUN 399 SER.#'d SETS
*GOLD REF: 2.5X TO 6X BASIC
GOLD ODDS 1:20 MINI BOXES
GOLD PRINT RUN 50 SER.#'d SETS
*GREEN REF: 1X TO 2.5X BASIC
GREEN ODDS 1:5 MINI BOXES
GREEN PRINT RUN 199 SER.#'d SETS
PRINTING PLATE ODDS 1:245 MINI BOXES
PLATE PRINT RUN 1 SET PER COLOR
BLACK-CYAN-MAGENTA-YELLOW ISSUED
NO PLATE PRICING DUE TO SCARCITY
AG Adrian Gonzalez .60 1.50
AP Andy Pettitte .60 1.50
APU Albert Pujols 1.25 3.00
AR Alex Rodriguez 1.25 3.00
AS Andy Sonnanstine .40 1.00
BP Brandon Phillips .40 1.00
BPB Brian Bannister .40 1.00
BW Brandon Webb .60 1.50
CB Clay Buchholz .60 1.50
CF Chone Figgins .40 1.00
CG Curtis Granderson .60 1.50
CH Cole Hamels .75 2.00
CP Carlos Pena .60 1.50
CS C.C. Sabathia .60 1.50
DH Dan Haren .40 1.00
DJ Derek Jeter 2.50 6.00
DL Derrek Lee .40 1.00
DO David Ortiz 1.00 2.50
DW David Wright .60 1.50
EB Eric Byrnes .40 1.00
FC Fausto Carmona .40 1.00
FH Felix Hernandez .60 1.50
FT Frank Thomas 1.00 2.50
HP Hunter Pence .60 1.50
HR Hanley Ramirez .60 1.50
IS Ichiro Suzuki 1.25 3.00
ISS Ichiro Suzuki 1.25 3.00
JAS Johan Santana .60 1.50
JMC Miguel Cabrera 1.00 2.50
JR Jose Reyes .60 1.50
JS John Smoltz 1.00 2.50
JSA Jarrod Saltalamacchia .40 1.00
JT Jim Thome .60 1.50
JV Justin Verlander 1.00 2.50
MB Mark Buehrle .60 1.50
ME Mark Ellis .40 1.00
MH Matt Holliday 1.00 2.50
MR Mark Reynolds .40 1.00
PF Prince Fielder .60 1.50
PM Pedro Martinez .60 1.50
RA Rick Ankiel .40 1.00
RB Ryan Braun .60 1.50
RH Ryan Howard .60 1.50
ROH Roy Halladay .60 1.50
SS Sammy Sosa 1.00 2.50
TG Tom Glavine .60 1.50
TH Trevor Hoffman .60 1.50
TOH Todd Helton .60 1.50
TT Troy Tulowitzki 1.00 2.50
VG Vladimir Guerrero .60 1.50

2008 Finest Finest Moments Refractors Red

STATED ODDS 1:39 MINI BOXES
STATED PRINT RUN 25 SER.#'d SETS
NO PRICING DUE TO SCARCITY

2008 Finest Finest Moments X-Fractors White Framed

STATED ODDS 1:982 MINI BOXES
STATED PRINT RUN 1 SER.#'d SET
NO PRICING DUE TO SCARCITY

2008 Finest Finest Moments Autographs

GROUP A ODDS 1:5 MINI BOXES
GROUP B ODDS 1:282 MINI BOXES
AR Alex Rios A 6.00 15.00
AS Andy Sonnanstine A 3.00 8.00
BP Brandon Phillips A 6.00 15.00
BPB Brian Bannister A 6.00 15.00
CG Curtis Granderson A 5.00 12.00
CH Cole Hamels A 3.00 8.00
CMW Chien-Ming Wang A 12.50 30.00
DW David Wright A 10.00 25.00
FC Fausto Carmona A 6.00 15.00
HR Hanley Ramirez A 4.00 10.00
JA Jeremy Accardo A 3.00 8.00
JC Jack Cust A 3.00 8.00
JD Justin Duchscherer A 6.00 15.00
JH Josh Hamilton A 6.00 15.00
JMC Miguel Cabrera A 20.00 50.00
JR Jose Reyes A 5.00 12.00
JS Jarrod Saltalamacchia A 3.00 8.00
ME Mark Ellis A 3.00 8.00
MR Mark Reynolds A 8.00 20.00
NM Nick Markakis A 6.00 15.00
PH Phil Hughes A 4.00 10.00
RB Ryan Braun A 10.00 25.00
RH Ryan Howard B 8.00 20.00
RZ Ryan Zimmerman A 6.00 15.00
VG Vladimir Guerrero A 10.00 25.00

2008 Finest Finest Moments Autographs Refractors Red

STATED ODDS 1:79 MINI BOXES
STATED PRINT RUN 25 SER.#'d SETS
NO PRICING DUE TO SCARCITY

2008 Finest Finest Moments Autographs X-Fractors White Framed

STATED ODDS 1:3260 MINI BOXES
STATED PRINT RUN 1 SER.#'d SET
NO PRICING DUE TO SCARCITY

2008 Finest Rookie Redemption

STATED ODDS 1:3 MINI BOXES
EXCHANGE DEADLINE 4/30/2009
1 Johnny Cueto 2.50 6.00
2 Jay Bruce AU 12.00 30.00
3 Kosuke Fukudome 3.00 8.00
4 Jeff Samardzija 3.00 8.00
5 Chris Davis 2.00 5.00
6 Justin Masterson 2.50 6.00
7 Clayton Kershaw 8.00 20.00
8 Daniel Murphy 4.00 10.00
9 Denard Span 1.50 4.00
10 Jed Lowrie AU 4.00 10.00

2008 Finest Topps Team Favorites

COMPLETE SET (8) 5.00 12.00
RANDOM INSERTS IN PACKS
*REF: .5X TO 1.2X BASIC
REF.ODDS 1:4 MINI BOXES
AS Alfonso Soriano 1.00 2.50
BC Bobby Crosby .60 1.50
DW David Wright 1.00 2.50
EC Eric Chavez .60 1.50
FP Felix Pie .60 1.50
JR Jose Reyes 1.00 2.50
MC Melky Cabrera .60 1.50
RC Robinson Cano 1.00 2.50

2008 Finest Topps Team Favorites Autographs

STATED PRINT RUN 100 SER.#'d SETS
AS Alfonso Soriano 20.00 50.00
BC Bobby Crosby 6.00 15.00
DW David Wright 20.00 50.00
EC Eric Chavez 6.00 15.00
FP Felix Pie 6.00 15.00
JR Jose Reyes 8.00 20.00
MC Melky Cabrera 4.00 10.00
RC Robinson Cano 15.00 40.00

2008 Finest Topps Team Favorites Autographs Refractors Red

STATED ODDS 1:164 MINI BOXES
STATED PRINT RUN 25 SER.#'d SETS
NO PRICING DUE TO SCARCITY

2008 Finest Topps Team Favorites Autographs X-Fractors White Framed

STATED ODDS 1:4092 MINI BOXES
STATED PRINT RUN 1 SER.#'d SET
NO PRICING DUE TO SCARCITY

2008 Finest Topps Team Favorites Dual

COMPLETE SET (4) 3.00 8.00
RANDOM INSERTS IN PACKS
*REF: .5X TO 1.2X BASIC
REF.RANDOMLY INSERTED
CC Melky Cabrera 1.00 2.50
Robinson Cano
EB Eric Chavez .60 1.50
Bobby Crosby
RW Jose Reyes 1.00 2.50
David Wright
SP Alfonso Soriano 1.00 2.50
Felix Pie

2008 Finest Topps Team Favorites Dual Autographs

STATED ODDS 1:166 MINI BOXES
STATED PRINT RUN 74 SER.#'d SETS
CC M.Cabrera/R.Cano 10.00 25.00
EB E.Chavez/B.Crosby 6.00 15.00
RW J.Reyes/D.Wright 25.00 60.00
SP A.Soriano/F.Pie 6.00 15.00

2008 Finest Topps Team Favorites Dual Autographs X-Fractors White Framed

STATED ODDS 1:4092 MINI BOXES
STATED PRINT RUN 1 SER.#'d SET
NO PRICING DUE TO SCARCITY

2008 Finest Topps Team Favorites Dual Autographs Cuts

STATED ODDS 1:9821 MINI BOXES
STATED PRINT RUN 1 SER.#'d SET
NO PRICING DUE TO SCARCITY

2008 Finest Topps TV Autographs

STATED ODDS 1:11 MINI BOXES
RM Alan Narz 4.00 10.00
RGF Felicia 4.00 10.00
RGH Hollie 4.00 10.00
RGR Rachael 4.00 10.00
RGLS Lindsey 4.00 10.00
Stephanie

2008 Finest Topps TV Autographs Red Ink

RANDOM INSERTS IN PACKS
PRINT RUNS B/WN 5-10 COPIES PER
NO PRICING DUE TO SCARCITY

2008 Finest Topps TV Autographs Refractors

STATED ODDS 1:392 MINI BOXES
STATED PRINT RUN 1 SER.#'d SET
NO PRICING DUE TO SCARCITY

2009 Finest

COMP.SET w/o AU's (150) 40.00 80.00
COMMON CARD (1-125) .15 .40
COMMON RC (126-150) .75 2.00
COMMON AU RC (151-164) 5.00 12.00
AU RC ODDS 1:2 MINI BOX
LETTERS SER.#'d B/W 170-285 COPIES PER
TOTAL PRINT RUNS LISTED BELOW
EXCHANGE DEADLINE 4/30/2012
1-150 PLATE ODDS 1:45 MINI BOX
PLATE PRINT RUN 1 SET PER COLOR
BLACK-CYAN-MAGENTA-YELLOW ISSUED
NO PLATE PRICING DUE TO SCARCITY
1 Kosuke Fukudome .25 .60
2 Derek Jeter 1.00 2.50
3 Evan Longoria .25 .60
4 Alex Gordon .25 .60
5 David Wright .30 .75
6 Ryan Howard .30 .75
7 Jose Reyes .25 .60
8 Ryan Braun .25 .60
9 Hunter Pence .25 .60
10 Chipper Jones .40 1.00
11 Jimmy Rollins .25 .60
12 Alfonso Soriano .25 .60
13 Alex Rodriguez .50 1.25
14 Paul Konerko .25 .60
15 Dustin Pedroia .40 1.00
16 Brian McCann .25 .60
17 Ken Griffey .75 2.00
18 Daisuke Matsuzaka .25 .60
19 Josh Beckett .15 .40
20 Jorge Posada .25 .60
21 Nick Markakis .30 .75
22 Xavier Nady .15 .40
23 Carlos Pena .25 .60
24 Grady Sizemore .25 .60
25 Mark Teixeira .25 .60
26 Chase Utley .25 .60
27 Vladimir Guerrero .25 .60
28 Prince Fielder .25 .60
29 Brian Roberts .15 .40
30 Magglio Ordonez .25 .60
31 Cliff Lee .25 .60
32 Josh Hamilton .25 .60
33 Justin Morneau .25 .60
34 David Ortiz .40 1.00
35 Cole Hamels .30 .75
36 Edinson Volquez .15 .40
37 Hanley Ramirez .25 .60
38 Carlos Zambrano .25 .60
39 Brett Myers .15 .40
40 Chien-Ming Wang .25 .60
41 John Lackey .25 .60
42 B.J. Upton .25 .60
43 Gary Sheffield .15 .40
44 Jake Peavy .15 .40
45 Carlos Lee .15 .40
46 Jacoby Ellsbury .30 .75
47 Francisco Liriano .15 .40
48 Torii Hunter .15 .40
49 Eric Chavez .15 .40
50 Jamie Moyer .15 .40
51 Ichiro Suzuki .50 1.25
52 CC Sabathia .25 .60
53 Matt Holliday .40 1.00
54 Ervin Santana .15 .40
55 Hideki Matsui .40 1.00
56 Mark Buehrle .25 .60
57 Johan Santana .25 .60
58 Francisco Rodriguez .25 .60
59 Jorge Cantu .15 .40
60 Joe Mauer .30 .75
61 Ian Kinsler .25 .60
62 Joba Chamberlain .15 .40
63 Stephen Drew .15 .40
64 J.D. Drew .15 .40
65 Justin Upton .25 .60
66 Troy Glaus .15 .40
67 Chone Figgins .15 .40
68 David DeJesus .15 .40
69 Joey Votto .40 1.00
70 Alex Rios .15 .40
71 Adam Jones .25 .60
72 Miguel Tejada .25 .60
73 Michael Young .15 .40
74 Vernon Wells .15 .40
75 Tim Lincecum .25 .60
76 Ryan Zimmerman .25 .60
77 Nate McLouth .15 .40
78 Carl Crawford .25 .60
79 Dan Haren .15 .40
80 Brandon Webb .25 .60
81 Tim Hudson .25 .60
82 Rafael Furcal .15 .40
83 Ryan Dempster .15 .40
84 Carlos Beltran .25 .60
85 Lance Berkman .25 .60
86 Jhonny Peralta .15 .40
87 Aramis Ramirez .15 .40
88 Aubrey Huff .15 .40
89 Johnny Damon .25 .60
90 Carlos Quentin .15 .40
91 Yunel Escobar .15 .40
92 Scott Kazmir .15 .40
93 Delmon Young .25 .60
94 Jermaine Dye .15 .40
95 Miguel Cabrera .40 1.00
96 Zack Greinke .40 1.00
97 Chris Young .15 .40
98 Derrek Lee .15 .40
99 Orlando Hudson .15 .40
100 Jay Bruce .25 .60
101 Garrett Atkins .15 .40
102 Curtis Granderson .30 .75
103 Adrian Gonzalez .30 .75
104 Raul Ibanez .25 .60
105 Roy Halladay .25 .60
106 Jon Lester .25 .60
107 Adam Dunn .25 .60
108 A.J. Burnett .15 .40
109 Gavin Floyd .15 .40
110 Russ Martin .15 .40
111 Dan Uggla .15 .40
112 Andre Ethier .25 .60
113 Casey Kotchman .15 .40
114 Matt Garza .15 .40
115 Kevin Youkilis .15 .40
116 Felix Hernandez .25 .60
117 Rich Harden .15 .40
118 Roy Oswalt .25 .60
119 Jason Bay .25 .60
120 Geovany Soto .25 .60
121 Ryan Ludwick .25 .60
122 Joe Saunders .15 .40
123 Gil Meche .15 .40
124 Jim Thome .25 .60
125 Albert Pujols .50 1.25
126 Andrew Carpenter RC 1.25 3.00
127 Aaron Cunningham RC .75 2.00
128 Phil Coke RC 1.25 3.00
129 Alcides Escobar RC 1.25 3.00
130 Dexter Fowler (RC) 1.25 3.00
131 Michael Hinckley (RC) .75 2.00
132 Brad Nelson (RC) .75 2.00
133 Scott Lewis (RC) .75 2.00
134 Juan Miranda RC 1.25 3.00
135 Jason Motte (RC) 1.25 3.00
136 Travis Snider RC 1.25 3.00
137 Wade LeBlanc RC 1.25 3.00
138 Matt Tuiasosopo (RC) .75 2.00
139 Humberto Sanchez (RC) .75 2.00
140 Freddy Sandoval (RC) .75 2.00
141 Chris Lambert (RC) .75 2.00
142 John Jaso RC .75 2.00
143 James McDonald RC 2.00 5.00
144 Luis Valbuena RC 1.25 3.00
145 Rich Rundles (RC) .75 2.00
146 Josh Whitesell RC 1.25 3.00
147 Jeff Baisley RC .75 2.00
148 Ramon Ramirez (RC) .75 2.00
149 Jason Bourgeois (RC) .75 2.00
150 Jesus Delgado RC 1.25 3.00
151 M.Gamel AU/1425 * RC 3.00 8.00
152 Travis Snider AU 5.00 12.00
153 Angel Salome AU/1308 * (RC) 5.00 12.00
154 Will Venable AU/1190 * RC 5.00 12.00
155 M.Bowden AU/1308 * (RC) 5.00 12.00
156 Conor Gillaspie AU/963 * RC 5.00 12.00
157 Matt Antonelli AU/963 * RC 5.00 12.00
158 Greg Golson AU/1308 * (RC) 5.00 12.00
159 Kila Ka'aihue AU/1190 * (RC) 4.00 10.00
160 Bobby Parnell AU/1190 * RC 5.00 12.00
161 Gaby Sanchez AU/1190 * RC 6.00 15.00
162 Jonathon Niese AU/1425 * RC 6.00 15.00
163 Dexter Fowler AU EXCH 3.00 8.00
164 David Price AU/1425 * RC 10.00 25.00

2009 Finest Refractors

*REF VET: 1.2X TO 3X BASIC
*REF RC: .5X TO 1.2X BASIC RC
1-150 RANDOMLY INSERTED
*REF AU: .5X TO 1.2X BASIC AU
151-164 ODDS 1:4 MINI BOXES
EACH LETTER AU SER.#'d TO 75
TOTAL PRINT RUNS LISTED BELOW
EXCHANGE DEADLINE 4/30/2012

2009 Finest Refractors Blue

*BLUE REF VET: 1.5X TO 4X BASIC
*BLUE REF RC: .6X TO 1.5X BASIC RC
1-150 RANDOMLY INSERTED
1-150 PRINT RUN 399 SER.#'d SETS
*BLUE REF AU: .6X TO 1.5X BASIC AU
151-164 ODDS 1:12 MINI BOXES
EACH LETTER AU SER.#'d TO 25
TOTAL PRINT RUNS LISTED BELOW
EXCHANGE DEADLINE 4/30/2012

2009 Finest Refractors Gold

*GOLD REF VET: 6X TO 15X BASIC
*GOLD REF RC: 1.5X TO 4X BASIC RC
1-150 STATED ODDS 1:4 MINI BOXES
1-150 PRINT RUN 50 SER.#'d SETS
*GOLD REF AU: .75X TO 2X BASIC AU
151-164 ODDS 1:30 MINI BOXES
EACH LETTER AU SER.#'d TO 10
TOTAL PRINT RUNS LISTED BELOW
EXCHANGE DEADLINE 4/30/2012

2009 Finest Refractors Green

*GREEN REF VET: 4X TO 10X BASIC
*GREEN REF RC: 1X TO 2.5X BASIC RC
1-150 STATED ODDS 1:2 MINI BOXES
STATED PRINT RUN 99 SER.#'d SETS

2009 Finest Refractors Red

*RED REF VET: 12X TO 30X BASIC
*RED REF RC: 2.5X TO 6X BASIC RC
1-150 STATED ODDS 1:8 MINI BOXES
1-150 PRINT RUN 25 SER.#'d SETS
*RED REF AU: 1.5X TO 4X BASIC AU
151-164 ODDS 1:60 MINI BOXES
EACH LETTER AU SER.#'d TO 5
TOTAL PRINT RUNS LISTED BELOW
EXCHANGE DEADLINE 4/30/2012

2009 Finest X-Fractors

1-150 ODDS 1:180 MINI BOX
151-164 AU ODDS 1:298 MINI BOX
STATED PRINT RUN 1 SER.#'d SET
NO PRICING DUE TO SCARCITY
EXCHANGE DEADLINE 4/30/2012

2009 Finest Finest Moments Autographs

GROUP A ODDS 1:10 MINI BOX
GROUP B ODDS 1:61 MINI BOX
REF.ODDS 1:68 MINI BOXES
REF.PRINT RUN 25 SER.#'d SETS
NO REF.PRICING DUE TO SCARCITY
X-F ODDS 1:1797 MINI BOX
X-F PRINT RUN 1 SER.#'d SET
NO X-F PRICING DUE TO SCARCITY
AC Asdrubal Cabrera A 5.00 12.00
AI Akinori Iwamura A 5.00 12.00
AR Alex Rodriguez B 100.00 175.00
DO David Ortiz B 30.00 80.00
DW David Wright A 8.00 20.00
EV Evan Longoria A 6.00 15.00
HP Hunter Pence A 6.00 15.00
JB Jay Bruce A 5.00 12.00
JC Joba Chamberlain A 8.00 20.00
JL Jon Lester A 5.00 12.00
JR Jose Reyes A 5.00 12.00
JT Jim Thome B 12.50 30.00
JV Joey Votto B 30.00 60.00
RC Robinson Cano A 10.00 25.00
RH Ryan Howard B 8.00 20.00
JBA Jason Bay B 5.00 12.00

2009 Finest Rookie Redemption

STATED ODDS 1:3 MINI BOXES
*REF: .5X TO 1.2X BASIC
REF.ODDS 1:14 MINI BOXES
*GOLD REF: 1.2X TO 3X BASIC
GOLD REF.ODDS 1:54 MINI BOXES
EXCHANGE DEADLINE 4/30/2010
1 Matt LaPorta 2.00 5.00
2 Tommy Hanson 3.00 8.00
3 Andrew Bailey 3.00 8.00
4 Julio Borbon 1.25 3.00
5 Colby Rasmus 2.00 5.00
6 Kyle Blanks 2.00 5.00
7 Neftali Feliz 2.00 5.00
8 Nolan Reimold 1.25 3.00
9 Rick Porcello 4.00 10.00
10 Tommy Hanson AU 6.00 15.00

2010 Finest

COMP.SET w/o AU's (150) 30.00 60.00
COMMON CARD (1-125) .15 .40
COMMON RC (126-150) .75 2.00
COMMON AU RC (151-164) 4.00 10.00
AU RC ODDS 1:2 MINI BOX
LETTERS SER.#'d B/W 106-284 COPIES PER
TOTAL PRINT RUNS LISTED BELOW
1-150 PLATE ODDS 1:50 MINI BOX
1 Tim Lincecum .25 .60
2 Evan Longoria .25 .60
3 Alex Rodriguez .50 1.25
4 Ryan Braun .25 .60
5 Grady Sizemore .25 .60
6 David Wright .30 .75
7 Albert Pujols .50 1.25
8 Derrek Lee .15 .40
9 Ichiro Suzuki .50 1.25
10 Justin Morneau .25 .60
11 Johan Santana .25 .60
12 Matt Kemp .30 .75
13 Daisuke Matsuzaka .25 .60
14 Derek Jeter 1.00 2.50
15 Mark Buehrle .25 .60
16 Chipper Jones .40 1.00
17 Prince Fielder .25 .60
18 Ryan Howard .30 .75
19 Vladimir Guerrero .25 .60
20 Alexei Ramirez .25 .60
21 Joba Chamberlain .15 .40
22 Russell Martin .15 .40
23 CC Sabathia .25 .60
24 Adam Dunn .25 .60
25 Jose Reyes .25 .60
26 Michael Young .15 .40
27 Joe Mauer .30 .75
28 Mark Teixeira .25 .60
29 Jason Bartlett .15 .40
30 Johnny Damon .25 .60
31 Miguel Cabrera .40 1.00
32 Adam Wainwright .25 .60
33 Brandon Webb .25 .60
34 Carlos Pena .25 .60
35 Jorge Posada .25 .60
36 Pablo Sandoval .25 .60
37 Manny Ramirez .40 1.00
38 Robinson Cano .25 .60
39 Nick Markakis .30 .75
40 Justin Upton .25 .60
41 Adrian Gonzalez .30 .75
42 Ian Kinsler .25 .60
43 Ryan Zimmerman .25 .60
44 Mark Reynolds .15 .40
45 Raul Ibanez .25 .60
46 Jason Bay .25 .60
47 Kendry Morales .15 .40
48 Todd Helton .25 .60
49 Dan Uggla .15 .40
50 Adam Lind .25 .60
51 Victor Martinez .25 .60
52 Mariano Rivera .50 1.25
53 Chase Utley .25 .60
54 Kevin Youkilis .15 .40
55 Carlos Lee .15 .40
56 Josh Hamilton .25 .60
57 Brad Hawpe .15 .40
58 Brandon Inge .25 .60
59 Bobby Abreu .15 .40
60 Nelson Cruz .40 1.00
61 James Loney .15 .40
62 Jason Kubel .15 .40
63 Russell Branyan .15 .40
64 Curtis Granderson .30 .75
65 Ken Griffey Jr. .75 2.00
66 Troy Tulowitzki .40 1.00
67 Jermaine Dye .15 .40
68 Paul Konerko .25 .60
69 Josh Johnson .25 .60
70 David Ortiz .40 1.00
71 Hideki Matsui .40 1.00
72 Dustin Pedroia .40 1.00
73 Jon Lester UER .25 .60
74 Joey Votto .40 1.00
75 Josh Beckett .15 .40
76 Billy Butler .15 .40
77 David DeJesus .15 .40
78 Nick Swisher .25 .60
79 Brian Roberts .15 .40
80 Felix Hernandez .25 .60
81 J.A. Happ .25 .60
82 Marco Scutaro .25 .60
83 Hanley Ramirez .25 .60
84 Lance Berkman .25 .60
85 Dan Haren .15 .40
86 Yunel Escobar .15 .40
87 Justin Verlander .40 1.00
88 Carlos Beltran .25 .60
89 Shane Victorino .25 .60
90 Carl Crawford .25 .60
91 Adam Jones .25 .60
92 Jason Marquis .15 .40
93 Everth Cabrera .15 .40
94 B.J. Upton .25 .60
95 Ted Lilly .15 .40
96 Ubaldo Jimenez .15 .40
97 Aaron Hill .15 .40
98 Kosuke Fukudome .25 .60
99 Jorge Cantu .15 .40
100 Jose Lopez .15 .40
101 Rick Porcello .25 .60
102 Matt Cain .25 .60
103 Chone Figgins .15 .40
104 Tommy Hanson .15 .40
105 Jacoby Ellsbury .30 .75
106 Clayton Kershaw .60 1.50
107 Miguel Tejada .25 .60
108 Yovani Gallardo .15 .40
109 Andrew McCutchen .40 1.00
110 Felipe Lopez .15 .40
111 Asdrubal Cabrera .25 .60
112 Roy Halladay .25 .60
113 Hunter Pence .25 .60
114 Gordon Beckham .15 .40
115 Cole Hamels .30 .75
116 Brian McCann .25 .60
117 Michael Cuddyer .15 .40
118 Cliff Lee .25 .60
119 Roy Oswalt .25 .60
120 A.J. Pierzynski .15 .40
121 Jayson Werth .25 .60
122 Mike Lowell .15 .40
123 John Lannan .15 .40
124 Luis Castillo .15 .40
125 Andy Pettitte .25 .60
126 Neil Walker (RC) 1.25 3.00
127 Brad Kilby RC .75 2.00
128 Chris Johnson RC 1.25 3.00
129 Tommy Manzella (RC) .75 2.00
130 Sergio Escalona (RC) .75 2.00
131 Chris Pettit RC .75 2.00
132 Kevin Richardson (RC) .75 2.00
133 Armando Gabino RC .75 2.00
134 Reid Gorecki (RC) 1.25 3.00
135 Justin Turner RC 6.00 15.00
136 Adam Moore RC .75 2.00
137 Kyle Phillips RC .75 2.00
138 John Hester RC .75 2.00
139 Dusty Hughes RC .75 2.00
140 Waldis Joaquin RC .75 2.00
141 Jeff Manship (RC) .75 2.00
142 Dan Runzler RC 1.25 3.00
143 Pedro Viola RC .75 2.00
144 Craig Gentry RC .75 2.00
145 Brent Dlugach (RC) .75 2.00
146 Esmil Rogers RC .75 2.00
147 Josh Butler RC .75 2.00
148 Dustin Richardson RC .75 2.00
149 Matt Carson (RC) .75 2.00
150 Henry Rodriguez RC .75 2.00
151 Brandon Allen AU/1420 * (RC) 4.00 10.00
152 Colvin AU/1302 * RC 4.00 10.00
153 Hudson AU/1302 * RC 4.00 10.00
154 Francisco AU/954 * RC 4.00 10.00
155 Stubbs AU/1302 * RC 4.00 10.00
156 Brantley AU/1072 * RC 6.00 15.00
157 Stoner AU/1302 * RC 4.00 10.00
158 Thole AU/1420 * RC 4.00 10.00
159 McCutchen AU/954 * RC 4.00 10.00
160 Eric Hacker AU/1302 * RC 4.00 10.00
161 Bumgarner AU/954 * RC 30.00 80.00
162 Posey AU/1420 * RC 50.00 120.00
163 Dan Runzler AU/1190 * 4.00 10.00
164 Desmond AU/1190 * (RC) 5.00 12.00
165 Richardson AU/2170 * 4.00 10.00

2010 Finest Rookie Logo Patch

STATED ODDS 1:26 MINI BOX
STATED PRINT RUN 50 SER.#'d SETS
PURPLE ODDS 1:1197 MINI BOX
PURPLE PRINT RUN 1 SER.#'d SET
126 Neil Walker 8.00 20.00
127 Brad Kilby 5.00 12.00
128 Chris Johnson 8.00 20.00
129 Tommy Manzella 5.00 12.00
130 Sergio Escalona 5.00 12.00
131 Chris Pettit 5.00 12.00
132 Kevin Richardson 5.00 12.00
133 Armando Gabino 5.00 12.00
134 Reid Gorecki 8.00 20.00
135 Justin Turner 40.00 100.00
136 Adam Moore 5.00 12.00
137 Kyle Phillips 5.00 12.00
138 John Hester 5.00 12.00
139 Dusty Hughes 5.00 12.00
140 Waldis Joaquin 5.00 12.00
141 Jeff Manship 5.00 12.00
142 Dan Runzler 8.00 20.00
143 Pedro Viola 5.00 12.00
144 Craig Gentry 5.00 12.00
145 Brent Dlugach 5.00 12.00
146 Esmil Rogers 5.00 12.00
147 Josh Butler 5.00 12.00
148 Dustin Richardson 5.00 12.00
149 Matt Carson 5.00 12.00
150 Henry Rodriguez 5.00 12.00

2010 Finest Refractors

*REF VET: 1.2X TO 3X BASIC
*REF RC: .5X TO 1.2X BASIC RC
1-150 RANDOMLY INSERTED
1-150 PRINT RUN 599 SER.#'d SETS
*REF AU: .5X TO 1.2X BASIC AU
151-165 ODDS 1:4 MINI BOX
EACH LETTER AU SER.#'d TO 75
TOTAL LETTER PRINT RUNS LISTED

2010 Finest Refractors Blue

*BLUE REF VET: 2.5X TO 6X BASIC
*BLUE REF RC: .6X TO 1.5X BASIC RC
1-150 STATED RANDOMLY INSERTED
1-150 PRINT RUN 299 SER.#'d SETS
*BLUE REF AU: .6X TO 1.5X BASIC AU
151-165 ODDS 1:13 MINI BOX
EACH LETTER AU SER.#'d TO 25
TOTAL LETTER PRINT RUNS LISTED

2010 Finest Refractors Gold

*GOLD REF VET: 10X TO 25X BASIC
*GOLD REF RC: 2X TO 5X BASIC RC
1-150 STATED ODDS 1:4 MINI BOX
1-150 PRINT RUN 50 SER.#'d SETS
*GOLD REF AU: 1X TO 2.5X BASIC AU
151-165 ODDS 1:32 MINI BOX
EACH LETTER AU SER.#'d TO 10
TOTAL LETTER PRINT RUNS LISTED

2010 Finest Refractors Green

*GREEN REF VET: 5X TO 12X BASIC
*GREEN REF RC: 1X TO 2.5X BASIC RC
STATED ODDS 1:3 MINI BOXES
STATED PRINT RUN 99 SER.#'d SETS

2010 Finest Refractors Red

*RED REF VET: 12X TO 30X BASIC
*RED REF RC: 2.5X TO 6X BASIC RC
1-150 STATED ODDS 1:8 MINI BOX
1-150 PRINT RUN 25 SER.#'d SETS
*RED REF AU: 1.5X TO 4X BASIC AU
151-165 ODDS 1:60 MINI BOX
EACH LETTER AU SER.#'d TO 5
TOTAL LETTER PRINT RUNS LISTED

2010 Finest Finest Moments Autographs

GROUP A ODDS 1:10 MINI BOX
GROUP B ODDS 1:58 MINI BOX
PURPLE ODDS 1:1662 MINI BOX
PURPLE PRINT RUN 1 SER.#'d SET
RED ODDS 1:67 MINI BOX
RED PRINT RUN 25 SER.#'d SETS
AE Andre Ethier A 6.00 15.00
AH Aaron Hill A 5.00 12.00
CF Chone Figgins A 4.00 10.00
CJ Chipper Jones B 40.00 80.00
CK Clayton Kershaw A 15.00 40.00
DP Dustin Pedroia A 12.50 30.00
DW David Wright B 15.00 40.00
JF Jeff Francoeur A 8.00 20.00
JM Justin Morneau B 12.50 30.00
JS Joe Saunders A 4.00 10.00
MS Max Scherzer A 20.00 50.00
PF Prince Fielder B 8.00 20.00
RC Robinson Cano A 10.00 25.00
RH Ryan Howard B 10.00 25.00
RP Rick Porcello B 4.00 10.00
UJ Ubaldo Jimenez A 8.00 20.00
YG Yovani Gallardo A 5.00 12.00
ZG Zack Greinke B 10.00 25.00

2010 Finest Rookie Redemption

COMPLETE SET (11) 175.00 350.00
STATED ODDS 1:3 MINI BOX
*BLUE REF: .6X TO 1.5X BASIC
BLUE REF.ODDS 1:15 MINI BOX
*GOLD REF: 2.5X TO 6X BASIC
GOLD REF.ODDS 1:60 MINI BOX
EXCHANGE DEADLINE 4/30/2011
1a Jason Heyward 2.50 6.00
1b Jason Heyward AU 40.00 80.00
2 Ike Davis 1.25 3.00

3 Starlin Castro 1.50 4.00
4 Mike Leake 2.00 5.00
5 Mike Stanton 8.00 20.00
6 Stephen Strasburg 4.00 10.00
7 Andrew Cashner AU 3.00 8.00
8 Dayan Viciedo 1.00 2.50
9 Domonic Brown 2.50 6.00
10 Ryan Kalish 1.00 2.50

2011 Finest

COMPLETE SET (100) 20.00 50.00
COMMON CARD (1-60) .15 .40
COMMON RC (61-100) .40 1.00
1-100 PLATE ODDS 1:103 MINI BOX
PLATE PRINT RUN 1 SET PER COLOR
BLACK-CYAN-MAGENTA-YELLOW ISSUED
NO PLATE PRICING DUE TO SCARCITY
1 Hanley Ramirez .25 .60
2 Jason Heyward .30 .75
3 Buster Posey .50 1.25
4 Mark Teixeira .25 .60
5 Evan Longoria .25 .60
6 Chase Utley .25 .60
7 Ryan Braun .25 .60
8 Felix Hernandez .25 .60
9 Hunter Pence .25 .60
10 Adrian Gonzalez .30 .75
11 Nick Markakis .30 .75
12 Miguel Cabrera .40 1.00
13 Paul Konerko .25 .60
14 Ryan Zimmerman .25 .60
15 Troy Tulowitzki .40 1.00
16 Chipper Jones .40 1.00
17 Torii Hunter .15 .40
18 B.J. Upton .25 .60
19 Michael Young .15 .40
20 Ryan Howard .30 .75
21 Andre Ethier .25 .60
22 Justin Verlander .40 1.00
23 Clay Buchholz .15 .40
24 Cole Hamels .30 .75
25 Albert Pujols .50 1.25
26 Adrian Beltre .40 1.00
27 Zack Greinke .40 1.00
28 Derek Jeter 1.00 2.50
29 Jacoby Ellsbury .30 .75
30 Dan Uggla .15 .40
31 Adam Dunn .25 .60
32 Matt Kemp .30 .75
33 Starlin Castro .25 .60
34 Brian McCann .25 .60
35 David Wright .30 .75
36 Tim Lincecum .25 .60
37 David Price .30 .75
38 Jayson Werth .25 .60
39 Roy Oswalt .25 .60
40 Ichiro Suzuki .50 1.25
41 Jose Bautista .25 .60
42 Robinson Cano .25 .60
43 David Ortiz .40 1.00
44 Mike Stanton .40 1.00
45 Roy Halladay .25 .60
46 Justin Upton .25 .60
47 Joey Votto .40 1.00
48 Andrew McCutchen .40 1.00
49 Matt Holliday .40 1.00
50 Alex Rodriguez .50 1.25
51 Jon Lester .25 .60
52 Jered Weaver .25 .60
53 Kevin Youkilis .15 .40
54 Ike Davis .15 .40
55 Joe Mauer .30 .75
56 Carl Crawford .25 .60
57 Cliff Lee .25 .60
58 Josh Hamilton .25 .60
59 Stephen Strasburg .40 1.00
60 Prince Fielder .25 .60
61 Sergio Santos .40 1.00
62 Randall Delgado RC .60 1.50
63 Eric Hosmer RC 2.50 6.00
64 Julio Teheran RC .60 1.50
65 Danny Duffy RC .60 1.50
66 J.P. Arencibia (RC) .40 1.00
67 Domonic Brown (RC) .75 2.00
68 Mike Minor (RC) .40 1.00
69 Brett Wallace (RC) .40 1.00
70 Jerry Sands RC 1.00 2.50
71 Mark Trumbo (RC) 1.00 2.50
72 Freddie Freeman RC 10.00 25.00
73 Tsuyoshi Nishioka RC 1.25 3.00
74 Jeremy Hellickson RC 1.00 2.50
75 Kyle Drabek RC .60 1.50
76 Dustin Ackley RC .60 1.50
77 Brandon Beachy RC 1.00 2.50
78 Brent Morel RC .40 1.00
79 Dillon Gee RC .60 1.50
80 Chris Sale RC 3.00 8.00
81 Alex Cobb RC .40 1.00
82 Dee Gordon RC .60 1.50
83 Brandon Belt RC 1.00 2.50
84 Zach Britton RC 1.00 2.50
85 Craig Kimbrel RC 1.00 2.50
86 Michael Pineda RC 1.00 2.50
87 Andrew Cashner (RC) .40 1.00
88 Jordan Walden RC .40 1.00
89 Alexi Ogando RC 1.00 2.50
90 Jake McGee (RC) .75 2.00
91 Hector Noesi RC .60 1.50
92 Darwin Barney RC 1.25 3.00
93 Ben Revere RC .60 1.50
94 Mike Trout RC 200.00 500.00
95 Danny Espinosa RC .40 1.00
96 Aaron Crow RC .60 1.50
97 Anthony Rizzo RC 4.00 10.00
98 Mike Moustakas RC 1.00 2.50
99 Eduardo Sanchez RC .60 1.50
100 Daniel Descalso RC .40 1.00

2011 Finest Refractors

*REF: 1.2X TO 3X BASIC
*REF RC: .5X TO 1.2X BASIC RC
STATED PRINT RUN 549 SER.#'d SETS
94 Mike Trout 400.00 1000.00

2011 Finest Gold Refractors

*GOLD: 6X TO 15X BASIC
*GOLD RC: 2.5X TO 6X BASIC RC
STATED ODDS 1:9 MINI BOX
STATED PRINT RUN 50 SER.#'d SETS
25 Albert Pujols 20.00 50.00
28 Derek Jeter 20.00 50.00
94 Mike Trout 2000.00 5000.00

2011 Finest Green Refractors

*GREEN: 2.5X TO 6X BASIC
*GREEN RC: 1X TO 2.5X BASIC RC
STATED ODDS 1:3 MINI BOX
STATED PRINT RUN 199 SER.#'d SETS
94 Mike Trout 750.00 2000.00

2011 Finest Orange Refractors

*ORANGE: 3X TO 8X BASIC
*ORANGE RC: 1.2X TO 3X BASIC RC
STATED ODDS 1:5 MINI BOX
STATED PRINT RUN 99 SER.#'d SETS
94 Mike Trout 1000.00 2500.00

2011 Finest X-Fractors

*XF: 2.5X TO 6X BASIC
*XF RC: 1X TO 2.5X BASIC RC
STATED ODDS 1:2 MINI BOX
STATED PRINT RUN 299 SER.#'d SETS
94 Mike Trout 600.00 1500.00

2011 Finest Foundations

STATED ODDS 1:6 MINI BOX
ORANGE ODDS 1:12 MINI BOX
PURPLE ODDS 1:96 MINI BOX
NO PURPLE PRICING DUE TO SCARCITY
FF1 Albert Pujols 1.25 3.00
FF2 Roy Halladay .60 1.50
FF3 Adrian Gonzalez .75 2.00
FF4 Ryan Howard .75 2.00
FF5 Alex Rodriguez 1.25 3.00
FF6 Evan Longoria .60 1.50
FF7 Buster Posey 1.25 3.00
FF8 Robinson Cano .60 1.50
FF9 Tim Lincecum .60 1.50
FF10 Jason Heyward .75 2.00
FF11 Troy Tulowitzki 1.00 2.50
FF12 Ichiro Suzuki 1.25 3.00
FF13 Stephen Strasburg 1.00 2.50
FF14 Hanley Ramirez .60 1.50
FF15 Derek Jeter 2.50 6.00

2011 Finest Foundations Orange Refractors

*ORANGE: .6X TO 1.5X BASIC
STATED ODDS 1:12 MINI BOX
FF12 Ichiro Suzuki 5.00 12.00
FF15 Derek Jeter 10.00 25.00

2011 Finest Freshmen

STATED ODDS 1:6 MINI BOX
*ORANGE: .6X TO 1.5X BASIC
ORANGE ODDS 1:12 MINI BOX
PURPLE ODDS 1:96 MINI BOX
NO PURPLE PRICING DUE TO SCARCITY
FFR1 Freddie Freeman 6.00 15.00
FFR2 Domonic Brown .75 2.00
FFR3 Jordan Walden .40 1.00
FFR4 Aroldis Chapman 1.25 3.00
FFR5 Zach Britton 1.00 2.50
FFR6 Mark Trumbo 1.00 2.50
FFR7 Brett Wallace .40 1.00
FFR8 Alexi Ogando 1.00 2.50
FFR9 Tsuyoshi Nishioka 1.25 3.00
FFR10 Jeremy Hellickson 1.00 2.50
FFR11 Brent Morel .40 1.00
FFR12 J.P. Arencibia .40 1.00
FFR13 Andrew Cashner .40 1.00
FFR14 Eric Hosmer 2.50 6.00
FFR15 Craig Kimbrel 1.00 2.50
FFR16 Kyle Drabek .60 1.50
FFR17 Michael Pineda 1.00 2.50

2011 Finest Moments

STATED ODDS 1:6 MINI BOX
*ORANGE: .6X TO 1.5X BASIC
ORANGE ODDS 1:12 MINI BOX
PURPLE ODDS 1:96 MINI BOX
NO PURPLE PRICING DUE TO SCARCITY
FM1 Joe Mauer .75 2.00
FM2 Carl Crawford .60 1.50
FM3 Robinson Cano .60 1.50
FM4 Andrew McCutchen 1.00 2.50
FM5 Cliff Lee .60 1.50
FM6 Nick Markakis .75 2.00
FM7 Roy Halladay .60 1.50
FM8 Ryan Howard .75 2.00
FM9 David Wright .75 2.00
FM10 Buster Posey 1.25 3.00
FM11 Jason Heyward .75 2.00
FM12 Josh Hamilton .60 1.50
FM13 Alex Rodriguez 1.25 3.00
FM14 Chase Utley .60 1.50
FM15 David Ortiz 1.00 2.50
FM16 CC Sabathia .60 1.50
FM17 Stephen Strasburg 1.00 2.50
FM18 Ike Davis .40 1.00

2011 Finest Moments Relic Autographs

GROUP A ODDS 1:25 MINI BOX
GROUP B ODDS 1:93 MINI BOX
GROUP C ODDS 1:342 MINI BOX
GROUP A PRINT RUN 274 SER.#'d SETS
GROUP B PRINT RUN 74 SER.#'d SETS
GROUP C PRINT RUN 24 SER.#'d SETS
NO PRICING ON QTY 25 OR LESS
EXCHANGE DEADLINE 10/31/2014
FMA1 Joe Mauer/274 10.00 25.00
FMA2 Carl Crawford/274 6.00 15.00
FMA3 Robinson Cano/274 15.00 40.00
FMA5 Cliff Lee/274 4.00 10.00
FMA6 Nick Markakis/274 6.00 15.00
FMA7 Roy Halladay/274 12.00 30.00
FMA8 Ryan Howard/74 12.50 30.00
FMA9 David Wright/74 15.00 40.00
FMA11 Jason Heyward/74 10.00 25.00
FMA12 Josh Hamilton/74 12.50 30.00
FMA13 Alex Rodriguez/74 50.00 100.00
FMA22 Adrian Gonzalez/74 10.00 25.00

2011 Finest Rookie Autographs Refractors

STATED ODDS 1:5 MINI BOX
STATED PRINT RUN 499 SER.#'d SETS
PRINTING PLATE ODDS 1:603 MINI BOX
PLATE PRINT RUN 1 SET PER COLOR
BLACK-CYAN-MAGENTA-YELLOW ISSUED
NO PLATE PRICING DUE TO SCARCITY
EXCHANGE DEADLINE 10/31/2014
62 Randall Delgado 4.00 10.00
66 Brandon Belt 4.00 10.00
69 Brett Wallace 5.00 12.00
70 Jerry Sands 4.00 10.00
71 Mark Trumbo 8.00 20.00
72 Freddie Freeman 30.00 80.00
76 Dustin Ackley 5.00 12.00
78 Brent Morel 4.00 10.00
79 Dillon Gee 4.00 10.00
82 Dee Gordon 4.00 10.00
83 Zach Britton 5.00 12.00
84 Mike Trout 1000.00 2000.00
86 Michael Pineda 4.00 10.00
88 Jordan Walden 4.00 10.00
93 Eric Sogard 4.00 10.00
96 Aaron Crow 5.00 12.00
97 Anthony Rizzo 30.00 80.00
98 Mike Moustakas EXCH 8.00 20.00
99 Eduardo Sanchez 4.00 10.00
100 Daniel Descalso 4.00 10.00
105 Eduardo Nunez 5.00 12.00

2011 Finest Rookie Autographs Gold Refractors

*GOLD: .75X TO 2X BASIC
STATED ODDS 1:33 MINI BOX
STATED PRINT RUN 75 SER.#'d SETS
EXCHANGE DEADLINE 10/31/2014

2011 Finest Rookie Autographs Green Refractors

*GREEN: .5X TO 1.2X BASIC
STATED ODDS 1:13 MINI BOX
STATED PRINT RUN 199 SER.#'d SETS
EXCHANGE DEADLINE 10/31/2014

2011 Finest Rookie Autographs Orange Refractors

*ORANGE: .6X TO 1.5X BASIC
STATED ODDS 1:25 MINI BOX
STATED PRINT RUN 99 SER.#'d SETS
EXCHANGE DEADLINE 10/31/2014

2011 Finest Rookie Autographs X-Fractors

*XF: .5X TO 1.2X BASIC
STATED ODDS 1:9 MINI BOX
STATED PRINT RUN 299 SER.#'d SETS
EXCHANGE DEADLINE 10/31/2014

2011 Finest Rookie Dual Relic Autographs Refractors

STATED ODDS 1:4 MINI BOX
STATED PRINT RUN 499 SER.#'d SETS
PRINTING PLATE ODDS 1:427 MINI BOX
PLATE PRINT RUN 1 SET PER COLOR
BLACK-CYAN-MAGENTA-YELLOW ISSUED
NO PLATE PRICING DUE TO SCARCITY
EXCHANGE DEADLINE 10/31/2014
62 Eduardo Nunez 4.00 10.00
63 Eric Hosmer 10.00 25.00
64 Julio Teheran 4.00 10.00
68 Mike Minor 6.00 15.00
72 Freddie Freeman 25.00 60.00
77 Brandon Beachy 8.00 20.00
79 Dillon Gee 4.00 10.00
82 Dee Gordon 10.00 25.00
84 Zach Britton 5.00 12.00
85 Craig Kimbrel 4.00 10.00
86 Michael Pineda 5.00 12.00
87 Andrew Cashner 4.00 10.00
88 Jordan Walden 4.00 10.00
89 Alexi Ogando 6.00 15.00
91 Hector Noesi 4.00 10.00
92 Darwin Barney 6.00 15.00
96 Aaron Crow 5.00 12.00
98A Mike Moustakas 10.00 25.00
98B Ivan DeJesus Jr. 4.00 10.00
100 Alex Cobb 4.00 10.00

2011 Finest Rookie Dual Relic Autographs Gold Refractors

*GOLD: .75X TO 2X BASIC
STATED ODDS 1:26 MINI BOX
STATED PRINT RUN 69 SER.#'d SETS
EXCHANGE DEADLINE 10/31/2014

2011 Finest Rookie Dual Relic Autographs Green Refractors

*GREEN: .4X TO 1X BASIC
STATED ODDS 1:12 MINI BOX
STATED PRINT RUN 149 SER.#'d SETS
EXCHANGE DEADLINE 10/31/2014

2011 Finest Rookie Dual Relic Autographs Orange Refractors

*ORANGE: .6X TO 1.5X BASIC
STATED ODDS 1:18 MINI BOX
STATED PRINT RUN 99 SER.#'d SETS
EXCHANGE DEADLINE 10/31/2014

2012 Finest

COMPLETE SET (100) 20.00 50.00
1-100 PLATE ODDS 1:90 MINI BOX
PLATE PRINT RUN 1 SET PER COLOR
BLACK-CYAN-MAGENTA-YELLOW ISSUED
NO PLATE PRICING DUE TO SCARCITY
1 Albert Pujols .50 1.25
2 Alex Rodriguez .50 1.25
3 Michael Pineda .25 .60
4 Jay Bruce .30 .75
5 Derek Jeter 1.00 2.50
6 Tom Milone RC .60 1.50
7 Justin Upton .30 .75
8 Cliff Lee .30 .75
9 Giancarlo Stanton .40 1.00
10 Justin Verlander .40 1.00
11 Ichiro Suzuki .50 1.25
12 Drew Pomeranz RC .60 1.50
13 Josh Hamilton .30 .75
14 David Freese .25 .60
15 Robinson Cano .30 .75
16 Wilin Rosario RC .60 1.50
17 Paul Goldschmidt .40 1.00
18 Drew Hutchison RC .75 2.00
19 Michael Young .25 .60
20 Ryan Braun .25 .60
21 David Price .30 .75
22 Jordan Pacheco RC .60 1.50
23 Ian Kennedy .25 .60
24 Jacoby Ellsbury .30 .75
25 Troy Tulowitzki .40 1.00
26 Evan Longoria .30 .75
27 Nelson Cruz .40 1.00
28 Jered Weaver .30 .75
29 Kirk Nieuwenhuis RC .60 1.50
30 Prince Fielder .30 .75
31 Mark Teixeira .30 .75
32 Ryan Zimmerman .30 .75
33 Steve Lombardozzi RC .60 1.50
34 Drew Smyly RC .60 1.50
35 Yu Darvish RC 1.50 4.00
36 Yovani Gallardo .30 .75
37 Felix Hernandez .30 .75
38 David Wright .30 .75
39 Dan Uggla .30 .75
40 Matt Kemp .30 .75
41 Zack Cozart .25 .60
42 Mariano Rivera .50 1.25
43 Jarrod Parker RC .75 2.00
44 Jon Lester .25 .60
45 Adrian Beltre .40 1.00
46 Lance Berkman .30 .75
47 Kevin Youkilis .40 1.00
48 CC Sabathia .30 .75
49 Dustin Pedroia .40 1.00
50 Clayton Kershaw .60 1.50
51 Brad Peacock RC .60 1.50
52 Tyler Pastornicky RC .60 1.50
53 Buster Posey .50 1.25
54 Chase Utley .30 .75
55 Hanley Ramirez .30 .75
56 Devin Mesoraco RC .60 1.50
57 Paul Konerko .25 .60
58 Chipper Jones .40 1.00
59 Mark Trumbo .25 .60
60 Jose Bautista .30 .75
61 Carlos Gonzalez .30 .75
62 Ryan Howard .30 .75
63 Eric Hosmer .30 .75
64 Matt Dominguez RC .75 2.00
65 Brett Lawrie .30 .75
66 Hisashi Iwakuma RC 1.25 3.00
67 Matt Moore RC 1.00 2.50
68 Wily Peralta RC .60 1.50
69 Pablo Sandoval .30 .75
70 Miguel Cabrera .40 1.00
71 Dellin Betances RC 1.00 2.50
72 Jesus Montero RC .60 1.50
73 Bryce Harper RC 6.00 15.00
74 Tsuyoshi Wada RC .60 1.50
75 Cole Hamels .30 .75
76 Wade Miley .30 .75
77 Liam Hendriks RC .60 1.50
78 Mike Trout 12.00 30.00
79 Ian Kinsler .30 .75
80 Joey Votto .40 1.00
81 Austin Romine RC .60 1.50
82 Starlin Castro .30 .75
83 Joe Mauer .30 .75
84 Tim Lincecum .30 .75
85 Curtis Granderson .30 .75
86 Addison Reed RC .60 1.50
87 Eric Surkamp RC 1.00 2.50
88 Chris Parmelee RC .60 1.50
89 Adrian Gonzalez .30 .75
90 Jose Reyes .25 .60
91 Brett Pill RC 1.00 2.50
92 Trevor Bauer RC 3.00 8.00
93 Leonys Martin RC .60 1.50
94 Josh Beckett .25 .60
95 Brian Wilson .40 1.00
96 Joe Benson RC .60 1.50
97 Yoenis Cespedes RC 1.50 4.00
98 Mike Napoli .25 .60
99 Alex Liddi RC .25 .60
100 Roy Halladay .30 .75

2012 Finest Refractors

*REF: 1.2X TO 3X BASIC
*REF RC: .5X TO 1.2X BASIC RC

2012 Finest Gold Refractors

*GOLD REF: 8X TO 20X BASIC
*GOLD REF RC: 3X TO 8X BASIC RC
STATED ODDS 1:8 MINI BOX
STATED PRINT RUN 50 SER.#'d SETS
78 Mike Trout 400.00 1000.00

2012 Finest Green Refractors

*GREEN REF: 2X TO 5X BASIC
*GREEN REF RC: .75X TO 2X BASIC RC
STATED ODDS 1:2 MINI BOX
STATED PRINT RUN 199 SER.#'d SETS
78 Mike Trout 100.00 250.00

2012 Finest Orange Refractors

*ORANGE REF: 3X TO 8X BASIC
*ORANGE REF RC: 1.2X TO 3X BASIC RC
STATED ODDS 1:4 MINI BOX
STATED PRINT RUN 99 SER.#'d SETS
78 Mike Trout 150.00 400.00

2012 Finest X-Fractors

*X-FRAC: 2X TO 5X BASIC
*X-FRAC RC: .75X TO 2X BASIC RC

2012 Finest Autograph Rookie Mystery Exchange

STATED ODDS 1:72 MINI BOX
EXCHANGE DEADLINE 08/22/2013
SM Starling Marte 20.00 50.00
BJ Brett Jackson 4.00 10.00
MT Mike Trout 500.00 1200.00
JR Josh Rutledge 4.00 10.00
JS Jean Segura 10.00 25.00

2012 Finest Faces of the Franchise

AM Andrew McCutchen 1.50 4.00
AP Albert Pujols 2.00 5.00
BP Buster Posey 2.00 5.00
CJ Chipper Jones 1.50 4.00
DJ Derek Jeter 4.00 10.00
DP Dustin Pedroia 1.50 4.00
DW David Wright 1.25 3.00
EH Eric Hosmer 1.25 3.00
EHO Eric Hosmer 1.25 3.00
EL Evan Longoria 1.25 3.00
FH Felix Hernandez 1.25 3.00
HR Hanley Ramirez 1.25 3.00
JB Jose Bautista 1.25 3.00
JH Josh Hamilton 1.25 3.00
JM Joe Mauer 1.25 3.00
JU Justin Upton 1.25 3.00
JV Justin Verlander 1.50 4.00
JVO Joey Votto 1.50 4.00
MK Matt Kemp 1.25 3.00
RB Ryan Braun 1.00 2.50
RH Roy Halladay 1.25 3.00
RZ Ryan Zimmerman .75 2.00
SC Starlin Castro 1.25 3.00
TL Tim Lincecum 1.25 3.00
TT Troy Tulowitzki 1.50 4.00

2012 Finest Game Changers

AG Adrian Gonzalez 1.25 3.00
AP Albert Pujols 2.00 5.00
BP Buster Posey 2.00 5.00
CG Carlos Gonzalez 1.25 3.00
CJ Chipper Jones 1.50 4.00
GS Giancarlo Stanton 1.50 4.00
JB Jose Bautista 1.25 3.00
JH Jason Heyward 1.25 3.00
JMA Joe Mauer 1.25 3.00
JV Justin Verlander 1.50 4.00
MC Miguel Cabrera 1.00 2.50
MT Mike Trout 20.00 50.00
PF Prince Fielder 1.25 3.00
RB Ryan Braun 1.00 2.50
RH Roy Halladay 1.25 3.00

2012 Finest Moments

AG Adrian Gonzalez .75 2.00
BL Brett Lawrie .75 2.00
CH Cole Hamels .75 2.00
CK Clayton Kershaw 1.50 4.00
DA Dustin Ackley .60 1.50
DF David Freese .60 1.50
DU Dan Uggla .75 2.00
IK Ian Kennedy .60 1.50
JH Jeremy Hellickson .60 1.50
JJ Josh Johnson .75 2.00
JM Jason Motte .60 1.50
JV Justin Verlander 1.00 2.50
MC Miguel Cabrera 1.00 2.50
MM Matt Moore 1.00 2.50
MP Michael Pineda .60 1.50
NC Nelson Cruz 1.00 2.50
RC Robinson Cano .75 2.00
SS Stephen Strasburg 1.00 2.50
UJ Ubaldo Jimenez .60 1.50
YD Yu Darvish 1.50 4.00

2012 Finest Rookie Autographs Refractors

STATED ODDS 1:9 MINI BOX
PRINTING PLATE ODDS 1:427 MINI BOX
PLATE PRINT RUN 1 SET PER COLOR
BLACK-CYAN-MAGENTA-YELLOW ISSUED
NO PLATE PRICING DUE TO SCARCITY
EXCHANGE DEADLINE 07/31/2015
ARAR Addison Reed 4.00 10.00
ARARO Austin Romine 4.00 10.00
ARBD Brian Dozier 20.00 50.00
ARBH Bryce Harper 125.00 300.00
ARBP Brad Peacock 4.00 10.00
ARDB Dellin Betances 5.00 12.00
ARDH Drew Hutchison 4.00 10.00
ARDM Devin Mesoraco 4.00 10.00
ARDS Drew Smyly 6.00 15.00
ARJM Jesus Montero 6.00 15.00
ARJP Jordan Pacheco 4.00 10.00
ARJPA Jarrod Parker 5.00 12.00
ARJT Jacob Turner 4.00 10.00
ARKS Kirk Nieuwenhuis 4.00 10.00
ARLH Liam Hendriks 4.00 10.00
ARMM Matt Moore 4.00 10.00
ARRL Ryan Lavarnway 5.00 12.00
ARTM Tom Milone 4.00 10.00
ARTW Tsuyoshi Wada 6.00 15.00
ARWP Wily Peralta 4.00 10.00
ARYD Yu Darvish 40.00 100.00

2012 Finest Rookie Autographs Gold Refractors

*GOLD REF: 1X TO 2.5X BASIC REF
STATED ODDS 1:35 MINI BOX
STATED PRINT RUN 50 SER.#'d SETS
EXCHANGED DEADLINE 07/31/2015
ARBH Bryce Harper 200.00 500.00
ARYD Yu Darvish 75.00 200.00

2012 Finest Rookie Autographs Green Refractors

*GREEN REF: .4X TO 1X BASIC REF
STATED ODDS 1:10 MINI BOX
STATED PRINT RUN 199 SER.#'d SETS
EXCHANGED DEADLINE 07/31/2015

2012 Finest Rookie Autographs Orange Refractors

*ORANGE REF: .5X TO 1.2X BASIC REF
STATED ODDS 1:18 MINI BOX
STATED PRINT RUN 99 SER.#'d SETS
EXCHANGED DEADLINE 07/31/2015
ARBH Bryce Harper 150.00 400.00
ARYD Yu Darvish 60.00 150.00

2012 Finest Rookie Autographs X-Fractors

*X-FRAC: .4X TO 1X BASIC REF
STATED ODDS 1:7 MINI BOX
STATED PRINT RUN 299 SER.#'d SETS
EXCHANGED DEADLINE 07/31/2015

2012 Finest Rookie Jumbo Relic Autographs Refractors

STATED ODDS 1:18 MINI BOX
1-100 PLATE ODDS 1:358 MINI BOX
PLATE PRINT RUN 1 SET PER COLOR
NO PLATE PRICING DUE TO SCARCITY
EXCHANGE DEADLINE 07/31/2015
ARO Austin Romine 4.00 10.00
BH Bryce Harper 100.00 250.00
BL Brett Lawrie 5.00 12.00
BP Brad Peacock 4.00 10.00
CP Chris Parmelee 5.00 12.00
DM Devin Mesoraco 5.00 12.00
DP Drew Pomeranz 4.00 10.00
JM Jesus Montero 6.00 15.00
JP Jordan Pacheco 4.00 10.00
JPA Jarrod Parker 8.00 20.00
JVN Jordany Valdespin 4.00 10.00
LH Liam Hendriks 4.00 10.00
LM Leonys Martin 4.00 10.00
MA Matt Adams 12.50 30.00
MD Matt Dominguez 4.00 10.00
MM Matt Moore 8.00 20.00
RL Ryan Lavarnway 5.00 12.00
TB Trevor Bauer 20.00 50.00
TM Tom Milone 5.00 12.00
TP Tyler Pastornicky 5.00 12.00
WMI Will Middlebrooks 6.00 15.00
YA Yonder Alonso 4.00 10.00
YC Yoenis Cespedes 20.00 50.00
YD Yu Darvish 75.00 150.00
ZC Zack Cozart 6.00 15.00

2012 Finest Rookie Jumbo Relic Autographs Gold Refractors

*GOLD REF: .6X TO 1.5X BASIC REF
STATED ODDS 1:30 MINI BOX
STATED PRINT RUN 50 SER.#'d SETS
EXCHANGE DEADLINE 07/31/2015
DP Drew Pomeranz 10.00 25.00
YD Yu Darvish 100.00 200.00

2012 Finest Rookie Jumbo Relic Autographs Green Refractors

*GREEN REF: .4X TO 1X BASIC REF
STATED ODDS 1:8 MINI BOX
STATED PRINT RUN 199 SER.#'d SETS
EXCHANGE DEADLINE 07/31/2015

2012 Finest Rookie Jumbo Relic Autographs Orange Refractors

*ORANGE REF: .5X TO 1.2X BASIC REF
STATED ODDS 1:15 MINI BOX
STATED PRINT RUN 99 SER.#'d SETS
EXCHANGE DEADLINE 07/31/2015
BH Bryce Harper 150.00 400.00
YD Yu Darvish 100.00 200.00

2012 Finest Rookie Jumbo Relic Autographs X-Fractors

*XFRAC: .4X TO 1X BASIC REF
STATED ODDS 1:6 MINI BOX
STATED PRINT RUN 299 SER.#'d SETS
EXCHANGE DEADLINE 07/31/2015

1993 Flair Promos

COMPLETE SET (8) 150.00 300.00
0 Will Clark 15.00 40.00
0 Darren Daulton 6.00 15.00
0 Andres Galarraga 8.00 20.00
0 Bryan Harvey 4.00 10.00
0 David Justice 8.00 20.00
0 Jody Reed 4.00 10.00
0 Nolan Ryan 125.00 250.00
0 Sammy Sosa 30.00 80.00

2013 Finest

COMPLETE SET (100) 15.00 40.00
1-100 PLATE ODDS 1:151 MINI BOX
PLATE PRINT RUN 1 SET PER COLOR
BLACK-CYAN-MAGENTA-YELLOW ISSUED
NO PLATE PRICING DUE TO SCARCITY
1 Mike Trout 2.00 5.00
2 Derek Jeter .60 1.50
3 Michael Wacha RC .40 1.00
4 Ryan Howard .20 .50
5 Adrian Beltre .25 .60
6 CC Sabathia .20 .50
7 Avisail Garcia RC .40 1.00
8 Prince Fielder .20 .50
9 David Price .20 .50
10 Clayton Kershaw .40 1.00
11 Roy Halladay .20 .50
12 Carlos Gonzalez .20 .50
13 Andrew McCutchen .40 1.00
14 Dustin Pedroia .25 .60
15 Allen Webster RC .40 1.00
16 Dylan Bundy RC .40 1.00
17 David Freese .15 .40
18 Johnny Cueto .20 .50
19 Yadier Molina .25 .60
20 Stephen Strasburg .30 .75
21 Kevin Gausman RC 1.00 2.50
22 Pablo Sandoval .20 .50
23 Adrian Gonzalez .20 .50
24 Jake Odorizzi RC .40 1.00
25 Matt Kemp .20 .50
26 Paul Goldschmidt .40 1.00
27 Tony Cingrani RC .60 1.50
28 Cliff Lee .30 .75
29 Will Middlebrooks .20 .50
30 Buster Posey .30 .75
31 Aroldis Chapman .25 .60
32 Mike Zunino RC .50 1.25
33 Wil Myers RC .50 1.25
34 Jason Heyward .20 .50
35 Troy Tulowitzki .40 1.00
36 Billy Butler .15 .40
37 Nolan Arenado RC 12.00 30.00
38 Adeiny Hechavarria RC .40 1.00
39 Jackie Bradley Jr. RC .75 2.00
40 Felix Hernandez .30 .75
41 Bruce Rondon RC .30 .75
42 Mariano Rivera .30 .75
43 Joey Votto .40 1.00
44 Kyuji Fujikawa RC .50 1.25
45 Didi Gregorius RC 1.25 3.00
46 Edwin Encarnacion .25 .60
47 Hyun-Jin Ryu RC .75 2.00
48 Cole Hamels .20 .50
49 Austin Jackson .15 .40
50 Justin Verlander .20 .50
51 Tyler Skaggs RC .50 1.25
52 Evan Longoria .30 .75
53 Chris Sale .40 1.00
54 Evan Gattis RC .60 1.50
55 David Wright .20 .50
56 Rob Brantly RC .30 .75
57 Kyle Gibson RC .50 1.25
58 Marcell Ozuna RC .75 2.00
59 Jose Fernandez RC .75 2.00
60 Yu Darvish .25 .60
61 Albert Pujols .50 1.25
62 Jurickson Profar RC .40 1.00
63 Jered Weaver .30 .75
64 Anthony Rendon RC 2.00 5.00
65 Robinson Cano .20 .50
66 Jose Bautista .20 .50
67 Joe Mauer .30 .75
68 Jose Reyes .20 .50
69 Shelby Miller RC .75 2.00
70 Miguel Cabrera .25 .60
71 Zack Wheeler RC .60 1.50
72 Anthony Rizzo .30 .75
73 Yoenis Cespedes .25 .60
74 R.A. Dickey .30 .75
75 Justin Upton .20 .50
76 Matt Harvey .20 .50
77 Carlos Beltran .20 .50
78 Jacoby Ellsbury .20 .50
79 Mike Olt RC .40 1.00
80 Manny Machado RC 2.00 5.00
81 Giancarlo Stanton .40 1.00
82 Oswaldo Arcia RC .30 .75
83 Freddie Freeman .50 1.25
84 Tim Lincecum .20 .50
85 Adam Wainwright .30 .75
86 Adam Jones .20 .50
87 Josh Hamilton .30 .75
88 Matt Cain .20 .50
89 Carlos Martinez RC .50 1.25
90 Ryan Braun .20 .50
91 Yasiel Puig RC 1.25 3.00
92 Mark Trumbo .25 .60
93 Nick Franklin RC .40 1.00
94 Adam Eaton RC .50 1.25
95 Trevor Rosenthal RC .60 1.50
96 Jedd Gyorko RC .40 1.00
97 Jeurys Familia RC .50 1.25
98 Starlin Castro .15 .40
99 Gerrit Cole RC 2.00 5.00
100 Bryce Harper .40 1.00

2013 Finest Gold Refractors

*GOLD REF: 10X TO 25X BASIC
*GOLD REF RC: 5X TO 12X BASIC RC
STATED ODDS 1:13 MINI BOX
STATED PRINT RUN 50 SER.#'d SETS
80 Manny Machado 30.00 60.00
91 Yasiel Puig 60.00 120.00

2013 Finest Green Refractors

*GREEN REF: 2.5X TO 6X BASIC
*GREEN REF RC: 1.2X TO 3X BASIC RC
STATED ODDS 1:4 MINI BOX
STATED PRINT RUN 199 SER.#'d SETS
91 Yasiel Puig 15.00 40.00

2013 Finest Orange Refractors

*ORANGE REF: 5X TO 12X BASIC
*ORANGE REF RC: 2.5X TO 6X BASIC RC
STATED ODDS 1:7 MINI BOX
STATED PRINT RUN 99 SER.#'d SETS
1 Mike Trout 12.50 30.00
2 Derek Jeter 12.50 30.00
91 Yasiel Puig 20.00 50.00

2013 Finest Refractors

*REF: 1.5X TO 4X BASIC
*REF RC: .75X TO 2X BASIC

2013 Finest X-Fractors

*X-FRACTOR: 2X TO 5X BASIC
*X-FRACTOR RC: 1X TO 2.5X BASIC
91 Yasiel Puig 10.00 25.00

2013 Finest 93 Finest

STATED ODDS 1:4 MINI BOX
AC Aroldis Chapman 1.50 4.00
AG Adrian Gonzalez 1.25 3.00
AJ Austin Jackson 1.00 2.50
AP Andy Pettitte 1.25 3.00
AR Alex Rodriguez 2.00 5.00
ARI Anthony Rizzo 2.00 5.00
AS Andrelton Simmons 1.00 2.50
AW Adam Wainwright 1.25 3.00
BB Billy Butler 1.00 2.50
BL Brett Lawrie 1.25 3.00
BP Brandon Phillips 1.00 2.50
CB Carlos Beltran 1.25 3.00
CD Chris Davis 1.25 3.00
CG Curtis Granderson 1.25 3.00
CH Cole Hamels 1.25 3.00
CK Clayton Kershaw 2.50 6.00
CL Cliff Lee 1.25 3.00
CR Carlos Ruiz 1.00 2.50
CS Carlos Santana 1.25 3.00
CU Chase Utley 1.25 3.00
DB Dylan Bundy 2.50 6.00
DO David Ortiz 1.50 4.00
DP David Price 1.25 3.00
DPE Dustin Pedroia 1.50 4.00
EE Edwin Encarnacion 1.50 4.00
EH Eric Hosmer 1.25 3.00
FF Freddie Freeman 2.00 5.00
GG Gio Gonzalez 1.25 3.00
HJR Hyun-Jin Ryu 2.50 6.00
HR Hanley Ramirez 1.25 3.00
IK Ian Kinsler 1.25 3.00
JB Jackie Bradley Jr. 2.50 6.00
JC Johnny Cueto 1.25 3.00
JE Jacoby Ellsbury 1.25 3.00
JF Jose Fernandez 2.50 6.00
JH Jason Heyward 1.25 3.00
JP Jurickson Profar 1.25 3.00
JR Josh Reddick 1.00 2.50
JRO Jimmy Rollins 1.25 3.00
JS James Shields 1.00 2.50
JSM Jeff Samardzija 1.00 2.50
JU Justin Upton 1.25 3.00
JV Joey Votto 1.50 4.00
JZ Jordan Zimmermann 1.25 3.00
KM Kris Medlen 1.25 3.00
MB Madison Bumgarner 1.25 3.00
MH Matt Holliday 1.50 4.00
MHA Matt Harvey 1.25 3.00
MK Matt Kemp 1.25 3.00
MM Manny Machado 6.00 15.00
MMO Matt Moore 1.25 3.00
MN Mike Napoli 1.00 2.50
MR Mariano Rivera 8.00 20.00

MT Mike Trout 20.00 50.00
MTE Mark Teixeira 1.25 3.00
MTR Mark Trumbo 1.00 2.50
RH Ryan Howard 1.25 3.00
RHA Roy Halladay 1.25 3.00
RZ Ryan Zimmerman 1.25 3.00
SC Starlin Castro 1.00 2.50
SP Salvador Perez 1.25 3.00
TH Torii Hunter 1.00 2.50
TL Tim Lincecum 1.25 3.00
WM Will Middlebrooks 1.00 2.50
YC Yoenis Cespedes 1.50 4.00
YM Yadier Molina 2.00 5.00
YP Yasiel Puig 12.50 30.00
ZG Zack Greinke 1.50 4.00

2013 Finest 93 Finest All-Star

STATED ODDS 1:12 MINI BOX
AB Adrian Beltre 3.00 8.00
AJ Adam Jones 2.50 6.00
AM Andrew McCutchen 3.00 8.00
AP Albert Pujols 4.00 10.00
BH Bryce Harper 20.00 50.00
BP Buster Posey 4.00 10.00
CC CC Sabathia 2.50 6.00
CG Carlos Gonzalez 2.50 6.00
CK Craig Kimbrel 2.50 6.00
CS Chris Sale 3.00 8.00
DF David Freese 2.00 5.00
DJ Derek Jeter 20.00 50.00
DW David Wright 2.50 6.00
EL Evan Longoria 2.50 6.00
FH Felix Hernandez 2.50 6.00
GS Giancarlo Stanton 3.00 8.00
JB Jose Bautista 2.50 6.00
JH Josh Hamilton 2.50 6.00
JM Joe Mauer 2.50 6.00
JR Jose Reyes 2.50 6.00
JV Justin Verlander 3.00 8.00
JW Jered Weaver 2.50 6.00
MC Matt Cain 2.50 6.00
MCA Miguel Cabrera 3.00 8.00
PF Prince Fielder 2.50 6.00
PS Pablo Sandoval 2.50 6.00
RB Ryan Braun 2.50 6.00
RC Robinson Cano 2.50 6.00
RD R.A. Dickey 2.50 6.00
SS Stephen Strasburg 3.00 8.00
TT Troy Tulowitzki 3.00 8.00
YD Yu Darvish 3.00 8.00

2013 Finest Autograph Rookie Mystery Exchange

STATED ODDS 1:201 MINI BOX
STATED PRINT RUN 100 SER.#'d SETS
EXCHANGE DEADLINE 9/30/2016
RR1 Wil Myers 10.00 25.00
RR2 Shelby Miller 5.00 12.00
RR3 Evan Gattis 12.00 30.00

2013 Finest Masters Refractors

STATED ODDS 1:61 MINI BOX
STATED PRINT RUN 50 SER.#'d SETS
AP Albert Pujols 8.00 20.00
BH Bryce Harper 10.00 25.00
BP Buster Posey 20.00 50.00
CG Carlos Gonzalez 5.00 12.00
CK Clayton Kershaw 10.00 25.00
DJ Derek Jeter 75.00 150.00
DP David Price 5.00 12.00
EL Evan Longoria 5.00 12.00
FH Felix Hernandez 5.00 12.00
GS Giancarlo Stanton 6.00 15.00
JH Josh Hamilton 5.00 12.00
JV Justin Verlander 6.00 15.00
JW Jered Weaver 5.00 12.00
MC Miguel Cabrera 8.00 20.00
MR Mariano Rivera 20.00 50.00
MT Mike Trout 50.00 125.00
RB Ryan Braun 5.00 12.00
RC Robinson Cano 5.00 12.00
SS Stephen Strasburg 6.00 15.00
YD Yu Darvish 6.00 15.00

2013 Finest Prodigies Die Cut Refractors

STATED ODDS 1:24 MINI BOX
PBH Bryce Harper 12.50 30.00
PGS Giancarlo Stanton 2.00 5.00
PJP Jurickson Profar 1.50 4.00
PMH Matt Harvey 1.50 4.00
PMM Manny Machado 8.00 20.00
PMT Mike Trout 12.50 30.00
PSS Stephen Strasburg 2.00 5.00
PYC Yoenis Cespedes 2.00 5.00
PYD Yu Darvish 2.00 5.00
PYP Yasiel Puig 25.00 60.00

2013 Finest Rookie Autographs Gold Refractors

*GOLD REF: .6X TO 1.5X BASIC
STATED ODDS 1:21 MINI BOX
STATED PRINT RUN 50 SER.#'d SETS
EXCHANGE DEADLINE 9/30/2016
DR Darin Ruf 12.50 30.00
MZ Mike Zunino 20.00 50.00

2013 Finest Rookie Autographs Green Refractors

*GREEN REF: .4X TO 1X BASIC
STATED ODDS 1:21 HOBBY
STATED PRINT RUN 125 SER.#'d SETS
EXCHANGE DEADLINE 9/30/2016

2013 Finest Rookie Autographs Orange Refractors

*ORANGE REF: .5X TO 1.2X BASIC
STATED ODDS 1:27 HOBBY
STATED PRINT RUN 99 SER.#'d SETS
EXCHANGE DEADLINE 9/30/2016

2013 Finest Rookie Autographs Refractors

PRINTING PLATE ODDS 1:655 MINI BOX
PLATE PRINT RUN 1 SET PER COLOR
BLACK-CYAN-MAGENTA-YELLOW ISSUED
NO PLATE PRICING DUE TO SCARCITY
EXCHANGE DEADLINE 09/30/2016
AE Adam Eaton 5.00 12.00
AG Avisail Garcia 4.00 10.00
AH Adeiny Hechavarria 3.00 8.00
AM Alfredo Marte 3.00 8.00
BM Brandon Maurer 3.00 8.00
CM Carlos Martinez 6.00 15.00
DB Dylan Bundy 6.00 15.00
DG Didi Gregorius 15.00 40.00
DR Darin Ruf 4.00 10.00
EG Evan Gattis 5.00 12.00
JF Jeurys Familia 3.00 8.00
JFZ Jose Fernandez 20.00 50.00
JG Jedd Gyorko 3.00 8.00
JO Jake Odorizzi 3.00 8.00
JP Jurickson Profar 5.00 12.00
KG Kyle Gibson 3.00 8.00
LH L.J. Hoes 3.00 8.00
MM Manny Machado 25.00 60.00
MO Mike Olt 4.00 10.00
MZ Mike Zunino 4.00 10.00
SM Shelby Miller 4.00 10.00
TCI Tony Cingrani 3.00 8.00
TS Tyler Skaggs 3.00 8.00
WM Wil Myers 8.00 20.00

2013 Finest Rookie Autographs X-Fractors

*X-FRACTORS: .4X TO 1X BASIC
STATED ODDS 1:18 HOBBY
STATED PRINT RUN 149 SER.#'d SETS
EXCHANGE DEADLINE 9/30/2016

2013 Finest Rookie Jumbo Relic Autographs Gold Refractors

*GOLD REF: .6X TO 1.5X BASIC
STATED ODDS 1:29 MINI BOX
STATED PRINT RUN 50 SER.#'d SETS
EXCHANGE DEADLINE 9/30/2016
YP Yasiel Puig 50.00 120.00

2013 Finest Rookie Jumbo Relic Autographs Green Refractors

*GREEN REF: .4X TO 1X BASIC
STATED ODDS 1:14 HOBBY
STATED PRINT RUN 125 SER.#'d SETS
EXCHANGE DEADLINE 9/30/2016

2013 Finest Rookie Jumbo Relic Autographs Orange Refractors

*ORANGE REF: .5X TO 1.2X BASIC
STATED ODDS 1:15 HOBBY
STATED PRINT RUN 99 SER.#'d SETS
EXCHANGE DEADLINE 9/30/2016
YP Yasiel Puig 40.00 100.00

2013 Finest Rookie Jumbo Relic Autographs Refractors

PRINTING PLATE ODDS 1:359 MINI BOX
PLATE PRINT RUN 1 SET PER COLOR
BLACK-CYAN-MAGENTA-YELLOW ISSUED
NO PLATE PRICING DUE TO SCARCITY
EXCHANGE DEADLINE 09/30/2016
AE Adam Eaton 4.00 10.00
AG Avisail Garcia 5.00 12.00
AG2 Avisail Garcia 4.00 10.00
AHI Aaron Hicks 5.00 12.00
AR Anthony Rendon 20.00 50.00
AR2 Anthony Rendon 20.00 50.00
AW Allen Webster 4.00 10.00
BM Brandon Maurer 4.00 10.00
BR Bruce Rondon 4.00 10.00
CK Casey Kelly 4.00 10.00
CM Carlos Martinez 8.00 20.00
CY Christian Yelich 75.00 200.00
DB Dylan Bundy 10.00 25.00
DG Didi Gregorius 4.00 10.00
DG2 Didi Gregorius 4.00 10.00
DR Darin Ruf 4.00 10.00
EG Evan Gattis 5.00 12.00
GC Gerrit Cole 20.00 50.00
HJR Hyun-Jin Ryu 12.00 30.00
JB Jackie Bradley Jr. 20.00 50.00
JC Jarred Cosart 4.00 10.00
JFE Jose Fernandez 20.00 50.00
JG Jedd Gyorko 4.00 10.00
JO Jake Odorizzi 4.00 10.00
JP Jurickson Profar 6.00 15.00
KF Kyuji Fujikawa 4.00 10.00
MM Manny Machado 30.00 80.00
MO Mike Olt 4.00 10.00
MO2 Mike Olt 4.00 10.00
MZ Mike Zunino 6.00 15.00
NA Nolan Arenado 60.00 150.00
OA Oswaldo Arcia EXCH 4.00 10.00
PR Paco Rodriguez 4.00 10.00
RB Rob Brantly 4.00 10.00
SM Shelby Miller 5.00 12.00
TC Tony Cingrani EXCH 5.00 12.00
TCL Tyler Cloyd 4.00 10.00
TR Trevor Rosenthal 6.00 15.00
TS Tyler Skaggs 4.00 10.00
WM Wil Myers 10.00 25.00
YP Yasiel Puig EXCH 30.00 80.00
ZW Zack Wheeler 6.00 15.00

2013 Finest Rookie Jumbo Relic Autographs X-Fractors

*X-FRACTORS: .4X TO 1X BASIC
STATED ODDS 1:12 HOBBY
STATED PRINT RUN 149 SER.#'d SETS
EXCHANGE DEADLINE 9/30/2016

2014 Finest

COMPLETE SET (100) 15.00 40.00
1-100 PLATE ODDS 1:110 MINI BOX
PLATE PRINT RUN 1 SET PER COLOR
BLACK-CYAN-MAGENTA-YELLOW ISSUED
NO PLATE PRICING DUE TO SCARCITY
1 Miguel Cabrera .30 .75
2 Adam Wainwright .25 .60
3 Luis Sardinas RC .40 1.00
4 Alex Rios .25 .60
5 Alex Guerrero RC .50 1.25
6 Michael Choice RC .40 1.00
7 Tim Beckham RC .60 1.50
8 Jay Bruce .25 .60
9 Matt Kemp .25 .60
10 Jimmy Nelson RC .40 1.00
11 Max Scherzer .30 .75
12 Buster Posey .40 1.00
13 Adrian Beltre .30 .75
14 Carlos Gomez .20 .50
15 Kolten Wong RC .50 1.25
16 Andre Rienzo RC .40 1.00
17 Matt Davidson RC .50 1.25
18 Chris Davis .20 .50
19 Madison Bumgarner .25 .60
20 Paul Goldschmidt .30 .75
21 Billy Hamilton RC .50 1.25
22 Jose Abreu RC 3.00 8.00
23 Prince Fielder .25 .60
24 Andrew McCutchen .30 .75
25 Clayton Kershaw .50 1.25
26 Rafael Montero RC .40 1.00
27 David Wright .25 .60
28 Chris Owings RC .40 1.00
29 Dustin Pedroia .30 .75
30 Carlos Gonzalez .25 .60
31 Marcus Semien RC 2.00 5.00
32 John Ryan Murphy RC .40 1.00
33 Ian Kinsler .25 .60
34 Enny Romero RC .40 1.00
35 Wil Myers .20 .50
36 C.J. Cron RC .40 1.00
37 Ryan Braun .25 .60
38 Yu Darvish .30 .75
39 George Springer RC 1.50 4.00
40 Rougned Odor RC 1.00 2.50
41 Jason Heyward .25 .60
42 Michael Wacha .25 .60
43 Joey Votto .30 .75
44 Josmil Pinto RC .40 1.00
45 Freddie Freeman .40 1.00
46 Cliff Lee .25 .60
47 Jacoby Ellsbury .25 .60
48 Bryce Harper .50 1.25
49 Gerrit Cole .30 .75
50 Yasiel Puig .30 .75
51 Taijuan Walker RC .40 1.00
52 Christian Bethancourt RC .40 1.00
53 Jose Bautista .25 .60
54 Derek Jeter .75 2.00
55 David Ortiz .30 .75
56 Manny Machado .30 .75
57 Felix Hernandez .25 .60
58 Adam Jones .25 .60
59 Jonathan Schoop RC .40 1.00
60 Joe Mauer .25 .60
61 Jason Kipnis .25 .60
62 Josh Donaldson .25 .60
63 Yangervis Solarte RC .40 1.00
64 David Price .25 .60
65 Ian Desmond .20 .50
66 Yadier Molina .40 1.00
67 Eric Hosmer .25 .60
68 Edwin Encarnacion .30 .75
69 Shin-Soo Choo .25 .60
70 Robinson Cano .25 .60
71 Aroldis Chapman .30 .75
72 Pedro Alvarez .20 .50
73 Craig Kimbrel .25 .60
74 Trevor Rosenthal .25 .60
75 Masahiro Tanaka RC 1.25 3.00
76 Erisbel Arruebarrena RC .40 1.00
77 Anthony Rizzo .40 1.00
78 Chris Sale .30 .75
79 Erik Johnson RC .40 1.00
80 Troy Tulowitzki .30 .75
81 Jose Ramirez RC 3.00 8.00
82 Yordano Ventura RC .50 1.25
83 Giancarlo Stanton .30 .75
84 Travis d'Arnaud RC .50 1.25
85 Justin Verlander .30 .75
86 Matt Holliday .30 .75
87 Carlos Santana .25 .60
88 Stephen Strasburg .30 .75
89 Xander Bogaerts RC 1.25 3.00
90 Marcus Stroman RC .60 1.50
91 Nick Castellanos .60 1.50
92 Evan Longoria .25 .60
93 Albert Pujols .40 1.00
94 Jake Marisnick RC .40 1.00
95 Jose Reyes .25 .60
96 Justin Upton .25 .60
97 Jose Fernandez .30 .75
98 Wilmer Flores RC .50 1.25
99 Hanley Ramirez .25 .60
100 Mike Trout 1.50 4.00

2014 Finest Black Refractors

*BLACK REF: 4X TO 10X BASIC
*BLACK REF RC: 2X TO 5X BASIC RC
STATED ODDS 1:5 MINI BOXES
STATED PRINT RUN 99 SER.#'d SETS
22 Jose Abreu 15.00 40.00
100 Mike Trout 15.00 40.00

2014 Finest Blue Refractors

*BLUE REF: 3X TO 8X BASIC
*BLUE REF RC: 1.5X TO 4X BASIC RC
STATED ODDS 1:4 MINI BOXES
STATED PRINT RUN 125 SER.#'d SETS

2014 Finest Gold Refractors

*GOLD REF: 5X TO 12X BASIC
*GOLD REF RC: 2.5X TO 6X BASIC RC
STATED ODDS 1:9 MINI BOXES
STATED PRINT RUN 50 SER.#'d SETS
22 Jose Abreu 20.00 50.00
54 Derek Jeter 15.00 40.00
100 Mike Trout 15.00 40.00

2014 Finest Green Refractors

*GREEN REF: 3X TO 8X BASIC
*GREEN REF RC: 1.5X TO 4X BASIC RC
STATED ODDS 1:3 MINI BOXES
STATED PRINT RUN 199 SER.#'d SETS
100 Mike Trout 12.00 30.00

2014 Finest Orange Refractors

*ORANGE REF: 2.5X TO 6X BASIC
*ORANGE REF RC: 1.2X TO 3X BASIC RC
RANDOM INSERTS IN HOT BOXES
54 Derek Jeter 10.00 25.00

2014 Finest Red Refractors

*RED REF: 8X TO 20X BASIC
*RED REF RC: 4X TO 10X BASIC RC
STATED ODDS 1:18 MINI BOXES
STATED PRINT RUN 25 SER.#'d SETS
100 Mike Trout 60.00 120.00

2014 Finest Refractors

*REF: 1X TO 2.5X BASIC
*REF RC: .5X TO 1.2X BASIC RC
RANDOM INSERTS IN MINI BOXES

2014 Finest X-Fractors

*X-FRACTOR: 1.5X TO 4X BASIC
*X-FRACTOR RC: .75X TO 2X BASIC RC
RANDOM INSERTS IN MINI BOXES

2014 Finest 94 Finest

RANDOM INSERTS IN PACKS
94FAJ Adam Jones .75 2.00
94FAM Andrew McCutchen 1.00 2.50
94FBH Bryce Harper 1.50 4.00
94FBHA Billy Hamilton .75 2.00
94FBP Buster Posey 1.25 3.00
94FCK Clayton Kershaw 1.50 4.00
94FDJ Derek Jeter 2.50 6.00
94FDP Dustin Pedroia 1.00 2.50
94FEL Evan Longoria .75 2.00
94FFH Felix Hernandez .75 2.00
94FGS George Springer 2.50 6.00
94FJA Jose Abreu 5.00 12.00
94FJF Jose Fernandez 1.00 2.50
94FJM Joe Mauer .75 2.00
94FJU Justin Upton .75 2.00
94FMC Miguel Cabrera 1.00 2.50
94FMM Manny Machado 1.00 2.50
94FMT Mike Trout 5.00 12.00
94FMTA Masahiro Tanaka 3.00 8.00
94FSS Stephen Strasburg 1.00 2.50
94FTT Troy Tulowitzki 1.00 2.50
94FTW Taijuan Walker .60 1.50
94FWM Wil Myers .60 1.50
94FXB Xander Bogaerts 2.00 5.00
94FYP Yasiel Puig 1.00 2.50

2014 Finest 94 Finest Refractors

*REFRACTORS: 10X TO 25X BASIC
STATED ODDS 1:71 MINI BOX
STATED PRINT RUN 25 SER.#'d SETS
94FDJ Derek Jeter 125.00 250.00
94FJA Jose Abreu 75.00 150.00
94FMT Mike Trout 125.00 250.00

2014 Finest Competitors Refractors

STATED ODDS 1:44 MINI BOX
FCAJ Adam Jones 4.00 10.00
FCAM Andrew McCutchen 5.00 12.00
FCBH Bryce Harper 10.00 25.00
FCBP Buster Posey 6.00 15.00
FCCK Clayton Kershaw 8.00 20.00
FCDO David Ortiz 5.00 12.00
FCDP Dustin Pedroia 5.00 12.00
FCDW David Wright 4.00 10.00
FCEL Evan Longoria 4.00 10.00
FCJE Jacoby Ellsbury 4.00 10.00
FCJF Jose Fernandez 5.00 12.00
FCJV Justin Verlander 5.00 12.00
FCMC Miguel Cabrera 5.00 12.00
FCMT Mike Trout 75.00 150.00
FCPG Paul Goldschmidt 5.00 12.00
FCRC Robinson Cano 4.00 10.00
FCTT Troy Tulowitzki 5.00 12.00
FCWM Wil Myers 3.00 8.00
FCYD Yu Darvish 5.00 12.00
FCYP Yasiel Puig 5.00 12.00

2014 Finest Competitors Gold Refractors

*GOLD REFRACTORS: 1X TO 2.5X BASIC
STATED ODDS 1:88 MINI BOX
STATED PRINT RUN 25 SER.#'d SETS
FCMT Mike Trout 150.00 300.00

2014 Finest Greats Autographs Black Refractors

STATED ODDS 1:222 MINI BOX
STATED PRINT RUN 99 SER.#'d SETS
FGAEB Ernie Banks 50.00 120.00
FGAMR Mariano Rivera 100.00 250.00
FGAMS Mike Schmidt 40.00 100.00
FGAOS Ozzie Smith 25.00 60.00
FGARY Robin Yount 30.00 80.00
FGASC Steve Carlton 15.00 40.00
FGASK Sandy Koufax 200.00 300.00

2014 Finest Greats Autographs Blue Refractors

STATED ODDS 1:176 MINI BOX
STATED PRINT RUN 125 SER.#'d SETS
FGABJ Bo Jackson 50.00 150.00
FGAEB Ernie Banks 50.00 120.00
FGAMS Mike Schmidt 40.00 100.00
FGAOS Ozzie Smith 25.00 60.00
FGASC Steve Carlton 15.00 40.00

2014 Finest Greats Autographs Gold Refractors

STATED ODDS 1:176 MINI BOX
STATED PRINT RUN 50 SER.#'d SETS
FGABJ Bo Jackson 60.00 150.00
FGAEB Ernie Banks 60.00 150.00
FGAKG Ken Griffey Jr. 200.00 300.00
FGALB Lou Brock 15.00 40.00
FGAMM Mark McGwire 100.00 250.00
FGAMR Mariano Rivera 125.00 300.00
FGAMS Mike Schmidt 50.00 120.00
FGAOS Ozzie Smith 40.00 100.00
FGARJ Randy Johnson 100.00 200.00
FGARY Robin Yount 40.00 100.00
FGASC Steve Carlton 20.00 50.00
FGASK Sandy Koufax 300.00 400.00

2014 Finest Greats Autographs Red Refractors

STATED ODDS 1:352 MINI BOX
STATED PRINT RUN 25 SER.#'d SETS
FGABJ Bo Jackson 75.00 200.00
FGAEB Ernie Banks 75.00 200.00
FGAKG Ken Griffey Jr. 250.00 400.00
FGALB Lou Brock 20.00 50.00
FGAMM Mark McGwire 150.00 300.00
FGAMR Mariano Rivera 150.00 400.00
FGAMS Mike Schmidt 60.00 150.00
FGAOS Ozzie Smith 50.00 120.00
FGARJ Randy Johnson 125.00 250.00
FGARY Robin Yount 60.00 150.00
FGASC Steve Carlton 25.00 60.00
FGASK Sandy Koufax 350.00 500.00

2014 Finest Greats Autographs X-Fractors

STATED ODDS 1:148 MINI BOX
STATED PRINT RUN 149 SER.#'d SETS
FGALB Lou Brock 12.00 30.00
FGAMR Mariano Rivera 100.00 250.00
FGARY Robin Yount 30.00 80.00

2014 Finest Rookie Autographs

OVERALL ONE AUTO PER MINI BOX
RAAG Alex Guerrero 4.00 10.00
RAAL Andrew Lambo 3.00 8.00
RACB Christian Bethancourt 3.00 8.00
RACO Chris Owings 3.00 8.00
RAEB Eddie Butler 3.00 8.00
RAEM Ethan Martin 3.00 8.00
RAER Enny Romero 3.00 8.00
RAGP Gregory Polanco 6.00 15.00
RAGS George Springer 20.00 50.00
RAJA Jose Abreu 20.00 50.00
RAJM J.R. Murphy 3.00 8.00
RAJMA Jake Marisnick 3.00 8.00
RAJPI Josmil Pinto 3.00 8.00
RAJR Jose Ramirez 40.00 100.00
RAJS Jonathan Schoop 3.00 8.00
RAKW Kolten Wong 4.00 10.00
RAMC Michael Choice 3.00 8.00
RAMD Matt Davidson 4.00 10.00
RANC Nick Castellanos 10.00 25.00
RAOG Onelki Garcia 3.00 8.00
RATM Tommy Medica 3.00 8.00
RATW Taijuan Walker 3.00 8.00
RAWF Wilmer Flores 4.00 10.00
RAYV Yordano Ventura 4.00 10.00

2014 Finest Rookie Autographs Refractors

*REF: .5X TO 1.2X BASIC
OVERALL ONE AUTO PER MINI BOX

2014 Finest Rookie Autographs Black Refractors

*BLACK REF: .6X TO 1.5X BASIC
STATED ODDS 1:18 MINI BOX
STATED PRINT RUN 99 SER.#'d SETS
RAAH Andrew Heaney 5.00 12.00
RAEA Erisbel Arruebarrena 20.00 50.00
RAOT Oscar Taveras 6.00 15.00
RAXB Xander Bogaerts 20.00 50.00

2014 Finest Rookie Autographs Blue Refractors

*BLUE REF: .6X TO 1.5X BASIC
STATED ODDS 1:14 MINI BOX
STATED PRINT RUN 125 SER.#'d SETS
RAAH Andrew Heaney 5.00 12.00
RAEA Erisbel Arruebarrena 20.00 50.00
RAOT Oscar Taveras 6.00 15.00
RAXB Xander Bogaerts 20.00 50.00

2014 Finest Rookie Autographs Gold Refractors

*GOLD REF: .75X TO 2X BASIC
STATED ODDS 1:34 MINI BOX
STATED PRINT RUN 50 SER.#'d SETS
RAAH Andrew Heaney 6.00 15.00
RAEA Erisbel Arruebarrena 25.00 60.00
RAOT Oscar Taveras 8.00 20.00
RAXB Xander Bogaerts 25.00 60.00

2014 Finest Rookie Autographs Red Refractors

*RED REF: 1X TO 2.5X BASIC
STATED ODDS 1:68 MINI BOX
STATED PRINT RUN 25 SER.#'d SETS
RAAH Andrew Heaney 8.00 20.00
RAEA Erisbel Arruebarrena 30.00 80.00
RAOT Oscar Taveras 10.00 25.00

2014 Finest Rookie Autographs X-Fractors

*X-FRACTORS: .6X TO 1.5X BASIC
STATED ODDS 1:12 MINI BOX
STATED PRINT RUN 149 SER.#'d SETS
RAAH Andrew Heaney 5.00 12.00
RAEA Erisbel Arruebarrena 15.00 40.00
RAOT Oscar Taveras 6.00 15.00
RAXB Xander Bogaerts 20.00 50.00

2014 Finest Rookie Autographs Mystery Exchange

RANDOM INSERTS IN PACKS
1 Sandy Koufax EXCH 150.00 300.00
2 Jacob deGrom EXCH
3 Kennys Vargas EXCH 15.00 40.00

2014 Finest Sterling Refractors

STATED ODDS 1:2 MINI BOX
TSAJ Adam Jones 1.00 2.50
TSAM Andrew McCutchen 1.25 3.00
TSBH Bryce Harper 2.00 5.00
TSBHA Billy Hamilton 1.00 2.50
TSBP Buster Posey 1.50 4.00
TSCD Chris Davis .75 2.00
TSCG Carlos Gonzalez 1.00 2.50
TSCK Clayton Kershaw 2.00 5.00
TSDJ Derek Jeter 3.00 8.00
TSDO David Ortiz 1.25 3.00
TSDW David Wright 1.00 2.50
TSFH Felix Hernandez 1.00 2.50
TSGS Giancarlo Stanton 1.25 3.00
TSJA Jose Abreu 6.00 15.00
TSJF Jose Fernandez 1.25 3.00
TSMC Miguel Cabrera 1.25 3.00
TSMM Manny Machado 1.25 3.00
TSMT Mike Trout 6.00 15.00
TSMTA Masahiro Tanaka 2.50 6.00
TSMW Michael Wacha 1.00 2.50
TSPG Paul Goldschmidt 1.25 3.00
TSRC Robinson Cano 1.00 2.50
TSTW Taijuan Walker .75 2.00
TSYD Yu Darvish 1.25 3.00
TSYP Yasiel Puig 1.25 3.00

2014 Finest Sterling Gold Refractors

*GOLD REF: 3X TO 8X BASIC
STATED ODDS 1:71 MINI BOX
STATED PRINT RUN 25 SER.#'d SETS
TSDJ Derek Jeter 150.00 250.00
TSJA Jose Abreu 75.00 150.00
TSMT Mike Trout 150.00 250.00

2014 Finest Vintage Refractors

STATED ODDS 1:2 MINI BOX
FVBG Bob Gibson .75 2.00
FVDS Duke Snider .75 2.00
FVGS Greg Maddux 1.25 3.00
FVHA Hank Aaron 2.00 5.00
FVJB Johnny Bench 1.00 2.50
FVMP Mike Piazza 1.00 2.50
FVMS Mike Schmidt 1.50 4.00
FVNR Nolan Ryan 3.00 8.00
FVOZ Ozzie Smith 1.25 3.00
FVRH Rickey Henderson 1.00 2.50
FVSK Sandy Koufax 2.00 5.00
FVTG Tony Gwynn 1.00 2.50
FVTS Tom Seaver .75 2.00
FVWM Willie Mays 2.00 5.00
FVYB Yogi Berra 1.00 2.50

2014 Finest Vintage Gold Refractors

*GOLD REF: 3X TO 8X BASIC
STATED ODDS 1:117 MINI BOX
STATED PRINT RUN 25 SER.#'d SETS

2014 Finest Warriors Die Cut Refractors

STATED ODDS 1:4 MINI BOX
FWBH Billy Hamilton 1.25 3.00
FWJA Jose Abreu 4.00 10.00
FWKW Kolten Wong 1.25 3.00
FWMC Michael Choice 1.00 2.50
FWMD Matt Davidson 1.25 3.00
FWMT Masahiro Tanaka 3.00 8.00
FWNC Nick Castellanos 3.00 8.00
FWTD Travis d'Arnaud 1.25 3.00
FWTW Taijuan Walker 1.00 2.50
FWXB Xander Bogaerts 3.00 8.00

2014 Finest Warriors Die Cut Gold Refractors

*GOLD: 2X TO 5X BASIC
STATED ODDS 1:176 MINI BOX
STATED PRINT RUN 25 SER.#'d SETS
FWJA Jose Abreu 40.00 100.00

2015 Finest

COMP.SET w/o SP's (100) 12.00 30.00
1-100 PLATE ODDS 1:114 MINI BOX
PLATE PRINT RUN 1 SET PER COLOR
BLACK-CYAN-MAGENTA-YELLOW ISSUED
NO PLATE PRICING DUE TO SCARCITY
1 Albert Pujols .40 1.00
2 Christian Yelich .40 1.00
3 Cory Spangenberg RC .30 .75
4 Mike Foltynewicz RC .30 .75
5 Miguel Cabrera .30 .75
6 Jonathan Lucroy .25 .60
7 Dustin Pedroia .30 .75
8 Samuel Tuivailala RC .30 .75
9 Hanley Ramirez .25 .60
10 Joe Mauer .25 .60
11 David Ortiz .30 .75
12 Michael Taylor RC .30 .75
13 Clayton Kershaw .50 1.25
14 Dalton Pompey RC .40 1.00
15 Eric Hosmer .25 .60
16 Jose Abreu .30 .75
17 Troy Tulowitzki .30 .75
18 Andrelton Simmons .20 .50
19 Giancarlo Stanton .30 .75
20 Jose Pirela RC .30 .75
21 Joc Pederson RC 1.25 3.00
22 Buster Posey .40 1.00
23 Josh Reddick .20 .50
24 Matt Barnes RC .30 .75
25 Stephen Strasburg .30 .75
26 David Peralta .20 .50
27 Jose Altuve .25 .60
28 Starling Marte .25 .60
29 Yu Darvish .30 .75
30 Jason Heyward .25 .60
31 Jose Fernandez .30 .75
32 Kyle Seager .20 .50
33 Michael Brantley .25 .60
34 Yoenis Cespedes .25 .60
35 Gregory Polanco .25 .60
36 Daniel Norris RC .30 .75
37 Jorge Soler RC .50 1.25
38 Nelson Cruz .30 .75
39 Buck Farmer RC .30 .75
40 Alex Gordon .25 .60
41 Yordano Ventura .25 .60
42 Bryce Harper .50 1.25
43 Chris Sale .30 .75
44 Javier Baez RC 2.50 6.00
45 Jacoby Ellsbury .25 .60
46 Cole Hamels .25 .60
47 Joey Votto .30 .75
48 Anthony Ranaudo RC .30 .75
49 Christian Walker RC .60 1.50
50 Rymer Liriano RC .30 .75
51 Freddie Freeman .40 1.00
52 Josh Harrison .20 .50
53 Justin Verlander .30 .75
54 Koji Uehara .20 .50
55 Evan Longoria .25 .60
56 Anthony Rendon .30 .75
57 Kolten Wong .25 .60
58 Brandon Phillips .20 .50
59 Elvis Andrus .25 .60
60 Rusney Castillo RC .40 1.00
61 Manny Machado .30 .75
62 Madison Bumgarner .25 .60
63 David Wright .25 .60
64 Anthony Rizzo .40 1.00
65 Josh Donaldson .25 .60
66 Phil Hughes .20 .50
67 Felix Hernandez .25 .60
68 Mike Trout 1.50 4.00
69 Salvador Perez .25 .60
70 Brandon Finnegan RC .30 .75
71 Brandon Crawford .25 .60
72 Edwin Escobar RC .30 .75
73 Max Scherzer .30 .75
74 Adam Jones .25 .60
75 Carlos Gonzalez .25 .60
76 Adrian Gonzalez .25 .60
77 Maikel Franco RC .40 1.00
78 Daniel Corcino RC .30 .75
79 Jake Lamb RC .50 1.25
80 Julio Teheran .25 .60
81 Matt Carpenter .30 .75
82 Trevor May RC .30 .75
83 Yasiel Puig .30 .75
84 Chase Utley .25 .60
85 Gary Brown RC .30 .75
86 Jose Bautista .25 .60
87 CC Sabathia .25 .60
88 George Springer .25 .60
89 Matt Kemp .25 .60
90 Yimi Garcia RC .30 .75
91 Dilson Herrera RC .40 1.00
92 Jacob deGrom .60 1.50
93 Zack Wheeler .25 .60
94 Sonny Gray .25 .60
95 Charlie Blackmon .30 .75
96 Masahiro Tanaka .25 .60
97 Joe Panik .25 .60
98 Corey Kluber .25 .60
99 Kennys Vargas .20 .50
100 Matt Adams .20 .50
101 Josh Hamilton SP 3.00 8.00
102 Wil Myers SP 3.00 8.00
103 Adam Wainwright SP 3.00 8.00
104 Edwin Encarnacion SP 4.00 10.00
105 Adrian Beltre SP 4.00 10.00
106 Andrew McCutchen SP 4.00 10.00
107 Paul Goldschmidt SP 4.00 10.00
108 Ryan Braun SP 3.00 8.00
109 Mark Teixeira SP 3.00 8.00
110 Robinson Cano SP 3.00 8.00
111 Kris Bryant SP RC 75.00 200.00

2015 Finest Black Refractors

*BLACK REF: 2X TO 5X BASIC
*BLACK REF RC: 1.2X TO 3X BASIC
RANDOM INSERTS IN MINI BOXES

2015 Finest Blue Refractors

*BLUE REF: 2.5X TO 6X BASIC
*BLUE REF RC: 1.5X TO 4X BASIC
STATED ODDS 1:4 MINI BOX
STATED PRINT RUN 150 SER.#'d SETS

2015 Finest Gold Refractors

*GOLD REF: 6X TO 15X BASIC
*GOLD REF RC: 4X TO 10X BASIC
STATED ODDS 1:10 MINI BOX
STATED PRINT RUN 50 SER.#'d SETS
68 Mike Trout 25.00 60.00

2015 Finest Green Refractors

*GREEN REF: 3X TO 8X BASIC
*GREEN REF RC: 2X TO 5X BASIC
STATED ODDS 1:5 MINI BOX
STATED PRINT RUN 99 SER.#'d SETS

2015 Finest Orange Refractors

*ORANGE REF: 8X TO 20X BASIC
*ORANGE REF RC: 5X TO 12X BASIC
STATED ODDS 1:19 MINI BOX
STATED PRINT RUN 25 SER.#'d SETS
68 Mike Trout 30.00 80.00

2015 Finest Prism Refractors

*PRISM REF: 1.2X TO 3X BASIC
*PRISM REF RC: .75X TO 2X BASIC
RANDOM INSERTS IN MINI BOXES

2015 Finest Purple Refractors

*PRPLE REF: 2X TO 5X BASIC
*PRPLE REF RC: 1.2X TO 3X BASIC
STATED ODDS 1:2 MINI BOX
STATED PRINT RUN 250 SER.#'d SETS

2015 Finest Refractors

*REF: 1X TO 2.5X BASIC
*REF RC: .6X TO 1.5X BASIC
RANDOM INSERTS IN MINI BOXES
*REF SP: .6X TO 1.5X BASIC
REF SP ODDS 1:183 MINI BOXES
REF SP PRINT RUN 25 SER.#'d SETS
106 Andrew McCutchen 20.00 50.00
111 Kris Bryant 250.00 400.00

2015 Finest '95 Topps Finest

COMPLETE SET (20) 6.00 15.00
RANDOM INSERTS IN MINI BOXES
*REF/25: 12X TO 30X BASIC
94F01 Clayton Kershaw 1.00 2.50
94F02 Jose Abreu .60 1.50
94F03 Mike Trout 3.00 8.00
94F04 Albert Pujols .75 2.00
94F05 Robinson Cano .50 1.25
94F06 Masahiro Tanaka .50 1.25
94F07 Adam Jones .50 1.25
94F08 Freddie Freeman .75 2.00
94F09 Matt Kemp .50 1.25
94F10 David Ortiz .60 1.50
94F11 Brandon Phillips .40 1.00
94F12 Troy Tulowitzki .60 1.50
94F13 Giancarlo Stanton .60 1.50
94F14 Ryan Braun .50 1.25
94F15 David Wright .50 1.25
94F16 Chase Utley .50 1.25
94F17 Madison Bumgarner .50 1.25
94F18 Adrian Beltre .60 1.50
94F19 Max Scherzer .60 1.50
94F20 Jose Bautista .50 1.25

2015 Finest Affiliations Autographs

STATED ODDS 1:92 MINI BOX
STATED PRINT RUN 50 SER.#'d SETS
EXCHANGE DEADLINE 5/31/2018
FAABSR J.Baez/J.Soler 125.00 300.00
FAACP D.Pedroia/R.Cano 25.00 60.00
FAAGS J.Smoltz/T.Glavine 50.00 120.00
FAAJM M.McGwire/R.Jackson 50.00 120.00
FAAKS C.Sale/C.Kershaw 40.00 100.00
FAAMP M.Mussina/J.Posada 40.00 100.00
FAASD R.Sandberg/A.Dawson 50.00 125.00
FAATA J.Abreu/F.Thomas 75.00 150.00

2015 Finest Autographs

RANDOM INSERTS IN PACKS
*BLUE REF/150: .5X TO 1.2X BASIC
*GREEN REF/99: .6X TO 1.5X BASIC

*GOLD REF/50: .75X TO 2X BASIC
*ORNGE REF/25: 1X TO 2.5X BASIC
PRINTING PLATE ODDS 1:197 MINI BOX
PLATE PRINT RUN 1 SET PER COLOR
BLACK-CYAN-MAGENTA-YELLOW ISSUED
NO PLATE PRICING DUE TO SCARCITY
EXCHANGE DEADLINE 5/31/2018
FAAR Anthony Rizzo 20.00 50.00
FABB Bryce Brentz 3.00 8.00
FABC Brandon Crawford 5.00 12.00
FABF Buck Farmer 3.00 8.00
FACR Carlos Rodon 8.00 20.00
FACSG Cory Spangenberg 3.00 8.00
FACW Christian Walker 6.00 15.00
FACY Christian Yelich 20.00 50.00
FADC Daniel Corcino 3.00 8.00
FADH Dilson Herrera 4.00 10.00
FAEE Edwin Escobar 3.00 8.00
FAGB Gary Brown 3.00 8.00
FAGSR George Springer 10.00 25.00
FAJDN Josh Donaldson 10.00 25.00
FAJF Jose Fernandez 25.00 60.00
FAJL Jake Lamb 5.00 12.00
FAJMN James McCann 5.00 12.00
FAJT Julio Teheran 4.00 10.00
FAKB Kris Bryant 75.00 200.00
FAKG Kendall Graveman 3.00 8.00
FAKL Kyle Lobstein 3.00 8.00
FAKW Kolten Wong 4.00 10.00
FAMA Matt Adams 3.00 8.00
FAMTR Michael Taylor 3.00 8.00
FARCA Rusney Castillo 4.00 10.00
FARCO Robinson Cano 5.00 12.00
FARL Rymer Liriano 3.00 8.00
FASG Sonny Gray 4.00 10.00
FASM Steven Moya 4.00 10.00
FAST Samuel Tuivailala 3.00 8.00
FATM Trevor May 3.00 8.00
FAXS Xavier Scruggs 3.00 8.00
FAYG Yimi Garcia 3.00 8.00

2015 Finest Autographs Blue Refractors

*BLUE REF: .5X TO 1.2X BASIC
STATED ODDS 1:7 MINI BOX
STATED PRINT RUN 150 SER.#'d SETS
EXCHANGE DEADLINE 5/31/2018
FAAG Adrian Gonzalez 10.00 25.00
FACSE Chris Sale 12.00 30.00
FADP Dustin Pedroia 12.00 3.00
FAFF Freddie Freeman 20.00 50.00
FAHR Hanley Ramirez 5.00 12.00
FAJDM Jacob deGrom 50.00 120.00
FARB Ryan Braun 8.00 20.00
FARCO Robinson Cano 6.00 15.00
FAYT Yasmany Tomas 6.00 15.00

2015 Finest Autographs Gold Refractors

*GOLD REF: .75X TO 2X BASIC
STATED ODDS 1:19 MINI BOX
STATED PRINT RUN 50 SER.#'d SETS
EXCHANGE DEADLINE 5/31/2018
FAAG Adrian Gonzalez 15.00 40.00
FAAJ Adam Jones 12.00 30.00
FACSE Chris Sale 20.00 50.00
FADP Dustin Pedroia 20.00 50.00
FAFF Freddie Freeman 30.00 80.00
FAHR Hanley Ramirez 8.00 20.00
FAJA Jose Abreu 30.00 80.00
FAJDM Jacob deGrom 75.00 200.00
FAKU Koji Uehara 8.00 20.00
FARB Ryan Braun 12.00 30.00
FARCO Robinson Cano 10.00 25.00
FAYT Yasmany Tomas 10.00 25.00

2015 Finest Autographs Green Refractors

*GREEN REF: .6X TO 1.5X BASIC
STATED ODDS 1:10 MINI BOX
STATED PRINT RUN 99 SER.#'d SETS
EXCHANGE DEADLINE 5/31/2018
FAAG Adrian Gonzalez 12.00 30.00
FAAJ Adam Jones 10.00 25.00
FACSE Chris Sale 15.00 40.00
FADP Dustin Pedroia 15.00 40.00
FAFF Freddie Freeman 25.00 60.00
FAHR Hanley Ramirez 6.00 15.00
FAJA Jose Abreu 25.00 60.00
FAJDM Jacob deGrom 60.00 -150.00
FAKU Koji Uehara 6.00 15.00
FARB Ryan Braun 10.00 25.00
FARCO Robinson Cano 8.00 20.00
FAYT Yasmany Tomas 8.00 20.00

2015 Finest Autographs Orange Refractors

*ORANGE REF: 1X TO 2.5X BASIC
STATED ODDS 1:32 MINI BOX
STATED PRINT RUN 25 SER.#'d SETS
EXCHANGE DEADLINE 5/31/2018
FAAG Adrian Gonzalez 20.00 50.00
FAAJ Adam Jones 15.00 40.00
FACK Clayton Kershaw 60.00 150.00
FACSE Chris Sale 25.00 60.00
FADP Dustin Pedroia 25.00 60.00
FAFF Freddie Freeman 40.00 100.00
FAHR Hanley Ramirez 10.00 25.00
FAJA Jose Abreu 40.00 100.00
FAJDM Jacob deGrom 100.00 250.00
FAJV Joey Votto 50.00 120.00
FAKB Kris Bryant 200.00 500.00
FAKU Koji Uehara 10.00 25.00
FAMTT Mike Trout 300.00 500.00
FARB Ryan Braun 15.00 40.00
FARCO Robinson Cano 60.00 150.00
FATT Troy Tulowitzki 20.00 50.00
FAYT Yasmany Tomas 12.00 30.00

2015 Finest Careers Die Cut

RANDOM INSERTS IN PACKS
*REF/25: 1.5X TO 4X BASIC
JETER1 Derek Jeter 8.00 20.00
JETER2 Derek Jeter 8.00 20.00
JETER3 Derek Jeter 8.00 20.00
JETER4 Derek Jeter 8.00 20.00
JETER5 Derek Jeter 8.00 20.00
JETER6 Derek Jeter 8.00 20.00
JETER7 Derek Jeter 8.00 20.00
JETER8 Derek Jeter 8.00 20.00
JETER9 Derek Jeter 8.00 20.00
JETER10 Derek Jeter 8.00 20.00

2015 Finest Firsts

RANDOM INSERTS IN MINI BOXES
*REF/25: 2.5X TO 6X BASIC
FF1 Joc Pederson 2.00 5.00
FF2 Maikel Franco .60 1.50
FF3 Anthony Ranaudo .50 1.25
FF4 Dalton Pompey .60 1.50
FF5 Brandon Finnegan .50 1.25
FF6 Javier Baez 4.00 10.00
FF7 Jorge Soler .75 2.00
FF8 Daniel Norris .50 1.25
FF9 Trevor May .50 1.25
FF10 Rusney Castillo .60 1.50

2015 Finest Firsts Autographs

STATED ODDS 1:25 MINI BOX
*BLUE REF/150: .5X TO 1.2X BASIC
*GREEN REF/99: .5X TO 1.2X BASIC
*GOLD REF/50: 1X TO 2.5X BASIC
*ORNGE REF/25: 1.2X TO 3X BASIC
PRINTING PLATE ODDS 1:1612 MINI BOX
PLATE PRINT RUN 1 SET PER COLOR
BLACK-CYAN-MAGENTA-YELLOW ISSUED
NO PLATE PRICING DUE TO SCARCITY
EXCHANGE DEADLINE 5/31/2018
FFABF Brandon Finnegan 5.00 12.00
FFADP Dalton Pompey 6.00 15.00
FFAJB Javier Baez 20.00 50.00
FFAJP Joc Pederson 8.00 20.00
FFAJS Jorge Soler 8.00 20.00
FFAMF Maikel Franco 8.00 20.00

2015 Finest Generations

COMPLETE SET (50) 30.00 80.00
RANDOM INSERTS IN MINI BOXES
*REF/25: 4X TO 10X BASIC
FG01 Stan Musial 1.25 3.00
FG02 Tom Glavine .60 1.50
FG03 Steve Carlton .60 1.50
FG04 Ozzie Smith 1.00 2.50
FG05 Ernie Banks .75 2.00
FG06 Frank Robinson .60 1.50
FG07 Barry Larkin .60 1.50
FG08 Chipper Jones .75 2.00
FG09 Mike Schmidt 1.25 3.00
FG10 Rickey Henderson .75 2.00
FG11 Mark McGwire 1.25 3.00
FG12 Nolan Ryan 2.50 6.00
FG13 Cal Ripken Jr. 2.50 6.00
FG14 Roger Clemens 1.00 2.50
FG15 Mike Piazza .75 2.00
FG16 Sandy Koufax 1.50 4.00
FG17 Johnny Bench .75 2.00
FG18 Ken Griffey Jr. 1.50 4.00
FG19 Tom Seaver .60 1.50
FG20 Robin Yount .75 2.00
FG21 Phil Niekro .60 1.50
FG22 Juan Marichal .60 1.50
FG23 Bo Jackson .75 2.00
FG24 Frank Thomas .75 2.00
FG25 Mariano Rivera 1.00 2.50
FG26 Lou Brock .60 1.50
FG27 Orlando Cepeda .60 1.50
FG28 Dennis Eckersley .60 1.50
FG29 Luis Aparicio .60 1.50
FG30 Andre Dawson .60 1.50
FG31 Rod Carew .60 1.50
FG32 Alex Rodriguez 1.00 2.50
FG33 Randy Johnson .75 2.00
FG34 Albert Pujols 1.00 2.50
FG35 Greg Maddux 1.00 2.50
FG36 Tony Gwynn .75 2.00
FG37 Chase Utley .60 1.50
FG38 Derek Jeter 2.00 5.00
FG39 Wade Boggs .60 1.50
FG40 Joe Morgan .60 1.50
FG41 Willie Mays 1.50 4.00
FG42 Clayton Kershaw 1.25 3.00
FG43 Mike Trout 4.00 10.00
FG44 Cole Hamels .60 1.50
FG45 David Price .60 1.50
FG46 Andrew McCutchen .75 2.00
FG47 Adrian Beltre .75 2.00
FG48 Giancarlo Stanton .75 2.00
FG49 Miguel Cabrera .75 2.00
FG50 Robinson Cano .60 1.50

2015 Finest Generations Autographs

STATED ODDS 1:122 MINI BOX
STATED PRINT RUN 25 SER.#'d SETS
EXCHANGE DEADLINE 5/31/2018
FGABL Barry Larkin 30.00 80.00
FGACR Cal Ripken Jr. 125.00 300.00
FGADE Dennis Eckersley 30.00 80.00
FGAFR Frank Robinson 30.00 80.00
FGAJB Johnny Bench 40.00 100.00
FGAKG Ken Griffey Jr. 200.00 400.00
FGALB Lou Brock 30.00 80.00
FGAMM Mark McGwire 125.00 250.00
FGAMP Mike Piazza 75.00 200.00
FGAMR Mariano Rivera 150.00 250.00
FGANR Nolan Ryan 125.00 300.00
FGAOS Ozzie Smith 30.00 80.00
FGARCS Roger Clemens 50.00 125.00
FGARH Rickey Henderson 60.00 150.00
FGASC Steve Carlton 30.00 80.00
FGASK Sandy Koufax 300.00 400.00
FGATG Tom Glavine 60.00 150.00

2015 Finest Greats Autographs

STATED ODDS 1:29 MINI BOX
PRINTING PLATE ODDS 1:764 MINI BOX
PLATE PRINT RUN 1 SET PER COLOR
BLACK-CYAN-MAGENTA-YELLOW ISSUED
NO PLATE PRICING DUE TO SCARCITY
EXCHANGE DEADLINE 5/31/2018
FGABL Barry Larkin 25.00 60.00
FGACF Carlton Fisk 12.00 30.00
FGACJ Chipper Jones 50.00 120.00
FGAFR Frank Robinson 15.00 40.00
FGAFT Frank Thomas 25.00 60.00
FGAJB Johnny Bench 20.00 50.00
FGALB Lou Brock 15.00 40.00
FGAOS Ozzie Smith 12.00 30.00
FGARH Rickey Henderson 50.00 120.00
FGATG Tom Glavine 15.00 40.00

2015 Finest Greats Autographs Gold Refractors

*GOLD REF: .5X TO 1.2X BASIC
STATED ODDS 1:61 MINI BOX
STATED PRINT RUN 50 SER.#'d SETS
EXCHANGE DEADLINE 5/31/2018
FGAGM Greg Maddux 40.00 100.00
FGAHA Hank Aaron 150.00 400.00
FGAKG Ken Griffey Jr. 125.00 300.00
FGANR Nolan Ryan 75.00 200.00

2015 Finest Greats Autographs Orange Refractors

*ORANGE REF: .6X TO 1.5X BASIC
STATED ODDS 1:122 MINI BOX
STATED PRINT RUN 25 SER.#'d SETS
EXCHANGE DEADLINE 5/31/2018
FGAGM Greg Maddux 50.00 120.00
FGAHA Hank Aaron 250.00 500.00
FGAKG Ken Griffey Jr. 200.00 400.00
FGANR Nolan Ryan 100.00 250.00
FGARC Roger Clemens 40.00 100.00
FGARJ Randy Johnson 60.00 150.00

2015 Finest Rookie Autographs Mystery Exchange

STATED ODDS 1:154 MINI BOX
EXCHANGE DEADLINE 5/31/2018
RR1 Byron Buxton 75.00 150.00
RR2 Joc Pederson 12.00 30.00
RR3 Francsico Lindor 75.00 200.00

2016 Finest

COMP.SET w/o SP's (100) 25.00 60.00
SP ODDS 1:5 MINI BOX
PRINTING PLATE ODDS 1:87 MINI BOX
BLACK-CYAN-MAGENTA-YELLOW ISSUED
PLATE PRINT RUN 1 SET PER COLOR
NO PLATE PRICING DUE TO SCARCITY
1 Mike Trout 1.50 4.00
2 Ryan Howard .25 .60
3 Edwin Encarnacion .30 .75
4 Dee Gordon .20 .50
5 Evan Longoria .25 .60
6 Jake Arrieta .25 .60
7 Jose Abreu .30 .75
8 Frankie Montas RC .40 1.00
9 Matt Harvey .25 .60
10 Ichiro Suzuki .40 1.00
11 A.J. Pollock .20 .50
12 Ian Kinsler .25 .60
13 Salvador Perez .25 .60
14 Buster Posey .40 1.00
15 Corey Kluber .25 .60
16 Jose Peraza RC .40 1.00
17 Greg Bird RC .40 1.00
18 Trea Turner RC 1.00 2.50
19 Joc Pederson .25 .60
20 J.D. Martinez .30 .75
21 Carl Edwards Jr. RC .40 1.00
22 Carlos Correa .30 .75
23 Cole Hamels .25 .60
24 Joey Votto .30 .75
25 Kenta Maeda RC .60 1.50
26 Dellin Betances .25 .60
27 Ketel Marte RC .60 1.50
28 Brian McCann .25 .60
29 Troy Tulowitzki .30 .75
30 Dallas Keuchel .25 .60
31 Byron Buxton .30 .75
32 David Ortiz .30 .75
33 Rob Refsnyder RC .40 1.00
34 Tyson Ross .20 .50
35 Mookie Betts .60 1.50
36 Charlie Blackmon .30 .75
37 Francisco Lindor .30 .75
38 Sonny Gray .25 .60
39 Jose Altuve .25 .60
40 Chris Sale .30 .75
41 Brian Dozier .25 .60
42 Luis Severino RC .40 1.00
43 Robinson Cano .25 .60
44 Josh Donaldson .25 .60
45 Adrian Beltre .30 .75
46 Jose Fernandez .30 .75
47 Andrew McCutchen .30 .75
48 Ryan Braun .25 .60
49 Noah Syndergaard .25 .60
50 Clayton Kershaw .50 1.25
51 Michael Brantley .25 .60
52 Felix Hernandez .25 .60
53 Yu Darvish .30 .75
54 Andrew Miller .25 .60
55 Eric Hosmer .25 .60
56 Peter O'Brien RC .30 .75
57 Wil Myers .25 .60
58 Corey Seager RC 2.50 6.00
59 George Springer .25 .60
60 Brandon Crawford .25 .60
61 Jacob deGrom .60 1.50
62 Alcides Escobar .25 .60
63 Yoenis Cespedes .30 .75
64 Gary Sanchez RC 1.00 2.50
65 Miguel Cabrera .30 .75
66 Gerrit Cole .30 .75
67 Kyle Schwarber RC 1.00 2.50
68 Jorge Soler .30 .75
69 Miguel Sano RC .50 1.25
70 Brandon Phillips .20 .50
71 Maikel Franco .25 .60
72 Craig Kimbrel .25 .60
73 Dustin Pedroia .30 .75
74 Matt Holliday .30 .75
75 Henry Owens RC .40 1.00
76 Anthony Rizzo .40 1.00
77 David Wright .25 .60
78 Giancarlo Stanton .30 .75
79 Nolan Arenado .50 1.25
80 Kyle Seager .20 .50
81 Mark Melancon .20 .50
82 Raul Mondesi Jr. RC .60 1.50
83 Carlos Carrasco .20 .50
84 Matt Carpenter .30 .75
85 David Price .25 .60
86 Todd Frazier .20 .50
87 Rusney Castillo .20 .50
88 Madison Bumgarner .25 .60
89 Starling Marte .25 .60
90 Zack Greinke .30 .75
91 Hector Olivera RC .40 1.00
92 Kolten Wong .25 .60
93 Christian Yelich .40 1.00
94 Max Kepler RC .50 1.25
95 Jason Kipnis .25 .60
96 Prince Fielder .25 .60
97 Stephen Piscotty RC .50 1.25
98 Jorge Lopez RC .30 .75
99 Jon Lester .25 .60
100 Bryce Harper .50 1.25
101 Adam Jones SP 8.00 20.00
102 Aroldis Chapman SP 10.00 25.00
103 Aaron Nola SP RC 12.00 30.00
104 Matt Harvey SP 8.00 20.00
105 Wade Davis SP 6.00 15.00
106 Paul Goldschmidt SP 10.00 25.00
107 Max Scherzer SP 10.00 25.00
108 Michael Conforto SP RC 8.00 20.00
109 Freddie Freeman SP 12.00 30.00
110 Kris Bryant SP 12.00 30.00

2016 Finest Blue Refractors

*BLUE REF: 2.5X TO 6X BASIC
*BLUE REF RC: 1.5X TO 4X BASIC
STATED ODDS 1:3 MINI BOX
STATED PRINT RUN 150 SER.#'d SETS

2016 Finest Gold Refractors

*GOLD REF: 6X TO 15X BASIC
*GOLD REF RC: 4X TO 10X BASIC
STATED ODDS 1:7 MINI BOX
STATED PRINT RUN 50 SER.#'d SETS

2016 Finest Green Refractors

*GREEN REF: 3X TO 8X BASIC
*GREEN REF RC: 2X TO 5X BASIC
STATED ODDS 1:4 MINI BOX
STATED PRINT RUN 99 SER.#'d SETS

2016 Finest Orange Refractors

*ORANGE REF: 8X TO 20X BASIC
*ORANGE REF RC: 5X TO 12X BASIC
*ORANGE REF SP: .75X TO 2X BASIC
STATED ODDS 1:14 MINI BOX
SP ODDS 1:139 MINI BOX
STATED PRINT RUN 25 SER.#'d SETS

2016 Finest Purple Refractors

*PRPLE REF: 2X TO 5X BASIC
*PRPLE REF RC: 1.2X TO 3X BASIC
STATED ODDS 1:2 MINI BOX
STATED PRINT RUN 250 SER.#'d SETS

2016 Finest Refractors

*REF: 1X TO 2.5X BASIC
*REF RC: .6X TO 1.5X BASIC
RANDOM INSERTS IN PACKS

2016 Finest '96 Finest Intimidators Autographs

STATED ODDS 1:136 MINI BOX
STATED PRINT RUN 25 SER.#'d SETS
PRINTING PLATE ODDS 1:847 MINI BOX
PLATE PRINT RUN 1 SET PER COLOR
NO PLATE PRICING DUE TO SCARCITY
EXCHANGE DEADLINE 4/30/2018
96FIABJ Bo Jackson 100.00 250.00
96FIAMM Mark McGwire
96FIANR Nolan Ryan
96FIARC Roger Clemens 30.00 80.00
96FIAYD Yu Darvish

2016 Finest '96 Finest Intimidators Refractors

RANDOM INSERTS IN PACKS
*ORANGE/25: 8X TO 20X BASIC
96FII Ichiro Suzuki .75 2.00
96FIAP Albert Pujols .75 2.00
96FIBJ Bo Jackson .60 1.50
96FICS Chris Sale .60 1.50
96FIDO David Ortiz .60 1.50
96FIEE Edwin Encarnacion .60 1.50
96FIEG Evan Gattis .40 1.00
96FIFT Frank Thomas .60 1.50
96FIGS Giancarlo Stanton .60 1.50
96FIJC Jose Canseco .50 1.25
96FIMH Matt Harvey .50 1.25
96FIMM Mark McGwire 1.00 2.50
96FIMP Mike Piazza .60 1.50
96FINR Nolan Ryan 2.00 5.00
96FIPF Prince Fielder .50 1.25
96FIRC Roger Clemens .75 2.00
96FIRJ Randy Johnson .60 1.50
96FIVG Vladimir Guerrero .50 1.25
96FIYC Yoenis Cespedes .60 1.50
96FIYD Yu Darvish .60 1.50

2016 Finest Autographs

OVERALL AUTO ODDS 1:1 MINI BOX
PRINTING PLATE ODDS 1:187 MINI BOX
PLATE PRINT RUN 1 SET PER COLOR
NO PLATE PRICING DUE TO SCARCITY
EXCHANGE DEADLINE 4/30/2018
FAAG Andres Galarraga 6.00 15.00
FAAJ Andruw Jones 5.00 12.00
FAAM Andrew Miller 4.00 10.00
FAAP A.J. Pollock 3.00 8.00
FABH Bryce Harper 50.00 120.00
FABPA Byung-Ho Park 40.00 100.00
FABPO Buster Posey 40.00 100.00
FABS Blake Swihart 4.00 10.00
FACB Craig Biggio 12.00 30.00
FACC Carlos Correa 60.00 150.00
FACD Carlos Delgado 3.00 8.00
FACDI Corey Dickerson 4.00 10.00
FACE Carl Edwards Jr. 4.00 10.00
FACKL Corey Kluber 5.00 12.00
FACM Carlos Martinez 4.00 10.00
FACR Cal Ripken Jr. 60.00 150.00
FADK Dallas Keuchel 10.00 25.00
FADN Daniel Norris 3.00 8.00
FAFF Freddie Freeman 12.00 30.00
FAFL Francisco Lindor 15.00 40.00
FAHO Hector Olivera 4.00 10.00
FAI Ichiro Suzuki 200.00 400.00
FAJAL Jose Altuve 12.00 30.00
FAJD Jacob deGrom 20.00 50.00
FAJKR John Kruk 5.00 12.00
FAJR J.T. Realmuto 12.00 30.00
FAKB Kris Bryant 40.00 100.00
FAKC Kole Calhoun 3.00 8.00
FAKMA Kenta Maeda 40.00 100.00
FAKW Kolten Wong 4.00 10.00
FAMC Matt Cain 4.00 10.00
FAMT Mike Trout 200.00 300.00
FAOV Omar Vizquel 4.00 10.00
FARB Ryan Braun 8.00 20.00
FARF Rollie Fingers 5.00 12.00
FARM Raul Mondesi Jr. 8.00 20.00
FARR Rob Refsnyder 4.00 10.00
FASM Starling Marte 4.00 10.00
FASMA Steven Matz 3.00 8.00
FASP Stephen Piscotty 5.00 12.00
FATT Trea Turner 12.00 30.00
FAWD Wade Davis 5.00 12.00
FAYD Yu Darvish 30.00 80.00

2016 Finest Autographs Blue Refractors

*BLUE REF: .5X TO 1.2X BASIC
STATED ODDS 1:8 MINI BOX
STATED PRINT RUN 150 SER.#'d SETS
EXCHANGE DEADLINE 4/30/2018

2016 Finest Autographs Gold Refractors

*GOLD REF: .75X TO 2X BASIC
STATED ODDS 1:18 MINI BOX
STATED PRINT RUN 50 SER.#'d SETS
EXCHANGE DEADLINE 4/30/2018
FAAJ Andruw Jones 10.00 25.00

2016 Finest Autographs Green Refractors

*GREEN REF: .6X TO 1.5X BASIC
STATED ODDS 1:11 MINI BOX
STATED PRINT RUN 99 SER.#'d SETS
EXCHANGE DEADLINE 4/30/2018

2016 Finest Autographs Orange Refractors

*ORANGE REF: 1X TO 2.5X BASIC
STATED ODDS 1:30 MINI BOX
STATED PRINT RUN 25 SER.#'d SETS
EXCHANGE DEADLINE 4/30/2018
FAAJ Andruw Jones 12.00 30.00

2016 Finest Autographs Purple Refractors

*PURPLE REF: 1X TO 2.5X BASIC
STATED ODDS 1:32 MINI BOX
STATED PRINT RUN 30 SER.#'d SETS
EXCHANGE DEADLINE 4/30/2018
FAAJ Andruw Jones 12.00 30.00

2016 Finest Careers Die Cut Refractors

STATED ODDS 1:16 MINI BOX
*ORANGE/25: 1X TO 2.5X BASIC
*RED/5: 3X TO 8X BASIC
FCAKG1 Ken Griffey Jr. 12.00 30.00
FCAKG2 Ken Griffey Jr. 12.00 30.00
FCAKG3 Ken Griffey Jr. 12.00 30.00
FCAKG4 Ken Griffey Jr. 12.00 30.00
FCAKG5 Ken Griffey Jr. 12.00 30.00
FCAKG6 Ken Griffey Jr. 12.00 30.00
FCAKG7 Ken Griffey Jr. 12.00 30.00
FCAKG8 Ken Griffey Jr. 12.00 30.00
FCAKG9 Ken Griffey Jr. 12.00 30.00
FCAKG10 Ken Griffey Jr. 12.00 30.00

2016 Finest Firsts Autographs

STATED ODDS 1:23 MINI BOX
PRINTING PLATE ODDS 1:1180 MINI BOX
PLATE PRINT RUN 1 SET PER COLOR
NO PLATE PRICING DUE TO SCARCITY
EXCHANGE DEADLINE 4/30/2018
FFAAN Aaron Nola 8.00 20.00
FFACS Corey Seager
FFAHOW Henry Owens EXCH 6.00 15.00
FFAKS Kyle Schwarber
FFALS Luis Severino 6.00 15.00
FFAMC Michael Conforto
FFAMS Miguel Sano 6.00 15.00

2016 Finest Firsts Autographs Blue Refractors

*BLUE REF: .5X TO 1.2X BASIC
STATED ODDS 1:38 MINI BOX
STATED PRINT RUN 150 SER.#'d SETS
EXCHANGE DEADLINE 4/30/2018

2016 Finest Firsts Autographs Gold Refractors

*GOLD REF: .75X TO 2X BASIC
STATED ODDS 1:97 MINI BOX
STATED PRINT RUN 50 SER.#'d SETS
EXCHANGE DEADLINE 4/30/2018
FFACS Corey Seager 125.00 300.00
FFAKS Kyle Schwarber 25.00 60.00
FFAMC Michael Conforto 15.00 40.00

2016 Finest Firsts Autographs Green Refractors

*GREEN REF: .6X TO 1.5X BASIC
STATED ODDS 1:49 MINI BOX
STATED PRINT RUN 99 SER.#'d SETS
EXCHANGE DEADLINE 4/30/2018
FFAKS Kyle Schwarber 20.00 50.00
FFAMC Michael Conforto 12.00 30.00

2016 Finest Firsts Autographs Orange Refractors

*ORANGE REF: 1.2X TO 3X BASIC
STATED ODDS 1:192 MINI BOX
STATED PRINT RUN 25 SER.#'d SETS
EXCHANGE DEADLINE 4/30/2018
FFACS Corey Seager 300.00 500.00
FFAKS Kyle Schwarber 40.00 100.00

2016 Finest Firsts Refractors

STATED ODDS 1:2 MINI BOX
*ORANGE/25: 6X TO 15X BASIC
FFAN Aaron Nola 1.00 2.50
FFCS Corey Seager 5.00 12.00
FFHO Hector Olivera .60 1.50
FFHOW Henry Owens .60 1.50
FFKS Kyle Schwarber 1.50 4.00
FFLS Luis Severino .60 1.50
FFMC Michael Conforto .60 1.50
FFMS Miguel Sano .75 2.00
FFSP Stephen Piscotty .75 2.00
FFTT Trea Turner 1.50 4.00

2016 Finest Franchise Finest Autographs

STATED ODDS 1:66 MINI BOX
PRINT RUNS B/WN 40-150 COPIES PER
PRINTING PLATE ODDS 1:1032 MINI BOX
PLATE PRINT RUN 1 SET PER COLOR
NO PLATE PRICING DUE TO SCARCITY
EXCHANGE DEADLINE 4/30/2018
*ORNGE REF: .6X TO 1.5X BASIC
FFIABP Buster Posey/40 40.00 100.00
FFIACK Clayton Kershaw/50 30.00 80.00
FFIAEL Evan Longoria/50 12.00 30.00
FFIAFH Felix Hernandez 30.00 80.00
FFIAJA Jose Altuve/150 15.00 40.00
FFIAMT Mike Trout/40 150.00 400.00
FFIAWM Wil Myers/100 8.00 20.00

2016 Finest Franchise Finest Refractors

RANDOM INSERTS IN PACKS
*ORANGE/25: 6X TO 15X BASIC
FFAJ Adam Jones .60 1.50
FFAM Andrew McCutchen .75 2.00
FFAR Anthony Rizzo 1.00 2.50
FFBD Brian Dozier .60 1.50
FFBH Bryce Harper 1.25 3.00
FFBM Brian McCann .60 1.50
FFBP Buster Posey 1.00 2.50
FFCK Clayton Kershaw 1.25 3.00
FFCS Chris Sale .75 2.00
FFDO David Ortiz .75 2.00
FFEH Eric Hosmer .60 1.50
FFEL Evan Longoria .60 1.50
FFFF Freddie Freeman 1.00 2.50
FFFH Felix Hernandez .60 1.50
FFGS Giancarlo Stanton .75 2.00
FFJA Jose Altuve .60 1.50
FFJD Josh Donaldson .60 1.50
FFJV Joey Votto .75 2.00
FFMB Michael Brantley .60 1.50
FFMC Miguel Cabrera .75 2.00
FFMCA Matt Carpenter .75 2.00
FFMH Matt Harvey .60 1.50
FFMT Mike Trout 4.00 10.00
FFNA Nolan Arenado 1.25 3.00
FFPF Prince Fielder .60 1.50
FFPG Paul Goldschmidt .75 2.00
FFRB Ryan Braun .60 1.50
FFRH Ryan Howard .60 1.50
FFSG Sonny Gray .60 1.50
FFWM Wil Myers .60 1.50

2016 Finest Greats Autographs

STATED ODDS 1:18 MINI BOX
PRINT RUNS B/WN 40-300 COPIES PER
PRINTING PLATE ODDS 1:702 MINI BOX
PLATE PRINT RUN 1 SET PER COLOR
NO PLATE PRICING DUE TO SCARCITY
EXCHANGE DEADLINE 4/30/2018
FGAAK Al Kaline/200 20.00 50.00
FGACR Cal Ripken Jr./60 50.00 120.00
FGADM Don Mattingly/60 25.00 60.00
FGAEM Edgar Martinez/300 10.00 25.00
FGAHA Hank Aaron/40 150.00 300.00
FGAJG Juan Gonzalez/300 8.00 20.00
FGAJS John Smoltz/90 20.00 50.00
FGAMP Mike Piazza/50 60.00 150.00
FGANR Nolan Ryan/60 75.00 200.00
FGARC Rod Carew/150 10.00 25.00
FGASK Sandy Koufax/40 150.00 300.00
FGAVG Vladimir Guerrero/150 15.00 40.00

2016 Finest Greats Autographs Gold Refractors

*GOLD REF: 1X TO 2.5X BASIC
STATED ODDS 1:75 MINI BOX
STATED PRINT RUN 50 SER.#'d SETS
EXCHANGE DEADLINE 4/30/2018
FGACR Cal Ripken Jr. 60.00 150.00
FGADM Don Mattingly 30.00 80.00
FGANR Nolan Ryan 100.00 250.00
FGARC Rod Carew 25.00 60.00

2016 Finest Greats Autographs Orange Refractors

*ORANGE REF: 1.2X TO 3X BASIC
STATED ODDS 1:135 MINI BOX
STATED PRINT RUN 25 SER.#'d SETS
EXCHANGE DEADLINE 4/30/2018
FGACR Cal Ripken Jr. 75.00 200.00
FGADM Don Mattingly 40.00 100.00
FGAMP Mike Piazza 100.00 250.00
FGANR Nolan Ryan 125.00 300.00
FGARC Rod Carew 30.00 80.00

2016 Finest Mystery Redemption Autograph

COMMON CARD 60.00 150.00
SEMISTARS 75.00 200.00
UNLISTED STARS 100.00 250.00
STATED ODDS 1:337 MINI BOX
EXCHANGE DEADLINE 4/30/2018
FMR1 Trevor Story
FMR2 Normar Mazara
FMR3 Julio Urias 60.00 150.00

2016 Finest Originals Buyback Autographs

STATED ODDS 1:170 MINI BOX
STATED PRINT RUN 20 SER.#'d SETS
EXCHANGE DEADLINE 4/30/2018
BW Billy Wagner 20.00 50.00
CJ Chipper Jones 60.00 150.00
CR Cal Ripken Jr.
JS John Smoltz
RJ Randy Johnson 30.00 120.00

2017 Finest

COMP.SET w/o SP's (100) 20.00 50.00
STATED SP ODDS 1:22 HOBBY
1 Mike Trout 1.50 4.00
2 Aaron Judge RC 6.00 15.00
3 Gregory Polanco .25 .60
4 Masahiro Tanaka .25 .60
5 Evan Longoria .25 .60
6 Todd Frazier .20 .50
7 Trea Turner .25 .60
8 Manny Machado .30 .75
9 Max Scherzer .30 .75
10 Edwin Encarnacion .30 .75
11 Jonathan Villar .20 .50
12 Hanley Ramirez .25 .60
13 Billy Hamilton .25 .60
14 Kenta Maeda .25 .60
15 Joey Votto .30 .75
16 Carlos Correa .30 .75
17 Carlos Santana .25 .60
18 Jose Bautista .25 .60
19 Seth Lugo RC .30 .75
20 Carlos Carrasco .20 .50
21 Christian Yelich .40 1.00
22 Tyler Austin RC .40 1.00
23 Jorge Alfaro RC .40 1.00
24 Yoan Moncada RC 1.00 2.50
25 Corey Seager .30 .75
26 Zack Greinke .30 .75
27 Ryan Braun .25 .60
28 Brian Dozier .30 .75
29 Giancarlo Stanton .30 .75
30 Carlos Martinez .25 .60
31 David Price .25 .60
32 Dansby Swanson RC .75 2.00
33 Willson Contreras .30 .75
34 Ryon Healy RC .40 1.00
35 Reynaldo Lopez RC .30 .75
36 Chris Archer .20 .50
37 D.J. LeMahieu .30 .75
38 Chris Sale .30 .75
39 Jean Segura .25 .60
40 Orlando Arcia RC .50 1.25
41 Braden Shipley RC .30 .75
42 Jon Lester .25 .60
43 Francisco Lindor .30 .75
44 Josh Donaldson .25 .60
45 Kenley Jansen .25 .60
46 Aroldis Chapman .30 .75
47 Adam Jones .25 .60
48 Jake Arrieta .25 .60
49 Stephen Strasburg .30 .75
50 Clayton Kershaw .50 1.25
51 Joe Musgrove RC 1.00 2.50
52 Rick Porcello .25 .60
53 Ichiro .40 1.00
54 Kyle Schwarber .30 .75
55 Manny Margot RC .30 .75
56 Dustin Pedroia .30 .75
57 Jose De Leon RC .30 .75
58 Alex Reyes RC .40 1.00
59 Kyle Seager .20 .50
60 Justin Verlander .30 .75
61 Miguel Cabrera .30 .75
62 Adrian Beltre .30 .75
63 Nelson Cruz .30 .75
64 Michael Fulmer .20 .50
65 Ian Kinsler .25 .60
66 Andrew Benintendi RC 1.00 2.50
67 Nolan Arenado .50 1.25
68 Jason Kipnis .25 .60
69 Stephen Piscotty .25 .60
70 Andrew Miller .25 .60
71 Mookie Betts .60 1.50
72 Yu Darvish .30 .75
73 J.D. Martinez .30 .75
74 Gerrit Cole .30 .75
75 Raimel Tapia RC .40 1.00
76 Robinson Cano .25 .60
77 Carlos Gonzalez .25 .60
78 Rougned Odor .25 .60
79 Bryce Harper .50 1.25
80 Noah Syndergaard .25 .60
81 Johnny Cueto .25 .60
82 Charlie Blackmon .30 .75
83 Buster Posey .40 1.00
84 Matt Harvey .25 .60
85 Freddie Freeman .40 1.00
86 Paul Goldschmidt .30 .75
87 Hunter Renfroe RC .40 1.00
88 Robert Gsellman RC .30 .75
89 Alex Bregman RC 1.50 4.00
90 Yulieski Gurriel RC .50 1.25
91 Wil Myers .25 .60
92 Justin Upton .25 .60
93 Matt Carpenter .30 .75
94 Starling Marte .25 .60
95 Craig Kimbrel .25 .60
96 Xander Bogaerts .30 .75
97 George Springer .25 .60
98 Roberto Osuna .20 .50
99 Dee Gordon .20 .50
100 Kris Bryant .40 1.00
101 Jose Altuve SP 5.00 12.00
102 Dellin Betances SP 5.00 12.00
103 Jackie Bradley Jr. SP 6.00 15.00
104 Yoenis Cespedes SP 6.00 15.00
105 Gavin Cecchini SP RC 4.00 10.00
106 Jharel Cotton SP RC 4.00 10.00
107 Albert Pujols SP 8.00 20.00
108 Daniel Murphy SP 5.00 12.00
109 Tyler Glasnow SP RC 15.00 40.00
110 Chris Davis SP 4.00 10.00
111 A.J. Pollock SP 4.00 10.00
112 Gary Sanchez SP 6.00 15.00
113 Kyle Hendricks SP 6.00 15.00
114 Eric Hosmer SP 5.00 12.00
115 Andrew McCutchen SP 6.00 15.00
116 Luke Weaver SP RC 5.00 12.00
117 Zach Britton SP 5.00 12.00
118 Jacob deGrom SP 12.00 30.00
119 Edwin Diaz SP 5.00 12.00
120 Corey Kluber SP 5.00 12.00
121 Danny Duffy SP 4.00 10.00
122 Jose Abreu SP 6.00 15.00
123 David Dahl SP RC 5.00 12.00
124 Trevor Story SP 6.00 15.00
125 Anthony Rizzo SP 8.00 20.00

2017 Finest Blue Refractors

*BLUE REF: 3X TO 8X BASIC
*BLUE REF RC: 2X TO 5X BASIC RC
STATED ODDS 1:19 HOBBY
STATED PRINT RUN 150 SER.#'d SETS

2017 Finest Gold Refractors

*GOLD REF: 6X TO 15X BASIC

*GOLD REF RC: 4X TO 10X BASIC RC
STATED ODDS 1:55 HOBBY
STATED PRINT RUN 50 SER.#'d SETS

2017 Finest Green Refractors

*GREEN REF: 4X TO 10X BASIC
*GREEN REF RC: 2.5X TO 6X BASIC RC
STATED ODDS 1:28 HOBBY
STATED PRINT RUN 99 SER.#'d SETS

2017 Finest Orange Refractors

*ORANGE REF: 8X TO 20X BASIC
*ORANGE REF RC: 5X TO 12X BASIC RC
*ORANGE REF SP: .6X TO 1.5X BASIC SP
STATED ODDS 1:110 HOBBY
STATED SP ODDS 1:438 HOBBY
STATED PRINT RUN 25 SER.#'d SETS

2017 Finest Purple Refractors

*PURPLE REF: 2.5X TO 6X BASIC
*PURPLE REF RC: 1.5X TO 4X BASIC RC
STATED ODDS 1:11 HOBBY
STATED PRINT RUN 250 SER.#'d SETS

2017 Finest Refractors

*REF: 1.2X TO 3X BASIC
*REF RC: .75X TO 2X BASIC RC
STATED ODDS 1:3 HOBBY

2017 Finest '94-'95 Finest Recreates

STATED ODDS 1:6 HOBBY
*ORANGE/25: 6X TO 15X BASIC
BRAG Andres Galarraga .50 1.25
BRAR Anthony Rizzo .75 2.00
BRBH Bryce Harper 1.00 2.50
BRBP Buster Posey .75 2.00
BRCJ Chipper Jones .60 1.50
BRCS Corey Seager .60 1.50
BRFL Francisco Lindor .60 1.50
BRGM Greg Maddux .75 2.00
BRIR Ivan Rodriguez .50 1.25
BRI Ichiro .75 2.00
BRJA Jose Altuve .50 1.25
BRKB Kris Bryant .75 2.00
BRKGJ Ken Griffey Jr. 1.25 3.00
BRMF Michael Fulmer .40 1.00
BRNA Nolan Arenado 1.00 2.50
BRNS Noah Syndergaard .50 1.25
BROV Omar Vizquel .50 1.25
BRSP Stephen Piscotty .50 1.25
BRTS Trevor Story .60 1.50
BRWC Willson Contreras .60 1.50

2017 Finest '94-'95 Finest Recreates Autographs

STATED ODDS 1:508 HOBBY
EXCHANGE DEADLINE 5/31/2019
*ORANGE/25: .6X TO 1.5X BASIC
BRAAG Andres Galarraga 12.00 30.00
BRAAR Anthony Rizzo 30.00 80.00
BRABP Buster Posey
BRACJ Chipper Jones
BRACS Corey Seager 60.00 150.00
BRAFL Francisco Lindor 30.00 80.00
BRAGM Greg Maddux 75.00 200.00
BRAIR Ivan Rodriguez 25.00 60.00
BRAJA Jose Altuve 40.00 100.00
BRAKB Kris Bryant EXCH 200.00 400.00
BRANS Noah Syndergaard EXCH 30.00 80.00
BRAOV Omar Vizquel EXCH 20.00 50.00
BRASP Stephen Piscotty 20.00 50.00
BRATS Trevor Story 12.00 30.00
BRAWC Willson Contreras 20.00 50.00

2017 Finest Autographs Refractors

STATED ODDS 1:22 HOBBY
EXCHANGE DEADLINE 5/31/2019
FAAB Andrew Benintendi 30.00 80.00
FAABR Alex Bregman 20.00 50.00
FAAD Adam Duvall 12.00 30.00
FAAJ Aaron Judge 250.00 500.00
FAAR Anthony Rizzo 20.00 50.00
FAARE Alex Reyes 5.00 12.00
FAARU Addison Russell 10.00 25.00
FABB Barry Bonds 200.00 400.00
FABH Bryce Harper 150.00 300.00
FABP Buster Posey 30.00 80.00
FABS Blake Snell 4.00 10.00
FACC Carlos Correa 30.00 80.00
FACJ Chipper Jones
FACK Clayton Kershaw 50.00 120.00
FACR Cody Reed 3.00 8.00
FACS Corey Seager 60.00 150.00
FADD Danny Duffy 3.00 8.00
FADDA David Dahl 4.00 10.00
FADJ Derek Jeter
FADP David Price 10.00 25.00
FADS Dansby Swanson 15.00 40.00
FAER Eddie Rosario 4.00 10.00
FAFL Francisco Lindor 20.00 50.00
FAHO Henry Owens 3.00 8.00
FAHR Hunter Renfroe 4.00 10.00
FAIR Ivan Rodriguez 12.00 30.00
FAJA Jose Altuve 30.00 80.00
FAJAL Jorge Alfaro 4.00 10.00
FAJDL Jose De Leon 3.00 8.00
FAJH Jason Heyward 8.00 20.00
FAJMU Joe Musgrove 12.00 30.00
FAJT Justin Turner 20.00 50.00
FAKB Kris Bryant 100.00 200.00
FAKGJ Ken Griffey Jr. EXCH 100.00 250.00
FAKM Kendrys Morales 3.00 8.00
FALG Lucas Giolito 4.00 10.00
FALS Luis Severino 5.00 12.00
FALW Luke Weaver 4.00 10.00
FAMF Michael Fulmer 8.00 20.00
FAMK Max Kepler 4.00 10.00
FAMT Mike Trout 300.00 600.00
FAMTA Masahiro Tanaka 75.00 200.00
FANM Nomar Mazara 3.00 8.00
FANS Noah Syndergaard 10.00 25.00
FAOA Orlando Arcia 5.00 12.00
FAOV Omar Vizquel 4.00 10.00
FARH Ryon Healy 4.00 10.00
FARS Rob Segedin 3.00 8.00
FASP Stephen Piscotty 4.00 10.00
FASW Steven Wright 3.00 8.00
FATA Tyler Austin 4.00 10.00
FATN Tyler Naquin 5.00 12.00
FATS Trevor Story 5.00 12.00
FATT Trea Turner 8.00 20.00
FAWC Willson Contreras 12.00 30.00
FAYG Yulieski Gurriel 8.00 20.00
FAYM Yoan Moncada 60.00 150.00

2017 Finest Autographs Blue Refractors

*BLUE REF: .5X TO 1.2X BASIC
STATED ODDS 1:36 HOBBY
STATED PRINT RUN 150 SER.#'d SETS
EXCHANGE DEADLINE 5/31/2019

2017 Finest Autographs Blue Wave Refractors

*BLUE WAVE REF: 1X TO 2.5X BASIC
STATED ODDS 1:214 HOBBY
STATED PRINT RUN 25 SER.#'d SETS
EXCHANGE DEADLINE 5/31/2019
FABH Bryce Harper 200.00 400.00
FACJ Chipper Jones 150.00 300.00
FACK Clayton Kershaw 60.00 150.00
FACS Corey Seager 75.00 200.00
FADP David Price 12.00 30.00
FAIR Ivan Rodriguez 15.00 40.00
FAJA Jose Altuve 40.00 100.00
FAJH Jason Heyward 10.00 25.00
FAKB Kris Bryant 250.00 500.00
FAKGJ Ken Griffey Jr. EXCH 200.00 500.00
FAMT Mike Trout 400.00 800.00
FAMTA Masahiro Tanaka 100.00 250.00
FAYM Yoan Moncada 100.00 250.00

2017 Finest Autographs Gold Refractors

*GOLD REF: .75X TO 2X BASIC
STATED ODDS 1:107 HOBBY
STATED PRINT RUN 50 SER.#'d SETS
EXCHANGE DEADLINE 5/31/2019

2017 Finest Autographs Green Refractors

*GREEN REF: .6X TO 1.5X BASIC
STATED ODDS 1:54 HOBBY
STATED PRINT RUN 99 SER.#'d SETS
EXCHANGE DEADLINE 5/31/2019

2017 Finest Autographs Orange Refractors

*ORANGE REF: 1X TO 2.5X BASIC
STATED ODDS 1:214 HOBBY
STATED PRINT RUN 25 SER.#'d SETS
EXCHANGE DEADLINE 5/31/2019
FABH Bryce Harper 200.00 400.00
FACJ Chipper Jones 150.00 300.00
FACK Clayton Kershaw 60.00 150.00
FACS Corey Seager 75.00 200.00
FADP David Price 12.00 30.00
FAIR Ivan Rodriguez 15.00 40.00
FAJA Jose Altuve 40.00 100.00
FAJH Jason Heyward 10.00 25.00
FAKB Kris Bryant 250.00 500.00
FAKGJ Ken Griffey Jr. EXCH 200.00 500.00
FAMT Mike Trout 400.00 800.00
FAMTA Masahiro Tanaka 100.00 250.00
FAYM Yoan Moncada 100.00 250.00

2017 Finest Autographs Red Wave Refractors

*RED WAVE REF: 1X TO 2.5X BASIC
STATED ODDS 1:214 HOBBY
STATED PRINT RUN 25 SER.#'d SETS
EXCHANGE DEADLINE 5/31/2019
FABH Bryce Harper 200.00 400.00
FACJ Chipper Jones 150.00 300.00
FACK Clayton Kershaw 60.00 150.00
FACS Corey Seager 75.00 200.00
FADP David Price 12.00 30.00
FAIR Ivan Rodriguez 15.00 40.00
FAJA Jose Altuve 40.00 100.00
FAJH Jason Heyward 10.00 25.00
FAKB Kris Bryant 250.00 500.00
FAKGJ Ken Griffey Jr. EXCH 200.00 500.00
FAMT Mike Trout 400.00 800.00
FAMTA Masahiro Tanaka 100.00 250.00
FAYM Yoan Moncada 100.00 250.00

2017 Finest Breakthroughs

STATED ODDS 1:3 HOBBY
*ORANGE/25: 4X TO 10X BASIC
FBAD Aledmys Diaz .50 1.25
FBAN Aaron Nola .50 1.25
FBAR Anthony Rizzo .75 2.00
FBARU Addison Russell .60 1.50
FBBH Bryce Harper 1.00 2.50
FBCC Carlos Correa .60 1.50
FBCS Corey Seager .60 1.50
FBFL Francisco Lindor .60 1.50
FBJA Jose Altuve .50 1.25
FBJD Jacob deGrom 1.25 3.00
FBKB Kris Bryant .75 2.00
FBKM Kenta Maeda .50 1.25
FBMT Mike Trout 3.00 8.00
FBNA Nolan Arenado 1.00 2.50
FBNM Nomar Mazara .40 1.00
FBNS Noah Syndergaard .50 1.25
FBSM Steven Matz .40 1.00
FBSP Stephen Piscotty .50 1.25
FBTS Trevor Story .60 1.50
FBWC Willson Contreras .60 1.50

2017 Finest Breakthroughs Autographs

STATED ODDS 1:356 HOBBY
PRINT RUNS B/WN 10-50 COPIES PER
NO PRICING ON QTY 20 OR LESS
EXCHANGE DEADLINE 5/31/2019
*ORANGE/25: .5X TO 1.2X BASIC
FBAAD Aledmys Diaz/50 8.00 20.00
FBAAR Anthony Rizzo/30 25.00 60.00
FBACS Corey Seager/30 75.00 200.00
FBAFL Francisco Lindor EXCH 25.00 60.00
FBAJA Jose Altuve/50 30.00 80.00
FBAKB Kris Bryant
FBANM Nomar Mazara/50 20.00 50.00
FBANS Noah Syndergaard EXCH
FBASP Stephen Piscotty/50 12.00 30.00
FBATS Trevor Story/50 12.00 30.00
FBAWC Willson Contreras/50 10.00 25.00

2017 Finest Careers Die Cut

STATED ODDS 1:48 HOBBY
*ORANGE/25: 2X TO 5X BASIC
FCID01 David Ortiz 2.00 5.00
FCID02 David Ortiz 2.00 5.00
FCID03 David Ortiz 2.00 5.00
FCID04 David Ortiz 2.00 5.00
FCID05 David Ortiz 2.00 5.00
FCID06 David Ortiz 2.00 5.00
FCID07 David Ortiz 2.00 5.00
FCID08 David Ortiz 2.00 5.00
FCID09 David Ortiz 2.00 5.00
FCID010 David Ortiz 2.00 5.00

2017 Finest Careers Die Cut Autographs

COMMON CARD 100.00 250.00
STATED ODDS 1:2666 HOBBY
STATED PRINT RUN 10 SER.#'d SETS
EXCHANGE DEADLINE 5/31/2019

2017 Finest Finishes Autographs

STATED ODDS 1:122 HOBBY
EXCHANGE DEADLINE 5/31/2019
*ORANGE/25: .6X TO 1.5X BASIC
FINABB Barry Bonds 100.00 250.00
FINACF Carlton Fisk 20.00 50.00
FINACRJ Cal Ripken Jr. 50.00 120.00
FINADJ Derek Jeter 400.00 700.00
FINAEM Edgar Martinez 12.00 30.00
FINAFL Francisco Lindor 10.00 25.00
FINAFV Fernando Valenzuela 15.00 40.00
FINAHA Hank Aaron
FINAIR Ivan Rodriguez 10.00 25.00
FINAJA Jake Arrieta EXCH 20.00 50.00
FINAKB Kris Bryant 100.00 200.00
FINAKGJ Ken Griffey Jr. EXCH 200.00 300.00
FINALG Luis Gonzalez 4.00 10.00
FINAMM Mark McGwire 60.00 150.00
FINANR Nolan Ryan
FINAOS Ozzie Smith 15.00 40.00
FINAOV Omar Vizquel 5.00 12.00
FINAPM Pedro Martinez 40.00 100.00
FINARJ Reggie Jackson 40.00 100.00
FINASK Sandy Koufax 100.00 250.00

2017 Finest Firsts

STATED ODDS 1:12 HOBBY
*ORANGE/25: 2.5X TO 6X BASIC
FFIAB Andrew Benintendi 1.50 4.00
FFIABR Alex Bregman 2.50 6.00
FFIAJ Aaron Judge 10.00 25.00
FFIAR Alex Reyes .60 1.50
FFIDD David Dahl .60 1.50
FFIDS Dansby Swanson 1.25 3.00
FFIOA Orlando Arcia .75 2.00
FFITG Tyler Glasnow 2.00 5.00
FFIYG Yulieski Gurriel .75 2.00
FFIYM Yoan Moncada 1.50 4.00

2017 Finest Firsts Autographs

STATED ODDS 1:77 HOBBY
EXCHANGE DEADLINE 5/31/2019
FFAB Andrew Benintendi 25.00 60.00
FFABR Alex Bregman 15.00 40.00
FFAJ Aaron Judge
FFAR Alex Reyes 5.00 12.00
FFDD David Dahl 5.00 12.00
FFDS Dansby Swanson 20.00 50.00
FFHR Hunter Renfroe 5.00 12.00
FFJDL Jose De Leon 4.00 10.00
FFOA Orlando Arcia
FFTA Tyler Austin 5.00 12.00
FFYG Yulieski Gurriel 6.00 15.00
FFYM Yoan Moncada 40.00 100.00

2017 Finest Firsts Autographs Blue Refractors

*BLUE REF: .5X TO 1.2X BASIC
STATED ODDS 1:178 HOBBY
STATED PRINT RUN 150 SER.#'d SETS
EXCHANGE DEADLINE 5/31/2019
FFAJ Aaron Judge 175.00 350.00

2017 Finest Firsts Autographs Blue Wave Refractors

*BLUE WAVE: 1X TO 2.5X BASIC
STATED ODDS 1:1067 HOBBY
STATED PRINT RUN 25 SER.#'d SETS
EXCHANGE DEADLINE 5/31/2019
FFAJ Aaron Judge 350.00 700.00
FFOA Orlando Arcia 20.00 50.00

2017 Finest Firsts Autographs Gold Refractors

*GOLD REF: .75X TO 2X BASIC
STATED ODDS 1:534 HOBBY
STATED PRINT RUN 50 SER.#'d SETS
EXCHANGE DEADLINE 5/31/2019
FFAJ Aaron Judge 250.00 500.00
FFOA Orlando Arcia 12.00 30.00

2017 Finest Firsts Autographs Green Refractors

*GREEN REF: .6X TO 1.5X BASIC
STATED ODDS 1:270 HOBBY
STATED PRINT RUN 99 SER.#'d SETS
EXCHANGE DEADLINE 5/31/2019
FFAJ Aaron Judge 200.00 400.00

2017 Finest Firsts Autographs Orange Refractors

*ORANGE REF: 1X TO 2.5X BASIC
STATED ODDS 1:1067 HOBBY
STATED PRINT RUN 25 SER.#'d SETS
EXCHANGE DEADLINE 5/31/2019
FFAJ Aaron Judge 350.00 700.00
FFOA Orlando Arcia 20.00 50.00

2017 Finest Firsts Autographs Red Wave Refractors

*RED WAVE: 1X TO 2.5X BASIC
STATED ODDS 1:1067 HOBBY
STATED PRINT RUN 25 SER.#'d SETS
EXCHANGE DEADLINE 5/31/2019
FFAJ Aaron Judge 350.00 700.00
FFOA Orlando Arcia 20.00 50.00

2017 Finest Mystery Redemption Autographs

STATED ODDS 1:898 HOBBY
EXCHANGE DEADLINE 5/31/2019
FMR1 Cody Bellinger 125.00 300.00
FMR2 Ian Happ 75.00 200.00
FMR3 Bradley Zimmer 75.00 200.00

2018 Finest

COMP.SET w/o SP's (100) 20.00 50.00
STATED SP ODDS 1:28 HOBBY
1 Aaron Judge .75 2.00
2 Francisco Lindor .30 .75
3 Brandon Woodruff RC 1.00 2.50
4 Rougned Odor .25 .60
5 Jose Abreu .30 .75
6 Chris Archer .20 .50
7 Andrew Benintendi .30 .75
8 Evan Longoria .25 .60
9 Joey Gallo .25 .60
10 Dallas Keuchel .25 .60
11 Austin Hays RC .50 1.25
12 Nicky Delmonico RC .30 .75
13 Elvis Andrus .25 .60
14 Jack Flaherty RC 1.25 3.00
15 Domingo Santana .25 .60
16 Anthony Rendon .30 .75
17 Alex Wood .20 .50
18 Eric Thames .25 .60
19 Jacob deGrom .60 1.50
20 Nomar Mazara .20 .50
21 Tommy Pham .20 .50
22 Didi Gregorius .25 .60
23 Tim Beckham .25 .60
24 Yadier Molina .40 1.00
25 Kris Bryant .40 1.00
26 Carlos Carrasco .20 .50
27 Jose Ramirez .25 .60
28 Lucas Sims RC .30 .75
29 Giancarlo Stanton .30 .75
30 Charlie Blackmon .30 .75
31 Albert Pujols .40 1.00
32 Ervin Santana .20 .50
33 Billy Hamilton .25 .60
34 Marcus Stroman .25 .60
35 Robinson Cano .25 .60
36 Dominic Smith RC .40 1.00
37 Anthony Rizzo .40 1.00
38 Mookie Betts .60 1.50
39 Wil Myers .25 .60
40 Clayton Kershaw .50 1.25
41 Travis Shaw .20 .50
42 Kevin Pillar .20 .50
43 Yuli Gurriel .25 .60
44 Paul DeJong .30 .75
45 George Springer .25 .60
46 Buster Posey .40 1.00
47 Craig Kimbrel .25 .60
48 Andrelton Simmons .20 .50
49 Justin Verlander .30 .75
50 Mike Trout 1.50 4.00
51 Adrian Beltre .30 .75
52 Raisel Iglesias .25 .60
53 Dustin Fowler RC .30 .75
54 Salvador Perez .25 .60
55 Stephen Strasburg .30 .75
56 Ryan McMahon RC .75 2.00
57 Edwin Encarnacion .30 .75
58 Noah Syndergaard .25 .60
59 Nolan Arenado .50 1.25
60 Maikel Franco .25 .60
61 Rafael Devers RC 1.00 2.50
62 Khris Davis .30 .75
63 J.P. Crawford RC .30 .75
64 Chris Sale .30 .75
65 Odubel Herrera .25 .60
66 Alex Bregman .30 .75
67 Justin Turner .30 .75
68 Michael Fulmer .20 .50
69 Brian Dozier .25 .60
70 Freddie Freeman .40 1.00
71 Avisail Garcia .25 .60
72 Adam Jones .25 .60
73 Jose Altuve .25 .60
74 Francisco Mejia RC .40 1.00
75 Rhys Hoskins RC 1.25 3.00
76 Max Scherzer .30 .75
77 Miguel Cabrera .30 .75
78 Corey Knebel .20 .50
79 Jackie Bradley Jr. .30 .75
80 Kenley Jansen .25 .60
81 Amed Rosario RC .40 1.00
82 Bryce Harper .50 1.25
83 Nick Williams RC .40 1.00
84 David Robertson .20 .50
85 Chance Sisco RC .40 1.00
86 Robbie Ray .20 .50
87 Nelson Cruz .30 .75
88 Ryan Braun .25 .60
89 Cody Bellinger .60 1.50
90 Miguel Andujar RC 1.25 3.00
91 Willson Contreras .30 .75
92 Andrew McCutchen .30 .75
93 Gary Sanchez .30 .75
94 Yoenis Cespedes .30 .75
95 Matt Olson .30 .75
96 Brett Gardner .25 .60
97 Paul Goldschmidt .30 .75
98 Manny Machado .30 .75
99 Alex Verdugo RC .50 1.25
100 Shohei Ohtani RC 6.00 15.00
101 Joey Votto SP 5.00 12.00
102 Yoan Moncada SP 5.00 12.00
103 Ozzie Albies SP RC 10.00 25.00
104 Corey Kluber SP 4.00 10.00
105 Jake Lamb SP 4.00 10.00
106 Aaron Altherr SP 3.00 8.00
107 Harrison Bader SP RC 5.00 12.00
108 Jose Berrios SP 4.00 10.00
109 Jonathan Schoop SP 3.00 8.00
110 Marcell Ozuna SP 5.00 12.00
111 J.D. Davis SP RC 4.00 10.00
112 Willie Calhoun SP RC 5.00 12.00
113 Hunter Renfroe SP 3.00 8.00
114 Michael Conforto SP 4.00 10.00
115 Brandon Crawford SP 4.00 10.00
116 Whit Merrifield SP 5.00 12.00
117 Josh Donaldson SP 4.00 10.00
118 Josh Bell SP 4.00 10.00
119 Clint Frazier SP RC 6.00 15.00
120 Nicholas Castellanos SP 5.00 12.00
121 Byron Buxton SP 5.00 12.00
122 Luis Severino SP 4.00 10.00
123 Corey Seager SP 5.00 12.00
124 Zack Greinke SP 5.00 12.00
125 Carlos Correa SP 5.00 12.00

2018 Finest Blue Refractors

*BLUE REF: 2X TO 5X BASIC
*BLUE REF RC: 1.2X TO 3X BASIC RC
STATED ODDS 1:28 HOBBY
STATED PRINT RUN 150 SER.#'d SETS
50 Mike Trout 10.00 25.00
100 Shohei Ohtani 40.00 100.00

2018 Finest Gold Refractors

*GOLD REF: 5X TO 12X BASIC
*GOLD REF RC: 3X TO 8X BASIC RC
*GOLD SP REF RC: .6X TO 1.5X BASIC RC
1-100 STATED ODDS 1:84 HOBBY
101-125 STATED ODDS 1:333 HOBBY
STATED PRINT RUN 50 SER.#'d SETS
50 Mike Trout 25.00 60.00
100 Shohei Ohtani 200.00 400.00

2018 Finest Green Refractors

*GREEN REF: 3X TO 8X BASIC
*GREEN REF RC: 2X TO 5X BASIC RC
STATED ODDS 1:43 HOBBY
STATED PRINT RUN 99 SER.#'d SETS
50 Mike Trout 15.00 40.00
100 Shohei Ohtani 60.00 150.00

2018 Finest Orange Refractors

*ORANGE REF: 6X TO 15X BASIC
*ORANGE REF RC: 4X TO 10X BASIC RC
STATED ODDS 1:167 HOBBY
STATED PRINT RUN 25 SER.#'d SETS
50 Mike Trout 30.00 80.00
100 Shohei Ohtani 250.00 500.00

2018 Finest Purple Refractors

*PURPLE REF: 1.5X TO 4X BASIC
*PURPLE REF RC: 1X TO 2.5X BASIC RC
STATED ODDS 1:11 HOBBY
STATED PRINT RUN 250 SER.#'d SETS
50 Mike Trout 8.00 20.00
100 Shohei Ohtani 25.00 60.00

2018 Finest Refractors

*REF: 1X TO 2.5X BASIC
*REF RC: .6X TO 1.5X BASIC RC
STATED ODDS 1:3 HOBBY

2018 Finest Autographs

STATED ODDS 1:14 HOBBY
EXCHANGE DEADLINE 5/31/2020
FAAB Adrian Beltre 20.00 50.00
FAABA Anthony Banda 2.50 6.00
FAAH Austin Hays 4.00 10.00
FAAP Andy Pettitte 12.00 30.00
FAAR Amed Rosario 3.00 8.00
FAAV Alex Verdugo 6.00 15.00
FABA Brian Anderson 5.00 12.00
FABD Brian Dozier 5.00 12.00
FABW Brandon Woodruff 8.00 20.00
FACA Christian Arroyo 2.50 6.00
FACS Chris Sale 10.00 25.00
FACT Chris Taylor 3.00 8.00
FADF Dustin Fowler 2.50 6.00
FADG Didi Gregorius 10.00 25.00
FADJ Derek Jeter 300.00 600.00
FADS Dominic Smith 3.00 8.00
FAFM Francisco Mejia 6.00 15.00
FAGA Greg Allen 2.50 6.00
FAGC Garrett Cooper 2.50 6.00
FAHB Harrison Bader 4.00 10.00
FAIH Ian Happ 5.00 12.00
FAJC J.P. Crawford 2.50 6.00
FAJF Jack Flaherty 15.00 40.00
FAJL Jake Lamb 3.00 8.00
FAJR Jose Ramirez 3.00 8.00
FAJT Jim Thome 50.00 120.00
FAKB Kris Bryant EXCH 60.00 150.00
FAKD Khris Davis 6.00 15.00
FALG Lucas Giolito 6.00 15.00
FALSI Lucas Sims 2.50 6.00
FAMA Miguel Andujar 10.00 25.00
FAMFR Max Fried 12.00 30.00
FAMM Manny Machado 15.00 40.00
FAMO Matt Olson 4.00 10.00
FAMR Mariano Rivera 100.00 250.00
FAMT Mike Trout
FAOA Ozzie Albies 12.00 30.00
FAPBL Paul Blackburn 2.50 6.00
FARD Rafael Devers 20.00 50.00
FARI Raisel Iglesias 3.00 8.00
FARM Ryan McMahon 6.00 15.00
FASA Sandy Alcantara 2.50 6.00
FASN Sean Newcomb 3.00 8.00
FASO Shohei Ohtani 250.00 600.00
FATM Tyler Mahle 3.00 8.00
FATP Tommy Pham 2.50 6.00
FATS Travis Shaw 3.00 8.00
FATW Tyler Wade 3.00 8.00
FATWL Tzu-Wei Lin 5.00 12.00
FAVR Victor Robles 12.00 30.00
FAWB Walker Buehler 25.00 60.00

2018 Finest Autographs Blue Refractors

*BLUE REF: .5X TO 1.2X BASIC
STATED ODDS 1:55 HOBBY
STATED PRINT RUN 150 SER.#'d SETS
EXCHANGE DEADLINE 5/31/2020
FABA Brian Anderson 10.00 25.00
FAWM Whit Merrifield 10.00 25.00

2018 Finest Autographs Gold Refractors

*GOLD REF: .75X TO 2X BASIC
STATED ODDS 1:164 HOBBY
STATED PRINT RUN 50 SER.#'d SETS
EXCHANGE DEADLINE 5/31/2020
FABA Brian Anderson 20.00 50.00
FACS Chris Sale 12.00 30.00
FACSI Chance Sisco 10.00 25.00
FAOA Ozzie Albies 25.00 60.00
FAPD Paul DeJong 12.00 30.00
FARD Rafael Devers 50.00 120.00
FASO Shohei Ohtani 500.00 1200.00
FATS Travis Shaw 10.00 25.00
FATWL Tzu-Wei Lin 25.00 60.00
FAWM Whit Merrifield 15.00 40.00

2018 Finest Autographs Green Refractors

*GREEN REF: .6X TO 1.5X BASIC
STATED ODDS 1:83 HOBBY
STATED PRINT RUN 99 SER.#'d SETS
EXCHANGE DEADLINE 5/31/2020
FABA Brian Anderson 12.00 30.00
FACSI Chance Sisco 8.00 20.00
FAPD Paul DeJong 8.00 20.00
FAWM Whit Merrifield 12.00 30.00

2018 Finest Autographs Green Wave Refractors

*GREEN WAVE REF: .6X TO 1.5X BASIC
STATED ODDS 1:83 HOBBY
STATED PRINT RUN 99 SER.#'d SETS
EXCHANGE DEADLINE 5/31/2020
FABA Brian Anderson 12.00 30.00
FACSI Chance Sisco 8.00 20.00
FAPD Paul DeJong 8.00 20.00
FAWM Whit Merrifield 12.00 30.00

2018 Finest Autographs Orange Refractors

*ORANGE REF: 1X TO 2.5X BASIC
STATED ODDS 1:370 HOBBY
STATED PRINT RUN 25 SER.#'d SETS
EXCHANGE DEADLINE 5/31/2020
FAAB Adrian Beltre 30.00 80.00
FAAV Alex Verdugo 30.00 80.00
FABA Brian Anderson 25.00 60.00
FACS Chris Sale 15.00 40.00
FACSI Chance Sisco 20.00 50.00
FADF Dustin Fowler 20.00 50.00
FADS Dominic Smith 10.00 25.00
FAFM Francisco Mejia 30.00 80.00
FAJT Jim Thome 60.00 150.00
FAKB Kris Bryant EXCH 125.00 300.00
FAOA Ozzie Albies 30.00 80.00
FAPD Paul DeJong 15.00 40.00
FARD Rafael Devers 60.00 150.00
FASN Sean Newcomb 20.00 50.00
FASO Shohei Ohtani 600.00 1500.00
FATS Travis Shaw 12.00 30.00
FATWL Tzu-Wei Lin 30.00 80.00
FAWM Whit Merrifield 20.00 50.00

2018 Finest Autographs Orange Wave Refractors

*ORANGE WAVE REF: 1X TO 2.5X BASIC
STATED ODDS 1:370 HOBBY
STATED PRINT RUN 25 SER.#'d SETS
EXCHANGE DEADLINE 5/31/2020
FAAB Adrian Beltre 30.00 80.00
FAAV Alex Verdugo 30.00 80.00
FABA Brian Anderson 25.00 60.00
FACS Chris Sale 15.00 40.00
FACSI Chance Sisco 20.00 50.00
FADF Dustin Fowler 20.00 50.00
FADS Dominic Smith 10.00 25.00
FAFM Francisco Mejia 30.00 80.00
FAJT Jim Thome 60.00 150.00
FAKB Kris Bryant EXCH 125.00 300.00
FAOA Ozzie Albies 30.00 80.00
FAPD Paul DeJong 15.00 40.00
FARD Rafael Devers 60.00 150.00
FASN Sean Newcomb 20.00 50.00
FASO Shohei Ohtani 600.00 1500.00
FATS Travis Shaw 12.00 30.00
FATWL Tzu-Wei Lin 30.00 80.00
FAWM Whit Merrifield 20.00 50.00

2018 Finest Careers Die Cut

STATED ODDS 1:48 HOBBY
*GOLD/50: 1.5X TO 4X BASIC
*RED/5: 5X TO 12X BASIC
FCCR1 Cal Ripken Jr. 4.00 10.00
FCCR2 Cal Ripken Jr. 4.00 10.00
FCCR3 Cal Ripken Jr. 4.00 10.00
FCCR4 Cal Ripken Jr. 4.00 10.00
FCCR5 Cal Ripken Jr. 4.00 10.00
FCCR6 Cal Ripken Jr. 4.00 10.00
FCCR7 Cal Ripken Jr. 4.00 10.00
FCCR8 Cal Ripken Jr. 4.00 10.00
FCCR9 Cal Ripken Jr. 4.00 10.00
FCCR10 Cal Ripken Jr. 4.00 10.00

2018 Finest Careers Die Cut Autographs

STATED ODDS 1:4056 HOBBY
STATED PRINT RUN 10 SER.#'d SETS
EXCHANGE DEADLINE 5/31/2020
FCACR1 Cal Ripken Jr. 80.00 200.00
FCACR2 Cal Ripken Jr. 80.00 200.00
FCACR3 Cal Ripken Jr. 80.00 200.00
FCACR4 Cal Ripken Jr. 80.00 200.00
FCACR5 Cal Ripken Jr. 80.00 200.00
FCACR6 Cal Ripken Jr. 80.00 200.00
FCACR7 Cal Ripken Jr. 80.00 200.00
FCACR8 Cal Ripken Jr. 80.00 200.00
FCACR9 Cal Ripken Jr. 80.00 200.00
FCACR10 Cal Ripken Jr. 80.00 200.00

2018 Finest Cornerstones

STATED ODDS 1:3 HOBBY
*GOLD/50: 2.5X TO 6X BASIC
FCAB Andrew Benintendi .60 1.50
FCAJ Aaron Judge 1.50 4.00
FCBH Bryce Harper 1.00 2.50
FCBP Buster Posey .75 2.00
FCCA Chris Archer .40 1.00
FCCB Cody Bellinger 1.25 3.00
FCCC Carlos Correa .60 1.50
FCFF Freddie Freeman .75 2.00
FCFL Francisco Lindor .60 1.50
FCJA Jose Abreu .60 1.50
FCJB Josh Bell .50 1.25
FCJD Josh Donaldson .50 1.25
FCJUB Justin Bour .40 1.00
FCJV Joey Votto .60 1.50
FCKB Kris Bryant .75 2.00
FCMC Miguel Cabrera .60 1.50
FCMM Manny Machado .60 1.50
FCMO Matt Olson .60 1.50
FCMS Miguel Sano .50 1.25
FCMT Mike Trout 3.00 8.00
FCNA Nolan Arenado 1.00 2.50
FCNM Nomar Mazara .40 1.00
FCNS Noah Syndergaard .50 1.25
FCPG Paul Goldschmidt .60 1.50
FCRB Ryan Braun .50 1.25
FCRC Robinson Cano .50 1.25
FCRH Rhys Hoskins 1.50 4.00
FCSP Salvador Perez .50 1.25
FCWM Wil Myers .50 1.25
FCYM Yadier Molina .75 2.00

2018 Finest Cornerstones Autographs

STATED ODDS 1:314 HOBBY
EXCHANGE DEADLINE 5/31/2020
FCABH Bryce Harper 125.00 300.00
FCAEL Evan Longoria 10.00 25.00
FCAFF Freddie Freeman 25.00 60.00
FCAJV Joey Votto 30.00 80.00
FCAKB Kris Bryant EXCH 125.00 300.00
FCAMM Manny Machado 25.00 60.00
FCAMO Matt Olson 8.00 20.00
FCAMT Mike Trout 250.00 500.00
FCAPG Paul Goldschmidt
FCARB Ryan Braun 10.00 25.00
FCAYM Yadier Molina 50.00 120.00

2018 Finest Cornerstones Autographs Orange Refractors

*ORANGE REF: .6X TO 1.5X BASIC
STATED ODDS 1:815 HOBBY
STATED PRINT RUN 25 SER.#'d SETS
EXCHANGE DEADLINE 5/31/2020
FCAPG Paul Goldschmidt 40.00 100.00

2018 Finest Finest Hour Autographs

STATED ODDS 1:156 HOBBY
EXCHANGE DEADLINE 5/31/2020
FHAABE Adrian Beltre 20.00 50.00
FHAAJ Aaron Judge 75.00 200.00
FHAAP Andy Pettitte 10.00 25.00
FHAAR Amed Rosario 5.00 12.00
FHABH Bryce Harper 150.00 400.00
FHABJ Bo Jackson 40.00 100.00
FHABL Barry Larkin 15.00 40.00
FHACF Clint Frazier 12.00 30.00
FHACK Clayton Kershaw
FHACS Chris Sale 10.00 25.00
FHADJ Derek Jeter 300.00 600.00
FHADS Dominic Smith 5.00 12.00
FHAFL Francisco Lindor 20.00 50.00
FHAFT Frank Thomas 25.00 60.00
FHAGS Gary Sanchez EXCH 15.00 40.00
FHAI Ichiro 150.00 300.00
FHAKB Kris Bryant EXCH 60.00 150.00
FHAMR Mariano Rivera 75.00 200.00
FHAMT Mike Trout 300.00 600.00
FHAOS Ozzie Smith 20.00 50.00
FHAPM Pedro Martinez 30.00 80.00
FHARD Rafael Devers 12.00 30.00
FHARH Rhys Hoskins 20.00 50.00
FHARHE Rickey Henderson
FHAVR Victor Robles 10.00 25.00

2018 Finest Finest Hour Autographs Gold Refractors

*GOLD REF: .5X TO 1.2X BASIC
STATED ODDS 1:407 HOBBY
STATED PRINT RUN 50 SER.#'d SETS
EXCHANGE DEADLINE 5/31/2020

2018 Finest Finest Hour Autographs Orange Refractors

*ORANGE REF: .6X TO 1.5X BASIC
STATED ODDS 1:813 HOBBY
STATED PRINT RUN 25 SER.#'d SETS
EXCHANGE DEADLINE 5/31/2020
FHACK Clayton Kershaw 60.00 150.00
FHARHE Rickey Henderson 40.00 100.00

2018 Finest Firsts

STATED ODDS 1:12 HOBBY
*GOLD/50: 4X TO 10X BASIC
FFAR Amed Rosario .60 1.50
FFAV Alex Verdugo .75 2.00
FFCF Clint Frazier 1.00 2.50
FFDS Dominic Smith .60 1.50
FFNW Nick Williams .60 1.50
FFOA Ozzie Albies 1.50 4.00
FFRD Rafael Devers 1.50 4.00
FFRH Rhys Hoskins 2.00 5.00
FFSO Shohei Ohtani 12.00 30.00
FFVR Victor Robles 1.25 3.00

2018 Finest Firsts Autographs

STATED ODDS 1:204 HOBBY
EXCHANGE DEADLINE 5/31/2020
*BLUE/150: .5X TO 1.2X BASIC
*GREEN/99: .6X TO 1.5X BASIC
*GREEN WAVE/99: .6X TO 1.5X BASIC
*GOLD/50: .75X TO 2X BASIC
*ORANGE/25: 1X TO 2.5X BASIC
*ORNGE WAVE/25: 1X TO 2.5X BASIC
FFAAR Amed Rosario 5.00 12.00
FFAAV Alex Verdugo 6.00 15.00
FFADS Dominic Smith 5.00 12.00
FFAFM Francisco Mejia 8.00 20.00
FFAHB Harrison Bader 6.00 15.00
FFAJC J.P. Crawford 4.00 10.00
FFAJF Jack Flaherty 15.00 40.00
FFAMA Miguel Andujar 15.00 40.00
FFAOA Ozzie Albies 12.00 30.00
FFARD Rafael Devers 254.00 60.00
FFAVR Victor Robles 12.00 30.00

2018 Finest Mystery Redemption Autographs

STATED ODDS 1:1390 HOBBY
EXCHANGE DEADLINE 5/31/2020
1 Shohei Ohtani 200.00 500.00
2 Gleyber Torres 50.00 120.00
3 Ronald Acuna Jr. 200.00 500.00

2018 Finest Sitting Red

STATED ODDS 1:6 HOBBY
*GOLD/50: 2.5X TO 6X BASIC
SRAJ Aaron Judge 1.50 4.00
SRBH Bryce Harper 1.00 2.50
SRCB Cody Bellinger 1.25 3.00
SREE Edwin Encarnacion .60 1.50

SRGS Gary Sanchez .60 1.50
SRGST Giancarlo Stanton .60 1.50
SRJD Josh Donaldson .50 1.25
SRJG Joey Gallo .50 1.25
SRJV Joey Votto .60 1.50
SRKB Kris Bryant .75 2.00
SRKD Khris Davis .60 1.50
SRMM Manny Machado .60 1.50
SRMO Matt Olson .60 1.50
SRMS Miguel Sano .50 1.25
SRMT Mike Trout 3.00 8.00
SRNA Nolan Arenado 1.00 2.50
SRNC Nelson Cruz .60 1.50
SRPG Paul Goldschmidt .60 1.50
SRRH Rhys Hoskins 1.50 4.00
SRYC Yoenis Cespedes .60 1.50

2018 Finest Sitting Red Autographs

STATED ODDS 1:544 HOBBY
STATED PRINT RUN 50 SER.#'d SETS
EXCHANGE DEADLINE 5/31/2020
SRABH Bryce Harper
SRAEE Edwin Encarnacion 10.00 25.00
SRAJV Joey Votto
SRAKB Kris Bryant EXCH
SRAKD Khris Davis 10.00 25.00
SRAMM Manny Machado
SRAMO Matt Olson 10.00 25.00
SRAMT Mike Trout
SRAPG Paul Goldschmidt
SRAYC Yoenis Cespedes 12.00 30.00

2018 Finest Sitting Red Autographs Orange Refractors

*ORANGE REF: .5X TO 1.2X BASIC
STATED ODDS 1:1089 HOBBY
STATED PRINT RUN 25 SER.#'d SETS
EXCHANGE DEADLINE 5/31/2020
SRAJV Joey Votto 60.00 150.00
SRAKB Kris Bryant EXCH 125.00 300.00
SRAMM Manny Machado 40.00 100.00
SRAPG Paul Goldschmidt 30.00 80.00

2019 Finest

COMP.SET w/o SP's (100) 20.00 50.00
STATED SP ODDS 1:30 HOBBY
1 Mookie Betts .60 1.50
2 Salvador Perez .25 .60
3 Kyle Tucker RC .75 2.00
4 Wil Myers .25 .60
5 Matt Chapman .30 .75
6 Aaron Nola .25 .60
7 Walker Buehler .40 1.00
8 Steven Duggar RC .40 1.00
9 Ryan O'Hearn RC .30 .75
10 Trevor Story .30 .75
11 Buster Posey .40 1.00
12 Albert Pujols .40 1.00
13 Javier Baez .40 1.00
14 Miguel Cabrera .30 .75
15 Marcus Stroman .25 .60
16 Michael Kopech RC 1.00 2.50
17 Maikel Franco .25 .60
18 Eloy Jimenez RC 1.25 3.00
19 Paul DeJong .30 .75
20 J.D. Martinez .30 .75
21 Paul Goldschmidt .30 .75
22 Ramon Laureano RC .60 1.50
23 Clayton Kershaw .50 1.25
24 Christin Stewart RC .40 1.00
25 Mike Trout 1.50 4.00
26 Joey Votto .30 .75
27 Kolby Allard RC .50 1.25
28 David Peralta .20 .50
29 Brandon Crawford .25 .60
30 Rhys Hoskins .40 1.00
31 Carlos Correa .30 .75
32 Jose Abreu .30 .75
33 Ronald Acuna Jr. 1.50 4.00
34 Robinson Cano .25 .60
35 Miguel Andujar .40 1.00
36 Blake Snell .25 .60
37 Chris Davis .20 .50
38 Francisco Lindor .30 .75
39 Corbin Burnes RC 2.50 6.00
40 Willy Adames .25 .60
41 Ryan Borucki RC .30 .75
42 Christian Yelich .40 1.00
43 Whit Merrifield .30 .75
44 Pete Alonso RC 2.50 6.00
45 Trey Mancini .25 .60
46 DJ Stewart RC .40 1.00
47 Yadier Molina .40 1.00
48 Josh Bell .25 .60
49 Brian Anderson .25 .60
50 Jacob deGrom .60 1.50
51 Aaron Judge .75 2.00
52 Rowdy Tellez RC .50 1.25
53 Gleyber Torres .60 1.50
54 Dee Gordon .20 .50
55 Jose Berrios .25 .60
56 Luis Urias RC .50 1.25
57 Mitch Haniger .25 .60
58 Scooter Gennett .25 .60
59 Ozzie Albies .30 .75
60 Lucas Giolito .25 .60
61 Starlin Castro .20 .50
62 Joey Gallo .25 .60
63 Charlie Blackmon .30 .75
64 Justus Sheffield RC .50 1.25
65 Anthony Rizzo .40 1.00
66 Tim Anderson .30 .75
67 Juan Soto 1.00 2.50
68 Xander Bogaerts .30 .75
69 Max Kepler .25 .60
70 Ronald Guzman .20 .50
71 Chris Shaw RC .30 .75
72 Corey Kluber .25 .60
73 Cedric Mullins RC .60 1.50
74 Kris Bryant .40 1.00
75 Nolan Arenado .50 1.25
76 Danny Jansen RC .30 .75
77 Eric Hosmer .25 .60
78 Byron Buxton .30 .75
79 Gregory Polanco .25 .60
80 Zack Greinke .30 .75
81 Trea Turner .25 .60
82 Justin Smoak .20 .50
83 Chance Adams RC .30 .75
84 Cody Bellinger .60 1.50
85 Fernando Tatis Jr. RC 15.00 40.00
86 Jake Bauers RC .50 1.25
87 Kyle Wright RC .50 1.25
88 Touki Toussaint RC .40 1.00
89 Jose Ramirez .25 .60
90 Jose Altuve .25 .60
91 Billy Hamilton .25 .60
92 Alex Bregman .30 .75
93 Matt Olson .30 .75
94 Josh Hader .25 .60
95 Noah Syndergaard .25 .60
96 Nicholas Castellanos .30 .75
97 Max Scherzer .30 .75
98 Dansby Swanson .30 .75
99 Willians Astudillo RC .30 .75
100 Shohei Ohtani .50 1.25
101 Vladimir Guerrero Jr. RC 6.00 15.00
101 Yusei Kikuchi SP RC 3.00 8.00
102 Eddie Rosario SP 2.50 6.00
103 Marcell Ozuna SP 3.00 8.00
104 Kevin Newman SP RC 3.00 8.00
105 Brad Keller SP RC 2.00 5.00
106 Heath Fillmyer SP RC 2.00 5.00
107 Justin Verlander SP 3.00 8.00
108 Freddie Freeman SP 4.00 10.00
109 Stephen Strasburg SP 3.00 8.00
110 Chris Sale SP 3.00 8.00
111 Jonathan Loaisiga SP RC 2.50 6.00
112 Anthony Rendon SP 3.00 8.00
113 Kevin Kramer SP RC 2.50 6.00
114 Andrew Benintendi SP 3.00 8.00
115 Taylor Ward SP RC 2.00 5.00
116 Starling Marte SP 2.50 6.00
117 George Springer SP 2.50 6.00
118 Daniel Ponce de Leon SP RC 3.00 8.00
119 Luis Severino SP 2.50 6.00
120 Dakota Hudson SP RC 2.50 6.00
121 Josh James SP RC 3.00 8.00
122 Khris Davis SP 3.00 8.00
123 Eugenio Suarez SP 2.50 6.00
124 Carlos Carrasco SP 2.00 5.00
125 Giancarlo Stanton SP 3.00 8.00

2019 Finest Blue Refractors

*BLUE REF: 3X TO 8X BASIC
*BLUE REF RC: 2X TO 5X BASIC RC
STATED ODDS 1:30 HOBBY
STATED PRINT RUN 150 SER.#'d SETS
33 Ronald Acuna Jr. 10.00 25.00
44 Pete Alonso 15.00 40.00

2019 Finest Gold Refractors

*GOLD REF: 6X TO 15X BASIC
*GOLD REF RC: 4X TO 10X BASIC RC
*GOLD SP REF RC: .75X TO 2X BASIC RC
1-100 STATED ODDS 1:88 HOBBY
101-125 STATED ODDS 1:350 HOBBY
STATED PRINT RUN 50 SER.#'d SETS
25 Mike Trout 40.00 100.00
33 Ronald Acuna Jr. 20.00 50.00
44 Pete Alonso 30.00 80.00

2019 Finest Green Refractors

*GREEN REF: 4X TO 10X BASIC
*GREEN REF RC: 2.5X TO 6X BASIC RC
STATED ODDS 1:45 HOBBY
STATED PRINT RUN 99 SER.#'d SETS
33 Ronald Acuna Jr. 12.00 30.00
44 Pete Alonso 20.00 50.00

2019 Finest Orange Refractors

*ORANGE REF: 8X TO 20X BASIC
*ORANGE REF RC: 5X TO 12X BASIC RC
STATED ODDS 1:176 HOBBY
STATED PRINT RUN 25 SER.#'d SETS
25 Mike Trout 50.00 120.00
33 Ronald Acuna Jr. 25.00 60.00
44 Pete Alonso 40.00 100.00

2019 Finest Purple Refractors

*PURPLE REF: 2.5X TO 6X BASIC
*PURPLE REF RC: 1.5X TO 4X BASIC RC
STATED ODDS 1:18 HOBBY
STATED PRINT RUN 250 SER.#'d SETS
44 Pete Alonso 12.00 30.00

2019 Finest Refractors

*REF: 1.5X TO 4X BASIC
*REF RC: 1X TO 2.5X BASIC RC
STATED ODDS 1:3 HOBBY

2019 Finest Autographs

STATED ODDS 1:12 HOBBY
EXCHANGE DEADLINE 5/31/2021
FAAB Alex Bregman 12.00 30.00
FAAJ Aaron Judge 75.00 200.00
FAAR Anthony Rizzo 20.00 50.00
FABK Brad Keller 2.50 6.00
FABL Brandon Lowe 6.00 15.00
FABN Brandon Nimmo 3.00 8.00
FABW Bryse Wilson 3.00 8.00
FACA Chance Adams 2.50 6.00
FACB Corbin Burnes 20.00 50.00
FACJ Chipper Jones 50.00 120.00
FACM Cedric Mullins 8.00 20.00
FACS Chris Shaw 2.50 6.00
FACSA Carlos Santana 3.00 8.00
FACST Christin Stewart 4.00 10.00
FACY Christian Yelich 40.00 100.00
FADJ Derek Jeter 150.00 400.00
FADJA Danny Jansen 2.50 6.00
FADL Dawel Lugo 4.00 10.00
FAEJ Eloy Jimenez 30.00 80.00
FAER Eddie Rosario 6.00 15.00
FAFA Francisco Arcia 4.00 10.00
FAFL Francisco Lindor 12.00 30.00
FAFR Franmil Reyes 10.00 25.00
FAFTJ Fernando Tatis Jr. 100.00 250.00
FAGS George Springer 12.00 30.00
FAI Ichiro 125.00 300.00
FAJA Jose Altuve 15.00 40.00
FAJAG Jesus Aguilar 3.00 8.00
FAJB Jake Bauers 4.00 10.00
FAJD Jacob deGrom 30.00 80.00
FAJM Jose Martinez 2.50 6.00
FAJMC Jeff McNeil 15.00 40.00
FAJP Jorge Posada 20.00 50.00
FAJS Juan Soto 50.00 120.00
FAJSH Justus Sheffield 4.00 10.00
FAKA Kolby Allard 4.00 10.00
FAKB Kris Bryant 50.00 120.00
FAKT Kyle Tucker 10.00 25.00
FAKW Kyle Wright 4.00 10.00
FALU Luis Urias 8.00 20.00
FALV Luke Voit 15.00 40.00
FAMA Miguel Andujar 10.00 25.00
FAMC Matt Chapman EXCH 6.00 15.00
FAMH Mitch Haniger 3.00 8.00
FAMK Michael Kopech 8.00 20.00
FAMR Mariano Rivera 75.00 200.00
FAMT Mike Trout 200.00 500.00
FANR Nolan Ryan 50.00 120.00
FAOA Ozzie Albies 12.00 30.00
FAPA Pete Alonso 75.00 200.00
FAPD Paul DeJong 5.00 12.00
FARAJ Ronald Acuna Jr. 50.00 120.00
FARB Ryan Borucki 2.50 6.00
FAROH Ryan O'Hearn 2.50 6.00
FART Rowdy Tellez 4.00 10.00
FASD Steven Duggar 3.00 8.00
FASO Shohei Ohtani 125.00 300.00
FATA Tim Anderson 8.00 20.00
FATHU Torii Hunter 8.00 20.00
FATON Tyler O'Neill 6.00 15.00
FATT Touki Toussaint 3.00 8.00
FAVGJ Vladimir Guerrero Jr. 100.00 250.00
FAWA Willians Astudillo 6.00 15.00
FAYK Yusei Kikuchi 12.00 30.00
FAYM Yadier Molina 30.00 80.00

2019 Finest Autographs Blue Refractors

*BLUE REF: .5X TO 1.2X BASIC
STATED ODDS 1:87 HOBBY
STATED PRINT RUN 150 SER.#'d SETS
EXCHANGE DEADLINE 5/31/2021

2019 Finest Autographs Gold Refractors

*GOLD REF: .75X TO 2X BASIC
STATED ODDS 1:176 HOBBY
STATED PRINT RUN 50 SER.#'d SETS
EXCHANGE DEADLINE 5/31/2021
FAAB Alex Bregman 25.00 60.00
FAEJ Eloy Jimenez 60.00 150.00
FAFL Francisco Lindor 20.00 50.00
FAJA Jose Altuve 20.00 50.00
FAJP Jorge Posada 25.00 60.00
FAJS Juan Soto 100.00 250.00
FAMA Miguel Andujar 15.00 40.00
FAYM Yadier Molina 40.00 100.00

2019 Finest Autographs Green Refractors

*GREEN REF: .6X TO 1.5X BASIC
STATED ODDS 1:112 HOBBY
STATED PRINT RUN 99 SER.#'d SETS
EXCHANGE DEADLINE 5/31/2021
FAEJ Eloy Jimenez 40.00 100.00

2019 Finest Autographs Green Wave Refractors

*GREEN WAVE REF: .6X TO 1.5X BASIC
STATED ODDS 1:112 HOBBY
STATED PRINT RUN 99 SER.#'d SETS
EXCHANGE DEADLINE 5/31/2021
FAEJ Eloy Jimenez 40.00 100.00

2019 Finest Autographs Orange Refractors

*ORANGE REF: 1X TO 2.5X BASIC
STATED ODDS 1:313 HOBBY
STATED PRINT RUN 25 SER.#'d SETS
EXCHANGE DEADLINE 5/31/2021
FAAB Alex Bregman 30.00 80.00
FAAJ Aaron Judge 125.00 300.00
FAAR Anthony Rizzo 30.00 80.00
FACJ Chipper Jones 75.00 200.00
FACY Christian Yelich 60.00 150.00
FAEJ Eloy Jimenez 75.00 200.00
FAFL Francisco Lindor 25.00 60.00
FAGS George Springer 20.00 50.00
FAJA Jose Altuve 30.00 80.00
FAJP Jorge Posada 30.00 80.00
FAJS Juan Soto 125.00 300.00
FAKB Kris Bryant 100.00 250.00
FAMA Miguel Andujar 20.00 50.00
FANR Nolan Ryan 75.00 200.00
FAYM Yadier Molina 50.00 120.00

2019 Finest Autographs Orange Wave Refractors

*ORANGE WAVE REF: 1X TO 2.5X BASIC
STATED ODDS 1:313 HOBBY
STATED PRINT RUN 25 SER.#'d SETS
EXCHANGE DEADLINE 5/31/2021
FAAB Alex Bregman 30.00 80.00
FAAJ Aaron Judge 125.00 300.00
FAAR Anthony Rizzo 30.00 80.00
FACJ Chipper Jones 75.00 200.00
FACY Christian Yelich 60.00 150.00
FAEJ Eloy Jimenez 75.00 200.00
FAFL Francisco Lindor 25.00 60.00
FAGS George Springer 20.00 50.00
FAJA Jose Altuve 30.00 80.00
FAJP Jorge Posada 30.00 80.00
FAJS Juan Soto 125.00 300.00
FAKB Kris Bryant 100.00 250.00
FAMA Miguel Andujar 20.00 50.00
FANR Nolan Ryan 75.00 200.00
FAYM Yadier Molina 50.00 120.00

2019 Finest Blue Chips

STATED ODDS 1:3 HOBBY
*GOLD/50: 2.5X TO 6X BASIC
FBCAB Alex Bregman .60 1.50
FBCABE Andrew Benintendi .60 1.50
FBCAJ Aaron Judge 1.50 4.00
FBCAM Austin Meadows .60 1.50
FBCAR Amed Rosario .50 1.25
FBCBN Brandon Nimmo .50 1.25
FBCBS Blake Snell .50 1.25
FBCFL Francisco Lindor .60 1.50
FBCGS Gary Sanchez .60 1.50
FBCGT Gleyber Torres 1.25 3.00
FBCIH Ian Happ .50 1.25
FBCJA Jesus Aguilar .50 1.25
FBCJH Josh Hader .50 1.25
FBCJM Jose Martinez .40 1.00
FBCJS Juan Soto 2.00 5.00
FBCLGJ Lourdes Gurriel Jr. .50 1.25
FBCLV Luke Voit 1.00 2.50
FBCMA Miguel Andujar .60 1.50
FBCMC Matt Chapman .60 1.50
FBCMH Mitch Haniger .50 1.25
FBCMM Miles Mikolas .60 1.50
FBCMO Matt Olson .60 1.50
FBCOA Ozzie Albies .60 1.50
FBCPD Paul DeJong .60 1.50
FBCRAJ Ronald Acuna Jr. 3.00 8.00
FBCRI Raisel Iglesias .40 1.00
FBCSK Scott Kingery .50 1.25
FBCSO Shohei Ohtani 1.00 2.50
FBCTM Trey Mancini .50 1.25
FBCWA Willy Adames .40 1.00

2019 Finest Blue Chips Autographs

STATED ODDS 1:284 HOBBY
PRINT RUNS B/WN 10-99 COPIES PER
NO PRICING ON QTY 15 OR LESS
EXCHANGE DEADLINE 5/31/2021
*ORANGE/25: .6X TO 1.5X p/r 99
*ORANGE/25: .5X TO 1.2X p/r 40
*ORANGE/25: .4X TO 1X p/r 25
FBCABN Brandon Nimmo/99 4.00 10.00
FBCABS Blake Snell/99 10.00 25.00
FBCAFL Francisco Lindor/25 40.00 100.00
FBCAGS Gary Sanchez/30 15.00 40.00
FBCAJA Jesus Aguilar/99 4.00 10.00
FBCAJH Josh Hader/99 4.00 10.00
FBCAJM Jose Martinez/99 6.00 15.00
FBCAJS Juan Soto/40 50.00 120.00
FBCALV Luke Voit/99 50.00 120.00
FBCAMA Miguel Andujar/25
FBCAMC Matt Chapman EXCH 10.00 25.00
FBCAMH Mitch Haniger/99 8.00 20.00
FBCAOA Ozzie Albies/99 12.00 30.00
FBCAPD Paul DeJong/99 5.00 12.00
FBCARAJ Ronald Acuna Jr./40 100.00 250.00
FBCARI Raisel Iglesias/99 3.00 8.00
FBCASK Scott Kingery/99 12.00 30.00
FBCAWA Willy Adames/99 3.00 8.00

2019 Finest Career Die Cuts

STATED ODDS 1:48 HOBBY
*GOLD/50: 2X TO 5X BASIC
*RED/5: 30X TO 80X BASIC
FCMR1 Mariano Rivera 1.50 4.00
FCMR2 Mariano Rivera 1.50 4.00
FCMR3 Mariano Rivera 1.50 4.00
FCMR4 Mariano Rivera 1.50 4.00
FCMR5 Mariano Rivera 1.50 4.00
FCMR6 Mariano Rivera 1.50 4.00
FCMR7 Mariano Rivera 1.50 4.00
FCMR8 Mariano Rivera 1.50 4.00
FCMR9 Mariano Rivera 1.50 4.00
FCMR10 Mariano Rivera 1.50 4.00

2019 Finest Career Die Cuts Autographs

STATED ODDS 1:4275 HOBBY
STATED PRINT RUN 10 SER.#'d SETS
EXCHANGE DEADLINE 5/31/2021
FCAMR1 Mariano Rivera 100.00 250.00
FCAMR2 Mariano Rivera 100.00 250.00
FCAMR3 Mariano Rivera 100.00 250.00
FCAMR4 Mariano Rivera 100.00 250.00
FCAMR5 Mariano Rivera 100.00 250.00
FCAMR6 Mariano Rivera 100.00 250.00
FCAMR7 Mariano Rivera 100.00 250.00
FCAMR8 Mariano Rivera 100.00 250.00
FCAMR9 Mariano Rivera 100.00 250.00
FCAMR10 Mariano Rivera 100.00 250.00

2019 Finest Firsts

STATED ODDS 1:12 HOBBY
*GOLD/50: 2.5X TO 6X BASIC
FFCB Corbin Burnes 3.00 8.00
FFCS Chris Shaw .40 1.00
FFJB Jake Bauers .60 1.50
FFJS Justus Sheffield .60 1.50
FFKT Kyle Tucker 1.00 2.50
FFLU Luis Urias .60 1.50
FFMK Michael Kopech 1.25 3.00
FFRB Ryan Borucki .40 1.00
FFRT Rowdy Tellez .60 1.50
FFYK Yusei Kikuchi .60 1.50

2019 Finest Firsts Autographs

STATED ODDS 1:117 HOBBY
EXCHANGE DEADLINE 5/31/2021
*BLUE/150: .5X TO 1.2X BASIC
*GREEN/99: .6X TO 1.5X BASIC
*GREEN WAVE/99: .6X TO 1.5X BASIC
*GOLD/50: .75X TO 2X BASIC
*ORANGE/25: 1X TO 2.5X BASIC
*ORNGE WAVE/25: 1X TO 2.5X BASIC
FFACB Corbin Burnes 20.00 50.00
FFACS Chris Shaw 3.00 8.00
FFADF David Fletcher 10.00 25.00
FFAJB Jake Bauers 5.00 12.00
FFAJM Jeff McNeil 12.00 30.00
FFAJS Justus Sheffield 5.00 12.00
FFAKT Kyle Tucker 20.00 50.00
FFALU Luis Urias 8.00 20.00
FFAMK Michael Kopech 10.00 25.00
FFARB Ryan Borucki 3.00 8.00
FFART Rowdy Tellez 5.00 12.00

2019 Finest Mystery Redemption Autographs

FMA1 Austin Riley 15.00 40.00
FMA2 Nick Senzel 25.00 60.00
FMA3 Vladimir Guerrero Jr 75.00 200.00

2019 Finest Origins Autographs

STATED ODDS 1:128 HOBBY
EXCHANGE DEADLINE 5/31/2021
*GOLD REF/50: .5X TO 1.2X BASIC
*ORANGE REF/25: .6X TO 1.5X BASIC
FOAABE Adrian Beltre 25.00 60.00
FOAAJ Aaron Judge 75.00 200.00
FOAAR Anthony Rizzo 25.00 60.00
FOACJ Chipper Jones 50.00 120.00
FOAEJ Eloy Jimenez 30.00 80.00
FOAFL Francisco Lindor 12.00 30.00
FOAHA Hank Aaron 250.00 500.00
FOAJA Jose Altuve 15.00 40.00
FOAJD Jacob deGrom 20.00 50.00
FOAJP Jorge Posada 20.00 50.00
FOAJS Juan Soto 60.00 150.00
FOAKB Kris Bryant 50.00 120.00
FOAMA Miguel Andujar 10.00 25.00
FOAMT Mike Trout 400.00 800.00
FOANR Nolan Ryan 100.00 250.00
FOAOS Ozzie Smith 15.00 40.00
FOARAJ Ronald Acuna Jr. 75.00 200.00
FOASC Steve Carlton 20.00 50.00
FOASO Shohei Ohtani 100.00 250.00
FOATH Todd Helton 15.00 40.00
FOAYM Yadier Molina 40.00 100.00

2019 Finest Prized Performers

STATED ODDS 1:6 HOBBY
*GOLD/50: 2.5X TO 6X BASIC
PPAR Anthony Rizzo .75 2.00
PPBH Bryce Harper 1.00 2.50
PPCK Corey Kluber .50 1.25
PPCKE Clayton Kershaw 1.00 2.50
PPCS Carlos Santana .50 1.25
PPCY Christian Yelich .75 2.00
PPDG Didi Gregorius .50 1.25
PPED Edwin Diaz .50 1.25
PPGS George Springer .50 1.25
PPJA Jose Altuve .50 1.25
PPJD Jacob deGrom 1.25 3.00
PPJS Justin Smoak .40 1.00
PPJU Justin Upton .50 1.25
PPJV Joey Votto .60 1.50
PPKB Kris Bryant .75 2.00
PPMT Mike Trout 3.00 8.00
PPNS Noah Syndergaard .50 1.25
PPPG Paul Goldschmidt .60 1.50
PPSP Salvador Perez .50 1.25
PPYM Yadier Molina .75 2.00

2019 Finest Prized Performers Autographs

STATED ODDS 1:659 HOBBY
STATED PRINT RUN 50 SER.#'d SETS
EXCHANGE DEADLINE 5/31/2021
*ORANGE/25: .5X TO 1.2X BASIC
PPAAR Anthony Rizzo 25.00 60.00
PPACK Corey Kluber 8.00 20.00
PPACS Carlos Santana 8.00 20.00
PPACY Christian Yelich 40.00 100.00
PPADG Didi Gregorius 10.00 25.00
PPAGS George Springer 8.00 20.00
PPAJA Jose Altuve 8.00 20.00
PPAJD Jacob deGrom 30.00 80.00
PPAJU Justin Upton 12.00 30.00
PPAKB Kris Bryant 50.00 120.00
PPAMT Mike Trout
PPAPG Paul Goldschmidt 10.00 25.00
PPASP Salvador Perez 10.00 25.00
PPAYM Yadier Molina 25.00 60.00

2020 Finest

STATED SP ODDS 1:32 HOBBY
1 Mike Trout 4.00 10.00
2 Ryan Braun .25 .60
3 Bryce Harper .50 1.25
4 Keston Hiura .40 1.00
5 Xander Bogaerts .30 .75
6 Vladimir Guerrero Jr. .50 1.25
7 Bobby Bradley RC .30 .75
8 Paul Goldschmidt .50 1.20
9 Jose Berrios .25 .60
10 Kris Bryant .40 1.00
11 Lucas Giolito .25 .60
12 Giancarlo Stanton .30 .75
13 Francisco Lindor .30 .75
14 Juan Soto 1.00 2.50
15 Jorge Polanco .25 .60
16 Dylan Cease RC .50 1.25
17 Noah Syndergaard .25 .60
18 Tim Anderson .30 .75
19 Brusdar Graterol RC .50 1.25
20 Trent Grisham RC 1.25 3.00
21 Aristides Aquino RC 2.00 5.00
22 Kyle Schwarber .30 .75
23 Charlie Blackmon .30 .75
24 Rafael Devers .40 1.00
25 Ronald Acuna Jr. 2.00 5.00
26 Trea Turner .25 .60
27 Bo Bichette RC 8.00 20.00
28 Yasmani Grandal .20 .50
29 Max Muncy .25 .60
30 A.J. Puk RC .50 1.25
31 Abraham Toro .25 .60
32 Franmil Reyes .20 .50
33 Matt Chapman .30 .75
34 Manny Machado .30 .75
35 Isan Diaz RC .50 1.25
36 Lorenzo Cain .20 .50
37 Gleyber Torres .60 1.50
38 Rhys Hoskins .40 1.00
39 Jorge Soler .30 .75
40 Shohei Ohtani .50 1.25
41 Kyle Lewis RC 2.50 6.00
42 Eric Hosmer .25 .60
43 Adbert Alzolay RC .40 1.00
44 Sean Murphy RC .50 1.25
45 Nico Hoerner RC 3.00 8.00
46 Will Smith .30 .75
47 Freddie Freeman .40 1.00
48 Zack Collins RC .40 1.00
49 J.D. Martinez .30 .75
50 Yordan Alvarez RC 8.00 20.00
51 Anthony Rizzo .40 1.00
52 Yu Darvish .30 .75
53 Yuli Gurriel .25 .60
54 Marcus Semien .30 .75
55 Jesus Luzardo RC .60 1.50
56 George Springer .25 .60
57 Eloy Jimenez .60 1.50
58 Cody Bellinger .60 1.50
59 Gerrit Cole .50 1.25
60 Dansby Swanson .30 .75
61 Austin Meadows .30 .75
62 Pete Alonso .75 2.00
63 Trevor Story .30 .75
64 Javier Baez .40 1.00
65 Whit Merrifield .30 .75
66 Anthony Rendon .30 .75
67 Charlie Morton .30 .75
68 Alex Bregman .30 .75
69 Stephen Strasburg .30 .75
70 Aaron Civale RC .60 1.50
71 Justin Verlander .30 .75
72 Sheldon Neuse RC .40 1.00
73 Mauricio Dubon RC .40 1.00
74 Jacob deGrom .60 1.50
75 Amed Rosario .25 .60
76 Dustin May RC 1.00 2.50
77 Gavin Lux RC 5.00 12.00
78 Max Scherzer .30 .75
79 Aaron Nola .25 .60
80 Josh Hader .25 .60
81 Justin Turner .30 .75
82 Jose Altuve .25 .60
83 Aaron Judge 1.50 4.00
84 Mookie Betts .60 1.50
85 J.T. Realmuto .30 .75
86 Nolan Arenado .50 1.25
87 Yoan Moncada .30 .75
88 Seth Brown RC .30 .75
89 Clayton Kershaw .50 1.25
90 Zack Greinke .30 .75
91 Masahiro Tanaka .30 .75
92 Michael Baez RC .30 .75
93 Nick Solak RC 1.25 3.00
94 Walker Buehler .40 1.00
95 Victor Robles .40 1.00
96 James Paxton .25 .60
97 Luis Robert RC 6.00 15.00
98 Mike Clevinger .25 .60
99 Adrian Morejon RC .40 1.00
100 Christian Yelich .40 1.00
101 Ozzie Albies SP 8.00 20.00
102 Khris Davis SP 12.00 30.00
103 DJ LeMahieu SP 12.00 30.00
104 Shane Bieber SP 3.00 8.00
105 Tommy Pham SP 6.00 15.00
106 Matt Olson SP 3.00 8.00
107 Paul DeJong SP 3.00 8.00
108 Josh Bell SP 2.50 6.00
109 Eddie Rosario SP 2.50 6.00
110 Gary Sanchez SP 10.00 25.00
111 Jeff McNeil SP 2.50 6.00
112 Trey Mancini SP 3.00 8.00
113 Kirby Yates SP 8.00 20.00
114 Mike Soroka SP 3.00 8.00
115 Michael Conforto SP 2.50 6.00
116 Adalberto Mondesi SP 2.50 6.00
117 Michael Brantley SP 8.00 20.00
118 Hyun-Jin Ryu SP 2.50 6.00
119 Jose Abreu SP 8.00 20.00
120 Didi Gregorius SP 6.00 15.00
121 Patrick Corbin SP 5.00 12.00
122 Carlos Santana SP 5.00 12.00
123 Andrew Benintendi SP 6.00 15.00
124 Jack Flaherty SP 5.00 12.00
125 Ketel Marte SP 2.50 6.00

2020 Finest Autographs

STATED ODDS 1:13 HOBBY
EXCHANGE DEADLINE 5/31/2022
FAAA Aristides Aquino 15.00 40.00
FAAJ Aaron Judge 60.00 150.00
FAAP A.J. Puk EXCH 4.00 10.00
FAAR Austin Riley 12.00 30.00
FAAT Abraham Toro 3.00 8.00
FABH Bryce Harper 125.00 300.00
FABM Brendan McKay 6.00 15.00
FABR Bryan Reynolds 5.00 12.00
FACB Cavan Biggio 15.00 40.00
FACC Carlos Carrasco 8.00 20.00
FACJ Chipper Jones 50.00 120.00
FACK Carter Kieboom 8.00 20.00
FACY Christian Yelich 30.00 80.00
FADC Dylan Cease 5.00 12.00
FADL Domingo Leyba 3.00 8.00
FADM Dustin May 20.00 50.00
FAEJ Eloy Jimenez 20.00 50.00
FAGL Gavin Lux 30.00 80.00
FAID Isan Diaz 10.00 25.00
FAI Ichiro
FAJA Jose Altuve 12.00 30.00
FAJB Jake Bauers 3.00 8.00
FAJL Jesus Luzardo 8.00 20.00
FAJM John Means 30.00 80.00
FAJR Jake Rogers 5.00 12.00
FAJS Juan Soto 100.00 250.00
FAJY Jordan Yamamoto 2.50 6.00
FAKB Kris Bryant 30.00 80.00
FAKH Keston Hiura 10.00 25.00
FALA Logan Allen 4.00 10.00
FAMC Michael Chavis 3.00 8.00
FAMD Mauricio Dubon 8.00 20.00
FAMK Mitch Keller 4.00 10.00
FAMM Mike Mussina 20.00 50.00
FAMT Mike Trout 400.00 800.00
FAMY Mike Yastrzemski 8.00 20.00
FANH Nico Hoerner 12.00 30.00
FANS Nick Solak 8.00 20.00
FAPA Pete Alonso 40.00 100.00
FAPD Paul DeJong 5.00 12.00
FARA Rogelio Armenteros 3.00 8.00
FARD Rafael Devers 12.00 30.00
FARG Robel Garcia 2.50 6.00
FARH Rhys Hoskins 20.00 50.00
FASN Sheldon Neuse 3.00 8.00
FASO Shohei Ohtani 100.00 250.00
FATA Tim Anderson 12.00 30.00
FATD Travis Demeritte 4.00 10.00
FATG Trent Grisham 12.00 30.00
FAWS Will Smith 12.00 30.00
FAZC Zack Collins 5.00 12.00
FAAAL Adbert Alzolay 3.00 8.00
FAAMU Andres Munoz 4.00 10.00
FABBR Bobby Bradley 5.00 12.00
FABBU Brock Burke 2.50 6.00
FAFTJ Fernando Tatis Jr. 100.00 250.00
FAJSO Jorge Soler 4.00 10.00
FAKGJ Ken Griffey Jr. 200.00 500.00
FALGJ Lourdes Gurriel Jr. 6.00 15.00
FAMBE Matt Beaty 5.00 12.00
FAMTH Matt Thaiss 5.00 12.00
FASBR Seth Brown 2.50 6.00
FASSC Shin-Soo Choo 12.00 30.00

2020 Finest Autographs Blue Refractors

*BLUE REF: .5X TO 1.2X BASIC
STATED ODDS 1:83 HOBBY
STATED PRINT RUN 150 SER.#'d SETS
EXCHANGE DEADLINE 5/31/2022
FADC Dylan Cease 10.00 25.00
FAGL Gavin Lux 60.00 150.00

2020 Finest Autographs Gold Refractors

*GOLD REF: .75X TO 2X BASIC
STATED ODDS 1:158 HOBBY
STATED PRINT RUN 50 SER.#'d SETS
EXCHANGE DEADLINE 5/31/2022
FABB Bo Bichette 100.00 250.00
FADC Dylan Cease 15.00 40.00
FAEJ Eloy Jimenez 40.00 100.00
FAGL Gavin Lux 100.00 250.00
FAMD Mauricio Dubon 20.00 50.00

2020 Finest Autographs Green Refractors

*GREEN REF: .6X TO 1.5X BASIC
STATED ODDS 1:103 HOBBY
STATED PRINT RUN 99 SER.#'d SETS
EXCHANGE DEADLINE 5/31/2022
FABB Bo Bichette 75.00 200.00
FADC Dylan Cease 12.00 30.00
FAGL Gavin Lux 75.00 200.00
FAMD Mauricio Dubon 15.00 40.00

2020 Finest Autographs Green Wave Refractors

*GREEN WAVE REF: .6X TO 1.5X BASIC
STATED ODDS 1:103 HOBBY
STATED PRINT RUN 99 SER.#'d SETS
EXCHANGE DEADLINE 5/31/2022
FABB Bo Bichette 75.00 200.00
FADC Dylan Cease 12.00 30.00
FAGL Gavin Lux 75.00 200.00
FAMD Mauricio Dubon 15.00 40.00

2020 Finest Autographs Orange Refractors

*ORANGE REF: 1X TO 2.5X BASIC
STATED ODDS 1:301 HOBBY
STATED PRINT RUN 25 SER.#'d SETS
EXCHANGE DEADLINE 5/31/2022
FABB Bo Bichette 200.00 500.00
FACK Carter Kieboom 30.00 80.00
FADC Dylan Cease 20.00 50.00
FAEJ Eloy Jimenez 50.00 120.00
FAGL Gavin Lux 150.00 400.00
FAMD Mauricio Dubon 40.00 100.00
FARD Rafael Devers 40.00 100.00
FAAMU Andres Munoz 15.00 40.00
FAMBE Matt Beaty 15.00 40.00
FASSC Shin-Soo Choo 50.00 120.00

2020 Finest Autographs Orange Wave Refractors

*ORANGE WAVE REF: 1X TO 2.5X BASIC
STATED ODDS 1:301 HOBBY
STATED PRINT RUN 25 SER.#'d SETS
EXCHANGE DEADLINE 5/31/2022
FABB Bo Bichette 200.00 500.00
FACK Carter Kieboom 30.00 80.00
FADC Dylan Cease 20.00 50.00
FAEJ Eloy Jimenez 50.00 120.00
FAGL Gavin Lux 150.00 400.00
FAMD Mauricio Dubon 40.00 100.00
FARD Rafael Devers 40.00 100.00
FAAMU Andres Munoz 15.00 40.00
FAMBE Matt Beaty 15.00 40.00
FASSC Shin-Soo Choo 50.00 120.00

2020 Finest Duals

STATED ODDS 1:6 HOBBY
FD1 S.Ohtani/M.Trout 5.00 12.00
FD2 M.Chavis/R.Devers .75 2.00
FD3 A.Riley/R.Acuna 2.50 6.00
FD4 S.Bieber/C.Carrasco .60 1.50
FD5 A.Rizzo/K.Bryant .75 2.00
FD6 I.Diaz/J.Yamamoto .60 1.50
FD7 J.Soto/C.Kieboom 2.00 5.00
FD8 C.Yelich/K.Hiura .75 2.00
FD9 B.Reynolds/M.Keller .60 1.50
FD10 S.Brown/A.Puk .60 1.50
FD11 W.Merrifield/J.Soler .60 1.50
FD12 B.Rodgers/N.Arenado 1.00 2.50
FD13 C.Paddack/F.Tatis Jr 3.00 8.00
FD14 T.Anderson/E.Jimenez 1.25 3.00
FD15 M.Muncy/W.Smith .60 1.50
FD16 B.Harper/R.Hoskins 1.00 2.50
FD17 Y.Alvarez/J.Altuve 4.00 10.00
FD18 V.Guerrero Jr/B.Bichette 3.00 8.00
FD19 N.Senzel/A.Aquino 1.00 2.50
FD20 A.Judge/G.Torres 1.50 4.00

2020 Finest Duals Gold Refractors

*GOLD REF: 3X TO 8X BASIC
STATED ODDS 1:468 HOBBY
STATED PRINT RUN 50 SER.#'d SETS
FD18 V.Guerrero Jr/B.Bichette 30.00 80.00

2020 Finest Duals Autographs

STATED ODDS 1:126 HOBBY
EXCHANGE DEADLINE 5/31/2022
FDAAJ T.Anderson/E.Jimenez 40.00 100.00
FDAAS N.Senzel/A.Aquino 50.00 120.00
FDADY J.Yamamoto/I.Diaz 20.00 50.00
FDARK B.Reynolds/M.Keller 20.00 50.00
FDASM M.Muncy/W.Smith 20.00 50.00
FDATP C.Paddack/F.Tatis Jr EXCH 125.00 300.00
FDASOM J.Soler/W.Merrifield 30.00 80.00

2020 Finest Duals Autographs Orange Refractors

*ORANGE REF/25: 1X TO 2.5X BASIC
STATED ODDS 1:964 HOBBY
STATED PRINT RUN 25 SER.#'d SETS
EXCHANGE DEADLINE 5/31/2022
FDAAA Y.Alvarez/J.Altuve 100.00 250.00
FDAAR A.Riley/R.Acuna 100.00 250.00
FDABR A.Rizzo/K.Bryant 100.00 250.00
FDAGB V.Guerrero Jr./B.Bichette EXCH
FDAHR R.Hoskins/B.Harper 200.00 500.00
FDAJT G.Torres/A.Judge 300.00 600.00

Card	Low	High
FDASK J.Soto/C.Kieboom	100.00	250.00
FDAYH K.Hiura/C.Yelich	125.00	300.00

2020 Finest Firsts

STATED ODDS 1:12 HOBBY

*GOLD REF: 3X TO 8X BASIC

Card	Low	High
FF1 Yordan Alvarez	4.00	10.00
FF2 A.J. Puk	.60	1.50
FF3 Gavin Lux	4.00	10.00
FF4 Kyle Lewis	3.00	8.00
FF5 Nico Hoerner	1.50	4.00
FF6 Dylan Cease	.60	1.50
FF7 Brendan McKay	.60	1.50
FF8 Dustin May	1.25	3.00
FF9 Aristides Aquino	1.00	2.50
FF10 Bo Bichette	3.00	8.00

2020 Finest Firsts Autographs

STATED ODDS 1:117 HOBBY

EXCHANGE DEADLINE 5/31/2022

*BLUE/150: .5X TO 1.2X BASIC

Card	Low	High
FFAAA Aristides Aquino	20.00	50.00
FFAAT Abraham Toro	4.00	10.00
FFABB Bo Bichette		
FFABM Brendan McKay	10.00	25.00
FFADC Dylan Cease	5.00	12.00
FFAGL Gavin Lux	60.00	150.00
FFAJY Jordan Yamamoto	3.00	8.00
FFANH Nico Hoerner	12.00	30.00
FFASB Seth Brown	3.00	8.00
FFAYA Yordan Alvarez	50.00	120.00
FFAAJP A.J. Puk EXCH	10.00	25.00

2020 Finest Firsts Autographs Gold Refractors

*GOLD REF: .75X TO 2X BASIC

STATED ODDS 1:762 HOBBY

STATED PRINT RUN 50 SER.#'d SETS

EXCHANGE DEADLINE 5/31/2022

Card	Low	High
FFABB Bo Bichette	100.00	250.00

2020 Finest Firsts Autographs Green Refractors

*GREEN REF: .6X TO 1.5X BASIC

STATED ODDS 1:385 HOBBY

STATED PRINT RUN 99 SER.#'d SETS

EXCHANGE DEADLINE 5/31/2022

Card	Low	High
FFABB Bo Bichette	75.00	200.00

2020 Finest Firsts Autographs Green Wave Refractors

*GREEN WAVE REF: .6X TO 1.5X BASIC

STATED ODDS 1:385 HOBBY

STATED PRINT RUN 99 SER.#'d SETS

EXCHANGE DEADLINE 5/31/2022

Card	Low	High
FFABB Bo Bichette	75.00	200.00

2020 Finest Firsts Autographs Orange Refractors

*ORANGE REF: 1X TO 2.5X BASIC

STATED ODDS 1:1520 HOBBY

STATED PRINT RUN 25 SER.#'d SETS

EXCHANGE DEADLINE 5/31/2022

Card	Low	High
FFABB Bo Bichette	125.00	300.00

2020 Finest Firsts Autographs Orange Wave Refractors

*ORANGE WAVE REF: 1X TO 2.5X BASIC

STATED ODDS 1:1520 HOBBY

STATED PRINT RUN 25 SER.#'d SETS

EXCHANGE DEADLINE 5/31/2022

Card	Low	High
FFABB Bo Bichette	125.00	300.00

2020 Finest Ichiro Careers

STATED ODDS 1:48 HOBBY

*GOLD REF: 2X TO 5X BASIC

Card	Low	High
FCI1 Ichiro	5.00	12.00
FCI2 Ichiro	5.00	12.00
FCI3 Ichiro	5.00	12.00
FCI4 Ichiro	5.00	12.00
FCI5 Ichiro	5.00	12.00
FCI6 Ichiro	5.00	12.00
FCI7 Ichiro	5.00	12.00
FCI8 Ichiro	5.00	12.00
FCI9 Ichiro	5.00	12.00
FCI10 Ichiro	5.00	12.00

2020 Finest Moments Autographs

STATED ODDS 1:126 HOBBY

EXCHANGE DEADLINE 5/31/2022

Card	Low	High
MOMAAA Aristides Aquino	10.00	25.00
MOMABB Bo Bichette EXCH	50.00	120.00
MOMABH Bryce Harper	125.00	300.00
MOMACJ Chipper Jones	50.00	120.00
MOMADO David Ortiz	40.00	100.00
MOMAFT Frank Thomas	30.00	80.00
MOMAHA Hank Aaron	125.00	300.00
MOMAJA Jose Altuve	15.00	40.00
MOMAKB Kris Bryant		
MOMAMM Mark McGwire	50.00	120.00
MOMAMT Mike Trout	400.00	800.00
MOMANR Nolan Ryan	100.00	250.00
MOMAOS Ozzie Smith	25.00	60.00
MOMAPA Pete Alonso	40.00	100.00
MOMARH Rhys Hoskins	15.00	40.00
MOMARJ Reggie Jackson	30.00	80.00
MOMASK Sandy Koufax	125.00	300.00
MOMASO Shohei Ohtani	100.00	250.00
MOMAVG Vladimir Guerrero	20.00	50.00
MOMAYA Yordan Alvarez	30.00	80.00
MOMACRJ Cal Ripken Jr.	75.00	200.00
MOMAKGJ Ken Griffey Jr.	200.00	500.00
MOMARAJ Ronald Acuna Jr.	100.00	250.00
MOMAVGJ Vladimir Guerrero Jr.	40.00	100.00

2020 Finest Moments Autographs Gold Refractors

*GOLD REF: .6X TO 1.5X BASIC

STATED ODDS 1:831 HOBBY

STATED PRINT RUN 50 SER.#'d SETS

EXCHANGE DEADLINE 5/31/2022

Card	Low	High
MOMAKB Kris Bryant	40.00	100.00

2020 Finest Moments Autographs Orange Refractors

*ORANGE REF/25: 1X TO 2.5X BASIC

STATED ODDS 1:1016 HOBBY

STATED PRINT RUN 25 SER.#'d SETS

EXCHANGE DEADLINE 5/31/2022

Card	Low	High
MOMABB Bo Bichette EXCH	150.00	400.00
MOMAKB Kris Bryant	75.00	200.00
MOMAPA Pete Alonso	125.00	300.00

2020 Finest The Man

STATED ODDS 1:3 HOBBY

Card	Low	High
FTM1 Mike Trout	15.00	40.00
FTM2 Bryan Reynolds	.50	1.25
FTM3 Carter Kieboom	.50	1.25
FTM4 Dustin May	1.25	3.00
FTM5 Will Smith	.60	1.50
FTM6 Jorge Soler	.60	1.50
FTM7 Juan Soto	6.00	15.00
FTM8 Gleyber Torres	2.50	6.00
FTM9 Luis Robert	15.00	40.00
FTM10 Gavin Lux	6.00	15.00
FTM11 Ronald Acuna Jr.	12.00	30.00
FTM12 Yordan Alvarez	4.00	10.00
FTM13 Rhys Hoskins	.75	2.00
FTM14 Matt Beaty	.50	1.25
FTM15 Austin Riley	2.00	5.00
FTM16 Keston Hiura	.75	2.00
FTM17 Bo Bichette	8.00	20.00
FTM18 Brendan McKay	.60	1.50
FTM19 Aristides Aquino	1.00	2.50
FTM20 Fernando Tatis Jr.	8.00	20.00
FTM21 Vladimir Guerrero Jr.	2.50	6.00
FTM22 Francisco Lindor	1.50	4.00
FTM23 Shane Bieber	.60	1.50
FTM24 Dylan Cease	.60	1.50
FTM25 Cavan Biggio	.75	2.00
FTM26 Tim Anderson	.60	1.50
FTM27 A.J. Puk	.60	1.50
FTM28 Pete Alonso	3.00	8.00
FTM29 Mike Yastrzemski	1.00	2.50
FTM30 Bryce Harper	3.00	8.00

2020 Finest The Man Gold Refractors

*GOLD REF: 3X TO 8X BASIC

STATED ODDS 1:312 HOBBY

STATED PRINT RUN 50 SER.#'d SETS

Card	Low	High
FTM1 Mike Trout	100.00	250.00
FTM7 Juan Soto	60.00	150.00
FTM8 Gleyber Torres	60.00	150.00
FTM11 Ronald Acuna Jr.	100.00	250.00
FTM13 Rhys Hoskins	15.00	40.00
FTM17 Bo Bichette	60.00	150.00
FTM25 Cavan Biggio	15.00	40.00
FTM30 Bryce Harper	30.00	80.00

2020 Finest The Man Autographs

STATED ODDS 1:325 HOBBY

PRINT RUNS B/NW 10-99 COPIES PER

NO PRICING ON QTY 15 OR LESS

EXCHANGE DEADLINE 5/31/2022

Card	Low	High
FTMAAA Aristides Aquino/99	30.00	80.00
FTMAAR Austin Riley/50	30.00	80.00
FTMABB Bo Bichette EXCH	125.00	300.00
FTMABH Bryce Harper/10		
FTMABM Brendan McKay/60	12.00	30.00
FTMACB Cavan Biggio/99	25.00	60.00
FTMACK Carter Kieboom/99	15.00	40.00
FTMADM Dustin May/99	15.00	40.00
FTMAGL Gavin Lux/99	60.00	150.00
FTMAGT Gleyber Torres/45	125.00	300.00
FTMAJB Jake Bauers/99	6.00	15.00
FTMAJS Juan Soto/40	100.00	250.00
FTMAMB Matt Beaty/99	8.00	20.00
FTMAMT Mike Trout/10		
FTMAPA Pete Alonso/30	60.00	150.00
FTMARH Rhys Hoskins/30	25.00	60.00
FTMATA Tim Anderson/99	12.00	30.00
FTMAWS Will Smith/99	12.00	30.00
FTMAYA Yordan Alvarez/75	75.00	200.00
FTMAFTJ Fernando Tatis Jr./50	125.00	300.00

2020 Finest The Man Autographs Orange Refractors

*ORANGE/25: .8X TO 2X p/r 60-99

*ORANGE/25: .5X TO 1.2X p/r 30-50

STATED ODDS 1:964 HOBBY

STATED PRINT RUN 25 SER.#'d SETS

EXCHANGE DEADLINE 5/31/2022

Card	Low	High
FTMABM Brendan McKay	40.00	100.00
FTMATA Tim Anderson	30.00	80.00

2020 Finest Flashbacks

Card	Low	High
1 Walker Buehler	2.00	5.00
2 John Means	1.00	2.50
3 Miguel Cabrera	4.00	10.00
4 Will Smith	1.00	2.50
5 Yu Chang RC	1.50	4.00
6 Charlie Blackmon	1.00	2.50
7 Andrelton Simmons	.60	1.50
8 Hunter Harvey	1.00	2.50
9 Whit Merrifield	1.00	2.50
10 Alex Young RC	1.00	2.50
11 Cedric Mullins	.75	2.00
12 Eloy Jimenez	2.00	5.00
13 Shohei Ohtani	1.50	4.00
14 Zack Collins RC	1.25	3.00
15 Tyler Alexander RC	1.50	4.00
16 Harold Ramirez	.60	1.50
17 Bobby Bradley	.60	1.50
18 Gavin Lux RC	10.00	25.00
19 Josh Reddick	.60	1.50
20 Carlos Correa	1.00	2.50
21 J.D. Martinez	1.00	2.50
22 Eduardo Escobar	.60	1.50
23 Jorge Soler	1.00	2.50
24 Austin Riley	1.25	3.00
25 Jake Rogers RC	1.00	2.50
26 Michael Chavis	.75	2.00
27 Hunter Dozier	.60	1.50
28 Nick Senzel	1.00	2.50
29 Isan Diaz RC	1.50	4.00
30 Bubba Starling RC	2.00	5.00
31 Matt Thaiss RC	1.25	3.00
32 Rafael Devers	1.25	3.00
33 A.J. Minter	.75	2.00
34 Robbie Ray	.60	1.50
35 Zack Greinke	1.00	2.50
36 Travis Demeritte RC	1.50	4.00
37 Yuli Gurriel	.75	2.00
38 Keston Hiura	1.25	3.00
39 Mookie Betts	2.00	5.00
40 Yordan Alvarez RC	10.00	25.00
41 Logan Allen	.60	1.50
42 Javier Baez	1.25	3.00
43 Ozzie Albies	1.00	2.50
44 Tim Anderson	1.00	2.50
45 Willi Castro	1.00	2.50
46 Aaron Civale	1.25	3.00
47 Albert Pujols	1.25	3.00
48 Trevor Bauer	1.25	3.00
49 Jon Lester	.75	2.00
50 Corey Seager	1.00	2.50
51 Ender Inciarte	.60	1.50
52 David Price	.75	2.00
53 Lorenzo Cain	.60	1.50
54 Zac Gallen RC	2.50	6.00
55 Trey Mancini	1.00	2.50
56 Jordan Yamamoto RC	1.00	2.50
57 Dylan Cease RC	1.50	4.00
58 Anthony Rendon	1.00	2.50
59 Luis Robert RC	40.00	100.00
60 Sandy Alcantara	.60	1.50
61 Kyle Schwarber	1.00	2.50
62 Max Muncy	.75	2.00
63 Sam Hilliard RC	1.50	4.00
64 Jose Altuve	.75	2.00
65 Mike Soroka	1.00	2.50
66 Robel Garcia RC	1.00	2.50
67 Nico Hoerner RC	4.00	10.00
68 Brandon Woodruff	1.00	2.50
69 Dustin May RC	3.00	8.00
70 Oscar Mercado RC	1.50	4.00
71 Aristides Aquino RC	2.00	5.00
72 Adalberto Mondesi	.75	2.00
73 Dwight Smith Jr.	.60	1.50
74 Brian Anderson	.60	1.50
75 Eugenio Suarez	.75	2.00
76 David Dahl	.60	1.50
77 Dom Nunez RC	1.25	3.00
78 Dansby Swanson	1.00	2.50
79 Raisel Iglesias	.60	1.50
80 Adbert Alzolay RC	1.25	3.00
81 Domingo Leyba RC	1.25	3.00
82 Trevor Story	1.00	2.50
83 Andrew Benintendi	1.00	2.50
84 Aroldis Chapman	1.00	2.50
85 Christian Yelich	1.25	3.00
86 Freddie Freeman	1.25	3.00
87 Carlos Santana	.75	2.00
88 Ketel Marte	.75	2.00
89 Javier Baez	1.25	3.00
90 Paul DeJong	1.00	2.50
91 Xander Bogaerts	1.00	2.50
92 DJ LeMahieu	1.00	2.50
93 Clayton Kershaw	1.50	4.00
94 Masahiro Tanaka	1.00	2.50
95 Max Scherzer	1.00	2.50
96 Jose Abreu	1.00	2.50
97 Pete Alonso	2.50	6.00
98 Gary Sanchez	1.00	2.50
99 Ronald Acuna Jr.	6.00	15.00
100 Alex Bregman	1.00	2.50
101 Nolan Arenado	1.50	4.00
102 Jacob deGrom	2.00	5.00
103 Justin Verlander	1.00	2.50
104 Willson Contreras	1.00	2.50
105 George Springer	.75	2.00
106 Michael Brantley	.75	2.00
107 Gleyber Torres	2.00	5.00
108 Cody Bellinger	2.00	5.00
109 J.T. Realmuto	1.00	2.50
110 Jorge Polanco	.75	2.00
111 Lucas Giolito	.75	2.00
112 Shane Bieber	1.00	2.50
113 Kris Bryant	1.25	3.00
114 Joey Gallo	1.00	2.50
115 Francisco Lindor	1.00	2.50
116 Mike Trout	15.00	40.00
117 Paul Goldschmidt	1.00	2.50
118 Willians Astudillo	.60	1.50
119 Tommy Pham	.60	1.50
120 Colin Moran	.60	1.50
121 Victor Robles	1.25	3.00
122 Jack Flaherty	1.00	2.50
123 Jeff McNeil	.75	2.00
124 Gerrit Cole	1.50	4.00
125 Lourdes Gurriel Jr.	.75	2.00
126 Brusdar Graterol RC	1.50	4.00
127 Rougned Odor	.75	2.00
128 Shin-Soo Choo	.75	2.00
129 Kean Wong RC	1.50	4.00
130 Tyler Glasnow	1.00	2.50
131 Bryan Reynolds	.75	2.00
132 Austin Nola RC	1.50	4.00
133 Kyle Lewis RC	15.00	40.00
134 Marcus Semien	1.00	2.50
135 Carter Kieboom	.75	2.00
136 Josh Bell	.75	2.00
137 Brandon Crawford	.75	2.00
138 Fernando Tatis Jr.	6.00	15.00
139 Tommy Edman	1.00	2.50
140 Justin Dunn RC	1.25	3.00
141 Stephen Strasburg	1.00	2.50
142 James Paxton	.75	2.00
143 Mike Minor	.60	1.50
144 Nelson Cruz	1.00	2.50
145 Trent Grisham RC	4.00	10.00
146 A.J. Puk RC	1.50	4.00
147 Blake Snell	.75	2.00
148 Max Kepler	.75	2.00
149 Yadier Molina	1.25	3.00
150 Adam Haseley	.75	2.00
151 Jose Berrios	.75	2.00
152 Patrick Corbin	.75	2.00
153 Jonathan Hernandez RC	1.00	2.50
154 Nick Solak RC	4.00	10.00
155 Trea Turner	.75	2.00
156 Buster Posey	1.25	3.00
157 Marcus Stroman	.75	2.00
158 Wilson Ramos	.60	1.50
159 Seth Brown	.60	1.50
160 Andres Munoz RC	1.50	4.00
161 Adam Ottavino	.75	2.00
162 Chris Archer	.60	1.50
163 Gio Urshela	1.00	2.50
164 Steven Matz	.60	1.50
165 Kevin Kiermaier	.75	2.00
166 Jeff Samardzija	.60	1.50
167 Juan Soto	4.00	10.00
168 Cavan Biggio	1.25	3.00
169 Mike Yastrzemski	1.50	4.00
170 Matt Chapman	1.00	2.50
171 Mitch Keller	1.00	2.50
172 Hyun-Jin Ryu	.75	2.00
173 Willy Adames	.60	1.50
174 Amed Rosario	.75	2.00
175 Rhys Hoskins	1.25	3.00
176 Junior Fernandez RC	1.00	2.50
177 Khris Davis	1.00	2.50
178 Mitch Haniger	.75	2.00
179 Ronald Guzman	.60	1.50
180 Brendan McKay RC	1.50	4.00
181 Ryan Braun	.75	2.00
182 Kevin Newman	1.00	2.50
183 Kirby Yates	.60	1.50
184 Didi Gregorius	.75	2.00
185 Josh Hader	.75	2.00
186 Bryce Harper	1.50	4.00
187 Jesus Luzardo RC	2.00	5.00
188 Austin Meadows	1.00	2.50
189 Miles Mikolas	.60	1.50
190 Bo Bichette RC	20.00	50.00
191 Manny Machado	1.00	2.50
192 J.D. Davis	.60	1.50
193 J.T. Realmuto	1.00	2.50
194 Eddie Rosario	.75	2.00
195 Brandon Belt	.75	2.00
196 Aaron Judge	2.50	6.00
197 Giancarlo Stanton	1.00	2.50
198 Vladimir Guerrero Jr.	1.50	4.00
199 Evan Longoria	.75	2.00

2020 Finest Flashbacks Black Refractors

*BLACK REF.: 5X TO 12X BASIC

*BLACK REF.RC: 3X TO 8X BASIC RC

STATED ODDS 1:36 HOBBY

STATED PRINT RUN 25 SER.#'d SETS

Card	Low	High
4 Will Smith	25.00	60.00
12 Eloy Jimenez	50.00	120.00
13 Shohei Ohtani	100.00	250.00
18 Gavin Lux	250.00	600.00
32 Rafael Devers	40.00	100.00
38 Keston Hiura	30.00	80.00
39 Mookie Betts	125.00	300.00
40 Yordan Alvarez	400.00	1000.00
42 Javier Baez	50.00	120.00
44 Tim Anderson	25.00	60.00
45 Willi Castro	40.00	100.00
47 Albert Pujols	125.00	300.00
54 Zac Gallen	40.00	100.00
59 Luis Robert	1000.00	2500.00
65 Mike Soroka	25.00	60.00
67 Nico Hoerner	75.00	200.00
69 Dustin May	50.00	120.00
83 Andrew Benintendi	20.00	50.00
85 Christian Yelich	60.00	150.00
86 Freddie Freeman	50.00	120.00
89 Javier Baez	60.00	150.00
90 Paul DeJong	20.00	50.00
93 Clayton Kershaw	60.00	150.00
97 Pete Alonso	60.00	150.00
99 Ronald Acuna Jr.	250.00	600.00
101 Nolan Arenado	50.00	120.00
107 Gleyber Torres	150.00	400.00
108 Cody Bellinger	100.00	250.00
113 Kris Bryant	60.00	150.00
116 Mike Trout	1000.00	2500.00
124 Gerrit Cole	25.00	60.00
125 Lourdes Gurriel Jr.	20.00	50.00
133 Kyle Lewis	200.00	500.00
138 Fernando Tatis Jr.	150.00	400.00
145 Trent Grisham	50.00	120.00
146 A.J. Puk	30.00	80.00
156 Buster Posey	30.00	80.00
167 Juan Soto	250.00	600.00
168 Cavan Biggio	30.00	80.00
169 Mike Yastrzemski	40.00	100.00
175 Rhys Hoskins	25.00	60.00
180 Brendan McKay	30.00	80.00
184 Didi Gregorius	15.00	40.00
186 Bryce Harper	125.00	300.00
187 Jesus Luzardo	50.00	120.00
190 Bo Bichette	400.00	1000.00
196 Aaron Judge	125.00	300.00
198 Vladimir Guerrero Jr.	75.00	200.00

2020 Finest Flashbacks Gold Refractors

*GOLD REF.: 4X TO 10X BASIC

*GOLD REF.RC: 2.5X TO 6X BASIC RC

STATED ODDS 1:18 HOBBY

STATED PRINT RUN 50 SER.#'d SETS

Card	Low	High
4 Will Smith	20.00	50.00
12 Eloy Jimenez	40.00	100.00
13 Shohei Ohtani	75.00	200.00
18 Gavin Lux	200.00	500.00
32 Rafael Devers	30.00	80.00
38 Keston Hiura	25.00	60.00
39 Mookie Betts	100.00	250.00
40 Yordan Alvarez	300.00	600.00
42 Javier Baez	40.00	100.00
47 Albert Pujols	100.00	250.00
54 Zac Gallen	30.00	80.00
59 Luis Robert	750.00	2000.00
67 Nico Hoerner	60.00	150.00
69 Dustin May	40.00	100.00
83 Andrew Benintendi	15.00	40.00
85 Christian Yelich	50.00	120.00
86 Freddie Freeman	40.00	100.00
89 Javier Baez	40.00	100.00
93 Clayton Kershaw	50.00	120.00
97 Pete Alonso	50.00	120.00
99 Ronald Acuna Jr.	200.00	500.00
101 Nolan Arenado	40.00	100.00
107 Gleyber Torres	125.00	300.00
108 Cody Bellinger	75.00	200.00
113 Kris Bryant	50.00	120.00
116 Mike Trout	750.00	2000.00
124 Gerrit Cole	20.00	50.00
133 Kyle Lewis	150.00	400.00
138 Fernando Tatis Jr.	125.00	300.00
145 Trent Grisham	40.00	100.00
146 A.J. Puk	25.00	60.00
156 Buster Posey	25.00	60.00
167 Juan Soto	200.00	500.00
168 Cavan Biggio	25.00	60.00
169 Mike Yastrzemski	30.00	80.00
175 Rhys Hoskins	20.00	50.00
180 Brendan McKay	25.00	60.00
186 Bryce Harper	100.00	250.00
187 Jesus Luzardo	40.00	100.00
190 Bo Bichette	300.00	800.00
196 Aaron Judge	100.00	250.00
198 Vladimir Guerrero Jr.	60.00	150.00

2020 Finest Flashbacks Refractors

*REF.: 3X TO 8X BASIC

*REF.RC: 2X TO 5X BASIC RC

STATED ODDS 1:18 HOBBY

Card	Low	High
4 Will Smith	15.00	40.00
12 Eloy Jimenez	30.00	80.00
13 Shohei Ohtani	60.00	150.00
18 Gavin Lux	150.00	400.00
32 Rafael Devers	25.00	60.00
38 Keston Hiura	20.00	50.00
39 Mookie Betts	75.00	200.00
40 Yordan Alvarez	250.00	500.00
42 Javier Baez	30.00	80.00
47 Albert Pujols	75.00	200.00
54 Zac Gallen	25.00	60.00
59 Luis Robert	600.00	1500.00
67 Nico Hoerner	50.00	120.00
69 Dustin May	30.00	80.00
83 Andrew Benintendi	12.00	30.00
85 Christian Yelich	40.00	100.00
86 Freddie Freeman	30.00	80.00
89 Javier Baez	30.00	80.00
93 Clayton Kershaw	40.00	100.00
97 Pete Alonso	40.00	100.00
99 Ronald Acuna Jr.	150.00	400.00
101 Nolan Arenado	30.00	80.00
107 Gleyber Torres	100.00	250.00
108 Cody Bellinger	60.00	150.00
113 Kris Bryant	40.00	100.00
116 Mike Trout	600.00	1500.00
124 Gerrit Cole	15.00	40.00
133 Kyle Lewis	125.00	300.00
138 Fernando Tatis Jr.	100.00	250.00
145 Trent Grisham	30.00	80.00
146 A.J. Puk	20.00	50.00
156 Buster Posey	20.00	50.00
167 Juan Soto	150.00	400.00
168 Cavan Biggio	20.00	50.00
169 Mike Yastrzemski	25.00	60.00
175 Rhys Hoskins	15.00	40.00
180 Brendan McKay	20.00	50.00
186 Bryce Harper	75.00	200.00
187 Jesus Luzardo	30.00	80.00
190 Bo Bichette	250.00	600.00
196 Aaron Judge	75.00	200.00
198 Vladimir Guerrero Jr.	50.00	120.00

1951-52 Fischer Baking Labels

One of the popular "Bread for Energy" end-labels sets, these labels are found with blue, red and yellow backgrounds. Each bread label measures 2 3/4" by 2 3/4". They were distributed mainly in the northeast section of the country and there may be an album associated with the set. These labels are unnumbered and we have sequenced them in alphabetical order. The catalog designation is D290-3.

Card	Low	High
COMPLETE SET (32)	3000.00	6000.00
1 Vern Bickford	125.00	250.00
2 Ralph Branca	150.00	300.00
3 Harry Brecheen	125.00	250.00
4 Chico Carrasquel	125.00	250.00
5 Cliff Chambers	125.00	250.00
6 Hoot Evers	125.00	250.00
7 Ned Garver	125.00	250.00
8 Billy Goodman	125.00	250.00
9 Gil Hodges	250.00	500.00
10 Larry Jansen	125.00	250.00
11 Willie Jones	125.00	250.00
12 Eddie Joost	125.00	250.00
13 George Kell	250.00	300.00
14 Alex Kellner	125.00	500.00
15 Ted Kluszewski	175.00	350.00
16 Jim Konstanty	150.00	300.00
17 Bob Lemon	250.00	500.00
18 Cass Michaels	125.00	250.00
19 Johnny Mize	250.00	500.00
20 Irv Noren	125.00	250.00
21 Andy Pafko	125.00	250.00
22 Joe Page	150.00	300.00
23 Mel Parnell	150.00	300.00
24 Johnny Sain	150.00	300.00
25 Red Schoendienst	150.00	300.00
26 Roy Sievers	150.00	300.00
27 Roy Smalley	125.00	250.00
28 Herm Wehmeier	125.00	250.00
29 Bill Werle	125.00	250.00
30 Wes Westrum	125.00	250.00
31 Early Wynn	250.00	500.00
32 Gus Zernial	150.00	300.00

1993 Flair

This 300-card standard-size set represents Fleer's entrance into the super-premium category of trading cards. Cards were distributed exclusively in specially encased "hardpacks". The cards are made from heavy 24 point board card stock, with an additional three points of high-gloss laminate on each side, and feature full-bleed color fronts that sport two photos of each player, one superposed upon the other. The cards are numbered alphabetically within teams with National League preceding American league. There are no key Rookie Cards in this set.

Card	Low	High
COMPLETE SET (300)	20.00	50.00
1 Steve Avery	.08	.25
2 Jeff Blauser	.08	.25
3 Ron Gant	.20	.50
4 Tom Glavine	.30	.75
5 David Justice	.20	.50
6 Mark Lemke	.08	.25
7 Greg Maddux	.75	2.00
8 Fred McGriff	.30	.75
9 Terry Pendleton	.20	.50
10 Deion Sanders	.30	.75
11 John Smoltz	.30	.75
12 Mike Stanton	.08	.25
13 Steve Buechele	.08	.25
14 Mark Grace	.30	.75
15 Greg Hibbard	.08	.25
16 Derrick May	.08	.25
17 Chuck McElroy	.08	.25
18 Mike Morgan	.08	.25
19 Randy Myers	.08	.25
20 Ryne Sandberg	.75	2.00
21 Dwight Smith	.08	.25
22 Sammy Sosa	.50	1.25
23 Jose Vizcaino	.08	.25
24 Tim Belcher	.08	.25
25 Rob Dibble	.20	.50
26 Roberto Kelly	.08	.25
27 Barry Larkin	.30	.75
28 Kevin Mitchell	.08	.25
29 Hal Morris	.08	.25
30 Joe Oliver	.08	.25
31 Jose Rijo	.08	.25
32 Bip Roberts	.08	.25
33 Chris Sabo	.08	.25
34 Reggie Sanders	.20	.50
35 Dante Bichette	.20	.50
36 Willie Blair	.08	.25
37 Jerald Clark	.08	.25
38 Alex Cole	.08	.25
39 Andres Galarraga	.20	.50
40 Joe Girardi	.08	.25
41 Charlie Hayes	.08	.25
42 Chris Jones	.08	.25
43 David Nied	.08	.25
44 Eric Young	.08	.25
45 Alex Arias	.08	.25
46 Jack Armstrong	.08	.25
47 Bret Barberie	.08	.25
48 Chuck Carr	.08	.25
49 Jeff Conine	.20	.50
50 Orestes Destrade	.08	.25
51 Chris Hammond	.08	.25
52 Bryan Harvey	.08	.25
53 Benito Santiago	.20	.50
54 Gary Sheffield	.20	.50
55 Walt Weiss	.08	.25
56 Eric Anthony	.08	.25
57 Jeff Bagwell	.30	.75
58 Craig Biggio	.30	.75
59 Ken Caminiti	.20	.50
60 Andujar Cedeno	.08	.25
61 Doug Drabek	.08	.25
62 Steve Finley	.20	.50
63 Luis Gonzalez	.20	.50
64 Pete Harnisch	.08	.25
65 Doug Jones	.08	.25
66 Darryl Kile	.20	.50
67 Greg Swindell	.08	.25
68 Brett Butler	.20	.50
69 Jim Gott	.08	.25
70 Orel Hershiser	.20	.50
71 Eric Karros	.20	.50
72 Pedro Martinez	1.00	2.50
73 Ramon Martinez	.08	.25
74 Roger McDowell	.08	.25
75 Mike Piazza	2.00	5.00
76 Jody Reed	.08	.25
77 Tim Wallach	.08	.25
78 Moises Alou	.20	.50
79 Greg Colbrunn	.08	.25
80 Wil Cordero	.08	.25
81 Delino DeShields	.08	.25
82 Jeff Fassero	.08	.25
83 Marquis Grissom	.20	.50
84 Ken Hill	.08	.25
85 Mike Lansing RC	.20	.50
86 Dennis Martinez	.20	.50
87 Larry Walker	.20	.50
88 John Wetteland	.20	.50
89 Bobby Bonilla	.20	.50
90 Vince Coleman	.08	.25
91 Dwight Gooden	.20	.50
92 Todd Hundley	.08	.25
93 Howard Johnson	.08	.25
94 Eddie Murray	.50	1.25
95 Joe Orsulak	.08	.25
96 Bret Saberhagen	.20	.50
97 Darren Daulton	.20	.50
98 Mariano Duncan	.08	.25
99 Len Dykstra	.20	.50
100 Jim Eisenreich	.08	.25
101 Tommy Greene	.08	.25
102 Dave Hollins	.08	.25
103 Pete Incaviglia	.08	.25
104 Danny Jackson	.08	.25
105 John Kruk	.20	.50
106 Terry Mulholland	.08	.25
107 Curt Schilling	.20	.50
108 Mitch Williams	.08	.25
109 Stan Belinda	.08	.25
110 Jay Bell	.20	.50
111 Steve Cooke	.08	.25
112 Carlos Garcia	.08	.25
113 Jeff King	.08	.25
114 Al Martin	.08	.25
115 Orlando Merced	.08	.25
116 Don Slaught	.08	.25
117 Andy Van Slyke	.30	.75
118 Tim Wakefield	.50	1.25
119 Rene Arocha RC	.20	.50
120 Bernard Gilkey	.08	.25
121 Gregg Jefferies	.08	.25
122 Ray Lankford	.20	.50
123 Donovan Osborne	.08	.25
124 Tom Pagnozzi	.08	.25
125 Erik Pappas	.08	.25
126 Geronimo Pena	.08	.25
127 Lee Smith	.20	.50
128 Ozzie Smith	.75	2.00
129 Bob Tewksbury	.08	.25
130 Mark Whiten	.08	.25
131 Derek Bell	.08	.25
132 Andy Benes	.08	.25
133 Tony Gwynn	.60	1.50
134 Gene Harris	.08	.25
135 Trevor Hoffman	.50	1.25
136 Phil Plantier	.08	.25
137 Rod Beck	.08	.25
138 Barry Bonds	1.25	3.00
139 John Burkett	.08	.25
140 Will Clark	.30	.75
141 Royce Clayton	.08	.25
142 Mike Jackson	.08	.25
143 Darren Lewis	.08	.25
144 Kirt Manwaring	.08	.25
145 Willie McGee	.20	.50
146 Bill Swift	.08	.25
147 Robby Thompson	.08	.25
148 Matt Williams	.20	.50
149 Brady Anderson	.20	.50
150 Mike Devereaux	.08	.25
151 Chris Hoiles	.08	.25
152 Ben McDonald	.08	.25
153 Mark McLemore	.08	.25
154 Mike Mussina	.30	.75
155 Gregg Olson	.08	.25
156 Harold Reynolds	.20	.50
157 Cal Ripken	1.50	4.00
158 Rick Sutcliffe	.20	.50
159 Fernando Valenzuela	.20	.50
160 Roger Clemens	1.00	2.50
161 Scott Cooper	.08	.25
162 Andre Dawson	.20	.50
163 Scott Fletcher	.08	.25
164 Mike Greenwell	.08	.25
165 Greg A. Harris	.08	.25
166 Billy Hatcher	.08	.25
167 Jeff Russell	.08	.25
168 Mo Vaughn	.20	.50
169 Frank Viola	.20	.50
170 Chad Curtis	.08	.25
171 Chili Davis	.20	.50
172 Gary DiSarcina	.08	.25
173 Damion Easley	.08	.25
174 Chuck Finley	.20	.50
175 Mark Langston	.08	.25
176 Luis Polonia	.08	.25
177 Tim Salmon	.30	.75
178 Scott Sanderson	.08	.25
179 J.T.Snow RC	.30	.75
180 Wilson Alvarez	.08	.25
181 Ellis Burks	.20	.50
182 Joey Cora	.08	.25
183 Alex Fernandez	.08	.25
184 Ozzie Guillen	.20	.50
185 Roberto Hernandez	.08	.25
186 Bo Jackson	.50	1.25
187 Lance Johnson	.08	.25
188 Jack McDowell	.08	.25
189 Frank Thomas	.50	1.25
190 Robin Ventura	.20	.50
191 Carlos Baerga	.08	.25
192 Albert Belle	.20	.50
193 Wayne Kirby	.08	.25
194 Derek Lilliquist	.08	.25
195 Kenny Lofton	.20	.50
196 Carlos Martinez	.08	.25
197 Jose Mesa	.08	.25
198 Eric Plunk	.08	.25
199 Paul Sorrento	.08	.25
200 John Doherty	.08	.25
201 Cecil Fielder	.20	.50
202 Travis Fryman	.20	.50
203 Kirk Gibson	.20	.50
204 Mike Henneman	.08	.25
205 Chad Kreuter	.08	.25
206 Scott Livingstone	.08	.25
207 Tony Phillips	.08	.25
208 Mickey Tettleton	.08	.25
209 Alan Trammell	.20	.50
210 David Wells	.20	.50
211 Lou Whitaker	.20	.50
212 Kevin Appier	.20	.50
213 George Brett	1.25	3.00
214 David Cone	.20	.50
215 Tom Gordon	.08	.25
216 Phil Hiatt	.08	.25
217 Felix Jose	.08	.25
218 Wally Joyner	.20	.50
219 Jose Lind	.08	.25
220 Mike Macfarlane	.08	.25
221 Brian McRae	.08	.25
222 Jeff Montgomery	.08	.25
223 Cal Eldred	.08	.25
224 Darryl Hamilton	.08	.25
225 John Jaha	.08	.25
226 Pat Listach	.08	.25
227 Graeme Lloyd RC	.20	.50
228 Kevin Reimer	.08	.25
229 Bill Spiers	.08	.25
230 B.J. Surhoff	.20	.50
231 Greg Vaughn	.08	.25
232 Robin Yount	.75	2.00
233 Rick Aguilera	.08	.25
234 Jim Deshaies	.08	.25
235 Brian Harper	.08	.25
236 Kent Hrbek	.20	.50
237 Chuck Knoblauch	.20	.50
238 Shane Mack	.08	.25
239 David McCarty	.08	.25
240 Pedro Munoz	.08	.25
241 Mike Pagliarulo	.08	.25
242 Kirby Puckett	.50	1.25
243 Dave Winfield	.20	.50
244 Jim Abbott	.30	.75
245 Wade Boggs	.30	.75
246 Pat Kelly	.08	.25
247 Jimmy Key	.20	.50
248 Jim Leyritz	.08	.25
249 Don Mattingly	1.25	3.00
250 Matt Nokes	.08	.25
251 Paul O'Neill	.30	.75
252 Mike Stanley	.08	.25
253 Danny Tartabull	.08	.25

254 Bob Wickman .08 .25
255 Bernie Williams .30 .75
256 Mike Bordick .08 .25
257 Dennis Eckersley .20 .50
258 Brent Gates .08 .25
259 Rich Gossage .20 .50
260 Rickey Henderson .50 1.25
261 Mark McGwire 1.25 3.00
262 Ruben Sierra .20 .50
263 Terry Steinbach .08 .25
264 Bob Welch .08 .25
265 Bobby Witt .08 .25
266 Rich Amaral .08 .25
267 Chris Bosio .08 .25
268 Jay Buhner .20 .50
269 Norm Charlton .08 .25
270 Ken Griffey Jr. 1.00 2.50
271 Erik Hanson .08 .25
272 Randy Johnson .50 1.25
273 Edgar Martinez .30 .75
274 Tino Martinez .30 .75
275 Dave Valle .08 .25
276 Omar Vizquel .30 .75
277 Kevin Brown .20 .50
278 Jose Canseco .30 .75
279 Julio Franco .20 .50
280 Juan Gonzalez .20 .50
281 Tom Henke .08 .25
282 David Hulse RC .08 .25
283 Rafael Palmeiro .30 .75
284 Dean Palmer .20 .50
285 Ivan Rodriguez .30 .75
286 Nolan Ryan 2.00 5.00
287 Roberto Alomar .30 .75
288 Pat Borders .08 .25
289 Joe Carter .20 .50
290 Juan Guzman .08 .25
291 Pat Hentgen .08 .25
292 Paul Molitor .20 .50
293 John Olerud .20 .50
294 Ed Sprague .08 .25
295 Dave Stewart .20 .50
296 Duane Ward .08 .25
297 Devon White .20 .50
298 Greg Maddux .08 .25
Bo Jackson CL
299 Barry Larkin .08 .25
Rafael Palmeiro CL
300 Roberto Alomar CL .08 .25

1993 Flair Wave of the Future

COMPLETE SET (20) 15.00 40.00
STATED ODDS 1:4
1 Jason Bere .40 1.00
2 Jeromy Burnitz .75 2.00
3 Russ Davis .75 2.00
4 Jim Edmonds 2.00 5.00
5 Cliff Floyd .75 2.00
6 Jeffrey Hammonds .40 1.00
7 Trevor Hoffman 1.50 4.00
8 Domingo Jean .40 1.00
9 David McCarty .40 1.00
10 Bobby Munoz .40 1.00
11 Brad Pennington .40 1.00
12 Mike Piazza 4.00 10.00
13 Manny Ramirez 1.50 4.00
14 John Roper .40 1.00
15 Tim Salmon 1.00 2.50
16 Aaron Sele .40 1.00
17 Allen Watson .40 1.00
18 Rondell White .75 2.00
19 Darrell Whitmore UER .40 1.00
20 Nigel Wilson UER .40 1.00

1994 Flair

For the second consecutive year Fleer issued their premium-level Flair brand. These cards were issued in 10-card packs which were issued 24 packs to a box and 18 boxes to a case. The set consists of 450 full bleed cards in two series of 250 and 200. The card stock is thicker than the traditional standard card. Card fronts feature two photos with the player's name and team name at the bottom in gold foil. The cards are grouped alphabetically by team within each league with AL preceding NL. Notable Rookie Cards include Chan Ho Park and Alex Rodriguez. An Aaron Sele promo card was distributed to dealers and hobby media to preview the product.

COMPLETE SET (450) 20.00 50.00
COMPLETE SERIES 1 (250) 4.00 10.00
COMPLETE SERIES 2 (200) 15.00 40.00
1 Harold Baines .20 .50
2 Jeffrey Hammonds .08 .25
3 Chris Hoiles .08 .25
4 Ben McDonald .08 .25
5 Mark McLemore .08 .25
6 Jamie Moyer .20 .50
7 Jim Poole .08 .25
8 Cal Ripken 1.50 4.00
9 Chris Sabo .08 .25
10 Scott Bankhead .08 .25
11 Scott Cooper .08 .25
12 Danny Darwin .08 .25
13 Andre Dawson .20 .50
14 Billy Hatcher .08 .25
15 Aaron Sele .08 .25
16 John Valentin .08 .25
17 Dave Valle .08 .25
18 Mo Vaughn .20 .50
19 Brian Anderson RC .20 .50
20 Gary DiSarcina .08 .25
21 Jim Edmonds .50 1.25
22 Chuck Finley .20 .50
23 Bo Jackson .50 1.25
24 Mark Leiter .08 .25
25 Greg Myers .08 .25
26 Eduardo Perez .08 .25
27 Tim Salmon .30 .75
28 Wilson Alvarez .08 .25
29 Jason Bere .08 .25
30 Alex Fernandez .08 .25
31 Ozzie Guillen .20 .50
32 Joe Hall RC .08 .25
33 Darrin Jackson .08 .25
34 Kirk McCaskill .08 .25
35 Tim Raines .20 .50
36 Frank Thomas .50 1.25
37 Carlos Baerga .08 .25
38 Albert Belle .20 .50
39 Mark Clark .08 .25
40 Wayne Kirby .08 .25
41 Dennis Martinez .20 .50
42 Charles Nagy .08 .25
43 Manny Ramirez .50 1.25
44 Paul Sorrento .08 .25
45 Jim Thome .30 .75
46 Eric Davis .20 .50
47 John Doherty .08 .25
48 Junior Felix .08 .25
49 Cecil Fielder .20 .50
50 Kirk Gibson .20 .50
51 Mike Moore .08 .25
52 Tony Phillips .08 .25
53 Alan Trammell .20 .50
54 Kevin Appier .20 .50
55 Stan Belinda .08 .25
56 Vince Coleman .08 .25
57 Greg Gagne .08 .25
58 Bob Hamelin .08 .25
59 Dave Henderson .08 .25
60 Wally Joyner .20 .50
61 Mike Macfarlane .08 .25
62 Jeff Montgomery .08 .25
63 Ricky Bones .08 .25
64 Jeff Bronkey .08 .25
65 Alex Diaz RC .08 .25
66 Cal Eldred .08 .25
67 Darryl Hamilton .08 .25
68 John Jaha .08 .25
69 Mark Kiefer .08 .25
70 Kevin Seitzer .08 .25
71 Turner Ward .08 .25
72 Rich Becker .08 .25
73 Scott Erickson .08 .25
74 Keith Garagozzo RC .08 .25
75 Kent Hrbek .20 .50
76 Scott Leius .08 .25
77 Kirby Puckett .50 1.25
78 Matt Walbeck .08 .25
79 Dave Winfield .20 .50
80 Mike Gallego .08 .25
81 Xavier Hernandez .08 .25
82 Jimmy Key .20 .50
83 Jim Leyritz .08 .25
84 Don Mattingly 1.25 3.00
85 Matt Nokes .08 .25
86 Paul O'Neill .30 .75
87 Melido Perez .08 .25
88 Danny Tartabull .08 .25
89 Mike Bordick .08 .25
90 Ron Darling .08 .25
91 Dennis Eckersley .20 .50
92 Stan Javier .08 .25
93 Steve Karsay .08 .25
94 Mark McGwire 1.25 3.00
95 Troy Neel .08 .25
96 Terry Steinbach .08 .25
97 Bill Taylor RC .20 .50
98 Eric Anthony .08 .25
99 Chris Bosio .08 .25
100 Tim Davis .08 .25
101 Felix Fermin .08 .25
102 Dave Fleming .08 .25
103 Ken Griffey Jr. 1.00 2.50
104 Greg Hibbard .08 .25
105 Reggie Jefferson .08 .25
106 Tino Martinez .30 .75
107 Jack Armstrong .08 .25
108 Will Clark .30 .75
109 Juan Gonzalez .20 .50
110 Rick Helling .08 .25
111 Tom Henke .08 .25
112 David Hulse .08 .25
113 Manuel Lee .08 .25
114 Doug Strange .08 .25
115 Roberto Alomar .30 .75
116 Joe Carter .20 .50
117 Carlos Delgado .30 .75
118 Pat Hentgen .08 .25
119 Paul Molitor .20 .50
120 John Olerud .20 .50
121 Dave Stewart .20 .50
122 Todd Stottlemyre .08 .25
123 Mike Timlin .08 .25
124 Jeff Blauser .08 .25
125 Tom Glavine .30 .75
126 David Justice .20 .50
127 Mike Kelly .08 .25
128 Ryan Klesko .20 .50
129 Javier Lopez .20 .50
130 Greg Maddux .75 2.00
131 Fred McGriff .30 .75
132 Kent Mercker .08 .25
133 Mark Wohlers .08 .25
134 Willie Banks .08 .25
135 Steve Buechele .08 .25
136 Shawon Dunston .08 .25
137 Jose Guzman .08 .25
138 Glenallen Hill .08 .25
139 Randy Myers .08 .25
140 Karl Rhodes .08 .25
141 Ryne Sandberg .75 2.00
142 Steve Trachsel .08 .25
143 Bret Boone .20 .50
144 Tom Browning .08 .25
145 Hector Carrasco .08 .25
146 Barry Larkin .30 .75
147 Hal Morris .08 .25
148 Jose Rijo .08 .25
149 Reggie Sanders .20 .50
150 John Smiley .08 .25
151 Dante Bichette .20 .50
152 Ellis Burks .20 .50
153 Joe Girardi .08 .25
154 Mike Harkey .08 .25
155 Roberto Mejia .08 .25
156 Marcus Moore .08 .25
157 Armando Reynoso .08 .25
158 Bruce Ruffin .08 .25
159 Eric Young .08 .25
160 Kurt Abbott RC .08 .25
161 Jeff Conine .20 .50
162 Orestes Destrade .08 .25
163 Chris Hammond .08 .25
164 Bryan Harvey .08 .25
165 Dave Magadan .08 .25
166 Gary Sheffield .20 .50
167 David Weathers .08 .25
168 Andujar Cedeno .08 .25
169 Tom Edens .08 .25
170 Luis Gonzalez .20 .50
171 Pete Harnisch .08 .25
172 Todd Jones .08 .25
173 Darryl Kile .20 .50
174 James Mouton .08 .25
175 Scott Servais .08 .25
176 Mitch Williams .08 .25
177 Pedro Astacio .08 .25
178 Orel Hershiser .20 .50
179 Raul Mondesi .20 .50
180 Jose Offerman .08 .25
181 Chan Ho Park RC .30 .75
182 Mike Piazza 1.00 2.50
183 Cory Snyder .08 .25
184 Tim Wallach .08 .25
185 Todd Worrell .08 .25
186 Sean Berry .08 .25
187 Wil Cordero .08 .25
188 Darrin Fletcher .08 .25
189 Cliff Floyd .20 .50
190 Marquis Grissom .20 .50
191 Rod Henderson .08 .25
192 Ken Hill .08 .25
193 Pedro Martinez .50 1.25
194 Kirk Rueter .08 .25
195 Jeromy Burnitz .20 .50
196 John Franco .20 .50
197 Dwight Gooden .20 .50
198 Todd Hundley .08 .25
199 Bobby Jones .08 .25
200 Jeff Kent .30 .75
201 Mike Maddux .08 .25
202 Ryan Thompson .08 .25
203 Jose Vizcaino .08 .25
204 Darren Daulton .20 .50
205 Lenny Dykstra .20 .50
206 Jim Eisenreich .08 .25
207 Dave Hollins .08 .25
208 Danny Jackson .08 .25
209 Doug Jones .08 .25
210 Jeff Juden .08 .25
211 Ben Rivera .08 .25
212 Kevin Stocker .08 .25
213 Milt Thompson .08 .25
214 Jay Bell .20 .50
215 Steve Cooke .08 .25
216 Mark Dewey .08 .25
217 Al Martin .08 .25
218 Orlando Merced .08 .25
219 Don Slaught .08 .25
220 Zane Smith .08 .25
221 Rick White RC .08 .25
222 Kevin Young .08 .25
223 Rene Arocha .08 .25
224 Rheal Cormier .08 .25
225 Brian Jordan .20 .50
226 Ray Lankford .20 .50
227 Mike Perez .08 .25
228 Ozzie Smith .75 2.00
229 Mark Whiten .08 .25
230 Todd Zeile .08 .25
231 Derek Bell .08 .25
232 Archi Cianfrocco .08 .25
233 Ricky Gutierrez .08 .25
234 Trevor Hoffman .30 .75
235 Phil Plantier .08 .25
236 Dave Staton .08 .25
237 Wally Whitehurst .08 .25
238 Todd Benzinger .08 .25
239 Barry Bonds 1.25 3.00
240 John Burkett .08 .25
241 Royce Clayton .08 .25
242 Bryan Hickerson .08 .25
243 Mike Jackson .08 .25
244 Darren Lewis .08 .25
245 Kirt Manwaring .08 .25
246 Mark Portugal .08 .25
247 Salomon Torres .08 .25
248 Checklist .08 .25
249 Checklist .08 .25
250 Checklist .08 .25
251 Brady Anderson .20 .50
252 Mike Devereaux .08 .25
253 Sid Fernandez .08 .25
254 Leo Gomez .08 .25
255 Mike Mussina .30 .75
256 Mike Oquist .08 .25
257 Rafael Palmeiro .30 .75
258 Lee Smith .20 .50
259 Damon Berryhill .08 .25
260 Wes Chamberlain .08 .25
261 Roger Clemens 1.00 2.50
262 Gar Finnvold RC .08 .25
263 Mike Greenwell .08 .25
264 Tim Naehring .08 .25
265 Otis Nixon .08 .25
266 Ken Ryan .08 .25
267 Chad Curtis .08 .25
268 Chili Davis .20 .50
269 Damion Easley .08 .25
270 Jorge Fabregas .08 .25
271 Mark Langston .08 .25
272 Phil Leftwich RC .08 .25
273 Harold Reynolds .20 .50
274 J.T. Snow .20 .50
275 Joey Cora .08 .25
276 Julio Franco .20 .50
277 Roberto Hernandez .08 .25
278 Lance Johnson .08 .25
279 Ron Karkovice .08 .25
280 Jack McDowell .08 .25
281 Robin Ventura .20 .50
282 Sandy Alomar Jr. .08 .25
283 Kenny Lofton .20 .50
284 Jose Mesa .08 .25
285 Jack Morris .20 .50
286 Eddie Murray .50 1.25
287 Chad Ogea .08 .25
288 Eric Plunk .08 .25
289 Paul Shuey .08 .25
290 Omar Vizquel .30 .75
291 Danny Bautista .08 .25
292 Travis Fryman .20 .50
293 Greg Gohr .08 .25
294 Chris Gomez .08 .25
295 Mickey Tettleton .08 .25
296 Lou Whitaker .20 .50
297 David Cone .20 .50
298 Gary Gaetti .20 .50
299 Tom Gordon .08 .25
300 Felix Jose .08 .25
301 Jose Lind .08 .25
302 Brian McRae .08 .25
303 Mike Fetters .08 .25
304 Brian Harper .08 .25
305 Pat Listach .08 .25
306 Matt Mieske .08 .25
307 Dave Nilsson .08 .25
308 Jody Reed .08 .25
309 Greg Vaughn .08 .25
310 Bill Wegman .08 .25
311 Rick Aguilera .08 .25
312 Alex Cole .08 .25
313 Denny Hocking .08 .25
314 Chuck Knoblauch .20 .50
315 Shane Mack .08 .25
316 Pat Meares .08 .25
317 Kevin Tapani .08 .25
318 Jim Abbott .30 .75
319 Wade Boggs .30 .75
320 Sterling Hitchcock .08 .25
321 Pat Kelly .08 .25
322 Terry Mulholland .08 .25
323 Luis Polonia .08 .25
324 Mike Stanley .08 .25
325 Bob Wickman .08 .25
326 Bernie Williams .30 .75
327 Mark Acre RC .08 .25
328 Geronimo Berroa .08 .25
329 Scott Brosius .20 .50
330 Brent Gates .08 .25
331 Rickey Henderson .50 1.25
332 Carlos Reyes RC .08 .25
333 Ruben Sierra .20 .50
334 Bobby Witt .08 .25
335 Bobby Ayala .08 .25
336 Jay Buhner .20 .50
337 Randy Johnson .50 1.25
338 Edgar Martinez .30 .75
339 Bill Risley .08 .25
340 Alex Rodriguez RC 6.00 15.00
341 Roger Salkeld .08 .25
342 Dan Wilson .08 .25
343 Kevin Brown .20 .50
344 Jose Canseco .30 .75
345 Dean Palmer .20 .50
346 Ivan Rodriguez .30 .75
347 Kenny Rogers .20 .50
348 Pat Borders .08 .25
349 Juan Guzman .08 .25
350 Ed Sprague .08 .25
351 Devon White .20 .50
352 Steve Avery .08 .25
353 Roberto Kelly .08 .25
354 Mark Lemke .08 .25
355 Greg McMichael .08 .25
356 Terry Pendleton .20 .50
357 John Smoltz .30 .75
358 Mike Stanton .08 .25
359 Tony Tarasco .08 .25
360 Mark Grace .30 .75
361 Derrick May .08 .25
362 Rey Sanchez .08 .25
363 Sammy Sosa .50 1.25
364 Rick Wilkins .08 .25
365 Jeff Brantley .08 .25
366 Tony Fernandez .08 .25
367 Chuck McElroy .08 .25
368 Kevin Mitchell .08 .25
369 John Roper .08 .25
370 Johnny Ruffin .08 .25
371 Deion Sanders .30 .75
372 Marvin Freeman .08 .25
373 Andres Galarraga .20 .50
374 Charlie Hayes .08 .25
375 Nelson Liriano .08 .25
376 David Nied .08 .25
377 Walt Weiss .08 .25
378 Bret Barberie .08 .25
379 Jerry Browne .08 .25
380 Chuck Carr .08 .25
381 Greg Colbrunn .08 .25
382 Charlie Hough .20 .50
383 Kurt Miller .08 .25
384 Benito Santiago .20 .50
385 Jeff Bagwell .30 .75
386 Craig Biggio .30 .75
387 Ken Caminiti .20 .50
388 Doug Drabek .08 .25
389 Steve Finley .20 .50
390 John Hudek RC .08 .25
391 Orlando Miller .08 .25
392 Shane Reynolds .08 .25
393 Brett Butler .20 .50
394 Tom Candiotti .08 .25
395 Delino DeShields .08 .25
396 Kevin Gross .08 .25
397 Eric Karros .20 .50
398 Ramon Martinez .08 .25
399 Henry Rodriguez .08 .25
400 Moises Alou .20 .50
401 Jeff Fassero .08 .25
402 Mike Lansing .08 .25
403 Mel Rojas .08 .25
404 Larry Walker .20 .50
405 John Wetteland .20 .50
406 Gabe White .08 .25
407 Bobby Bonilla .20 .50
408 Josias Manzanillo .08 .25
409 Bret Saberhagen .20 .50
410 David Segui .08 .25
411 Mariano Duncan .08 .25
412 Tommy Greene .08 .25
413 Billy Hatcher .08 .25
414 Ricky Jordan .08 .25
415 John Kruk .20 .50
416 Bobby Munoz .08 .25
417 Curt Schilling .20 .50
418 Fernando Valenzuela .20 .50
419 David West .08 .25
420 Carlos Garcia .08 .25
421 Brian Hunter .08 .25
422 Jeff King .08 .25
423 Jon Lieber .20 .50
424 Ravelo Manzanillo .08 .25
425 Denny Neagle .20 .50
426 Andy Van Slyke .30 .75
427 Bryan Eversgerd RC .08 .25
428 Bernard Gilkey .08 .25
429 Gregg Jefferies .08 .25
430 Tom Pagnozzi .08 .25
431 Bob Tewksbury .08 .25
432 Allen Watson .08 .25
433 Andy Ashby .08 .25
434 Andy Benes .08 .25
435 Donnie Elliott .08 .25
436 Tony Gwynn .60 1.50
437 Joey Hamilton .08 .25
438 Tim Hyers RC .08 .25
439 Luis Lopez .08 .25
440 Bip Roberts .08 .25
441 Scott Sanders .08 .25
442 Rod Beck .08 .25
443 Dave Burba .08 .25
444 Darryl Strawberry .20 .50
445 Bill Swift .08 .25
446 Robby Thompson .08 .25
447 W.VanLandingham RC .08 .25
448 Matt Williams .20 .50
449 Checklist .08 .25
450 Checklist .08 .25
P15 Aaron Sele Promo .40 1.00

1994 Flair Hot Gloves

COMPLETE SET (10) 20.00 50.00
RANDOM INSERTS IN SER.2 PACKS
1 Barry Bonds 3.00 8.00
2 Will Clark 1.00 2.50
3 Ken Griffey Jr. 8.00 20.00
4 Kenny Lofton .60 1.50
5 Greg Maddux 2.50 6.00
6 Don Mattingly 3.00 8.00
7 Kirby Puckett 1.50 4.00
8 Cal Ripken 5.00 12.00
9 Tim Salmon .60 1.50
10 Matt Williams .60 1.50

1994 Flair Hot Numbers

COMPLETE SET (10) 20.00 50.00
SER.1 STATED ODDS 1:24
1 Roberto Alomar 2.00 5.00
2 Carlos Baerga .60 1.50
3 Will Clark 2.00 5.00
4 Fred McGriff 2.00 5.00
5 Paul Molitor 1.25 3.00
6 John Olerud 1.25 3.00
7 Mike Piazza 6.00 15.00
8 Cal Ripken 10.00 25.00
9 Ryne Sandberg 5.00 12.00
10 Frank Thomas 3.00 8.00

1994 Flair Infield Power

COMPLETE SET (10) 6.00 15.00
STATED ODDS 1:5
1 Jeff Bagwell .50 1.25
2 Will Clark .50 1.25
3 Darren Daulton .30 .75
4 Don Mattingly 2.00 5.00
5 Fred McGriff .50 1.25
6 Rafael Palmeiro .50 1.25
7 Mike Piazza 1.50 4.00
8 Cal Ripken 2.50 6.00
9 Frank Thomas .75 2.00
10 Matt Williams .30 .75

1994 Flair Outfield Power

COMPLETE SET (10) 8.00 20.00
STATED ODDS 1:5
1 Albert Belle .40 1.00
2 Barry Bonds 2.50 6.00
3 Joe Carter .40 1.00
4 Lenny Dykstra .40 1.00
5 Juan Gonzalez .40 1.00
6 Ken Griffey Jr. 2.00 5.00
7 David Justice .40 1.00
8 Kirby Puckett 1.00 2.50
9 Tim Salmon .60 1.50
10 Dave Winfield .40 1.00

1994 Flair Wave of the Future

COMPLETE SERIES 1 (10) 6.00 15.00
COMPLETE SERIES 2 (10) 15.00 40.00
A1-A10 SER.1 STATED ODDS 1:5
B1-B19 SER.2 STATED ODDS 1:5
A1 Kurt Abbott .40 1.00
A2 Carlos Delgado 1.00 2.50
A3 Steve Karsay .40 1.00
A4 Ryan Klesko .75 2.00
A5 Javier Lopez .75 2.00
A6 Raul Mondesi .75 2.00
A7 James Mouton .40 1.00
A8 Chan Ho Park 1.00 2.50
A9 Dave Staton .40 1.00
A10 Rick White .40 1.00
B1 Mark Acre .40 1.00
B2 Chris Gomez .40 1.00
B3 Joey Hamilton .40 1.00
B4 John Hudek .40 1.00
B5 Jon Lieber .75 2.00
B6 Matt Mieske .40 1.00
B7 Orlando Miller .40 1.00
B8 Alex Rodriguez 6.00 15.00
B9 Tony Tarasco .40 1.00
B10 W.VanLandingham .40 1.00

1995 Flair

This set (produced by Fleer) was issued in two series of 216 cards for a total of 432 standard-size cards. Horizontally designed fronts have a 100 percent etched foil surface containing two player photos. The backs feature a full-bleed photo with yearly statistics superimposed. The checklist is arranged alphabetically by league with AL preceding NL. Rookie Cards include Bobby Higginson and Hideo Nomo.

COMPLETE SET (432) 20.00 50.00
COMPLETE SERIES 1 (216) 12.50 30.00
COMPLETE SERIES 2 (216) 8.00 20.00
1 Brady Anderson .20 .50
2 Harold Baines .20 .50
3 Leo Gomez .08 .25
4 Alan Mills .08 .25
5 Jamie Moyer .20 .50
6 Mike Mussina .30 .75
7 Mike Oquist .08 .25
8 Arthur Rhodes .08 .25
9 Cal Ripken 1.50 4.00
10 Roger Clemens 1.00 2.50
11 Scott Cooper .08 .25
12 Mike Greenwell .08 .25
13 Aaron Sele .08 .25
14 John Valentin .08 .25
15 Mo Vaughn .20 .50
16 Chad Curtis .08 .25
17 Gary DiSarcina .08 .25
18 Chuck Finley .20 .50
19 Andrew Lorraine .08 .25
20 Spike Owen .08 .25
21 Tim Salmon .30 .75
22 J.T. Snow .20 .50
23 Wilson Alvarez .08 .25
24 Jason Bere .08 .25
25 Ozzie Guillen .20 .50
26 Mike LaValliere .08 .25
27 Frank Thomas .50 1.25
28 Robin Ventura .20 .50
29 Carlos Baerga .08 .25
30 Albert Belle .20 .50
31 Jason Grimsley .08 .25
32 Dennis Martinez .20 .50
33 Eddie Murray .50 1.25
34 Charles Nagy .08 .25
35 Manny Ramirez .30 .75
36 Paul Sorrento .08 .25
37 John Doherty .08 .25
38 Cecil Fielder .20 .50
39 Travis Fryman .20 .50
40 Chris Gomez .08 .25
41 Tony Phillips .08 .25
42 Lou Whitaker .20 .50
43 David Cone .20 .50
44 Gary Gaetti .20 .50
45 Mark Gubicza .08 .25
46 Bob Hamelin .08 .25
47 Wally Joyner .20 .50
48 Rusty Meacham .08 .25
49 Jeff Montgomery .08 .25
50 Ricky Bones .08 .25
51 Cal Eldred .08 .25
52 Pat Listach .08 .25
53 Matt Mieske .08 .25
54 Dave Nilsson .08 .25
55 Greg Vaughn .08 .25
56 Bill Wegman .08 .25
57 Chuck Knoblauch .20 .50
58 Scott Leius .08 .25
59 Pat Mahomes .08 .25
60 Pat Meares .08 .25
61 Pedro Munoz .08 .25
62 Kirby Puckett .50 1.25
63 Wade Boggs .30 .75
64 Jimmy Key .20 .50
65 Jim Leyritz .08 .25
66 Don Mattingly 1.25 3.00
67 Paul O'Neill .30 .75
68 Melido Perez .08 .25
69 Danny Tartabull .08 .25
70 John Briscoe .08 .25
71 Scott Brosius .20 .50
72 Ron Darling .08 .25
73 Brent Gates .08 .25
74 Rickey Henderson .50 1.25
75 Stan Javier .08 .25
76 Mark McGwire 1.25 3.00
77 Todd Van Poppel .08 .25
78 Bobby Ayala .08 .25
79 Mike Blowers .08 .25
80 Jay Buhner .20 .50
81 Ken Griffey Jr. 1.00 2.50
82 Randy Johnson .50 1.25
83 Tino Martinez .30 .75
84 Jeff Nelson .08 .25
85 Alex Rodriguez 1.25 3.00
86 Will Clark .30 .75
87 Jeff Frye .08 .25
88 Juan Gonzalez .20 .50
89 Rusty Greer .20 .50
90 Darren Oliver .08 .25
91 Dean Palmer .20 .50
92 Ivan Rodriguez .30 .75
93 Matt Whiteside .08 .25
94 Roberto Alomar .30 .75
95 Joe Carter .20 .50
96 Tony Castillo .08 .25
97 Juan Guzman .08 .25
98 Pat Hentgen .08 .25
99 Mike Huff .08 .25
100 John Olerud .20 .50
101 Woody Williams .08 .25
102 Roberto Kelly .08 .25
103 Ryan Klesko .20 .50
104 Javier Lopez .20 .50
105 Greg Maddux .75 2.00
106 Fred McGriff .30 .75
107 Jose Oliva .08 .25
108 John Smoltz .30 .75
109 Tony Tarasco .08 .25
110 Mark Wohlers .08 .25
111 Jim Bullinger .08 .25
112 Shawon Dunston .08 .25
113 Derrick May .08 .25
114 Randy Myers .08 .25
115 Karl Rhodes .08 .25
116 Rey Sanchez .08 .25
117 Steve Trachsel .08 .25
118 Eddie Zambrano .08 .25
119 Bret Boone .20 .50
120 Brian Dorsett .08 .25
121 Hal Morris .08 .25
122 Jose Rijo .08 .25
123 John Roper .08 .25
124 Reggie Sanders .20 .50
125 Pete Schourek .08 .25
126 John Smiley .08 .25
127 Ellis Burks .20 .50
128 Vinny Castilla .20 .50
129 Marvin Freeman .08 .25
130 Andres Galarraga .20 .50
131 Mike Munoz .08 .25
132 David Nied .08 .25
133 Bruce Ruffin .08 .25
134 Walt Weiss .08 .25
135 Eric Young .08 .25
136 Greg Colbrunn .08 .25
137 Jeff Conine .20 .50
138 Jeremy Hernandez .08 .25
139 Charles Johnson .20 .50
140 Robb Nen .20 .50
141 Gary Sheffield .20 .50
142 Dave Weathers .08 .25
143 Jeff Bagwell .30 .75
144 Craig Biggio .30 .75
145 Tony Eusebio .08 .25
146 Luis Gonzalez .20 .50
147 John Hudek .08 .25
148 Darryl Kile .20 .50
149 Dave Veres .08 .25
150 Billy Ashley .08 .25
151 Pedro Astacio .08 .25
152 Rafael Bournigal .08 .25
153 Delino DeShields .08 .25
154 Raul Mondesi .20 .50
155 Mike Piazza .75 2.00
156 Rudy Seanez .08 .25
157 Ismael Valdes .08 .25
158 Tim Wallach .08 .25
159 Todd Worrell .08 .25
160 Moises Alou .20 .50
161 Cliff Floyd .20 .50
162 Gil Heredia .08 .25
163 Mike Lansing .08 .25
164 Pedro Martinez .30 .75
165 Kirk Rueter .08 .25
166 Tim Scott .08 .25
167 Jeff Shaw .08 .25
168 Rondell White .20 .50
169 Bobby Bonilla .20 .50
170 Rico Brogna .08 .25
171 Todd Hundley .08 .25
172 Jeff Kent .20 .50
173 Jim Lindeman .08 .25
174 Joe Orsulak .08 .25
175 Bret Saberhagen .20 .50
176 Toby Borland .08 .25
177 Darren Daulton .20 .50
178 Lenny Dykstra .20 .50
179 Jim Eisenreich .08 .25
180 Tommy Greene .08 .25
181 Tony Longmire .08 .25
182 Bobby Munoz .08 .25
183 Kevin Stocker .08 .25
184 Jay Bell .20 .50
185 Steve Cooke .08 .25
186 Ravelo Manzanillo .08 .25
187 Al Martin .08 .25
188 Denny Neagle .20 .50
189 Don Slaught .08 .25
190 Paul Wagner .08 .25
191 Rene Arocha .08 .25
192 Bernard Gilkey .08 .25
193 Jose Oquendo .08 .25
194 Tom Pagnozzi .08 .25
195 Ozzie Smith .75 2.00
196 Allen Watson .08 .25
197 Mark Whiten .08 .25
198 Andy Ashby .08 .25
199 Donnie Elliott .08 .25
200 Bryce Florie .08 .25
201 Tony Gwynn .60 1.50
202 Trevor Hoffman .20 .50
203 Brian Johnson .08 .25
204 Tim Mauser .08 .25
205 Bip Roberts .08 .25
206 Rod Beck .08 .25
207 Barry Bonds 1.25 3.00
208 Royce Clayton .08 .25
209 Darren Lewis .08 .25
210 Mark Portugal .08 .25
211 Kevin Rogers .08 .25
212 Wm. VanLandingham .08 .25
213 Matt Williams .20 .50
214 Checklist .08 .25
215 Checklist .08 .25
216 Checklist .08 .25
217 Bret Barberie .08 .25
218 Armando Benitez .08 .25
219 Kevin Brown .20 .50
220 Sid Fernandez .08 .25
221 Chris Hoiles .08 .25
222 Doug Jones .08 .25
223 Ben McDonald .08 .25
224 Rafael Palmeiro .30 .75
225 Andy Van Slyke .30 .75
226 Jose Canseco .30 .75
227 Vaughn Eshelman .08 .25
228 Mike Macfarlane .08 .25
229 Tim Naehring .08 .25
230 Frank Rodriguez .08 .25
231 Lee Tinsley .08 .25
232 Mark Whiten .08 .25
233 Garret Anderson .20 .50
234 Chili Davis .20 .50
235 Jim Edmonds .30 .75
236 Mark Langston .08 .25
237 Troy Percival .20 .50
238 Tony Phillips .08 .25

239 Lee Smith .20 .50
240 Jim Abbott .30 .75
241 James Baldwin .08 .25
242 Mike Devereaux .08 .25
243 Ray Durham .20 .50
244 Alex Fernandez .08 .25
245 Roberto Hernandez .08 .25
246 Lance Johnson .08 .25
247 Ron Karkovice .08 .25
248 Tim Raines .20 .50
249 Sandy Alomar Jr. .08 .25
250 Orel Hershiser .20 .50
251 Julian Tavarez .08 .25
252 Jim Thome .30 .75
253 Omar Vizquel .30 .75
254 Dave Winfield .20 .50
255 Chad Curtis .08 .25
256 Kirk Gibson .20 .50
257 Mike Henneman .08 .25
258 Bob Higginson RC .40 1.00
259 Felipe Lira .08 .25
260 Rudy Pemberton .08 .25
261 Alan Trammell .20 .50
262 Kevin Appier .20 .50
263 Pat Borders .08 .25
264 Tom Gordon .08 .25
265 Jose Lind .08 .25
266 Jon Nunnally .08 .25
267 Dilson Torres RC .08 .25
268 Michael Tucker .08 .25
269 Jeff Cirillo .08 .25
270 Darryl Hamilton .08 .25
271 David Hulse .08 .25
272 Mark Kiefer .08 .25
273 Graeme Lloyd .08 .25
274 Joe Oliver .08 .25
275 Al Reyes RC .08 .25
276 Kevin Seitzer .08 .25
277 Rick Aguilera .08 .25
278 Marty Cordova .08 .25
279 Scott Erickson .08 .25
280 LaTroy Hawkins .08 .25
281 Brad Radke RC .40 1.00
282 Kevin Tapani .08 .25
283 Tony Fernandez .08 .25
284 Sterling Hitchcock .08 .25
285 Pat Kelly .08 .25
286 Jack McDowell .08 .25
287 Andy Pettitte .30 .75
288 Mike Stanley .08 .25
289 John Wetteland .20 .50
290 Bernie Williams .30 .75
291 Mark Acre .08 .25
292 Geronimo Berroa .08 .25
293 Dennis Eckersley .20 .50
294 Steve Ontiveros .08 .25
295 Ruben Sierra .20 .50
296 Terry Steinbach .08 .25
297 Dave Stewart .20 .50
298 Todd Stottlemyre .08 .25
299 Darren Bragg .08 .25
300 Joey Cora .08 .25
301 Edgar Martinez .30 .75
302 Bill Risley .08 .25
303 Ron Villone .08 .25
304 Dan Wilson .08 .25
305 Benji Gil .08 .25
306 Wilson Heredia .08 .25
307 Mark McLemore .08 .25
308 Otis Nixon .08 .25
309 Kenny Rogers .20 .50
310 Jeff Russell .08 .25
311 Mickey Tettleton .08 .25
312 Bob Tewksbury .08 .25
313 David Cone .20 .50
314 Carlos Delgado .20 .50
315 Alex Gonzalez .08 .25
316 Shawn Green .20 .50
317 Paul Molitor .20 .50
318 Ed Sprague .08 .25
319 Devon White .20 .50
320 Steve Avery .08 .25
321 Jeff Blauser .08 .25
322 Brad Clontz .08 .25
323 Tom Glavine .30 .75
324 Marquis Grissom .20 .50
325 Chipper Jones .50 1.25
326 David Justice .20 .50
327 Mark Lemke .08 .25
328 Kent Mercker .08 .25
329 Jason Schmidt .50 1.25
330 Steve Buechele .08 .25
331 Kevin Foster .08 .25
332 Mark Grace .30 .75
333 Brian McRae .08 .25
334 Sammy Sosa .50 1.25
335 Ozzie Timmons .08 .25
336 Rick Wilkins .08 .25
337 Hector Carrasco .08 .25
338 Ron Gant .20 .50
339 Barry Larkin .30 .75
340 Deion Sanders .30 .75
341 Benito Santiago .20 .50
342 Roger Bailey .08 .25
343 Jason Bates .08 .25
344 Dante Bichette .20 .50
345 Joe Girardi .08 .25
346 Bill Swift .08 .25
347 Mark Thompson .08 .25
348 Larry Walker .20 .50
349 Kurt Abbott .08 .25
350 John Burkett .08 .25
351 Chuck Carr .08 .25
352 Andre Dawson .20 .50
353 Chris Hammond .08 .25
354 Charles Johnson .20 .50
355 Terry Pendleton .20 .50
356 Quilvio Veras .08 .25
357 Derek Bell .08 .25
358 Jim Dougherty RC .08 .25
359 Doug Drabek .08 .25
360 Todd Jones .08 .25
361 Orlando Miller .08 .25
362 James Mouton .08 .25
363 Phil Plantier .08 .25
364 Shane Reynolds .08 .25
365 Todd Hollandsworth .08 .25
366 Eric Karros .20 .50
367 Ramon Martinez .08 .25
368 Hideo Nomo RC 1.50 4.00
369 Jose Offerman .08 .25
370 Antonio Osuna .08 .25
371 Todd Williams .08 .25
372 Shane Andrews .08 .25
373 Wil Cordero .08 .25
374 Jeff Fassero .08 .25
375 Darrin Fletcher .08 .25
376 Mark Grudzielanek RC .40 1.00
377 Carlos Perez RC .20 .50
378 Mel Rojas .08 .25
379 Tony Tarasco .08 .25
380 Edgardo Alfonzo .08 .25
381 Brett Butler .20 .50
382 Carl Everett .20 .50
383 John Franco .20 .50
384 Pete Harnisch .08 .25
385 Bobby Jones .08 .25
386 Dave Mlicki .08 .25
387 Jose Vizcaino .08 .25
388 Ricky Bottalico .08 .25
389 Tyler Green .08 .25
390 Charlie Hayes .08 .25
391 Dave Hollins .08 .25
392 Gregg Jefferies .08 .25
393 Michael Mimbs RC .08 .25
394 Mickey Morandini .08 .25
395 Curt Schilling .20 .50
396 Heathcliff Slocumb .08 .25
397 Jason Christiansen RC .08 .25
398 Midre Cummings .08 .25
399 Carlos Garcia .08 .25
400 Mark Johnson RC .08 .25
401 Jeff King .08 .25
402 Jon Lieber .08 .25
403 Esteban Loaiza .08 .25
404 Orlando Merced .08 .25
405 Gary Wilson RC .08 .25
406 Scott Cooper .08 .25
407 Tom Henke .08 .25
408 Ken Hill .08 .25
409 Danny Jackson .08 .25
410 Brian Jordan .20 .50
411 Ray Lankford .20 .50
412 John Mabry .08 .25
413 Todd Zeile .08 .25
414 Andy Benes .08 .25
415 Andres Berumen .08 .25
416 Ken Caminiti .20 .50
417 Andujar Cedeno .08 .25
418 Steve Finley .20 .50
419 Joey Hamilton .08 .25
420 Dustin Hermanson .08 .25
421 Melvin Nieves .08 .25
422 Robert Petagine .08 .25
423 Eddie Williams .08 .25
424 Glenallen Hill .08 .25
425 Kirt Manwaring .08 .25
426 Terry Mulholland .08 .25
427 J.R. Phillips .08 .25
428 Joe Rosselli .08 .25
429 Robby Thompson .08 .25
430 Checklist .08 .25
431 Checklist .08 .25
432 Checklist .08 .25
86P Will Clark PROMO

1995 Flair Hot Gloves

COMPLETE SET (12) 12.00 30.00
SER.2 STATED ODDS 1:25
1 Roberto Alomar .60 1.50
2 Barry Bonds 1.50 4.00
3 Ken Griffey Jr. 2.00 5.00
4 Marquis Grissom .40 1.00
5 Barry Larkin .60 1.50
6 Darren Lewis .40 1.00
7 Kenny Lofton .40 1.00
8 Don Mattingly 2.00 5.00
9 Cal Ripken 3.00 8.00
10 Ivan Rodriguez .60 1.50
11 Devon White .40 1.00
12 Matt Williams .40 1.00

1995 Flair Hot Numbers

COMPLETE SET (10) 20.00 50.00
SER.1 STATED ODDS 1:9
1 Jeff Bagwell 1.00 2.50
2 Albert Belle .60 1.50
3 Barry Bonds 4.00 10.00
4 Ken Griffey Jr. 3.00 8.00
5 Kenny Lofton 1.50 4.00
6 Greg Maddux 2.50 6.00
7 Mike Piazza 2.50 6.00
8 Cal Ripken 5.00 12.00
9 Frank Thomas 1.50 4.00
10 Matt Williams .60 1.50

1995 Flair Infield Power

COMPLETE SET (10) 5.00 12.00
SER.2 STATED ODDS 1:6
1 Jeff Bagwell .50 1.25
2 Darren Daulton .30 .75
3 Cecil Fielder .30 .75
4 Andres Galarraga .30 .75
5 Fred McGriff .50 1.25
6 Rafael Palmeiro .50 1.25
7 Mike Piazza 1.25 3.00
8 Frank Thomas .75 2.00
9 Mo Vaughn .30 .75
10 Matt Williams .30 .75

1995 Flair Outfield Power

COMPLETE SET (10) 5.00 12.00
SER.1 STATED ODDS 1:6
1 Albert Belle .30 .75
2 Dante Bichette .30 .75
3 Barry Bonds 2.00 5.00
4 Jose Canseco .50 1.25
5 Joe Carter .30 .75
6 Juan Gonzalez .30 .75
7 Ken Griffey Jr. 1.50 4.00
8 Kirby Puckett .75 2.00
9 Gary Sheffield .30 .75
10 Ruben Sierra .30 .75

1995 Flair Ripken

COMPLETE SET (10) 30.00 80.00
COMMON CARD (1-10) 4.00 10.00
SER.2 STATED ODDS 1:12
COMMON MAIL-IN (11-15) 2.00 5.00
MAIL-IN CARDS DIST.VIA WRAPPER EXCH.

1995 Flair Today's Spotlight

COMPLETE SET (12) 40.00 100.00
SER.1 STATED ODDS 1:25
1 Jeff Bagwell 3.00 8.00
2 Jason Bere 1.00 2.50
3 Cliff Floyd 2.00 5.00
4 Chuck Knoblauch 2.00 5.00
5 Kenny Lofton 5.00 12.00
6 Javier Lopez 2.00 5.00
7 Raul Mondesi 2.00 5.00
8 Mike Mussina 3.00 8.00
9 Mike Piazza 8.00 20.00
10 Manny Ramirez 3.00 8.00
11 Tim Salmon 3.00 8.00
12 Frank Thomas 5.00 12.00

1995 Flair Wave of the Future

COMPLETE SET (10) 10.00 25.00
SER.2 STATED ODDS 1:9
1 Jason Bates .40 1.00
2 Armando Benitez .40 1.00
3 Marty Cordova .40 1.00
4 Ray Durham .60 1.50
5 Vaughn Eshelman .40 1.00
6 Carl Everett .60 1.50
7 Shawn Green .60 1.50
8 Dustin Hermanson .40 1.00
9 Chipper Jones 1.50 4.00
10 Hideo Nomo 2.00 5.00

1996 Flair

Released in July, 1996, this 400-card set (produced by Fleer) was issued in one series and sold in seven-card packs at a suggested retail price of $4.99. Gold and Silver etched foil front variations exist for all cards. The 1996 Flair base cards have the players name in gold on the front, while the 1996 Flair Gold cards have the player's name in silver on the front. These color variations were printed in similar quantities and are valued equally. This checklist is for the silver version. The fronts and backs each carry a color action player cut-out on a player portrait background with player statistics on the backs. The cards are grouped alphabetically within teams and checklisted below alphabetically according to teams for each league. Notable Rookie Cards include Tony Batista.

COMPLETE SET (400) 40.00 100.00
GOLD AND SILVER EQUAL VALUE
1 Roberto Alomar .60 1.50
2 Brady Anderson .40 1.00
3 Bobby Bonilla .40 1.00
4 Scott Erickson .40 1.00
5 Jeffrey Hammonds .40 1.00
6 Jimmy Haynes .40 1.00
7 Chris Hoiles .40 1.00
8 Kent Mercker .40 1.00
9 Mike Mussina .60 1.50
10 Randy Myers .40 1.00
11 Rafael Palmeiro .60 1.50
12 Cal Ripken 3.00 8.00
13 B.J. Surhoff .40 1.00
14 David Wells .40 1.00
15 Jose Canseco .60 1.50
16 Roger Clemens 2.00 5.00
17 Wil Cordero .40 1.00
18 Tom Gordon .40 1.00
19 Mike Greenwell .40 1.00
20 Dwayne Hosey .40 1.00
21 Jose Malave .40 1.00
22 Tim Naehring .40 1.00
23 Troy O'Leary .40 1.00
24 Aaron Sele .40 1.00
25 Heathcliff Slocumb .40 1.00
26 Mike Stanley .40 1.00
27 Jeff Suppan .40 1.00
28 John Valentin .40 1.00
29 Mo Vaughn .40 1.00
30 Tim Wakefield .40 1.00
31 Jim Abbott .60 1.50
32 Garret Anderson .40 1.00
33 George Arias .40 1.00
34 Chili Davis .40 1.00
35 Gary DiSarcina .40 1.00
36 Jim Edmonds .40 1.00
37 Chuck Finley .40 1.00
38 Todd Greene .40 1.00
39 Mark Langston .40 1.00
40 Troy Percival .40 1.00
41 Tim Salmon .60 1.50
42 Lee Smith .40 1.00
43 J.T. Snow .40 1.00
44 Randy Velarde .40 1.00
45 Tim Wallach .40 1.00
46 Wilson Alvarez .40 1.00
47 Harold Baines .40 1.00
48 Jason Bere .40 1.00
49 Ray Durham .40 1.00
50 Alex Fernandez .40 1.00
51 Ozzie Guillen .40 1.00
52 Roberto Hernandez .40 1.00
53 Ron Karkovice .40 1.00
54 Darren Lewis .40 1.00
55 Lyle Mouton .40 1.00
56 Tony Phillips .40 1.00
57 Chris Snopek .40 1.00
58 Kevin Tapani .40 1.00
59 Danny Tartabull .40 1.00
60 Frank Thomas 1.00 2.50
61 Robin Ventura .40 1.00
62 Sandy Alomar Jr. .40 1.00
63 Carlos Baerga .40 1.00
64 Albert Belle .40 1.00
65 Julio Franco .40 1.00
66 Orel Hershiser .40 1.00
67 Kenny Lofton .40 1.00
68 Dennis Martinez .40 1.00
69 Jack McDowell .40 1.00
70 Jose Mesa .40 1.00
71 Eddie Murray 1.00 2.50
72 Charles Nagy .40 1.00
73 Tony Pena .40 1.00
74 Manny Ramirez .60 1.50
75 Julian Tavarez .40 1.00
76 Jim Thome .60 1.50
77 Omar Vizquel .60 1.50
78 Chad Curtis .40 1.00
79 Cecil Fielder .40 1.00
80 Travis Fryman .40 1.00
81 Chris Gomez .40 1.00
82 Bob Higginson .40 1.00
83 Mark Lewis .40 1.00
84 Felipe Lira .40 1.00
85 Alan Trammell .40 1.00
86 Kevin Appier .40 1.00
87 Johnny Damon .60 1.50
88 Tom Goodwin .40 1.00
89 Mark Gubicza .40 1.00
90 Bob Hamelin .40 1.00
91 Keith Lockhart .40 1.00
92 Jeff Montgomery .40 1.00
93 Jon Nunnally .40 1.00
94 Bip Roberts .40 1.00
95 Michael Tucker .40 1.00
96 Joe Vitiello .40 1.00
97 Ricky Bones .40 1.00
98 Chuck Carr .40 1.00
99 Jeff Cirillo .40 1.00
100 Mike Fetters .40 1.00
101 John Jaha .40 1.00
102 Mike Matheny .40 1.00
103 Ben McDonald .40 1.00
104 Matt Mieske .40 1.00
105 Dave Nilsson .40 1.00
106 Kevin Seitzer .40 1.00
107 Steve Sparks .40 1.00
108 Jose Valentin .40 1.00
109 Greg Vaughn .40 1.00
110 Rick Aguilera .40 1.00
111 Rich Becker .40 1.00
112 Marty Cordova .40 1.00
113 LaTroy Hawkins .40 1.00
114 Dave Hollins .40 1.00
115 Roberto Kelly .40 1.00
116 Chuck Knoblauch .40 1.00
117 Matt Lawton RC .40 1.00
118 Pat Meares .40 1.00
119 Paul Molitor .40 1.00
120 Kirby Puckett 1.00 2.50
121 Brad Radke .40 1.00
122 Frank Rodriguez .40 1.00
123 Scott Stahoviak .40 1.00
124 Matt Walbeck .40 1.00
125 Wade Boggs .60 1.50
126 David Cone .40 1.00
127 Joe Girardi .40 1.00
128 Dwight Gooden .40 1.00
129 Derek Jeter 2.50 6.00
130 Jimmy Key .40 1.00
131 Jim Leyritz .40 1.00
132 Tino Martinez .60 1.50
133 Paul O'Neill .60 1.50
134 Andy Pettitte .60 1.50
135 Tim Raines .40 1.00
136 Ruben Rivera .40 1.00
137 Kenny Rogers .40 1.00
138 Ruben Sierra .40 1.00
139 John Wetteland .40 1.00
140 Bernie Williams .60 1.50
141 Tony Batista RC .60 1.50
142 Allen Battle .40 1.00
143 Geronimo Berroa .40 1.00
144 Mike Bordick .40 1.00
145 Scott Brosius .40 1.00
146 Steve Cox .40 1.00
147 Brent Gates .40 1.00
148 Jason Giambi .40 1.00
149 Doug Johns .40 1.00
150 Mark McGwire 2.50 6.00
151 Pedro Munoz .40 1.00
152 Ariel Prieto .40 1.00
153 Terry Steinbach .40 1.00
154 Todd Van Poppel .40 1.00
155 Bobby Ayala .40 1.00
156 Chris Bosio .40 1.00
157 Jay Buhner .40 1.00
158 Joey Cora .40 1.00
159 Russ Davis .40 1.00
160 Ken Griffey Jr. 2.00 5.00
161 Sterling Hitchcock .40 1.00
162 Randy Johnson 1.00 2.50
163 Edgar Martinez .60 1.50
164 Alex Rodriguez 2.00 5.00
165 Paul Sorrento .40 1.00
166 Dan Wilson .40 1.00
167 Will Clark .60 1.50
168 Benji Gil .40 1.00
169 Juan Gonzalez .40 1.00
170 Rusty Greer .40 1.00
171 Kevin Gross .40 1.00
172 Darryl Hamilton .40 1.00
173 Mike Henneman .40 1.00
174 Ken Hill .40 1.00
175 Mark McLemore .40 1.00
176 Dean Palmer .40 1.00
177 Roger Pavlik .40 1.00
178 Ivan Rodriguez .60 1.50
179 Mickey Tettleton .40 1.00
180 Bobby Witt .40 1.00
181 Joe Carter .40 1.00
182 Felipe Crespo .40 1.00
183 Alex Gonzalez .40 1.00
184 Shawn Green .40 1.00
185 Juan Guzman .40 1.00
186 Erik Hanson .40 1.00
187 Pat Hentgen .40 1.00
188 Sandy Martinez .40 1.00
189 Otis Nixon .40 1.00
190 John Olerud .40 1.00
191 Paul Quantrill .40 1.00
192 Bill Risley .40 1.00
193 Ed Sprague .40 1.00
194 Steve Avery .40 1.00
195 Jeff Blauser .40 1.00
196 Brad Clontz .40 1.00
197 Jermaine Dye .40 1.00
198 Tom Glavine .60 1.50
199 Marquis Grissom .40 1.00
200 Chipper Jones 1.00 2.50
201 David Justice .40 1.00
202 Ryan Klesko .40 1.00
203 Mark Lemke .40 1.00
204 Javier Lopez .40 1.00
205 Greg Maddux 1.50 4.00
206 Fred McGriff .60 1.50
207 Greg McMichael .40 1.00
208 Wonderful Monds RC .40 1.00
209 Jason Schmidt .60 1.50
210 John Smoltz .60 1.50
211 Mark Wohlers .40 1.00
212 Jim Bullinger .40 1.00
213 Frank Castillo .40 1.00
214 Kevin Foster .40 1.00
215 Luis Gonzalez .40 1.00
216 Mark Grace .60 1.50
217 Robin Jennings .40 1.00
218 Doug Jones .40 1.00
219 Dave Magadan .40 1.00
220 Brian McRae .40 1.00
221 Jaime Navarro .40 1.00
222 Rey Sanchez .40 1.00
223 Ryne Sandberg 1.50 4.00
224 Scott Servais .40 1.00
225 Sammy Sosa 1.00 2.50
226 Ozzie Timmons .40 1.00
227 Bret Boone .40 1.00
228 Jeff Branson .40 1.00
229 Jeff Brantley .40 1.00
230 Dave Burba .40 1.00
231 Vince Coleman .40 1.00
232 Steve Gibralter .40 1.00
233 Mike Kelly .40 1.00
234 Barry Larkin .60 1.50
235 Hal Morris .40 1.00
236 Mark Portugal .40 1.00
237 Jose Rijo .40 1.00
238 Reggie Sanders .40 1.00
239 Pete Schourek .40 1.00
240 John Smiley .40 1.00
241 Eddie Taubensee .40 1.00
242 Jason Bates .40 1.00
243 Dante Bichette .40 1.00
244 Ellis Burks .40 1.00
245 Vinny Castilla .40 1.00
246 Andres Galarraga .40 1.00
247 Darren Holmes .40 1.00
248 Curt Leskanic .40 1.00
249 Steve Reed .40 1.00
250 Kevin Rtiz .40 1.00
251 Bret Saberhagen .40 1.00
252 Bill Swift .40 1.00
253 Larry Walker .40 1.00
254 Walt Weiss .40 1.00
255 Eric Young .40 1.00
256 Kurt Abbott .40 1.00
257 Kevin Brown .40 1.00
258 John Burkett .40 1.00
259 Greg Colbrunn .40 1.00
260 Jeff Conine .40 1.00
261 Andre Dawson .40 1.00
262 Chris Hammond .40 1.00
263 Charles Johnson .40 1.00
264 Al Leiter .40 1.00
265 Robb Nen .40 1.00
266 Terry Pendleton .40 1.00
267 Pat Rapp .40 1.00
268 Gary Sheffield .40 1.00
269 Quilvio Veras .40 1.00
270 Devon White .40 1.00
271 Bob Abreu 1.00 2.50
272 Jeff Bagwell .60 1.50
273 Derek Bell .40 1.00
274 Sean Berry .40 1.00
275 Craig Biggio .60 1.50
276 Doug Drabek .40 1.00
277 Tony Eusebio .40 1.00
278 Richard Hidalgo .40 1.00
279 Brian L.Hunter .40 1.00
280 Todd Jones .40 1.00
281 Derrick May .40 1.00
282 Orlando Miller .40 1.00
283 James Mouton .40 1.00
284 Shane Reynolds .40 1.00
285 Greg Swindell .40 1.00
286 Mike Blowers .40 1.00
287 Brett Butler .40 1.00
288 Tom Candiotti .40 1.00
289 Roger Cedeno .40 1.00
290 Delino DeShields .40 1.00
291 Greg Gagne .40 1.00
292 Karim Garcia .40 1.00
293 Todd Hollandsworth .40 1.00
294 Eric Karros .40 1.00
295 Ramon Martinez .40 1.00
296 Raul Mondesi .40 1.00
297 Hideo Nomo 1.00 2.50
298 Mike Piazza 1.50 4.00
299 Ismael Valdes .40 1.00
300 Todd Worrell .40 1.00
301 Moises Alou .40 1.00
302 Shane Andrews .40 1.00
303 Yamil Benitez .40 1.00
304 Jeff Fassero .40 1.00
305 Darrin Fletcher .40 1.00
306 Cliff Floyd .40 1.00
307 Mark Grudzielanek .40 1.00
308 Mike Lansing .40 1.00
309 Pedro Martinez .60 1.50
310 Ryan McGuire .40 1.00
311 Carlos Perez .40 1.00
312 Mel Rojas .40 1.00
313 David Segui .40 1.00
314 Rondell White .40 1.00
315 Edgardo Alfonzo .40 1.00
316 Rico Brogna .40 1.00
317 Carl Everett .40 1.00
318 John Franco .40 1.00
319 Bernard Gilkey .40 1.00
320 Todd Hundley .40 1.00
321 Jason Isringhausen .40 1.00
322 Lance Johnson .40 1.00
323 Bobby Jones .40 1.00
324 Jeff Kent .40 1.00
325 Rey Ordonez .40 1.00
326 Bill Pulsipher .40 1.00
327 Jose Vizcaino .40 1.00
328 Paul Wilson .40 1.00
329 Ricky Bottalico .40 1.00
330 Darren Daulton .40 1.00
331 David Doster .40 1.00
332 Lenny Dykstra .40 1.00
333 Jim Eisenreich .40 1.00
334 Sid Fernandez .40 1.00
335 Gregg Jefferies .40 1.00
336 Mickey Morandini .40 1.00
337 Benito Santiago .40 1.00
338 Curt Schilling .40 1.00
339 Kevin Stocker .40 1.00
340 David West .40 1.00
341 Mark Whiten .40 1.00
342 Todd Zeile .40 1.00
343 Jay Bell .40 1.00
344 John Ericks .40 1.00
345 Carlos Garcia .40 1.00
346 Charlie Hayes .40 1.00
347 Jason Kendall .40 1.00
348 Jeff King .40 1.00
349 Mike Kingery .40 1.00
350 Al Martin .40 1.00
351 Orlando Merced .40 1.00
352 Dan Miceli .40 1.00
353 Denny Neagle .40 1.00
354 Alan Benes .40 1.00
355 Andy Benes .40 1.00
356 Royce Clayton .40 1.00
357 Dennis Eckersley .40 1.00
358 Gary Gaetti .40 1.00
359 Ron Gant .40 1.00
360 Brian Jordan .40 1.00
361 Ray Lankford .40 1.00
362 John Mabry .40 1.00
363 T.J. Mathews .40 1.00
364 Mike Morgan .40 1.00
365 Donovan Osborne .40 1.00
366 Tom Pagnozzi .40 1.00
367 Ozzie Smith 1.50 4.00
368 Todd Stottlemyre .40 1.00
369 Andy Ashby .40 1.00
370 Brad Ausmus .40 1.00
371 Ken Caminiti .40 1.00
372 Andujar Cedeno .40 1.00
373 Steve Finley .40 1.00
374 Tony Gwynn 1.25 3.00
375 Joey Hamilton .40 1.00
376 Rickey Henderson 1.00 2.50
377 Trevor Hoffman .40 1.00
378 Wally Joyner .40 1.00
379 Marc Newfield .40 1.00
380 Jody Reed .40 1.00
381 Bob Tewksbury .40 1.00
382 Fernando Valenzuela .40 1.00
383 Rod Beck .40 1.00
384 Barry Bonds 2.50 6.00
385 Mark Carreon .40 1.00
386 Shawon Dunston .40 1.00
387 Osvaldo Fernandez RC .40 1.00
388 Glenallen Hill .40 1.00
389 Stan Javier .40 1.00
390 Mark Leiter .40 1.00
391 Kirt Manwaring .40 1.00
392 Robby Thompson .40 1.00
393 William VanLandingham .40 1.00
394 Allen Watson .40 1.00
395 Matt Williams .40 1.00
396 Checklist (1-92) .40 1.00
397 Checklist (93-180) .40 1.00
398 Checklist (181-272) .40 1.00
399 Checklist (273-365) .40 1.00
400 Checklist (366-400 Inserts) .40 1.00
P12 Cal Ripken Jr PROMO

1996 Flair Diamond Cuts

COMPLETE SET (12) 12.00 30.00
STATED ODDS 1:20
1 Jeff Bagwell 1.00 2.50
2 Albert Belle .60 1.50
3 Barry Bonds 2.50 6.00
4 Juan Gonzalez .60 1.50
5 Ken Griffey Jr. 3.00 8.00
6 Greg Maddux 2.50 6.00
7 Eddie Murray 1.00 2.50
8 Mike Piazza 1.50 4.00
9 Cal Ripken 5.00 12.00
10 Frank Thomas 1.50 4.00
11 Mo Vaughn .60 1.50
12 Matt Williams .60 1.50

1996 Flair Hot Gloves

COMPLETE SET (10) 100.00 200.00
STATED ODDS 1:90 HOBBY
1 Roberto Alomar 2.00 5.00
2 Barry Bonds 5.00 12.00
3 Will Clark 2.00 5.00
4 Ken Griffey Jr. 75.00 150.00
5 Kenny Lofton 1.25 3.00
6 Greg Maddux 5.00 12.00
7 Mike Piazza 3.00 8.00
8 Cal Ripken 10.00 25.00
9 Ivan Rodriguez 2.00 5.00
10 Matt Williams 1.25 3.00

1996 Flair Powerline

COMPLETE SET (10) 12.50 30.00
STATED ODDS 1:6
1 Albert Belle .40 1.00
2 Barry Bonds 2.50 6.00
3 Juan Gonzalez .40 1.00
4 Ken Griffey Jr. 2.00 5.00
5 Mark McGwire 2.50 6.00
6 Mike Piazza 1.50 4.00
7 Manny Ramirez .60 1.50
8 Sammy Sosa 1.00 2.50
9 Frank Thomas 1.00 2.50
10 Matt Williams .40 1.00

1996 Flair Wave of the Future

COMPLETE SET (20) 100.00 200.00
STATED ODDS 1:72
1 Bob Abreu 6.00 15.00
2 George Arias 4.00 10.00
3 Tony Batista 6.00 15.00
4 Alan Benes 4.00 10.00
5 Yamil Benitez 4.00 10.00
6 Steve Cox 4.00 10.00
7 David Doster 4.00 10.00
8 Jermaine Dye 4.00 10.00
9 Osvaldo Fernandez 4.00 10.00
10 Karim Garcia 4.00 10.00
11 Steve Gibralter 4.00 10.00
12 Todd Greene 4.00 10.00
13 Richard Hidalgo 4.00 10.00
14 Robin Jennings 4.00 10.00
15 Jason Kendall 4.00 10.00
16 Jose Malave 4.00 10.00
17 Wonderful Monds 4.00 10.00
18 Rey Ordonez 4.00 10.00
19 Ruben Rivera 4.00 10.00
20 Paul Wilson 4.00 10.00

2002 Flair

COMP.SET w/o SP's (100) 10.00 25.00
COMMON CARD (1-100) .20 .50
COMMON CARD (101-138) 2.00 5.00
101-138 RANDOM INSERTS IN PACKS
101-138 PRINT RUN 1750 SERIAL #'d SETS
1 Scott Rolen .30 .75
2 Derek Jeter 1.25 3.00
3 Sean Casey .20 .50
4 Hideo Nomo .50 1.25
5 Craig Biggio .30 .75
6 Randy Johnson .50 1.25
7 J.D. Drew .20 .50
8 Greg Maddux .75 2.00
9 Paul LoDuca .20 .50
10 John Olerud .20 .50
11 Barry Larkin .30 .75
12 Mark Grace .30 .75
13 Jimmy Rollins .20 .50
14 Todd Helton .30 .75
15 Jim Edmonds .20 .50
16 Roy Oswalt .20 .50
17 Phil Nevin .20 .50
18 Tim Salmon .30 .75
19 Magglio Ordonez .20 .50
20 Roger Clemens 1.00 2.50
21 Raul Mondesi .20 .50
22 Edgar Martinez .30 .75
23 Pedro Martinez .30 .75
24 Edgardo Alfonzo .20 .50
25 Bernie Williams .30 .75
26 Gary Sheffield .20 .50
27 D'Angelo Jimenez .20 .50
28 Toby Hall .20 .50
29 Joe Mays .20 .50
30 Alfonso Soriano .20 .50
31 Mike Piazza .75 2.00
32 Lance Berkman .20 .50
33 Jim Thome .30 .75
34 Ben Sheets .20 .50
35 Brandon Inge .20 .50
36 Luis Gonzalez .20 .50
37 Jeff Kent .20 .50
38 Ben Grieve .20 .50
39 Carlos Delgado .20 .50
40 Pat Burrell .20 .50
41 Mark Buehrle .20 .50
42 Cristian Guzman .20 .50
43 Shawn Green .20 .50
44 Nomar Garciaparra .75 2.00
45 Carlos Beltran .20 .50
46 Troy Glaus .20 .50
47 Paul Konerko .20 .50
48 Moises Alou .20 .50
49 Kerry Wood .20 .50
50 Jose Vidro .20 .50
51 Juan Encarnacion .20 .50
52 Bobby Abreu .20 .50
53 C.C. Sabathia .20 .50
54 Alex Rodriguez .60 1.50
55 Albert Pujols 1.00 2.50
56 Bret Boone .20 .50
57 Orlando Hernandez .20 .50
58 Jason Kendall .20 .50
59 Tim Hudson .20 .50
60 Darin Erstad .20 .50
61 Mike Mussina .30 .75
62 Ken Griffey Jr. 1.00 2.50
63 Adrian Beltre .20 .50
64 Jeff Bagwell .30 .75
65 Vladimir Guerrero .50 1.25
66 Mike Sweeney .20 .50
67 Sammy Sosa .50 1.25
68 Andruw Jones .30 .75
69 Richie Sexson .20 .50
70 Matt Morris .20 .50
71 Ivan Rodriguez .30 .75
72 Shannon Stewart .20 .50
73 Barry Bonds 1.25 3.00
74 Matt Williams .20 .50
75 Jason Giambi .20 .50
76 Brian Giles .20 .50
77 Cliff Floyd .20 .50
78 Tino Martinez .30 .75
79 Juan Gonzalez .20 .50
80 Frank Thomas .50 1.25
81 Ichiro Suzuki 1.00 2.50
82 Barry Zito .20 .50
83 Chipper Jones .50 1.25
84 Adam Dunn .20 .50
85 Kazuhiro Sasaki .20 .50
86 Mark Quinn .20 .50
87 Rafael Palmeiro .30 .75
88 Jeromy Burnitz .20 .50
89 Curt Schilling .20 .50
90 Chris Richard .20 .50

91 Jon Lieber .20 .50
92 Doug Mientkiewicz .20 .50
93 Roberto Alomar .30 .75
94 Rich Aurilia .20 .50
95 Eric Chavez .20 .50
96 Larry Walker .20 .50
97 Manny Ramirez .30 .75
98 Tony Clark .20 .50
99 Tsuyoshi Shinjo .20 .50
100 Josh Beckett .20 .50
101 Dewon Brazelton FF 2.00 5.00
102 Jeremy Lambert FF RC 2.00 5.00
103 Andres Torres FF 2.00 5.00
104 Matt Childers FF RC 2.00 5.00
105 Wilson Betemit FF 2.00 5.00
106 Willie Harris FF 2.00 5.00
107 Drew Henson FF 2.00 5.00
108 Rafael Soriano FF 2.00 5.00
109 Carlos Valderrama FF 2.00 5.00
110 Victor Martinez FF 3.00 8.00
111 Juan Rivera FF 2.00 5.00
112 Felipe Lopez FF 2.00 5.00
113 Brandon Duckworth FF 2.00 5.00
114 Jeremy Owens FF 2.00 5.00
115 Aaron Cook FF RC 2.00 5.00
116 Derrick Lewis FF 2.00 5.00
117 Mark Teixeira FF 3.00 8.00
118 Ken Harvey FF 2.00 5.00
119 Tim Spooneybarger FF 2.00 5.00
120 Bill Hall FF 2.00 5.00
121 Adam Pettyjohn FF 2.00 5.00
122 Ramon Castro FF 2.00 5.00
123 Marlon Byrd FF 2.00 5.00
124 Matt White FF 2.00 5.00
125 Eric Cyr FF 2.00 5.00
126 Morgan Ensberg FF 2.00 5.00
127 Horacio Ramirez FF 2.00 5.00
128 Ron Calloway FF RC 2.00 5.00
129 Nick Punto FF 2.00 5.00
130 Joe Kennedy FF 2.00 5.00
131 So Taguchi FF RC 3.00 8.00
132 Austin Kearns FF 2.00 5.00
133 Mark Prior FF 3.00 8.00
134 Kazuhisa Ishii FF RC 3.00 8.00
135 Steve Torrealba FF 2.00 5.00
136 Adam Walker FF RC 2.00 5.00
137 Travis Hafner FF 2.00 5.00
138 Zach Day FF 2.00 5.00

2002 Flair Collection
*COLLECTION 1-100: 3X TO 8X BASIC
1-100 PRINT RUN 175 SERIAL #'d SETS
*COLLECTION 101-138: 1X TO 2.5X BASIC
101-138 PRINT RUN 50 SERIAL #'d SETS

2002 Flair Jersey Heights
STATED ODDS 1:18 HOBBY, 1:100 RETAIL
SP INFO PROVIDED BY FLEER
SP'S ARE ONLY SLIGHTLY LOWER QUANTITY
ASTERISKS PERCEIVED AS LARGER SUPPLY
1 Edgardo Alfonzo 1.00 2.50
2 Jeff Bagwell * 1.50 4.00
3 Craig Biggio 1.50 4.00
4 Barry Bonds SP 4.00 10.00
5 Sean Casey 1.00 2.50
6 Roger Clemens SP 3.00 8.00
7 Carlos Delgado 1.00 2.50
8 J.D. Drew SP 1.00 2.50
9 Jim Edmonds * 1.50 4.00
10 Nomar Garciaparra 1.50 4.00
11 Shawn Green 1.00 2.50
12 Todd Helton 1.50 4.00
13 Derek Jeter * 8.00 20.00
14 Randy Johnson * 2.50 6.00
15 Chipper Jones * 2.50 6.00
16 Barry Larkin 1.50 4.00
17 Greg Maddux SP 4.00 10.00
18 Pedro Martinez 1.50 4.00
19 Rafael Palmeiro 1.50 4.00
20 Mike Piazza 2.50 6.00
21 Manny Ramirez 1.50 4.00
22 Alex Rodriguez SP 3.00 8.00
23 Ivan Rodriguez * 1.50 4.00
24 Curt Schilling * 1.50 4.00
25 Larry Walker * 1.50 4.00

2002 Flair Jersey Heights Dual Swatch
RANDOM INSERTS IN PACKS
STATED PRINT RUN 100 SERIAL #'d SETS
1 R.Johnson/C.Schilling 8.00 20.00
2 P.Martinez/N.Garciaparra 5.00 12.00
3 E.Alfonzo/M.Piazza 8.00 20.00
4 D.Jeter/R.Clemens 20.00 50.00
5 G.Maddux/C.Jones 12.00 30.00
6 J.Edmonds/J.Drew 5.00 12.00
7 J.Bagwell/C.Biggio 5.00 12.00
8 R.Palmeiro/I.Rodriguez 5.00 12.00
9 C.Delgado/S.Green 3.00 8.00
10 T.Helton/L.Walker 5.00 12.00
11 S.Casey/B.Larkin 5.00 12.00
12 A.Rodriguez/M.Ramirez 10.00 25.00

2002 Flair Jersey Heights Hot Numbers Patch
RANDOM INSERTS IN PACKS
STATED PRINT RUN 100 SERIAL #'d SETS
1 Edgardo Alfonzo 10.00 25.00
2 Jeff Bagwell 15.00 40.00
3 Craig Biggio 15.00 40.00
4 Sean Casey 10.00 25.00
6 Carlos Delgado 10.00 25.00
7 J.D. Drew 10.00 25.00
8 Jim Edmonds 10.00 25.00
9 Nomar Garciaparra 40.00 80.00
10 Shawn Green 10.00 25.00
11 Todd Helton 15.00 40.00
12 Derek Jeter 30.00 80.00
13 Randy Johnson 15.00 40.00
14 Chipper Jones 15.00 40.00
15 Barry Larkin 15.00 40.00
16 Greg Maddux 20.00 50.00
17 Pedro Martinez 15.00 40.00
18 Rafael Palmeiro 15.00 40.00
19 Mike Piazza 30.00 60.00
20 Manny Ramirez 15.00 40.00
21 Alex Rodriguez 30.00 60.00
22 Ivan Rodriguez 15.00 40.00
23 Curt Schilling 10.00 25.00
24 Larry Walker 10.00 25.00

2002 Flair Power Tools Bats
STATED ODDS 1:19 HOBBY, 1:123 RETAIL
SP PRINT RUNS PROVIDED BY FLEER
SP'S ARE NOT SERIAL-NUMBERED
ASTERISKS PERCEIVED AS LARGER SUPPLY
GOLD RANDOM INSERTS IN PACKS
GOLD PRINT RUN 100 SERIAL #'d SETS
1 Roberto Alomar 3.00 8.00
2 Jeff Bagwell SP/150 6.00 15.00
3 Craig Biggio 3.00 8.00
4 Barry Bonds 6.00 15.00
5 Bret Boone * 3.00 8.00
6 Pat Burrell SP/225 6.00 15.00
7 Eric Chavez 3.00 8.00
8 J.D. Drew SP/150 6.00 15.00
9 Jim Edmonds 3.00 8.00
10 Juan Gonzalez 3.00 8.00
11 Luis Gonzalez 3.00 8.00
12 Shawn Green 3.00 8.00
13 Derek Jeter 8.00 20.00
14 Doug Mientkiewicz 3.00 8.00
15 Magglio Ordonez 3.00 8.00
16 Rafael Palmeiro SP/100 6.00 15.00
17 Mike Piazza 6.00 15.00
18 Alex Rodriguez 6.00 15.00
19 Ivan Rodriguez * 3.00 8.00
21 Reggie Sanders SP/120 6.00 15.00
22 Gary Sheffield 3.00 8.00
23 Tsuyoshi Shinjo * 3.00 8.00
24 Miguel Tejada 3.00 8.00
25 Frank Thomas 4.00 10.00
26 Jim Thome SP/225 6.00 15.00
27 Larry Walker 3.00 8.00
28 Bernie Williams 3.00 8.00

2002 Flair Power Tools Dual Bats
STATED ODDS 1:40 HOBBY, 1:150 RETAIL
SP PRINT RUNS PROVIDED BY FLEER
SP'S ARE NOT SERIAL-NUMBERED
*GOLD: 1X TO 2.5X BASIC DUAL BAT
GOLD RANDOM INSERTS IN PACKS
GOLD PRINT RUN 50 SERIAL #'d SETS
GOLD CARDS 7 AND 13 DO NOT EXIST
1 E.Chavez/M.Tejada 6.00 15.00
2 B.Bonds/T.Shinjo 12.50 30.00
3 J.Edmonds/J.Drew 6.00 15.00
4 J.Bagwell/C.Biggio 10.00 25.00
5 B.Williams/D.Jeter 10.00 25.00
6 R.Alomar/M.Piazza 10.00 25.00
8 P.Burrell/S.Rolen 6.00 15.00
9 G.Sheffield/S.Green 6.00 15.00
10 I.Rodriguez/A.Rodriguez 10.00 25.00
11 J.Gonzalez/R.Palmeiro 6.00 15.00
12 M.Ordonez/F.Thomas 8.00 20.00
13 L.Walker/T.Helton SP/225 6.00 15.00
14 L.Gonzalez/R.Sanders 6.00 15.00
15 D.Mientkiewicz/B.Boone 6.00 15.00

2002 Flair Sweet Swatch
ONE SWATCH PER HOBBY BOX
STATED PRINT RUNS LISTED BELOW
1 Jeff Bagwell/490 6.00 15.00
2 Josh Beckett/500 6.00 15.00
3 Darin Erstad/525 6.00 15.00
4 Freddy Garcia/620 6.00 15.00
5 Brian Giles Pants/445 6.00 15.00
6 Juan Gonzalez/505 6.00 15.00
7 Mark Grace/795 6.00 15.00
8 Derek Jeter/525 15.00 40.00
9 Jason Kendall/990 6.00 15.00
10 Paul LoDuca/440 6.00 15.00
11 Greg Maddux/475 6.00 15.00
12 Magglio Ordonez/495 6.00 15.00
13 Rafael Palmeiro/535 6.00 15.00
14 Mike Piazza/1000 6.00 15.00
15 Alex Rodriguez/550 10.00 25.00
16 Ivan Rodriguez/475 6.00 15.00
17 Tim Salmon/465 6.00 15.00
18 Kazuhiro Sasaki/770 6.00 15.00
19 Alfonso Soriano/775 6.00 15.00
20 Larry Walker/430 6.00 15.00
21 Ted Williams/250 50.00 100.00

2002 Flair Sweet Swatch Bat Autograph
STATED PRINT RUNS LISTED BELOW
APPX. 45% OF HENSON'S ARE EXCH.CARDS
GOLD PRINT RUN 15 SERIAL #'d SETS
GOLD NOT PRICED DUE TO SCARCITY
1 Barry Bonds/35 150.00 250.00
2 Dewon Brazelton/185 8.00 20.00
3 Marlon Byrd/185 8.00 20.00
4 Ron Cey/285 10.00 25.00
5 David Espinosa/485 8.00 20.00
6 Drew Henson/785 8.00 20.00
7 Kazuhisa Ishii/335 8.00 20.00
8 Derek Jeter/375 100.00 200.00
9 Al Kaline/285 30.00 80.00
10 Don Mattingly/85 100.00 200.00
11 Paul Molitor/85 20.00 50.00
12 Dale Murphy/285 10.00 25.00
13 Tony Perez/115 20.00 50.00
14 Mark Prior/285 10.00 25.00
16 Brooks Robinson/185 15.00 40.00
17 Dane Sardinha/485 8.00 20.00
18 Ben Sheets/85 20.00 50.00
19 Ozzie Smith/185 20.00 50.00
20 So Taguchi/335 10.00 25.00
21 Mark Teixeira/185 20.00 50.00
22 Maury Wills/285 10.00 25.00

2002 Flair Sweet Swatch Patch
*PREMIUM PATCHES: 2X LISTED PRICES
RANDOMLY INSERTED HOBBY BOX-TOPPER
STATED PRINT RUNS LISTED BELOW
NO PRICING ON QTY OF 25 OR LESS
NO 1 OF 1 PRICING DUE TO SCARCITY
1 Jeff Bagwell/45 30.00 60.00
2 Josh Beckett/60 15.00 40.00
3 Darin Erstad/50 15.00 40.00
4 Freddy Garcia/50 15.00 40.00
5 Juan Gonzalez/55 15.00 40.00
6 Mark Grace/75 30.00 60.00
8 Jason Kendall/120 6.00 15.00
9 Paul LoDuca/50 15.00 40.00
10 Greg Maddux/50 50.00 100.00
11 Magglio Ordonez/55 15.00 40.00
12 Rafael Palmeiro/60 30.00 60.00
13 Mike Piazza/95 40.00 80.00
14 Alex Rodriguez/50 50.00 100.00
15 Ivan Rodriguez/50 30.00 60.00
16 Tim Salmon/40 30.00 60.00
17 Kazuhiro Sasaki/80 15.00 40.00
18 Alfonso Soriano/35 15.00 40.00
19 Larry Walker/60 15.00 40.00

2003 Flair
COMP.LO SET w/o SP's (90) 10.00 25.00
COMMON CARD (1-90) .20 .50
COMMON CARD (91-135) 1.00 2.50
91-125 RANDOM INSERTS IN PACKS
126-135 RANDOM IN FLEER R/G PACKS
91-135 PRINT RUN 500 SERIAL #'d SETS
1 Hideo Nomo .50 1.25
2 Derek Jeter 1.25 3.00
3 Junior Spivey .20 .50
4 Rich Aurilia .20 .50
5 Luis Gonzalez .20 .50
6 Sean Burroughs .20 .50
7 Pedro Martinez .30 .75
8 Randy Winn .20 .50
9 Carlos Delgado .20 .50
10 Pat Burrell .20 .50
11 Barry Larkin .30 .75
12 Roberto Alomar .30 .75
13 Tony Batista .20 .50
14 Barry Bonds .75 2.00
15 Craig Biggio .30 .75
16 Ivan Rodriguez .30 .75
17 Javier Vazquez .20 .50
18 Joe Borchard .20 .50
19 Josh Phelps .20 .50
20 Omar Vizquel .30 .75
21 Tom Glavine .30 .75
22 Darin Erstad .20 .50
23 Hee Seop Choi .20 .50
24 Roger Clemens .60 1.50
25 Michael Cuddyer .20 .50
26 Mike Sweeney .20 .50
27 Phil Nevin .20 .50
28 Torii Hunter .20 .50
29 Vladimir Guerrero .30 .75
30 Ellis Burks .20 .50
31 Jimmy Rollins .30 .75
32 Ken Griffey Jr. 1.00 2.50
33 Magglio Ordonez .30 .75
34 Mark Prior .30 .75
35 Mike Lieberthal .20 .50
36 Jorge Posada .30 .75
37 Rodrigo Lopez .20 .50
38 Todd Helton .30 .75
39 Adam Kennedy .20 .50
40 Curt Schilling .30 .75
41 Jim Thome .30 .75
42 Josh Beckett .20 .50
43 Carlos Pena .30 .75
44 Jason Kendall .20 .50
45 Sammy Sosa .50 1.25
46 Scott Rolen .30 .75
47 Alex Rodriguez .60 1.50
48 Aubrey Huff .20 .50
49 Bobby Abreu .20 .50
50 Jeff Kent .20 .50
51 Joe Randa .20 .50
52 Lance Berkman .30 .75
53 Orlando Cabrera .20 .50
54 Richie Sexson .20 .50
55 Albert Pujols .60 1.50
56 Alfonso Soriano .30 .75
57 Greg Maddux .60 1.50
58 Jason Giambi .20 .50
59 Jeff Bagwell .30 .75
60 Kerry Wood .20 .50
61 Manny Ramirez .50 1.25
62 Eric Chavez .20 .50
63 Preston Wilson .20 .50
64 Shawn Green .20 .50
65 Shea Hillenbrand .20 .50
66 Austin Kearns .20 .50
67 Cliff Floyd .20 .50
68 Edgardo Alfonzo .20 .50
69 J.D. Drew .20 .50
70 Larry Walker .30 .75
71 Mike Piazza .50 1.25
72 Andruw Jones .20 .50
73 Ben Grieve .20 .50
74 Eric Hinske .20 .50
75 Geoff Jenkins .20 .50
76 Kazuhiro Sasaki .20 .50
77 Matt Morris .20 .50
78 Miguel Tejada .30 .75
79 Aramis Ramirez .20 .50
80 Troy Glaus .20 .50
81 Ichiro Suzuki .60 1.50
82 Mark Teixeira .30 .75
83 Nomar Garciaparra .30 .75
84 Chipper Jones .50 1.25
85 Frank Thomas .50 1.25
86 Paul Lo Duca .20 .50
87 Bernie Williams .30 .75
88 Adam Dunn .30 .75
89 Randy Johnson .50 1.25
90 Barry Zito .30 .75
91 Lew Ford FF RC 1.00 2.50
92 Joe Valentine FF RC 1.00 2.50
93 Jhonny Peralta FF 1.00 2.50
94 Hideki Matsui FF RC 5.00 12.00
95 Francisco Rosario FF RC 1.00 2.50
96 Adam LaRoche FF 1.00 2.50
97 Josh Hall FF RC 1.00 2.50
98 Chien-Ming Wang FF RC 4.00 10.00
99 Josh Willingham FF RC 3.00 8.00
100 Guillermo Quiroz FF RC 1.00 2.50
101 Termel Sledge FF RC 1.00 2.50
102 Prentice Redman FF RC 1.00 2.50
103 Matt Bruback FF RC 1.00 2.50
104 Alejandro Machado FF RC 1.00 2.50
105 Shane Victorino FF RC 3.00 8.00
106 Chris Waters FF RC 1.00 2.50
107 Jose Contreras FF RC 2.50 6.00
108 Pete LaForest FF RC 1.00 2.50
109 Nook Logan FF RC 1.00 2.50
110 Hector Luna FF RC 1.00 2.50
111 Daniel Cabrera FF RC 1.50 4.00
112 Matt Kata FF RC 1.00 2.50
113 Rontrez Johnson FF RC 1.00 2.50
114 Josh Stewart FF RC 1.00 2.50
115 Michael Hessman FF RC 1.00 2.50
116 Felix Sanchez FF RC 1.00 2.50
117 Michel Hernandez FF RC 1.00 2.50
118 Arnaldo Munoz FF RC 1.00 2.50
119 Ian Ferguson FF RC 1.00 2.50
120 Clint Barmes FF RC 2.50 6.00
121 Brian Stokes FF RC 1.00 2.50
122 Craig Brazell FF RC 1.00 2.50
123 John Webb FF 1.00 2.50
124 Tim Olson FF RC 1.00 2.50
125 Jeremy Bonderman FF RC 4.00 10.00
126 Jeff Duncan RC 1.00 2.50
127 Rickie Weeks RC 3.00 8.00
128 Brandon Webb RC 3.00 8.00
129 Robby Hammock RC 1.00 2.50
130 Jon Leicester RC 1.00 2.50
131 Ryan Wagner RC 1.00 2.50
132 Bo Hart RC 1.00 2.50
133 Edwin Jackson RC 1.50 4.00
134 Sergio Mitre RC 1.00 2.50
135 Delmon Young RC 6.00 15.00

2003 Flair Collection Row 1
*ROW 1 1-90: 1.25X TO 3X BASIC
*ROW 1 91-125: .6X TO 1.5X BASIC
RANDOM INSERTS IN PACKS
STATED PRINT RUN 150 SERIAL #'d SETS

2003 Flair Collection Row 2
STATED PRINT RUN 25 SERIAL #'d SETS
NO PRICING DUE TO SCARCITY

2003 Flair Diamond Cuts Jersey
STATED ODDS 1:10
*GOLD: 1X TO 2.5X BASIC
GOLD RANDOM INSERTS IN PACKS
GOLD PRINT RUN 100 SERIAL #'d SETS
AR Alex Rodriguez 4.00 10.00
AS Alfonso Soriano 2.00 5.00
BZ Barry Zito 2.00 5.00
CJ Chipper Jones 3.00 8.00
DJ Derek Jeter 10.00 25.00
GM Greg Maddux 4.00 10.00
JD J.D. Drew 2.00 5.00
MP Mike Piazza 4.00 10.00
PB Pat Burrell 2.00 5.00
RA Roberto Alomar 3.00 8.00
RC Roger Clemens 4.00 10.00
RO Roy Oswalt 2.00 5.00
SR Scott Rolen 3.00 8.00
TG Troy Glaus 2.00 5.00
VG Vladimir Guerrero 3.00 8.00

2003 Flair Hot Numbers Patch
RANDOM INSERTS IN PACKS
STATED PRINT RUN 100 SERIAL #'d SETS
AR Alex Rodriguez 20.00 50.00
AS Alfonso Soriano 10.00 25.00
BZ Barry Zito 10.00 25.00
CJ Chipper Jones 12.50 30.00
DJ Derek Jeter 25.00 60.00
GM Greg Maddux 15.00 40.00
JD J.D. Drew 10.00 25.00
MP Mike Piazza 12.50 30.00
PB Pat Burrell 10.00 25.00
RA Roberto Alomar 12.50 30.00
RO Roy Oswalt 10.00 25.00
SR Scott Rolen 12.50 30.00
TG Troy Glaus 10.00 25.00
VG Vladimir Guerrero 12.50 30.00

2003 Flair Power Tools Bats
STATED PRINT RUN 500 SERIAL #'d SETS
*GOLD: .6X TO 1.5X BASIC
GOLD PRINT RUN 100 SERIAL #'d SETS
AD Adam Dunn 3.00 8.00
AJ Andruw Jones 4.00 10.00
AK Austin Kearns 3.00 8.00
AR Alex Rodriguez 6.00 15.00
AS Alfonso Soriano 3.00 8.00
BW Bernie Williams 4.00 10.00
DJ Derek Jeter 8.00 20.00
HSC Hee-Seop Choi 3.00 8.00
JB Jeff Bagwell 4.00 10.00
JGI Jason Giambi 3.00 8.00
JGO Juan Gonzalez 3.00 8.00
JT Jim Thome 4.00 10.00
LB Lance Berkman 3.00 8.00
MP Mike Piazza 6.00 15.00
MT Miguel Tejada 3.00 8.00
NG Nomar Garciaparra 6.00 15.00
SR Scott Rolen 4.00 10.00
SS Sammy Sosa 4.00 10.00

2003 Flair Power Tools Dual Bats
RANDOM INSERTS IN PACKS
STATED PRINT RUN 200 SERIAL #'d SETS
ADAK A.Dunn/A.Kearns 2.50 6.00
ARNG A.Rodriguez/N.Garciaparra 5.00 12.00
DJAS D.Jeter/A.Soriano 10.00 25.00
JGBW J.Giambi/B.Williams 2.50 6.00
JGMP J.Giambi/M.Piazza 4.00 10.00
JTSS J.Thome/S.Sosa 4.00 10.00
LBJB L.Berkman/J.Bagwell 2.50 6.00
MTAR M.Tejada/A.Rodriguez 5.00 12.00
NBDJ N.Garciaparra/D.Jeter 10.00 25.00

2003 Flair Sweet Swatch Autos Jumbo
PRINT RUNS B/WN 30-224 COPIES PER
GOLD PRINT RUN 25 SERIAL #'d SETS
NO GOLD PRICING DUE TO SCARCITY
MASTERPIECE PRINT 1 SERIAL #'d SET
NO M'PIECE PRICING DUE TO SCARCITY
AD Adam Dunn/218 15.00 40.00
DJ Derek Jeter/312 75.00 150.00
JB Jeff Bagwell/218 20.00 50.00
RJ Randy Johnson/218 15.00 40.00
TG Troy Glaus/116 20.00 50.00

2003 Flair Sweet Swatch Jersey
RANDOM INSERTS IN PACKS
PRINT RUN 250 SERIAL #'d SETS
*JUMBO 50: 1X TO 2.5X BASIC
JUMBO 50 PRINT RUN 50 SERIAL #'d SETS
*JUMBO 150: .6X TO 1.5X BASIC
JUMBO 150 PRINT RUN 150 SERIAL #'d SETS
JUMBO MASTERPIECE 1 SERIAL #'d SET
NO JUMBO M'PIECE PRICING AVAILABLE
SSAD Adam Dunn 3.00 8.00
SSAR Alex Rodriguez 6.00 15.00
SSAS Alfonso Soriano 3.00 8.00
SSBW Bernie Williams 4.00 10.00
SSCJ Chipper Jones 4.00 10.00
SSDJ Derek Jeter 8.00 20.00
SSHN Hideo Nomo 6.00 15.00
SSJG Jason Giambi 3.00 8.00
SSKS Kazuhiro Sasaki 3.00 8.00
SSLB Lance Berkman 3.00 8.00
SSMP Mark Prior 4.00 10.00
SSMT Miguel Tejada 3.00 8.00
SSNG Nomar Garciaparra 6.00 15.00
SSPM Pedro Martinez 4.00 10.00
SSRC Roger Clemens 6.00 15.00
SSRJ Randy Johnson 4.00 10.00
SSSS Sammy Sosa 4.00 10.00
SSVG Vladimir Guerrero 4.00 10.00

2003 Flair Sweet Swatch Jersey Jumbo
ONE PER JUMBO PACK
PRINT RUNS B/WN 46-1480 COPIES PER
ADSSJ Adam Dunn/1090 3.00 8.00
ARSSJ Alex Rodriguez/55 15.00 40.00
BWSSJ Bernie Williams/1420 10.00 25.00
CJSSJ Chipper Jones/80 10.00 25.00
DJSSJ Derek Jeter/47 20.00 50.00
HNSSJ Hideo Nomo/970 4.00 10.00
JGSSJ Jason Giambi/350 4.00 10.00
KSSSJ Kazuhiro Sasaki/505 4.00 10.00
LBSSJ Lance Berkman/1465 3.00 8.00
MPSSJ Mark Prior/1195 4.00 10.00
MTSSJ Miguel Tejada/518 4.00 10.00
NGSSJ Nomar Garciaparra/727 8.00 20.00
PMSSJ Pedro Martinez/1480 4.00 10.00
RCSSJ Roger Clemens/97 12.50 30.00
RJSSJ Randy Johnson/274 6.00 15.00
SSSSJ Sammy Sosa/279 6.00 15.00
VGSSJ Vladimir Guerrero/46 15.00 40.00

2003 Flair Sweet Swatch Jersey Dual Jumbo
RANDOM INSERTS IN JUMBO PACKS
STATED PRINT RUN 25 SERIAL #'d SETS
NO PRICING DUE TO SCARCITY

2003 Flair Sweet Swatch Patch
RANDOM INSERTS IN PACKS
STATED PRINT RUN 50 SERIAL #'d SETS
SSPAR Alex Rodriguez 20.00 50.00
SSPAS Alfonso Soriano 12.50 30.00
SSPBW Bernie Williams 15.00 40.00
SSPCJ Chipper Jones 15.00 40.00
SSPDJ Derek Jeter 30.00 80.00
SSPHN Hideo Nomo 15.00 40.00
SSPJG Jason Giambi 12.50 30.00
SSPKS Kazuhiro Sasaki 12.50 30.00
SSPLB Lance Berkman 12.50 30.00
SSPMP Mark Prior 15.00 40.00
SSPMT Miguel Tejada 12.50 30.00
SSPNG Nomar Garciaparra 20.00 50.00
SSPPM Pedro Martinez 15.00 40.00
SSPRC Roger Clemens 25.00 60.00
SSPRJ Randy Johnson 15.00 40.00
SSPSS Sammy Sosa 15.00 40.00
SSPVG Vladimir Guerrero 15.00 40.00

2003 Flair Sweet Swatch Patch Jumbo
PRINT RUNS B/WN 1-298 COPIES PER
ADSSPE Adam Dunn/130 12.50 30.00
ARSSPE Alex Rodriguez/298 12.50 30.00
BWSSPE Bernie Williams/123 15.00 40.00
CJSSPE Chipper Jones/284 12.50 30.00
HNSSPE Hideo Nomo/114 25.00 60.00
KSSSPE Kazuhiro Sasaki/90 12.50 30.00
LBSSPE Lance Berkman/287 10.00 25.00
MPSSPE Mark Prior/290 12.50 30.00
MTSSPE Miguel Tejada/183 10.00 25.00
NGSSPE Nomar Garciaparra/124 20.00 50.00
PMSSPE Pedro Martinez/185 12.50 30.00
RJSSPE Randy Johnson/46 20.00 50.00
SSSSPE Sammy Sosa/190 12.50 30.00
VGSSPE Vladimir Guerrero/290 12.50 30.00

2003 Flair Wave of the Future Memorabilia
STATED PRINT RUN 500 SERIAL #'d SETS
*GOLD: .6X TO 1.5X BASIC
GOLD PRINT RUN 100 SERIAL #'d SETS
AH Aubrey Huff Bat 3.00 8.00
AK Austin Kearns Jsy 3.00 8.00
CC Carl Crawford Bat 3.00 8.00
HB Hank Blalock Bat 3.00 8.00
JP Josh Phelps Jsy 3.00 8.00
SB Sean Burroughs Jsy 3.00 8.00

2004 Flair
COMMON CARD (1-60) .40 1.00
COMMON CARD (61-82) .75 2.00
61-82 ODDS 1:1 HOBBY, 1:200 RETAIL
62-82 PRINT RUN 799 SERIAL #'d SETS
1 Brandon Webb .40 1.00
2 Todd Helton .60 1.50
3 Jeff Bagwell .60 1.50
4 Shawn Green .40 1.00
5 Vladimir Guerrero .60 1.50
6 Tom Glavine .60 1.50
7 Jason Giambi .40 1.00
8 Barry Zito .60 1.50
9 Jason Kendall .40 1.00
10 Carlos Delgado .40 1.00
11 Curt Schilling .60 1.50
12 Ken Griffey Jr. 2.00 5.00
13 Mike Piazza 1.00 2.50
14 Alfonso Soriano .60 1.50
15 Albert Pujols 1.25 3.00
16 Chipper Jones 1.00 2.50
17 Alex Rodriguez 1.25 3.00
18 Miguel Tejada .60 1.50
19 Pedro Martinez .60 1.50
20 Mark Prior .60 1.50
21 Magglio Ordonez .60 1.50
22 Scott Podsednik .40 1.00
23 Shannon Stewart .40 1.00
24 Rocco Baldelli .40 1.00
25 Darin Erstad .40 1.00
26 Omar Vizquel .60 1.50
27 Angel Berroa .40 1.00
28 Jose Vidro .40 1.00
29 Rich Harden .40 1.00
30 Andruw Jones .40 1.00
31 Troy Glaus .40 1.00
32 Sammy Sosa 1.00 2.50
33 Dontrelle Willis .40 1.00
34 Ivan Rodriguez .60 1.50
35 Nomar Garciaparra .60 1.50
36 Josh Beckett .40 1.00
37 Jose Reyes .60 1.50
38 Scott Rolen .60 1.50
39 Greg Maddux 1.25 3.00
40 Andy Pettitte .60 1.50
41 Jason Schmidt .40 1.00
42 Edgar Martinez .60 1.50
43 Manny Ramirez 1.00 2.50
44 Torii Hunter .40 1.00
45 Mark Teixeira .60 1.50
46 Hideo Nomo 1.00 2.50
47 Brian Giles .40 1.00
48 Adam Dunn .60 1.50
49 Fernando Vina .40 1.00
50 Hideki Matsui 1.50 4.00
51 Jim Thome .60 1.50
52 Hank Blalock .40 1.00
53 Miguel Cabrera 1.00 2.50
54 Randy Johnson 1.00 2.50
55 Javy Lopez .40 1.00
56 Frank Thomas 1.00 2.50
57 Roger Clemens 1.25 3.00
58 Marlon Byrd .40 1.00
59 Derek Jeter 2.50 6.00
60 Ichiro Suzuki 1.25 3.00
61 Kaz Matsui C04 RC 1.25 3.00
62 Chad Bentz C04 RC .75 2.00
63 Greg Dobbs C04 RC .75 2.00
64 John Gall C04 RC .75 2.00
65 Cory Sullivan C04 RC .75 2.00
66 Hector Gimenez C04 RC .75 2.00
67 Graham Koonce C04 .75 2.00
68 Jason Bartlett C04 RC 2.50 6.00
69 Angel Chavez C04 RC .75 2.00
70 Ronny Cedeno C04 RC .75 2.00
71 Don Kelly C04 RC 1.25 3.00
72 Ivan Ochoa C04 RC .75 2.00
73 Ruddy Yan C04 .75 2.00
74 Mike Gosling C04 RC .75 2.00
75 Alfredo Simon C04 RC 1.25 3.00
76 Jerome Gamble C04 RC .75 2.00
77 Chris Aguila C04 RC .75 2.00
78 Mike Rouse C04 RC .75 2.00
79 Justin Leone C04 RC .75 2.00
80 Merkin Valdez C04 RC .75 2.00
81 Aaron Baldiris C04 RC .75 2.00
82 Chris Shelton C04 RC .75 2.00

2004 Flair Collection Row 1
*ROW 1 1-60: 1.25X TO 3X BASIC
*ROW 1 61-82: .6X TO 1.5X BASIC
OVERALL PARALLEL ODDS 1:6 HOBBY
ROW 1 STATED ODDS 1:55 RETAIL
STATED PRINT RUN 100 SERIAL #'d SETS

2004 Flair Collection Row 2
OVERALL PARALLEL ODDS 1:6 HOBBY
STATED PRINT RUN 1 SERIAL #'d SET
NO PRICING DUE TO SCARCITY

2004 Flair Autograph
PRINT RUNS B/WN 60-280 COPIES PER
*CROWN: .4X TO 1X p/r 122-280
*CROWN: .4X TO 1X p/r 60-96
CROWN PRINT RUN 100 SERIAL #'d SETS
MASTERPIECE PRINT RUN 1 SER.#'d SET
NO M'PIECE PRICING DUE TO SCARCITY
*PARCHMENT: .75X TO 2X p/r 122-280
*PARCHMENT: .6X TO 1.5X p/r 60-96
PARCHMENT PRINT RUN 25 SER.#'d SETS
NO RC YR PARCHMENT PRICING AVAIL.
PLATINUM PRINT RUN 10 SERIAL #'d SETS
NO PLATINUM PRICING DUE TO SCARCITY
OVERALL AU ODDS 1:1 HOBBY
OVERALL AU-GU ODDS 1:24 RETAIL
AB1 Aarom Baldiris/180 4.00 10.00
AB2 Angel Berroa/178 4.00 10.00
AJ Andruw Jones/163 10.00 25.00
ALR Adam LaRoche/280 4.00 10.00
AR Alexis Rios/185 6.00 15.00
BC Bobby Crosby/87 10.00 25.00
BN Bubba Nelson/185 4.00 10.00
BW Brandon Webb/122 4.00 10.00
CMW Chien-Ming Wang/178 12.50 30.00
CP Corey Patterson/172 4.00 10.00
CS Chris Shelton/170 4.00 10.00
DH Dan Haren/195 6.00 15.00
DW Dontrelle Willis/73 15.00 40.00
DY Delmon Young/177 6.00 15.00
EJ Edwin Jackson/193 4.00 10.00
GA Garrett Atkins/195 4.00 10.00
GK Graham Koonce/175 4.00 10.00
GS Grady Sizemore/197 4.00 10.00
JB1 Jason Bartlett/95 6.00 15.00
JB2 Josh Beckett/65 6.00 15.00
JE Jim Edmonds/73 8.00 20.00
JG John Gall/94 6.00 15.00
JL Josh Labandeira/166 4.00 10.00
JP Juan Pierre/94 6.00 15.00
JUL Justin Leone/180 6.00 15.00
JV Javier Vazquez/187 6.00 15.00
KG Khalil Greene/195 10.00 25.00
KWO Kerry Wood/73 6.00 15.00
MC Miguel Cabrera/172 20.00 50.00
MM Mike Mussina/69 15.00 40.00
MN Michael Nakamura/180 4.00 10.00
MP Mark Prior/60 12.50 30.00
MR Mike Rouse/185 4.00 10.00
MV Merkin Valdez/179 4.00 10.00
RB Rocco Baldelli/180 6.00 15.00
RH Ryan Howard/185 10.00 25.00
RM Ryan Meaux/180 4.00 10.00
RW1 Ryan Wagner/175 4.00 10.00
RW2 Rickie Weeks/169 6.00 15.00
SP Scott Podsednik/96 15.00 40.00

2004 Flair Autograph Die Cut
OVERALL AU ODDS 1:1 HOBBY
PRINT RUNS B/WN 10-113 COPIES PER
NO PRICING ON QTY OF 19 OR LESS
BC Bobby Crosby/102 10.00 25.00
JB1 Jason Bartlett/113 6.00 15.00
JG John Gall/94 6.00 15.00
JP Juan Pierre/80 10.00 25.00
SP Scott Podsednik/84 15.00 40.00

2004 Flair Cuts and Glory 100
STATED PRINT RUN 100 SERIAL #'d SETS
*CUTS/GLORY 50: .5X TO 1X BASIC
CUTS/GLORY 50 PRINT RUN 50 #'d SETS
CUTS/GLORY 15 PRINT RUN 15 #'d SETS
C/G 15 NO PRICING DUE TO SCARCITY
CUTS/GLORY 3 PRINT RUN 3 #'d SETS
C/G 3 NO PRICING DUE TO SCARCITY
CUTS/GLORY 1 PRINT RUN 1 #'d SETS
C/G 1 NO PRICING DUE TO SCARCITY
OVERALL AU ODDS 1:1 HOBBY
OVERALL AU-GU ODDS 1:24 RETAIL
EXCHANGE DEADLINE INDEFINITE
AD Adam Dunn 15.00 40.00
AK Austin Kearns 6.00 15.00
AP Albert Pujols 50.00 100.00
CD Carlos Delgado 15.00 40.00
CJ Chipper Jones 30.00 60.00
EG Eric Gagne 8.00 20.00
EM Edgar Martinez 15.00 40.00
FT Frank Thomas 30.00 60.00
GA Garret Anderson 10.00 25.00
HB Hank Blalock 10.00 25.00
JR Jose Reyes 10.00 25.00
LG Luis Gonzalez 10.00 25.00
MB Marlon Byrd 6.00 15.00
MO Magglio Ordonez 10.00 25.00
MT Mark Teixeira 15.00 40.00
RH Rickey Henderson 40.00 80.00
RJ Randy Johnson 30.00 60.00
SR Scott Rolen 10.00 25.00
TH Torii Hunter 10.00 25.00
VG Vladimir Guerrero 10.00 25.00

2004 Flair Diamond Cuts Game Used Blue
STATED PRINT RUN 250 SERIAL #'d SETS
*BLUE DC: 1X TO 2.5X BLUE
BLUE DC PRINT RUN 25 SERIAL #'d SETS
*COPPER: .6X TO 1.5X BLUE
COPPER PRINT RUN 75 SERIAL #'d SETS
COPPER DC PRINT RUN 8 SERIAL #'d SETS
NO COPPER DC PRICING DUE TO SCARCITY
*GOLD p/r 38-55: 1.25X TO 3X BLUE
*GOLD p/r 21-35: 1.5X TO 4X BLUE
GOLD PRINT RUNS B/WN 2-55 COPIES PER
NO GOLD PRICING ON QTY OF 10 OR LESS
GOLD DC PRINT RUN 3 SERIAL #'d SETS
NO GOLD DC PRICING DUE TO SCARCITY
GREEN ODDS 1:48 RETAIL
*PEWTER: .5X TO 1.2X BLUE
PEWTER PRINT RUN 125 SERIAL #'d SETS
PEWTER DC PRINT RUN 13 SER.#'d SETS
NO PEWTER DC PRICING DUE TO SCARCITY
*PLATINUM p/r 36-43: 1.25X TO 3X BLUE
*PLATINUM p/r 21-29: 1.5X TO 4X BLUE
*PLATINUM p/r 16-18: 2X TO 5X BLUE
PLAT.PRINT RUNS B/WN 5-43 COPIES PER
NO PLAT.PRICING ON QTY OF 14 OR LESS
PLATINUM DC PRINT RUN 1 SERIAL #'d SET
NO PLAT.DC PRICING DUE TO SCARCITY
PURPLE PRINT RUN 1 SERIAL #'d SET
NO PURPLE PRICING DUE TO SCARCITY
*RED: .4X TO 1X BLUE
RED PRINT RUN 175 SERIAL #'d SETS
RED DC: 1.25X TO 3X BLUE
RED DC PRINT RUN 18 SERIAL #'d SETS
*SILVER: 1.25X TO 3X BLUE
SILVER PRINT RUN 50 SERIAL #'d SETS
SILVER DC PRINT RUN 5 SERIAL #'d SETS
NO SILVER DC PRICING DUE TO SCARCITY
OVERALL GU ODDS 3 PER HOBBY PACK
ALL ARE JERSEY CARDS UNLESS NOTED
AJ Andruw Jones 3.00 8.00
ALP Albert Pujols 6.00 15.00
ANP Andy Pettitte 3.00 8.00
CJ Chipper Jones 3.00 8.00
CS Curt Schilling 3.00 8.00
DJ Derek Jeter 6.00 15.00
DW Dontrelle Willis 3.00 8.00
HB Hank Blalock 2.00 5.00
HM Hideki Matsui Base 6.00 15.00
IS Ichiro Suzuki Base 6.00 15.00
JB Josh Beckett 2.00 5.00
JR Jose Reyes 2.00 5.00
MAP Mark Prior 3.00 8.00
MIP Mike Piazza 5.00 12.00
MT Mark Teixeira 3.00 8.00
NG Nomar Garciaparra 3.00 8.00
PM Pedro Martinez 3.00 8.00
RC Roger Clemens 6.00 15.00
SR Scott Rolen 3.00 8.00
SS Sammy Sosa 3.00 8.00

2004 Flair Diamond Cuts Game Used Gold
OVERALL GU ODDS 3 PER HOBBY PACK
STATED PRINT RUN 10 SERIAL #'d SETS
NO PRICING DUE TO SCARCITY

2004 Flair Hot Numbers
STATED ODDS 1:16 RETAIL
STATED PRINT RUN 500 SERIAL #'d SETS
*GOLD p/r 51-75: .75X TO 2X BASIC
*GOLD p/r 38-48: 1X TO 2.5X BASIC
*GOLD p/r 21-35: 1.25X TO 3X BASIC

*GOLD p/r 17: 1.5X TO 4X BASIC
GOLD ODDS 1:275 RETAIL
GOLD PRINT RUNS B/WN 2-75 COPIES PER
NO GOLD PRICING ON QTY OF 13 OR LESS
1 Chipper Jones 1.50 4.00
2 Derek Jeter 4.00 10.00
3 Alex Rodriguez 2.00 5.00
4 Torii Hunter .60 1.50
5 Nomar Garciaparra 1.00 2.50
6 Troy Glaus .60 1.50
7 Tom Glavine 1.00 2.50
8 Albert Pujols 2.00 5.00
9 Kerry Wood .60 1.50
10 Hideo Nomo 1.50 4.00
11 Rocco Baldelli .60 1.50
12 Mark Prior 1.00 2.50
13 Hank Blalock .60 1.50
14 Mark Teixeira 1.00 2.50
15 Curt Schilling 1.00 2.50
16 Randy Johnson 1.50 4.00
17 Barry Larkin 1.00 2.50
18 Vladimir Guerrero 1.00 2.50
19 Brandon Webb .60 1.50
20 Todd Helton 1.00 2.50
21 Jeff Bagwell 1.00 2.50
22 Barry Zito 1.00 2.50
23 Sammy Sosa 1.50 4.00
24 Pedro Martinez 1.00 2.50
25 Jim Thome 1.00 2.50
26 Frank Thomas 1.50 4.00
27 Greg Maddux 2.00 5.00
28 Jason Giambi .60 1.50
29 Manny Ramirez 1.50 4.00
30 Josh Beckett .60 1.50
31 Mike Piazza 1.50 4.00
32 Hideki Matsui 2.50 6.00
33 Ichiro Suzuki 2.00 5.00
34 Ken Griffey Jr. 3.00 8.00
35 Mike Mussina 1.00 2.50

2004 Flair Hot Numbers Game Used Blue

STATED PRINT RUN 250 SERIAL #'d SETS
*BLUE DC: 1X TO 2.5X BLUE
BLUE DC PRINT RUN 25 SERIAL #'d SETS
COPPER: .6X TO 1.5X BLUE
COPPER PRINT RUN 75 SERIAL #'d SETS
COPPER DC PRINT RUN 8 SERIAL #'d SETS
NO COPPER DC PRICING DUE TO SCARCITY
*GOLD p/r 38-55: 1.25X TO 3X BLUE
*GOLD p/r 21-35: 1.5X TO 4X BLUE
*GOLD p/r 17: 2X TO 5X BLUE
GOLD PRINT RUNS B/WN 2-55 COPIES PER
NO GOLD PRICING ON QTY OF 13 OR LESS
GOLD DC PRINT RUN 3 SERIAL #'d SETS
NO GOLD DC PRICING DUE TO SCARCITY
GREEN STATED ODDS 1:24 RETAIL
*PEWTER: .5X TO 1.2X BLUE
PEWTER PRINT RUN 125 SERIAL #'d SETS
PEWTER DC PRINT RUN 13 SER.#'d SETS
NO PEWTER DC PRICING DUE TO SCARCITY
*PLATINUM p/r 37-47: 1.25X TO 3X BLUE
*PLATINUM p/r 25-33: 1.5X TO 4X BLUE
*PLATINUM p/r 16-18: 2X TO 5X BLUE
PLAT.PRINT RUNS B/WN 2-47 COPIES PER
NO PLAT.PRICING ON QTY OF 14 OR LESS
PLATINUM DC PRINT RUN 1 SERIAL #'d SET
NO PLAT.DC PRICING DUE TO SCARCITY
PURPLE PRINT RUN 1 SERIAL #'d SET
NO PURPLE PRICING DUE TO SCARCITY
*RED: .4X TO 1X BLUE
RED PRINT RUN 175 SERIAL #'d SETS
*RED DC: 1.25X TO 3X BLUE
RED DC PRINT RUN 18 SERIAL #'d SETS
*SILVER: 1.25X TO 3X BLUE
SILVER PRINT RUN 50 SERIAL #'d SETS
SILVER DC PRINT RUN 5 SERIAL #'d SETS
NO SILVER DC PRICING DUE TO SCARCITY
OVERALL GU ODDS 3 PER HOBBY PACK
AP Albert Pujols 6.00 15.00
AR Alex Rodriguez 6.00 15.00
BL Barry Larkin 3.00 8.00
BW Brandon Webb 2.00 5.00
CJ Chipper Jones 3.00 8.00
CS Curt Schilling 3.00 8.00
DJ Derek Jeter 6.00 15.00
FT Frank Thomas 3.00 8.00
GM Greg Maddux 5.00 12.00
HB Hank Blalock 2.00 5.00
HN Hideo Nomo 3.00 8.00
JEB Jeff Bagwell 3.00 8.00
JG Jason Giambi 2.00 5.00
JOB Josh Beckett 2.00 5.00
JT Jim Thome 3.00 8.00
KW Kerry Wood 2.00 5.00
MAP Mark Prior 3.00 8.00
MIP Mike Piazza 5.00 12.00
MM Mike Mussina 3.00 8.00
MR Manny Ramirez 3.00 8.00
MT Mark Teixeira 3.00 8.00
NG Nomar Garciaparra 5.00 12.00
PM Pedro Martinez 3.00 8.00
RB Rocco Baldelli 2.00 5.00
RJ Randy Johnson 3.00 8.00
SS Sammy Sosa 3.00 8.00
TH Todd Helton 3.00 8.00
TOG Tom Glavine 3.00 8.00
TRG Troy Glaus 2.00 5.00
VG Vladimir Guerrero 3.00 8.00

2004 Flair Lettermen

OVERALL GU ODDS 3 PER HOBBY PACK
PRINT RUNS B/WN 4-11 COPIES PER
NO PRICING DUE TO SCARCITY

2004 Flair Power Tools Game Used Blue

STATED PRINT RUN 250 SERIAL #'d SETS
*BLUE DC: 1X TO 2.5X BLUE
BLUE DC PRINT RUN 25 SERIAL #'d SETS
*COPPER: .75X TO 2X BLUE
COPPER PRINT RUN 75 SERIAL #'d SETS
COPPER DC PRINT RUN 8 SERIAL #'d SETS
NO COPPER DC PRICING DUE TO SCARCITY
*GOLD p/r 44: 1.5X TO 4X BLUE
*GOLD p/r 20-31: 2X TO 5X BLUE
GOLD PRINT RUNS B/WN 2-44 COPIES PER
NO GOLD PRICING ON QTY OF 13 OR LESS
GOLD DC PRINT RUN 3 SERIAL #'d SETS
NO GOLD DC PRICING DUE TO SCARCITY
*PEWTER: .75X TO 2X BLUE
PEWTER PRINT RUN 125 SERIAL #'d SETS
PEWTER DC 13 SERIAL #'d SETS
NO PEWTER DC PRICING DUE TO SCARCITY
*PLATINUM p/r 37-47: 1.5X TO 4X BLUE
*PLATINUM p/r 25-30: 2X TO 5X BLUE
PLAT.PRINT RUN B/WN 10-47 COPIES PER
NO PLAT.PRICING ON QTY OF 11 OR LESS
PLATINUM DC PRINT RUN 1 SERIAL #'d SET
NO PLAT.DC PRICING DUE TO SCARCITY
PURPLE PRINT RUN 1 SERIAL #'d SET
NO PURPLE PRICING DUE TO SCARCITY
*RED: .4X TO 1X BLUE
RED PRINT RUN 175 SERIAL #'d SETS
*RED DC: 1.25X TO 3X BLUE
RED DC PRINT RUN 18 SERIAL #'d SETS
*SILVER: 1X TO 2.5X BLUE
SILVER PRINT RUN 50 SERIAL #'d SETS
SILVER DC PRINT RUN 5 SERIAL #'d SETS
NO SILVER DC PRICING DUE TO SCARCITY
OVERALL GU ODDS 3 PER HOBBY PACK
AD Adam Dunn 2.00 5.00
AP Albert Pujols 6.00 15.00
AR Alex Rodriguez 6.00 15.00
AS Alfonso Soriano 2.00 5.00
CJ Chipper Jones 3.00 8.00
DJ Derek Jeter 6.00 15.00
JG Jason Giambi 2.00 5.00
JP Jorge Posada 3.00 8.00
JT Jim Thome 3.00 8.00
MP Mike Piazza 5.00 12.00
MR Manny Ramirez 3.00 8.00
NG Nomar Garciaparra 5.00 12.00
RB Rocco Baldelli 2.00 5.00
SS Sammy Sosa 3.00 8.00
VG Vladimir Guerrero 3.00 8.00

2004 Flair Significant Cuts

OVERALL AU ODDS 1:1 HOBBY
PRINT RUNS B/WN 1-200 COPIES PER
NO PRICING ON QTY OF 10 OR LESS
AP1 Andy Pettitte/50 10.00 25.00
BL Barry Larkin/75 20.00 50.00
CR Cal Ripken/25 50.00 120.00
DE Dennis Eckersley/75 10.00 25.00
DM Don Mattingly/25 20.00 60.00
GS Gary Sheffield/50 10.00 25.00
IR Ivan Rodriguez/50 20.00 50.00
JB2 Johnny Bench/25 15.00 60.00
JR Jose Reyes/25 12.00 30.00
JS John Smoltz/75 25.00 60.00
MR Mariano Rivera/50 50.00 120.00
MS Mike Schmidt/25 60.00 150.00
MT Miguel Tejada/25 20.00 50.00
NR Nolan Ryan/25 50.00 120.00
PM Paul Molitor/75 10.00 25.00
RA Roberto Alomar/50 15.00 40.00
RH Roy Halladay/50 30.00 80.00
RP Rafael Palmeiro/25 8.00 20.00
VC Vince Carter/200 12.00 40.00

2005 Flair

COMMON CARD (1-50) .40 1.00
COMMON CARD (51-80) .40 1.00
51-80 ODDS 1:1 HOBBY, 1:130 RETAIL
51-80 PRINT RUN 699 SERIAL #'d SETS
COMMON CARD (81-90) .40 1.00
81-90 ODDS 1:2 HOBBY, 1:240 RETAIL
81-90 PRINT RUN 699 SERIAL #'d SETS
1 Curt Schilling .60 1.50
2 Jim Thome .60 1.50
3 Miguel Cabrera 1.00 2.50
4 Randy Johnson 1.00 2.50
5 David Ortiz 1.00 2.50
6 Vladimir Guerrero .60 1.50
7 Nomar Garciaparra .60 1.50
8 Ivan Rodriguez .60 1.50
9 Jason Schmidt .40 1.00
10 Khalil Greene .40 1.00
11 Jose Vidro .40 1.00
12 Lyle Overbay .40 1.00
13 Todd Helton .60 1.50
14 Vernon Wells .40 1.00
15 B.J. Upton .60 1.50
16 Hideki Matsui 1.50 4.00
17 Pedro Martinez .60 1.50
18 Victor Martinez .60 1.50
19 Adam Dunn .60 1.50
20 Andruw Jones .40 1.00
21 Jeff Bagwell .60 1.50
22 Mike Sweeney .40 1.00
23 Mike Piazza 1.00 2.50
24 Ben Sheets .40 1.00
25 Adrian Beltre 1.00 2.50
26 Chipper Jones 1.00 2.50
27 Greg Maddux 1.25 3.00
28 Manny Ramirez 1.00 2.50
29 Roger Clemens 1.25 3.00
30 Johan Santana .60 1.50
31 Derek Jeter 2.50 6.00
32 Jason Bay .40 1.00
33 Ken Griffey Jr. 2.00 5.00
34 Miguel Tejada .60 1.50
35 Richie Sexson .40 1.00
36 Scott Rolen .60 1.50
37 Alfonso Soriano .60 1.50
38 Ichiro Suzuki 1.25 3.00
39 Sammy Sosa 1.00 2.50
40 Barry Zito .60 1.50
41 Kaz Matsui .40 1.00
42 Mark Teixeira .60 1.50
43 Carlos Beltran .60 1.50
44 Mark Prior .60 1.50
45 Travis Hafner .40 1.00
46 Alex Rodriguez 1.25 3.00
47 Lew Ford .40 1.00
48 Albert Pujols 1.25 3.00
49 Frank Thomas 1.00 2.50
50 Juan Pierre .40 1.00
51 David Aardsma C05 .40 1.00
52 J.D. Durbin C05 .40 1.00
53 Zack Greinke C05 1.25 3.00
54 Dioner Navarro C05 .40 1.00
55 Edwin Encarnacion C05 1.00 2.50
56 Luis Hernandez C05 RC .40 1.00
57 Jeff Baker C05 .40 1.00
58 Victor Diaz C05 .40 1.00
59 Joey Gathright C05 .40 1.00
60 Casey Kotchman C05 .40 1.00
61 David Wright C05 .75 2.00
62 Jon Knott C05 .40 1.00
63 Charlton Jimerson C05 .40 1.00
64 Nick Swisher C05 .60 1.50
65 Ryan Raburn C05 .40 1.00
66 Josh Kroeger C05 .40 1.00
67 Kelly Johnson C05 .40 1.00
68 Justin Verlander C05 RC 8.00 20.00
69 Taylor Buchholz C05 .40 1.00
70 Ubaldo Jimenez C05 RC 1.00 2.50
71 Russ Adams C05 .40 1.00
72 Ronny Cedeno C05 .40 1.00
73 Bobby Jenks C05 .40 1.00
74 Dan Meyer C05 .40 1.00
75 Jeff Francis C05 .40 1.00
76 Scott Kazmir C05 1.00 2.50
77 Sean Burnett C05 .40 1.00
78 Jose Lopez C05 .40 1.00
79 Andres Blanco C05 .40 1.00
80 Gavin Floyd C05 .40 1.00
81 Tom Seaver RET .60 1.50
82 Steve Carlton RET .60 1.50
83 Al Kaline RET 1.00 2.50
84 Cal Ripken RET 3.00 8.00
85 Willie McCovey RET .60 1.50
86 Johnny Bench RET 1.00 2.50
87 Nolan Ryan RET 3.00 8.00
88 Mike Schmidt RET 1.50 4.00
89 Carlton Fisk RET .60 1.50
90 Don Mattingly RET 2.00 5.00

2005 Flair Row 1

*ROW 1 1-50: 2X TO 5X BASIC
*ROW 1 51-80: 1X TO 2.5X BASIC
*ROW 1 81-90: 1.5X TO 4X BASIC
OVERALL PARALLEL ODDS 1:6 H, 1:55 R
STATED PRINT RUN 100 SERIAL #'d SETS

2005 Flair Row 2

OVERALL PARALLEL ODDS 1:6 HOBBY
STATED PRINT RUN 1 SERIAL #'d SET
NO PRICING DUE TO SCARCITY

2005 Flair Cuts and Glory Jersey

STATED PRINT RUN 100 SERIAL #'d SETS
LOGO PRINT RUN 1 SERIAL #'d SET
NO LOGO PRICING DUE TO SCARCITY
PATCH-JSY PRINT RUN 15 #'d SETS
NO PATCH-JSY PRICING DUE TO SCARCITY
OVERALL AU ODDS 1:1 H, AU-GU 1:24 R
BS Ben Sheets 10.00 25.00
CC Carl Crawford 10.00 25.00
JB Johnny Bench 30.00 60.00
JL Javy Lopez 10.00 25.00
JP Josh Phelps 6.00 15.00
SS Shannon Stewart 10.00 25.00

2005 Flair Cuts and Glory Patch

*PATCH: .6X TO 1.5X JSY
OVERALL AU ODDS 1:1 H, AU-GU 1:24 R
STATED PRINT RUN 50 SERIAL #'d SETS
HA Hank Aaron 175.00 300.00

2005 Flair Diamond Cuts Jersey

STATED PRINT RUN 150 SERIAL #'d SETS
*BLUE FOIL: .4X TO 1X BASIC
BLUE FOIL ODDS 1:48 RETAIL
BLUE FOIL CARDS ARE NOT SERIAL #'d
*DIE CUT: .5X TO 1.2X BASIC
DIE CUT PRINT RUN 75 SERIAL #'d SETS
*PATCH: 1X TO 2.5X BASIC
PATCH PRINT RUN 50 SERIAL #'d SETS
*PATCH DIE CUT: 1.5X TO 4X BASIC
PATCH DC PRINT RUN 25 SERIAL #'d SETS
PATCH MLB LOGO PRINT RUN 1 #'d SET
NO PATCH MLB LOGO PRICING AVAILABLE
PATCH SUPER PRINT RUN 20 #'d SETS
NO PATCH SUPER PRICING AVAILABLE
PATCH SUPER DC PRINT RUN 10 #'d SETS
NO PATCH SUPER DC PRICING AVAILABLE
OVERALL GU ODDS 2:1 HOBBY
AD Adam Dunn 3.00 8.00
AJ Andruw Jones 3.00 8.00
AK Austin Kearns 3.00 8.00
AP Albert Pujols 6.00 15.00
AS Alfonso Soriano 3.00 8.00
BU B.J. Upton 3.00 8.00
CB Carlos Beltran 3.00 8.00
CJ Chipper Jones 4.00 10.00
CS Curt Schilling 3.00 8.00
DO David Ortiz 3.00 8.00
GS Gary Sheffield 3.00 8.00
HB Hank Blalock 3.00 8.00
HM Hideki Matsui 10.00 25.00
HN Hideo Nomo 4.00 10.00
JB Jeff Bagwell 3.00 8.00
JT Jim Thome 3.00 8.00
KW Kerry Wood 3.00 8.00
MC Miguel Cabrera 3.00 8.00
MP Mike Piazza 4.00 10.00
MP2 Mark Prior 3.00 8.00
MR Manny Ramirez 3.00 8.00
MT Mark Teixeira 3.00 8.00
PM Pedro Martinez 3.00 8.00
RC Roger Clemens 4.00 10.00
RJ Randy Johnson 4.00 10.00
SR Scott Rolen 3.00 8.00
SS Sammy Sosa 4.00 10.00
TH Todd Helton 3.00 8.00
VG Vladimir Guerrero 4.00 10.00
VM Victor Martinez 3.00 8.00

2005 Flair Diamond Cuts Dual Jersey

STATED PRINT RUN 99 SERIAL #'d SETS
*DIE CUT: .5X TO 1.2X BASIC
DIE CUT PRINT RUN 50 SERIAL #'d SETS
PATCH PRINT RUN 15 SERIAL #'d SETS
NO PATCH PRICING DUE TO SCARCITY
PATCH DIE CUT PRINT RUN 5 #'d SETS
NO PATCH DC PRICING DUE TO SCARCITY
OVERALL GU ODDS 2:1 HOBBY
BC J.Bagwell/R.Clemens 6.00 15.00
BM C.Beltran/P.Martinez 4.00 10.00
BS H.Blalock/A.Soriano 4.00 10.00
CH M.Cabrera/T.Helton 4.00 10.00
DK A.Dunn/A.Kearns 4.00 10.00
JJ C.Jones/A.Jones 6.00 15.00
JS R.Johnson/C.Schilling 6.00 15.00
MS H.Matsui/G.Sheffield 12.50 30.00
MT V.Martinez/M.Teixeira 4.00 10.00
NU H.Nomo/B.J.Upton 6.00 15.00
OR D.Ortiz/M.Ramirez 4.00 10.00
PR A.Pujols/S.Rolen 10.00 25.00
PT M.Piazza/J.Thome 6.00 15.00
PW M.Prior/K.Wood 4.00 10.00
SG S.Sosa/V.Guerrero 6.00 15.00

2005 Flair Dynasty Cornerstones Signatures

OVERALL AU ODDS 1:1 HOBBY
PRINT RUNS B/WN 3-75 COPIES PER
NO PRICING ON QTY OF 16 OR LESS
DG Dwight Gooden/25 10.00 25.00
DO David Ortiz/75 20.00 50.00
JB Jeremy Bonderman/75 10.00 25.00
JV Jason Varitek/75 30.00 60.00
JV2 Justin Verlander/75 40.00 80.00

2005 Flair Dynasty Cornerstones Dual Signatures

OVERALL AU ODDS 1:1 HOBBY
PRINT RUNS B/WN 2-30 COPIES PER
NO PRICING ON QTY OF 15 OR LESS
BV Bonderman/Verlander/30 50.00 100.00

2005 Flair Dynasty Foundations

STATED PRINT RUN 500 SERIAL #'d SETS
*GOLD p/r 61-98: .75X TO 2X BASIC
GOLD PRINT RUNS B/WN 1-98 COPIES PER
NO GOLD PRICING ON QTY OF 1
OVERALL ODDS 1:25 RETAIL
1 Guer 6.00 15.00
And
Erst
Carew
Ryan
2 Rip 6.00 15.00
Teja
Javy
Palm
Brooks
3 Manny 4.00 10.00
Ted
Ortiz
Dam
Yaz
4 Sos 4.00 10.00
Bank
Ryno
Mad
Prior
5 Dunn 2.00 5.00
Kea
Mor
Ben
Perez
6 Mart 1.25 3.00
Haf
Saba
Doby
Feller
7 Helton 2.00 5.00
Atk
Wils
Miles
Holl
8 Cab 2.00 5.00
Beck
Willis
Pier
Leit
9 Bag 2.50 6.00
Berk
Bigg
Clem
Osw
10 Jenk 2.00 5.00
Moli
Shee
Over
Yount
11 Johan 2.00 5.00
Kill
Torii
Stew
Ford
12 Piaz 6.00 15.00
Seav
Ryan
Mart
Glav
13 Zito 1.25 3.00
Chav
Regg
Crosb
Eck
14 Thom 3.00 8.00
Abr
Floyd
Rob
Schm
15 C.Wil 1.25 3.00
J.Wil
Bay
Starg
Maz
16 J.Sch 1.25 3.00
Mari
McCov
Cep
Dur
17 Rol 3.00 8.00
Pujols
Edm
Muld
Musial
18 Upt 2.00 5.00
Craw
Kaz
Huff
Rocco
19 Sor 6.00 15.00
Teix
Blal
Ryan
Young
20 Hud 2.00 5.00
Wells
Rios
Moli
Halla

2005 Flair Dynasty Foundations Level 1 Jersey

OVERALL AU-GU ODDS 1:24 RETAIL
STATED PRINT RUN 150 SERIAL #'d SETS
ACTUAL PRINT RUNS B/WN 140-150 PER
*PATCH: 1X TO 2.5X BASIC
PATCH ODDS OVERALL GU 2:1 HOBBY
PATCH PRINT RUN 99 SERIAL #'d SETS
ACTUAL PATCH PRINT B/WN 98-99 PER
BR David Ortiz 3.00 8.00
CI Victor Martinez 3.00 8.00
CR1 Adam Dunn/140 UER 3.00 8.00
CR2 Todd Helton 3.00 8.00
FM Miguel Cabrera/140 UER 3.00 8.00
HA Jeff Bagwell/146 UER 3.00 8.00
LA Vladimir Guerrero 4.00 10.00
MB Lyle Overbay 3.00 8.00
MT Johan Santana 4.00 10.00
NM Mike Piazza 4.00 10.00
OA Barry Zito 3.00 8.00
PP Jim Thome 3.00 8.00
PT Jason Bay 3.00 8.00
SC Albert Pujols 6.00 15.00
SG Jason Schmidt 3.00 8.00
TD B.J. Upton 3.00 8.00
TR Michael Young 3.00 8.00

2005 Flair Dynasty Foundations Level 2 Jersey

STATED PRINT RUN 150 SERIAL #'d SETS
*PATCH: 1X TO 2.5X BASIC
PATCH PRINT RUN 50 SERIAL #'d SETS
OVERALL GU ODDS 2:1 HOBBY
BR M.Ramirez/D.Ortiz 4.00 10.00
CI V.Martinez/T.Hafner 4.00 10.00
CR1 A.Dunn/A.Kearns 4.00 10.00
CR2 T.Helton/P.Wilson 5.00 12.00
FM M.Cabrera/J.Pierre 4.00 10.00
HA J.Bagwell/L.Berkman 4.00 10.00
LA V.Guerrero/G.Anderson 6.00 15.00
MT J.Santana/T.Hunter 6.00 15.00
NM M.Piazza/T.Glavine 6.00 15.00
OA B.Zito/E.Chavez 4.00 10.00
PP J.Thome/B.Abreu 4.00 10.00
SC S.Rolen/A.Pujols 10.00 25.00
TD B.Upton/S.Kazmir 4.00 10.00
TR M.Teixeira/M.Young 4.00 10.00

2005 Flair Dynasty Foundations Level 3 Jersey

OVERALL GU ODDS 2:1 HOBBY
STATED PRINT RUN 99 SERIAL #'d SETS
CR1 Dunn/Kearns/Morgan 6.00 15.00
FM Cabrera/Beckett/Pierre 6.00 15.00
HA Bagwell/Berkman/Clemens 12.50 30.00
LA Guerrero/Anderson/Erstad 10.00 25.00
MT Santana/Hunter/Stewart 10.00 25.00
NM Piazza/Martinez/Glavine 10.00 25.00
SC Rolen/Pujols/Edmonds 20.00 50.00
TR Soriano/Teixeira/Young 6.00 15.00

2005 Flair Dynasty Foundations Level 3 Patch

*PATCH: 1X TO 2.5X L3 JSY
OVERALL GU ODDS 2:1 HOBBY
STATED PRINT RUN 25 SERIAL #'d SETS

2005 Flair Dynasty Foundations Level 4 Jersey

STATED PRINT RUN 40 SERIAL #'d SETS
PATCH PRINT RUN 15 SERIAL #'d SETS
NO PATCH PRICING DUE TO SCARCITY
OVERALL GU ODDS 2:1 HOBBY
CR1 Dunn/Kearns/Morg/Bench 15.00 40.00
FM Cabr/Beckett/Willis/Pierre 10.00 25.00
HA Bag/Berk/Clemens/Oswalt 15.00 40.00
NM Piazza/Ryan/Pedro/Glavine 30.00 60.00
SC Rolen/Pujols/Edm/Mulder 30.00 60.00
TR Soriano/Teix/Ryan/Young 15.00 40.00

2005 Flair Dynasty Foundations Level 5 Jersey

STATED PRINT RUN 25 SERIAL #'d SETS
MLB LOGO PRINT RUN 1 SERIAL #'d SET
NO MLB LOGO PRICING DUE TO SCARCITY
PATCH PRINT RUN 9 SERIAL #'d SETS
NO PATCH PRICING DUE TO SCARCITY
OVERALL GU ODDS 2:1 HOBBY
FM Cab/Beck/Willis/Pier/Leit 15.00 40.00
LA Guer/And/Erst/Carew/Ryan 40.00 80.00
NM Piaz/Seav/Ryan/Mart/Glav 75.00 150.00
TR Sor/Teix/Blal/Ryan/Young 40.00 80.00

2005 Flair Head of the Class Triple Jersey

PRINT RUNS B/WN 1-99 COPIES PER
NO PRICING ON QTY OF 3 OR LESS
LOGO PRINT RUN 1 SERIAL #'d SET
NO LOGO PRICING DUE TO SCARCITY
OVERALL GU ODDS 2:1 HOBBY
AGJ Abreu/Vlad/Andruw/96 6.00 15.00
BGB Beltran/Glaus/Beltre/98 6.00 15.00
BTR Bagwell/Thome/I.Rod/91 6.00 15.00
GBH Gagne/Burnett/Hudson/99 6.00 15.00
JDR Chipper/Delg/Manny/93 6.00 15.00
OHS Ortiz/Torii/Sexson/97 6.00 15.00
SNP J.Schmidt/Nomo/Pettite/95 10.00 25.00

2005 Flair Head of the Class Triple Patch

*PATCH: 1.25X TO 3X BASIC p/r 91-99
OVERALL GU ODDS 2:1 HOBBY
STATED PRINT RUN 33 SERIAL #'d SETS
BMK Blalock/V.Mart/Kearns 20.00 50.00
CGB Cabrera/Greene/Bay 20.00 50.00
SMZ Johan/Mulder/Zito 20.00 50.00

2005 Flair Letterman

OVERALL GU ODDS 2:1 HOBBY
PRINT RUNS B/WN 4-8 COPIES PER
NO PRICING DUE TO SCARCITY

2005 Flair Significant Signings Blue

PRINT RUNS B/WN 4-250 COPIES PER
NO PRICING ON QTY OF 20 OR LESS
JSY TAG OVERALL AU ODDS 1:1 HOBBY
JSY TAG PRINT RUN 1 SERIAL #'d SET
NO JSY TAG PRICING DUE TO SCARCITY
PATCH PRINT RUN 15 SERIAL #'d SETS
ACTUAL HAFNER PATCH QTY 8 COPIES
NO PATCH PRICING DUE TO SCARCITY
OVERALL AU ODDS 1:1 H, AU-GU 1:24 R
AB Adrian Beltre/30 10.00 25.00
BC Bobby Crosby/93 6.00 15.00
BU B.J. Upton/250 6.00 15.00
CK Casey Kotchman/250 6.00 15.00
DM Don Mattingly/103 30.00 60.00
DW David Wright/250 20.00 50.00
GF Gavin Floyd/221 4.00 10.00
JB Jason Bay/250 6.00 15.00
JM Justin Morneau/225 6.00 15.00
JP Jake Peavy UER 200/198 * 8.00 20.00
JR Jeremy Reed/250 4.00 10.00
KW Kerry Wood/200 10.00 25.00
LF Lew Ford/230 4.00 10.00
MC Miguel Cabrera/250 20.00 50.00
MT Mark Teixeira/160 10.00 25.00
NR Nolan Ryan/92 50.00 100.00
PM Pedro Martinez/101 40.00 80.00
RC Roger Clemens UER 43/33 * 75.00 150.00
SC Steve Carlton/59 8.00 20.00
SK Scott Kazmir/250 8.00 20.00
TH T.Hafner UER 250/249 * 6.00 15.00
VM Victor Martinez/224 6.00 15.00
ZG Zack Greinke/250 6.00 15.00

2005 Flair Significant Signings Die Cut Silver

*DC SIL: .5X TO 1.2X BLUE p/r 160-250
*DC SIL: .5X TO 1.2X BLUE p/r 92-101
*DC SIL: .4X TO 1X BLUE p/r 43-59
*DC SIL: .3X TO .8X BLUE p/r 30
OVERALL AU ODDS 1:1 HOBBY
STATED PRINT RUN 50 SERIAL #'d SETS
CB Carlos Beltran 8.00 20.00
CR Cal Ripken 100.00 175.00
MS Mike Schmidt 40.00 80.00

2005 Flair Significant Signings Jersey Gold

*JSY GOLD: .75X TO 2X BLUE p/r 160-250
*JSY GOLD: .75X TO 2X BLUE p/r 92-103
OVERALL AU ODDS 1:1 H, AU-GU 1:24 R
STATED PRINT RUN 25 SERIAL #'d SETS
ACTUAL CLEMENS PRINT RUN 6 COPIES
NO PRICING ON CLEMENS
KG Khalil Greene 20.00 50.00
KW Kerry Wood 20.00 50.00
NR Nolan Ryan 75.00 150.00
PM Pedro Martinez 60.00 120.00

2005 Flair Significant Signings Dual

STATED PRINT RUN 40 SERIAL #'d SETS
ACTUAL UPTON/KAZMIR QTY 33 COPIES
JSY PRINT RUN 15 SERIAL #'d SETS
NO JSY PRICING DUE TO SCARCITY
PATCH PRINT RUN 5 SERIAL #'d SETS
NO PATCH PRICING DUE TO SCARCITY
OVERALL AU ODDS 1:1 HOBBY
BR A.Beltre 10.00 25.00
J.Reed
CF S.Carlton/G.Floyd 20.00 50.00
FM L.Ford/J.Morneau 8.00 20.00
MH V.Martinez/T.Hafner 20.00 50.00
SR M.Schmidt/C.Ripken 150.00 250.00
UK B.Upton/S.Kazmir/33 UER 20.00 50.00

2003 Flair Greats

COMP.SET w/o SP's (95) 15.00 40.00
COMMON CARD (1-95) .40 1.00
COMMON CARD (96-133) 1.50 4.00
96-133 ODDS FOUR PER HOME TEAM BOX
1 Ozzie Smith 1.25 3.00
2 Red Schoendienst .60 1.50
3 Harmon Killebrew 1.00 2.50
4 Ralph Kiner .60 1.50
5 Johnny Bench 1.00 2.50
6 Al Kaline .60 1.50
7 Bobby Doerr .60 1.50
8 Cal Ripken 3.00 8.00
9 Enos Slaughter .60 1.50
10 Phil Rizzuto .60 1.50
11 Luis Aparicio .60 1.50
12 Pee Wee Reese .60 1.50
13 Richie Ashburn .60 1.50
14 Ernie Banks 1.00 2.50
15 Earl Weaver .60 1.50
16 Whitey Ford .60 1.50
17 Brooks Robinson .60 1.50
18 Lou Boudreau .60 1.50
19 Robin Yount 1.00 2.50
20 Mike Schmidt 1.50 4.00
21 Bob Lemon .60 1.50
22 Stan Musial 1.50 4.00
23 Joe Morgan .60 1.50
24 Early Wynn .60 1.50
25 Willie Stargell .60 1.50
26 Yogi Berra 1.00 2.50
27 Juan Marichal .60 1.50
28 Rick Ferrell .40 1.00
29 Rod Carew .60 1.50
30 Jim Bunning .60 1.50
31 Ferguson Jenkins .60 1.50
32 Steve Carlton .60 1.50
33 Larry Doby .60 1.50
34 Nolan Ryan 3.00 8.00
35 Phil Niekro .60 1.50
36 Billy Williams .60 1.50
37 Hal Newhouser .60 1.50
38 Bob Feller .60 1.50
39 Lou Brock .60 1.50
40 Monte Irvin .60 1.50
41 Eddie Mathews 1.00 2.50
42 Rollie Fingers .60 1.50
43 Gaylord Perry .60 1.50
44 Reggie Jackson .60 1.50
45 Bob Gibson .60 1.50
46 Robin Roberts .60 1.50
47 Tom Seaver .60 1.50
48 Willie McCovey .60 1.50
49 Hoyt Wilhelm .60 1.50
50 George Kell .60 1.50
51 Warren Spahn .60 1.50
52 Catfish Hunter .60 1.50
53 Dom DiMaggio .40 1.00
54 Joe Medwick .40 1.00
55 Johnny Pesky .40 1.00
56 Steve Garvey .40 1.00
57 Harry Heilmann .60 1.50
58 Dave Winfield .60 1.50
59 Andre Dawson .60 1.50
60 Jimmie Foxx 1.00 2.50
61 Buddy Bell .40 1.00
62 Gabby Hartnett .40 1.00
63 Babe Ruth 2.50 6.00
64 Dizzy Dean .60 1.50
65 Hank Greenberg 1.00 2.50
66 Don Drysdale .60 1.50
67 Gary Carter .60 1.50
68 Wade Boggs .60 1.50
69 Tony Perez .60 1.50
70 Mickey Cochrane .60 1.50
71 Bill Dickey .40 1.00
72 George Brett 2.00 5.00
73 Honus Wagner 1.00 2.50
74 George Sisler .60 1.50
75 Walter Johnson 1.00 2.50
76 Ron Santo .60 1.50
77 Roy Campanella 1.00 2.50
78 Roger Maris 1.00 2.50
79 Kirby Puckett 1.00 2.50
80 Alan Trammell .60 1.50
81 Don Mattingly 2.00 5.00
82 Ty Cobb 1.50 4.00
83 Lou Gehrig 2.00 5.00
84 Jackie Robinson 1.00 2.50
85 Billy Martin .60 1.50
86 Paul Molitor 1.00 2.50
87 Duke Snider .60 1.50
88 Thurman Munson 1.00 2.50
89 Luke Appling .60 1.50
90 Ernie Lombardi .40 1.00
91 Rube Waddell .40 1.00
92 Travis Jackson .40 1.00
93 Joe Sewell .60 1.50
94 King Kelly .40 1.00
95 Heinie Manush .40 1.00
96 Bobby Doerr HT 2.50 6.00
97 Johnny Pesky HT 1.50 4.00
98 Wade Boggs HT 2.50 6.00
99 Tony Conigliaro HT 1.50 4.00
100 Carlton Fisk HT 2.50 6.00
101 Rico Petrocelli HT 1.50 4.00
102 Jim Rice HT 2.50 6.00
103 Al Lopez HT 1.50 4.00
104 Pee Wee Reese HT 2.50 6.00
105 Tommy Lasorda HT 2.50 6.00
106 Gil Hodges HT 2.50 6.00
107 Jackie Robinson HT 4.00 10.00
108 Duke Snider HT 2.50 6.00
109 Don Drysdale HT 2.50 6.00
110 Steve Garvey HT 1.50 4.00
111 Hoyt Wilhelm HT 2.50 6.00
112 Juan Marichal HT 2.50 6.00
113 Monte Irvin HT 2.50 6.00
114 Willie McCovey HT 2.50 6.00
115 Travis Jackson HT 1.50 4.00
116 Bobby Bonds HT 1.50 4.00
117 Orlando Cepeda HT 2.50 6.00
118 Whitey Ford HT 2.50 6.00
119 Phil Rizzuto HT 2.50 6.00
120 Reggie Jackson HT 2.50 6.00
121 Yogi Berra HT 4.00 10.00
122 Roger Maris HT 4.00 10.00
123 Don Mattingly HT 8.00 20.00
124 Babe Ruth HT 10.00 25.00
125 Dave Winfield HT 2.50 6.00
126 Bob Gibson HT 2.50 6.00
127 Enos Slaughter HT 2.50 6.00
128 Joe Medwick HT 1.50 4.00
129 Lou Brock HT 2.50 6.00
130 Ozzie Smith HT 5.00 12.00
131 Stan Musial HT 6.00 15.00
132 Steve Carlton HT 2.50 6.00
133 Dizzy Dean HT 2.50 6.00
P6 Al Kaline Sample 2.50 6.00
NNO Checklist .40 1.00

2003 Flair Greats Ballpark Heroes

COMPLETE SET (9) 10.00 25.00
STATED ODDS 1:10
1 Nolan Ryan 3.00 8.00
2 Babe Ruth 2.50 6.00
3 Honus Wagner 1.00 2.50
4 Ty Cobb 1.50 4.00
5 Ernie Banks 1.00 2.50
6 Mike Schmidt 1.50 4.00
7 Duke Snider .60 1.50
8 Cal Ripken 3.00 8.00
9 Stan Musial 1.50 4.00

2003 Flair Greats Bat Rack Classics Quads

RANDOM INSERTS IN PACKS
STATED PRINT RUN 150 SERIAL #'d SETS
1 Mattin/Morg/Ripken/B.Rob 20.00 50.00
2 Murray/Math/Reggie/McCov 20.00 50.00
3 Perez/Mattin/G'berg/Starg 40.00 80.00

4 Ryno/Santo/B.Will/Dawson 15.00 40.00
5 Winf/Ripken/Molitor/Yount 12.50 30.00

2003 Flair Greats Bat Rack Classics Trios
RANDOM INSERTS IN PACKS
STATED PRINT RUN 300 SERIAL #'d SETS
1 Agee/Grote/Harrelson 10.00 25.00
2 Bench/Morgan/Perez 15.00 40.00
3 Greenberg/Heilman/Kell 20.00 50.00
4 Reggie/Mattingly/Winfield 20.00 50.00
5 Mathews/Molitor/Yount 12.00 30.00
6 Murray/Ripken/B.Rob 15.00 40.00
7 D.Parker/W.Stargell 10.00 25.00
8 Ryno/Santo/B.Williams 12.50 30.00

2003 Flair Greats Classic Numbers
STATED ODDS 1:20
1 Jackie Robinson 1.00 2.50
2 Willie McCovey .60 1.50
3 Brooks Robinson .60 1.50
4 Reggie Jackson .60 1.50
5 Ozzie Smith 1.25 3.00
6 Johnny Bench 1.00 2.50
7 Yogi Berra 1.00 2.50
8 Cal Ripken 3.00 8.00
9 George Brett 2.00 5.00
10 Thurman Munson 1.00 2.50
11 Joe Morgan .60 1.50
12 Nolan Ryan 3.00 8.00
13 Steve Carlton .60 1.50

2003 Flair Greats Classic Numbers Game Used
STATED ODDS 1:24 HOBBY, 1:27 HOME TEAM
SP PRINT RUNS PROVIDED BY FLEER
SP'S ARE NOT SERIAL-NUMBERED
PATCH RANDOM INSERTS IN PACKS
PATCH PRINT RUN 25 SERIAL #'d SETS
NO PATCH PRICING DUE TO SCARCITY
1 Johnny Bench Jsy 8.00 20.00
2 Yogi Berra Pants SP/75 10.00 25.00
3 George Brett Jsy 6.00 15.00
4 Steve Carlton Jsy 8.00 20.00
5 Willie McCovey Jsy SP/125 6.00 15.00
6 Joe Morgan Pants SP/200 6.00 15.00
7 Thurman Munson Pants 12.50 30.00
8 Cal Ripken Jsy 12.50 30.00
9 Nolan Ryan Jsy 10.00 25.00
10 Ryne Sandberg Jsy 10.00 25.00
11 Ozzie Smith Jsy 8.00 20.00

2003 Flair Greats Classic Numbers Game Used Dual
RANDOM INSERTS IN PACKS
STATED PRINT RUN 250 SERIAL #'d SETS
1 Bench Jsy/Munson Pants 15.00 40.00
2 Berra Pants/Munson Pants 15.00 40.00
3 Berra Pants/Ripken Jsy 30.00 60.00
4 Brett Jsy/Ryan Jsy 12.00 30.00
5 McCovey Jsy/Bench Jsy 10.00 25.00
6 Morgan Pants/Sandberg Jsy 10.00 25.00
7 Ripken Pants/Ozzie Jsy 8.00 20.00
8 Ryan Jsy/Carlton Jsy 12.00 30.00

2003 Flair Greats Cut of History Autographs
RANDOM INSERTS IN PACKS
STATED PRINT RUNS LISTED BELOW
1 Johnny Bench/161 50.00 120.00
2 Steve Carlton/506 10.00 25.00
3 Dom DiMaggio/402 20.00 50.00
4 Tony Kubek/161 20.00 50.00
5 Cal Ripken/155 40.00 100.00
6 Alan Trammell/211 10.00 25.00

2003 Flair Greats Cut of History Game Used
STATED ODDS 1:10
SP PRINT RUNS PROVIDED BY FLEER
SP'S ARE NOT SERIAL-NUMBERED
1 Luis Aparicio Jsy 3.00 8.00
2 Frank Baker Bat SP/50* 20.00 50.00
3 Buddy Bell Bat 3.00 8.00
4 Wade Boggs Jsy SP/250* 8.00 20.00
5 Steve Carlton Pants 3.00 8.00
6 Gary Carter Jsy 5.00 12.00
7 Dennis Eckersley Jsy 3.00 8.00
8 Hank Greenberg Bat SP/100* 10.00 25.00
9 Catfish Hunter Jsy SP/200* 8.00 20.00
10 Reggie Jackson Bat 4.00 10.00
11 Ferguson Jenkins Pants 3.00 8.00
12 Roger Maris Jsy SP/250* 12.50 30.00
13 Billy Martin Pants 4.00 10.00
14 Willie McCovey Pants 3.00 8.00
15 Joe Medwick Bat 8.00 20.00
16 Eddie Murray Jsy 4.00 10.00
17 Graig Nettles Bat 3.00 8.00
18 Phil Niekro Pants 3.00 8.00
19 Paul O'Neill Jsy 4.00 10.00
20 Jim Palmer Pants 3.00 8.00
21 Kirby Puckett Bat 4.00 10.00
22 Cal Ripken Pants 10.00 25.00
23 Tom Seaver Pants 4.00 10.00
24A Alan Trammell Bat 3.00 8.00
24B Alan Trammell Jsy 3.00 8.00
25 Hoyt Wilhelm Jsy 3.00 8.00
26 Early Wynn Jsy 3.00 8.00

2003 Flair Greats Cut of History Game Used Gold
*GOLD: .75X TO 2X BASIC
*GOLD: .5X TO 1.2X BASIC SP'S
RANDOM INSERTS IN PACKS
STATED PRINT RUN 100 SERIAL #'d SETS

2003 Flair Greats of the Grain
RANDOM INSERTS IN PACKS
STATED PRINT RUN 50 SERIAL #'d SETS
CARD DO NOT FEATURE GAME-USED WOOD
1 George Brett 20.00 50.00
2 Ty Cobb 15.00 40.00
3 Lou Gehrig 20.00 50.00
4 Eddie Mathews 10.00 25.00
5 Don Mattingly 20.00 50.00
6 Stan Musial 15.00 40.00
7 Cal Ripken 30.00 80.00
8 Babe Ruth 25.00 60.00
9 Mike Schmidt 15.00 40.00

2003 Flair Greats Hall of Fame Postmark
RANDOM INSERTS IN PACKS
STATED PRINT RUNS LISTED BELOW
1 Ozzie Smith/2002 8.00 20.00
2 Ozzie Smith AU/202 50.00 100.00

2003 Flair Greats Home Team Cuts Game Used
SINGLE-DUAL ODDS 1:20 HOME TEAM
SP PRINT RUNS PROVIDED BY FLEER
SP'S ARE NOT SERIAL-NUMBERED
1 Wade Boggs Jsy SP/250 8.00 20.00
2 Bobby Bonds Bat 4.00 10.00
3 Carlton Fisk Jsy 6.00 15.00
4 Steve Garvey Jsy 4.00 10.00
5 Reggie Jackson Bat 6.00 15.00
6 Tom Lasorda Jsy SP/150 6.00 15.00
7 Juan Marichal Pants 4.00 10.00
8 Roger Maris Jsy SP/150 15.00 40.00
9 Billy Martin Pants 6.00 15.00
10 W.McCovey Pants SP/200 6.00 15.00
11 Joe Medwick Bat SP/250 10.00 25.00
12 P.Reese Pants SP/75 8.00 20.00
13 Jim Rice Bat 4.00 10.00
14 R.Schoen Pants SP/200 6.00 15.00
15 Ozzie Smith Bat 8.00 20.00
16 Duke Snider Pants 6.00 15.00
17 Dave Winfield Bat 4.00 10.00

2003 Flair Greats Home Team Cuts Game Used Dual
SINGLE-DUAL ODDS 1:20 HOME TEAM
STATED PRINT RUNS LISTED BELOW
CARDS ARE NOT SERIAL-NUMBERED
PRINT RUNS PROVIDED BY FLEER
1 Bonds Bat/McCov Pants/100 15.00 40.00
2 Fisk Jsy/Rice Bat/100 12.50 30.00
3 Martin Pants/Reggie Bat/175 12.50 30.00
4 Reese Pants/Snider Pants/100 12.50 30.00
5 Schoen Pants/Medw Bat/125 10.00 25.00

2003 Flair Greats Sweet Swatch Classic Bat
STATED PRINT RUNS LISTED BELOW
1 Johnny Bench/175 10.00 25.00
2 George Brett/320 15.00 40.00
3 Jose Canseco/175 10.00 25.00
4 Orlando Cepeda/165 8.00 20.00
5 Andre Dawson/310 6.00 15.00
6 Reggie Jackson/155 10.00 25.00
7 Eddie Mathews/185 10.00 25.00
8 Don Mattingly/340 15.00 40.00
9 Willie McCovey/155 8.00 20.00
10 Kirby Puckett/165 10.00 25.00
11 Pee Wee Reese/165 10.00 25.00
12 Cal Ripken/305 12.00 30.00

2003 Flair Greats Sweet Swatch Classic Bat Image
STATED PRINT RUNS LISTED BELOW
1 Johnny Bench/36 40.00 80.00
2 Tony Kubek/35 30.00 60.00
3 Cal Ripken/42 75.00 150.00
4 Alan Trammell/44 30.00 60.00

2003 Flair Greats Sweet Swatch Classic Bat Image Autographs
RANDOM INSERTS IN JUMBO PACKS
STATED PRINT RUN 40 SERIAL #'d SETS
1 Johnny Bench 60.00 150.00
2 Tony Kubek 50.00 100.00
3 Cal Ripken 150.00 250.00
4 Alan Trammell 40.00 80.00

2003 Flair Greats Sweet Swatch Classic Jersey
STATED PRINT RUNS LISTED BELOW
1 Johnny Bench Jsy/410 8.00 20.00
2 George Brett Jsy/384 30.00 60.00
3 Jose Canseco Jsy/1329 6.00 15.00
4 Jerry Coleman Jsy/528 8.00 20.00
5 Andre Dawson Jsy/335 8.00 20.00
6 Carlton Fisk Jsy/1200 6.00 15.00
7 Gil Hodges Jsy/545 8.00 20.00
8 Juan Marichal Jsy/385 8.00 20.00
9 Don Mattingly Jsy/880 10.00 25.00
10 Paul Molitor Jsy/592 8.00 20.00
11 Jim Palmer Jsy/335 8.00 20.00
12 Kirby Puckett Jsy/445 8.00 20.00
13 Cal Ripken Jsy/557 15.00 40.00
14 Nolan Ryan Jsy/590 10.00 25.00
15 Ryne Sandberg Jsy/374 12.50 30.00
17 Robin Yount Jsy/340 8.00 20.00
19 Tom Seaver Jsy/385 6.00 15.00

2003 Flair Greats Sweet Swatch Classic Patch
STATED PRINT RUNS LISTED BELOW
PATCH MASTERPIECE PRINT RUN 1 #'d SET
NO PATCH MP PRICING DUE TO SCARCITY
1 Johnny Bench/59 40.00 80.00
2 George Brett/53 75.00 150.00
3 Jose Canseco/177 30.00 60.00
4 Jerry Coleman/37 20.00 50.00
5 Andre Dawson/58 20.00 50.00
6 Carlton Fisk/51 40.00 80.00
7 Juan Marichal/48 20.00 50.00
8 Don Mattingly/106 60.00 120.00
9 Paul Molitor/96 30.00 60.00
10 Jim Palmer/63 30.00 60.00
11 Kirby Puckett/72 40.00 80.00
12 Cal Ripken/69 75.00 150.00
13 Nolan Ryan/60 30.00 60.00
14 Ryne Sandberg/40 75.00 150.00
15 Tom Seaver/66 30.00 60.00
16 Robin Yount/66 40.00 80.00

1997 Flair Showcase Rodriguez Sample Strip
NNO Alex Rodriguez Promo Strip

1997 Flair Showcase Row 2
The 1997 Flair Showcase set (produced by Fleer) was issued in one series totalling 540 cards and was distributed in five-card packs with a suggested retail price of $4.99. Three groups of 60 cards were inserted at different rates: Cards numbered from one through 60 were inserted 1.5 cards per pack, cards numbered from 61 through 120 were inserted one every 1.5 packs and cards numbered from 61 through 120 were inserted at a rate of one per pack. This hobby exclusive set is divided into three 180-card sets (Row 2/Style, Row 1/Grace, and Row 0/Showcase) and features holographic foil fronts with an action photo of the player silhouetted over a larger black-and-white head-shot image in the background. The thick card stock is laminated with a shiny glossy coating for a super-premium "feel." Also inserted one in every pack was a Million Dollar Moments card. Rookie Cards include Brian Giles. Finally, 25 serial-numbered Alex Rodriguez Emerald Exchange cards (good for a signed Rodriguez glove) were randomly seeded into packs. The card fronts were very similar in design to the regular Row 2 Rodriguez, except for green foil accents. The card back, however, consisted entirely of text explaining prize guidelines. The deadline to exchange the card was 8/1/98.

COMPLETE SET (180) 30.00 80.00
COMMON CARD (1-60) .20 .50
ROW 2 1-60 ODDS 1.5:1
COMMON CARD (61-120) .30 .75
ROW 2 61-120 ODDS 1:1.5
COMMON CARD (121-180) .25 .60
ROW 2 121-180 STATED ODDS 1:1
A.ROD GLOVE EXCH RANDOM IN PACKS
A.ROD GLOVE EXCH.DEADLINE: 8/1/98
1 Andruw Jones .30 .75
2 Derek Jeter 1.25 3.00
3 Alex Rodriguez .75 2.00
4 Paul Molitor .20 .50
5 Jeff Bagwell .30 .75
6 Scott Rolen .30 .75
7 Kenny Lofton .20 .50
8 Cal Ripken 1.50 4.00
9 Brady Anderson .20 .50
10 Chipper Jones .50 1.25
11 Todd Greene .20 .50
12 Todd Walker .20 .50
13 Billy Wagner .20 .50
14 Craig Biggio .30 .75
15 Kevin Orie .20 .50
16 Hideo Nomo .50 1.25
17 Kevin Appier .20 .50
18 Bubba Trammell RC .20 .50
19 Juan Gonzalez .20 .50
20 Randy Johnson .50 1.25
21 Roger Clemens 1.00 2.50
22 Johnny Damon .30 .75
23 Ryne Sandberg .75 2.00
24 Ken Griffey Jr. 1.00 2.50
25 Barry Bonds 1.25 3.00
26 Nomar Garciaparra .75 2.00
27 Vladimir Guerrero .50 1.25
28 Ron Gant .20 .50
29 Joe Carter .20 .50
30 Tim Salmon .30 .75
31 Mike Piazza .75 2.00
32 Barry Larkin .30 .75
33 Manny Ramirez .30 .75
34 Sammy Sosa .50 1.25
35 Frank Thomas .50 1.25
36 Melvin Nieves .20 .50
37 Tony Gwynn .60 1.50
38 Gary Sheffield .20 .50
39 Darin Erstad .20 .50
40 Ken Caminiti .20 .50
41 Jermaine Dye .20 .50
42 Mo Vaughn .20 .50
43 Raul Mondesi .20 .50
44 Greg Maddux .75 2.00
45 Chuck Knoblauch .20 .50
46 Andy Pettitte .30 .75
47 Deion Sanders .30 .75
48 Albert Belle .20 .50
49 Jamey Wright .20 .50
50 Rey Ordonez .20 .50
51 Bernie Williams .30 .75
52 Mark McGwire 1.25 3.00
53 Mike Mussina .30 .75
54 Bob Abreu .30 .75
55 Reggie Sanders .20 .50
56 Brian Jordan .20 .50
57 Ivan Rodriguez .30 .75
58 Roberto Alomar .30 .75
59 Tim Naehring .20 .50
60 Edgar Renteria .20 .50
61 Dean Palmer .30 .75
62 Benito Santiago .30 .75
63 David Cone .30 .75
64 Carlos Delgado .30 .75
65 Brian Giles RC .75 2.00
66 Alex Ochoa .30 .75
67 Rondell White .30 .75
68 Robin Ventura .30 .75
69 Eric Karros .30 .75
70 Jose Valentin .30 .75
71 Rafael Palmeiro .50 1.25
72 Chris Snopek .30 .75
73 David Justice .30 .75
74 Tom Glavine .50 1.25
75 Rudy Pemberton .30 .75
76 Larry Walker .30 .75
77 Jim Thome .50 1.25
78 Charles Johnson .30 .75
79 Dante Powell .30 .75
80 Derrek Lee .50 1.25
81 Jason Kendall .30 .75
82 Todd Hollandsworth .30 .75
83 Bernard Gilkey .30 .75
84 Mel Rojas .30 .75
85 Dmitri Young .30 .75
86 Bret Boone .30 .75
87 Pat Hentgen .30 .75
88 Bobby Bonilla .30 .75
89 John Wetteland .30 .75
90 Todd Hundley .30 .75
91 Wilton Guerrero .30 .75
92 Geronimo Berroa .30 .75
93 Al Martin .30 .75
94 Danny Tartabull .30 .75
95 Brian McRae .30 .75
96 Steve Finley .30 .75
97 Todd Stottlemyre .30 .75
98 John Smoltz .50 1.25
99 Matt Williams .30 .75
100 Eddie Murray .75 2.00
101 Henry Rodriguez .30 .75
102 Marty Cordova .30 .75
103 Juan Guzman .30 .75
104 Chili Davis .30 .75
105 Eric Young .30 .75
106 Jeff Abbott .30 .75
107 Shannon Stewart .30 .75
108 Rocky Coppinger .30 .75
109 Jose Canseco .50 1.25
110 Dante Bichette .30 .75
111 Dwight Gooden .30 .75
112 Scott Brosius .30 .75
113 Steve Avery .30 .75
114 Andres Galarraga .30 .75
115 Sandy Alomar Jr. .30 .75
116 Ray Lankford .30 .75
117 Jorge Posada .50 1.25
118 Ryan Klesko .30 .75
119 Jay Buhner .30 .75
120 Jose Guillen .30 .75
121 Paul O'Neill .40 1.00
122 Jimmy Key .25 .60
123 Hal Morris .25 .60
124 Travis Fryman .25 .60
125 Jim Edmonds .25 .60
126 Jeff Cirillo .25 .60
127 Fred McGriff .40 1.00
128 Alan Benes .25 .60
129 Derek Bell .25 .60
130 Tony Graffanino .25 .60
131 Shawn Green .25 .60
132 Denny Neagle UER .25 .60
Debut in '91 not '92
133 Alex Fernandez .25 .60
134 Mickey Morandini .25 .60
135 Royce Clayton .25 .60
136 Jose Mesa .25 .60
137 Edgar Martinez .40 1.00
138 Curt Schilling .25 .60
139 Lance Johnson .25 .60
140 Andy Benes .25 .60
141 Charles Nagy .25 .60
142 Mariano Rivera .60 1.50
143 Mark Wohlers .25 .60
144 Ken Hill .25 .60
145 Jay Bell .25 .60
146 Bob Higginson .25 .60
147 Mark Grudzielanek .25 .60
148 Ray Durham .25 .60
149 John Olerud .25 .60
150 Joey Hamilton .25 .60
151 Trevor Hoffman .25 .60
152 Dan Wilson .25 .60
153 J.T. Snow .25 .60
154 Marquis Grissom .25 .60
155 Yamil Benitez .25 .60
156 Rusty Greer .25 .60
157 Darryl Kile .25 .60
158 Ismael Valdes .25 .60
159 Jeff Conine .25 .60
160 Darren Daulton .25 .60
161 Chan Ho Park .25 .60
162 Troy Percival .25 .60
163 Wade Boggs .40 1.00
164 Dave Nilsson .25 .60
165 Vinny Castilla .25 .60
166 Kevin Brown .25 .60
167 Dennis Eckersley .25 .60
168 Wendell Magee Jr. .25 .60
169 John Jaha .25 .60
170 Garret Anderson .25 .60
171 Jason Giambi .25 .60
172 Mark Grace .40 1.00
173 Tony Clark .25 .60
174 Moises Alou .25 .60
175 Brett Butler .25 .60
176 Cecil Fielder .25 .60
177 Chris Widger .25 .60
178 Doug Drabek .25 .60
179 Ellis Burks .25 .60
180 Shigetoshi Hasegawa RC .40 1.00
NNO A.Rod. Glove/25 .75 2.00

1997 Flair Showcase Row 1
*STARS 1-60: .75X TO 2X ROW 2
ROW 1 1-60 ODDS 1:2.5
*STARS 61-120: .4X TO 1X ROW 2
*ROOKIES 61-120: .5X TO 1.25X ROW 2
ROW 1 61-120 ODDS 1:2
*ROOKIES 61-120: .5X TO 1.25X ROW 2
ROW 1 121-180 ODDS 1:3

1997 Flair Showcase Row 0
*STARS 1-60: 4X TO 10X ROW 2
ROW 0 1-60 ODDS 1:24
*STARS 61-120: 1.25X TO 3X ROW 2
*ROOKIES 61-120: 1.5X TO 4X ROW 2
ROW 0 61-120 ODDS 1:12
*STARS 121-180: 1X TO 2.5X ROW 2
ROW 0 121-180 ODDS 1:5

1997 Flair Showcase Legacy Collection Row 2
*LC ROW 2 1-60: 25X TO 60X BASIC
*LC ROW 2 61-120: 15X TO 40X BASIC
*LC ROW 2 RC'S 61-120: 12.5X TO 30X BASIC
*LC ROW 2 121-180: 20X TO 50X BASIC
STATED ODDS 1:30
STATED PRINT RUN 100 SERIAL #'d SETS
24 Ken Griffey Jr. 125.00 300.00

1997 Flair Showcase Legacy Collection Row 1
*LC ROW 1 1-60: 25X TO 60X BASIC
*LC ROW 1 61-120: 15X TO 40X BASIC
*LC ROW 1 RC'S 61-120: 12.5X TO 30X BASIC
*LC ROW 1 121-180: 20X TO 50X BASIC
STATED ODDS 1:30
STATED PRINT RUN 100 SERIAL #'d SETS
24 Ken Griffey Jr. 125.00 300.00

1997 Flair Showcase Legacy Collection Row 0
*LC ROW 0 1-60: 30X TO 80X BASIC
*LC ROW 0 61-120: 20X TO 50X BASIC
*LC ROW 0 RC'S 61-120: 15X TO 40X BASIC
*LC ROW 0 121-180: 25X TO 60X BASIC
STATED ODDS 1:30
STATED PRINT RUN 100 SERIAL #'d SETS
24 Ken Griffey Jr. 125.00 300.00

1997 Flair Showcase Diamond Cuts
COMPLETE SET (20) 30.00 60.00
STATED ODDS 1:20
1 Jeff Bagwell 1.50 4.00
2 Albert Belle 1.00 2.50
3 Ken Caminiti 1.00 2.50
4 Juan Gonzalez 1.00 2.50
5 Ken Griffey Jr. 20.00 50.00
6 Tony Gwynn 2.50 6.00
7 Todd Hundley 1.00 2.50
8 Andruw Jones 1.00 2.50
9 Chipper Jones 2.50 6.00
10 Greg Maddux 4.00 10.00
11 Mark McGwire 4.00 10.00
12 Mike Piazza 2.50 6.00
13 Derek Jeter 12.00 30.00
14 Manny Ramirez 1.50 4.00
15 Cal Ripken 8.00 20.00
16 Alex Rodriguez 3.00 8.00
17 Frank Thomas 2.50 6.00
18 Mo Vaughn 1.00 2.50
19 Bernie Williams 1.50 4.00
20 Matt Williams 1.00 2.50

1997 Flair Showcase Hot Gloves
STATED ODDS 1:90
1 Roberto Alomar 3.00 8.00
2 Barry Bonds 8.00 20.00
3 Juan Gonzalez 2.00 5.00
4 Ken Griffey Jr. 60.00 150.00
5 Marquis Grissom 2.00 5.00
6 Derek Jeter 20.00 50.00
7 Chipper Jones 5.00 12.00
8 Barry Larkin 3.00 8.00
9 Kenny Lofton 2.00 5.00
10 Greg Maddux 8.00 20.00
11 Mike Piazza 5.00 12.00
12 Cal Ripken 12.00 30.00
13 Alex Rodriguez 6.00 15.00
14 Ivan Rodriguez 3.00 8.00
15 Frank Thomas 12.00 30.00

1997 Flair Showcase Wave of the Future
COMPLETE SET (27) 15.00 40.00
COMMON RC YR .40 1.00
STATED ODDS 1:4
1 Todd Greene .40 1.00
2 Andruw Jones .75 2.00
3 Randall Simon .60 1.50
4 Wady Almonte .40 1.00
5 Pat Cline .40 1.00
6 Jeff Abbott .40 1.00
7 Justin Towle .40 1.00
8 Richie Sexson .60 1.50
9 Bubba Trammell .60 1.50
10 Bob Abreu .75 2.00
11 David Arias-Ortiz 8.00 20.00
12 Todd Walker .40 1.00
13 Orlando Cabrera 1.50 4.00
14 Vladimir Guerrero 1.25 3.00
15 Ricky Ledee .60 1.50
16 Jorge Posada .75 2.00
17 Ruben Rivera .40 1.00
18 Scott Spiezio .40 1.00
19 Scott Rolen .75 2.00
20 Emil Brown .40 1.00
21 Jose Guillen .60 1.50
22 T.J. Staton .40 1.00
23 Eli Marrero .40 1.00
24 Fernando Tatis .40 1.00
25 Ryan Jones .40 1.00
WF1 Hideki Irabu .60 1.50
WF2 Jose Cruz Jr. .60 1.50

1998 Flair Showcase Ripken Sample Strip
NNO Cal Ripken Promo Strip 1.25 3.00

1998 Flair Showcase Row 3
This set (produced by Fleer) was issued in five card packs which retailed for $4.99 per pack and were released in July, 1998. Each player was featured in four rows with Row 3 being the easiest to obtain from opening packs. This 120 card set features two photos of the player on the front. The Row 3 cards were inserted in different ratios depending on which numbers they are. The complete odds are listed below for each group of 30 cards. Cards numbered 1-30 were seeded one every 9/10th of a pack; cards numbered 31-60 were seeded one every 1.1 packs; cards numbered 61-90 were seeded one every 1.5 packs and cards 91-120 were seeded one every two packs. Rookie Cards include Magglio Ordonez.

COMPLETE SET (120) 25.00 60.00
COMMON CARD (1-30) .20 .50
ROW 3 1-30 STATED ODDS 1:0.9
COMMON CARD (31-60) .20 .50
ROW 3 31-60 STATED ODDS 1:1.1
COMMON CARD (61-90) .25 .60
ROW 3 61-90 STATED ODDS 1:1.5
COMMON CARD (91-120) .30 .75
ROW 3 91-120 STATED ODDS 1:2
1 Ken Griffey Jr. 1.00 2.50
2 Travis Lee .20 .50
3 Frank Thomas .50 1.25
4 Ben Grieve .20 .50
5 Nomar Garciaparra .75 2.00
6 Jose Cruz Jr. .20 .50
7 Alex Rodriguez .75 2.00
8 Cal Ripken 1.50 4.00
9 Mark McGwire 1.25 3.00
10 Chipper Jones .50 1.25
11 Paul Konerko .20 .50
12 Todd Helton .30 .75
13 Greg Maddux .75 2.00
14 Derek Jeter 1.25 3.00
15 Jaret Wright .20 .50
16 Livan Hernandez .20 .50
17 Mike Piazza .75 2.00
18 Juan Encarnacion .20 .50
19 Tony Gwynn .60 1.50
20 Scott Rolen .30 .75
21 Roger Clemens 1.00 2.50
22 Tony Clark .20 .50
23 Albert Belle .20 .50
24 Mo Vaughn .20 .50
25 Andruw Jones .30 .75
26 Jason Dickson .20 .50
27 Fernando Tatis .20 .50
28 Ivan Rodriguez .30 .75
29 Ricky Ledee .20 .50
30 Darin Erstad .20 .50
31 Brian Rose .20 .50
32 Magglio Ordonez RC 2.50 6.00
33 Larry Walker .20 .50
34 Bobby Higginson .20 .50
35 Chili Davis .20 .50
36 Barry Bonds 1.25 3.00
37 Vladimir Guerrero .50 1.25
38 Jeff Bagwell .30 .75
39 Kenny Lofton .20 .50
40 Ryan Klesko .20 .50
41 Mike Cameron .20 .50
42 Charles Johnson .20 .50
43 Andy Pettitte .30 .75
44 Juan Gonzalez .20 .50
45 Tim Salmon .30 .75
46 Hideki Irabu .20 .50
47 Paul Molitor .20 .50
48 Edgar Renteria .20 .50
49 Manny Ramirez .30 .75
50 Jim Edmonds .20 .50
51 Bernie Williams .30 .75
52 Roberto Alomar .30 .75
53 David Justice .20 .50
54 Rey Ordonez .20 .50
55 Ken Caminiti .20 .50
56 Jose Guillen .20 .50
57 Randy Johnson .50 1.25
58 Brady Anderson .20 .50
59 Hideo Nomo .50 1.25
60 Tino Martinez .30 .75
61 John Smoltz .40 1.00
62 Joe Carter .25 .60
63 Matt Williams .25 .60
64 Robin Ventura .25 .60
65 Barry Larkin .40 1.00
66 Dante Bichette .25 .60
67 Travis Fryman .25 .60
68 Gary Sheffield .25 .60
69 Eric Karros .25 .60
70 Matt Stairs .25 .60
71 Al Martin .25 .60
72 Jay Buhner .25 .60
73 Ray Lankford .25 .60
74 Carlos Delgado .25 .60
75 Edgardo Alfonzo .25 .60
76 Rondell White .25 .60
77 Chuck Knoblauch .25 .60
78 Raul Mondesi .25 .60
79 Johnny Damon .40 1.00
80 Matt Morris .25 .60
81 Tom Glavine .40 1.00
82 Kevin Brown .40 1.00
83 Garret Anderson .25 .60
84 Mike Mussina .40 1.00
85 Pedro Martinez .40 1.00
86 Craig Biggio .40 1.00
87 Darryl Kile .25 .60
88 Rafael Palmeiro .40 1.00
89 Jim Thome .40 1.00
90 Andres Galarraga .25 .60
91 Sammy Sosa .50 1.25
92 Willie Greene .30 .75
93 Vinny Castilla .30 .75
94 Justin Thompson .30 .75
95 Jeff King .30 .75
96 Jeff Cirillo .30 .75
97 Mark Grudzielanek .30 .75
98 Brad Radke .30 .75
99 John Olerud .30 .75
100 Curt Schilling .30 .75
101 Steve Finley .30 .75
102 J.T. Snow .30 .75
103 Edgar Martinez .50 1.25
104 Wilson Alvarez .30 .75
105 Rusty Greer .30 .75
106 Pat Hentgen .30 .75
107 David Cone .30 .75
108 Fred McGriff .50 1.25
109 Jason Giambi .30 .75
110 Tony Womack .30 .75
111 Bernard Gilkey .30 .75
112 Alan Benes .30 .75
113 Mark Grace .50 1.25
114 Reggie Sanders .30 .75
115 Moises Alou .30 .75
116 John Jaha .30 .75
117 Henry Rodriguez .30 .75
118 Dean Palmer .30 .75
119 Mike Lieberthal .30 .75
120 Shawn Estes .30 .75
NNO Checklist .10 .25

1998 Flair Showcase Row 2
COMPLETE SET (120) 40.00 100.00
*STARS 1-30: .5X TO 1.5X ROW 3
ROW 2 1-30 STATED ODDS 1:3
*STARS 31-60: .5X TO 1.25X ROW 3
ROW 2 31-60 STATED ODDS 1:2.5
*STARS 61-90: .6X TO 1.5X ROW 3
ROW 2 61-90 STATED ODDS 1:4
*STARS 91-120: .5X TO 1.25X ROW 3
ROW 2 91-120 STATED ODDS 1:3.5

1998 Flair Showcase Row 1
*STARS 1-30: 2X TO 5X ROW 3
ROW 1 1-30 STATED ODDS 1:6
*STARS 31-60: 2.5X TO 6X ROW 3
*ROOKIES 31-60: 2.5X TO 6X ROW 3
ROW 1 31-60 STATED ODDS 1:24
*STARS 61-90: .75X TO 2X ROW 3
ROW 1 61-90 STATED ODDS 1:6
*STARS 91-120: 1X TO 2.5X ROW 3
ROW 1 91-120 STATED ODDS 1:10

1998 Flair Showcase Row 0
COMPLETE SET (120) 750.00 1500.00
*STARS 1-30: 6X TO 15X ROW 3
ROW 0 1-30 PRINT RUN 250 SERIAL #'d SETS
*STARS 31-60: 5X TO 12X ROW 3
*ROOKIES 31-60: 5X TO 12X ROW 3
ROW 0 31-60 PRINT RUN 500 SERIAL #'d SETS
*STARS 61-90: 3X TO 8X ROW 3
ROW 0 61-90 PR.RUN 1000 SERIAL #'d SETS
*STARS 91-120: 1.5X TO 4X ROW 3
ROW 0 91-120 PR.RUN 2000 SERIAL #'d SETS
1 Ken Griffey Jr. 100.00 250.00

1998 Flair Showcase Legacy Collection Row 3
*STARS 1-30: 12.5X TO 30X BASIC ROW 3
*STARS 31-60: 12.5X TO 30X BASIC ROW 3
*ROOKIES 31-60: 6X TO 20X BASIC ROW 3
*STARS 61-90: 10X TO 25X BASIC ROW 3
*STARS 91-120: 8X TO 20X BASIC ROW 3
RANDOM INSERTS IN PACKS
STATED PRINT RUN 100 SERIAL #'d SETS
1 Ken Griffey Jr. 125.00 300.00

1998 Flair Showcase Legacy Collection Row 2
*STARS 1-30: 12.5X TO 30X BASIC ROW 3
*STARS 31-60: 12.5X TO 30X BASIC ROW 3
*ROOKIES 31-60: 8X TO 20X BASIC ROW 2
*STARS 61-90: 10X TO 25X BASIC ROW 3
*STARS 91-120: 8X TO 20X BASIC ROW 3
RANDOM INSERTS IN PACKS
STATED PRINT RUN 100 SERIAL #'d SETS
1 Ken Griffey Jr. 125.00 300.00

1998 Flair Showcase Legacy Collection Row 1
*STARS 1-30: 12.5X TO 30X BASIC ROW 3
*STARS 31-60: 12.5X TO 30X BASIC ROW 3
*ROOKIES 31-60: 8X TO 20X BASIC ROW 1
*STARS 61-90: 10X TO 25X BASIC ROW 3
*STARS 91-120: 8X TO 20X BASIC ROW 3
RANDOM INSERTS IN PACKS
STATED PRINT RUN 100 SERIAL #'d SETS
1 Ken Griffey Jr. 125.00 300.00

1998 Flair Showcase Legacy Collection Row 0
*STARS 1-30: 12.5X TO 30X BASIC ROW 3
*STARS 31-60: 12.5X TO 30X BASIC ROW 3
*ROOKIES 31-60: 8X TO 20X BASIC ROW 3
*STARS 61-90: 10X TO 25X BASIC ROW 3
*STARS 91-120: 8X TO 20X BASIC ROW 3
RANDOM INSERTS IN PACKS
STATED PRINT RUN 100 SERIAL #'d SETS
1 Ken Griffey Jr. 125.00 300.00

1998 Flair Showcase Wave of the Future
COMPLETE SET (12) 10.00 25.00
STATED ODDS 1:20
1 Travis Lee .75 2.00
2 Todd Helton 1.25 3.00
3 Ben Grieve .75 2.00
4 Juan Encarnacion .75 2.00
5 Brad Fullmer .75 2.00
6 Ruben Rivera .75 2.00
7 Paul Konerko .75 2.00
8 Derrek Lee 1.25 3.00
9 Mike Lowell 3.00 8.00
10 Magglio Ordonez 1.50 4.00
11 Rich Butler .75 2.00
12 Eli Marrero .75 2.00

1999 Flair Showcase Samples
COMPLETE SET (3) 1.25 3.00
COMMON ROLEN (1-3) .40 1.00

1999 Flair Showcase Row 3
This 144-card set was distributed in five-card packs with a suggested retail price of $4.99 and features two color player photos on the front with full rainbow holofoil, silver foil and embossing. This base set is considered the "Power" level. The set was broken into three separate tiers of 28 card subsets as follows: Cards numbered from 1 through 48 were seeded one every .9 packs; cards numbered 49 through 96 were seeded one every 1.1 packs and cards numbered 97 through 144 were seeded one every 1.2 packs. Rookie Cards include Pat Burrell.

COMPLETE SET (144) 25.00 60.00
COMMON CARD (1-48) .20 .50
ROW 3 1-48 STATED ODDS 1:0.9
COMMON CARD (49-96) .20 .50
ROW 3 49-96 STATED ODDS 1:1
COMMON CARD (97-144) .25 .60
ROW 3 97-144 STATED ODDS 1:1.2
1 Mark McGwire 1.25 3.00
2 Sammy Sosa .50 1.25
3 Ken Griffey Jr. 1.00 2.50
4 Chipper Jones .50 1.25
5 Ben Grieve .20 .50
6 J.D. Drew .20 .50
7 Jeff Bagwell .30 .75
8 Cal Ripken 1.50 4.00
9 Tony Gwynn .60 1.50
10 Nomar Garciaparra .75 2.00
11 Travis Lee .20 .50
12 Troy Glaus .30 .75
13 Mike Piazza .75 2.00
14 Alex Rodriguez .75 2.00
15 Kevin Brown .30 .75
16 Darin Erstad .20 .50
17 Scott Rolen .30 .75
18 Micah Bowie RC .20 .50
19 Juan Gonzalez .20 .50
20 Kerry Wood .20 .50
21 Roger Clemens 1.00 2.50
22 Derek Jeter 1.25 3.00
23 Pat Burrell RC 1.25 3.00
24 Tim Salmon .30 .75
25 Barry Bonds 1.25 3.00
26 Roosevelt Brown RC .20 .50

27 Vladimir Guerrero .50 1.25
28 Randy Johnson .50 1.25
29 Mo Vaughn .20 .50
30 Fernando Seguignol .20 .50
31 Greg Maddux .75 2.00
32 Tony Clark .20 .50
33 Eric Chavez .20 .50
34 Kris Benson .20 .50
35 Frank Thomas .50 1.25
36 Mario Encarnacion RC .20 .50
37 Gabe Kapler .20 .50
38 Jeremy Giambi .20 .50
39 Peter Tucci .20 .50
40 Manny Ramirez .30 .75
41 Albert Belle .20 .50
42 Warren Morris .20 .50
43 Michael Barrett .20 .50
44 Andruw Jones .30 .75
45 Carlos Delgado .20 .50
46 Jaret Wright .20 .50
47 Juan Encarnacion .20 .50
48 Scott Hunter RC .20 .50
49 Tino Martinez .30 .75
50 Craig Biggio .30 .75
51 Jim Thome .30 .75
52 Vinny Castilla .20 .50
53 Tom Glavine .30 .75
54 Bob Higginson .20 .50
55 Moises Alou .20 .50
56 Robin Ventura .20 .50
57 Bernie Williams .30 .75
58 Pedro Martinez .30 .75
59 Greg Vaughn .20 .50
60 Ray Lankford .20 .50
61 Jose Canseco .30 .75
62 Ivan Rodriguez .30 .75
63 Shawn Green .20 .50
64 Rafael Palmeiro .30 .75
65 Ellis Burks .20 .50
66 Jason Kendall .20 .50
67 David Wells .20 .50
68 Rondell White .20 .50
69 Gary Sheffield .20 .50
70 Ken Caminiti .20 .50
71 Cliff Floyd .20 .50
72 Larry Walker .20 .50
73 Bartolo Colon .20 .50
74 Barry Larkin .30 .75
75 Calvin Pickering .20 .50
76 Jim Edmonds .20 .50
77 Henry Rodriguez .20 .50
78 Roberto Alomar .30 .75
79 Andres Galarraga .20 .50
80 Richie Sexson .20 .50
81 Todd Helton .30 .75
82 Damion Easley .20 .50
83 Livan Hernandez .20 .50
84 Carlos Beltran .30 .75
85 Todd Hundley .20 .50
86 Todd Walker .20 .50
87 Scott Brosius .20 .50
88 Bob Abreu .20 .50
89 Corey Koskie .20 .50
90 Ruben Rivera .20 .50
91 Edgar Renteria .20 .50
92 Quinton McCracken .20 .50
93 Bernard Gilkey .20 .50
94 Shannon Stewart .20 .50
95 Dustin Hermanson .20 .50
96 Mike Caruso .20 .50
97 Alex Gonzalez .25 .60
98 Raul Mondesi .25 .60
99 David Cone .25 .60
100 Curt Schilling .25 .60
101 Brian Giles .25 .60
102 Edgar Martinez .40 1.00
103 Rolando Arrojo .25 .60
104 Derek Bell .25 .60
105 Denny Neagle .25 .60
106 Marquis Grissom .25 .60
107 Bret Boone .25 .60
108 Mike Mussina .40 1.00
109 John Smoltz .40 1.00
110 Brett Tomko .25 .60
111 David Justice .25 .60
112 Andy Pettitte .40 1.00
113 Eric Karros .25 .60
114 Dante Bichette .25 .60
115 Jeromy Burnitz .25 .60
116 Paul Konerko .25 .60
117 Steve Finley .25 .60
118 Ricky Ledee .25 .60
119 Edgardo Alfonzo .25 .60
120 Dean Palmer .25 .60
121 Rusty Greer .25 .60
122 Luis Gonzalez .25 .60
123 Randy Winn .25 .60
124 Jeff Kent .25 .60
125 Doug Glanville .25 .60
126 Justin Thompson .25 .60
127 Bret Saberhagen .25 .60
128 Wade Boggs .40 1.00
129 Al Leiter .25 .60
130 Paul O'Neill .40 1.00
131 Chan Ho Park .25 .60
132 Johnny Damon .40 1.00
133 Darryl Kile .25 .60
134 Reggie Sanders .25 .60
135 Kevin Millwood .25 .60
136 Charles Johnson .25 .60
137 Ray Durham .25 .60
138 Rico Brogna .25 .60
139 Matt Williams .25 .60
140 Sandy Alomar Jr. .25 .60
141 Jeff Cirillo .25 .60
142 Devon White .25 .60
143 Andy Benes .25 .60
144 Mike Stanley .25 .60

1999 Flair Showcase Row 2

*STARS 1-48: 1X TO 2.5X ROW 3
*ROOKIES 1-48: 1.25X TO 3X ROW 3
ROW 2 1-48 STATED ODDS 1:3
*STARS 49-96: .5X TO 1.25X ROW 3
ROW 2 49-96 STATED ODDS 1:1.33
*STARS 97-144: .5X TO 1.25X ROW 3
ROW 2 97-144 STATED ODDS 1:2

1999 Flair Showcase Row 1

*STARS 1-48: 4X TO 10X ROW 3
*ROOKIES 1-48: 4X TO 10X ROW 3
1-48 PRINT RUN 1500 SERIAL #'d SETS
*STARS 49-96: 2.5X TO 6X ROW 3
49-96 PRINT RUN 3000 SERIAL #'d SETS
*STARS 97-144: 1.25X TO 3X ROW 3
97-144 PRINT RUN 6000 SERIAL #'d SETS
RANDOM INSERTS IN PACKS

1999 Flair Showcase Legacy Collection

*STARS 1-48: 12.5X TO 30X ROW 3
*ROOKIES 1-48: 8X TO 20X ROW 3
*STARS 49-96: 12.5X TO 30X ROW 3
*STARS 97-144: 10X TO 25X ROW 3
RANDOM INSERTS IN PACKS
STATED PRINT RUN 99 SERIAL #'d SETS
THREE CARDS PER PLAYER

1999 Flair Showcase Masterpiece

PRINT RUN 1 SERIAL #'d SET FOR EACH ROW
NOT PRICED DUE TO SCARCITY

1999 Flair Showcase Measure of Greatness

COMPLETE SET (15) 50.00 100.00
RANDOM INSERTS IN PACKS
STATED PRINT RUN 500 SERIAL #'d SETS
1 Roger Clemens 2.50 6.00
2 Nomar Garciaparra 1.25 3.00
3 Juan Gonzalez .75 2.00
4 Ken Griffey Jr. 8.00 20.00
5 Vladimir Guerrero 1.25 3.00
6 Tony Gwynn 2.00 5.00
7 Derek Jeter 15.00 40.00
8 Chipper Jones 2.00 5.00
9 Mark McGwire 3.00 8.00
10 Mike Piazza 2.00 5.00
11 Manny Ramirez 2.00 5.00
12 Cal Ripken 6.00 15.00
13 Alex Rodriguez 2.50 6.00
14 Sammy Sosa 2.00 5.00
15 Frank Thomas 2.00 5.00

1999 Flair Showcase Wave of the Future

COMPLETE SET (15) 40.00 100.00
RANDOM INSERTS IN PACKS
STATED PRINT RUN 1000 SERIAL #'d SETS
1 Kerry Wood 2.00 5.00
2 Ben Grieve 2.00 5.00
3 J.D. Drew 2.00 5.00
4 Juan Encarnacion 2.00 5.00
5 Travis Lee 2.00 5.00
6 Todd Helton 3.00 8.00
7 Troy Glaus 3.00 8.00
8 Ricky Ledee 2.00 5.00
9 Eric Chavez 2.00 5.00
10 Ben Davis 2.00 5.00
11 George Lombard 2.00 5.00
12 Jeremy Giambi 2.00 5.00
13 Roosevelt Brown 2.00 5.00
14 Pat Burrell 6.00 15.00
15 Preston Wilson 2.00 5.00

2006 Flair Showcase

COMP.SET w/o SP's (100) 15.00 40.00
101-150 STATED ODDS 1:4 H, 1:8 R
151-200 STATED ODDS 1:8 H, 1:16 R
PLATE ODDS: 1-2 PER HOBBY CASE
PLATE PRINT RUN 1 SET PER COLOR
BLACK-CYAN-MAGENTA-YELLOW ISSUED
NO PLATE PRICING DUE TO SCARCITY
1 Jeremy Hermida UD (RC) .40 1.00
2 Albert Pujols UD 1.00 2.50
3 Ryan Shealy UD (RC) .40 1.00
4 Mark Prior UD .50 1.25
5 Chuck James UD (RC) .40 1.00
6 Shawn Green UD .30 .75
7 Rickie Weeks UD .30 .75
8 Roy Halladay UD .50 1.25
9 Luis Gonzalez UD .30 .75
10 David Ortiz UD .75 2.00
11 Josh Beckett UD .30 .75
12 Gary Sheffield UD .30 .75
13 Jose Reyes UD .50 1.25
14 Brandon Watson UD (RC) .40 1.00
15 Tadahito Iguchi UD .30 .75
16 Rich Harden UD .30 .75
17 Skip Schumaker UD (RC) .40 1.00
18 Vladimir Guerrero UD .50 1.25
19 Chris Carpenter UD .50 1.25
20 Brian Roberts UD .30 .75
21 Roy Oswalt UD .50 1.25
22 Ben Johnson UD (RC) .40 1.00
23 Todd Helton UD .50 1.25
24 Wil Nieves UD (RC) .40 1.00
25 Michael Young UD .30 .75
26 A.J. Burnett UD .30 .75
27 J.D. Drew UD .30 .75
28 Adrian Beltre UD .75 2.00
29 Tim Hudson UD .50 1.25
30 Jake Peavy UD .30 .75
31 Magglio Ordonez UD .50 1.25
32 Brad Wilkerson UD .30 .75
33 Ryan Freel UD .30 .75
34 Javier Vazquez UD .30 .75
35 Tom Glavine UD .50 1.25
36 Jason Bergmann UD RC .40 1.00
37 Marcus Giles UD .30 .75
38 Jim Thome UD .50 1.25
39 Ichiro Suzuki UD 1.00 2.50
40 Jeff Harris UD RC .30 .75
41 Miguel Cabrera UD .75 2.00
42 Nomar Garciaparra UD .50 1.25
43 Brian Giles UD .30 .75
44 Jeremy Accardo UD RC .40 1.00
45 Taylor Buchholz UD (RC) .40 1.00
46 Mike Jacobs UD (RC) .40 1.00
47 Chris Denorfia UD (RC) .40 1.00
48 Ivan Rodriguez UD .50 1.25
49 Mike Piazza UD .75 2.00
50 Curt Schilling UD .50 1.25
51 Kelly Shoppach UD (RC) .40 1.00
52 Jason Kubel UD (RC) .40 1.00
53 Craig Biggio UD .50 1.25
54 Livan Hernandez UD .30 .75
55 Joe Mauer UD .50 1.25
56 Scott Feldman UD RC .40 1.00
57 Garret Anderson UD .30 .75
58 Steve Stemle UD RC .40 1.00
59 Boof Bonser UD (RC) .60 1.50
60 Jose Guillen UD .30 .75
61 Rafael Furcal UD .30 .75
62 John Van Benschoten UD (RC) .40 1.00
63 Dontrelle Willis UD .30 .75
64 Jose Vidro UD .30 .75
65 David Wright UD .60 1.50
66 Alfonso Soriano UD .50 1.25
67 Scott Podsednik UD .30 .75
68 Felix Hernandez UD .50 1.25
69 Richie Sexson UD .30 .75
70 Jeff Francoeur UD .75 2.00
71 Conor Jackson UD .50 1.25
72 Javy Lopez UD .30 .75
73 Jonathan Papelbon UD (RC) 2.00 5.00
74 Frank Thomas UD .75 2.00
75 Greg Maddux UD 1.00 2.50
76 Josh Rupe UD (RC) .40 1.00
77 Eric Chavez UD .30 .75
78 Ben Sheets UD .30 .75
79 Chase Utley UD .50 1.25
80 Derrek Lee UD .30 .75
81 Manny Ramirez UD .75 2.00
82 Pedro Martinez UD .50 1.25
83 Hideki Matsui UD .75 2.00
84 Jeremy Bonderman UD .30 .75
85 Ronny Cedeno UD .30 .75
86 Trevor Hoffman UD .50 1.25
87 Mark Buehrle UD .50 1.25
88 Jason Bay UD .30 .75
89 Reggie Sanders UD .30 .75
90 Brian Anderson UD (RC) .40 1.00
91 Travis Hafner UD .30 .75
92 Carlos Beltran UD .50 1.25
93 Cody Ross UD (RC) 1.00 2.50
94 Melvin Mora UD .30 .75
95 Chris Duffy UD .30 .75
96 Vernon Wells UD .30 .75
97 Bartolo Colon UD .30 .75
98 Aubrey Huff UD .30 .75
99 Paul Konerko UD .50 1.25
100 Cesar Izturis UD .30 .75
101 Josh Willingham FB (RC) 1.25 3.00
102 Matt Cain FB (RC) 5.00 12.00
103 Macay McBride FB (RC) .75 2.00
104 Jeff Mathis FB .75 2.00
105 Alex Rodriguez FB 2.50 6.00
106 Justin Morneau FB 1.25 3.00
107 Felipe Lopez FB .75 2.00
108 Justin Verlander FB (RC) 6.00 15.00
109 Ryan Howard FB 1.50 4.00
110 Mike Sweeney FB .75 2.00
111 Scott Rolen FB 1.25 3.00
112 Hank Blalock FB .75 2.00
113 Kerry Wood FB .75 2.00
114 B.J. Ryan FB .75 2.00
115 Garrett Atkins FB .75 2.00
116 Carlos Delgado FB .75 2.00
117 Zack Greinke FB 2.00 5.00
118 Chad Cordero FB .75 2.00
119 Julio Lugo FB .75 2.00
120 Bobby Crosby FB .75 2.00
121 Barry Zito FB 1.25 3.00
122 Jhonny Peralta FB .75 2.00
123 Miguel Tejada FB 1.25 3.00
124 Grady Sizemore FB 1.25 3.00
125 Derek Jeter FB 5.00 12.00
126 Cliff Lee FB 1.25 3.00
127 Khalil Greene FB .75 2.00
128 Lance Berkman FB 1.25 3.00
129 Huston Street FB .75 2.00
130 Jermaine Dye FB .75 2.00
131 Chone Figgins FB .75 2.00
132 Torii Hunter FB .75 2.00
133 Jorge Cantu FB .75 2.00
134 Jason Giambi FB .75 2.00
135 Johan Santana FB 1.25 3.00
136 Chad Tracy FB .75 2.00
137 Troy Glaus FB .75 2.00
138 Moises Alou FB .75 2.00
139 Jason Schmidt FB .75 2.00
140 Ken Griffey Jr. FB 4.00 10.00
141 Jason Varitek FB 2.00 5.00
142 John Smoltz FB 2.00 5.00
143 Andy Pettitte FB 1.25 3.00
144 Jeff Kent FB .75 2.00
145 Coco Crisp FB .75 2.00
146 Jonny Gomes FB .75 2.00
147 Aaron Rowand FB .75 2.00
148 Mike Mussina FB 1.25 3.00
149 Johnny Damon FB 1.25 3.00
150 Edgar Renteria FB .75 2.00
151 Scott Kazmir SL 2.00 5.00
152 Lyle Overbay SL 1.25 3.00
153 Placido Polanco SL 1.25 3.00
154 Mariano Rivera SL 4.00 10.00
155 Hanley Ramirez SL (RC) 2.00 5.00
156 Morgan Ensberg SL 1.25 3.00
157 Kenny Rogers SL 1.25 3.00
158 Brad Lidge SL 1.25 3.00
159 A.J. Pierzynski SL 1.25 3.00
160 Aramis Ramirez SL 1.25 3.00
161 Mark Teixeira SL 2.00 5.00
162 Carl Crawford SL 2.00 5.00
163 Ryan Zimmerman SL (RC) 4.00 10.00
164 Adam Dunn SL 2.00 5.00
165 Joe Nathan SL 1.25 3.00
166 Juan Pierre SL 1.25 3.00
167 Pat Burrell SL 1.25 3.00
168 Carlos Lee SL 1.25 3.00
169 Billy Wagner SL 1.25 3.00
170 Prince Fielder SL (RC) 6.00 15.00
171 Randy Johnson SL 3.00 8.00
172 Andruw Jones SL 1.25 3.00
173 Francisco Rodriguez SL 2.00 5.00
174 Robinson Cano SL 2.00 5.00
175 Matt Holliday SL 3.00 8.00
176 Jim Edmonds SL 2.00 5.00
177 Josh Barfield SL (RC) 1.25 3.00
178 Chipper Jones SL 3.00 8.00
179 Bobby Jenks SL 1.25 3.00
180 Carlos Zambrano SL 2.00 5.00
181 Bobby Abreu SL 1.25 3.00
182 Brandon Webb SL 2.00 5.00
183 Kevin Millwood SL 1.25 3.00
184 Zach Duke SL 1.25 3.00
185 Randy Winn SL 1.25 3.00
186 Eric Gagne SL 1.25 3.00
187 Kenji Johjima SL RC 3.00 8.00
188 John Patterson SL 1.25 3.00
189 Mark Loretta SL 1.25 3.00
190 Anderson Hernandez SL (RC) 1.25 3.00
191 Chris Resop SL (RC) 1.25 3.00
192 Ian Kinsler SL (RC) 4.00 10.00
193 Francisco Liriano SL (RC) 3.00 8.00
194 Noah Lowry SL 1.25 3.00
195 Brett Myers SL 1.25 3.00
196 Rocco Baldelli SL 1.25 3.00
197 Cliff Floyd SL 1.25 3.00
198 Sean Casey SL 1.25 3.00
199 Geoff Jenkins SL 1.25 3.00
200 Clint Barmes SL 1.25 3.00

2006 Flair Showcase Legacy Blue

*BLUE 1-100: 1.5X TO 4X BASIC
*BLUE 1-100: 1.25X TO 3X BASIC RC's
*BLUE 101-150: .6X TO 1.5X BASIC
*BLUE 151-200: .4X TO 1X BASIC
STATED ODDS 1:18 HOBBY
STATED PRINT RUN 150 SERIAL #'d SETS

2006 Flair Showcase Legacy Emerald

*EMERALD 1-100: 1.5X TO 4X BASIC
*EMERALD 1-100: 1.25X TO 3X BASIC RC's
*EMERALD 101-150: .6X TO 1.5X BASIC
*EMERALD 151-200: .4X TO 1X BASIC
STATED ODDS 1:18 HOBBY
STATED PRINT RUN 150 SERIAL #'d SETS

2006 Flair Showcase Autographics

STATED ODDS 1:36 H, 1:576 R
SP PRINT RUNS PROVIDED BY UD
SP'S ARE NOT SERIAL-NUMBERED
NO SP PRICING ON QTY OF 46 OR LESS
PLATE ODDS: 1-2 PER HOBBY CASE
PLATE PRINT RUN 1 SET PER COLOR
BLACK-CYAN-MAGENTA-YELLOW ISSUED
PLATES DO NOT FEATURE AUTOS
NO PLATE PRICING DUE TO SCARCITY
AH Aaron Harang 6.00 15.00
AR Aaron Rowand 6.00 15.00
BA Bronson Arroyo 10.00 25.00
BC Brandon Claussen 4.00 10.00
BO Jeremy Bonderman 6.00 15.00
CA Carl Crawford 8.00 20.00
CC Coco Crisp 8.00 20.00
CH Chad Cordero 4.00 10.00
CI Cesar Izturis 4.00 10.00
CL Cliff Lee 6.00 15.00
CO Craig Counsell 6.00 15.00
CU Chase Utley SP/100 * 20.00 50.00
GC Gustavo Chacin 4.00 10.00
HB Hank Blalock 6.00 15.00
JB Jason Bay 6.00 15.00
JG Jose Guillen 4.00 10.00
JH Jhonny Peralta 6.00 15.00
JM Justin Morneau 6.00 15.00
JP Joel Pineiro 4.00 10.00
JV Javier Vazquez 6.00 15.00
KG Ken Griffey Jr. 25.00 60.00
LH Livan Hernandez 4.00 10.00
MK Mark Kotsay 4.00 10.00
OV Omar Vizquel 6.00 15.00
RA Aramis Ramirez 6.00 15.00
RO Roy Oswalt 6.00 15.00
RZ Ryan Zimmerman 8.00 20.00
SC Sean Casey 6.00 15.00
TH Travis Hafner 6.00 15.00
WP Wily Mo Pena 6.00 15.00
XN Xavier Nady 4.00 10.00

2006 Flair Showcase Fresh Ink

STATED ODDS 1:36 H, 1:576 R
SP PRINT RUNS PROVIDED BY UD
SP'S ARE NOT SERIAL-NUMBERED
NO SP PRICING ON QTY OF 43
PLATE ODDS: 1-2 PER HOBBY CASE
PLATE PRINT RUN 1 SET PER COLOR
BLACK-CYAN-MAGENTA-YELLOW ISSUED
PLATES DO NOT FEATURE AUTOS
NO PLATE PRICING DUE TO SCARCITY
BC Bobby Crosby 6.00 15.00
BM Brandon McCarthy 4.00 10.00
BR Brian Roberts 6.00 15.00
CB Clint Barmes 4.00 10.00
CK Casey Kotchman 4.00 10.00
CS Chris Shelton 6.00 15.00
DD David DeJesus 4.00 10.00
DH Danny Haren 4.00 10.00
DW Dontrelle Willis 6.00 15.00
ES Ervin Santana 6.00 15.00
GA Garrett Atkins 4.00 10.00
GF Gavin Floyd 4.00 10.00
HA Rich Harden 6.00 15.00
HS Huston Street 6.00 15.00
JB Joe Blanton 4.00 10.00
JG Jonny Gomes 4.00 10.00
JS Johan Santana 15.00 40.00
KG Khalil Greene 10.00 25.00
KY Kevin Youkilis 6.00 15.00
MA Matt Cain 10.00 25.00
MC Miguel Cabrera 12.50 30.00
MT Mark Teahen 4.00 10.00
MY Michael Young SP/100 * 10.00 25.00
NL Noah Lowry 6.00 15.00
OP Odalis Perez 4.00 10.00
RE Jeremy Reed 4.00 10.00
RH Rich Hill 4.00 10.00
SK Scott Kazmir 8.00 20.00
TI Tadahito Iguchi 8.00 20.00
VM Victor Martinez 6.00 15.00
WR David Wright SP/100 * 30.00 60.00
ZG Zack Greinke 4.00 10.00

2006 Flair Showcase Hot Gloves

STATED ODDS 1:108 H, 1:576 R
ANNOUNCED PRINT RUN 125-150
PRINT RUN INFO PROVIDED BY UD
CARDS ARE NOT SERIAL-NUMBERED
PLATE ODDS: 1-2 PER HOBBY CASE
UNPRICED PRINT PLATE PRINT RUN 1
BLACK-CYAN-MAGENTA-YELLOW ISSUED
1 Derrek Lee 4.00 10.00
2 Andruw Jones 4.00 10.00
3 Bobby Abreu 4.00 10.00
4 Luis Castillo 4.00 10.00
5 Mike Matheny 4.00 10.00
6 Cesar Izturis 4.00 10.00
7 Craig Biggio 6.00 15.00
8 Darin Erstad 4.00 10.00
9 Derek Jeter 25.00 60.00
10 Eric Chavez 4.00 10.00
11 Greg Maddux 12.00 30.00
12 Ichiro Suzuki 12.00 30.00
13 Ivan Rodriguez 6.00 15.00
14 J.T. Snow 4.00 10.00
15 Jim Edmonds 6.00 15.00
16 Steve Finley 4.00 10.00
17 Kenny Rogers 4.00 10.00
18 Jason Varitek 10.00 25.00
19 Ken Griffey Jr. 20.00 50.00
20 Mark Teixeira 6.00 15.00
21 Orlando Hudson 4.00 10.00
22 Mike Hampton 4.00 10.00
23 Mike Mussina 6.00 15.00
24 Vernon Wells 4.00 10.00
25 Omar Vizquel 6.00 15.00
26 Alex Rodriguez 12.00 30.00
27 Mike Cameron 4.00 10.00
28 Scott Rolen 6.00 15.00
29 Todd Helton 6.00 15.00
30 Torii Hunter 4.00 10.00

2006 Flair Showcase Hot Numbers

STATED ODDS 1:6 H, 1:36 R
PLATE ODDS: 1-2 PER HOBBY CASE
PLATE PRINT RUN 1 SET PER COLOR
BLACK-CYAN-MAGENTA-YELLOW ISSUED
NO PLATE PRICING DUE TO SCARCITY
1 Albert Pujols 2.00 5.00
2 Alex Rodriguez 2.00 5.00
3 Andruw Jones .60 1.50
4 Bobby Abreu .60 1.50
5 Chipper Jones 1.50 4.00
6 Curt Schilling 1.00 2.50
7 David Ortiz 1.50 4.00
8 David Wright 1.25 3.00
9 Derek Jeter 4.00 10.00
10 Derrek Lee .60 1.50
11 Eric Gagne .60 1.50
12 Greg Maddux 2.00 5.00
13 Hideki Matsui 1.50 4.00
14 Ichiro Suzuki 2.00 5.00
15 Ivan Rodriguez 1.00 2.50
16 Johan Santana 1.00 2.50
17 Johnny Damon 1.00 2.50
18 Ken Griffey Jr. 3.00 8.00
19 Manny Ramirez 1.50 4.00
20 Mark Prior 1.00 2.50
21 Mark Teixeira 1.00 2.50
22 Miguel Cabrera 1.50 4.00
23 Miguel Tejada 1.00 2.50
24 Pedro Martinez 1.00 2.50
25 Randy Johnson 1.50 4.00
26 Rickie Weeks .60 1.50
27 Roger Clemens 2.00 5.00
28 Todd Helton 1.00 2.50
29 Torii Hunter .60 1.50
30 Vladimir Guerrero 1.00 2.50

2006 Flair Showcase Lettermen

RANDOM INSERTS IN HOBBY PACKS
PRINT RUNS B/WN 3-9 #'d COPIES PER
NO PRICING DUE TO SCARCITY

2006 Flair Showcase Signatures

RANDOM INSERTS IN HOBBY PACKS
STATED PRINT RUN 35 SERIAL #'d SETS
NO PRICING DUE TO SCARCITY
PLATE ODDS: 1-2 PER HOBBY CASE
PLATE PRINT RUN 1 SET PER COLOR
BLACK-CYAN-MAGENTA-YELLOW ISSUED
PLATES DO NOT FEATURE AUTOS
NO PLATE PRICING DUE TO SCARCITY

2006 Flair Showcase Stitches

OVERALL GU ODDS 1:9 H, 1:18 R
AB Adrian Beltre Jsy 3.00 8.00
AD Adam Dunn Jsy 3.00 8.00
AJ Andruw Jones Jsy 4.00 10.00
AN Andy Pettitte Jsy 4.00 10.00
AP Albert Pujols Pants 8.00 20.00
AR Aramis Ramirez Jsy 3.00 8.00
AS Alfonso Soriano Jsy 3.00 8.00
BA Bobby Abreu Jsy 3.00 8.00
BC Bobby Crosby Jsy 3.00 8.00
BG Brian Giles Jsy 3.00 8.00
BO Jeremy Bonderman Jsy 3.00 8.00
BR Brian Roberts Jsy 3.00 8.00
BS Ben Sheets Jsy 3.00 8.00
BZ Barry Zito Jsy 3.00 8.00
CA Carl Crawford Jsy 3.00 8.00
CB Carlos Beltran Jsy 3.00 8.00
CC C.C. Sabathia Jsy 3.00 8.00
CD Carlos Delgado Jsy 3.00 8.00
CJ Chipper Jones Jsy 4.00 10.00
CL Carlos Lee Jsy 3.00 8.00
CO Michael Collins Jsy 3.00 8.00
CS Curt Schilling Jsy 4.00 10.00
DJ Derek Jeter Pants 8.00 20.00
DL Derrek Lee Jsy 3.00 8.00
DM Daisuke Matsuzaka Jsy 8.00 20.00
DO David Ortiz Jsy 4.00 10.00
DR J.D. Drew Jsy 3.00 8.00
DW Dontrelle Willis Jsy 3.00 8.00
EC Eric Chavez Jsy 3.00 8.00
EG Eric Gagne Jsy 3.00 8.00
FG Freddy Garcia Jsy 3.00 8.00
FR Francisco Rodriguez Jsy 3.00 8.00
FT Frank Thomas Jsy 4.00 10.00
GM Greg Maddux Jsy 4.00 10.00
GR Khalil Greene Jsy 3.00 8.00
GS Gary Sheffield Jsy 3.00 8.00
HA J.J. Hardy Jsy 3.00 8.00
HB Hank Blalock Jsy 3.00 8.00
HO Trevor Hoffman Jsy 3.00 8.00
HU Tim Hudson Jsy 3.00 8.00
IR Ivan Rodriguez Jsy 4.00 10.00
JA Jason Schmidt Jsy 3.00 8.00
JC Jorge Cantu Jsy 3.00 8.00
JD Johnny Damon Jsy 4.00 10.00
JE Jim Edmonds Jsy 3.00 8.00
JG Jason Giambi Jsy 3.00 8.00
JJ Jacque Jones Jsy 3.00 8.00
JK Jeff Kent Jsy 3.00 8.00
JL Javy Lopez Jsy 3.00 8.00
JM Joe Mauer Jsy 4.00 10.00
JO Josh Beckett Jsy 3.00 8.00
JP Jake Peavy Jsy 3.00 8.00
JR Jose Reyes Jsy 3.00 8.00
JS Johan Santana Jsy 4.00 10.00
JT Jim Thome Jsy 4.00 10.00
JU Juan Uribe Jsy 3.00 8.00
JV Jason Varitek Jsy 4.00 10.00
KE Kevin Millwood Jsy 3.00 8.00
KG Ken Griffey Jr. Jsy 6.00 15.00
KM Kazuo Matsui Jsy 3.00 8.00
KW Kerry Wood Jsy 3.00 8.00
LB Lance Berkman Jsy 3.00 8.00
LG Luis Gonzalez Jsy 3.00 8.00
MA Moises Alou Jsy 3.00 8.00
MB Mark Buehrle Jsy 3.00 8.00
MC Miguel Cabrera Jsy 4.00 10.00
MH Matt Holliday Jsy 4.00 10.00
MI Mike Piazza Jsy 4.00 10.00
MM Mike Mussina Jsy 4.00 10.00
MP Mark Prior Jsy 3.00 8.00
MR Manny Ramirez Jsy 4.00 10.00
MT Mark Teixeira Jsy 4.00 10.00
MY Michael Young Jsy 3.00 8.00
OV Omar Vizquel Jsy 4.00 10.00
PL Paul Lo Duca Jsy 3.00 8.00
PM Pedro Martinez Jsy 4.00 10.00
PW Preston Wilson Jsy 3.00 8.00
RB Rocco Baldelli Jsy 3.00 8.00
RC Robinson Cano Jsy 6.00 15.00
RE Jeremy Reed Jsy 3.00 8.00
RF Rafael Furcal Jsy 3.00 8.00
RH Roy Halladay Jsy 3.00 8.00
RI Rich Harden Jsy 3.00 8.00
RJ Randy Johnson Jsy 4.00 10.00
RS Richie Sexson Jsy 3.00 8.00
RW Rickie Weeks Jsy 3.00 8.00
SK Scott Kazmir Jsy 3.00 8.00
SM John Smoltz Jsy 4.00 10.00
SR Scott Rolen Jsy 4.00 10.00
SW Mike Sweeney Jsy 3.00 8.00
TE Miguel Tejada Jsy 3.00 8.00
TG Tom Glavine Jsy 4.00 10.00
TH Todd Helton Jsy 4.00 10.00
TN Trot Nixon Jsy 3.00 8.00
TO Torii Hunter Jsy 3.00 8.00
TR Travis Hafner Jsy 3.00 8.00
VG Vladimir Guerrero Jsy 4.00 10.00
VW Vernon Wells Jsy 3.00 8.00
WR David Wright Jsy 4.00 10.00

2006 Flair Showcase Wave of the Future

STATED ODDS 1:3 H, 1:36 R
PLATE ODDS: 1-2 PER HOBBY CASE
PLATE PRINT RUN 1 SET PER COLOR
BLACK-CYAN-MAGENTA-YELLOW ISSUED
NO PLATE PRICING DUE TO SCARCITY
1 Jeremy Hermida .40 1.00
2 Kelly Shoppach .40 1.00
3 Adam Wainwright .60 1.50
4 Ryan Zimmerman 1.25 3.00
5 Josh Willingham .60 1.50
6 Brandon McCarthy .40 1.00
7 Conor Jackson .60 1.50
8 Grady Sizemore .60 1.50
9 Curtis Granderson .75 2.00
10 Jose Capellan .40 1.00
11 Mike Jacobs .40 1.00
12 Gavin Floyd .40 1.00
13 Hanley Ramirez .60 1.50
14 Jason Kubel .40 1.00
15 Nate McLouth .40 1.00
16 Felix Hernandez .60 1.50
17 Jeff Francoeur 1.00 2.50
18 Wil Nieves .40 1.00
19 Cody Ross 1.00 2.50
20 Justin Verlander 3.00 8.00
21 Ben Johnson .40 1.00
22 Guillermo Quiroz .40 1.00
23 Jonathan Papelbon 2.00 5.00
24 Prince Fielder 2.00 5.00
25 Rickie Weeks .40 1.00
26 Robinson Cano .60 1.50
27 Kenji Johjima 1.00 2.50
28 Anderson Hernandez .40 1.00
29 Yuniesky Betancourt .40 1.00
30 Zach Duke .40 1.00

2006 Flair Showcase World Baseball Classic

STATED ODDS 1:8 H, 1:36 R
PLATE ODDS: 1-2 PER HOBBY CASE
PLATE PRINT RUN 1 SET PER COLOR
BLACK-CYAN-MAGENTA-YELLOW ISSUED
NO PLATE PRICING DUE TO SCARCITY
1 Adam Stern .75 2.00
2 Jason Bay .75 2.00
3 Wei Wang .75 2.00
4 Yung Chi Chen 1.25 3.00
5 Pedro Lazo 1.25 3.00
6 Yoandy Garlobo .75 2.00
7 Ormari Romero .75 2.00
8 Frederich Cepeda .75 2.00
9 Yulieski Gourriel 2.50 6.00
10 Yadel Marti .75 2.00
11 David Ortiz 2.00 5.00
12 Albert Pujols 2.50 6.00
13 Adrian Beltre .75 2.00
14 Alberto Castillo .75 2.00
15 Odalis Perez .75 2.00
16 Jason Grilli .75 2.00
17 Daisuke Matsuzaka 2.50 6.00
18 Sadaharu Oh 5.00 12.00
19 Nobuhiko Matsunaka 1.25 3.00
20 Ichiro Suzuki 2.50 6.00
21 Akinori Otsuka .75 2.00
22 Koji Uehara 2.50 6.00
23 Kosuke Fukudome 2.50 6.00
24 Daisuke Matsuzaka 2.50 6.00
25 Ichiro Suzuki 2.50 6.00
26 Seung Yeop Lee 1.25 3.00
27 Seung Yeop Lee 1.25 3.00
28 Jong Beom Lee .75 2.00
29 Jae Seo .75 2.00
30 Chan Ho Park 1.25 3.00
31 Hee Seop Choi .75 2.00
32 Jorge Cantu .75 2.00
33 Oliver Perez .75 2.00
34 Vinny Castilla .75 2.00
35 Esteban Loaiza .75 2.00
36 Shairon Martis .75 2.00
37 Bernie Williams 1.25 3.00
38 Javier Vazquez .75 2.00
39 Carlos Beltran 1.25 3.00
40 Bernie Williams 1.25 3.00
41 Roger Clemens 2.50 6.00
42 Ken Griffey Jr. 4.00 10.00
43 Alex Rodriguez 2.50 6.00
44 Derrek Lee .75 2.00
45 Derek Jeter 5.00 12.00
46 Chipper Jones 2.00 5.00
47 Miguel Cabrera 2.00 5.00
48 Francisco Rodriguez 1.25 3.00
49 Victor Martinez 1.25 3.00
50 Freddy Garcia .75 2.00

1959 Fleer Ted Williams

The cards in this 80-card set measure 2 1/2" by 3 1/2". The 1959 Fleer set, with a catalog designation of R418-1, portrays the life of Ted Williams. The wording of the wrapper, "Baseball's Greatest Series," has led to speculation that Fleer contemplated similar sets honoring other baseball immortals, but chose to develop instead the format of the 1960 and 1961 issues. These packs contained either six or eight cards. The packs cost a nickel and were packed 24 to a box which were packed 24 to a case. Card number 68, which was withdrawn early in production, is considered scarce and has even been counterfeited; the fake has a rosy coloration and a cross-hatch pattern visible over the picture area. The card numbering is arranged essentially in chronological order.

COMPLETE SET (80) 900.00 1500.00
WRAPPER (6-CARD) 100.00 125.00
WRAPPER (8-CARD) 100.00 150.00
1 The Early Years 60.00 100.00
2 Ted's Idol Babe Ruth 60.00 100.00
3 Practice Makes Perfect 7.50 15.00
4 Learns Fine Points 7.50 15.00
5 Ted's Fame Spreads 7.50 15.00
6 Ted Turns Pro 12.50 25.00
7 From Mound to Plate 7.50 15.00
8 1937 First Full Season 7.50 15.00
9 Williams 10.00 20.00
E.Collins
10 Gunning as Pastime 7.50 15.00
11 T.Williams 20.00 40.00
J.Foxx
12 Burning Up Minors 10.00 20.00
13 1939 Shows Will Stay 7.50 15.00
14 Outstanding Rookie '39 7.50 15.00
15 Licks Sophomore Jinx 10.00 20.00
16 1941 Greatest Year 7.50 15.00
17 How Ted Hit .400 20.00 40.00
18 1941 All Star Hero 10.00 20.00
19 Ted Wins Triple Crown 7.50 15.00
20 On to Naval Training 7.50 15.00
21 Honors for Williams 7.50 15.00
22 1944 Ted Solos 7.50 15.00
23 Williams Wins Wings 7.50 15.00
24 1945 Sharpshooter# 7.50 15.00
25 1945 Ted Discharged 7.50 15.00
26 Off to Flying Start 7.50 15.00
27 7/9/46 One Man Show 7.50 15.00
28 The Williams Shift 7.50 15.00
29 Ted Hits for Cycle 10.00 20.00
30 Beating Williams Shift 7.50 15.00
31 Sox Lose Series 10.00 20.00
32 Most Valuable Player 7.50 15.00
33 Another Triple Crown 7.50 15.00
34 Runs Scored Record 7.50 15.00
35 Sox Miss Pennant 7.50 15.00
36 Banner Year for Ted 7.50 15.00
37 1949 Sox Miss Again 7.50 15.00
38 1949 Power Rampage 7.50 15.00
39 1950 Great Start 12.50 25.00
40 Ted Crashes into Wall 7.50 15.00
41 1950 Ted Recovers 7.50 15.00
42 Williams 7.50 15.00
Tom Yawkey
43 Double Play Lead 7.50 15.00
44 Back to Marines 7.50 15.00
45 Farewell to Baseball 7.50 15.00
46 Ready for Combat 7.50 15.00
47 Ted Crash Lands Jet 7.50 15.00
48 1953 Ted Returns 10.00 20.00
49 Smash Return 7.50 15.00
50 1954 Spring Injury 12.50 25.00
51 Ted is Patched Up 7.50 15.00
52 1954 Ted's Comeback 10.00 20.00
53 Comeback is Success 7.50 15.00
54 Ted Hooks Big One 7.50 15.00
55 Retirement No Go 10.00 20.00
56 2,000th Hit 8/11/55 7.50 15.00
57 400th Homer 10.00 20.00
58 Williams Hits .388 7.50 15.00
59 Hot September for Ted 7.50 15.00
60 More Records for Ted 7.50 15.00
61 1957 Outfielder Ted 10.00 20.00

62 1958 Sixth Batting Title 7.50 15.00
63 AS Record w 50.00 80.00
Auto
64 Daughter and Daddy 7.50 15.00
65 1958 August 30 10.00 20.00
66 1958 Powerhouse 7.50 15.00
67 Fam.Fishermen w 20.00 40.00
Snead
68 Signs for 1959 SP 400.00 700.00
69 A Future Ted Williams 7.50 15.00
70 T.Williams 20.00 40.00
J.Thorpe
71 Hitting Fundamental 1 7.50 15.00
72 Hitting Fundamental 2 7.50 15.00
73 Hitting Fundamental 3 7.50 15.00
74 Here's How 7.50 15.00
75 Williams' Value to Sox 30.00 50.00
76 On Base Record 7.50 15.00
77 Ted Relaxes 7.50 15.00
78 Honors for Williams 7.50 15.00
79 Where Ted Stands 12.50 25.00
80 Ted's Goals for 1959 20.00 40.00

1960 Fleer

The cards in this 79-card set measure 2 1/2" by 3 1/2". The cards from the 1960 Fleer series of Baseball Greats are sometimes mistaken for 1930s cards by collectors not familiar with this set. The cards each contain a tinted photo of a baseball immortal, and were issued in one series. There are no known scarcities, although a number 80 card (Pepper Martin reverse with Eddie Collins, Joe Tinker or Lefty Grove obverse) exists (this is not considered part of the set). The catalog designation for 1960 Fleer is R418-2. The cards were printed on a 96-card sheet with 17 double prints. These are noted in the checklist below by DP. On the sheet the second Eddie Collins card is typically found in the number 80 position. According to correspondence sent from Fleers at the time -- no card 80 was issued because of contract problems. Some cards have been discovered with wrong backs. The cards were issued in nickel packs which were packed 24 to a box.

COMPLETE SET (79) 250.00 600.00
WRAPPER (5-CENT) 50.00 100.00
1 Napoleon Lajoie DP 12.50 30.00
2 Christy Mathewson 8.00 20.00
3 Babe Ruth 75.00 150.00
4 Carl Hubbell 3.00 8.00
5 Grover C. Alexander 3.00 8.00
6 Walter Johnson DP 4.00 10.00
7 Chief Bender 1.50 4.00
8 Roger Bresnahan 1.50 4.00
9 Mordecai Brown 1.50 4.00
10 Tris Speaker 3.00 8.00
11 Arky Vaughan DP 1.50 4.00
12 Zach Wheat 1.50 4.00
13 George Sisler 1.50 4.00
14 Connie Mack 3.00 8.00
15 Clark Griffith 1.50 4.00
16 Lou Boudreau DP 3.00 8.00
17 Ernie Lombardi 1.50 4.00
18 Heinie Manush 1.50 4.00
19 Marty Marion 2.50 6.00
20 Eddie Collins DP 1.50 4.00
21 Rabbit Maranville DP 1.50 4.00
22 Joe Medwick 1.50 4.00
23 Ed Barrow 1.50 4.00
24 Mickey Cochrane 2.50 6.00
25 Jimmy Collins 1.50 4.00
26 Bob Feller DP 6.00 15.00
27 Luke Appling 2.50 6.00
28 Lou Gehrig 30.00 80.00
29 Gabby Hartnett 1.50 4.00
30 Chuck Klein 1.50 4.00
31 Tony Lazzeri DP 2.50 6.00
32 Al Simmons 1.50 4.00
33 Wilbert Robinson 1.50 4.00
34 Sam Rice 1.50 4.00
35 Herb Pennock 1.50 4.00
36 Mel Ott DP 3.00 8.00
37 Lefty O'Doul 1.50 4.00
38 Johnny Mize 3.00 8.00
39 Edmund (Bing) Miller 1.50 4.00
40 Joe Tinker 1.50 4.00
41 Frank Baker DP 1.50 4.00
42 Ty Cobb 25.00 60.00
43 Paul Derringer 1.50 4.00
44 Cap Anson 1.50 4.00
45 Jim Bottomley 1.50 4.00
46 Eddie Plank DP 1.50 4.00
47 Denton (Cy) Young 12.00 30.00
48 Hack Wilson 2.50 6.00
49 Ed Walsh UER 1.50 4.00
50 Frank Chance 1.50 4.00
51 Dazzy Vance DP 1.50 4.00
52 Bill Terry 2.50 6.00
53 Jimmie Foxx 4.00 10.00
54 Lefty Gomez 3.00 8.00
55 Branch Rickey 1.50 4.00
56 Ray Schalk DP 1.50 4.00
57 Johnny Evers 1.50 4.00
58 Charley Gehringer 2.50 6.00
59 Burleigh Grimes 1.50 4.00
60 Lefty Grove 3.00 8.00
61 Rube Waddell DP 1.50 4.00
62 Honus Wagner 15.00 40.00
63 Red Ruffing 1.50 4.00
64 Kenesaw M. Landis 1.50 4.00
65 Harry Heilmann 1.50 4.00
66 John McGraw DP 1.50 4.00
67 Hughie Jennings 1.50 4.00
68 Hal Newhouser 2.50 6.00
69 Waite Hoyt 1.50 4.00
70 Bobo Newsom 1.50 4.00
71 Earl Averill DP 1.50 4.00
72 Ted Williams 40.00 100.00
73 Warren Giles 2.50 6.00
74 Ford Frick 2.50 6.00
75 Kiki Cuyler 1.50 4.00
76 Paul Waner DP 2.50 6.00
77 Pie Traynor 1.50 4.00
78 Lloyd Waner 1.50 4.00
79 Ralph Kiner 4.00 10.00
80A P.Martin SP/Eddie Collins 1250.00 2500.00
80B P.Martin SP/Lefty Grove 1000.00 2000.00
80C P.Martin SP/Joe Tinker 1000.00 2000.00

1960 Fleer Stickers

This 20-sticker set measures the standard size. The fronts feature a cartoon depicting the title of the card. The pictures are framed with red and black stars and the words "All Star" printed in blue. First names are printed below and are used to place in the blank box of each sticker to represent the person the sticker depicts. The stickers are unnumbered and checklisted below in alphabetical order.

COMPLETE SET (20) 20.00 50.00
COMMON CARD (1-20) 1.25 3.00

1961 Fleer

The cards in this 154-card set measure 2 1/2" by 3 1/2". In 1961, Fleer continued its Baseball Greats format by issuing this series of cards. The set was released in two distinct series, 1-88 and 89-154 (of which the latter is more difficult to obtain). The players within each series are conveniently numbered in alphabetical order. The catalog number for this set is F418-3. In each first series pack Fleer inserted a Major League team decal and a pennant sticker honoring past World Series winners. The cards were issued in nickel packs which were issued 24 to a box.

COMPLETE SET (154) 400.00 1000.00
COMMON CARD (1-88) 1.25 3.00
COMMON CARD (89-154) 3.00 8.00
WRAPPER (5-CENT) 50.00 100.00
1 Baker/Cobb/Wheat 20.00 50.00
2 Grover C. Alexander 2.50 6.00
3 Nick Altrock 1.25 3.00
4 Cap Anson 1.50 4.00
5 Earl Averill 1.50 4.00
6 Frank Baker 1.50 4.00
7 Dave Bancroft 1.50 4.00
8 Chief Bender 1.50 4.00
9 Jim Bottomley 1.50 4.00
10 Roger Bresnahan 1.50 4.00
11 Mordecai Brown 1.50 4.00
12 Max Carey 1.50 4.00
13 Jack Chesbro 1.50 4.00
14 Ty Cobb 20.00 50.00
15 Mickey Cochrane 1.50 4.00
16 Eddie Collins 2.50 6.00
17 Earle Combs 1.50 4.00
18 Charles Comiskey 1.50 4.00
19 Kiki Cuyler 1.50 4.00
20 Paul Derringer 1.25 3.00
21 Howard Ehmke 1.25 3.00
22 Billy Evans UMP 1.50 4.00
23 Johnny Evers 1.50 4.00
24 Urban Faber 1.50 4.00
25 Bob Feller 5.00 12.00
26 Wes Ferrell 1.25 3.00
27 Lew Fonseca 1.25 3.00
28 Jimmie Foxx 2.50 6.00
29 Ford Frick 1.25 3.00
30 Frankie Frisch 1.50 4.00
31 Lou Gehrig 40.00 100.00
32 Charley Gehringer 1.50 4.00
33 Warren Giles 1.25 3.00
34 Lefty Gomez 1.50 4.00
35 Goose Goslin 1.50 4.00
36 Clark Griffith 1.50 4.00
37 Burleigh Grimes 1.50 4.00
38 Lefty Grove 2.50 6.00
39 Chick Hafey 1.50 4.00
40 Jesse Haines 1.50 4.00
41 Gabby Hartnett 1.50 4.00
42 Harry Heilmann 1.50 4.00
43 Rogers Hornsby 2.50 6.00
44 Waite Hoyt 1.50 4.00
45 Carl Hubbell 2.50 6.00
46 Miller Huggins 1.50 4.00
47 Hughie Jennings 1.50 4.00
48 Ban Johnson 1.50 4.00
49 Walter Johnson 5.00 12.00
50 Ralph Kiner 2.50 6.00
51 Chuck Klein 1.50 4.00
52 Johnny Kling 1.25 3.00
53 Kenesaw M. Landis 1.50 4.00
54 Tony Lazzeri 1.50 4.00
55 Ernie Lombardi 1.50 4.00
56 Dolf Luque 1.25 3.00
57 Heinie Manush 1.50 4.00
58 Marty Marion 1.25 3.00
59 Christy Mathewson 5.00 12.00
60 John McGraw 1.50 4.00
61 Joe Medwick 1.50 4.00
62 Edmund (Bing) Miller 1.25 3.00
63 Johnny Mize 1.50 4.00
64 John Mostil 1.25 3.00
65 Art Nehf 1.25 3.00
66 Hal Newhouser 1.50 4.00
67 Bobo Newsom 1.25 3.00
68 Mel Ott 2.50 6.00
69 Allie Reynolds 1.25 3.00
70 Sam Rice 1.50 4.00
71 Eppa Rixey 1.50 4.00
72 Edd Roush 1.50 4.00
73 Schoolboy Rowe 1.25 3.00
74 Red Ruffing 1.50 4.00
75 Babe Ruth 100.00 250.00
76 Joe Sewell 1.50 4.00
77 Al Simmons 1.50 4.00
78 George Sisler 1.50 4.00
79 Tris Speaker 1.50 4.00
80 Fred Toney 1.25 3.00
81 Dazzy Vance 1.50 4.00
82 Hippo Vaughn 1.25 3.00
83 Ed Walsh 1.50 4.00
84 Lloyd Waner 1.50 4.00
85 Paul Waner 1.50 4.00
86 Zack Wheat 1.50 4.00
87 Hack Wilson 1.50 4.00
88 Jimmy Wilson 1.25 3.00
89 G.Sisler/P.Traynor 30.00 60.00
90 Babe Adams 3.00 8.00
91 Dale Alexander 3.00 8.00
92 Jim Bagby 3.00 8.00
93 Ossie Bluege 3.00 8.00
94 Lou Boudreau 4.00 10.00
95 Tommy Bridges 3.00 8.00
96 Donie Bush 3.00 8.00
97 Dolph Camilli 3.00 8.00
98 Frank Chance 4.00 10.00
99 Jimmy Collins 4.00 10.00
100 Stan Coveleskie 4.00 10.00
101 Hugh Critz 3.00 8.00
102 Alvin Crowder 3.00 8.00
103 Joe Dugan 3.00 8.00
104 Bibb Falk 3.00 8.00
105 Rick Ferrell 4.00 10.00
106 Art Fletcher 3.00 8.00
107 Dennis Galehouse 3.00 8.00
108 Chick Galloway 3.00 8.00
109 Mule Haas 3.00 8.00
110 Stan Hack 3.00 8.00
111 Bump Hadley 3.00 8.00
112 Billy Hamilton 4.00 10.00
113 Joe Hauser 3.00 8.00
114 Babe Herman 3.00 8.00
115 Travis Jackson 4.00 10.00
116 Eddie Joost 3.00 8.00
117 Addie Joss 4.00 10.00
118 Joe Judge 3.00 8.00
119 Joe Kuhel 3.00 8.00
120 Napoleon Lajoie 5.00 12.00
121 Dutch Leonard 3.00 8.00
122 Ted Lyons 4.00 10.00
123 Connie Mack 5.00 12.00
124 Rabbit Maranville 4.00 10.00
125 Fred Marberry 3.00 8.00
126 Joe McGinnity 4.00 10.00
127 Oscar Melillo 3.00 8.00
128 Ray Mueller 3.00 8.00
129 Kid Nichols 4.00 10.00
130 Lefty O'Doul 4.00 10.00
131 Bob O'Farrell 3.00 8.00
132 Roger Peckinpaugh 3.00 8.00
133 Herb Pennock 4.00 10.00
134 George Pipgras 3.00 8.00
135 Eddie Plank 4.00 10.00
136 Ray Schalk 4.00 10.00
137 Hal Schumacher 3.00 8.00
138 Luke Sewell 3.00 8.00
139 Bob Shawkey 3.00 8.00
140 Riggs Stephenson 3.00 8.00
141 Billy Sullivan 3.00 8.00
142 Bill Terry 5.00 12.00
143 Joe Tinker 4.00 10.00
144 Pie Traynor 4.00 10.00
145 Hal Trosky 3.00 8.00
146 George Uhle 3.00 8.00
147 Johnny VanderMeer 4.00 10.00
148 Arky Vaughan 4.00 10.00
149 Rube Waddell 4.00 10.00
150 Honus Wagner 20.00 50.00
151 Dixie Walker 3.00 8.00
152 Ted Williams 40.00 100.00
153 Cy Young 15.00 40.00
154 Ross Youngs 15.00 40.00

1963 Fleer

The Fleer set of current baseball players was marketed in 1963 in a gum card-style waxed wrapper package which contained a cherry cookie instead of gum. The five cent packs were packaged 24 to a box. The cards were printed in sheets of 66 with the scarce card of Joe Adcock (number 46) replaced by the unnumbered checklist card for the final press run. The complete set price includes the checklist card. The catalog designation for this set is R418-4. The key Rookie Card in this set is Maury Wills. The set is basically arranged numerically in alphabetical order by teams which are also in alphabetical order.

COMPLETE SET (67) 600.00 1500.00
WRAPPER (5-CENT) 50.00 100.00
1 Steve Barber 10.00 25.00
2 Ron Hansen 6.00 15.00
3 Milt Pappas 8.00 20.00
4 Brooks Robinson 30.00 80.00
5 Willie Mays 75.00 200.00
6 Lou Clinton 6.00 15.00
7 Bill Monbouquette 6.00 15.00
8 Carl Yastrzemski 25.00 60.00
9 Ray Herbert 6.00 15.00
10 Jim Landis 6.00 15.00
11 Dick Donovan 6.00 15.00
12 Tito Francona 6.00 15.00
13 Jerry Kindall 6.00 15.00
14 Frank Lary 8.00 20.00
15 Dick Howser 8.00 20.00
16 Jerry Lumpe 6.00 15.00
17 Norm Siebern 6.00 15.00
18 Don Lee 6.00 15.00
19 Albie Pearson 8.00 20.00
20 Bob Rodgers 8.00 20.00
21 Leon Wagner 6.00 15.00
22 Jim Kaat 10.00 25.00
23 Vic Power 8.00 20.00
24 Rich Rollins 8.00 20.00
25 Bobby Richardson 10.00 25.00
26 Ralph Terry 8.00 20.00
27 Tom Cheney 6.00 15.00
28 Chuck Cottier 6.00 15.00
29 Jimmy Piersall 8.00 20.00
30 Dave Stenhouse 6.00 15.00
31 Glen Hobbie 6.00 15.00
32 Ron Santo 15.00 40.00
33 Gene Freese 6.00 15.00
34 Vada Pinson 10.00 25.00
35 Bob Purkey 6.00 15.00
36 Joe Amalfitano 6.00 15.00
37 Bob Aspromonte 6.00 15.00
38 Dick Farrell 6.00 15.00
39 Al Spangler 6.00 15.00
40 Tommy Davis 8.00 20.00
41 Don Drysdale 20.00 50.00
42 Sandy Koufax 50.00 120.00
43 Maury Wills RC 40.00 100.00
44 Frank Bolling 6.00 15.00
45 Warren Spahn 25.00 60.00
46 Joe Adcock SP 25.00 60.00
47 Roger Craig 8.00 20.00
48 Al Jackson 8.00 20.00
49 Rod Kanehl 8.00 20.00
50 Ruben Amaro 6.00 15.00
51 Johnny Callison 8.00 20.00
52 Clay Dalrymple 6.00 15.00
53 Don Demeter 6.00 15.00
54 Art Mahaffey 6.00 15.00
55 Smoky Burgess 8.00 20.00
56 Roberto Clemente 75.00 200.00
57 Roy Face 8.00 20.00
58 Vern Law 8.00 20.00
59 Bill Mazeroski 8.00 20.00
60 Ken Boyer 10.00 25.00
61 Bob Gibson 25.00 60.00
62 Gene Oliver 6.00 15.00
63 Bill White 8.00 20.00
64 Orlando Cepeda 12.00 30.00
65 Jim Davenport 6.00 15.00
66 Billy O'Dell 10.00 25.00
NNO Checklist SP 250.00 500.00

1966 Fleer AS Match Game

The 1966 Fleer All-Star Match Baseball Game set consists of 66 standard-size cards. The front of each card has nine rectangular boxes, one for each inning of a baseball game. These boxes are either blue (for American All Stars) or yellow (for National All Stars). In the lower right corner, a tie breaker rule is listed. When properly placed, the backs of all the cards form a composite black and white photo of Don Drysdale. The cards are numbered on the front. This is a rare instance where the set is worth much more than any individual part.

COMPLETE SET (66) 150.00 300.00
COMMON PLAYER (1-66) 3.00 8.00

1968-72 Fleer Cloth Stickers

This set was issued over a period of four years. This can be determined by the inclusion of the Seattle Pilots, who only played in 1969, as well as the Texas Rangers who did not move to Texas until 1972. This sticker set measures 2 1/2" by 3 1/4" and is comprised of two different types of stickers. The first group (1-24) are all the same design with the team city printed in a banner across the top and the official team logo in a circular design below. Both are designed to peel off. The second group (25-48) are of a different design with the team logo letter being the top portion and the city left off. The team name makes up the bottom section. Again, both are designed to be peeled off. The stickers are unnumbered and checklisted below in alphabetical order within each sticker type.

COMPLETE SET (48) 40.00 80.00
1 Atlanta Braves .75 2.00
2 Baltimore Orioles .75 2.00
3 Boston Red Sox .75 2.00
4 California Angels .75 2.00
5 Chicago Cubs .75 2.00
6 Chicago White Sox .75 2.00
7 Cincinnati Reds .75 2.00
8 Cleveland Indians .75 2.00
9 Detroit Tigers .75 2.00
10 Houston Astros .75 2.00
11 Kansas City Royals .75 2.00
12 Los Angeles Dodgers .75 2.00
13 Minnesota Twins .75 2.00
14 Montreal Expos .75 2.00
15 New York Mets .75 2.00
16 New York Yankees .75 2.00
17 Oakland A's .75 2.00
18 Philadelphia Phillies .75 2.00
19 Pittsburgh Pirates .75 2.00
20 St. Louis Cardinals .75 2.00
21 San Francisco Giants .75 2.00
22 Seattle Pilots 2.00 5.00
23 Texas Rangers .75 2.00
24 Washington Senators .75 2.00
25 California Angels .75 2.00
26 Houston Astros .75 2.00
27 Atlanta Braves .75 2.00
28 St. Louis Cardinals .75 2.00
29 Chicago Cubs .75 2.00
30 Los Angeles Dodgers .75 2.00
31 Montreal Expos .75 2.00
32 San Francisco Giants .75 2.00
33 Cleveland Indians .75 2.00
34 New York Mets .75 2.00
35 Oakland A's .75 2.00
36 Baltimore Orioles .75 2.00
37 Philadelphia Phillies .75 2.00
38 Seattle Pilots .75 2.00
39 Pittsburgh Pirates .75 2.00
40 Texas Rangers .75 2.00
41 Reds .75 2.00
42 Red Sox .75 2.00
43 Royals .75 2.00
44 Senators .75 2.00
45 Sox .75 2.00
46 Tigers .75 2.00
47 Twins .75 2.00
48 Yankees .75 2.00

1970 Fleer Laughlin World Series Blue Backs

This set of 66 standard-size cards was distributed by Fleer in 1970 although the cards carry a copyright date of 1968 on the back. The cards are in crude color on the front with light blue printing on white card stock on the back. All the years are represented except for 1904 when no World Series was played. In the list below, the winning series team is listed first. The year of the Series on the obverse is inside a white baseball. The original art for the cards in this set was drawn by sports artist R.G. Laughlin.

COMPLETE SET (66) 75.00 150.00
1 1903 Red Sox .60 1.50
Pirates
2 1905 Giants 1.50 4.00
A's/(Christy Mathewson)
3 1906 White Sox .60 1.50
Cubs
4 1907 Cubs .60 1.50
Tigers
5 1908 Cubs 1.50 4.00
Tigers/(Joe Tinker&
Johnny Evers&
and
6 1909 Pirates/Tigers 2.50 6.00
7 1910 A's 1.00 2.50
Cubs/(Chief Bender
and Jack Coombs)
8 1911 A's 1.00 2.50
Giants/(John McGraw)
9 1912 Red Sox .60 1.50
Giants
10 1913 A's .60 1.50
Giants
11 1914 Braves .60 1.50
A's
12 1915 Red Sox 3.00 8.00
Phillies/(Babe Ruth)
13 1916 Red Sox 3.00 8.00
Dodgers/(Babe Ruth)
14 1917 White Sox .60 1.50
Giants
15 1918 Red Sox .60 1.50
Cubs
16 1919 Reds 3.00 8.00
White Sox
17 1920 Indians 1.00 2.50
Dodgers/(Stan Coveleski)
18 1921 Giants .60 1.50
Yankees/(Commissioner Landis)
19 1922 Giants .60 1.50
Yankees
20 1923 Yankees 3.00 8.00
Giants/(Babe Ruth)
21 1924 Senators 1.00 2.50
Giants/(John McGraw)
22 1925 Pirates 1.50 4.00
Senators/(Walter Johnson)
23 1926 Cardinals 1.00 2.50
Yankees/(Grover C. Alexander
and
24 1927 Yankees .60 1.50
Pirates
25 1928 Yankees 3.00 8.00
Cardinals/(Babe Ruth
and Lou Gehrig
26 1929 A's .60 1.50
Cubs
27 1930 A's .60 1.50
Cardinals
28 1931 Cardinals .60 1.50
A's/(Pepper Martin)
29 1932 Yankees 3.00 8.00
Cubs/(Babe Ruth
and Lou Gehrig)
30 1933 Giants 1.00 2.50
Senators/(Mel Ott)
31 1934 Cardinals .60 1.50
Tigers
32 1935 Tigers 1.00 2.50
Cubs/(Charlie Gehringer
and Tommy Br
33 1936 Yankees .60 1.50
Giants
34 1937 Yankees 1.00 2.50
Giants/(Carl Hubbell)
35 1938 Yankees 2.50 6.00
Cubs/(Lou Gehrig)
36 1939 Yankees .60 1.50
Reds
37 1940 Reds .60 1.50
Tigers
38 1941 Yankees .60 1.50
Dodgers
39 1942 Cardinals .60 1.50
Yankees
40 1943 Yankees .60 1.50
Cardinals
41 1944 Cardinals .60 1.50
Browns
42 1945 Tigers 1.50 4.00
Cubs/(Hank Greenberg)
43 1946 Cardinals 1.00 2.50
Red Sox/(Enos Slaughter)
44 1947 Yankees .60 1.50
Dodgers/(Al Gionfriddo)
45 1948 Indians .60 1.50
Braves
46 1949 Yankees .60 1.50
Dodgers/(Allie Reynolds
and Preache
47 1950 Yankees .60 1.50
Phillies
48 1951 Yankees .60 1.50
Giants
49 1952 Yankees 2.50 6.00
Dodgers/(Johnny Mize
and Duke Snide
50 1953 Yankees .60 1.50
Dodgers/(Carl Erskine)
51 1954 Giants .60 1.50
Indians/(Johnny Antonelli)
52 1955 Dodgers .60 1.50
Yankees/(Johnny Podres)
53 1956 Yankees .60 1.50
Dodgers
54 1957 Braves .60 1.50
Yankees/(Lew Burdette)
55 1958 Yankees .60 1.50
Braves/(Bob Turley)
56 1959 Dodgers .60 1.50
White Sox/(Chuck Essegian)
57 1960 Pirates .60 1.50
Yankees
58 1961 Yankees 1.00 2.50
Reds/(Whitey Ford)
59 1962 Yankees .60 1.50
Giants
60 1963 Dodgers .60 1.50
Yankees/(Moose Skowron)
61 1964 Cardinals 1.00 2.50
Yankees/(Bobby Richardson)
62 1965 Dodgers .60 1.50
Twins
63 1966 Orioles .60 1.50
Dodgers
64 1967 Cardinals .60 1.50
Red Sox
65 1968 Tigers .60 1.50
Cardinals
66 1969 Mets 1.00 2.50
Orioles

1971 Fleer Laughlin World Series Black Backs

This set of standard-size cards was distributed by Fleer in 1971 as a 68-card set. The cards were printed in crude color on the front with black printing on white card stock on the back. All the years since 1903 are represented in this set including 1904, when no World Series was played. While the copyright line on the card back references the year of issue as 1968, these black backed card first appeared in 1971. In 1978, Fleer reissued the entire 68-card set along with 7-update cards for the World Series' 1971-1977.

COMPLETE SET (68) 250.00 500.00
1 1903 Red Sox 1.50 4.00
Pirates/(Cy Young)
2 1904 NO Series/(John McGraw) 1.00 2.50
3 1905 Giants 1.50 4.00
A's/(Christy Mathewson&
Chief Bender
4 1906 White Sox .60 1.50
Cubs/(Fielder Jones)
5 1907 Cubs .60 1.50
Tigers
6 1908 Cubs/Tigers 2.00 5.00
7 1909 Pirates .60 1.50
Tigers
8 1910 A's 1.00 2.50
Cubs/(Eddie Collins)
9 1911 A's 1.00 2.50
Giants/(Home Run Baker)
10 1912 Red Sox .60 1.50
Giants
11 1913 A's 1.50 4.00
Giants/(Christy Mathewson)
12 1914 Braves .60 1.50
A's
13 1915 Red Sox 1.00 2.50
Phillies/(Grover Alexander)
14 1916 Red Sox .60 1.50
Dodgers
15 1917 White Sox 1.00 2.50
Giants/(Red Faber)
16 1918 Red Sox 3.00 8.00
Cubs/(Babe Ruth)
17 1919 Reds 3.00 8.00
White Sox
18 1920 Indians .60 1.50
Dodgers
19 1921 Giants 1.00 2.50
Yankees/(Waite Hoyt)
20 1922 Giants .60 1.50
Yankees
21 1923 Yankees 1.00 2.50
Giants/(Herb Pennock)
22 1924 Senators 1.50 4.00
Giants/(Walter Johnson)
23 1925 Pirates 1.00 2.50
Senators/(Kiki Cuyler and
Walter Jo
24 1926 Cardinals 1.50 4.00
Yankees/(Rogers Hornsby)
25 1927 Yankees .60 1.50
Pirates
26 1928 Yankees 2.00 5.00
Cardinals/(Lou Gehrig)
27 1929 A's .60 1.50
Cubs/(Howard Ehmke)
28 1930 A's 1.50 4.00
Cardinals/(Jimmie Foxx)
29 1931 Cardinals .60 1.50
A's/(Pepper Martin)
30 1932 Yankees 3.00 8.00
Cubs/(Babe Ruth)
31 1933 Giants 1.00 2.50
Senators/(Carl Hubbell)
32 1934 Cardinals .60 1.50
Tigers
33 1935 Tigers 1.00 2.50
Cubs/(Mickey Cochrane)
34 1936 Yankees .60 1.50
Giants/(Red Rolfe)
35 1937 Yankees 1.00 2.50
Giants/(Tony Lazzeri)
36 1938 Yankees .60 1.50
Cubs
37 1939 Yankees .60 1.50
Reds
38 1940 Reds .60 1.50
Tigers
39 1941 Yankees .60 1.50
Dodgers
40 1942 Cardinals .60 1.50
Yankees
41 1943 Yankees .60 1.50
Cardinals
42 1944 Cardinals .60 1.50
Browns
43 1945 Tigers 1.50 4.00
Cubs/(Hank Greenberg)
44 1946 Cardinals 1.00 2.50
Red Sox/(Enos Slaughter)
45 1947 Yankees .60 1.50
Dodgers
46 1948 Indians .60 1.50
Braves
47 1949 Yankees .60 1.50
Dodgers/(Preacher Roe)
48 1950 Yankees .60 1.50
Phillies/(Allie Reynolds)
49 1951 Yankees .60 1.50
Giants/(Ed Lopat)
50 1952 Yankees 1.00 2.50
Dodgers/(Johnny Mize)
51 1953 Yankees .60 1.50
Dodgers
52 1954 Giants .60 1.50
Indians
53 1955 Dodgers 1.00 2.50
Yankees/(Duke Snider)
54 1956 Yankees .60 1.50
Dodgers
55 1957 Braves .60 1.50
Yankees
56 1958 Yankees .60 1.50
Braves/(Hank Bauer)
57 1959 Dodgers 1.00 2.50
Wh.Sox/(Duke Snider)
58 1960 Pirates .60 1.50
Yankees
59 1961 Yankees 1.00 2.50
Reds/(Whitey Ford)
60 1962 Yankees .60 1.50
Giants
61 1963 Dodgers .60 1.50
Yankees
62 1964 Cardinals .60 1.50
Yankees
63 1965 Dodgers .60 1.50
Twins
64 1966 Orioles .60 1.50
Dodgers
65 1967 Cardinals .60 1.50
Red Sox
66 1968 Tigers .60 1.50
Cardinals
67 1969 Mets .60 1.50
Orioles
68 1970 Orioles 1.00 2.50
Reds
69 1971 Pirates 100.00 200.00
Orioles
Roberto Clemente
70 1972 A's 40.00 80.00
Reds
71 1973 A's 40.00 80.00
Mets
72 1974 A's 40.00 80.00
Dodgers
73 1975 Reds 40.00 80.00
Red Sox
74 1976 Reds 40.00 80.00
Yankees
75 1977 Yankees 40.00 80.00
Dodgers

1972 Fleer Famous Feats

This Fleer set of 40 cards features the artwork of sports artist R.G. Laughlin. The set is titled "Baseball's Famous Feats." The cards are numbered both on the front and back. The backs are printed in light blue on white card stock. The cards measure approximately 2 1/2" by 4". This set was licensed by Major League Baseball.

COMPLETE SET (40) 60.00 120.00
1 Joe McGinnity .75 2.00
2 Rogers Hornsby 1.25 3.00
3 Christy Mathewson 2.50 6.00
4 Dazzy Vance .75 2.00
5 Lou Gehrig 5.00 12.00
6 Jim Bottomley .75 2.00
7 Johnny Evers .75 2.00
8 Walter Johnson 2.50 6.00
9 Hack Wilson .75 2.00
10 Wilbert Robinson .75 2.00
11 Cy Young 1.25 3.00
12 Rudy York .50 1.25
13 Grover C. Alexander .75 2.00
14 Fred Toney and .50 1.25
Hippo Vaughan
15 Ty Cobb 5.00 12.00
16 Jimmie Foxx 2.50 6.00
17 Hub Leonard .50 1.25
18 Eddie Collins .75 2.00
19 Joe Oeschger and .50 1.25
Leon Cadore
20 Babe Ruth 10.00 25.00
21 Honus Wagner 1.25 3.00
22 Red Rolfe .50 1.25
23 Ed Walsh .75 2.00
24 Paul Waner .75 2.00
25 Mel Ott 1.00 2.50
26 Eddie Plank .75 2.00
27 Sam Crawford .75 2.00
28 Napoleon Lajoie 1.00 2.50
29 Ed Reulbach .50 1.25
30 Pinky Higgins .50 1.25
31 Bill Klem .75 2.00
32 Tris Speaker 1.00 2.50
33 Hank Gowdy .50 1.25
34 Lefty O'Doul .50 1.25
35 Lloyd Waner .75 2.00
36 Chuck Klein .75 2.00
37 Deacon Phillippe .50 1.25
38 Ed Delahanty .75 2.00
39 Jack Chesbro .75 2.00
40 Willie Keeler .75 2.00

1973 Fleer Wildest Days

This Fleer set of 42 cards is titled "Baseball's Wildest Days and Plays" and features the artwork of sports artist R.G. Laughlin. The sets were available from Bob Laughlin for $3. The backs are printed in dark red on white card stock. The cards measure approximately 2 1/2" by 4". This set was not licensed by Major League Baseball.

COMPLETE SET (42) 60.00 120.00
1 Cubs and Phillies 1.25 3.00
Score 49 Runs in Game
2 Frank Chance .60 1.50
Five HBP's in One Day
3 Jim Thorpe 4.00 10.00
Homered into 3 States
4 Eddie Gaedel 1.50 4.00
Midget in Majors
5 Most Tied Game Ever .60 1.50
6 Seven Errors in .60 1.50
One Inning
7 Four 20-Game Winners .60 1.50
But No Pennant
8 Dummy Hoy 1.25 3.00
Umpires Signal Strikes
9 Fourteen Hits in .60 1.50
One Inning
10 Yankees Not Shut Out .60 1.50
For Two Years
11 Buck Weaver 1.50 4.00
17 Straight Fouls

12 George Sisler Greatest Thrill Was as a Pitcher .60 1.50
13 Wrong-Way Baserunner .60 1.50
14 Kiki Cuyler Sits Out Series .60 1.50
15 Grounder Climbed Wall .60 1.50
16 Gabby Street Washington Monument .60 1.50
17 Mel Ott Ejected Twice 3.00 8.00
18 Shortest Pitching Career .60 1.50
19 Three Homers in One Inning .60 1.50
20 Bill Byron Singing Umpire .60 1.50
21 Fred Clarke Walking Steal of Home .60 1.50
22 Christy Mathewson 373rd Win Discovered 3.00 8.00
23 Hitting Through the Unglaub Arc .60 1.50
24 Jim O'Rourke Catching at 52 .60 1.50
25 Fired for Striking Out in Series .60 1.50
26 Eleven Run Inning on One Hit .60 1.50
27 58 Innings in 3 Days .60 1.50
28 Homer on Warm-Up Pitch .60 1.50
29 Giants Win 26 Straight But Finish Fourth .60 1.50
30 Player Who Stole First Base .60 1.50
31 Ernie Shore Perfect Game in Relief .60 1.50
32 Greatest Comeback .60 1.50
33 All-Time Flash-In-The-Pan .60 1.50
34 Hub Pruett Fanned Ruth 19 out of 31 1.50 4.00
35 Fixed Batting Race Cobb/Lajoie 3.00 8.00
36 Wild-Pitch Rebound Play .60 1.50
37 17 Straight Scoring Innings .60 1.50
38 Wildest Opening Day .60 1.50
39 Baseball's Strike One .60 1.50
40 Opening Day No Hitter That Didn't Count .60 1.50
41 Jimmie Foxx Six Straight Walks in One Game 3.00 8.00
42 Entire Team Hit and Scored in Inning 1.25 3.00

1974 Fleer Baseball Firsts

This Fleer set of 42 cards is titled "Baseball Firsts" and features the artwork of sports artist R.G. Laughlin. The cards are numbered on the back. The backs are printed in black on gray card stock. The cards measure approximately 2 1/2" by 4". This set was not licensed by Major League Baseball.

COMPLETE SET (42) 50.00 100.00
COMMON PLAYER (1-42) .60 1.50
1 Slide 1.00 2.50
2 Spring Training .60 1.50
3 Bunt .60 1.50
4 Catcher's Mask .60 1.50
5 Lou Gehrig Four straight Homers 8.00 20.00
6 Radio Broadcast .60 1.50
7 Numbered Uniforms .60 1.50
8 Shin Guards .60 1.50
9 Players Association .60 1.50
10 Knuckleball .60 1.50
11 Player With Glasses .60 1.50
12 Baseball Cards 6.00 15.00
13 Standardized Rules .60 1.50
14 Grand Slam .60 1.50
15 Player Fined .60 1.50
16 Presidential Opener .60 1.50
17 Player Transaction .60 1.50
18 All-Star Game .60 1.50
19 Scoreboard .60 1.50
20 Cork Center Ball .60 1.50
21 Scorekeeping .60 1.50
22 Domed Stadium .60 1.50
23 Batting Helmet .60 1.50
24 Fatality .60 1.50
25 Unassisted Triple Play .60 1.50
26 Home Run At Night .60 1.50
27 Black Major Leaguer 1.00 2.50
28 Pinch Hitter .60 1.50
29 Million-Dollar World Series .60 1.50
30 Tarpaulin .60 1.50
31 Team Initials .60 1.50
32 Pennant Playoff .60 1.50
33 Glove .60 1.50
34 Curve Ball .60 1.50
35 Night Game .60 1.50
36 Admission Charge .60 1.50
37 Farm System .60 1.50
38 Telecast .60 1.50
39 Commissioner .60 1.50
40 .400 Hitter .60 1.50
41 World Series .60 1.50
42 Player Into Service 1.00 2.50

1975 Fleer Pioneers

This 28-card set of brown and white sepia-toned photos of old timers is subtitled "Pioneers of Baseball." The graphics artwork was done by R.G. Laughlin. The cards measure approximately 2 1/2" X 4". The card backs are a narrative about the particular player.

COMPLETE SET (28) 15.00 40.00
1 Cap Anson 1.25 3.00
2 Harry Wright .75 2.00
3 Buck Ewing .75 2.00
4 Al G. Spalding .75 2.00
5 Old Hoss Radbourn .75 2.00
6 Dan Brouthers .75 2.00
7 Roger Bresnahan .75 2.00
8 Mike Kelly .75 2.00
9 Ned Hanlon .75 2.00
10 Ed Delahanty .75 2.00
11 Pud Galvin .75 2.00
12 Amos Rusie .75 2.00
13 Tommy McCarthy .75 2.00
14 Ty Cobb 4.00 10.00
15 John McGraw .75 2.00
16 Home Run Baker .75 2.00
17 Johnny Evers .75 2.00
18 Nap Lajoie 1.00 2.50
19 Cy Young 1.25 3.00
20 Eddie Collins 1.00 2.50
21 John Glasscock .60 1.50
22 Hal Chase .60 1.50
23 Mordecai Brown .75 2.00
24 Jake Daubert .60 1.50
25 Mike Donlin .60 1.50
26 John Clarkson .75 2.00
27 Buck Herzog .60 1.50
28 Art Nehf .60 1.50

1981 Fleer

This issue of cards marks Fleer's first modern era entry into the current player baseball card market since 1963. Unopened packs contained 17 cards as well as a piece of gum. Unopened boxes contained 38 packs. As a matter of fact, the boxes actually told the retailer there was extra profit as they were charged as if there were 36 packs in the box. These cards were packed 20 boxes to a case. Cards are grouped in team order and teams are ordered based upon their standings from the 1980 season with the World Series champion Philadelphia Phillies starting off the set. Cards 638-660 feature specials and checklists. The cards of pitchers in this set erroneously show a heading (on the card backs) of "Batting Record" over their career pitching statistics. There were three distinct printings: the two following the primary run were designed to correct numerous errors. The variations caused by these multiple printings are noted in the checklist below (P1, P2, or P3). The Craig Nettles variation was corrected before the end of the first printing and thus is not included in the complete set consideration due to scarcity. The key Rookie Cards in this set are Danny Ainge, Harold Baines, Kirk Gibson, Jeff Reardon, and Fernando Valenzuela, whose first name was erroneously spelled Fernand on the card front.

COMPLETE SET (660) 15.00 40.00
1 Pete Rose 1.25 3.00
2 Larry Bowa .08 .25
3 Manny Trillo .02 .10
4 Bob Boone .08 .25
5A M.Schmidt Batting 1.00 2.50
5B M.Schmidt Portrait P1 1.00 2.50
6 Steve Carlton P1 .20 .50
6B Steve Carlton P2 .60 1.50
6C Steve Carlton P3 .75 2.00
7 Tug McGraw .08 .25
8 Larry Christenson .02 .10
9 Bake McBride .08 .25
10 Greg Luzinski .08 .25
11 Ron Reed .02 .10
12 Dickie Noles .02 .10
13 Keith Moreland RC .08 .25
14 Bob Walk RC .20 .50
15 Lonnie Smith .08 .25
16 Dick Ruthven .02 .10
17 Sparky Lyle .08 .25
18 Greg Gross .02 .10
19 Garry Maddox .02 .10
20 Nino Espinosa .02 .10
21 George Vukovich RC .02 .10
22 John Vukovich .02 .10
23 Ramon Aviles .02 .10
24A Kevin Saucier P1 .02 .10
24B Kevin Saucier P3 .20 .50
25 Randy Lerch .02 .10
26 Del Unser .02 .10
27 Tim McCarver .08 .25
28A George Brett 1.00 2.50
28B George Brett (MVP Third Base) 1.00 2.50
29A Willie Wilson .08 .25
29B Willie Wilson Outfield .08 .25
30 Paul Splittorff .02 .10
31 Dan Quisenberry .02 .10
32A Amos Otis P1 Batting .08 .25
32B Amos Otis P2 Portrait .08 .25
33 Steve Busby .02 .10
34 U.L. Washington .02 .10
35 Dave Chalk .02 .10
36 Darrell Porter .02 .10
37 Marty Pattin .02 .10
38 Larry Gura .02 .10
39 Renie Martin .02 .10
40 Rich Gale .02 .10
41A Hal McRae P1 .20 .50
41B Hal McRae P2 .08 .25
42 Dennis Leonard .02 .10
43 Willie Aikens .02 .10
44 Frank White .08 .25
45 Clint Hurdle .02 .10
46 John Wathan .02 .10
47 Pete LaCock .02 .10
48 Rance Mulliniks .02 .10
49 Jeff Twitty RC .02 .10
50 Jamie Quirk .02 .10
51 Art Howe .02 .10
52 Ken Forsch .02 .10
53 Vern Ruhle .02 .10
54 Joe Niekro .02 .10
55 Frank LaCorte .02 .10
56 J.R. Richard .08 .25
57 Nolan Ryan 2.00 5.00
58 Enos Cabell .02 .10
59 Cesar Cedeno .08 .25
60 Jose Cruz .08 .25
61 Bill Virdon MG .02 .10
62 Terry Puhl .02 .10
63 Joaquin Andujar .08 .25
64 Alan Ashby .02 .10
65 Joe Sambito .02 .10
66 Denny Walling .02 .10
67 Jeff Leonard .08 .25
68 Luis Pujols .02 .10
69 Bruce Bochy .02 .10
70 Rafael Landestoy .02 .10
71 Dave Smith RC .20 .50
72 Danny Heep RC .02 .10
73 Julio Gonzalez .02 .10
74 Craig Reynolds .02 .10
75 Gary Woods .02 .10
76 Dave Bergman .02 .10
77 Randy Niemann .02 .10
78 Joe Morgan .20 .50
79A Reggie Jackson .40 1.00
79B Reggie Jackson Mr.Baseball .40 1.00
80 Bucky Dent .08 .25
81 Tommy John .08 .25
82 Luis Tiant .08 .25
83 Rick Cerone .02 .10
84 Dick Howser MG .02 .10
85 Lou Piniella .08 .25
86 Ron Davis .02 .10
87A Craig Nettles P1 2.00 5.00
87B Graig Nettles COR .08 .25
88 Ron Guidry .08 .25
89 Rich Gossage .08 .25
90 Rudy May .02 .10
91 Gaylord Perry .08 .25
92 Eric Soderholm .02 .10
93 Bob Watson .08 .25
94 Bobby Murcer .08 .25
95 Bobby Brown .02 .10
96 Jim Spencer .02 .10
97 Tom Underwood .02 .10
98 Oscar Gamble .02 .10
99 Johnny Oates .08 .25
100 Fred Stanley .02 .10
101 Ruppert Jones .02 .10
102 Dennis Werth RC .02 .10
103 Joe Lefebvre RC .02 .10
104 Brian Doyle .02 .10
105 Aurelio Rodriguez .02 .10
106 Doug Bird .02 .10
107 Mike Griffin RC .05 .15
108 Tim Lollar RC .02 .10
109 Willie Randolph .08 .25
110 Steve Garvey .20 .50
111 Reggie Smith .08 .25
112 Don Sutton .08 .25
113 Burt Hooton .02 .10
114A Dave Lopes P1 .20 .50
114B Dave Lopes P2 .08 .25
115 Dusty Baker .08 .25
116 Tom Lasorda MG .20 .50
117 Bill Russell .08 .25
118 Jerry Reuss UER .08 .25
119 Terry Forster .08 .25
120A Bob Welch .08 .25
120B Bob Welch (Robert) .08 .25
121 Don Stanhouse .02 .10
122 Rick Monday .08 .25
123 Derrel Thomas .02 .10
124 Joe Ferguson .02 .10
125 Rick Sutcliffe .08 .25
126A Ron Cey P1 .08 .25
126B Ron Cey P2 .08 .25
127 Dave Goltz .02 .10
128 Jay Johnstone .02 .10
129 Steve Yeager .08 .25
130 Gary Weiss RC .02 .10
131 Mike Scioscia RC .60 1.50
132 Vic Davalillo .02 .10
133 Doug Rau .02 .10
134 Pepe Frias .02 .10
135 Mickey Hatcher .02 .10
136 Steve Howe RC .20 .50
137 Robert Castillo RC .02 .10
138 Gary Thomasson .02 .10
139 Rudy Law .02 .10
140 Fernando Valenzuela RC 2.50 6.00
141 Manny Mota .08 .25
142 Gary Carter .20 .50
143 Steve Rogers .08 .25
144 Warren Cromartie .02 .10
145 Andre Dawson .20 .50
146 Larry Parrish .02 .10
147 Rowland Office .02 .10
148 Ellis Valentine .02 .10
149 Dick Williams MG .02 .10
150 Bill Gullickson RC .20 .50
151 Elias Sosa .02 .10
152 John Tamargo .02 .10
153 Chris Speier .02 .10
154 Ron LeFlore .08 .25
155 Rodney Scott .02 .10
156 Stan Bahnsen .02 .10
157 Bill Lee .08 .25
158 Fred Norman .02 .10
159 Woodie Fryman .02 .10
160 David Palmer .02 .10
161 Jerry White .02 .10
162 Roberto Ramos RC .02 .10
163 John D'Acquisto .02 .10
164 Tommy Hutton .02 .10
165 Charlie Lea RC .02 .10
166 Scott Sanderson .02 .10
167 Ken Macha .02 .10
168 Tony Bernazard .02 .10
169 Jim Palmer .20 .50
170 Steve Stone .02 .10
171 Mike Flanagan .02 .10
172 Al Bumbry .02 .10
173 Doug DeCinces .02 .10
174 Scott McGregor .02 .10
175 Mark Belanger .02 .10
176 Tim Stoddard .02 .10
177A Rick Dempsey P1 .08 .25
177B Rick Dempsey P2 .02 .10
178 Earl Weaver MG .08 .25
179 Tippy Martinez .02 .10
180 Dennis Martinez .08 .25
181 Sammy Stewart .02 .10
182 Rich Dauer .02 .10
183 Lee May .02 .10
184 Eddie Murray .60 1.50
185 Benny Ayala .02 .10
186 John Lowenstein .02 .10
187 Gary Roenicke .02 .10
188 Ken Singleton .08 .25
189 Dan Graham .02 .10
190 Terry Crowley .02 .10
191 Kiko Garcia .02 .10
192 Dave Ford .02 .10
193 Mark Corey .02 .10
194 Lenn Sakata .02 .10
195 Doug DeCinces .02 .10
196 Johnny Bench .40 1.00
197 Dave Concepcion .08 .25
198 Ray Knight .08 .25
199 Ken Griffey .08 .25
200 Tom Seaver .40 1.00
201 Dave Collins .08 .25
202 George Foster .20 .50
203 Junior Kennedy .02 .10
204 Frank Pastore .02 .10
205 Dan Driessen .02 .10
206 Hector Cruz .02 .10
207 Paul Moskau .02 .10
208 Charlie Leibrandt RC .20 .50
209 Harry Spilman .02 .10
210 Joe Price RC .02 .10
211 Tom Hume .02 .10
212 Joe Nolan RC .02 .10
213 Doug Bair .02 .10
214 Mario Soto .08 .25
215A Bill Bonham P1 .20 .50
215B Bill Bonham P2 .02 .10
216A George Foster SLG .08 .25
216B George Foster P2 .20 .50
217 Paul Householder RC .02 .10
218 Ron Oester .02 .10
219 Sam Mejias .02 .10
220 Sheldon Burnside RC .02 .10
221 Carl Yastrzemski .60 1.50
222 Jim Rice .08 .25
223 Fred Lynn .08 .25
224 Carlton Fisk .20 .50
225 Rick Burleson .02 .10
226 Dennis Eckersley .20 .50
227 Butch Hobson .02 .10
228 Tom Burgmeier .02 .10
229 Garry Hancock .02 .10
230 Don Zimmer MG .08 .25
231 Steve Renko .02 .10
232 Dwight Evans .20 .50
233 Mike Torrez .02 .10
234 Bob Stanley .02 .10
235 Jim Dwyer .02 .10
236 Dave Stapleton RC .02 .10
237 Glenn Hoffman RC .02 .10
238 Jerry Remy .02 .10
239 Dick Drago .02 .10
240 Bill Campbell .02 .10
241 Tony Perez .20 .50
242 Phil Niekro .08 .25
243 Dale Murphy .20 .50
244 Bob Horner .08 .25
245 Jeff Burroughs .08 .25
246 Rick Camp .02 .10
247 Bobby Cox MG .08 .25
248 Bruce Benedict .02 .10
249 Gene Garber .02 .10
250 Jerry Royster .02 .10
251A Gary Matthews P1 .20 .50
251B Gary Matthews P2 .08 .25
252 Chris Chambliss .08 .25
253 Luis Gomez .02 .10
254 Bill Nahorodny .02 .10
255 Doyle Alexander .02 .10
256 Brian Asselstine .02 .10
257 Biff Pocoroba .02 .10
258 Mike Lum .02 .10
259 Charlie Spikes .02 .10
260 Glenn Hubbard .02 .10
261 Tommy Boggs .02 .10
262 Al Hrabosky .02 .10
263 Rick Matula .02 .10
264 Preston Hanna .02 .10
265 Larry Bradford .02 .10
266 Rafael Ramirez RC .02 .10
267 Larry McWilliams .02 .10
268 Rod Carew .20 .50
269 Bobby Grich .08 .25
270 Carney Lansford .08 .25
271 Don Baylor .08 .25
272 Joe Rudi .08 .25
273 Dan Ford .02 .10
274 Jim Fregosi MG .02 .10
275 Dave Frost .02 .10
276 Frank Tanana .08 .25
277 Dickie Thon .02 .10
278 Jason Thompson .02 .10
279 Rick Miller .02 .10
280 Bert Campaneris .08 .25
281 Tom Donohue .02 .10
282 Brian Downing .08 .25
283 Fred Patek .08 .25
284 Bruce Kison .02 .10
285 Dave LaRoche .02 .10
286 Don Aase .02 .10
287 Jim Barr .02 .10
288 Alfredo Martinez RC .02 .10
289 Larry Harlow .02 .10
290 Andy Hassler .02 .10
291 Dave Kingman .08 .25
292 Bill Buckner .08 .25
293 Rick Reuschel .08 .25
294 Bruce Sutter .20 .50
295 Jerry Martin .02 .10
296 Scot Thompson .02 .10
297 Ivan DeJesus .02 .10
298 Steve Dillard .02 .10
299 Dick Tidrow .02 .10
300 Randy Martz RC .02 .10
301 Lenny Randle .02 .10
302 Lynn McGlothen .02 .10
303 Cliff Johnson .02 .10
304 Tim Blackwell .02 .10
305 Dennis Lamp .02 .10
306 Bill Caudill .02 .10
307 Carlos Lezcano RC .02 .10
308 Jim Tracy RC .40 1.00
309 Doug Capilla UER .02 .10
310 Willie Hernandez .02 .10
311 Mike Vail .02 .10
312 Mike Krukow RC .02 .10
313 Barry Foote .02 .10
314 Larry Biittner .02 .10
315 Mike Tyson .02 .10
316 Lee Mazzilli .08 .25
317 John Stearns .02 .10
318 Alex Trevino .02 .10
319 Craig Swan .02 .10
320 Frank Taveras .02 .10
321 Steve Henderson .02 .10
322 Neil Allen .02 .10
323 Mark Bomback RC .02 .10
324 Mike Jorgensen .02 .10
325 Joe Torre MG .08 .25
326 Elliott Maddox .02 .10
327 Pete Falcone .02 .10
328 Ray Burris .02 .10
329 Claudell Washington .02 .10
330 Doug Flynn .02 .10
331 Joel Youngblood .02 .10
332 Bill Almon .02 .10
333 Tom Hausman .02 .10
334 Pat Zachry .02 .10
335 Jeff Reardon RC .40 1.00
336 Wally Backman RC .20 .50
337 Dan Norman .02 .10
338 Jerry Morales .02 .10
339 Ed Farmer .02 .10
340 Bob Molinaro .02 .10
341 Todd Cruz .02 .10
342A Britt Burns P1 .20 .50
342B Britt Burns P2 RC .08 .25
343 Kevin Bell .02 .10
344 Tony LaRussa MG .08 .25
345 Steve Trout .02 .10
346 Harold Baines RC .75 2.00
347 Richard Wortham .02 .10
348 Wayne Nordhagen .02 .10
349 Mike Squires .02 .10
350 Lamar Johnson .02 .10
351 Rickey Henderson SB 1.25 3.00
352 Francisco Barrios .02 .10
353 Thad Bosley .02 .10
354 Chet Lemon .08 .25
355 Bruce Kimm .02 .10
356 Richard Dotson RC .02 .10
357 Jim Morrison .02 .10
358 Mike Proly .02 .10
359 Greg Pryor .02 .10
360 Dave Parker .08 .25
361 Omar Moreno .02 .10
362A Kent Tekulve P1 .02 .10
362B Kent Tekulve P2 .02 .10
363 Willie Stargell .20 .50
364 Phil Garner .08 .25
365 Ed Ott .02 .10
366 Don Robinson .02 .10
367 Chuck Tanner MG .02 .10
368 Jim Rooker .02 .10
369 Dale Berra .02 .10
370 Jim Bibby .02 .10
371 Steve Nicosia .02 .10
372 Mike Easler .02 .10
373 Bill Robinson .02 .10
374 Lee Lacy .02 .10
375 John Candelaria .08 .25
376 Manny Sanguillen .08 .25
377 Rick Rhoden .02 .10
378 Grant Jackson .02 .10
379 Tim Foli .02 .10
380 Rod Scurry RC .02 .10
381 Bill Madlock .08 .25
382A Kurt Bevacqua P1 .08 .25
382B Kurt Bevacqua P2 .02 .10
383 Bert Blyleven .08 .25
384 Eddie Solomon .02 .10
385 Enrique Romo .02 .10
386 John Milner .02 .10
387 Mike Hargrove .02 .10
388 Jorge Orta .02 .10
389 Toby Harrah .08 .25
390 Tom Veryzer .02 .10
391 Miguel Dilone .02 .10
392 Dan Spillner .02 .10
393 Jack Brohamer .02 .10
394 Wayne Garland .02 .10
395 Sid Monge .02 .10
396 Rick Waits .02 .10
397 Joe Charboneau RC .40 1.00
398 Gary Alexander .02 .10
399 Jerry Dybzinski RC .02 .10
400 Mike Stanton RC .02 .10
401 Mike Paxton .02 .10
402 Gary Gray RC .02 .10
403 Rick Manning .02 .10
404 Bo Diaz .02 .10
405 Ron Hassey .02 .10
406 Ross Grimsley .02 .10
407 Victor Cruz .02 .10
408 Len Barker .08 .25
409 Bob Bailor .02 .10
410 Otto Velez .02 .10
411 Ernie Whitt .02 .10
412 Jim Clancy .02 .10
413 Barry Bonnell .02 .10
414 Dave Stieb .08 .25
415 Damaso Garcia RC .08 .25
416 John Mayberry .02 .10
417 Roy Howell .02 .10
418 Danny Ainge RC 1.25 3.00
419A Jesse Jefferson P1 .02 .10
419B Jesse Jefferson P3 .20 .50
420 Joey McLaughlin .02 .10
421 Lloyd Moseby RC .20 .50
422 Alvis Woods .02 .10
423 Garth Iorg .02 .10
424 Doug Ault .02 .10
425 Ken Schrom RC .02 .10
426 Mike Willis .02 .10
427 Steve Braun .02 .10
428 Bob Davis .02 .10
429 Jerry Garvin .02 .10
430 Alfredo Griffin .02 .10
431 Bob Mattick MG RC .02 .10
432 Vida Blue .08 .25
433 Jack Clark .08 .25
434 Willie McCovey .20 .50
435 Mike Ivie .02 .10
436A Darrel Evans P1 ERR .20 .50
436B Darrell Evans P2 COR .20 .50
437 Terry Whitfield .02 .10
438 Rennie Stennett .02 .10
439 John Montefusco .02 .10
440 Jim Wohlford .02 .10
441 Bill North .02 .10
442 Milt May .02 .10
443 Max Venable RC .02 .10
444 Ed Whitson .02 .10
445 Al Holland RC .02 .10
446 Randy Moffitt .02 .10
447 Bob Knepper .02 .10
448 Gary Lavelle .02 .10
449 Greg Minton .02 .10
450 Johnnie LeMaster .02 .10
451 Larry Herndon .02 .10
452 Rich Murray RC .02 .10
453 Joe Pettini RC .02 .10
454 Allen Ripley .02 .10
455 Dennis Littlejohn .02 .10
456 Tom Griffin .02 .10
457 Alan Hargesheimer RC .02 .10
458 Joe Strain .02 .10
459 Steve Kemp .02 .10
460 Sparky Anderson MG .08 .25
461 Alan Trammell .20 .50
462 Mark Fidrych .08 .25
463 Lou Whitaker .20 .50
464 Dave Rozema .02 .10
465 Milt Wilcox .02 .10
466 Champ Summers .02 .10
467 Lance Parrish .08 .25
468 Dan Petry .02 .10
469 Pat Underwood .02 .10
470 Rick Peters RC .02 .10
471 Al Cowens .02 .10
472 John Wockenfuss .02 .10
473 Tom Brookens .02 .10
474 Richie Hebner .02 .10
475 Jack Morris .20 .50
476 Jim Lentine RC .02 .10
477 Bruce Robbins .02 .10
478 Mark Wagner .02 .10
479 Tim Corcoran .02 .10
480A Stan Papi P1 .08 .25
480B Stan Papi P2 .02 .10
481 Kirk Gibson RC 2.00 5.00
482 Dan Schatzeder .02 .10
483 Amos Otis .08 .25
484 Dave Winfield .20 .50
485 Rollie Fingers .08 .25
486 Gene Richards .02 .10
487 Randy Jones .02 .10
488 Ozzie Smith 1.25 3.00
489 Gene Tenace .08 .25
490 Bill Fahey .02 .10
491 John Curtis .02 .10
492 Dave Cash .02 .10
493A Tim Flannery P1 .08 .25
493B Tim Flannery P2 .02 .10
494 Jerry Mumphrey .02 .10
495 Bob Shirley .02 .10
496 Steve Mura .02 .10
497 Eric Rasmussen .02 .10
498 Broderick Perkins .02 .10
499 Barry Evans RC .02 .10
500 Chuck Baker .02 .10
501 Luis Salazar RC .20 .50
502 Gary Lucas RC .02 .10
503 Mike Armstrong RC .02 .10
504 Jerry Turner .02 .10
505 Dennis Kinney RC .02 .10
506 Willie Montanez UER .02 .10
507 Gorman Thomas .08 .25
508 Ben Oglivie .08 .25
509 Larry Hisle .02 .10
510 Sal Bando .08 .25
511 Robin Yount .60 1.50
512 Mike Caldwell .02 .10
513 Sixto Lezcano .02 .10
514A Bill Travers P1 ERR .08 .25
514B Bill Travers P2 COR .02 .10
515 Paul Molitor .40 1.00
516 Moose Haas .02 .10
517 Bill Castro .02 .10
518 Jim Slaton .02 .10
519 Lary Sorensen .02 .10
520 Bob McClure .02 .10
521 Charlie Moore .02 .10
522 Jim Gantner .02 .10
523 Reggie Cleveland .02 .10
524 Don Money .02 .10
525 Bill Travers .02 .10
526 Buck Martinez .02 .10
527 Dick Davis .02 .10
528 Ted Simmons .08 .25
529 Garry Templeton .08 .25
530 Ken Reitz .02 .10
531 Tony Scott .02 .10
532 Ken Oberkfell .02 .10
533 Bob Sykes .02 .10
534 Keith Smith .02 .10
535 John Littlefield RC .02 .10
536 Jim Kaat .08 .25
537 Bob Forsch .02 .10
538 Mike Phillips .02 .10
539 Terry Landrum RC .02 .10
540 Leon Durham RC .20 .50
541 Terry Kennedy .02 .10
542 George Hendrick .08 .25
543 Dane Iorg .02 .10
544 Mark Littell .02 .10
545 Keith Hernandez .08 .25
546 Silvio Martinez .02 .10
547A Don Hood P1 ERR .08 .25
547B Don Hood P2 COR .02 .10
548 Bobby Bonds .08 .25
549 Mike Ramsey RC .05 .15
550 Tom Herr .02 .10
551 Roy Smalley .02 .10
552 Jerry Koosman .08 .25
553 Ken Landreaux .02 .10
554 John Castino .02 .10
555 Doug Corbett RC .02 .10
556 Bombo Rivera .02 .10
557 Ron Jackson .02 .10
558 Butch Wynegar .02 .10
559 Hosken Powell .02 .10
560 Pete Redfern .02 .10
561 Roger Erickson .02 .10
562 Glenn Adams .02 .10
563 Rick Sofield .02 .10
564 Geoff Zahn .02 .10
565 Pete Mackanin .02 .10
566 Mike Cubbage .02 .10
567 Darrell Jackson .02 .10
568 Dave Edwards .02 .10
569 Rob Wilfong .02 .10
570 Sal Butera RC .02 .10
571 Jose Morales .02 .10
572 Rick Langford .02 .10
573 Mike Norris .02 .10
574 Rickey Henderson 2.50 6.00
575 Tony Armas .08 .25
576 Dave Revering .02 .10
577 Jeff Newman .02 .10
578 Bob Lacey .02 .10
579 Brian Kingman .02 .10
580 Mitchell Page .02 .10
581 Billy Martin MG .20 .50
582 Rob Picciolo .02 .10
583 Mike Heath .02 .10
584 Mickey Klutts .02 .10
585 Orlando Gonzalez .02 .10
586 Mike Davis RC .20 .50
587 Wayne Gross .02 .10
588 Matt Keough .02 .10
589 Steve McCatty .02 .10
590 Dwayne Murphy .02 .10
591 Mario Guerrero .02 .10
592 Dave McKay RC .02 .10
593 Jim Essian .02 .10
594 Dave Heaverlo .02 .10
595 Maury Wills MG .08 .25
596 Juan Beniquez .02 .10
597 Rodney Craig .02 .10
598 Jim Anderson .02 .10
599 Floyd Bannister .02 .10
600 Bruce Bochte .02 .10
601 Julio Cruz .02 .10
602 Ted Cox .02 .10
603 Dan Meyer .02 .10
604 Larry Cox .02 .10
605 Bill Stein .02 .10
606 Steve Garvey .20 .50
607 Dave Roberts .02 .10
608 Leon Roberts .02 .10
609 Reggie Walton RC .02 .10
610 Dave Edler RC .02 .10
611 Larry Milbourne .02 .10
612 Kim Allen RC .02 .10
613 Mario Mendoza .02 .10
614 Tom Paciorek .02 .10
615 Glenn Abbott .02 .10
616 Joe Simpson .02 .10
617 Mickey Rivers .02 .10
618 Jim Kern .02 .10
619 Jim Sundberg .08 .25
620 Richie Zisk .02 .10
621 Jon Matlack .02 .10
622 Fergie Jenkins .08 .25
623 Pat Corrales MG .02 .10
624 Ed Figueroa .02 .10
625 Buddy Bell .08 .25
626 Al Oliver .08 .25
627 Doc Medich .02 .10
628 Bump Wills .02 .10
629 Rusty Staub .08 .25
630 Pat Putnam .02 .10
631 John Grubb .02 .10
632 Danny Darwin .02 .10
633 Ken Clay .02 .10
634 Jim Norris .02 .10
635 John Butcher RC .02 .10
636 Dave Roberts .02 .10
637 Billy Sample .02 .10
638 Carl Yastrzemski .60 1.50
639 Cecil Cooper .08 .25
640 M.Schmidt Portrait P2 1.00 2.50
641A CL: Phils/Royals P1 .08 .25
641B CL: Phils/Royals P2 .08 .25
642 CL: Astros Yankees .02 .10
643 CL: Expos Dodgers .02 .10
644A CL: Reds/Orioles P1 .08 .25
644B CL: Reds/Orioles P2 .08 .25
645A Rose/Bowa/Schmidt .60 1.50
645B Rose/Bowa/Schmidt 1.00 2.50
646 CL: Braves Red Sox .02 .10
647 CL: Cubs Angels .02 .10
648 CL: Mets White Sox .02 .10
649 CL: Indians Pirates .02 .10
650 Reggie Jackson Mr. BB .40 1.00
651 CL: Giants Blue Jays .02 .10
652A CL: Tigers/Padres P1 .08 .25
652B CL: Tigers/Padres P2 .08 .25
653 Willie Wilson Most Hits .08 .25
654A CL:Brewers/Cards P1 .08 .25
654B CL:Brewers/Cards P2 .08 .25
655 George Brett .390 Avg. 1.00 2.50
656 CL: Twins/Oakland A's .08 .25
657 T.McGraw Saver P2 .08 .25
658 CL: Rangers Mariners .02 .10
659A Checklist P1 .02 .10
659B Checklist P2 .02 .10
660A S.Carlton Gold Arm P1 .20 .50
660B S.Carlton Golden Arm .75 2.00

1981 Fleer Star Stickers

The stickers in this 128-sticker standard-size set were distributed in wax packs. The 1981 Fleer Baseball Star

Stickers consist of numbered cards with peelable, full-color sticker fronts and three unnumbered checklists. The backs of the numbered player cards are the same as the 1981 Fleer regular issue cards except for the numbers, while the checklist cards (cards 126-128 below) have sticker fronts of Jackson (1-42), Brett (43-83), and Schmidt (84-125).

COMPLETE SET (128) 10.00 25.00
1 Steve Garvey .20 .50
2 Ron LeFlore .02 .10
3 Ron Cey .05 .15
4 Dave Revering .02 .10
5 Tony Armas .02 .10
6 Mike Norris .02 .10
7 Steve Kemp .02 .10
8 Bruce Bochte .02 .10
9 Mike Schmidt 1.00 2.50
10 Scott McGregor .02 .10
11 Buddy Bell .05 .15
12 Carney Lansford .05 .15
13 Carl Yastrzemski .40 1.00
14 Ben Oglivie .02 .10
15 Willie Stargell .20 .50
16 Cecil Cooper .05 .15
17 Gene Richards .02 .10
18 Jim Kern .02 .10
19 Jerry Koosman .05 .15
20 Larry Bowa .05 .15
21 Kent Tekulve .05 .15
22 Dan Driessen .02 .10
23 Phil Niekro .20 .50
24 Dan Quisenberry .05 .15
25 Dave Winfield .40 1.00
26 Dave Parker .05 .15
27 Rick Langford .02 .10
28 Amos Otis .05 .15
29 Bill Buckner .05 .15
30 Al Bumbry .02 .10
31 Bake McBride .02 .10
32 Mickey Rivers .05 .15
33 Rick Burleson .02 .10
34 Dennis Eckersley .20 .50
35 Cesar Cedeno .05 .15
36 Enos Cabell .02 .10
37 Johnny Bench .40 1.00
38 Robin Yount .40 1.00
39 Mark Belanger .05 .15
40 Rod Carew .30 .75
41 George Foster .05 .15
42 Lee Mazzilli .02 .10
43 Triple Threat: .75 2.00
Pete Rose
Larry Bowa
Mike Schmid
44 J.R. Richard .02 .10
45 Lou Piniella .05 .15
46 Ken Landreaux .02 .10
47 Rollie Fingers .20 .50
48 Joaquin Andujar .05 .15
49 Tom Seaver .40 1.00
50 Bobby Grich .05 .15
51 Jon Matlack .02 .10
52 Jack Clark .05 .15
53 Jim Rice .05 .15
54 Rickey Henderson 1.50 4.00
55 Roy Smalley .02 .10
56 Mike Flanagan .02 .10
57 Steve Rogers .02 .10
58 Carlton Fisk .60 1.50
59 Don Sutton .20 .50
60 Ken Griffey .05 .15
61 Burt Hooton .02 .10
62 Dusty Baker .05 .15
63 Vida Blue .05 .15
64 Al Oliver .05 .15
65 Jim Bibby .02 .10
66 Tony Perez .10 .30
67 Davey Lopes .05 .15
68 Bill Russell .05 .15
69 Larry Parrish .02 .10
70 Garry Maddox .02 .10
71 Phil Garner .05 .15
72 Graig Nettles .07 .20
73 Gary Carter .30 .75
74 Pete Rose .60 1.50
75 Greg Luzinski .05 .15
76 Ron Guidry .05 .15
77 Gorman Thomas .02 .10
78 Jose Cruz .05 .15
79 Bob Boone .05 .15
80 Bruce Sutter .05 .15
81 Chris Chambliss .05 .15
82 Paul Molitor .75 2.00
83 Tug McGraw .05 .15
84 Ferguson Jenkins .10 .30
85 Steve Carlton .30 .75
86 Miguel Dilone .02 .10
87 Reggie Smith .05 .15
88 Rick Cerone .02 .10
89 Alan Trammell .20 .50
90 Doug DeCinces .02 .10
91 Sparky Lyle .05 .15
92 Warren Cromartie .02 .10
93 Rick Reuschel .05 .15
94 Larry Hisle .02 .10
95 Paul Splittorff .02 .10
96 Manny Trillo .02 .10
97 Frank White .05 .15
98 Fred Lynn .05 .15
99 Bob Horner .02 .10
100 Omar Moreno .02 .10
101 Dave Concepcion .05 .15
102 Larry Gura .02 .10
103 Ken Singleton .05 .15
104 Steve Stone .02 .10
105 Richie Zisk .05 .15
106 Willie Wilson .05 .15
107 Willie Randolph .05 .15
108 Nolan Ryan 3.00 8.00
109 Joe Morgan .30 .75
110 Bucky Dent .05 .15
111 Dave Kingman .07 .20
112 John Castino .02 .10
113 Joe Rudi .02 .10
114 Ed Farmer .02 .10
115 Reggie Jackson .40 1.00
116 George Brett 1.25 3.00
117 Eddie Murray .75 2.00
118 Rich Gossage .20 .50
119 Dale Murphy .30 .75
120 Ted Simmons .05 .15
121 Tommy John .08 .25
122 Don Baylor .07 .20
123 Andre Dawson .30 .75
124 Jim Palmer .30 .75
125 Garry Templeton .02 .10
126 Reggie Jackson CL 1 .20 .50
Unnumbered
127 George Brett CL 2 .60 1.50
Unnumbered
128 Mike Schmidt CL3 .40 1.00
Unnumbered

1982 Fleer

The 1982 Fleer set contains 660-card standard-size cards, of which are grouped in team order based upon standings from the previous season. Cards numbered 628 through 646 are special cards highlighting some of the stars and leaders of the 1981 season. The last 14 cards in the set (647-660) are checklist cards. The backs feature player statistics and a full-color team logo in the upper right-hand corner of each card. The complete set price below does not include any of the more valuable variation cards listed. Fleer was not allowed to insert bubble gum or other confectionary products into these packs; therefore logo stickers were included in these 15-card packs. Those 15-card packs with an SRP of 30 cents were packed 36 packs to a box and 20 boxes to a case. Notable Rookie Cards in this set include Cal Ripken Jr., Lee Smith, and Dave Stewart.

COMPLETE SET (660) 20.00 50.00
1 Dusty Baker .07 .20
2 Robert Castillo .02 .10
3 Ron Cey .07 .20
4 Terry Forster .07 .20
5 Steve Garvey .07 .20
6 Dave Goltz .02 .10
7 Pedro Guerrero .07 .20
8 Burt Hooton .02 .10
9 Steve Howe .02 .10
10 Jay Johnstone .02 .10
11 Ken Landreaux .02 .10
12 Dave Lopes .07 .20
13 Mike A. Marshall RC .20 .50
14 Bobby Mitchell .02 .10
15 Rick Monday .07 .20
16 Tom Niedenfuer RC .20 .50
17 Ted Power RC .05 .15
18 Jerry Reuss UER .02 .10
19 Ron Roenicke .02 .10
20 Bill Russell .07 .20
21 Steve Sax RC .40 1.00
22 Mike Scioscia .07 .20
23 Reggie Smith .07 .20
24 Dave Stewart RC .60 1.50
25 Rick Sutcliffe .07 .20
26 Derrel Thomas .02 .10
27 Fernando Valenzuela .30 .75
28 Bob Welch .07 .20
29 Steve Yeager .07 .20
30 Bobby Brown .02 .10
31 Rick Cerone .02 .10
32 Ron Davis .02 .10
33 Bucky Dent .07 .20
34 Barry Foote .02 .10
35 George Frazier .02 .10
36 Oscar Gamble .02 .10
37 Rich Gossage .07 .20
38 Ron Guidry .07 .20
39 Reggie Jackson .15 .40
40 Tommy John .07 .20
41 Rudy May .02 .10
42 Larry Milbourne .02 .10
43 Jerry Mumphrey .02 .10
44 Bobby Murcer .07 .20
45 Gene Nelson .02 .10
46 Graig Nettles .07 .20
47 Johnny Oates .07 .20
48 Lou Piniella .07 .20
49 Willie Randolph .07 .20
50 Rick Reuschel .07 .20
51 Dave Revering .02 .10
52 Dave Righetti RC .60 1.50
53 Aurelio Rodriguez .02 .10
54 Bob Watson .02 .10
55 Dennis Werth .02 .10
56 Dave Winfield .07 .20
57 Johnny Bench .30 .75
58 Bruce Berenyi .02 .10
59 Larry Biittner .02 .10
60 Scott Brown .02 .10
61 Dave Collins .02 .10
62 Geoff Combe .02 .10
63 Dave Concepcion .07 .20
64 Dan Driessen .02 .10
65 Joe Edelen .02 .10
66 George Foster .07 .20
67 Ken Griffey .07 .20
68 Paul Householder .02 .10
69 Tom Hume .02 .10
70 Junior Kennedy .02 .10
71 Ray Knight .07 .20
72 Mike LaCoss .02 .10
73 Rafael Landestoy .02 .10
74 Charlie Leibrandt .02 .10
75 Sam Mejias .02 .10
76 Paul Moskau .02 .10
77 Joe Nolan .02 .10
78 Mike O'Berry .02 .10
79 Ron Oester .02 .10
80 Frank Pastore .02 .10
81 Joe Price .02 .10
82 Tom Seaver .30 .75
83 Mario Soto .07 .20
84 Mike Vail .02 .10
85 Tony Armas .07 .20
86 Shooty Babitt .02 .10
87 Dave Beard .02 .10
88 Rick Bosetti .02 .10
89 Keith Drumwright .02 .10
90 Wayne Gross .02 .10
91 Mike Heath .02 .10
92 Rickey Henderson 1.00 2.50
93 Cliff Johnson .02 .10
94 Jeff Jones .02 .10
95 Matt Keough .02 .10
96 Brian Kingman .02 .10
97 Mickey Klutts .02 .10
98 Rick Langford .02 .10
99 Steve McCatty .02 .10
100 Dave McKay .02 .10
101 Dwayne Murphy .02 .10
102 Jeff Newman .02 .10
103 Mike Norris .02 .10
104 Bob Owchinko .02 .10
105 Mitchell Page .02 .10
106 Rob Picciolo .02 .10
107 Jim Spencer .02 .10
108 Fred Stanley .02 .10
109 Tom Underwood .02 .10
110 Joaquin Andujar .07 .20
111 Steve Braun .02 .10
112 Bob Forsch .02 .10
113 George Hendrick .07 .20
114 Keith Hernandez .07 .20
115 Tom Herr .02 .10
116 Dane Iorg .02 .10
117 Jim Kaat .07 .20
118 Tito Landrum .02 .10
119 Sixto Lezcano .02 .10
120 Mark Littell .02 .10
121 John Martin RC .05 .15
122 Silvio Martinez .02 .10
123 Ken Oberkfell .02 .10
124 Darrell Porter .02 .10
125 Mike Ramsey .02 .10
126 Orlando Sanchez .02 .10
127 Bob Shirley .02 .10
128 Lary Sorensen .02 .10
129 Bruce Sutter .15 .40
130 Bob Sykes .02 .10
131 Garry Templeton .07 .20
132 Gene Tenace .07 .20
133 Jerry Augustine .02 .10
134 Sal Bando .07 .20
135 Mark Brouhard .02 .10
136 Mike Caldwell .02 .10
137 Reggie Cleveland .02 .10
138 Cecil Cooper .07 .20
139 Jamie Easterly .02 .10
140 Marshall Edwards .02 .10
141 Rollie Fingers .07 .20
142 Jim Gantner .02 .10
143 Moose Haas .02 .10
144 Larry Hisle .02 .10
145 Roy Howell .02 .10
146 Rickey Keeton .02 .10
147 Randy Lerch .02 .10
148 Paul Molitor .07 .20
149 Don Money .02 .10
150 Charlie Moore .02 .10
151 Ben Oglivie .07 .20
152 Ted Simmons .07 .20
153 Jim Slaton .02 .10
154 Gorman Thomas .07 .20
155 Robin Yount .50 1.25
156 Pete Vuckovich .02 .10
Should precede Yount
in the team order
157 Benny Ayala .02 .10
158 Mark Belanger .02 .10
159 Al Bumbry .02 .10
160 Terry Crowley .02 .10
161 Rich Dauer .02 .10
162 Doug DeCinces .02 .10
163 Rick Dempsey .02 .10
164 Jim Dwyer .02 .10
165 Mike Flanagan .02 .10
166 Dave Ford .02 .10
167 Dan Graham .02 .10
168 Wayne Krenchicki .02 .10
169 John Lowenstein .02 .10
170 Dennis Martinez .07 .20
171 Tippy Martinez .02 .10
172 Scott McGregor .02 .10
173 Jose Morales .02 .10
174 Eddie Murray .30 .75
175 Jim Palmer .07 .20
176 Cal Ripken RC 15.00 40.00
177 Gary Roenicke .02 .10
178 Lenn Sakata .02 .10
179 Ken Singleton .07 .20
180 Sammy Stewart .02 .10
181 Tim Stoddard .02 .10
182 Steve Stone .02 .10
183 Stan Bahnsen .02 .10
184 Ray Burris .02 .10
185 Gary Carter .07 .20
186 Warren Cromartie .02 .10
187 Andre Dawson .07 .20
188 Terry Francona RC 1.25 3.00
189 Woodie Fryman .02 .10
190 Bill Gullickson .02 .10
191 Grant Jackson .02 .10
192 Wallace Johnson .02 .10
193 Charlie Lea .02 .10
194 Bill Lee .07 .20
195 Jerry Manuel .02 .10
196 Brad Mills .02 .10
197 John Milner .02 .10
198 Rowland Office .02 .10
199 David Palmer .02 .10
200 Larry Parrish .02 .10
201 Mike Phillips .02 .10
202 Tim Raines .15 .40
203 Bobby Ramos .02 .10
204 Jeff Reardon .07 .20
205 Steve Rogers .07 .20
206 Scott Sanderson .02 .10
207 Rodney Scott UER .15 .40
Photo actually
Tim Raines
208 Elias Sosa .02 .10
209 Chris Speier .02 .10
210 Tim Wallach RC .40 1.00
211 Jerry White .02 .10
212 Alan Ashby .02 .10
213 Cesar Cedeno .07 .20
214 Jose Cruz .07 .20
215 Kiko Garcia .02 .10
216 Phil Garner .07 .20
217 Danny Heep .02 .10
218 Art Howe .02 .10
219 Bob Knepper .02 .10
220 Frank LaCorte .02 .10
221 Joe Niekro .02 .10
222 Joe Pittman .02 .10
223 Terry Puhl .02 .10
224 Luis Pujols .02 .10
225 Craig Reynolds .02 .10
226 J.R. Richard .07 .20
227 Dave Roberts .02 .10
228 Vern Ruhle .02 .10
229 Nolan Ryan 1.50 4.00
230 Joe Sambito .02 .10
231 Tony Scott .02 .10
232 Dave Smith .02 .10
233 Harry Spilman .02 .10
234 Don Sutton .07 .20
235 Dickie Thon .02 .10
236 Denny Walling .02 .10
237 Gary Woods .02 .10
238 Luis Aguayo .02 .10
239 Ramon Aviles .02 .10
240 Bob Boone .07 .20
241 Larry Bowa .07 .20
242 Warren Brusstar .02 .10
243 Steve Carlton .15 .40
244 Larry Christenson .02 .10
245 Dick Davis .02 .10
246 Greg Gross .02 .10
247 Sparky Lyle .07 .20
248 Garry Maddox .02 .10
249 Gary Matthews .07 .20
250 Bake McBride .07 .20
251 Tug McGraw .07 .20
252 Keith Moreland .02 .10
253 Dickie Noles .02 .10
254 Mike Proly .02 .10
255 Ron Reed .02 .10
256 Pete Rose 1.00 2.50
257 Dick Ruthven .02 .10
258 Mike Schmidt .75 2.00
259 Lonnie Smith .02 .10
260 Manny Trillo .02 .10
261 Del Unser .02 .10
262 George Vukovich .02 .10
263 Tom Brookens .02 .10
264 George Cappuzzello .02 .10
265 Marty Castillo .02 .10
266 Al Cowens .02 .10
267 Kirk Gibson .30 .75
268 Richie Hebner .02 .10
269 Ron Jackson .02 .10
270 Lynn Jones .02 .10
271 Steve Kemp .02 .10
272 Rick Leach .02 .10
273 Aurelio Lopez .02 .10
274 Jack Morris .07 .20
275 Kevin Saucier .02 .10
276 Lance Parrish .07 .20
277 Rick Peters .02 .10
278 Dan Petry .02 .10
279 Dave Rozema .02 .10
280 Stan Papi .02 .10
281 Dan Schatzeder .02 .10
282 Champ Summers .02 .10
283 Alan Trammell .07 .20
284 Lou Whitaker .07 .20
285 Milt Wilcox .02 .10
286 John Wockenfuss .02 .10
287 Gary Allenson .02 .10
288 Tom Burgmeier .02 .10
289 Bill Campbell .02 .10
290 Mark Clear .02 .10
291 Steve Crawford .02 .10
292 Dennis Eckersley .15 .40
293 Dwight Evans .15 .40
294 Rich Gedman .20 .50
295 Garry Hancock .02 .10
296 Glenn Hoffman .02 .10
297 Bruce Hurst .02 .10
298 Carney Lansford .07 .20
299 Rick Miller .02 .10
300 Reid Nichols .02 .10
301 Bob Ojeda RC .20 .50
302 Tony Perez .15 .40
303 Chuck Rainey .02 .10
304 Jerry Remy .02 .10
305 Jim Rice .07 .20
306 Joe Rudi .07 .20
307 Bob Stanley .02 .10
308 Dave Stapleton .02 .10
309 Frank Tanana .07 .20
310 Mike Torrez .02 .10
311 John Tudor .07 .20
312 Carl Yastrzemski .50 1.25
313 Buddy Bell .07 .20
314 Steve Comer .02 .10
315 Danny Darwin .02 .10
316 John Ellis .02 .10
317 John Grubb .02 .10
318 Rick Honeycutt .02 .10
319 Charlie Hough .07 .20
320 Ferguson Jenkins .07 .20
321 John Henry Johnson .02 .10
322 Jim Kern .02 .10
323 Jon Matlack .02 .10
324 Doc Medich .02 .10
325 Mario Mendoza .02 .10
326 Al Oliver .07 .20
327 Pat Putnam .02 .10
328 Mickey Rivers .02 .10
329 Leon Roberts .02 .10
330 Billy Sample .02 .10
331 Bill Stein .02 .10
332 Jim Sundberg .07 .20
333 Mark Wagner .02 .10
334 Bump Wills .02 .10
335 Bill Almon .02 .10
336 Harold Baines .07 .20
337 Ross Baumgarten .02 .10
338 Tony Bernazard .02 .10
339 Britt Burns .02 .10
340 Richard Dotson .02 .10
341 Jim Essian .02 .10
342 Ed Farmer .02 .10
343 Carlton Fisk .15 .40
344 Kevin Hickey RC .05 .15
345 LaMarr Hoyt .02 .10
346 Lamar Johnson .02 .10
347 Jerry Koosman .07 .20
348 Rusty Kuntz .02 .10
349 Dennis Lamp .02 .10
350 Ron LeFlore .07 .20
351 Chet Lemon .07 .20
352 Greg Luzinski .07 .20
353 Bob Molinaro .02 .10
354 Jim Morrison .02 .10
355 Wayne Nordhagen .02 .10
356 Greg Pryor .02 .10
357 Mike Squires .02 .10
358 Steve Trout .02 .10
359 Alan Bannister .02 .10
360 Len Barker .02 .10
361 Bert Blyleven .07 .20
362 Joe Charboneau .07 .20
363 John Denny .02 .10
364 Bo Diaz .02 .10
365 Miguel Dilone .02 .10
366 Jerry Dybzinski .02 .10
367 Wayne Garland .02 .10
368 Mike Hargrove .02 .10
369 Toby Harrah .07 .20
370 Ron Hassey .02 .10
371 Von Hayes RC .20 .50
372 Pat Kelly .02 .10
373 Duane Kuiper .02 .10
374 Rick Manning .02 .10
375 Sid Monge .02 .10
376 Jorge Orta .02 .10
377 Dave Rosello .02 .10
378 Dan Spillner .02 .10
379 Mike Stanton .02 .10
380 Andre Thornton .02 .10
381 Tom Veryzer .02 .10
382 Rick Waits .02 .10
383 Doyle Alexander .02 .10
384 Vida Blue .07 .20
385 Fred Breining .02 .10
386 Enos Cabell .02 .10
387 Jack Clark .07 .20
388 Darrell Evans .07 .20
389 Tom Griffin .02 .10
390 Larry Herndon .02 .10
391 Al Holland .02 .10
392 Gary Lavelle .02 .10
393 Johnnie LeMaster .02 .10
394 Jerry Martin .02 .10
395 Milt May .02 .10
396 Greg Minton .02 .10
397 Joe Morgan .07 .20
398 Joe Pettini .02 .10
399 Allen Ripley .02 .10
400 Billy Smith .02 .10
401 Rennie Stennett .02 .10
402 Ed Whitson .02 .10
403 Jim Wohlford .02 .10
404 Willie Aikens .02 .10
405 George Brett .75 2.00
406 Ken Brett .02 .10
407 Dave Chalk .02 .10
408 Rich Gale .02 .10
409 Cesar Geronimo .02 .10
410 Larry Gura .02 .10
411 Clint Hurdle .02 .10
412 Mike Jones .02 .10
413 Dennis Leonard .02 .10
414 Renie Martin .02 .10
415 Lee May .02 .10
416 Hal McRae .07 .20
417 Darryl Motley .02 .10
418 Rance Mulliniks .02 .10
419 Amos Otis .07 .20
420 Ken Phelps .02 .10
421 Jamie Quirk .02 .10
422 Dan Quisenberry .02 .10
423 Paul Splittorff .02 .10
424 U.L. Washington .02 .10
425 John Wathan .02 .10
426 Frank White .07 .20
427 Willie Wilson .07 .20
428 Brian Asselstine .02 .10
429 Bruce Benedict .02 .10
430 Tommy Boggs .02 .10
431 Larry Bradford .02 .10
432 Rick Camp .02 .10
433 Chris Chambliss .07 .20
434 Gene Garber .02 .10
435 Preston Hanna .02 .10
436 Bob Horner .07 .20
437 Glenn Hubbard .02 .10
438A All Hrabosky ERR 3.00 8.00
438B Al Hrabosky ERR .15 .40
Height 5'1
438C Al Hrabosky .07 .20
Height 5'10
439 Rufino Linares .02 .10
440 Rick Mahler .02 .10
441 Ed Miller .02 .10
442 John Montefusco .02 .10
443 Dale Murphy .15 .40
444 Phil Niekro .07 .20
445 Gaylord Perry .07 .20
446 Biff Pocoroba .02 .10
447 Rafael Ramirez .02 .10
448 Jerry Royster .02 .10
449 Claudell Washington .02 .10
450 Don Aase .02 .10
451 Don Baylor .07 .20
452 Juan Beniquez .02 .10
453 Rick Burleson .02 .10
454 Bert Campaneris .07 .20
455 Rod Carew .15 .40
456 Bob Clark .02 .10
457 Brian Downing .07 .20
458 Dan Ford .02 .10
459 Ken Forsch .02 .10
460A Dave Frost 5 mm .02 .10
space before ERA
460B Dave Frost .02 .10
1 mm space
461 Bobby Grich .07 .20
462 Larry Harlow .02 .10
463 John Harris .02 .10
464 Andy Hassler .02 .10
465 Butch Hobson .02 .10
466 Jesse Jefferson .02 .10
467 Bruce Kison .02 .10
468 Fred Lynn .07 .20
469 Angel Moreno .02 .10
470 Ed Ott .02 .10
471 Fred Patek .02 .10
472 Steve Renko .02 .10
473 Mike Witt .20 .50
474 Geoff Zahn .02 .10
475 Gary Alexander .02 .10
476 Dale Berra .02 .10
477 Kurt Bevacqua .02 .10
478 Jim Bibby .02 .10
479 John Candelaria .02 .10
480 Victor Cruz .02 .10
481 Mike Easler .02 .10
482 Tim Foli .02 .10
483 Lee Lacy .02 .10
484 Vance Law .02 .10
485 Bill Madlock .07 .20
486 Willie Montanez .02 .10
487 Omar Moreno .02 .10
488 Steve Nicosia .02 .10
489 Dave Parker .07 .20
490 Tony Pena .07 .20
491 Pascual Perez .02 .10
492 Johnny Ray RC .20 .50
493 Rick Rhoden .02 .10
494 Bill Robinson .02 .10
495 Don Robinson .02 .10
496 Enrique Romo .02 .10
497 Rod Scurry .02 .10
498 Eddie Solomon .02 .10
499 Willie Stargell .15 .40
500 Kent Tekulve .02 .10
501 Jason Thompson .02 .10
502 Glenn Abbott .02 .10
503 Jim Anderson .02 .10
504 Floyd Bannister .02 .10
505 Bruce Bochte .02 .10
506 Jeff Burroughs .02 .10
507 Bryan Clark RC .05 .15
508 Ken Clay .02 .10
509 Julio Cruz .02 .10
510 Dick Drago .02 .10
511 Gary Gray .02 .10
512 Dan Meyer .02 .10
513 Jerry Narron .02 .10
514 Tom Paciorek .02 .10
515 Casey Parsons .02 .10
516 Lenny Randle .02 .10
517 Shane Rawley .02 .10
518 Joe Simpson .02 .10
519 Richie Zisk .02 .10
520 Neil Allen .02 .10
521 Bob Bailor .02 .10
522 Hubie Brooks .02 .10
523 Mike Cubbage .02 .10
524 Pete Falcone .02 .10
525 Doug Flynn .02 .10
526 Tom Hausman .02 .10
527 Ron Hodges .02 .10
528 Randy Jones .02 .10
529 Mike Jorgensen .02 .10
530 Dave Kingman .07 .20
531 Ed Lynch .02 .10
532 Mike G. Marshall .02 .10
533 Lee Mazzilli .07 .20
534 Dyar Miller .02 .10
535 Mike Scott .07 .20
536 Rusty Staub .07 .20
537 John Stearns .02 .10
538 Craig Swan .02 .10
539 Frank Taveras .02 .10
540 Alex Trevino .02 .10
541 Ellis Valentine .02 .10
542 Mookie Wilson .07 .20
543 Joel Youngblood .02 .10
544 Pat Zachry .02 .10
545 Glenn Adams .02 .10
546 Fernando Arroyo .02 .10
547 John Verhoeven .02 .10
548 Sal Butera .02 .10
549 John Castino .02 .10
550 Don Cooper .02 .10
551 Doug Corbett .02 .10
552 Dave Engle .02 .10
553 Roger Erickson .02 .10
554 Danny Goodwin .02 .10
555A Darrell Jackson .15 .40
Black cap
555B Darrell Jackson .07 .20
Red cap with T
555C Darrell Jackson 1.25 3.00
556 Pete Mackanin .02 .10
557 Jack O'Connor .02 .10
558 Hosken Powell .02 .10
559 Pete Redfern .02 .10
560 Roy Smalley .02 .10
561 Chuck Baker UER .02 .10
Shortshop on front
562 Gary Ward .02 .10
563 Rob Wilfong .02 .10
564 Al Williams .02 .10
565 Butch Wynegar .02 .10
566 Randy Bass .20 .50
567 Juan Bonilla RC .05 .15
568 Danny Boone .02 .10
569 John Curtis .02 .10
570 Juan Eichelberger .02 .10
571 Barry Evans .02 .10
572 Tim Flannery .02 .10
573 Ruppert Jones .02 .10
574 Terry Kennedy .02 .10
575 Joe Lefebvre .02 .10
576A John Littlefield ERR 30.00 60.00
576B John Littlefield COR .07 .20
Right handed
577 Gary Lucas .02 .10
578 Steve Mura .02 .10
579 Broderick Perkins .02 .10
580 Gene Richards .02 .10
581 Luis Salazar .02 .10
582 Ozzie Smith .60 1.50
583 John Urrea .02 .10
584 Chris Welsh .02 .10
585 Rick Wise .02 .10
586 Doug Bird .02 .10
587 Tim Blackwell .02 .10
588 Bobby Bonds .07 .20
589 Bill Buckner .07 .20
590 Bill Caudill .02 .10
591 Hector Cruz .02 .10
592 Jody Davis RC .02 .10
593 Ivan DeJesus .02 .10
594 Steve Dillard .02 .10
595 Leon Durham .02 .10
596 Rawly Eastwick .07 .20
597 Steve Henderson .02 .10
598 Mike Krukow .02 .10
599 Mike Lum .02 .10
600 Randy Martz .02 .10
601 Jerry Morales .02 .10
602 Ken Reitz .02 .10
603 Lee Smith RC ERR .75 2.00
603B Lee Smith RC COR 2.50 6.00
604 Dick Tidrow .02 .10
605 Jim Tracy .07 .20
606 Mike Tyson .02 .10
607 Ty Waller .02 .10
608 Danny Ainge .07 .20
609 Jorge Bell RC .40 1.00
George Bell
610 Mark Bomback .02 .10
611 Barry Bonnell .02 .10
612 Jim Clancy .02 .10
613 Damaso Garcia .02 .10
614 Jerry Garvin .02 .10
615 Alfredo Griffin .02 .10
616 Garth Iorg .02 .10
617 Luis Leal .02 .10
618 Ken Macha .02 .10
619 John Mayberry .02 .10
620 Joey McLaughlin .02 .10
621 Lloyd Moseby .02 .10
622 Dave Stieb .07 .20
623 Jackson Todd .02 .10
624 Willie Upshaw .20 .50
625 Otto Velez .02 .10
626 Ernie Whitt .02 .10
627 Alvis Woods .02 .10
628 All Star Game .07 .20
Cleveland, Ohio
629 Frank White .07 .20
Bucky Dent
630 Dan Driessen .07 .20
Dave Concepcion
George Foster
631 Bruce Sutter .07 .20
Top NL Relief Pitcher
632 Steve Carlton .07 .20
Carlton Fisk
633 Carl Yastrzemski .30 .75
3000th Game
634 Johnny Bench .30 .75
Tom Seaver
635 Fernando Valenzuela .02 .10
Gary Carter
636A Fernando Valenzuela: .15 .40
NL SO King 'he' NL
636B Fernando Valenzuela .15 .40
NL SO King 'the' NL
637 Mike Schmidt .30 .75
Home Run King
638 Gary Carter .02 .10
Dave Parker
639 Perfect Game UER .07 .20
Len Barker
Bo Diaz
Catcher actually
Ron Hassey
640 Pete Rose .30 .75
Pete Rose Jr.
641 Lonnie Smith .30 .75
Mike Schmidt
Steve Carlton
642 Fred Lynn .15 .40
Dwight Evans
643 Rickey Henderson .50 1.25
644 Rollie Fingers .07 .20
Most Saves AL
645 Tom Seaver .07 .20
Most 1981 Wins
646 Yankee Powerhouse .07 .20
Reggie Jackson
Dave Winfield
Comma on back
after outfielder
646B Yankee Powerhouse .07 .20
Reggie Jackson
Dave Winfield
No comma
647 CL: Yankees .02 .10
Dodgers
648 CL: A's .02 .10
Reds
649 CL: Cards .02 .10
Brewers
650 CL: Expos .02 .10
Orioles
651 CL: Astros .02 .10
Phillies

652 CL: Tigers .02 .10
Red Sox
653 CL: Rangers .02 .10
White Sox
654 CL: Giants .02 .10
Indians
655 CL: Royals .02 .10
Braves
656 CL: Angels .02 .10
Pirates
657 CL: Mariners .02 .10
Mets
658 CL: Padres .02 .10
Twins
659 CL: Blue Jays .02 .10
Cubs
660 Specials Checklist .02 .10

1982 Fleer Stamps

The stamps in this 242-piece set measure 1 13/16" by 2 1/2". The 1982 Fleer stamp set consists of different individual stamps issued in strips of 10 stamps each. The stamps were issued in packages with the Fleer team logo stickers. The backs are blank and an inexpensive album is available in which to place the stamps. A checklist is provided in the back of the album which lists 25 strips of 10 stamps. The checklist below lists the individual stamps plus the strip (with prefix G) to which the stamps are supposed to belong based on the album strip checklist. Complete strips have equal value to the sum of the individual stamps on the strip. Eight stamps have been doubly printed and are noted by two different strip numbers below. The numbering is essentially in team order.

COMPLETE SET (242) 8.00 20.00
COMMON SHEET .30 .75
1 Fern. Valenzuela G20 .20 .50
2 Rick Monday G16 .01 .05
3 Ron Cey G9 .02 .10
4 Dusty Baker G20 .02 .10
5 Burt Hooton G10 .01 .05
6 Pedro Guerrero G23 .02 .10
7 Jerry Reuss G12 .01 .05
8 Bill Russell G7 .01 .05
9 Steve Garvey G21 .05 .15
10 Davey Lopes G19 .02 .10
11 Tom Seaver G7 .40 1.00
12 George Foster G17 .02 .10
13 Frank Pastore G12 .01 .05
14 Dave Collins G5 .01 .05
15 Dave Concepcion G21 .02 .10
16 Ken Griffey G6 .02 .10
17 Johnny Bench G20 .40 1.00
18 Ray Knight G16 .01 .05
19 Mario Soto G9 .01 .05
20 Ron Oester G19 .01 .05
21 Ken Oberkfell G21 .01 .05
22 Bob Forsch G4 .01 .05
23 Keith Hernandez G19 .02 .10
24 Dane Iorg G9 .01 .05
25 George Hendrick G2 .01 .05
26 Gene Tenace G24 .01 .05
27 Garry Templeton G12 .01 .05
28 Bruce Sutter G18 .02 .10
29 Darrell Porter G14 .01 .05
30 Tom Herr G3 .01 .05
31 Tim Raines G11 .20 .50
32 Chris Speier G13 .01 .05
33 Warren Cromartie G22 .01 .05
34 Larry Parrish G15 .01 .05
35 Andre Dawson G10 .30 .75
36 Steve Rogers G1 .01 .05
G25
37 Jeff Reardon G23 .05 .15
38 Rodney Scott G12 .01 .05
39 Gary Carter G14 .25 .60
40 Scott Sanderson G6 .01 .05
41 Cesar Cedeno G7 .01 .05
42 Nolan Ryan G10 2.50 6.00
43 Don Sutton G24 .08 .25
44 Terry Puhl G15 .01 .05
45 Joe Niekro G13 .02 .10
46 Tony Scott G16 .01 .05
47 Joe Sambito G1 .01 .05
48 Art Howe G9 .01 .05
49 Bob Knepper G18 .01 .05
50 Jose Cruz G22 .02 .10
51 Pete Rose G16 .75 2.00
52 Dick Ruthven G12 .01 .05
53 Mike Schmidt G14 .75 2.00
54 Steve Carlton G17 .40 1.00
55 Tug McGraw G4 .02 .10
56 Larry Bowa G4 .02 .10
57 Garry Maddox G18 .01 .05
58 Gary Matthews G4 .01 .05
59 Manny Trillo G15 .01 .05
60 Lonnie Smith G20 .01 .05
61 Vida Blue G11 .02 .10
62 Milt May G12 .01 .05
63 Joe Morgan G16 .20 .50
64 Enos Cabell G8 .01 .05
65 Jack Clark G18 .02 .10
66 Claud.Washington G19 .01 .05
67 Gaylord Perry G16 .20 .50
68 Phil Niekro G22 .20 .50
69 Bob Horner G7 .20 .50
70 Chris Chambliss G11 .01 .05
71 Dave Parker G15 .05 .15
72 Tony Pena G11 .02 .10
73 Kent Tekulve G23 .01 .05
74 Mike Easler G18 .01 .05
75 Tim Foli G13 .01 .05
76 Willie Stargell G21 .20 .50
77 Bill Madlock G5 .02 .10
78 Jim Bibby G14 .01 .05
79 Omar Moreno G17 .01 .05
80 Lee Lacy G2 .01 .05
81 Hubie Brooks G24 .01 .05
82 Rusty Staub G4 .02 .10
83 Ellis Valentine G13 .01 .05
84 Neil Allen G1 .01 .05
85 Dave Kingman G9 .05 .15
86 Mookie Wilson G3 .05 .15
87 Doug Flynn G11 .01 .05
88 Pat Zachry G8 .01 .05
89 John Stearns G6 .01 .05
90 Lee Mazzilli G2 .01 .05
91 Ken Reitz G23 .01 .05
92 Mike Krukow G11 .01 .05
93 Jerry Morales G10 .01 .05
94 Leon Durham G22 .01 .05
95 Ivan DeJesus G2 .01 .05
96 Bill Buckner G17 .01 .05
97 Jim Tracy G12 .01 .05
98 Steve Henderson G14 .01 .05
99 Dick Tidrow G14 .01 .05
100 Mike Tyson G5 .01 .05
101 Ozzie Smith G12 1.00 2.50
102 Ruppert Jones G24 .01 .05
103 Brod Perkins G10 .01 .05
104 Gene Richards G15 .01 .05
105 Terry Kennedy G22 .01 .05
106 Jim Bibby and .05 .15
Willie Stargell G4
107 Pete Rose and .30 .75
Larry Bowa G21
108 Fern.Valenzuela and .08 .25
Warren Spahn G1
G25
109 Pete Rose and .30 .75
Dave Concepcion G8
110 Reggie Jackson and .60 1.50
Dave Winfield G3
111 Fernando Valenzuela .05 .15
and Tom Lasorda G4
112 Reggie Jackson G6 .75 2.00
113 Dave Winfield G3 .60 1.50
114 Lou Piniella G2 .02 .10
115 Tommy John G9 .02 .10
116 Rich Gossage G1 .02 .10
G25
117 Ron Davis G10 .01 .05
118 Rick Cerone G5 .01 .05
119 Graig Nettles G8 .02 .10
120 Ron Guidry G24 .02 .10
121 Willie Randolph G24 .02 .10
122 Dwayne Murphy G15 .01 .05
123 Rickey Henderson G16 1.00 2.50
124 Wayne Gross G6 .01 .05
125 Mike Norris G8 .01 .05
126 Rick Langford G20 .01 .05
127 Jim Spencer G17 .01 .05
128 Tony Armas G12 .01 .05
129 Matt Keough G7 .01 .05
130 Jeff Jones G19 .01 .05
131 Steve McCatty G3 .01 .05
132 Rollie Fingers G7 .10 .30
133 Jim Gantner G15 .01 .05
134 Gorman Thomas G6 .01 .05
135 Robin Yount G13 .40 1.00
136 Paul Molitor G22 .60 1.50
137 Ted Simmons G10 .02 .10
138 Ben Oglivie G23 .01 .05
139 Moose Haas G21 .01 .05
140 Cecil Cooper G24 .02 .10
141 Pete Vuckovich G10 .01 .05
142 Doug DeCinces G21 .01 .05
143 Jim Palmer G9 .20 .50
144 Steve Stone G16 .01 .05
145 Mike Flanagan G19 .01 .05
146 Rick Dempsey G9 .01 .05
147 Al Bumbry G14 .01 .05
148 Mark Belanger G8 .01 .05
149 Scott McGregor G23 .01 .05
150 Ken Singleton G10 .01 .05
151 Eddie Murray G5 1.00 2.50
152 Lance Parrish G20 .05 .15
153 Dave Rozema G15 .01 .05
154 Champ Summers G13 .01 .05
155 Alan Trammell G2 .20 .50
156 Lou Whitaker G1 .08 .25
G25
157 Milt Wilcox G5 .01 .05
158 Kevin Saucier G24 .01 .05
159 Jack Morris G14 .02 .10
160 Steve Kemp G7 .01 .05
161 Kirk Gibson G3 .08 .25
162 Carl Yastrzemski G3 .30 .75
163 Jim Rice G21 .05 .15
164 Carney Lansford G15 .01 .05
165 Dennis Eckersley G6 .20 .50
166 Mike Torrez G5 .01 .05
167 Dwight Evans G19 .02 .10
168 Glenn Hoffman G18 .01 .05
169 Bob Stanley G20 .01 .05
170 Tony Perez G16 .08 .25
171 Jerry Remy G13 .01 .05
172 Buddy Bell G5 .02 .10
173 Fergie Jenkins G17 .08 .25
174 Mickey Rivers G9 .01 .05
175 Bump Wills G2 .01 .05
176 Jon Matlack G20 .01 .05
177 Steve Comer G23 .01 .05
178 Al Oliver G1 .02 .10
G25
179 Bill Stein G3 .01 .05
180 Pat Putnam G14 .01 .05
181 Jim Sundberg G4 .01 .05
182 Ron LeFlore G4 .02 .10
183 Carlton Fisk G11 .40 1.00
184 Harold Baines G18 .08 .25
185 Bill Almon G2 .01 .05
186 Richard Dotson G9 .01 .05
187 Greg Luzinski G14 .02 .10
188 Mike Squires G13 .01 .05
189 Britt Burns G19 .01 .05
190 LaMarr Hoyt G6 .01 .05
191 Chet Lemon G22 .01 .05
192 Joe Charboneau G20 .01 .05
193 Toby Harrah G16 .01 .05
194 John Denny G22 .01 .05
195 Rick Manning G8 .01 .05
196 Miguel Dilone G15 .01 .05
197 Bo Diaz G13 .01 .05
198 Mike Hargrove G17 .02 .10
199 Bert Blyleven G11 .02 .10
200 Len Barker G7 .01 .05
201 Andre Thornton G18 .01 .05
202 George Brett G24 .75 2.00
203 U.L. Washington G25 .01 .05
204 Dan Quisenberry G17 .01 .05
205 Larry Gura G17 .01 .05
206 Willie Aikens G22 .01 .05
207 Willie Wilson G21 .01 .05
208 Dennis Leonard G8 .01 .05
209 Frank White G6 .02 .10
210 Hal McRae G23 .02 .10
211 Amos Otis G18 .01 .05
212 Don Aase G23 .02 .10
213 Butch Hobson G6 .01 .05
214 Fred Lynn G18 .02 .10
215 Brian Downing G10 .01 .05
216 Dan Ford G5 .01 .05
217 Rod Carew G5 .30 .75
218 Bobby Grich G19 .02 .10
219 Rick Burleson G11 .01 .05
220 Don Baylor G3 .02 .10
221 Ken Forsch G17 .01 .05
222 Bruce Bochte .01 .05
223 Richie Zisk .01 .05
224 Tom Paciorek .01 .05
225 Julio Cruz .01 .05
226 Jeff Burroughs .01 .05
227 Doug Corbett .01 .05
228 Roy Smalley .01 .05
229 Gary Ward .01 .05
230 John Castino .01 .05
231 Rob Wilfong .01 .05
232 Dave Stieb .02 .10
233 Otto Velez .01 .05
234 Damaso Garcia .01 .05
235 John Mayberry .01 .05
236 Alfredo Griffin .01 .05
237 Ted Williams .75 2.00
Carl Yastrzemski
238 Rick Cerone .02 .10
Graig Nettles
239 Buddy Bell .60 1.50
George Brett
240 Steve Carlton .08 .25
Jim Kaat
241 Steve Carlton .08 .25
Dave Parker
242 Ron Davis 1.50 4.00
Nolan Ryan
XX Stamp Album .75 2.00

1983 Fleer Promo Sheet

This sheet, which measures approximately 7 1/2" by 10 1/2" featured information on the 1983 Fleer wax, cello and rack packs. The cards shown on the sheet are the same as their regular card from the set. Six different players are featured on this set.

1 Rod Carew 1.25 3.00
Tom Paciorek
Jerry Dybzinski
Dan Drie

1983 Fleer

In 1983, for the third straight year, Fleer produced a baseball series of 660 standard-size cards. Of these, 1-628 are player cards, 629-646 are special cards, and 647-660 are checklist cards. The player cards are again ordered alphabetically within team and teams seeded in descending order based upon the previous season's standings. The front of each card has a colorful team logo at bottom left and the player's name and position at lower right. The reverses are done in shades of brown on white. Wax packs consisted of 15 cards plus logo stickers in a 38-pack box. Notable Rookie Cards include Wade Boggs, Tony Gwynn and Ryne Sandberg.

COMPLETE SET (660) 25.00 60.00
1 Joaquin Andujar .07 .20
2 Doug Bair .02 .10
3 Steve Braun .02 .10
4 Glenn Brummer .02 .10
5 Bob Forsch .02 .10
6 David Green RC .20 .50
7 George Hendrick .07 .20
8 Keith Hernandez .07 .20
9 Tom Herr .07 .20
10 Dane Iorg .02 .10
11 Jim Kaat .07 .20
12 Jeff Lahti .02 .10
13 Tito Landrum .02 .10
14 Dave LaPoint .02 .10
15 Willie McGee RC .60 1.50
16 Steve Mura .02 .10
17 Ken Oberkfell .02 .10
18 Darrell Porter .02 .10
19 Mike Ramsey .02 .10
20 Gene Roof .02 .10
21 Lonnie Smith .02 .10
22 Ozzie Smith .50 1.25
23 John Stuper .02 .10
24 Bruce Sutter .15 .40
25 Gene Tenace .07 .20
26 Jerry Augustine .02 .10
27 Dwight Bernard .02 .10
28 Mark Brouhard .02 .10
29 Mike Caldwell .02 .10
30 Cecil Cooper .07 .20
31 Jamie Easterly .02 .10
32 Marshall Edwards .02 .10
33 Rollie Fingers .07 .20
34 Jim Gantner .02 .10
35 Moose Haas .02 .10
36 Roy Howell .02 .10
37 Pete Ladd .02 .10
38 Bob McClure .02 .10
39 Doc Medich .02 .10
40 Paul Molitor .07 .20
41 Don Money .02 .10
42 Charlie Moore .02 .10
43 Ben Oglivie .07 .20
44 Ed Romero .02 .10
45 Ted Simmons .07 .20
46 Jim Slaton .02 .10
47 Don Sutton .07 .20
48 Gorman Thomas .07 .20
49 Pete Vuckovich .02 .10
50 Ned Yost .02 .10
51 Robin Yount .50 1.25
52 Benny Ayala .02 .10
53 Bob Bonner .02 .10
54 Al Bumbry .02 .10
55 Terry Crowley .02 .10
56 Storm Davis RC .20 .50
57 Rich Dauer .02 .10
58 Rick Dempsey UER .02 .10
Posing batting lefty
59 Jim Dwyer .02 .10
60 Mike Flanagan .02 .10
61 Dan Ford .02 .10
62 Glenn Gulliver .02 .10
63 John Lowenstein .02 .10
64 Dennis Martinez .07 .20
65 Tippy Martinez .02 .10
66 Scott McGregor .02 .10
67 Eddie Murray .30 .75
68 Joe Nolan .02 .10
69 Jim Palmer .07 .20
70 Cal Ripken 2.50 6.00
71 Gary Roenicke .02 .10
72 Lenn Sakata .02 .10
73 Ken Singleton .07 .20
74 Sammy Stewart .02 .10
75 Tim Stoddard .02 .10
76 Don Aase .02 .10
77 Don Baylor .07 .20
78 Juan Beniquez .02 .10
79 Bob Boone .07 .20
80 Rick Burleson .02 .10
81 Rod Carew .15 .40
82 Bobby Clark .02 .10
83 Doug Corbett .02 .10
84 John Curtis .02 .10
85 Doug DeCinces .02 .10
86 Brian Downing .07 .20
87 Joe Ferguson .02 .10
88 Tim Foli .02 .10
89 Ken Forsch .02 .10
90 Dave Goltz .02 .10
91 Bobby Grich .07 .20
92 Andy Hassler .02 .10
93 Reggie Jackson .15 .40
94 Ron Jackson .02 .10
95 Tommy John .07 .20
96 Bruce Kison .02 .10
97 Fred Lynn .07 .20
98 Ed Ott .02 .10
99 Steve Renko .02 .10
100 Luis Sanchez .02 .10
101 Rob Wilfong .02 .10
102 Mike Witt .02 .10
103 Geoff Zahn .02 .10
104 Willie Aikens .02 .10
105 Mike Armstrong .02 .10
106 Vida Blue .07 .20
107 Bud Black RC .20 .50
108 George Brett .75 2.00
109 Bill Castro .02 .10
110 Onix Concepcion .02 .10
111 Dave Frost .02 .10
112 Cesar Geronimo .02 .10
113 Larry Gura .02 .10
114 Steve Hammond .02 .10
115 Don Hood .02 .10
116 Dennis Leonard .02 .10
117 Jerry Martin .02 .10
118 Lee May .02 .10
119 Hal McRae .07 .20
120 Amos Otis .07 .20
121 Greg Pryor .02 .10
122 Dan Quisenberry .07 .20
123 Don Slaught RC .20 .50
124 Paul Splittorff .02 .10
125 U.L. Washington .02 .10
126 John Wathan .02 .10
127 Frank White .07 .20
128 Willie Wilson .07 .20
129 Steve Bedrosian UER .02 .10
Height 6'33
130 Bruce Benedict .02 .10
131 Tommy Boggs .02 .10
132 Brett Butler .07 .20
133 Rick Camp .02 .10
134 Chris Chambliss .07 .20
135 Ken Dayley .02 .10
136 Gene Garber .02 .10
137 Terry Harper .02 .10
138 Bob Horner .07 .20
139 Glenn Hubbard .02 .10
140 Rufino Linares .02 .10
141 Rick Mahler .02 .10
142 Dale Murphy .15 .40
143 Phil Niekro .07 .20
144 Pascual Perez .02 .10
145 Biff Pocoroba .02 .10
146 Rafael Ramirez .02 .10
147 Jerry Royster .02 .10
148 Ken Smith .02 .10
149 Bob Walk .02 .10
150 Claudell Washington .02 .10
151 Bob Watson .02 .10
152 Larry Whisenton .02 .10
153 Porfirio Altamirano .02 .10
154 Marty Bystrom .02 .10
155 Steve Carlton .15 .40
156 Larry Christenson .02 .10
157 Ivan DeJesus .02 .10
158 John Denny .02 .10
159 Bob Dernier .02 .10
160 Bo Diaz .02 .10
161 Ed Farmer .02 .10
162 Greg Gross .02 .10
163 Mike Krukow .02 .10
164 Garry Maddox .02 .10
165 Gary Matthews .07 .20
166 Tug McGraw .07 .20
167 Bob Molinaro .02 .10
168 Sid Monge .02 .10
169 Ron Reed .02 .10
170 Bill Robinson .02 .10
171 Pete Rose 1.00 2.50
172 Dick Ruthven .02 .10
173 Mike Schmidt .75 2.00
174 Manny Trillo .02 .10
175 Ozzie Virgil .02 .10
176 George Vukovich .02 .10
177 Gary Allenson .02 .10
178 Luis Aponte .02 .10
179 Wade Boggs RC 8.00 20.00
180 Tom Burgmeier .02 .10
181 Mark Clear .02 .10
182 Dennis Eckersley .15 .40
183 Dwight Evans .15 .40
184 Rich Gedman .02 .10
185 Glenn Hoffman .02 .10
186 Bruce Hurst .02 .10
187 Carney Lansford .07 .20
188 Rick Miller .02 .10
189 Reid Nichols .02 .10
190 Bob Ojeda .02 .10
191 Tony Perez .15 .40
192 Chuck Rainey .02 .10
193 Jerry Remy .02 .10
194 Jim Rice .07 .20
195 Bob Stanley .02 .10
196 Dave Stapleton .02 .10
197 Mike Torrez .02 .10
198 John Tudor .07 .20
199 Julio Valdez .02 .10
200 Carl Yastrzemski .50 1.25
201 Dusty Baker .07 .20
202 Joe Beckwith .02 .10
203 Greg Brock .02 .10
204 Ron Cey .07 .20
205 Terry Forster .07 .20
206 Steve Garvey .07 .20
207 Pedro Guerrero .07 .20
208 Burt Hooton .02 .10
209 Steve Howe .02 .10
210 Ken Landreaux .02 .10
211 Mike Marshall .02 .10
212 Candy Maldonado RC .20 .50
213 Rick Monday .07 .20
214 Tom Niedenfuer .02 .10
215 Jorge Orta .02 .10
216 Jerry Reuss UER .02 .10
217 Ron Roenicke .02 .10
218 Vicente Romo .02 .10
219 Bill Russell .07 .20
220 Steve Sax .07 .20
221 Mike Scioscia .07 .20
222 Dave Stewart .07 .20
223 Derrel Thomas .02 .10
224 Fernando Valenzuela .07 .20
225 Bob Welch .07 .20
226 Ricky Wright .02 .10
227 Steve Yeager .07 .20
228 Bill Almon .02 .10
229 Harold Baines .07 .20
230 Salome Barojas .02 .10
231 Tony Bernazard .02 .10
232 Britt Burns .02 .10
233 Richard Dotson .02 .10
234 Ernesto Escarrega .02 .10
235 Carlton Fisk .15 .40
236 Jerry Hairston .02 .10
237 Kevin Hickey .02 .10
238 LaMarr Hoyt .02 .10
239 Steve Kemp .02 .10
240 Jim Kern .02 .10
241 Ron Kittle RC .40 1.00
242 Jerry Koosman .07 .20
243 Dennis Lamp .02 .10
244 Rudy Law .02 .10
245 Vance Law .02 .10
246 Ron LeFlore .07 .20
247 Greg Luzinski .07 .20
248 Tom Paciorek .07 .20
249 Aurelio Rodriguez .02 .10
250 Mike Squires .02 .10
251 Steve Trout .02 .10
252 Jim Barr .02 .10
253 Dave Bergman .02 .10
254 Fred Breining .02 .10
255 Bob Brenly .02 .10
256 Jack Clark .07 .20
257 Chili Davis .07 .20
258 Darrell Evans .07 .20
259 Alan Fowlkes .02 .10
260 Rich Gale .02 .10
261 Atlee Hammaker .02 .10
262 Al Holland .02 .10
263 Duane Kuiper .02 .10
264 Bill Laskey .02 .10
265 Gary Lavelle .02 .10
266 Johnnie LeMaster .02 .10
267 Renie Martin .02 .10
268 Milt May .02 .10
269 Greg Minton .02 .10
270 Joe Morgan .07 .20
271 Tom O'Malley .02 .10
272 Reggie Smith .07 .20
273 Guy Sularz .02 .10
274 Champ Summers .02 .10
275 Max Venable .02 .10
276 Jim Wohlford .02 .10
277 Ray Burris .02 .10
278 Gary Carter .07 .20
279 Warren Cromartie .02 .10
280 Andre Dawson .07 .20
281 Terry Francona .07 .20
282 Doug Flynn .02 .10
283 Woodie Fryman .02 .10
284 Bill Gullickson .02 .10
285 Wallace Johnson .02 .10
286 Charlie Lea .02 .10
287 Randy Lerch .02 .10
288 Brad Mills .02 .10
289 Dan Norman .02 .10
290 Al Oliver .07 .20
291 David Palmer .02 .10
292 Tim Raines .07 .20
293 Jeff Reardon .07 .20
294 Steve Rogers .07 .20
295 Scott Sanderson .02 .10
296 Dan Schatzeder .02 .10
297 Bryn Smith .02 .10
298 Chris Speier .02 .10
299 Tim Wallach .07 .20
300 Jerry White .02 .10
301 Joel Youngblood .02 .10
302 Ross Baumgarten .02 .10
303 Dale Berra .02 .10
304 John Candelaria .02 .10
305 Dick Davis .02 .10
306 Mike Easler .02 .10
307 Richie Hebner .02 .10
308 Lee Lacy .02 .10
309 Bill Madlock .07 .20
310 Larry McWilliams .02 .10
311 John Milner .02 .10
312 Omar Moreno .02 .10
313 Jim Morrison .02 .10
314 Steve Nicosia .02 .10
315 Dave Parker .07 .20
316 Tony Pena .02 .10
317 Johnny Ray .02 .10
318 Rick Rhoden .02 .10
319 Don Robinson .02 .10
320 Enrique Romo .02 .10
321 Manny Sarmiento .02 .10
322 Rod Scurry .02 .10
323 Jimmy Smith .02 .10
324 Willie Stargell .15 .40
325 Jason Thompson .02 .10
326 Kent Tekulve .02 .10
327A Tom Brookens .02 .10
Short .375-inch brown box
shaded in on card back
327B Tom Brookens .02 .10
Longer 1.25-inch brown box
shaded in on card back
328 Enos Cabell .02 .10
329 Kirk Gibson .07 .20
330 Larry Herndon .02 .10
331 Mike Ivie .02 .10
332 Howard Johnson RC .40 1.00
333 Lynn Jones .02 .10
334 Rick Leach .02 .10
335 Chet Lemon .07 .20
336 Jack Morris .07 .20
337 Lance Parrish .07 .20
338 Larry Pashnick .02 .10
339 Dan Petry .02 .10
340 Dave Rozema .02 .10
341 Dave Rucker .02 .10
342 Elias Sosa .02 .10
343 Dave Tobik .02 .10
344 Alan Trammell .07 .20
345 Jerry Turner .02 .10
346 Jerry Ujdur .02 .10
347 Pat Underwood .02 .10
348 Lou Whitaker .07 .20
349 Milt Wilcox .02 .10
350 Glenn Wilson .20 .50
351 John Wockenfuss .02 .10
352 Kurt Bevacqua .02 .10
353 Juan Bonilla .02 .10
354 Floyd Chiffer .02 .10
355 Luis DeLeon .02 .10
356 Dave Dravecky RC .40 1.00
357 Dave Edwards .02 .10
358 Juan Eichelberger .02 .10
359 Tim Flannery .02 .10
360 Tony Gwynn RC 12.00 30.00
361 Ruppert Jones .02 .10
362 Terry Kennedy .02 .10
363 Joe Lefebvre .02 .10
364 Sixto Lezcano .02 .10
365 Tim Lollar .02 .10
366 Gary Lucas .02 .10
367 John Montefusco .02 .10
368 Broderick Perkins .02 .10
369 Joe Pittman .02 .10
370 Gene Richards .02 .10
371 Luis Salazar .02 .10
372 Eric Show RC .20 .50
373 Garry Templeton .07 .20
374 Chris Welsh .02 .10
375 Alan Wiggins .02 .10
376 Rick Cerone .02 .10
377 Dave Collins .02 .10
378 Roger Erickson .02 .10
379 George Frazier .02 .10
380 Oscar Gamble .02 .10
381 Rich Gossage .07 .20
382 Ken Griffey .07 .20
383 Ron Guidry .07 .20
384 Dave LaRoche .02 .10
385 Rudy May .02 .10
386 John Mayberry .02 .10
387 Lee Mazzilli .07 .20
388 Mike Morgan .02 .10
389 Jerry Mumphrey .02 .10
390 Bobby Murcer .07 .20
391 Graig Nettles .07 .20
392 Lou Piniella .07 .20
393 Willie Randolph .07 .20
394 Shane Rawley .02 .10
395 Dave Righetti .07 .20
396 Andre Robertson .02 .10
397 Roy Smalley .02 .10
398 Dave Winfield .07 .20
399 Butch Wynegar .02 .10
400 Chris Bando .02 .10
401 Alan Bannister .02 .10
402 Len Barker .02 .10
403 Tom Brennan .02 .10
404 Carmelo Castillo .02 .10
405 Miguel Dilone .02 .10
406 Jerry Dybzinski .02 .10
407 Mike Fischlin .02 .10
408 Ed Glynn UER .02 .10
Photo actually
Bud Anderson
409 Mike Hargrove .02 .10
410 Toby Harrah .07 .20
411 Ron Hassey .02 .10
412 Von Hayes .07 .20
413 Rick Manning .02 .10
414 Bake McBride .07 .20
415 Larry Milbourne .02 .10
416 Bill Nahorodny .02 .10
417 Jack Perconte .02 .10
418 Lary Sorensen .02 .10
419 Dan Spillner .02 .10
420 Rick Sutcliffe .07 .20
421 Andre Thornton .02 .10
422 Rick Waits .02 .10
423 Eddie Whitson .02 .10
424 Jesse Barfield .07 .20
425 Barry Bonnell .02 .10
426 Jim Clancy .02 .10
427 Damaso Garcia .02 .10
428 Jerry Garvin .02 .10
429 Alfredo Griffin .02 .10
430 Garth Iorg .02 .10
431 Roy Lee Jackson .02 .10
432 Luis Leal .02 .10
433 Buck Martinez .02 .10
434 Joey McLaughlin .02 .10
435 Lloyd Moseby .02 .10
436 Rance Mulliniks .02 .10
437 Dale Murray .02 .10
438 Wayne Nordhagen .02 .10
439 Geno Petralli .20 .50
440 Hosken Powell .02 .10
441 Dave Stieb .07 .20
442 Willie Upshaw .02 .10
443 Ernie Whitt .02 .10
444 Alvis Woods .02 .10
445 Alan Ashby .02 .10
446 Jose Cruz .07 .20
447 Kiko Garcia .02 .10
448 Phil Garner .07 .20
449 Danny Heep .02 .10
450 Art Howe .02 .10
451 Bob Knepper .02 .10
452 Alan Knicely .02 .10
453 Ray Knight .07 .20
454 Frank LaCorte .02 .10
455 Mike LaCoss .02 .10
456 Randy Moffitt .02 .10
457 Joe Niekro .02 .10
458 Terry Puhl .02 .10
459 Luis Pujols .02 .10
460 Craig Reynolds .02 .10
461 Bert Roberge .02 .10
462 Vern Ruhle .02 .10
463 Nolan Ryan 1.50 4.00
464 Joe Sambito .02 .10
465 Tony Scott .02 .10
466 Dave Smith .02 .10
467 Harry Spilman .02 .10
468 Dickie Thon .02 .10
469 Denny Walling .02 .10
470 Larry Andersen .02 .10
471 Floyd Bannister .02 .10
472 Jim Beattie .02 .10
473 Bruce Bochte .02 .10
474 Manny Castillo .02 .10
475 Bill Caudill .02 .10
476 Bryan Clark .02 .10
477 Al Cowens .02 .10
478 Julio Cruz .02 .10
479 Todd Cruz .02 .10
480 Gary Gray .02 .10
481 Dave Henderson .02 .10
482 Mike Moore RC .20 .50
483 Gaylord Perry .07 .20
484 Dave Revering .02 .10
485 Joe Simpson .02 .10
486 Mike Stanton .02 .10
487 Rick Sweet .02 .10
488 Ed VandeBerg .02 .10
489 Richie Zisk .02 .10
490 Doug Bird .02 .10
491 Larry Bowa .07 .20
492 Bill Buckner .07 .20
493 Bill Campbell .02 .10
494 Jody Davis .02 .10
495 Leon Durham .02 .10
496 Steve Henderson .02 .10
497 Willie Hernandez .07 .20
498 Ferguson Jenkins .07 .20
499 Jay Johnstone .02 .10
500 Junior Kennedy .02 .10
501 Randy Martz .02 .10
502 Jerry Morales .02 .10
503 Keith Moreland .02 .10
504 Dickie Noles .02 .10
505 Mike Proly .02 .10
506 Allen Ripley .02 .10
507 Ryne Sandberg RC UER 10.00 25.00
508 Lee Smith .15 .40
509 Pat Tabler .02 .10
510 Dick Tidrow .02 .10
511 Bump Wills .02 .10
512 Gary Woods .02 .10
513 Tony Armas .07 .20
514 Dave Beard .02 .10
515 Jeff Burroughs .02 .10
516 John D'Acquisto .02 .10
517 Wayne Gross .02 .10
518 Mike Heath .02 .10
519 Rickey Henderson UER .60 1.50
520 Cliff Johnson .02 .10
521 Matt Keough .02 .10
522 Brian Kingman .02 .10
523 Rick Langford .02 .10
524 Dave Lopes .07 .20
525 Steve McCatty .02 .10
526 Dave McKay .02 .10
527 Dan Meyer .02 .10
528 Dwayne Murphy .02 .10
529 Jeff Newman .02 .10
530 Mike Norris .02 .10
531 Bob Owchinko .02 .10
532 Joe Rudi .07 .20
533 Jimmy Sexton .02 .10
534 Fred Stanley .02 .10
535 Tom Underwood .02 .10
536 Neil Allen .02 .10
537 Wally Backman .02 .10
538 Bob Bailor .02 .10
539 Hubie Brooks .02 .10
540 Carlos Diaz RC .08 .25
541 Pete Falcone .02 .10

Card	Low	High
542 George Foster	.07	.20
543 Ron Gardenhire	.02	.10
544 Brian Giles	.02	.10
545 Ron Hodges	.02	.10
546 Randy Jones	.02	.10
547 Mike Jorgensen	.02	.10
548 Dave Kingman	.07	.20
549 Ed Lynch	.02	.10
550 Jesse Orosco	.02	.10
551 Rick Ownbey	.02	.10
552 Charlie Puleo	.02	.10
553 Gary Rajsich	.02	.10
554 Mike Scott	.07	.20
555 Rusty Staub	.07	.20
556 John Stearns	.02	.10
557 Craig Swan	.02	.10
558 Ellis Valentine	.02	.10
559 Tom Veryzer	.02	.10
560 Mookie Wilson	.07	.20
561 Pat Zachry	.02	.10
562 Buddy Bell	.07	.20
563 John Butcher	.02	.10
564 Steve Comer	.02	.10
565 Danny Darwin	.02	.10
566 Bucky Dent	.07	.20
567 John Grubb	.02	.10
568 Rick Honeycutt	.02	.10
569 Dave Hostetler RC	.02	.10
570 Charlie Hough	.07	.20
571 Lamar Johnson	.02	.10
572 Jon Matlack	.02	.10
573 Paul Mirabella	.02	.10
574 Larry Parrish	.02	.10
575 Mike Richardt	.02	.10
576 Mickey Rivers	.02	.10
577 Billy Sample	.02	.10
578 Dave Schmidt	.02	.10
579 Bill Stein	.02	.10
580 Jim Sundberg	.07	.20
581 Frank Tanana	.07	.20
582 Mark Wagner	.02	.10
583 George Wright RC	.20	.50
584 Johnny Bench	.30	.75
585 Bruce Berenyi	.02	.10
586 Larry Biittner	.02	.10
587 Cesar Cedeno	.07	.20
588 Dave Concepcion	.07	.20
589 Dan Driessen	.02	.10
590 Greg Harris	.02	.10
591 Ben Hayes	.02	.10
592 Paul Householder	.02	.10
593 Tom Hume	.02	.10
594 Wayne Krenchicki	.02	.10
595 Rafael Landestoy	.02	.10
596 Charlie Leibrandt	.02	.10
597 Eddie Milner	.02	.10
598 Ron Oester	.02	.10
599 Frank Pastore	.02	.10
600 Joe Price	.02	.10
601 Tom Seaver	.30	.75
602 Bob Shirley	.02	.10
603 Mario Soto	.07	.20
604 Alex Trevino	.02	.10
605 Mike Vail	.02	.10
606 Duane Walker RC	.02	.10
607 Tom Brunansky	.07	.20
608 Bobby Castillo	.02	.10
609 John Castino	.02	.10
610 Ron Davis	.02	.10
611 Lenny Faedo	.02	.10
612 Terry Felton	.02	.10
613 Gary Gaetti RC	.40	1.00
614 Mickey Hatcher	.02	.10
615 Brad Havens	.02	.10
616 Kent Hrbek	.07	.20
617 Randy Johnson RC	.02	.10
618 Tim Laudner	.02	.10
619 Jeff Little	.02	.10
620 Bobby Mitchell	.02	.10
621 Jack O'Connor	.02	.10
622 John Pacella	.02	.10
623 Pete Redfern	.02	.10
624 Jesus Vega	.02	.10
625 Frank Viola RC	.60	1.50
626 Ron Washington RC	.10	.25
627 Gary Ward	.02	.10
628 Al Williams	.02	.10
629 Carl Yastrzemski	.30	.75
Dennis Eckersley		
Mark Clear		
630 Gaylord Perry	.02	.10
Terry Bulling		
631 Dave Concepcion	.07	.20
Manny Trillo		
632 Robin Yount	.30	.75
Buddy Bell		
633 Dave Winfield	.02	.10
Kent Hrbek		
634 Willie Stargell	.30	.75
Pete Rose		
635 Toby Harrah	.07	.20
Andre Thornton		
636 Ozzie Smith	.30	.75
Lonnie Smith		
637 Bo Diaz	.02	.10
Gary Carter		
638 Carlton Fisk	.07	.20
Gary Carter		
639 Rickey Henderson IA	.30	.75
640 Ben Oglivie	.15	.40
Reggie Jackson		
641 Joel Youngblood	.02	.10
4-Aug-82		
642 Ron Hassey	.07	.20
Len Barker		
643 Black and Blue	.07	.20
Vida Blue		
644 Black and Blue	.02	.10
Bud Black		
645 Reggie Jackson Power	.07	.20
646 Rickey Henderson Speed	.30	.75
647 CL: Cards	.02	.10
Brewers		
648 CL: Orioles	.02	.10
Angels		
649 CL: Royals	.02	.10
Braves		
650 CL: Phillies	.02	.10
Red Sox		
651 CL: Dodgers	.02	.10
White Sox		
652 CL: Giants	.02	.10
Expos		
653 CL: Pirates	.02	.10
Tigers		
654 CL: Padres	.02	.10
Yankees		
655 CL: Indians	.02	.10
Blue Jays		
656 CL: Astros	.02	.10
Mariners		
657 CL: Cubs	.02	.10
A's		
658 CL: Mets	.02	.10
Rangers		
659 CL: Reds	.02	.10
Twins		
660 CL: Specials	.02	.10
Teams		

1983 Fleer Stamps

This 250-stamp set features color photos of players and team logos on stamps measuring approximately 1 1/4" by 1 13/16" each. The stamps were issued on four different sheets of 72 stamps each. There are 224 player stamps and 26 team logo stamps. The team logo stamps have double and triple prints. Baseball trivia quiz questions were also included with the stamps. The stamps are unnumbered and checklisted below in alphabetical order. Stamps were issued in three different colored Vend-A-Strip dispensors. Each row in a dispensor consisted of 18 stamps and 11 quizes.

Card	Low	High
COMPLETE SET (250)	4.00	10.00
1 Willie Aikens	.01	.05
2 Neil Allen	.01	.05
3 Joaquin Andujar	.01	.05
4 Alan Ashby	.01	.05
5 Bob Bailor	.01	.05
6 Harold Baines	.05	.15
7 Dusty Baker	.02	.10
8 Floyd Bannister	.01	.05
9 Len Barker	.01	.05
10 Don Baylor	.02	.10
11 Dave Beard	.01	.05
12 Jim Beattie	.01	.05
13 Buddy Bell	.02	.10
14 Johnny Bench	.30	.75
15 Dale Berra	.01	.05
16 Larry Biittner	.01	.05
17 Vida Blue	.02	.10
18 Bruce Bochte	.01	.05
19 Wade Boggs	2.50	6.00
20 Bob Boone	.02	.10
21 Larry Bowa	.01	.05
22 George Brett	.75	2.00
23 Hubie Brooks	.01	.05
24 Tom Brunansky	.01	.05
25 Bill Buckner	.02	.10
26 Al Bumbry	.01	.05
27 Jeff Burroughs	.01	.05
28 Enos Cabell	.01	.05
29 Rod Carew	.20	.50
30 Steve Carlton	.15	.40
31 Gary Carter	.15	.40
32 Bobby Castillo	.01	.05
33 Bill Caudill	.01	.05
34 Cesar Cedeno	.02	.10
35 Rick Cerone	.01	.05
36 Ron Cey	.02	.10
37 Chris Chambliss	.02	.10
38 Larry Christenson	.01	.05
39 Jim Clancy	.01	.05
40 Jack Clark	.02	.10
41 Mark Clear	.01	.05
42 Dave Concepcion	.02	.10
43 Cecil Cooper	.02	.10
44 Warren Cromartie	.01	.05
45 Jose Cruz	.02	.10
46 Danny Darwin	.01	.05
47 Rich Dauer	.01	.05
48 Ron Davis	.01	.05
49 Andre Dawson	.20	.50
50 Doug DeCinces	.01	.05
51 Ivan DeJesus	.01	.05
52 Luis DeLeon	.01	.05
53 Bo Diaz	.01	.05
54 Brian Downing	.02	.10
55 Dan Driessen	.01	.05
56 Leon Durham	.01	.05
57 Mike Easler	.01	.05
58 Dennis Eckersley	.20	.50
59 Dwight Evans	.05	.15
60 Rollie Fingers	.15	.40
61 Carlton Fisk	.20	.50
62 Mike Flanagan	.01	.05
63 Bob Forsch	.01	.05
64 Ken Forsch	.01	.05
65 George Foster	.02	.10
66 Gene Garber	.01	.05
67 Damaso Garcia	.01	.05
68 Phil Garner	.01	.05
69 Steve Garvey	.05	.15
70 Goose Gossage	.05	.15
71 Ken Griffey	.02	.10
72 John Grubb	.01	.05
73 Ron Guidry	.02	.10
74 Atlee Hammaker	.01	.05
75 Mike Hargrove	.02	.10
76 Toby Harrah	.01	.05
77 Rickey Henderson	.75	2.00
78 Keith Hernandez	.05	.15
79 Larry Herndon	.01	.05
80 Tom Herr	.01	.05
81 Al Holland	.01	.05
82 Burt Hooton	.01	.05
83 Bob Horner	.01	.05
84 Art Howe	.01	.05
85 Steve Howe	.01	.05
86 LaMarr Hoyt	.01	.05
87 Kent Hrbek	.08	.25
88 Tom Hume	.01	.05
89 Garth Iorg	.01	.05
90 Reggie Jackson	.30	.75
91 Ferguson Jenkins	.10	.30
92 Tommy John	.05	.15
93 Ruppert Jones	.01	.05
94 Steve Kemp	.01	.05
95 Bruce Kison	.01	.05
96 Ray Knight	.01	.05
97 Jerry Koosman	.02	.10
98 Duane Kuiper	.01	.05
99 Ken Landreaux	.01	.05
100 Carney Lansford	.01	.05
101 Bill Laskey	.01	.05
102 Gary Lavelle	.01	.05
103 Charlie Lea	.01	.05
104 Ron LeFlore	.01	.05
105 Dennis Leonard	.01	.05
106 Sixto Lezcano	.01	.05
107 Davey Lopes	.02	.10
108 John Lowenstein	.01	.05
109 Greg Luzinski	.02	.10
110 Fred Lynn	.05	.15
111 Garry Maddox	.01	.05
112 Bill Madlock	.02	.10
113 Rick Manning	.01	.05
114 Dennis Martinez	.02	.10
115 Tippy Martinez	.01	.05
116 Randy Martz	.01	.05
117 John Matlack	.01	.05
118 Gary Matthews	.02	.10
119 Milt May	.01	.05
120 Lee Mazzilli	.02	.10
121 Bob McClure	.01	.05
122 Tug McGraw	.02	.10
123 Scott McGregor	.01	.05
124 Hal McRae	.02	.10
125 Eddie Milner	.01	.05
126 Greg Minton	.01	.05
127 Paul Molitor	.30	.75
128 Rick Monday	.01	.05
129 John Montefusco	.01	.05
130 Keith Moreland	.01	.05
131 Joe Morgan	.20	.50
132 Jerry Mumphrey	.01	.05
133 Steve Mura	.01	.05
134 Dale Murphy	.15	.40
135 Dwayne Murphy	.01	.05
136 Eddie Murray	.20	.50
137 Graig Nettles	.05	.15
138 Joe Niekro	.02	.10
139 Phil Niekro	.10	.30
140 Ken Oberkfell	.01	.05
141 Ben Oglivie	.01	.05
142 Al Oliver	.05	.15
143 Amos Otis	.01	.05
144 Tom Paciorek	.01	.05
145 Jim Palmer	.15	.40
146 Dave Parker	.02	.10
147 Lance Parrish	.05	.15
148 Larry Parrish	.01	.05
149 Tony Pena	.01	.05
150 Gaylord Perry	.10	.30
151 Lou Piniella	.02	.10
152 Darrell Porter	.01	.05
153 Hosken Powell	.01	.05
154 Dan Quisenberry	.02	.10
155 Tim Raines	.08	.25
156 Rafael Ramirez	.01	.05
157 Willie Randolph	.02	.10
158 Johnny Ray	.01	.05
159 Jeff Reardon	.02	.10
160 Ron Reed	.01	.05
161 Jerry Reuss	.02	.10
162 Rick Rhoden	.01	.05
163 Jim Rice	.02	.10
164 Mike Richardt	.01	.05
165 Cal Ripken Jr.	1.50	4.00
166 Ron Roenicke	.01	.05
167 Steve Rogers	.01	.05
168 Pete Rose	.40	1.00
169 Jerry Royster	.01	.05
170 Nolan Ryan	1.50	4.00
171 Manny Sarmiento	.01	.05
172 Steve Sax	.01	.05
173 Mike Schmidt	.40	1.00
174 Tom Seaver	.20	.50
175 Eric Show	.01	.05
176 Ted Simmons	.05	.15
177 Ken Singleton	.01	.05
178 Roy Smalley	.01	.05
179 Lonnie Smith	.01	.05
180 Ozzie Smith	.75	2.00
181 Reggie Smith	.02	.10
182 Mario Soto	.01	.05
183 Chris Speier	.01	.05
184 Dan Spillner	.01	.05
185 Bob Stanley	.01	.05
186 Willie Stargell	.10	.30
187 Rusty Staub	.05	.15
188 Dave Stieb	.02	.10
189 Jim Sundberg	.01	.05
190 Rick Sutcliffe	.01	.05
191 Bruce Sutter	.02	.10
192 Don Sutton	.10	.30
193 Craig Swan	.01	.05
194 Kent Tekulve	.01	.05
195 Gorman Thomas	.01	.05
196 Jason Thompson	.01	.05
197 Dickie Thon	.01	.05
198 Andre Thornton	.01	.05
199 Dick Tidrow	.01	.05
200 Manny Trillo	.01	.05
201 John Tudor	.01	.05
202 Tom Underwood	.01	.05
203 Willie Upshaw	.01	.05
204 Ellis Valentin	.01	.05
205 Fernando Valenzuela	.10	.30
206 Ed VandeBerg	.01	.05
207 Pete Vuckovich	.01	.05
208 Gary Ward	.01	.05
209 Claudell Washington	.01	.05
210 U.L. Washington	.01	.05
211 Bob Watson	.02	.10
212 Lou Whitaker	.08	.25
213 Frank White	.01	.05
214 Milt Wilcox	.01	.05
215 Al Williams	.01	.05
216 Bump Wills	.01	.05
217 Mookie Wilson	.02	.10
218 Willie Wilson	.01	.05
219 Dave Winfield	.30	.75
220 John Wockenfuss	.01	.05
221 Carl Yastrzemski	.20	.50
222 Robin Yount	.20	.50
223 Pat Zachry	.01	.05
224 Richie Zisk	.01	.05
225 Atlanta Braves TP	.01	.05
226 Baltimore Orioles DP	.01	.05
227 Boston Red Sox DP	.01	.05
228 California Angels TP	.01	.05
229 Chicago Cubs DP	.01	.05
230 Chicago White Sox TP	.01	.05
231 Cincinnati Reds TP	.01	.05
232 Cleveland Indians TP	.01	.05
233 Detroit Tigers DP	.01	.05
234 Houston Astros DP	.01	.05
235 Los Angeles Dodgers TP	.01	.05
236 Kansas City Royals TP	.01	.05
237 Milwaukee Brewers DP	.01	.05
238 Minnesota Twins TP	.01	.05
239 Montreal Expos TP	.01	.05
240 New York Mets DP	.01	.05
241 New York Yankees DP	.01	.05
242 Oakland A's DP	.01	.05
243 Philadelphia Phillies TP	.01	.05
244 Pittsburgh Pirates TP	.01	.05
245 St. Louis Cardinals DP	.01	.05
246 San Diego Padres DP	.01	.05
247 San Francisco Giants TP	.01	.05
248 Seattle Mariners DP	.01	.05
249 Texas Rangers DP	.01	.05
250 Toronto Blue Jays DP	.01	.05

1983 Fleer Stickers

The stickers in this 270-sticker set measure approximately 1 13/16" by 2 1/2". The 1983 Fleer stickers set was issued in strips of ten stickers plus two team logos per strip. No album was issued for the stickers. The fronts contain player photos surrounded by a blue border with two red stars on the upper portion of a yellow frameline. While all of the players could be attained on 27 different strips, it was necessary to have 30 different strips to obtain all of the team logos. There are a few instances where the logo pictured on the front of the card relates to a different team checklisted on the back of the card. The backs of the logo stamps feature either a team checklist (CL) or poster offer (PO).

Card	Low	High
COMPLETE SET	5.00	12.00
1 Bruce Sutter	.02	.10
2 Willie McGee	.10	.30
3 Darrell Porter	.01	.05
4 Lonnie Smith	.01	.05
5 Dane Iorg	.01	.05
6 Keith Hernandez	.02	.10
7 Joaquin Andujar	.01	.05
8 Ken Oberkfell	.01	.05
9 John Stuper	.01	.05
10 Ozzie Smith	.60	1.50
11 Bob Forsch	.01	.05
12 Jim Gantner	.01	.05
13 Rollie Fingers	.10	.30
14 Pete Vuckovich	.01	.05
15 Ben Oglivie	.01	.05
16 Don Sutton	.10	.30
17 Bob McClure	.01	.05
18 Robin Yount	.15	.40
19 Paul Molitor	.20	.50
20 Gorman Thomas	.01	.05
21 Mike Caldwell	.01	.05
22 Ted Simmons	.02	.10
23 Cecil Cooper	.02	.10
24 Steve Renko	.01	.05
25 Tommy John	.05	.15
26 Rod Carew	.15	.40
27 Bruce Kison	.01	.05
28 Ken Forsch	.01	.05
29 Geoff Zahn	.01	.05
30 Doug DeCinces	.01	.05
31 Fred Lynn	.02	.10
32 Reggie Jackson	.30	.75
33 Don Baylor	.02	.10
34 Bob Boone	.02	.10
35 Brian Downing	.01	.05
36 Rich Gossage	.05	.15
37 Roy Smalley	.01	.05
38 Graig Nettles	.05	.15
39 Dave Winfield	.20	.50
40 Lee Mazzilli	.02	.10
41 Jerry Mumphrey	.01	.05
42 Dave Collins	.01	.05
43 Rick Cerone	.01	.05
44 Willie Randolph	.02	.10
45 Lou Piniella	.02	.10
46 Ken Griffey	.02	.10
47 Ron Guidry	.02	.10
48 Jack Clark	.02	.10
49 Reggie Smith	.02	.10
50 Atlee Hammaker	.01	.05
51 Fred Breining	.01	.05
52 Gary Lavelle	.01	.05
53 Chili Davis	.08	.25
54 Greg Minton	.01	.05
55 Joe Morgan	.10	.30
56 Al Holland	.01	.05
57 Bill Laskey	.01	.05
58 Duane Kuiper	.01	.05
59 Tom Burgmeier	.01	.05
60 Carl Yastrzemski	.20	.50
61 Mark Clear	.01	.05
62 Mike Torrez	.01	.05
63 Dennis Eckersley	.10	.30
64 Wade Boggs	1.50	4.00
65 Bob Stanley	.01	.05
66 Jim Rice	.02	.10
67 Carney Lansford	.01	.05
68 Jerry Remy	.01	.05
69 Dwight Evans	.05	.15
70 John Candelaria	.01	.05
71 Bill Madlock	.02	.10
72 Dave Parker	.02	.10
73 Kent Tekulve	.01	.05
74 Tony Pena	.02	.10
75 Manny Sarmiento	.01	.05
76 Johnny Ray	.01	.05
77 Dale Berra	.01	.05
78 Lee Lacy	.01	.05
79 Jason Thompson	.01	.05
80 Mike Easler	.01	.05
81 Willie Stargell	.10	.30
82 Rick Camp	.01	.05
83 Bob Watson	.02	.10
84 Bob Horner	.01	.05
85 Rafael Ramirez	.01	.05
86 Chris Chambliss	.02	.10
87 Gene Garber	.02	.10
88 Claudell Washington	.01	.05
89 Steve Bedrosian	.01	.05
90 Dale Murphy	.20	.50
91 Phil Niekro	.10	.30
92 Jerry Royster	.01	.05
93 Bob Walk	.01	.05
94 Frank White	.01	.05
95 Dennis Leonard	.01	.05
96 Vida Blue	.02	.10
97 U.L. Washington	.01	.05
98 George Brett	1.25	3.00
99 Amos Otis	.01	.05
100 Dan Quisenberry	.01	.05
101 Willie Aikens	.01	.05
102 Hal McRae	.01	.05
103 Larry Gura	.01	.05
104 Willie Wilson	.01	.05
105 Damaso Garcia	.01	.05
106 Hosken Powell	.01	.05
107 Joey McLaughlin	.01	.05
108 Jim Clancy	.01	.05
109 Barry Bonnell	.01	.05
110 Garth Iorg	.01	.05
111 Dave Stieb	.02	.10
112 Fernando Valenzuela	.05	.15
113 Steve Garvey	.08	.25
114 Rick Monday	.01	.05
115 Burt Hooton	.01	.05
116 Bill Russell	.01	.05
117 Pedro Guerrero	.02	.10
118 Steve Sax	.01	.05
119 Steve Howe	.01	.05
120 Ken Landreaux	.01	.05
121 Dusty Baker	.02	.10
122 Ron Cey	.02	.10
123 Jerry Reuss	.02	.10
124 Bump Wills	.01	.05
125 Keith Moreland	.01	.05
126 Dick Tidrow	.01	.05
127 Bill Campbell	.01	.05
128 Larry Bowa	.01	.05
129 Randy Martz	.01	.05
130 Ferguson Jenkins	.10	.30
131 Leon Durham	.01	.05
132 Bill Buckner	.02	.10
133 Ron Davis	.01	.05
134 Jack O'Connor	.01	.05
135 Kent Hrbek	.02	.10
136 Gary Ward	.01	.05
137 Al Williams	.01	.05
138 Tom Brunansky	.01	.05
139 Bobby Castillo	.01	.05
140 Dusty Baker	.05	.15
Dale Murphy		
141 Nolan Ryan	1.00	2.50
Alan Ashby		
142 Omar Moreno	.01	.05
Lee Lacy		
sic, Lacey		
143 Al Oliver	.20	.50
Pete Rose		
144 Rickey Henderson	.30	.75
145 Ray Knight	.20	.50
Mike Schmidt		
Pete Rose		
146 Ben Oglivie	.01	.05
Hal McRae		
147 Ray Knight	.01	.05
Tom Hume		
148 Buddy Bell	.08	.25
Carlton Fisk		
149 Steve Kemp	.01	.05
150 Rudy Law	.01	.05
151 Ron LeFlore	.01	.05
152 Jerry Koosman	.05	.15
153 Carlton Fisk	.20	.50
154 Salome Barojas	.01	.05
155 Harold Baines	.02	.10
156 Britt Burns	.01	.05
157 Tom Paciorek	.01	.05
158 Greg Luzinski	.01	.05
159 LaMarr Hoyt	.01	.05
160 George Wright	.01	.05
161 Danny Darwin	.01	.05
162 Lamar Johnson	.01	.05
163 Charlie Hough	.02	.10
164 Buddy Bell	.02	.10
165 Jon Matlack	.01	.05
166 Billy Sample	.01	.05
167 Johnny Grubb	.01	.05
168 Larry Parrish	.02	.10
169 Ivan DeJesus	.01	.05
170 Mike Schmidt	.40	1.00
171 Tug McGraw	.01	.05
172 Ron Reed	.01	.05
173 Garry Maddox	.01	.05
174 Pete Rose	.60	1.50
175 Manny Trillo	.01	.05
176 Steve Carlton	.30	.75
177 Bo Diaz	.01	.05
178 Gary Matthews	.01	.05
179 Bill Caudill	.01	.05
180 Ed VandeBerg	.01	.05
181 Gaylord Perry	.10	.30
182 Floyd Bannister	.01	.05
183 Richie Zisk	.01	.05
184 Al Cowens	.01	.05
185 Bruce Bochte	.01	.05
186 Jeff Burroughs	.01	.05
187 Dave Beard	.01	.05
188 Dave Lopes	.01	.05
189 Dwayne Murphy	.01	.05
190 Rick Langford	.01	.05
191 Tom Underwood	.01	.05
192 Rickey Henderson	.75	2.00
193 Mike Flanagan	.01	.05
194 Scott McGregor	.01	.05
195 Ken Singleton	.01	.05
196 Rich Dauer	.01	.05
197 John Lowenstein	.01	.05
198 Cal Ripken	2.00	5.00
199 Dennis Martinez	.02	.10
200 Jim Palmer	.20	.50
201 Tippy Martinez	.01	.05
202 Eddie Murray	.40	1.00
203 Al Bumbry	.01	.05
204 Dickie Thon	.01	.05
205 Phil Garner	.02	.10
206 Jose Cruz	.02	.10
207 Nolan Ryan	2.00	5.00
208 Ray Knight	.01	.05
209 Terry Puhl	.01	.05
210 Joe Niekro	.01	.05
211 Art Howe	.01	.05
212 Alan Ashby	.01	.05
213 Tom Hume	.01	.05
214 Johnny Bench	.20	.50
215 Larry Biittner	.01	.05
216 Mario Soto	.01	.05
217 Dan Driessen	.01	.05
218 Tom Seaver	.20	.50
219 Dave Concepcion	.02	.10
220 Wayne Krenchicki	.01	.05
221 Cesar Cedeno	.01	.05
222 Ruppert Jones	.01	.05
223 Terry Kennedy	.01	.05
224 Luis DeLeon	.01	.05
225 Eric Show	.01	.05
226 Tim Flannery	.01	.05
227 Garry Templeton	.01	.05
228 Tim Lollar	.01	.05
229 Sixto Lezcano	.01	.05
230 Bob Bailor	.01	.05
231 Craig Swan	.01	.05
232 Dave Kingman	.02	.10
233 Mookie Wilson	.02	.10
234 John Stearns	.01	.05
235 Ellis Valentine	.01	.05
236 Neil Allen	.01	.05
237 Pat Zachry	.01	.05
238 Rusty Staub	.02	.10
239 George Foster	.01	.05
240 Rick Sutcliffe	.01	.05
241 Andre Thornton	.01	.05
242 Mike Hargrove	.02	.10
243 Dan Spillner	.01	.05
244 Lary Sorensen	.01	.05
245 Len Barker	.01	.05
246 Rick Manning	.01	.05
247 Toby Harrah	.01	.05
248 Milt Wilcox	.01	.05
249 Lou Whitaker	.02	.10
250 Tom Brookens	.01	.05
251 Chet Lemon	.01	.05
252 Jack Morris	.02	.10
253 Alan Trammell	.08	.25
254 Johnny Wockenfuss	.01	.05
255 Lance Parrish	.05	.15
256 Larry Herndon	.01	.05
257 Chris Speier	.01	.05
258 Woodie Fryman	.01	.05
259 Scott Sanderson	.01	.05
260 Steve Rogers	.01	.05
261 Warren Cromartie	.01	.05
262 Gary Carter	.15	.40
263 Bill Gullickson	.01	.05
264 Andre Dawson	.10	.30
265 Tim Raines	.05	.15
266 Charlie Lea	.01	.05
267 Jeff Reardon	.02	.10
268 Al Oliver	.02	.10
269 George Hendrick	.01	.05
270 John Montefusco	.01	.05
NNO Oakland A's CL	.01	.05
NNO Pittsburgh Pirates PO	.01	.05
NNO St. Louis Cardinals CL	.01	.05
NNO Los Angeles Dodgers CL	.01	.05
NNO St. Louis Cardinals PO	.01	.05
NNO Baltimore Orioles CL	.01	.05
NNO Montreal Expos PO	.01	.05
NNO Philadelphia Phillies CL	.01	.05
NNO Chicago White Sox PO	.01	.05
NNO New York Yankees PO	.01	.05
NNO San Diego Padres PO	.01	.05
NNO Atlanta Braves PO	.01	.05
NNO Texas Rangers CL	.01	.05
NNO Los Angeles Dodgers PO	.01	.05
NNO Detroit Tigers CL	.01	.05
NNO Milwaukee Brewers PO	.01	.05
NNO Toronto Blue Jays PO	.01	.05
NNO Kansas City Royals CL	.01	.05
NNO Montreal Expos CL	.01	.05
NNO Boston Red Sox CL	.01	.05
NNO California Angels PO	.01	.05
NNO California Angels CL	.01	.05
NNO Minnesota Twins PO	.01	.05
NNO Pittsburgh Pirates CL	.01	.05
NNO San Diego Padres CL	.01	.05
NNO Cleveland Indians PO	.01	.05
NNO Baltimore Orioles PO	.01	.05
NNO New York Mets PO	.01	.05
NNO Cincinnati Reds CL	.01	.05
NNO Houston Astros PO	.01	.05
NNO San Francisco Giants PO	.01	.05
NNO Atlanta Braves CL	.01	.05
NNO Toronto Blue Jays CL	.01	.05
NNO Minnesota Twins CL	.01	.05
NNO Chicago Cubs CL	.01	.05
NNO Boston Red Sox PO	.01	.05
NNO Kansas City Royals PO	.01	.05
NNO New York Yankees CL	.01	.05
NNO Philadelphia Phillies PO	.01	.05
NNO Cincinnati Reds PO	.01	.05
NNO Detroit Tigers PO	.01	.05
NNO New York Mets CL	.01	.05
NNO Milwaukee Brewers CL	.01	.05
NNO Cleveland Indians CL	.01	.05
NNO Seattle Mariners CL	.01	.05
NNO Seattle Mariners PO	.01	.05

1984 Fleer

The 1984 Fleer card 660-card standard-size set featured fronts with full-color team logos along with the player's name and position and the Fleer identification. Wax packs again consisted of 15 cards plus logo stickers. The set features many imaginative photos, several multi-player cards, and many more action shots than the 1983 card set. The backs are quite similar to the 1983 backs except that blue rather than brown ink is used. The player cards are alphabetized within team and the teams are ordered by their 1983 season finish and won-lost record. Specials (626-646) and checklist cards (647-660) make up the end of the set. The key Rookie Cards in this set are Don Mattingly, Darryl Strawberry and Andy Van Slyke.

Card	Low	High
COMPLETE SET (660)	20.00	50.00
1 Mike Boddicker	.05	.15
2 Al Bumbry	.05	.15
3 Todd Cruz	.05	.15
4 Rich Dauer	.05	.15
5 Storm Davis	.05	.15
6 Rick Dempsey	.05	.15
7 Jim Dwyer	.05	.15
8 Mike Flanagan	.05	.15
9 Dan Ford	.05	.15
10 John Lowenstein	.05	.15
11 Dennis Martinez	.15	.40
12 Tippy Martinez	.05	.15
13 Scott McGregor	.05	.15
14 Eddie Murray	.60	1.50
15 Joe Nolan	.05	.15
16 Jim Palmer	.15	.40
17 Cal Ripken	4.00	10.00
18 Gary Roenicke	.05	.15
19 Lenn Sakata	.05	.15
20 John Shelby	.05	.15
21 Ken Singleton	.15	.40
22 Sammy Stewart	.05	.15
23 Tim Stoddard	.05	.15
24 Marty Bystrom	.05	.15
25 Steve Carlton	.30	.75
26 Ivan DeJesus	.05	.15
27 John Denny	.05	.15
28 Bob Dernier	.05	.15
29 Bo Diaz	.05	.15
30 Kiko Garcia	.05	.15
31 Greg Gross	.05	.15
32 Kevin Gross RC	.20	.50
33 Von Hayes	.05	.15
34 Willie Hernandez	.05	.15
35 Al Holland	.05	.15
36 Charles Hudson	.05	.15
37 Joe Lefebvre	.05	.15
38 Sixto Lezcano	.05	.15
39 Garry Maddox	.05	.15
40 Gary Matthews	.15	.40
41 Len Matuszek	.05	.15
42 Tug McGraw	.15	.40
43 Joe Morgan	.15	.40
44 Tony Perez	.30	.75
45 Ron Reed	.05	.15
46 Pete Rose	2.00	5.00
47 Juan Samuel RC	.40	1.00
48 Mike Schmidt	1.50	4.00
49 Ozzie Virgil	.05	.15
50 Juan Agosto	.05	.15
51 Harold Baines	.15	.40
52 Floyd Bannister	.05	.15
53 Salome Barojas	.05	.15
54 Britt Burns	.05	.15
55 Julio Cruz	.05	.15
56 Richard Dotson	.05	.15
57 Jerry Dybzinski	.05	.15
58 Carlton Fisk	.30	.75
59 Scott Fletcher	.05	.15
60 Jerry Hairston	.05	.15
61 Kevin Hickey	.05	.15
62 Marc Hill	.05	.15
63 LaMarr Hoyt	.05	.15
64 Ron Kittle	.05	.15
65 Jerry Koosman	.15	.40
66 Dennis Lamp	.05	.15
67 Rudy Law	.05	.15
68 Vance Law	.05	.15
69 Greg Luzinski	.15	.40
70 Tom Paciorek	.05	.15
71 Mike Squires	.05	.15
72 Dick Tidrow	.05	.15
73 Greg Walker	.20	.50
74 Glenn Abbott	.05	.15
75 Howard Bailey	.05	.15
76 Doug Bair	.05	.15
77 Juan Berenguer	.05	.15
78 Tom Brookens	.15	.40
79 Enos Cabell	.05	.15
80 Kirk Gibson	.60	1.50
81 John Grubb	.05	.15
82 Larry Herndon	.15	.40
83 Wayne Krenchicki	.05	.15
84 Rick Leach	.05	.15
85 Chet Lemon	.15	.40
86 Aurelio Lopez	.05	.15
87 Jack Morris	.15	.40
88 Lance Parrish	.30	.75
89 Dan Petry	.15	.40
90 Dave Rozema	.05	.15
91 Alan Trammell	.15	.40
92 Lou Whitaker	.15	.40
93 Milt Wilcox	.05	.15
94 Glenn Wilson	.15	.40
95 John Wockenfuss	.05	.15
96 Dusty Baker	.15	.40
97 Joe Beckwith	.05	.15
98 Greg Brock	.05	.15
99 Jack Fimple	.05	.15

100 Pedro Guerrero .15 .40
101 Rick Honeycutt .05 .15
102 Burt Hooton .05 .15
103 Steve Howe .05 .15
104 Ken Landreaux .05 .15
105 Mike Marshall .05 .15
106 Rick Monday .15 .40
107 Jose Morales .05 .15
108 Tom Niedenfuer .05 .15
109 Alejandro Pena RC* .40 1.00
110 Jerry Reuss UER .05 .15
111 Bill Russell .15 .40
112 Steve Sax .05 .15
113 Mike Scioscia .15 .40
114 Derrel Thomas .05 .15
115 Fernando Valenzuela .15 .40
116 Bob Welch .15 .40
117 Steve Yeager .15 .40
118 Pat Zachry .05 .15
119 Don Baylor .15 .40
120 Bert Campaneris .15 .40
121 Rick Cerone .05 .15
122 Ray Fontenot .05 .15
123 George Frazier .05 .15
124 Oscar Gamble .05 .15
125 Rich Gossage .15 .40
126 Ken Griffey .15 .40
127 Ron Guidry .15 .40
128 Jay Howell .05 .15
129 Steve Kemp .05 .15
130 Matt Keough .05 .15
131 Don Mattingly RC 15.00 40.00
132 John Montefusco .05 .15
133 Omar Moreno .05 .15
134 Dale Murray .05 .15
135 Graig Nettles .15 .40
136 Lou Piniella .15 .40
137 Willie Randolph .15 .40
138 Shane Rawley .05 .15
139 Dave Righetti .15 .40
140 Andre Robertson .05 .15
141 Bob Shirley .05 .15
142 Roy Smalley .05 .15
143 Dave Winfield .15 .40
144 Butch Wynegar .05 .15
145 Jim Acker .05 .15
146 Doyle Alexander .05 .15
147 Jesse Barfield .15 .40
148 Jorge Bell .15 .40
149 Barry Bonnell .05 .15
150 Jim Clancy .05 .15
151 Dave Collins .05 .15
152 Tony Fernandez RC .40 1.00
153 Damaso Garcia .05 .15
154 Dave Geisel .05 .15
155 Jim Gott .05 .15
156 Alfredo Griffin .05 .15
157 Garth Iorg .05 .15
158 Roy Lee Jackson .05 .15
159 Cliff Johnson .05 .15
160 Luis Leal .05 .15
161 Buck Martinez .05 .15
162 Joey McLaughlin .05 .15
163 Randy Moffitt .05 .15
164 Lloyd Moseby .05 .15
165 Rance Mulliniks .05 .15
166 Jorge Orta .05 .15
167 Dave Stieb .15 .40
168 Willie Upshaw .05 .15
169 Ernie Whitt .05 .15
170 Len Barker .05 .15
171 Steve Bedrosian .05 .15
172 Bruce Benedict .05 .15
173 Brett Butler .15 .40
174 Rick Camp .05 .15
175 Chris Chambliss .15 .40
176 Ken Dayley .05 .15
177 Pete Falcone .05 .15
178 Terry Forster .15 .40
179 Gene Garber .05 .15
180 Terry Harper .05 .15
181 Bob Horner .15 .40
182 Glenn Hubbard .05 .15
183 Randy Johnson .05 .15
184 Craig McMurtry .05 .15
185 Donnie Moore .05 .15
186 Dale Murphy .30 .75
187 Phil Niekro .15 .40
188 Pascual Perez .05 .15
189 Biff Pocoroba .05 .15
190 Rafael Ramirez .05 .15
191 Jerry Royster .05 .15
192 Claudell Washington .05 .15
193 Bob Watson .05 .15
194 Jerry Augustine .05 .15
195 Mark Brouhard .05 .15
196 Mike Caldwell .05 .15
197 Tom Candiotti RC .40 1.00
198 Cecil Cooper .15 .40
199 Rollie Fingers .15 .40
200 Jim Gantner .05 .15
201 Bob L. Gibson RC .08 .25
202 Moose Haas .05 .15
203 Roy Howell .05 .15
204 Pete Ladd .05 .15
205 Rick Manning .05 .15
206 Bob McClure .05 .15
207 Paul Molitor UER .15 .40
'83 stats should say
.270 BA and 608 AB
208 Don Money .05 .15
209 Charlie Moore .05 .15
210 Ben Oglivie .15 .40
211 Chuck Porter .05 .15
212 Ed Romero .05 .15
213 Ted Simmons .15 .40
214 Jim Slaton .05 .15
215 Don Sutton .15 .40
216 Tom Tellmann .05 .15
217 Pete Vuckovich .05 .15
218 Ned Yost .05 .15
219 Robin Yount 1.00 2.50
220 Alan Ashby .05 .15
221 Kevin Bass .05 .15
222 Jose Cruz .15 .40
223 Bill Dawley .05 .15
224 Frank DiPino .05 .15
225 Bill Doran RC .20 .50
226 Phil Garner .15 .40
227 Art Howe .05 .15
228 Bob Knepper .05 .15
229 Ray Knight .15 .40
230 Frank LaCorte .05 .15
231 Mike LaCoss .05 .15
232 Mike Madden .05 .15
233 Jerry Mumphrey .05 .15
234 Joe Niekro .05 .15
235 Terry Puhl .05 .15
236 Luis Pujols .05 .15
237 Craig Reynolds .05 .15
238 Vern Ruhle .05 .15
239 Nolan Ryan 4.00 10.00
240 Mike Scott .15 .40
241 Tony Scott .05 .15
242 Dave Smith .05 .15
243 Dickie Thon .05 .15
244 Denny Walling .05 .15
245 Dale Berra .05 .15
246 Jim Bibby .05 .15
247 John Candelaria .05 .15
248 Jose DeLeon RC .20 .50
249 Mike Easler .05 .15
250 Cecilio Guante .05 .15
251 Richie Hebner .05 .15
252 Lee Lacy .05 .15
253 Bill Madlock .15 .40
254 Milt May .05 .15
255 Lee Mazzilli .15 .40
256 Larry McWilliams .05 .15
257 Jim Morrison .05 .15
258 Dave Parker .15 .40
259 Tony Pena .05 .15
260 Johnny Ray .05 .15
261 Rick Rhoden .05 .15
262 Don Robinson .05 .15
263 Manny Sarmiento .05 .15
264 Rod Scurry .05 .15
265 Kent Tekulve .05 .15
266 Gene Tenace .15 .40
267 Jason Thompson .05 .15
268 Lee Tunnell .05 .15
269 Marvell Wynne .20 .50
270 Ray Burris .05 .15
271 Gary Carter .15 .40
272 Warren Cromartie .05 .15
273 Andre Dawson .15 .40
274 Doug Flynn .05 .15
275 Terry Francona .15 .40
276 Bill Gullickson .05 .15
277 Bob James .05 .15
278 Charlie Lea .05 .15
279 Bryan Little .05 .15
280 Al Oliver .15 .40
281 Tim Raines .15 .40
282 Bobby Ramos .05 .15
283 Jeff Reardon .15 .40
284 Steve Rogers .15 .40
285 Scott Sanderson .05 .15
286 Dan Schatzeder .05 .15
287 Bryn Smith .05 .15
288 Chris Speier .05 .15
289 Manny Trillo .05 .15
290 Mike Vail .05 .15
291 Tim Wallach .15 .40
292 Chris Welsh .05 .15
293 Jim Wohlford .05 .15
294 Kurt Bevacqua .05 .15
295 Juan Bonilla .05 .15
296 Bobby Brown .05 .15
297 Luis DeLeon .05 .15
298 Dave Dravecky .05 .15
299 Tim Flannery .05 .15
300 Steve Garvey .15 .40
301 Tony Gwynn 2.50 6.00
302 Andy Hawkins .05 .15
303 Ruppert Jones .05 .15
304 Terry Kennedy .05 .15
305 Tim Lollar .05 .15
306 Gary Lucas .05 .15
307 Kevin McReynolds RC .40 1.00
308 Sid Monge .05 .15
309 Mario Ramirez .05 .15
310 Gene Richards .05 .15
311 Luis Salazar .05 .15
312 Eric Show .05 .15
313 Elias Sosa .05 .15
314 Garry Templeton .15 .40
315 Mark Thurmond .05 .15
316 Ed Whitson .05 .15
317 Alan Wiggins .05 .15
318 Neil Allen .05 .15
319 Joaquin Andujar .15 .40
320 Steve Braun .05 .15
321 Glenn Brummer .05 .15
322 Bob Forsch .05 .15
323 David Green .05 .15
324 George Hendrick .15 .40
325 Tom Herr .05 .15
326 Dane Iorg .05 .15
327 Jeff Lahti .05 .15
328 Dave LaPoint .05 .15
329 Willie McGee .15 .40
330 Ken Oberkfell .05 .15
331 Darrell Porter .05 .15
332 Jamie Quirk .05 .15
333 Mike Ramsey .05 .15
334 Floyd Rayford .05 .15
335 Lonnie Smith .05 .15
336 Ozzie Smith 1.00 2.50
337 John Stuper .05 .15
338 Bruce Sutter .30 .75
339 A.Van Slyke RC UER 1.00 2.50
340 Dave Von Ohlen .05 .15
341 Willie Aikens .05 .15
342 Mike Armstrong .05 .15
343 Bud Black .05 .15
344 George Brett 1.50 4.00
345 Onix Concepcion .05 .15
346 Keith Creel .05 .15
347 Larry Gura .05 .15
348 Don Hood .05 .15
349 Dennis Leonard .05 .15
350 Hal McRae .15 .40
351 Amos Otis .15 .40
352 Gaylord Perry .15 .40
353 Greg Pryor .05 .15
354 Dan Quisenberry .05 .15
355 Steve Renko .15 .40
356 Leon Roberts .05 .15
357 Pat Sheridan .05 .15
358 Joe Simpson .05 .15
359 Don Slaught .15 .40
360 Paul Splittorff .05 .15
361 U.L. Washington .05 .15
362 John Wathan .05 .15
363 Frank White .15 .40
364 Willie Wilson .15 .40
365 Jim Barr .05 .15
366 Dave Bergman .05 .15
367 Fred Breining .05 .15
368 Bob Brenly .05 .15
369 Jack Clark .15 .40
370 Chili Davis .15 .40
371 Mark Davis .05 .15
372 Darrell Evans .15 .40
373 Atlee Hammaker .05 .15
374 Mike Krukow .05 .15
375 Duane Kuiper .05 .15
376 Bill Laskey .05 .15
377 Gary Lavelle .05 .15
378 Johnnie LeMaster .05 .15
379 Jeff Leonard .05 .15
380 Randy Lerch .05 .15
381 Renie Martin .05 .15
382 Andy McGaffigan .05 .15
383 Greg Minton .05 .15
384 Tom O'Malley .05 .15
385 Max Venable .05 .15
386 Brad Wellman .05 .15
387 Joel Youngblood .05 .15
388 Gary Allenson .05 .15
389 Luis Aponte .05 .15
390 Tony Armas .15 .40
391 Doug Bird .05 .15
392 Wade Boggs 1.50 4.00
393 Dennis Boyd .15 .40
394 Mike G. Brown UER .08 .25
shown with record
of 31-104
395 Mark Clear .05 .15
396 Dennis Eckersley .30 .75
397 Dwight Evans .30 .75
398 Rich Gedman .05 .15
399 Glenn Hoffman .05 .15
400 Bruce Hurst .05 .15
401 John Henry Johnson .05 .15
402 Ed Jurak .05 .15
403 Rick Miller .05 .15
404 Jeff Newman .05 .15
405 Reid Nichols .05 .15
406 Bob Ojeda .05 .15
407 Jerry Remy .05 .15
408 Jim Rice .15 .40
409 Bob Stanley .05 .15
410 Dave Stapleton .05 .15
411 John Tudor .15 .40
412 Carl Yastrzemski .60 1.50
413 Buddy Bell .15 .40
414 Larry Biittner .05 .15
415 John Butcher .05 .15
416 Danny Darwin .05 .15
417 Bucky Dent .15 .40
418 Dave Hostetler .05 .15
419 Charlie Hough .15 .40
420 Bobby Johnson .05 .15
421 Odell Jones .05 .15
422 Jon Matlack .05 .15
423 Pete O'Brien RC* .20 .50
424 Larry Parrish .05 .15
425 Mickey Rivers .05 .15
426 Billy Sample .05 .15
427 Dave Schmidt .05 .15
428 Mike Smithson .05 .15
429 Bill Stein .05 .15
430 Dave Stewart .15 .40
431 Jim Sundberg .15 .40
432 Frank Tanana .15 .40
433 Dave Tobik .05 .15
434 Wayne Tolleson .05 .15
435 George Wright .05 .15
436 Bill Almon .05 .15
437 Keith Atherton .05 .15
438 Dave Beard .05 .15
439 Tom Burgmeier .05 .15
440 Jeff Burroughs .05 .15
441 Chris Codiroli .05 .15
442 Tim Conroy .05 .15
443 Mike Davis .05 .15
444 Wayne Gross .05 .15
445 Garry Hancock .05 .15
446 Mike Heath .05 .15
447 Rickey Henderson 1.00 2.50
448 Donnie Hill .05 .15
449 Bob Kearney .05 .15
450 Bill Krueger RC .08 .25
451 Rick Langford .05 .15
452 Carney Lansford .15 .40
453 Dave Lopes .15 .40
454 Steve McCatty .05 .15
455 Dan Meyer .05 .15
456 Dwayne Murphy .05 .15
457 Mike Norris .05 .15
458 Ricky Peters .05 .15
459 Tony Phillips RC .40 1.00
460 Tom Underwood .05 .15
461 Mike Warren .05 .15
462 Johnny Bench .60 1.50
463 Bruce Berenyi .05 .15
464 Dann Bilardello .05 .15
465 Cesar Cedeno .15 .40
466 Dave Concepcion .15 .40
467 Dan Driessen .05 .15
468 Nick Esasky .05 .15
469 Rich Gale .05 .15
470 Ben Hayes .05 .15
471 Paul Householder .05 .15
472 Tom Hume .05 .15
473 Alan Knicely .05 .15
474 Eddie Milner .05 .15
475 Ron Oester .05 .15
476 Kelly Paris .05 .15
477 Frank Pastore .05 .15
478 Ted Power .05 .15
479 Joe Price .05 .15
480 Charlie Puleo .05 .15
481 Gary Redus RC* .20 .50
482 Bill Scherrer .05 .15
483 Mario Soto .15 .40
484 Alex Trevino .05 .15
485 Duane Walker .05 .15
486 Larry Bowa .15 .40
487 Warren Brusstar .05 .15
488 Bill Buckner .15 .40
489 Bill Campbell .05 .15
490 Ron Cey .15 .40
491 Jody Davis .05 .15
492 Leon Durham .05 .15
493 Mel Hall .15 .40
494 Ferguson Jenkins .15 .40
495 Jay Johnstone .05 .15
496 Craig Lefferts RC .08 .25
497 Carmelo Martinez .05 .15
498 Jerry Morales .05 .15
499 Keith Moreland .05 .15
500 Dickie Noles .05 .15
501 Mike Proly .05 .15
502 Chuck Rainey .05 .15
503 Dick Ruthven .05 .15
504 Ryne Sandberg 2.50 6.00
505 Lee Smith .15 .40
506 Steve Trout .05 .15
507 Gary Woods .05 .15
508 Juan Beniquez .05 .15
509 Bob Boone .15 .40
510 Rick Burleson .05 .15
511 Rod Carew .30 .75
512 Bobby Clark .05 .15
513 John Curtis .05 .15
514 Doug DeCinces .05 .15
515 Brian Downing .15 .40
516 Tim Foli .05 .15
517 Ken Forsch .05 .15
518 Bobby Grich .15 .40
519 Andy Hassler .05 .15
520 Reggie Jackson .30 .75
521 Ron Jackson .05 .15
522 Tommy John .15 .40
523 Bruce Kison .05 .15
524 Steve Lubratich .05 .15
525 Fred Lynn .15 .40
526 Gary Pettis .05 .15
527 Luis Sanchez .05 .15
528 Daryl Sconiers .05 .15
529 Ellis Valentine .05 .15
530 Rob Wilfong .05 .15
531 Mike Witt .05 .15
532 Geoff Zahn .05 .15
533 Bud Anderson .05 .15
534 Chris Bando .05 .15
535 Alan Bannister .05 .15
536 Bert Blyleven .15 .40
537 Tom Brennan .05 .15
538 Jamie Easterly .05 .15
539 Juan Eichelberger .05 .15
540 Jim Essian .05 .15
541 Mike Fischlin .05 .15
542 Julio Franco .15 .40
543 Mike Hargrove .05 .15
544 Toby Harrah .15 .40
545 Ron Hassey .05 .15
546 Neal Heaton .05 .15
547 Bake McBride .05 .15
548 Broderick Perkins .05 .15
549 Lary Sorensen .05 .15
550 Dan Spillner .05 .15
551 Rick Sutcliffe .15 .40
552 Pat Tabler .05 .15
553 Gorman Thomas .15 .40
554 Andre Thornton .05 .15
555 George Vukovich .05 .15
556 Darrell Brown .05 .15
557 Tom Brunansky .05 .15
558 Randy Bush .05 .15
559 Bobby Castillo .05 .15
560 John Castino .05 .15
561 Ron Davis .05 .15
562 Dave Engle .05 .15
563 Lenny Faedo .05 .15
564 Pete Filson .05 .15
565 Gary Gaetti .30 .75
566 Mickey Hatcher .05 .15
567 Kent Hrbek .15 .40
568 Rusty Kuntz .05 .15
569 Tim Laudner .05 .15
570 Rick Lysander .05 .15
571 Bobby Mitchell .05 .15
572 Ken Schrom .05 .15
573 Ray Smith .05 .15
574 Tim Teufel RC .20 .50
575 Frank Viola .30 .75
576 Gary Ward .05 .15
577 Ron Washington .05 .15
578 Len Whitehouse .05 .15
579 Al Williams .05 .15
580 Bob Bailor .05 .15
581 Mark Bradley .05 .15
582 Hubie Brooks .05 .15
583 Carlos Diaz .05 .15
584 George Foster .15 .40
585 Brian Giles .05 .15
586 Danny Heep .05 .15
587 Keith Hernandez .15 .40
588 Ron Hodges .05 .15
589 Scott Holman .05 .15
590 Dave Kingman .15 .40
591 Ed Lynch .05 .15
592 Jose Oquendo RC .20 .50
593 Jesse Orosco .05 .15
594 Junior Ortiz .05 .15
595 Tom Seaver .60 1.50
596 Doug Sisk .05 .15
597 Rusty Staub .15 .40
598 John Stearns .05 .15
599 Darryl Strawberry RC 2.50 6.00
600 Craig Swan .05 .15
601 Walt Terrell .05 .15
602 Mike Torrez .05 .15
603 Mookie Wilson .15 .40
604 Jamie Allen .05 .15
605 Jim Beattie .05 .15
606 Tony Bernazard .05 .15
607 Manny Castillo .05 .15
608 Bill Caudill .05 .15
609 Bryan Clark .05 .15
610 Al Cowens .05 .15
611 Dave Henderson .15 .40
612 Steve Henderson .05 .15
613 Orlando Mercado .05 .15
614 Mike Moore .05 .15
615 Ricky Nelson UER .05 .15
Jamie Nelson's
stats on back
616 Spike Owen RC .20 .50
617 Pat Putnam .05 .15
618 Ron Roenicke .05 .15
619 Mike Stanton .05 .15
620 Bob Stoddard .05 .15
621 Rick Sweet .05 .15
622 Roy Thomas .05 .15
623 Ed VandeBerg .05 .15
624 Matt Young RC .20 .50
625 Richie Zisk .05 .15
626 Fred Lynn IA .15 .40
627 Manny Trillo IA .05 .15
628 Steve Garvey IA .15 .40
629 Rod Carew IA .15 .40
630 Wade Boggs IA .60 1.50
631 Tim Raines IA .05 .15
632 Al Oliver .15 .40
Double Trouble
633 Steve Sax IA .05 .15
634 Dickie Thon IA .05 .15
635 Dan Quisenberry .05 .15
Tippy Martinez
636 Joe Morgan .60 1.50
Pete Rose
Tony Perez
637 Lance Parrish .30 .75
Bob Boone
638 George Brett .75 2.00
Gaylord Perry
639 Dave Righetti .30 .75
Mike Warren
Bob Forsch
640 Johnny Bench .60 1.50
Carl Yastrzemski
641 Gaylord Perry IA .05 .15
642 Steve Carlton IA .15 .40
643 Joe Altobelli MG .05 .15
Paul Owens MG
644 Rick Dempsey WS .05 .15
645 Mike Boddicker WS .05 .15
646 Scott McGregor WS .05 .15
647 CL: Orioles .05 .15
Royals
Joe Altobelli MG
648 CL: Phillies .05 .15
Giants
Paul Owens MG
649 CL: White Sox .30 .75
Red Sox
Tony LaRussa MG
650 CL: Tigers .30 .75
Rangers
Sparky Anderson MG
651 CL: Dodgers .30 .75
A's
Tommy Lasorda MG
652 CL: Yankees .30 .75
Reds
Billy Martin MG
653 CL: Blue Jays .15 .40
Cubs
Bobby Cox MG
654 CL: Braves .30 .75
Angels
Joe Torre MG
655 CL: Brewers .05 .15
Indians
Rene Lachemann MG
656 CL: Astros .05 .15
Twins
Bob Lillis MG
657 CL: Pirates .05 .15
Mets
Chuck Tanner MG
658 CL: Expos .05 .15
Mariners
Bill Virdon MG
659 CL: Padres .15 .40
Specials
Dick Williams MG
660 CL: Cardinals .30 .75
Teams
Whitey Herzog MG

1984 Fleer Update

This set was Fleer's first update set and portrayed players with their proper team for the current year and rookies who were not in their regular issue. Like the Topps Traded sets of the time, the Fleer Update sets were distributed in factory set form through hobby dealers only. The set was quite popular with collectors, and, apparently, the print run was relatively short, as the set was quickly in short supply and exhibited a rapid and dramatic price increase in the mid to late 1980's. The cards are numbered on the back with a U prefix and placed in alphabetical order by player name. The key (extended) Rookie Cards in this set are Roger Clemens, John Franco, Dwight Gooden, Jimmy Key, Mark Langston, Kirby Puckett, and Bret Saberhagen. Collectors are urged to be careful if purchasing single cards of Clemens, Darling, Gooden, Puckett, Rose, or Saberhagen as these specific cards have been illegally reprinted. These fakes are blurry when compared to the real cards and have noticeably different printing dot patterns under 8X or greater magnification.

COMP.FACT.SET (132) 125.00 250.00
1 Willie Aikens .40 1.00
2 Luis Aponte .40 1.00
3 Mark Bailey .40 1.00
4 Bob Bailor .40 1.00
5 Dusty Baker .60 1.50
6 Steve Balboni .40 1.00
7 Alan Bannister .40 1.00
8 Marty Barrett XRC .75 2.00
9 Dave Beard .40 1.00
10 Joe Beckwith .40 1.00
11 Dave Bergman .40 1.00
12 Tony Bernazard .40 1.00
13 Bruce Bochte .40 1.00
14 Barry Bonnell .40 1.00
15 Phil Bradley .75 2.00
16 Fred Breining .40 1.00
17 Mike C. Brown .40 1.00
18 Bill Buckner .60 1.50
19 Ray Burris .40 1.00
20 John Butcher .40 1.00
21 Brett Butler .60 1.50
22 Enos Cabell .40 1.00
23 Bill Campbell .40 1.00
24 Bill Caudill .40 1.00
25 Bobby Clark .40 1.00
26 Bryan Clark .40 1.00
27 Roger Clemens XRC 75.00 200.00
28 Jaime Cocanower .40 1.00
29 Ron Darling XRC 2.00 5.00
30 Alvin Davis XRC .75 2.00
31 Bob Dernier .40 1.00
32 Carlos Diaz .40 1.00
33 Mike Easler .40 1.00
34 Dennis Eckersley 1.00 2.50
35 Jim Essian .40 1.00
36 Darrell Evans .60 1.50
37 Mike Fitzgerald .40 1.00
38 Tim Foli .40 1.00
39 John Franco XRC 2.00 5.00
40 George Frazier .40 1.00
41 Rich Gale .40 1.00
42 Barbaro Garbey .40 1.00
43 Dwight Gooden XRC 30.00 80.00
44 Rich Gossage .60 1.50
45 Wayne Gross .40 1.00
46 Mark Gubicza XRC .75 2.00
47 Jackie Gutierrez .40 1.00
48 Toby Harrah .60 1.50
49 Ron Hassey .40 1.00
50 Richie Hebner .40 1.00
51 Willie Hernandez .40 1.00
52 Ed Hodge .40 1.00
53 Ricky Horton .40 1.00
54 Art Howe .40 1.00
55 Dane Iorg .40 1.00
56 Brook Jacoby .75 2.00
57 Dion James XRC .40 1.00
58 Mike Jeffcoat XRC .40 1.00
59 Ruppert Jones .40 1.00
60 Bob Kearney .40 1.00
61 Jimmy Key XRC 2.00 5.00
62 Dave Kingman .60 1.50
63 Brad Komminsk XRC .40 1.00
64 Jerry Koosman .60 1.50
65 Wayne Krenchicki .40 1.00
66 Rusty Kuntz .40 1.00
67 Frank LaCorte .40 1.00
68 Dennis Lamp .40 1.00
69 Tito Landrum .40 1.00
70 Mark Langston XRC 2.00 5.00
71 Rick Leach .40 1.00
72 Craig Lefferts .40 1.00
73 Gary Lucas .40 1.00
74 Jerry Martin .40 1.00
75 Carmelo Martinez .40 1.00
76 Mike Mason XRC .40 1.00
77 Gary Matthews .60 1.50
78 Andy McGaffigan .40 1.00
79 Joey McLaughlin .40 1.00
80 Joe Morgan .60 1.50
81 Darryl Motley .40 1.00
82 Graig Nettles .60 1.50
83 Phil Niekro .60 1.50
84 Ken Oberkfell .40 1.00
85 Al Oliver .60 1.50
86 Jorge Orta .40 1.00
87 Amos Otis .60 1.50
88 Bob Owchinko .40 1.00
89 Dave Parker .60 1.50
90 Jack Perconte .40 1.00
91 Tony Perez 1.00 2.50
92 Gerald Perry .75 2.00
93 Kirby Puckett XRC 100.00 250.00
94 Shane Rawley .40 1.00
95 Floyd Rayford .40 1.00
96 Ron Reed .40 1.00
97 R.J. Reynolds .40 1.00
98 Gene Richards .40 1.00
99 Jose Rijo XRC 2.00 5.00
100 Jeff D. Robinson .40 1.00
101 Ron Romanick .40 1.00
102 Pete Rose 5.00 12.00
103 Bret Saberhagen XRC 4.00 10.00
104 Scott Sanderson .40 1.00
105 Dick Schofield XRC .75 2.00
106 Tom Seaver 1.50 4.00
107 Jim Slaton .40 1.00
108 Mike Smithson .40 1.00
109 Lary Sorensen .40 1.00
110 Tim Stoddard .40 1.00
111 Jeff Stone XRC .40 1.00
112 Champ Summers .40 1.00
113 Jim Sundberg .60 1.50
114 Rick Sutcliffe .60 1.50
115 Craig Swan .40 1.00
116 Derrel Thomas .40 1.00
117 Gorman Thomas .60 1.50
118 Alex Trevino .40 1.00
119 Manny Trillo .40 1.00
120 John Tudor .60 1.50
121 Tom Underwood .40 1.00
122 Mike Vail .40 1.00
123 Tom Waddell .40 1.00
124 Gary Ward .40 1.00
125 Terry Whitfield .40 1.00
126 Curtis Wilkerson .40 1.00
127 Frank Williams .40 1.00
128 Glenn Wilson .60 1.50
129 John Wockenfuss .40 1.00
130 Ned Yost .40 1.00
131 Mike Young XRC .40 1.00
132 Checklist 1-132 .40 1.00

1984 Fleer Stickers

The stickers in this 126-sticker set measure approximately 1 15/16" by 2 1/2". The 1984 Fleer sticker set is a very attractive set with a beige border. Many players are featured more than once in the set due to the fact that the album issued to house the set contains league leader categories in which to place the stickers. The checklist below is ordered by categories, e.g., Game Winning RBI's (1-5), Batting Average (6-15), Home Runs (16-23), Hits (24-31), Slugging Percentage (32-39), Pinch Hits (40-43), Designated Hitter's Hits (44-47), On Base Percentage (48-55), Won/Lost Percentage (56-64), Earned Run Average (65-66), Saves (67-77), Strikeouts (78-87), Stolen Bases (88-95), Future Hall of Famers (96-103), Rookie Stars (104-113), World Series Batting (114-122) and Playoff Managers (123-126). These stickers were originally issued in packs of six for 25 cents plus a team logo.

COMPLETE SET (126) 5.00 12.00
1 Dickie Thon .01 .05
2 Ken Landreaux .01 .05
3 Darrell Evans .05 .15
4 Harold Baines .05 .15
5 Dave Winfield .20 .50
6 Bill Madlock .01 .05
7 Lonnie Smith .01 .05
8 Jose Cruz .05 .15
9 George Hendrick .01 .05
10 Ray Knight .01 .05
11 Wade Boggs .25 .60
12 Rod Carew .20 .50
13 Lou Whitaker .08 .25
14 Alan Trammell .15 .40
15 Cal Ripken .75 2.00
16 Mike Schmidt .30 .75
17 Dale Murphy .15 .40
18 Andre Dawson .15 .40
19 Pedro Guerrero .05 .15
20 Jim Rice .05 .15
21 Tony Armas .01 .05
22 Ron Kittle .01 .05
23 Eddie Murray .20 .50
24 Jose Cruz .05 .15
25 Andre Dawson .15 .40
26 Rafael Ramirez .01 .05
27 Al Oliver .05 .15
28 Wade Boggs .30 .75
29 Cal Ripken .75 2.00
30 Lou Whitaker .05 .15
31 Cecil Cooper .05 .15
32 Dale Murphy .15 .40
33 Andre Dawson .15 .40
34 Pedro Guerrero .05 .15
35 Mike Schmidt .25 .60
36 George Brett .40 1.00
37 Jim Rice .05 .15
38 Eddie Murray .15 .40
39 Carlton Fisk .15 .40
40 Rusty Staub .05 .15
41 Duane Walker .01 .05
42 Steve Braun .01 .05
43 Kurt Bevacqua .01 .05
44 Hal McRae .05 .15
45 Don Baylor .05 .15
46 Ken Singleton .01 .05
47 Greg Luzinski .05 .15
48 Mike Schmidt .15 .40
49 Keith Hernandez .05 .15
50 Dale Murphy .15 .40
51 Tim Raines .08 .25
52 Wade Boggs .30 .75
53 Rickey Henderson .30 .75
54 Rod Carew .20 .50
55 Ken Singleton .01 .05
56 John Denny .01 .05
57 John Candelaria .01 .05
58 Larry McWilliams .01 .05
59 Pascual Perez .01 .05
60 Jesse Orosco .05 .15
61 Moose Haas .01 .05
62 Richard Dotson .01 .05
63 Mike Flanagan .01 .05
64 Scott McGregor .01 .05
65 Atlee Hammaker .01 .05
66 Rick Honeycutt .01 .05
67 Lee Smith .15 .40
68 Al Holland .01 .05
69 Greg Minton .01 .05
70 Bruce Sutter .05 .15
71 Jeff Reardon .05 .15
72 Frank DiPino .01 .05
73 Dan Quisenberry .05 .15
74 Bob Stanley .01 .05
75 Ron Davis .01 .05
76 Bill Caudill .01 .05
77 Peter Ladd .01 .05
78 Steve Carlton .15 .40
79 Mario Soto .01 .05
80 Larry McWilliams .01 .05
81 Fernando Valenzuela .05 .15
82 Nolan Ryan .75 2.00
83 Jack Morris .08 .25
84 Floyd Bannister .01 .05
85 Dave Stieb .01 .05
86 Dave Righetti .01 .05
87 Rick Sutcliffe .05 .15
88 Tim Raines .08 .25
89 Alan Wiggins .01 .05
90 Steve Sax .05 .15

91 Mookie Wilson .08 .25
92 Rickey Henderson .30 .75
93 Rudy Law .01 .05
94 Willie Wilson .05 .15
95 Julio Cruz .01 .05
96 Johnny Bench .20 .50
97 Carl Yastrzemski .20 .50
98 Gaylord Perry .15 .40
99 Pete Rose .30 .75
100 Joe Morgan .20 .50
101 Steve Carlton .20 .50
102 Jim Palmer .20 .50
103 Rod Carew .20 .50
104 Darryl Strawberry .25 .60
105 Craig McMurtry .01 .05
106 Mel Hall .01 .05
107 Lee Tunnell .01 .05
108 Bill Dawley .01 .05
109 Ron Kittle .01 .05
110 Mike Boddicker .01 .05
111 Julio Franco .15 .40
112 Daryl Sconiers .01 .05
113 Neal Heaton .01 .05
114 John Shelby .01 .05
115 Rick Dempsey .05 .15
116 John Lowenstein .01 .05
117 Jim Dwyer .01 .05
118 Bo Diaz .01 .05
119 Pete Rose .30 .75
120 Joe Morgan .20 .50
121 Gary Matthews .01 .05
122 Garry Maddox .01 .05
123 Paul Owens MG .01 .05
124 Tom Lasorda MG .08 .25
125 Joe Altobelli MG .01 .05
126 Tony LaRussa MG .05 .15

1985 Fleer

The 1985 Fleer set consists of 660 standard-size cards. Wax packs contained 15 cards plus logo stickers. Card fronts feature a full color photo, team logo along with the player's name and position. The borders enclosing the photo are color-coded to correspond to the player's team. The cards are ordered alphabetically within team. The teams are ordered based on their respective performance during the prior year. Subsets include Specials (626-643) and Major League Prospects (644-653). The black and white photo on the reverse is included for the third straight year. Rookie Cards include Roger Clemens, Eric Davis, Shawon Dunston, John Franco, Dwight Gooden, Orel Hershiser, Jimmy Key, Mark Langston, Terry Pendleton, Kirby Puckett and Bret Saberhagen

COMPLETE SET (660) 25.00 60.00
COMP.FACT.SET (660) 50.00 100.00
1 Doug Bair .05 .15
2 Juan Berenguer .05 .15
3 Dave Bergman .05 .15
4 Tom Brookens .05 .15
5 Marty Castilio .05 .15
6 Darrell Evans .15 .40
7 Barbaro Garbey .05 .15
8 Kirk Gibson .15 .40
9 John Grubb .05 .15
10 Willie Hernandez .05 .15
11 Larry Herndon .05 .15
12 Howard Johnson .15 .40
13 Ruppert Jones .05 .15
14 Rusty Kuntz .05 .15
15 Chet Lemon .15 .40
16 Aurelio Lopez .05 .15
17 Sid Monge .05 .15
18 Jack Morris .15 .40
19 Lance Parrish .15 .40
20 Dan Petry .05 .15
21 Dave Rozema .05 .15
22 Bill Scherrer .05 .15
23 Alan Trammell .15 .40
24 Lou Whitaker .15 .40
25 Milt Wilcox .05 .15
26 Kurt Bevacqua .05 .15
27 Greg Booker .05 .15
28 Bobby Brown .05 .15
29 Luis DeLeon .05 .15
30 Dave Dravecky .05 .15
31 Tim Flannery .05 .15
32 Steve Garvey .15 .40
33 Rich Gossage .15 .40
34 Tony Gwynn 1.00 2.50
35 Greg Harris .05 .15
36 Andy Hawkins .05 .15
37 Terry Kennedy .05 .15
38 Craig Lefferts .05 .15
39 Tim Lollar .05 .15
40 Carmelo Martinez .05 .15
41 Kevin McReynolds .15 .40
42 Graig Nettles .15 .40
43 Luis Salazar .05 .15
44 Eric Show .05 .15
45 Garry Templeton .15 .40
46 Mark Thurmond .05 .15
47 Ed Whitson .05 .15
48 Alan Wiggins .05 .15
49 Rich Bordi .05 .15
50 Larry Bowa .15 .40
51 Warren Brusstar .05 .15
52 Ron Cey .15 .40
53 Henry Cotto RC .08 .25
54 Jody Davis .05 .15
55 Bob Dernier .05 .15
56 Leon Durham .05 .15
57 Dennis Eckersley .30 .75
58 George Frazier .05 .15
59 Richie Hebner .05 .15
60 Dave Lopes .15 .40
61 Gary Matthews .15 .40
62 Keith Moreland .05 .15
63 Rick Reuschel .15 .40
64 Dick Ruthven .05 .15
65 Ryne Sandberg 1.00 2.50
66 Scott Sanderson .05 .15
67 Lee Smith .15 .40
68 Tim Stoddard .05 .15
69 Rick Sutcliffe .15 .40
70 Steve Trout .05 .15
71 Gary Woods .05 .15
72 Wally Backman .05 .15
73 Bruce Berenyi .05 .15
74 Hubie Brooks UER .05 .15
 Kelvin Chapman's
 stats on card back
75 Kelvin Chapman .05 .15
76 Ron Darling .15 .40
77 Sid Fernandez .15 .40
78 Mike Fitzgerald .05 .15
79 George Foster .15 .40
80 Brent Gaff .05 .15
81 Ron Gardenhire .05 .15
82 Dwight Gooden RC 1.25 3.00
83 Tom Gorman .05 .15
84 Danny Heep .05 .15
85 Keith Hernandez .15 .40
86 Ray Knight .15 .40
87 Ed Lynch .05 .15
88 Jose Oquendo .05 .15
89 Jesse Orosco .05 .15
90 Rafael Santana .05 .15
91 Doug Sisk .05 .15
92 Rusty Staub .15 .40
93 Darryl Strawberry .50 1.25
94 Walt Terrell .05 .15
95 Mookie Wilson .15 .40
96 Jim Acker .05 .15
97 Willie Aikens .05 .15
98 Doyle Alexander .05 .15
99 Jesse Barfield .15 .40
100 George Bell .15 .40
101 Jim Clancy .05 .15
102 Dave Collins .05 .15
103 Tony Fernandez .15 .40
104 Damaso Garcia .05 .15
105 Jim Gott .05 .15
106 Alfredo Griffin .05 .15
107 Garth Iorg .05 .15
108 Roy Lee Jackson .05 .15
109 Cliff Johnson .05 .15
110 Jimmy Key RC .40 1.00
111 Dennis Lamp .05 .15
112 Rick Leach .05 .15
113 Luis Leal .05 .15
114 Buck Martinez .05 .15
115 Lloyd Moseby .05 .15
116 Rance Mulliniks .05 .15
117 Dave Stieb .15 .40
118 Willie Upshaw .05 .15
119 Ernie Whitt .05 .15
120 Mike Armstrong .05 .15
121 Don Baylor .15 .40
122 Marty Bystrom .05 .15
123 Rick Cerone .05 .15
124 Joe Cowley .05 .15
125 Brian Dayett .05 .15
126 Tim Foli .05 .15
127 Ray Fontenot .05 .15
128 Ken Griffey .15 .40
129 Ron Guidry .15 .40
130 Toby Harrah .15 .40
131 Jay Howell .05 .15
132 Steve Kemp .05 .15
133 Don Mattingly 2.00 5.00
134 Bobby Meacham .05 .15
135 John Montefusco .05 .15
136 Omar Moreno .05 .15
137 Dale Murray .05 .15
138 Phil Niekro .15 .40
139 Mike Pagliarulo .05 .15
140 Willie Randolph .15 .40
141 Dennis Rasmussen .05 .15
142 Dave Righetti .15 .40
143 Jose Rijo RC .40 1.00
144 Andre Robertson .05 .15
145 Bob Shirley .05 .15
146 Dave Winfield .15 .40
147 Butch Wynegar .05 .15
148 Gary Allenson .05 .15
149 Tony Armas .15 .40
150 Marty Barrett .05 .15
151 Wade Boggs .50 1.25
152 Dennis Boyd .05 .15
153 Bill Buckner .15 .40
154 Mark Clear .05 .15
155 Roger Clemens RC 10.00 25.00
156 Steve Crawford .05 .15
157 Mike Easler .05 .15
158 Dwight Evans .30 .75
159 Rich Gedman .05 .15
160 Jackie Gutierrez .15 .40
 Wade Boggs
 shown on deck
161 Bruce Hurst .05 .15
162 John Henry Johnson .05 .15
163 Rick Miller .05 .15
164 Reid Nichols .05 .15
165 Al Nipper .05 .15
166 Bob Ojeda .05 .15
167 Jerry Remy .05 .15
168 Jim Rice .15 .40
169 Bob Stanley .05 .15
170 Mike Boddicker .05 .15
171 Al Bumbry .05 .15
172 Todd Cruz .05 .15
173 Rich Dauer .05 .15
174 Storm Davis .05 .15
175 Rick Dempsey .05 .15
176 Jim Dwyer .05 .15
177 Mike Flanagan .05 .15
178 Dan Ford .05 .15
179 Wayne Gross .05 .15
180 John Lowenstein .05 .15
181 Dennis Martinez .15 .40
182 Tippy Martinez .05 .15
183 Scott McGregor .05 .15
184 Eddie Murray .50 1.25
185 Joe Nolan .05 .15
186 Floyd Rayford .05 .15
187 Cal Ripken 2.00 5.00
188 Gary Roenicke .05 .15
189 Lenn Sakata .05 .15
190 John Shelby .05 .15
191 Ken Singleton .15 .40
192 Sammy Stewart .05 .15
193 Bill Swaggerty .05 .15
194 Tom Underwood .05 .15
195 Mike Young .05 .15
196 Steve Balboni .05 .15
197 Joe Beckwith .05 .15
198 Bud Black .05 .15
199 George Brett 1.25 3.00
200 Onix Concepcion .05 .15
201 Mark Gubicza RC .20 .50
202 Larry Gura .05 .15
203 Mark Huismann .05 .15
204 Dane Iorg .05 .15
205 Danny Jackson .05 .15
206 Charlie Leibrandt .05 .15
207 Hal McRae .15 .40
208 Darryl Motley .05 .15
209 Jorge Orta .05 .15
210 Greg Pryor .05 .15
211 Dan Quisenberry .05 .15
212 Bret Saberhagen RC .60 1.50
213 Pat Sheridan .05 .15
214 Don Slaught .05 .15
215 U.L. Washington .05 .15
216 John Wathan .05 .15
217 Frank White .15 .40
218 Willie Wilson .15 .40
219 Neil Allen .05 .15
220 Joaquin Andujar .15 .40
221 Steve Braun .05 .15
222 Danny Cox .05 .15
223 Bob Forsch .05 .15
224 David Green .05 .15
225 George Hendrick .15 .40
226 Tom Herr .05 .15
227 Ricky Horton .05 .15
228 Art Howe .05 .15
229 Mike Jorgensen .05 .15
230 Kurt Kepshire .05 .15
231 Jeff Lahti .05 .15
232 Tito Landrum .05 .15
233 Dave LaPoint .05 .15
234 Willie McGee .15 .40
235 Tom Nieto .05 .15
236 Terry Pendleton RC .40 1.00
237 Darrell Porter .05 .15
238 Dave Rucker .05 .15
239 Lonnie Smith .05 .15
240 Ozzie Smith .75 2.00
241 Bruce Sutter .15 .40
242 Andy Van Slyke UER .30 .75
 Bats Right,
 Throws Left
243 Dave Von Ohlen .05 .15
244 Larry Andersen .05 .15
245 Bill Campbell .05 .15
246 Steve Carlton .15 .40
247 Tim Corcoran .05 .15
248 Ivan DeJesus .05 .15
249 John Denny .05 .15
250 Bo Diaz .05 .15
251 Greg Gross .05 .15
252 Kevin Gross .05 .15
253 Von Hayes .05 .15
254 Al Holland .05 .15
255 Charles Hudson .05 .15
256 Jerry Koosman .15 .40
257 Joe Lefebvre .05 .15
258 Sixto Lezcano .05 .15
259 Garry Maddox .05 .15
260 Len Matuszek .05 .15
261 Tug McGraw .15 .40
262 Al Oliver .15 .40
263 Shane Rawley .05 .15
264 Juan Samuel .05 .15
265 Mike Schmidt 1.25 3.00
266 Jeff Stone RC .05 .15
267 Ozzie Virgil .05 .15
268 Glenn Wilson .05 .15
269 John Wockenfuss .05 .15
270 Darrell Brown .05 .15
271 Tom Brunansky .05 .15
272 Randy Bush .05 .15
273 John Butcher .05 .15
274 Bobby Castillo .05 .15
275 Ron Davis .05 .15
276 Dave Engle .05 .15
277 Pete Filson .05 .15
278 Gary Gaetti .15 .40
279 Mickey Hatcher .05 .15
280 Ed Hodge .05 .15
281 Kent Hrbek .15 .40
282 Houston Jimenez .05 .15
283 Tim Laudner .05 .15
284 Rick Lysander .05 .15
285 Dave Meier .05 .15
286 Kirby Puckett RC 12.00 30.00
287 Pat Putnam .05 .15
288 Ken Schrom .05 .15
289 Mike Smithson .05 .15
290 Tim Teufel .05 .15
291 Frank Viola .15 .40
292 Ron Washington .05 .15
293 Don Aase .05 .15
294 Juan Beniquez .05 .15
295 Bob Boone .15 .40
296 Mike C. Brown .05 .15
297 Rod Carew .30 .75
298 Doug Corbett .05 .15
299 Doug DeCinces .05 .15
300 Brian Downing .15 .40
301 Ken Forsch .05 .15
302 Bobby Grich .15 .40
303 Reggie Jackson .30 .75
304 Tommy John .15 .40
305 Curt Kaufman .05 .15
306 Bruce Kison .05 .15
307 Fred Lynn .15 .40
308 Gary Pettis .05 .15
309 Ron Romanick .05 .15
310 Luis Sanchez .05 .15
311 Dick Schofield .05 .15
312 Daryl Sconiers .05 .15
313 Jim Slaton .05 .15
314 Derrel Thomas .05 .15
315 Rob Wilfong .05 .15
316 Mike Witt .05 .15
317 Geoff Zahn .05 .15
318 Len Barker .05 .15
319 Steve Bedrosian .05 .15
320 Bruce Benedict .05 .15
321 Rick Camp .05 .15
322 Chris Chambliss .15 .40
323 Jeff Dedmon .05 .15
324 Terry Forster .15 .40
325 Gene Garber .05 .15
326 Albert Hall .05 .15
327 Terry Harper .05 .15
328 Bob Horner .15 .40
329 Glenn Hubbard .05 .15
330 Randy Johnson .05 .15
331 Brad Komminsk .05 .15
332 Rick Mahler .05 .15
333 Craig McMurtry .05 .15
334 Donnie Moore .05 .15
335 Dale Murphy .30 .75
336 Ken Oberkfell .05 .15
337 Pascual Perez .05 .15
338 Gerald Perry .05 .15
339 Rafael Ramirez .05 .15
340 Jerry Royster .05 .15
341 Alex Trevino .05 .15
342 Claudell Washington .05 .15
343 Alan Ashby .05 .15
344 Mark Bailey .05 .15
345 Kevin Bass .05 .15
346 Enos Cabell .05 .15
347 Jose Cruz .15 .40
348 Bill Dawley .05 .15
349 Frank DiPino .05 .15
350 Bill Doran .05 .15
351 Phil Garner .15 .40
352 Bob Knepper .05 .15
353 Mike LaCoss .05 .15
354 Jerry Mumphrey .05 .15
355 Joe Niekro .05 .15
356 Terry Puhl .05 .15
357 Craig Reynolds .05 .15
358 Vern Ruhle .05 .15
359 Nolan Ryan 2.50 6.00
360 Joe Sambito .05 .15
361 Mike Scott .15 .40
362 Dave Smith .05 .15
363 Julio Solano .05 .15
364 Dickie Thon .05 .15
365 Denny Walling .05 .15
366 Dave Anderson .05 .15
367 Bob Bailor .05 .15
368 Greg Brock .05 .15
369 Carlos Diaz .05 .15
370 Pedro Guerrero .15 .40
371 Orel Hershiser RC 1.25 3.00
372 Rick Honeycutt .05 .15
373 Burt Hooton .05 .15
374 Ken Howell .05 .15
375 Ken Landreaux .05 .15
376 Candy Maldonado .05 .15
377 Mike Marshall .05 .15
378 Tom Niedenfuer .05 .15
379 Alejandro Pena .05 .15
380 Jerry Reuss UER .05 .15
381 R.J. Reynolds .05 .15
382 German Rivera .05 .15
383 Bill Russell .15 .40
384 Steve Sax .05 .15
385 Mike Scioscia .15 .40
386 Franklin Stubbs .05 .15
387 Fernando Valenzuela .15 .40
388 Bob Welch .15 .40
389 Terry Whitfield .05 .15
390 Steve Yeager .15 .40
391 Pat Zachry .05 .15
392 Fred Breining .05 .15
393 Gary Carter .15 .40
394 Andre Dawson .15 .40
395 Miguel Dilone .05 .15
396 Dan Driessen .05 .15
397 Doug Flynn .05 .15
398 Terry Francona .15 .40
399 Bill Gullickson .05 .15
400 Bob James .05 .15
401 Charlie Lea .05 .15
402 Bryan Little .05 .15
403 Gary Lucas .05 .15
404 David Palmer .05 .15
405 Tim Raines .15 .40
406 Mike Ramsey .05 .15
407 Jeff Reardon .15 .40
408 Steve Rogers .15 .40
409 Dan Schatzeder .05 .15
410 Bryn Smith .05 .15
411 Mike Stenhouse .05 .15
412 Tim Wallach .05 .15
413 Jim Wohlford .05 .15
414 Bill Almon .05 .15
415 Keith Atherton .05 .15
416 Bruce Bochte .05 .15
417 Tom Burgmeier .05 .15
418 Ray Burris .05 .15
419 Bill Caudill .05 .15
420 Chris Codiroli .05 .15
421 Tim Conroy .05 .15
422 Mike Davis .05 .15
423 Jim Essian .05 .15
424 Mike Heath .05 .15
425 Rickey Henderson .60 1.50
426 Donnie Hill .05 .15
427 Dave Kingman .15 .40
428 Bill Krueger .05 .15
429 Carney Lansford .15 .40
430 Steve McCatty .05 .15
431 Joe Morgan .15 .40
432 Dwayne Murphy .05 .15
433 Tony Phillips .05 .15
434 Lary Sorensen .05 .15
435 Mike Warren .05 .15
436 Curt Young .05 .15
437 Luis Aponte .05 .15
438 Chris Bando .05 .15
439 Tony Bernazard .05 .15
440 Bert Blyleven .15 .40
441 Brett Butler .15 .40
442 Ernie Camacho .05 .15
443 Joe Carter .50 1.25
444 Carmelo Castillo .05 .15
445 Jamie Easterly .05 .15
446 Steve Farr RC .20 .50
447 Mike Fischlin .05 .15
448 Julio Franco .15 .40
449 Mel Hall .05 .15
450 Mike Hargrove .05 .15
451 Neal Heaton .05 .15
452 Brook Jacoby .05 .15
453 Mike Jeffcoat .05 .15
454 Don Schulze .05 .15
455 Roy Smith .05 .15
456 Pat Tabler .05 .15
457 Andre Thornton .05 .15
458 George Vukovich .05 .15
459 Tom Waddell .05 .15
460 Jerry Willard .05 .15
461 Dale Berra .05 .15
462 John Candelaria .05 .15
463 Jose DeLeon .05 .15
464 Doug Frobel .05 .15
465 Cecilio Guante .05 .15
466 Brian Harper .05 .15
467 Lee Lacy .05 .15
468 Bill Madlock .15 .40
469 Lee Mazzilli .15 .40
470 Larry McWilliams .05 .15
471 Jim Morrison .05 .15
472 Tony Pena .05 .15
473 Johnny Ray .05 .15
474 Rick Rhoden .05 .15
475 Don Robinson .05 .15
476 Rod Scurry .05 .15
477 Kent Tekulve .05 .15
478 Jason Thompson .05 .15
479 John Tudor .15 .40
480 Lee Tunnell .05 .15
481 Marvell Wynne .05 .15
482 Salome Barojas .05 .15
483 Dave Beard .05 .15
484 Jim Beattie .05 .15
485 Barry Bonnell .05 .15
486 Phil Bradley .20 .50
487 Al Cowens .05 .15
488 Alvin Davis RC .20 .50
489 Dave Henderson .05 .15
490 Steve Henderson .05 .15
491 Bob Kearney .05 .15
492 Mark Langston RC .40 1.00
493 Larry Milbourne .05 .15
494 Paul Mirabella .05 .15
495 Mike Moore .05 .15
496 Edwin Nunez .05 .15
497 Spike Owen .05 .15
498 Jack Perconte .05 .15
499 Ken Phelps .05 .15
500 Jim Presley .20 .50
501 Mike Stanton .05 .15
502 Bob Stoddard .05 .15
503 Gorman Thomas .15 .40
504 Ed VandeBerg .05 .15
505 Matt Young .05 .15
506 Juan Agosto .05 .15
507 Harold Baines .15 .40
508 Floyd Bannister .05 .15
509 Britt Burns .05 .15
510 Julio Cruz .05 .15
511 Richard Dotson .05 .15
512 Jerry Dybzinski .05 .15
513 Carlton Fisk .30 .75
514 Scott Fletcher .05 .15
515 Jerry Hairston .05 .15
516 Marc Hill .05 .15
517 LaMarr Hoyt .05 .15
518 Ron Kittle .05 .15
519 Rudy Law .05 .15
520 Vance Law .05 .15
521 Greg Luzinski .15 .40
522 Gene Nelson .05 .15
523 Tom Paciorek .05 .15
524 Ron Reed .05 .15
525 Bert Roberge .05 .15
526 Tom Seaver .30 .75
527 Roy Smalley .05 .15
528 Dan Spillner .05 .15
529 Mike Squires .05 .15
530 Greg Walker .05 .15
531 Cesar Cedeno .15 .40
532 Dave Concepcion .15 .40
533 Eric Davis RC 1.25 3.00
534 Nick Esasky .05 .15
535 Tom Foley .05 .15
536 John Franco UER RC .40 1.00
 Koufax misspelled
 as Kofax on back
537 Brad Gulden .05 .15
538 Tom Hume .05 .15
539 Wayne Krenchicki .05 .15
540 Andy McGaffigan .05 .15
541 Eddie Milner .05 .15
542 Ron Oester .05 .15
543 Bob Owchinko .05 .15
544 Dave Parker .15 .40
545 Frank Pastore .05 .15
546 Tony Perez .30 .75
547 Ted Power .05 .15
548 Joe Price .05 .15
549 Gary Redus .05 .15
550 Pete Rose 1.50 4.00
551 Jeff Russell .05 .15
552 Mario Soto .15 .40
553 Jay Tibbs .05 .15
554 Duane Walker .05 .15
555 Alan Bannister .05 .15
556 Buddy Bell .15 .40
557 Danny Darwin .05 .15
558 Charlie Hough .15 .40
559 Bobby Jones .05 .15
560 Odell Jones .05 .15
561 Jeff Kunkel .05 .15
562 Mike Mason RC .08 .25
563 Pete O'Brien .05 .15
564 Larry Parrish .05 .15
565 Mickey Rivers .05 .15
566 Billy Sample .05 .15
567 Dave Schmidt .05 .15
568 Donnie Scott .05 .15
569 Dave Stewart .15 .40
570 Frank Tanana .15 .40
571 Wayne Tolleson .05 .15
572 Gary Ward .05 .15
573 Curtis Wilkerson .05 .15
574 George Wright .05 .15
575 Ned Yost .05 .15
576 Mark Brouhard .05 .15
577 Mike Caldwell .05 .15
578 Bobby Clark .05 .15
579 Jaime Cocanower .05 .15
580 Cecil Cooper .15 .40
581 Rollie Fingers .15 .40
582 Jim Gantner .05 .15
583 Moose Haas .05 .15
584 Dion James .05 .15
585 Pete Ladd .05 .15
586 Rick Manning .05 .15
587 Bob McClure .05 .15
588 Paul Molitor .15 .40
589 Charlie Moore .05 .15
590 Ben Oglivie .15 .40
591 Chuck Porter .05 .15
592 Randy Ready RC .08 .25
593 Ed Romero .05 .15
594 Bill Schroeder .05 .15
595 Ray Searage .05 .15
596 Ted Simmons .15 .40
597 Jim Sundberg .15 .40
598 Don Sutton .15 .40
599 Tom Tellmann .05 .15
600 Rick Waits .05 .15
601 Robin Yount .75 2.00
602 Dusty Baker .15 .40
603 Bob Brenly .05 .15
604 Jack Clark .15 .40
605 Chili Davis .15 .40
606 Mark Davis .05 .15
607 Dan Gladden RC .20 .50
608 Atlee Hammaker .05 .15
609 Mike Krukow .05 .15
610 Duane Kuiper .05 .15
611 Bob Lacey .05 .15
612 Bill Laskey .05 .15
613 Gary Lavelle .05 .15
614 Johnnie LeMaster .05 .15
615 Jeff Leonard .05 .15
616 Randy Lerch .05 .15
617 Greg Minton .05 .15
618 Steve Nicosia .05 .15
619 Gene Richards .05 .15
620 Jeff D. Robinson .05 .15
621 Scot Thompson .05 .15
622 Manny Trillo .05 .15
623 Brad Wellman .05 .15
624 Frank Williams .05 .15
625 Joel Youngblood .05 .15
626 Cal Ripken IA 1.25 3.00
627 Mike Schmidt IA .50 1.25
628 Sparky Anderson IA .15 .40
629 Dave Winfield .15 .40
 Rickey Henderson
630 Mike Schmidt .75 2.00
 Ryne Sandberg
631 Darryl Strawberry .50 1.25
 Gary Carter
 Steve Garvey
 Ozzie Smith
632 Gary Carter .05 .15
 Charlie Lea
633 Steve Garvey .15 .40
 Rich Gossage
634 Dwight Gooden .50 1.25
 Juan Samuel
635 Willie Upshaw IA .05 .15
636 Lloyd Moseby IA .05 .15
637 Al Holland .05 .15
638 Lee Tunnell .05 .15
639 Reggie Jackson IA .15 .40
640 Pete Rose .50 1.25
 4000th Hit IA
641 Cal Ripken Jr. 1.25 3.00
 Cal Ripken Sr.
642 Cubs Division Champs .15 .40
643 Two Perfect Games .15 .40
 and One No-Hitter:
 Mike Witt
 David Palmer
 Jack Morris
644 W.Lozado RC/V.Mata RC .05 .15
645 K.Gruber RC/R.O'Neal RC .20 .50
646 J.Roman RC/J.Skinner .05 .15
647 S.Kiefer RC/D.Tartabull RC .40 1.00
648 R.Deer RC/A.Sanchez RC .20 .50
649 B.Hatcher RC/S.Dunston RC .40 1.00
650 R.Robinson RC/M.Bielecki RC .05 .15
651 Z.Smith RC/P.Zuvella RC .20 .50
652 J.Hesketh RC/G.Davis RC .20 .50
653 J.Russell RC/S.Jeltz RC .05 .15
654 CL: Tigers .05 .15
 Padres
 and Cubs
 Mets
655 CL: Blue Jays .05 .15
 Yankees
 and Red Sox
 Orioles
656 CL: Royals .05 .15
 Cardinals
 and Phillies
 Twins
657 CL: Angels .05 .15
 Braves
 and Astros
 Dodgers
658 CL: Expos .05 .15
 A's
 and Indians
 Pirates
659 CL: Mariners .05 .15
 White Sox
 and Reds
 Rangers
660 CL: Brewers .05 .15
 Giants
 and Special Cards

1985 Fleer Update

This 132-card standard-size update set was issued in factory set form exclusively through hobby dealers. Design is identical to the regular-issue 1985 Fleer cards except for the U prefixed card numbers on back. Cards are ordered alphabetically by the player's name. This set features the extended Rookie Cards of Vince Coleman, Darren Daulton, Ozzie Guillen and Mickey Tettleton.

COMP.FACT.SET (132) 3.00 8.00
1 Don Aase .05 .15
2 Bill Almon .05 .15
3 Dusty Baker .15 .40
4 Dale Berra .05 .15
5 Karl Best .05 .15
6 Tim Birtsas .05 .15
7 Vida Blue .15 .40
8 Rich Bordi .05 .15
9 Daryl Boston XRC .08 .25
10 Hubie Brooks .05 .15
11 Chris Brown XRC .08 .25
12 Tom Browning XRC .20 .50
13 Al Bumbry .05 .15
14 Tim Burke .05 .15
15 Ray Burris .05 .15
16 Jeff Burroughs .05 .15
17 Ivan Calderon XRC .20 .50
18 Jeff Calhoun .05 .15
19 Bill Campbell .05 .15
20 Don Carman .05 .15
21 Gary Carter .15 .40
22 Bobby Castillo .05 .15
23 Bill Caudill .05 .15
24 Rick Cerone .05 .15
25 Jack Clark .15 .40
26 Pat Clements .05 .15
27 Stu Cliburn .05 .15
28 Vince Coleman XRC .40 1.00
29 Dave Collins .05 .15
30 Fritz Connally .05 .15
31 Henry Cotto .08 .25
32 Danny Darwin .05 .15
33 Darren Daulton XRC .40 1.00
34 Jerry Davis .05 .15
35 Brian Dayett .05 .15
36 Ken Dixon .05 .15
37 Tommy Dunbar .05 .15
38 Mariano Duncan XRC .20 .50
39 Bob Fallon .05 .15
40 Brian Fisher XRC .08 .25
41 Mike Fitzgerald .05 .15
42 Ray Fontenot .05 .15
43 Greg Gagne XRC .20 .50
44 Oscar Gamble .05 .15
45 Jim Gott .05 .15
46 David Green .05 .15
47 Alfredo Griffin .05 .15
48 Ozzie Guillen XRC 2.00 5.00
49 Toby Harrah .15 .40
50 Ron Hassey .05 .15
51 Rickey Henderson 1.00 2.50
52 Steve Henderson .05 .15
53 George Hendrick .15 .40
54 Teddy Higuera XRC .20 .50
55 Al Holland .05 .15
56 Burt Hooton .05 .15
57 Jay Howell .05 .15
58 LaMarr Hoyt .05 .15
59 Tim Hulett XRC .08 .25
60 Bob James .05 .15
61 Cliff Johnson .05 .15
62 Howard Johnson .15 .40
63 Ruppert Jones .05 .15
64 Steve Kemp .05 .15
65 Bruce Kison .05 .15
66 Mike LaCoss .05 .15
67 Lee Lacy .05 .15
68 Dave LaPoint .05 .15
69 Gary Lavelle .05 .15
70 Vance Law .05 .15
71 Manuel Lee XRC .08 .25
72 Sixto Lezcano .05 .15
73 Tim Lollar .05 .15
74 Urbano Lugo .05 .15
75 Fred Lynn .15 .40
76 Steve Lyons XRC .20 .50
77 Mickey Mahler .05 .15
78 Ron Mathis .05 .15
79 Len Matuszek .05 .15
80 Oddibe McDowell XRC .20 .50
81 Roger McDowell UER XRC .20 .50
82 Donnie Moore .05 .15
83 Ron Musselman .05 .15
84 Al Oliver .15 .40
85 Joe Orsulak XRC .20 .50
86 Dan Pasqua XRC .20 .50
87 Chris Pittaro .05 .15
88 Rick Reuschel .15 .40
89 Earnie Riles .05 .15
90 Jerry Royster .05 .15

91 Dave Rozema .05 .15
92 Dave Rucker .05 .15
93 Vern Ruhle .05 .15
94 Mark Salas .05 .15
95 Luis Salazar .05 .15
96 Joe Sambito .05 .15
97 Billy Sample .05 .15
98 Alejandro Sanchez XRC .08 .25
99 Calvin Schiraldi XRC .20 .50
100 Rick Schu .05 .15
101 Larry Sheets XRC .08 .25
102 Ron Shephard .05 .15
103 Nelson Simmons .05 .15
104 Don Slaught .05 .15
105 Roy Smalley .05 .15
106 Lonnie Smith .05 .15
107 Nate Snell .05 .15
108 Lary Sorensen .05 .15
109 Chris Speier .05 .15
110 Mike Stenhouse .05 .15
111 Tim Stoddard .05 .15
112 John Stuper .05 .15
113 Jim Sundberg .15 .40
114 Bruce Sutter .15 .40
115 Don Sutton .15 .40
116 Bruce Tanner .05 .15
117 Kent Tekulve .05 .15
118 Walt Terrell .05 .15
119 Mickey Tettleton XRC .20 .50
120 Rich Thompson .05 .15
121 Louis Thornton .05 .15
122 Alex Trevino .05 .15
123 John Tudor .15 .40
124 Jose Uribe .05 .15
125 Dave Valle XRC .20 .50
126 Dave Von Ohlen .05 .15
127 Curt Wardle .05 .15
128 U.L. Washington .05 .15
129 Ed Whitson .05 .15
130 Herm Winningham .05 .15
131 Rich Yett .05 .15
132 Checklist U1-U132 .05 .15

1985 Fleer Limited Edition

This 44-card set features standard size cards which were distributed in a colorful box as a complete set. The back of the box gives a complete checklist of the cards in the set. The cards are ordered alphabetically by the player's name. Backs of the cards are yellow and white whereas the fronts show a picture of the player inside a red banner-type border.

COMP. FACT. SET (44) 3.00 8.00
1 Buddy Bell .01 .05
2 Bert Blyleven .02 .10
3 Wade Boggs .20 .50
4 George Brett .50 1.25
5 Rod Carew .15 .40
6 Steve Carlton .15 .40
7 Alvin Davis .01 .05
8 Andre Dawson .08 .25
9 Steve Garvey .05 .15
10 Rich Gossage .02 .10
11 Tony Gwynn .60 1.50
12 Keith Hernandez .02 .10
13 Kent Hrbek .02 .10
14 Reggie Jackson .20 .50
15 Dave Kingman .02 .10
16 Ron Kittle .01 .05
17 Mark Langston .02 .10
18 Jeff Leonard .01 .05
19 Bill Madlock .01 .05
20 Don Mattingly .50 1.25
21 Jack Morris .02 .10
22 Dale Murphy .08 .25
23 Eddie Murray .20 .50
24 Tony Pena .02 .10
25 Dan Quisenberry .01 .05
26 Tim Raines .02 .10
27 Jim Rice .02 .10
28 Cal Ripken 1.00 2.50
29 Pete Rose .30 .75
30 Nolan Ryan 1.00 2.50
31 Ryne Sandberg .40 1.00
32 Steve Sax .01 .05
33 Mike Schmidt .20 .50
34 Tom Seaver .15 .40
35 Ozzie Smith .40 1.00
36 Mario Soto .01 .05
37 Dave Stieb .01 .05
38 Darryl Strawberry .02 .10
39 Rick Sutcliffe .01 .05
40 Alan Trammell .05 .15
41 Willie Upshaw .01 .05
42 Fernando Valenzuela .02 .10
43 Dave Winfield .10 .30
44 Robin Yount .20 .50

1985 Fleer Star Stickers

The stickers in this 126-sticker set measure approximately 1 15/16" by 2 1/2". The 1985 Fleer stickers set can be housed in a Fleer sticker album. Stickers are numbered on the fronts. A distinctive feature of the set is the inclusion of stop-action (designated SA in the checklist below) photos on cards 62 through 79. These photos are actually a series of six consecutive stickers which depict a player in action through the course of an activity; e.g., Eddie Murray's swing, Tom Seaver's wind-up and Mike Schmidt fielding. The backs of these stickers are blue and similar in design to past years. Player selection is highlighted by RC-year stickers of superstars Roger Clemens and Kirby Puckett.

COMPLETE SET (126) 20.00 50.00
1 Pete Rose 1.25 3.00
2 Pete Rose 1.25 3.00
3 Pete Rose 1.25 3.00
4 Don Mattingly 3.00 8.00
5 Dave Winfield .50 1.25
6 Wade Boggs 1.00 2.50
7 Buddy Bell .07 .20
8 Tony Gwynn 3.00 8.00
9 Lee Lacy .02 .10
10 Chili Davis .07 .20
11 Ryne Sandberg 1.50 4.00
12 Tony Armas .02 .10
13 Jim Rice .07 .20
14 Dave Kingman .07 .20
15 Alvin Davis .07 .20
16 Gary Carter 1.25
17 Mike Schmidt 1.00 2.50
18 Dale Murphy .20 .50
19 Ron Cey .07 .20
20 Eddie Murray .60 1.50
21 Harold Baines .07 .20
22 Kirk Gibson .07 .20
23 Jim Rice .07 .20
24 Gary Matthews .02 .10
25 Keith Hernandez .07 .20
26 Gary Carter 1.25
27 George Hendrick .02 .10
28 Tony Armas .02 .10
29 Dave Kingman .07 .20
30 Dwayne Murphy .02 .10
31 Lance Parrish .07 .20
32 Andre Thornton .02 .10
33 Dale Murphy .20 .50
34 Mike Schmidt 1.00 2.50
35 Gary Carter 1.25
36 Darryl Strawberry .07 .20
37 Don Mattingly 3.00 8.00
38 Larry Parrish .02 .10
39 George Bell .07 .20
40 Dwight Evans .07 .20
41 Cal Ripken 3.00 8.00
42 Tim Raines .07 .20
43 Johnny Ray .02 .10
44 Juan Samuel .02 .10
45 Ryne Sandberg 1.50 4.00
46 Mike Easler .02 .10
47 Andre Thornton .02 .10
48 Dave Kingman .07 .20
49 Don Baylor .07 .20
50 Rusty Staub .07 .20
51 Steve Braun .02 .10
52 Kevin Bass .02 .10
53 Greg Gross .02 .10
54 Rickey Henderson 2.00 5.00
55 Dave Collins .02 .10
56 Brett Butler .07 .20
57 Gary Pettis .02 .10
58 Tim Raines .07 .20
59 Juan Samuel .02 .10
60 Alan Wiggins .02 .10
61 Lonnie Smith .02 .10
62 Eddie Murray SA .30 .75
63 Eddie Murray SA .30 .75
64 Eddie Murray SA .30 .75
65 Eddie Murray SA .30 .75
66 Eddie Murray SA .30 .75
67 Eddie Murray SA .30 .75
68 Tom Seaver SA .40 1.00
69 Tom Seaver SA .40 1.00
70 Tom Seaver SA .40 1.00
71 Tom Seaver SA .40 1.00
72 Tom Seaver SA .40 1.00
73 Tom Seaver SA .40 1.00
74 Mike Schmidt SA .50 1.25
75 Mike Schmidt SA .50 1.25
76 Mike Schmidt SA .50 1.25
77 Mike Schmidt SA .50 1.25
78 Mike Schmidt SA .50 1.25
79 Mike Schmidt SA .50 1.25
80 Mike Boddicker .02 .10
81 Bert Blyleven .07 .20
82 Jack Morris .07 .20
83 Dan Petry .02 .10
84 Frank Viola .07 .20
85 Joaquin Andujar .02 .10
86 Mario Soto .02 .10
87 Dwight Gooden 1.00 2.50
88 Joe Niekro .02 .10
89 Rick Sutcliffe .02 .10
90 Mike Boddicker .02 .10
91 Dave Stieb .02 .10
92 Bert Blyleven .07 .20
93 Phil Niekro .25 .60
94 Alejandro Pena .02 .10
95 Dwight Gooden 1.00 2.50
96 Orel Hershiser 1.00 2.50
97 Rick Rhoden .02 .10
98 John Candelaria .02 .10
99 Dan Quisenberry .02 .10
100 Bill Caudill .02 .10
101 Willie Hernandez .02 .10
102 Dave Righetti .07 .20
103 Ron Davis .02 .10
104 Bruce Sutter .07 .20
105 Lee Smith .10 .30
106 Jesse Orosco .07 .20
107 Al Holland .02 .10
108 Goose Gossage .07 .20
109 Mark Langston .30 .75
110 Dave Stieb .07 .20
111 Mike Witt .02 .10
112 Bert Blyleven .07 .20
113 Dwight Gooden 1.00 2.50
114 Fernando Valenzuela .07 .20
115 Nolan Ryan 3.00 8.00
116 Mario Soto .02 .10
117 Ron Darling .07 .20
118 Dan Gladden .02 .10
119 Jeff Stone .02 .10
120 John Franco .30 .75
121 Barbaro Garbey .02 .10
122 Kirby Puckett 4.00 10.00
123 Roger Clemens 8.00 20.00
124 Bret Saberhagen .30 .75
125 Sparky Anderson MG .10 .30
126 Dick Williams MG .02 .10
NNO Sticker Album 4.00 10.00

1986 Fleer

The 1986 Fleer set consists of 660-card standard-size cards. Wax packs included 15 cards plus logo stickers. Card fronts feature dark blue borders (resulting in extremely condition sensitive cards commonly found with chipped edges), a team logo along with the player's name and position. The player cards are alphabetized within team and the teams are ordered by their 1985 season finish and won-lost record. Subsets include Specials (626-643) and Major League Prospects (644-653). The Dennis and Tippy Martinez cards were apparently switched in the set numbering, as their adjacent numbers (279 and 280) were reversed on the Orioles checklist card. The set includes the Rookie Cards of Rick Aguilera, Jose Canseco, Darren Daulton, Len Dykstra, Cecil Fielder, Andres Galarraga and Paul O'Neill.

COMPLETE SET (660) 15.00 40.00
COMP.FACT.SET (660) 15.00 40.00
1 Steve Balboni .05 .15
2 Joe Beckwith .05 .15
3 Buddy Biancalana .05 .15
4 Bud Black .05 .15
5 George Brett .75 2.00
6 Onix Concepcion .05 .15
7 Steve Farr .05 .15
8 Mark Gubicza .05 .15
9 Dane Iorg .05 .15
10 Danny Jackson .05 .15
11 Lynn Jones .05 .15
12 Mike Jones .05 .15
13 Charlie Leibrandt .05 .15
14 Hal McRae .08 .25
15 Omar Moreno .05 .15
16 Darryl Motley .05 .15
17 Jorge Orta .05 .15
18 Dan Quisenberry .05 .15
19 Bret Saberhagen .08 .25
20 Pat Sheridan .05 .15
21 Lonnie Smith .05 .15
22 Jim Sundberg .08 .25
23 John Wathan .05 .15
24 Frank White .08 .25
25 Willie Wilson .08 .25
26 Joaquin Andujar .08 .25
27 Steve Braun .05 .15
28 Bill Campbell .05 .15
29 Cesar Cedeno .08 .25
30 Jack Clark .08 .25
31 Vince Coleman RC .40 1.00
32 Danny Cox .05 .15
33 Ken Dayley .05 .15
34 Ivan DeJesus .05 .15
35 Bob Forsch .05 .15
36 Brian Harper .05 .15
37 Tom Herr .05 .15
38 Ricky Horton .05 .15
39 Kurt Kepshire .05 .15
40 Jeff Lahti .05 .15
41 Tito Landrum .05 .15
42 Willie McGee .08 .25
43 Tom Nieto .05 .15
44 Terry Pendleton .08 .25
45 Darrell Porter .05 .15
46 Ozzie Smith .50 1.25
47 John Tudor .08 .25
48 Andy Van Slyke .20 .50
49 Todd Worrell RC .20 .50
50 Jim Acker .05 .15
51 Doyle Alexander .05 .15
52 Jesse Barfield .08 .25
53 George Bell .08 .25
54 Jeff Burroughs .05 .15
55 Bill Caudill .05 .15
56 Jim Clancy .05 .15
57 Tony Fernandez .05 .15
58 Tom Filer .05 .15
59 Damaso Garcia .05 .15
60 Tom Henke .08 .25
61 Garth Iorg .05 .15
62 Cliff Johnson .05 .15
63 Jimmy Key .08 .25
64 Dennis Lamp .05 .15
65 Gary Lavelle .05 .15
66 Buck Martinez .05 .15
67 Lloyd Moseby .05 .15
68 Rance Mulliniks .05 .15
69 Al Oliver .08 .25
70 Dave Stieb .08 .25
71 Louis Thornton .05 .15
72 Willie Upshaw .05 .15
73 Ernie Whitt .05 .15
74 Rick Aguilera RC .20 .50
75 Wally Backman .05 .15
76 Gary Carter .08 .25
77 Ron Darling .08 .25
78 Len Dykstra RC .60 1.50
79 Sid Fernandez .05 .15
80 George Foster .08 .25
81 Dwight Gooden .30 .75
82 Tom Gorman .05 .15
83 Danny Heep .05 .15
84 Keith Hernandez .08 .25
85 Howard Johnson .08 .25
86 Ray Knight .08 .25
87 Terry Leach .05 .15
88 Ed Lynch .05 .15
89 Roger McDowell RC* .20 .50
90 Jesse Orosco .05 .15
91 Tom Paciorek .05 .15
92 Ronn Reynolds .05 .15
93 Rafael Santana .05 .15
94 Doug Sisk .05 .15
95 Rusty Staub .08 .25
96 Darryl Strawberry .20 .50
97 Mookie Wilson .08 .25
98 Neil Allen .05 .15
99 Don Baylor .08 .25
100 Dale Berra .05 .15
101 Rich Bordi .05 .15
102 Marty Bystrom .05 .15
103 Joe Cowley .05 .15
104 Brian Fisher RC .05 .15
105 Ken Griffey .08 .25
106 Ron Guidry .08 .25
107 Ron Hassey .05 .15
108 Rickey Henderson .30 .75
109 Don Mattingly 1.00 2.50
110 Bobby Meacham .05 .15
111 John Montefusco .05 .15
112 Phil Niekro .08 .25
113 Mike Pagliarulo .05 .15
114 Dan Pasqua .05 .15
115 Willie Randolph .08 .25
116 Dave Righetti .08 .25
117 Andre Robertson .05 .15
118 Billy Sample .05 .15
119 Bob Shirley .05 .15
120 Ed Whitson .05 .15
121 Dave Winfield .08 .25
122 Butch Wynegar .05 .15
123 Dave Anderson .05 .15
124 Bob Bailor .05 .15
125 Greg Brock .05 .15
126 Enos Cabell .05 .15
127 Bobby Castillo .05 .15
128 Carlos Diaz .05 .15
129 Mariano Duncan RC .20 .50
130 Pedro Guerrero .08 .25
131 Orel Hershiser .30 .75
132 Rick Honeycutt .05 .15
133 Ken Howell .05 .15
134 Ken Landreaux .05 .15
135 Bill Madlock .08 .25
136 Candy Maldonado .05 .15
137 Mike Marshall .05 .15
138 Len Matuszek .05 .15
139 Tom Niedenfuer .05 .15
140 Alejandro Pena .05 .15
141 Jerry Reuss .05 .15
142 Bill Russell .08 .25
143 Steve Sax .05 .15
144 Mike Scioscia .08 .25
145 Fernando Valenzuela .08 .25
146 Bob Welch .08 .25
147 Terry Whitfield .05 .15
148 Juan Beniquez .05 .15
149 Bob Boone .08 .25
150 John Candelaria .05 .15
151 Rod Carew .20 .50
152 Stu Cliburn .05 .15
153 Doug DeCinces .05 .15
154 Brian Downing .08 .25
155 Ken Forsch .05 .15
156 Craig Gerber .05 .15
157 Bobby Grich .08 .25
158 George Hendrick .08 .25
159 Al Holland .05 .15
160 Reggie Jackson .20 .50
161 Ruppert Jones .05 .15
162 Urbano Lugo .05 .15
163 Kirk McCaskill RC .20 .50
164 Donnie Moore .05 .15
165 Gary Pettis .05 .15
166 Ron Romanick .05 .15
167 Dick Schofield .05 .15
168 Daryl Sconiers .05 .15
169 Jim Slaton .05 .15
170 Don Sutton .08 .25
171 Mike Witt .05 .15
172 Buddy Bell .08 .25
173 Tom Browning .05 .15
174 Dave Concepcion .08 .25
175 Eric Davis .30 .75
176 Bo Diaz .05 .15
177 Nick Esasky .05 .15
178 John Franco .08 .25
179 Tom Hume .05 .15
180 Wayne Krenchicki .05 .15
181 Andy McGaffigan .05 .15
182 Eddie Milner .05 .15
183 Ron Oester .05 .15
184 Dave Parker .08 .25
185 Frank Pastore .05 .15
186 Tony Perez .20 .50
187 Ted Power .05 .15
188 Joe Price .05 .15
189 Gary Redus .05 .15
190 Ron Robinson .05 .15
191 Pete Rose 1.00 2.50
192 Mario Soto .08 .25
193 John Stuper .05 .15
194 Jay Tibbs .05 .15
195 Dave Van Gorder .05 .15
196 Max Venable .05 .15
197 Juan Agosto .05 .15
198 Harold Baines .08 .25
199 Floyd Bannister .05 .15
200 Britt Burns .05 .15
201 Julio Cruz .05 .15
202 Joel Davis .05 .15
203 Richard Dotson .05 .15
204 Carlton Fisk .20 .50
205 Scott Fletcher .05 .15
206 Ozzie Guillen RC .75 2.00
207 Jerry Hairston .05 .15
208 Tim Hulett .05 .15
209 Bob James .05 .15
210 Ron Kittle .05 .15
211 Rudy Law .05 .15
212 Bryan Little .05 .15
213 Gene Nelson .05 .15
214 Reid Nichols .05 .15
215 Luis Salazar .05 .15
216 Tom Seaver .20 .50
217 Dan Spillner .05 .15
218 Bruce Tanner .05 .15
219 Greg Walker .05 .15
220 Dave Wehrmeister .05 .15
221 Juan Berenguer .05 .15
222 Dave Bergman .05 .15
223 Tom Brookens .05 .15
224 Darrell Evans .08 .25
225 Barbaro Garbey .05 .15
226 Kirk Gibson .08 .25
227 John Grubb .05 .15
228 Willie Hernandez .05 .15
229 Larry Herndon .05 .15
230 Chet Lemon .08 .25
231 Aurelio Lopez .05 .15
232 Jack Morris .08 .25
233 Randy O'Neal .05 .15
234 Lance Parrish .08 .25
235 Dan Petry .05 .15
236 Alejandro Sanchez .05 .15
237 Bill Scherrer .05 .15
238 Nelson Simmons .05 .15
239 Frank Tanana .08 .25
240 Walt Terrell .05 .15
241 Alan Trammell .08 .25
242 Lou Whitaker .08 .25
243 Milt Wilcox .05 .15
244 Hubie Brooks .05 .15
245 Tim Burke .05 .15
246 Andre Dawson .08 .25
247 Mike Fitzgerald .05 .15
248 Terry Francona .08 .25
249 Bill Gullickson .05 .15
250 Joe Hesketh .05 .15
251 Bill Laskey .05 .15
252 Vance Law .05 .15
253 Charlie Lea .05 .15
254 Gary Lucas .05 .15
255 David Palmer .05 .15
256 Tim Raines .08 .25
257 Jeff Reardon .08 .25
258 Bert Roberge .05 .15
259 Dan Schatzeder .05 .15
260 Bryn Smith .05 .15
261 Randy St.Claire .05 .15
262 Scot Thompson .05 .15
263 Tim Wallach .05 .15
264 U.L. Washington .05 .15
265 Mitch Webster .05 .15
266 Herm Winningham .05 .15
267 Floyd Youmans .05 .15
268 Don Aase .05 .15
269 Mike Boddicker .05 .15
270 Rich Dauer .05 .15
271 Storm Davis .05 .15
272 Rick Dempsey .05 .15
273 Ken Dixon .05 .15
274 Jim Dwyer .05 .15
275 Mike Flanagan .05 .15
276 Wayne Gross .05 .15
277 Lee Lacy .05 .15
278 Fred Lynn .08 .25
279 Tippy Martinez .05 .15
280 Dennis Martinez .08 .25
281 Scott McGregor .05 .15
282 Eddie Murray .30 .75
283 Floyd Rayford .05 .15
284 Cal Ripken 1.25 3.00
285 Gary Roenicke .05 .15
286 Larry Sheets .05 .15
287 John Shelby .05 .15
288 Nate Snell .05 .15
289 Sammy Stewart .05 .15
290 Alan Wiggins .05 .15
291 Mike Young .05 .15
292 Alan Ashby .05 .15
293 Mark Bailey .05 .15
294 Kevin Bass .05 .15
295 Jeff Calhoun .05 .15
296 Jose Cruz .08 .25
297 Glenn Davis .05 .15
298 Bill Dawley .05 .15
299 Frank DiPino .05 .15
300 Bill Doran .05 .15
301 Phil Garner .08 .25
302 Jeff Heathcock .05 .15
303 Charlie Kerfeld .05 .15
304 Bob Knepper .05 .15
305 Ron Mathis .05 .15
306 Jerry Mumphrey .05 .15
307 Jim Pankovits .05 .15
308 Terry Puhl .05 .15
309 Craig Reynolds .05 .15
310 Nolan Ryan 1.50 4.00
311 Mike Scott .08 .25
312 Dave Smith .05 .15
313 Dickie Thon .05 .15
314 Denny Walling .05 .15
315 Kurt Bevacqua .05 .15
316 Al Bumbry .05 .15
317 Jerry Davis .05 .15
318 Luis DeLeon .05 .15
319 Dave Dravecky .05 .15
320 Tim Flannery .05 .15
321 Steve Garvey .08 .25
322 Rich Gossage .08 .25
323 Tony Gwynn .50 1.25
324 Andy Hawkins .05 .15
325 LaMarr Hoyt .05 .15
326 Roy Lee Jackson .05 .15
327 Terry Kennedy .05 .15
328 Craig Lefferts .05 .15
329 Carmelo Martinez .05 .15
330 Lance McCullers .05 .15
331 Kevin McReynolds .05 .15
332 Graig Nettles .08 .25
333 Jerry Royster .05 .15
334 Eric Show .05 .15
335 Tim Stoddard .05 .15
336 Garry Templeton .08 .25
337 Mark Thurmond .05 .15
338 Ed Wojna .05 .15
339 Tony Armas .08 .25
340 Marty Barrett .05 .15
341 Wade Boggs .20 .50
342 Dennis Boyd .05 .15
343 Bill Buckner .08 .25
344 Mark Clear .05 .15
345 Roger Clemens 2.00 5.00
346 Steve Crawford .05 .15
347 Mike Easler .05 .15
348 Dwight Evans .20 .50
349 Rich Gedman .05 .15
350 Jackie Gutierrez .05 .15
351 Glenn Hoffman .05 .15
352 Bruce Hurst .05 .15
353 Bruce Kison .05 .15
354 Tim Lollar .05 .15
355 Steve Lyons .05 .15
356 Al Nipper .05 .15
357 Bob Ojeda .05 .15
358 Jim Rice .08 .25
359 Bob Stanley .05 .15
360 Mike Trujillo .05 .15
361 Thad Bosley .05 .15
362 Warren Brusstar .05 .15
363 Ron Cey .08 .25
364 Jody Davis .05 .15
365 Bob Dernier .05 .15
366 Shawon Dunston .08 .25
367 Leon Durham .05 .15
368 Dennis Eckersley .20 .50
369 Ray Fontenot .05 .15
370 George Frazier .05 .15
371 Billy Hatcher .05 .15
372 Dave Lopes .08 .25
373 Gary Matthews .08 .25
374 Ron Meridith .05 .15
375 Keith Moreland .05 .15
376 Reggie Patterson .05 .15
377 Dick Ruthven .05 .15
378 Ryne Sandberg .60 1.50
379 Scott Sanderson .05 .15
380 Lee Smith .08 .25
381 Lary Sorensen .05 .15
382 Chris Speier .05 .15
383 Rick Sutcliffe .08 .25
384 Steve Trout .05 .15
385 Gary Woods .05 .15
386 Bert Blyleven .08 .25
387 Tom Brunansky .05 .15
388 Randy Bush .05 .15
389 John Butcher .05 .15
390 Ron Davis .05 .15
391 Dave Engle .05 .15
392 Frank Eufemia .05 .15
393 Pete Filson .05 .15
394 Gary Gaetti .08 .25
395 Greg Gagne .05 .15
396 Mickey Hatcher .05 .15
397 Kent Hrbek .08 .25
398 Tim Laudner .05 .15
399 Rick Lysander .05 .15
400 Dave Meier .05 .15
401 Kirby Puckett .75 2.00
402 Mark Salas .05 .15
403 Ken Schrom .05 .15
404 Roy Smalley .05 .15
405 Mike Smithson .05 .15
406 Mike Stenhouse .05 .15
407 Tim Teufel .05 .15
408 Frank Viola .08 .25
409 Ron Washington .05 .15
410 Keith Atherton .05 .15
411 Dusty Baker .08 .25
412 Tim Birtsas .05 .15
413 Bruce Bochte .05 .15
414 Chris Codiroli .05 .15
415 Dave Collins .05 .15
416 Mike Davis .05 .15
417 Alfredo Griffin .05 .15
418 Mike Heath .05 .15
419 Steve Henderson .05 .15
420 Donnie Hill .05 .15
421 Jay Howell .05 .15
422 Tommy John .08 .25
423 Dave Kingman .08 .25
424 Bill Krueger .05 .15
425 Rick Langford .05 .15
426 Carney Lansford .08 .25
427 Steve McCatty .05 .15
428 Dwayne Murphy .05 .15
429 Steve Ontiveros RC .05 .15
430 Tony Phillips .05 .15
431 Jose Rijo .08 .25
432 Mickey Tettleton RC .20 .50
433 Luis Aguayo .05 .15
434 Larry Andersen .05 .15
435 Steve Carlton .08 .25
436 Don Carman .05 .15
437 Tim Corcoran .05 .15
438 Darren Daulton RC .40 1.00
439 John Denny .05 .15
440 Tom Foley .05 .15
441 Greg Gross .05 .15
442 Kevin Gross .05 .15
443 Von Hayes .05 .15
444 Charles Hudson .05 .15
445 Garry Maddox .05 .15
446 Shane Rawley .05 .15
447 Dave Rucker .05 .15
448 John Russell .05 .15
449 Juan Samuel .05 .15
450 Mike Schmidt .75 2.00
451 Rick Schu .05 .15
452 Dave Shipanoff .05 .15
453 Dave Stewart .08 .25
454 Jeff Stone .05 .15
455 Kent Tekulve .05 .15
456 Ozzie Virgil .05 .15
457 Glenn Wilson .05 .15
458 Jim Beattie .05 .15
459 Karl Best .05 .15
460 Barry Bonnell .05 .15
461 Phil Bradley .05 .15
462 Ivan Calderon RC* .20 .50
463 Al Cowens .05 .15
464 Alvin Davis .05 .15
465 Dave Henderson .05 .15
466 Bob Kearney .05 .15
467 Mark Langston .08 .25
468 Bob Long .05 .15
469 Mike Moore .05 .15
470 Edwin Nunez .05 .15
471 Spike Owen .05 .15
472 Jack Perconte .05 .15
473 Jim Presley .05 .15
474 Donnie Scott .05 .15
475 Bill Swift .05 .15
476 Danny Tartabull .08 .25
477 Gorman Thomas .08 .25
478 Roy Thomas .05 .15
479 Ed VandeBerg .05 .15
480 Frank Wills .05 .15
481 Matt Young .05 .15
482 Ray Burris .05 .15
483 Jaime Cocanower .05 .15
484 Cecil Cooper .08 .25
485 Danny Darwin .05 .15
486 Rollie Fingers .08 .25
487 Jim Gantner .05 .15
488 Bob L. Gibson .05 .15
489 Moose Haas .05 .15
490 Teddy Higuera RC* .20 .50
491 Paul Householder .05 .15
492 Pete Ladd .05 .15
493 Rick Manning .05 .15
494 Bob McClure .05 .15
495 Paul Molitor .08 .25
496 Charlie Moore .05 .15
497 Ben Oglivie .08 .25
498 Randy Ready .05 .15
499 Earnie Riles .05 .15
500 Ed Romero .05 .15
501 Bill Schroeder .05 .15
502 Ray Searage .05 .15
503 Ted Simmons .08 .25
504 Pete Vuckovich .05 .15
505 Rick Waits .05 .15
506 Robin Yount .50 1.25
507 Len Barker .05 .15
508 Steve Bedrosian .05 .15
509 Bruce Benedict .05 .15
510 Rick Camp .05 .15
511 Rick Cerone .05 .15
512 Chris Chambliss .08 .25
513 Jeff Dedmon .05 .15
514 Terry Forster .08 .25
515 Gene Garber .05 .15
516 Terry Harper .05 .15
517 Bob Horner .08 .25
518 Glenn Hubbard .05 .15
519 Joe Johnson .05 .15
520 Brad Komminsk .05 .15
521 Rick Mahler .05 .15
522 Dale Murphy .20 .50
523 Ken Oberkfell .05 .15
524 Pascual Perez .05 .15
525 Gerald Perry .05 .15
526 Rafael Ramirez .05 .15
527 Steve Shields .05 .15
528 Zane Smith .05 .15
529 Bruce Sutter .08 .25
530 Milt Thompson RC .20 .50
531 Claudell Washington .05 .15
532 Paul Zuvella .05 .15
533 Vida Blue .08 .25
534 Bob Brenly .05 .15
535 Chris Brown RC .05 .15
536 Chili Davis .08 .25
537 Mark Davis .05 .15
538 Rob Deer .05 .15
539 Dan Driessen .05 .15
540 Scott Garrelts .05 .15
541 Dan Gladden .05 .15
542 Jim Gott .05 .15
543 David Green .05 .15
544 Atlee Hammaker .05 .15
545 Mike Jeffcoat .05 .15
546 Mike Krukow .05 .15
547 Dave LaPoint .05 .15
548 Jeff Leonard .05 .15
549 Greg Minton .05 .15
550 Alex Trevino .05 .15
551 Manny Trillo .05 .15
552 Jose Uribe .05 .15
553 Brad Wellman .05 .15
554 Frank Williams .05 .15
555 Joel Youngblood .05 .15
556 Alan Bannister .05 .15
557 Glenn Brummer .05 .15
558 Steve Buechele RC .20 .50
559 Jose Guzman RC .05 .15
560 Toby Harrah .08 .25
561 Greg Harris .05 .15
562 Dwayne Henry .05 .15
563 Burt Hooton .05 .15
564 Charlie Hough .08 .25
565 Mike Mason .05 .15
566 Oddibe McDowell .05 .15
567 Dickie Noles .05 .15
568 Pete O'Brien .05 .15
569 Larry Parrish .05 .15
570 Dave Rozema .05 .15
571 Dave Schmidt .05 .15
572 Don Slaught .05 .15
573 Wayne Tolleson .05 .15
574 Duane Walker .05 .15
575 Gary Ward .05 .15
576 Chris Welsh .05 .15
577 Curtis Wilkerson .05 .15
578 George Wright .05 .15
579 Chris Bando .05 .15
580 Tony Bernazard .05 .15
581 Brett Butler .08 .25
582 Ernie Camacho .05 .15
583 Joe Carter .08 .25
584 Carmen Castillo .05 .15
585 Jamie Easterly .05 .15
586 Julio Franco .08 .25
587 Mel Hall .05 .15
588 Mike Hargrove .05 .15
589 Neal Heaton .05 .15
590 Brook Jacoby .05 .15
591 Otis Nixon RC .40 1.00
592 Jerry Reed .05 .15
593 Vern Ruhle .05 .15
594 Pat Tabler .05 .15
595 Rich Thompson .05 .15
596 Andre Thornton .05 .15
597 Dave Von Ohlen .05 .15
598 George Vukovich .05 .15
599 Tom Waddell .05 .15
600 Curt Wardle .05 .15
601 Jerry Willard .05 .15
602 Bill Almon .05 .15
603 Mike Bielecki .05 .15
604 Sid Bream .05 .15
605 Mike C. Brown .05 .15
606 Pat Clements .05 .15
607 Jose DeLeon .05 .15
608 Denny Gonzalez .05 .15
609 Cecilio Guante .05 .15
610 Steve Kemp .05 .15
611 Sammy Khalifa .05 .15
612 Lee Mazzilli .08 .25
613 Larry McWilliams .05 .15
614 Jim Morrison .05 .15
615 Joe Orsulak RC* .20 .50
616 Tony Pena .05 .15
617 Johnny Ray .05 .15
618 Rick Reuschel .08 .25
619 R.J. Reynolds .05 .15
620 Rick Rhoden .05 .15
621 Don Robinson .05 .15
622 Jason Thompson .05 .15
623 Lee Tunnell .05 .15
624 Jim Winn .05 .15

625 Marvell Wynne .05 .15
626 Dwight Gooden IA .20 .50
627 Don Mattingly IA .50 1.25
628 Pete Rose 4192 .20 .50
629 Rod Carew 3000 Hits .08 .25
630 T.Seaver .08 .25
P.Niekro
631 Don Baylor Ouch .08 .25
632 Tim Raines .08 .25
Strawberry
633 C.Ripken .60 1.50
A.Trammell
634 Wade Boggs .40 1.00
G.Brett
635 B.Horner .20 .50
D.Murphy
636 W.McGee .08 .25
V.Coleman
637 Vince Coleman IA .08 .25
638 Pete Rose .30 .75
D.Gooden
639 Wade Boggs .50 1.25
D.Mattingly
640 Murphy .20 .50
Garvey
Parker
641 D.Gooden .20 .50
F.Valenzuela
642 Jimmy Key .08 .25
D.Stieb
643 C.Fisk .08 .25
R.Gedman
644 Benito Santiago RC .75 2.00
645 M.Woodard .05 .15
C.Ward RC
646 Paul O'Neill RC 1.50 4.00
647 Andres Galarraga RC .60 1.50
648 B.Kipper .05 .15
C.Ford RC
649 Jose Canseco RC 3.00 8.00
650 Mark McLemore RC .40 1.00
651 R.Woodward .05 .15
M.Brantley RC
652 B.Robidoux .05 .15
M.Funderburk RC
653 Cecil Fielder RC .75 2.00
654 CL: Royals .05 .15
Cardinals
Blue Jays
Mets
655 CL: Yankees .05 .15
Dodgers
Angels
Reds UER/(168 Darly S
656 CL: White Sox .05 .15
Tigers
Expos
Orioles/(279 Dennis&#
657 CL: Astros .05 .15
Padres
Red Sox
Cubs
658 CL: Twins .05 .15
A's
Phillies
Mariners
659 CL: Brewers .05 .15
Braves
Giants
Rangers
660 CL: Indians .05 .15
Pirates
Special Cards

1986 Fleer All-Stars

COMPLETE SET (12) 10.00 25.00
RANDOM INSERTS IN PACKS 1.25 2.50
1 Don Mattingly 3.00 8.00
2 Tom Herr .20 .50
3 George Brett 2.50 6.00
4 Gary Carter .30 .75
5 Cal Ripken 4.00 10.00
6 Dave Parker .30 .75
7 Rickey Henderson 1.00 2.50
8 Pedro Guerrero .30 .75
9 Dan Quisenberry .20 .50
10 Dwight Gooden 1.00 2.50
11 Gorman Thomas .30 .75
12 John Tudor .30 .75

1986 Fleer Future Hall of Famers

COMPLETE SET (6) 6.00 15.00
SEMISTARS .25 .60
ONE PER RACK PACK
1 Pete Rose 2.50 6.00
2 Steve Carlton .25 .60
3 Tom Seaver .50 1.25
4 Rod Carew .50 1.25
5 Nolan Ryan 4.00 10.00
6 Reggie Jackson .50 1.25

1986 Fleer Wax Box Cards

COMPLETE SET (8) 2.50 6.00
C1 Royals Logo .08 .25
C2 George Brett 1.25 3.00
C3 Ozzie Guillen .30 .75
C4 Dale Murphy .30 .75
C5 Cardinals Logo .08 .25
C6 Tom Browning .08 .25
C7 Gary Carter .40 1.00
C8 Carlton Fisk .40 1.00

1986 Fleer Update

This 132-card standard-size set was distributed in factory set form through hobby dealers. These sets were distributed in 50-set cases. In addition to the complete set of 132 cards, the box also contains 25 Team Logo Stickers.The card fronts look very similar to the 1986 Fleer regular issue. These cards are just as condition sensitive with most cards having chipped edges straight out of the box. The cards are numbered (with a U prefix) alphabetically according to player's last name. The extended Rookie Cards in this set include Barry Bonds, Bobby Bonilla, Will Clark, Wally Joyner and John Kruk.

COMP.FACT.SET (132) 12.50 30.00
1 Mike Aldrete XRC .05 .15
2 Andy Allanson XRC .05 .15
3 Neil Allen .05 .15
4 Joaquin Andujar .08 .25
5 Paul Assenmacher XRC .20 .50
6 Scott Bailes XRC .05 .15
7 Jay Baller XRC .05 .15
8 Scott Bankhead .05 .15
9 Bill Bathe XRC .05 .15
10 Don Baylor .08 .25
11 Billy Beane XRC .40 1.00
12 Steve Bedrosian .05 .15
13 Juan Beniquez .05 .15
14 Barry Bonds XRC 8.00 20.00
15 Bobby Bonilla XRC .40 1.00
16 Rich Bordi .05 .15
17 Bill Campbell .05 .15
18 Tom Candiotti .05 .15
19 John Cangelosi XRC .20 .50
20 Jose Canseco 1.50 4.00
21 Chuck Cary XRC .05 .15
22 Juan Castillo XRC .05 .15
23 Rick Cerone .05 .15
24 John Cerutti XRC .05 .15
25 Will Clark XRC .75 2.00
26 Mark Clear .05 .15
27 Darnell Coles .05 .15
28 Dave Collins .05 .15
29 Tim Conroy .05 .15
30 Ed Correa .05 .15
31 Joe Cowley .05 .15
32 Bill Dawley .05 .15
33 Rob Deer .05 .15
34 John Denny .05 .15
35 Jim Deshaies XRC .05 .15
36 Doug Drabek XRC .40 1.00
37 Mike Easler .05 .15
38 Mark Eichhorn .05 .15
39 Dave Engle .05 .15
40 Mike Fischlin .05 .15
41 Scott Fletcher .05 .15
42 Terry Forster .08 .25
43 Terry Francona .08 .25
44 Andres Galarraga .60 1.50
45 Lee Guetterman .05 .15
46 Bill Gullickson .05 .15
47 Jackie Gutierrez .05 .15
48 Moose Haas .05 .15
49 Billy Hatcher .05 .15
50 Mike Heath .05 .15
51 Guy Hoffman .05 .15
52 Tom Hume .05 .15
53 Pete Incaviglia XRC .20 .50
54 Dane Iorg .05 .15
55 Chris James XRC .05 .15
56 Stan Javier XRC* .20 .50
57 Tommy John .08 .25
58 Tracy Jones .05 .15
59 Wally Joyner XRC .40 1.00
60 Wayne Krenchicki .05 .15
61 John Kruk XRC .60 1.50
62 Mike LaCoss .05 .15
63 Pete Ladd .05 .15
64 Dave LaPoint .05 .15
65 Mike LaValliere XRC .20 .50
66 Rudy Law .05 .15
67 Dennis Leonard .05 .15
68 Steve Lombardozzi .05 .15
69 Aurelio Lopez .05 .15
70 Mickey Mahler .05 .15
71 Candy Maldonado .05 .15
72 Roger Mason XRC* .20 .50
73 Greg Mathews .05 .15
74 Andy McGaffigan .05 .15
75 Joel McKeon .05 .15
76 Kevin Mitchell XRC .40 1.00
77 Bill Mooneyham .05 .15
78 Omar Moreno .05 .15
79 Jerry Mumphrey .05 .15
80 Al Newman XRC .08 .25
81 Phil Niekro .08 .25
82 Randy Niemann .05 .15
83 Juan Nieves .05 .15
84 Bob Ojeda .05 .15
85 Rick Ownbey .05 .15
86 Tom Paciorek .05 .15
87 David Palmer .05 .15
88 Jeff Parrett XRC .05 .15
89 Pat Perry .05 .15
90 Dan Plesac .05 .15
91 Darrell Porter .05 .15
92 Luis Quinones .05 .15
93 Rey Quinones UER/(Misspelled Quinonez) .05
.15
94 Gary Redus .05 .15
95 Jeff Reed .05 .15
96 Bip Roberts XRC .20 .50
97 Billy Joe Robidoux .05 .15
98 Gary Roenicke .05 .15
99 Ron Roenicke .05 .15
100 Angel Salazar .05 .15
101 Joe Sambito .05 .15
102 Billy Sample .05 .15
103 Dave Schmidt .05 .15
104 Ken Schrom .05 .15
105 Ruben Sierra XRC .60 1.50
106 Ted Simmons .08 .25
107 Sammy Stewart .05 .15
108 Kurt Stillwell .05 .15
109 Dale Sveum .05 .15
110 Tim Teufel .05 .15
111 Bob Tewksbury XRC .20 .50
112 Andres Thomas .05 .15
113 Jason Thompson .05 .15
114 Milt Thompson .20 .50
115 Robby Thompson XRC .20 .50
116 Jay Tibbs .05 .15
117 Fred Toliver .05 .15
118 Wayne Tolleson .05 .15
119 Alex Trevino .05 .15
120 Manny Trillo .05 .15
121 Ed VandeBerg .05 .15
122 Ozzie Virgil .05 .15
123 Tony Walker .05 .15
124 Gene Walter .05 .15
125 Duane Ward XRC .20 .50
126 Jerry Willard .05 .15
127 Mitch Williams XRC .20 .50
128 Reggie Williams .05 .15
129 Bobby Witt XRC .20 .50
130 Marvell Wynne .05 .15
131 Steve Yeager .08 .25
132 Checklist 1-132 .05 .15

1986 Fleer League Leaders

This 44-card standard-size set is also sometimes referred to as the Walgreen's set. Although the set was distributed through Walgreen's, there is no mention on the cards or box of that fact. The cards are easily recognizable by the fact that they contain the phrase "Fleer League Leaders" at the top of the obverse. Both sides of the cards are designed with a blue stripe on white pattern. The checklist for the set is given on the outside of the red, white, blue, and gold box in which the set was packaged. A first year card of Jose Canseco highlights the set.

COMP.FACT. SET (44) 2.50 6.00
1 Wade Boggs .20 .50
2 George Brett .30 .75
3 Jose Canseco .75 2.00
4 Rod Carew .07 .20
5 Gary Carter .20 .50
6 Jack Clark .02 .10
7 Vince Coleman .02 .10
8 Jose Cruz .02 .10
9 Alvin Davis .01 .05
10 Mariano Duncan .01 .05
11 Leon Durham .01 .05
12 Carlton Fisk .15 .40
13 Julio Franco .02 .10
14 Scott Garrelts .01 .05
15 Steve Garvey .05 .15
16 Dwight Gooden .05 .15
17 Ozzie Guillen .05 .15
18 Willie Hernandez .01 .05
19 Bob Horner .01 .05
20 Kent Hrbek .02 .10
21 Charlie Leibrandt .01 .05
22 Don Mattingly .20 .50
23 Oddibe McDowell .01 .05
24 Willie McGee .02 .10
25 Keith Moreland .01 .05
26 Lloyd Moseby .01 .05
27 Dale Murphy .07 .20
28 Phil Niekro .15 .40
29 Joe Orsulak .01 .05
30 Dave Parker .02 .10
31 Lance Parrish .02 .10
32 Kirby Puckett .20 .50
33 Tim Raines .02 .10
34 Earnie Riles .01 .05
35 Cal Ripken .60 1.50
36 Pete Rose .20 .50
37 Bret Saberhagen .02 .10
38 Juan Samuel .01 .05
39 Ryne Sandberg .20 .50
40 Tom Seaver .15 .40
41 Lee Smith .05 .15
42 Ozzie Smith .30 .75
43 Dave Stieb .01 .05
44 Robin Yount .10 .30

1986 Fleer Limited Edition

The 44-card boxed standard-size set was produced by Fleer for McCrory's. The cards have green and yellow borders. Card backs are printed in red and black on white card stock. The back of the original box gives a complete checklist of the players in the set. The set box also contains six logo stickers.

COMP.FACT. SET (44) 2.50 6.00
1 Doyle Alexander .01 .05
2 Joaquin Andujar .01 .05
3 Harold Baines .05 .15
4 Wade Boggs .15 .40
5 Phil Bradley .01 .05
6 George Brett .20 .50
7 Hubie Brooks .01 .05
8 Chris Brown .01 .05
9 Tom Brunansky .01 .05
10 Gary Carter .15 .40
11 Vince Coleman .02 .10
12 Cecil Cooper .02 .10
13 Jose Cruz .02 .10
14 Mike Davis .01 .05
15 Carlton Fisk .15 .40
16 Julio Franco .02 .10
17 Damaso Garcia .01 .05
18 Rich Gedman .01 .05
19 Kirk Gibson .02 .10
20 Dwight Gooden .05 .15
21 Pedro Guerrero .01 .05
22 Tony Gwynn .30 .75
23 Rickey Henderson .30 .75
24 Orel Hershiser .05 .15
25 LaMarr Hoyt .01 .05
26 Reggie Jackson .20 .50
27 Don Mattingly .30 .75
28 Oddibe McDowell .01 .05
29 Willie McGee .02 .10
30 Paul Molitor .15 .40
31 Dale Murphy .07 .20
32 Eddie Murray .15 .40
33 Dave Parker .02 .10
34 Tony Pena .02 .10
35 Jeff Reardon .01 .05
36 Cal Ripken .60 1.50
37 Pete Rose .20 .50
38 Bret Saberhagen .02 .10
39 Juan Samuel .01 .05
40 Ryne Sandberg .20 .50
41 Mike Schmidt .20 .50
42 Lee Smith .05 .15
43 Don Sutton .15 .40
44 Lou Whitaker .02 .10

1986 Fleer Mini

The Fleer "Classic Miniatures" set consists of 120 small cards with all new pictures of the players as compared to the 1986 Fleer regular issue. The cards are only 1 13/16" by 2 9/16", making them some of the smallest (in size) produced in the 1980's. Card backs provide career year-by-year statistics. The complete set was distributed in a red, white, and silver factory box along with 18 logo stickers. The card numbering is done in the same team order as the 1986 Fleer regular set. An early card of Jose Canseco is featured in this set.

COMP.FACT.SET (120) 3.00 8.00
1 George Brett .30 .75
2 Dan Quisenberry .01 .05
3 Bret Saberhagen .02 .10
4 Lonnie Smith .01 .05
5 Willie Wilson .01 .05
6 Jack Clark .02 .10
7 Vince Coleman .02 .10
8 Tom Herr .01 .05
9 Willie McGee .02 .10
10 Ozzie Smith .30 .75
11 John Tudor .01 .05
12 Jesse Barfield .01 .05
13 George Bell .02 .10
14 Tony Fernandez .02 .10
15 Damaso Garcia .01 .05
16 Dave Stieb .01 .05
17 Gary Carter .15 .40
18 Ron Darling .01 .05
19A Dwight Gooden/(R on Mets logo) .10 .30
19B Dwight Gooden/(No R on Mets logo) .10 .30
20 Keith Hernandez .02 .10
21 Darryl Strawberry .02 .10
22 Ron Guidry .02 .10
23 Rickey Henderson .25 .60
24 Don Mattingly .30 .75
25 Dave Righetti .01 .05
26 Dave Winfield .15 .40
27 Mariano Duncan .01 .05
28 Pedro Guerrero .02 .10
29 Bill Madlock .02 .10
30 Mike Marshall .01 .05
31 Fernando Valenzuela .05 .15
32 Reggie Jackson .20 .50
33 Gary Pettis .01 .05
34 Ron Romanick .01 .05
35 Don Sutton .10 .30
36 Mike Witt .01 .05
37 Buddy Bell .02 .10
38 Tom Browning .01 .05
39 Dave Parker .02 .10
40 Pete Rose .20 .50
41 Mario Soto .01 .05
42 Harold Baines .05 .15
43 Carlton Fisk .16 .40
44 Ozzie Guillen .05 .15
45 Ron Kittle .01 .05
46 Tom Seaver .15 .40
47 Kirk Gibson .02 .10
48 Jack Morris .02 .10
49 Lance Parrish .02 .10
50 Alan Trammell .05 .15
51 Lou Whitaker .02 .10
52 Hubie Brooks .01 .05
53 Andre Dawson .15 .40
54 Tim Raines .02 .10
55 Bryn Smith .01 .05
56 Tim Wallach .01 .05
57 Mike Boddicker .01 .05
58 Eddie Murray .15 .40
59 Cal Ripken .60 1.50
60 John Shelby .01 .05
61 Mike Young .01 .05
62 Jose Cruz .02 .10
63 Glenn Davis .01 .05
64 Phil Garner .02 .10
65 Nolan Ryan .60 1.50
66 Mike Scott .02 .10
67 Steve Garvey .02 .10
68 Rich Gossage .02 .10
69 Tony Gwynn .40 1.00
70 Andy Hawkins .01 .05
71 Garry Templeton .01 .05
72 Wade Boggs .15 .40
73 Roger Clemens .40 1.00
74 Dwight Evans .02 .10
75 Rich Gedman .01 .05
76 Jim Rice .02 .10
77 Shawon Dunston .01 .05
78 Leon Durham .01 .05
79 Keith Moreland .01 .05
80 Ryne Sandberg .20 .50
81 Rick Sutcliffe .01 .05
82 Bert Blyleven .02 .10
83 Tom Brunansky .01 .05
84 Kent Hrbek .02 .10
85 Kirby Puckett .20 .50
86 Bruce Bochte .01 .05
87 Jose Canseco .30 .75
88 Mike Davis .01 .05
89 Jay Howell .01 .05
90 Dwayne Murphy .01 .05
91 Steve Carlton .15 .40
92 Von Hayes .01 .05
93 Juan Samuel .01 .05
94 Mike Schmidt .15 .40
95 Glenn Wilson .01 .05
96 Phil Bradley .01 .05
97 Alvin Davis .01 .05
98 Jim Presley .01 .05
99 Danny Tartabull .01 .05
100 Cecil Cooper .02 .10
101 Paul Molitor .15 .40
102 Ernie Riles .01 .05
103 Robin Yount .15 .40
104 Bob Horner .01 .05
105 Dale Murphy .07 .20
106 Bruce Sutter .02 .10
107 Claudell Washington .01 .05
108 Chris Brown .01 .05
109 Chili Davis .02 .10
110 Scott Garrelts .01 .05
111 Oddibe McDowell .01 .05
112 Pete O'Brien .01 .05
113 Gary Ward .01 .05
114 Brett Butler .02 .10
115 Julio Franco .02 .10
116 Brook Jacoby .01 .05
117 Mike C. Brown .01 .05
118 Joe Orsulak .01 .05
119 Tony Pena .02 .10
120 R.J. Reynolds .01 .05

1986 Fleer Sluggers/Pitchers

Fleer produced this 44-card boxed standard-size set although it was primarily distributed by Kress, McCrory, Newberry, T.G.Y., and other similar stores. The set features 22 sluggers and 22 pitchers and is subtitled "Baseball's Best". The set was packaged in a red, white, blue, and yellow custom box along with six logo stickers. The set checklist is given on the back of the box. The card numbering is in alphabetical order by the player's name. The Will Clark and Bobby Witt cards were the first major league cards produced of those players. In addition, an early card of Jose Canseco is featured in this set.

COMP.FACT.SET (44) 2.50 6.00
1 Bert Blyleven .02 .10
2 Wade Boggs .15 .40
3 George Brett .30 .75
4 Tom Browning .01 .05
5 Jose Canseco .40 1.00
6 Will Clark .40 1.00
7 Roger Clemens .30 .75
8 Alvin Davis .01 .05
9 Julio Franco .02 .10
10 Kirk Gibson .02 .10
11 Dwight Gooden .02 .10
12 Rich Gossage .02 .10
13 Pedro Guerrero .01 .05
14 Ron Guidry .02 .10
15 Tony Gwynn .30 .75
16 Orel Hershiser .07 .20
17 Kent Hrbek .01 .05
18 Reggie Jackson .15 .40
19 Wally Joyner .15 .40
20 Charlie Leibrandt .01 .05
21 Don Mattingly .30 .75
22 Willie McGee .02 .10
23 Jack Morris .02 .10
24 Dale Murphy .07 .20
25 Eddie Murray .15 .40
26 Jeff Reardon .01 .05
27 Rick Reuschel .01 .05
28 Cal Ripken .60 1.50
29 Pete Rose .20 .50
30 Nolan Ryan .60 1.50
31 Bret Saberhagen .02 .10
32 Ryne Sandberg .20 .50
33 Mike Schmidt .20 .50
34 Tom Seaver .15 .40
35 Bryn Smith .01 .05
36 Mario Soto .01 .05
37 Dave Stieb .01 .05
38 Darryl Strawberry .02 .10
39 Rick Sutcliffe .01 .05
40 John Tudor .01 .05
41 Fernando Valenzuela .02 .10
42 Bobby Witt .02 .10
43 Mike Witt .01 .05
44 Robin Yount .15 .40

1986 Fleer Sluggers/Pitchers Box Cards

COMPLETE SET (6) 4.00 10.00
M1 Harold Baines .60 1.50
M2 Steve Carlton 1.50 4.00
M3 Gary Carter 1.25 3.00
M4 Vince Coleman .30 .75
M5 Kirby Puckett 2.50 6.00
NNO New York Mets .20 .50

1986 Fleer Star Stickers

The standard-size stickers (made of card stock) 132-card set were distributed in wax packs and feature card photos on the front surrounded by a yellow border and a cranberry frame. The backs are printed in blue and black on white card stock. The backs contain year-by-year statistical information. They are numbered on the back in the upper left-hand corner. The card numbering is in alphabetical order by the player's name. A first year card of slugger Jose Canseco is featured in this set.

COMPLETE SET (132) 6.00 15.00
1 Harold Baines .05 .15
2 Jesse Barfield .01 .05
3 Don Baylor .02 .10
4 Juan Beniquez .01 .05
5 Tim Birtsas .01 .05
6 Bert Blyleven .02 .10
7 Bruce Bochte .01 .05
8 Wade Boggs .20 .50
9 Dennis Boyd .01 .05
10 Phil Bradley .01 .05
11 George Brett .50 1.25
12 Hubie Brooks .01 .05
13 Chris Brown .01 .05
14 Tom Browning .01 .05
15 Tom Brunansky .01 .05
16 Bill Buckner .02 .10
17 Britt Burns .01 .05
18 Brett Butler .02 .10
19 Jose Canseco .75 2.00
20 Rod Carew .15 .40
21 Steve Carlton .15 .40
22 Don Carman .01 .05
23 Gary Carter .20 .50
24 Jack Clark .02 .10
25 Vince Coleman .02 .10
26 Cecil Cooper .02 .10
27 Jose Cruz .02 .10
28 Ron Darling .01 .05
29 Alvin Davis .01 .05
30 Jody Davis .01 .05
31 Mike Davis .01 .05
32 Andre Dawson .07 .20
33 Mariano Duncan .01 .05
34 Shawon Dunston .01 .05
35 Leon Durham .01 .05
36 Darrell Evans .02 .10
37 Tony Fernandez .02 .10
38 Carlton Fisk .15 .40
39 John Franco .07 .20
40 Julio Franco .02 .10
41 Damaso Garcia .01 .05
42 Scott Garrelts .01 .05
43 Steve Garvey .07 .20
44 Rich Gedman .01 .05
45 Kirk Gibson .02 .10
46 Dwight Gooden .05 .15
47 Pedro Guerrero .02 .10
48 Ron Guidry .02 .10
49 Ozzie Guillen .20 .50
50 Tony Gwynn .50 1.25
51 Andy Hawkins .01 .05
52 Von Hayes .01 .05
53 Rickey Henderson .30 1.00
54 Tom Henke .01 .05
55 Keith Hernandez .02 .10
56 Willie Hernandez .01 .05
57 Tommy Herr .01 .05
58 Orel Hershiser .05 .15
59 Teddy Higuera .01 .05
60 Bob Horner .01 .05
61 Charlie Hough .02 .10
62 Jay Howell .01 .05
63 LaMarr Hoyt .01 .05
64 Kent Hrbek .02 .10
65 Reggie Jackson .20 .50
66 Bob James .01 .05
67 Dave Kingman .02 .10
68 Ron Kittle .01 .05
69 Charlie Leibrandt .01 .05
70 Fred Lynn .02 .10
71 Mike Marshall .01 .05
72 Don Mattingly .50 1.25
73 Oddibe McDowell .01 .05
74 Willie McGee .02 .10
75 Scott McGregor .01 .05
76 Paul Molitor .20 .50
77 Donnie Moore .01 .05
78 Keith Moreland .01 .05
79 Jack Morris .02 .10
80 Dale Murphy .07 .20
81 Eddie Murray .20 .50
82 Phil Niekro .15 .40
83 Joe Orsulak .01 .05
84 Dave Parker .02 .10
85 Lance Parrish .02 .10
86 Larry Parrish .01 .05
87 Tony Pena .02 .10
88 Gary Pettis .01 .05
89 Jim Presley .01 .05
90 Kirby Puckett 1.00 1.00
91 Dan Quisenberry .01 .05
92 Tim Raines .02 .10
93 Johnny Ray .01 .05
94 Jeff Reardon .02 .10
95 Rick Reuschel .02 .10
96 Jim Rice .02 .10
97 Dave Righetti .01 .05
98 Earnie Riles .01 .05
99 Cal Ripken 1.00 2.50
100 Ron Romanick .01 .05
101 Pete Rose .30 .75
102 Nolan Ryan 1.00 2.50
103 Bret Saberhagen .02 .10
104 Mark Salas .01 .05
105 Juan Samuel .01 .05
106 Ryne Sandberg .30 .75
107 Mike Schmidt .20 .50
108 Mike Scott .01 .05
109 Tom Seaver .15 .40
110 Bryn Smith .01 .05
111 Dave Smith .02 .10
112 Lee Smith .05 .15
113 Ozzie Smith .30 .75
114 Mario Soto .01 .05
115 Dave Stieb .01 .05
116 Darryl Strawberry .02 .10
117 Bruce Sutter .02 .10
118 Garry Templeton .01 .05
119 Gorman Thomas .01 .05
120 Andre Thornton .01 .05
121 Alan Trammell .05 .15
122 John Tudor .01 .05
123 Fernando Valenzuela .07 .20
124 Frank Viola .02 .10
125 Gary Ward .01 .05
126 Lou Whitaker .02 .10
127 Frank White .02 .10
128 Glenn Wilson .01 .05
129 Willie Wilson .01 .05
130 Dave Winfield .15 .40
131 Robin Yount .15 .40
132 Checklist Card .07 .20
Dwight Gooden
Dale Murphy

1986 Fleer Stickers Wax Box Cards

COMPLETE SET (4) 1.50 4.00
S1 Dodgers Team Logo/(Checklist back) .08 .25
S2 Wade Boggs .75 2.00
S3 Steve Garvey .30 .75
S4 Dave Winfield .60 1.50

1987 Fleer

This set consists of 660 standard-size cards. Cards were primarily issued in 17-card wax packs, rack packs and hobby and retail factory sets. The wax packs were packed 36 to a box and 20 boxes to a case. The rack packs were packed 24 to a box and 3 boxes to a case and had 51 regular cards and three sticker card per pack. Card fronts feature a distinctive light blue and white blended border encasing a color photo. Cards are again organized numerically by teams with team ordering based on the previous seasons record. The last 36 cards in the set consist of Specials (625-643), Rookie Pairs (644-653), and checklists (654-660). The key Rookie Cards in this set are Barry Bonds, Bobby Bonilla, Will Clark, Chuck Finley, Bo Jackson, Wally Joyner, John Kruk, Barry Larkin and Devon White.

COMPLETE SET (660) 12.50 30.00
COMP.FACT.SET (672) 15.00 40.00
1 Rick Aguilera .05 .15
2 Richard Anderson .05 .15
3 Wally Backman .05 .15
4 Gary Carter .08 .25
5 Ron Darling .08 .25
6 Len Dykstra .08 .25
7 Kevin Elster RC .20 .50
8 Sid Fernandez .05 .15
9 Dwight Gooden .15 .40
10 Ed Hearn RC .05 .15
11 Danny Heep .05 .15
12 Keith Hernandez .08 .25
13 Howard Johnson .08 .25
14 Ray Knight .08 .25
15 Lee Mazzilli .08 .25
16 Roger McDowell .05 .15
17 Kevin Mitchell RC .50 1.25
18 Randy Niemann .05 .15
19 Bob Ojeda .05 .15
20 Jesse Orosco .05 .15
21 Rafael Santana .05 .15
22 Doug Sisk .05 .15
23 Darryl Strawberry .08 .25
24 Tim Teufel .05 .15
25 Mookie Wilson .08 .25
26 Tony Armas .08 .25
27 Marty Barrett .05 .15
28 Don Baylor .08 .25
29 Wade Boggs .15 .40
30 Oil Can Boyd .05 .15
31 Bill Buckner .08 .25
32 Roger Clemens 1.25 3.00
33 Steve Crawford .05 .15
34 Dwight Evans .15 .40
35 Rich Gedman .05 .15
36 Dave Henderson .05 .15
37 Bruce Hurst .05 .15
38 Tim Lollar .05 .15
39 Al Nipper .05 .15
40 Spike Owen .05 .15
41 Jim Rice .08 .25
42 Ed Romero .05 .15
43 Joe Sambito .05 .15
44 Calvin Schiraldi .05 .15
45 Tom Seaver UER .15 .40
Lifetime saves total 0, should be 1
46 Jeff Sellers .05 .15
47 Bob Stanley .05 .15
48 Sammy Stewart .05 .15
49 Larry Andersen .05 .15
50 Alan Ashby .05 .15
51 Kevin Bass .05 .15
52 Jeff Calhoun .05 .15
53 Jose Cruz .08 .25
54 Danny Darwin .05 .15
55 Glenn Davis .05 .15
56 Jim Deshaies RC .08 .25
57 Bill Doran .05 .15
58 Phil Garner .08 .25
59 Billy Hatcher .05 .15
60 Charlie Kerfeld .05 .15
61 Bob Knepper .05 .15
62 Dave Lopes .08 .25
63 Aurelio Lopez .05 .15
64 Jim Pankovits .05 .15
65 Terry Puhl .05 .15
66 Craig Reynolds .05 .15
67 Nolan Ryan 1.25 3.00
68 Mike Scott .08 .25
69 Dave Smith .05 .15
70 Dickie Thon .05 .15
71 Tony Walker .05 .15
72 Denny Walling .05 .15
73 Bob Boone .08 .25
74 Rick Burleson .05 .15
75 John Candelaria .05 .15
76 Doug Corbett .05 .15
77 Doug DeCinces .05 .15
78 Brian Downing .08 .25
79 Chuck Finley RC .50 1.25
80 Terry Forster .08 .25
81 Bob Grich .08 .25
82 George Hendrick .08 .25
83 Jack Howell .05 .15
84 Reggie Jackson .15 .40
85 Ruppert Jones .05 .15
86 Wally Joyner RC .50 1.25
87 Gary Lucas .05 .15
88 Kirk McCaskill .05 .15
89 Donnie Moore .05 .15
90 Gary Pettis .05 .15
91 Vern Ruhle .05 .15
92 Dick Schofield .05 .15
93 Don Sutton .08 .25
94 Rob Wilfong .05 .15
95 Mike Witt .05 .15
96 Doug Drabek RC .50 1.25
97 Mike Easler .05 .15
98 Mike Fischlin .05 .15
99 Brian Fisher .05 .15
100 Ron Guidry .08 .25
101 Rickey Henderson .25 .60
102 Tommy John .08 .25
103 Ron Kittle .05 .15
104 Don Mattingly .75 2.00
105 Bobby Meacham .05 .15
106 Joe Niekro .05 .15
107 Mike Pagliarulo .05 .15
108 Dan Pasqua .05 .15
109 Willie Randolph .08 .25
110 Dennis Rasmussen .05 .15
111 Dave Righetti .08 .25
112 Gary Roenicke .05 .15
113 Rod Scurry .05 .15
114 Bob Shirley .05 .15
115 Joel Skinner .05 .15
116 Tim Stoddard .05 .15
117 Bob Tewksbury RC .20 .50
118 Wayne Tolleson .05 .15
119 Claudell Washington .05 .15
120 Dave Winfield .08 .25
121 Steve Buechele .05 .15
122 Ed Correa .05 .15
123 Scott Fletcher .05 .15
124 Jose Guzman .05 .15
125 Toby Harrah .08 .25
126 Greg Harris .05 .15
127 Charlie Hough .08 .25

128 Pete Incaviglia RC .20 .50
129 Mike Mason .05 .15
130 Oddibe McDowell .05 .15
131 Dale Mohorcic .05 .15
132 Pete O'Brien .05 .15
133 Tom Paciorek .05 .15
134 Larry Parrish .05 .15
135 Geno Petralli .05 .15
136 Darrell Porter .05 .15
137 Jeff Russell .05 .15
138 Ruben Sierra RC .75 2.00
139 Don Slaught .05 .15
140 Gary Ward .05 .15
141 Curtis Wilkerson .05 .15
142 Mitch Williams RC .20 .50
143 Bobby Witt RC UER .20 .50
Tulsa misspelled as
Tusla; ERA should
be 6.43, not .643
144 Dave Bergman .05 .15
145 Tom Brookens .05 .15
146 Bill Campbell .05 .15
147 Chuck Cary .05 .15
148 Darnell Coles .05 .15
149 Dave Collins .05 .15
150 Darrell Evans .08 .25
151 Kirk Gibson .08 .25
152 John Grubb .05 .15
153 Willie Hernandez .05 .15
154 Larry Herndon .05 .15
155 Eric King .05 .15
156 Chet Lemon .08 .25
157 Dwight Lowry .05 .15
158 Jack Morris .08 .25
159 Randy O'Neal .05 .15
160 Lance Parrish .08 .25
161 Dan Petry .05 .15
162 Pat Sheridan .05 .15
163 Jim Slaton .05 .15
164 Frank Tanana .08 .25
165 Walt Terrell .05 .15
166 Mark Thurmond .05 .15
167 Alan Trammell .08 .25
168 Lou Whitaker .08 .25
169 Luis Aguayo .05 .15
170 Steve Bedrosian .05 .15
171 Don Carman .05 .15
172 Darren Daulton .08 .25
173 Greg Gross .05 .15
174 Kevin Gross .05 .15
175 Von Hayes .05 .15
176 Charles Hudson .05 .15
177 Tom Hume .05 .15
178 Steve Jeltz .05 .15
179 Mike Maddux RC .05 .15
180 Shane Rawley .05 .15
181 Gary Redus .05 .15
182 Ron Roenicke .05 .15
183 Bruce Ruffin RC .08 .25
184 John Russell .05 .15
185 Juan Samuel .05 .15
186 Dan Schatzeder .05 .15
187 Mike Schmidt .60 1.50
188 Rick Schu .05 .15
189 Jeff Stone .05 .15
190 Kent Tekulve .05 .15
191 Milt Thompson .05 .15
192 Glenn Wilson .05 .15
193 Buddy Bell .08 .25
194 Tom Browning .05 .15
195 Sal Butera .05 .15
196 Dave Concepcion .08 .25
197 Kal Daniels .05 .15
198 Eric Davis .15 .40
199 John Denny .05 .15
200 Bo Diaz .05 .15
201 Nick Esasky .05 .15
202 John Franco .08 .25
203 Bill Gullickson .05 .15
204 Barry Larkin RC 4.00 10.00
205 Eddie Milner .05 .15
206 Rob Murphy .05 .15
207 Ron Oester .05 .15
208 Dave Parker .08 .25
209 Tony Perez .15 .40
210 Ted Power .05 .15
211 Joe Price .05 .15
212 Ron Robinson .05 .15
213 Pete Rose .75 2.00
214 Mario Soto .08 .25
215 Kurt Stillwell .05 .15
216 Max Venable .05 .15
217 Chris Welsh .05 .15
218 Carl Willis RC .08 .25
219 Jesse Barfield .08 .25
220 George Bell .08 .25
221 Bill Caudill .05 .15
222 John Cerutti .05 .15
223 Jim Clancy .05 .15
224 Mark Eichhorn .05 .15
225 Tony Fernandez .05 .15
226 Damaso Garcia .05 .15
227 Kelly Gruber ERR .05 .15
Wrong birth year
228 Tom Henke .05 .15
229 Garth Iorg .05 .15
230 Joe Johnson .05 .15
231 Cliff Johnson .05 .15
232 Jimmy Key .08 .25
233 Dennis Lamp .05 .15
234 Rick Leach .05 .15
235 Buck Martinez .05 .15
236 Lloyd Moseby .05 .15
237 Rance Mulliniks .05 .15
238 Dave Stieb .08 .25
239 Willie Upshaw .05 .15
240 Ernie Whitt .05 .15
241 Andy Allanson RC .05 .15
242 Scott Bailes .05 .15
243 Chris Bando .05 .15
244 Tony Bernazard .05 .15
245 John Butcher .05 .15
246 Brett Butler .08 .25
247 Ernie Camacho .05 .15
248 Tom Candiotti .05 .15
249 Joe Carter .08 .25
250 Carmen Castillo .05 .15
251 Julio Franco .08 .25
252 Mel Hall .05 .15
253 Brook Jacoby .05 .15
254 Phil Niekro .08 .25
255 Otis Nixon .05 .15
256 Dickie Noles .05 .15
257 Bryan Oelkers .05 .15
258 Ken Schrom .05 .15
259 Don Schulze .05 .15
260 Cory Snyder .05 .15
261 Pat Tabler .05 .15
262 Andre Thornton .05 .15
263 Rich Yett .05 .15
264 Mike Aldrete .05 .15
265 Juan Berenguer .05 .15
266 Vida Blue .08 .25
267 Bob Brenly .05 .15
268 Chris Brown .05 .15
269 Will Clark RC 1.25 3.00
270 Chili Davis .08 .25
271 Mark Davis .05 .15
272 Kelly Downs RC .08 .25
273 Scott Garrelts .05 .15
274 Dan Gladden .05 .15
275 Mike Krukow .05 .15
276 Randy Kutcher .05 .15
277 Mike LaCoss .05 .15
278 Jeff Leonard .05 .15
279 Candy Maldonado .05 .15
280 Roger Mason .05 .15
281 Bob Melvin .05 .15
282 Greg Minton .05 .15
283 Jeff D. Robinson .05 .15
284 Harry Spilman .05 .15
285 Robby Thompson RC .20 .50
286 Jose Uribe .05 .15
287 Frank Williams .05 .15
288 Joel Youngblood .05 .15
289 Jack Clark .08 .25
290 Vince Coleman .05 .15
291 Tim Conroy .05 .15
292 Danny Cox .05 .15
293 Ken Dayley .05 .15
294 Curt Ford .05 .15
295 Bob Forsch .05 .15
296 Tom Herr .05 .15
297 Ricky Horton .05 .15
298 Clint Hurdle .05 .15
299 Jeff Lahti .05 .15
300 Steve Lake .05 .15
301 Tito Landrum .05 .15
302 Mike LaValliere RC .20 .50
303 Greg Mathews .05 .15
304 Willie McGee .08 .25
305 Jose Oquendo .05 .15
306 Terry Pendleton .08 .25
307 Pat Perry .05 .15
308 Ozzie Smith .40 1.00
309 Ray Soff .05 .15
310 John Tudor .08 .25
311 Andy Van Slyke UER .15 .40
Bats R, Throws L
312 Todd Worrell .05 .15
313 Dann Bilardello .05 .15
314 Hubie Brooks .05 .15
315 Tim Burke .05 .15
316 Andre Dawson .08 .25
317 Mike Fitzgerald .05 .15
318 Tom Foley .05 .15
319 Andres Galarraga .08 .25
320 Joe Hesketh .05 .15
321 Wallace Johnson .05 .15
322 Wayne Krenchicki .05 .15
323 Vance Law .05 .15
324 Dennis Martinez .08 .25
325 Bob McClure .05 .15
326 Andy McGaffigan .05 .15
327 Al Newman RC .05 .15
328 Tim Raines .08 .25
329 Jeff Reardon .08 .25
330 Luis Rivera RC .08 .25
331 Bob Sebra .05 .15
332 Bryn Smith .05 .15
333 Jay Tibbs .05 .15
334 Tim Wallach .05 .15
335 Mitch Webster .05 .15
336 Jim Wohlford .05 .15
337 Floyd Youmans .05 .15
338 Chris Bosio RC .20 .50
339 Glenn Braggs RC .08 .25
340 Rick Cerone .05 .15
341 Mark Clear .05 .15
342 Bryan Clutterbuck .05 .15
343 Cecil Cooper .08 .25
344 Rob Deer .05 .15
345 Jim Gantner .05 .15
346 Ted Higuera .05 .15
347 John Henry Johnson .05 .15
348 Tim Leary .05 .15
349 Rick Manning .05 .15
350 Paul Molitor .08 .25
351 Charlie Moore .05 .15
352 Juan Nieves .05 .15
353 Ben Oglivie .08 .25
354 Dan Plesac .05 .15
355 Ernest Riles .05 .15
356 Billy Joe Robidoux .05 .15
357 Bill Schroeder .05 .15
358 Dale Sveum .05 .15
359 Gorman Thomas .08 .25
360 Bill Wegman .05 .15
361 Robin Yount .40 1.00
362 Steve Balboni .05 .15
363 Scott Bankhead .05 .15
364 Buddy Biancalana .05 .15
365 Bud Black .05 .15
366 George Brett .60 1.50
367 Steve Farr .05 .15
368 Mark Gubicza .05 .15
369 Bo Jackson RC 5.00 12.00
370 Danny Jackson .05 .15
371 Mike Kingery RC .08 .25
372 Rudy Law .05 .15
373 Charlie Leibrandt .05 .15
374 Dennis Leonard .05 .15
375 Hal McRae .08 .25
376 Jorge Orta .05 .15
377 Jamie Quirk .05 .15
378 Dan Quisenberry .05 .15
379 Bret Saberhagen .08 .25
380 Angel Salazar .05 .15
381 Lonnie Smith .05 .15
382 Jim Sundberg .08 .25
383 Frank White .08 .25
384 Willie Wilson .08 .25
385 Joaquin Andujar .08 .25
386 Doug Bair .05 .15
387 Dusty Baker .08 .25
388 Bruce Bochte .05 .15
389 Jose Canseco .60 1.50
390 Chris Codiroli .05 .15
391 Mike Davis .05 .15
392 Alfredo Griffin .05 .15
393 Moose Haas .05 .15
394 Donnie Hill .05 .15
395 Jay Howell .05 .15
396 Dave Kingman .08 .25
397 Carney Lansford .08 .25
398 Dave Leiper .05 .15
399 Bill Mooneyham .05 .15
400 Dwayne Murphy .05 .15
401 Steve Ontiveros .05 .15
402 Tony Phillips .05 .15
403 Eric Plunk .05 .15
404 Jose Rijo .08 .25
405 Terry Steinbach RC .50 1.25
406 Dave Stewart .08 .25
407 Mickey Tettleton .05 .15
408 Dave Von Ohlen .05 .15
409 Jerry Willard .05 .15
410 Curt Young .05 .15
411 Bruce Bochy .05 .15
412 Dave Dravecky .05 .15
413 Tim Flannery .05 .15
414 Steve Garvey .08 .25
415 Rich Gossage .08 .25
416 Tony Gwynn .40 1.00
417 Andy Hawkins .05 .15
418 LaMarr Hoyt .05 .15
419 Terry Kennedy .05 .15
420 John Kruk RC .75 2.00
421 Dave LaPoint .05 .15
422 Craig Lefferts .05 .15
423 Carmelo Martinez .05 .15
424 Lance McCullers .05 .15
425 Kevin McReynolds .05 .15
426 Graig Nettles .08 .25
427 Bip Roberts RC .20 .50
428 Jerry Royster .05 .15
429 Benito Santiago .08 .25
430 Eric Show .05 .15
431 Bob Stoddard .05 .15
432 Garry Templeton .08 .25
433 Gene Walter .05 .15
434 Ed Whitson .05 .15
435 Marvell Wynne .05 .15
436 Dave Anderson .05 .15
437 Greg Brock .05 .15
438 Enos Cabell .05 .15
439 Mariano Duncan .05 .15
440 Pedro Guerrero .08 .25
441 Orel Hershiser .15 .40
442 Rick Honeycutt .05 .15
443 Ken Howell .05 .15
444 Ken Landreaux .05 .15
445 Bill Madlock .08 .25
446 Mike Marshall .05 .15
447 Len Matuszek .05 .15
448 Tom Niedenfuer .05 .15
449 Alejandro Pena .05 .15
450 Dennis Powell .05 .15
451 Jerry Reuss .05 .15
452 Bill Russell .08 .25
453 Steve Sax .05 .15
454 Mike Scioscia .08 .25
455 Franklin Stubbs .05 .15
456 Alex Trevino .05 .15
457 Fernando Valenzuela .08 .25
458 Ed VandeBerg .05 .15
459 Bob Welch .08 .25
460 Reggie Williams .05 .15
461 Don Aase .05 .15
462 Juan Beniquez .05 .15
463 Mike Boddicker .05 .15
464 Juan Bonilla .05 .15
465 Rich Bordi .05 .15
466 Storm Davis .05 .15
467 Rick Dempsey .05 .15
468 Ken Dixon .05 .15
469 Jim Dwyer .05 .15
470 Mike Flanagan .05 .15
471 Jackie Gutierrez .05 .15
472 Brad Havens .05 .15
473 Lee Lacy .05 .15
474 Fred Lynn .08 .25
475 Scott McGregor .05 .15
476 Eddie Murray .25 .60
477 Tom O'Malley .05 .15
478 Cal Ripken Jr. 1.00 2.50
479 Larry Sheets .05 .15
480 John Shelby .05 .15
481 Nate Snell .05 .15
482 Jim Traber .05 .15
483 Mike Young .05 .15
484 Neil Allen .05 .15
485 Harold Baines .08 .25
486 Floyd Bannister .05 .15
487 Daryl Boston .05 .15
488 Ivan Calderon .05 .15
489 John Cangelosi .05 .15
490 Steve Carlton .08 .25
491 Joe Cowley .05 .15
492 Julio Cruz .05 .15
493 Bill Dawley .05 .15
494 Jose DeLeon .05 .15
495 Richard Dotson .05 .15
496 Carlton Fisk .15 .40
497 Ozzie Guillen .15 .40
498 Jerry Hairston .05 .15
499 Ron Hassey .05 .15
500 Tim Hulett .05 .15
501 Bob James .05 .15
502 Steve Lyons .05 .15
503 Joel McKeon .05 .15
504 Gene Nelson .05 .15
505 Dave Schmidt .05 .15
506 Ray Searage .05 .15
507 Bobby Thigpen RC .20 .50
508 Greg Walker .05 .15
509 Jim Acker .05 .15
510 Doyle Alexander .05 .15
511 Paul Assenmacher .20 .50
512 Bruce Benedict .05 .15
513 Chris Chambliss .08 .25
514 Jeff Dedmon .05 .15
515 Gene Garber .05 .15
516 Ken Griffey .08 .25
517 Terry Harper .05 .15
518 Bob Horner .08 .25
519 Glenn Hubbard .05 .15
520 Rick Mahler .05 .15
521 Omar Moreno .05 .15
522 Dale Murphy .15 .40
523 Ken Oberkfell .05 .15
524 Ed Olwine .05 .15
525 David Palmer .05 .15
526 Rafael Ramirez .05 .15
527 Billy Sample .05 .15
528 Ted Simmons .08 .25
529 Zane Smith .05 .15
530 Bruce Sutter .08 .25
531 Andres Thomas .05 .15
532 Ozzie Virgil .05 .15
533 Allan Anderson RC .05 .15
534 Keith Atherton .05 .15
535 Billy Beane .08 .25
536 Bert Blyleven .08 .25
537 Tom Brunansky .05 .15
538 Randy Bush .05 .15
539 George Frazier .05 .15
540 Gary Gaetti .08 .25
541 Greg Gagne .05 .15
542 Mickey Hatcher .05 .15
543 Neal Heaton .05 .15
544 Kent Hrbek .08 .25
545 Roy Lee Jackson .05 .15
546 Tim Laudner .05 .15
547 Steve Lombardozzi .05 .15
548 Mark Portugal RC .20 .50
549 Kirby Puckett .40 1.00
550 Jeff Reed .05 .15
551 Mark Salas .05 .15
552 Roy Smalley .05 .15
553 Mike Smithson .05 .15
554 Frank Viola .08 .25
555 Thad Bosley .05 .15
556 Ron Cey .08 .25
557 Jody Davis .05 .15
558 Ron Davis .05 .15
559 Bob Dernier .05 .15
560 Frank DiPino .05 .15
561 Shawon Dunston UER .05 .15
Wrong birth year
listed on card back
562 Leon Durham .05 .15
563 Dennis Eckersley .15 .40
564 Terry Francona .08 .25
565 Dave Gumpert .05 .15
566 Guy Hoffman .05 .15
567 Ed Lynch .05 .15
568 Gary Matthews .08 .25
569 Keith Moreland .05 .15
570 Jamie Moyer RC .75 2.00
571 Jerry Mumphrey .05 .15
572 Ryne Sandberg .50 1.25
573 Scott Sanderson .05 .15
574 Lee Smith .08 .25
575 Chris Speier .05 .15
576 Rick Sutcliffe .08 .25
577 Manny Trillo .05 .15
578 Steve Trout .05 .15
579 Karl Best .05 .15
580 Scott Bradley .05 .15
581 Phil Bradley .05 .15
582 Mickey Brantley .05 .15
583 Mike G. Brown P .05 .15
584 Alvin Davis .05 .15
585 Lee Guetterman .05 .15
586 Mark Huismann .05 .15
587 Bob Kearney .05 .15
588 Pete Ladd .05 .15
589 Mark Langston .05 .15
590 Mike Moore .05 .15
591 Mike Morgan .05 .15
592 John Moses .05 .15
593 Ken Phelps .05 .15
594 Jim Presley .05 .15
595 Rey Quinones UER .05 .15
Quinonez on front
596 Harold Reynolds .08 .25
597 Billy Swift .05 .15
598 Danny Tartabull .05 .15
599 Steve Yeager .08 .25
600 Matt Young .05 .15
601 Bill Almon .05 .15
602 Rafael Belliard RC .20 .50
603 Mike Bielecki .05 .15
604 Barry Bonds RC 6.00 15.00
605 Bobby Bonilla RC .50 1.25
606 Sid Bream .05 .15
607 Mike C. Brown .05 .15
608 Pat Clements .05 .15
609 Mike Diaz .05 .15
610 Cecilio Guante .05 .15
611 Barry Jones .05 .15
612 Bob Kipper .05 .15
613 Larry McWilliams .05 .15
614 Jim Morrison .05 .15
615 Joe Orsulak .05 .15
616 Junior Ortiz .05 .15
617 Tony Pena .05 .15
618 Johnny Ray .05 .15
619 Rick Reuschel .08 .25
620 R.J. Reynolds .05 .15
621 Rick Rhoden .05 .15
622 Don Robinson .05 .15
623 Bob Walk .05 .15
624 Jim Winn .05 .15
625 P.Incaviglia/J.Canseco .30 .75
626 Don Sutton .08 .25
Phil Niekro
627 Dave Righetti .05 .15
Don Aase
628 W.Joyner/J.Canseco .30 .75
629 Gary Carter .15 .40
Sid Fernandez
Dwight Gooden
Keith Hernandez
Darryl Strawberry
630 Mike Scott .05 .15
Mike Krukow
631 Fernando Valenzuela .05 .15
John Franco
632 Count'Em .05 .15
Bob Horner
633 Canseco/Rice/Puckett .30 .75
634 Gary Carter .25 .60
Roger Clemens
635 Steve Carlton 4000K's .08 .25
636 Glenn Davis .25 .60
Eddie Murray
637 Wade Boggs .08 .25
Keith Hernandez
638 D.Mattingly/D.Strawberry .40 1.00
639 Dave Parker .25 .60
Ryne Sandberg
640 Dwight Gooden .25 .60
Roger Clemens
641 Mike Witt .05 .15
Charlie Hough
642 Juan Samuel .08 .25
Tim Raines
643 Harold Baines .08 .25
Jesse Barfield
644 Dave Clark RC .20 .50
Greg Swindell RC
645 Ron Karkovice RC .20 .50
Russ Morman RC
646 Devon White RC .50 1.25
Willie Fraser RC
647 Mike Stanley RC .20 .50
Jerry Browne RC
648 Dave Magadan RC .20 .50
Phil Lombardi RC
649 Jose Gonzalez RC .08 .25
Ralph Bryant RC
650 Jimmy Jones RC .08 .25
Randy Asadoor RC
651 Tracy Jones RC .08 .25
Marvin Freeman RC
652 John Stefero .20 .50
Kevin Seitzer RC
653 Rob Nelson RC .08 .25
Steve Fireovid RC
654 CL: Mets .05 .15
Red Sox
Astros
Angels
655 CL: Yankees .05 .15
Rangers
Tigers
Phillies
656 CL: Reds .05 .15
Blue Jays
Indians
Giants
ERR 230
231 wrong
657 CL: Cardinals .05 .15
Expos
Brewers
Royals
658 CL: A's .05 .15
Padres
Dodgers
Orioles
659 CL: White Sox .05 .15
Braves
Twins
Cubs
660 CL: Mariners .05 .15
Pirates
Special Cards
ER 580
581 wrong

1987 Fleer Glossy

COMP.FACT.SET (672) 15.00 40.00
*STARS: .5X TO 1.2X BASIC CARDS
*ROOKIES: .5X TO 1.2X BASIC CARDS
DISTRIBUTED ONLY IN FACTORY SET FORM
FACTORY SET PRICE IS FOR SEALED SETS
OPENED SETS SELL FOR 50-60% OF SEALED
604 Barry Bonds 6.00 15.00

1987 Fleer All-Stars

COMPLETE SET (12) 8.00 20.00
RANDOM INSERTS IN PACKS
1 Don Mattingly 2.50 6.00
2 Gary Carter .30 .75
3 Tony Fernandez .20 .50
4 Steve Sax .20 .50
5 Kirby Puckett 1.25 3.00
6 Mike Schmidt 2.00 5.00
7 Mike Easler .20 .50
8 Todd Worrell .20 .50
9 George Bell .30 .75
10 Fernando Valenzuela .30 .75
11 Roger Clemens 4.00 10.00
12 Tim Raines .30 .75

1987 Fleer Headliners

COMPLETE SET (6) 2.50 6.00
ONE PER RACK PACK
1 Wade Boggs .25 .60
2 Jose Canseco 1.00 2.50
3 Dwight Gooden .25 .60
4 Rickey Henderson .40 1.00
5 Keith Hernandez .15 .40
6 Jim Rice .15 .40

1987 Fleer Wax Box Cards

COMPLETE SET (16) 4.00 10.00
C1 Mets Logo .02 .10
C2 Jesse Barfield .02 .10
C3 George Brett 1.25 3.00
C4 Dwight Gooden .20 .50
C5 Boston Logo .02 .10
C6 Keith Hernandez .08 .25
C7 Wally Joyner .30 .75
C8 Dale Murphy .30 .75
C9 Astros Logo .02 .10
C10 Dave Parker .08 .25
C11 Kirby Puckett .80 1.00
C12 Dave Righetti .02 .10
C13 Angels Logo .02 .10
C14 Ryne Sandberg .75 2.00
C15 Mike Schmidt .60 1.50
C16 Robin Yount .30 .75

1987 Fleer World Series

COMPLETE SET (12) .75 2.00
ONE SET PER FACTORY SET
1 Bruce Hurst .05 .15
2 Keith Hernandez and .08 .25
Wade Boggs
3 Roger Clemens 1.25 3.00
4 Gary Carter .08 .25
5 Ron Darling .08 .25
6 Marty Barrett .05 .15
7 Dwight Gooden .15 .40
8 Strategy at Work/(Mets Conference) .08 .25
9 Dwight Evans .15 .40
Congratulated by Rich Gedman
10 Dave Henderson .05 .15
11 Ray Knight .08 .25
Darryl Strawberry
12 Ray Knight .08 .25

1987 Fleer World Series Glossy

*GLOSSY: .5X TO 1.2X BASIC WS
DISTRIBUTED ONLY IN FACTORY SET FORM

1987 Fleer Update

This 132-card standard-size set was distributed exclusively in factory set form through hobby dealers. In addition to the complete set of 132 cards, the box also contained 25 Team Logo stickers. The cards look very similar to the 1987 Fleer regular issue except for the U-prefixed numbering on back. Cards are ordered alphabetically according to player's last name. The key extended Rookie Cards in this set are Ellis Burks, Greg Maddux, Fred McGriff and Matt Williams. In addition an early card of legendary slugger Mark McGwire highlights this set.

COMP.FACT.SET (132) 5.00 12.00
1 Scott Bankhead .02 .10
2 Eric Bell .05 .15
3 Juan Beniquez .02 .10
4 Juan Berenguer .02 .10
5 Mike Birkbeck .05 .15
6 Randy Bockus .02 .10
7 Rod Booker .02 .10
8 Thad Bosley .02 .10
9 Greg Brock .02 .10
10 Bob Brower .02 .10
11 Chris Brown .02 .10
12 Jerry Browne .05 .15
13 Ralph Bryant .02 .10
14 DeWayne Buice .02 .10
15 Ellis Burks XRC .30 .75
16 Casey Candaele .02 .10
17 Steve Carlton .05 .15
18 Juan Castillo .05 .15
19 Chuck Crim .02 .10
20 Mark Davidson .02 .10
21 Mark Davis .02 .10
22 Storm Davis .02 .10
23 Bill Dawley .02 .10
24 Andre Dawson .05 .15
25 Brian Dayett .02 .10
26 Rick Dempsey .02 .10
27 Ken Dowell .02 .10
28 Dave Dravecky .02 .10
29 Mike Dunne .02 .10
30 Dennis Eckersley .08 .25
31 Cecil Fielder .05 .15
32 Brian Fisher .02 .10
33 Willie Fraser .05 .15
34 Ken Gerhart .02 .10
35 Jim Gott .02 .10
36 Dan Gladden .02 .10
37 Mike Greenwell XRC .10 .30
38 Cecilio Guante .02 .10
39 Albert Hall .02 .10
40 Atlee Hammaker .02 .10
41 Mickey Hatcher .02 .10
42 Mike Heath .02 .10
43 Neal Heaton .02 .10
44 Mike Henneman XRC .10 .30
45 Guy Hoffman .02 .10
46 Charles Hudson .02 .10
47 Chuck Jackson .02 .10
48 Mike Jackson XRC .10 .30
49 Reggie Jackson .08 .25
50 Chris James .02 .10
51 Dion James .02 .10
52 Stan Javier .02 .10
53 Stan Jefferson .02 .10
54 Jimmy Jones .05 .15
55 Tracy Jones .02 .10
56 Terry Kennedy .02 .10
57 Mike Kingery .05 .15
58 Ray Knight .05 .15
59 Gene Larkin XRC .10 .30
60 Mike LaValliere .10 .30
61 Jack Lazorko .02 .10
62 Terry Leach .02 .10
63 Rick Leach .02 .10
64 Craig Lefferts .02 .10
65 Jim Lindeman .05 .15
66 Bill Long .02 .10
67 Mike Loynd XRC .05 .15
68 Greg Maddux XRC 6.00 15.00
69 Bill Madlock .05 .15
70 Dave Magadan .10 .30
71 Joe Magrane XRC .05 .15
72 Fred Manrique .02 .10
73 Mike Mason .02 .10
74 Lloyd McClendon XRC .10 .30
75 Fred McGriff .40 1.00
76 Mark McGwire 2.50 6.00
77 Mark McLemore .05 .15
78 Kevin McReynolds .02 .10
79 Dave Meads .02 .10
80 Greg Minton .02 .10
81 John Mitchell XRC .05 .15
82 Kevin Mitchell .08 .25
83 John Morris .02 .10
84 Jeff Musselman .02 .10
85 Randy Myers XRC .30 .75
86 Gene Nelson .02 .10
87 Joe Niekro .02 .10
88 Tom Nieto .02 .10
89 Reid Nichols .02 .10
90 Matt Nokes XRC .10 .30
91 Dickie Noles .02 .10
92 Edwin Nunez .02 .10
93 Jose Nunez XRC .02 .10
94 Paul O'Neill .15 .40
95 Jim Paciorek .02 .10
96 Lance Parrish .05 .15
97 Bill Pecota XRC .05 .15
98 Tony Pena .02 .10
99 Luis Polonia XRC .10 .30
100 Randy Ready .02 .10
101 Jeff Reardon .05 .15
102 Gary Redus .02 .10
103 Rick Rhoden .02 .10
104 Wally Ritchie .02 .10
105 Jeff M. Robinson UER/(Wrong Jeff's.02 .10
stats on back
106 Mark Salas .02 .10
107 Dave Schmidt .02 .10
108 Kevin Seitzer UER .10 .30
109 John Shelby .02 .10
110 John Smiley XRC .10 .30
111 Lary Sorensen .02 .10
112 Chris Speier .02 .10
113 Randy St.Claire .02 .10
114 Jim Sundberg .05 .15
115 B.J. Surhoff XRC .30 .75
116 Greg Swindell .10 .30
117 Danny Tartabull .02 .10
118 Dorn Taylor .02 .10
119 Lee Tunnell .02 .10
120 Ed VandeBerg .02 .10
121 Andy Van Slyke .08 .25
122 Gary Ward .02 .10
123 Devon White .30 .75
124 Alan Wiggins .02 .10
125 Bill Wilkinson .02 .10
126 Jim Winn .02 .10
127 Frank Williams .02 .10
128 Ken Williams .02 .10
129 Matt Williams XRC .60 1.50
130 Herm Winningham .02 .10
131 Matt Young .02 .10
132 Checklist 1-132 .02 .10

1987 Fleer Update Glossy

COMP.FACT.SET (132) 6.00 15.00
*STARS: .4X TO 1X BASIC CARDS
*ROOKIES: .4X TO 1X BASIC CARDS
DISTRIBUTED ONLY IN FACTORY SET FORM

1987 Fleer Award Winners

This small set of 44 standard-size cards was produced for 7-Eleven stores by Fleer. The cards feature full color fronts and yellow, white, and black backs. The card fronts are distinguished by their yellow frame around the player's full-color photo. The box for the cards describes the set as the "1987 Limited Edition Baseball's Award Winners." The checklist for the set is given on the back of the set box. The card numbering is in alphabetical order by player's name.

COMP.FACT SET (44) 2.00 5.00
1 Marty Barrett .01 .05
2 George Bell .01 .05
3 Bert Blyleven .02 .10
4 Bob Boone .02 .10
5 John Candelaria .01 .05
6 Jose Canseco .20 .50
7 Gary Carter .05 .15
8 Joe Carter .07 .20
9 Roger Clemens .30 .75
10 Cecil Cooper .02 .10
11 Eric Davis .05 .15
12 Tony Fernandez .02 .10
13 Scott Fletcher .01 .05
14 Bob Forsch .01 .05
15 Dwight Gooden .05 .15
16 Ron Guidry .02 .10
17 Ozzie Guillen .02 .10
18 Bill Gullickson .01 .05
19 Tony Gwynn .30 .75
20 Bob Knepper .01 .05
21 Ray Knight .01 .05
22 Mark Langston .01 .05
23 Candy Maldonado .01 .05
24 Don Mattingly .30 .75
25 Roger McDowell .01 .05
26 Dale Murphy .07 .20
27 Dave Parker .02 .10
28 Lance Parrish .02 .10
29 Gary Pettis .01 .05
30 Kirby Puckett .20 .50
31 Johnny Ray .01 .05
32 Dave Righetti .01 .05
33 Cal Ripken .60 1.50
34 Bret Saberhagen .02 .10
35 Ryne Sandberg .20 .50
36 Mike Schmidt .20 .50
37 Mike Scott .01 .05
38 Ozzie Smith .30 .75
39 Robby Thompson .02 .10
40 Fernando Valenzuela .02 .10

41 Mitch Webster UER/(Mike on front) .01 .05
42 Frank White .02 .10
43 Mike Witt .01 .05
44 Todd Worrell .02 .10

1987 Fleer Baseball All-Stars

This small set of 44 standard-size cards was produced for Ben Franklin stores by Fleer. The cards feature full color fronts and red, white, and blue backs. The card fronts are easily distinguished by their white vertical stripes over a bright red background. The box for the cards proclaims "Limited Edition Baseball All-Stars" and is styled in the same manner and color scheme as the cards themselves. The checklist for the set is given on the back of the set box. The card numbering is in alphabetical order by player's name.

COMP. FACT. SET (44) 2.50 6.00
1 Harold Baines .05 .15
2 Jesse Barfield .01 .05
3 Wade Boggs .20 .50
4 Dennis Boyd .01 .05
5 Scott Bradley .01 .05
6 Jose Canseco .20 .50
7 Gary Carter .15 .40
8 Joe Carter .07 .20
9 Mark Clear .01 .05
10 Roger Clemens .30 .75
11 Jose Cruz .02 .10
12 Chili Davis .05 .15
13 Jody Davis .01 .05
14 Rob Deer .01 .05
15 Brian Downing .01 .05
16 Sid Fernandez .01 .05
17 John Franco .02 .10
18 Andres Galarraga .15 .40
19 Dwight Gooden .05 .15
20 Tony Gwynn .30 .75
21 Charlie Hough .01 .05
22 Bruce Hurst .01 .05
23 Wally Joyner .07 .20
24 Carney Lansford .02 .10
25 Fred Lynn .02 .10
26 Don Mattingly .30 .75
27 Willie McGee .02 .10
28 Jack Morris .02 .10
29 Dale Murphy .07 .20
30 Bob Ojeda .01 .05
31 Tony Pena .02 .10
32 Kirby Puckett .20 .50
33 Dan Quisenberry .01 .05
34 Tim Raines .02 .10
35 Willie Randolph .02 .10
36 Cal Ripken .60 1.50
37 Pete Rose .20 .50
38 Nolan Ryan .60 1.50
39 Juan Samuel .01 .05
40 Mike Schmidt .20 .50
41 Ozzie Smith .30 .75
42 Andres Thomas .01 .05
43 Fernando Valenzuela .02 .10
44 Mike Witt .01 .05

1987 Fleer Exciting Stars

This small 44-card boxed standard-size set was produced by Fleer for distribution by the Cumberland Farm stores. The cards feature full color fronts. The set is titled "Baseball's Exciting Stars." Each individual boxed set includes the 44 cards and six logo stickers. The checklist for the set is found on the back panel of the box. The card numbering is in alphabetical order by player's name.

COMP.FACT SET (44) 2.00 5.00
1 Don Aase .01 .05
2 Rick Aguilera .02 .10
3 Jesse Barfield .01 .05
4 Wade Boggs .15 .40
5 Oil Can Boyd .01 .05
6 Sid Bream .01 .05
7 Jose Canseco .20 .50
8 Steve Carlton .15 .40
9 Gary Carter .15 .40
10 Will Clark .30 .75
11 Roger Clemens .30 .75
12 Danny Cox .01 .05
13 Alvin Davis .01 .05
14 Eric Davis .05 .15
15 Rob Deer .01 .05
16 Brian Downing .01 .05
17 Gene Garber .01 .05
18 Steve Garvey .05 .15
19 Dwight Gooden .05 .15
20 Mark Gubicza .01 .05
21 Mel Hall .01 .05
22 Terry Harper .01 .05
23 Von Hayes .01 .05
24 Rickey Henderson .25 .60
25 Tom Henke .01 .05
26 Willie Hernandez .01 .05
27 Ted Higuera .01 .05
28 Rick Honeycutt .01 .05
29 Kent Hrbek .02 .10
30 Wally Joyner .07 .20
31 Charlie Kerfeld .01 .05
32 Fred Lynn .02 .10
33 Don Mattingly .30 .75
34 Tim Raines .02 .10
35 Dennis Rasmussen .01 .05
36 Johnny Ray .01 .05
37 Jim Rice .02 .10
38 Pete Rose .20 .50
39 Lee Smith .05 .15
40 Cory Snyder .01 .05
41 Darryl Strawberry .02 .10
42 Kent Tekulve .01 .05
43 Willie Wilson .02 .10
44 Bobby Witt .01 .05

1987 Fleer Game Winners

This small 44-card boxed standard-size set was produced by Fleer for distribution by several store chains, including Bi-Mart, Pay'n'Save, Mott's, M.E.Moses, and Winn's. The cards feature full color fronts. The set is titled "Baseball's Game Winners." Each individual boxed set includes the 44 cards and six logo stickers. The checklist for the set is found on the back panel of the box. The card numbering is in alphabetical order by player's name.

COMP.FACT SET (44) 2.50 6.00
1 Harold Baines .05 .15
2 Don Baylor .02 .10
3 George Bell .01 .05
4 Tony Bernazard .01 .05
5 Wade Boggs .20 .50
6 George Brett .30 .75
7 Hubie Brooks .01 .05
8 Jose Canseco .30 .75
9 Gary Carter .15 .40
10 Roger Clemens .30 .75
11 Eric Davis .02 .10
12 Glenn Davis .01 .05
13 Shawon Dunston .01 .05
14 Mark Eichhorn .01 .05
15 Gary Gaetti .02 .10
16 Steve Garvey .05 .15
17 Kirk Gibson .02 .10
18 Dwight Gooden .05 .15
19 Von Hayes .01 .05
20 Willie Hernandez .01 .05
21 Ted Higuera .01 .05
22 Wally Joyner .07 .20
23 Bob Knepper .01 .05
24 Mike Krukow .01 .05
25 Jeff Leonard .01 .05
26 Don Mattingly .30 .75
27 Kirk McCaskill .01 .05
28 Kevin McReynolds .01 .05
29 Jim Morrison .01 .05
30 Dale Murphy .07 .20
31 Pete O'Brien .01 .05
32 Bob Ojeda .01 .05
33 Larry Parrish .01 .05
34 Ken Phelps .01 .05
35 Dennis Rasmussen .01 .05
36 Ernest Riles .01 .05
37 Cal Ripken .60 1.50
38 Ron Robinson .01 .05
39 Steve Sax .01 .05
40 Mike Schmidt .20 .50
41 John Tudor .01 .05
42 Fernando Valenzuela .02 .10
43 Mike Witt .01 .05
44 Curt Young .01 .05

1987 Fleer Hottest Stars

COMP.FACT.SET (44) 10.00 25.00
DISTRIBUTED IN FACTORY SET FORM
FACTORY SET PRICE IS FOR SEALED SETS
1 Joaquin Andujar .02 .10
2 Harold Baines .05 .15
3 Kevin Bass .02 .10
4 Don Baylor .05 .15
5 Barry Bonds 10.00 25.00
6 George Brett .40 1.00
7 Tom Brunansky .02 .10
8 Brett Butler .05 .15
9 Jose Canseco .40 1.00
10 Roger Clemens 1.25 3.00
11 Ron Darling .02 .10
12 Eric Davis .08 .25
13 Andre Dawson .05 .15
14 Doug DeCinces .02 .10
15 Leon Durham .02 .10
16 Mark Eichhorn .02 .10
17 Scott Garrelts .02 .10
18 Dwight Gooden .08 .25
19 Dave Henderson .02 .10
20 Rickey Henderson .15 .40
21 Keith Hernandez .05 .15
22 Ted Higuera .02 .10
23 Bob Horner .05 .15
24 Pete Incaviglia .05 .15
25 Wally Joyner .08 .25
26 Mark Langston .02 .10
27 Don Mattingly UER .50 1.25
28 Dale Murphy .08 .25
29 Kirk McCaskill .02 .10
30 Willie McGee .05 .15
31 Dave Righetti .05 .15
32 Pete Rose .50 1.25
33 Bruce Ruffin .02 .10
34 Steve Sax .02 .10
35 Mike Schmidt .40 1.00
36 Larry Sheets .02 .10
37 Eric Show .02 .10
38 Dave Smith .02 .10
39 Cory Snyder .02 .10
40 Frank Tanana .05 .15
41 Alan Trammell .05 .15
42 Reggie Williams .02 .10
43 Mookie Wilson .05 .15
44 Todd Worrell .05 .15

1987 Fleer League Leaders

This small set of 44 standard-size cards was produced for Walgreens by Fleer. The cards feature full color fronts and red, white, and blue backs. The card fronts are easily distinguished by their light blue vertical stripes over a white background. The box for the cards proclaims a "Walgreens Exclusive" and is styled in the same manner and color scheme as the cards themselves. The checklist for the set is given on the back of the set box. The card numbering is in alphabetical order by player's name.

COMP.FACT SET (44) 2.50 6.00
1 Jesse Barfield .01 .05
2 Mike Boddicker .01 .05
3 Wade Boggs .20 .50
4 Phil Bradley .01 .05
5 George Brett .30 .75
6 Hubie Brooks .01 .05
7 Chris Brown .01 .05
8 Jose Canseco .30 .75
9 Joe Carter .07 .20
10 Roger Clemens .30 .75
11 Vince Coleman .01 .05
12 Joe Cowley .01 .05
13 Kal Daniels .01 .05
14 Glenn Davis .01 .05
15 Jody Davis .01 .05
16 Darrell Evans .02 .10
17 Dwight Evans .02 .10
18 John Franco .02 .10
19 Julio Franco .02 .10
20 Dwight Gooden .05 .15
21 Rich Gossage .02 .10
22 Tom Herr .01 .05
23 Ted Higuera .01 .05
24 Bob Horner .01 .05
25 Pete Incaviglia .02 .10
26 Wally Joyner .07 .20
27 Dave Kingman .02 .10
28 Don Mattingly .30 .75
29 Willie McGee .02 .10
30 Donnie Moore .01 .05
31 Keith Moreland .01 .05
32 Eddie Murray .20 .50
33 Mike Pagliarulo .01 .05
34 Larry Parrish .01 .05
35 Tony Pena .02 .10
36 Kirby Puckett .20 .50
37 Pete Rose .20 .50
38 Juan Samuel .01 .05
39 Ryne Sandberg .30 .75
40 Mike Schmidt .20 .50
41 Darryl Strawberry .02 .10
42 Greg Walker .01 .05
43 Bob Welch .01 .05
44 Todd Worrell .01 .05

1987 Fleer Limited Edition

This 44-card boxed standard-size set was (mass) produced by Fleer for distribution by McCrory's and is sometimes referred to as the McCrory's set. The numerical checklist on the back of the box shows that the set is numbered alphabetically.

COMP.FACT SET (44) 2.00 5.00
1 Floyd Bannister .01 .05
2 Marty Barrett .01 .05
3 Steve Bedrosian .01 .05
4 George Bell .01 .05
5 George Brett .30 .75
6 Jose Canseco .20 .50
7 Joe Carter .07 .20
8 Will Clark .40 1.00
9 Roger Clemens .20 .50
10 Vince Coleman .01 .05
11 Glenn Davis .01 .05
12 Mike Davis .01 .05
13 Len Dykstra .05 .15
14 John Franco .02 .10
15 Julio Franco .02 .10
16 Steve Garvey .05 .15
17 Kirk Gibson .02 .10
18 Dwight Gooden .05 .15
19 Tony Gwynn .30 .75
20 Keith Hernandez .02 .10
21 Teddy Higuera .01 .05
22 Kent Hrbek .02 .10
23 Wally Joyner .07 .20
24 Mike Krukow .01 .05
25 Mike Marshall .01 .05
26 Don Mattingly .30 .75
27 Oddibe McDowell .01 .05
28 Jack Morris .02 .10
29 Lloyd Moseby .01 .05
30 Dale Murphy .07 .20
31 Eddie Murray .20 .50
32 Tony Pena .02 .10
33 Jim Presley .01 .05
34 Jeff Reardon .02 .10
35 Jim Rice .02 .10
36 Pete Rose .20 .50
37 Mike Schmidt .20 .50
38 Mike Scott .01 .05
39 Lee Smith .05 .15
40 Lonnie Smith .01 .05
41 Gary Ward .01 .05
42 Dave Winfield .15 .40
43 Todd Worrell .02 .10
44 Robin Yount .15 .40

1987 Fleer Limited Box Cards

The cards in this six-card set each measure the standard size. Cards have essentially the same design as the 1987 Fleer Limited Edition cards which were distributed by McCrory's. The cards were printed on the bottom of the counter display box which held 24 small boxed sets; hence theoretically these box cards are 1/24 as plentiful as the regular boxed set cards. These six cards, numbered C1 to C6, are considered a separate set in their own right and are not typically included in a complete set of the 1987 Fleer Limited Edition set of 44. The value of the panels uncut is slightly greater, perhaps by 25 percent greater, than the value of the individual cards cut up carefully.

COMPLETE SET (6) .75 2.00
C1 Ron Darling .08 .25
C2 Bill Buckner .20 .50
C3 John Candelaria .08 .25
C4 Jack Clark .20 .50
C5 Bret Saberhagen .20 .50
C6 Houston Astros .08 .25

1987 Fleer Mini

The 1987 Fleer "Classic Miniatures" set consists of 120 small cards with all new pictures of the players as compared to the 1987 Fleer regular issue. The cards are only 1 13/16" by 2 9/16", making them one of the smallest cards issued in the 1980's. Card backs provide career year-by-year statistics. The complete set was distributed in a blue, red, white, and silver factory box along with 18 logo stickers. The card numbering is by alphabetical order.

COMP.FACT SET (120) 2.50 6.00
1 Don Aase .01 .05
2 Joaquin Andujar .01 .05
3 Harold Baines .05 .15
4 Jesse Barfield .01 .05
5 Kevin Bass .01 .05
6 Don Baylor .02 .10
7 George Bell .01 .05
8 Tony Bernazard .01 .05
9 Bert Blyleven .02 .10
10 Wade Boggs .15 .40
11 Phil Bradley .01 .05
12 Sid Bream .01 .05
13 George Brett .30 .75
14 Hubie Brooks .01 .05
15 Chris Brown .01 .05
16 Tom Candiotti .01 .05
17 Jose Canseco .20 .50
18 Gary Carter .05 .15
19 Joe Carter .07 .20
20 Roger Clemens .30 .75
21 Vince Coleman .01 .05
22 Cecil Cooper .02 .10
23 Ron Darling .01 .05
24 Alvin Davis .01 .05
25 Chili Davis .05 .15
26 Eric Davis .02 .10
27 Glenn Davis .01 .05
28 Mike Davis .01 .05
29 Doug DeCinces .01 .05
30 Rob Deer .01 .05
31 Jim Deshaies .01 .05
32 Bo Diaz .01 .05
33 Richard Dotson .01 .05
34 Brian Downing .01 .05
35 Shawon Dunston .01 .05
36 Mark Eichhorn .01 .05
37 Dwight Evans .02 .10
38 Tony Fernandez .02 .10
39 Julio Franco .02 .10
40 Gary Gaetti .02 .10
41 Andres Galarraga .15 .40
42 Scott Garrelts .01 .05
43 Steve Garvey .05 .15
44 Kirk Gibson .02 .10
45 Dwight Gooden .05 .15
46 Ken Griffey Sr. .02 .10
47 Mark Gubicza .01 .05
48 Ozzie Guillen .02 .10
49 Bill Gullickson .01 .05
50 Tony Gwynn .30 .75
51 Von Hayes .01 .05
52 Rickey Henderson .30 .75
53 Keith Hernandez .02 .10
54 Willie Hernandez .01 .05
55 Ted Higuera .01 .05
56 Charlie Hough .01 .05
57 Kent Hrbek .02 .10
58 Pete Incaviglia .02 .10
59 Wally Joyner .10 .30
60 Bob Knepper .01 .05
61 Mike Krukow .01 .05
62 Mark Langston .01 .05
63 Carney Lansford .02 .10
64 Jim Lindeman .01 .05
65 Bill Madlock .02 .10
66 Don Mattingly .30 .75
67 Kirk McCaskill .01 .05
68 Lance McCullers .01 .05
69 Keith Moreland .01 .05
70 Jack Morris .02 .10
71 Jim Morrison .01 .05
72 Lloyd Moseby .01 .05
73 Jerry Mumphrey .01 .05
74 Dale Murphy .07 .20
75 Eddie Murray .20 .50
76 Pete O'Brien .01 .05
77 Bob Ojeda .01 .05
78 Jesse Orosco .02 .10
79 Dan Pasqua .01 .05
80 Dave Parker .02 .10
81 Larry Parrish .01 .05
82 Jim Presley .01 .05
83 Kirby Puckett .20 .50
84 Dan Quisenberry .01 .05
85 Tim Raines .02 .10
86 Dennis Rasmussen .01 .05
87 Johnny Ray .01 .05
88 Jeff Reardon .02 .10
89 Jim Rice .02 .10
90 Dave Righetti .01 .05
91 Earnest Riles .01 .05
92 Cal Ripken .60 1.50
93 Ron Robinson .01 .05
94 Juan Samuel .01 .05
95 Ryne Sandberg .25 .60
96 Steve Sax .01 .05
97 Mike Schmidt .15 .40
98 Ken Schrom .01 .05
99 Mike Scott .01 .05
100 Ruben Sierra .15 .40
101 Lee Smith .05 .15
102 Ozzie Smith .30 .75
103 Cory Snyder .01 .05
104 Kent Tekulve .01 .05
105 Andres Thomas .01 .05
106 Robby Thompson .02 .10
107 Alan Trammell .05 .15
108 John Tudor .01 .05
109 Fernando Valenzuela .02 .10
110 Greg Walker .01 .05
111 Mitch Webster .01 .05
112 Lou Whitaker .02 .10
113 Frank White .02 .10
114 Reggie Williams .01 .05
115 Glenn Wilson .01 .05
116 Willie Wilson .02 .10
117 Dave Winfield .20 .50
118 Mike Witt .01 .05
119 Todd Worrell .02 .10
120 Floyd Youmans .01 .05

1987 Fleer Record Setters

This 44-card boxed standard-size set was produced by Fleer for distribution by Eckerd's Drug Stores and is sometimes referred to as the Eckerd's set. Six team logo stickers are included in the box with the complete set. The numerical checklist on the back of the box shows that the set is numbered alphabetically.

COMP.FACT SET (44) 2.00 5.00
1 George Brett .20 .50
2 Chris Brown .01 .05
3 Jose Canseco UER/(3 of 444 on back) .20 .50
4 Roger Clemens .20 .50
5 Alvin Davis UER/(5 of 441 on back, upside down o .01 .05
6 Shawon Dunston .01 .05
7 Tony Fernandez .02 .10
8 Carlton Fisk UER/(8 of 44' on back) .15 .40
9 Gary Gaetti UER/(9 of 444 on back) .02 .10
10 Gene Garber .01 .05
11 Rich Gedman .01 .05
12 Dwight Gooden .05 .15
13 Ozzie Guillen .02 .10
14 Bill Gullickson .01 .05
15 Billy Hatcher .01 .05
16 Orel Hershiser .02 .10
17 Wally Joyner .10 .30
18 Ray Knight .01 .05
19 Craig Lefferts .01 .05
20 Don Mattingly .30 .75
21 Kevin Mitchell .05 .15
22 Lloyd Moseby .01 .05
23 Dale Murphy .07 .20
24 Eddie Murray .15 .40
25 Phil Niekro .10 .30
26 Ben Oglivie .01 .05
27 Jesse Orosco .02 .10
28 Joe Orsulak .01 .05
29 Larry Parrish .01 .05
30 Tim Raines .02 .10
31 Shane Rawley .01 .05
32 Dave Righetti .01 .05
33 Pete Rose .20 .50
34 Steve Sax .01 .05
35 Mike Schmidt .20 .50
36 Mike Scott .01 .05
37 Don Sutton .10 .30
38 Alan Trammell .05 .15
39 John Tudor .01 .05
40 Gary Ward .01 .05
41 Lou Whitaker .02 .10
42 Willie Wilson .02 .10
43 Todd Worrell .02 .10
44 Floyd Youmans .01 .05

1987 Fleer Sluggers/Pitchers

Fleer produced this 44-card boxed standard-size set although it was primarily distributed by McCrory, McLellan, Newberry, H.L.Green, T.G.Y., and other similar stores. The set features 28 sluggers and 16 pitchers and is subtitled "Baseball's Best". The set was packaged in a red, white, blue, and yellow custom box along with six logo stickers. The set checklist is given on the back of the box. The checklist on the back of the set box misspells McGwire as McGuire. The card numbering is in alphabetical order by player's name.

COMP.FACT. SET (44) 4.00 10.00
1 Kevin Bass .01 .05
2 Jesse Barfield .01 .05
3 George Bell .01 .05
4 Wade Boggs .20 .50
5 Sid Bream .01 .05
6 George Brett .30 .75
7 Ivan Calderon .01 .05
8 Jose Canseco .20 .50
9 Jack Clark .02 .10
10 Roger Clemens .40 1.00
11 Eric Davis .02 .10
12 Andre Dawson .08 .25
13 Sid Fernandez .01 .05
14 John Franco .02 .10
15 Dwight Gooden .05 .15
16 Pedro Guerrero .01 .05
17 Tony Gwynn .30 .75
18 Rickey Henderson .30 .75
19 Tom Henke .01 .05
20 Ted Higuera .01 .05
21 Pete Incaviglia .02 .10
22 Wally Joyner .10 .30
23 Jeff Leonard .01 .05
24 Joe Magrane .01 .05
25 Don Mattingly .30 .75
26 Mark McGwire 1.25 3.00
27 Jack Morris .02 .10
28 Dale Murphy .08 .25
29 Dave Parker .02 .10
30 Ken Phelps .01 .05
31 Kirby Puckett .20 .50
32 Tim Raines .02 .10
33 Jeff Reardon .02 .10
34 Dave Righetti .01 .05
35 Cal Ripken .75 2.00
36 Bret Saberhagen .02 .10
37 Mike Schmidt .20 .50
38 Mike Scott .01 .05
39 Kevin Seitzer .08 .25
40 Darryl Strawberry .02 .10
41 Rick Sutcliffe .01 .05
42 Pat Tabler .01 .05
43 Fernando Valenzuela .02 .10
44 Mike Witt .01 .05

1987 Fleer Sluggers/Pitchers Box Cards

COMPLETE SET (6) 8.00 20.00
M1 Steve Bedrosian .40 1.00
M2 Will Clark 4.00 10.00
M3 Vince Coleman .40 1.00
M4 Bo Jackson 4.00 10.00
M5 Cory Snyder .40 1.00
NNO Team Logo/(Blank back) .40 1.00

1987 Fleer Star Stickers

These Star Stickers were distributed as a separate issue by Fleer with five star stickers and a logo sticker in each wax pack. The 132-card (sticker) set features 2 1/2" by 3 1/2" full-color fronts and even statistics on the sticker back, which is an indication that the Fleer Company understands that these stickers are rarely used as stickers but more like traditional cards. The fronts are surrounded by a green border and the backs are printed in green and yellow on white card stock. The numbering is in alphabetical order by player's name.

COMPLETE SET (132) 6.00 15.00
1 Don Aase .01 .05
2 Harold Baines .07 .20
3 Floyd Bannister .01 .05
4 Jesse Barfield .01 .05
5 Marty Barrett .01 .05
6 Kevin Bass .01 .05
7 Don Baylor .02 .10
8 Steve Bedrosian .01 .05
9 George Bell .01 .05
10 Bert Blyleven .02 .10
11 Mike Boddicker .01 .05
12 Wade Boggs .15 .40
13 Phil Bradley .01 .05
14 Sid Bream .01 .05
15 George Brett .50 1.25
16 Hubie Brooks .01 .05
17 Tom Brunansky .01 .05
18 Tom Candiotti .01 .05
19 Jose Canseco .30 .75
20 Gary Carter .15 .40
21 Joe Carter .10 .30
22 Will Clark .50 1.25
23 Mark Clear .01 .05
24 Roger Clemens .40 1.00
25 Vince Coleman .01 .05
26 Jose Cruz .02 .10
27 Ron Darling .01 .05
28 Alvin Davis .01 .05
29 Chili Davis .07 .20
30 Eric Davis .07 .20
31 Glenn Davis .01 .05
32 Mike Davis .01 .05
33 Andre Dawson .10 .30
34 Doug DeCinces .01 .05
35 Brian Downing .01 .05
36 Shawon Dunston .01 .05
37 Mark Eichhorn .01 .05
38 Dwight Evans .02 .10
39 Tony Fernandez .02 .10
40 Bob Forsch .01 .05
41 John Franco .02 .10
42 Julio Franco .02 .10
43 Gary Gaetti .02 .10
44 Gene Garber .01 .05
45 Scott Garrelts .01 .05
46 Steve Garvey .07 .20
47 Kirk Gibson .02 .10
48 Dwight Gooden .07 .20
49 Ken Griffey Sr. .02 .10
50 Ozzie Guillen .02 .10
51 Bill Gullickson .01 .05
52 Tony Gwynn .50 1.25
53 Mel Hall .01 .05
54 Greg A. Harris .01 .05
55 Von Hayes .01 .05
56 Rickey Henderson .30 .75
57 Tom Henke .01 .05
58 Keith Hernandez .02 .10
59 Willie Hernandez .01 .05
60 Ted Higuera .01 .05
61 Bob Horner .01 .05
62 Charlie Hough .01 .05
63 Jay Howell .01 .05
64 Kent Hrbek .02 .10
65 Bruce Hurst .01 .05
66 Pete Incaviglia .02 .10
67 Bob James .01 .05
68 Wally Joyner .15 .40
69 Mike Krukow .01 .05
70 Mark Langston .01 .05
71 Carney Lansford .02 .10
72 Fred Lynn .02 .10
73 Bill Madlock .02 .10
74 Don Mattingly .50 1.25
75 Kirk McCaskill .01 .05
76 Lance McCullers .01 .05
77 Oddibe McDowell .01 .05
78 Paul Molitor .20 .50
79 Keith Moreland .01 .05
80 Jack Morris .02 .10
81 Jim Morrison .01 .05
82 Jerry Mumphrey .01 .05
83 Dale Murphy .10 .30
84 Eddie Murray .20 .50
85 Ben Oglivie .01 .05
86 Bob Ojeda .01 .05
87 Jesse Orosco .02 .10
88 Dave Parker .02 .10
89 Larry Parrish .01 .05
90 Tony Pena .02 .10
91 Jim Presley .01 .05
92 Kirby Puckett .20 .50
93 Dan Quisenberry .01 .05
94 Tim Raines .02 .10
95 Dennis Rasmussen .01 .05
96 Shane Rawley .01 .05
97 Johnny Ray .01 .05
98 Jeff Reardon .02 .10
99 Jim Rice .02 .10
100 Dave Righetti .01 .05
101 Cal Ripken 1.00 2.50
102 Pete Rose .40 1.00
103 Nolan Ryan 1.00 2.50
104 Juan Samuel .01 .05
105 Ryne Sandberg .40 1.00
106 Steve Sax .01 .05
107 Mike Schmidt .20 .50
108 Mike Scott .01 .05
109 Dave Smith .01 .05
110 Lee Smith .07 .20
111 Lonnie Smith .01 .05
112 Ozzie Smith .40 1.00
113 Cory Snyder .01 .05
114 Darryl Strawberry .02 .10
115 Don Sutton .20 .50
116 Kent Tekulve .01 .05
117 Andres Thomas .01 .05
118 Alan Trammell .07 .20
119 John Tudor .01 .05
120 Fernando Valenzuela .02 .10
121 Bob Welch .02 .10
122 Lou Whitaker .02 .10
123 Frank White .02 .10
124 Reggie Williams .01 .05
125 Willie Wilson .02 .10
126 Dave Winfield .15 .40
127 Mike Witt .01 .05
128 Todd Worrell .02 .10
129 Curt Young .01 .05
130 Robin Yount .15 .40
131 Jose Canseco CL .30 .75
Don Mattingly
132 Bo Jackson CL .15 .40
Eric Davis

1987 Fleer Stickers Wax Box Cards

COMPLETE SET (8) 2.50 6.00
S1 Detroit Logo .02 .10
S2 Wade Boggs .60 1.50
S3 Bert Blyleven .08 .25
S4 Jose Cruz .08 .25
S5 Glenn Davis .02 .10
S6 Phillies Logo .02 .10
S7 Bob Horner .02 .10
S8 Don Mattingly 1.50 4.00

1988 Fleer

This set consists of 660 standard-size cards. Cards were primarily issued in 15-card wax packs and hobby and retail factory sets. Each wax pack contained one of 26 different "Stadium Card" stickers. Card fronts feature a distinctive white background with red and blue diagonal stripes across the card. As in years past cards are organized numerically by teams and team order is based upon the previous season's record. Subsets include Specials (622-640), Rookie Pairs (641-653), and checklists (654-660). Rookie Cards in this set include Jay Bell, Ellis Burks, Ken Caminiti, Ron Gant, Tom Glavine, Mark Grace, Edgar Martinez, Jack McDowell and Matt Williams.

COMPLETE SET (660) 6.00 15.00
COMP.RETAIL SET (660) 6.00 15.00
COMP.HOBBY SET (672) 6.00 15.00
1 Keith Atherton .02 .10
2 Don Baylor .05 .15
3 Juan Berenguer .02 .10
4 Bert Blyleven .05 .15
5 Tom Brunansky .02 .10
6 Randy Bush .02 .10
7 Steve Carlton .05 .15
8 Mark Davidson .02 .10
9 George Frazier .02 .10
10 Gary Gaetti .05 .15
11 Greg Gagne .02 .10
12 Dan Gladden .02 .10
13 Kent Hrbek .05 .15
14 Gene Larkin RC .15 .40
15 Tim Laudner .02 .10
16 Steve Lombardozzi .02 .10
17 Al Newman .02 .10
18 Joe Niekro .02 .10
19 Kirby Puckett .10 .30
20 Jeff Reardon .05 .15
21A Dan Schatzeder ERR .05 .15
21B Dan Schatzeder COR .02 .10
22 Roy Smalley .02 .10
23 Mike Smithson .02 .10
24 Les Straker .02 .10
25 Frank Viola .05 .15
26 Jack Clark .05 .15
27 Vince Coleman .02 .10
28 Danny Cox .02 .10
29 Bill Dawley .02 .10
30 Ken Dayley .02 .10
31 Doug DeCinces .02 .10
32 Curt Ford .02 .10
33 Bob Forsch .02 .10
34 David Green .02 .10
35 Tom Herr .02 .10
36 Ricky Horton .02 .10
37 Lance Johnson RC .15 .40
38 Steve Lake .02 .10
39 Jim Lindeman .02 .10
40 Joe Magrane RC .15 .40
41 Greg Mathews .02 .10
42 Willie McGee .05 .15
43 John Morris .02 .10
44 Jose Oquendo .02 .10
45 Tony Pena .02 .10
46 Terry Pendleton .05 .15
47 Ozzie Smith .20 .50
48 John Tudor .05 .15
49 Lee Tunnell .02 .10
50 Todd Worrell .02 .10
51 Doyle Alexander .02 .10
52 Dave Bergman .02 .10
53 Tom Brookens .02 .10
54 Darrell Evans .05 .15
55 Kirk Gibson .10 .30
56 Mike Heath .02 .10
57 Mike Henneman RC .15 .40
58 Willie Hernandez .02 .10
59 Larry Herndon .02 .10
60 Eric King .02 .10
61 Chet Lemon .05 .15
62 Scott Lusader .02 .10
63 Bill Madlock .05 .15
64 Jack Morris .05 .15
65 Jim Morrison .02 .10
66 Matt Nokes RC .15 .40
67 Dan Petry .02 .10
68A Jeff M. Robinson .07 .20
ERR, Stats for Jeff D. Robinson
on card back
Born 12-13-60
68B Jeff M. Robinson .02 .10
COR, Born 12-14-61
69 Pat Sheridan .02 .10
70 Nate Snell .02 .10
71 Frank Tanana .05 .15
72 Walt Terrell .02 .10
73 Mark Thurmond .02 .10
74 Alan Trammell .05 .15
75 Lou Whitaker .05 .15
76 Mike Aldrete .02 .10
77 Bob Brenly .02 .10
78 Will Clark .10 .30
79 Chili Davis .05 .15
80 Kelly Downs .02 .10
81 Dave Dravecky .02 .10
82 Scott Garrelts .02 .10
83 Atlee Hammaker .02 .10
84 Dave Henderson .02 .10
85 Mike Krukow .02 .10
86 Mike LaCoss .02 .10
87 Craig Lefferts .02 .10
88 Jeff Leonard .02 .10
89 Candy Maldonado .02 .10

90 Eddie Milner .02 .10
91 Bob Melvin .02 .10
92 Kevin Mitchell .05 .15
93 Jon Perlman RC .02 .10
94 Rick Reuschel .05 .15
95 Don Robinson .02 .10
96 Chris Speier .02 .10
97 Harry Spilman .02 .10
98 Robby Thompson .02 .10
99 Jose Uribe .02 .10
100 Mark Wasinger .02 .10
101 Matt Williams RC .60 1.50
102 Jesse Barfield .05 .15
103 George Bell .05 .15
104 Juan Beniquez .02 .10
105 John Cerutti .02 .10
106 Jim Clancy .02 .10
107 Rob Ducey RC .02 .10
108 Mark Eichhorn .02 .10
109 Tony Fernandez .02 .10
110 Cecil Fielder .05 .15
111 Kelly Gruber .02 .10
112 Tom Henke .02 .10
113A Garth Iorg ERR .07 .20
Misspelled Iorq
on card front
113B Garth Iorg COR .02 .10
114 Jimmy Key .05 .15
115 Rick Leach .02 .10
116 Manny Lee .02 .10
117 Nelson Liriano RC .02 .10
118 Fred McGriff .10 .30
119 Lloyd Moseby .02 .10
120 Rance Mulliniks .02 .10
121 Jeff Musselman .02 .10
122 Jose Nunez .02 .10
123 Dave Stieb .05 .15
124 Willie Upshaw .02 .10
125 Duane Ward .02 .10
126 Ernie Whitt .02 .10
127 Rick Aguilera .02 .10
128 Wally Backman .02 .10
129 Mark Carreon RC .05 .15
130 Gary Carter .05 .15
131 David Cone .05 .15
132 Ron Darling .05 .15
133 Len Dykstra .05 .15
134 Sid Fernandez .02 .10
135 Dwight Gooden .05 .15
136 Keith Hernandez .05 .15
137 Gregg Jefferies RC .15 .40
138 Howard Johnson .05 .15
139 Terry Leach .02 .10
140 Barry Lyons .02 .10
141 Dave Magadan .02 .10
142 Roger McDowell .02 .10
143 Kevin McReynolds .02 .10
144 Keith A. Miller RC .15 .40
145 John Mitchell RC .05 .15
146 Randy Myers .05 .15
147 Bob Ojeda .02 .10
148 Jesse Orosco .02 .10
149 Rafael Santana .02 .10
150 Doug Sisk .02 .10
151 Darryl Strawberry .05 .15
152 Tim Teufel .02 .10
153 Gene Walter .02 .10
154 Mookie Wilson .05 .15
155 Jay Aldrich .02 .10
156 Chris Bosio .02 .10
157 Glenn Braggs .02 .10
158 Greg Brock .02 .10
159 Juan Castillo .02 .10
160 Mark Clear .02 .10
161 Cecil Cooper .05 .15
162 Chuck Crim .02 .10
163 Rob Deer .02 .10
164 Mike Felder .02 .10
165 Jim Gantner .02 .10
166 Ted Higuera .02 .10
167 Steve Kiefer .02 .10
168 Rick Manning .02 .10
169 Paul Molitor .05 .15
170 Juan Nieves .02 .10
171 Dan Plesac .02 .10
172 Earnest Riles .02 .10
173 Bill Schroeder .02 .10
174 Steve Stanicek .02 .10
175 B.J. Surhoff .05 .15
176 Dale Sveum .02 .10
177 Bill Wegman .02 .10
178 Robin Yount .20 .50
179 Hubie Brooks .02 .10
180 Tim Burke .02 .10
181 Casey Candaele .02 .10
182 Mike Fitzgerald .02 .10
183 Tom Foley .02 .10
184 Andres Galarraga .05 .15
185 Neal Heaton .02 .10
186 Wallace Johnson .02 .10
187 Vance Law .02 .10
188 Dennis Martinez .05 .15
189 Bob McClure .02 .10
190 Andy McGaffigan .02 .10
191 Reid Nichols .02 .10
192 Pascual Perez .02 .10
193 Tim Raines .05 .15
194 Jeff Reed .02 .10
195 Bob Sebra .02 .10
196 Bryn Smith .02 .10
197 Randy St.Claire .02 .10
198 Tim Wallach .02 .10
199 Mitch Webster .02 .10
200 Herm Winningham .02 .10
201 Floyd Youmans .02 .10
202 Brad Arnsberg .02 .10
203 Rick Cerone .02 .10
204 Pat Clements .02 .10
205 Henry Cotto .02 .10
206 Mike Easler .02 .10
207 Ron Guidry .05 .15
208 Bill Gullickson .02 .10
209 Rickey Henderson .10 .30
210 Charles Hudson .02 .10
211 Tommy John .05 .15
212 Roberto Kelly RC .15 .40

213 Ron Kittle .02 .10
214 Don Mattingly .40 1.00
215 Bobby Meacham .02 .10
216 Mike Pagliarulo .02 .10
217 Dan Pasqua .02 .10
218 Willie Randolph .05 .15
219 Rick Rhoden .02 .10
220 Dave Righetti .05 .15
221 Jerry Royster .02 .10
222 Tim Stoddard .02 .10
223 Wayne Tolleson .02 .10
224 Gary Ward .02 .10
225 Claudell Washington .02 .10
226 Dave Winfield .05 .15
227 Buddy Bell .05 .15
228 Tom Browning .02 .10
229 Dave Concepcion .05 .15
230 Kal Daniels .02 .10
231 Eric Davis .05 .15
232 Bo Diaz .02 .10
233 Nick Esasky .02 .10
Has a dollar sign
before '87 SB totals
234 John Franco .05 .15
235 Guy Hoffman .02 .10
236 Tom Hume .02 .10
237 Tracy Jones .02 .10
238 Bill Landrum .02 .10
239 Barry Larkin .07 .20
240 Terry McGriff .02 .10
241 Rob Murphy .02 .10
242 Ron Oester .02 .10
243 Dave Parker .05 .15
244 Pat Perry .02 .10
245 Ted Power .02 .10
246 Dennis Rasmussen .02 .10
247 Ron Robinson .02 .10
248 Kurt Stillwell .02 .10
249 Jeff Treadway RC .15 .40
250 Frank Williams .02 .10
251 Steve Balboni .02 .10
252 Bud Black .02 .10
253 Thad Bosley .02 .10
254 George Brett .30 .75
255 John Davis RC .02 .10
256 Steve Farr .02 .10
257 Gene Garber .02 .10
258 Jerry Don Gleaton .02 .10
259 Mark Gubicza .02 .10
260 Bo Jackson .10 .30
261 Danny Jackson .02 .10
262 Ross Jones .02 .10
263 Charlie Leibrandt .02 .10
264 Bill Pecota RC .05 .15
265 Melido Perez RC .15 .40
266 Jamie Quirk .02 .10
267 Dan Quisenberry .02 .10
268 Bret Saberhagen .05 .15
269 Angel Salazar .02 .10
270 Kevin Seitzer UER .05 .15
Wrong birth year
271 Danny Tartabull .02 .10
272 Gary Thurman RC .02 .10
273 Frank White .05 .15
274 Willie Wilson .05 .15
275 Tony Bernazard .02 .10
276 Jose Canseco .30 .75
277 Mike Davis .02 .10
278 Storm Davis .02 .10
279 Dennis Eckersley .07 .20
280 Alfredo Griffin .02 .10
281 Rick Honeycutt .02 .10
282 Jay Howell .02 .10
283 Reggie Jackson .07 .20
284 Dennis Lamp .02 .10
285 Carney Lansford .05 .15
286 Mark McGwire 1.00 2.50
287 Dwayne Murphy .02 .10
288 Gene Nelson .02 .10
289 Steve Ontiveros .02 .10
290 Tony Phillips .02 .10
291 Eric Plunk .02 .10
292 Luis Polonia RC .15 .40
293 Rick Rodriguez .02 .10
294 Terry Steinbach .05 .15
295 Dave Stewart .05 .15
296 Curt Young .02 .10
297 Luis Aguayo .02 .10
298 Steve Bedrosian .02 .10
299 Jeff Calhoun .02 .10
300 Don Carman .02 .10
301 Todd Frohwirth .02 .10
302 Greg Gross .02 .10
303 Kevin Gross .02 .10
304 Von Hayes .02 .10
305 Keith Hughes RC .02 .10
306 Mike Jackson RC .15 .40
307 Chris James .02 .10
308 Steve Jeltz .02 .10
309 Mike Maddux .02 .10
310 Lance Parrish .05 .15
311 Shane Rawley .02 .10
312 Wally Ritchie .02 .10
313 Bruce Ruffin .02 .10
314 Juan Samuel .02 .10
315 Mike Schmidt .30 .75
316 Rick Schu .02 .10
317 Jeff Stone .02 .10
318 Kent Tekulve .02 .10
319 Milt Thompson .02 .10
320 Glenn Wilson .02 .10
321 Rafael Belliard .02 .10
322 Barry Bonds 1.00 2.50
323 Bobby Bonilla UER .05 .15
Wrong birth year
324 Sid Bream .02 .10
325 John Cangelosi .02 .10
326 Mike Diaz .02 .10
327 Doug Drabek .02 .10
328 Mike Dunne .02 .10
329 Brian Fisher .02 .10
330 Brett Gideon .02 .10
331 Terry Harper .02 .10
332 Bob Kipper .02 .10
333 Mike LaValliere .02 .10
334 Jose Lind RC .15 .40

335 Junior Ortiz .02 .10
336 Vicente Palacios RC .02 .10
337 Bob Patterson .02 .10
338 Al Pedrique .02 .10
339 R.J. Reynolds .02 .10
340 John Smiley RC .15 .40
341 Andy Van Slyke UER .07 .20
Wrong batting and
throwing listed
342 Bob Walk .02 .10
343 Marty Barrett .02 .10
344 Todd Benzinger RC .15 .40
345 Wade Boggs .07 .20
346 Tom Bolton .02 .10
347 Oil Can Boyd .02 .10
348 Ellis Burks RC .20 .50
349 Roger Clemens .60 1.50
350 Steve Crawford .02 .10
351 Dwight Evans .07 .20
352 Wes Gardner .02 .10
353 Rich Gedman .02 .10
354 Mike Greenwell .02 .10
355 Sam Horn RC .05 .15
356 Bruce Hurst .02 .10
357 John Marzano .02 .10
358 Al Nipper .02 .10
359 Spike Owen .02 .10
360 Jody Reed RC .15 .40
361 Jim Rice .05 .15
362 Ed Romero .02 .10
363 Kevin Romine RC .02 .10
364 Joe Sambito .02 .10
365 Calvin Schiraldi .02 .10
366 Jeff Sellers .02 .10
367 Bob Stanley .02 .10
368 Scott Bankhead .02 .10
369 Phil Bradley .02 .10
370 Scott Bradley .02 .10
371 Mickey Brantley .02 .10
372 Mike Campbell RC .02 .10
373 Alvin Davis .02 .10
374 Lee Guetterman .02 .10
375 Dave Hengel .02 .10
376 Mike Kingery .02 .10
377 Mark Langston .02 .10
378 Edgar Martinez RC 2.50 6.00
379 Mike Moore .02 .10
380 Mike Morgan .02 .10
381 John Moses .02 .10
382 Donell Nixon .02 .10
383 Edwin Nunez .02 .10
384 Ken Phelps .02 .10
385 Jim Presley .02 .10
386 Rey Quinones .02 .10
387 Jerry Reed .02 .10
388 Harold Reynolds .05 .15
389 Dave Valle .02 .10
390 Bill Wilkinson .02 .10
391 Harold Baines .05 .15
392 Floyd Bannister .02 .10
393 Daryl Boston .02 .10
394 Ivan Calderon .02 .10
395 Jose DeLeon .02 .10
396 Richard Dotson .02 .10
397 Carlton Fisk .07 .20
398 Ozzie Guillen .05 .15
399 Ron Hassey .02 .10
400 Donnie Hill .02 .10
401 Bob James .02 .10
402 Dave LaPoint .02 .10
403 Bill Lindsey .02 .10
404 Bill Long .02 .10
405 Steve Lyons .02 .10
406 Fred Manrique .02 .10
407 Jack McDowell RC .20 .50
408 Gary Redus .02 .10
409 Ray Searage .02 .10
410 Bobby Thigpen .02 .10
411 Greg Walker .02 .10
412 Ken Williams RC .02 .10
413 Jim Winn .02 .10
414 Jody Davis .02 .10
415 Andre Dawson .05 .15
416 Brian Dayett .02 .10
417 Bob Dernier .02 .10
418 Frank DiPino .02 .10
419 Shawon Dunston .02 .10
420 Leon Durham .02 .10
421 Les Lancaster .02 .10
422 Ed Lynch .02 .10
423 Greg Maddux .60 1.50
424 Dave Martinez .02 .10
425A Keith Moreland ERR .60 1.50
425B Keith Moreland COR .05 .15
Bat on shoulder
426 Jamie Moyer .05 .15
427 Jerry Mumphrey .02 .10
428 Paul Noce .02 .10
429 Rafael Palmeiro .25 .60
430 Wade Rowdon .02 .10
431 Ryne Sandberg .25 .60
432 Scott Sanderson .02 .10
433 Lee Smith .05 .15
434 Jim Sundberg .05 .15
435 Rick Sutcliffe .05 .15
436 Manny Trillo .02 .10
437 Juan Agosto .02 .10
438 Larry Andersen .02 .10
439 Alan Ashby .02 .10
440 Kevin Bass .02 .10
441 Ken Caminiti RC 1.25 3.00
442 Rocky Childress .02 .10
443 Jose Cruz .05 .15
444 Danny Darwin .02 .10
445 Glenn Davis .02 .10
446 Jim Deshaies .02 .10
447 Bill Doran .02 .10
448 Ty Gainey .02 .10
449 Billy Hatcher .02 .10
450 Jeff Heathcock .02 .10
451 Bob Knepper .02 .10
452 Rob Mallicoat .02 .10
453 Dave Meads .02 .10
454 Craig Reynolds .02 .10
455 Nolan Ryan .60 1.50
456 Mike Scott .05 .15

457 Dave Smith .02 .10
458 Denny Walling .02 .10
459 Robbie Wine .02 .10
460 Gerald Young .02 .10
461 Bob Brower .02 .10
462A Jerry Browne ERR .60 1.50
462B Jerry Browne COR .05 .15
Posed with bat
463 Steve Buechele .02 .10
464 Edwin Correa .02 .10
465 Cecil Espy RC .02 .10
466 Scott Fletcher .02 .10
467 Jose Guzman .02 .10
468 Greg Harris .02 .10
469 Charlie Hough .05 .15
470 Pete Incaviglia .02 .10
471 Paul Kilgus .02 .10
472 Mike Loynd .02 .10
473 Oddibe McDowell .02 .10
474 Dale Mohorcic .02 .10
475 Pete O'Brien .02 .10
476 Larry Parrish .02 .10
477 Geno Petralli .02 .10
478 Jeff Russell .02 .10
479 Ruben Sierra .05 .15
480 Mike Stanley .02 .10
481 Curtis Wilkerson .02 .10
482 Mitch Williams .02 .10
483 Bobby Witt .02 .10
484 Tony Armas .05 .15
485 Bob Boone .05 .15
486 Bill Buckner .05 .15
487 DeWayne Buice .02 .10
488 Brian Downing .05 .15
489 Chuck Finley .05 .15
490 Willie Fraser UER .02 .10
Wrong bio stats,
for George Hendrick
491 Jack Howell .02 .10
492 Ruppert Jones .02 .10
493 Wally Joyner .05 .15
494 Jack Lazorko .02 .10
495 Gary Lucas .02 .10
496 Kirk McCaskill .02 .10
497 Mark McLemore .02 .10
498 Darrell Miller .02 .10
499 Greg Minton .02 .10
500 Donnie Moore .02 .10
501 Gus Polidor .02 .10
502 Johnny Ray .02 .10
503 Mark Ryal .02 .10
504 Dick Schofield .02 .10
505 Don Sutton .05 .15
506 Devon White .05 .15
507 Mike Witt .02 .10
508 Dave Anderson .02 .10
509 Tim Belcher .02 .10
510 Ralph Bryant .02 .10
511 Tim Crews RC .15 .40
512 Mike Devereaux RC .15 .40
513 Mariano Duncan .02 .10
514 Pedro Guerrero .05 .15
515 Jeff Hamilton .02 .10
516 Mickey Hatcher .02 .10
517 Brad Havens .02 .10
518 Orel Hershiser .05 .15
519 Shawn Hillegas RC .02 .10
520 Ken Howell .02 .10
521 Tim Leary .02 .10
522 Mike Marshall .02 .10
523 Steve Sax .02 .10
524 Mike Scioscia .05 .15
525 Mike Sharperson .02 .10
526 John Shelby .02 .10
527 Franklin Stubbs .02 .10
528 Fernando Valenzuela .05 .15
529 Bob Welch .05 .15
530 Matt Young .02 .10
531 Jim Acker .02 .10
532 Paul Assenmacher .02 .10
533 Jeff Blauser RC .15 .40
534 Joe Boever .02 .10
535 Martin Clary .02 .10
536 Kevin Coffman .02 .10
537 Jeff Dedmon .02 .10
538 Ron Gant RC .20 .50
539 Tom Glavine RC 1.25 3.00
540 Ken Griffey .05 .15
541 Albert Hall .02 .10
542 Glenn Hubbard .02 .10
543 Dion James .02 .10
544 Dale Murphy .07 .20
545 Ken Oberkfell .02 .10
546 David Palmer .02 .10
547 Gerald Perry .02 .10
548 Charlie Puleo .02 .10
549 Ted Simmons .05 .15
550 Zane Smith .02 .10
551 Andres Thomas .02 .10
552 Ozzie Virgil .02 .10
553 Don Aase .02 .10
554 Jeff Ballard RC .02 .10
555 Eric Bell .02 .10
556 Mike Boddicker .02 .10
557 Ken Dixon .02 .10
558 Jim Dwyer .02 .10
559 Ken Gerhart .02 .10
560 Rene Gonzales RC .05 .15
561 Mike Griffin .02 .10
562 John Habyan UER .02 .10
Misspelled Hayban on
both sides of card
563 Terry Kennedy .02 .10
564 Ray Knight .05 .15
565 Lee Lacy .02 .10
566 Fred Lynn .05 .15
567 Eddie Murray .10 .30
568 Tom Niedenfuer .02 .10
569 Bill Ripken RC .15 .40
570 Cal Ripken .50 1.25
571 Dave Schmidt .02 .10
572 Larry Sheets .02 .10
573 Pete Stanicek RC .02 .10
574 Mark Williamson .02 .10
575 Mike Young .02 .10
576 Shawn Abner .02 .10

577 Greg Booker .02 .10
578 Chris Brown .02 .10
579 Keith Comstock .02 .10
580 Joey Cora RC .15 .40
581 Mark Davis .02 .10
582 Tim Flannery .07 .20
With surfboard
583 Goose Gossage .05 .15
584 Mark Grant .02 .10
585 Tony Gwynn .20 .50
586 Andy Hawkins .02 .10
587 Stan Jefferson .02 .10
588 Jimmy Jones .02 .10
589 John Kruk .05 .15
590 Shane Mack .02 .10
591 Carmelo Martinez .02 .10
592 Lance McCullers UER .02 .10
6'11 tall
593 Eric Nolte .02 .10
594 Randy Ready .02 .10
595 Luis Salazar .02 .10
596 Benito Santiago .05 .15
597 Eric Show .02 .10
598 Garry Templeton .05 .15
599 Ed Whitson .02 .10
600 Scott Bailes .02 .10
601 Chris Bando .02 .10
602 Jay Bell RC .20 .50
603 Brett Butler .05 .15
604 Tom Candiotti .02 .10
605 Joe Carter .05 .15
606 Carmen Castillo .02 .10
607 Brian Dorsett .02 .10
608 John Farrell RC .05 .15
609 Julio Franco .05 .15
610 Mel Hall .02 .10
611 Tommy Hinzo .02 .10
612 Brook Jacoby .02 .10
613 Doug Jones RC .15 .40
614 Ken Schrom .02 .10
615 Cory Snyder .02 .10
616 Sammy Stewart .02 .10
617 Greg Swindell .02 .10
618 Pat Tabler .02 .10
619 Ed VandeBerg .02 .10
620 Eddie Williams RC .05 .15
621 Rich Yett .02 .10
622 Wally Joyner .05 .15
Cory Snyder
623 George Bell .02 .10
Pedro Guerrero
624 M.McGwire/J.Canseco .60 1.50
625 Dave Righetti .02 .10
Dan Plesac
626 Bret Saberhagen .05 .15
Mike Witt
Jack Morris
627 John Franco .02 .10
Steve Bedrosian
628 Ozzie Smith .10 .30
Ryne Sandberg
629 Mark McGwire HL .50 1.25
630 Mike Greenwell .10 .30
Ellis Burks
Todd Benzinger
631 Tony Gwynn .07 .20
Tim Raines
632 Mike Scott .05 .15
Orel Hershiser
633 P.Tabler/M.McGwire .50 1.25
634 Tony Gwynn .07 .20
Vince Coleman
635 Fernandez/Ripken/Trammell .20 .50
636 Mike Schmidt .10 .30
Gary Carter
637 Darryl Strawberry .05 .15
Eric Davis
638 Matt Nokes .07 .20
Kirby Puckett
639 Keith Hernandez .05 .15
Dale Murphy
640 B.Ripken/C.Ripken .30 .75
641 M.Grace RC 1.25 3.00
D.Jackson
642 Damon Berryhill RC .15 .40
Jeff Montgomery RC
643 Felix Fermin .05 .15
Jesse Reid RC
644 Greg Myers .15 .40
Greg Tabor RC
645 Joey Meyer .05 .15
Jim Eppard RC
646 Adam Peterson RC .15 .40
Randy Velarde RC
647 Pete Smith RC .15 .40
Chris Gwynn RC
648 Tom Newell .05 .15
Greg Jelks RC
649 Mario Diaz .05 .15
Clay Parker RC
650 Jack Savage .05 .15
Todd Simmons RC
651 John Burkett .15 .40
Kirt Manwaring RC
652 Dave Otto .20 .50
Walt Weiss RC
653 Jeff King .15 .40
Randell Byers RC
654 CL: Twins/Cards .02 .10
Tigers/Giants UER
90 Bob Melvin,
91 Eddie Milner
655 CL: Blue Jays/Mets .02 .10
Brewers/Expos UER
Mets listed before
Blue Jays on card
656 CL: Yankees/Reds .02 .10
Royals/A's
657 CL: Phillies/Pirates .02 .10
Red Sox/Mariners
658 CL: White Sox/Cubs .02 .10
Astros/Rangers
659 CL: Angels/Dodgers .02 .10
Braves/Orioles
660 CL: Padres/Indians .02 .10
Rookies/Specials

1988 Fleer Glossy

COMP.FACT.SET (672) 8.00 25.00
*STARS: .6X TO 1.5X BASIC CARDS
*ROOKIES: .75X TO 2X BASIC CARDS
DISTRIBUTED ONLY IN FACTORY SET FORM
378 Edgar Martinez 12.00 30.00

1988 Fleer All-Stars

COMPLETE SET (12) 2.50 6.00
RANDOM INSERTS IN PACKS .40 .75
1 Matt Nokes .60 1.50
2 Tom Henke .15 .40
3 Ted Higuera .15 .40
4 Roger Clemens 2.50 6.00
5 George Bell .25 .60
6 Andre Dawson .25 .60
7 Eric Davis .25 .60
8 Wade Boggs .30 .75
9 Alan Trammell .25 .60
10 Juan Samuel .15 .40
11 Jack Clark .25 .60
12 Paul Molitor .25 .60

1988 Fleer Headliners

COMPLETE SET (6) 2.50 6.00
ONE PER RACK PACK .10 .20
1 Don Mattingly .50 1.25
2 Mark McGwire 1.50 4.00
3 Jack Morris .07 .20
4 Darryl Strawberry .07 .20
5 Dwight Gooden .10 .20
6 Tim Raines .07 .20

1988 Fleer Wax Box Cards

COMPLETE SET (16) 3.00 8.00
C1 Cardinals Logo .02 .10
C2 Dwight Evans .08 .25
C3 Andres Galarraga .40 1.00
C4 Wally Joyner .08 .25
C5 Twins Logo .02 .10
C6 Dale Murphy .40 1.00
C7 Kirby Puckett .50 1.25
C8 Shane Rawley .02 .10
C9 Giants Logo .02 .10
C10 Ryne Sandberg 1.00 2.50
C11 Mike Schmidt .50 1.25
C12 Kevin Seitzer .02 .10
C13 Tigers Logo .02 .10
C14 Dave Stewart .08 .25
C15 Tim Wallach .02 .10
C16 Todd Worrell .08 .25

1988 Fleer World Series

COMPLETE SET (12) .75 2.00
ONE SET PER FACTORY SET
1 Dan Gladden .02 .10
2 Randy Bush .02 .10
3 John Tudor .05 .15
4 Ozzie Smith .20 .50
5 T.Worrell .02 .10
T.Pena
6 Vince Coleman .02 .10
7 T.Herr .02 .10
D.Driessen
8 Kirby Puckett .10 .30
9 Kent Hrbek .05 .15
10 Tom Herr .02 .10
11 Don Baylor .05 .15
12 Frank Viola .05 .15

1988 Fleer World Series Glossy

*GLOSSY: .5X TO 1.2X BASIC WS
DISTRIBUTED ONLY IN FACTORY SET FORM

1988 Fleer Update

This 132-card standard-size set was distributed exclusively in factory set form in a red, white and blue, cellophane-wrapped box through hobby dealers. In addition to the complete set of 132 cards, the box also contained 25 Team Logo stickers. The cards look very similar to the 1988 Fleer regular issue except for the U-prefixed numbering on back. Cards are ordered alphabetically by player's last name. This was the first Fleer Update set to adopt the Fleer "alphabetical within team" numbering system. The key extended Rookie Cards in this set are Roberto Alomar, Craig Biggio Al Leiter, John Smoltz and David Wells.

COMP.FACT.SET (132) 4.00 10.00
1 Jose Bautista XRC .08 .25
2 Joe Orsulak .02 .10
3 Doug Sisk .02 .10
4 Craig Worthington .02 .10
5 Mike Boddicker .02 .10
6 Rick Cerone .02 .10
7 Larry Parrish .02 .10
8 Lee Smith .07 .20
9 Mike Smithson .02 .10
10 John Trautwein .02 .10
11 Sherman Corbett XRC .02 .10
12 Chili Davis .07 .20
13 Jim Eppard .02 .10
14 Bryan Harvey XRC .20 .50
15 John Davis .02 .10
16 Dave Gallagher .02 .10
17 Ricky Horton .02 .10
18 Dan Pasqua .02 .10
19 Melido Perez .02 .10
20 Jose Segura .02 .10
21 Andy Allanson .02 .10
22 Jon Perlman XRC .02 .10
23 Domingo Ramos .02 .10
24 Rick Rodriguez .02 .10
25 Willie Upshaw .02 .10
26 Paul Gibson .02 .10
27 Don Heinkel .02 .10
28 Ray Knight .07 .20
29 Gary Pettis .02 .10
30 Luis Salazar .02 .10
31 Mike Macfarlane XRC .20 .50
32 Jeff Montgomery .20 .50
33 Ted Power .02 .10
34 Israel Sanchez .02 .10
35 Kurt Stillwell .02 .10
36 Pat Tabler .02 .10
37 Don August .02 .10
38 Darryl Hamilton XRC .20 .50
39 Jeff Leonard .02 .10
40 Joey Meyer .02 .10
41 Allan Anderson .02 .10
42 Brian Harper .02 .10
43 Tom Herr .02 .10
44 Charlie Lea .02 .10
45 John Moses .02 .10
Listed as Hohn on
checklist card
46 John Candelaria .02 .10
47 Jack Clark .07 .20
48 Richard Dotson .02 .10
49 Al Leiter XRC .40 1.00
50 Rafael Santana .02 .10
51 Don Slaught .02 .10
52 Todd Burns .02 .10
53 Dave Henderson .02 .10
54 Doug Jennings XRC .02 .10
55 Dave Parker .07 .20
56 Walt Weiss .30 .75
57 Bob Welch .07 .20
58 Henry Cotto .02 .10
59 Mario Diaz UER .02 .10
Listed as Marion
on card front
60 Mike Jackson .07 .20
61 Bill Swift .02 .10
62 Jose Cecena .02 .10
63 Ray Hayward .02 .10
64 Jim Steels UER .02 .10
Listed as Jim Steele
on card back
65 Pat Borders XRC .20 .50
66 Sil Campusano .02 .10
67 Mike Flanagan .02 .10
68 Todd Stottlemyre XRC .20 .50
69 David Wells XRC .60 1.50
70 Jose Alvarez XRC .08 .25
71 Paul Runge .02 .10
72 Cesar Jimenez .02 .10
Card was intended
for German Jiminez&
it's his photo
73 Pete Smith .02 .10
74 John Smoltz XRC 2.50 6.00
75 Damon Berryhill .08 .25
76 Goose Gossage .07 .20
77 Mark Grace .75 2.00
78 Darrin Jackson .08 .25
79 Vance Law .02 .10
80 Jeff Pico .02 .10
81 Gary Varsho .02 .10
82 Tim Birtsas .02 .10
83 Rob Dibble XRC .30 .75
84 Danny Jackson .02 .10
85 Paul O'Neill .10 .30
86 Jose Rijo .07 .20
87 Chris Sabo XRC .30 .75
88 John Fishel XRC .02 .10
89 Craig Biggio XRC 2.50 6.00
90 Terry Puhl .02 .10
91 Rafael Ramirez .02 .10
92 Louie Meadows XRC .02 .10
93 Kirk Gibson .20 .50
94 Alfredo Griffin .02 .10
95 Jay Howell .02 .10
96 Jesse Orosco .02 .10
97 Alejandro Pena .02 .10
98 Tracy Woodson XRC .08 .25
99 John Dopson .02 .10
100 Brian Holman XRC .08 .25
101 Rex Hudler .02 .10
102 Jeff Parrett .02 .10
103 Nelson Santovenia .02 .10
104 Kevin Elster .02 .10
105 Jeff Innis .02 .10
106 Mackey Sasser XRC .20 .50
107 Phil Bradley .02 .10
108 Danny Clay XRC .02 .10
109 Greg A.Harris .02 .10
110 Ricky Jordan XRC .20 .50
111 David Palmer .02 .10
112 Jim Gott .02 .10
113 Tommy Gregg UER .02 .10
Photo actually
Randy Milligan
114 Barry Jones .02 .10
115 Randy Milligan XRC .08 .25
116 Luis Alicea XRC .20 .50
117 Tom Brunansky .02 .10
118 John Costello XRC .02 .10
119 Jose DeLeon .02 .10
120 Bob Horner .07 .20
121 Scott Terry .02 .10
122 Roberto Alomar XRC .75 2.00
123 Dave Leiper .02 .10
124 Keith Moreland .02 .10
125 Mark Parent XRC .02 .10
126 Dennis Rasmussen .02 .10
127 Randy Bockus .02 .10
128 Brett Butler .07 .20
129 Donell Nixon .02 .10
130 Earnest Riles .02 .10
131 Roger Samuels .02 .10
132 Checklist U1-U132 .02 .10

1988 Fleer Update Glossy

COMP.FACT.SET (132) 10.00 25.00
*STARS: .75X TO 2X BASIC CARDS
*ROOKIES: .75X TO 2X BASIC CARDS
DISTRIBUTED ONLY IN FACTORY SET FORM

1988 Fleer Award Winners

This small set of 44 standard-size cards was produced for 7-Eleven stores by Fleer. The cards feature full color fronts and red, white, and blue backs. The card fronts are distinguished by the red, white, and blue frame around the player's full-color photo. The box for the cards describes the set as the "1988 Limited Edition Baseball Award Winners." The checklist for the set is given on the back of the set box. The card numbering is in alphabetical order by player's name.

COMP.FACT SET (44) 3.00 8.00
1 Steve Bedrosian .01 .05
2 George Bell .01 .05
3 Wade Boggs .15 .40
4 Jose Canseco .15 .40
5 Will Clark .20 .50
6 Roger Clemens .25 .60
7 Kal Daniels .01 .05
8 Eric Davis .02 .10
9 Andre Dawson .10 .30
10 Mike Dunne .01 .05
11 Dwight Evans .02 .10
12 Carlton Fisk .15 .40
13 Julio Franco .01 .05
14 Dwight Gooden .02 .10
15 Pedro Guerrero .01 .05
16 Tony Gwynn .30 .75
17 Orel Hershiser .02 .10
18 Tom Henke .01 .05
19 Ted Higuera .01 .05
20 Charlie Hough .02 .10
21 Wally Joyner .02 .10
22 Jimmy Key .02 .10
23 Don Mattingly .30 .75
24 Mark McGwire .40 1.00
25 Paul Molitor .20 .50
26 Jack Morris .02 .10
27 Dale Murphy .10 .30
28 Terry Pendleton .02 .10
29 Kirby Puckett .15 .40
30 Tim Raines .02 .10
31 Jeff Reardon .02 .10
32 Harold Reynolds .02 .10
33 Dave Righetti .01 .05
34 Benito Santiago .02 .10
35 Mike Schmidt .20 .50
36 Mike Scott .01 .05
37 Kevin Seitzer .02 .10
38 Larry Sheets .01 .05
39 Ozzie Smith .30 .75
40 Darryl Strawberry .02 .10
41 Rick Sutcliffe .01 .05
42 Danny Tartabull .01 .05
43 Alan Trammell .07 .20
44 Tim Wallach .01 .05

1988 Fleer Baseball All-Stars

This small boxed set of 44 standard-size cards was produced exclusively for Ben Franklin Stores. The cards feature full color fronts and white and blue backs. The card fronts are distinguished by the yellow and blue striped background behind the player's full-color photo. The box for the cards describes the set as the "1988 Fleer Baseball All-Stars." The checklist for the set is given on the back of the set box. The card numbering is in alphabetical order by player's name.

COMP.FACT SET (44) 2.50 6.00
1 George Bell .01 .05
2 Wade Boggs .15 .40
3 Bobby Bonilla .02 .10
4 George Brett .20 .50
5 Jose Canseco .15 .40
6 Jack Clark .02 .10
7 Will Clark .20 .50
8 Roger Clemens .30 .75
9 Eric Davis .02 .10
10 Andre Dawson .07 .20
11 Julio Franco .01 .05
12 Dwight Gooden .02 .10
13 Tony Gwynn .30 .75
14 Orel Hershiser .02 .10
15 Teddy Higuera .01 .05
16 Charlie Hough .02 .10
17 Kent Hrbek .02 .10
18 Bruce Hurst .01 .05
19 Wally Joyner .02 .10
20 Mark Langston .01 .05
21 Dave LaPoint .01 .05
22 Candy Maldonado .01 .05
23 Don Mattingly .30 .75
24 Roger McDowell .01 .05
25 Mark McGwire .40 1.00
26 Jack Morris .02 .10
27 Dale Murphy .07 .20
28 Eddie Murray .15 .40
29 Matt Nokes .01 .05
30 Kirby Puckett .15 .40
31 Tim Raines .02 .10
32 Willie Randolph .02 .10
33 Jeff Reardon .02 .10
34 Nolan Ryan .60 1.50
35 Juan Samuel .01 .05
36 Mike Schmidt .15 .40
37 Mike Scott .01 .05
38 Kevin Seitzer .02 .10
39 Ozzie Smith .30 .75
40 Darryl Strawberry .02 .10
41 Rick Sutcliffe .01 .05
42 Alan Trammell .05 .15
43 Tim Wallach .01 .05
44 Dave Winfield .15 .40

1988 Fleer Baseball MVP's

This small 44-card boxed standard-size set was produced by Fleer for distribution by the Toys'r'Us stores. The cards feature full color fronts. The set is titled "Baseball MVP." Each individual boxed set includes the 44 cards and six logo stickers. The checklist for the set is found on the back panel of the box. The card fronts have a vanilla-yellow and blue border. The box refers to Toys'r'Us but there is no mention of Toys'r'Us anywhere on the cards themselves. The card numbering is in alphabetical order by player's name.

COMP.FACT SET (44) 3.00 8.00
1 George Bell .01 .05
2 Wade Boggs .15 .40
3 Jose Canseco .15 .40
4 Ivan Calderon .01 .05
5 Will Clark .20 .50
6 Roger Clemens .30 .75
7 Vince Coleman .01 .05
8 Eric Davis .02 .10
9 Andre Dawson .07 .20
10 Dave Dravecky .02 .10
11 Mike Dunne .01 .05
12 Dwight Evans .02 .10
13 Sid Fernandez .01 .05
14 Tony Fernandez .01 .05
15 Julio Franco .02 .10
16 Dwight Gooden .02 .10
17 Tony Gwynn .30 .75
18 Ted Higuera .01 .05
19 Charlie Hough .02 .10
20 Wally Joyner .05 .15
21 Mark Langston .01 .05
22 Don Mattingly .30 .75
23 Mark McGwire .40 1.00
24 Jack Morris .02 .10
25 Dale Murphy .07 .20
26 Kirby Puckett .10 .30
27 Tim Raines .02 .10
28 Willie Randolph .02 .10
29 Ryne Sandberg .20 .50
30 Benito Santiago .02 .10
31 Mike Schmidt .20 .50
32 Mike Scott .01 .05
33 Kevin Seitzer .01 .05
34 Larry Sheets .01 .05
35 Ozzie Smith .30 .75
36 Dave Stewart .02 .10
37 Darryl Strawberry .02 .10
38 Rick Sutcliffe .01 .05
39 Alan Trammell .05 .15
40 Fernando Valenzuela .02 .10
41 Frank Viola .01 .05
42 Tim Wallach .01 .05
43 Dave Winfield .20 .50
44 Robin Yount .15 .40

1988 Fleer Exciting Stars

This small boxed set of 44 standard-size cards was produced exclusively for Cumberland Farm Stores. The cards feature full color fronts and red, white, and blue backs. The card fronts are distinguished by the framing of the player's full-color photo with a blue border with a red and white bar stripe across the middle. The box for the cards describes the set as the "1988 Fleer Baseball's Exciting Stars." The checklist for the set is given on the back of the set box. The card numbering is in alphabetical order by player's name.

COMP.FACT SET (44) 2.00 5.00
1 Harold Baines .05 .15
2 Kevin Bass .01 .05
3 George Bell .01 .05
4 Wade Boggs .15 .40
5 Mickey Brantley .01 .05
6 Sid Bream .01 .05
7 Jose Canseco .10 .30
8 Jack Clark .02 .10
9 Will Clark .20 .50
10 Roger Clemens .30 .75
11 Vince Coleman .01 .05
12 Eric Davis .02 .10
13 Andre Dawson .07 .20
14 Julio Franco .02 .10
15 Dwight Gooden .02 .10
16 Mike Greenwell .01 .05
17 Tony Gwynn .30 .75
18 Von Hayes .01 .05
19 Tom Henke .01 .05
20 Orel Hershiser .02 .10
21 Teddy Higuera .01 .05
22 Brook Jacoby .01 .05
23 Wally Joyner .05 .15
24 Jimmy Key .02 .10
25 Don Mattingly .30 .75
26 Mark McGwire .40 1.00
27 Jack Morris .02 .10
28 Dale Murphy .07 .20
29 Matt Nokes .01 .05
30 Kirby Puckett .10 .30
31 Tim Raines .02 .10
32 Ryne Sandberg .20 .50
33 Benito Santiago .02 .10
34 Mike Schmidt .20 .50
35 Mike Scott .01 .05
36 Kevin Seitzer .02 .10
37 Larry Sheets .01 .05
38 Ruben Sierra .02 .10
39 Darryl Strawberry .02 .10
40 Rick Sutcliffe .01 .05
41 Danny Tartabull .01 .05
42 Alan Trammell .05 .15
43 Fernando Valenzuela .02 .10
44 Devon White .01 .05

1988 Fleer Hottest Stars

This 44-card boxed standard-size set was produced by Fleer for exclusive distribution by Revco Discount Drug stores all over the country. The cards feature full color fronts and red, white, and blue backs. The card fronts are easily distinguished by the flaming baseball in the lower right corner which says "Fleer Baseball's Hottest Stars." The player's picture is framed in red fading from orange down to yellow. The box for the cards proclaims "1988 Limited Edition Baseball's Hottest Stars" and is styled in blue, red, and yellow. The checklist for the set is given on the back of the set box. The box refers to Revco but there is no mention of Revco anywhere on the cards themselves. The card numbering is in alphabetical order by player's name.

COMP.FACT SET (44) 2.00 5.00
1 George Bell .01 .05
2 Wade Boggs .15 .40
3 Bobby Bonilla .02 .10
4 George Brett .20 .50
5 Jose Canseco .10 .30
6 Will Clark .20 .50
7 Roger Clemens .30 .75
8 Eric Davis .02 .10
9 Andre Dawson .07 .20
10 Tony Fernandez .02 .10
11 Julio Franco .02 .10
12 Gary Gaetti .02 .10
13 Dwight Gooden .02 .10
14 Mike Greenwell .01 .05
15 Tony Gwynn .30 .75
16 Rickey Henderson .25 .60
17 Keith Hernandez .02 .10
18 Tom Herr .01 .05
19 Orel Hershiser .02 .10
20 Ted Higuera .01 .05
21 Wally Joyner .02 .10
22 Jimmy Key .02 .10
23 Mark Langston .01 .05
24 Don Mattingly .30 .75
25 Jack McDowell .05 .15
26 Mark McGwire .40 1.00
27 Kevin Mitchell .02 .10
28 Jack Morris .02 .10
29 Dale Murphy .07 .20
30 Kirby Puckett .10 .30
31 Tim Raines .02 .10
32 Shane Rawley .01 .05
33 Benito Santiago .02 .10
34 Mike Schmidt .20 .50
35 Mike Scott .01 .05
36 Kevin Seitzer .01 .05
37 Larry Sheets .01 .05
38 Ruben Sierra .02 .10
39 Dave Smith .01 .05
40 Ozzie Smith .30 .75
41 Darryl Strawberry .02 .10
42 Rick Sutcliffe .01 .05
43 Pat Tabler .01 .05
44 Alan Trammell .05 .15

1988 Fleer League Leaders

This small boxed set of 44 standard-size cards was produced exclusively for Walgreen Drug Stores. The cards feature full color fronts and pink, white, and blue backs. The card fronts are distinguished by the blue solid and striped background behind the player's full-color photo. The box for the cards describes the set as the "1988 Fleer Baseball's League Leaders." The checklist for the set is given on the back of the set box. The card numbering is in alphabetical order by player's name.

COMP.FACT SET (44) 2.00 5.00
1 George Bell .01 .05
2 Wade Boggs .15 .40
3 Ivan Calderon .01 .05
4 Jose Canseco .15 .40
5 Will Clark .20 .50
6 Roger Clemens .30 .75
7 Vince Coleman .01 .05
8 Eric Davis .02 .10
9 Andre Dawson .10 .30
10 Bill Doran .01 .05
11 Dwight Evans .02 .10
12 Julio Franco .02 .10
13 Gary Gaetti .02 .10
14 Andres Galarraga .10 .30
15 Dwight Gooden .02 .10
16 Tony Gwynn .30 .75
17 Tom Henke .01 .05
18 Keith Hernandez .02 .10
19 Orel Hershiser .02 .10
20 Ted Higuera .01 .05
21 Kent Hrbek .02 .10
22 Wally Joyner .07 .20
23 Jimmy Key .02 .10
24 Mark Langston .01 .05
25 Don Mattingly .30 .75
26 Mark McGwire .40 1.00
27 Paul Molitor .20 .50
28 Jack Morris .02 .10
29 Dale Murphy .10 .30
30 Kirby Puckett .15 .40
31 Tim Raines .02 .10
32 Rick Reuschel .01 .05
33 Bret Saberhagen .02 .10
34 Benito Santiago .02 .10
35 Mike Schmidt .20 .50
36 Mike Scott .01 .05
37 Kevin Seitzer .02 .10
38 Larry Sheets .01 .05
39 Ruben Sierra .02 .10
40 Darryl Strawberry .02 .10
41 Rick Sutcliffe .01 .05
42 Alan Trammell .07 .20
43 Andy Van Slyke .02 .10
44 Todd Worrell .02 .10

1988 Fleer Mini

The 1988 Fleer "Classic Miniatures" set consists of 120 small cards with all new pictures of the players as compared to the 1988 Fleer regular issue. The cards are only 1 13/16" by 2 9/16", making them one of the smallest cards issued in the 1980's. Card backs provide career year-by-year statistics. The complete set was distributed in a green, red, white, and silver box along with 18 logo stickers. The card numbering is by alphabetical team order within league and alphabetically within each team. A rookie year card of Mark Grace highlights the set.

COMP.FACT SET (120) 4.00 10.00
1 Eddie Murray .20 .50
2 Dave Schmidt .01 .05
3 Larry Sheets .01 .05
4 Wade Boggs .20 .50
5 Roger Clemens .30 .75
6 Dwight Evans .02 .10
7 Mike Greenwell .01 .05
8 Sam Horn .01 .05
9 Lee Smith .02 .10
10 Brian Downing .01 .05
11 Wally Joyner .02 .10
12 Devon White .01 .05
13 Mike Witt .01 .05
14 Ivan Calderon .01 .05
15 Ozzie Guillen .02 .10
16 Jack McDowell .05 .15
17 Kenny Williams .08 .25
18 Joe Carter .07 .20
19 Julio Franco .02 .10
20 Pat Tabler .01 .05
21 Doyle Alexander .01 .05
22 Jack Morris .02 .10
23 Matt Nokes .01 .05
24 Walt Terrell .01 .05
25 Alan Trammell .05 .15
26 Bret Saberhagen .02 .10
27 Kevin Seitzer .02 .10
28 Danny Tartabull .01 .05
29 Gary Thurman .01 .05
30 Ted Higuera .01 .05
31 Paul Molitor .20 .50
32 Dan Plesac .01 .05
33 Robin Yount .10 .30
34 Gary Gaetti .02 .10
35 Kent Hrbek .02 .10
36 Kirby Puckett .10 .30
37 Jeff Reardon .02 .10
38 Frank Viola .01 .05
39 Jack Clark .02 .10
40 Rickey Henderson .25 .60
41 Don Mattingly .30 .75
42 Willie Randolph .02 .10
43 Dave Righetti .01 .05
44 Dave Winfield .15 .40
45 Jose Canseco .15 .40
46 Mark McGwire .40 1.00
47 Dave Parker .02 .10
48 Dave Stewart .02 .10
49 Walt Weiss .07 .20
50 Bob Welch .01 .05
51 Mickey Brantley .01 .05
52 Mark Langston .01 .05
53 Harold Reynolds .02 .10
54 Scott Fletcher .01 .05
55 Charlie Hough .02 .10
56 Pete Incaviglia .01 .05
57 Larry Parrish .01 .05
58 Ruben Sierra .02 .10
59 George Bell .01 .05
60 Mark Eichhorn .01 .05
61 Tony Fernandez .02 .10
62 Tom Henke .02 .10
63 Jimmy Key .02 .10
64 Dion James .01 .05
65 Dale Murphy .07 .20
66 Zane Smith .01 .05
67 Andre Dawson .07 .20
68 Mark Grace .60 1.50
69 Jerry Mumphrey .01 .05
70 Ryne Sandberg .30 .75
71 Rick Sutcliffe .01 .05
72 Kal Daniels .01 .05
73 Eric Davis .02 .10
74 John Franco .02 .10
75 Ron Robinson .01 .05
76 Jeff Treadway .01 .05
77 Kevin Bass .01 .05
78 Glenn Davis .01 .05
79 Nolan Ryan .60 1.50
80 Mike Scott .01 .05
81 Dave Smith .01 .05
82 Kirk Gibson .02 .10
83 Pedro Guerrero .01 .05
84 Orel Hershiser .02 .10
85 Steve Sax .01 .05
86 Fernando Valenzuela .02 .10
87 Tim Burke .01 .05
88 Andres Galarraga .07 .20
89 Neal Heaton .01 .05
90 Tim Raines .02 .10
91 Tim Wallach .01 .05
92 Dwight Gooden .02 .10
93 Keith Hernandez .02 .10
94 Gregg Jefferies .05 .15
95 Howard Johnson .01 .05
96 Roger McDowell .01 .05
97 Darryl Strawberry .02 .10
98 Steve Bedrosian .01 .05
99 Von Hayes .01 .05
100 Shane Rawley .01 .05
101 Juan Samuel .01 .05
102 Mike Schmidt .10 .30
103 Bobby Bonilla .02 .10
104 Mike Dunne .01 .05
105 Andy Van Slyke .02 .10
106 Vince Coleman .01 .05
107 Bob Horner .01 .05
108 Willie McGee .02 .10
109 Ozzie Smith .30 .75
110 John Tudor .01 .05
111 Todd Worrell .02 .10
112 Tony Gwynn .30 .75
113 John Kruk .02 .10
114 Lance McCullers .01 .05
115 Benito Santiago .02 .10
116 Will Clark .20 .50
117 Jeff Leonard .01 .05
118 Candy Maldonado .01 .05
119 Kirt Manwaring .01 .05
120 Don Robinson .01 .05

1988 Fleer Record Setters

This small boxed set of 44 standard-size cards was produced exclusively for Eckerd's Drug Stores. The cards feature full color fronts and red, white, and blue backs. The card fronts are distinguished by the red and blue frame around the player's full-color photo. The box for the cards describes the set as the "1988 Baseball Record Setters." The checklist for the set is given on the back of the set box. The card numbering is in alphabetical order by player's name.

COMP.FACT SET (44) 2.50 6.00
1 Jesse Barfield .01 .05
2 George Bell .01 .05
3 Wade Boggs .15 .40
4 Jose Canseco .10 .30
5 Jack Clark .02 .10
6 Will Clark .20 .50
7 Roger Clemens .30 .75
8 Alvin Davis .01 .05
9 Eric Davis .02 .10
10 Andre Dawson .07 .20
11 Mike Dunne .01 .05
12 John Franco .02 .10
13 Julio Franco .02 .10
14 Dwight Gooden .02 .10
15 Mark Gubicza .01 .05
Listed as Gubiczo
on box checklist
16 Ozzie Guillen .02 .10
17 Tony Gwynn .30 .75
18 Orel Hershiser .02 .10
19 Teddy Higuera .01 .05
20 Howard Johnson UER .01 .05
Missing '87 stats
on card back
21 Wally Joyner .05 .15
22 Jimmy Key .02 .10
23 Jeff Leonard .01 .05
24 Don Mattingly .30 .75
25 Mark McGwire .40 1.00
26 Jack Morris .02 .10
27 Dale Murphy .07 .20
28 Larry Parrish .01 .05
29 Kirby Puckett .10 .30
30 Tim Raines .02 .10
31 Harold Reynolds .02 .10
32 Dave Righetti .01 .05
33 Cal Ripken .60 1.50
34 Benito Santiago .02 .10
35 Mike Schmidt .20 .50
36 Mike Scott .01 .05
37 Kevin Seitzer .02 .10
38 Ozzie Smith .30 .75
39 Darryl Strawberry .02 .10
40 Rick Sutcliffe .01 .05
41 Alan Trammell .05 .15
42 Frank Viola .01 .05
43 Mitch Williams .01 .05
44 Todd Worrell .02 .10

1988 Fleer Sluggers/Pitchers

Fleer produced this 44-card boxed standard-size set although it was primarily distributed by McCrory, McLellan, J.J Newberry, H.L.Green, T.G.Y., and other similar stores. The set is subtitled "Baseball's Best". The set was packaged in a green custom box along with six logo stickers. The set checklist is given on the back of the box. The bottoms of the boxes which held the individual set boxes also contained a panel of six cards; these box bottom cards were numbered C1 through C6. The card numbering is in alphabetical order by player's name.

COMP.FACT SET (44) 2.50 6.00
1 George Bell .01 .05
2 Wade Boggs .15 .40
3 Bobby Bonilla .02 .10
4 Tom Brunansky .01 .05
5 Ellis Burks .15 .40
6 Jose Canseco .10 .30
7 Joe Carter .07 .20
8 Will Clark .20 .50
9 Roger Clemens .30 .75
10 Eric Davis .02 .10
11 Glenn Davis .01 .05
12 Andre Dawson .07 .20
13 Dennis Eckersley .15 .40
14 Andres Galarraga .07 .20
15 Dwight Gooden .02 .10
16 Pedro Guerrero .01 .05
17 Tony Gwynn .30 .75
18 Orel Hershiser .02 .10
19 Ted Higuera .01 .05
20 Pete Incaviglia .01 .05
21 Danny Jackson .01 .05
22 Doug Jennings .01 .05
23 Mark Langston .01 .05
24 Dave LaPoint .01 .05
25 Mike LaValliere .01 .05
26 Don Mattingly .30 .75
27 Mark McGwire .40 1.00
28 Dale Murphy .07 .20
29 Ken Phelps .01 .05
30 Kirby Puckett .10 .30
31 Johnny Ray .01 .05
32 Jeff Reardon .02 .10
33 Dave Righetti .01 .05
34 Cal Ripken UER/(Misspelled Ripkin .60 1.50
on card front)
35 Chris Sabo .02 .10
36 Mike Schmidt .20 .50
37 Mike Scott .02 .05
38 Kevin Seitzer .02 .10
39 Dave Stewart .02 .10
40 Darryl Strawberry .02 .10
41 Greg Swindell .01 .05
42 Frank Tanana .01 .05
43 Dave Winfield .20 .50
44 Todd Worrell .02 .10

1988 Fleer Sluggers/Pitchers Box Cards

COMPLETE SET (6) 3.00 8.00
C1 Ron Darling .40 1.00
C2 Rickey Henderson 1.25 3.00
C3 Carney Lansford .40 1.00
C4 Rafael Palmeiro 1.25 3.00
C5 Frank Viola .40 1.00
C6 Twins Logo/(Checklist back) .40 1.00

1988 Fleer Star Stickers

These Star Stickers were distributed as a separate issue by Fleer, with five star stickers and a logo sticker in each wax pack. The 132-card (sticker) set features 2 1/2" by 3 1/2" full-color fronts and even statistics on the sticker back, which is an indication that the Fleer Company understands that these stickers are rarely used as stickers but more like traditional cards. The fronts are surrounded by a silver-gray border and the backs are printed in red and black on white card stock. The set numbering is in alphabetical order within team and alphabetically by team within each league.

COMPLETE SET (132) 6.00 15.00
1 Mike Boddicker .01 .05
2 Eddie Murray .20 .50
3 Cal Ripken 1.00 2.50
4 Larry Sheets .01 .05
5 Wade Boggs .20 .50
6 Ellis Burks .20 1.00
7 Roger Clemens .40 1.25
8 Dwight Evans .02 .10
9 Mike Greenwell .01 .05
10 Bruce Hurst .01 .05
11 Brian Downing .01 .05
12 Wally Joyner .02 .10
13 Mike Witt .01 .05
14 Ivan Calderon .01 .05
15 Jose DeLeon .01 .05
16 Ozzie Guillen .60 1.50
17 Bobby Thigpen .01 .05
18 Joe Carter .07 .20
19 Julio Franco .02 .10
20 Brook Jacoby .01 .05
21 Cory Snyder .01 .05
22 Pat Tabler .01 .05
23 Doyle Alexander .01 .05
24 Kirk Gibson .02 .10
25 Mike Henneman .02 .10
26 Jack Morris .02 .10
27 Matt Nokes .01 .05
28 Walt Terrell .01 .05
29 Alan Trammell .05 .15
30 George Brett .40 1.25
31 Charlie Leibrandt .01 .05
32 Bret Saberhagen .02 .10
33 Kevin Seitzer .01 .05
34 Danny Tartabull .01 .05
35 Frank White .02 .10
36 Rob Deer .01 .05
37 Ted Higuera .01 .05
38 Paul Molitor .20 .50
39 Dan Plesac .01 .05
40 Robin Yount .15 .40
41 Bert Blyleven .02 .10
42 Tom Brunansky .01 .05
43 Gary Gaetti .02 .10
44 Kent Hrbek .02 .10
45 Kirby Puckett .20 .50
46 Jeff Reardon .02 .10
47 Frank Viola .01 .05
48 Don Mattingly .50 1.25
49 Mike Pagliarulo .01 .05
50 Willie Randolph .02 .10
51 Rick Rhoden .01 .05
52 Dave Righetti .01 .05
53 Dave Winfield .15 .40
54 Jose Canseco .15 .40
55 Carney Lansford .02 .10
56 Mark McGwire .60 1.50
57 Dave Stewart .02 .10
58 Curt Young .01 .05
59 Alvin Davis .01 .05
60 Mark Langston .01 .05
61 Ken Phelps .01 .05
62 Harold Reynolds .02 .10
63 Scott Fletcher .01 .05
64 Charlie Hough .02 .10
65 Pete Incaviglia .01 .05
66 Oddibe McDowell .01 .05
67 Pete O'Brien .01 .05
68 Larry Parrish .01 .05
69 Ruben Sierra .02 .10
70 Jesse Barfield .01 .05
71 George Bell .01 .05
72 Tony Fernandez .02 .10
73 Tom Henke .01 .05
74 Jimmy Key .01 .05
75 Lloyd Moseby .01 .05
76 Dion James .01 .05
77 Dale Murphy .07 .20
78 Zane Smith .01 .05
79 Andre Dawson .07 .20
80 Ryne Sandberg .40 1.00
81 Rick Sutcliffe .01 .05
82 Kal Daniels .01 .05
83 Eric Davis .02 .10
84 John Franco .02 .10
85 Kevin Bass .01 .05
86 Glenn Davis .01 .05
87 Bill Doran .01 .05
88 Nolan Ryan 1.00 2.50
89 Mike Scott .01 .05
90 Dave Smith .01 .05
91 Pedro Guerrero .01 .05
92 Orel Hershiser .02 .10
93 Steve Sax .01 .05
94 Fernando Valenzuela .02 .10
95 Tim Burke .01 .05
96 Andres Galarraga .07 .20
97 Tim Raines .02 .10
98 Tim Wallach .01 .05
99 Mitch Webster .01 .05
100 Ron Darling .01 .05
101 Sid Fernandez .01 .05
102 Dwight Gooden .02 .10
103 Keith Hernandez .02 .10
104 Howard Johnson .01 .05
105 Roger McDowell .01 .05
106 Darryl Strawberry .02 .10
107 Steve Bedrosian .01 .05
108 Von Hayes .01 .05
109 Shane Rawley .01 .05
110 Juan Samuel .01 .05
111 Mike Schmidt .20 .50
112 Milt Thompson .01 .05
113 Sid Bream .01 .05
114 Bobby Bonilla .01 .05
115 Mike Dunne .01 .05
116 Andy Van Slyke .02 .10
117 Vince Coleman .01 .05
118 Willie McGee .02 .10
119 Terry Pendleton .02 .10
120 Ozzie Smith .40 1.00
121 John Tudor .01 .05
122 Todd Worrell .02 .10
123 Tony Gwynn .50 1.25
124 John Kruk .08 .25
125 Benito Santiago .02 .10
126 Will Clark .20 .50
127 Dave Dravecky .02 .10
128 Jeff Leonard .01 .05
129 Candy Maldonado .01 .05
130 Rick Reuschel .01 .05
131 Don Robinson .01 .05
132 Checklist Card .01 .05

1988 Fleer Stickers Wax Box Cards

COMPLETE SET (8) 1.50 4.00
S1 Mark McGwire 1.50 4.00
Eric Davis
S2 Gary Carter .40 1.00
S3 Kevin Mitchell .30 .75
S4 Ron Guidry .30 .75
S5 Rickey Henderson .75 2.00
S6 Don Baylor .30 .75
S7 Giants Logo .20 .50
S8 Detroit Logo .20 .50

1988 Fleer Superstars

Fleer produced this 44-card boxed standard-size set although it was primarily distributed by McCrory, McLellan, J.J Newberry, H.L.Green, T.G.Y., and other similar stores. The set is subtitled "Fleer Superstars." The set was packaged in a red, white, blue, and yellow custom box along with six logo stickers. The set checklist is given on the back of the box. The bottoms of the boxes which held the individual set boxes also contained a panel of six cards; these box bottom cards were numbered C1 through C6. The card numbering is in alphabetical order by player's name.

COMP.FACT SET (44) 2.50 6.00
1 Steve Bedrosian .01 .05
2 George Bell .01 .05
3 Wade Boggs .15 .40
4 Barry Bonds .30 1.00
5 Jose Canseco .10 .30
6 Joe Carter .07 .20
7 Jack Clark .02 .10
8 Will Clark .20 .50
9 Roger Clemens .30 .75
10 Alvin Davis .01 .05
11 Eric Davis .02 .10
12 Glenn Davis .01 .05
13 Andre Dawson .07 .20
14 Dwight Gooden .02 .10
15 Orel Hershiser .02 .10
16 Teddy Higuera .01 .05
17 Kent Hrbek .02 .10
18 Wally Joyner .02 .10
19 Jimmy Key .01 .05
20 John Kruk .02 .10
21 Jeff Leonard .01 .05
22 Don Mattingly .30 .75
23 Mark McGwire .40 1.00
24 Kevin McReynolds .01 .05
25 Dale Murphy .07 .20
26 Matt Nokes .01 .05
27 Terry Pendleton .02 .10
28 Kirby Puckett .15 .40
29 Tim Raines .02 .10
30 Rick Rhoden .01 .05
31 Cal Ripken .60 1.50
32 Benito Santiago .02 .10
33 Mike Schmidt .15 .40
34 Mike Scott .01 .05
35 Kevin Seitzer .02 .10
36 Ruben Sierra .02 .10
37 Cory Snyder .01 .05
38 Darryl Strawberry .02 .10
39 Rick Sutcliffe .01 .05
40 Danny Tartabull .01 .05
41 Alan Trammell .05 .15
42 Kenny Williams .08 .25
43 Mike Witt .01 .05
44 Robin Yount .15 .40

1988 Fleer Superstars Box Cards

COMPLETE SET (6) 4.00 10.00
C1 Pete Incaviglia .20 .50
C2 Rickey Henderson 2.00 5.00
C3 Tony Fernandez .20 .50
C4 Shane Rawley .20 .50
C5 Ryne Sandberg 2.00 5.00
C6 Cardinals Logo/(Checklist back) .20 .50

1988 Fleer Team Leaders

This 44-card boxed standard-size set was produced by Fleer for exclusive distribution by Kay Bee Toys and is sometimes referred to as the Fleer Kay Bee set. Six team logo stickers are included in the box with the complete set. The numerical checklist on the back of the box shows that the set is numbered alphabetically. The cards have a distinctive red border on the fronts. The Kay Bee logo is printed in the lower right corner of the obverse of each card.

COMP.FACT SET (44) 3.00 8.00
1 George Bell .01 .05
2 Wade Boggs .20 .50
3 Jose Canseco .15 .40
4 Will Clark .25 .60
5 Roger Clemens .30 .75
6 Eric Davis .02 .10
7 Andre Dawson .10 .30
8 Julio Franco .02 .10
9 Andres Galarraga .10 .30
10 Dwight Gooden .02 .10
11 Tony Gwynn .30 .75
12 Tom Henke .01 .05
13 Orel Hershiser .02 .10
14 Kent Hrbek .02 .10
15 Ted Higuera .01 .05
16 Wally Joyner .07 .20
17 Jimmy Key .01 .05
18 Mark Langston .01 .05
19 Don Mattingly .30 .75
20 Willie McGee .02 .10
21 Mark McGwire .40 1.00
22 Paul Molitor .20 .50
23 Jack Morris .02 .10
24 Dale Murphy .10 .30
25 Larry Parrish .01 .05
26 Kirby Puckett .15 .40
27 Tim Raines .02 .10
28 Jeff Reardon .02 .10
29 Dave Righetti .01 .05
30 Cal Ripken .60 1.50
31 Don Robinson .01 .05
32 Bret Saberhagen .02 .10
33 Juan Samuel .01 .05
34 Mike Schmidt .20 .50
35 Mike Scott .01 .05
36 Kevin Seitzer .02 .10
37 Dave Smith .01 .05
38 Ozzie Smith .30 .75
39 Zane Smith .01 .05

40 Darryl Strawberry .02 .10
41 Rick Sutcliffe .01 .05
42 Bobby Thigpen .01 .05
43 Alan Trammell .07 .20
44 Andy Van Slyke .01 .05

1989 Fleer

This set consists of 660 standard-size cards. Cards were primarily issued in 15-card wax packs, rack packs and hobby and retail factory sets. Card fronts feature a distinctive gray border background with white and yellow trim. Cards are again organized alphabetically within teams and teams ordered by previous season record. The last 33 cards in the set consist of Specials (628-639), Rookie Pairs (640-653), and checklists (654-660). Approximately half of the California Angels players have white rather than yellow halos. Certain Oakland A's player cards have red instead of green lines for front photo borders. Checklist cards are available either with or without positions listed for each player. Rookie Cards in this set include Craig Biggio, Ken Griffey Jr., Randy Johnson, Gary Sheffield, and John Smoltz. An interesting variation was discovered in late 1999 by Beckett Grading Services on the Randy Johnson RC (card number 381). It seems the most common version features a crudely-blacked out image of an outfield billboard. A scarcer version clearly reveals the words "Marlboro" on the billboard. One of the hobby's most notorious errors and variations hails from this product. Card number 616, Billy Ripken, was originally published with a four-letter word imprinted on the bat. Needless to say, this caused quite a stir in 1989 and the card was quickly reprinted. Because of this, several different variations were printed with the final solution (and the most common version of this card) being a black box covering the bat knob. The first variation is still actively sought after in the hobby and the other versions are still sought after by collectors seeking a "master" set.

COMPLETE SET (660) 6.00 15.00
COMP.FACT.SET (672) 6.00 15.00
1 Don Baylor .02 .10
2 Lance Blankenship RC .02 .10
3 Todd Burns UER .01 .05
Wrong birthdate, before after All-Star stats missing
4 Greg Cadaret UER .01 .05
All-Star Break stats show 3 losses, should be 2
5 Jose Canseco .08 .25
6 Storm Davis .01 .05
7 Dennis Eckersley .05 .15
8 Mike Gallego .01 .05
9 Ron Hassey .01 .05
10 Dave Henderson .01 .05
11 Rick Honeycutt .01 .05
12 Glenn Hubbard .01 .05
13 Stan Javier .01 .05
14 Doug Jennings RC .01 .05
15 Felix Jose RC .02 .10
16 Carney Lansford .02 .10
17 Mark McGwire .40 1.00
18 Gene Nelson .01 .05
19 Dave Parker .02 .10
20 Eric Plunk .01 .05
21 Luis Polonia .01 .05
22 Terry Steinbach .02 .10
23 Dave Stewart .02 .10
24 Walt Weiss .01 .05
25 Bob Welch .02 .10
26 Curt Young .01 .05
27 Rick Aguilera .01 .05
28 Wally Backman .01 .05
29 Mark Carreon UER .01 .05
After All-Star Break batting 7.14
30 Gary Carter .02 .10
31 David Cone .02 .10
32 Ron Darling .02 .10
33 Len Dykstra .02 .10
34 Kevin Elster .01 .05
35 Sid Fernandez .01 .05
36 Dwight Gooden .02 .10
37 Keith Hernandez .02 .10
38 Gregg Jefferies .02 .10
39 Howard Johnson .02 .10
40 Terry Leach .01 .05
41 Dave Magadan UER .01 .05
Bio says 15 doubles, should be 13
42 Bob McClure .01 .05
43 Roger McDowell UER .01 .05
Led Mets with 58 should be 62
44 Kevin McReynolds .01 .05
45 Keith A. Miller .01 .05
46 Randy Myers .02 .10
47 Bob Ojeda .01 .05
48 Mackey Sasser .01 .05
49 Darryl Strawberry .02 .10
50 Tim Teufel .01 .05
51 Dave West RC .02 .10
52 Mookie Wilson .02 .10
53 Dave Anderson .01 .05
54 Tim Belcher .01 .05
55 Mike Davis .01 .05
56 Mike Devereaux .01 .05
57 Kirk Gibson .02 .10
58 Alfredo Griffin .01 .05
59 Chris Gwynn .01 .05
60 Jeff Hamilton .01 .05
61A Danny Heep ERR .08 .25
Lake Hills
61B Danny Heep COR .01 .05
San Antonio
62 Orel Hershiser .02 .10
63 Brian Holton .01 .05
64 Jay Howell .01 .05
65 Tim Leary .01 .05
66 Mike Marshall .01 .05
67 Ramon Martinez RC .08 .25
68 Jesse Orosco .01 .05
69 Alejandro Pena .01 .05
70 Steve Sax .01 .05
71 Mike Scioscia .02 .10
72 Mike Sharperson .01 .05
73 John Shelby .01 .05
74 Franklin Stubbs .01 .05
75 John Tudor .02 .10
76 Fernando Valenzuela .02 .10
77 Tracy Woodson .01 .05
78 Marty Barrett .01 .05
79 Todd Benzinger .01 .05
80 Mike Boddicker UER .01 .05
Rochester in '76, should be '78
81 Wade Boggs .05 .15
82 Oil Can Boyd .01 .05
83 Ellis Burks .02 .10
84 Rick Cerone .01 .05
85 Roger Clemens .40 1.00
86 Steve Curry .01 .05
87 Dwight Evans .05 .15
88 Wes Gardner .01 .05
89 Rich Gedman .01 .05
90 Mike Greenwell .01 .05
91 Bruce Hurst .01 .05
92 Dennis Lamp .01 .05
93 Spike Owen .01 .05
94 Larry Parrish UER .01 .05
Before All-Star Break batting 1.90
95 Carlos Quintana RC .02 .10
96 Jody Reed .01 .05
97 Jim Rice .02 .10
98A Kevin Romine ERR .08 .25
Photo actually Randy Kutcher batting
98B Kevin Romine COR .01 .05
Arms folded
99 Lee Smith .02 .10
100 Mike Smithson .01 .05
101 Bob Stanley .01 .05
102 Allan Anderson .01 .05
103 Keith Atherton .01 .05
104 Juan Berenguer .01 .05
105 Bert Blyleven .02 .10
106 Eric Bullock UER .01 .05
Bats Throws Right, should be Left
107 Randy Bush .01 .05
108 John Christensen .01 .05
109 Mark Davidson .01 .05
110 Gary Gaetti .02 .10
111 Greg Gagne .01 .05
112 Dan Gladden .01 .05
113 German Gonzalez .01 .05
114 Brian Harper .01 .05
115 Tom Herr .01 .05
116 Kent Hrbek .02 .10
117 Gene Larkin .01 .05
118 Tim Laudner .01 .05
119 Charlie Lea .01 .05
120 Steve Lombardozzi .01 .05
121A John Moses ERR .08 .25
Tempe
121B John Moses COR .01 .05
Phoenix
122 Al Newman .01 .05
123 Mark Portugal .01 .05
124 Kirby Puckett .08 .25
125 Jeff Reardon .02 .10
126 Fred Toliver .01 .05
127 Frank Viola .02 .10
128 Doyle Alexander .01 .05
129 Dave Bergman .01 .05
130A Tom Brookens ERR .30 .75
130B Tom Brookens COR .01 .05
131 Paul Gibson .01 .05
132A Mike Heath ERR .30 .75
132B Mike Heath COR .01 .05
133 Don Heinkel .01 .05
134 Mike Henneman .01 .05
135 Guillermo Hernandez .01 .05
136 Eric King .01 .05
137 Chet Lemon .02 .10
138 Fred Lynn UER .02 .10
'74 and '75 stats missing
139 Jack Morris .02 .10
140 Matt Nokes .01 .05
141 Gary Pettis .01 .05
142 Ted Power .01 .05
143 Jeff M. Robinson .01 .05
144 Luis Salazar .01 .05
145 Steve Searcy .01 .05
146 Pat Sheridan .01 .05
147 Frank Tanana .02 .10
148 Alan Trammell .02 .10
149 Walt Terrell .01 .05
150 Jim Walewander .01 .05
151 Lou Whitaker .02 .10
152 Tim Birtsas .01 .05
153 Tom Browning .01 .05
154 Keith Brown .01 .05
155 Norm Charlton RC .08 .25
156 Dave Concepcion .02 .10
157 Kal Daniels .01 .05
158 Eric Davis .02 .10
159 Bo Diaz .01 .05
160 Rob Dibble RC .15 .40
161 Nick Esasky .01 .05
162 John Franco .02 .10
163 Danny Jackson .01 .05
164 Barry Larkin .05 .15
165 Rob Murphy .01 .05
166 Paul O'Neill .05 .15
167 Jeff Reed .01 .05
168 Jose Rijo .02 .10
169 Ron Robinson .01 .05
170 Chris Sabo RC .15 .40
171 Candy Sierra .01 .05
172 Van Snider .01 .05
173A Jeff Treadway 10.00 25.00
173B Jeff Treadway .01 .05
No target on front
174 Frank Williams UER .01 .05
After All-Star Break stats are jumbled
175 Herm Winningham .01 .05
176 Jim Adduci .01 .05
177 Don August .01 .05
178 Mike Birkbeck .01 .05
179 Chris Bosio .01 .05
180 Glenn Braggs .01 .05
181 Greg Brock .01 .05
182 Mark Clear .01 .05
183 Chuck Crim .01 .05
184 Rob Deer .01 .05
185 Tom Filer .01 .05
186 Jim Gantner .01 .05
187 Darryl Hamilton RC .08 .25
188 Ted Higuera .01 .05
189 Odell Jones .01 .05
190 Jeffrey Leonard .01 .05
191 Joey Meyer .01 .05
192 Paul Mirabella .01 .05
193 Paul Molitor .02 .10
194 Charlie O'Brien .01 .05
195 Dan Plesac .01 .05
196 Gary Sheffield RC .60 1.50
197 B.J. Surhoff .02 .10
198 Dale Sveum .01 .05
199 Bill Wegman .01 .05
200 Robin Yount .15 .40
201 Rafael Belliard .01 .05
202 Barry Bonds .60 1.50
203 Bobby Bonilla .02 .10
204 Sid Bream .01 .05
205 Benny Distefano .01 .05
206 Doug Drabek .01 .05
207 Mike Dunne .01 .05
208 Felix Fermin .01 .05
209 Brian Fisher .01 .05
210 Jim Gott .01 .05
211 Bob Kipper .01 .05
212 Dave LaPoint .01 .05
213 Mike LaValliere .01 .05
214 Jose Lind .01 .05
215 Junior Ortiz .01 .05
216 Vicente Palacios .01 .05
217 Tom Prince .01 .05
218 Gary Redus .01 .05
219 R.J. Reynolds .01 .05
220 Jeff D. Robinson .01 .05
221 John Smiley .01 .05
222 Andy Van Slyke .05 .15
223 Bob Walk .01 .05
224 Glenn Wilson .01 .05
225 Jesse Barfield .02 .10
226 George Bell .02 .10
227 Pat Borders RC .08 .25
228 John Cerutti .01 .05
229 Jim Clancy .01 .05
230 Mark Eichhorn .01 .05
231 Tony Fernandez .01 .05
232 Cecil Fielder .02 .10
233 Mike Flanagan .01 .05
234 Kelly Gruber .01 .05
235 Tom Henke .01 .05
236 Jimmy Key .02 .10
237 Rick Leach .01 .05
238 Manny Lee UER .01 .05
Bio says regular shortstop, sic, Tony Fernandez
239 Nelson Liriano .01 .05
240 Fred McGriff .05 .15
241 Lloyd Moseby .01 .05
242 Rance Mulliniks .01 .05
243 Jeff Musselman .01 .05
244 Dave Stieb .02 .10
245 Todd Stottlemyre .01 .05
246 Duane Ward .01 .05
247 David Wells .02 .10
248 Ernie Whitt UER .01 .05
HR total 21, should be 121
249 Luis Aquayo .01 .05
250A Neil Allen ERR .30 .75
250B Neil Allen COR .01 .05
Syosset, NY
251 John Candelaria .01 .05
252 Jack Clark .02 .10
253 Richard Dotson .01 .05
254 Rickey Henderson .08 .25
255 Tommy John .02 .10
256 Roberto Kelly .01 .05
257 Al Leiter .08 .25
258 Don Mattingly .25 .60
259 Dale Mohorcic .01 .05
260 Hal Morris RC .08 .25
261 Scott Nielsen .01 .05
262 Mike Pagliarulo UER .01 .05
Wrong birthdate
263 Hipolito Pena .01 .05
264 Ken Phelps .01 .05
265 Willie Randolph .02 .10
266 Rick Rhoden .01 .05
267 Dave Righetti .02 .10
268 Rafael Santana .01 .05
269 Steve Shields .01 .05
270 Joel Skinner .01 .05
271 Don Slaught .01 .05
272 Claudell Washington .01 .05
273 Gary Ward .01 .05
274 Dave Winfield .02 .10
275 Luis Aquino .01 .05
276 Floyd Bannister .01 .05
277 George Brett .25 .60
278 Bill Buckner .02 .10
279 Nick Capra .01 .05
280 Jose DeJesus .01 .05
281 Steve Farr .01 .05
282 Jerry Don Gleaton .01 .05
283 Mark Gubicza .01 .05
284 T.Gordon RC UER .20 .50
285 Bo Jackson .08 .25
286 Charlie Leibrandt .01 .05
287 Mike Macfarlane RC .08 .25
288 Jeff Montgomery .01 .05
289 Bill Pecota UER .01 .05
Photo actually Brad Wellman
290 Jamie Quirk .01 .05
291 Bret Saberhagen .02 .10
292 Kevin Seitzer .01 .05
293 Kurt Stillwell .01 .05
294 Pat Tabler .01 .05
295 Danny Tartabull .01 .05
296 Gary Thurman .01 .05
297 Frank White .02 .10
298 Willie Wilson .02 .10
299 Roberto Alomar .08 .25
300 S.Alomar Jr. RC UER .15 .40
Wrong birthdate, says 6/16/66, should say 6/18/66
301 Chris Brown .01 .05
302 Mike Brumley UER .01 .05
133 hits in '88, should be 134
303 Mark Davis .01 .05
304 Mark Grant .01 .05
305 Tony Gwynn .10 .30
306 Greg W. Harris RC .02 .10
307 Andy Hawkins .01 .05
308 Jimmy Jones .01 .05
309 John Kruk .02 .10
310 Dave Leiper .01 .05
311 Carmelo Martinez .01 .05
312 Lance McCullers .01 .05
313 Keith Moreland .01 .05
314 Dennis Rasmussen .01 .05
315 Randy Ready UER .01 .05
1214 games in '88, should be 114
316 Benito Santiago .02 .10
317 Eric Show .01 .05
318 Todd Simmons .01 .05
319 Garry Templeton .02 .10
320 Dickie Thon .01 .05
321 Ed Whitson .01 .05
322 Marvell Wynne .01 .05
323 Mike Aldrete .01 .05
324 Brett Butler .02 .10
325 Will Clark UER .05 .15
Three consecutive 100 RBI seasons
326 Kelly Downs UER .01 .05
'88 stats missing
327 Dave Dravecky .01 .05
328 Scott Garrelts .01 .05
329 Atlee Hammaker .01 .05
330 Charlie Hayes RC .08 .25
331 Mike Krukow .01 .05
332 Craig Lefferts .01 .05
333 Candy Maldonado .01 .05
334 Kirt Manwaring UER .01 .05
Bats Rights
335 Bob Melvin .01 .05
336 Kevin Mitchell .02 .10
337 Donell Nixon .01 .05
338 Tony Perezchica .01 .05
339 Joe Price .01 .05
340 Rick Reuschel .02 .10
341 Earnest Riles .01 .05
342 Don Robinson .01 .05
343 Chris Speier .01 .05
344 Robby Thompson UER .01 .05
West Plam Beach
345 Jose Uribe .01 .05
346 Matt Williams .08 .25
347 Trevor Wilson RC .02 .10
348 Juan Agosto .01 .05
349 Larry Andersen .01 .05
350A Alan Ashby ERR .75 2.00
350B Alan Ashby COR .01 .05
351 Kevin Bass .01 .05
352 Buddy Bell .02 .10
353 Craig Biggio RC 1.00 2.50
354 Danny Darwin .01 .05
355 Glenn Davis .01 .05
356 Jim Deshaies .01 .05
357 Bill Doran .01 .05
358 John Fishel RC .01 .05
359 Billy Hatcher .01 .05
360 Bob Knepper .01 .05
361 Louie Meadows UER RC .01 .05
Bio says 10 EBH's and 6 SB's in '88, should be 3 and 4
362 Dave Meads .01 .05
363 Jim Pankovits .01 .05
364 Terry Puhl .01 .05
365 Rafael Ramirez .01 .05
366 Craig Reynolds .01 .05
367 Mike Scott .02 .10
Card number listed as 368 on Astros CL
368 Nolan Ryan .40 1.00
369 Dave Smith .01 .05
370 Gerald Young .01 .05
371 Hubie Brooks .01 .05
372 Tim Burke .01 .05
373 John Dopson .01 .05
374 Mike R. Fitzgerald .01 .05
375 Tom Foley .01 .05
376 Andres Galarraga UER .02 .10
Home: Caracus
377 Neal Heaton .01 .05
378 Joe Hesketh .01 .05
379 Brian Holman RC .02 .10
380 Rex Hudler .01 .05
381 Randy Johnson RC UER 1.00 2.50
381B R.Johnson Marlboro ERR 15.00 40.00
381C R.Johnson Red Tint
381D R.Johnson Black Box
381E R.Johnson Green Tint
382 Wallace Johnson .01 .05
383 Tracy Jones .01 .05
384 Dave Martinez .01 .05
385 Dennis Martinez .02 .10
386 Andy McGaffigan .01 .05
387 Otis Nixon .01 .05
388 Johnny Paredes .01 .05
389 Jeff Parrett .01 .05
390 Pascual Perez .01 .05
391 Tim Raines .02 .10
392 Luis Rivera .01 .05
393 Nelson Santovenia .01 .05
394 Bryn Smith .01 .05
395 Tim Wallach .01 .05
396 Andy Allanson UER .01 .05
1214 hits in '88, should be 114
397 Rod Allen RC .01 .05
398 Scott Bailes .01 .05
399 Tom Candiotti .01 .05
400 Joe Carter .02 .10
401 Carmen Castillo UER .01 .05
After All-Star Break batting 2.50
402 Dave Clark UER .01 .05
Card front shows position as Rookie; after All-Star Break batting 3.14
403 John Farrell UER .01 .05
Typo in runs allowed in '88
404 Julio Franco .02 .10
405 Don Gordon .01 .05
406 Mel Hall .01 .05
407 Brad Havens .01 .05
408 Brook Jacoby .01 .05
409 Doug Jones .01 .05
410 Jeff Kaiser .01 .05
411 Luis Medina .01 .05
412 Cory Snyder .01 .05
413 Greg Swindell .01 .05
414 Ron Tingley UER .01 .05
Hit HR in first ML at-bat, should be first AL at-bat
415 Willie Upshaw .01 .05
416 Ron Washington .01 .05
417 Rich Yett .01 .05
418 Damon Berryhill .01 .05
419 Mike Bielecki .01 .05
420 Doug Dascenzo .01 .05
421 Jody Davis UER .01 .05
Braves stats for '88 missing
422 Andre Dawson .02 .10
423 Frank DiPino .01 .05
424 Shawon Dunston .01 .05
425 Rich Gossage .02 .10
426 Mark Grace UER .08 .25
Minor League stats for '88 missing
427 Mike Harkey RC .02 .10
428 Darrin Jackson .02 .10
429 Les Lancaster .01 .05
430 Vance Law .01 .05
431 Greg Maddux .20 .50
432 Jamie Moyer .02 .10
433 Al Nipper .01 .05
434 Rafael Palmeiro UER .08 .25
170 hits in '88, should be 178
435 Pat Perry .01 .05
436 Jeff Pico .01 .05
437 Ryne Sandberg .15 .40
438 Calvin Schiraldi .01 .05
439 Rick Sutcliffe .02 .10
440A Manny Trillo ERR .75 2.00
440B Manny Trillo COR .01 .05
441 Gary Varsho UER .01 .05
Wrong birthdate; .303 should be .302; 11/28 should be 9/19
442 Mitch Webster .01 .05
443 Luis Alicea RC .08 .25
444 Tom Brunansky .01 .05
445 Vince Coleman UER .01 .05
Third straight with 83 should be fourth straight with 81
446 John Costello UER RC .01 .05
Home California, should be New York
447 Danny Cox .01 .05
448 Ken Dayley .01 .05
449 Jose DeLeon .01 .05
450 Curt Ford .01 .05
451 Pedro Guerrero .02 .10
452 Bob Horner .02 .10
453 Tim Jones .01 .05
454 Steve Lake .01 .05
455 Joe Magrane UER .01 .05
Des Moines,IO
456 Greg Mathews .01 .05
457 Willie McGee .02 .10
458 Larry McWilliams .01 .05
459 Jose Oquendo .01 .05
460 Tony Pena .01 .05
461 Terry Pendleton .02 .10
462 Steve Peters UER .01 .05
Lives in Harrah, not Harah
463 Ozzie Smith .15 .40
464 Scott Terry .01 .05
465 Denny Walling .01 .05
466 Todd Worrell .01 .05
467 Tony Armas UER .02 .10
Before All-Star Break batting 2.39
468 Dante Bichette RC .15 .40
469 Bob Boone .02 .10
470 Terry Clark .01 .05
471 Stu Cliburn .01 .05
472 Mike Cook UER .01 .05
TM near Angels logo missing from front
473 Sherman Corbett RC .01 .05
474 Chili Davis .02 .10
475 Brian Downing .02 .10
476 Jim Eppard .01 .05
477 Chuck Finley .02 .10
478 Willie Fraser .01 .05
479 Bryan Harvey UER RC .08 .25
ML record shows 0-0, should be 7-5
480 Jack Howell .01 .05
481 Wally Joyner UER .02 .10
Yorba Linda, GA
482 Jack Lazorko .01 .05
483 Kirk McCaskill .01 .05
484 Mark McLemore .01 .05
485 Greg Minton .01 .05
486 Dan Petry .01 .05
487 Johnny Ray .01 .05
488 Dick Schofield .01 .05
489 Devon White .02 .10
490 Mike Witt .01 .05
491 Harold Baines .02 .10
492 Daryl Boston .01 .05
493 Ivan Calderon UER .01 .05
'80 stats shifted
494 Mike Diaz .01 .05
495 Carlton Fisk .05 .15
496 Dave Gallagher .01 .05
497 Ozzie Guillen .02 .10
498 Shawn Hillegas .01 .05
499 Lance Johnson .01 .05
500 Barry Jones .01 .05
501 Bill Long .01 .05
502 Steve Lyons .01 .05
503 Fred Manrique .01 .05
504 Jack McDowell .02 .10
505 Donn Pall .01 .05
506 Kelly Paris .01 .05
507 Dan Pasqua .01 .05
508 Ken Patterson .01 .05
509 Melido Perez .01 .05
510 Jerry Reuss .01 .05
511 Mark Salas .01 .05
512 Bobby Thigpen UER .01 .05
'86 ERA 4.69, should be 4.68
513 Mike Woodard .01 .05
514 Bob Brower .01 .05
515 Steve Buechele .01 .05
516 Jose Cecena .01 .05
517 Cecil Espy .01 .05
518 Scott Fletcher .01 .05
519 Cecilio Guante .01 .05
'87 Yankee stats are off-centered
520 Jose Guzman .01 .05
521 Ray Hayward .01 .05
522 Charlie Hough .02 .10
523 Pete Incaviglia .01 .05
524 Mike Jeffcoat .01 .05
525 Paul Kilgus .01 .05
526 Chad Kreuter RC .08 .25
527 Jeff Kunkel .01 .05
528 Oddibe McDowell .01 .05
529 Pete O'Brien .01 .05
530 Geno Petralli .01 .05
531 Jeff Russell .01 .05
532 Ruben Sierra .02 .10
533 Mike Stanley .01 .05
534A Ed VandeBerg ERR .75 2.00
534B Ed VandeBerg COR .01 .05
535 Curtis Wilkerson ERR .01 .05
Pitcher headings at bottom
536 Mitch Williams .01 .05
537 Bobby Witt UER .01 .05
'85 ERA .643, should be 6.43
538 Steve Balboni .01 .05
539 Scott Bankhead .01 .05
540 Scott Bradley .01 .05
541 Mickey Brantley .01 .05
542 Jay Buhner .02 .10
543 Mike Campbell .01 .05
544 Darnell Coles .01 .05
545 Henry Cotto .01 .05
546 Alvin Davis .01 .05
547 Mario Diaz .01 .05
548 Ken Griffey Jr. RC 6.00 15.00
549 Erik Hanson RC .08 .25
550 Mike Jackson UER .01 .05
Lifetime ERA 3.345, should be 3.45
551 Mark Langston .01 .05
552 Edgar Martinez .08 .25
553 Bill McGuire .01 .05
554 Mike Moore .01 .05
555 Jim Presley .01 .05
556 Rey Quinones .01 .05
557 Jerry Reed .01 .05
558 Harold Reynolds .02 .10
559 Mike Schooler .01 .05
560 Bill Swift .01 .05
561 Dave Valle .01 .05
562 Steve Bedrosian .01 .05
563 Phil Bradley .01 .05
564 Don Carman .01 .05
565 Bob Dernier .01 .05
566 Marvin Freeman .01 .05
567 Todd Frohwirth .01 .05
568 Greg Gross .01 .05
569 Kevin Gross .01 .05
570 Greg A. Harris .01 .05
571 Von Hayes .01 .05
572 Chris James .01 .05
573 Steve Jeltz .01 .05
574 Ron Jones UER .02 .10
Led IL in '88 with 85, should be 75
575 Ricky Jordan RC .08 .25
576 Mike Maddux .01 .05
577 David Palmer .01 .05
578 Lance Parrish .02 .10
579 Shane Rawley .01 .05
580 Bruce Ruffin .01 .05
581 Juan Samuel .01 .05
582 Mike Schmidt .20 .50
583 Kent Tekulve .01 .05
584 Milt Thompson UER .01 .05
19 hits in '88, should be 109
585 Jose Alvarez RC .02 .10
586 Paul Assenmacher .01 .05
587 Bruce Benedict .01 .05
588 Jeff Blauser .01 .05
589 Terry Blocker .01 .05
590 Ron Gant .02 .10
591 Tom Glavine .08 .25
592 Tommy Gregg .01 .05
593 Albert Hall .01 .05
594 Dion James .01 .05
595 Rick Mahler .01 .05
596 Dale Murphy .05 .15
597 Gerald Perry .01 .05
598 Charlie Puleo .01 .05
599 Ted Simmons .02 .10
600 Pete Smith .01 .05
601 Zane Smith .01 .05
602 John Smoltz RC .60 1.50
603 Bruce Sutter .02 .10
604 Andres Thomas .01 .05
605 Ozzie Virgil .01 .05
606 Brady Anderson RC .15 .40
607 Jeff Ballard .01 .05
608 Jose Bautista RC .02 .10
609 Ken Gerhart .01 .05
610 Terry Kennedy .01 .05
611 Eddie Murray .08 .25
612 Carl Nichols UER .01 .05
Before All-Star Break batting 1.86
613 Tom Niedenfuer .01 .05
614 Joe Orsulak .01 .05
615 Oswald Peraza UER RC .01 .05
(Shown as Oswaldo
616A B.Ripken Rick Face 8.00 20.00
616B B.Ripken White Out 60.00 120.00
616C Ripken Wht Scribble 40.00 100.00
616D Ripken Blk Scribble 3.00 8.00
616E B.Ripken Blk Box 2.50 6.00
617 Cal Ripken .30 .75
618 Dave Schmidt .01 .05
619 Rick Schu .01 .05
620 Larry Sheets .01 .05
621 Doug Sisk .01 .05
622 Pete Stanicek .01 .05
623 Mickey Tettleton .01 .05
624 Jay Tibbs .01 .05
625 Jim Traber .01 .05
626 Mark Williamson .01 .05
627 Craig Worthington .01 .05
628 Jose Canseco 40 .08 .25
40
629 Tom Browning Perfect .01 .05
630 R.Alomar/S.Alomar .08 .25
631 W.Clark/R.Palmeiro .05 .15
632 D.Strawberry/W.Clark .02 .10
633 W.Boggs/C.Lansford .02 .10
634 McGwire/Cans/Stein .30 .75
635 M.Davis/D.Gooden .01 .05
636 D.Jackson/D.Cone UER .01 .05
637 C.Sabo/B.Bonilla UER .02 .10
638 A.Galarraga/G.Perry UER .01 .05
639 K.Puckett/E.Davis .05 .15
640 S.Wilson/C.Drew .01 .05
641 K.Brown/K.Reimer .08 .25
642 B.Pounders RC/J.Clark .02 .10
643 M.Capel/D.Hall .01 .05
644 J.Girardi RC/R.Roomes .15 .40
645 L.Harris RC/M.Brown .08 .25
646 L.De Los Santos/J.Campbell .01 .05
647 R.Kramer/M.Garcia .01 .05
648 T.Lovullo RC/R.Palacios .02 .10
649 J.Corsi/B.Milacki .01 .05
650 G.Hall/M.Rochford .01 .05
651 T.Taylor/V.Lovelace RC .02 .10
652 K.Hill RC/D.Cook .08 .25
653 S.Service/S.Turner .01 .05
654 CL: Oakland .01 .05
Mets
Dodgers
Red Sox
10 Henderson;
68 Jess Orosco
655A CL: Twins .01 .05
Tigers ERR
Reds
Brewers
179 Boslo and
Twins
Tigers positions
listed
655B CL: Twins .01 .05
Tigers COR
Reds
Brewers
179 Boslo but
Twins
Tigers positions
not listed
656 CL: Pirates .01 .05
Blue Jays
Yankees
Royals
225 Jess Barfield
657 CL: Padres .01 .05
Giants
Astros
Expos
367
368 wrong
658 CL: Indians .01 .05
Cubs
Cardinals
Angels
449 Deleon
659 CL: White Sox .01 .05
Rangers
Mariners
Phillies
660 CL: Braves .01 .05
Orioles
Specials
Checklists

632 hyphenated diff-
erently and 650 Hali;
595 Rich Mahler;
619 Rich Schu

1989 Fleer Glossy

COMP.FACT.SET (672) 40.00 100.00
*STARS: 2X TO 5X BASIC CARDS
*ROOKIES: 2X TO 5X BASIC CARDS
DISTRIBUTED ONLY IN FACTORY SET FORM

1989 Fleer All-Stars

COMPLETE SET (12) 2.00 5.00
RANDOM INSERTS IN PACKS 1.00 2.00
1 Bobby Bonilla .30 .75
2 Jose Canseco .75 2.00
3 Will Clark .50 1.25
4 Dennis Eckersley .50 1.25
5 Julio Franco .30 .75
6 Mike Greenwell .15 .40
7 Orel Hershiser .30 .75
8 Paul Molitor .30 .75
9 Mike Scioscia .30 .75
10 Darryl Strawberry .30 .75
11 Alan Trammell .30 .75
12 Frank Viola .30 .75

1989 Fleer For The Record

COMPLETE SET (6) 3.00 8.00
ONE PER RACK PACK .50 1.00
1 Wade Boggs .40 1.00
2 Roger Clemens 2.50 6.00
3 Andres Galarraga .25 .60
4 Kirk Gibson .25 .60
5 Greg Maddux 1.25 3.00
6 Don Mattingly 1.50 4.00

1989 Fleer Wax Box Cards

COMPLETE SET (28) 4.00 10.00
C1 Mets Logo .05 .15
C2 Wade Boggs .30 .75
C3 George Brett .60 1.50
C4 Jose Canseco UER .60 1.50
'88 strikeouts 121
and career strike-
outs 49, should
be 128 and 491
C5 A's Logo .05 .15
C6 Will Clark .40 1.00
C7 David Cone .25 .60
C8 Andres Galarraga UER .25 .60
Career average .289
should be .269
C9 Dodgers Logo .05 .15
C10 Kirk Gibson .08 .25
C11 Mike Greenwell .05 .15
C12 Tony Gwynn 1.00 2.50
C13 Tigers Logo .05 .15
C14 Orel Hershiser .08 .25
C15 Danny Jackson .05 .15
C16 Wally Joyner .08 .25
C17 Red Sox Logo .05 .15
C18 Yankees Logo .05 .15
C19 Fred McGriff UER .40 1.00
Career BA of .289
should be .269
C20 Kirby Puckett .75 2.00
C21 Chris Sabo .05 .15
C22 Kevin Seitzer .05 .15
C23 Pirates Logo .05 .15
C24 Astros Logo .05 .15
C25 Darryl Strawberry .08 .25
C26 Alan Trammell .15 .40
C27 Andy Van Slyke .05 .15
C28 Frank Viola .05 .15

1989 Fleer World Series

COMPLETE SET (12) .75 2.00
ONE SET PER FACTORY SET
1 Mickey Hatcher .01 .05
2 Tim Belcher .01 .05
3 Jose Canseco .08 .25
4 Mike Scioscia .02 .10
5 Kirk Gibson .02 .10
6 Orel Hershiser .02 .10
7 Mike Marshall .01 .05
8 Mark McGwire .40 1.00
9 Steve Sax .01 .05
10 Walt Weiss .01 .05
11 Orel Hershiser .02 .10
12 Dodger Blue World Champs .02 .10

1989 Fleer Glossy World Series

*GLOSSY: .5X TO 1.2X BASIC WS
DISTRIBUTED ONLY IN FACTORY SET FORM

1989 Fleer Update

The 1989 Fleer Update set contains 132 standard-size cards. The cards were distributed exclusively in factory set form in grey and white, cellophane wrapped boxes through hobby dealers. The cards are identical in design to regular issue 1989 Fleer cards except for the U-prefixed numbering on back. The set numbering is in team order with players within teams ordered alphabetically. The set includes special cards for Nolan Ryan's 5,000th strikeout and Mike Schmidt's retirement. Rookie Cards include Kevin Appier, Joey (Albert) Belle, Deion Sanders, Greg Vaughn, Robin Ventura and Todd Zeile.

COMP.FACT.SET (132) 2.00 5.00
1 Phil Bradley .01 .05
2 Mike Devereaux .01 .05
3 Steve Finley RC .30 .75
4 Kevin Hickey .01 .05
5 Brian Holton .01 .05
6 Bob Milacki .01 .05
7 Randy Milligan .01 .05
8 John Dopson .01 .05
9 Nick Esasky .01 .05
10 Rob Murphy .01 .05
11 Jim Abbott RC .40 1.00
12 Bert Blyleven .02 .10
13 Jeff Manto RC .02 .10
14 Bob McClure .01 .05
15 Lance Parrish .02 .10
16 Lee Stevens RC .08 .25
17 Claudell Washington .01 .05
18 Mark Davis RC .08 .25
19 Eric King .01 .05
20 Ron Kittle .01 .05
21 Matt Merullo .01 .05
22 Steve Rosenberg .01 .05
23 Robin Ventura RC .30 .75
24 Keith Atherton .01 .05
25 Albert Belle RC .40 1.00
26 Jerry Browne .01 .05
27 Felix Fermin .01 .05
28 Brad Komminsk .01 .05
29 Pete O'Brien .01 .05
30 Mike Brumley .01 .05
31 Tracy Jones .01 .05
32 Mike Schwabe .01 .05
33 Gary Ward .01 .05
34 Frank Williams .01 .05
35 Kevin Appier RC .20 .50
36 Bob Boone .02 .10
37 Luis DeLosSantos .01 .05
38 Jim Eisenreich .01 .05
39 Jaime Navarro RC .02 .10
40 Billy Spiers RC .08 .25
41 Greg Vaughn RC .15 .40
42 Randy Veres .01 .05
43 Wally Backman .01 .05
44 Shane Rawley .01 .05
45 Steve Balboni .01 .05
46 Jesse Barfield .02 .10
47 Alvaro Espinoza .01 .05
48 Bob Geren RC .01 .05
49 Mel Hall .01 .05
50 Andy Hawkins .01 .05
51 Hensley Meulens RC .02 .10
52 Steve Sax .01 .05
53 Deion Sanders RC .60 1.50
54 Rickey Henderson .08 .25
55 Mike Moore .01 .05
56 Tony Phillips .01 .05
57 Greg Briley .02 .10
58 Gene Harris RC .02 .10
59 Randy Johnson 1.25 3.00
60 Jeffrey Leonard .01 .05
61 Dennis Powell .01 .05
62 Omar Vizquel RC .40 1.00
63 Kevin Brown .08 .25
64 Julio Franco .02 .10
65 Jamie Moyer .02 .10
66 Rafael Palmeiro .08 .25
67 Nolan Ryan .60 1.50
68 Francisco Cabrera RC .02 .10
69 Junior Felix RC .02 .10
70 Al Leiter .08 .25
71 Alex Sanchez RC .01 .05
72 Geronimo Berroa .01 .05
73 Derek Lilliquist RC .02 .10
74 Lonnie Smith .01 .05
75 Jeff Treadway .01 .05
76 Paul Kilgus .01 .05
77 Lloyd McClendon .01 .05
78 Scott Sanderson .01 .05
79 Dwight Smith RC .08 .25
80 Jerome Walton RC .08 .25
81 Mitch Williams .01 .05
82 Steve Wilson .02 .10
83 Todd Benzinger .01 .05
84 Ken Griffey Sr. .02 .10
85 Rick Mahler .01 .05
86 Rolando Roomes .01 .05
87 Scott Scudder RC .02 .10
88 Jim Clancy .01 .05
89 Rick Rhoden .01 .05
90 Dan Schatzeder .01 .05
91 Mike Morgan .01 .05
92 Eddie Murray .08 .25
93 Willie Randolph .02 .10
94 Ray Searage .01 .05
95 Mike Aldrete .01 .05
96 Kevin Gross .01 .05
97 Mark Langston .01 .05
98 Spike Owen .01 .05
99 Zane Smith .01 .05
100 Don Aase .01 .05
101 Barry Lyons .01 .05
102 Juan Samuel .01 .05
103 Wally Whitehurst RC .02 .10
104 Dennis Cook .01 .05
105 Len Dykstra .02 .10
106 Charlie Hayes .08 .25
107 Tommy Herr .01 .05
108 Ken Howell .01 .05
109 John Kruk .02 .10
110 Roger McDowell .01 .05
111 Terry Mulholland .01 .05
112 Jeff Parrett .01 .05
113 Neal Heaton .01 .05
114 Jeff King .01 .05
115 Randy Kramer .01 .05
116 Bill Landrum .01 .05
117 Cris Carpenter RC * .02 .10
118 Frank DiPino .01 .05
119 Ken Hill .08 .25
120 Dan Quisenberry .01 .05
121 Milt Thompson .01 .05
122 Todd Zeile RC .15 .40
123 Jack Clark .02 .10
124 Bruce Hurst .01 .05
125 Mark Parent RC .01 .05
126 Bip Roberts .01 .05
127 Jeff Brantley UER RC .08 .25
128 Terry Kennedy .01 .05
129 Mike LaCoss .01 .05
130 Greg Litton .01 .05
131 Mike Schmidt SPEC .30 .75
132 Checklist 1-132 .01 .05

1989 Fleer Baseball All-Stars

The 1989 Fleer Baseball All-Stars set contains 44 standard-size cards. The fronts are yellowish beige with salmon pinstripes; the vertically oriented backs are red, white and pink and feature career stats. The card numbering of this set is ordered alphabetically by player's name. The cards were distributed through Ben Franklin stores as a boxed set.

COMP.FACT SET (44) 2.50 6.00
1 Doyle Alexander .01 .05
2 George Bell .01 .05
3 Wade Boggs .15 .40
4 Bobby Bonilla .02 .10
5 Jose Canseco .15 .40
6 Will Clark .30 .75
7 Roger Clemens .30 .75
8 Vince Coleman .01 .05
9 David Cone .07 .20
10 Mark Davis .01 .05
11 Andre Dawson .07 .20
12 Dennis Eckersley .15 .40
13 Andres Galarraga .07 .20
14 Kirk Gibson .02 .10
15 Dwight Gooden .02 .10
16 Mike Greenwell .01 .05
17 Mark Gubicza .01 .05
18 Ozzie Guillen .02 .10
19 Tony Gwynn .30 .75
20 Rickey Henderson .25 .60
21 Orel Hershiser .02 .10
22 Danny Jackson .01 .05
23 Doug Jones .01 .05
24 Ricky Jordan .01 .05
25 Bob Knepper .01 .05
26 Barry Larkin .20 .50
27 Vance Law .01 .05
28 Don Mattingly .30 .75
29 Mark McGwire .40 1.00
30 Paul Molitor .15 .40
31 Gerald Perry .01 .05
32 Kirby Puckett .15 .40
33 Johnny Ray .01 .05
34 Harold Reynolds .02 .10
35 Cal Ripken .60 1.50
36 Don Robinson .01 .05
37 Ruben Sierra .02 .10
38 Dave Smith .01 .05
39 Darryl Strawberry .02 .10
40 Dave Stieb .01 .05
41 Alan Trammell .05 .15
42 Andy Van Slyke .01 .05
43 Frank Viola .01 .05
44 Dave Winfield .15 .40

1989 Fleer Baseball MVP's

The 1989 Fleer Baseball MVP's set contains 44 standard-size cards. The fronts and backs are green and yellow. The horizontally oriented backs feature career stats. The card numbering of this set is ordered alphabetically by player's name. The cards were distributed through Toys 'R' Us stores as a boxed set.

COMP.FACT SET (44) 3.00 8.00
1 Steve Bedrosian .01 .05
2 George Bell .01 .05
3 Wade Boggs .15 .40
4 George Brett .20 .50
5 Hubie Brooks .01 .05
6 Jose Canseco .10 .30
7 Will Clark .20 .50
8 Roger Clemens .20 .50
9 Eric Davis .02 .10
10 Glenn Davis .01 .05
11 Andre Dawson .07 .20
12 Andres Galarraga .07 .20
13 Kirk Gibson .02 .10
14 Dwight Gooden .02 .10
15 Mark Grace .20 .50
16 Mike Greenwell .01 .05
17 Tony Gwynn .30 .75
18 Bryan Harvey .01 .05
19 Orel Hershiser .02 .10
20 Ted Higuera .01 .05
21 Danny Jackson .01 .05
22 Mike Jackson .02 .10
23 Doug Jones .01 .05
24 Greg Maddux .60 1.00
25 Mike Marshall .01 .05
26 Don Mattingly .30 .75
27 Fred McGriff .20 .50
28 Mark McGwire .40 1.00
29 Kevin McReynolds .01 .05
30 Jack Morris .02 .10
31 Gerald Perry .01 .05
32 Kirby Puckett .15 .40
33 Chris Sabo .01 .05
34 Mike Scott .01 .05
35 Ruben Sierra .02 .10
36 Darryl Strawberry .02 .10
37 Danny Tartabull .01 .05
38 Bobby Thigpen .01 .05
39 Alan Trammell .05 .15
40 Andy Van Slyke .02 .10
41 Frank Viola .01 .05
42 Walt Weiss .01 .05
43 Dave Winfield .15 .40
44 Todd Worrell .02 .10

1989 Fleer Exciting Stars

The 1989 Fleer Exciting Stars set contains 44 standard-size cards. The fronts have baby blue borders; the backs are pink and blue. The vertically oriented backs feature career stats. The card numbering of this set is ordered alphabetically by player's name. The cards were distributed as a boxed set.

COMP.FACT SET (44) 2.50 6.00
1 Harold Baines .05 .15
2 Wade Boggs .15 .40
3 Jose Canseco .10 .30
4 Joe Carter .05 .15
5 Will Clark .20 .50
6 Roger Clemens .30 .75
7 Vince Coleman .01 .05
8 David Cone .07 .20
9 Eric Davis .02 .10
10 Glenn Davis .01 .05
11 Andre Dawson .07 .20
12 Dwight Evans .02 .10
13 Andres Galarraga .07 .20
14 Kirk Gibson .02 .10
15 Dwight Gooden .02 .10
16 Jim Gott .01 .05
17 Mark Grace .30 .75
18 Mike Greenwell .01 .05
19 Mark Gubicza .01 .05
20 Tony Gwynn .30 .75
21 Rickey Henderson .25 .60
22 Tom Henke .01 .05
23 Mike Henneman .01 .05
24 Orel Hershiser .02 .10
25 Danny Jackson .01 .05
26 Gregg Jefferies .01 .05
27 Ricky Jordan .01 .05
28 Wally Joyner .02 .10
29 Mark Langston .01 .05
30 Tim Leary .01 .05
31 Don Mattingly .30 .75
32 Mark McGwire .40 1.00
33 Dale Murphy .07 .20
34 Kirby Puckett .15 .40
35 Chris Sabo .01 .05
36 Kevin Seitzer .01 .05
37 Ruben Sierra .02 .10
38 Ozzie Smith .30 .75
39 Dave Stewart .02 .10
40 Darryl Strawberry .02 .10
41 Alan Trammell .05 .15
42 Frank Viola .01 .05
43 Dave Winfield .15 .40
44 Robin Yount .15 .40

1989 Fleer Heroes of Baseball

The 1989 Fleer Heroes of Baseball set contains 44 standard-size cards. The fronts and backs are red, white and blue. The vertically oriented backs feature career stats. The card numbering of this set is ordered alphabetically by player's name. The cards were distributed through Woolworth stores as a boxed set.

COMP.FACT SET (44) 2.50 6.00
1 George Bell .01 .05
2 Wade Boggs .20 .50
3 Barry Bonds .40 1.00
4 Tom Brunansky .01 .05
5 Jose Canseco .15 .40
6 Joe Carter .05 .15
7 Will Clark .20 .50
8 Roger Clemens .40 1.00
9 David Cone .07 .20
10 Eric Davis .02 .10
11 Glenn Davis .01 .05
12 Andre Dawson .07 .20
13 Dennis Eckersley .15 .40
14 John Franco .02 .10
15 Gary Gaetti .02 .10
16 Andres Galarraga .07 .20
17 Kirk Gibson .02 .10
18 Dwight Gooden .02 .10
19 Mike Greenwell .01 .05
20 Tony Gwynn .30 .75
21 Bryan Harvey .01 .05
22 Orel Hershiser .02 .10
23 Ted Higuera .01 .05
24 Danny Jackson .01 .05
25 Ricky Jordan .01 .05
26 Don Mattingly .30 .75
27 Fred McGriff .15 .40
28 Mark McGwire .40 1.00
29 Kevin McReynolds .01 .05
30 Gerald Perry .01 .05
31 Kirby Puckett .20 .50
32 Johnny Ray .01 .05
33 Harold Reynolds .02 .10
34 Cal Ripken .60 1.50
35 Ryne Sandberg .20 .50
36 Kevin Seitzer .01 .05
37 Ruben Sierra .02 .10
38 Darryl Strawberry .02 .10
39 Bobby Thigpen .01 .05
40 Alan Trammell .05 .15
41 Andy Van Slyke .02 .10
42 Frank Viola .01 .05
43 Dave Winfield .15 .40
44 Robin Yount .20 .50

1989 Fleer League Leaders

The 1989 Fleer League Leaders set contains 44 standard-size cards. The fronts are red and yellow; the horizontally oriented backs are light blue and red, and feature career stats. The card numbering of this set is ordered alphabetically by player's name. The cards were distributed through Woolworth stores as a boxed set.

COMP.FACT SET (44) 2.50 6.00
1 Allan Anderson .01 .05
2 Wade Boggs .15 .40
3 Jose Canseco .10 .30
4 Will Clark .20 .50
5 Roger Clemens .30 .75
6 Vince Coleman .01 .05
7 David Cone .07 .20
8 Kal Daniels .01 .05
9 Chili Davis .02 .10
10 Eric Davis .02 .10
11 Glenn Davis .01 .05
12 Andre Dawson .07 .20
13 John Franco .02 .10
14 Andres Galarraga .07 .20
15 Kirk Gibson .02 .10
16 Dwight Gooden .02 .10
17 Mark Grace .30 .75
18 Mike Greenwell .01 .05
19 Tony Gwynn .30 .75
20 Orel Hershiser .02 .10
21 Pete Incaviglia .01 .05
22 Danny Jackson .01 .05
23 Gregg Jefferies .01 .05
24 Joe Magrane .01 .05
25 Don Mattingly .30 .75
26 Fred McGriff .15 .40
27 Mark McGwire .40 1.00
28 Dale Murphy .07 .20
29 Dan Plesac .01 .05
30 Kirby Puckett .20 .50
31 Harold Reynolds .02 .10
32 Cal Ripken .60 1.50
33 Jeff M. Robinson .01 .05
34 Mike Scott .01 .05
35 Ozzie Smith .30 .75
36 Dave Stewart .02 .10
37 Darryl Strawberry .02 .10
38 Greg Swindell .01 .05
39 Bobby Thigpen .01 .05
40 Alan Trammell .05 .15
41 Andy Van Slyke .01 .05
42 Frank Viola .01 .05
43 Dave Winfield .15 .40
44 Robin Yount .20 .50

1989 Fleer Superstars

The 1989 Fleer Superstars set contains 44 standard-size cards. The fronts are red and beige; the horizontally oriented backs are yellow, and feature career stats. The card numbering of this set is ordered alphabetically by player's name. The cards were distributed as a boxed set. The back panel of the box contains the complete set checklist.

COMP.FACT SET (44) 2.50 6.00
1 Roberto Alomar .30 .75
2 Harold Baines .02 .10
3 Tim Belcher .01 .05
4 Wade Boggs .15 .40
5 George Brett .30 .75
6 Jose Canseco .10 .30
7 Gary Carter .05 .15
8 Will Clark .20 .50
9 Roger Clemens .30 .75
10 Kal Daniels UER/(Reverse negative .01 .05
photo on front
11 Eric Davis .02 .10
12 Andre Dawson .07 .20
13 Tony Fernandez .02 .10
14 Scott Fletcher .01 .05
15 Andres Galarraga .07 .20
16 Kirk Gibson .02 .10
17 Dwight Gooden .02 .10
18 Jim Gott .01 .05
19 Mark Grace .30 .75
20 Mike Greenwell .01 .05
21 Tony Gwynn .30 .75
22 Rickey Henderson .25 .60
23 Orel Hershiser .02 .10
24 Ted Higuera .01 .05
25 Gregg Jefferies .01 .05
26 Wally Joyner .02 .10
27 Mark Langston .01 .05
28 Greg Maddux .60 1.50
29 Don Mattingly .30 .75
30 Fred McGriff .15 .40
31 Mark McGwire .40 1.00
32 Dan Plesac .01 .05
33 Kirby Puckett .15 .40
34 Jeff Reardon .02 .10
35 Chris Sabo .01 .05
36 Mike Schmidt .20 .50
37 Mike Scott .01 .05
38 Cory Snyder .01 .05
39 Darryl Strawberry .02 .10
40 Alan Trammell .05 .15
41 Frank Viola .01 .05
42 Walt Weiss .01 .05
43 Dave Winfield .20 .50
44 Todd Worrell UER/(Statistical headings.01 .05
on back f

1990 Fleer

The 1990 Fleer set contains 660 standard-size cards. Cards were primarily issued in wax packs, cello packs, rack packs and hobby and retail factory sets. Card fronts feature white outer borders with ribbon-like, colored inner borders. The set is again ordered numerically by teams based upon the previous season's record. Subsets include Decade Greats (621-630), Superstar Combinations (631-639), Rookie Prospects (640-653) and checklists (654-660). Rookie Cards of note include Moises Alou, Juan Gonzalez, David Justice, Sammy Sosa and Larry Walker.

COMPLETE SET (660) 6.00 15.00
COMP.RETAIL SET (660) 6.00 15.00
COMP.HOBBY SET (672) 6.00 15.00
1 Lance Blankenship .01 .05
2 Todd Burns .01 .05
3 Jose Canseco .05 .15
4 Jim Corsi .01 .05
5 Storm Davis .01 .05
6 Dennis Eckersley .02 .10
7 Mike Gallego .01 .05
8 Ron Hassey .01 .05
9 Dave Henderson .01 .05
10 Rickey Henderson .08 .25
11 Rick Honeycutt .01 .05
12 Stan Javier .01 .05
13 Felix Jose .01 .05
14 Carney Lansford .02 .10
15 Mark McGwire .40 1.00
16 Mike Moore .01 .05
17 Gene Nelson .01 .05
18 Dave Parker .02 .10
19 Tony Phillips .01 .05
20 Terry Steinbach .01 .05
21 Dave Stewart .02 .10
22 Walt Weiss .01 .05
23 Bob Welch .01 .05
24 Curt Young .01 .05
25 Paul Assenmacher .01 .05
26 Damon Berryhill .01 .05
27 Mike Bielecki .01 .05
28 Kevin Blankenship .01 .05
29 Andre Dawson .02 .10
30 Shawon Dunston .01 .05
31 Joe Girardi .05 .15
32 Mark Grace .05 .15
33 Mike Harkey .01 .05
34 Paul Kilgus .01 .05
35 Les Lancaster .01 .05
36 Vance Law .01 .05
37 Greg Maddux .15 .40
38 Lloyd McClendon .01 .05
39 Jeff Pico .01 .05
40 Ryne Sandberg .15 .40
41 Scott Sanderson .01 .05
42 Dwight Smith .01 .05
43 Rick Sutcliffe .02 .10
44 Jerome Walton .01 .05
45 Mitch Webster .01 .05
46 Curt Wilkerson .01 .05
47 Dean Wilkins RC .01 .05
48 Mitch Williams .01 .05
49 Steve Wilson .01 .05
50 Steve Bedrosian .01 .05
51 Mike Benjamin RC .02 .10
52 Jeff Brantley .01 .05
53 Brett Butler .02 .10
54 Will Clark UER .02 .10
55 Kelly Downs .01 .05
56 Scott Garrelts .01 .05
57 Atlee Hammaker .01 .05
58 Terry Kennedy .01 .05
59 Mike LaCoss .01 .05
60 Craig Lefferts .01 .05
61 Greg Litton .01 .05
62 Candy Maldonado .01 .05
63 Kirt Manwaring UER/(No '88 Phoenix stats/as note
.01 .05
64 Randy McCament RC .01 .05
65 Kevin Mitchell .01 .05
66 Donell Nixon .01 .05
67 Ken Oberkfell .01 .05
68 Rick Reuschel .01 .05
69 Ernest Riles .01 .05
70 Don Robinson .01 .05
71 Pat Sheridan .01 .05
72 Chris Speier .01 .05
73 Robby Thompson .01 .05
74 Jose Uribe .01 .05
75 Matt Williams .02 .10
76 George Bell .01 .05
77 Pat Borders .01 .05
78 John Cerutti .01 .05
79 Junior Felix .01 .05
80 Tony Fernandez .01 .05
81 Mike Flanagan .01 .05
82 Mauro Gozzo RC .01 .05
83 Kelly Gruber .01 .05
84 Tom Henke .01 .05
85 Jimmy Key .02 .10
86 Manny Lee .01 .05
87 Nelson Liriano UER .01 .05
88 Lee Mazzilli .01 .05
89 Fred McGriff .08 .25
90 Lloyd Moseby .01 .05
91 Rance Mulliniks .01 .05
92 Alex Sanchez .01 .05
93 Dave Stieb .02 .10
94 Todd Stottlemyre .02 .10
95 Duane Ward UER .01 .05
96 David Wells .02 .10
97 Ernie Whitt .01 .05
98 Frank Wills .01 .05
99 Mookie Wilson .02 .10
100 Kevin Appier .02 .10
101 Luis Aquino .01 .05
102 Bob Boone .02 .10
103 George Brett .25 .60
104 Jose DeJesus .01 .05
105 Luis De Los Santos .01 .05
106 Jim Eisenreich .01 .05
107 Steve Farr .01 .05
108 Tom Gordon .02 .10
109 Mark Gubicza .01 .05
110 Bo Jackson .08 .25
111 Terry Leach .01 .05
112 Charlie Leibrandt .01 .05
113 Rick Luecken RC .01 .05
114 Mike Macfarlane .01 .05
115 Jeff Montgomery .02 .10
116 Bret Saberhagen .02 .10
117 Kevin Seitzer .01 .05
118 Kurt Stillwell .01 .05
119 Pat Tabler .01 .05
120 Danny Tartabull .01 .05
121 Gary Thurman .01 .05
122 Frank White .02 .10
123 Willie Wilson .01 .05
124 Matt Winters RC .01 .05
125 Jim Abbott .05 .15
126 Tony Armas .01 .05
127 Dante Bichette .02 .10
128 Bert Blyleven .02 .10
129 Chili Davis .02 .10
130 Brian Downing .01 .05
131 Mike Fetters RC .08 .25
132 Chuck Finley .02 .10
133 Willie Fraser .01 .05
134 Bryan Harvey .01 .05
135 Jack Howell .01 .05
136 Wally Joyner .02 .10
137 Jeff Manto .01 .05
138 Kirk McCaskill .01 .05
139 Bob McClure .01 .05
140 Greg Minton .01 .05
141 Lance Parrish .01 .05
142 Dan Petry .01 .05
143 Johnny Ray .01 .05
144 Dick Schofield .01 .05
145 Lee Stevens .02 .10
146 Claudell Washington .01 .05
147 Devon White .02 .10
148 Mike Witt .01 .05
149 Roberto Alomar .05 .15
150 Sandy Alomar Jr. .02 .10
151 Andy Benes .02 .10
152 Jack Clark .02 .10
153 Pat Clements .01 .05
154 Joey Cora .02 .10
155 Mark Davis .01 .05
156 Mark Grant .01 .05
157 Tony Gwynn .10 .30
158 Greg W. Harris .01 .05
159 Bruce Hurst .01 .05
160 Darrin Jackson .01 .05
161 Chris James .01 .05
162 Carmelo Martinez .01 .05
163 Mike Pagliarulo .01 .05
164 Mark Parent .01 .05
165 Dennis Rasmussen .01 .05
166 Bip Roberts .01 .05
167 Benito Santiago .02 .10
168 Calvin Schiraldi .01 .05
169 Eric Show .01 .05
170 Garry Templeton .01 .05
171 Ed Whitson .01 .05
172 Brady Anderson .02 .10
173 Jeff Ballard .01 .05
174 Phil Bradley .01 .05
175 Mike Devereaux .01 .05
176 Steve Finley .02 .10
177 Pete Harnisch .01 .05
178 Kevin Hickey .01 .05
179 Brian Holton .01 .05
180 Ben McDonald RC .08 .25
181 Bob Melvin .01 .05
182 Bob Milacki .01 .05
183 Randy Milligan UER .01 .05
184 Gregg Olson .02 .10
185 Joe Orsulak .01 .05
186 Bill Ripken .01 .05
187 Cal Ripken .30 .75
188 Dave Schmidt .01 .05
189 Larry Sheets .01 .05
190 Mickey Tettleton .01 .05
191 Mark Thurmond .01 .05
192 Jay Tibbs .01 .05
193 Jim Traber .01 .05
194 Mark Williamson .01 .05
195 Craig Worthington .01 .05
196 Don Aase .01 .05
197 Blaine Beatty RC .01 .05
198 Mark Carreon .01 .05
199 Gary Carter .02 .10
200 David Cone .02 .10
201 Ron Darling .01 .05
202 Kevin Elster .01 .05
203 Sid Fernandez .01 .05
204 Dwight Gooden .02 .10
205 Keith Hernandez .02 .10
206 Jeff Innis RC .01 .05
207 Gregg Jefferies .02 .10
208 Howard Johnson .01 .05
209 Barry Lyons UER .01 .05
210 Dave Magadan .01 .05
211 Kevin McReynolds .01 .05
212 Jeff Musselman .01 .05
213 Randy Myers .02 .10
214 Bob Ojeda .01 .05
215 Juan Samuel .01 .05
216 Mackey Sasser .01 .05
217 Darryl Strawberry .02 .10
218 Tim Teufel .01 .05
219 Frank Viola .01 .05
220 Juan Agosto .01 .05
221 Larry Andersen .01 .05
222 Eric Anthony RC .02 .10
223 Kevin Bass .01 .05
224 Craig Biggio .08 .25
225 Ken Caminiti .02 .10
226 Jim Clancy .01 .05
227 Danny Darwin .01 .05
228 Glenn Davis .01 .05
229 Jim Deshaies .01 .05
230 Bill Doran .01 .05
231 Bob Forsch .01 .05
232 Brian Meyer .01 .05
233 Terry Puhl .01 .05
234 Rafael Ramirez .01 .05
235 Rick Rhoden .01 .05
236 Dan Schatzeder .01 .05
237 Mike Scott .01 .05
238 Dave Smith .01 .05
239 Alex Trevino .01 .05
240 Glenn Wilson .01 .05
241 Gerald Young .01 .05
242 Tom Brunansky .01 .05
243 Cris Carpenter .01 .05
244 Alex Cole RC .02 .10
245 Vince Coleman .01 .05
246 John Costello .01 .05
247 Ken Dayley .01 .05
248 Jose DeLeon .01 .05
249 Frank DiPino .01 .05
250 Pedro Guerrero .01 .05
251 Ken Hill .02 .10
252 Joe Magrane .01 .05
253 Willie McGee UER .02 .10
254 John Morris .01 .05
255 Jose Oquendo .01 .05
256 Tony Pena .01 .05
257 Terry Pendleton .02 .10
258 Ted Power .01 .05
259 Dan Quisenberry .01 .05
260 Ozzie Smith .15 .40
261 Scott Terry .01 .05
262 Milt Thompson .01 .05
263 Denny Walling .01 .05
264 Todd Worrell .01 .05
265 Todd Zeile .02 .10
266 Marty Barrett .01 .05
267 Mike Boddicker .01 .05
268 Wade Boggs .05 .15
269 Ellis Burks .05 .15
270 Rick Cerone .01 .05
271 Roger Clemens .40 1.00
272 John Dopson .01 .05
273 Nick Esasky .01 .05
274 Dwight Evans .05 .15
275 Wes Gardner .01 .05
276 Rich Gedman .01 .05
277 Mike Greenwell .01 .05
278 Danny Heep .01 .05
279 Eric Hetzel .01 .05
280 Dennis Lamp .01 .05
281 Rob Murphy UER .01 .05
282 Joe Price .01 .05
283 Carlos Quintana .01 .05
284 Jody Reed .01 .05
285 Luis Rivera .01 .05
286 Kevin Romine .01 .05
287 Lee Smith .02 .10
288 Mike Smithson .01 .05
289 Bob Stanley .01 .05
290 Harold Baines .02 .10
291 Kevin Brown .02 .10
292 Steve Buechele .01 .05
293 Scott Coolbaugh RC .01 .05
294 Jack Daugherty RC .01 .05

295 Cecil Espy .01 .05
296 Julio Franco .02 .10
297 Juan Gonzalez RC .40 1.00
298 Cecilio Guante .01 .05
299 Drew Hall .01 .05
300 Charlie Hough .02 .10
301 Pete Incaviglia .01 .05
302 Mike Jeffcoat .01 .05
303 Chad Kreuter .01 .05
304 Jeff Kunkel .01 .05
305 Rick Leach .01 .05
306 Fred Manrique .01 .05
307 Jamie Moyer .02 .10
308 Rafael Palmeiro .05 .15
309 Geno Petralli .01 .05
310 Kevin Reimer .01 .05
311 Kenny Rogers .02 .10
312 Jeff Russell .01 .05
313 Nolan Ryan .40 1.00
314 Ruben Sierra .02 .10
315 Bobby Witt .01 .05
316 Chris Bosio .01 .05
317 Glenn Braggs UER .01 .05
318 Greg Brock .01 .05
319 Chuck Crim .01 .05
320 Rob Deer .01 .05
321 Mike Felder .01 .05
322 Tom Filer .01 .05
323 Tony Fossas RC .01 .05
324 Jim Gantner .01 .05
325 Darryl Hamilton .01 .05
326 Teddy Higuera .01 .05
327 Mark Knudson .01 .05
328 Bill Krueger UER .01 .05
329 Tim McIntosh RC .02 .10
330 Paul Molitor .02 .10
331 Jaime Navarro .01 .05
332 Charlie O'Brien .01 .05
333 Jeff Peterek RC .01 .05
334 Dan Plesac .01 .05
335 Jerry Reuss .01 .05
336 Gary Sheffield UER .08 .25
337 Bill Spiers .01 .05
338 B.J. Surhoff .02 .10
339 Greg Vaughn .01 .05
340 Robin Yount .15 .40
341 Hubie Brooks .01 .05
342 Tim Burke .01 .05
343 Mike Fitzgerald .01 .05
344 Tom Foley .01 .05
345 Andres Galarraga .02 .10
346 Damaso Garcia .01 .05
347 Marquis Grissom RC .15 .40
348 Kevin Gross .01 .05
349 Joe Hesketh .01 .05
350 Jeff Huson RC .01 .05
351 Wallace Johnson .01 .05
352 Mark Langston .01 .05
353A Dave Martinez Yellow .75 2.00
353B Dave Martinez .01 .05
Red on front
354 Dennis Martinez UER .02 .10
355 Andy McGaffigan .01 .05
356 Otis Nixon .01 .05
357 Spike Owen .01 .05
358 Pascual Perez .01 .05
359 Tim Raines .02 .10
360 Nelson Santovenia .01 .05
361 Bryn Smith .01 .05
362 Zane Smith .01 .05
363 Larry Walker RC .40 1.00
364 Tim Wallach .01 .05
365 Rick Aguilera .02 .10
366 Allan Anderson .01 .05
367 Wally Backman .01 .05
368 Doug Baker .01 .05
369 Juan Berenguer .01 .05
370 Randy Bush .01 .05
371 Carmelo Castillo .01 .05
372 Mike Dyer RC .01 .05
373 Gary Gaetti .02 .10
374 Greg Gagne .01 .05
375 Dan Gladden .01 .05
376 German Gonzalez UER .01 .05
377 Brian Harper .01 .05
378 Kent Hrbek .02 .10
379 Gene Larkin .01 .05
380 Tim Laudner UER .01 .05
381 John Moses .01 .05
382 Al Newman .01 .05
383 Kirby Puckett .08 .25
384 Shane Rawley .01 .05
385 Jeff Reardon .02 .10
386 Roy Smith .01 .05
387 Gary Wayne .01 .05
388 Dave West .01 .05
389 Tim Belcher .01 .05
390 Tim Crews UER .01 .05
391 Mike Davis .01 .05
392 Rick Dempsey .01 .05
393 Kirk Gibson .02 .10
394 Jose Gonzalez .01 .05
395 Alfredo Griffin .01 .05
396 Jeff Hamilton .01 .05
397 Lenny Harris .01 .05
398 Mickey Hatcher .01 .05
399 Orel Hershiser .02 .10
400 Jay Howell .01 .05
401 Mike Marshall .01 .05
402 Ramon Martinez .01 .05
403 Mike Morgan .01 .05
404 Eddie Murray .08 .25
405 Alejandro Pena .01 .05
406 Willie Randolph .02 .10
407 Mike Scioscia .01 .05
408 Ray Searage .01 .05
409 Fernando Valenzuela .02 .10
410 Jose Vizcaino RC .08 .25
411 John Wetteland .08 .25
412 Jack Armstrong .01 .05
413 Todd Benzinger UER .01 .05
414 Tim Birtsas .01 .05
415 Tom Browning .01 .05
416 Norm Charlton .01 .05
417 Eric Davis .02 .10
418 Rob Dibble .02 .10
419 John Franco .02 .10
420 Ken Griffey Sr. .02 .10
421 Chris Hammond RC .02 .10
422 Danny Jackson .01 .05
423 Barry Larkin .05 .15
424 Tim Leary .01 .05
425 Rick Mahler .01 .05
426 Joe Oliver .01 .05
427 Paul O'Neill .05 .15
428 Luis Quinones UER .01 .05
429 Jeff Reed .01 .05
430 Jose Rijo .01 .05
431 Ron Robinson .01 .05
432 Rolando Roomes .01 .05
433 Chris Sabo .01 .05
434 Scott Scudder .01 .05
435 Herm Winningham .01 .05
436 Steve Balboni .01 .05
437 Jesse Barfield .01 .05
438 Mike Blowers RC .02 .10
439 Tom Brookens .01 .05
440 Greg Cadaret .01 .05
441 Alvaro Espinoza UER .01 .05
442 Bob Geren .01 .05
443 Lee Guetterman .01 .05
444 Mel Hall .01 .05
445 Andy Hawkins .01 .05
446 Roberto Kelly .01 .05
447 Don Mattingly .25 .60
448 Lance McCullers .01 .05
449 Hensley Meulens .01 .05
450 Dale Mohorcic .01 .05
451 Clay Parker .01 .05
452 Eric Plunk .01 .05
453 Dave Righetti .01 .05
454 Deion Sanders .08 .25
455 Steve Sax .01 .05
456 Don Slaught .01 .05
457 Walt Terrell .01 .05
458 Dave Winfield .02 .10
459 Jay Bell .02 .10
460 Rafael Belliard .01 .05
461 Barry Bonds .40 1.00
462 Bobby Bonilla .02 .10
463 Sid Bream .01 .05
464 Benny Distefano .01 .05
465 Doug Drabek .01 .05
466 Jim Gott .01 .05
467 Billy Hatcher UER .01 .05
468 Neal Heaton .01 .05
469 Jeff King .01 .05
470 Bob Kipper .01 .05
471 Randy Kramer .01 .05
472 Bill Landrum .01 .05
473 Mike LaValliere .01 .05
474 Jose Lind .01 .05
475 Junior Ortiz .01 .05
476 Gary Redus .01 .05
477 Rick Reed RC .08 .25
478 R.J. Reynolds .01 .05
479 Jeff D. Robinson .01 .05
480 John Smiley .01 .05
481 Andy Van Slyke .05 .15
482 Bob Walk .01 .05
483 Andy Allanson .01 .05
484 Scott Bailes .01 .05
485 Albert Belle .08 .25
486 Bud Black .01 .05
487 Jerry Browne .01 .05
488 Tom Candiotti .01 .05
489 Joe Carter .02 .10
490 Dave Clark .01 .05
No '84 stats
491 John Farrell .01 .05
492 Felix Fermin .01 .05
493 Brook Jacoby .01 .05
494 Dion James .01 .05
495 Doug Jones .01 .05
496 Brad Komminsk .01 .05
497 Rod Nichols .01 .05
498 Pete O'Brien .01 .05
499 Steve Olin RC .02 .10
500 Jesse Orosco .01 .05
501 Joel Skinner .01 .05
502 Cory Snyder .01 .05
503 Greg Swindell .01 .05
504 Rich Yett .01 .05
505 Scott Bankhead .01 .05
506 Scott Bradley .01 .05
507 Greg Briley UER .01 .05
508 Jay Buhner .02 .10
509 Darnell Coles .01 .05
510 Keith Comstock .01 .05
511 Henry Cotto .01 .05
512 Alvin Davis .01 .05
513 Ken Griffey Jr. .40 1.00
514 Erik Hanson .01 .05
515 Gene Harris .01 .05
516 Brian Holman .01 .05
517 Mike Jackson .01 .05
518 Randy Johnson .20 .50
519 Jeffrey Leonard .01 .05
520 Edgar Martinez .05 .15
521 Dennis Powell .01 .05
522 Jim Presley .01 .05
523 Jerry Reed .01 .05
524 Harold Reynolds .02 .10
525 Mike Schooler .01 .05
526 Bill Swift .01 .05
527 Dave Valle .01 .05
528 Omar Vizquel .08 .25
529 Ivan Calderon .01 .05
530 Carlton Fisk UER .05 .15
531 Scott Fletcher .01 .05
532 Dave Gallagher .01 .05
533 Ozzie Guillen .02 .10
534 Greg Hibbard RC .02 .10
535 Shawn Hillegas .01 .05
536 Lance Johnson .01 .05
537 Eric King .01 .05
538 Ron Kittle .01 .05
539 Steve Lyons .01 .05
540 Carlos Martinez .01 .05
541 Tom McCarthy .01 .05
542 Matt Merullo .01 .05
543 Donn Pall UER .01 .05
544 Dan Pasqua .01 .05
545 Ken Patterson .01 .05
546 Melido Perez .01 .05
547 Steve Rosenberg .01 .05
548 Sammy Sosa RC 1.00 2.50
549 Bobby Thigpen .01 .05
550 Robin Ventura .08 .25
551 Greg Walker .01 .05
552 Don Carman .01 .05
553 Pat Combs .01 .05
554 Dennis Cook .01 .05
555 Darren Daulton .02 .10
556 Len Dykstra .02 .10
557 Curt Ford .01 .05
558 Charlie Hayes .01 .05
559 Von Hayes .01 .05
560 Tommy Herr .01 .05
561 Ken Howell .01 .05
562 Steve Jeltz .01 .05
563 Ron Jones .01 .05
564 Ricky Jordan UER .01 .05
565 John Kruk .02 .10
566 Steve Lake .01 .05
567 Roger McDowell .01 .05
568 Terry Mulholland UER .01 .05
569 Dwayne Murphy .01 .05
570 Jeff Parrett .01 .05
571 Randy Ready .01 .05
572 Bruce Ruffin .01 .05
573 Dickie Thon .01 .05
574 Jose Alvarez UER .01 .05
575 Geronimo Berroa .01 .05
576 Jeff Blauser .01 .05
577 Joe Boever .01 .05
578 Marty Clary UER .01 .05
579 Jody Davis .01 .05
580 Mark Eichhorn .01 .05
581 Darrell Evans .02 .10
582 Ron Gant .02 .10
583 Tom Glavine .05 .15
584 Tommy Greene RC .02 .10
585 Tommy Gregg .01 .05
586 David Justice RC .20 .50
587 Mark Lemke .01 .05
588 Derek Lilliquist .01 .05
589 Oddibe McDowell .01 .05
590 Kent Mercker RC .01 .05
591 Dale Murphy .05 .15
592 Gerald Perry .01 .05
593 Lonnie Smith .01 .05
594 Pete Smith .01 .05
595 John Smoltz .08 .25
596 Mike Stanton UER RC .08 .25
597 Andres Thomas .01 .05
598 Jeff Treadway .01 .05
599 Doyle Alexander .01 .05
600 Dave Bergman .01 .05
601 Brian DuBois RC .01 .05
602 Paul Gibson .01 .05
603 Mike Heath .01 .05
604 Mike Henneman .01 .05
605 Guillermo Hernandez .01 .05
606 Shawn Holman RC .01 .05
607 Tracy Jones .01 .05
608 Chet Lemon .01 .05
609 Fred Lynn .01 .05
610 Jack Morris .02 .10
611 Matt Nokes .01 .05
612 Gary Pettis .01 .05
613 Kevin Ritz RC .01 .05
614 Jeff M. Robinson .01 .05
615 Steve Searcy .01 .05
616 Frank Tanana .01 .05
617 Alan Trammell .02 .10
618 Gary Ward .01 .05
619 Lou Whitaker .02 .10
620 Frank Williams .01 .05
621A George Brett '80 ERR .75 2.00
621B George Brett '80 .10 .30
622 Fern.Valenzuela '81 .01 .05
623 Dale Murphy '82 .05 .15
624A Cal Ripkin '83 ERR 2.00 5.00
624B Cal Ripken '83 COR .15 .40
625 Ryne Sandberg '84 .08 .25
626 Don Mattingly '85 .07 .20
627 Roger Clemens '86 .20 .50
628 George Bell '87 .01 .05
629 Jose Canseco '88 UER .02 .10
630A Will Clark '89 ERR 32 .40 1.00
630B Will Clark '89 COR 321 .05 .15
631 M.Davis/M.Williams .01 .05
632 W.Boggs/M.Greenwell .02 .10
633 M.Gubicza/J.Russell .01 .05
634 C.Ripken/T.Fernandez .08 .25
635 K.Puckett/Bo Jackson .05 .15
636 N.Ryan/M.Scott .15 .40
637 W.Clark/K.Mitchell .02 .10
638 M.McGwire/D.Mattingly .10 .30
639 R.Sandberg/H.Johnson .08 .25
640 R.Seanez RC/C.Charland RC .02 .10
641 G.Canale RC/K.Maas RC .08 .25
642 Kelly Mann RC/D.Hansen RC .08 .25
643 G.Smith RC/S.Tate RC .02 .10
644 T.Drees RC/D.Howitt RC .02 .10
645 M.Roesler RC/D.May RC .02 .10
646 S.Hemond RC/M.Gardner RC .02 .10
647 John Orton RC/S.Leius RC .02 .10
648 R.Monteleone RC/D.Williams RC .02 .10
649 M.Huff RC/S.Frey RC .02 .10
650 C.McElroy RC/M.Alou RC .30 .75
651 B.Rose RC/M.Hartley RC .08 .25
652 M.Kinzer RC/W.Edwards RC .02 .10
653 D.DeShields RC/J.Grimsley RC .08 .25
654 CL: A's .01 .05
Cubs
Giants
Blue Jays
655 CL: Royals .01 .05
Angels
Padres
Orioles
656 CL: Mets .01 .05
Astros
Cards
Red Sox
657 CL: Rangers .01 .05
Brewers
Expos
Twins
658 CL: Dodgers .01 .05
Reds
Yankees
Pirates
659 CL: Indians .01 .05
Mariners
White Sox
Phillies
660A CL: Braves/Tigers
Specials/Checklists/(Checklist .01 .05
660B CL: Braves/Tigers/Specials
Checklists/(Checklist .01 .05
NNO 10th Anniversary Pin .75 2.00

1990 Fleer Canadian

STARS: 4X to 10X BASIC CARDS
YOUNG STARS: 4X to 10X BASIC CARDS
*ROOKIES: 4X to 10X BASIC CARDS

1990 Fleer All-Stars

COMPLETE SET (12) 1.25 3.00
RANDOM INSERTS IN PACKS
1 Harold Baines .08 .25
2 Will Clark .08 .25
3 Mark Davis .05 .15
4 Howard Johnson UER .05 .15
5 Joe Magrane .05 .15
6 Kevin Mitchell .05 .15
7 Kirby Puckett .25 .60
8 Cal Ripken .75 2.00
9 Ryne Sandberg .40 1.00
10 Mike Scott .05 .15
11 Ruben Sierra .08 .25
12 Mickey Tettleton .05 .15

1990 Fleer League Standouts

COMPLETE SET (6) 3.00 8.00
ONE PER RACK PACK .60 1.25
1 Barry Larkin .50 1.25
2 Don Mattingly 2.00 5.00
3 Darryl Strawberry .30 .75
4 Jose Canseco .50 1.25
5 Wade Boggs .50 1.25
6 Mark Grace .50 1.25

1990 Fleer Soaring Stars

COMPLETE SET (12) 6.00 15.00
RANDOM INSERTS IN JUMBO PACKS
1 Todd Zeile .40 1.00
2 Mike Stanton .20 .50
3 Larry Walker .75 2.00
4 Robin Ventura .75 2.00
5 Scott Coolbaugh .20 .50
6 Ken Griffey Jr. 2.50 6.00
7 Tom Gordon .40 1.00
8 Jerome Walton .20 .50
9 Junior Felix .20 .50
10 Jim Abbott .60 1.50
11 Ricky Jordan .20 .50
12 Dwight Smith .20 .50

1990 Fleer Wax Box Cards

COMPLETE SET (28) 5.00 12.00
C1 Giants Logo .02 .10
C2 Tim Belcher .02 .10
C3 Roger Clemens 1.00 2.50
C4 Eric Davis .08 .25
C5 Glenn Davis .02 .10
C6 Cubs Logo .02 .10
C7 John Franco .08 .25
C8 Mike Greenwell .02 .10
C9 A's Logo .02 .10
C10 Ken Griffey Jr. 1.50 4.00
C11 Pedro Guerrero .02 .10
C12 Tony Gwynn 1.00 2.50
C13 Blue Jays Logo .02 .10
C14 Orel Hershiser .08 .25
C15 Bo Jackson .30 .75
C16 Howard Johnson .02 .10
C17 Mets Logo .02 .10
C18 Cardinals Logo .02 .10
C19 Don Mattingly 1.00 2.50
C20 Mark McGwire .75 2.00
C21 Kevin Mitchell .02 .10
C22 Kirby Puckett .40 1.00
C23 Royals Logo .02 .10
C24 Orioles Logo .02 .10
C25 Ruben Sierra .08 .25
C26 Dave Stewart .08 .25
C27 Jerome Walton .02 .10
C28 Robin Yount .50 1.25

1990 Fleer World Series

COMPLETE SET (12) .40 1.00
ONE SET PER FACTORY SET
1 Mike Moore .01 .05
2 Kevin Mitchell .01 .05
3 Terry Steinbach .01 .05
4 Will Clark .02 .10
5 Jose Canseco .05 .15
6 Walt Weiss .01 .05
7 Terry Steinbach .01 .05
8 Dave Stewart .02 .10
9 Dave Parker .02 .10
10 D.Parker/J.Canseco/W.Clark .02 .10
11 Rickey Henderson .08 .25
12 Oakland A's Celebrate .02 .10

1990 Fleer Update

The 1990 Fleer Update set contains 132 standard-size cards. This set marked the seventh consecutive year Fleer issued an end of season Update set. The set was issued exclusively as a boxed set through hobby dealers. The set is checklisted alphabetically by team for each league and then alphabetically within each team. The fronts are styled the same as the 1990 Fleer regular issue set. The backs are numbered with the prefix "U" for Update. Rookie Cards in this set include Travis Fryman, Todd Hundley, John Olerud and Frank Thomas.

COMP.FACT.SET (132) 1.50 4.00
U PREFIX ON CARD NUMBERS
1 Steve Avery .01 .05
2 Francisco Cabrera .01 .05
3 Nick Esasky .01 .05
4 Jim Kremers RC .01 .05
5 Greg Olson (C) RC .02 .10
6 Jim Presley .01 .05
7 Shawn Boskie RC .02 .10
8 Joe Kraemer RC .01 .05
9 Luis Salazar .01 .05
10 Hector Villanueva RC .01 .05
11 Glenn Braggs .01 .05
12 Mariano Duncan .01 .05
13 Billy Hatcher .01 .05
14 Tim Layana RC .01 .05
15 Hal Morris .01 .05
16 Javier Ortiz RC .01 .05
17 Dave Rohde RC .01 .05
18 Eric Yelding RC .01 .05
19 Hubie Brooks .01 .05
20 Kal Daniels .01 .05
21 Dave Hansen RC .01 .05
22 Mike Hartley .01 .05
23 Stan Javier .01 .05
24 Jose Offerman RC .08 .25
25 Juan Samuel .01 .05
26 Dennis Boyd .01 .05
27 Delino DeShields .08 .25
28 Steve Frey .01 .05
29 Mark Gardner .01 .05
30 Chris Nabholz RC .02 .10
31 Bill Sampen RC .01 .05
32 Dave Schmidt .01 .05
33 Daryl Boston .01 .05
34 Chuck Carr RC .02 .10
35 John Franco .02 .10
36 Todd Hundley RC .08 .25
37 Julio Machado RC .01 .05
38 Alejandro Pena .01 .05
39 Darren Reed RC .01 .05
40 Kelvin Torve .01 .05
41 Darrel Akerfelds .01 .05
42 Jose DeJesus .01 .05
43 Dave Hollins UER RC .08 .25
44 Carmelo Martinez .01 .05
45 Brad Moore .01 .05
46 Dale Murphy .05 .15
47 Wally Backman .01 .05
48 Stan Belinda RC .02 .10
49 Bob Patterson .01 .05
50 Ted Power .01 .05
51 Don Slaught .01 .05
52 Geronimo Pena RC .02 .10
53 Lee Smith .02 .10
54 John Tudor .01 .05
55 Joe Carter .02 .10
56 Thomas Howard .01 .05
57 Craig Lefferts .01 .05
58 Rafael Valdez RC .01 .05
59 Dave Anderson .01 .05
60 Kevin Bass .01 .05
61 John Burkett .01 .05
62 Gary Carter .02 .10
63 Rick Parker RC .01 .05
64 Trevor Wilson .01 .05
65 Chris Hoiles RC .08 .25
66 Tim Hulett .01 .05
67 Dave Wayne Johnson RC .01 .05
68 Curt Schilling .40 1.00
69 David Segui RC .15 .40
70 Tom Brunansky .01 .05
71 Greg A. Harris .01 .05
72 Dana Kiecker RC .01 .05
73 Tim Naehring RC .02 .10
74 Tony Pena .01 .05
75 Jeff Reardon .02 .10
76 Jerry Reed .01 .05
77 Mark Eichhorn .01 .05
78 Mark Langston .01 .05
79 John Orton .01 .05
80 Luis Polonia .01 .05
81 Dave Winfield .02 .10
82 Cliff Young RC .01 .05
83 Wayne Edwards RC .01 .05
84 Alex Fernandez RC .08 .25
85 Craig Grebeck RC .02 .10
86 Scott Radinsky RC .02 .10
87 Frank Thomas RC 1.00 2.50
88 Beau Allred RC .01 .05
89 Sandy Alomar Jr. .02 .10
90 Carlos Baerga RC .08 .25
91 Kevin Bearse RC .01 .05
92 Chris James .01 .05
93 Candy Maldonado .01 .05
94 Jeff Manto .01 .05
95 Cecil Fielder .02 .10
96 Travis Fryman RC .15 .40
97 Lloyd Moseby .01 .05
98 Edwin Nunez .01 .05
99 Tony Phillips .01 .05
100 Larry Sheets .01 .05
101 Mark Davis .01 .05
102 Storm Davis .01 .05
103 Gerald Perry .01 .05
104 Terry Shumpert RC .01 .05
105 Edgar Diaz RC .01 .05
106 Dave Parker .02 .10
107 Tim Drummond RC .01 .05
108 Junior Ortiz .01 .05
109 Park Pittman RC .01 .05
110 Kevin Tapani RC .08 .25
111 Oscar Azocar RC .01 .05
112 Jim Leyritz RC .08 .25
113 Kevin Maas .02 .10
114 Alan Mills RC .02 .10
115 Matt Nokes .01 .05
116 Pascual Perez .01 .05
117 Ozzie Canseco .01 .05
118 Scott Sanderson .01 .05
119 Tino Martinez .20 .50
120 Jeff Schaefer RC .01 .05
121 Matt Young .01 .05
122 Brian Bohanon RC .02 .10
123 Jeff Huson .01 .05
124 Ramon Manon RC .01 .05
125 Gary Mielke RC .01 .05
126 Willie Blair RC .02 .10
127 Glenallen Hill .01 .05
128 John Olerud RC .20 .50
129 Luis Sojo RC .01 .05
130 Mark Whiten RC .08 .25
131 Nolan Ryan SPEC .40 1.00
132 Checklist U1-U132 .01 .05

1990 Fleer Award Winners

The 1990 Fleer Award Winners set was printed by Fleer for Hills stores (as well as for some 7/Eleven's) and released early in the summer of 1990. The original suggested retail price for the set at Hills was 2.49. The set features a player photo within a trophy design with the player's name, team and position at the base. This 44-card standard-size set is numbered in alphabetical order, although Will Clark erroneously precedes Jack Clark. Card number 10 is listed on the box checklist as being Ron Darling, but Darling is not in the set. Consequently the numbers on the box checklist between 10 and 37 are off by one. Darryl Strawberry (38) is not listed on the box, but is included in the set.

COMP.FACT SET (44) 5.00 12.00
1 Jeff Ballard .01 .05
2 Tim Belcher .01 .05
3 Bert Blyleven .02 .10
4 Wade Boggs .15 .40
5 Bob Boone .02 .10
6 Jose Canseco .15 .40
7 Will Clark .20 .50
8 Jack Clark .02 .10
9 Vince Coleman .01 .05
10 Eric Davis .02 .10
11 Jose DeLeon .01 .05
12 Tony Fernandez .02 .10
13 Carlton Fisk .15 .40
14 Scott Garrelts .01 .05
15 Tom Gordon .05 .15
16 Ken Griffey Jr. 1.50 4.00
17 Von Hayes .01 .05
18 Rickey Henderson .30 .75
19 Bo Jackson .25 .60
20 Howard Johnson .01 .05
21 Don Mattingly .40 1.00
22 Fred McGriff .15 .40
23 Kevin Mitchell .01 .05
24 Gregg Olson .01 .05
25 Gary Pettis .01 .05
26 Kirby Puckett .20 .50
27 Harold Reynolds .02 .10
28 Jeff Russell .01 .05
29 Nolan Ryan .75 2.00
30 Bret Saberhagen .02 .10
31 Ryne Sandberg .30 .75
32 Benito Santiago .02 .10
33 Mike Scott .01 .05
34 Ruben Sierra .02 .10
35 Lonnie Smith .01 .05
36 Ozzie Smith .40 1.00
37 Dave Stewart .02 .10
38 Darryl Strawberry .02 .10
39 Greg Swindell .01 .05
40 Andy Van Slyke .01 .05
41 Tim Wallach .01 .05
42 Jerome Walton .01 .05
43 Mitch Williams .01 .05
44 Robin Yount .15 .40

1990 Fleer Baseball All-Stars

The 1990 Fleer Baseball All-Stars Set was produced by Fleer for the Ben Franklin chain and released early in the summer of 1990. This standard-size 44-card set features some of the best of today's players in alphabetical order. The design of the cards has vertical stripes on the front of the card. The set's custom box gives the set checklist on the back panel. The box also includes six peel-off team logo stickers each with a trivia quiz on back.

COMP.FACT SET (44) 5.00 12.00
1 Wade Boggs .15 .40
2 Bobby Bonilla .01 .05
3 Tim Burke .01 .05
4 Jose Canseco .15 .40
5 Will Clark .20 .50
6 Eric Davis .02 .10
7 Glenn Davis .01 .05
8 Julio Franco .02 .10
9 Tony Fernandez .02 .10
10 Gary Gaetti .02 .10
11 Scott Garrelts .01 .05
12 Mark Grace .20 .50
13 Mike Greenwell .01 .05
14 Ken Griffey Jr. 1.50 4.00
15 Mark Gubicza .01 .05
16 Pedro Guerrero .01 .05
17 Von Hayes .01 .05
18 Orel Hershiser .02 .10
19 Bruce Hurst .01 .05
20 Bo Jackson .20 .50
21 Howard Johnson .01 .05
22 Doug Jones .01 .05
23 Barry Larkin .20 .50
24 Don Mattingly .40 1.00
25 Mark McGwire .50 1.25
26 Kevin McReynolds .01 .05
27 Kevin Mitchell .01 .05
28 Dan Plesac .01 .05
29 Kirby Puckett .20 .50
30 Cal Ripken .75 2.00
31 Bret Saberhagen .02 .10
32 Ryne Sandberg .40 1.00
33 Steve Sax .01 .05
34 Ruben Sierra .02 .10
35 Ozzie Smith .40 1.00
36 John Smoltz .05 .15
37 Darryl Strawberry .02 .10
38 Terry Steinbach .01 .05
39 Dave Stewart .02 .10
40 Bobby Thigpen .01 .05
41 Alan Trammell .05 .15
42 Devon White .01 .05
43 Mitch Williams .01 .05
44 Robin Yount .15 .40

1990 Fleer Baseball MVP's

The 1990 Fleer Baseball MVP's were produced by Fleer exclusively for the Toys'R'Us chain and released early in the summer of 1990. This set has a multi-colored border, is standard size, and has 44 players arranged in alphabetical order. The set's custom box gives the set checklist on the back panel. The box also includes six peel-off team logo stickers.

COMP.FACT SET (44) 5.00 12.00
1 George Bell .01 .05
2 Bert Blyleven .02 .10
3 Wade Boggs .15 .40
4 Bobby Bonilla .01 .05
5 George Brett .40 1.00
6 Jose Canseco .15 .40
7 Will Clark .20 .50
8 Roger Clemens .40 1.00
9 Eric Davis .02 .10
10 Glenn Davis .01 .05
11 Tony Fernandez .02 .10
12 Dwight Gooden .02 .10
13 Mike Greenwell .01 .05
14 Ken Griffey Jr. 1.25 3.00
15 Pedro Guerrero .01 .05
16 Tony Gwynn .40 1.00
17 Rickey Henderson .25 .60
18 Tom Herr .01 .05
19 Orel Hershiser .02 .10
20 Kent Hrbek .02 .10
21 Bo Jackson .20 .50
22 Howard Johnson .01 .05
23 Don Mattingly .40 1.00
24 Fred McGriff .15 .40
25 Mark McGwire .50 1.25
26 Kevin Mitchell .01 .05
27 Paul Molitor .15 .40
28 Dale Murphy .07 .20
29 Kirby Puckett .20 .50
30 Tim Raines .02 .10
31 Cal Ripken .75 2.00
32 Bret Saberhagen .02 .10
33 Ryne Sandberg .30 .75
34 Ruben Sierra .02 .10
35 Dwight Smith .01 .05
36 Ozzie Smith .40 1.00
37 Darryl Strawberry .02 .10
38 Dave Stewart .02 .10
39 Greg Swindell .01 .05
40 Bobby Thigpen .01 .05
41 Alan Trammell .05 .15
42 Jerome Walton .01 .05
43 Mitch Williams .01 .05
44 Robin Yount .15 .40

1990 Fleer League Leaders

The 1990 Fleer League Leader set was issued by Fleer for Walgreen stores. This set design features solid blue borders with the players photo inset within the middle of the card. This 44-card, standard-size set is numbered in alphabetical order. The set's custom box gives the set checklist on the back panel. The box also includes six peel-off team logo stickers. The original suggested retail price for the set at Walgreen's was 2.49.

COMP.FACT SET (44) 5.00 12.00
1 Roberto Alomar .30 .75
2 Tim Belcher .01 .05
3 George Bell .01 .05
4 Wade Boggs .15 .40
5 Jose Canseco .20 .50
6 Will Clark .20 .50
7 David Cone .07 .20
8 Eric Davis .02 .10
9 Glenn Davis .01 .05
10 Nick Esasky .01 .05
11 Dennis Eckersley .15 .40
12 Mark Grace .20 .50
13 Mike Greenwell .01 .05
14 Ken Griffey Jr. 1.50 4.00
15 Mark Gubicza .01 .05
16 Pedro Guerrero .01 .05
17 Tony Gwynn .40 1.00
18 Rickey Henderson .25 .60
19 Bo Jackson .20 .50
20 Doug Jones .01 .05
21 Ricky Jordan .01 .05
22 Barry Larkin .20 .50
23 Don Mattingly .40 1.00
24 Fred McGriff .15 .40
25 Mark McGwire .50 1.25
26 Kevin Mitchell .01 .05
27 Jack Morris .02 .10
28 Gregg Olson .01 .05
29 Dan Plesac .01 .05
30 Kirby Puckett .20 .50
31 Nolan Ryan .75 2.00
32 Bret Saberhagen .02 .10
33 Ryne Sandberg .40 1.00
34 Steve Sax .01 .05
35 Mike Scott .01 .05
36 Ruben Sierra .02 .10
37 Lonnie Smith .01 .05
38 Darryl Strawberry .02 .10
39 Bobby Thigpen .01 .05
40 Andy Van Slyke .02 .10
41 Tim Wallach .01 .05
42 Jerome Walton UER/(Photo actually .01 .05
Eric Yelding)
43 Devon White .01 .05
44 Robin Yount .15 .40

1991 Fleer

The 1991 Fleer set consists of 720 standard-size cards. Cards were primarily issued in wax packs, cello packs and factory sets. This set does not have what had been a Fleer tradition in prior years, the two-player Rookie Cards and there are less two-player special cards than in prior years. The design features bright yellow borders with the information in black indicating name, position, and team. The set is again ordered numerically by teams, followed by combination cards, rookie prospect pairs, and checklists. There are no notable Rookie Cards in this set. A number of the cards in the set can be found with photos cropped (very slightly) differently as Fleer used two separate

printers in their attempt to maximize production.
COMPLETE SET (720) 3.00 8.00
COMP.RETAIL SET (732) 4.00 10.00
COMP.HOBBY SET (732) 4.00 10.00
1 Troy Afenir RC .01 .05
2 Harold Baines .02 .10
3 Lance Blankenship .01 .05
4 Todd Burns .01 .05
5 Jose Canseco .05 .15
6 Dennis Eckersley .02 .10
7 Mike Gallego .01 .05
8 Ron Hassey .01 .05
9 Dave Henderson .01 .05
10 Rickey Henderson .08 .25
11 Rick Honeycutt .01 .05
12 Doug Jennings .01 .05
13 Joe Klink .01 .05
14 Carney Lansford .02 .10
15 Darren Lewis .01 .05
16 Willie McGee UER .02 .10
17 Mark McGwire UER .30 .75
18 Mike Moore .01 .05
19 Gene Nelson .01 .05
20 Dave Otto .01 .05
21 Jamie Quirk .01 .05
22 Willie Randolph .02 .10
23 Scott Sanderson .01 .05
24 Terry Steinbach .01 .05
25 Dave Stewart .02 .10
26 Walt Weiss .01 .05
27 Bob Welch .01 .05
28 Curt Young .01 .05
29 Wally Backman .01 .05
30 Stan Belinda UER .01 .05
31 Jay Bell .02 .10
32 Rafael Belliard .01 .05
33 Barry Bonds .40 1.00
34 Bobby Bonilla .02 .10
35 Sid Bream .01 .05
36 Doug Drabek .01 .05
37 Carlos Garcia RC .02 .10
38 Neal Heaton .01 .05
39 Jeff King .01 .05
40 Bob Kipper .01 .05
41 Bill Landrum .01 .05
42 Mike LaValliere .01 .05
43 Jose Lind .01 .05
44 Carmelo Martinez .01 .05
45 Bob Patterson .01 .05
46 Ted Power .01 .05
47 Gary Redus .01 .05
48 R.J. Reynolds .01 .05
49 Don Slaught .01 .05
50 John Smiley .01 .05
51 Zane Smith .01 .05
52 Randy Tomlin RC .02 .10
53 Andy Van Slyke .05 .15
54 Bob Walk .01 .05
55 Jack Armstrong .01 .05
56 Todd Benzinger .01 .05
57 Glenn Braggs .01 .05
58 Keith Brown .01 .05
59 Tom Browning .01 .05
60 Norm Charlton .01 .05
61 Eric Davis .02 .10
62 Rob Dibble .02 .10
63 Bill Doran .01 .05
64 Mariano Duncan .01 .05
65 Chris Hammond .01 .05
66 Billy Hatcher .01 .05
67 Danny Jackson .01 .05
68 Barry Larkin .05 .15
69 Tim Layana UER .01 .05
70 Terry Lee RC .01 .05
71 Rick Mahler .01 .05
72 Hal Morris .01 .05
73 Randy Myers .01 .05
74 Ron Oester .01 .05
75 Joe Oliver .01 .05
76 Paul O'Neill .05 .15
77 Luis Quinones .01 .05
78 Jeff Reed .01 .05
79 Jose Rijo .01 .05
80 Chris Sabo .01 .05
81 Scott Scudder .01 .05
82 Herm Winningham .01 .05
83 Larry Andersen .01 .05
84 Marty Barrett .01 .05
85 Mike Boddicker .01 .05
86 Wade Boggs .05 .15
87 Tom Bolton .01 .05
88 Tom Brunansky .01 .05
89 Ellis Burks .02 .10
90 Roger Clemens .30 .75
91 Scott Cooper .01 .05
92 John Dopson .01 .05
93 Dwight Evans .05 .15
94 Wes Gardner .01 .05
95 Jeff Gray .01 .05
96 Mike Greenwell .01 .05
97 Greg A. Harris .01 .05
98 Daryl Irvine RC .01 .05
99 Dana Kiecker .01 .05
100 Randy Kutcher .01 .05
101 Dennis Lamp .01 .05
102 Mike Marshall .01 .05
103 John Marzano .01 .05
104 Rob Murphy .01 .05
105 Tim Naehring .01 .05
106 Tony Pena .01 .05
107 Phil Plantier RC .08 .25
108 Carlos Quintana .01 .05
109 Jeff Reardon .02 .10
110 Jerry Reed .01 .05
111 Jody Reed .01 .05
112 Luis Rivera UER .01 .05
Born 1/3/84
113 Kevin Romine .01 .05
114 Phil Bradley .01 .05
115 Ivan Calderon .01 .05
116 Wayne Edwards .01 .05
117 Alex Fernandez .01 .05
118 Carlton Fisk .05 .15
119 Scott Fletcher .01 .05
120 Craig Grebeck .01 .05
121 Ozzie Guillen .02 .10
122 Greg Hibbard .01 .05
123 Lance Johnson UER .01 .05
Born Cincinnati, should
be Lincoln Heights
124 Barry Jones .01 .05
125 Ron Karkovice .01 .05
126 Eric King .01 .05
127 Steve Lyons .01 .05
128 Carlos Martinez .01 .05
129 Jack McDowell UER .01 .05
Stanford misspelled
as Standford on back
130 Donn Pall .01 .05
No dots over any
i's in text
131 Dan Pasqua .01 .05
132 Ken Patterson .01 .05
133 Melido Perez .01 .05
134 Adam Peterson .01 .05
135 Scott Radinsky .01 .05
136 Sammy Sosa .08 .25
137 Bobby Thigpen .01 .05
138 Frank Thomas .08 .25
139 Robin Ventura .02 .10
140 Daryl Boston .01 .05
141 Chuck Carr .01 .05
142 Mark Carreon .01 .05
143 David Cone .02 .10
144 Ron Darling .01 .05
145 Kevin Elster .01 .05
146 Sid Fernandez .01 .05
147 John Franco .02 .10
148 Dwight Gooden .02 .10
149 Tom Herr .01 .05
150 Todd Hundley .01 .05
151 Gregg Jefferies .01 .05
152 Howard Johnson .01 .05
153 Dave Magadan .01 .05
154 Kevin McReynolds .01 .05
155 Keith Miller UER .01 .05
Text says Rochester in
'87, stats say Tide-
water, mixed up with
other Keith Miller
156 Bob Ojeda .01 .05
157 Tom O'Malley .01 .05
158 Alejandro Pena .01 .05
159 Darren Reed .01 .05
160 Mackey Sasser .01 .05
161 Darryl Strawberry .02 .10
162 Tim Teufel .01 .05
163 Kelvin Torve .01 .05
164 Julio Valera .01 .05
165 Frank Viola .02 .10
166 Wally Whitehurst .01 .05
167 Jim Acker .01 .05
168 Derek Bell .02 .10
169 George Bell .01 .05
170 Willie Blair .01 .05
171 Pat Borders .01 .05
172 John Cerutti .01 .05
173 Junior Felix .01 .05
174 Tony Fernandez .01 .05
175 Kelly Gruber UER .01 .05
Born in Houston,
should be Bellaire
176 Tom Henke .01 .05
177 Glenallen Hill .01 .05
178 Jimmy Key .02 .10
179 Manny Lee .01 .05
180 Fred McGriff .05 .15
181 Rance Mulliniks .01 .05
182 Greg Myers .01 .05
183 John Olerud UER .02 .10
Listed as throwing
right, should be left
184 Luis Sojo .01 .05
185 Dave Stieb .01 .05
186 Todd Stottlemyre .01 .05
187 Duane Ward .01 .05
188 David Wells .02 .10
189 Mark Whiten .01 .05
190 Ken Williams .01 .05
191 Frank Wills .01 .05
192 Mookie Wilson .02 .10
193 Don Aase .01 .05
194 Tim Belcher UER .01 .05
Born Sparta, Ohio,
should say Mt. Gilead
195 Hubie Brooks .01 .05
196 Dennis Cook .01 .05
197 Tim Crews .01 .05
198 Kal Daniels .01 .05
199 Kirk Gibson .02 .10
200 Jim Gott .01 .05
201 Alfredo Griffin .01 .05
202 Chris Gwynn .01 .05
203 Dave Hansen .01 .05
204 Lenny Harris .01 .05
205 Mike Hartley .01 .05
206 Mickey Hatcher .01 .05
207 Carlos Hernandez .01 .05
208 Orel Hershiser .02 .10
209 Jay Howell UER .01 .05
No 1982 Yankee stats
210 Mike Huff .01 .05
211 Stan Javier .01 .05
212 Ramon Martinez .01 .05
213 Mike Morgan .01 .05
214 Eddie Murray .08 .25
215 Jim Neidlinger RC .01 .05
216 Jose Offerman .01 .05
217 Jim Poole .01 .05
218 Juan Samuel .01 .05
219 Mike Scioscia .01 .05
220 Ray Searage .01 .05
221 Mike Sharperson .01 .05
222 Fernando Valenzuela .02 .10
223 Jose Vizcaino .01 .05
224 Mike Aldrete .01 .05
225 Scott Anderson RC .01 .05
226 Dennis Boyd .01 .05
227 Tim Burke .01 .05
228 Delino DeShields .02 .10
229 Mike Fitzgerald .01 .05
230 Tom Foley .01 .05
231 Steve Frey .01 .05
232 Andres Galarraga .02 .10
233 Mark Gardner .01 .05
234 Marquis Grissom .02 .10
235 Kevin Gross .01 .05
No date given for
first Expos win
236 Drew Hall .01 .05
237 Dave Martinez .01 .05
238 Dennis Martinez .02 .10
239 Dale Mohorcic .01 .05
240 Chris Nabholz .01 .05
241 Otis Nixon .01 .05
242 Junior Noboa .01 .05
243 Spike Owen .01 .05
244 Tim Raines .02 .10
245 Mel Rojas UER .01 .05
Stats show 3.60 ERA,
bio says 3.19 ERA
246 Scott Ruskin .01 .05
247 Bill Sampen .01 .05
248 Nelson Santovenia .01 .05
249 Dave Schmidt .01 .05
250 Larry Walker .08 .25
251 Tim Wallach .01 .05
252 Dave Anderson .01 .05
253 Kevin Bass .01 .05
254 Steve Bedrosian .01 .05
255 Jeff Brantley .01 .05
256 John Burkett .01 .05
257 Brett Butler .02 .10
258 Gary Carter .02 .10
259 Will Clark .05 .15
260 Steve Decker RC .02 .10
261 Kelly Downs .01 .05
262 Scott Garrelts .01 .05
263 Terry Kennedy .01 .05
264 Mike LaCoss .01 .05
265 Mark Leonard RC .01 .05
266 Greg Litton .01 .05
267 Kevin Mitchell .01 .05
268 Randy O'Neal .01 .05
269 Rick Parker .01 .05
270 Rick Reuschel .01 .05
271 Ernest Riles .01 .05
272 Don Robinson .01 .05
273 Robby Thompson .01 .05
274 Mark Thurmond .01 .05
275 Jose Uribe .01 .05
276 Matt Williams .02 .10
277 Trevor Wilson .01 .05
278 Gerald Alexander RC .01 .05
279 Brad Arnsberg .01 .05
280 Kevin Belcher RC .01 .05
281 Joe Bitker RC .01 .05
282 Kevin Brown .02 .10
283 Steve Buechele .01 .05
284 Jack Daugherty .01 .05
285 Julio Franco .02 .10
286 Juan Gonzalez .08 .25
287 Bill Haselman RC .01 .05
288 Charlie Hough .02 .10
289 Jeff Huson .01 .05
290 Pete Incaviglia .01 .05
291 Mike Jeffcoat .01 .05
292 Jeff Kunkel .01 .05
293 Gary Mielke .01 .05
294 Jamie Moyer .02 .10
295 Rafael Palmeiro .05 .15
296 Geno Petralli .01 .05
297 Gary Pettis .01 .05
298 Kevin Reimer .01 .05
299 Kenny Rogers .02 .10
300 Jeff Russell .01 .05
301 John Russell .01 .05
302 Nolan Ryan .40 1.00
303 Ruben Sierra .02 .10
304 Bobby Witt .01 .05
305 Jim Abbott UER .05 .15
Text on back states he won
Sullivan Award outstanding amateur
athlete in 1989;should be '88
306 Kent Anderson .01 .05
307 Dante Bichette .02 .10
308 Bert Blyleven .02 .10
309 Chili Davis .02 .10
310 Brian Downing .01 .05
311 Mark Eichhorn .01 .05
312 Mike Fetters .01 .05
313 Chuck Finley .02 .10
314 Willie Fraser .01 .05
315 Bryan Harvey .01 .05
316 Donnie Hill .01 .05
317 Wally Joyner .02 .10
318 Mark Langston .01 .05
319 Kirk McCaskill .01 .05
320 John Orton .01 .05
321 Lance Parrish .02 .10
322 Luis Polonia UER .01 .05
1984 Madfison,
should be Madison
323 Johnny Ray .01 .05
324 Bobby Rose .01 .05
325 Dick Schofield .01 .05
326 Rick Schu .01 .05
327 Lee Stevens .01 .05
328 Devon White .02 .10
329 Dave Winfield .02 .10
330 Cliff Young .01 .05
331 Dave Bergman .01 .05
332 Phil Clark RC .02 .10
333 Darnell Coles .01 .05
334 Milt Cuyler .01 .05
335 Cecil Fielder .02 .10
336 Travis Fryman .02 .10
337 Paul Gibson .01 .05
338 Jerry Don Gleaton .01 .05
339 Mike Heath .01 .05
340 Mike Henneman .01 .05
341 Chet Lemon .01 .05
342 Lance McCullers .01 .05
343 Jack Morris .02 .10
344 Lloyd Moseby .01 .05
345 Edwin Nunez .01 .05
346 Clay Parker .01 .05
347 Dan Petry .01 .05
348 Tony Phillips .01 .05
349 Jeff M. Robinson .01 .05
350 Mark Salas .01 .05
351 Mike Schwabe .01 .05
352 Larry Sheets .01 .05
353 John Shelby .01 .05
354 Frank Tanana .01 .05
355 Alan Trammell .02 .10
356 Gary Ward .01 .05
357 Lou Whitaker .02 .10
358 Beau Allred .01 .05
359 Sandy Alomar Jr. .01 .05
360 Carlos Baerga .01 .05
361 Kevin Bearse .01 .05
362 Tom Brookens .01 .05
363 Jerry Browne UER .01 .05
No dot over i in
first text line
364 Tom Candiotti .01 .05
365 Alex Cole .01 .05
366 John Farrell UER .01 .05
Born in Neptune,
should be Monmouth
367 Felix Fermin .01 .05
368 Keith Hernandez .02 .10
369 Brook Jacoby .01 .05
370 Chris James .01 .05
371 Dion James .01 .05
372 Doug Jones .01 .05
373 Candy Maldonado .01 .05
374 Steve Olin .01 .05
375 Jesse Orosco .01 .05
376 Rudy Seanez .01 .05
377 Joel Skinner .01 .05
378 Cory Snyder .01 .05
379 Greg Swindell .01 .05
380 Sergio Valdez .01 .05
381 Mike Walker .01 .05
382 Colby Ward RC .01 .05
383 Turner Ward RC .08 .25
384 Mitch Webster .01 .05
385 Kevin Wickander .01 .05
386 Darrel Akerfelds .01 .05
387 Joe Boever .01 .05
388 Rod Booker .01 .05
389 Sil Campusano .01 .05
390 Don Carman .01 .05
391 Wes Chamberlain RC .08 .25
392 Pat Combs .01 .05
393 Darren Daulton .02 .10
394 Jose DeJesus .01 .05
395A Len Dykstra .02 .10
Name spelled Lenny on back
395B Len Dykstra .02 .10
Name spelled Len on back
396 Jason Grimsley .01 .05
397 Charlie Hayes .01 .05
398 Von Hayes .01 .05
399 David Hollins UER .01 .05
Atl-bats& should
say at-bats
400 Ken Howell .01 .05
401 Ricky Jordan .01 .05
402 John Kruk .02 .10
403 Steve Lake .01 .05
404 Chuck Malone .01 .05
405 Roger McDowell UER .01 .05
Says Phillies is
saves, should say in
406 Chuck McElroy .01 .05
407 Mickey Morandini .01 .05
408 Terry Mulholland .01 .05
409 Dale Murphy .05 .15
410A Randy Ready ERR .01 .05
No Brewers stats
listed for 1983
410B Randy Ready COR .01 .05
411 Bruce Ruffin .01 .05
412 Dickie Thon .01 .05
413 Paul Assenmacher .01 .05
414 Damon Berryhill .01 .05
415 Mike Bielecki .01 .05
416 Shawn Boskie .01 .05
417 Dave Clark .01 .05
418 Doug Dascenzo .01 .05
419A Andre Dawson ERR .02 .10
No stats for 1976
419B Andre Dawson COR .02 .10
420 Shawon Dunston .01 .05
421 Joe Girardi .01 .05
422 Mark Grace .05 .15
423 Mike Harkey .01 .05
424 Les Lancaster .01 .05
425 Bill Long .01 .05
426 Greg Maddux .15 .40
427 Derrick May .01 .05
428 Jeff Pico .01 .05
429 Domingo Ramos .01 .05
430 Luis Salazar .01 .05
431 Ryne Sandberg .15 .40
432 Dwight Smith .01 .05
433 Greg Smith .01 .05
434 Rick Sutcliffe .02 .10
435 Gary Varsho .01 .05
436 Hector Villanueva .01 .05
437 Jerome Walton .01 .05
438 Curtis Wilkerson .01 .05
439 Mitch Williams .01 .05
440 Steve Wilson .01 .05
441 Marvell Wynne .01 .05
442 Scott Bankhead .01 .05
443 Scott Bradley .01 .05
444 Greg Briley .01 .05
445 Mike Brumley UER .01 .05
Text 40 SB's in 1988,
stats say 41
446 Jay Buhner .02 .10
447 Dave Burba RC .08 .25
448 Henry Cotto .01 .05
449 Alvin Davis .01 .05
450 Ken Griffey Jr. .25 .60
Bat around .300
450A Ken Griffey Jr. .50 1.25
Bat .300
451 Erik Hanson .01 .05
452 Gene Harris UER .01 .05
63 career runs,
should be 73
453 Brian Holman .01 .05
454 Mike Jackson .01 .05
455 Randy Johnson .10 .30
456 Jeffrey Leonard .01 .05
457 Edgar Martinez .05 .15
458 Tino Martinez .08 .25
459 Pete O'Brien UER .01 .05
1987 BA .266,
should be .286
460 Harold Reynolds .02 .10
461 Mike Schooler .01 .05
462 Bill Swift .01 .05
463 David Valle .01 .05
464 Omar Vizquel .05 .15
465 Matt Young .01 .05
466 Brady Anderson .02 .10
467 Jeff Ballard UER .01 .05
Missing top of right
parenthesis after
Saberhagen in last
text line
468 Juan Bell .01 .05
469A Mike Devereaux .02 .10
First line of text
ends with six
469B Mike Devereaux .02 .10
First line of text
ends with runs
470 Steve Finley .02 .10
471 Dave Gallagher .01 .05
472 Leo Gomez .01 .05
473 Rene Gonzales .01 .05
474 Pete Harnisch .01 .05
475 Kevin Hickey .01 .05
476 Chris Hoiles .01 .05
477 Sam Horn .01 .05
478 Tim Hulett .01 .05
Photo shows National
Leaguer sliding into
second base
479 Dave Johnson .01 .05
480 Ron Kittle UER .01 .05
Edmonton misspelled
as Edmundton
481 Ben McDonald .01 .05
482 Bob Melvin .01 .05
483 Bob Milacki .01 .05
484 Randy Milligan .01 .05
485 John Mitchell .01 .05
486 Gregg Olson .01 .05
487 Joe Orsulak .01 .05
488 Joe Price .01 .05
489 Bill Ripken .01 .05
490 Cal Ripken .30 .75
491 Curt Schilling .08 .25
492 David Segui .01 .05
493 Anthony Telford RC .01 .05
494 Mickey Tettleton .01 .05
495 Mark Williamson .01 .05
496 Craig Worthington .01 .05
497 Juan Agosto .01 .05
498 Eric Anthony .01 .05
499 Craig Biggio .05 .15
500 Ken Caminiti UER .02 .10
Born 4
4, should
be 4
21
501 Casey Candaele .01 .05
502 Andujar Cedeno .01 .05
503 Danny Darwin .01 .05
504 Mark Davidson .01 .05
505 Glenn Davis .01 .05
506 Jim Deshaies .01 .05
507 Luis Gonzalez RC .20 .50
508 Bill Gullickson .01 .05
509 Xavier Hernandez .01 .05
510 Brian Meyer .01 .05
511 Ken Oberkfell .01 .05
512 Mark Portugal .01 .05
513 Rafael Ramirez .01 .05
514 Karl Rhodes .01 .05
515 Mike Scott .01 .05
516 Mike Simms RC .01 .05
517 Dave Smith .01 .05
518 Franklin Stubbs .01 .05
519 Glenn Wilson .01 .05
520 Eric Yelding UER .01 .05
Text has 63 steals,
stats have 64,
which is correct
521 Gerald Young .01 .05
522 Shawn Abner .01 .05
523 Roberto Alomar .05 .15
524 Andy Benes .01 .05
525 Joe Carter .02 .10
526 Jack Clark .02 .10
527 Joey Cora .01 .05
528 Paul Faries RC .01 .05
529 Tony Gwynn .10 .30
530 Atlee Hammaker .01 .05
531 Greg W. Harris .01 .05
532 Thomas Howard .01 .05
533 Bruce Hurst .01 .05
534 Craig Lefferts .01 .05
535 Derek Lilliquist .01 .05
536 Fred Lynn .01 .05
537 Mike Pagliarulo .01 .05
538 Mark Parent .01 .05
539 Dennis Rasmussen .01 .05
540 Bip Roberts .01 .05
541 Richard Rodriguez RC .01 .05
542 Benito Santiago .02 .10
543 Calvin Schiraldi .01 .05
544 Eric Show .01 .05
545 Phil Stephenson .01 .05
546 Garry Templeton UER .01 .05
Born 3/24/57,
should be 3/24/56
547 Ed Whitson .01 .05
548 Eddie Williams .01 .05
549 Kevin Appier .02 .10
550 Luis Aquino .01 .05
551 Bob Boone .02 .10
552 George Brett .25 .60
553 Jeff Conine RC .15 .40
554 Steve Crawford .01 .05
555 Mark Davis .01 .05
556 Storm Davis .01 .05
557 Jim Eisenreich .01 .05
558 Steve Farr .01 .05
559 Tom Gordon .01 .05
560 Mark Gubicza .01 .05
561 Bo Jackson .08 .25
562 Mike Macfarlane .01 .05
563 Brian McRae RC .08 .25
564 Jeff Montgomery .01 .05
565 Bill Pecota .01 .05
566 Gerald Perry .01 .05
567 Bret Saberhagen .02 .10
568 Jeff Schulz RC .01 .05
569 Kevin Seitzer .01 .05
570 Terry Shumpert .01 .05
571 Kurt Stillwell .01 .05
572 Danny Tartabull .01 .05
573 Gary Thurman .01 .05
574 Frank White .02 .10
575 Willie Wilson .01 .05
576 Chris Bosio .01 .05
577 Greg Brock .01 .05
578 George Canale .01 .05
579 Chuck Crim .01 .05
580 Rob Deer .01 .05
581 Edgar Diaz .01 .05
582 Tom Edens RC .01 .05
583 Mike Felder .01 .05
584 Jim Gantner .01 .05
585 Darryl Hamilton .01 .05
586 Ted Higuera .01 .05
587 Mark Knudson .01 .05
588 Bill Krueger .01 .05
589 Tim McIntosh .01 .05
590 Paul Mirabella .01 .05
591 Paul Molitor .02 .10
592 Jaime Navarro .01 .05
593 Dave Parker .02 .10
594 Dan Plesac .01 .05
595 Ron Robinson .01 .05
596 Gary Sheffield .02 .10
597 Bill Spiers .01 .05
598 B.J. Surhoff .02 .10
599 Greg Vaughn .01 .05
600 Randy Veres .01 .05
601 Robin Yount .15 .40
602 Rick Aguilera .02 .10
603 Allan Anderson .01 .05
604 Juan Berenguer .01 .05
605 Randy Bush .01 .05
606 Carmelo Castillo .01 .05
607 Tim Drummond .01 .05
608 Scott Erickson .01 .05
609 Gary Gaetti .02 .10
610 Greg Gagne .01 .05
611 Dan Gladden .01 .05
612 Mark Guthrie .01 .05
613 Brian Harper .01 .05
614 Kent Hrbek .02 .10
615 Gene Larkin .01 .05
616 Terry Leach .01 .05
617 Nelson Liriano .01 .05
618 Shane Mack .01 .05
619 John Moses .01 .05
620 Pedro Munoz RC .02 .10
621 Al Newman .01 .05
622 Junior Ortiz .01 .05
623 Kirby Puckett .08 .25
624 Roy Smith .01 .05
625 Kevin Tapani .01 .05
626 Gary Wayne .01 .05
627 David West .01 .05
628 Cris Carpenter .01 .05
629 Vince Coleman .01 .05
630 Ken Dayley .01 .05
631A Jose DeLeon ERR .01 .05
(missing '79 Bradenton stats
631B Jose DeLeon COR .01 .05
(with '79 Bradenton stats
632 Frank DiPino .01 .05
633 Bernard Gilkey .01 .05
634A Pedro Guerrero ERR .02 .10
634B Pedro Guerrero COR .02 .10
635 Ken Hill .01 .05
636 Felix Jose .01 .05
637 Ray Lankford .02 .10
638 Joe Magrane .01 .05
639 Tom Niedenfuer .01 .05
640 Jose Oquendo .01 .05
641 Tom Pagnozzi .01 .05
642 Terry Pendleton .02 .10
643 Mike Perez RC .02 .10
644 Bryn Smith .01 .05
645 Lee Smith .02 .10
646 Ozzie Smith .15 .40
647 Scott Terry .01 .05
648 Bob Tewksbury .01 .05
649 Milt Thompson .01 .05
650 John Tudor .01 .05
651 Denny Walling .01 .05
652 Craig Wilson RC .01 .05
653 Todd Worrell .01 .05
654 Todd Zeile .01 .05
655 Oscar Azocar .01 .05
656 Steve Balboni UER .01 .05
Born 1/5/57,
should be 1/16
657 Jesse Barfield .01 .05
658 Greg Cadaret .01 .05
659 Chuck Cary .01 .05
660 Rick Cerone .01 .05
661 Dave Eiland .01 .05
662 Alvaro Espinoza .01 .05
663 Bob Geren .01 .05
664 Lee Guetterman .01 .05
665 Mel Hall .01 .05
666 Andy Hawkins .01 .05
667 Jimmy Jones .01 .05
668 Roberto Kelly .01 .05
669 Dave LaPoint UER .01 .05
No '81 Brewers stats,
totals also are wrong
670 Tim Leary .01 .05
671 Jim Leyritz .01 .05
672 Kevin Maas .01 .05
673 Don Mattingly .25 .60
674 Matt Nokes .01 .05
675 Pascual Perez .01 .05
676 Eric Plunk .01 .05
677 Dave Righetti .02 .10
678 Jeff D. Robinson .01 .05
679 Steve Sax .01 .05
680 Mike Witt .01 .05
681 Steve Avery UER .01 .05
Born in New Jersey,
should say Michigan
682 Mike Bell RC .01 .05
683 Jeff Blauser .01 .05
684 Francisco Cabrera UER .01 .05
Born 10/16,
should say 10/10
685 Tony Castillo .01 .05
686 Marty Clary UER .01 .05
Shown pitching righty,
but bio has left
687 Nick Esasky .01 .05
688 Ron Gant .02 .10
689 Tom Glavine .05 .15
690 Mark Grant .01 .05
691 Tommy Gregg .01 .05
692 Dwayne Henry .01 .05
693 Dave Justice .02 .10
694 Jimmy Kremers .01 .05
695 Charlie Leibrandt .01 .05
696 Mark Lemke .01 .05
697 Oddibe McDowell .01 .05
698 Greg Olson .01 .05
699 Jeff Parrett .01 .05
700 Jim Presley .01 .05
701 Victor Rosario RC .01 .05
702 Lonnie Smith .01 .05
703 Pete Smith .01 .05
704 John Smoltz .05 .15
705 Mike Stanton .01 .05
706 Andres Thomas .01 .05
707 Jeff Treadway .01 .05
708 Jim Vatcher RC .01 .05
709 Ryne Sandberg .08 .25
Cecil Fielder
710 Barry Bonds .50 1.25
Ken Griffey Jr.
711 Bobby Bonilla .02 .10
Barry Larkin
712 Bobby Thigpen .01 .05
John Franco
713 Andre Dawson .08 .25
Ryne Sandberg UER
Ryno misspelled Rhino
714 CL:A's .01 .05
Pirates
Reds
Red Sox
715 CL:White Sox .01 .05
Mets
Blue Jays
Dodgers
716 CL:Expos .01 .05
Giants
Rangers
Angels
717 CL:Tigers .01 .05
Indians
Phillies
Cubs
718 CL:Mariners .01 .05
Orioles
Astros
Padres
719 CL:Royals .01 .05
Brewers
Twins
Cardinals
720 CL:Yankees .01 .05
Braves
Superstars
Specials

1991 Fleer All-Stars

COMPLETE SET (10) 6.00 15.00
RANDOM INSERTS IN CELLO PACKS
1 Ryne Sandberg 1.25 3.00
2 Barry Larkin .50 1.25
3 Matt Williams .30 .75
4 Cecil Fielder .30 .75
5 Barry Bonds 3.00 8.00
6 Rickey Henderson .75 2.00
7 Ken Griffey Jr. 2.00 5.00
8 Jose Canseco .50 1.25
9 Benito Santiago .30 .75
10 Roger Clemens 2.50 6.00

1991 Fleer Pro-Visions

COMP.WAX SET (12) 1.50 4.00
COMP.FACT.SET (4) 1.00 2.00
1-12: RANDOM INSERTS IN PACKS
F1-F4: ONE SET PER FACT.SET
1 Kirby Puckett UER .30 .75
.326 average,
should be .328
2 Will Clark UER .20 .50
On tenth line, pennant
misspelled pennent
3 Ruben Sierra UER .10 .30
No apostrophe
in hasn't
4 Mark McGwire UER 1.00 2.50
Fisk won ROY in
'72, not '82
5 Bo Jackson .30 .75
Bio says 6', others
have him at 6'1"
6 Jose Canseco UER .20 .50
Bio 6'3", 230
text has 6'4", 240
7 Dwight Gooden UER .10 .30
2.80 ERA in Lynchburg,
should be 2.50
8 Mike Greenwell UER .05 .15
.328 BA and 87 RBI,

should be .325 and 95
9 Roger Clemens 1.00 2.50
10 Eric Davis .10 .30
11 Don Mattingly .75 2.00
12 Darryl Strawberry .10 .30
1 Barry Bonds 1.25 3.00
Factory set exclusive
2 Rickey Henderson .30 .75
Factory set exclusive
3 Ryne Sandberg .50 1.25
Factory set exclusive
4 Dave Stewart .10 .30
Factory set exclusive

1991 Fleer Wax Box Cards

COMPLETE SET (9) 1.50 4.00
1 Mark Langston .02 .10
and Mike Witt
2 Randy Johnson .40 1.00
3 Nolan Ryan 1.25 3.00
4 Dave Stewart .07 .20
5 Fernando Valenzuela .07 .20
6 Andy Hawkins .02 .10
7 Melido Perez .02 .10
8 Terry Mulholland .02 .10
9 Dave Stieb .07 .20

1991 Fleer World Series

COMPLETE SET (8) .30 .75
ONE COMPLETE SET PER FACTORY SET
1 Eric Davis .02 .10
2 Billy Hatcher .01 .05
3 Jose Canseco .05 .15
4 Rickey Henderson .08 .25
5 Chris Sabo .01 .05
6 Dave Stewart .02 .10
7 Jose Rijo .01 .05
8 Reds Celebrate .01 .05

1991 Fleer Update

The 1991 Fleer Update set contains 132 standard-size cards. The cards were distributed exclusively in factory set form through hobby dealers. Card design is identical to regular issue 1991 Fleer cards with the notable bright yellow borders except for the U-prefixed numbering on back. The cards are ordered alphabetically by team. The key Rookie Cards in this set are Jeff Bagwell and Ivan Rodriguez.

COMP.FACT.SET (132) 2.00 5.00
1 Glenn Davis .01 .05
2 Dwight Evans .05 .15
3 Jose Mesa .01 .05
4 Jack Clark .02 .10
5 Danny Darwin .01 .05
6 Steve Lyons .01 .05
7 Mo Vaughn .02 .10
8 Floyd Bannister .01 .05
9 Gary Gaetti .02 .10
10 Dave Parker .02 .10
11 Joey Cora .01 .05
12 Charlie Hough .02 .10
13 Matt Merullo .01 .05
14 Warren Newson RC .01 .05
15 Tim Raines .02 .10
16 Albert Belle .02 .10
17 Glenallen Hill .01 .05
18 Shawn Hillegas .01 .05
19 Mark Lewis .01 .05
20 Charles Nagy .01 .05
21 Mark Whiten .01 .05
22 John Cerutti .01 .05
23 Rob Deer .01 .05
24 Mickey Tettleton .01 .05
25 Warren Cromartie .01 .05
26 Kirk Gibson .02 .10
27 David Howard RC .01 .05
28 Brent Mayne .01 .05
29 Dante Bichette .02 .10
30 Mark Lee RC .01 .05
31 Julio Machado .01 .05
32 Edwin Nunez .01 .05
33 Willie Randolph .02 .10
34 Franklin Stubbs .01 .05
35 Bill Wegman .01 .05
36 Chili Davis .02 .10
37 Chuck Knoblauch .02 .10
38 Scott Leius .01 .05
39 Jack Morris .02 .10
40 Mike Pagliarulo .01 .05
41 Lenny Webster .01 .05
42 John Habyan .01 .05
43 Steve Howe .01 .05
44 Jeff Johnson RC .01 .05
45 Scott Kamieniecki RC .01 .05
46 Pat Kelly RC .01 .05
47 Hensley Meulens .01 .05
48 Wade Taylor RC .01 .05
49 Bernie Williams .08 .25
50 Kirk Dressendorfer RC .01 .05
51 Ernest Riles .01 .05
52 Rich DeLucia RC .01 .05
53 Tracy Jones .01 .05
54 Bill Krueger .01 .05
55 Alonzo Powell RC .01 .05
56 Jeff Schaefer .01 .05
57 Russ Swan .01 .05
58 John Barfield .01 .05
59 Rich Gossage .02 .10
60 Jose Guzman .01 .05
61 Dean Palmer .02 .10
62 Ivan Rodriguez RC .75 2.00
63 Roberto Alomar .05 .15
64 Tom Candiotti .01 .05
65 Joe Carter .02 .10
66 Ed Sprague .01 .05
67 Pat Tabler .01 .05
68 Mike Timlin RC .02 .10
69 Devon White .02 .10
70 Rafael Belliard .01 .05
71 Juan Berenguer .01 .05
72 Sid Bream .01 .05
73 Marvin Freeman .01 .05
74 Kent Mercker .01 .05
75 Otis Nixon .01 .05
76 Terry Pendleton .02 .10
77 George Bell .01 .05
78 Danny Jackson .01 .05
79 Chuck McElroy .01 .05
80 Gary Scott RC .01 .05
81 Heathcliff Slocumb RC .02 .10
82 Dave Smith .01 .05
83 Rick Wilkins RC .01 .05
84 Freddie Benavides RC .01 .05
85 Ted Power .01 .05
86 Mo Sanford RC .01 .05
87 Jeff Bagwell RC .60 1.50
88 Steve Finley .02 .10
89 Pete Harnisch .01 .05
90 Darryl Kile .02 .10
91 Brett Butler .02 .10
92 John Candelaria .01 .05
93 Gary Carter .02 .10
94 Kevin Gross .01 .05
95 Bob Ojeda .01 .05
96 Darryl Strawberry .02 .10
97 Ivan Calderon .01 .05
98 Ron Hassey .01 .05
99 Gilberto Reyes .01 .05
100 Hubie Brooks .01 .05
101 Rick Cerone .01 .05
102 Vince Coleman .01 .05
103 Jeff Innis .01 .05
104 Pete Schourek RC .01 .05
105 Andy Ashby RC .08 .25
106 Wally Backman .01 .05
107 Darrin Fletcher .01 .05
108 Tommy Greene .01 .05
109 John Morris .01 .05
110 Mitch Williams .01 .05
111 Lloyd McClendon .01 .05
112 Orlando Merced RC .01 .05
113 Vicente Palacios .01 .05
114 Gary Varsho .01 .05
115 John Wehner RC .01 .05
116 Rex Hudler .01 .05
117 Tim Jones .01 .05
118 Geronimo Pena .01 .05
119 Gerald Perry .01 .05
120 Larry Andersen .01 .05
121 Jerald Clark .01 .05
122 Scott Coolbaugh .01 .05
123 Tony Fernandez .01 .05
124 Darrin Jackson .01 .05
125 Fred McGriff .05 .15
126 Jose Mota RC .01 .05
127 Tim Teufel .01 .05
128 Bud Black .01 .05
129 Mike Felder .01 .05
130 Willie McGee .02 .10
131 Dave Righetti .02 .10
132 Checklist U1-U132 .01 .05

1992 Fleer

The 1992 Fleer set contains 720 standard-size cards issued in one comprehensive series. The cards were distributed in plastic wrapped packs, 35-card cello packs, 42-card rack packs and factory sets. The card fronts shade from metallic pale green to white as one moves down the face. The team logo and player's name appear to the right of the picture, running the length of the card. The cards are ordered alphabetically within and according to teams for each league with AL preceding NL. Topical subsets feature Major League Prospects (652-680), Record Setters (681-687), League Leaders (688-697), Super Star Specials (698-707) and Pro Visions (708-713). Rookie Cards include Scott Brosius and Vinny Castilla.

COMPLETE SET (720) 4.00 10.00
COMP.HOBBY SET (732) 8.00 20.00
COMP.RETAIL SET (732) 8.00 20.00
1 Brady Anderson .02 .10
2 Jose Bautista .02 .10
3 Juan Bell .02 .10
4 Glenn Davis .02 .10
5 Mike Devereaux .02 .10
6 Dwight Evans .05 .15
7 Mike Flanagan .02 .10
8 Leo Gomez .02 .10
9 Chris Hoiles .02 .10
10 Sam Horn .02 .10
11 Tim Hulett .02 .10
12 Dave Johnson .02 .10
13 Chito Martinez .02 .10
14 Ben McDonald .02 .10
15 Bob Melvin .02 .10
16 Luis Mercedes .02 .10
17 Jose Mesa .02 .10
18 Bob Milacki .02 .10
19 Randy Milligan .02 .10
20 Mike Mussina UER .08 .25
Card back refers
to him as Jeff
21 Gregg Olson .02 .10
22 Joe Orsulak .02 .10
23 Jim Poole .02 .10
24 Arthur Rhodes .02 .10
25 Billy Ripken .02 .10
26 Cal Ripken .30 .75
27 David Segui .02 .10
28 Roy Smith .02 .10
29 Anthony Telford .02 .10
30 Mark Williamson .02 .10
31 Craig Worthington .02 .10
32 Wade Boggs .05 .15
33 Tom Bolton .02 .10
34 Tom Brunansky .02 .10
35 Ellis Burks .02 .10
36 Jack Clark .02 .10
37 Roger Clemens .20 .50
38 Danny Darwin .02 .10
39 Mike Greenwell .02 .10
40 Joe Hesketh .02 .10
41 Daryl Irvine .02 .10
42 Dennis Lamp .02 .10
43 Tony Pena .02 .10
44 Phil Plantier .02 .10
45 Carlos Quintana .02 .10
46 Jeff Reardon .02 .10
47 Jody Reed .02 .10
48 Luis Rivera .02 .10
49 Mo Vaughn .02 .10
50 Jim Abbott .05 .15
51 Kyle Abbott .02 .10
52 Ruben Amaro .02 .10
53 Scott Bailes .02 .10
54 Chris Beasley .02 .10
55 Mark Eichhorn .02 .10
56 Mike Fetters .02 .10
57 Chuck Finley .02 .10
58 Gary Gaetti .02 .10
59 Dave Gallagher .02 .10
60 Donnie Hill .02 .10
61 Bryan Harvey UER .02 .10
Lee Smith led the
Majors with 47 saves
62 Wally Joyner .02 .10
63 Mark Langston .02 .10
64 Kirk McCaskill .02 .10
65 John Orton .02 .10
66 Lance Parrish .02 .10
67 Luis Polonia .02 .10
68 Bobby Rose .02 .10
69 Dick Schofield .02 .10
70 Luis Sojo .02 .10
71 Lee Stevens .02 .10
72 Dave Winfield .02 .10
73 Cliff Young .02 .10
74 Wilson Alvarez .02 .10
75 Esteban Beltre .02 .10
76 Joey Cora .02 .10
77 Brian Drahman .02 .10
78 Alex Fernandez .02 .10
79 Carlton Fisk .05 .15
80 Scott Fletcher .02 .10
81 Craig Grebeck .02 .10
82 Ozzie Guillen .02 .10
83 Greg Hibbard .02 .10
84 Charlie Hough .02 .10
85 Mike Huff .02 .10
86 Bo Jackson .08 .25
87 Lance Johnson .02 .10
88 Ron Karkovice .02 .10
89 Jack McDowell .02 .10
90 Matt Merullo .02 .10
91 Warren Newson .02 .10
92 Donn Pall UER .02 .10
Called Dunn on
card back
93 Dan Pasqua .02 .10
94 Ken Patterson .02 .10
95 Melido Perez .02 .10
96 Scott Radinsky .02 .10
97 Tim Raines .02 .10
98 Sammy Sosa .08 .25
99 Bobby Thigpen .02 .10
100 Frank Thomas .08 .25
101 Robin Ventura .02 .10
102 Mike Aldrete .02 .10
103 Sandy Alomar Jr. .02 .10
104 Carlos Baerga .02 .10
105 Albert Belle .02 .10
106 Willie Blair .02 .10
107 Jerry Browne .02 .10
108 Alex Cole .02 .10
109 Felix Fermin .02 .10
110 Glenallen Hill .02 .10
111 Shawn Hillegas .02 .10
112 Chris James .02 .10
113 Reggie Jefferson .02 .10
114 Doug Jones .02 .10
115 Eric King .02 .10
116 Mark Lewis .02 .10
117 Carlos Martinez .02 .10
118 Charles Nagy UER .02 .10
Throws right, but
card says left
119 Rod Nichols .02 .10
120 Steve Olin .02 .10
121 Jesse Orosco .02 .10
122 Rudy Seanez .02 .10
123 Joel Skinner .02 .10
124 Greg Swindell .02 .10
125 Jim Thome .08 .25
126 Mark Whiten .02 .10
127 Scott Aldred .02 .10
128 Andy Allanson .02 .10
129 John Cerutti .02 .10
130 Milt Cuyler .02 .10
131 Mike Dalton .02 .10
132 Rob Deer .02 .10
133 Cecil Fielder .02 .10
134 Travis Fryman .02 .10
135 Dan Gakeler .02 .10
136 Paul Gibson .02 .10
137 Bill Gullickson .02 .10
138 Mike Henneman .02 .10
139 Pete Incaviglia .02 .10
140 Mark Leiter .02 .10
141 Scott Livingstone .02 .10
142 Lloyd Moseby .02 .10
143 Tony Phillips .02 .10
144 Mark Salas .02 .10
145 Frank Tanana .02 .10
146 Walt Terrell .02 .10
147 Mickey Tettleton .02 .10
148 Alan Trammell .02 .10
149 Lou Whitaker .02 .10
150 Kevin Appier .02 .10
151 Luis Aquino .02 .10
152 Todd Benzinger .02 .10
153 Mike Boddicker .02 .10
154 George Brett .25 .60
155 Storm Davis .02 .10
156 Jim Eisenreich .02 .10
157 Kirk Gibson .02 .10
158 Tom Gordon .02 .10
159 Mark Gubicza .02 .10
160 David Howard .02 .10
161 Mike Macfarlane .02 .10
162 Brent Mayne .02 .10
163 Brian McRae .02 .10
164 Jeff Montgomery .02 .10
165 Bill Pecota .02 .10
166 Harvey Pulliam .02 .10
167 Bret Saberhagen .02 .10
168 Kevin Seitzer .02 .10
169 Terry Shumpert .02 .10
170 Kurt Stillwell .02 .10
171 Danny Tartabull .02 .10
172 Gary Thurman .02 .10
173 Dante Bichette .02 .10
174 Kevin D. Brown .02 .10
175 Chuck Crim .02 .10
176 Jim Gantner .02 .10
177 Darryl Hamilton .02 .10
178 Ted Higuera .02 .10
179 Darren Holmes .02 .10
180 Mark Lee .02 .10
181 Julio Machado .02 .10
182 Paul Molitor .02 .10
183 Jaime Navarro .02 .10
184 Edwin Nunez .02 .10
185 Dan Plesac .02 .10
186 Willie Randolph .02 .10
187 Ron Robinson .02 .10
188 Gary Sheffield .02 .10
189 Bill Spiers .02 .10
190 B.J. Surhoff .02 .10
191 Dale Sveum .02 .10
192 Greg Vaughn .02 .10
193 Bill Wegman .02 .10
194 Robin Yount .15 .40
195 Rick Aguilera .02 .10
196 Allan Anderson .02 .10
197 Steve Bedrosian .02 .10
198 Randy Bush .02 .10
199 Larry Casian .02 .10
200 Chili Davis .02 .10
201 Scott Erickson .02 .10
202 Greg Gagne .02 .10
203 Dan Gladden .02 .10
204 Brian Harper .02 .10
205 Kent Hrbek .02 .10
206 Chuck Knoblauch UER .02 .10
Career hit total
of 59 is wrong
207 Gene Larkin .02 .10
208 Terry Leach .02 .10
209 Scott Leius .02 .10
210 Shane Mack .02 .10
211 Jack Morris .02 .10
212 Pedro Munoz .02 .10
213 Denny Neagle .02 .10
214 Al Newman .02 .10
215 Junior Ortiz .02 .10
216 Mike Pagliarulo .02 .10
217 Kirby Puckett .08 .25
218 Paul Sorrento .02 .10
219 Kevin Tapani .02 .10
220 Lenny Webster .02 .10
221 Jesse Barfield .02 .10
222 Greg Cadaret .02 .10
223 Dave Eiland .02 .10
224 Alvaro Espinoza .02 .10
225 Steve Farr .02 .10
226 Bob Geren .02 .10
227 Lee Guetterman .02 .10
228 John Habyan .02 .10
229 Mel Hall .02 .10
230 Steve Howe .02 .10
231 Mike Humphreys .02 .10
232 Scott Kamieniecki .02 .10
233 Pat Kelly .02 .10
234 Roberto Kelly .02 .10
235 Tim Leary .02 .10
236 Kevin Maas .02 .10
237 Don Mattingly .25 .60
238 Hensley Meulens .02 .10
239 Matt Nokes .02 .10
240 Pascual Perez .02 .10
241 Eric Plunk .02 .10
242 John Ramos .02 .10
243 Scott Sanderson .02 .10
244 Steve Sax .02 .10
245 Wade Taylor .02 .10
246 Randy Velarde .02 .10
247 Bernie Williams .05 .15
248 Troy Afenir .02 .10
249 Harold Baines .02 .10
250 Lance Blankenship .02 .10
251 Mike Bordick .02 .10
252 Jose Canseco .05 .15
253 Steve Chitren .02 .10
254 Ron Darling .02 .10
255 Dennis Eckersley .02 .10
256 Mike Gallego .02 .10
257 Dave Henderson .02 .10
258 Rickey Henderson UER .08 .25
Wearing 24 on front
and 22 on back
259 Rick Honeycutt .02 .10
260 Brook Jacoby .02 .10
261 Carney Lansford .02 .10
262 Mark McGwire .25 .60
263 Mike Moore .02 .10
264 Gene Nelson .02 .10
265 Jamie Quirk .02 .10
266 Joe Slusarski .02 .10
267 Terry Steinbach .02 .10
268 Dave Stewart .02 .10
269 Todd Van Poppel .02 .10
270 Walt Weiss .02 .10
271 Bob Welch .02 .10
272 Curt Young .02 .10
273 Scott Bradley .02 .10
274 Greg Briley .02 .10
275 Jay Buhner .02 .10
276 Henry Cotto .02 .10
277 Alvin Davis .02 .10
278 Rich DeLucia .02 .10
279 Ken Griffey Jr. .20 .50
280 Erik Hanson .02 .10
281 Brian Holman .02 .10
282 Mike Jackson .02 .10
283 Randy Johnson .08 .25
284 Tracy Jones .02 .10
285 Bill Krueger .02 .10
286 Edgar Martinez .05 .15
287 Tino Martinez .05 .15
288 Rob Murphy .02 .10
289 Pete O'Brien .02 .10
290 Alonzo Powell .02 .10
291 Harold Reynolds .02 .10
292 Mike Schooler .02 .10
293 Russ Swan .02 .10
294 Bill Swift .02 .10
295 Dave Valle .02 .10
296 Omar Vizquel .05 .15
297 Gerald Alexander .02 .10
298 Brad Arnsberg .02 .10
299 Kevin Brown .02 .10
300 Jack Daugherty .02 .10
301 Mario Diaz .02 .10
302 Brian Downing .02 .10
303 Julio Franco .02 .10
304 Juan Gonzalez .05 .15
305 Rich Gossage .02 .10
306 Jose Guzman .02 .10
307 Jose Hernandez RC .08 .25
308 Jeff Huson .02 .10
309 Mike Jeffcoat .02 .10
310 Terry Mathews .02 .10
311 Rafael Palmeiro .05 .15
312 Dean Palmer .02 .10
313 Geno Petralli .02 .10
314 Gary Pettis .02 .10
315 Kevin Reimer .02 .10
316 Ivan Rodriguez .08 .25
317 Kenny Rogers .02 .10
318 Wayne Rosenthal .02 .10
319 Jeff Russell .02 .10
320 Nolan Ryan .40 1.00
321 Ruben Sierra .02 .10
322 Jim Acker .02 .10
323 Roberto Alomar .05 .15
324 Derek Bell .02 .10
325 Pat Borders .02 .10
326 Tom Candiotti .02 .10
327 Joe Carter .02 .10
328 Rob Ducey .02 .10
329 Kelly Gruber .02 .10
330 Juan Guzman .02 .10
331 Tom Henke .02 .10
332 Jimmy Key .02 .10
333 Manny Lee .02 .10
334 Al Leiter .02 .10
335 Bob MacDonald .02 .10
336 Candy Maldonado .02 .10
337 Rance Mulliniks .02 .10
338 Greg Myers .02 .10
339 John Olerud UER .02 .10
1991 BA has .256,
but text says .258
340 Ed Sprague .02 .10
341 Dave Stieb .02 .10
342 Todd Stottlemyre .02 .10
343 Mike Timlin .02 .10
344 Duane Ward .02 .10
345 David Wells .02 .10
346 Devon White .02 .10
347 Mookie Wilson .02 .10
348 Eddie Zosky .02 .10
349 Steve Avery .02 .10
350 Mike Bell .02 .10
351 Rafael Belliard .02 .10
352 Juan Berenguer .02 .10
353 Jeff Blauser .02 .10
354 Sid Bream .02 .10
355 Francisco Cabrera .02 .10
356 Marvin Freeman .02 .10
357 Ron Gant .02 .10
358 Tom Glavine .05 .15
359 Brian Hunter .02 .10
360 Dave Justice .02 .10
361 Charlie Leibrandt .02 .10
362 Mark Lemke .02 .10
363 Kent Mercker .02 .10
364 Keith Mitchell .02 .10
365 Greg Olson .02 .10
366 Terry Pendleton .02 .10
367 Armando Reynoso RC .08 .25
368 Deion Sanders .05 .15
369 Lonnie Smith .02 .10
370 Pete Smith .02 .10
371 John Smoltz .05 .15
372 Mike Stanton .02 .10
373 Jeff Treadway .02 .10
374 Mark Wohlers .02 .10
375 Paul Assenmacher .02 .10
376 George Bell .02 .10
377 Shawn Boskie .02 .10
378 Frank Castillo .02 .10
379 Andre Dawson .02 .10
380 Shawon Dunston .02 .10
381 Mark Grace .05 .15
382 Mike Harkey .02 .10
383 Danny Jackson .02 .10
384 Les Lancaster .02 .10
385 Ced Landrum .02 .10
386 Greg Maddux .15 .40
387 Derrick May .02 .10
388 Chuck McElroy .02 .10
389 Ryne Sandberg .15 .40
390 Heathcliff Slocumb .02 .10
391 Dave Smith .02 .10
392 Dwight Smith .02 .10
393 Rick Sutcliffe .02 .10
394 Hector Villanueva .02 .10
395 Chico Walker .02 .10
396 Jerome Walton .02 .10
397 Rick Wilkins .02 .10
398 Jack Armstrong .02 .10
399 Freddie Benavides .02 .10
400 Glenn Braggs .02 .10
401 Tom Browning .02 .10
402 Norm Charlton .02 .10
403 Eric Davis .02 .10
404 Rob Dibble .02 .10
405 Bill Doran .02 .10
406 Mariano Duncan .02 .10
407 Kip Gross .02 .10
408 Chris Hammond .02 .10
409 Billy Hatcher .02 .10
410 Chris Jones .02 .10
411 Barry Larkin .05 .15
412 Hal Morris .02 .10
413 Randy Myers .02 .10
414 Joe Oliver .02 .10
415 Paul O'Neill .05 .15
416 Ted Power .02 .10
417 Luis Quinones .02 .10
418 Jeff Reed .02 .10
419 Jose Rijo .02 .10
420 Chris Sabo .02 .10
421 Reggie Sanders .02 .10
422 Scott Scudder .02 .10
423 Glenn Sutko .02 .10
424 Eric Anthony .02 .10
425 Jeff Bagwell .08 .25
426 Craig Biggio .05 .15
427 Ken Caminiti .02 .10
428 Casey Candaele .02 .10
429 Mike Capel .02 .10
430 Andujar Cedeno .02 .10
431 Jim Corsi .02 .10
432 Mark Davidson .02 .10
433 Steve Finley .02 .10
434 Luis Gonzalez .02 .10
435 Pete Harnisch .02 .10
436 Dwayne Henry .02 .10
437 Xavier Hernandez .02 .10
438 Jimmy Jones .02 .10
439 Darryl Kile .02 .10
440 Rob Mallicoat .02 .10
441 Andy Mota .02 .10
442 Al Osuna .02 .10
443 Mark Portugal .02 .10
444 Scott Servais .02 .10
445 Mike Simms .02 .10
446 Gerald Young .02 .10
447 Tim Belcher .02 .10
448 Brett Butler .02 .10
449 John Candelaria .02 .10
450 Gary Carter .02 .10
451 Dennis Cook .02 .10
452 Tim Crews .02 .10
453 Kal Daniels .02 .10
454 Jim Gott .02 .10
455 Alfredo Griffin .02 .10
456 Kevin Gross .02 .10
457 Chris Gwynn .02 .10
458 Lenny Harris .02 .10
459 Orel Hershiser .02 .10
460 Jay Howell .02 .10
461 Stan Javier .02 .10
462 Eric Karros .02 .10
463 Ramon Martinez UER .02 .10
Card says bats right,
should be left
464 Roger McDowell UER .02 .10
Wins add up to 54,
totals have 51
465 Mike Morgan .02 .10
466 Eddie Murray .08 .25
467 Jose Offerman .02 .10
468 Bob Ojeda .02 .10
469 Juan Samuel .02 .10
470 Mike Scioscia .02 .10
471 Darryl Strawberry .02 .10
472 Bret Barberie .02 .10
473 Brian Barnes .02 .10
474 Eric Bullock .02 .10
475 Ivan Calderon .02 .10
476 Delino DeShields .02 .10
477 Jeff Fassero .02 .10
478 Mike Fitzgerald .02 .10
479 Steve Frey .02 .10
480 Andres Galarraga .05 .15
481 Mark Gardner .02 .10
482 Marquis Grissom .02 .10
483 Chris Haney .02 .10
484 Barry Jones .02 .10
485 Dave Martinez .02 .10
486 Dennis Martinez .02 .10
487 Chris Nabholz .02 .10
488 Spike Owen .02 .10
489 Gilberto Reyes .02 .10
490 Mel Rojas .02 .10
491 Scott Ruskin .02 .10
492 Bill Sampen .02 .10
493 Larry Walker .05 .15
494 Tim Wallach .02 .10
495 Daryl Boston .02 .10
496 Hubie Brooks .02 .10
497 Tim Burke .02 .10
498 Mark Carreon .02 .10
499 Tony Castillo .02 .10
500 Vince Coleman .02 .10
501 David Cone .02 .10
502 Kevin Elster .02 .10
503 Sid Fernandez .05 .15
504 John Franco .02 .10
505 Dwight Gooden .02 .10
506 Todd Hundley .02 .10
507 Jeff Innis .02 .10
508 Gregg Jefferies .02 .10
509 Howard Johnson .02 .10
510 Dave Magadan .02 .10
511 Terry McDaniel .02 .10
512 Kevin McReynolds .02 .10
513 Keith Miller .02 .10
514 Charlie O'Brien .02 .10
515 Mackey Sasser .02 .10
516 Pete Schourek .02 .10
517 Julio Valera .02 .10
518 Frank Viola .02 .10
519 Wally Whitehurst .02 .10
520 Anthony Young .02 .10
521 Andy Ashby .02 .10
522 Kim Batiste .02 .10
523 Joe Boever .02 .10
524 Wes Chamberlain .02 .10
525 Pat Combs .02 .10
526 Danny Cox .02 .10
527 Darren Daulton .02 .10
528 Jose DeJesus .02 .10
529 Len Dykstra .02 .10
530 Darrin Fletcher .02 .10
531 Tommy Greene .02 .10
532 Jason Grimsley .02 .10
533 Charlie Hayes .02 .10
534 Von Hayes .02 .10
535 Dave Hollins .02 .10
536 Ricky Jordan .02 .10
537 John Kruk .02 .10
538 Jim Lindeman .02 .10
539 Mickey Morandini .02 .10
540 Terry Mulholland .02 .10
541 Dale Murphy .05 .15
542 Randy Ready .02 .10
543 Wally Ritchie UER .02 .10
Letters in data are
cut off on card
544 Bruce Ruffin .02 .10
545 Steve Searcy .02 .10
546 Dickie Thon .02 .10
547 Mitch Williams .02 .10
548 Stan Belinda .02 .10
549 Jay Bell .02 .10
550 Barry Bonds .40 1.00
551 Bobby Bonilla .02 .10
552 Steve Buechele .02 .10
553 Doug Drabek .02 .10
554 Neal Heaton .02 .10
555 Jeff King .02 .10
556 Bob Kipper .02 .10
557 Bill Landrum .02 .10
558 Mike LaValliere .02 .10
559 Jose Lind .02 .10
560 Lloyd McClendon .02 .10
561 Orlando Merced .02 .10
562 Bob Patterson .02 .10
563 Joe Redfield .02 .10
564 Gary Redus .02 .10
565 Rosario Rodriguez .02 .10
566 Don Slaught .02 .10
567 John Smiley .02 .10
568 Zane Smith .02 .10
569 Randy Tomlin .02 .10
570 Andy Van Slyke .05 .15
571 Gary Varsho .02 .10
572 Bob Walk .02 .10
573 John Wehner UER .02 .10
Actually played for
Carolina in 1991,
not Cards
574 Juan Agosto .02 .10
575 Cris Carpenter .02 .10
576 Jose DeLeon .02 .10
577 Rich Gedman .02 .10
578 Bernard Gilkey .02 .10
579 Pedro Guerrero .02 .10
580 Ken Hill .02 .10
581 Rex Hudler .02 .10
582 Felix Jose .02 .10
583 Ray Lankford .02 .10
584 Omar Olivares .02 .10
585 Jose Oquendo .02 .10
586 Tom Pagnozzi .02 .10
587 Geronimo Pena .02 .10
588 Mike Perez .02 .10
589 Gerald Perry .02 .10
590 Bryn Smith .02 .10
591 Lee Smith .02 .10
592 Ozzie Smith .15 .40
593 Scott Terry .02 .10
594 Bob Tewksbury .02 .10
595 Milt Thompson .02 .10
596 Todd Zeile .02 .10
597 Larry Andersen .02 .10
598 Oscar Azocar .02 .10
599 Andy Benes .02 .10
600 Ricky Bones .02 .10
601 Jerald Clark .02 .10
602 Pat Clements .02 .10
603 Paul Faries .02 .10
604 Tony Fernandez .02 .10
605 Tony Gwynn .10 .30
606 Greg W. Harris .02 .10
607 Thomas Howard .02 .10
608 Bruce Hurst .02 .10
609 Darrin Jackson .02 .10
610 Tom Lampkin .02 .10
611 Craig Lefferts .02 .10
612 Jim Lewis RC .02 .10
613 Mike Maddux .02 .10
614 Fred McGriff .05 .15
615 Jose Melendez .02 .10
616 Jose Mota .02 .10
617 Dennis Rasmussen .02 .10
618 Bip Roberts .02 .10
619 Rich Rodriguez .02 .10
620 Benito Santiago .02 .10
621 Craig Shipley .02 .10
622 Tim Teufel .02 .10
623 Kevin Ward .02 .10
624 Ed Whitson .02 .10
625 Dave Anderson .02 .10
626 Kevin Bass .02 .10
627 Rod Beck RC .15 .40
628 Bud Black .02 .10
629 Jeff Brantley .02 .10
630 John Burkett .02 .10
631 Will Clark .05 .15
632 Royce Clayton .02 .10
633 Steve Decker .02 .10
634 Kelly Downs .02 .10
635 Mike Felder .02 .10
636 Scott Garrelts .02 .10
637 Eric Gunderson .02 .10
638 Bryan Hickerson RC .02 .10
639 Darren Lewis .02 .10
640 Greg Litton .02 .10
641 Kirt Manwaring .02 .10
642 Paul McClellan .02 .10
643 Willie McGee .02 .10
644 Kevin Mitchell .02 .10
645 Francisco Oliveras .02 .10
646 Mike Remlinger .02 .10
647 Dave Righetti .02 .10
648 Robby Thompson .02 .10
649 Jose Uribe .02 .10

650 Matt Williams .02 .10
651 Trevor Wilson .02 .10
652 Tom Goodwin MLP UER .02 .10
Timed in 3.5,
should be be timed
653 Terry Bross MLP .02 .10
654 Mike Christopher MLP .02 .10
655 Kenny Lofton MLP .05 .15
656 Chris Cron MLP .02 .10
657 Willie Banks MLP .02 .10
658 Pat Rice MLP .02 .10
659A R.Maurer MLP ERR RC .30 .75
659B Rob Maurer MLP COR RC .02 .10
660 Don Harris MLP .02 .10
661 Henry Rodriguez MLP .02 .10
662 Cliff Brantley MLP .02 .10
663 Mike Linskey MLP UER .02 .10
220 pounds in data,
200 in text
664 Gary DiSarcina MLP .02 .10
665 Gil Heredia RC .08 .25
666 Vinny Castilla RC .40 1.00
667 Paul Abbott MLP .02 .10
668 Monty Fariss MLP UER .02 .10
Called Paul on back
669 Jarvis Brown MLP .02 .10
670 Wayne Kirby RC .02 .10
671 Scott Brosius RC .15 .40
672 Bob Hamelin MLP .02 .10
673 Joel Johnston MLP .02 .10
674 Tim Spehr MLP .02 .10
675A J.Gardner MLP ERR .30 .75
675B Jeff Gardner MLP COR .02 .10
676 Rico Rossy MLP .02 .10
677 Roberto Hernandez MLP RC .02 .10
678 Ted Wood MLP .02 .10
679 Cal Eldred MLP .02 .10
680 Sean Berry MLP .02 .10
681 Rickey Henderson RS .05 .15
682 Nolan Ryan RS .20 .50
683 Dennis Martinez RS .02 .10
684 Wilson Alvarez RS .02 .10
685 Joe Carter RS .02 .10
686 Dave Winfield RS .02 .10
687 David Cone RS .02 .10
688 Jose Canseco LL UER .02 .10
Text on back has 42 stolen
bases in 88; should be 40
689 Howard Johnson LL .02 .10
690 Julio Franco LL .02 .10
691 Terry Pendleton LL .02 .10
692 Cecil Fielder LL .02 .10
693 Scott Erickson LL .02 .10
694 Tom Glavine LL .02 .10
695 Dennis Martinez LL .02 .10
696 Bryan Harvey LL .02 .10
697 Lee Smith LL .02 .10
698 Roberto Alomar .02 .10
Sandy Alomar Jr.
699 Bobby Bonilla .02 .10
Will Clark
700 Wohlers/Mercker/Pena .02 .10
701 B.Jackson/F.Thomas .05 .15
702 Paul Molitor .02 .10
Brett Butler
703 C.Ripken/J.Carter .15 .40
704 Barry Larkin .05 .15
Kirby Puckett
705 M.Vaughn/C.Fielder .02 .10
706 Ramon Martinez .02 .10
Ozzie Guillen
707 Harold Baines .02 .10
Wade Boggs
708 Robin Yount PV .08 .25
709 Ken Griffey Jr. PV UER .10 .30
Missing quotations on
back; BA has .322, but
was actually .327
710 Nolan Ryan PV .20 .50
711 Cal Ripken PV .15 .40
712 Frank Thomas PV .05 .15
713 Dave Justice PV .02 .10
714 Checklist 1-101 .02 .10
715 Checklist 102-194 .02 .10
716 Checklist 195-296 .02 .10
717 Checklist 297-397 .02 .10
718 Checklist 398-494 .02 .10
719 Checklist 495-596 .02 .10
720A CL 597-720 ERR .02 .10
659 Rob Mauer
720B CL 597-720 COR .02 .10
659 Rob Maurer

1992 Fleer All-Stars

COMPLETE SET (24) 12.50 30.00
RANDOM INSERTS IN WAX PACKS
1 Felix Jose .30 .75
2 Tony Gwynn 1.00 2.50
3 Barry Bonds 3.00 8.00
4 Bobby Bonilla .30 .75
5 Mike LaValliere .30 .75
6 Tom Glavine .50 1.25
7 Ramon Martinez .30 .75
8 Lee Smith .30 .75
9 Mickey Tettleton .30 .75
10 Scott Erickson .30 .75
11 Frank Thomas .75 2.00
12 Danny Tartabull .30 .75
13 Will Clark .50 1.25
14 Ryne Sandberg 1.25 3.00
15 Terry Pendleton .30 .75
16 Barry Larkin .50 1.25
17 Rafael Palmeiro .50 1.25
18 Julio Franco .30 .75
19 Robin Ventura .30 .75
20 Cal Ripken 2.50 6.00
21 Joe Carter .30 .75
22 Kirby Puckett .75 2.00
23 Ken Griffey Jr. 1.50 4.00
24 Jose Canseco .50 1.25

1992 Fleer Clemens

COMPLETE SET (12) 5.00 12.00
COMMON CLEMENS (1-12) .40 1.00
RANDOM INSERTS IN PACKS
COMMON MAIL-IN (13-15) .40 1.00
MAIL-IN CARDS DIST.VIA WRAPPER EXCH.
AU CARD RANDOM INSERT IN PACKS
AUTOGRAPH CARD IS NOT CERTIFIED
AU Roger Clemens AU/2000 30.00 60.00
NNO R.Clemens 2.50 6.00
P.Mullan Promo

1992 Fleer Lumber Company

COMPLETE SET (9) 4.00 10.00
ONE SET PER HOBBY FACTORY SET
L1 Cecil Fielder .30 .75
L2 Mickey Tettleton .30 .75
L3 Darryl Strawberry .30 .75
L4 Ryne Sandberg 1.25 3.00
L5 Jose Canseco .50 1.25
L6 Matt Williams .30 .75
L7 Cal Ripken 2.50 6.00
L8 Barry Bonds 3.00 8.00
L9 Ron Gant .30 .75

1992 Fleer Rookie Sensations

COMPLETE SET (20) 10.00 25.00
RANDOM INSERTS IN CELLO PACKS
1 Frank Thomas 8.00 20.00
2 Todd Van Poppel .60 1.50
3 Orlando Merced .60 1.50
4 Jeff Bagwell 3.00 8.00
5 Jeff Fassero .60 1.50
6 Darren Lewis .60 1.50
7 Milt Cuyler .60 1.50
8 Mike Timlin .60 1.50
9 Brian McRae .60 1.50
10 Chuck Knoblauch .75 2.00
11 Rich DeLucia .60 1.50
12 Ivan Rodriguez 2.00 5.00
13 Juan Guzman .60 1.50
14 Steve Chitren .60 1.50
15 Mark Wohlers .60 1.50
16 Wes Chamberlain .60 1.50
17 Ray Lankford .75 2.00
18 Chito Martinez .60 1.50
19 Phil Plantier .60 1.50
20 Scott Leius UER .60 1.50

1992 Fleer Smoke 'n Heat

COMPLETE SET (12) 4.00 10.00
ONE SET PER RETAIL FACTORY SET
S1 Lee Smith .30 .75
S2 Jack McDowell .30 .75
S3 David Cone .30 .75
S4 Roger Clemens 1.50 4.00
S5 Nolan Ryan 3.00 8.00
S6 Scott Erickson .30 .75
S7 Tom Glavine .50 1.25
S8 Andy Benes .30 .75
S10 Steve Avery .30 .75
S11 Randy Johnson .75 2.00
S12 Jim Abbott .50 1.25

1992 Fleer Team Leaders

COMPLETE SET (20) 10.00 25.00
ONE TL OR CLEMENS PER RACK PACK
1 Don Mattingly 4.00 10.00
2 Howard Johnson .60 1.50
3 Chris Sabo UER .60 1.50
4 Carlton Fisk 1.00 2.50
5 Kirby Puckett 1.50 4.00
6 Cecil Fielder .60 1.50
7 Tony Gwynn 2.00 5.00
8 Will Clark 1.00 2.50
9 Bobby Bonilla .60 1.50
10 Len Dykstra .60 1.50
11 Tom Glavine 1.00 2.50
12 Rafael Palmeiro 1.00 2.50
13 Wade Boggs 1.00 2.50
14 Joe Carter .60 1.50
15 Ken Griffey Jr. 3.00 8.00
16 Darryl Strawberry .60 1.50
17 Cal Ripken 5.00 12.00
18 Danny Tartabull .60 1.50
19 Jose Canseco 1.00 2.50
20 Andre Dawson .60 1.50

1992 Fleer Update

The 1992 Fleer Update set contains 132 standard-size cards. Cards were distributed exclusively in factory sets through hobby dealers. Factory sets included a four-card, black-bordered "92 Headliners" insert set for a total of 136 cards. Due to lackluster retail response for previous Fleer Update sets, wholesale orders for this product were low, resulting in a short print run. As word got out that the cards were in short supply, the secondary market prices soared soon after release. The basic card design is identical to the regular issue 1992 Fleer cards except for the U-prefixed numbering on back. The cards are checklisted alphabetically within and according to teams for each league with AL preceding NL. Rookie Cards in this set include Jeff Kent and Mike Piazza. The Piazza card is widely recognized as one of the more desirable singles issued in the 1990's.

COMP.FACT.SET (136) 30.00 60.00
COMPLETE SET (132) 30.00 60.00
U PREFIX ON REG.CARD NUMBERS
1 Todd Frohwirth .20 .50
2 Alan Mills .20 .50
3 Rick Sutcliffe .40 1.00
4 John Valentin RC .60 1.50
5 Frank Viola .40 1.00
6 Bob Zupcic RC .20 .50
7 Mike Butcher .20 .50
8 Chad Curtis RC .60 1.50
9 Damion Easley RC .60 1.50
10 Tim Salmon .60 1.50
11 Julio Valera .20 .50
12 George Bell .20 .50
13 Roberto Hernandez .20 .50
14 Shawn Jeter RC .20 .50
15 Thomas Howard .20 .50
16 Jesse Levis .20 .50
17 Kenny Lofton .60 1.50
18 Paul Sorrento .20 .50
19 Rico Brogna .20 .50
20 John Doherty RC .20 .50
21 Dan Gladden .20 .50
22 Buddy Groom RC .20 .50
23 Shawn Hare RC .20 .50
24 John Kiely .20 .50
25 Kurt Knudsen .20 .50
26 Gregg Jefferies .20 .50
27 Wally Joyner .40 1.00
28 Kevin Koslofski .20 .50
29 Kevin McReynolds .20 .50
30 Rusty Meacham .20 .50
31 Keith Miller .20 .50
32 Hipolito Pichardo RC .20 .50
33 Jim Austin .20 .50
34 Scott Fletcher .20 .50
35 John Jaha RC .60 1.50
36 Pat Listach RC .60 1.50
37 Dave Nilsson .20 .50
38 Kevin Seitzer .20 .50
39 Tom Edens .20 .50
40 Pat Mahomes RC .60 1.50
41 John Smiley .20 .50
42 Charlie Hayes .20 .50
43 Sam Militello .20 .50
44 Andy Stankiewicz .20 .50
45 Danny Tartabull .20 .50
46 Bob Wickman 1.00 2.50
47 Jerry Browne .20 .50
48 Kevin Campbell .20 .50
49 Vince Horsman .20 .50
50 Troy Neel RC .20 .50
51 Ruben Sierra .40 1.00
52 Bruce Walton .20 .50
53 Willie Wilson .20 .50
54 Bret Boone .60 1.50
55 Dave Fleming .20 .50
56 Kevin Mitchell .20 .50
57 Jeff Nelson RC 1.00 2.50
58 Shane Turner .20 .50
59 Jose Canseco .60 1.50
60 Jeff Frye RC .20 .50
61 Danny Leon .20 .50
62 Roger Pavlik RC .20 .50
63 David Cone .40 1.00
64 Pat Hentgen .20 .50
65 Randy Knorr .20 .50
66 Jack Morris .40 1.00
67 Dave Winfield .40 1.00
68 David Nied RC .20 .50
69 Otis Nixon .20 .50
70 Alejandro Pena .20 .50
71 Jeff Reardon .40 1.00
72 Alex Arias RC .20 .50
73 Jim Bullinger .20 .50
74 Mike Morgan .20 .50
75 Rey Sanchez RC .60 1.50
76 Bob Scanlan .20 .50
77 Sammy Sosa Cubs 1.50 4.00
78 Scott Bankhead .20 .50
79 Tim Belcher .20 .50
80 Steve Foster .20 .50
81 Willie Greene .20 .50
82 Bip Roberts .20 .50
83 Scott Ruskin .20 .50
84 Greg Swindell .20 .50
85 Juan Guerrero .20 .50
86 Butch Henry .20 .50
87 Doug Jones .20 .50
88 Brian Williams RC .20 .50
89 Tom Candiotti .20 .50
90 Eric Davis .40 1.00
91 Carlos Hernandez .20 .50
92 Mike Piazza RC 30.00 80.00
93 Mike Sharperson .20 .50
94 Eric Young RC .60 1.50
95 Moises Alou .40 1.00
96 Greg Colbrunn .20 .50
97 Wil Cordero .20 .50
98 Ken Hill .20 .50
99 John Vander Wal RC .60 1.50
100 John Wetteland .40 1.00
101 Bobby Bonilla .40 1.00
102 Eric Hillman RC .20 .50
103 Pat Howell .20 .50
104 Jeff Kent RC 10.00 25.00
105 Dick Schofield .20 .50
106 Ryan Thompson RC .20 .50
107 Chico Walker .20 .50
108 Juan Bell .20 .50
109 Mariano Duncan .20 .50
110 Jeff Grotewold .20 .50
111 Ben Rivera .20 .50
112 Curt Schilling .60 1.50
113 Victor Cole RC .20 .50
114 Al Martin RC .60 1.50
115 Roger Mason .20 .50
116 Blas Minor .20 .50
117 Tim Wakefield RC 4.00 10.00
118 Mark Clark RC .20 .50
119 Rheal Cormier .20 .50
120 Donovan Osborne .20 .50
121 Todd Worrell .20 .50
122 Jeremy Hernandez RC .20 .50
123 Randy Myers .20 .50
124 Frank Seminara RC .20 .50
125 Gary Sheffield .40 1.00
126 Dan Walters .20 .50
127 Steve Hosey .20 .50
128 Mike Jackson .20 .50
129 Jim Pena .20 .50
130 Cory Snyder .20 .50
131 Bill Swift .20 .50
132 Checklist U1-U132 .20 .50

1992 Fleer Update Headliners

COMPLETE SET (4) 3.00 8.00
ONE SET PER FACTORY SET
1 Ken Griffey Jr. 1.50 4.00
2 Robin Yount 1.25 3.00
3 Jeff Reardon .30 .75
4 Cecil Fielder .30 .75

1992 Fleer Citgo The Performer

This 24-card standard-size set was produced by Fleer for 7-Eleven. During April and May at any of the 1,600 participating 7-Eleven stores, customers who purchased eight gallons or more of mid-grade or premium Citgo-brand gasoline received a packet of five trading cards. During June or while supplies last, customers who wanted additional cards could receive three trading cards of their choice per eight gallon or more fill-up by sending in a self-addressed envelope with 1.00 to cover postage and handling. The front design has color action player photos, with a metallic blue-green border that fades to white as one moves down the card face. The card front prominently features "The Performer". The team logo, player's name, and his position appear in the wider right border. The top half of the backs have close-up photos, while the bottom half carry biography and complete career statistics.

COMPLETE SET (24) 3.00 8.00
1 Nolan Ryan .50 1.25
2 Frank Thomas .15 .40
3 Ryne Sandberg .20 .50
4 Ken Griffey Jr. .50 1.25
5 Cal Ripken .50 1.25
6 Roger Clemens .20 .50
7 Cecil Fielder .05 .15
8 Dave Justice .10 .30
9 Wade Boggs .15 .40
10 Tony Gwynn .30 .75
11 Kirby Puckett .15 .40
12 Darryl Strawberry .05 .15
13 Jose Canseco .15 .40
14 Barry Larkin .10 .30
15 Terry Pendleton .02 .10
16 Don Mattingly .25 .60
17 Rickey Henderson .25 .60
18 Ruben Sierra .05 .15
19 Jeff Bagwell .30 .75
20 Tom Glavine .10 .30
21 Ramon Martinez .05 .15
22 Will Clark .10 .30
23 Barry Bonds .25 .60
24 Roberto Alomar .10 .30

1992 Fleer Gwynn Casa de Amparo

This one card set was produced by the Fleer Corporation for Casa de Amparo (Spanish for house of refuge) which provided care for over 600 children each year. Tony Gwynn served as a spokesperson for the house. The front features a color picture of Tony Gwynn hold Casa's Poster Child for 1992. The back displays information about Casa de Amparo.

1 Tony Gwynn 2.00 5.00

1993 Fleer

The 720-card 1993 Fleer baseball set contains two series of 360 standard-size cards. Cards were distributed in plastic wrapped packs, cello packs, jumbo packs and rack packs. For the first time in years, Fleer did not issue a factory set. In fact, Fleer discontinued issuing factory sets from 1993 through 1998. The cards are checklisted below alphabetically within and according to teams for each league with NL preceding AL. Topical subsets include League Leaders (344-348/704-708), Round Trippers (349-353/709-713), and Super Star Specials (354-357/714-717). Each series concludes with checklists (358-360/718-720). There are no key Rookie Cards in this set.

COMPLETE SET (720) 15.00 40.00
COMPLETE SERIES 1 (360) 8.00 20.00
COMPLETE SERIES 2 (360) 8.00 20.00
1 Steve Avery .02 .10
2 Sid Bream .02 .10
3 Ron Gant .07 .20
4 Tom Glavine .10 .30
5 Brian Hunter .02 .10
6 Ryan Klesko .07 .20
7 Charlie Leibrandt .02 .10
8 Kent Mercker .02 .10
9 David Nied .02 .10
10 Otis Nixon .02 .10
11 Greg Olson .02 .10
12 Terry Pendleton .07 .20
13 Deion Sanders .10 .30
14 John Smoltz .10 .30
15 Mike Stanton .02 .10
16 Mark Wohlers .02 .10
17 Paul Assenmacher .02 .10
18 Steve Buechele .02 .10
19 Shawon Dunston .02 .10
20 Mark Grace .10 .30
21 Derrick May .02 .10
22 Chuck McElroy .02 .10
23 Mike Morgan .02 .10
24 Rey Sanchez .02 .10
25 Ryne Sandberg .30 .75
26 Bob Scanlan .02 .10
27 Sammy Sosa .20 .50
28 Rick Wilkins .02 .10
29 Bobby Ayala RC .02 .10
30 Tim Belcher .02 .10
31 Jeff Branson .02 .10
32 Norm Charlton .02 .10
33 Steve Foster .02 .10
34 Willie Greene .02 .10
35 Chris Hammond .02 .10
36 Milt Hill .02 .10
37 Hal Morris .02 .10
38 Joe Oliver .02 .10
39 Paul O'Neill .10 .30
40 Tim Pugh RC .02 .10
41 Jose Rijo .02 .10
42 Bip Roberts .02 .10
43 Chris Sabo .02 .10
44 Reggie Sanders .07 .20
45 Eric Anthony .02 .10
46 Jeff Bagwell .10 .30
47 Craig Biggio .10 .30
48 Joe Boever .02 .10
49 Casey Candaele .02 .10
50 Steve Finley .07 .20
51 Luis Gonzalez .07 .20
52 Pete Harnisch .02 .10
53 Xavier Hernandez .02 .10
54 Doug Jones .02 .10
55 Eddie Taubensee .02 .10
56 Brian Williams .02 .10
57 Pedro Astacio .02 .10
58 Todd Benzinger .02 .10
59 Brett Butler .07 .20
60 Tom Candiotti .02 .10
61 Lenny Harris .02 .10
62 Carlos Hernandez .02 .10
63 Orel Hershiser .07 .20
64 Eric Karros .07 .20
65 Ramon Martinez .02 .10
66 Jose Offerman .02 .10
67 Mike Scioscia .02 .10
68 Mike Sharperson .02 .10
69 Eric Young .02 .10
70 Moises Alou .07 .20
71 Ivan Calderon .02 .10
72 Archi Cianfrocco .02 .10
73 Wil Cordero .02 .10
74 Delino DeShields .02 .10
75 Mark Gardner .02 .10
76 Ken Hill .02 .10
77 Tim Laker RC .02 .10
78 Chris Nabholz .02 .10
79 Mel Rojas .02 .10
80 John Vander Wal UER(Misspelled Vander Wall .02 .10
in l
81 Larry Walker .07 .20
82 Tim Wallach .02 .10
83 John Wetteland .07 .20
84 Bobby Bonilla .07 .20
85 Daryl Boston .02 .10
86 Sid Fernandez .02 .10
87 Eric Hillman .02 .10
88 Todd Hundley .02 .10
89 Howard Johnson .02 .10
90 Jeff Kent .20 .50
91 Eddie Murray .20 .50
92 Bill Pecota .02 .10
93 Bret Saberhagen .07 .20
94 Dick Schofield .02 .10
95 Pete Schourek .02 .10
96 Anthony Young .02 .10
97 Ruben Amaro .02 .10
98 Juan Bell .02 .10
99 Wes Chamberlain .02 .10
100 Darren Daulton .07 .20
101 Mariano Duncan .02 .10
102 Mike Hartley .02 .10
103 Ricky Jordan .02 .10
104 John Kruk .07 .20
105 Mickey Morandini .02 .10
106 Terry Mulholland .02 .10
107 Ben Rivera .02 .10
108 Curt Schilling .07 .20
109 Keith Shepherd RC .02 .10
110 Stan Belinda .02 .10
111 Jay Bell .07 .20
112 Barry Bonds .60 1.50
113 Jeff King .02 .10
114 Mike LaValliere .02 .10
115 Jose Lind .02 .10
116 Roger Mason .02 .10
117 Orlando Merced .02 .10
118 Bob Patterson .02 .10
119 Don Slaught .02 .10
120 Zane Smith .02 .10
121 Randy Tomlin .02 .10
122 Andy Van Slyke .10 .30
123 Tim Wakefield .20 .50
124 Rheal Cormier .02 .10
125 Bernard Gilkey .02 .10
126 Felix Jose .02 .10
127 Ray Lankford .07 .20
128 Bob McClure .02 .10
129 Donovan Osborne .02 .10
130 Tom Pagnozzi .02 .10
131 Geronimo Pena .02 .10
132 Mike Perez .02 .10
133 Lee Smith .07 .20
134 Bob Tewksbury .02 .10
135 Todd Worrell .02 .10
136 Todd Zeile .02 .10
137 Jerald Clark .02 .10
138 Tony Gwynn .25 .60
139 Greg W. Harris .02 .10
140 Jeremy Hernandez .02 .10
141 Darrin Jackson .02 .10
142 Mike Maddux .02 .10
143 Fred McGriff .10 .30
144 Jose Melendez .02 .10
145 Rich Rodriguez .02 .10
146 Frank Seminara .02 .10
147 Gary Sheffield .07 .20
148 Kurt Stillwell .02 .10
149 Dan Walters .02 .10
150 Rod Beck .02 .10
151 Bud Black .02 .10
152 Jeff Brantley .02 .10
153 John Burkett .02 .10
154 Will Clark .10 .30
155 Royce Clayton .02 .10
156 Mike Jackson .02 .10
157 Darren Lewis .02 .10
158 Kirt Manwaring .02 .10
159 Willie McGee .07 .20
160 Cory Snyder .02 .10
161 Bill Swift .02 .10
162 Trevor Wilson .02 .10
163 Brady Anderson .07 .20
164 Glenn Davis .02 .10
165 Mike Devereaux .02 .10
166 Todd Frohwirth .02 .10
167 Leo Gomez .02 .10
168 Chris Hoiles .02 .10
169 Ben McDonald .02 .10
170 Randy Milligan .02 .10
171 Alan Mills .02 .10
172 Mike Mussina .10 .30
173 Gregg Olson .02 .10
174 Arthur Rhodes .02 .10
175 David Segui .02 .10
176 Ellis Burks .07 .20
177 Roger Clemens .40 1.00
178 Scott Cooper .02 .10
179 Danny Darwin .02 .10
180 Tony Fossas .02 .10
181 Paul Quantrill .02 .10
182 Jody Reed .02 .10
183 John Valentin .02 .10
184 Mo Vaughn .07 .20
185 Frank Viola .07 .20
186 Bob Zupcic .02 .10
187 Jim Abbott .10 .30
188 Gary DiSarcina .02 .10
189 Damion Easley .02 .10
190 Junior Felix .02 .10
191 Chuck Finley .07 .20
192 Joe Grahe .02 .10
193 Bryan Harvey .02 .10
194 Mark Langston .02 .10
195 John Orton .02 .10
196 Luis Polonia .02 .10
197 Tim Salmon .10 .30
198 Luis Sojo .02 .10
199 Wilson Alvarez .02 .10
200 George Bell .02 .10
201 Alex Fernandez .02 .10
202 Craig Grebeck .02 .10
203 Ozzie Guillen .07 .20
204 Lance Johnson .02 .10
205 Ron Karkovice .02 .10
206 Kirk McCaskill .02 .10
207 Jack McDowell .02 .10
208 Scott Radinsky .02 .10
209 Tim Raines .07 .20
210 Frank Thomas .20 .50
211 Robin Ventura .07 .20
212 Sandy Alomar Jr. .02 .10
213 Carlos Baerga .02 .10
214 Dennis Cook .02 .10
215 Thomas Howard .02 .10
216 Mark Lewis .02 .10
217 Derek Lilliquist .02 .10
218 Kenny Lofton .07 .20
219 Charles Nagy .02 .10
220 Steve Olin .02 .10
221 Paul Sorrento .02 .10
222 Jim Thome .10 .30
223 Mark Whiten .02 .10
224 Milt Cuyler .02 .10
225 Rob Deer .02 .10
226 John Doherty .02 .10
227 Cecil Fielder .07 .20
228 Travis Fryman .07 .20
229 Mike Henneman .02 .10
230 John Kiely UER(Card has batting .02 .10
stats of Pat Ke
231 Kurt Knudsen .02 .10
232 Scott Livingstone .02 .10
233 Tony Phillips .02 .10
234 Mickey Tettleton .02 .10
235 Kevin Appier .07 .20
236 George Brett .50 1.25
237 Tom Gordon .02 .10
238 Gregg Jefferies .02 .10
239 Wally Joyner .07 .20
240 Kevin Koslofski .02 .10
241 Mike Macfarlane .02 .10
242 Brian McRae .02 .10
243 Rusty Meacham .02 .10
244 Keith Miller .02 .10
245 Jeff Montgomery .02 .10
246 Hipolito Pichardo .02 .10
247 Ricky Bones .02 .10
248 Cal Eldred .02 .10
249 Mike Fetters .02 .10
250 Darryl Hamilton .02 .10
251 Doug Henry .02 .10
252 John Jaha .02 .10
253 Pat Listach .02 .10
254 Paul Molitor .07 .20
255 Jaime Navarro .02 .10
256 Kevin Seitzer .02 .10
257 B.J. Surhoff .07 .20
258 Greg Vaughn .02 .10
259 Bill Wegman .02 .10
260 Robin Yount .30 .75
261 Rick Aguilera .02 .10
262 Chili Davis .07 .20
263 Scott Erickson .02 .10
264 Greg Gagne .02 .10
265 Mark Guthrie .02 .10
266 Brian Harper .02 .10
267 Kent Hrbek .07 .20
268 Terry Jorgensen .02 .10
269 Gene Larkin .02 .10
270 Scott Leius .02 .10
271 Pat Mahomes .02 .10
272 Pedro Munoz .02 .10
273 Kirby Puckett .20 .50
274 Kevin Tapani .02 .10
275 Carl Willis .02 .10
276 Steve Farr .02 .10
277 John Habyan .02 .10
278 Mel Hall .02 .10
279 Charlie Hayes .02 .10
280 Pat Kelly .02 .10
281 Don Mattingly .50 1.25
282 Sam Militello .02 .10
283 Matt Nokes .02 .10
284 Melido Perez .02 .10
285 Andy Stankiewicz .02 .10
286 Danny Tartabull .02 .10
287 Randy Velarde .02 .10
288 Bob Wickman .07 .20
289 Bernie Williams .10 .30
290 Lance Blankenship .02 .10
291 Mike Bordick .02 .10
292 Jerry Browne .02 .10
293 Dennis Eckersley .07 .20
294 Rickey Henderson .20 .50
295 Vince Horsman .02 .10
296 Mark McGwire .50 1.25
297 Jeff Parrett .02 .10
298 Ruben Sierra .07 .20
299 Terry Steinbach .02 .10
300 Walt Weiss .02 .10
301 Bob Welch .02 .10
302 Willie Wilson .02 .10
303 Bobby Witt .02 .10
304 Bret Boone .07 .20
305 Jay Buhner .07 .20
306 Dave Fleming .02 .10
307 Ken Griffey Jr. .40 1.00
308 Erik Hanson .02 .10
309 Edgar Martinez .10 .30
310 Tino Martinez .10 .30
311 Jeff Nelson .02 .10
312 Dennis Powell .02 .10
313 Mike Schooler .02 .10
314 Russ Swan .02 .10
315 Dave Valle .02 .10
316 Omar Vizquel .10 .30
317 Kevin Brown .07 .20
318 Todd Burns .02 .10
319 Jose Canseco .10 .30
320 Julio Franco .07 .20
321 Jeff Frye .02 .10
322 Juan Gonzalez .07 .20
323 Jose Guzman .02 .10
324 Jeff Huson .02 .10
325 Dean Palmer .07 .20
326 Kevin Reimer .02 .10
327 Ivan Rodriguez .10 .30
328 Kenny Rogers .07 .20
329 Dan Smith .02 .10
330 Roberto Alomar .10 .30
331 Derek Bell .02 .10
332 Pat Borders .02 .10
333 Joe Carter .07 .20
334 Kelly Gruber .02 .10
335 Tom Henke .02 .10
336 Jimmy Key .07 .20
337 Manuel Lee .02 .10
338 Candy Maldonado .02 .10
339 John Olerud .07 .20
340 Todd Stottlemyre .02 .10
341 Duane Ward .02 .10
342 Devon White .07 .20
343 Dave Winfield .07 .20
344 Edgar Martinez LL .07 .20
345 Cecil Fielder LL .07 .20
346 Kenny Lofton LL .02 .10
347 Jack Morris LL .02 .10
348 Roger Clemens LL .20 .50
349 Fred McGriff RT .07 .20
350 Barry Bonds RT .30 .75
351 Gary Sheffield RT .02 .10
352 Darren Daulton RT .02 .10
353 Dave Hollins RT .02 .10
354 P.Martinez .20 .50
R.Martinez
355 K.Puckett .10 .30
I.Rodriguez
356 Sandberg .20 .50
Sheffield
357 R.Alomar .07 .20
Knoblauch
Baerg
358 Checklist 1-120 .02 .10
359 Checklist 121-240 .02 .10
360 Checklist 241-360 .02 .10
361 Rafael Belliard .02 .10
362 Damon Berryhill .02 .10
363 Mike Bielecki .02 .10
364 Jeff Blauser .02 .10
365 Francisco Cabrera .02 .10
366 Marvin Freeman .02 .10
367 David Justice .07 .20
368 Mark Lemke .02 .10
369 Alejandro Pena .02 .10
370 Jeff Reardon .07 .20
371 Lonnie Smith .02 .10
372 Pete Smith .02 .10
373 Shawn Boskie .02 .10
374 Jim Bullinger .02 .10
375 Frank Castillo .02 .10
376 Doug Dascenzo .02 .10
377 Andre Dawson .07 .20
378 Mike Harkey .02 .10
379 Greg Hibbard .02 .10
380 Greg Maddux .30 .75
381 Ken Patterson .02 .10
382 Jeff D. Robinson .02 .10
383 Luis Salazar .02 .10
384 Dwight Smith .02 .10
385 Jose Vizcaino .02 .10
386 Scott Bankhead .02 .10
387 Tom Browning .02 .10
388 Darnell Coles .02 .10
389 Rob Dibble .07 .20
390 Bill Doran .02 .10
391 Dwayne Henry .02 .10
392 Cesar Hernandez .02 .10
393 Roberto Kelly .02 .10
394 Barry Larkin .10 .30
395 Dave Martinez .02 .10
396 Kevin Mitchell .02 .10
397 Jeff Reed .02 .10
398 Scott Ruskin .02 .10
399 Greg Swindell .02 .10
400 Dan Wilson .07 .20
401 Andy Ashby .02 .10
402 Freddie Benavides .02 .10
403 Dante Bichette .07 .20
404 Willie Blair .02 .10
405 Denis Boucher .02 .10
406 Vinny Castilla .10 .30
407 Braulio Castillo .02 .10
408 Alex Cole .02 .10
409 Andres Galarraga .07 .20
410 Joe Girardi .02 .10
411 Butch Henry .02 .10
412 Darren Holmes .02 .10
413 Calvin Jones .02 .10
414 Steve Reed RC .02 .10
415 Kevin Ritz .02 .10
416 Jim Tatum RC .02 .10
417 Jack Armstrong .02 .10

418 Bret Barberie .02 .10
419 Ryan Bowen .02 .10
420 Cris Carpenter .02 .10
421 Chuck Carr .02 .10
422 Scott Chiamparino .02 .10
423 Jeff Conine .07 .20
424 Jim Corsi .02 .10
425 Steve Decker .02 .10
426 Chris Donnels .02 .10
427 Monty Fariss .02 .10
428 Bob Natal .02 .10
429 Pat Rapp .02 .10
430 Dave Weathers .02 .10
431 Nigel Wilson .02 .10
432 Ken Caminiti .07 .20
433 Andujar Cedeno .02 .10
434 Tom Edens .02 .10
435 Juan Guerrero .02 .10
436 Pete Incaviglia .02 .10
437 Jimmy Jones .02 .10
438 Darryl Kile .07 .20
439 Rob Murphy .02 .10
440 Al Osuna .02 .10
441 Mark Portugal .02 .10
442 Scott Servais .02 .10
443 John Candelaria .02 .10
444 Tim Crews .02 .10
445 Eric Davis .07 .20
446 Tom Goodwin .02 .10
447 Jim Gott .02 .10
448 Kevin Gross .02 .10
449 Dave Hansen .02 .10
450 Jay Howell .02 .10
451 Roger McDowell .02 .10
452 Bob Ojeda .02 .10
453 Henry Rodriguez .02 .10
454 Darryl Strawberry .07 .20
455 Mitch Webster .02 .10
456 Steve Wilson .02 .10
457 Brian Barnes .02 .10
458 Sean Berry .02 .10
459 Jeff Fassero .02 .10
460 Darrin Fletcher .02 .10
461 Marquis Grissom .07 .20
462 Dennis Martinez .07 .20
463 Spike Owen .02 .10
464 Matt Stairs .02 .10
465 Sergio Valdez .02 .10
466 Kevin Bass .02 .10
467 Vince Coleman .02 .10
468 Mark Dewey .02 .10
469 Kevin Elster .02 .10
470 Tony Fernandez .02 .10
471 John Franco .07 .20
472 Dave Gallagher .02 .10
473 Paul Gibson .02 .10
474 Dwight Gooden .07 .20
475 Lee Guetterman .02 .10
476 Jeff Innis .02 .10
477 Dave Magadan .02 .10
478 Charlie O'Brien .02 .10
479 Willie Randolph .07 .20
480 Mackey Sasser .02 .10
481 Ryan Thompson .02 .10
482 Chico Walker .02 .10
483 Kyle Abbott .02 .10
484 Bob Ayrault .02 .10
485 Kim Batiste .02 .10
486 Cliff Brantley .02 .10
487 Jose DeLeon .02 .10
488 Len Dykstra .07 .20
489 Tommy Greene .02 .10
490 Jeff Grotewold .02 .10
491 Dave Hollins .02 .10
492 Danny Jackson .02 .10
493 Stan Javier .02 .10
494 Tom Marsh .02 .10
495 Greg Mathews .02 .10
496 Dale Murphy .10 .30
497 Todd Pratt RC .07 .20
498 Mitch Williams .02 .10
499 Danny Cox .02 .10
500 Doug Drabek .02 .10
501 Carlos Garcia .02 .10
502 Lloyd McClendon .02 .10
503 Denny Neagle .07 .20
504 Gary Redus .02 .10
505 Bob Walk .02 .10
506 John Wehner .02 .10
507 Luis Alicea .02 .10
508 Mark Clark .02 .10
509 Pedro Guerrero .07 .20
510 Rex Hudler .02 .10
511 Brian Jordan .07 .20
512 Omar Olivares .02 .10
513 Jose Oquendo .02 .10
514 Gerald Perry .02 .10
515 Bryn Smith .02 .10
516 Craig Wilson .02 .10
517 Tracy Woodson .02 .10
518 Larry Andersen .02 .10
519 Andy Benes .02 .10
520 Jim Deshaies .02 .10
521 Bruce Hurst .02 .10
522 Randy Myers .02 .10
523 Benito Santiago .07 .20
524 Tim Scott .02 .10
525 Tim Teufel .02 .10
526 Mike Benjamin .02 .10
527 Dave Burba .02 .10
528 Craig Colbert .02 .10
529 Mike Felder .02 .10
530 Bryan Hickerson .02 .10
531 Chris James .02 .10
532 Mark Leonard .02 .10
533 Greg Litton .02 .10
534 Francisco Oliveras .02 .10
535 John Patterson .02 .10
536 Jim Pena .02 .10
537 Dave Righetti .07 .20
538 Robby Thompson .02 .10
539 Jose Uribe .02 .10
540 Matt Williams .07 .20
541 Storm Davis .02 .10
542 Sam Horn .02 .10
543 Tim Hulett .02 .10
544 Craig Lefferts .02 .10
545 Chito Martinez .02 .10
546 Mark McLemore .02 .10
547 Luis Mercedes .02 .10
548 Bob Milacki .02 .10
549 Joe Orsulak .02 .10
550 Billy Ripken .02 .10
551 Cal Ripken .60 1.50
552 Rick Sutcliffe .07 .20
553 Jeff Tackett .02 .10
554 Wade Boggs .10 .30
555 Tom Brunansky .02 .10
556 Jack Clark .07 .20
557 John Dopson .02 .10
558 Mike Gardiner .02 .10
559 Mike Greenwell .02 .10
560 Greg A. Harris .02 .10
561 Billy Hatcher .02 .10
562 Joe Hesketh .02 .10
563 Tony Pena .02 .10
564 Phil Plantier .02 .10
565 Luis Rivera .02 .10
566 Herm Winningham .02 .10
567 Matt Young .02 .10
568 Bert Blyleven .07 .20
569 Mike Butcher .02 .10
570 Chuck Crim .02 .10
571 Chad Curtis .02 .10
572 Tim Fortugno .02 .10
573 Steve Frey .02 .10
574 Gary Gaetti .07 .20
575 Scott Lewis .02 .10
576 Lee Stevens .02 .10
577 Ron Tingley .02 .10
578 Julio Valera .02 .10
579 Shawn Abner .02 .10
580 Joey Cora .02 .10
581 Chris Cron .02 .10
582 Carlton Fisk .10 .30
583 Roberto Hernandez .02 .10
584 Charlie Hough .07 .20
585 Terry Leach .02 .10
586 Donn Pall .02 .10
587 Dan Pasqua .02 .10
588 Steve Sax .02 .10
589 Bobby Thigpen .02 .10
590 Albert Belle .07 .20
591 Felix Fermin .02 .10
592 Glenallen Hill .02 .10
593 Brook Jacoby .02 .10
594 Reggie Jefferson .02 .10
595 Carlos Martinez .02 .10
596 Jose Mesa .02 .10
597 Rod Nichols .02 .10
598 Junior Ortiz .02 .10
599 Eric Plunk .02 .10
600 Ted Power .02 .10
601 Scott Scudder .02 .10
602 Kevin Wickander .02 .10
603 Skeeter Barnes .02 .10
604 Mark Carreon .02 .10
605 Dan Gladden .02 .10
606 Bill Gullickson .02 .10
607 Chad Kreuter .02 .10
608 Mark Leiter .02 .10
609 Mike Munoz .02 .10
610 Rich Rowland .02 .10
611 Frank Tanana .02 .10
612 Walt Terrell .02 .10
613 Alan Trammell .07 .20
614 Lou Whitaker .07 .20
615 Luis Aquino .02 .10
616 Mike Boddicker .02 .10
617 Jim Eisenreich .02 .10
618 Mark Gubicza .02 .10
619 David Howard .02 .10
620 Mike Magnante .02 .10
621 Brent Mayne .02 .10
622 Kevin McReynolds .02 .10
623 Eddie Pierce RC .02 .10
624 Bill Sampen .02 .10
625 Steve Shifflett .02 .10
626 Gary Thurman .02 .10
627 Curt Wilkerson .02 .10
628 Chris Bosio .02 .10
629 Scott Fletcher .02 .10
630 Jim Gantner .02 .10
631 Dave Nilsson .02 .10
632 Jesse Orosco .02 .10
633 Dan Plesac .02 .10
634 Ron Robinson .02 .10
635 Bill Spiers .02 .10
636 Franklin Stubbs .02 .10
637 Willie Banks .02 .10
638 Randy Bush .02 .10
639 Chuck Knoblauch .07 .20
640 Shane Mack .02 .10
641 Mike Pagliarulo .02 .10
642 Jeff Reboulet .02 .10
643 John Smiley .02 .10
644 Mike Trombley .02 .10
645 Gary Wayne .02 .10
646 Lenny Webster .02 .10
647 Tim Burke .02 .10
648 Mike Gallego .02 .10
649 Dion James .02 .10
650 Jeff Johnson .02 .10
651 Scott Kamieniecki .02 .10
652 Kevin Maas .02 .10
653 Rich Monteleone .02 .10
654 Jerry Nielsen .02 .10
655 Scott Sanderson .02 .10
656 Mike Stanley .02 .10
657 Gerald Williams .02 .10
658 Curt Young .02 .10
659 Harold Baines .07 .20
660 Kevin Campbell .02 .10
661 Ron Darling .02 .10
662 Kelly Downs .02 .10
663 Eric Fox .02 .10
664 Dave Henderson .02 .10
665 Rick Honeycutt .02 .10
666 Mike Moore .02 .10
667 Jamie Quirk .02 .10
668 Jeff Russell .02 .10
669 Dave Stewart .07 .20
670 Greg Briley .02 .10
671 Dave Cochrane .02 .10
672 Henry Cotto .02 .10
673 Rich DeLucia .02 .10
674 Brian Fisher .02 .10
675 Mark Grant .02 .10
676 Randy Johnson .20 .50
677 Tim Leary .02 .10
678 Pete O'Brien .02 .10
679 Lance Parrish .07 .20
680 Harold Reynolds .07 .20
681 Shane Turner .02 .10
682 Jack Daugherty .02 .10
683 David Hulse RC .02 .10
684 Terry Mathews .02 .10
685 Al Newman .02 .10
686 Edwin Nunez .02 .10
687 Rafael Palmeiro .10 .30
688 Roger Pavlik .02 .10
689 Geno Petralli .02 .10
690 Nolan Ryan .75 2.00
691 David Cone .07 .20
692 Alfredo Griffin .02 .10
693 Juan Guzman .02 .10
694 Pat Hentgen .02 .10
695 Randy Knorr .02 .10
696 Bob MacDonald .02 .10
697 Jack Morris .07 .20
698 Ed Sprague .02 .10
699 Dave Stieb .02 .10
700 Pat Tabler .02 .10
701 Mike Timlin .02 .10
702 David Wells .07 .20
703 Eddie Zosky .02 .10
704 Gary Sheffield LL .02 .10
705 Darren Daulton LL .02 .10
706 Marquis Grissom LL .02 .10
707 Greg Maddux LL .20 .50
708 Bill Swift LL .02 .10
709 Juan Gonzalez RT .02 .10
710 Mark McGwire RT .25 .60
711 Cecil Fielder RT .02 .10
712 Albert Belle RT .07 .20
713 Joe Carter RT .02 .10
714 F.Thomas .10 .30
C.Fielder
715 L.Walker .07 .20
D.Daulton SS
716 E.Martinez .07 .20
R.Ventura SS
717 R.Clemens .20 .50
D.Eckersley
718 Checklist 361-480 .02 .10
719 Checklist 481-600 .02 .10
720 Checklist 601-720 .02 .10

1993 Fleer All-Stars

COMPLETE SET (24) 15.00 40.00
COMPLETE SERIES 1 (12) 10.00 25.00
COMPLETE SERIES 2 (12) 6.00 15.00
AL: RANDOM INSERTS IN SER.1 PACKS
NL: RANDOM INSERTS IN SER.2 PACKS
AL1 Frank Thomas AL 1.25 3.00
AL2 Roberto Alomar AL .75 2.00
AL3 Edgar Martinez AL .75 2.00
AL4 Pat Listach AL .25 .60
AL5 Cecil Fielder AL .50 1.25
AL6 Juan Gonzalez AL .50 1.25
AL7 Ken Griffey Jr. AL 2.50 6.00
AL8 Joe Carter AL .50 1.25
AL9 Kirby Puckett AL 1.25 3.00
AL10 Brian Harper AL .25 .60
AL11 Dave Fleming AL .25 .60
AL12 Jack McDowell AL .25 .60
NL1 Fred McGriff NL .75 2.00
NL2 Delino DeShields NL .25 .60
NL3 Gary Sheffield NL .50 1.25
NL4 Barry Larkin NL .75 2.00
NL5 Felix Jose NL .25 .60
NL6 Larry Walker NL .50 1.25
NL7 Barry Bonds NL 4.00 10.00
NL8 Andy Van Slyke NL .75 2.00
NL9 Darren Daulton NL .50 1.25
NL10 Greg Maddux NL 2.00 5.00
NL11 Tom Glavine NL .75 2.00
NL12 Lee Smith NL .50 1.25

1993 Fleer Glavine

COMPLETE SET (12) 1.50 4.00
COMMON GLAVINE (1-12) .20 .50
RANDOM INSERTS IN ALL PACKS
COMMON MAIL-IN (13-15) .75 2.00
MAIL-IN CARDS DIST.VIA WRAPPER EXCH.
AU Tom Glavine AU 30.00 60.00

1993 Fleer Golden Moments

COMPLETE SET (6) 5.00 12.00
COMPLETE SERIES 1 (3) 1.50 4.00
COMPLETE SERIES 2 (3) 3.00 8.00
RANDOM INSERTS IN WAX PACKS
A1 George Brett 2.50 6.00
A2 Mickey Morandini .20 .50
A3 Dave Winfield .40 1.00
B1 Dennis Eckersley .40 1.00
B2 Bip Roberts .20 .50
B3 J.Gonzalez 1.00 2.50
F.Thomas

1993 Fleer Major League Prospects

COMPLETE SET (36) 12.50 30.00
COMPLETE SERIES 1 (18) 8.00 20.00
COMPLETE SERIES 2 (18) 4.00 10.00
RANDOM INSERTS IN WAX PACKS
1 Melvin Nieves .20 .50
Series 1
2 Sterling Hitchcock .30 .75
Series 1
3 Tim Costo .20 .50
Series 1
4 Manny Alexander .20 .50
Series 1
5 Alan Embree .20 .50
Series 1
6 Kevin Young .30 .75
Series 1
7 J.T. Snow .50 1.25
Series 1
8 Russ Springer .20 .50
Series 1
9 Billy Ashley .20 .50
Series 1
10 Kevin Rogers .20 .50
Series 1
11 Steve Hosey .20 .50
Series 1
12 Eric Wedge .20 .50
Series 1
13 M.Piazza Ser 1 3.00 8.00
14 Jesse Levis .20 .50
Series 1
15 Rico Brogna .20 .50
Series 1
16 Alex Arias .20 .50
Series 1
17 Rod Brewer .20 .50
Series 1
18 Troy Neel .20 .50
Series 1
1 Scooter Tucker .20 .50
Series 2
2 Kerry Woodson .20 .50
Series 2
3 Greg Colbrunn .20 .50
Series 2
4 P.Martinez Ser.2 2.50 6.00
5 Dave Silvestri .20 .50
Series 2
6 Kent Bottenfield .20 .50
Series 2
7 Rafael Bournigal .20 .50
Series 2
8 J.T. Bruett .20 .50
Series 2
9 Dave Mlicki .20 .50
Series 2
10 Paul Wagner .20 .50
Series 2
11 Mike Williams .20 .50
Series 2
12 Henry Mercedes .20 .50
Series 2
13 Scott Taylor .20 .50
Series 2
14 Dennis Moeller .20 .50
Series 2
15 Javy Lopez .50 1.25
Series 2
16 Steve Cooke .20 .50
Series 2
17 Pete Young .20 .50
Series 2
18 Ken Ryan .20 .50
Series 2

1993 Fleer Pro-Visions

COMPLETE SET (6) 2.00 5.00
COMPLETE SERIES 1 (3) 1.25 3.00
COMPLETE SERIES 2 (3) .75 2.00
RANDOM INSERTS IN WAX PACKS
A1 Roberto Alomar .75 2.00
A2 Dennis Eckersley .50 1.25
A3 Gary Sheffield .50 1.25
B1 Andy Van Slyke .75 2.00
B2 Tom Glavine .75 2.00
B3 Cecil Fielder .50 1.25

1993 Fleer Rookie Sensations

COMPLETE SET (20) 8.00 20.00
COMPLETE SERIES 1 (10) 4.00 10.00
COMPLETE SERIES 2 (10) 4.00 10.00
RANDOM INSERTS IN CELLO PACKS
RSA1 Kenny Lofton .75 2.00
RSA2 Cal Eldred .40 1.00
RSA3 Pat Listach .40 1.00
RSA4 Roberto Hernandez .40 1.00
RSA5 Dave Fleming .40 1.00
RSA6 Eric Karros .75 2.00
RSA7 Reggie Sanders .75 2.00
RSA8 Derrick May .40 1.00
RSA9 Mike Perez .40 1.00
RSA10 Donovan Osborne .40 1.00
RSB1 Moises Alou .75 2.00
RSB2 Pedro Astacio .40 1.00
RSB3 Jim Austin .40 1.00
RSB4 Chad Curtis .40 1.00
RSB5 Gary DiSarcina .40 1.00
RSB6 Scott Livingstone .40 1.00
RSB7 Sam Militello .40 1.00
RSB8 Arthur Rhodes .40 1.00
RSB9 Tim Wakefield 2.00 5.00
RSB10 Bob Zupcic .40 1.00

1993 Fleer Team Leaders

COMPLETE SET (20) 30.00 80.00
COMPLETE SERIES 1 (10) 20.00 50.00
COMPLETE SERIES 2 (10) 8.00 20.00
ONE TL OR GLAVINE PER RACK PACK
AL: RANDOM INSERTS IN SER.1 PACKS
NL: RANDOM INSERTS IN SER.2 PACKS
AL1 Kirby Puckett 2.00 5.00
AL2 Mark McGwire 5.00 12.00
AL3 Pat Listach .40 1.00
AL4 Roger Clemens 4.00 10.00
AL5 Frank Thomas 2.00 5.00
AL6 Carlos Baerga .40 1.00
AL7 Brady Anderson .75 2.00
AL8 Juan Gonzalez .75 2.00
AL9 Roberto Alomar 1.25 3.00
AL10 Ken Griffey Jr. 4.00 10.00
NL1 Will Clark 1.25 3.00
NL2 Terry Pendleton .75 2.00
NL3 Ray Lankford .75 2.00
NL4 Eric Karros .75 2.00
NL5 Gary Sheffield .75 2.00
NL6 Ryne Sandberg 3.00 8.00
NL7 Marquis Grissom .75 2.00
NL8 John Kruk .75 2.00
NL9 Jeff Bagwell 1.25 3.00
NL10 Andy Van Slyke 1.25 3.00

1993 Fleer Final Edition

This 300-card standard-size set was issued exclusively in factory set form (along with ten Diamond Tribute inserts) to update and feature rookies not in the regular 1993 Fleer set. The cards are identical in design to regular issue 1993 Fleer cards except for the F-prefixed numbering. Cards are ordered alphabetically within teams with NL preceding AL. The set closes with checklist cards (298-300). The only key Rookie Card in this set features Jim Edmonds.

CCMP.FACT.SET (310) 4.00 10.00
COMPLETE SET (300) 3.00 8.00
F PREFIX ON REG.CARD NUMBERS
1 Steve Bedrosian .02 .10
2 Jay Howell .02 .10
3 Greg Maddux .30 .75
4 Greg McMichael RC .05 .15
5 Tony Tarasco RC .05 .15
6 Jose Bautista .02 .10
7 Jose Guzman .02 .10
8 Greg Hibbard .02 .10
9 Candy Maldonado .02 .10
10 Randy Myers .02 .10
11 Matt Walbeck RC .15 .40
12 Turk Wendell .02 .10
13 Willie Wilson .02 .10
14 Greg Cadaret .02 .10
15 Roberto Kelly .02 .10
16 Randy Milligan .02 .10
17 Kevin Mitchell .02 .10
18 Jeff Reardon .07 .20
19 John Roper .02 .10
20 John Smiley .02 .10
21 Andy Ashby .02 .10
22 Dante Bichette .07 .20
23 Willie Blair .02 .10
24 Pedro Castellano .02 .10
25 Vinny Castilla .20 .50
26 Jerald Clark .02 .10
27 Alex Cole .02 .10
28 Scott Fredrickson RC .05 .15
29 Jay Gainer RC .05 .15
30 Andres Galarraga .07 .20
31 Joe Girardi .02 .10
32 Ryan Hawblitzel .02 .10
33 Charlie Hayes .02 .10
34 Darren Holmes .02 .10
35 Chris Jones .02 .10
36 David Nied .02 .10
37 Jayhawk Owens RC .05 .15
38 Lance Painter RC .15 .40
39 Jeff Parrett .02 .10
40 Steve Reed .02 .10
41 Armando Reynoso .02 .10
42 Bruce Ruffin .02 .10
43 Danny Sheaffer RC .05 .15
44 Keith Shepherd .02 .10
45 Jim Tatum .02 .10
46 Gary Wayne .02 .10
47 Eric Young .02 .10
48 Luis Aquino .02 .10
49 Alex Arias .02 .10
50 Jack Armstrong .02 .10
51 Bret Barberie .02 .10
52 Geronimo Berroa .02 .10
53 Ryan Bowen .02 .10
54 Greg Briley .02 .10
55 Cris Carpenter .02 .10
56 Chuck Carr .02 .10
57 Jeff Conine .07 .20
58 Jim Corsi .02 .10
59 Orestes Destrade .02 .10
60 Junior Felix .02 .10
61 Chris Hammond .02 .10
62 Bryan Harvey .02 .10
63 Charlie Hough .07 .20
64 Joe Klink .02 .10
65 Richie Lewis RC UER .05 .15
Refers to place of birth and residence as Illinois instead of Indiana
66 Mitch Lyden RC .05 .15
67 Bob Natal .02 .10
68 Scott Pose RC .05 .15
69 Rich Renteria .02 .10
70 Benito Santiago .07 .20
71 Gary Sheffield .07 .20
72 Matt Turner RC .05 .15
73 Walt Weiss .02 .10
74 Darrell Whitmore RC .05 .15
75 Nigel Wilson .02 .10
76 Kevin Bass .02 .10
77 Doug Drabek .02 .10
78 Tom Edens .02 .10
79 Chris James .02 .10
80 Greg Swindell .02 .10
81 Omar Daal RC .05 .15
82 Raul Mondesi .07 .20
83 Jody Reed .02 .10
84 Cory Snyder .02 .10
85 Rick Trlicek .02 .10
86 Tim Wallach .02 .10
87 Todd Worrell .02 .10
88 Tavo Alvarez .02 .10
89 Frank Bolick .02 .10
90 Kent Bottenfield .02 .10
91 Greg Colbrunn .02 .10
92 Cliff Floyd .07 .20
93 Lou Frazier RC .05 .15
94 Mike Gardiner .02 .10
95 Mike Lansing RC .15 .40
96 Bill Risley .02 .10
97 Jeff Shaw .02 .10
98 Kevin Baez .02 .10
99 Tim Bogar RC .05 .15
100 Jeromy Burnitz .07 .20
101 Mike Draper .02 .10
102 Darrin Jackson .02 .10
103 Mike Maddux .02 .10
104 Joe Orsulak .02 .10
105 Doug Saunders RC .05 .15
106 Frank Tanana .02 .10
107 Dave Telgheder RC .05 .15
108 Larry Andersen .02 .10
109 Jim Eisenreich .02 .10
110 Pete Incaviglia .02 .10
111 Danny Jackson .02 .10
112 David West .02 .10
113 Al Martin .02 .10
114 Blas Minor .02 .10
115 Dennis Moeller .02 .10
116 William Pennyfeather .02 .10
117 Rich Robertson RC .05 .15
118 Ben Shelton .02 .10
119 Lonnie Smith .02 .10
120 Freddie Toliver .02 .10
121 Paul Wagner .02 .10
122 Kevin Young .07 .20
123 Rene Arocha RC .15 .40
124 Gregg Jefferies .02 .10
125 Paul Kilgus .02 .10
126 Les Lancaster .02 .10
127 Joe Magrane .02 .10
128 Rob Murphy .02 .10
129 Erik Pappas .02 .10
130 Stan Royer .02 .10
131 Ozzie Smith .30 .75
132 Tom Urbani RC .05 .15
133 Mark Whiten .02 .10
134 Derek Bell .02 .10
135 Doug Brocail .02 .10
136 Phil Clark .02 .10
137 Mark Ettles RC .05 .15
138 Jeff Gardner .02 .10
139 Pat Gomez RC .05 .15
140 Ricky Gutierrez .02 .10
141 Gene Harris .02 .10
142 Kevin Higgins .02 .10
143 Trevor Hoffman .20 .50
144 Phil Plantier .02 .10
145 Kerry Taylor RC .05 .15
146 Guillermo Velasquez .02 .10
147 Wally Whitehurst .02 .10
148 Tim Worrell RC .15 .40
149 Todd Benzinger .02 .10
150 Barry Bonds .60 1.50
151 Greg Brummett RC .05 .15
152 Mark Carreon .02 .10
153 Dave Martinez .02 .10
154 Jeff Reed .02 .10
155 Kevin Rogers .02 .10
156 Harold Baines .07 .20
157 Damon Buford .02 .10
158 Paul Carey RC .05 .15
159 Jeffrey Hammonds .02 .10
160 Jamie Moyer .07 .20
161 Sherman Obando RC .05 .15
162 John O'Donoghue RC .05 .15
163 Brad Pennington .02 .10
164 Jim Poole .02 .10
165 Harold Reynolds .07 .20
166 Fernando Valenzuela .07 .20
167 Jack Voigt RC .05 .15
168 Mark Williamson .02 .10
169 Scott Bankhead .02 .10
170 Greg Blosser .02 .10
171 Jim Byrd RC .05 .15
172 Ivan Calderon .02 .10
173 Andre Dawson .07 .20
174 Scott Fletcher .02 .10
175 Jose Melendez .02 .10
176 Carlos Quintana .02 .10
177 Jeff Russell .02 .10
178 Aaron Sele .02 .10
179 Rod Correia RC .05 .15
180 Chili Davis .07 .20
181 Jim Edmonds RC 1.25 3.00
182 Rene Gonzales .02 .10
183 Hilly Hathaway RC .05 .15
184 Torey Lovullo .02 .10
185 Greg Myers .02 .10
186 Gene Nelson .02 .10
187 Troy Percival .10 .30
188 Scott Sanderson .02 .10
189 Darryl Scott RC .05 .15
190 J.T.Snow RC .25 .60
191 Russ Springer .02 .10
192 Jason Bere .02 .10
193 Rodney Bolton .02 .10
194 Ellis Burks .07 .20
195 Bo Jackson .20 .50
196 Mike LaValliere .02 .10
197 Scott Ruffcorn .02 .10
198 Jeff Schwarz .02 .10
199 Jerry DiPoto .02 .10
200 Alvaro Espinoza .02 .10
201 Wayne Kirby .02 .10
202 Tom Kramer RC .05 .15
203 Jesse Levis .02 .10
204 Manny Ramirez .30 .75
205 Jeff Treadway .02 .10
206 Bill Wertz RC .05 .15
207 Cliff Young .02 .10
208 Matt Young .02 .10
209 Kirk Gibson .07 .20
210 Greg Gohr .02 .10
211 Bill Krueger .02 .10
212 Bob MacDonald .02 .10
213 Mike Moore .02 .10
214 David Wells .07 .20
215 Billy Brewer .02 .10
216 David Cone .07 .20
217 Greg Gagne .02 .10
218 Mark Gardner .02 .10
219 Chris Haney .02 .10
220 Phil Hiatt .02 .10
221 Jose Lind .02 .10
222 Juan Bell .02 .10
223 Tom Brunansky .02 .10
224 Mike Ignasiak .02 .10
225 Joe Kmak .02 .10
226 Tom Lampkin .02 .10
227 Graeme Lloyd RC .15 .40
228 Carlos Maldonado .02 .10
229 Matt Mieske .02 .10
230 Angel Miranda .02 .10
231 Troy O'Leary RC .15 .40
232 Kevin Reimer .02 .10
233 Larry Casian .02 .10
234 Jim Deshaies .02 .10
235 Eddie Guardado RC .25 .60
236 Chip Hale .02 .10
237 Mike Maksudian RC .05 .15
238 David McCarty .02 .10
239 Pat Meares RC .15 .40
240 George Tsamis RC .05 .15
241 Dave Winfield .07 .20
242 Jim Abbott .10 .30
243 Wade Boggs .10 .30
244 Andy Cook RC .05 .15
245 Russ Davis RC .05 .15
246 Mike Humphreys .02 .10
247 Jimmy Key .07 .20
248 Jim Leyritz .02 .10
249 Bobby Munoz .02 .10
250 Paul O'Neill .10 .30
251 Spike Owen .02 .10
252 Dave Silvestri .02 .10
253 Marcos Armas RC .05 .15
254 Brent Gates .02 .10
255 Rich Gossage .07 .20
256 Scott Lydy RC .05 .15
257 Henry Mercedes .02 .10
258 Mike Mohler RC .15 .40
259 Troy Neel .02 .10
260 Edwin Nunez .02 .10
261 Craig Paquette .02 .10
262 Kevin Seitzer .02 .10
263 Rich Amaral .02 .10
264 Mike Blowers .02 .10
265 Chris Bosio .02 .10
266 Norm Charlton .02 .10
267 Jim Converse RC .05 .15
268 John Cummings RC .05 .15
269 Mike Felder .02 .10
270 Mike Hampton .07 .20
271 Bill Haselman .02 .10
272 Dwayne Henry .02 .10
273 Greg Litton .02 .10
274 Mackey Sasser .02 .10
275 Lee Tinsley .02 .10
276 David Wainhouse .02 .10
277 Jeff Bronkey .02 .10
278 Benji Gil .02 .10
279 Tom Henke .02 .10
280 Charlie Leibrandt .02 .10
281 Robb Nen .07 .20
282 Bill Ripken .02 .10
283 Jon Shave RC .05 .15
284 Doug Strange .02 .10
285 Matt Whiteside RC .05 .15
286 Scott Brow RC .05 .15
287 Willie Canate RC .05 .15
288 Tony Castillo .02 .10
289 Domingo Cedeno RC .05 .15
290 Darnell Coles .02 .10
291 Danny Cox .02 .10
292 Mark Eichhorn .02 .10
293 Tony Fernandez .02 .10
294 Al Leiter .07 .20
295 Paul Molitor .07 .20
296 Dave Stewart .07 .20
297 Woody Williams RC .25 .60
298 Checklist F1-F100 .02 .10
299 Checklist F101-F200 .02 .10
300 Checklist F201-F300 .02 .10

1993 Fleer Final Edition Diamond Tribute

COMPLETE SET (10) 1.50 4.00
ONE SET PER FINAL EDITION FACTORY SET
1 Wade Boggs .20 .50
2 George Brett .75 2.00
3 Andre Dawson .10 .30
4 Carlton Fisk .20 .50
5 Paul Molitor .10 .30
6 Nolan Ryan 1.25 3.00
7 Lee Smith .10 .30
8 Ozzie Smith .50 1.25
9 Dave Winfield .10 .30
10 Robin Yount .50 1.25

1993 Fleer Atlantic

This standard-size set of 25 cards features 24 high-profile players plus a checklist and was offered free in packs of five cards with a minimum purchase of eight gallons of Atlantic gasoline. The cards were available from June 14 to July 25, 1993, at participating Atlantic retailers in New York and Pennsylvania. The Atlantic Collector's Edition logo appears in the lower left. The cards are sequenced in alphabetical order. This set features one of the earliest cards picturing Barry Bonds as a member of the San Francisco Giants.

COMPLETE SET (25) 3.00 8.00
1 Roberto Alomar .15 .40
2 Barry Bonds .50 1.25
3 Bobby Bonilla .02 .10
4 Will Clark .20 .50
5 Roger Clemens .50 1.25
6 Darren Daulton .07 .20
7 Dennis Eckersley .20 .50
8 Cecil Fielder .07 .20
9 Tom Glavine .20 .50
10 Juan Gonzalez .15 .40
11 Ken Griffey Jr. .75 2.00
12 John Kruk .07 .20
13 Greg Maddux .50 1.25
14 Don Mattingly .50 1.25
15 Fred McGriff .10 .30
16 Mark McGwire .60 1.50
17 Terry Pendleton .02 .10
18 Kirby Puckett .20 .50
19 Cal Ripken 1.00 2.50
20 Nolan Ryan 1.00 2.50
21 Ryne Sandberg .40 1.00
22 Gary Sheffield .20 .50
23 Frank Thomas .20 .50
24 Andy Van Slyke .02 .10
25 Checklist 1-25 .02 .10

1993 Fleer Fruit of the Loom

The 1993 Fleer Fruit of the Loom set consists of 66 cards measuring the standard size. Six-card packs were inserted in three-packs of Fruit of the Loom boys briefs. The cards have the same design as the regular issue 1993 Fleer. The only exception is the Fruit of the Loom logo which appears on the front. The cards are numbered on the back ordered alphabetically by player's name.

COMPLETE SET (66) 60.00 120.00
1 Roberto Alomar .60 1.50
2 Brady Anderson .30 .75
3 Jeff Bagwell 1.50 4.00
4 Albert Belle .30 .75
5 Craig Biggio .40 1.00
6 Barry Bonds 3.00 8.00
7 George Brett 3.00 8.00
8 Brett Butler .30 .75
9 Jose Canseco 1.00 2.50
10 Joe Carter .30 .75
11 Will Clark .60 1.50
12 Roger Clemens 3.00 8.00
13 Darren Daulton .30 .75
14 Andre Dawson .60 1.50
15 Delino DeShields .20 .50
16 Rob Dibble .30 .75
17 Doug Drabek .20 .50
18 Dennis Eckersley 1.00 2.50
19 Cecil Fielder .20 .50
20 Travis Fryman .30 .75
21 Tom Glavine .60 1.50
22 Juan Gonzalez .60 1.50
23 Dwight Gooden .30 .75
24 Mark Grace .40 1.00
25 Ken Griffey Jr. 4.00 10.00
26 Marquis Grissom .30 .75
27 Juan Guzman .20 .50
28 Tony Gwynn 3.00 8.00
29 Rickey Henderson 2.00 5.00
30 David Justice .60 1.50
31 Eric Karros .40 1.00
32 Chuck Knoblauch .60 1.50
33 John Kruk .30 .75
34 Ray Lankford .30 .75
35 Barry Larkin .60 1.50
36 Pat Listach .20 .50
37 Kenny Lofton .40 1.00
38 Shane Mack .20 .50
39 Greg Maddux 3.00 8.00
40 Dennis Martinez .30 .75
41 Edgar Martinez .40 1.00
42 Ramon Martinez .20 .50
43 Don Mattingly 3.00 8.00
44 Jack McDowell .20 .50
45 Fred McGriff .40 1.00
46 Mark McGwire 4.00 10.00
47 Jeff Montgomery .30 .75
48 Eddie Murray 1.25 3.00
49 Charles Nagy .20 .50
50 Tom Pagnozzi .20 .50
51 Terry Pendleton .20 .50
52 Kirby Puckett 1.50 4.00
53 Jose Rijo .20 .50
54 Cal Ripken 6.00 15.00
55 Nolan Ryan 6.00 15.00
56 Ryne Sandberg 2.00 5.00
57 Gary Sheffield 1.25 3.00
58 Bill Swift .20 .50
59 Danny Tartabull .20 .50
60 Mickey Tettleton .20 .50
61 Frank Thomas 1.00 2.50
62 Andy Van Slyke .20 .50
63 Robin Ventura .40 1.00
64 Larry Walker .60 1.50
65 Robin Yount 1.00 2.50
66 Checklist 1-66 .20 .50

1994 Fleer

The 1994 Fleer baseball set consists of 720 standard-size cards. Cards were distributed in hobby, retail, and jumbo packs. The cards are numbered on the back, grouped alphabetically within teams, and checklisted below alphabetically according to teams for each league with AL preceding NL. The set closes with a Superstar Specials (706-713) subset. There are no key Rookie Cards in this set.

COMPLETE SET (720) 20.00 50.00
1 Brady Anderson .10 .30
2 Harold Baines .10 .30
3 Mike Devereaux .05 .15
4 Todd Frohwirth .05 .15
5 Jeffrey Hammonds .05 .15
6 Chris Hoiles .05 .15
7 Tim Hulett .05 .15
8 Ben McDonald .05 .15
9 Mark McLemore .05 .15
10 Alan Mills .05 .15
11 Jamie Moyer .10 .30
12 Mike Mussina .20 .50
13 Gregg Olson .05 .15
14 Mike Pagliarulo .05 .15
15 Brad Pennington .05 .15
16 Jim Poole .05 .15
17 Harold Reynolds .10 .30
18 Arthur Rhodes .05 .15
19 Cal Ripken Jr. 1.00 2.50
20 David Segui .05 .15
21 Rick Sutcliffe .10 .30
22 Fernando Valenzuela .10 .30
23 Jack Voigt .05 .15
24 Mark Williamson .05 .15
25 Scott Bankhead .05 .15
26 Roger Clemens .60 1.50
27 Scott Cooper .05 .15
28 Danny Darwin .05 .15
29 Andre Dawson .10 .30
30 Rob Deer .05 .15
31 John Dopson .05 .15
32 Scott Fletcher .05 .15
33 Mike Greenwell .05 .15
34 Greg A. Harris .05 .15
35 Billy Hatcher .05 .15
36 Bob Melvin .05 .15
37 Tony Pena .05 .15
38 Paul Quantrill .05 .15
39 Carlos Quintana .05 .15
40 Ernest Riles .05 .15
41 Jeff Russell .05 .15
42 Ken Ryan .05 .15
43 Aaron Sele .05 .15
44 John Valentin .05 .15
45 Mo Vaughn .10 .30
46 Frank Viola .10 .30
47 Bob Zupcic .05 .15
48 Mike Butcher .05 .15
49 Rod Correia .05 .15
50 Chad Curtis .05 .15
51 Chili Davis .10 .30
52 Gary DiSarcina .05 .15
53 Damion Easley .05 .15
54 Jim Edmonds .30 .75
55 Chuck Finley .10 .30
56 Steve Frey .05 .15
57 Rene Gonzales .05 .15
58 Joe Grahe .05 .15
59 Hilly Hathaway .05 .15
60 Stan Javier .05 .15
61 Mark Langston .05 .15
62 Phil Leftwich RC .05 .15
63 Torey Lovullo .05 .15
64 Joe Magrane .05 .15
65 Greg Myers .05 .15
66 Ken Patterson .05 .15
67 Eduardo Perez .05 .15
68 Luis Polonia .05 .15
69 Tim Salmon .20 .50
70 J.T.Snow .10 .30
71 Ron Tingley .05 .15
72 Julio Valera .05 .15
73 Wilson Alvarez .05 .15
74 Tim Belcher .05 .15
75 George Bell .05 .15
76 Jason Bere .05 .15
77 Rod Bolton .05 .15
78 Ellis Burks .10 .30
79 Joey Cora .05 .15
80 Alex Fernandez .05 .15
81 Craig Grebeck .05 .15
82 Ozzie Guillen .10 .30
83 Roberto Hernandez .05 .15
84 Bo Jackson .30 .75
85 Lance Johnson .05 .15
86 Ron Karkovice .05 .15
87 Mike LaValliere .05 .15
88 Kirk McCaskill .05 .15
89 Jack McDowell .05 .15
90 Warren Newson .05 .15
91 Dan Pasqua .05 .15
92 Scott Radinsky .05 .15
93 Tim Raines .10 .30
94 Steve Sax .05 .15
95 Jeff Schwarz .05 .15
96 Frank Thomas .30 .75
97 Robin Ventura .10 .30
98 Sandy Alomar Jr. .05 .15
99 Carlos Baerga .05 .15
100 Albert Belle .10 .30
101 Mark Clark .05 .15
102 Jerry DiPoto .05 .15
103 Alvaro Espinoza .05 .15
104 Felix Fermin .05 .15
105 Jeremy Hernandez .05 .15
106 Reggie Jefferson .05 .15
107 Wayne Kirby .05 .15
108 Tom Kramer .05 .15
109 Mark Lewis .05 .15
110 Derek Lilliquist .05 .15
111 Kenny Lofton .10 .30
112 Candy Maldonado .05 .15
113 Jose Mesa .05 .15
114 Jeff Mutis .05 .15
115 Charles Nagy .05 .15
116 Bob Ojeda .05 .15
117 Junior Ortiz .05 .15
118 Eric Plunk .05 .15
119 Manny Ramirez .30 .75
120 Paul Sorrento .05 .15
121 Jim Thome .20 .50
122 Jeff Treadway .05 .15
123 Bill Wertz .05 .15
124 Skeeter Barnes .05 .15
125 Milt Cuyler .05 .15
126 Eric Davis .10 .30
127 John Doherty .05 .15
128 Cecil Fielder .10 .30
129 Travis Fryman .10 .30
130 Kirk Gibson .10 .30
131 Dan Gladden .05 .15
132 Greg Gohr .05 .15
133 Chris Gomez .05 .15
134 Bill Gullickson .05 .15
135 Mike Henneman .05 .15
136 Kurt Knudsen .05 .15
137 Chad Kreuter .05 .15
138 Bill Krueger .05 .15
139 Scott Livingstone .05 .15
140 Bob MacDonald .05 .15
141 Mike Moore .05 .15
142 Tony Phillips .05 .15
143 Mickey Tettleton .05 .15
144 Alan Trammell .10 .30
145 David Wells .10 .30
146 Lou Whitaker .10 .30
147 Kevin Appier .10 .30
148 Stan Belinda .05 .15
149 George Brett .75 2.00
150 Billy Brewer .05 .15
151 Hubie Brooks .05 .15
152 David Cone .10 .30
153 Gary Gaetti .10 .30
154 Greg Gagne .05 .15
155 Tom Gordon .05 .15
156 Mark Gubicza .05 .15
157 Chris Gwynn .05 .15
158 John Habyan .05 .15
159 Chris Haney .05 .15
160 Phil Hiatt .05 .15
161 Felix Jose .05 .15
162 Wally Joyner .10 .30
163 Jose Lind .05 .15
164 Mike Macfarlane .05 .15
165 Mike Magnante .05 .15
166 Brent Mayne .05 .15
167 Brian McRae .05 .15
168 Kevin McReynolds .05 .15
169 Keith Miller .05 .15
170 Jeff Montgomery .05 .15
171 Hipolito Pichardo .05 .15
172 Rico Rossy .05 .15
173 Juan Bell .05 .15
174 Ricky Bones .05 .15
175 Cal Eldred .05 .15
176 Mike Fetters .05 .15
177 Darryl Hamilton .05 .15
178 Doug Henry .05 .15
179 Mike Ignasiak .05 .15
180 John Jaha .05 .15
181 Pat Listach .05 .15
182 Graeme Lloyd .05 .15
183 Matt Mieske .05 .15
184 Angel Miranda .05 .15
185 Jaime Navarro .05 .15
186 Dave Nilsson .05 .15
187 Troy O'Leary .05 .15
188 Jesse Orosco .05 .15
189 Kevin Reimer .05 .15
190 Kevin Seitzer .05 .15
191 Bill Spiers .05 .15
192 B.J. Surhoff .10 .30
193 Dickie Thon .05 .15
194 Jose Valentin .05 .15
195 Greg Vaughn .05 .15
196 Bill Wegman .05 .15
197 Robin Yount .50 1.25
198 Rick Aguilera .05 .15
199 Willie Banks .05 .15
200 Bernardo Brito .05 .15
201 Larry Casian .05 .15
202 Scott Erickson .05 .15
203 Eddie Guardado .10 .30
204 Mark Guthrie .05 .15
205 Chip Hale .05 .15
206 Brian Harper .05 .15
207 Mike Hartley .05 .15
208 Kent Hrbek .10 .30
209 Terry Jorgensen .05 .15
210 Chuck Knoblauch .10 .30
211 Gene Larkin .05 .15
212 Shane Mack .05 .15
213 David McCarty .05 .15
214 Pat Meares .05 .15
215 Pedro Munoz .05 .15
216 Derek Parks .05 .15
217 Kirby Puckett .30 .75
218 Jeff Reboulet .05 .15
219 Kevin Tapani .05 .15
220 Mike Trombley .05 .15
221 George Tsamis .05 .15
222 Carl Willis .05 .15
223 Dave Winfield .10 .30
224 Jim Abbott .20 .50
225 Paul Assenmacher .05 .15
226 Wade Boggs .20 .50
227 Russ Davis .05 .15
228 Steve Farr .05 .15
229 Mike Gallego .05 .15
230 Paul Gibson .05 .15
231 Steve Howe .05 .15
232 Dion James .05 .15
233 Domingo Jean .05 .15
234 Scott Kamieniecki .05 .15
235 Pat Kelly .05 .15
236 Jimmy Key .10 .30
237 Jim Leyritz .05 .15
238 Kevin Maas .05 .15
239 Don Mattingly .75 2.00
240 Rich Monteleone .05 .15
241 Bobby Munoz .05 .15
242 Matt Nokes .05 .15
243 Paul O'Neill .20 .50
244 Spike Owen .05 .15
245 Melido Perez .05 .15
246 Lee Smith .10 .30
247 Mike Stanley .05 .15
248 Danny Tartabull .05 .15
249 Randy Velarde .05 .15
250 Bob Wickman .05 .15
251 Bernie Williams .20 .50
252 Mike Aldrete .05 .15
253 Marcos Armas .05 .15
254 Lance Blankenship .05 .15
255 Mike Bordick .05 .15
256 Scott Brosius .10 .30
257 Jerry Browne .05 .15
258 Ron Darling .05 .15
259 Kelly Downs .05 .15
260 Dennis Eckersley .10 .30
261 Brent Gates .05 .15
262 Rich Gossage .10 .30
263 Scott Hemond .05 .15
264 Dave Henderson .05 .15
265 Rick Honeycutt .05 .15
266 Vince Horsman .05 .15
267 Scott Lydy .05 .15
268 Mark McGwire .75 2.00
269 Mike Mohler .05 .15
270 Troy Neel .05 .15
271 Edwin Nunez .05 .15
272 Craig Paquette .05 .15
273 Ruben Sierra .10 .30
274 Terry Steinbach .05 .15
275 Todd Van Poppel .05 .15
276 Bob Welch .05 .15
277 Bobby Witt .05 .15
278 Rich Amaral .05 .15
279 Mike Blowers .05 .15
280 Bret Boone UER .10 .30
Name spelled Brett on front
281 Chris Bosio .05 .15
282 Jay Buhner .10 .30
283 Norm Charlton .05 .15
284 Mike Felder .05 .15
285 Dave Fleming .05 .15
286 Ken Griffey Jr. .60 1.50
287 Erik Hanson .05 .15
288 Bill Haselman .05 .15
289 Brad Holman RC .05 .15
290 Randy Johnson .30 .75
291 Tim Leary .05 .15
292 Greg Litton .05 .15
293 Dave Magadan .05 .15
294 Edgar Martinez .20 .50
295 Tino Martinez .20 .50
296 Jeff Nelson .05 .15
297 Erik Plantenberg RC .05 .15
298 Mackey Sasser .05 .15
299 Brian Turang RC .05 .15
300 Dave Valle .05 .15
301 Omar Vizquel .20 .50
302 Brian Bohanon .05 .15
303 Kevin Brown .10 .30
304 Jose Canseco UER .20 .50
Back mentions 1991 as his
40
40 MVP season; should be '88
305 Mario Diaz .05 .15
306 Julio Franco .10 .30
307 Juan Gonzalez .10 .30
308 Tom Henke .05 .15
309 David Hulse .05 .15
310 Manuel Lee .05 .15
311 Craig Lefferts .05 .15
312 Charlie Leibrandt .05 .15
313 Rafael Palmeiro .20 .50
314 Dean Palmer .10 .30
315 Roger Pavlik .05 .15
316 Dan Peltier .05 .15
317 Gene Petralli .05 .15
318 Gary Redus .05 .15
319 Ivan Rodriguez .20 .50
320 Kenny Rogers .10 .30
321 Nolan Ryan 1.25 3.00
322 Doug Strange .05 .15
323 Matt Whiteside .05 .15
324 Roberto Alomar .20 .50
325 Pat Borders .05 .15
326 Joe Carter .10 .30
327 Tony Castillo .05 .15
328 Darnell Coles .05 .15
329 Danny Cox .05 .15
330 Mark Eichhorn .05 .15
331 Tony Fernandez .05 .15
332 Alfredo Griffin .05 .15
333 Juan Guzman .05 .15
334 Rickey Henderson .30 .75
335 Pat Hentgen .05 .15
336 Randy Knorr .05 .15
337 Al Leiter .10 .30
338 Paul Molitor .10 .30
339 Jack Morris .10 .30
340 John Olerud .10 .30
341 Dick Schofield .05 .15
342 Ed Sprague .05 .15
343 Dave Stewart .10 .30
344 Todd Stottlemyre .05 .15
345 Mike Timlin .05 .15
346 Duane Ward .05 .15
347 Turner Ward .05 .15
348 Devon White .10 .30
349 Woody Williams .10 .30
350 Steve Avery .05 .15
351 Steve Bedrosian .05 .15
352 Rafael Belliard .05 .15
353 Damon Berryhill .05 .15
354 Jeff Blauser .05 .15
355 Sid Bream .05 .15
356 Francisco Cabrera .05 .15
357 Marvin Freeman .05 .15
358 Ron Gant .10 .30
359 Tom Glavine .20 .50
360 Jay Howell .05 .15
361 David Justice .10 .30
362 Ryan Klesko .10 .30
363 Mark Lemke .05 .15
364 Javier Lopez .10 .30
365 Greg Maddux .50 1.25
366 Fred McGriff .20 .50
367 Greg McMichael .05 .15
368 Kent Mercker .05 .15
369 Otis Nixon .05 .15
370 Greg Olson .05 .15
371 Bill Pecota .05 .15
372 Terry Pendleton .10 .30
373 Deion Sanders .20 .50
374 Pete Smith .05 .15
375 John Smoltz .20 .50
376 Mike Stanton .05 .15
377 Tony Tarasco .05 .15
378 Mark Wohlers .05 .15
379 Jose Bautista .05 .15
380 Shawn Boskie .05 .15
381 Steve Buechele .05 .15
382 Frank Castillo .05 .15
383 Mark Grace .20 .50
384 Jose Guzman .05 .15
385 Mike Harkey .05 .15
386 Greg Hibbard .05 .15
387 Glenallen Hill .05 .15
388 Steve Lake .05 .15
389 Derrick May .05 .15
390 Chuck McElroy .05 .15
391 Mike Morgan .05 .15
392 Randy Myers .05 .15
393 Dan Plesac .05 .15
394 Kevin Roberson .05 .15
395 Rey Sanchez .05 .15
396 Ryne Sandberg .50 1.25
397 Bob Scanlan .05 .15
398 Dwight Smith .05 .15
399 Sammy Sosa .30 .75
400 Jose Vizcaino .05 .15
401 Rick Wilkins .05 .15
402 Willie Wilson .05 .15
403 Eric Yelding .05 .15
404 Bobby Ayala .05 .15
405 Jeff Branson .05 .15
406 Tom Browning .05 .15
407 Jacob Brumfield .05 .15
408 Tim Costo .05 .15
409 Rob Dibble .10 .30
410 Willie Greene .05 .15
411 Thomas Howard .05 .15
412 Roberto Kelly .05 .15
413 Bill Landrum .05 .15
414 Barry Larkin .20 .50
415 Larry Luebbers RC .05 .15
416 Kevin Mitchell .05 .15
417 Hal Morris .05 .15
418 Joe Oliver .05 .15
419 Tim Pugh .05 .15
420 Jeff Reardon .10 .30
421 Jose Rijo .05 .15
422 Bip Roberts .05 .15
423 John Roper .05 .15
424 Johnny Ruffin .05 .15
425 Chris Sabo .05 .15
426 Juan Samuel .05 .15
427 Reggie Sanders .10 .30
428 Scott Service .05 .15
429 John Smiley .05 .15
430 Jerry Spradlin RC .05 .15
431 Kevin Wickander .05 .15
432 Freddie Benavides .05 .15
433 Dante Bichette .10 .30
434 Willie Blair .05 .15
435 Daryl Boston .05 .15
436 Kent Bottenfield .05 .15
437 Vinny Castilla .10 .30
438 Jerald Clark .05 .15
439 Alex Cole .05 .15
440 Andres Galarraga .10 .30
441 Joe Girardi .05 .15
442 Greg W. Harris .05 .15
443 Charlie Hayes .05 .15
444 Darren Holmes .05 .15
445 Chris Jones .05 .15
446 Roberto Mejia .05 .15
447 David Nied .05 .15
448 Jayhawk Owens .05 .15
449 Jeff Parrett .05 .15
450 Steve Reed .05 .15
451 Armando Reynoso .05 .15
452 Bruce Ruffin .05 .15
453 Mo Sanford .05 .15
454 Danny Sheaffer .05 .15
455 Jim Tatum .05 .15
456 Gary Wayne .05 .15
457 Eric Young .05 .15
458 Luis Aquino .05 .15
459 Alex Arias .05 .15
460 Jack Armstrong .05 .15
461 Bret Barberie .05 .15
462 Ryan Bowen .05 .15
463 Chuck Carr .05 .15
464 Jeff Conine .10 .30
465 Henry Cotto .05 .15
466 Orestes Destrade .05 .15
467 Chris Hammond .05 .15
468 Bryan Harvey .05 .15
469 Charlie Hough .10 .30
470 Joe Klink .05 .15
471 Richie Lewis .05 .15
472 Bob Natal .05 .15
473 Pat Rapp .05 .15
474 Rich Renteria .05 .15
475 Rich Rodriguez .05 .15
476 Benito Santiago .10 .30
477 Gary Sheffield .10 .30
478 Matt Turner .05 .15
479 David Weathers .05 .15
480 Walt Weiss .05 .15
481 Darrell Whitmore .05 .15
482 Eric Anthony .05 .15
483 Jeff Bagwell .20 .50
484 Kevin Bass .05 .15
485 Craig Biggio .20 .50
486 Ken Caminiti .10 .30
487 Andujar Cedeno .05 .15
488 Chris Donnels .05 .15
489 Doug Drabek .05 .15
490 Steve Finley .10 .30
491 Luis Gonzalez .10 .30
492 Pete Harnisch .05 .15
493 Xavier Hernandez .05 .15
494 Doug Jones .05 .15
495 Todd Jones .05 .15
496 Darryl Kile .10 .30
497 Al Osuna .05 .15
498 Mark Portugal .05 .15
499 Scott Servais .05 .15
500 Greg Swindell .05 .15
501 Eddie Taubensee .05 .15
502 Jose Uribe .05 .15
503 Brian Williams .05 .15
504 Billy Ashley .05 .15
505 Pedro Astacio .05 .15
506 Brett Butler .10 .30
507 Tom Candiotti .05 .15
508 Omar Daal .05 .15
509 Jim Gott .05 .15
510 Kevin Gross .05 .15
511 Dave Hansen .05 .15
512 Carlos Hernandez .05 .15
513 Orel Hershiser .10 .30
514 Eric Karros .10 .30
515 Pedro Martinez .30 .75
516 Ramon Martinez .05 .15
517 Roger McDowell .05 .15
518 Raul Mondesi .10 .30
519 Jose Offerman .05 .15
520 Mike Piazza .60 1.50
521 Jody Reed .05 .15
522 Henry Rodriguez .05 .15
523 Mike Sharperson .05 .15
524 Cory Snyder .05 .15
525 Darryl Strawberry .10 .30
526 Rick Trlicek .05 .15
527 Tim Wallach .05 .15
528 Mitch Webster .05 .15
529 Steve Wilson .05 .15
530 Todd Worrell .05 .15
531 Moises Alou .10 .30
532 Brian Barnes .05 .15
533 Sean Berry .05 .15
534 Greg Colbrunn .05 .15
535 Delino DeShields .05 .15
536 Jeff Fassero .05 .15
537 Darrin Fletcher .05 .15
538 Cliff Floyd .10 .30
539 Lou Frazier .05 .15
540 Marquis Grissom .10 .30
541 Butch Henry .05 .15
542 Ken Hill .05 .15
543 Mike Lansing .05 .15
544 Brian Looney RC .05 .15
545 Dennis Martinez .10 .30
546 Chris Nabholz .05 .15
547 Randy Ready .05 .15
548 Mel Rojas .05 .15
549 Kirk Rueter .05 .15
550 Tim Scott .05 .15
551 Jeff Shaw .05 .15
552 Tim Spehr .05 .15
553 John Vander Wal .05 .15
554 Larry Walker .10 .30
555 John Wetteland .10 .30
556 Rondell White .10 .30
557 Tim Bogar .05 .15
558 Bobby Bonilla .10 .30
559 Jeromy Burnitz .10 .30
560 Sid Fernandez .05 .15
561 John Franco .10 .30
562 Dave Gallagher .05 .15
563 Dwight Gooden .10 .30
564 Eric Hillman .05 .15
565 Todd Hundley .05 .15
566 Jeff Innis .05 .15
567 Darrin Jackson .05 .15
568 Howard Johnson .05 .15
569 Bobby Jones .05 .15
570 Jeff Kent .20 .50
571 Mike Maddux .05 .15
572 Jeff McKnight .05 .15
573 Eddie Murray .30 .75
574 Charlie O'Brien .05 .15
575 Joe Orsulak .05 .15
576 Bret Saberhagen .10 .30
577 Pete Schourek .05 .15
578 Dave Telgheder .05 .15
579 Ryan Thompson .05 .15
580 Anthony Young .05 .15
581 Ruben Amaro .05 .15
582 Larry Andersen .05 .15
583 Kim Batiste .05 .15
584 Wes Chamberlain .05 .15
585 Darren Daulton .10 .30
586 Mariano Duncan .05 .15
587 Lenny Dykstra .10 .30
588 Jim Eisenreich .05 .15
589 Tommy Greene .05 .15
590 Dave Hollins .05 .15
591 Pete Incaviglia .05 .15
592 Danny Jackson .05 .15
593 Ricky Jordan .05 .15
594 John Kruk .10 .30
595 Roger Mason .05 .15
596 Mickey Morandini .05 .15
597 Terry Mulholland .05 .15
598 Todd Pratt .05 .15
599 Ben Rivera .05 .15
600 Curt Schilling .10 .30
601 Kevin Stocker .05 .15
602 Milt Thompson .05 .15
603 David West .05 .15
604 Mitch Williams .05 .15
605 Jay Bell .10 .30
606 Dave Clark .05 .15
607 Steve Cooke .05 .15
608 Tom Foley .05 .15
609 Carlos Garcia .05 .15
610 Joel Johnston .05 .15
611 Jeff King .05 .15
612 Al Martin .05 .15
613 Lloyd McClendon .05 .15
614 Orlando Merced .05 .15
615 Blas Minor .05 .15
616 Denny Neagle .10 .30
617 Mark Petkovsek RC .05 .15
618 Tom Prince .05 .15
619 Don Slaught .05 .15
620 Zane Smith .05 .15
621 Randy Tomlin .05 .15
622 Andy Van Slyke .20 .50
623 Paul Wagner .05 .15
624 Tim Wakefield .20 .50
625 Bob Walk .05 .15
626 Kevin Young .05 .15
627 Luis Alicea .05 .15
628 Rene Arocha .05 .15
629 Rod Brewer .05 .15
630 Rheal Cormier .05 .15
631 Bernard Gilkey .05 .15
632 Lee Guetterman .05 .15
633 Gregg Jefferies .05 .15
634 Brian Jordan .10 .30
635 Les Lancaster .05 .15
636 Ray Lankford .10 .30
637 Rob Murphy .05 .15
638 Omar Olivares .05 .15
639 Jose Oquendo .05 .15
640 Donovan Osborne .05 .15
641 Tom Pagnozzi .05 .15
642 Erik Pappas .05 .15
643 Geronimo Pena .05 .15
644 Mike Perez .05 .15
645 Gerald Perry .05 .15
646 Ozzie Smith .50 1.25
647 Bob Tewksbury .05 .15
648 Allen Watson .05 .15
649 Mark Whiten .05 .15
650 Tracy Woodson .05 .15
651 Todd Zeile .05 .15
652 Andy Ashby .05 .15
653 Brad Ausmus .20 .50
654 Billy Bean .05 .15
655 Derek Bell .05 .15
656 Andy Benes .05 .15
657 Doug Brocail .05 .15
658 Jarvis Brown .05 .15
659 Archi Cianfrocco .05 .15
660 Phil Clark .05 .15
661 Mark Davis .05 .15
662 Jeff Gardner .05 .15
663 Pat Gomez .05 .15
664 Ricky Gutierrez .05 .15
665 Tony Gwynn .40 1.00
666 Gene Harris .05 .15
667 Kevin Higgins .05 .15
668 Trevor Hoffman .20 .50
669 Pedro Martinez RC .05 .15
670 Tim Mauser .05 .15
671 Melvin Nieves .05 .15
672 Phil Plantier .05 .15
673 Frank Seminara .05 .15
674 Craig Shipley .05 .15
675 Kerry Taylor .05 .15
676 Tim Teufel .05 .15
677 Guillermo Velasquez .05 .15
678 Wally Whitehurst .05 .15
679 Tim Worrell .05 .15
680 Rod Beck .05 .15
681 Mike Benjamin .05 .15
682 Todd Benzinger .05 .15
683 Bud Black .05 .15
684 Barry Bonds .75 2.00
685 Jeff Brantley .05 .15
686 Dave Burba .05 .15
687 John Burkett .05 .15
688 Mark Carreon .05 .15
689 Will Clark .20 .50
690 Royce Clayton .05 .15
691 Bryan Hickerson .05 .15
692 Mike Jackson .05 .15
693 Darren Lewis .05 .15
694 Kirt Manwaring .05 .15
695 Dave Martinez .05 .15
696 Willie McGee .10 .30
697 John Patterson .05 .15
698 Jeff Reed .05 .15
699 Kevin Rogers .05 .15
700 Scott Sanderson .05 .15
701 Steve Scarsone .05 .15
702 Billy Swift .05 .15
703 Robby Thompson .05 .15
704 Matt Williams .10 .30
705 Trevor Wilson .05 .15
706 Fred McGriff .10 .30
Ron Gant
David Justice
707 John Olerud .10 .30
Paul Molitor
708 Mike Mussina .10 .30
Jack McDowell
709 Lou Whitaker .10 .30
Alan Trammell
710 Rafael Palmeiro .10 .30
Juan Gonzalez
711 Brett Butler .20 .50
Tony Gwynn
712 Kirby Puckett .20 .50
Chuck Knoblauch
713 Mike Piazza .30 .75
Eric Karros
714 Checklist 1 .05 .15
715 Checklist 2 .05 .15
716 Checklist 3 .05 .15
717 Checklist 4 .05 .15
718 Checklist 5 .05 .15
719 Checklist 6 .05 .15
720 Checklist 7 .05 .15
P69 Tim Salmon Promo .40 1.00

1994 Fleer All-Rookies

COMPLETE SET (9) 3.00 8.00
ONE SET PER EXCHANGE CARD VIA MAIL
M1 Kurt Abbott .20 .50
M2 Rich Becker .20 .50
M3 Carlos Delgado .60 1.50
M4 Jorge Fabregas .20 .50
M5 Bob Hamelin .20 .50
M6 John Hudek .20 .50
M7 Tim Hyers .20 .50
M8 Luis Lopez .20 .50
M9 James Mouton .20 .50
NNO Expired All-Rookie Exch. .20 .50

1994 Fleer All-Stars

COMPLETE SET (50) 10.00 25.00
STATED ODDS 1:2
1 Roberto Alomar .25 .60
2 Carlos Baerga .07 .20
3 Albert Belle .15 .40
4 Wade Boggs .25 .60
5 Joe Carter .15 .40
6 Scott Cooper .07 .20
7 Cecil Fielder .15 .40
8 Travis Fryman .15 .40
9 Juan Gonzalez .15 .40
10 Ken Griffey Jr. .75 2.00
11 Pat Hentgen .07 .20
12 Randy Johnson .40 1.00
13 Jimmy Key .15 .40
14 Mark Langston .07 .20
15 Jack McDowell .07 .20
16 Paul Molitor .15 .40
17 Jeff Montgomery .07 .20
18 Mike Mussina .25 .60
19 John Olerud .15 .40
20 Kirby Puckett .40 1.00
21 Cal Ripken 1.25 3.00
22 Ivan Rodriguez .25 .60
23 Frank Thomas .40 1.00
24 Greg Vaughn .07 .20
25 Duane Ward .07 .20
26 Steve Avery .10 .20
27 Rod Beck .07 .20
28 Jay Bell .15 .40
29 Andy Benes .07 .20
30 Jeff Blauser .07 .20
31 Barry Bonds 1.00 2.50
32 Bobby Bonilla .15 .40
33 John Burkett .07 .20
34 Darren Daulton .15 .40
35 Andres Galarraga .15 .40
36 Tom Glavine .25 .60

37 Mark Grace .25 .60
38 Marquis Grissom .15 .40
39 Tony Gwynn .50 1.25
40 Bryan Harvey .07 .20
41 Dave Hollins .07 .20
42 David Justice .15 .40
43 Darryl Kile .15 .40
44 John Kruk .15 .40
45 Barry Larkin .25 .60
46 Terry Mulholland .07 .20
47 Mike Piazza .75 2.00
48 Ryne Sandberg .60 1.50
49 Gary Sheffield .15 .40
50 John Smoltz .25 .60

1994 Fleer Award Winners

COMPLETE SET (6) 3.00 8.00
STATED ODDS 1:37
1 Frank Thomas .50 1.25
2 Barry Bonds 1.25 3.00
3 Jack McDowell .08 .25
4 Greg Maddux .75 2.00
5 Tim Salmon .30 .75
6 Mike Piazza 1.00 2.50

1994 Fleer Golden Moments

COMPLETE SET (10) 12.50 30.00
ONE PER BLUE RETAIL JUMBO PACK
*JUMBOS: .4X TO 1X BASIC GM
ONE JUMBO SET PER HOBBY CASE
JUMBOS ALSO REPACKAGED FOR RETAIL
1 Mark Whiten .25 .60
2 Carlos Baerga .25 .60
3 Dave Winfield .50 1.25
4 Ken Griffey Jr. 2.50 6.00
5 Bo Jackson 1.25 3.00
6 George Brett 3.00 8.00
7 Nolan Ryan 5.00 12.00
8 Fred McGriff .75 2.00
9 Frank Thomas 1.25 3.00
10 Bosio .25 .60
Abbott
Kile

1994 Fleer League Leaders

COMPLETE SET (12) 2.00 5.00
STATED ODDS 1:17
1 John Olerud .15 .40
2 Albert Belle .15 .40
3 Rafael Palmeiro .20 .50
4 Kenny Lofton .15 .40
5 Jack McDowell .08 .25
6 Kevin Appier .15 .40
7 Andres Galarraga .15 .40
8 Barry Bonds .60 1.50
9 Len Dykstra .15 .40
10 Chuck Carr .08 .25
11 Tom Glavine UER NNO .20 .50
12 Greg Maddux 1.00 2.50

1994 Fleer Lumber Company

COMPLETE SET (10) 4.00 10.00
STATED ODDS 1:5 JUMBO
1 Albert Belle .20 .50
2 Barry Bonds 1.25 3.00
3 Ron Gant .20 .50
4 Juan Gonzalez .20 .50
5 Ken Griffey Jr. 1.00 2.50
6 David Justice .20 .50
7 Fred McGriff .30 .75
8 Rafael Palmeiro .30 .75
9 Frank Thomas .50 1.25
10 Matt Williams .20 .50

1994 Fleer Major League Prospects

COMPLETE SET (35) 6.00 15.00
STATED ODDS 1:6
1 Kurt Abbott .08 .25
2 Brian Anderson .30 .75
3 Rich Aude .08 .25
4 Cory Bailey .08 .25
5 Danny Bautista .08 .25
6 Marty Cordova .08 .25
7 Tripp Cromer .08 .25
8 Midre Cummings .08 .25
9 Carlos Delgado .50 1.25
10 Steve Dreyer .08 .25
11 Steve Dunn .08 .25
12 Jeff Granger .08 .25
13 Tyrone Hill .08 .25
14 Denny Hocking .08 .25
15 John Hope .08 .25
16 Butch Huskey .08 .25
17 Miguel Jimenez .08 .25
18 Chipper Jones .75 2.00
19 Steve Karsay .08 .25
20 Mike Kelly .08 .25
21 Mike Lieberthal .30 .75
22 Albie Lopez .08 .25
23 Jeff McNeely .08 .25
24 Danny Miceli .08 .25
25 Nate Minchey .08 .25
26 Marc Newfield .08 .25
27 Darren Oliver .30 .75
28 Luis Ortiz .08 .25
29 Curtis Pride .30 .75
30 Roger Salkeld .08 .25
31 Scott Sanders .08 .25
32 Dave Staton .08 .25
33 Salomon Torres .08 .25
34 Steve Trachsel .08 .25
35 Chris Turner .08 .25

1994 Fleer Pro-Visions

COMPLETE SET (9) 1.50 4.00
STATED ODDS 1:12
1 Darren Daulton .15 .40
2 John Olerud .15 .40
3 Matt Williams .15 .40
4 Carlos Baerga .07 .20
5 Ozzie Smith .60 1.50
6 Juan Gonzalez .15 .40
7 Jack McDowell .07 .20
8 Mike Piazza .75 2.00
9 Tony Gwynn .50 1.25

1994 Fleer Rookie Sensations

COMPLETE SET (20) 8.00 20.00
STATED ODDS 1:4 JUMBO
1 Rene Arocha .40 1.00
2 Jason Bere .40 1.00
3 Jeromy Burnitz .75 2.00
4 Chuck Carr .40 1.00
5 Jeff Conine .75 2.00
6 Steve Cooke .40 1.00
7 Cliff Floyd .75 2.00
8 Jeffrey Hammonds .40 1.00
9 Wayne Kirby .40 1.00
10 Mike Lansing .40 1.00
11 Al Martin .40 1.00
12 Greg McMichael .40 1.00
13 Troy Neel .40 1.00
14 Mike Piazza 3.00 8.00
15 Armando Reynoso .40 1.00
16 Kirk Rueter .40 1.00
17 Tim Salmon 1.25 3.00
18 Aaron Sele .40 1.00
19 J.T.Snow .75 2.00
20 Kevin Stocker .40 1.00

1994 Fleer Salmon

COMPLETE SET (12) 6.00 15.00
COMMON CARD (1-12) .40 1.00
1-12 STATED ODDS 1:8
COMMON MAIL-IN (13-15) .40 1.00
13-15 DISTRIBUTED VIA WRAPPER EXCH.
AU Tim Salmon AU/2000 6.00 15.00

1994 Fleer Smoke 'n Heat

COMPLETE SET (12) 25.00 60.00
STATED ODDS 1:36
1 Roger Clemens 4.00 10.00
2 David Cone .75 2.00
3 Juan Guzman .40 1.00
4 Pete Harnisch .40 1.00
5 Randy Johnson 2.00 5.00
6 Mark Langston .40 1.00
7 Greg Maddux 3.00 8.00
8 Mike Mussina 1.25 3.00
9 Jose Rijo .40 1.00
10 Nolan Ryan 8.00 20.00
11 Curt Schilling .75 2.00
12 John Smoltz 1.25 3.00

1994 Fleer Team Leaders

COMPLETE SET (28) 10.00 25.00
RANDOM INSERTS IN ALL PACKS
1 Cal Ripken 1.50 4.00
2 Mo Vaughn .20 .50
3 Tim Salmon .30 .75
4 Frank Thomas .50 1.25
5 Carlos Baerga .08 .25
6 Cecil Fielder .20 .50
7 Brian McRae .08 .25
8 Greg Vaughn .08 .25
9 Kirby Puckett .50 1.25
10 Don Mattingly 1.25 3.00
11 Mark McGwire 1.25 3.00
12 Ken Griffey Jr. 1.00 2.50
13 Juan Gonzalez .20 .50
14 Paul Molitor .20 .50
15 David Justice .20 .50
16 Ryne Sandberg .75 2.00
17 Barry Larkin .30 .75
18 Andres Galarraga .20 .50
19 Gary Sheffield .20 .50
20 Jeff Bagwell .30 .75
21 Mike Piazza 1.00 2.50
22 Marquis Grissom .20 .50
23 Bobby Bonilla .20 .50
24 Len Dykstra .20 .50
25 Jay Bell .20 .50
26 Gregg Jefferies .08 .25
27 Tony Gwynn .60 1.50
28 Will Clark .30 .75

1994 Fleer Update

This 200-card standard-size set highlights traded players in their new uniforms and promising young rookies. The Update set was exclusively distributed in factory set form through hobby dealers. Each hobby case contained 20 cases. A ten card Diamond Tribute set was included in each factory set for a total of 210 cards. The cards are numbered on the back, grouped alphabetically by team by league with AL preceding NL. Key Rookie Cards include Chan Ho Park and Alex Rodriguez.

COMP.FACT.SET (210) 12.50 30.00
U PREFIX ON REG.CARD NUMBERS
1 Mark Eichhorn .08 .25
2 Sid Fernandez .08 .25
3 Leo Gomez .08 .25
4 Mike Oquist .08 .25
5 Rafael Palmeiro .30 .75
6 Chris Sabo .08 .25
7 Dwight Smith .08 .25
8 Lee Smith .20 .50
9 Damon Berryhill .08 .25
10 Wes Chamberlain .08 .25
11 Gar Finnvold .08 .25
12 Chris Howard .08 .25
13 Tim Naehring .08 .25
14 Otis Nixon .08 .25
15 Brian Anderson RC .20 .50
16 Jorge Fabregas .08 .25
17 Rex Hudler .08 .25
18 Bo Jackson .50 1.25
19 Mark Leiter .08 .25
20 Spike Owen .08 .25
21 Harold Reynolds .20 .50
22 Chris Turner .08 .25
23 Dennis Cook .08 .25
24 Jose DeLeon .08 .25
25 Julio Franco .20 .50
26 Joe Hall .08 .25
27 Darrin Jackson .08 .25
28 Dane Johnson .08 .25
29 Norberto Martin .08 .25
30 Scott Sanderson .08 .25
31 Jason Grimsley .08 .25
32 Dennis Martinez .20 .50
33 Jack Morris .20 .50
34 Eddie Murray .50 1.25
35 Chad Ogea .08 .25
36 Tony Pena .08 .25
37 Paul Shuey .08 .25
38 Omar Vizquel .30 .75
39 Danny Bautista .08 .25
40 Tim Belcher .08 .25
41 Joe Boever .08 .25
42 Storm Davis .08 .25
43 Junior Felix .08 .25
44 Mike Gardiner .08 .25
45 Buddy Groom .08 .25
46 Juan Samuel .08 .25
47 Vince Coleman .08 .25
48 Bob Hamelin .08 .25
49 Dave Henderson .08 .25
50 Rusty Meacham .08 .25
51 Terry Shumpert .08 .25
52 Jeff Bronkey .08 .25
53 Alex Diaz .08 .25
54 Brian Harper .08 .25
55 Jose Mercedes .08 .25
56 Jody Reed .08 .25
57 Bob Scanlan .08 .25
58 Turner Ward .08 .25
59 Rich Becker .08 .25
60 Alex Cole .08 .25
61 Denny Hocking .08 .25
62 Scott Leius .08 .25
63 Pat Mahomes .08 .25
64 Carlos Pulido .08 .25
65 Dave Stevens .08 .25
66 Matt Walbeck .08 .25
67 Xavier Hernandez .08 .25
68 Sterling Hitchcock .08 .25
69 Terry Mulholland .08 .25
70 Luis Polonia .08 .25
71 Gerald Williams .08 .25
72 Mark Acre RC .08 .25
73 Geronimo Berroa .08 .25
74 Rickey Henderson .50 1.25
75 Stan Javier .08 .25
76 Steve Karsay .08 .25
77 Carlos Reyes .08 .25
78 Bill Taylor RC .20 .50
79 Eric Anthony .08 .25
80 Bobby Ayala .08 .25
81 Tim Davis .08 .25
82 Felix Fermin .08 .25
83 Reggie Jefferson .08 .25
84 Keith Mitchell .08 .25
85 Bill Risley .08 .25
86 Alex Rodriguez RC ! 8.00 20.00
87 Roger Salkeld .08 .25
88 Dan Wilson .08 .25
89 Cris Carpenter .08 .25
90 Will Clark .30 .75
91 Jeff Frye .08 .25
92 Rick Helling .08 .25
93 Chris James .08 .25
94 Oddibe McDowell .08 .25
95 Billy Ripken .08 .25
96 Carlos Delgado .30 .75
97 Alex Gonzalez .08 .25
98 Shawn Green .50 1.25
99 Darren Hall .08 .25
100 Mike Huff .08 .25
101 Mike Kelly .08 .25
102 Roberto Kelly .08 .25
103 Charlie O'Brien .08 .25
104 Jose Oliva .08 .25
105 Gregg Olson .08 .25
106 Willie Banks .08 .25
107 Jim Bullinger .08 .25
108 Chuck Crim .08 .25
109 Shawon Dunston .08 .25
110 Karl Rhodes .08 .25
111 Steve Trachsel .08 .25
112 Anthony Young .08 .25
113 Eddie Zambrano .08 .25
114 Bret Boone .20 .50
115 Jeff Brantley .08 .25
116 Hector Carrasco .08 .25
117 Tony Fernandez .08 .25
118 Tim Fortugno .08 .25
119 Erik Hanson .08 .25
120 Chuck McElroy .08 .25
121 Deion Sanders .30 .75
122 Ellis Burks .20 .50
123 Marvin Freeman .08 .25
124 Mike Harkey .08 .25
125 Howard Johnson .08 .25
126 Mike Kingery .08 .25
127 Nelson Liriano .08 .25
128 Marcus Moore .08 .25
129 Mike Munoz .08 .25
130 Kevin Ritz .08 .25
131 Walt Weiss .08 .25
132 Kurt Abbott RC .08 .25
133 Jerry Browne .08 .25
134 Greg Colbrunn .08 .25
135 Jeremy Hernandez .08 .25
136 Dave Magadan .08 .25
137 Kurt Miller .08 .25
138 Robb Nen .20 .50
139 Jesus Tavarez RC .08 .25
140 Sid Bream .08 .25
141 Tom Edens .08 .25
142 Tony Eusebio .08 .25
143 John Hudek RC .08 .25
144 Brian L.Hunter .08 .25
145 Orlando Miller .08 .25
146 James Mouton .08 .25
147 Shane Reynolds .08 .25
148 Rafael Bournigal .08 .25
149 Delino DeShields .08 .25
150 Garey Ingram RC .08 .25
151 Chan Ho Park RC .30 .75
152 Wil Cordero .08 .25
153 Pedro Martinez .50 1.25
154 Randy Milligan .08 .25
155 Lenny Webster .08 .25
156 Rico Brogna .08 .25
157 Josias Manzanillo .08 .25
158 Kevin McReynolds .08 .25
159 Mike Remlinger .08 .25
160 David Segui .08 .25
161 Pete Smith .08 .25
162 Kelly Stinnett RC .20 .50
163 Jose Vizcaino .08 .25
164 Billy Hatcher .08 .25
165 Doug Jones .08 .25
166 Mike Lieberthal .20 .50
167 Tony Longmire .08 .25
168 Bobby Munoz .08 .25
169 Paul Quantrill .08 .25
170 Heathcliff Slocumb .08 .25
171 Fernando Valenzuela .20 .50
172 Mark Dewey .08 .25
173 Brian R. Hunter .08 .25
174 Jon Lieber .20 .50
175 Ravelo Manzanillo .08 .25
176 Dan Miceli .08 .25
177 Rick White .08 .25
178 Bryan Eversgerd .08 .25
179 John Habyan .08 .25
180 Terry McGriff .08 .25
181 Vicente Palacios .08 .25
182 Rich Rodriguez .08 .25
183 Rick Sutcliffe .20 .50
184 Donnie Elliott .08 .25
185 Joey Hamilton .08 .25
186 Tim Hyers RC .08 .25
187 Luis Lopez .08 .25
188 Ray McDavid .08 .25
189 Bip Roberts .08 .25
190 Scott Sanders .08 .25
191 Eddie Williams .08 .25
192 Steve Frey .08 .25
193 Pat Gomez .08 .25
194 Rich Monteleone .08 .25
195 Mark Portugal .08 .25
196 Darryl Strawberry .20 .50
197 Salomon Torres .08 .25
198 W.VanLandingham RC .08 .25
199 Checklist .08 .25
200 Checklist .08 .25

1994 Fleer Update Diamond Tribute

COMPLETE SET (10) .75 2.00
ONE SET PER UPDATE FACTORY SET
1 Barry Bonds .40 1.00
2 Joe Carter .05 .15
3 Will Clark .08 .25
4 Roger Clemens .30 .75
5 Tony Gwynn .20 .50
6 Don Mattingly .40 1.00
7 Fred McGriff .08 .25
8 Eddie Murray .15 .40
9 Kirby Puckett .15 .40
10 Cal Ripken .50 1.25

1994 Fleer Sunoco

These 25 standard-size cards feature white-bordered color player action shots on their fronts. The cards are numbered on the back as "X of 25."

COMPLETE SET (25) 2.50 6.00
1 Roberto Alomar .08 .25
2 Carlos Baerga .02 .10
3 Jeff Bagwell .20 .50
4 Jay Bell .02 .10
5 Barry Bonds .40 1.00
6 Joe Carter .05 .15
7 Roger Clemens .40 1.00
8 Darren Daulton .05 .15
9 Len Dykstra .05 .15
10 Cecil Fielder .05 .15
11 Tom Glavine .08 .25
12 Juan Gonzalez .15 .40
13 Ken Griffey Jr. .50 1.25
14 David Justice .08 .25
15 John Kruk .05 .15
16 Greg Maddux .50 1.25
17 Don Mattingly .40 1.00
18 Jack McDowell .02 .10
19 John Olerud .05 .15
20 Mike Piazza .60 1.50
21 Kirby Puckett .15 .40
22 Tim Salmon .08 .25
23 Frank Thomas .20 .50
24 Andy Van Slyke .02 .10
25 Checklist .02 .10

1995 Fleer

The 1995 Fleer set consists of 600 standard-size cards issued as one series. Each pack contained at least one insert card with some "Hot Packs" containing nothing but insert cards. Full-bleed fronts have two player photos and, atypical of baseball cards fronts, biographical information such as height, weight, etc. The backgrounds are multi-colored. The backs are horizontal and contain year-by-year statistics along with a photo. There was a different design for each of baseball's six divisions. The checklist is arranged alphabetically by teams within each league with AL preceding NL. To preview the product prior to it's public release, Fleer printed up additional quantities of cards 26, 78, 155, 235, 285, 351, 509 and 514 and mailed them to dealers and hobby media.

COMPLETE SET (600) 20.00 50.00
1 Brady Anderson .10 .30
2 Harold Baines .10 .30
3 Damon Buford .05 .15
4 Mike Devereaux .05 .15
5 Mark Eichhorn .05 .15
6 Sid Fernandez .05 .15
7 Leo Gomez .05 .15
8 Jeffrey Hammonds .05 .15
9 Chris Hoiles .05 .15
10 Rick Krivda .05 .15
11 Ben McDonald .05 .15
12 Mark McLemore .05 .15
13 Alan Mills .05 .15
14 Jamie Moyer .10 .30
15 Mike Mussina .20 .50
16 Mike Oquist .05 .15
17 Rafael Palmeiro .20 .50
18 Arthur Rhodes .05 .15
19 Cal Ripken 1.00 2.50
20 Chris Sabo .05 .15
21 Lee Smith .10 .30
22 Jack Voigt .05 .15
23 Damon Berryhill .05 .15
24 Tom Brunansky .05 .15
25 Wes Chamberlain .05 .15
26 Roger Clemens .60 1.50
27 Scott Cooper .05 .15
28 Andre Dawson .10 .30
29 Gar Finnvold .05 .15
30 Tony Fossas .05 .15
31 Mike Greenwell .05 .15
32 Joe Hesketh .05 .15
33 Chris Howard .05 .15
34 Chris Nabholz .05 .15
35 Tim Naehring .05 .15
36 Otis Nixon .05 .15
37 Carlos Rodriguez .05 .15
38 Rich Rowland .05 .15
39 Ken Ryan .05 .15
40 Aaron Sele .05 .15
41 John Valentin .05 .15
42 Mo Vaughn .10 .30
43 Frank Viola .10 .30
44 Danny Bautista .05 .15
45 Joe Boever .05 .15
46 Milt Cuyler .05 .15
47 Storm Davis .05 .15
48 John Doherty .05 .15
49 Junior Felix .05 .15
50 Cecil Fielder .10 .30
51 Travis Fryman .10 .30
52 Mike Gardiner .05 .15
53 Kirk Gibson .10 .30
54 Chris Gomez .05 .15
55 Buddy Groom .05 .15
56 Mike Henneman .05 .15
57 Chad Kreuter .05 .15
58 Mike Moore .05 .15
59 Tony Phillips .05 .15
60 Juan Samuel .05 .15
61 Mickey Tettleton .05 .15
62 Alan Trammell .10 .30
63 David Wells .10 .30
64 Lou Whitaker .10 .30
65 Jim Abbott .20 .50
66 Joe Ausanio .05 .15
67 Wade Boggs .20 .50
68 Mike Gallego .05 .15
69 Xavier Hernandez .05 .15
70 Sterling Hitchcock .05 .15
71 Steve Howe .05 .15
72 Scott Kamieniecki .05 .15
73 Pat Kelly .05 .15
74 Jimmy Key .10 .30
75 Jim Leyritz .05 .15
76 Don Mattingly .75 2.00
77 Terry Mulholland .05 .15
78 Paul O'Neill .20 .50
79 Melido Perez .05 .15
80 Luis Polonia .05 .15
81 Mike Stanley .05 .15
82 Danny Tartabull .05 .15
83 Randy Velarde .05 .15
84 Bob Wickman .05 .15
85 Bernie Williams .20 .50
86 Gerald Williams .05 .15
87 Roberto Alomar .20 .50
88 Pat Borders .05 .15
89 Joe Carter .10 .30
90 Tony Castillo .05 .15
91 Brad Cornett RC .05 .15
92 Carlos Delgado .10 .30
93 Alex Gonzalez .05 .15
94 Shawn Green .10 .30
95 Juan Guzman .05 .15
96 Darren Hall .05 .15
97 Pat Hentgen .05 .15
98 Mike Huff .05 .15
99 Randy Knorr .05 .15
100 Al Leiter .10 .30
101 Paul Molitor .10 .30
102 John Olerud .10 .30
103 Dick Schofield .05 .15
104 Ed Sprague .05 .15
105 Dave Stewart .10 .30
106 Todd Stottlemyre .05 .15
107 Devon White .10 .30
108 Woody Williams .05 .15
109 Wilson Alvarez .05 .15
110 Paul Assenmacher .05 .15
111 Jason Bere .05 .15
112 Dennis Cook .05 .15
113 Joey Cora .05 .15
114 Jose DeLeon .05 .15
115 Alex Fernandez .05 .15
116 Julio Franco .10 .30
117 Craig Grebeck .05 .15
118 Ozzie Guillen .10 .30
119 Roberto Hernandez .05 .15
120 Darrin Jackson .05 .15
121 Lance Johnson .05 .15
122 Ron Karkovice .05 .15
123 Mike LaValliere .05 .15
124 Norberto Martin .05 .15
125 Kirk McCaskill .05 .15
126 Jack McDowell .05 .15
127 Tim Raines .10 .30
128 Frank Thomas .30 .75
129 Robin Ventura .10 .30
130 Sandy Alomar Jr. .05 .15
131 Carlos Baerga .05 .15
132 Albert Belle .10 .30
133 Mark Clark .05 .15
134 Alvaro Espinoza .05 .15
135 Jason Grimsley .05 .15
136 Wayne Kirby .05 .15
137 Kenny Lofton .10 .30
138 Albie Lopez .05 .15
139 Dennis Martinez .10 .30
140 Jose Mesa .05 .15
141 Eddie Murray .30 .75
142 Charles Nagy .05 .15
143 Tony Pena .05 .15
144 Eric Plunk .05 .15
145 Manny Ramirez .20 .50
146 Jeff Russell .05 .15
147 Paul Shuey .05 .15
148 Paul Sorrento .05 .15
149 Jim Thome .20 .50
150 Omar Vizquel .20 .50
151 Dave Winfield .10 .30
152 Kevin Appier .10 .30
153 Billy Brewer .05 .15
154 Vince Coleman .05 .15
155 David Cone .10 .30
156 Gary Gaetti .10 .30
157 Greg Gagne .05 .15
158 Tom Gordon .05 .15
159 Mark Gubicza .05 .15
160 Bob Hamelin .05 .15
161 Dave Henderson .05 .15
162 Felix Jose .05 .15
163 Wally Joyner .10 .30
164 Jose Lind .05 .15
165 Mike Macfarlane .05 .15
166 Mike Magnante .05 .15
167 Brent Mayne .05 .15
168 Brian McRae .05 .15
169 Rusty Meacham .05 .15
170 Jeff Montgomery .05 .15
171 Hipolito Pichardo .05 .15
172 Terry Shumpert .05 .15
173 Michael Tucker .05 .15
174 Ricky Bones .05 .15
175 Jeff Cirillo .05 .15
176 Alex Diaz .05 .15
177 Cal Eldred .05 .15
178 Mike Fetters .05 .15
179 Darryl Hamilton .05 .15
180 Brian Harper .05 .15
181 John Jaha .05 .15
182 Pat Listach .05 .15
183 Graeme Lloyd .05 .15
184 Jose Mercedes .05 .15
185 Matt Mieske .05 .15
186 Dave Nilsson .05 .15
187 Jody Reed .05 .15
188 Bob Scanlan .05 .15
189 Kevin Seitzer .05 .15
190 Bill Spiers .05 .15
191 B.J. Surhoff .10 .30
192 Jose Valentin .05 .15
193 Greg Vaughn .05 .15
194 Turner Ward .05 .15
195 Bill Wegman .05 .15
196 Rick Aguilera .05 .15
197 Rich Becker .05 .15
198 Alex Cole .05 .15
199 Marty Cordova .05 .15
200 Steve Dunn .05 .15
201 Scott Erickson .05 .15
202 Mark Guthrie .05 .15
203 Chip Hale .05 .15
204 LaTroy Hawkins .05 .15
205 Denny Hocking .05 .15
206 Chuck Knoblauch .10 .30
207 Scott Leius .05 .15
208 Shane Mack .05 .15
209 Pat Mahomes .05 .15
210 Pat Meares .05 .15
211 Pedro Munoz .05 .15
212 Kirby Puckett .30 .75
213 Jeff Reboulet .05 .15
214 Dave Stevens .05 .15
215 Kevin Tapani .05 .15
216 Matt Walbeck .05 .15
217 Carl Willis .05 .15
218 Brian Anderson .05 .15
219 Chad Curtis .05 .15
220 Chili Davis .10 .30
221 Gary DiSarcina .05 .15
222 Damion Easley .05 .15
223 Jim Edmonds .20 .50
224 Chuck Finley .10 .30
225 Joe Grahe .05 .15
226 Rex Hudler .05 .15
227 Bo Jackson .30 .75
228 Mark Langston .05 .15
229 Phil Leftwich .05 .15
230 Mark Leiter .05 .15
231 Spike Owen .05 .15
232 Bob Patterson .05 .15
233 Troy Percival .10 .30
234 Eduardo Perez .05 .15
235 Tim Salmon .20 .50
236 J.T. Snow .10 .30
237 Chris Turner .05 .15
238 Mark Acre .05 .15
239 Geronimo Berroa .05 .15
240 Mike Bordick .05 .15
241 John Briscoe .05 .15
242 Scott Brosius .10 .30
243 Ron Darling .05 .15
244 Dennis Eckersley .10 .30
245 Brent Gates .05 .15
246 Rickey Henderson .30 .75
247 Stan Javier .05 .15
248 Steve Karsay .05 .15
249 Mark McGwire .75 2.00
250 Troy Neel .05 .15
251 Steve Ontiveros .05 .15
252 Carlos Reyes .05 .15
253 Ruben Sierra .10 .30
254 Terry Steinbach .05 .15
255 Bill Taylor .05 .15
256 Todd Van Poppel .05 .15
257 Bobby Witt .05 .15
258 Rich Amaral .05 .15
259 Eric Anthony .05 .15
260 Bobby Ayala .05 .15
261 Mike Blowers .05 .15
262 Chris Bosio .05 .15
263 Jay Buhner .10 .30
264 John Cummings .05 .15
265 Tim Davis .05 .15
266 Felix Fermin .05 .15
267 Dave Fleming .05 .15
268 Goose Gossage .10 .30
269 Ken Griffey Jr. .60 1.50
270 Reggie Jefferson .05 .15
271 Randy Johnson .30 .75
272 Edgar Martinez .20 .50
273 Tino Martinez .20 .50
274 Greg Pirkl .05 .15
275 Bill Risley .05 .15
276 Roger Salkeld .05 .15
277 Luis Sojo .05 .15
278 Mac Suzuki .05 .15
279 Dan Wilson .05 .15
280 Kevin Brown .10 .30
281 Jose Canseco .20 .50
282 Cris Carpenter .05 .15
283 Will Clark .20 .50
284 Jeff Frye .05 .15
285 Juan Gonzalez .10 .30
286 Rick Helling .05 .15
287 Tom Henke .05 .15
288 David Hulse .05 .15
289 Chris James .05 .15
290 Manuel Lee .05 .15
291 Oddibe McDowell .05 .15
292 Dean Palmer .10 .30
293 Roger Pavlik .05 .15
294 Bill Ripken .05 .15
295 Ivan Rodriguez .20 .50
296 Kenny Rogers .10 .30
297 Doug Strange .05 .15
298 Matt Whiteside .05 .15
299 Steve Avery .05 .15
300 Steve Bedrosian .05 .15
301 Rafael Belliard .05 .15
302 Jeff Blauser .05 .15
303 Dave Gallagher .05 .15
304 Tom Glavine .20 .50
305 David Justice .10 .30
306 Mike Kelly .05 .15
307 Roberto Kelly .05 .15
308 Ryan Klesko .10 .30
309 Mark Lemke .05 .15
310 Javier Lopez .10 .30
311 Greg Maddux .50 1.25
312 Fred McGriff .20 .50
313 Greg McMichael .05 .15
314 Kent Mercker .05 .15
315 Charlie O'Brien .05 .15
316 Jose Oliva .05 .15
317 Terry Pendleton .10 .30
318 John Smoltz .20 .50
319 Mike Stanton .05 .15
320 Tony Tarasco .05 .15
321 Terrell Wade .05 .15
322 Mark Wohlers .05 .15
323 Kurt Abbott .05 .15
324 Luis Aquino .05 .15
325 Bret Barberie .05 .15
326 Ryan Bowen .05 .15
327 Jerry Browne .05 .15
328 Chuck Carr .05 .15
329 Matias Carrillo .05 .15
330 Greg Colbrunn .05 .15
331 Jeff Conine .10 .30
332 Mark Gardner .05 .15
333 Chris Hammond .05 .15
334 Bryan Harvey .05 .15
335 Richie Lewis .05 .15
336 Dave Magadan .05 .15
337 Terry Mathews .05 .15
338 Robb Nen .10 .30
339 Yorkis Perez .05 .15
340 Pat Rapp .05 .15
341 Benito Santiago .10 .30
342 Gary Sheffield .10 .30
343 Dave Weathers .05 .15
344 Moises Alou .10 .30
345 Sean Berry .05 .15
346 Wil Cordero .05 .15
347 Joey Eischen .05 .15
348 Jeff Fassero .05 .15
349 Darrin Fletcher .05 .15
350 Cliff Floyd .10 .30
351 Marquis Grissom .10 .30
352 Butch Henry .05 .15
353 Gil Heredia .05 .15
354 Ken Hill .05 .15
355 Mike Lansing .05 .15
356 Pedro Martinez .20 .50
357 Mel Rojas .05 .15
358 Kirk Rueter .05 .15
359 Tim Scott .05 .15
360 Jeff Shaw .05 .15
361 Larry Walker .10 .30
362 Lenny Webster .05 .15
363 John Wetteland .10 .30
364 Rondell White .10 .30
365 Bobby Bonilla .10 .30
366 Rico Brogna .05 .15
367 Jeromy Burnitz .10 .30
368 John Franco .10 .30
369 Dwight Gooden .10 .30
370 Todd Hundley .05 .15
371 Jason Jacome .05 .15
372 Bobby Jones .05 .15
373 Jeff Kent .10 .30
374 Jim Lindeman .05 .15
375 Josias Manzanillo .05 .15
376 Roger Mason .05 .15
377 Kevin McReynolds .05 .15
378 Joe Orsulak .05 .15
379 Bill Pulsipher .05 .15
380 Bret Saberhagen .10 .30
381 David Segui .05 .15
382 Pete Smith .05 .15
383 Kelly Stinnett .05 .15
384 Ryan Thompson .05 .15
385 Jose Vizcaino .05 .15
386 Toby Borland .05 .15
387 Ricky Bottalico .05 .15
388 Darren Daulton .10 .30
389 Mariano Duncan .05 .15
390 Lenny Dykstra .10 .30
391 Jim Eisenreich .05 .15
392 Tommy Greene .05 .15
393 Dave Hollins .05 .15
394 Pete Incaviglia .05 .15

395 Danny Jackson .05 .15
396 Doug Jones .05 .15
397 Ricky Jordan .05 .15
398 John Kruk .10 .30
399 Mike Lieberthal .10 .30
400 Tony Longmire .05 .15
401 Mickey Morandini .05 .15
402 Bobby Munoz .05 .15
403 Curt Schilling .10 .30
404 Heathcliff Slocumb .05 .15
405 Kevin Stocker .05 .15
406 Fernando Valenzuela .10 .30
407 David West .05 .15
408 Willie Banks .05 .15
409 Jose Bautista .05 .15
410 Steve Buechele .05 .15
411 Jim Bullinger .05 .15
412 Chuck Crim .05 .15
413 Shawon Dunston .05 .15
414 Kevin Foster .05 .15
415 Mark Grace .20 .50
416 Jose Hernandez .05 .15
417 Glenallen Hill .05 .15
418 Brooks Kieschnick .05 .15
419 Derrick May .05 .15
420 Randy Myers .05 .15
421 Dan Plesac .05 .15
422 Karl Rhodes .05 .15
423 Rey Sanchez .05 .15
424 Sammy Sosa .30 .75
425 Steve Trachsel .05 .15
426 Rick Wilkins .05 .15
427 Anthony Young .05 .15
428 Eddie Zambrano .05 .15
429 Bret Boone .10 .30
430 Jeff Branson .05 .15
431 Jeff Brantley .05 .15
432 Hector Carrasco .05 .15
433 Brian Dorsett .05 .15
434 Tony Fernandez .05 .15
435 Tim Fortugno .05 .15
436 Erik Hanson .05 .15
437 Thomas Howard .05 .15
438 Kevin Jarvis .05 .15
439 Barry Larkin .20 .50
440 Chuck McElroy .05 .15
441 Kevin Mitchell .05 .15
442 Hal Morris .05 .15
443 Jose Rijo .05 .15
444 John Roper .05 .15
445 Johnny Ruffin .05 .15
446 Deion Sanders .20 .50
447 Reggie Sanders .10 .30
448 Pete Schourek .05 .15
449 John Smiley .05 .15
450 Eddie Taubensee .05 .15
451 Jeff Bagwell .20 .50
452 Kevin Bass .05 .15
453 Craig Biggio .20 .50
454 Ken Caminiti .10 .30
455 Andujar Cedeno .05 .15
456 Doug Drabek .05 .15
457 Tony Eusebio .05 .15
458 Mike Felder .05 .15
459 Steve Finley .10 .30
460 Luis Gonzalez .10 .30
461 Mike Hampton .10 .30
462 Pete Harnisch .05 .15
463 John Hudek .05 .15
464 Todd Jones .05 .15
465 Darryl Kile .10 .30
466 James Mouton .05 .15
467 Shane Reynolds .05 .15
468 Scott Servais .05 .15
469 Greg Swindell .05 .15
470 Dave Veres RC .15 .40
471 Brian Williams .05 .15
472 Jay Bell .10 .30
473 Jacob Brumfield .05 .15
474 Dave Clark .05 .15
475 Steve Cooke .05 .15
476 Midre Cummings .05 .15
477 Mark Dewey .05 .15
478 Tom Foley .05 .15
479 Carlos Garcia .05 .15
480 Jeff King .05 .15
481 Jon Lieber .05 .15
482 Ravelo Manzanillo .05 .15
483 Al Martin .05 .15
484 Orlando Merced .05 .15
485 Danny Miceli .05 .15
486 Denny Neagle .10 .30
487 Lance Parrish .10 .30
488 Don Slaught .05 .15
489 Zane Smith .05 .15
490 Andy Van Slyke .20 .50
491 Paul Wagner .05 .15
492 Rick White .05 .15
493 Luis Alicea .05 .15
494 Rene Arocha .05 .15
495 Rheal Cormier .05 .15
496 Bryan Eversgerd .05 .15
497 Bernard Gilkey .05 .15
498 John Habyan .05 .15
499 Gregg Jefferies .05 .15
500 Brian Jordan .10 .30
501 Ray Lankford .10 .30
502 John Mabry .05 .15
503 Terry McGriff .05 .15
504 Tom Pagnozzi .05 .15
505 Vicente Palacios .05 .15
506 Geronimo Pena .05 .15
507 Gerald Perry .05 .15
508 Rich Rodriguez .05 .15
509 Ozzie Smith .50 1.25
510 Bob Tewksbury .05 .15
511 Allen Watson .05 .15
512 Mark Whiten .05 .15
513 Todd Zeile .05 .15
514 Dante Bichette .10 .30
515 Willie Blair .05 .15
516 Ellis Burks .10 .30
517 Marvin Freeman .05 .15
518 Andres Galarraga .10 .30
519 Joe Girardi .05 .15
520 Greg W. Harris .05 .15
521 Charlie Hayes .05 .15
522 Mike Kingery .05 .15
523 Nelson Liriano .05 .15
524 Mike Munoz .05 .15
525 David Nied .05 .15
526 Steve Reed .05 .15
527 Kevin Ritz .05 .15
528 Bruce Ruffin .05 .15
529 John Vander Wal .05 .15
530 Walt Weiss .05 .15
531 Eric Young .05 .15
532 Billy Ashley .05 .15
533 Pedro Astacio .05 .15
534 Rafael Bournigal .05 .15
535 Brett Butler .10 .30
536 Tom Candiotti .05 .15
537 Omar Daal .05 .15
538 Delino DeShields .05 .15
539 Darren Dreifort .05 .15
540 Kevin Gross .05 .15
541 Orel Hershiser .10 .30
542 Garey Ingram .05 .15
543 Eric Karros .10 .30
544 Ramon Martinez .05 .15
545 Raul Mondesi .10 .30
546 Chan Ho Park .10 .30
547 Mike Piazza .50 1.25
548 Henry Rodriguez .05 .15
549 Rudy Seanez .05 .15
550 Ismael Valdes .05 .15
551 Tim Wallach .05 .15
552 Todd Worrell .05 .15
553 Andy Ashby .05 .15
554 Brad Ausmus .10 .30
555 Derek Bell .05 .15
556 Andy Benes .05 .15
557 Phil Clark .05 .15
558 Donnie Elliott .05 .15
559 Ricky Gutierrez .05 .15
560 Tony Gwynn .40 1.00
561 Joey Hamilton .05 .15
562 Trevor Hoffman .10 .30
563 Luis Lopez .05 .15
564 Pedro A. Martinez .05 .15
565 Tim Mauser .05 .15
566 Phil Plantier .05 .15
567 Bip Roberts .05 .15
568 Scott Sanders .05 .15
569 Craig Shipley .05 .15
570 Jeff Tabaka .05 .15
571 Eddie Williams .05 .15
572 Rod Beck .05 .15
573 Mike Benjamin .05 .15
574 Barry Bonds .75 2.00
575 Dave Burba .05 .15
576 John Burkett .05 .15
577 Mark Carreon .05 .15
578 Royce Clayton .05 .15
579 Steve Frey .05 .15
580 Bryan Hickerson .05 .15
581 Mike Jackson .05 .15
582 Darren Lewis .05 .15
583 Kirt Manwaring .05 .15
584 Rich Monteleone .05 .15
585 John Patterson .05 .15
586 J.R. Phillips .05 .15
587 Mark Portugal .05 .15
588 Joe Rosselli .05 .15
589 Darryl Strawberry .10 .30
590 Bill Swift .05 .15
591 Robby Thompson .05 .15
592 William VanLandingham .05 .15
593 Matt Williams .10 .30
594 Checklist .05 .15
595 Checklist .05 .15
596 Checklist .05 .15
597 Checklist .05 .15
598 Checklist .05 .15
599 Checklist .05 .15
600 Checklist .05 .15

1995 Fleer All-Fleer

COMPLETE SET (9) 4.00 10.00
SETS WERE AVAILABLE VIA WRAPPER OFFER
1 Mike Piazza .50 1.25
2 Frank Thomas .30 .75
3 Roberto Alomar .20 .50
4 Cal Ripken 1.00 2.50
5 Matt Williams .10 .30
6 Barry Bonds .75 2.00
7 Ken Griffey Jr. .60 1.50
8 Tony Gwynn .40 1.00
9 Greg Maddux .50 1.25

1995 Fleer All-Rookies

COMPLETE SET (9) 1.25 3.00
ONE SET PER EXCHANGE CARD VIA MAIL
M1 Edgardo Alfonzo .08 .25
M2 Jason Bates .08 .25
M3 Brian Boehringer .08 .25
M4 Darren Bragg .08 .25
M5 Brad Clontz .08 .25
M6 Jim Dougherty .08 .25
M7 Todd Hollandsworth .08 .25
M8 Rudy Pemberton .08 .25
M9 Frank Rodriguez .08 .25
NNO Expired All-Rookie Exch. .08 .25

1995 Fleer All-Stars

COMPLETE SET (25) 4.00 10.00
STATED ODDS 1:3
1 M.Piazza .60 1.50
I.Rodriguez
2 F.Thomas .40 1.00
G.Jefferies
3 R.Alomar .25 .60
M.Duncan
4 W.Boggs .25 .60
M.Williams
5 C.Ripken 1.25 3.00
O.Smith
6 B.Bonds 1.00 2.50
J.Carter
7 K.Griffey .75 2.00
T.Gwynn
8 K.Puckett .40 1.00
D.Justice
9 G.Maddux .60 1.50
J.Key
10 C.Knoblauch .15 .40
W.Cordero
11 S.Cooper .15 .40
K.Caminiti
12 W.Clark .25 .60
C.Garcia
13 J.Bagwell .25 .60
P.Molitor
14 T.Fryman .25 .60
C.Biggio
15 M.Tettleton .25 .60
F.McGriff
16 K.Lofton .15 .40
M.Alou
17 A.Belle .15 .40
M.Grissom
18 P.O'Neill .25 .60
D.Bichette
19 D.Cone .15 .40
K.Hill
20 M.Mussina .25 .60
D.Drabek
21 R.Johnson .40 1.00
J.Hudek
22 P.Hentgen .07 .20
D.Jackson
23 W.Alvarez .07 .20
R.Beck
24 L.Smith .15 .40
R.Myers
25 J.Bere .07 .20
D.Jones

1995 Fleer Award Winners

COMPLETE SET (6) 2.00 5.00
STATED ODDS 1:24
1 Frank Thomas .50 1.25
2 Jeff Bagwell .30 .75
3 David Cone .20 .50
4 Greg Maddux .75 2.00
5 Bob Hamelin .08 .25
6 Raul Mondesi .20 .50

1995 Fleer League Leaders

COMPLETE SET (10) 3.00 8.00
STATED ODDS 1:12
1 Paul O'Neill .30 .75
2 Ken Griffey Jr. 1.00 2.50
3 Kirby Puckett .50 1.25
4 Jimmy Key .20 .50
5 Randy Johnson .50 1.25
6 Tony Gwynn .60 1.50
7 Matt Williams .20 .50
8 Jeff Bagwell .30 .75
9 G.Maddux .75 2.00
K.Hill
10 Andy Benes .08 .25

1995 Fleer Lumber Company

COMPLETE SET (10) 12.50 30.00
STATED ODDS 1:24 RETAIL
1 Jeff Bagwell 1.00 2.50
2 Albert Belle .60 1.50
3 Barry Bonds 4.00 10.00
4 Jose Canseco 1.00 2.50
5 Joe Carter .60 1.50
6 Ken Griffey Jr. 3.00 8.00
7 Fred McGriff 1.00 2.50
8 Kevin Mitchell .30 .75
9 Frank Thomas 1.50 4.00
10 Matt Williams .60 1.50

1995 Fleer Major League Prospects

COMPLETE SET (10) 4.00 10.00
STATED ODDS 1:6
1 Garret Anderson .20 .50
2 James Baldwin .08 .25
3 Alan Benes .08 .25
4 Armando Benitez .08 .25
5 Ray Durham .20 .50
6 Brian L.Hunter .08 .25
7 Derek Jeter 1.50 4.00
8 Charles Johnson .20 .50
9 Orlando Miller .08 .25
10 Alex Rodriguez 1.50 4.00

1995 Fleer Pro-Visions

COMPLETE SET (6) 1.25 3.00
STATED ODDS 1:9
1 Mike Mussina .20 .50
2 Raul Mondesi .10 .30
3 Jeff Bagwell .20 .50
4 Greg Maddux .50 1.25
5 Tim Salmon .20 .50
6 Manny Ramirez .20 .50

1995 Fleer Rookie Sensations

COMPLETE SET (20) 15.00 40.00
RANDOM INSERTS IN JUMBO PACKS
1 Kurt Abbott .75 2.00
2 Rico Brogna .75 2.00
3 Hector Carrasco .75 2.00
4 Kevin Foster .75 2.00
5 Chris Gomez .75 2.00
6 Darren Hall .75 2.00
7 Bob Hamelin .75 2.00
8 Joey Hamilton .75 2.00
9 John Hudek .75 2.00
10 Ryan Klesko 1.50 4.00
11 Javier Lopez 1.50 4.00
12 Matt Mieske .75 2.00
13 Raul Mondesi 1.50 4.00
14 Manny Ramirez 2.00 5.00
15 Shane Reynolds .75 2.00
16 Bill Risley .75 2.00
17 Johnny Ruffin .75 2.00
18 Steve Trachsel .75 2.00
19 William VanLandingham .75 2.00
20 Rondell White 1.50 4.00

1995 Fleer Team Leaders

COMPLETE SET (28) 40.00 100.00
STATED ODDS 1:24 HOBBY
1 C.Ripken 10.00 25.00
M.Mussina
2 R.Clemens 6.00 15.00
M.Vaughn
3 T.Salmon 2.00 5.00
C.Finley
4 F.Thomas 3.00 8.00
J.McDowell
5 A.Belle 1.25 3.00
D.Martinez
6 C.Fielder 1.25 3.00
M.Moore
7 B.Hamelin 1.25 3.00
D.Cone
8 G.Vaughn .60 1.50
R.Bones
9 K.Puckett 3.00 8.00
R.Aguilera
10 D.Mattingly 8.00 20.00
J.Key
11 R.Sierra 1.25 3.00
D.Eckersley
12 K.Griffey 6.00 15.00
R.Johnson
13 J.Canseco 2.00 5.00
K.Rogers
14 J.Carter 1.25 3.00
P.Hentgen
15 G.Maddux 5.00 12.00
D.Justice
16 S.Sosa 3.00 8.00
S.Trachsel
17 K.Mitchell .60 1.50
J.Rijo
18 D.Bichette 1.25 3.00
B.Ruffin
19 J.Conine 1.25 3.00
R.Nen
20 J.Bagwell 2.00 5.00
D.Drabek
21 M.Piazza 5.00 12.00
R.Martinez
22 M.Alou 1.25 3.00
K.Hill
23 B.Bonilla 1.25 3.00
B.Saberhagen
24 D.Daulton 1.25 3.00
D.Jackson
25 J.Bell 1.25 3.00
Z.Smith
26 G.Jefferies .60 1.50
B.Tewksbury
27 T.Gwynn 4.00 10.00
A.Benes
28 M.Williams 1.25 3.00
R.Beck

1995 Fleer Update

This 200-card standard-size set features many players who were either rookies in 1995 or played for new teams. These cards were issued in either 12-card packs with a suggested retail price of $1.49 or 18-card packs that had a suggested retail price of $2.29. Each Fleer Update pack included one card from several insert sets produced with this product. Hot packs featuring only these insert cards were included one every 72 packs. The full-bleed fronts have two player photos and, atypical of baseball card fronts, biographical information such as height, weight, etc. The backgrounds are multi-colored. The backs are horizontal, have yearly statistics, a photo, and are numbered with the prefix "U". The checklist is arranged alphabetically by team within each league's divisions. Key Rookie Cards in this set include Bobby Higginson and Hideo Nomo.

COMPLETE SET (200) 6.00 15.00
ONE INSERT PER PACK
U PREFIX ON CARD NUMBERS
1 Manny Alexander .02 .10
2 Bret Barberie .02 .10
3 Armando Benitez .02 .10
4 Kevin Brown .07 .20
5 Doug Jones .02 .10
6 Sherman Obando .02 .10
7 Andy Van Slyke .10 .30
8 Stan Belinda .02 .10
9 Jose Canseco .10 .30
10 Vaughn Eshelman .02 .10
11 Mike Macfarlane .02 .10
12 Troy O'Leary .02 .10
13 Steve Rodriguez .02 .10
14 Lee Tinsley .02 .10
15 Tim Vanegmond .02 .10
16 Mark Whiten .02 .10
17 Sean Bergman .02 .10
18 Chad Curtis .02 .10
19 John Flaherty .02 .10
20 Bob Higginson RC .30 .75
21 Felipe Lira .02 .10
22 Shannon Penn .02 .10
23 Todd Steverson .02 .10
24 Sean Whiteside .02 .10
25 Tony Fernandez .02 .10
26 Jack McDowell .02 .10
27 Andy Pettitte .10 .30
28 John Wetteland .07 .20
29 David Cone .07 .20
30 Mike Timlin .02 .10
31 Duane Ward .02 .10
32 Jim Abbott .10 .30
33 James Baldwin .02 .10
34 Mike Devereaux .02 .10
35 Ray Durham .07 .20
36 Tim Fortugno .02 .10
37 Scott Ruffcorn .02 .10
38 Chris Sabo .02 .10
39 Paul Assenmacher .02 .10
40 Bud Black .02 .10
41 Orel Hershiser .07 .20
42 Julian Tavarez .02 .10
43 Dave Winfield .07 .20
44 Pat Borders .02 .10
45 Melvin Bunch RC .02 .10
46 Tom Goodwin .02 .10
47 Jon Nunnally .02 .10
48 Joe Randa .07 .20
49 Dilson Torres RC .02 .10
50 Joe Vitiello .02 .10
51 David Hulse .02 .10
52 Scott Karl .02 .10
53 Mark Kiefer .02 .10
54 Derrick May .02 .10
55 Joe Oliver .02 .10
56 Al Reyes RC .02 .10
57 Steve Sparks RC .15 .40
58 Jerald Clark .02 .10
59 Eddie Guardado .02 .10
60 Kevin Maas .02 .10
61 David McCarty .02 .10
62 Brad Radke RC .30 .75
63 Scott Stahoviak .02 .10
64 Garret Anderson .07 .20
65 Shawn Boskie .02 .10
66 Mike James .02 .10
67 Tony Phillips .02 .10
68 Lee Smith .07 .20
69 Mitch Williams .02 .10
70 Jim Corsi .02 .10
71 Mike Harkey .02 .10
72 Dave Stewart .07 .20
73 Todd Stottlemyre .02 .10
74 Joey Cora .02 .10
75 Chad Kreuter .02 .10
76 Jeff Nelson .02 .10
77 Alex Rodriguez .50 1.25
78 Ron Villone .02 .10
79 Bob Wells RC .15 .40
80 Jose Alberro RC .02 .10
81 Terry Burrows .02 .10
82 Kevin Gross .02 .10
83 Wilson Heredia .02 .10
84 Mark McLemore .02 .10
85 Otis Nixon .02 .10
86 Jeff Russell .02 .10
87 Mickey Tettleton .02 .10
88 Bob Tewksbury .02 .10
89 Pedro Borbon .02 .10
90 Marquis Grissom .07 .20
91 Chipper Jones .20 .50
92 Mike Mordecai .02 .10
93 Jason Schmidt .20 .50
94 John Burkett .02 .10
95 Andre Dawson .07 .20
96 Matt Dunbar RC .02 .10
97 Charles Johnson .07 .20
98 Terry Pendleton .07 .20
99 Rich Scheid .02 .10
100 Quilvio Veras .02 .10
101 Bobby Witt .02 .10
102 Eddie Zosky .02 .10
103 Shane Andrews .02 .10
104 Reid Cornelius .02 .10
105 Chad Fonville RC .02 .10
106 Mark Grudzielanek RC .30 .75
107 Roberto Kelly .02 .10
108 Carlos Perez RC .15 .40
109 Tony Tarasco .02 .10
110 Brett Butler .07 .20
111 Carl Everett .07 .20
112 Pete Harnisch .02 .10
113 Doug Henry .02 .10
114 Kevin Lomon RC .02 .10
115 Blas Minor .02 .10
116 Dave Mlicki .02 .10
117 Ricky Otero RC .02 .10
118 Norm Charlton .02 .10
119 Tyler Green .02 .10
120 Gene Harris .02 .10
121 Charlie Hayes .02 .10
122 Gregg Jefferies .02 .10
123 Michael Mimbs RC .02 .10
124 Paul Quantrill .02 .10
125 Frank Castillo .02 .10
126 Brian McRae .02 .10
127 Jaime Navarro .02 .10
128 Mike Perez .02 .10
129 Tanyon Sturtze .02 .10
130 Ozzie Timmons .02 .10
131 John Courtright .02 .10
132 Ron Gant .07 .20
133 Xavier Hernandez .02 .10
134 Brian Hunter .02 .10
135 Benito Santiago .07 .20
136 Pete Smith .02 .10
137 Scott Sullivan .02 .10
138 Derek Bell .02 .10
139 Doug Brocail .02 .10
140 Ricky Gutierrez .02 .10
141 Pedro A.Martinez .02 .10
142 Orlando Miller .02 .10
143 Phil Plantier .02 .10
144 Craig Shipley .02 .10
145 Rich Aude .02 .10
146 Jason Christiansen RC .02 .10
147 Freddy Adrian Garcia RC .02 .10
148 Jim Gott .02 .10
149 Mark Johnson RC .15 .40
150 Esteban Loaiza .02 .10
151 Dan Plesac .02 .10
152 Gary Wilson RC .02 .10
153 Allen Battle .02 .10
154 Terry Bradshaw .02 .10
155 Scott Cooper .02 .10
156 Tripp Cromer .02 .10
157 John Frascatore RC .02 .10
158 John Habyan .02 .10
159 Tom Henke .02 .10
160 Ken Hill .02 .10
161 Danny Jackson .02 .10
162 Donovan Osborne .02 .10
163 Tom Urbani .02 .10
164 Roger Bailey .02 .10
165 Jorge Brito RC .02 .10
166 Vinny Castilla .07 .20
167 Darren Holmes .02 .10
168 Roberto Mejia .02 .10
169 Bill Swift .02 .10
170 Mark Thompson .02 .10
171 Larry Walker .07 .20
172 Greg Hansell .02 .10
173 Dave Hansen .02 .10
174 Carlos Hernandez .02 .10
175 Hideo Nomo RC .75 2.00
176 Jose Offerman .02 .10
177 Antonio Osuna .02 .10
178 Reggie Williams .02 .10
179 Todd Williams .02 .10
180 Andres Berumen .02 .10
181 Ken Caminiti .07 .20
182 Andujar Cedeno .02 .10
183 Steve Finley .07 .20
184 Bryce Florie .02 .10
185 Dustin Hermanson .02 .10
186 Ray Holbert .02 .10
187 Melvin Nieves .02 .10
188 Roberto Petagine .02 .10
189 Jody Reed .02 .10
190 Fernando Valenzuela .07 .20
191 Brian Williams .02 .10
192 Mark Dewey .02 .10
193 Glenallen Hill .02 .10
194 Chris Hook RC .02 .10
195 Terry Mulholland .02 .10
196 Steve Scarsone .02 .10
197 Trevor Wilson .02 .10
198 Checklist .02 .10
199 Checklist .02 .10
200 Checklist .02 .10

1995 Fleer Update Diamond Tribute

COMPLETE SET (10) 3.00 8.00
STATED ODDS 1:5 HOB/RET
1 Jeff Bagwell .20 .50
2 Albert Belle .10 .30
3 Barry Bonds .75 2.00
4 David Cone .10 .30
5 Dennis Eckersley .10 .30
6 Ken Griffey Jr. .60 1.50
7 Rickey Henderson .30 .75
8 Greg Maddux .50 1.25
9 Frank Thomas .30 .75
10 Matt Williams .10 .30

1995 Fleer Update Headliners

COMPLETE SET (20) 5.00 12.00
STATED ODDS 1:3
1 Jeff Bagwell .20 .50
2 Albert Belle .10 .30
3 Barry Bonds .75 2.00
4 Jose Canseco .20 .50
5 Joe Carter .10 .30
6 Will Clark .20 .50
7 Roger Clemens .60 1.50
8 Lenny Dykstra .10 .30
9 Cecil Fielder .10 .30
10 Juan Gonzalez .10 .30
11 Ken Griffey Jr. .60 1.50
12 Kenny Lofton .10 .30
13 Greg Maddux .50 1.25
14 Fred McGriff .20 .50
15 Mike Piazza .50 1.25
16 Kirby Puckett .30 .75
17 Tim Salmon .20 .50
18 Frank Thomas .30 .75
19 Mo Vaughn .10 .30
20 Matt Williams .10 .30

1995 Fleer Update Rookie Update

COMPLETE SET (10) 4.00 10.00
STATED ODDS 1:4
1 Shane Andrews .08 .25
2 Ray Durham .20 .50
3 Shawn Green .20 .50
4 Charles Johnson .20 .50
5 Chipper Jones .60 1.50
6 Esteban Loaiza .08 .25
7 Hideo Nomo .75 2.00
8 Jon Nunnally .08 .25
9 Alex Rodriguez 1.50 4.00
10 Julian Tavarez .08 .25

1995 Fleer Update Smooth Leather

COMPLETE SET (10) 10.00 25.00
STATED ODDS 1:5 JUMBO
1 Roberto Alomar .60 1.50
2 Barry Bonds 2.50 6.00
3 Ken Griffey Jr. 2.00 5.00
4 Marquis Grissom .40 1.00
5 Darren Lewis .20 .50
6 Kenny Lofton .40 1.00
7 Don Mattingly 2.50 6.00
8 Cal Ripken 3.00 8.00
9 Ivan Rodriguez .60 1.50
10 Matt Williams .40 1.00

1995 Fleer Update Soaring Stars

COMPLETE SET (10) 10.00 25.00
STATED ODDS 1:36
1 Moises Alou 1.00 2.50
2 Jason Bere .50 1.25
3 Jeff Conine 1.00 2.50
4 Cliff Floyd 1.00 2.50
5 Pat Hentgen .50 1.25
6 Kenny Lofton 1.00 2.50
7 Raul Mondesi 1.00 2.50
8 Mike Piazza 4.00 10.00
9 Tim Salmon 1.50 4.00

1996 Fleer

The 1996 Fleer baseball set consists of 600 standard-size cards issued in one series. Cards were issued in 11-card packs with a suggested retail price of $1.49. Borderless fronts are matte-finished and have full-color action shots with the player's name, team and position stamped in gold foil. Backs contain a biography and career stats on the top and a full-color head shot with a 1995 synopsis on the bottom. The matte finish on the cards was designed so collectors could have an easier surface for cards to be autographed. Fleer included in each pack a "Thanks a Million" scratch-off game card redeemable for instant-win prizes and a chance to bat for a million-dollar prize in a Major League park. Rookie Cards in this set include Matt Lawton and Mike Sweeney. A Cal Ripken promo was distributed to dealers and hobby media to preview the set.

COMPLETE SET (600) 20.00 50.00
1 Manny Alexander .10 .30
2 Brady Anderson .10 .30
3 Harold Baines .10 .30
4 Armando Benitez .10 .30
5 Bobby Bonilla .10 .30
6 Kevin Brown .10 .30
7 Scott Erickson .10 .30
8 Curtis Goodwin .10 .30
9 Jeffrey Hammonds .10 .30
10 Jimmy Haynes .10 .30
11 Chris Hoiles .10 .30
12 Doug Jones .10 .30
13 Rick Krivda .10 .30
14 Jeff Manto .10 .30
15 Ben McDonald .10 .30
16 Jamie Moyer .10 .30
17 Mike Mussina .20 .50
18 Jesse Orosco .10 .30
19 Rafael Palmeiro .20 .50
20 Cal Ripken 1.00 2.50
21 Rick Aguilera .10 .30
22 Luis Alicea .10 .30
23 Stan Belinda .10 .30
24 Jose Canseco .20 .50
25 Roger Clemens .60 1.50
26 Vaughn Eshelman .10 .30
27 Mike Greenwell .10 .30
28 Erik Hanson .10 .30
29 Dwayne Hosey .10 .30
30 Mike Macfarlane UER .10 .30
31 Tim Naehring .10 .30
32 Troy O'Leary .10 .30
33 Aaron Sele .10 .30
34 Zane Smith .10 .30
35 Jeff Suppan .10 .30
36 Lee Tinsley .10 .30
37 John Valentin .10 .30
38 Mo Vaughn .10 .30
39 Tim Wakefield .10 .30
40 Jim Abbott .20 .50
41 Brian Anderson .10 .30
42 Garret Anderson .10 .30
43 Chili Davis .10 .30
44 Gary DiSarcina .10 .30
45 Damion Easley .10 .30
46 Jim Edmonds .10 .30
47 Chuck Finley .10 .30
48 Todd Greene .10 .30
49 Mike Harkey .10 .30
50 Mike James .10 .30
51 Mark Langston .10 .30
52 Greg Myers .10 .30
53 Orlando Palmeiro .10 .30
54 Bob Patterson .10 .30
55 Troy Percival .10 .30
56 Tony Phillips .10 .30
57 Tim Salmon .20 .50
58 Lee Smith .10 .30
59 J.T. Snow .10 .30
60 Randy Velarde .10 .30
61 Wilson Alvarez .10 .30
62 Luis Andujar .10 .30
63 Jason Bere .10 .30
64 Ray Durham .10 .30
65 Alex Fernandez .10 .30
66 Ozzie Guillen .10 .30
67 Roberto Hernandez .10 .30
68 Lance Johnson .10 .30
69 Matt Karchner .10 .30
70 Ron Karkovice .10 .30
71 Norberto Martin .10 .30
72 Dave Martinez .10 .30
73 Kirk McCaskill .10 .30
74 Lyle Mouton .10 .30
75 Tim Raines .10 .30
76 Mike Sirotka RC .10 .30
77 Frank Thomas .30 .75
78 Larry Thomas .10 .30
79 Robin Ventura .10 .30
80 Sandy Alomar Jr. .10 .30
81 Paul Assenmacher .10 .30
82 Carlos Baerga .10 .30
83 Albert Belle .10 .30
84 Mark Clark .10 .30
85 Alan Embree .10 .30
86 Alvaro Espinoza .10 .30
87 Orel Hershiser .10 .30
88 Ken Hill .10 .30
89 Kenny Lofton .10 .30
90 Dennis Martinez .10 .30
91 Jose Mesa .10 .30
92 Eddie Murray .30 .75
93 Charles Nagy .10 .30
94 Chad Ogea .10 .30
95 Tony Pena .10 .30
96 Herb Perry .10 .30
97 Eric Plunk .10 .30
98 Jim Poole .10 .30
99 Manny Ramirez .20 .50
100 Paul Sorrento .10 .30
101 Julian Tavarez .10 .30

102 Jim Thome .20 .50
103 Omar Vizquel .20 .50
104 Dave Winfield .10 .30
105 Danny Bautista .10 .30
106 Joe Boever .10 .30
107 Chad Curtis .10 .30
108 John Doherty .10 .30
109 Cecil Fielder .10 .30
110 John Flaherty .10 .30
111 Travis Fryman .10 .30
112 Chris Gomez .10 .30
113 Bob Higginson .10 .30
114 Mark Lewis .10 .30
115 Jose Lima .10 .30
116 Felipe Lira .10 .30
117 Brian Maxcy .10 .30
118 C.J. Nitkowski .10 .30
119 Phil Plantier .10 .30
120 Clint Sodowsky .10 .30
121 Alan Trammell .10 .30
122 Lou Whitaker .10 .30
123 Kevin Appier .10 .30
124 Johnny Damon .20 .50
125 Gary Gaetti .10 .30
126 Tom Goodwin .10 .30
127 Tom Gordon .10 .30
128 Mark Gubicza .10 .30
129 Bob Hamelin .10 .30
130 David Howard .10 .30
131 Jason Jacome .10 .30
132 Wally Joyner .10 .30
133 Keith Lockhart .10 .30
134 Brent Mayne .10 .30
135 Jeff Montgomery .10 .30
136 Jon Nunnally .10 .30
137 Juan Samuel .10 .30
138 Mike Sweeney RC .40 1.00
139 Michael Tucker .10 .30
140 Joe Vitiello .10 .30
141 Ricky Bones .10 .30
142 Chuck Carr .10 .30
143 Jeff Cirillo .10 .30
144 Mike Fetters .10 .30
145 Darryl Hamilton .10 .30
146 David Hulse .10 .30
147 John Jaha .10 .30
148 Scott Karl .10 .30
149 Mark Kiefer .10 .30
150 Pat Listach .10 .30
151 Mark Loretta .10 .30
152 Mike Matheny .10 .30
153 Matt Mieske .10 .30
154 Dave Nilsson .10 .30
155 Joe Oliver .10 .30
156 Al Reyes .10 .30
157 Kevin Seitzer .10 .30
158 Steve Sparks .10 .30
159 B.J. Surhoff .10 .30
160 Jose Valentin .10 .30
161 Greg Vaughn .10 .30
162 Fernando Vina .10 .30
163 Rich Becker .10 .30
164 Ron Coomer .10 .30
165 Marty Cordova .10 .30
166 Chuck Knoblauch .10 .30
167 Matt Lawton RC .20 .50
168 Pat Meares .10 .30
169 Paul Molitor .10 .30
170 Pedro Munoz .10 .30
171 Jose Parra .10 .30
172 Kirby Puckett .30 .75
173 Brad Radke .10 .30
174 Jeff Reboulet .10 .30
175 Rich Robertson .10 .30
176 Frank Rodriguez .10 .30
177 Scott Stahoviak .10 .30
178 Dave Stevens .10 .30
179 Matt Walbeck .10 .30
180 Wade Boggs .20 .50
181 David Cone .10 .30
182 Tony Fernandez .10 .30
183 Joe Girardi .10 .30
184 Derek Jeter 1.25 3.00
185 Scott Kamieniecki .10 .30
186 Pat Kelly .10 .30
187 Jim Leyritz .10 .30
188 Tino Martinez .20 .50
189 Don Mattingly .75 2.00
190 Jack McDowell .10 .30
191 Jeff Nelson .10 .30
192 Paul O'Neill .20 .50
193 Melido Perez .10 .30
194 Andy Pettitte .20 .50
195 Mariano Rivera .60 1.50
196 Ruben Sierra .10 .30
197 Mike Stanley .10 .30
198 Darryl Strawberry .10 .30
199 John Wetteland .10 .30
200 Bob Wickman .10 .30
201 Bernie Williams .20 .50
202 Mark Acre .10 .30
203 Geronimo Berroa .10 .30
204 Mike Bordick .10 .30
205 Scott Brosius .10 .30
206 Dennis Eckersley .10 .30
207 Brent Gates .10 .30
208 Jason Giambi .10 .30
209 Rickey Henderson .30 .75
210 Jose Herrera .10 .30
211 Stan Javier .10 .30
212 Doug Johns .10 .30
213 Mark McGwire .75 2.00
214 Steve Ontiveros .10 .30
215 Craig Paquette .10 .30
216 Ariel Prieto .10 .30
217 Carlos Reyes .10 .30
218 Terry Steinbach .10 .30
219 Todd Stottlemyre .10 .30
220 Danny Tartabull .10 .30
221 Todd Van Poppel .10 .30
222 John Wasdin .10 .30
223 George Williams .10 .30
224 Steve Wojciechowski .10 .30
225 Rich Amaral .10 .30
226 Bobby Ayala .10 .30
227 Tim Belcher .10 .30
228 Andy Benes .10 .30
229 Chris Bosio .10 .30
230 Darren Bragg .10 .30
231 Jay Buhner .10 .30
232 Norm Charlton .10 .30
233 Vince Coleman .10 .30
234 Joey Cora .10 .30
235 Russ Davis .10 .30
236 Alex Diaz .10 .30
237 Felix Fermin .10 .30
238 Ken Griffey Jr. .60 1.50
239 Sterling Hitchcock .10 .30
240 Randy Johnson .30 .75
241 Edgar Martinez .20 .50
242 Bill Risley .10 .30
243 Alex Rodriguez .60 1.50
244 Luis Sojo .10 .30
245 Dan Wilson .10 .30
246 Bob Wolcott .10 .30
247 Will Clark .20 .50
248 Jeff Frye .10 .30
249 Benji Gil .10 .30
250 Juan Gonzalez .10 .30
251 Rusty Greer .10 .30
252 Kevin Gross .10 .30
253 Roger McDowell .10 .30
254 Mark McLemore .10 .30
255 Otis Nixon .10 .30
256 Luis Ortiz .10 .30
257 Mike Pagliarulo .10 .30
258 Dean Palmer .10 .30
259 Roger Pavlik .10 .30
260 Ivan Rodriguez .20 .50
261 Kenny Rogers .10 .30
262 Jeff Russell .10 .30
263 Mickey Tettleton .10 .30
264 Bob Tewksbury .10 .30
265 Dave Valle .10 .30
266 Matt Whiteside .10 .30
267 Roberto Alomar .20 .50
268 Joe Carter .10 .30
269 Tony Castillo .10 .30
270 Domingo Cedeno .10 .30
271 Tim Crabtree UER .10 .30
272 Carlos Delgado .10 .30
273 Alex Gonzalez .10 .30
274 Shawn Green .10 .30
275 Juan Guzman .10 .30
276 Pat Hentgen .10 .30
277 Al Leiter .10 .30
278 Sandy Martinez .10 .30
279 Paul Menhart .10 .30
280 John Olerud .10 .30
281 Paul Quantrill .10 .30
282 Ken Robinson .10 .30
283 Ed Sprague .10 .30
284 Mike Timlin .10 .30
285 Steve Avery .10 .30
286 Rafael Belliard .10 .30
287 Jeff Blauser .10 .30
288 Pedro Borbon .10 .30
289 Brad Clontz .10 .30
290 Mike Devereaux .10 .30
291 Tom Glavine .20 .50
292 Marquis Grissom .10 .30
293 Chipper Jones .30 .75
294 David Justice .10 .30
295 Mike Kelly .10 .30
296 Ryan Klesko .10 .30
297 Mark Lemke .10 .30
298 Javier Lopez .10 .30
299 Greg Maddux .50 1.25
300 Fred McGriff .20 .50
301 Greg McMichael .10 .30
302 Kent Mercker .10 .30
303 Mike Mordecai .10 .30
304 Charlie O'Brien .10 .30
305 Eduardo Perez .10 .30
306 Luis Polonia .10 .30
307 Jason Schmidt .20 .50
308 John Smoltz .20 .50
309 Terrell Wade .10 .30
310 Mark Wohlers .10 .30
311 Scott Bullett .10 .30
312 Jim Bullinger .10 .30
313 Larry Casian .10 .30
314 Frank Castillo .10 .30
315 Shawon Dunston .10 .30
316 Kevin Foster .10 .30
317 Matt Franco RC .10 .30
318 Luis Gonzalez .10 .30
319 Mark Grace .20 .50
320 Jose Hernandez .10 .30
321 Mike Hubbard .10 .30
322 Brian McRae .10 .30
323 Randy Myers .10 .30
324 Jaime Navarro .10 .30
325 Mark Parent .10 .30
326 Mike Perez .10 .30
327 Rey Sanchez .10 .30
328 Ryne Sandberg .50 1.25
329 Scott Servais .10 .30
330 Sammy Sosa .30 .75
331 Ozzie Timmons .10 .30
332 Steve Trachsel .10 .30
333 Todd Zeile .10 .30
334 Bret Boone .10 .30
335 Jeff Branson .10 .30
336 Jeff Brantley .10 .30
337 Dave Burba .10 .30
338 Hector Carrasco .10 .30
339 Mariano Duncan .10 .30
340 Ron Gant .10 .30
341 Lenny Harris .10 .30
342 Xavier Hernandez .10 .30
343 Thomas Howard .10 .30
344 Mike Jackson .10 .30
345 Barry Larkin .20 .50
346 Darren Lewis .10 .30
347 Hal Morris .10 .30
348 Eric Owens .10 .30
349 Mark Portugal .10 .30
350 Jose Rijo .10 .30
351 Reggie Sanders .10 .30
352 Benito Santiago .10 .30
353 Pete Schourek .10 .30
354 John Smiley .10 .30
355 Eddie Taubensee .10 .30
356 Jerome Walton .10 .30
357 David Wells .10 .30
358 Roger Bailey .10 .30
359 Jason Bates .10 .30
360 Dante Bichette .10 .30
361 Ellis Burks .10 .30
362 Vinny Castilla .10 .30
363 Andres Galarraga .10 .30
364 Darren Holmes .10 .30
365 Mike Kingery .10 .30
366 Curt Leskanic .10 .30
367 Quinton McCracken .10 .30
368 Mike Munoz .10 .30
369 David Nied .10 .30
370 Steve Reed .10 .30
371 Bryan Rekar .10 .30
372 Kevin Ritz .10 .30
373 Bruce Ruffin .10 .30
374 Bret Saberhagen .10 .30
375 Bill Swift .10 .30
376 John Vander Wal .10 .30
377 Larry Walker .10 .30
378 Walt Weiss .10 .30
379 Eric Young .10 .30
380 Kurt Abbott .10 .30
381 Alex Arias .10 .30
382 Jerry Browne .10 .30
383 John Burkett .10 .30
384 Greg Colbrunn .10 .30
385 Jeff Conine .10 .30
386 Andre Dawson .10 .30
387 Chris Hammond .10 .30
388 Charles Johnson .10 .30
389 Terry Mathews .10 .30
390 Robb Nen .10 .30
391 Joe Orsulak .10 .30
392 Terry Pendleton .10 .30
393 Pat Rapp .10 .30
394 Gary Sheffield .10 .30
395 Jesus Tavarez .10 .30
396 Marc Valdes .10 .30
397 Quilvio Veras .10 .30
398 Randy Veres .10 .30
399 Devon White .10 .30
400 Jeff Bagwell .20 .50
401 Derek Bell .10 .30
402 Craig Biggio .20 .50
403 John Cangelosi .10 .30
404 Jim Dougherty .10 .30
405 Doug Drabek .10 .30
406 Tony Eusebio .10 .30
407 Ricky Gutierrez .10 .30
408 Mike Hampton .10 .30
409 Dean Hartgraves .10 .30
410 John Hudek .10 .30
411 Brian Hunter .10 .30
412 Todd Jones .10 .30
413 Darryl Kile .10 .30
414 Dave Magadan .10 .30
415 Derrick May .10 .30
416 Orlando Miller .10 .30
417 James Mouton .10 .30
418 Shane Reynolds .10 .30
419 Greg Swindell .10 .30
420 Jeff Tabaka .10 .30
421 Dave Veres .10 .30
422 Billy Wagner .10 .30
423 Donne Wall .10 .30
424 Rick Wilkins .10 .30
425 Billy Ashley .10 .30
426 Mike Blowers .10 .30
427 Brett Butler .10 .30
428 Tom Candiotti .10 .30
429 Juan Castro .10 .30
430 John Cummings .10 .30
431 Delino DeShields .10 .30
432 Joey Eischen .10 .30
433 Chad Fonville .10 .30
434 Greg Gagne .10 .30
435 Dave Hansen .10 .30
436 Carlos Hernandez .10 .30
437 Todd Hollandsworth .10 .30
438 Eric Karros .10 .30
439 Roberto Kelly .10 .30
440 Ramon Martinez .10 .30
441 Raul Mondesi .10 .30
442 Hideo Nomo .30 .75
443 Antonio Osuna .10 .30
444 Chan Ho Park .10 .30
445 Mike Piazza .50 1.25
446 Felix Rodriguez .10 .30
447 Kevin Tapani .10 .30
448 Ismael Valdes .10 .30
449 Todd Worrell .10 .30
450 Moises Alou .10 .30
451 Shane Andrews .10 .30
452 Yamil Benitez .10 .30
453 Sean Berry .10 .30
454 Wil Cordero .10 .30
455 Jeff Fassero .10 .30
456 Darrin Fletcher .10 .30
457 Cliff Floyd .10 .30
458 Mark Grudzielanek .10 .30
459 Gil Heredia .10 .30
460 Tim Laker .10 .30
461 Mike Lansing .10 .30
462 Pedro Martinez .20 .50
463 Carlos Perez .10 .30
464 Curtis Pride .10 .30
465 Mel Rojas .10 .30
466 Kirk Rueter .10 .30
467 F.P. Santangelo .10 .30
468 Tim Scott .10 .30
469 David Segui .10 .30
470 Tony Tarasco .10 .30
471 Rondell White .10 .30
472 Edgardo Alfonzo .10 .30
473 Tim Bogar .10 .30
474 Rico Brogna .10 .30
475 Damon Buford .10 .30
476 Paul Byrd .10 .30
477 Carl Everett .10 .30
478 John Franco .10 .30
479 Todd Hundley .10 .30
480 Butch Huskey .10 .30
481 Jason Isringhausen .10 .30
482 Bobby Jones .10 .30
483 Chris Jones .10 .30
484 Jeff Kent .10 .30
485 Dave Mlicki .10 .30
486 Robert Person .10 .30
487 Bill Pulsipher .10 .30
488 Kelly Stinnett .10 .30
489 Ryan Thompson .10 .30
490 Jose Vizcaino .10 .30
491 Howard Battle .10 .30
492 Toby Borland .10 .30
493 Ricky Bottalico .10 .30
494 Darren Daulton .10 .30
495 Lenny Dykstra .10 .30
496 Jim Eisenreich .10 .30
497 Sid Fernandez .10 .30
498 Tyler Green .10 .30
499 Charlie Hayes .10 .30
500 Gregg Jefferies .10 .30
501 Kevin Jordan .10 .30
502 Tony Longmire .10 .30
503 Tom Marsh .10 .30
504 Michael Mimbs .10 .30
505 Mickey Morandini .10 .30
506 Gene Schall .10 .30
507 Curt Schilling .10 .30
508 Heathcliff Slocumb .10 .30
509 Kevin Stocker .10 .30
510 Andy Van Slyke .20 .50
511 Lenny Webster .10 .30
512 Mark Whiten .10 .30
513 Mike Williams .10 .30
514 Jay Bell .10 .30
515 Jacob Brumfield .10 .30
516 Jason Christiansen .10 .30
517 Dave Clark .10 .30
518 Midre Cummings .10 .30
519 Angelo Encarnacion .10 .30
520 John Ericks .10 .30
521 Carlos Garcia .10 .30
522 Mark Johnson .10 .30
523 Jeff King .10 .30
524 Nelson Liriano .10 .30
525 Esteban Loaiza .10 .30
526 Al Martin .10 .30
527 Orlando Merced .10 .30
528 Dan Miceli .10 .30
529 Ramon Morel .10 .30
530 Denny Neagle .10 .30
531 Steve Parris .10 .30
532 Dan Plesac .10 .30
533 Don Slaught .10 .30
534 Paul Wagner .10 .30
535 John Wehner .10 .30
536 Kevin Young .10 .30
537 Allen Battle .10 .30
538 David Bell .10 .30
539 Alan Benes .10 .30
540 Scott Cooper .10 .30
541 Tripp Cromer .10 .30
542 Tony Fossas .10 .30
543 Bernard Gilkey .10 .30
544 Tom Henke .10 .30
545 Brian Jordan .10 .30
546 Ray Lankford .10 .30
547 John Mabry .10 .30
548 T.J. Mathews .10 .30
549 Mike Morgan .10 .30
550 Jose Oliva .10 .30
551 Jose Oquendo .10 .30
552 Donovan Osborne .10 .30
553 Tom Pagnozzi .10 .30
554 Mark Petkovsek .10 .30
555 Danny Sheaffer .10 .30
556 Ozzie Smith .50 1.25
557 Mark Sweeney .10 .30
558 Allen Watson .10 .30
559 Andy Ashby .10 .30
560 Brad Ausmus .10 .30
561 Willie Blair .10 .30
562 Ken Caminiti .10 .30
563 Andujar Cedeno .10 .30
564 Glenn Dishman .10 .30
565 Steve Finley .10 .30
566 Bryce Florie .10 .30
567 Tony Gwynn .40 1.00
568 Joey Hamilton .10 .30
569 Dustin Hermanson UER .10 .30
570 Trevor Hoffman .10 .30
571 Brian Johnson .10 .30
572 Marc Kroon .10 .30
573 Scott Livingstone .10 .30
574 Marc Newfield .10 .30
575 Melvin Nieves .10 .30
576 Jody Reed .10 .30
577 Bip Roberts .10 .30
578 Scott Sanders .10 .30
579 Fernando Valenzuela .10 .30
580 Eddie Williams .10 .30
581 Rod Beck .10 .30
582 Marvin Benard RC .10 .30
583 Barry Bonds .75 2.00
584 Jamie Brewington RC .10 .30
585 Mark Carreon .10 .30
586 Royce Clayton .10 .30
587 Shawn Estes .10 .30
588 Glenallen Hill .10 .30
589 Mark Leiter .10 .30
590 Kirt Manwaring .10 .30
591 David McCarty .10 .30
592 Terry Mulholland .10 .30
593 John Patterson .10 .30
594 J.R. Phillips .10 .30
595 Deion Sanders .20 .50
596 Steve Scarsone .10 .30
597 Robby Thompson .10 .30
598 Sergio Valdez .10 .30
599 William Van Landingham .10 .30
600 Matt Williams .10 .30
P20 Cal Ripken Promo 1.25 3.00

1996 Fleer Tiffany

COMPLETE SET (600) 75.00 150.00
*STARS: 2X TO 5X BASIC CARDS
*ROOKIES: 4X TO 10X BASIC CARDS
ONE PER PACK

1996 Fleer Checklists

COMPLETE SET (10) 1.50 4.00
STATED ODDS 1:6
1 Barry Bonds .40 1.00
2 Ken Griffey Jr. .30 .75
3 Chipper Jones .15 .40
4 Greg Maddux .25 .60
5 Mike Piazza .25 .60
6 Manny Ramirez .08 .25
7 Cal Ripken .50 1.25
8 Frank Thomas .15 .40
9 Mo Vaughn .05 .15
10 Matt Williams .05 .15

1996 Fleer Golden Memories

COMPLETE SET (10) 3.00 8.00
STATED ODDS 1:10
1 Albert Belle .15 .40
2 B.Bonds S.Sosa .40 1.00
3 Greg Maddux .60 1.50
4 Edgar Martinez .25 .60
5 Ramon Martinez .15 .40
6 Mark McGwire 1.00 2.50
7 Eddie Murray .40 1.00
8 Cal Ripken 1.25 3.00
9 Frank Thomas .40 1.00
10 A.Trammell L.Whitaker .15 .40

1996 Fleer Lumber Company

COMPLETE SET (12) 10.00 25.00
STATED ODDS 1:9 RETAIL
1 Albert Belle .40 1.00
2 Dante Bichette .40 1.00
3 Barry Bonds 2.50 6.00
4 Ken Griffey Jr. 2.00 5.00
5 Mark McGwire 2.50 6.00
6 Mike Piazza 1.50 4.00
7 Manny Ramirez .60 1.50
8 Tim Salmon .60 1.50
9 Sammy Sosa 1.00 2.50
10 Frank Thomas 1.00 2.50
11 Mo Vaughn .40 1.00
12 Matt Williams .40 1.00

1996 Fleer Postseason Glory

COMPLETE SET (5) .75 2.00
STATED ODDS 1:5
1 Tom Glavine .08 .25
2 Ken Griffey Jr. .30 .75
3 Orel Hershiser .05 .15
4 Randy Johnson .15 .40
5 Jim Thome .08 .25

1996 Fleer Prospects

COMPLETE SET (10) 1.50 4.00
STATED ODDS 1:6
1 Yamil Benitez .20 .50
2 Roger Cedeno .20 .50
3 Tony Clark .20 .50
4 Micah Franklin .20 .50
5 Karim Garcia .20 .50
6 Todd Greene .20 .50
7 Alex Ochoa .20 .50
8 Ruben Rivera .20 .50
9 Chris Snopek .20 .50
10 Shannon Stewart .40 1.00

1996 Fleer Road Warriors

COMPLETE SET (10) 5.00 12.00
STATED ODDS 1:13
1 Derek Bell .20 .50
2 Tony Gwynn .60 1.50
3 Greg Maddux .75 2.00
4 Mark McGwire 1.25 3.00
5 Mike Piazza .75 2.00
6 Manny Ramirez .30 .75
7 Tim Salmon .30 .75
8 Frank Thomas .50 1.25
9 Mo Vaughn .20 .50
10 Matt Williams .20 .50

1996 Fleer Rookie Sensations

COMPLETE SET (15) 6.00 15.00
STATED ODDS 1:11
1 Garret Anderson .50 1.25
2 Marty Cordova .50 1.25
3 Johnny Damon .75 2.00
4 Ray Durham .50 1.25
5 Carl Everett .50 1.25
6 Shawn Green .50 1.25
7 Brian L.Hunter .50 1.25
8 Jason Isringhausen .50 1.25
9 Charles Johnson .50 1.25
10 Chipper Jones 1.25 3.00
11 John Mabry .50 1.25
12 Hideo Nomo 1.25 3.00
13 Troy Percival .50 1.25
14 Andy Pettitte .75 2.00
15 Quilvio Veras .50 1.25

1996 Fleer Smoke 'n Heat

COMPLETE SET (10) 2.50 6.00
STATED ODDS 1:9
1 Kevin Appier .20 .50
2 Roger Clemens 1.00 2.50
3 David Cone .20 .50
4 Chuck Finley .20 .50
5 Randy Johnson .50 1.25
6 Greg Maddux .75 2.00
7 Pedro Martinez .30 .75
8 Hideo Nomo .50 1.25
9 John Smoltz .30 .75
10 Todd Stottlemyre .20 .50

1996 Fleer Team Leaders

COMPLETE SET (28) 25.00 60.00
STATED ODDS 1:9 HOBBY
1 Cal Ripken 4.00 10.00
2 Mo Vaughn .50 1.25
3 Jim Edmonds .50 1.25
4 Frank Thomas 1.25 3.00
5 Kenny Lofton .50 1.25
6 Travis Fryman .50 1.25
7 Gary Gaetti .50 1.25
8 B.J. Surhoff .50 1.25
9 Kirby Puckett 1.25 3.00
10 Don Mattingly 3.00 8.00
11 Mark McGwire 3.00 8.00
12 Ken Griffey Jr. 2.50 6.00
13 Juan Gonzalez .50 1.25
14 Joe Carter .50 1.25
15 Greg Maddux 2.00 5.00
16 Sammy Sosa 1.25 3.00
17 Barry Larkin .75 2.00
18 Dante Bichette .50 1.25
19 Jeff Conine .50 1.25
20 Jeff Bagwell .75 2.00
21 Mike Piazza 2.00 5.00
22 Rondell White .50 1.25
23 Rico Brogna .50 1.25
24 Darren Daulton .50 1.25
25 Jeff King .50 1.25
26 Ray Lankford .50 1.25
27 Tony Gwynn 1.50 4.00
28 Barry Bonds 3.00 8.00

1996 Fleer Tomorrow's Legends

COMPLETE SET (10) 4.00 10.00
STATED ODDS 1:13
1 Garret Anderson .30 .75
2 Jim Edmonds .30 .75
3 Brian L.Hunter .30 .75
4 Jason Isringhausen .30 .75
5 Charles Johnson .30 .75
6 Chipper Jones .75 2.00
7 Ryan Klesko .30 .75
8 Hideo Nomo .75 2.00
9 Manny Ramirez .50 1.25
10 Rondell White .30 .75

1996 Fleer Zone

COMPLETE SET (12) 15.00 40.00
STATED ODDS 1:90
1 Albert Belle 1.00 2.50
2 Barry Bonds 4.00 10.00
3 Ken Griffey Jr. 5.00 12.00
4 Tony Gwynn 2.50 6.00
5 Randy Johnson 2.50 6.00
6 Kenny Lofton 1.00 2.50
7 Greg Maddux 4.00 10.00
8 Edgar Martinez 1.50 4.00
9 Mike Piazza 2.50 6.00
10 Frank Thomas 2.50 6.00
11 Mo Vaughn 1.00 2.50
12 Matt Williams 1.00 2.50

1996 Fleer Update

The 1996 Fleer Update set was issued in one series totalling 250 cards. The 11-card packs retailed for $1.49 each. The fronts feature color action player photos. The backs carry complete player stats and a "Did you know?" fact. The cards are grouped alphabetically within teams and checklisted below alphabetically according to teams for each league with AL preceding NL. The set contains the subset: Encore (U211-U245). Notable Rookie Cards include Tony Batista, Mike Cameron, Matt Mantei and Chris Singleton.

COMPLETE SET (250) 12.50 30.00
U1 Roberto Alomar .20 .50
U2 Mike Devereaux .10 .30
U3 Scott McClain RC .10 .30
U4 Roger McDowell .10 .30
U5 Kent Mercker .10 .30
U6 Jimmy Myers RC .10 .30
U7 Randy Myers .10 .30
U8 B.J. Surhoff .10 .30
U9 Tony Tarasco .10 .30
U10 David Wells .10 .30
U11 Wil Cordero .10 .30
U12 Tom Gordon .10 .30
U13 Reggie Jefferson .10 .30
U14 Jose Malave .10 .30
U15 Kevin Mitchell .10 .30
U16 Jamie Moyer .10 .30
U17 Heathcliff Slocumb .10 .30
U18 Mike Stanley .10 .30
U19 George Arias .10 .30
U20 Jorge Fabregas .10 .30
U21 Don Slaught .10 .30
U22 Randy Velarde .10 .30
U23 Harold Baines .10 .30
U24 Mike Cameron RC .30 .75
U25 Darren Lewis .10 .30
U26 Tony Phillips .10 .30
U27 Bill Simas .10 .30
U28 Chris Snopek .10 .30
U29 Kevin Tapani .10 .30
U30 Danny Tartabull .10 .30
U31 Julio Franco .10 .30
U32 Jack McDowell .10 .30
U33 Kimera Bartee .10 .30
U34 Mark Lewis .10 .30
U35 Melvin Nieves .10 .30
U36 Mark Parent .10 .30
U37 Eddie Williams .10 .30
U38 Tim Belcher .10 .30
U39 Sal Fasano .10 .30
U40 Chris Haney .10 .30
U41 Mike Macfarlane .10 .30
U42 Jose Offerman .10 .30
U43 Joe Randa .10 .30
U44 Bip Roberts .10 .30
U45 Chuck Carr .10 .30
U46 Bobby Hughes .10 .30
U47 Graeme Lloyd .10 .30
U48 Ben McDonald .10 .30
U49 Kevin Wickander .10 .30
U50 Rick Aguilera .10 .30
U51 Mike Durant .10 .30
U52 Chip Hale .10 .30
U53 LaTroy Hawkins .10 .30
U54 Dave Hollins .10 .30
U55 Roberto Kelly .10 .30
U56 Paul Molitor .10 .30
U57 Dan Naulty RC .10 .30
U58 Mariano Duncan .10 .30
U59 Andy Fox .10 .30
U60 Joe Girardi .10 .30
U61 Dwight Gooden .10 .30
U62 Jimmy Key .10 .30
U63 Matt Luke .10 .30
U64 Tino Martinez .20 .50
U65 Jeff Nelson .10 .30
U66 Tim Raines .10 .30
U67 Ruben Rivera .10 .30
U68 Kenny Rogers .10 .30
U69 Gerald Williams .10 .30
U70 Tony Batista RC .30 .75
U71 Allen Battle .10 .30
U72 Jim Corsi .10 .30
U73 Steve Cox .10 .30
U74 Pedro Munoz .10 .30
U75 Phil Plantier .10 .30
U76 Scott Spiezio .10 .30
U77 Ernie Young .10 .30
U78 Russ Davis .10 .30
U79 Sterling Hitchcock .10 .30
U80 Edwin Hurtado .10 .30
U81 Raul Ibanez RC 1.00 2.50
U82 Mike Jackson .10 .30
U83 Ricky Jordan .10 .30
U84 Paul Sorrento .10 .30
U85 Doug Strange .10 .30
U86 Mark Brandenberg RC .10 .30
U87 Damon Buford .10 .30
U88 Kevin Elster .10 .30
U89 Darryl Hamilton .10 .30
U90 Ken Hill .10 .30
U91 Ed Vosberg .10 .30
U92 Craig Worthington .10 .30
U93 Tilson Brito RC .10 .30
U94 Giovanni Carrara RC .10 .30
U95 Felipe Crespo .10 .30
U96 Erik Hanson .10 .30
U97 Marty Janzen RC .10 .30
U98 Otis Nixon .10 .30
U99 Charlie O'Brien .10 .30
U100 Robert Perez .10 .30
U101 Paul Quantrill .10 .30
U102 Bill Risley .10 .30
U103 Juan Samuel .10 .30
U104 Jermaine Dye .10 .30
U105 Wonderful Monds RC .10 .30
U106 Dwight Smith .10 .30
U107 Jerome Walton .10 .30
U108 Terry Adams .10 .30
U109 Leo Gomez .10 .30
U110 Robin Jennings .10 .30
U111 Doug Jones .10 .30
U112 Brooks Kieschnick .10 .30
U113 Dave Magadan .10 .30
U114 Jason Maxwell RC .10 .30
U115 Rodney Myers RC .10 .30
U116 Eric Anthony .10 .30
U117 Vince Coleman .10 .30
U118 Eric Davis .10 .30
U119 Steve Gibralter .10 .30
U120 Curtis Goodwin .10 .30
U121 Willie Greene .10 .30
U122 Mike Kelly .10 .30
U123 Marcus Moore .10 .30
U124 Chad Mottola .10 .30
U125 Chris Sabo .10 .30
U126 Roger Salkeld .10 .30
U127 Pedro Castellano .10 .30
U128 Trenidad Hubbard .10 .30
U129 Jayhawk Owens .10 .30
U130 Jeff Reed .10 .30
U131 Kevin Brown .10 .30
U132 Al Leiter .10 .30
U133 Matt Mantei RC .20 .50
U134 Dave Weathers .10 .30
U135 Devon White .10 .30
U136 Bob Abreu .30 .75
U137 Sean Berry .10 .30
U138 Doug Brocail .10 .30
U139 Richard Hidalgo .10 .30
U140 Alvin Morman .10 .30
U141 Mike Blowers .10 .30
U142 Roger Cedeno .10 .30
U143 Greg Gagne .10 .30
U144 Karim Garcia .10 .30
U145 Wilton Guerrero RC .10 .30
U146 Israel Alcantara RC .10 .30
U147 Omar Daal .10 .30
U148 Ryan McGuire .10 .30
U149 Sherman Obando .10 .30
U150 Jose Paniagua .10 .30
U151 Henry Rodriguez .10 .30
U152 Andy Stankiewicz .10 .30
U153 Dave Veres .10 .30
U154 Juan Acevedo .10 .30
U155 Mark Clark .10 .30
U156 Bernard Gilkey .10 .30
U157 Pete Harnisch .10 .30
U158 Lance Johnson .10 .30
U159 Brent Mayne .10 .30
U160 Rey Ordonez .10 .30
U161 Kevin Roberson .10 .30
U162 Paul Wilson .10 .30
U163 David Doster RC .10 .30
U164 Mike Grace RC .10 .30
U165 Rich Hunter RC .10 .30
U166 Pete Incaviglia .10 .30
U167 Mike Lieberthal .10 .30
U168 Terry Mulholland .10 .30
U169 Ken Ryan .10 .30
U170 Benito Santiago .10 .30
U171 Kevin Sefcik RC .10 .30
U172 Lee Tinsley .10 .30
U173 Todd Zeile .10 .30
U174 Francisco Cordova RC .20 .50
U175 Danny Darwin .10 .30
U176 Charlie Hayes .10 .30
U177 Jason Kendall .10 .30
U178 Mike Kingery .10 .30
U179 Jon Lieber .10 .30
U180 Zane Smith .10 .30
U181 Luis Alicea .10 .30
U182 Cory Bailey .10 .30
U183 Andy Benes .10 .30
U184 Pat Borders .10 .30
U185 Mike Busby RC .10 .30
U186 Royce Clayton .10 .30
U187 Dennis Eckersley .10 .30
U188 Gary Gaetti .10 .30
U189 Ron Gant .10 .30
U190 Aaron Holbert .10 .30
U191 Willie McGee .10 .30
U192 Miguel Mejia RC .10 .30

- U193 Jeff Parrett .10 .30
- U194 Todd Stottlemyre .10 .30
- U195 Sean Bergman .10 .30
- U196 Archi Cianfrocco .10 .30
- U197 Rickey Henderson .30 .75
- U198 Wally Joyner .10 .30
- U199 Craig Shipley .10 .30
- U200 Bob Tewksbury .10 .30
- U201 Tim Worrell .10 .30
- U202 Rich Aurilia RC .20 .50
- U203 Doug Creek .10 .30
- U204 Shawon Dunston .10 .30
- U205 Osvaldo Fernandez RC .10 .30
- U206 Mark Gardner .10 .30
- U207 Stan Javier .10 .30
- U208 Marcus Jensen .10 .30
- U209 Chris Singleton RC .20 .50
- U210 Allen Watson .10 .30
- U211 Jeff Bagwell ENC .20 .50
- U212 Derek Bell ENC .10 .30
- U213 Albert Belle ENC .10 .30
- U214 Wade Boggs ENC .20 .50
- U215 Barry Bonds ENC .75 2.00
- U216 Jose Canseco ENC .20 .50
- U217 Marty Cordova ENC .10 .30
- U218 Jim Edmonds ENC .10 .30
- U219 Cecil Fielder ENC .10 .30
- U220 Andres Galarraga ENC .10 .30
- U221 Juan Gonzalez ENC .10 .30
- U222 Mark Grace ENC .20 .50
- U223 Ken Griffey Jr. ENC .60 1.50
- U224 Tony Gwynn ENC .40 1.00
- U225 Jason Isringhausen ENC .10 .30
- U226 Derek Jeter ENC .75 2.00
- U227 Randy Johnson ENC .30 .75
- U228 Chipper Jones ENC .30 .75
- U229 Ryan Klesko ENC .10 .30
- U230 Barry Larkin ENC .20 .50
- U231 Kenny Lofton ENC .10 .30
- U232 Greg Maddux ENC .50 1.25
- U233 Raul Mondesi ENC .10 .30
- U234 Hideo Nomo ENC .30 .75
- U235 Mike Piazza ENC .50 1.25
- U236 Manny Ramirez ENC .20 .50
- U237 Cal Ripken ENC .60 1.50
- U238 Tim Salmon ENC .20 .50
- U239 Ryne Sandberg ENC .50 1.25
- U240 Reggie Sanders ENC .10 .30
- U241 Gary Sheffield ENC .10 .30
- U242 Sammy Sosa ENC .30 .75
- U243 Frank Thomas ENC .30 .75
- U244 Mo Vaughn ENC .10 .30
- U245 Matt Williams ENC .10 .30
- U246 Barry Bonds CL .40 1.00
- U247 Ken Griffey Jr. CL .40 1.00
- U248 Rey Ordonez CL .10 .30
- U249 Ryne Sandberg CL .30 .75
- U250 Frank Thomas CL .20 .50

1996 Fleer Update Tiffany

COMPLETE SET (250) 60.00 120.00
*STARS: 1.25X TO 3X BASIC CARDS
*ROOKIES: 2X TO 5X BASIC CARDS
ONE TIFFANY PER PACK

1996 Fleer Update Diamond Tribute

COMPLETE SET (10) 75.00 150.00
STATED ODDS 1:100

- 1 Wade Boggs 2.50 6.00
- 2 Barry Bonds 10.00 25.00
- 3 Ken Griffey Jr. 8.00 20.00
- 4 Tony Gwynn 5.00 12.00
- 5 Rickey Henderson 4.00 10.00
- 6 Greg Maddux 6.00 15.00
- 7 Eddie Murray 4.00 10.00
- 8 Cal Ripken 12.50 30.00
- 9 Ozzie Smith 6.00 15.00
- 10 Frank Thomas 4.00 10.00

1996 Fleer Update Headliners

COMPLETE SET (20) 15.00 40.00
STATED ODDS 1:5 RETAIL

- 1 Roberto Alomar .50 1.25
- 2 Jeff Bagwell .50 1.25
- 3 Albert Belle .30 .75
- 4 Barry Bonds 2.00 5.00
- 5 Cecil Fielder .30 .75
- 6 Juan Gonzalez .30 .75
- 7 Ken Griffey Jr. 1.50 4.00
- 8 Tony Gwynn 1.00 2.50
- 9 Randy Johnson .75 2.00
- 10 Chipper Jones .75 2.00
- 11 Ryan Klesko .30 .75
- 12 Kenny Lofton .30 .75
- 13 Greg Maddux 1.25 3.00
- 14 Hideo Nomo .75 2.00
- 15 Mike Piazza 1.25 3.00
- 16 Manny Ramirez .50 1.25
- 17 Cal Ripken 2.50 6.00
- 18 Tim Salmon .50 1.25
- 19 Frank Thomas .75 2.00
- 20 Matt Williams .30 .75

1996 Fleer Update New Horizons

COMPLETE SET (20) 6.00 15.00
STATED ODDS 1:5 HOBBY

- 1 Bob Abreu .60 1.50
- 2 George Arias .20 .50
- 3 Tony Batista .40 1.00
- 4 Steve Cox .20 .50
- 5 Jermaine Dye .20 .50
- 6 Andy Fox .20 .50
- 7 Mike Grace .20 .50
- 8 Todd Greene .20 .50
- 9 Wilton Guerrero .20 .50
- 10 Richard Hidalgo .20 .50
- 11 Raul Ibanez .50 1.25
- 12 Robin Jennings .20 .50
- 13 Marcus Jensen .20 .50
- 14 Jason Kendall .20 .50
- 15 Jason Maxwell .20 .50
- 16 Ryan McGuire .20 .50
- 17 Miguel Mejia .20 .50
- 18 Wonderful Monds .20 .50
- 19 Rey Ordonez .20 .50
- 20 Paul Wilson .20 .50

1996 Fleer Update Smooth Leather

COMPLETE SET (10) 4.00 10.00
STATED ODDS 1:5

- 1 Roberto Alomar .25 .60
- 2 Barry Bonds 1.00 2.50
- 3 Will Clark .25 .60
- 4 Ken Griffey Jr. .75 2.00
- 5 Kenny Lofton .15 .40
- 6 Greg Maddux .60 1.50
- 7 Raul Mondesi .15 .40
- 8 Rey Ordonez .15 .40
- 9 Cal Ripken 1.25 3.00
- 10 Matt Williams .15 .40

1996 Fleer Update Soaring Stars

COMPLETE SET (10) 10.00 25.00
STATED ODDS 1:11

- 1 Jeff Bagwell .50 1.25
- 2 Barry Bonds 2.00 5.00
- 3 Juan Gonzalez .30 .75
- 4 Ken Griffey Jr. 1.50 4.00
- 5 Chipper Jones .75 2.00
- 6 Greg Maddux 1.25 3.00
- 7 Mike Piazza 1.25 3.00
- 8 Manny Ramirez .50 1.25
- 9 Frank Thomas .75 2.00
- 10 Matt Williams .30 .75

1997 Fleer

The 1997 Fleer set was issued in two series totaling 761 cards and distributed in 10-card packs with a suggested retail price of $1.49. The fronts feature color action player photos with a matte finish and gold foil printing. The backs carry another player photo with player information and career statistics. Cards 491-500 are a Checklist subset of Series one and feature black-and-white or sepia tone photos of big-name players. Series two contains the following subsets: Encore (696-720) which are redesigned cards of the big-name players from Series one, and Checklists (721-748). Cards 749 and 750 are expansion team logo cards with the insert checklists on the backs. Many dealers believe that cards numbered 751-761 were shortprinted. An Andruw Jones autographed Circa card numbered to 200 was also randomly inserted into packs. Rookie Cards in this set include Jose Cruz Jr., Brian Giles and Fernando Tatis.

COMPLETE SET (761) 30.00 80.00
COMPLETE SERIES 1 (500) 12.50 30.00
COMPLETE SERIES 2 (261) 15.00 40.00
COMMON CARD (1-750) .10 .30
COMMON CARD (751-761) .20 .50
751-761 BELIEVED TO BE SHORT-PRINTED
A.JONES CIRCA AU RANDOM IN PACKS
SUBSET CARDS HALF VALUE OF BASE CARDS

- 1 Roberto Alomar .20 .50
- 2 Brady Anderson .10 .30
- 3 Bobby Bonilla .10 .30
- 4 Rocky Coppinger .10 .30
- 5 Cesar Devarez .10 .30
- 6 Scott Erickson .10 .30
- 7 Jeffrey Hammonds .10 .30
- 8 Chris Hoiles .10 .30
- 9 Eddie Murray .30 .75
- 10 Mike Mussina .20 .50
- 11 Randy Myers .10 .30
- 12 Rafael Palmeiro .20 .50
- 13 Cal Ripken 1.00 2.50
- 14 B.J. Surhoff .10 .30
- 15 David Wells .10 .30
- 16 Todd Zeile .10 .30
- 17 Darren Bragg .10 .30
- 18 Jose Canseco .20 .50
- 19 Roger Clemens .60 1.50
- 20 Wil Cordero .10 .30
- 21 Jeff Frye .10 .30
- 22 Nomar Garciaparra .50 1.25
- 23 Tom Gordon .10 .30
- 24 Mike Greenwell .10 .30
- 25 Reggie Jefferson .10 .30
- 26 Jose Malave .10 .30
- 27 Tim Naehring .10 .30
- 28 Troy O'Leary .10 .30
- 29 Heathcliff Slocumb .10 .30
- 30 Mike Stanley .10 .30
- 31 John Valentin .10 .30
- 32 Mo Vaughn .10 .30
- 33 Tim Wakefield .10 .30
- 34 Garret Anderson .10 .30
- 35 George Arias .10 .30
- 36 Shawn Boskie .10 .30
- 37 Chili Davis .10 .30
- 38 Jason Dickson .10 .30
- 39 Gary DiSarcina .10 .30
- 40 Jim Edmonds .10 .30
- 41 Darin Erstad .10 .30
- 42 Jorge Fabregas .10 .30
- 43 Chuck Finley .10 .30
- 44 Todd Greene .10 .30
- 45 Mike Holtz .10 .30
- 46 Rex Hudler .10 .30
- 47 Mike James .10 .30
- 48 Mark Langston .10 .30
- 49 Troy Percival .10 .30
- 50 Tim Salmon .20 .50
- 51 Jeff Schmidt .10 .30
- 52 J.T. Snow .10 .30
- 53 Randy Velarde .10 .30
- 54 Wilson Alvarez .10 .30
- 55 Harold Baines .10 .30
- 56 James Baldwin .10 .30
- 57 Jason Bere .10 .30
- 58 Mike Cameron .10 .30
- 59 Ray Durham .10 .30
- 60 Alex Fernandez .10 .30
- 61 Ozzie Guillen .10 .30
- 62 Roberto Hernandez .10 .30
- 63 Ron Karkovice .10 .30
- 64 Darren Lewis .10 .30
- 65 Dave Martinez .10 .30
- 66 Lyle Mouton .10 .30
- 67 Greg Norton .10 .30
- 68 Tony Phillips .10 .30
- 69 Chris Snopek .10 .30
- 70 Kevin Tapani .10 .30
- 71 Danny Tartabull .10 .30
- 72 Frank Thomas .30 .75
- 73 Robin Ventura .10 .30
- 74 Sandy Alomar Jr. .10 .30
- 75 Albert Belle .10 .30
- 76 Mark Carreon .10 .30
- 77 Julio Franco .10 .30
- 78 Brian Giles RC .60 1.50
- 79 Orel Hershiser .10 .30
- 80 Kenny Lofton .10 .30
- 81 Dennis Martinez .10 .30
- 82 Jack McDowell .10 .30
- 83 Jose Mesa .10 .30
- 84 Charles Nagy .10 .30
- 85 Chad Ogea .10 .30
- 86 Eric Plunk .10 .30
- 87 Manny Ramirez .20 .50
- 88 Kevin Seitzer .10 .30
- 89 Julian Tavarez .10 .30
- 90 Jim Thome .20 .50
- 91 Jose Vizcaino .10 .30
- 92 Omar Vizquel .20 .50
- 93 Brad Ausmus .10 .30
- 94 Kimera Bartee .10 .30
- 95 Raul Casanova .10 .30
- 96 Tony Clark .10 .30
- 97 John Cummings .10 .30
- 98 Travis Fryman .10 .30
- 99 Bob Higginson .10 .30
- 100 Mark Lewis .10 .30
- 101 Felipe Lira .10 .30
- 102 Phil Nevin .10 .30
- 103 Melvin Nieves .10 .30
- 104 Curtis Pride .10 .30
- 105 A.J. Sager .10 .30
- 106 Ruben Sierra .10 .30
- 107 Justin Thompson .10 .30
- 108 Alan Trammell .10 .30
- 109 Kevin Appier .10 .30
- 110 Tim Belcher .10 .30
- 111 Jaime Bluma .10 .30
- 112 Johnny Damon .20 .50
- 113 Tom Goodwin .10 .30
- 114 Chris Haney .10 .30
- 115 Keith Lockhart .10 .30
- 116 Mike Macfarlane .10 .30
- 117 Jeff Montgomery .10 .30
- 118 Jose Offerman .10 .30
- 119 Craig Paquette .10 .30
- 120 Joe Randa .10 .30
- 121 Bip Roberts .10 .30
- 122 Jose Rosado .10 .30
- 123 Mike Sweeney .10 .30
- 124 Michael Tucker .10 .30
- 125 Jeromy Burnitz .10 .30
- 126 Jeff Cirillo .10 .30
- 127 Jeff D'Amico .10 .30
- 128 Mike Fetters .10 .30
- 129 John Jaha .10 .30
- 130 Scott Karl .10 .30
- 131 Jesse Levis .10 .30
- 132 Mark Loretta .10 .30
- 133 Mike Matheny .10 .30
- 134 Ben McDonald .10 .30
- 135 Matt Mieske .10 .30
- 136 Marc Newfield .10 .30
- 137 Dave Nilsson .10 .30
- 138 Jose Valentin .10 .30
- 139 Fernando Vina .10 .30
- 140 Bob Wickman .10 .30
- 141 Gerald Williams .10 .30
- 142 Rick Aguilera .10 .30
- 143 Rich Becker .10 .30
- 144 Ron Coomer .10 .30
- 145 Marty Cordova .10 .30
- 146 Roberto Kelly .10 .30
- 147 Chuck Knoblauch .10 .30
- 148 Matt Lawton .10 .30
- 149 Pat Meares .10 .30
- 150 Travis Miller .10 .30
- 151 Paul Molitor .10 .30
- 152 Greg Myers .10 .30
- 153 Dan Naulty .10 .30
- 154 Kirby Puckett .30 .75
- 155 Brad Radke .10 .30
- 156 Frank Rodriguez .10 .30
- 157 Scott Stahoviak .10 .30
- 158 Dave Stevens .10 .30
- 159 Matt Walbeck .10 .30
- 160 Todd Walker .10 .30
- 161 Wade Boggs .20 .50
- 162 David Cone .10 .30
- 163 Mariano Duncan .10 .30
- 164 Cecil Fielder .10 .30
- 165 Joe Girardi .10 .30
- 166 Dwight Gooden .10 .30
- 167 Charlie Hayes .10 .30
- 168 Derek Jeter .75 2.00
- 169 Jimmy Key .10 .30
- 170 Jim Leyritz .10 .30
- 171 Tino Martinez .20 .50
- 172 Ramiro Mendoza RC .10 .30
- 173 Jeff Nelson .10 .30
- 174 Paul O'Neill .20 .50
- 175 Andy Pettitte .20 .50
- 176 Mariano Rivera .30 .75
- 177 Ruben Rivera .10 .30
- 178 Kenny Rogers .10 .30
- 179 Darryl Strawberry .10 .30
- 180 John Wetteland .10 .30
- 181 Bernie Williams .20 .50
- 182 Willie Adams .10 .30
- 183 Tony Batista .10 .30
- 184 Geronimo Berroa .10 .30
- 185 Mike Bordick .10 .30
- 186 Scott Brosius .10 .30
- 187 Bobby Chouinard .10 .30
- 188 Jim Corsi .10 .30
- 189 Brent Gates .10 .30
- 190 Jason Giambi .10 .30
- 191 Jose Herrera .10 .30
- 192 Damon Mashore .10 .30
- 193 Mark McGwire .75 2.00
- 194 Mike Mohler .10 .30
- 195 Scott Spiezio .10 .30
- 196 Terry Steinbach .10 .30
- 197 Bill Taylor .10 .30
- 198 John Wasdin .10 .30
- 199 Steve Wojciechowski .10 .30
- 200 Ernie Young .10 .30
- 201 Rich Amaral .10 .30
- 202 Jay Buhner .10 .30
- 203 Norm Charlton .10 .30
- 204 Joey Cora .10 .30
- 205 Russ Davis .10 .30
- 206 Ken Griffey Jr. .60 1.50
- 207 Sterling Hitchcock .10 .30
- 208 Brian Hunter .10 .30
- 209 Raul Ibanez .10 .30
- 210 Randy Johnson .30 .75
- 211 Edgar Martinez .20 .50
- 212 Jamie Moyer .10 .30
- 213 Alex Rodriguez .50 1.25
- 214 Paul Sorrento .10 .30
- 215 Matt Wagner .10 .30
- 216 Bob Wells .10 .30
- 217 Dan Wilson .10 .30
- 218 Damon Buford .10 .30
- 219 Will Clark .20 .50
- 220 Kevin Elster .10 .30
- 221 Juan Gonzalez .10 .30
- 222 Rusty Greer .10 .30
- 223 Kevin Gross .10 .30
- 224 Darryl Hamilton .10 .30
- 225 Mike Henneman .10 .30
- 226 Ken Hill .10 .30
- 227 Mark McLemore .10 .30
- 228 Darren Oliver .10 .30
- 229 Dean Palmer .10 .30
- 230 Roger Pavlik .10 .30
- 231 Ivan Rodriguez .20 .50
- 232 Mickey Tettleton .10 .30
- 233 Bobby Witt .10 .30
- 234 Jacob Brumfield .10 .30
- 235 Joe Carter .10 .30
- 236 Tim Crabtree .10 .30
- 237 Carlos Delgado .10 .30
- 238 Huck Flener .10 .30
- 239 Alex Gonzalez .10 .30
- 240 Shawn Green .10 .30
- 241 Juan Guzman .10 .30
- 242 Pat Hentgen .10 .30
- 243 Marty Janzen .10 .30
- 244 Sandy Martinez .10 .30
- 245 Otis Nixon .10 .30
- 246 Charlie O'Brien .10 .30
- 247 John Olerud .10 .30
- 248 Robert Perez .10 .30
- 249 Ed Sprague .10 .30
- 250 Mike Timlin .10 .30
- 251 Steve Avery .10 .30
- 252 Jeff Blauser .10 .30
- 253 Brad Clontz .10 .30
- 254 Jermaine Dye .10 .30
- 255 Tom Glavine .20 .50
- 256 Marquis Grissom .10 .30
- 257 Andruw Jones .20 .50
- 258 Chipper Jones .30 .75
- 259 David Justice .10 .30
- 260 Ryan Klesko .10 .30
- 261 Mark Lemke .10 .30
- 262 Javier Lopez .10 .30
- 263 Greg Maddux .50 1.25
- 264 Fred McGriff .20 .50
- 265 Greg McMichael .10 .30
- 266 Denny Neagle .10 .30
- 267 Terry Pendleton .10 .30
- 268 Eddie Perez .10 .30
- 269 John Smoltz .20 .50
- 270 Terrell Wade .10 .30
- 271 Mark Wohlers .10 .30
- 272 Terry Adams .10 .30
- 273 Brant Brown .10 .30
- 274 Leo Gomez .10 .30
- 275 Luis Gonzalez .10 .30
- 276 Mark Grace .20 .50
- 277 Tyler Houston .10 .30
- 278 Robin Jennings .10 .30
- 279 Brooks Kieschnick .10 .30
- 280 Brian McRae .10 .30
- 281 Jaime Navarro .10 .30
- 282 Ryne Sandberg .50 1.25
- 283 Scott Servais .10 .30
- 284 Sammy Sosa .30 .75
- 285 Dave Swartzbaugh .10 .30
- 286 Amaury Telemaco .10 .30
- 287 Steve Trachsel .10 .30
- 288 Pedro Valdes .10 .30
- 289 Turk Wendell .10 .30
- 290 Bret Boone .10 .30
- 291 Jeff Branson .10 .30
- 292 Jeff Brantley .10 .30
- 293 Eric Davis .10 .30
- 294 Willie Greene .10 .30
- 295 Thomas Howard .10 .30
- 296 Barry Larkin .20 .50
- 297 Kevin Mitchell .10 .30
- 298 Hal Morris .10 .30
- 299 Chad Mottola .10 .30
- 300 Joe Oliver .10 .30
- 301 Mark Portugal .10 .30
- 302 Roger Salkeld .10 .30
- 303 Reggie Sanders .10 .30
- 304 Pete Schourek .10 .30
- 305 John Smiley .10 .30
- 306 Eddie Taubensee .10 .30
- 307 Dante Bichette .10 .30
- 308 Ellis Burks .10 .30
- 309 Vinny Castilla .10 .30
- 310 Andres Galarraga .10 .30
- 311 Curt Leskanic .10 .30
- 312 Quinton McCracken .10 .30
- 313 Neifi Perez .10 .30
- 314 Jeff Reed .10 .30
- 315 Steve Reed .10 .30
- 316 Armando Reynoso .10 .30
- 317 Kevin Ritz .10 .30
- 318 Bruce Ruffin .10 .30
- 319 Larry Walker .10 .30
- 320 Walt Weiss .10 .30
- 321 Jamey Wright .10 .30
- 322 Eric Young .10 .30
- 323 Kurt Abbott .10 .30
- 324 Alex Arias .10 .30
- 325 Kevin Brown .10 .30
- 326 Luis Castillo .10 .30
- 327 Greg Colbrunn .10 .30
- 328 Jeff Conine .10 .30
- 329 Andre Dawson .10 .30
- 330 Charles Johnson .10 .30
- 331 Al Leiter .10 .30
- 332 Ralph Milliard .10 .30
- 333 Robb Nen .10 .30
- 334 Pat Rapp .10 .30
- 335 Edgar Renteria .10 .30
- 336 Gary Sheffield .10 .30
- 337 Devon White .10 .30
- 338 Bob Abreu .20 .50
- 339 Jeff Bagwell .20 .50
- 340 Derek Bell .10 .30
- 341 Sean Berry .10 .30
- 342 Craig Biggio .20 .50
- 343 Doug Drabek .10 .30
- 344 Tony Eusebio .10 .30
- 345 Ricky Gutierrez .10 .30
- 346 Mike Hampton .10 .30
- 347 Brian Hunter .10 .30
- 348 Todd Jones .10 .30
- 349 Darryl Kile .10 .30
- 350 Derrick May .10 .30
- 351 Orlando Miller .10 .30
- 352 James Mouton .10 .30
- 353 Shane Reynolds .10 .30
- 354 Billy Wagner .10 .30
- 355 Donne Wall .10 .30
- 356 Mike Blowers .10 .30
- 357 Brett Butler .10 .30
- 358 Roger Cedeno .10 .30
- 359 Chad Curtis .10 .30
- 360 Delino DeShields .10 .30
- 361 Greg Gagne .10 .30
- 362 Karim Garcia .10 .30
- 363 Wilton Guerrero .10 .30
- 364 Todd Hollandsworth .10 .30
- 365 Eric Karros .10 .30
- 366 Ramon Martinez .10 .30
- 367 Raul Mondesi .10 .30
- 368 Hideo Nomo .30 .75
- 369 Antonio Osuna .10 .30
- 370 Chan Ho Park .10 .30
- 371 Mike Piazza .50 1.25
- 372 Ismael Valdes .10 .30
- 373 Todd Worrell .10 .30
- 374 Moises Alou .10 .30
- 375 Shane Andrews .10 .30
- 376 Yamil Benitez .10 .30
- 377 Jeff Fassero .10 .30
- 378 Darrin Fletcher .10 .30
- 379 Cliff Floyd .10 .30
- 380 Mark Grudzielanek .10 .30
- 381 Mike Lansing .10 .30
- 382 Barry Manuel .10 .30
- 383 Pedro Martinez .20 .50
- 384 Henry Rodriguez .10 .30
- 385 Mel Rojas .10 .30
- 386 F.P. Santangelo .10 .30
- 387 David Segui .10 .30
- 388 Ugueth Urbina .10 .30
- 389 Rondell White .10 .30
- 390 Edgardo Alfonzo .10 .30
- 391 Carlos Baerga .10 .30
- 392 Mark Clark .10 .30
- 393 Alvaro Espinoza .10 .30
- 394 John Franco .10 .30
- 395 Bernard Gilkey .10 .30
- 396 Pete Harnisch .10 .30
- 397 Todd Hundley .10 .30
- 398 Butch Huskey .10 .30
- 399 Jason Isringhausen .10 .30
- 400 Lance Johnson .10 .30
- 401 Bobby Jones .10 .30
- 402 Alex Ochoa .10 .30
- 403 Rey Ordonez .10 .30
- 404 Robert Person .10 .30
- 405 Paul Wilson .10 .30
- 406 Matt Beech .10 .30
- 407 Ron Blazier .10 .30
- 408 Ricky Bottalico .10 .30
- 409 Lenny Dykstra .10 .30
- 410 Jim Eisenreich .10 .30
- 411 Bobby Estalella .10 .30
- 412 Mike Grace .10 .30
- 413 Gregg Jefferies .10 .30
- 414 Mike Lieberthal .10 .30
- 415 Wendell Magee .10 .30
- 416 Mickey Morandini .10 .30
- 417 Ricky Otero .10 .30
- 418 Scott Rolen .20 .50
- 419 Ken Ryan .10 .30
- 420 Benito Santiago .10 .30
- 421 Curt Schilling .10 .30
- 422 Kevin Sefcik .10 .30
- 423 Jermaine Allensworth .10 .30
- 424 Trey Beamon .10 .30
- 425 Jay Bell .10 .30
- 426 Francisco Cordova .10 .30
- 427 Carlos Garcia .10 .30
- 428 Mark Johnson .10 .30
- 429 Jason Kendall .10 .30
- 430 Jeff King .10 .30
- 431 Jon Lieber .10 .30
- 432 Al Martin .10 .30
- 433 Orlando Merced .10 .30
- 434 Ramon Morel .10 .30
- 435 Matt Ruebel .10 .30
- 436 Jason Schmidt .10 .30
- 437 Marc Wilkins .10 .30
- 438 Alan Benes .10 .30
- 439 Andy Benes .10 .30
- 440 Royce Clayton .10 .30
- 441 Dennis Eckersley .10 .30
- 442 Gary Gaetti .10 .30
- 443 Ron Gant .10 .30
- 444 Aaron Holbert .10 .30
- 445 Brian Jordan .10 .30
- 446 Ray Lankford .10 .30
- 447 John Mabry .10 .30
- 448 T.J. Mathews .10 .30
- 449 Willie McGee .10 .30
- 450 Donovan Osborne .10 .30
- 451 Tom Pagnozzi .10 .30
- 452 Ozzie Smith .50 1.25
- 453 Todd Stottlemyre .10 .30
- 454 Mark Sweeney .10 .30
- 455 Dmitri Young .10 .30
- 456 Andy Ashby .10 .30
- 457 Ken Caminiti .10 .30
- 458 Archi Cianfrocco .10 .30
- 459 Steve Finley .10 .30
- 460 John Flaherty .10 .30
- 461 Chris Gomez .10 .30
- 462 Tony Gwynn .40 1.00
- 463 Joey Hamilton .10 .30
- 464 Rickey Henderson .30 .75
- 465 Trevor Hoffman .10 .30
- 466 Brian Johnson .10 .30
- 467 Wally Joyner .10 .30
- 468 Jody Reed .10 .30
- 469 Scott Sanders .10 .30
- 470 Bob Tewksbury .10 .30
- 471 Fernando Valenzuela .10 .30
- 472 Greg Vaughn .10 .30
- 473 Tim Worrell .10 .30
- 474 Rich Aurilia .10 .30
- 475 Rod Beck .10 .30
- 476 Marvin Benard .10 .30
- 477 Barry Bonds .75 2.00
- 478 Jay Canizaro .10 .30
- 479 Shawon Dunston .10 .30
- 480 Shawn Estes .10 .30
- 481 Mark Gardner .10 .30
- 482 Glenallen Hill .10 .30
- 483 Stan Javier .10 .30
- 484 Marcus Jensen .10 .30
- 485 Bill Mueller RC .50 1.25
- 486 Wm. VanLandingham .10 .30
- 487 Allen Watson .10 .30
- 488 Rick Wilkins .10 .30
- 489 Matt Williams .10 .30
- 490 Desi Wilson .10 .30
- 491 Albert Belle CL .10 .30
- 492 Ken Griffey Jr. CL .40 1.00
- 493 Andruw Jones CL .10 .30
- 494 Chipper Jones CL .20 .50
- 495 Mark McGwire CL .40 1.00
- 496 Paul Molitor CL .10 .30
- 497 Mike Piazza CL .30 .75
- 498 Cal Ripken CL .50 1.25
- 499 Alex Rodriguez CL .30 .75
- 500 Frank Thomas CL .20 .50
- 501 Kenny Lofton .10 .30
- 502 Carlos Perez .10 .30
- 503 Tim Raines .10 .30
- 504 Danny Patterson .10 .30
- 505 Derrick May .10 .30
- 506 Dave Hollins .10 .30
- 507 Felipe Crespo .10 .30
- 508 Brian Banks .10 .30
- 509 Jeff Kent .10 .30
- 510 Bubba Trammell RC .15 .40
- 511 Robert Person .10 .30
- 512 David Arias-Ortiz RC 75.00 200.00
- 513 Ryan Jones .10 .30
- 514 David Justice .10 .30
- 515 Will Cunnane .10 .30
- 516 Russ Johnson .10 .30
- 517 John Burkett .10 .30
- 518 Robinson Checo RC .10 .30
- 519 Ricardo Rincon RC .10 .30
- 520 Woody Williams .10 .30
- 521 Rick Helling .10 .30
- 522 Jorge Posada .20 .50
- 523 Kevin Orie .10 .30
- 524 Fernando Tatis RC .10 .30
- 525 Jermaine Dye .10 .30
- 526 Brian Hunter .10 .30
- 527 Greg McMichael .10 .30
- 528 Matt Wagner .10 .30
- 529 Richie Sexson .10 .30
- 530 Scott Ruffcorn .10 .30
- 531 Luis Gonzalez .10 .30
- 532 Mike Johnson RC .10 .30
- 533 Mark Petkovsek .10 .30
- 534 Doug Drabek .10 .30
- 535 Jose Canseco .20 .50
- 536 Bobby Bonilla .10 .30
- 537 J.T. Snow .10 .30
- 538 Shawon Dunston .10 .30
- 539 John Ericks .10 .30
- 540 Terry Steinbach .10 .30
- 541 Jay Bell .10 .30
- 542 Joe Borowski RC .15 .40
- 543 David Wells .10 .30
- 544 Justin Towle RC .10 .30
- 545 Mike Blowers .10 .30
- 546 Shannon Stewart .10 .30
- 547 Rudy Pemberton .10 .30
- 548 Bill Swift .10 .30
- 549 Osvaldo Fernandez .10 .30
- 550 Eddie Murray .30 .75
- 551 Don Wengert .10 .30
- 552 Brad Ausmus .10 .30
- 553 Carlos Garcia .10 .30
- 554 Jose Guillen .10 .30
- 555 Rheal Cormier .10 .30
- 556 Doug Brocail .10 .30
- 557 Rex Hudler .10 .30
- 558 Armando Benitez .10 .30
- 559 Eli Marrero .10 .30
- 560 Ricky Ledee RC .15 .40
- 561 Bartolo Colon .10 .30
- 562 Quilvio Veras .10 .30
- 563 Alex Fernandez .10 .30
- 564 Darren Dreifort .10 .30
- 565 Benji Gil .10 .30
- 566 Kent Mercker .10 .30
- 567 Glendon Rusch .10 .30
- 568 Ramon Tatis RC .10 .30
- 569 Roger Clemens .60 1.50
- 570 Mark Lewis .10 .30
- 571 Emil Brown RC .10 .30
- 572 Jaime Navarro .10 .30
- 573 Sherman Obando .10 .30
- 574 John Wasdin .10 .30
- 575 Calvin Maduro .10 .30
- 576 Todd Jones .10 .30
- 577 Orlando Merced .10 .30
- 578 Cal Eldred .10 .30
- 579 Mark Gubicza .10 .30
- 580 Michael Tucker .10 .30
- 581 Tony Saunders RC .10 .30
- 582 Garvin Alston .10 .30
- 583 Joe Roa .10 .30
- 584 Brady Raggio RC .10 .30
- 585 Jimmy Key .10 .30
- 586 Marc Sagmoen RC .10 .30
- 587 Jim Bullinger .10 .30
- 588 Yorkis Perez .10 .30
- 589 Jose Cruz Jr. RC .15 .40
- 590 Mike Stanton .10 .30
- 591 Deivi Cruz RC .15 .40
- 592 Steve Karsay .10 .30
- 593 Mike Trombley .10 .30
- 594 Doug Glanville .10 .30
- 595 Scott Sanders .10 .30
- 596 Thomas Howard .10 .30
- 597 T.J. Staton RC .10 .30
- 598 Garrett Stephenson .10 .30
- 599 Rico Brogna .10 .30
- 600 Albert Belle .10 .30
- 601 Jose Vizcaino .10 .30
- 602 Chili Davis .10 .30
- 603 Shane Mack .10 .30
- 604 Jim Eisenreich .10 .30
- 605 Todd Zeile .10 .30
- 606 Brian Boehringer RC .10 .30
- 607 Paul Shuey .10 .30
- 608 Kevin Tapani .10 .30
- 609 John Wetteland .10 .30
- 610 Jim Leyritz .10 .30
- 611 Ray Montgomery RC .10 .30
- 612 Doug Bochtler .10 .30
- 613 Wady Almonte RC .10 .30
- 614 Danny Tartabull .10 .30
- 615 Orlando Miller .10 .30
- 616 Bobby Ayala .10 .30
- 617 Tony Graffanino .10 .30
- 618 Marc Valdes .10 .30
- 619 Ron Villone .10 .30
- 620 Derrek Lee .20 .50
- 621 Greg Colbrunn .10 .30
- 622 Felix Heredia RC .15 .40
- 623 Carl Everett .10 .30
- 624 Mark Thompson .10 .30
- 625 Jeff Granger .10 .30
- 626 Damian Jackson .10 .30
- 627 Mark Leiter .10 .30
- 628 Chris Holt .10 .30
- 629 Dario Veras RC .10 .30
- 630 Dave Burba .10 .30
- 631 Darryl Hamilton .10 .30
- 632 Mark Acre .10 .30
- 633 Fernando Hernandez RC .10 .30
- 634 Terry Mulholland .10 .30
- 635 Dustin Hermanson .10 .30
- 636 Delino DeShields .10 .30
- 637 Steve Avery .10 .30
- 638 Tony Womack RC .15 .40
- 639 Mark Whiten .10 .30
- 640 Marquis Grissom .10 .30
- 641 Xavier Hernandez .10 .30
- 642 Eric Davis .10 .30
- 643 Bob Tewksbury .10 .30
- 644 Dante Powell .10 .30
- 645 Carlos Castillo RC .10 .30
- 646 Chris Widger .10 .30
- 647 Moises Alou .10 .30
- 648 Pat Listach .10 .30
- 649 Edgar Ramos RC .10 .30
- 650 Deion Sanders .20 .50
- 651 John Olerud .10 .30
- 652 Todd Dunwoody .10 .30
- 653 Randall Simon RC .15 .40
- 654 Dan Carlson .10 .30
- 655 Matt Williams .10 .30
- 656 Jeff King .10 .30
- 657 Luis Alicea .10 .30
- 658 Brian Moehler RC .15 .40
- 659 Ariel Prieto .10 .30
- 660 Kevin Elster .10 .30
- 661 Mark Hutton .10 .30
- 662 Aaron Sele .10 .30
- 663 Graeme Lloyd .10 .30
- 664 John Burke .10 .30
- 665 Mel Rojas .10 .30
- 666 Sid Fernandez .10 .30
- 667 Pedro Astacio .10 .30
- 668 Jeff Abbott .10 .30
- 669 Darren Daulton .10 .30
- 670 Mike Bordick .10 .30
- 671 Sterling Hitchcock .10 .30
- 672 Damion Easley .10 .30
- 673 Armando Reynoso .10 .30
- 674 Pat Cline .10 .30
- 675 Orlando Cabrera RC .30 .75
- 676 Alan Embree .10 .30
- 677 Brian Bevil .10 .30
- 678 David Weathers .10 .30
- 679 Cliff Floyd .10 .30
- 680 Joe Randa .10 .30
- 681 Bill Haselman .10 .30
- 682 Jeff Fassero .10 .30
- 683 Matt Morris .10 .30
- 684 Mark Portugal .10 .30
- 685 Lee Smith .10 .30
- 686 Pokey Reese .10 .30
- 687 Benito Santiago .10 .30
- 688 Brian Johnson .10 .30
- 689 Brent Brede RC .10 .30
- 690 Shigetoshi Hasegawa RC .20 .50

691 Julio Santana .10 .30
692 Steve Kline .10 .30
693 Julian Tavarez .10 .30
694 John Hudek .10 .30
695 Manny Alexander .10 .30
696 Roberto Alomar ENC .10 .30
697 Jeff Bagwell ENC .10 .30
698 Barry Bonds ENC .40 1.00
699 Ken Caminiti ENC .10 .30
700 Juan Gonzalez ENC .10 .30
701 Ken Griffey Jr. ENC .40 1.00
702 Tony Gwynn ENC .20 .50
703 Derek Jeter ENC .40 1.00
704 Andruw Jones ENC .20 .50
705 Chipper Jones ENC .20 .50
706 Barry Larkin ENC .10 .30
707 Greg Maddux ENC .30 .75
708 Mark McGwire ENC .40 1.00
709 Paul Molitor ENC .10 .30
710 Hideo Nomo ENC .10 .30
711 Andy Pettitte ENC .10 .30
712 Mike Piazza ENC .30 .75
713 Manny Ramirez ENC .20 .50
714 Cal Ripken ENC .50 1.25
715 Alex Rodriguez ENC .30 .75
716 Ryne Sandberg ENC .30 .75
717 John Smoltz ENC .10 .30
718 Frank Thomas ENC .20 .50
719 Mo Vaughn ENC .10 .30
720 Bernie Williams ENC .10 .30
721 Tim Salmon CL .10 .30
722 Greg Maddux CL .30 .75
723 Cal Ripken CL .50 1.25
724 Mo Vaughn CL .10 .30
725 Ryne Sandberg CL .30 .75
726 Frank Thomas CL .20 .50
727 Barry Larkin CL .10 .30
728 Manny Ramirez CL .10 .30
729 Andres Galarraga CL .10 .30
730 Tony Clark CL .10 .30
731 Gary Sheffield CL .10 .30
732 Jeff Bagwell CL .10 .30
733 Kevin Appier CL .10 .30
734 Mike Piazza CL .30 .75
735 Jeff Cirillo CL .10 .30
736 Paul Molitor CL .10 .30
737 Henry Rodriguez CL .10 .30
738 Todd Hundley CL .10 .30
739 Derek Jeter CL .40 1.00
740 Mark McGwire CL .40 1.00
741 Curt Schilling CL .10 .30
742 Jason Kendall CL .10 .30
743 Tony Gwynn CL .20 .50
744 Barry Bonds CL .40 1.00
745 Ken Griffey Jr. CL .40 1.00
746 Brian Jordan CL .10 .30
747 Juan Gonzalez CL .10 .30
748 Joe Carter CL .10 .30
749 Arizona Diamondbacks CL .10 .30
750 Tampa Bay Devil Rays CL .10 .30
751 Hideki Irabu RC .30 .75
752 Jeremi Gonzalez RC .20 .50
753 Mario Valdez RC .20 .50
754 Aaron Boone .30 .75
755 Brett Tomko .20 .50
756 Jaret Wright RC .30 .75
757 Ryan McGuire .20 .50
758 Jason McDonald .20 .50
759 Adrian Brown RC .20 .50
760 Keith Foulke RC .75 2.00
761 Bonus Checklist (751-761) .20 .50
P489 Matt Williams Promo .40 1.00
NNO A.Jones Circa AU/200 10.00 25.00

1997 Fleer Tiffany
*TIFFANY 1-750: 10X TO 25X BASIC CARDS
*TIFFANY RC's 1-750: 6X TO 15X BASIC
*TIFFANY 751-761: 4X TO 10X BASIC
*TIFFANY 751-761: 3X TO 8X BASIC RC'S
STATED ODDS 1:20
512 David Arias-Ortiz 300.00 800.00
675 Orlando Cabrera 5.00 12.00
760 Keith Foulke 6.00 15.00

1997 Fleer Bleacher Blasters
COMPLETE SET(10) 20.00 50.00
SER.2 STATED ODDS 1:36 RETAIL
1 Albert Belle 1.25 3.00
2 Barry Bonds 5.00 12.00
3 Juan Gonzalez 1.25 3.00
4 Ken Griffey Jr. 12.00 30.00
5 Mark McGwire 5.00 12.00
6 Mike Piazza 3.00 8.00
7 Alex Rodriguez 4.00 10.00
8 Frank Thomas 3.00 8.00
9 Mo Vaughn 1.25 3.00
10 Matt Williams 1.25 3.00

1997 Fleer Decade of Excellence
COMPLETE SET (12) 10.00 25.00
SER.2 STATED ODDS 1:36 HOBBY
*RARE TRAD: 2X TO 5X BASIC DECADE
RARE TRAD.STATED ODDS 1:360 HOBBY
1 Wade Boggs .60 1.50
2 Barry Bonds 1.50 4.00
3 Roger Clemens 1.25 3.00
4 Tony Gwynn 1.00 2.50
5 Rickey Henderson 1.00 2.50
6 Greg Maddux 1.50 4.00
7 Mark McGwire 1.50 4.00
8 Paul Molitor 1.00 2.50
9 Eddie Murray .60 1.50
10 Cal Ripken 3.00 8.00
11 Ryne Sandberg 1.50 4.00
12 Matt Williams .40 1.00

1997 Fleer Diamond Tribute
SER.2 STATED ODDS 1:288
1 Albert Belle 1.00 2.50
2 Barry Bonds 4.00 10.00
3 Juan Gonzalez 1.00 2.50
4 Ken Griffey Jr. 20.00 50.00
5 Tony Gwynn 2.50 6.00
6 Greg Maddux 4.00 10.00
7 Mark McGwire 4.00 10.00
8 Eddie Murray 1.50 4.00
9 Mike Piazza 2.50 6.00
10 Cal Ripken 8.00 20.00
11 Alex Rodriguez 3.00 8.00
12 Frank Thomas 2.50 6.00

1997 Fleer Golden Memories
COMPLETE SET (10) 4.00 10.00
SER.1 STATED ODDS 1:16 HOBBY
1 Barry Bonds 1.25 3.00
2 Dwight Gooden .20 .50
3 Todd Hundley .20 .50
4 Mark McGwire 1.25 3.00
5 Paul Molitor .20 .50
6 Eddie Murray .50 1.25
7 Hideo Nomo .50 1.25
8 Mike Piazza .75 2.00
9 Cal Ripken 1.50 4.00
10 Ozzie Smith w kids .75 2.00

1997 Fleer Goudey Greats
COMPLETE SET (15) 6.00 15.00
SER.2 STATED ODDS 1:8
*FOIL CARDS: 6X TO 15X BASIC GOUDEY
FOIL SER.2 STATED ODDS 1:800
1 Barry Bonds 1.25 3.00
2 Ken Griffey Jr. 1.00 2.50
3 Tony Gwynn .60 1.50
4 Derek Jeter 1.25 3.00
5 Chipper Jones .50 1.25
6 Kenny Lofton .20 .50
7 Greg Maddux .75 2.00
8 Mark McGwire 1.25 3.00
9 Eddie Murray .50 1.25
10 Mike Piazza .75 2.00
11 Cal Ripken 1.50 4.00
12 Alex Rodriguez .75 2.00
13 Ryne Sandberg .75 2.00
14 Frank Thomas .50 1.25
15 Mo Vaughn .20 .50

1997 Fleer Headliners
COMPLETE SET (20) 4.00 10.00
SER.2 STATED ODDS 1:2
1 Jeff Bagwell .10 .30
2 Albert Belle .07 .20
3 Barry Bonds .50 1.25
4 Ken Caminiti .07 .20
5 Juan Gonzalez .07 .20
6 Ken Griffey Jr. .40 1.00
7 Tony Gwynn .25 .60
8 Derek Jeter .50 1.25
9 Andruw Jones .10 .30
10 Chipper Jones .20 .50
11 Greg Maddux .30 .75
12 Mark McGwire .50 1.25
13 Paul Molitor .07 .20
14 Eddie Murray .20 .50
15 Mike Piazza .30 .75
16 Cal Ripken .60 1.50
17 Alex Rodriguez .30 .75
18 Ryne Sandberg .30 .75
19 John Smoltz .10 .30
20 Frank Thomas .20 .50

1997 Fleer Lumber Company
COMPLETE SET (18) 25.00 60.00
SER.1 STATED ODDS 1:48 RETAIL
1 Brady Anderson 1.00 2.50
2 Jeff Bagwell 1.50 4.00
3 Albert Belle 1.00 2.50
4 Barry Bonds 4.00 10.00
5 Jay Buhner 1.00 2.50
6 Ellis Burks 1.00 2.50
7 Andres Galarraga 1.50 4.00
8 Juan Gonzalez 1.00 2.50
9 Ken Griffey Jr. 5.00 12.00
10 Todd Hundley 1.00 2.50
11 Ryan Klesko 1.00 2.50
12 Mark McGwire 4.00 10.00
13 Mike Piazza 2.50 6.00
14 Alex Rodriguez 3.00 8.00
15 Gary Sheffield 1.00 2.50
16 Sammy Sosa 1.50 4.00
17 Frank Thomas 2.50 6.00
18 Mo Vaughn 1.00 2.50

1997-98 Fleer Million Dollar Moments
COMPLETE SET (45) 3.00 8.00
1-45 SET REDEEMABLE FOR 1-50 EXCH.SET
EXCHANGE DEADLINE: 7/31/98
1 Checklist .02 .10
2 Derek Jeter .25 .60
3 Babe Ruth .60 1.50
4 Barry Bonds .25 .60
5 Brooks Robinson .08 .25
6 Todd Hundley .02 .10
7 Johnny Vander Meer .02 .10
8 Cal Ripken .30 .75
9 Bill Mazeroski .05 .15
10 Chipper Jones .08 .25
11 Frank Robinson .05 .15
12 Roger Clemens .20 .50
13 Bob Feller .05 .15
14 Mike Piazza .15 .40
15 Joe Nuxhall .02 .10
16 Hideo Nomo .08 .25
17 Jackie Robinson .08 .25
18 Orel Hershiser .02 .10
19 Bobby Thomson .02 .10
20 Joe Carter .02 .10
21 Al Kaline .08 .25
22 Bernie Williams .05 .15
23 Don Larsen .05 .15
24 Rickey Henderson .08 .25
25 Maury Wills .02 .10
26 Andruw Jones .05 .15
27 Bobby Richardson .02 .10
28 Alex Rodriguez .15 .40
29 Jim Bunning .05 .15
30 Ken Caminiti .02 .10
31 Bob Gibson .05 .15
32 Frank Thomas .08 .25
33 Mickey Lolich .02 .10
34 John Smoltz .05 .15
35 Ron Swoboda .02 .10
36 Albert Belle .02 .10
37 Chris Chambliss .02 .10
38 Juan Gonzalez .02 .10
39 Ron Blomberg .02 .10
40 John Wetteland .02 .10
41 Carlton Fisk .08 .25
42 Mo Vaughn .02 .10
43 Bucky Dent .02 .10
44 Greg Maddux .15 .40
45 Willie Stargell .02 .10
46 Tony Gwynn SP
47 Joel Youngblood SP
48 Andy Pettitte SP
49 Mookie Wilson SP
50 Jeff Bagwell SP

1997-98 Fleer Million Dollar Moments Redemption
COMPLETE SET (45) 3.00 8.00
1 Checklist .25 .60
2 Derek Jeter 1.50 4.00
3 Babe Ruth 1.50 4.00
4 Barry Bonds 1.25 3.00
5 Brooks Robinson .40 1.00
6 Todd Hundley .25 .60
7 Johnny Vander Meer .25 .60
8 Cal Ripken 2.00 5.00
9 Bill Mazeroski .40 1.00
10 Chipper Jones .60 1.50
11 Frank Robinson .40 1.00
12 Roger Clemens .75 2.00
13 Bob Feller .40 1.00
14 Mike Piazza .60 1.50
15 Joe Nuxhall .25 .60
16 Hideo Nomo .60 1.50
17 Jackie Robinson .60 1.50
18 Orel Hershiser .25 .60
19 Bobby Thomson .40 1.00
20 Joe Carter .25 .60
21 Al Kaline .60 1.50
22 Bernie Williams .40 1.00
23 Don Larsen .40 1.00
24 Rickey Henderson .60 1.50
25 Maury Wills .25 .60
26 Andruw Jones .25 .60
27 Bobby Richardson .25 .60
28 Alex Rodriguez 1.00 2.50
29 Jim Bunning .40 1.00
30 Ken Caminiti .25 .60
31 Bob Gibson .40 1.00
32 Frank Thomas .60 1.50
33 Mickey Lolich .25 .60
34 John Smoltz .60 1.50
35 Ron Swoboda .25 .60
36 Albert Belle .25 .60
37 Chris Chambliss .25 .60
38 Juan Gonzalez .25 .60
39 Ron Blomberg .25 .60
40 John Wetteland .25 .60
41 Carlton Fisk .40 1.00
42 Mo Vaughn .25 .60
43 Bucky Dent .25 .60
44 Greg Maddux .75 2.00
45 Willie Stargell .40 1.00
46 Tony Gwynn .60 1.50
47 Joel Youngblood .25 .60
48 Andy Pettitte .40 1.00
49 Mookie Wilson .25 .60
50 Jeff Bagwell .40 1.00

1997 Fleer New Horizons
COMPLETE SET (15) 3.00 8.00
SER.2 STATED ODDS 1:4
1 Bob Abreu .30 .75
2 Jose Cruz Jr. .25 .60
3 Darin Erstad .20 .50
4 Nomar Garciaparra .75 2.00
5 Vladimir Guerrero .50 1.25
6 Wilton Guerrero .20 .50
7 Jose Guillen .20 .50
8 Hideki Irabu .50 1.25
9 Andruw Jones .30 .75
10 Kevin Orie .20 .50
11 Scott Rolen .30 .75
12 Scott Spiezio .20 .50
13 Bubba Trammell .25 .60
14 Todd Walker .20 .50
15 Dmitri Young .20 .50

1997 Fleer Night and Day
COMPLETE SET (10) 25.00 60.00
SER.1 STATED ODDS 1:240
1 Barry Bonds 4.00 10.00
2 Ellis Burks 1.00 2.50
3 Juan Gonzalez 1.00 2.50
4 Ken Griffey Jr. 10.00 25.00
5 Mark McGwire 4.00 10.00
6 Mike Piazza 2.50 6.00
7 Manny Ramirez 1.50 4.00
8 Alex Rodriguez 3.00 8.00
9 John Smoltz 1.50 4.00
10 Frank Thomas 5.00 12.00

1997 Fleer Rookie Sensations
COMPLETE SET (20) 8.00 20.00
SER.1 STATED ODDS 1:6
1 Jermaine Allensworth .30 .75
2 James Baldwin .30 .75
3 Alan Benes .30 .75
4 Jermaine Dye .30 .75
5 Darin Erstad .30 .75
6 Todd Hollandsworth .30 .75
7 Derek Jeter 2.00 5.00
8 Jason Kendall .30 .75
9 Alex Ochoa .30 .75
10 Rey Ordonez .30 .75
11 Edgar Renteria .30 .75
12 Bob Abreu .50 1.25
13 Nomar Garciaparra 1.25 3.00
14 Wilton Guerrero .30 .75
15 Andruw Jones .50 1.25
16 Wendell Magee .30 .75
17 Neifi Perez .30 .75
18 Scott Rolen .50 1.25
19 Scott Spiezio .30 .75
20 Todd Walker .30 .75

1997 Fleer Soaring Stars
COMPLETE SET (12) 12.50 30.00
SER.2 STATED ODDS 1:12
*GLOWING: 4X TO 10X BASIC SOARING
GLOWING: RANDOM INS.IN SER.2 PACKS
LAST 20% OF PRINT RUN WAS GLOWING
1 Albert Belle .25 .60
2 Barry Bonds 1.50 4.00
3 Juan Gonzalez .25 .60
4 Ken Griffey Jr. 1.25 3.00
5 Derek Jeter 1.50 4.00
6 Andruw Jones .40 1.00
7 Chipper Jones .60 1.50
8 Greg Maddux 1.00 2.50
9 Mark McGwire 1.50 4.00
10 Mike Piazza 1.00 2.50
11 Alex Rodriguez 1.00 2.50
12 Frank Thomas .60 1.50

1997 Fleer Team Leaders
COMPLETE SET (28) 15.00 40.00
SER.1 STATED ODDS 1:20
1 Cal Ripken 3.00 8.00
2 Mo Vaughn .40 1.00
3 Jim Edmonds .40 1.00
4 Frank Thomas 1.00 2.50
5 Albert Belle .40 1.00
6 Bob Higginson .40 1.00
7 Kevin Appier .40 1.00
8 John Jaha .40 1.00
9 Paul Molitor 1.00 2.50
10 Andy Pettitte .60 1.50
11 Mark McGwire 1.50 4.00
12 Ken Griffey Jr. 2.00 5.00
13 Juan Gonzalez .40 1.00
14 Pat Hentgen .40 1.00
15 Chipper Jones 1.00 2.50
16 Mark Grace .60 1.50
17 Barry Larkin .60 1.50
18 Ellis Burks .40 1.00
19 Gary Sheffield .40 1.00
20 Jeff Bagwell .60 1.50
21 Mike Piazza 1.00 2.50
22 Henry Rodriguez .40 1.00
23 Todd Hundley .40 1.00
24 Curt Schilling .40 1.00
25 Jeff King .40 1.00
26 Brian Jordan .40 1.00
27 Tony Gwynn 1.00 2.50
28 Barry Bonds 1.50 4.00

1997 Fleer Zone
COMPLETE SET (20) 100.00 200.00
SER.1 STATED ODDS 1:80 HOBBY
1 Jeff Bagwell 2.50 6.00
2 Albert Belle 1.50 4.00
3 Barry Bonds 10.00 25.00
4 Ken Caminiti 1.50 4.00
5 Andres Galarraga 1.50 4.00
6 Juan Gonzalez 1.50 4.00
7 Ken Griffey Jr. 8.00 20.00
8 Tony Gwynn 5.00 12.00
9 Chipper Jones 4.00 10.00
10 Greg Maddux 6.00 15.00
11 Mark McGwire 10.00 25.00
12 Dean Palmer 1.50 4.00
13 Andy Pettitte 2.50 6.00
14 Mike Piazza 6.00 15.00
15 Alex Rodriguez 6.00 15.00
16 Gary Sheffield 1.50 4.00
17 John Smoltz 2.50 6.00
18 Frank Thomas 4.00 10.00
19 Jim Thome 2.50 6.00
20 Matt Williams 1.50 4.00

1997 Fleer Firestone
This one-card set features a color portrait with gold foil printing of Roy Firestone, the host of ESPN's "Up Close Prime Time." The back displays information about the interviewer.
1 Roy Firestone .75 2.00

1998 Fleer Diamond Skills Commemorative Sheet
This attractive eight-card unperforated sheet was distributed nationwide by hobby shops that participated in Fleer's Diamond Skills youth baseball program. Each shop that enrolled with Fleer in early April, 1998 received 25 sheets to give away to young baseball fans participating in the contest. From April 1st through June 30th, 1998, MLB and Fleer/SkyBox distributed more than 600,000 questionaire surveys. Each survey was then filled out and brought into a local card shop, where the participating youth had to buy two packs of Fleer/SkyBox trading cards. In exchange for the two wrappers from those packs and the completed survey, the youth received one of these commemorative sheets.
NNO Commemorative Sheet 2.00 5.00

1998 Fleer Mantle and Sons
This special one-shot standard-sized card was distributed at Fleer's booth at the Sportsfest '98 show in Philadelphia as well as the National Convention in Chicago in the Summer of 1998. In conjunction with their licensing agreement with the Mantle family and accompanying 1998 Mantle promotions, Fleer brought Mantle's sons Danny and David to the aforementioned trade shows to sign this special card for collectors. The back of the card outlines Mickey Mantle's various card appearances in Fleer's 1998 products. Pricing is provided below for both signed and unsigned versions of this card.
NNO Mickey Mantle w sons AU 4.00 10.00
NNO Mickey Mantle w sons 1.25 3.00

1998 Fleer National Promos
NC1 Mickey Mantle 2.00 5.00
NC2 Mickey Mantle 2.00 5.00
David Mantle
Danny Mantle

1998 Fleer Postcard Mantle Promo
This one-card set features a color photo of Mickey Mantle as the A.L. Most Valuable Player in 1962 with a white border and measuring approximately 4 1/4" by 5 1/2". The white back has a date of August 5, 1998, and the words "Isn't it about time your customers complete their '63 set?" Only 3,500 of the cards were printed and are serially numbered.
1 Mickey Mantle 2.00 5.00

1998 Fleer/SkyBox Player's Choice Sheet
This one-card set was given out at stadiums during the final weekend of the 1998 season and measures approximately 8 1/2" by 11". The card features color action player images of nominees for Outstanding Player, Pitcher and Rookie, Comeback Player of the Year, Man of the Year, and Player of the Year. One side displays the NL nominees and the other the AL ones. The players are checklisted below in alphabetical order.
NNO Player's Choice AL/NL 2.00 5.00

1999 Fleer Stan Musial NSCC Commemorative
This five-card over-sized (3 1/2" by 5") set was distributed to attendees of the 20th Annual National Sports Collectors Convention held in Atlanta in July, 1999. The cards were packaged in complete set form within a sealed clear plastic cello wrapper. An unnumbered Cover Card (bereft of any player images) displays the 20th National Convention logo on front and a checklist on back. This was the top card in each cello wrapped set. Card NC1 was a straight parallel of the basic issue 1999 Fleer Stan Musial card (number 6 within the basic Fleer set, but renumbered as NC1 for this set) and is the only standard-sized card in the set. Cards NC2-NC4 are quasi-reprints of selected cards from the 1999 Fleer Stan Musial Monumental Moments set - taking those standard sized cards and incorporating them into an over-sized card format with the famous Arch of St.Louis in the background.
COMPLETE SET (5) 10.00 25.00
COMMON CARD (NC1-NC4) 2.00 5.00

1999 Fleer 23K McGwire
This card was issued by Fleer and commemorated the breaking of the single season homer record by Mark McGwire. The front has a relief photo of McGwire and a fascimile autograph. The back has information about the homer as well as the date listed on top. The card is also serial numbered on the back. However, it is possible that more of these cards were issued so any further information about this set is appreciated.
1 Mark McGwire 4.00 10.00

1999 Fleer Diamond Skills Commemorative Sheet
For the second year running, Fleer issued an attractive eight-card unperforated sheet. The sheet was distributed nationwide by hobby shops that participated in Fleer's Diamond Skills youth baseball program.
NNO Diamond Skills Sheet 2.00 5.00

1999 Fleer Spectra Star
These six cards of baseball's leading superstars were issued by Fleer along with a kite. These cards are in the design of the 1999 Fleer set but are numbered "x" of 6. The kites were issued by Spectra Star.
COMPLETE SET (6) 12.50 30.00
1 Mark McGwire 2.50 6.00
2 Ken Griffey Jr. 3.00 8.00
3 Derek Jeter 4.00 10.00
4 Greg Maddux 2.00 5.00
5 Mike Piazza 2.50 6.00
6 Sammy Sosa 1.50 4.00

1999 Fleer White Rose
These 30 cards were issued along with a special truck in a combo package. The cards are sequenced thusly: Cards 1-14 are American League teams in alphabetical order; 15-26 are National League teams in alpha order, 27 and 28 are 1993 Expansion teams and 29 and 30 and 1998 Expansion teams. The cards have the 1999 Fleer fronts and are specially numbered for this set. We are only pricing the cards here.
COMPLETE SET (30) 30.00 80.00
1 Cal Ripken Jr 4.00 10.00
2 Nomar Garciaparra 2.00 5.00
3 Tim Salmon .60 1.50
4 Frank Thomas 1.25 3.00
5 Jim Thome 1.00 2.50
6 Tony Clark .40 1.00
7 Johnny Damon 1.00 2.50
8 Jeromy Burnitz .60 1.50
9 Brad Radke .40 1.00
10 Derek Jeter 4.00 10.00
11 Ben Grieve .60 1.50
12 Ken Griffey Jr. 3.00 8.00
13 Ivan Rodriguez 1.25 3.00
14 Carlos Delgado 1.00 2.50
15 Greg Maddux 2.50 6.00
16 Sammy Sosa 1.50 4.00
17 Sean Casey .60 1.50
18 Jeff Bagwell 1.25 3.00
19 Raul Mondesi .40 1.00
20 Vladimir Guerrero 1.50 4.00
21 Mike Piazza 2.50 6.00
22 Scott Rolen 1.00 2.50
23 Jose Guillen .75 2.00
24 Mark McGwire 2.50 6.00
25 Tony Gwynn 2.00 5.00
26 Barry Bonds 2.00 5.00
27 Larry Walker 1.00 2.50
28 Livan Hernandez .40 1.00
29 Matt Williams .60 1.50
30 Wade Boggs 1.00 2.50

2000 Fleer Club 3000
COMPLETE SET (14) 15.00 40.00
COMP.FLEER SET (3) 3.00 8.00
COMP.FOCUS SET (3) 2.50 6.00
COMP.MYSTIQUE SET (3) 4.00 10.00
COMP.SHOWCASE SET (2) 3.00 8.00
COMP.ULTRA SET (3) 2.50 6.00
FLEER STATED ODDS 1:36
FOCUS STATED ODDS 1:36
MYSTIQUE STATED ODDS 1:20
SHOWCASE STATED ODDS 1:24
ULTRA STATED ODDS 1:24
SHOW SUFFIX ON SHOWCASE DISTRIBUTION
ACTUAL CARDS ARE ALL UNNUMBERED
BG Bob Gibson MYST .75 2.00
CR Cal Ripken MYST 4.00 10.00
CY Carl Yastrzemski ULT 2.00 5.00
DW Dave Winfield MYST .75 2.00
GB George Brett FLE 2.50 6.00
LB Lou Brock SHOW .75 2.00
NR Nolan Ryan SHOW 4.00 10.00
PM Paul Molitor FOCUS 1.25 3.00
RC Rod Carew FLE .75 2.00
RY Robin Yount FLE 1.25 3.00
SC Steve Carlton FOCUS .50 1.25
SM Stan Musial FOCUS 2.00 5.00
TG Tony Gwynn ULT 1.25 3.00
WB Wade Boggs ULT .75 2.00

2000 Fleer Club 3000 Memorabilia
B/WN 225-335 OF EACH BAT PRODUCED
B/WN 55-115 OF EACH HAT PRODUCED
700-1000 OF EACH JSY UNLESS STATED
100 #'d COPIES OF EACH BAT-JSY MADE
25 #'d COPIES OF EACH BAT-HAT-JSY MADE
PRINT RUNS LISTED BELOW
ACTUAL CARDS ARE ALL UNNUMBERED
NO PRICING ON QTY OF 25 OR LESS
BG1 B.Gibson Bat/265 10.00 25.00
BG2 B.Gibson Hat/55 30.00 60.00
BG3 B.Gibson Jersey/825 6.00 15.00
BG4 B.Gibson Bat-Jersey/100 20.00 50.00
CR1 C.Ripken Bat/265 30.00 80.00
CR2 C.Ripken Hat/55 60.00 150.00
CR3 C.Ripken Jersey/825 10.00 25.00
CR4 C.Ripken Bat-Jersey/100 20.00 50.00
CY1 C.Yaz Bat/250 15.00 40.00
CY2 C.Yaz Hat/100 20.00 50.00
CY3 C.Yaz Jersey/440 10.00 25.00
CY4 C.Yaz Bat-Jersey/100 10.00 25.00
DW1 D.Winfield Bat/270 6.00 15.00
DW2 D.Winfield Hat/55 20.00 50.00
DW3 D.Winfield Jersey/825 8.00 20.00
DW4 D.Winfield Bat-Jersey/100 15.00 40.00
GB1 G.Brett Bat/240 12.00 30.00
GB2 G.Brett Hat/105 30.00 60.00
GB3 G.Brett Jersey/445 10.00 25.00
GB4 G.Brett Bat-Jersey/100 30.00 60.00
LB1 L.Brock Bat/270 10.00 25.00
LB2 L.Brock Hat/60 30.00 60.00
LB3 L.Brock Jersey/680 6.00 15.00
LB4 L.Brock Bat-Jersey/100 15.00 40.00
NR1 N.Ryan Bat/265 10.00 25.00
NR2 N.Ryan Hat/65 60.00 120.00
NR3 N.Ryan Jersey/780 10.00 25.00
NR4 N.Ryan Bat-Jersey/100 60.00 150.00
PM1 P.Molitor Bat/335 10.00 25.00
PM2 P.Molitor Hat/65 15.00 40.00
PM3 P.Molitor Jersey/975 10.00 25.00
PM4 P.Molitor Bat-Jersey/100 10.00 25.00
RC1 R.Carew Bat/225 10.00 25.00
RC2 R.Carew Hat/105 30.00 60.00
RC3 R.Carew Jersey/395 6.00 15.00
RC4 R.Carew Bat-Jersey/100 15.00 40.00
RY1 R.Yount Bat/230 12.00 30.00
RY2 R.Yount Hat/105 40.00 80.00
RY3 R.Yount Jersey/445 6.00 15.00
RY4 R.Yount Bat-Jersey/100 40.00 80.00
SC1 S.Carlton Bat/325 6.00 15.00
SC2 S.Carlton Hat/65 20.00 50.00
SC3 S.Carlton Jersey/750 10.00 25.00
SC4 S.Carlton Bat-Jersey/100 20.00 50.00
SM1 S.Musial Bat/325 10.00 25.00
SM2 S.Musial Hat/65 50.00 100.00
SM3 S.Musial Jersey/975 12.00 30.00
SM4 S.Musial Bat-Jersey/100 30.00 60.00
TG1 T.Gwynn Bat/260 10.00 25.00
TG2 T.Gwynn Hat/115 40.00 80.00
TG3 T.Gwynn Jersey/450 10.00 25.00
TG4 T.Gwynn Bat-Jersey/100 40.00 80.00
WB1 W.Boggs Bat/250 10.00 25.00
WB2 W.Boggs Hat/100 10.00 25.00
WB3 W.Boggs Jersey/440 8.00 20.00
WB4 W.Boggs Bat-Jersey/100 10.00 25.00

2000 Fleer Japan Sheet
1 Sammy Sosa 2.00 5.00
Mike Piazza
Chipper Jones
Ivan Rodri

2000 Fleer Oreo
COMPLETE SET (2) 2.50 6.00
1 Ken Griffey Jr. 2.00 5.00
2 Derek Jeter 2.50 6.00

2000 Fleer Twizzlers
COMPLETE SET (12) 6.00 15.00
1 Mark McGwire 1.00 2.50
2 Cal Ripken Jr. 2.00 5.00
3 Chipper Jones .60 1.50
4 Bernie Williams .40 1.00
5 Alex Rodriguez .75 2.00
6 Curt Schilling .40 1.00
7 Ken Griffey Jr. 1.25 3.00
8 Sammy Sosa .60 1.50
9 Mike Piazza .60 1.50
10 Pedro Martinez .40 1.00
11 Kenny Lofton .25 .60
12 Larry Walker .40 1.00

2001 Fleer Autographics
FOCUS: AUTO OR FEEL GAME 1:72
GENUINE: STATED ODDS 1:24
PREMIUM: STATED ODDS 1:96 RETAIL
SHOWCASE: STATED ODDS 1:96 RETAIL
'02 PLATINUM: AUTO OR BAT 1:1 RACK
'02 GENUINE: 1:18 HOB.DIR., 1:30 HOB.DIST.
FC SUFFIX ON FOCUS DISTRIBUTION
FS SUFFIX ON SHOWCASE DISTRIBUTION
FP'02 SUFFIX ON ULTRA DISTRIBUTION
GN SUFFIX ON GENUINE DISTRIBUTION
PM SUFFIX ON PREMIUM DISTRIBUTION
TC SUFFIX ON TRIPLE CROWN DISTRIBUTION
UL SUFFIX ON ULTRA DISTRIBUTION
1 Roberto Alomar 10.00 25.00
2 Jimmy Anderson 3.00 8.00
3 Ryan Anderson 3.00 8.00
4 Rick Ankiel 3.00 8.00
6 Carlos Beltran 12.00 30.00
7 Adrian Beltre 6.00 15.00
8 Peter Bergeron 3.00 8.00
9 Lance Berkman 3.00 8.00
10 Barry Bonds 25.00 60.00
11 Milton Bradley 3.00 8.00
12 Ryan Bradley 3.00 8.00
13 Dee Brown 3.00 8.00
14 Roosevelt Brown 3.00 8.00
15 Jeromy Burnitz 3.00 8.00
16 Pat Burrell 3.00 8.00
17 Alex Cabrera 10.00 25.00
18 Sean Casey 3.00 8.00
19 Eric Chavez 3.00 8.00
20 Giuseppe Chiaramonte 3.00 8.00
21 Joe Crede 3.00 8.00
22 Jose Cruz Jr. 3.00 8.00
23 Johnny Damon 5.00 12.00
24 Carlos Delgado 3.00 8.00
25 Ryan Dempster 3.00 8.00
26 J.D. Drew 3.00 8.00
27 Adam Dunn 5.00 12.00
28 Erubiel Durazo 3.00 8.00
29 Jermaine Dye 3.00 8.00
30 David Eckstein 3.00 8.00
31 Jim Edmonds 5.00 12.00
32 Alex Escobar 3.00 8.00
33 Seth Etherton 3.00 8.00
34 Adam Everett 3.00 8.00
35 Carlos Febles 3.00 8.00
36 Troy Glaus 10.00 25.00
37 Chad Green 3.00 8.00
38 Ben Grieve 3.00 8.00
39 Wilton Guerrero 3.00 8.00
40 Tony Gwynn 20.00 50.00
41 Toby Hall 3.00 8.00
42 Todd Helton 5.00 12.00
43 Chad Hermansen 3.00 8.00
44 Dustin Hermanson 3.00 8.00
45 Shea Hillenbrand 3.00 8.00
46 Aubrey Huff 3.00 8.00
47 Derek Jeter 150.00 300.00
48 D'Angelo Jimenez 3.00 8.00
49 Randy Johnson 40.00 100.00
50 Chipper Jones 20.00 50.00
51 Cesar King 3.00 8.00
52 Paul Konerko 5.00 12.00
53 Corey Koskie 3.00 8.00
54 Mike Lamb 3.00 8.00
55 Matt Lawton 3.00 8.00
56 Corey Lee 3.00 8.00
57 Derrek Lee 3.00 8.00
58 Mike Lieberthal 3.00 8.00
59 Cole Liniak 3.00 8.00
60 Steve Lomasney 3.00 8.00
61 Terrence Long 3.00 8.00
62 Mike Lowell 3.00 8.00
63 Julio Lugo 3.00 8.00
64 Greg Maddux 40.00 100.00
65 Jason Marquis 3.00 8.00
66 Edgar Martinez 5.00 12.00
67 Justin Miller 3.00 8.00
68 Kevin Millwood 3.00 8.00
69 Eric Milton 3.00 8.00
70 Bengie Molina 3.00 8.00
71 Mike Mussina 5.00 12.00
72 David Ortiz 20.00 50.00
73 Russ Ortiz 3.00 8.00
74 Pablo Ozuna 3.00 8.00
75 Corey Patterson 3.00 8.00
76 Carl Pavano 3.00 8.00
77 Jay Payton 3.00 8.00
78 Wily Pena 3.00 8.00
79 Josh Phelps 3.00 8.00
80 Adam Piatt 3.00 8.00
81 Juan Pierre 3.00 8.00
82 Brad Radke 3.00 8.00
83 Mark Redman 3.00 8.00
84 Matt Riley 3.00 8.00
85 Cal Ripken 50.00 120.00
86 John Rocker 10.00 25.00
87 Alex Rodriguez 40.00 100.00
88 Scott Rolen 5.00 12.00
89 Alex Sanchez 3.00 8.00
90 Fernando Seguignol 3.00 8.00
91 Richie Sexson 3.00 8.00
92 Gary Sheffield 3.00 8.00
93 Alfonso Soriano 5.00 12.00
94 Dernell Stenson 3.00 8.00
95 Garrett Stephenson 3.00 8.00
96 Shannon Stewart 3.00 8.00
97 Fernando Tatis 3.00 8.00
98 Miguel Tejada 10.00 25.00
99 Jorge Toca 3.00 8.00
100 Robin Ventura 3.00 8.00
101 Jose Vidro 3.00 8.00
102 Billy Wagner 3.00 8.00
103 Kip Wells 3.00 8.00
104 Vernon Wells 3.00 8.00
105 Rondell White 3.00 8.00
106 Bernie Williams 30.00 80.00
107 Scott Williamson 3.00 8.00
108 Preston Wilson 3.00 8.00
109 Kerry Wood 3.00 8.00
110 Jamey Wright 3.00 8.00
111 Julio Zuleta 3.00 8.00

2001 Fleer Autographics Gold
*GOLD: .75X TO 2X BASIC AUTOS
STATED PRINT RUN 50 SERIAL #'d SETS

2001 Fleer Autographics Silver
*SILVER: .6X TO 1.5X BASIC AUTOS
STATED PRINT RUN 250 SERIAL #'d SETS

2001 Fleer Feel the Game
*GOLD: 1.25X TO 2.5X BASIC FEEL GAME
GOLD PRINT RUN 50 SERIAL #'d SETS
1 Moises Alou Bat 2.00 5.00
2 Brady Anderson Bat 2.00 5.00
3 Adrian Beltre Bat 5.00 12.00
4 Dante Bichette Bat 2.00 5.00
5 Roger Cedeno Bat 2.00 5.00
6 Ben Davis Bat 2.00 5.00
7 Carlos Delgado Bat 2.00 5.00
8 J.D. Drew Bat 2.00 5.00

9 Jermaine Dye Bat 2.00 5.00
10 Jason Giambi Bat 2.00 5.00
11 Brian Giles Bat 2.00 5.00
12 Juan Gonzalez Bat 2.00 5.00
13 Rickey Henderson Bat 5.00 12.00
14 Richard Hidalgo Bat 2.00 5.00
15 Chipper Jones Bat 5.00 12.00
16 Eric Karros Bat 2.00 5.00
17 Javy Lopez Bat 2.00 5.00
18 Tino Martinez Bat 3.00 8.00
19 Raul Mondesi Bat 2.00 5.00
20 Phil Nevin Bat 2.00 5.00
21 Chan Ho Park Bat 3.00 8.00
22 Ivan Rodriguez Bat 3.00 8.00
23 Matt Stairs Bat 2.00 5.00
24 Shannon Stewart Bat 2.00 5.00
25 Frank Thomas Bat 5.00 12.00
26 Jose Vidro Bat 2.00 5.00
27 Matt Williams Bat 2.00 5.00
28 Preston Wilson Bat 2.00 5.00

2001 Fleer Bonds Home Run King Jumbo

BBHRK Barry Bonds 1.50 4.00

2001 Fleer Ripken Cal to Greatness Jumbo

NNO Cal Ripken 4.00 10.00

2001 Fleer Ripken Commemorative 50000

COMPLETE SET 4.00 10.00
COMMON CARD .20 .50

2001 Fleer Cal Ripken Career Highlights 2632

COMP.FACT SET
COMMON CARD

2002 Fleer

COMPLETE SET (540) 15.00 40.00
COMMON CARD (1-540) .08 .25
COMMON CARD (492-531) .20 .50
1 Darin Erstad FP .25 .60
2 Randy Johnson FP .25 .60
3 Chipper Jones FP .25 .60
4 Jay Gibbons FP .08 .25
5 Nomar Garciaparra FP .40 1.00
6 Sammy Sosa FP .25 .60
7 Frank Thomas FP .25 .60
8 Ken Griffey Jr. FP .50 1.25
9 Jim Thome FP .15 .40
10 Todd Helton FP .15 .40
11 Jeff Weaver FP .08 .25
12 Cliff Floyd FP .08 .25
13 Jeff Bagwell FP .15 .40
14 Mike Sweeney FP .08 .25
15 Adrian Beltre FP .08 .25
16 Richie Sexson FP .08 .25
17 Brad Radke FP .08 .25
18 Vladimir Guerrero FP .15 .40
19 Mike Piazza FP .40 1.00
20 Derek Jeter FP .50 1.25
21 Eric Chavez FP .08 .25
22 Pat Burrell FP .08 .25
23 Brian Giles FP .08 .25
24 Trevor Hoffman FP .08 .25
25 Barry Bonds FP .40 1.00
26 Ichiro Suzuki FP .40 1.00
27 Albert Pujols FP .40 1.00
28 Ben Grieve FP .08 .25
29 Alex Rodriguez FP .30 .75
30 Carlos Delgado FP .08 .25
31 Miguel Tejada .15 .40
32 Todd Hollandsworth .08 .25
33 Marlon Anderson .08 .25
34 Kerry Robinson .08 .25
35 Chris Richard .08 .25
36 Jamey Wright .08 .25
37 Ray Lankford .15 .40
38 Mike Bordick .15 .40
39 Danny Graves .08 .25
40 A.J. Pierzynski .15 .40
41 Shannon Stewart .15 .40
42 Tony Armas Jr. .08 .25
43 Brad Ausmus .15 .40
44 Alfonso Soriano .15 .40
45 Junior Spivey .08 .25
46 Brent Mayne .08 .25
47 Jim Thome .25 .60
48 Dan Wilson .08 .25
49 Geoff Jenkins .08 .25
50 Kris Benson .08 .25
51 Rafael Furcal .15 .40
52 Wiki Gonzalez .08 .25
53 Jeff Kent .15 .40
54 Curt Schilling .15 .40
55 Ken Harvey .08 .25
56 Roosevelt Brown .08 .25
57 David Segui .08 .25
58 Mario Valdez .08 .25
59 Adam Dunn .15 .40
60 Bob Howry .08 .25
61 Michael Barrett .08 .25
62 Garret Anderson .15 .40
63 Kelvim Escobar .08 .25
64 Ben Grieve .08 .25
65 Randy Johnson .40 1.00
66 Jose Offerman .08 .25
67 Jason Kendall .15 .40
68 Joel Pineiro .08 .25
69 Alex Escobar .08 .25
70 Chris George .08 .25
71 Bobby Higginson .15 .40
72 Nomar Garciaparra .60 1.50
73 Pat Burrell .15 .40
74 Lee Stevens .08 .25
75 Felipe Lopez .08 .25
76 Al Leiter .15 .40
77 Jim Edmonds .15 .40
78 Al Levine .08 .25
79 Raul Mondesi .15 .40
80 Jose Valentin .08 .25
81 Matt Clement .15 .40
82 Richard Hidalgo .08 .25
83 Jamie Moyer .15 .40
84 Brian Schneider .08 .25
85 John Franco .15 .40
86 Brian Buchanan .08 .25
87 Roy Oswalt .15 .40
88 Johnny Estrada .08 .25
89 Marcus Giles .15 .40
90 Carlos Valderrama .08 .25
91 Mark Mulder .15 .40
92 Mark Grace .25 .60
93 Andy Ashby .08 .25
94 Woody Williams .08 .25
95 Ben Petrick .08 .25
96 Roy Halladay .15 .40
97 Fred McGriff .25 .60
98 Shawn Green .15 .40
99 Todd Hundley .08 .25
100 Carlos Febles .08 .25
101 Jason Marquis .08 .25
102 Mike Redmond .08 .25
103 Shane Halter .08 .25
104 Trot Nixon .15 .40
105 Jeremy Giambi .08 .25
106 Carlos Delgado .15 .40
107 Richie Sexson .15 .40
108 Russ Ortiz .08 .25
109 David Ortiz .40 1.00
110 Curtis Leskanic .08 .25
111 Jay Payton .08 .25
112 Travis Phelps .08 .25
113 J.T. Snow .15 .40
114 Edgar Renteria .15 .40
115 Freddy Garcia .15 .40
116 Cliff Floyd .15 .40
117 Charles Nagy .08 .25
118 Tony Batista .08 .25
119 Rafael Palmeiro .25 .60
120 Darren Dreifort .08 .25
121 Warren Morris .08 .25
122 Augie Ojeda .08 .25
123 Rusty Greer .15 .40
124 Esteban Yan .08 .25
125 Corey Patterson .08 .25
126 Matt Ginter .08 .25
127 Matt Lawton .08 .25
128 Miguel Batista .08 .25
129 Randy Winn .08 .25
130 Eric Milton .08 .25
131 Jack Wilson .08 .25
132 Sean Casey .15 .40
133 Mike Sweeney .15 .40
134 Jason Tyner .08 .25
135 Carlos Hernandez .08 .25
136 Shea Hillenbrand .15 .40
137 Shawn Wooten .08 .25
138 Peter Bergeron .08 .25
139 Travis Lee .08 .25
140 Craig Wilson .08 .25
141 Carlos Guillen .15 .40
142 Chipper Jones .40 1.00
143 Gabe Kapler .15 .40
144 Raul Ibanez .08 .25
145 Eric Chavez .15 .40
146 D'Angelo Jimenez .08 .25
147 Chad Hermansen .08 .25
148 Joe Kennedy .08 .25
149 Mariano Rivera .40 1.00
150 Jeff Bagwell .25 .60
151 Joe McEwing .08 .25
152 Ronnie Belliard .08 .25
153 Desi Relaford .08 .25
154 Vinny Castilla .15 .40
155 Tim Hudson .15 .40
156 Wilton Guerrero .08 .25
157 Raul Casanova .08 .25
158 Edgardo Alfonzo .08 .25
159 Derrek Lee .25 .60
160 Phil Nevin .15 .40
161 Roger Clemens .75 2.00
162 Jason LaRue .08 .25
163 Brian Lawrence .08 .25
164 Adrian Beltre .15 .40
165 Troy Glaus .15 .40
166 Jeff Weaver .08 .25
167 B.J. Surhoff .15 .40
168 Eric Byrnes .08 .25
169 Mike Sirotka .08 .25
170 Bill Haselman .08 .25
171 Javier Vazquez .15 .40
172 Sidney Ponson .08 .25
173 Adam Everett .08 .25
174 Bubba Trammell .08 .25
175 Robb Nen .15 .40
176 Barry Larkin .25 .60
177 Tony Graffanino .08 .25
178 Rich Garces .08 .25
179 Juan Uribe .08 .25
180 Tom Glavine .25 .60
181 Eric Karros .15 .40
182 Michael Cuddyer .08 .25
183 Wade Miller .08 .25
184 Matt Williams .15 .40
185 Matt Morris .15 .40
186 Rickey Henderson .40 1.00
187 Trevor Hoffman .15 .40
188 Wilson Betemit .08 .25
189 Steve Karsay .08 .25
190 Frank Catalanotto .08 .25
191 Jason Schmidt .15 .40
192 Roger Cedeno .08 .25
193 Magglio Ordonez .15 .40
194 Pat Hentgen .08 .25
195 Mike Lieberthal .15 .40
196 Andy Pettitte .25 .60
197 Jay Gibbons .08 .25
198 Rolando Arrojo .08 .25
199 Joe Mays .08 .25
200 Aubrey Huff .15 .40
201 Nelson Figueroa .08 .25
202 Paul Konerko .15 .40
203 Ken Griffey Jr. .75 2.00
204 Brandon Duckworth .08 .25
205 Sammy Sosa .40 1.00
206 Carl Everett .15 .40
207 Scott Rolen .25 .60
208 Orlando Hernandez .15 .40
209 Todd Helton .25 .60
210 Preston Wilson .15 .40
211 Gil Meche .08 .25
212 Bill Mueller .15 .40
213 Craig Biggio .25 .60
214 Dean Palmer .15 .40
215 Randy Wolf .08 .25
216 Jeff Suppan .08 .25
217 Jimmy Rollins .15 .40
218 Alexis Gomez .08 .25
219 Ellis Burks .15 .40
220 Ramon E. Martinez .08 .25
221 Ramiro Mendoza .08 .25
222 Einar Diaz .08 .25
223 Brent Abernathy .08 .25
224 Darin Erstad .15 .40
225 Reggie Taylor .08 .25
226 Jason Jennings .08 .25
227 Ray Durham .15 .40
228 John Parrish .08 .25
229 Kevin Young .08 .25
230 Xavier Nady .08 .25
231 Juan Cruz .08 .25
232 Greg Norton .08 .25
233 Barry Bonds 1.00 2.50
234 Kip Wells .08 .25
235 Paul LoDuca .15 .40
236 Javy Lopez .15 .40
237 Luis Castillo .08 .25
238 Tom Gordon .08 .25
239 Mike Mordecai .08 .25
240 Damian Rolls .08 .25
241 Julio Lugo .08 .25
242 Ichiro Suzuki .75 2.00
243 Tony Womack .08 .25
244 Matt Anderson .08 .25
245 Carlos Lee .15 .40
246 Alex Rodriguez .50 1.50
247 Bernie Williams .25 .60
248 Scott Sullivan .08 .25
249 Mike Hampton .15 .40
250 Orlando Cabrera .15 .40
251 Benito Santiago .15 .40
252 Steve Finley .15 .40
253 Dave Williams .08 .25
254 Adam Kennedy .08 .25
255 Omar Vizquel .25 .60
256 Garrett Stephenson .08 .25
257 Fernando Tatis .08 .25
258 Mike Piazza .60 1.50
259 Scott Spiezio .08 .25
260 Jacque Jones .15 .40
261 Russell Branyan .08 .25
262 Mark McLemore .08 .25
263 Mitch Meluskey .08 .25
264 Marlon Byrd .08 .25
265 Kyle Farnsworth .08 .25
266 Billy Sylvester .08 .25
267 C.C. Sabathia .15 .40
268 Mark Buehrle .15 .40
269 Geoff Blum .08 .25
270 Bret Prinz .08 .25
271 Placido Polanco .08 .25
272 John Olerud .15 .40
273 Pedro Martinez .25 .60
274 Doug Mientkiewicz .15 .40
275 Jason Bere .08 .25
276 Bud Smith .08 .25
277 Terrence Long .08 .25
278 Troy Percival .15 .40
279 Derek Jeter 1.00 2.50
280 Eric Owens .08 .25
281 Jay Bell .15 .40
282 Mike Cameron .08 .25
283 Joe Randa .15 .40
284 Brian Roberts .15 .40
285 Ryan Klesko .15 .40
286 Ryan Dempster .15 .40
287 Cristian Guzman .08 .25
288 Tim Salmon .25 .60
289 Mark Johnson .08 .25
290 Brian Giles .15 .40
291 Jon Lieber .08 .25
292 Fernando Vina .08 .25
293 Mike Mussina .25 .60
294 Juan Pierre .15 .40
295 Carlos Beltran .15 .40
296 Vladimir Guerrero .40 1.00
297 Orlando Merced .08 .25
298 Jose Hernandez .08 .25
299 Mike Lamb .08 .25
300 David Eckstein .15 .40
301 Mark Loretta .08 .25
302 Greg Vaughn .08 .25
303 Jose Vidro .08 .25
304 Jose Ortiz .08 .25
305 Mark Grudzielanek .08 .25
306 Rob Bell .08 .25
307 Elmer Dessens .08 .25
308 Tomas Perez .08 .25
309 Jerry Hairston Jr. .08 .25
310 Mike Stanton .08 .25
311 Todd Walker .08 .25
312 Jason Varitek .40 1.00
313 Masato Yoshii .08 .25
314 Ben Sheets .15 .40
315 Roberto Hernandez .08 .25
316 Eli Marrero .08 .25
317 Josh Beckett .15 .40
318 Robert Fick .08 .25
319 Aramis Ramirez .15 .40
320 Bartolo Colon .15 .40
321 Kenny Kelly .08 .25
322 Luis Gonzalez .15 .40
323 John Smoltz .25 .60
324 Homer Bush .08 .25
325 Kevin Millwood .15 .40
326 Manny Ramirez .25 .60
327 Armando Benitez .08 .25
328 Luis Alicea .08 .25
329 Mark Kotsay .15 .40
330 Felix Rodriguez .08 .25
331 Eddie Taubensee .08 .25
332 John Burkett .08 .25
333 Ramon Ortiz .08 .25
334 Daryle Ward .08 .25
335 Jarrod Washburn .08 .25
336 Benji Gil .08 .25
337 Mike Lowell .15 .40
338 Larry Walker .15 .40
339 Andruw Jones .25 .60
340 Scott Elarton .08 .25
341 Tony McKnight .08 .25
342 Frank Thomas .40 1.00
343 Kevin Brown .15 .40
344 Jermaine Dye .15 .40
345 Luis Rivas .08 .25
346 Jeff Conine .15 .40
347 Bobby Kielty .08 .25
348 Jeffrey Hammonds .08 .25
349 Keith Foulke .15 .40
350 Dave Martinez .08 .25
351 Adam Eaton .08 .25
352 Brandon Inge .08 .25
353 Tyler Houston .08 .25
354 Bobby Abreu .15 .40
355 Ivan Rodriguez .25 .60
356 Doug Glanville .08 .25
357 Jorge Julio .08 .25
358 Kerry Wood .15 .40
359 Eric Munson .08 .25
360 Joe Crede .08 .25
361 Denny Neagle .08 .25
362 Vance Wilson .08 .25
363 Neifi Perez .08 .25
364 Darryl Kile .15 .40
365 Jose Macias .08 .25
366 Michael Coleman .08 .25
367 Erubiel Durazo .08 .25
368 Darrin Fletcher .08 .25
369 Matt White .08 .25
370 Marvin Benard .08 .25
371 Brad Penny .08 .25
372 Chuck Finley .15 .40
373 Delino DeShields .08 .25
374 Adrian Brown .08 .25
375 Corey Koskie .08 .25
376 Kazuhiro Sasaki .15 .40
377 Brent Butler .08 .25
378 Paul Wilson .08 .25
379 Scott Williamson .08 .25
380 Mike Young .40 1.00
381 Toby Hall .08 .25
382 Shane Reynolds .08 .25
383 Tom Goodwin .08 .25
384 Seth Etherton .08 .25
385 Billy Wagner .15 .40
386 Josh Phelps .08 .25
387 Kyle Lohse .08 .25
388 Jeremy Fikac .08 .25
389 Jorge Posada .25 .60
390 Bret Boone .15 .40
391 Angel Berroa .08 .25
392 Matt Mantei .08 .25
393 Alex Gonzalez .08 .25
394 Scott Strickland .08 .25
395 Charles Johnson .08 .25
396 Ramon Hernandez .08 .25
397 Damian Jackson .08 .25
398 Albert Pujols .75 2.00
399 Gary Bennett .08 .25
400 Edgar Martinez .25 .60
401 Carl Pavano .15 .40
402 Chris Gomez .08 .25
403 Jaret Wright .08 .25
404 Lance Berkman .15 .40
405 Robert Person .08 .25
406 Brook Fordyce .08 .25
407 Adam Pettyjohn .08 .25
408 Chris Carpenter .15 .40
409 Rey Ordonez .08 .25
410 Eric Gagne .15 .40
411 Damion Easley .08 .25
412 A.J. Burnett .15 .40
413 Aaron Boone .15 .40
414 J.D. Drew .15 .40
415 Kelly Stinnett .08 .25
416 Mark Quinn .08 .25
417 Brad Radke .15 .40
418 Jose Cruz Jr. .08 .25
419 Greg Maddux .60 1.50
420 Steve Cox .08 .25
421 Torii Hunter .15 .40
422 Sandy Alomar Jr. .08 .25
423 Barry Zito .15 .40
424 Bill Hall .15 .40
425 Marquis Grissom .15 .40
426 Rich Aurilia .08 .25
427 Royce Clayton .08 .25
428 Travis Fryman .15 .40
429 Pablo Ozuna .08 .25
430 David Dellucci .08 .25
431 Vernon Wells .15 .40
432 Gregg Zaun CP .08 .25
433 Alex Gonzalez CP .08 .25
434 Hideo Nomo CP .40 1.00
435 Jeromy Burnitz CP .15 .40
436 Gary Sheffield CP .15 .40
437 Tino Martinez CP .25 .60
438 Tsuyoshi Shinjo CP .15 .40
439 Chan Ho Park CP .15 .40
440 Tony Clark CP .08 .25
441 Brad Fullmer CP .08 .25
442 Jason Giambi CP .15 .40
443 Billy Koch CP .08 .25
444 Mo Vaughn CP .15 .40
445 Alex Ochoa CP .08 .25
446 Darren Lewis CP .08 .25
447 John Rocker CP .15 .40
448 Scott Hatteberg CP .08 .25
449 Brady Anderson CP .15 .40
450 Chuck Knoblauch CP .15 .40
451 Pokey Reese CP .08 .25
452 Brian Jordan CP .15 .40
453 Albie Lopez CP .08 .25
454 David Bell CP .08 .25
455 Juan Gonzalez CP .15 .40
456 Terry Adams CP .08 .25
457 Kenny Lofton CP .15 .40
458 Shawn Estes CP .08 .25
459 Josh Fogg CP .08 .25
460 Dmitri Young CP .15 .40
461 Johnny Damon Sox CP .25 .60
462 Chris Singleton CP .08 .25
463 Ricky Ledee CP .08 .25
464 Dustin Hermanson CP .08 .25
465 Aaron Sele CP .08 .25
466 Chris Stynes CP .08 .25
467 Matt Stairs CP .08 .25
468 Kevin Appier CP .15 .40
469 Omar Daal CP .08 .25
470 Moises Alou CP .15 .40
471 Juan Encarnacion CP .08 .25
472 Robin Ventura CP .15 .40
473 Eric Hinske CP .08 .25
474 Rondell White CP .15 .40
475 Carlos Pena CP .08 .25
476 Craig Paquette CP .08 .25
477 Marty Cordova CP .08 .25
478 Brett Tomko CP .08 .25
479 Reggie Sanders CP .08 .25
480 Roberto Alomar CP .25 .60
481 Jeff Cirillo CP .08 .25
482 Todd Zeile CP .15 .40
483 John Vander Wal CP .08 .25
484 Rick Helling CP .08 .25
485 Jeff D'Amico CP .08 .25
486 David Justice CP .15 .40
487 Jason Isringhausen CP .15 .40
488 Shigetoshi Hasegawa CP .15 .40
489 Eric Young CP .08 .25
490 David Wells CP .15 .40
491 Ruben Sierra CP .08 .25
492 Aaron Cook FF RC .30 .75
493 Takahito Nomura FF RC .30 .75
494 Austin Kearns FF .20 .50
495 Kazuhisa Ishii FF RC .50 1.25
496 Mark Teixeira FF .75 2.00
497 Rene Reyes FF RC .30 .75
498 Tim Spooneybarger FF .20 .50
499 Ben Broussard FF .20 .50
500 Eric Cyr FF .20 .50
501 Anastacio Martinez FF RC .30 .75
502 Morgan Ensberg FF .30 .75
503 Steve Kent FF RC .30 .75
504 Franklin Nunez FF RC .30 .75
505 Adam Walker FF RC .30 .75
506 Anderson Machado FF RC .30 .75
507 Ryan Drese FF .20 .50
508 Luis Ugueto FF RC .30 .75
509 Jorge Nunez FF RC .30 .75
510 Colby Lewis FF .20 .50
511 Ron Calloway FF RC .30 .75
512 Hansel Izquierdo FF RC .30 .75
513 Jason Lane FF .20 .50
514 Rafael Soriano FF .20 .50
515 Jackson Melian FF .20 .50
516 Edwin Almonte FF RC .30 .75
517 Satoru Komiyama FF RC .30 .75
518 Corey Thurman FF RC .30 .75
519 Jorge De La Rosa FF RC .30 .75
520 Victor Martinez FF .75 2.00
521 Dewon Brazelton FF .20 .50
522 Marlon Byrd FF .20 .50
523 Jae Seo FF .20 .50
524 Orlando Hudson FF .20 .50
525 Sean Burroughs FF .20 .50
526 Ryan Langerhans FF .30 .75
527 David Kelton FF .20 .50
528 So Taguchi FF RC .50 1.25
529 Tyler Walker FF .20 .50
530 Hank Blalock FF .50 1.25
531 Mark Prior FF .50 1.25
532 Yankee Stadium CL .15 .40
533 Fenway Park CL .15 .40
534 Wrigley Field CL .15 .40
535 Dodger Stadium CL .15 .40
536 Camden Yards CL .15 .40
537 PacBell Park CL .08 .25
538 Jacobs Field CL .08 .25
539 SAFECO Field CL .08 .25
540 Miller Field CL .08 .25

2002 Fleer Gold Backs

*GOLD BACK: .75X TO 2X BASIC
*GOLD BACK 492-531: .75X TO 2X BASIC
RANDOM INSERTS IN PACKS
15% OF PRINT RUN ARE GOLD BACKS

2002 Fleer Mini

*MINI: 10X TO 25X BASIC
*MINI 492-531: 5X TO 12X BASIC
RANDOM INSERTS IN RETAIL PACKS
STATED PRINT RUN 50 SERIAL #'d SETS

2002 Fleer Tiffany

*TIFFANY: 4X TO 10X BASIC
*TIFFANY 492-531: 2X TO 5X BASIC
RANDOM INSERTS IN HOBBY PACKS
STATED PRINT RUN 200 SERIAL #'d SETS

2002 Fleer Barry Bonds Career Highlights

COMPLETE SET (10) 15.00 40.00
COMMON CARD (1-3) 1.50 4.00
COMMON CARD (4-6) 2.00 5.00
COMMON CARD (7-9) 3.00 8.00
COMMON CARD (10) 2.00 5.00
1-3 ODDS 1:65 HOBBY, 1:225 RETAIL
4-6 ODDS 1:125 HOBBY, 1:400 RETAIL
7-9 ODDS 1:250 HOBBY, 1:500 RETAIL
10 ODDS 1:383 HOBBY, 1:800 RETAIL
OVERALL ODDS 1:12 HOBBY, 1:36 RETAIL

2002 Fleer Barry Bonds Career Highlights Autographs

COMMON CARD (1-10) 125.00 200.00
RANDOM INSERTS IN ALL PACKS
STATED PRINT RUN 25 SERIAL #'d SETS

2002 Fleer Classic Cuts Autographs

STATED ODDS 1:432 HOBBY
SP PRINT RUNS PROVIDED BY FLEER
SP'S ARE NOT SERIAL NUMBERED
BRA Brooks Robinson SP/200 10.00 25.00
GPA Gaylord Perry SP/225 6.00 15.00
HKA Harmon Killebrew 15.00 40.00
JMA Juan Marichal 8.00 20.00
LAA Luis Aparicio 6.00 15.00
PRA Phil Rizzuto SP/125 20.00 50.00
RCA Ron Cey 6.00 15.00
RFA Rollie Fingers SP/35 6.00 15.00
TLA Tommy Lasorda SP/35 40.00 100.00

2002 Fleer Classic Cuts Game Used

STATED ODDS 1:24 HOBBY
SP PRINT RUNS PROVIDED BY FLEER
SP'S ARE NOT SERIAL NUMBERED
NO PRICING ON QTY OF 110 OR LESS
ADJ Andre Dawson Jsy 4.00 10.00
ATB Alan Trammell Bat 4.00 10.00
BBB Bobby Bonds Bat 4.00 10.00
BBJ Bobby Bonds Jsy 4.00 10.00
BDB Bill Dickey Bat/200 * 6.00 15.00
BJJ Bo Jackson Jsy 4.00 10.00
BMB Billy Martin Bat/65 * 10.00 25.00
BRB Brooks Robinson Bat/250 * 6.00 15.00
BTB Bill Terry Bat/65 * 15.00 40.00
CFB Carlton Fisk Bat 6.00 15.00
CFJ Carlton Fisk Jsy/150 * 6.00 15.00
CHJ Jim Hunter Jsy 6.00 15.00
CRBG Cal Ripken Btg Glv/100 * 12.00 30.00
CRFG Cal Ripken Fld Glv/60 * 12.00 30.00
CRJ Cal Ripken Jsy 8.00 20.00
CRP Cal Ripken Pants/200 * 10.00 25.00
DEB Dwight Evans Bat/250 * 6.00 15.00
DEJ Dwight Evans Jsy 6.00 15.00
DMB Don Mattingly Bat/200 * 10.00 25.00
DMJ Don Mattingly Jsy 10.00 25.00
DPB Dave Parker Bat 4.00 10.00
DWB Dave Winfield Bat 4.00 10.00
DWJ Dave Winfield Jsy/231 * 4.00 10.00
DWP Dave Winfield Pants 4.00 10.00
DZJ Don Zimmer Jsy/90 * 6.00 15.00
EMB Eddie Mathews Bat/200 * 4.00 10.00
EMB Eddie Murray Bat 6.00 15.00
EMJ Eddie Murray Jsy 6.00 15.00
EMP Eddie Murray Patch/45 * 15.00 40.00
EWJ Earl Weaver Jsy 4.00 10.00
GBB George Brett Bat/250 * 10.00 25.00
GBJ George Brett Jsy/250 * 10.00 25.00
GHB Gil Hodges Bat/200 * 6.00 15.00
GKB George Kell Bat/150 * 6.00 15.00
HBB Hank Bauer Bat 6.00 15.00
HWP Hoyt Wilhelm Pants/150 * 4.00 10.00
JBB Johnny Bench Bat/100 * 10.00 25.00
JBJ Johnny Bench Jsy 6.00 15.00
JMB Joe Morgan Bat/250 * 4.00 10.00
JPJ Jim Palmer Jsy/273 * 4.00 10.00
JRB Jim Rice Bat/225 * 4.00 10.00
JRJ Jim Rice Jsy/90 * 6.00 15.00
JTJ Joe Torre Jsy/125 * 6.00 15.00
KGB Kirk Gibson Bat 4.00 10.00
KPJ Kirby Puckett Jsy 6.00 15.00
LDB Larry Doby Bat/250 * 10.00 25.00
LPP Lou Piniella Pants 4.00 10.00
NFB Nellie Fox Bat/200 * 6.00 15.00
NRJ Nolan Ryan Jsy 15.00 40.00
NRP Nolan Ryan Pants/200 * 15.00 40.00
OCB Orlando Cepeda Bat/45 * 6.00 15.00
OCP Orlando Cepeda Pants 4.00 10.00
OSJ Ozzie Smith Jsy/250 * 10.00 25.00
PBB Paul Blair Bat 4.00 10.00
PMB Paul Molitor Bat/250 * 4.00 10.00
PMP Paul Molitor Patch/110 * 6.00 15.00
RFJ Rollie Fingers Jsy 4.00 10.00
RJB Reggie Jackson Bat/50 * 12.50 30.00
RJP Reggie Jackson Pants 6.00 15.00
RKB Ralph Kiner Bat/47 * 6.00 15.00
RMP Roger Maris Pants/200 * 12.00 50.00
RSB Ryne Sandberg Bat 6.00 15.00
RYB Robin Yount Bat 4.00 10.00
SAP Sparky Anderson Pants 4.00 10.00
SCP Steve Carlton Pants 4.00 10.00
SGB Steve Garvey Bat 4.00 10.00
TJJ Tommy John Jsy/55 * 6.00 15.00
TKB Ted Kluszewski Bat/200 * 6.00 15.00
TKP Ted Kluszewski Pants 6.00 15.00
TPB Tony Perez Bat/250 * 4.00 10.00
TPJ Tony Perez Jsy 4.00 10.00
TWB Ted Williams Bat 20.00 50.00
TWP Ted Williams Pants 12.50 30.00
WBB Wade Boggs Bat/99 * 10.00 25.00
WBJ Wade Boggs Jsy 4.00 10.00
WBP Wade Boggs Patch/50 * 15.00 40.00
WMJ Willie McCovey Jsy/300 * 4.00 10.00
WSB Willie Stargell Bat/250 * 6.00 15.00
YBB Yogi Berra Bat/72 * 10.00 25.00
RCCB Rod Carew Bat 4.00 10.00

2002 Fleer Classic Cuts Game Used Autographs

RANDOM INSERTS IN HOBBY PACKS
STATED PRINT RUNS LISTED BELOW
BRB Brooks Robinson Bat/45 30.00 60.00
LAB Luis Aparicio Bat/45 15.00 40.00
RFJ Rollie Fingers Jsy/35 5.00 12.00

2002 Fleer Diamond Standouts

COMPLETE SET (10) 30.00 80.00
RANDOM INSERTS IN HOBBY PACKS
STATED PRINT RUN 1200 SERIAL #'d SETS
1 Mike Piazza 3.00 8.00
2 Derek Jeter 5.00 12.00
3 Ken Griffey Jr. 4.00 10.00
4 Barry Bonds 5.00 12.00
5 Sammy Sosa 3.00 8.00
6 Alex Rodriguez 2.50 6.00
7 Ichiro Suzuki 4.00 10.00
8 Greg Maddux 3.00 8.00
9 Jason Giambi 3.00 8.00
10 Nomar Garciaparra 3.00 8.00

2002 Fleer Golden Memories

COMPLETE SET (15) 15.00 40.00
STATED ODDS 1:24 HOBBY/RETAIL
1 Frank Thomas 1.00 2.50
2 Derek Jeter 2.50 6.00
3 Albert Pujols 2.00 5.00
4 Barry Bonds 2.50 6.00
5 Alex Rodriguez 1.25 3.00
6 Randy Johnson 1.00 2.50
7 Jeff Bagwell .60 1.50
8 Greg Maddux 1.50 4.00
9 Ivan Rodriguez .60 1.50
10 Ichiro Suzuki 2.00 5.00
11 Mike Piazza 1.50 4.00
12 Pat Burrell .60 1.50
13 Rickey Henderson 1.00 2.50
14 Vladimir Guerrero 1.00 2.50
15 Sammy Sosa 1.00 2.50

2002 Fleer Headliners

COMPLETE SET (20) 10.00 25.00
STATED ODDS 1:8 HOBBY, 1:12 RETAIL
1 Randy Johnson .50 1.25
2 Alex Rodriguez .60 1.50
3 Todd Helton .40 1.00
4 Pedro Martinez .40 1.00
5 Ichiro Suzuki 1.00 2.50
6 Vladimir Guerrero .50 1.25
7 Derek Jeter 1.25 3.00
8 Adam Dunn .40 1.00
9 Luis Gonzalez .40 1.00
10 Kazuhiro Sasaki .40 1.00
11 Sammy Sosa .50 1.25
12 Jason Giambi .40 1.00
13 Ken Griffey Jr. 1.00 2.50
14 Roger Clemens 1.00 2.50
15 Brandon Duckworth .40 1.00
16 Nomar Garciaparra .75 2.00
17 Bud Smith .40 1.00
18 Juan Gonzalez .40 1.00
19 Chipper Jones .50 1.25
20 Barry Bonds 1.25 3.00

2002 Fleer Rookie Flashbacks

COMPLETE SET (20) 10.00 25.00
STATED ODDS 1:3 RETAIL
1 Bret Prinz .40 1.00
2 Albert Pujols 1.50 4.00
3 C.C. Sabathia .40 1.00
4 Ichiro Suzuki 1.50 4.00
5 Juan Cruz .40 1.00
6 Jay Gibbons .40 1.00
7 Bud Smith .40 1.00
8 Johnny Estrada .40 1.00
9 Roy Oswalt .40 1.00
10 Tsuyoshi Shinjo .40 1.00
11 Brandon Duckworth .40 1.00
12 Jackson Melian .40 1.00
13 Josh Beckett .40 1.00
14 Morgan Ensberg .40 1.00
15 Brian Lawrence .40 1.00
16 Eric Hinske .40 1.00
17 Juan Uribe .40 1.00
18 Matt White .40 1.00
19 Junior Spivey .40 1.00
20 Wilson Betemit .40 1.00

2002 Fleer Rookie Sensations

COMPLETE SET (20) 20.00 50.00
RANDOM INSERTS IN HOBBY PACKS
STATED PRINT RUN 1500 SERIAL #'d SETS
1 Bret Prinz 2.00 5.00
2 Albert Pujols 10.00 25.00
3 C.C. Sabathia 2.00 5.00
4 Ichiro Suzuki 10.00 25.00
5 Juan Cruz 2.00 5.00
6 Jay Gibbons 2.00 5.00
7 Bud Smith 2.00 5.00
8 Johnny Estrada 2.00 5.00
9 Roy Oswalt 2.00 5.00
10 Tsuyoshi Shinjo 2.00 5.00
11 Brandon Duckworth 2.00 5.00
12 Jackson Melian 2.00 5.00
13 Josh Beckett 2.00 5.00
14 Morgan Ensberg 2.00 5.00
15 Brian Lawrence 2.00 5.00
16 Eric Hinske 2.00 5.00
17 Juan Uribe 2.00 5.00
18 Matt White 2.00 5.00
19 Junior Spivey 2.00 5.00
20 Wilson Betemit 2.00 5.00

2002 Fleer Then and Now

COMPLETE SET (10) 60.00 150.00
RANDOM INSERTS IN HOBBY PACKS
STATED PRINT RUN 275 SERIAL #'d SETS
1 E.Mathews 6.00 15.00
C.Jones
2 W.McCovey 12.50 30.00
B.Bonds
3 J.Bench 8.00 20.00
M.Piazza
4 E.Banks 6.00 15.00
A.Rodriguez
5 R.Henderson 10.00 25.00
I.Suzuki
6 T.Seaver 10.00 25.00
R.Clemens
7 J.Marichal 6.00 15.00
P.Martinez
8 R.Jackson 12.50 30.00
D.Jeter
9 N.Ryan 20.00 50.00
K.Wood
10 J.Morgan 10.00 25.00
K.Griffey Jr.

2002 Fleer Collection

COMPLETE SET 40.00 100.00
1 Troy Glaus 1.00 2.50
2 Luis Gonzalez 1.00 2.50
3 Chipper Jones 2.00 5.00
4 Cal Ripken Jr. 4.00 10.00
5 Nomar Garciaparra 2.00 5.00
6 Sammy Sosa 1.50 4.00
7 Frank Thomas 1.25 3.00
8 Ken Griffey Jr. 3.00 8.00
9 Jim Thome 1.00 2.50
10 Todd Helton 1.00 2.50
11 Tony Clark .40 1.00
12 A.J. Burnett .40 1.00
13 Jeff Bagwell 1.00 2.50

14 Mike Sweeney 1.00 2.50
15 Shawn Green 1.00 2.50
16 Ben Sheets .60 1.50
17 Doug Mientkiewicz .40 1.00
18 Vladimir Guerrero 1.50 4.00
19 Mike Piazza 2.00 5.00
20 Derek Jeter 4.00 10.00
21 Tim Hudson 1.00 2.50
22 Pat Burrell .60 1.50
23 Jason Kendall .60 1.50
24 Phil Nevin .60 1.50
25 Barry Bonds 2.00 5.00
26 Ichiro Suzuki 4.00 10.00
27 Albert Pujols 3.00 8.00
28 Ben Grieve .40 1.00
29 Alex Rodriguez 1.50 4.00
30 Carlos Delgado 1.25 3.00

2002 Fleer Bonds 4X MVP Jumbo

NNO Barry Bonds 6.00 15.00

2002 Fleer Barry Bonds 600 Home Run Chasing History

1 Barry Bonds 75.00 150.00

2002 Fleer Barry Bonds 600 Home Run Jumbo

BB600 Barry Bonds 2.00 5.00

2002 Fleer Barry Bonds 600 Home Run Jumbo Game Used Autographed

1 Barry Bonds 40.00 80.00

2002 Fleer Jeter Turn 2

COMPLETE SET 2.00 5.00
COMMON CARD .75 2.00

2003 Fleer 3D

COMPLETE SET 10.00 20.00
1 Derek Jeter 1.00 2.50
2 Barry Bonds .60 1.50
3 Ichiro Suzuki .50 1.25
4 Jason Giambi .15 .40
5 Chipper Jones .40 1.00
6 Alfonso Soriano .25 .60
7 Miguel Tejada .25 .60
8 Nomar Garciaparra .25 .60
9 Alex Rodriguez .50 1.25
10 Ken Griffey Jr .75 2.00
11 Sammy Sosa .40 1.00
12 Albert Pujols .50 1.25
13 Nomar Garciaparra H .25 .60
14 Nomar Garciaparra A .25 .60
15 Derek Jeter H 1.00 2.50
16 Derek Jeter A 1.00 2.50
17 Sammy Sosa .40 1.00
18 Chipper Jones .40 1.00
19 Alfonso Soriano H .25 .60
20 Alfonso Soriano A .25 .60
21 Alex Rodriguez H .50 1.25
22 Alex Rodriguez A .50 1.25
23 Miguel Tejada .25 .60
24 Albert Pujols .50 1.25
25 Derek Jeter H 1.00 2.50
26 Derek Jeter A 1.00 2.50
27 Sammy Sosa H .40 1.00
28 Sammy Sosa A .40 1.00
29 Chipper Jones .40 1.00
30 Alfonso Soriano H .25 .60
31 Alfonso Soriano A .25 .60
32 Miguel Tejada .25 .60
33 Nomar Garciaparra .25 .60
34 Alex Rodriguez .50 1.25
35 Albert Pujols H .50 1.25
36 Albert Pujols A .50 1.25
37 Jason Giambi H .15 .40
38 Jason Giambi A .15 .40
39 Jason Giambi ALT .15 .40
40 Ken Griffey Jr H .75 2.00
41 Ken Griffey Jr A .75 2.00
42 Ken Griffey Jr ALT .75 2.00
43 Barry Bonds H .60 1.50
44 Barry Bonds A .60 1.50
45 Barry Bonds ALT .60 1.50
46 Ichiro Suzuki H .50 1.25
47 Ichiro Suzuki A .50 1.25
48 Ichiro Suzuki ALT .50 1.25
49 Derek Jeter H 1.00 2.50
50 Derek Jeter A 1.00 2.50
51 Sammy Sosa H .40 1.00
52 Sammy Sosa A .40 1.00
53 Chipper Jones .40 1.00
54 Alfonso Soriano H .25 .60
55 Alfonso Soriano A .25 .60
56 Miguel Tejada .25 .60
57 Nomar Garciaparra .25 .60
58 Alex Rodriguez .50 1.25
59 Albert Pujols H .50 1.25
60 Albert Pujols A .50 1.25
61 Roger Clemens H .50 1.25
62 Roger Clemens A .50 1.25
63 Curt Schilling H .25 .60
64 Curt Schilling A .25 .60
65 Pedro Martinez H .25 .60
66 Pedro Martinez A .25 .60
67 Greg Maddux H .50 1.25
68 Greg Maddux A .50 1.25
69 Mark Prior H .25 .60
70 Mark Prior A .25 .60
71 Mariano Rivera H .50 1.25
72 Mariano Rivera A .50 1.25

2003 Fleer Barry Bonds 5 Time MVP

1 Barry Bonds AU/613 50.00 100.00

2003 Fleer Cub Foods

COMPLETE SET (10) 6.00 15.00
1 Ichiro Suzuki .60 1.50
2 Kerry Wood .20 .50
3 Mike Piazza .50 1.25
4 Randy Johnson .50 1.25
5 Maggio Ordonez .30 .75
6 Brad Radke .20 .50
7 Omar Vizquel .30 .75
8 Ben Sheets .20 .50
9 Barry Zito .30 .75
10 Ken Griffey Jr 1.00 2.50

2003 Fleer Die Cast

COMPLETE SET 15.00 40.00
1 Josh Beckett .40 1.00
2 Lance Berkman .60 1.50
3 Barry Bonds 1.50 4.00
4 Pat Burrell .40 1.00
5 Carlos Delgado .40 1.00
6 Adam Dunn .60 1.50
7 Robert Fick .40 1.00
8 Jason Giambi .40 1.00
9 Nomar Garciaparra .60 1.50
10 Jay Gibbons .40 1.00
11 Brian Giles .40 1.00
12 Troy Glaus .40 1.00
13 Tom Glavine .60 1.50
14 Shawn Green .40 1.00
15 Ben Grieve .40 1.00
16 Vladimir Guerrero .60 1.50
17 Todd Helton .60 1.50
18 Trevor Hoffman .60 1.50
19 Torii Hunter .40 1.00
20 Derek Jeter 2.50 6.00
21 Randy Johnson 1.00 2.50
22 Chipper Jones 1.00 2.50
23 Magglio Ordonez .60 1.50
24 Mike Piazza 1.00 2.50
25 Albert Pujols 1.25 3.00
26 Alex Rodriguez 1.25 3.00
27 Richie Sexson .40 1.00
28 Sammy Sosa 1.00 2.50
29 Ichiro Suzuki 1.25 3.00
30 Mike Sweeney .40 1.00
31 Miguel Tejada .60 1.50
32 Jim Thome .60 1.50
33 Omar Vizquel .60 1.50

2006 Fleer

COMP.FACT.SET (430) 20.00 50.00
COMPLETE SET (400) 15.00 40.00
COMMON CARD (1-400) .15 .40
COMMON ROOKIE .20 .50
COMMON ROOKIE (401-430) .25 .60
401-430 AVAIL. IN FLEER FACT.SET
1 Adam Kennedy .15 .40
2 Bartolo Colon .15 .40
3 Bengie Molina .15 .40
4 Chone Figgins .15 .40
5 Dallas McPherson .15 .40
6 Darin Erstad .15 .40
7 Francisco Rodriguez .25 .60
8 Garret Anderson .15 .40
9 Jarrod Washburn .15 .40
10 John Lackey .25 .60
11 Orlando Cabrera .15 .40
12 Ryan Theriot RC .60 1.50
13 Steve Finley .15 .40
14 Vladimir Guerrero .25 .60
15 Adam Everett .15 .40
16 Andy Pettitte .25 .60
17 Charlton Jimerson (RC) .20 .50
18 Brad Lidge .15 .40
19 Chris Burke .15 .40
20 Craig Biggio .25 .60
21 Jason Lane .15 .40
22 Jeff Bagwell .25 .60
23 Lance Berkman .25 .60
24 Morgan Ensberg .15 .40
25 Roger Clemens .50 1.25
26 Roy Oswalt .25 .60
27 Willy Taveras .15 .40
28 Barry Zito .25 .60
29 Bobby Crosby .15 .40
30 Bobby Kielty .15 .40
31 Dan Johnson .15 .40
32 Danny Haren .15 .40
33 Eric Chavez .15 .40
34 Huston Street .15 .40
35 Jason Kendall .15 .40
36 Jay Payton .15 .40
37 Joe Blanton .15 .40
38 Mark Kotsay .15 .40
39 Nick Swisher .25 .60
40 Rich Harden .15 .40
41 Ron Flores RC .20 .50
42 Alex Rios .15 .40
43 John-Ford Griffin (RC) .20 .50
44 Dave Bush .15 .40
45 Eric Hinske .15 .40
46 Frank Catalanotto .15 .40
47 Gustavo Chacin .15 .40
48 Josh Towers .15 .40
49 Miguel Batista .15 .40
50 Orlando Hudson .15 .40
51 Roy Halladay .25 .60
52 Shea Hillenbrand .15 .40
53 Shaun Marcum (RC) .20 .50
54 Vernon Wells .15 .40
55 Adam LaRoche .15 .40
56 Andruw Jones .15 .40
57 Chipper Jones .40 1.00
58 Anthony Lerew (RC) .20 .50
59 Jeff Francoeur .40 1.00
60 John Smoltz .40 1.00
61 Johnny Estrada .15 .40
62 Julio Franco .15 .40
63 Joey Devine RC .20 .50
64 Marcus Giles .15 .40
65 Mike Hampton .15 .40
66 Rafael Furcal .15 .40
67 Chuck James (RC) .20 .50
68 Tim Hudson .25 .60
69 Ben Sheets .15 .40
70 Bill Hall .15 .40
71 Brady Clark .15 .40
72 Carlos Lee .15 .40
73 Chris Capuano .15 .40
74 Nelson Cruz (RC) .75 2.00
75 Derrick Turnbow .15 .40
76 Doug Davis .15 .40
77 Geoff Jenkins .15 .40
78 J.J. Hardy .15 .40
79 Lyle Overbay .15 .40
80 Prince Fielder .75 2.00
81 Rickie Weeks .15 .40
82 Albert Pujols .50 1.25
83 Chris Carpenter .25 .60
84 David Eckstein .15 .40
85 Jason Isringhausen .15 .40
86 Tyler Johnson (RC) .20 .50
87 Adam Wainwright (RC) .30 .75
88 Jim Edmonds .25 .60
89 Chris Duncan (RC) .30 .75
90 Mark Grudzielanek .15 .40
91 Mark Mulder .15 .40
92 Matt Morris .15 .40
93 Reggie Sanders .15 .40
94 Scott Rolen .25 .60
95 Yadier Molina .50 1.25
96 Aramis Ramirez .15 .40
97 Carlos Zambrano .25 .60
98 Corey Patterson .15 .40
99 Derrek Lee .15 .40
100 Glendon Rusch .15 .40
101 Greg Maddux .50 1.25
102 Jeromy Burnitz .15 .40
103 Kerry Wood .15 .40
104 Mark Prior .25 .60
105 Michael Barrett .15 .40
106 Geovany Soto (RC) .50 1.25
107 Nomar Garciaparra .25 .60
108 Ryan Dempster .15 .40
109 Todd Walker .15 .40
110 Alex S. Gonzalez .15 .40
111 Aubrey Huff .15 .40
112 Victor Diaz .15 .40
113 Carl Crawford .25 .60
114 Danys Baez .15 .40
115 Joey Gathright .15 .40
116 Jonny Gomes .15 .40
117 Jorge Cantu .15 .40
118 Julio Lugo .15 .40
119 Rocco Baldelli .15 .40
120 Scott Kazmir .25 .60
121 Toby Hall .15 .40
122 Tim Corcoran RC .20 .50
123 Alex Cintron .15 .40
124 Brandon Webb .25 .60
125 Chad Tracy .15 .40
126 Dustin Nippert (RC) .20 .50
127 Claudio Vargas .15 .40
128 Craig Counsell .15 .40
129 Javier Vazquez .15 .40
130 Jose Valverde .15 .40
131 Luis Gonzalez .15 .40
132 Royce Clayton .15 .40
133 Russ Ortiz .15 .40
134 Shawn Green .15 .40
135 Tony Clark .15 .40
136 Troy Glaus .15 .40
137 Brad Penny .15 .40
138 Cesar Izturis .15 .40
139 Derek Lowe .15 .40
140 Eric Gagne .15 .40
141 Hee Seop Choi .15 .40
142 J.D. Drew .15 .40
143 Jason Phillips .15 .40
144 Jayson Werth .25 .60
145 Jeff Kent .15 .40
146 Jeff Weaver .15 .40
147 Milton Bradley .15 .40
148 Odalis Perez .15 .40
149 Hong-Chih Kuo (RC) .50 1.25
150 Brian Myrow RC .20 .50
151 Armando Benitez .15 .40
152 Edgardo Alfonzo .15 .40
153 J.T. Snow .15 .40
154 Jason Schmidt .15 .40
155 Lance Niekro .15 .40
156 Doug Clark (RC) .20 .50
157 Dan Ortmeier (RC) .20 .50
158 Moises Alou .15 .40
159 Noah Lowry .15 .40
160 Omar Vizquel .25 .60
161 Pedro Feliz .15 .40
162 Randy Winn .15 .40
163 Jeremy Accardo RC .20 .50
164 Aaron Boone .15 .40
165 Ryan Garko (RC) .20 .50
166 C.C. Sabathia .25 .60
167 Casey Blake .15 .40
168 Cliff Lee .25 .60
169 Coco Crisp .15 .40
170 Grady Sizemore .25 .60
171 Jake Westbrook .15 .40
172 Jhonny Peralta .15 .40
173 Kevin Millwood .15 .40
174 Scott Elarton .15 .40
175 Travis Hafner .15 .40
176 Victor Martinez .25 .60
177 Adrian Beltre .40 1.00
178 Eddie Guardado .15 .40
179 Felix Hernandez .25 .60
180 Gil Meche .15 .40
181 Ichiro Suzuki .50 1.25
182 Jamie Moyer .15 .40
183 Jeremy Reed .15 .40
184 Jaime Bubela (RC) .20 .50
185 Raul Ibanez .25 .60
186 Richie Sexson .15 .40
187 Ryan Franklin .15 .40
188 Jeff Harris RC .15 .40
189 A.J. Burnett .15 .40
190 Josh Wilson (RC) .20 .50
191 Josh Johnson (RC) .50 1.25
192 Carlos Delgado .15 .40
193 Dontrelle Willis .15 .40
194 Bernie Castro (RC) .20 .50
195 Josh Beckett .15 .40
196 Juan Encarnacion .15 .40
197 Juan Pierre .15 .40
198 Robert Andino RC .20 .50
199 Miguel Cabrera .40 1.00
200 Ryan Jorgensen RC .20 .50
201 Paul Lo Duca .15 .40
202 Todd Jones .15 .40
203 Braden Looper .15 .40
204 Carlos Beltran .25 .60
205 Cliff Floyd .15 .40
206 David Wright .30 .75
207 Doug Mientkiewicz .15 .40
208 Jae Seo .15 .40
209 Jose Reyes .25 .60
210 Anderson Hernandez (RC) .20 .50
211 Miguel Cairo .15 .40
212 Mike Cameron .15 .40
213 Mike Piazza .40 1.00
214 Pedro Martinez .25 .60
215 Tom Glavine .25 .60
216 Tim Hamulack (RC) .20 .50
217 Brad Wilkerson .15 .40
218 Darrell Rasner (RC) .20 .50
219 Chad Cordero .15 .40
220 Cristian Guzman .15 .40
221 Jason Bergmann RC .20 .50
222 John Patterson .15 .40
223 Jose Guillen .15 .40
224 Jose Vidro .15 .40
225 Livan Hernandez .15 .40
226 Nick Johnson .15 .40
227 Preston Wilson .15 .40
228 Ryan Zimmerman (RC) .60 1.50
229 Vinny Castilla .15 .40
230 B.J. Ryan .15 .40
231 B.J. Surhoff .15 .40
232 Brian Roberts .15 .40
233 Walter Young (RC) .20 .50
234 Daniel Cabrera .15 .40
235 Erik Bedard .15 .40
236 Javy Lopez .15 .40
237 Jay Gibbons .15 .40
238 Luis Matos .15 .40
239 Melvin Mora .15 .40
240 Miguel Tejada .25 .60
241 Rafael Palmeiro .25 .60
242 Alejandro Freire RC .20 .50
243 Sammy Sosa .40 1.00
244 Adam Eaton .15 .40
245 Brian Giles .15 .40
246 Brian Lawrence .15 .40
247 Dave Roberts .25 .60
248 Jake Peavy .15 .40
249 Khalil Greene .15 .40
250 Mark Loretta .15 .40
251 Ramon Hernandez .15 .40
252 Ryan Klesko .15 .40
253 Trevor Hoffman .25 .60
254 Woody Williams .15 .40
255 Craig Breslow RC .20 .50
256 Billy Wagner .15 .40
257 Bobby Abreu .15 .40
258 Brett Myers .15 .40
259 Chase Utley .25 .60
260 David Bell .15 .40
261 Jim Thome .25 .60
262 Jimmy Rollins .25 .60
263 Jon Lieber .15 .40
264 Danny Sandoval RC .20 .50
265 Mike Lieberthal .15 .40
266 Pat Burrell .15 .40
267 Randy Wolf .15 .40
268 Ryan Howard .30 .75
269 J.J. Furmaniak (RC) .20 .50
270 Ronny Paulino (RC) .20 .50
271 Craig Wilson .15 .40
272 Bryan Bullington (RC) .20 .50
273 Jack Wilson .15 .40
274 Jason Bay .15 .40
275 Matt Capps (RC) .20 .50
276 Oliver Perez .15 .40
277 Rob Mackowiak .15 .40
278 Tom Gorzelanny (RC) .20 .50
279 Zach Duke .15 .40
280 Alfonso Soriano .25 .60
281 Chris R. Young .15 .40
282 David Dellucci .15 .40
283 Francisco Cordero .15 .40
284 Jason Botts (RC) UER .20 .50
285 Hank Blalock .15 .40
286 Josh Rupe (RC) .20 .50
287 Kevin Mench .15 .40
288 Laynce Nix .15 .40
289 Mark Teixeira .25 .60
290 Michael Young .15 .40
291 Richard Hidalgo .15 .40
292 Scott Feldman RC .20 .50
293 Bill Mueller .15 .40
294 Hanley Ramirez (RC) .30 .75
295 Curt Schilling .25 .60
296 David Ortiz .40 1.00
297 Alejandro Machado (RC) .20 .50
298 Edgar Renteria .15 .40
299 Jason Varitek .40 1.00
300 Johnny Damon .25 .60
301 Keith Foulke .15 .40
302 Manny Ramirez .40 1.00
303 Matt Clement .15 .40
304 Craig Hansen RC .50 1.25
305 Tim Wakefield .25 .60
306 Trot Nixon .15 .40
307 Aaron Harang .15 .40
308 Adam Dunn .25 .60
309 Austin Kearns .15 .40
310 Brandon Claussen .15 .40
311 Chris Booker (RC) .20 .50
312 Edwin Encarnacion .40 1.00
313 Chris Denorfia (RC) .20 .50
314 Felipe Lopez .15 .40
315 Miguel Perez (RC) .20 .50
316 Ken Griffey Jr. .75 2.00
317 Ryan Freel .15 .40
318 Sean Casey .15 .40
319 Wily Mo Pena .15 .40
320 Mike Esposito (RC) .20 .50
321 Aaron Miles .15 .40
322 Brad Hawpe .15 .40
323 Brian Fuentes .15 .40
324 Clint Barmes .15 .40
325 Cory Sullivan .15 .40
326 Garrett Atkins .15 .40
327 J.D. Closser .15 .40
328 Jeff Francis .15 .40
329 Luis Gonzalez .15 .40
330 Matt Holliday .40 1.00
331 Todd Helton .25 .60
332 Angel Berroa .15 .40
333 David DeJesus .15 .40
334 Emil Brown .15 .40
335 Jeremy Affeldt .15 .40
336 Chris Demaria RC .20 .50
337 Mark Teahen .15 .40
338 Matt Stairs .15 .40
339 Steve Stemle RC .20 .50
340 Mike Sweeney .15 .40
341 Runelvys Hernandez .15 .40
342 Jonah Bayliss RC .20 .50
343 Zack Greinke .40 1.00
344 Brandon Inge .15 .40
345 Carlos Guillen .15 .40
346 Carlos Pena .25 .60
347 Chris Shelton .15 .40
348 Craig Monroe .15 .40
349 Dmitri Young .15 .40
350 Ivan Rodriguez .25 .60
351 Jeremy Bonderman .15 .40
352 Magglio Ordonez .25 .60
353 Mark Woodyard (RC) .20 .50
354 Omar Infante .15 .40
355 Placido Polanco .15 .40
356 Rondell White .15 .40
357 Brad Radke .15 .40
358 Carlos Silva .15 .40
359 Jacque Jones .15 .40
360 Joe Mauer .25 .60
361 Chris Heintz RC .20 .50
362 Joe Nathan .15 .40
363 Johan Santana .25 .60
364 Justin Morneau .25 .60
365 Francisco Liriano (RC) .50 1.25
366 Travis Bowyer (RC) .20 .50
367 Michael Cuddyer .15 .40
368 Scott Baker .15 .40
369 Shannon Stewart .15 .40
370 Torii Hunter .15 .40
371 A.J. Pierzynski .15 .40
372 Aaron Rowand .15 .40
373 Carl Everett .15 .40
374 Dustin Hermanson .15 .40
375 Frank Thomas .40 1.00
376 Freddy Garcia .15 .40
377 Jermaine Dye .15 .40
378 Joe Crede .15 .40
379 Jon Garland .15 .40
380 Jose Contreras .15 .40
381 Juan Uribe .15 .40
382 Mark Buehrle .25 .60
383 Orlando Hernandez .15 .40
384 Paul Konerko .25 .60
385 Scott Podsednik .15 .40
386 Tadahito Iguchi .15 .40
387 Alex Rodriguez .50 1.25
388 Bernie Williams .25 .60
389 Chien-Ming Wang .25 .60
390 Derek Jeter 1.00 2.50
391 Gary Sheffield .15 .40
392 Hideki Matsui .40 1.00
393 Jason Giambi .15 .40
394 Jorge Posada .25 .60
395 Mike Vento (RC) .20 .50
396 Mariano Rivera .50 1.25
397 Mike Mussina .25 .60
398 Randy Johnson .40 1.00
399 Robinson Cano .25 .60
400 Tino Martinez .15 .40
401 Alay Soler RC .25 .60
402 Boof Bonser (RC) .40 1.00
403 Cole Hamels (RC) .75 2.00
404 Ian Kinsler (RC) .75 2.00
405 Jason Kubel (RC) .25 .60
406 Joel Zumaya (RC) .60 1.50
407 Jonathan Papelbon (RC) 1.25 3.00
408 Jered Weaver (RC) .75 2.00
409 Kendry Morales (RC) .60 1.50
410 Lastings Milledge (RC) .25 .60
411 Matt Kemp (RC) .60 1.50
412 Taylor Buchholz (RC) .25 .60
413 Andre Ethier (RC) .75 2.00
414 Dan Uggla (RC) .40 1.00
415 Jeremy Sowers (RC) .25 .60
416 Chad Billingsley (RC) .40 1.00
417 Josh Barfield (RC) .25 .60
418 Matt Cain (RC) 1.50 4.00
419 Fausto Carmona (RC) .25 .60
420 Josh Willingham (RC) .40 1.00
421 Jeremy Hermida (RC) .25 .60
422 Conor Jackson (RC) .40 1.00
423 Dave Gassner (RC) .25 .60
424 Brian Bannister (RC) .25 .60
425 Fernando Nieve (RC) .25 .60
426 Justin Verlander (RC) 2.00 5.00
427 Scott Olsen (RC) .25 .60
428 Takashi Saito RC .40 1.00
429 Willie Eyre (RC) .25 .60
430 Travis Ishikawa (RC) .40 1.00

2006 Fleer Glossy Gold

STATED ODDS 1:144 HOBBY, 1:144 RETAIL
NO PRICING DUE TO SCARCITY

2006 Fleer Glossy Silver

*GLOSSY SILVER: 2X TO 5X BASIC
*GLOSSY SILVER: 1.5X TO 4X BASIC RC
STATED ODDS 1:12 HOBBY, 1:24 RETAIL

2006 Fleer Autographics

STATED ODDS 1:432 HOBBY, 1:432 RETAIL
SP PRINT RUNS PROVIDED BY UD
SP'S ARE NOT SERIAL-NUMBERED
NO SP PRICING ON QTY OF 25 OR LESS
AN Garret Anderson 6.00 15.00
CS Chris Shelton 6.00 15.00
EC Eric Chavez 6.00 15.00
GA Garrett Atkins 6.00 15.00
JB Joe Blanton 6.00 15.00
KG Ken Griffey Jr.SP/150 * 50.00 120.00
KY Kevin Youkilis 6.00 15.00
NS Nick Swisher 6.00 15.00
TI Tadahito Iguchi 6.00 15.00

2006 Fleer Award Winners

COMPLETE SET (6) 6.00 15.00
OVERALL INSERT ODDS ONE PER PACK
AW1 Albert Pujols 1.25 3.00
AW2 Alex Rodriguez 1.25 3.00
AW3 Chris Carpenter .60 1.50
AW4 Bartolo Colon .40 1.00
AW5 Ryan Howard .75 2.00
AW6 Huston Street .40 1.00

2006 Fleer Fabrics

STATED ODDS 1:36 HOBBY, 1:72 RETAIL
SP INFO PROVIDED BY UPPER DECK
AJ Andruw Jones Jsy 3.00 8.00
AP Albert Pujols Jsy 6.00 15.00
AR Aramis Ramirez Jsy 3.00 8.00
AS Alfonso Soriano Jsy 3.00 8.00
BA Bobby Abreu Jsy 3.00 8.00
CB Carlos Beltran Jsy 3.00 8.00
CJ Chipper Jones Jsy 4.00 10.00
CS Curt Schilling Jsy 3.00 8.00
DJ Derek Jeter Jsy 10.00 25.00
DL Derrek Lee Jsy 3.00 8.00
DO David Ortiz Pants 4.00 10.00
DW Dontrelle Willis Jsy SP 4.00 10.00
EC Eric Chavez Jsy 3.00 8.00
EG Eric Gagne Jsy 3.00 8.00
GM Greg Maddux Jsy 4.00 10.00
GR Khalil Greene Jsy 4.00 10.00
GS Gary Sheffield Jsy SP 4.00 10.00
IR Ivan Rodriguez Jsy 3.00 8.00
JE Jim Edmonds Jsy 3.00 8.00
JM Joe Mauer Jsy 4.00 10.00
JP Jake Peavy Jsy 3.00 8.00
JS Johan Santana Jsy 4.00 10.00
JT Jim Thome Jsy 4.00 10.00
KG Ken Griffey Jr. Jsy 6.00 15.00
LG Luis Gonzalez Jsy 3.00 8.00
MC Miguel Cabrera Jsy 4.00 10.00
MP Mark Prior Jsy 4.00 10.00
MR Manny Ramirez Jsy 4.00 10.00
MT Mark Teixeira Jsy 4.00 10.00
MY Michael Young Jsy 3.00 8.00
PM Pedro Martinez Jsy 4.00 10.00
RC Roger Clemens Jsy 6.00 15.00
RH Roy Halladay Jsy 3.00 8.00
RJ Randy Johnson Jsy 4.00 10.00
RW Rickie Weeks Jsy 3.00 8.00
SM John Smoltz Jsy 4.00 10.00
TE Miguel Tejada Jsy 3.00 8.00
TH Todd Helton Jsy 4.00 10.00
VG Vladimir Guerrero Jsy 4.00 10.00
WR David Wright Jsy 4.00 10.00

2006 Fleer Lumber Company

COMPLETE SET (25) 10.00 25.00
OVERALL INSERT ODDS ONE PER PACK
LC1 Adam Dunn .60 1.50
LC2 Albert Pujols 1.25 3.00
LC3 Alex Rodriguez 1.25 3.00
LC4 Alfonso Soriano .60 1.50
LC5 Andruw Jones .40 1.00
LC6 Aramis Ramirez .40 1.00
LC7 Bobby Abreu .40 1.00
LC8 Carlos Delgado .40 1.00
LC9 Carlos Lee .40 1.00
LC10 David Ortiz 1.00 2.50
LC11 David Wright .75 2.00
LC12 Derrek Lee .40 1.00
LC13 Eric Chavez .40 1.00
LC14 Gary Sheffield .40 1.00
LC15 Jeff Kent .40 1.00
LC16 Ken Griffey Jr. 2.00 5.00
LC17 Manny Ramirez 1.00 2.50
LC18 Mark Teixeira .60 1.50
LC19 Miguel Cabrera 1.00 2.50
LC20 Miguel Tejada .60 1.50
LC21 Paul Konerko .60 1.50
LC22 Richie Sexson .40 1.00
LC23 Todd Helton .60 1.50
LC24 Troy Glaus .40 1.00
LC25 Vladimir Guerrero .60 1.50

2006 Fleer Smoke 'n Heat

COMPLETE SET (15) 8.00 20.00
OVERALL INSERT ODDS ONE PER PACK
SH1 Carlos Zambrano .60 1.50
SH2 Chris Carpenter .60 1.50
SH3 Curt Schilling .60 1.50
SH4 Dontrelle Willis .40 1.00
SH5 Felix Hernandez .60 1.50
SH6 Jake Peavy .40 1.00
SH7 Johan Santana .60 1.50
SH8 John Smoltz 1.00 2.50
SH9 Mark Prior .60 1.50
SH10 Pedro Martinez .60 1.50
SH11 Randy Johnson 1.00 2.50
SH12 Roger Clemens 1.25 3.00
SH13 Roy Halladay .60 1.50
SH14 Roy Oswalt .60 1.50
SH15 Scott Kazmir .60 1.50

2006 Fleer Smooth Leather

COMPLETE SET (14) 10.00 25.00
OVERALL INSERT ODDS ONE PER PACK
SL1 Alex Rodriguez 1.25 3.00
SL2 Andruw Jones .40 1.00
SL3 Derek Jeter 2.50 6.00
SL4 Derrek Lee .40 1.00
SL5 Eric Chavez .40 1.00
SL6 Greg Maddux 1.25 3.00
SL7 Ichiro Suzuki 1.25 3.00
SL8 Ivan Rodriguez .60 1.50
SL9 Jim Edmonds .60 1.50
SL10 Mike Mussina .60 1.50
SL11 Omar Vizquel .60 1.50
SL12 Scott Rolen .60 1.50
SL13 Todd Helton .60 1.50
SL14 Torii Hunter .40 1.00

2006 Fleer Stars of Tomorrow

COMPLETE SET (10) 6.00 15.00
OVERALL INSERT ODDS ONE PER PACK
ST1 David Wright .75 2.00
ST2 Ryan Howard .75 2.00
ST3 Felix Hernandez .60 1.50
ST4 Jeff Francoeur 1.00 2.50
ST5 Joe Mauer .60 1.50
ST6 Mark Prior .60 1.50
ST7 Mark Teixeira .60 1.50
ST8 Miguel Cabrera 1.00 2.50
ST9 Prince Fielder 2.00 5.00
ST10 Rickie Weeks .40 1.00

2006 Fleer Team Fleer

OVERALL INSERT ODDS ONE PER PACK
TF1 Albert Pujols 6.00 15.00
TF2 Alex Rodriguez 6.00 15.00
TF3 Alfonso Soriano 3.00 8.00
TF4 Andruw Jones 2.00 5.00
TF5 Bobby Abreu 2.00 5.00
TF6 David Ortiz 5.00 12.00
TF7 David Wright 4.00 10.00
TF8 Eric Gagne 2.00 5.00
TF9 Ichiro Suzuki 6.00 15.00
TF10 Jason Varitek 5.00 12.00
TF11 Jeff Kent 2.00 5.00
TF12 Johan Santana 3.00 8.00
TF13 Jose Reyes 3.00 8.00
TF14 Manny Ramirez 5.00 12.00
TF15 Mariano Rivera 6.00 15.00
TF16 Miguel Cabrera 5.00 12.00
TF17 Miguel Tejada 3.00 8.00
TF18 Mike Piazza 5.00 12.00
TF19 Roger Clemens 6.00 15.00
TF20 Torii Hunter 2.00 5.00

2006 Fleer Team Leaders

COMPLETE SET (30) 15.00 40.00
OVERALL INSERT ODDS ONE PER PACK
TL1 Troy Glaus .60 1.50
Brandon Webb
TL2 Andruw Jones 1.00 2.50
John Smoltz
TL3 Miguel Tejada .60 1.50
Erik Bedard
TL4 David Ortiz 1.00 2.50
Curt Schilling
TL5 Derrek Lee .60 1.50
Mark Prior
TL6 Paul Konerko .60 1.50
Mark Buehrle
TL7 Ken Griffey Jr. 2.00 5.00
Aaron Harang
TL8 Travis Hafner .60 1.50
Cliff Lee
TL9 Todd Helton .60 1.50
Jeff Francis
TL10 Ivan Rodriguez .60 1.50
Jeremy Bonderman
TL11 Miguel Cabrera 1.00 2.50
Dontrelle Willis
TL12 Lance Berkman 1.25 3.00
Roger Clemens
TL13 Mike Sweeney 1.00 2.50
Zack Greinke
TL14 Jeff Kent .40 1.00
Derek Lowe
TL15 Carlos Lee .40 1.00
Ben Sheets
TL16 Torii Hunter .60 1.50
Johan Santana
TL17 David Wright .75 2.00
Pedro Martinez
TL18 Derek Jeter 2.50 6.00
Randy Johnson
TL19 Eric Chavez .60 1.50
Barry Zito
TL20 Bobby Abreu .40 1.00
Brett Myers
TL21 Jason Bay .40 1.00
Zach Duke
TL22 Brian Giles .40 1.00
Jake Peavy
TL23 Moises Alou .40 1.00
Jason Schmidt
TL24 Ichiro Suzuki 1.25 3.00
Felix Hernandez
TL25 Albert Pujols 1.25 3.00
Chris Carpenter
TL26 Carl Crawford .60 1.50
Scott Kazmir
TL27 Mark Teixeira .60 1.50
Kenny Rogers
TL28 Vernon Wells .60 1.50
Roy Halladay
TL29 Jose Guillen .40 1.00
Livan Hernandez
TL30 Vladimir Guerrero .60 1.50
Bartolo Colon

2006 Fleer Top 40

STATED ODDS 2:1 FAT PACKS
1 Ken Griffey Jr. 2.00 5.00
2 Derek Jeter 2.50 6.00
3 Albert Pujols 1.25 3.00
4 Alex Rodriguez 1.25 3.00
5 Vladimir Guerrero .60 1.50
6 Roger Clemens 1.25 3.00
7 Derrek Lee .40 1.00
8 David Ortiz 1.00 2.50
9 Miguel Cabrera 1.00 2.50
10 Bobby Abreu .40 1.00
11 Mark Teixeira .60 1.50
12 Johan Santana .60 1.50
13 Hideki Matsui 1.00 2.50
14 Ichiro Suzuki 1.25 3.00
15 Andruw Jones .40 1.00
16 Eric Chavez .40 1.00
17 Roy Oswalt .60 1.50
18 Curt Schilling .60 1.50
19 Randy Johnson 1.00 2.50
20 Ivan Rodriguez .60 1.50
21 Chipper Jones 1.00 2.50
22 Mark Prior .60 1.50
23 Jason Bay .40 1.00
24 Pedro Martinez .60 1.50
25 David Wright .75 2.00
26 Carlos Beltran .60 1.50
27 Jim Edmonds .60 1.50
28 Chris Carpenter .60 1.50
29 Roy Halladay .60 1.50
30 Jake Peavy .40 1.00

31 Paul Konerko	.60	1.50
32 Travis Hafner	.40	1.00
33 Barry Zito	.60	1.50
34 Miguel Tejada	.60	1.50
35 Josh Beckett	.40	1.00
36 Todd Helton	.60	1.50
37 Dontrelle Willis	.40	1.00
38 Manny Ramirez	1.00	2.50
39 Mariano Rivera	1.25	3.00
40 Jeff Kent	.40	1.00

2007 Fleer

COMPLETE SET (400)	30.00	60.00
COMP.FACT.SET (430)	30.00	60.00
COMMON CARD (1-430)	.12	.30
COMMON RC	.25	.60

401-430 ISSUED IN FACT.SET
OVERALL PRINTING PLATE ODDS 1:720
PLATE PRINT RUN 1 SET PER COLOR
BLACK-CYAN-MAGENTA-YELLOW ISSUED
NO PLATE PRICING DUE TO SCARCITY

1 Chad Cordero	.12	.30
2 Alfonso Soriano	.20	.50
3 Nick Johnson	.12	.30
4 Austin Kearns	.12	.30
5 Ramon Ortiz	.12	.30
6 Brian Schneider	.12	.30
7 Ryan Zimmerman	.20	.50
8 Jose Vidro	.12	.30
9 Felipe Lopez	.12	.30
10 Cristian Guzman	.12	.30
11 B.J. Ryan	.12	.30
12 Alex Rios	.12	.30
13 Vernon Wells	.12	.30
14 Roy Halladay	.20	.50
15 A.J. Burnett	.12	.30
16 Lyle Overbay	.12	.30
17 Troy Glaus	.12	.30
18 Bengie Molina	.12	.30
19 Gustavo Chacin	.12	.30
20 Aaron Hill	.12	.30
21 Vicente Padilla	.12	.30
22 Kevin Millwood	.12	.30
23 Akinori Otsuka	.12	.30
24 Adam Eaton	.12	.30
25 Hank Blalock	.12	.30
26 Mark Teixeira	.20	.50
27 Michael Young	.12	.30
28 Mark DeRosa	.12	.30
29 Gary Matthews	.12	.30
30 Ian Kinsler	.20	.50
31 Carlos Lee	.12	.30
32 James Shields	.12	.30
33 Scott Kazmir	.20	.50
34 Carl Crawford	.20	.50
35 Jonny Gomes	.12	.30
36 Tim Corcoran	.12	.30
37 B.J. Upton	.12	.30
38 Rocco Baldelli	.12	.30
39 Jae Seo	.12	.30
40 Jorge Cantu	.12	.30
41 Ty Wigginton	.12	.30
42 Chris Carpenter	.20	.50
43 Albert Pujols	.40	1.00
44 Scott Rolen	.20	.50
45 Jim Edmonds	.20	.50
46 Jason Isringhausen	.12	.30
47 Yadier Molina	.40	1.00
48 Adam Wainwright	.20	.50
49 Mark Mulder	.12	.30
50 Jason Marquis	.12	.30
51 Juan Encarnacion	.12	.30
52 Aaron Miles	.12	.30
53 Ichiro Suzuki	.40	1.00
54 Felix Hernandez	.20	.50
55 Kenji Johjima	.30	.75
56 Richie Sexson	.12	.30
57 Yuniesky Betancourt	.12	.30
58 J.J. Putz	.12	.30
59 Jarrod Washburn	.12	.30
60 Ben Broussard	.12	.30
61 Adrian Beltre	.30	.75
62 Raul Ibanez	.20	.50
63 Jose Lopez	.12	.30
64 Matt Cain	.20	.50
65 Noah Lowry	.12	.30
66 Jason Schmidt	.12	.30
67 Pedro Feliz	.12	.30
68 Matt Morris	.12	.30
69 Ray Durham	.12	.30
70 Steve Finley	.12	.30
71 Randy Winn	.12	.30
72 Moises Alou	.12	.30
73 Eliezer Alfonzo	.12	.30
74 Armando Benitez	.12	.30
75 Omar Vizquel	.20	.50
76 Chris R. Young	.12	.30
77 Adrian Gonzalez	.25	.60
78 Khalil Greene	.12	.30
79 Mike Piazza	.30	.75
80 Josh Barfield	.12	.30
81 Brian Giles	.12	.30
82 Jake Peavy	.12	.30
83 Trevor Hoffman	.20	.50
84 Mike Cameron	.12	.30
85 Dave Roberts	.20	.50
86 David Wells	.12	.30
87 Zach Duke	.12	.30
88 Ian Snell	.12	.30
89 Jason Bay	.20	.50
90 Freddy Sanchez	.12	.30
91 Jack Wilson	.12	.30
92 Tom Gorzelanny	.12	.30
93 Chris Duffy	.12	.30
94 Jose Castillo	.12	.30
95 Matt Capps	.12	.30
96 Mike Gonzalez	.12	.30
97 Chase Utley	.20	.50
98 Jimmy Rollins	.20	.50
99 Aaron Rowand	.12	.30
100 Ryan Howard	.25	.60
101 Cole Hamels	.25	.60
102 Pat Burrell	.12	.30
103 Shane Victorino	.12	.30
104 Jamie Moyer	.12	.30
105 Mike Lieberthal	.12	.30
106 Tom Gordon	.12	.30
107 Brett Myers	.12	.30
108 Nick Swisher	.20	.50
109 Barry Zito	.20	.50
110 Jason Kendall	.12	.30
111 Milton Bradley	.12	.30
112 Bobby Crosby	.12	.30
113 Huston Street	.12	.30
114 Eric Chavez	.12	.30
115 Frank Thomas	.30	.75
116 Dan Haren	.12	.30
117 Jay Payton	.12	.30
118 Randy Johnson	.30	.75
119 Mike Mussina	.20	.50
120 Bobby Abreu	.12	.30
121 Jason Giambi	.12	.30
122 Derek Jeter	.75	2.00
123 Alex Rodriguez	.40	1.00
124 Jorge Posada	.20	.50
125 Robinson Cano	.20	.50
126 Mariano Rivera	.40	1.00
127 Chien-Ming Wang	.20	.50
128 Hideki Matsui	.30	.75
129 Gary Sheffield	.12	.30
130 Lastings Milledge	.20	.50
131 Tom Glavine	.20	.50
132 Billy Wagner	.12	.30
133 Pedro Martinez	.20	.50
134 Paul LoDuca	.12	.30
135 Carlos Delgado	.12	.30
136 Carlos Beltran	.20	.50
137 David Wright	.25	.60
138 Jose Reyes	.20	.50
139 Julio Franco	.12	.30
140 Michael Cuddyer	.12	.30
141 Justin Morneau	.20	.50
142 Johan Santana	.20	.50
143 Francisco Liriano	.12	.30
144 Joe Mauer	.25	.60
145 Torii Hunter	.12	.30
146 Luis Castillo	.12	.30
147 Joe Nathan	.12	.30
148 Carlos Silva	.12	.30
149 Boof Bonser	.12	.30
150 Ben Sheets	.12	.30
151 Prince Fielder	.20	.50
152 Bill Hall	.12	.30
153 Rickie Weeks	.12	.30
154 Geoff Jenkins	.12	.30
155 Kevin Mench	.12	.30
156 Francisco Cordero	.12	.30
157 Chris Capuano	.12	.30
158 Brady Clark	.12	.30
159 Tony Gwynn Jr.	.12	.30
160 Chad Billingsley	.20	.50
161 Russell Martin	.12	.30
162 Wilson Betemit	.12	.30
163 Nomar Garciaparra	.20	.50
164 Kenny Lofton	.12	.30
165 Rafael Furcal	.12	.30
166 Julio Lugo	.12	.30
167 Brad Penny	.12	.30
168 Jeff Kent	.12	.30
169 Greg Maddux	.40	1.00
170 Derek Lowe	.12	.30
171 Andre Ethier	.20	.50
172 Chone Figgins	.12	.30
173 Francisco Rodriguez	.20	.50
174 Garret Anderson	.12	.30
175 Orlando Cabrera	.12	.30
176 Adam Kennedy	.12	.30
177 John Lackey	.20	.50
178 Vladimir Guerrero	.20	.50
179 Bartolo Colon	.12	.30
180 Jered Weaver	.20	.50
181 Juan Rivera	.12	.30
182 Howie Kendrick	.12	.30
183 Ervin Santana	.12	.30
184 Mark Redman	.12	.30
185 David DeJesus	.12	.30
186 Joey Gathright	.12	.30
187 Mike Sweeney	.12	.30
188 Mark Teahen	.12	.30
189 Angel Berroa	.12	.30
190 Ambiorix Burgos	.12	.30
191 Luke Hudson	.12	.30
192 Mark Grudzielanek	.12	.30
193 Roger Clemens	.40	1.00
194 Willy Taveras	.12	.30
195 Craig Biggio	.20	.50
196 Andy Pettitte	.20	.50
197 Roy Oswalt	.20	.50
198 Lance Berkman	.20	.50
199 Morgan Ensberg	.12	.30
200 Brad Lidge	.12	.30
201 Chris Burke	.12	.30
202 Miguel Cabrera	.30	.75
203 Dontrelle Willis	.12	.30
204 Josh Johnson	.30	.75
205 Ricky Nolasco	.12	.30
206 Dan Uggla	.12	.30
207 Jeremy Hermida	.12	.30
208 Scott Olsen	.12	.30
209 Josh Willingham	.20	.50
210 Joe Borowski	.12	.30
211 Hanley Ramirez	.20	.50
212 Mike Jacobs	.12	.30
213 Kenny Rogers	.12	.30
214 Justin Verlander	.30	.75
215 Ivan Rodriguez	.20	.50
216 Magglio Ordonez	.20	.50
217 Todd Jones	.12	.30
218 Joel Zumaya	.12	.30
219 Jeremy Bonderman	.12	.30
220 Nate Robertson	.12	.30
221 Brandon Inge	.12	.30
222 Craig Monroe	.12	.30
223 Carlos Guillen	.12	.30
224 Jeff Francis	.12	.30
225 Brian Fuentes	.12	.30
226 Todd Helton	.20	.50
227 Matt Holliday	.30	.75
228 Garrett Atkins	.12	.30
229 Clint Barmes	.12	.30
230 Jason Jennings	.12	.30
231 Aaron Cook	.12	.30
232 Brad Hawpe	.12	.30
233 Cory Sullivan	.12	.30
234 Aaron Boone	.12	.30
235 C.C. Sabathia	.20	.50
236 Grady Sizemore	.20	.50
237 Travis Hafner	.12	.30
238 Jhonny Peralta	.12	.30
239 Jake Westbrook	.12	.30
240 Jeremy Sowers	.12	.30
241 Andy Marte	.12	.30
242 Victor Martinez	.20	.50
243 Jason Michaels	.12	.30
244 Cliff Lee	.20	.50
245 Bronson Arroyo	.12	.30
246 Aaron Harang	.12	.30
247 Ken Griffey Jr.	.60	1.50
248 Adam Dunn	.20	.50
249 Rich Aurilia	.12	.30
250 Eric Milton	.12	.30
251 David Ross	.12	.30
252 Brandon Phillips	.12	.30
253 Ryan Freel	.12	.30
254 Eddie Guardado	.12	.30
255 Jose Contreras	.12	.30
256 Freddy Garcia	.12	.30
257 Jon Garland	.12	.30
258 Mark Buehrle	.20	.50
259 Bobby Jenks	.12	.30
260 Paul Konerko	.20	.50
261 Jermaine Dye	.12	.30
262 Joe Crede	.12	.30
263 Jim Thome	.20	.50
264 Javier Vazquez	.12	.30
265 A.J. Pierzynski	.12	.30
266 Tadahito Iguchi	.12	.30
267 Carlos Zambrano	.20	.50
268 Derrek Lee	.12	.30
269 Aramis Ramirez	.12	.30
270 Ryan Theriot	.12	.30
271 Juan Pierre	.12	.30
272 Rich Hill	.12	.30
273 Ryan Dempster	.12	.30
274 Jacque Jones	.12	.30
275 Mark Prior	.20	.50
276 Kerry Wood	.12	.30
277 Josh Beckett	.12	.30
278 David Ortiz	.30	.75
279 Kevin Youkilis	.12	.30
280 Jason Varitek	.30	.75
281 Manny Ramirez	.30	.75
282 Curt Schilling	.20	.50
283 Jon Lester	.20	.50
284 Jonathan Papelbon	.30	.75
285 Alex Gonzalez	.12	.30
286 Mike Lowell	.12	.30
287 Kyle Snyder	.12	.30
288 Miguel Tejada	.20	.50
289 Erik Bedard	.12	.30
290 Ramon Hernandez	.12	.30
291 Melvin Mora	.12	.30
292 Nick Markakis	.25	.60
293 Brian Roberts	.12	.30
294 Corey Patterson	.12	.30
295 Kris Benson	.12	.30
296 Jay Gibbons	.12	.30
297 Rodrigo Lopez	.12	.30
298 Chris Ray	.12	.30
299 Andruw Jones	.12	.30
300 Brian McCann	.12	.30
301 Jeff Francoeur	.30	.75
302 Chuck James	.12	.30
303 John Smoltz	.30	.75
304 Bob Wickman	.12	.30
305 Edgar Renteria	.12	.30
306 Adam LaRoche	.12	.30
307 Marcus Giles	.12	.30
308 Tim Hudson	.20	.50
309 Chipper Jones	.30	.75
310 Miguel Batista	.12	.30
311 Claudio Vargas	.12	.30
312 Brandon Webb	.20	.50
313 Luis Gonzalez	.12	.30
314 Livan Hernandez	.12	.30
315 Stephen Drew	.12	.30
316 Johnny Estrada	.12	.30
317 Orlando Hudson	.12	.30
318 Conor Jackson	.12	.30
319 Chad Tracy	.12	.30
320 Carlos Quentin	.12	.30
321 Alvin Colina RC	.60	1.50
322 Miguel Montero (RC)	.25	.60
323 Jeff Fiorentino (RC)	.25	.60
324 Jeff Baker (RC)	.25	.60
325 Brian Burres (RC)	.25	.60
326 David Murphy (RC)	.25	.60
327 Francisco Cruceta (RC)	.25	.60
328 Beltran Perez (RC)	.25	.60
329 Scott Moore (RC)	.25	.60
330 Sean Henn (RC)	.25	.60
331 Ryan Sweeney (RC)	.25	.60
332 Josh Fields (RC)	.25	.60
333 Jerry Owens (RC)	.25	.60
334 Vinny Rottino (RC)	.25	.60
335 Kevin Kouzmanoff (RC)	.25	.60
336 Alexi Casilla RC	.40	1.00
337 Justin Hampson (RC)	.25	.60
338 Troy Tulowitzki (RC)	.75	2.00
339 Jose Garcia RC	.25	.60
340 Andrew Miller RC	1.00	2.50
341 Glen Perkins (RC)	.25	.60
342 Ubaldo Jimenez (RC)	.75	2.00
343 Doug Slaten RC	.25	.60
344 Angel Sanchez RC	.25	.60
345 Mitch Maier RC	.25	.60
346 Ryan Braun RC	.25	.60
347 Joselo Diaz (RC)	.25	.60
348 Delwyn Young (RC)	.25	.60
349 Kevin Hooper (RC)	.25	.60
350 Dennis Sarfate (RC)	.25	.60
351 Andy Cannizaro RC	.25	.60
352 Devern Hansack RC	.25	.60
353 Michael Bourn (RC)	.40	1.00
354 Carlos Maldonado (RC)	.25	.60
355 Shane Youman RC	.25	.60
356 Philip Humber (RC)	.25	.60
357 Hector Gimenez (RC)	.25	.60
358 Fred Lewis (RC)	.40	1.00
359 Ryan Feierabend (RC)	.25	.60
360 Juan Morillo (RC)	.25	.60
361 Travis Chick (RC)	.25	.60
362 Oswaldo Navarro RC	.25	.60
363 Cesar Jimenez RC	.25	.60
364 Brian Stokes (RC)	.25	.60
365 Delmon Young (RC)	.40	1.00
366 Juan Salas (RC)	.25	.60
367 Shawn Riggans (RC)	.25	.60
368 Adam Lind (RC)	.25	.60
369 Joaquin Arias (RC)	.25	.60
370 Eric Stults RC	.25	.60
371 Brandon Webb CL	.20	.50
372 John Smoltz CL	.30	.75
373 Miguel Tejada CL	.20	.50
374 David Ortiz CL	.30	.75
375 Carlos Zambrano CL	.20	.50
376 Jermaine Dye CL	.12	.30
377 Ken Griffey Jr. CL	.60	1.50
378 Victor Martinez CL	.20	.50
379 Todd Helton CL	.20	.50
380 Ivan Rodriguez CL	.20	.50
381 Miguel Cabrera CL	.30	.75
382 Lance Berkman CL	.20	.50
383 Mike Sweeney CL	.12	.30
384 Vladimir Guerrero CL	.20	.50
385 Derek Lowe CL	.12	.30
386 Bill Hall CL	.12	.30
387 Johan Santana CL	.20	.50
388 Carlos Beltran CL	.20	.50
389 Derek Jeter CL	.75	2.00
390 Nick Swisher CL	.20	.50
391 Ryan Howard CL	.25	.60
392 Jason Bay CL	.20	.50
393 Trevor Hoffman CL	.20	.50
394 Omar Vizquel CL	.20	.50
395 Ichiro Suzuki CL	.40	1.00
396 Albert Pujols CL	.40	1.00
397 Carl Crawford CL	.20	.50
398 Mark Teixeira CL	.20	.50
399 Roy Halladay CL	.20	.50
400 Ryan Zimmerman CL	.20	.50
401 Mark Reynolds RC	.75	2.00
402 Micah Owings (RC)	.25	.60
403 Jarrod Saltalamacchia (RC)	.40	1.00
404 Daisuke Matsuzaka RC	1.00	2.50
405 Hideki Okajima RC	1.25	3.00
406 Felix Pie (RC)	.25	.60
407 Mike Fontenot (RC)	.25	.60
408 John Danks RC	.40	1.00
409 Josh Hamilton (RC)	.75	2.00
410 Homer Bailey (RC)	.40	1.00
411 Alejandro De Aza RC	.40	1.00
412 Matt Lindstrom (RC)	.25	.60
413 Hunter Pence (RC)	.75	2.00
414 Alex Gordon RC	.75	2.00
415 Billy Butler (RC)	.40	1.00
416 Brandon Wood (RC)	.25	.60
417 Andy LaRoche (RC)	.25	.60
418 Ryan Bruan (RC)	1.25	3.00
419 Joe Smith RC	.25	.60
420 Carlos Gomez RC	.50	1.25
421 Tyler Clippard (RC)	.40	1.00
422 Matt DeSalvo (RC)	.25	..60
423 Phil Hughes (RC)	.60	1.50
424 Kei Igawa RC	.60	1.50
425 Chase Wright RC	.60	1.50
426 Travis Buck (RC)	.25	.60
427 Zack Segovia (RC)	.25	.60
428 Tim Lincecum RC	1.25	3.00
429 Elijah Dukes RC	.40	1.00
430 Akinori Iwamura RC	.60	1.50

2007 Fleer Mini Die Cuts

*MINI: 1.25X TO 3X BASIC
*MINI RC: .6X TO 1.5X BASIC RC
STATED ODDS 1:2 HOBBY, 1:2 RETAIL

2007 Fleer Mini Die Cuts Gold

STATED ODDS 1:576 HOBBY, 1:576 RETAIL
NO PRICING DUE TO SCARCITY

2007 Fleer Autographics

STATED ODDS 1:720
NO PRICING ON MOST DUE TO SCARCITY

BH Bill Hall	20.00	50.00
CB Chris Booker	6.00	15.00
CK Casey Kotchman	6.00	15.00
DJ Dan Johnson	6.00	15.00
JJ Jorge Julio	6.00	15.00
KH Koyie Hill	6.00	15.00
NS Nick Swisher	6.00	15.00

2007 Fleer Crowning Achievement

COMPLETE SET (20)	6.00	15.00

STATED ODDS 1:5
OVERALL PRINTING PLATE ODDS 1:720
PLATE PRINT RUN 1 SET PER COLOR
BLACK-CYAN-MAGENTA-YELLOW ISSUED
NO PLATE PRICING DUE TO SCARCITY

AP Albert Pujols	1.25	3.00
BZ Barry Zito	.60	1.50
CD Carlos Delgado	.40	1.00
CS Curt Schilling	.60	1.50
DJ Derek Jeter	2.50	6.00
DO David Ortiz	1.00	2.50
FT Frank Thomas	1.00	2.50
GM Greg Maddux	1.25	3.00
IS Ichiro Suzuki	1.25	3.00
JS Johan Santana	.60	1.50
JT Jim Thome	.60	1.50
KG Ken Griffey Jr.	2.00	5.00
MC Miguel Cabrera	1.00	2.50
MP Mike Piazza	1.00	2.50
MR Manny Ramirez	1.00	2.50
PM Pedro Martinez	.60	1.50
RC Roger Clemens	1.25	3.00
RH Ryan Howard	.75	2.00
TG Tom Glavine	.60	1.50
TH Trevor Hoffman	.60	1.50

2007 Fleer Fresh Ink

STATED ODDS 1:720
NO PRICING ON MOST DUE TO SCARCITY

CC Craig Counsell	6.00	15.00
GQ Guillermo Quiroz	6.00	15.00
JB Joe Blanton	6.00	15.00
KG Khalil Greene	10.00	25.00
LN Leo Nunez	6.00	15.00
MM Matt Murton	15.00	40.00
SD Scott Dunn	6.00	15.00
SR Saul Rivera	6.00	15.00

2007 Fleer Genuine Coverage

STATED ODDS 1:720
MANY NOT PRICED DUE TO SCARCITY

AP Albert Pujols	8.00	20.00
AR Aramis Ramirez	4.00	10.00
BE Adrian Beltre	4.00	10.00
BR Brian Roberts	4.00	10.00
BS Ben Sheets	4.00	10.00
CB Carlos Beltran	6.00	15.00
CS C.C. Sabathia	4.00	10.00
DJ Derek Jeter	10.00	25.00
DW Dontrelle Willis	4.00	10.00
GJ Geoff Jenkins	4.00	10.00
HA Rich Harden	4.00	10.00
IS Ian Snell	4.00	10.00
JM Justin Morneau	5.00	12.00
JP Jake Peavy	4.00	10.00
KG Ken Griffey Jr.	8.00	20.00
MR Manny Ramirez	6.00	15.00
PK Paul Konerko	4.00	10.00
RS Richie Sexson	4.00	10.00
TH Torii Hunter	4.00	10.00

2007 Fleer In the Zone

COMPLETE SET (10)	5.00	12.00

STATED ODDS 1:10 HOBBY, 1:10 RETAIL
OVERALL PRINTING PLATE ODDS 1:720
PLATE PRINT RUN 1 SET PER COLOR
BLACK-CYAN-MAGENTA-YELLOW ISSUED
NO PLATE PRICING DUE TO SCARCITY

AJ Andruw Jones	.40	1.00
AP Albert Pujols	1.25	3.00
AR Alex Rodriguez	1.25	3.00
DO David Ortiz	1.00	2.50
DW David Wright	.75	2.00
KG Ken Griffey Jr.	2.00	5.00
MC Miguel Cabrera	1.00	2.50
MT Mark Teixeira	.60	1.50
RH Ryan Howard	.75	2.00
VG Vladimir Guerrero	.60	1.50

2007 Fleer Perfect 10

COMPLETE SET (20)	6.00	15.00

STATED ODDS 1:5
OVERALL PRINTING PLATE ODDS 1:720
PLATE PRINT RUN 1 SET PER COLOR
BLACK-CYAN-MAGENTA-YELLOW ISSUED
NO PLATE PRICING DUE TO SCARCITY

AP Albert Pujols	1.25	3.00
AS Alfonso Soriano	.60	1.50
BH Bill Hall	.40	1.00
CB Carlos Beltran	.60	1.50
CC Carl Crawford	.60	1.50
CJ Chipper Jones	1.00	2.50
CU Chase Utley	.60	1.50
DJ Derek Jeter	2.50	6.00
DO David Ortiz	1.00	2.50
IR Ivan Rodriguez	.60	1.50
JB Jason Bay	.60	1.50
JD Jermaine Dye	.40	1.00
JS Johan Santana	.60	1.50
MC Miguel Cabrera	1.00	2.50
MM Mike Mussina	.60	1.50
MY Michael Young	.40	1.00
RC Roger Clemens	1.25	3.00
RH Roy Halladay	.60	1.50
RH Ryan Howard	.75	2.00
VG Vladimir Guerrero	.60	1.50

2007 Fleer Rookie Sensations

COMPLETE SET (25)	6.00	15.00

STATED ODDS APPX 1:1 HOBBY, 1:1 RETAIL
OVERALL PRINTING PLATE ODDS 1:720
PLATE PRINT RUN 1 SET PER COLOR
BLACK-CYAN-MAGENTA-YELLOW ISSUED
NO PLATE PRICING DUE TO SCARCITY

BB Boof Bonser	.40	1.00
CB Chad Billingsley	.60	1.50
CH Cole Hamels	.75	2.00
CJ Conor Jackson	.40	1.00
DU Dan Uggla	.40	1.00
FL Francisco Liriano	.40	1.00
HR Hanley Ramirez	.60	1.50
IK Ian Kinsler	.60	1.50
JB Josh Barfield	.40	1.00
JH Jeremy Hermida	.40	1.00
JJ Josh Johnson	1.00	2.50
JL Jon Lester	.60	1.50
JP Jonathan Papelbon	1.00	2.50
JS Jeremy Sowers	.40	1.00
JV Justin Verlander	1.00	2.50
JW Jered Weaver	.60	1.50
KJ Kenji Johjima	1.00	2.50
LO James Loney	.40	1.00
MK Matt Kemp	.75	2.00
NM Nick Markakis	.75	2.00
PF Prince Fielder	.60	1.50
RG Matt Garza	.40	1.00
RN Ricky Nolasco	.40	1.00
RZ Ryan Zimmerman	.60	1.50
SO Scott Olsen	.40	1.00

2007 Fleer Soaring Stars

STATED ODDS 1:2 FAT PACKS
OVERALL PRINTING PLATE ODDS 1:720
PLATE PRINT RUN 1 SET PER COLOR
BLACK-CYAN-MAGENTA-YELLOW ISSUED
NO PLATE PRICING DUE TO SCARCITY

AD Adam Dunn	.60	1.50
AJ Andruw Jones	.40	1.00
AL Alex Rodriguez	1.25	3.00
AP Albert Pujols	1.25	3.00
AR Alex Rios	.40	1.00
AS Alfonso Soriano	.60	1.50
BW Brandon Webb	.60	1.50
BZ Barry Zito	.60	1.50
CB Carlos Beltran	.60	1.50
CJ Chipper Jones	1.00	2.50
CU Chase Utley	.60	1.50
DA Johnny Damon	.60	1.50
DJ Derek Jeter	2.50	6.00
DL Derrek Lee	.40	1.00
DO David Ortiz	1.00	2.50
DW David Wright	.75	2.00
HA Roy Halladay	.60	1.50
IR Ivan Rodriguez*	.60	1.50
IS Ichiro Suzuki	1.25	3.00
JB Jason Bay	.40	1.00
JD Jermaine Dye	.40	1.00
JG Jon Garland	.40	1.00
JM Joe Mauer	.75	2.00
JS Johan Santana	.60	1.50
JV Justin Verlander	1.00	2.50
KG Ken Griffey Jr.	2.00	5.00
LB Lance Berkman	.60	1.50
MC Miguel Cabrera	1.00	2.50
MP Mike Piazza	1.00	2.50
MR Manny Ramirez	1.00	2.50
MT Mark Teixeira	.60	1.50
NG Nomar Garciaparra	.60	1.50
PF Prince Fielder	.60	1.50
PM Pedro Martinez	.60	1.50
RH Ryan Howard	.75	2.00
RI Mariano Rivera	1.25	3.00
RO Roy Oswalt	.60	1.50
TE Miguel Tejada	.60	1.50
TG Tom Glavine	.60	1.50
TH Travis Hafner	.40	1.00
VG Vladimir Guerrero	.60	1.50
WI Dontrelle Willis	.40	1.00

2007 Fleer Year in Review

COMPLETE SET (20)	6.00	15.00

STATED ODDS 1:5
OVERALL PRINTING PLATE ODDS 1:720
PLATE PRINT RUN 1 SET PER COLOR
BLACK-CYAN-MAGENTA-YELLOW ISSUED
NO PLATE PRICING DUE TO SCARCITY

AP Albert Pujols	1.25	3.00
AR Alex Rodriguez	1.25	3.00
AS Alfonso Soriano	.60	1.50
BA Bobby Abreu	.40	1.00
CU Chase Utley	.60	1.50
DJ Derek Jeter	2.50	6.00
DO David Ortiz	1.00	2.50
FL Francisco Liriano	.40	1.00
FS Freddy Sanchez	.40	1.00
HO Ryan Howard	.75	2.00
JD Jermaine Dye	.40	1.00
JM Joe Mauer	.75	2.00
JR Jose Reyes	.60	1.50
JV Justin Verlander	1.00	2.50
JW Jered Weaver	.60	1.50
KG Ken Griffey Jr.	2.00	5.00
MD Mark DeRosa	.40	1.00
MO Justin Morneau	.60	1.50
RH Roy Halladay	.60	1.50
TH Travis Hafner	.40	1.00

2004 Fleer Authentic Player Autographs

AVAIL.VIA MAIL REDEMPTION
STATED PRINT RUN 300 SERIAL #'d CARDS

RJ Randy Johnson/300	20.00	50.00

2005 Fleer Authentic Player Autographs

NO PRICING ON QTY OF 25 OR LESS

DW1 David Wright AU/300	15.00	40.00
DW2 David Wright Jsy AU/100	15.00	40.00
JF1 Jennie Finch AU/500	12.00	30.00
JF2 Jennie Finch AU/300	12.00	30.00
JF3 Jennie Finch AU/150	15.00	40.00
JF4 Jennie Finch AU/50	20.00	50.00
JV1 Justin Verlander AU/300	20.00	50.00
JV2 Justin Verlander AU/150	25.00	60.00
JV3 Justin Verlander AU/50	30.00	80.00
KS1 Kurt Suzuki AU/300	3.00	8.00
KW1 Kerry Wood Jsy AU/100	5.00	12.00
MC1 Miguel Cabrera AU/300	10.00	25.00
MC2 Miguel Cabrera AU/150	12.00	30.00
MC3 Miguel Cabrera AU/50	15.00	40.00
MC4 Miguel Cabrera Jsy AU/100	15.00	40.00
RJ1 Randy Johnson AU/150	25.00	60.00
RJ2 Randy Johnson AU/50	25.00	60.00

2002 Fleer Authentix

COMP.SET w/o SP's (150)	15.00	40.00
COMMON CARD (1-135)	.15	.40
COMMON CARD (136-150)	.25	.60
COMMON CARD (151-170)	1.50	4.00

151-170 RANDOM INSERTS IN PACKS
151-170 PRINT RUN 1850 SERIAL #'d SETS

1 Derek Jeter	1.00	2.50
2 Tim Hudson	.15	.40
3 Robert Fick	.15	.40
4 Javy Lopez	.15	.40
5 Alfonso Soriano	.15	.40
6 Ken Griffey Jr.	.75	2.00
7 Rafael Palmeiro	.25	.60
8 Bernie Williams	.25	.60
9 Adam Dunn	.15	.40
10 Ivan Rodriguez	.25	.60
11 Vladimir Guerrero	.40	1.00
12 Pedro Martinez	.25	.60
13 Bret Boone	.15	.40
14 Paul LoDuca	.15	.40
15 Tony Batista	.15	.40
16 Barry Bonds	1.00	2.50
17 Craig Biggio	.25	.60
18 Garret Anderson	.15	.40
19 Mark Mulder	.15	.40
20 Frank Thomas	.40	1.00
21 Alex Rodriguez	.50	1.50
22 Cristian Guzman	.15	.40
23 Sammy Sosa	.40	1.00
24 Ichiro Suzuki	.75	2.00
25 Carlos Beltran	.15	.40
26 Edgardo Alfonzo	.15	.40
27 Josh Beckett	.15	.40
28 Eric Chavez	.15	.40
29 Roberto Alomar	.25	.60
30 Raul Mondesi	.15	.40
31 Mike Piazza	.60	1.50
32 Barry Larkin	.25	.60
33 Ruben Sierra	.15	.40
34 Tsuyoshi Shinjo	.15	.40
35 Magglio Ordonez	.15	.40
36 Ben Grieve	.15	.40
37 Richie Sexson	.15	.40
38 Manny Ramirez	.25	.60
39 Jeff Kent	.15	.40
40 Shawn Green	.15	.40
41 Andruw Jones	.25	.60
42 Aramis Ramirez	.15	.40
43 Cliff Floyd	.15	.40
44 Juan Pierre	.15	.40
45 Jose Vidro	.15	.40
46 Paul Konerko	.15	.40
47 Greg Vaughn	.15	.40
48 Geoff Jenkins	.15	.40
49 Greg Maddux	.60	1.50
50 Ryan Klesko	.15	.40
51 Corey Koskie	.15	.40
52 Nomar Garciaparra	.60	1.50
53 Edgar Martinez	.25	.60
54 Gary Sheffield	.15	.40
55 Randy Johnson	.40	1.00
56 Bobby Abreu	.15	.40
57 Mike Sweeney	.15	.40
58 Chipper Jones	.40	1.00
59 Brian Giles	.15	.40
60 Charles Johnson	.15	.40
61 Ben Sheets	.15	.40
62 Jason Giambi	.15	.40
63 Todd Helton	.25	.60
64 David Eckstein	.15	.40
65 Troy Glaus	.15	.40
66 Sean Casey	.15	.40
67 Gabe Kapler	.15	.40
68 Doug Mientkiewicz	.15	.40
69 Curt Schilling	.15	.40
70 Pat Burrell	.15	.40
71 Albert Pujols	.75	2.00
72 Jermaine Dye	.15	.40
73 Miguel Tejada	.15	.40
74 Jim Thome	.25	.60
75 Carlos Delgado	.15	.40
76 Fred McGriff	.25	.60
77 Mike Cameron	.15	.40
78 Jeromy Burnitz	.15	.40
79 Jay Gibbons	.15	.40
80 Rich Aurilia	.15	.40
81 Lance Berkman	.15	.40
82 Brian Jordan	.15	.40
83 Phil Nevin	.15	.40
84 Moises Alou	.15	.40
85 Reggie Sanders	.15	.40
86 Scott Rolen	.25	.60
87 Larry Walker	.15	.40
88 Matt Williams	.15	.40
89 Roger Clemens	.75	2.00
90 Juan Gonzalez	.15	.40
91 Jose Cruz Jr.	.15	.40
92 Tino Martinez	.25	.60
93 Kerry Wood	.15	.40
94 Freddy Garcia	.15	.40
95 Jeff Bagwell	.25	.60
96 Luis Gonzalez	.15	.40
97 Jimmy Rollins	.15	.40
98 Bobby Higginson	.15	.40
99 Rondell White	.15	.40
100 Jorge Posada	.25	.60
101 Trot Nixon	.15	.40
102 Jason Kendall	.15	.40
103 Preston Wilson	.15	.40
104 Corey Patterson	.15	.40
105 Jose Valentin	.15	.40
106 Carlos Lee	.15	.40
107 Chris Richard	.15	.40
108 Todd Walker	.15	.40
109 Ellis Burks	.15	.40
110 Brady Anderson	.15	.40
111 Kazuhiro Sasaki	.15	.40
112 Roy Oswalt	.15	.40
113 Kevin Brown	.15	.40
114 Jeff Weaver	.15	.40
115 Todd Hollandsworth	.15	.40
116 Joe Crede	.15	.40
117 Tom Glavine	.25	.60
118 Mike Lieberthal	.15	.40
119 Tim Salmon	.25	.60
120 Johnny Damon Sox	.25	.60
121 Brad Fullmer	.15	.40
122 Mo Vaughn	.15	.40
123 Torii Hunter	.15	.40
124 Jamie Moyer	.15	.40
125 Terrence Long	.15	.40
126 Travis Lee	.15	.40
127 Jacque Jones	.15	.40
128 Lee Stevens	.15	.40
129 Russ Ortiz	.15	.40
130 Jeremy Giambi	.15	.40
131 Mike Mussina	.25	.60
132 Orlando Cabrera	.15	.40
133 Barry Zito	.15	.40
134 Robert Person	.15	.40
135 Andy Pettitte	.25	.60
136 Drew Henson FS	.25	.60
137 Mark Teixeira FS	.60	1.50
138 David Espinosa FS	.25	.60
139 Orlando Hudson FS	.25	.60
140 Colby Lewis FS	.25	.60
141 Bill Hall FS	.25	.60
142 Michael Restovich FS	.25	.60
143 Angel Berroa FS	.25	.60
144 Dewon Brazelton FS	.25	.60
145 Joe Thurston FS	.25	.60

146 Mark Prior FS .60 1.50
147 Dane Sardinha FS .25 .60
148 Marlon Byrd FS .25 .60
149 Jeff Deardorff FS .25 .60
150 Austin Kearns FS .25 .60
151 Anderson Machado TM RC 1.50 4.00
152 Kazuhisa Ishii TM RC 2.00 5.00
153 Eric Junge TM RC 1.50 4.00
154 Mark Corey TM RC 1.50 4.00
155 So Taguchi TM RC 2.00 5.00
156 Jorge Padilla TM RC 1.50 4.00
157 Steve Kent TM RC 1.50 4.00
158 Jaime Cerda TM RC 1.50 4.00
159 Hansel Izquierdo TM RC 1.50 4.00
160 Rene Reyes TM RC 1.50 4.00
161 Jorge Nunez TM RC 1.50 4.00
162 Corey Thurman TM RC 1.50 4.00
163 Jorge Sosa TM RC 2.00 5.00
164 Franklin Nunez TM RC 1.50 4.00
165 Adam Walker TM RC 1.50 4.00
166 Ryan Baerlocher TM RC 1.50 4.00
167 Ron Calloway TM RC 1.50 4.00
168 Miguel Asencio TM RC 1.50 4.00
169 Luis Ugueto TM RC 1.50 4.00
170 Felix Escalona TM RC 1.50 4.00

2002 Fleer Authentix Front Row

*FRONT ROW 1-135: 4X TO 10X BASIC
*FRONT ROW 136-150: 4X TO 10X BASIC
*FRONT ROW 151-170: .75X TO 2X BASIC
RANDOM INSERTS IN PACKS
STATED PRINT RUN 150 SERIAL #'d SETS

2002 Fleer Authentix Second Row

*2ND ROW 1-135: 2.5X TO 6X BASIC
*2ND ROW 136-150: 2.5X TO 6X BASIC
*2ND ROW 151-170: .6X TO 1.5X BASIC
RANDOM INSERTS IN PACKS
STATED PRINT RUN 250 SERIAL #'d SETS

2002 Fleer Authentix Autograph AuthenTIX

STATED ODDS 1:780 HOBBY, 1:2200 RETAIL
SP PRINT RUNS LISTED BELOW
SP'S ARE NOT SERIAL NUMBERED
SP PRINT RUNS PROVIDED BY FLEER
NO PRICING ON QUANTITIES OF 25 OR LESS
UNRIPPED PRINT RUN 25 #'d SETS
NO UNRIPPED PRICE DUE TO SCARCITY
AABR Brooks Robinson SP/145 10.00 25.00
AADE David Espinosa 6.00 15.00
AADS Dane Sardinha 6.00 15.00
AAKI Kazuhisa Ishii 10.00 25.00
AAMP Mark Prior SP/145 20.00 50.00
AAST So Taguchi SP/150 6.00 15.00

2002 Fleer Authentix Ballpark Classics

COMPLETE SET (15) 40.00 80.00
STATED ODDS 1:22 HOBBY, 1:24 RETAIL
1 Reggie Jackson 1.50 4.00
2 Don Mattingly 3.00 8.00
3 Duke Snider 1.50 4.00
4 Carlton Fisk 1.50 4.00
5 Cal Ripken 5.00 12.00
6 Willie McCovey 1.50 4.00
7 Robin Yount 1.50 4.00
8 Paul Molitor 1.50 4.00
9 George Brett 3.00 8.00
10 Ryne Sandberg 2.50 6.00
11 Nolan Ryan 4.00 10.00
12 Thurman Munson 1.50 4.00
13 Joe Morgan 1.50 4.00
14 Jim Rice 1.50 4.00
15 Babe Ruth 6.00 15.00

2002 Fleer Authentix Ballpark Classics Memorabilia

STATED ODDS 1:83 HOBBY, 1:440 RETAIL
ALL CARDS FEATURE SEAT SWATCHES
SP'S ARE NOT SERIAL NUMBERED
SP PRINT RUNS PROVIDED BY FLEER
CF Carlton Fisk Jsy 6.00 15.00
CR Cal Ripken Jsy 10.00 25.00
DM Don Mattingly Jsy 10.00 25.00
DS Duke Snider Bat SP/249 10.00 25.00
GB George Brett Jsy SP/482 10.00 25.00
JM Joe Morgan Bat 6.00 15.00
JR Jim Rice Jsy SP/487 6.00 15.00
NR Nolan Ryan Jsy 8.00 20.00
PM Paul Molitor Jsy 6.00 15.00
RJ Reggie Jackson Jsy SP/230 10.00 25.00
RS Ryne Sandberg Bat SP/82 30.00 60.00
RY Robin Yount Jsy SP/83 10.00 25.00
TM Thur Munson Cap SP/83 30.00 60.00
WM Willie McCovey Jsy SP/359 10.00 25.00

2002 Fleer Authentix Ballpark Classics Memorabilia Gold

RANDOM INSERTS IN PACKS
STATED PRINT RUN 100 SERIAL #'d SETS
BR Babe Ruth Bat Seat 125.00 200.00
CF Carlton Fisk Jsy Seat 10.00 25.00
CR Cal Ripken Jsy Seat 20.00 50.00
DM Don Mattingly Jsy Seat 20.00 50.00
DS Duke Snider Bat Seat 10.00 25.00
GB George Brett Jsy Seat 20.00 50.00
JM Joe Morgan Bat Seat 10.00 25.00
JR Jim Rice Jsy Seat 10.00 25.00
NR Nolan Ryan Jsy Seat 12.50 30.00
PM Paul Molitor Jsy Seat 10.00 25.00
RJ Reggie Jackson Jsy Seat 10.00 25.00
RS Ryne Sandberg Bat Seat 20.00 50.00
RY Robin Yount Jsy Seat 15.00 40.00
TM Thurman Munson Cap Seat 20.00 50.00
WM Willie McCovey Jsy Seat 10.00 25.00

2002 Fleer Authentix Bat AuthenTIX

STATED ODDS 1:68 HOBBY
SP PRINT RUNS LISTED BELOW
SP'S ARE NOT SERIAL NUMBERED
PRINT RUNS PROVIDED BY FLEER
BAAJ Andruw Jones SP/171 6.00 15.00
BABB Barry Bonds SP/437 10.00 25.00
BADH Drew Henson 4.00 10.00
BADJ Derek Jeter SP/197 12.50 30.00
BAJG Juan Gonzalez SP/213 6.00 15.00
BAJR Jimmy Rollins SP/409 6.00 15.00
BAMR Manny Ramirez 6.00 15.00
BANG Nomar Garciaparra 10.00 25.00
BAOH Orlando Hernandez 4.00 10.00
BAPB Pat Burrell SP/468 6.00 15.00

2002 Fleer Authentix Jersey AuthenTIX

STATED ODDS 1:27 HOBBY, 1:43 RETAIL
SP'S: 50% LESS PRODUCED THAN NON SP'S
SP INFORMATION PROVIDED BY FLEER
JAAJ Andruw Jones SP 2.50 6.00
JAAR Alex Rodriguez 4.00 10.00
JABB Barry Bonds 5.00 12.00
JABW Bernie Williams SP 4.00 10.00
JABZ Barry Zito 1.25 3.00
JACJ Chipper Jones 3.00 8.00
JADE Darin Erstad SP 2.50 6.00
JADJ Derek Jeter 8.00 20.00
JAEC Eric Chavez 1.25 3.00
JAFG Freddy Garcia 1.25 3.00
JAFT Frank Thomas 3.00 8.00
JAGM Greg Maddux 5.00 12.00
JAIR Ivan Rodriguez 2.00 5.00
JAJB Jeff Bagwell 2.00 5.00
JAJD J.D. Drew SP 2.50 6.00
JAJE Jim Edmonds SP 4.00 10.00
JAJT Jim Thome SP 4.00 10.00
JALG Luis Gonzalez SP 2.50 6.00
JAMO Magglio Ordonez 2.00 5.00
JAMP Mike Piazza 3.00 8.00
JAMR Manny Ramirez SP 4.00 10.00
JANG Nomar Garciaparra SP 4.00 10.00
JAPL Paul LoDuca 1.25 3.00
JAPM Pedro Martinez 2.00 5.00
JARA Roberto Alomar 2.00 5.00
JARJ Randy Johnson 3.00 8.00
JASG Shawn Green 1.25 3.00
JASR Scott Rolen SP 4.00 10.00
JATH Todd Helton 2.00 5.00
JACS Curt Schilling SP 4.00 10.00

2002 Fleer Authentix Jersey Autograph AuthenTIX

STATED ODDS 1:1387 HOBBY, 1:8800 RETAIL
STATED PRINT RUN 50 SETS
CARDS ARE NOT SERIAL-NUMBERED
PRINT RUN INFO PROVIDED BY FLEER
UNRIPPED PRINT RUN 1 SERIAL #'d SET
NO UNRIPPED PRICE DUE TO SCARCITY
AJADJ Derek Jeter 150.00 250.00

2002 Fleer Authentix Derek Jeter '96 Autographics

RANDOM INSERT IN PACKS
STATED PRINT RUN 100 CARDS
CARDS ARE NOT SERIAL-NUMBERED
PRINT RUN PROVIDED BY FLEER
NNO Derek Jeter/100 * 150.00 300.00

2002 Fleer Authentix Power Alley

COMPLETE SET (15) 15.00 40.00
STATED ODDS 1:11 HOBBY, 1:12 RETAIL
1 Sammy Sosa 1.00 2.50
2 Ken Griffey Jr. 2.00 5.00
3 Luis Gonzalez .75 2.00
4 Alex Rodriguez 1.25 3.00
5 Shawn Green .75 2.00
6 Barry Bonds 2.50 6.00
7 Todd Helton .75 2.00
8 Jim Thome .75 2.00
9 Troy Glaus .75 2.00
10 Manny Ramirez .75 2.00
11 Jeff Bagwell .75 2.00
12 Jason Giambi .75 2.00
13 Chipper Jones 1.00 2.50
14 Mike Piazza 1.50 4.00
15 Albert Pujols 2.00 5.00

2003 Fleer Authentix

COMP.LO SET w/o SP's (110) 10.00 25.00
COMMON CARD (1-100) .15 .40
COMMON CARD (101-110) .25 .60
COMMON (111-125/161-175) .75 2.00
111-125 RANDOM INSERTS IN PACKS
161-175 RANDOM IN FLEER R/G PACKS
111-125 PRINT RUN 1850 SERIAL #'d SETS
161-175 PRINT RUN 1250 SERIAL #'d SETS
COMMON CARD (126-132) .75 2.00
126-132 STATED PRINT RUN 1700 SETS
COMMON CARD (133-139) 1.50 4.00
133-139 STATED PRINT RUN 210 SETS
COMMON CARD (140-153) 1.25 3.00
140-153 STATED PRINT RUN 560 SETS
COMMON CARD (154-160) 1.50 4.00
154-160 STATED PRINT RUN 280 SETS
126-160 FOUR PER HOME TEAM PACK
ONE HT PACK PER HOME TEAM BOX
1 IN 12 HOBBY BOXES IS HOME TEAM
126-160 PRINT RUNS PROVIDED BY FLEER
126-160 ARE NOT SERIAL-NUMBERED
1 Derek Jeter 1.00 2.50
2 Tom Glavine .25 .60
3 Jason Jennings .15 .40
4 Craig Biggio .25 .60
5 Miguel Tejada .25 .60
6 Barry Bonds .60 1.50
7 Juan Gonzalez .15 .40
8 Luis Gonzalez .15 .40
9 Johnny Damon .25 .60
10 Ellis Burks .15 .40
11 Frank Thomas .40 1.00
12 Richie Sexson .15 .40
13 Roger Clemens .50 1.25
14 Matt Morris .15 .40
15 Troy Glaus .15 .40
16 Tony Batista .15 .40
17 Magglio Ordonez .25 .60
18 Jose Vidro .15 .40
19 Barry Zito .25 .60
20 Chipper Jones .40 1.00
21 Moises Alou .15 .40
22 Lance Berkman .25 .60
23 Jacque Jones .15 .40
24 Alfonso Soriano .25 .60
25 Sean Burroughs .15 .40
26 Scott Rolen .25 .60
27 Mark Grace .25 .60
28 Manny Ramirez .40 1.00
29 Ken Griffey Jr. .75 2.00
30 Josh Beckett .15 .40
31 Kazuhisa Ishii .15 .40
32 Pat Burrell .15 .40
33 Edgar Martinez .25 .60
34 Tim Salmon .15 .40
35 Raul Ibanez .25 .60
36 Vladimir Guerrero .25 .60
37 Jermaine Dye .15 .40
38 Rich Aurilia .15 .40
39 Rafael Palmeiro .25 .60
40 Kerry Wood .15 .40
41 Omar Vizquel .25 .60
42 Fred McGriff .25 .60
43 Ben Sheets .15 .40
44 Bernie Williams .25 .60
45 Brian Giles .15 .40
46 Jim Edmonds .25 .60
47 Garret Anderson .15 .40
48 Pedro Martinez .25 .60
49 Adam Dunn .25 .60
50 A.J. Burnett .15 .40
51 Eric Gagne .15 .40
52 Mo Vaughn .15 .40
53 Bobby Abreu .15 .40
54 Bret Boone .15 .40
55 Carlos Delgado .15 .40
56 Gary Sheffield .15 .40
57 Sammy Sosa .40 1.00
58 Jim Thome .25 .60
59 Jeff Bagwell .25 .60
60 David Eckstein .15 .40
61 Jason Kendall .15 .40
62 Albert Pujols .50 1.25
63 Curt Schilling .25 .60
64 Nomar Garciaparra .25 .60
65 Sean Casey .15 .40
66 Shawn Green .15 .40
67 Mike Piazza .40 1.00
68 Ichiro Suzuki .50 1.25
69 Eric Hinske .15 .40
70 Greg Maddux .50 1.25
71 Larry Walker .25 .60
72 Roy Oswalt .25 .60
73 Alex Rodriguez .50 1.25
74 Austin Kearns .15 .40
75 Cliff Floyd .15 .40
76 Kevin Brown .15 .40
77 Jason Giambi .15 .40
78 Jorge Julio .15 .40
79 Carlos Lee .15 .40
80 Mike Sweeney .15 .40
81 Edgardo Alfonzo .15 .40
82 Eric Chavez .15 .40
83 Andruw Jones .15 .40
84 Mark Prior .25 .60
85 Todd Helton .25 .60
86 Torii Hunter .15 .40
87 Ryan Klesko .15 .40
88 Aubrey Huff .15 .40
89 Randy Johnson .40 1.00
90 Barry Larkin .25 .60
91 Mike Lowell .15 .40
92 Jimmy Rollins .25 .60
93 Darin Erstad .15 .40
94 Jay Gibbons .15 .40
95 Paul Konerko .25 .60
96 Bobby Higginson .15 .40
97 Carlos Beltran .25 .60
98 Bartolo Colon .15 .40
99 Jeff Kent .15 .40
100 Ivan Rodriguez .25 .60
101 Joe Borchard FS .25 .60
102 Mark Teixeira FS .40 1.00
103 Francisco Rodriguez FS .40 1.00
104 Chris Snelling FS .25 .60
105 Hee Seop Choi FS .25 .60
106 Hank Blalock FS .25 .60
107 Marlon Byrd FS .25 .60
108 Michael Restovich FS .25 .60
109 Victor Martinez FS .40 1.00
110 Lyle Overbay FS .25 .60
111 Brian Stokes TM RC .75 2.00
112 Josh Hall TM RC .75 2.00
113 Chris Waters TM RC .75 2.00
114 Lew Ford TM RC .75 2.00
115 Ian Ferguson TM RC .75 2.00
116 Josh Willingham TM RC 2.50 6.00
117 Josh Stewart TM RC .75 2.00
118 Pete LaForest TM RC .75 2.00
119 Jose Contreras TM RC 2.00 5.00
120 Termel Sledge TM RC .75 2.00
121 Guillermo Quiroz TM RC .75 2.00
122 Alejandro Machado TM RC .75 2.00
123 Nook Logan TM RC .75 2.00
124 Rontrez Johnson TM RC .75 2.00
125 Hideki Matsui TM RC 4.00 10.00
126 Phil Rizzuto HT 1.25 3.00
127 Robin Ventura HT .75 2.00
128 Andy Pettitte HT 1.25 3.00
129 Mike Mussina HT 1.25 3.00
130 Mariano Rivera HT 2.50 6.00
131 Jeff Weaver HT .75 2.00
132 David Wells HT .75 2.00
133 Tommy Lasorda HT 2.50 6.00
134 Pee Wee Reese HT 2.50 6.00
135 Hideo Nomo HT 4.00 10.00
136 Adrian Beltre HT 4.00 10.00
137 Chin-Feng Chen HT 1.50 4.00
138 Odalis Perez HT 1.50 4.00
139 Dave Roberts HT 2.50 6.00
140 Bobby Doerr HT 2.00 5.00
141 Jason Varitek HT 3.00 8.00
142 Trot Nixon HT 1.25 3.00
143 Tim Wakefield HT 2.00 5.00
144 John Burkett HT 1.25 3.00
145 Jeremy Giambi HT 1.25 3.00
146 Casey Fossum HT 1.25 3.00
147 Phil Niekro HT 2.00 5.00
148 Warren Spahn HT 2.00 5.00
149 Rafael Furcal HT 1.25 3.00
150 Vinny Castilla HT 1.25 3.00
151 Javy Lopez HT 1.25 3.00
152 Jason Marquis HT 1.25 3.00
153 Mike Hampton HT 1.25 3.00
154 Gaylord Perry HT 2.50 6.00
155 Ruben Sierra HT 1.50 4.00
156 Mike Cameron HT 1.50 4.00
157 Freddy Garcia HT 1.50 4.00
158 Joel Pineiro HT 1.50 4.00
159 Jamie Moyer HT 1.50 4.00
160 Carlos Guillen HT 1.50 4.00
161 Chien-Ming Wang TM RC 3.00 8.00
162 Rickie Weeks TM RC 2.50 6.00
163 Brandon Webb TM RC 2.50 6.00
164 Craig Brazell TM RC .75 2.00
165 Michael Hessman TM RC .75 2.00
166 Ryan Wagner TM RC .75 2.00
167 Matt Kata TM RC .75 2.00
168 Edwin Jackson TM RC 1.25 3.00
169 Mike Ryan TM RC .75 2.00
170 Delmon Young TM RC 5.00 12.00
171 Bo Hart TM RC .75 2.00
172 Jeff Duncan TM RC .75 2.00
173 Robby Hammock TM RC .75 2.00
174 Jeremy Bonderman TM RC 3.00 8.00
175 Clint Barmes TM RC 2.00 5.00

2003 Fleer Authentix Balcony

*BALCONY 1-100: 2X TO 5X BASIC
*BALCONY 101-110: 1.2X TO 3X BASIC
*BALCONY 111-125: .5X TO 1.2X BASIC
RANDOM INSERTS IN PACKS
STATED PRINT RUN 250 SERIAL #'d SETS

2003 Fleer Authentix Club Box

*CLUB BOX 1-100: 4X TO 10X BASIC
*CLUB BOX 101-110: 2.5X TO 6X BASIC
*CLUB BOX 111-125: .75X TO 2X BASIC
RANDOM INSERTS IN PACKS
STATED PRINT RUN 100 SERIAL #'d SETS

2003 Fleer Authentix Autograph Front Row

RANDOM INSERTS IN PACKS
STATED PRINT RUN 50 SERIAL #'d SETS
BB Barry Bonds 100.00 175.00
DJ Derek Jeter 125.00 300.00

2003 Fleer Authentix Autograph Second Row

RANDOM INSERT IN PACKS
STATED PRINT RUN 150 SERIAL #'d SETS
DJ Derek Jeter 100.00 200.00

2003 Fleer Authentix Autograph Third Row

RANDOM INSERTS IN PACKS
STATED PRINT RUN 250 SERIAL #'d SETS
BB Barry Bonds 75.00 200.00
DJ Derek Jeter 75.00 200.00

2003 Fleer Authentix Ballpark Classics

COMPLETE SET (10) 8.00 20.00
STATED ODDS 1:12 HOBBY, 1:18 RETAIL
1 Derek Jeter 2.50 6.00
2 Randy Johnson 1.00 2.50
3 Nomar Garciaparra .60 1.50
4 Barry Bonds 1.50 4.00
5 Alfonso Soriano .60 1.50
6 Alex Rodriguez 1.25 3.00
7 Jim Thome .60 1.50
8 Chipper Jones 1.00 2.50
9 Mike Piazza 1.00 2.50
10 Ichiro Suzuki 1.25 3.00

2003 Fleer Authentix Game Bat

STATED ODDS 1:78 HOBBY, 1:202 RETAIL
SP INFO PROVIDED BY FLEER
*UNRIPPED: .75X TO 2X BASIC GAME BAT
UNRIPPED PRINT RUN 50 SERIAL #'d SETS
AD Adam Dunn 3.00 8.00
CJ Chipper Jones 4.00 10.00
DJ Derek Jeter 10.00 25.00
JG Jason Giambi SP 3.00 8.00
JT Jim Thome 4.00 10.00
MR Manny Ramirez 4.00 10.00
NG Nomar Garciaparra 6.00 15.00
SS Sammy Sosa 4.00 10.00
VG Vladimir Guerrero 4.00 10.00

2003 Fleer Authentix Game Jersey

STATED ODDS 1:10 HOBBY, 1:41 RETAIL
SP QTY 1/2 BASIC GAME JERSEY
SP INFO PROVIDED BY FLEER
*UNRIPPED: .75X TO 2X BASIC GAME JSY
UNRIPPED PRINT RUN 50 SERIAL #'d SETS
AD Adam Dunn 3.00 8.00
AR Alex Rodriguez 6.00 15.00
AS Alfonso Soriano 3.00 8.00
CD Carlos Delgado 3.00 8.00
CJ Chipper Jones 4.00 10.00
DJ Derek Jeter SP 12.50 30.00
EH Eric Hinske 3.00 8.00
GM Greg Maddux 4.00 10.00
JB Jeff Bagwell 4.00 10.00
JB2 Josh Beckett 3.00 8.00
KW Kerry Wood 3.00 8.00
LB Lance Berkman 3.00 8.00
MB Mark Buehrle 3.00 8.00
MP Mike Piazza 4.00 10.00
MR Manny Ramirez 4.00 10.00
MT Miguel Tejada 3.00 8.00
NG Nomar Garciaparra 6.00 15.00
PB Pat Burrell 3.00 8.00
RC Roger Clemens 6.00 15.00
RJ Randy Johnson SP 4.00 10.00
SB Sean Burroughs 3.00 8.00
SS Sammy Sosa 4.00 10.00
TH Torii Hunter 3.00 8.00
VG Vladimir Guerrero 4.00 10.00

2003 Fleer Authentix Game Jersey All-Star

STATED PRINT RUNS LISTED BELOW
NO PRICING ON QTY OF 25 OR LESS
AD Adam Dunn/91 6.00 15.00
AR Alex Rodriguez/111 15.00 40.00
DJ Derek Jeter/81 25.00 60.00
LB Lance Berkman/103 6.00 15.00
MB Mark Buehrle/88 6.00 15.00
MP Mike Piazza/109 12.50 30.00
MR Manny Ramirez/78 10.00 25.00
MT Miguel Tejada/52 15.00 40.00
NG Nomar Garciaparra/53 25.00 60.00
TH Torii Hunter/64 12.50 30.00
VG Vladimir Guerrero/66 15.00 40.00

2003 Fleer Authentix Game Jersey Autograph Front Row

RANDOM INSERTS IN PACKS
STATED PRINT RUN 100 SERIAL #'d SETS
DJ Derek Jeter 200.00 500.00
NR Nolan Ryan 60.00 120.00

2003 Fleer Authentix Game Jersey Autograph Second Row

RANDOM INSERTS IN PACKS
STATED PRINT RUN 200 SERIAL #'d SETS
DJ Derek Jeter 150.00 400.00
NR Nolan Ryan 60.00 120.00

2003 Fleer Authentix Game Jersey Autograph Third Row

RANDOM INSERT IN PACKS
STATED PRINT RUN 300 SERIAL #'d SETS
DJ Derek Jeter 125.00 300.00

2003 Fleer Authentix Game Jersey Game of the Week

STATED ODDS 1:240 HOBBY, 1:420 RETAIL
GROUP A 2X SCARCER THAN GROUP B
GROUP INFO PROVIDED BY FLEER
*UNRIPPED: 1X TO 2.5X BASIC GAME A
*UNRIPPED: .75X TO 2X BASIC GAME B
UNRIPPED PRINT RUN 50 SERIAL #'d SETS
ADLB A.Dunn/L.Berkman A 6.00 15.00
ARMT A.Rodriguez/M.Tejada A 6.00 15.00
ASSS A.Soriano/S.Sosa A 6.00 15.00
CJPB C.Jones/P.Burrell B 10.00 25.00
DJMT D.Jeter/M.Tejada A 10.00 25.00
DJNG D.Jeter/N.Garciaparra A 15.00 40.00
EHTH E.Hinske/T.Hunter A 6.00 15.00
GMRJ G.Maddux/R.Johnson B 12.50 30.00
MPSS M.Piazza/S.Sosa A 6.00 15.00
THAS T.Hunter/A.Soriano A 6.00 15.00

2003 Fleer Authentix Hometown Heroes Memorabilia

STATED ODDS ONE PER HOME TEAM PACK
ONE HT PACK PER HOME TEAM BOX
ONE IN EVERY 12 BOXES ARE HOME TEAM
SP PRINT RUNS PROVIDED BY FLEER
SP'S ARE NOT SERIAL-NUMBERED
I Ichiro Suzuki Base SP/100 5.00 12.00
AJ Andruw Jones Jsy SP/150 1.50 4.00
AS Alfonso Soriano Jsy 2.50 6.00
BB Bret Boone Jsy SP/200 1.50 4.00
CC Chin-Feng Chen Jsy SP/150 12.00 30.00
CJ Chipper Jones Jsy 4.00 10.00
DJ Derek Jeter Jsy 10.00 25.00
EM Edgar Martinez Jsy SP/200 2.50 6.00
FG Freddy Garcia Jsy SP/200 1.50 4.00
GM Greg Maddux Jsy 5.00 12.00
GS Gary Sheffield Jsy SP/100 1.50 4.00
JD Johnny Damon Jsy SP/100 2.50 6.00
JG Jason Giambi Bat SP/300 1.50 4.00
KB Kevin Brown Jsy SP/150 1.50 4.00
KI Kazuhisa Ishii Jsy SP/100 1.50 4.00
MR Manny Ramirez Jsy 4.00 10.00
NG Nomar Garciaparra Jsy 2.50 6.00
PM Pedro Martinez Jsy SP/100 2.50 6.00
RC Roger Clemens Jsy 5.00 12.00
SG Shawn Green Jsy SP/100 1.50 4.00

2003 Fleer Authentix Ticket Studs

COMPLETE SET (15) 10.00 25.00
STATED ODDS 1:6
1 Curt Schilling .60 1.50
2 Greg Maddux 1.25 3.00
3 Torii Hunter .40 1.00
4 Mike Piazza 1.00 2.50
5 Pedro Martinez .60 1.50
6 Nomar Garciaparra .60 1.50
7 Derek Jeter 2.50 6.00
8 Alex Rodriguez 1.25 3.00
9 Alfonso Soriano .60 1.50
10 Pat Burrell .40 1.00
11 Barry Bonds 1.50 4.00
12 Jason Giambi .40 1.00
13 Sammy Sosa 1.00 2.50
14 Vladimir Guerrero .60 1.50
15 Ichiro Suzuki 1.25 3.00

2004 Fleer Authentix

COMP.SET w/o SP's (100) 10.00 25.00
COMMON CARD (1-100) .15 .40
COMMON CARD (101-130) .75 2.00
101-130 ODDS 1:11 HOBBY, 1:34 RETAIL
101-130 PRINT RUN 999 SERIAL #'d SETS
COMMON CARD (131-140) 1.25 3.00
131-140 FOUR PER YANKS HOME TM PACK
131-140 STATED PRINT RUN APPX. 800 SETS
131-140 PRINT RUN PROVIDED BY FLEER
131-140 ARE NOT SERIAL-NUMBERED
1 Albert Pujols .50 1.25
2 Derek Jeter 1.00 2.50
3 Jody Gerut .15 .40
4 Mark Teixeira .25 .60
5 Tom Glavine .25 .60
6 Kerry Wood .15 .40
7 Ichiro Suzuki .50 1.25
8 Jose Vidro .15 .40
9 Mark Prior .25 .60
10 Jim Edmonds .25 .60
11 Richie Sexson .15 .40
12 Jay Gibbons .15 .40
13 Jason Kendall .15 .40
14 Lance Berkman .25 .60
15 Andruw Jones .15 .40
16 Jim Thome .25 .60
17 Josh Beckett .15 .40
18 Troy Glaus .15 .40
19 Jason Giambi .15 .40
20 Sammy Sosa .40 1.00
21 Bret Boone .15 .40
22 Eric Gagne .15 .40
23 Nomar Garciaparra .25 .60
24 Geoff Jenkins .15 .40
25 Ivan Rodriguez .25 .60
26 Preston Wilson .15 .40
27 Alex Rodriguez .50 1.25
28 Jorge Posada .25 .60
29 Ken Griffey Jr. .75 2.00
30 Rocco Baldelli .15 .40
31 Shannon Stewart .15 .40
32 Frank Thomas .40 1.00
33 Edgar Renteria .15 .40
34 Torii Hunter .15 .40
35 Corey Patterson .15 .40
36 Edgar Martinez .25 .60
37 Jeff Bagwell .25 .60
38 Greg Maddux .50 1.25
39 Mike Lieberthal .15 .40
40 Craig Biggio .25 .60
41 Randy Johnson .40 1.00
42 Marlon Byrd .15 .40
43 Jay Payton .15 .40
44 Carlos Delgado .15 .40
45 Scott Podsednik .15 .40
46 Pedro Martinez .25 .60
47 Carlos Beltran .25 .60
48 Mike Sweeney .15 .40
49 Gary Sheffield .15 .40
50 Pat Burrell .15 .40
51 Shawn Green .15 .40
52 Tony Batista .15 .40
53 Brian Giles .15 .40
54 Roy Oswalt .25 .60
55 Brandon Webb .15 .40
56 Miguel Tejada .25 .60
57 Miguel Cabrera .40 1.00
58 Luis Gonzalez .15 .40
59 Billy Wagner .15 .40
60 Craig Monroe .15 .40
61 Vernon Wells .15 .40
62 Bernie Williams .25 .60
63 Austin Kearns .15 .40
64 Aubrey Huff .15 .40
65 Mike Piazza .40 1.00
66 Magglio Ordonez .25 .60
67 Bo Hart .15 .40
68 Hideo Nomo .40 1.00
69 Curt Schilling .25 .60
70 Barry Zito .25 .60
71 Todd Helton .25 .60
72 Roy Halladay .25 .60
73 Alfonso Soriano .25 .60
74 Roberto Alomar .25 .60
75 Scott Rolen .25 .60
76 Manny Ramirez .40 1.00
77 Sean Burroughs .15 .40
78 Angel Berroa .15 .40
79 Javy Lopez .15 .40
80 Reggie Sanders .15 .40
81 Juan Pierre .15 .40
82 Chipper Jones .40 1.00
83 Bobby Abreu .15 .40
84 Dontrelle Willis .15 .40
85 Tim Salmon .15 .40
86 Eric Chavez .15 .40
87 Adam Dunn .25 .60
88 Rafael Palmeiro .25 .60
89 Hideki Matsui .60 1.50
90 Esteban Loaiza .15 .40
91 Darin Erstad .15 .40
92 Vladimir Guerrero .25 .60
93 David Ortiz .40 1.00
94 Jason Schmidt .15 .40
95 Dmitri Young .15 .40
96 Garret Anderson .15 .40
97 Mark Mulder .15 .40
98 Omar Vizquel .25 .60
99 Hank Blalock .15 .40
100 Jose Reyes .25 .60
101 Rickie Weeks TM .75 2.00
102 Chad Gaudin TM .75 2.00
103 Ryan Wagner TM .75 2.00
104 Koyie Hill TM .75 2.00
105 Rich Harden TM .75 2.00
106 Edwin Jackson TM .75 2.00
107 Khalil Greene TM 1.25 3.00
108 Chien-Ming Wang TM 3.00 8.00
109 Matt Kata TM .75 2.00
110 Chin-Hui Tsao TM .75 2.00
111 Dan Haren TM .75 2.00
112 Delmon Young TM 1.25 3.00
113 Mike Hessman TM .75 2.00
114 Bobby Crosby TM .75 2.00
115 Cory Sullivan TM RC .75 2.00
116 Brandon Watson TM .75 2.00
117 Aaron Miles TM .75 2.00
118 Jonny Gomes TM .75 2.00
119 Graham Koonce TM .75 2.00
120 Shawn Hill TM RC .75 2.00
121 Garrett Atkins TM .75 2.00
122 John Gall TM RC .75 2.00
123 Chad Bentz TM RC .75 2.00
124 Alfredo Simon TM RC 1.25 3.00
125 Josh Labandeira TM RC .75 2.00
126 Ryan Howard TM 1.50 4.00
127 Jason Bartlett TM RC 2.50 6.00
128 Dallas McPherson TM .75 2.00
129 Greg Dobbs TM RC .75 2.00
130 Jerry Gil TM RC .75 2.00
131 Aaron Boone EXT 1.25 3.00
132 Javier Vazquez EXT 1.25 3.00
133 Mariano Rivera EXT 4.00 10.00
134 Kevin Brown EXT 1.25 3.00
135 Mike Mussina EXT 2.00 5.00
136 Ruben Sierra EXT 1.25 3.00
137 Enrique Wilson EXT 1.25 3.00
138 Erick Almonte EXT 1.25 3.00
139 Jose Contreras EXT 1.25 3.00
140 Drew Henson EXT 1.25 3.00

2004 Fleer Authentix Balcony

*BALCONY 1-100: 4X TO 10X BASIC
*BALCONY 101-130: .6X TO 1.5X BASIC
*BALCONY 101-130: .6X TO 1.5X BASIC RC
OVERALL PARALLEL ODDS 1:6 H, 1:48 R
STATED PRINT RUN 100 SERIAL #'d SETS

2004 Fleer Authentix Club Box

OVERALL PARALLEL ODDS 1:6 H, 1:48 R
STATED PRINT RUN 25 SERIAL #'d SETS
NO PRICING DUE TO SCARCITY

2004 Fleer Authentix Standing Room Only

OVERALL PARALLEL ODDS 1:6 H, 1:48 R
STATED PRINT RUN 5 SERIAL #'d SETS
NO PRICING DUE TO SCARCITY

2004 Fleer Authentix Ticket to the Majors Autograph Boosters

STATED ODDS 1:200 HOBBY, 1:1560 RETAIL
STATED PRINT RUN 50 SERIAL #'d SETS
LISTED PRICES ARE FOR NON-TORN CARDS
FOUR AUTOS PER NON-TORN CARD
EXCHANGE DEADLINE INDEFINITE
101 Rickie Weeks 15.00 40.00
103 Ryan Wagner 10.00 25.00
105 Rich Harden 10.00 25.00
106 Edwin Jackson 10.00 25.00
107 Khalil Greene 30.00 60.00
112 Delmon Young 40.00 80.00
115 Cory Sullivan 10.00 25.00
117 Aaron Miles 10.00 25.00
118 Jonny Gomes 15.00 40.00
119 Graham Koonce 10.00 25.00
121 Garrett Atkins 10.00 25.00
122 John Gall 15.00 40.00
123 Chad Bentz 10.00 25.00
125 John Labandeira 10.00 25.00
126 Ryan Howard 125.00 200.00
127 Jason Bartlett 15.00 40.00
128 Dallas McPherson 15.00 40.00

2004 Fleer Authentix Autograph All-Star

STATED PRINT RUN 75 SERIAL #'d SETS
CHAMPIONSHIP PRINT RUN 25 #'d SETS
NO CHAMP.PRICING DUE TO SCARCITY
RANDOM INSERTS IN PACKS
EXCHANGE DEADLINE INDEFINITE
AP Albert Pujols 100.00 175.00
EG Eric Gagne 15.00 40.00
JP Juan Pierre 10.00 25.00
MB Marlon Byrd 6.00 15.00
RB Rocco Baldelli 10.00 25.00
RH Roy Halladay 30.00 60.00
TN Trot Nixon 10.00 25.00
VW Vernon Wells 10.00 25.00

2004 Fleer Authentix Ballpark Classics

STATED ODDS 1:12 HOBBY, 1:18 RETAIL
1 Nomar Garciaparra .60 1.50
2 Alfonso Soriano .60 1.50
3 Chipper Jones 1.00 2.50
4 Albert Pujols 1.25 3.00
5 Jason Giambi .40 1.00
6 Mark Prior .60 1.50
7 Sammy Sosa 1.00 2.50
8 Derek Jeter 2.50 6.00
9 Greg Maddux 1.25 3.00
10 Alex Rodriguez 1.25 3.00

2004 Fleer Authentix Ballpark Classics Jersey

STATED ODDS 1:37 HOBBY, 1:240 RETAIL
AP Albert Pujols 6.00 15.00
AR Alex Rodriguez 4.00 10.00
AS Alfonso Soriano 3.00 8.00
CJ Chipper Jones 4.00 10.00
DJ Derek Jeter 8.00 20.00
GM Greg Maddux 4.00 10.00
JG Jason Giambi 3.00 8.00
MP Mark Prior 4.00 10.00
NG Nomar Garciaparra 6.00 15.00
SS Sammy Sosa 4.00 10.00

2004 Fleer Authentix Game Jersey

STATED ODDS 1:16 HOBBY, 1:71 RETAIL
*UNRIPPED: .6X TO 1.5X BASIC
UNRIPPED RANDOM INSERTS IN PACKS
UNRIPPED PRINT RUN 50 SERIAL #'d SETS
*GOLD p/r 51-89: .6X TO 1.5X BASIC
*GOLD p/r 38-44: .75X TO 2X BASIC
GOLD RANDOM INSERTS IN PACKS
GOLD PRINT B/WN 25-89 COPIES PER
NO GOLD PRICING ON QTY OF 25 OR LESS
GOLD UNRIPPED PRINT 1 SERIAL #'d SET
NO GOLD UNRIPPED PRICING AVAILABLE
AK Austin Kearns 3.00 8.00
AP Albert Pujols 6.00 15.00
AR Alex Rodriguez 4.00 10.00
AS Alfonso Soriano 3.00 8.00
BZ Barry Zito 3.00 8.00
CJ Chipper Jones 4.00 10.00
DJ Derek Jeter 8.00 20.00
DW Dontrelle Willis 4.00 10.00
GM Greg Maddux 4.00 10.00
HC Hee Seop Choi 3.00 8.00
IR Ivan Rodriguez 4.00 10.00
JB Josh Beckett 3.00 8.00
JB2 Jeff Bagwell 4.00 10.00
JG Jason Giambi 3.00 8.00
JP Juan Pierre 3.00 8.00
JR Jose Reyes 3.00 8.00
JT Jim Thome 4.00 10.00
KW Kerry Wood 3.00 8.00

MC Miguel Cabrera 4.00 10.00
MP Mark Prior 4.00 10.00
MT Mark Teixeira 4.00 10.00
NG Nomar Garciaparra 6.00 15.00
RJ Randy Johnson 4.00 10.00
SS Sammy Sosa 4.00 10.00
TH Torii Hunter 3.00 8.00

2004 Fleer Authentix Game Jersey Autograph Regular Season

STATED PRINT RUN 100 SERIAL #'d SETS
*ALL-STAR: .5X TO 1.2X BASIC
ALL-STAR PRINT RUN 50 SERIAL #'d SETS
CHAMPIONSHIP PRINT 10 SERIAL #'d SETS
NO CHAMP.PRICING DUE TO SCARCITY
RANDOM INSERTS IN PACKS
EXCHANGE DEADLINE INDEFINITE
AP Albert Pujols 150.00 250.00
EG Eric Gagne 4.00 10.00
JP Juan Pierre 10.00 25.00
MB Marlon Byrd 6.00 15.00
RB Rocco Baldelli 10.00 25.00
RH Roy Halladay 30.00 60.00
TN Trot Nixon 10.00 25.00
VW Vernon Wells 10.00 25.00

2004 Fleer Authentix Game Jersey Dual

STATED ODDS 1:120 HOBBY, 1:420 RETAIL
*UNRIPPED: .6X TO 1.5X BASIC
UNRIPPED RANDOM INSERTS IN PACKS
UNRIPPED PRINT RUN 50 SERIAL #'d SETS
ARDJ A.Rodriguez/D.Jeter 12.00 30.00
CJAP C.Jones/A.Pujols 8.00 20.00
DWKW D.Willis/K.Wood 4.00 10.00
JBAK J.Bagwell/A.Kearns 6.00 15.00
JBMP J.Beckett/M.Prior 6.00 15.00
JGBZ J.Giambi/B.Zito 4.00 10.00
JRJP J.Reyes/J.Pierre 4.00 10.00
JTIR J.Thome/I.Rodriguez 6.00 15.00
MCMT M.Cabrera/M.Teixeira 6.00 15.00
NGAS N.Garciaparra/A.Soriano 6.00 15.00

2004 Fleer Authentix Ticket for Four

RANDOM INSERTS IN PACKS
STATED PRINT RUN 100 SERIAL #'d SETS
GJBH Giambi 8.00 20.00
Randy
Bag
Torii
GRJR Nomar 20.00 50.00
A.Rod
Jeter
Reyes
GSJP Nomar 10.00 25.00
A.Sor
Chip
Pujols
GTTB Giambi 5.00 12.00
Thome
Teix
Bag
JPSH Chip 10.00 25.00
Pujols
Sosa
Torii
MJWZ Madd 10.00 25.00
Randy
Wood
Zito
PMKR Prior 10.00 25.00
Madd
Kea
I.Rod
RCCP I.Rod 8.00 20.00
M.Cab
Choi
Pierre
SJRT Sosa 20.00 50.00
Jeter
A.Rod
Thome
WBPW Willis 5.00 12.00
Beck
Prior
Wood

2004 Fleer Authentix Ticket Studs

STATED ODDS 1:6 HOBBY, 1:8 RETAIL
1 Nomar Garciaparra .60 1.50
2 Josh Beckett .40 1.00
3 Derek Jeter 2.50 6.00
4 Mark Prior .60 1.50
5 Albert Pujols 1.25 3.00
6 Alfonso Soriano .60 1.50
7 Jim Thome .60 1.50
8 Ichiro Suzuki 1.25 3.00
9 Hideki Matsui 1.50 4.00
10 Dontrelle Willis .40 1.00
11 Mike Schmidt 1.50 4.00
12 Nolan Ryan 3.00 8.00
13 Reggie Jackson .60 1.50
14 Tom Seaver .60 1.50
15 Brooks Robinson .60 1.50

2004 Fleer Authentix Yankees Game Used Unripped

NE GU YANKS CARD PER YANKS HT PACK
NRIPPED 50 RANDOM IN YANKS HOME TM
NRIPPED 50 PRINT 50 SERIAL #'d SETS
J Derek Jeter Jsy 8.00 20.00
M Don Mattingly Jsy 10.00 25.00
R Phil Rizzuto Pants 6.00 15.00
J Reggie Jackson Jsy 6.00 15.00

2004 Fleer Authentix Yankees Game Used Dual Unripped

NE GU YANKS CARD PER YANKS HT PACK
ATED PRINT RUN 25 SERIAL #'d SETS
) PRICING DUE TO SCARCITY

2005 Fleer Authentix

COMP.SET w/o SP's (100) 10.00 25.00
COMMON CARD (1-100) .15 .40
COMMON CARD (101-125) 4.00 10.00
101-125 STATED ODDS 1:45 H, 1:1600 R
101-125 PRINT RUN 250 SERIAL #'d SETS
CARD 124 DOES NOT EXIST
EXCHANGE DEADLINE 02/16/08
1 Albert Pujols .50 1.25
2 Bernie Williams .25 .60
3 Vinny Castilla .15 .40
4 Rocco Baldelli .15 .40
5 Mike Piazza .40 1.00
6 Sean Casey .15 .40
7 Oliver Perez .15 .40
8 Tony Batista .15 .40
9 Paul Konerko .25 .60
10 Scott Rolen .25 .60
11 Justin Morneau .25 .60
12 Nomar Garciaparra .25 .60
13 Lance Berkman .25 .60
14 Mike Sweeney .15 .40
15 Miguel Tejada .25 .60
16 Craig Wilson .15 .40
17 Craig Biggio .25 .60
18 Shea Hillenbrand .15 .40
19 Mark Mulder .15 .40
20 Juan Pierre .15 .40
21 Troy Glaus .15 .40
22 Eric Chavez .15 .40
23 Jeromy Burnitz .15 .40
24 Carl Crawford .25 .60
25 Kaz Matsui .15 .40
26 Ivan Rodriguez .25 .60
27 Aubrey Huff .15 .40
28 Derek Jeter 1.00 2.50
29 Casey Blake .15 .40
30 Mark Teixeira .25 .60
31 Brad Wilkerson .15 .40
32 Austin Kearns .15 .40
33 Jim Edmonds .25 .60
34 Johan Santana .25 .60
35 Kerry Wood .15 .40
36 Ichiro Suzuki .50 1.25
37 Lyle Overbay .15 .40
38 Melvin Mora .15 .40
39 Jason Bay .15 .40
40 Jake Westbrook .15 .40
41 Andruw Jones .15 .40
42 Chase Utley .25 .60
43 Carl Pavano .15 .40
44 Luis Gonzalez .15 .40
45 Bobby Crosby .15 .40
46 Carlos Guillen .15 .40
47 Carlos Delgado .15 .40
48 Alex Rodriguez .50 1.25
49 Todd Helton .25 .60
50 Michael Young .15 .40
51 Geoff Jenkins .15 .40
52 Pedro Martinez .25 .60
53 Brian Giles .15 .40
54 Ken Harvey .15 .40
55 Johnny Estrada .15 .40
56 Billy Wagner .15 .40
57 Roger Clemens .50 1.25
58 Chipper Jones .40 1.00
59 Jim Thome .25 .60
60 Miguel Cabrera .40 1.00
61 Vladimir Guerrero .25 .60
62 Gary Sheffield .15 .40
63 Travis Hafner .15 .40
64 Alfonso Soriano .25 .60
65 Richard Hidalgo .15 .40
66 Adam Dunn .25 .60
67 Garret Anderson .15 .40
68 Lew Ford .15 .40
69 Mark Prior .25 .60
70 Bret Boone .15 .40
71 Ben Sheets .15 .40
72 David Ortiz .40 1.00
73 Mark Loretta .15 .40
74 Eric Gagne .15 .40
75 Curt Schilling .25 .60
76 Jason Schmidt .15 .40
77 Adrian Beltre .40 1.00
78 Javy Lopez .15 .40
79 Jack Wilson .15 .40
80 Carlos Beltran .25 .60
81 J.D. Drew .15 .40
82 Bobby Abreu .15 .40
83 Jeff Bagwell .25 .60
84 Randy Johnson .40 1.00
85 Tim Hudson .25 .60
86 Carlos Pena .25 .60
87 Vernon Wells .15 .40
88 Tom Glavine .25 .60
89 Victor Martinez .25 .60
90 Hank Blalock .15 .40
91 Jose Vidro .15 .40
92 Magglio Ordonez .25 .60
93 Jake Peavy .15 .40
94 Torii Hunter .15 .40
95 Sammy Sosa .40 1.00
96 Hideki Matsui .60 1.50
97 Shawn Green .15 .40
98 Manny Ramirez .40 1.00
99 Khalil Greene .15 .40
100 Jason Marquis .15 .40
101 B.J. Upton TM AU 6.00 15.00
102 Scott Kazmir TM AU 8.00 20.00
106 Zack Greinke TM AU 12.00 30.00
107 David Wright TM AU 12.50 30.00
108 David Aardsma TM AU 4.00 10.00
109 Josh Kroeger TM AU 4.00 10.00
111 Jason Kubel TM AU 4.00 10.00
112 Casey Kotchman TM AU 6.00 15.00
113 Joey Gathright TM AU 4.00 10.00
115 J.D. Durbin TM AU 4.00 10.00
117 Charlton Jimerson TM AU 4.00 10.00
118 Sean Burnett TM AU 4.00 10.00
120 Justin Verlander TM AU RC 25.00 60.00
121 Mike Gosling TM AU 4.00 10.00
122 Jeff Keppinger TM AU 4.00 10.00
123 Dave Krynzel TM AU 4.00 10.00

2005 Fleer Authentix Club Box

*CLUB BOX 1-100: 5X TO 12X BASIC
*CLUB BOX 101-125: .5X TO 1.2X BASIC
OVERALL PARALLEL ODDS 1:12 H, 1:72 R
STATED PRINT RUN 50 SERIAL #'d SETS
CARD 124 DOES NOT EXIST
EXCHANGE DEADLINE 02/16/08

2005 Fleer Authentix General Admission

*GEN ADM 1-100: 4X TO 10X BASIC
*GEN ADM 101-125: .4X TO 1X BASIC
OVERALL PARALLEL ODDS 1:12 H, 1:72 R
STATED PRINT RUN 100 SERIAL #'d SETS
CARD 124 DOES NOT EXIST
EXCHANGE DEADLINE 02/16/08

2005 Fleer Authentix Mezzanine

*MEZZ 1-100: 4X TO 10X BASIC
*MEZZ 101-125: .4X TO 1X BASIC
OVERALL PARALLEL ODDS 1:12 H, 1:72 R
STATED PRINT RUN 75 SERIAL #'d SETS
CARD 124 DOES NOT EXIST
EXCHANGE DEADLINE 02/16/08

2005 Fleer Authentix Standing Room Only

OVERALL PARALLEL ODDS 1:12 H, 1:72 R
STATED PRINT RUN 10 SERIAL #'d SETS
NO PRICING DUE TO SCARCITY

2005 Fleer Authentix Auto General Admission

STATED PRINT RUN 100 SERIAL #'d SETS
CLUB BOX PRINT RUN 5 SERIAL #'d SETS
NO CLUB BOX PRICING DUE TO SCARCITY
*MEZZANINE: .6X TO 1.5X BASIC
MEZZANINE PRINT RUN 40 #'d SETS
STANDING ROOM PRINT RUN 1 #'d SET
NO STANDING ROOM PRICING AVAILABLE
OVERALL AU-GU ODDS 1:6
EXCHANGE DEADLINE 02/16/08
BS Ben Sheets 10.00 25.00
CF Chone Figgins 6.00 15.00
CU Chase Utley 10.00 25.00
JB Jason Bay 6.00 15.00
JM Justin Morneau 6.00 15.00
JW Jack Wilson 6.00 15.00
KG Khalil Greene 10.00 25.00
LF Lew Ford 4.00 10.00
TH Travis Hafner 6.00 15.00

2005 Fleer Authentix Auto Jersey General Admission

STATED PRINT RUN 75 SERIAL #'d SETS
CLUB BOX PRINT RUN 5 SERIAL #'d SETS
NO CLUB BOX PRICING DUE TO SCARCITY
MEZZANINE PRINT RUN 15 #'d SETS
NO MEZZ.PRICING DUE TO SCARCITY
STANDING ROOM PRINT RUN 1 #'d SET
NO STANDING ROOM PRICING AVAILABLE
OVERALL AU-GU ODDS 1:6
EXCHANGE DEADLINE 02/16/08
BS Ben Sheets 15.00 40.00
JB Jason Bay 10.00 25.00
JM Justin Morneau 10.00 25.00
KG Khalil Greene 15.00 40.00
MS Mike Schmidt 40.00 80.00
TH Travis Hafner 10.00 25.00

2005 Fleer Authentix Auto Patch General Admission

STATED PRINT RUN 40 SERIAL #'d SETS
CLUB BOX PRINT RUN 5 SERIAL #'d SETS
NO CLUB BOX PRICING DUE TO SCARCITY
MEZZANINE PRINT RUN 10 #'d SETS
NO MEZZ.PRICING DUE TO SCARCITY
STANDING ROOM PRINT RUN 1 #'d SET
NO STANDING ROOM PRICING AVAILABLE
OVERALL AU-GU ODDS 1:6
EXCHANGE DEADLINE 02/16/08
BS Ben Sheets 30.00 60.00
CR Cal Ripken 175.00 300.00
JB Jason Bay 15.00 40.00
JM Justin Morneau 15.00 40.00
JT Jim Thome 40.00 80.00
KG Khalil Greene 30.00 60.00
MP Mike Piazza 125.00 200.00
MS Mike Schmidt 40.00 80.00
NR Nolan Ryan 125.00 200.00
TH Travis Hafner 15.00 40.00

2005 Fleer Authentix Game of the Week Jersey

PRINT RUNS B/WN 10-200 COPIES PER
NO PRICING ON QTY OF 10
PATCH PRINT RUN 10 SERIAL #'d SETS
NO PATCH PRICING DUE TO SCARCITY
OVERALL AU-GU ODDS 1:6
CG E.Chavez/T.Glaus/150 4.00 10.00
CJ2 M.Cabrera/C.Jones/90 6.00 15.00
GG S.Green/V.Guerrero/180 6.00 15.00
GS V.Guerrero/A.Soriano/100 6.00 15.00
KG S.Kazmir/Z.Greinke/80 4.00 10.00
MM K.Matsui/H.Matsui/30 40.00 80.00
MR P.Martinez/M.Rivera/60 10.00 25.00
OP D.Ortiz/A.Pujols/200 8.00 20.00
OS M.Ordonez/S.Sosa/160 6.00 15.00
RH M.Ramirez/T.Hunter/140 6.00 15.00
SS J.Santana/C.Schilling/40 10.00 25.00
WO K.Wood/R.Oswalt/50 6.00 15.00

2005 Fleer Authentix Hot Ticket

STATED ODDS 1:12 HOBBY, 1:24 RETAIL
*DIE CUTS: .75X TO 2X BASIC
DC RANDOM INSERTS IN EXCEL RETAIL
1 Derek Jeter 2.50 6.00
2 Roger Clemens 1.25 3.00
3 Vladimir Guerrero .60 1.50
4 Manny Ramirez 1.00 2.50
5 Alex Rodriguez 1.25 3.00
6 Albert Pujols 1.25 3.00
7 Mike Piazza 1.00 2.50
8 Hideki Matsui 1.50 4.00
9 Sammy Sosa 1.00 2.50
10 Chipper Jones 1.00 2.50

2005 Fleer Authentix Hot Ticket Jersey

STATED ODDS 1:87 HOBBY, 1:120 RETAIL
MLB LOGO PRINT RUN 1 SERIAL #'d SET
NO MLB LOGO PRICING DUE TO SCARCITY
*PATCH p/r 55: 1.25X TO 3X BASIC
*PATCH p/r 21-31: 1.5X TO 4X BASIC
PATCH PRINT RUNS B/WN 5-55 PER
NO PATCH PRICING ON QTY 10 OR LESS
OVERALL AU-GU ODDS 1:6
AP Albert Pujols 6.00 15.00
CJ Chipper Jones 4.00 10.00
HM Hideki Matsui 10.00 25.00
MP Mike Piazza 4.00 10.00
MR Manny Ramirez 4.00 10.00
RC Roger Clemens 4.00 10.00
SS Sammy Sosa 4.00 10.00
VG Vladimir Guerrero 4.00 10.00

2005 Fleer Authentix Jersey General Admission

STATED ODDS 1:16 HOBBY, 1:80 RETAIL
*CLUB BOX: 1X TO 2.5X BASIC
CLUB BOX PRINT RUN 25 SERIAL #'d SETS
*MEZZANINE: .6X TO 1.5X BASIC
MEZZANINE PRINT RUN 75 #'d SETS
STANDING ROOM PRINT RUN 10 #'d SETS
NO STANDING ROOM PRICING AVAILABLE
PATCH CLUB BOX PRINT RUN 10 #'d SETS
NO PATCH CB PRICING DUE TO SCARCITY
*PATCH GEN ADM: 1.25X TO 3X BASIC
PATCH GEN ADM PRINT RUN 75 #'d SETS
PATCH MEZZ PRINT RUN 15 #'d SETS
NO PATCH MZ PRICING DUE TO SCARCITY
PATCH STAND.ROOM PRINT RUN 1 #'d SET
NO PATCH SR PRICING DUE TO SCARCITY
OVERALL AU-GU ODDS 1:6
AB Adrian Beltre 3.00 8.00
AD Adam Dunn 3.00 8.00
AP Albert Pujols 6.00 15.00
AS Alfonso Soriano 3.00 8.00
BU B.J. Upton 4.00 10.00
BW Bernie Williams 4.00 10.00
CB Carlos Beltran 3.00 8.00
CJ Chipper Jones 4.00 10.00
CS Curt Schilling 4.00 10.00
DO David Ortiz 4.00 10.00
DW David Wright 6.00 15.00
EG Eric Gagne 3.00 8.00
GS Gary Sheffield 3.00 8.00
HB Hank Blalock 3.00 8.00
HM Hideki Matsui 8.00 20.00
HN Hideo Nomo 5.00 12.00
IR Ivan Rodriguez 4.00 10.00
JM Joe Mauer 4.00 10.00
JS Johan Santana 4.00 10.00
JT Jim Thome 4.00 10.00
KG Khalil Greene 4.00 10.00
KM Kaz Matsui 3.00 8.00
KW Kerry Wood 3.00 8.00
LB Lance Berkman 3.00 8.00
MC Miguel Cabrera 4.00 10.00
MP Mike Piazza 4.00 10.00
MR Manny Ramirez 4.00 10.00
MR2 Mariano Rivera 4.00 10.00
PM Pedro Martinez 4.00 10.00
RC Roger Clemens 4.00 10.00
RJ Randy Johnson 4.00 10.00
SR Scott Rolen 4.00 10.00
SS Sammy Sosa 4.00 10.00
TH Todd Helton 4.00 10.00
VG Vladimir Guerrero 4.00 10.00

2005 Fleer Authentix Showstoppers

STATED ODDS 1:8 HOBBY, 1:12 RETAIL
1 Nomar Garciaparra .60 1.50
2 Ichiro Suzuki 1.25 3.00
3 Ken Griffey Jr. 2.00 5.00
4 Alex Rodriguez 1.25 3.00
5 Albert Pujols 1.25 3.00
6 Derek Jeter 2.50 6.00
7 Roger Clemens 1.25 3.00
8 Randy Johnson 1.00 2.50
9 Hideo Nomo 1.00 2.50
10 Jim Thome .60 1.50
11 Mike Piazza 1.00 2.50
12 Hideki Matsui 1.50 4.00
13 Sammy Sosa 1.00 2.50
14 Kerry Wood .40 1.00
15 Eric Gagne .40 1.00

2005 Fleer Authentix Teammate Trios Jersey

STATED PRINT RUN 75 SERIAL #'d SETS
*HOMETOWN 25: .6X TO 1.5X BASIC
HOMETOWN 25 PRINT RUN 25 #'d SETS
HOMETOWN 5 PRINT RUN 5 #'d SETS
NO HOMETOWN 5 PRICING AVAILABLE
OVERALL AU-GU ODDS 1:6
BR Ortiz/Manny/Pedro 10.00 25.00
CC Sosa/Prior/Nomar Bat 10.00 25.00
LD Beltre/Finley/Green 6.00 15.00
NM Wright/Kaz/Piazza 15.00 40.00
OA Mulder/Zito/Hudson 6.00 15.00
PP Thome/Burrell/Abreu 10.00 25.00
SC Rolen/Pujols/Edmonds 15.00 40.00
TD Rocco/Upton/Kazmir 6.00 15.00
TR Soriano/Blalock/Teixiera 10.00 25.00

2001 Fleer Authority

COMP.SET w/o SP's (100) 10.00 25.00
COMMON CARD (1-100) .15 .40
COMMON CARD (101-150) 2.00 5.00
101-150 RANDOM INSERTS IN PACKS
101-150 PRINT RUN 2001 SERIAL #'d SETS
JETER MM'S RANDOM INSERTS IN PACKS
JETER 93 AU RANDOM INSERT IN PACKS
1 Mark Grace .25 .60
2 Paul Konerko .15 .40
3 Sean Casey .15 .40
4 Jim Thome .25 .60
5 Todd Helton .25 .60
6 Tony Clark .15 .40
7 Jeff Bagwell .25 .60
8 Mike Sweeney .15 .40
9 Eric Karros .15 .40
10 Richie Sexson .15 .40
11 Doug Mientkiewicz .15 .40
12 Ryan Klesko .15 .40
13 John Olerud .15 .40
14 Mark McGwire 1.00 2.50
15 Fred McGriff .25 .60
16 Rafael Palmeiro .25 .60
17 Carlos Delgado .15 .40
18 Roberto Alomar .25 .60
19 Craig Biggio .25 .60
20 Jose Vidro .15 .40
21 Edgardo Alfonzo .15 .40
22 Jeff Kent .15 .40
23 Bret Boone .15 .40
24 Rafael Furcal .15 .40
25 Nomar Garciaparra .60 1.50
26 Barry Larkin .25 .60
27 Cristian Guzman .15 .40
28 Derek Jeter 1.00 2.50
29 Miguel Tejada .15 .40
30 Jimmy Rollins .15 .40
31 Rich Aurilia .15 .40
32 Alex Rodriguez .50 1.25
33 Cal Ripken 1.25 3.00
34 Troy Glaus .15 .40
35 Matt Williams .15 .40
36 Chipper Jones .40 1.00
37 Jeff Cirillo .15 .40
38 Robin Ventura .15 .40
39 Eric Chavez .15 .40
40 Scott Rolen .25 .60
41 Phil Nevin .15 .40
42 Mike Piazza .60 1.50
43 Jorge Posada .25 .60
44 Jason Kendall .15 .40
45 Ivan Rodriguez .25 .60
46 Frank Thomas .40 1.00
47 Edgar Martinez .25 .60
48 Darin Erstad .15 .40
49 Tim Salmon .25 .60
50 Luis Gonzalez .15 .40
51 Andruw Jones .25 .60
52 Carl Everett .15 .40
53 Manny Ramirez Sox .25 .60
54 Sammy Sosa .40 1.00
55 Rondell White .15 .40
56 Magglio Ordonez .15 .40
57 Ken Griffey Jr. .75 2.00
58 Juan Gonzalez .15 .40
59 Larry Walker .15 .40
60 Bobby Higginson .15 .40
61 Cliff Floyd .15 .40
62 Preston Wilson .15 .40
63 Moises Alou .15 .40
64 Lance Berkman .15 .40
65 Richard Hidalgo .15 .40
66 Jermaine Dye .15 .40
67 Mark Quinn .15 .40
68 Shawn Green .15 .40
69 Gary Sheffield .15 .40
70 Jeromy Burnitz .15 .40
71 Geoff Jenkins .15 .40
72 Vladimir Guerrero .40 1.00
73 Bernie Williams .25 .60
74 Johnny Damon .25 .60
75 Jason Giambi .15 .40
76 Bobby Abreu .15 .40
77 Pat Burrell .15 .40
78 Brian Giles .15 .40
79 Tony Gwynn .50 1.25
80 Barry Bonds 1.00 2.50
81 J.D. Drew .15 .40
82 Jim Edmonds .15 .40
83 Greg Vaughn .15 .40
84 Raul Mondesi .15 .40
85 Shannon Stewart .15 .40
86 Randy Johnson .40 1.00
87 Curt Schilling .15 .40
88 Tom Glavine .25 .60
89 Greg Maddux .60 1.50
90 Pedro Martinez .25 .60
91 Kerry Wood .15 .40
92 David Wells .15 .40
93 Bartolo Colon .15 .40
94 Mike Hampton .15 .40
95 Kevin Brown .15 .40
96 Al Leiter .15 .40
97 Roger Clemens .75 2.00
98 Mike Mussina .25 .60
99 Tim Hudson .15 .40
100 Kazuhiro Sasaki .15 .40
101 Ichiro Suzuki RC 12.00 30.00
102 Albert Pujols RC 25.00 50.00
103 Drew Henson RC 2.50 6.00
104 Adam Pettyjohn RC 2.00 5.00
105 Adrian Hernandez RC 2.00 5.00
106 Andy Morales RC 2.00 5.00
107 Tsuyoshi Shinjo RC 2.50 6.00
108 Juan Uribe RC 2.50 6.00
109 Jack Wilson RC 2.50 6.00
110 Jason Smith RC 2.00 5.00
111 Junior Spivey RC 2.50 6.00
112 Wilson Betemit RC 2.00 5.00
113 Elpidio Guzman RC 2.00 5.00
114 Esix Snead RC 2.00 5.00
115 Winston Abreu RC 2.00 5.00
116 Jeremy Owens RC 2.00 5.00
117 Jay Gibbons RC 2.50 6.00
118 Luis Lopez 2.00 5.00
119 Ryan Freel RC 2.00 5.00
120 Rafael Soriano RC 2.00 5.00
121 Johnny Estrada RC 2.50 6.00
122 Bud Smith RC 2.00 5.00
123 Jackson Melian RC 2.00 5.00
124 Matt White RC 2.00 5.00
125 Travis Hafner RC 4.00 10.00
126 Morgan Ensberg RC 2.00 5.00
127 Endy Chavez RC 2.00 5.00
128 Brett Prinz RC 2.00 5.00
129 Juan Diaz RC 2.00 5.00
130 Erick Almonte RC 2.00 5.00
131 Rob Mackowiak RC 2.50 6.00
132 Carlos Valderrama RC 2.00 5.00
133 Wilkin Ruan RC 2.00 5.00
134 Angel Berroa RC 2.50 6.00
135 Henry Mateo RC 2.00 5.00
136 Bill Ortega RC 2.00 5.00
137 Billy Sylvester RC 2.00 5.00
138 Andres Torres RC 2.00 5.00
139 Nate Frese RC 2.00 5.00
140 Casey Fossum RC 2.00 5.00
141 Ricardo Rodriguez RC 2.00 5.00
142 Brian Roberts RC 2.00 5.00
143 Carlos Garcia RC 2.00 5.00
144 Brian Lawrence RC 2.00 5.00
145 Cory Aldridge RC 2.00 5.00
146 Mark Teixeira RC 5.00 12.00
147 Juan Cruz RC 2.00 5.00
148 Brandon Duckworth RC 2.00 5.00
149 Dewon Brazelton RC 2.00 5.00
150 Mark Prior RC 4.00 10.00
MM4 Derek Jeter MM/2000 6.00 15.00
MM4AU D.Jeter MM AU/100 150.00 250.00

2001 Fleer Authority Prominence 125/75

COMMON CARD (101-100) 1.50 4.00
*STARS 1-100: 5X TO 12X BASIC
1-100 PRINT RUN 125 SERIAL #'d SETS
COMMON CARD (101-150) 3.00 8.00
*ROOKIES 101-150: 1.25X TO 3X BASIC
101-150 PRINT RUN 75 SERIAL #'d SETS

2001 Fleer Authority Diamond Cuts Memorabilia

STATED ODDS 1:10 HOBBY, 1:36 RETAIL
BASE PRINT RUN 250 SETS
BAT PRINT RUN 800 SETS
BATTING GLOVE PRINT RUN 100-200 SETS
SHOES PRINT RUN 400 SETS
CARDS ARE NOT SERIAL NUMBERED
PRINT RUNS PROVIDED BY FLEER
ALL BASE CARDS ARE RETAIL ONLY
NO PRICING ON QTY OF 25 OR LESS
1 Rick Ankiel Shoes/400 3.00 8.00
2 Jeff Bagwell Jsy/1000 4.00 10.00
3 Adrian Beltre Hat/240 4.00 10.00
4 Craig Biggio Bat/800 4.00 10.00
5 Barry Bonds Hat/240 15.00 40.00
6 Barry Bonds Jsy/1000 10.00 25.00
7 Barry Bonds Pants/800 10.00 25.00
8 Barry Bonds Shoes/400 10.00 25.00
9 Barry Bonds Wristband/100 20.00 50.00
10 Kevin Brown Hat/240 4.00 10.00
11 Kevin Brown Pants/800 3.00 8.00
12 Eric Byrnes Bat/800 3.00 8.00
13 Sean Casey Jsy/1000 3.00 8.00
14 Eric Chavez Hat/240 4.00 10.00
15 Bartolo Colon Hat/240 4.00 10.00
16 Erubiel Durazo Bat/800 3.00 8.00
17 Ray Durham Bat/800 3.00 8.00
18 Jim Edmonds Hat/240 4.00 10.00
19 Jim Edmonds Shoes/400 3.00 8.00
20 Darin Erstad Hat/240 4.00 10.00
21 Carlos Febles Bat/800 3.00 8.00
22 Carlos Febles Shoes/400 3.00 8.00
23 Rafael Furcal Hat/240 4.00 10.00
24 Brian Giles Pants/800 3.00 8.00
25 Juan Gonzalez Btg Glv/100 4.00 10.00
26 Juan Gonzalez Hat/240 4.00 10.00
27 Luis Gonzalez Hat/240 4.00 10.00
28 Shawn Green Bat/800 3.00 8.00
29 Shawn Green Btg Glv/100 4.00 10.00
30 Vladimir Guerrero Bat/800 4.00 10.00
31 Tony Gwynn Bat/975 6.00 15.00
32 Jerry Hairston Jr. Hat/240 4.00 10.00
33 Mike Hampton Hat/240 4.00 10.00
34 Mike Hampton Shoes/400 3.00 8.00
35 Jason Hart Bat/800 3.00 8.00
36 Todd Helton Jsy/1000 4.00 10.00
37 Todd Helton Pants/800 4.00 10.00
38 Orlando Hernandez Bat/800 3.00 8.00
39 Richard Hidalgo Bat/800 3.00 8.00
40 Richard Hidalgo Btg Glv/200 4.00 10.00
41 Derek Jeter Bat/800 8.00 20.00
42 Derek Jeter Btg Glv/150 20.00 50.00
43 Derek Jeter Jsy/1000 10.00 25.00
44 Derek Jeter Pants/800 10.00 25.00
45 Derek Jeter Shoes/400 15.00 40.00
46 Randy Johnson Hat/240 6.00 15.00
47 Chipper Jones Bat/800 4.00 10.00
48 Chipper Jones Jsy/1000 4.00 10.00
49 Andruw Jones Bat/800 4.00 10.00
50 Andruw Jones Hat/240 6.00 15.00
51 Jason Kendall Hat/240 4.00 10.00
52 Jason Kendall Base/250 4.00 10.00
53 Barry Larkin Base/250 6.00 15.00
54 Barry Larkin Jsy/1000 4.00 10.00
55 Matt Lawton Hat/240 4.00 10.00
56 Mike Lieberthal Btg Glv/100 4.00 10.00
58 Kenny Lofton Bat/800 3.00 8.00
59 Edgar Martinez Btg Glv/200 6.00 15.00
60 Pedro Martinez Shoes/400 4.00 10.00
61 Raul Mondesi Bat/800 3.00 8.00
62 Raul Mondesi Btg Glv/100 4.00 10.00
63 Hideo Nomo Bat/800 4.00 10.00
64 Hideo Nomo Hat/240 10.00 25.00
65 Magglio Ordonez Base/250 4.00 10.00
66 Magglio Ordonez Btg Glv/200 4.00 10.00
67 Magglio Ordonez Hat/240 4.00 10.00
68 David Ortiz Base/250 8.00 20.00
69 David Ortiz Bat/800 5.00 12.00
70 Rafael Palmeiro Bat/800 4.00 10.00
71 Rafael Palmeiro Hat/240 6.00 15.00
72 Rafael Palmeiro Hat/240 6.00 15.00
73 Chan Ho Park Hat/240 4.00 10.00
74 Mike Piazza Bat/800 6.00 15.00
75 Mike Piazza Jsy/1000 6.00 15.00
76 Mike Piazza Shoes/400 6.00 15.00
77 Albert Pujols Pants/800 12.00 30.00
78 Manny Ramirez Sox Bat/800 4.00 10.00
79 Manny Ramirez Sox Btg Glv/200 6.00 15.00
80 Manny Ramirez Sox Hat/240 6.00 15.00
81 Manny Ramirez Sox Hat/240 6.00 15.00
82 Cal Ripken Btg Glv/100 30.00 60.00
83 Cal Ripken Pants/800 15.00 40.00
84 Ivan Rodriguez Base/250 6.00 15.00
85 Ivan Rodriguez Btg Glv/100 6.00 15.00
86 Ivan Rodriguez Hat/240 6.00 15.00
87 Ivan Rodriguez Pants/800 4.00 10.00
88 Ivan Rodriguez Shoes/400 4.00 10.00
90 Scott Rolen Base/250 6.00 15.00
91 Scott Rolen Hat/240 6.00 15.00
92 Jared Sandberg Bat/800 3.00 8.00
93 Deion Sanders Jsy/1000 4.00 10.00
94 Tsuy Shinjo Bat/800 4.00 10.00
95 Tsuy Shinjo Wristband/150 6.00 15.00
96 J.T. Snow Bat/800 3.00 8.00
97 J.T. Snow Jsy/1000 3.00 8.00
98 Alfonso Soriano Hat/240 6.00 15.00
99 Ichiro Suzuki Bat/350 20.00 50.00
100 Ichiro Suzuki Hat/240 20.00 50.00
101 Mike Sweeney Hat/240 4.00 10.00
103 Miguel Tejada Hat/240 4.00 10.00
104 Frank Thomas Base/250 6.00 15.00
105 Frank Thomas Bat/800 4.00 10.00
106 Frank Thomas Hat/240 6.00 15.00
107 Jim Thome Bat/800 4.00 10.00
109 Larry Walker Bat/800 3.00 8.00
110 Larry Walker Jsy/1000 3.00 8.00
111 Bernie Williams Bat/800 4.00 10.00

2001 Fleer Authority Figures

COMPLETE SET (20) 75.00 150.00
STATED PRINT RUN 1750 SERIAL #'d SETS
1 M.McGwire 8.00 20.00
A.Pujols
2 K.Sasaki 8.00 20.00
I.Suzuki
3 D.Jeter 5.00 12.00
D.Henson
4 K.Griffey Jr. 5.00 12.00
J.Melian
5 C.Jones 3.00 8.00
W.Betemit
6 J.Bagwell 3.00 8.00
M.Ensberg
7 C.Ripken 12.50 30.00
J.Gibbons
8 M.Piazza 3.00 8.00
T.Shinjo
9 L.Gonzalez 1.50 4.00
J.Spivey
10 B.Bonds 6.00 15.00
C.Valderrama
11 T.Helton 1.50 4.00
J.Uribe
12 R.Clemens 5.00 12.00
A.Hernandez
13 A.Rodriguez 4.00 10.00
T.Hafner
14 S.Rolen 1.50 4.00
J.Estrada
15 B.Giles 1.50 4.00
R.Mackowiak
16 R.Johnson 2.50 6.00
B.Prinz
17 C.Delgado 1.25 3.00
L.Lopez
18 M.Ramirez Sox 1.50 4.00
J.Diaz
19 M.Sweeney 1.25 3.00
E.Chavez
20 S.Sosa 2.50 6.00
J.Randolph

2001 Fleer Authority Seal of Approval

COMPLETE SET (15) 60.00 120.00
STATED ODDS 1:20
1 Derek Jeter 5.00 12.00
2 Alex Rodriguez 2.50 6.00
3 Nomar Garciaparra 3.00 8.00
4 Cal Ripken 6.00 15.00
5 Mike Piazza 3.00 8.00
6 Mark McGwire 5.00 12.00
7 Tony Gwynn 2.50 6.00
8 Barry Bonds 5.00 12.00
9 Greg Maddux 3.00 8.00
10 Chipper Jones 2.00 5.00
11 Roger Clemens 4.00 10.00
12 Ken Griffey Jr. 4.00 10.00
13 Vladimir Guerrero 2.00 5.00
14 Sammy Sosa 2.00 5.00
15 Todd Helton 2.00 5.00

2003 Fleer Avant

COMP.SET w/o SP's (65) 20.00 50.00
COMMON CARD (1-65) .40 1.00
COMMON CARD (66-75) .60 1.50
66-75 PRINT RUN 799 SERIAL #'d SETS
COMMON CARD (76-90) 1.25 3.00
76-90 PRINT RUN 699 SERIAL #'d SETS
66-90 RANDOM INSERTS IN PACKS
1 Adam Dunn .60 1.50
2 Barry Zito .60 1.50
3 Preston Wilson .40 1.00
4 Barry Bonds 1.50 4.00
5 Hank Blalock .40 1.00
6 Omar Vizquel .60 1.50
7 Brian Giles .40 1.00
8 Kerry Wood .40 1.00
9 Miguel Tejada .60 1.50
10 Magglio Ordonez .60 1.50
11 Randy Johnson 1.00 2.50
12 Jeff Bagwell .60 1.50
13 Pat Burrell .40 1.00
14 Jason Giambi .40 1.00
15 Mark Prior .60 1.50
16 Roger Clemens 1.25 3.00
17 Sammy Sosa 1.00 2.50
18 Jay Gibbons .40 1.00

19 Torii Hunter .40 1.00
20 Ichiro Suzuki 1.25 3.00
21 Derek Jeter 2.50 6.00
22 Tom Glavine .60 1.50
23 Alfonso Soriano .60 1.50
24 Manny Ramirez 1.00 2.50
25 Frank Thomas 1.00 2.50
26 Carlos Pena .60 1.50
27 Alex Rodriguez 1.25 3.00
28 Edgar Martinez .60 1.50
29 Larry Walker .60 1.50
30 Rafael Palmeiro .60 1.50
31 Mike Piazza 1.00 2.50
32 Nomar Garciaparra .60 1.50
33 Lance Berkman .60 1.50
34 Vladimir Guerrero .60 1.50
35 Troy Glaus .40 1.00
36 Ivan Rodriguez .60 1.50
37 Mark Mulder .40 1.00
38 Curt Schilling .60 1.50
39 Mike Sweeney .40 1.00
40 Albert Pujols 1.25 3.00
41 Tim Hudson .60 1.50
42 Greg Maddux 1.25 3.00
43 Shawn Green .40 1.00
44 Scott Rolen .60 1.50
45 Gary Sheffield .40 1.00
46 Richie Sexson .40 1.00
47 Aubrey Huff .40 1.00
48 Luis Gonzalez .40 1.00
49 Todd Helton .60 1.50
50 Xavier Nady .40 1.00
51 Juan Gonzalez .40 1.00
52 Pedro Martinez .60 1.50
53 Garret Anderson .40 1.00
54 Craig Biggio .60 1.50
55 Bret Boone .40 1.00
56 Ken Griffey Jr. 2.00 5.00
57 Kevin Millwood .40 1.00
58 Carlos Delgado .40 1.00
59 Chipper Jones 1.00 2.50
60 Hideo Nomo 1.00 2.50
61 Jim Edmonds .60 1.50
62 Austin Kearns .40 1.00
63 Jim Thome .60 1.50
64 Vernon Wells .40 1.00
65 Mike Lowell .40 1.00
66 Whitey Ford RET 1.00 2.50
67 Bob Gibson RET 1.00 2.50
68 Reggie Jackson RET 1.00 2.50
69 Willie McCovey RET 1.00 2.50
70 Phil Rizzuto RET 1.00 2.50
71 Al Kaline RET 1.00 2.50
72 Brooks Robinson RET 1.00 2.50
73 Nolan Ryan RET 5.00 12.00
74 Mike Schmidt RET 2.50 6.00
75 Tom Seaver RET 1.00 2.50
76 Hideki Matsui ROO RC 6.00 15.00
77 Rocco Baldelli ROO 1.25 3.00
78 Jose Contreras ROO RC 3.00 8.00
79 Hee Seop Choi ROO 1.25 3.00
80 Jeremy Bonderman ROO RC 5.00 12.00
81 Bo Hart ROO RC 1.25 3.00
82 Brandon Webb ROO RC 4.00 10.00
83 Ron Calloway ROO 1.25 3.00
84 Jesse Foppert ROO 1.25 3.00
85 Kyle Snyder ROO 1.25 3.00
86 Mark Teixeira ROO 2.00 5.00
87 Jose Reyes ROO 3.00 8.00
88 Dontrelle Willis ROO 1.25 3.00
89 Reed Johnson ROO 1.25 3.00
90 Rickie Weeks ROO RC 4.00 10.00
P39 Derek Jeter Promo .75 2.00

2003 Fleer Avant Black and White

*B/W 1-65: 1.25X TO 3X BASIC
*B/W 66-75: .75X TO 2X BASIC
*B/W 76-90: .6X TO 1.2X BASIC
*B/W 76-90: .6X TO 1.2X BASIC RC'S
RANDOM INSERTS IN PACKS
STATED PRINT RUN 199 SERIAL #'d SETS

2003 Fleer Avant Autograph Blue

PRINT RUNS B/WN 246-300 COPIES PER
AH Aubrey Huff/300 6.00 15.00
AK Al Kaline/200 8.00 20.00
BG Bob Gibson/250 12.50 30.00
BH Bo Hart/300 6.00 15.00
BR Brooks Robinson/300 10.00 25.00
BW Brandon Webb/300 10.00 25.00
CB Craig Biggio/250 10.00 25.00
DW Dontrelle Willis/300 5.00 12.00
EM Edgar Martinez/246 8.00 20.00
HB Hank Blalock/300 6.00 15.00
JR Jose Reyes/300 6.00 15.00
RB Rocco Baldelli/250 6.00 15.00
VW Vernon Wells/250 6.00 15.00

2003 Fleer Avant Autograph Copper

*ACTIVE: .5X TO 1.2X BLUE AUTOS
*ROOKIES: .5X TO 1.2X BLUE AUTOS
*RETIRED: .5X TO 1.2X BLUE AUTOS
PRINT RUNS B/WN 100-150 COPIES PER
BZ Barry Zito/150 6.00 15.00
CP Carlos Pena/150 8.00 20.00
ML Mike Lowell/150 8.00 20.00
MR Manny Ramirez/100 20.00 50.00
MT Miguel Tejada/150 12.50 30.00

2003 Fleer Avant Autograph Gold

STATED PRINT RUN 25 SERIAL #'d SETS
NO PRICING DUE TO SCARCITY

2003 Fleer Avant Autograph Silver

*SILVER: .5X TO 1.2X COPPER AUTO
RANDOM INSERTS IN PACKS
STATED PRINT RUN 75 SERIAL #'d SETS
DJ Derek Jeter 100.00 200.00

2003 Fleer Avant Material

RANDOM INSERTS IN PACKS
STATED PRINT RUN 50 SERIAL #'d SETS
AR Alex Rodriguez Jsy 10.00 25.00
AS Alfonso Soriano Jsy 6.00 15.00
CJ Chipper Jones Jsy 8.00 20.00
GM Greg Maddux Jsy 8.00 20.00
JG Jason Giambi Jsy 6.00 15.00
JT Jim Thome Jsy 8.00 20.00
MT Miguel Tejada Jsy 6.00 15.00
NG Nomar Garciaparra Jsy 10.00 25.00
RB Rocco Baldelli Jsy 6.00 15.00
RJ Randy Johnson Jsy 8.00 20.00
SS Sammy Sosa Jsy 8.00 20.00
VG Vladimir Guerrero Jsy 8.00 20.00

2003 Fleer Avant Candid Collection

RANDOM INSERTS IN PACKS
STATED PRINT RUN 500 SERIAL #'d SETS
1 Derek Jeter 4.00 10.00
2 Mike Piazza 1.50 4.00
3 Albert Pujols 2.00 5.00
4 Randy Johnson 1.50 4.00
5 Alex Rodriguez 2.00 5.00
6 Vladimir Guerrero 1.00 2.50
7 Troy Glaus .60 1.50
8 Ichiro Suzuki 2.00 5.00
9 Barry Zito 1.00 2.50
10 Jim Thome 1.00 2.50
11 Sammy Sosa 1.50 4.00
12 Greg Maddux 2.00 5.00
13 Barry Bonds 2.50 6.00
14 Jason Giambi .60 1.50
15 Nomar Garciaparra 1.00 2.50

2003 Fleer Avant Candid Collection Game Jersey

RANDOM INSERTS IN PACKS
STATED PRINT RUN 150 SERIAL #'d SETS
AR Alex Rodriguez 8.00 20.00
BZ Barry Zito 4.00 10.00
DJ Derek Jeter 12.50 30.00
GM Greg Maddux 6.00 15.00
JG Jason Giambi 4.00 10.00
JT Jim Thome 6.00 15.00
MP Mike Piazza 6.00 15.00
NG Nomar Garciaparra 8.00 20.00
RJ Randy Johnson 6.00 15.00
SS Sammy Sosa 6.00 15.00

2003 Fleer Avant Hall of Frame

RANDOM INSERTS IN PACKS
STATED PRINT RUN 299 SERIAL #'d SETS
1 Richie Ashburn 1.25 3.00
2 Rod Carew 1.25 3.00
3 Whitey Ford 1.25 3.00
4 Bob Gibson 1.25 3.00
5 Reggie Jackson 1.25 3.00
6 Harmon Killebrew 2.00 5.00
7 Willie McCovey 1.25 3.00
8 Phil Rizzuto 1.25 3.00
9 Al Kaline 1.25 3.00
10 Brooks Robinson 1.25 3.00
11 Nolan Ryan 6.00 15.00
12 Mike Schmidt 3.00 8.00
13 Tom Seaver 1.25 3.00
14 Warren Spahn 1.25 3.00

2003 Fleer Avant Hall of Frame Game Used

RANDOM INSERTS IN PACKS
STATED PRINT RUN 99 SERIAL #'d SETS
AK Al Kaline Jsy 12.50 30.00
MS Mike Schmidt Bat 15.00 40.00
NR Nolan Ryan Patch 40.00 80.00
RJ Reggie Jackson Pants 10.00 25.00
WM Willie McCovey Jsy 8.00 20.00

2003 Fleer Avant On Display

RANDOM INSERTS IN PACKS
STATED PRINT RUN 399 SERIAL #'d SETS
1 Derek Jeter 5.00 12.00
2 Barry Bonds 3.00 8.00
3 Rocco Baldelli .75 2.00
4 Alex Rodriguez 2.50 6.00
5 Alfonso Soriano 1.25 3.00
6 Sammy Sosa 2.00 5.00
7 Nomar Garciaparra 1.25 3.00
8 Hideki Matsui 4.00 10.00
9 Miguel Tejada 1.25 3.00
10 Chipper Jones 2.00 5.00

2003 Fleer Avant On Display Game Used

RANDOM INSERTS IN PACKS
STATED PRINT RUN 250 SERIAL #'d SETS
AR Alex Rodriguez Jsy 6.00 15.00
AS Alfonso Soriano Jsy 3.00 8.00
BB Barry Bonds Base 6.00 15.00
CJ Chipper Jones Jsy 4.00 10.00
DJ Derek Jeter Jsy 10.00 25.00
HM Hideki Matsui Base 6.00 15.00
MT Miguel Tejada Jsy 3.00 8.00
NG Nomar Garciaparra Jsy 8.00 20.00
RB Rocco Baldelli Jsy 3.00 8.00
SS Sammy Sosa Jsy 4.00 10.00

2002 Fleer Box Score

COMP.SET w/o SP's (125) 10.00 25.00
COMMON CARD (1-125) .15 .40
COMMON CARD (126-150) 2.00 5.00
126-150 RANDOM INSERTS IN BASIC PACKS
126-150 PRINT RUN 2499 SERIAL #'d SETS
COMP.RISING STAR SET (40) 10.00 25.00
COMMON CARD (151-190) .75 2.00
151-190 ONE FULL SUBSET PER RS BOX
COMP.INT'L SET (40) 10.00 25.00
COMMON CARD (191-230) .75 2.00
191-230 ONE FULL SUBSET PER IRT BOX
COMP.ALL-STAR SET (40) 10.00 25.00
COMMON CARD (231-270) .75 2.00
231-270 ONE FULL SUBSET PER AS BOX
COMP.COOPERSTOWN SET (40) 15.00 40.00
COMMON CARD (271-310) .75 2.00
271-310 ONE FULL SUBSET PER CT BOX
151-310 PRINT RUN 2950 SERIAL #'d SETS
1 Derek Jeter 1.00 2.50
2 Kevin Brown .15 .40
3 Nomar Garciaparra .60 1.50
4 Mark Buehrle .15 .40
5 Mike Piazza .60 1.50
6 David Justice .15 .40
7 Tino Martinez .25 .60
8 Paul Konerko .15 .40
9 Larry Walker .15 .40
10 Ben Sheets .15 .40
11 Mike Cameron .15 .40
12 David Wells .15 .40
13 Barry Zito .15 .40
14 Pat Burrell .15 .40
15 Mike Mussina .25 .60
16 Bud Smith .15 .40
17 Brian Jordan .15 .40
18 Chris Singleton .15 .40
19 Daryle Ward .15 .40
20 Russ Ortiz .15 .40
21 Jason Kendall .15 .40
22 Kerry Wood .15 .40
23 Jeff Weaver .15 .40
24 Tony Armas Jr. .15 .40
25 Toby Hall .15 .40
26 Brian Giles .15 .40
27 Juan Pierre .15 .40
28 Ken Griffey Jr. .75 2.00
29 Mike Sweeney .15 .40
30 John Smoltz .25 .60
31 Sean Casey .15 .40
32 Jeremy Giambi .15 .40
33 Mike Lieberthal .15 .40
34 Rich Aurilia .15 .40
35 Matt Lawton .15 .40
36 Dmitri Young .15 .40
37 Wade Miller .15 .40
38 Jason Giambi .15 .40
39 Jeff Cirillo .15 .40
40 Mark Grace .25 .60
41 Frank Thomas .40 1.00
42 Preston Wilson .15 .40
43 Brad Radke .15 .40
44 Greg Maddux .60 1.50
45 Adam Dunn .15 .40
46 Roy Oswalt .15 .40
47 Troy Glaus .15 .40
48 Edgar Martinez .25 .60
49 Billy Koch .15 .40
50 Chipper Jones .40 1.00
51 Lance Berkman .15 .40
52 Shannon Stewart .15 .40
53 Eddie Guardado .15 .40
54 C.C. Sabathia .15 .40
55 Craig Biggio .25 .60
56 Roger Clemens .75 2.00
57 Jimmy Rollins .15 .40
58 Carlos Delgado .15 .40
59 Tony Clark .15 .40
60 Mike Hampton .15 .40
61 Jeromy Burnitz .15 .40
62 Jorge Posada .25 .60
63 Todd Helton .25 .60
64 Richie Sexson .15 .40
65 Ryan Klesko .15 .40
66 Cliff Floyd .15 .40
67 Eric Milton .15 .40
68 Scott Rolen .25 .60
69 Steve Finley .15 .40
70 Ray Durham .15 .40
71 Jeff Bagwell .25 .60
72 Geoff Jenkins .15 .40
73 Jamie Moyer .15 .40
74 David Eckstein .15 .40
75 Johnny Damon Sox .25 .60
76 Pokey Reese .15 .40
77 Mo Vaughn .15 .40
78 Trevor Hoffman .15 .40
79 Albert Pujols .75 2.00
80 Ben Grieve .15 .40
81 Matt Morris .15 .40
82 Aubrey Huff .15 .40
83 Darin Erstad .15 .40
84 Garret Anderson .15 .40
85 Jacque Jones .15 .40
86 Matt Anderson .15 .40
87 Jose Vidro .15 .40
88 Carlos Lee .15 .40
89 Jeff Suppan .15 .40
90 Al Leiter .15 .40
91 Jeff Kent .15 .40
92 Randy Johnson .40 1.00
93 Moises Alou .15 .40
94 Bobby Higginson .15 .40
95 Phil Nevin .15 .40
96 Alex Rodriguez .50 1.50
97 Luis Gonzalez .15 .40
98 A.J. Burnett .15 .40
99 Torii Hunter .15 .40
100 Ivan Rodriguez .25 .60
101 Pedro Martinez .25 .60
102 Brady Anderson .15 .40
103 Paul LoDuca .15 .40
104 Eric Chavez .15 .40
105 Tim Salmon .25 .60
106 Javier Vazquez .15 .40
107 Bret Boone .15 .40
108 Greg Vaughn .15 .40
109 J.D. Drew .15 .40
110 Jay Gibbons .15 .40
111 Jim Thome .25 .60
112 Shawn Green .15 .40
113 Tim Hudson .15 .40
114 John Olerud .15 .40
115 Raul Mondesi .15 .40
116 Curt Schilling .15 .40
117 Corey Patterson .15 .40
118 Robert Fick .15 .40
119 Corey Koskie .15 .40
120 Juan Gonzalez .15 .40
121 Jerry Hairston Jr. .15 .40
122 Gary Sheffield .15 .40
123 Mark Mulder .15 .40
124 Barry Bonds 1.00 2.50
125 Jim Edmonds .15 .40
126 Franklyn German RP RC 2.00 5.00
127 Rodrigo Rosario RP RC 2.00 5.00
128 Ryan Ludwick RP 2.00 5.00
129 Jorge De La Rosa RP RC 2.00 5.00
130 Jason Lane RP 2.00 5.00
131 Brian Mallette RP RC 2.00 5.00
132 Chris Baker RP RC 2.00 5.00
133 Kyle Kane RP RC 2.00 5.00
134 Doug Devore RP RC 2.00 5.00
135 Raul Chavez RP RC 2.00 5.00
136 Miguel Asencio RP RC 2.00 5.00
137 Luis C.Garcia RP RC 2.00 5.00
138 Nick Johnson RP 2.00 5.00
139 Mike Crudale RP RC 2.00 5.00
140 P.J. Bevis RP RC 2.00 5.00
141 Josh Hancock RP RC 2.50 6.00
142 Jeremy Lambert RP RC 2.00 5.00
143 Ben Broussard RP 2.00 5.00
144 John Ennis RP RC 2.00 5.00
145 Wilson Valdez RP RC 2.00 5.00
146 Eric Good RP RC 2.00 5.00
147 Elio Serrano RP RC 2.00 5.00
148 Jaime Cerda RP RC 2.00 5.00
149 Hank Blalock RP 3.00 8.00
150 Brandon Duckworth RP 2.00 5.00
151 Drew Henson RS .75 2.00
152 Kazuhisa Ishii RS RC 1.25 3.00
153 Earl Snyder RS RC .75 2.00
154 J.M. Gold RS .75 2.00
155 Satoru Komiyama RS RC .75 2.00
156 Marlon Byrd RS .75 2.00
157 So Taguchi RS RC 1.25 3.00
158 Eric Hinske RS .75 2.00
159 Mark Prior RS 1.25 3.00
160 Jorge Padilla RS RC .75 2.00
161 Rene Reyes RS RC .75 2.00
162 Jorge Nunez RS RC .75 2.00
163 Nelson Castro RS RC .75 2.00
164 Anderson Machado RS RC .75 2.00
165 Mark Teixeira RS 1.25 3.00
166 Orlando Hudson RS .75 2.00
167 Edwin Almonte RS RC .75 2.00
168 Luis Ugueto RS RC .75 2.00
169 Felix Escalona RS RC .75 2.00
170 Ron Calloway RS RC .75 2.00
171 Kevin Mench RS .75 2.00
172 Takahito Nomura RS RC .75 2.00
173 Sean Burroughs RS .75 2.00
174 Steve Kent RS RC .75 2.00
175 Jorge Sosa RS RC 1.25 3.00
176 Mike Moriarty RS RC .75 2.00
177 Carlos Pena RS .75 2.00
178 Anastacio Martinez RS RC .75 2.00
179 Reed Johnson RS RC 1.25 3.00
180 Juan Brito RS RC .75 2.00
181 Wilson Betemit RS .75 2.00
182 Mike Rivera RS .75 2.00
183 David Espinosa RS .75 2.00
184 Todd Donovan RS RC .75 2.00
185 Morgan Ensberg RS .75 2.00
186 Dewon Brazelton RS .75 2.00
187 Ben Howard RS RC .75 2.00
188 Austin Kearns RS .75 2.00
189 Josh Beckett RS .75 2.00
190 Brandon Backe RS RC 1.25 3.00
191 Ichiro Suzuki IRT 3.00 8.00
192 Tsuyoshi Shinjo IRT .75 2.00
193 Hideo Nomo IRT 1.50 4.00
194 Kazuhiro Sasaki IRT .75 2.00
195 Edgardo Alfonzo IRT .75 2.00
196 Chan Ho Park IRT .75 2.00
197 Carlos Hernandez IRT .75 2.00
198 Byung-Hyun Kim IRT .75 2.00
199 Omar Vizquel IRT 1.00 2.50
200 Freddy Garcia IRT .75 2.00
201 Richard Hidalgo IRT .75 2.00
202 Magglio Ordonez IRT .75 2.00
203 Bob Abreu IRT .75 2.00
204 Roger Cedeno IRT .75 2.00
205 Andruw Jones IRT 1.00 2.50
206 Mariano Rivera IRT 1.50 4.00
207 Jose Macias IRT .75 2.00
208 Orlando Hernandez IRT .75 2.00
209 Rafael Palmeiro IRT 1.00 2.50
210 Danys Baez IRT .75 2.00
211 Bernie Williams IRT 1.00 2.50
212 Carlos Beltran IRT .75 2.00
213 Roberto Alomar IRT 1.00 2.50
214 Jose Cruz Jr. IRT .75 2.00
215 Ryan Dempster IRT .75 2.00
216 Erubiel Durazo IRT .75 2.00
217 Carlos Pena IRT .75 2.00
218 Sammy Sosa IRT 1.50 4.00
219 Adrian Beltre IRT .75 2.00
220 Aramis Ramirez IRT .75 2.00
221 Alfonso Soriano IRT .75 2.00
222 Vladimir Guerrero IRT 1.50 4.00
223 Juan Uribe IRT .75 2.00
224 Cristian Guzman IRT .75 2.00
225 Manny Ramirez IRT 1.00 2.50
226 Juan Cruz IRT .75 2.00
227 Ramon Ortiz IRT .75 2.00
228 Juan Encarnacion IRT .75 2.00
229 Bartolo Colon IRT .75 2.00
230 Miguel Tejada IRT .75 2.00
231 Cal Ripken AS 5.00 12.00
232 Derek Jeter AS 4.00 10.00
233 Pedro Martinez AS 1.00 2.50
234 Roberto Alomar AS 1.00 2.50
235 Sandy Alomar Jr. AS .75 2.00
236 Mike Piazza AS 2.50 6.00
237 Jeff Conine AS .75 2.00
238 Fred McGriff AS 1.00 2.50
239 Kirby Puckett AS 1.50 4.00
240 Ken Griffey Jr. AS 3.00 8.00
241 Roger Clemens AS 3.00 8.00
242 Joe Morgan AS .75 2.00
243 Willie McCovey AS .75 2.00
244 Brooks Robinson AS 1.00 2.50
245 Juan Marichal AS .75 2.00
246 Todd Helton AS 1.00 2.50
247 Alex Rodriguez AS 2.00 5.00
248 Barry Bonds AS 4.00 10.00
249 Nomar Garciaparra AS 2.50 6.00
250 Jeff Bagwell AS 1.00 2.50
251 Kenny Lofton AS .75 2.00
252 Barry Larkin AS 1.00 2.50
253 Tom Glavine AS 1.00 2.50
254 Magglio Ordonez AS .75 2.00
255 Randy Johnson AS 1.50 4.00
256 Chipper Jones AS 1.50 4.00
257 Kevin Brown AS .75 2.00
258 Rickey Henderson AS 1.50 4.00
259 Greg Maddux AS 2.50 6.00
260 Jim Thome AS 1.00 2.50
261 Rafael Palmeiro AS 1.00 2.50
262 Frank Thomas AS 1.50 4.00
263 Manny Ramirez AS 1.00 2.50
264 Travis Fryman AS .75 2.00
265 Gary Sheffield AS .75 2.00
266 Bernie Williams AS 1.00 2.50
267 Matt Williams AS .75 2.00
268 Ivan Rodriguez AS 1.00 2.50
269 Mike Mussina AS 1.00 2.50
270 Larry Walker AS .75 2.00
271 Jim Palmer CT .75 2.00
272 Cal Ripken CT 6.00 15.00
273 Brooks Robinson CT 1.25 3.00
274 Bobby Doerr CT .75 2.00
275 Ernie Banks CT 2.00 5.00
276 Fergie Jenkins CT .75 2.00
277 Luis Aparicio CT .75 2.00
278 Hoyt Wilhelm CT .75 2.00
279 Tom Seaver CT 1.25 3.00
280 Joe Morgan CT .75 2.00
281 Lou Boudreau CT .75 2.00
282 Larry Doby CT .75 2.00
283 Jim Bunning CT .75 2.00
284 George Kell CT .75 2.00
285 Pee Wee Reese CT 1.25 3.00
286 Eddie Mathews CT 2.00 5.00
287 Robin Yount CT 2.00 5.00
288 Rod Carew CT 1.25 3.00
289 Monte Irvin CT .75 2.00
290 Yogi Berra CT 2.00 5.00
291 Whitey Ford CT 1.25 3.00
292 Reggie Jackson CT 1.25 3.00
293 Rollie Fingers CT .75 2.00
294 Catfish Hunter CT 1.25 3.00
295 Richie Ashburn CT 1.25 3.00
296 Willie Stargell CT 1.25 3.00
297 Ralph Kiner CT 1.25 3.00
298 Orlando Cepeda CT .75 2.00
299 Juan Marichal CT .75 2.00
300 Gaylord Perry CT .75 2.00
301 Willie McCovey CT .75 2.00
302 Red Schoendienst CT .75 2.00
303 Nolan Ryan CT 5.00 12.00
304 Bob Gibson CT 1.25 3.00
305 Al Kaline CT 2.00 5.00
306 Harmon Killebrew CT 2.00 5.00
307 Stan Musial CT 3.00 8.00
308 Phil Rizzuto CT 1.25 3.00
309 Mike Schmidt CT 5.00 12.00
310 Enos Slaughter CT .75 2.00
P124 Barry Bonds Promo .75 2.00

2002 Fleer Box Score Classic Miniatures

COMPLETE SET (40) 10.00 25.00
ONE SET PER CLASSIC MINI BOX
STATED PRINT RUN 2950 SERIAL #'d SETS
40-CARD SKIP-NUMBERED SET
SEE BECKETT.COM FOR FULL CHECKLIST
1 Derek Jeter 4.00 10.00
3 Nomar Garciaparra 2.50 6.00
5 Mike Piazza 2.50 6.00
9 Larry Walker .60 1.50
11 Mike Cameron .60 1.50
14 Pat Burrell .60 1.50
26 Brian Giles .60 1.50
28 Ken Griffey Jr. 3.00 8.00
29 Mike Sweeney .60 1.50
38 Jason Giambi .60 1.50
41 Frank Thomas 1.50 4.00
44 Greg Maddux 2.50 6.00
45 Adam Dunn .60 1.50
46 Roy Oswalt .60 1.50
47 Troy Glaus .60 1.50
50 Chipper Jones 1.50 4.00
51 Lance Berkman .60 1.50
56 Roger Clemens 3.00 8.00
57 Jimmy Rollins .60 1.50
58 Carlos Delgado .60 1.50
63 Todd Helton 1.00 2.50
64 Richie Sexson .60 1.50
66 Cliff Floyd .60 1.50
71 Jeff Bagwell 1.00 2.50
79 Albert Pujols 3.00 8.00
92 Randy Johnson 1.50 4.00
95 Phil Nevin .60 1.50
96 Alex Rodriguez 2.00 5.00
97 Luis Gonzalez .60 1.50
99 Torii Hunter .60 1.50
100 Ivan Rodriguez 1.00 2.50
101 Pedro Martinez 1.00 2.50
104 Eric Chavez .60 1.50
107 Bret Boone .60 1.50
109 J.D. Drew .60 1.50
111 Jim Thome 1.00 2.50
112 Shawn Green .60 1.50
113 Tim Hudson .60 1.50
116 Curt Schilling .60 1.50
124 Barry Bonds 4.00 10.00

2002 Fleer Box Score Classic Miniatures First Edition

*CLASSIC MINIS 1ST ED: 4X TO 10X BASIC
ONE SET PER CLASSIC MINI 1ST ED. BOX
STATED PRINT RUN 100 SERIAL #'d SETS
40-CARD SKIP-NUMBERED SET

2002 Fleer Box Score Classic Miniatures Game Used

ONE PER CLASSIC MINI BOX
1 Derek Jeter Bat 10.00 25.00
2 Mike Piazza Jsy 6.00 15.00
3 Adam Dunn Jsy 6.00 15.00
4 Chipper Jones Bat 8.00 20.00
5 Roger Clemens Jsy 8.00 20.00
6 Alex Rodriguez Jsy 6.00 15.00
7 Pedro Martinez Jsy 6.00 15.00
8 Jim Thome Bat 6.00 15.00
9 Curt Schilling Jsy 6.00 15.00
10 Barry Bonds Bat 10.00 25.00

2002 Fleer Box Score First Edition

*1ST ED. 1-125: 4X TO 10X BASIC CARDS
*1ST ED. 126-150: .5X TO 1.2X BASIC
*1ST ED. 151-190: 1X TO 2.5X BASIC
*1ST ED. 191-230: 1X TO 2.5X BASIC
*1ST ED. 231-270: 1X TO 2.5X BASIC
*1ST ED. 271-310: 1X TO 2.5X BASIC
1-150 RANDOM INSERTS IN BASIC PACKS
151-190 ONE SUBSET PER RS 1ST ED. BOX
191-230 ONE SUBSET PER IRT 1ST ED. BOX
231-270 ONE SUBSET PER AS 1ST ED. BOX
271-310 ONE SUBSET PER CT 1ST ED. BOX
STATED PRINT RUN 100 SERIAL #'d SETS

2002 Fleer Box Score All-Star Lineup Game Used

ONE PER ALL-STARS BOX
1 Jeter/Nomar/A.Rod 20.00 50.00
1A Jeter/Nomar/A.Rod 20.00 50.00
2 Morgan/McCovey/Brooks 5.00 12.00
3 I.Rod/Palmeiro/A.Rod 10.00 25.00
4 Bernie/Jeter/Mussina 20.00 50.00
5 Bonds/Ripken/Thomas 25.00 60.00
6 Ripken/Jeter/Pedro/Alomar 25.00 60.00
7 Piazza/Bonds/Grif/Bagwell 15.00 40.00
8 Clem/Madd/Randy/Pedro 12.00 30.00
9 Helton/Alomar/A.Rod/Chip 10.00 25.00
10 Grif/Bonds/Manny/Walker 15.00 40.00

2002 Fleer Box Score Amazing Greats

COMPLETE SET (20) 15.00 40.00
STATED ODDS 1:5
1 Derek Jeter 2.50 6.00
2 Barry Bonds 2.50 6.00
3 Mike Piazza 1.50 4.00
4 Ivan Rodriguez .60 1.50
5 Todd Helton .60 1.50
6 Nomar Garciaparra 1.50 4.00
7 Jim Thome .60 1.50
8 Bernie Williams .60 1.50
9 Kazuhiro Sasaki .60 1.50
10 Torii Hunter .60 1.50
11 Bret Boone .60 1.50
12 Tim Hudson .60 1.50
13 Randy Johnson 1.00 2.50
14 Rafael Palmeiro .60 1.50
15 Scott Rolen .60 1.50
16 Carlos Delgado .60 1.50
17 Chipper Jones 1.00 2.50
18 Lance Berkman .60 1.50
19 Frank Thomas 1.00 2.50
20 Greg Maddux 1.50 4.00

2002 Fleer Box Score Amazing Greats Single Swatch

STATED ODDS 1:13
1 Lance Berkman 4.00 10.00
2 Barry Bonds 10.00 25.00
3 Bret Boone 4.00 10.00
4 Carlos Delgado 4.00 10.00
5 Nomar Garciaparra 8.00 20.00
6 Torii Hunter 4.00 10.00
7 Derek Jeter 10.00 25.00
8 Greg Maddux 6.00 15.00
9 Rafael Palmeiro 6.00 15.00
10 Mike Piazza 6.00 15.00
11 Ivan Rodriguez 6.00 15.00
12 Scott Rolen 6.00 15.00
13 Kazuhiro Sasaki 4.00 10.00
14 Frank Thomas 6.00 15.00
15 Jim Thome Bat 6.00 15.00
16 Bernie Williams 6.00 15.00

2002 Fleer Box Score Amazing Greats Dual Swatch

STATED ODDS 1:90
1 Lance Berkman 6.00 15.00
2 Barry Bonds 15.00 40.00
3 Bret Boone 6.00 15.00
4 Carlos Delgado 6.00 15.00
5 Nomar Garciaparra 12.50 30.00
6 Torii Hunter 6.00 15.00
7 Derek Jeter 15.00 40.00
8 Greg Maddux 10.00 25.00
9 Rafael Palmeiro 10.00 25.00
10 Mike Piazza 10.00 25.00
11 Ivan Rodriguez 10.00 25.00
12 Scott Rolen 10.00 25.00
13 Kazuhiro Sasaki 6.00 15.00
14 Frank Thomas 10.00 25.00
15 Bernie Williams 10.00 25.00

2002 Fleer Box Score Amazing Greats Patch

RANDOM INSERTS IN PACKS
STATED PRINT RUN 150 SERIAL #'d SETS
1 Lance Berkman 10.00 25.00
2 Barry Bonds 30.00 60.00
3 Bret Boone 10.00 25.00
4 Carlos Delgado 10.00 25.00
5 Nomar Garciaparra 20.00 50.00
6 Torii Hunter 10.00 25.00
7 Derek Jeter 30.00 60.00
8 Greg Maddux 15.00 40.00
9 Rafael Palmeiro 15.00 40.00
10 Mike Piazza 15.00 40.00
11 Ivan Rodriguez 15.00 40.00
12 Scott Rolen 15.00 40.00
13 Kazuhiro Sasaki 10.00 25.00
14 Frank Thomas 15.00 40.00
15 Bernie Williams 15.00 40.00

2002 Fleer Box Score Bat Rack Quads

RANDOM INSERTS IN PACKS
STATED PRINT RUN 150 SERIAL #'d SETS
1 Torii Hunter 15.00 40.00
Cristian Guzman
Frank Thomas
Magglio Ordonez
2 Arod/Irod/Chav/Tej 15.00 40.00
3 Jeter/Sor/Piazza/Alom 30.00 60.00
4 Bonds/Berk/Arod/Nomar 60.00 120.00
5 Irod/Piazza/Chipper/Bonds 60.00 120.00
6 Arod/Nomar/Jeter/Tej 60.00 120.00
7 Roberto Alomar 15.00 40.00
Mo Vaughn
Jeff Bagwell
Craig Biggio
8 Rafael Palmeiro 15.00 40.00
Carlos Delgado
Jim Thome
Frank Thomas
9 Magglio Ordonez 15.00 40.00
Bernie Williams
Juan Gonzalez
Manny Ramirez
10 Chipper Jones 15.00 40.00
Adam Dunn
Jeff Bagwell
Mo Vaughn
11 Arod/Palm/Willms/Soriano 30.00 60.00
12 Carlos Pena 15.00 40.00
Eric Chavez
Carlos Delgado
Juan Gonzalez
13 Adam Dunn 15.00 40.00
Lance Berkman
Jim Thome
Manny Ramirez

2002 Fleer Box Score Bat Rack Trios

RANDOM INSERTS IN PACKS
STATED PRINT RUN 300 SERIAL #'d SETS
1 Jeter/Soriano/Bernie 40.00 80.00
2 Piazza/Alomar/Vaughn 15.00 40.00
3 Bagwell/Berkman/Biggio 15.00 40.00
4 Chavez/Tejada/C.Pena 10.00 25.00
5 ARod/IRod/Palmeiro 20.00 50.00
6 Chipper/Sheffield/Andruw 10.00 25.00
7 Delgado/Thome/Thomas 10.00 25.00
8 Jeter/Nomar/A.Rodriguez 40.00 80.00
9 Bonds/Dunn/Chipper 20.00 50.00
10 Maggio/J.Gonz/Manny 10.00 25.00

2002 Fleer Box Score Debuts

COMPLETE SET (15) 50.00 100.00
RANDOM INSERTS IN PACKS
STATED PRINT RUN 2002 SERIAL #'d SETS
1 Hank Blalock 3.00 8.00
2 Eric Hinske 2.00 5.00
3 Kazuhisa Ishii 3.00 8.00
4 Sean Burroughs 2.00 5.00
5 Andres Torres 2.00 5.00
6 Satoru Komiyama 2.00 5.00
7 Mark Prior 3.00 8.00
8 Kevin Mench 2.00 5.00
9 Austin Kearns 2.00 5.00
10 Earl Snyder 2.00 5.00
11 Jon Rauch 2.00 5.00
12 Jason Lane 2.00 5.00
13 Ben Howard 2.00 5.00
14 Bobby Hill 2.00 5.00
15 Dennis Tankersley 2.00 5.00

2002 Fleer Box Score Hall of Fame Material

ONE PER COOPERSTOWN BOX
1 Jim Palmer Jsy 6.00 15.00
2 Cal Ripken Jsy 15.00 40.00
3 Brooks Robinson Bat 6.00 15.00
4 Joe Morgan Bat 6.00 15.00
5 Eddie Mathews Bat 6.00 15.00
6 Robin Yount Jsy 6.00 15.00
7 Reggie Jackson Jsy 6.00 15.00
8 Catfish Hunter Jsy 6.00 15.00
9 Willie McCovey Jsy 6.00 15.00
10 Nolan Ryan Jsy 20.00 50.00

2002 Fleer Box Score Press Clippings

COMPLETE SET (20) 80.00 200.00
STATED ODDS 1:90
1 Mark Mulder 3.00 8.00
2 Curt Schilling 3.00 8.00
3 Alfonso Soriano 3.00 8.00
4 Jeff Bagwell 3.00 8.00
5 J.D. Drew 3.00 8.00
6 Pedro Martinez 3.00 8.00
7 Bob Abreu 3.00 8.00
8 Alex Rodriguez 5.00 12.00
9 Mike Sweeney 3.00 8.00
10 Carlos Pena 3.00 8.00
11 Josh Beckett 3.00 8.00
12 Roger Clemens 8.00 20.00
13 Manny Ramirez 3.00 8.00
14 Adam Dunn 3.00 8.00
15 Kazuhisa Ishii 3.00 8.00
16 Ken Griffey Jr. 8.00 20.00
17 Sammy Sosa 4.00 10.00
18 Ichiro Suzuki 6.00 15.00
19 Albert Pujols 6.00 15.00
20 Troy Glaus 3.00 8.00

2002 Fleer Box Score Press Clippings Game Used

STATED ODDS 1:13
SP PRINT RUNS PROVIDED BY FLEER
SP'S ARE NOT SERIAL-NUMBERED
1 Bob Abreu Jsy 4.00 10.00
2 Jeff Bagwell Jsy 6.00 15.00
3 Josh Beckett Jsy 4.00 10.00
5 J.D. Drew Jsy 4.00 10.00
6 Adam Dunn Jsy 4.00 10.00
7 Troy Glaus Base 4.00 10.00
8 Ken Griffey Jr. Base 6.00 15.00
9 Kazuhisa Ishii Jsy SP/350 4.00 10.00
10 Pedro Martinez Jsy 6.00 15.00
11 Mark Mulder Jsy 4.00 10.00
12 Carlos Pena Jsy 4.00 10.00
13 Albert Pujols Base 6.00 15.00
14 Manny Ramirez Jsy 6.00 15.00
15 Alex Rodriguez Jsy 6.00 15.00
16 Curt Schilling Jsy 4.00 10.00
17 Alfonso Soriano Bat 4.00 10.00
18 Sammy Sosa Base 6.00 15.00
19 Ichiro Suzuki Base 10.00 25.00
20 Mike Sweeney Jsy 4.00 10.00

2002 Fleer Box Score Wave of the Future Game Used

ONE PER RISING STARS BOX
SP PRINT RUNS PROVIDED BY FLEER
SP'S ARE NOT SERIAL-NUMBERED
1 Drew Henson Bat 3.00 8.00
2 Kazuhisa Ishii Bat 4.00 10.00
3 Marlon Byrd Pants 3.00 8.00
4 So Taguchi Bat 4.00 10.00
5 Jorge Padilla Pants SP/75 6.00 15.00
6 Rene Reyes Pants 3.00 8.00
7 Mark Teixeira Pants SP/100 8.00 20.00
8 Carlos Pena Bat 3.00 8.00

9 Austin Kearns Pants 3.00 8.00
10 Josh Beckett Jsy SP/50 8.00 20.00

2002 Fleer Box Score World Piece Game Used

ONE PER INTERNATIONAL BOX
1 Ichiro Suzuki Base 10.00 25.00
2 Tsuyoshi Shinjo Bat 4.00 10.00
3 Hideo Nomo Jsy 12.50 30.00
4 Kazuhiro Sasaki Jsy 4.00 10.00
5 Chan Ho Park Jsy 4.00 10.00
6 Magglio Ordonez Jsy 4.00 10.00
7 Andruw Jones Jsy 6.00 15.00
8 Rafael Palmeiro Jsy 6.00 15.00
9 Bernie Williams Jsy 6.00 15.00
10 Roberto Alomar Bat 6.00 15.00

2003 Fleer Box Score

COMP.SET w/o SP's (100) 10.00 25.00
COMMON CARD (1-100) .15 .40
COMMON CARD (101-110) 1.25 3.00
101-110 PRINT RUN 599 SERIAL #'d SETS
COMMON CARD (111-125) .40 1.00
111-125 STATED ODDS 1:6
COMP.RS SET (30) 10.00 25.00
COMMON CARD (126-155) .50 1.25
126-155 ONE FULL RS SUBSET PER RS BOX
COMP.AS SET (30) 10.00 25.00
COMMON CARD (156-185) .50 1.25
156-185 ONE FULL SUBSET PER AS BOX
COMP.IRT SET (30) 10.00 25.00
COMMON CARD (186-215) .50 1.25
186-215 ONE FULL SUBSET PER IRT BOX
COMP.BRX SET (29) 15.00 40.00
COMMON CARD (216-245) .50 1.25
216-245 ONE FULL SUBSET PER BRX BOX
CARD 224 DOES NOT EXIST
126-245 PRINT RUN 2400 SETS
1 Troy Glaus .15 .40
2 Derek Jeter 1.00 2.50
3 Alex Rodriguez .50 1.25
4 Barry Zito .25 .60
5 Darin Erstad .15 .40
6 Tim Hudson .25 .60
7 Josh Beckett .15 .40
8 Adam Dunn .25 .60
9 Tim Salmon .15 .40
10 Ivan Rodriguez .25 .60
11 Mark Buehrle .25 .60
12 Sammy Sosa .40 1.00
13 Vicente Padilla .15 .40
14 Randy Johnson .40 1.00
15 Lance Berkman .25 .60
16 Jim Thome .25 .60
17 Luis Gonzalez .15 .40
18 Craig Biggio .25 .60
19 Cliff Floyd .15 .40
20 Pat Burrell .15 .40
21 Matt Morris .15 .40
22 Torii Hunter .15 .40
23 Curt Schilling .25 .60
24 Paul Konerko .25 .60
25 Jeff Bagwell .25 .60
26 Mike Piazza .40 1.00
27 A.J. Burnett .15 .40
28 Jimmy Rollins .25 .60
29 Greg Maddux .50 1.25
30 Jeff Kent .15 .40
31 Bobby Abreu .15 .40
32 Chipper Jones .40 1.00
33 Mike Sweeney .15 .40
34 Jason Kendall .15 .40
35 Gary Sheffield .15 .40
36 Carlos Beltran .25 .60
37 Brian Giles .15 .40
38 Jim Edmonds .25 .60
39 Roger Clemens .50 1.25
40 Andruw Jones .15 .40
41 Paul Lo Duca .15 .40
42 Ryan Klesko .15 .40
43 Jay Gibbons .15 .40
44 Shawn Green .15 .40
45 Sean Burroughs .15 .40
46 Magglio Ordonez .25 .60
47 Tony Batista .15 .40
48 J.D. Drew .15 .40
49 Hideo Nomo .40 1.00
50 Edgardo Alfonzo .15 .40
51 Nomar Garciaparra .25 .60
52 Frank Thomas .40 1.00
53 Kazuhisa Ishii .15 .40
54 Rich Aurilia .15 .40
55 Shea Hillenbrand .15 .40
56 Tom Glavine .25 .60
57 Richie Sexson .15 .40
58 Mo Vaughn .15 .40
59 Barry Bonds .60 1.50
60 Carlos Delgado .15 .40
61 Pedro Martinez .25 .60
62 Jacque Jones .15 .40
63 Edgar Martinez .25 .60
64 Manny Ramirez .40 1.00
65 Bret Boone .15 .40
66 Kerry Wood .15 .40
67 Roy Oswalt .25 .60
68 Cristian Guzman .15 .40
69 Moises Alou .15 .40
70 Bartolo Colon .15 .40
71 Ichiro Suzuki .50 1.25
72 Jose Vidro .15 .40
73 Scott Rolen .25 .60
74 Mark Prior .25 .60
75 Vladimir Guerrero .25 .60
76 Albert Pujols .50 1.25
77 Aubrey Huff .15 .40
78 Ken Griffey Jr. .75 2.00
79 Roberto Alomar .25 .60
80 Ben Grieve .15 .40
81 Miguel Tejada .25 .60
82 Austin Kearns .15 .40
83 Jason Giambi .15 .40
84 John Olerud .15 .40
85 Omar Vizquel .25 .60
86 Juan Gonzalez .15 .40
87 Larry Walker .25 .60
88 Jorge Posada .25 .60
89 Rafael Palmeiro .25 .60
90 Todd Helton .25 .60
91 Bernie Williams .25 .60
92 Garret Anderson .15 .40
93 Eric Hinske .15 .40
94 Mike Lowell .15 .40
95 Jason Jennings .15 .40
96 Eric Chavez .15 .40
97 Alfonso Soriano .25 .60
98 David Eckstein .15 .40
99 Bobby Higginson .15 .40
100 Roy Halladay .25 .60
101 Robby Hammock BSD RC 1.25 3.00
102 Hideki Matsui BSD RC 6.00 15.00
103 Chase Utley BSD 2.00 5.00
104 Oscar Villarreal BSD RC 1.25 3.00
105 Jose Contreras BSD RC 3.00 8.00
106 Rocco Baldelli BSD 1.25 3.00
107 Jesse Foppert BSD 1.25 3.00
108 Jeremy Bonderman BSD RC 5.00 12.00
109 Shane Victorino BSD RC 4.00 10.00
110 Ron Calloway BSD 1.25 3.00
111 Brandon Webb ROO RC 1.25 3.00
112 Guillermo Quiroz ROO RC .40 1.00
113 Clint Barmes ROO RC 1.00 2.50
114 Pete LaForest ROO RC .40 1.00
115 Craig Brazell ROO RC .40 1.00
116 Todd Wellemeyer ROO RC .40 1.00
117 Bernie Castro ROO RC .40 1.00
118 Alejandro Machado ROO RC .40 1.00
119 Termel Sledge ROO RC .40 1.00
120 Ian Ferguson ROO RC .40 1.00
121 Lew Ford ROO RC .40 1.00
122 Nook Logan ROO RC .40 1.00
123 Mike Nicolas ROO RC .40 1.00
124 Jeff Duncan ROO RC .40 1.00
125 Tim Olson ROO RC .40 1.00
126 Michael Hessman RS RC .50 1.25
127 Francisco Rosario RS RC .50 1.25
128 Felix Sanchez RS RC .50 1.25
129 Andrew Brown RS RC .50 1.25
130 Matt Bruback RS RC .50 1.25
131 Diegomar Markwell RS RC .50 1.25
132 Josh Willingham RS RC 1.50 4.00
133 Wes Obermueller RS .50 1.25
134 Phil Seibel RS RC .50 1.25
135 Arnie Munoz RS RC .50 1.25
136 Matt Kata RS RC .50 1.25
137 Joe Valentine RS RC .50 1.25
138 Ricardo Rodriguez RS .50 1.25
139 Lyle Overbay RS .50 1.25
140 Brian Stokes RS RC .50 1.25
141 Josh Hall RS RC .50 1.25
142 Kevin Hooper RS .50 1.25
143 Chien-Ming Wang RS RC 2.00 5.00
144 Prentice Redman RS RC .50 1.25
145 Chris Waters RS RC .50 1.25
146 Jon Leicester RS RC .50 1.25
147 Daniel Cabrera RS RC .75 2.00
148 Alfredo Gonzalez RS RC .50 1.25
149 Doug Waechter RS RC .50 1.25
150 Brandon Larson RS .50 1.25
151 Beau Kemp RS RC .50 1.25
152 Cory Stewart RS RC .50 1.25
153 Francisco Rodriguez RS .75 2.00
154 Hee Seop Choi RS .50 1.25
155 Mike Neu RS RC .50 1.25
156 Derek Jeter AS 3.00 8.00
157 Alex Rodriguez AS 1.50 4.00
158 Nomar Garciaparra AS .75 2.00
159 Barry Bonds AS 2.00 5.00
160 Sammy Sosa AS 1.25 3.00
161 Vladimir Guerrero AS .75 2.00
162 Roger Clemens AS 1.50 4.00
163 Randy Johnson AS 1.25 3.00
164 Greg Maddux AS 1.50 4.00
165 Ken Griffey Jr. AS 2.50 6.00
166 Mike Piazza AS 1.25 3.00
167 Ichiro Suzuki AS 1.50 4.00
168 Barry Larkin AS .75 2.00
169 Lance Berkman AS .75 2.00
170 Jim Thome AS .75 2.00
171 Jason Giambi AS .50 1.25
172 Gary Sheffield AS .50 1.25
173 Ivan Rodriguez AS .75 2.00
174 Miguel Tejada AS .75 2.00
175 Manny Ramirez AS 1.25 3.00
176 Mike Sweeney AS .50 1.25
177 Larry Walker AS .75 2.00
178 Jeff Bagwell AS .75 2.00
179 Chipper Jones AS 1.25 3.00
180 Craig Biggio AS .75 2.00
181 Curt Schilling AS .75 2.00
182 Pedro Martinez AS .75 2.00
183 Roberto Alomar AS .75 2.00
184 Bernie Williams AS .75 2.00
185 Magglio Ordonez AS .75 2.00
186 Jose Contreras IRT 1.25 3.00
187 Rafael Palmeiro IRT .75 2.00
188 Andruw Jones IRT .50 1.25
189 Bartolo Colon IRT .50 1.25
190 Vladimir Guerrero IRT .75 2.00
191 Pedro Martinez IRT .75 2.00
192 Albert Pujols IRT 1.50 4.00
193 Manny Ramirez IRT 1.25 3.00
194 Felix Rodriguez IRT .50 1.25
195 Alfonso Soriano IRT .75 2.00
196 Sammy Sosa IRT 1.25 3.00
197 Miguel Tejada IRT .75 2.00
198 Kazuhisa Ishii IRT .50 1.25
199 Hideki Matsui IRT 2.50 6.00
200 Hideo Nomo IRT 1.25 3.00
201 Tomo Ohka IRT .50 1.25
202 Kazuhiro Sasaki IRT .50 1.25
203 Tsuyoshi Shinjo IRT .50 1.25
204 Ichiro Suzuki IRT 1.50 4.00
205 Vicente Padilla IRT .50 1.25
206 Carlos Beltran IRT .75 2.00
207 Jose Cruz Jr. IRT .50 1.25
208 Carlos Delgado IRT .50 1.25
209 Juan Gonzalez IRT .50 1.25
210 Jorge Posada IRT .75 2.00
211 Ivan Rodriguez IRT .75 2.00
212 Hee Seop Choi IRT .50 1.25
213 Bobby Abreu IRT .50 1.25
214 Magglio Ordonez IRT .75 2.00
215 Francisco Rodriguez IRT .75 2.00
216 Juan Acevedo BRX .50 1.25
217 Erick Almonte BRX .50 1.25
218 Yogi Berra BRX 1.25 3.00
219 Brandon Claussen BRX .50 1.25
220 Roger Clemens BRX 1.50 4.00
221 Jose Contreras BRX 1.25 3.00
222 Whitey Ford BRX .75 2.00
223 Jason Giambi BRX .50 1.25
225 Michel Hernandez BRX RC .50 1.25
226 Sterling Hitchcock BRX .50 1.25
227 Catfish Hunter BRX .75 2.00
228 Reggie Jackson BRX .75 2.00
229 Derek Jeter BRX 3.00 8.00
230 Nick Johnson BRX .50 1.25
231 Hideki Matsui BRX 2.50 6.00
232 Raul Mondesi BRX .50 1.25
233 Mike Mussina BRX .75 2.00
234 Andy Pettitte BRX .75 2.00
235 Jorge Posada BRX .75 2.00
236 Mariano Rivera BRX 1.50 4.00
237 Phil Rizzuto BRX .75 2.00
238 Enos Slaughter BRX .75 2.00
239 Alfonso Soriano BRX .75 2.00
240 Robin Ventura BRX .50 1.25
241 Chien-Ming Wang BRX RC 2.00 5.00
242 Jeff Weaver BRX .50 1.25
243 David Wells BRX .50 1.25
244 Bernie Williams BRX .75 2.00
245 Todd Zeile BRX .50 1.25

2003 Fleer Box Score Classic Miniatures

COMPLETE SET (30) 10.00 25.00
ONE SET PER CLASSIC MINI BOX
STATED PRINT RUN 2400 SETS
1 Jim Thome .75 2.00
2 Jason Giambi .50 1.25
3 Miguel Tejada .75 2.00
4 Alfonso Soriano .75 2.00
5 Ivan Rodriguez .75 2.00
6 Troy Glaus .50 1.25
7 Mike Piazza 1.25 3.00
8 Barry Bonds 2.00 5.00
9 Sammy Sosa 1.25 3.00
10 Lance Berkman .75 2.00
11 Pat Burrell .50 1.25
12 Chipper Jones 1.25 3.00
13 Shawn Green .50 1.25
14 Manny Ramirez 1.25 3.00
15 Ichiro Suzuki 1.50 4.00
16 Vladimir Guerrero .75 2.00
17 Albert Pujols 1.50 4.00
18 Ken Griffey Jr. 2.50 6.00
19 Bernie Williams .75 2.00
20 Austin Kearns .50 1.25
21 Randy Johnson 1.25 3.00
22 Greg Maddux 1.50 4.00
23 Roger Clemens 1.50 4.00
24 Hideo Nomo 1.25 3.00
25 Pedro Martinez .75 2.00
26 Kerry Wood .50 1.25
27 Mark Prior .75 2.00
28 Derek Jeter 3.00 8.00
29 Alex Rodriguez 1.50 4.00
30 Nomar Garciaparra .75 2.00

2003 Fleer Box Score Classic Miniatures First Edition

*CLASSIC MINIS 1ST ED: .75X TO 2X BASIC
ONE SET PER CLASSIC MINI 1ST ED. BOX
STATED PRINT RUN 100 SERIAL #'d SETS

2003 Fleer Box Score Classic Miniatures Game Jersey

ONE PER CLASSIC MINI BOX
SP PRINT RUNS PROVIDED BY FLEER
SP'S ARE NOT SERIAL-NUMBERED
AK Austin Kearns 3.00 8.00
DJ Derek Jeter 10.00 25.00
GM Greg Maddux 4.00 10.00
HN Hideo Nomo 6.00 15.00
JG Jason Giambi 3.00 8.00
JT Jim Thome SP/150 4.00 10.00
MP Mark Prior SP/150 4.00 10.00
MT Miguel Tejada 3.00 8.00
NG Nomar Garciaparra 6.00 15.00
VG Vladimir Guerrero SP/250 4.00 10.00

2003 Fleer Box Score First Edition

*1ST ED. 1-100: 4X TO 10X BASIC
*1ST ED. 101-110: .5X TO 1.2X BASIC
*1ST ED. 111-125: 1.5X TO 4X BASIC
*1ST ED. 126-155: 1.2X TO 3X BASIC
*1ST ED. 156-185: 1.2X TO 3X BASIC
*1ST ED. 186-215: 1.2X TO 3X BASIC
*1ST ED. 216-245: 1.2X TO 3X BASIC
1-125 RANDOM INSERTS IN PACKS
126-155 ONE SUBSET PER RS 1ST ED. BOX
156-185 ONE SUBSET PER AS 1ST ED. BOX
186-215 ONE SUBSET PER IRT 1ST ED. BOX
216-245 ONE SUBSET PER BRX 1ST ED. BOX
1-125 PRINT RUN 150 SERIAL #'d SETS
126-245 PRINT RUN 100 SERIAL #'d SETS
CARD 224 DOES NOT EXIST

2003 Fleer Box Score All-Star Line Up Autographs

PRINT RUNS B/WN 170-270 COPIES PER
*GOLD: .6X TO 1.5X BASIC
GOLD PRINT RUN 50 SERIAL #'d SETS
CJ Chipper Jones/170 20.00 50.00
JT Jim Thome/260 15.00 40.00
RJ Randy Johnson/270 40.00 80.00

2003 Fleer Box Score All-Star Lineup Game Used

ONE PER ALL-STARS BOX
SP PRINT RUNS PROVIDED BY FLEER
SP'S ARE NOT SERIAL-NUMBERED
CARDS BSG AND BGRS BONDS HAS NO GU
APSG Alom/Piaz/Sori/Giambi 20.00 50.00
BBB Biggio 10.00 25.00
Bagw
Berkman/150
BGRS Bonds 10.00 25.00
Grif
Ram
Ichiro/175
BSG Bonds 8.00 20.00
Sosa
Guerrero/200
CJM Clemens 15.00 40.00
R.John
Maddux
GSJ Giambi 12.00 30.00
Soriano
Jeter/50
JRG Jeter 12.50 30.00
A-Rod
Nomar
JSM Chipper 15.00 40.00
Sheff
Maddux
RPJC I.Rod/Piaz/Randy/Clem 20.00 50.00
TARG Thome/Alo/A.Rod/Gar/100 20.00 50.00

2003 Fleer Box Score Bat Rack Quads

RANDOM INSERTS IN PACKS
STATED PRINT RUN 50 SERIAL #'d SETS
1 Jeter/Torii/Glaus/Tejada 25.00 60.00
2 Jeter/Piazza/Nomar/Chip 20.00 50.00
3 Vlad/Berk/Sosa/Rolen 15.00 40.00
4 Giambi/Sor/A.Rod/Glaus 20.00 50.00
5 A.Rod/Thome/Sosa/Rolen 20.00 50.00
6 Giambi/Thome/Piaz/Chip 20.00 50.00

2003 Fleer Box Score Bat Rack Trios

RANDOM INSERTS IN PACKS
STATED PRINT RUN 250 SERIAL #'d SETS
1 Jeter/Soriano/Giambi 20.00 50.00
2 Rolen/Tejada/Glaus 8.00 20.00
3 Thome/Chipper/Piazza 10.00 25.00
4 Glaus/Nomar/Soriano 15.00 40.00
5 Berkman/Guerrero/Sosa 8.00 20.00
6 Chipper/Berkman/Guerrero 8.00 20.00
7 Torii/Giambi/Nomar 8.00 20.00
8 Jeter/Tejada/A.Rod 15.00 40.00
9 Rolen/Sosa/A.Rod 15.00 40.00
10 Torii/Thome/Piazza 8.00 20.00

2003 Fleer Box Score Bronx Bombers Game Jersey

ONE PER BRONX BOMBERS BOX
SP PRINT RUNS PROVIDED BY FLEER
SP'S ARE NOT SERIAL-NUMBERED
AS Alfonso Soriano 4.00 10.00
BW Bernie Williams 6.00 15.00
DJ Derek Jeter 20.00 50.00
JG Jason Giambi 4.00 10.00
JP Jorge Posada 6.00 15.00
MM Mike Mussina 8.00 20.00
NJ Nick Johnson SP/150 4.00 10.00
RC Roger Clemens 8.00 20.00
RV Robin Ventura 4.00 10.00

2003 Fleer Box Score Jersey Rack Trios

RANDOM INSERTS IN PACKS
STATED PRINT RUN 350 SERIAL #'d SETS
1 Jeter/Soriano/Giambi 20.00 50.00
2 Schilling/Randy/Maddux 10.00 25.00
3 Clemens/Pedro/Zito 10.00 25.00
4 A.Rod/Guerrero/Sosa 15.00 40.00
5 Jeter/Nomar/A.Rod 10.00 25.00
6 Berkman/Sosa/Torii 8.00 20.00
7 Guerrero/Thome/A.Rod 10.00 25.00
8 Jeter/Tejada/Nomar 15.00 40.00
9 Soriano/Chavez/Thome 8.00 20.00
10 Tejada/Chavez/Zito 8.00 20.00

2003 Fleer Box Score Jersey Rack Quads

RANDOM INSERTS IN PACKS
STATED PRINT RUN 150 SERIAL #'d SETS
1 Jeter/A.Rod/Nomar/Tejada 25.00 60.00
2 Clem/Giambi/Soriano/Jeter 12.50 30.00
3 Randy/Maddux/Clem/Pedro 30.00 80.00
4 Schilling/Vlad/Randy/A.Rod 15.00 40.00
7 Zito/Maddux/Pedro/Schilling 10.00 25.00
8 Nomar/Tejada/Zito/Chavez 15.00 40.00

2003 Fleer Box Score Press Clippings

STATED ODDS 1:18
1 Derek Jeter 2.50 6.00
2 Nomar Garciaparra .60 1.50
3 Miguel Tejada .60 1.50
4 Barry Bonds 1.50 4.00
5 Alex Rodriguez 1.25 3.00
6 Sammy Sosa 1.00 2.50
7 Lance Berkman .60 1.50
8 Torii Hunter .40 1.00
9 Troy Glaus .40 1.00
10 Eric Chavez .40 1.00
11 Tim Hudson .60 1.50
12 Randy Johnson 1.00 2.50
13 Mike Piazza 1.00 2.50
14 Roberto Alomar .60 1.50
15 Jim Thome .60 1.50
16 Alfonso Soriano .60 1.50
17 Roger Clemens 1.25 3.00
18 Pedro Martinez .60 1.50
19 Mark Prior .60 1.50
20 Curt Schilling .60 1.50

2003 Fleer Box Score Press Clippings Dual

RANDOM INSERTS IN PACKS
STATED PRINT RUN 250 SERIAL #'d SETS
1 D.Jeter 6.00 15.00
N.Garciaparra
2 M.Tejada/B.Bonds 4.00 10.00
3 A.Rodriguez/S.Sosa 3.00 8.00
4 L.Berkman/T.Hunter 1.50 4.00
5 T.Glaus/E.Chavez 1.00 2.50
6 T.Hudson/R.Johnson 2.50 6.00
7 M.Piazza/R.Alomar 2.50 6.00
8 J.Thome/A.Soriano 1.50 4.00
9 R.Clemens/P.Martinez 3.00 8.00
10 M.Prior/C.Schilling 1.50 4.00

2003 Fleer Box Score Press Clippings Dual Patch

RANDOM INSERTS IN PACKS
PRINT RUNS B/WN 100-150 COPIES PER
1 D.Jeter 40.00 100.00
N.Garciaparra/100
2 M.Tejada/T.Glaus/150 10.00 25.00
3 A.Rodriguez/S.Sosa/150 10.00 25.00
4 L.Berkman/T.Hunter/150 10.00 25.00
5 T.Glaus/E.Chavez/150 10.00 25.00
6 T.Hudson/R.Johnson/150 10.00 25.00
7 M.Piazza/R.Alomar/150 20.00 50.00
8 J.Thome/A.Soriano/100 10.00 25.00
9 R.Clemens/P.Martinez/100 20.00 50.00
10 M.Prior/C.Schilling/150 10.00 25.00
11 K.Wood/K.Benson/150 10.00 25.00
12 R.Palmeiro/J.Bagwell/150 10.00 25.00
13 A.Jones/G.Sheffield/150 10.00 25.00
14 M.Ramirez/C.Beltran/150 10.00 25.00
15 T.Helton/E.Durazo/150 10.00 25.00

2003 Fleer Box Score Press Clippings Game Jersey

STATED ODDS 1:12
SP PRINT RUNS PROVIDED BY FLEER
SP'S ARE NOT SERIAL-NUMBERED
AJ Andruw Jones 3.00 8.00
AR Alex Rodriguez 4.00 10.00
AS Alfonso Soriano 2.00 5.00
CB Carlos Beltran SP/250 2.00 5.00
CS Curt Schilling 2.00 5.00
DJ Derek Jeter 8.00 20.00
EC Eric Chavez 2.00 5.00
ED Erubiel Durazo SP/250 2.00 5.00
GS Gary Sheffield SP/250 2.00 5.00
JB Jeff Bagwell 3.00 8.00
JT Jim Thome 3.00 8.00
KB Kris Benson SP/250 2.00 5.00
KW Kerry Wood SP/250 2.00 5.00
LB Lance Berkman SP/250 2.00 5.00
MP1 Mike Piazza 4.00 10.00
MP2 Mark Prior 3.00 8.00
MR Manny Ramirez SP/250 3.00 8.00
MT Miguel Tejada 2.00 5.00
NG Nomar Garciaparra 6.00 15.00
PM Pedro Martinez 3.00 8.00
RA Roberto Alomar 3.00 8.00
RC Roger Clemens 6.00 15.00
RJ Randy Johnson 3.00 8.00
RP Rafael Palmeiro 3.00 8.00
SS Sammy Sosa 3.00 8.00
TG Troy Glaus 2.00 5.00
TH1 Todd Helton SP/250 3.00 8.00
TH2 Tim Hudson 2.00 5.00
TH3 Torii Hunter 2.00 5.00

2003 Fleer Box Score Wave of the Future Game Used

ONE PER RISING STARS BOX
SP PRINT RUNS PROVIDED BY FLEER
SP'S ARE NOT SERIAL-NUMBERED
BL Brandon Larson Bat 3.00 8.00
CU Chase Utley Jsy 6.00 15.00
FR Fran Rodriguez Jsy SP/125 4.00 10.00
HC Hee Seop Choi Jsy 3.00 8.00
JB Jeremy Bonderman Bat 5.00 12.00
LO Lyle Overbay Bat 3.00 8.00
RC Ron Calloway Jsy 3.00 8.00
RR Ricardo Rodriguez Jsy 3.00 8.00

2003 Fleer Box Score World Piece Game Jersey

ONE PER INTERNATIONAL BOX
SP PRINT RUNS PROVIDED BY FLEER
SP'S ARE NOT SERIAL-NUMBERED
FR Francisco Rodriguez SP/100 3.00 8.00
HC Hee Seop Choi 3.00 8.00
HN Hideo Nomo 4.00 10.00
IR Ivan Rodriguez 4.00 10.00
JC Jose Cruz Jr. SP/100 3.00 8.00
KS Kazuhiro Sasaki 3.00 8.00
MT Miguel Tejada 3.00 8.00
PM Pedro Martinez 4.00 10.00
SS Sammy Sosa 4.00 10.00
VG Vladimir Guerrero SP/200 4.00 10.00

1999 Fleer Brilliants

The 1999 Fleer Brilliants set was issued in June 1999 in one series for a total of 175 cards. The set was distributed in five-card packs with an original SRP of $4.99. The fronts feature color action player images on a black-and-white, high-contrast, super-bright mirror background printed on 24-point styrene card stock and laminated with radial-etched mirror foil. The set contains the Rookie subset (126-175) with an insertion rate in packs of 1:2. A promotional sample card featuring J.D. Drew was distributed to dealer accounts and hobby media a few months prior to the product's national release. This card can be easily identified by the "PROMOTIONAL SAMPLE" text running diagonally across the front and back. Notable Rookie Cards include Pat Burrell and Freddy Garcia.

COMPLETE SET (175) 25.00 60.00
COMP.SET w/o SP's (125) 12.00 30.00
CARDS 126-175 STATED ODDS 1:2
1 Mark McGwire .75 2.00
2 Derek Jeter 1.25 3.00
3 Nomar Garciaparra .30 .75
4 Travis Lee .20 .50
5 Jeff Bagwell .30 .75
6 Andres Galarraga .30 .75
7 Pedro Martinez .30 .75
8 Cal Ripken 1.50 4.00
9 Vladimir Guerrero .30 .75
10 Chipper Jones .50 1.25
11 Rusty Greer .20 .50
12 Omar Vizquel .30 .75
13 Quinton McCracken .20 .50
14 Jaret Wright .20 .50
15 Mike Mussina .30 .75
16 Jason Giambi .20 .50
17 Tony Clark .20 .50
18 Troy O'Leary .20 .50
19 Troy Percival .20 .50
20 Kerry Wood .20 .50
21 Vinny Castilla .20 .50
22 Chris Carpenter .20 .50
23 Richie Sexson .20 .50
24 Ken Griffey Jr. 1.00 2.50
25 Barry Bonds .75 2.00
26 Carlos Delgado .20 .50
27 Frank Thomas .50 1.25
28 Manny Ramirez .50 1.25
29 Shawn Green .20 .50
30 Mike Piazza .50 1.25
31 Tino Martinez .20 .50
32 Dante Bichette .20 .50
33 Scott Rolen .30 .75
34 Gabe Alvarez .20 .50
35 Raul Mondesi .20 .50
36 Damion Easley .20 .50
37 Jeff Kent .20 .50
38 Al Leiter .20 .50
39 Alex Rodriguez .60 1.50
40 Jeff King .20 .50
41 Mark Grace .30 .75
42 Larry Walker .30 .75
43 Moises Alou .20 .50
44 Juan Gonzalez .20 .50
45 Rolando Arrojo .20 .50
46 Tom Glavine .30 .75
47 Johnny Damon .30 .75
48 Livan Hernandez .20 .50
49 Craig Biggio .30 .75
50 Dmitri Young .20 .50
51 Chan Ho Park .30 .75
52 Todd Walker .20 .50
53 Derrek Lee .20 .50
54 Todd Helton .30 .75
55 Ray Lankford .20 .50
56 Jim Thome .30 .75
57 Matt Lawton .20 .50
58 Matt Anderson .20 .50
59 Jose Offerman .20 .50
60 Eric Karros .20 .50
61 Orlando Hernandez .20 .50
62 Ben Grieve .20 .50
63 Bobby Abreu .20 .50
64 Kevin Young .20 .50
65 John Olerud .20 .50
66 Sammy Sosa .50 1.25
67 Andy Ashby .20 .50
68 Juan Encarnacion .20 .50
69 Shane Reynolds .20 .50
70 Bernie Williams .30 .75
71 Mike Cameron .20 .50
72 Troy Glaus .20 .50
73 Gary Sheffield .20 .50
74 Jeromy Burnitz .20 .50
75 Mike Caruso .20 .50
76 Chuck Knoblauch .20 .50
77 Kenny Rogers .20 .50
78 David Cone .20 .50
79 Tony Gwynn .50 1.25
80 Jay Buhner .20 .50
81 Paul O'Neill .30 .75
82 Charles Nagy .20 .50
83 Javy Lopez .20 .50
84 Scott Erickson .20 .50
85 Trevor Hoffman .30 .75
86 Andruw Jones .20 .50
87 Ray Durham .20 .50
88 Jorge Posada .30 .75
89 Edgar Martinez .30 .75
90 Tim Salmon .20 .50
91 Bobby Higginson .20 .50
92 Adrian Beltre .50 1.25
93 Jason Kendall .20 .50
94 Henry Rodriguez .20 .50
95 Greg Maddux .60 1.50
96 David Justice .20 .50
97 Ivan Rodriguez .30 .75
98 Curt Schilling .20 .50
99 Matt Williams .20 .50
100 Darin Erstad .20 .50
101 Rafael Palmeiro .30 .75
102 David Wells .20 .50
103 Barry Larkin .30 .75
104 Robin Ventura .20 .50
105 Edgar Renteria .20 .50
106 Andy Pettitte .30 .75
107 Albert Belle .20 .50
108 Steve Finley .20 .50
109 Fernando Vina .20 .50
110 Rondell White .20 .50
111 Kevin Brown .20 .50
112 Jose Canseco .30 .75
113 Roger Clemens .60 1.50
114 Todd Hundley .20 .50
115 Will Clark .30 .75
116 Jim Edmonds .30 .75
117 Randy Johnson .50 1.25
118 Denny Neagle .20 .50
119 Brian Jordan .20 .50
120 Dean Palmer .20 .50
121 Roberto Alomar .30 .75
122 Ken Caminiti .20 .50
123 Brian Giles .20 .50
124 Todd Stottlemyre .20 .50
125 Mo Vaughn .20 .50
126 J.D. Drew .30 .75
127 Ryan Minor .30 .75
128 Gabe Kapler .30 .75
129 Jeremy Giambi .30 .75
130 Eric Chavez .30 .75
131 Ben Davis .30 .75
132 Rob Fick .30 .75
133 George Lombard .30 .75
134 Calvin Pickering .30 .75
135 Preston Wilson .30 .75
136 Corey Koskie .30 .75
137 Russell Branyan .30 .75
138 Bruce Chen .30 .75
139 Matt Clement .30 .75
140 Pat Burrell RC 1.25 3.00
141 Freddy Garcia RC .75 2.00
142 Brian Simmons .30 .75
143 Carlos Febles .30 .75
144 Carlos Guillen .30 .75
145 Fernando Seguignol .30 .75
146 Carlos Beltran .50 1.25
147 Edgard Clemente .30 .75
148 Mitch Meluskey .30 .75
149 Ryan Bradley .30 .75
150 Marlon Anderson .30 .75
151 A.J. Burnett RC .50 1.25
152 Scott Hunter RC .30 .75
153 Mark Johnson .30 .75
154 Angel Pena .30 .75
155 Roy Halladay .50 1.25
156 Chad Allen RC .30 .75
157 Trot Nixon .30 .75
158 Ricky Ledee .30 .75
159 Gary Bennett RC .30 .75
160 Micah Bowie RC .30 .75
161 Doug Mientkiewicz RC .50 1.25
162 Danny Klassen .30 .75
163 Willis Otanez .30 .75
164 Jin Ho Cho .30 .75
165 Mike Lowell .30 .75
166 Armando Rios .30 .75
167 Warren Morris .30 .75
168 Michael Barrett .30 .75
169 Alex Gonzalez .30 .75
170 Masao Kida RC .30 .75
171 Peter Tucci .30 .75
172 Luis Saturria RC .30 .75
173 Kris Benson .30 .75
174 Mario Encarnacion RC .30 .75
175 Roosevelt Brown RC .30 .75
NNO J.D. Drew Sample .40 1.00

1999 Fleer Brilliants 24-Karat Gold

*STARS 1-125: 20X TO 50X BASIC
*ROOKIES: 126-175: 12.5X TO 30X BASIC
RANDOM INSERTS IN PACKS
STATED PRINT RUN 24 SERIAL #'d SETS
NO RC PRICING DUE TO SCARCITY
1 Mark McGwire 600.00 1500.00
2 Derek Jeter 3000.00 5000.00
8 Cal Ripken 200.00 500.00
10 Chipper Jones 400.00 1000.00
24 Ken Griffey Jr. 1500.00 4000.00
25 Barry Bonds 600.00 1500.00
27 Frank Thomas 400.00 1000.00
28 Manny Ramirez 400.00 1000.00
30 Mike Piazza 400.00 1000.00
39 Alex Rodriguez 500.00 1200.00
79 Tony Gwynn 400.00 1000.00
92 Adrian Beltre 200.00 500.00
95 Greg Maddux 500.00 1200.00
113 Roger Clemens 500.00 1200.00
117 Randy Johnson 400.00 1000.00

1999 Fleer Brilliants Blue

*STARS 1-125: 1.25X TO 3X BASIC CARDS
*ROOKIES: 126-175: .75X TO 2X BASIC
STARS 1-125 STATED ODDS 1:3
ROOKIES 126-175 STATED ODDS 1:6

1999 Fleer Brilliants Gold

*STARS 1-125: 10X TO 25X BASIC
*ROOKIES 126-175: 6X TO 15X BASIC
STATED PRINT RUN 99 SERIAL #'d SETS
1 Mark McGwire 60.00 150.00
2 Derek Jeter 200.00 500.00
8 Cal Ripken 100.00 250.00
10 Chipper Jones 40.00 100.00
24 Ken Griffey Jr. 150.00 400.00
25 Barry Bonds 60.00 150.00
27 Frank Thomas 40.00 100.00
28 Manny Ramirez 40.00 100.00
30 Mike Piazza 40.00 100.00
39 Alex Rodriguez 50.00 120.00
79 Tony Gwynn 40.00 100.00
92 Adrian Beltre 20.00 50.00
95 Greg Maddux 50.00 120.00
113 Roger Clemens 50.00 120.00
117 Randy Johnson 40.00 100.00

1999 Fleer Brilliants Illuminators

COMPLETE SET (15) 4.00 10.00
STATED ODDS 1:10
1 Kerry Wood .40 1.00
2 Ben Grieve .40 1.00
3 J.D. Drew .40 1.00
4 Juan Encarnacion .40 1.00
5 Travis Lee .40 1.00
6 Todd Helton .60 1.50
7 Troy Glaus .40 1.00
8 Ricky Ledee .40 1.00
9 Eric Chavez .40 1.00
10 Ben Davis .40 1.00
11 George Lombard .40 1.00
12 Jeremy Giambi .40 1.00
13 Richie Sexson .40 1.00
14 Corey Koskie .40 1.00
15 Russell Branyan .40 1.00

1999 Fleer Brilliants Shining Stars

COMPLETE SET (15) 12.00 30.00
STATED ODDS 1:20
*PULSAR: 2X TO 5X BASIC SHINING STAR
PULSAR STATED ODDS 1:400
1 Ken Griffey Jr. 2.00 5.00
2 Mark McGwire 1.50 4.00
3 Sammy Sosa 1.00 2.50
4 Derek Jeter 2.50 6.00
5 Nomar Garciaparra .60 1.50
6 Alex Rodriguez 1.25 3.00

7 Mike Piazza 1.00 2.50
8 Juan Gonzalez .40 1.00
9 Chipper Jones 1.00 2.50
10 Cal Ripken 3.00 8.00
11 Frank Thomas 1.00 2.50
12 Greg Maddux 1.25 3.00
13 Roger Clemens 1.25 3.00
14 Vladimir Guerrero .60 1.50
15 Manny Ramirez 1.00 2.50

2003 Fleer Double Header

COMPLETE SET (240) 30.00 80.00
COMMON CARD (1-180) .15 .40
COMMON CARD (181-270) .15 .40
COMMON CARD (271-300) .40 1.00
181-300 COMPRISED OF 60 TOTAL CARDS
181-300 FEATURE DUAL-NUMBERING
1 Ramon Vazquez .15 .40
2 Derek Jeter 1.00 2.50
3 Orlando Hudson .15 .40
4 Miguel Tejada .25 .60
5 Steve Finley .15 .40
6 Brad Wilkerson .15 .40
7 Craig Biggio .25 .60
8 Marlon Anderson .15 .40
9 Phil Nevin .15 .40
10 Hideo Nomo .40 1.00
11 Barry Larkin .25 .60
12 Alfonso Soriano .25 .60
13 Rodrigo Lopez .15 .40
14 Paul Konerko .25 .60
15 Carlos Beltran .25 .60
16 Garret Anderson .15 .40
17 Kazuhisa Ishii .15 .40
18 Eddie Guardado .15 .40
19 Juan Gonzalez .15 .40
20 Mark Mulder .15 .40
21 Sammy Sosa .40 1.00
22 Kazuhiro Sasaki .15 .40
23 Jose Cruz Jr. .15 .40
24 Tomo Ohka .15 .40
25 Barry Bonds .60 1.50
26 Carlos Delgado .15 .40
27 Scott Rolen .25 .60
28 Steve Cox .15 .40
29 Mike Sweeney .15 .40
30 Ryan Klesko .15 .40
31 Greg Maddux .50 1.25
32 Derek Lowe .15 .40
33 David Wells .15 .40
34 Kerry Wood .15 .40
35 Randall Simon .15 .40
36 Ben Howard .15 .40
37 Jeff Suppan .15 .40
38 Curt Schilling .25 .60
39 Eric Gagne .15 .40
40 Raul Mondesi .15 .40
41 Jeffrey Hammonds .15 .40
42 Mo Vaughn .15 .40
43 Sidney Ponson .15 .40
44 Adam Dunn .25 .60
45 Pedro Martinez .25 .60
46 Jason Simontacchi .15 .40
47 Tom Glavine .25 .60
48 Torii Hunter .15 .40
49 Gabe Kapler .15 .40
50 Andy Van Hekken .15 .40
51 Ichiro Suzuki .50 1.25
52 Andruw Jones .15 .40
53 Bobby Abreu .15 .40
54 Junior Spivey .15 .40
55 Ray Durham .15 .40
56 Mark Buehrle .25 .60
57 Drew Henson .15 .40
58 Brandon Duckworth .15 .40
59 Rob Mackowiak .15 .40
60 Josh Beckett .15 .40
61 Chan Ho Park .25 .60
62 John Smoltz .40 1.00
63 Jimmy Rollins .25 .60
64 Orlando Cabrera .15 .40
65 Johnny Damon .25 .60
66 Austin Kearns .15 .40
67 Tsuyoshi Shinjo .15 .40
68 Tim Hudson .25 .60
69 Coco Crisp .15 .40
70 Darin Erstad .15 .40
71 Jacque Jones .15 .40
72 Vicente Padilla .15 .40
73 Hee Seop Choi .15 .40
74 Shea Hillenbrand .15 .40
75 Edgardo Alfonzo .15 .40
76 Pat Burrell .15 .40
77 Ben Sheets .15 .40
78 Ivan Rodriguez .25 .60
79 Josh Phelps .15 .40
80 Adam Kennedy .15 .40
81 Eric Chavez .15 .40
82 Bobby Higginson .15 .40
83 Nomar Garciaparra .25 .60
84 J.D. Drew .15 .40
85 Carl Crawford .25 .60
86 Matt Morris .15 .40
87 Chipper Jones .40 1.00
88 Luis Gonzalez .15 .40
89 Richie Sexson .15 .40
90 Eric Milton .15 .40
91 Andres Galarraga .25 .60
92 Paul Lo Duca .15 .40
93 Mark Grace .25 .60
94 Ben Grieve .15 .40
95 Mike Lowell .15 .40
96 Roberto Alomar .25 .60
97 Wade Miller .15 .40
98 Sean Casey .15 .40
99 Roger Clemens .50 1.25
100 Matt Williams .15 .40
101 Brian Giles .15 .40
102 Jim Thome .25 .60
103 Troy Glaus .15 .40
104 Joe Borchard .15 .40
105 Vladimir Guerrero .25 .60
106 Kevin Mench .15 .40
107 Omar Vizquel .25 .60
108 Magglio Ordonez .25 .60
109 Ken Griffey Jr. .75 2.00
110 Mike Piazza .40 1.00
111 Mark Teixeira .25 .60
112 Jason Jennings .15 .40
113 Ellis Burks .15 .40
114 Jason Varitek .40 1.00
115 Larry Walker .25 .60
116 Frank Thomas .40 1.00
117 Ramon Ortiz .15 .40
118 Mark Quinn .15 .40
119 Preston Wilson .15 .40
120 Carlos Lee .15 .40
121 Brian Lawrence .15 .40
122 Tim Salmon .15 .40
123 Shawn Green .15 .40
124 Randy Johnson .40 1.00
125 Jeff Bagwell .25 .60
126 C.C. Sabathia .25 .60
127 Bernie Williams .25 .60
128 Roy Oswalt .25 .60
129 Albert Pujols .50 1.25
130 Reggie Sanders .15 .40
131 Jeff Conine .15 .40
132 John Olerud .15 .40
133 Lance Berkman .25 .60
134 Geoff Jenkins .15 .40
135 Jim Edmonds .25 .60
136 Todd Helton .25 .60
137 Jason Kendall .15 .40
138 Robin Ventura .15 .40
139 Randy Winn .15 .40
140 Carl Everett .15 .40
141 Jose Vidro .15 .40
142 Pokey Reese .15 .40
143 Edgar Renteria .15 .40
144 Alex Rodriguez .50 1.25
145 Doug Mientkiewicz .15 .40
146 Aramis Ramirez .15 .40
147 Bobby Hill .15 .40
148 Jorge Posada .25 .60
149 Sean Burroughs .15 .40
150 Jeff Kent .15 .40
151 Tino Martinez .15 .40
152 Mark Prior .25 .60
153 Brad Radke .15 .40
154 Al Leiter .15 .40
155 Eric Karros .15 .40
156 Manny Ramirez .40 1.00
157 Jason Lane .15 .40
158 Mike Lieberthal .15 .40
159 Shannon Stewart .15 .40
160 Robert Fick .15 .40
161 Derrek Lee .15 .40
162 Jason Giambi .15 .40
163 Rafael Palmeiro .25 .60
164 Jay Payton .15 .40
165 Adrian Beltre .40 1.00
166 Marlon Byrd .15 .40
167 Bret Boone .15 .40
168 Roy Halladay .25 .60
169 Freddy Garcia .15 .40
170 Rich Aurilia .15 .40
171 Jared Sandberg .15 .40
172 Paul Byrd .15 .40
173 Gary Sheffield .15 .40
174 Edgar Martinez .25 .60
175 Eric Hinske .15 .40
176 Milton Bradley .15 .40
177 David Eckstein .15 .40
178 Jay Gibbons .15 .40
179 Corey Patterson .15 .40
180 Barry Zito .25 .60
181-82 D.Erstad .15 .40
T.Glaus
183-84 C.Schilling .40 1.00
R.Johnson
185-86 A.Jones .40 1.00
C.Jones
187-88 T.Batista .15 .40
J.Gibbons
189-90 P.Martinez .25 .60
N.Garciaparra
191-92 S.Sosa .40 1.00
K.Wood
193-94 P.Konerko .25 .60
J.Borchard
195-96 A.Kearns .25 .60
A.Dunn
197-98 O.Vizquel .25 .60
J.Thome
199-00 L.Walker .25 .60
T.Helton
201-02 J.Beckett .15 .40
L.Castillo
203-04 C.Biggio .25 .60
J.Bagwell
205-06 P.Byrd .15 .40
M.Sweeney
207-08 A.Beltre .40 1.00
S.Green
209-10 J.Hernandez .15 .40
R.Sexson
211-12 J.Jones .15 .40
T.Hunter
213-14 V.Guerrero .25 .60
J.Vidro
215-16 E.Alfonzo .40 1.00
M.Piazza
217-18 R.Clemens 1.00 2.50
D.Jeter
219-20 E.Chavez .25 .60
M.Tejada
221-22 M.Byrd .15 .40
P.Burrell
223-24 J.Kendall .15 .40
B.Giles
225-26 P.Nevin .15 .40
S.Burroughs
227-28 J.Kent .60 1.50
B.Bonds
229-30 K.Sasaki .50 1.25
I.Suzuki
231-32 A.Pujols .50 1.25
J.Drew
233-34 J.Gonzalez .25 .60
I.Rodriguez
235-36 E.Hinske .15 .40
O.Hudson
237-38 L.Berkman .40 1.00
C.Jones
239-40 A.Rodriguez 1.00 2.50
D.Jeter
241-42 I.Suzuki .50 1.25
H.Nomo
243-44 M.Ramirez .40 1.00
B.Williams
245-46 T.Glavine .50 1.25
R.Clemens
247-48 K.Griffey Jr. .75 2.00
B.Larkin
249-50 M.Teixeira .25 .60
M.Prior
251-52 A.Pujols .50 1.25
D.Henson
253-54 J.Giambi .25 .60
T.Helton AS
255-56 J.Vidro .25 .60
A.Soriano AS
257-58 S.Hillenbrand .25 .60
S.Rolen AS
259-60 J.Rollins .50 1.25
A.Rodriguez AS
261-62 T.Hunter .25 .60
V.Guerrero AS
263-64 I.Suzuki .50 1.25
S.Sosa AS
265-66 B.Bonds .60 1.50
M.Ramirez AS
267-68 M.Piazza .40 1.00
J.Posada AS
269-70 R.Yount .50 1.25
O.Smith AS
271-72 J.Hancock .40 1.00
F.Sanchez OD
273-74 R.Bukvich .40 1.00
S.Sedlacek OD
275-76 D.Devore .40 1.00
R.Reyes OD
277-78 H.Blalock .40 1.00
T.Hafner OD
279-80 E.Junge .40 1.00
B.Myers OD
281-82 B.Lidge .40 1.00
J.Robertson OD
283-84 M.Asencio .40 1.00
R.Hernandez OD
285-86 F.Rodney .40 1.00
B.Wesson OD
287-88 V.Alvarez .40 1.00
D.Ross OD
289-90 T.Torcato .40 1.00
C.Snelling OD
291-92 K.Saarloos .40 1.00
M.Ensberg OD
293-94 J.Bard .40 1.00
W.Nieves OD
295-96 J.Bong .40 1.00
T.Hodges OD
297-98 K.Cash .40 1.00
R.Johnson OD
299-00 C.Figgins .60 1.50
J.Lackey OD
P2 Derek Jeter Promo 1.25 3.00

2003 Fleer Double Header Flip Card Game Used

STATED ODDS 1:20
SP PRINT RUNS PROVIDED BY FLEER
SP'S ARE NOT SERIAL-NUMERED
*GOLD: .75X TO 2X BASIC GAME USED
*GOLD: .6X TO 1.5X BASIC GAME USED SP
GOLD RANDOM INSERTS IN PACKS
GOLD PRINT RUN 100 SERIAL #'d SETS
AB Adrian Beltre Jsy 3.00 8.00
AD Adam Dunn Jsy SP/200 4.00 10.00
AR Alex Rodriguez Jsy 6.00 15.00
AS Alfonso Soriano Jsy 3.00 8.00
BB Barry Bonds Bat SP/200 10.00 25.00
BL Barry Larkin Jsy SP/200 6.00 15.00
BW Bernie Williams Jsy SP/200 6.00 15.00
CJ Chipper Jones Jsy 4.00 10.00
CS Curt Schilling Jsy SP/200 4.00 10.00
DJ Derek Jeter Jsy SP/200 10.00 25.00
EK Eric Karros Jsy 3.00 8.00
GM Greg Maddux Jsy SP/200 6.00 15.00
HN Hideo Nomo Jsy SP/200 6.00 15.00
JB Jeff Bagwell Jsy 4.00 10.00
JD J.D. Drew Jsy 3.00 8.00
JP Jorge Posada Jsy SP/200 6.00 15.00
JT Jim Thome Jsy SP/200 6.00 15.00
KI Kazuhisa Ishii Jsy 3.00 8.00
KS Kazuhiro Sasaki Jsy SP/200 4.00 10.00
KW Kerry Wood Jsy SP/200 4.00 10.00
MG Mark Grace Jsy 4.00 10.00
MP Mike Piazza Jsy SP/200 6.00 15.00
MP Mark Prior Jsy SP/200 6.00 15.00
MT Miguel Tejada Jsy 3.00 8.00
NG N.Garciaparra Jsy SP/200 8.00 20.00
RA Roberto Alomar Bat SP/200 6.00 15.00
RC Roger Clemens Jsy SP/200 8.00 20.00
RJ Randy Johnson Jsy SP/200 6.00 15.00
RV Robin Ventura Jsy 3.00 8.00
TH Todd Helton Jsy SP/200 6.00 15.00

2003 Fleer Double Header Keystone Combinations

STATED ODDS 1:10
1 D.Jeter 2.50 6.00
B.Boone
2 M.Tejada .60 1.50
J.Kent
3 N.Garciaparra .60 1.50
R.Durham
4 O.Vizquel .60 1.50
R.Alomar
5 P.Reese .60 1.50
J.Morgan
6 A.Rodriguez 1.25 3.00
C.Biggio
7 O.Hudson .40 1.00
J.Vidro
8 P.Rizzuto .60 1.50
A.Soriano
9 A.Rodriguez 1.25 3.00
M.Tejada
10 N.Garciaparra 2.50 6.00
D.Jeter

2003 Fleer Double Header Keystone Combinations Memorabilia

STATED ODDS 1:40
SP PRINT RUNS PROVIDED BY FLEER
SP'S ARE NOT SERIAL-NUMBERED
1 R.Alomar Jsy-Vizquel 4.00 10.00
2 C.Biggio Jsy-A.Rod 4.00 10.00
3 B.Boone Jsy-Jeter 3.00 8.00
4 N.Garc Jsy-Durham SP/175 8.00 20.00
5 N.Garc Jsy-Jeter SP/175 8.00 20.00
6 D.Jeter Jsy-Boone SP/175 10.00 25.00
7 D.Jeter Jsy-Nomar SP/175 10.00 25.00
8 J.Kent Jsy-Tejada 3.00 8.00
9 A.Rod Jsy-Biggio SP/200 6.00 15.00
10 A.Rodriguez Bat-Tejada 6.00 15.00
11 A.Soriano Jsy-Rizzuto SP/75 4.00 10.00
12 M.Tejada Jsy-Kent 3.00 8.00
13 M.Tejada Jsy-A.Rod 3.00 8.00
14 J.Vidro Jsy-Hudson 3.00 8.00

2003 Fleer Double Header Let's Play Too

COMPLETE SET (15) 6.00 15.00
STATED ODDS 1:5
1 Chris Snelling .40 1.00
2 Kevin Mench .40 1.00
3 Brett Myers .40 1.00
4 Julius Matos .40 1.00
5 Drew Henson .40 1.00
6 Joe Borchard .40 1.00
7 Felix Escalona .40 1.00
8 Kirk Saarloos .40 1.00
9 Ben Howard .40 1.00
10 Hee Seop Choi .40 1.00
11 Rene Reyes .40 1.00
12 Josh Bard .40 1.00
13 Marlon Byrd .40 1.00
14 Coco Crisp .40 1.00
15 Reed Johnson .40 1.00

2003 Fleer Double Header Matinee Idols

STATED ODDS 1:20
1 Yogi Berra 1.00 2.50
2 Richie Ashburn .60 1.50
3 Whitey Ford .60 1.50
4 Eddie Mathews 1.00 2.50
5 Jim Palmer .60 1.50
6 Al Kaline .60 1.50
7 Brooks Robinson .60 1.50
8 Willie McCovey .60 1.50
9 Billy Williams .60 1.50
10 Willie Stargell .60 1.50
11 Nolan Ryan 3.00 8.00
12 Rod Carew .60 1.50
13 Reggie Jackson .60 1.50
14 Tom Seaver .60 1.50
15 Mike Schmidt 1.50 4.00

2003 Fleer Double Header Twin Bill

STATED ODDS 1:10
1A Barry Bonds 1.50 4.00
1B Lance Berkman .60 1.50
2A Derek Jeter 2.50 6.00
2B Alex Rodriguez 1.25 3.00
3A Roger Clemens 1.25 3.00
3B Pedro Martinez .60 1.50
4A Roberto Alomar .60 1.50
4B Chipper Jones 1.00 2.50
5A Barry Zito .60 1.50
5B Ichiro Suzuki 1.25 3.00
6A Sammy Sosa 1.00 2.50
6B Ken Griffey Jr. 2.00 5.00
7A Bernie Williams .60 1.50
7B Manny Ramirez 1.00 2.50
8A Nomar Garciaparra .60 1.50
8B Derek Jeter 2.50 6.00
9A Randy Johnson 1.00 2.50
9B Greg Maddux 1.25 3.00
10A Albert Pujols 1.25 3.00
10B Adam Dunn .60 1.50

2003 Fleer Double Header Twin Bill Single Swatch

STATED ODDS 1:200
SP PRINT RUNS PROVIDED BY FLEER
SP'S ARE NOT SERIAL-NUMBERED
ALL CARDS FEATURE GAME USED CAPS
1 Roberto Alomar 6.00 15.00
2 Barry Bonds SP/100 10.00 25.00
3 Roger Clemens SP/100 10.00 25.00
4 Adam Dunn SP/100 8.00 20.00
5 Nomar Garciaparra SP/100 10.00 25.00
6 Derek Jeter SP/100 10.00 25.00
7 Randy Johnson SP/100 8.00 20.00
8 Pedro Martinez SP/100 8.00 20.00
9 Manny Ramirez SP/75 8.00 20.00
10 Alex Rodriguez SP/100 10.00 25.00
11 Bernie Williams SP/100 8.00 20.00
12 Barry Zito SP/100 8.00 20.00

1994 Fleer Extra Bases

Measuring 2 1/2" by 4 3/4", this 400 card set was issued by Fleer. Each pack contained at least one insert card. Full-bleed fronts contain a large color photo with the player's name and Extra Bases logo at the bottom. The backs are also full-bleed with a large player photo and statistics. The checklist was arranged alphabetically by team and league starting with the American League. Within each team, the player listings are alphabetical. Rookie Cards include Ray Durham and Chan Ho Park.

COMPLETE SET (400) 15.00 40.00
ONE INSERT PER PACK
1 Brady Anderson .10 .30
2 Harold Baines .10 .30
3 Mike Devereaux .05 .15
4 Sid Fernandez .05 .15
5 Jeffrey Hammonds .05 .15
6 Chris Hoiles .05 .15
7 Ben McDonald .05 .15
8 Mark McLemore .05 .15
9 Mike Mussina .20 .50
10 Mike Oquist .05 .15
11 Rafael Palmeiro .20 .50
12 Cal Ripken 1.00 2.50
13 Chris Sabo .05 .15
14 Lee Smith .10 .30
15 Wes Chamberlain .05 .15
16 Roger Clemens .60 1.50
17 Scott Cooper .05 .15
18 Danny Darwin .05 .15
19 Andre Dawson .10 .30
20 Mike Greenwell .05 .15
21 Tim Naehring .05 .15
22 Otis Nixon .05 .15
23 Jeff Russell .05 .15
24 Ken Ryan .05 .15
25 Aaron Sele .05 .15
26 John Valentin .05 .15
27 Mo Vaughn .10 .30
28 Frank Viola .10 .30
29 Brian Anderson RC .10 .30
30 Chad Curtis .05 .15
31 Chili Davis .10 .30
32 Gary DiSarcina .05 .15
33 Damion Easley .05 .15
34 Jim Edmonds .30 .75
35 Chuck Finley .10 .30
36 Bo Jackson .30 .75
37 Mark Langston .05 .15
38 Harold Reynolds .10 .30
39 Tim Salmon .20 .50
40 Wilson Alvarez .05 .15
41 James Baldwin .05 .15
42 Jason Bere .05 .15
43 Joey Cora .05 .15
44 Ray Durham RC .40 1.00
45 Alex Fernandez .05 .15
46 Julio Franco .10 .30
47 Ozzie Guillen .10 .30
48 Darrin Jackson .05 .15
49 Lance Johnson .05 .15
50 Ron Karkovice .05 .15
51 Jack McDowell .05 .15
52 Tim Raines .10 .30
53 Frank Thomas .30 .75
54 Robin Ventura .10 .30
55 Sandy Alomar Jr. .05 .15
56 Carlos Baerga .05 .15
57 Albert Belle .10 .30
58 Mark Clark .05 .15
59 Wayne Kirby .05 .15
60 Kenny Lofton .10 .30
61 Dennis Martinez .10 .30
62 Jose Mesa .05 .15
63 Jack Morris .10 .30
64 Eddie Murray .30 .75
65 Charles Nagy .05 .15
66 Manny Ramirez .30 .75
67 Paul Shuey .05 .15
68 Paul Sorrento .05 .15
69 Jim Thome .20 .50
70 Omar Vizquel .20 .50
71 Eric Davis .10 .30
72 John Doherty .05 .15
73 Cecil Fielder .10 .30
74 Travis Fryman .10 .30
75 Kirk Gibson .10 .30
76 Gene Harris .05 .15
77 Mike Henneman .05 .15
78 Mike Moore .05 .15
79 Tony Phillips .05 .15
80 Mickey Tettleton .05 .15
81 Alan Trammell .10 .30
82 Lou Whitaker .10 .30
83 Kevin Appier .10 .30
84 Vince Coleman .05 .15
85 David Cone .10 .30
86 Gary Gaetti .10 .30
87 Greg Gagne .05 .15
88 Tom Gordon .05 .15
89 Jeff Granger .05 .15
90 Bob Hamelin .05 .15
91 Dave Henderson .05 .15
92 Felix Jose .05 .15
93 Wally Joyner .10 .30
94 Jose Lind .05 .15
95 Mike Macfarlane .05 .15
96 Brian McRae .05 .15
97 Jeff Montgomery .05 .15
98 Ricky Bones .05 .15
99 Jeff Bronkey .05 .15
100 Alex Diaz RC .05 .15
101 Cal Eldred .05 .15
102 Darryl Hamilton .05 .15
103 Brian Harper .05 .15
104 John Jaha .05 .15
105 Pat Listach .05 .15
106 Dave Nilsson .05 .15
107 Jody Reed .05 .15
108 Kevin Seitzer .05 .15
109 Greg Vaughn .05 .15
110 Turner Ward .05 .15
111 Wes Weger RC .05 .15
112 Bill Wegman .05 .15
113 Rick Aguilera .10 .30
114 Rich Becker .05 .15
115 Alex Cole .05 .15
116 Scott Erickson .05 .15
117 Kent Hrbek .10 .30
118 Chuck Knoblauch .10 .30
119 Scott Leius .05 .15
120 Shane Mack .05 .15
121 Pat Mahomes .05 .15
122 Pat Meares .05 .15
123 Kirby Puckett .30 .75
124 Kevin Tapani .05 .15
125 Matt Walbeck .05 .15
126 Dave Winfield .10 .30
127 Jim Abbott .20 .50
128 Wade Boggs .20 .50
129 Mike Gallego .05 .15
130 Xavier Hernandez .05 .15
131 Pat Kelly .05 .15
132 Jimmy Key .10 .30
133 Don Mattingly .75 2.00
134 Terry Mulholland .05 .15
135 Matt Nokes .05 .15
136 Paul O'Neill .20 .50
137 Melido Perez .05 .15
138 Luis Polonia .05 .15
139 Mike Stanley .05 .15
140 Danny Tartabull .05 .15
141 Randy Velarde .05 .15
142 Bernie Williams .20 .50
143 Mark Acre RC .05 .15
144 Geronimo Berroa .05 .15
145 Mike Bordick .10 .30
146 Scott Brosius .10 .30
147 Ron Darling .05 .15
148 Dennis Eckersley .10 .30
149 Brent Gates .05 .15
150 Rickey Henderson .30 .75
151 Stan Javier .05 .15
152 Steve Karsay .05 .15
153 Mark McGwire .75 2.00
154 Troy Neel .05 .15
155 Ruben Sierra .10 .30
156 Terry Steinbach .05 .15
157 Bill Taylor RC .10 .30
158 Rich Amaral .05 .15
159 Eric Anthony .05 .15
160 Bobby Ayala .05 .15
161 Chris Bosio .05 .15
162 Jay Buhner .10 .30
163 Tim Davis .05 .15
164 Felix Fermin .05 .15
165 Dave Fleming .05 .15
166 Ken Griffey Jr. .60 1.50
167 Reggie Jefferson .05 .15
168 Randy Johnson .30 .75
169 Edgar Martinez .20 .50
170 Tino Martinez .20 .50
171 Bill Risley .05 .15
172 Roger Salkeld .05 .15
173 Mac Suzuki RC .30 .75
174 Dan Wilson .05 .15
175 Kevin Brown .10 .30
176 Jose Canseco .20 .50
177 Will Clark .20 .50
178 Juan Gonzalez .10 .30
179 Rick Helling .05 .15
180 Tom Henke .05 .15
181 Chris James .05 .15
182 Manuel Lee .05 .15
183 Dean Palmer .10 .30
184 Ivan Rodriguez .20 .50
185 Kenny Rogers .10 .30
186 Roberto Alomar .20 .50
187 Pat Borders .05 .15
188 Joe Carter .10 .30
189 Carlos Delgado .20 .50
190 Juan Guzman .05 .15
191 Pat Hentgen .05 .15
192 Paul Molitor .10 .30
193 John Olerud .10 .30
194 Ed Sprague .05 .15
195 Dave Stewart .10 .30
196 Todd Stottlemyre .05 .15
197 Duane Ward .05 .15
198 Devon White .10 .30
199 Steve Avery .05 .15
200 Jeff Blauser .05 .15
201 Tom Glavine .20 .50
202 David Justice .10 .30
203 Mike Kelly .05 .15
204 Roberto Kelly .05 .15
205 Ryan Klesko .10 .30
206 Mark Lemke .05 .15
207 Javier Lopez .10 .30
208 Greg Maddux .50 1.25
209 Fred McGriff .20 .50
210 Greg McMichael .05 .15
211 Kent Mercker .05 .15
212 Terry Pendleton .10 .30
213 John Smoltz .20 .50
214 Tony Tarasco .05 .15
215 Willie Banks .05 .15
216 Steve Buechele .05 .15
217 Shawon Dunston .05 .15
218 Mark Grace .20 .50
219 Brooks Kieschnick RC .05 .15
220 Derrick May .05 .15
221 Randy Myers .10 .30
222 Karl Rhodes .05 .15
223 Rey Sanchez .05 .15
224 Sammy Sosa .30 .75
225 Steve Trachsel .05 .15
226 Rick Wilkins .05 .15
227 Bret Boone .10 .30
228 Jeff Brantley .05 .15
229 Tom Browning .05 .15
230 Hector Carrasco .05 .15
231 Rob Dibble .10 .30
232 Erik Hanson .05 .15
233 Barry Larkin .20 .50
234 Kevin Mitchell .05 .15
235 Hal Morris .05 .15
236 Joe Oliver .05 .15
237 Jose Rijo .05 .15
238 Johnny Ruffin .05 .15
239 Deion Sanders .20 .50
240 Reggie Sanders .10 .30
241 John Smiley .05 .15
242 Dante Bichette .10 .30
243 Ellis Burks .10 .30
244 Andres Galarraga .10 .30
245 Joe Girardi .05 .15
246 Greg Harris .05 .15
247 Charlie Hayes .05 .15
248 Howard Johnson .05 .15
249 Roberto Mejia .05 .15
250 Marcus Moore .05 .15
251 David Nied .05 .15
252 Armando Reynoso .05 .15
253 Bruce Ruffin .05 .15
254 Mark Thompson .05 .15
255 Walt Weiss .05 .15
256 Kurt Abbott RC .05 .15
257 Bret Barberie .05 .15
258 Chuck Carr .05 .15
259 Jeff Conine .10 .30
260 Chris Hammond .05 .15
261 Bryan Harvey .05 .15
262 Jeremy Hernandez .05 .15
263 Charlie Hough .10 .30
264 Dave Magadan .05 .15
265 Benito Santiago .10 .30
266 Gary Sheffield .10 .30
267 David Weathers .05 .15
268 Jeff Bagwell .20 .50
269 Craig Biggio .20 .50
270 Ken Caminiti .10 .30
271 Andujar Cedeno .05 .15
272 Doug Drabek .05 .15
273 Steve Finley .10 .30
274 Luis Gonzalez .10 .30
275 Pete Harnisch .05 .15
276 John Hudek RC .05 .15
277 Darryl Kile .10 .30
278 Orlando Miller .05 .15
279 James Mouton .05 .15
280 Shane Reynolds .05 .15
281 Scott Servais .05 .15
282 Greg Swindell .05 .15
283 Pedro Astacio .05 .15
284 Brett Butler .10 .30
285 Tom Candiotti .05 .15
286 Delino DeShields .05 .15
287 Kevin Gross .05 .15
288 Orel Hershiser .10 .30
289 Eric Karros .10 .30
290 Ramon Martinez .05 .15
291 Raul Mondesi .10 .30
292 Jose Offerman .05 .15
293 Chan Ho Park RC .20 .50
294 Mike Piazza .50 1.25
295 Henry Rodriguez .05 .15
296 Cory Snyder .05 .15
297 Tim Wallach .05 .15
298 Todd Worrell .05 .15
299 Moises Alou .10 .30
300 Sean Berry .05 .15
301 Wil Cordero .05 .15
302 Joey Eischen .05 .15
303 Jeff Fassero .05 .15
304 Darrin Fletcher .05 .15
305 Cliff Floyd .10 .30
306 Marquis Grissom .10 .30
307 Ken Hill .05 .15
308 Mike Lansing .05 .15
309 Pedro Martinez .30 .75
310 Mel Rojas .05 .15
311 Kirk Rueter .05 .15
312 Larry Walker .10 .30
313 John Wetteland .10 .30
314 Rondell White .10 .30
315 Bobby Bonilla .10 .30
316 John Franco .10 .30
317 Dwight Gooden .10 .30
318 Todd Hundley .05 .15
319 Bobby Jones .05 .15
320 Jeff Kent .20 .50
321 Kevin McReynolds .05 .15
322 Bill Pulsipher .05 .15
323 Bret Saberhagen .10 .30
324 David Segui .05 .15
325 Pete Smith .05 .15
326 Kelly Stinnett RC .05 .15
327 Ryan Thompson .05 .15
328 Jose Vizcaino .05 .15
329 Ricky Bottalico RC .05 .15
330 Darren Daulton .10 .30
331 Mariano Duncan .05 .15
332 Lenny Dykstra .10 .30
333 Tommy Greene .05 .15
334 Billy Hatcher .05 .15
335 Dave Hollins .05 .15
336 Pete Incaviglia .05 .15
337 Danny Jackson .05 .15
338 Doug Jones .05 .15
339 Ricky Jordan .05 .15
340 John Kruk .10 .30
341 Curt Schilling .10 .30
342 Kevin Stocker .05 .15
343 Jay Bell .10 .30
344 Steve Cooke .05 .15
345 Carlos Garcia .05 .15
346 Brian Hunter .05 .15
347 Jeff King .05 .15
348 Al Martin .05 .15
349 Orlando Merced .05 .15
350 Denny Neagle .05 .15
351 Don Slaught .05 .15
352 Andy Van Slyke .20 .50
353 Paul Wagner .05 .15
354 Rick White RC .05 .15
355 Luis Alicea .05 .15
356 Rene Arocha .05 .15
357 Rheal Cormier .05 .15
358 Bernard Gilkey .05 .15
359 Gregg Jefferies .05 .15
360 Ray Lankford .10 .30
361 Tom Pagnozzi .05 .15
362 Mike Perez .05 .15
363 Ozzie Smith .50 1.25
364 Bob Tewksbury .05 .15
365 Mark Whiten .05 .15
366 Todd Zeile .10 .30
367 Andy Ashby .05 .15
368 Brad Ausmus .20 .50
369 Derek Bell .05 .15
370 Andy Benes .05 .15
371 Archi Cianfrocco .05 .15
372 Tony Gwynn .40 1.00
373 Trevor Hoffman .20 .50
374 Tim Hyers RC .05 .15
375 Pedro A.Martinez RC .05 .15
376 Phil Plantier .05 .15
377 Bip Roberts .05 .15
378 Scott Sanders .05 .15
379 Dave Staton .05 .15
380 Wally Whitehurst .05 .15
381 Rod Beck .05 .15
382 Todd Benzinger .05 .15
383 Barry Bonds .75 2.00
384 John Burkett .05 .15
385 Royce Clayton .05 .15
386 Bryan Hickerson .05 .15
387 Mike Jackson .05 .15
388 Darren Lewis .05 .15

389 Kirt Manwaring .05 .15
390 Willie McGee .10 .30
391 Mark Portugal .05 .15
392 Bill Swift .05 .15
393 Robby Thompson .05 .15
394 Salomon Torres .05 .15
395 Matt Williams .10 .30
396 Checklist .05 .15
397 Checklist .05 .15
398 Checklist .05 .15
399 Checklist .05 .15
400 Checklist .05 .15
P1 Paul Molitor Promo .75 2.00

1994 Fleer Extra Bases Game Breakers

COMPLETE SET (30) 8.00 20.00
STATED ODDS 3:8
1 Jeff Bagwell .40 1.00
2 Rod Beck .20 .50
3 Albert Belle .30 .75
4 Barry Bonds 1.50 4.00
5 Jose Canseco .40 1.00
6 Joe Carter .30 .75
7 Roger Clemens 1.25 3.00
8 Darren Daulton .30 .75
9 Lenny Dykstra .30 .75
10 Cecil Fielder .30 .75
11 Tom Glavine .40 1.00
12 Juan Gonzalez .30 .75
13 Mark Grace .40 1.00
14 Ken Griffey Jr. 1.25 3.00
15 David Justice .30 .75
16 Greg Maddux 1.00 2.50
17 Don Mattingly 1.50 4.00
18 Ben McDonald .20 .50
19 Fred McGriff .40 1.00
20 Paul Molitor .30 .75
21 John Olerud .30 .75
22 Mike Piazza 1.00 2.50
23 Kirby Puckett .60 1.50
24 Cal Ripken 2.00 5.00
25 Tim Salmon .40 1.00
26 Gary Sheffield .30 .75
27 Frank Thomas .60 1.50
28 Mo Vaughn .30 .75
29 Matt Williams .30 .75
30 Dave Winfield .30 .75

1994 Fleer Extra Bases Major League Hopefuls

COMPLETE SET (10) 3.00 8.00
STATED ODDS 1:8
1 James Baldwin .20 .50
2 Ricky Bottalico .20 .50
3 Ray Durham .60 1.50
4 Joey Eischen .20 .50
5 Brooks Kieschnick .20 .50
6 Orlando Miller .20 .50
7 Bill Pulsipher .20 .50
8 Mac Suzuki .60 1.50
9 Mark Thompson .20 .50
10 Wes Weger .20 .50

1994 Fleer Extra Bases Pitchers Duel

COMPLETE SET (10) 5.00 12.00
SETS WERE AVAILABLE VIA WRAPPER OFFER
1 R.Clemens 1.25 3.00
J.McDowell
2 B.McDonald .40 1.00
R.Johnson
3 David Cone .30 .75
Jimmy Key
4 M.Mussina .40 1.00
A.Sele
5 C.Finley .30 .75
W.Alvarez
6 C.Schilling .30 .75
S.Avery
7 G.Maddux 1.00 2.50
J.Rijo
8 B.Tewks .30 .75
B.Saberhagen
9 T.Glavine .40 1.00
B.Swift
10 D.Drabek .30 .75
O.Hershiser

1994 Fleer Extra Bases Rookie Standouts

COMPLETE SET (20) 5.00 12.00
STATED ODDS 1:4
1 Kurt Abbott .20 .50
2 Brian Anderson .30 .75
3 Hector Carrasco .20 .50
4 Tim Davis .20 .50
5 Carlos Delgado .40 1.00
6 Cliff Floyd .30 .75
7 Bob Hamelin .20 .50
8 Jeffrey Hammonds .20 .50
9 Rick Helling .20 .50
10 Steve Karsay .20 .50
11 Ryan Klesko .30 .75
12 Javier Lopez .30 .75
13 Raul Mondesi .30 .75
14 James Mouton .20 .50
15 Chan Ho Park .40 1.00
16 Manny Ramirez .60 1.50
17 Tony Tarasco .20 .50
18 Steve Trachsel .20 .50
19 Rick White .20 .50
20 Rondell White .30 .75

1994 Fleer Extra Bases Second Year Stars

COMPLETE SET (20) 4.00 10.00
STATED ODDS 1:4
1 Bobby Ayala .20 .50
2 Jason Bere .20 .50
3 Chuck Carr .20 .50
4 Jeff Conine .30 .75
5 Steve Cooke .20 .50
6 Wil Cordero .20 .50
7 Carlos Garcia .20 .50
8 Brent Gates .20 .50
9 Trevor Hoffman .40 1.00
10 Wayne Kirby .20 .50
11 Al Martin .20 .50
12 Pedro Martinez .60 1.50
13 Greg McMichael .20 .50
14 Troy Neel .20 .50
15 David Nied .20 .50
16 Mike Piazza 1.00 2.50
17 Kirk Rueter .20 .50
18 Tim Salmon .40 1.00
19 Aaron Sele .20 .50
20 Kevin Stocker .20 .50

2002 Fleer Fall Classics

COMPLETE SET (100) 12.50 30.00
COMMON CARD (1-100) .20 .50
COMMON SP 2.00 5.00
SP STATED ODDS 1:18 HOBBY, 1:24 RETAIL
1 Rabbit Maranville .20 .50
2 Tris Speaker .30 .75
3 Harmon Killebrew .50 1.25
4 Lou Gehrig 1.00 2.50
5 Lou Boudreau .20 .50
6 Al Kaline .50 1.25
7A Paul Molitor Blue Jays .20 .50
7B Paul Molitor Brewers SP 2.00 5.00
8 Cal Ripken 1.50 4.00
9 Yogi Berra .50 1.25
10 Phil Rizzuto .30 .75
11A Luis Aparicio W.Sox .20 .50
11B Luis Aparicio O's SP 2.00 5.00
12 Stan Musial .75 2.00
13 Mel Ott .50 1.25
14 Larry Doby .20 .50
15 Ozzie Smith .75 2.00
16A Babe Ruth Yankees 2.00 5.00
16B Babe Ruth Red Sox SP 6.00 15.00
17A Red Schoendienst Braves .20 .50
17B Red Schoendienst Cards SP 2.00 5.00
18 Rollie Fingers .20 .50
19 Thurman Munson .50 1.25
20 Lou Brock .30 .75
21A Paul O'Neill Yankees .30 .75
21B Paul O'Neill Reds SP 3.00 8.00
22 Jim Palmer .20 .50
23 Kirby Puckett .50 1.25
24A Tony Perez Reds .20 .50
24B Tony Perez Phils SP 2.00 5.00
25 Don Larsen .20 .50
26A Steve Garvey Dodgers .20 .50
26B Steve Garvey Padres SP 2.00 5.00
27A Jim Hunter A's .30 .75
27B Jim Hunter Yankees SP 3.00 8.00
28 Juan Marichal .20 .50
29 Pee Wee Reese .30 .75
30 Orlando Cepeda .20 .50
31 Goose Gossage .20 .50
32 Ray Knight .20 .50
33 Eddie Murray .50 1.25
34 Nolan Ryan 1.25 3.00
35 Alan Trammell .20 .50
36 Grover Alexander .50 1.25
37 Joe Carter .20 .50
38 Rogers Hornsby .50 1.25
39 Jimmie Foxx .50 1.25
40 Mike Schmidt 1.00 2.50
41 Eddie Mathews .50 1.25
42 Jackie Robinson .50 1.25
43A Eddie Collins A's .20 .50
43B Eddie Collins White Sox SP 2.00 5.00
44 Willie McCovey .20 .50
45 Bob Gibson .30 .75
46A Keith Hernandez Mets .20 .50
46B Keith Hernandez Cards SP 2.00 5.00
47 Brooks Robinson .30 .75
48 Mordecai Brown .20 .50
49 Gary Carter .20 .50
50A Kirk Gibson Dodgers .20 .50
50B Kirk Gibson Tigers SP 2.00 5.00
51 Johnny Mize .20 .50
52 Johnny Podres .20 .50
53 Darrell Porter .20 .50
54 Willie Stargell .30 .75
55A Lenny Dykstra Mets .20 .50
55B Lenny Dykstra Phillies SP 2.00 5.00
56 Christy Mathewson .50 1.25
57 Walter Johnson .50 1.25
58 Whitey Ford .30 .75
59 Lefty Grove .30 .75
60 Duke Snider .30 .75
61 Cy Young .50 1.25
62A Dave Winfield Blue Jays .20 .50
62B Dave Winfield Yankees SP 2.00 5.00
63 Robin Yount .50 1.25
64 Fred Lynn .20 .50
65 Ty Cobb .75 2.00
66 Joe Morgan .20 .50
67 Bill Mazeroski .20 .50
68 Frank Baker .20 .50
69 Chief Bender .20 .50
70 Carlton Fisk .30 .75
71 Jerry Coleman .20 .50
72 Frankie Frisch .20 .50
73A Wade Boggs Red Sox .30 .75
73B Wade Boggs Yankees SP 3.00 8.00
74 Johnny Bench .50 1.25
75A Roger Maris Yankees .50 1.25
75B Roger Maris Cards SP 4.00 10.00
76 Dom DiMaggio .20 .50
77 George Brett 1.00 2.50
78A Dave Parker Pirates .20 .50
78B Dave Parker A's SP 2.00 5.00
79 Hank Greenberg .50 1.25
80 Pepper Martin .30 .75
81A Graig Nettles Yankees .20 .50
81B Graig Nettles Padres SP 2.00 5.00
82 Dennis Eckersley .20 .50
83 Don Clendenon .20 .50
84 Tom Seaver .30 .75
85 Honus Wagner .75 2.00
86A Reggie Jackson Yankees .30 .75
86B Reggie Jackson A's SP 3.00 8.00
87A Goose Goslin Senators .20 .50
87B Goose Goslin Tigers SP 2.00 5.00
88 Tony Kubek .30 .75
89 Roy Campanella .50 1.25
90A Steve Carlton Phillies .20 .50
90B Steve Carlton Cards SP 2.00 5.00
91 L.Gehrig .60 1.50
M.Ott
92 E.Collins .20 .50
J.Morgan
93 G.Brett 1.00 2.50
M.Schmidt
94 C.Ripken 1.00 2.50
O.Smith
95 T.Munson .50 1.25
J.Bench
96 Stargell .50 1.25
Musial
Martin
97 Ruth 1.00 2.50
Puckett
Reggie
98 C.Young .30 .75
B.Gibson
99 W.Ford .30 .75
S.Carlton
100 P.Molitor .30 .75
L.Brock

2002 Fleer Fall Classics Championship Gold

*GOLD POST-WAR: 8X TO 20X BASIC
*GOLD PRE-WAR: 5X TO 12X BASIC
*GOLD POST-WAR: .75X TO 2X BASIC SP's
*GOLD PRE-WAR: .5X TO 1.2X BASIC SP's
RANDOM INSERTS IN PACKS
STATED PRINT RUN 50 SERIAL #'d SETS

2002 Fleer Fall Classics HOF Plaque

COMPLETE SET (30) 50.00 120.00
RANDOM INSERTS IN PACKS
STATED PRINT RUN BASED ON HOF YEAR
1 Babe Ruth/1936 6.00 15.00
2 Christy Mathewson/1936 2.00 5.00
3 Honus Wagner/1936 3.00 8.00
4 Ty Cobb/1936 3.00 8.00
5 Walter Johnson/1936 2.00 5.00
6 Cy Young/1937 2.00 5.00
7 Tris Speaker/1937 1.25 3.00
8 Eddie Collins/1939 1.25 3.00
9 Lou Gehrig/1939 4.00 10.00
10 Jimmie Foxx/1951 2.00 5.00
11 Jackie Robinson/1962 2.00 5.00
12 Stan Musial/1969 3.00 8.00
13 Yogi Berra/1972 2.00 5.00
14 Duke Snider/1980 1.25 3.00
15 Juan Marichal/1983 1.25 3.00
16 Luis Aparicio/1984 1.25 3.00
17 Pee Wee Reese/1984 1.25 3.00
18 Willie McCovey/1986 1.25 3.00
19 Willie Stargell/1988 1.25 3.00
20 Johnny Bench/1989 2.00 5.00
21 Joe Morgan/1990 1.25 3.00
22 Jim Palmer/1990 1.25 3.00
23 Tom Seaver/1992 1.25 3.00
24 Reggie Jackson/1993 1.25 3.00
25 Steve Carlton/1994 1.25 3.00
26 George Brett/1999 4.00 10.00
27 Nolan Ryan/1999 5.00 12.00
28 Robin Yount/1999 2.00 5.00
29 Kirby Puckett/2001 2.00 5.00
30 Ozzie Smith/2002 3.00 8.00

2002 Fleer Fall Classics MVP Collection Game Used

STATED ODDS 1:100 HOBBY, 1:240 RETAIL
SP PRINT RUNS PROVIDED BY FLEER
SP'S ARE NOT SERIAL-NUMBERED
AT Alan Trammell Jsy 4.00 10.00
BR Brooks Robinson Bat SP/250 6.00 15.00
DC Donn Clendenon Pants 4.00 10.00
DP Darrell Porter Bat SP/250 4.00 10.00
JB Johnny Bench Jsy SP/200 10.00 25.00
PM Paul Molitor Bat SP/250 4.00 10.00
RF Rollie Fingers Jsy SP/200 4.00 10.00
RJNY Reg Jackson Yanks Jsy 6.00 15.00
RJOK Reg Jackson A's Jsy SP/50 12.50 30.00
RK Ray Knight Bat 4.00 10.00
WS Willie Stargell Jsy SP/200 6.00 15.00

2002 Fleer Fall Classics MVP Collection Game Used Patch

RANDOM INSERTS IN PACKS
STATED PRINT RUNS BASED ON WS MVP
AT Alan Trammell Jsy /84 10.00 25.00
BR Brooks Robinson Bat/70 12.00 30.00
JB Johnny Bench Jsy/76 10.00 25.00
RF Rollie Fingers Jsy/74 10.00 25.00
RJNY Reg Jackson Yanks Jsy/77 8.00 20.00

2002 Fleer Fall Classics October Legends Game Used

STATED ODDS 1:48 HOBBY, 1:200 RETAIL
SP PRINT RUNS PROVIDED BY FLEER
SP'S ARE NOT SERIAL-NUMBERED
DE Dennis Eckersley Jsy 4.00 10.00
DP Dave Parker Bat SP/50 8.00 20.00
DP Darrell Porter Bat SP/150 4.00 10.00
DS Duke Snider Pants SP/200 8.00 20.00
EM Eddie Murray Jsy 6.00 15.00
GB George Brett Jsy 10.00 25.00
GC Gary Carter Jsy SP/200 6.00 15.00
JM Joe Morgan Bat 4.00 10.00
JMA Juan Marichal Jsy 4.00 10.00
KH Keith Hernandez Bat SP/100 6.00 15.00
KHJ Keith Hernandez Jsy SP/150 6.00 15.00
LD Lenny Dykstra Bat SP/200 6.00 15.00
PM Pepper Martin Bat 10.00 25.00
PM Paul Molitor Bat SP/150 6.00 15.00
PO Paul O'Neill Jsy 6.00 15.00
PWR Pee Wee Pants SP/200 8.00 20.00
RF Rollie Fingers Jsy 4.00 10.00
RM Roger Maris Jsy 15.00 40.00
RS Red Schoen Pants SP/210 6.00 15.00
RY Robin Yount Bat 6.00 15.00
TP Tony Perez Jsy 4.00 10.00
WB Wade Boggs Jsy 6.00 15.00
WM Willie McCovey Jsy SP/150 6.00 15.00
WS Willie Stargell Jsy SP/225 8.00 20.00

2002 Fleer Fall Classics October Legends Game Used Gold

*GOLD: .6X TO 1.5X BASIC OCT.LGD
*GOLD: .5X TO 1.2X BASIC OCT.LGD SP
*GOLD: .4X TO 1X BASIC OCT.LGD SP/50
RANDOM INSERTS IN PACKS
STATED PRINT RUN 100 SERIAL #'d SETS

2002 Fleer Fall Classics October Legends Game Used Dual

STATED ODDS 1:60 HOBBY, 1:244 RETAIL
SP PRINT RUNS PROVIDED BY FLEER
SP'S ARE NOT SERIAL-NUMBERED
1 Ripken Jsy/Murray Jsy/100 12.00 30.00
2 Ripken Bat/Murray Jsy/200 12.00 30.00
3 Snider Pnts/Reese Pnts/200 15.00 40.00
4 Brett Jsy/Porter Bat/150 12.00 30.00
5 G.Carter Jsy/K.Hern Bat 8.00 20.00
6 Marichal Jsy/McCovey Jsy 8.00 20.00
7 Morgan Bat/T.Perez Jsy 8.00 20.00
8 K.Hern Jsy/R.Schoen Pants 8.00 20.00
9 Dykstra Bat/G.Carter Jsy 8.00 20.00
10 P.Martin Bat/Frisch Pants 20.00 50.00
11 Fingers Jsy/Eckersley Jsy 8.00 20.00
12 Maris Jsy/O'Neill Jsy/200 10.00 25.00
13 Yount Bat/Molitor Bat/150 20.00 50.00
14 Boggs Jsy/K.Hernandez Jsy 8.00 20.00
15 Stargell Jsy/Parker Bat 8.00 20.00

2002 Fleer Fall Classics Pennant Chase Game Used

STATED ODDS 1:48 HOBBY, 1:200 RETAIL
SP PRINT RUNS PROVIDED BY FLEER
SP'S ARE NOT SERIAL-NUMBERED
CF Carlton Fisk Bat 6.00 15.00
DW Dave Winfield Bat 6.00 15.00
FL Fred Lynn Bat 6.00 15.00
RJ Reggie Jackson Jsy 6.00 15.00
TM Thurman Munson Bat 10.00 25.00
WB Wade Boggs Jsy 6.00 15.00
YB Yogi Berra Pants SP/150 10.00 25.00

2002 Fleer Fall Classics Pennant Chase Game Used Dual

RANDOM INSERTS IN PACKS
STATED PRINT RUN 50 SERIAL #'d SETS
CFRJ Fisk Bat/Jackson Jsy 15.00 40.00
FLTM Lynn Bat/Munson Bat 30.00 60.00
WBDW Boggs Jsy/Winf Bat 15.00 40.00

2002 Fleer Fall Classics Rival Factions

1-24 PRINT RUN 1000 SERIAL #'d SETS
25-34 PRINT RUN 500 SERIAL #'d SETS
37-43 PRINT RUN 50 SERIAL #'d SETS
1 C.Fisk 2.50 6.00
T.Munson
2 F.Baker 8.00 20.00
B.Ruth
3 J.Foxx 4.00 10.00
L.Gehrig
4 S.Carlton 6.00 15.00
N.Ryan
5 M.Brown 4.00 10.00
H.Wagner
6 F.Frisch 1.50 4.00
D.Snider
7 O.Smith 4.00 10.00
A.Trammell
8 L.Doby 2.50 6.00
J.Robinson
9 S.Garvey 1.50 4.00
T.Perez
10 J.Bench 2.50 6.00
W.Stargell
11 T.Cobb 4.00 10.00
E.Collins
12 R.Jackson 1.50 4.00
B.Robinson
13 Y.Berra 2.50 6.00
R.Campanella
14 O.Cepeda 1.50 4.00
W.McCovey
15 A.Kaline 2.50 6.00
J.Palmer
16 G.Brett 4.00 10.00
K.Puckett
17 B.Gibson 1.50 4.00
T.Seaver
18 C.Ripken 8.00 20.00
R.Yount
19 J.Mize 2.50 6.00
M.Ott
20 S.Musial 4.00 10.00
P.Reese
21 H.Greenberg 2.50 6.00
L.Grove
22 D.Parker 5.00 12.00
M.Schmidt
23 B.Mazeroski 1.50 4.00
J.Morgan
24 J.Bench 2.50 6.00
C.Fisk
25 G.Brett 6.00 15.00
M.Schmidt
26 P.Reese 2.00 5.00
P.Rizzuto
27 C.Ripken 10.00 25.00
A.Trammell
28 C.Hunter 2.00 5.00
T.Seaver
29 T.Cobb 5.00 12.00
H.Wagner
30 S.Carlton 2.00 5.00
L.Grove
31 O.Smith 5.00 12.00
R.Yount
32 F.Frisch 2.00 5.00
J.Morgan
33 H.Greenberg 3.00 8.00
J.Robinson
34 J.Foxx 3.00 8.00
P.Martin
35 L.Gehrig 40.00 80.00
C.Ripken
36 O.Smith 15.00 40.00
H.Wagner
37 R.Jackson 10.00 25.00
D.Winfield
38 T.Cobb 15.00 40.00
R.Hornsby
39 B.Ruth 30.00 60.00
R.Maris
40 Y.Berra 10.00 25.00
T.Munson
41 N.Ryan 30.00 60.00
T.Seaver
42 J.Morgan 10.00 25.00
J.Robinson
43 J.Foxx 10.00 25.00
M.Ott

2002 Fleer Fall Classics Rival Factions Game Used

STATED ODDS 1:32 HOBBY, 1:121 RETAIL
SP PRINT RUNS PROVIDED BY FLEER
SP'S ARE NOT SERIAL-NUMBERED
NO PRICING ON QTY OF 25 OR LESS
1 Frank Baker Bat-Ruth 15.00 40.00
2 Johnny Bench Jsy-Fisk/75 12.50 30.00
3 Johnny Bench Jsy-Starg/55 12.50 30.00
4 Yogi Berra Pants-Campy/225 8.00 20.00
5 Yogi Berra Pants-Munson 8.00 20.00
6 George Brett Jsy-Kirby/200 10.00 25.00
7 George Brett Jsy-Schmidt 10.00 25.00
8 Steve Carlton Pants-Grove 6.00 15.00
9 S.Carlton Pants-Ryan/225 8.00 20.00
10 Orl Cepeda Bat-McCovey 6.00 15.00
11 Larry Doby Bat-Jackie 12.50 30.00
12 Carlton Fisk Jsy-Bench/200 8.00 20.00
13 Carlt Fisk Jsy-Munson/200 8.00 20.00
14 Jimmie Foxx Bat-Gehrig/100 20.00 50.00
15 Jimmie Foxx Bat-Martin/50 12.50 30.00
16 Jimmie Foxx Bat-Ott/100 20.00 50.00
17 Fra Frisch Pants-Morgan/75 12.50 30.00
18 Fra Frisch Pants-Snider/200 10.00 25.00
19 Steve Garvey Jsy-Perez 6.00 15.00
20 H.Greenberg Bat-Grove/45 20.00 50.00
21 H.Greenberg Bat-Jackie/75 15.00 40.00
22 Jim Hunter Jsy-Seaver 8.00 20.00
23 Reg Jackson Jsy-Brooks/50 12.50 30.00
24 Reg Jackson Jsy-Winf/100 10.00 25.00
25 Roger Maris Jsy-Ruth 12.50 30.00
26 Pepper Martin Bat-Foxx/50 12.50 30.00
27 W.McCovey Jsy-Cepeda/200 8.00 20.00
28 Johnny Mize Bat-Ott/95 6.00 15.00
29 Joe Morgan Pants-Frisch 8.00 20.00
30 Joe Morgan Pants-J.Rob/275 8.00 20.00
31 Joe Morgan Pants-Maz/200 8.00 20.00
32 Thur Munson Jsy-Berra/50 15.00 40.00
33 Thur Munson Jsy-Fisk/50 15.00 40.00
34 Jim Palmer Pants-Kaline 6.00 15.00
35 Dave Parker Bat-Schm/100 6.00 15.00
36 Tony Perez Jsy-Garvey/250 8.00 20.00
37 Kirby Puckett Bat-Brett/250 8.00 20.00
38 Pee Wee Pants-Musial 8.00 20.00
39 Pee Wee Pants-Rizzuto/250 8.00 20.00
40 Cal Ripken Jsy-Gehrig 8.00 20.00
41 Cal Ripken Jsy-Trammell/225 15.00 40.00
42 Cal Ripken Jsy-Yount/200 15.00 40.00
43 Brooks Robinson Bat-Reggie 8.00 20.00
44 J.Robinson Pants-Doby/50 20.00 50.00
45 J.Robinson Pants-G'berg/75 20.00 50.00
46 J.Robinson Pants-Morg/75 20.00 50.00
47 Nolan Ryan Jsy-Carlton/200 15.00 40.00
49 Nolan Ryan Jsy-Carlton/200 15.00 40.00
50 Nolan Ryan Jsy-Seaver/200 8.00 20.00
51 Tom Seaver Pants-Gibson 8.00 20.00
52 Tom Seaver Pants-Hunt/225 8.00 20.00
53 Tom Seaver Pants-Ryan/150 8.00 20.00
54 Ozzie Smith Jsy-Tram/100 10.00 25.00
55 Ozzie Smith Jsy-Wagner 8.00 20.00
56 Ozzie Smith Jsy-Yount/175 8.00 20.00
57 D.Snider Pants-Frisch/200 8.00 20.00
58 Willie Stargell Jsy-Bench/200 8.00 20.00
59 Alan Trammell Jsy-Ozzie/250 8.00 20.00
60 Alan Trammell Jsy-Ripken 6.00 15.00
61 D.Winfield Jsy-Reggie/100 6.00 15.00
62 Robin Yount Jsy-Ozzie/250 8.00 20.00
63 Robin Yount Jsy-Ripken/200 8.00 20.00

2002 Fleer Fall Classics Rival Factions Game Used Dual

STATED ODDS 1:60 HOBBY, 1:244 RETAIL
SP PRINT RUNS PROVIDED BY FLEER
SP'S ARE NOT SERIAL-NUMBERED
2 Fisk Jsy/Munson Jsy 12.00 30.00
3 Hunter Jsy/Seaver Pants 10.00 25.00
4 Ripken Jsy/Trammell Jsy 10.00 25.00
5 Ripken Jsy/Yount Jsy 10.00 25.00
7 Frisch Pants/Snider Pants 10.00 25.00
8 Frisch Pants/Morgan Pants 10.00 25.00
9 Brett Jsy/Puckett Bat 12.00 30.00
10 G'berg Bat/Jackie Pants/50 25.00 60.00
11 Bench Jsy/Fisk Jsy 12.00 30.00
12 Bench Jsy/Stargell Jsy 12.00 30.00
13 Foxx Bat/P.Martin Bat/200 12.00 30.00
14 Morg Pants/J.Rob Pants/50 12.00 30.00
15 Doby Bat/J.Rob Pants/75 20.00 50.00
16 Ryan Jsy/Seaver Pants 12.00 30.00
17 Cepeda Bat/McCov Jsy/200 10.00 25.00
18 Ozzie Jsy/Trammell Jsy 15.00 40.00
19 Ozzie Jsy/Yount Jsy 12.00 30.00
20 Reggie Jsy/Brooks Bat 10.00 25.00
21 Reggie Jsy/Winfield Jsy/150 10.00 25.00
22 Carlton Pants/Ryan Jsy 10.00 25.00
23 Garvey Jsy/Perez Jsy 8.00 20.00
24 Berra Pants/Munson Jsy 15.00 40.00

2002 Fleer Fall Classics Rival Factions Game Used Dual Patch

RANDOM INSERTS IN PACKS
STATED PRINT RUN 50 SERIAL #'d SETS
CFTM C.Fisk/T.Munson 30.00 60.00
CRAT C.Ripken/A.Trammell 30.00 60.00
CRRY C.Ripken/R.Yount 30.00 60.00
JBCF J.Bench/C.Fisk 30.00 60.00
JBWS J.Bench/W.Stargell 30.00 60.00
OSAT O.Smith/A.Trammell 30.00 60.00
OSRY O.Smith/R.Yount 30.00 60.00
RJDW R.Jackson/D.Winfield 15.00 40.00
SCNR S.Carlton/N.Ryan 60.00 120.00
SGTP S.Garvey/T.Perez 15.00 40.00

2002 Fleer Fall Classics Series of Champions

COMPLETE SET (19) 15.00 40.00
STATED ODDS 1:6 HOBBY, 1:6 RETAIL
1 Yogi Berra 1.25 3.00
2 Wade Boggs .75 2.00
3 Dave Parker .75 2.00
4 Joe Carter .75 2.00
5 Kirk Gibson .75 2.00
6 Reggie Jackson .75 2.00
7 Tony Kubek .75 2.00
8 Don Larsen .75 2.00
9 Bill Mazeroski .75 2.00
10 Eddie Murray 1.25 3.00
11 Graig Nettles .75 2.00
12 Tony Perez .75 2.00
13 Phil Rizzuto .75 2.00
14 Mike Schmidt 2.50 6.00
15 Red Schoendienst .75 2.00
16 Duke Snider .75 2.00
17 Ty Cobb 2.00 5.00
18 Lou Gehrig 2.50 6.00
19 Babe Ruth 4.00 10.00

2002 Fleer Fall Classics Series of Champions Game Used

STATED ODDS 1:36 HOBBY, 1:135 RETAIL
SP PRINT RUNS PROVIDED BY FLEER
SP'S ARE NOT SERIAL-NUMBERED
DP Dave Parker Bat 4.00 10.00
DS Duke Snider Bat 6.00 15.00
EM Eddie Murray Bat 6.00 15.00
GN Graig Nettles Bat 4.00 10.00
JC Joe Carter Bat 4.00 10.00
KG Kirk Gibson Bat 4.00 10.00
RJ Reggie Jackson Bat 6.00 15.00
RS Red Schoendienst Pants 4.00 10.00
TK Tony Kubek Bat 6.00 15.00
TP Tony Perez Bat 4.00 10.00
WB Wade Boggs Jsy 6.00 15.00
YB Yogi Berra Bat 6.00 15.00

2002 Fleer Fall Classics Series of Champions Game Used Gold

*GOLD: .6X TO 1.5X BASIC CHAMPIONS
RANDOM INSERTS IN PACKS
STATED PRINT RUN 100 SERIAL #'d SETS
BR Babe Ruth Bat 100.00 200.00

2003 Fleer Fall Classics

COMP. SET w/o SP's (87) 10.00 25.00
COMMON CARD (1-87) .20 .50
COMMON SP1 .60 1.50
SP1 STATED ODDS 1:18 H, 1:36 R
COMMON SP2 .60 1.50
SP2 UNLISTED STARS 1.50 4.00
SP2 STATED ODDS 1:1 LGD STAR
1 Rod Carew .30 .75
2 Bobby Doerr .30 .75
3A Eddie Mathews Braves .50 1.25
3B Eddie Mathews Tigers SP2 1.50 4.00
4 Tom Seaver .30 .75
5 Lou Brock .30 .75
6A Nolan Ryan Mets 1.50 4.00
6B Nolan Ryan Astros SP2 5.00 12.00
7 Pee Wee Reese .30 .75
8 Robin Yount .50 1.25
9 Bob Feller .30 .75
10 Harmon Killebrew .50 1.25
11 Hal Newhouser .30 .75
12 Al Kaline .50 1.25
13 Hoyt Wilhelm .30 .75
14 Early Wynn .30 .75
15A Yogi Berra Yanks .50 1.25
15B Yogi Berra Mets SP2 1.50 4.00
16 Billy Williams .30 .75
17 Rollie Fingers .30 .75
18A Sparky Anderson Tigers .30 .75
18B Sparky Anderson Reds SP1 1.00 2.50
19 Lou Boudreau .30 .75
20 Warren Spahn .30 .75
21 Enos Slaughter .30 .75
22 Luis Aparicio .30 .75
23 Phil Rizzuto .30 .75
24 Willie McCovey .30 .75
25 Joe Morgan .30 .75
26 Alan Trammell .30 .75
27 Eddie Plank .30 .75
28 Lefty Grove .30 .75
29 Walter Johnson .50 1.25
30 Roy Campanella .50 1.25
31 Carlton Fisk .30 .75
32 Bill Dickey .20 .50
33A Rogers Hornsby Cards .30 .75
33B Rogers Hornsby Cubs SP1 1.00 2.50
34 Wade Boggs .30 .75
35 Chick Stahl .20 .50
36A Don Drysdale Brooklyn .30 .75
36B Don Drysdale LA SP1 1.00 2.50
37 Jose Canseco .30 .75
38A Roger Maris Cards .50 1.25
38B Roger Maris Yanks SP2 1.50 4.00
39 Cal Ripken 1.50 4.00
40A Kiki Cuyler Pirates .30 .75
40B Kiki Cuyler Cubs SP1 1.00 2.50
41 Hank Greenberg .50 1.25
42 Bud Harrelson .20 .50
43A Eddie Murray O's .30 .75
43B Eddie Murray Indians SP2 1.00 2.50
44 Jimmy Sebring .20 .50
45 Ozzie Smith .60 1.50
46A Darryl Strawberry Mets .20 .50
46B Darryl Strawberry Yanks SP2 .60 1.50
47 Dave Parker .20 .50
48A Gil Hodges Dodgers .30 .75
48B Gil Hodges Mets SP2 1.00 2.50
49 Joe Carter .20 .50
50A Leo Durocher Cards .20 .50
50B Leo Durocher Giants SP1 .60 1.50
51 Christy Mathewson .50 1.25
52 Elston Howard .20 .50
53 Hughie Jennings .40 1.00
54 Nellie Fox .30 .75
55 Carl Yastrzemski .75 2.00
56A Frank Robinson O's .30 .75
56B Frank Robinson Reds SP2 1.00 2.50
57 Dennis Eckersley .30 .75
58A Grover Alexander Phils .30 .75
58B Grover Alexander Cards SP1 1.00 2.50
59 Carl Hubbell .30 .75
60 Dave Winfield .30 .75
61 Honus Wagner .50 1.25
62A Duke Snider Brooklyn .30 .75
62B Duke Snider LA SP2 1.00 2.50
63A Frankie Frisch Giants .30 .75
63B Frankie Frisch Cards SP1 1.00 2.50
64 Dizzy Dean DF .30 .75
65 Bob Gibson DF .30 .75
66 Johnny Bench DF .50 1.25
67 Ty Cobb DF .75 2.00
68 Lou Gehrig DF 1.00 2.50
69 Catfish Hunter DF .30 .75
70 Willie Stargell DF .30 .75
71A Reggie Jackson A's GC .30 .75
71B Reggie Jackson Yanks GC SP2 1.00 2.50
72 George Brett GC 1.00 2.50
73A Babe Ruth Sox GC 1.25 3.00
73B Babe Ruth Yanks GC SP1 4.00 10.00
74 Cy Young GC .30 .75
75 Jim Palmer GC .30 .75
76 Mickey Lolich GC .20 .50
77 Stan Musial GC .75 2.00
78 Steve Carlton GC .30 .75
79 Roberto Clemente GC 1.25 3.00
80 John McGraw GC .30 .75
81 Paul Molitor GC .50 1.25
82 Red Ruffing GC .20 .50
83 Connie Mack GC .20 .50
84 Mike Schmidt GC .75 2.00
85A Mickey Cochrane A's GC .30 .75
85B Mickey Cochrane Tigers GC SP1 1.00 2.50
86 Brooks Robinson GC .30 .75
87 Whitey Ford GC .30 .75

2003 Fleer Fall Classics Championship Gold

*GOLD POST-WAR: 5X TO 12X BASIC
*GOLD PRE-WAR: 5X TO 12X BASIC
*GOLD POST-WAR: 1.5X TO 4X BASIC SP1
*GOLD PRE-WAR: 1.5X TO 4X BASIC SP1
*GOLD POST-WAR: 1.5X TO 4X BASIC SP2
RANDOM INSERTS IN PACKS
STATED PRINT RUN 50 SERIAL #'d SETS

2003 Fleer Fall Classics All-American Autographs

PRINT RUNS B/WN 75-450 COPIES PER
AK Al Kaline/325 12.00 30.00
AT Alan Trammell/150 6.00 15.00
BF Bob Feller/300 8.00 20.00
BM Bill Mazeroski/75 8.00 20.00
BR Brooks Robinson/325 8.00 20.00
BS Moose Skowron/150 6.00 15.00
CF Carlton Fisk/75 8.00 20.00
FL Fred Lynn/275 6.00 15.00
HK Harmon Killebrew/150 10.00 25.00
LA Luis Aparicio/150 6.00 15.00
PR Preacher Roe/450 6.00 15.00
RB Rick Burleson/250 4.00 10.00
VB Vida Blue/450 4.00 10.00
WS Warren Spahn/75 15.00 40.00

2003 Fleer Fall Classics All-American Autographs 100

RANDOM INSERTS IN PACKS
STATED PRINT RUN 100 SERIAL #'d SETS
AK Al Kaline 20.00 50.00
AT Alan Trammell 8.00 20.00
BF Bob Feller 10.00 25.00
BM Bill Mazeroski 8.00 20.00
BR Brooks Robinson 12.00 30.00
BS Moose Skowron 8.00 20.00
CF Carlton Fisk 12.00 30.00
DS Duke Snider 8.00 20.00
FL Fred Lynn 8.00 20.00
HK Harmon Killebrew 12.00 30.00
JP Jim Palmer 8.00 20.00
LA Luis Aparicio 8.00 20.00
PR Preacher Roe 8.00 20.00
RB Rick Burleson 6.00 15.00
SC Steve Carlton 8.00 20.00
VB Vida Blue 6.00 15.00
WS Warren Spahn 15.00 40.00

2003 Fleer Fall Classics All-American Autographs 50

*AUTO 50: .5X TO 1.2X AUTO 100
RANDOM INSERTS IN PACKS
STATED PRINT RUN 50 SERIAL #'d SETS
MS Mike Schmidt 40.00 80.00
OS Ozzie Smith 40.00 80.00

2003 Fleer Fall Classics All-American Game Used

RANDOM INSERTS IN PACKS
STATED PRINT RUN 100 SERIAL #'d SETS
AK Al Kaline Bat 10.00 25.00
AT Alan Trammell Jsy 6.00 15.00
BM Bill Mazeroski Bat 6.00 15.00
BR Brooks Robinson Bat 10.00 25.00
CR Cal Ripken Jsy 40.00 80.00
DS Duke Snider Pants 10.00 25.00
EMA Eddie Mathews Bat 10.00 25.00
EMU Eddie Murray Jsy 10.00 25.00
FR Frank Robinson Bat 6.00 15.00
LA Luis Aparicio Jsy 6.00 15.00
OS Ozzie Smith Jsy 15.00 40.00
RJ Reggie Jackson Jsy 10.00 25.00
SM Stan Musial Jsy 20.00 50.00
TS Tom Seaver Jsy 10.00 25.00
WB Wade Boggs Patch 10.00 25.00
YB Yogi Berra Pants 10.00 25.00

2003 Fleer Fall Classics Legendary Collection Memorabilia

STATED ODDS 1:1 LGD STAR
SP INFO PROVIDED BY FLEER
DS Duke Snider Pants 4.00 10.00
DSY Darryl Strawberry Bat 4.00 10.00
EM Eddie Mathews Bat SP 8.00 20.00
EMY Eddie Murray Bat 4.00 10.00

FR Frank Robinson Bat 4.00 10.00
GH Gil Hodges Jsy SP 6.00 15.00
NR Nolan Ryan Jsy 10.00 25.00
RJ Reggie Jackson Jsy 4.00 10.00
RM Roger Maris Pants SP 10.00 25.00
YB Yogi Berra Pants 4.00 10.00

2003 Fleer Fall Classics Pennant Aggression

RANDOM INSERTS IN PACKS
PRINT RUNS B/WN 1908-1985 COPIES PER
1 Ty Cobb/1908 2.50 6.00
2 Honus Wagner/1909 1.50 4.00
3 Walter Johnson/1924 1.50 4.00
4 Jimmie Foxx/1930 1.50 4.00
5 Frankie Frisch/1931 1.00 2.50
6 Pee Wee Reese/1947 1.00 2.50
7 Yogi Berra/1951 1.50 4.00
8 Roy Campanella/1953 1.50 4.00
9 Whitey Ford/1961 1.00 2.50
10 Frank Robinson/1966 1.00 2.50
11 Carl Yastrzemski/1967 2.50 6.00
12 Brooks Robinson/1970 1.00 2.50
13 Johnny Bench/1972 1.50 4.00
14 Reggie Jackson/1973 1.00 2.50
15 Catfish Hunter/1974 1.00 2.50
16 Joe Morgan/1975 1.00 2.50
17 Thurman Munson/1976 1.50 4.00
18 Willie Stargell/1979 1.00 2.50
19 Mike Schmidt/1980 2.50 6.00
20 George Brett/1985 3.00 8.00

2003 Fleer Fall Classics Pennant Aggression Game Used

STATED PRINT RUN 100 SERIAL #'d SETS
*PATCH: 1X TO 2X BASIC
PATCH PRINT RUN 50 SERIAL #'d SETS
BR Brooks Robinson Bat 10.00 25.00
CH Catfish Hunter Jsy 10.00 25.00
CM Joe Morgan Jsy 6.00 15.00
CY Carl Yastrzemski Jsy 15.00 40.00
FR Frank Robinson Jsy 6.00 15.00
GB George Brett Jsy 20.00 50.00
JB Johnny Bench Jsy 10.00 25.00
MS Mike Schmidt Jsy 15.00 40.00
RJ Reggie Jackson Jsy 10.00 25.00
TM Thurman Munson Jsy 6.00 15.00
WS Willie Stargell Jsy 6.00 15.00
YB Yogi Berra Jsy 10.00 25.00

2003 Fleer Fall Classics Postseason Glory

1-15 PRINT RUN 1500 SERIAL #'d SETS
16-25 PRINT RUN 750 SERIAL #'d SETS
26-30 PRINT RUN 100 SERIAL #'d SETS
CARD 17 DOES NOT EXIST
1 C.Fisk 2.50 6.00
C.Yastrzemski
2 E.Slaughter 2.50 6.00
S.Musial
3 R.Jackson 1.50 4.00
T.Munson
4 E.Plank 1.50 4.00
C.Mathewson
5 C.Young 1.00 2.50
J.Sebring
6 Y.Berra 1.50 4.00
W.Ford
7 M.Lolich 1.00 2.50
A.Trammell
8 E.Mathews 1.50 4.00
R.Schoendienst
9 R.Campanella 1.50 4.00
P.Reese
10 J.Carter 1.00 2.50
B.Mazeroski
11 B.Robinson 1.00 2.50
F.Robinson
12 T.Seaver 1.00 2.50
G.Hodges
13 R.Yount 1.50 4.00
P.Molitor
14 D.Parker 1.00 2.50
W.Stargell
15 C.Ripken 5.00 12.00
J.Palmer
16 B.Ruth 5.00 12.00
W.Ford
18 L.Brock 1.25 3.00
B.Gibson
19 M.Schmidt 3.00 8.00
B.Robinson
20 J.Bench 2.00 5.00
T.Munson
21 N.Ryan 6.00 15.00
W.Johnson
22 D.Drysdale 1.25 3.00
D.Snider
23 J.Carter 2.00 5.00
P.Molitor
24 H.Jennings 3.00 8.00
T.Cobb
25 C.Ripken 6.00 15.00
E.Murray
26 M.Schmidt 8.00 20.00
S.Carlton
27 R.Clemente 12.00 30.00
W.Stargell
28 J.Palmer 15.00 40.00
N.Ryan
29 J.Morgan 5.00 12.00
J.Bench
30 L.Gehrig 12.00 30.00
B.Ruth

2003 Fleer Fall Classics Postseason Glory Dual Patch

*PATCH: 1X TO 2X BASIC DUAL JSY
RANDOM INSERTS IN PACKS
STATED PRINT RUN 50 SERIAL #'d SETS
LBBG L.Brock/B.Gibson 30.00 60.00

2003 Fleer Fall Classics Postseason Glory Dual Swatch

RANDOM INSERTS IN PACKS
STATED PRINT RUN 100 SERIAL #'d SETS
BRFR B.Rob Bat/F.Rob Bat 6.00 15.00
CFCY Fisk Jsy/Yastrzemski Jsy 10.00 25.00
CREM Ripken Jsy/Murray Jsy 15.00 40.00
DDDS Drysdale Jsy/Snider Pants 12.50 30.00
JMJB Morgan Jsy/Bench Jsy 6.00 15.00
JPNR Palmer Jsy/Ryan Jsy 12.00 30.00
MSSC Schmidt Jsy/Carlton Jsy 6.00 15.00
RJTM Reggie Jsy/Munson Pants 12.50 30.00
RYPM Yount Jsy/Molitor Jsy 12.50 30.00
YBWF Berra Pants/Ford Jsy 12.50 30.00

2003 Fleer Fall Classics Postseason Glory Single Patch

RANDOM INSERTS IN PACKS
STATED PRINT RUN 75 SERIAL #'d SETS
BG Bob Gibson-Brock 15.00 40.00
CF Carlton Fisk-Yaz 15.00 40.00
CR Cal Ripken-Murray 40.00 80.00
CY Carl Yastrzemski-Fisk 15.00 40.00
EM Eddie Murray-Ripken 15.00 40.00
JB Johnny Bench-Morgan 15.00 40.00
JM Joe Morgan-Bench 10.00 25.00
JP Jim Palmer-Ryan 10.00 25.00
LB Lou Brock-Gibson 15.00 40.00
MS Mike Schmidt-Carlton 12.00 30.00
NR Nolan Ryan-Palmer 15.00 40.00
PM Paul Molitor-Yount 10.00 25.00
RY Robin Yount-Molitor 15.00 40.00
SC Steve Carlton-Schmidt 10.00 25.00

2003 Fleer Fall Classics Postseason Glory Single Swatch

RANDOM INSERTS IN PACKS
STATED PRINT RUN 150 SERIAL #'d SETS
BG Bob Gibson Jsy-Brock 6.00 15.00
BRO Brooks Robinson Bat-F.Rob 6.00 15.00
BRU Babe Ruth Bat-Gehrig 50.00 100.00
CF Carlton Fisk Jsy-Yaz 6.00 15.00
CR Cal Ripken Jsy-Murray 20.00 50.00
CY Carl Yastrzemski Jsy-Fisk 15.00 40.00
DD Don Drysdale Jsy-Snider 6.00 15.00
DP Dave Parker Bat-Stargell 4.00 10.00
DS Duke Snider Pants-Drysdale 6.00 15.00
EM Eddie Murray Jsy-Ripken 10.00 25.00
FR Frank Robinson Bat-Brooks 4.00 10.00
JB Johnny Bench Jsy-Morgan 6.00 15.00
JC Joe Carter Bat-Molitor 4.00 10.00
JM Joe Morgan Jsy-Bench 4.00 10.00
JP Jim Palmer Jsy-Ryan 6.00 15.00
LB Lou Brock Jsy-Gibson 6.00 15.00
MS Mike Schmidt Jsy-Carlton 12.50 30.00
NR Nolan Ryan Jsy-Palmer 20.00 50.00
PMC Paul Molitor Bat-Carter 4.00 10.00
PMY Paul Molitor Jsy-Yount 10.00 25.00
RJ Reggie Jackson Jsy-Munson 6.00 15.00
RY Robin Yount Jsy-Molitor 6.00 15.00
SC Steve Carlton Jsy-Schmidt 4.00 10.00
TM T.Munson Pants-Reggie 10.00 25.00
WF Whitey Ford Jsy-Berra 6.00 15.00
WS Willie Stargell Bat-Parker 6.00 15.00
YB Yogi Berra Pants-Ford 6.00 15.00

2003 Fleer Fall Classics Series Contenders Bat

STATED ODDS 1:111 RETAIL
KNOBS PRINT RUN B/WN 9-10 COPIES PER
NO KNOBS PRICING DUE TO SCARCITY
AK Al Kaline 10.00 25.00
BD Bill Dickey 6.00 15.00
CF Carlton Fisk 6.00 15.00
DM Don Mattingly 15.00 40.00
DS Darryl Strawberry 4.00 10.00
HK Harmon Killebrew 10.00 25.00
JC Jose Canseco 6.00 15.00
PR Phil Rizzuto SP 6.00 15.00
WM Willie McCovey SP 6.00 15.00

2003 Fleer Fall Classics Yankees Penstripes Autographs Anniversary

STATED PRINT RUN 100 SERIAL #'d SETS
WS PRINT RUN 26 SERIAL #'d SETS
NO WS PRICING DUE TO SCARCITY
BS Moose Skowron 10.00 25.00
DM Don Mattingly 20.00 50.00
DW Dave Winfield 15.00 40.00
RJ Reggie Jackson 20.00 50.00
WB Wade Boggs 15.00 40.00

2000 Fleer Focus

COMP.MASTER SET (275) 100.00 200.00
COMPLETE SET w/2999's (250) 20.00 50.00
COMP.SET w/o SP's (225) 6.00 15.00
COMMON CARD (1-225) .12 .30
COMMON ROOKIE (226-250) 1.25 3.00
226-250 ACTIONS SERIAL #'d 1000-3999
COMMON PORT (226P-250P) 2.00 5.00
226-250 PORTRAITS SERIAL #'d 1-999
CARDS 226-250 RANDOM INSERTS IN PACKS
1 Nomar Garciaparra .20 .50
2 Adrian Beltre .30 .75
3 Miguel Tejada .20 .50
4 Joe Randa .12 .30
5 Larry Walker .20 .50
6 Jeff Weaver .12 .30
7 Jay Bell .12 .30
8 Ivan Rodriguez .20 .50
9 Edgar Martinez .20 .50
10 Desi Relaford .12 .30
11 Derek Jeter .75 2.00
12 Delino Deshields .12 .30
13 Craig Biggio .20 .50
14 Chuck Knoblauch .12 .30
15 Chuck Finley .12 .30
16 Brett Tomko .12 .30
17 Bobby Higginson .12 .30
18 Pedro Martinez .20 .50
19 Troy O'Leary .12 .30
20 Rickey Henderson .30 .75
21 Robb Nen .12 .30
22 Rolando Arrojo .12 .30
23 Rondell White .12 .30
24 Royce Clayton .12 .30
25 Rusty Greer .12 .30
26 Stan Spencer .12 .30
27 Steve Finley .12 .30
28 Tom Goodwin .12 .30
29 Troy Percival .12 .30
30 Wilton Guerrero .12 .30
31 Roberto Alomar .20 .50
32 Mike Hampton .12 .30
33 Michael Barrett .12 .30
34 Curt Schilling .20 .50
35 Bill Mueller .12 .30
36 Bernie Williams .20 .50
37 John Smoltz .30 .75
38 B.J. Surhoff .12 .30
39 Pete Harnisch .12 .30
40 Juan Encarnacion .12 .30
41 Derrek Lee .12 .30
42 Jeff Shaw .12 .30
43 David Cone .12 .30
44 Jason Christiansen .12 .30
45 Jeff Kent .12 .30
46 Randy Johnson .30 .75
47 Todd Walker .12 .30
48 Jose Lima .12 .30
49 Jason Giambi .12 .30
50 Ken Griffey Jr. Reds .60 1.50
51 Bartolo Colon .12 .30
52 Mike Lieberthal .12 .30
53 Shane Reynolds .12 .30
54 Travis Lee .12 .30
55 Travis Fryman .12 .30
56 John Valentin .12 .30
57 Joey Hamilton .12 .30
58 Jay Buhner .12 .30
59 Brad Radke .12 .30
60 A.J. Burnett .12 .30
61 Roy Halladay .20 .50
62 Raul Mondesi .12 .30
63 Matt Mantei .12 .30
64 Mark Grace .20 .50
65 David Justice .12 .30
66 Billy Wagner .12 .30
67 Eric Milton .12 .30
68 Eric Chavez .12 .30
69 Doug Glanville .12 .30
70 Ray Durham .12 .30
71 Mike Sirotka .12 .30
72 Greg Vaughn .12 .30
73 Brian Jordan .12 .30
74 Alex Gonzalez .12 .30
75 Alex Rodriguez .40 1.00
76 David Nilsson .12 .30
77 Robin Ventura .12 .30
78 Kevin Young .12 .30
79 Wilson Alvarez .12 .30
80 Matt Williams .12 .30
81 Ismael Valdes .12 .30
82 Kenny Lofton .12 .30
83 Carlos Beltran .20 .50
84 Doug Mientkiewicz .12 .30
85 Wally Joyner .12 .30
86 J.D. Drew .12 .30
87 Carlos Delgado .12 .30
88 Tony Womack .12 .30
89 Eric Young .12 .30
90 Manny Ramirez .30 .75
91 Johnny Damon .20 .50
92 Torii Hunter .12 .30
93 Kenny Rogers .12 .30
94 Trevor Hoffman .20 .50
95 John Wetteland .12 .30
96 Ray Lankford .12 .30
97 Tom Glavine .20 .50
98 Carlos Lee .12 .30
99 Richie Sexson .12 .30
100 Carlos Febles .12 .30
101 Chad Allen .12 .30
102 Sterling Hitchcock .12 .30
103 Joe McEwing .12 .30
104 Justin Thompson .12 .30
105 Jim Edmonds .12 .30
106 Kerry Wood .12 .30
107 Jim Thome .20 .50
108 Jeremy Giambi .12 .30
109 Mike Piazza .30 .75
110 Darryl Kile .12 .30
111 Darin Erstad .12 .30
112 Kyle Farnsworth .12 .30
113 Omar Vizquel .20 .50
114 Orber Moreno .12 .30
115 Al Leiter .12 .30
116 John Olerud .12 .30
117 Aaron Sele .12 .30
118 Chipper Jones .30 .75
119 Paul Konerko .12 .30
120 Chris Singleton .12 .30
121 Fernando Vina .12 .30
122 Andy Ashby .12 .30
123 Eli Marrero .12 .30
124 Edgar Renteria .12 .30
125 Roberto Hernandez .12 .30
126 Andruw Jones .12 .30
127 Maggio Ordonez .20 .50
128 Bob Wickman .12 .30
129 Tony Gwynn .30 .75
130 Mark McGwire .50 1.25
131 Albert Belle .12 .30
132 Pokey Reese .12 .30
133 Tony Clark .12 .30
134 Jeff Bagwell .20 .50
135 Mark Grudzielanek .12 .30
136 Dustin Hermanson .12 .30
137 Reggie Sanders .12 .30
138 Ryan Rupe .12 .30
139 Kevin Millwood .12 .30
140 Bret Saberhagen .12 .30
141 Juan Guzman .12 .30
142 Alex Gonzalez .12 .30
143 Gary Sheffield .12 .30
144 Roger Clemens .40 1.00
145 Ben Grieve .12 .30
146 Bobby Abreu .12 .30
147 Brian Giles .12 .30
148 Quinton McCracken .12 .30
149 Freddy Garcia .12 .30
150 Erubiel Durazo .12 .30
151 Sidney Ponson .12 .30
152 Scott Williamson .12 .30
153 Ken Caminiti .12 .30
154 Vladimir Guerrero .20 .50
155 Andy Pettitte .20 .50
156 Edwards Guzman .12 .30
157 Shannon Stewart .12 .30
158 Greg Maddux .40 1.00
159 Mike Stanley .12 .30
160 Sean Casey .12 .30
161 Cliff Floyd .12 .30
162 Devon White .12 .30
163 Scott Brosius .12 .30
164 Marlon Anderson .12 .30
165 Jason Kendall .12 .30
166 Ryan Klesko .12 .30
167 Sammy Sosa .30 .75
168 Frank Thomas .30 .75
169 Geoff Jenkins .12 .30
170 Jason Schmidt .12 .30
171 Dan Wilson .12 .30
172 Jose Canseco .20 .50
173 Troy Glaus .12 .30
174 Mariano Rivera .40 1.00
175 Scott Rolen .20 .50
176 J.T. Snow .12 .30
177 Rafael Palmeiro .20 .50
178 A.J. Hinch .12 .30
179 Jose Offerman .12 .30
180 Jeff Cirillo .12 .30
181 Dean Palmer .12 .30
182 Jose Rosado .12 .30
183 Armando Benitez .12 .30
184 Brady Anderson .12 .30
185 Cal Ripken 1.00 2.50
186 Barry Larkin .20 .50
187 Damion Easley .12 .30
188 Moises Alou .12 .30
189 Todd Hundley .12 .30
190 Tim Hudson .20 .50
191 Livan Hernandez .12 .30
192 Fred McGriff .20 .50
193 Orlando Hernandez .12 .30
194 Tim Salmon .12 .30
195 Mike Mussina .20 .50
196 Todd Helton .20 .50
197 Juan Gonzalez .12 .30
198 Kevin Brown .12 .30
199 Ugueth Urbina .12 .30
200 Matt Stairs .12 .30
201 Shawn Estes .12 .30
202 Gabe Kapler .12 .30
203 Javy Lopez .12 .30
204 Henry Rodriguez .12 .30
205 Dante Bichette .12 .30
206 Jeromy Burnitz .12 .30
207 Todd Zeile .12 .30
208 Rico Brogna .12 .30
209 Warren Morris .12 .30
210 David Segui .12 .30
211 Vinny Castilla .12 .30
212 Mo Vaughn .12 .30
213 Charles Johnson .12 .30
214 Neifi Perez .12 .30
215 Shawn Green .12 .30
216 Carl Pavano .12 .30
217 Tino Martinez .12 .30
218 Barry Bonds .50 1.25
219 David Wells .12 .30
220 Paul O'Neill .20 .50
221 Masato Yoshii .12 .30
222 Kris Benson .12 .30
223 Fernando Tatis .12 .30
224 Lee Stevens .12 .30
225 Jose Cruz Jr. .12 .30
226 Rick Ankiel 2.00 5.00
226P Rick Ankiel PORT 3.00 8.00
227 Matt Riley 1.25 3.00
227P Matt Riley PORT 2.00 5.00
228 Norm Hutchins 1.25 3.00
228P Norm Hutchins PORT 2.00 5.00
229 Ruben Mateo 1.25 3.00
229P Ruben Mateo PORT 2.00 5.00
230 Ben Petrick 1.25 3.00
230P Ben Petrick PORT 2.00 5.00
231 Mario Encarnacion 1.25 3.00
231P Mario Encarnacion PORT 2.00 5.00
232 Nick Johnson 1.25 3.00
232P Nick Johnson PORT 2.00 5.00
233 Adam Piatt 1.25 3.00
233P Adam Piatt PORT 2.00 5.00
234 Mike Darr 1.25 3.00
234P Mike Darr PORT 2.00 5.00
235 Chad Hermansen 1.25 3.00
235P Chad Hermansen PORT 2.00 5.00
236 Wily Pena 1.25 3.00
236P Wily Pena PORT 2.00 5.00
237 Octavio Dotel 1.25 3.00
237P Octavio Dotel PORT 2.00 5.00
238 Vernon Wells 1.25 3.00
238P Vernon Wells PORT 2.00 5.00
239 Daryle Ward 1.25 3.00
239P Daryle Ward PORT 2.00 5.00
240 Adam Kennedy 1.25 3.00
240P Adam Kennedy PORT 2.00 5.00
241 Angel Pena 1.25 3.00
241P Angel Pena PORT 2.00 5.00
242 Lance Berkman 2.00 5.00
242P Lance Berkman PORT 3.00 8.00
243 Gabe Molina 1.25 3.00
243P Gabe Molina PORT 2.00 5.00
244 Steve Lomasney 1.25 3.00
244P Steve Lomasney PORT 2.00 5.00
245 Jacob Cruz 1.25 3.00
245P Jacob Cruz PORT 2.00 5.00
246 Mark Quinn 1.25 3.00
246P Mark Quinn PORT 2.00 5.00
247 Eric Munson 1.25 3.00
247P Eric Munson PORT 2.00 5.00
248 Alfonso Soriano 3.00 8.00
248P Alfonso Soriano PORT 5.00 12.00
249 Kip Wells 1.25 3.00
249P Kip Wells PORT 2.00 5.00
250 Josh Beckett 2.50 6.00
250P Josh Beckett PORT 4.00 10.00

2000 Fleer Focus Masterpiece Errors

50 Ken Griffey Jr. Reds 8.00 20.00
202 Gabe Kapler 1.50 4.00
203 Javy Lopez 1.50 4.00
204 Henry Rodriguez 1.50 4.00
205 Dante Bichette 1.50 4.00
206 Jeromy Burnitz 1.50 4.00
207 Todd Zeile 1.50 4.00
208 Rico Brogna 1.50 4.00
209 Warren Morris 1.50 4.00
210 David Segui 1.50 4.00
211 Vinny Castilla 1.50 4.00
212 Mo Vaughn 1.50 4.00
213 Charles Johnson 1.50 4.00
214 Neifi Perez 1.50 4.00
215 Shawn Green 1.50 4.00
216 Carl Pavano 1.50 4.00
217 Tino Martinez 1.50 4.00
218 Barry Bonds 6.00 15.00
219 David Wells 1.50 4.00
220 Paul O'Neill 2.50 6.00
221 Masato Yoshii 1.50 4.00
222 Kris Benson 1.50 4.00
223 Fernando Tatis 1.50 4.00
224 Lee Stevens 1.50 4.00
225 Jose Cruz Jr. 1.50 4.00

2000 Fleer Focus Masterpiece Mania

*STARS 1-225: 6X TO 15X BASIC CARDS
*ROOKIES 226-250: .5X TO 1.2X BASIC

2000 Fleer Focus Feel the Game

STATED ODDS 1:288
ALL CARDS FEATURE JERSEY PATCHES
1 Cal Ripken 8.00 20.00
2 Randy Johnson 6.00 15.00
3 Alex Rodriguez 6.00 15.00
4 Scott Rolen 6.00 15.00
5 Javy Lopez 4.00 10.00
6 Vladimir Guerrero 6.00 15.00
7 Tom Glavine 6.00 15.00
8 Tim Salmon 6.00 15.00
9 Adrian Beltre 4.00 10.00
10 Miguel Tejada 4.00 10.00

2000 Fleer Focus Focal Points

COMPLETE SET (15) 8.00 20.00
STATED ODDS 1:6
*STRIKING: 12X TO 30X BASIC FOCAL
STRIKING RANDOM IN HOBBY PACKS
STRIKING PRINT RUN 50 SERIAL #'d SETS
1 Mark McGwire .75 2.00
2 Tony Gwynn .50 1.25
3 Nomar Garciaparra .30 .75
4 Juan Gonzalez .20 .50
5 Jeff Bagwell .30 .75
6 Chipper Jones .50 1.25
7 Cal Ripken 1.50 4.00
8 Alex Rodriguez .60 1.50
9 Scott Rolen .30 .75
10 Vladimir Guerrero .30 .75
11 Mike Piazza .50 1.25
12 Frank Thomas .50 1.25
13 Ken Griffey Jr. 1.00 2.50
14 Sammy Sosa .50 1.25
15 Derek Jeter 1.25 3.00

2000 Fleer Focus Fresh Ink

STATED ODDS 1:96
EXCHANGE DEADLINE 5/31/2001
1 Chad Allen 4.00 10.00
2 Michael Barrett 4.00 10.00
3 Josh Beckett 6.00 15.00
4 Rob Bell 4.00 10.00
5 Adrian Beltre 8.00 20.00
6 Milton Bradley 6.00 15.00
7 Rico Brogna 4.00 10.00
8 Mike Cameron 6.00 15.00
9 Eric Chavez 6.00 15.00
10 Bruce Chen 4.00 10.00
11 Johnny Damon 5.00 12.00
12 Ben Davis 4.00 10.00
13 J.D. Drew 6.00 15.00
14 Erubiel Durazo 4.00 10.00
15 Jeremy Giambi 4.00 10.00
16 Jason Giambi 6.00 15.00
17 Doug Glanville 6.00 15.00
18 Troy Glaus 10.00 25.00
19 Shawn Green 6.00 15.00
20 Tony Gwynn 40.00 100.00
21 Mike Hampton 6.00 15.00
22 Tim Hudson 10.00 25.00
23 John Jaha 4.00 10.00
24 Derek Jeter SP/100 * 125.00 250.00
25 D'Angelo Jimenez 4.00 10.00
26 Nick Johnson 6.00 15.00
27 Randy Johnson SP 50.00 100.00
28 Andruw Jones 6.00 15.00
29 Jason Kendall 6.00 15.00
30 Adam Kennedy 6.00 15.00
31 Mike Lieberthal 6.00 15.00
32 Edgar Martinez 10.00 25.00
33 Aaron McNeal 4.00 10.00
34 Kevin Millwood 6.00 15.00
35 Mike Mussina 10.00 25.00
36 Magglio Ordonez 6.00 15.00
37 Eric Owens 4.00 10.00
38 Rafael Palmeiro 20.00 50.00
39 Wily Pena 12.50 30.00
40 Adam Piatt 4.00 10.00
41 Cal Ripken 50.00 100.00
42 Alex Rodriguez 20.00 50.00
43 Tim Salmon 4.00 10.00
44 Chris Singleton 4.00 10.00
45 Mike Sweeney 6.00 15.00
46 Jose Vidro 4.00 10.00
47 Rondell White 6.00 15.00
48 Jaret Wright 4.00 10.00

2000 Fleer Focus Future Vision

COMPLETE SET (15) 5.00 12.00
STATED ODDS 1:9
1 Rick Ankiel .60 1.50
2 Matt Riley .40 1.00
3 Ruben Mateo .40 1.00
4 Ben Petrick .40 1.00
5 Mario Encarnacion .40 1.00
6 Octavio Dotel .40 1.00
7 Vernon Wells .40 1.00
8 Adam Kennedy .40 1.00
9 Lance Berkman .60 1.50
10 Chad Hermansen .40 1.00
11 Mark Quinn .40 1.00
12 Eric Munson .40 1.00
13 Alfonso Soriano 1.00 2.50
14 Kip Wells .40 1.00
15 Josh Beckett .75 2.00

2000 Fleer Focus Pocus

COMPLETE SET (10) 20.00 50.00
STATED ODDS 1:14
1 Cal Ripken 5.00 12.00
2 Tony Gwynn 1.50 4.00
3 Nomar Garciaparra 1.00 2.50
4 Juan Gonzalez .60 1.50
5 Mike Piazza 1.50 4.00
6 Mark McGwire 2.50 6.00
7 Chipper Jones 1.50 4.00
8 Ken Griffey Jr. 3.00 8.00
9 Derek Jeter 4.00 10.00
10 Alex Rodriguez 2.00 5.00

2001 Fleer Focus

COMP.SET w/o SP's (200) 10.00 25.00
COMMON CARD (1-200) .10 .30
COMMON CARD (201-240) 2.00 5.00
201-207 PRINT RUN 2499 SERIAL #'d CARDS
208-211 PRINT RUN 2999 SERIAL #'d CARDS
212 PRINT RUN 3499 SERIAL #'d CARDS
213-224 PRINT RUN 1999 SERIAL #'d CARDS
225-235 PRINT RUN 4999 SERIAL #'d CARDS
236-240 PRINT RUN 3999 SERIAL #'d CARDS
CARDS 201-240 RANDOM INSERTS IN PACKS
COMMON CARD (241-250) 4.00 10.00
241-250 DIST.IN FLEER PLAT.RC HOB/RET
241-250 PRINT RUN 999 SERIAL #'d SETS
1 Derek Jeter .75 2.00
2 Manny Ramirez .20 .50
3 Ken Griffey Jr. .60 1.50
4 Ken Caminiti .10 .30
5 Joe Randa .10 .30
6 Jason Kendall .10 .30
7 Ron Coomer .10 .30
8 Rondell White .10 .30
9 Tino Martinez .20 .50
10 Nomar Garciaparra .50 1.25
11 Tony Batista .10 .30
12 Todd Stottlemyre .10 .30
13 Ryan Klesko .10 .30
14 Darin Erstad .10 .30
15 Todd Walker .10 .30
16 Al Leiter .10 .30
17 Carl Everett .10 .30
18 Bobby Abreu .10 .30
19 Raul Mondesi .10 .30
20 Vladimir Guerrero .30 .75
21 Mike Bordick .10 .30
22 Aaron Sele .10 .30
23 Ray Lankford .10 .30
24 Roger Clemens .60 1.50
25 Kevin Young .10 .30
26 Brad Radke .10 .30
27 Todd Hundley .10 .30
28 Ellis Burks .10 .30
29 Lee Stevens .10 .30
30 Eric Karros .10 .30
31 Darren Dreifort .10 .30
32 Ivan Rodriguez .20 .50
33 Pedro Martinez .20 .50
34 Travis Fryman .10 .30
35 Garret Anderson .10 .30
36 Rafael Palmeiro .20 .50
37 Jason Giambi .10 .30
38 Jeromy Burnitz .10 .30
39 Robin Ventura .10 .30
40 Derek Bell .10 .30
41 Carlos Guillen .10 .30
42 Albert Belle .10 .30
43 Henry Rodriguez .10 .30
44 Brian Jordan .10 .30
45 Mike Sweeney .10 .30
46 Ruben Rivera .10 .30
47 Greg Maddux .50 1.25
48 Corey Koskie .10 .30
49 Sandy Alomar Jr. .10 .30
50 Mike Mussina .20 .50
51 Tom Glavine .20 .50
52 Aaron Boone .10 .30
53 Frank Thomas .30 .75
54 Kenny Lofton .10 .30
55 Danny Graves .10 .30
56 Jose Valentin .10 .30
57 Travis Lee .10 .30
58 Jim Edmonds .10 .30
59 Jim Thome .20 .50
60 Steve Finley .10 .30
61 Shawn Green .10 .30
62 Lance Berkman .10 .30
63 Mark Quinn .10 .30
64 Randy Johnson .30 .75
65 Dmitri Young .10 .30
66 Andy Pettitte .20 .50
67 Paul O'Neill .20 .50
68 Gil Heredia .10 .30
69 Russell Branyan .10 .30
70 Alex Rodriguez .40 1.00
71 Geoff Jenkins .10 .30
72 Eric Chavez .10 .30
73 Cal Ripken 1.00 2.50
74 Mark Kotsay .10 .30
75 Jeff D'Amico .10 .30
76 Tony Womack .10 .30
77 Eric Milton .10 .30
78 Joe Girardi .10 .30
79 Peter Bergeron .10 .30
80 Miguel Tejada .10 .30
81 Luis Gonzalez .10 .30
82 Doug Glanville .10 .30
83 Gerald Williams .10 .30
84 Troy O'Leary .10 .30
85 Brian Giles .10 .30
86 Miguel Cairo .10 .30
87 Magglio Ordonez .10 .30
88 Rick Helling .10 .30
89 Bruce Chen .10 .30
90 Jason Varitek .30 .75
91 Mike Lieberthal .10 .30
92 Shawn Estes .10 .30
93 Rick Ankiel .10 .30
94 Tim Salmon .20 .50
95 Jacque Jones .10 .30
96 Johnny Damon .20 .50
97 Larry Walker .10 .30
98 Ruben Mateo .10 .30
99 Brad Fullmer .10 .30
100 Edgardo Alfonzo .10 .30
101 Mark Mulder .10 .30
102 Tony Gwynn .40 1.00
103 Mike Cameron .10 .30
104 Richie Sexson .10 .30
105 Barry Larkin .20 .50
106 Mike Piazza .50 1.25
107 Eric Young .10 .30
108 Edgar Renteria .10 .30
109 Todd Zeile .10 .30
110 Luis Castillo .10 .30
111 Sammy Sosa .30 .75
112 David Justice .10 .30
113 Delino DeShields .10 .30
114 Mariano Rivera .30 .75
115 Edgar Martinez .20 .50
116 Ray Durham .10 .30
117 Brady Anderson .10 .30
118 Eric Owens .10 .30
119 Alex Gonzalez .10 .30
120 Jay Buhner .10 .30
121 Greg Vaughn .10 .30
122 Mike Lowell .10 .30
123 Marquis Grissom .10 .30
124 Matt Williams .10 .30
125 Dean Palmer .10 .30
126 Troy Glaus .10 .30
127 Bret Boone .10 .30
128 David Ortiz .30 .75
129 Glenallen Hill .10 .30
130 Chipper Jones .30 .75
131 Tony Clark .10 .30
132 Terrence Long .10 .30
133 Chuck Finley .10 .30
134 Jeff Bagwell .20 .50
135 J.T. Snow .10 .30
136 Andruw Jones .20 .50
137 Carlos Delgado .10 .30
138 Mo Vaughn .10 .30
139 Derrek Lee .20 .50
140 Bobby Estalella .10 .30
141 Kerry Wood .10 .30
142 Jose Vidro .10 .30
143 Ben Grieve .10 .30
144 Barry Bonds .75 2.00
145 Javy Lopez .10 .30
146 Adam Kennedy .10 .30
147 Jeff Cirillo .10 .30
148 Cliff Floyd .10 .30
149 Carl Pavano .10 .30
150 Bobby Higginson .10 .30
151 Kevin Brown .10 .30
152 Fernando Tatis .10 .30
153 Matt Lawton .10 .30
154 Damion Easley .10 .30
155 Curt Schilling .10 .30
156 Mark McGwire .75 2.00
157 Mark Grace .20 .50
158 Adrian Beltre .10 .30
159 Jorge Posada .20 .50
160 Richard Hidalgo .10 .30
161 Vinny Castilla .10 .30
162 Bernie Williams .20 .50
163 John Olerud .10 .30
164 Todd Helton .20 .50
165 Craig Biggio .20 .50
166 David Wells .10 .30
167 Phil Nevin .10 .30
168 Andres Galarraga .10 .30
169 Moises Alou .10 .30
170 Denny Neagle .10 .30
171 Jeffrey Hammonds .10 .30
172 Sean Casey .10 .30
173 Gary Sheffield .10 .30
174 Carlos Lee .10 .30
175 Juan Encarnacion .10 .30
176 Roberto Alomar .20 .50
177 Kenny Rogers .10 .30
178 Charles Johnson .10 .30
179 Shannon Stewart .10 .30
180 B.J. Surhoff .10 .30
181 Paul Konerko .10 .30
182 Jermaine Dye .10 .30
183 Scott Rolen .20 .50
184 Fred McGriff .20 .50
185 Juan Gonzalez .10 .30
186 Carlos Beltran .10 .30
187 Jay Payton .10 .30
188 Chad Hermansen .10 .30
189 Pat Burrell .10 .30
190 Omar Vizquel .20 .50
191 Trot Nixon .10 .30
192 Mike Hampton .10 .30
193 Kris Benson .10 .30
194 Gabe Kapler .10 .30
195 Rickey Henderson .30 .75
196 J.D. Drew .10 .30
197 Pokey Reese .10 .30
198 Jeff Kent .10 .30
199 Jose Cruz Jr. .10 .30
200 Preston Wilson .10 .30
201 Eric Munson/2499 2.00 5.00
202 Alex Cabrera/2499 2.00 5.00
203 Nate Rolison/2499 2.00 5.00
204 Julio Zuleta/2499 2.00 5.00
205 Chris Richard/2499 2.00 5.00
206 Dernell Stenson/2499 2.00 5.00
207 Aaron McNeal/2499 2.00 5.00
208 Aubrey Huff/2999 2.00 5.00
209 Mike Lamb/2999 2.00 5.00
210 Xavier Nady/2999 2.00 5.00
211 Joe Crede/2999 3.00 8.00
212 Ben Petrick/3499 2.00 5.00

213 Morgan Burkhart/1999 2.00 5.00
214 Jason Tyner/1999 2.00 5.00
215 Juan Pierre/1999 2.00 5.00
216 Adam Dunn/1999 3.00 8.00
217 Adam Piatt/1999 2.00 5.00
218 Eric Byrnes/1999 2.00 5.00
219 Corey Patterson/1999 2.00 5.00
220 Kenny Kelly/1999 2.00 5.00
221 Tike Redman/1999 2.00 5.00
222 Luis Matos/1999 2.00 5.00
223 Timo Perez/1999 2.00 5.00
224 Vernon Wells/1999 2.00 5.00
225 Barry Zito/4999 3.00 8.00
226 Adam Bernero/4999 2.00 5.00
227 Kazuhiro Sasaki/4999 2.00 5.00
228 Oswaldo Mairena/4999 2.00 5.00
229 Mark Buehrle/4999 3.00 8.00
230 Ryan Dempster/4999 2.00 5.00
231 Tim Hudson/4999 2.00 5.00
232 Scott Downs/4999 2.00 5.00
233 A.J. Burnett/4999 2.00 5.00
234 Adam Eaton/4999 2.00 5.00
235 Paxton Crawford/4999 2.00 5.00
236 Jace Brewer/3999 2.00 5.00
237 Jose Ortiz/3999 2.00 5.00
238 Rafael Furcal/3999 2.00 5.00
239 Julio Lugo/3999 2.00 5.00
240 Tomas De la Rosa/3999 2.00 5.00
241 Tsuyoshi Shinjo/999 RC 4.00 10.00
242 Wilson Betemit/999 RC 4.00 10.00
243 Jeremy Owens/999 RC 4.00 10.00
244 Drew Henson/999 RC 3.00 8.00
245 Albert Pujols/999 RC 40.00 100.00
246 Travis Hafner/999 RC 6.00 15.00
247 Ichiro Suzuki/999 RC 25.00 60.00
248 Elpidio Guzman/999 RC 4.00 10.00
249 Matt White/999 RC 4.00 10.00
250 Junior Spivey/999 RC 4.00 10.00

2001 Fleer Focus Green

*1-200 PRINT RUN b/wn 401-600: 3X TO 8X
*1-200 PRINT RUN b/wn 250-400: 4X TO 10X
*1-200 PRINT RUN b/wn 201-250: 5X TO 12X
*1-200 PRINT RUN b/wn 151-200: 6X TO 15X
PRINT RUNS BASED ON 2000 BAT.AVG/ERA
PRINTS b/wn 1-15 TOO SCARCE TO PRICE

2001 Fleer Focus Bat Company

COMPLETE SET (10) 40.00 80.00
STATED ODDS 1:24
*VIP: 3X TO 6X BASIC BAT CO.
VIP PRINT RUN 50 SERIAL #'d SETS
1 Barry Bonds 5.00 12.00
2 Mark McGwire 5.00 12.00
3 Sammy Sosa 2.00 5.00
4 Ken Griffey Jr. 4.00 10.00
5 Mike Piazza 3.00 8.00
6 Derek Jeter 5.00 12.00
7 Gary Sheffield 1.50 4.00
8 Frank Thomas 2.00 5.00
9 Chipper Jones 2.00 5.00
10 Alex Rodriguez 2.50 6.00

2001 Fleer Focus Big Innings

COMPLETE SET (25) 20.00 40.00
STATED ODDS 1:6
*VIP: 6X TO 12X BASIC BIG.INN.
VIP PRINT RUN 50 SERIAL #'d SETS
1 Rick Ankiel .60 1.50
2 Andruw Jones .60 1.50
3 Brian Giles .60 1.50
4 Derek Jeter 2.50 6.00
5 Rafael Furcal .60 1.50
6 Richie Sexson .60 1.50
7 Jay Payton .60 1.50
8 Carlos Delgado .60 1.50
9 Jermaine Dye .60 1.50
10 Darin Erstad .60 1.50
11 Pat Burrell .60 1.50
12 Richard Hidalgo .60 1.50
13 Adrian Beltre .60 1.50
14 Todd Helton .60 1.50
15 Vladimir Guerrero 1.00 2.50
16 Nomar Garciaparra 1.50 4.00
17 Gabe Kapler .60 1.50
18 Carlos Lee .60 1.50
19 J.D. Drew .60 1.50
20 Troy Glaus .60 1.50
21 Scott Rolen .60 1.50
22 Alex Rodriguez 1.25 3.00
23 Magglio Ordonez .60 1.50
24 Miguel Tejada .60 1.50
25 Ruben Mateo .60 1.50

2001 Fleer Focus Diamond Vision

COMPLETE SET (15) 30.00 60.00
STATED ODDS 1:12
*VIP: 6X TO 12X BASIC DIAM.VIS.
VIP PRINT RUN 50 SERIAL #'d SETS
1 Derek Jeter 2.50 6.00
2 Nomar Garciaparra 1.50 4.00
3 Cal Ripken 3.00 8.00
4 Jeff Bagwell .75 2.00
5 Mark McGwire 2.50 6.00
6 Ken Griffey Jr. 2.00 5.00
7 Pedro Martinez .75 2.00
8 Carlos Delgado .75 2.00
9 Chipper Jones 1.00 2.50
10 Barry Bonds 2.50 6.00
11 Mike Piazza 1.50 4.00
12 Sammy Sosa 1.00 2.50
13 Alex Rodriguez 1.25 3.00
14 Frank Thomas 1.00 2.50
15 Randy Johnson 1.00 2.50

2001 Fleer Focus Feel the Game

STATED ODDS 1:72
SEE 2001 FLEER FEEL GAME FOR PRICES

2001 Fleer Focus ROY Collection

COMPLETE SET (25) 25.00 60.00
STATED ODDS 1:24
1 Luis Aparicio 1.00 2.50
2 Johnny Bench 1.50 4.00
3 Joe Black .60 1.50
4 Rod Carew 1.00 2.50
5 Orlando Cepeda 1.00 2.50
6 Carlton Fisk 1.00 2.50
7 Ben Grieve .60 1.50
8 Frank Howard .60 1.50
9 Derek Jeter 4.00 10.00
10 Fred Lynn .60 1.50
11 Willie Mays 3.00 8.00
12 Willie McCovey 1.00 2.50
13 Mark McGwire 2.50 6.00
14 Raul Mondesi .60 1.50
15 Thurman Munson 1.50 4.00
16 Eddie Murray 1.00 2.50
17 Mike Piazza 1.50 4.00
18 Cal Ripken 5.00 12.00
19 Frank Robinson 1.00 2.50
20 Jackie Robinson 1.50 4.00
21 Scott Rolen 1.00 2.50
22 Tom Seaver 1.00 2.50
23 Kerry Wood .60 1.50
24 David Justice .60 1.50
25 Billy Williams 1.00 2.50

2001 Fleer Focus ROY Collection Memorabilia

STATED ODDS 1:288 HOB, 1:576 RET
ROY1 Luis Aparicio Bat 6.00 15.00
ROY2 Johnny Bench Jsy 10.00 25.00
ROY3 Orlando Cepeda Bat 6.00 15.00
ROY4 Carlton Fisk Jsy 10.00 25.00
ROY5 Ben Grieve Jsy 6.00 15.00
ROY6 Frank Howard Bat 6.00 15.00
ROY7 Derek Jeter Jsy 10.00 25.00
ROY8 Fred Lynn Bat 6.00 15.00
ROY9 Willie Mays Jsy 40.00 80.00
ROY10 Willie McCovey Bat 6.00 15.00
ROY11 Mark McGwire Ball 10.00 25.00
ROY12 Raul Mondesi Bat 6.00 15.00
ROY13 Thurman Munson Bat 15.00 40.00
ROY14 Eddie Murray Jsy 10.00 25.00
ROY15 Mike Piazza Base 6.00 15.00
ROY16 Cal Ripken Jsy 20.00 50.00
ROY17 Frank Robinson Bat 10.00 25.00
ROY18 Jackie Robinson Pants 30.00 60.00
ROY19 Scott Rolen Bat 10.00 25.00
ROY20 Tom Seaver Jsy 10.00 25.00
ROY22 David Justice Jsy 6.00 15.00

2001 Fleer Focus ROY Collection Memorabilia Autograph

PRINT RUNS LISTED BELOW
1 Luis Aparicio Bat/56 20.00 50.00
2 Johnny Bench Jsy/68 50.00 100.00
3 Orlando Cepeda Bat/58 20.00 50.00
4 Carlton Fisk Jsy/72 20.00 50.00
5 Ben Grieve Jsy/98 20.00 50.00
6 Frank Howard Bat/60 20.00 50.00
7 Derek Jeter Jsy/96 250.00 350.00
8 Fred Lynn Bat/75 20.00 50.00
9 Willie Mays Jsy/51 250.00 500.00
10 Willie McCovey Bat/59 40.00 80.00
11 Raul Mondesi Bat/94 20.00 50.00
12 Eddie Murray Jsy/77 50.00 100.00
13 Cal Ripken Jsy/82 150.00 250.00
14 Frank Robinson Bat/56 40.00 80.00
15 Scott Rolen Bat/97 20.00 50.00
16 Tom Seaver Jsy/67 50.00 120.00
18 David Justice Jsy/90 20.00 50.00

2002 Fleer Focus JE

COMPLETE SET (260) 50.00 100.00
COMP.SET w/o SP's (225) 10.00 25.00
COMMON CARD (1-225) .10 .30
COMMON CARD (226-260) .75 2.00
226-260 STATED ODDS 1:4 HOB, 1:8 RET
1 Mike Piazza .50 1.25
2 Jason Giambi .10 .30
3 Jim Thome .20 .50
4 John Olerud .10 .30
5 J.D. Drew .10 .30
6 Richard Hidalgo .10 .30
7 Rusty Greer .10 .30
8 Tony Batista .10 .30
9 Omar Vizquel .20 .50
10 Randy Johnson .30 .75
11 Cristian Guzman .10 .30
12 Mark Grace .20 .50
13 Jeff Cirillo .10 .30
14 Mike Cameron .10 .30
15 Jeromy Burnitz .10 .30
16 Pokey Reese .10 .30
17 Richie Sexson .10 .30
18 Joe Randa .10 .30
19 Aramis Ramirez .10 .30
20 Pedro Martinez .20 .50
21 Todd Hollandsworth .10 .30
22 Rondell White .10 .30
23 Tsuyoshi Shinjo .10 .30
24 Melvin Mora .10 .30
25 Tim Hudson .10 .30
26 Darrin Fletcher .10 .30
27 Bill Mueller .10 .30
28 Jeff Weaver .10 .30
29 Tony Clark .10 .30
30 Tom Glavine .20 .50
31 Jarrod Washburn .10 .30
32 Greg Vaughn .10 .30
33 Lee Stevens .10 .30
34 Charles Johnson .10 .30
35 Lance Berkman .10 .30
36 Bud Smith .10 .30
37 Keith Foulke .10 .30
38 Ben Davis .10 .30
39 Daryle Ward .10 .30
40 Bernie Williams .20 .50
41 Dean Palmer .10 .30
42 Mark Mulder .10 .30
43 Jason LaRue .10 .30
44 Jay Gibbons .10 .30
45 Brandon Duckworth .10 .30
46 Carlos Delgado .10 .30
47 Barry Zito .10 .30
48 Matt Morris .10 .30
49 J.T. Snow .10 .30
50 Albert Pujols .60 1.50
51 Brad Fullmer .10 .30
52 Damion Easley .10 .30
53 Pat Burrell .10 .30
54 Kevin Brown .10 .30
55 Todd Walker .10 .30
56 Rich Garces .10 .30
57 Carlos Pena .10 .30
58 Paul LoDuca .10 .30
59 Mike Lieberthal .10 .30
60 Barry Larkin .20 .50
61 Jon Lieber .10 .30
62 Jose Cruz Jr. .10 .30
63 Mo Vaughn .10 .30
64 Ivan Rodriguez .20 .50
65 Jorge Posada .20 .50
66 Magglio Ordonez .10 .30
67 Juan Encarnacion .10 .30
68 Shawn Estes .10 .30
69 Kevin Appier .10 .30
70 Jeff Bagwell .20 .50
71 Tim Wakefield .10 .30
72 Shannon Stewart .10 .30
73 Scott Rolen .20 .50
74 Bobby Higginson .10 .30
75 Jim Edmonds .10 .30
76 Adam Dunn .10 .30
77 Eric Chavez .10 .30
78 Adrian Beltre .10 .30
79 Jason Varitek .30 .75
80 Barry Bonds .75 2.00
81 Edgar Renteria .10 .30
82 Raul Mondesi .10 .30
83 Eric Karros .10 .30
84 Ken Griffey Jr. .60 1.50
85 Jermaine Dye .10 .30
86 Carlos Beltran .10 .30
87 Mark Quinn .10 .30
88 Terrence Long .10 .30
89 Shawn Green .10 .30
90 Nomar Garciaparra .50 1.25
91 Sean Casey .10 .30
92 Homer Bush .10 .30
93 Bob Abreu .10 .30
94 Jamey Wright .10 .30
95 Tony Womack .10 .30
96 Larry Walker .10 .30
97 Doug Mientkiewicz .10 .30
98 Jimmy Rollins .10 .30
99 Brady Anderson .10 .30
100 Derek Jeter .75 2.00
101 Kevin Young .10 .30
102 Juan Pierre .10 .30
103 Edgar Martinez .20 .50
104 Corey Koskie .10 .30
105 Jeffrey Hammonds .10 .30
106 Luis Gonzalez .10 .30
107 Travis Fryman .10 .30
108 Kerry Wood .10 .30
109 Rafael Palmeiro .20 .50
110 Ichiro Suzuki .60 1.50
111 Russ Ortiz .10 .30
112 Jeff Kent .10 .30
113 Scott Erickson .10 .30
114 Bruce Chen .10 .30
115 Craig Biggio .20 .50
116 Robin Ventura .10 .30
117 Alex Rodriguez .40 1.00
118 Roy Oswalt .10 .30
119 Fred McGriff .20 .50
120 Juan Gonzalez .10 .30
121 David Justice .10 .30
122 Pat Hentgen .10 .30
123 Hideo Nomo .30 .75
124 Ramon Ortiz .10 .30
125 David Ortiz .30 .75
126 Phil Nevin .10 .30
127 Ryan Dempster .10 .30
128 Toby Hall .10 .30
129 Vladimir Guerrero .30 .75
130 Chipper Jones .30 .75
131 Russell Branyan .10 .30
132 Jose Vidro .10 .30
133 Bubba Trammell .10 .30
134 Tino Martinez .20 .50
135 Greg Maddux .50 1.25
136 Derrek Lee .20 .50
137 Troy Glaus .10 .30
138 Joe Crede .10 .30
139 Steve Cox .10 .30
140 Sammy Sosa .30 .75
141 Corey Patterson .10 .30
142 Vernon Wells .10 .30
143 Matt Lawton .10 .30
144 Gabe Kapler .10 .30
145 Johnny Damon Sox .20 .50
146 Marty Cordova .10 .30
147 Moises Alou .10 .30
148 Fernando Tatis .10 .30
149 Tanyon Sturtze .10 .30
150 Roger Clemens .60 1.50
151 Paul Konerko .10 .30
152 Chan Ho Park .10 .30
153 Marcus Giles .10 .30
154 David Eckstein .10 .30
155 Mike Lowell .10 .30
156 Preston Wilson .10 .30
157 John Vander Wal .10 .30
158 Tim Salmon .20 .50
159 Andy Pettitte .20 .50
160 Mike Mussina .20 .50
161 Doug Davis .10 .30
162 Peter Bergeron .10 .30
163 Rich Aurilia .10 .30
164 Eric Milton .10 .30
165 Geoff Jenkins .10 .30
166 Todd Helton .20 .50
167 Bret Boone .10 .30
168 Kris Benson .10 .30
169 Brian Anderson .10 .30
170 Roberto Alomar .20 .50
171 Javier Vazquez .10 .30
172 Scott Schoeneweis .10 .30
173 Ryan Klesko .10 .30
174 Jacque Jones .10 .30
175 Andruw Jones .20 .50
176 Aubrey Huff .10 .30
177 Mark Buehrle .10 .30
178 Josh Beckett .10 .30
179 Ben Sheets .10 .30
180 Curt Schilling .10 .30
181 C.C. Sabathia .10 .30
182 Denny Neagle .10 .30
183 Jamie Moyer .10 .30
184 Jason Kendall .10 .30
185 Dee Brown .10 .30
186 Frank Thomas .30 .75
187 Damian Rolls .10 .30
188 Carlos Lee .10 .30
189 Kevin Jarvis .10 .30
190 Manny Ramirez .20 .50
191 Cliff Floyd .10 .30
192 Freddy Garcia .10 .30
193 Orlando Cabrera .10 .30
194 Mike Sweeney .10 .30
195 Gary Sheffield .10 .30
196 Rafael Furcal .10 .30
197 Esteban Loaiza .10 .30
198 Mike Hampton .10 .30
199 Brian Giles .10 .30
200 Darin Erstad .10 .30
201 David Wells .10 .30
202 Kenny Lofton .10 .30
203 Aaron Sele .10 .30
204 Jason Schmidt .10 .30
205 Javy Lopez .10 .30
206 Dmitri Young .10 .30
207 Darryl Kile .10 .30
208 Matt Williams .10 .30
209 Joe Kennedy .10 .30
210 Chuck Knoblauch .10 .30
211 Brian Jordan .10 .30
212 Robert Person .10 .30
213 Alex Ochoa .10 .30
214 Steve Finley .10 .30
215 Ben Petrick .10 .30
216 Al Leiter .10 .30
217 Mark Kotsay .10 .30
218 Miguel Tejada .10 .30
219 David Segui .10 .30
220 A.J. Burnett .10 .30
221 Marlon Anderson .10 .30
222 Wiki Gonzalez .10 .30
223 Jeff Suppan .10 .30
224 Dave Roberts .10 .30
225 Jose Hernandez .10 .30
226 Angel Berroa ROO .75 2.00
227 Sean Burroughs ROO .75 2.00
228 Luis Martinez ROO RC .75 2.00
229 Adrian Burnside ROO RC .75 2.00
230 John Ennis ROO RC .75 2.00
231 Anastacio Martinez ROO RC .75 2.00
232 Hank Blalock ROO 1.25 3.00
233 Eric Hinske ROO .75 2.00
234 Chris Booker ROO RC .75 2.00
235 Colin Young ROO RC .75 2.00
236 Mark Corey ROO RC .75 2.00
237 Satoru Komiyama ROO RC .75 2.00
238 So Taguchi ROO RC 1.25 3.00
239 Elio Serrano ROO RC .75 2.00
240 Reed Johnson ROO RC 1.25 3.00
241 Jeremy Lambert ROO RC .75 2.00
242 Chris Baker ROO RC .75 2.00
243 Orlando Hudson ROO .75 2.00
244 Travis Hughes ROO RC .75 2.00
245 Kevin Frederick ROO RC .75 2.00
246 Rodrigo Rosario ROO RC .75 2.00
247 Jeremy Ward ROO RC .75 2.00
248 Kazuhisa Ishii ROO RC 1.25 3.00
249 Austin Kearns ROO .75 2.00
250 Kyle Kane ROO RC .75 2.00
251 Cam Esslinger ROO RC .75 2.00
252 Jeff Austin ROO RC .75 2.00
253 Brian Mallette ROO RC .75 2.00
254 Mark Prior ROO 1.25 3.00
255 Mark Teixeira ROO 1.25 3.00
256 Carlos Valderrama ROO .75 2.00
257 Jason Hart ROO .75 2.00
258 Takahito Nomura ROO RC .75 2.00
259 Matt Thornton ROO RC .75 2.00
260 Marlon Byrd ROO .75 2.00

2002 Fleer Focus JE Century Parallel

*CENTURY 1-225: 6X TO 15X BASIC
*CENTURY 226-260: 1X TO 2.5X BASIC
RANDOM INSERTS IN HOBBY PACKS
PRINT RUNS RANGE FROM 101-199 OF EACH
SEE BECKETT.COM FOR ALL PRINT RUNS

2002 Fleer Focus JE Jersey Parallel

*1-225 PRINT RUN b/wn 26-35 20X TO 50X
*1-225 PRINT RUN b/wn 36-50 15X TO 40X
*1-225 PRINT RUN b/wn 51-65 12.5X TO 30X
*1-225 PRINT RUN b/wn 66-80 10X TO 25X
COMMON (226-260) p/r 81-99 2.50 6.00
UNLISTED 226-260 p/r 81-99 6.00 15.00
COMMON (226-260) p/r 66-80 3.00 8.00
UNLISTED 226-260 p/r 66-80 8.00 20.00
COMMON (226-260) p/r 51-65 4.00 10.00
SEMIS 226-260 p/r 51-65 6.00 15.00
COMMON (226-260) p/r 36-50 5.00 12.00
UNLISTED 226-260 p/r 26-35 15.00 40.00
PRINT RUNS BASED ON UNIFORM NUMBER
SEE BECKETT.COM FOR PRINT RUNS
NO PRICING ON QUANTITIES OF 25 OR LESS

2002 Fleer Focus JE Blue Chips

COMPLETE SET (15) 6.00 15.00
STATED ODDS 1:6 HOBBY, 1:12 RETAIL
1 Albert Pujols 2.00 5.00
2 Sean Burroughs .40 1.00
3 Vernon Wells .40 1.00
4 Adam Dunn .40 1.00
5 Pat Burrell .40 1.00
6 Juan Pierre .40 1.00
7 Russell Branyan .40 1.00
8 Carlos Pena .40 1.00
9 Toby Hall .40 1.00
10 Hank Blalock .60 1.50
11 Alfonso Soriano .40 1.00
12 Jimmy Rollins .40 1.00
13 Jose Ortiz .40 1.00
14 Eric Hinske .40 1.00
15 Nick Johnson .40 1.00

2002 Fleer Focus JE Blue Chips Game Used

STATED ODDS 1:96 HOBBY, 1:180 RETAIL
1 Russell Branyan Pants 4.00 10.00
2 Nick Johnson Jsy 4.00 10.00

2002 Fleer Focus JE Blue Chips Game Used Patch

RANDOM INSERTS IN PACKS
STATED PRINT RUN 100 SERIAL #'d SETS
1 Nick Johnson 10.00 25.00

2002 Fleer Focus JE Intl Diamond Co.

COMPLETE SET (25) 15.00 40.00
STATED ODDS 1:8 HOBBY, 1:12 RETAIL
1 Bobby Abreu .75 2.00
2 Adrian Beltre .75 2.00
3 Jorge Posada .75 2.00
4 Vladimir Guerrero 1.25 3.00
5 Rafael Palmeiro .75 2.00
6 Sammy Sosa 1.25 3.00
7 Larry Walker .75 2.00
8 Manny Ramirez .75 2.00
9 Ichiro Suzuki 2.50 6.00
10 Jose Cruz Jr. .75 2.00
11 Juan Gonzalez .75 2.00
12 Bernie Williams .75 2.00
13 Ivan Rodriguez .75 2.00
14 Moises Alou .75 2.00
15 Cristian Guzman .75 2.00
16 Andruw Jones .75 2.00
17 Aramis Ramirez .75 2.00
18 Raul Mondesi .75 2.00
19 Edgar Martinez .75 2.00
20 Magglio Ordonez .75 2.00
21 Roberto Alomar .75 2.00
22 Chan Ho Park .75 2.00
23 Kazuhiro Sasaki .75 2.00
24 Tsuyoshi Shinjo .75 2.00
25 Hideo Nomo 1.25 3.00

2002 Fleer Focus JE Intl Diamond Co. Game Used

STATED ODDS 1:144 HOBBY, 1:180 RETAIL
SP PRINT RUNS PROVIDED BY FLEER
SP'S ARE NOT SERIAL-NUMBERED
1 Andruw Jones Jsy 6.00 15.00
2 Edgar Martinez Jsy 6.00 15.00
3 Raul Mondesi Jsy 4.00 10.00
4 Hideo Nomo Jsy 15.00 40.00
5 Rafael Palmeiro Jsy 6.00 15.00
6 Chan Ho Park Jsy 4.00 10.00
7 Aramis Ramirez Pants 4.00 10.00
8 Manny Ramirez Jsy 6.00 15.00
9 Ivan Rodriguez Jsy 6.00 15.00
10 Kazuhiro Sasaki Jsy SP/307 4.00 10.00

2002 Fleer Focus JE Intl Diamond Co. Game Used Patch

RANDOM INSERTS IN PACKS
STATED PRINT RUN 100 SERIAL #'d SETS
1 Edgar Martinez 12.50 30.00
2 Raul Mondesi 10.00 25.00
3 Hideo Nomo 75.00 150.00
4 Chan Ho Park 10.00 25.00
5 Manny Ramirez 12.50 30.00
6 Ivan Rodriguez 12.50 30.00

2002 Fleer Focus JE K Corps

COMPLETE SET (15) 10.00 25.00
STATED ODDS 1:12 HOBBY/RETAIL
1 Roger Clemens 2.00 5.00
2 Randy Johnson 1.00 2.50
3 Tom Glavine .60 1.50
4 Josh Beckett .60 1.50
5 Matt Morris .60 1.50
6 Curt Schilling .60 1.50
7 Greg Maddux 1.50 4.00
8 Tim Hudson .60 1.50
9 Roy Oswalt .60 1.50
10 Kerry Wood .60 1.50
11 Barry Zito .60 1.50
12 Kevin Brown .60 1.50
13 Ryan Dempster .60 1.50
14 Ben Sheets .60 1.50
15 Pedro Martinez .60 1.50

2002 Fleer Focus JE K Corps Game Used

STATED ODDS 1:96 HOBBY, 1:180 RETAIL
SP PRINT RUNS PROVIDED BY FLEER
SP'S ARE NOT SERIAL-NUMBERED
1 Kevin Brown Jsy 4.00 10.00
2 Randy Johnson Jsy SP/316 6.00 15.00
3 Greg Maddux Jsy 6.00 15.00
4 Pedro Martinez Jsy 6.00 15.00
5 Curt Schilling Jsy 4.00 10.00
6 Barry Zito Jsy SP/220 4.00 10.00

2002 Fleer Focus JE K Corps Game Used Patch

RANDOM INSERTS IN PACKS
STATED PRINT RUN 100 SERIAL #'d SETS
1 Kevin Brown 10.00 25.00
2 Pedro Martinez 12.50 30.00
3 Curt Schilling 10.00 25.00

2002 Fleer Focus JE Kings of Swing

COMPLETE SET (20) 75.00 150.00
STATED ODDS 1:48 HOBBY/RETAIL
1 Barry Bonds 6.00 15.00
2 Mike Piazza 4.00 10.00
3 Albert Pujols 5.00 12.00
4 Todd Helton 2.00 5.00
5 Ken Griffey Jr. 5.00 12.00
6 Alex Rodriguez 3.00 8.00
7 Sammy Sosa 2.50 6.00
8 Troy Glaus 2.00 5.00
9 Derek Jeter 6.00 15.00
10 Ichiro Suzuki 5.00 12.00
11 Manny Ramirez 2.00 5.00
12 Roberto Alomar 2.00 5.00
13 Juan Gonzalez 2.00 5.00
14 Shawn Green 2.00 5.00
15 Vladimir Guerrero 2.50 6.00
16 Nomar Garciaparra 4.00 10.00
17 Adam Dunn 2.00 5.00
18 Jason Giambi 2.00 5.00
19 Edgar Martinez 2.00 5.00
20 Chipper Jones 2.50 6.00

2002 Fleer Focus JE Kings of Swing Game Used

STATED ODDS 1:108 HOBBY, 1:180 RETAIL
SP PRINT RUNS PROVIDED BY FLEER
SP'S ARE NOT SERIAL-NUMBERED
1 Shawn Green Jsy 6.00 15.00
2 Todd Helton Jsy 6.00 15.00
3 Derek Jeter Jsy SP/348 12.00 30.00
4 Chipper Jones Jsy 6.00 15.00
5 Edgar Martinez Jsy 6.00 15.00
6 Mike Piazza Jsy 6.00 15.00
7 Manny Ramirez Jsy 6.00 15.00
8 Alex Rodriguez Jsy 6.00 15.00

2002 Fleer Focus JE Kings of Swing Game Used Patch

RANDOM INSERTS IN PACKS
STATED PRINT RUN 100 SERIAL #'d SETS
1 Shawn Green 12.50 30.00
2 Todd Helton 12.50 30.00
3 Edgar Martinez 12.50 30.00
4 Mike Piazza 20.00 50.00
5 Manny Ramirez 12.50 30.00

2002 Fleer Focus JE Larger than Life

STATED ODDS 1:240 HOBBY/RETAIL
1 Jason Giambi 4.00 10.00
2 Carlos Delgado 4.00 10.00
3 Alex Rodriguez 8.00 20.00
4 Preston Wilson 4.00 10.00
5 Frank Thomas 6.00 15.00
6 Nomar Garciaparra 10.00 25.00
7 Jim Edmonds 4.00 10.00
8 Jim Thome 6.00 15.00
9 Barry Bonds 15.00 40.00
10 Mo Vaughn 4.00 10.00
11 Ichiro Suzuki 12.50 30.00
12 Ivan Rodriguez 6.00 15.00
13 Gary Sheffield 4.00 10.00
14 Derek Jeter 15.00 40.00
15 Jeff Bagwell 6.00 15.00
16 Mike Piazza 10.00 25.00
17 J.D. Drew 4.00 10.00
18 Sammy Sosa 6.00 15.00
19 Albert Pujols 12.50 30.00
20 Luis Gonzalez 4.00 10.00

2002 Fleer Focus JE Larger than Life Game Used

STATED ODDS 1:144 HOBBY, 1:180 RETAIL
SP PRINT RUNS PROVIDED BY FLEER
SP'S ARE NOT SERIAL-NUMBERED
2 Jim Edmonds Jsy 4.00 10.00
3 Luis Gonzalez Jsy 4.00 10.00
4 Derek Jeter Jsy 12.50 30.00
5 Mike Piazza Jsy 8.00 20.00
6 Alex Rodriguez Jsy 8.00 20.00
7 Ivan Rodriguez Jsy 6.00 15.00
8 Frank Thomas Jsy 6.00 15.00
9 Mo Vaughn Jsy 4.00 10.00
10 Preston Wilson Jsy 4.00 10.00

2002 Fleer Focus JE Larger than Life Game Used Patch

RANDOM INSERTS IN PACKS
STATED PRINT RUN 100 SERIAL #'d SETS
1 Jim Edmonds 10.00 25.00
2 Luis Gonzalez 10.00 25.00
3 Mike Piazza 20.00 50.00
4 Ivan Rodriguez 12.50 30.00
5 Frank Thomas 15.00 40.00
6 Preston Wilson 10.00 25.00

2002 Fleer Focus JE Lettermen Jumbos

ONE CARD PER LETTER IN PLAYER'S NAME
NO PRICING DUE TO SCARCITY

2002 Fleer Focus JE Materialistic Away

COMPLETE SET (15) 50.00 120.00
STATED ODDS 1:24 HOBBY/RETAIL
*HOME: 1.5X TO 4X BASIC
HOME RANDOM INSERTS IN PACKS
HOME PRINT RUN 50 SERIAL #'d SETS
*JUMBO AWAY: .5X TO 1.2X BASIC
JUMBO AWAY ONE PER HOBBY BOX
*JUMBO HOME: 1.5X TO 4X BASIC
JUMBO HOME PRINT RUN 50 #'d SETS
1 Derek Jeter 6.00 15.00
2 Alex Rodriguez 3.00 8.00
3 Mike Piazza 4.00 10.00
4 Ivan Rodriguez 1.50 4.00
5 Chipper Jones 2.50 6.00
6 Todd Helton 1.50 4.00
7 Nomar Garciaparra 4.00 10.00
8 Barry Bonds 6.00 15.00
9 Ichiro Suzuki 5.00 12.00
10 Ken Griffey Jr. 5.00 12.00
11 Jason Giambi 1.50 4.00
12 Sammy Sosa 2.50 6.00
13 Albert Pujols 5.00 12.00
14 Pedro Martinez 1.50 4.00
15 Vladimir Guerrero 2.50 6.00

2003 Fleer Focus JE

COMPLETE SET (180) 20.00 50.00
COMP.SET w/o SP's (160) 8.00 20.00
COMMON CARD (1-160) .10 .30
COMMON CARD (161-180) .40 1.00
161-180 STATED ODDS 1:4
1 Derek Jeter .75 2.00
2 Preston Wilson .12 .30
3 Trevor Hoffman .20 .50
4 Moises Alou .12 .30
5 Roberto Alomar .20 .50
6 Tim Salmon .12 .30
7 Mike Lowell .12 .30
8 Barry Bonds .50 1.25
9 Fred McGriff .20 .50
10 Mo Vaughn .12 .30
11 Junior Spivey .12 .30
12 Roy Oswalt .20 .50
13 Ichiro Suzuki .40 1.00
14 Magglio Ordonez .20 .50
15 Adam Kennedy .12 .30
16 Randy Johnson .30 .75
17 Carlos Beltran .20 .50
18 John Olerud .12 .30
19 Joe Borchard .12 .30
20 Alfonso Soriano .20 .50
21 Curt Schilling .20 .50
22 Mike Sweeney .12 .30
23 Tino Martinez .12 .30
24 Barry Larkin .20 .50
25 Miguel Tejada .20 .50
26 Chipper Jones .30 .75
27 Kevin Brown .12 .30
28 J.D. Drew .12 .30
29 Sean Casey .12 .30
30 Bernie Williams .20 .50
31 Troy Percival .12 .30
32 Jeff Bagwell .20 .50
33 Kenny Lofton .12 .30
34 Kerry Wood .12 .30
35 Armando Benitez .12 .30
36 David Eckstein .12 .30
37 Wade Miller .12 .30
38 Edgar Martinez .20 .50
39 Mark Prior .20 .50
40 Mike Piazza .30 .75
41 Shea Hillenbrand .12 .30
42 Bartolo Colon .12 .30
43 Darin Erstad .12 .30
44 A.J. Burnett .12 .30
45 Jeff Kent .12 .30
46 Corey Patterson .12 .30
47 Ty Wigginton .12 .30
48 Troy Glaus .12 .30
49 Josh Beckett .12 .30
50 Brian Lawrence .12 .30
51 Frank Thomas .30 .75
52 Jason Giambi .12 .30
53 Luis Gonzalez .12 .30
54 Raul Ibanez .20 .50
55 Kazuhiro Sasaki .12 .30
56 Mark Buehrle .20 .50
57 Roger Clemens .40 1.00
58 Matt Williams .12 .30
59 Joe Randa .12 .30
60 Jamie Moyer .12 .30
61 Paul Konerko .20 .50
62 Mike Mussina .20 .50
63 Javy Lopez .12 .30
64 Brian Jordan .12 .30
65 Scott Rolen .20 .50
66 Aaron Boone .12 .30
67 Eric Chavez .12 .30
68 Mark Grace .20 .50
69 Shawn Green .12 .30
70 Albert Pujols .40 1.00
71 Sammy Sosa .30 .75
72 Edgardo Alfonzo .12 .30
73 Garret Anderson .12 .30
74 Lance Berkman .20 .50
75 Bret Boone .12 .30
76 Joe Crede .12 .30
77 Al Leiter .12 .30
78 Jarrod Washburn .12 .30
79 Craig Biggio .20 .50
80 Rich Aurilia .12 .30
81 Adam Dunn .20 .50
82 Jermaine Dye .12 .30
83 Tom Glavine .20 .50
84 Eric Gagne .12 .30
85 Jared Sandberg .12 .30
86 Jim Thome .20 .50
87 Barry Zito .20 .50
88 Gary Sheffield .12 .30
89 Paul Lo Duca .12 .30
90 Matt Morris .12 .30
91 Juan Pierre .12 .30
92 Randy Wolf .12 .30
93 Jay Gibbons .12 .30
94 Brad Radke .12 .30
95 Carlos Delgado .12 .30
96 Carlos Pena .20 .50
97 Brian Giles .12 .30
98 Rodrigo Lopez .12 .30
99 Jacque Jones .12 .30
100 Juan Gonzalez .12 .30
101 Randall Simon .12 .30
102 Mike Williams .12 .30
103 Derek Lowe .12 .30
104 Brad Wilkerson .12 .30
105 Eric Hinske .12 .30
106 Luis Castillo .12 .30
107 Phil Nevin .12 .30
108 Manny Ramirez .30 .75
109 Vladimir Guerrero .20 .50
110 Roy Halladay .20 .50
111 Ellis Burks .12 .30
112 Bobby Abreu .12 .30
113 Tony Batista .12 .30
114 Richie Sexson .12 .30
115 Rafael Palmeiro .20 .50
116 Todd Helton .20 .50
117 Pat Burrell .12 .30
118 John Smoltz .30 .75
119 Ben Sheets .12 .30
120 Aubrey Huff .12 .30
121 Andruw Jones .12 .30
122 Kazuhisa Ishii .12 .30
123 Jim Edmonds .20 .50
124 Austin Kearns .12 .30
125 Mark Mulder .12 .30
126 Greg Maddux .40 1.00
127 Jose Hernandez .12 .30
128 Ben Grieve .12 .30
129 Ken Griffey Jr. .60 1.50
130 Tim Hudson .20 .50
131 Jorge Julio .12 .30

132 Torii Hunter	.12	.30
133 Ivan Rodriguez	.20	.50
134 Jason Jennings	.12	.30
135 Jason Kendall	.12	.30
136 Nomar Garciaparra	.20	.50
137 Michael Cuddyer	.12	.30
138 Shannon Stewart	.12	.30
139 Larry Walker	.20	.50
140 Aramis Ramirez	.12	.30
141 Johnny Damon	.20	.50
142 Orlando Cabrera	.12	.30
143 Vernon Wells	.12	.30
144 Bobby Higginson	.12	.30
145 Sean Burroughs	.12	.30
146 Pedro Martinez	.20	.50
147 Jose Vidro	.12	.30
148 Orlando Hudson	.12	.30
149 Robert Fick	.12	.30
150 Ryan Klesko	.12	.30
151 Kevin Millwood	.12	.30
152 Alex Sanchez	.12	.30
153 Randy Winn	.12	.30
154 Omar Vizquel	.20	.50
155 Mike Lieberthal	.12	.30
156 Marty Cordova	.12	.30
157 Cristian Guzman	.12	.30
158 Alex Rodriguez	.40	1.00
159 C.C. Sabathia	.20	.50
160 Jimmy Rollins	.20	.50
161 Josh Willingham HP RC	1.25	3.00
162 Lance Niekro HP	.40	1.00
163 Nook Logan HP RC	.40	1.00
164 Chase Utley HP	.60	1.50
165 Pete LaForest HP RC	.40	1.00
166 Victor Martinez HP	.60	1.50
167 Adam LaRoche HP	.40	1.00
168 Ian Ferguson HP RC	.40	1.00
169 Mark Teixeira HP	.60	1.50
170 Chris Waters HP RC	.40	1.00
171 Hideki Matsui HP RC	2.00	5.00
172 Alejandro Machado HP RC	.40	1.00
173 Francisco Rosario HP RC	.40	1.00
174 Termel Sledge HP RC	.40	1.00
175 Guillermo Quiroz HP RC	.40	1.00
176 Lew Ford HP RC	.40	1.00
177 Hank Blalock HP	.40	1.00
178 Lyle Overbay HP	.40	1.00
179 Matt Bruback HP RC	.40	1.00
180 Jose Contreras HP RC	1.00	2.50

2003 Fleer Focus JE Century Parallel

*CENTURY 1-160: 6X TO 15X BASIC		
*CENTURY 161-180: 1X TO 2.5X BASIC		
RANDOM INSERTS IN PACKS		
PRINT RUNS BASED ON JSY NUMBER +100		

2003 Fleer Focus JE Franchise Focus

COMPLETE SET (20)	6.00	15.00
STATED ODDS 1:4		
1 Troy Glaus	.40	1.00
2 Randy Johnson	1.00	2.50
3 Chipper Jones	1.00	2.50
4 Nomar Garciaparra	.60	1.50
5 Sammy Sosa	1.00	2.50
6 Ken Griffey Jr.	2.00	5.00
7 Jeff Bagwell	.60	1.50
8 Mike Sweeney	.40	1.00
9 Shawn Green	.40	1.00
10 Torii Hunter	.40	1.00
11 Vladimir Guerrero	.60	1.50
12 Mike Piazza	1.00	2.50
13 Jason Giambi	.40	1.00
14 Barry Zito	.60	1.50
15 Pat Burrell	.40	1.00
16 Barry Bonds	1.50	4.00
17 Ichiro Suzuki	1.25	3.00
18 Albert Pujols	1.25	3.00
19 Alex Rodriguez	1.25	3.00
20 Carlos Delgado	.40	1.00

2003 Fleer Focus JE Home and Aways Game Jersey

STATED ODDS 1:288		
AR Alex Rodriguez	12.50	30.00
AS Alfonso Soriano	6.00	15.00
CJ Chipper Jones	6.00	15.00
DJ Derek Jeter	10.00	25.00
GM Greg Maddux	8.00	20.00
JD J.D. Drew	6.00	15.00
LB Lance Berkman	6.00	15.00
NG Nomar Garciaparra	8.00	20.00
RO Roy Oswalt	6.00	15.00

2003 Fleer Focus JE Materialistic Action Away

STATED ODDS 1:192		
*HOME: .75X TO 2X BASIC AWAY		
HOME RANDOM INSERTS IN PACKS		
HOME PRINT RUN 50 SERIAL #'d SETS		
I Ichiro Suzuki	5.00	12.00
AD Adam Dunn	2.50	6.00
AP Albert Pujols	5.00	12.00
AR Alex Rodriguez	5.00	12.00
AS Alfonso Soriano	2.50	6.00
CJ Chipper Jones	4.00	10.00
DJ Derek Jeter	10.00	25.00
GM Greg Maddux	5.00	12.00
JG Jason Giambi	1.50	4.00
KG Ken Griffey Jr.	8.00	20.00
MP Mike Piazza	4.00	10.00
NG Nomar Garciaparra	2.50	6.00
PB Pat Burrell	1.50	4.00
RC Roger Clemens	5.00	12.00
SS Sammy Sosa	4.00	10.00

2003 Fleer Focus JE Materialistic Oversized

ONE PER SEALED BOX		
I Ichiro Suzuki	2.00	5.00
AD Adam Dunn	1.00	2.50
AP Albert Pujols	2.00	5.00
AR Alex Rodriguez	2.00	5.00
AS Alfonso Soriano	1.00	2.50
CJ Chipper Jones	1.50	4.00
DJ Derek Jeter	4.00	10.00
GM Greg Maddux	2.00	5.00
JG Jason Giambi	.60	1.50
KG Ken Griffey Jr.	3.00	8.00
MP Mike Piazza	1.50	4.00
NG Nomar Garciaparra	1.00	2.50
PB Pat Burrell	.60	1.50
RC Roger Clemens	2.00	5.00
RJ Reggie Jackson	1.00	2.50
SS Sammy Sosa	1.50	4.00

2003 Fleer Focus JE Materialistic Oversized Autographs

STATED PRINT RUNS LISTED BELOW		
CJ Chipper Jones/80 *	30.00	60.00
DJ Derek Jeter/360 *	75.00	200.00
RJ Reggie Jackson/360 *	15.00	40.00

2003 Fleer Focus JE Materialistic Plus Game Jersey

RANDOM INSERTS IN PACKS		
STATED PRINT RUN 250 SERIAL #'d SETS		
AD Adam Dunn	4.00	10.00
AR Alex Rodriguez	8.00	20.00
AS Alfonso Soriano	4.00	10.00
CJ Chipper Jones	6.00	15.00
DJ Derek Jeter	8.00	20.00
GM Greg Maddux	10.00	25.00
MP Mike Piazza	10.00	25.00
NG Nomar Garciaparra	10.00	25.00
RC Roger Clemens	6.00	15.00

2003 Fleer Focus JE Materialistic Portrait Away

STATED ODDS 1:576		
HOME RANDOM INSERTS IN PACKS		
HOME PRINT RUN 1 SERIAL #'d SET		
NO HOME PRICING DUE TO SCARCITY		
I Ichiro Suzuki	6.00	15.00
AD Adam Dunn	3.00	8.00
AP Albert Pujols	6.00	15.00
AR Alex Rodriguez	6.00	15.00
AS Alfonso Soriano	3.00	8.00
CJ Chipper Jones	5.00	12.00
DJ Derek Jeter	12.00	30.00
GM Greg Maddux	6.00	15.00
JG Jason Giambi	2.00	5.00
KG Ken Griffey Jr.	10.00	25.00
MP Mike Piazza	5.00	12.00
NG Nomar Garciaparra	3.00	8.00
PB Pat Burrell	2.00	5.00
RC Roger Clemens	6.00	15.00
SS Sammy Sosa	5.00	12.00

2003 Fleer Focus JE MLB Shirtified

STATED ODDS 1:24		
1 Manny Ramirez	1.00	2.50
2 Jarrod Washburn	.40	1.00
3 Greg Maddux	1.25	3.00
4 Austin Kearns	.40	1.00
5 Jim Thome	.60	1.50
6 Kazuhisa Ishii	.40	1.00
7 Mike Piazza	1.00	2.50
8 Alfonso Soriano	.60	1.50
9 Pat Burrell	.40	1.00
10 Derek Jeter	2.50	6.00
11 Miguel Tejada	.60	1.50
12 Roger Clemens	1.25	3.00
13 Alex Rodriguez	1.25	3.00
14 Roy Oswalt	.60	1.50
15 Richie Sexson	.40	1.00

2003 Fleer Focus JE MLB Shirtified Game Jersey

STATED ODDS 1:35		
AR Alex Rodriguez	6.00	15.00
AS Alfonso Soriano	3.00	8.00
DJ Derek Jeter	10.00	25.00
GM Greg Maddux	4.00	10.00
MP Mike Piazza	4.00	10.00
MR Manny Ramirez	4.00	10.00
MT Miguel Tejada	3.00	8.00
RC Roger Clemens	6.00	15.00
RO Roy Oswalt	3.00	8.00
RS Richie Sexson	3.00	8.00

2003 Fleer Focus JE MLB Shirtified Patch

*PREMIUM LOGOS: 2X HI COLUMN		
*4 OR MORE COLORS: 1.5X HI COLUMN		
RANDOM INSERTS IN PACKS		
STATED PRINT RUN 200 SERIAL #'d SETS		
AR Alex Rodriguez	10.00	25.00
AS Alfonso Soriano	8.00	20.00
DJ Derek Jeter	30.00	60.00
GM Greg Maddux	15.00	40.00
MP Mike Piazza	15.00	40.00
MR Manny Ramirez	10.00	25.00
MT Miguel Tejada	8.00	20.00
RC Roger Clemens	15.00	40.00
RO Roy Oswalt	8.00	20.00
RS Richie Sexson	8.00	20.00

2003 Fleer Focus JE Team Colors

STATED ODDS 1:12		
1 Alex Rodriguez	1.25	3.00
2 Mark Prior	.60	1.50
3 Derek Jeter	2.50	6.00
4 Curt Schilling	.60	1.50
5 Pat Burrell	.40	1.00
6 Josh Beckett	.40	1.00
7 Sean Burroughs	.40	1.00
8 Troy Glaus	.40	1.00
9 Torii Hunter	.40	1.00
10 Jeff Bagwell	.60	1.50
11 Pedro Martinez	.60	1.50
12 Mike Piazza	1.00	2.50
13 Lance Berkman	.60	1.50
14 Nomar Garciaparra	.60	1.50
15 Chipper Jones	1.00	2.50
16 Eric Chavez	.40	1.00
17 Barry Zito	.60	1.50
18 Barry Bonds	1.50	4.00
19 Adam Dunn	.60	1.50
20 Randy Johnson	1.00	2.50

2003 Fleer Focus JE Team Colors Game Jersey

STATED ODDS 1:28		
AD Adam Dunn	3.00	8.00
CJ Chipper Jones	4.00	10.00
CS Curt Schilling	3.00	8.00
DJ Derek Jeter	10.00	25.00
EC Eric Chavez	3.00	8.00
JBA Jeff Bagwell	4.00	10.00
JBE Josh Beckett	3.00	8.00
LB Lance Berkman	3.00	8.00
NG Nomar Garciaparra	6.00	15.00
PM Pedro Martinez	4.00	10.00
RJ Randy Johnson	4.00	10.00
TG Troy Glaus	3.00	8.00

2003 Fleer Focus JE Team Colors Game Jersey Multi Color

*4 OR MORE COLORS: 1.5X HI COLUMN		
RANDOM INSERTS IN PACKS		
STATED PRINT RUN 250 SERIAL #'d SETS		
AD Adam Dunn	8.00	20.00
AR Alex Rodriguez	15.00	40.00
CJ Chipper Jones	10.00	25.00
CS Curt Schilling	8.00	20.00
DJ Derek Jeter	20.00	50.00
EC Eric Chavez	8.00	20.00
JBA Jeff Bagwell	10.00	25.00
JBE Josh Beckett	8.00	20.00
LB Lance Berkman	8.00	20.00
MP Mike Piazza	15.00	40.00
NG Nomar Garciaparra	15.00	40.00
PM Pedro Martinez	10.00	25.00
RJ Randy Johnson	10.00	25.00
TG Troy Glaus	8.00	20.00

2001 Fleer Futures

COMPLETE SET (220)	10.00	25.00
COMMON CARD (1-220)	.10	.30
COMMON CARD (221-230)	2.00	5.00
221-230 DIST.IN FLEER PLAT.RC HOB/RET		
221-230 PRINT RUN 2499 SERIAL #'d SETS		
1 Darin Erstad	.10	.30
2 Manny Ramirez	.20	.50
3 Darryl Kile	.10	.30
4 Troy O'Leary	.10	.30
5 Mark Quinn	.10	.30
6 Brian Giles	.10	.30
7 Randy Johnson	.30	.75
8 Todd Walker	.10	.30
9 Mike Piazza	.30	.75
10 Fred McGriff	.20	.50
11 Sammy Sosa	.30	.75
12 Chan Ho Park	.10	.30
13 John Rocker	.10	.30
14 Luis Castillo	.10	.30
15 Eric Chavez	.10	.30
16 Carlos Delgado	.10	.30
17 Sean Casey	.10	.30
18 Corey Koskie	.10	.30
19 John Olerud	.10	.30
20 Nomar Garciaparra	.30	.75
21 Craig Biggio	.20	.50
22 Pat Burrell	.10	.30
23 Ben Molina	.10	.30
24 Jim Thome	.20	.50
25 Rey Ordonez	.10	.30
26 Fernando Tatis	.10	.30
27 Eric Young	.10	.30
28 Eric Karros	.10	.30
29 Adam Eaton	.10	.30
30 Brian Jordan	.10	.30
31 Jorge Posada	.20	.50
32 Gabe Kapler	.10	.30
33 Keith Foulke	.10	.30
34 Ron Coomer	.10	.30
35 Chipper Jones	.30	.75
36 Miguel Tejada	.10	.30
37 David Wells	.10	.30
38 Carlos Lee	.10	.30
39 Barry Bonds	.75	2.00
40 Derrek Lee	.20	.50
41 Tim Hudson	.10	.30
42 Billy Koch	.10	.30
43 Dmitri Young	.10	.30
44 Vladimir Guerrero	.30	.75
45 Rickey Henderson	.30	.75
46 Jeff Bagwell	.20	.50
47 Robert Person	.10	.30
48 Brady Anderson	.10	.30
49 Lance Berkman	.10	.30
50 Mike Lieberthal	.10	.30
51 Adam Kennedy	.10	.30
52 Russell Branyan	.10	.30
53 Robin Ventura	.10	.30
54 Mark McGwire	.75	2.00
55 Tony Gwynn	.40	1.00
56 Matt Williams	.10	.30
57 Jeff Cirillo	.10	.30
58 Roger Clemens	.60	1.50
59 Ivan Rodriguez	.20	.50
60 Brad Radke	.10	.30
61 Kazuhiro Sasaki	.10	.30
62 Cal Ripken	1.00	2.50
63 Ken Caminiti	.10	.30
64 Bob Abreu	.10	.30
65 Troy Glaus	.10	.30
66 Sandy Alomar Jr.	.10	.30
67 Jose Vidro	.10	.30
68 Pedro Martinez	.20	.50
69 Kevin Young	.10	.30
70 Jay Bell	.10	.30
71 Larry Walker	.10	.30
72 Derek Jeter	.75	2.00
73 Miguel Cairo	.10	.30
74 Magglio Ordonez	.10	.30
75 Jeromy Burnitz	.10	.30
76 J.T. Snow	.10	.30
77 Andres Galarraga	.10	.30
78 Ryan Dempster	.10	.30
79 Ken Griffey Jr.	.60	1.50
80 Aaron Sele	.10	.30
81 Tom Glavine	.20	.50
82 Hideo Nomo	.30	.75
83 Orlando Hernandez	.10	.30
84 Tony Batista	.10	.30
85 Aaron Boone	.10	.30
86 Jacque Jones	.10	.30
87 Delino DeShields	.10	.30
88 Garret Anderson	.10	.30
89 Fernando Seguignol	.10	.30
90 Jim Edmonds	.10	.30
91 Frank Thomas	.30	.75
92 Adrian Beltre	.10	.30
93 Ellis Burks	.10	.30
94 Andruw Jones	.20	.50
95 Tony Clark	.10	.30
96 Danny Graves	.10	.30
97 Alex Rodriguez	.40	1.00
98 Mike Mussina	.20	.50
99 Scott Elarton	.10	.30
100 Jason Giambi	.10	.30
101 Jay Payton	.10	.30
102 Gerald Williams	.10	.30
103 Kerry Wood	.10	.30
104 Shawn Green	.10	.30
105 Greg Maddux	.50	1.25
106 Juan Encarnacion	.10	.30
107 Bernie Williams	.20	.50
108 Mike Lamb	.10	.30
109 Charles Johnson	.10	.30
110 Richie Sexson	.10	.30
111 Jeff Kent	.10	.30
112 Albert Belle	.10	.30
113 Cliff Floyd	.10	.30
114 Ben Grieve	.10	.30
115 Tim Salmon	.20	.50
116 Carl Pavano	.10	.30
117 Rick Ankiel	.10	.30
118 Dante Bichette	.10	.30
119 Johnny Damon	.20	.50
120 Brian Anderson	.10	.30
121 Roberto Alomar	.20	.50
122 Mike Hampton	.10	.30
123 Greg Vaughn	.10	.30
124 Carl Everett	.10	.30
125 Moises Alou	.10	.30
126 Jason Kendall	.10	.30
127 Omar Vizquel	.20	.50
128 Mark Grace	.20	.50
129 Kevin Brown	.10	.30
130 Phil Nevin	.10	.30
131 Kevin Millwood	.10	.30
132 Bobby Higginson	.10	.30
133 Ruben Mateo	.10	.30
134 Luis Gonzalez	.10	.30
135 Dean Palmer	.10	.30
136 Mariano Rivera	.30	.75
137 Rick Helling	.10	.30
138 Paul Konerko	.10	.30
139 Marquis Grissom	.10	.30
140 Robb Nen	.10	.30
141 Javy Lopez	.10	.30
142 Preston Wilson	.10	.30
143 Terrence Long	.10	.30
144 Shannon Stewart	.10	.30
145 Barry Larkin	.20	.50
146 Cristian Guzman	.10	.30
147 Jay Buhner	.10	.30
148 Jermaine Dye	.10	.30
149 Kris Benson	.10	.30
150 Curt Schilling	.10	.30
151 Todd Helton	.20	.50
152 Paul O'Neill	.20	.50
153 Rafael Palmeiro	.20	.50
154 Ray Durham	.10	.30
155 Geoff Jenkins	.10	.30
156 Livan Hernandez	.10	.30
157 Rafael Furcal	.10	.30
158 Juan Gonzalez	.10	.30
159 Tino Martinez	.20	.50
160 Raul Mondesi	.10	.30
161 Matt Lawton	.10	.30
162 Edgar Martinez	.20	.50
163 Richard Hidalgo	.10	.30
164 Scott Rolen	.20	.50
165 Chuck Finley	.10	.30
166 Edgardo Alfonzo	.10	.30
167 J.D. Drew	.10	.30
168 Trot Nixon	.10	.30
169 Carlos Beltran	.10	.30
170 Ryan Klesko	.10	.30
171 Mo Vaughn	.10	.30
172 Kenny Lofton	.10	.30
173 Al Leiter	.10	.30
174 Rondell White	.10	.30
175 Mike Sweeney	.10	.30
176 Trevor Hoffman	.10	.30
177 Steve Finley	.10	.30
178 Jeffrey Hammonds	.10	.30
179 David Justice	.10	.30
180 Gary Sheffield	.10	.30
181 Eric Munson BF	.10	.30
182 Luis Matos BF	.10	.30
183 Alex Cabrera BF	.10	.30
184 Randy Keisler BF	.10	.30
185 Nate Rolison BF	.10	.30
186 Jason Hart BF	.10	.30
187 Timo Perez BF	.10	.30
188 Adam Bernero BF	.10	.30
189 Barry Zito BF	.20	.50
190 Ryan Kohlmeier BF	.10	.30
191 Joey Nation BF	.10	.30
192 Oswaldo Mairena BF	.10	.30
193 Aubrey Huff BF	.10	.30
194 Mark Buehrle BF	.20	.50
195 Jace Brewer BF	.10	.30
196 Julio Zuleta BF	.10	.30
197 Xavier Nady BF	.10	.30
198 Vernon Wells BF	.10	.30
199 Joe Crede BF	.30	.75
200 Scott Downs BF	.10	.30
201 Ben Petrick BF	.10	.30
202 A.J. Burnett BF	.10	.30
203 Esix Snead BF RC	.10	.30
204 Dernell Stenson BF	.10	.30
205 Jose Ortiz BF	.10	.30
206 Paxton Crawford BF	.10	.30
207 Jason Tyner BF	.10	.30
208 Jimmy Rollins BF	.10	.30
209 Juan Pierre BF	.10	.30
210 Keith Ginter BF	.10	.30
211 Adam Dunn BF	.20	.50
212 Larry Barnes BF	.10	.30
213 Adam Piatt BF	.10	.30
214 Rodney Lindsey BF	.10	.30
215 Eric Byrnes BF	.10	.30
216 Julio Lugo BF	.10	.30
217 Corey Patterson BF	.10	.30
218 Reggie Taylor BF	.10	.30
219 Kenny Kelly BF	.10	.30
220 Tike Redman BF	.10	.30
221 Drew Henson/2499 RC	2.00	5.00
222 Johnny Estrada/2499 RC	2.00	5.00
223 Elpidio Guzman/2499 RC	2.00	5.00
224 Albert Pujols/2499 RC	15.00	40.00
225 Wilson Betemit/2499 RC	2.00	5.00
226 Mark Teixeira/2499 RC	6.00	15.00
227 Tsuyoshi Shinjo/2499 RC	2.00	5.00
228 Matt White/2499 RC	2.00	5.00
229 Adrian Hernandez/2499 RC	2.00	5.00
230 Ichiro Suzuki/2499 RC	12.00	30.00

2001 Fleer Futures Black Gold

*STARS 1-180: 3X TO 8X BASE HI		
*BF 181-220: 3X TO 8X BASE HI		
*BF RC'S 181-220: 3X TO 8X BASE HI		
STATED PRINT RUN 499 SERIAL #'d SETS		

2001 Fleer Futures September Call-Ups Memorabilia

STATED PRINT RUN 200 SERIAL #'d SETS		
SKIP-NUMBERED SET		
184 Randy Keisler Cap Cleat	3.00	8.00
185 Nate Rolison Bat	3.00	8.00
187 Timo Perez Bat	3.00	8.00
191 Joey Nation Glove	3.00	8.00
192 Oswaldo Mairena Glove	3.00	8.00
195 Jace Brewer Bat	3.00	8.00
197 Xavier Nady Glove	3.00	8.00
199 Joe Crede Bat	6.00	15.00
205 Jose Ortiz Bat	3.00	8.00
208 Jimmy Rollins Glove	3.00	8.00
210 Keith Ginter Bat	3.00	8.00
214 Rodney Lindsey Bat	3.00	8.00
217 Corey Patterson Bat	3.00	8.00
218 Reggie Taylor Bat	3.00	8.00
219 Kenny Kelly Bat	3.00	8.00

2001 Fleer Futures Bases Loaded

STATED ODDS 1:134 HOBBY		
BL1 Ken Griffey Jr.	6.00	15.00
BL2 Mark McGwire	15.00	40.00
BL3 Carlos Delgado	3.00	8.00
BL4 Chipper Jones	4.00	10.00
BL5 Nomar Garciaparra	6.00	15.00
BL6 Cal Ripken	10.00	25.00
BL7 Sammy Sosa	4.00	10.00
BL8 Jeff Bagwell	4.00	10.00
BL9 Vladimir Guerrero	4.00	10.00
BL10 Tony Gwynn	4.00	10.00
BL11 Frank Thomas	4.00	10.00
BL12 Mike Piazza	4.00	10.00
BL13 Jason Giambi	3.00	8.00
BL14 Troy Glaus	3.00	8.00
BL15 Pat Burrell	3.00	8.00

2001 Fleer Futures Bats to the Future

COMPLETE SET (25)	125.00	200.00
STATED ODDS 1:28		
BF1 Mike Schmidt	6.00	15.00
BF2 Carlton Fisk	2.00	5.00
BF3 Paul Molitor	2.00	5.00
BF4 Vladimir Guerrero	2.50	6.00
BF5 Dave Parker	2.00	5.00
BF6 Chipper Jones	2.50	6.00
BF7 Carlos Delgado	2.00	5.00
BF8 Tony Gwynn	3.00	8.00
BF9 Reggie Jackson	2.00	5.00
BF10 Eddie Murray	2.50	6.00
BF11 Robin Yount	2.50	6.00
BF12 Alan Trammell	2.00	5.00
BF13 Frank Thomas	2.50	6.00
BF14 Cal Ripken	8.00	20.00
BF15 Don Mattingly	6.00	15.00
BF16 Jim Rice	2.00	5.00
BF17 Juan Gonzalez	2.00	5.00
BF18 Todd Helton	2.00	5.00
BF19 George Brett	6.00	15.00
BF20 Barry Bonds	6.00	15.00
BF21 Kirk Gibson	2.00	5.00
BF22 Matt Williams	2.00	5.00
BF23 Dave Winfield	2.00	5.00
BF24 Ryne Sandberg	6.00	15.00
BF25 Ivan Rodriguez	2.00	5.00

2001 Fleer Futures Bats to the Future Game Bat

STATED ODDS 1:114		
1 Barry Bonds	5.00	12.00
2 George Brett	6.00	15.00
3 Carlos Delgado	1.25	3.00
4 Carlton Fisk	2.00	5.00
5 Kirk Gibson	1.25	3.00
6 Juan Gonzalez	1.25	3.00
7 Vladimir Guerrero	3.00	8.00
8 Tony Gwynn	3.00	8.00
9 Todd Helton	2.00	5.00
10 Reggie Jackson	2.50	6.00
11 Chipper Jones	3.00	8.00
12 Don Mattingly	6.00	15.00
13 Paul Molitor	3.00	8.00
14 Eddie Murray	2.00	5.00
15 Dave Parker	1.25	3.00
16 Jim Rice	2.00	5.00
17 Cal Ripken	10.00	25.00
18 Ivan Rodriguez	2.00	5.00
19 Ryne Sandberg	6.00	15.00
20 Mike Schmidt	5.00	12.00
21 Frank Thomas	3.00	8.00
22 Alan Trammell	2.00	5.00
23 Matt Williams	1.25	3.00
24 Dave Winfield	2.00	5.00
25 Robin Yount	3.00	8.00

2001 Fleer Futures Bats to the Future Game Bat Autograph

STATED PRINT RUN 50 SERIAL #'d SETS		
1 Barry Bonds	125.00	200.00
2 George Brett	75.00	150.00
3 Carlos Delgado	15.00	40.00
4 Carlton Fisk	30.00	60.00
5 Kirk Gibson	15.00	40.00
6 Juan Gonzalez	15.00	40.00
7 Vladimir Guerrero	20.00	50.00
8 Tony Gwynn	50.00	100.00
9 Todd Helton	20.00	50.00
10 Reggie Jackson	50.00	100.00
11 Chipper Jones	40.00	80.00
12 Don Mattingly	75.00	150.00
13 Paul Molitor	15.00	40.00
14 Eddie Murray	50.00	100.00
15 Dave Parker	15.00	40.00
16 Jim Rice	15.00	40.00
17 Cal Ripken	100.00	200.00
18 Ivan Rodriguez	40.00	80.00
19 Ryne Sandberg	75.00	150.00
20 Mike Schmidt	50.00	100.00
21 Frank Thomas	40.00	80.00
22 Alan Trammell	15.00	40.00
23 Matt Williams	10.00	25.00
24 Dave Winfield	30.00	60.00
25 Robin Yount	75.00	150.00

2001 Fleer Futures Characteristics

COMPLETE SET (15)	15.00	40.00
STATED ODDS 1:9		
C1 Derek Jeter	2.00	5.00
C2 Mark McGwire	2.00	5.00
C3 Nomar Garciaparra	1.25	3.00
C4 Sammy Sosa	.75	2.00
C5 Pedro Martinez	.60	1.50
C6 Chipper Jones	.75	2.00
C7 Cal Ripken	2.50	6.00
C8 Todd Helton	.60	1.50
C9 Jim Edmonds	.60	1.50
C10 Ken Griffey Jr.	1.50	4.00
C11 Alex Rodriguez	1.00	2.50
C12 Mike Piazza	1.25	3.00
C13 Vladimir Guerrero	.75	2.00
C14 Frank Thomas	.75	2.00
C15 Carlos Delgado	.60	1.50

2001 Fleer Futures Hot Commodities

COMPLETE SET (10)	15.00	40.00
STATED ODDS 1:14		
HC1 Mark McGwire	2.00	5.00
HC2 Ken Griffey Jr.	1.50	4.00
HC3 Derek Jeter	2.00	5.00
HC4 Cal Ripken	2.50	6.00
HC5 Chipper Jones	.75	2.00
HC6 Barry Bonds	2.00	5.00
HC7 Mike Piazza	1.25	3.00
HC8 Sammy Sosa	.75	2.00
HC9 Alex Rodriguez	1.00	2.50
HC10 Frank Thomas	.75	2.00

2001 Fleer Game Time

COMP.SET w/o SP's (90)	10.00	25.00
COMMON CARD (1-90)	.15	.40
COMMON NG (91-121)	1.50	4.00
NG 91-121 RANDOM INSERTS IN PACKS		
NG 91-121 PRINT RUN 2000 SERIAL #'d SETS		
JETER MM'S RANDOMLY INSERTED IN PACKS		
1 Derek Jeter	1.00	2.50
2 Nomar Garciaparra	.60	1.50
3 Alex Rodriguez	.50	1.25
4 Jason Kendall	.15	.40
5 Barry Bonds	1.00	2.50
6 David Wells	.15	.40
7 Craig Biggio	.25	.60
8 Adrian Beltre	.15	.40
9 Pat Burrell	.15	.40
10 Rafael Palmeiro	.25	.60
11 Jim Thome	.25	.60
12 Mike Lowell	.15	.40
13 Trevor Hoffman	.15	.40
14 Pokey Reese	.15	.40
15 Juan Encarnacion	.15	.40
16 Shawn Green	.15	.40
17 Kerry Wood	.15	.40
18 Richard Hidalgo	.15	.40
19 Scott Rolen	.25	.60
20 Jeff Kent	.15	.40
21 Alex Gonzalez	.15	.40
22 Matt Williams	.15	.40
23 Mike Sweeney	.15	.40
24 Edgar Martinez	.25	.60
25 Sammy Sosa	.40	1.00
26 Bobby Higginson	.15	.40
27 Kevin Brown	.15	.40
28 Mike Lieberthal	.15	.40
29 Pedro Martinez	.25	.60
30 Jeff Weaver	.15	.40
31 Greg Maddux	.60	1.50
32 Mike Hampton	.15	.40
33 Vladimir Guerrero	.40	1.00
34 Greg Vaughn	.15	.40
35 Manny Ramirez Sox	.25	.60
36 Carlos Beltran	.15	.40
37 Eric Chavez	.15	.40
38 Troy Glaus	.15	.40
39 Todd Helton	.25	.60
40 Gary Sheffield	.15	.40
41 Brady Anderson	.15	.40
42 Juan Gonzalez	.15	.40
43 Tim Hudson	.15	.40
44 Kenny Lofton	.15	.40
45 Al Leiter	.15	.40
46 Eric Owens	.15	.40
47 Roberto Alomar	.25	.60
48 Preston Wilson	.15	.40
49 Tony Gwynn	.50	1.25
50 Cal Ripken	1.25	3.00
51 Ben Petrick	.15	.40
52 Jason Giambi	.15	.40
53 Ben Grieve	.15	.40
54 Albert Belle	.15	.40
55 Jose Vidro	.15	.40
56 Barry Zito	.25	.60
57 Ivan Rodriguez	.25	.60
58 Jeff Bagwell	.25	.60
59 Geoff Jenkins	.15	.40
60 Roger Clemens	.75	2.00
61 John Olerud	.15	.40
62 Randy Johnson	.40	1.00
63 Matt Lawton	.15	.40
64 Mark McGwire	1.00	2.50
65 Brad Radke	.15	.40
66 Frank Thomas	.40	1.00
67 Edgardo Alfonzo	.15	.40
68 Brian Giles	.15	.40
69 J.T. Snow	.15	.40
70 Carlos Delgado	.15	.40
71 Chipper Jones	.40	1.00
72 Mark Quinn	.15	.40
73 Mike Mussina	.25	.60
74 Rick Ankiel	.15	.40
75 Rafael Furcal	.15	.40
76 Jim Edmonds	.15	.40
77 Vinny Castilla	.15	.40
78 Sean Casey	.15	.40
79 Derrek Lee	.25	.60
80 Mike Piazza	.60	1.50
81 Warren Morris	.15	.40
82 Tim Salmon	.25	.60
83 Jeromy Burnitz	.15	.40
84 Freddy Garcia	.15	.40
85 Ken Griffey Jr.	.75	2.00
86 Andruw Jones	.25	.60
87 Darryl Kile	.15	.40
88 Magglio Ordonez	.15	.40
89 Bernie Williams	.25	.60
90 Timo Perez	.15	.40
91 Ichiro Suzuki NG RC	15.00	40.00
92 L.Barnes D.Erstad NG	1.50	4.00
93 Jaisen Randolph NG RC	1.50	4.00
94 Paul Phillips NG RC	1.50	4.00
95 Esix Snead NG RC	1.50	4.00
96 Matt White NG RC	1.50	4.00
97 Ryan Freel NG RC	2.00	5.00
98 Winston Abreu NG RC	1.50	4.00
99 Junior Spivey NG RC	2.00	5.00
100 R.Keisler R.Clemens NG	3.00	8.00
101 M.Piazza B.Cole NG	2.50	6.00
102 A.Huff C.Jones NG	2.00	5.00
103 C.Patterson S.Sosa NG	2.00	5.00
104 S.Kim P.Martinez NG	2.00	5.00
105 Drew Henson NG RC	2.00	5.00
106 Claudio Vargas NG RC	1.50	4.00
107 R.Furcal C.Izturis NG	1.50	4.00
108 P.Crawford P.Martinez NG	2.00	5.00
109 Adrian Hernandez NG RC	1.50	4.00
110 J.Brewer D.Jeter NG	4.00	10.00
111 Andy Morales NG RC	1.50	4.00
112 Wilson Betemit NG RC	2.00	5.00
113 Juan Diaz NG RC	1.50	4.00
114 Erick Almonte NG RC	1.50	4.00
115 Nick Punto NG RC	1.50	4.00
116 Tsuyoshi Shinjo NG RC	2.00	5.00
117 Jay Gibbons NG RC	2.00	5.00
118 Andres Torres NG RC	1.50	4.00
119 Alexis Gomez NG RC	1.50	4.00
120 Wilkin Ruan NG RC	1.50	4.00
121 Albert Pujols NG RC	10.00	25.00
MM2 Derek Jeter/1996	5.00	12.00
MM2 Derek Jeter AU/96	75.00	150.00

2001 Fleer Game Time Next Game Extra

COMMON CARD (91-121)	6.00	15.00
*EXTRA: .75X TO 2X BASIC CARDS		
STATED PRINT RUN 200 SERIAL #'d SETS		
91 Ichiro Suzuki	30.00	80.00
121 Albert Pujols	15.00	40.00

2001 Fleer Game Time Famers Lumber

STATED PRINT RUN 100 SERIAL #'d SETS		
1 Luis Aparicio	6.00	15.00
2 Hank Bauer	6.00	15.00
3 Paul Blair	6.00	15.00
4 Bobby Bonds	6.00	15.00
5 Orlando Cepeda	6.00	15.00
6 Roberto Clemente	30.00	60.00
7 Rocky Colavito	10.00	25.00
8 Bucky Dent	6.00	15.00
9 Bill Dickey	10.00	25.00
10 Larry Doby	6.00	15.00
12 Carlton Fisk	10.00	25.00
13 Hank Greenberg	30.00	60.00
14 Elston Howard	10.00	25.00
15 Frank Howard	6.00	15.00
16 Reggie Jackson	10.00	25.00
17 Harmon Killebrew	10.00	25.00
18 Tony Lazzeri	15.00	40.00
19 Roger Maris	20.00	50.00
20 Johnny Mize	6.00	15.00
21 Thurman Munson	15.00	40.00
22 Tony Perez	6.00	15.00
23 Jim Rice	6.00	15.00
24 Phil Rizzuto	10.00	25.00
25 Bill Skowron	10.00	25.00
26 Enos Slaughter	6.00	15.00
27 Duke Snider	10.00	25.00
28 Willie Stargell	20.00	50.00
29 Bill Terry	10.00	25.00
30 Ted Williams	20.00	50.00

2001 Fleer Game Time Let's Play Two

COMPLETE SET (15)	50.00	120.00
STATED ODDS 1:24		
1 N.Garciaparra D.Jeter	4.00	10.00

2 M.McGwire 5.00 12.00
S.Sosa
3 P.Martinez 2.00 5.00
R.Johnson
4 V.Guerrero 2.00 5.00
C.Delgado
5 M.Piazza 5.00 12.00
R.Clemens
6 A.Rodriguez 2.50 6.00
M.Tejada
7 C.Jones 2.00 5.00
T.Glaus
8 A.Rodriguez 4.00 10.00
D.Jeter
9 C.Ripken 6.00 15.00
D.Jeter
10 J.Giambi 5.00 12.00
M.McGwire
11 J.Bagwell 2.00 5.00
C.Biggio
12 T.Glavine 3.00 8.00
G.Maddux
13 K.Griffey Jr. 6.00 15.00
B.Bonds
14 M.Ramirez Sox 2.00 5.00
P.Martinez
15 I.Rodriguez 2.50 6.00
A.Rodriguez

2001 Fleer Game Time Lumber

STATED ODDS 1:40
1 Roberto Alomar 6.00 15.00
2 Rick Ankiel 4.00 10.00
3 Adrian Beltre 4.00 10.00
4 Barry Bonds 10.00 25.00
5 Kevin Brown 4.00 10.00
6 Ken Caminiti 4.00 10.00
7 Eric Chavez 4.00 10.00
8 Carlos Delgado 4.00 10.00
9 J.D. Drew 4.00 10.00
10 Erubiel Durazo 4.00 10.00
11 Carl Everett 4.00 10.00
12 Rafael Furcal 4.00 10.00
13 Nomar Garciaparra 6.00 15.00
14 Brian Giles 4.00 10.00
15 Juan Gonzalez 4.00 10.00
16 Todd Helton 6.00 15.00
17 Randy Johnson 6.00 15.00
18 Chipper Jones 6.00 15.00
19 Pedro Martinez 6.00 15.00
20 Tino Martinez 6.00 15.00
21 Dean Palmer 4.00 10.00
22 Cal Ripken SP/275 15.00 40.00
23 Ivan Rodriguez 6.00 15.00
24 Frank Thomas 6.00 15.00
25 Jim Thome 6.00 15.00
26 Bernie Williams 6.00 15.00

2001 Fleer Game Time New Order

COMPLETE SET (15) 15.00 40.00
STATED ODDS 1:12
1 Derek Jeter 2.50 6.00
2 Nomar Garciaparra 1.50 4.00
3 Alex Rodriguez 1.25 3.00
4 Mark McGwire 2.50 6.00
5 Sammy Sosa 1.00 2.50
6 Carlos Delgado .60 1.50
7 Troy Glaus .60 1.50
8 Jason Giambi .60 1.50
9 Mike Piazza 1.50 4.00
10 Todd Helton .60 1.50
11 Vladimir Guerrero 1.00 2.50
12 Manny Ramirez Sox .60 1.50
13 Frank Thomas 1.00 2.50
14 Ken Griffey Jr. 2.00 5.00
15 Chipper Jones 1.00 2.50

2001 Fleer Game Time Sticktoitness

COMPLETE SET (20) 20.00 50.00
STATED ODDS 1:8
1 Derek Jeter 1.50 4.00
2 Nomar Garciaparra 1.00 2.50
3 Alex Rodriguez .80 2.00
4 Jeff Bagwell .40 1.00
5 Bernie Williams .40 1.00
6 Eric Chavez .40 1.00
7 Richard Hidalgo .40 1.00
8 Ichiro Suzuki 5.00 12.00
9 Troy Glaus .40 1.00
10 Magglio Ordonez .40 1.00
11 Corey Patterson .40 1.00
12 Todd Helton .40 1.00
13 Jim Edmonds .40 1.00
14 Rafael Furcal .40 1.00
15 Mo Vaughn .40 1.00
16 Pat Burrell .40 1.00
17 Adrian Beltre .40 1.00
18 Andruw Jones .40 1.00
19 Manny Ramirez Sox .40 1.00
20 Sean Casey .40 1.00

2001 Fleer Game Time Uniformity

STATED ODDS 1:25
1 Barry Bonds 6.00 15.00
2 Kevin Brown 1.50 4.00
3 Jay Buhner 1.50 4.00
4 Jeromy Burnitz 1.50 4.00
5 Andres Galarraga 2.50 6.00
6 Troy Glaus 1.50 4.00
7 Vladimir Guerrero 4.00 10.00
8 Carlos Guillen 1.50 4.00
9 Tony Gwynn 4.00 10.00
10 Brian Jordan 1.50 4.00
11 Greg Maddux 6.00 15.00
12 Fred McGriff 2.50 6.00
13 John Olerud 1.50 4.00
14 Magglio Ordonez 1.50 4.00
15 Ben Petrick 1.50 4.00
16 Brad Radke 1.50 4.00
17 Ivan Rodriguez 2.50 6.00
18 Fernando Seguignol 1.50 4.00
19 Gary Sheffield 1.50 4.00
20 Robin Ventura 1.50 4.00
21 Larry Walker 2.50 6.00

22 Rondell White 1.50 4.00
23 Matt Williams 1.50 4.00

2000 Fleer Gamers

COMPLETE SET (120) 30.00 80.00
COMP.SET w/o SP's (90) 10.00 25.00
COMMON CARD (1-90) .12 .30
COMMON NG (91-110) .40 1.00
NG STATED ODDS 1:3
COMMON FG (111-120) .40 1.00
FG STATED ODDS 1:8
1 Cal Ripken 1.00 2.50
2 Derek Jeter .75 2.00
3 Alex Rodriguez .40 1.00
4 Alex Gonzalez .12 .30
5 Nomar Garciaparra .20 .50
6 Brian Giles .12 .30
7 Chris Singleton .12 .30
8 Kevin Brown .12 .30
9 J.D. Drew .12 .30
10 Raul Mondesi .12 .30
11 Sammy Sosa .30 .75
12 Carlos Beltran .20 .50
13 Eric Chavez .12 .30
14 Gabe Kapler .12 .30
15 Tim Salmon .12 .30
16 Manny Ramirez .30 .75
17 Orlando Hernandez .12 .30
18 Jeff Kent .12 .30
19 Juan Gonzalez .12 .30
20 Moises Alou .12 .30
21 Jason Giambi .12 .30
22 Ivan Rodriguez .20 .50
23 Geoff Jenkins .12 .30
24 Ken Griffey Jr. .60 1.50
25 Mark McGwire .50 1.25
26 Jose Canseco .20 .50
27 Roberto Alomar .20 .50
28 Craig Biggio .20 .50
29 Scott Rolen .20 .50
30 Vinny Castilla .12 .30
31 Greg Maddux .40 1.00
32 Pedro Martinez .20 .50
33 Mike Piazza .30 .75
34 Albert Belle .12 .30
35 Frank Thomas .30 .75
36 Bobby Abreu .12 .30
37 Edgar Martinez .20 .50
38 Pokey Reese .12 .30
39 Preston Wilson .12 .30
40 Mike Lieberthal .12 .30
41 Andruw Jones .12 .30
42 Damion Easley .12 .30
43 Mike Cameron .12 .30
44 Todd Walker .12 .30
45 Jason Kendall .12 .30
46 Sean Casey .12 .30
47 Corey Koskie .12 .30
48 Warren Morris .12 .30
49 Andres Galarraga .20 .50
50 Dean Palmer .12 .30
51 Jose Vidro .12 .30
52 Brian Jordan .12 .30
53 Tony Clark .12 .30
54 Vladimir Guerrero .20 .50
55 Mo Vaughn .12 .30
56 Richie Sexson .12 .30
57 Tino Martinez .12 .30
58 Eric Owens .12 .30
59 Matt Williams .12 .30
60 Omar Vizquel .20 .50
61 Rickey Henderson .30 .75
62 J.T. Snow .12 .30
63 Mark Grace .20 .50
64 Carlos Febles .12 .30
65 Paul O'Neill .20 .50
66 Randy Johnson .30 .75
67 Kenny Lofton .12 .30
68 Roger Cedeno .12 .30
69 Shawn Green .12 .30
70 Chipper Jones .30 .75
71 Jeff Cirillo .12 .30
72 Robin Ventura .12 .30
73 Paul Konerko .12 .30
74 Jeromy Burnitz .12 .30
75 Ben Grieve .12 .30
76 Troy Glaus .12 .30
77 Jim Thome .20 .50
78 Bernie Williams .20 .50
79 Barry Bonds .50 1.25
80 Ray Durham .12 .30
81 Adrian Beltre .30 .75
82 Ray Lankford .12 .30
83 Carlos Delgado .12 .30
84 Erubiel Durazo .12 .30
85 Larry Walker .20 .50
86 Edgardo Alfonzo .12 .30
87 Rafael Palmeiro .20 .50
88 Magglio Ordonez .20 .50
89 Jeff Bagwell .20 .50
90 Tony Gwynn .30 .75
91 Norm Hutchins NG .40 1.00
92 Derrick Turnbow NG RC .40 1.00
93 Matt Riley NG .40 1.00
94 David Eckstein NG .40 1.00
95 Dernell Stenson NG .40 1.00
96 Joe Crede NG .40 1.00
97 Ben Petrick NG .40 1.00
98 Eric Munson NG .40 1.00
99 Pablo Ozuna NG .40 1.00
100 Josh Beckett NG .75 2.00
101 Aaron McNeal NG RC .40 1.00
102 Milton Bradley NG .40 1.00
103 Alex Escobar NG .40 1.00
104 Alfonso Soriano NG 1.00 2.50
105 Wily Pena NG .40 1.00
106 Nick Johnson NG .40 1.00
107 Adam Piatt NG .40 1.00
108 Pat Burrell NG .40 1.00
109 Rick Ankiel NG .60 1.50
110 Vernon Wells NG .40 1.00
111 Alex Rodriguez FG 1.25 3.00
112 Cal Ripken FG 3.00 8.00
113 Mark McGwire FG 1.50 4.00
114 Ken Griffey Jr. FG 2.00 5.00
115 Mike Piazza FG 1.00 2.50
116 Nomar Garciaparra FG .60 1.50

117 Derek Jeter FG 2.50 6.00
118 Chipper Jones FG 1.00 2.50
119 Sammy Sosa FG 1.00 2.50
120 Tony Gwynn FG 1.00 2.50
S3 Alex Rodriguez Sample .60 1.50

2000 Fleer Gamers Extra

*EXTRA 1-90: 6X TO 15X BASIC 1-90
BASIC 1-90 STATED ODDS 1:24
*EXTRA 91-110: .75X TO 2X BASIC 91-110
NG 91-110 STATED ODDS 1:36
*EXTRA 111-120: .75X TO 2X BASIC 111-120
FG 111-120 STATED ODDS 1:36

2000 Fleer Gamers Cal to Greatness

COMPLETE SET (15) 40.00 100.00
COMMON CARD (CTA1-CTA5) 1.50 4.00
COMMON CARD (CTA6-CTA10) 3.00 8.00
COMMON CARD (CTA11-CTA15) 8.00 20.00
CTA1-CTA5 STATED ODDS 1:9
CTA6-CTA10 STATED ODDS 1:25
CTA11-CTA15 STATED ODDS 1:144

2000 Fleer Gamers Change the Game

COMPLETE SET (15) 20.00 50.00
STATED ODDS 1:24
1 Alex Rodriguez 2.00 5.00
2 Cal Ripken 5.00 12.00
3 Chipper Jones 1.50 4.00
4 Derek Jeter 4.00 10.00
5 Ken Griffey Jr. 3.00 8.00
6 Mark McGwire 2.50 6.00
7 Mike Piazza 1.50 4.00
8 Nomar Garciaparra 1.00 2.50
9 Sammy Sosa 1.50 4.00
10 Tony Gwynn 1.50 4.00
11 Ivan Rodriguez 1.00 2.50
12 Pedro Martinez 1.00 2.50
13 Juan Gonzalez .60 1.50
14 Vladimir Guerrero 1.00 2.50
15 Manny Ramirez 1.50 4.00

2000 Fleer Gamers Determined

COMPLETE SET (15) 15.00 40.00
STATED ODDS 1:12
1 Nomar Garciaparra .60 1.50
2 Chipper Jones 1.00 2.50
3 Derek Jeter 2.50 6.00
4 Mike Piazza 1.00 2.50
5 Jeff Bagwell .60 1.50
6 Mark McGwire 1.50 4.00
7 Greg Maddux 1.25 3.00
8 Sammy Sosa 1.00 2.50
9 Ken Griffey Jr. 2.00 5.00
10 Alex Rodriguez 1.25 3.00
11 Tony Gwynn 1.00 2.50
12 Cal Ripken 3.00 8.00
13 Barry Bonds 1.50 4.00
14 Juan Gonzalez .40 1.00
15 Sean Casey .40 1.00

2000 Fleer Gamers Lumber

STATED ODDS 1:36
1 Edgardo Alfonzo 1.50 4.00
2 Roberto Alomar 2.50 6.00
3 Moises Alou 1.50 4.00
4 Carlos Beltran 2.50 6.00
5 Adrian Beltre 4.00 10.00
6 Wade Boggs 2.50 6.00
7 Barry Bonds 6.00 15.00
8 Jeromy Burnitz 1.50 4.00
9 Mike Cameron 1.50 4.00
10 Sean Casey 1.50 4.00
11 Roger Cedeno 1.50 4.00
12 Eric Chavez 1.50 4.00
13 Tony Clark 1.50 4.00
14 Carlos Delgado 1.50 4.00
15 J.D. Drew 1.50 4.00
16 Erubiel Durazo 1.50 4.00
17 Ray Durham 1.50 4.00
18 Damion Easley 1.50 4.00
19 Carlos Febles 1.50 4.00
20 Jason Giambi 1.50 4.00
21 Shawn Green 1.50 4.00
22 Vladimir Guerrero 2.50 6.00
23 Norm Hutchins 1.50 4.00
24 Derek Jeter 10.00 25.00
25 Chipper Jones 4.00 10.00
26 Gabe Kapler 1.50 4.00
27 Jason Kendall 1.50 4.00
28 Paul Konerko 1.50 4.00
29 Ray Lankford 1.50 4.00
30 Mike Lieberthal 1.50 4.00
31 Edgar Martinez 2.50 6.00
32 Raul Mondesi 1.50 4.00
33 Warren Morris 1.50 4.00
34 Magglio Ordonez 2.50 6.00
35 Rafael Palmeiro 2.50 6.00
36 Pokey Reese 1.50 4.00
37 Cal Ripken 12.00 30.00
38 Alex Rodriguez 5.00 12.00
39 Ivan Rodriguez 2.50 6.00
40 Scott Rolen 2.50 6.00
41 Chris Singleton 1.50 4.00
42 Alfonso Soriano 4.00 10.00
43 Frank Thomas 4.00 10.00
44 Jim Thome 2.50 6.00
45 Robin Ventura 1.50 4.00
46 Jose Vidro 1.50 4.00
47 Bernie Williams 2.50 6.00
48 Matt Williams 1.50 4.00

2000 Fleer Gamers Signed Lumber

STATED ODDS 1:287
EXCHANGE DEADLINE 05/01/01
1 Roberto Alomar 15.00 40.00
2 Sean Casey 10.00 25.00
3 Eric Chavez 10.00 25.00
4 Tony Clark 6.00 15.00
5 Erubiel Durazo 6.00 15.00
6 Shawn Green 8.00 20.00
7 Derek Jeter 250.00 350.00
8 Paul Konerko 10.00 25.00
9 Rafael Palmeiro 10.00 25.00
10 Alex Rodriguez 40.00 80.00
11 Alfonso Soriano 10.00 25.00
12 Robin Ventura 10.00 25.00

2001 Fleer Genuine

COMP.SET w/o SP's (100) 10.00 25.00
COMMON CARD (1-100) .20 .50
COMMON CARD (101-130) 2.00 5.00
101-130 GU RANDOM INSERTS IN PACKS
101-130 GU PRINT RUN 1500 #'d SETS
JETER AU SHEET AVAIL.VIA MAIL EXCH.
JETER SHEET EXCH. RANDOM IN PACKS
1 Derek Jeter 1.25 3.00
2 Nomar Garciaparra .75 2.00
3 Alex Rodriguez .60 1.50
4 Frank Thomas .50 1.25
5 Travis Fryman .20 .50
6 Gary Sheffield .20 .50
7 Jason Giambi .20 .50
8 Trevor Hoffman .20 .50
9 Todd Helton .30 .75
10 Ivan Rodriguez .30 .75
11 Roberto Alomar .30 .75
12 Barrry Zito .30 .75
13 Kevin Brown .20 .50
14 Shawn Green .20 .50
15 Kenny Lofton .20 .50
16 Jeff Weaver .20 .50
17 Geoff Jenkins .20 .50
18 Carlos Delgado .20 .50
19 Mark Grace .30 .75
20 Ken Griffey Jr. 1.00 2.50
21 David Justice .20 .50
22 Brian Giles .20 .50
23 Scott Williamson .20 .50
24 Richie Sexson .20 .50
25 John Olerud .20 .50
26 Sammy Sosa .50 1.25
27 Bobby Higginson .20 .50
28 Matt Lawton .20 .50
29 Vinny Castilla .20 .50
30 Alex Gonzalez .20 .50
31 Manny Ramirez Sox .30 .75
32 Brad Radke .20 .50
33 Cal Ripken 1.50 4.00
34 Richard Hidalgo .20 .50
35 Al Leiter .20 .50
36 Freddy Garcia .20 .50
37 Juan Encarnacion .20 .50
38 Corey Koskie .20 .50
39 Greg Vaughn .20 .50
40 Rafael Palmeiro .30 .75
41 Vladimir Guerrero .50 1.25
42 Troy Glaus .20 .50
43 Mike Hampton .20 .50
44 Jose Vidro .20 .50
45 Ryan Rupe .20 .50
46 Troy O'Leary .20 .50
47 Ben Petrick .20 .50
48 Mike Lieberthal .20 .50
49 Mike Sweeney .20 .50
50 Scott Rolen .30 .75
51 Albert Belle .20 .50
52 Mark Quinn .20 .50
53 Mike Piazza .75 2.00
54 Mark McGwire 1.25 3.00
55 Brady Anderson .20 .50
56 Carlos Beltran .20 .50
57 Michael Barrett .20 .50
58 Jason Kendall .20 .50
59 Jim Edmonds .20 .50
60 Matt Williams .20 .50
61 Pokey Reese .20 .50
62 Bernie Williams .30 .75
63 Barry Bonds 1.25 3.00
64 David Wells .20 .50
65 Chipper Jones .50 1.25
66 Jim Parque .20 .50
67 Derrek Lee .30 .75
68 Darin Erstad .20 .50
69 Edgar Martinez .30 .75
70 Kerry Wood .20 .50
71 Omar Vizquel .30 .75
72 Jeromy Burnitz .20 .50
73 Warren Morris .20 .50
74 Rick Ankiel .20 .50
75 Andruw Jones .30 .75
76 Paul Konerko .20 .50
77 Mike Lowell .20 .50
78 Roger Clemens 1.00 2.50
79 Tim Hudson .20 .50
80 Rafael Furcal .20 .50
81 Craig Biggio .30 .75
82 Edgardo Alfonzo .20 .50
83 Pat Burrell .20 .50
84 Adrian Beltre .20 .50
85 Tony Gwynn .60 1.50
86 J.T. Snow .20 .50
87 Randy Johnson .50 1.25
88 Sean Casey .20 .50
89 Preston Wilson .20 .50
90 Mike Mussina .30 .75
91 Eric Chavez .20 .50
92 Tim Salmon .30 .75
93 Pedro Martinez .30 .75
94 Darryl Kile .20 .50
95 Greg Maddux .75 2.00
96 Magglio Ordonez .20 .50
97 Jeff Bagwell .30 .75
98 Timo Perez .20 .50
99 Jeff Kent .20 .50
100 Eric Owens .20 .50
101 Ichiro Suzuki GU RC 10.00 25.00
102 Elpidio Guzman GU RC 2.00 5.00
103 Tsuyoshi Shinjo GU RC 2.50 6.00
104 Travis Hafner GU RC 6.00 15.00
105 Larry Barnes GU 2.00 5.00
106 Jaisen Randolph GU RC 2.00 5.00
107 Paul Phillips GU RC 2.00 5.00
108 Erick Almonte GU RC 2.00 5.00
109 Nick Punto GU RC 2.00 5.00
110 Jack Wilson GU RC 2.50 6.00
111 Jeremy Owens GU RC 2.00 5.00
112 Esix Snead GU RC 2.00 5.00
113 Jay Gibbons GU RC 2.50 6.00
114 Adrian Hernandez GU RC 2.00 5.00
115 Matt White GU RC 2.00 5.00
116 Ryan Freel GU RC 2.00 5.00
117 Martin Vargas GU RC 2.00 5.00
118 Winston Abreu GU RC 2.00 5.00
119 Junior Spivey GU RC 2.50 6.00
120 Paxton Crawford GU 2.00 5.00
121 Randy Keisler GU 2.00 5.00
122 Juan Diaz GU RC 2.00 5.00
123 Aaron Rowand GU 2.00 5.00
124 Toby Hall GU 2.00 5.00
125 Brian Cole GU 2.00 5.00
126 Aubrey Huff GU 2.00 5.00
127 Corey Patterson GU 2.00 5.00
128 Sun Woo Kim GU 2.00 5.00
129 Jace Brewer GU 2.00 5.00
130 Cesar Izturis GU 2.00 5.00
NNO D.Jeter AU Sheet/500 60.00 120.00

2001 Fleer Genuine At Large

COMPLETE SET (15) 60.00 120.00
STATED ODDS 1:23
1 Derek Jeter 5.00 12.00
2 Nomar Garciaparra 3.00 8.00
3 Mark McGwire 5.00 12.00
4 Pedro Martinez 1.25 3.00
5 Tony Gwynn 2.50 6.00
6 Roger Clemens 4.00 10.00
7 Ivan Rodriguez 1.25 3.00
8 Sammy Sosa 2.00 5.00
9 Magglio Ordonez 1.25 3.00
10 Jason Giambi 1.25 3.00
11 Carlos Delgado 1.25 3.00
12 Chipper Jones 2.00 5.00
13 Mike Piazza 3.00 8.00
14 Cal Ripken 6.00 15.00
15 Ken Griffey Jr. 4.00 10.00

2001 Fleer Genuine Coverage Plus

STATED PRINT RUN 150 SERIAL #'d SETS
1 Barry Bonds 10.00 25.00
2 Darin Erstad 6.00 15.00
3 Troy Glaus 6.00 15.00
4 Tony Gwynn 10.00 25.00
5 Derek Jeter 20.00 50.00
6 Randy Johnson 8.00 20.00
7 Andruw Jones 8.00 20.00
8 Chipper Jones 8.00 20.00
9 Cal Ripken 20.00 50.00
10 Frank Thomas 8.00 20.00

2001 Fleer Genuine Final Cut

*MULTI-COLOR PATCH: .75X TO 2X BASIC
STATED ODDS 1:30
SP PRINT RUNS PROVIDED BY FLEER
SP'S ARE NOT SERIAL-NUMBERED
1 Wade Boggs 6.00 15.00
2 Barry Bonds SP/330 30.00 60.00
3 George Brett 10.00 25.00
4 Sean Casey 4.00 10.00
5 J.D. Drew SP/75 10.00 25.00
6 Bob Gibson SP/200 15.00 40.00
7 Troy Glaus 4.00 10.00
9 Tony Gwynn 6.00 15.00
11 Andruw Jones SP/135 15.00 40.00
12 Chipper Jones 6.00 15.00
14 Greg Maddux 6.00 15.00
15 Edgar Martinez SP/130 15.00 40.00
17 Pokey Reese 4.00 10.00
19 Cal Ripken 10.00 25.00
20 Ivan Rodriguez SP/120 15.00 40.00
21 Scott Rolen 6.00 15.00
22 Tim Salmon 6.00 15.00
23 Miguel Tejada SP/170 10.00 25.00
24 Frank Thomas 6.00 15.00
25 Robin Ventura 4.00 10.00
26 Larry Walker 4.00 10.00
27 Matt Williams 4.00 10.00
28 Robin Yount 6.00 15.00

2001 Fleer Genuine High Interest

COMPLETE SET (15) 50.00 100.00
STATED ODDS 1:23
1 Derek Jeter 5.00 12.00
2 Nomar Garciaparra 3.00 8.00
3 Greg Maddux 3.00 8.00
4 Todd Helton 1.25 3.00
5 Sammy Sosa 2.00 5.00
6 Jeff Bagwell 1.25 3.00
7 Jason Giambi 1.25 3.00
8 Frank Thomas 2.00 5.00
9 Andruw Jones 1.25 3.00
10 Jim Edmonds 1.25 3.00
11 Bernie Williams 1.25 3.00
12 Randy Johnson 2.00 5.00
13 Ken Griffey Jr. 4.00 10.00
14 Pedro Martinez 1.25 3.00
15 Mark McGwire 5.00 12.00

2001 Fleer Genuine Material Issue

*MULTI-COLOR PATCH: 1X TO 2.5X BASIC
STATED ODDS 1:30 HOBBY
SP PRINT RUNS PROVIDED BY FLEER
SP'S ARE NOT SERIAL-NUMBERED
CJ Chipper Jones 6.00 15.00
CR Cal Ripken 10.00 25.00
CS Curt Schilling SP/120 * 10.00 25.00
DE Darin Erstad 4.00 10.00
EM Edgar Martinez SP * 12.50 30.00
FT Frank Thomas 6.00 15.00
GM Greg Maddux 6.00 15.00
JD J.D. Drew 4.00 10.00
KM Kevin Millwood 4.00 10.00
NR Nolan Ryan 10.00 25.00
PM1 Pedro Martinez SP/60 * 20.00 50.00
PM2 Paul Molitor SP * 10.00 25.00
RJ Randy Johnson 6.00 15.00
RV Robin Ventura 4.00 10.00
SC Steve Carlton SP * 10.00 25.00
SR Scott Rolen 6.00 15.00
TG1 Troy Glaus 4.00 10.00
TG2 Tom Glavine 6.00 15.00
TG3 Tony Gwynn 6.00 15.00

2001 Fleer Genuine Names Of The Game

STATED PRINT RUN 50 SERIAL #'d SETS
1 Yogi Berra Bat 15.00 40.00
2 Orlando Cepeda Bat 10.00 25.00
3 Rocky Colavito Bat 15.00 40.00
4 Andre Dawson Jsy 10.00 25.00
5 Bucky Dent Bat 10.00 25.00
6 Rollie Fingers Jsy 10.00 25.00
7 Carlton Fisk Bat 15.00 40.00
8 Whitey Ford Jsy 10.00 25.00
9 Jimmie Foxx Bat 40.00 80.00
10 Hank Greenberg Bat 40.00 80.00
11 Catfish Hunter Jsy 15.00 40.00
12 Reggie Jackson Jsy 10.00 25.00
13 Randy Johnson Jsy 15.00 40.00
14 Chipper Jones Bat 15.00 40.00
15 Harmon Killebrew Bat 15.00 40.00
16 Tony Lazzeri Bat 10.00 25.00
17 Don Mattingly Bat 15.00 40.00
19 Willie McCovey Bat 10.00 25.00
20 Johnny Mize Bat 10.00 25.00
21 Pee Wee Reese Jsy 10.00 25.00
22 Cal Ripken Bat 30.00 60.00
23 Phil Rizzuto Bat 30.00 60.00
24 Ivan Rodriguez Bat 15.00 40.00
25 Preacher Roe Jsy 15.00 40.00
26 Babe Ruth Bat 125.00 250.00
27 Nolan Ryan Jsy 30.00 60.00
28 Tom Seaver Jsy 15.00 40.00
29 Bill Skowron Bat 15.00 40.00
30 Enos Slaughter Bat 10.00 25.00
31 Duke Snider Bat 15.00 40.00
32 Willie Stargell Bat 15.00 40.00
33 Bill Terry Bat 10.00 25.00
34 Ted Williams Bat 20.00 50.00
35 Hack Wilson Bat 40.00 80.00

2001 Fleer Genuine Names Of The Game Autographs

STATED PRINT RUN 100 SERIAL #'d SETS
1 Yogi Berra Bat 40.00 100.00
2 Orlando Cepeda Bat 10.00 25.00
3 Rocky Colavito Bat 40.00 80.00
4 Andre Dawson Jsy 30.00 60.00
5 Bucky Dent Bat 10.00 25.00
6 Rollie Fingers Jsy 10.00 25.00
7 Carlton Fisk Bat 30.00 60.00
8 Whitey Ford Jsy 15.00 40.00
9 Reggie Jackson Jsy 30.00 60.00
10 Randy Johnson Jsy 40.00 80.00
11 Chipper Jones Bat 30.00 60.00
12 Harmon Killebrew Bat 30.00 80.00
13 Don Mattingly Bat 50.00 100.00
14 Willie McCovey Bat 15.00 40.00
16 Cal Ripken Bat 75.00 150.00
18 Ivan Rodriguez Bat 15.00 40.00
19 Preacher Roe Jsy 10.00 25.00
20 Nolan Ryan Jsy 100.00 250.00
21 Tom Seaver Jsy 40.00 100.00
22 Bill Skowron Bat 10.00 25.00
23 Enos Slaughter Bat 30.00 60.00
24 Duke Snider Bat 30.00 80.00

2001 Fleer Genuine Pennant Aggression

COMPLETE SET (10) 30.00 60.00
STATED ODDS 1:23
1 Derek Jeter 4.00 10.00
2 Alex Rodriguez 2.00 5.00
3 Nomar Garciaparra 2.50 6.00
4 Mark McGwire 4.00 10.00
5 Ken Griffey Jr. 3.00 8.00
6 Mike Piazza 2.50 6.00
7 Sammy Sosa 1.50 4.00
8 Barry Bonds 4.00 10.00
9 Chipper Jones 1.50 4.00
10 Pedro Martinez 1.50 4.00

2001 Fleer Genuine Tip Of The Cap

STATED PRINT RUN 150 SERIAL #'d SETS
1 Roberto Alomar 10.00 25.00
2 Barry Bonds 12.00 30.00
3 Eric Chavez 6.00 15.00
5 Shawn Green 6.00 15.00
6 Vladimir Guerrero 10.00 25.00
7 Randy Johnson 10.00 25.00
8 Andruw Jones 10.00 25.00
9 Javy Lopez 6.00 15.00
10 Pedro Martinez 10.00 25.00
11 Rafael Palmeiro 10.00 25.00
12 Ivan Rodriguez 10.00 25.00
13 Miguel Tejada 6.00 15.00

2002 Fleer Genuine

COMP.SET w/o SP's (100) 10.00 25.00
COMMON CARD (1-100) .20 .50
COMMON CARD (101-140) 2.00 5.00
101-140 RANDOM INSERTS IN PACKS
101-140 PRINT RUN 2002 SERIAL #'d SETS
1 Alex Rodriguez .60 1.50
2 Manny Ramirez .30 .75
3 Jim Thome .30 .75
4 Eric Milton .20 .50
5 Todd Helton .30 .75
6 Mike Mussina .30 .75
7 Ichiro Suzuki 1.00 2.50
8 Randy Johnson .50 1.25
9 Mark Mulder .20 .50
10 Johnny Damon Sox .30 .75
11 Sean Casey .20 .50
12 Albert Pujols 1.00 2.50
13 Mark Grace .30 .75
14 Moises Alou .20 .50
15 Raul Mondesi .20 .50
16 Cliff Floyd .20 .50
17 Vladimir Guerrero .50 1.25
18 Pat Burrell .20 .50
19 Ryan Klesko .20 .50
20 Mike Hampton .20 .50
21 Shawn Green .20 .50
22 Rich Aurilia .20 .50
23 Matt Morris .20 .50
24 Curt Schilling .20 .50
25 Kevin Brown .20 .50
26 Adrian Beltre .20 .50
27 Joe Mays .20 .50
28 Luis Gonzalez .20 .50
29 Barry Larkin .30 .75
30 A.J. Burnett .20 .50
31 Eric Munson .20 .50
32 Juan Gonzalez .20 .50
33 Lance Berkman .20 .50
34 Fred McGriff .30 .75
35 Paul Konerko .20 .50
36 Pedro Martinez .30 .75
37 Adam Dunn .20 .50
38 Jeromy Burnitz .20 .50
39 Mike Sweeney .20 .50
40 Bret Boone .20 .50
41 Ken Griffey Jr. 1.00 2.50
42 Eric Chavez .20 .50
43 Mark Quinn .20 .50
44 Roberto Alomar .30 .75
45 Bobby Abreu .20 .50
46 Bartolo Colon .20 .50
47 Jimmy Rollins .20 .50
48 Chipper Jones .50 1.25
49 Ben Sheets .20 .50
50 Freddy Garcia .20 .50
51 Sammy Sosa .50 1.25
52 Rafael Palmeiro .30 .75
53 Preston Wilson .20 .50
54 Troy Glaus .20 .50
55 Josh Beckett .20 .50
56 C.C. Sabathia .20 .50
57 Magglio Ordonez .20 .50
58 Brian Giles .20 .50
59 Darin Erstad .20 .50
60 Gary Sheffield .20 .50
61 Paul LoDuca .20 .50
62 Derek Jeter 1.25 3.00
63 Greg Maddux .75 2.00
64 Kerry Wood .20 .50
65 Toby Hall .20 .50
66 Barry Bonds 1.25 3.00
67 Jeff Bagwell .30 .75
68 Jason Kendall .20 .50
69 Richard Hidalgo .20 .50
70 J.D. Drew .20 .50
71 Tom Glavine .30 .75
72 Javier Vazquez .20 .50
73 Doug Mientkiewicz .20 .50
74 Jason Giambi .20 .50
75 Carlos Delgado .20 .50
76 Aramis Ramirez .20 .50
77 Torii Hunter .20 .50
78 Ivan Rodriguez .30 .75
79 Charles Johnson .20 .50
80 Jeff Kent .20 .50
81 Jacque Jones .20 .50
82 Larry Walker .20 .50
83 Cristian Guzman .20 .50
84 Jermaine Dye .20 .50
85 Roger Clemens 1.00 2.50
86 Mike Piazza .75 2.00
87 Craig Biggio .30 .75
88 Phil Nevin .20 .50
89 Jeff Cirillo .20 .50
90 Barry Zito .20 .50
91 Ryan Dempster .20 .50
92 Mark Buehrle .20 .50
93 Nomar Garciaparra .75 2.00
94 Frank Thomas .50 1.25
95 Jim Edmonds .20 .50
96 Geoff Jenkins .20 .50
97 Scott Rolen .30 .75
98 Tim Hudson .20 .50
99 Shannon Stewart .20 .50
100 Richie Sexson .20 .50
101 Orlando Hudson UP 2.00 5.00
102 Doug Devore UP RC 2.00 5.00
103 Rene Reyes UP RC 2.00 5.00
104 Steve Bechler UP RC 2.00 5.00
105 Jorge Nunez UP RC 2.00 5.00
106 Mitch Wylie UP RC 2.00 5.00
107 Jaime Cerda UP RC 2.00 5.00
108 Brandon Puffer UP RC 2.00 5.00
109 Tyler Yates UP RC 2.00 5.00
110 Bill Hall UP 2.00 5.00
111 Pete Zamora UP RC 2.00 5.00
112 Jeff Deardorff UP 2.00 5.00
113 J.J. Putz UP RC 2.00 5.00
114 Scotty Layfield UP RC 2.00 5.00
115 Brandon Backe UP RC 3.00 8.00
116 Andy Pratt UP RC 2.00 5.00
117 Mark Prior UP 3.00 8.00
118 Franklyn German UP RC 2.00 5.00
119 Todd Donovan UP RC 2.00 5.00
120 Franklin Nunez UP RC 2.00 5.00
121 Adam Walker UP RC 2.00 5.00
122 Ron Calloway UP RC 2.00 5.00
123 Tim Kalita UP RC 2.00 5.00
124 Kazuhisa Ishii UP RC 3.00 8.00
125 Mark Teixeira UP 3.00 8.00
126 Nate Field UP RC 2.00 5.00
127 Nelson Castro UP RC 2.00 5.00
128 So Taguchi UP RC 3.00 8.00
129 Marlon Byrd UP 2.00 5.00
130 Drew Henson UP 2.00 5.00
131 Kenny Kelly UP 2.00 5.00
132 John Ennis UP RC 2.00 5.00
133 Anastacio Martinez UP RC 2.00 5.00
134 Matt Guerrier UP 2.00 5.00
135 Tom Wilson UP RC 2.00 5.00
136 Ben Howard UP RC 2.00 5.00
137 Chris Baker UP RC 2.00 5.00
138 Kevin Frederick UP RC 2.00 5.00
139 Wilson Valdez UP RC 2.00 5.00
140 Austin Kearns UP 2.00 5.00

2002 Fleer Genuine Bats Incredible

COMPLETE SET (25) 40.00 100.00
STATED ODDS 1:10 HOBBY, 1:20 RETAIL
1 Todd Helton 1.00 2.50
2 Chipper Jones 1.50 4.00
3 Luis Gonzalez 1.00 2.50
4 Barry Bonds 4.00 10.00

5 Jason Giambi 1.00 2.50
6 Alex Rodriguez 2.00 5.00
7 Manny Ramirez 1.00 2.50
8 Jeff Bagwell 1.00 2.50
9 Shawn Green 1.00 2.50
10 Albert Pujols 3.00 8.00
11 Paul LoDuca 1.00 2.50
12 Mike Piazza 2.50 6.00
13 Derek Jeter 4.00 10.00
14 Edgar Martinez 1.00 2.50
BI15 Juan Gonzalez 1.00 2.50
16 Magglio Ordonez 1.00 2.50
17 Jermaine Dye 1.00 2.50
18 Larry Walker 1.00 2.50
19 Phil Nevin 1.00 2.50
20 Ivan Rodriguez 1.00 2.50
21 Ichiro Suzuki 3.00 8.00
22 J.D. Drew 1.00 2.50
23 Vladimir Guerrero 1.50 4.00
24 Sammy Sosa 1.50 4.00
25 Ken Griffey Jr. 3.00 8.00

2002 Fleer Genuine Bats Incredible Game Used

STATED ODDS 1:18 HOBBY, 1:90 RETAIL
1 Todd Helton 4.00 10.00
2 Chipper Jones 6.00 15.00
3 J.D. Drew 4.00 10.00
4 Alex Rodriguez 6.00 15.00
5 Manny Ramirez 4.00 10.00
6 Shawn Green 4.00 10.00
7 Derek Jeter 12.50 30.00
8 Edgar Martinez 4.00 10.00
9 Juan Gonzalez 4.00 10.00
10 Jermaine Dye 3.00 8.00
11 Phil Nevin 3.00 8.00
12 Ivan Rodriguez 4.00 10.00

2002 Fleer Genuine Ink

RANDOM INSERTS IN HOBBY PACKS
STATED PRINT RUNS LISTED BELOW
1 Barry Bonds/150 25.00 60.00
2 Ron Cey/975 6.00 15.00
3 Derek Jeter/150 100.00 200.00
4 Al Kaline/300 12.00 30.00
5 Don Mattingly/50 50.00 100.00
6 Paul Molitor/365 6.00 15.00
7 Dale Murphy/700 6.00 15.00
8 Phil Rizzuto/700 20.00 50.00
9 Brooks Robinson/140 20.00 50.00
10 Maury Wills/975 6.00 15.00

2002 Fleer Genuine Leaders

COMPLETE SET (15) 15.00 40.00
STATED ODDS 1:6 HOBBY, 1:8 RETAIL
1 Sammy Sosa 1.00 2.50
2 Todd Helton .60 1.50
3 Alex Rodriguez 1.25 3.00
4 Roger Clemens 2.00 5.00
5 Barry Bonds 2.50 6.00
6 Randy Johnson 1.00 2.50
7 Albert Pujols 2.00 5.00
8 Curt Schilling .60 1.50
9 Bernie Williams .60 1.50
10 Ken Griffey Jr. 2.00 5.00
11 Pedro Martinez .60 1.50
12 Juan Gonzalez .60 1.50
13 Hideo Nomo 1.00 2.50
14 Bret Boone .60 1.50
15 Ichiro Suzuki 2.00 5.00

2002 Fleer Genuine Leaders Game Jersey

STATED ODDS 1:11 HOBBY, 1:566 RETAIL
1 Todd Helton 6.00 15.00
2 Alex Rodriguez 6.00 15.00
3 Roger Clemens 8.00 20.00
4 Barry Bonds 10.00 25.00
5 Randy Johnson 6.00 15.00
6 Bernie Williams 6.00 15.00
7 Curt Schilling 6.00 15.00
8 Hideo Nomo 8.00 20.00
9 Pedro Martinez 6.00 15.00

2002 Fleer Genuine Names of the Game

COMPLETE SET (30) 50.00 120.00
STATED ODDS 1:10 HOBBY, 1:20 RETAIL
1 Mike Piazza 3.00 8.00
2 Chipper Jones 2.00 5.00
3 Jim Edmonds 1.25 3.00
4 Barry Larkin 1.25 3.00
5 Frank Thomas 2.00 5.00
6 Manny Ramirez 1.25 3.00
7 Carlos Delgado 1.25 3.00
8 Brian Giles 1.25 3.00
9 Kerry Wood 1.25 3.00
10 Derek Jeter 5.00 12.00
11 Adam Dunn 1.25 3.00
12 Gary Sheffield 1.25 3.00
13 Luis Gonzalez 1.25 3.00
14 Mark Mulder 1.25 3.00
15 Roberto Alomar 1.25 3.00
16 Scott Rolen 1.25 3.00
17 Tom Glavine 1.25 3.00
18 Bobby Abreu 1.25 3.00
19 Nomar Garciaparra 3.00 8.00
20 Darin Erstad 1.25 3.00
21 Cliff Floyd 1.25 3.00
22 Tim Hudson 1.25 3.00
23 Jim Thome 1.25 3.00
24 Nolan Ryan 5.00 12.00
25 Reggie Jackson 1.25 3.00
26 Rafael Palmeiro 1.25 3.00
27 Ken Griffey Jr. 4.00 10.00
28 Sammy Sosa 2.00 5.00
29 Vladimir Guerrero 2.00 5.00
30 Ichiro Suzuki 4.00 10.00

2002 Fleer Genuine Names of the Game Memorabilia

STATED ODDS 1:24 HOBBY, 1:100 RETAIL
SP'S ARE NOT SERIAL NUMBERED
SP PRINT RUNS PROVIDED BY FLEER
1 Roberto Alomar 6.00 15.00
2 Carlos Delgado 4.00 10.00
3 Jim Edmonds 4.00 10.00
4 Darin Erstad 4.00 10.00
5 Cliff Floyd 4.00 10.00
7 Brian Giles 4.00 10.00
8 Luis Gonzalez 4.00 10.00
9 Tim Hudson 4.00 10.00
10 Derek Jeter 12.50 30.00
11 Chipper Jones 6.00 15.00
12 Barry Larkin 6.00 15.00
13 Mark Mulder 4.00 10.00
14 Rafael Palmeiro 6.00 15.00
15 Mike Piazza 6.00 15.00
16 Manny Ramirez 6.00 15.00
17 Scott Rolen 6.00 15.00
18 Nolan Ryan 10.00 25.00
19 Jim Thome 6.00 15.00

2002 Fleer Genuine Tip of the Cap

COMPLETE SET (25) 25.00 60.00
STATED ODDS 1:6 HOBBY, 1:8 RETAIL
1 Alex Rodriguez 1.50 4.00
2 Derek Jeter 3.00 8.00
3 Kazuhiro Sasaki .75 2.00
4 Barry Bonds 3.00 8.00
5 J.D. Drew .75 2.00
6 Tsuyoshi Shinjo .75 2.00
7 Alfonso Soriano .75 2.00
8 Albert Pujols 2.50 6.00
9 Tom Seaver .75 2.00
10 Drew Henson .75 2.00
11 Dave Winfield .75 2.00
12 Carlos Delgado .75 2.00
13 Lou Boudreau .75 2.00
14 Shawn Green .75 2.00
15 Roger Clemens 2.50 6.00
16 Randy Johnson 1.25 3.00
17 Sammy Sosa 1.25 3.00
18 Rafael Palmeiro .75 2.00
19 Ken Griffey Jr. 2.50 6.00
20 Ichiro Suzuki 2.50 6.00
21 Eric Chavez .75 2.00
22 Andruw Jones .75 2.00
23 Miguel Tejada .75 2.00
24 Pedro Martinez .75 2.00
25 Tim Salmon .75 2.00

2002 Fleer Genuine Tip of the Cap Game Used

RANDOM INSERTS IN PACKS
STATED PRINT RUNS LISTED BELOW
NO PRICING ON QTY OF 40 OR LESS
3 Lou Boudreau/303 10.00 25.00
7 Carlos Delgado/219 8.00 20.00
15 Drew Henson/361 8.00 20.00
21 Rafael Palmeiro/300 10.00 25.00
22 Alex Rodriguez/670 10.00 25.00
24 Tom Seaver/224 10.00 25.00
26 Miguel Tejada/225 8.00 20.00
27 Dave Winfield/363 8.00 20.00

2002 Fleer Genuine Touch Em All

COMPLETE SET (25) 40.00 100.00
STATED ODDS 1:10 HOBBY, 1:20 RETAIL
1 Derek Jeter 4.00 10.00
2 Sammy Sosa 1.50 4.00
3 Albert Pujols 3.00 8.00
4 Vladimir Guerrero 1.50 4.00
5 Ken Griffey Jr. 3.00 8.00
6 Nomar Garciaparra 2.50 6.00
7 Luis Gonzalez 1.00 2.50
8 Barry Bonds 4.00 10.00
9 Manny Ramirez 1.00 2.50
10 Jason Giambi 1.00 2.50
11 Chipper Jones 1.50 4.00
12 Ichiro Suzuki 3.00 8.00
13 Alex Rodriguez 2.00 5.00
14 Juan Gonzalez 1.00 2.50
15 Todd Helton 1.00 2.50
16 Roberto Alomar 1.00 2.50
17 Jeff Bagwell 1.00 2.50
18 Mike Piazza 2.50 6.00
19 Gary Sheffield 1.00 2.50
20 Ivan Rodriguez 1.00 2.50
21 Frank Thomas 1.50 4.00
22 Bobby Abreu 1.00 2.50
23 J.D. Drew 1.00 2.50
24 Scott Rolen 1.00 2.50
25 Darin Erstad 1.00 2.50

2002 Fleer Genuine Touch Em All Game Base

RANDOM INSERTS IN HOBBY PACKS
STATED PRINT RUN 350 SERIAL #'d SETS
1 Derek Jeter 6.00 15.00
2 Sammy Sosa 2.50 6.00
3 Albert Pujols 5.00 12.00
4 Vladimir Guerrero 1.50 4.00
5 Ken Griffey Jr. 5.00 12.00
6 Nomar Garciaparra 1.50 4.00
7 Luis Gonzalez 1.00 2.50
8 Barry Bonds 4.00 10.00
9 Manny Ramirez 1.50 4.00
10 Jason Giambi 1.00 2.50
11 Chipper Jones 2.50 6.00
12 Ichiro Suzuki 3.00 8.00
13 Alex Rodriguez 3.00 8.00
14 Juan Gonzalez 1.00 2.50
15 Todd Helton 1.50 4.00
16 Roberto Alomar 1.50 4.00
17 Jeff Bagwell 1.50 4.00
18 Mike Piazza 2.50 6.00
19 Gary Sheffield 1.00 2.50
20 Ivan Rodriguez 1.50 4.00
21 Frank Thomas 2.50 6.00
22 Bobby Abreu 1.00 2.50
23 J.D. Drew 1.00 2.50
24 Scott Rolen 1.50 4.00
25 Darin Erstad 1.00 2.50

2003 Fleer Genuine

COMP.LO SET w/o SP's (100) 10.00 25.00
COMMON CARD (1-100) .20 .50
COMMON CARD (101-145) .75 2.00
101-130 RANDOM INSERTS IN PACKS
131-145 RANDOM IN FLEER R/G PACKS
101-130 PRINT RUN 799 SERIAL #'d SETS
131-145 PRINT RUN 1000 SERIAL #'d SETS
1 Derek Jeter 1.25 3.00
2 Mo Vaughn .20 .50
3 Adam Dunn .30 .75
4 Aubrey Huff .20 .50
5 Jacque Jones .20 .50
6 Kerry Wood .20 .50
7 Barry Bonds .75 2.00
8 Kevin Brown .20 .50
9 Sammy Sosa .50 1.25
10 Ray Durham .20 .50
11 Carlos Beltran .30 .75
12 Tony Batista .20 .50
13 Bobby Abreu .20 .50
14 Craig Biggio .30 .75
15 Gary Sheffield .20 .50
16 Jermaine Dye .20 .50
17 Carlos Pena .30 .75
18 Tim Salmon .20 .50
19 Mike Piazza .50 1.25
20 Moises Alou .20 .50
21 Edgardo Alfonzo .20 .50
22 Mike Sweeney .20 .50
23 Jay Gibbons .20 .50
24 Kevin Millwood .20 .50
25 A.J. Burnett .20 .50
26 Austin Kearns .20 .50
27 Rafael Palmeiro .30 .75
28 Vladimir Guerrero .30 .75
29 Paul Konerko .30 .75
30 Scott Rolen .30 .75
31 Fred McGriff .30 .75
32 Frank Thomas .50 1.25
33 John Olerud .20 .50
34 Eric Gagne .20 .50
35 Nomar Garciaparra .30 .75
36 Ryan Klesko .20 .50
37 Lance Berkman .30 .75
38 Andruw Jones .20 .50
39 Pat Burrell .20 .50
40 Juan Encarnacion .20 .50
41 Curt Schilling .30 .75
42 Jason Giambi .20 .50
43 Barry Larkin .30 .75
44 Alex Rodriguez .60 1.50
45 Kazuhisa Ishii .20 .50
46 Pedro Martinez .30 .75
47 Sean Burroughs .20 .50
48 Roy Oswalt .30 .75
49 Chipper Jones .50 1.25
50 Barry Zito .30 .75
51 Jeff Kent .20 .50
52 Rodrigo Lopez .20 .50
53 Jim Thome .30 .75
54 Ivan Rodriguez .30 .75
55 Luis Gonzalez .20 .50
56 Alfonso Soriano .30 .75
57 Josh Beckett .20 .50
58 Junior Spivey .20 .50
59 Bernie Williams .30 .75
60 Omar Vizquel .30 .75
61 Eric Hinske .20 .50
62 Jose Vidro .20 .50
63 Bartolo Colon .20 .50
64 Jim Edmonds .30 .75
65 Ben Sheets .20 .50
66 Mark Prior .30 .75
67 Edgar Martinez .30 .75
68 Raul Ibanez .30 .75
69 Darin Erstad .20 .50
70 Roger Clemens .60 1.50
71 C.C. Sabathia .30 .75
72 Carlos Delgado .20 .50
73 Tom Glavine .30 .75
74 Magglio Ordonez .30 .75
75 Ichiro Suzuki .60 1.50
76 Johnny Damon .30 .75
77 Brian Giles .20 .50
78 Jeff Bagwell .30 .75
79 Greg Maddux .60 1.50
80 Eric Chavez .20 .50
81 Larry Walker .30 .75
82 Randy Johnson .50 1.25
83 Miguel Tejada .30 .75
84 Todd Helton .30 .75
85 Jarrod Washburn .20 .50
86 Troy Glaus .20 .50
87 Ken Griffey Jr. 1.00 2.50
88 Albert Pujols .60 1.50
89 Torii Hunter .20 .50
90 Joe Crede .20 .50
91 Matt Morris .20 .50
92 Shawn Green .20 .50
93 Manny Ramirez .50 1.25
94 Jason Kendall .20 .50
95 Preston Wilson .20 .50
96 Garret Anderson .20 .50
97 Cliff Floyd .20 .50
98 Sean Casey .20 .50
99 Juan Gonzalez .20 .50
100 Richie Sexson .20 .50
101 Joe Borchard GU .75 2.00
102 Josh Stewart GU RC .75 2.00
103 Francisco Rodriguez GU 1.25 3.00
104 Jeremy Bonderman GU RC 3.00 8.00
105 Walter Young GU .75 2.00
106 Brandon Webb GU RC 2.50 6.00
107 Lyle Overbay GU .75 2.00
108 Jose Contreras GU RC 2.00 5.00
109 Victor Martinez GU 1.25 3.00
110 Hideki Matsui GU RC 4.00 10.00
111 Brian Stokes GU RC .75 2.00
112 Daniel Cabrera GU RC 1.25 3.00
113 Josh Willingham GU RC 2.50 6.00
114 Mark Teixeira GU 1.25 3.00
115 Pete LaForest GU RC .75 2.00
116 Chris Waters GU RC .75 2.00
117 Chien-Ming Wang GU RC 3.00 8.00
118 Ian Ferguson GU RC .75 2.00
119 Rocco Baldelli GU .75 2.00
120 Termel Sledge GU RC .75 2.00
121 Hank Blalock GU .75 2.00
122 Alejandro Machado GU RC .75 2.00
123 Hee Seop Choi GU .75 2.00
124 Guillermo Quiroz GU RC .75 2.00
125 Chase Utley GU 1.25 3.00
126 Nook Logan GU RC .75 2.00
127 Josh Hall GU RC .75 2.00
128 Ryan Church GU .75 2.00
129 Lew Ford GU RC .75 2.00
130 Francisco Rosario GU RC .75 2.00
131 Dan Haren GU RC 4.00 10.00
132 Rickie Weeks GU RC 2.50 6.00
133 Prentice Redman GU RC .75 2.00
134 Craig Brazell GU RC .75 2.00
135 Jon Leicester GU RC .75 2.00
136 Ryan Wagner GU RC .75 2.00
137 Matt Kata GU RC .75 2.00
138 Edwin Jackson GU RC 1.25 3.00
139 Mike Ryan GU RC .75 2.00
140 Delmon Young GU RC 5.00 12.00
141 Bo Hart GU RC .75 2.00
142 Jeff Duncan GU RC .75 2.00
143 Robby Hammock GU RC .75 2.00
144 Michael Hessman GU RC .75 2.00
145 Clint Barmes GU RC 2.00 5.00

2003 Fleer Genuine Reflection Ascending

*1-100 PRINT RUN b/wn 26-35: 8X TO 20X
*1-100 PRINT RUN b/wn 36-50: 6X TO 15X
*1-100 PRINT RUN b/wn 51-65: 5X TO 12X
*1-100 PRINT RUN b/wn 66-80: 4X TO 10X
*1-100 PRINT RUN b/wn 81-100: 3X TO 8X
*101-130 P/R b/wn 101-130: .75X TO 2X
*101-130 P/R b/wn 101-130: .75X TO 2X RC
PRINT RUNS B/WN 1-130 COPIES PER CARD
1-25 NOT PRICED DUE TO SCARCITY

2003 Fleer Genuine Reflection Descending

*1-100 PRINT RUN b/wn 130-101: 2.5X TO 6X
*1-100 PRINT RUN b/wn 100-81: 3X TO 8X
*1-100 PRINT RUN b/wn 80-66: 4X TO 10X
*1-100 PRINT RUN b/wn 65-51: 5X TO 12X
*1-100 PRINT RUN b/wn 50-36: 6X TO 15X
*1-100 PRINT RUN b/wn 35-31: 8X TO 20X
*101-130 P/R b/wn 30-26: 1.25X TO 3X
PRINT RUNS B/WN 1-130 COPIES PER CARD
101-105 RC'S NOT PRICED DUE TO SCARCITY
106-130 NOT PRICED DUE TO SCARCITY

2003 Fleer Genuine Article Insider Game Jersey

STATED ODDS 1:24
SP PRINT RUNS PROVIDED BY FLEER
SP'S ARE NOT SERIAL-NUMBERED
AD Adam Dunn 3.00 8.00
AJ Andruw Jones SP/200 4.00 10.00
AS Alfonso Soriano SP/300 3.00 8.00
CJ Chipper Jones 4.00 10.00
CS Curt Schilling 3.00 8.00
DJ Derek Jeter SP/450 10.00 25.00
DM Don Mattingly Pants 10.00 25.00
JB Jeff Bagwell 4.00 10.00
LB Lance Berkman 3.00 8.00
MO Magglio Ordonez 3.00 8.00
MP Mike Piazza SP/100 8.00 20.00
MS Greg Maddux 4.00 10.00
MT Miguel Tejada SP/100 6.00 15.00
NG Nomar Garciaparra 6.00 15.00
PG Pat Burrell 3.00 8.00
PM Pedro Martinez 4.00 10.00
RJ Randy Johnson 4.00 10.00
SG Shawn Green 3.00 8.00
SS Sammy Sosa SP/300 4.00 10.00
TG Troy Glaus 3.00 8.00
TH Torii Hunter 3.00 8.00
TH2 Todd Helton 4.00 10.00
VG Vladimir Guerrero SP/100 8.00 20.00

2003 Fleer Genuine Article Insider Game Jersey Autographs

RANDOM INSERTS IN PACKS
PRINTS B/WN 165-170 COPIES PER CARD
GADM D.Matt Pants/170 30.00 80.00
GALB Lance Berkman/165 8.00 20.00

2003 Fleer Genuine Article Insider Game Jersey Autographs VIP Blue

RANDOM INSERTS IN PACKS
STATED PRINT RUN 50 SERIAL #'d SETS
GADM Don Mattingly Pants 50.00 120.00
GALB Lance Berkman 15.00 40.00

2003 Fleer Genuine Article Insider Game Jersey Autographs VIP Red

RANDOM INSERTS IN PACKS
STATED PRINT RUN 100 SERIAL #'d SETS
GADJ Derek Jeter 75.00 150.00
GADM Don Mattingly Pants 40.00 100.00
GALB Lance Berkman 12.50 30.00

2003 Fleer Genuine Longball Threats

COMPLETE SET (15) 10.00 25.00
STATED ODDS 1:8
1 D.Jeter / N.Garciaparra 2.50 6.00
2 J.Thome / P.Burrell .60 1.50
3 A.Rodriguez / R.Palmeiro 1.25 3.00
4 A.Soriano / H.Matsui 2.00 5.00
5 T.Hunter / V.Guerrero .60 1.50
6 M.Sweeney / P.Nevin .40 1.00
7 M.Piazza / S.Sosa 1.00 2.50
8 S.Green / J.Giambi .40 1.00
9 M.Ordonez / A.Jones .60 1.50
10 E.Chavez / C.Delgado .40 1.00
11 M.Ramirez / J.Bagwell 1.00 2.50
12 S.Rolen / T.Glaus .60 1.50
13 B.Bonds / M.Tejada 1.50 4.00
14 A.Pujols / L.Berkman 1.25 3.00
15 C.Jones / T.Helton 1.00 2.50

2003 Fleer Genuine Longball Threats Dual Patch

PRINT RUNS B/WN 36-100 COPIES PER CARD
1 D.Jeter/N.Garciaparra/42 50.00 100.00
2 J.Thome/P.Burrell/89 10.00 25.00
3 A.Rodriguez/R.Palmeiro/100 20.00 50.00
5 T.Hunter/V.Guerrero/68 15.00 40.00
6 M.Sweeney/P.Nevin/36 15.00 40.00
7 M.Piazza/S.Sosa/82 10.00 25.00
8 S.Green/J.Giambi/83 6.00 15.00
9 M.Ordonez/A.Jones/73 10.00 25.00
11 M.Ramirez/J.Bagwell/64 15.00 40.00
12 S.Rolen/T.Glaus/61 15.00 40.00
15 C.Jones/T.Helton/56 15.00 40.00

2003 Fleer Genuine Longball Threats Dual Swatch

STATED ODDS 1:72
1 D.Jeter / N.Garciaparra 15.00 40.00
2 J.Thome/P.Burrell 6.00 15.00
3 A.Rodriguez/R.Palmeiro 10.00 25.00
5 T.Hunter/V.Guerrero 6.00 15.00
6 M.Sweeney/P.Nevin 4.00 10.00
7 M.Piazza/S.Sosa 6.00 15.00
8 S.Green/J.Giambi 4.00 10.00
9 M.Ordonez/A.Jones 6.00 15.00
11 M.Ramirez/J.Bagwell 6.00 15.00
12 S.Rolen/T.Glaus 6.00 15.00
15 C.Jones/T.Helton 6.00 15.00

2003 Fleer Genuine Longball Threats Single Swatch

STATED ODDS 1:13
SP PRINT RUNS PROVIDED BY FLEER
SP'S ARE NOT SERIAL-NUMBERED
1A D.Jeter Jsy-Nomar SP/300 10.00 25.00
1B N.Garciaparra Jsy-Jeter 6.00 15.00
2A J.Thome Jsy-Burrell 4.00 10.00
2B P.Burrell Jsy-Thome 3.00 8.00
3B R.Palmeiro Jsy-A.Rod 4.00 10.00
4A A.Soriano Jsy-Matsui SP/250 10.00 25.00
5A T.Hunter Jsy-Guerrero 3.00 8.00
5B V.Guerrero Jsy-Torii 4.00 10.00
6A M.Sweeney Jsy-Nevin 3.00 8.00
6B P.Nevin Jsy-Sweeney SP/300 3.00 8.00
7A M.Piazza Jsy-Sosa 4.00 10.00
7B S.Sosa Jsy-Piazza SP/100 8.00 20.00
8A S.Green Jsy-Giambi 3.00 8.00
9A M.Ordonez Jsy-Andruw 4.00 10.00
9B A.Jones Jsy-Magglio SP/200 4.00 10.00
10B C.Delgado Jsy-Chavez 3.00 8.00
11A M.Ramirez Jsy-Bagwell 4.00 10.00
11B J.Bagwell Jsy-Manny SP/450 4.00 10.00
12A S.Rolen Jsy-Glaus 4.00 10.00
12B T.Glaus Jsy-Rolen 3.00 8.00
13B M.Tejada Jsy-Bonds 3.00 8.00
14B L.Berkman Jsy-Pujols 3.00 8.00
15A C.Jones Jsy-Helton 4.00 10.00
15B T.Helton Jsy-Chipper 4.00 10.00

2003 Fleer Genuine Tools of the Game

STATED ODDS 1:20
1 Adam Dunn .60 1.50
2 Chipper Jones 1.00 2.50
3 Torii Hunter .40 1.00
4 Mike Piazza 1.00 2.50
5 Hideki Matsui 2.00 5.00
6 Nomar Garciaparra .60 1.50
7 Derek Jeter 2.50 6.00
8 Alex Rodriguez 1.25 3.00
9 Alfonso Soriano .60 1.50
10 Pat Burrell .40 1.00
11 Barry Bonds 1.50 4.00
12 Jason Giambi .40 1.00
13 Sammy Sosa 1.00 2.50
14 Vladimir Guerrero .60 1.50
15 Ichiro Suzuki 1.25 3.00

2003 Fleer Genuine Tools of the Game Bat

STATED ODDS 1:42
AD Adam Dunn 2.00 5.00
AR Alex Rodriguez 5.00 12.00
AS Alfonso Soriano 2.00 5.00
DJ Derek Jeter 8.00 20.00
JG Jason Giambi 2.00 5.00
MP Mike Piazza 5.00 12.00
SS Sammy Sosa 3.00 8.00
VG Vladimir Guerrero 3.00 8.00

2003 Fleer Genuine Tools of the Game Bat-Jersey

RANDOM INSERTS IN PACKS
STATED PRINT RUN 250 SERIAL #'d SETS
AD Adam Dunn 4.00 10.00
AS Alfonso Soriano 4.00 10.00
DJ Derek Jeter 15.00 40.00
JG Jason Giambi 4.00 10.00
MP Mike Piazza 10.00 25.00
SS Sammy Sosa 6.00 15.00
VG Vladimir Guerrero 6.00 15.00

2003 Fleer Genuine Tools of the Game Bat-Jersey-Cap

RANDOM INSERTS IN PACKS
STATED PRINT RUN 100 SERIAL #'d SETS
AD Adam Dunn 8.00 20.00
AR Alex Rodriguez 10.00 25.00
AS Alfonso Soriano 8.00 20.00
DJ Derek Jeter 30.00 80.00
JG Jason Giambi 8.00 20.00
MP Mike Piazza 10.00 25.00
SS Sammy Sosa 8.00 20.00
VG Vladimir Guerrero 8.00 20.00

2004 Fleer Genuine Insider

COMP.SET w/o SP's (90) 10.00 25.00
COMMON CARD (1-90) .20 .50
COMMON CARD (91-100) 1.00 2.50
91-100 PRINT RUN 499 SERIAL #'d SETS
COMMON CARD (101-120) .75 2.00
101-120 PRINT RUN 799 SERIAL #'d SETS
91-120 STATED ODDS 1:14 HOB, 1:72 RET
COMMON CARD (121-130) 1.00 2.50
121-130 SEEDED WITHIN RI 91-100 CARDS
121-130 PRINT RUN 350 SERIAL #'d SETS
121-130 ARE MINI-SIZED CARDS
1 Troy Glaus .20 .50
2 Eric Chavez .20 .50
3 Lance Berkman .30 .75
4 Pedro Martinez .30 .75
5 Jim Edmonds .30 .75
6 Tom Glavine .30 .75
7 Ken Griffey Jr. 1.00 2.50
8 Vernon Wells .20 .50
9 Hideki Matsui .75 2.00
10 Jeff Bagwell .30 .75
11 Rafael Palmeiro .30 .75
12 Edgar Martinez .30 .75
13 Bernie Williams .30 .75
14 Josh Beckett .20 .50
15 Javy Lopez .20 .50
16 Ichiro Suzuki .60 1.50
17 Scott Podsednik .20 .50
18 Sammy Sosa .50 1.25
19 Mark Teixeira .30 .75
20 Jorge Posada .30 .75
21 Miguel Cabrera .50 1.25
22 Chipper Jones .50 1.25
23 Sean Burroughs .20 .50
24 Dmitri Young .20 .50
25 Brandon Webb .20 .50
26 Bobby Abreu .20 .50
27 Hideo Nomo .50 1.25
28 Frank Thomas .50 1.25
29 Alex Rodriguez .60 1.50
30 Derek Jeter 1.25 3.00
31 Todd Helton .30 .75
32 Andruw Jones .20 .50
33 Jason Kendall .20 .50
34 Eric Gagne .20 .50
35 Omar Vizquel .30 .75
36 Vladimir Guerrero .30 .75
37 Jim Thome .30 .75
38 Mike Sweeney .20 .50
39 Manny Ramirez .50 1.25
40 Scott Rolen .30 .75
41 Jose Vidro .20 .50
42 Adam Dunn .30 .75
43 Garret Anderson .20 .50
44 Mike Lieberthal .20 .50
45 Roy Oswalt .30 .75
46 Geoff Jenkins .20 .50
47 Magglio Ordonez .30 .75
48 Hank Blalock .20 .50
49 Barry Zito .30 .75
50 Dontrelle Willis .20 .50
51 Greg Maddux .60 1.50
52 Brian Giles .20 .50
53 Shawn Green .20 .50
54 Carlos Lee .20 .50
55 Carlos Delgado .20 .50
56 Alfonso Soriano .30 .75
57 Angel Berroa .20 .50
58 Kerry Wood .20 .50
59 Rocco Baldelli .20 .50
60 Gary Sheffield .20 .50
61 Ivan Rodriguez .30 .75
62 Richie Sexson .20 .50
63 Marlon Byrd .20 .50
64 Carlos Beltran .30 .75
65 Mark Prior .30 .75
66 Aubrey Huff .20 .50
67 Jason Giambi .20 .50
68 Curt Schilling .30 .75
69 Reggie Sanders .20 .50
70 Mike Piazza .50 1.25
71 Craig Monroe .20 .50
72 Randy Johnson .50 1.25
73 Pat Burrell .20 .50
74 Craig Biggio .30 .75
75 Nomar Garciaparra .30 .75
76 Albert Pujols .60 1.50
77 Jose Reyes .30 .75
78 Preston Wilson .20 .50
79 Miguel Tejada .30 .75
80 Bret Boone .20 .50
81 Shannon Stewart .20 .50
82 Jody Gerut .20 .50
83 Tim Salmon .20 .50
84 Tim Hudson .30 .75
85 Juan Pierre .20 .50
86 Jay Gibbons .20 .50
87 Jason Schmidt .20 .50
88 Torii Hunter .20 .50
89 Austin Kearns .20 .50
90 Roy Halladay .30 .75
91 John Gall RI RC 1.00 2.50
92 Kaz Matsui RI RC 1.50 4.00
93 Merkin Valdez RI RC 1.00 2.50
94 William Bergolla RI RC 1.00 2.50
95 Angel Chavez RI RC 1.00 2.50
96 Hector Gimenez RI RC 1.00 2.50
97 Aarom Baldiris RI RC 1.00 2.50
98 Justin Leone RI RC 1.00 2.50
99 Onil Joseph RI RC 1.00 2.50
100 Freddy Guzman RI RC 1.00 2.50
101 Rickie Weeks UP .75 2.00
102 Chad Bentz UP RC .75 2.00
103 Bobby Crosby UP .75 2.00
104 Dallas McPherson UP .75 2.00
105 Brandon Watson UP .75 2.00
106 Garrett Atkins UP .75 2.00
107 Graham Koonce UP .75 2.00
108 Chien-Ming Wang UP 3.00 8.00
109 Jonny Gomes UP .75 2.00
110 Edwin Jackson UP .75 2.00
111 Alfredo Simon UP RC 1.25 3.00
112 Delmon Young UP 1.25 3.00
113 Angel Guzman UP .75 2.00
114 Ryan Howard UP 1.50 4.00
115 Scott Hairston UP .75 2.00
116 Edwin Encarnacion UP 2.00 5.00
117 Byron Gettis UP .75 2.00
118 Kevin Youkilis UP .75 2.00
119 Grady Sizemore UP 1.25 3.00
120 Corey Hart UP .75 2.00
121 Greg Dobbs MRI RC 1.00 2.50
122 Jerry Gil MRI RC 1.00 2.50
123 Shawn Hill MRI RC 1.00 2.50
124 John Labandeira MRI RC 1.00 2.50
125 Jason Bartlett MRI RC 3.00 8.00
126 Ronny Cedeno MRI RC 1.00 2.50
127 Don Kelly MRI RC 1.50 4.00
128 Ivan Ochoa MRI RC 1.00 2.50
129 Mariano Gomez MRI RC 1.00 2.50
130 Ruddy Yan MRI 1.00 2.50

2004 Fleer Genuine Insider Mini Parallel 137

*PARA.137: .6X TO 1.5X BASIC
RANDOM WITHIN ROOKIE INSIDER CARDS
STATED PRINT RUN 137 SERIAL #'d SETS

2004 Fleer Genuine Insider Reflections

*REFL 1-90: 3X TO 8X BASIC
*REFL 101-120: .6X TO 1.5X BASIC
STATED ODDS 1:24 HOBBY, 1:200 RETAIL
STATED PRINT RUN 99 SERIAL #'d SETS

2004 Fleer Genuine Insider Article Jersey

STATED PRINT RUN 250 SERIAL #'d SETS
*ARTICLE BAT: .5X TO 1.2X BASIC
ARTICLE BAT PRINT RUN 100 #'d SETS
*ARTICLE BAT-JSY: 1X TO 2.5X BASIC
ARTICLE BAT-JSY PRINT RUN 50 #'d SETS
ARTICLE JSY TAG PRINT RUN 5 #'d SETS
NO ART.JSY TAG PRICE DUE TO SCARCITY
OVERALL ODDS GU 1:9 H, AU-GU 1:48 R
AD Adam Dunn 2.00 5.00
AP Albert Pujols 6.00 15.00
AR Alex Rodriguez 6.00 15.00
AS Alfonso Soriano 2.00 5.00
CD Carlos Delgado 2.00 5.00
CJ Chipper Jones 3.00 8.00
DJ Derek Jeter 8.00 20.00
GS Gary Sheffield 2.00 5.00
HB Hank Blalock 2.00 5.00
JG Jason Giambi 2.00 5.00
JR Jose Reyes 2.00 5.00
JT Jim Thome 3.00 8.00
LB Lance Berkman 2.00 5.00
MC Miguel Cabrera 3.00 8.00
MO Magglio Ordonez 2.00 5.00
MP Mike Piazza 5.00 12.00
MR Manny Ramirez 3.00 8.00
MT Mark Teixeira 3.00 8.00
NG Nomar Garciaparra 5.00 12.00
RB Rocco Baldelli 2.00 5.00
RP Rafael Palmeiro 3.00 8.00
SS Sammy Sosa 3.00 8.00
TG Troy Glaus 2.00 5.00
TH Todd Helton 3.00 8.00
VG Vladimir Guerrero 3.00 8.00

2004 Fleer Genuine Insider Autograph

OVERALL ODDS AU 1:18 H, AU-GU 1:48 R
PRINT RUNS B/WN 27-550 COPIES PER
AH Aubrey Huff/550 6.00 15.00
AK Austin Kearns/350 4.00 10.00
BW Brandon Webb/450 4.00 10.00
DE David Eckstein/350 12.00 30.00
IR Ivan Rodriguez/150 10.00 25.00
JG Jody Gerut/550 4.00 10.00
JG2 Jay Gibbons/350 4.00 10.00
JR Jose Reyes/350 6.00 15.00
JR2 Jimmy Rollins/350 10.00 25.00
JS Jason Schmidt/300 6.00 15.00
JS2 John Smoltz/150 6.00 15.00
MB Marlon Byrd/550 4.00 10.00
MC Miguel Cabrera/250 20.00 50.00
MO Magglio Ordonez/250 6.00 15.00
MR Mariano Rivera/150 60.00 120.00
MT Mark Teixeira/350 10.00 25.00
OH Orlando Hudson/550 4.00 10.00
RA Roberto Alomar/150 8.00 20.00
RJ Randy Johnson/51 20.00 50.00
RP Rafael Palmeiro/150 6.00 15.00
SP Scott Podsednik/550 4.00 10.00
VG Vladimir Guerrero/27 15.00 60.00

2004 Fleer Genuine Insider Autograph-Jersey

STATED PRINT RUN 100 SERIAL #'d SETS
AUTO BALL PRINT RUN 10 #'d SETS
NO AUTO BALL PRICING DUE TO SCARCITY
*AUTO BAT: .5X TO 1.2X BASIC
AUTO BAT PRINT RUN 50 SERIAL #'d SETS
OVERALL ODDS AU 1:18 H, AU-GU 1:48 R
AH Aubrey Huff 6.00 15.00
AK Austin Kearns 6.00 15.00
AP Albert Pujols 75.00 150.00
BW Brandon Webb 6.00 15.00
DE David Eckstein 12.50 30.00
IR Ivan Rodriguez 15.00 40.00
JG Jody Gerut 6.00 15.00
JG2 Jay Gibbons 6.00 15.00
JR Jose Reyes 6.00 15.00
JR2 Jimmy Rollins 10.00 25.00
JS Jason Schmidt 6.00 15.00
JS2 John Smoltz 15.00 40.00
MB Marlon Byrd 6.00 15.00
MC Miguel Cabrera 20.00 50.00
MO Magglio Ordonez 6.00 15.00
MR Mariano Rivera 30.00 60.00
MT Mark Teixeira 10.00 25.00
OH Orlando Hudson 6.00 15.00
RA Roberto Alomar 10.00 25.00
RP Rafael Palmeiro 10.00 25.00
SP Scott Podsednik 10.00 25.00

2004 Fleer Genuine Insider Classic Confrontations

STATED ODDS 1:18 HOBBY, 1:24 RETAIL
1 M.Piazza / R.Clemens 1.25 3.00
2 P.Martinez / D.Jeter 2.50 6.00

3 R.Johnson 1.00 2.50
J.Bagwell
4 M.Prior 1.25 3.00
A.Pujols
5 J.Beckett 1.00 2.50
S.Sosa
6 E.Gagne .40 1.00
H.Blalock
7 M.Rivera 1.25 3.00
N.Garciaparra
8 C.Schilling 1.00 2.50
C.Jones
9 K.Wood .60 1.50
J.Edmonds
10 B.Zito .60 1.50
A.Soriano
11 R.Johnson 2.00 5.00
K.Griffey Jr.
12 D.Jeter 2.50 6.00
J.Smoltz
13 R.Oswalt 2.00 5.00
K.Griffey Jr.
14 D.Willis 1.50 4.00
H.Matsui
15 H.Nomo 1.25 3.00
I.Suzuki

2004 Fleer Genuine Insider Classic Confrontations Dual Swatch

STATED PRINT RUN 100 SERIAL #'d SETS
DUAL PATCH PRINT RUN 10 #'d SETS
NO DUAL PATCH PRICE DUE TO SCARCITY
OVERALL ODDS GU 1:9 H, AU-GU 1:48 R
BZAS B.Zito/A.Soriano 4.00 10.00
CSCJ C.Schilling/C.Jones 6.00 15.00
EGHB E.Gagne/H.Blalock 4.00 10.00
JBSS J.Beckett/S.Sosa 6.00 15.00
KWJE K.Wood/J.Edmonds 4.00 10.00
MPAP M.Prior/A.Pujols 10.00 25.00
MRNG M.Rivera/N.Garciaparra 6.00 15.00
PMDJ P.Martinez/D.Jeter 10.00 25.00
RJJB R.Johnson/J.Bagwell 6.00 15.00

2004 Fleer Genuine Insider Classic Confrontations Swatch

OVERALL ODDS GU 1:9 H, AU-GU 1:48 R
STATED PRINT RUN 400 SERIAL #'d SETS
AP A.Pujols Jsy w/Prior 5.00 12.00
AS A.Soriano Jsy w/Zito 2.00 5.00
BZ B.Zito Jsy w/Soriano 2.00 5.00
CJ C.Jones Jsy w/Schilling 3.00 8.00
CS C.Schilling Jsy w/Chipper 3.00 8.00
DJ D.Jeter Jsy w/Pedro 6.00 15.00
DW D.Willis Jsy w/Matsui 3.00 8.00
EG E.Gagne Jsy w/Blalock 2.00 5.00
HB H.Blalock Jsy w/Gagne 2.00 5.00
HN H.Nomo Jsy w/Ichiro 3.00 8.00
JB J.Bagwell Jsy w/Randy 3.00 8.00
JB2 J.Beckett Jsy w/Sosa 2.00 5.00
JE J.Edmonds Jsy w/Wood 2.00 5.00
JS J.Smoltz Jsy w/Jeter 3.00 8.00
KW K.Wood Jsy w/Edmonds 2.00 5.00
MP M.Piazza Jsy w/Clemens 4.00 10.00
MP2 M.Prior Jsy w/Pujols 4.00 10.00
MR M.Rivera Jsy w/Nomar 3.00 8.00
NG N.Garciaparra Jsy w/Rivera 4.00 10.00
PM P.Martinez Jsy w/Jeter 3.00 8.00
RC R.Clemens Jsy w/Piazza 5.00 12.00
RJ1 R.Johnson Jsy w 3.00 8.00
Bagwell
RJ2 R.Johnson Jsy w/Griffey Jr. 3.00 8.00
RO R.Oswalt Jsy w/Griffey Jr. 2.00 5.00
SS S.Sosa Jsy w/Beckett 3.00 8.00

2004 Fleer Genuine Insider Tools of the Game

STATED ODDS 1:6 HOBBY, 1:12 RETAIL
1 Jason Giambi .40 1.00
2 Torii Hunter .40 1.00
3 Derek Jeter 2.50 6.00
4 Nomar Garciaparra .60 1.50
5 Albert Pujols 1.25 3.00
6 Jim Thome .60 1.50
7 Alex Rodriguez 1.25 3.00
8 Chipper Jones 1.00 2.50
9 Sammy Sosa 1.00 2.50
10 Jose Reyes .60 1.50
11 Pedro Martinez .60 1.50
12 Greg Maddux 1.25 3.00
13 Randy Johnson 1.00 2.50
14 Curt Schilling .60 1.50
15 Mark Prior .60 1.50
16 Ichiro Suzuki 1.25 3.00
17 Hideki Matsui 1.50 4.00
18 Kaz Matsui .60 1.50
19 Ken Griffey Jr. 2.00 5.00
20 Josh Beckett .40 1.00

2004 Fleer Genuine Insider Tools of the Game Jersey

STATED PRINT RUN 250 SERIAL #'d SETS
*TOOLS 2-PIECE: .75X TO 2X BASIC
TOOLS 2-PIECE PRINT RUN 125 #'d SETS
TOOLS 2-PIECE ARE BAT-JSY CARDS
*TOOLS 3-PIECE: 1.5X TO 4X BASIC
TOOLS 3-PIECE PRINT RUN 75 #'d SETS
TOOLS 3-PIECE ARE BAT-CAP-JSY CARDS
OVERALL ODDS GU 1:9 H, AU-GU 1:48 R
AP Albert Pujols Jsy 6.00 15.00
AR Alex Rodriguez Jsy 6.00 15.00
CJ Chipper Jones Jsy 3.00 8.00
CS Curt Schilling Jsy 3.00 8.00
DJ Derek Jeter Jsy 8.00 20.00
GM Greg Maddux Jsy 5.00 12.00
JG Jason Giambi Jsy 2.00 5.00
JR Jose Reyes Jsy 2.00 5.00
JT Jim Thome Jsy 3.00 8.00
MP Mark Prior Jsy 3.00 8.00
NG Nomar Garciaparra Jsy 5.00 12.00
PM Pedro Martinez Jsy 3.00 8.00
RJ Randy Johnson Jsy 3.00 8.00
SS Sammy Sosa Jsy 3.00 8.00
TH Torii Hunter Jsy 2.00 5.00

2003 Fleer Hardball

COMPLETE SET (280) 90.00 150.00
COMP.SET w/o SP's (240) 40.00 80.00
COMMON CARD (1-240) .15 .40
COMMON CARD (241-265) .25 .60
COMMON CARD (266-280) .40 1.00
241-280 STATED ODDS 1:2 H 1:4 R 1:5 BL
1 Barry Bonds .60 1.50
2 Derek Jeter 1.00 2.50
3 Jason Varitek .40 1.00
4 Magglio Ordonez .25 .60
5 Ryan Dempster .15 .40
6 Adam Everett .15 .40
7 Paul LoDuca .15 .40
8 Brad Wilkerson .15 .40
9 Al Leiter .15 .40
10 Jermaine Dye .15 .40
11 Rob Mackowiak .15 .40
12 J.T. Snow .15 .40
13 Juan Gonzalez .15 .40
14 Eric Hinske .15 .40
15 Greg Maddux .50 1.25
16 Moises Alou .15 .40
17 Carlos Lee .15 .40
18 Richard Hidalgo .15 .40
19 Jorge Posada .25 .60
20 Mike Lieberthal .15 .40
21 Jeff Cirillo .15 .40
22 Corey Patterson .15 .40
23 C.C. Sabathia .25 .60
24 Brian Giles .15 .40
25 Edgar Martinez .25 .60
26 Trot Nixon .15 .40
27 Kerry Wood .15 .40
28 Austin Kearns .15 .40
29 Lance Berkman .25 .60
30 Hideo Nomo .40 1.00
31 Brad Radke .15 .40
32 John Valentin .15 .40
33 Tim Hudson .25 .60
34 Aramis Ramirez .15 .40
35 Kevin Mench .15 .40
36 Kevin Appier .15 .40
37 Chris Richard .15 .40
38 Ruben Mateo .15 .40
39 Juan Pierre .15 .40
40 Nick Neugebauer .15 .40
41 Mike Mussina .25 .60
42 Rich Aurilia .15 .40
43 Albert Pujols .50 1.25
44 Carlos Delgado .15 .40
45 Junior Spivey .15 .40
46 Marcus Giles .15 .40
47 Johnny Damon .25 .60
48 Mark Prior .25 .60
49 Omar Vizquel .25 .60
50 Craig Biggio .25 .60
51 Chuck Knoblauch .15 .40
52 Eric Milton .15 .40
53 Jeromy Burnitz .15 .40
54 Jim Thome .25 .60
55 Steve Finley .15 .40
56 Kevin Millwood .15 .40
57 Alex Gonzalez .15 .40
58 Ben Broussard .15 .40
59 Derrek Lee .15 .40
60 Joe Randa .15 .40
61 Doug Mientkiewicz .15 .40
62 Jason Phillips .15 .40
63 Brett Myers .15 .40
64 Josh Fogg .15 .40
65 Reggie Sanders .15 .40
66 Chipper Jones .40 1.00
67 Roosevelt Brown .15 .40
68 Matt Lawton .15 .40
69 Charles Johnson .15 .40
70 Mark Quinn .15 .40
71 Jacque Jones .15 .40
72 Armando Benitez .15 .40
73 Bobby Abreu .15 .40
74 Jason Kendall .15 .40
75 Jeff Kent .15 .40
76 Mark Teixeira .25 .60
77 Garret Anderson .15 .40
78 Jerry Hairston Jr. .15 .40
79 Tony Graffanino .15 .40
80 Josh Beckett .15 .40
81 Eric Gagne .15 .40
82 Fernando Tatis .15 .40
83 Brett Tomko .15 .40
84 Fernando Vina .15 .40
85 Rafael Palmeiro .25 .60
86 Luis Gonzalez .15 .40
87 Javy Lopez .15 .40
88 Shea Hillenbrand .15 .40
89 Hee Seop Choi .15 .40
90 Preston Wilson .15 .40
91 Neifi Perez .15 .40
92 Ray Lankford .15 .40
93 Tsuyoshi Shinjo .15 .40
94 Ben Grieve .15 .40
95 Jarrod Washburn .15 .40
96 Gary Sheffield .15 .40
97 Derek Lowe .15 .40
98 Tony Womack .15 .40
99 Milton Bradley .15 .40
100 Brad Penny .15 .40
101 Mike Sweeney .15 .40
102 A.J. Pierzynski .15 .40
103 Edgardo Alfonzo .15 .40
104 Marlon Byrd .15 .40
105 Sean Burroughs .15 .40
106 Kazuhiro Sasaki .15 .40
107 Damian Rolls .15 .40
108 Troy Glaus .15 .40
109 Rafael Furcal .15 .40
110 Nomar Garciaparra .25 .60
111 Josh Bard .15 .40
112 Alex Gonzalez .15 .40
113 Cristian Guzman .15 .40
114 Roger Cedeno .15 .40
115 Freddy Garcia .15 .40
116 Travis Phelps .15 .40
117 Juan Cruz .15 .40
118 Frank Thomas .40 1.00
119 Jaret Wright .15 .40
120 Carlos Beltran .25 .60
121 Ronnie Belliard .15 .40
122 Roger Clemens .50 1.25
123 Vicente Padilla .15 .40
124 Joel Pineiro .15 .40
125 Jared Sandberg .15 .40
126 Tom Glavine .25 .60
127 Matt Clement .15 .40
128 Aaron Rowand .15 .40
129 Alex Escobar .15 .40
130 Randy Wolf .15 .40
131 Ichiro Suzuki .50 1.25
132 Toby Hall .15 .40
133 Scott Spiezio .15 .40
134 Bobby Higginson .15 .40
135 A.J. Burnett .15 .40
136 Cesar Izturis .15 .40
137 Roberto Alomar .25 .60
138 Trevor Hoffman .25 .60
139 Edgar Renteria .15 .40
140 Rusty Greer .15 .40
141 David Eckstein .15 .40
142 Pedro Martinez .25 .60
143 Joe Crede .15 .40
144 Robert Fick .15 .40
145 Mike Lowell .15 .40
146 Brian Jordan .15 .40
147 Mark Mulder .15 .40
148 Scott Rolen .25 .60
149 Eddie Guardado .15 .40
150 Adam Kennedy .15 .40
151 Ken Griffey Jr. .75 2.00
152 Larry Walker .25 .60
153 Carlos Pena .25 .60
154 Geoff Jenkins .15 .40
155 Bartolo Colon .15 .40
156 Mariano Rivera .50 1.25
157 Robb Nen .15 .40
158 Bret Boone .15 .40
159 Shannon Stewart .15 .40
160 Chris Singleton .15 .40
161 Todd Walker .15 .40
162 Jay Payton .15 .40
163 Zach Day .15 .40
164 Bernie Williams .25 .60
165 Bubba Trammell .15 .40
166 Matt Morris .15 .40
167 Jose Cruz Jr. .15 .40
168 Mark Grace .25 .60
169 Andruw Jones .15 .40
170 Cliff Floyd .15 .40
171 Antonio Alfonseca .15 .40
172 Jeff Bagwell .25 .60
173 Shawn Green .15 .40
174 Joe Mays .15 .40
175 Mike Piazza .40 1.00
176 Adam Piatt .15 .40
177 Pokey Reese .15 .40
178 Carl Everett .15 .40
179 Tim Salmon .15 .40
180 Rodrigo Lopez .15 .40
181 Brandon Inge .15 .40
182 Kazuhisa Ishii .15 .40
183 Jose Vidro .15 .40
184 Barry Zito .25 .60
185 Phil Nevin .15 .40
186 J.D. Drew .15 .40
187 Vernon Wells .15 .40
188 Darin Erstad .15 .40
189 Barry Larkin .25 .60
190 Jason Jennings .15 .40
191 Luis Castillo .15 .40
192 Adrian Beltre .40 1.00
193 Tony Armas .15 .40
194 Terrence Long .15 .40
195 Mark Kotsay .15 .40
196 Tino Martinez .15 .40
197 Jayson Werth .25 .60
198 Eric Chavez .15 .40
199 Matt Williams .15 .40
200 Jon Lieber .15 .40
201 Eddie Taubensee .15 .40
202 Shane Reynolds .15 .40
203 Alex Sanchez .15 .40
204 Jason Giambi .15 .40
205 Jimmy Rollins .25 .60
206 Jamie Moyer .15 .40
207 Francisco Rodriguez .25 .60
208 Marty Cordova .15 .40
209 Aaron Boone .15 .40
210 Mike Hampton .15 .40
211 Mark Redman .15 .40
212 Richie Sexson .15 .40
213 Andy Pettitte .25 .60
214 Livan Hernandez .15 .40
215 Jason Isringhausen .15 .40
216 Curt Schilling .25 .60
217 Manny Ramirez .40 1.00
218 Jose Valentin .15 .40
219 Brent Butler .15 .40
220 Billy Wagner .15 .40
221 Ben Sheets .15 .40
222 Jeff Weaver .15 .40
223 Brent Abernathy .15 .40
224 Jay Gibbons .15 .40
225 Sean Casey .15 .40
226 Greg Norton .15 .40
227 Andy Van Hekken .15 .40
228 Kevin Brown .15 .40
229 Orlando Cabrera .15 .40
230 Scott Hatteberg .15 .40
231 Ryan Klesko .15 .40
232 Roy Halladay .25 .60
233 Randy Johnson .40 1.00
234 Mark Buehrle .25 .60
235 Todd Helton .25 .60
236 Jeffrey Hammonds .15 .40
237 Sidney Ponson .15 .40
238 Kip Wells .15 .40
239 John Olerud .15 .40
240 Aubrey Huff .15 .40
241 Derek Jeter AAS 1.50 4.00
242 Barry Bonds AAS 1.00 2.50
243 Ichiro Suzuki AAS .75 2.00
244 Troy Glaus AAS .25 .60
245 Alex Rodriguez AAS .75 2.00
246 Sammy Sosa AAS .60 1.50
247 Lance Berkman AAS .40 1.00
248 Jason Giambi AAS .25 .60
249 Nomar Garciaparra AAS .40 1.00
250 Miguel Tejada AAS .40 1.00
251 Albert Pujols AAS .75 2.00
252 Mike Piazza AAS .60 1.50
253 Vladimir Guerrero AAS .40 1.00
254 Shawn Green AAS .25 .60
255 Todd Helton AAS .40 1.00
256 Ken Griffey Jr. AAS 1.25 3.00
257 Torii Hunter AAS .25 .60
258 Chipper Jones AAS .60 1.50
259 Alfonso Soriano AAS .40 1.00
260 Luis Gonzalez AAS .25 .60
261 Pedro Martinez AAS .40 1.00
262 Tim Hudson AAS .40 1.00
263 Roger Clemens AAS .75 2.00
264 Greg Maddux AAS .75 2.00
265 Randy Johnson AAS .60 1.50
266 Vinny Chulk OD .40 1.00
267 Jose Castillo OD .40 1.00
268 Craig Brazell OD RC .40 1.00
269 Felix Sanchez OD RC .40 1.00
270 John Webb OD .40 1.00
271 Josh Hall OD RC .40 1.00
272 Alexis Rios OD .40 1.00
273 Phil Seibel OD RC .40 1.00
274 Prentice Redman OD RC .40 1.00
275 Walter Young OD .40 1.00
276 Nic Jackson OD .40 1.00
277 Adam Morrissey OD .40 1.00
278 Bobby Jenks OD .40 1.00
279 Rodrigo Rosario OD .40 1.00
280 Chin-Feng Chen OD .40 1.00

2003 Fleer Hardball Gold

*GOLD 1-240: 1.5X TO 4X BASIC
*GOLD 241-265: 1X TO 2.5X BASIC
*GOLD 266-280: .6X TO 1.5X BASIC
1-260 STATED ODDS 1:4 H; 1:6 R; 1:10 BL

2003 Fleer Hardball Platinum

*PLATINUM 1-240: 8X TO 20X BASIC
*PLATINUM 241-265: 5X TO 12X BASIC
*PLATINUM 266-280: 3X TO 8X BASIC
RANDOM INSERTS IN HOBBY PACKS
STATED PRINT RUN 50 SERIAL #'d SETS

2003 Fleer Hardball Discs

STATED ODDS 1:24 H; 1:24 R; 1:50 BL
1 Derek Jeter 2.50 6.00
2 Barry Bonds 1.50 4.00
3 Ichiro Suzuki 1.25 3.00
4 Sammy Sosa 1.00 2.50
5 Nomar Garciaparra .60 1.50
6 Lance Berkman .60 1.50
7 Jason Giambi .40 1.00
8 Mike Piazza 1.00 2.50
9 Shawn Green .40 1.00
10 Barry Zito .60 1.50
11 Albert Pujols 1.25 3.00
12 Alex Rodriguez 1.25 3.00
13 Tim Salmon .40 1.00
14 Eric Chavez .40 1.00
15 Ken Griffey Jr. 2.00 5.00
16 Alfonso Soriano .60 1.50
17 Vladimir Guerrero .60 1.50
18 Francisco Rodriguez .60 1.50
19 Miguel Tejada .60 1.50
20 Randy Johnson 1.00 2.50

2003 Fleer Hardball On the Ball

STATED ODDS 1:12 H; 1:18 R; 1:20 BL
1 Derek Jeter 2.50 6.00
2 Barry Bonds 1.50 4.00
3 Nomar Garciaparra .60 1.50
4 Alfonso Soriano .60 1.50
5 Mike Piazza 1.00 2.50
6 Alex Rodriguez 1.25 3.00
7 Chipper Jones 1.00 2.50
8 Randy Johnson 1.00 2.50
9 Pedro Martinez .60 1.50
10 Albert Pujols 1.25 3.00
11 Vladimir Guerrero .60 1.50
12 Sammy Sosa 1.00 2.50
13 Ichiro Suzuki 1.25 3.00
14 Troy Glaus .40 1.00
15 Jason Giambi .40 1.00

2003 Fleer Hardball On the Ball Game Used

STATED ODDS 1:18 H; 1:30 R; 1:10 BL
AR Alex Rodriguez Jsy 4.00 10.00
AS Alfonso Soriano Jsy 2.00 5.00
BB Barry Bonds Jsy 5.00 12.00
CJ Chipper Jones Bat 3.00 8.00
DJ Derek Jeter Bat 8.00 20.00
MP Mike Piazza Jsy 3.00 8.00
NG Nomar Garciaparra Jsy 2.00 5.00
PM Pedro Martinez Jsy 2.00 5.00
RJ Randy Johnson Jsy 3.00 8.00
TG Troy Glaus Jsy 1.25 3.00

2003 Fleer Hardball Round Numbers

RANDOM INSERTS IN PACKS
STATED PRINT RUN 1000 SERIAL #'d SETS
1 Nolan Ryan 5.00 12.00
2 Al Kaline 1.00 2.50
3 Mike Schmidt 2.50 6.00
4 Yogi Berra 1.50 4.00
5 Brooks Robinson 1.00 2.50
6 Tom Seaver 1.00 2.50
7 Willie McCovey 1.00 2.50
8 Harmon Killebrew 1.50 4.00
9 Richie Ashburn 1.00 2.50
10 Lou Brock 1.00 2.50
11 Jim Palmer 1.00 2.50
12 Willie Stargell 1.00 2.50
13 Whitey Ford 1.00 2.50
14 Robin Yount 1.50 4.00

2003 Fleer Hardball Round Numbers Game Used

STATED ODDS 1:288 HOBBY, 1:566 RETAIL
ASTERISKS PERCEIVED AS LARGER SUPPLY
AK Al Kaline Jsy * 6.00 15.00
HK Harmon Killebrew Bat 10.00 25.00
LB Lou Brock Jsy 8.00 20.00
MS Mike Schmidt Jsy * 6.00 15.00

2003 Fleer Hardball Round Trippers

STATED ODDS 1:8 H; 1:12 R; 1:20 BL
1 Alfonso Soriano .60 1.50
2 Alex Rodriguez 1.25 3.00
3 Lance Berkman .60 1.50
4 Shawn Green .40 1.00
5 Pat Burrell .40 1.00
6 Andruw Jones .40 1.00
7 Garret Anderson .40 1.00
8 Miguel Tejada .60 1.50
9 Mike Piazza 1.00 2.50
10 Eric Chavez .40 1.00
11 Rafael Palmeiro .60 1.50
12 Chipper Jones 1.00 2.50
13 Manny Ramirez 1.00 2.50
14 Jeff Bagwell .60 1.50
15 Torii Hunter .40 1.00
16 Nomar Garciaparra .60 1.50
17 Sammy Sosa 1.00 2.50
18 Vladimir Guerrero .60 1.50
19 Troy Glaus .40 1.00
20 Jason Giambi .40 1.00

2003 Fleer Hardball Round Trippers Rounding First

STATED PRINT RUNS LISTED BELOW
NO PRICING ON QTY OF 40 OR LESS
2 Jeff Bagwell Bat/344 4.00 10.00
3 Lance Berkman Jsy/529 3.00 8.00
4 Pat Burrell Bat/502 3.00 8.00
5 Eric Chavez Jsy/572 3.00 8.00
6 Nomar Garciaparra Bat/529 6.00 15.00
7 Shawn Green Bat/249 3.00 8.00
8 Andruw Jones Jsy/569 4.00 10.00
9 Chipper Jones Jsy/570 4.00 10.00
10 Rafael Palmeiro Jsy/515 4.00 10.00
11 Mike Piazza Bat/289 10.00 25.00
12 Manny Ramirez Jsy/530 4.00 10.00
13 Alex Rodriguez Jsy/536 8.00 20.00
14 Alfonso Soriano Jsy/228 3.00 8.00
15 Miguel Tejada Jsy/524 3.00 8.00

2003 Fleer Hardball Signatures

RANDOM INSERTS IN HOBBY/RETAIL
STATED PRINT RUNS PROVIDED BY FLEER
CARDS ARE NOT SERIAL NUMBERED
BONDS BASIC AU PRINT RUN 255 CARDS
BONDS 600 HR PRINT RUN 100 CARDS
BONDS #25 PRINT RUN 25 CARDS
BB1 Barry Bonds/255 * 40.00 80.00
BB2 Barry Bonds HR 600/100 * 50.00 100.00
DJ Derek Jeter/500 * 100.00 200.00

2004 Fleer InScribed

COMP.SET w/o SP's (75) 10.00 25.00
COMMON CARD (1-75) .15 .40
COMMON CARD (76-85) .40 1.00
76-85 ODDS 1:20 HOBBY, 1:200 RETAIL
76-85 PRINT RUN 1000 SERIAL #'d SETS
COMMON CARD (86-100) .40 1.00
86-100 ODDS 1:12 HOBBY, 1:100 RETAIL
86-100 ARE ALL SERIAL #'d TO 750
86-100 ACTUAL PRINT RUNS B/WN 325-750
86-100 W/ASTERISK = ACTUAL PRINT RUN
ACTUAL PRINT RUNS PROVIDED BY FLEER
86-100: ON MANY, 1ST 75-425 #'d ARE AU'S
SEE AUTO PARALLEL SETS FOR AU PRICES
1 Vladimir Guerrero .25 .60
2 Bartolo Colon .15 .40
3 Troy Glaus .15 .40
4 Richie Sexson .15 .40
5 Randy Johnson .40 1.00
6 Luis Gonzalez .15 .40
7 J.D. Drew .15 .40
8 Chipper Jones .40 1.00
9 Andruw Jones .15 .40
10 Melvin Mora .15 .40
11 Miguel Tejada .25 .60
12 Curt Schilling .25 .60
13 Pedro Martinez .25 .60
14 Nomar Garciaparra .25 .60
15 Kerry Wood .15 .40
16 Mark Prior .25 .60
17 Sammy Sosa .40 1.00
18 Frank Thomas .40 1.00
19 Magglio Ordonez .25 .60
20 Sean Casey .15 .40
21 Ken Griffey Jr. .75 2.00
22 Adam Dunn .25 .60
23 Jody Gerut .15 .40
24 Omar Vizquel .25 .60
25 Todd Helton .25 .60
26 Vinny Castilla .15 .40
27 Alex Sanchez .15 .40
28 Ivan Rodriguez .25 .60
29 Dontrelle Willis .15 .40
30 Josh Beckett .15 .40
31 Miguel Cabrera .40 1.00
32 Roger Clemens .50 1.25
33 Andy Pettitte .25 .60
34 Jeff Bagwell .25 .60
35 Ken Harvey .15 .40
36 Carlos Beltran .25 .60
37 Shawn Green .15 .40
38 Hideo Nomo .40 1.00
39 Scott Podsednik .15 .40
40 Ben Sheets .15 .40
41 Torii Hunter .15 .40
42 Jacque Jones .15 .40
43 Jose Vidro .15 .40
44 Mike Piazza .40 1.00
45 Tom Glavine .25 .60
46 Derek Jeter 1.00 2.50
47 Alex Rodriguez .50 1.25
48 Jason Giambi .15 .40
49 Hideki Matsui .60 1.50
50 Eric Chavez .15 .40
51 Barry Zito .25 .60
52 Tim Hudson .25 .60
53 Mark Mulder .15 .40
54 Jim Thome .25 .60
55 Pat Burrell .15 .40
56 Chase Utley .25 .60
57 Jason Kendall .15 .40
58 Jack Wilson .15 .40
59 Khalil Greene .25 .60
60 Brian Giles .15 .40
61 Jason Schmidt .15 .40
62 Marquis Grissom .15 .40
63 Ichiro Suzuki .50 1.25
64 Bret Boone .15 .40
65 Albert Pujols .50 1.25
66 Scott Rolen .25 .60
67 Jim Edmonds .25 .60
68 Tino Martinez .25 .60
69 Rocco Baldelli .15 .40
70 Alfonso Soriano .25 .60
71 Michael Young .15 .40
72 Hank Blalock .15 .40
73 Roy Halladay .25 .60
74 Carlos Delgado .15 .40
75 Vernon Wells .15 .40
76 Johnny Bench RET 1.00 2.50
77 Reggie Jackson RET .60 1.50
78 Al Kaline RET 1.00 2.50
79 Nolan Ryan RET 3.00 8.00
80 Tom Seaver RET .60 1.50
81 Robin Yount RET 1.00 2.50
82 Mike Schmidt RET 1.50 4.00
83 Jim Palmer RET .60 1.50
84 Harmon Killebrew RET 1.00 2.50
85 Joe Morgan RET .60 1.50
86 Kaz Matsui ROO/675 RC * .60 1.50
87 L.Gonzalez ROO/435 RC * .40 1.00
88 Yadier Molina ROO/750 RC 100.00 250.00
89 Jon Knott ROO/675 RC * .40 1.00
90 Kevin Youkilis ROO/640 * .40 1.00
91 Chris Saenz ROO/325 RC * .40 1.00
92 A.Blanco ROO/675 RC * .40 1.00
93 D.Aardsma ROO/750 RC .40 1.00
94 Merkin Valdez ROO/500 RC * .40 1.00
95 Jason Bartlett ROO/675 RC * 1.25 3.00
96 John Gall ROO/325 RC * .40 1.00
97 Zack Greinke ROO/675 * 1.50 4.00
98 Scott Hairston ROO/675 * .40 1.00
99 Matt Holliday ROO/750 1.00 2.50
100 C.Kotchman ROO/375 * .40 1.00

2004 Fleer InScribed Gold

*GOLD 1-75: 3X TO 8X BASIC
*GOLD 76-85: .6X TO 1.5X BASIC
*GOLD 86-100: .6X TO 1.5X BASIC
OVERALL PARALLEL ODDS 1:18 H, 1:96 R
STATED PRINT RUN 199 SERIAL #'d SETS
BLACK BORDERED CARDS W/GOLD FOIL

2004 Fleer InScribed Autographs Purple

*PUR p/r 38-52: .5X TO 1.2X SILV p/r 235-322
*PUR p/r 38-52: .5X TO 1.2X SILV p/r 134-195
*PUR p/r 38-52: .4X TO 1X SILV p/r 55-57
*PUR p/r 38-52: .3X TO .8X SILV 20-34
*PUR p/r 20-35: .6X TO 1.5X SILV p/r 235-322
*PUR p/r 20-35: .6X TO 1.5X SILV 134-195
*PUR p/r 20-35: .5X TO 1.2X SILV p/r 55-57
*PUR p/r 15-18: .75X TO 2X SILV p/r 235-322
OVERALL AU ODDS 1:12 H, AU-GU 1:48 R
PRINT RUNS B/WN 3-52 COPIES PER
NO PRICING ON QTY OF 11 OR LESS
40 COPIES ACTUALLY MADE OF R.JOHNSON
ACTUAL R.JOHNSON QTY FROM FLEER

2004 Fleer InScribed Autographs Red

*RED: .6X TO 1.5X SILVER p/r 235-322
*RED: .6X TO 1.5X SILVER p/r 134-195
*RED: .5X TO 1.2X SILVER p/r 55-57
*RED: .4X TO 1X SILVER p/r 20-34
OVERALL AU ODDS 1:12 H, AU-GU 1:48 R
STATED PRINT RUN 25 SERIAL #'d SETS
UER'S ARE #'d OF 25 BUT 10-15 PER MADE
ACTUAL UER QTY PROVIDED BY FLEER
NO PUJOLS UER/10 PRICING AVAILABLE
AB Angel Berroa 6.00 15.00
RJ Randy Johnson/15 UER 50.00 100.00

2004 Fleer InScribed Autographs Silver

OVERALL AU ODDS 1:12 H, AU-GU 1:48 R
PRINT RUNS B/WN 5-322 COPIES PER
CARDS ARE NOT SERIAL-NUMBERED
PRINT RUN INFO PROVIDED BY FLEER
NO PRICING ON QTY OF 11 OR LESS
BG Brian Giles/134 4.00 10.00
BL Barry Larkin/140 15.00 40.00
BR Brad Radke/168 6.00 15.00
CB Carlos Beltran/296 6.00 15.00
DW Dontrelle Willis/290 10.00 25.00
EC Eric Chavez/322 6.00 15.00
EG Eric Gagne/57 12.50 30.00
JB Jeremy Bonderman/287 6.00 15.00
JL Javy Lopez/257 6.00 15.00
LG Luis Gonzalez/55 5.00 12.00
LO Lyle Overbay/240 4.00 10.00
RB Rocco Baldelli/34 10.00 25.00
RHL Roy Halladay/139 30.00 60.00
RHR Rich Harden/235 6.00 15.00
RJ Randy Johnson/20 40.00 80.00
SP Scott Podsednik/280 4.00 10.00
TH Trevor Hoffman/174 10.00 25.00
TN Trot Nixon/318 6.00 15.00
WM Wade Miller/195 4.00 10.00

2004 Fleer InScribed Rookie Autographs

OVERALL AU ODDS 1:12 H, AU-GU 1:48 R
CARDS ARE SERIAL #'d TO 750
ACTUAL PRINT RUNS B/WN 34-646 PER
ACTUAL PRINT RUNS PROVIDED BY FLEER
HENN/MCPHERSON AVAIL.ONLY AS AU'S
87 Luis A. Gonzalez/240 * 3.00 8.00
90 Kevin Youkilis/34 * 6.00 15.00
91 Chris Saenz/350 * 3.00 8.00
94 Merkin Valdez/175 * 4.00 10.00
96 John Gall/350 * 4.00 10.00
100 Casey Kotchman/300 * 5.00 12.00
DM Dallas McPherson/646 * 6.00 15.00
SH Sean Henn/526 * 3.00 8.00

2004 Fleer InScribed Rookie Autographs Notation

OVERALL AU ODDS 1:12 H, AU-GU 1:48 R
CARDS ARE SERIAL #'d TO 750
ACTUAL PRINT RUN 75 COPIES PER
J.GALL PRINT RUNS B/WN 25-50 PER
NOTATIONS ARE 1ST 75 #'d CARDS
NO GALL-STAR PRICING DUE TO SCARCITY
87 Luis A. Gonzalez 4/6/04 6.00 15.00
89 Jon Knott 5/30/04 6.00 15.00
90 Kevin Youkilis 5/15/04 6.00 15.00
91 Chris Saenz 4/24/04 6.00 15.00
92 Andres Blanco 4/17/04 6.00 15.00
94 Merkin Valdez Go Giants 8.00 20.00
95 Jason Bartlett Go Twins 8.00 20.00
96B John Gall Go Cards/50 * 8.00 20.00
98 Scott Hairston 5/17/04 6.00 15.00
100 Casey Kotchman 5/9/04 6.00 15.00

2004 Fleer InScribed Award Winners

OVERALL INSERT ODDS 1:12 H, 1:12 R
STATED PRINT RUN 150 SERIAL #'d SETS
1 Alex Rodriguez 2.50 6.00
2 Eric Gagne .75 2.00
3 Miguel Tejada 1.25 3.00
4 Roy Halladay 1.25 3.00
5 Randy Johnson 2.00 5.00
6 Barry Zito 1.25 3.00
7 Chipper Jones 2.00 5.00
8 Ivan Rodriguez 1.25 3.00
9 Pedro Martinez 1.25 3.00
10 Barry Larkin 1.25 3.00
11 Dontrelle Willis .75 2.00
12 Angel Berroa .75 2.00
13 Kerry Wood .75 2.00
14 Albert Pujols 2.50 6.00
15 Hideo Nomo 2.00 5.00

2004 Fleer InScribed Award Winners Autographs

OVERALL AU ODDS 1:12 H, AU-GU 1:48 R
PRINT RUNS B/WN 15-103 COPIES PER
UER SERIAL # LISTED BEFORE ACTUAL QTY
ACTUAL UER QTY PROVIDED BY FLEER
EXCHANGE DEADLINE INDEFINITE
AB Angel Berroa/103 6.00 15.00
BL Barry Larkin UER 95/50 40.00 80.00
BZ Barry Zito UER 99/35 12.50 30.00
CJ Chipper Jones UER 99/35 30.00 60.00
DW Dontrelle Willis/103 15.00 40.00
IR Ivan Rodriguez UER 99/35 30.00 60.00
RH Roy Halladay/102 15.00 40.00

2004 Fleer InScribed Award Winners Jersey Silver

STATED PRINT RUN 175 SERIAL #'d SETS
*BLUE: 1.25X TO 3X SILVER
BLUE PRINT RUN 15 SERIAL #'d SETS
*COPPER: .4X TO 1X SILVER
COPPER PRINT RUN 99 SERIAL #'d SETS
*PURPLE PATCH: 1X TO 2.5X SILVER
PURPLE PATCH PRINT RUN 49 #'d SETS
OVERALL GU ODDS 1:6 H, AU-GU 1:48 R
AB Angel Berroa 2.50 6.00
AP Albert Pujols 8.00 20.00
BL Barry Larkin 4.00 10.00
BZ Barry Zito 2.50 6.00
CJ Chipper Jones 4.00 10.00
DW Dontrelle Willis 4.00 10.00
EG Eric Gagne 2.50 6.00
HN Hideo Nomo 4.00 10.00
IR Ivan Rodriguez 4.00 10.00
KW Kerry Wood 2.50 6.00
MT Miguel Tejada 2.50 6.00
PM Pedro Martinez 4.00 10.00
RH Roy Halladay 2.50 6.00
RJ Randy Johnson 4.00 10.00

2004 Fleer InScribed Induction Ceremony

OVERALL INSERT ODDS 1:12 H, 1:12 R
PRINT RUNS B/WN 80-101 COPIES PER
1 Carlton Fisk/100 2.00 5.00
2 Tony Perez/100 2.00 5.00
3 Nolan Ryan/99 10.00 25.00
4 Robin Yount/99 3.00 8.00
5 Orlando Cepeda/99 2.00 5.00
6 Bill Mazeroski/101 2.00 5.00
7 Larry Doby/98 2.00 5.00
8 Phil Niekro/97 2.00 5.00
9 Jim Bunning/96 2.00 5.00
10 Sparky Anderson/100 2.00 5.00
11 Phil Rizzuto/94 2.00 5.00
12 Rollie Fingers/92 2.00 5.00
13 Hal Newhouser/92 2.00 5.00
14 Rod Carew/91 2.00 5.00
15 Reggie Jackson/93 2.00 5.00
16 Tom Seaver/92 2.00 5.00
17 Bob Gibson/81 2.00 5.00
18 Jim Palmer/90 2.00 5.00
19 Joe Morgan/90 2.00 5.00
20 Al Kaline/80 3.00 8.00

2004 Fleer InScribed Induction Ceremony Autographs Bronze

OVERALL AU ODDS 1:12 H, AU-GU 1:48 R
STATED PRINT RUN 50 SERIAL #'d SETS
UER'S ARE #'d OF 50 BUT 30-40 PER MADE
ACTUAL UER QTY PROVIDED BY FLEER
EXCHANGE DEADLINE INDEFINITE
AK Al Kaline 15.00 40.00
BG Bob Gibson 15.00 40.00
CF Carlton Fisk 15.00 40.00
JB Jim Bunning 15.00 40.00
NR Nolan Ryan/35 UER 60.00 120.00
OC Orlando Cepeda/40 UER 10.00 25.00
PN Phil Niekro/35 UER 20.00 50.00
RF Rollie Fingers 10.00 25.00
RJ Reggie Jackson/30 UER 40.00 80.00
TP Tony Perez 15.00 40.00
TS Tom Seaver/30 UER 30.00 80.00

2004 Fleer InScribed Induction Ceremony Autographs Gold

OVERALL AU ODDS 1:12 H, AU-GU 1:48 R
STATED PRINT RUN 5 SERIAL #'d SETS

EXCHANGE DEADLINE INDEFINITE
NO PRICING DUE TO SCARCITY

2004 Fleer InScribed Induction Ceremony Autographs Silver

*SILVER: .6X TO 1.5X BRONZE
OVERALL AU ODDS 1:12 H, AU-GU 1:48 R
STATED PRINT RUN 15 SERIAL #'d SETS
UER'S ARE #'d OF 15 BUT 10-12 PER MADE
ACTUAL UER QTY PROVIDED BY FLEER
NO UER PRICING DUE TO SCARCITY
UER CL: CF/NR/OC/PN/RJ/RY/TP/TS
EXCHANGE DEADLINE INDEFINITE

2004 Fleer InScribed Induction Ceremony Material Silver

PRINT RUNS B/WN 80-101 COPIES PER
MASTERPIECE PRINT RUN 1 #'d SET
NO M'PIECE PRICING DUE TO SCARCITY
OVERALL GU ODDS 1:6 H, AU-GU 1:48 R
AK Al Kaline Pants/80 8.00 20.00
BM Bill Mazeroski Bat/101 6.00 15.00
CF Carlton Fisk Jsy/100 6.00 15.00
JM Joe Morgan Bat/90 4.00 10.00
JP Jim Palmer Jsy/90 4.00 10.00
LD Larry Doby Bat/98 4.00 10.00
NR Nolan Ryan Jsy/99 12.50 30.00
OC Orlando Cepeda Bat/99 4.00 10.00
PN Phil Niekro Jsy/97 4.00 10.00
PR Phil Rizzuto Bat/94 6.00 15.00
RC Rod Carew Jsy/91 6.00 15.00
RF Rollie Fingers Jsy/92 4.00 10.00
RJ Reggie Jackson Pants/93 6.00 15.00
RY Robin Yount Jsy/99 8.00 20.00
SA Sparky Anderson Jsy/100 4.00 10.00
TP Tony Perez Bat/100 4.00 10.00
TS Tom Seaver Jsy/92 6.00 15.00

2004 Fleer InScribed Names of the Game

OVERALL INSERT ODDS 1:12 H, 1:12 R
STATED PRINT RUN 299 SERIAL #'d SETS
1 Nomar Garciaparra 1.25 3.00
2 Randy Johnson 2.00 5.00
3 Hideki Matsui 3.00 8.00
4 Frank Thomas 2.00 5.00
5 Ivan Rodriguez 1.25 3.00
6 Roger Clemens 2.50 6.00
7 Chipper Jones 2.00 5.00
8 Dontrelle Willis .75 2.00
9 Luis Gonzalez .75 2.00
10 Alex Rodriguez 2.50 6.00
11 Eric Gagne .75 2.00
12 Juan Gonzalez .75 2.00
13 Hideo Nomo 2.00 5.00
14 Sean Casey .75 2.00
15 Greg Maddux 2.50 6.00
16 Cal Ripken 6.00 15.00
17 Carl Yastrzemski 2.00 5.00
18 Tony Perez 1.25 3.00
19 Joe Morgan 1.25 3.00
20 Carlton Fisk 1.25 3.00
21 Willie McCovey 1.25 3.00
22 Al Kaline 2.00 5.00
23 Dennis Eckersley 1.25 3.00
24 Ted Williams 4.00 10.00
25 Willie Stargell 1.25 3.00
26 Rollie Fingers 1.25 3.00
27 Yogi Berra 2.00 5.00
28 Reggie Jackson 1.25 3.00
29 Harmon Killebrew 2.00 5.00
30 Nolan Ryan 6.00 15.00

2004 Fleer InScribed Names of the Game Autographs Silver

OVERALL AU ODDS 1:12 H, AU-GU 1:48 R
CARDS ARE SERIAL #'d TO 99
UER'S ARE #'d OF 99 BUT 20-90 PER MADE
ACTUAL UER QTY PROVIDED BY FLEER
EXCHANGE DEADLINE INDEFINITE
AK Al Kaline/90 UER 12.00 30.00
CF Carlton Fisk/50 UER 15.00 40.00
CJ Chipper Jones/40 UER 30.00 60.00
DE Dennis Eckersley/90 UER 10.00 25.00
DW Dontrelle Willis 15.00 40.00
IR Ivan Rodriguez/40 UER 30.00 60.00
LG Luis Gonzalez/75 UER 6.00 15.00
NR Nolan Ryan/35 UER 75.00 150.00
RF Rollie Fingers/90 UER 10.00 25.00
RJ Reggie Jackson/35 UER 40.00 80.00
SC Sean Casey 10.00 25.00

2004 Fleer InScribed Names of the Game Autographs Gold

*GOLD p/r 25: .6X TO 1.5X SILVER p/r 75-99
*GOLD p/r 25: .5X TO 1.2X SILVER p/r 40-50
OVERALL AU ODDS 1:12 H, AU-GU 1:48 R
CARDS ARE SERIAL #'d TO 25
UER'S ARE #'d TO 25 BUT 1-22 PER MADE
ACTUAL UER QTY PROVIDED BY FLEER
UER p/r 15's ARE NOMO, REGGIE & RYAN
NO PRICING ON UER QTY B/WN 1-10 PER
EXCHANGE DEADLINE INDEFINITE

2004 Fleer InScribed Names of the Game Material Copper

STATED PRINT RUN 250 SERIAL #'d SETS
*BLUE: 1.25X TO 3X COPPER
BLUE PRINT RUN 20 SERIAL #'d SETS
*GOLD: .4X TO 1X COPPER
GOLD PRINT RUN 150 SERIAL #'d SETS
*PURPLE BAT-PANTS: 1X TO 2.5X COPPER
*PURPLE PATCH: 1.5X TO 4X COPPER
PURPLE PRINT RUN 33 SERIAL #'d SETS
*RED: .5X TO 1.2X COPPER
RED PRINT RUN 79 SERIAL #'d SETS
*SILVER: .4X TO 1X COPPER
SILVER ODDS AU-GU 1:48 RETAIL
SILVER PRINT RUN 150 SETS
SILVER ARE NOT SERIAL-NUMBERED
SILVER PRINT RUN PROVIDED BY FLEER
OVERALL GU ODDS 1:6 H, AU-GU 1:48 R
AK Al Kaline Pants 6.00 15.00
CF Carlton Fisk Jsy 4.00 10.00
CJ Chipper Jones Jsy 3.00 8.00
CR Cal Ripken Jsy 10.00 25.00
CY Carl Yastrzemski Jsy 6.00 15.00
DE Dennis Eckersley Jsy 3.00 8.00
DW Dontrelle Willis Jsy 3.00 8.00
EG Eric Gagne Jsy 2.00 5.00
FT Frank Thomas Jsy 3.00 8.00
GM Greg Maddux Jsy 4.00 10.00
HK Harmon Killebrew Bat 6.00 15.00
HM Hideki Matsui Jsy 10.00 25.00
HN Hideo Nomo Jsy 3.00 8.00
IR Ivan Rodriguez Jsy 3.00 8.00
JG Juan Gonzalez Jsy 2.00 5.00
JM Joe Morgan Bat 3.00 8.00
LG Luis Gonzalez Jsy 2.00 5.00
NR Nolan Ryan Jsy 10.00 25.00
RC Roger Clemens Jsy 4.00 10.00
RF Rollie Fingers Jsy 3.00 8.00
RJA Reggie Jackson Pants 4.00 10.00
RJO Randy Johnson Jsy 3.00 8.00
SC Sean Casey Jsy 2.00 5.00
TP Tony Perez Bat 3.00 8.00
TW Ted Williams Bat 20.00 50.00
WM Willie McCovey Pants 4.00 10.00
WS Willie Stargell Jsy 4.00 10.00
YB Yogi Berra Bat 6.00 15.00

2001 Fleer Legacy

COMP.SET w/o SP's (90) 15.00 40.00
COMMON CARD (1-90) .40 1.00
COMMON AUTO (91-100) 4.00 10.00
COMMON CARD (101-105) 3.00 8.00
91-105 RANDOM INSERTS IN PACKS
91-105 PRINT RUN 799 SERIAL #'d SETS
1ST 300 #'d PUJOLS ARE AUTO CARDS
CARD NUMBER 98 DOES NOT EXIST
1 Pedro Martinez .60 1.50
2 Andruw Jones .60 1.50
3 Mike Hampton .40 1.00
4 Gary Sheffield .40 1.00
5 Barry Zito .60 1.50
6 J.D. Drew .40 1.00
7 Charles Johnson .40 1.00
8 David Wells .40 1.00
9 Kazuhiro Sasaki .40 1.00
10 Vladimir Guerrero 1.00 2.50
11 Pat Burrell .40 1.00
12 Ruben Mateo .40 1.00
13 Greg Maddux 1.50 4.00
14 Sean Casey .40 1.00
15 Craig Biggio .60 1.50
16 Bernie Williams .60 1.50
17 Jeff Kent .40 1.00
18 Nomar Garciaparra 1.50 4.00
19 Cal Ripken 3.00 8.00
20 Larry Walker .40 1.00
21 Adrian Beltre .40 1.00
22 Johnny Damon .60 1.50
23 Rick Ankiel .40 1.00
24 Matt Williams .40 1.00
25 Magglio Ordonez .40 1.00
26 Richard Hidalgo .40 1.00
27 Robin Ventura .40 1.00
28 Jason Kendall .40 1.00
29 Tony Batista .40 1.00
30 Chipper Jones 1.00 2.50
31 Jim Thome .60 1.50
32 Kevin Brown .40 1.00
33 Mike Mussina .60 1.50
34 Mark McGwire 2.50 6.00
35 Darin Erstad .40 1.00
36 Manny Ramirez Sox .60 1.50
37 Bobby Higginson .40 1.00
38 Richie Sexson .40 1.00
39 Jason Giambi .40 1.00
40 Alex Rodriguez 1.25 3.00
41 Mark Grace .60 1.50
42 Ken Griffey Jr. 2.00 5.00
43 Moises Alou .40 1.00
44 Edgardo Alfonzo .40 1.00
45 Phil Nevin .40 1.00
46 Rafael Palmeiro .60 1.50
47 Javy Lopez .40 1.00
48 Juan Gonzalez .40 1.00
49 Jermaine Dye .40 1.00
50 Roger Clemens 2.00 5.00
51 Barry Bonds 2.50 6.00
52 Carl Everett .40 1.00
53 Ben Sheets .60 1.50
54 Juan Encarnacion .40 1.00
55 Jeromy Burnitz .40 1.00
56 Miguel Tejada .40 1.00
57 Ben Grieve .40 1.00
58 Randy Johnson 1.00 2.50
59 Frank Thomas 1.00 2.50
60 Preston Wilson .40 1.00
61 Mike Piazza 1.50 4.00
62 Brian Giles .40 1.00
63 Carlos Delgado .40 1.00
64 Tom Glavine .60 1.50
65 Roberto Alomar .60 1.50
66 Mike Sweeney .40 1.00
67 Orlando Hernandez .40 1.00
68 Edgar Martinez .60 1.50
69 Tim Salmon .60 1.50
70 Kerry Wood .40 1.00
71 Jack Wilson RC .60 1.50
72 Matt Lawton .40 1.00
73 Scott Rolen .60 1.50
74 Ivan Rodriguez .60 1.50
75 Steve Finley .40 1.00
76 Barry Larkin .60 1.50
77 Jeff Bagwell .60 1.50
78 Derek Jeter 2.50 6.00
79 Tony Gwynn 1.25 3.00
80 Raul Mondesi .40 1.00
81 Rafael Furcal .40 1.00
82 Todd Helton .60 1.50
83 Shawn Green .40 1.00
84 Tim Hudson .40 1.00
85 Jim Edmonds .40 1.00
86 Troy Glaus .40 1.00
87 Sammy Sosa 1.00 2.50
88 Cliff Floyd .40 1.00
89 Jose Vidro .40 1.00
90 Bob Abreu .40 1.00
91 Drew Henson AU RC 6.00 15.00
92 Andy Morales AU RC 4.00 10.00
93 Wilson Betemit AU RC 10.00 25.00
94 Elpidio Guzman AU RC 4.00 10.00
95 Esix Snead AU RC 4.00 10.00
96 Winston Abreu AU RC 4.00 10.00
97 Jeremy Owens AU RC 4.00 10.00
99 Junior Spivey AU RC 6.00 15.00
100 Jaisen Randolph AU RC 4.00 10.00
101 Ichiro Suzuki RC 30.00 80.00
102 Albert Pujols/499 RC 60.00 150.00
102AU Albert Pujols AU/300 150.00 400.00
103 Tsuyoshi Shinjo RC 4.00 10.00
104 Jay Gibbons RC 4.00 10.00
105 Juan Uribe RC 4.00 10.00

2001 Fleer Legacy Ultimate

*STARS 1-90: 2.5X TO 6X BASIC CARDS
*ROOKIES 91-100: .2X TO .5X BASE HI
*ROOKIES 101-105: .4X TO 1X BASIC
STATED PRINT RUN 250 SERIAL #'d SETS

2001 Fleer Legacy Hit Kings

STATED ODDS 1:13
1 Rick Ankiel 4.00 10.00
2 Tony Batista 4.00 10.00
3 Carlos Beltran 4.00 10.00
4 Adrian Beltre 4.00 10.00
5 Barry Bonds 12.50 30.00
6 George Brett 10.00 25.00
7 Jose Canseco 6.00 15.00
8 Roger Cedeno 4.00 10.00
9 Johnny Damon 6.00 15.00
10 Erubiel Durazo 4.00 10.00
11 Juan Encarnacion 4.00 10.00
12 Troy Glaus 4.00 10.00
13 Shawn Green 4.00 10.00
14 Vladimir Guerrero 6.00 15.00
15 Reggie Jackson 6.00 15.00
16 Andruw Jones 6.00 15.00
17 Jason Kendall 4.00 10.00
18 Ralph Kiner 6.00 15.00
19 Billy Martin 6.00 15.00
20 Ruben Mateo 4.00 10.00
21 Stan Musial 10.00 25.00
22 Troy O'Leary 4.00 10.00
23 Magglio Ordonez 4.00 10.00
24 Corey Patterson 4.00 10.00
25 Juan Pierre 4.00 10.00
26 Ivan Rodriguez 6.00 15.00
27 Tim Salmon 6.00 15.00
28 Jim Thome 6.00 15.00
29 Jose Vidro 4.00 10.00

2001 Fleer Legacy Hit Kings Short Prints

STATED PRINT RUN 100 SERIAL #'d SETS
1 Johnny Bench 15.00 40.00
2 Wade Boggs 15.00 40.00
3 Roger Clemens 40.00 80.00
4 Steve Garvey 10.00 25.00
5 Tony Gwynn 20.00 50.00
6 Eddie Mathews 15.00 40.00
7 Joe Morgan 10.00 25.00
8 Scott Rolen 15.00 40.00
9 Frank Thomas 15.00 40.00
10 Robin Yount 15.00 40.00

2001 Fleer Legacy Hot Gloves

*REDEMPTION CARDS: .25X VALUE
STATED ODDS 1:180
ALL ARE EXCHANGE CARDS
LISTINGS REFER TO REDEEMED CARDS
1 Andruw Jones 12.00 30.00
2 Mike Mussina 8.00 20.00
3 Roberto Alomar 12.00 30.00
4 Tony Gwynn 15.00 40.00
5 Bernie Williams 12.00 30.00
6 Ivan Rodriguez 12.00 30.00
7 Ken Griffey Jr. 30.00 80.00
8 Robin Ventura 8.00 20.00
9 Cal Ripken 30.00 80.00
10 Jeff Bagwell 8.00 20.00
11 Mark McGwire 50.00 120.00
12 Rafael Palmeiro 12.00 30.00
13 Scott Rolen 12.00 30.00
14 Barry Bonds 12.00 30.00
15 Greg Maddux 20.00 50.00

2001 Fleer Legacy Derek Jeter Collection

COMMON JETER (1-22) 5.00 12.00
1-22 PRINT RUN 1000 SER.#'d SETS
ULTRA AU ISSUED VIA MAIL EXCH.IN 2004
FLEER PRINT RUN 500 CARDS
FLEER PRINT INFO PROVIDED BY FLEER
FLEER AU IS NOT SERIAL-NUMBERED
NNO Derek Jeter WS Ball
NNO D.Jeter 00 Grts AU 300.00 500.00
NNO D.Jeter 96 Autographics AU 300.00 500.00
NNO D.Jeter 93 Ultra AU 300.00 500.00
NNO D.Jeter 93 Fleer AU/500 300.00 500.00

2001 Fleer Legacy MLB Autograph Fitted Caps

ONE PER BOX
NO MORE THAN 500 OF EACH CAP SIGNED
SP PRINT RUNS PROVIDED BY FLEER
SP'S ARE NOT SERIAL-NUMBERED
1 Edgardo Alfonzo 15.00 40.00
2 Roberto Alomar 20.00 50.00
3 Ernie Banks SP/100 75.00 150.00
4 Adrian Beltre 20.00 50.00
5 Johnny Bench SP/100 75.00 150.00
6 Lance Berkman 20.00 50.00
7 Yogi Berra SP/200 50.00 120.00
8 Craig Biggio 20.00 50.00
9 Barry Bonds 100.00 200.00
10 Jeromy Burnitz 15.00 40.00
11 Pat Burrell 15.00 40.00
12 Steve Carlton 15.00 40.00
13 Sean Casey 15.00 40.00
14 Orlando Cepeda 15.00 40.00
15 Eric Chavez 15.00 40.00
16 Tony Clark 10.00 25.00
17 Roger Clemens SP/100 175.00 300.00
18 Johnny Damon 20.00 50.00
19 Dom DiMaggio SP/200 50.00 100.00
20 J.D. Drew 15.00 40.00
21 Jermaine Dye 15.00 40.00
22 Darin Erstad 15.00 40.00
23 Carlton Fisk SP/150 40.00 80.00
24 Rafael Furcal 15.00 40.00
25 Nomar Garciaparra SP/150 75.00 150.00
26 Jason Giambi 15.00 40.00
27 Troy Glaus 20.00 50.00
28 Tom Glavine 40.00 80.00
29 Juan Gonzalez 15.00 40.00
30 Luis Gonzalez 15.00 40.00
31 Tony Gwynn 60.00 120.00
32 Drew Henson 10.00 25.00
33 Derek Jeter 200.00 300.00
34 Andruw Jones 20.00 50.00
35 David Justice 15.00 40.00
36 Paul Konerko 20.00 50.00
37 Don Mattingly 75.00 150.00
38 Willie McCovey 20.00 50.00
39 Paul Molitor 15.00 40.00
40 Stan Musial SP/200 75.00 150.00
41 Mike Mussina 30.00 80.00
42 Jim Palmer 15.00 40.00
43 Corey Patterson 10.00 25.00
44 Kirby Puckett SP/200 75.00 150.00
45 Cal Ripken SP/200 175.00 300.00
46 Brooks Robinson 20.00 50.00
47 Ivan Rodriguez 40.00 80.00
48 Scott Rolen 20.00 50.00
49 Nolan Ryan SP/150 150.00 250.00
50 Mike Schmidt SP/150 75.00 150.00
51 Tom Seaver SP/100 100.00 250.00
52 Ben Sheets 20.00 50.00
53 Ozzie Smith 60.00 120.00
54 Duke Snider 20.00 50.00
55 Miguel Tejada 20.00 50.00
56 Jim Thome 40.00 80.00
57 Matt Williams 20.00 50.00
58 Dave Winfield SP/150 40.00 80.00
59 Carl Yastrzemski SP/150 60.00 120.00
60 Robin Yount 60.00 120.00
61 Barry Zito 20.00 50.00

2001 Fleer Legacy MLB Game Issue Base

STATED ODDS 1:52
1 Barry Bonds 6.00 15.00
2 Pat Burrell 1.50 4.00
3 Troy Glaus 1.50 4.00
4 Ken Griffey Jr. 8.00 20.00
5 Tony Gwynn 4.00 10.00
6 Todd Helton 2.50 6.00
7 Derek Jeter 10.00 25.00
8 Chipper Jones 4.00 10.00
9 Mark McGwire 6.00 15.00
10 Mike Piazza 4.00 10.00
11 Cal Ripken 12.00 30.00
12 Alex Rodriguez 5.00 12.00
13 Scott Rolen 2.50 6.00
14 Sammy Sosa 2.50 6.00
15 Frank Thomas 4.00 10.00

2001 Fleer Legacy MLB Game Issue Base-Ball

STATED PRINT RUN 100 SERIAL #'d SETS
1 Barry Bonds 10.00 25.00
2 Pat Burrell 2.50 6.00
3 Troy Glaus 2.50 6.00
4 Ken Griffey Jr. 12.00 30.00
5 Tony Gwynn 6.00 15.00
6 Todd Helton 4.00 10.00
7 Derek Jeter 15.00 40.00
8 Chipper Jones 6.00 15.00
9 Mark McGwire 10.00 25.00
10 Mike Piazza 6.00 15.00
11 Cal Ripken 20.00 50.00
12 Scott Rolen 4.00 10.00
13 Alex Rodriguez 8.00 20.00
14 Sammy Sosa 4.00 10.00
15 Frank Thomas 6.00 15.00

2001 Fleer Legacy MLB Game Issue Base-Ball-Jersey

STATED PRINT RUN 50 SERIAL #'d SETS
1A Barry Bonds 20.00 50.00
1B Barry Bonds EXCH 12.00 30.00
2A Pat Burrell 5.00 12.00
2B Pat Burrell EXCH 3.00 8.00
3 Troy Glaus 5.00 12.00
4A Tony Gwynn 12.00 30.00
4B Tony Gwynn EXCH 8.00 20.00
5 Todd Helton 8.00 20.00
6 Derek Jeter 30.00 80.00
7 Chipper Jones 12.00 30.00
8A Cal Ripken 40.00 100.00
8B Cal Ripken EXCH 25.00 60.00
9A Scott Rolen 8.00 20.00
9B Scott Rolen EXCH 5.00 12.00
10A Frank Thomas 12.00 30.00
10B Frank Thomas EXCH 8.00 20.00

2001 Fleer Legacy Tailor Made

*MULTI-COLOR PATCH: .75X TO 2X BASIC
STATED ODDS 1:15
1 Edgardo Alfonzo 4.00 10.00
2 Rick Ankiel 4.00 10.00
3 Barry Bonds 15.00 40.00
4 Kevin Brown 4.00 10.00
5 Orlando Cepeda 4.00 10.00
6 Carlos Delgado 4.00 10.00
7 J.D. Drew 4.00 10.00
9 Shawn Green 4.00 10.00
10 Todd Helton 6.00 15.00
11 Reggie Jackson 8.00 20.00
12 Jason Kendall 4.00 10.00
13 Greg Maddux 6.00 15.00
14 Don Mattingly 15.00 40.00
15 Willie McCovey 4.00 10.00
16 Rafael Palmeiro 6.00 15.00
17 Lou Piniella 4.00 10.00
18 Manny Ramirez Sox 6.00 15.00
19 Cal Ripken 20.00 50.00
20 Ivan Rodriguez 6.00 15.00
21 Nolan Ryan 12.50 30.00
22 Curt Schilling 4.00 10.00
23 Rondell White 4.00 10.00
24 Dave Winfield 4.00 10.00

2004 Fleer Legacy

COMP.SET w/o SP's (60) 30.00 60.00
COMMON CARD (1-60) .40 1.00
COMMON CARD (61-75) .75 2.00
61-75 ODDS 1:1 HOBBY, 1:96 RETAIL
61-75 PRINT RUN 599 SERIAL #'d SETS
1 Angel Berroa .40 1.00
2 Derek Jeter 2.50 6.00
3 Jody Gerut .40 1.00
4 Curt Schilling .60 1.50
5 Khalil Greene .60 1.50
6 Manny Ramirez 1.00 2.50
7 Rocco Baldelli .40 1.00
8 Sammy Sosa 1.00 2.50
9 Shawn Green .40 1.00
10 Austin Kearns .40 1.00
11 Frank Thomas 1.00 2.50
12 Alfonso Soriano .60 1.50
13 Alex Rodriguez 1.25 3.00
14 Carlos Delgado .40 1.00
15 Chipper Jones 1.00 2.50
16 Edgar Martinez .60 1.50
17 Ivan Rodriguez .60 1.50
18 Mark Prior .60 1.50
19 Mike Piazza 1.00 2.50
20 Orlando Cabrera .40 1.00
21 Adam Dunn .60 1.50
22 Andruw Jones .40 1.00
23 Eric Chavez .40 1.00
24 Mark Teixeira .60 1.50
25 Scott Podsednik .40 1.00
26 Torii Hunter .40 1.00
27 Miguel Cabrera 1.00 2.50
28 Hideki Matsui 1.50 4.00
29 Jose Reyes .60 1.50
30 Vladimir Guerrero .60 1.50
31 Albert Pujols 1.25 3.00
32 Greg Maddux 1.25 3.00
33 Jason Giambi .40 1.00
34 Randy Johnson 1.00 2.50
35 Roger Clemens 1.25 3.00
36 Casey Kotchman .40 1.00
37 Ken Griffey Jr. 2.00 5.00
38 Todd Helton .60 1.50
39 Javy Lopez .40 1.00
40 Jim Thome .60 1.50
41 Josh Beckett .40 1.00
42 Kerry Wood .40 1.00
43 Scott Rolen .60 1.50
44 Pat Burrell .40 1.00
45 Pedro Martinez .60 1.50
46 Barry Zito .60 1.50
47 Hank Blalock .40 1.00
48 Hideo Nomo 1.00 2.50
49 Jeff Bagwell .60 1.50
50 Magglio Ordonez .60 1.50
51 Ichiro Suzuki 1.25 3.00
52 Joe Mauer .75 2.00
53 Richie Sexson .40 1.00
54 Shannon Stewart .40 1.00
55 Craig Wilson .40 1.00
56 Miguel Tejada .60 1.50
57 Sean Casey .40 1.00
58 Tom Glavine .60 1.50
59 Jason Schmidt .40 1.00
60 Nomar Garciaparra .60 1.50
61 Kaz Matsui FL RC 1.25 3.00
62 Justin Leone FL RC .75 2.00
63 Merkin Valdez FL RC .75 2.00
64 Shingo Takatsu FL RC .75 2.00
65 Andres Blanco FL RC .75 2.00
66 Angel Chavez FL RC .75 2.00
67 Hector Gimenez FL RC .75 2.00
68 Akinori Otsuka FL RC .75 2.00
69 Jason Bartlett FL RC 2.50 6.00
70 Luis Gonzalez FL RC .75 2.00
71 Sean Henn FL RC .75 2.00
72 Mike Rouse FL RC .75 2.00
73 Chris Aguila FL RC .75 2.00
74 Aarom Baldiris FL RC .75 2.00
75 Jerry Gil FL RC .75 2.00

2004 Fleer Legacy Gold

*GOLD 1-60: 1.5X TO 4X BASIC
*GOLD 61-75: .75X TO 2X BASIC
OVERALL PARALLEL ODDS 1:3 H, 1:240 R
STATED PRINT RUN 50 SERIAL #'d SETS

2004 Fleer Legacy Franchise Patch 99

STATED PRINT RUN 99 SERIAL #'d SETS
PATCH 1 PRINT RUN 1 SERIAL #'d SET
NO PATCH 1 PRICING DUE TO SCARCITY
OVERALL PATCH ODDS 1:1 HOBBY
PRICES BELOW REFER TO NON LOGO/TAG
LOGO/TAG CARDS COMMAND 2X-3X HI
AP Albert Pujols 15.00 40.00
CJ Chipper Jones 6.00 15.00
CR Cal Ripken 20.00 50.00
DM Don Mattingly 10.00 25.00
GM Greg Maddux 10.00 25.00
HM Hideki Matsui 20.00 50.00
HN Hideo Nomo 10.00 25.00
IR Ivan Rodriguez 6.00 15.00
JBA Jeff Bagwell 6.00 15.00
JBE Josh Beckett 4.00 10.00
JL Javy Lopez 4.00 10.00
JT Jim Thome 6.00 15.00
KM Kaz Matsui 10.00 25.00
KW Kerry Wood 6.00 15.00
MP Mike Piazza 10.00 25.00
MPR Mark Prior 6.00 15.00
MT Miguel Tejada 4.00 10.00
NR Nolan Ryan 20.00 50.00
PM Pedro Martinez 6.00 15.00
RC Roger Clemens 10.00 25.00
RJ Randy Johnson 6.00 15.00
SS Sammy Sosa 6.00 15.00
VG Vladimir Guerrero 6.00 15.00

2004 Fleer Legacy Franchise Patch 50

*PATCH 50: .5X TO 1.2X BASIC
OVERALL PATCH ODDS 1:1 HOBBY
STATED PRINT RUN 50 SERIAL #'d SETS
PRICES BELOW REFER TO NON LOGO/TAG
LOGO/TAG CARDS COMMAND 2X-3X HI

2004 Fleer Legacy Franchise Patch 25

*PATCH 25: .75X TO 2X BASIC
OVERALL PATCH ODDS 1:1 HOBBY
STATED PRINT RUN 25 SERIAL #'d SETS
PRICES BELOW REFER TO NON LOGO/TAG
LOGO/TAG CARDS COMMAND 2X-3X HI

2004 Fleer Legacy Franchise Dual Patch

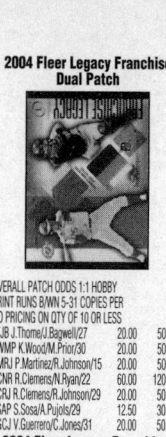

OVERALL PATCH ODDS 1:1 HOBBY
PRINT RUNS B/WN 5-31 COPIES PER
NO PRICING ON QTY OF 10 OR LESS
JTJB J.Thome/J.Bagwell/27 20.00 50.00
KWMP K.Wood/M.Prior/30 20.00 50.00
PMRJ P.Martinez/R.Johnson/15 20.00 50.00
RCNR R.Clemens/N.Ryan/22 60.00 120.00
RCRJ R.Clemens/R.Johnson/29 20.00 50.00
SSAP S.Sosa/A.Pujols/29 12.50 30.00
VGCJ V.Guerrero/C.Jones/31 20.00 50.00

2004 Fleer Legacy Franchise Quad Patch

OVERALL PATCH ODDS 1:1 HOBBY
PRINT RUNS B/WN 2-22 COPIES PER
NO PRICING ON QTY OF 14 OR LESS
GJSP Vlad/Chip/Sos/Puj/22 25.00 60.00
MMMP Matt/Hid/Kaz/Piaz/16 125.00 200.00
MSWP Mad/Sos/Woo/Prior/21 50.00 100.00
WPNM Woo/Prior/Mart/Nom/19 40.00 80.00

2004 Fleer Legacy Hit Kings

STATED ODDS 1:8 RETAIL
1 Sammy Sosa 1.00 2.50
2 Hideki Matsui 1.50 4.00
3 Vladimir Guerrero .60 1.50
4 Mike Piazza 1.00 2.50
5 Jeff Bagwell .60 1.50
6 Miguel Cabrera 1.00 2.50
7 Scott Rolen .60 1.50
8 Lance Berkman .60 1.50
9 Jason Giambi .40 1.00
10 Mark Teixeira .60 1.50
11 Jim Thome .60 1.50
12 Albert Pujols 1.25 3.00
13 Chipper Jones 1.00 2.50
14 Manny Ramirez 1.00 2.50
15 Adam Dunn .60 1.50

2004 Fleer Legacy Hit Kings Jersey Copper

STATED ODDS 1:24 RETAIL
AD Adam Dunn 2.00 5.00
AK Austin Kearns 2.00 5.00
AP Albert Pujols 6.00 15.00
CD Carlos Delgado 2.00 5.00
CJ Chipper Jones 3.00 8.00
FT Frank Thomas 3.00 8.00
GS Gary Sheffield 2.00 5.00
HB Hank Blalock 2.00 5.00
HM Hideki Matsui 8.00 20.00
JB Jeff Bagwell 3.00 8.00
JG Jason Giambi 2.00 5.00
JT Jim Thome 3.00 8.00
LB Lance Berkman 2.00 5.00
MC Miguel Cabrera 3.00 8.00
MP Mike Piazza 4.00 10.00
MR Manny Ramirez 3.00 8.00
MS Mike Schmidt 6.00 15.00
MT Mark Teixeira 3.00 8.00
RS Richie Sexson 2.00 5.00
SR Scott Rolen 3.00 8.00
SS Sammy Sosa 3.00 8.00
VG Vladimir Guerrero 3.00 8.00

2004 Fleer Legacy Hit Kings Dual Patch

OVERALL PATCH ODDS 1:1 HOBBY
PRINT RUNS B/WN 7-21 COPIES PER
NO PRICING ON QTY OF 13 OR LESS
AKAD Kearns/Dunn/20 15.00 40.00
HBMT Blalock/Teixeira/17 20.00 50.00
JBLB Bagwell/Berkman/21 20.00 50.00
MRGS Manny/Sheffield/19 20.00 50.00
SRAB Rolen/Pujols/16 50.00 100.00
SSFT Sosa/Thomas/20 20.00 50.00

2002 Fleer Maximum

COMP.SET w/o SP's (200) 15.00 40.00
COMP.IMPACT SET (20) 10.00 25.00
COMMON CARD (1-200) .15 .40
COMMON CARD (201-250) 4.00 10.00
201-250 RANDOM INSERTS IN PACKS
201-250 PRINT RUN 500 SERIAL #'d SETS
COMMON CARD (251-270) .30 .75
251-270 ONE PER HOBBY PACK
1 Barry Bonds 1.00 2.50
2 Alex Rodriguez .50 1.50
3 Jim Edmonds .15 .40
4 Manny Ramirez .25 .60
5 Jeff Bagwell .25 .60
6 Kazuhiro Sasaki .15 .40
7 Jason Giambi .15 .40
8 J.D. Drew .15 .40
9 Barry Larkin .25 .60
10 Chipper Jones .40 1.00
11 Rafael Palmeiro .25 .60
12 Roberto Alomar .25 .60
13 Randy Johnson .40 1.00
14 Juan Gonzalez .15 .40
15 Gary Sheffield .15 .40
16 Larry Walker .15 .40
17 Todd Helton .25 .60
18 Ivan Rodriguez .25 .60
19 Greg Maddux .60 1.50
20 Mike Piazza .60 1.50
21 Tsuyoshi Shinjo .15 .40
22 Luis Gonzalez .15 .40
23 Pedro Martinez .25 .60
24 Albert Pujols .75 2.00
25 Jose Canseco .25 .60
26 Edgar Martinez .25 .60
27 Moises Alou .15 .40
28 Vladimir Guerrero .40 1.00
29 Shawn Green .15 .40
30 Miguel Tejada .15 .40
31 Bernie Williams .25 .60
32 Frank Thomas .40 1.00
33 Jim Thome .25 .60
34 Derek Jeter 1.00 2.50
35 Julio Lugo .15 .40
36 Mo Vaughn .15 .40
37 Steve Cox .15 .40
38 Brad Radke .15 .40
39 Brian Jordan .15 .40
40 Garret Anderson .15 .40
41 Ichiro Suzuki .75 2.00
42 Mike Lieberthal .15 .40
43 Preston Wilson .15 .40
44 Bud Smith .15 .40
45 Curt Schilling .15 .40
46 Eric Chavez .15 .40
47 Javier Vazquez .15 .40
48 Jose Ortiz .15 .40
49 Mike Sweeney .15 .40
50 Travis Fryman .15 .40
51 Brady Anderson .15 .40
52 Chan Ho Park .15 .40
53 C.C. Sabathia .15 .40
54 Jack Wilson .15 .40
55 Joe Crede .15 .40
56 Mike Mussina .25 .60
57 Sean Casey .15 .40
58 Bobby Abreu .15 .40
59 Joe Randa .15 .40
60 Jose Vidro .15 .40
61 Juan Uribe .15 .40
62 Mark Grace .25 .60
63 Matt Morris .15 .40
64 Omar Vizquel .25 .60
65 Darryl Kile .15 .40
66 Dee Brown .15 .40
67 Fernando Tatis .15 .40
68 Jeff Cirillo .15 .40
69 Johnny Damon .25 .60
70 Milton Bradley .15 .40
71 Reggie Sanders .15 .40
72 Al Leiter .15 .40
73 Andres Galarraga .15 .40
74 Ellis Burks .15 .40
75 Jermaine Dye .15 .40
76 Juan Pierre .15 .40
77 Junior Spivey .15 .40
78 Mark Quinn .15 .40
79 Ben Sheets .15 .40
80 Brad Fullmer .15 .40
81 Bubba Trammell .15 .40
82 Dante Bichette .15 .40
83 Ken Griffey Jr. .75 2.00
84 Paul O'Neill .25 .60
85 Robert Fick .15 .40
86 Bret Boone .15 .40
87 Raul Mondesi .15 .40
88 Josh Beckett .15 .40
89 Geoff Jenkins .15 .40
90 Ramon Ortiz .15 .40
91 Robin Ventura .15 .40
92 Tom Glavine .25 .60
93 Jimmy Rollins .15 .40
94 Jamie Moyer .15 .40
95 Magglio Ordonez .15 .40
96 Mike Lowell .15 .40
97 Ryan Dempster .15 .40
98 Scott Schoeneweis .15 .40
99 Todd Zeile .15 .40
100 A.J. Burnett .15 .40
101 Aaron Sele .15 .40
102 Cal Ripken 1.25 3.00
103 Carlos Beltran .15 .40
104 David Eckstein .15 .40
105 Jason Marquis .15 .40
106 Matt Lawton .15 .40
107 Ben Grieve .15 .40
108 Brian Giles .15 .40
109 Josh Towers .15 .40
110 Lance Berkman .15 .40
111 Sammy Sosa .40 1.00
112 Torii Hunter .15 .40
113 Aubrey Huff .15 .40
114 Craig Biggio .25 .60
115 Doug Mientkiewicz .15 .40
116 Fred McGriff .25 .60
117 Jason Johnson .15 .40
118 Pat Burrell .15 .40
119 Aaron Boone .15 .40
120 Carlos Delgado .15 .40
121 Nomar Garciaparra .60 1.50
122 Richie Sexson .15 .40
123 Russ Ortiz .15 .40
124 Tim Hudson .15 .40
125 Tony Clark .15 .40
126 Jeromy Burnitz .15 .40
127 Jose Cruz .15 .40
128 Juan Encarnacion .15 .40
129 Mark Mulder .15 .40
130 Mike Hampton .15 .40
131 Rich Aurilia .15 .40
132 Trot Nixon .15 .40
133 Greg Vaughn .15 .40
134 Jacque Jones .15 .40
135 Jason Kendall .15 .40
136 Jay Gibbons .15 .40
137 Mark Buehrle .15 .40
138 Richard Hidalgo .15 .40
139 Rondell White .15 .40
140 Cristian Guzman .15 .40
141 Andy Pettitte .25 .60
142 Chris Richard .15 .40
143 Paul LoDuca .15 .40
144 Phil Nevin .15 .40
145 Ray Durham .15 .40
146 Todd Walker .15 .40
147 Bartolo Colon .15 .40
148 Ben Petrick .15 .40
149 Freddy Garcia .15 .40
150 Jon Lieber .15 .40
151 Jose Hernandez .15 .40
152 Matt Williams .15 .40
153 Shannon Stewart .15 .40
154 Adrian Beltre .15 .40

155 Carlos Lee .15 .40
156 Frank Catalanotto .15 .40
157 Jorge Posada .25 .60
158 Pokey Reese .15 .40
159 Ryan Klesko .15 .40
160 Ugueth Urbina .15 .40
161 Adam Dunn .15 .40
162 Alfonso Soriano .15 .40
163 Ben Davis .15 .40
164 Paul Konerko .15 .40
165 Eric Karros .15 .40
166 Jeff Weaver .15 .40
167 Ruben Sierra .15 .40
168 Bobby Higginson .15 .40
169 Eric Milton .15 .40
170 Kerry Wood .15 .40
171 Roy Oswalt .15 .40
172 Scott Rolen .25 .60
173 Tim Salmon .25 .60
174 Aramis Ramirez .15 .40
175 Jason Tyner .15 .40
176 Juan Cruz .15 .40
177 Keith Foulke .15 .40
178 Kevin Brown .15 .40
179 Roger Clemens .75 2.00
180 Tony Batista .15 .40
181 Andruw Jones .25 .60
182 Cliff Floyd .15 .40
183 Darin Erstad .15 .40
184 Joe Mays .15 .40
185 Mike Cameron .15 .40
186 Robert Person .15 .40
187 Jeff Kent .15 .40
188 Gabe Kapler .15 .40
189 Jason Jennings .15 .40
190 Jason Varitek .40 1.00
191 Barry Zito .15 .40
192 Rickey Henderson .40 1.00
193 Tino Martinez .25 .60
194 Brandon Duckworth .15 .40
195 Corey Koskie .15 .40
196 Derrek Lee .25 .60
197 Javy Lopez .15 .40
198 John Olerud .15 .40
199 Terrence Long .15 .40
200 Troy Glaus .15 .40
201 Scott MacRae RHW 4.00 10.00
202 Scott Chiasson RHW 4.00 10.00
203 Bart Miadich RHW 4.00 10.00
204 Brian Bowles RHW 4.00 10.00
205 David Williams RHW 4.00 10.00
206 Victor Zambrano RHW 4.00 10.00
207 Joe Beimel RHW 4.00 10.00
208 Scott Stewart RHW 4.00 10.00
209 Bob File RHW 4.00 10.00
210 Ryan Jensen RHW 4.00 10.00
211 Jason Karnuth RHW 4.00 10.00
212 Brandon Knight RHW 4.00 10.00
213 Andy Shibilo RHW RC 4.00 10.00
214 Chad Ricketts RHW RC 4.00 10.00
215 Mark Prior RHW 3.00 8.00
216 Chad Paronto RHW 4.00 10.00
217 Corky Miller RHW 4.00 10.00
218 Luis Pineda RHW 4.00 10.00
219 Ramon Vazquez RHW 4.00 10.00
220 Tony Cogan RHW 4.00 10.00
221 Roy Smith RHW 4.00 10.00
222 Mark Lukasiewicz RHW 4.00 10.00
223 Mike Rivera RHW 4.00 10.00
224 Brad Voyles RHW 4.00 10.00
225 Jamie Burke RHW RC 4.00 10.00
226 Justin Duchscherer RTC 4.00 10.00
227 Eric Cyr RTC 4.00 10.00
228 Mark Lukasiewicz RTC 4.00 10.00
229 Marlon Byrd RTC 4.00 10.00
230 Chris Piersoll RTC RC 4.00 10.00
231 Ramon Vazquez RTC 4.00 10.00
232 Tony Cogan RTC 4.00 10.00
233 Roy Smith RTC 4.00 10.00
234 Franklin Nunez RTC RC 4.00 10.00
235 Corky Miller RTC 4.00 10.00
236 Jorge Nunez RTC RC 4.00 10.00
237 Joe Beimel RTC 4.00 10.00
238 Eric Knott RTC 4.00 10.00
239 Victor Zambrano RTC 4.00 10.00
240 Jason Karnuth RTC 4.00 10.00
241 Jason Middlebrook RTC 4.00 10.00
242 Scott Stewart RTC 4.00 10.00
243 Tim Spooneybarger RTC 4.00 10.00
244 David Williams RTC 4.00 10.00
245 Bart Miadich RTC 4.00 10.00
246 Mike Koplove RTC 4.00 10.00
247 Ryan Jensen RTC 4.00 10.00
248 Jeremy Fikac RTC 4.00 10.00
249 Bob File RTC 4.00 10.00
250 Craig Monroe RTC 4.00 10.00
251 Albert Pujols MI 1.25 3.00
252 Ichiro Suzuki MI 1.25 3.00
253 Nomar Garciaparra MI 1.00 2.50
254 Barry Bonds MI 1.50 4.00
255 Jason Giambi MI .30 .75
256 Derek Jeter MI 1.50 4.00
257 Roberto Alomar MI .40 1.00
258 Roger Clemens MI 1.25 3.00
259 Mike Piazza MI 1.00 2.50
260 Vladimir Guerrero MI .60 1.50
261 Todd Helton MI .40 1.00
262 Shawn Green MI .30 .75
263 Chipper Jones MI .60 1.50
264 Pedro Martinez MI .40 1.00
265 Pat Burrell MI .30 .75
266 Sammy Sosa MI .60 1.50
267 Ken Griffey Jr. MI 1.25 3.00
268 Cal Ripken MI 2.00 5.00
269 Kerry Wood MI .30 .75
270 Alex Rodriguez MI .75 2.00
NNO Derek Jeter Promo 1.25 3.00

2002 Fleer Maximum To the Max

*1-200 PRINT RUN b/wn 201-417 4X TO 10X
*1-200 PRINT RUN b/wn 151-200 5X TO 12X
*1-200 PRINT RUN b/wn 121-150 6X TO 15X
*1-200 PRINT RUN b/wn 81-120 8X TO 20X
*1-200 PRINT RUN b/wn 66-80 10X TO 25X
*1-200 PRINT RUN b/wn 51-65 12.5X TO 30X
*1-200 PRINT RUN b/wn 36-50 15X TO 40X
*1-200 PRINT RUN b/wn 26-35 20X TO 50X
*1-200 PRINT RUN b/wn 21-25 25X TO 60X
1-200 PRINT RUN b/wn 24-417 OF EACH
*ROOKIES 151-200: 4X TO 1X BASIC
151-200 PRINT RUN 100 SERIAL #'d SETS
*IMPACT 251-270: 2.5X TO 6X BASIC
251-270 PRINT RUN b/wn 233-372 OF EACH
SEE BECKETT.COM FOR EXACT PRINT RUNS

2002 Fleer Maximum Americas Game

COMPLETE SET (25) 30.00 60.00
STATED ODDS 1:10 RETAIL
1 Pedro Martinez .75 2.00
2 Miguel Tejada .50 1.25
3 Randy Johnson 1.25 3.00
4 Barry Bonds 3.00 8.00
5 Rafael Palmeiro .75 2.00
6 Mike Piazza 2.00 5.00
7 Greg Maddux 2.00 5.00
8 Jeff Bagwell .75 2.00
9 Edgar Martinez .75 2.00
10 Albert Pujols 2.50 6.00
11 Todd Helton .75 2.00
12 Chipper Jones 1.25 3.00
13 Luis Gonzalez .50 1.25
14 Jason Giambi .50 1.25
15 Kazuhiro Sasaki .50 1.25
16 Dave Winfield .50 1.25
17 Reggie Jackson .75 2.00
18 Tom Glavine .75 2.00
19 Carlos Delgado .50 1.25
20 Bobby Abreu .50 1.25
21 Larry Walker .50 1.25
22 J.D. Drew .50 1.25
23 Alex Rodriguez 1.50 4.00
24 Frank Thomas 1.25 3.00
25 C.C. Sabathia .50 1.25

2002 Fleer Maximum Americas Game Jersey

STATED ODDS 1:24 HOBBY, 1:72 RETAIL
ASTERISKS PERCEIVED SP'S
CARDS CHECKLISTED ALPHABETICALLY
*GOLD: .75X TO 2X BASIC AMERICA JERSEY
GOLD RANDOM INSERTS IN PACKS
GOLD PRINT RUN 100 SERIAL #'d SETS
1 Jeff Bagwell 6.00 15.00
2 Craig Biggio * 6.00 15.00
3 Barry Bonds Pants 10.00 25.00
4 Carlos Delgado 4.00 10.00
5 J.D. Drew 4.00 10.00
6 Jason Giambi * 4.00 10.00
7 Tom Glavine * 6.00 15.00
8 Luis Gonzalez 4.00 10.00
9 Todd Helton 6.00 15.00
10 Reggie Jackson Pants* 6.00 15.00
11 Randy Johnson 6.00 15.00
12 Chipper Jones 6.00 15.00
13 Greg Maddux 6.00 15.00
14 Edgar Martinez 6.00 15.00
15 Pedro Martinez * 6.00 15.00
16 Rafael Palmeiro 6.00 15.00
17 Chan Ho Park 4.00 10.00
18 Mike Piazza 6.00 15.00
19 Albert Pujols 10.00 25.00
20 Kazuhiro Sasaki 4.00 10.00
21 Miguel Tejada * 4.00 10.00
22 Frank Thomas 6.00 15.00
23 Larry Walker 4.00 10.00
24 Dave Winfield * 4.00 10.00

2002 Fleer Maximum Coverage

RANDOM INSERTS IN ALL PACKS
STATED PRINT RUN 100 SERIAL #'d SETS
CARDS CHECKLISTED ALPHABETICALLY
1 Roberto Alomar Bat 6.00 15.00
2 Jeff Bagwell Jsy 6.00 15.00
3 Barry Bonds Bat 40.00 80.00
4 Jose Canseco Bat 6.00 15.00
6 Jim Edmonds Bat 4.00 10.00
7 Jason Giambi Bat 4.00 10.00
8 Juan Gonzalez Bat 4.00 10.00
9 Luis Gonzalez Jsy 4.00 10.00
10 Todd Helton Jsy 6.00 15.00
11 Randy Johnson Jsy 6.00 15.00
12 Chipper Jones Bat 6.00 15.00
13 Greg Maddux Jsy 20.00 50.00
14 Pedro Martinez Jsy 6.00 15.00
16 Albert Pujols Jsy 40.00 80.00
17 Manny Ramirez Bat 6.00 15.00
19 Ivan Rodriguez Bat 6.00 15.00
21 Gary Sheffield Bat 4.00 10.00
22 Tsuyoshi Shinjo Bat 4.00 10.00

2002 Fleer Maximum Coverage Autographs

PRINT RUNS B/WN 50-100 COPIES PER
CARDS CHECKLISTED ALPHABETICALLY
ALL WERE EXCHANGE CARDS
1 Barry Bonds Pants/50 75.00 150.00
2 J.D. Drew Bat/100 10.00 25.00
3 Jim Edmonds Bat/100 15.00 40.00
4 Drew Henson Bat/100 10.00 25.00
5 Chipper Jones Bat/50 40.00 80.00
6 Albert Pujols Jsy/100 75.00 200.00
7 Gary Sheffield Bat/100 6.00 15.00

2002 Fleer Maximum Derek Jeter Legacy Collection

BAT-JSY STATED ODDS 1:236
AUTOS RANDOM INSERTS IN ALL PACKS
BRONX AUTO PRINT RUN LISTED BELOW
LESS THAN 100 COLUMBUS AUTOS MADE
1 D.Jeter Bronx Bat 12.00 30.00
2 D.Jeter Bronx Bat AU/222 300.00 600.00
3 D.Jeter Columbus Jsy 20.00 50.00
4 D.Jeter Columbus Jsy AU 200.00 400.00

2002 Fleer Maximum Power

COMPLETE SET (25) 50.00 100.00
STATED ODDS 1:20 RETAIL
1 Luis Gonzalez .75 2.00
2 Jimmy Rollins .75 2.00
3 Larry Walker .75 2.00
4 Frank Thomas 2.00 5.00
5 Manny Ramirez 1.25 3.00
6 Barry Bonds 5.00 12.00
7 Jim Thome 1.25 3.00
8 Tsuyoshi Shinjo .75 2.00
9 Bernie Williams 1.25 3.00
10 Chipper Jones 2.00 5.00
11 Shawn Green .75 2.00
12 Drew Henson .75 2.00
13 Juan Gonzalez .75 2.00
14 Jim Edmonds .75 2.00
15 Moises Alou .75 2.00
16 Roberto Alomar 1.25 3.00
17 Jose Canseco 1.25 3.00
18 Ivan Rodriguez 1.25 3.00
19 Barry Larkin 1.25 3.00
20 Mike Piazza 3.00 8.00
21 Gary Sheffield .75 2.00
22 J.D. Drew .75 2.00
23 Alex Rodriguez 2.50 6.00
24 Jason Giambi .75 2.00
25 Todd Helton 1.25 3.00

2002 Fleer Maximum Power Bat

STATED ODDS 1:24 HOBBY, 1:72 RETAIL
SP PRINT RUNS PROVIDED BY FLEER
SP'S ARE NOT SERIAL NUMBERED
CARDS CHECKLISTED ALPHABETICALLY
ASTERISK = 's 50% EXCH, 50% IN PACKS
GOLD RANDOM INSERTS IN PACKS
GOLD PRINT RUN 25 SERIAL #'d SETS
GOLD NO PRICING DUE TO SCARCITY
1 Roberto Alomar 6.00 15.00
3 Barry Bonds * 10.00 25.00
4 Jose Canseco 6.00 15.00
5 J.D. Drew SP/200 4.00 10.00
6 Jim Edmonds 4.00 10.00
7 Jason Giambi 4.00 10.00
8 Juan Gonzalez 4.00 10.00
9 Luis Gonzalez 4.00 10.00
10 Shawn Green 4.00 10.00
11 Todd Helton 6.00 15.00
12 Chipper Jones * 6.00 15.00
14 Mike Piazza * 6.00 15.00
15 Manny Ramirez 6.00 15.00
16 Alex Rodriguez * 6.00 15.00
17 Ivan Rodriguez 6.00 15.00
18 Gary Sheffield 4.00 10.00
19 Tsuyoshi Shinjo 4.00 10.00
20 Frank Thomas 6.00 15.00
21 Jim Thome 6.00 15.00
22 Larry Walker 4.00 10.00

1999 Fleer Mystique

This 160-card set features color action player photos with a palette name box and shadowed "Mystique" in the background. The cards were issued in four-card packs with an SRP of $4.99 per pack. The backs carry player statistics. The set included the following two subsets: Rookies (101-150) serially numbered to 2,999, and Stars (151-160) serially numbered to 2,500. The cards with "SP" following the player's name in our checklist were distributed only as peel offs. Peel off cards were seeded at a rate of one per pack. Collectors had to peel off the sparkling foil coating off the front and back of the card to reveal what it was (hence the name "Mystique"). Peel off cards were either short printed super stars from the basic set (1-100), a serial numbered Prospect or Star card (101-160) or an insert card. A promo card featuring J.D. Drew was distributed to dealers and hobby media several weeks prior to the product's release. This Drew card is easily identified by the text "PROMOTIONAL SAMPLE" running diagonally across the front and back of the card. This set contains Pat Burrell's "Best" Rookie Card. The Phillies player had 25 Rookie Cards issued in 1999 and the Fleer Mystique was the only one that was serial numbered. That, in large part, boosted this card to the top of many collectors wantlists after the product's release.

COMPLETE SET (160) 125.00 250.00
COMP.SHORT SET (100) 15.00 40.00
COMMON CARD (1-100) .15 .40
COMMON SP (1-100) .40 1.00
SP CARDS ISSUED ONLY AS PEEL OFFS
COMMON CARD (101-150) 2.00 5.00
101-150 PRINT RUN 2999 SERIAL #'d SETS
COMMON CARD (151-160) 2.00 5.00
151-160 PRINT RUN 2500 SERIAL #'d SETS
101-160 RANDOM INSERTS IN PACKS
1 Ken Griffey Jr. SP 1.25 3.00
2 Livan Hernandez .15 .40
3 Jeff Kent .15 .40
4 Brian Jordan .15 .40
5 Kevin Young .15 .40
6 Vinny Castilla .15 .40
7 Orlando Hernandez SP .40 1.00
8 Bobby Abreu .15 .40
9 Vladimir Guerrero SP .60 1.50
10 Chuck Knoblauch .15 .40
11 Nomar Garciaparra SP 1.00 2.50
12 Jeff Bagwell .25 .60
13 Todd Walker .15 .40
14 Johnny Damon .25 .60
15 Mike Caruso .15 .40
16 Cliff Floyd .15 .40
17 Andy Pettitte .25 .60
18 Cal Ripken SP 2.00 5.00
19 Brian Giles .15 .40
20 Robin Ventura .15 .40
21 Alex Gonzalez .15 .40
22 Randy Johnson .40 1.00
23 Raul Mondesi .15 .40
24 Ken Caminiti .15 .40
25 Tom Glavine .25 .60
26 Derek Jeter SP 1.50 4.00
27 Carlos Delgado .15 .40
28 Adrian Beltre .15 .40
29 Tino Martinez .25 .60
30 Todd Helton .25 .60
31 Juan Gonzalez SP .40 1.00
32 Henry Rodriguez .15 .40
33 Jim Thome .25 .60
34 Paul O'Neill .25 .60
35 Scott Rolen SP .40 1.00
36 Rafael Palmeiro .25 .60
37 Will Clark .25 .60
38 Todd Hundley .15 .40
39 Andruw Jones SP .40 1.00
40 Rolando Arrojo .15 .40
41 Barry Larkin .25 .60
42 Tim Salmon .25 .60
43 Rondell White .15 .40
44 Curt Schilling .15 .40
45 Chipper Jones SP .60 1.50
46 Jeromy Burnitz .15 .40
47 Mo Vaughn .15 .40
48 Tony Clark .15 .40
49 Fernando Tatis .15 .40
50 Dmitri Young .15 .40
51 Wade Boggs .25 .60
52 Rickey Henderson .40 1.00
53 Manny Ramirez SP .40 1.00
54 Edgar Martinez .25 .60
55 Jason Giambi .15 .40
56 Jason Kendall .15 .40
57 Eric Karros .15 .40
58 Jose Canseco SP .40 1.00
59 Shawn Green .15 .40
60 Ellis Burks .15 .40
61 Derek Bell .15 .40
62 Shannon Stewart .15 .40
63 Roger Clemens SP 1.25 3.00
64 Sean Casey SP .40 1.00
65 Jose Offerman .15 .40
66 Sammy Sosa SP .60 1.50
67 Frank Thomas SP .60 1.50
68 Tony Gwynn SP .60 1.50
69 Roberto Alomar .25 .60
70 Mark McGwire SP 1.50 4.00
71 Troy Glaus .25 .60
72 Ray Durham .15 .40
73 Jeff Cirillo .15 .40
74 Alex Rodriguez SP 1.00 2.50
75 Jose Cruz Jr. .15 .40
76 Juan Encarnacion .15 .40
77 Mark Grace .25 .60
78 Barry Bonds SP 1.50 4.00
79 Ivan Rodriguez SP .40 1.00
80 Greg Vaughn .15 .40
81 Greg Maddux SP 1.00 2.50
82 Albert Belle .15 .40
83 John Olerud .15 .40
84 Kenny Lofton .15 .40
85 Bernie Williams .25 .60
86 Matt Williams .15 .40
87 Ray Lankford .15 .40
88 Darin Erstad .15 .40
89 Ben Grieve .15 .40
90 Craig Biggio .25 .60
91 Dean Palmer .15 .40
92 Reggie Sanders .15 .40
93 Dante Bichette .15 .40
94 Pedro Martinez SP .40 1.00
95 Larry Walker .15 .40
96 David Wells .15 .40
97 Travis Lee SP .40 1.00
98 Mike Piazza SP 1.00 2.50
99 Mike Mussina .25 .60
100 Kevin Brown .25 .60
101 Ruben Mateo PROS 2.00 5.00
102 Roberto Ramirez PROS RC 2.00 5.00
103 Glen Barker PROS RC 2.00 5.00
104 Clay Bellinger PROS RC 2.00 5.00
105 Carlos Guillen PROS 2.00 5.00
106 Scott Schoeneweis PROS 2.00 5.00
107 C.Gubanich PROS RC 2.00 5.00
108 Scott Williamson PROS 2.00 5.00
109 Edwards Guzman PROS RC 2.00 5.00
110 A.J. Burnett PROS RC 5.00 12.00
111 Jeremy Giambi PROS 2.00 5.00
112 Trot Nixon PROS 2.00 5.00
113 J.D. Drew PROS 2.00 5.00
114 Roy Halladay PROS 10.00 25.00
115 Jose Macias PROS RC 2.00 5.00
116 Corey Koskie PROS 2.00 5.00
117 Ryan Rupe PROS RC 2.00 5.00
118 Scott Hunter PROS RC 2.00 5.00
119 Rob Fick PROS 2.00 5.00
120 M.Christensen PROS 2.00 5.00
121 Carlos Febles PROS 2.00 5.00
122 Gabe Kapler PROS 2.00 5.00
123 Jeff Liefer PROS 2.00 5.00
124 Warren Morris PROS 2.00 5.00
125 Chris Pritchett PROS 2.00 5.00
126 Torii Hunter PROS 2.00 5.00
127 Armando Rios PROS 2.00 5.00
128 Ricky Ledee PROS 2.00 5.00
129 Kelly Dransfeldt PROS RC 2.00 5.00
130 Jeff Zimmerman PROS RC 2.00 5.00
131 Eric Chavez PROS 2.00 5.00
132 Freddy Garcia PROS RC 4.00 10.00
133 Jose Jimenez PROS 2.00 5.00
134 Pat Burrell PROS RC 12.50 30.00
135 Joe McEwing PROS RC 2.00 5.00
136 Kris Benson PROS 2.00 5.00
137 Joe Mays PROS RC 2.00 5.00
138 Rafael Roque PROS RC 2.00 5.00
139 Cristian Guzman PROS 2.00 5.00
140 Michael Barrett PROS 2.00 5.00
141 D.Mientkiewicz PROS RC 3.00 8.00
142 Jeff Weaver PROS RC 3.00 8.00
143 Mike Lowell PROS 2.00 5.00
144 Jason Phillips PROS RC 2.00 5.00
145 Marlon Anderson PROS 2.00 5.00
146 Brett Hinchliffe PROS RC 2.00 5.00
147 Matt Clement PROS 2.00 5.00
148 Terrence Long PROS 2.00 5.00
149 Carlos Beltran PROS 3.00 8.00
150 Preston Wilson PROS 2.00 5.00
151 Ken Griffey Jr. STAR 4.00 10.00
152 Mark McGwire STAR 5.00 12.00
153 Sammy Sosa STAR 2.00 5.00
154 Mike Piazza STAR 3.00 8.00
155 Alex Rodriguez STAR 3.00 8.00
156 Nomar Garciaparra STAR 3.00 8.00
157 Cal Ripken STAR 6.00 15.00
158 Greg Maddux STAR 3.00 8.00
159 Derek Jeter STAR 5.00 12.00
160 Juan Gonzalez STAR 2.00 5.00
P113 J.D. Drew Promo .40 1.00

1999 Fleer Mystique Gold

*GOLD: 1.5X TO 4X BASIC CARDS
*GOLD: 1X TO 2.5X BASIC SP's
STATED ODDS 1:8

1999 Fleer Mystique Destiny

COMPLETE SET (10) 60.00 120.00
RANDOM INSERTS IN PACKS
STATED PRINT RUN 999 SERIAL #'d SETS
1 Tony Gwynn 5.00 12.00
2 Juan Gonzalez 3.00 8.00
3 Scott Rolen 3.00 8.00
4 Nomar Garciaparra 8.00 20.00
5 Orlando Hernandez 3.00 8.00
6 Andruw Jones 3.00 8.00
7 Vladimir Guerrero 5.00 12.00
8 Darin Erstad 1.25 3.00
9 Manny Ramirez 3.00 8.00
10 Roger Clemens 10.00 25.00

1999 Fleer Mystique Established

RANDOM INSERTS IN PACKS
STATED PRINT RUN 100 SERIAL #'d SETS
1 Ken Griffey Jr. 60.00 150.00
2 Derek Jeter 125.00 300.00
3 Chipper Jones 30.00 80.00
4 Greg Maddux 40.00 100.00
5 Mark McGwire 50.00 120.00
6 Mike Piazza 30.00 80.00
7 Cal Ripken 100.00 250.00
8 Alex Rodriguez 40.00 100.00
9 Sammy Sosa 30.00 80.00
10 Frank Thomas 30.00 80.00

1999 Fleer Mystique Feel the Game

RANDOM INSERTS IN PACKS
PRINT RUNS B/WN 415-450 COPIES PER
1 A.Beltre Shoe/430 6.00 15.00
2 J.Drew Jersey/450 2.50 6.00
3 J.Gonzalez Btg.Glove/415 2.50 6.00
4 T.Gwynn Jersey/435 6.00 15.00
5 K.Millwood Jersey/435 2.50 6.00
6 A.Rodriguez Btg.Glove/345 8.00 20.00
7 F.Thomas Jersey/450 6.00 15.00

1999 Fleer Mystique Fresh Ink

STATED ODDS 1:48
PRINT RUNS B/WN 140-1000 COPIES PER
NNO CARDS LISTED IN ALPH.ORDER
1 Roberto Alomar/500 10.00 25.00
2 Michael Barrett/1000 4.00 10.00
3 Kris Benson/500 6.00 15.00
4 Micah Bowie/1000 4.00 10.00
5 A.J. Burnett/1000 10.00 25.00
6 Pat Burrell/500 6.00 15.00
7 Ken Caminiti/250 20.00 50.00
8 Jose Canseco/250 12.00 30.00
9 Sean Casey/1000 6.00 15.00
10 Edgard Clemente/1000 4.00 10.00
11 Bartolo Colon/500 6.00 15.00
12 J.D. Drew/400 6.00 15.00
13 Juan Encarnacion/1000 6.00 15.00
14 Troy Glaus/400 6.00 15.00
15 Juan Gonzalez/250 6.00 15.00
16 Shawn Green/250 6.00 15.00
17 Tony Gwynn/250 20.00 50.00
18 Chipper Jones/500 25.00 60.00
19 Gabe Kapler/750 6.00 15.00
20 Barry Larkin/250 30.00 60.00
21 Doug Mientkiewicz/500 4.00 10.00
22 Alex Rodriguez/200 40.00 100.00
23 Scott Rolen/140 15.00 40.00
24 Fernando Tatis/750 4.00 10.00
25 Robin Ventura/500 6.00 15.00
26 Todd Walker/1000 6.00 15.00

1999 Fleer Mystique Prophetic

COMPLETE SET (10) 20.00 50.00
RANDOM INSERTS IN PACKS
STATED PRINT RUN 1999 SERIAL #'d SETS
1 Eric Chavez 1.25 3.00
2 J.D. Drew 1.25 3.00
3 A.J. Burnett 1.50 4.00
4 Ben Grieve 1.25 3.00
5 Gabe Kapler 1.25 3.00
6 Todd Helton 2.00 5.00
7 Troy Glaus 2.00 5.00
8 Travis Lee 1.25 3.00
9 Pat Burrell 3.00 8.00
10 Kerry Wood 1.25 3.00

2000 Fleer Mystique

COMP.SET w/o SP's (125) 15.00 40.00
COMMON CARD (1-125) .20 .50
COMMON CARD (126-175) .40 1.00
126-175 RANDOM INSERTS IN PACKS
126-175 PRINT RUN 2000 SERIAL #'d SETS
WINFIELD HELMET EXCH.RANDOM IN PACKS
WINFIELD EXCH.DEADLINE 07/01/01
1 Derek Jeter 1.25 3.00
2 David Justice .20 .50
3 Kevin Brown .20 .50
4 Jason Giambi .20 .50
5 Jose Canseco .30 .75
6 Mark Grace .30 .75
7 Hideo Nomo .50 1.25
8 Edgardo Alfonzo .20 .50
9 Barry Bonds .75 2.00
10 Pedro Martinez .30 .75
11 Juan Gonzalez .20 .50
12 Vladimir Guerrero .30 .75
13 Chuck Finley .20 .50
14 Brian Jordan .20 .50
15 Richie Sexson .20 .50
16 Chan Ho Park .30 .75
17 Tim Hudson .30 .75
18 Fred McGriff .30 .75
19 Darin Erstad .20 .50
20 Chris Singleton .20 .50
21 Jeff Bagwell .30 .75
22 David Cone .20 .50
23 Edgar Martinez .30 .75
24 Greg Maddux .60 1.50
25 Jim Thome .30 .75
26 Eric Karros .20 .50
27 Bob Abreu .20 .50
28 Greg Vaughn .20 .50
29 Kevin Millwood .20 .50
30 Omar Vizquel .30 .75
31 Marquis Grissom .20 .50
32 Mike Lieberthal .20 .50
33 Gabe Kapler .20 .50
34 Brady Anderson .20 .50
35 Jeff Cirillo .20 .50
36 Geoff Jenkins .20 .50
37 Scott Rolen .30 .75
38 Rafael Palmeiro .30 .75
39 Randy Johnson .50 1.25
40 Barry Larkin .30 .75
41 Johnny Damon .30 .75
42 Andy Pettitte .30 .75
43 Mark McGwire .75 2.00
44 Albert Belle .20 .50
45 Derrick Gibson .20 .50
46 Corey Koskie .20 .50
47 Curt Schilling .30 .75
48 Ivan Rodriguez .30 .75
49 Mike Mussina .30 .75
50 Todd Helton .30 .75
51 Matt Lawton .20 .50
52 Jason Kendall .20 .50
53 Kenny Rogers .20 .50
54 Cal Ripken 1.50 4.00
55 Larry Walker .30 .75
56 Eric Milton .20 .50
57 Warren Morris .20 .50
58 Carlos Delgado .20 .50
59 Kerry Wood .20 .50
60 Cliff Floyd .20 .50
61 Mike Piazza .50 1.25
62 Jeff Kent .20 .50
63 Sammy Sosa .50 1.25
64 Alex Fernandez .20 .50
65 Mike Hampton .20 .50
66 Livan Hernandez .20 .50
67 Matt Williams .20 .50
68 Roberto Alomar .30 .75
69 Jermaine Dye .20 .50
70 Bernie Williams .30 .75
71 Edgar Renteria .20 .50
72 Tom Glavine .30 .75
73 Bartolo Colon .20 .50
74 Jason Varitek .50 1.25
75 Eric Chavez .20 .50
76 Fernando Tatis .20 .50
77 Adrian Beltre .50 1.25
78 Paul Konerko .20 .50
79 Mike Lowell .20 .50
80 Robin Ventura .20 .50
81 Russ Ortiz .20 .50
82 Troy Glaus .20 .50
83 Frank Thomas .50 1.25
84 Craig Biggio .30 .75
85 Orlando Hernandez .20 .50
86 John Olerud .20 .50
87 Chipper Jones .50 1.25
88 Manny Ramirez .50 1.25
89 Shawn Green .20 .50
90 Ben Grieve .20 .50
91 Vinny Castilla .20 .50
92 Tim Salmon .20 .50
93 Dante Bichette .20 .50
94 Ken Caminiti .20 .50
95 Andruw Jones .20 .50
96 Alex Rodriguez .60 1.50
97 Erubiel Durazo .20 .50
98 Sean Casey .20 .50
99 Carlos Beltran .30 .75
100 Paul O'Neill .30 .75
101 Ray Lankford .20 .50
102 Troy O'Leary .20 .50
103 Bobby Higginson .20 .50
104 Rondell White .20 .50
105 Tony Gwynn .50 1.25
106 Jim Edmonds .30 .75
107 Magglio Ordonez .30 .75
108 Preston Wilson .20 .50
109 Roger Clemens .60 1.50
110 Ken Griffey Jr. 1.00 2.50
111 Nomar Garciaparra .30 .75
112 Juan Encarnacion .20 .50
113 Michael Barrett .20 .50
114 Matt Clement .20 .50
115 David Wells .20 .50
116 Mo Vaughn .20 .50
117 Mike Cameron .20 .50
118 Jose Lima .20 .50
119 Tino Martinez .20 .50
120 J.D. Drew .20 .50
121 Carl Everett .20 .50
122 Tony Clark .20 .50
123 Brad Radke .20 .50
124 Kevin Young .20 .50
125 Raul Mondesi .20 .50
126 Cole Liniak PROS .40 1.00
127 Alfonso Soriano PROS 1.00 2.50
128 Lance Berkman PROS .60 1.50
129 Danny Young PROS RC .40 1.00
130 Francisco Cordero PROS .40 1.00
131 Robert Fick PROS .40 1.00
132 Matt LeCroy PROS .40 1.00
133 Adam Piatt PROS .40 1.00
134 Derrick Turnbow PROS RC .40 1.00
135 Mark Quinn PROS .40 1.00
136 Kip Wells PROS .40 1.00
137 Rob Bell PROS .40 1.00
138 Brad Penny PROS .40 1.00
139 Pat Burrell PROS .40 1.00
140 Danys Baez PROS RC .40 1.00
141 Chad Hermansen PROS .40 1.00
142 Steve Lomasney PROS .40 1.00
143 Peter Bergeron PROS .40 1.00
144 Jimmy Anderson PROS .40 1.00
145 Mike Darr PROS .40 1.00
146 Jacob Cruz PROS .40 1.00
147 Kazuhiro Sasaki PROS RC 1.00 2.50
148 Ben Petrick PROS .40 1.00
149 Rick Ankiel PROS .60 1.50
150 Aaron McNeal PROS RC .40 1.00
151 Octavio Dotel PROS .40 1.00
152 Juan Pena PROS .40 1.00
153 Nick Johnson PROS .40 1.00
154 Wilton Veras PROS .40 1.00
155 Willy Pena PROS .40 1.00
156 Mark Mulder PROS .40 1.00
157 Daryle Ward PROS .40 1.00
158 Chad Durbin PROS RC .40 1.00
159 Angel Pena PROS .40 1.00
160 DeWayne Wise PROS .40 1.00
161 Tarrik Brock PROS .40 1.00
162 Marcus Jensen PROS .40 1.00
163 Kevin Barker PROS .40 1.00
164 B.J. Ryan PROS .40 1.00
165 Cesar King PROS .40 1.00
166 Geoff Blum PROS .40 1.00
167 Ruben Mateo PROS .40 1.00
168 Ramon Ortiz PROS .40 1.00
169 Eric Munson PROS .40 1.00
170 Josh Beckett PROS .75 2.00
171 Rafael Furcal PROS .60 1.50
172 Matt Riley PROS .40 1.00
173 Johan Santana PROS RC 6.00 15.00
174 Mark Johnson PROS .40 1.00
175 Adam Kennedy PROS .40 1.00
P54 Cal Ripken PROMO 1.00 2.50
DW2 D.Winfield Helmet/40 50.00 100.00

2000 Fleer Mystique Gold

*STARS 1-125: 2.5X TO 6X BASIC CARDS
*PROSPECTS 126-175: 1.25X TO 3X BASIC
STATED ODDS 1:20

2000 Fleer Mystique Diamond Dominators

COMPLETE SET (10) 5.00 12.00
STATED ODDS 1:5
1 Manny Ramirez .60 1.50
2 Pedro Martinez .40 1.00
3 Sean Casey .25 .60
4 Vladimir Guerrero .40 1.00
5 Sammy Sosa .60 1.50
6 Nomar Garciaparra .40 1.00
7 Mark McGwire 1.00 2.50
8 Ken Griffey Jr. 1.25 3.00
9 Derek Jeter 1.50 4.00
10 Alex Rodriguez .75 2.00

2000 Fleer Mystique Feel the Game

STATED ODDS 1:120
1 Michael Barrett Bat 3.00 8.00
2 Carlos Beltran Bat 4.00 10.00
3 Barry Bonds Bat 15.00 40.00
4 Pat Burrell Bat 4.00 10.00
5 Shawn Green Bat 4.00 10.00
6 Vladimir Guerrero Bat 6.00 15.00
7 Tony Gwynn Jsy 6.00 15.00
8 Derek Jeter Pants 12.00 30.00
9 Chipper Jones Jsy 6.00 15.00
10 Rafael Palmeiro Bat 6.00 15.00
11 Cal Ripken Jsy 15.00 40.00
12 Alex Rodriguez Bat 10.00 25.00
13 Alex Rodriguez Jsy 10.00 25.00
14 Frank Thomas Bat 6.00 15.00

2000 Fleer Mystique Fresh Ink

STATED ODDS 1:40
1 Chad Allen 4.00 10.00
2 Glen Barker 4.00 10.00
3 Michael Barrett 4.00 10.00
4 Josh Beckett 15.00 40.00
5 Lance Berkman SP 6.00 15.00
6 Kent Bottenfield 4.00 10.00
7 Milton Bradley 6.00 15.00
8 Orlando Cabrera 6.00 15.00
9 Sean Casey 6.00 15.00
10 Roger Cedeno 4.00 10.00
11 Will Clark 10.00 25.00
12 Russ Davis 4.00 10.00
13 Carlos Delgado 6.00 15.00
14 Einar Diaz 4.00 10.00
15 J.D. Drew 6.00 15.00
16 Damion Easley 4.00 10.00
17 Carlos Febles 4.00 10.00
18 Doug Glanville 6.00 15.00
19 Alex Gonzalez 4.00 10.00
20 Tony Gwynn 20.00 50.00
21 Mike Hampton 6.00 15.00
22 Bobby Howry 4.00 10.00
23 John Jaha 4.00 10.00
24 Nick Johnson 6.00 15.00
25 Andruw Jones 6.00 15.00
26 Adam Kennedy 6.00 15.00
27 Mike Lieberthal 6.00 15.00
28 Jose Macias 4.00 10.00
29 Raul Mondesi 6.00 15.00
30 Heath Murray 4.00 10.00
31 Mike Mussina 6.00 15.00
32 Hideo Nomo 250.00 500.00
33 Magglio Ordonez 6.00 15.00
34 Eric Owens 4.00 10.00
35 Adam Piatt 4.00 10.00
36 Cal Ripken 50.00 100.00
37 Tim Salmon 5.00 12.00
38 Chris Singleton 4.00 10.00
39 J.T. Snow 6.00 15.00
40 Mike Sweeney 6.00 15.00
41 Wilton Veras 4.00 10.00
42 Jose Vidro 4.00 10.00
43 Rondell White 6.00 15.00
44 Jaret Wright 4.00 10.00

2000 Fleer Mystique High Praise

COMPLETE SET (10) 10.00 25.00
STATED ODDS 1:20
1 Mark McGwire 1.50 4.00
2 Ken Griffey Jr. 2.00 5.00
3 Alex Rodriguez 1.25 3.00
4 Derek Jeter 2.50 6.00
5 Sammy Sosa 1.00 2.50
6 Mike Piazza 1.00 2.50
7 Nomar Garciaparra .60 1.50
8 Cal Ripken 3.00 8.00

9 Tony Gwynn 1.00 2.50
10 Shawn Green .40 1.00

2000 Fleer Mystique Rookie I.P.O.

COMPLETE SET (10) 4.00 10.00
STATED ODDS 1:10
1 Josh Beckett .75 2.00
2 Eric Munson .40 1.00
3 Pat Burrell .40 1.00
4 Alfonso Soriano 1.00 2.50
5 Rick Ankiel .60 1.50
6 Ruben Mateo .40 1.00
7 Mark Quinn .40 1.00
8 Kip Wells .40 1.00
9 Ben Petrick .40 1.00
10 Nick Johnson .40 1.00

2000 Fleer Mystique Seismic Activity

COMPLETE SET (10) 10.00 25.00
STATED ODDS 1:40
*RICHTER 100: 1.5X TO 4X BASIC SEISMIC
RICHTER 100 PRINT RUN 100 SERIAL #'d SETS
1 Ken Griffey Jr. 2.00 5.00
2 Sammy Sosa 1.00 2.50
3 Derek Jeter 2.50 6.00
4 Mark McGwire 1.50 4.00
5 Manny Ramirez 1.00 2.50
6 Mike Piazza 1.00 2.50
7 Vladimir Guerrero .60 1.50
8 Chipper Jones 1.00 2.50
9 Alex Rodriguez 1.25 3.00
10 Jeff Bagwell .60 1.50

2000 Fleer Mystique Supernaturals

COMPLETE SET (10) 5.00 12.00
STATED ODDS 1:10
1 Alex Rodriguez .60 1.50
2 Chipper Jones .50 1.25
3 Derek Jeter 1.25 3.00
4 Ivan Rodriguez .30 .75
5 Ken Griffey Jr. 1.00 2.50
6 Mark McGwire .75 2.00
7 Mike Piazza .50 1.25
8 Nomar Garciaparra .30 .75
9 Sammy Sosa .50 1.25
10 Vladimir Guerrero .30 .75

2003 Fleer Mystique

COMP.SET w/o SP's (80) 15.00 40.00
COMMON CARD (1-80) .20 .50
COMMON CARD (81-130) 2.00 5.00
81-130 STATED ODDS 1:5
81-130 PRINT RUN 699 SERIAL #'d SETS
1 Alex Rodriguez .60 1.50
2 Derek Jeter 1.25 3.00
3 Jose Vidro .20 .50
4 Miguel Tejada .30 .75
5 Albert Pujols .60 1.50
6 Rocco Baldelli .20 .50
7 Jose Reyes .50 1.25
8 Hideo Nomo .50 1.25
9 Hank Blalock .20 .50
10 Chipper Jones .50 1.25
11 Barry Larkin .30 .75
12 Alfonso Soriano .30 .75
13 Aramis Ramirez .20 .50
14 Darin Erstad .20 .50
15 Jim Edmonds .30 .75
16 Garret Anderson .20 .50
17 Todd Helton .30 .75
18 Jason Kendall .20 .50
19 Aubrey Huff .20 .50
20 Troy Glaus .20 .50
21 Sammy Sosa .50 1.25
22 Roger Clemens .60 1.50
23 Mark Teixeira .30 .75
24 Barry Bonds .75 2.00
25 Jim Thome .30 .75
26 Carlos Delgado .20 .50
27 Vladimir Guerrero .30 .75
28 Austin Kearns .20 .50
29 Pat Burrell .20 .50
30 Ken Griffey Jr. 1.00 2.50
31 Greg Maddux .60 1.50
32 Corey Patterson .20 .50
33 Larry Walker .30 .75
34 Kerry Wood .20 .50
35 Frank Thomas .50 1.25
36 Dontrelle Willis .20 .50
37 Randy Johnson .50 1.25
38 Curt Schilling .30 .75
39 Jay Gibbons .20 .50
40 Dmitri Young .20 .50
41 Edgar Martinez .30 .75
42 Kevin Brown .20 .50
43 Scott Rolen .30 .75
44 Adam Dunn .30 .75
45 Pedro Martinez .30 .75
46 Corey Koskie .20 .50
47 Tom Glavine .30 .75
48 Torii Hunter .20 .50
49 Shawn Green .20 .50
50 Nomar Garciaparra .30 .75
51 Bernie Williams .30 .75
52 Milton Bradley .20 .50
53 Jason Giambi .20 .50
54 Mike Lieberthal .20 .50
55 Jeff Bagwell .30 .75
56 Carlos Pena .30 .75
57 Lance Berkman .30 .75
58 Jose Cruz Jr. .20 .50
59 Josh Beckett .20 .50
60 Mark Mulder .20 .50
61 Mike Piazza .50 1.25
62 Mark Prior .30 .75
63 Sean Burroughs .20 .50
64 Angel Berroa .20 .50
65 Geoff Jenkins .20 .50
66 Magglio Ordonez .30 .75
67 Craig Biggio .30 .75
68 Roberto Alomar .30 .75
69 Hee Seop Choi .20 .50
70 J.D. Drew .20 .50
71 Richie Sexson .20 .50
72 Brian Giles .20 .50
73 Gary Sheffield .20 .50
74 Manny Ramirez .50 1.25
75 Barry Zito .30 .75
76 Andruw Jones .20 .50
77 Ivan Rodriguez .30 .75
78 Ichiro Suzuki .60 1.50
79 Mike Sweeney .20 .50
80 Vernon Wells .20 .50
81 Craig Brazell RU RC 1.25 3.00
82 Wilfredo Ledezma RU RC 1.25 3.00
83 Josh Willingham RU RC 4.00 10.00
84 Chien-Ming Wang RU RC 5.00 12.00
85 Mike Ryan RU RC 1.25 3.00
86 Mike Gallo RU RC 1.25 3.00
87 Rickie Weeks RU RC 4.00 10.00
88 Brian Stokes RU RC 1.25 3.00
89 Humberto Quintero RU RC 1.25 3.00
90 Ramon Nivar RU RC 1.25 3.00
91 Jeremy Griffiths RU RC 1.25 3.00
92 Termel Sledge RU RC 1.25 3.00
93 Brandon Webb RU RC 4.00 10.00
94 David DeJesus RU RC 3.00 8.00
95 Doug Waechter RU RC 1.25 3.00
96 Jeremy Bonderman RU RC 5.00 12.00
97 Felix Sanchez RU RC 1.25 3.00
98 Colin Porter RU RC 1.25 3.00
99 Francisco Cruceta RU RC 1.25 3.00
100 Hideki Matsui RU RC 6.00 15.00
101 Chris Waters RU RC 1.25 3.00
102 Dan Haren RU RC 6.00 15.00
103 Lew Ford RU RC 1.25 3.00
104 Oscar Villarreal RU RC 1.25 3.00
105 Ryan Wagner RU RC 1.25 3.00
106 Prentice Redman RU RC 1.25 3.00
107 Josh Stewart RU RC 1.25 3.00
108 Carlos Mendez RU RC 1.25 3.00
109 Michael Hessman RU RC 1.25 3.00
110 Josh Hall RU RC 1.25 3.00
111 Daniel Garcia RU RC 1.25 3.00
112 Matt Kata RU RC 1.25 3.00
113 Michel Hernandez RU RC 1.25 3.00
114 Sergio Mitre RU RC 1.25 3.00
115 Pete LaForest RU RC 1.25 3.00
116 Edwin Jackson RU RC 2.00 5.00
117 Matt Diaz RU RC 2.00 5.00
118 Greg Aquino RU RC 1.25 3.00
119 Jose Contreras RU RC 3.00 8.00
120 Jeff Duncan RU RC 1.25 3.00
121 Richard Fischer RU RC 1.25 3.00
122 Todd Wellemeyer RU RC 1.25 3.00
123 Robby Hammock RU RC 1.25 3.00
124 Delmon Young RU RC 4.00 10.00
125 Clint Barmes RU RC 3.00 8.00
126 Phil Seibel RU RC 1.25 3.00
127 Bo Hart RU RC 1.25 3.00
128 Jon Leicester RU RC 1.25 3.00
129 Chad Gaudin RU RC 1.25 3.00
130 Guillermo Quiroz RU RC 1.25 3.00

2003 Fleer Mystique Blue Die Cuts

*BLUE DIE CUTS: .4X TO 1X BASIC
TWO PER MYSTERY PACK
STATED PRINT RUN 200 SERIAL #'d SETS

2003 Fleer Mystique Gold

*GOLD: 4X TO 10X BASIC
STATED ODDS 1:18
1-80 PRINT RUN 75 SERIAL #'d SETS
81-130 PRINT RUN 25 SERIAL #'d SETS
81-130 NO PRICING DUE TO SCARCITY

2003 Fleer Mystique Awe Pairs

OVERALL #'d INSERT ODDS 1:10
STATED PRINT RUN 250 SERIAL #'d SETS
*GOLD: .75X TO 2X BASIC AWE
OVERALL #'d INSERT PARALLEL ODDS 1:30
GOLD PRINT RUNS B/WN 63-101 COPIES PER
1 N.Garciaparra 1.00 2.50
P.Martinez
2 D.Jeter 4.00 10.00
A.Soriano
3 R.Baldelli .60 1.50
A.Huff
4 C.Delgado .60 1.50
V.Wells
5 T.Glaus .60 1.50
G.Anderson
6 I.Suzuki 2.00 5.00
B.Boone
7 A.Rodriguez 2.00 5.00
H.Blalock
8 C.Jones 1.50 4.00
A.Jones
9 D.Willis .60 1.50
M.Lowell
10 V.Guerrero 1.00 2.50
O.Cabrera
11 T.Glavine 1.50 4.00
M.Piazza
12 J.Thome 1.00 2.50
M.Lieberthal
13 S.Sosa 1.50 4.00
C.Patterson
14 J.Bagwell 1.00 2.50
L.Berkman
15 G.Jenkins .60 1.50
R.Sexson
16 A.Pujols 2.00 5.00
J.Edmonds
17 T.Helton 1.00 2.50
L.Walker
18 P.LoDuca .60 1.50
S.Green
19 R.Klesko .60 1.50
S.Burroughs
20 B.Bonds 2.50 6.00
R.Aurilia

2003 Fleer Mystique Awe Pairs Memorabilia

OVERALL #'d GU INSERT ODDS 1:20
STATED PRINT RUN 100 SERIAL #'d SETS
OVERALL #'d GU PARALLEL ODDS 1:350
GOLD PRINT RUN 10 SERIAL #'d SETS
NO GOLD PRICING DUE TO SCARCITY
APJE Pujols Jsy/Edmonds Jsy 10.00 25.00
ARHB A.Rod Jsy/Blalock Bat 8.00 20.00
CDVW Delgado Jsy/V.Wells Bat 4.00 10.00
CJAJ Chipper Jsy/Andruw Jsy 6.00 15.00
DJAS Jeter Jsy/Soriano Jsy 12.50 30.00
DWML D.Willis Jsy/Lowell Bat 6.00 15.00
GJRS Jenkins Bat/Sexson Bat 4.00 10.00
JBLB Bagwell Jsy/Berkman Jsy 6.00 15.00
JTML Thome Jsy/Lieberthal Bat 6.00 15.00
NGPM Nomar Jsy/Pedro Jsy 8.00 20.00
PLDSG Lo Duca Jsy/S.Green Jsy 4.00 10.00
RBAH Baldelli Jsy/Huff Bat 4.00 10.00
RKSB Klesko Bat/Burroughs Jsy 4.00 10.00
SSCP Sosa Jsy/Patterson Jsy 6.00 15.00
TGGA Glaus Jsy/Anderson Bat 4.00 10.00
TGMP Glavine Jsy/Piazza Jsy 6.00 15.00
THLW Helton Jsy/Walker Jsy 6.00 15.00
VGOC Guerrero Jsy/Cabrera Bat 6.00 15.00

2003 Fleer Mystique Diamond Dominators

OVERALL #'d INSERT ODDS 1:10
STATED PRINT RUN 100 SERIAL #'d SETS
*GOLD p/r 51-75: .6X TO 1.5X BASIC
*GOLD p/r 44-45: .75X TO 2X BASIC
*GOLD p/r 31: 1.25X TO 3X BASIC
OVERALL #'d INSERT PARALLEL ODDS 1:30
GOLD PRINT RUNS B/WN 3-75 COPIES PER
NO GOLD PRICING ON QTY OF 25 OR LESS
1 Mike Piazza 1.50 4.00
2 Greg Maddux 2.00 5.00
3 Alfonso Soriano 1.00 2.50
4 Barry Zito 1.00 2.50
5 Alex Rodriguez 2.00 5.00
6 Roger Clemens 2.00 5.00
7 Sammy Sosa 1.50 4.00
8 Adam Dunn 1.00 2.50
9 Randy Johnson 1.50 4.00
10 Pedro Martinez 1.00 2.50

2003 Fleer Mystique Diamond Dominators Memorabilia

OVERALL #'d GU INSERT ODDS 1:20
STATED PRINT RUN 75 SERIAL #'d SETS
OVERALL #'d GU PARALLEL ODDS 1:350
GOLD PRINT RUN 10 SERIAL #'d SETS
NO GOLD PRICING DUE TO SCARCITY
AD Adam Dunn Bat 5.00 12.00
AR Alex Rodriguez Jsy 8.00 20.00
AS Alfonso Soriano Jsy 5.00 12.00
BZ Barry Zito Jsy 5.00 12.00
GM Greg Maddux Jsy 8.00 20.00
MP Mike Piazza Jsy 8.00 20.00
PM Pedro Martinez Jsy 6.00 15.00
RC Roger Clemens Jsy 10.00 25.00
RJ Randy Johnson Jsy 6.00 15.00
SS Sammy Sosa Jsy 6.00 15.00

2003 Fleer Mystique Ink Appeal

OVERALL INK APPEAL ODDS 1:150
STATED PRINT RUN 50 SERIAL #'d SETS
AH Aubrey Huff 10.00 25.00
BH Bo Hart 6.00 15.00
CP Corey Patterson 6.00 15.00
DW Dontrelle Willis 10.00 25.00
HB Hank Blalock 10.00 25.00
JR Jose Reyes 10.00 25.00
JW Josh Willingham 12.50 30.00
MR Mike Ryan 6.00 15.00
RB Rocco Baldelli 10.00 25.00
TH Torii Hunter 10.00 25.00

2003 Fleer Mystique Ink Appeal Gold

OVERALL INK APPEAL ODDS 1:150
PRINT RUNS B/WN 2-70 COPIES PER
NO PRICING ON QTY OF 25 OR LESS
DW Dontrelle Willis/35 10.00 25.00
JW Josh Willingham/70 12.50 30.00
MR Mike Ryan/54 6.00 15.00
TH Torii Hunter/48 10.00 25.00

2003 Fleer Mystique Ink Appeal Dual

STATED PRINT RUN 20 SERIAL #'d SETS
GOLD PRINT RUN 5 SERIAL #'d SETS
OVERALL INK APPEAL ODDS 1:150
NO PRICING DUE TO SCARCITY

2003 Fleer Mystique Rare Finds

OVERALL #'d INSERT ODDS 1:10
STATED PRINT RUN 250 SERIAL #'d SETS
1 Giambi 4.00 10.00
Clemens
Jeter
2 Randy 2.00 5.00
Schilling
Webb
3 Nomar 1.50 4.00
Pedro
Manny
4 Prior 1.50 4.00
Wood
Sosa
5 Bagwell 1.00 2.50
Biggio
Berkman
6 Kearns 1.00 2.50
Dunn
Larkin
7 Edmonds 1.00 2.50
Rolen
Drew
8 Chipper 2.00 5.00
Andruw
Maddux
9 Zito 1.00 2.50
Tejada
Mulder
10 A.Rod 2.00 5.00
Teixeira
Palmeiro

2003 Fleer Mystique Rare Finds Single Swatch

OVERALL RF SWATCH ODDS 1:1 MYSTERY
STATED PRINT RUN 150 SERIAL #'d SETS
GOLD RANDOM IN MYSTERY PACKS
GOLD PRINT RUN 15 SERIAL #'d SETS
NO GOLD PRICING DUE TO SCARCITY
AK Austin Kearns Jsy 3.00 8.00
AR Alex Rodriguez Jsy 6.00 15.00
BL Barry Larkin Jsy 4.00 10.00
BW Brandon Webb Jsy 4.00 10.00
CJ Chipper Jones Jsy 4.00 10.00
DJ Derek Jeter Jsy 8.00 20.00
GM Greg Maddux Jsy 4.00 10.00
JB Jeff Bagwell Jsy 4.00 10.00
JD J.D. Drew Jsy 3.00 8.00
JG Jason Giambi Jsy 3.00 8.00
MM Mark Mulder Jsy 3.00 8.00
MP Mark Prior Jsy 4.00 10.00
MTJ Miguel Tejada Jsy 3.00 8.00
MTX Mark Teixeira Jsy 4.00 10.00
NG Nomar Garciaparra Jsy 6.00 15.00
PM Pedro Martinez Jsy 4.00 10.00
RC Roger Clemens Jsy 6.00 15.00
RJ Randy Johnson Jsy 4.00 10.00
SR Scott Rolen Jsy 4.00 10.00
SS Sammy Sosa Jsy 4.00 10.00

2003 Fleer Mystique Rare Finds Double Swatch

OVERALL RF SWATCH ODDS 1:1 MYSTERY
STATED PRINT RUN 75 SERIAL #'d SETS
GOLD RANDOM IN MYSTERY PACKS
GOLD PRINT RUN 10 SERIAL #'d SETS
NO GOLD PRICING DUE TO SCARCITY
AJGM Andruw Jsy/Maddux Jsy 6.00 15.00
AKAD Kearns Jsy/Dunn Jsy 4.00 10.00
ARMT A.Rod Jsy/Teixeira Jsy 10.00 25.00
BZMT Zito Jsy/Tejada Jsy 4.00 10.00
CJGM Chipper Jsy/Maddux Jsy 10.00 25.00
JBCB Bagwell Jsy/Biggio Jsy 6.00 15.00
JESR Edmonds Jsy/Rolen Jsy 6.00 15.00
JGDJ Giambi Jsy/Jeter Jsy 12.50 30.00
MPKW Prior Jsy/K.Wood Jsy 6.00 15.00
MPSS Prior Jsy/Sosa Jsy 6.00 15.00
NGMR Nomar Jsy/Manny Jsy 12.50 30.00
PMMR Pedro Jsy/Manny Jsy 6.00 15.00
RCDJ Clemens Jsy/Jeter Jsy 20.00 50.00
RJBW Randy Jsy/B.Webb Jsy 6.00 15.00
RJCS Randy Jsy/Schilling Jsy 6.00 15.00

2003 Fleer Mystique Rare Finds Triple Swatch

OVERALL RF SWATCH ODDS 1:1 MYSTERY
STATED PRINT RUN 50 SERIAL #'d SETS
GOLD RANDOM IN MYSTERY PACKS
GOLD PRINT RUN 5 SERIAL #'d SETS
NO GOLD PRICING DUE TO SCARCITY
AAB Kearns/Dunn/Larkin 6.00 15.00
AMR A.Rod/Teixeira/Palmeiro 15.00 40.00
BMM Zito/Tejada/Mulder 6.00 15.00
CAG Chipper/Andruw/Maddux 30.00 60.00
JCL Bagwell/Biggio/Berkman 10.00 25.00
JRD Giambi/Clemens/Jeter 40.00 80.00
JSJ Edmonds/Rolen/Drew 15.00 40.00
MKS Prior/Wood/Sosa 10.00 25.00
NPM Nomar/Pedro/Manny 40.00 80.00
RCB Randy/Schilling/Webb 10.00 25.00

2003 Fleer Mystique Rare Finds Autograph

STATED PRINT RUN 15 SERIAL #'d SETS
AU JSY PRINT RUN 5 SERIAL #'d SETS
OVERALL RF AUTO ODDS 1:650 MYSTERY
NO PRICING DUE TO SCARCITY

2003 Fleer Mystique Secret Weapons

OVERALL #'d INSERT ODDS 1:10
STATED PRINT RUN 250 SERIAL #'d SETS
*GOLD p/r 224-307: .4X TO 1X BASIC SW
*GOLD p/r 100: .6X TO 1.5X BASIC SW
OVERALL #'d INSERT PARALLEL ODDS 1:30
GOLD PRINT RUNS B/WN 100-307 COPIES PER
1 Hank Blalock .60 1.50
2 Dontrelle Willis .60 1.50
3 Jose Reyes 1.50 4.00
4 Bo Hart .60 1.50
5 Corey Patterson .60 1.50
6 Hideki Matsui 3.00 8.00
7 Mark Teixeira 1.00 2.50
8 Brandon Webb 2.00 5.00
9 Rocco Baldelli .60 1.50
10 Mark Prior 1.00 2.50

2003 Fleer Mystique Shining Stars

OVERALL #'d INSERT ODDS 1:10
STATED PRINT RUN 300 SERIAL #'d SETS
*GOLD p/r 419-658: .3X TO .8X BASIC SS
*GOLD p/r 269-381: .4X TO 1X BASIC SS
*GOLD p/r 173-234: .5X TO 1.2X BASIC SS
*GOLD p/r 114-127: .6X TO 1.5X BASIC SS
*GOLD p/r 96: .75X TO 2X BASIC SS
*GOLD p/r 28-29: 2X TO 5X BASIC SS
OVERALL #'d INSERT PARALLEL ODDS 1:30
GOLD PRINT RUNS B/WN 28-658 COPIES PER
1 Derek Jeter 4.00 10.00
2 Barry Bonds 2.50 6.00
3 Nomar Garciaparra 1.00 2.50
4 Austin Kearns .60 1.50
5 Vladimir Guerrero 1.00 2.50
6 Jim Thome 1.00 2.50
7 Ichiro Suzuki 2.00 5.00
8 Jason Giambi .60 1.50
9 Albert Pujols 2.00 5.00
10 Ken Griffey Jr. 3.00 8.00
11 Chipper Jones 1.50 4.00
12 Scott Rolen 1.00 2.50
13 Manny Ramirez 1.50 4.00
14 Jeff Bagwell 1.00 2.50
15 Torii Hunter .60 1.50

2003 Fleer Mystique Shining Stars Jersey

STATED PRINT RUN 100 SERIAL #'d SETS
*PATCH: .75X TO 2X BASIC SS JSY
PATCH PRINT RUN 50 SERIAL #'d SETS
OVERALL #'d GU INSERT ODDS 1:20
AJ Andruw Jones 5.00 12.00
AK Austin Kearns 4.00 10.00
AP Albert Pujols 8.00 20.00
CD Carlos Delgado 4.00 10.00
CJ Chipper Jones 5.00 12.00
DJ Derek Jeter 10.00 25.00
JB Jeff Bagwell 5.00 12.00
JG Jason Giambi 4.00 10.00
JT Jim Thome 5.00 12.00
MR Manny Ramirez 5.00 12.00
NG Nomar Garciaparra 8.00 20.00
SR Scott Rolen 5.00 12.00
THE Todd Helton 5.00 12.00
THU Torii Hunter 4.00 10.00
VG Vladimir Guerrero 5.00 12.00

2003 Fleer Patchworks

COMP.SET w/o SP's (90) 6.00 15.00
COMMON CARD (1-90) .15 .40
COMMON CARD (91-115) .75 2.00
91-115 RANDOM INSERTS IN PACKS
91-115 PRINT RUN 1500 SERIAL #'d SETS
1 Luis Castillo .15 .40
2 Derek Jeter 1.00 2.50
3 Vladimir Guerrero .25 .60
4 Bobby Higginson .15 .40
5 Pat Burrell .15 .40
6 Ivan Rodriguez .25 .60
7 Craig Biggio .25 .60
8 Troy Glaus .15 .40
9 Barry Bonds .60 1.50
10 Hideo Nomo .40 1.00
11 Barry Larkin .25 .60
12 Roberto Alomar .25 .60
13 Rodrigo Lopez .15 .40
14 Eric Chavez .15 .40
15 Shawn Green .15 .40
16 Joe Randa .15 .40
17 Mark Grace .25 .60
18 Jason Kendall .15 .40
19 Hee Seop Choi .15 .40
20 Luis Gonzalez .15 .40
21 Sammy Sosa .40 1.00
22 Larry Walker .25 .60
23 Phil Nevin .15 .40
24 Manny Ramirez .40 1.00
25 Jim Thome .25 .60
26 Randy Johnson .40 1.00
27 Jose Vidro .15 .40
28 Austin Kearns .15 .40
29 Mike Sweeney .15 .40
30 Magglio Ordonez .25 .60
31 Mike Piazza .40 1.00
32 Eric Hinske .15 .40
33 Alex Rodriguez .50 1.25
34 Kerry Wood .15 .40
35 Matt Morris .15 .40
36 Lance Berkman .25 .60
37 Michael Cuddyer .15 .40
38 Curt Schilling .25 .60
39 Sean Burroughs .15 .40
40 Ken Griffey Jr. .75 2.00
41 Edgardo Alfonzo .15 .40
42 Carlos Pena .25 .60
43 Adam Dunn .25 .60
44 Pedro Martinez .25 .60
45 Miguel Tejada .25 .60
46 Tom Glavine .25 .60
47 Torii Hunter .15 .40
48 Jason Giambi .15 .40
49 Tony Batista .15 .40
50 Ben Grieve .15 .40
51 Ichiro Suzuki .50 1.25
52 Bobby Abreu .15 .40
53 Todd Helton .25 .60
54 Kazuhiro Sasaki .15 .40
55 Nomar Garciaparra .25 .60
56 Francisco Rodriguez .25 .60
57 Ellis Burks .15 .40
58 Frank Thomas .40 1.00
59 Greg Maddux .50 1.25
60 Josh Beckett .15 .40
61 Brad Wilkerson .15 .40
62 Joe Borchard .15 .40
63 Carlos Delgado .15 .40
64 Alfonso Soriano .25 .60
65 Chipper Jones .40 1.00
66 J.D. Drew .15 .40
67 Mark Prior .25 .60
68 Rafael Palmeiro .25 .60
69 Jeff Kent .15 .40
70 Adrian Beltre .40 1.00
71 Marlon Byrd .15 .40
72 Orlando Hudson .15 .40
73 Junior Spivey .15 .40
74 Jeff Bagwell .25 .60
75 Barry Zito .25 .60
76 Roger Clemens .50 1.25
77 Aubrey Huff .15 .40
78 Geoff Jenkins .15 .40
79 Andruw Jones .15 .40
80 Scott Rolen .25 .60
81 Omar Vizquel .25 .60
82 Darin Erstad .15 .40
83 Bernie Williams .25 .60
84 Freddy Garcia .15 .40
85 Richie Sexson .15 .40
86 Josh Phelps .15 .40
87 Albert Pujols .50 1.25
88 Aramis Ramirez .15 .40
89 Shea Hillenbrand .15 .40
90 Cristian Guzman .15 .40
91 Adam LaRoche RR .75 2.00
92 David Pember RR RC .75 2.00
93 Termel Sledge RR RC .75 2.00
94 Hideki Matsui RR RC 4.00 10.00
95 Nook Logan RR RC .75 2.00
96 Jose Contreras RR RC 2.00 5.00
97 Pete LaForest RR RC .75 2.00
98 Rich Fischer RR RC .75 2.00
99 Francisco Rosario RR RC .75 2.00
100 Josh Willingham RR RC 2.50 6.00
101 Alejandro Machado RR RC .75 2.00
102 Lew Ford RR RC .75 2.00
103 Joe Valentine RR RC .75 2.00
104 Guillermo Quiroz RR RC .75 2.00
105 Chien-Ming Wang RR RC 3.00 8.00
106 Jhonny Peralta RR .75 2.00
107 Shane Victorino RR RC 2.50 6.00
108 Prentice Redman RR RC .75 2.00
109 Matt Bruback RR RC .75 2.00
110 Lance Niekro RR .75 2.00
111 Travis Hughes RR .75 2.00
112 Nic Jackson RR .75 2.00
113 Hector Luna RR RC .75 2.00
114 Cliff Lee RR 5.00 12.00
115 Tim Olson RR RC .75 2.00

2003 Fleer Patchworks Star Ruby

*RUBY 1-90: 4X TO 10X BASIC
*RUBY 91-115: .75X TO 2X BASIC
RANDOM INSERTS IN PACKS
STATED PRINT RUN 100 SERIAL #'d SETS

2003 Fleer Patchworks Diamond Ink

RANDOM INSERTS IN PACKS
STATED PRINT RUNS LISTED BELOW
DJ1 Derek Jeter Black/210 100.00 200.00
DJ2 Derek Jeter Blue/101 100.00 200.00
DJ3 Derek Jeter Red/50 100.00 200.00
MP Mark Prior/88 15.00 40.00
MS Mike Schmidt/194 20.00 50.00
TG Troy Glaus/351 10.00 25.00

2003 Fleer Patchworks Game-Worn Patch 100

ISSUED IN 04 AS QLTY CONTROL EXCH
STATED PRINT RUN 100 SERIAL #'d SETS
AB2 Adrian Beltre 6.00 15.00
AJ2 Andruw Jones 10.00 25.00
AK2 Austin Kearns 6.00 15.00
CB2 Carlos Beltran 6.00 15.00
KW2 Kerry Wood 10.00 25.00
RO2 Roy Oswalt 6.00 15.00
AR2 Alex Rodriguez 10.00 25.00
GM2 Greg Maddux 10.00 25.00
MM2 Mark Mulder 6.00 15.00

2003 Fleer Patchworks Game-Worn Patch 300

ISSUED IN 04 AS QLTY CONTROL EXCH
STATED PRINT RUN 300 SERIAL #'d SETS
AB2 Bob Abreu 4.00 10.00
AK2 Austin Kearns 4.00 10.00
CD2 Carlos Delgado 4.00 10.00
DE2 Darin Erstad 6.00 15.00
HC2 Hee Seop Choi 4.00 10.00

2003 Fleer Patchworks Game-Worn Patch Level 1 Single

RANDOM INSERTS IN PACKS
STATED PRINT RUN 250 SERIAL #'d SETS
AB Adrian Beltre 4.00 10.00
AJ Andruw Jones 6.00 15.00
BA Bob Abreu 4.00 10.00
BW Bernie Williams 6.00 15.00
EC Eric Chavez 4.00 10.00
FT Frank Thomas 6.00 15.00
GM Greg Maddux 6.00 15.00
JB Josh Beckett 4.00 10.00
KS Kazuhiro Sasaki 4.00 10.00
KW Kerry Wood 4.00 10.00
LB Lance Berkman 4.00 10.00
MG Mark Grace 6.00 15.00
RA Roberto Alomar 6.00 15.00
RO Roy Oswalt 4.00 10.00
VG Vladimir Guerrero 6.00 15.00

2003 Fleer Patchworks Game-Worn Patch Level 2 Dual

RANDOM INSERTS IN PACKS
STATED PRINT RUN 100 SERIAL #'d SETS
AB Adrian Beltre 10.00 25.00
AJ Andruw Jones 12.50 30.00
AR Alex Rodriguez 20.00 50.00
BA Bob Abreu 10.00 25.00
BW Bernie Williams 12.50 30.00
CD Carlos Delgado 10.00 25.00
CS Curt Schilling 10.00 25.00
EC Eric Chavez 10.00 25.00
FT Frank Thomas 12.50 30.00
GM Greg Maddux 15.00 40.00
JB Josh Beckett 10.00 25.00
KS Kazuhiro Sasaki 10.00 25.00
KW Kerry Wood 10.00 25.00
LB Lance Berkman 10.00 25.00
MG Mark Grace 12.50 30.00
RA Roberto Alomar 12.50 30.00
RO Roy Oswalt 10.00 25.00
VG Vladimir Guerrero 12.50 30.00

2003 Fleer Patchworks Game-Worn Patch Level 3 Multi

RANDOM INSERTS IN PACKS
STATED PRINT RUN 50 SERIAL #'d SETS
AB Adrian Beltre 12.50 30.00
AJ Andruw Jones 15.00 40.00
AR Alex Rodriguez 30.00 60.00
BA Bob Abreu 12.50 30.00
BW Bernie Williams 15.00 40.00
CD Carlos Delgado 12.50 30.00
CS Curt Schilling 12.50 30.00
EC Eric Chavez 12.50 30.00
FT Frank Thomas 15.00 40.00
GM Greg Maddux 12.50 30.00
JB Josh Beckett 12.50 30.00
KS Kazuhiro Sasaki 12.50 30.00
KW Kerry Wood 12.50 30.00
LB Lance Berkman 12.50 30.00
MG Mark Grace 15.00 40.00
RA Roberto Alomar 15.00 40.00
RO Roy Oswalt 12.50 30.00
VG Vladimir Guerrero 15.00 40.00

2003 Fleer Patchworks Licensed Apparel Jersey

STATED PRINT RUN 500 SERIAL #'d SETS
*ONE-COLOR PATCH: .75X TO 2X BASIC APP
*MULTI-COLOR PATCH: 1.25 TO 3X BASIC APP
PATCH PRINT RUN 300 SERIAL #'d SETS
AD Adam Dunn 3.00 8.00
CB Carlos Beltran 3.00 8.00
CJ Chipper Jones 4.00 10.00
DE Darin Erstad 3.00 8.00
DJ Derek Jeter 10.00 25.00
JD J.D. Drew 3.00 8.00
JR Jimmy Rollins 3.00 8.00
KB Kevin Brown 3.00 8.00
MM Mike Mussina 6.00 15.00
MO Magglio Ordonez 3.00 8.00
MP Mike Piazza 6.00 15.00
PK Paul Konerko 3.00 8.00
SG Shawn Green 3.00 8.00
SS Shannon Stewart 3.00 8.00
TH Todd Helton 4.00 10.00

2003 Fleer Patchworks Licensed Apparel Patch

RANDOM INSERTS IN PACKS
STATED PRINT RUN 300 SERIAL #'d SETS

2003 Fleer Patchworks National Pastime

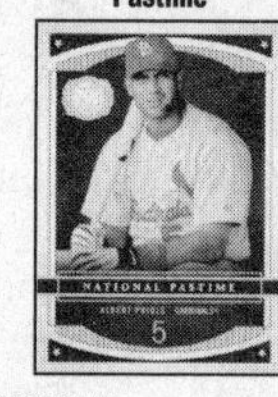

STATED ODDS 1:12
1 Barry Bonds 1.50 4.00
2 Kazuhiro Sasaki .40 1.00
3 Mike Piazza 1.00 2.50
4 Barry Zito .60 1.50
5 Sammy Sosa 1.00 2.50
6 Pedro Martinez .60 1.50
7 Craig Biggio .60 1.50
8 Rafael Palmeiro .60 1.50
9 Greg Maddux 1.25 3.00
10 Manny Ramirez 1.00 2.50
11 Adam Dunn .60 1.50
12 Omar Vizquel .60 1.50
13 Hideo Nomo 1.00 2.50
14 Alex Rodriguez 1.25 3.00
15 Pat Burrell .40 1.00
16 Nomar Garciaparra .60 1.50
17 Randy Johnson 1.00 2.50
18 Juan Gonzalez .40 1.00
19 Chipper Jones 1.00 2.50
20 Frank Thomas 1.00 2.50
21 Vladimir Guerrero .60 1.50
22 Troy Glaus .40 1.00
23 Albert Pujols 1.25 3.00
24 Ichiro Suzuki 1.25 3.00
25 Ken Griffey Jr. 2.00 5.00

2003 Fleer Patchworks National Patchtime Nameplate

RANDOM INSERTS IN PACKS
STATED PRINT RUN 50 SERIAL #'d SETS
AR Alex Rodriguez 20.00 50.00
BZ Barry Zito 12.50 30.00
CB Craig Biggio 15.00 40.00
CJ Chipper Jones 15.00 40.00
FT Frank Thomas 15.00 40.00
GM Greg Maddux 15.00 40.00
HN Hideo Nomo 40.00 80.00
MP Mike Piazza 15.00 40.00
NG Nomar Garciaparra 30.00 60.00
PB Pat Burrell 12.50 30.00
RJ Randy Johnson 15.00 40.00
RP Rafael Palmeiro 15.00 40.00
SS Sammy Sosa 15.00 40.00
TG Troy Glaus 12.50 30.00
VG Vladimir Guerrero 15.00 40.00

2003 Fleer Patchworks National Patchtime Number

RANDOM INSERTS IN PACKS
STATED PRINT RUN 75 SERIAL #'d SETS
AR Alex Rodriguez 15.00 40.00
BZ Barry Zito 10.00 25.00
CB Craig Biggio 12.50 30.00
CJ Chipper Jones 12.50 30.00
FT Frank Thomas 12.50 30.00
GM Greg Maddux 12.50 30.00
HN Hideo Nomo 30.00 60.00
MP Mike Piazza 12.50 30.00
MR Manny Ramirez 12.50 30.00
NG Nomar Garciaparra 20.00 50.00
PB Pat Burrell 10.00 25.00
PM Pedro Martinez 12.50 30.00
RJ Randy Johnson 12.50 30.00
RP Rafael Palmeiro 12.50 30.00
SS Sammy Sosa 12.50 30.00
VG Vladimir Guerrero 12.50 30.00

2003 Fleer Patchworks National Patchtime Team Name

RANDOM INSERTS IN PACKS
STATED PRINT RUN 100 SERIAL #'d SETS
AR Alex Rodriguez 15.00 40.00
BZ Barry Zito 10.00 25.00
CJ Chipper Jones 12.50 30.00
FT Frank Thomas 12.50 30.00
GM Greg Maddux 15.00 40.00
HN Hideo Nomo 30.00 60.00
MP Mike Piazza 15.00 40.00
NG Nomar Garciaparra 20.00 50.00
OV Omar Vizquel 12.50 30.00
PB Pat Burrell 10.00 25.00
RJ Randy Johnson 12.50 30.00
RP Rafael Palmeiro 12.50 30.00
SS Sammy Sosa 12.50 30.00
TG Troy Glaus 10.00 25.00
VG Vladimir Guerrero 12.50 30.00

2003 Fleer Patchworks National Patchtime Trim

RANDOM INSERTS IN PACKS
STATED PRINT RUN 200 SERIAL #'d SETS
COMMEMORATIVE PRINT RUN 25 #'d SETS
NO COMMEMORATIVE PRICING AVAILABLE
MLB LOGO PRINT RUN 1 SERIAL #'d SET
NO MLB LOGO PRICING AVAILABLE
NAMEPLATE PRINT RUN 50 #'d SETS

NUMBER PRINT RUN 75 #'d SETS
AR Alex Rodriguez 12.50 30.00
CJ Chipper Jones 10.00 25.00
FT Frank Thomas 10.00 25.00
GM Greg Maddux 12.50 30.00
HN Hideo Nomo 20.00 50.00
MP Mike Piazza 12.50 30.00
MR Manny Ramirez 10.00 25.00
NG Nomar Garciaparra 15.00 40.00
PM Pedro Martinez 10.00 25.00
RP Rafael Palmeiro 10.00 25.00
VG Vladimir Guerrero 10.00 25.00

2003 Fleer Patchworks National Patchtime 100

ISSUED IN 04 AS QLTY CONTROL EXCH
STATED PRINT RUN 100 SERIAL #'d SETS
JG2 Juan Gonzalez 10.00 25.00
KB2 Kris Benson 6.00 15.00
NG2 Nomar Garciaparra 15.00 40.00
CB2 Craig Biggio 6.00 15.00
MP2 Mike Piazza 15.00 40.00

2003 Fleer Patchworks National Patchtime 300

ISSUED IN 04 AS QLTY CONTROL EXCH
STATED PRINT RUN 300 SERIAL #'d SETS
AD2 Adam Dunn 4.00 10.00
BZ2 Barry Zito 4.00 10.00
MP2 Mike Piazza 10.00 25.00
NG2 Nomar Garciaparra 10.00 25.00
PB2 Pat Burrell 4.00 10.00
TH2 Tim Hudson 4.00 10.00
EH2 Eric Hinkse 4.00 10.00
RJ2 Randy Johnson 6.00 15.00
RP2 Rafael Palmeiro 6.00 15.00
VG2 Vladimir Guerrero 6.00 15.00

2003 Fleer Patchworks Numbers Game

STATED ODDS 1:24
1 Ichiro Suzuki 1.25 3.00
2 Derek Jeter 2.50 6.00
3 Alex Rodriguez 1.25 3.00
4 Miguel Tejada .60 1.50
5 Nomar Garciaparra .60 1.50
6 Jason Giambi .40 1.00
7 J.D. Drew .40 1.00
8 Barry Bonds 1.50 4.00
9 Alfonso Soriano .60 1.50
10 Jeff Bagwell .60 1.50
11 Barry Larkin .60 1.50
12 Roberto Alomar .60 1.50
13 Larry Walker .60 1.50
14 Roger Clemens 1.25 3.00
15 Ken Griffey Jr. 2.00 5.00

2003 Fleer Patchworks Numbers Game Jersey

STATED ODDS 1:33
PATCH RANDOM IN PACKS
PATCH PRINT RUN 300 SERIAL #'d SETS
AR Alex Rodriguez 8.00 20.00
AS Alfonso Soriano 3.00 8.00
BL Barry Larkin 3.00 8.00
DJ Derek Jeter 6.00 15.00
JB Jeff Bagwell 3.00 8.00
JG Jason Giambi 3.00 8.00
LW Larry Walker 3.00 8.00
MT Miguel Tejada 3.00 8.00
RA Roberto Alomar 3.00 8.00
RC Roger Clemens 6.00 15.00

2003 Fleer Patchworks Numbers Game Patch

RANDOM INSERTS IN PACKS
STATED PRINT RUN 300 SERIAL #'d SETS
AR Alex Rodriguez 10.00 25.00
AS Alfonso Soriano 6.00 15.00
BL Barry Larkin 10.00 25.00
DJ Derek Jeter 15.00 40.00
JB Jeff Bagwell 10.00 25.00
JG Jason Giambi 6.00 15.00
LW Larry Walker 6.00 15.00
MT Miguel Tejada 6.00 15.00
RA Roberto Alomar 10.00 25.00
RC Roger Clemens 15.00 40.00

2003 Fleer Patchworks Past Present Future

STATED ODDS 1:72
1 Mathews 2.00 5.00
Palmeiro
A-Rod
2 Rizzuto 4.00 10.00
Jeter
Soriano
3 R.Jackson 2.50 6.00
Bonds
Sosa
4 B.Williams 1.50 4.00
Sosa
Choi
5 Morgan 1.00 2.50
R.Alomar
Soriano
6 Berra 1.50 4.00
Piazza
Phelps
7 Ryan 5.00 12.00
Clemens
Wood
8 Schmidt 2.50 6.00
Rolen
Hinske
9 Bonds 2.50 6.00
A-Rod
Soriano
10 Berra 4.00 10.00
Jeter
Matsui

2003 Fleer Patchworks Patch Present Future Single

RANDOM INSERTS IN PACKS
STATED PRINT RUN 200 SERIAL #'d SETS
AR1 A.Rod w 15.00 40.00
Mathews-Raffy
AS1 A.Soriano w 6.00 15.00
Rizzuto-Jeter
AS2 A.Soriano w 6.00 15.00
Morg-Alom
AS3 A.Soriano w 6.00 15.00
Bonds-A.Rod
BB B.Bonds w 10.00 25.00
Reggie-Sosa
DJ1 D.Jeter w 30.00 60.00
Rizzuto-Soriano
DJ2 D.Jeter w 30.00 60.00
Berra-Matsui
EH E.Hinske w 6.00 15.00
Schmidt-Rolen
KW K.Wood w 15.00 40.00
Ryan-Clemens
MP M.Piazza w 15.00 40.00
Berra-Phelps
RA R.Alomar w 10.00 25.00
Morg-Soriano
RC R.Clemens w 30.00 60.00
Ryan-Wood
RP R.Palmeiro w 10.00 25.00
Math-A.Rod
SS1 S.Sosa w 15.00 40.00
Reggie-Bonds
SS2 S.Sosa w 15.00 40.00
Williams-Choi

2003 Fleer Patchworks Patch Present Future Dual

RANDOM INSERTS IN PACKS
STATED PRINT RUN 100 SERIAL #'d SETS
ARAS A.Rodriguez/A.Soriano 10.00 25.00
DJAS D.Jeter/A.Soriano 15.00 40.00
RAAS R.Alomar/A.Soriano 4.00 10.00
RCKW R.Clemens/K.Wood 20.00 50.00
RPAR R.Palmeiro/A.Rodriguez 8.00 20.00
SREH S.Rolen/E.Hinske 10.00 25.00

2004 Fleer Patchworks

COMP.SET w/o SP's (90) 10.00 25.00
COMMON CARD (1-90) .15 .40
COMMON CARD (91-110) .60 1.50
91-110 ODDS 1:24 HOBBY, 1:48 RETAIL
91-110 PRINT RUN 799 SERIAL #'d SETS
1 Kerry Wood .15 .40
2 Brian Giles .15 .40
3 Tino Martinez .25 .60
4 Mark Mulder .15 .40
5 Andy Pettitte .25 .60
6 Gary Sheffield .15 .40
7 Mark Teixeira .25 .60
8 Garret Anderson .15 .40
9 Craig Biggio .25 .60
10 Alfonso Soriano .25 .60
11 Bret Boone .15 .40
12 Mike Piazza .40 1.00
13 Todd Helton .25 .60
14 Jay Gibbons .15 .40
15 Eric Chavez .15 .40
16 Andruw Jones .15 .40
17 Adam Dunn .25 .60
18 Corey Koskie .15 .40
19 Rafael Palmeiro .25 .60
20 Ivan Rodriguez .25 .60
21 Tom Glavine .25 .60
22 Luis Gonzalez .15 .40
23 Miguel Tejada .25 .60
24 Jose Vidro .15 .40
25 Richie Sexson .15 .40
26 Roy Halladay .25 .60
27 Vladimir Guerrero .25 .60
28 Randy Johnson .40 1.00
29 Vernon Wells .15 .40
30 Pat Burrell .15 .40
31 Jason Schmidt .15 .40
32 Casey Blake .15 .40
33 Greg Maddux .50 1.25
34 Mike Lowell .15 .40
35 Hideo Nomo .40 1.00
36 Carlos Delgado .15 .40
37 Dontrelle Willis .15 .40
38 Shawn Green .15 .40
39 Pedro Martinez .25 .60
40 Josh Beckett .15 .40
41 Eric Gagne .15 .40
42 Manny Ramirez .40 1.00
43 Jim Edmonds .25 .60
44 Curt Schilling .25 .60
45 Mike Sweeney .15 .40
46 Albert Pujols .50 1.25
47 Nomar Garciaparra .25 .60
48 Alex Rodriguez Yanks .50 1.25
49 Angel Berroa .15 .40
50 Jim Thome .25 .60
51 Edgardo Alfonzo .15 .40
52 Jeremy Bonderman .15 .40
53 Miguel Cabrera .40 1.00
54 Bobby Higginson .15 .40
55 John Smoltz .40 1.00
56 Jason Kendall .15 .40
57 Torii Hunter .15 .40
58 Troy Glaus .15 .40
59 Rafael Furcal .15 .40
60 Austin Kearns .15 .40
61 Esteban Loaiza .15 .40
62 Darin Erstad .15 .40
63 Jose Reyes .25 .60
64 Preston Wilson .15 .40
65 Rocco Baldelli .15 .40
66 Barry Zito .25 .60
67 Ken Griffey Jr. .75 2.00
68 Frank Thomas .40 1.00
69 Roger Clemens .50 1.25
70 Brett Myers .15 .40
71 Billy Wagner .15 .40
72 Scott Podsednik .15 .40
73 Jody Gerut .15 .40
74 Bartolo Colon .15 .40
75 Jeff Bagwell .25 .60
76 Jason Giambi .15 .40
77 Edgar Martinez .25 .60
78 Chipper Jones .40 1.00
79 Jason Bay .25 .60
80 Doug Mientkiewicz .15 .40
81 Hank Blalock .15 .40
82 Sammy Sosa .40 1.00
83 Derek Jeter 1.00 2.50
84 Ichiro Suzuki .50 1.25
85 Ben Sheets .15 .40
86 Magglio Ordonez .25 .60
87 Carlos Beltran .25 .60
88 Mark Prior .25 .60
89 Sean Burroughs .15 .40
90 Tim Hudson .25 .60
91 Hector Gimenez ROO RC .60 1.50
92 Khalil Greene ROO 1.00 2.50
93 Rickie Weeks ROO .60 1.50
94 Delmon Young ROO 1.00 2.50
95 Don Kelly ROO RC 1.00 2.50
96 Chad Bentz ROO RC .60 1.50
97 Greg Dobbs ROO RC .60 1.50
98 John Gall ROO RC .60 1.50
99 Cory Sullivan ROO RC .60 1.50
100 Kazuo Matsui ROO RC 1.00 2.50
101 Graham Koonce ROO .60 1.50
102 Jason Bartlett ROO RC 2.00 5.00
103 Angel Chavez ROO RC .60 1.50
104 Ronny Cedeno ROO RC .60 1.50
105 Jerry Gil ROO RC .60 1.50
106 Ivan Ochoa ROO RC .60 1.50
107 Ruddy Yan ROO .60 1.50
108 Mike Gosling ROO RC .60 1.50
109 Alfredo Simon ROO RC 1.00 2.50
110 Koyie Hill ROO .60 1.50

2004 Fleer Patchworks Star Ruby

*RUBY 1-90: 5X TO 12X BASIC
*RUBY 91-110: .75X TO 2X BASIC
STATED ODDS 1:48 HOBBY, 1:96 RETAIL
STATED PRINT RUN 50 SERIAL #'d SETS

2004 Fleer Patchworks Autoworks Black

PRINT RUNS B/WN 145-376 COPIES PER
*BLUE: .4X TO 1X BLACK p/r 263-376
*BLUE: .4X TO 1X BLACK p/r 145-193
RED PATCH PRINT RUN 10 SERIAL #'d SETS
NO RED PATCH PRICING DUE TO SCARCITY
ALL RED PATCH ARE EXCHANGE CARDS
RED PATCH EXCH.DEADLINE IS INDEFINITE
OVERALL AU ODDS 1:54 HOB, 1:120 RET
AB Angel Berroa/145 4.00 10.00
AP1 Andy Pettitte/148 10.00 25.00
AP2 Albert Pujols/193 60.00 120.00
EG Eric Gagne/193 10.00 25.00
GA Garret Anderson/145 6.00 15.00
GS Grady Sizemore/263 6.00 15.00
JB Josh Beckett/148 10.00 25.00
JG Jody Gerut/376 4.00 10.00
MM Mark Mulder/190 6.00 15.00
MT Miguel Tejada/164 10.00 25.00
RH Roy Halladay/286 15.00 40.00
SP Scott Podsednik/146 10.00 25.00

2004 Fleer Patchworks By the Numbers

STATED ODDS 1:24 HOBBY, 1:12 RETAIL
1 Albert Pujols 1.25 3.00
2 Derek Jeter 2.50 6.00
3 Mike Piazza 1.00 2.50
4 Nomar Garciaparra .60 1.50
5 Eric Gagne .40 1.00
6 Sammy Sosa 1.00 2.50
7 Josh Beckett .40 1.00
8 Vladimir Guerrero .60 1.50
9 Jose Reyes .60 1.50
10 Bret Boone .40 1.00
11 Alex Rodriguez Yanks 1.25 3.00
12 Randy Johnson 1.00 2.50
13 Chipper Jones 1.00 2.50
14 Tim Hudson .60 1.50
15 Rocco Baldelli .40 1.00

2004 Fleer Patchworks By the Numbers Patch

OVERALL GU ODDS 1:6 HOBBY, 1:36 RETAIL
STATED PRINT RUN 100 SERIAL #'d SETS
AP Albert Pujols 12.50 30.00
AR Alex Rodriguez 10.00 25.00
BB Bret Boone 6.00 15.00
CJ Chipper Jones 10.00 25.00
DJ Derek Jeter 10.00 25.00
EG Eric Gagne 6.00 15.00
JB Josh Beckett 6.00 15.00
JR Jose Reyes 6.00 15.00
MP Mike Piazza 10.00 25.00
NG Nomar Garciaparra 10.00 25.00
RB Rocco Baldelli 6.00 15.00
RJ Randy Johnson 10.00 25.00
SS Sammy Sosa 10.00 25.00
TH Tim Hudson 6.00 15.00
VG Vladimir Guerrero 10.00 25.00

2004 Fleer Patchworks Game Used Level 1

STATED PRINT RUN 200 SERIAL #'d SETS
*LEVEL 2: .5X TO 1.2X BASIC
LEVEL 2 PRINT RUN 100 SERIAL #'d SETS
*PATCH: 1.25X TO 3X BASIC
PATCH PRINT RUN 50 SERIAL #'d SETS
OVERALL GU ODDS 1:6 HOBBY, 1:36 RETAIL
AJ Andruw Jones 4.00 10.00
AP1 Andy Pettitte 4.00 10.00
AP2 Albert Pujols 6.00 15.00
AS Alfonso Soriano 3.00 8.00
BB Bret Boone 3.00 8.00
BW Bernie Williams 4.00 10.00
BZ Barry Zito 3.00 8.00
CD Carlos Delgado 3.00 8.00
DW Dontrelle Willis 4.00 10.00
GA Garret Anderson 3.00 8.00
HB Hank Blalock 3.00 8.00
JR Jose Reyes 3.00 8.00
LW Larry Walker 3.00 8.00
MP1 Mike Piazza 5.00 12.00
MP2 Mark Prior 4.00 10.00
RH Roy Halladay 3.00 8.00
SG Shawn Green 3.00 8.00
TG Troy Glaus 3.00 8.00
TH Torii Hunter 3.00 8.00

2004 Fleer Patchworks Licensed Apparel

STATED PRINT RUN 300 SERIAL #'d SETS
JSY TAG PRINT RUN 10 SERIAL #'d SETS
NO JSY TAG PRICING DUE TO SCARCITY
MLB LOGO PRINT RUN 1 SERIAL #'d SET
NO MLB LOGO PRICING DUE TO SCARCITY
*NAMEPLATE: 1.25X TO 3X BASIC
NAMEPLATE PRINT RUN 50 SERIAL #'d SETS
*NUMBER: .75X TO 2X BASIC
NUMBER PRINT RUN 100 SERIAL #'d SETS
*TEAM NAME: .75X TO 2X BASIC
TEAM NAME PRINT RUN 150 SER.#'d SETS
OVERALL GU ODDS 1:6 HOBBY, 1:36 RETAIL
AJ Andruw Jones 4.00 10.00
AK Austin Kearns 3.00 8.00
AP Albert Pujols 6.00 15.00
AR Alex Rodriguez 5.00 12.00
BB Bret Boone 3.00 8.00
DJ Derek Jeter 8.00 20.00
DW Dontrelle Willis 4.00 10.00
JB Jeff Bagwell 4.00 10.00
JT Jim Thome 4.00 10.00
MP1 Mike Piazza 5.00 12.00
MP2 Mark Prior 4.00 10.00
SS Sammy Sosa 4.00 10.00
TG Troy Glaus 3.00 8.00
TH1 Tim Hudson 3.00 8.00
TH2 Torii Hunter 3.00 8.00

2004 Fleer Patchworks National Pastime

STATED ODDS 1:72 HOBBY, 1:144 RETAIL
STATED PRINT RUN 250 SERIAL #'d SETS
1 Albert Pujols 1.50 4.00
2 Alex Rodriguez Yanks 1.50 4.00
3 Derek Jeter 3.00 8.00
4 Nomar Garciaparra .75 2.00
5 Jim Thome .75 2.00
6 Chipper Jones 1.25 3.00
7 Mark Prior .75 2.00
8 Ichiro Suzuki 1.50 4.00
9 Jeff Bagwell .75 2.00
10 Troy Glaus .50 1.25
11 Randy Johnson 1.25 3.00
12 Sammy Sosa 1.25 3.00
13 Austin Kearns .50 1.25
14 Miguel Cabrera 1.25 3.00
15 Vladimir Guerrero .75 2.00

2004 Fleer Patchworks National Patchtime

STATED PRINT RUN 350 SERIAL #'d SETS
*GOLD: 4X TO 1X BASIC
GOLD PRINT RUN 200 SERIAL #'d SETS
*PATCH: .75X TO 2X BASIC
PATCH PRINT RUN 100 SERIAL #'d SETS
OVERALL GU ODDS 1:6 HOBBY, 1:36 RETAIL
AK Austin Kearns 3.00 8.00
AP Albert Pujols 6.00 15.00
AR Alex Rodriguez 5.00 12.00
CJ Chipper Jones 4.00 10.00
DJ Derek Jeter 8.00 20.00
JB Jeff Bagwell 4.00 10.00
JT Jim Thome 4.00 10.00
MC Miguel Cabrera 4.00 10.00
MP Mark Prior 4.00 10.00
NG Nomar Garciaparra 5.00 12.00
RJ Randy Johnson 4.00 10.00
SS Sammy Sosa 4.00 10.00
TG Troy Glaus 3.00 8.00
VG Vladimir Guerrero 4.00 10.00

2004 Fleer Patchworks Stitches In Time

STATED ODDS 1:12 HOBBY, 1:6 RETAIL
1 Albert Pujols 1.25 3.00
2 Alex Rodriguez Yanks 1.25 3.00
3 Derek Jeter 2.50 6.00
4 Nomar Garciaparra .60 1.50
5 Jim Thome .60 1.50
6 Chipper Jones 1.00 2.50
7 Mark Prior .60 1.50
8 Eric Gagne .40 1.00
9 Jeff Bagwell .60 1.50
10 Troy Glaus .40 1.00
11 Randy Johnson 1.00 2.50
12 Sammy Sosa 1.00 2.50
13 Austin Kearns .40 1.00
14 Miguel Cabrera 1.00 2.50
15 Vladimir Guerrero .60 1.50
16 Mike Piazza 1.00 2.50
17 Jason Giambi .40 1.00
18 Tim Hudson .60 1.50
19 Carlos Delgado .40 1.00
20 Rocco Baldelli .40 1.00
21 Ichiro Suzuki 1.25 3.00
22 Barry Zito .60 1.50
23 Pedro Martinez .60 1.50
24 Torii Hunter .40 1.00
25 Andruw Jones .40 1.00

2004 Fleer Patchworks Stitches in Time Jersey

STATED PRINT RUN 350 SERIAL #'d SETS
*PATCH: .75X TO 2X BASIC
PATCH PRINT RUN 150 SERIAL #'d SETS
OVERALL GU ODDS 1:6 HOBBY, 1:36 RETAIL
AJ Andruw Jones 4.00 10.00
AK Austin Kearns 3.00 8.00
AP Albert Pujols 6.00 15.00
AR Alex Rodriguez 5.00 12.00
BZ Barry Zito 3.00 8.00
CD Carlos Delgado 3.00 8.00
CJ Chipper Jones 8.00 20.00
DJ Derek Jeter 8.00 20.00
EG Eric Gagne 3.00 8.00
JB Jeff Bagwell 4.00 10.00
JG Jason Giambi 3.00 8.00
JT Jim Thome 4.00 10.00
MC Miguel Cabrera 4.00 10.00
MP Mike Piazza 5.00 12.00
MP Mark Prior 4.00 10.00
NG Nomar Garciaparra 5.00 12.00
PM Pedro Martinez 4.00 10.00
RB Rocco Baldelli 3.00 8.00
RJ Randy Johnson 4.00 10.00
SS Sammy Sosa 4.00 10.00
TG Troy Glaus 3.00 8.00
TH1 Tim Hudson 3.00 8.00
TH2 Torii Hunter 3.00 8.00
VG Vladimir Guerrero 4.00 10.00

2005 Fleer Patchworks

COMP.SET w/o SP's (70) 15.00 40.00
COMMON (1-70) .30 .75
COMMON (71-90) .40 1.00
71-90 PRINT RUN 499 SERIAL #'d SETS
COMMON (91-100) .40 1.00
91-100 PRINT RUN 999 SERIAL #'d SETS
71-100 ODDS 1:8 HOBBY
1 Bobby Abreu .30 .75
2 Miguel Cabrera .75 2.00
3 J.D. Drew .30 .75
4 Justin Morneau .50 1.25
5 David Ortiz .75 2.00
6 Ivan Rodriguez .50 1.25
7 Jason Schmidt .30 .75
8 Frank Thomas .75 2.00
9 Travis Hafner .30 .75
10 Curt Schilling .50 1.25
11 Jim Edmonds .50 1.25
12 Randy Johnson .75 2.00
13 Jose Vidro .30 .75
14 Vernon Wells .30 .75
15 Lance Berkman .50 1.25
16 Khalil Greene .30 .75
17 Andruw Jones .30 .75
18 Mark Prior .50 1.25
19 Mark Teixeira .50 1.25
20 Jack Wilson .30 .75
21 Adrian Beltre .75 2.00
22 Lew Ford .30 .75
23 Shawn Green .30 .75
24 Juan Pierre .30 .75
25 Alfonso Soriano .50 1.25
26 Mike Sweeney .30 .75
27 Chipper Jones .75 2.00
28 Javy Lopez .30 .75
29 Victor Martinez .50 1.25
30 Kaz Matsui .30 .75
31 Bernie Williams .50 1.25
32 Kerry Wood .30 .75
33 Barry Zito .50 1.25
34 Austin Kearns .30 .75
35 Todd Helton .50 1.25
36 B.J. Upton .50 1.25
37 Jeff Bagwell .50 1.25
38 Pedro Martinez .50 1.25
39 Lyle Overbay .30 .75
40 Ichiro Suzuki 1.00 2.50
41 Jason Bay .30 .75
42 Bobby Crosby .30 .75
43 Vladimir Guerrero .50 1.25
44 Richie Sexson .30 .75
45 Johan Santana .50 1.25
46 Magglio Ordonez .50 1.25
47 Derek Jeter 2.00 5.00
48 Eric Gagne .30 .75
49 Albert Pujols 1.00 2.50
50 Jim Thome .50 1.25
51 Hideki Matsui 1.25 3.00
52 Torii Hunter .30 .75
53 Greg Maddux 1.00 2.50
54 Michael Young .30 .75
55 Carlos Beltran .50 1.25
56 Carl Crawford .50 1.25
57 Adam Dunn .50 1.25
58 Nomar Garciaparra .50 1.25
59 Mike Piazza .75 2.00
60 Alex Rodriguez 1.00 2.50
61 Scott Rolen .50 1.25
62 Ben Sheets .30 .75
63 Sammy Sosa .75 2.00
64 Hank Blalock .30 .75
65 Carlos Delgado .30 .75
66 Ken Griffey Jr. 1.50 4.00
67 Manny Ramirez .75 2.00
68 Miguel Tejada .50 1.25
69 Roger Clemens 1.00 2.50
70 Gary Sheffield .30 .75
71 Jon Knott PO .40 1.00
72 Ryan Raburn PO .40 1.00
73 Zack Greinke PO 1.25 3.00
74 David Aardsma PO .40 1.00
75 Justin Verlander PO RC 8.00 20.00
76 Andres Blanco PO .40 1.00
77 David Wright PO .75 2.00
78 Jeff Baker PO .40 1.00
79 Charlton Jimerson PO .40 1.00
80 Sean Burnett PO .40 1.00
81 Joey Gathright PO .40 1.00
82 Victor Diaz PO .40 1.00
83 Scott Kazmir PO 1.00 2.50
84 Edwin Encarnacion PO 1.00 2.50
85 J.D. Durbin PO .40 1.00
86 Nick Swisher PO .60 1.50
87 Casey Kotchman PO .40 1.00
88 Gavin Floyd PO .40 1.00
89 Josh Kroeger PO .40 1.00
90 Taylor Buchholz PO .40 1.00
91 Reggie Jackson LS .60 1.50
92 Nolan Ryan LS 3.00 8.00
93 Eddie Murray LS .60 1.50
94 Carlton Fisk LS .60 1.50
95 Mike Schmidt LS 1.50 4.00
96 Joe Morgan LS .60 1.50
97 Rod Carew LS .60 1.50
98 Harmon Killebrew LS 1.00 2.50
99 Tom Seaver LS .60 1.50
100 Brooks Robinson LS .60 1.50

2005 Fleer Patchworks Gold

*GOLD 1-70: 1.5X TO 4X BASIC
*GOLD 71-90: .6X TO 1.5X BASIC
*GOLD 91-100: .6X TO 1.5X BASIC
OVERALL PARALLEL ODDS 1:16 H
STATED PRINT RUN 99 SERIAL #'d SETS

2005 Fleer Patchworks Autoworks Copper

OVERALL AU ODDS 1:18 H
PRINT RUNS B/WN 75-250 COPIES PER
BL Brad Lidge/75 8.00 20.00
BU B.J. Upton/150 6.00 15.00
CC Carl Crawford/175 10.00 25.00
DW David Wright/250 6.00 15.00
JB Jason Bay/150 6.00 15.00
JBO Jeremy Bonderman/100 6.00 15.00
JD J.D. Durbin/100 4.00 10.00
JM Justin Morneau/175 6.00 15.00
JV Justin Verlander/100 20.00 50.00
MC Miguel Cabrera/75 20.00 50.00
RB Rocco Baldelli/100 6.00 15.00
SB Sean Burnett/100 4.00 10.00
TH Travis Hafner/150 6.00 15.00
VM Victor Martinez/100 6.00 15.00
ZG Zack Greinke/200 6.00 15.00

2005 Fleer Patchworks Autoworks Gold

*GOLD: .5X TO 1.2X COPPER p/r 150-250
OVERALL AU ODDS 1:18 H
STATED PRINT RUN 49 SERIAL #'d SETS
BS Ben Sheets 8.00 20.00
EB Ernie Banks 30.00 60.00
GF Gavin Floyd 5.00 12.00
HA Hank Aaron 150.00 250.00
JP Josh Phelps 5.00 12.00
LB Lance Berkman 12.50 30.00
LF Lew Ford 5.00 12.00
MCA Mike Cameron 5.00 12.00
MY Michael Young 8.00 20.00

2005 Fleer Patchworks Autoworks Silver

*SILVER: .4X TO 1X COPPER p/r 150-250
OVERALL AU ODDS 1:18 H
STATED PRINT RUN 99 SERIAL #'d SETS
BS Ben Sheets 6.00 15.00
JP Josh Phelps 4.00 10.00
LF Lew Ford 4.00 10.00
MCA Mike Cameron 4.00 10.00

2005 Fleer Patchworks By the Numbers

STATED ODDS 1:18 H, 1:24 R
1 Roy Oswalt .60 1.50
2 Hideki Matsui 1.50 4.00
3 Curt Schilling .60 1.50
4 Mike Piazza 1.00 2.50
5 Alex Rodriguez 1.25 3.00
6 Vladimir Guerrero .60 1.50
7 Victor Martinez .60 1.50
8 Adrian Beltre 1.00 2.50
9 Johnny Estrada .40 1.00
10 Ken Griffey Jr. 2.00 5.00
11 Sammy Sosa 1.00 2.50
12 Ichiro Suzuki 1.25 3.00
13 Roger Clemens 1.25 3.00
14 David Ortiz 1.00 2.50
15 Johan Santana .60 1.50
16 Pedro Martinez .60 1.50
17 Austin Kearns .40 1.00
18 Randy Johnson 1.00 2.50
19 Nomar Garciaparra .60 1.50
20 Albert Pujols 1.25 3.00

2005 Fleer Patchworks By the Numbers Jersey Die Cut

STATED PRINT RUN 199 SERIAL #'d SETS
*JERSEY: .4X TO 1X JSY DC
JERSEY RANDOM IN RETAIL PACKS
NO CLEMENS JSY PRICE DUE TO SCARCITY
JERSEY TAG PRINT RUN 1 #'d SET
NO JSY TAG PRICING DUE TO SCARCITY
OVERALL GAME-USED ODDS 1:9 H
AB Adrian Beltre 2.00 5.00
AP Albert Pujols 6.00 15.00
CS Curt Schilling 3.00 8.00
DO David Ortiz 3.00 8.00
HM Hideki Matsui 8.00 20.00
JE Johnny Estrada 2.00 5.00
JS Johan Santana 4.00 10.00
MP Mike Piazza/116 UER 4.00 10.00
PM Pedro Martinez 3.00 8.00
RC Roger Clemens 4.00 10.00
RJ Randy Johnson 4.00 10.00
RO Roy Oswalt 2.00 5.00
SS Sammy Sosa 4.00 10.00
VG Vladimir Guerrero 4.00 10.00

2005 Fleer Patchworks By the Numbers Patch

*PATCH: .75X TO 2X JSY DC
OVERALL GAME-USED ODDS 1:9 H
STATED PRINT RUN 99 SERIAL #'d SETS
AK Austin Kearns/78 UER 4.00 10.00

2005 Fleer Patchworks By the Numbers Patch Die Cut

*PATCH DC: 1.25X TO 3X JSY DC
OVERALL GAME-USED ODDS 1:9 H
STATED PRINT RUN 25 SERIAL #'d SETS
AK Austin Kearns 6.00 15.00

2005 Fleer Patchworks Heart of the Team

STATED ODDS 1:108 H, 1:360 R
1 Braves 1.25 3.00
Marlins
2 Red Sox 3.00 8.00
Yankees
3 Cardinals 1.50 4.00
Astros
4 Angels .75 2.00
A's
5 Phillies 1.25 3.00
Mets
6 Twins 1.25 3.00
White Sox
7 Reds 2.50 6.00
Cubs
8 Mariners 1.50 4.00
Rangers
9 Orioles .75 2.00
Nationals
10 Blue Jays .75 2.00
Devil Rays

2005 Fleer Patchworks Heart of the Team Jersey

STATED PRINT RUN 199 SERIAL #'d SETS
PATCH PRINT RUN 15 SERIAL #'d SETS
NO PATCH PRICING DUE TO SCARCITY
OVERALL GAME-USED ODDS 1:9 H
ABFM Braves 10.00 25.00
Marlins/132 UER
PPNM Phillies 10.00 25.00
Mets/132 UER
SCHA Cardinals 15.00 40.00
Astros/132 UER

2005 Fleer Patchworks Jersey

*JERSEY: .2X TO .5X PATCH
RANDOM INSERTS IN RETAIL PACKS
GS Gary Sheffield 2.00 5.00

2005 Fleer Patchworks Patch

STATED PRINT RUN 99 SERIAL #'d SETS
*PATCH DC: .6X TO 1.5X PATCH
PATCH DC PRINT RUN 49 SERIAL #'d SETS
OVERALL GAME-USED ODDS 1:9 H
AS Alfonso Soriano/73 UER 4.00 10.00
BW Bernie Williams 6.00 15.00
DO David Ortiz/51 UER 6.00 15.00
DW Dontrelle Willis 4.00 10.00
DWR David Wright 15.00 40.00
JB Josh Beckett 4.00 10.00
KW Kerry Wood 4.00 10.00
MARK Mark Prior 6.00 15.00
MIKE Mike Piazza 8.00 20.00
MR Manny Ramirez 6.00 15.00
MY Michael Young 4.00 10.00
SS Shannon Stewart 4.00 10.00
TH Torii Hunter 4.00 10.00

2005 Fleer Patchworks Dual Jersey Die Cut

STATED PRINT RUN 199 SERIAL #'d SETS
*DUAL JSY: .4X TO 1X DUAL JSY DC
DUAL JSY RANDOM IN RETAIL PACKS
GSBW JSY NOT PRICED DUE TO SCARCITY
DUAL MLB LOGO PRINT RUN 1 #'d SET
NO DUAL MLB LOGO PRICING AVAILABLE
DUAL PATCH PRINT RUN 25 #'d SETS
NO DUAL PATCH PRICING AVAILABLE
DUAL PATCH DC PRINT RUN 15 #'d SETS
NO DUAL PATCH DC PRICING AVAILABLE
DWJB D.Willis/J.Beckett 3.00 8.00
DWMP D.Wright/M.Piazza 6.00 15.00
GSBW G.Sheffield/B.Williams 4.00 10.00
KWMP K.Wood/M.Prior 4.00 10.00
MRDO M.Ramirez/D.Ortiz 6.00 15.00
MYAS M.Young/A.Soriano 3.00 8.00
SSTH S.Stewart/T.Hunter 3.00 8.00

2005 Fleer Patchworks Property of

STATED ODDS 1:6 H, 1:6 R
1 Vladimir Guerrero .60 1.50
2 Luis Gonzalez .40 1.00
3 Chipper Jones 1.00 2.50
4 Miguel Tejada .60 1.50
5 David Ortiz 1.00 2.50
6 Kerry Wood .40 1.00
7 Frank Thomas 1.00 2.50
8 Adam Dunn .60 1.50
9 Victor Martinez .60 1.50
10 Todd Helton .60 1.50
11 Ivan Rodriguez .60 1.50
12 Miguel Cabrera 1.00 2.50
13 Jeff Bagwell .60 1.50
14 Mike Sweeney .40 1.00
15 Eric Gagne .40 1.00
16 Lyle Overbay .40 1.00
17 Johan Santana .60 1.50
18 Mike Piazza 1.00 2.50
19 Derek Jeter 2.50 6.00
20 Bobby Crosby .40 1.00
21 Jim Thome .60 1.50
22 Jason Bay .40 1.00
23 Khalil Greene .40 1.00
24 Jason Schmidt .40 1.00
25 Ichiro Suzuki 1.25 3.00
26 Albert Pujols 1.25 3.00
27 B.J. Upton .60 1.50
28 Hank Blalock .40 1.00
29 Vernon Wells .40 1.00
30 Jose Vidro .40 1.00

2005 Fleer Patchworks Property of Jersey Die Cut

STATED PRINT RUN 199 SERIAL #'d SETS
*JERSEY: .4X TO 1X JSY DC
JERSEY RANDOM IN RETAIL PACKS
MLB LOGO PRINT RUN 1 SERIAL #'d SET
NO MLB LOGO PRICING AVAILABLE
OVERALL GAME-USED ODDS 1:9 H
AP Albert Pujols 6.00 15.00
BU B.J. Upton 2.00 5.00
CJ Chipper Jones 4.00 10.00
DO David Ortiz 4.00 10.00
EG Eric Gagne 2.00 5.00
FT Frank Thomas 4.00 10.00
HB Hank Blalock 2.00 5.00
IR Ivan Rodriguez 3.00 8.00
JB Jeff Bagwell 3.00 8.00
JBA Jason Bay 2.00 5.00
JS Johan Santana 4.00 10.00
JSC Jason Schmidt 2.00 5.00
JT Jim Thome 3.00 8.00
KG Khalil Greene 3.00 8.00
KW Kerry Wood 2.00 5.00
LG Luis Gonzalez 2.00 5.00
LO Lyle Overbay/86 UER 2.00 5.00
MC Miguel Cabrera 3.00 8.00
MP Mike Piazza 4.00 10.00
MT Miguel Tejada 2.00 5.00
VG Vladimir Guerrero 4.00 10.00
VW Vernon Wells 2.00 5.00

2005 Fleer Patchworks Property of Patch

*PATCH: .75X TO 2X JSY DC
OVERALL GAME-USED ODDS 1:9 H
STATED PRINT RUN 99 SERIAL #'d SETS
AD Adam Dunn/42 UER 4.00 10.00
MS Mike Sweeney/77 UER 4.00 10.00

2005 Fleer Patchworks Property of Patch Die Cut

*DIE CUT: 1.25X TO 3X JSY DC
OVERALL GAME-USED ODDS 1:9 H
STATED PRINT RUN 25 SERIAL #'d SETS
NO PRICING DUE TO SCARCITY
AD Adam Dunn 6.00 15.00
MS Mike Sweeney 6.00 15.00

2005 Fleer Patchworks Property of Patch Nameplate

*PATCH NAMEPLATE: 1.25X TO 3X JSY DC
OVERALL GAME-USED ODDS 1:9 H
STATED PRINT RUN 49 SERIAL #'d SETS
MS Mike Sweeney 6.00 15.00

2001 Fleer Platinum

COMPLETE SERIES 1 (301) 100.00 200.00
COMPLETE SERIES 2 (300) 100.00 200.00
COMP.SER.1 w/o SP's (250) 15.00 40.00
COMP.SER.2 w/o SP's (200) 15.00 40.00
COMMON (1-250/302-501) .10 .30
COMMON PROSPECT (251-280) .75 2.00
COMMON AS (281-300) .75 2.00
251-300 ODDS 1:6 HOB, 1:2 JUM, 1:1 RACK
CARD 301 RANDOM IN HOBBY/JUMBO
CARD 301 PR.RUN 1500 SERIAL #'d COPIES
COMMON CARD (502-601) .75 2.00
502-601 ODDS 1:3 H, 1:2 J, 1:1 RACK, 1:6 R
CARDS 402 AND 529 SWITCHED ON SHEETS
SER.2 SET w/o SP's EXCLUDES CARD 402
SER.2 SET w/o SP's INCLUDES CARD 529
1 Bobby Abreu .10 .30
2 Brad Radke .10 .30
3 Bill Mueller .10 .30
4 Adam Eaton .10 .30
5 Antonio Alfonseca .10 .30
6 Manny Ramirez Sox .20 .50
7 Adam Kennedy .10 .30
8 Jose Valentin .10 .30
9 Jaret Wright .10 .30
10 Aramis Ramirez .10 .30
11 Jeff Kent .10 .30
12 Juan Encarnacion .10 .30
13 Sandy Alomar Jr. .10 .30
14 Joe Randa .10 .30
15 Darryl Kile .10 .30
16 Darren Dreifort .10 .30
17 Matt Kinney .10 .30
18 Pokey Reese .10 .30
19 Ryan Klesko .10 .30
20 Shawn Estes .10 .30
21 Moises Alou .10 .30
22 Edgar Renteria .10 .30
23 Chuck Knoblauch .10 .30
24 Carl Everett .10 .30
25 Garret Anderson .10 .30
26 Shane Reynolds .10 .30
27 Billy Koch .10 .30
28 Carlos Febles .10 .30
29 Brian Anderson .10 .30
30 Armando Rios .10 .30
31 Ryan Kohlmeier .10 .30
32 Steve Finley .10 .30
33 Brady Anderson .10 .30
34 Cal Ripken 1.00 2.50
35 Paul Konerko .10 .30
36 Chuck Finley .10 .30
37 Rick Ankiel .10 .30
38 Mariano Rivera .30 .75
39 Corey Koskie .10 .30
40 Cliff Floyd .10 .30
41 Kevin Appier .10 .30
42 Henry Rodriguez .10 .30
43 Mark Kotsay .10 .30
44 Brook Fordyce .10 .30
45 Brad Ausmus .10 .30
46 Alfonso Soriano .20 .50
47 Ray Lankford .10 .30
48 Keith Foulke .10 .30
49 Rich Aurilia .10 .30
50 Alex Rodriguez .50 1.25
51 Eric Byrnes .10 .30
52 Travis Fryman .10 .30
53 Jeff Bagwell .20 .50
54 Scott Rolen .20 .50
55 Matt Lawton .10 .30
56 Brad Fullmer .10 .30
57 Tony Batista .10 .30
58 Nate Rolison .10 .30
59 Carlos Lee .10 .30
60 Rafael Furcal .10 .30
61 Jay Bell .10 .30
62 Jimmy Rollins .10 .30
63 Derrek Lee .20 .50
64 Andres Galarraga .10 .30
65 Derek Bell .10 .30
66 Tim Salmon .20 .50
67 Travis Lee .10 .30
68 Kevin Millwood .10 .30
69 Albert Belle .10 .30
70 Kazuhiro Sasaki .10 .30
71 Al Leiter .10 .30
72 Britt Reames .10 .30
73 Carlos Beltran .10 .30
74 Curt Schilling .10 .30
75 Curtis Leskanic .10 .30
76 Jeremy Giambi .10 .30
77 Adrian Beltre .10 .30
78 David Segui .10 .30
79 Mike Lieberthal .10 .30
80 Brian Giles .10 .30
81 Marvin Benard .10 .30
82 Aaron Sele .10 .30
83 Kenny Lofton .10 .30
84 Doug Glanville .10 .30
85 Kris Benson .10 .30
86 Richie Sexson .10 .30
87 Javy Lopez .10 .30
88 Doug Mientkiewicz .10 .30
89 Peter Bergeron .10 .30
90 Gary Sheffield .10 .30
91 Derek Lowe .10 .30
92 Tom Glavine .20 .50
93 Lance Berkman .10 .30
94 Chris Singleton .10 .30
95 Mike Lowell .10 .30
96 Luis Gonzalez .10 .30
97 Dante Bichette .10 .30
98 Mike Sirotka .10 .30
99 Julio Lugo .10 .30
100 Juan Gonzalez .10 .30
101 Craig Biggio .20 .50
102 Armando Benitez .10 .30
103 Greg Maddux .50 1.25
104 Mark Grace .20 .50
105 John Smoltz .20 .50
106 J.T. Snow .10 .30
107 Al Martin .10 .30
108 Danny Graves .10 .30
109 Barry Bonds .75 2.00
110 Lee Stevens .10 .30
111 Pedro Martinez .20 .50
112 Shawn Green .10 .30
113 Bret Boone .10 .30
114 Matt Stairs .10 .30
115 Tino Martinez .20 .50
116 Rusty Greer .10 .30
117 Mike Bordick .10 .30
118 Garrett Stephenson .10 .30
119 Edgar Martinez .20 .50
120 Ben Grieve .10 .30
121 Milton Bradley .10 .30
122 Aaron Boone .10 .30
123 Ruben Mateo .10 .30
124 Ken Griffey Jr. .60 1.50
125 Russell Branyan .10 .30
126 Shannon Stewart .10 .30
127 Fred McGriff .20 .50
128 Ben Petrick .10 .30
129 Kevin Brown .10 .30
130 B.J. Surhoff .10 .30
131 Mark McGwire .75 2.00
132 Carlos Guillen .10 .30
133 Adrian Brown .10 .30
134 Mike Sweeney .10 .30
135 Eric Milton .10 .30
136 Cristian Guzman .10 .30
137 Ellis Burks .10 .30
138 Fernando Tatis .10 .30
139 Bengie Molina .10 .30
140 Tony Gwynn .40 1.00
141 Jeromy Burnitz .10 .30
142 Miguel Tejada .10 .30
143 Raul Mondesi .10 .30
144 Jeffrey Hammonds .10 .30
145 Pat Burrell .10 .30
146 Frank Thomas .30 .75
147 Eric Munson .10 .30
148 Mike Hampton .10 .30
149 Mike Cameron .10 .30
150 Jim Thome .20 .50
151 Mike Mussina .20 .50
152 Rick Helling .10 .30
153 Ken Caminiti .10 .30
154 John VanderWal .10 .30
155 Denny Neagle .10 .30
156 Robb Nen .10 .30
157 Jose Canseco .20 .50
158 Mo Vaughn .10 .30
159 Phil Nevin .10 .30
160 Pat Hentgen .10 .30
161 Sean Casey .10 .30
162 Greg Vaughn .10 .30
163 Trot Nixon .10 .30
164 Roberto Hernandez .10 .30
165 Vinny Castilla .10 .30
166 Robin Ventura .10 .30
167 Alex Ochoa .10 .30
168 Orlando Hernandez .10 .30
169 Luis Castillo .10 .30
170 Quilvio Veras .10 .30
171 Troy O'Leary .10 .30
172 Livan Hernandez .10 .30
173 Roger Cedeno .10 .30
174 Jose Vidro .10 .30
175 John Olerud .10 .30
176 Richard Hidalgo .10 .30
177 Eric Chavez .10 .30
178 Fernando Vina .10 .30
179 Chris Stynes .10 .30
180 Bobby Higginson .10 .30
181 Bruce Chen .10 .30
182 Omar Vizquel .20 .50
183 Rey Ordonez .10 .30
184 Trevor Hoffman .10 .30
185 Jeff Cirillo .10 .30
186 Billy Wagner .10 .30
187 David Ortiz .30 .75
188 Tim Hudson .10 .30
189 Tony Clark .10 .30
190 Larry Walker .10 .30
191 Eric Owens .10 .30
192 Aubrey Huff .10 .30
193 Royce Clayton .10 .30
194 Todd Walker .10 .30
195 Rafael Palmeiro .20 .50
196 Todd Hundley .10 .30
197 Roger Clemens .60 1.50
198 Jeff Weaver .10 .30
199 Dean Palmer .10 .30
200 Geoff Jenkins .10 .30
201 Matt Clement .10 .30
202 David Wells .10 .30
203 Chan Ho Park .10 .30
204 Hideo Nomo .30 .75
205 Bartolo Colon .10 .30
206 John Wetteland .10 .30
207 Corey Patterson .10 .30
208 Freddy Garcia .10 .30
209 David Cone .10 .30
210 Rondell White .10 .30
211 Carl Pavano .10 .30
212 Charles Johnson .10 .30
213 Ron Coomer .10 .30
214 Matt Williams .10 .30
215 Jay Payton .10 .30
216 Nick Johnson .10 .30
217 Deivi Cruz .10 .30
218 Scott Elarton .10 .30
219 Neifi Perez .10 .30
220 Jason Isringhausen .10 .30
221 Jose Cruz Jr. .10 .30
222 Gerald Williams .10 .30
223 Timo Perez .10 .30
224 Damion Easley .10 .30
225 Jeff D'Amico .10 .30
226 Preston Wilson .10 .30
227 Robert Person .10 .30
228 Jacque Jones .10 .30
229 Johnny Damon .20 .50
230 Tony Womack .10 .30
231 Adam Piatt .10 .30
232 Brian Jordan .10 .30
233 Ben Davis .10 .30
234 Kerry Wood .10 .30
235 Mike Piazza .50 1.25
236 David Justice .10 .30
237 Dave Veres .10 .30
238 Eric Young .10 .30
239 Juan Pierre .10 .30
240 Gabe Kapler .10 .30
241 Ryan Dempster .10 .30
242 Dmitri Young .10 .30
243 Jorge Posada .20 .50
244 Eric Karros .10 .30
245 J.D. Drew .10 .30
246 Todd Zeile .10 .30
247 Mark Quinn .10 .30
248 Kenny Kelly .10 .30
249 Jermaine Dye .10 .30
250 Barry Zito .20 .50
251 J.Hart .75 2.00
L.Barnes
252 Ichiro Suzuki RC 10.00 25.00
253 Tsuyoshi Shinjo RC 1.25 3.00
254 A.Hernandez RC .75 2.00
J.Barnes
255 J.Tyner .75 2.00
J.Brewer
256 B.Buchanan .75 2.00
L.Rivas
257 B.Abernathy .75 2.00
J.Ortiz
258 M.Giles .75 2.00
K.Ginter
259 J.Randolph RC .75 2.00
T.Redman
260 D.Sardinha .75 2.00
D.Espinosa
261 J.Beckett 1.25 3.00
C.House
262 J.Cust .75 2.00
H.Bocachica
263 E.Snead RC .75 2.00
A.Escobar
264 C.Richard .75 2.00
V.Wells
265 P.Feliz .75 2.00
X.Nady
266 B.Inge 1.50 4.00
J.Crede
267 B.Sheets 1.50 4.00
R.Oswalt
268 Drew Henson RC 1.25 3.00
269 C.Sabathia .75 2.00
J.Miller
270 D.Eckstein .75 2.00
J.Grabowski
271 D.Brown .75 2.00
C.Wakeland
272 Junior Spivey RC .75 2.00
273 J.Uribe RC 1.25 3.00
E.Pena
274 C.Pena .75 2.00
J.Romano
275 W.Betemit RC 1.50 4.00
W.Abreu RC
276 J.Mieses RC .75 2.00
N.Neugebauer
277 S.Hillenbrand .75 2.00
D.Stenson
278 J.Sandberg .75 2.00
T.Hall
279 Jay Gibbons RC 1.25 3.00
280 P.Ozuna .75 2.00
S.Perez
281 Nomar Garciaparra AS 3.00 8.00
282 Derek Jeter AS 5.00 12.00
283 Jason Giambi AS .75 2.00
284 Magglio Ordonez AS .75 2.00
285 Ivan Rodriguez AS 1.25 3.00
286 Troy Glaus AS .75 2.00
287 Carlos Delgado AS .75 2.00
288 Darin Erstad AS .75 2.00
289 Bernie Williams AS 1.25 3.00
290 Roberto Alomar AS 1.25 3.00
291 Barry Larkin AS 1.25 3.00
292 Chipper Jones AS 2.00 5.00
293 Vladimir Guerrero AS 2.00 5.00
294 Sammy Sosa AS 2.00 5.00
295 Todd Helton AS 1.25 3.00
296 Randy Johnson AS 2.00 5.00
297 Jason Kendall AS .75 2.00
298 Jim Edmonds AS .75 2.00
299 Andruw Jones AS 1.25 3.00
300 Edgardo Alfonzo AS .75 2.00
301 Albert Pujols/1500 RC 20.00 50.00
302 Shawn Wooten .10 .30
303 Todd Walker .10 .30
304 Brian Buchanan .10 .30
305 Jim Edmonds .10 .30
306 Jarrod Washburn .10 .30
307 Jose Rijo .10 .30
308 Tim Raines .10 .30
309 Matt Morris .10 .30
310 Troy Glaus .10 .30
311 Barry Larkin .20 .50
312 Javier Vazquez .10 .30
313 Placido Polanco .10 .30
314 Darin Erstad .10 .30
315 Marty Cordova .10 .30
316 Vladimir Guerrero .30 .75
317 Kerry Robinson .10 .30
318 Byung-Hyun Kim .10 .30
319 C.C. Sabathia .10 .30
320 Edgardo Alfonzo .10 .30
321 Jason Tyner .10 .30
322 Reggie Sanders .10 .30
323 Roberto Alomar .20 .50
324 Matt Lawton .10 .30
325 Brent Abernathy .10 .30
326 Randy Johnson .30 .75
327 Todd Helton .20 .50
328 Andy Pettitte .20 .50
329 Josh Beckett .20 .50
330 Mark DeRosa .10 .30
331 Jose Ortiz .10 .30
332 Derek Jeter .75 2.00
333 Toby Hall .10 .30
334 Wes Helms .10 .30
335 Jose Macias .10 .30
336 Bernie Williams .20 .50
337 Ivan Rodriguez .20 .50
338 Chipper Jones .30 .75
339 Brandon Inge .10 .30
340 Jason Giambi .10 .30
341 Frank Catalanotto .10 .30
342 Andruw Jones .20 .50
343 Carlos Hernandez .10 .30
344 Jermaine Dye .10 .30
345 Mike Lamb .10 .30
346 Ken Caminiti .10 .30
347 A.J. Burnett .10 .30
348 Terrence Long .10 .30
349 Ruben Sierra .10 .30
350 Marcus Giles .10 .30
351 Wade Miller .10 .30
352 Mark Mulder .10 .30
353 Carlos Delgado .10 .30
354 Chris Richard .10 .30
355 Daryle Ward .10 .30
356 Brad Penny .10 .30
357 Vernon Wells .10 .30
358 Jason Johnson .10 .30
359 Tim Redding .10 .30
360 Marlon Anderson .10 .30
361 Carlos Pena .10 .30
362 Nomar Garciaparra .50 1.25
363 Roy Oswalt .30 .75
364 Todd Ritchie .10 .30
365 Jose Mesa .10 .30
366 Shea Hillenbrand .10 .30
367 Dee Brown .10 .30
368 Jason Kendall .10 .30
369 Vinny Castilla .10 .30
370 Fred McGriff .20 .50
371 Neifi Perez .10 .30
372 Xavier Nady .10 .30
373 Abraham Nunez .10 .30
374 Jon Lieber .10 .30
375 Paul LoDuca .10 .30
376 Bubba Trammell .10 .30
377 Brady Clark .10 .30
378 Joel Pineiro .10 .30
379 Mark Grudzielanek .10 .30
380 D'Angelo Jimenez .10 .30
381 Junior Herndon .10 .30
382 Magglio Ordonez .10 .30
383 Ben Sheets .20 .50
384 John Vander Wal .10 .30
385 Pedro Astacio .10 .30
386 Jose Canseco .20 .50
387 Jose Hernandez .10 .30
388 Eric Davis .10 .30
389 Sammy Sosa .30 .75
390 Mark Buehrle .20 .50
391 Mark Loretta .10 .30
392 Andres Galarraga .10 .30
393 Scott Spiezio .10 .30
394 Joe Crede .30 .75
395 Luis Rivas .10 .30
396 David Bell .10 .30
397 Einar Diaz .10 .30
398 Adam Dunn .20 .50
399 A.J. Pierzynski .10 .30
400 Jamie Moyer .10 .30
401 Nick Johnson .10 .30
402 Freddy Garcia CT SP 4.00 10.00
403 Hideo Nomo CT .10 .30
404 Mark Mulder CT .10 .30
405 Steve Sparks CT .10 .30
406 Mariano Rivera CT .20 .50
407 M.Buerhle .10 .30
M.Mussina CT
408 Randy Johnson CT .20 .50
409 Randy Johnson CT .20 .50
410 C.Schilling .10 .30
M.Morris CT
411 Greg Maddux CT .30 .75
412 Robb Nen CT .10 .30
413 Randy Johnson CT .20 .50
414 Barry Bonds CT .40 1.00
415 Jason Giambi CT .10 .30
416 Ichiro Suzuki CT 2.50 6.00
417 Ichiro Suzuki CT 2.50 6.00
418 Alex Rodriguez CT .25 .60
419 Bret Boone CT .10 .30
420 Ichiro Suzuki CT 2.50 6.00
421 Alex Rodriguez CT .25 .60
422 Jason Giambi CT .10 .30
423 Alex Rodriguez CT .25 .60
424 Larry Walker CT .10 .30
425 Rich Aurilia CT .10 .30
426 Barry Bonds CT .40 1.00
427 Sammy Sosa CT .20 .50
428 J.Rollins .10 .30
J.Pierre CT
429 Sammy Sosa CT .20 .50
430 Lance Berkman CT .10 .30
431 Sammy Sosa CT .20 .50
432 Carlos Delgado TL .10 .30
433 Alex Rodriguez TL .25 .60
434 Greg Vaughn TL .10 .30
435 Albert Pujols TL 8.00 20.00
436 Ichiro Suzuki TL 2.50 6.00
437 Barry Bonds TL .40 1.00
438 Phil Nevin TL .10 .30
439 Brian Giles TL .10 .30
440 Bobby Abreu TL .10 .30
441 Jason Giambi TL .10 .30
442 Derek Jeter TL .40 1.00
443 Mike Piazza TL .30 .75
444 Vladimir Guerrero TL .20 .50
445 Corey Koskie TL .10 .30
446 Richie Sexson TL .10 .30
447 Shawn Green TL .10 .30
448 Mike Sweeney TL .10 .30
449 Jeff Bagwell TL .10 .30
450 Cliff Floyd TL .10 .30
451 Roger Cedeno TL .10 .30
452 Todd Helton TL .10 .30
453 Juan Gonzalez TL .10 .30
454 Sean Casey TL .10 .30
455 Magglio Ordonez TL .10 .30
456 Sammy Sosa TL .20 .50
457 Manny Ramirez Sox TL .20 .50
458 Jeff Conine TL .10 .30
459 Chipper Jones TL .20 .50
460 Luis Gonzalez TL .10 .30
461 Troy Glaus TL .10 .30
462 I.Rodriguez .10 .30
J.Romano FF
463 L.Gonzalez .10 .30
J.Cust FF
464 J.Thome .10 .30
C.Sabathia FF
465 J.Giambi .10 .30
J.Hart FF
466 J.Bagwell .30 .75
R.Oswalt FF
467 S.Sosa .20 .50
C.Patterson FF
468 M.Piazza .30 .75
A.Escobar FF
469 K.Griffey Jr. .40 1.00
A.Dunn FF
470 R.Clemens .30 .75
N.Johnson FF
471 C.Floyd .10 .30
J.Beckett FF
472 C.Ripken .50 1.25
J.Hairston Jr. FF
473 P.Nevin .10 .30
X.Nady FF
474 S.Rolen .10 .30
J.Rollins FF
475 B.Larkin .10 .30
D.Espinosa FF
476 L.Walker .10 .30
J.Ortiz FF
477 C.Jones .20 .50
M.Giles FF
478 C.Biggio .10 .30
K.Ginter FF
479 M.Ordonez .10 .30
A.Rowand FF
480 A.Rodriguez .25 .60
C.Pena FF
481 D.Jeter .40 1.00
A.Soriano FF
482 Erubiel Durazo PG .10 .30
483 Bernie Williams PG .10 .30
484 Team Photo PG .10 .30
485 Team Photo PG .10 .30
486 Andy Pettitte PG .10 .30
487 Curt Schilling PG .10 .30
488 Randy Johnson PG .20 .50
489 Rudolph Guiliani PG .30 .75
490 George Bush PG 2.00 5.00
491 Roger Clemens PG .30 .75
492 Mariano Rivera PG .20 .50
493 Tino Martinez PG .10 .30
494 Derek Jeter PG .40 1.00
495 Scott Brosius PG .10 .30
496 Alfonso Soriano PG .10 .30
497 Matt Williams PG .10 .30
498 Tony Womack PG .10 .30
499 Luis Gonzalez PG .10 .30
500 Arizona Diamondbacks PG .30 .75
501 Johnson .20 .50
Schilling MVP PG
502 Josh Fogg RC .75 2.00
503 Elpidio Guzman .75 2.00
504 Corky Miller RC .75 2.00
505 Cesar Crespo RC .75 2.00
506 Carlos Garcia RC .75 2.00
507 Carlos Valderrama RC .75 2.00
508 Joe Kennedy RC 1.25 3.00
509 Henry Mateo RC .75 2.00
510 Brandon Duckworth RC .75 2.00
511 Ichiro Suzuki 8.00 20.00
512 Zach Day RC .75 2.00
513 Ryan Freel RC 1.25 3.00
514 Brian Lawrence RC .75 2.00
515 Alexis Gomez RC .75 2.00
516 Will Ohman RC .75 2.00
517 Juan Diaz RC .75 2.00
518 Juan Moreno RC .75 2.00
519 Rob Mackowiak RC 1.25 3.00
520 Horacio Ramirez RC 1.25 3.00
521 Albert Pujols 15.00 40.00
522 Tsuyoshi Shinjo 1.25 3.00
523 Ryan Drese RC 1.25 3.00
524 Angel Berroa RC 1.25 3.00
525 Josh Towers RC 1.25 3.00
526 Junior Spivey 1.25 3.00
527 Greg Miller RC .75 2.00
528 Esix Snead .75 2.00
529 Mark Prior DP RC 3.00 8.00
530 Drew Henson 1.25 3.00
531 Brian Reith RC .75 2.00
532 Andres Torres RC .75 2.00
533 Casey Fossum RC .75 2.00
534 Wilmy Caceres RC .75 2.00
535 Matt White RC .75 2.00
536 Wilkin Ruan RC .75 2.00
537 Rick Bauer RC .75 2.00
538 Morgan Ensberg RC 1.50 4.00
539 Geronimo Gil RC .75 2.00
540 Dewon Brazelton RC .75 2.00
541 Johnny Estrada RC 1.25 3.00
542 Claudio Vargas RC .75 2.00
543 Donaldo Mendez .75 2.00
544 Kyle Lohse RC 1.25 3.00
545 Nate Frese RC .75 2.00
546 Christian Parker RC .75 2.00
547 Blaine Neal RC .75 2.00
548 Travis Hafner RC 4.00 10.00
549 Billy Sylvester RC .75 2.00
550 Adam Pettyjohn RC .75 2.00
551 Bill Ortega RC .75 2.00
552 Jose Acevedo RC .75 2.00
553 Steve Green RC .75 2.00
554 Jay Gibbons 1.25 3.00
555 Bert Snow RC .75 2.00
556 Erick Almonte RC .75 2.00
557 Jeremy Owens RC .75 2.00
558 Sean Douglass RC .75 2.00
559 Jason Smith RC .75 2.00
560 Ricardo Rodriguez RC .75 2.00
561 Mark Teixeira RC 5.00 12.00
562 Tyler Walker RC .75 2.00
563 Juan Uribe 1.25 3.00
564 Bud Smith RC .75 2.00
565 Angel Santos RC .75 2.00
566 Brandon Lyon RC .75 2.00
567 Eric Hinske RC 1.25 3.00
568 Nick Punto RC .75 2.00
569 Winston Abreu .75 2.00
570 Jason Phillips RC .75 2.00
571 Rafael Soriano RC .75 2.00
572 Wilson Betemit 1.50 4.00
573 Endy Chavez RC .75 2.00
574 Juan Cruz RC .75 2.00
575 Cory Aldridge RC .75 2.00
576 Adrian Hernandez .75 2.00
577 Brandon Larson RC .75 2.00
578 Bret Prinz RC .75 2.00
579 Jackson Melian RC .75 2.00
580 Dave Maurer RC .75 2.00
581 Jason Michaels RC .75 2.00
582 Travis Phelps RC .75 2.00
583 Cody Ransom RC .75 2.00
584 Benito Baez RC .75 2.00
585 Brian Roberts RC 1.50 4.00
586 Nate Teut RC .75 2.00
587 Jack Wilson RC 1.25 3.00
588 Willie Harris RC .75 2.00
589 Martin Vargas RC .75 2.00
590 Steve Torrealba RC .75 2.00
591 Stubby Clapp RC .75 2.00
592 Dan Wright .75 2.00
593 Mike Rivera RC .75 2.00
594 Luis Pineda RC .75 2.00
595 Lance Davis RC .75 2.00
596 Ramon Vazquez RC .75 2.00
597 Dustan Mohr RC .75 2.00
598 Troy Mattes RC .75 2.00
599 Grant Balfour RC .75 2.00
600 Jared Fernandez RC .75 2.00
601 Jorge Julio RC .75 2.00

2001 Fleer Platinum Parallel

*STARS 1-250/302-501: 2.5X TO 6X BASIC
*SUBSET RC'S 402-501: 2X TO 5X BASIC
1-250/302-501 PRINT 201 SERIAL #'d SETS
251-300/502-601 PRINT 21 SERIAL #'d SETS
251-300 NO PRICING DUE TO SCARCITY
502-601 NO PRICING DUE TO SCARCITY
CARD 301 DOES NOT EXIST IN PARALLEL SET
435 Albert Pujols TL 75.00 200.00

2001 Fleer Platinum 20th Anniversary Reprints

COMPLETE SET (18) 30.00 60.00
SER.1 ODDS 1:8 HOB, 1:4 JUM, 1:2 RACK
1 Cal Ripken 82F 5.00 12.00
2 Wade Boggs 83F 1.00 2.50
3 Ryne Sandberg 83F 2.50 6.00
4 Tony Gwynn 83F 2.00 5.00
5 Don Mattingly 84F 4.00 10.00
6 Roger Clemens 85F 3.00 8.00
7 Kirby Puckett 85F 1.50 4.00
8 Jose Canseco 86LL 1.00 2.50
9 Barry Bonds 87F 4.00 10.00
10 Ken Griffey Jr. 89F 3.00 8.00
11 Sammy Sosa 90F 1.50 4.00
12 Ivan Rodriguez 91UU 1.00 2.50
13 Jeff Bagwell 91UU 1.00 2.50
14 J.D. Drew 98UPD 1.00 2.50
15 Troy Glaus 98UPD 1.00 2.50
16 Rick Ankiel 99UPD 1.00 2.50
17 Xavier Nady 00GL 1.00 2.50
18 Jose Ortiz 00GL 1.00 2.50

2001 Fleer Platinum Classic Combinations

1-10 STATED PRINT RUN 250 SETS
11-20 STATED PRINT RUN 500 SETS
21-30 STATED PRINT RUN 1000 SETS
31-40 STATED PRINT RUN 2000 SETS
1 D.Jeter 6.00 15.00
A.Rodriguez
2 W.Mays 5.00 12.00
W.McCovey
3 L.Gehrig 6.00 15.00
B.Ruth
4 M.McGwire 5.00 12.00
K.Griffey Jr.
5 J.Bench 2.50 6.00
R.Campanella
6 T.Williams 5.00 12.00
N.Garciaparra
7 Y.Berra 2.50 6.00
M.Piazza
8 E.Banks 2.50 6.00
S.Sosa
9 N.Ryan 8.00 20.00
R.Johnson
10 R.Clemente 6.00 15.00
V.Guerrero
11 S.Musial 4.00 10.00
L.Gehrig
12 B.Mazeroski 5.00 12.00
R.Clemente
13 E.Banks 2.50 6.00
A.Rodriguez
14 P.Rizzuto 5.00 12.00
D.Jeter
15 M.Piazza 2.00 5.00
J.Bench
16 M.McGwire 3.00 8.00
S.Sosa
17 T.Williams 4.00 10.00
T.Gwynn
18 E.Mathews 3.00 8.00
M.Schmidt
19 B.Bonds 4.00 10.00
W.Mays
20 N.Ryan 6.00 15.00
P.Martinez
21 B.Bonds 3.00 8.00
K.Griffey Jr.
22 W.McCovey 1.25 3.00
R.Jackson
23 R.Clemente 4.00 10.00
S.Sosa
24 W.Mays 3.00 8.00
E.Banks
25 E.Mathews 1.50 4.00
C.Jones
26 M.Schmidt 2.50 6.00
B.Robinson
27 S.Musial 2.50 6.00
M.McGwire
28 T.Williams 3.00 8.00
R.Maris
29 Y.Berra 1.50 4.00
R.Campanella
30 J.Bench 1.50 4.00
T.Perez
31 B.Mazeroski 1.00 2.50
J.Carter
32 M.Piazza 1.50 4.00
R.Campanella
33 E.Banks 1.50 4.00
C.Biggio
34 F.Robinson 1.00 2.50
B.Robinson
35 M.Schmidt 2.50 6.00
S.Rolen
36 R.Maris 2.50 6.00
M.McGwire
37 S.Musial 2.50 6.00
T.Gwynn
38 T.Williams 3.00 8.00
B.Terry
39 D.Jeter 4.00 10.00
R.Jackson
40 Y.Berra 1.50 4.00
B.Dickey

2001 Fleer Platinum Classic Combinations Retail

COMPLETE SET (40) 60.00 150.00
SER.1 STATED ODDS 1:20 RETAIL
1 D.Jeter 3.00 8.00
A.Rodriguez
2 W.Mays 2.50 6.00
W.McCovey
3 L.Gehrig 3.00 8.00
B.Ruth
4 M.McGwire 2.50 6.00
K.Griffey Jr.
5 J.Bench 1.25 3.00
R.Campanella
6 T.Williams 2.50 6.00
N.Garciaparra
7 Y.Berra 1.25 3.00
M.Piazza
8 E.Banks 1.25 3.00
S.Sosa
9 N.Ryan 4.00 10.00
R.Johnson
10 R.Clemente 3.00 8.00
V.Guerrero
11 S.Musial 2.50 6.00
L.Gehrig
12 B.Mazeroski 3.00 8.00
R.Clemente
13 E.Banks 1.50 4.00
A.Rodriguez
14 P.Rizzuto 3.00 8.00
D.Jeter
15 M.Piazza 1.25 3.00
J.Bench
16 M.McGwire 2.00 5.00
S.Sosa
17 T.Williams 2.50 6.00
T.Gwynn
18 E.Mathews 2.00 5.00
M.Schmidt
19 B.Bonds 2.50 6.00
W.Mays
20 N.Ryan 4.00 10.00
P.Martinez
21 B.Bonds 2.50 6.00
K.Griffey Jr.
22 W.McCovey 1.00 2.50
R.Jackson
23 R.Clemente 3.00 8.00
S.Sosa
24 W.Mays 2.50 6.00
E.Banks
25 E.Mathews 1.25 3.00
C.Jones
26 M.Schmidt 2.00 5.00
B.Robinson
27 S.Musial 2.00 5.00
M.McGwire
28 T.Williams 2.50 6.00
R.Maris
29 Y.Berra 1.25 3.00
R.Campanella
30 J.Bench 1.25 3.00
T.Perez
31 B.Mazeroski .75 2.00
J.Carter
32 M.Piazza 1.25 3.00
R.Campanella
33 E.Banks 1.25 3.00
C.Biggio
34 F.Robinson .75 2.00
B.Robinson
35 M.Schmidt 2.00 5.00
S.Rolen
36 R.Maris 2.00 5.00
M.McGwire
37 S.Musial 2.00 5.00
T.Gwynn
38 T.Williams 2.50 6.00

B.Terry
39 D.Jeter 3.00 8.00
R.Jackson
40 Y.Berra 1.25 3.00
B.Dickey

2001 Fleer Platinum Grandstand Greats
COMPLETE SET (20) 40.00 80.00
SER.1 ODDS 1:12 HOB, 1:6 JUM, 1:3 RACK
1 Chipper Jones 1.25 3.00
2 Alex Rodriguez 1.50 4.00
3 Jeff Bagwell .75 2.00
4 Troy Glaus .75 2.00
5 Manny Ramirez Sox .75 2.00
6 Derek Jeter 3.00 8.00
7 Tony Gwynn 1.50 4.00
8 Greg Maddux 2.00 5.00
9 Nomar Garciaparra 2.00 5.00
10 Sammy Sosa 1.25 3.00
11 Mike Piazza 2.00 5.00
12 Barry Bonds 3.00 8.00
13 Mark McGwire 3.00 8.00
14 Vladimir Guerrero 1.25 3.00
15 Ivan Rodriguez .75 2.00
16 Ken Griffey Jr. 2.50 6.00
17 Todd Helton .75 2.00
18 Cal Ripken 4.00 10.00
19 Pedro Martinez .75 2.00
20 Frank Thomas 1.25 3.00

2001 Fleer Platinum Lumberjacks
SER.2 STATED ODDS 1:1 RACK
1 Roberto Alomar 6.00 15.00
2 Moises Alou 4.00 10.00
3 Adrian Beltre 4.00 10.00
4 Lance Berkman 4.00 10.00
5 Barry Bonds 10.00 25.00
6 Bret Boone 4.00 10.00
8 Adam Dunn 6.00 15.00
9 Darin Erstad 4.00 10.00
10 Cliff Floyd 4.00 10.00
11 Brian Giles 4.00 10.00
12 Luis Gonzalez 4.00 10.00
13 Vladimir Guerrero 6.00 15.00
14 Cristian Guzman 4.00 10.00
15 Tony Gwynn 6.00 15.00
16 Todd Helton 6.00 15.00
17 Drew Henson 6.00 15.00
18 Derek Jeter 10.00 25.00
19 Chipper Jones 6.00 15.00
20 Mike Piazza 6.00 15.00
21 Albert Pujols 20.00 50.00
22 Manny Ramirez Sox 6.00 15.00
24 Ivan Rodriguez 6.00 15.00
25 Gary Sheffield 4.00 10.00
26 Mike Sweeney 4.00 10.00
27 Larry Walker 4.00 10.00

2001 Fleer Platinum Lumberjacks Autographs
STATED PRINT RUN 100 SETS
UNNUMBERED 8-CARD SET
6 Barry Bonds 100.00 250.00
8 Adam Dunn 10.00 25.00
12 Luis Gonzalez 10.00 25.00
18 Derek Jeter 175.00 350.00
21 Albert Pujols 400.00 1000.00
23 Cal Ripken 40.00 80.00

2001 Fleer Platinum Nameplates
SER.1 STATED ODDS 1:12 JUMBO
PRINT RUNS LISTED BELOW
NO PRICING ON QTY OF 25 OR LESS
ASTERISK CARDS LACK SERIAL #ING
1 Carlos Beltran/90 10.00 25.00
2 Adrian Beltre/55 * 10.00 25.00
4 J.D. Drew/170 10.00 25.00
5 Darin Erstad/39 10.00 25.00
6 Troy Glaus/85 10.00 25.00
7 Tom Glavine/125 15.00 40.00
8 Vladimir Guerrero/80 10.00 25.00
9 Vladimir Guerrero/90 10.00 25.00
10 Tony Gwynn/35 40.00 80.00
11 Tony Gwynn/65 20.00 50.00
12 Tony Gwynn/70 20.00 50.00
13 Jeffrey Hammonds/135 10.00 25.00
14 Randy Johnson/99 10.00 25.00
15 Chipper Jones/95 15.00 40.00
16 Javy Lopez/49 * 10.00 25.00
17 Greg Maddux/180 20.00 50.00
18 Edgar Martinez/87 10.00 25.00
19 Pedro Martinez/120 10.00 25.00
20 Kevin Millwood/130 10.00 25.00
21 Stan Musial/30 60.00 120.00
22 Mike Mussina/91 15.00 40.00
23 Manny Ramirez Sox/75 15.00 40.00
24 Manny Ramirez Sox/105 15.00 40.00
28 Cal Ripken/110 30.00 60.00
29 Ivan Rodriguez/177 10.00 25.00
30 Scott Rolen/65 10.00 25.00
31 Scott Rolen/125 15.00 40.00
32 Nolan Ryan/40 30.00 60.00
33 Nolan Ryan/55 30.00 60.00
34 Curt Schilling/110 * 10.00 25.00
35 Frank Thomas/35 10.00 25.00
36 Frank Thomas/75 10.00 25.00
37 Frank Thomas/80 10.00 25.00
38 Robin Ventura/99 10.00 25.00
39 Larry Walker/79 10.00 25.00
40 Larry Walker/85 10.00 25.00
41 Matt Williams/175 10.00 25.00
42 Dave Winfield/80 10.00 25.00

2001 Fleer Platinum National Patch Time
SER.1 AND 2 ODDS 1:24 HOBBY, 1:36 RETAIL
MUSSINA & RICE NOT INTENDED FOR RELEASE
1 Edgardo Alfonzo S1 1.25 3.00
2 Brady Anderson Pants S1 1.25 3.00
3 Jeff Bagwell S2 2.00 5.00
4 Adrian Beltre S2 3.00 8.00
5 Wade Boggs S1 2.00 5.00
6 Barry Bonds S2 5.00 12.00
7 George Brett S1 6.00 15.00
8 Eric Chavez S2 1.25 3.00
9 Jeff Cirillo S1 1.25 3.00
10 Roger Clemens Gray S1 5.00 12.00
11 Roger Clemens White S2 5.00 12.00
12 Pedro Martinez S1 2.00 5.00
12 J.D. Drew S2 1.25 3.00
13 Darin Erstad S2 1.25 3.00
14 Carl Everett S1 1.25 3.00
15 Rollie Fingers Pants S1 2.00 5.00
16 Freddy Garcia White S1 1.25 3.00
17 Freddy Garcia White S2 1.25 3.00
18 Jason Giambi SP S2 1.25 3.00
19 Juan Gonzalez SP S2 1.25 3.00
20 Mark Grace S2 2.00 5.00
21 Shawn Green S2 1.25 3.00
22 Ben Grieve S2 1.25 3.00
23 Vladimir Guerrero S2 3.00 8.00
24 Tony Gwynn White S1 3.00 8.00
25 Tony Gwynn White S2 3.00 8.00
26 Todd Helton S2 2.00 5.00
27 Randy Johnson S2 3.00 8.00
28 Chipper Jones S2 3.00 8.00
29 David Justice S2 1.25 3.00
30 Jason Kendall S1 1.25 3.00
31 Jeff Kent S2 1.25 3.00
32 Paul LoDuca S2 1.25 3.00
33 Greg Maddux White S1 5.00 12.00
34 Greg Maddux Gray-White S2 5.00 12.00
36 Fred McGriff S1 2.00 5.00
37 Eddie Murray S1 2.00 5.00
38 Mike Mussina S2 SP 2.00 5.00
39 John Olerud S2 1.25 3.00
40 Magglio Ordonez Gray S1 1.25 3.00
41 Magglio Ordonez Gray SP S2 1.25 3.00
42 Adam Piatt S1 1.25 3.00
43 Jorge Posada S2 2.00 5.00
44 Manny Ramirez Sox S1 3.00 8.00
45 Cal Ripken Black S1 8.00 20.00
46 Cal Ripken Gray-White S2 8.00 20.00
47 Mariano Rivera S2 3.00 8.00
48 Ivan Rodriguez Blue S1 2.00 5.00
49 Ivan Rodriguez Blue-WhiteS2 2.00 5.00
50 Scott Rolen S2 2.00 5.00
51 Nolan Ryan S1 8.00 20.00
52 Kazuhiro Sasaki S2 1.25 3.00
53 Mike Schmidt S1 5.00 12.00
54 Tom Seaver S1 2.00 5.00
55 Aaron Sele S2 1.25 3.00
56 Gary Sheffield S2 1.25 3.00
57 Ozzie Smith S1 4.00 10.00
58 John Smoltz S2 2.00 5.00
59 Frank Thomas S2 3.00 8.00
60 Mo Vaughn S2 1.25 3.00
61 Robin Ventura S2 1.25 3.00
62 Rondell White S1 1.25 3.00
63 Bernie Williams S2 2.00 5.00
64 Dave Winfield S1 2.00 5.00
65 Carl Yastrzemski Mail-In SP 5.00 12.00
NNO Todd Walker 1.25 3.00
NNO Jim Rice 2.00 5.00

2001 Fleer Platinum Prime Numbers
SER.2 STATED ODDS 1:12 JUMBO
1 Jeff Bagwell 6.00 15.00
2 Cal Ripken 30.00 60.00
3 Barry Bonds 20.00 50.00
5 Derek Jeter 20.00 50.00
6 Tony Gwynn 10.00 25.00
7 Kazuhiro Sasaki 4.00 10.00
8 Chan Ho Park 4.00 10.00
10 Chipper Jones 6.00 15.00
11 Pedro Martinez 6.00 15.00
12 Mike Piazza 12.50 30.00
13 Carlos Delgado 4.00 10.00
15 Roger Clemens 15.00 40.00

2001 Fleer Platinum Rack Pack Autographs
ONE AU OR 99-01 AUTO.PER SER.1 RACK
1998 E-X SIGNATURE 2001 ALSO INSERTED
1992 CLEMENS AU'S ALSO INSERTED
PRINT RUNS LISTED BELOW AS AVAILABLE
ASTERISK CARDS LACK SERIAL NUMBERING
NO PRICING ON QTY OF 25 OR LESS
1 H.Aaron 1997 SI/90 125.00 200.00
3 R.Clemens 1998 SITN/125 50.00 100.00
4 J.Cruz Jr. 1997 No Brand 2.00 5.00
7 B.Gibson 1998 SITN/300 10.00 25.00
8 B.Grieve No Brand/100 * 2.00 5.00
9 T.Gwynn 1998 SITN/125 20.00 50.00
10 W.Helms 1997 No Brand 2.00 5.00
11 H.Killebrew 1998 SITN/300 20.00 50.00
12 P.Konerko No Brand/135 * 10.00 25.00
13 W.Mays 1997 SI/115 75.00 150.00
14 W.Mays 1998 SITN/120 75.00 150.00
15 K.Puckett 1997 SI/105 50.00 100.00
17 B.Robinson 1998 SITN/40 30.00 60.00
18 F.Robinson 1997 SI/115 10.00 25.00
19 S.Rolen 1998 SITN/150 10.00 25.00
20 A.Rodriguez 1997 SI/94 40.00 80.00
21 A.Rod 1998 Promo/150 40.00 80.00

2001 Fleer Platinum Tickets Autographs
3 S.Carlton 300 Win 9/23/83 15.00 30.00

2001 Fleer Platinum Winning Combinations
STATED PRINT RUNS LISTED BELOW
1 D.Jeter 4.00 10.00
O.Smith/2000
2 B.Bonds 3.00 8.00
M.McGwire/500
3 I.Suzuki 25.00 60.00
A.Pujols/250
4 T.Williams 3.00 8.00
M.Ramirez Sox/1000
5 T.Gwynn 8.00 20.00
C.Ripken/250
6 M.Piazza 5.00 12.00
D.Jeter/500
7 D.Winfield 1.50 4.00
T.Gwynn/2000
8 H.Nomo 6.00 15.00
I.Suzuki/2000
9 C.Ripken 5.00 12.00
O.Smith/1000
10 M.McGwire 8.00 20.00
A.Pujols/2000
11 J.Bagwell 1.00 2.50
C.Biggio/1000
12 B.Bonds 4.00 10.00
B.Bonds/250
13 T.Williams 5.00 12.00
S.Musial/250
14 B.Ruth 5.00 12.00
R.Jackson/500
15 K.Sasaki 8.00 20.00
I.Suzuki/500
16 N.Ryan 6.00 15.00
R.Clemens/500
17 R.Clemens 6.00 15.00
D.Jeter/250
18 M.Piazza 1.50 4.00
I.Rodriguez/1000
19 V.Guerrero 1.50 4.00
S.Sosa/2000
20 B.Bonds 4.00 10.00
S.Sosa/250
21 R.Clemens 2.50 6.00
G.Maddux/1000
22 J.Gonzalez 1.50 4.00
M.Ramirez Sox/2000
23 T.Helton 1.00 2.50
J.Giambi/2000
24 J.Bagwell 1.00 2.50
L.Berkman/2000
25 M.Sweeney 3.00 8.00
G.Brett/1000
26 L.Gonzalez 4.00 10.00
B.Ruth/2000
27 B.Skowron 5.00 12.00
D.Mattingly/250
28 Y.Berra 5.00 12.00
C.Ripken/2000
29 P.Martinez 1.25 3.00
Nomar/500
30 T.Kluszewski 1.00 2.50
F.Rob/1000
31 C.Schilling 1.50 4.00
R.Johnson/1000
32 K.Griffey Jr. 6.00 15.00
C.Ripken/500
33 M.Piazza 1.50 4.00
J.Bench/1000
34 S.Musial 10.00 25.00
A.Pujols/500
35 J.Robinson 2.00 5.00
N.Fox/500
36 L.Grove 1.50 4.00
S.Carlton/250
37 T.Cobb 4.00 10.00
T.Gwynn/250
38 A.Pujols 8.00 20.00
F.Robinson/1000
39 R.Sandberg 4.00 10.00
S.Sosa/500
40 C.Ripken 8.00 20.00
L.Gehrig/250

2001 Fleer Platinum Winning Combinations Blue
SER.2 ODDS 1:12 JUM, 1:6 RACK, 1:20 RET
CARDS FEATURE BLUE BORDERS
1 D.Jeter 2.50 6.00
O.Smith
2 B.Bonds 1.50 4.00
M.McGwire
3 I.Suzuki 20.00 50.00
A.Pujols
4 T.Williams 2.00 5.00
M.Ramirez Sox
5 T.Gwynn 3.00 8.00
C.Ripken
6 M.Piazza 2.50 6.00
D.Jeter
7 D.Winfield 1.00 2.50
T.Gwynn
8 H.Nomo 4.00 10.00
I.Suzuki
9 C.Ripken 3.00 8.00
O.Smith
10 M.McGwire 5.00 12.00
A.Pujols
11 J.Bagwell .60 1.50
C.Biggio
12 B.Bonds 1.50 4.00
B.Bonds
13 T.Williams 2.00 5.00
S.Musial
14 B.Ruth 2.50 6.00
R.Jackson
15 K.Sasaki 5.00 12.00
I.Suzuki
16 N.Ryan 3.00 8.00
R.Clemens
17 R.Clemens 2.50 6.00
D.Jeter
18 M.Piazza 1.00 2.50
I.Rodriguez
19 V.Guerrero 1.00 2.50
S.Sosa
20 B.Bonds 1.50 4.00
S.Sosa
21 R.Clemens 1.50 4.00
G.Maddux
22 J.Gonzalez 1.00 2.50
M.Ramirez Sox
23 T.Helton .60 1.50
J.Giambi
24 J.Bagwell .60 1.50
L.Berkman
25 M.Sweeney 2.00 5.00
G.Brett
26 L.Gonzalez 2.50 6.00
B.Ruth
27 B.Skowron 2.00 5.00
D.Mattingly
28 Y.Berra 3.00 8.00
C.Ripken
29 P.Martinez .60 1.50
Nomar
30 T.Kluszewski .60 1.50
F.Robinson
31 C.Schilling 1.00 2.50
R.Johnson
32 K.Griffey Jr. 3.00 8.00
C.Ripken
33 M.Piazza 1.00 2.50
J.Bench
34 S.Musial 6.00 15.00
A.Pujols
35 J.Robinson 1.00 2.50
N.Fox
36 L.Grove .60 1.50
S.Carlton
37 T.Cobb 1.50 4.00
T.Gwynn
38 A.Pujols 5.00 12.00
F.Robinson
39 R.Sandberg 2.00 5.00
S.Sosa
40 C.Ripken 3.00 8.00
L.Gehrig

2002 Fleer Platinum
COMPLETE SET (301) 100.00 200.00
COMP.SET w/o SP's (250) 10.00 25.00
COMMON CARD (1-250) .10 .30
COMMON CARD (251-260) 1.25 3.00
COMMON CARD (261-270) 1.25 3.00
COMMON CARD (271-302) 1.25 3.00
251-300 ODDS 1:3 HOBBY, 1:2 JUMBO
251-300 ODDS 1:1 RACK, 1:6 RETAIL
301-302 2X TOUGHER THAN 251-300
280 NOT INTENDED FOR PUBLIC RELEASE
1986 BONDS EXCH.RANDOM IN HOB/RET
1986 BONDS EXCH.DEADLINE 04/30/03
1 Garret Anderson .10 .30
2 Randy Johnson .30 .75
3 Chipper Jones .30 .75
4 David Cone .10 .30
5 Corey Patterson .10 .30
6 Carlos Lee .10 .30
7 Barry Larkin .20 .50
8 Jim Thome .20 .50
9 Larry Walker .10 .30
10 Randall Simon .10 .30
11 Charles Johnson .10 .30
12 Richard Hidalgo .10 .30
13 Mark Quinn .10 .30
14 Paul LoDuca .10 .30
15 Cristian Guzman .10 .30
16 Orlando Cabrera .10 .30
17 Al Leiter .10 .30
18 Nick Johnson .10 .30
19 Eric Chavez .10 .30
20 Miguel Tejada .10 .30
21 Mike Lieberthal .10 .30
22 Rob Mackowiak .10 .30
23 Ryan Klesko .10 .30
24 Jeff Kent .10 .30
25 Edgar Martinez .20 .50
26 Steve Kline .10 .30
27 Toby Hall .10 .30
28 Rusty Greer .10 .30
29 Jose Cruz Jr. .10 .30
30 Darin Erstad .10 .30
31 Reggie Sanders .10 .30
32 Javy Lopez .10 .30
33 Carl Everett .10 .30
34 Sammy Sosa .30 .75
35 Magglio Ordonez .10 .30
36 Todd Walker .10 .30
37 Omar Vizquel .20 .50
38 Matt Anderson .10 .30
39 Jeff Weaver .10 .30
40 Derrek Lee .20 .50
41 Julio Lugo .10 .30
42 Joe Randa .10 .30
43 Chan Ho Park .10 .30
44 Torii Hunter .10 .30
45 Vladimir Guerrero .30 .75
46 Rey Ordonez .10 .30
47 Tino Martinez .20 .50
48 Johnny Damon Sox .20 .50
49 Barry Zito .10 .30
50 Robert Person .10 .30
51 Aramis Ramirez .10 .30
52 Mark Kotsay .10 .30
53 Jason Schmidt .10 .30
54 Jamie Moyer .10 .30
55 David Justice .10 .30
56 Aubrey Huff .10 .30
57 Rick Helling .10 .30
58 Carlos Delgado .10 .30
59 Troy Glaus .10 .30
60 Curt Schilling .10 .30
61 Greg Maddux .50 1.25
62 Nomar Garciaparra .50 1.25
63 Kerry Wood .10 .30
64 Frank Thomas .30 .75
65 Dmitri Young .10 .30
66 Alex Ochoa .10 .30
67 Jose Macias .10 .30
68 Antonio Alfonseca .10 .30
69 Mike Lowell .10 .30
70 Wade Miller .10 .30
71 Mike Sweeney .10 .30
72 Gary Sheffield .10 .30
73 Corey Koskie .10 .30
74 Lee Stevens .10 .30
75 Jay Payton .10 .30
76 Mike Mussina .20 .50
77 Jermaine Dye .10 .30
78 Bobby Abreu .10 .30
79 Scott Rolen .20 .50
80 Todd Ritchie .10 .30
81 D'Angelo Jimenez .10 .30
82 Robb Nen .10 .30
83 John Olerud .10 .30
84 Matt Morris .10 .30
85 Joe Kennedy .10 .30
86 Gabe Kapler .10 .30
87 Chris Carpenter .10 .30
88 David Eckstein .10 .30
89 Matt Williams .10 .30
90 John Smoltz .20 .50
91 Pedro Martinez .20 .50
92 Eric Young .10 .30
93 Jose Valentin .10 .30
94 Erubiel Durazo .10 .30
95 Jeff Cirillo .10 .30
96 Brandon Inge .10 .30
97 Josh Beckett .10 .30
98 Preston Wilson .10 .30
99 Damian Jackson .10 .30
100 Adrian Beltre .10 .30
101 Jeromy Burnitz .10 .30
102 Joe Mays .10 .30
103 Michael Barrett .10 .30
104 Mike Piazza .50 1.25
105 Brady Anderson .10 .30
106 Jason Giambi Yankees .10 .30
107 Marlon Anderson .10 .30
108 Jimmy Rollins .10 .30
109 Jack Wilson .10 .30
110 Brian Lawrence .10 .30
111 Russ Ortiz .10 .30
112 Kazuhiro Sasaki .10 .30
113 Placido Polanco .10 .30
114 Damian Rolls .10 .30
115 Rafael Palmeiro .20 .50
116 Brad Fullmer .10 .30
117 Tim Salmon .20 .50
118 Tony Womack .10 .30
119 Tony Batista .10 .30
120 Trot Nixon .10 .30
121 Mark Buehrle .10 .30
122 Derek Jeter .75 2.00
123 Ellis Burks .10 .30
124 Mike Hampton .10 .30
125 Roger Cedeno .10 .30
126 A.J. Burnett .10 .30
127 Moises Alou .10 .30
128 Billy Wagner .10 .30
129 Kevin Brown .10 .30
130 Jose Hernandez .10 .30
131 Doug Mientkiewicz .10 .30
132 Javier Vazquez .10 .30
133 Tsuyoshi Shinjo .10 .30
134 Andy Pettitte .20 .50
135 Tim Hudson .10 .30
136 Pat Burrell .10 .30
137 Brian Giles .10 .30
138 Kevin Young .10 .30
139 Xavier Nady .10 .30
140 J.T. Snow .10 .30
141 Aaron Sele .10 .30
142 Albert Pujols .60 1.50
143 Jason Tyner .10 .30
144 Ivan Rodriguez .20 .50
145 Raul Mondesi .10 .30
146 Matt Lawton .10 .30
147 Rafael Furcal .10 .30
148 Jeff Conine .10 .30
149 Hideo Nomo .30 .75
150 Jose Canseco .20 .50
151 Aaron Boone .10 .30
152 Bartolo Colon .10 .30
153 Todd Helton .20 .50
154 Tony Clark .10 .30
155 Pablo Ozuna .10 .30
156 Jeff Bagwell .20 .50
157 Carlos Beltran .10 .30
158 Shawn Green .10 .30
159 Geoff Jenkins .10 .30
160 Eric Milton .10 .30
161 Jose Vidro .10 .30
162 Robin Ventura .10 .30
163 Jorge Posada .20 .50
164 Terrence Long .10 .30
165 Brandon Duckworth .10 .30
166 Chad Hermansen .10 .30
167 Ben Davis .10 .30
168 Phil Nevin .10 .30
169 Bret Boone .10 .30
170 J.D. Drew .10 .30
171 Edgar Renteria .10 .30
172 Randy Winn .10 .30
173 Alex Rodriguez .40 1.00
174 Shannon Stewart .10 .30
175 Steve Finley .10 .30
176 Marcus Giles .10 .30
177 Jay Gibbons .10 .30
178 Manny Ramirez .20 .50
179 Ray Durham .10 .30
180 Sean Casey .10 .30
181 Travis Fryman .10 .30
182 Denny Neagle .10 .30
183 Deivi Cruz .10 .30
184 Luis Castillo .10 .30
185 Lance Berkman .10 .30
186 Dee Brown .10 .30
187 Jeff Shaw .10 .30
188 Mark Loretta .10 .30
189 David Ortiz .30 .75
190 Edgardo Alfonzo .10 .30
191 Roger Clemens .60 1.50
192 Mariano Rivera .30 .75
193 Jeremy Giambi .10 .30
194 Johnny Estrada .10 .30
195 Craig Wilson .10 .30
196 Adam Eaton .10 .30
197 Rich Aurilia .10 .30
198 Mike Cameron .10 .30
199 Jim Edmonds .10 .30
200 Fernando Vina .10 .30
201 Greg Vaughn .10 .30
202 Mike Young .30 .75
203 Vernon Wells .10 .30
204 Luis Gonzalez .10 .30
205 Tom Glavine .20 .50
206 Chris Richard .10 .30
207 Jon Lieber .10 .30
208 Keith Foulke .10 .30
209 Rondell White .10 .30
210 Bernie Williams .20 .50
211 Juan Pierre .10 .30
212 Juan Encarnacion .10 .30
213 Ryan Dempster .10 .30
214 Tim Redding .10 .30
215 Jeff Suppan .10 .30
216 Mark Grudzielanek .10 .30
217 Richie Sexson .10 .30
218 Brad Radke .10 .30
219 Armando Benitez .10 .30
220 Orlando Hernandez .10 .30
221 Alfonso Soriano .10 .30
222 Mark Mulder .10 .30
223 Travis Lee .10 .30
224 Jason Kendall .10 .30
225 Trevor Hoffman .10 .30
226 Barry Bonds .75 2.00
227 Freddy Garcia .10 .30
228 Darryl Kile .10 .30
229 Ben Grieve .10 .30
230 Frank Catalanotto .10 .30
231 Ruben Sierra .10 .30
232 Homer Bush .10 .30
233 Mark Grace .20 .50
234 Andruw Jones .20 .50
235 Brian Roberts .10 .30
236 Fred McGriff .20 .50
237 Paul Konerko .10 .30
238 Ken Griffey Jr. .60 1.50
239 John Burkett .10 .30
240 Juan Uribe .10 .30
241 Bobby Higginson .10 .30
242 Cliff Floyd .10 .30
243 Craig Biggio .20 .50
244 Neifi Perez .10 .30
245 Eric Karros .10 .30
246 Ben Sheets .10 .30
247 Tony Armas Jr. .10 .30
248 Mo Vaughn .10 .30
249 David Wells .10 .30
250 Juan Gonzalez .10 .30
251 Barry Bonds DD 3.00 8.00
252 Sammy Sosa DD 1.25 3.00
253 Ken Griffey Jr. DD 2.50 6.00
254 Roger Clemens DD 2.50 6.00
255 Greg Maddux DD 2.00 5.00
256 Chipper Jones DD 1.25 3.00
257 A.Rod 2.00 5.00
Jeter
Nomar DD
258 Roberto Alomar DD 1.25 3.00
259 Jeff Bagwell DD 1.25 3.00
260 Mike Piazza DD 2.00 5.00
261 Mark Teixeira BB 1.50 4.00
262 Mark Prior BB 1.50 4.00
263 Alex Escobar BB 1.25 3.00
264 C.C. Sabathia BB 1.25 3.00
265 Drew Henson BB 1.25 3.00
266 Wilson Betemit BB 1.25 3.00
267 Roy Oswalt BB 1.25 3.00
268 Adam Dunn BB 1.25 3.00
269 Bud Smith BB 1.25 3.00
270 Dewon Brazelton BB 1.25 3.00
271 B.Backe RC 1.25 3.00
J.Standridge
272 W.Rodriguez 1.25 3.00
C.Hernandez
273 G.Gil 1.25 3.00
L.Rivera
274 C.Pena 1.25 3.00
J.Cedeno
275 A.Kearns 1.25 3.00
B.Broussard
276 J.De La Rosa RC 1.25 3.00
K.Kelly
277 R.Drese 1.50 4.00
V.Martinez
278 J.Pinero 1.25 3.00
N.Cornejo
279 D.Kelton 1.25 3.00
C.Zambrano
281 D.Bridges 1.25 3.00
W.Ruan
282 W.Pena 1.25 3.00
B.Claussen
283 J.Jennings 1.25 3.00
R.Reyes RC
284 S.Green 1.25 3.00
A.Amezaga
285 E.Hinske 1.25 3.00
F.Lopez
286 A.Machado RC 1.25 3.00
B.Baisley
287 C.Garcia 1.25 3.00
S.Douglass
288 P.Strange 1.25 3.00
J.Seo
289 M.Thames 1.25 3.00
A.Graman
290 M.Childers RC 1.25 3.00
H.Izquierdo RC
291 R.Calloway RC 1.25 3.00
A.Walker RC
292 J.House 1.25 3.00
J.Davis
293 R.Anderson 1.25 3.00
R.Soriano
294 M.Bynum 1.25 3.00
D.Tankersley
295 K.Ainsworth 1.25 3.00
C.Valderrama
296 B.Hall 1.25 3.00
C.Guerrero
297 M.Olivo 1.25 3.00
D.Wright
298 M.Byrd 1.25 3.00
J.Padilla RC
299 J.Cruz 1.25 3.00
B.Christensen
300 A.Johnson 1.25 3.00
M.Restovich
301 So Taguchi SP RC 1.25 3.00
302 Kazuhisa Ishii SP RC 1.25 3.00
NNO B.Bonds 1986 AU/73 250.00 400.00

2002 Fleer Platinum Parallel
*PARALLEL 1-250: 2.5X TO 6X BASIC
1-250 PRINT RUN 202 SERIAL #'d SETS
251-302 PRINT RUN 22 SERIAL #'d SETS
251-302 NO PRICING DUE TO SCARCITY
CARD NUMBER 280 DOES NOT EXIST

2002 Fleer Platinum Clubhouse Memorabilia
STATED ODDS 1:32 HOBBY, 1:44 RETAIL
STATED PRINT RUNS LISTED BELOW
CARDS ARE NOT SERIAL-NUMBERED
PRINT RUNS PROVIDED BY FLEER
1 Edgardo Alfonzo Jsy/1000 * 1.50 4.00
2 Rick Ankiel Jsy/500 *
3 Adrian Beltre Jsy/875 * 4.00 10.00
4 Craig Biggio Bat/600 * 2.50 6.00
5 Barry Bonds Jsy/1000 * 6.00 15.00
6 Sean Casey Jsy/800 * 1.50 4.00
7 Eric Chavez Jsy/1000 * 1.50 4.00
8 Roger Clemens Jsy/1000 * 5.00 12.00
9 J.Damon Sox Bat/700 * 2.50 6.00
10 Carlos Delgado Jsy/750 * 1.50 4.00
11 J.D. Drew Jsy/1000 * 1.50 4.00
12 Darin Erstad Jsy/850 * 1.50 4.00
13 Nomar Garciaparra Jsy/750 * 2.50 6.00
14 Juan Gonzalez Bat/1000 * 1.50 4.00
15 Todd Helton Jsy/925 * 2.50 6.00
16 Tim Hudson Jsy/825 * 2.50 6.00
17 Derek Jeter Pants/1000 * 10.00 25.00
18 Randy Johnson Jsy/1000 * 4.00 10.00
19 Andruw Jones Jsy/1000 * 1.50 4.00
20 Jason Kendall Jsy/1000 * 1.50 4.00
21 Paul LoDuca Jsy/1000 * 1.50 4.00
22 Greg Maddux Jsy/875 * 6.00 15.00
23 Pedro Martinez Jsy/775 * 2.50 6.00
24 Raul Mondesi Bat/575 * 1.50 4.00
25 Magglio Ordonez Jsy/575 * 2.50 6.00
26 Mike Piazza Jsy/950 * 4.00 10.00
27 Mike Piazza Pants/1000 * 4.00 10.00
28 Manny Ramirez Jsy/1000 * 2.50 6.00
29 Mariano Rivera Jsy/725 * 4.00 10.00
30 Alex Rodriguez Jsy/850 * 5.00 12.00
31 Ivan Rodriguez Jsy/1000 * 2.50 6.00
32 Scott Rolen Jsy/120 * 2.50 6.00
33 Kazuhiro Sasaki Jsy/1000 * 1.50 4.00
34 Curt Schilling Jsy/1000 * 2.50 6.00
35 Gary Sheffield Bat/775 * 1.50 4.00
36 Gary Sheffield Jsy/800 * 1.50 4.00
37 Frank Thomas Jsy/850 * 4.00 10.00
38 Jim Thome Bat/750 * 2.50 6.00
39 Omar Vizquel Jsy/1000 * 2.50 6.00

2002 Fleer Platinum Clubhouse Memorabilia Combos
STATED ODDS 1:96 HOBBY, 1:192 RETAIL
STATED PRINT RUNS LISTED BELOW
CARDS ARE NOT SERIAL-NUMBERED
PRINT RUNS PROVIDED BY FLEER
1 Edgardo Alfonzo Ball-Jsy/125 6.00 15.00
2 Rick Ankiel Bat-Jsy/200 6.00 15.00
3 Adrian Beltre Ball-Jsy/125 6.00 15.00
5 Barry Bonds Glove-Jsy/275 20.00 50.00
6 Sean Casey Ball-Jsy/125 6.00 15.00
7 Eric Chavez Base-Jsy/125 6.00 15.00
8 Roger Clemens Base-Jsy/325 15.00 40.00
9 J.Damon Sox Base-Bat/175 10.00 25.00
10 Carlos Delgado Bat-Jsy/325 6.00 15.00
11 J.D. Drew Ball-Jsy/125 6.00 15.00
12 Darin Erstad Bat-Jsy/125 6.00 15.00
13 N Garciaparra Base-Jsy/275 15.00 40.00
14 Juan Gonzalez Jsy-Bat/75 6.00 15.00
16 Tim Hudson Bat-Jsy/200 6.00 15.00
17 D.Jeter Btg Glv-Pants/200 20.00 50.00
18 Randy Johnson Bat-Jsy/125 10.00 25.00
19 And Jones Btg Glv-Jsy/100 10.00 25.00
21 Paul LoDuca Ball-Jsy/125 6.00 15.00
22 Greg Maddux Ball-Jsy/275 10.00 25.00
23 Pedro Martinez Base-Jsy/300 10.00 25.00
25 Magglio Ordonez Bat-Jsy/325 6.00 15.00
26 Mike Piazza Ball-Jsy/125 15.00 40.00
27 Mike Piazza Pants-Jsy/125 15.00 40.00
28 Manny Ramirez Base-Jsy/350 10.00 25.00
29 Mariano Rivera Base-Jsy/175 10.00 25.00
30 Alex Rodriguez Base-Jsy/300 12.50 30.00
31 I Rodriguez Btg Glv-Jsy/100 10.00 25.00
32 Scott Rolen Ball-Jsy/125 10.00 25.00
33 Kaz Sasaki Base-Jsy/350 6.00 15.00
34 Curt Schilling Ball-Jsy/125 6.00 15.00
35 Gary Sheffield Ball-Bat/125 6.00 15.00
36 Gary Sheffield Ball-Jsy/125 6.00 15.00
37 Frank Thomas Base-Jsy/275 10.00 25.00
38 Jim Thome Base-Bat/275 10.00 25.00
39 Omar Vizquel Base-Jsy/300 10.00 25.00

2002 Fleer Platinum Cornerstones
COMPLETE SET (40) 20.00 50.00
STATED ODDS 1:12 JUM, 1:6 RACK, 1:20 RET
1 B.Terry .60 1.50
J.Mize
2 C.Ripken 3.00 8.00
E.Murray
3 E.Mathews 1.00 2.50
C.Jones
4 A.Pujols 2.00 5.00
G.Sisler
5 S.Casey .60 1.50
T.Perez
6 J.Foxx 1.00 2.50
S.Rolen
7 W.Boggs 2.00 5.00
G.Brett
8 R.Carew .40 1.00
T.Glaus
9 J.Bagwell .60 1.50
R.Palmeiro
10 W.Stargell .60 1.50
P.Traynor
11 C.Ripken 3.00 8.00
B.Robinson
12 T.Perez .60 1.50
T.Kluszewski
13 J.Giambi 2.00 5.00
D.Mattingly
14 H.Greenberg 1.00 2.50
J.Foxx

15 E.Banks W.McCovey 1.00 2.50
16 J.Thome T.Fryman .60 1.50
17 T.Kluszewski S.Casey .60 1.50
18 G.Hodges J.Mize .60 1.50
19 B.Robinson B.Powell .60 1.50
20 B.Terry G.Sisler .40 1.00
21 W.Boggs D.Mattingly 2.00 5.00
22 J.Giambi Yanks C.Delgado .40 1.00
23 W.Stargell B.Madlock .60 1.50
24 M.Grace M.Williams .60 1.50
25 P.Molitor G.Brett 2.00 5.00
26 C.Delgado M.Vaughn .40 1.00
27 B.Terry W.McCovey .60 1.50
28 M.Sweeney G.Brett 2.00 5.00
29 E.Mathews E.Banks 1.00 2.50
30 E.Karros G.Hodges .60 1.50
31 P.Molitor D.Mattingly 2.00 5.00
32 B.Robinson R.Carew .60 1.50
33 C.Jones A.Pujols 2.00 5.00
34 H.Heilmann H.Greenberg 1.00 2.50
35 F.Thomas C.Delgado 1.00 2.50
36 J.Bagwell T.Helton .60 1.50
37 R.Palmeiro F.McGriff .60 1.50
38 C.Ripken W.Boggs 3.00 8.00
39 O.Cepeda W.McCovey .60 1.50
40 J.Olerud M.Grace .60 1.50

2002 Fleer Platinum Cornerstones Numbered

1-10 PRINT RUN 250 SERIAL #'d SETS
11-20 PRINT RUN 500 SERIAL #'d SETS
21-30 PRINT RUN 1000 SERIAL #'d SETS
31-40 PRINT RUN 2000 SERIAL #'d SETS
1 B.Terry J.Mize 1.25 3.00
2 C.Ripken E.Murray 6.00 15.00
3 E.Mathews C.Jones 2.00 5.00
4 A.Pujols G.Sisler 4.00 10.00
5 S.Casey T.Perez 1.25 3.00
6 J.Foxx S.Rolen 2.00 5.00
7 W.Boggs G.Brett 4.00 10.00
8 R.Carew T.Glaus .75 2.00
9 J.Bagwell R.Palmeiro 1.25 3.00
10 W.Stargell P.Traynor 1.25 3.00
11 C.Ripken B.Robinson 5.00 12.00
12 T.Perez T.Kluszewski 1.00 2.50
13 J.Giambi D.Mattingly 3.00 8.00
14 H.Greenberg J.Foxx 1.50 4.00
15 E.Banks W.McCovey 1.50 4.00
16 J.Thome T.Fryman 1.00 2.50
17 T.Kluszewski S.Casey 1.00 2.50
18 G.Hodges J.Mize 1.00 2.50
19 B.Robinson B.Powell 1.00 2.50
20 B.Terry G.Sisler .60 1.50
21 W.Boggs D.Mattingly 2.50 6.00
22 J.Giambi Yanks C.Delgado .50 1.25
23 W.Stargell B.Madlock .75 2.00
24 M.Grace M.Williams .75 2.00
25 P.Molitor G.Brett 2.50 6.00
26 C.Delgado M.Vaughn .50 1.25
27 B.Terry W.McCovey .75 2.00
28 M.Sweeney G.Brett 2.50 6.00
29 E.Mathews E.Banks 1.25 3.00
30 E.Karros G.Hodges .75 2.00
31 P.Molitor D.Mattingly 2.50 6.00
32 B.Robinson R.Carew .75 2.00
33 C.Jones A.Pujols 2.50 6.00
34 H.Heilmann H.Greenberg 1.25 3.00
35 F.Thomas C.Delgado 1.25 3.00
36 J.Bagwell T.Helton .75 2.00
37 R.Palmeiro F.McGriff .75 2.00
38 C.Ripken W.Boggs 4.00 10.00
39 O.Cepeda W.McCovey .75 2.00
40 J.Olerud M.Grace .75 2.00

2002 Fleer Platinum Fence Busters

ONE FENCEBUSTER OR AUTO PER RACK
STATED PRINT RUNS LISTED BELOW
CARDS ARE NOT SERIAL-NUMBERED
PRINT RUNS PROVIDED BY FLEER
1 Roberto Alomar/800 * 4.00 10.00
2 Moises Alou/800 * 3.00 8.00
3 Jeff Bagwell/400 * 4.00 10.00
4 Barry Bonds/700 * 10.00 25.00
5 J.D. Drew/800 * 3.00 8.00
6 Jim Edmonds/500 * 3.00 8.00
7 Brian Giles/700 * 3.00 8.00
8 Luis Gonzalez/625 * 3.00 8.00
9 Shawn Green/800 * 3.00 8.00
10 Todd Helton/675 * 4.00 10.00
11 Derek Jeter/400 * 10.00 25.00
12 Andruw Jones/800 * 4.00 10.00
13 Chipper Jones/800 * 4.00 10.00
14 Tino Martinez/800 * 4.00 10.00
15 Rafael Palmeiro/800 * 4.00 10.00
16 Mike Piazza/800 * 6.00 15.00
17 Manny Ramirez/800 * 4.00 10.00
18 Alex Rodriguez/675 * 6.00 15.00
19 Miguel Tejada/700 * 3.00 8.00
20 Frank Thomas/800 * 4.00 10.00
21 Jim Thome/800 * 4.00 10.00
22 Larry Walker/750 * 3.00 8.00

2002 Fleer Platinum Fence Busters Autographs

RANDOM INSERTS IN RACK PACKS
SERIAL #'d TO PLAYER'S 2001 HR TOTAL
ALL ARE EXCHANGE CARDS
2 Barry Bonds/73 50.00 100.00

2002 Fleer Platinum National Patch Time

STATED ODDS 1:12 JUMBO
STATED PRINT RUNS LISTED BELOW
1 Barry Bonds/75 25.00 60.00
2 Pat Burrell/285 8.00 20.00
3 Jose Canseco/150 12.00 30.00
4 Carlos Delgado/70 8.00 20.00
5 J.D. Drew/210 8.00 20.00
6 Adam Dunn/75 12.00 30.00
7 Darin Erstad/315 8.00 20.00
8 Juan Gonzalez/50 8.00 20.00
9 Todd Helton/110 12.00 30.00
10 Derek Jeter/65 40.00 80.00
11 Greg Maddux/775 15.00 40.00
12 Pedro Martinez/45 12.00 30.00
13 Magglio Ordonez/85 12.00 30.00
14 Manny Ramirez/100 12.00 30.00
15 Cal Ripken/350 30.00 60.00
16 Alex Rodriguez/325 25.00 60.00
17 Ivan Rodriguez/225 12.00 30.00
18 Kazuhiro Sasaki/310 8.00 20.00
19 Miguel Tejada/55 12.00 30.00

2002 Fleer Platinum Wheelhouse

COMPLETE SET (20) 40.00 80.00
STATED ODDS 1:12 HOBBY, 1:20 RETAIL
1 Derek Jeter 3.00 8.00
2 Barry Bonds 3.00 8.00
3 Luis Gonzalez 1.25 3.00
4 Jason Giambi 1.25 3.00
5 Ivan Rodriguez 1.25 3.00
6 Mike Piazza 2.00 5.00
7 Troy Glaus 1.25 3.00
8 Nomar Garciaparra 2.00 5.00
9 Juan Gonzalez 1.25 3.00
10 Sammy Sosa 1.25 3.00
11 Albert Pujols 2.50 6.00
12 Ken Griffey Jr. 2.50 6.00
13 Scott Rolen 1.25 3.00
14 Jeff Bagwell 1.25 3.00
15 Ichiro Suzuki 2.50 6.00
16 Todd Helton 1.25 3.00
17 Chipper Jones 1.25 3.00
18 Alex Rodriguez 1.50 4.00
19 Vladimir Guerrero 1.25 3.00
20 Manny Ramirez 1.25 3.00

2003 Fleer Platinum

COMP.SET w/o SP's (220) 10.00 25.00
COMMON CARD (1-220) .10 .30
COMMON CARD (221-235) .40 1.00
221-235 ODDS 1:4 WAX, 1:2 JUM, 1:1 RACK
COMMON CARD (236-240) .40 1.00
236-240 ODDS 1:12 WAX
COMMON CARD (241-245) .60 1.50
241-245 ODDS 1:6 JUMBO
COMMON CARD (246-250) .60 1.50
246-250 ODDS 1:2 RACK
1 Barry Bonds .50 1.25
2 Sean Casey .12 .30
3 Todd Walker .12 .30
4 Tony Batista .12 .30
5 Todd Zeile .12 .30
6 Ruben Sierra .12 .30
7 Jose Cruz Jr. .12 .30
8 Ben Grieve .12 .30
9 Rob Mackowiak .12 .30
10 Gary Sheffield .12 .30
11 Armando Benitez .12 .30
12 Tim Hudson .20 .50
13 Eric Milton .12 .30
14 Andy Pettitte .20 .50
15 Jeff Bagwell .20 .50
16 Jeff Kent .12 .30
17 Joe Randa .12 .30
18 Benito Santiago .12 .30
19 Russell Branyan .12 .30
20 Cliff Floyd .12 .30
21 Chris Richard .12 .30
22 Randy Winn .12 .30
23 Freddy Garcia .12 .30
24 Derek Lowe .12 .30
25 Ben Sheets .12 .30
26 Fred McGriff .20 .50
27 Bret Boone .12 .30
28 Jose Hernandez .12 .30
29 Phil Nevin .12 .30
30 Mike Piazza .30 .75
31 Bobby Abreu .12 .30
32 Darin Erstad .12 .30
33 Andruw Jones .12 .30
34 Brad Wilkerson .12 .30
35 Brian Lawrence .12 .30
36 Vladimir Nunez .12 .30
37 Kazuhiro Sasaki .12 .30
38 Carlos Delgado .12 .30
39 Steve Cox .12 .30
40 Adrian Beltre .30 .75
41 Josh Bard .12 .30
42 Randall Simon .12 .30
43 Johnny Damon .20 .50
44 Ken Griffey Jr. .60 1.50
45 Sammy Sosa .30 .75
46 Kevin Brown .12 .30
47 Kazuhisa Ishii .12 .30
48 Matt Morris .12 .30
49 Mark Prior .20 .50
50 Kip Wells .12 .30
51 Hee Seop Choi .12 .30
52 Craig Biggio .20 .50
53 Derek Jeter .75 2.00
54 Albert Pujols .40 1.00
55 Joe Borchard .12 .30
56 Robert Fick .12 .30
57 Jacque Jones .12 .30
58 Juan Pierre .12 .30
59 Bernie Williams .20 .50
60 Elmer Dessens .12 .30
61 Al Leiter .12 .30
62 Curt Schilling .20 .50
63 Carlos Pena .12 .30
64 Tino Martinez .20 .50
65 Fernando Vina .12 .30
66 Aaron Boone .12 .30
67 Michael Barrett .12 .30
68 Frank Thomas .30 .75
69 J.D. Drew .12 .30
70 Vladimir Guerrero .20 .50
71 Shannon Stewart .12 .30
72 Mark Buehrle .20 .50
73 Jamie Moyer .12 .30
74 Brad Radke .12 .30
75 Mike Williams .12 .30
76 Ryan Klesko .12 .30
77 Roberto Alomar .20 .50
78 Edgardo Alfonzo .12 .30
79 Matt Williams .12 .30
80 Edgar Martinez .20 .50
81 Shawn Green .12 .30
82 Kenny Lofton .12 .30
83 Josh Beckett .12 .30
84 Trevor Hoffman .20 .50
85 Kevin Millwood .12 .30
86 Odalis Perez .12 .30
87 Jarrod Washburn .12 .30
88 Jason Giambi .12 .30
89 Eric Young .12 .30
90 Barry Larkin .20 .50
91 Aramis Ramirez .12 .30
92 Ivan Rodriguez .20 .50
93 Steve Finley .12 .30
94 Brian Jordan .12 .30
95 Manny Ramirez .30 .75
96 Preston Wilson .12 .30
97 Rodrigo Lopez .12 .30
98 Ramon Ortiz .12 .30
99 Jim Thome .20 .50
100 Luis Castillo .12 .30
101 Alex Rodriguez .40 1.00
102 Jared Sandberg .12 .30
103 Ellis Burks .12 .30
104 Pat Burrell .12 .30
105 Brian Giles .12 .30
106 Mark Kotsay .12 .30
107 Dave Roberts .20 .50
108 Roy Halladay .20 .50
109 Chan Ho Park .20 .50
110 Erubiel Durazo .12 .30
111 Bobby Hill .12 .30
112 Cristian Guzman .12 .30
113 Troy Glaus .12 .30
114 Lance Berkman .20 .50
115 Juan Encarnacion .12 .30
116 Chipper Jones .30 .75
117 Corey Patterson .12 .30
118 Vernon Wells .12 .30
119 Matt Clement .12 .30
120 Billy Koch .12 .30
121 Hideo Nomo .30 .75
122 Derrek Lee .12 .30
123 Todd Helton .20 .50
124 Sean Burroughs .12 .30
125 Jason Kendall .12 .30
126 Dmitri Young .12 .30
127 Adam Dunn .20 .50
128 Bobby Higginson .12 .30
129 Raul Mondesi .12 .30
130 Bubba Trammell .12 .30
131 A.J. Burnett .12 .30
132 Randy Johnson .30 .75
133 Mark Mulder .12 .30
134 Mariano Rivera .40 1.00
135 Kerry Wood .12 .30
136 Mo Vaughn .12 .30
137 Jimmy Rollins .20 .50
138 Jose Valentin .12 .30
139 Brad Fullmer .12 .30
140 Mike Cameron .12 .30
141 Luis Gonzalez .12 .30
142 Kevin Appier .12 .30
143 Mike Hampton .12 .30
144 Pedro Martinez .20 .50
145 Javier Vazquez .12 .30
146 Doug Mientkiewicz .12 .30
147 Adam Kennedy .12 .30
148 Rafael Furcal .12 .30
149 Eric Chavez .12 .30
150 Mike Lieberthal .12 .30
151 Moises Alou .12 .30
152 Jermaine Dye .12 .30
153 Torii Hunter .12 .30
154 Trot Nixon .12 .30
155 Larry Walker .20 .50
156 Jorge Julio .12 .30
157 Mike Mussina .20 .50
158 Kirk Rueter .12 .30
159 Rafael Palmeiro .20 .50
160 Pokey Reese .12 .30
161 Miguel Tejada .20 .50
162 Robin Ventura .12 .30
163 Raul Ibanez .20 .50
164 Roger Cedeno .12 .30
165 Juan Gonzalez .12 .30
166 Carlos Lee .12 .30
167 Tim Salmon .12 .30
168 Orlando Hernandez .12 .30
169 Wade Miller .12 .30
170 Troy Percival .12 .30
171 Billy Wagner .12 .30
172 Jeff Conine .12 .30
173 Junior Spivey .12 .30
174 Edgar Renteria .12 .30
175 Scott Rolen .20 .50
176 Jason Varitek .30 .75
177 Ben Broussard .12 .30
178 Jeremy Giambi .12 .30
179 Gabe Kapler .12 .30
180 Armando Rios .12 .30
181 Ichiro Suzuki .40 1.00
182 Tom Glavine .20 .50
183 Greg Maddux .40 1.00
184 Roy Oswalt .20 .50
185 John Smoltz .30 .75
186 Eric Karros .12 .30
187 Alfonso Soriano .20 .50
188 Nomar Garciaparra .20 .50
189 Joe Crede .12 .30
190 Javy Lopez .12 .30
191 Carlos Beltran .20 .50
192 Jim Edmonds .20 .50
193 Geoff Jenkins .12 .30
194 Magglio Ordonez .20 .50
195 Daryle Ward .12 .30
196 Roger Clemens .40 1.00
197 Byung-Hyun Kim .12 .30
198 Robb Nen .12 .30
199 C.C. Sabathia .20 .50
200 Barry Zito .20 .50
201 Mark Grace UH .20 .50
202 Paul Konerko UH .20 .50
203 Mike Sweeney UH .12 .30
204 John Olerud UH .12 .30
205 Jose Vidro UH .12 .30
206 Ray Durham UH .12 .30
207 Omar Vizquel UH .20 .50
208 Shea Hillenbrand UH .12 .30
209 Mike Lowell UH .12 .30
210 Aubrey Huff UH .12 .30
211 Eric Hinske UH .12 .30
212 Paul Lo Duca UH .12 .30
213 Jay Gibbons UH .12 .30
214 Austin Kearns UH .12 .30
215 Richie Sexson UH .12 .30
216 Garret Anderson UH .12 .30
217 Eric Gagne UH .12 .30
218 Jason Jennings UH .12 .30
219 Damian Moss UH .12 .30
220 David Eckstein UH .12 .30
221 Mark Teixeira PROS .60 1.50
222 Bill Hall PROS .40 1.00
223 Bobby Jenks PROS .40 1.00
224 Adam Morrissey PROS .40 1.00
225 Rodrigo Rosario PROS .40 1.00
226 Brett Myers PROS .40 1.00
227 Tony Alvarez PROS .40 1.00
228 Willie Bloomquist PROS .40 1.00
229 Ben Howard PROS .40 1.00
230 Nic Jackson PROS .40 1.00
231 Carl Crawford PROS .60 1.50
232 Omar Infante PROS .40 1.00
233 Francisco Rodriguez PROS .60 1.50
234 Andy Van Hekken PROS .40 1.00
235 Kirk Saarloos PROS .40 1.00
236 Dusty Wathan PROS RC .40 1.00
237 Jamey Carroll PROS .40 1.00
238 Jason Phillips PROS .40 1.00
239 Jose Castillo PROS .40 1.00
240 Arnaldo Munoz PROS RC .40 1.00
241 Orlando Hudson PROS .60 1.50
242 Drew Henson PROS .60 1.50
243 Jason Lane PROS .60 1.50
244 Vinny Chulk PROS .60 1.50
245 Prentice Redman PROS RC .60 1.50
246 Marlon Byrd PROS .60 1.50
247 Chin-Feng Chen PROS .60 1.50
248 Craig Brazell PROS RC .60 1.50
249 John Webb PROS .60 1.50
250 Adam LaRoche PROS .60 1.50

2003 Fleer Platinum Finish

*FINISH 1-220: 3X TO 8X BASIC
*FINISH 221-235: 1X TO 2.5X BASIC
*FINISH 236-240: 1X TO 2.5X BASIC
*FINISH 241-245: .5X TO 1.2X BASIC
*FINISH 2446-250: .5X TO 1.2X BASIC
RANDOM INSERTS IN ALL PACKS
STATED PRINT RUN 100 SERIAL #'d SETS

2003 Fleer Platinum Barry Bonds Chasing History Game Used

RANDOM INSERTS IN WAX PACKS
DUAL-PLAYER PRINT RUN 250 #'d SETS
FIVE-PLAYER PRINT RUN 25 #'d SETS
FIVE PLAYER CARD TOO SCARCE TO PRICE
BB B.Bonds Jsy/Bo.Bonds Bat 12.00 30.00
BR B.Bonds Jsy/B.Ruth Bat 125.00 200.00
RM B.Bonds Jsy/R.Maris Pants 10.00 25.00
WM B.Bonds Jsy/W.McCovey Jsy 10.00 25.00

2003 Fleer Platinum Guts and Glory

COMPLETE SET (20) 10.00 25.00
STAT.ODDS 1:4 WAX, 1:2 JUMBO, 1:1 RACK
1 Jason Giambi .40 1.00
2 Alfonso Soriano .60 1.50
3 Scott Rolen .60 1.50
4 Ivan Rodriguez .60 1.50
5 Barry Bonds 1.50 4.00
6 Jim Edmonds .60 1.50
7 Darin Erstad .40 1.00
8 Brian Giles .40 1.00
9 Luis Gonzalez .40 1.00
10 Adam Dunn .60 1.50
11 Torii Hunter .40 1.00
12 Andruw Jones .40 1.00
13 Sammy Sosa 1.00 2.50
14 Ichiro Suzuki 1.25 3.00
15 Miguel Tejada .60 1.50
16 Roger Clemens 1.25 3.00
17 Curt Schilling .60 1.50
18 Nomar Garciaparra .60 1.50
19 Derek Jeter 2.50 6.00
20 Alex Rodriguez 1.25 3.00

2003 Fleer Platinum Heart of the Order

STAT.ODDS 1:12 WAX, 1:6 JUMBO, 1:3 RACK
1 Giambi Jeter Soriano 2.50 6.00
2 Helton Wilson Walker .60 1.50
3 Palmeiro A.Rod I.Rod 1.25 3.00
4 Dunn Griffey Kearns 2.00 5.00
5 Bagwell Biggio Berkman .60 1.50
6 Chavez Tejada Dye .60 1.50
7 Glaus Anderson Erstad .40 1.00
8 Piazza Vaughn Alomar 1.00 2.50
9 Torii Jones Koskie .40 1.00
10 Bonds Kent Aurilia 1.50 4.00
11 Burrell Abreu Rollins .60 1.50
12 Green Beltre LoDuca 1.00 2.50
13 Guerrero Wilkerson Vidro .60 1.50
14 Chipper Andruw Sheffield 1.00 2.50
15 Ichiro Boone Edgar 1.25 3.00
16 Pujols Rolen Drew 1.25 3.00
17 Sosa McGriff Alou 1.00 2.50
18 Nomar Hillenbrand Manny 1.00 2.50
19 Thomas Magglio Konerko 1.00 2.50
20 Kendall Giles Ramirez .40 1.00

2003 Fleer Platinum Heart of the Order Game Used

STATED ODDS 1:2 RACK
STATED PRINT RUN 400 SERIAL #'d SETS
AB Adrian Beltre Mem 3.00 8.00
AD Adam Dunn Mem
AK Austin Kearns Mem 3.00 8.00
AR Alex Rodriguez Mem
AS Alfonso Soriano Mem 3.00 8.00
BB Bret Boone Mem 3.00 8.00
BG Brian Giles Mem 3.00 8.00
CJ Chipper Jones Mem 6.00 15.00
DE Darin Erstad Mem 3.00 8.00
EM Edgar Martinez Mem
FT Frank Thomas Mem 6.00 15.00
JD J.D. Drew Mem 3.00 8.00
JK Jeff Kent Mem 3.00 8.00
JR Jimmy Rollins Mem 3.00 8.00
JV Jose Vidro Mem 3.00 8.00
LB Lance Berkman Mem 3.00 8.00
LW Larry Walker Mem
MP Mike Piazza Mem 6.00 15.00
MR Manny Ramirez Mem 4.00 10.00
RA Roberto Alomar Mem
RP Rafael Palmeiro Mem 4.00 10.00
SG Shawn Green Mem
SH Shea Hillenbrand Mem
SS Sammy Sosa Mem 6.00 15.00
TH Todd Helton Mem 4.00 10.00

2003 Fleer Platinum MLB Scouting Report

RANDOM INSERTS IN ALL PACKS
STATED PRINT RUN 400 SERIAL #'d SETS
1 Jason Giambi .60 1.50
2 Paul Konerko 1.00 2.50
3 Jim Thome 1.00 2.50
4 Alfonso Soriano 1.00 2.50
5 Troy Glaus .60 1.50
6 Eric Hinske .60 1.50
7 Paul Lo Duca .60 1.50
8 Mike Piazza 1.50 4.00
9 Marlon Byrd .60 1.50
10 Garret Anderson .60 1.50
11 Barry Bonds 2.50 6.00
12 Pat Burrell .60 1.50
13 Joe Crede .60 1.50
14 J.D. Drew .60 1.50
15 Ken Griffey Jr. 3.00 8.00
16 Vladimir Guerrero 1.00 2.50
17 Torii Hunter .60 1.50
18 Chipper Jones 1.50 4.00
19 Austin Kearns .60 1.50
20 Albert Pujols 2.00 5.00
21 Manny Ramirez 1.50 4.00
22 Gary Sheffield .60 1.50
23 Sammy Sosa 1.50 4.00
24 Ichiro Suzuki 2.00 5.00
25 Bernie Williams 1.00 2.50
26 Randy Johnson 1.50 4.00
27 Greg Maddux 2.00 5.00
28 Hideo Nomo 1.50 4.00
29 Nomar Garciaparra 1.00 2.50
30 Derek Jeter 4.00 10.00
31 Alex Rodriguez 2.00 5.00
32 Miguel Tejada 1.00 2.50

2003 Fleer Platinum MLB Scouting Report Game Used

RANDOM INSERTS IN WAX PACKS
STATED PRINT RUN 250 SERIAL #'d SETS
AK Austin Kearns Pants 4.00 10.00
AS Alfonso Soriano Bat 4.00 10.00
BB Barry Bonds Jsy 10.00 25.00
CJ Chipper Jones Jsy 6.00 15.00
DJ Derek Jeter Jsy 10.00 25.00
GM Greg Maddux Jsy 6.00 15.00
HN Hideo Nomo Jsy 12.50 30.00
JD J.D. Drew Jsy 4.00 10.00
JT Jim Thome Jsy 6.00 15.00
MP Mike Piazza Jsy 6.00 15.00
MR Manny Ramirez Jsy 6.00 15.00
RJ Randy Johnson Jsy 6.00 15.00
SS Sammy Sosa Jsy 6.00 15.00

2003 Fleer Platinum Nameplates

STATED ODDS 1:8 JUMBO
STATED PRINT RUNS LISTED BELOW
AD Adam Dunn/117 10.00 25.00
AJ Andruw Jones/170 10.00 25.00
AR Alex Rodriguez/248 20.00 50.00
BB Barry Bonds/251 12.00 30.00
BL Barry Larkin/97 15.00 40.00
BZ Barry Zito/248 10.00 25.00
CB Craig Biggio/152 10.00 25.00
CC Chin-Feng Chen/110 60.00 120.00
CJ Chipper Jones/251 12.00 30.00
CK Corey Koskie/130 10.00 25.00
EH Eric Hinske/173 10.00 25.00
EM Edgar Martinez/176 10.00 25.00
FT Frank Thomas/58 20.00 50.00
FT Frank Thomas/93 20.00 50.00
GM Greg Maddux/248 15.00 40.00
IR Ivan Rodriguez/189 10.00 25.00
JB Jeff Bagwell/121 10.00 25.00
JD Johnny Damon/35 30.00 60.00
JO John Olerud/180 10.00 25.00
JR Jimmy Rollins/74 10.00 25.00
JT Jim Thome/158 10.00 25.00
KI Kazuhisa Ishii/35 20.00 50.00
KS Kazuhiro Sasaki/82 10.00 25.00
KW Kerry Wood/49 20.00 50.00
LB Lance Berkman/176 10.00 25.00
LW Larry Walker/161 10.00 25.00
MP Mike Piazza/200 10.00 25.00
MP2 Mark Prior/123 10.00 25.00
MR Manny Ramirez/94 10.00 25.00
MS Mike Sweeney/175 10.00 25.00
MT Miguel Tejada/225 10.00 25.00
NG Nomar Garciaparra/258 15.00 40.00
PB Pat Burrell/176 10.00 25.00
PM Pedro Martinez/244 10.00 25.00
RC Roger Clemens/141 30.00 60.00
RO Roy Oswalt/155 10.00 25.00
RP Rafael Palmeiro/245 10.00 25.00
RS Richie Sexson/160 10.00 25.00
VG Vladimir Guerrero/102 20.00 50.00

2003 Fleer Platinum Portraits

STAT.ODDS 1:20 WAX, 1:10 JUMBO, 1:5 RACK
1 Josh Beckett .40 1.00
2 Roberto Alomar .60 1.50
3 Alfonso Soriano .60 1.50
4 Mike Piazza 1.00 2.50
5 Ivan Rodriguez .60 1.50
6 Edgar Martinez .60 1.50
7 Barry Bonds 1.50 4.00
8 Adam Dunn .60 1.50
9 Juan Gonzalez .40 1.00
10 Chipper Jones 1.00 2.50
11 Albert Pujols 1.25 3.00
12 Magglio Ordonez .60 1.50
13 Shea Hillenbrand .40 1.00
14 Larry Walker .60 1.50
15 Pedro Martinez .60 1.50
16 Kerry Wood .40 1.00
17 Barry Zito .60 1.50
18 Nomar Garciaparra .60 1.50
19 Derek Jeter 2.50 6.00
20 Alex Rodriguez 1.00 2.50

2003 Fleer Platinum Portraits Game Jersey

STATED ODDS 1:86 WAX
SP INFO PROVIDED BY FLEER
SP'S ARE NOT SERIAL-NUMBERED
PPAD Adam Dunn 2.00 5.00
PPBB Barry Bonds 5.00 12.00
PPBZ Barry Zito 2.00 5.00
PPCJ Chipper Jones 3.00 8.00
PPDJ Derek Jeter SP/150 8.00 20.00
PPEM Edgar Martinez
PPIR Ivan Rodriguez 2.00 5.00
PPJB Josh Beckett 1.25 3.00
PPKW Kerry Wood 1.25 3.00
PPLW Larry Walker
PPMP Mike Piazza 3.00 8.00
PPNG Nomar Garciaparra 2.00 5.00
PPPM Pedro Martinez 2.00 5.00

2003 Fleer Platinum Portraits Game Patch

RANDOM INSERTS IN WAX PACKS
STATED PRINT RUN 100 SERIAL #'d SETS
AD Adam Dunn 15.00 40.00
BB Barry Bonds 12.50 30.00
BZ Barry Zito 15.00 40.00
CJ Chipper Jones 15.00 40.00
IR Ivan Rodriguez 15.00 40.00
KW Kerry Wood 15.00 40.00
MP Mike Piazza 30.00 60.00
NG Nomar Garciaparra 30.00 60.00
PM Pedro Martinez 15.00 40.00

2004 Fleer Platinum

COMP.SET w/o SP's (178) 10.00 25.00
COMMON (1-135/158-182) .10 .30
COMMON CARD (183-200) .40 1.00
183-200 ARE NOT SHORT-PRINTS
COMMON CARD (136-143) .40 1.00
136-143 ODDS 1:3 WAX, 1:12 RETAIL
COMMON CARD (144-151) .40 1.00
144-151 ODDS ONE PER JUMBO
COMMON CARD (152-157) 3.00 8.00
152-157 ODDS ONE PER RACK PACK
152-157 STATED PRINT RUN APPX.1000 SETS
152-157 PRINT RUN PROVIDED BY FLEER
152-157 ARE NOT SERIAL-NUMBERED
1 Luis Castillo .12 .30
2 Preston Wilson .12 .30
3 Johan Santana .20 .50
4 Fred McGriff .12 .30
5 Albert Pujols .40 1.00
6 Reggie Sanders .12 .30
7 Ivan Rodriguez .20 .50
8 Roy Halladay .20 .50
9 Brian Giles .12 .30
10 Bernie Williams .20 .50
11 Barry Larkin .20 .50
12 Marlon Anderson .12 .30
13 Ramon Ortiz .12 .30
14 Luis Matos .12 .30
15 Esteban Loaiza .12 .30
16 Orlando Cabrera .12 .30
17 Jamie Moyer .12 .30
18 Tino Martinez .20 .50
19 Josh Beckett .12 .30
20 Derek Jeter .75 2.00
21 Derek Lowe .12 .30
22 Jack Wilson .12 .30
23 Bret Boone .12 .30
24 Matt Morris .12 .30
25 Javier Vazquez .12 .30
26 Joe Crede .12 .30
27 Jose Vidro .12 .30
28 Mike Piazza .30 .75
29 Curt Schilling .20 .50
30 Alex Rodriguez .40 1.00
31 John Olerud .12 .30
32 Dontrelle Willis .12 .30
33 Larry Walker .20 .50
34 Joe Randa .12 .30
35 Paul Lo Duca .12 .30
36 Marlon Byrd .12 .30
37 Bo Hart .12 .30
38 Rafael Palmeiro .20 .50
39 Garret Anderson .12 .30
40 Tom Glavine .20 .50
41 Ichiro Suzuki .40 1.00
42 Derrek Lee .12 .30
43 Lance Berkman .20 .50
44 Nomar Garciaparra .20 .50
45 Mike Sweeney .12 .30
46 A.J. Burnett .12 .30
47 Sean Casey .12 .30
48 Eric Gagne .12 .30
49 Joel Pineiro .12 .30
50 Russ Ortiz .12 .30
51 Placido Polanco .12 .30
52 Sammy Sosa .30 .75
53 Mark Teixeira .20 .50
54 Randy Wolf .12 .30
55 Vladimir Guerrero .20 .50
56 Tim Hudson .20 .50
57 Lew Ford .12 .30
58 Carlos Delgado .12 .30
59 Darin Erstad .12 .30
60 Mike Lieberthal .12 .30
61 Craig Biggio .20 .50
62 Ryan Klesko .12 .30
63 C.C. Sabathia .20 .50
64 Carlos Lee .12 .30
65 Al Leiter .12 .30
66 Brandon Webb .12 .30
67 Jacque Jones .12 .30
68 Kerry Wood .12 .30
69 Omar Vizquel .20 .50
70 Jeremy Bonderman .12 .30
71 Kevin Brown .12 .30
72 Richie Sexson .12 .30
73 Zach Day .12 .30
74 Mike Mussina .20 .50
75 Sidney Ponson .12 .30
76 Andruw Jones .12 .30
77 Woody Williams .12 .30
78 Kazuhiro Sasaki .12 .30
79 Matt Clement .12 .30
80 Shea Hillenbrand .12 .30
81 Bartolo Colon .12 .30
82 Ken Griffey Jr. .60 1.50
83 Todd Helton .20 .50

84 Dmitri Young .12 .30
85 Richard Hidalgo .12 .30
86 Carlos Beltran .20 .50
87 Brad Wilkerson .12 .30
88 Andy Pettitte .20 .50
89 Miguel Tejada .20 .50
90 Edgar Martinez .20 .50
91 Vernon Wells .12 .30
92 Magglio Ordonez .20 .50
93 Tony Batista .12 .30
94 Jose Reyes .20 .50
95 Matt Stairs .12 .30
96 Manny Ramirez .30 .75
97 Carlos Pena .20 .50
98 A.J. Pierzynski .12 .30
99 Jim Thome .20 .50
100 Aubrey Huff .12 .30
101 Roberto Alomar .20 .50
102 Luis Gonzalez .12 .30
103 Chipper Jones .30 .75
104 Jay Gibbons .12 .30
105 Adam Dunn .20 .50
106 Jay Payton .12 .30
107 Scott Podsednik .12 .30
108 Roy Oswalt .20 .50
109 Milton Bradley .12 .30
110 Shawn Green .12 .30
111 Ryan Wagner .12 .30
112 Eric Chavez .12 .30
113 Pat Burrell .12 .30
114 Frank Thomas .30 .75
115 Jason Kendall .12 .30
116 Jake Peavy .12 .30
117 Mike Cameron .12 .30
118 Jim Edmonds .20 .50
119 Hank Blalock .12 .30
120 Troy Glaus .12 .30
121 Jeff Kent .12 .30
122 Jason Schmidt .12 .30
123 Corey Patterson .12 .30
124 Austin Kearns .12 .30
125 Edwin Jackson .12 .30
126 Alfonso Soriano .20 .50
127 Bobby Abreu .12 .30
128 Scott Rolen .20 .50
129 Jeff Bagwell .20 .50
130 Shannon Stewart .12 .30
131 Rich Aurilia .12 .30
132 Ty Wigginton .12 .30
133 Randy Johnson .30 .75
134 Rocco Baldelli .12 .30
135 Hideo Nomo .30 .75
136 Greg Maddux WE 1.25 3.00
137 Johnny Damon WE .60 1.50
138 Mark Prior WE .60 1.50
139 Corey Koskie WE .40 1.00
140 Miguel Cabrera WE 1.00 2.50
141 Hideki Matsui WE 1.50 4.00
142 Jose Cruz Jr. WE .40 1.00
143 Barry Zito WE .60 1.50
144 Javy Lopez JE .40 1.00
145 Jason Varitek JE 1.00 2.50
146 Moises Alou JE .40 1.00
147 Torii Hunter JE .40 1.00
148 Juan Encarnacion JE .40 1.00
149 Jorge Posada JE .60 1.50
150 Marquis Grissom JE .40 1.00
151 Rich Harden JE .40 1.00
152 Gary Sheffield RE .40 1.00
153 Pedro Martinez RE .60 1.50
154 Brad Radke RE .40 1.00
155 Mike Lowell RE .40 1.00
156 Jason Giambi RE .40 1.00
157 Mark Mulder RE .40 1.00
158 Ben Weber UH .12 .30
159 Mark DeRosa UH .12 .30
160 Melvin Mora UH .12 .30
161 Bill Mueller UH .12 .30
162 Jon Garland UH .12 .30
163 Jody Gerut UH .12 .30
164 Javier Lopez UH .12 .30
165 Craig Monroe UH .12 .30
166 Juan Pierre UH .12 .30
167 Morgan Ensberg UH .12 .30
168 Angel Berroa UH .12 .30
169 Geoff Jenkins UH .12 .30
170 Matt LeCroy UH .12 .30
171 Livan Hernandez UH .12 .30
172 Jason Phillips UH .12 .30
173 Mariano Rivera UH .40 1.00
174 Erubiel Durazo UH .12 .30
175 Jason Michaels UH .12 .30
176 Kip Wells UH .12 .30
177 Ray Durham UH .12 .30
178 Randy Winn UH .12 .30
179 Edgar Renteria UH .12 .30
180 Carl Crawford UH .20 .50
181 Laynce Nix UH .12 .30
182 Greg Myers UH .12 .30
183 D.Young .60 1.50
C.Gaudin
184 H.Quintero .40 1.00
B.Castro
185 C.Brazell .40 1.00
D.Garcia
186 R.Wing RC .40 1.00
F.Cruceta
187 W.Bergolla RC .40 1.00
J.Hall
188 C.Barmes .60 1.50
G.Atkins
189 C.Bootcheck .40 1.00
R.Fischer
190 E.Gonzalez .40 1.00
M.Kata
191 A.Brown .40 1.00
K.Hill
192 J.Gall RC .40 1.00
D.Haren
193 C.Bentz RC .40 1.00
L.Ayala
194 H.Gimenez RC .40 1.00
E.Bruntlett
195 B.Bonser .40 1.00
R.Bowen
196 C.Snelling .40 1.00
R.Johnson
197 R.Weeks .40 1.00
A.Morrissey
198 N.Lowry .40 1.00
T.Linden
199 C.Waters .40 1.00
B.Evert
200 J.De Paula 1.50 4.00
C.Wang

2004 Fleer Platinum Finish

*FINISH 1-135/158-182: 3X TO 8X BASIC
*FINISH 183-200: 1X TO 2.5X BASIC
*FINISH 136-143: 1.25X TO 3X BASIC
*FINISH 144-151: .75X TO 2X BASIC
*FINISH 152-157: .25X TO .6X BASIC
STATED ODDS 1:15 WAX
STATED PRINT RUN 100 SERIAL #'d SETS

2004 Fleer Platinum Big Signs

COMPLETE SET (15) 10.00 25.00
ODDS 1:9 WAX, 1:2 JUMBO, 1:8 RETAIL
1 Albert Pujols 1.25 3.00
2 Derek Jeter 2.50 6.00
3 Mike Piazza 1.00 2.50
4 Jason Giambi .40 1.00
5 Ichiro Suzuki 1.25 3.00
6 Nomar Garciaparra .60 1.50
7 Mark Prior .60 1.50
8 Randy Johnson 1.00 2.50
9 Greg Maddux 1.25 3.00
10 Sammy Sosa 1.00 2.50
11 Ken Griffey Jr. 2.00 5.00
12 Dontrelle Willis .40 1.00
13 Alex Rodriguez 1.25 3.00
14 Chipper Jones 1.00 2.50
15 Hank Blalock .40 1.00

2004 Fleer Platinum Big Signs Autographs

RANDOM INSERTS IN WAX PACKS
STATED PRINT RUN 100 SERIAL #'d SETS
EXCHANGE DEADLINE INDEFINITE
AP Albert Pujols 40.00 100.00
DW Dontrelle Willis 10.00 25.00
HB Hank Blalock 6.00 15.00

2004 Fleer Platinum Classic Combinations

STATED ODDS 1:108 WAX, 1:270 RETAIL
1 I.Rodriguez 2.50 6.00
M.Piazza
2 A.Rodriguez 3.00 8.00
S.Sosa
3 D.Willis 1.00 2.50
A.Berroa
4 N.Garciaparra 6.00 15.00
D.Jeter
5 I.Suzuki 3.00 8.00
H.Nomo
6 J.Beckett 1.00 2.50
K.Wood
7 A.Pujols 3.00 8.00
C.Delgado
8 A.Soriano 1.50 4.00
J.Morgan
9 J.Giambi 1.50 4.00
R.Jackson
10 N.Ryan 8.00 20.00
T.Seaver

2004 Fleer Platinum Clubhouse Memorabilia

STATED ODDS 1:24 WAX, 1:96 RETAIL
SP INFO PROVIDED BY FLEER
*DUAL: 1X TO 2.5X BASIC
*DUAL: .75X TO 2X BASIC SP
DUAL RANDOM IN WAX AND RETAIL
DUAL PRINT RUN 50 SERIAL #'d SETS
DUAL FEATURE TWO JSY SWATCHES
AK Austin Kearns 3.00 8.00
AP Albert Pujols SP 8.00 20.00
AR Alex Rodriguez 4.00 10.00
AS Alfonso Soriano SP 3.00 8.00
CJ Chipper Jones SP 4.00 10.00
DJ Derek Jeter 8.00 20.00
DW Dontrelle Willis 4.00 10.00
GM Greg Maddux 4.00 10.00
HB Hank Blalock 3.00 8.00
HN Hideo Nomo 6.00 15.00
JB Josh Beckett 3.00 8.00
JG Jason Giambi 3.00 8.00
JT Jim Thome 4.00 10.00
MPI Mike Piazza 4.00 10.00
MPR Mark Prior SP 4.00 10.00
MT Miguel Tejada 3.00 8.00
NG Nomar Garciaparra 4.00 10.00
RB Rocco Baldelli 3.00 8.00
RS Richie Sexson 3.00 8.00
SS Sammy Sosa 4.00 10.00
THE Todd Helton 4.00 10.00
THU Torii Hunter 3.00 8.00
VG Vladimir Guerrero 4.00 10.00

2004 Fleer Platinum Inscribed

ONE PER RACK PACK
PRINT RUNS B/WN 20-315 COPIES PER
EXCH PRINT RUNS PROVIDED BY FLEER
EXCHANGE DEADLINE INDEFINITE
NO PRICING ON QTY OF 25 OR LESS
AB Angel Berroa/210 4.00 10.00
AP Albert Pujols/100 60.00 120.00
BWE Brandon Webb/150 6.00 15.00
CBE Chad Bentz/310 4.00 10.00
CBO Chris Bootcheck/210 4.00 10.00
CSN Chris Snelling/310 4.00 10.00
DH Dan Haren/200 4.00 10.00
DM Dallas McPherson/160 6.00 15.00
DY Delmon Young/210 10.00 25.00
EG Eric Gagne/130 5.00 12.00
EJ Edwin Jackson/200 4.00 10.00
JV Javier Vazquez/160 6.00 15.00
KG Khalil Greene/310 10.00 25.00
KH Koyie Hill/300 4.00 10.00
LN Laynce Nix/200 4.00 10.00
MB Marlon Byrd/255 4.00 10.00
MC Miguel Cabrera/200 15.00 40.00
MK Matt Kata/315 4.00 10.00
RB Rocco Baldelli/100 10.00 25.00
RHA Rich Harden/200 6.00 15.00
RHO Ryan Howard/160 15.00 40.00
RWE Rickie Weeks/200 6.00 15.00
SP Scott Podsednik/180 10.00 25.00
VW Vernon Wells/200 6.00 15.00

2004 Fleer Platinum MLB Scouting Report

ODDS 1:45 WAX, 1:96 JUMBO, 1:190 RETAIL
STATED PRINT RUN 400 SERIAL #'d SETS
1 Josh Beckett .75 2.00
2 Todd Helton 1.25 3.00
3 Rocco Baldelli .75 2.00
4 Pedro Martinez 1.25 3.00
5 Jeff Bagwell 1.25 3.00
6 Mark Prior 1.25 3.00
7 Ichiro Suzuki 2.50 6.00
8 Barry Zito 1.25 3.00
9 Manny Ramirez 2.00 5.00
10 Miguel Cabrera 2.00 5.00
11 Richie Sexson .75 2.00
12 Hideki Matsui 3.00 8.00
13 Magglio Ordonez 1.25 3.00
14 Brandon Webb .75 2.00
15 Kerry Wood .75 2.00

2004 Fleer Platinum MLB Scouting Report Game Jersey

RANDOM IN WAX AND RETAIL PACKS
STATED PRINT RUN 250 SERIAL #'d SETS
BW Brandon Webb 4.00 10.00
JB Josh Beckett 4.00 10.00
JBAG Jeff Bagwell 6.00 15.00
KW Kerry Wood 4.00 10.00
MP Mark Prior 6.00 15.00
MR Manny Ramirez 6.00 15.00
PM Pedro Martinez 6.00 15.00
RB Rocco Baldelli 4.00 10.00
TH Todd Helton 6.00 15.00

2004 Fleer Platinum Nameplates Player

OVERALL NAMEPLATES ODDS 1:4 JUMBO
PRINT RUNS B/WN 25-320 COPIES PER
NO PRICING ON QTY OF 25 OR LESS
AK Austin Kearns/310 4.00 10.00
AP Albert Pujols/190 15.00 40.00
AR Alex Rodriguez/225 10.00 25.00
BZ Barry Zito/170 6.00 15.00
CJ Chipper Jones/150 10.00 25.00
CS Curt Schilling/260 8.00 20.00
GS Gary Sheffield/115 8.00 20.00
HB Hank Blalock/200 6.00 15.00
HN Hideo Nomo/85 20.00 50.00
HSC Hee Seop Choi/70 8.00 20.00
JB Josh Beckett/255 6.00 15.00
JP Juan Pierre/50 10.00 25.00
JR Jose Reyes/310 6.00 15.00
KB Kevin Brown/80 6.00 15.00
KW Kerry Wood/290 6.00 15.00
LC Luis Castillo/75 6.00 15.00
MB Marlon Byrd/75 6.00 15.00
MC Miguel Cabrera/75 10.00 25.00
MR Manny Ramirez/210 8.00 20.00
MT Mark Teixeira/250 8.00 20.00
NG Nomar Garciaparra/320 10.00 25.00
RJ Randy Johnson/200 8.00 20.00
RS Richie Sexson/165 6.00 15.00
SS Sammy Sosa/260 8.00 20.00

2004 Fleer Platinum Nameplates Team

OVERALL NAMEPLATES ODDS 1:4 JUMBO
PRINT RUNS B/WN 105-515 COPIES PER
AK Austin Kearns/515 4.00 10.00
AP Albert Pujols/470 12.50 30.00
AR Alex Rodriguez/510 10.00 25.00
BZ Barry Zito/515 4.00 10.00
CJ Chipper Jones/420 10.00 25.00
CS Curt Schilling/250 8.00 20.00
GS Gary Sheffield/500 4.00 10.00
HB Hank Blalock/515 4.00 10.00
HN Hideo Nomo/390 8.00 20.00
HSC Hee Seop Choi/220 6.00 15.00
JB Josh Beckett/390 4.00 10.00
JP Juan Pierre/110 8.00 20.00
JR Jose Reyes/510 4.00 10.00
KB Kevin Brown/220 4.00 10.00
KW Kerry Wood/510 4.00 10.00
LC Luis Castillo/225 4.00 10.00
MB Marlon Byrd/470 4.00 10.00
MC Miguel Cabrera/105 10.00 25.00
MR Manny Ramirez/480 6.00 15.00
MT Mark Teixeira/505 6.00 15.00
NG Nomar Garciaparra/250 10.00 25.00
RJ Randy Johnson/290 8.00 20.00
RS Richie Sexson/420 4.00 10.00
SS Sammy Sosa/490 6.00 15.00

2004 Fleer Platinum Portraits

ODDS 1:18 WAX, 1:4 JUMBO, 1:24 RETAIL
1 Jason Giambi .40 1.00
2 Nomar Garciaparra .60 1.50
3 Vladimir Guerrero .60 1.50
4 Mark Prior .60 1.50
5 Jim Thome .60 1.50
6 Derek Jeter 2.50 6.00
7 Sammy Sosa 1.00 2.50
8 Alex Rodriguez 1.25 3.00
9 Greg Maddux 1.25 3.00
10 Albert Pujols 1.25 3.00

2004 Fleer Platinum Portraits Game Jersey

STATED ODDS 1:48 WAX, 1:120 RETAIL
SP INFO PROVIDED BY FLEER
*PATCH: .75X TO 2X BASIC
*PATCH: .6X TO 1.5X BASIC SP
PATCH RANDOM IN WAX AND RETAIL
PATCH PRINT RUN 100 SERIAL #'d SETS
AP Albert Pujols 6.00 15.00
AR Alex Rodriguez 4.00 10.00
DJ Derek Jeter 10.00 25.00
GM Greg Maddux SP 6.00 15.00
JG Jason Giambi 3.00 8.00
JT Jim Thome 4.00 10.00
MP Mark Prior SP 6.00 15.00
NG Nomar Garciaparra 4.00 10.00
SS Sammy Sosa 4.00 10.00
VG Vladimir Guerrero 4.00 10.00

2005 Fleer Platinum

COMP.SET w/o SP's (100) 10.00 25.00
COMMON CARD (1-100) .10 .30
COMMON CARD (101-125) .60 1.50
101-125 ODDS 1:18 HOBBY, 1:60 RETAIL
101-125 PRINT RUN 1000 SERIAL #'d SETS
1 Nomar Garciaparra .20 .50
2 Matt Holliday .30 .75
3 Rickie Weeks .12 .30
4 Jim Thome .20 .50
5 Roy Halladay .20 .50
6 Paul Konerko .20 .50
7 Lance Berkman .20 .50
8 Ichiro Suzuki .40 1.00
9 Kerry Wood .12 .30
10 Lew Ford .12 .30
11 Omar Vizquel .20 .50
12 Manny Ramirez .30 .75
13 Carlos Beltran .20 .50
14 Lyle Overbay .12 .30
15 Billy Wagner .12 .30
16 Jose Vidro .12 .30
17 Vladimir Guerrero .20 .50
18 Miguel Tejada .20 .50
19 Alex Rodriguez .40 1.00
20 Rocco Baldelli .12 .30
21 David Ortiz .30 .75
22 Victor Martinez .20 .50
23 Shawn Green .12 .30
24 Jason Bay .12 .30
25 Pedro Martinez .20 .50
26 Travis Hafner .12 .30
27 Eric Gagne .12 .30
28 Jack Wilson .12 .30
29 Ivan Rodriguez .20 .50
30 Jody Gerut .12 .30
31 Adrian Beltre .30 .75
32 Craig Wilson .12 .30
33 J.D. Drew .12 .30
34 Craig Biggio .20 .50
35 Mark Mulder .12 .30
36 Mark Teixeira .20 .50
37 Melvin Mora .12 .30
38 Ken Griffey Jr. .60 1.50
39 Mike Sweeney .12 .30
40 Khalil Greene .12 .30
41 Rafael Palmeiro .20 .50
42 Austin Kearns .12 .30
43 Garret Anderson .12 .30
44 Trevor Hoffman .20 .50
45 Andruw Jones .12 .30
46 Adam Dunn .20 .50
47 Angel Berroa .12 .30
48 Ryan Klesko .12 .30
49 Sean Casey .12 .30
50 Kaz Matsui .12 .30
51 Jim Edmonds .20 .50
52 Magglio Ordonez .20 .50
53 Tom Glavine .20 .50
54 Larry Walker .20 .50
55 Johnny Estrada .12 .30
56 Brad Lidge .12 .30
57 Barry Zito .20 .50
58 Michael Young .12 .30
59 Chipper Jones .30 .75
60 Andy Pettitte .20 .50
61 Eric Chavez .12 .30
62 Carlos Delgado .12 .30
63 David Eckstein .12 .30
64 Dmitri Young .12 .30
65 Mike Piazza .30 .75
66 Albert Pujols .40 1.00
67 Luis Gonzalez .12 .30
68 Hideki Matsui .50 1.25
69 Gary Sheffield .12 .30
70 Carl Crawford .20 .50
71 Curt Schilling .20 .50
72 Todd Helton .20 .50
73 Ben Sheets .12 .30
74 Bobby Abreu .12 .30
75 Jose Guillen .12 .30
76 Richie Sexson .12 .30
77 Miguel Cabrera .30 .75
78 Bernie Williams .20 .50
79 Aubrey Huff .12 .30
80 John Smoltz .30 .75
81 Jeff Bagwell .20 .50
82 Tim Hudson .20 .50
83 Alfonso Soriano .20 .50
84 Freddy Garcia .12 .30
85 Johan Santana .20 .50
86 Bret Boone .12 .30
87 Troy Glaus .12 .30
88 Carlos Guillen .12 .30
89 Derek Jeter .75 2.00
90 Scott Rolen .20 .50
91 Sammy Sosa .30 .75
92 Jacque Jones .12 .30
93 Jason Schmidt .12 .30
94 Randy Johnson .30 .75
95 Dontrelle Willis .12 .30
96 Mariano Rivera .40 1.00
97 Hank Blalock .12 .30
98 Mark Prior .20 .50
99 Torii Hunter .12 .30
100 Roger Clemens .40 1.00
101 David Wright ROO 1.25 3.00
102 Justin Morneau ROO 1.00 2.50
103 Scott Kazmir ROO 1.50 4.00
104 Gavin Floyd ROO .60 1.50
105 Justin Verlander ROO RC 12.00 30.00
106 Zack Greinke ROO 2.00 5.00
107 David Aardsma ROO .60 1.50
108 Ryan Raburn ROO .60 1.50
109 Joey Gathright ROO .60 1.50
110 J.D. Durbin ROO .60 1.50
111 Sean Burnett ROO .60 1.50
112 Jose Lopez ROO .60 1.50
113 Nick Swisher ROO 1.00 2.50
114 Bobby Jenks ROO .60 1.50
115 Kelly Johnson ROO .60 1.50
116 B.J. Upton ROO 1.00 2.50
117 Ronny Cedeno ROO .60 1.50
118 Edwin Encarnacion ROO 1.50 4.00
119 Jeff Baker ROO .60 1.50
120 Taylor Buchholz ROO .60 1.50
121 Luis Hernandez ROO RC .60 1.50
122 Dioner Navarro ROO .60 1.50
123 Victor Diaz ROO .60 1.50
124 Jon Knott ROO .60 1.50
125 Russ Adams ROO .60 1.50

2005 Fleer Platinum Finish

*FINISH 1-100: 2.5X TO 6X BASIC
*FINISH 101-125: .4X TO 1X BASIC
OVERALL PARALLEL ODDS 1:9 H, 1:114 R
STATED PRINT RUN 199 SERIAL #'d SETS

2005 Fleer Platinum Autograph Die Cuts

STATED ODDS 1:184 HOBBY
PRINT RUNS B/WN 10-99 COPIES PER
CARDS ARE NOT SERIAL-NUMBERED
PRINT RUN INFO PROVIDED BY FLEER
NO PRICING ON QTY OF 20 OR LESS
1 Lew Ford/99 * 4.00 10.00
3 Jason Bay/50 * 6.00 15.00
4 Travis Hafner/99 * 6.00 15.00
6 Brad Lidge/99 * 15.00 40.00
7 Michael Young/99 * 6.00 15.00
8 David Eckstein/99 * 12.50 30.00
9 Carl Crawford/50 * 6.00 15.00
10 Miguel Cabrera/50 * 20.00 50.00
11 David Wright ROO/50 * 20.00 50.00
13 Scott Kazmir ROO/99 * 8.00 20.00
14 Gavin Floyd ROO/99 * 4.00 10.00
15 Justin Verlander ROO/99 * 20.00 50.00
18 Joey Gathright ROO/50 * 4.00 10.00

2005 Fleer Platinum Decade of Excellence

STATED ODDS 1:99 HOBBY, 1:125 RETAIL
1 Albert Pujols 1.25 3.00
2 Derek Jeter 2.50 6.00
3 Randy Johnson 1.00 2.50
4 Ichiro Suzuki 1.25 3.00
5 Alex Rodriguez 1.25 3.00
6 Mike Piazza 1.00 2.50
7 Greg Maddux 1.25 3.00
8 Curt Schilling .60 1.50
9 Frank Thomas 1.00 2.50
10 Torii Hunter .40 1.00
11 Al Kaline 1.00 2.50
12 Travis Hafner .40 1.00
13 Ivan Rodriguez .60 1.50
14 Rafael Palmeiro .60 1.50
15 Mike Schmidt 1.50 4.00
16 Johnny Bench 1.00 2.50
17 Jim Edmonds .60 1.50
18 Pedro Martinez .60 1.50
19 Robin Yount 1.00 2.50
20 Sammy Sosa 1.00 2.50

2005 Fleer Platinum Decade of Excellence Jersey Silver

STATED ODDS 1:54 HOBBY
*GOLD: .5X TO 1.2X BASIC
GOLD PRINT RUN 99 SERIAL #'d SETS
PATCH PLATINUM PRINT 10 #'d SETS
NO PATCH PLT.PRICING DUE TO SCARCITY
OVERALL GU ODDS 1:9 H, AU-GU 1:48 R
AK Al Kaline 6.00 15.00
AP Albert Pujols 6.00 15.00
CS Curt Schilling 4.00 10.00
FT Frank Thomas 4.00 10.00
GM Greg Maddux 4.00 10.00
IR Ivan Rodriguez 4.00 10.00
JB Johnny Bench 6.00 15.00
JE Jim Edmonds 3.00 8.00
MP Mike Piazza 4.00 10.00
MS Mike Schmidt 6.00 15.00
PM Pedro Martinez 4.00 10.00
RJ Randy Johnson 4.00 10.00
RP Rafael Palmeiro 4.00 10.00
RY Robin Yount 6.00 15.00
SS Sammy Sosa 4.00 10.00
TF Travis Hafner 3.00 8.00
TH Torii Hunter 3.00 8.00

2005 Fleer Platinum Diamond Dominators

*DOM: .4X TO 1X METAL DOM
STATED ODDS 1:12 RETAIL

2005 Fleer Platinum Diamond Dominators Jersey Silver

STATED ODDS 1:45 HOBBY
*GOLD: .4X TO 1X BASIC
OVERALL GU ODDS 1:9H, AU-GU 1:48 R
GOLD PRINT RUN 199 SERIAL #'d SETS
*RED: .4X TO 1X BASIC
RED STATED ODDS 1:50 RETAIL
AB Adrian Beltre 3.00 8.00
AP Albert Pujols 6.00 15.00
AS Alfonso Soriano 3.00 8.00
CJ Chipper Jones 4.00 10.00
CS Curt Schilling 4.00 10.00
DO David Ortiz 4.00 10.00
EG Eric Gagne 3.00 8.00
IR Ivan Rodriguez 4.00 10.00
JG Jason Giambi 3.00 8.00
KG Khalil Greene 4.00 10.00
KM Kaz Matsui 3.00 8.00
MC Miguel Cabrera 4.00 10.00
MP Mike Piazza 4.00 10.00
RB Rocco Baldelli 3.00 8.00
RJ Randy Johnson 4.00 10.00
SR Scott Rolen 4.00 10.00
SS Sammy Sosa 4.00 10.00
TH Tim Hudson 3.00 8.00
VG Vladimir Guerrero 4.00 10.00

2005 Fleer Platinum Diamond Dominators Metal

STATED ODDS 1:18 HOBBY
1 Albert Pujols 1.25 3.00
2 Curt Schilling .60 1.50
3 Adrian Beltre 1.00 2.50
4 Randy Johnson 1.00 2.50
5 Ivan Rodriguez .60 1.50
6 Mike Piazza 1.00 2.50
7 Chipper Jones 1.00 2.50
8 Sammy Sosa 1.00 2.50
9 Tim Hudson .60 1.50
10 Rocco Baldelli .40 1.00
11 Alfonso Soriano .60 1.50
12 David Ortiz 1.00 2.50
13 Kaz Matsui .40 1.00
14 Khalil Greene .40 1.00
15 Eric Gagne .40 1.00
16 Vladimir Guerrero .60 1.50
17 Jason Giambi .40 1.00
18 Scott Rolen .60 1.50
19 Miguel Cabrera 1.00 2.50

2005 Fleer Platinum Lumberjacks

STATED ODDS 1:6 HOBBY, 1:8 RETAIL
1 Albert Pujols 1.25 3.00
2 Jim Thome .60 1.50
3 Andruw Jones .40 1.00
4 Kaz Matsui .40 1.00
5 Adam Dunn .60 1.50
6 Bernie Williams .60 1.50
7 Hank Blalock .40 1.00
8 Bobby Abreu .40 1.00
9 Rocco Baldelli .40 1.00
10 Jacque Jones .40 1.00
11 Mark Teixeira .60 1.50
12 Ichiro Suzuki 1.25 3.00
13 Gary Sheffield .40 1.00
14 Sean Casey .40 1.00
15 Carl Crawford .60 1.50

2005 Fleer Platinum Lumberjacks Bat Silver

OVERALL GU ODDS 1:9 HOBBY
*GOLD: .4X TO 1X BASIC
GOLD PRINT RUN 250 SERIAL #'d SETS
BAT-PATCH PLATINUM PRINT 20 #'d SETS
NO BAT-PATCH PLT.PRICING AVAILABLE
AD Adam Dunn 3.00 8.00
AJ Andruw Jones 4.00 10.00
AP Albert Pujols 6.00 15.00
BA Bobby Abreu 3.00 8.00
BW Bernie Williams 4.00 10.00
CC Carl Crawford 3.00 8.00
GS Gary Sheffield 3.00 8.00
HB Hank Blalock 3.00 8.00
JJ Jacque Jones 3.00 8.00
JT Jim Thome 4.00 10.00
KM Kaz Matsui 3.00 8.00
MT Mark Teixeira 4.00 10.00
RB Rocco Baldelli 3.00 8.00
SC Sean Casey 3.00 8.00

2001 Fleer Premium

COMP.SET w/o SP's (200) 12.50 30.00
COMMON CARD (1-200) .15 .40
COMMON CARD (201-230) 2.00 5.00
COMMON EXCH. (231-235) 3.00 8.00
201-235 PRINT RUN 1999 SERIAL #'d SETS
231-235 EXCHANGE DEADLINE 05/01/02
JETER MM'S RANDOMLY INSERTED IN PACKS
1 Cal Ripken 1.25 3.00
2 Derek Jeter 1.00 2.50
3 Edgardo Alfonzo .15 .40
4 Luis Castillo .15 .40
5 Mike Lieberthal .15 .40
6 Kazuhiro Sasaki .15 .40
7 Jeff Kent .15 .40
8 Eric Karros .15 .40
9 Tom Glavine .25 .60
10 Jeromy Burnitz .15 .40
11 Travis Fryman .15 .40
12 Ron Coomer .15 .40
13 Jeff D'Amico .15 .40
14 Carlos Febles .15 .40
15 Kevin Brown .15 .40
16 Deivi Cruz .15 .40
17 Tino Martinez .25 .60
18 Bobby Abreu .15 .40
19 Roger Clemens .75 2.00
20 Jeffrey Hammonds .15 .40
21 Peter Bergeron .15 .40
22 Ray Lankford .15 .40
23 Scott Rolen .25 .60
24 Jermaine Dye .15 .40
25 Rusty Greer .15 .40
26 Frank Thomas .40 1.00
27 Jeff Bagwell .25 .60
28 Cliff Floyd .15 .40
29 Chris Singleton .15 .40
30 Steve Finley .15 .40
31 Orlando Hernandez .15 .40
32 Tom Goodwin .15 .40
33 Larry Walker .15 .40
34 Mike Sweeney .15 .40
35 Tim Hudson .15 .40
36 Kerry Wood .15 .40
37 Mike Lowell .15 .40
38 Andruw Jones .30 .75
39 Alex Gonzalez .15 .40
40 Juan Gonzalez .30 .75
41 J.D. Drew .15 .40
42 Mark McLemore .15 .40
43 Royce Clayton .15 .40
44 Paul O'Neill .25 .60
45 Carlos Beltran .15 .40
46 Phil Nevin .15 .40
47 Rondell White .15 .40
48 Gerald Williams .15 .40
49 Geoff Jenkins .15 .40
50 Marvin Benard .15 .40
51 Alex Rodriguez .50 1.25
52 Moises Alou .15 .40
53 Mike Lansing .15 .40
54 Omar Vizquel .25 .60
55 Eric Chavez .15 .40
56 Mark Quinn .15 .40
57 Mike Lamb .15 .40
58 Rick Ankiel .15 .40
59 Lance Berkman .15 .40
60 Jeff Conine .15 .40
61 B.J. Surhoff .15 .40
62 Todd Helton .25 .60
63 J.T. Snow .15 .40
64 John VanderWal .15 .40
65 Johnny Damon .25 .60
66 Bobby Higginson .15 .40
67 Carlos Delgado .30 .75
68 Shawn Green .15 .40
69 Mike Redmond .15 .40
70 Mike Piazza .60 1.50
71 Adrian Beltre .15 .40
72 Juan Encarnacion .15 .40
73 Chipper Jones .40 1.00
74 Garret Anderson .15 .40
75 Paul Konerko .15 .40
76 Barry Larkin .25 .60
77 Tony Gwynn .50 1.25
78 Rafael Palmeiro .25 .60
79 Randy Johnson .40 1.00
80 Mark Grace .30 .75
81 Javy Lopez .15 .40
82 Gabe Kapler .15 .40
83 Henry Rodriguez .15 .40
84 Raul Mondesi .15 .40
85 Adam Piatt .15 .40
86 Marquis Grissom .15 .40
87 Charles Johnson .15 .40
88 Sean Casey .15 .40
89 Manny Ramirez .25 .60
90 Curt Schilling .15 .40
91 Fernando Tatis .15 .40
92 Derek Bell .15 .40
93 Tony Clark .15 .40
94 Homer Bush .15 .40
95 Nomar Garciaparra .60 1.50
96 Vinny Castilla .15 .40
97 Ben Davis .15 .40
98 Carl Everett .15 .40
99 Damion Easley .15 .40
100 Craig Biggio .25 .60
101 Todd Hollandsworth .15 .40
102 Jay Payton .15 .40
103 Gary Sheffield .15 .40
104 Sandy Alomar Jr. .15 .40
105 Doug Glanville .15 .40
106 Barry Bonds 1.00 2.50
107 Tim Salmon .25 .60
108 Terrence Long .15 .40
109 Jorge Posada .25 .60
110 Jose Offerman .15 .40
111 Edgar Martinez .25 .60
112 Jeremy Giambi .15 .40
113 Dean Palmer .15 .40
114 Roberto Alomar .30 .75
115 Aaron Boone .15 .40
116 Adam Kennedy .15 .40
117 Joe Randa .15 .40
118 Jose Vidro .15 .40
119 Tony Batista .15 .40
120 Kevin Young .15 .40
121 Preston Wilson .15 .40
122 Jason Kendall .15 .40
123 Mark Kotsay .15 .40
124 Timo Perez .15 .40
125 Eric Young .15 .40
126 Greg Maddux .60 1.50
127 Richard Hidalgo .15 .40
128 Brian Giles .15 .40
129 Fred McGriff .25 .60
130 Troy Glaus .15 .40
131 Todd Walker .15 .40
132 Brady Anderson .15 .40
133 Jim Edmonds .15 .40
134 Ben Grieve .15 .40
135 Greg Vaughn .15 .40
136 Robin Ventura .15 .40
137 Sammy Sosa .40 1.00
138 Rich Aurilia .15 .40
139 Jose Valentin .15 .40
140 Trot Nixon .15 .40
141 Troy Percival .15 .40
142 Bernie Williams .25 .60
143 Warren Morris .15 .40
144 Jacque Jones .15 .40
145 Danny Bautista .15 .40
146 A.J. Pierzynski .15 .40
147 Mark McGwire 1.00 2.50
148 Rafael Furcal .15 .40
149 Ray Durham .15 .40
150 Mike Mussina .30 .75
151 Jay Bell .15 .40
152 David Wells .15 .40
153 Ken Caminiti .15 .40
154 Jim Thome .25 .60
155 Ivan Rodriguez .25 .60
156 Milton Bradley .15 .40
157 Ken Griffey Jr. .75 2.00
158 Al Leiter .15 .40
159 Corey Koskie .15 .40
160 Shannon Stewart .15 .40
161 Mo Vaughn .15 .40
162 Pedro Martinez .25 .60
163 Todd Hundley .15 .40
164 Darin Erstad .30 .75
165 Ruben Rivera .15 .40
166 Richie Sexson .15 .40
167 Andres Galarraga .15 .40
168 Darryl Kile .15 .40
169 Jose Cruz Jr. .15 .40
170 David Justice .15 .40
171 Vladimir Guerrero .40 1.00
172 Jeff Cirillo .15 .40
173 John Olerud .15 .40
174 Devon White .15 .40
175 Ron Belliard .15 .40
176 Pokey Reese .15 .40
177 Mike Hampton .15 .40
178 David Ortiz .40 1.00
179 Magglio Ordonez .15 .40

180 Ruben Mateo .15 .40
181 Carlos Lee .15 .40
182 Matt Williams .15 .40
183 Miguel Tejada .15 .40
184 Scott Elarton .15 .40
185 Bret Boone .15 .40
186 Pat Burrell .15 .40
187 Brad Radke .15 .40
188 Brian Jordan .15 .40
189 Matt Lawton .15 .40
190 Al Martin .15 .40
191 Albert Belle .15 .40
192 Tony Womack .15 .40
193 Roger Cedeno .15 .40
194 Travis Lee .15 .40
195 Dmitri Young .15 .40
196 Jay Buhner .15 .40
197 Jason Giambi .30 .75
198 Jason Tyner .15 .40
199 Ben Petrick .15 .40
200 Jose Canseco .30 .75
201 Nick Johnson 2.00 5.00
202 Jace Brewer 2.00 5.00
203 Ryan Freel RC 2.00 5.00
204 Jaisen Randolph RC 2.00 5.00
205 Marcus Giles 2.00 5.00
206 Claudio Vargas RC 2.00 5.00
207 Brian Cole 2.00 5.00
208 Scott Hodges 2.00 5.00
209 Winston Abreu RC 2.00 5.00
210 Shea Hillenbrand 2.00 5.00
211 Larry Barnes 2.00 5.00
212 Paul Phillips RC 2.00 5.00
213 Pedro Santana RC 2.00 5.00
214 Ivanon Coffie 2.00 5.00
215 Junior Spivey RC 3.00 8.00
216 Donzell McDonald 2.00 5.00
217 Vernon Wells 2.00 5.00
218 Corey Patterson 2.00 5.00
219 Sang-Hoon Lee 2.00 5.00
220 Jack Cust 2.00 5.00
221 Jason Romano 2.00 5.00
222 Jack Wilson RC 3.00 8.00
223 Adam Everett 2.00 5.00
224 Esix Snead RC 2.00 5.00
225 Jason Hart 2.00 5.00
226 Joe Lawrence 2.00 5.00
227 Brandon Inge 2.00 5.00
228 Alex Escobar 2.00 5.00
229 Abraham Nunez 2.00 5.00
230 Jared Sandberg 2.00 5.00
231 Ichiro Suzuki RC 12.00 30.00
232 Tsuyoshi Shinjo RC 4.00 10.00
233 Albert Pujols RC 40.00 100.00
234 Wilson Betemit RC 4.00 10.00
235 Drew Henson RC 4.00 10.00
MM1 Derek Jeter MM/1995 5.00 12.00
NNO Derek Jeter MM AU/95 150.00 300.00

2001 Fleer Premium Star Ruby

*RUBY 1-200: 5X TO 12X BASE HI
*RUBY 201-230: .3X TO .8X BASE HI
STATED PRINT RUN 125 SERIAL #'d SETS

2001 Fleer Premium A Time for Heroes

COMPLETE SET (20) 40.00 80.00
STATED ODDS 1:20
1 Darin Erstad .75 2.00
2 Alex Rodriguez 2.00 5.00
3 Shawn Green .75 2.00
4 Jeff Bagwell 1.00 2.50
5 Sammy Sosa 1.50 4.00
6 Derek Jeter 4.00 10.00
7 Nomar Garciaparra 2.50 6.00
8 Carlos Delgado .75 2.00
9 Pat Burrell .75 2.00
10 Tony Gwynn 2.00 5.00
11 Chipper Jones 1.50 4.00
12 Jason Giambi .75 2.00
13 Magglio Ordonez .75 2.00
14 Troy Glaus .75 2.00
15 Ivan Rodriguez 1.00 2.50
16 Andruw Jones 1.00 2.50
17 Vladimir Guerrero 1.50 4.00
18 Ken Griffey Jr. 3.00 8.00
19 J.D. Drew .75 2.00
20 Todd Helton 1.00 2.50

2001 Fleer Premium Brother Wood

STATED ODDS 1:108
BW1 Vladimir Guerrero 6.00 15.00
BW2 Andruw Jones 6.00 15.00
BW3 Corey Patterson 4.00 10.00
BW4 Magglio Ordonez 4.00 10.00
BW5 Jason Giambi 4.00 10.00
BW6 Rafael Palmeiro 6.00 15.00
BW7 Eric Chavez 4.00 10.00
BW8 Pat Burrell 4.00 10.00
BW9 Adrian Beltre 4.00 10.00

2001 Fleer Premium Decades of Excellence

STATED ODDS 1:12
CARD NUMBER 17 DOES NOT EXIST
1 L.Gehrig 8.00 20.00
B.Ruth
2 Lloyd Waner 1.25 3.00
3 Jimmie Foxx 2.00 5.00
4 Hank Greenberg 2.00 5.00
5 Ted Williams 5.00 12.00
6 Johnny Mize 1.25 3.00
7 Enos Slaughter 1.25 3.00
8 Jackie Robinson 2.00 5.00
9 Stan Musial 3.00 8.00
10 Duke Snider 1.25 3.00
11 Eddie Mathews 2.00 5.00
12 Roy Campanella 2.00 5.00
13 Yogi Berra 2.00 5.00
14 Pee Wee Reese 2.00 5.00
15 Phil Rizzuto 2.00 5.00
16 Al Kaline 2.00 5.00
18 Frank Howard 1.25 3.00
19 Roberto Clemente 6.00 15.00
20 Bob Gibson 1.25 3.00
21 Roger Maris 2.00 5.00
22 Don Drysdale 1.25 3.00
23 Maury Wills 1.25 3.00
24 Tom Seaver 1.25 3.00
25 Reggie Jackson 1.25 3.00
26 Johnny Bench 2.00 5.00
27 Carlton Fisk 1.25 3.00
28 Rod Carew 1.25 3.00
29 Steve Carlton 1.25 3.00
30 Mike Schmidt 5.00 12.00
31 Nolan Ryan 6.00 15.00
32 Rickey Henderson 2.00 5.00
33 Roger Clemens 4.00 10.00
34 Don Mattingly 5.00 12.00
35 George Brett 5.00 12.00
36 Greg Maddux 3.00 8.00
37 Cal Ripken 6.00 15.00
38 Chipper Jones 2.00 5.00
39 Barry Bonds 5.00 12.00
40 Ivan Rodriguez 1.25 3.00
41 M.McGwire 6.00 15.00
S.Sosa
42 Ken Griffey Jr. 4.00 10.00
43 Tony Gwynn 2.50 6.00
44 Vladimir Guerrero 2.00 5.00
45 Shawn Green 1.25 3.00
46 A-Rod 4.00 10.00
Jeter
Nomar
47 Pat Burrell 1.25 3.00
48 Rick Ankiel 1.25 3.00
49 Eric Chavez 1.25 3.00
50 Troy Glaus 1.25 3.00

2001 Fleer Premium Decades of Excellence Autograph

STATED PRINT RUNS LISTED BELOW
1 Rick Ankiel/99 15.00 40.00
2 Johnny Bench/67 40.00 80.00
3 Barry Bonds/86 60.00 120.00
4 George Brett/73 60.00 120.00
5 Rod Carew/67 30.00 60.00
6 Steve Carlton/65 15.00 40.00
7 Eric Chavez/98 15.00 40.00
8 Carlton Fisk/69 30.00 60.00
9 Bob Gibson/59 30.00 60.00
10 Tony Gwynn/82 30.00 60.00
11 Reggie Jackson/67 40.00 80.00
12 Chipper Jones/93 40.00 80.00
13 Al Kaline/53 40.00 100.00
14 Don Mattingly/82 30.00 80.00
15 Cal Ripken/81 50.00 100.00
16 Nolan Ryan/66 75.00 150.00
17 Mike Schmidt/72 30.00 80.00
18 Tom Seaver/67 30.00 80.00
19 Enos Slaughter/38 30.00 60.00
20 Maury Wills/59 15.00 40.00

2001 Fleer Premium Decades of Excellence Memorabilia

STATED ODDS 1:217 HOBBY
SP PRINT RUNS PROVIDED BY FLEER
SP'S ARE NOT SERIAL-NUMBERED
1 Rick Ankiel Jsy 4.00 10.00
2 Barry Bonds Jsy 30.00 60.00
3 Pat Burrell Jsy 6.00 15.00
4 Roy Campanella Bat SP/50 20.00 50.00
5 Eric Chavez Bat 6.00 15.00
6 R.Clemente Bat SP/50 50.00 100.00
7 Carlton Fisk Uniform 10.00 25.00
8 Jimmie Foxx Bat SP/50 50.00 100.00
9 Shawn Green Bat 6.00 15.00
10 Tony Gwynn Jsy 10.00 25.00
11 Reggie Jackson Jsy 10.00 25.00
12 Greg Maddux Jsy 10.00 25.00
13 Roger Maris Uni 30.00 60.00
14 Pee Wee Reese Jsy 10.00 25.00
16 Ivan Rodriguez Bat 10.00 25.00
20 Duke Snider Bat 10.00 25.00
21 Ted Williams Jsy SP/50 50.00 100.00

2001 Fleer Premium Diamond Dominators Game Jersey

STATED ODDS 1:51
DD1 Troy Glaus 2.00 5.00
DD2 Darin Erstad 2.00 5.00
DD3 J.D. Drew 2.00 5.00
DD4 Barry Bonds 8.00 20.00
DD5 Roger Clemens 8.00 20.00
DD6 Vladimir Guerrero 5.00 12.00
DD7 Tony Gwynn 5.00 12.00
DD8 Greg Maddux 8.00 20.00
DD9 Cal Ripken 10.00 25.00
DD10 Ivan Rodriguez 3.00 8.00
DD11 Frank Thomas 5.00 12.00
DD12 Bernie Williams 3.00 8.00
DD13 Jeromy Burnitz 2.00 5.00
DD14 Juan Gonzalez 2.00 5.00

2001 Fleer Premium Diamond Patches

STATED PRINT RUN 100 SERIAL #'d SETS
DD1 Troy Glaus 20.00 50.00
DD2 Darin Erstad 20.00 50.00
DD3 J.D. Drew 20.00 50.00
DD4 Barry Bonds 20.00 50.00
DD5 Roger Clemens 50.00 100.00
DD6 Vladimir Guerrero 40.00 80.00
DD7 Tony Gwynn 40.00 80.00
DD8 Greg Maddux 40.00 80.00
DD9 Cal Ripken 40.00 80.00
DD10 Ivan Rodriguez 40.00 80.00
DD11 Frank Thomas 40.00 80.00
DD12 Bernie Williams 40.00 80.00
DD13 Jeromy Burnitz 20.00 50.00
DD14 Juan Gonzalez 20.00 50.00

2001 Fleer Premium Grip It and Rip It

COMPLETE SET (15) 8.00 20.00
STATED ODDS 1:6
1 R.Clemens 1.25 3.00
D.Jeter
2 S.Rolen .40 1.00
P.Burrell
3 G.Maddux .75 2.00
A.Jones
4 S.Stewart .40 1.00
C.Delgado
5 S.Estes 1.25 3.00
B.Bonds
6 C.Eldred .50 1.25
F.Thomas
7 M.McGwire 1.25 3.00
J.Edmonds
8 J.Vidro .50 1.25
V.Guerrero
9 P.Martinez .75 2.00
N.Garciaparra
10 T.Glavine .50 1.25
C.Jones
11 K.Griffey Jr. 1.00 2.50
S.Casey
12 J.Bagwell .40 1.00
M.Alou
13 T.Glaus .40 1.00
D.Erstad
14 M.Piazza .75 2.00
R.Ventura
15 E.Chavez .40 1.00
J.Giambi

2001 Fleer Premium Grip It and Rip It Plus

PRINT RUNS LISTED BELOW
200 OF EACH BASE-BAT CARD PRODUCED
100 OF EACH BALL-BAT CARD PRODUCED
1 R.Clemens 30.00 80.00
D.Jeter/100
2 S.Rolen 10.00 25.00
P.Burrell/200
3 G.Maddux 15.00 40.00
A.Jones/100
4 S.Stewart 6.00 15.00
C.Delgado/200
5 S.Estes 20.00 50.00
B.Bonds/100
6 C.Eldred 10.00 25.00
F.Thomas/200
7 McGwire 40.00 80.00
Edmonds/100
8 J.Vidro 10.00 25.00
V.Guerrero/200
9 Pedro 40.00 80.00
Nomar/100
10 T.Glavine 10.00 25.00
C.Jones/200
11 K.Griffey Jr. 15.00 40.00
S.Casey/200
12 J.Bagwell 10.00 25.00
M.Alou/200
13 T.Glaus 6.00 15.00
D.Erstad/200
14 M.Piazza 40.00 80.00
R.Ventura/100
15 E.Chavez 6.00 15.00
J.Giambi/200

2001 Fleer Premium Heroes Game Jersey

STATED ODDS 1:101 HOBBY
1 Pat Burrell 1.50 4.00
2 J.D. Drew 1.50 4.00
3 Jason Giambi 1.50 4.00
4 Troy Glaus 1.50 4.00
5 Shawn Green 1.50 4.00
6 Todd Helton 2.50 6.00
7 Derek Jeter 10.00 25.00
8 Andruw Jones 2.50 6.00
9 Chipper Jones 4.00 10.00
10 Ivan Rodriguez 2.50 6.00

2001 Fleer Premium Home Field Advantage

COMPLETE SET (15) 30.00 80.00
STATED ODDS 1:72 HOB, 1:144 RET
1 Mike Piazza 2.50 6.00
2 Derek Jeter 6.00 15.00
3 Ken Griffey Jr. 5.00 12.00
4 Carlos Delgado 1.00 2.50
5 Chipper Jones 2.50 6.00
6 Alex Rodriguez 3.00 8.00
7 Sammy Sosa 1.50 4.00
8 Scott Rolen 1.50 4.00
9 Nomar Garciaparra 1.50 4.00
10 Todd Helton 1.50 4.00
11 Vladimir Guerrero 2.50 6.00
12 Jeff Bagwell 1.50 4.00
13 Barry Bonds 4.00 10.00
14 Cal Ripken 8.00 20.00
15 Mark McGwire 4.00 10.00

2001 Fleer Premium Home Field Advantage Game Wall

STATED PRINT RUN 100 SERIAL #'d SETS
1 Mike Piazza 15.00 40.00
2 Derek Jeter 12.00 60.00
3 Ken Griffey Jr. 15.00 40.00
4 Carlos Delgado 6.00 15.00
5 Chipper Jones 10.00 25.00
6 Alex Rodriguez 15.00 40.00
7 Sammy Sosa 10.00 25.00
8 Scott Rolen 10.00 25.00
9 Nomar Garciaparra 15.00 40.00
10 Todd Helton 10.00 25.00
11 Vladimir Guerrero 10.00 25.00
12 Jeff Bagwell 10.00 25.00
13 Barry Bonds 10.00 25.00
14 Cal Ripken 30.00 80.00
15 Mark McGwire 30.00 80.00

2001 Fleer Premium Performers Game Base

STATED PRINT RUN 150 SERIAL #'d SETS
SP1 Mark McGwire 10.00 25.00
SP2 Alex Rodriguez 8.00 20.00
SP3 Nomar Garciaparra 4.00 10.00
SP4 Derek Jeter 15.00 40.00
SP5 Vladimir Guerrero 6.00 15.00
SP6 Todd Helton 4.00 10.00
SP7 Chipper Jones 6.00 15.00
SP8 Mike Piazza 6.00 15.00
SP9 Ivan Rodriguez 4.00 10.00
SP10 Tony Gwynn 6.00 15.00
SP11 Cal Ripken 20.00 50.00
SP12 Barry Bonds 10.00 25.00
SP13 Jeff Bagwell 4.00 10.00
SP14 Ken Griffey Jr. 12.00 30.00
SP15 Sammy Sosa 4.00 10.00

2001 Fleer Premium Solid Performers

COMPLETE SET (15) 40.00 80.00
STATED ODDS 1:20
1 Mark McGwire 3.00 8.00
2 Alex Rodriguez 1.50 4.00
3 Nomar Garciaparra 2.00 5.00
4 Derek Jeter 3.00 8.00
5 Vladimir Guerrero 1.25 3.00
6 Todd Helton 1.25 3.00
7 Chipper Jones 1.25 3.00
8 Mike Piazza 2.00 5.00
9 Ivan Rodriguez 1.25 3.00
10 Tony Gwynn 1.50 4.00
11 Cal Ripken 4.00 10.00
12 Barry Bonds 3.00 8.00
13 Jeff Bagwell 1.25 3.00
14 Ken Griffey Jr. 2.50 6.00
15 Sammy Sosa 1.25 3.00

2002 Fleer Premium

COMP.MASTER SET (250) 50.00 120.00
COMPLETE SET (240) 30.00 80.00
COMP.SET w/o SP'S (200) 12.50 30.00
COMP.UPDATE SET (10) 15.00 40.00
COMMON CARD (1-200) .15 .40
COMMON CARD (201-240) .75 2.00
201-240 STATED ODDS 1:2
COMMON CARD (241-250) 1.50 4.00
241-250 AVAIL.VIA MAIL EXCH.PROGRAM
241-250 PRINT RUN 2002 SERIAL #'d SETS
1 Garret Anderson .15 .40
2 Derek Jeter 1.00 2.50
3 Ken Griffey Jr. .75 2.00
4 Luis Castillo .15 .40
5 Richie Sexson .15 .40
6 Mike Mussina .25 .60
7 Rickey Henderson .40 1.00
8 Bud Smith .15 .40
9 David Eckstein .15 .40
10 Nomar Garciaparra .60 1.50
11 Barry Larkin .25 .60
12 Cliff Floyd .15 .40
13 Ben Sheets .15 .40
14 Jorge Posada .25 .60
15 Phil Nevin .15 .40
16 Fernando Vina .15 .40
17 Darin Erstad .15 .40
18 Shea Hillenbrand .15 .40
19 Todd Walker .15 .40
20 Charles Johnson .15 .40
21 Cristian Guzman .15 .40
22 Mariano Rivera .40 1.00
23 Bubba Trammell .15 .40
24 Brent Abernathy .15 .40
25 Troy Glaus .15 .40
26 Pedro Martinez .25 .60
27 Dmitri Young .15 .40
28 Derrek Lee .25 .60
29 Torii Hunter .15 .40
30 Alfonso Soriano .15 .40
31 Rich Aurilia .15 .40
32 Ben Grieve .15 .40
33 Tim Salmon .25 .60
34 Trot Nixon .15 .40
35 Roberto Alomar .25 .60
36 Mike Lowell .15 .40
37 Jacque Jones .15 .40
38 Bernie Williams .25 .60
39 Barry Bonds 1.00 2.50
40 Toby Hall .15 .40
41 Mo Vaughn .15 .40
42 Hideo Nomo .40 1.00
43 Travis Fryman .15 .40
44 Preston Wilson .15 .40
45 Corey Koskie .15 .40
46 Eric Chavez .15 .40
47 Andres Galarraga .15 .40
48 Greg Vaughn .15 .40
49 Shawn Wooten .15 .40
50 Manny Ramirez .25 .60
51 Juan Gonzalez .15 .40
52 Moises Alou .15 .40
53 Joe Mays .15 .40
54 Johnny Damon .25 .60
55 Jeff Kent .15 .40
56 Frank Catalanotto .15 .40
57 Steve Finley .15 .40
58 Jason Varitek .40 1.00
59 Kenny Lofton .15 .40
60 Jeff Bagwell .25 .60
61 Doug Mientkiewicz .15 .40
62 Jermaine Dye .15 .40
63 John Vander Wal .15 .40
64 Gabe Kapler .15 .40
65 Luis Gonzalez .15 .40
66 Jon Lieber .15 .40
67 C.C. Sabathia .15 .40
68 Lance Berkman .15 .40
69 Eric Milton .15 .40
70 Jason Giambi Yankees .15 .40
71 Ichiro Suzuki .75 2.00
72 Rafael Palmeiro .25 .60
73 Mark Grace .25 .60
74 Fred McGriff .25 .60
75 Jim Thome .25 .60
76 Craig Biggio .25 .60
77 A.J. Pierzynski .15 .40
78 Ramon Hernandez .15 .40
79 Paul Abbott .15 .40
80 Alex Rodriguez .50 1.50
81 Randy Johnson .40 1.00
82 Corey Patterson .15 .40
83 Omar Vizquel .25 .60
84 Richard Hidalgo .15 .40
85 Luis Rivas .15 .40
86 Tim Hudson .15 .40
87 Bret Boone .15 .40
88 Ivan Rodriguez .25 .60
89 Junior Spivey .15 .40
90 Sammy Sosa .40 1.00
91 Jeff Cirillo .15 .40
92 Roy Oswalt .15 .40
93 Orlando Cabrera .15 .40
94 Terrence Long .15 .40
95 Mike Cameron .15 .40
96 Homer Bush .15 .40
97 Reggie Sanders .15 .40
98 Rondell White .15 .40
99 Mike Hampton .15 .40
100 Carlos Beltran .15 .40
101 Vladimir Guerrero .40 1.00
102 Miguel Tejada .15 .40
103 Freddy Garcia .15 .40
104 Jose Cruz Jr. .15 .40
105 Curt Schilling .15 .40
106 Kerry Wood .15 .40
107 Todd Helton .25 .60
108 Neifi Perez .15 .40
109 Javier Vazquez .15 .40
110 Barry Zito .15 .40
111 Edgar Martinez .25 .60
112 Carlos Delgado .15 .40
113 Matt Williams .15 .40
114 Eric Young .15 .40
115 Alex Ochoa .15 .40
116 Mark Quinn .15 .40
117 Jose Vidro .15 .40
118 Bobby Abreu .15 .40
119 David Bell .15 .40
120 Brad Fullmer .15 .40
121 Rafael Furcal .15 .40
122 Ray Durham .15 .40
123 Jose Ortiz .15 .40
124 Joe Randa .15 .40
125 Edgardo Alfonzo .15 .40
126 Marlon Anderson .15 .40
127 Jamie Moyer .15 .40
128 Alex Gonzalez .15 .40
129 Marcus Giles .15 .40
130 Keith Foulke .15 .40
131 Juan Pierre .15 .40
132 Mike Sweeney .15 .40
133 Matt Lawton .15 .40
134 Pat Burrell .15 .40
135 John Olerud .15 .40
136 Raul Mondesi .15 .40
137 Tom Glavine .25 .60
138 Paul Konerko .15 .40
139 Larry Walker .15 .40
140 Adrian Beltre .15 .40
141 Al Leiter .15 .40
142 Mike Lieberthal .15 .40
143 Kazuhiro Sasaki .15 .40
144 Shannon Stewart .15 .40
145 Andruw Jones .25 .60
146 Carlos Lee .15 .40
147 Roger Cedeno .15 .40
148 Kevin Brown .15 .40
149 Jay Payton .15 .40
150 Scott Rolen .25 .60
151 J.D. Drew .15 .40
152 Chipper Jones .40 1.00
153 Magglio Ordonez .15 .40
154 Tony Clark .15 .40
155 Shawn Green .15 .40
156 Mike Piazza .60 1.50
157 Jimmy Rollins .15 .40
158 Jim Edmonds .15 .40
159 Javy Lopez .15 .40
160 Chris Singleton .15 .40
161 Juan Encarnacion .15 .40
162 Eric Karros .15 .40
163 Tsuyoshi Shinjo .15 .40
164 Brian Giles .15 .40
165 Darryl Kile .15 .40
166 Greg Maddux .60 1.50
167 Frank Thomas .40 1.00
168 Shane Halter .15 .40
169 Paul LoDuca .15 .40
170 Robin Ventura .15 .40
171 Jason Kendall .15 .40
172 Jason Hart .15 .40
173 Brady Anderson .15 .40
174 Jose Valentin .15 .40
175 Bobby Higginson .15 .40
176 Gary Sheffield .15 .40
177 Roger Clemens .75 2.00
178 Aramis Ramirez .15 .40
179 Matt Morris .15 .40
180 Jeff Conine .15 .40
181 Aaron Boone .15 .40
182 Jose Macias .15 .40
183 Jeromy Burnitz .15 .40
184 Carl Everett .15 .40
185 Trevor Hoffman .15 .40
186 Placido Polanco .15 .40
187 Jay Gibbons .15 .40
188 Sean Casey .15 .40
189 Josh Beckett .15 .40
190 Jeffrey Hammonds .15 .40
191 Chuck Knoblauch .15 .40
192 Ryan Klesko .15 .40
193 Albert Pujols .75 2.00
194 Chris Richard .15 .40
195 Adam Dunn .15 .40
196 A.J. Burnett .15 .40
197 Geoff Jenkins .15 .40
198 Tino Martinez .25 .60
199 Ray Lankford .15 .40
200 Edgar Renteria .15 .40
201 Eric Cyr PROS .75 2.00
202 Travis Phelps PROS .75 2.00
203 Rick Bauer PROS .75 2.00
204 Mark Prior PROS 1.50 4.00
205 Wilson Betemit PROS .75 2.00
206 Dewon Brazelton PROS .75 2.00
207 Cody Ransom PROS .75 2.00
208 Donnie Bridges PROS .75 2.00
209 Justin Duchscherer PROS .75 2.00
210 Nate Cornejo PROS .75 2.00
211 Jason Romano PROS .75 2.00
212 Juan Cruz PROS .75 2.00
213 Pedro Santana PROS .75 2.00
214 Ryan Drese PROS .75 2.00
215 Bert Snow PROS .75 2.00
216 Nate Frese PROS .75 2.00
217 Rafael Soriano PROS .75 2.00
218 Franklin Nunez PROS RC .75 2.00
219 Tim Spooneybarger PROS .75 2.00
220 Willie Harris PROS .75 2.00
221 Billy Sylvester PROS .75 2.00
222 Carlos Hernandez PROS .75 2.00
223 Mark Teixeira PROS 1.50 4.00
224 Adrian Hernandez PROS .75 2.00
225 Andres Torres PROS .75 2.00
226 Marlon Byrd PROS .75 2.00
227 Juan Rivera PROS .75 2.00
228 Adam Johnson PROS .75 2.00
229 Justin Kaye PROS .75 2.00
230 Kyle Kessel PROS .75 2.00
231 Horacio Ramirez PROS .75 2.00
232 Brandon Larson PROS .75 2.00
233 Luis Lopez PROS .75 2.00
234 Rob Mackowiak PROS .75 2.00
235 Henry Mateo PROS .75 2.00
236 Corky Miller PROS .75 2.00
237 Greg Miller PROS .75 2.00
238 Dustan Mohr PROS .75 2.00
239 Bill Ortega PROS .75 2.00
240 Billy Hall PROS .75 2.00
241 Kazuhisa Ishii UPD RC 2.00 5.00
242 So Taguchi UPD RC 2.00 5.00
243 Takahito Nomura UPD RC 1.50 4.00
244 Satoru Komiyama UPD RC 1.50 4.00
245 Jorge Padilla UPD RC 1.50 4.00
246 Anastacio Martinez UPD RC 1.50 4.00
247 Rodrigo Rosario UPD RC 1.50 4.00
248 Ben Howard UPD RC 1.50 4.00
249 Reed Johnson UPD RC 2.00 5.00
250 Mike Crudale UPD RC 1.50 4.00
P2 Derek Jeter Promo 1.00 2.50

2002 Fleer Premium Star Ruby

*STARS 1-200: 5X TO 12X BASIC
*PROSPECTS 201-240: 1X TO 2.5X BASIC
1-240 RANDOM INSERTS IN PACKS
241-250 AVAIL.VIA MAIL EXCH.PROGRAM
1-240 PRINT RUN 125 SERIAL #'d SETS
241-250 PRINT RUN 50 SERIAL #'d SETS

2002 Fleer Premium Diamond Stars

COMPLETE SET (20) 100.00 200.00
STATED ODDS 1:72
1 Pedro Martinez 2.00 5.00
2 Derek Jeter 8.00 20.00
3 Sammy Sosa 3.00 8.00
4 Ken Griffey Jr. 6.00 15.00
5 Chipper Jones 3.00 8.00
6 Roger Clemens 6.00 15.00
7 Ichiro Suzuki 6.00 15.00
8 Jeff Bagwell 2.00 5.00
9 Luis Gonzalez 2.00 5.00
10 Manny Ramirez 2.00 5.00
11 Alex Rodriguez 4.00 10.00
12 Kazuhiro Sasaki 2.00 5.00
13 Mike Piazza 5.00 12.00
14 Vladimir Guerrero 3.00 8.00
15 Randy Johnson 3.00 8.00
16 Ivan Rodriguez 2.00 5.00
17 Nomar Garciaparra 5.00 12.00
18 Barry Bonds 8.00 20.00
19 Todd Helton 2.00 5.00
20 Greg Maddux 5.00 12.00

2002 Fleer Premium Diamond Stars Autograph

RANDOM INSERT IN PACKS
STATED PRINT RUN 100 CARDS
1 Derek Jeter/100 * 150.00 400.00

2002 Fleer Premium Diamond Stars Game Used

STATED ODDS 1:105
SP PRINT RUNS PROVIDED BY FLEER
SP'S ARE NOT SERIAL-NUMBERED
1 Barry Bonds Jsy 5.00 12.00
2 Manny Ramirez Jsy 2.00 5.00
3 Ivan Rodriguez Jsy 2.00 5.00
4 Kazuhiro Sasaki Jsy 1.25 3.00
5 Roger Clemens Jsy 4.00 10.00
6 Alex Rodriguez Jsy 4.00 10.00
7 Derek Jeter Bat 8.00 20.00
8 Chipper Jones Jsy 3.00 8.00
9 Todd Helton Pants 2.00 5.00
10 Luis Gonzalez Jsy 1.25 3.00
11 Mike Piazza Jsy 3.00 8.00
12 N.Garciaparra Bat SP/150 15.00 40.00

2002 Fleer Premium Diamond Stars Game Used Premium

RANDOM INSERTS IN PACKS
STATED PRINT RUN 75 SERIAL #'d SETS
ALL CARDS FEATURE JERSEY PATCHES
1 Barry Bonds 20.00 50.00
2 Roger Clemens 40.00 100.00
3 Todd Helton 20.00 50.00
4 Chipper Jones 20.00 50.00
5 Manny Ramirez 20.00 50.00
6 Alex Rodriguez 30.00 80.00
7 Ivan Rodriguez 20.00 50.00
8 Luis Gonzalez 15.00 40.00
9 Mike Piazza 20.00 50.00
10 Kazuhiro Sasaki 15.00 40.00

2002 Fleer Premium Diamond Stars Dual Game Used

STATED PRINT RUN 100 SERIAL #'d SETS
PREMIUM PRINT RUN 25 #'d SETS
NO PREMIUM PRICING DUE TO SCARCITY
1 Barry Bonds Jsy-Pants 10.00 25.00
2 Todd Helton Jsy-Bat 10.00 25.00
3 Derek Jeter Jsy-Bat 40.00 80.00
4 Chipper Jones Jsy-Bat 10.00 25.00
5 Mike Piazza Bat-Jsy 20.00 50.00
6 Manny Ramirez Jsy-Jsy 10.00 25.00
7 Alex Rodriguez Jsy-Hat 25.00 60.00

2002 Fleer Premium International Pride

COMPLETE SET (15) 10.00 25.00
STATED ODDS 1:6
1 Larry Walker .75 2.00
2 Albert Pujols 1.50 4.00
3 Juan Gonzalez .75 2.00
4 Ichiro Suzuki 1.50 4.00
5 Rafael Palmeiro .75 2.00
6 Carlos Delgado .75 2.00
7 Kazuhiro Sasaki .75 2.00
8 Vladimir Guerrero .75 2.00
9 Bobby Abreu .75 2.00
10 Ivan Rodriguez .75 2.00
11 Tsuyoshi Shinjo .75 2.00
12 Pedro Martinez .75 2.00
13 Andruw Jones .75 2.00
14 Sammy Sosa .75 2.00
15 Chan Ho Park .75 2.00

2002 Fleer Premium International Pride Game Used

STATED ODDS 1:90
1 Carlos Delgado Jsy 6.00 15.00
2 Juan Gonzalez Jsy 6.00 15.00
3 Andruw Jones Bat 6.00 15.00
4 Pedro Martinez Jsy 6.00 15.00
5 Rafael Palmeiro Jsy 6.00 15.00
6 Chan Ho Park Jsy 6.00 15.00
7 Albert Pujols Jsy 10.00 25.00
8 Ivan Rodriguez Bat 6.00 15.00
9 Kazuhiro Sasaki Jsy 6.00 15.00
10 Tsuyoshi Shinjo Jsy 6.00 15.00

2002 Fleer Premium International Pride Game Used Premium

RANDOM INSERTS IN PACKS
STATED PRINT RUN 75 SERIAL #'d SETS
ALL CARDS FEATURE JERSEY PATCHES
1 Carlos Delgado 15.00 40.00
2 Juan Gonzalez 15.00 40.00
3 Andruw Jones 20.00 50.00
4 Pedro Martinez 20.00 50.00
5 Chan Ho Park 15.00 40.00
6 Ivan Rodriguez 20.00 50.00
7 Tsuyoshi Shinjo 15.00 40.00
8 Rafael Palmeiro 20.00 50.00
9 Albert Pujols 30.00 80.00
10 Kazuhiro Sasaki 15.00 40.00

2002 Fleer Premium Legendary Dynasties

STATED ODDS 1:18
*GOLD: .6X TO 1.5X BASIC DYNASTY
GOLD RANDOM INSERT IN PACKS
GOLD PRINT RUN 300 SERIAL #'d SETS
1 Honus Wagner 4.00 10.00
2 Christy Mathewson 4.00 10.00
3 Lou Gehrig 5.00 12.00
4 Babe Ruth 8.00 20.00
5 Jimmie Foxx 4.00 10.00
6 Lefty Grove 3.00 8.00
7 Al Simmons 2.00 5.00
8 Bill Dickey 3.00 8.00
9 Stan Musial 4.00 10.00
10 Enos Slaughter 2.00 5.00
11 Johnny Mize 2.00 5.00
12 Yogi Berra 4.00 10.00
13 Whitey Ford 3.00 8.00
14 Jackie Robinson 2.00 5.00
15 Duke Snider 3.00 8.00
16 Roger Maris 4.00 10.00
17 Jim Palmer 2.00 5.00
18 Don Drysdale 3.00 8.00
19 Brooks Robinson 3.00 8.00
20 Rollie Fingers 2.00 5.00
21 Reggie Jackson 3.00 8.00
22 Joe Morgan 2.00 5.00
23 Johnny Bench 4.00 10.00
24 Thurman Munson 2.00 5.00
25 Jose Canseco 2.00 5.00
26 Tom Glavine 2.00 5.00
27 Chipper Jones 2.00 5.00
28 Greg Maddux 3.00 8.00
29 Roberto Alomar 2.00 5.00
30 David Cone 2.00 5.00
31 Jim Thome 2.00 5.00
32 Manny Ramirez 2.00 5.00
33 Roger Clemens 4.00 10.00
34 Derek Jeter 8.00 20.00
35 Bernie Williams 2.00 5.00
36 Alfonso Soriano 2.00 5.00

2002 Fleer Premium Legendary Dynasties Autographs

RANDOM INSERTS IN HOBBY PACKS
SERIAL #'d TO WORLD SERIES YEAR
ALL WERE EXCHANGE CARDS
6 Derek Jeter/96 100.00 250.00

2002 Fleer Premium Legendary Dynasties Game Used

STATED ODDS 1:120
SP PRINT RUNS PROVIDED BY FLEER
SP'S ARE NOT SERIAL-NUMBERED
1 Roberto Alomar Jsy 8.00 20.00
2 Johnny Bench Jsy 8.00 20.00
4 Roger Clemens Jsy 10.00 25.00
5 Bill Dickey Bat SP/200 10.00 25.00
6 Rollie Fingers Jsy 6.00 15.00
8 Reggie Jackson Bat SP/250 15.00 40.00
9 Derek Jeter Bat 10.00 25.00
10 Chipper Jones Jsy 8.00 20.00
11 Roger Maris Bat SP/225 12.50 30.00
12 Johnny Mize Bat SP/225 10.00 25.00
13 Joe Morgan Bat 6.00 15.00
14 Thurman Munson Bat SP/250 12.00 30.00
15 Jim Palmer Jsy 6.00 15.00
16 Manny Ramirez Jsy 8.00 20.00
17 Brooks Robinson Bat SP/200 6.00 15.00
18 J.Robinson Pants SP/150 15.00 40.00
19 Babe Ruth Bat SP/60 125.00 200.00
20 Duke Snider Bat SP/250 15.00 40.00
21 Alfonso Soriano Jsy 6.00 15.00
22 Bernie Williams Jsy 8.00 20.00

2002 Fleer Premium Legendary Dynasties Game Used Premium
RANDOM INSERTS IN PACKS
SERIAL #'d TO HIGHEST WIN TOTAL
ALL CARDS FEATURE JERSEY PATCHES
1 Rollie Fingers/93 6.00 15.00
2 Roger Clemens/114 30.00 80.00
3 Roger Maris/109 40.00 100.00
4 Roberto Alomar/96 10.00 25.00
5 Reggie Jackson/93 10.00 25.00
6 Manny Ramirez/99 10.00 25.00
7 Johnny Bench/108 15.00 40.00
8 Jim Palmer/109 6.00 15.00
9 Derek Jeter/114 30.00 60.00
10 Alfonso Soriano/99 6.00 15.00
11 Chipper Jones/106 15.00 40.00
12 Bernie Williams/114 10.00 25.00

2002 Fleer Premium On Base!
COMPLETE SET (30) 100.00 250.00
RANDOM INSERTS IN PACKS
SERIAL #'d TO ON-BASE PERCENTAGE
1 Frank Thomas/316 3.00 8.00
2 Ivan Rodriguez/347 2.00 5.00
3 Nomar Garciaparra/352 5.00 12.00
4 Ken Griffey Jr./365 6.00 15.00
5 Juan Gonzalez/370 2.00 5.00
6 Shawn Green/372 2.00 5.00
7 Vladimir Guerrero/377 3.00 8.00
8 Derek Jeter/377 8.00 20.00
9 Scott Rolen/378 2.00 5.00
10 Ichiro Suzuki/381 6.00 15.00
11 Mike Piazza/384 5.00 12.00
12 Bernie Williams/395 2.00 5.00
13 Moises Alou/396 2.00 5.00
14 Jeff Bagwell/397 2.00 5.00
15 Alex Rodriguez/399 4.00 10.00
16 Albert Pujols/403 6.00 15.00
17 Manny Ramirez/405 2.00 5.00
18 Carlos Delgado/408 2.00 5.00
19 Jim Edmonds/410 2.00 5.00
20 Roberto Alomar/415 2.00 5.00
21 Jim Thome/416 2.00 5.00
22 Gary Sheffield/417 2.00 5.00
23 Chipper Jones/427 3.00 8.00
24 Luis Gonzalez/429 2.00 5.00
25 Lance Berkman/430 2.00 5.00
26 Todd Helton/432 2.00 5.00
27 Sammy Sosa/437 3.00 8.00
28 Larry Walker/449 2.00 5.00
29 Jason Giambi/477 2.00 5.00
30 Barry Bonds/515 8.00 20.00

2002 Fleer Premium On Base! Game Used
RANDOM INSERTS IN PACKS
STATED PRINT RUN 100 SERIAL #'d SETS
1 Luis Gonzalez 4.00 10.00
2 Chipper Jones 6.00 15.00
3 Gary Sheffield 4.00 10.00
4 Nomar Garciaparra 10.00 25.00
5 Manny Ramirez 6.00 15.00
6 Moises Alou 4.00 10.00
7 Sammy Sosa 6.00 15.00
8 Frank Thomas 6.00 15.00
9 Ken Griffey Jr. 15.00 40.00
10 Jim Thome 6.00 15.00
11 Todd Helton 6.00 15.00
12 Larry Walker 4.00 10.00
13 Jeff Bagwell 6.00 15.00
14 Lance Berkman 4.00 10.00
15 Shawn Green 4.00 10.00
16 Vladimir Guerrero 6.00 15.00
17 Roberto Alomar 6.00 15.00
18 Mike Piazza 10.00 25.00
19 Jason Giambi 4.00 10.00
20 Derek Jeter 15.00 40.00
21 Bernie Williams 6.00 15.00
22 Scott Rolen 6.00 15.00
23 Barry Bonds 15.00 40.00
24 Ichiro Suzuki 15.00 40.00
25 Jim Edmonds 4.00 10.00
26 Albert Pujols 12.50 30.00
27 Juan Gonzalez 4.00 10.00
28 Alex Rodriguez 12.50 30.00
29 Ivan Rodriguez 6.00 15.00
30 Carlos Delgado 4.00 10.00

2013 Fleer Precious Metal Gems Industry Summit
LV1 Mike Trout Red/100 20.00 50.00
LV1 Mike Trout Blue/50 60.00 120.00
LV1 Mike Trout Green/10

2001 Fleer Red Sox 100th
COMPLETE SET (100) 10.00 25.00
FIELD GAME EXCH.RANDOM IN PACKS
FIELD THE GAME EXCH.DEADLINE 08/01/02
1 Carl Yastrzemski 1.25 3.00
2 Mel Parnell .20 .50
3 Birdie Tebbetts .20 .50
4 Tex Hughson .20 .50
5 Nomar Garciaparra 1.25 3.00
6 Fred Lynn .30 .75
7 John Valentin .20 .50
8 Rico Petrocelli .20 .50
9 Ted Williams 2.00 5.00
10 Roger Clemens 1.50 4.00
11 Luis Aparicio .30 .75
12 Cy Young .75 2.00
13 Carlton Fisk .50 1.25
14 Pedro Martinez .50 1.25
15 Joe Dobson .20 .50
16 Babe Ruth 2.50 6.00
17 Doc Cramer .20 .50
18 Pete Runnels .20 .50
19 Tony Conigliaro .50 1.25
20 Bill Monbouquette .20 .50
21 Boo Ferriss .20 .50
22 Harry Hooper .50 1.25
23 Tony Armas .20 .50
24 Joe Cronin .30 .75
25 Rick Ferrell .30 .75
26 Wade Boggs .50 1.25
27 Don Baylor .30 .75
28 Jeff Reardon .30 .75
29 Joe Wood .50 1.25
30 Mo Vaughn .30 .75
31 Walt Dropo .20 .50
32 Vern Stephens .20 .50
33 Bernie Carbo .20 .50
34 George Scott .20 .50
35 Lefty Grove .75 2.00
36 Dom DiMaggio .75 2.00
37 Dennis Eckersley .30 .75
38 Johnny Pesky .30 .75
39 Jim Lonborg .20 .50
40 Jimmy Piersall .30 .75
41 Tris Speaker .75 2.00
42 Frank Malzone .20 .50
43 Bobby Doerr .50 1.25
44 Jimmie Foxx .75 2.00
45 Tony Pena .20 .50
46 Billy Goodman .20 .50
47 Jim Rice .30 .75
48 Reggie Smith .30 .75
49 Bill Buckner .30 .75
50 Earl Wilson .20 .50
51 Rick Burleson .20 .50
52 George Kell .30 .75
53 Dick Radatz .20 .50
54 Dwight Evans .50 1.25
55 Luis Tiant .30 .75
56 Elijah Green .20 .50
57 Gene Conley .20 .50
58 Jackie Jensen .30 .75
59 Mike Fornieles .20 .50
60 Dutch Leonard .20 .50
61 Jake Stahl .20 .50
62 Don Schwall .20 .50
63 Jimmy Collins .30 .75
64 Herb Pennock .50 1.25
65 Red Ruffing .50 1.25
66 Carney Lansford .30 .75
67 Dick Stuart .20 .50
68 Dave Morehead .20 .50
69 Harry Agganis .30 .75
70 Lou Boudreau MGR .50 1.25
71 Joe Morgan MGR .20 .50
72 Don Zimmer MGR .30 .75
73 Tom Yawkey OWN .30 .75
74 Jean Yawkey OWN .20 .50
75 Boston Red Sox .30 .75
76 Boston Red Sox .30 .75
77 Boston Red Sox .30 .75
78 Carl Yastrzemski BB .75 2.00
79 Carlton Fisk BB .30 .75
80 Dom DiMaggio BB .30 .75
81 Wade Boggs BB .30 .75
82 Nomar Garciaparra BB .75 2.00
83 Pedro Martinez BB .50 1.25
84 Ted Williams BB 1.00 2.50
85 Jim Rice BB .20 .50
86 Fred Lynn BB .20 .50
87 Mo Vaughn BB .20 .50
88 Bobby Doerr BB .30 .75
89 Bernie Carbo BB .20 .50
90 Dennis Eckersley BB .30 .75
91 Jimmy Piersall BB .20 .50
92 Luis Tiant BB .20 .50
93 Fenway Park .20 .50
94 Fenway Park .20 .50
95 Fenway Park .20 .50
96 Fenway Park .20 .50
97 Fenway Park .20 .50
98 Fenway Park .20 .50
99 Fenway Park .20 .50
100 Fenway Park .20 .50
NNO Field the Game/7150 12.50 30.00

2001 Fleer Red Sox 100th BoSox Sigs
STATED ODDS 1:96
EXCHANGE DEADLINE 07/31/02
1 Wade Boggs 20.00 50.00
2 Bill Buckner 12.00 30.00
3 Bernie Carbo 10.00 25.00
4 Roger Clemens SP/100 175.00 300.00
5 Dom DiMaggio 30.00 60.00
6 Bobby Doerr 40.00 80.00
7 Dennis Eckersley 20.00 50.00
8 Dwight Evans 20.00 50.00
9 Carlton Fisk 50.00 80.00
10 Nomar Garciaparra 60.00 100.00
11 Jim Lonborg 10.00 25.00
12 Fred Lynn 15.00 40.00
13 Rico Petrocelli 10.00 25.00
14 Jim Rice 10.00 25.00
15 Luis Tiant 20.00 50.00
16 Carl Yastrzemski SP/200 90.00 150.00

2001 Fleer Red Sox 100th MLB Autographed Fitted Caps
ONE CAP PER DELUXE BOX
2 Bill Buckner 20.00 50.00
3 Bernie Carbo 15.00 40.00
5 Bobby Doerr 20.00 50.00
6 Dennis Eckersley 30.00 60.00
7 Dwight Evans 30.00 60.00
8 Nomar Garciaparra 60.00 120.00
9 Jim Lonborg 15.00 40.00
10 Johnny Pesky 15.00 40.00
11 Rico Petrocelli 15.00 40.00
12 Jim Rice 15.00 40.00
13 Luis Tiant 15.00 40.00

2001 Fleer Red Sox 100th Splendid Splinters
COMPLETE SET (15) 12.50 30.00
STATED ODDS 1:10
SS1 Babe Ruth 3.00 8.00
SS2 Dom DiMaggio 1.00 2.50
SS3 Carlton Fisk .60 1.50
SS4 Carl Yastrzemski 1.50 4.00
SS5 Nomar Garciaparra 2.00 5.00
SS6 Wade Boggs .60 1.50
SS7 Ted Williams 3.00 8.00
SS8 Jim Rice .40 1.00
SS9 Mo Vaughn .40 1.00
SS10 Tris Speaker 1.00 2.50
SS11 Dwight Evans .60 1.50
SS12 Jimmie Foxx 1.25 3.00
SS13 Bobby Doerr .60 1.50
SS14 Fred Lynn .40 1.00
SS15 Johnny Pesky .40 1.00

2001 Fleer Red Sox 100th Splendid Splinters Game Bat
STATED ODDS 1:96
SP PRINT RUNS PROVIDED BY FLEER
SP'S ARE NOT SERIAL-NUMBERED
1 Wade Boggs 15.00 40.00
2 Dwight Evans 10.00 25.00
3 Jimmie Foxx SP/100 * 125.00 200.00
4 Nomar Garciaparra 10.00 25.00
5 Jim Rice 10.00 25.00
6 Babe Ruth SP/100 * 150.00 300.00
7 Ted Williams SP/100 * 125.00 200.00
8 Carl Yastrzemski 10.00 25.00

2001 Fleer Red Sox 100th Threads
STATED ODDS 1:96
SP PRINT RUNS PROVIDED BY FLEER
SP'S ARE NOT SERIAL-NUMBERED
1 Wade Boggs 15.00 40.00
2 Roger Clemens 10.00 25.00
3 Dwight Evans 15.00 40.00
4 Carlton Fisk SP/100 30.00 60.00
5 Pedro Martinez SP/100 10.00 25.00
6 Jim Rice 10.00 25.00
7 Ted Williams SP/100 125.00 200.00
8 Carl Yastrzemski 15.00 40.00
9 Don Zimmer 10.00 25.00

2001 Fleer Red Sox 100th Yawkey's Heroes
COMPLETE SET (20) 6.00 15.00
STATED ODDS 1:4
YH1 Bobby Doerr .50 1.25
YH2 Dom DiMaggio .75 2.00
YH3 Jim Rice .30 .75
YH4 Wade Boggs .50 1.25
YH5 Carlton Fisk .50 1.25
YH6 Nomar Garciaparra 1.25 3.00
YH7 Dennis Eckersley .30 .75
YH8 Carl Yastrzemski 1.25 3.00
YH9 Ted Williams 2.00 5.00
YH10 Tony Conigliaro .50 1.25
YH11 Tony Armas .30 .75
YH12 Joe Cronin .75 2.00
YH13 Mo Vaughn .30 .75
YH14 Johnny Pesky .30 .75
YH15 Jim Lonborg .30 .75
YH16 Luis Tiant .30 .75
YH17 Tony Pena .30 .75
YH18 Dwight Evans .50 1.25
YH19 Fred Lynn .30 .75
YH20 Jimmy Piersall .30 .75

2003 Fleer Rookies and Greats
COMPLETE SET (75) 10.00 25.00
COMMON CARD (1-60) .15 .40
COMMON CARD (61-75) .15 .40
1 Troy Glaus .15 .40
2 Gary Sheffield .15 .40
3 Sammy Sosa .40 1.00
4 Mark Prior .25 .60
5 Dontrelle Willis .15 .40
6 Shawn Green .15 .40
7 Vladimir Guerrero .25 .60
8 Jose Reyes .40 1.00
9 Miguel Tejada .25 .60
10 Bret Boone .15 .40
11 Rocco Baldelli .15 .40
12 Rafael Palmeiro .25 .60
13 Ichiro Suzuki .50 1.25
14 Carlos Delgado .15 .40
15 Garret Anderson .15 .40
16 Richie Sexson .15 .40
17 Roger Clemens .50 1.25
18 Barry Zito .25 .60
19 Jim Thome .25 .60
20 Alex Rodriguez .50 1.25
21 Randy Johnson .40 1.00
22 Chipper Jones .40 1.00
23 Kerry Wood .15 .40
24 Ken Griffey Jr. .75 2.00
25 Ivan Rodriguez .25 .60
26 Jeff Kent .15 .40
27 Todd Helton .25 .60
28 Jeff Bagwell .25 .60
29 Hideo Nomo .40 1.00
30 Torii Hunter .15 .40
31 Brian Giles .15 .40
32 Albert Pujols .50 1.25
33 Vernon Wells .15 .40
34 Nomar Garciaparra .25 .60
35 Magglio Ordonez .25 .60
36 C.C. Sabathia .25 .60
37 Preston Wilson .15 .40
38 Mike Sweeney .15 .40
39 Jose Vidro .15 .40
40 Jason Giambi .15 .40
41 Derek Jeter 1.00 2.50
42 Mike Piazza .40 1.00
43 Rich Harden .25 .60
44 Jason Kendall .15 .40
45 Barry Bonds .60 1.50
46 Barry Larkin .25 .60
47 Dmitri Young .15 .40
48 Craig Biggio .25 .60
49 Angel Berroa .15 .40
50 Alfonso Soriano .25 .60
51 Kevin Millwood .15 .40
52 Edgar Martinez .25 .60
53 Jim Edmonds .25 .60
54 Curt Schilling .25 .60
55 Jay Gibbons .15 .40
56 Pedro Martinez .25 .60
57 Greg Maddux .50 1.25
58 Manny Ramirez .40 1.00
59 Frank Thomas .40 1.00
60 Adam Dunn .25 .60
61 Babe Ruth GR 1.00 2.50
62 Bob Gibson GR .25 .60
63 Willie Stargell GR .25 .60
64 Mike Schmidt GR .60 1.50
65 Nolan Ryan GR 1.25 3.00
66 Tom Seaver GR .25 .60
67 Brooks Robinson GR .25 .60
68 Willie McCovey GR .25 .60
69 Harmon Killebrew GR .40 1.00
70 Al Kaline GR .25 .60
71 Reggie Jackson GR .25 .60
72 Eddie Mathews GR .40 1.00
73 Ralph Kiner GR .25 .60
74 Cal Ripken GR 1.25 3.00
75 Phil Rizzuto GR .25 .60

2003 Fleer Rookies and Greats Blue
*BLUE 1-60: 2X TO 5X BASIC
*BLUE 61-75: 2X TO 5X BASIC
STATED ODDS 1:10
STATED PRINT RUN 250 SERIAL #'d SETS

2003 Fleer Rookies and Greats Boyhood Idols Game Used
OVERALL AU-GU ODDS 1:7
STATED PRINT RUN 615 SERIAL #'d SETS
BD Bucky Dent Jsy 1.25 3.00
BR Brooks Robinson Jsy 2.00 5.00
CF Carlton Fisk Jsy 2.00 5.00
CR Cal Ripken Jsy 10.00 25.00
DM Don Mattingly Jsy 6.00 15.00
FH Frank Howard Bat 1.25 3.00
HK Harmon Killebrew Pants 3.00 8.00
JC Joe Carter Bat 1.25 3.00
JM Joe Morgan Jsy 2.00 5.00
JP Jim Palmer Jsy 2.00 5.00
MS Mike Schmidt Jsy 5.00 12.00
MS2 Moose Skowron Pants 1.25 3.00
NR Nolan Ryan Jsy 10.00 25.00
RY Robin Yount Jsy 3.00 8.00

2003 Fleer Rookies and Greats Boyhood Idols Game Used Autograph
OVERALL AU-GU ODDS 1:7
PRINT RUNS B/WN 40-50 COPIES PER
BD Bucky Dent Jsy/50 12.50 30.00
BR Brooks Robinson Jsy/50 20.00 50.00
CF Carlton Fisk Jsy/50 12.50 30.00
FH Frank Howard Bat/50 12.50 30.00
HK Harmon Killebrew Pants/40 40.00 80.00
JC Joe Carter Bat/50 12.50 30.00
JP Jim Palmer Jsy/50 12.50 30.00
MS2 Moose Skowron Pants/50 12.50 30.00

2003 Fleer Rookies and Greats Dynamic Debuts
STATED ODDS 1:10
1 Rickie Weeks 1.25 3.00
2 Brandon Webb 1.25 3.00
3 Jose Reyes 1.00 2.50
4 Bo Hart .40 1.00
5 Dontrelle Willis .40 1.00
6 Rich Harden .60 1.50
7 Ryan Wagner .40 1.00
8 Rocco Baldelli .40 1.00
9 Mark Teixeira .60 1.50
10 Hideki Matsui 2.00 5.00

2003 Fleer Rookies and Greats Dynamic Debuts Autograph
OVERALL AU-GU ODDS 1:7
STATED PRINT RUN 100 SERIAL #'d SETS
BH Bo Hart 4.00 10.00
DW Dontrelle Willis 5.00 12.00
JR Jose Reyes 10.00 25.00
RW Rickie Weeks 15.00 40.00
RW2 Ryan Wagner 4.00 10.00

2003 Fleer Rookies and Greats Looming Large
STATED PRINT RUN 500 SERIAL #'d SETS
RARE PRINT RUN 15 SERIAL #'d SETS
NO RARE PRICING DUE TO SCARCITY
*UNCOMMON: .75X TO 2X BASIC
UNCOMMON PRINT RUN 150 SER. #'d SETS
BH Bo Hart .60 1.50
BW Brandon Webb 2.00 5.00
CB Clint Barmes 1.50 4.00
CW Chien-Ming Wang 2.50 6.00
DY Delmon Young 4.00 10.00
EJ Edwin Jackson 1.00 2.50
HM Hideki Matsui 3.00 8.00
JB Jeremy Bonderman 2.50 6.00
JC Jose Contreras 1.50 4.00
JD Jeff Duncan .60 1.50
MH Michael Hessman .60 1.50
MK Matt Kata .60 1.50
RH Robby Hammock .60 1.50
RW Rickie Weeks 2.00 5.00
RW2 Ryan Wagner .60 1.50

2003 Fleer Rookies and Greats Naturals
STATED ODDS 1:5
*UNCOMMON: 1.5X TO 4X BASIC
UNCOMMON PRINT RUN 75 SERIAL #'d SETS
TN1 Cal Ripken 3.00 8.00
TN2 Mike Schmidt 1.50 4.00
TN3 Derek Jeter 2.50 6.00
TN4 Joe Carter .40 1.00
TN5 Nomar Garciaparra .60 1.50
TN6 Frank Howard .40 1.00
TN7 Al Kaline .60 1.50
TN8 Albert Pujols 1.25 3.00
TN9 Nolan Ryan 3.00 8.00
TN10 Duke Snider .60 1.50
TN11 Alex Rodriguez 1.25 3.00
TN12 Brooks Robinson .60 1.50
TN13 Roger Clemens 1.25 3.00
TN14 Sammy Sosa 1.00 2.50
TN15 Jim Palmer .60 1.50
TN16 Alfonso Soriano .60 1.50
TN17 Don Mattingly 2.00 5.00
TN18 Harmon Killebrew 1.00 2.50
TN19 Bob Feller .60 1.50
TN20 Reggie Jackson .60 1.50
TN21 Ichiro Suzuki 1.25 3.00
TN22 Barry Bonds 1.50 4.00
TN23 Hideki Matsui 2.00 5.00
TN24 Willie Stargell .60 1.50
TN25 Pee Wee Reese .60 1.50

2003 Fleer Rookies and Greats Naturals Autograph
OVERALL AU-GU ODDS 1:7
STATED PRINT RUN 50 SERIAL #'d SETS
AK Al Kaline 15.00 40.00
BF Bob Feller 10.00 25.00
BR Brooks Robinson 15.00 40.00
CR Cal Ripken 40.00 80.00
DS Duke Snider 15.00 40.00
FH Frank Howard 15.00 40.00
HK Harmon Killebrew 30.00 60.00
JC Joe Carter 10.00 25.00
JP Jim Palmer 10.00 25.00
NR Nolan Ryan 60.00 120.00

2003 Fleer Rookies and Greats Naturals Game Used
PRINT RUNS B/WN 250-400 COPIES PER
PATCH PRINT RUN 25 SERIAL #'d SETS
NO PATCH PRICING DUE TO SCARCITY
OVERALL AU-GU ODDS 1:7
AK Al Kaline Bat/250 6.00 15.00
AP Albert Pujols Jsy/250 8.00 20.00
AR Alex Rodriguez Jsy/250 4.00 10.00
AS Alfonso Soriano Jsy/250 3.00 8.00
BR Brooks Robinson Jsy/400 6.00 15.00
CR Cal Ripken Jsy/250 12.50 30.00
DJ Derek Jeter Jsy/250 10.00 25.00
DM Don Mattingly Jsy/250 8.00 20.00
DS Duke Snider Jsy/250 6.00 15.00
FH Frank Howard Bat/400 4.00 10.00
HK Harmon Killebrew Pants/400 6.00 15.00
JC Joe Carter Bat/250 4.00 10.00
JP Jim Palmer Jsy/250 4.00 10.00
MS Mike Schmidt Jsy/250 8.00 20.00
NG Nomar Garciaparra Jsy/250 6.00 15.00
NR Nolan Ryan Jsy/400 10.00 25.00
RC Roger Clemens Jsy/400 6.00 15.00
RJ Reggie Jackson Jsy/400 6.00 15.00
SS Sammy Sosa Jsy/250 4.00 10.00

2003 Fleer Rookies and Greats Naturals Game Used Autograph
OVERALL AU-GU ODDS 1:7
STATED PRINT RUN 30 SERIAL #'d SETS
AU PATCH PRINT RUN 5 SERIAL #'d SETS
NO AU PATCH PRICING DUE TO SCARCITY
AK Al Kaline Bat 40.00 100.00
BR Brooks Robinson Jsy 12.00 30.00
CR Cal Ripken Jsy 125.00 200.00
DS Duke Snider Jsy 30.00 60.00
FH Frank Howard Bat 15.00 40.00
HK Harmon Killebrew Pants 25.00 60.00
JC Joe Carter Bat 10.00 25.00
JP Jim Palmer Jsy 10.00 25.00
NR Nolan Ryan Jsy 50.00 100.00

2003 Fleer Rookies and Greats Through the Years Game Used Dual
STATED PRINT RUN 360 SERIAL #'d SETS
PATCH PRINT RUN 25 SERIAL #'d SETS
NO PATCH PRICING DUE TO SCARCITY
OVERALL AU-GU ODDS 1:7
ALL ARE DUAL JSY UNLESS NOTED
ARMT A.Rodriguez/M.Teixeira 6.00 15.00
BHLB B.Hart Pants/L.Brock 4.00 10.00
BLJM B.Larkin/J.Morgan 6.00 15.00
DJPR D.Jeter/P.Rizzuto Pants 10.00 25.00
EMCJ E.Mathews Pants/C.Jones 8.00 20.00
HKTH H.Killebrew Pants/T.Hunter 6.00 15.00
JCMM J.Contreras/M.Mussina 6.00 15.00
JGRJ J.Giambi/R.Jackson 6.00 15.00
JTMS J.Thome/M.Schmidt 12.50 30.00
MHCJ M.Hessman Pants/C.Jones 6.00 15.00
MPJR M.Piazza/J.Reyes 6.00 15.00
NGBD N.Garciaparra/B.Doerr Bat 10.00 25.00
NRHB N.Ryan/H.Blalock 15.00 40.00
PRJR P.Rizzuto Pants/J.Reyes 8.00 20.00
RCCW R.Clemens/C.Wang Pants 15.00 40.00
RJBW R.Johnson/B.Webb 6.00 15.00
RYSP R.Yount/S.Podsednik Bat 6.00 15.00
SCKM S.Carlton/K.Millwood 4.00 10.00
SSMP S.Sosa/M.Prior 6.00 15.00
WMBB McCov Pants/Bonds Base 10.00 25.00

2000 Fleer Showcase
COMP.SET w/o SP's (100) 10.00 25.00
COMMON CARD (1-100) .20 .50
COMMON CARD (101-115) 1.25 3.00
101-115 PRINT RUN 1000 SERIAL #'d SETS
COMMON CARD (116-140) 1.00 2.50
116-140 PRINT RUN 2000 SERIAL #'d SETS
101-140 RANDOM INSERTS IN PACKS
1 Alex Rodriguez .60 1.50
2 Derek Jeter 1.25 3.00
3 Jeromy Burnitz .20 .50
4 John Olerud .20 .50
5 Paul Konerko .20 .50
6 Johnny Damon .30 .75
7 Curt Schilling .30 .75
8 Barry Larkin .30 .75
9 Adrian Beltre .50 1.25
10 Scott Rolen .30 .75
11 Carlos Delgado .20 .50
12 Pedro Martinez .30 .75
13 Todd Helton .30 .75
14 Jacque Jones .20 .50
15 Jeff Kent .20 .50
16 Darin Erstad .20 .50
17 Juan Encarnacion .20 .50
18 Roger Clemens .60 1.50
19 Tony Gwynn .50 1.25
20 Nomar Garciaparra .30 .75
21 Roberto Alomar .30 .75
22 Matt Lawton .20 .50
23 Rich Aurilia .20 .50
24 Charles Johnson .20 .50
25 Jim Thome .30 .75
26 Eric Milton .20 .50
27 Barry Bonds .75 2.00
28 Albert Belle .20 .50
29 Travis Fryman .20 .50
30 Ken Griffey Jr. 1.00 2.50
31 Phil Nevin .20 .50
32 Chipper Jones .50 1.25
33 Craig Biggio .30 .75
34 Mike Hampton .20 .50
35 Fred McGriff .30 .75
36 Cal Ripken 1.50 4.00
37 Manny Ramirez .50 1.25
38 Jose Vidro .20 .50
39 Trevor Hoffman .30 .75
40 Tom Glavine .30 .75
41 Frank Thomas .50 1.25
42 Chris Widger .20 .50
43 J.D. Drew .20 .50
44 Andres Galarraga .30 .75
45 Pokey Reese .20 .50
46 Mike Piazza .50 1.25
47 Kevin Young .20 .50
48 Sean Casey .20 .50
49 Carlos Beltran .30 .75
50 Jason Kendall .20 .50
51 Vladimir Guerrero .30 .75
52 Jermaine Dye .20 .50
53 Brian Giles .20 .50
54 Andruw Jones .20 .50
55 Richard Hidalgo .20 .50
56 Robin Ventura .20 .50
57 Ivan Rodriguez .30 .75
58 Greg Maddux .60 1.50
59 Billy Wagner .20 .50
60 Ruben Mateo .20 .50
61 Troy Glaus .20 .50
62 Dean Palmer .20 .50
63 Eric Chavez .20 .50
64 Edgar Martinez .30 .75
65 Randy Johnson .50 1.25
66 Preston Wilson .20 .50
67 Orlando Hernandez .20 .50
68 Jim Edmonds .20 .50
69 Carl Everett .20 .50
70 Larry Walker .30 .75
71 Ron Belliard .20 .50
72 Sammy Sosa .50 1.25
73 Matt Williams .20 .50
74 Cliff Floyd .20 .50
75 Bernie Williams .30 .75
76 Fernando Tatis .20 .50
77 Steve Finley .20 .50
78 Jeff Bagwell .30 .75
79 Edgardo Alfonzo .20 .50
80 Jose Canseco .30 .75
81 Magglio Ordonez .30 .75
82 Shawn Green .20 .50
83 Bobby Abreu .20 .50
84 Tony Batista .20 .50
85 Mo Vaughn .20 .50
86 Juan Gonzalez .20 .50
87 Paul O'Neill .30 .75
88 Mark McGwire .75 2.00
89 Mark Grace .30 .75
90 Kevin Brown .20 .50
91 Ben Grieve .20 .50
92 Shannon Stewart .20 .50
93 Erubiel Durazo .20 .50
94 Antonio Alfonseca .20 .50
95 Jeff Cirillo .20 .50
96 Greg Vaughn .20 .50
97 Kerry Wood .20 .50
98 Geoff Jenkins .20 .50
99 Jason Giambi .20 .50
100 Rafael Palmeiro .30 .75
101 Rafael Furcal PROS 2.00 5.00
102 Pablo Ozuna PROS 1.25 3.00
103 Brad Penny PROS 1.25 3.00
104 Mark Mulder PROS 1.25 3.00
105 Adam Piatt PROS 1.25 3.00
106 Mike Lamb PROS RC 1.25 3.00
107 Kazuhiro Sasaki PROS RC 3.00 8.00
108 Aaron McNeal PROS RC 1.25 3.00
109 Pat Burrell PROS 1.25 3.00
110 Rick Ankiel PROS 2.00 5.00
111 Eric Munson PROS 1.25 3.00
112 Josh Beckett PROS 2.50 6.00
113 Adam Kennedy PROS 1.25 3.00
114 Alex Escobar PROS 1.25 3.00
115 Chad Hermansen PROS 1.25 3.00
116 Kip Wells PROS 1.00 2.50
117 Matt LeCroy PROS 1.00 2.50
118 Julio Ramirez PROS 1.00 2.50
119 Ben Petrick PROS 1.00 2.50
120 Nick Johnson PROS 1.00 2.50
121 Gookie Dawkins PROS 1.00 2.50
122 Julio Zuleta PROS RC 1.00 2.50
123 Alfonso Soriano PROS 2.50 6.00
124 Keith McDonald PROS RC 1.00 2.50
125 Kory DeHaan PROS 1.00 2.50
126 Vernon Wells PROS 1.00 2.50
127 Dernell Stenson PROS 1.00 2.50
128 David Eckstein PROS 1.00 2.50
129 Robert Fick PROS 1.00 2.50
130 Cole Liniak PROS 1.00 2.50
131 Mark Quinn PROS 1.00 2.50
132 Eric Gagne PROS 1.00 2.50
133 Wily Mo Pena PROS 1.00 2.50
134 Andy Thompson PROS RC 1.00 2.50
135 Steve Sisco PROS RC 1.00 2.50
136 Paul Rigdon PROS RC 1.00 2.50
137 Rob Bell PROS 1.00 2.50
138 Carlos Guillen PROS 1.00 2.50
139 Jimmy Rollins PROS 1.50 4.00
140 Jason Conti PROS 1.00 2.50

2000 Fleer Showcase Legacy Collection
*STARS 1-100: 25X TO 60X BASIC
STATED PRINT RUN 20 SERIAL #'d SETS
101-140 NO PRICING DUE TO SCARCITY

2000 Fleer Showcase Prospect Showcase First
STATED PRINT RUN 500 SERIAL #'d SETS
1 Rafael Furcal 3.00 8.00
2 Pablo Ozuna 2.00 5.00
3 Brad Penny 2.00 5.00
4 Mark Mulder 2.00 5.00
5 Adam Piatt 2.00 5.00
6 Mike Lamb 2.00 5.00
7 Kazuhiro Sasaki 5.00 12.00
8 Aaron McNeal 2.00 5.00
9 Pat Burrell 2.00 5.00
10 Rick Ankiel 3.00 8.00
11 Eric Munson 2.00 5.00
12 Josh Beckett 4.00 10.00
13 Adam Kennedy 2.00 5.00
14 Alex Escobar 2.00 5.00
15 Chad Hermansen 2.00 5.00
16 Kip Wells 2.00 5.00
17 Matt LeCroy 2.00 5.00
18 Julio Ramirez 2.00 5.00
19 Ben Petrick 2.00 5.00
20 Nick Johnson 2.00 5.00
21 Gookie Dawkins 2.00 5.00
22 Julio Zuleta 2.00 5.00
23 Alfonso Soriano 5.00 12.00
24 Keith McDonald 2.00 5.00
25 Kory DeHaan 2.00 5.00
26 Vernon Wells 2.00 5.00
27 Dernell Stenson 2.00 5.00
28 David Eckstein 2.00 5.00
29 Robert Fick 2.00 5.00
30 Cole Liniak 2.00 5.00
31 Mark Quinn 2.00 5.00
32 Eric Gagne 2.00 5.00
33 Wily Mo Pena 2.00 5.00
34 Andy Thompson 2.00 5.00
35 Steve Sisco 2.00 5.00
36 Paul Rigdon 2.00 5.00
37 Rob Bell 2.00 5.00
38 Carlos Guillen 2.00 5.00
39 Jimmy Rollins 3.00 8.00
40 Jason Conti 2.00 5.00

2000 Fleer Showcase Consummate Prose
COMPLETE SET (15) 8.00 20.00
STATED ODDS 1:6
1 Jeff Bagwell .40 1.00
2 Alex Rodriguez .75 2.00
3 Chipper Jones .60 1.50
4 Derek Jeter 1.50 4.00
5 Manny Ramirez .60 1.50
6 Tony Gwynn .60 1.50
7 Sammy Sosa .60 1.50
8 Ivan Rodriguez .40 1.00
9 Greg Maddux .75 2.00
10 Ken Griffey Jr. 1.25 3.00
11 Rick Ankiel .40 1.00
12 Cal Ripken 2.00 5.00
13 Pedro Martinez .40 1.00
14 Mike Piazza .60 1.50
15 Mark McGwire 1.00 2.50

2000 Fleer Showcase Feel the Game
STATED ODDS 1:72
1 Barry Bonds 10.00 25.00
2 Gookie Dawkins 3.00 8.00
3 Darin Erstad 4.00 10.00
4 Troy Glaus 4.00 10.00
5 Scott Rolen 6.00 15.00
6 Alex Rodriguez 10.00 25.00
7 Andruw Jones 6.00 15.00
8 Robin Ventura 4.00 10.00
9 Sean Casey 4.00 10.00
10 Cal Ripken 10.00 25.00

2000 Fleer Showcase Final Answer
COMPLETE SET (10) 12.50 30.00
STATED ODDS 1:10
1 Alex Rodriguez 1.25 3.00
2 Vladimir Guerrero .60 1.50
3 Cal Ripken 3.00 8.00
4 Sammy Sosa 1.00 2.50
5 Barry Bonds 1.50 4.00
6 Derek Jeter 2.50 6.00
7 Ken Griffey Jr. 2.00 5.00
8 Mike Piazza 1.00 2.50
9 Nomar Garciaparra .60 1.50
10 Mark McGwire 1.50 4.00

2000 Fleer Showcase Fresh Ink
STATED ODDS 1:24
EXCH.DEADLINE 07/01/01
1 Rick Ankiel 5.00 12.00
2 Josh Beckett 6.00 15.00
3 Barry Bonds 40.00 80.00
4 A.J. Burnett 3.00 8.00
5 Pat Burrell 3.00 8.00
6 Ken Caminiti 3.00 8.00
7 Sean Casey 3.00 8.00
8 Jose Cruz Jr. 3.00 8.00
9 Gookie Dawkins 3.00 8.00
10 Erubiel Durazo 3.00 8.00
11 Juan Encarnacion 3.00 8.00
12 Darin Erstad 3.00 8.00
13 Rafael Furcal 5.00 12.00
14 Nomar Garciaparra 12.50 30.00
15 Jason Giambi 3.00 8.00
16 Jeremy Giambi 3.00 8.00
17 Brian Giles 3.00 8.00
18 Troy Glaus 3.00 8.00
19 Vladimir Guerrero 10.00 25.00
20 Chad Hermansen 3.00 8.00
21 Randy Johnson 40.00 80.00
22 Andruw Jones 3.00 8.00
23 Jason Kendall 3.00 8.00
24 Paul Konerko 3.00 8.00
25 Mike Lowell 3.00 8.00
26 Aaron McNeal 3.00 8.00
27 Warren Morris 3.00 8.00
28 Paul O'Neill 10.00 25.00

29 Magglio Ordonez 5.00 12.00
30 Pablo Ozuna 3.00 8.00
31 Brad Penny 3.00 8.00
32 Ben Petrick 3.00 8.00
33 Pokey Reese 3.00 8.00
34 Cal Ripken 40.00 100.00
35 Alex Rodriguez 30.00 60.00
36 Scott Rolen 5.00 12.00
37 Jose Vidro 3.00 8.00
38 Kip Wells 3.00 8.00

2000 Fleer Showcase License to Skill

COMPLETE SET (10) 12.50 30.00
STATED ODDS 1:20
1 Vladimir Guerrero 1.00 2.50
2 Pedro Martinez 1.00 2.50
3 Nomar Garciaparra 1.00 2.50
4 Ivan Rodriguez 1.00 2.50
5 Mark McGwire 2.50 6.00
6 Derek Jeter 4.00 10.00
7 Ken Griffey Jr. 3.00 8.00
8 Randy Johnson 1.50 4.00
9 Sammy Sosa 1.50 4.00
10 Alex Rodriguez 2.00 5.00

2000 Fleer Showcase Long Gone

COMPLETE SET (10) 10.00 25.00
STATED ODDS 1:20
1 Sammy Sosa 1.00 2.50
2 Derek Jeter 2.50 6.00
3 Nomar Garciaparra .60 1.50
4 Juan Gonzalez .40 1.00
5 Vladimir Guerrero .60 1.50
6 Barry Bonds 1.50 4.00
7 Jeff Bagwell .60 1.50
8 Alex Rodriguez 1.25 3.00
9 Ken Griffey Jr. 2.00 5.00
10 Mark McGwire 1.50 4.00

2000 Fleer Showcase Noise of Summer

COMPLETE SET (10) 10.00 25.00
STATED ODDS 1:10
1 Chipper Jones 1.00 2.50
2 Jeff Bagwell .60 1.50
3 Manny Ramirez 1.00 2.50
4 Mark McGwire 1.50 4.00
5 Ken Griffey Jr. 2.00 5.00
6 Mike Piazza 1.00 2.50
7 Pedro Martinez .60 1.50
8 Alex Rodriguez 1.25 3.00
9 Derek Jeter 2.50 6.00
10 Randy Johnson 1.00 2.50

2000 Fleer Showcase Sweet Sigs

STATED ODDS 1:250
SP'S ARE NOT SERIAL-NUMBERED
SP INFO PROVIDED BY FLEER
SS1 Nomar Garciaparra SP/53 30.00 60.00
SS2 Alex Rodriguez SP/67 100.00 200.00
SS3 Tony Gwynn 25.00 60.00
SS4 Roger Clemens SP/79 40.00 80.00
SS5 Scott Rolen 6.00 15.00
SS6 Greg Maddux 50.00 100.00
SS7 Jose Cruz Jr. 6.00 15.00
SS8 Tony Womack 6.00 15.00
SS9 Jay Buhner 6.00 15.00
SS10 Nolan Ryan 40.00 100.00

2001 Fleer Showcase

COMP.SET w/o SP's (100) 12.50 30.00
COMMON CARD (1-100) .20 .50
COMMON CARD (101-115) 2.00 5.00
101-115 RANDOM INSERTS IN PACKS
COMMON CARD (116-125) 3.00 8.00
116-125 RANDOM INSERTS IN PACKS
116-125 PRINT RUN 500 SERIAL #'d SETS
COMMON CARD (126 -160) 2.00 5.00
126-160 RANDOM INSERTS IN PACKS
126-145 PRINT RUN 1500 SERIAL #'d SETS
146-160 PRINT RUN 2000 SERIAL #'d SETS
1 Tony Gwynn .60 1.50
2 Barry Larkin .30 .75
3 Chan Ho Park .20 .50
4 Darin Erstad .20 .50
5 Rafael Furcal .20 .50
6 Roger Cedeno .20 .50
7 Timo Perez .20 .50
8 Rick Ankiel .20 .50
9 Pokey Reese .20 .50
10 Jeromy Burnitz .20 .50
11 Phil Nevin .20 .50
12 Matt Williams .20 .50
13 Mike Hampton .20 .50
14 Fernando Tatis .20 .50
15 Kazuhiro Sasaki .20 .50
16 Jim Thome .30 .75
17 Geoff Jenkins .20 .50
18 Jeff Kent .20 .50
19 Tom Glavine .30 .75
20 Dean Palmer .20 .50
21 Todd Zeile .20 .50
22 Edgar Renteria .20 .50
23 Andruw Jones .30 .75
24 Juan Encarnacion .20 .50
25 Robin Ventura .20 .50
26 J.D. Drew .20 .50
27 Ray Durham .20 .50
28 Richard Hidalgo .20 .50
29 Eric Chavez .20 .50
30 Rafael Palmeiro .30 .75
31 Steve Finley .20 .50
32 Jeff Weaver .20 .50
33 Al Leiter .20 .50
34 Jim Edmonds .20 .50
35 Garret Anderson .20 .50
36 Larry Walker .20 .50
37 Jose Vidro .20 .50
38 Mike Cameron .20 .50
39 Brady Anderson .20 .50
40 Mike Lowell .20 .50
41 Bernie Williams .30 .75
42 Gary Sheffield .20 .50
43 John Smoltz .30 .75
44 Mike Mussina .30 .75
45 Greg Vaughn .20 .50
46 Juan Gonzalez .20 .50
47 Matt Lawton .20 .50
48 Robb Nen .20 .50
49 Brad Radke .20 .50
50 Edgar Martinez .30 .75
51 Mike Bordick .20 .50
52 Shawn Green .20 .50
53 Carl Everett .20 .50
54 Adrian Beltre .20 .50
55 Kerry Wood .20 .50
56 Kevin Brown .20 .50
57 Brian Giles .20 .50
58 Greg Maddux .75 2.00
59 Preston Wilson .20 .50
60 Orlando Hernandez .20 .50
61 Ben Grieve .20 .50
62 Jermaine Dye .20 .50
63 Travis Lee .20 .50
64 Jose Cruz Jr. .20 .50
65 Rondell White .20 .50
66 Carlos Beltran .20 .50
67 Scott Rolen .30 .75
68 Brad Fullmer .20 .50
69 David Wells .20 .50
70 Mike Sweeney .20 .50
71 Barry Zito .30 .75
72 Tony Batista .20 .50
73 Curt Schilling .20 .50
74 Jeff Cirillo .20 .50
75 Edgardo Alfonzo .20 .50
76 John Olerud .20 .50
77 Carlos Lee .20 .50
78 Moises Alou .20 .50
79 Tim Hudson .20 .50
80 Andres Galarraga .20 .50
81 Roberto Alomar .30 .75
82 Richie Sexson .20 .50
83 Trevor Hoffman .20 .50
84 Omar Vizquel .30 .75
85 Jacque Jones .20 .50
86 J.T. Snow .20 .50
87 Sean Casey .20 .50
88 Craig Biggio .30 .75
89 Mariano Rivera .50 1.25
90 Rusty Greer .20 .50
91 Barry Bonds 1.25 3.00
92 Pedro Martinez .30 .75
93 Cal Ripken 1.50 4.00
94 Pat Burrell .20 .50
95 Chipper Jones .50 1.25
96 Magglio Ordonez .20 .50
97 Jeff Bagwell .30 .75
98 Randy Johnson .50 1.25
99 Frank Thomas .50 1.25
100 Jason Kendall .20 .50
101 Nomar Garciaparra AC 5.00 12.00
102 Mark McGwire AC 8.00 20.00
103 Troy Glaus AC 2.00 5.00
104 Ivan Rodriguez AC 2.00 5.00
105 Manny Ramirez Sox AC 2.00 5.00
106 Derek Jeter AC 8.00 20.00
107 Alex Rodriguez AC 4.00 10.00
108 Ken Griffey Jr. AC 6.00 15.00
109 Todd Helton AC 2.00 5.00
110 Sammy Sosa AC 3.00 8.00
111 Vladimir Guerrero AC 3.00 8.00
112 Mike Piazza AC 5.00 12.00
113 Roger Clemens AC 6.00 15.00
114 Jason Giambi AC 2.00 5.00
115 Carlos Delgado AC 2.00 5.00
116 Ichiro Suzuki AC RC 50.00 120.00
117 Morgan Ensberg AC RC 5.00 12.00
118 Carlos Valderrama AC RC 3.00 8.00
119 Erick Almonte AC RC 3.00 8.00
120 Tsuyoshi Shinjo AC RC 5.00 12.00
121 Albert Pujols AC RC 75.00 200.00
122 Wilson Betemit AC RC 5.00 12.00
123 Adrian Hernandez AC RC 3.00 8.00
124 Jackson Melian AC RC 3.00 8.00
125 Drew Henson AC RC 5.00 12.00
126 Paul Phillips RS RC 2.00 5.00
127 Esix Snead RS RC 2.00 5.00
128 Ryan Freel RS RC 2.00 5.00
129 Junior Spivey RS RC 3.00 8.00
130 Elpidio Guzman RS RC 2.00 5.00
131 Juan Diaz RS RC 2.00 5.00
132 Andres Torres RS RC 2.00 5.00
133 Jay Gibbons RS RC 3.00 8.00
134 Bill Ortega RS RC 2.00 5.00
135 Alexis Gomez RS RC 2.00 5.00
136 Wilkin Ruan RS RC 2.00 5.00
137 Henry Mateo RS RC 2.00 5.00
138 Juan Uribe RS RC 3.00 8.00
139 Johnny Estrada RS RC 3.00 8.00
140 Jaisen Randolph RS RC 2.00 5.00
141 Eric Hinske RS RC 3.00 8.00
142 Jack Wilson RS RC 3.00 8.00
143 Cody Ransom RS RC 2.00 5.00
144 Nate Frese RS RC 2.00 5.00
145 John Grabow RS RC 2.00 5.00
146 Christian Parker RS RC 2.00 5.00
147 Brian Lawrence RS RC 2.00 5.00
148 Brandon Duckworth RS RC 2.00 5.00
149 Winston Abreu RS RC 2.00 5.00
150 Horacio Ramirez RS RC 3.00 8.00
151 Nick Maness RS RC 2.00 5.00
152 Blaine Neal RS RC 2.00 5.00
153 Billy Sylvester RS RC 2.00 5.00
154 David Elder RS RC 2.00 5.00
155 Bert Snow RS RC 2.00 5.00
156 Claudio Vargas RS RC 2.00 5.00
157 Martin Vargas RS RC 2.00 5.00
158 Grant Balfour RS RC 2.00 5.00
159 Randy Keisler RS 2.00 5.00
160 Zach Day RS RC 2.00 5.00
P1 Tony Gwynn Promo .75 2.00
MM3 Derek Jeter MM/2000 5.00 12.00
NNO Derek Jeter MM AU/100 150.00 250.00

2001 Fleer Showcase Legacy

*STARS 1-100: 8X TO 20X BASIC 1-100
*AVANT 101-115: 1.25X TO 3X BASIC 101-115
*AVANT 116-125: .75X TO 2X BASIC 116-125
*RS 126-145: 1.25X TO 3X BASIC 126-145
*RS 146-160: 1.5X TO 4X BASIC 146-160
STATED PRINT RUN 50 SERIAL #'d SETS

2001 Fleer Showcase Awards Showcase

COMPLETE SET (20) 30.00 60.00
STATED ODDS 1:20 RETAIL
1 Derek Jeter 3.00 8.00
2 Derek Jeter 3.00 8.00
3 Jason Giambi .50 1.25
4 Jeff Kent .50 1.25
5 Pedro Martinez .75 2.00
6 Randy Johnson 1.25 3.00
7 Kazuhiro Sasaki .50 1.25
8 Rafael Furcal .50 1.25
9 Carlos Delgado .50 1.25
10 Todd Helton .75 2.00
11 Ivan Rodriguez .75 2.00
12 Darin Erstad .50 1.25
13 Bernie Williams .75 2.00
14 Greg Maddux 2.00 5.00
15 Jim Edmonds .50 1.25
16 Andruw Jones .75 2.00
17 Nomar Garciaparra 2.00 5.00
18 Todd Helton .75 2.00
19 Troy Glaus .50 1.25
20 Sammy Sosa 1.25 3.00

2001 Fleer Showcase Awards Showcase Memorabilia

STATED PRINT RUN 100 SERIAL #'d SETS
1 Johnny Bench Jsy 10.00 25.00
2 Yogi Berra Bat 10.00 25.00
3 George Brett Jsy 15.00 40.00
4 Lou Brock Bat 10.00 25.00
5 Roy Campanella Bat 10.00 25.00
6 Steve Carlton Jsy 6.00 15.00
7 Roger Clemens Jsy 15.00 40.00
9 Andre Dawson Jsy 6.00 15.00
10 Whitey Ford Jsy 10.00 25.00
12 Jimmie Foxx Bat 20.00 50.00
14 Kirk Gibson Bat 6.00 15.00
15 Tom Glavine Jsy 10.00 25.00
16 Juan Gonzalez Bat 6.00 15.00
17 Elston Howard Bat 10.00 25.00
18 Jim Hunter Jsy 10.00 25.00
19 Reggie Jackson Bat 10.00 25.00
20 Randy Johnson Jsy 10.00 25.00
21 Chipper Jones Bat 10.00 25.00
22 Harmon Killebrew Bat 10.00 25.00
23 Fred Lynn Bat 6.00 15.00
24 Greg Maddux Jsy 10.00 25.00
25 Don Mattingly Bat 10.00 25.00
27 Willie McCovey Jsy 6.00 15.00
28 Jim Palmer Jsy 6.00 15.00
29 Jim Rice Bat 6.00 15.00
30 Brooks Robinson Bat 10.00 25.00
31 Frank Robinson Bat 10.00 25.00
32 Jackie Robinson Pants 15.00 40.00
33 Ivan Rodriguez Jsy 10.00 25.00
34 Mike Schmidt Jsy 10.00 25.00
35 Tom Seaver Jsy 10.00 25.00
36 Willie Stargell Jsy 10.00 25.00
37 Ted Williams Jsy 50.00 100.00
38 Robin Yount Jsy 10.00 25.00

2001 Fleer Showcase Sticks

STATED ODDS 1:24 HOBBY
I.SUZUKI/R.ALOMAR 25% SHORTER SUPPLY
1 Roberto Alomar 6.00 15.00
2 Rick Ankiel 4.00 10.00
3 Adrian Beltre 4.00 10.00
4 Barry Bonds 10.00 25.00
5 Pat Burrell 4.00 10.00
6 Roger Cedeno 4.00 10.00
7 Tony Clark 4.00 10.00
8 Roger Clemens 6.00 15.00
9 Carlos Delgado 4.00 10.00
10 J.D. Drew 4.00 10.00
11 Steve Finley 4.00 10.00
12 Rafael Furcal 4.00 10.00
13 Alex Gonzalez 4.00 10.00
14 Juan Gonzalez 4.00 10.00
15 Shawn Green 4.00 10.00
16 Vladimir Guerrero 6.00 15.00
17 Richard Hidalgo 4.00 10.00
18 Reggie Jackson 6.00 15.00
19 Randy Johnson 6.00 15.00
20 Andruw Jones 6.00 15.00
21 Chipper Jones 6.00 15.00
22 Al Kaline 6.00 15.00
23 George Kell 6.00 15.00
24 Jason Kendall 4.00 10.00
25 Magglio Ordonez 4.00 10.00
26 Adam Piatt 4.00 10.00
27 Jorge Posada 6.00 15.00
28 Ivan Rodriguez 6.00 15.00
29 Scott Rolen 6.00 15.00
30 Tsuyoshi Shinjo 6.00 15.00
31 Shannon Stewart 4.00 10.00
32 Ichiro Suzuki 20.00 50.00
33 Frank Thomas 6.00 15.00
34 Jim Thome 6.00 15.00
35 Jose Vidro 4.00 10.00
36 Preston Wilson 4.00 10.00

2001 Fleer Showcase Sweet Sigs Leather

OVERALL SIGS STATED ODDS 1:24 HOBBY
SP PRINT PRINT RUNS LISTED BELOW
1 Bob Abreu SP/100 * 15.00 40.00
2 Wilson Betemit 10.00 25.00
3 Russell Branyan 6.00 15.00
4 Pat Burrell SP/75 * 15.00 40.00
5 Sean Casey SP/75 * 10.00 25.00
6 Eric Chavez SP/100 * 15.00 40.00
7 Rafael Furcal 6.00 15.00
8 N.Garciaparra SP/55 * 30.00 60.00
9 Brian Giles SP/75 * 15.00 40.00
10 Juan Gonzalez SP/75 * 15.00 40.00
11 Elpidio Guzman 6.00 15.00
12 Drew Henson SP/75 * 10.00 25.00
13 Brandon Inge 6.00 15.00
14 Derek Jeter SP/75 * 100.00 200.00
15 Andruw Jones SP/85 * 20.00 50.00
16 Willie Mays SP/60 * 125.00 200.00
17 Jackson Melian 6.00 15.00
18 Xavier Nady 6.00 15.00
19 Jose Ortiz 6.00 15.00
20 Albert Pujols SP/75 * 400.00 1000.00
21 Ben Sheets 8.00 20.00
22 Mike Sweeney 6.00 15.00
23 Miguel Tejada SP/75 * 6.00 15.00

2001 Fleer Showcase Sweet Sigs Lumber

OVERALL SIGS STATED ODDS 1:24 HOBBY
SP PRINT PRINT RUNS LISTED BELOW
1 Bob Abreu 6.00 15.00
2 Wilson Betemit 10.00 25.00
3 Russell Branyan 6.00 15.00
4 Pat Burrell SP/300 * 10.00 25.00
5 Sean Casey SP/300 * 6.00 15.00
6 Eric Chavez 6.00 15.00
7 Rafael Furcal 6.00 15.00
8 N.Garciaparra SP/155 * 50.00 100.00
9 Brian Giles SP/155 * 10.00 25.00
10 Juan Gonzalez SP/300 * 10.00 25.00
11 Elpidio Guzman 6.00 15.00
12 Drew Henson SP/145 * 10.00 25.00
13 Brandon Inge 6.00 15.00
14 Derek Jeter SP/300 * 100.00 175.00
15 Andruw Jones SP/300 * 6.00 15.00
16 Willie Mays SP/155 * 100.00 200.00
17 Jackson Melian 6.00 15.00
18 Xavier Nady 6.00 15.00
19 Jose Ortiz 6.00 15.00
20 Albert Pujols SP/150 * 250.00 600.00
21 Ben Sheets 8.00 20.00
22 Mike Sweeney 6.00 15.00
23 Miguel Tejada SP/300 * 12.50 30.00

2001 Fleer Showcase Sweet Sigs Wall

OVERALL SIGS STATED ODDS 1:24 HOBBY
SP PRINT PRINT RUNS LISTED BELOW
1 Bob Abreu 6.00 15.00
2 Wilson Betemit 10.00 25.00
3 Russell Branyan 6.00 15.00
4 Pat Burrell SP/93 * 12.50 30.00
5 Sean Casey SP/98 * 12.50 30.00
6 Eric Chavez 6.00 15.00
7 Rafael Furcal 6.00 15.00
8 N.Garciaparra SP/80 * 20.00 50.00
9 Brian Giles SP/100 * 12.50 30.00
10 Juan Gonzalez SP/30 * 15.00 40.00
11 Elpidio Guzman 6.00 15.00
12 Drew Henson SP/100 * 12.50 30.00
13 Brandon Inge 6.00 15.00
14 Derek Jeter SP/90 * 150.00 300.00
15 Andruw Jones SP/200 * 15.00 40.00
16 Willie Mays SP/85 * 125.00 200.00
17 Jackson Melian 6.00 15.00
18 Xavier Nady 6.00 15.00
19 Jose Ortiz 6.00 15.00
20 Albert Pujols SP/80 * 300.00 800.00
21 Ben Sheets 8.00 20.00
23 Miguel Tejada SP/120 * 15.00 40.00

2002 Fleer Showcase

COMP.SET w/o SP's (125) 12.50 30.00
COMMON CARD (1-125) .20 .50
COMMON CARD (126-135) 3.00 8.00
126-135 STATED ODDS 1:12
COMMON CARD (136-141) 4.00 10.00
136-141 PRINT RUN 500 SERIAL #'d SETS
COMMON CARD (142-166) 3.00 8.00
142-156 PRINT RUN 1000 SERIAL #'d SETS
157-166 PRINT RUN 1500 SERIAL #'d SETS
136-166 RANDOM INSERTS IN PACKS
1 Albert Pujols 1.00 2.50
2 Pedro Martinez .30 .75
3 Frank Thomas .50 1.25
4 Gary Sheffield .20 .50
5 Roberto Alomar .30 .75
6 Luis Gonzalez .20 .50
7 Bobby Abreu .20 .50
8 Carlos Lee .20 .50
9 Preston Wilson .20 .50
10 Todd Helton .30 .75
11 Juan Gonzalez .20 .50
12 Chuck Knoblauch .20 .50
13 Jason Kendall .20 .50
14 Aaron Sele .20 .50
15 Greg Vaughn .20 .50
16 Fred McGriff .30 .75
17 Doug Mientkiewicz .20 .50
18 Richard Hidalgo .20 .50
19 Alfonso Soriano .20 .50
20 Matt Williams .20 .50
21 Bobby Higginson .20 .50
22 Mo Vaughn .20 .50
23 Andruw Jones .30 .75
24 Omar Vizquel .30 .75
25 Bret Boone .20 .50
26 Bernie Williams .30 .75
27 Rafael Furcal .20 .50
28 Jeff Bagwell .30 .75
29 Marty Cordova .20 .50
30 Lance Berkman .20 .50
31 Vernon Wells .20 .50
32 Garret Anderson .20 .50
33 Larry Bigbie .20 .50
34 Steve Finley .20 .50
35 Barry Bonds 1.25 3.00
36 Eric Chavez .20 .50
37 Tony Clark .20 .50
38 Roger Clemens 1.00 2.50
39 Adam Dunn .20 .50
40 Roger Cedeno .20 .50
41 Carlos Delgado .20 .50
42 Jermaine Dye .20 .50
43 Brian Jordan .20 .50
44 Darin Erstad .20 .50
45 Paul LoDuca .20 .50
46 Jim Edmonds .20 .50
47 Tom Glavine .30 .75
48 Cliff Floyd .20 .50
49 Jon Lieber .20 .50
50 Adrian Beltre .20 .50
51 Joel Pineiro .20 .50
52 Jim Thome .30 .75
53 Jimmy Rollins .20 .50
54 Pat Burrell .20 .50
55 Jeromy Burnitz .20 .50
56 Larry Walker .20 .50
57 Damon Minor .20 .50
58 John Olerud .20 .50
59 Carlos Beltran .20 .50
60 Vladimir Guerrero .50 1.25
61 David Justice .20 .50
62 Phil Nevin .20 .50
63 Tino Martinez .30 .75
64 Curt Schilling .20 .50
65 Corey Patterson .20 .50
66 Aubrey Huff .20 .50
67 Mark Grace .30 .75
68 Rafael Palmeiro .30 .75
69 Jorge Posada .30 .75
70 Craig Biggio .30 .75
71 Manny Ramirez .30 .75
72 Mark Quinn .20 .50
73 Raul Mondesi .20 .50
74 Shawn Green .20 .50
75 Brian Giles .20 .50
76 Paul Konerko .20 .50
77 Troy Glaus .20 .50
78 Mike Mussina .30 .75
79 Greg Maddux .75 2.00
80 Edgar Martinez .30 .75
81 Jose Vidro .20 .50
82 Scott Rolen .30 .75
83 Ben Grieve .20 .50
84 Jeff Kent .20 .50
85 Magglio Ordonez .20 .50
86 Freddy Garcia .20 .50
87 Ivan Rodriguez .30 .75
88 Pokey Reese .20 .50
89 Shannon Stewart .20 .50
90 Randy Johnson .50 1.25
91 Cristian Guzman .20 .50
92 Tsuyoshi Shinjo .20 .50
93 Steve Cox .20 .50
94 Mike Sweeney .20 .50
95 Robert Fick .20 .50
96 Sean Casey .20 .50
97 Tim Hudson .20 .50
98 Bud Smith .20 .50
99 Corey Koskie .20 .50
100 Richie Sexson .20 .50
101 Aramis Ramirez .20 .50
102 Barry Larkin .30 .75
103 Rich Aurilia .20 .50
104 Charles Johnson .20 .50
105 Ryan Klesko .20 .50
106 Ben Sheets .20 .50
107 J.D. Drew .20 .50
108 Jay Gibbons .20 .50
109 Kerry Wood .20 .50
110 C.C. Sabathia .20 .50
111 Eric Munson .20 .50
112 Josh Beckett .20 .50
113 Javier Vazquez .20 .50
114 Barry Zito .20 .50
115 Kazuhiro Sasaki .20 .50
116 Bubba Trammell .20 .50
117 Russell Branyan .20 .50
118 Todd Walker .20 .50
119 Mike Hampton .20 .50
120 Jeff Weaver .20 .50
121 Geoff Jenkins .20 .50
122 Edgardo Alfonzo .20 .50
123 Mike Lieberthal .20 .50
124 Mike Lowell .20 .50
125 Kevin Brown .20 .50
126 Derek Jeter AC 8.00 20.00
127 Ichiro Suzuki AC 6.00 15.00
128 Nomar Garciaparra AC 5.00 12.00
129 Ken Griffey Jr. AC 6.00 15.00
130 Jason Giambi AC 3.00 8.00
131 Alex Rodriguez AC 4.00 10.00
132 Chipper Jones AC 3.00 8.00
133 Mike Piazza AC 5.00 12.00
134 Sammy Sosa AC 3.00 8.00
135 Hideo Nomo AC 3.00 8.00
136 Kazuhisa Ishii AC RC 6.00 15.00
137 Satoru Komiyama AC RC 4.00 10.00
138 So Taguchi AC RC 6.00 15.00
139 Jorge Padilla AC RC 4.00 10.00
140 Rene Reyes AC RC 4.00 10.00
141 Jorge Nunez AC RC 4.00 10.00
142 Nelson Castro RS 3.00 8.00
143 Anderson Machado RS RC 3.00 8.00
144 Edwin Almonte RS RC 3.00 8.00
145 Luis Ugueto RS RC 3.00 8.00
146 Felix Escalona RS RC 3.00 8.00
147 Ron Calloway RS RC 3.00 8.00
148 Hansel Izquierdo RS RC 3.00 8.00
149 Mark Teixeira RS 4.00 10.00
150 Orlando Hudson RS 3.00 8.00
151 Aaron Cook RS RC 3.00 8.00
152 Aaron Taylor RS RC 3.00 8.00
153 Takahito Nomura RS RC 3.00 8.00
154 Matt Thornton RS RC 3.00 8.00
155 Mark Prior RS 4.00 10.00
156 Reed Johnson RS RC 4.00 10.00
157 Doug DeVore RS RC 3.00 8.00
158 Ben Howard RS RC 3.00 8.00
159 Francis Beltran RS RC 3.00 8.00
160 Brian Mallette RS RC 3.00 8.00
161 Sean Burroughs RS 3.00 8.00
162 Michael Restovich RS 3.00 8.00
163 Austin Kearns RS 3.00 8.00
164 Marlon Byrd RS 3.00 8.00
165 Hank Blalock RS 4.00 10.00
166 Mike Rivera RS 3.00 8.00

2002 Fleer Showcase Legacy

*LEGACY 1-125: 2.5X TO 6X BASIC
*LEGACY 126-135: .5X TO 1.2X BASIC
*LEGACY 136-141: .4X TO 1X BASIC
*LEGACY 142-166: .5X TO 1.2X BASIC
ONE PER HOBBY BOX
STATED PRINT RUN 175 SERIAL #'d SETS

2002 Fleer Showcase Baseball's Best

COMPLETE SET (20) 25.00 60.00
STATED ODDS 1:8 HOBBY, 1:10 RETAIL
1 Derek Jeter 3.00 8.00
2 Barry Bonds 3.00 8.00
3 Mike Piazza 2.00 5.00
4 Alex Rodriguez 1.50 4.00
5 Pat Burrell .75 2.00
6 Rafael Palmeiro .75 2.00
7 Nomar Garciaparra 2.00 5.00
8 Todd Helton .75 2.00
9 Roger Clemens 2.50 6.00
10 Shawn Green .75 2.00
11 Chipper Jones 1.25 3.00
12 Pedro Martinez .75 2.00
13 Luis Gonzalez .75 2.00
14 Randy Johnson 1.25 3.00
15 Ichiro Suzuki 2.50 6.00
16 Ken Griffey Jr. 2.50 6.00
17 Vladimir Guerrero 1.25 3.00
18 Sammy Sosa 1.25 3.00
19 Jason Giambi .75 2.00
20 Albert Pujols 2.50 6.00

2002 Fleer Showcase Baseball's Best Memorabilia

*MULTI-COLOR PATCH: 1X TO 2.5X BASIC
STATED ODDS 1:12 HOBBY, 1:36 RETAIL
SP PRINT RUNS PROVIDED BY FLEER
SP'S ARE NOT SERIAL-NUMBERED
BASE CARDS IN GREATER SUPPLY
CARD NUMBER 5 DOES NOT EXIST
*GOLD: 1X TO 2.5X BASIC
GOLD RANDOM INSERTS IN PACKS
GOLD PRINT RUN 100 SERIAL #'d SETS
1 Derek Jeter Jsy 12.00 30.00
2 Barry Bonds Jsy 6.00 15.00
3 Mike Piazza Jsy 4.00 10.00
4 Alex Rodriguez Bat 6.00 15.00
6 Rafael Palmeiro Jsy 4.00 10.00
7 Nomar Garciaparra Jsy 6.00 15.00
8 Todd Helton Bat SP/350 4.00 10.00
9 Roger Clemens Jsy 6.00 15.00
10 Shawn Green Jsy 3.00 8.00
11 Chipper Jones Jsy 4.00 10.00
12 Pedro Martinez Jsy 4.00 10.00
13 Luis Gonzalez Jsy 3.00 8.00
14 Randy Johnson Jsy 4.00 10.00
15 Ichiro Suzuki Base 8.00 20.00
16 Ken Griffey Jr. Base 6.00 15.00
17 Vladimir Guerrero Base 3.00 8.00
18 Sammy Sosa Base 4.00 10.00
19 Jason Giambi Base 3.00 8.00
20 Albert Pujols Base 6.00 15.00

2002 Fleer Showcase Baseball's Best Memorabilia Autographs Silver

STATED PRINT RUN 400 SERIAL #'d SETS
*GOLD: .6X TO 1.2X SILVER AU
GOLD PRINT RUN 100 SERIAL #'d SETS
1 Derek Jeter Jsy 125.00 300.00
2 Barry Bonds Jsy 75.00 200.00

2002 Fleer Showcase Derek Jeter Legacy Collection

COMPLETE SET (22) 40.00 100.00
COMMON CARD (1-22) 3.00 8.00
RANDOM INSERTS IN PACKS
STATED PRINT RUN 1000 SERIAL #'d SETS

2002 Fleer Showcase Derek Jeter Legacy Collection Memorabilia

RANDOM INSERTS IN PACKS
PRINT RUNS PROVIDED BY FLEER
CARDS ARE NOT SERIAL-NUMBERED
1 D.Jeter YC Jsy/300 * 75.00 150.00
2 D.Jeter YC Combo Jsy/175 * 75.00 150.00
3 D.Jeter WS Ball/50 * 125.00 250.00
4 D.Jeter Fldg Glv/425 * 40.00 80.00

2002 Fleer Showcase Sweet Sigs Leather

CARDS DISPLAY CUMULATIVE PRINT RUNS
ACTUAL PRINT RUNS LISTED BELOW
LEATHER ON CARDS IS NOT GAME-USED
NO PRICING ON QTY OF 37 OR LESS
2 Russell Branyan/90 6.00 15.00
6 Rafael Furcal/92 6.00 15.00
8 Brandon Inge/122 5.00 12.00
10 Xavier Nady/301 6.00 15.00
11 Jose Ortiz/50 8.00 20.00
12 Ben Sheets/60 12.50 30.00
13 Mike Sweeney/103 8.00 20.00

2002 Fleer Showcase Sweet Sigs Lumber

CARDS DISPLAY CUMULATIVE PRINT RUNS
ACTUAL PRINT RUNS LISTED BELOW
NO PRICING ON QTY OF 25 OR LESS
1 Bobby Abreu/231 6.00 15.00
2 Russell Branyan/425 4.00 10.00
3 Pat Burrell/115 8.00 20.00
4 Sean Casey/64 12.50 30.00
5 Eric Chavez/256 6.00 15.00
6 Rafael Furcal/530 4.00 10.00
8 Brandon Inge/528 4.00 10.00
9 Jackson Melian/636 4.00 10.00
10 Xavier Nady/589 4.00 10.00
11 Jose Ortiz/515 4.00 10.00
12 Ben Sheets/458 6.00 15.00
13 Mike Sweeney/495 6.00 15.00

2002 Fleer Showcase Sweet Sigs Wall

CARDS DISPLAY CUMULATIVE PRINT RUNS
ACTUAL PRINT RUNS LISTED BELOW
WALL ON CARDS IS GAME-USED
NO PRICING ON QTY OF 35 OR LESS
1 Bobby Abreu/70 12.50 30.00
2 Russell Branyan/200 4.00 10.00
5 Eric Chavez/108 8.00 20.00
6 Rafael Furcal/207 4.00 10.00
8 Brandon Inge/187 5.00 12.00
9 Jackson Melian/146 5.00 12.00
10 Xavier Nady/286 4.00 10.00
11 Jose Ortiz/116 5.00 12.00
12 Ben Sheets/150 8.00 20.00
13 Mike Sweeney/371 6.00 15.00

2003 Fleer Showcase

COMP.LO SET w/o SP's (105) 10.00 25.00
COMMON CARD (1-95) .20 .50
COMMON CARD (96-105) .20 .50
COMMON CARD (106-135) .40 1.00
106-135 ODDS 1:3 HOBBY, 1:12 RETAIL
106-115 DIST IN JERSEY & RETAIL PACKS
116-125 DIST IN LEATHER & RETAIL PACKS
126-135 DIST IN LUMBER & RETAIL PACKS
COMMON CARD (136-145) 1.00 2.50
136-145 RANDOM IN FLEER R/G PACKS
136-145 PRINT RUN 750 SERIAL #'d SETS
1 David Eckstein .20 .50
2 Curt Schilling .30 .75
3 Jay Gibbons .20 .50
4 Kerry Wood .20 .50
5 Jeff Bagwell .30 .75
6 Hideo Nomo .50 1.25
7 Tim Hudson .30 .75
8 J.D. Drew .20 .50
9 Josh Phelps .20 .50
10 Bartolo Colon .20 .50
11 Bobby Abreu .20 .50
12 Matt Morris .20 .50
13 Kazuhiro Sasaki .20 .50
14 Sean Burroughs .20 .50
15 Vicente Padilla .20 .50
16 Jorge Posada .30 .75
17 Torii Hunter .20 .50
18 Richie Sexson .20 .50
19 Lance Berkman .30 .75
20 Todd Helton .30 .75
21 Paul Konerko .30 .75
22 Pedro Martinez .30 .75
23 Rodrigo Lopez .20 .50
24 Gary Sheffield .20 .50
25 Darin Erstad .20 .50
26 Nomar Garciaparra .30 .75
27 Adam Dunn .30 .75
28 Jason Giambi .20 .50
29 Miguel Tejada .30 .75
30 Chipper Jones .50 1.25
31 Alex Rodriguez .60 1.50
32 Barry Bonds .75 2.00
33 Roger Clemens .60 1.50
34 Sammy Sosa .50 1.25
35 Randy Johnson .50 1.25
36 Tim Salmon .20 .50
37 Shea Hillenbrand .20 .50
38 Larry Walker .30 .75
39 A.J. Burnett .20 .50
40 Shawn Green .20 .50
41 Cristian Guzman .20 .50
42 Bernie Williams .30 .75
43 Mark Mulder .20 .50
44 Brian Giles .20 .50
45 Bret Boone .20 .50
46 Juan Gonzalez .20 .50
47 Roy Halladay .30 .75
48 Wade Miller .20 .50
49 Jeff Kent .20 .50
50 Carlos Delgado .20 .50
51 Mike Lowell .20 .50
52 Jim Edmonds .30 .75
53 Ivan Rodriguez .30 .75
54 Aubrey Huff .20 .50
55 Ryan Klesko .20 .50
56 Paul Lo Duca .20 .50
57 Roy Oswalt .30 .75
58 Omar Vizquel .30 .75
59 Manny Ramirez .50 1.25
60 Andruw Jones .20 .50
61 Troy Glaus .20 .50
62 Ichiro Suzuki .60 1.50
63 Albert Pujols .60 1.50
64 Derek Jeter 1.25 3.00
65 Mark Prior .30 .75
66 Ken Griffey Jr. 1.00 2.50
67 Vladimir Guerrero .30 .75
68 Mike Piazza .50 1.25
69 Alfonso Soriano .30 .75
70 Greg Maddux .60 1.50
71 Adam Kennedy .20 .50
72 Junior Spivey .20 .50
73 Tom Glavine .30 .75
74 Derek Lowe .20 .50
75 Magglio Ordonez .30 .75
76 Jim Thome .30 .75
77 Robert Fick .20 .50
78 Josh Beckett .20 .50
79 Mike Sweeney .20 .50
80 Kazuhisa Ishii .20 .50
81 Roberto Alomar .30 .75
82 Barry Zito .30 .75
83 Pat Burrell .20 .50
84 Scott Rolen .30 .75
85 John Olerud .20 .50
86 Eric Hinske .20 .50
87 Rafael Palmeiro .30 .75
88 Edgar Martinez .30 .75
89 Eric Chavez .20 .50
90 Jose Vidro .20 .50
91 Craig Biggio .30 .75
92 Rich Aurilia .20 .50
93 Austin Kearns .20 .50
94 Luis Gonzalez .20 .50
95 Garret Anderson .20 .50
96 Yogi Berra .50 1.25
97 Al Kaline .30 .75
98 Robin Yount .50 1.25
99 Reggie Jackson .30 .75
100 Harmon Killebrew .50 1.25
101 Eddie Mathews .50 1.25
102 Willie McCovey .30 .75
103 Nolan Ryan 1.50 4.00
104 Mike Schmidt .75 2.00
105 Tom Seaver .30 .75
106 Francisco Rodriguez ST .60 1.50
107 Carl Crawford ST .60 1.50
108 Ben Howard ST .40 1.00
109 Hank Blalock ST .40 1.00
110 Hee Seop Choi ST .40 1.00

111 Kirk Saarloos ST .40 1.00
112 Lew Ford ST RC .40 1.00
113 Andy Van Hekken ST .40 1.00
114 Drew Henson ST .40 1.00
115 Marlon Byrd ST .40 1.00
116 Jayson Werth ST .60 1.50
117 Willie Bloomquist ST .40 1.00
118 Joe Borchard ST .40 1.00
119 Mark Teixeira ST .60 1.50
120 Bobby Hill ST .40 1.00
121 Jason Lane ST .40 1.00
122 Omar Infante ST .40 1.00
123 Victor Martinez ST .60 1.50
124 Jorge Padilla ST .40 1.00
125 John Lackey ST .60 1.50
126 Anderson Machado ST .40 1.00
127 Rodrigo Rosario ST .40 1.00
128 Freddy Sanchez ST .40 1.00
129 Tony Alvarez ST .40 1.00
130 Matt Thornton ST .40 1.00
131 Joe Thurston ST .40 1.00
132 Brett Myers ST .40 1.00
133 Nook Logan ST RC .40 1.00
134 Chris Snelling ST .40 1.00
135 Termel Sledge ST RC .40 1.00
136 Chien-Ming Wang ST RC 4.00 10.00
137 Rickie Weeks ST RC 3.00 8.00
138 Brandon Webb ST RC 3.00 8.00
139 Hideki Matsui ST RC 5.00 12.00
140 Michael Hessman ST RC 1.00 2.50
141 Ryan Wagner ST RC 1.00 2.50
142 Bo Hart ST RC 1.00 2.50
143 Edwin Jackson ST RC 1.50 4.00
144 Jose Contreras ST RC 2.50 6.00
145 Delmon Young ST RC 6.00 15.00

2003 Fleer Showcase Legacy
*LEGACY 1-95: 2.5X TO 6X BASIC
*LEGACY 96-105: 2.5X TO 6X BASIC
*LEGACY 106-135: 1.2X TO 3X BASIC
RANDOM INSERTS IN HOBBY PACKS
STATED PRINT RUN 150 SERIAL #'d SETS

2003 Fleer Showcase Baseball's Best
STATED ODDS 1:8 LEATHER, 1:24 RETAIL
1 Curt Schilling .60 1.50
2 Barry Zito .60 1.50
3 Torii Hunter .40 1.00
4 Pedro Martinez .60 1.50
5 Bernie Williams .60 1.50
6 Magglio Ordonez .60 1.50
7 Alfonso Soriano .60 1.50
8 Hideo Nomo 1.00 2.50
9 Jason Giambi .40 1.00
10 Sammy Sosa 1.00 2.50
11 Vladimir Guerrero .60 1.50
12 Ken Griffey Jr. 2.00 5.00
13 Troy Glaus .40 1.00
14 Ichiro Suzuki 1.25 3.00
15 Albert Pujols 1.25 3.00

2003 Fleer Showcase Baseball's Best Game Jersey
STATED ODDS 1:27 LEATHER, 1:24 RETAIL
AS Alfonso Soriano 3.00 8.00
BW Bernie Williams 4.00 10.00
BZ Barry Zito 3.00 8.00
CS Curt Schilling 3.00 8.00
HN Hideo Nomo Sox 4.00 10.00
JG Jason Giambi 3.00 8.00
MO Magglio Ordonez 3.00 8.00
PM Pedro Martinez 4.00 10.00
SS Sammy Sosa 4.00 10.00
TH Torii Hunter 3.00 8.00

2003 Fleer Showcase Hot Gloves
STATED ODDS 1:144 LEATHER, 1:288 RETAIL
1 Greg Maddux 6.00 15.00
2 Ivan Rodriguez 3.00 8.00
3 Derek Jeter 12.00 30.00
4 Mike Piazza 5.00 12.00
5 Nomar Garciaparra 3.00 8.00
6 Andruw Jones 2.00 5.00
7 Scott Rolen 3.00 8.00
8 Barry Bonds 8.00 20.00
9 Roger Clemens 6.00 15.00
10 Alex Rodriguez 6.00 15.00

2003 Fleer Showcase Hot Gloves Game Jersey
RANDOM INSERTS IN LUMBER PACKS
STATED PRINT RUN 350 SERIAL #'d SETS
ALL ARE GAME USED GLOVE UNLESS NOTED
AJ Andruw Jones 10.00 25.00
AR Alex Rodriguez 8.00 20.00
BB Barry Bonds 10.00 25.00
DJ Derek Jeter 15.00 40.00
GM Greg Maddux 8.00 20.00
IR Ivan Rodriguez 6.00 15.00
MP Mike Piazza 8.00 20.00
NG Nomar Garciaparra 8.00 20.00
RC Roger Clemens 10.00 25.00
SR Scott Rolen 6.00 15.00

2003 Fleer Showcase Sweet Sigs
RANDOM IN LEATHER AND RETAIL PACKS
STATED PRINT RUNS LISTED BELOW
NO PRICING ON QTY OF 25 OR LESS
BB1 Barry Bonds 90 MVP/150 50.00 120.00
BB2 Barry Bonds 92 MVP/100 50.00 120.00
BB3 Barry Bonds 93 MVP/75 50.00 120.00
BB4 Barry Bonds 01 MVP/50 60.00 150.00
DJ2 Derek Jeter Blue Ink/250 100.00 250.00
DJ3 Derek Jeter Red Ink/50 125.00 300.00

2003 Fleer Showcase Sweet Stitches
STATED ODDS 1:8 JERSEY, 1:24 RETAIL
1 Derek Jeter 3.00 8.00
2 Randy Johnson 1.25 3.00
3 Jeff Bagwell 1.25 3.00
4 Nomar Garciaparra 2.00 5.00
5 Roger Clemens 2.50 6.00
6 Todd Helton 1.25 3.00
7 Barry Bonds 3.00 8.00
8 Alfonso Soriano 1.25 3.00
9 Miguel Tejada 1.25 3.00
10 Mark Prior 1.25 3.00

2003 Fleer Showcase Sweet Stitches Game Jersey
RANDOM INSERTS IN JERSEY PACKS
STATED PRINT RUNS LISTED BELOW
AR Alex Rodriguez/899 5.00 12.00
AS Alfonso Soriano/599 2.50 6.00
BB Barry Bonds/899 6.00 15.00
DJ Derek Jeter/599 10.00 25.00
JB Jeff Bagwell/899 2.50 6.00
JD J.D. Drew/899 1.50 4.00
MP Mike Piazza/899 4.00 10.00
MP Mark Prior/899 2.50 6.00
MT Miguel Tejada/899 2.50 6.00
NG Nomar Garciaparra/899 2.50 6.00
RC Roger Clemens/599 5.00 12.00
RJ Randy Johnson/899 4.00 10.00
SS Sammy Sosa/899 4.00 10.00
TH Todd Helton/899 2.50 6.00

2003 Fleer Showcase Sweet Stitches Patch
STATED PRINT RUNS LISTED BELOW
2 Randy Johnson/150 15.00 40.00
3 Jeff Bagwell/150 15.00 40.00
4 Nomar Garciaparra/150 30.00 60.00
6 Todd Helton/75 20.00 50.00
7 Barry Bonds/150 10.00 25.00
8 Alfonso Soriano/50 10.00 25.00
9 Miguel Tejada/150 10.00 25.00
10 Mark Prior/150 15.00 40.00
11 Sammy Sosa/150 15.00 40.00
12 J.D. Drew/150 10.00 25.00
13 Alex Rodriguez/150 30.00 60.00
14 Mike Piazza/150 30.00 60.00

2003 Fleer Showcase Thunder Sticks
STATED ODDS 1:8 LUMBER, 1:24 RETAIL
1 Adam Dunn .60 1.50
2 Alex Rodriguez 1.25 3.00
3 Barry Bonds 1.50 4.00
4 Jim Thome .60 1.50
5 Chipper Jones 1.00 2.50
6 Manny Ramirez 1.00 2.50
7 Carlos Delgado .40 1.00
8 Mike Piazza 1.00 2.50
9 Shawn Green .40 1.00
10 Pat Burrell .40 1.00

2003 Fleer Showcase Thunder Sticks Game Bat
STATED PRINT RUNS LISTED BELOW
GOLD PRINT RUN 99 SERIAL #'d SETS
AD Adam Dunn/799 2.50 6.00
AR Alex Rodriguez/799 5.00 12.00
BB Barry Bonds/899 6.00 15.00
CJ Chipper Jones/799 4.00 10.00
JT Jim Thome/799 2.50 6.00
MR Manny Ramirez/799 4.00 10.00
PB Pat Burrell/799 1.50 4.00
SG Shawn Green/799 1.50 4.00
TG Troy Glaus/799 1.50 4.00
VG Vladimir Guerrero/799 2.50 6.00

2004 Fleer Showcase
COMP.SET w/o SP's (100) 10.00 25.00
COMMON CARD (1-100) .20 .50
COMMON CARD (101-130) .75 2.00
101-130 ODDS 1:6 HOBBY, 1:12 RETAIL
1 Corey Patterson .20 .50
2 Ken Griffey Jr. 1.00 2.50
3 Preston Wilson .20 .50
4 Juan Pierre .20 .50
5 Jose Reyes .30 .75
6 Jason Schmidt .20 .50
7 Rocco Baldelli .20 .50
8 Carlos Delgado .20 .50
9 Hideki Matsui .75 2.00
10 Nomar Garciaparra .30 .75
11 Brian Giles .20 .50
12 Darin Erstad .20 .50
13 Larry Walker .30 .75
14 Bernie Williams .30 .75
15 Laynce Nix .20 .50
16 Manny Ramirez .50 1.25
17 Magglio Ordonez .30 .75
18 Khalil Greene .30 .75
19 Jim Edmonds .30 .75
20 Troy Glaus .20 .50
21 Curt Schilling .30 .75
22 Chipper Jones .50 1.25
23 Sammy Sosa .50 1.25
24 Frank Thomas .50 1.25
25 Todd Helton .30 .75
26 Craig Biggio .30 .75
27 Shannon Stewart .20 .50
28 Mark Mulder .20 .50
29 Mike Lieberthal .20 .50
30 Reggie Sanders .20 .50
31 Edgar Martinez .30 .75
32 Bo Hart .20 .50
33 Mark Teixeira .30 .75
34 Jay Gibbons .20 .50
35 Roberto Alomar .30 .75
36 Kip Wells .20 .50
37 J.D. Drew .20 .50
38 Jason Varitek .50 1.25
39 Craig Monroe .20 .50
40 Roy Oswalt .30 .75
41 Edgardo Alfonzo .20 .50
42 Roy Halladay .30 .75
43 Gary Sheffield .20 .50
44 Lance Berkman .30 .75
45 Torii Hunter .20 .50
46 Vladimir Guerrero .30 .75
47 Marlon Byrd .20 .50
48 Austin Kearns .20 .50
49 Angel Berroa .20 .50
50 Geoff Jenkins .20 .50
51 Aubrey Huff .20 .50
52 Dontrelle Willis .20 .50
53 Tony Batista .20 .50
54 Shawn Green .20 .50
55 Jason Kendall .20 .50
56 Garret Anderson .20 .50
57 Andruw Jones .20 .50
58 Dmitri Young .20 .50
59 Richie Sexson .20 .50
60 Jorge Posada .30 .75
61 Bobby Abreu .20 .50
62 Vernon Wells .20 .50
63 Javy Lopez .20 .50
64 Josh Beckett .20 .50
65 Eric Chavez .20 .50
66 Tim Salmon .20 .50
67 Brandon Webb .20 .50
68 Pedro Martinez .30 .75
69 Kerry Wood .20 .50
70 Jose Vidro .20 .50
71 Alfonso Soriano .30 .75
72 Barry Zito .30 .75
73 Sean Burroughs .20 .50
74 Jamie Moyer .20 .50
75 Luis Gonzalez .20 .50
76 Adam Dunn .30 .75
77 Mike Piazza .50 1.25
78 Pat Burrell .20 .50
79 Scott Rolen .30 .75
80 Milton Bradley .20 .50
81 Mike Sweeney .20 .50
82 Hank Blalock .20 .50
83 Esteban Loaiza .20 .50
84 Hideo Nomo .50 1.25
85 Derek Jeter 1.25 3.00
86 Albert Pujols .60 1.50
87 Greg Maddux .60 1.50
88 Mark Prior .30 .75
89 Mike Lowell .20 .50
90 Jeff Bagwell .30 .75
91 Scott Podsednik .20 .50
92 Tom Glavine .30 .75
93 Jason Giambi .20 .50
94 Jim Thome .30 .75
95 Ichiro Suzuki .60 1.50
96 Randy Johnson .50 1.25
97 Omar Vizquel .30 .75
98 Ivan Rodriguez .30 .75
99 Miguel Tejada .30 .75
100 Alex Rodriguez .60 1.50
101 Rickie Weeks ST .40 1.00
102 Chad Gaudin ST .40 1.00
103 Rich Harden ST .40 1.00
104 Edwin Jackson ST .40 1.00
105 Chien-Ming Wang ST 1.50 4.00
106 Matt Kata ST .40 1.00
107 Delmon Young ST .60 1.50
108 Ryan Wagner ST .40 1.00
109 Jeff Duncan ST .40 1.00
110 Prentice Redman ST .40 1.00
111 Clint Barmes ST .60 1.50
112 Jeremy Guthrie ST .40 1.00
113 Brian Stokes ST .40 1.00
114 David DeJesus ST .40 1.00
115 Felix Sanchez ST .40 1.00
116 Josh Stewart ST .40 1.00
117 Daniel Garcia ST .40 1.00
118 Jon Leicester ST .40 1.00
119 Francisco Cruceta ST .40 1.00
120 Oscar Villarreal ST .40 1.00
121 Michael Hessman ST .40 1.00
122 Michel Hernandez ST .40 1.00
123 Richard Fischer ST .40 1.00
124 Robby Hammock ST .40 1.00
125 Guillermo Quiroz ST .40 1.00
126 Craig Brazell ST .40 1.00
127 Wilfredo Ledezma ST .40 1.00
128 Josh Willingham ST .60 1.50
129 Ramon Nivar ST .40 1.00
130 Matt Diaz ST .60 1.50

2004 Fleer Showcase Legacy
*LEGACY 1-100: 6X TO 15X BASIC
*LEGACY 101-130: 1.5X TO 4X BASIC
OVERALL PARALLEL ODDS 1:24
STATED PRINT RUN 99 SERIAL #'d SETS

2004 Fleer Showcase Baseballs Best
STATED ODDS 1:24 HOBBY, 1:12 RETAIL
1 Derek Jeter 2.50 6.00
2 Mark Prior .60 1.50
3 Mike Piazza 1.00 2.50
4 Jeff Bagwell .60 1.50
5 Kerry Wood .40 1.00
6 Ivan Rodriguez .60 1.50
7 Albert Pujols 1.25 3.00
8 Jim Thome .60 1.50
9 Sammy Sosa 1.00 2.50
10 Vladimir Guerrero .60 1.50
11 Eric Gagne .40 1.00
12 Randy Johnson 1.00 2.50
13 Todd Helton .60 1.50
14 Chipper Jones 1.00 2.50
15 Alex Rodriguez 1.25 3.00

2004 Fleer Showcase Baseballs Best Game Used
STATED ODDS 1:72 HOBBY, 1:48 RETAIL
*PATCH: 1.5X TO 4X BASIC
PATCH RANDOM INSERTS IN PACKS
PATCH PRINT RUN 50 SERIAL #'d SETS
*GOLD: .5X TO 1.2X BASIC
GOLD RANDOM INSERTS IN PACKS
GOLD PRINT RUN 150 SERIAL #'d SETS
*REWARD: 1X TO 2.5X BASIC
REWARD ISSUED ONLY IN DEALER PACKS
REWARD PRINTS B/WN 29-44 COPIES PER
AP Albert Pujols Jsy 6.00 15.00
AR Alex Rodriguez Jsy 4.00 10.00
CJ Chipper Jones Jsy 4.00 10.00
DJ Derek Jeter Bat 8.00 20.00
EG Eric Gagne Jsy 3.00 8.00
IR Ivan Rodriguez Jsy 4.00 10.00
JB Jeff Bagwell Jsy 4.00 10.00
JT Jim Thome Jsy 4.00 10.00
KW Kerry Wood Jsy 3.00 8.00
MPI Mike Piazza Jsy 4.00 10.00
MPR Mark Prior Jsy 4.00 10.00
RJ Randy Johnson Jsy 4.00 10.00
SS Sammy Sosa Jsy 4.00 10.00
TH Todd Helton Jsy 4.00 10.00
VG Vladimir Guerrero Jsy 4.00 10.00

2004 Fleer Showcase Grace
STATED ODDS 1:12 HOBBY/RETAIL
1 Kerry Wood .40 1.00
2 Derek Jeter 2.50 6.00
3 Nomar Garciaparra .60 1.50
4 Mike Piazza 1.00 2.50
5 Mark Prior .60 1.50
6 Jose Reyes .60 1.50
7 Dontrelle Willis .40 1.00
8 Pedro Martinez .60 1.50
9 Tim Hudson .60 1.50
10 Troy Glaus .40 1.00
11 Hank Blalock .40 1.00
12 Albert Pujols 1.25 3.00
13 Juan Pierre .40 1.00
14 Angel Berroa .40 1.00
15 Rocco Baldelli .40 1.00
16 Carlos Delgado .40 1.00
17 Manny Ramirez 1.00 2.50
18 Alex Rodriguez 1.25 3.00
19 Andruw Jones .40 1.00
20 Luis Gonzalez .40 1.00

2004 Fleer Showcase Grace Game Used
STATED ODDS 1:48 HOBBY/RETAIL
*PATCH: 1.5X TO 4X BASIC
PATCH RANDOM INSERTS IN PACKS
PATCH PRINT RUN 50 SERIAL #'d SETS
*GOLD: .5X TO 1.2X BASIC
GOLD RANDOM INSERTS IN PACKS
GOLD PRINT RUN 150 SERIAL #'d SETS
*REWARD p/r 44-55: 1X TO 2.5X BASIC
REWARD ISSUED ONLY IN DEALER PACKS
REWARD PRINTS B/WN 23-55 COPIES PER
NO REWARD PRICING ON QTY OF 23
AP Albert Pujols Jsy 6.00 15.00
AR Alex Rodriguez Jsy 4.00 10.00
DJ Derek Jeter Bat 8.00 20.00
DW Dontrelle Willis Jsy 4.00 10.00
MPI Mike Piazza Jsy 4.00 10.00
MPR Mark Prior Jsy 4.00 10.00
MR Manny Ramirez Jsy 4.00 10.00
NG Nomar Garciaparra Jsy 4.00 10.00
PM Pedro Martinez Jsy 4.00 10.00
RB Rocco Baldelli Jsy 3.00 8.00

2004 Fleer Showcase Hot Gloves
STATED ODDS 1:288 HOBBY, 1:576 RETAIL
NO MORE THAN 120 SETS PRODUCED
PRINT RUN INFO PROVIDED BY FLEER
CARDS ARE NOT SERIAL-NUMBERED
1 Derek Jeter 15.00 40.00
2 Nomar Garciaparra 4.00 10.00
3 Alex Rodriguez 8.00 20.00
4 Chipper Jones 6.00 15.00
5 Torii Hunter 2.50 6.00
6 Ichiro Suzuki 8.00 20.00
7 Mark Prior 4.00 10.00
8 Vladimir Guerrero 4.00 10.00
9 Albert Pujols 8.00 20.00
10 Ivan Rodriguez 4.00 10.00
11 Hideki Matsui 10.00 25.00
12 Sammy Sosa 6.00 15.00
13 Jim Thome 4.00 10.00
14 Rocco Baldelli 2.50 6.00
15 Jeff Bagwell 4.00 10.00

2004 Fleer Showcase Hot Gloves Game Used
RANDOM INSERTS IN PACKS
STATED PRINT RUN 50 SERIAL #'d SETS
AP Albert Pujols Jsy 30.00 60.00
AR Alex Rodriguez Jsy 20.00 50.00
CJ Chipper Jones Jsy 12.50 30.00
DJ Derek Jeter Jsy 40.00 80.00
HM Hideki Matsui Base 50.00 100.00
IR Ivan Rodriguez Jsy 12.50 30.00
IS Ichiro Suzuki Base 60.00 120.00
JB Jeff Bagwell Jsy 12.50 30.00
JT Jim Thome Jsy 12.50 30.00
MP Mark Prior Jsy 12.50 30.00
NG Nomar Garciaparra Jsy 10.00 25.00
RB Rocco Baldelli Jsy 12.50 30.00
SS Sammy Sosa Jsy 12.50 30.00
TH Torii Hunter Jsy 12.50 30.00
VG Vladimir Guerrero Jsy 12.50 30.00

2004 Fleer Showcase Pujols Legacy Collection
COMMON CARD (1-10) 3.00 8.00
STATED ODDS 1:24
STATED PRINT RUN 1000 SERIAL #'d SETS

2004 Fleer Showcase Pujols Legacy Collection Game Jersey
RANDOM INSERTS IN PACKS
PRINT RUNS B/WN 10-100 COPIES PER
NO PRICING ON QTY OF 40 OR LESS
5 Albert Pujols NL Records/50 12.50 30.00
6 Albert Pujols 2X AS/60 12.50 30.00
7 Albert Pujols HR Record/70 10.00 25.00
8 Albert Pujols 300-100-100/60 10.00 25.00
9 Albert Pujols 03 Btg Champ/90 10.00 25.00
10 Albert Pujols 03 POY/100 10.00 25.00

2004 Fleer Showcase Sweet Sigs
OVERALL AUTOGRAPH ODDS 1:24
PRINT RUNS B/WN 26-1000 COPIES PER
EXCH.PRINT RUNS PROVIDED BY FLEER
EXCHANGE DEADLINE INDEFINITE
AK Austin Kearns/224 4.00 10.00
AP Albert Pujols/150 60.00 120.00
AP1 Albert Pujols 60.00 120.00
BH Bo Hart/667 4.00 10.00
BW Brandon Webb/1000 4.00 10.00
BZ Barry Zito/248 6.00 15.00
CPA Corey Patterson/176 6.00 15.00
CPE Carlos Pena/48 8.00 20.00
CW Chien Mien-Wang/35 125.00 200.00
DW Dontrelle Willis/26 30.00 60.00
HB Hank Blalock/824 6.00 15.00
JR Jose Reyes/115 8.00 20.00
JW Josh Willingham/180 6.00 15.00
ML Mike Lowell/44 10.00 25.00
MR Michael Ryan/288 4.00 10.00
MT Miguel Tejada/52 15.00 40.00
RWE Rickie Weeks/416 6.00 15.00
SR Scott Rolen/200 10.00 25.00
TH Torii Hunter/294 6.00 15.00
WL Wilfredo Ledezma/376 4.00 10.00

2005 Fleer Showcase
COMP.SET w/o SP's (100) 15.00 40.00
COMMON CARD (1-100) .30 .75
COMP.ST SUBSET (10) 6.00 15.00
COMMON CARD (101-110) .60 1.50
101-110 ODDS 1:5 HOBBY, 1:12 RETAIL
COMMON CARD (111-135) .60 1.50
111-135 ODDDS 1:20 HOBBY, 1:48 RETAIL
1 Albert Pujols 1.00 2.50
2 Rocco Baldelli .30 .75
3 Bernie Williams .50 1.25
4 Shawn Green .30 .75
5 Garret Anderson .30 .75
6 Paul Konerko .50 1.25
7 Mike Sweeney .30 .75
8 Jim Thome .50 1.25
9 Mark Teixeira .50 1.25
10 Mark Prior .50 1.25
11 Angel Berroa .30 .75
12 Barry Zito .50 1.25
13 Carlos Delgado .30 .75
14 Troy Glaus .30 .75
15 Travis Hafner .30 .75
16 Lyle Overbay .30 .75
17 David Ortiz .75 2.00
18 Ivan Rodriguez .50 1.25
19 Jack Wilson .30 .75
20 Jason Schmidt .30 .75
21 Mike Piazza .75 2.00
22 David Eckstein .30 .75
23 Ben Sheets .30 .75
24 Randy Johnson .75 2.00
25 Jacque Jones .30 .75
26 Jody Gerut .30 .75
27 Kris Benson .30 .75
28 Luis Gonzalez .30 .75
29 Victor Martinez .50 1.25
30 Torii Hunter .30 .75
31 Gary Sheffield .30 .75
32 Miguel Tejada .50 1.25
33 Dontrelle Willis .30 .75
34 Bret Boone .30 .75
35 Kaz Matsui .30 .75
36 Shea Hillenbrand .30 .75
37 Wily Mo Pena .30 .75
38 Johan Santana .50 1.25
39 Derek Jeter 2.00 5.00
40 Chipper Jones .75 2.00
41 Sean Casey .30 .75
42 Corey Koskie .30 .75
43 Alex Rodriguez 1.00 2.50
44 Andruw Jones .30 .75
45 Austin Kearns .30 .75
46 Jose Vidro .30 .75
47 Adam Dunn .50 1.25
48 Adrian Beltre .75 2.00
49 Bobby Abreu .30 .75
50 Michael Young .30 .75
51 Freddy Garcia .30 .75
52 Eric Gagne .30 .75
53 Chase Utley .50 1.25
54 Alfonso Soriano .50 1.25
55 Nick Johnson .30 .75
56 Johnny Estrada .30 .75
57 Jeff Bagwell .50 1.25
58 Randy Winn .30 .75
59 Roy Halladay .50 1.25
60 J.D. Drew .30 .75
61 Craig Biggio .50 1.25
62 Scott Rolen .50 1.25
63 Nomar Garciaparra .50 1.25
64 Matt Holliday .75 2.00
65 Billy Wagner .30 .75
66 Carl Crawford .50 1.25
67 Pedro Martinez .50 1.25
68 Jeremy Bonderman .30 .75
69 Jason Bay .30 .75
70 A.J. Pierzynski .30 .75
71 Vladimir Guerrero .50 1.25
72 Rickie Weeks .30 .75
73 Mark Loretta .30 .75
74 Todd Helton .50 1.25
75 Manny Ramirez .75 2.00
76 Carlos Guillen .30 .75
77 Khalil Greene .30 .75
78 Javy Lopez .30 .75
79 Josh Beckett .30 .75
80 Ichiro Suzuki 1.00 2.50
81 Magglio Ordonez .50 1.25
82 Ken Harvey .30 .75
83 Mark Mulder .30 .75
84 Hank Blalock .30 .75
85 Richard Hidalgo .30 .75
86 Curt Schilling .50 1.25
87 Jeromy Burnitz .30 .75
88 Craig Wilson .30 .75
89 Aubrey Huff .30 .75
90 Kerry Wood .30 .75
91 Andy Pettitte .50 1.25
92 Tim Hudson .50 1.25
93 Jim Edmonds .50 1.25
94 Melvin Mora .30 .75
95 Miguel Cabrera .75 2.00
96 Trevor Hoffman .50 1.25
97 J.T. Snow .30 .75
98 Sammy Sosa .75 2.00
99 Roger Clemens 1.00 2.50
100 Eric Chavez .30 .75
101 B.J. Upton ST 1.00 2.50
102 Gavin Floyd ST .60 1.50
103 Casey Kotchman ST .60 1.50
104 David Wright ST 1.25 3.00
105 Dioner Navarro ST .60 1.50
106 Scott Kazmir ST 1.50 4.00
107 Andres Blanco ST .60 1.50
108 Joey Gathright ST .60 1.50
109 Jon Knott ST .60 1.50
110 Charlton Jimerson ST .60 1.50
111 Larry Doby SH 1.00 2.50
112 Reggie Jackson SH 1.00 2.50
113 Enos Slaughter SH 1.00 2.50
114 Bill Skowron SH .60 1.50
115 Duke Snider SH 1.00 2.50
116 Harmon Killebrew SH 1.50 4.00
117 Willie McCovey SH 1.00 2.50
118 Rollie Fingers SH 1.00 2.50
119 Preacher Roe SH .60 1.50
120 Carlton Fisk SH 1.00 2.50
121 Andre Dawson SH 1.00 2.50
122 Orlando Cepeda SH 1.00 2.50
123 Bucky Dent SH .60 1.50
124 Cal Ripken SH 5.00 12.00
125 Nolan Ryan SH 5.00 12.00
126 Tony Perez SH 1.00 2.50
127 Mike Schmidt SH 2.50 6.00
128 Johnny Bench SH 1.50 4.00
129 Sparky Anderson SH 1.00 2.50
130 Ted Williams SH 3.00 8.00
131 Al Kaline SH 1.50 4.00
132 Carl Yastrzemski SH 2.00 5.00
133 Eddie Murray SH 1.00 2.50
134 Roberto Clemente SH 4.00 10.00
135 Yogi Berra SH 1.50 4.00

2005 Fleer Showcase Showtime
*SHOWDOWN 1-100: 2.5X TO 6X BASIC
*SHOWDOWN 101-110: 1X TO 2.5X BASIC
*SHOWDOWN 111-135: .75X TO 2X BASIC
BASIC PARALLEL ODDS 1:10 HOBBY
STATED PRINT RUN 99 SERIAL #'d SETS

2005 Fleer Showcase Autographed Legacy
LEGACY PARALLEL ODDS 1:20 HOBBY
PRINT RUNS B/WN 7-460 COPIES PER
NO PRICING ON QTY OF 19 OR LESS
SKIP-NUMBERED 58-CARD SET
EXCHANGE DEADLINE 01/15/08
8 Jim Thome/34 30.00 60.00
10 Mark Prior/43 15.00 40.00
12 Barry Zito/45 15.00 40.00
18 Ivan Rodriguez/217 10.00 25.00
19 Jack Wilson/298 6.00 15.00
20 Jason Schmidt/127 6.00 15.00
21 Mike Piazza/26 60.00 120.00
22 David Eckstein/40 20.00 50.00
23 Ben Sheets/427 6.00 15.00
40 Chipper Jones/41 30.00 60.00
45 Austin Kearns/460 4.00 10.00
47 Adam Dunn/52 15.00 40.00
48 Adrian Beltre/180 8.00 20.00
50 Michael Young/80 8.00 20.00
52 Eric Gagne/310 10.00 25.00
59 Roy Halladay/99 6.00 15.00
68 Jeremy Bonderman/97 8.00 20.00
72 Rickie Weeks/453 6.00 15.00
75 Manny Ramirez/31 40.00 80.00
77 Khalil Greene/299 10.00 25.00
88 Craig Wilson/40 8.00 20.00
89 Aubrey Huff/453 6.00 15.00
90 Kerry Wood/28 15.00 40.00
92 Tim Hudson/183 10.00 25.00
95 Miguel Cabrera/32 20.00 50.00
99 Roger Clemens/64 60.00 120.00
100 Eric Chavez/204 10.00 25.00
103 Casey Kotchman ST/454 6.00 15.00
104 David Wright ST/298 10.00 25.00
106 Scott Kazmir ST/458 8.00 20.00
107 Andres Blanco ST/23 8.00 20.00
109 Jon Knott ST/402 4.00 10.00
114 Bill Skowron SH/64 10.00 25.00
119 Preacher Roe SH/304 10.00 25.00
120 Carlton Fisk SH/86 12.50 30.00
123 Bucky Dent SH/99 8.00 20.00
135 Yogi Berra SH/25 40.00 100.00

2005 Fleer Showcase Legacy
*LEGACY 1-100: 2.5X TO 6X BASIC
*LEGACY 101-110: 1X TO 2.5X BASIC
*LEGACY 111-135: .75X TO 2X BASIC
LEGACY PARALLEL ODDS 1:20 HOBBY
STATED PRINT RUN 99 SERIAL #'d SETS
SKIP-NUMBERED 50-CARD SET

2005 Fleer Showcase Measure of Greatness
STATED ODDS 1:5 HOBBY, 1:5 RETAIL
1 Albert Pujols 1.25 3.00
2 Mike Piazza 1.00 2.50
3 Vladimir Guerrero .60 1.50
4 Jim Thome .60 1.50
5 Pedro Martinez .60 1.50
6 Rafael Palmeiro .60 1.50
7 Adrian Beltre 1.00 2.50
8 Sammy Sosa 1.00 2.50
9 Todd Helton .60 1.50
10 Randy Johnson 1.00 2.50
11 Jeff Bagwell .60 1.50
12 Jason Giambi .40 1.00
13 Scott Rolen .60 1.50
14 Greg Maddux 1.25 3.00
15 Alfonso Soriano .60 1.50
16 Mariano Rivera 1.25 3.00
17 Curt Schilling .60 1.50
18 Derek Jeter 2.50 6.00
19 Chipper Jones 1.00 2.50
20 Roger Clemens 1.25 3.00

2005 Fleer Showcase Measure of Greatness Jersey Red
STATED PRINT RUN 340 SERIAL #'d SETS
*GREEN: .6X TO 1.5X BASIC
GREEN ODDS 1:144 RETAIL
PATCH PRINT RUN 10 SERIAL #'d SETS
NO PATCH PRICING DUE TO SCARCITY
PATCH MP PRINT RUN 1 SERIAL #'d SET
NO PATCH MP PRICING DUE TO SCARCITY
OVERALL GAME-USED ODDS 1:10 HOBBY
AB Adrian Beltre 3.00 8.00
AP Albert Pujols 8.00 20.00
AS Alfonso Soriano 3.00 8.00
CJ Chipper Jones 4.00 10.00
JT Jim Thome 4.00 10.00
MP Mike Piazza 4.00 10.00
MR Mariano Rivera 4.00 10.00
PM Pedro Martinez 4.00 10.00
RC Roger Clemens 6.00 15.00
RJ Randy Johnson 4.00 10.00
RP Rafael Palmeiro 4.00 10.00
SR Scott Rolen 4.00 10.00
SS Sammy Sosa 4.00 10.00
TH Todd Helton 4.00 10.00
VG Vladimir Guerrero 4.00 10.00

2005 Fleer Showcase Swing Time
STATED ODDS 1:45 HOBBY, 1:96 RETAIL
1 Ivan Rodriguez 1.00 2.50
2 Gary Sheffield .60 1.50
3 Bernie Williams 1.00 2.50
4 Vladimir Guerrero 1.00 2.50
5 Jim Edmonds 1.00 2.50
6 Manny Ramirez 1.50 4.00
7 Todd Helton 1.00 2.50
8 Hank Blalock .60 1.50
9 Hideki Matsui 2.50 6.00
10 David Ortiz 1.50 4.00
11 Albert Pujols 2.00 5.00
12 Miguel Tejada 1.00 2.50
13 Miguel Cabrera 1.50 4.00
14 Alex Rodriguez 2.00 5.00
15 Ichiro Suzuki 2.00 5.00

2005 Fleer Showcase Swing Time Jersey Red
STATED PRINT RUN 610 SERIAL #'d SETS
*GREEN: .75X TO 2X BASIC
GREEN ODDS 1:444 RETAIL
*PATCH: 1.25X TO 3X BASIC
PATCH PRINT RUN 50 SERIAL #'d SETS
PATCH MP PRINT RUN 1 SERIAL #'d SET
NO PATCH MP PRICING DUE TO SCARCITY
OVERALL GAME-USED ODDS 1:10 HOBBY
AP Albert Pujols 6.00 15.00
BW Bernie Williams 3.00 8.00
DO David Ortiz 3.00 8.00
HB Hank Blalock 2.00 5.00
HM Hideki Matsui 8.00 20.00
IR Ivan Rodriguez 3.00 8.00
JE Jim Edmonds 2.00 5.00
MC Miguel Cabrera 3.00 8.00
MR Manny Ramirez 3.00 8.00
TH Todd Helton 3.00 8.00

2005 Fleer Showcase Wave of the Future
STATED ODDS 1:15 HOBBY, 1:15 RETAIL
1 Kaz Matsui .40 1.00
2 Johan Santana .60 1.50
3 Khalil Greene .40 1.00
4 Dontrelle Willis .40 1.00
5 Mark Teixeira .60 1.50
6 Travis Hafner .40 1.00
7 Jason Bay .40 1.00
8 Angel Berroa .40 1.00
9 Miguel Cabrera 1.00 2.50
10 Joe Mauer .75 2.00
11 Adam Dunn .60 1.50
12 B.J. Upton .60 1.50
13 Victor Martinez .60 1.50
14 Michael Young .40 1.00
15 David Wright .75 2.00

2005 Fleer Showcase Wave of the Future Jersey Red
STATED PRINT RUN 610 SERIAL #'d SETS
*GREEN: .4X TO 1X BASIC
GREEN ODDS 1:48 RETAIL
*PATCH: 1.25X TO 3X BASIC
PATCH PRINT RUN 50 SERIAL #'d SETS
PATCH MP PRINT RUN 1 SERIAL #'d SET
NO PATCH MP PRICING DUE TO SCARCITY
OVERALL GAME-USED ODDS 1:10 HOBBY
AB Angel Berroa 2.00 5.00
AD Adam Dunn 2.00 5.00
BU B.J. Upton 3.00 8.00
DW David Wright 8.00 20.00
DW Dontrelle Willis 2.00 5.00
JB Jason Bay 2.00 5.00
JM Joe Mauer 3.00 8.00
JS Johan Santana 3.00 8.00
KG Khalil Greene 3.00 8.00
KM Kaz Matsui 2.00 5.00
MC Miguel Cabrera 3.00 8.00
MT Mark Teixeira 3.00 8.00
MY Michael Young 2.00 5.00
TH Travis Hafner 2.00 5.00
VM Victor Martinez 2.00 5.00

2003 Fleer Splendid Splinters
COMP.SET w/o SP's (90) 6.00 15.00
COMMON CARD (1-90) .12 .30
COMMON CARD (91-110) .75 2.00
91-110 RANDOM INSERTS IN PACKS
91-110 PRINT RUN 499 SERIAL #'d SETS
COMMON CARD (111-140) .40 1.00
111-140 STATED ODDS 1:6
COMMON CARD (141-150) 1.25 3.00
141-150 RANDOM INSERTS IN PACKS
141-150 PRINT RUN B/WN 499-999 #'d SETS
1 David Eckstein .12 .30
2 Barry Larkin .20 .50
3 Edgardo Alfonzo .12 .30
4 Darin Erstad .12 .30
5 Ellis Burks .12 .30
6 Omar Vizquel .20 .50
7 Bartolo Colon .12 .30
8 Roberto Alomar .20 .50
9 Garret Anderson .12 .30
10 Al Leiter .12 .30
11 Tim Salmon .12 .30
12 Larry Walker .20 .50
13 Jorge Posada .20 .50
14 Curt Schilling .20 .50
15 Jason Jennings .12 .30
16 Jason Giambi .12 .30
17 Robert Fick .12 .30
18 Kazuhiro Sasaki .12 .30
19 Bernie Williams .20 .50
20 Junior Spivey .12 .30
21 Mike Lowell .12 .30
22 Luis Gonzalez .12 .30
23 Josh Beckett .12 .30
24 John Smoltz .30 .75
25 Mike Mussina .20 .50
26 Gary Sheffield .12 .30
27 Tom Glavine .20 .50
28 Tim Hudson .20 .50
29 Austin Kearns .12 .30
30 Andruw Jones .12 .30

Card	Low	High
31 Roger Clemens	.40	1.00
32 Mark Mulder	.12	.30
33 Jay Gibbons	.12	.30
34 Jeff Kent	.12	.30
35 Barry Zito	.20	.50
36 Rodrigo Lopez	.12	.30
37 Jeff Bagwell	.20	.50
38 Eric Chavez	.12	.30
39 Pedro Martinez	.20	.50
40 Lance Berkman	.20	.50
41 Bobby Abreu	.12	.30
42 Wade Miller	.12	.30
43 Bret Boone	.12	.30
44 Vicente Padilla	.12	.30
45 Shea Hillenbrand	.12	.30
46 Roy Oswalt	.20	.50
47 Pat Burrell	.12	.30
48 Manny Ramirez	.30	.75
49 Craig Biggio	.20	.50
50 Randy Wolf	.12	.30
51 Kerry Wood	.12	.30
52 Mike Sweeney	.12	.30
53 Brian Giles	.12	.30
54 Kazuhisa Ishii	.12	.30
55 Jason Kendall	.12	.30
56 Hideo Nomo	.30	.75
57 Josh Phelps	.12	.30
58 Sean Burroughs	.12	.30
59 Paul Konerko	.20	.50
60 Shawn Green	.12	.30
61 Ryan Klesko	.12	.30
62 Magglio Ordonez	.20	.50
63 Paul Lo Duca	.12	.30
64 Edgar Martinez	.20	.50
65 J.D. Drew	.12	.30
66 Phil Nevin	.12	.30
67 Jim Edmonds	.20	.50
68 Matt Morris	.12	.30
69 Aubrey Huff	.12	.30
70 Adam Dunn	.20	.50
71 John Olerud	.12	.30
72 Juan Gonzalez	.12	.30
73 Scott Rolen	.20	.50
74 Rafael Palmeiro	.20	.50
75 Roy Halladay	.20	.50
76 Kevin Brown	.12	.30
77 Ivan Rodriguez	.20	.50
78 Eric Hinske	.12	.30
79 Frank Thomas	.30	.75
80 Carlos Delgado	.12	.30
81 Bobby Higginson	.12	.30
82 Trevor Hoffman	.20	.50
83 Cliff Floyd	.12	.30
84 Derek Lowe	.12	.30
85 Richie Sexson	.12	.30
86 Rich Aurilia	.12	.30
87 Sean Casey	.12	.30
88 Cristian Guzman	.12	.30
89 Randy Winn	.12	.30
90 Jose Vidro	.12	.30
91 Mark Prior Wood	1.25	3.00
92 Derek Jeter Wood	5.00	12.00
93 Alex Rodriguez Wood	2.50	6.00
94 Greg Maddux Wood	2.50	6.00
95 Troy Glaus Wood	.75	2.00
96 Vladimir Guerrero Wood	1.25	3.00
97 Todd Helton Wood	1.25	3.00
98 Albert Pujols Wood	2.50	6.00
99 Torii Hunter Wood	.75	2.00
100 Mike Piazza Wood	2.00	5.00
101 Ichiro Suzuki Wood	2.50	6.00
102 Sammy Sosa Wood	2.00	5.00
103 Ken Griffey Jr. Wood	4.00	10.00
104 Nomar Garciaparra Wood	1.25	3.00
105 Barry Bonds Wood	3.00	8.00
106 Chipper Jones Wood	2.00	5.00
107 Jim Thome Wood	1.25	3.00
108 Miguel Tejada Wood	1.25	3.00
109 Randy Johnson Wood	2.00	5.00
110 Alfonso Soriano Wood	1.25	3.00
111 Guillermo Quiroz BB RC	.40	1.00
112 Josh Willingham BB RC	1.25	3.00
113 Alejandro Machado BB RC	.40	1.00
114 Chris Waters BB RC	.40	1.00
115 Adam LaRoche BB	.40	1.00
116 Prentice Redman BB RC	.40	1.00
117 Jhonny Peralta BB	.40	1.00
118 Francisco Rosario BB RC	.40	1.00
119 Shane Victorino BB RC	1.25	3.00
120 Chien-Ming Wang BB RC	1.50	4.00
121 Matt Bruback BB RC	.40	1.00
122 Rontrez Johnson BB RC	.40	1.00
123 Josh Hall BB RC	.40	1.00
124 Matt Kata BB RC	.40	1.00
125 Hector Luna BB RC	.40	1.00
126 Josh Stewart BB RC	.40	1.00
127 Craig Brazell BB RC	.40	1.00
128 Tim Olson BB RC	.40	1.00
129 Michel Hernandez BB RC	.40	1.00
130 Michael Hessman BB RC	.40	1.00
131 Clint Barmes BB RC	1.00	2.50
132 Justin Morneau BB	.60	1.50
133 Chris Snelling BB	.40	1.00
134 Bobby Jenks BB	.40	1.00
135 Tim Hummell BB	.40	1.00
136 Adam Morrissey BB	.40	1.00
137 Carl Crawford BB	.60	1.50
138 Garrett Atkins BB	.40	1.00
139 Jung Bong BB	.40	1.00
140 Ken Harvey BB	.40	1.00
141 Chin-Feng Chen Wood	1.25	3.00
142 Hee Seop Choi Wood	1.25	3.00
143 Lance Niekro Wood	1.25	3.00
144 Mark Teixeira Wood	2.00	5.00
145 Nook Logan Wood RC	1.25	3.00
146 Termel Sledge Wood RC	1.25	3.00
147 Lew Ford Wood RC	1.25	3.00
148 Ian Ferguson Wood RC	1.25	3.00
149 Hid Matsui Wood/499 RC	6.00	15.00
150 Jose Contreras Wood RC	3.00	8.00

2003 Fleer Splendid Splinters Bat Chips

RANDOM INSERTS IN PACKS

STATED PRINT RUN 425 SERIAL #'d SETS

Card	Low	High
16 Jason Giambi	3.00	8.00
19 Bernie Williams	4.00	10.00
26 Gary Sheffield	3.00	8.00
37 Jeff Bagwell	4.00	10.00
48 Manny Ramirez	4.00	10.00
61 Ryan Klesko	3.00	8.00
70 Adam Dunn	3.00	8.00
87 Sean Casey	3.00	8.00
92 Derek Jeter	10.00	25.00
93 Alex Rodriguez	6.00	15.00
95 Troy Glaus	3.00	8.00
96 Vladimir Guerrero	4.00	10.00
100 Mike Piazza	6.00	15.00
102 Sammy Sosa	4.00	10.00
104 Nomar Garciaparra	6.00	15.00
105 Barry Bonds	10.00	25.00
107 Jim Thome	4.00	10.00
108 Miguel Tejada	3.00	8.00
110 Alfonso Soriano	3.00	8.00

2003 Fleer Splendid Splinters Family Tree

Card	Low	High
COMPLETE SET (10)	5.00	12.00
STATED ODDS 1:12		
1 L.Niekro	.60	1.50
P.Niekro		
2 B.Boone	.40	1.00
B.Boone		
3 S.Alomar Jr.	.60	1.50
R.Alomar		
4 K.Griffey Sr.	2.00	5.00
K.Griffey Jr.		
5 J.Giambi	.40	1.00
J.Giambi		
6 B.Bonds	1.50	4.00
B.Bonds		
7 T.Perez	.60	1.50
E.Perez		
8 B.Giles	.40	1.00
M.Giles		
9 F.Alou	.40	1.00
M.Alou		
10 P.Martinez	.60	1.50
R.Martinez		

2003 Fleer Splendid Splinters Home Run Club

STATED ODDS 1:72

Card	Low	High
1 Barry Bonds	4.00	10.00
2 Jason Giambi	1.00	2.50
3 Sammy Sosa	2.50	6.00
4 Jim Thome	1.50	4.00
5 Lance Berkman	1.50	4.00
6 Alfonso Soriano	1.50	4.00
7 Vladimir Guerrero	1.50	4.00
8 Shawn Green	1.00	2.50
9 Troy Glaus	1.00	2.50
10 Pat Burrell	1.00	2.50
11 Alex Rodriguez	3.00	8.00
12 Mike Piazza	2.50	6.00

2003 Fleer Splendid Splinters Home Run Club Autographs

RANDOM INSERTS IN PACKS

STATED PRINT RUNS LISTED BELOW

Card	Low	High
BB1 B.Bonds Black Ink/150	40.00	100.00
CR1 Cal Ripken Black Ink/300	25.00	60.00
CR2 Cal Ripken Blue Ink/150	30.00	80.00
CR3 Cal Ripken Red Ink/50	40.00	100.00
DJ1 Derek Jeter Black Ink/400	75.00	200.00
DJ2 Derek Jeter Blue Ink/250	100.00	250.00
DJ3 Derek Jeter Red Ink/50	125.00	300.00

2003 Fleer Splendid Splinters Home Run Club Memorabilia

RANDOM INSERTS IN PACKS

STATED PRINT RUN 599 SERIAL #'d SETS

Card	Low	High
1 Barry Bonds Jsy	10.00	25.00
2 Jason Giambi Bat	3.00	8.00
3 Sammy Sosa Jsy	4.00	10.00
4 Jim Thome Bat	4.00	10.00
5 Lance Berkman Bat	3.00	8.00
6 Alfonso Soriano Jsy	3.00	8.00
7 Vladimir Guerrero Jsy	4.00	10.00
8 Shawn Green Jsy	3.00	8.00
9 Troy Glaus Bat	3.00	8.00
10 Pat Burrell Bat	3.00	8.00
11 Alex Rodriguez Jsy	6.00	15.00
12 Mike Piazza Jsy	6.00	15.00
13 Todd Helton Jsy	4.00	10.00
14 Rafael Palmeiro Jsy	4.00	10.00

2003 Fleer Splendid Splinters Knothole Gang

STATED ODDS 1:24

Card	Low	High
1 Derek Jeter	2.50	6.00
2 Barry Bonds	1.50	4.00
3 Sammy Sosa	1.00	2.50
4 Jason Giambi	.40	1.00
5 Alfonso Soriano	.60	1.50
6 Roger Clemens	1.25	3.00
7 Miguel Tejada	.60	1.50
8 Greg Maddux	1.25	3.00
9 Randy Johnson	1.00	2.50
10 Chipper Jones	1.00	2.50
11 Nomar Garciaparra	.60	1.50
12 Alex Rodriguez	1.25	3.00
13 Ichiro Suzuki	1.25	3.00
14 Vladimir Guerrero	.60	1.50
15 Albert Pujols	1.25	3.00

2003 Fleer Splendid Splinters Knothole Gang Game Jersey

STATED ODDS 1:40

Card	Low	High
AR Alex Rodriguez	5.00	12.00
AS Alfonso Soriano	2.50	6.00
BB Barry Bonds	6.00	15.00
CJ Chipper Jones	4.00	10.00
DJ Derek Jeter	10.00	25.00
GM Greg Maddux	5.00	12.00
LB Lance Berkman	2.50	6.00
MO Magglio Ordonez	2.50	6.00
MT Miguel Tejada	2.50	6.00
NG Nomar Garciaparra	2.50	6.00
RC Roger Clemens	5.00	12.00
RJ Randy Johnson	4.00	10.00
SS Sammy Sosa	4.00	10.00
TH Torii Hunter	1.50	4.00
VG Vladimir Guerrero	2.50	6.00

2003 Fleer Splendid Splinters Knothole Gang Patch

RANDOM INSERTS IN PACKS

STATED PRINT RUN 99 SERIAL #'d SETS

Card	Low	High
AR Alex Rodriguez	15.00	40.00
AS Alfonso Soriano	10.00	25.00
BB Barry Bonds	12.00	30.00
CJ Chipper Jones	8.00	20.00
DJ Derek Jeter	12.00	30.00
GM Greg Maddux	15.00	40.00
MT Miguel Tejada	10.00	25.00
NG Nomar Garciaparra	10.00	25.00
RC Roger Clemens	8.00	20.00
RJ Randy Johnson	8.00	20.00
SS Sammy Sosa	8.00	20.00
VG Vladimir Guerrero	10.00	25.00

2003 Fleer Splendid Splinters Wood

Card	Low	High
COMPLETE SET (10)	12.50	30.00
STATED ODDS 1:24		
1 Derek Jeter	4.00	10.00
2 Barry Bonds	2.50	6.00
3 Scott Rolen	1.00	2.50
4 Nomar Garciaparra	1.00	2.50
5 Sammy Sosa	1.50	4.00
6 Alfonso Soriano	1.00	2.50
7 Alex Rodriguez	2.00	5.00
8 Mike Piazza	1.50	4.00
9 Manny Ramirez	1.50	4.00
10 Jeff Bagwell	1.00	2.50

2003 Fleer Splendid Splinters Wood Game Bat

RANDOM INSERTS IN PACKS

STATED PRINT RUN 349 SERIAL #'d SETS

Card	Low	High
AR Alex Rodriguez	6.00	15.00
AS Alfonso Soriano	3.00	8.00
BB Barry Bonds	10.00	25.00
DJ Derek Jeter	10.00	25.00
JB Jeff Bagwell	4.00	10.00
MP Mike Piazza	6.00	15.00
MR Manny Ramirez	4.00	10.00
NG Nomar Garciaparra	6.00	15.00
SS Sammy Sosa	4.00	10.00

2003 Fleer Splendid Splinters Wood Game Bat Dual

RANDOM INSERTS IN PACKS

STATED PRINT RUN 99 SERIAL #'d SETS

Card	Low	High
ARNG A.Rodriguez/N.Garciaparra	12.00	30.00
BBSS B.Bonds/S.Sosa	15.00	40.00
DJAS D.Jeter/A.Soriano	20.00	50.00
MPJB M.Piazza/J.Bagwell	15.00	40.00

2004 Fleer Sweet Sigs

Card	Low	High
COMP.SET w/o SP's (75)	10.00	25.00
COMMON CARD (1-75)	.20	.50
COMMON CARD (76-100)	.60	1.50
76-100 ODDS 1:7 HOBBY, 1:48 RETAIL		
76-100 PRINT RUN 999 SERIAL #'d SETS		
1 Manny Ramirez	.50	1.25
2 Frank Thomas	.50	1.25
3 Josh Beckett	.20	.50
4 Shawn Green	.20	.50
5 Tom Glavine	.30	.75
6 Marquis Grissom	.20	.50
7 Nomar Garciaparra	.30	.75
8 Magglio Ordonez	.30	.75
9 Alex Rodriguez	.60	1.50
10 Chipper Jones	.50	1.25
11 Jody Gerut	.20	.50
12 Dontrelle Willis	.20	.50
13 Lance Berkman	.30	.75
14 Jose Vidro	.20	.50
15 Barry Zito	.30	.75
16 Jason Kendall	.20	.50
17 Scott Rolen	.30	.75
18 Troy Glaus	.20	.50
19 Brandon Webb	.20	.50
20 Tim Hudson	.30	.75
21 Shannon Stewart	.20	.50
22 Darin Erstad	.20	.50
23 Curt Schilling	.30	.75
24 Bret Boone	.20	.50
25 Richie Sexson	.20	.50
26 Hideki Matsui	.75	2.00
27 Albert Pujols	.60	1.50
28 Greg Maddux	.60	1.50
29 Austin Kearns	.20	.50
30 Todd Helton	.30	.75
31 Miguel Cabrera	.50	1.25
32 Jeff Bagwell	.30	.75
33 Marlon Byrd	.20	.50
34 Ichiro Suzuki	.60	1.50
35 Rocco Baldelli	.20	.50
36 Garret Anderson	.20	.50
37 Javy Lopez	.20	.50
38 Kerry Wood	.20	.50
39 Adam Dunn	.30	.75
40 Geoff Jenkins	.20	.50
41 Derek Jeter	1.25	3.00
42 Rich Harden	.20	.50
43 Alfonso Soriano	.30	.75
44 Ken Griffey Jr.	1.00	2.50
45 Ivan Rodriguez	.30	.75
46 Pedro Martinez	.30	.75
47 Andy Pettitte	.30	.75
48 Gary Sheffield	.20	.50
49 Brian Giles	.20	.50
50 Carlos Delgado	.20	.50
51 Mike Piazza	.50	1.25
52 Hank Blalock	.20	.50
53 Roger Clemens	.60	1.50
54 Scott Podsednik	.20	.50
55 Torii Hunter	.20	.50
56 Jose Reyes	.30	.75
57 Jim Thome	.30	.75
58 Jason Schmidt	.20	.50
59 Jose Cruz Jr.	.20	.50
60 Mark Teixeira	.30	.75
61 Randy Johnson	.50	1.25
62 Miguel Tejada	.30	.75
63 Sammy Sosa	.50	1.25
64 Larry Walker	.30	.75
65 Carl Everett	.20	.50
66 Luis Castillo	.20	.50
67 Jason Giambi	.20	.50
68 Mike Sweeney	.20	.50
69 Andruw Jones	.20	.50
70 Vladimir Guerrero	.30	.75
71 J.D. Drew	.20	.50
72 Mark Prior	.30	.75
73 Angel Berroa	.20	.50
74 Hideo Nomo	.50	1.25
75 Roy Halladay	.30	.75
76 John Gall FS RC	.60	1.50
77 Angel Chavez FS RC	.60	1.50
78 Alfredo Simon FS RC	1.00	2.50
79 Merkin Valdez FS RC	.60	1.50
80 Chad Bentz FS RC	.60	1.50
81 Justin Leone FS RC	.60	1.50
82 Mike Rouse FS RC	.60	1.50
83 Aarom Baldiris FS RC	.60	1.50
84 Chris Shelton FS RC	.60	1.50
85 Akinori Otsuka FS RC	.60	1.50
86 Ruddy Yan FS	.60	1.50
87 Ramon Ramirez FS RC	.60	1.50
88 Hector Gimenez FS RC	.60	1.50
89 Mike Gosling FS RC	.60	1.50
90 Greg Dobbs FS RC	.60	1.50
91 Kaz Matsui FS RC	1.00	2.50
92 Don Kelly FS RC	1.00	2.50
93 Shingo Takatsu FS RC	.60	1.50
94 Ivan Ochoa FS RC	.60	1.50
95 Chris Aguila FS RC	.60	1.50
96 Jason Bartlett FS RC	2.00	5.00
97 Graham Koonce FS	.60	1.50
98 Ronny Cedeno FS RC	.60	1.50
99 Jerome Gamble FS RC	.60	1.50
100 Onil Joseph FS RC	.60	1.50

2004 Fleer Sweet Sigs Gold

*GOLD 1-75: 2X TO 5X BASIC

*GOLD 76-100: .6X TO 1.5X BASIC

OVERALL PARALLEL ODDS 1:18 H, 1:96 R

STATED PRINT RUN 99 SERIAL #'d SETS

2004 Fleer Sweet Sigs Autograph Gold

*GOLD: .6X TO 1.5X RED p/r 150-163

*GOLD: .6X TO 1.5X RED p/r 73-100

*GOLD: .5X TO 1.2X RED p/r 44-52

*GOLD: .4X TO 1X RED p/r 28

*GOLD: .4X TO 1X RED p/r 25

OVERALL AU ODDS 1:12 H, AU-GU 1:24 R

STATED PRINT RUN 30 SERIAL #'d SETS

EXCHANGE DEADLINE INDEFINITE

Card	Low	High
HN Hideo Nomo/10	250.00	400.00
SM Stan Musial	75.00	150.00

2004 Fleer Sweet Sigs Autograph Platinum

*PLAT p/r 75: .3X TO .8X RED p/r 44

*PLAT p/r 38-61: .3X TO .8X RED p/r 28

*PLAT p/r 38-61: .4X TO 1X RED p/r 50

*PLAT p/r 38-61: .5X TO 1.2X RED p/r 75-100

*PLAT p/r 38-61: .5X TO 1.2X RED p/r 150

*PLAT p/r 27-35: .5X TO 1.2X RED p/r 50

*PLAT p/r 27-35: .6X TO 1.5X RED p/r 75-100

*PLAT p/r 27-35: .6X TO 1.5X RED p/r 150

OVERALL AU ODDS 1:12 H, AU-GU 1:24 R

PRINT RUNS B/WN 3-75 COPIES PER

NO PRICING ON QTY OF 24 OR LESS

EXCHANGE DEADLINE INDEFINITE

2004 Fleer Sweet Sigs Autograph Red

OVERALL AU ODDS 1:12 H, AU-GU 1:24 R

PRINT RUNS B/WN 5-163 COPIES PER

NO PRICING ON QTY OF 5 OR LESS

MASTERPIECE PRINT RUN 1 #'d SET

NO M'PIECE PRICING DUE TO SCARCITY

EXCHANGE DEADLINE INDEFINITE

Card	Low	High
AB Angel Berroa/75	6.00	15.00
AE Adam Everett/150	6.00	15.00
AP1 Andy Pettitte/50	20.00	50.00
AP2 Albert Pujols/73	75.00	150.00
BL Barry Larkin/50	30.00	60.00
BP Brad Penny/150	6.00	15.00
BW Bernie Williams/50	40.00	80.00
BZ Barry Zito/44	6.00	15.00
CB Carlos Beltran/75	6.00	15.00
CJ Chipper Jones/50	30.00	60.00
CL Carlos Lee/150	6.00	15.00
CY Carl Yastrzemski/50	50.00	100.00
DE Dennis Eckersley/75	6.00	15.00
DW Dontrelle Willis/150	10.00	25.00
EJ Edwin Jackson/75	6.00	15.00
GA Garret Anderson/100	10.00	25.00
JB1 Josh Beckett/75	10.00	25.00
JD1 Johnny Damon/100	15.00	40.00
JD2 J.D. Drew/75	6.00	15.00
JF Julio Franco/150	12.50	30.00
JO John Olerud/75	15.00	40.00
JS Johan Santana/150	6.00	15.00
JV Jason Varitek/75	12.50	30.00
KG Khalil Greene/150	10.00	25.00
KL Kenny Lofton/50	15.00	40.00
KW Kerry Wood/75	10.00	25.00
LB Lance Berkman/150	10.00	25.00
LG Luis Gonzalez/150	6.00	15.00
LN Lance Niekro/150	6.00	15.00
MC1 Miguel Cabrera/150	15.00	40.00
MC2 Mike Cameron/150	6.00	15.00
MK Matt Kata/150	6.00	15.00
MM Mike Mussina/50	15.00	40.00
MO Magglio Ordonez/150	6.00	15.00
MP Mike Piazza/50	75.00	150.00
PM1 Pedro Martinez/75	50.00	100.00
PM2 Paul Molitor/75	6.00	15.00
RB Rocco Baldelli/75	6.00	15.00
RJ Randy Johnson/28	50.00	100.00
RO1 Russ Ortiz/150	6.00	15.00
RO2 Roy Oswalt/150	6.00	15.00
SM Stan Musial/25	50.00	100.00
TS Tim Salmon/100	8.00	20.00
TW1 Tim Wakefield/150	100.00	200.00
VG Vladimir Guerrero/75	30.00	60.00
VW Vernon Wells/150	6.00	15.00
WM Wade Miller/150	6.00	15.00

2004 Fleer Sweet Sigs Ballpark Heroes

STATED ODDS 1:6 HOBBY/RETAIL

Card	Low	High
1 Rocco Baldelli	.40	1.00
2 Adam Dunn	.60	1.50
3 Nomar Garciaparra	.60	1.50
4 Ken Griffey Jr.	2.00	5.00
5 Vladimir Guerrero	.60	1.50
6 Torii Hunter	.40	1.00
7 Andruw Jones	.40	1.00
8 Mike Piazza	1.00	2.50
9 Alfonso Soriano	.60	1.50
10 Frank Thomas	1.00	2.50
11 Dontrelle Willis	.40	1.00
12 Barry Zito	.60	1.50
13 Javy Lopez	.40	1.00
14 Miguel Cabrera	1.00	2.50
15 Kaz Matsui	.60	1.50
16 Josh Beckett	.40	1.00
17 Derek Jeter	2.50	6.00
18 Greg Maddux	1.25	3.00
19 Pedro Martinez	.60	1.50
20 Hideo Nomo	1.00	2.50
21 Mark Prior	.60	1.50
22 Albert Pujols	1.25	3.00
23 Alex Rodriguez	1.25	3.00
24 Scott Rolen	.60	1.50
25 Ichiro Suzuki	1.25	3.00

2004 Fleer Sweet Sigs Ballpark Heroes Jersey Red

STATED ODDS 1:108 RETAIL

LOGO MASTERPIECE PRINT RUN 1 #'d SET

OVERALL GU ODDS 1:8 H, AU-GU 1:24 R

Card	Low	High
AD Adam Dunn	2.50	6.00
AP Albert Pujols	8.00	20.00
AR Alex Rodriguez	5.00	12.00
AS Alfonso Soriano	2.50	6.00
BZ Barry Zito	2.50	6.00
DW Dontrelle Willis	4.00	10.00
FT Frank Thomas	4.00	10.00
GM Greg Maddux	6.00	15.00
HN Hideo Nomo	4.00	10.00
JB Josh Beckett	2.50	6.00
KM Kaz Matsui	3.00	8.00
MC Miguel Cabrera	4.00	10.00
MP1 Mike Piazza	6.00	15.00
MP2 Mark Prior	4.00	10.00
PM Pedro Martinez	4.00	10.00
RB Rocco Baldelli	2.50	6.00
SR Scott Rolen	4.00	10.00
VG Vladimir Guerrero	4.00	10.00

2004 Fleer Sweet Sigs Ballpark Heroes Jersey Silver

*SILVER p/r 163-250: .3X TO .8X RED

*SILVER p/r 39: 1X TO 2.5X RED

*SILVER p/r 35: 1X TO 2.5X RED

OVERALL GU ODDS 1:8 H, AU-GU 1:24 R

PRINT RUNS B/WN 35-250 COPIES PER

Card	Low	High
KM Kaz Matsui/39	8.00	20.00

2004 Fleer Sweet Sigs Ballpark Heroes Jersey-Patch

*JSY-PATCH p/r 20-29: 1.25X TO 3X RED

*JSY-PATCH p/r 15-19: 1.5X TO 4X RED

OVERALL GU ODDS 1:8 H, AU-GU 1:24 R

PRINT RUNS B/WN 10-29 COPIES PER

NO PRICING ON QTY OF 10 OR LESS

Card	Low	High
KM Kaz Matsui/25	15.00	40.00

2004 Fleer Sweet Sigs Ballpark Heroes Patch Black

*PATCH BLACK p/r 75: .75X TO 2X RED

*PATCH BLACK p/r 44-45: .75X TO 2X RED

*PATCH BLACK p/r 21-35: 1X TO 2.5X RED

OVERALL GU ODDS 1:8 H, AU-GU 1:24 R

PRINT RUNS B/WN 5-75 COPIES PER

NO PRICING ON QTY OF 13 OR LESS

Card	Low	High
KM Kaz Matsui/25	12.50	30.00

2004 Fleer Sweet Sigs Ballpark Heroes Patch Gold

*GOLD PATCH: .75X TO 2X RED

OVERALL GU ODDS 1:8 H, AU-GU 1:24 R

STATED PRINT RUN 50 SERIAL #'d SETS

Card	Low	High
KM Kaz Matsui	10.00	25.00

2004 Fleer Sweet Sigs Ballpark Heroes Quad Patch

OVERALL GU ODDS 1:8 H, AU-GU 1:24 R

PRINT RUNS B/WN 9-42 COPIES PER

NO PRICING ON QTY OF 9 OR LESS

Card	Low	High
BMMP Beck/Mad/Pedro/Prior/42	30.00	60.00
PGPR Puj/Vlad/Piaz/A.Rod/37	50.00	100.00
WBJR Will/Beck/Jet/A.Rod/32	30.00	60.00
WMCB Willis/Kaz/Cabr/Bald/26	15.00	40.00

2004 Fleer Sweet Sigs Sweet Stitches Jersey Red

STATED ODDS 1:108 RETAIL

STATED PRINT RUN 125 SERIAL #'d SETS

LOGO MASTERPIECE PRINT RUN 1 #'d SET

NO LOGO M'PIECE PRICE DUE TO SCARCITY

OVERALL GU ODDS 1:8 H, AU-GU 1:24 R

Card	Low	High
AJ Andruw Jones	4.00	10.00
AP Albert Pujols	8.00	20.00
AR Alex Rodriguez	5.00	12.00
AS Alfonso Soriano	2.50	6.00
FT Frank Thomas	4.00	10.00
GM Greg Maddux	6.00	15.00
GS Gary Sheffield	2.50	6.00
HB Hank Blalock	2.50	6.00
HN Hideo Nomo	4.00	10.00
JB Josh Beckett	2.50	6.00
JG Jason Giambi	2.50	6.00
JR Jose Reyes	2.50	6.00
JT Jim Thome	4.00	10.00
KM Kaz Matsui	3.00	8.00
KW Kerry Wood	2.50	6.00
MC Miguel Cabrera	4.00	10.00
MO Magglio Ordonez	2.50	6.00
MP1 Mike Piazza	6.00	15.00
MP2 Mark Prior	4.00	10.00
MR Manny Ramirez	4.00	10.00
MT1 Mark Teixeira	4.00	10.00
MT2 Miguel Tejada	2.50	6.00
RB Rocco Baldelli	2.50	6.00
RC Roger Clemens	6.00	15.00
RJ Randy Johnson	4.00	10.00
SR Scott Rolen	4.00	10.00
SS Sammy Sosa	4.00	10.00
VG Vladimir Guerrero	4.00	10.00

2004 Fleer Sweet Sigs Sweet Stitches Jersey Silver

*SILVER p/r 134-175: .3X TO .8X RED

*SILVER p/r 88-125: .4X TO 1X RED

*SILVER p/r 23: 1X TO 2.5X RED

OVERALL GU ODDS 1:8 H, AU-GU 1:24 R

PRINT RUNS B/WN 8-175 COPIES PER

NO PRICING ON QTY OF 10 OR LESS

Card	Low	High
KM Kaz Matsui/175	3.00	8.00

2004 Fleer Sweet Sigs Sweet Stitches Patch Black

*PATCH BLACK p/r 36-48: .75X TO 2X RED

*PATCH BLACK p/r 21-33: 1X TO 2.5X RED

*PATCH BLACK p/r 15-19: 1.25X TO 3X RED

OVERALL GU ODDS 1:8 H, AU-GU 1:24 R

PRINT RUNS B/WN 2-48 COPIES PER

NO PRICING ON QTY 14 OR LESS

Card	Low	High
KM Kaz Matsui/19	15.00	40.00

2004 Fleer Sweet Sigs Sweet Stitches Patch Gold

*PATCH GOLD: .75X TO 2X RED

OVERALL GU ODDS 1:8 H, AU-GU 1:24 R

STATED PRINT RUN 50 SERIAL #'d SETS

Card	Low	High
KM Kaz Matsui	10.00	25.00

2004 Fleer Sweet Sigs Sweet Stitches Quad Patch

OVERALL GU ODDS 1:8 H, AU-GU 1:24 R

PRINT RUNS B/WN 2-33 COPIES PER

NO PRICING ON QTY OF 10 OR LESS

Card	Low	High
CPBW Clem/Prior/Bec/Wood/24	40.00	80.00
GRPR Giam/A.Rod/Piaz/Rey/22	30.00	60.00
GSCR Giam/Sori/Cab/A.Rod/29	30.00	60.00
JCPS Andruw/Cab/Puj/Sosa/31	40.00	80.00
MSPW Madd/Sosa/Prior/Wood/33	50.00	100.00
RSBG Manny/Shef/Bald/Vlad/16	12.50	30.00
SRTM Sori/Reyes/Teja/Kaz/26	12.50	30.00
TRMR Thome/Rey/Kaz/Rolen/32	12.50	30.00

2004 Fleer Sweet Sigs Sweet Swing

STATED ODDS 1:12 HOBBY/RETAIL

Card	Low	High
1 Sammy Sosa	1.00	2.50
2 Vladimir Guerrero	.60	1.50
3 Jason Giambi	.40	1.00
4 Chipper Jones	1.00	2.50
5 Alfonso Soriano	.60	1.50
6 Manny Ramirez	1.00	2.50
7 Todd Helton	.60	1.50
8 Alex Rodriguez	1.25	3.00
9 Albert Pujols	1.25	3.00
10 Jeff Bagwell	.60	1.50
11 Mike Piazza	1.00	2.50
12 Hank Blalock	.40	1.00
13 Jim Thome	.60	1.50
14 Carlos Delgado	.40	1.00
15 Nomar Garciaparra	.60	1.50

2004 Fleer Sweet Sigs Sweet Swing Jersey Red

STATED ODDS 1:108 RETAIL

STATED PRINT RUN 200 SERIAL #'d SETS

*BAT SILVER p/r 213-250: .4X TO 1X RED

*BAT SILVER p/r 15: 1.5X TO 4X RED

BAT SILVER PRINT RUNS B/WN 15-250 PER

*BAT-JSY GOLD: .75X TO 2X RED

BAT-JSY GOLD PRINT RUN 50 #'d SETS

BAT LOGO M'PIECE PRINT RUN 1 #'d SET

NO BAT LOGO MP PRICE DUE TO SCARCITY

*BAT-PATCH BLK p/r 66: 1X TO 2.5X RED

*BAT-PATCH BLK p/r 39-57: 1.25X TO 3X RED

*BAT-PATCH BLK p/r 29: 1.5X TO 4X RED

BAT-PATCH BLACK PRINT B/WN 29-66 PER

OVERALL GU ODDS 1:8 H, AU-GU 1:24 R

Card	Low	High
AP Albert Pujols	6.00	15.00
AR Alex Rodriguez	4.00	10.00
AS Alfonso Soriano	2.00	5.00
CJ Chipper Jones	3.00	8.00
HB Hank Blalock	2.00	5.00
JG Jason Giambi	2.00	5.00
JT Jim Thome	3.00	8.00
MP Mike Piazza	5.00	12.00
MR Manny Ramirez	3.00	8.00
SS Sammy Sosa	3.00	8.00
VG Vladimir Guerrero	3.00	8.00

2004 Fleer Sweet Sigs Sweet Swing Quad Patch

OVERALL GU ODDS 1:8 H, AU-GU 1:24 R

PRINT RUNS B/WN 12-35 COPIES PER

NO PRICING ON QTY OF 12 OR LESS

Card	Low	High
GPJS Vlad/Pujols/Chip/Sosa/27	50.00	100.00
GRBR Giam/A.Rod/Bag/Ram/35	40.00	80.00
PSHB Piaz/Sori/Helt/Blalock/32	40.00	80.00
RDTP A.Rod/Del/Thome/Puj/22	50.00	100.00

1998 Fleer Tradition

The 600-card 1998 Fleer set was issued in two series. Series one consists of 350 cards and Series two consists of 250 cards. The packs for either series consisted of 12 cards and had a SRP of $1.49. Card fronts feature borderless color action player photos with UV-coating and foil stamping. The backs display player information and career statistics. The set contains the following topical subsets: Smoke 'N Heat (301-310), Golden Memories (311-320), Tale of the Tape (321-340) and Unforgettable Moments (576-600). The Golden Memories (1:6 packs), Tale of the Tape (1:4 packs) and Unforgettable Moments (1:4 packs) cards are shortprinted. An Alex Rodriguez Promo card was distributed to dealers along with their 1998 Fleer series one order forms. The card can be readily distinguished by the "Promotional Sample" text running diagonally across both the front and back of the card. 50 Fleer Flashback Exchange cards were hand-numbered and randomly inserted into packs. Each of these cards could be exchanged for a framed, uncut press sheet from one of Fleer's baseball sets dating anywhere from 1981 to 1993.

Card	Low	High
COMPLETE SET (600)	75.00	150.00
COMPLETE SERIES 1 (350)	40.00	100.00
COMPLETE SERIES 2 (250)	25.00	60.00
COMMON CARD (1-600)	.10	.30
COMMON GM (311-320)	.20	.50
GOLDEN MOMENT SER.1 ODDS 1:6		
COMMON TT (321-340)	.25	.60
TALE OF TAPE SER.1 ODDS 1:4		
COMMON UM (576-600)	.30	.75
UNF.MOMENTS SER.2 ODDS 1:4		
1 Ken Griffey Jr.	.60	1.50
2 Derek Jeter	.75	2.00
3 Gerald Williams	.10	.30
4 Carlos Delgado	.10	.30
5 Nomar Garciaparra	.50	1.25
6 Gary Sheffield	.10	.30
7 Jeff King	.10	.30
8 Cal Ripken	1.00	2.50
9 Matt Williams	.10	.30
10 Chipper Jones	.30	.75
11 Chuck Knoblauch	.10	.30
12 Mark Grudzielanek	.10	.30
13 Edgardo Alfonzo	.10	.30
14 Andres Galarraga	.10	.30
15 Tim Salmon	.20	.50
16 Reggie Sanders	.10	.30
17 Tony Clark	.10	.30
18 Jason Kendall	.10	.30
19 Juan Gonzalez	.10	.30
20 Ben Grieve	.10	.30
21 Roger Clemens	.60	1.50
22 Raul Mondesi	.10	.30
23 Robin Ventura	.10	.30
24 Derrek Lee	.20	.50
25 Mark McGwire	.75	2.00
26 Luis Gonzalez	.10	.30
27 Kevin Brown	.20	.50
28 Kirk Rueter	.10	.30
29 Bobby Estalella	.10	.30
30 Shawn Green	.10	.30
31 Greg Maddux	.50	1.25
32 Jorge Velandia	.10	.30
33 Larry Walker	.10	.30
34 Joey Cora	.10	.30
35 Frank Thomas	.30	.75
36 Curtis King RC	.10	.30
37 Aaron Boone	.10	.30
38 Curt Schilling	.10	.30
39 Bruce Aven	.10	.30
40 Ben McDonald	.10	.30
41 Andy Ashby	.10	.30
42 Jason McDonald	.10	.30
43 Eric Davis	.10	.30
44 Mark Grace	.20	.50
45 Pedro Martinez	.20	.50
46 Lou Collier	.10	.30
47 Chan Ho Park	.10	.30
48 Shane Halter	.10	.30
49 Brian Hunter	.10	.30
50 Jeff Bagwell	.20	.50
51 Bernie Williams	.20	.50
52 J.T. Snow	.10	.30
53 Todd Greene	.10	.30
54 Shannon Stewart	.10	.30
55 Darren Bragg	.10	.30
56 Fernando Tatis	.10	.30
57 Darryl Kile	.10	.30
58 Chris Stynes	.10	.30
59 Javier Valentin	.10	.30
60 Brian McRae	.10	.30
61 Tom Evans	.10	.30
62 Randall Simon	.10	.30
63 Darrin Fletcher	.10	.30
64 Jaret Wright	.10	.30
65 Luis Ordaz	.10	.30
66 Jose Canseco	.20	.50
67 Edgar Renteria	.10	.30
68 Jay Buhner	.10	.30
69 Paul Konerko	.10	.30
70 Adrian Brown	.10	.30
71 Chris Carpenter	.10	.30
72 Mike Lieberthal	.10	.30
73 Dean Palmer	.10	.30
74 Jorge Fabregas	.10	.30
75 Stan Javier	.10	.30
76 Damion Easley	.10	.30
77 David Cone	.10	.30
78 Aaron Sele	.10	.30
79 Antonio Alfonseca	.10	.30
80 Bobby Jones	.10	.30
81 David Justice	.10	.30
82 Jeffrey Hammonds	.10	.30
83 Doug Glanville	.10	.30
84 Jason Dickson	.10	.30
85 Brad Radke	.10	.30
86 David Segui	.10	.30
87 Greg Vaughn	.10	.30
88 Mike Cather RC	.10	.30
89 Alex Fernandez	.10	.30
90 Billy Taylor	.10	.30
91 Jason Schmidt	.10	.30
92 Mike DeJean RC	.15	.40
93 Domingo Cedeno	.10	.30
94 Jeff Cirillo	.10	.30
95 Manny Aybar RC	.15	.40
96 Jaime Navarro	.10	.30
97 Dennis Reyes	.10	.30
98 Barry Larkin	.20	.50
99 Troy O'Leary	.10	.30
100 Alex Rodriguez	.50	1.25
101 Pat Hentgen	.10	.30
102 Bubba Trammell	.10	.30
103 Glendon Rusch	.10	.30
104 Kenny Lofton	.10	.30
105 Craig Biggio	.20	.50
106 Kelvim Escobar	.10	.30
107 Mark Kotsay	.10	.30
108 Rondell White	.10	.30
109 Darren Oliver	.10	.30
110 Jim Thome	.20	.50
111 Rich Becker	.10	.30
112 Chad Curtis	.10	.30

113 Dave Hollins .10 .30
114 Bill Mueller .10 .30
115 Antone Williamson .10 .30
116 Tony Womack .10 .30
117 Randy Myers .10 .30
118 Rico Brogna .10 .30
119 Pat Watkins .10 .30
120 Eli Marrero .10 .30
121 Jay Bell .10 .30
122 Kevin Tapani .10 .30
123 Todd Erdos RC .10 .30
124 Neifi Perez .10 .30
125 Todd Hundley .10 .30
126 Jeff Abbott .10 .30
127 Todd Zeile .10 .30
128 Travis Fryman .10 .30
129 Sandy Alomar Jr. .10 .30
130 Fred McGriff .20 .50
131 Richard Hidalgo .10 .30
132 Scott Spiezio .10 .30
133 John Valentin .10 .30
134 Quilvio Veras .10 .30
135 Mike Lansing .10 .30
136 Paul Molitor .10 .30
137 Randy Johnson .30 .75
138 Harold Baines .10 .30
139 Doug Jones .10 .30
140 Abraham Nunez .10 .30
141 Alan Benes .10 .30
142 Matt Perisho .10 .30
143 Chris Clemons .10 .30
144 Andy Pettitte .20 .50
145 Jason Giambi .10 .30
146 Moises Alou .10 .30
147 Chad Fox RC .10 .30
148 Felix Martinez .10 .30
149 Carlos Mendoza RC .10 .30
150 Scott Rolen .20 .50
151 Jose Cabrera RC .10 .30
152 Justin Thompson .10 .30
153 Ellis Burks .10 .30
154 Pokey Reese .10 .30
155 Bartolo Colon .10 .30
156 Ray Durham .10 .30
157 Ugueth Urbina .10 .30
158 Tom Goodwin .10 .30
159 Dave Dellucci RC .25 .60
160 Rod Beck .10 .30
161 Ramon Martinez .10 .30
162 Joe Carter .10 .30
163 Kevin Orie .10 .30
164 Trevor Hoffman .10 .30
165 Emil Brown .10 .30
166 Robb Nen .10 .30
167 Paul O'Neill .20 .50
168 Ryan Long .10 .30
169 Ray Lankford .10 .30
170 Ivan Rodriguez .20 .50
171 Rick Aguilera .10 .30
172 Deivi Cruz .10 .30
173 Ricky Bottalico .10 .30
174 Garret Anderson .10 .30
175 Jose Vizcaino .10 .30
176 Omar Vizquel .20 .50
177 Jeff Blauser .10 .30
178 Orlando Cabrera .10 .30
179 Russ Johnson .10 .30
180 Matt Stairs .10 .30
181 Will Cunnane .10 .30
182 Adam Riggs .10 .30
183 Matt Morris .10 .30
184 Mario Valdez .10 .30
185 Larry Sutton .10 .30
186 Marc Pisciotta RC .10 .30
187 Dan Wilson .10 .30
188 John Franco .10 .30
189 Darren Daulton .10 .30
190 Todd Helton .20 .50
191 Brady Anderson .10 .30
192 Ricardo Rincon .10 .30
193 Kevin Stocker .10 .30
194 Jose Valentin .10 .30
195 Ed Sprague .10 .30
196 Ryan McGuire .10 .30
197 Scott Eyre .10 .30
198 Steve Finley .10 .30
199 T.J. Mathews .10 .30
200 Mike Piazza .50 1.25
201 Mark Wohlers .10 .30
202 Brian Giles .10 .30
203 Eduardo Perez .10 .30
204 Shigetoshi Hasegawa .10 .30
205 Mariano Rivera .30 .75
206 Jose Rosado .10 .30
207 Michael Coleman .10 .30
208 James Baldwin .10 .30
209 Russ Davis .10 .30
210 Billy Wagner .10 .30
211 Sammy Sosa .30 .75
212 Frank Catalanotto RC .25 .60
213 Delino DeShields .10 .30
214 John Olerud .10 .30
215 Heath Murray .10 .30
216 Jose Vidro .10 .30
217 Jim Edmonds .10 .30
218 Shawon Dunston .10 .30
219 Homer Bush .10 .30
220 Midre Cummings .10 .30
221 Tony Saunders .10 .30
222 Jeromy Burnitz .10 .30
223 Enrique Wilson .10 .30
224 Chili Davis .10 .30
225 Jerry DiPoto .10 .30
226 Dante Powell .10 .30
227 Javier Lopez .10 .30
228 Kevin Polcovich .10 .30
229 Deion Sanders .20 .50
230 Jimmy Key .10 .30
231 Rusty Greer .10 .30
232 Reggie Jefferson .10 .30
233 Ron Coomer .10 .30
234 Bobby Higginson .10 .30
235 Magglio Ordonez RC 1.00 2.50
236 Miguel Tejada .30 .75
237 Rick Gorecki .10 .30
238 Charles Johnson .10 .30
239 Lance Johnson .10 .30
240 Derek Bell .10 .30
241 Will Clark .20 .50
242 Brady Raggio .10 .30
243 Orel Hershiser .10 .30
244 Vladimir Guerrero .30 .75
245 John LeRoy .10 .30
246 Shawn Estes .10 .30
247 Brett Tomko .10 .30
248 Dave Nilsson .10 .30
249 Edgar Martinez .20 .50
250 Tony Gwynn .40 1.00
251 Mark Bellhorn .10 .30
252 Jed Hansen .10 .30
253 Butch Huskey .10 .30
254 Eric Young .10 .30
255 Vinny Castilla .10 .30
256 Hideki Irabu .10 .30
257 Mike Cameron .10 .30
258 Juan Encarnacion .10 .30
259 Brian Rose .10 .30
260 Brad Ausmus .10 .30
261 Dan Serafini .10 .30
262 Willie Greene .10 .30
263 Troy Percival .10 .30
264 Jeff Wallace .10 .30
265 Richie Sexson .10 .30
266 Rafael Palmeiro .20 .50
267 Brad Fullmer .10 .30
268 Jeremi Gonzalez .10 .30
269 Rob Stanifer RC .10 .30
270 Mickey Morandini .10 .30
271 Andruw Jones .20 .50
272 Royce Clayton .10 .30
273 Takashi Kashiwada RC .15 .40
274 Steve Woodard .10 .30
275 Jose Cruz Jr. .10 .30
276 Keith Foulke .10 .30
277 Brad Rigby .10 .30
278 Tino Martinez .20 .50
279 Todd Jones .10 .30
280 John Wetteland .10 .30
281 Alex Gonzalez .10 .30
282 Ken Cloude .10 .30
283 Jose Guillen .10 .30
284 Danny Clyburn .10 .30
285 David Ortiz .40 1.00
286 John Thomson .10 .30
287 Kevin Appier .10 .30
288 Ismael Valdes .10 .30
289 Gary DiSarcina .10 .30
290 Todd Dunwoody .10 .30
291 Wally Joyner .10 .30
292 Charles Nagy .10 .30
293 Jeff Shaw .10 .30
294 Kevin Millwood RC .40 1.00
295 Rigo Beltran RC .10 .30
296 Jeff Frye .10 .30
297 Oscar Henriquez .10 .30
298 Mike Thurman .10 .30
299 Garrett Stephenson .10 .30
300 Barry Bonds .75 2.00
301 Roger Clemens SH .30 .75
302 David Cone SH .10 .30
303 Hideki Irabu SH .10 .30
304 Randy Johnson SH .20 .50
305 Greg Maddux SH .30 .75
306 Pedro Martinez SH .20 .50
307 Mike Mussina SH .10 .30
308 Andy Pettitte SH .10 .30
309 Curt Schilling SH .10 .30
310 John Smoltz SH .10 .30
311 Roger Clemens GM 1.00 2.50
312 Jose Cruz JR. GM .20 .50
313 Nomar Garciaparra GM .75 2.00
314 Ken Griffey Jr. GM 1.00 2.50
315 Tony Gwynn GM .60 1.50
316 Hideki Irabu GM .20 .50
317 Randy Johnson GM .50 1.25
318 Mark McGwire GM 1.25 3.00
319 Curt Schilling GM .20 .50
320 Larry Walker GM .20 .50
321 Jeff Bagwell TT .40 1.00
322 Albert Belle TT .25 .60
323 Barry Bonds TT 1.50 4.00
324 Jay Buhner TT .25 .60
325 Tony Clark TT .25 .60
326 Jose Cruz Jr. TT .25 .60
327 Andres Galarraga TT .25 .60
328 Juan Gonzalez TT .25 .60
329 Ken Griffey Jr. TT 1.25 3.00
330 Andruw Jones TT .40 1.00
331 Tino Martinez TT .40 1.00
332 Mark McGwire TT 1.50 4.00
333 Rafael Palmeiro TT .40 1.00
334 Mike Piazza TT 1.00 2.50
335 Manny Ramirez TT .40 1.00
336 Alex Rodriguez TT 1.00 2.50
337 Frank Thomas TT .60 1.50
338 Jim Thome TT .40 1.00
339 Mo Vaughn TT .25 .60
340 Larry Walker TT .25 .60
341 Jose Cruz Jr. CL .10 .30
342 Ken Griffey Jr. CL .40 1.00
343 Derek Jeter CL .40 1.00
344 Andruw Jones CL .10 .30
345 Chipper Jones CL .20 .50
346 Greg Maddux CL .30 .75
347 Mike Piazza CL .30 .75
348 Cal Ripken CL .50 1.25
349 Alex Rodriguez CL .30 .75
350 Frank Thomas CL .20 .50
351 Mo Vaughn .10 .30
352 Andres Galarraga .10 .30
353 Roberto Alomar .20 .50
354 Darin Erstad .10 .30
355 Albert Belle .10 .30
356 Matt Williams .10 .30
357 Darryl Kile .10 .30
358 Kenny Lofton .10 .30
359 Orel Hershiser .10 .30
360 Bob Abreu .10 .30
361 Chris Widger .10 .30
362 Glenallen Hill .10 .30
363 Chili Davis .10 .30
364 Kevin Brown .20 .50
365 Marquis Grissom .10 .30
366 Livan Hernandez .10 .30
367 Moises Alou .10 .30
368 Matt Lawton .10 .30
369 Rey Ordonez .10 .30
370 Kenny Rogers .10 .30
371 Lee Stevens .10 .30
372 Wade Boggs .20 .50
373 Luis Gonzalez .10 .30
374 Jeff Conine .10 .30
375 Esteban Loaiza .10 .30
376 Jose Canseco .20 .50
377 Henry Rodriguez .10 .30
378 Dave Burba .10 .30
379 Todd Hollandsworth .10 .30
380 Ron Gant .10 .30
381 Pedro Martinez .20 .50
382 Ryan Klesko .10 .30
383 Derrek Lee .20 .50
384 Doug Glanville .10 .30
385 David Wells .10 .30
386 Ken Caminiti .10 .30
387 Damon Hollins .10 .30
388 Manny Ramirez .20 .50
389 Mike Mussina .20 .50
390 Jay Bell .10 .30
391 Mike Piazza .50 1.25
392 Mike Lansing .10 .30
393 Mike Hampton .10 .30
394 Geoff Jenkins .10 .30
395 Jimmy Haynes .10 .30
396 Scott Servais .10 .30
397 Kent Mercker .10 .30
398 Jeff Kent .10 .30
399 Kevin Elster .10 .30
400 Masato Yoshii RC .15 .40
401 Jose Vizcaino .10 .30
402 Javier Martinez RC .10 .30
403 David Segui .10 .30
404 Tony Saunders .10 .30
405 Karim Garcia .10 .30
406 Armando Benitez .10 .30
407 Joe Randa .10 .30
408 Vic Darensbourg .10 .30
409 Sean Casey .10 .30
410 Eric Milton .10 .30
411 Trey Moore .10 .30
412 Mike Stanley .10 .30
413 Tom Gordon .10 .30
414 Hal Morris .10 .30
415 Braden Looper .10 .30
416 Mike Kelly .10 .30
417 John Smoltz .20 .50
418 Roger Cedeno .10 .30
419 Al Leiter .10 .30
420 Chuck Knoblauch .10 .30
421 Felix Rodriguez .10 .30
422 Bip Roberts .10 .30
423 Ken Hill .10 .30
424 Jermaine Allensworth .10 .30
425 Esteban Yan RC .15 .40
426 Scott Karl .10 .30
427 Sean Berry .10 .30
428 Rafael Medina .10 .30
429 Javier Vazquez .10 .30
430 Rickey Henderson .30 .75
431 Adam Butler .10 .30
432 Todd Stottlemyre .10 .30
433 Yamil Benitez .10 .30
434 Sterling Hitchcock .10 .30
435 Paul Sorrento .10 .30
436 Bobby Ayala .10 .30
437 Tim Raines .10 .30
438 Chris Hoiles .10 .30
439 Rod Beck .10 .30
440 Donnie Sadler .10 .30
441 Charles Johnson .10 .30
442 Russ Ortiz .10 .30
443 Pedro Astacio .10 .30
444 Wilson Alvarez .10 .30
445 Mike Blowers .10 .30
446 Todd Zeile .10 .30
447 Mel Rojas .10 .30
448 F.P. Santangelo .10 .30
449 Dmitri Young .10 .30
450 Brian Anderson .10 .30
451 Cecil Fielder .10 .30
452 Roberto Hernandez .10 .30
453 Todd Walker .10 .30
454 Tyler Green .10 .30
455 Jorge Posada .20 .50
456 Geronimo Berroa .10 .30
457 Jose Silva .10 .30
458 Bobby Bonilla .10 .30
459 Walt Weiss .10 .30
460 Darren Dreifort .10 .30
461 B.J. Surhoff .10 .30
462 Quinton McCracken .10 .30
463 Derek Lowe .10 .30
464 Jorge Fabregas .10 .30
465 Joey Hamilton .10 .30
466 Brian Jordan .10 .30
467 Allen Watson .10 .30
468 John Jaha .10 .30
469 Heathcliff Slocumb .10 .30
470 Gregg Jefferies .10 .30
471 Scott Brosius .10 .30
472 Chad Ogea .10 .30
473 A.J. Hinch .10 .30
474 Bobby Smith .10 .30
475 Brian Moehler .10 .30
476 DaRond Stovall .10 .30
477 Kevin Young .10 .30
478 Jeff Suppan .10 .30
479 Marty Cordova .10 .30
480 John Halama RC .15 .40
481 Bubba Trammell .10 .30
482 Mike Caruso .10 .30
483 Eric Karros .10 .30
484 Jamey Wright .10 .30
485 Mike Sweeney .10 .30
486 Aaron Sele .10 .30
487 Cliff Floyd .10 .30
488 Jeff Brantley .10 .30
489 Jim Leyritz .10 .30
490 Denny Neagle .10 .30
491 Travis Fryman .10 .30
492 Carlos Baerga .10 .30
493 Eddie Taubensee .10 .30
494 Darryl Strawberry .10 .30
495 Brian Johnson .10 .30
496 Randy Myers .10 .30
497 Jeff Blauser .10 .30
498 Jason Wood .10 .30
499 Rolando Arrojo RC .15 .40
500 Johnny Damon .20 .50
501 Jose Mercedes .10 .30
502 Tony Batista .10 .30
503 Mike Piazza Mets .50 1.25
504 Hideo Nomo .30 .75
505 Chris Gomez .10 .30
506 Jesus Sanchez RC .10 .30
507 Al Martin .10 .30
508 Brian Edmondson .10 .30
509 Joe Girardi .10 .30
510 Shayne Bennett .10 .30
511 Joe Carter .10 .30
512 Dave Mlicki .10 .30
513 Rich Butler RC .10 .30
514 Dennis Eckersley .10 .30
515 Travis Lee .10 .30
516 John Mabry .10 .30
517 Jose Mesa .10 .30
518 Phil Nevin .10 .30
519 Raul Casanova .10 .30
520 Mike Fetters .10 .30
521 Gary Sheffield .10 .30
522 Terry Steinbach .10 .30
523 Steve Trachsel .10 .30
524 Josh Booty .10 .30
525 Darryl Hamilton .10 .30
526 Mark McLemore .10 .30
527 Kevin Stocker .10 .30
528 Bret Boone .10 .30
529 Shane Andrews .10 .30
530 Robb Nen .10 .30
531 Carl Everett .10 .30
532 LaTroy Hawkins .10 .30
533 Fernando Vina .10 .30
534 Michael Tucker .10 .30
535 Mark Langston .10 .30
536 Mickey Mantle 2.00 5.00
537 Bernard Gilkey .10 .30
538 Francisco Cordova .10 .30
539 Mike Bordick .10 .30
540 Fred McGriff .20 .50
541 Cliff Politte .10 .30
542 Jason Varitek .30 .75
543 Shawon Dunston .10 .30
544 Brian Meadows .10 .30
545 Pat Meares .10 .30
546 Carlos Perez .10 .30
547 Desi Relaford .10 .30
548 Antonio Osuna .10 .30
549 Devon White .10 .30
550 Sean Runyan .10 .30
551 Mickey Morandini .10 .30
552 Dave Martinez .10 .30
553 Jeff Fassero .10 .30
554 Ryan Jackson RC .10 .30
555 Stan Javier .10 .30
556 Jaime Navarro .10 .30
557 Jose Offerman .10 .30
558 Mike Lowell RC .60 1.50
559 Darrin Fletcher .10 .30
560 Mark Lewis .10 .30
561 Dante Bichette .10 .30
562 Chuck Finley .10 .30
563 Kerry Wood .15 .40
564 Andy Benes .10 .30
565 Freddy Garcia .10 .30
566 Tom Glavine .20 .50
567 Jon Nunnally .10 .30
568 Miguel Cairo .10 .30
569 Shane Reynolds .10 .30
570 Roberto Kelly .10 .30
571 Jose Cruz Jr. CL .10 .30
572 Ken Griffey Jr. CL .40 1.00
573 Mark McGwire CL .40 1.00
574 Cal Ripken CL .50 1.25
575 Frank Thomas CL .20 .50
576 Jeff Bagwell UM .50 1.25
577 Barry Bonds UM 2.00 5.00
578 Tony Clark UM .30 .75
579 Roger Clemens UM 1.50 4.00
580 Jose Cruz Jr. UM .30 .75
581 Nomar Garciaparra UM 1.25 3.00
582 Juan Gonzalez UM .30 .75
583 Ben Grieve UM .30 .75
584 Ken Griffey Jr. UM 1.50 4.00
585 Tony Gwynn UM 1.00 2.50
586 Derek Jeter UM 2.00 5.00
587 Randy Johnson UM .75 2.00
588 Chipper Jones UM .75 2.00
589 Greg Maddux UM 1.25 3.00
590 Mark McGwire UM 2.00 5.00
591 Andy Pettitte UM .50 1.25
592 Paul Molitor UM .30 .75
593 Cal Ripken UM 2.50 6.00
594 Alex Rodriguez UM 1.25 3.00
595 Scott Rolen UM .50 1.25
596 Curt Schilling UM .30 .75
597 Frank Thomas UM .75 2.00
598 Jim Thome UM .50 1.25
599 Larry Walker UM .30 .75
600 Bernie Williams UM .50 1.25
P100 Alex Rodriguez Promo .60 1.50

1998 Fleer Tradition Vintage '63

COMPLETE SET (128) 30.00 60.00
COMPLETE SERIES 1 (64) 15.00 40.00
STATED ODDS 1:1 HOBBY
*'63 CLASSIC: 12.5X TO 30X VINTAGE '63
63 CLASSIC RANDOM INS.IN HOBBY PACKS
63 CLASSIC PRINT RUN 63 SERIAL #'d SETS
1 Jason Dickson .15 .40
2 Tim Salmon .25 .60
3 Andruw Jones .25 .60
4 Chipper Jones .40 1.00
5 Kenny Lofton .15 .40
6 Greg Maddux .60 1.50
7 Rafael Palmeiro .25 .60
8 Cal Ripken 1.25 3.00
9 Nomar Garciaparra .60 1.50
10 Mark Grace .25 .60
11 Sammy Sosa .40 1.00
12 Frank Thomas .40 1.00
13 Deion Sanders .25 .60
14 Sandy Alomar Jr. .15 .40
15 David Justice .15 .40
16 Jim Thome .25 .60
17 Matt Williams .15 .40
18 Jaret Wright .15 .40
19 Vinny Castilla .15 .40
20 Andres Galarraga .15 .40
21 Todd Helton .25 .60
22 Larry Walker .15 .40
23 Tony Clark .15 .40
24 Moises Alou .15 .40
25 Kevin Brown .25 .60
26 Charles Johnson .15 .40
27 Edgar Renteria .15 .40
28 Gary Sheffield .15 .40
29 Jeff Bagwell .25 .60
30 Craig Biggio .25 .60
31 Raul Mondesi .15 .40
32 Mike Piazza .60 1.50
33 Chuck Knoblauch .15 .40
34 Paul Molitor .15 .40
35 Vladimir Guerrero .40 1.00
36 Pedro Martinez .25 .60
37 Todd Hundley .15 .40
38 Derek Jeter 1.00 2.50
39 Tino Martinez .25 .60
40 Paul O'Neill .25 .60
41 Andy Pettitte .25 .60
42 Mariano Rivera .40 1.00
43 Bernie Williams .25 .60
44 Ben Grieve .15 .40
45 Scott Rolen .25 .60
46 Curt Schilling .15 .40
47 Jason Kendall .15 .40
48 Tony Womack .15 .40
49 Ray Lankford .15 .40
50 Mark McGwire 1.00 2.50
51 Matt Morris .15 .40
52 Tony Gwynn .50 1.25
53 Barry Bonds 1.00 2.50
54 Jay Buhner .15 .40
55 Ken Griffey Jr. .75 2.00
56 Randy Johnson .40 1.00
57 Edgar Martinez .25 .60
58 Alex Rodriguez .60 1.50
59 Juan Gonzalez .15 .40
60 Rusty Greer .15 .40
61 Ivan Rodriguez .25 .60
62 Roger Clemens .75 2.00
63 Jose Cruz Jr. .15 .40
64 Darin Erstad .15 .40
65 Jay Bell .15 .40
66 Andy Benes .15 .40
67 Mickey Mantle 2.50 6.00
68 Karim Garcia .15 .40
69 Travis Lee .15 .40
70 Matt Williams .15 .40
71 Andres Galarraga .15 .40
72 Tom Glavine .25 .60
73 Ryan Klesko .15 .40
74 Denny Neagle .15 .40
75 John Smoltz .25 .60
76 Roberto Alomar .25 .60
77 Joe Carter .15 .40
78 Mike Mussina .25 .60
79 B.J. Surhoff .15 .40
80 Dennis Eckersley .15 .40
81 Pedro Martinez .25 .60
82 Mo Vaughn .15 .40
83 Henry Rodriguez .15 .40
84 Kerry Wood .20 .50
85 Albert Belle .15 .40
86 Sean Casey .15 .40
87 Travis Fryman .15 .40
88 Kenny Lofton .15 .40
89 Darryl Kile .15 .40
90 Mike Lansing .15 .40
91 Bobby Bonilla .15 .40
92 Cliff Floyd .15 .40
93 Livan Hernandez .15 .40
94 Derrek Lee .25 .60
95 Moises Alou .15 .40
96 Shane Reynolds .15 .40
97 Mike Piazza .60 1.50
98 Johnny Damon .25 .60
99 Eric Karros .15 .40
100 Hideo Nomo .40 1.00
101 Marquis Grissom .15 .40
102 Matt Lawton .15 .40
103 Todd Walker .15 .40
104 Gary Sheffield .15 .40
105 Bernard Gilkey .15 .40
106 Rey Ordonez .15 .40
107 Chili Davis .15 .40
108 Chuck Knoblauch .15 .40
109 Charles Johnson .15 .40
110 Rickey Henderson .40 1.00
111 Bob Abreu .15 .40
112 Doug Glanville .15 .40
113 Gregg Jefferies .15 .40
114 Al Martin .15 .40
115 Kevin Young .15 .40
116 Ron Gant .15 .40
117 Kevin Brown .25 .60
118 Ken Caminiti .15 .40
119 Joey Hamilton .15 .40
120 Jeff Kent .15 .40
121 Wade Boggs .25 .60
122 Quinton McCracken .15 .40
123 Fred McGriff .25 .60
124 Paul Sorrento .15 .40
125 Jose Canseco .25 .60
126 Randy Myers .15 .40
NNO Checklist 1 .15 .40
NNO Checklist 2 .15 .40

1998 Fleer Tradition Decade of Excellence

COMPLETE SET (12) 60.00 120.00
STATED ODDS 1:72 HOBBY
*RARE TRAD: 2X TO 5X BASIC DECADES
RARE TRAD. STATED ODDS 1:720 HOBBY
1 Roberto Alomar 1.50 4.00
2 Barry Bonds 6.00 15.00
3 Roger Clemens 5.00 12.00
4 David Cone 1.00 2.50
5 Andres Galarraga 1.00 2.50
6 Mark Grace 1.50 4.00
7 Tony Gwynn 3.00 8.00
8 Randy Johnson 2.50 6.00
9 Greg Maddux 4.00 10.00
10 Mark McGwire 6.00 15.00
11 Paul O'Neill 1.50 4.00
12 Cal Ripken 8.00 20.00

1998 Fleer Tradition Diamond Ink

ONE PER FLEER 1 AND ULTRA 1 PACK
PRICES LISTED WERE PER POINT
EXCHANGE 500 PTS. FOR SIGNED BALL

1998 Fleer Tradition Diamond Standouts

COMPLETE SET (20) 20.00 50.00
STATED ODDS 1:12
1 Jeff Bagwell .50 1.25
2 Barry Bonds 2.00 5.00
3 Roger Clemens 1.50 4.00
4 Jose Cruz Jr. .30 .75
5 Andres Galarraga .30 .75
6 Nomar Garciaparra 1.25 3.00
7 Juan Gonzalez .30 .75
8 Ken Griffey Jr. 1.50 4.00
9 Derek Jeter 2.00 5.00
10 Randy Johnson .75 2.00
11 Chipper Jones .75 2.00
12 Kenny Lofton .30 .75
13 Greg Maddux 1.25 3.00
14 Pedro Martinez .50 1.25
15 Mark McGwire 2.00 5.00
16 Mike Piazza 1.25 3.00
17 Alex Rodriguez 1.25 3.00
18 Curt Schilling .30 .75
19 Frank Thomas .75 2.00
20 Larry Walker .30 .75

1998 Fleer Tradition Diamond Tribute

COMPLETE SET (10) 100.00 200.00
SER.2 STATED ODDS 1:300
DT1 Jeff Bagwell 1.25 3.00
DT2 Roger Clemens 2.50 6.00
DT3 Nomar Garciaparra 1.25 3.00
DT4 Juan Gonzalez .75 2.00
DT5 Ken Griffey Jr. 12.00 30.00
DT6 Mark McGwire 3.00 8.00
DT7 Mike Piazza 2.00 5.00
DT8 Cal Ripken 6.00 15.00
DT9 Alex Rodriguez 2.50 6.00
DT10 Frank Thomas 2.00 5.00

1998 Fleer Tradition In The Clutch

COMPLETE SET (15) 10.00 25.00
SER.2 STATED ODDS 1:20
IC1 Jeff Bagwell .60 1.50
IC2 Barry Bonds 1.50 4.00
IC3 Roger Clemens 1.25 3.00
IC4 Jose Cruz Jr. .40 1.00
IC5 Nomar Garciaparra .60 1.50
IC6 Juan Gonzalez .40 1.00
IC7 Ken Griffey Jr. 2.00 5.00
IC8 Tony Gwynn 1.00 2.50
IC9 Derek Jeter 2.50 6.00
IC10 Chipper Jones 1.00 2.50
IC11 Greg Maddux 1.25 3.00
IC12 Mark McGwire 1.50 4.00
IC13 Mike Piazza 1.00 2.50
IC14 Frank Thomas 1.00 2.50
IC15 Larry Walker .60 1.50

1998 Fleer Tradition Lumber Company

COMPLETE SET (15) 60.00 120.00
STATED ODDS 1:36 RETAIL
1 Jeff Bagwell 1.50 4.00
2 Barry Bonds 6.00 15.00
3 Jose Cruz Jr. 1.00 2.50
4 Nomar Garciaparra 4.00 10.00
5 Juan Gonzalez 1.00 2.50
6 Ken Griffey Jr. 5.00 12.00
7 Tony Gwynn 3.00 8.00
8 Chipper Jones 2.50 6.00
9 Tino Martinez 1.50 4.00
10 Mark McGwire 6.00 15.00
11 Mike Piazza 4.00 10.00
12 Cal Ripken 8.00 20.00
13 Alex Rodriguez 4.00 10.00
14 Frank Thomas 2.50 6.00
15 Larry Walker 1.00 2.50

1998 Fleer Tradition Mickey Mantle Monumental Moments

COMPLETE SET (10) 12.50 30.00
COMMON CARD (1-10) 2.00 5.00
SER.2 STATED ODDS 1:68
*GOLD: 1.5X TO 4X BASIC MANTLE
GOLD: RANDOM INSERTS IN SER.2 PACKS
GOLD PRINT RUN 51 SERIAL #'d SETS

1998 Fleer Tradition Power Game

COMPLETE SET (20) 30.00 80.00
STATED ODDS 1:36
1 Jeff Bagwell 1.50 4.00
2 Albert Belle 1.00 2.50
3 Barry Bonds 4.00 10.00
4 Tony Clark 1.00 2.50
5 Roger Clemens 3.00 8.00
6 Jose Cruz Jr. 1.00 2.50
7 Andres Galarraga 1.50 4.00
8 Nomar Garciaparra 1.50 4.00
9 Juan Gonzalez 1.00 2.50
10 Ken Griffey Jr. 5.00 12.00
11 Randy Johnson 2.50 6.00
12 Greg Maddux 3.00 8.00
13 Pedro Martinez 1.50 4.00
14 Tino Martinez 1.00 2.50
15 Mark McGwire 4.00 10.00
16 Mike Piazza 2.50 6.00
17 Curt Schilling 1.50 4.00
18 Frank Thomas 2.50 6.00
19 Jim Thome 1.50 4.00
20 Larry Walker 1.50 4.00

1998 Fleer Tradition Promising Forecast

COMPLETE SET (20) 6.00 15.00
SER.2 STATED ODDS 1:12
PF1 Rolando Arrojo .50 1.25
PF2 Sean Casey .40 1.00
PF3 Brad Fullmer .40 1.00
PF4 Karim Garcia .40 1.00
PF5 Ben Grieve .40 1.00
PF6 Todd Helton .60 1.50
PF7 Richard Hidalgo .40 1.00
PF8 A.J. Hinch .40 1.00
PF9 Paul Konerko .40 1.00
PF10 Mark Kotsay .40 1.00
PF11 Derrek Lee .60 1.50
PF12 Travis Lee .40 1.00
PF13 Eric Milton .40 1.00
PF14 Magglio Ordonez 1.00 2.50
PF15 David Ortiz 1.25 3.00
PF16 Brian Rose .40 1.00
PF17 Miguel Tejada 1.00 2.50
PF18 Jason Varitek 1.00 2.50
PF19 Enrique Wilson .40 1.00
PF20 Kerry Wood .50 1.25

1998 Fleer Tradition Rookie Sensations

COMPLETE SET (20) 15.00 40.00
STATED ODDS 1:18
1 Mike Cameron .60 1.50
2 Jose Cruz Jr. .60 1.50
3 Jason Dickson .60 1.50
4 Kelvim Escobar .60 1.50
5 Nomar Garciaparra 2.50 6.00
6 Ben Grieve .60 1.50
7 Vladimir Guerrero 1.50 4.00
8 Wilton Guerrero .60 1.50
9 Jose Guillen .60 1.50
10 Todd Helton 1.00 2.50
11 Livan Hernandez .60 1.50
12 Hideki Irabu .60 1.50
13 Andruw Jones 1.00 2.50
14 Matt Morris .60 1.50
15 Magglio Ordonez 3.00 8.00
16 Neifi Perez .60 1.50
17 Scott Rolen 1.00 2.50
18 Fernando Tatis .60 1.50
19 Brett Tomko .60 1.50
20 Jaret Wright .60 1.50

1998 Fleer Tradition Zone

COMPLETE SET (15) 125.00 250.00
STATED ODDS 1:288
1 Jeff Bagwell 4.00 10.00
2 Barry Bonds 15.00 40.00
3 Roger Clemens 12.50 30.00
4 Jose Cruz Jr. 2.50 6.00
5 Nomar Garciaparra 10.00 25.00
6 Juan Gonzalez 2.50 6.00
7 Ken Griffey Jr. 12.50 30.00
8 Tony Gwynn 8.00 20.00
9 Chipper Jones 6.00 15.00
10 Greg Maddux 10.00 25.00
11 Mark McGwire 15.00 40.00
12 Mike Piazza 10.00 25.00
13 Alex Rodriguez 10.00 25.00
14 Frank Thomas 6.00 15.00
15 Larry Walker 2.50 6.00

1998 Fleer Tradition Update

The 1998 Fleer Update set was issued exclusively in factory set form. This set, issued in November, 1998, was created in large part to get the first J.D. Drew Rookie Card on the market. The set also took advantage of the "retro" themes that were popular in 1998 and represented the return of Fleer Update factory sets that had a rich history from 1984 through 1994. In addition to the aforementioned Drew, other notable RC's in this set include Troy Glaus, Orlando Hernandez and Gabe Kapler.

COMP.FACT.SET (100) 6.00 15.00
U1 Mark McGwire HL .50 1.25
U2 Sammy Sosa HL .10 .30
U3 Roger Clemens HL .40 1.00
U4 Barry Bonds HL .60 1.50
U5 Kerry Wood HL .08 .25
U6 Paul Molitor HL .07 .20
U7 Ken Griffey Jr. HL .40 1.00
U8 Cal Ripken HL .60 1.50
U9 David Wells HL .07 .20
U10 Alex Rodriguez HL .30 .75
U11 Angel Pena RC .15 .40
U12 Bruce Chen .07 .20
U13 Craig Wilson .07 .20
U14 Orlando Hernandez RC .75 2.00
U15 Aramis Ramirez .07 .20
U16 Aaron Boone .07 .20
U17 Bob Henley .07 .20
U18 Juan Guzman .07 .20
U19 Darryl Hamilton .07 .20
U20 Jay Payton .07 .20
U21 Jeremy Powell .07 .20
U22 Ben Davis .07 .20
U23 Preston Wilson .07 .20
U24 Jim Parque RC .25 .60
U25 Odalis Perez RC .60 1.50
U26 Ronnie Belliard .07 .20
U27 Royce Clayton .07 .20
U28 George Lombard .07 .20
U29 Tony Phillips .07 .20
U30 Fernando Seguignol RC .15 .40
U31 Armando Rios RC .25 .60

U32 Jerry Hairston Jr. RC .25 .60
U33 Justin Baughman RC .15 .40
U34 Seth Greisinger .07 .20
U35 Alex Gonzalez .07 .20
U36 Michael Barrett .07 .20
U37 Carlos Beltran .40 1.00
U38 Ellis Burks .07 .20
U39 Jose Jimenez RC .40 1.00
U40 Carlos Guillen .07 .20
U41 Marlon Anderson .07 .20
U42 Scott Elarton .07 .20
U43 Glenallen Hill .07 .20
U44 Shane Monahan .07 .20
U45 Dennis Martinez .07 .20
U46 Carlos Febles RC .25 .60
U47 Carlos Perez .07 .20
U48 Wilton Guerrero .07 .20
U49 Randy Johnson .20 .50
U50 Brian Simmons RC .15 .40
U51 Carlton Loewer .07 .20
U52 Mark DeRosa RC .40 1.00
U53 Tim Young RC .15 .40
U54 Gary Gaetti .07 .20
U55 Eric Chavez .07 .20
U56 Carl Pavano .07 .20
U57 Mike Stanley .07 .20
U58 Todd Stottlemyre .07 .20
U59 Gabe Kapler RC .40 1.00
U60 Mike Jerzembeck RC .15 .40
U61 Mitch Meluskey RC .25 .60
U62 Bill Pulsipher .07 .20
U63 Derrick Gibson .07 .20
U64 John Rocker RC .40 1.00
U65 Calvin Pickering .07 .20
U66 Blake Stein .07 .20
U67 Fernando Tatis .07 .20
U68 Gabe Alvarez .07 .20
U69 Jeffrey Hammonds .07 .20
U70 Adrian Beltre .07 .20
U71 Ryan Bradley RC .15 .40
U72 Edgard Clemente .07 .20
U73 Rick Croushore RC .15 .40
U74 Matt Clement .07 .20
U75 Dermal Brown .07 .20
U76 Paul Bako .07 .20
U77 Placido Polanco RC .40 1.00
U78 Jay Tessmer .07 .20
U79 Jarrod Washburn .07 .20
U80 Kevin Witt .07 .20
U81 Mike Metcalfe .07 .20
U82 Daryle Ward .07 .20
U83 Benj Sampson RC .15 .40
U84 Mike Kinkade RC .15 .40
U85 Randy Winn .07 .20
U86 Jeff Shaw .07 .20
U87 Troy Glaus RC 1.25 3.00
U88 Hideo Nomo .20 .50
U89 Mark Grudzielanek .07 .20
U90 Mike Frank RC .15 .40
U91 Bobby Howry RC .15 .40
U92 Ryan Minor RC .15 .40
U93 Corey Koskie RC .40 1.00
U94 Matt Anderson RC .15 .40
U95 Joe Carter .07 .20
U96 Paul Konerko .07 .20
U97 Sidney Ponson .07 .20
U98 Jeremy Giambi RC .25 .60
U99 Jeff Kubenka RC .15 .40
U100 J.D. Drew RC 1.00 2.50

1999 Fleer Tradition

The 1999 Fleer set was issued in one series totalling 600 cards and was distributed in 10-card packs with a suggested retail price of $1.59. The fronts feature color action photos with gold foil player names. The backs carry another player photo with biographical information and career statistics. The set includes the following subsets: Franchise Futures (576-590) and Checklists (591-600).

COMPLETE SET (600) 25.00 60.00
1 Mark McGwire .75 2.00
2 Sammy Sosa .30 .75
3 Ken Griffey Jr. .60 1.50
4 Kerry Wood .10 .30
5 Derek Jeter .75 2.00
6 Stan Musial .60 1.50
7 J.D. Drew .10 .30
8 Cal Ripken 1.00 2.50
9 Alex Rodriguez .50 1.25
10 Travis Lee .07 .20
11 Andres Galarraga .10 .30
12 Nomar Garciaparra .50 1.25
13 Albert Belle .10 .30
14 Barry Larkin .20 .50
15 Dante Bichette .10 .30
16 Tony Clark .07 .20
17 Moises Alou .10 .30
18 Rafael Palmeiro .20 .50
19 Raul Mondesi .10 .30
20 Vladimir Guerrero .30 .75
21 John Olerud .10 .30
22 Bernie Williams .20 .50
23 Ben Grieve .07 .20
24 Scott Rolen .20 .50
25 Jeromy Burnitz .10 .30
26 Ken Caminiti .10 .30
27 Barry Bonds .75 2.00
28 Todd Helton .20 .50
29 Juan Gonzalez .10 .30
30 Roger Clemens .60 1.50
31 Andruw Jones .20 .50
32 Mo Vaughn .10 .30
33 Larry Walker .10 .30
34 Frank Thomas .30 .75
35 Manny Ramirez .20 .50
36 Randy Johnson .30 .75
37 Vinny Castilla .10 .30
38 Juan Encarnacion .07 .20
39 Jeff Bagwell .20 .50
40 Gary Sheffield .10 .30
41 Mike Piazza .50 1.25
42 Richie Sexson .10 .30
43 Tony Gwynn .40 1.00
44 Chipper Jones .30 .75
45 Jim Thome .20 .50
46 Craig Biggio .20 .50
47 Carlos Delgado .10 .30
48 Greg Vaughn .07 .20
49 Greg Maddux .50 1.25
50 Troy Glaus .20 .50
51 Roberto Alomar .20 .50
52 Dennis Eckersley .10 .30
53 Mike Caruso .07 .20
54 Bruce Chen .07 .20
55 Aaron Boone .10 .30
56 Bartolo Colon .10 .30
57 Derrick Gibson .07 .20
58 Brian Anderson .07 .20
59 Gabe Alvarez .07 .20
60 Todd Dunwoody .07 .20
61 Rod Beck .07 .20
62 Derek Bell .07 .20
63 Francisco Cordova .07 .20
64 Johnny Damon .20 .50
65 Adrian Beltre .10 .30
66 Garret Anderson .10 .30
67 Armando Benitez .07 .20
68 Edgardo Alfonzo .07 .20
69 Ryan Bradley .07 .20
70 Eric Chavez .10 .30
71 Bobby Abreu .10 .30
72 Andy Ashby .07 .20
73 Ellis Burks .10 .30
74 Jeff Cirillo .07 .20
75 Jay Buhner .10 .30
76 Ron Gant .10 .30
77 Rolando Arrojo .07 .20
78 Will Clark .20 .50
79 Chris Carpenter .10 .30
80 Jim Edmonds .10 .30
81 Tony Batista .07 .20
82 Shane Andrews .07 .20
83 Mark DeRosa .07 .20
84 Brady Anderson .10 .30
85 Tom Gordon .07 .20
86 Brant Brown .07 .20
87 Ray Durham .10 .30
88 Ron Coomer .07 .20
89 Bret Boone .10 .30
90 Travis Fryman .10 .30
91 Darryl Kile .10 .30
92 Paul Bako .07 .20
93 Cliff Floyd .10 .30
94 Scott Elarton .07 .20
95 Jeremy Giambi .07 .20
96 Darren Dreifort .07 .20
97 Marquis Grissom .10 .30
98 Marty Cordova .07 .20
99 Fernando Seguignol .07 .20
100 Orlando Hernandez .10 .30
101 Jose Cruz Jr. .07 .20
102 Jason Giambi .10 .30
103 Damion Easley .07 .20
104 Freddy Garcia .07 .20
105 Marlon Anderson .07 .20
106 Kevin Brown .20 .50
107 Joe Carter .10 .30
108 Russ Davis .07 .20
109 Brian Jordan .10 .30
110 Wade Boggs .20 .50
111 Tom Goodwin .07 .20
112 Scott Brosius .10 .30
113 Darin Erstad .10 .30
114 Jay Bell .10 .30
115 Tom Glavine .20 .50
116 Pedro Martinez .20 .50
117 Mark Grace .20 .50
118 Russ Ortiz .07 .20
119 Magglio Ordonez .10 .30
120 Sean Casey .10 .30
121 Rafael Roque RC .07 .20
122 Brian Giles .10 .30
123 Mike Lansing .07 .20
124 David Cone .10 .30
125 Alex Gonzalez .07 .20
126 Carl Everett .10 .30
127 Jeff King .07 .20
128 Charles Johnson .10 .30
129 Geoff Jenkins .07 .20
130 Corey Koskie .07 .20
131 Brad Fullmer .07 .20
132 Al Leiter .10 .30
133 Rickey Henderson .30 .75
134 Rico Brogna .07 .20
135 Jose Guillen .10 .30
136 Matt Clement .10 .30
137 Carlos Guillen .10 .30
138 Orel Hershiser .10 .30
139 Ray Lankford .10 .30
140 Miguel Cairo .07 .20
141 Chuck Finley .10 .30
142 Rusty Greer .10 .30
143 Kelvim Escobar .07 .20
144 Ryan Klesko .10 .30
145 Andy Benes .07 .20
146 Eric Davis .10 .30
147 David Wells .10 .30
148 Trot Nixon .10 .30
149 Jose Hernandez .07 .20
150 Mark Johnson .07 .20
151 Mike Frank .07 .20
152 Joey Hamilton .07 .20
153 David Justice .10 .30
154 Mike Mussina .20 .50
155 Neifi Perez .07 .20
156 Luis Gonzalez .10 .30
157 Livan Hernandez .10 .30
158 Dermal Brown .07 .20
159 Jose Lima .07 .20
160 Eric Karros .10 .30
161 Ronnie Belliard .07 .20
162 Matt Lawton .07 .20
163 Dustin Hermanson .07 .20
164 Brian McRae .07 .20
165 Mike Kinkade .07 .20
166 A.J. Hinch .07 .20
167 Doug Glanville .07 .20
168 Hideo Nomo .30 .75
169 Jason Kendall .10 .30
170 Steve Finley .10 .30
171 Jeff Kent .10 .30
172 Ben Davis .07 .20
173 Edgar Martinez .20 .50
174 Eli Marrero .07 .20
175 Quinton McCracken .07 .20
176 Rick Helling .07 .20
177 Tom Evans .07 .20
178 Carl Pavano .10 .30
179 Todd Greene .07 .20
180 Omar Daal .07 .20
181 George Lombard .07 .20
182 Ryan Minor .07 .20
183 Troy O'Leary .07 .20
184 Robb Nen .10 .30
185 Mickey Morandini .07 .20
186 Robin Ventura .10 .30
187 Pete Harnisch .07 .20
188 Kenny Lofton .10 .30
189 Eric Milton .07 .20
190 Bobby Higginson .10 .30
191 Jamie Moyer .10 .30
192 Mark Kotsay .10 .30
193 Shane Reynolds .07 .20
194 Carlos Febles .07 .20
195 Jeff Kubenka .07 .20
196 Chuck Knoblauch .10 .30
197 Kenny Rogers .10 .30
198 Bill Mueller .10 .30
199 Shane Monahan .07 .20
200 Matt Morris .07 .20
201 Fred McGriff .20 .50
202 Ivan Rodriguez .20 .50
203 Kevin Witt .07 .20
204 Troy Percival .10 .30
205 David Dellucci .07 .20
206 Kevin Millwood .10 .30
207 Jerry Hairston Jr. .07 .20
208 Mike Stanley .07 .20
209 Henry Rodriguez .07 .20
210 Trevor Hoffman .10 .30
211 Craig Wilson .07 .20
212 Reggie Sanders .10 .30
213 Carlton Loewer .07 .20
214 Omar Vizquel .20 .50
215 Gabe Kapler .10 .30
216 Derrek Lee .20 .50
217 Billy Wagner .10 .30
218 Dean Palmer .10 .30
219 Chan Ho Park .10 .30
220 Fernando Vina .07 .20
221 Roy Halladay .30 .75
222 Paul Molitor .10 .30
223 Ugueth Urbina .07 .20
224 Rey Ordonez .07 .20
225 Ricky Ledee .07 .20
226 Scott Spiezio .07 .20
227 Wendell Magee .07 .20
228 Aramis Ramirez .07 .20
229 Brian Simmons .07 .20
230 Fernando Tatis .07 .20
231 Bobby Smith .07 .20
232 Aaron Sele .07 .20
233 Shawn Green .10 .30
234 Mariano Rivera .30 .75
235 Tim Salmon .20 .50
236 Andy Fox .07 .20
237 Denny Neagle .07 .20
238 John Valentin .07 .20
239 Kevin Tapani .07 .20
240 Paul Konerko .10 .30
241 Robert Fick .07 .20
242 Edgar Renteria .10 .30
243 Brett Tomko .07 .20
244 Daryle Ward .07 .20
245 Carlos Beltran .20 .50
246 Angel Pena .07 .20
247 Steve Woodard .07 .20
248 David Ortiz .30 .75
249 Justin Thompson .07 .20
250 Rondell White .10 .30
251 Jaret Wright .07 .20
252 Ed Sprague .07 .20
253 Jay Payton .07 .20
254 Mike Lowell .10 .30
255 Orlando Cabrera .10 .30
256 Jason Schmidt .10 .30
257 David Segui .07 .20
258 Paul Sorrento .07 .20
259 John Wetteland .10 .30
260 Devon White .10 .30
261 Odalis Perez .07 .20
262 Calvin Pickering .07 .20
263 Tyler Green .07 .20
264 Preston Wilson .10 .30
265 Brad Radke .10 .30
266 Walt Weiss .07 .20
267 Tim Young .07 .20
268 Tino Martinez .20 .50
269 Matt Stairs .07 .20
270 Curt Schilling .10 .30
271 Tony Womack .07 .20
272 Ismael Valdes .07 .20
273 Wally Joyner .10 .30
274 Armando Rios .07 .20
275 Andy Pettitte .20 .50
276 Bubba Trammell .07 .20
277 Todd Zeile .10 .30
278 Shannon Stewart .10 .30
279 Matt Williams .10 .30
280 John Rocker .10 .30
281 B.J. Surhoff .10 .30
282 Eric Young .07 .20
283 Dmitri Young .10 .30
284 John Smoltz .20 .50
285 Todd Walker .07 .20
286 Paul O'Neill .20 .50
287 Blake Stein .07 .20
288 Kevin Young .10 .30
289 Quilvio Veras .07 .20
290 Kirk Rueter .07 .20
291 Randy Winn .07 .20
292 Miguel Tejada .10 .30
293 J.T. Snow .10 .30
294 Michael Tucker .07 .20
295 Jay Tessmer .07 .20
296 Scott Erickson .07 .20
297 Tim Wakefield .10 .30
298 Jeff Abbott .07 .20
299 Eddie Taubensee .07 .20
300 Darryl Hamilton .07 .20
301 Kevin Orie .07 .20
302 Jose Offerman .07 .20
303 Scott Karl .07 .20
304 Chris Widger .07 .20
305 Todd Hundley .07 .20
306 Desi Relaford .07 .20
307 Sterling Hitchcock .07 .20
308 Delino DeShields .07 .20
309 Alex Gonzalez .07 .20
310 Justin Baughman .07 .20
311 Jamey Wright .07 .20
312 Wes Helms .07 .20
313 Dante Powell .07 .20
314 Jim Abbott .20 .50
315 Manny Alexander .07 .20
316 Harold Baines .10 .30
317 Danny Graves .07 .20
318 Sandy Alomar Jr. .07 .20
319 Pedro Astacio .07 .20
320 Jermaine Allensworth .07 .20
321 Matt Anderson .07 .20
322 Chad Curtis .07 .20
323 Antonio Osuna .07 .20
324 Brad Ausmus .10 .30
325 Steve Trachsel .07 .20
326 Mike Blowers .07 .20
327 Brian Bohanon .07 .20
328 Chris Gomez .07 .20
329 Valerio De Los Santos .07 .20
330 Rich Aurilia .07 .20
331 Michael Barrett .07 .20
332 Rick Aguilera .07 .20
333 Adrian Brown .07 .20
334 Bill Spiers .07 .20
335 Matt Beech .07 .20
336 David Bell .07 .20
337 Juan Acevedo .07 .20
338 Jose Canseco .20 .50
339 Wilson Alvarez .07 .20
340 Luis Alicea .07 .20
341 Jason Dickson .07 .20
342 Mike Bordick .07 .20
343 Ben Ford .07 .20
344 Javy Lopez .10 .30
345 Jason Christiansen .07 .20
346 Darren Bragg .07 .20
347 Doug Brocail .07 .20
348 Jeff Blauser .07 .20
349 James Baldwin .07 .20
350 Jeffrey Hammonds .07 .20
351 Ricky Bottalico .07 .20
352 Russ Branyan .07 .20
353 Mark Brownson RC .07 .20
354 Dave Berg .07 .20
355 Sean Bergman .07 .20
356 Jeff Conine .10 .30
357 Shayne Bennett .07 .20
358 Bobby Bonilla .10 .30
359 Bob Wickman .07 .20
360 Carlos Baerga .07 .20
361 Chris Fussell .07 .20
362 Chili Davis .10 .30
363 Jerry Spradlin .07 .20
364 Carlos Hernandez .07 .20
365 Roberto Hernandez .07 .20
366 Marvin Benard .07 .20
367 Ken Cloude .07 .20
368 Tony Fernandez .07 .20
369 John Burkett .07 .20
370 Gary DiSarcina .07 .20
371 Alan Benes .07 .20
372 Karim Garcia .07 .20
373 Carlos Perez .07 .20
374 Damon Buford .07 .20
375 Mark Clark .07 .20
376 Edgard Clemente .07 .20
377 Chad Bradford RC .07 .20
378 Frank Catalanotto .07 .20
379 Vic Darensbourg .07 .20
380 Sean Berry .07 .20
381 Dave Burba .07 .20
382 Sal Fasano .07 .20
383 Steve Parris .07 .20
384 Roger Cedeno .07 .20
385 Chad Fox .07 .20
386 Wilton Guerrero .07 .20
387 Dennis Cook .07 .20
388 Joe Girardi .07 .20
389 LaTroy Hawkins .07 .20
390 Ryan Christenson .07 .20
391 Paul Byrd .07 .20
392 Lou Collier .07 .20
393 Jeff Fassero .07 .20
394 Jim Leyritz .07 .20
395 Shawn Estes .07 .20
396 Mike Kelly .07 .20
397 Rich Croushore .07 .20
398 Royce Clayton .07 .20
399 Rudy Seanez .07 .20
400 Darrin Fletcher .07 .20
401 Shigetoshi Hasegawa .10 .30
402 Bernard Gilkey .07 .20
403 Juan Guzman .07 .20
404 Jeff Frye .07 .20
405 Donovan Osborne .07 .20
406 Alex Fernandez .07 .20
407 Gary Gaetti .07 .20
408 Dan Miceli .07 .20
409 Mike Cameron .07 .20
410 Mike Remlinger .07 .20
411 Joey Cora .07 .20
412 Mark Gardner .07 .20
413 Aaron Ledesma .07 .20
414 Jerry Dipoto .07 .20
415 Ricky Gutierrez .07 .20
416 John Franco .10 .30
417 Mendy Lopez .07 .20
418 Hideki Irabu .07 .20
419 Mark Grudzielanek .07 .20
420 Bobby Hughes .07 .20
421 Pat Meares .07 .20
422 Jimmy Haynes .07 .20
423 Bob Henley .07 .20
424 Bobby Estalella .07 .20
425 Jon Lieber .07 .20
426 Giomar Guevara RC .07 .20
427 Jose Jimenez .07 .20
428 Deivi Cruz .07 .20
429 Jonathan Johnson .07 .20
430 Ken Hill .07 .20
431 Craig Grebeck .07 .20
432 Jose Rosado .07 .20
433 Danny Klassen .07 .20
434 Bobby Howry .07 .20
435 Gerald Williams .07 .20
436 Omar Olivares .07 .20
437 Chris Hoiles .07 .20
438 Seth Greisinger .07 .20
439 Scott Hatteberg .07 .20
440 Jeremi Gonzalez .07 .20
441 Wil Cordero .07 .20
442 Jeff Montgomery .07 .20
443 Chris Stynes .07 .20
444 Tony Saunders .07 .20
445 Einar Diaz .07 .20
446 Lariel Gonzalez .07 .20
447 Ryan Jackson .07 .20
448 Mike Hampton .10 .30
449 Todd Hollandsworth .07 .20
450 Gabe White .07 .20
451 John Jaha .07 .20
452 Bret Saberhagen .10 .30
453 Otis Nixon .07 .20
454 Steve Kline .07 .20
455 Butch Huskey .07 .20
456 Mike Jerzembeck .07 .20
457 Wayne Gomes .07 .20
458 Mike Macfarlane .07 .20
459 Jesus Sanchez .07 .20
460 Al Martin .07 .20
461 Dwight Gooden .10 .30
462 Ruben Rivera .07 .20
463 Pat Hentgen .07 .20
464 Jose Valentin .07 .20
465 Vladimir Nunez .07 .20
466 Charlie Hayes .07 .20
467 Jay Powell .07 .20
468 Raul Ibanez .07 .20
469 Kent Mercker .07 .20
470 John Mabry .07 .20
471 Woody Williams .07 .20
472 Roberto Kelly .07 .20
473 Jim Mecir .07 .20
474 Dave Hollins .07 .20
475 Rafael Medina .07 .20
476 Darren Lewis .07 .20
477 Felix Heredia .07 .20
478 Brian Hunter .07 .20
479 Matt Mantei .07 .20
480 Richard Hidalgo .07 .20
481 Bobby Jones .07 .20
482 Hal Morris .07 .20
483 Ramiro Mendoza .07 .20
484 Matt Luke .07 .20
485 Esteban Loaiza .07 .20
486 Mark Loretta .07 .20
487 A.J. Pierzynski .10 .30
488 Charles Nagy .07 .20
489 Kevin Sefcik .07 .20
490 Jason McDonald .07 .20
491 Jeremy Powell .07 .20
492 Scott Servais .07 .20
493 Abraham Nunez .07 .20
494 Stan Spencer .07 .20
495 Stan Javier .07 .20
496 Jose Paniagua .07 .20
497 Gregg Jefferies .07 .20
498 Gregg Olson .07 .20
499 Derek Lowe .10 .30
500 Willis Otanez .07 .20
501 Brian Moehler .07 .20
502 Glenallen Hill .07 .20
503 Bobby M. Jones .07 .20
504 Greg Norton .07 .20
505 Mike Jackson .07 .20
506 Kirt Manwaring .07 .20
507 Eric Weaver RC .07 .20
508 Mitch Meluskey .07 .20
509 Todd Jones .07 .20
510 Mike Matheny .07 .20
511 Benj Sampson .07 .20
512 Tony Phillips .07 .20
513 Mike Thurman .07 .20
514 Jorge Posada .20 .50
515 Bill Taylor .07 .20
516 Mike Sweeney .10 .30
517 Jose Silva .07 .20
518 Mark Lewis .07 .20
519 Chris Peters .07 .20
520 Brian Johnson .07 .20
521 Mike Timlin .07 .20
522 Mark McLemore .07 .20
523 Dan Plesac .07 .20
524 Kelly Stinnett .07 .20
525 Sidney Ponson .07 .20
526 Jim Parque .07 .20
527 Tyler Houston .07 .20
528 John Thomson .07 .20
529 Reggie Jefferson .07 .20
530 Robert Person .07 .20
531 Marc Newfield .07 .20
532 Javier Vazquez .10 .30
533 Terry Steinbach .07 .20
534 Turk Wendell .07 .20
535 Tim Raines .10 .30
536 Brian Meadows .07 .20
537 Mike Lieberthal .07 .20
538 Ricardo Rincon .07 .20
539 Dan Wilson .07 .20
540 John Johnstone .07 .20
541 Todd Stottlemyre .07 .20
542 Kevin Stocker .07 .20
543 Ramon Martinez .07 .20
544 Mike Simms .07 .20
545 Paul Quantrill .07 .20
546 Matt Walbeck .07 .20
547 Turner Ward .07 .20
548 Bill Pulsipher .07 .20
549 Donnie Sadler .07 .20
550 Lance Johnson .07 .20
551 Bill Simas .07 .20
552 Jeff Reed .07 .20
553 Jeff Shaw .07 .20
554 Joe Randa .10 .30
555 Paul Shuey .07 .20
556 Mike Redmond RC .07 .20
557 Sean Runyan .07 .20
558 Enrique Wilson .07 .20
559 Scott Radinsky .07 .20
560 Larry Sutton .07 .20
561 Masato Yoshii .07 .20
562 David Nilsson .07 .20
563 Mike Trombley .07 .20
564 Darryl Strawberry .10 .30
565 Dave Mlicki .07 .20
566 Placido Polanco .07 .20
567 Yorkis Perez .07 .20
568 Esteban Yan .07 .20
569 Lee Stevens .07 .20
570 Steve Sinclair .07 .20
571 Jarrod Washburn .07 .20
572 Lenny Webster .07 .20
573 Mike Sirotka .07 .20
574 Jason Varitek .30 .75
575 Terry Mulholland .07 .20
576 Adrian Beltre FF .07 .20
577 Eric Chavez FF .07 .20
578 J.D. Drew FF .07 .20
579 Juan Encarnacion FF .07 .20
580 Nomar Garciaparra FF .30 .75
581 Troy Glaus FF .10 .30
582 Ben Grieve FF .07 .20
583 Vladimir Guerrero FF .20 .50
584 Todd Helton FF .10 .30
585 Derek Jeter FF .40 1.00
586 Travis Lee FF .07 .20
587 Alex Rodriguez FF .30 .75
588 Scott Rolen FF .10 .30
589 Richie Sexson FF .07 .20
590 Kerry Wood FF .07 .20
591 Ken Griffey Jr. CL .40 1.00
592 Chipper Jones CL .20 .50
593 Alex Rodriguez CL .30 .75
594 Sammy Sosa CL .20 .50
595 Mark McGwire CL .40 1.00
596 Cal Ripken CL .50 1.25
597 Nomar Garciaparra CL .30 .75
598 Derek Jeter CL .40 1.00
599 Kerry Wood CL .07 .20
600 J.D. Drew CL .07 .20
P7 J.D. Drew Promo .40 1.00

1999 Fleer Tradition Millenium

COMP.FACT.SET (620) 30.00 80.00
*STARS 1-600: 1X TO 2.5X BASIC CARDS
*ROOKIES 1-600: 1X TO 2.5X BASIC CARDS
SET DIST.ONLY IN FACTORY SET FORM
STATED PRINT RUN 5000 SETS
601 Rick Ankiel 1.00 2.50
602 Peter Bergeron .30 .75
603 Pat Burrell 3.00 8.00
604 Eric Munson .60 1.50
605 Alfonso Soriano 6.00 15.00
606 Tim Hudson 3.00 8.00
607 Erubiel Durazo .60 1.50
608 Chad Hermansen .30 .75
609 Jeff Zimmerman .60 1.50
610 Jesus Pena .30 .75
611 Wade Boggs HL .50 1.25
612 Jose Canseco HL .50 1.25
613 Roger Clemens HL 1.50 4.00
614 David Cone HL .30 .75
615 Tony Gwynn HL 1.00 2.50
616 Mark McGwire HL 2.00 5.00
617 Cal Ripken HL 2.50 6.00
618 Alex Rodriguez HL 1.25 3.00
619 Fernando Tatis HL .20 .50
620 Robin Ventura HL .30 .75

1999 Fleer Tradition Starting 9

RANDOM INSERTS IN HOBBY PACKS
STATED PRINT RUN 9 SERIAL #'d SETS
NO PRICING DUE TO SCARCITY

1999 Fleer Tradition Warning Track

*STARS: 2.5X TO 6X BASIC CARDS
ONE PER RETAIL PACK

1999 Fleer Tradition Vintage '61

COMPLETE SET (50) 10.00 25.00
*SINGLES: .4X TO 1X BASE CARD HI
ONE PER HOBBY PACK

1999 Fleer Tradition Date With Destiny

STATED PRINT RUN 100 SERIAL #'d SETS
1 Barry Bonds 15.00 40.00
2 Roger Clemens 12.00 30.00
3 Ken Griffey Jr. 20.00 50.00
4 Tony Gwynn 10.00 25.00
5 Greg Maddux 12.00 30.00
6 Mark McGwire 15.00 40.00
7 Mike Piazza 10.00 25.00
8 Cal Ripken 30.00 80.00
9 Alex Rodriguez 12.00 30.00
10 Frank Thomas 10.00 25.00

1999 Fleer Tradition Diamond Magic

COMPLETE SET (15) 20.00 50.00
STATED ODDS 1:96
1 Barry Bonds 2.50 6.00
2 Roger Clemens 2.00 5.00
3 Nomar Garciaparra 1.00 2.50
4 Ken Griffey Jr. 3.00 8.00
5 Tony Gwynn 1.50 4.00
6 Orlando Hernandez .60 1.50
7 Derek Jeter 4.00 10.00
8 Randy Johnson 1.50 4.00
9 Chipper Jones 1.50 4.00
10 Greg Maddux 2.00 5.00
11 Mark McGwire 2.50 6.00
12 Alex Rodriguez 2.00 5.00
13 Sammy Sosa 1.50 4.00
14 Bernie Williams 1.00 2.50
15 Kerry Wood .60 1.50

1999 Fleer Tradition Going Yard

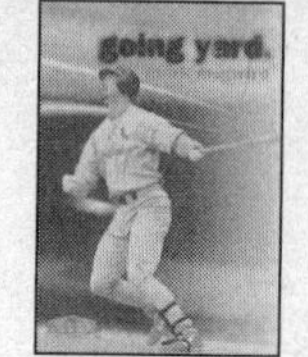

COMPLETE SET (15) 15.00 40.00
STATED ODDS 1:18
1 Moises Alou .40 1.00
2 Albert Belle .40 1.00
3 Jose Canseco .60 1.50
4 Vinny Castilla .40 1.00
5 Andres Galarraga .40 1.00
6 Juan Gonzalez .40 1.00
7 Ken Griffey Jr. 2.00 5.00
8 Chipper Jones 1.00 2.50
9 Mark McGwire 2.50 6.00
10 Rafael Palmeiro .60 1.50
11 Mike Piazza 1.50 4.00
12 Alex Rodriguez 1.50 4.00
13 Sammy Sosa 1.00 2.50
14 Greg Vaughn .25 .60
15 Mo Vaughn .40 1.00

1999 Fleer Tradition Golden Memories

COMPLETE SET (15) 75.00 150.00
STATED ODDS 1:54
1 Albert Belle 1.00 2.50
2 Barry Bonds 6.00 15.00
3 Roger Clemens 5.00 12.00
4 Nomar Garciaparra 4.00 10.00
5 Juan Gonzalez 1.00 2.50
6 Ken Griffey Jr. 5.00 12.00
7 Randy Johnson 2.50 6.00
8 Greg Maddux 4.00 10.00
9 Mark McGwire 6.00 15.00
10 Mike Piazza 4.00 10.00
11 Cal Ripken 8.00 20.00
12 Alex Rodriguez 4.00 10.00
13 Sammy Sosa 2.50 6.00
14 David Wells 1.00 2.50
15 Kerry Wood 1.00 2.50

1999 Fleer Tradition Stan Musial Monumental Moments

COMPLETE SET (10) 10.00 25.00
COMMON CARD (1-10) 1.00 2.50
STATED ODDS 1:36

1999 Fleer Tradition Stan Musial Monumental Moments Autographs

COMMON CARD (1-10) 30.00 60.00
RANDOM INSERTS IN PACKS
STATED PRINT RUN 50 SERIAL #'d SETS

1999 Fleer Tradition Rookie Flashback

COMPLETE SET (15) 4.00 10.00
STATED ODDS 1:6
1 Matt Anderson .20 .50
2 Rolando Arrojo .20 .50
3 Adrian Beltre .30 .75
4 Mike Caruso .20 .50
5 Eric Chavez .30 .75
6 J.D. Drew .30 .75
7 Juan Encarnacion .20 .50
8 Brad Fullmer .20 .50
9 Troy Glaus .50 1.25
10 Ben Grieve .20 .50
11 Todd Helton .50 1.25
12 Orlando Hernandez .30 .75
13 Travis Lee .20 .50
14 Richie Sexson .30 .75
15 Kerry Wood .30 .75

1999 Fleer Tradition Update

The 1999 Fleer Update set was issued in one series totalling 150 cards and distributed only as a factory boxed set. The fronts feature color action player photos. The backs carry player information. The set features the Season Highlights subset (Cards 141-150). Over 100 Rookie Cards are featured in this set. Among these Rookie Cards are Rick Ankiel, Josh Beckett, Pat Burrell, Tim Hudson, Eric Munson, Wily Mo Pena and Alfonso Soriano.

COMP.FACT.SET (150) 10.00 25.00
DISTRIBUTED ONLY IN FACTORY SET FORM
U1 Rick Ankiel RC 3.00 8.00
U2 Peter Bergeron RC .08 .25
U3 Pat Burrell RC .75 2.00
U4 Eric Munson RC .15 .40
U5 Alfonso Soriano RC 2.00 5.00
U6 Tim Hudson RC .75 2.00
U7 Erubiel Durazo RC .15 .40
U8 Chad Hermansen .07 .20
U9 Jeff Zimmerman RC .08 .25
U10 Jesus Pena RC .08 .25
U11 Ramon Hernandez .08 .25
U12 Trent Durrington RC .08 .25
U13 Tony Armas Jr. .07 .20
U14 Mike Fyhrie RC .08 .25
U15 Danny Kolb RC .30 .75
U16 Mike Porzio RC .08 .25
U17 Will Brunson RC .08 .25
U18 Mike Duvall RC .08 .25
U19 Doug Mientkiewicz RC .30 .75
U20 Gabe Molina RC .08 .25
U21 Luis Vizcaino RC .08 .25
U22 Robinson Cancel RC .08 .25
U23 Brett Laxton RC .08 .25
U24 Joe McEwing RC .08 .25
U25 Justin Speier RC .08 .25
U26 Kip Wells RC .15 .40
U27 Armando Almanza RC .08 .25
U28 Joe Davenport RC .08 .25
U29 Yamid Haad RC .08 .25
U30 John Halama .07 .20
U31 Adam Kennedy .07 .20
U32 Micah Bowie RC .08 .25

U33 Gookie Dawkins RC .15 .40
U34 Ryan Rupe RC .08 .25
U35 B.J. Ryan RC .75 2.00
U36 Chance Sanford RC .08 .25
U37 Anthony Shumaker RC .08 .25
U38 Ryan Glynn RC .08 .25
U39 Roosevelt Brown RC .08 .25
U40 Ben Molina RC .60 1.50
U41 Scott Williamson .07 .20
U42 Eric Gagne RC 1.50 4.00
U43 John McDonald RC .08 .25
U44 Scott Sauerbeck RC .08 .25
U45 Mike Venafro RC .08 .25
U46 Edwards Guzman RC .08 .25
U47 Richard Barker RC .08 .25
U48 Braden Looper .07 .20
U49 Chad Meyers RC .08 .25
U50 Scott Strickland RC .08 .25
U51 Billy Koch .07 .20
U52 David Newhan RC .15 .40
U53 David Riske RC .08 .25
U54 Jose Santiago RC .08 .25
U55 Miguel Del Toro RC .08 .25
U56 Orber Moreno RC .08 .25
U57 Dave Roberts RC .30 .75
U58 Tim Byrdak RC .08 .25
U59 David Lee RC .08 .25
U60 Guillermo Mota RC .08 .25
U61 Wilton Veras RC .08 .25
U62 Joe Mays RC .15 .40
U63 Jose Fernandez RC .08 .25
U64 Ray King RC .08 .25
U65 Chris Petersen RC .08 .25
U66 Vernon Wells .07 .20
U67 Ruben Mateo .07 .20
U68 Ben Petrick .07 .20
U69 Chris Tremie RC .08 .25
U70 Lance Berkman .07 .20
U71 Dan Smith RC .08 .25
U72 Carlos Eduardo Hernandez RC .15 .40
U73 Chad Harville RC .08 .25
U74 Damaso Marte RC .08 .25
U75 Aaron Myette RC .08 .25
U76 Willis Roberts RC .08 .25
U77 Erik Sabel RC .08 .25
U78 Hector Almonte RC .08 .25
U79 Kris Benson .07 .20
U80 Pat Daneker RC .08 .25
U81 Freddy Garcia RC .40 1.00
U82 Byung-Hyun Kim RC .40 1.00
U83 Wily Pena RC 1.25 3.00
U84 Dan Wheeler RC .15 .40
U85 Tim Harikkala RC .08 .25
U86 Derrin Ebert RC .08 .25
U87 Horacio Estrada RC .08 .25
U88 Liu Rodriguez RC .08 .25
U89 Jordan Zimmerman RC .08 .25
U90 A.J. Burnett RC .40 1.00
U91 Doug Davis RC .40 1.00
U92 Rob Ramsay RC .08 .25
U93 Clay Bellinger RC .08 .25
U94 Charlie Greene RC .08 .25
U95 Bo Porter RC .08 .25
U96 Jorge Toca RC .15 .40
U97 Casey Blake RC .50 1.25
U98 Amaury Garcia RC .08 .25
U99 Jose Molina RC .15 .40
U100 Melvin Mora RC 1.00 2.50
U101 Joe Nathan RC .50 1.25
U102 Juan Pena RC .08 .25
U103 Dave Borkowski RC .08 .25
U104 Eddie Gaillard RC .08 .25
U105 Glen Barker RC .08 .25
U106 Brett Hinchliffe RC .08 .25
U107 Carlos Lee .07 .20
U108 Rob Ryan RC .08 .25
U109 Jeff Weaver RC .30 .75
U110 Ed Yarnall .07 .20
U111 Nelson Cruz RC .08 .25
U112 Cleatus Davidson RC .08 .25
U113 Tim Kubinski RC .08 .25
U114 Sean Spencer RC .08 .25
U115 Joe Winkelsas RC .08 .25
U116 Mike Colangelo RC .08 .25
U117 Tom Davey RC .08 .25
U118 Warren Morris .07 .20
U119 Dan Murray RC .08 .25
U120 Jose Nieves RC .08 .25
U121 Mark Quinn RC .08 .25
U122 Josh Beckett RC 4.00 10.00
U123 Chad Allen RC .08 .25
U124 Mike Figga .08 .25
U125 Beiker Graterol RC .08 .25
U126 Aaron Scheffer RC .08 .25
U127 Wiki Gonzalez RC .15 .40
U128 Ramon E.Martinez RC .08 .25
U129 Matt Riley RC .15 .40
U130 Chris Woodward RC .08 .25
U131 Albert Belle .07 .20
U132 Roger Cedeno .07 .20
U133 Roger Clemens .40 1.00
U134 Brian Giles .07 .20
U135 Rickey Henderson .20 .50
U136 Randy Johnson .20 .50
U137 Brian Jordan .07 .20
U138 Paul Konerko .07 .20
U139 Hideo Nomo .20 .50
U140 Kenny Rogers .07 .20
U141 Wade Boggs HL .10 .30
U142 Jose Canseco HL .07 .20
U143 Roger Clemens HL .40 1.00
U144 David Cone HL .07 .20
U145 Tony Gwynn HL .25 .60
U146 Mark McGwire HL .50 1.25
U147 Cal Ripken HL .60 1.50
U148 Alex Rodriguez HL .30 .75
U149 Fernando Tatis HL .07 .20
U150 Robin Ventura HL .07 .20

2000 Fleer Tradition

COMPLETE SET (450) 20.00 50.00
COMMON CARD (1-450) .12 .30
COMMON RC .12 .30
1 AL Home Run LL .60 1.50
2 NL Home Run LL .50 1.25
3 AL RBI LL .60 1.50
4 NL RBI LL .50 1.25
5 AL Avg LL .75 2.00
6 NL Avg LL .20 .50
7 AL Wins LL .20 .50
8 NL Wins LL .40 1.00
9 AL ERA LL .20 .50
10 NL ERA LL .30 .75
11 Matt Mantei .12 .30
12 John Rocker .12 .30
13 Kyle Farnsworth .12 .30
14 Juan Guzman .12 .30
15 Manny Ramirez .30 .75
16 M.Riley .12 .30
C.Pickering
17 Tony Clark .12 .30
18 Brian Meadows .12 .30
19 Orber Moreno .12 .30
20 Eric Karros .12 .30
21 Steve Woodard .12 .30
22 Scott Brosius .12 .30
23 Gary Bennett .12 .30
24 J.Wood .12 .30
D.Borkowski
25 Joe McEwing .12 .30
26 Juan Gonzalez .12 .30
27 Roy Halladay .20 .50
28 Trevor Hoffman .20 .50
29 Arizona Diamondbacks .10 .30
30 Domingo Guzman RC .12 .30
31 Bret Boone .12 .30
32 Nomar Garciaparra .20 .50
33 Bo Porter .12 .30
34 Eddie Taubensee .12 .30
35 Pedro Astacio .12 .30
36 Derek Bell .12 .30
37 Jacque Jones .12 .30
38 Ricky Ledee .12 .30
39 Jeff Kent .12 .30
40 Matt Williams .12 .30
41 A.Soriano .30 .75
D.Jimenez
42 B.J. Surhoff .12 .30
43 Denny Neagle .12 .30
44 Omar Vizquel .20 .50
45 Jeff Bagwell .20 .50
46 Mark Grudzielanek .12 .30
47 LaTroy Hawkins .12 .30
48 Orlando Hernandez .12 .30
49 Checklist .60 1.50
K.Griffey Jr.
50 Fernando Tatis .12 .30
51 Quilvio Veras .12 .30
52 Wayne Gomes .12 .30
53 Rick Helling .12 .30
54 Shannon Stewart .12 .30
55 D.Brown .12 .30
M.Quinn
56 Randy Johnson .30 .75
57 Greg Maddux .40 1.00
58 Mike Cameron .12 .30
59 Matt Anderson .12 .30
60 Milwaukee Brewers .10 .30
61 Derrek Lee .12 .30
62 Mike Sweeney .12 .30
63 Fernando Vina .12 .30
64 Orlando Cabrera .12 .30
65 Doug Glanville .12 .30
66 Stan Spencer .12 .30
67 Ray Lankford .12 .30
68 Kelly Dransfeldt .12 .30
69 Alex Gonzalez .12 .30
70 R.Branyan .12 .30
D.Peoples
71 Jim Edmonds .12 .30
72 Brady Anderson .12 .30
73 Mike Stanley .12 .30
74 Travis Fryman .12 .30
75 Carlos Febles .12 .30
76 Bobby Higginson .12 .30
77 Carlos Perez .12 .30
78 S.Cox .12 .30
A.Sanchez
79 Dustin Hermanson .12 .30
80 Kenny Rogers .12 .30
81 Miguel Tejada .20 .50
82 Ben Davis .12 .30
83 Reggie Sanders .12 .30
84 Eric Davis .12 .30
85 J.D. Drew .12 .30
86 Ryan Rupe .12 .30
87 Bobby Smith .12 .30
88 Jose Cruz Jr. .12 .30
89 Carlos Delgado .12 .30
90 Toronto Blue Jays .10 .30
91 D.Stark RC .12 .30
G.Meche
92 Randy Velarde .12 .30
93 Aaron Boone .12 .30
94 Javy Lopez .12 .30
95 Johnny Damon .20 .50
96 Jon Lieber .12 .30
97 Montreal Expos .10 .30
98 Mark Kotsay .12 .30
99 Luis Gonzalez .12 .30
100 Larry Walker .20 .50
101 Adrian Beltre .30 .75
102 Alex Ochoa .12 .30
103 Michael Barrett .12 .30
104 Tampa Bay Devil Rays .10 .30
105 Rey Ordonez .12 .30
106 Derek Jeter .75 2.00
107 Mike Lieberthal .12 .30
108 Ellis Burks .12 .30
109 Steve Finley .12 .30
110 Ryan Klesko .12 .30
111 Steve Avery .12 .30
112 Dave Veres .12 .30
113 Cliff Floyd .12 .30
114 Shane Reynolds .12 .30
115 Kevin Brown .12 .30
116 Dave Nilsson .12 .30
117 Mike Trombley .12 .30
118 Todd Walker .12 .30
119 John Olerud .12 .30
120 Chuck Knoblauch .12 .30
121 Checklist .20 .50
N.Garciaparra
122 Trot Nixon .12 .30
123 Erubiel Durazo .12 .30
124 Edwards Guzman .12 .30
125 Curt Schilling .20 .50
126 Brian Jordan .12 .30
127 Cleveland Indians .10 .30
128 Benito Santiago .12 .30
129 Frank Thomas .30 .75
130 Neifi Perez .12 .30
131 Alex Fernandez .12 .30
132 Jose Lima .12 .30
133 J.Toca .12 .30
M.Mora
134 Scott Karl .12 .30
135 Brad Radke .12 .30
136 Paul O'Neill .20 .50
137 Kris Benson .12 .30
138 Colorado Rockies .10 .30
139 Jason Phillips .12 .30
140 Robb Nen .12 .30
141 Ken Hill .12 .30
142 Charles Johnson .12 .30
143 Paul Konerko .12 .30
144 Dmitri Young .12 .30
145 Justin Thompson .12 .30
146 Mark Loretta .12 .30
147 Edgardo Alfonzo .12 .30
148 Armando Benitez .12 .30
149 Octavio Dotel .12 .30
150 Wade Boggs .20 .50
151 Ramon Hernandez .12 .30
152 Freddy Garcia .12 .30
153 Edgar Martinez .20 .50
154 Ivan Rodriguez .20 .50
155 Kansas City Royals .10 .30
156 C.Davidson .12 .30
C.Guzman
157 Andy Benes .12 .30
158 Todd Dunwoody .12 .30
159 Pedro Martinez .20 .50
160 Mike Caruso .12 .30
161 Mike Sirotka .12 .30
162 Houston Astros .10 .30
163 Darryl Kile .12 .30
164 Chipper Jones .30 .75
165 Carl Everett .12 .30
166 Geoff Jenkins .12 .30
167 Dan Perkins .12 .30
168 Andy Pettitte .20 .50
169 Francisco Cordova .12 .30
170 Jay Buhner .12 .30
171 Jay Bell .12 .30
172 Andruw Jones .12 .30
173 Bobby Howry .12 .30
174 Chris Singleton .12 .30
175 Todd Helton .20 .50
176 A.J. Burnett .12 .30
177 Marquis Grissom .12 .30
178 Eric Milton .12 .30
179 Los Angeles Dodgers .10 .30
180 Kevin Appier .12 .30
181 Brian Giles .12 .30
182 Tom Davey .12 .30
183 Mo Vaughn .12 .30
184 Jose Hernandez .12 .30
185 Jim Parque .12 .30
186 Derrick Gibson .12 .30
187 Bruce Aven .12 .30
188 Jeff Cirillo .12 .30
189 Doug Mientkiewicz .12 .30
190 Eric Chavez .12 .30
191 Al Martin .12 .30
192 Tom Glavine .20 .50
193 Butch Huskey .12 .30
194 Ray Durham .12 .30
195 Greg Vaughn .12 .30
196 Vinny Castilla .12 .30
197 Ken Caminiti .12 .30
198 Joe Mays .12 .30
199 Chicago White Sox .10 .30
200 Mariano Rivera .40 1.00
201 Checklist .50 1.25
M.McGwire
202 Pat Meares .12 .30
203 Andres Galarraga .20 .50
204 Tom Gordon .12 .30
205 Henry Rodriguez .12 .30
206 Brett Tomko .12 .30
207 Dante Bichette .12 .30
208 Craig Biggio .20 .50
209 Matt Lawton .12 .30
210 Tino Martinez .12 .30
211 A.Myette .12 .30
J.Paul
212 Warren Morris .12 .30
213 San Diego Padres .10 .30
214 Ramon E. Martinez .12 .30
215 Troy Percival .12 .30
216 Jason Johnson .12 .30
217 Carlos Lee .12 .30
218 Scott Williamson .12 .30
219 Jeff Weaver .12 .30
220 Ronnie Belliard .12 .30
221 Jason Giambi .12 .30
222 Ken Griffey Jr. .60 1.50
223 John Halama .12 .30
224 Brett Hinchliffe .12 .30
225 Wilson Alvarez .12 .30
226 Rolando Arrojo .12 .30
227 Ruben Mateo .12 .30
228 Rafael Palmeiro .20 .50
229 David Wells .12 .30
230 E.Gagne RC/J.Williams RC .12 .30
231 Tim Salmon .12 .30
232 Mike Mussina .20 .50
233 Magglio Ordonez .20 .50
234 Ron Villone .12 .30
235 Antonio Alfonseca .12 .30
236 Jeromy Burnitz .12 .30
237 Ben Grieve .12 .30
238 Giomar Guevara .12 .30
239 Garret Anderson .12 .30
240 John Smoltz .30 .75
241 Mark Grace .20 .50
242 C.Liniak .12 .30
J.Molina
243 Damion Easley .12 .30
244 Jeff Montgomery .12 .30
245 Kenny Lofton .12 .30
246 Masato Yoshii .12 .30
247 Philadelphia Phillies .10 .30
248 Raul Mondesi .12 .30
249 Marlon Anderson .12 .30
250 Shawn Green .12 .30
251 Sterling Hitchcock .12 .30
252 R.Wolf .12 .30
A.Shumaker
253 Jeff Fassero .12 .30
254 Eli Marrero .12 .30
255 Cincinnati Reds .10 .30
256 Rick Ankiel .20 .50
257 Darin Erstad .12 .30
258 Albert Belle .12 .30
259 Bartolo Colon .12 .30
260 Bret Saberhagen .12 .30
261 Carlos Beltran .20 .50
262 Glenallen Hill .12 .30
263 Gregg Jefferies .12 .30
264 Matt Clement .12 .30
265 Miguel Del Toro .10 .30
266 R.Cancel .12 .30
K.Barker
267 San Francisco Giants .10 .30
268 Kent Bottenfield .12 .30
269 Fred McGriff .20 .50
270 Chris Carpenter .20 .50
271 Atlanta Braves .10 .30
272 Tomo Ohka RC .12 .30
273 Will Clark .20 .50
274 Troy O'Leary .12 .30
275 Checklist .30 .75
S.Sosa
276 Travis Lee .12 .30
277 Sean Casey .12 .30
278 Ron Gant .12 .30
279 Roger Clemens .40 1.00
280 Phil Nevin .12 .30
281 Mike Piazza .30 .75
282 Mike Lowell .12 .30
283 Kevin Millwood .12 .30
284 Joe Randa .12 .30
285 Jeff Shaw .12 .30
286 Jason Varitek .30 .75
287 Harold Baines .20 .50
288 Gabe Kapler .12 .30
289 Chuck Finley .12 .30
290 Carl Pavano .12 .30
291 Brad Ausmus .12 .30
292 Brad Fullmer .12 .30
293 Boston Red Sox .10 .30
294 Bob Wickman .12 .30
295 Billy Wagner .12 .30
296 Shawn Estes .12 .30
297 Gary Sheffield .12 .30
298 Fernando Seguignol .12 .30
299 Omar Olivares .12 .30
300 Baltimore Orioles .10 .30
301 Matt Stairs .12 .30
302 Andy Ashby .12 .30
303 Todd Greene .12 .30
304 Jesse Garcia .12 .30
305 Kerry Wood .12 .30
306 Roberto Alomar .20 .50
307 New York Mets .10 .30
308 Dean Palmer .12 .30
309 Mike Hampton .12 .30
310 Devon White .12 .30
311 Mike Garcia RC .12 .30
312 Tim Hudson .20 .50
313 John Franco .12 .30
314 Jason Schmidt .12 .30
315 J.T. Snow .12 .30
316 Ed Sprague .12 .30
317 Chris Widger .12 .30
318 Luther Hackman RC .12 .30
319 Jose Mesa .12 .30
320 Jose Canseco .20 .50
321 John Wetteland .12 .30
322 Minnesota Twins .10 .30
323 Jeff DaVanon RC .12 .30
324 Tony Womack .12 .30
325 Rod Beck .12 .30
326 Mickey Morandini .12 .30
327 Pokey Reese .12 .30
328 Jaret Wright .12 .30
329 Glen Barker .12 .30
330 Darren Dreifort .12 .30
331 Torii Hunter .12 .30
332 T.Armas .12 .30
P.Bergeron
333 Hideki Irabu .12 .30
334 Desi Relaford .12 .30
335 Barry Bonds .50 1.25
336 Gary DiSarcina .12 .30
337 Gerald Williams .12 .30
338 John Valentin .12 .30
339 David Justice .12 .30
340 Juan Encarnacion .12 .30
341 Jeremy Giambi .12 .30
342 Chan Ho Park .20 .50
343 Vladimir Guerrero .20 .50
344 Robin Ventura .12 .30
345 Bob Abreu .12 .30
346 Tony Gwynn .30 .75
347 Jose Jimenez .12 .30
348 Royce Clayton .12 .30
349 Kelvim Escobar .12 .30
350 Chicago Cubs .10 .30
351 T.Dawkins .12 .30
J.LaRue
352 Barry Larkin .20 .50
353 Cal Ripken 1.00 2.50
354 Checklist .40 1.00
A.Rodriguez
355 Todd Stottlemyre .12 .30
356 Terry Adams .12 .30
357 Pittsburgh Pirates .10 .30
358 Jim Thome .20 .50
359 C.Lee .12 .30
D.Davis
360 Moises Alou .12 .30
361 Todd Hollandsworth .12 .30
362 Marty Cordova .12 .30
363 David Cone .12 .30
364 J.Nathan .12 .30
W.Delgado
365 Paul Byrd .12 .30
366 Edgar Renteria .12 .30
367 Rusty Greer .12 .30
368 David Segui .12 .30
369 New York Yankees .20 .50
370 D.Ward .12 .30
C.Hernandez
371 Troy Glaus .12 .30
372 Delion DeShields .12 .30
373 Jose Offerman .12 .30
374 Sammy Sosa .30 .75
375 Sandy Alomar Jr. .12 .30
376 Masao Kida .12 .30
377 Richard Hidalgo .12 .30
378 Ismael Valdes .12 .30
379 Ugueth Urbina .12 .30
380 Darryl Hamilton .12 .30
381 John Jaha .12 .30
382 St. Louis Cardinals .10 .30
383 Scott Sauerbeck .12 .30
384 Russ Ortiz .12 .30
385 Jamie Moyer .12 .30
386 Dave Martinez .12 .30
387 Todd Zeile .12 .30
388 Anaheim Angels .10 .30
389 R.Ryan .12 .30
N.Bierbrodt
390 Rickey Henderson .30 .75
391 Alex Rodriguez .40 1.00
392 Texas Rangers .10 .30
393 Roberto Hernandez .12 .30
394 Tony Batista .12 .30
395 Oakland Athletics .10 .30
396 Dave Cortes RC .12 .30
397 Gregg Olson .12 .30
398 Sidney Ponson .12 .30
399 Micah Bowie .12 .30
400 Mark McGwire .50 1.25
401 Florida Marlins .10 .30
402 Chad Allen .12 .30
403 C.Blake .12 .30
V.Wells
404 Pete Harnisch .12 .30
405 Preston Wilson .12 .30
406 Richie Sexson .12 .30
407 Rico Brogna .12 .30
408 Todd Hundley .12 .30
409 Wally Joyner .12 .30
410 Tom Goodwin .12 .30
411 Joey Hamilton .12 .30
412 Detroit Tigers .10 .30
413 Michael Tejera RC .12 .30
414 Alex Gonzalez .12 .30
415 Jermaine Dye .12 .30
416 Jose Rosada .12 .30
417 Wilton Guerrero .12 .30
418 Rondell White .12 .30
419 Al Leiter .12 .30
420 Bernie Williams .20 .50
421 A.J. Hinch .12 .30
422 Pat Burrell .12 .30
423 Scott Rolen .20 .50
424 Jason Kendall .12 .30
425 Kevin Young .12 .30
426 Eric Owens .12 .30
427 Checklist .75 2.00
D.Jeter
428 Livan Hernandez .12 .30
429 Russ Davis .12 .30
430 Dan Wilson .12 .30
431 Quinton McCracken .12 .30
432 Homer Bush .12 .30
433 Seattle Mariners .10 .30
434 C.Harville .12 .30
L.Vizcaino
435 Carlos Beltran AW .20 .50
436 Scott Williamson AW .12 .30
437 Pedro Martinez AW .20 .50
438 Randy Johnson AW .30 .75
439 Ivan Rodriguez AW .20 .50
440 Chipper Jones AW .30 .75
441 Bernie Williams DIV .20 .50
442 Pedro Martinez DIV .20 .50
443 Derek Jeter DIV .75 2.00
444 Brian Jordan DIV .12 .30
445 Todd Pratt DIV .12 .30
446 Kevin Millwood DIV .12 .30
447 Orlando Hernandez WS .12 .30
448 Derek Jeter WS .75 2.00
449 Chad Curtis WS .12 .30
450 Roger Clemens WS .40 1.00
P353 Cal Ripken Promo 1.00 2.50

2000 Fleer Tradition Glossy

COMP.FACT.SET (455) 25.00 50.00
*GLOSSY 1-450: .75X TO 2X BASIC
FIVE 451-500 CARDS PER GLOSSY FACTORY
451-500 PRINT RUN 1000 SERIAL #'d SETS
451 Carlos Casimiro RC .75 2.00
452 Adam Melhuse RC .75 2.00
453 Adam Bernero RC .75 2.00
454 Dusty Allen RC .75 2.00
455 Chan Perry RC .75 2.00
456 Damian Rolls RC .75 2.00
457 Josh Phelps RC .75 2.00
458 Barry Zito 6.00 15.00
459 Hector Ortiz RC .75 2.00
460 Juan Pierre RC 4.00 10.00
461 Jose Ortiz RC .75 2.00
462 Chad Zerbe RC .75 2.00
463 Julio Zuleta RC .75 2.00
464 Eric Byrnes .75 2.00
465 Wilfredo Rodriguez RC .75 2.00
466 Wascar Serrano RC .75 2.00
467 Aaron McNeal RC .75 2.00
468 Paul Rigdon RC .75 2.00
469 John Snyder RC .75 2.00
470 J.C. Romero RC .75 2.00
471 Talmadge Nunnari RC .75 2.00
472 Mike Lamb .75 2.00
473 Ryan Kohlmeier RC .75 2.00
474 Rodney Lindsey RC .75 2.00
475 Elvis Pena RC .75 2.00
476 Alex Cabrera .75 2.00
477 Chris Richard .75 2.00
478 Pedro Feliz RC 2.00 5.00
479 Ross Gload RC .75 2.00
480 Timo Perez RC 1.25 3.00
481 Jason Woolf RC .75 2.00
482 Kenny Kelly RC .75 2.00
483 Sang-Hoon Lee .75 2.00
484 John Riedling RC .75 2.00
485 Chris Wakeland RC .75 2.00
486 Britt Reames RC .75 2.00
487 Greg LaRocca RC .75 2.00
488 Randy Keisler RC .75 2.00
489 Xavier Nady RC 2.00 5.00
490 Keith Ginter RC .75 2.00
491 Joey Nation RC .75 2.00
492 Kazuhiro Sasaki 2.00 5.00
493 Lesli Brea RC .75 2.00
494 Jace Brewer .75 2.00
495 Yohanny Valera RC .75 2.00
496 Adam Piatt .75 2.00
497 Nate Rolison .75 2.00
498 Aubrey Huff .75 2.00
499 Jason Tyner .75 2.00
500 Corey Patterson .75 2.00

2000 Fleer Tradition Glossy Hawaii

STATED PRINT RUN 1 SERIAL #'d SET

2000 Fleer Tradition Dividends

COMPLETE SET (15) 4.00 10.00
STATED ODDS 1:6
D1 Alex Rodriguez .40 1.00
D2 Ben Grieve .12 .30
D3 Cal Ripken 1.00 2.50
D4 Chipper Jones .30 .75
D5 Derek Jeter .75 2.00
D6 Frank Thomas .30 .75
D7 Jeff Bagwell .20 .50
D8 Sammy Sosa .30 .75
D9 Tony Gwynn .30 .75
D10 Scott Rolen .20 .50
D11 Nomar Garciaparra .20 .50
D12 Mike Piazza .30 .75
D13 Mark McGwire .50 1.25
D14 Ken Griffey Jr. .60 1.50
D15 Juan Gonzalez .12 .30

2000 Fleer Tradition Fresh Ink

STATED ODDS 1:144 HOBBY
1 Rick Ankiel 4.00 10.00
2 Carlos Beltran 8.00 20.00
3 Pat Burrell 4.00 10.00
4 Miguel Cairo 4.00 10.00
5 Sean Casey 6.00 15.00
6 Will Clark 10.00 25.00
7 Mike Darr 6.00 15.00
8 J.D. Drew 6.00 15.00
9 Erubiel Durazo 4.00 10.00
10 Carlos Febles 4.00 10.00
11 Freddy Garcia 4.00 10.00
12 Jason Grilli 4.00 10.00
13 Vladimir Guerrero 15.00 40.00
14 Tony Gwynn 20.00 50.00
15 Jerry Hairston Jr. 4.00 10.00
16 Tim Hudson 6.00 15.00
17 John Jaha 4.00 10.00
18 D'Angelo Jimenez 4.00 10.00
19 Andruw Jones 6.00 15.00
20 Gabe Kapler 6.00 15.00
21 Cesar King 4.00 10.00
22 Jason LaRue 4.00 10.00
23 Mike Lieberthal 6.00 15.00
24 Greg Maddux 100.00 200.00
25 Pedro Martinez 40.00 80.00
26 Gary Matthews Jr. 4.00 10.00
27 Orber Moreno 4.00 10.00
28 Eric Munson 4.00 10.00
29 Rafael Palmeiro 10.00 25.00
30 Jim Parque 4.00 10.00
31 Wily Pena 12.50 30.00
32 Cal Ripken 50.00 120.00
33 Alex Rodriguez 50.00 100.00
34 Tim Salmon 10.00 25.00
35 Chris Singleton 4.00 10.00
36 Alfonso Soriano 6.00 15.00
37 Ed Yarnall 4.00 10.00

2000 Fleer Tradition Grasskickers

COMPLETE SET (15) 15.00 40.00
STATED ODDS 1:30
GK1 Tony Gwynn 1.00 2.50
GK2 Scott Rolen .60 1.50
GK3 Nomar Garciaparra .60 1.50
GK4 Mike Piazza 1.00 2.50
GK5 Mark McGwire 1.50 4.00
GK6 Frank Thomas 1.00 2.50
GK7 Cal Ripken 3.00 8.00
GK8 Chipper Jones 1.00 2.50
GK9 Greg Maddux 1.25 3.00
GK10 Ken Griffey Jr. 2.00 5.00
GK11 Juan Gonzalez .40 1.00
GK12 Derek Jeter 2.50 6.00
GK13 Sammy Sosa 1.00 2.50
GK14 Roger Clemens 1.25 3.00
GK15 Alex Rodriguez 1.25 3.00

2000 Fleer Tradition Hall's Well

COMPLETE SET (15) 15.00 40.00
STATED ODDS 1:30
HW1 Mark McGwire 2.50 6.00
HW2 Alex Rodriguez 2.00 5.00
HW3 Cal Ripken 5.00 12.00
HW4 Chipper Jones 1.50 4.00
HW5 Derek Jeter 4.00 10.00
HW6 Frank Thomas 1.50 4.00
HW7 Greg Maddux 2.00 5.00
HW8 Juan Gonzalez .60 1.50
HW9 Ken Griffey Jr. 3.00 8.00
HW10 Mike Piazza 1.50 4.00
HW11 Nomar Garciaparra 1.00 2.50
HW12 Sammy Sosa 1.50 4.00
HW13 Roger Clemens 2.00 5.00
HW14 Ivan Rodriguez 1.00 2.50
HW15 Tony Gwynn 1.50 4.00

2000 Fleer Tradition Ripken Collection

COMPLETE SET (10) 1.50 30.00
COMMON CARD (1-10) 2.00 5.00
STATED ODDS 1:30

2000 Fleer Tradition Ten-4

COMPLETE SET (10) 8.00 20.00
STATED ODDS 1:18
TF1 Sammy Sosa .75 2.00
TF2 Nomar Garciaparra .50 1.25
TF3 Mike Piazza .75 2.00
TF4 Mark McGwire 1.25 3.00
TF5 Ken Griffey Jr. 1.50 4.00
TF6 Juan Gonzalez .30 .75
TF7 Derek Jeter 2.00 5.00
TF8 Chipper Jones .75 2.00
TF9 Cal Ripken 2.50 6.00
TF10 Alex Rodriguez 1.00 2.50

2000 Fleer Tradition Who To Watch

COMPLETE SET (15) 2.00 5.00
STATED ODDS 1:3
WW1 Rick Ankiel .30 .75
WW2 Matt Riley .20 .50
WW3 Wilton Veras .20 .50
WW4 Ben Petrick .20 .50
WW5 Chad Hermansen .20 .50
WW6 Peter Bergeron .20 .50
WW7 Mark Quinn .20 .50
WW8 Russell Branyan .20 .50
WW9 Alfonso Soriano .50 1.25
WW10 Randy Wolf .20 .50
WW11 Ben Davis .20 .50
WW12 Jeff DaVanon .20 .50
WW13 D'Angelo Jimenez .20 .50
WW14 Vernon Wells .20 .50
WW15 Adam Kennedy .20 .50

2000 Fleer Tradition Glossy Lumberjacks

ONE PER GLOSSY FACTORY SET
STATED PRINT RUNS LISTED BELOW
NO PRICING ON QTY OF 40 OR LESS
1 Edgardo Alfonzo/145 5.00 12.00
2 Roberto Alomar/627 6.00 15.00
3 Moises Alou/529 4.00 10.00
4 Carlos Beltran/489 4.00 10.00
5 Adrian Beltre/127 5.00 12.00
7 Barry Bonds/305 15.00 40.00
11 Eric Chavez/259 4.00 10.00
12 Tony Clark/70 6.00 15.00
13 Carlos Delgado/70 6.00 15.00
14 J.D. Drew/135 5.00 12.00
15 Erubiel Durazo/70 6.00 15.00
17 Carlos Febles/120 5.00 12.00
18 Jason Giambi/220 4.00 10.00
19 Shawn Green/429 4.00 10.00
20 Vladimir Guerrero/809 6.00 15.00
21 Derek Jeter/180 25.00 60.00
22 Chipper Jones/725 6.00 15.00
23 Gabe Kapler/160 5.00 12.00
25 Paul Konerko/70 6.00 15.00
28 Edgar Martinez/211 6.00 15.00
29 Raul Mondesi/458 4.00 10.00
31 Magglio Ordonez/190 5.00 12.00
33 Pokey Reese/110 5.00 12.00
34 Cal Ripken/235 30.00 80.00
35 Alex Rodriguez/292 15.00 40.00
36 Ivan Rodriguez/602 6.00 15.00
37 Scott Rolen/502 6.00 15.00
38 Chris Singleton/68 6.00 15.00
39 Alfonso Soriano/285 6.00 15.00
40 Frank Thomas/489 6.00 15.00
41 Jim Thome/479 6.00 15.00
42 Robin Ventura/114 5.00 12.00
43 Jose Vidro/60 6.00 15.00
44 Bernie Williams/215 6.00 15.00
45 Matt Williams/152 5.00 12.00

2000 Fleer Tradition Update

COMP.FACT.SET (149) 10.00 25.00
COMMON CARD (1-49/51-150) .12 .30
COMMON RC .12 .30
CARD NUMBER 50 DOES NOT EXIST
MANTLE JERSEY STATED ODDS 1:80 SETS
1 Ken Griffey Jr. SH .60 1.50
2 Cal Ripken SH 1.00 2.50
3 Randy Velarde SH .12 .30
4 Fred McGriff SH .20 .50
5 Derek Jeter SH .75 2.00
6 Tom Glavine SH .20 .50
7 Brent Mayne SH .12 .30
8 Alex Ochoa SH .12 .30
9 Scott Sheldon SH .12 .30
10 Randy Johnson SH .30 .75
11 Daniel Garibay RC .12 .30
12 Brad Fullmer .12 .30
13 Kazuhiro Sasaki RC .30 .75
14 Andy Tracy RC .12 .30
15 Bret Boone .12 .30
16 Chad Durbin RC .12 .30
17 Mark Buehrle RC 2.00 5.00
18 Julio Zuleta RC .12 .30
19 Jeremy Giambi .12 .30
20 Gene Stechschulte RC .12 .30

21 L.Pote .12 .30
B.Molina
22 Darrell Einertson RC .12 .30
23 Ken Griffey Jr. .60 1.50
24 J.Sparks RC .12 .30
D.Wheeler
25 Aaron Fultz RC .12 .30
26 Derek Bell .12 .30
27 R.Bell .12 .30
D.Cromer
28 Robert Fick .12 .30
29 Darryl Kile .12 .30
30 C.Andrews .12 .30
J.Bale RC
31 Dave Veres .12 .30
32 Hector Mercado RC .12 .30
33 Willie Morales RC .12 .30
34 K.Wunsch .12 .30
K.Wells
35 Hideki Irabu .12 .30
36 Sean DePaula RC .12 .30
37 D.Wise .12 .30
C.Woodward
38 Curt Schilling .20 .50
39 Mark Johnson .12 .30
40 Mike Cameron .12 .30
41 S.Sheldon .12 .30
T.Evans
42 Brett Tomko .12 .30
43 Johan Santana RC 2.00 5.00
44 Andy Benes .12 .30
45 M.LeCroy .12 .30
M.Redman
46 Ryan Klesko .12 .30
47 Andy Ashby .12 .30
48 Octavio Dotel .12 .30
49 Eric Byrnes RC .12 .30
51 Kenny Rogers .12 .30
52 Ben Weber RC .12 .30
53 M.Blank .12 .30
S.Strickland
54 Tom Goodwin .12 .30
55 Jim Edmonds Cards .12 .30
56 Derrick Turnbow RC .12 .30
57 Mark Mulder .12 .30
58 T.Brock .12 .30
R.Quevedo
59 Danny Young RC .12 .30
60 Fernando Vina .12 .30
61 Justin Brunette RC .12 .30
62 Jimmy Anderson .12 .30
63 Reggie Sanders .12 .30
64 Adam Kennedy .12 .30
65 J.Garcia .12 .30
B.Ryan
66 Al Martin .12 .30
67 Kevin Walker RC .12 .30
68 Brad Penny .12 .30
69 B.J. Surhoff .12 .30
70 G.Blum .12 .30
T.Coquillette RC
71 Jose Jimenez .12 .30
72 Chuck Finley .12 .30
73 V.De Los Santos .12 .30
E.Stull
74 Terry Adams
75 Rafael Furcal .20 .50
76 J.Roskos .12 .30
M.Darr
77 Quilvio Veras .12 .30
78 A.Almanza .12 .30
N.Rolison
79 Greg Vaughn .12 .30
80 Keith McDonald RC .12 .30
81 Eric Cammack RC .12 .30
82 H.Estrada .12 .30
R.King
83 Kory DeHaan .12 .30
84 Kevin Hodges RC .12 .30
85 Mike Lamb RC .12 .30
86 Shawn Green .12 .30
87 D.Reichert .12 .30
J.Rakers
88 Adam Piatt .12 .30
89 Mike Garcia .12 .30
90 Rodrigo Lopez RC .12 .30
91 John Olerud .12 .30
92 B.Zito RC 1.00 2.50
T.Long
93 Jimmy Rollins .20 .50
94 Denny Neagle .12 .30
95 Rickey Henderson .30 .75
96 A.Eaton .12 .30
B.Carlyle
97 Brian O'Connor RC .12 .30
98 Andy Thompson RC .12 .30
99 Jason Boyd RC .12 .30
100 J.Pineiro RC 1.50 4.00
C.Guillen
101 Raul Gonzalez RC .12 .30
102 Brandon Kolb RC .12 .30
103 J.Maxwell .12 .30
M.Lincoln
104 Luis Matos RC .12 .30
105 Morgan Burkhart RC .12 .30
106 I.Villegas .12 .30
S.Sisco RC
107 David Justice Yankees .12 .30
108 Pablo Ozuna .12 .30
109 Jose Canseco Yankees .20 .50
110 A.Cora .20 .50
S.Gilbert
111 Will Clark Cardinals .20 .50
112 K.Luuloa .12 .30
E.Weaver
113 Bruce Chen .12 .30
114 Adam Hyzdu .12 .30
115 S.Forster .12 .30
Y.Lara RC
116 A.McDill RC .12 .30
J.Macias
117 Kevin Nicholson .12 .30
118 I.Alcantara .12 .30
T.Young
119 Juan Alvarez RC .12 .30
120 J.Lugo .12 .30
M.Meluskey
121 B.J. Waszgis RC .12 .30
122 J.D'Amico RC .12 .30
B.Laxton
123 Ricky Ledee .12 .30
124 M.DeRosa .12 .30
J.Marquis
125 Alex Cabrera RC .12 .30
126 A.Ojeda RC .12 .30
G.Matthews Jr.
127 Richie Sexson .12 .30
128 S.Perez .12 .30
H.Ramirez RC
129 Rondell White .12 .30
130 Craig House RC .12 .30
131 K.Beirne .12 .30
J.Garland
132 Wayne Franklin RC .12 .30
133 Henry Rodriguez .12 .30
134 J.Payton .12 .30
J.Mann
135 Ron Gant .12 .30
136 P.Crawford .12 .30
S.Lee RC
137 Kent Bottenfield .12 .30
138 Rocky Biddle RC .12 .30
139 Travis Lee .12 .30
140 Ryan Vogelsong RC 1.25 3.00
141 J.Conti .12 .30
G.Guzman RC
142 M.Watson RC .12 .30
T.Drew
143 J.Parrish .12 .30
C.Richard RC
144 J.Cardona .12 .30
B.Villafuerte RC
145 T.Redman .12 .30
S.Sparks RC
146 B.Schneider .12 .30
M.Skrmetta RC
147 Pasqual Coco RC .12 .30
Leo Estrella RC
148 L.Barcelo RC .12 .30
J.Crede
149 Jace Brewer RC .12 .30
150 T.De La Rosa RC .12 .30
M.Bradley
MP1 Mickey Mantle Pants 30.00 80.00

2001 Fleer Tradition

COMP.FACT.SET (485) 30.00 60.00
COMPLETE SET (450) 15.00 40.00
COMMON CARD (1-450) .10 .30
COMMON CARD (451-485) .20 .50
451-485 DIST.ONLY IN FACTORY SETS
SHEET EXCHANGE DEADLINE: 03/01/02
1 Andres Galarraga .10 .30
2 Armando Rios .10 .30
3 Julio Lugo .10 .30
4 Darryl Hamilton .10 .30
5 Dave Veres .10 .30
6 Edgardo Alfonzo .10 .30
7 Brook Fordyce .10 .30
8 Eric Karros .10 .30
9 Neifi Perez .10 .30
10 Jim Edmonds .10 .30
11 Barry Larkin .20 .50
12 Trot Nixon .10 .30
13 Andy Pettitte .20 .50
14 Jose Guillen .10 .30
15 David Wells .10 .30
16 Magglio Ordonez .10 .30
17 David Segui .10 .30
17A David Segui ERR .10 .30
Card has no number on the back
18 Juan Encarnacion .10 .30
19 Robert Person .10 .30
20 Quilvio Veras .10 .30
21 Mo Vaughn .10 .30
22 B.J. Surhoff .10 .30
23 Ken Caminiti .10 .30
24 Frank Catalanotto .10 .30
25 Luis Gonzalez .10 .30
26 Pete Harnisch .10 .30
27 Alex Gonzalez .10 .30
28 Mark Quinn .10 .30
29 Luis Castillo .10 .30
30 Rick Helling .10 .30
31 Barry Bonds .75 2.00
32 Warren Morris .10 .30
33 Aaron Boone .10 .30
34 Ricky Gutierrez .10 .30
35 Preston Wilson .10 .30
36 Erubiel Durazo .10 .30
37 Jermaine Dye .10 .30
38 John Rocker .10 .30
39 Mark Grudzielanek .10 .30
40 Pedro Martinez .20 .50
41 Phil Nevin .10 .30
42 Luis Matos .10 .30
43 Orlando Hernandez .10 .30
44 Steve Cox .10 .30
45 James Baldwin .10 .30
46 Rafael Furcal .10 .30
47 Todd Zeile .10 .30
48 Elmer Dessens .10 .30
49 Russell Branyan .10 .30
50 Juan Gonzalez .10 .30
51 Mac Suzuki .10 .30
52 Adam Kennedy .10 .30
53 Randy Velarde .10 .30
54 David Bell .10 .30
55 Royce Clayton .10 .30
56 Greg Colbrunn .10 .30
57 Rey Ordonez .10 .30
58 Kevin Millwood .10 .30
59 Fernando Vina .10 .30
60 Eddie Taubensee .10 .30
61 Enrique Wilson .10 .30
62 Jay Bell .10 .30
63 Brian Moehler .10 .30
64 Brad Fullmer .10 .30
65 Ben Petrick .10 .30
66 Orlando Cabrera .10 .30
67 Shane Reynolds .10 .30
68 Mitch Meluskey .10 .30
69 Jeff Shaw .10 .30
70 Chipper Jones .30 .75
71 Tomo Ohka .10 .30
72 Ruben Rivera .10 .30
73 Mike Sirotka .10 .30
74 Scott Rolen .20 .50
75 Glendon Rusch .10 .30
76 Miguel Tejada .10 .30
77 Brady Anderson .10 .30
78 Bartolo Colon .10 .30
79 Ron Coomer .10 .30
80 Gary DiSarcina .10 .30
81 Geoff Jenkins .10 .30
82 Billy Koch .10 .30
83 Mike Lamb .10 .30
84 Alex Rodriguez .40 1.00
85 Denny Neagle .10 .30
86 Michael Tucker .10 .30
87 Edgar Renteria .10 .30
88 Brian Anderson .10 .30
89 Glenallen Hill .10 .30
90 Aramis Ramirez .10 .30
91 Rondell White .10 .30
92 Tony Womack .10 .30
93 Jeffrey Hammonds .10 .30
94 Freddy Garcia .10 .30
95 Bill Mueller .10 .30
96 Mike Lieberthal .10 .30
97 Michael Barrett .10 .30
98 Derrek Lee .20 .50
99 Bill Spiers .10 .30
100 Derek Lowe .10 .30
101 Javy Lopez .10 .30
102 Adrian Beltre .10 .30
103 Jim Parque .10 .30
104 Marquis Grissom .10 .30
105 Eric Chavez .10 .30
106 Todd Jones .10 .30
107 Eric Owens .10 .30
108 Roger Clemens .60 1.50
109 Denny Hocking .10 .30
110 Roberto Hernandez .10 .30
111 Albert Belle .10 .30
112 Troy Glaus .10 .30
113 Ivan Rodriguez .20 .50
114 Carlos Guillen .10 .30
115 Chuck Finley .10 .30
116 Dmitri Young .10 .30
117 Paul Konerko .10 .30
118 Damon Buford .10 .30
119 Fernando Tatis .10 .30
120 Larry Walker .10 .30
121 Jason Kendall .10 .30
122 Matt Williams .10 .30
123 Henry Rodriguez .10 .30
124 Placido Polanco .10 .30
125 Bobby Estalella .10 .30
126 Pat Burrell .10 .30
127 Mark Loretta .10 .30
128 Moises Alou .10 .30
129 Tino Martinez .20 .50
130 Milton Bradley .10 .30
131 Todd Hundley .10 .30
132 Keith Foulke .10 .30
133 Robert Fick .10 .30
134 Cristian Guzman .10 .30
135 Rusty Greer .10 .30
136 John Olerud .10 .30
137 Mariano Rivera .30 .75
138 Jeromy Burnitz .10 .30
139 Dave Burba .10 .30
140 Ken Griffey Jr. .60 1.50
141 Tony Gwynn .40 1.00
142 Carlos Delgado .10 .30
143 Edgar Martinez .20 .50
144 Ramon Hernandez .10 .30
145 Pedro Astacio .10 .30
146 Ray Lankford .10 .30
147 Mike Mussina .20 .50
148 Ray Durham .10 .30
149 Lee Stevens .10 .30
150 Jay Canizaro .10 .30
151 Adrian Brown .10 .30
152 Mike Piazza .50 1.25
153 Cliff Floyd .10 .30
154 Jose Vidro .10 .30
155 Jason Giambi .10 .30
156 Andruw Jones .20 .50
157 Robin Ventura .10 .30
158 Gary Sheffield .10 .30
159 Jeff D'Amico .10 .30
160 Chuck Knoblauch .10 .30
161 Roger Cedeno .10 .30
162 Jim Thome .20 .50
163 Peter Bergeron .10 .30
164 Kerry Wood .10 .30
165 Gabe Kapler .10 .30
166 Corey Koskie .10 .30
167 Doug Glanville .10 .30
168 Brent Mayne .10 .30
169 Scott Spiezio .10 .30
170 Steve Karsay .10 .30
171 Al Martin .10 .30
172 Fred McGriff .20 .50
173 Gabe White .10 .30
174 Alex Gonzalez .10 .30
175 Mike Darr .10 .30
176 Bengie Molina .10 .30
177 Ben Grieve .10 .30
178 Marlon Anderson .10 .30
179 Brian Giles .10 .30
180 Jose Valentin .10 .30
181 Brian Jordan .10 .30
182 Randy Johnson .30 .75
183 Ricky Ledee .10 .30
184 Russ Ortiz .10 .30
185 Mike Lowell .10 .30
186 Curtis Leskanic .10 .30
187 Bob Abreu .10 .30
188 Derek Jeter .75 2.00
189 Lance Berkman .10 .30
190 Roberto Alomar .20 .50
191 Darin Erstad .10 .30
192 Richie Sexson .10 .30
193 Alex Ochoa .10 .30
194 Carlos Febles .10 .30
195 David Ortiz .30 .75
196 Shawn Green .10 .30
197 Mike Sweeney .10 .30
198 Vladimir Guerrero .30 .75
199 Jose Jimenez .10 .30
200 Travis Lee .10 .30
201 Rickey Henderson .30 .75
202 Bob Wickman .10 .30
203 Miguel Cairo .10 .30
204 Steve Finley .10 .30
205 Tony Batista .10 .30
206 Jamey Wright .10 .30
207 Terrence Long .10 .30
208 Trevor Hoffman .10 .30
209 John VanderWal .10 .30
210 Greg Maddux .50 1.25
211 Tim Salmon .20 .50
212 Herbert Perry .10 .30
213 Marvin Benard .10 .30
214 Jose Offerman .10 .30
215 Jay Payton .10 .30
216 Jon Lieber .10 .30
217 Mark Kotsay .10 .30
218 Scott Brosius .10 .30
219 Scott Williamson .10 .30
220 Omar Vizquel .20 .50
221 Mike Hampton .10 .30
222 Richard Hidalgo .10 .30
223 Rey Sanchez .10 .30
224 Matt Lawton .10 .30
225 Bruce Chen .10 .30
226 Ryan Klesko .10 .30
227 Garret Anderson .10 .30
228 Kevin Brown .10 .30
229 Mike Cameron .10 .30
230 Tony Clark .10 .30
231 Curt Schilling .10 .30
232 Vinny Castilla .10 .30
233 Carl Pavano .10 .30
234 Eric Davis .10 .30
235 Darrin Fletcher .10 .30
236 Matt Stairs .10 .30
237 Octavio Dotel .10 .30
238 Mark Grace .20 .50
239 John Smoltz .20 .50
240 Matt Clement .10 .30
241 Ellis Burks .10 .30
242 Charles Johnson .10 .30
243 Jeff Bagwell .20 .50
244 Derek Bell .10 .30
245 Nomar Garciaparra .50 1.25
246 Jorge Posada .20 .50
247 Ryan Dempster .10 .30
248 J.T. Snow .10 .30
249 Eric Young .10 .30
250 Daryle Ward .10 .30
251 Joe Randa .10 .30
252 Travis Fryman .10 .30
253 Mike Williams .10 .30
254 Jacque Jones .10 .30
255 Scott Elarton .10 .30
256 Mark McGwire .75 2.00
257 Jay Buhner .10 .30
258 Randy Wolf .10 .30
259 Sammy Sosa .30 .75
260 Chan Ho Park .10 .30
261 Damion Easley .10 .30
262 Rick Ankiel .10 .30
263 Frank Thomas .30 .75
264 Kris Benson .10 .30
265 Luis Alicea .10 .30
266 Jeromy Giambi .10 .30
267 Geoff Blum .10 .30
268 Joe Girardi .10 .30
269 Livan Hernandez .10 .30
270 Jeff Conine .10 .30
271 Danny Graves .10 .30
272 Craig Biggio .20 .50
273 Jose Canseco .20 .50
274 Tom Glavine .20 .50
275 Ruben Mateo .10 .30
276 Jeff Kent .10 .30
277 Kevin Young .10 .30
278 A.J. Burnett .10 .30
279 Dante Bichette .10 .30
280 Sandy Alomar Jr. .10 .30
281 John Wetteland .10 .30
282 Torii Hunter .10 .30
283 Jarrod Washburn .10 .30
284 Rich Aurilia .10 .30
285 Jeff Cirillo .10 .30
286 Fernando Seguignol .10 .30
287 Darren Dreifort .10 .30
288 Deivi Cruz .10 .30
289 Pokey Reese .10 .30
290 Garrett Stephenson .10 .30
291 Bret Boone .10 .30
292 Tim Hudson .10 .30
293 John Flaherty .10 .30
294 Shannon Stewart .10 .30
295 Shawn Estes .10 .30
296 Wilton Guerrero .10 .30
297 Delino DeShields .10 .30
298 David Justice .10 .30
299 Harold Baines .10 .30
300 Al Leiter .10 .30
301 Wil Cordero .10 .30
302 Antonio Alfonseca .10 .30
303 Sean Casey .10 .30
304 Carlos Beltran .10 .30
305 Brad Radke .10 .30
306 Jason Varitek .30 .75
307 Shigetoshi Hasegawa .10 .30
308 Todd Stottlemyre .10 .30
309 Raul Mondesi .10 .30
310 Mike Bordick .10 .30
311 Darryl Kile .10 .30
312 Dean Palmer .10 .30
313 Johnny Damon .20 .50
314 Todd Helton .20 .50
315 Chad Hermansen .10 .30
316 Kevin Appier .10 .30
317 Greg Vaughn .10 .30
318 Robb Nen .10 .30
319 Jose Cruz Jr. .10 .30
320 Ron Belliard .10 .30
321 Bernie Williams .20 .50
322 Melvin Mora .10 .30
323 Kenny Lofton .10 .30
324 Armando Benitez .10 .30
325 Carlos Lee .10 .30
326 Damian Jackson .10 .30
327 Eric Milton .10 .30
328 J.D. Drew .10 .30
329 Byung-Hyun Kim .10 .30
330 Chris Stynes .10 .30
331 Kazuhiro Sasaki .10 .30
332 Troy O'Leary .10 .30
333 Pat Hentgen .10 .30
334 Brad Ausmus .10 .30
335 Todd Walker .10 .30
336 Jason Isringhausen .10 .30
337 Gerald Williams .10 .30
338 Aaron Sele .10 .30
339 Paul O'Neill .20 .50
340 Cal Ripken 1.00 2.50
341 Manny Ramirez .20 .50
342 Will Clark .20 .50
343 Mark Redman .10 .30
344 Bubba Trammell .10 .30
345 Troy Percival .10 .30
346 Chris Singleton .10 .30
347 Rafael Palmeiro .20 .50
348 Carl Everett .10 .30
349 Andy Benes .10 .30
350 Bobby Higginson .10 .30
351 Alex Cabrera .10 .30
352 Barry Zito .20 .50
353 Jace Brewer .10 .30
354 Paxton Crawford .10 .30
355 Oswaldo Mairena .10 .30
356 Joe Crede .30 .75
357 A.J. Pierzynski .10 .30
358 Daniel Garibay .10 .30
359 Jason Tyner .10 .30
360 Nate Rolison .10 .30
361 Scott Downs .10 .30
362 Keith Ginter .10 .30
363 Juan Pierre .10 .30
364 Adam Bernero .10 .30
365 Chris Richard .10 .30
366 Joey Nation .10 .30
367 Aubrey Huff .10 .30
368 Adam Eaton .10 .30
369 Jose Ortiz .10 .30
370 Eric Munson .10 .30
371 Matt Kinney .10 .30
372 Eric Byrnes .10 .30
373 Keith McDonald .10 .30
374 Matt Wise .10 .30
375 Timo Perez .10 .30
376 Julio Zuleta .10 .30
377 Jimmy Rollins .10 .30
378 Xavier Nady .10 .30
379 Ryan Kohlmeier .10 .30
380 Corey Patterson .10 .30
381 Todd Helton LL .10 .30
382 Moises Alou LL .10 .30
383 Vladimir Guerrero LL .20 .50
384 Luis Castillo LL .10 .30
385 Jeffrey Hammonds LL .10 .30
386 Nomar Garciaparra LL .30 .75
387 Carlos Delgado LL .10 .30
388 Darin Erstad LL .10 .30
389 Manny Ramirez LL .10 .30
390 Mike Sweeney LL .10 .30
391 Sammy Sosa LL .20 .50
392 Barry Bonds LL .40 1.00
393 Jeff Bagwell LL .10 .30
394 Richard Hidalgo LL .10 .30
395 Vladimir Guerrero LL .20 .50
396 Troy Glaus LL .10 .30
397 Frank Thomas LL .20 .50
398 Carlos Delgado LL .10 .30
399 David Justice LL .10 .30
400 Jason Giambi LL .10 .30
401 Randy Johnson LL .20 .50
402 Kevin Brown LL .10 .30
403 Greg Maddux LL .30 .75
404 Al Leiter LL .10 .30
405 Mike Hampton LL .10 .30
406 Pedro Martinez LL .20 .50
407 Roger Clemens LL .30 .75
408 Mike Sirotka LL .10 .30
409 Mike Mussina LL .10 .30
410 Bartolo Colon LL .10 .30
411 Subway Series WS .20 .50
412 Jose Vizcaino WS .20 .50
413 Jose Vizcaino WS .20 .50
414 Roger Clemens WS .30 .75
415 Benitez .10 .30
Alfonzo
Perez WS
416 Al Leiter WS .20 .50
417 Luis Sojo WS .20 .50
418 Yankees 3-Peat WS .30 .75
419 Derek Jeter WS .40 1.00
420 Toast of the Town WS .20 .50
421 Atlanta Braves CL .10 .30
422 New York Mets CL .30 .75
423 Florida Marlins CL .10 .30
424 Philadelphia Phillies CL .10 .30
425 Montreal Expos CL .10 .30
426 St. Louis Cardinals CL .10 .30
427 Cincinnati Reds CL .15 .40
428 Chicago Cubs CL .20 .50
429 Milwaukee Brewers CL .10 .30
430 Houston Astros CL .10 .30
431 Pittsburgh Pirates CL .20 .50
432 San Francisco Giants CL .10 .30
433 Arizona Diamondbacks CL .10 .30
434 Los Angeles Dodgers CL UER .10 .30
435 Colorado Rockies CL UER .10 .30
436 San Diego Padres CL .10 .30
437 New York Yankees CL .30 .75
438 Boston Red Sox CL .20 .50
439 Baltimore Orioles CL .10 .30
440 Toronto Blue Jays CL .10 .30
441 Tampa Bay Devil Rays CL .10 .30
442 Chicago White Sox CL .20 .50
443 Cleveland Indians CL .10 .30
444 Detoit Tigers CL .10 .30
445 Kansas City Royals CL .10 .30
446 Minnesota Twins CL .10 .30
447 Seattle Mariners CL .10 .30
448 Oakland Athletics CL .10 .30
449 Anaheim Angels CL .10 .30
450 Texas Rangers CL .10 .30
451 Albert Pujols RC 15.00 40.00
452 Ichiro Suzuki RC 12.00 30.00
453 Tsuyoshi Shinjo RC .30 .75
454 Johnny Estrada RC .30 .75
455 Elpidio Guzman RC .20 .50
456 Adrian Hernandez RC .20 .50
457 Rafael Soriano RC .20 .50
458 Drew Henson RC .30 .75
459 Juan Uribe RC .30 .75
460 Matt White RC .20 .50
461 Endy Chavez RC .20 .50
462 Bud Smith RC .20 .50
463 Morgan Ensberg RC 1.00 2.50
464 Jay Gibbons RC .30 .75
465 Jackson Melian RC .20 .50
466 Junior Spivey RC .30 .75
467 Juan Cruz RC .20 .50
468 Wilson Betemit RC 1.00 2.50
469 Alexis Gomez RC .20 .50
470 Mark Teixeira RC 5.00 12.00
471 Erick Almonte RC .20 .50
472 Travis Hafner RC 3.00 8.00
473 Carlos Valderrama RC .20 .50
474 Brandon Duckworth RC .20 .50
475 Ryan Freel RC .60 1.50
476 Wilkin Ruan RC .20 .50
477 Andres Torres RC .20 .50
478 Josh Towers RC .30 .75
479 Kyle Lohse RC .30 .75
480 Jason Michaels RC .20 .50
481 Alfonso Soriano .30 .75
482 C.C. Sabathia .20 .50
483 Roy Oswalt .50 1.25
484 Ben Sheets .30 .75
485 Adam Dunn .30 .75

2001 Fleer Tradition Diamond Tributes

COMPLETE SET (30) 30.00 60.00
STATED ODDS 1:7
DT1 Jackie Robinson .60 1.50
DT2 Mike Piazza 1.00 2.50
DT3 Alex Rodriguez .75 2.00
DT4 Barry Bonds 1.50 4.00
DT5 Nomar Garciaparra 1.00 2.50
DT6 Roger Clemens 1.25 3.00
DT7 Ivan Rodriguez .40 1.00
DT8 Cal Ripken 2.00 5.00
DT9 Manny Ramirez .40 1.00
DT10 Chipper Jones .60 1.50
DT11 Barry Larkin .40 1.00
DT12 Carlos Delgado .40 1.00
DT13 J.D. Drew .40 1.00
DT14 Carl Everett .40 1.00
DT15 Todd Helton .40 1.00
DT16 Greg Maddux 1.00 2.50
DT17 Scott Rolen .40 1.00
DT18 Troy Glaus .40 1.00
DT19 Brian Giles .40 1.00
DT20 Jeff Bagwell .40 1.00
DT21 Sammy Sosa .60 1.50
DT22 Randy Johnson .60 1.50
DT23 Andruw Jones .40 1.00
DT24 Ken Griffey Jr. 1.25 3.00
DT25 Mark McGwire 1.50 4.00
DT26 Derek Jeter 1.50 4.00
DT27 Vladimir Guerrero .60 1.50
DT28 Frank Thomas .60 1.50
DT29 Pedro Martinez .40 1.00
DT30 Bernie Williams .40 1.00

2001 Fleer Tradition Grass Roots

COMPLETE SET (15) 30.00 60.00
STATED ODDS 1:18
GR1 Derek Jeter 2.50 6.00
GR2 Greg Maddux 1.50 4.00
GR3 Sammy Sosa 1.00 2.50
GR4 Alex Rodriguez 1.25 3.00
GR5 Vladimir Guerrero 1.00 2.50
GR6 Scott Rolen .60 1.50
GR7 Frank Thomas 1.00 2.50
GR8 Nomar Garciaparra 1.50 4.00
GR9 Cal Ripken 3.00 8.00
GR10 Mike Piazza 1.50 4.00
GR11 Ivan Rodriguez .60 1.50
GR12 Chipper Jones 1.00 2.50
GR13 Tony Gwynn 1.25 3.00
GR14 Ken Griffey Jr. 2.00 5.00
GR15 Mark McGwire 2.50 6.00

2001 Fleer Tradition Lumber Company

COMPLETE SET (20) 25.00 50.00
STATED ODDS 1:12
LC1 Vladimir Guerrero .75 2.00
LC2 Mo Vaughn .40 1.00
LC3 Ken Griffey Jr. 1.50 4.00
LC4 Juan Gonzalez .40 1.00
LC5 Tony Gwynn 1.00 2.50
LC6 Jim Edmonds .40 1.00
LC7 Jason Giambi .40 1.00
LC8 Alex Rodriguez 1.00 2.50
LC9 Derek Jeter 2.00 5.00
LC10 Darin Erstad .40 1.00
LC11 Andruw Jones .50 1.25
LC12 Cal Ripken 2.50 6.00
LC13 Magglio Ordonez .40 1.00
LC14 Nomar Garciaparra 1.25 3.00
LC15 Chipper Jones .75 2.00
LC16 Sean Casey .40 1.00
LC17 Shawn Green .40 1.00
LC18 Mike Piazza 1.25 3.00
LC19 Sammy Sosa .75 2.00
LC20 Barry Bonds 2.00 5.00

2001 Fleer Tradition Stitches in Time

COMPLETE SET (24) 15.00 40.00
STATED ODDS 1:18
ST2 Ernie Banks 2.00 5.00
ST3 Cool Papa Bell 2.00 5.00
ST4 Joe Black 1.25 3.00
ST5 Roy Campanella 2.50 6.00
ST6 Ray Dandridge 1.25 3.00
ST7 Leon Day 1.25 3.00
ST8 Larry Doby 1.25 3.00
ST9 Josh Gibson 2.00 5.00
ST10 Elston Howard 1.25 3.00
ST11 Monte Irvin 1.25 3.00
ST12 Buck Leonard 1.25 3.00
ST13 Max Manning 1.25 3.00
ST14 Willie Mays 4.00 10.00
ST15 Buck O'Neil 1.25 3.00
ST16 Satchel Paige 2.00 5.00
ST17 Ted Radcliffe 1.25 3.00
ST18 Jackie Robinson 2.00 5.00
ST19 Bill Perkins 1.25 3.00
ST20 Rube Foster 2.00 5.00
ST21 Judy Johnson 1.25 3.00
ST22 Oscar Charleston 1.25 3.00
ST23 Pop Lloyd 1.25 3.00
ST24 Artie Wilson 1.25 3.00
ST25 Sam Jethroe 1.25 3.00
NNO Henry Kimbro 1.25 3.00

2001 Fleer Tradition Stitches in Time Autographs

GAME-USED OR AUTO CARD 1:4 BOXES
1 Ernie Banks 40.00 100.00
2 Joe Black 12.50 30.00
3 Monte Irvin 12.00 30.00
4 Willie Mays 100.00 200.00
5 Buck O'Neil 15.00 40.00
6 Ted Radcliffe 10.00 25.00
7 Artie Wilson 10.00 25.00

2001 Fleer Tradition Stitches in Time Memorabilia

GAME-USED OR AUTO CARD 1:4 BOXES
1 Roy Campanella Bat 15.00 40.00
2 Larry Doby Bat 15.00 40.00
3 Elston Howard Bat 20.00 50.00
4 Willie Mays Pants 25.00 60.00
5 Jackie Robinson Pants 60.00 120.00

2001 Fleer Tradition Turn Back the Clock Game Jersey

GAME-USED OR AUTO CARD 1:4 BOXES
TBC1 Tom Glavine 6.00 15.00
TBC2 Greg Maddux 15.00 40.00
TBC3 Sean Casey 4.00 10.00
TBC4 Pokey Reese 4.00 10.00
TBC5 Jason Giambi 4.00 10.00
TBC6 Tim Hudson 4.00 10.00
TBC7 Larry Walker 4.00 10.00
TBC8 Jeffrey Hammonds 4.00 10.00
TBC9 Scott Rolen 6.00 15.00
TBC10 Pat Burrell 4.00 10.00
TBC11 Chipper Jones 6.00 15.00
TBC12 Greg Maddux 15.00 40.00
TBC13 Troy Glaus 4.00 10.00
TBC14 Tony Gwynn 10.00 25.00
TBC15 Cal Ripken 10.00 25.00
TBC16 T.Glavine/G.Maddux 40.00 80.00
TBC17 S.Casey/P.Reese 15.00 40.00
TBC18 C.Jones/G.Maddux 15.00 40.00
TBC19 L.Walker/J.Hammonds 15.00 40.00
TBC20 S.Rolen/P.Burrell 15.00 40.00
TBC21 J.Giambi/T.Hudson 10.00 25.00

2001 Fleer Tradition Warning Track

COMPLETE SET (23) 150.00 250.00
STATED ODDS 1:72
WT1 Josh Gibson 4.00 10.00
WT3 Willie Mays 6.00 15.00
WT4 Mark McGwire 8.00 20.00
WT7 Jose Canseco 2.00 5.00
WT8 Ken Griffey Jr. 6.00 15.00
WT9 Cal Ripken 10.00 25.00
WT10 Rafael Palmeiro 2.00 5.00
WT11 Sammy Sosa 3.00 8.00
WT12 Juan Gonzalez 2.00 5.00
WT13 Frank Thomas 3.00 8.00
WT14 Jeff Bagwell 2.00 5.00
WT15 Gary Sheffield 2.00 5.00
WT16 Larry Walker 2.00 5.00
WT17 Mike Piazza 5.00 12.00
WT18 Larry Doby 2.00 5.00
WT19 Roy Campanella 4.00 10.00
WT20 Manny Ramirez 2.00 5.00
WT21 Chipper Jones 3.00 8.00
WT22 Alex Rodriguez 4.00 10.00
WT23 Ivan Rodriguez 2.00 5.00
WT24 Vladimir Guerrero 3.00 8.00
WT25 Nomar Garciaparra 5.00 12.00

2002 Fleer Tradition

COMPLETE SET (500) 30.00 60.00
COMP.SET w/o SP's (400) 10.00 25.00
COMMON CARD (101-500) .10 .30
COMMON SP (1-100) 1.25 3.00
1-100 SP STATED ODDS 1:2
COMMON CARD (436-470) .20 .50
1 Barry Bonds SP 5.00 12.00
2 Cal Ripken SP 6.00 15.00
3 Tony Gwynn SP 2.50 6.00
4 Brad Radke SP 1.25 3.00
5 Jose Ortiz SP 1.25 3.00
6 Mark Mulder SP 1.25 3.00
7 Jon Lieber SP 1.25 3.00
8 John Olerud SP 1.25 3.00
9 Phil Nevin SP 1.25 3.00
10 Craig Biggio SP 1.25 3.00
11 Pedro Martinez SP 1.25 3.00
12 Fred McGriff SP 1.25 3.00
13 Vladimir Guerrero SP 2.00 5.00
14 Jason Giambi SP 1.25 3.00
15 Mark Kotsay SP 1.25 3.00
16 Bud Smith SP 1.25 3.00
17 Kevin Brown SP 1.25 3.00
18 Darin Erstad SP 1.25 3.00
19 Julio Franco SP 1.25 3.00
20 C.C. Sabathia SP 1.25 3.00
21 Larry Walker SP 1.25 3.00
22 Doug Mientkiewicz SP 1.25 3.00
23 Luis Gonzalez SP 1.25 3.00
24 Albert Pujols SP 4.00 10.00
25 Brian Lawrence SP 1.25 3.00
26 Al Leiter SP 1.25 3.00
27 Mike Sweeney SP 1.25 3.00

28 Jeff Weaver SP 1.25 3.00
29 Matt Morris SP 1.25 3.00
30 Hideo Nomo SP 2.00 5.00
31 Tom Glavine SP 1.25 3.00
32 Magglio Ordonez SP 1.25 3.00
33 Roberto Alomar SP 1.25 3.00
34 Roger Cedeno SP 1.25 3.00
35 Greg Vaughn SP 1.25 3.00
36 Chan Ho Park SP 1.25 3.00
37 Rich Aurilia SP 1.25 3.00
38 Tsuyoshi Shinjo SP 1.25 3.00
39 Eric Young SP 1.25 3.00
40 Bobby Higginson SP 1.25 3.00
41 Marlon Anderson SP 1.25 3.00
42 Mark Grace SP 1.25 3.00
43 Steve Cox SP 1.25 3.00
44 Cliff Floyd SP 1.25 3.00
45 Brian Roberts SP 1.25 3.00
46 Paul Konerko SP 1.25 3.00
47 Brandon Duckworth SP 1.25 3.00
48 Josh Beckett SP 1.25 3.00
49 David Ortiz SP 2.00 5.00
50 Geoff Jenkins SP 1.25 3.00
51 Ruben Sierra SP 1.25 3.00
52 John Franco SP 1.25 3.00
53 Einar Diaz SP 1.25 3.00
54 Luis Castillo SP 1.25 3.00
55 Mark Quinn SP 1.25 3.00
56 Shea Hillenbrand SP 1.25 3.00
57 Rafael Palmeiro SP 1.25 3.00
58 Paul O'Neill SP 1.25 3.00
59 Andruw Jones SP 1.25 3.00
60 Lance Berkman SP 1.25 3.00
61 Jimmy Rollins SP 1.25 3.00
62 Jose Hernandez SP 1.25 3.00
63 Rusty Greer SP 1.25 3.00
64 Wade Miller SP 1.25 3.00
65 David Eckstein SP 1.25 3.00
66 Jose Valentin SP 1.25 3.00
67 Javier Vazquez SP 1.25 3.00
68 Roger Clemens SP 4.00 10.00
69 Omar Vizquel SP 1.25 3.00
70 Roy Oswalt SP 1.25 3.00
71 Shannon Stewart SP 1.25 3.00
72 Byung-Hyun Kim SP 1.25 3.00
73 Jay Gibbons SP 1.25 3.00
74 Barry Larkin SP 1.25 3.00
75 Brian Giles SP 1.25 3.00
76 Andres Galarraga SP 1.25 3.00
77 Sammy Sosa SP 2.00 5.00
78 Manny Ramirez SP 1.25 3.00
79 Carlos Delgado SP 1.25 3.00
80 Jorge Posada SP 1.25 3.00
81 Todd Ritchie SP 1.25 3.00
82 Russ Ortiz SP 1.25 3.00
83 Brent Mayne SP 1.25 3.00
84 Mike Mussina SP 1.25 3.00
85 Raul Mondesi SP 1.25 3.00
86 Mark Loretta SP 1.25 3.00
87 Tim Raines SP 1.25 3.00
88 Ichiro Suzuki SP 4.00 10.00
89 Juan Pierre SP 1.25 3.00
90 Adam Dunn SP 1.25 3.00
91 Jason Tyner SP 1.25 3.00
92 Miguel Tejada SP 1.25 3.00
93 Elpidio Guzman SP 1.25 3.00
94 Freddy Garcia SP 1.25 3.00
95 Marcus Giles SP 1.25 3.00
96 Junior Spivey SP 1.25 3.00
97 Aramis Ramirez SP 1.25 3.00
98 Jose Rijo SP 1.25 3.00
99 Paul LoDuca SP 1.25 3.00
100 Mike Cameron SP 1.25 3.00
101 Alex Hernandez .10 .30
102 Benji Gil .10 .30
103 Benito Santiago .10 .30
104 Bobby Abreu .10 .30
105 Brad Penny .10 .30
106 Calvin Murray .10 .30
107 Chad Durbin .10 .30
108 Chris Singleton .10 .30
109 Chris Carpenter .10 .30
110 David Justice .10 .30
111 Eric Chavez .10 .30
112 Fernando Tatis .10 .30
113 Frank Castillo .10 .30
114 Jason LaRue .10 .30
115 Jim Edmonds .10 .30
116 Joe Kennedy .10 .30
117 Jose Jimenez .10 .30
118 Josh Towers .10 .30
119 Junior Herndon .10 .30
120 Luke Prokopec .10 .30
121 Mac Suzuki .10 .30
122 Mark DeRosa .10 .30
123 Marty Cordova .10 .30
124 Michael Tucker .10 .30
125 Michael Young .30 .75
126 Robin Ventura .10 .30
127 Shane Halter .10 .30
128 Shane Reynolds .10 .30
129 Tony Womack .10 .30
130 A.J. Pierzynski .10 .30
131 Aaron Rowand .10 .30
132 Antonio Alfonseca .10 .30
133 Arthur Rhodes .10 .30
134 Bob Wickman .10 .30
135 Brady Clark .10 .30
136 Chad Hermansen .10 .30
137 Marlon Byrd .10 .30
138 Dan Wilson .10 .30
139 David Cone .10 .30
140 Dean Palmer .10 .30
141 Denny Neagle .10 .30
142 Derek Jeter .75 2.00
143 Erubiel Durazo .10 .30
144 Felix Rodriguez .10 .30
145 Jason Hart .10 .30
146 Jay Bell .10 .30
147 Jeff Suppan .10 .30
148 Jeff Zimmerman .10 .30
149 Kerry Wood .10 .30
150 Kerry Robinson .10 .30
151 Kevin Appier .10 .30
152 Michael Barrett .10 .30
153 Mo Vaughn .10 .30
154 Rafael Furcal .10 .30
155 Sidney Ponson .10 .30
156 Terry Adams .10 .30
157 Tim Redding .10 .30
158 Toby Hall .10 .30
159 Aaron Sele .10 .30
160 Bartolo Colon .10 .30
161 Brad Ausmus .10 .30
162 Carlos Pena .10 .30
163 Jace Brewer .10 .30
164 David Wells .10 .30
165 David Segui .10 .30
166 Derek Lowe .10 .30
167 Derek Bell .10 .30
168 Jason Grabowski .10 .30
169 Johnny Damon .20 .50
170 Jose Mesa .10 .30
171 Juan Encarnacion .10 .30
172 Ken Caminiti .10 .30
173 Ken Griffey Jr. .60 1.50
174 Luis Rivas .10 .30
175 Mariano Rivera .30 .75
176 Mark Grudzielanek .10 .30
177 Mark McGwire .75 2.00
178 Mike Bordick .10 .30
179 Mike Hampton .10 .30
180 Nick Bierbrodt .10 .30
181 Paul Byrd .10 .30
182 Robb Nen .10 .30
183 Ryan Dempster .10 .30
184 Ryan Klesko .10 .30
185 Scott Spiezio .10 .30
186 Scott Strickland .10 .30
187 Todd Zeile .10 .30
188 Tom Gordon .10 .30
189 Troy Glaus .10 .30
190 Matt Williams .10 .30
191 Wes Helms .10 .30
192 Jerry Hairston Jr. .10 .30
193 Brook Fordyce .10 .30
194 Nomar Garciaparra .50 1.25
195 Kevin Tapani .10 .30
196 Mark Buehrle .10 .30
197 Dmitri Young .10 .30
198 John Rocker .10 .30
199 Juan Uribe .10 .30
200 Matt Anderson .10 .30
201 Alex Gonzalez .10 .30
202 Julio Lugo .10 .30
203 Roberto Hernandez .10 .30
204 Richie Sexson .10 .30
205 Corey Koskie .10 .30
206 Tony Armas Jr. .10 .30
207 Rey Ordonez .10 .30
208 Orlando Hernandez .10 .30
209 Pokey Reese .10 .30
210 Mike Lieberthal .10 .30
211 Kris Benson .10 .30
212 Jermaine Dye .10 .30
213 Livan Hernandez .10 .30
214 Bret Boone .10 .30
215 Dustin Hermanson .10 .30
216 Placido Polanco .10 .30
217 Jesus Colome .10 .30
218 Alex Gonzalez .10 .30
219 Adam Everett .10 .30
220 Adam Piatt .10 .30
221 Brad Fullmer .10 .30
222 Brian Buchanan .10 .30
223 Chipper Jones .30 .75
224 Chuck Finley .10 .30
225 David Bell .10 .30
226 Jack Wilson .10 .30
227 Jason Bere .10 .30
228 Jeff Conine .10 .30
229 Jeff Bagwell .20 .50
230 Joe McEwing .10 .30
231 Kip Wells .10 .30
232 Mike Lansing .10 .30
233 Neifi Perez .10 .30
234 Omar Daal .10 .30
235 Reggie Sanders .10 .30
236 Shawn Wooten .10 .30
237 Shawn Chacon .10 .30
238 Shawn Estes .10 .30
239 Steve Sparks .10 .30
240 Steve Kline .10 .30
241 Tino Martinez .20 .50
242 Tyler Houston .10 .30
243 Xavier Nady .10 .30
244 Bengie Molina .10 .30
245 Ben Davis .10 .30
246 Casey Fossum .10 .30
247 Chris Stynes .10 .30
248 Danny Graves .10 .30
249 Pedro Feliz .10 .30
250 Darren Oliver .10 .30
251 Dave Veres .10 .30
252 Deivi Cruz .10 .30
253 Desi Relaford .10 .30
254 Devon White .10 .30
255 Edgar Martinez .20 .50
256 Eric Munson .10 .30
257 Eric Karros .10 .30
258 Homer Bush .10 .30
259 Jason Kendall .10 .30
260 Javy Lopez .10 .30
261 Keith Foulke .10 .30
262 Keith Ginter .10 .30
263 Nick Johnson .10 .30
264 Pat Burrell .10 .30
265 Ricky Gutierrez .10 .30
266 Russ Johnson .10 .30
267 Steve Finley .10 .30
268 Terrence Long .10 .30
269 Tony Batista .10 .30
270 Torii Hunter .10 .30
271 Vinny Castilla .10 .30
272 A.J. Burnett .10 .30
273 Adrian Beltre .10 .30
274 Alex Rodriguez .40 1.00
275 Armando Benitez .10 .30
276 Billy Koch .10 .30
277 Brady Anderson .10 .30
278 Brian Jordan .10 .30
279 Carlos Febles .10 .30
280 Daryle Ward .10 .30
281 Eli Marrero .10 .30
282 Garret Anderson .10 .30
283 Jack Cust .10 .30
284 Jacque Jones .10 .30
285 Jamie Moyer .10 .30
286 Jeffrey Hammonds .10 .30
287 Jim Thome .20 .50
288 Jon Garland .10 .30
289 Jose Offerman .10 .30
290 Matt Stairs .10 .30
291 Orlando Cabrera .10 .30
292 Ramiro Mendoza .10 .30
293 Ray Durham .10 .30
294 Rickey Henderson .30 .75
295 Rob Mackowiak .10 .30
296 Scott Rolen .20 .50
297 Tim Hudson .10 .30
298 Todd Helton .20 .50
299 Tony Clark .10 .30
300 B.J. Surhoff .10 .30
301 Bernie Williams .20 .50
302 Bill Mueller .10 .30
303 Chris Richard .10 .30
304 Craig Paquette .10 .30
305 Curt Schilling .10 .30
306 Damian Jackson .10 .30
307 Derrek Lee .20 .50
308 Eric Milton .10 .30
309 Frank Catalanotto .10 .30
310 J.T. Snow .10 .30
311 Jared Sandberg .10 .30
312 Jason Varitek .30 .75
313 Jeff Cirillo .10 .30
314 Jeromy Burnitz .10 .30
315 Joe Crede .10 .30
316 Joel Pineiro .10 .30
317 Jose Cruz Jr. .10 .30
318 Kevin Young .10 .30
319 Marquis Grissom .10 .30
320 Moises Alou .10 .30
321 Randall Simon .10 .30
322 Royce Clayton .10 .30
323 Tim Salmon .20 .50
324 Travis Fryman .10 .30
325 Travis Lee .10 .30
326 Vance Wilson .10 .30
327 Jarrod Washburn .10 .30
328 Ben Petrick .10 .30
329 Ben Grieve .10 .30
330 Carl Everett .10 .30
331 Eric Byrnes .10 .30
332 Doug Glanville .10 .30
333 Edgardo Alfonzo .10 .30
334 Ellis Burks .10 .30
335 Gabe Kapler .10 .30
336 Gary Sheffield .10 .30
337 Greg Maddux .50 1.25
338 J.D. Drew .10 .30
339 Jamey Wright .10 .30
340 Jeff Kent .10 .30
341 Jeremy Giambi .10 .30
342 Joe Randa .10 .30
343 Joe Mays .10 .30
344 Jose Macias .10 .30
345 Kazuhiro Sasaki .10 .30
346 Mike Kinkade .10 .30
347 Mike Lowell .10 .30
348 Randy Johnson .30 .75
349 Randy Wolf .10 .30
350 Richard Hidalgo .10 .30
351 Ron Coomer .10 .30
352 Sandy Alomar Jr. .10 .30
353 Sean Casey .10 .30
354 Trevor Hoffman .10 .30
355 Adam Eaton .10 .30
356 Alfonso Soriano .10 .30
357 Barry Zito .10 .30
358 Billy Wagner .10 .30
359 Brent Abernathy .10 .30
360 Bret Prinz .10 .30
361 Carlos Beltran .10 .30
362 Carlos Guillen .10 .30
363 Charles Johnson .10 .30
364 Cristian Guzman .10 .30
365 Damion Easley .10 .30
366 Darryl Kile .10 .30
367 Delino DeShields .10 .30
368 Eric Davis .10 .30
369 Frank Thomas .30 .75
370 Ivan Rodriguez .20 .50
371 Jay Payton .10 .30
372 Jeff D'Amico .10 .30
373 John Burkett .10 .30
374 Melvin Mora .10 .30
375 Ramon Ortiz .10 .30
376 Robert Person .10 .30
377 Russell Branyan .10 .30
378 Shawn Green .10 .30
379 Todd Hollandsworth .10 .30
380 Tony McKnight .10 .30
381 Trot Nixon .10 .30
382 Vernon Wells .10 .30
383 Troy Percival .10 .30
384 Albie Lopez .10 .30
385 Alex Ochoa .10 .30
386 Andy Pettitte .20 .50
387 Brandon Inge .10 .30
388 Bubba Trammell .10 .30
389 Corey Patterson .10 .30
390 Damian Rolls .10 .30
391 Dee Brown .10 .30
392 Edgar Renteria .10 .30
393 Eric Gagne .10 .30
394 Jason Johnson .10 .30
395 Jeff Nelson .10 .30
396 John Vander Wal .10 .30
397 Johnny Estrada .10 .30
398 Jose Canseco .20 .50
399 Juan Gonzalez .10 .30
400 Kevin Millwood .10 .30
401 Lee Stevens .10 .30
402 Matt Lawton .10 .30
403 Mike Lamb .10 .30
404 Octavio Dotel .10 .30
405 Ramon Hernandez .10 .30
406 Ruben Quevedo .10 .30
407 Todd Walker .10 .30
408 Troy O'Leary .10 .30
409 Wascar Serrano .10 .30
410 Aaron Boone .10 .30
411 Aubrey Huff .10 .30
412 Ben Sheets .10 .30
413 Carlos Lee .10 .30
414 Chuck Knoblauch .10 .30
415 Steve Karsay .10 .30
416 Dante Bichette .10 .30
417 David Dellucci .10 .30
418 Esteban Loaiza .10 .30
419 Fernando Vina .10 .30
420 Ismael Valdes .10 .30
421 Jason Isringhausen .10 .30
422 Jeff Shaw .10 .30
423 John Smoltz .20 .50
424 Jose Vidro .10 .30
425 Kenny Lofton .10 .30
426 Mark Little .10 .30
427 Mark McLemore .10 .30
428 Marvin Benard .10 .30
429 Mike Piazza .50 1.25
430 Pat Hentgen .10 .30
431 Preston Wilson .10 .30
432 Rick Helling .10 .30
433 Robert Fick .10 .30
434 Rondell White .10 .30
435 Adam Kennedy .10 .30
436 David Espinosa PROS .20 .50
437 Dewon Brazelton PROS .20 .50
438 Drew Henson PROS .20 .50
439 Juan Cruz PROS .20 .50
440 Jason Jennings PROS .20 .50
441 Carlos Garcia PROS .20 .50
442 Carlos Hernandez PROS .20 .50
443 Wilkin Ruan PROS .20 .50
444 Wilson Betemit PROS .20 .50
445 Horacio Ramirez PROS .20 .50
446 Danys Baez PROS .20 .50
447 Abraham Nunez PROS .20 .50
448 Josh Hamilton .40 1.00
449 Chris George PROS .20 .50
450 Rick Bauer PROS .20 .50
451 Donnie Bridges PROS .20 .50
452 Erick Almonte PROS .20 .50
453 Cory Aldridge PROS .20 .50
454 Ryan Drese PROS .20 .50
455 Jason Romano PROS .20 .50
456 Corky Miller PROS .20 .50
457 Rafael Soriano PROS .20 .50
458 Mark Prior PROS .50 1.25
459 Mark Teixeira PROS .50 1.25
460 Adrian Hernandez PROS .20 .50
461 Tim Spooneybarger PROS .20 .50
462 Bill Ortega PROS .20 .50
463 D'Angelo Jimenez PROS .20 .50
464 Andres Torres PROS .20 .50
465 Alexis Gomez PROS .20 .50
466 Angel Berroa PROS .20 .50
467 Henry Mateo PROS .20 .50
468 Endy Chavez PROS .20 .50
469 Billy Sylvester PROS .20 .50
470 Nate Frese PROS .20 .50
471 Luis Gonzalez BNR .10 .30
472 Barry Bonds BNR .75 2.00
473 Rich Aurilia BNR .10 .30
474 Albert Pujols BNR .60 1.50
475 Todd Helton BNR .20 .50
476 Moises Alou BNR .10 .30
477 Lance Berkman BNR .10 .30
478 Brian Giles BNR .10 .30
479 Cliff Floyd BNR .10 .30
480 Sammy Sosa BNR .30 .75
481 Shawn Green BNR .10 .30
482 Jon Lieber BNR .10 .30
483 Matt Morris BNR .10 .30
484 Curt Schilling BNR .10 .30
485 Randy Johnson BNR .20 .50
486 Manny Ramirez BNR .20 .50
487 Ichiro Suzuki BNR .60 1.50
488 Juan Gonzalez BNR .10 .30
489 Derek Jeter BNR .75 2.00
490 Alex Rodriguez BNR .40 1.00
491 Bret Boone BNR .10 .30
492 Roberto Alomar BNR .20 .50
493 Jason Giambi BNR .10 .30
494 Rafael Palmeiro BNR .20 .50
495 Doug Mientkiewicz BNR .10 .30
496 Jim Thome BNR .10 .30
497 Freddy Garcia BNR .10 .30
498 Mark Buehrle BNR .10 .30
499 Mark Mulder BNR .10 .30
500 Roger Clemens BNR .60 1.50

2002 Fleer Tradition Glossy

*GLOSSY 1-100: .5X TO 1.2X BASIC
*GLOSSY 101-435/471-500: 3X TO 8X BASIC
*GLOSSY 436-470: 2X TO 5X BASIC
RANDOM INSERTS IN UPDATE PACKS
STATED PRINT RUN 200 SERIAL #'d SETS

2002 Fleer Tradition Diamond Tributes

COMPLETE SET (15) 8.00 20.00
STATED ODDS 1:6 HOBBY, 1:10 RETAIL
1 Cal Ripken 1.50 4.00
2 Tony Gwynn .60 1.50
3 Derek Jeter 1.25 3.00
4 Pedro Martinez .50 1.25
5 Mark McGwire 1.25 3.00
6 Sammy Sosa .50 1.25
7 Barry Bonds 1.25 3.00
8 Roger Clemens 1.00 2.50
9 Mike Piazza .75 2.00
10 Alex Rodriguez .60 1.50
11 Randy Johnson .50 1.25
12 Chipper Jones .50 1.25
13 Nomar Garciaparra .75 2.00
14 Ichiro Suzuki 1.00 2.50
15 Jason Giambi .50 1.25

2002 Fleer Tradition Grass Patch

RANDOM INSERTS IN PACKS
STATED PRINT RUN 50 SETS
CARDS ARE NOT SERIAL-NUMBERED
CARDS CHECKLISTED ALPHABETICALLY
1 Jeff Bagwell/50 * 15.00 40.00
2 Barry Bonds/50 * 20.00 50.00
4 Greg Maddux/50 * 30.00 60.00
5 Cal Ripken/50 * 75.00 150.00
6 Alex Rodriguez/50 * 30.00 60.00
7 Ivan Rodriguez/50 * 15.00 40.00
8 Scott Rolen/50 * 15.00 40.00
9 Larry Walker/50 * 15.00 40.00
10 Bernie Williams/50 * 15.00 40.00

2002 Fleer Tradition Grass Roots

COMPLETE SET (10) 12.50 30.00
STATED ODDS 1:18 HOBBY, 1:20 RETAIL
1 Barry Bonds 2.50 6.00
2 Alex Rodriguez 1.25 3.00
3 Derek Jeter 2.50 6.00
4 Greg Maddux 1.50 4.00
5 Ivan Rodriguez .60 1.50
6 Cal Ripken 3.00 8.00
7 Bernie Williams .60 1.50
8 Jeff Bagwell .60 1.50
9 Scott Rolen .60 1.50
10 Larry Walker .60 1.50

2002 Fleer Tradition Heads Up

COMPLETE SET (10) 30.00 80.00
STATED ODDS 1:36 HOBBY, 1:40 RETAIL
1 Derek Jeter 4.00 10.00
2 Ichiro Suzuki 3.00 8.00
3 Sammy Sosa 2.50 6.00
4 Mike Piazza 2.50 6.00
5 Ken Griffey Jr. 3.00 8.00
6 Alex Rodriguez 2.00 5.00
7 Barry Bonds 4.00 10.00
8 Nomar Garciaparra 2.50 6.00
9 Mark McGwire 4.00 10.00
10 Cal Ripken 5.00 12.00

2002 Fleer Tradition Lumber Company

COMPLETE SET (30) 25.00 60.00
STATED ODDS 1:12 HOBBY, 1:20 RETAIL
1 Moises Alou .60 1.50
2 Luis Gonzalez .60 1.50
3 Todd Helton .60 1.50
4 Mike Piazza 1.50 4.00
5 J.D. Drew .60 1.50
6 Albert Pujols 2.00 5.00
7 Chipper Jones 1.00 2.50
8 Manny Ramirez .60 1.50
9 Miguel Tejada .60 1.50
10 Curt Schilling .60 1.50
11 Alex Rodriguez 1.25 3.00
12 Barry Larkin .60 1.50
13 Nomar Garciaparra 1.50 4.00
14 Cliff Floyd .60 1.50
15 Alfonso Soriano .60 1.50
16 Sean Casey .60 1.50
17 Scott Rolen .60 1.50
18 Jose Ortiz .60 1.50
19 Corey Patterson .60 1.50
20 Joe Crede .60 1.50
21 Jace Brewer .60 1.50
22 Derek Jeter 2.50 6.00
23 Jim Thome .60 1.50
24 Frank Thomas 1.00 2.50
25 Shawn Green .60 1.50
26 Drew Henson .60 1.50
27 Jimmy Rollins .60 1.50
28 David Justice .60 1.50
29 Roberto Alomar .60 1.50
30 Bernie Williams .60 1.50

2002 Fleer Tradition Lumber Company Game Bat

STATED ODDS 1:72 HOBBY, 1:108 RETAIL
SP PRINT RUNS PROVIDED BY FLEER
SP'S ARE NOT SERIAL-NUMBERED
CARDS CHECKLISTED ALPHABETICALLY
1 Roberto Alomar 6.00 15.00
2 Moises Alou 4.00 10.00
3 Jace Brewer SP/250 4.00 10.00
4 Sean Casey SP/250 4.00 10.00
5 Joe Crede SP/250 4.00 10.00
6 J.D. Drew 4.00 10.00
7 Cliff Floyd 4.00 10.00
8 Nomar Garciaparra 8.00 20.00
9 Luis Gonzalez 4.00 10.00
10 Shawn Green 4.00 10.00
11 Todd Helton 6.00 15.00
12 Drew Henson 4.00 10.00
13 Derek Jeter SP/250 10.00 25.00
14 Chipper Jones 6.00 15.00
15 David Justice 4.00 10.00
16 Barry Larkin 6.00 15.00
17 Jose Ortiz SP/250 4.00 10.00
18 Corey Patterson SP/250 4.00 10.00
19 Mike Piazza 6.00 15.00
20 Albert Pujols 10.00 25.00
21 Manny Ramirez 6.00 15.00
22 Alex Rodriguez 8.00 20.00
23 Scott Rolen SP/250 6.00 15.00
24 Jimmy Rollins 4.00 10.00
25 Curt Schilling 4.00 10.00
26 Alfonso Soriano 4.00 10.00
27 Miguel Tejada 4.00 10.00
28 Frank Thomas 6.00 15.00
29 Jim Thome 6.00 15.00
30 Bernie Williams 6.00 15.00

2002 Fleer Tradition This Day in History

COMPLETE SET (29) 25.00 60.00
STATED ODDS 1:18 HOBBY, 1:20 RETAIL
CARD NUMBER 24 DOES NOT EXIST
1 Cal Ripken 3.00 8.00
2 Barry Bonds 1.50 4.00
3 George Brett 2.00 5.00
4 Tony Gwynn 1.00 2.50
5 Nolan Ryan 3.00 8.00
6 Reggie Jackson .60 1.50
7 Paul Molitor 1.00 2.50
8 Ichiro Suzuki 1.25 3.00
9 Alex Rodriguez 1.25 3.00
10 Don Mattingly 2.00 5.00
11 Sammy Sosa 1.00 2.50
12 Mark McGwire 1.50 4.00
13 Derek Jeter 2.50 6.00
14 Roger Clemens 1.25 3.00
15 Jim Hunter .60 1.50
16 Greg Maddux 1.50 4.00
17 Ken Griffey Jr. 2.00 5.00
18 Gil Hodges .60 1.50
19 Edgar Martinez .60 1.50
20 Mike Piazza 1.00 2.50
21 Jimmie Foxx 1.00 2.50
22 Albert Pujols 2.00 5.00
23 Chipper Jones 1.00 2.50
25 Jeff Bagwell .60 1.50
26 Nomar Garciaparra .60 1.50
27 Randy Johnson 1.00 2.50
28 Todd Helton .60 1.50
29 Ted Kluszewski .60 1.50
30 Ivan Rodriguez .60 1.50

2002 Fleer Tradition This Day in History Autographs

RANDOM INSERTS IN PACKS
PRINT RUNS LISTED BELOW
PRINT RUN INFO PROVIDED BY FLEER
CARDS ARE NOT SERIAL-NUMBERED
CARDS CHECKLISTED ALPHABETICALLY
3 Derek Jeter/100 * 150.00 400.00
4 Randy Johnson/75 * 40.00 80.00
5 Don Mattingly/50 * 50.00 100.00
7 Albert Pujols/50 * 150.00 250.00
8 Cal Ripken/50 * 75.00 150.00

2002 Fleer Tradition This Day in History Game Used

RANDOM INSERTS IN PACKS
PRINT RUNS LISTED BELOW
PRINT RUN INFO PROVIDED BY FLEER
CARDS ARE NOT SERIAL-NUMBERED
CARDS CHECKLISTED ALPHABETICALLY
1 Jeff Bagwell Bat/100 * 10.00 25.00
2 Barry Bonds Jsy/250 * 30.00 80.00
4 Roger Clemens Jsy/150 * 15.00 40.00
5 Jimmie Foxx Bat/250 * 10.00 25.00
6 Todd Helton Bat/150 * 10.00 25.00
8 Jim Hunter Jsy/250 * 10.00 25.00
11 Derek Jeter Jsy/250 * 12.50 30.00
15 Greg Maddux Jsy/100 * 12.50 30.00
18 Mike Piazza Bat/150 * 10.00 25.00
21 Alex Rodriguez Hat/250 * 15.00 40.00

2002 Fleer Tradition Update

COMPLETE SET (400) 30.00 60.00
COMP.SET w/o SP's (300) 8.00 20.00
COMMON CARD (U101-U400) .10 .30
COMMON CARD (U1-U100) .40 1.00
1-100 STATED ODDS ONE PER PACK
U1 P.J. Bevis SP RC .40 1.00
U2 Mike Crudale SP RC .40 1.00
U3 Ben Howard SP RC .40 1.00
U4 Travis Driskill SP RC .40 1.00
U5 Reed Johnson SP RC .60 1.50
U6 Kyle Kane SP RC .40 1.00
U7 Deivis Santos SP .40 1.00
U8 Tim Kalita SP RC .40 1.00
U9 Brandon Puffer SP RC .40 1.00
U10 Chris Snelling SP RC .60 1.50
U11 Juan Brito SP RC .40 1.00
U12 Tyler Yates SP RC .40 1.00
U13 Victor Alvarez SP RC .40 1.00
U14 Takahito Nomura SP RC .40 1.00
U15 Ron Calloway SP RC .40 1.00
U16 Satoru Komiyama SP RC .40 1.00
U17 Julius Matos SP RC .40 1.00
U18 Jorge Nunez SP RC .40 1.00
U19 Anderson Machado SP RC .40 1.00
U20 Scott Layfield SP RC .40 1.00
U21 Aaron Cook SP RC .40 1.00
U22 Alex Pelaez SP RC .40 1.00
U23 Corey Thurman SP RC .40 1.00
U24 Nelson Castro SP RC .40 1.00
U25 Jeff Austin SP RC .40 1.00
U26 Felix Escalona SP RC .40 1.00
U27 Luis Ugueto SP RC .40 1.00
U28 Jaime Cerda SP RC .40 1.00
U29 J.J. Trujillo SP RC .40 1.00
U30 Rodrigo Rosario SP RC .40 1.00
U31 Jorge Padilla SP RC .40 1.00
U32 Shawn Sedlacek SP RC .40 1.00
U33 Nate Field SP RC .40 1.00
U34 Earl Snyder SP RC .40 1.00
U35 Miguel Asencio SP RC .40 1.00
U36 Ken Huckaby SP RC .40 1.00
U37 Valentino Pascucci SP .40 1.00
U38 So Taguchi SP RC .50 1.25
U39 Brian Mallette SP RC .40 1.00
U40 Kazuhisa Ishii SP RC .50 1.25
U41 Matt Thornton SP RC .40 1.00
U42 Mark Corey SP RC .40 1.00
U43 Kirk Saarloos SP RC .40 1.00
U44 Josh Bard SP RC .40 1.00
U45 Hansel Izquierdo SP RC .40 1.00
U46 Rene Reyes SP RC .40 1.00
U47 Luis Garcia SP .40 1.00
U48 Jason Simontacchi SP RC .40 1.00
U49 John Ennis SP RC .40 1.00
U50 Franklyn German SP RC .40 1.00
U51 Aaron Guiel SP RC .40 1.00
U52 Howie Clark SP RC .40 1.00
U53 David Ross SP RC .50 1.25
U54 Jason Davis SP RC .40 1.00
U55 Francis Beltran SP RC .40 1.00
U56 Barry Wesson SP RC .40 1.00
U57 Runelvys Hernandez SP RC .40 1.00
U58 Oliver Perez SP RC .60 1.50
U59 Ryan Bukvich SP RC .40 1.00
U60 Steve Kent SP RC .40 1.00
U61 Julio Mateo SP RC .40 1.00
U62 Jason Jimenez SP RC .40 1.00
U63 Jayson Durocher SP RC .40 1.00
U64 Kevin Frederick SP RC .40 1.00
U65 Kevin Gryboski SP RC .40 1.00
U66 Edwin Almonte SP RC .40 1.00
U67 John Foster SP RC .40 1.00
U68 Doug Devore SP RC .40 1.00
U69 Tom Shearn SP RC .40 1.00
U70 Colin Young SP RC .40 1.00
U71 Jon Adkins SP RC .40 1.00
U72 Wilbert Nieves SP RC .40 1.00
U73 Matt Duff SP RC .40 1.00
U74 Carl Sadler SP RC .40 1.00
U75 Jason Kershner SP RC .40 1.00
U76 Brandon Backe SP RC .50 1.25
U77 Josh Hancock SP RC .50 1.25
U78 Chris Baker SP RC .40 1.00
U79 Travis Hughes SP RC .40 1.00
U80 Steve Bechler SP RC .40 1.00
U81 Allan Simpson SP RC .40 1.00
U82 Aaron Taylor SP RC .40 1.00
U83 Kevin Cash SP RC .40 1.00
U84 Chone Figgins SP RC .75 2.00
U85 Clay Condrey SP RC .40 1.00
U86 Shane Nance SP RC .40 1.00
U87 Freddy Sanchez SP RC 1.25 3.00
U88 Jim Rushford SP RC .40 1.00
U89 Jeriome Robertson SP RC .40 1.00
U90 Trey Lunsford SP RC .40 1.00
U91 Cody McKay SP RC .40 1.00
U92 Trey Hodges SP RC .40 1.00
U93 Hee Seop Choi SP .40 1.00
U94 Joe Borchard SP .40 1.00
U95 Orlando Hudson SP .40 1.00
U96 Carl Crawford SP .40 1.00
U97 Mark Prior SP .75 2.00
U98 Brett Myers SP .40 1.00
U99 Kenny Lofton SP .40 1.00
U100 Cliff Floyd SP .40 1.00
U101 Randy Winn .10 .30
U102 Ryan Dempster .10 .30
U103 Josh Phelps .10 .30
U104 Marcus Giles .10 .30
U105 Rickey Henderson .30 .75
U106 Jose Leon .10 .30
U107 Tino Martinez .20 .50
U108 Greg Norton .10 .30
U109 Odalis Perez .10 .30
U110 J.C. Romero .10 .30
U111 Gary Sheffield .10 .30
U112 Ismael Valdes .10 .30
U113 Juan Acevedo .10 .30
U114 Ben Broussard .10 .30
U115 Deivi Cruz .10 .30
U116 Geronimo Gil .10 .30
U117 Eric Hinske .10 .30
U118 Ted Lilly .10 .30
U119 Quinton McCracken .10 .30
U120 Antonio Alfonseca .10 .30
U121 Brent Abernathy .10 .30
U122 Johnny Damon Sox .20 .50
U123 Francisco Cordero .10 .30
U124 Sterling Hitchcock .10 .30
U125 Vladimir Nunez .10 .30
U126 Andres Galarraga .10 .30
U127 Timo Perez .10 .30
U128 Tsuyoshi Shinjo .10 .30
U129 Joe Girardi .10 .30
U130 Roberto Alomar .20 .50
U131 Ellis Burks .10 .30
U132 Mike DeJean .10 .30
U133 Alex Gonzalez .10 .30
U134 Johan Santana .50 1.25
U135 Kenny Lofton .10 .30
U136 Juan Encarnacion .10 .30
U137 Dewon Brazelton .10 .30
U138 Jeromy Burnitz .10 .30
U139 Elmer Dessens .10 .30
U140 Juan Gonzalez .10 .30
U141 Todd Hundley .10 .30
U142 Tomo Ohka .10 .30
U143 Robin Ventura .10 .30
U144 Rodrigo Lopez .10 .30
U145 Ruben Sierra .10 .30
U146 Jason Phillips .10 .30
U147 Ryan Rupe .10 .30
U148 Kevin Appier .10 .30
U149 Sean Burroughs .10 .30
U150 Masato Yoshii .10 .30
U151 Juan Diaz .10 .30
U152 Tony Graffanino .10 .30
U153 Raul Ibanez .10 .30
U154 Kevin Mench .10 .30
U155 Pedro Astacio .10 .30
U156 Brent Butler .10 .30
U157 Kirk Rueter .10 .30
U158 Eddie Guardado .10 .30
U159 Hideki Irabu .10 .30
U160 Wendell Magee .10 .30
U161 Antonio Osuna .10 .30
U162 Jose Vizcaino .10 .30
U163 Danny Bautista .10 .30
U164 Vinny Castilla .10 .30
U165 Chris Singleton .10 .30
U166 Mark Redman .10 .30
U167 Olmedo Saenz .10 .30
U168 Scott Erickson .10 .30
U169 Ty Wigginton .10 .30
U170 Jason Isringhausen .10 .30
U171 Andy Van Hekken .10 .30
U172 Chris Magruder .10 .30
U173 Brandon Berger .10 .30
U174 Roger Cedeno .10 .30
U175 Kelvim Escobar .10 .30
U176 Jose Guillen .10 .30
U177 Damian Jackson .10 .30
U178 Eric Owens .10 .30
U179 Angel Berroa .10 .30

U180 Alex Cintron .10 .30
U181 Jeff Weaver .10 .30
U182 Damon Minor .10 .30
U183 Bobby Estalella .10 .30
U184 David Justice .10 .30
U185 Roy Halladay .10 .30
U186 Brian Jordan .10 .30
U187 Mike Maroth .10 .30
U188 Pokey Reese .10 .30
U189 Rey Sanchez .10 .30
U190 Hank Blalock .20 .50
U191 Jeff Cirillo .10 .30
U192 Dmitri Young .10 .30
U193 Carl Everett .10 .30
U194 Joey Hamilton .10 .30
U195 Jorge Julio .10 .30
U196 Pablo Ozuna .10 .30
U197 Jason Marquis .10 .30
U198 Dustan Mohr .10 .30
U199 Joe Borowski .10 .30
U200 Tony Clark .10 .30
U201 David Wells .10 .30
U202 Josh Fogg .10 .30
U203 Aaron Harang .10 .30
U204 John McDonald .10 .30
U205 John Stephens .10 .30
U206 Chris Reitsma .10 .30
U207 Alex Sanchez .10 .30
U208 Milton Bradley .10 .30
U209 Matt Clement .10 .30
U210 Brad Fullmer .10 .30
U211 Shigetoshi Hasegawa .10 .30
U212 Austin Kearns .10 .30
U213 Damaso Marte .10 .30
U214 Vicente Padilla .10 .30
U215 Raul Mondesi .10 .30
U216 Russell Branyan .10 .30
U217 Bartolo Colon .10 .30
U218 Moises Alou .10 .30
U219 Scott Hatteberg .10 .30
U220 Bobby Kielty .10 .30
U221 Kip Wells .10 .30
U222 Scott Stewart .10 .30
U223 Victor Martinez .30 .75
U224 Marty Cordova .10 .30
U225 Desi Relaford .10 .30
U226 Reggie Sanders .10 .30
U227 Jason Giambi .10 .30
U228 Jimmy Haynes .10 .30
U229 Billy Koch .10 .30
U230 Damian Moss .10 .30
U231 Chan Ho Park .10 .30
U232 Cliff Floyd .10 .30
U233 Todd Zeile .10 .30
U234 Jeremy Giambi .10 .30
U235 Rick Helling .10 .30
U236 Matt Lawton .10 .30
U237 Ramon Martinez .10 .30
U238 Rondell White .10 .30
U239 Scott Sullivan .10 .30
U240 Hideo Nomo .30 .75
U241 Todd Ritchie .10 .30
U242 Ramon Santiago .10 .30
U243 Jake Peavy .20 .50
U244 Brad Wilkerson .10 .30
U245 Reggie Taylor .10 .30
U246 Carlos Pena .10 .30
U247 Willis Roberts .10 .30
U248 Jason Schmidt .10 .30
U249 Mike Williams .10 .30
U250 Alan Zinter .10 .30
U251 Michael Tejera .10 .30
U252 Dave Roberts .10 .30
U253 Scott Schoeneweis .10 .30
U254 Woody Williams .10 .30
U255 John Thomson .10 .30
U256 Ricardo Rodriguez .10 .30
U257 Aaron Sele .10 .30
U258 Paul Wilson .10 .30
U259 Brett Tomko .10 .30
U260 Kenny Rogers .10 .30
U261 Mo Vaughn .10 .30
U262 John Burkett .10 .30
U263 Dennis Stark .10 .30
U264 Ray Durham .10 .30
U265 Scott Rolen .20 .50
U266 Gabe Kapler .10 .30
U267 Todd Hollandsworth .10 .30
U268 Bud Smith .10 .30
U269 Jay Payton .10 .30
U270 Tyler Houston .10 .30
U271 Brian Moehler .10 .30
U272 David Espinosa .10 .30
U273 Placido Polanco .10 .30
U274 John Patterson .10 .30
U275 Adam Hyzdu .10 .30
U276 Albert Pujols DS .30 .75
U277 Larry Walker DS .10 .30
U278 Magglio Ordonez DS .10 .30
U279 Ryan Klesko DS .10 .30
U280 Darin Erstad DS .10 .30
U281 Jeff Kent DS .10 .30
U282 Paul Lo Duca DS .10 .30
U283 Jim Edmonds DS .10 .30
U284 Chipper Jones DS .20 .50
U285 Bernie Williams DS .10 .30
U286 Pat Burrell DS .10 .30
U287 Cliff Floyd DS .10 .30
U288 Troy Glaus DS .10 .30
U289 Brian Giles DS .10 .30
U290 Jim Thome DS .10 .30
U291 Greg Maddux DS .30 .75
U292 Roberto Alomar DS .10 .30
U293 Jeff Bagwell DS .10 .30
U294 Rafael Furcal DS .10 .30
U295 Josh Beckett DS .10 .30
U296 Carlos Delgado DS .10 .30
U297 Ken Griffey Jr. DS .40 1.00
U298 Jason Giambi AS .10 .30
U299 Paul Konerko AS .10 .30
U300 Mike Sweeney AS .10 .30
U301 Alfonso Soriano AS .10 .30
U302 Shea Hillenbrand AS .10 .30
U303 Tony Batista AS .10 .30
U304 Robin Ventura AS .10 .30
U305 Alex Rodriguez AS .25 .60
U306 Nomar Garciaparra AS .30 .75
U307 Derek Jeter AS .40 1.00
U308 Miguel Tejada AS .10 .30
U309 Omar Vizquel AS .10 .30
U310 Jorge Posada AS .10 .30
U311 A.J. Pierzynski AS .10 .30
U312 Ichiro Suzuki AS .30 .75
U313 Manny Ramirez AS .20 .50
U314 Torii Hunter AS .10 .30
U315 Garret Anderson AS .10 .30
U316 Robert Fick AS .10 .30
U317 Randy Winn AS .10 .30
U318 Mark Buehrle AS .10 .30
U319 Freddy Garcia AS .10 .30
U320 Eddie Guardado AS .10 .30
U321 Roy Halladay AS .10 .30
U322 Derek Lowe AS .10 .30
U323 Pedro Martinez AS .20 .50
U324 Mariano Rivera AS .20 .50
U325 Kazuhiro Sasaki AS .10 .30
U326 Barry Zito AS .10 .30
U327 Johnny Damon Sox AS .20 .50
U328 Ugueth Urbina AS .10 .30
U329 Todd Helton AS .10 .30
U330 Richie Sexson AS .10 .30
U331 Jose Vidro AS .10 .30
U332 Luis Castillo AS .10 .30
U333 Junior Spivey AS .10 .30
U334 Scott Rolen AS .10 .30
U335 Mike Lowell AS .10 .30
U336 Jimmy Rollins AS .10 .30
U337 Jose Hernandez AS .10 .30
U338 Mike Piazza AS .30 .75
U339 Benito Santiago AS .10 .30
U340 Sammy Sosa AS .20 .50
U341 Barry Bonds AS .40 1.00
U342 Vladimir Guerrero AS .20 .50
U343 Lance Berkman AS .10 .30
U344 Adam Dunn AS .10 .30
U345 Shawn Green AS .10 .30
U346 Luis Gonzalez AS .10 .30
U347 Eric Gagne AS .10 .30
U348 Tom Glavine AS .10 .30
U349 Trevor Hoffman AS .10 .30
U350 Randy Johnson AS .20 .50
U351 Byung-Hyun Kim AS .10 .30
U352 Matt Morris AS .10 .30
U353 Odalis Perez AS .10 .30
U354 Curt Schilling AS .10 .30
U355 John Smoltz AS .10 .30
U356 Mike Williams AS .10 .30
U357 Andruw Jones AS .10 .30
U358 Vicente Padilla AS .10 .30
U359 Mike Remlinger AS .10 .30
U360 Robb Nen AS .10 .30
U361 Shawn Green CC .10 .30
U362 Derek Jeter CC .40 1.00
U363 Troy Glaus CC .10 .30
U364 Ken Griffey Jr. CC .40 1.00
U365 Mike Piazza CC .30 .75
U366 Jason Giambi CC .10 .30
U367 Greg Maddux CC .30 .75
U368 Albert Pujols CC .30 .75
U369 Pedro Martinez CC .20 .50
U370 Barry Zito CC .10 .30
U371 Ichiro Suzuki CC .30 .75
U372 Nomar Garciaparra CC .30 .75
U373 Vladimir Guerrero CC .20 .50
U374 Randy Johnson CC .20 .50
U375 Barry Bonds CC .40 1.00
U376 Sammy Sosa CC .20 .50
U377 Hideo Nomo CC .20 .50
U378 Jeff Bagwell CC .10 .30
U379 Curt Schilling CC .10 .30
U380 Jim Thome CC .10 .30
U381 Todd Helton CC .10 .30
U382 Roger Clemens CC .30 .75
U383 Chipper Jones CC .20 .50
U384 Alex Rodriguez CC .25 .60
U385 Manny Ramirez CC .20 .50
U386 Barry Bonds TT .40 1.00
U387 Jim Thome TT .10 .30
U388 Adam Dunn TT .10 .30
U389 Alex Rodriguez TT .25 .60
U390 Shawn Green TT .10 .30
U391 Jason Giambi TT .10 .30
U392 Lance Berkman TT .10 .30
U393 Pat Burrell TT .10 .30
U394 Eric Chavez TT .10 .30
U395 Mike Piazza TT .30 .75
U396 Vladimir Guerrero TT .20 .50
U397 Paul Konerko TT .10 .30
U398 Sammy Sosa TT .20 .50
U399 Richie Sexson TT .10 .30
U400 Torii Hunter TT .10 .30

2002 Fleer Tradition Update Glossy

*GLOSSY 1-100: 1X TO 2.5X BASIC
*GLOSSY 101-275: 3X TO 8X BASIC
*GLOSSY 276-400: 6X TO 15X BASIC
RANDOM INSERTS IN PACKS
STATED PRINT RUN 200 SERIAL #'d SETS

2002 Fleer Tradition Update Diamond Debuts

COMPLETE SET (15) 6.00 15.00
STATED ODDS 1:6
U1 Mark Prior .50 1.25
U2 Eric Hinske .40 1.00
U3 Kazuhisa Ishii .50 1.25
U4 Ben Broussard .40 1.00
U5 Sean Burroughs .40 1.00
U6 Austin Kearns .40 1.00
U7 Hee Seop Choi .40 1.00
U8 Kirk Saarloos .40 1.00
U9 Orlando Hudson .40 1.00
U10 So Taguchi .50 1.25
U11 Kevin Mench .40 1.00
U12 Carl Crawford .40 1.00
U13 Marlon Byrd .40 1.00
U14 Hank Blalock .50 1.25
U15 Brett Myers .40 1.00

2002 Fleer Tradition Update Grass Patch

RANDOM INSERTS IN PACKS
STATED PRINT RUN 50 SERIAL #'d SETS
1 Roberto Alomar 15.00 40.00
2 Jim Edmonds 10.00 25.00
3 Nomar Garciaparra 40.00 80.00
4 Shawn Green 10.00 25.00
5 Torii Hunter 10.00 25.00
6 Andruw Jones 15.00 40.00
7 Alfonso Soriano 10.00 25.00

2002 Fleer Tradition Update Grass Roots

COMPLETE SET (10) 6.00 15.00
STATED ODDS 1:18
U1 Alfonso Soriano .75 2.00
U2 Torii Hunter .75 2.00
U3 Andruw Jones .75 2.00
U4 Jim Edmonds .75 2.00
U5 Shawn Green .75 2.00
U6 Todd Helton .75 2.00
U7 Nomar Garciaparra 1.50 4.00
U8 Roberto Alomar .75 2.00
U9 Vladimir Guerrero 1.00 2.50
U10 Ichiro Suzuki 2.00 5.00

2002 Fleer Tradition Update Heads Up

STATED ODDS 1:36
U1 Roger Clemens 3.00 8.00
U2 Adam Dunn 1.25 3.00
U3 Kazuhisa Ishii 1.25 3.00
U4 Barry Zito 1.25 3.00
U5 Pedro Martinez 1.25 3.00
U6 Alfonso Soriano 1.25 3.00
U7 Mark Prior 1.50 4.00
U8 Chipper Jones 1.50 4.00
U9 Randy Johnson 1.50 4.00
U10 Lance Berkman 1.25 3.00

2002 Fleer Tradition Update Heads Up Game Used Caps

RANDOM INSERTS IN PACKS
STATED PRINT RUN 150 SERIAL #'D SETS
1 Lance Berkman 8.00 20.00
2 Barry Bonds 12.50 30.00
3 Roger Clemens 20.00 50.00
4 Adam Dunn 8.00 20.00
5 Kazuhisa Ishii 6.00 15.00
6 Randy Johnson 10.00 25.00
7 Chipper Jones 10.00 25.00
8 Mike Piazza 12.50 30.00
9 Mark Prior 10.00 25.00
10 Alfonso Soriano 8.00 20.00
11 Barry Zito 8.00 20.00

2002 Fleer Tradition Update New York's Finest

STATED ODDS 1:83
1 Edgardo Alfonzo 3.00 8.00
2 Roberto Alomar 3.00 8.00
3 Jeromy Burnitz 3.00 8.00
4 Satoru Komiyama 3.00 8.00
5 Rey Ordonez 3.00 8.00
6 Mike Piazza 5.00 12.00
7 Mo Vaughn 3.00 8.00
8 Roger Clemens 6.00 15.00
9 Jason Giambi 3.00 8.00
10 Derek Jeter 8.00 20.00
11 Mike Mussina 3.00 8.00
12 Jorge Posada 3.00 8.00
13 Alfonso Soriano 3.00 8.00
14 Robin Ventura 3.00 8.00
15 Bernie Williams 3.00 8.00

2002 Fleer Tradition Update New York's Finest Dual Swatch

RANDOM INSERTS IN PACKS
STATED PRINT RUN 100 SERIAL #'d SETS
1 D.Jeter/R.Ordonez 15.00 40.00
2 A.Soriano/R.Alomar 15.00 40.00
3 R.Clemens/M.Piazza 60.00 120.00
4 M.Mussina/M.Vaughn 10.00 25.00
5 B.Williams/J.Burnitz 10.00 25.00
6 R.Ventura/E.Alfonzo 10.00 25.00

2002 Fleer Tradition Update New York's Finest Single Swatch

STATED ODDS 1:112
1 D.Jeter Jsy Ordonez 12.50 30.00
2 A.Soriano Jsy Alomar 6.00 15.00
3 R.Clemens Jsy Piazza 8.00 20.00
4 M.Mussina Jsy Vaughn 6.00 15.00
5 B.Williams Jsy Burnitz 6.00 15.00
6 D.Jeter Jsy Komiyama 12.50 30.00
7 R.Ventura Jsy Alfonzo 4.00 10.00
8 J.Posada Jsy Piazza 6.00 15.00
9 J.Giambi Base Vaughn 4.00 10.00
10 A.Soriano Jsy Alfonzo 4.00 10.00
11 R.Ordonez Jsy Jeter 4.00 10.00
12 R.Alomar Jsy Soriano 6.00 15.00
13 M.Piazza Jsy Clemens 6.00 15.00
14 M.Vaughn Jsy Mussina 4.00 10.00
15 J.Burnitz Jsy B.Williams 4.00 10.00
16 S.Komiyama Bat Jeter 6.00 15.00
17 E.Alfonzo Jsy Ventura 4.00 10.00
18 M.Piazza Jsy Posada 6.00 15.00
19 M.Vaughn Jsy Giambi 4.00 10.00
20 E.Alfonzo Jsy Soriano 4.00 10.00

2002 Fleer Tradition Update Plays of the Week

STATED ODDS 1:12
1 Troy Glaus .60 1.50
2 Andruw Jones .60 1.50
3 Curt Schilling .60 1.50
4 Manny Ramirez .60 1.50
5 Sammy Sosa 1.00 2.50
6 Magglio Ordonez .60 1.50
7 Ken Griffey Jr. 2.00 5.00
8 Jim Thome .60 1.50
9 Larry Walker .60 1.50
10 Robert Fick .60 1.50
11 Josh Beckett .60 1.50
12 Roy Oswalt .60 1.50
13 Mike Sweeney .60 1.50
14 Shawn Green .60 1.50
15 Torii Hunter .60 1.50
16 Vladimir Guerrero 1.00 2.50
17 Mike Piazza 1.50 4.00
18 Jason Giambi .60 1.50
19 Eric Chavez .60 1.50
20 Pat Burrell .60 1.50
21 Brian Giles .60 1.50
22 Ryan Klesko .60 1.50
23 Barry Bonds 2.50 6.00
24 Mike Cameron .60 1.50
25 Albert Pujols 2.00 5.00
26 Alex Rodriguez 1.25 3.00
27 Carlos Delgado .60 1.50
28 Richie Sexson .60 1.50
29 Jay Gibbons .60 1.50
30 Randy Winn .60 1.50

2002 Fleer Tradition Update This Day In History

STATED ODDS 1:12
U1 Shawn Green .40 1.00
U2 Ozzie Smith 1.25 3.00
U3 Derek Lowe .40 1.00
U4 Ken Griffey Jr. 2.00 5.00
U5 Barry Bonds 1.50 4.00
U6 Juan Gonzalez .40 1.00
U7 Wade Boggs .60 1.50
U8 Mark Prior .60 1.50
U9 Thurman Munson 1.00 2.50
U10 Curt Schilling .60 1.50
U11 Jason Giambi .40 1.00
U12 Cal Ripken 3.00 8.00
U13 Craig Biggio .60 1.50
U14 Drew Henson .40 1.00
U15 Steve Carlton .60 1.50
U16 Greg Maddux 1.50 4.00
U17 Adam Dunn .60 1.50
U18 Vladimir Guerrero .60 1.50
U19 Alex Rodriguez 1.25 3.00
U20 Carlton Fisk .60 1.50
U21 Ichiro Suzuki 1.25 3.00
U22 Johnny Bench 1.00 2.50
U23 Kazuhisa Ishii .60 1.50
U24 Derek Jeter 2.50 6.00
U25 Jim Thome .60 1.50

2002 Fleer Tradition Update This Day In History Autographs

STATED ODDS 1:582
SP PRINT RUNS PROVIDED BY FLEER
SP'S ARE NOT SERIAL-NUMBERED
1 Barry Bonds SP/150 100.00 175.00
2 Mark Prior SP/64 10.00 25.00
4 Drew Henson 8.00 20.00
5 Greg Maddux SP/99 125.00 200.00
6 Derek Jeter 125.00 250.00

2002 Fleer Tradition Update This Day In History Game Used

STATED ODDS 1:28
SP PRINT RUNS PROVIDED BY FLEER
SP'S ARE NOT SERIAL-NUMBERED
2 Craig Biggio Jsy 6.00 15.00
3 Wade Boggs Jsy 6.00 15.00
4 Wade Boggs Pants 6.00 15.00
5 Barry Bonds Bat 8.00 20.00
6 Barry Bonds Jsy 8.00 20.00
7 Adam Dunn Jsy 4.00 10.00
8 Carlton Fisk Bat 6.00 15.00
9 Juan Gonzalez Bat 4.00 10.00
10 Shawn Green Jsy 4.00 10.00
11 Kazuhisa Ishii Bat 4.00 10.00
12 Derek Jeter Pants 10.00 25.00
13 Greg Maddux Jsy 6.00 15.00
15 Alex Rodriguez Bat 6.00 15.00
16 Alex Rodriguez Jsy 6.00 15.00
17 Curt Schilling Jsy 4.00 10.00
18 Ozzie Smith Jsy 6.00 15.00
20 Jim Thome Jsy 6.00 15.00

2003 Fleer Tradition

COMPLETE SET (485) 12.50 30.00
COMP.SET w/o SP's (385) 8.00 20.00
COMMON CARD (1-30) .40 1.00
COMM.SP (31-66/86-100) .40 1.00
COMMON ML (67-85) .40 1.00
1-100 SP ODDS 1:1 HOBBY, 1:12 RETAIL
COMMON CARD (101-485) .12 .30
COMMON PR (426-460) .12 .30
1 Wash Glaus And Ortiz TL .40 1.00
2 L.Gonzalez R.Johnson TL 1.00 2.50
3 Andruw Chip Glav Mill TL 1.00 2.50
4 T.Batista R.Lopez TL .40 1.00
5 Ram Nomar Lowe Pedro TL 1.00 2.50
6 Sosa Clement Wood TL 1.00 2.50
7 Buehrle Magglio Wright TL .60 1.50
8 Dunn Boone Haynes TL .60 1.50
9 C.Sabathia J.Thome TL .60 1.50
10 T.Helton J.Jennings TL .60 1.50
11 Simon Sparks Redman TL .40 1.00
12 Lee Lowell Burnett TL .40 1.00
13 L.Berkman R.Oswalt TL .60 1.50
14 P.Byrd C.Beltran TL .60 1.50
15 S.Green H.Nomo TL 1.00 2.50
16 R.Sexson B.Sheets TL .40 1.00
17 Hunter Lohse Santana TL .60 1.50
18 Vladdie Ohka Vazquez TL .60 1.50
19 M.Piazza A.Leiter TL 1.00 2.50
20 Giambi Wells Clemens TL 1.25 3.00
21 Chavez Tejada Zito TL .60 1.50
22 Burrell Padilla Wolf TL .40 1.00
23 Giles Fogg Wells TL .40 1.00
24 R.Klesko B.Lawrence TL .40 1.00
25 Bonds Ortiz Schmidt TL 1.50 4.00
26 Cameron Boone Garcia TL .40 1.00
27 A.Pujols M.Morris TL 1.25 3.00
28 Huff Winn Kenn Sturtze TL .40 1.00
29 A-Rod Rogers Park TL 1.25 3.00
30 C.Delgado R.Halladay TL .60 1.50
31 Greg Maddux SP 1.25 3.00
32 Nick Neugebauer SP .40 1.00
33 Larry Walker SP .60 1.50
34 Freddy Garcia SP .40 1.00
35 Rich Aurilia SP .40 1.00
36 Craig Wilson SP .40 1.00
37 Jeff Suppan SP .40 1.00
38 Joel Pineiro SP .40 1.00
39 Pedro Feliz SP .40 1.00
40 Bartolo Colon SP .40 1.00
41 Pete Walker SP .40 1.00
42 Mo Vaughn SP .40 1.00
43 Sidney Ponson SP .40 1.00
44 Jason Isringhausen SP .40 1.00
45 Hideki Irabu SP .40 1.00
46 Pedro Martinez SP .60 1.50
47 Tom Glavine SP .60 1.50
48 Matt Lawton SP .40 1.00
49 Kyle Lohse SP .40 1.00
50 Corey Patterson SP .40 1.00
51 Ichiro Suzuki SP 1.25 3.00
52 Wade Miller SP .40 1.00
53 Ben Diggins SP .40 1.00
54 Jayson Werth SP .60 1.50
55 Masato Yoshii SP .40 1.00
56 Mark Buehrle SP .60 1.50
57 Drew Henson SP .40 1.00
58 Dave Williams SP .40 1.00
59 Juan Rivera SP .40 1.00
60 Scott Schoeneweis SP .40 1.00
61 Josh Beckett SP .40 1.00
62 Vinny Castilla SP .40 1.00
63 Barry Zito SP .60 1.50
64 Jose Valentin SP .40 1.00
65 Jon Lieber SP .40 1.00
66 Jorge Padilla SP .40 1.00
67 Luis Aparicio ML SP .60 1.50
68 Boog Powell ML SP .40 1.00
69 Dick Radatz ML SP .40 1.00
70 Frank Malzone ML SP .40 1.00
71 Lou Brock ML SP .60 1.50
72 Billy Williams ML SP .60 1.50
73 Early Wynn ML SP .60 1.50
74 Jim Bunning ML SP .60 1.50
75 Al Kaline ML SP .60 1.50
76 Eddie Mathews ML SP 1.00 2.50
77 Harmon Killebrew ML SP 1.00 2.50
78 Gil Hodges ML SP .60 1.50
79 Duke Snider ML SP .60 1.50
80 Yogi Berra ML SP 1.00 2.50
81 Whitey Ford ML SP .60 1.50
82 Willie Stargell ML SP .60 1.50
83 Willie McCovey ML SP .60 1.50
84 Gaylord Perry ML SP .60 1.50
85 Red Schoendienst ML SP .60 1.50
86 Luis Castillo SP .40 1.00
87 Derek Jeter SP 2.50 6.00
88 Orlando Hudson SP .40 1.00
89 Bobby Higginson SP .40 1.00
90 Brent Butler SP .40 1.00
91 Brad Wilkerson SP .40 1.00
92 Craig Biggio SP .60 1.50
93 Marlon Anderson SP .40 1.00
94 Ty Wigginton SP .40 1.00
95 Hideo Nomo SP 1.00 2.50
96 Barry Larkin SP .60 1.50
97 Roberto Alomar SP .60 1.50
98 Omar Vizquel SP .60 1.50
99 Andres Galarraga SP .60 1.50
100 Shawn Green SP .40 1.00
101 Rafael Furcal .12 .30
102 Bill Selby .12 .30
103 Brent Abernathy .12 .30
104 Nomar Garciaparra .20 .50
105 Michael Barrett .12 .30
106 Travis Hafner .12 .30
107 Carl Crawford .20 .50
108 Jeff Cirillo .12 .30
109 Mike Hampton .12 .30
110 Kip Wells .12 .30
111 Luis Alicea .12 .30
112 Ellis Burks .12 .30
113 Matt Anderson .12 .30
114 Carlos Beltran .20 .50
115 Paul Lo Duca .12 .30
116 Lance Berkman .20 .50
117 Moises Alou .12 .30
118 Roger Cedeno .12 .30
119 Brad Fullmer .12 .30
120 Sean Burroughs .12 .30
121 Eric Byrnes .12 .30
122 Milton Bradley .12 .30
123 Jason Giambi .12 .30
124 Brook Fordyce .12 .30
125 Kevin Appier .12 .30
126 Steve Cox .12 .30
127 Danny Bautista .12 .30
128 Edgardo Alfonzo .12 .30
129 Matt Clement .12 .30
130 Robb Nen .12 .30
131 Roy Halladay .20 .50
132 Brian Jordan .12 .30
133 A.J. Burnett .12 .30
134 Aaron Cook .12 .30
135 Paul Byrd .12 .30
136 Ramon Ortiz .12 .30
137 Adam Hyzdu .12 .30
138 Rafael Soriano .12 .30
139 Marty Cordova .12 .30
140 Nelson Cruz .12 .30
141 Jamie Moyer .12 .30
142 Raul Mondesi .12 .30
143 Josh Bard .12 .30
144 Elmer Dessens .12 .30
145 Rickey Henderson .30 .75
146 Joe McEwing .12 .30
147 Luis Rivas .12 .30
148 Armando Benitez .12 .30
149 Keith Foulke .12 .30
150 Zach Day .12 .30
151 Trey Lunsford .12 .30
152 Bobby Abreu .12 .30
153 Juan Cruz .12 .30
154 Ramon Hernandez .12 .30
155 Brandon Duckworth .12 .30
156 Matt Ginter .12 .30
157 Rob Mackowiak .12 .30
158 Josh Pearce .12 .30
159 Marlon Byrd .12 .30
160 Todd Walker .12 .30
161 Chad Hermansen .12 .30
162 Felix Escalona .12 .30
163 Ruben Mateo .12 .30
164 Mark Johnson .12 .30
165 Juan Pierre .12 .30
166 Gary Sheffield .12 .30
167 Edgar Martinez .20 .50
168 Randy Winn .12 .30
169 Pokey Reese .12 .30
170 Kevin Mench .12 .30
171 Albert Pujols .40 1.00
172 J.T. Snow .12 .30
173 Dean Palmer .12 .30
174 Jay Payton .12 .30
175 Abraham Nunez .12 .30
176 Richie Sexson .12 .30
177 Jose Vidro .12 .30
178 Geoff Jenkins .12 .30
179 Dan Wilson .12 .30
180 John Olerud .12 .30
181 Javy Lopez .12 .30
182 Carl Everett .12 .30
183 Vernon Wells .12 .30
184 Juan Gonzalez .12 .30
185 Jorge Posada .20 .50
186 Mike Sweeney .12 .30
187 Cesar Izturis .12 .30
188 Jason Schmidt .12 .30
189 Chris Richard .12 .30
190 Jason Phillips .12 .30
191 Fred McGriff .20 .50
192 Shea Hillenbrand .12 .30
193 Ivan Rodriguez .20 .50
194 Mike Lowell .12 .30
195 Neifi Perez .12 .30
196 Kenny Lofton .12 .30
197 A.J. Pierzynski .12 .30
198 Larry Bigbie .12 .30
199 Juan Uribe .12 .30
200 Jeff Bagwell .20 .50
201 Timo Perez .12 .30
202 Jeremy Giambi .12 .30
203 Deivi Cruz .12 .30
204 Marquis Grissom .12 .30
205 Chipper Jones .30 .75
206 Alex Gonzalez .12 .30
207 Steve Finley .12 .30
208 Ben Davis .12 .30
209 Mike Bordick .12 .30
210 Casey Fossum .12 .30
211 Aramis Ramirez .12 .30
212 Aaron Boone .12 .30
213 Orlando Cabrera .12 .30
214 Hee Seop Choi .12 .30
215 Jeromy Burnitz .12 .30
216 Todd Hollandsworth .12 .30
217 Rey Sanchez .12 .30
218 Jose Cruz .12 .30
219 Roosevelt Brown .12 .30
220 Odalis Perez .12 .30
221 Carlos Delgado .12 .30
222 Orlando Hernandez .12 .30
223 Adam Everett .12 .30
224 Adrian Beltre .30 .75
225 Ken Griffey Jr. .60 1.50
226 Brad Penny .12 .30
227 Carlos Lee .12 .30
228 J.C. Romero .12 .30
229 Ramon Martinez .12 .30
230 Matt Morris .12 .30
231 Ben Howard .12 .30
232 Damon Minor .12 .30
233 Jason Marquis .12 .30
234 Paul Wilson .12 .30
235 Ryan Dempster .12 .30
236 Jeffrey Hammonds .12 .30
237 Jaret Wright .12 .30
238 Carlos Pena .20 .50
239 Toby Hall .12 .30
240 Rick Helling .12 .30
241 Alex Escobar .12 .30
242 Trevor Hoffman .20 .50
243 Bernie Williams .20 .50
244 Jorge Julio .12 .30
245 Byung-Hyun Kim .12 .30
246 Mike Redmond .12 .30
247 Tony Armas .12 .30
248 Aaron Rowand .12 .30
249 Rusty Greer .12 .30
250 Aaron Harang .12 .30
251 Jeremy Fikac .12 .30
252 Jay Gibbons .12 .30
253 Brandon Puffer .12 .30
254 Dewayne Wise .12 .30
255 Chan Ho Park .20 .50
256 David Bell .12 .30
257 Kenny Rogers .12 .30
258 Mark Quinn .12 .30
259 Greg LaRocca .12 .30
260 Reggie Taylor .12 .30
261 Brett Tomko .12 .30
262 Jack Wilson .12 .30
263 Billy Wagner .12 .30
264 Greg Norton .12 .30
265 Tim Salmon .12 .30
266 Joe Randa .12 .30
267 Geronimo Gil .12 .30
268 Johnny Damon .20 .50
269 Robin Ventura 12 30
270 Frank Thomas .30 .75
271 Terrence Long .12 .30
272 Mark Redman .12 .30
273 Mark Kotsay .12 .30
274 Ben Sheets .12 .30
275 Reggie Sanders .12 .30
276 Mark Grace .20 .50
277 Eddie Guardado .12 .30
278 Julio Mateo .12 .30
279 Bengie Molina .12 .30
280 Bill Hall .12 .30
281 Eric Chavez .12 .30
282 Joe Kennedy .12 .30
283 John Valentin .12 .30
284 Ray Durham .12 .30
285 Trot Nixon .12 .30
286 Rondell White .12 .30
287 Alex Gonzalez .12 .30
288 Tomas Perez .12 .30
289 Jared Sandberg .12 .30
290 Jacque Jones .12 .30
291 Cliff Floyd .12 .30
292 Ryan Klesko .12 .30
293 Morgan Ensberg .12 .30
294 Jerry Hairston .12 .30
295 Doug Mientkiewicz .12 .30
296 Darin Erstad .12 .30
297 Jeff Conine .12 .30
298 Johnny Estrada .12 .30
299 Mark Mulder .12 .30
300 Jeff Kent .12 .30
301 Roger Clemens .40 1.00
302 Endy Chavez .12 .30
303 Joe Crede .12 .30
304 J.D. Drew .12 .30
305 David Dellucci .12 .30
306 Eli Marrero .12 .30
307 Josh Fogg .12 .30
308 Mike Crudale .12 .30
309 Bret Boone .12 .30
310 Mariano Rivera .40 1.00
311 Mike Piazza .30 .75
312 Jason Jennings .12 .30
313 Jason Varitek .30 .75
314 Vicente Padilla .12 .30
315 Kevin Millwood .12 .30
316 Nick Johnson .12 .30
317 Shane Reynolds .12 .30
318 Joe Thurston .12 .30
319 Mike Lamb .12 .30
320 Aaron Sele .12 .30
321 Fernando Tatis .12 .30
322 Randy Wolf .12 .30
323 David Justice .12 .30
324 Andy Pettitte .20 .50
325 Freddy Sanchez .12 .30
326 Scott Spiezio .12 .30
327 Randy Johnson .30 .75
328 Karim Garcia .12 .30
329 Eric Milton .12 .30
330 Jermaine Dye .12 .30
331 Kevin Brown .12 .30
332 Adam Pettyjohn .12 .30
333 Jason Lane .12 .30
334 Mark Prior .20 .50
335 Mike Lieberthal .12 .30
336 Matt White .12 .30
337 John Patterson .12 .30
338 Marcus Giles .12 .30
339 Kazuhisa Ishii .12 .30
340 Willie Harris .12 .30
341 Travis Phelps .12 .30
342 Randall Simon .12 .30
343 Manny Ramirez .30 .75
344 Kerry Wood .12 .30
345 Shannon Stewart .12 .30
346 Mike Mussina .20 .50
347 Joe Borchard .12 .30
348 Tyler Walker .12 .30

349 Preston Wilson .12 .30
350 Damian Moss .12 .30
351 Eric Karros .12 .30
352 Bobby Kielty .12 .30
353 Jason LaRue .12 .30
354 Phil Nevin .12 .30
355 Tony Graffanino .12 .30
356 Antonio Alfonseca .12 .30
357 Eddie Taubensee .12 .30
358 Luis Ugueto .12 .30
359 Greg Vaughn .12 .30
360 Corey Thurman .12 .30
361 Omar Infante .12 .30
362 Alex Cintron .12 .30
363 Esteban Loaiza .12 .30
364 Tino Martinez .12 .30
365 David Eckstein .12 .30
366 Dave Pember RC .12 .30
367 Damian Rolls .12 .30
368 Richard Hidalgo .12 .30
369 Brad Radke .12 .30
370 Alex Sanchez .12 .30
371 Ben Grieve .12 .30
372 Brandon Inge .12 .30
373 Adam Piatt .12 .30
374 Charles Johnson .12 .30
375 Rafael Palmeiro .20 .50
376 Joe Mays .12 .30
377 Derrek Lee .12 .30
378 Fernando Vina .12 .30
379 Andruw Jones .12 .30
380 Troy Glaus .12 .30
381 Bobby Hill .12 .30
382 C.C. Sabathia .20 .50
383 Jose Hernandez .12 .30
384 Al Leiter .12 .30
385 Jarrod Washburn .12 .30
386 Cody Ransom .12 .30
387 Matt Stairs .12 .30
388 Edgar Renteria .12 .30
389 Tsuyoshi Shinjo .12 .30
390 Matt Williams .12 .30
391 Bubba Trammell .12 .30
392 Jason Kendall .12 .30
393 Scott Rolen .20 .50
394 Chuck Knoblauch .12 .30
395 Jimmy Rollins .20 .50
396 Gary Bennett .12 .30
397 David Wells .12 .30
398 Ronnie Belliard .12 .30
399 Austin Kearns .12 .30
400 Tim Hudson .20 .50
401 Andy Van Hekken .12 .30
402 Ray Lankford .12 .30
403 Todd Helton .20 .50
404 Jeff Weaver .12 .30
405 Gabe Kapler .12 .30
406 Luis Gonzalez .12 .30
407 Sean Casey .12 .30
408 Kazuhiro Sasaki .12 .30
409 Mark Teixeira .20 .50
410 Brian Giles .12 .30
411 Robert Fick .12 .30
412 Wilkin Ruan .12 .30
413 Jose Rijo .12 .30
414 Ben Broussard .12 .30
415 Aubrey Huff .12 .30
416 Magglio Ordonez .20 .50
417 Barry Bonds AW .50 1.25
418 Miguel Tejada AW .20 .50
419 Randy Johnson AW .30 .75
420 Barry Zito AW .20 .50
421 Jason Jennings AW .12 .30
422 Eric Hinske AW .12 .30
423 Benito Santiago AW .12 .30
424 Adam Kennedy AW .12 .30
425 Troy Glaus AW .12 .30
426 Brandon Phillips PR .12 .30
427 Jake Peavy PR .12 .30
428 Jason Romano PR .12 .30
429 Jeriome Robertson PR .12 .30
430 Aaron Guiel PR .12 .30
431 Hank Blalock PR .12 .30
432 Brad Lidge PR .12 .30
433 Francisco Rodriguez PR .20 .50
434 Jaime Cerda PR .12 .30
435 Jung Bong PR .12 .30
436 Reed Johnson PR .12 .30
437 Rene Reyes PR .12 .30
438 Chris Snelling PR .12 .30
439 Miguel Olivo PR .12 .30
440 Brian Banks PR .12 .30
441 Eric Junge PR .12 .30
442 Kirk Saarloos PR .12 .30
443 Jamey Carroll PR .12 .30
444 Josh Hancock PR .12 .30
445 Michael Restovich PR .12 .30
446 Willie Bloomquist PR .12 .30
447 John Lackey PR .20 .50
448 Marcus Thames PR .12 .30
449 Victor Martinez PR .20 .50
450 Brett Myers PR .12 .30
451 Wes Obermueller PR .12 .30
452 Hansel Izquierdo PR .12 .30
453 Brian Tallet PR .12 .30
454 Craig Monroe PR .12 .30
455 Doug Devore PR .12 .30
456 John Buck PR .12 .30
457 Tony Alvarez PR .12 .30
458 Wily Mo Pena PR .12 .30
459 John Stephens PR .12 .30
460 Tony Torcato PR .12 .30
461 Adam Kennedy BNR .12 .30
462 Alex Rodriguez BNR .40 1.00
463 Derek Lowe BNR .12 .30
464 Garret Anderson BNR .12 .30
465 Pat Burrell BNR .12 .30
466 Eric Gagne BNR .12 .30
467 Tomo Ohka BNR .12 .30
468 Josh Phelps BNR .12 .30
469 Sammy Sosa BNR .30 .75
470 Jim Thome BNR .20 .50
471 Vladimir Guerrero BNR .20 .50
472 Jason Simontacchi BNR .12 .30
473 Adam Dunn BNR .20 .50
474 Jim Edmonds BNR .20 .50
475 Barry Bonds BNR .50 1.25
476 Paul Konerko BNR .20 .50
477 Alfonso Soriano BNR .20 .50
478 Curt Schilling BNR .20 .50
479 John Smoltz BNR .30 .75
480 Torii Hunter BNR .12 .30
481 Rodrigo Lopez BNR .12 .30
482 Miguel Tejada BNR .20 .50
483 Eric Hinske BNR .12 .30
484 Roy Oswalt BNR .20 .50
485 Junior Spivey BNR .12 .30
P1 Barry Bonds Pin 1.50 4.00
P87 Derek Jeter Promo 1.25 3.00

2003 Fleer Tradition Glossy

*GLOSSY 1-100: 1.5X TO 4X BASIC
*GLOSSY 101-485: 5X TO 12X BASIC
RANDOM IN HOBBY UPDATE PACKS
STATED ODDS 1:24 RETAIL
STATED PRINT RUN 100 SERIAL #'d SETS

2003 Fleer Tradition Game Used

STATED ODDS 1:35 HOBBY, 1:90 RETAIL
SP PRINT RUNS PROVIDED BY FLEER
SP'S ARE NOT SERIAL-NUMBERED
*GOLD: .75X TO 2X BASIC GU
*GOLD: .6X TO 1.5X GU p/r 150-200
*GOLD ML: .6X TO 1.5X GU p/r 150-200
*GOLD: .4X TO 1X GU p/r 50-60
GOLD RANDOM INSERTS IN PACKS
GOLD PRINT RUN 100 SERIAL #'d SETS
2 Adrian Beltre Jsy 4.00 10.00
7 Andruw Jones Bat SP/150 2.00 5.00
10 Barry Bonds AW Jsy SP/50 12.00 30.00
11 Barry Larkin Jsy SP/200 3.00 8.00
22 Barry Zito Jsy 2.50 6.00
31 Craig Biggio Bat 2.50 6.00
42 Chipper Jones Jsy 4.00 10.00
46 Darin Erstad Jsy 1.50 4.00
63 Derek Jeter Jsy SP/150 15.00 40.00
67 Edg Alfonzo Jsy SP/200 2.00 5.00
97 Eric Karros Jsy 1.50 4.00
104 Frank Thomas Jsy 4.00 10.00
128 Greg Maddux Jsy 5.00 12.00
180 Hideo Nomo Jsy SP/200 5.00 12.00
184 Ivan Rodriguez Jsy 2.50 6.00
185 Jeromy Burnitz Jsy SP/200 2.00 5.00
192 Jeff Bagwell Jsy SP/200 3.00 8.00
193 J.D. Drew Jsy 1.50 4.00
194 Juan Gonzalez Bat SP/200 2.00 5.00
200 Jason Jennings AW Pants 1.50 4.00
205 Jason Kendall Pants 1.50 4.00
215 John Olerud Jsy 2.00 5.00
224 Jorge Posada Bat 3.00 8.00
269 Jimmy Rollins Jsy 2.50 6.00
270 Kazuhisa Ishii Jsy 1.50 4.00
276 Kazuhiro Sasaki Jsy SP/200 2.00 5.00
296 Kerry Wood Jsy SP/200 2.00 5.00
301 Luis Aparicio ML Jsy SP/150 3.00 8.00
304 Mark Grace Jsy 2.50 6.00
311 Mike Lowell Bat 1.50 4.00
327 Mike Mussina Jsy 2.50 6.00
334 Mike Piazza Jsy SP/150 6.00 15.00
339 Mark Prior Jsy SP/200 3.00 8.00
343 Manny Ramirez Jsy SP/150 5.00 12.00
344 M.Tejada AW Bat SP/150 3.00 8.00
346 Mo Vaughn Jsy SP/60 3.00 8.00
351 N.Garciaparra Jsy SP/200 3.00 8.00
375 Pedro Martinez Jsy SP/200 3.00 8.00
379 Roger Clemens Jsy SP/150 6.00 15.00
392 Randy Johnson Jsy SP/150 5.00 12.00
395 Rafael Palmeiro Jsy 2.50 6.00
402 Robin Ventura Jsy 1.50 4.00
403 Shea Hillenbrand Bat 1.50 4.00
406 W.Stargell ML Pants SP/150 3.00 8.00

2003 Fleer Tradition Game Used Gold

RANDOM INSERTS IN PACKS
STATED PRINT RUN 100 SERIAL #'d SETS

2003 Fleer Tradition Black-White Goudey

RANDOM INSERTS IN HOBBY PACKS
STATED PRINT RUN 1936 SERIAL #'d SETS
*GOLD: 2.5X TO 6X BASIC B/W GOUDEY
GOLD RANDOM INSERTS IN HOBBY PACKS
GOLD PRINT RUN 36 SERIAL #'d SETS
*RED: .75X TO 2X BASIC B/W GOUDEY
RED RANDOM INSERTS IN RETAIL PACKS
RED PRINT RUN 500 SERIAL #'d SETS
1 Jim Thome 1.00 2.50
2 Derek Jeter 4.00 10.00
3 Alex Rodriguez 2.00 5.00
4 Mark Prior 1.00 2.50
5 Nomar Garciaparra 1.00 2.50
6 Curt Schilling 1.00 2.50
7 Pat Burrell .60 1.50
8 Frank Thomas 1.50 4.00
9 Roger Clemens 2.00 5.00
10 Chipper Jones 1.50 4.00
11 Barry Larkin 1.00 2.50
12 Hideo Nomo 1.50 4.00
13 Pedro Martinez 1.00 2.50
14 Jeff Bagwell 1.00 2.50
15 Greg Maddux 2.00 5.00
16 Vladimir Guerrero 1.00 2.50
17 Ichiro Suzuki 2.00 5.00
18 Mike Piazza 1.50 4.00
19 Drew Henson .60 1.50
20 Albert Pujols 2.00 5.00
21 Sammy Sosa 1.50 4.00
22 Jason Giambi .60 1.50
23 Randy Johnson 1.50 4.00
24 Ken Griffey Jr. 3.00 8.00
25 Barry Bonds 2.50 6.00

2003 Fleer Tradition Checklists

COMP.JETER PUZZLE (9) 3.00 8.00
COMMON JETER .40 1.00
COMP.BONDS PUZZLE (9) 3.00 8.00
COMMON BONDS .40 1.00
STATED ODDS 1:4

2003 Fleer Tradition Hardball Preview

STATED ODDS 1:400 HOBBY, 1:480 RETAIL
1 Miguel Tejada 4.00 10.00
2 Derek Jeter 15.00 40.00
3 Mike Piazza 6.00 15.00
4 Barry Bonds 10.00 25.00
5 Mark Prior 4.00 10.00
6 Ichiro Suzuki 8.00 20.00
7 Alex Rodriguez 8.00 20.00
8 Nomar Garciaparra 4.00 10.00
9 Alfonso Soriano 4.00 10.00
10 Ken Griffey Jr. 12.00 30.00

2003 Fleer Tradition Lumber Company

COMPLETE SET (30) 15.00 40.00
STATED ODDS 1:10 HOBBY, 1:12 RETAIL
1 Mike Piazza 1.00 2.50
2 Derek Jeter 2.50 6.00
3 Alex Rodriguez 1.25 3.00
4 Miguel Tejada .60 1.50
5 Nomar Garciaparra .60 1.50
6 Andruw Jones .40 1.00
7 Pat Burrell .40 1.00
8 Albert Pujols 1.25 3.00
9 Jeff Bagwell .60 1.50
10 Chipper Jones 1.00 2.50
11 Ichiro Suzuki 1.25 3.00
12 Alfonso Soriano .60 1.50
13 Eric Chavez .40 1.00
14 Brian Giles .40 1.00
15 Shawn Green .40 1.00
16 Jim Thome .60 1.50
17 Lance Berkman .60 1.50
18 Bernie Williams .60 1.50
19 Manny Ramirez 1.00 2.50
20 Vladimir Guerrero .60 1.50
21 Carlos Delgado .40 1.00
22 Scott Rolen .60 1.50
23 Sammy Sosa 1.00 2.50
24 Ken Griffey Jr. 2.00 5.00
25 Barry Bonds 1.50 4.00
26 Todd Helton .60 1.50
27 Jason Giambi .40 1.00
28 Austin Kearns .40 1.00
29 Jeff Kent .40 1.00
30 Magglio Ordonez .60 1.50

2003 Fleer Tradition Lumber Company Game Used

STATED ODDS 1:108 HOBBY, 1:195 RETAIL
GOLD RANDOM INSERTS IN PACKS
GOLD #'d PRINT RUN BASED ON 02 HR'S
NO GOLD PRICING ON QTY OF 40 OR LESS
AJ Andruw Jones 4.00 10.00
AK Austin Kearns SP/75 6.00 15.00
AS Alfonso Soriano SP/200 4.00 10.00
BB Barry Bonds SP/150 12.50 30.00
BG Brian Giles SP/200 4.00 10.00
BW Bernie Williams 4.00 10.00
CD Carlos Delgado SP/200 4.00 10.00
CJ Chipper Jones 6.00 15.00
DJ Derek Jeter SP/96 15.00 40.00
EC Eric Chavez SP/125 4.00 10.00
JB Jeff Bagwell SP/200 6.00 15.00
JK Jeff Kent SP/200 4.00 10.00
JT Jim Thome SP/200 6.00 15.00
LB Lance Berkman SP/200 4.00 10.00
MO Magglio Ordonez 3.00 8.00
MP Mike Piazza SP/200 10.00 25.00
MR Manny Ramirez 4.00 10.00
MT Miguel Tejada 3.00 8.00
NG Nomar Garciaparra SP/200 8.00 20.00
PB Pat Burrell SP/75 6.00 15.00
RA Alex Rodriguez 6.00 15.00
SG Shawn Green SP/200 4.00 10.00
SR Scott Rolen SP/80 10.00 25.00
TH Todd Helton 4.00 10.00

2003 Fleer Tradition Lumber Company Game Used Gold

RANDOM INSERTS IN PACKS
SERIAL #'d PRINT RUN BASED ON 02 HR'S
NO PRICING ON QTY OF 31 OR LESS
AJ Andruw Jones/35 15.00 40.00
AR Alex Rodriguez/57 20.00 50.00
AS Alfonso Soriano/39 10.00 25.00
BB Barry Bonds/46 15.00 40.00
BG Brian Giles/38 10.00 25.00
CD Carlos Delgado/33 10.00 25.00
CJ Chipper Jones/26 15.00 40.00
EC Eric Chavez/34 10.00 25.00
JK Jeff Kent/37 10.00 25.00
JT Jim Thome/52 15.00 40.00
LB Lance Berkman/42 10.00 25.00
MO Magglio Ordonez/38 10.00 25.00
MP Mike Piazza/33 12.00 30.00
MR Manny Ramirez/33 15.00 40.00
MT Miguel Tejada/34 10.00 25.00
PB Pat Burrell/37 10.00 25.00
SG Shawn Green/42 10.00 25.00
SR Scott Rolen/31 15.00 40.00
TH Todd Helton/30 15.00 40.00

2003 Fleer Tradition Milestones

COMPLETE SET (25) 12.50 30.00
STATED ODDS 1:5 HOBBY, 1:4 RETAIL
1 Eddie Mathews 1.00 2.50
2 Rickey Henderson 1.00 2.50
3 Harmon Killebrew 1.00 2.50
4 Al Kaline .60 1.50
5 Willie McCovey .60 1.50
6 Tom Seaver .60 1.50
7 Reggie Jackson .60 1.50
8 Mike Schmidt 1.50 4.00
9 Nolan Ryan 3.00 8.00
10 Mike Piazza 1.00 2.50
11 Randy Johnson 1.00 2.50
12 Bernie Williams .60 1.50
13 Rafael Palmeiro .60 1.50
14 Juan Gonzalez .40 1.00
15 Ken Griffey Jr. 2.00 5.00
16 Derek Jeter 2.50 6.00
17 Roger Clemens 1.25 3.00
18 Roberto Alomar .60 1.50
19 Manny Ramirez 1.00 2.50
20 Luis Gonzalez .40 1.00
21 Barry Bonds 1.50 4.00
22 Nomar Garciaparra .60 1.50
23 Fred McGriff .60 1.50
24 Greg Maddux 1.25 3.00
25 Barry Bonds 1.50 4.00

2003 Fleer Tradition Milestones Game Used

STATED ODDS 1:143 HOBBY, 1:270 RETAIL
SP PRINT RUNS PROVIDED BY FLEER
SP'S ARE NOT SERIAL-NUMBERED
*GOLD: .75X TO 2X BASIC MILE
*GOLD: .6X TO 1.5X MILE SP/150-200
*GOLD: .5X TO 1.2X MILE SP/100
GOLD RANDOM INSERTS IN PACKS
GOLD PRINT RUN 100 SERIAL #'d SETS
BB1 B.Bonds 5 MVP Jsy SP/200 12.50 30.00
BB2 B.Bonds 600 HR Bat SP/100 15.00 40.00
BW Bernie Williams Jsy SP/200 6.00 15.00
DJ Derek Jeter Jsy SP/150 12.50 30.00
FM Fred McGriff Bat 4.00 10.00
GM Greg Maddux Jsy 6.00 15.00
JG Juan Gonzalez Bat SP/250 4.00 10.00
MP Mike Piazza Jsy SP/100 10.00 25.00
MR Manny Ramirez Jsy SP/150 6.00 15.00
NG N.Garciaparra Jsy SP/200 8.00 20.00
RA Roberto Alomar Bat SP/200 6.00 15.00
RC Roger Clemens Jsy SP/150 10.00 25.00
RJ Randy Johnson Jsy SP/100 6.00 15.00
RP Rafael Palmeiro Jsy SP/200 6.00 15.00

2003 Fleer Tradition Standouts

STATED ODDS 1:40 HOBBY, 1:72 RETAIL
CARDS ARE LISTED ALPHABETICALLY
1 Barry Bonds 2.50 6.00
2 Pat Burrell .60 1.50
3 Roger Clemens 2.00 5.00
4 Adam Dunn 1.00 2.50
5 Nomar Garciaparra 1.00 2.50
6 Ken Griffey Jr. 3.00 8.00
7 Vladimir Guerrero 1.00 2.50
8 Derek Jeter 4.00 10.00
9 Greg Maddux 2.00 5.00
10 Mike Piazza 1.50 4.00
11 Alex Rodriguez 2.00 5.00
12 Alfonso Soriano 1.00 2.50
13 Sammy Sosa 1.50 4.00
14 Ichiro Suzuki 2.00 5.00
15 Miguel Tejada 1.00 2.50

2003 Fleer Tradition Update

COMP.SET w/o SP's (285) 15.00 40.00
COMMON CARD (1-285) .12 .30
COMMON CARD (286-299) .40 1.00
COMMON RC (286-299) .40 1.00
286-299 STATED ODDS 1:4 HOB/RET
COMMON CARD (300-398) .40 1.00
COMMON RC (300-398) .40 1.00
300-398 ISSUED IN MINI-BOXES
ONE MINI-BOX PER UPDATE BOX
25 CARDS PER MINI-BOX
1 Aaron Boone .12 .30
2 Carl Everett .12 .30
3 Eduardo Perez .12 .30
4 Jason Michaels .12 .30
5 Karim Garcia .12 .30
6 Rainer Olmedo .12 .30
7 Scott Williamson .12 .30
8 Adam Kennedy .12 .30
9 Carl Pavano .12 .30
10 Eli Marrero .12 .30
11 Jason Simontacchi .12 .30
12 Keith Foulke .12 .30
13 Preston Wilson .12 .30
14 Scott Hatteberg .12 .30
15 Adam Dunn .20 .50
16 Carlos Baerga .12 .30
17 Elmer Dessens .12 .30
18 Javier Vazquez .12 .30
19 Kenny Rogers .12 .30
20 Quinton McCracken .12 .30
21 Shane Reynolds .12 .30
22 Adam Eaton .12 .30
23 Carlos Zambrano .20 .50
24 Enrique Wilson .12 .30
25 Jeff DaVanon .12 .30
26 Kenny Lofton .12 .30
27 Ramon Castro .12 .30
28 Shannon Stewart .12 .30
29 Al Martin .12 .30
30 Carlos Guillen .12 .30
31 Eric Karros .12 .30
32 Tim Worrell .12 .30
33 Kevin Millwood .12 .30
34 Randall Simon .12 .30
35 Shawn Chacon .12 .30
36 Alex Rodriguez .40 1.00
37 Casey Blake .12 .30
38 Eric Munson .12 .30
39 Jeff Kent .12 .30
40 Kris Benson .12 .30
41 Randy Winn .12 .30
42 Shea Hillenbrand .12 .30
43 Alfonso Soriano .20 .50
44 Chris George .12 .30
45 Eric Bruntlett .12 .30
46 Jeromy Burnitz .12 .30
47 Kyle Farnsworth .12 .30
48 Torii Hunter .12 .30
49 Sidney Ponson .12 .30
50 Andres Galarraga .20 .50
51 Chris Singleton .12 .30
52 Eric Gagne .12 .30
53 Jesse Foppert .12 .30
54 Lance Carter .12 .30
55 Ray Durham .12 .30
56 Tanyon Sturtze .12 .30
57 Andy Ashby .12 .30
58 Cliff Floyd .12 .30
59 Eric Young .12 .30
60 Jhonny Peralta .12 .30
61 Livan Hernandez .12 .30
62 Reggie Sanders .12 .30
63 Tim Spooneybarger .12 .30
64 Angel Berroa .12 .30
65 Coco Crisp .12 .30
66 Eric Hinske .12 .30
67 Jim Edmonds .20 .50
68 Luis Matos .12 .30
69 Rickey Henderson .30 .75
70 Todd Walker .12 .30
71 Antonio Alfonseca .12 .30
72 Corey Koskie .12 .30
73 Erubiel Durazo .12 .30
74 Jim Thome .20 .50
75 Lyle Overbay .12 .30
76 Robert Fick .12 .30
77 Todd Hollandsworth .12 .30
78 Aramis Ramirez .12 .30
79 Cristian Guzman .12 .30
80 Esteban Loaiza .12 .30
81 Jody Gerut .12 .30
82 Mark Grudzielanek .12 .30
83 Roberto Alomar .20 .50
84 Todd Hundley .12 .30
85 Mike Hampton .12 .30
86 Curt Schilling .20 .50
87 Francisco Rodriguez .20 .50
88 John Lackey .20 .50
89 Mark Redman .12 .30
90 Robin Ventura .12 .30
91 Todd Zeile .12 .30
92 B.J. Surhoff .12 .30
93 Raul Mondesi .12 .30
94 Frank Catalanotto .12 .30
95 John Smoltz .30 .75
96 Mark Ellis .12 .30
97 Rocco Baldelli .12 .30
98 Todd Pratt .12 .30
99 Barry Bonds .50 1.25
100 Danny Graves .12 .30
101 Fred McGriff .20 .50
102 John Burkett .12 .30
103 Marquis Grissom .12 .30
104 Rocky Biddle .12 .30
105 Tom Glavine .20 .50
106 Bartolo Colon .12 .30
107 Darren Bragg .12 .30
108 Gabe Kapler .12 .30
109 John Franco .12 .30
110 Matt Mantei .12 .30
111 Rod Beck .12 .30
112 Tomo Ohka .12 .30
113 Ben Petrick .12 .30
114 Darren Dreifort .12 .30
115 Garret Anderson .12 .30
116 John Vander Wal .12 .30
117 Melvin Mora .12 .30
118 Rodrigo Lopez .12 .30
119 Raul Ibanez .20 .50
120 Benito Santiago .12 .30
121 David Ortiz Sox .30 .75
122 Gary Bennett .12 .30
123 Jon Garland .12 .30
124 Michael Young .12 .30
125 Rodrigo Rosario .12 .30
126 Travis Lee .12 .30
127 Bill Mueller .12 .30
128 Derek Lowe .12 .30
129 Gil Meche .12 .30
130 Jose Guillen .12 .30
131 Miguel Cabrera 1.50 4.00
132 Ron Calloway .12 .30
133 Troy Percival .12 .30
134 Billy Koch .12 .30
135 Dmitri Young .12 .30
136 Glendon Rusch .12 .30
137 Jose Jimenez .12 .30
138 Miguel Tejada .20 .50
139 John Thomson .12 .30
140 Troy O'Leary .12 .30
141 Bobby Kielty .12 .30
142 Dontrelle Willis .12 .30
143 Greg Myers .12 .30
144 Jose Vizcaino .12 .30
145 Mike MacDougal .12 .30
146 Ronnie Belliard .12 .30
147 Tyler Houston .12 .30
148 Brady Clark .12 .30
149 Edgardo Alfonzo .12 .30
150 Guillermo Mota .12 .30
151 Jose Lima .12 .30
152 Mike Williams .12 .30
153 Roy Oswalt .20 .50
154 Scott Podsednik .12 .30
155 Brandon Lyon .12 .30
156 Henry Mateo .12 .30
157 Jose Macias .12 .30
158 Mike Bordick .12 .30
159 Royce Clayton .12 .30
160 Vance Wilson .12 .30
161 Brent Abernathy .12 .30
162 Horacio Ramirez .12 .30
163 Jose Reyes .30 .75
164 Nick Punto .12 .30
165 Ruben Sierra .12 .30
166 Victor Zambrano .12 .30
167 Brett Tomko .12 .30
168 Ivan Rodriguez .20 .50
169 Jose Mesa .12 .30
170 Octavio Dotel .12 .30
171 Russ Ortiz .12 .30
172 Vladimir Guerrero .20 .50
173 Brian Lawrence .12 .30
174 Jae Weong Seo .12 .30
175 Jose Cruz Jr. .12 .30
176 Pat Burrell .12 .30
177 Russell Branyan .12 .30
178 Warren Morris .12 .30
179 Brian Boehringer .12 .30
180 Jason Johnson .12 .30
181 Josh Phelps .12 .30
182 Paul Konerko .20 .50
183 Ryan Franklin .12 .30
184 Wes Helms .12 .30
185 Brooks Kieschnick .12 .30
186 Jason Davis .12 .30
187 Juan Pierre .12 .30
188 Paul Wilson .12 .30
189 Sammy Sosa .30 .75
190 Wil Cordero .12 .30
191 Byung-Hyun Kim .12 .30
192 Juan Encarnacion .12 .30
193 Placido Polanco .12 .30
194 Sandy Alomar Jr. .12 .30
195 Julio Lugo .12 .30
196 Junior Spivey .12 .30
197 Woody Williams .12 .30
198 Xavier Nady .12 .30
199 Mark Loretta .12 .30
200 Deivi Cruz .12 .30
201 Jorge Posada AS .20 .50
202 Carlos Delgado AS .12 .30
203 Alfonso Soriano AS .20 .50
204 Alex Rodriguez AS .40 1.00
205 Troy Glaus AS .12 .30
206 Garret Anderson AS .12 .30
207 Hideki Matsui AS .60 1.50
208 Ichiro Suzuki AS .40 1.00
209 Esteban Loaiza AS .12 .30
210 Manny Ramirez AS .30 .75
211 Roger Clemens AS .40 1.00
212 Roy Halladay AS .20 .50
213 Jason Giambi AS .12 .30
214 Edgar Martinez AS .20 .50
215 Bret Boone AS .12 .30
216 Hank Blalock AS .12 .30
217 Nomar Garciaparra AS .20 .50
218 Vernon Wells AS .12 .30
219 Melvin Mora AS .12 .30
220 Magglio Ordonez AS .20 .50
221 Mike Sweeney AS .12 .30
222 Barry Zito AS .20 .50
223 Carl Everett AS .12 .30
224 Shigetoshi Hasegawa AS .12 .30
225 Jamie Moyer AS .12 .30
226 Mark Mulder AS .12 .30
227 Eddie Guardado AS .12 .30
228 Ramon Hernandez AS .12 .30
229 Keith Foulke AS .12 .30
230 Javy Lopez AS .12 .30
231 Todd Helton AS .20 .50
232 Marcus Giles AS .12 .30
233 Edgar Renteria AS .12 .30
234 Scott Rolen AS .20 .50
235 Barry Bonds AS .50 1.25
236 Albert Pujols AS .40 1.00
237 Gary Sheffield AS .12 .30
238 Jim Edmonds AS .20 .50
239 Jason Schmidt AS .12 .30
240 Mark Prior AS .20 .50
241 Dontrelle Willis AS .12 .30
242 Kerry Wood AS .12 .30
243 Kevin Brown AS .12 .30
244 Woody Williams AS .12 .30
245 Paul Lo Duca AS .12 .30
246 Richie Sexson AS .12 .30
247 Jose Vidro AS .12 .30
248 Luis Castillo AS .12 .30
249 Aaron Boone AS .12 .30
250 Mike Lowell AS .12 .30
251 Rafael Furcal AS .12 .30
252 Andruw Jones AS .12 .30
253 Preston Wilson AS .12 .30
254 John Smoltz AS .30 .75
255 Eric Gagne AS .12 .30
256 Randy Wolf AS .12 .30
257 Billy Wagner AS .12 .30
258 Luis Gonzalez AS .12 .30
259 Russ Ortiz AS .12 .30
260 J.Thome P.Martinez IL .20 .50
261 A.Soriano J.Bagwell IL .20 .50
262 D.Willis R.Baldelli IL .12 .30
263 C.Delgado V.Guerrero IL .20 .50
264 S.Sosa M.Ordonez IL .30 .75
265 J.Giambi A.Dunn IL .20 .50
266 M.Sweeney A.Pujols IL .40 1.00
267 B.Bonds T.Hunter IL .50 1.25
268 I.Suzuki A.Jones IL .40 1.00
269 C.Jones H.Blalock IL .30 .75
270 M.Prior V.Wells IL .20 .50
271 N.Garciaparra S.Rolen IL .20 .50
272 A.Rodriguez L.Berkman IL .40 1.00
273 R.Clemens K.Wood IL .40 1.00
274 D.Jeter J.Reyes IL .75 2.00
275 G.Maddux B.Zito IL .40 1.00
276 Carlos Delgado TT .12 .30
277 J.D. Drew TT .12 .30
278 Barry Bonds TT .50 1.25
279 Albert Pujols TT .40 1.00
280 Jim Thome TT .20 .50
281 Sammy Sosa TT .30 .75
282 Alfonso Soriano TT .20 .50
283 Hideki Matsui TT .60 1.50
284 Mike Piazza TT .30 .75
285 Vladimir Guerrero TT .20 .50
286 Rich Harden ROO .60 1.50
287 Chin-Hui Tsao ROO .40 1.00
288 Edwin Jackson ROO RC .60 1.50
289 Chien-Ming Wang ROO RC 1.50 4.00
290 Josh Willingham ROO RC 1.25 3.00
291 Matt Kata ROO RC .40 1.00
292 Jose Contreras ROO RC 1.00 2.50
293 Chris Bootcheck ROO .40 1.00
294 Javier A. Lopez ROO RC .40 1.00
295 Delmon Young ROO RC 2.50 6.00
296 Pedro Liriano ROO .40 1.00
297 Noah Lowry ROO .40 1.00
298 Khalil Greene ROO .60 1.50
299 Rob Bowen ROO .40 1.00
300 Bo Hart ROO RC .40 1.00
301 Beau Kemp ROO RC .40 1.00
302 Gerald Laird ROO .40 1.00
303 Miguel Ojeda ROO RC .40 1.00
304 Todd Wellemeyer ROO RC .40 1.00
305 Ryan Wagner ROO RC .40 1.00
306 Jeff Duncan ROO RC .40 1.00
307 Wilfredo Ledezma ROO RC .40 1.00
308 Wes Obermueller ROO .40 1.00
309 Bernie Castro ROO RC .40 1.00
310 Tim Olson ROO RC .40 1.00
311 Colin Porter ROO RC .40 1.00
312 Francisco Cruceta ROO RC .40 1.00
313 Guillermo Quiroz ROO RC .40 1.00
314 Brian Stokes ROO RC .40 1.00
315 Robby Hammock ROO RC .40 1.00
316 Lew Ford ROO RC .40 1.00
317 Todd Linden ROO .40 1.00
318 Mike Gallo ROO RC .40 1.00
319 Francisco Rosario ROO RC .40 1.00
320 Rosman Garcia ROO RC .40 1.00
321 Felix Sanchez ROO RC .40 1.00
322 Chad Gaudin ROO RC .40 1.00
323 Phil Seibel ROO RC .40 1.00
324 Jason Gilfillan ROO RC .40 1.00
325 Termel Sledge ROO RC .40 1.00
326 Alfredo Gonzalez ROO RC .40 1.00
327 Josh Stewart ROO RC .40 1.00
328 Jeremy Griffiths ROO RC .40 1.00
329 Cory Stewart ROO RC .40 1.00
330 Josh Hall ROO RC .40 1.00
331 Arnie Munoz ROO RC .40 1.00
332 Garrett Atkins ROO .40 1.00
333 Neal Cotts ROO .40 1.00
334 Dan Haren ROO RC 2.00 5.00
335 Shane Victorino ROO RC 1.25 3.00
336 David Sanders ROO RC .40 1.00
337 Oscar Villarreal ROO RC .40 1.00
338 Michael Hessman ROO RC .40 1.00
339 Andrew Brown ROO RC .40 1.00
340 Kevin Hooper ROO .40 1.00
341 Prentice Redman ROO RC .40 1.00
342 Brandon Webb ROO RC 1.25 3.00
343 Jimmy Gobble ROO .40 1.00
344 Pete LaForest ROO RC .40 1.00
345 Chris Waters ROO RC .40 1.00
346 Hideki Matsui ROO RC 2.00 5.00
347 Chris Capuano ROO RC .40 1.00
348 Jon Leicester ROO RC .40 1.00
349 Mike Nicolas ROO RC .40 1.00
350 Nook Logan ROO RC .40 1.00
351 Craig Brazell ROO RC .40 1.00
352 Aaron Looper ROO RC .40 1.00
353 D.J. Carrasco ROO RC .40 1.00
354 Clint Barmes ROO RC 1.00 2.50
355 Doug Waechter ROO RC .40 1.00
356 Julio Manon ROO RC .40 1.00
357 Jeremy Bonderman ROO RC 1.50 4.00
358 Diegomar Markwell ROO RC .40 1.00
359 Dave Matranga ROO RC .40 1.00
360 Luis Ayala ROO RC .40 1.00
361 Jason Stanford ROO .40 1.00
362 Roger Deago ROO RC .40 1.00
363 Geoff Geary ROO RC .40 1.00
364 Edgar Gonzalez ROO RC .40 1.00
365 Michel Hernandez ROO RC .40 1.00
366 Aquilino Lopez ROO RC .40 1.00
367 David Manning ROO .40 1.00
368 Carlos Mendez ROO RC .40 1.00
369 Matt Miller ROO RC .40 1.00
370 Michael Nakamura ROO RC .40 1.00
371 Mike Neu ROO RC .40 1.00
372 Ramon Nivar ROO RC .40 1.00
373 Kevin Ohme ROO RC .40 1.00
374 Alex Prieto ROO RC .40 1.00
375 Stephen Randolph ROO RC .40 1.00
376 Brian Sweeney ROO RC .40 1.00
377 Matt Diaz ROO RC .60 1.50
378 Mike Gonzalez ROO .40 1.00
379 Daniel Cabrera ROO RC .60 1.50
380 Fernando Cabrera ROO RC .40 1.00
381 David DeJesus ROO RC 1.00 2.50
382 Mike Ryan ROO RC .40 1.00
383 Rick Roberts ROO RC .40 1.00
384 Seung Song ROO .40 1.00
385 Rickie Weeks ROO RC 1.25 3.00
386 Humberto Quintero ROO RC .40 1.00
387 Alexis Rios ROO .40 1.00
388 Aaron Miles ROO RC .40 1.00
389 Tom Gregorio ROO RC .40 1.00
390 Anthony Ferrari ROO RC .40 1.00
391 Kevin Correia ROO RC .40 1.00
392 Rafael Betancourt ROO RC .40 1.00
393 Rett Johnson ROO RC .40 1.00
394 Richard Fischer ROO RC .40 1.00
395 Greg Aquino ROO RC .40 1.00
396 Daniel Garcia ROO RC .40 1.00
397 Sergio Mitre ROO RC .40 1.00
398 Edwin Almonte ROO .40 1.00

2003 Fleer Tradition Update Glossy

*GLOSSY 1-285: 5X TO 12X BASIC
*GLOSSY MATSUI 207/283: 1.5X TO 4X BASIC
*GLOSSY 286-299: 1.5X TO 4X BASIC
*GLOSSY 286-299: 1.5X TO 4X BASIC RC's
*GLOSSY 300-398: 1.5X TO 4X BASIC
*GLOSSY 300-398: 1.5X TO 4X BASIC RC's
RANDOM INSERTS IN HOBBY PACKS
STATED ODDS 1:24 RETAIL
STATED PRINT RUN 100 SERIAL #'d SETS

2003 Fleer Tradition Update Diamond Debuts

STATED ODDS 1:10 HOBBY, 1:8 RETAIL
1 Dontrelle Willis .40 1.00
2 Bo Hart .40 1.00
3 Jose Reyes 1.00 2.50
4 Chin-Hui Tsao .40 1.00
5 Brandon Webb 1.25 3.00
6 Rich Harden .60 1.50
7 Jesse Foppert .40 1.00
8 Rocco Baldelli .40 1.00
9 Hideki Matsui 2.00 5.00
10 Ron Calloway .40 1.00
11 Jeremy Bonderman 1.50 4.00
12 Mark Teixeira .60 1.50
13 Ryan Wagner .40 1.00
14 Jose Contreras 1.00 2.50
15 Miguel Cabrera 5.00 12.00
16 Lew Ford .40 1.00
17 Jeff Duncan .40 1.00
18 Matt Kata .40 1.00
19 Jeremy Griffiths .40 1.00
20 Todd Wellemeyer .40 1.00
21 Robby Hammock .40 1.00
22 Dave Matranga .40 1.00
23 Laynce Nix .40 1.00
24 Jhonny Peralta .40 1.00
25 Oscar Villareal .40 1.00

2003 Fleer Tradition Update Long Gone!

RANDOM INSERTS IN HOBBY PACKS
STATED ODDS 1:72 RETAIL
PRINT RUNS B/WN 410-536 COPIES PER
1 Barry Bonds/475 2.50 6.00
2 Jason Giambi/440 .60 1.50
3 Albert Pujols/452 2.00 5.00
4 Chipper Jones/420 1.50 4.00
5 Manny Ramirez/430 1.50 4.00
6 Sammy Sosa/536 1.50 4.00
7 Alfonso Soriano/440 1.00 2.50
8 Alex Rodriguez/430 2.00 5.00
9 Jim Thome/445 1.00 2.50
10 Vladimir Guerrero/502 1.00 2.50
11 Austin Kearns/430 .60 1.50
12 Jeff Bagwell/420 1.00 2.50
13 Andruw Jones/430 .60 1.50
14 Carlos Delgado/451 .60 1.50
15 Nomar Garciaparra/440 1.00 2.50
16 Adam Dunn/464 1.00 2.50
17 Mike Piazza/450 1.50 4.00
18 Derek Jeter/410 4.00 10.00
19 Ken Griffey Jr./430 3.00 8.00
20 Hank Blalock/424 .60 1.50

2003 Fleer Tradition Update Milestones

STATED ODDS 1:8 HOBBY, 1:6 RETAIL
1 Roger Clemens 1.25 3.00
2 Rafael Palmeiro .60 1.50
3 Jeff Bagwell .60 1.50
4 Barry Bonds 1.50 4.00
5 Sammy Sosa 1.00 2.50
6 Albert Pujols 1.25 3.00
7 Ichiro Suzuki 1.25 3.00
8 Alfonso Soriano .60 1.50
9 Alex Rodriguez 1.25 3.00
10 Randy Johnson 1.00 2.50
11 Manny Ramirez 1.00 2.50
12 Chipper Jones 1.00 2.50
13 Todd Helton .60 1.50
14 Ken Griffey Jr. 2.00 5.00
15 Jim Thome .60 1.50
16 Frank Thomas 1.00 2.50
17 Pedro Martinez .60 1.50
18 Hideo Nomo 1.00 2.50
19 Jason Schmidt .40 1.00
20 Carlos Delgado .40 1.00

2003 Fleer Tradition Update Milestones Game Jersey

STATED ODDS 1:20 HOBBY, 1:96 RETAIL
*GOLD: .75X TO 2X BASIC
GOLD RANDOM IN HOB/RET PACKS
GOLD PRINT RUN 100 SERIAL #'d SETS
AR Alex Rodriguez 4.00 10.00
AS Alfonso Soriano 3.00 8.00
CD Carlos Delgado 3.00 8.00
CJ Chipper Jones 4.00 10.00
FT Frank Thomas 4.00 10.00
HN Hideo Nomo 4.00 10.00
JB Jeff Bagwell 4.00 10.00
JS Jason Schmidt 3.00 8.00
JT Jim Thome 4.00 10.00
MR Manny Ramirez 4.00 10.00
PM Pedro Martinez 4.00 10.00
RC Roger Clemens 6.00 15.00
RJ Randy Johnson 4.00 10.00
RP Rafael Palmeiro 4.00 10.00
SS Sammy Sosa 4.00 10.00
TH Todd Helton 4.00 10.00

2003 Fleer Tradition Update Throwback Threads

STATED ODDS 1:64 HOBBY, 1:288 RETAIL
*PATCH: 1X TO 2.5X BASIC
PATCH RANDOM INSERTS IN PACKS
PATCH PRINT RUN 100 SERIAL #'d SETS
AL Al Leiter 3.00 8.00
KM Kevin Millwood 3.00 8.00
MP Mike Piazza 6.00 15.00
TG Troy Glaus 3.00 8.00
VG Vladimir Guerrero 4.00 10.00

2003 Fleer Tradition Update Throwback Threads Dual

RANDOM INSERTS IN HOB/RET PACKS
STATED PRINT RUN 100 SERIAL #'d SETS
MPAL M.Piazza/A.Leiter 10.00 25.00
VGTG V.Guerrero/T.Glaus 8.00 20.00

2003 Fleer Tradition Update Turn Back the Clock

STATED ODDS 1:160 HOBBY, 1:288 RETAIL
1 Yogi Berra 2.50 6.00
2 Mike Schmidt 4.00 10.00
3 Tom Seaver 1.50 4.00
4 Reggie Jackson 1.50 4.00
5 Pee Wee Reese 1.50 4.00
6 Phil Rizzuto 1.50 4.00
7 Jim Palmer 1.50 4.00
8 Robin Yount 2.50 6.00
9 Nolan Ryan 8.00 20.00
10 Al Kaline 1.50 4.00

2004 Fleer Tradition

COMPLETE SET (500) 25.00 60.00
COMP.SET w/o SP's (400) 8.00 20.00
COMMON CARD (1-400) .10 .30
COMMON CARD (401-470) .40 1.00
COMMON CARD (471-500) .40 1.00
401-445 STATED ODDS 1:2
446-461 STATED ODDS 1:6
462-470 STATED ODDS 1:9
471-500 STATED ODDS 1:3
1 Juan Pierre WS .12 .30
2 Josh Beckett WS .12 .30
3 Ivan Rodriguez WS .20 .50
4 Miguel Cabrera WS .30 .75
5 Dontrelle Willis WS .12 .30
6 Derek Jeter WS .75 2.00
7 Jason Giambi WS .12 .30
8 Bernie Williams WS .20 .50
9 Alfonso Soriano WS .20 .50
10 Hideki Matsui WS .50 1.25
11 Anderson Ortiz Lackey TL .20 .50
12 Gonzalez Webb Schilling TL .20 .50
13 Lopez Sheffield Ortiz TL .12 .30
14 Batista Gibb Ponson John TL .12 .30
15 Manny Nomar Lowe Pedro TL .30 .75
16 Sosa Prior Wood TL .30 .75
17 Thomas Lee Loaiza TL .30 .75
18 Dunn Casey Reit Wilson TL .20 .50
19 Gerut Sabathia TL .20 .50
20 Wilson Oliver Jennings TL .12 .30
21 Young Maroth Bonderman TL .12 .30
22 Lowell Willis Beckett TL .12 .30
23 Bagwell Robertson Miller TL .20 .50
24 Beltran May TL .20 .50
25 Beltre Green Nomo Brown TL .30 .75
26 Sexson Sheets TL .12 .30
27 Hunter Radke Santana TL .20 .50
28 Vlad Cabrera Livan Vazq TL .20 .50
29 Floyd Wigg Trach Leiter TL .12 .30
30 Giambi Pettitte Mussina TL .20 .50
31 Chavez Tejada Hudson TL .20 .50
32 Thome Wolf TL .20 .50
33 Sanders Fogg Wells TL .12 .30
34 Klesko Loretta Peavy TL .12 .30
35 Cruz Jr. Alfonzo Schmidt TL .12 .30
36 Boone Moyer Pineiro TL .12 .30
37 Pujols Williams TL .40 1.00
38 Huff Zambrano TL .12 .30
39 A.Rodriguez Thomson TL .40 1.00
40 Delgado Halladay TL .20 .50
41 Greg Maddux .40 1.00
42 Ben Grieve .12 .30
43 Darin Erstad .12 .30
44 Ruben Sierra .12 .30
45 Byung-Hyung Kim .12 .30
46 Freddy Garcia .12 .30
47 Richard Hidalgo .12 .30
48 Tike Redman .12 .30
49 Kevin Millwood .12 .30
50 Marquis Grissom .12 .30
51 Jae Weong Seo .12 .30
52 Wil Cordero .12 .30
53 LaTroy Hawkins .12 .30
54 Jolbert Cabrera .12 .30
55 Kevin Appier .12 .30
56 John Lackey .20 .50
57 Garret Anderson .12 .30
58 R.A. Dickey .20 .50
59 David Segui .12 .30
60 Erubiel Durazo .12 .30
61 Bobby Abreu .12 .30
62 Travis Hafner .12 .30
63 Victor Zambrano .12 .30
64 Randy Johnson .30 .75
65 Bernie Williams .20 .50
66 J.T. Snow .12 .30
67 Sammy Sosa .30 .75
68 Al Leiter .12 .30
69 Jason Jennings .12 .30
70 Matt Morris .12 .30
71 Mike Hampton .12 .30
72 Juan Encarnacion .12 .30
73 Alex Gonzalez .12 .30
74 Bartolo Colon .12 .30
75 Brett Myers .12 .30
76 Michael Young .12 .30
77 Ichiro Suzuki .40 1.00
78 Jason Johnson .12 .30
79 Brad Ausmus .12 .30
80 Ted Lilly .12 .30
81 Ken Griffey Jr. .60 1.50
82 Chone Figgins .12 .30
83 Edgar Martinez .20 .50
84 Adam Eaton .12 .30
85 Ken Harvey .12 .30
86 Francisco Rodriguez .20 .50
87 Bill Mueller .12 .30
88 Mike Maroth .12 .30
89 Charles Johnson .12 .30
90 Jhonny Peralta .12 .30
91 Kip Wells .12 .30
92 Cesar Izturis .12 .30
93 Matt Clement .12 .30
94 Lyle Overbay .12 .30
95 Kirk Rueter .12 .30
96 Cristian Guzman .12 .30
97 Garrett Stephenson .12 .30
98 Lance Berkman .20 .50
99 Brett Tomko .12 .30
100 Chris Stynes .12 .30
101 Nate Cornejo .12 .30
102 Aaron Rowand .12 .30
103 Javier Vazquez .12 .30
104 Jason Kendall .12 .30
105 Mark Redman .12 .30
106 Benito Santiago .12 .30
107 C.C. Sabathia .20 .50
108 David Wells .12 .30
109 Mark Ellis .12 .30
110 Casey Blake .12 .30
111 Sean Burroughs .12 .30
112 Carlos Beltran .20 .50
113 Ramon Hernandez .12 .30
114 Eric Hinske .12 .30
115 Luis Gonzalez .12 .30
116 Jarrod Washburn .12 .30
117 Ronnie Belliard .12 .30
118 Troy Percival .12 .30
119 Jose Valentin .12 .30
120 Chase Utley .20 .50
121 Odalis Perez .12 .30
122 Steve Finley .12 .30
123 Bret Boone .12 .30
124 Jeff Conine .12 .30
125 Josh Fogg .12 .30
126 Neifi Perez .12 .30
127 Ben Sheets .12 .30
128 Randy Winn .12 .30
129 Matt Stairs .12 .30
130 Carlos Delgado .12 .30
131 Morgan Ensberg .12 .30
132 Vinny Castilla .12 .30
133 Matt Mantei .12 .30
134 Alex Rodriguez .40 1.00
135 Matthew LeCroy .12 .30
136 Woody Williams .12 .30
137 Frank Catalanotto .12 .30
138 Rondell White .12 .30
139 Scott Rolen .20 .50
140 Cliff Floyd .12 .30
141 Chipper Jones .30 .75
142 Robin Ventura .12 .30
143 Mariano Rivera .40 1.00
144 Brady Clark .12 .30
145 Ramon Ortiz .12 .30
146 Omar Infante .12 .30
147 Mike Matheny .12 .30
148 Pedro Martinez .20 .50
149 Carlos Baerga .12 .30
150 Shannon Stewart .12 .30
151 Travis Lee .12 .30
152 Eric Byrnes .12 .30
153 Rafael Furcal .12 .30
154 B.J. Surhoff .12 .30
155 Zach Day .12 .30
156 Marlon Anderson .12 .30
157 Mark Hendrickson .12 .30
158 Mike Mussina .20 .50
159 Randall Simon .12 .30
160 Jeff DaVanon .12 .30
161 Joel Pineiro .12 .30
162 Vernon Wells .12 .30
163 Adam Kennedy .12 .30
164 Trot Nixon .12 .30
165 Rodrigo Lopez .12 .30
166 Curt Schilling .20 .50
167 Horacio Ramirez .12 .30
168 Jason Marquis .12 .30
169 Magglio Ordonez .20 .50
170 Scott Schoeneweis .12 .30
171 Andruw Jones .12 .30
172 Tino Martinez .20 .50
173 Moises Alou .12 .30
174 Kelvim Escobar .12 .30
175 Xavier Nady .12 .30
176 Ramon Martinez .12 .30
177 Pat Hentgen .12 .30
178 Austin Kearns .12 .30
179 D'Angelo Jimenez .12 .30
180 Deivi Cruz .12 .30
181 John Smoltz .30 .75
182 Toby Hall .12 .30
183 Mark Buehrle .20 .50
184 Howie Clark .12 .30
185 David Ortiz .30 .75
186 Raul Mondesi .12 .30
187 Milton Bradley .12 .30
188 Jorge Julio .12 .30
189 Victor Martinez .20 .50
190 Gabe Kapler .12 .30
191 Julio Franco .12 .30
192 Ryan Freel .12 .30
193 Brad Fullmer .12 .30
194 Joe Borowski .12 .30
195 Darren Oliver .12 .30
196 Jason Varitek .30 .75
197 Greg Myers .12 .30
198 Eric Munson .12 .30
199 Tim Wakefield .20 .50
200 Kyle Farnsworth .12 .30
201 Johnny Vander Wal .12 .30
202 Alex Escobar .12 .30
203 Sean Casey .12 .30
204 John Thomson .12 .30
205 Carlos Zambrano .20 .50
206 Kenny Lofton .12 .30
207 Marcus Giles .12 .30
208 Wade Miller .12 .30
209 Geoff Blum .12 .30
210 Jason LaRue .12 .30
211 Omar Vizquel .20 .50
212 Carlos Pena .20 .50
213 Adam Dunn .20 .50
214 Oscar Villarreal .12 .30
215 Paul Konerko .20 .50
216 Hideo Nomo .30 .75
217 Mike Sweeney .12 .30
218 Coco Crisp .12 .30
219 Shawn Chacon .12 .30
220 Brook Fordyce .12 .30
221 Josh Beckett .12 .30
222 Paul Wilson .12 .30
223 Josh Towers .12 .30
224 Geoff Jenkins .12 .30
225 Shawn Green .12 .30
226 Derrek Lee .12 .30
227 Karim Garcia .12 .30
228 Preston Wilson .12 .30
229 Dane Sardinha .12 .30
230 Aramis Ramirez .12 .30
231 Doug Mientkiewicz .12 .30
232 Jay Gibbons .12 .30
233 Adam Everett .12 .30
234 Brooks Kieschnick .12 .30
235 Dmitri Young .12 .30
236 Brad Penny .12 .30
237 Todd Zeile .12 .30
238 Eric Gagne .12 .30
239 Esteban Loaiza .12 .30
240 Billy Wagner .12 .30
241 Nomar Garciaparra .20 .50
242 Desi Relaford .12 .30
243 Luis Rivas .12 .30
244 Andy Pettitte .20 .50
245 Ty Wigginton .12 .30
246 Edgar Gonzalez .12 .30
247 Brian Anderson .12 .30
248 Richie Sexson .12 .30
249 Russell Branyan .12 .30
250 Jose Guillen .12 .30
251 Chin-Hui Tsao .12 .30
252 Jose Hernandez .12 .30
253 Kevin Brown .12 .30
254 Pete LaForest .12 .30
255 Adrian Beltre .30 .75
256 Jacque Jones .12 .30
257 Jimmy Rollins .20 .50
258 Brandon Phillips .12 .30
259 Derek Jeter .75 2.00
260 Carl Everett .12 .30
261 Wes Helms .12 .30
262 Kyle Lohse .12 .30
263 Jason Phillips .12 .30
264 Jake Peavy .12 .30
265 Orlando Hernandez .12 .30
266 Keith Foulke .12 .30
267 Brad Wilkerson .12 .30
268 Corey Koskie .12 .30
269 Josh Hall .12 .30
270 Bobby Higginson .12 .30
271 Andres Galarraga .20 .50
272 Alfonso Soriano .20 .50
273 Carlos Rivera .12 .30
274 Steve Trachsel .12 .30
275 David Bell .12 .30
276 Endy Chavez .12 .30
277 Jay Payton .12 .30
278 Mark Mulder .12 .30
279 Terrence Long .12 .30
280 A.J. Burnett .12 .30
281 Pokey Reese .12 .30
282 Phil Nevin .12 .30
283 Jose Contreras .12 .30
284 Jim Thome .20 .50
285 Pat Burrell .12 .30
286 Luis Castillo .12 .30
287 Juan Uribe .12 .30
288 Raul Ibanez .20 .50
289 Sidney Ponson .12 .30
290 Scott Hatteberg .12 .30
291 Jack Wilson .12 .30
292 Reggie Sanders .12 .30
293 Brian Giles .12 .30
294 Craig Biggio .20 .50
295 Kazuhisa Ishii .12 .30
296 Jim Edmonds .20 .50
297 Trevor Hoffman .20 .50
298 Ray Durham .12 .30
299 Mike Lieberthal .12 .30
300 Tim Worrell .12 .30
301 Chris George .12 .30
302 Jamie Moyer .12 .30
303 Mike Cameron .12 .30
304 Matt Kinney .12 .30
305 Aubrey Huff .12 .30
306 Brian Lawrence .12 .30
307 Carlos Guillen .12 .30
308 J.D. Drew .12 .30
309 Paul Lo Duca .12 .30
310 Tim Salmon .12 .30
311 Jason Schmidt .12 .30
312 A.J. Pierzynski .12 .30
313 Lance Carter .12 .30
314 Julio Lugo .12 .30
315 Johan Santana .20 .50
316 Laynce Nix .12 .30
317 John Olerud .12 .30
318 Robb Quinlan .12 .30
319 Scott Spiezio .12 .30
320 Tony Clark .12 .30
321 Jose Vidro .12 .30
322 Shea Hillenbrand .12 .30
323 Doug Glanville .12 .30
324 Orlando Palmeiro .12 .30
325 Juan Gonzalez .12 .30
326 Jason Giambi .12 .30
327 Junior Spivey .12 .30
328 Tom Glavine .20 .50
329 Reed Johnson .12 .30
330 David Eckstein .12 .30
331 Damian Jackson .12 .30
332 Orlando Hudson .12 .30
333 Barry Zito .20 .50
334 Robert Fick .12 .30
335 Aaron Boone .12 .30
336 Rafael Palmeiro .20 .50
337 Bobby Kielty .12 .30
338 Tony Batista .12 .30
339 Ryan Dempster .12 .30
340 Derek Lowe .12 .30
341 Alex Cintron .12 .30
342 Jermaine Dye .12 .30
343 John Burkett .12 .30
344 Javy Lopez .12 .30
345 Eric Karros .12 .30
346 Corey Patterson .12 .30
347 Josh Phelps .12 .30
348 Ryan Klesko .12 .30
349 Craig Wilson .12 .30
350 Brian Roberts .12 .30
351 Roberto Alomar .20 .50
352 Frank Thomas .30 .75
353 Gary Sheffield .12 .30
354 Alex Gonzalez .12 .30
355 Jose Cruz Jr. .12 .30
356 Jerome Williams .12 .30
357 Mark Kotsay .12 .30
358 Chris Reitsma .12 .30
359 Carlos Lee .12 .30
360 Todd Helton .20 .50
361 Gil Meche .12 .30
362 Ryan Franklin .12 .30
363 Josh Bard .12 .30
364 Juan Pierre .12 .30
365 Barry Larkin .20 .50
366 Edgar Renteria .12 .30
367 Alex Sanchez .12 .30
368 Jeff Bagwell .20 .50
369 Ben Broussard .12 .30
370 Chan-Ho Park .20 .50
371 Darrell May .12 .30
372 Roy Oswalt .20 .50
373 Craig Monroe .12 .30
374 Fred McGriff .12 .30
375 Bengie Molina .12 .30
376 Aaron Guiel .12 .30
377 Jeriome Robertson .12 .30
378 Kenny Rogers .12 .30
379 Colby Lewis .12 .30
380 Jeromy Burnitz .12 .30
381 Orlando Cabrera .12 .30
382 Joe Randa .12 .30
383 Miguel Batista .12 .30
384 Brad Radke .12 .30
385 Jeremy Giambi .12 .30
386 Vladimir Guerrero .20 .50
387 Melvin Mora .12 .30
388 Royce Clayton .12 .30
389 Danny Garcia .12 .30
390 Manny Ramirez .30 .75
391 Dave McCarty .12 .30
392 Mark Grudzielanek .12 .30
393 Mike Piazza .30 .75
394 Jorge Posada .20 .50
395 Tim Hudson .20 .50
396 Placido Polanco .12 .30
397 Mark Loretta .12 .30
398 Jesse Foppert .12 .30
399 Albert Pujols .40 1.00
400 Jeremi Gonzalez .12 .30
401 Paul Bako SP .40 1.00
402 Luis Matos SP .40 1.00
403 Johnny Damon SP .60 1.50
404 Kerry Wood SP .40 1.00
405 Joe Crede SP .40 1.00
406 Jason Davis SP .40 1.00
407 Larry Walker SP .60 1.50
408 Ivan Rodriguez SP .60 1.50
409 Nick Johnson SP .40 1.00
410 Jose Lima SP .40 1.00
411 Brian Jordan SP .40 1.00
412 Eddie Guardado SP .40 1.00
413 Ron Calloway SP .40 1.00
414 Aaron Heilman SP .40 1.00
415 Eric Chavez SP .40 1.00
416 Randy Wolf SP .40 1.00
417 Jason Bay SP .60 1.50
418 Edgardo Alfonzo SP .40 1.00
419 Kazuhiro Sasaki SP .40 1.00
420 Eduardo Perez SP .40 1.00
421 Carl Crawford SP .60 1.50
422 Troy Glaus SP .40 1.00
423 Joaquin Benoit SP .40 1.00
424 Russ Ortiz SP .40 1.00
425 Larry Bigbie SP .40 1.00
426 Todd Walker SP .40 1.00
427 Kris Benson SP .40 1.00
428 Sandy Alomar Jr. SP .40 1.00
429 Jody Gerut SP .40 1.00
430 Rene Reyes SP .40 1.00
431 Mike Lowell SP .40 1.00
432 Jeff Kent SP .40 1.00
433 Mike MacDougal SP .40 1.00
434 Dave Roberts SP .60 1.50
435 Torii Hunter SP .40 1.00
436 Tomo Ohka SP .40 1.00
437 Jeremy Griffiths SP .40 1.00
438 Miguel Tejada SP .60 1.50
439 Vicente Padilla SP .40 1.00
440 Bobby Hill SP .40 1.00
441 Rich Aurilia SP .40 1.00
442 Shigetoshi Hasegawa SP .40 1.00
443 So Taguchi SP .40 1.00
444 Damian Rolls SP .40 1.00
445 Roy Halladay SP .60 1.50
446 Rocco Baldelli SO SP .40 1.00
447 Dontrelle Willis SO SP .40 1.00
448 Mark Prior SO SP .60 1.50
449 Jason Lane SO SP .40 1.00
450 Angel Berroa SO SP .40 1.00

2004 Fleer Tradition

451 Jose Reyes SO SP .60 1.50
452 Ryan Wagner SO SP .40 1.00
453 Marlon Byrd SO SP .40 1.00
454 Hee Seop Choi SO SP .40 1.00
455 Brandon Webb SO SP .40 1.00
456 Bo Hart SO SP .40 1.00
457 Hank Blalock SO SP .40 1.00
458 Mark Teixeira SO SP .60 1.50
459 Hideki Matsui SO SP 1.50 4.00
460 Scott Podsednik SO SP .40 1.00
461 Miguel Cabrera SO SP 1.00 2.50
462 Josh Beckett AW SP .40 1.00
463 Mariano Rivera AW SP 1.25 3.00
464 Ivan Rodriguez AW SP .60 1.50
465 Alex Rodriguez AW SP 1.25 3.00
466 Albert Pujols AW SP 1.25 3.00
467 Roy Halladay AW SP .60 1.50
468 Eric Gagne AW SP .40 1.00
469 Angel Berroa AW SP .40 1.00
470 Dontrelle Willis AW SP .40 1.00
471 Boot Gregorio#{Fischer SP .40 1.00
472 Kata Olson#{Hammock SP .40 1.00
473 Hessman Waters#{Aquino SP .40 1.00
474 Mendez Cabrera#{Guthrie SP .40 1.00
475 Almonte Seibel#{Sanchez SP .40 1.00
476 Wellemeyer Leicester#{Mitre SP .40 1.00
477 Stewart Cotts#{Miles SP .40 1.00
478 Sledge Hall#{Claussen SP .40 1.00
479 Cruceta Stanford#{Betan SP .40 1.00
480 Lopez Atkins#{Barmes SP .60 1.50
481 Ledez Logan#{Bonderman SP .40 1.00
482 Willingham Hoop#{Roberts SP .60 1.50
483 Porter Gallo#{Matranga SP .40 1.00
484 DeJesus Gilfillan#{Gobble SP .40 1.00
485 Hill Gonzalez#{Brown SP .40 1.00
486 Weeks Liriano#{Oberm SP .40 1.00
487 Prieto Ryan#{Ford SP .40 1.00
488 Manon Ayala#{Song SP .40 1.00
489 Duncan Redman#{Brazell SP .40 1.00
490 Wang M.Hern#{M.Gonz SP 1.50 4.00
491 Harden Neu#{Geary SP .40 1.00
492 Markwell Gaudin#{Sanders SP .40 1.00
493 Kemp Nakamura#{Carrasco SP .40 1.00
494 Greene Ojeda#{Castro SP .60 1.50
495 Lowry Linden#{Correia SP .40 1.00
496 Looper Sweeney#{R.John SP .40 1.00
497 J.Gall RC Haren#{Ohme SP .40 1.00
498 Young Waechter#{Diaz SP .60 1.50
499 Laird Garcia#{Nivar SP .40 1.00
500 Rios Quiroz#{Rosario SP .40 1.00

2004 Fleer Tradition Career Tributes

PRINT RUNS B/WN 1956-1993 COPIES PER
*DIE CUT: 1.25X TO 3X BASIC
DIE CUT PRINTS B/WN 56-93 COPIES PER
OVERALL CAREER TRIBUTE ODDS 1:36
1 Mike Schmidt/1989 2.50 6.00
2 Nolan Ryan/1993 5.00 12.00
3 Tom Seaver/1986 1.00 2.50
4 Reggie Jackson/1987 1.00 2.50
5 Bob Gibson/1975 1.00 2.50
6 Harmon Killebrew/1975 1.50 4.00
7 Phil Rizzuto/1956 1.00 2.50
8 Lou Brock/1979 1.00 2.50
9 Eddie Mathews/1968 1.50 4.00
10 Al Kaline/1974 1.50 4.00

2004 Fleer Tradition Diamond Tributes

COMPLETE SET (20) 8.00 20.00
STATED ODDS 1:6
1 Derek Jeter 2.50 6.00
2 Chipper Jones 1.00 2.50
3 Vladimir Guerrero .60 1.50
4 Kerry Wood .40 1.00
5 Jim Thome .60 1.50
6 Nomar Garciaparra .60 1.50
7 Alex Rodriguez 1.25 3.00
8 Mike Piazza 1.00 2.50
9 Jason Giambi .40 1.00
10 Barry Zito .60 1.50
11 Dontrelle Willis .40 1.00
12 Albert Pujols 1.25 3.00
13 Todd Helton .60 1.50
14 Richie Sexson .40 1.00
15 Randy Johnson 1.00 2.50
16 Pedro Martinez .60 1.50
17 Josh Beckett .40 1.00
18 Manny Ramirez 1.00 2.50
19 Roy Halladay .60 1.50
20 Mark Prior .60 1.50

2004 Fleer Tradition Diamond Tributes Game Jersey

STATED ODDS 1:36
*PATCH: 1X TO 2.5X BASIC
PATCH RANDOM INSERTS IN PACKS
PATCH PRINT RUN 50 SERIAL #'d SETS
AP Albert Pujols 6.00 15.00
AR Alex Rodriguez 4.00 10.00
BZ Barry Zito 3.00 8.00
CJ Chipper Jones 4.00 10.00
DJ Derek Jeter 12.50 30.00
DW Dontrelle Willis 4.00 10.00
JB Josh Beckett 3.00 8.00
JG Jason Giambi 3.00 8.00
JT Jim Thome 4.00 10.00
KW Kerry Wood 3.00 8.00
MP Mike Piazza 4.00 10.00
MP2 Mark Prior 4.00 10.00
MR Manny Ramirez 4.00 10.00
NG Nomar Garciaparra 4.00 10.00
PM Pedro Martinez 4.00 10.00
RH Roy Halladay 3.00 8.00
RJ Randy Johnson 4.00 10.00
RS Richie Sexson 3.00 8.00
TH Todd Helton 4.00 10.00
VG Vladimir Guerrero 4.00 10.00

2004 Fleer Tradition Retrospection

STATED ODDS 1:360
1 Rickie Weeks 2.00 5.00
2 Delmon Young 3.00 8.00
3 Torii Hunter 2.00 5.00
4 Aubrey Huff 2.00 5.00
5 Rocco Baldelli 2.00 5.00
6 Mike Lowell 2.00 5.00
7 Dontrelle Willis 2.00 5.00
8 Albert Pujols 6.00 15.00
9 Bo Hart 2.00 5.00
10 Brandon Webb 2.00 5.00

2004 Fleer Tradition Retrospection Autographs

OVERALL AUTO ODDS 1:720
STATED PRINT RUN 60 SERIAL #'d SETS
EXCHANGE DEADLINE INDEFINITE
AH Aubrey Huff 10.00 25.00
AK Austin Kearns 10.00 25.00
BO Bo Hart 10.00 25.00
BW Brandon Webb 10.00 25.00
CP Corey Patterson 10.00 25.00
DW Dontrelle Willis 15.00 40.00
HB Hank Blalock 10.00 25.00
JR Jose Reyes 10.00 25.00
JW Josh Willingham 10.00 25.00
MR Mike Ryan 10.00 25.00
RW Rickie Weeks 10.00 25.00
SR Scott Rolen 15.00 40.00
TH Torii Hunter 10.00 25.00

2004 Fleer Tradition Retrospection Autographs Dual

OVERALL AUTO ODDS 1:720
STATED PRINT RUN 19 SERIAL #'d SETS
NO PRICING DUE TO SCARCITY
EXCHANGE DEADLINE INDEFINITE

2004 Fleer Tradition Stand Outs Game Used

STATED ODDS 1:41
GOLD RANDOM INSERTS IN PACKS
GOLD PRINTS B/WN 20-27 COPIES PER
NO GOLD PRICING DUE TO SCARCITY
AB Angel Berroa Pants 3.00 8.00
BH Bo Hart Jsy 3.00 8.00
BW Brandon Webb Pants 3.00 8.00
DW Dontrelle Willis Jsy 4.00 10.00
HB Hank Blalock Jsy 3.00 8.00
HC Hee Seop Choi Jsy 3.00 8.00
JR Jose Reyes Jsy 3.00 8.00
MB Marlon Byrd Jsy 3.00 8.00
MC Miguel Cabrera Jsy 4.00 10.00
MT Mark Teixeira Jsy 4.00 10.00
RB Rocco Baldelli Jsy 3.00 8.00

2004 Fleer Tradition This Day in History

STATED ODDS 1:18
1 Josh Beckett .40 1.00
2 Carlos Delgado .40 1.00
3 Javy Lopez .40 1.00
4 Greg Maddux 1.25 3.00
5 Rafael Palmeiro .60 1.50
6 Sammy Sosa 1.00 2.50
7 Jeff Bagwell .60 1.50
8 Frank Thomas 1.00 2.50
9 Kevin Millwood .40 1.00
10 Jose Reyes .60 1.50
11 Rafael Furcal .40 1.00
12 Alfonso Soriano .60 1.50
13 Eric Gagne .40 1.00
14 Hideki Matsui 1.50 4.00
15 Hank Blalock .40 1.00

2004 Fleer Tradition This Day in History Game Used

STATED ODDS 1:288
AS Alfonso Soriano Jsy 4.00 10.00
CD Carlos Delgado Jsy 4.00 10.00
FT Frank Thomas Jsy 6.00 15.00
GM Greg Maddux Jsy 6.00 15.00
JB Josh Beckett Jsy 4.00 10.00
JB Jeff Bagwell Jsy 6.00 15.00
JL Javy Lopez Jsy 4.00 10.00
JR Jose Reyes Jsy 4.00 10.00
RP Rafael Palmeiro Jsy 6.00 15.00
SS Sammy Sosa Bat 6.00 15.00

2004 Fleer Tradition This Day in History Game Used Dual

STATED PRINT RUN 25 SERIAL #'d SETS
NO PRICING DUE TO SCARCITY

2005 Fleer Tradition

COMPLETE SET (350) 30.00 60.00
COMP.SET w/o SP's (300) 15.00 40.00
COMMON CARD (1-300) .10 .30
COMMON CARD (301-330) .40 1.00
COMMON CARD (331-350) .40 1.00
301-350 STATED ODDS 1:2 H, 1:4 R
1 Johan Schil#{Westbrook SL .20 .50
2 Sheets Peavy#{Randy SL .30 .75
3 Johan Colon#{Schilling SL .20 .50
4 Pavano Oswalt#{Clemens SL .40 1.00
5 Johan Pedro#{Schilling SL .20 .50
6 Schmidt Randy#{Sheets SL .30 .75
7 Mora Guerrero#{Ichiro SL .40 1.00
8 Beltre Helton#{Loretta SL .30 .75
9 Manny Konerko#{Ortiz SL .30 .75
10 Pujols Beltre#{Dunn SL .40 1.00
11 Ortiz Manny#{Tejada SL .30 .75
12 Pujols Castilla#{Rolen SL .40 1.00
13 Jason Bay .12 .30
14 Greg Maddux .40 1.00
15 Melvin Mora .12 .30
16 Matt Stairs .12 .30
17 Scott Podsednik .12 .30
18 Bartolo Colon .12 .30
19 Roger Clemens .40 1.00
20 Eric Hinske .12 .30
21 Johnny Estrada .12 .30
22 Brett Tomko .12 .30
23 John Buck .12 .30
24 Nomar Garciaparra .20 .50
25 Milton Bradley .12 .30
26 Craig Biggio .20 .50
27 Kyle Denney .12 .30
28 Brad Penny .12 .30
29 Todd Helton .20 .50
30 Luis Gonzalez .12 .30
31 Bill Hall .12 .30
32 Ruben Sierra .12 .30
33 Zack Greinke .40 1.00
34 Sandy Alomar Jr. .12 .30
35 Jason Giambi .12 .30
36 Ben Sheets .12 .30
37 Edgardo Alfonzo .12 .30
38 Kenny Rogers .12 .30
39 Coco Crisp .12 .30
40 Randy Choate .12 .30
41 Braden Looper .12 .30
42 Adam Dunn .20 .50
43 Adam Eaton .12 .30
44 Luis Castillo .12 .30
45 Casey Fossum .12 .30
46 Mike Piazza .30 .75
47 Juan Pierre .12 .30
48 Doug Davis .12 .30
49 Manny Ramirez .30 .75
50 Travis Hafner .12 .30
51 Jack Wilson .12 .30
52 Mike Maroth .12 .30
53 Ken Harvey .12 .30
54 Brooks Kieschnick .12 .30
55 Brad Fullmer .12 .30
56 Octavio Dotel .12 .30
57 Mike Matheny .12 .30
58 Andruw Jones .12 .30
59 Alfonso Soriano .20 .50
60 Royce Clayton .12 .30
61 Jon Garland .12 .30
62 John Mabry .12 .30
63 Rafael Palmeiro .20 .50
64 Garett Atkins .12 .30
65 Brian Meadows .12 .30
66 Tony Armas Jr. .12 .30
67 Toby Hall .12 .30
68 Carlos Baerga .12 .30
69 Barry Larkin .20 .50
70 Jody Gerut .12 .30
71 Brent Mayne .12 .30
72 Shigetoshi Hasegawa .12 .30
73 Jose Cruz Jr. .12 .30
74 Dan Wilson .12 .30
75 Sidney Ponson .12 .30
76 Jason Jennings .12 .30
77 A.J. Burnett .12 .30
78 Tony Batista .12 .30
79 Kris Benson .12 .30
80 Sean Burroughs .12 .30
81 Eric Young .12 .30
82 Casey Kotchman .12 .30
83 Derrek Lee .12 .30
84 Mariano Rivera .40 1.00
85 Julio Franco .12 .30
86 Corey Patterson .12 .30
87 Carlos Beltran .20 .50
88 Trevor Hoffman .20 .50
89 Danny Garcia .12 .30
90 Marcos Scutaro .20 .50
91 Marquis Grissom .12 .30
92 Aubrey Huff .12 .30
93 Tony Womack .12 .30
94 Placido Polanco .12 .30
95 Bengie Molina .12 .30
96 Roger Cedeno .12 .30
97 Geoff Jenkins .12 .30
98 Kip Wells .12 .30
99 Derek Jeter .75 2.00
100 Omar Infante .12 .30
101 Phil Nevin .12 .30
102 Edgar Renteria .12 .30
103 B.J. Surhoff .12 .30
104 David DeJesus .12 .30
105 Raul Ibanez .20 .50
106 Hank Blalock .12 .30
107 Shawn Estes .12 .30
108 Wily Mo Pena .12 .30
109 Shawn Green .12 .30
110 David Wright .25 .60
111 Kenny Lofton .12 .30
112 Matt Clement .12 .30
113 Cesar Izturis .12 .30
114 John Lackey .20 .50
115 Torii Hunter .12 .30
116 Charles Johnson .12 .30
117 Ray Durham .12 .30
118 Luke Hudson .12 .30
119 Jeremy Bonderman .12 .30
120 Sean Casey .12 .30
121 Johnny Damon .20 .50
122 Eric Milton .12 .30
123 Shea Hillenbrand .12 .30
124 Johan Santana .20 .50
125 Jim Edmonds .20 .50
126 Javier Vazquez .12 .30
127 Jon Adkins .12 .30
128 Mike Lowell .12 .30
129 Khalil Greene .12 .30
130 Quinton McCracken .12 .30
131 Edgar Martinez .20 .50
132 Matt Lawton .12 .30
133 Jeff Weaver .12 .30
134 Marlon Byrd .12 .30
135 John Smoltz .30 .75
136 Grady Sizemore .20 .50
137 Brian Roberts .12 .30
138 Dee Brown .12 .30
139 Joel Pineiro .12 .30
140 David Dellucci .12 .30
141 Bobby Higginson .12 .30
142 Ryan Madson .12 .30
143 Scott Hatteberg .12 .30
144 Greg Zaun .12 .30
145 Brian Jordan .12 .30
146 Jason Isringhausen .12 .30
147 Vinnie Chulk .12 .30
148 Al Leiter .12 .30
149 Pedro Martinez .20 .50
150 Carlos Guillen .12 .30
151 Randy Wolf .12 .30
152 Vernon Wells .12 .30
153 Barry Zito .20 .50
154 Pedro Feliz .12 .30
155 Omar Vizquel .20 .50
156 Chone Figgins .12 .30
157 David Ortiz .30 .75
158 Sunny Kim .12 .30
159 Adam Kennedy .12 .30
160 Carlos Lee .12 .30
161 Rick Ankiel .12 .30
162 Roy Oswalt .20 .50
163 Armando Benitez .12 .30
164 Erubiel Durazo .12 .30
165 Adam Hyzdu .12 .30
166 Esteban Yan .12 .30
167 Victor Santos .12 .30
168 Kevin Millwood .12 .30
169 Andy Pettitte .20 .50
170 Mike Cameron .12 .30
171 Scott Rolen .20 .50
172 Trot Nixon .12 .30
173 Eric Munson .12 .30
174 Roy Halladay .20 .50
175 Juan Encarnacion .12 .30
176 Eric Chavez .12 .30
177 Termel Sledge .12 .30
178 Jason Schmidt .12 .30
179 Endy Chavez .12 .30
180 Carlos Zambrano .20 .50
181 Carlos Delgado .12 .30
182 Dewon Brazelton .12 .30
183 J.D. Drew .12 .30
184 Orlando Cabrera .12 .30
185 Craig Wilson .12 .30
186 Chin-Hui Tsao .12 .30
187 Jolbert Cabrera .12 .30
188 Rod Barajas .12 .30
189 Craig Monroe .12 .30
190 Dave Berg .12 .30
191 Carlos Silva .12 .30
192 Eric Gagne .12 .30
193 Marcus Giles .12 .30
194 Nick Johnson .12 .30
195 Kelvim Escobar .12 .30
196 Wade Miller .12 .30
197 David Bell .12 .30
198 Rondell White .12 .30
199 Brian Giles .12 .30
200 Jeromy Burnitz .12 .30
201 Carl Pavano .12 .30
202 Alex Rios .12 .30
203 Ryan Freel .12 .30
204 R.A. Dickey .20 .50
205 Miguel Cairo .12 .30
206 Kerry Wood .12 .30
207 C.C. Sabathia .20 .50
208 Jaime Cerda .12 .30
209 Jerome Williams .12 .30
210 Ryan Wagner .12 .30
211 Javy Lopez .12 .30
212 Tike Redman .12 .30
213 Richie Sexson .12 .30
214 Shannon Stewart .12 .30
215 Ben Davis .12 .30
216 Jeff Bagwell .20 .50
217 David Wells .12 .30
218 Justin Leone .12 .30
219 Brad Radke .12 .30
220 Ramon Santiago .12 .30
221 Richard Hidalgo .12 .30
222 Aaron Miles .12 .30
223 Mark Loretta .12 .30
224 Aaron Boone .12 .30
225 Steve Trachsel .12 .30
226 Geoff Blum .12 .30
227 Shingo Takatsu .12 .30
228 Kevin Youkilis .12 .30
229 Laynce Nix .12 .30
230 Daniel Cabrera .12 .30
231 Kyle Lohse .12 .30
232 Todd Pratt .12 .30
233 Reed Johnson .12 .30
234 Lance Berkman .20 .50
235 Hideki Matsui .50 1.25
236 Randy Winn .12 .30
237 Joe Randa .12 .30
238 Bob Howry .12 .30
239 Jason LaRue .12 .30
240 Jose Valentin .12 .30
241 Livan Hernandez .12 .30
242 Jamie Moyer .12 .30
243 Garret Anderson .12 .30
244 Brad Ausmus .12 .30
245 Russell Branyan .12 .30
246 Paul Wilson .12 .30
247 Tim Wakefield .20 .50
248 Roberto Alomar .20 .50
249 Kazuhisa Ishii .12 .30
250 Tino Martinez .20 .50
251 Tomo Ohka .12 .30
252 Mark Redman .12 .30
253 Paul Byrd .12 .30
254 Greg Aquino .12 .30
255 Adrian Beltre .30 .75
256 Ricky Ledee .12 .30
257 Josh Fogg .12 .30
258 Derek Lowe .12 .30
259 Lew Ford .12 .30
260 Bobby Crosby .12 .30
261 Jim Thome .20 .50
262 Jaret Wright .12 .30
263 Chin-Feng Chen .12 .30
264 Troy Glaus .12 .30
265 Jorge Sosa .12 .30
266 Mike Lamb .12 .30
267 Russ Ortiz .12 .30
268 Reggie Sanders .12 .30
269 Orlando Hudson .12 .30
270 Rodrigo Lopez .12 .30
271 Jose Vidro .12 .30
272 Akinori Otsuka .12 .30
273 Victor Martinez .20 .50
274 Carl Crawford .20 .50
275 Roberto Novoa .12 .30
276 Brian Lawrence .12 .30
277 Angel Berroa .12 .30
278 Josh Beckett .12 .30
279 Lyle Overbay .12 .30
280 Dustin Hermanson .12 .30
281 Jeff Conine .12 .30
282 Mark Prior .20 .50
283 Kevin Brown .12 .30
284 Magglio Ordonez .20 .50
285 Dontrelle Willis .12 .30
286 Dallas McPherson .12 .30
287 Rafael Furcal .12 .30
288 Ty Wigginton .12 .30
289 Moises Alou .12 .30
290 A.J. Pierzynski .12 .30
291 Todd Walker .12 .30
292 Hideo Nomo .30 .75
293 Larry Walker .20 .50
294 Choo Freeman .12 .30
295 Eduardo Perez .12 .30
296 Miguel Tejada .20 .50
297 Corey Koskie .12 .30
298 Jermaine Dye .12 .30
299 John Riedling .12 .30
300 John Olerud .12 .30
301 Bittner Woods#{Jenks TP .40 1.00
302 Kroeger Daigle#{Medders TP .40 1.00
303 K.Johnson Thom#{Meyer TP .40 1.00
304 E.Rod Hannam#{Maine TP .40 1.00
306 Cedeno Vasquez#{Pinto TP .40 1.00
307 Munoz Wing#{Diaz TP .40 1.00
308 Bergolla Olmedo#{E.Enc TP 1.00 2.50
309 Gomez Ochoa#{Tadano TP .40 1.00
310 Miller Baker#{Holliday TP 1.00 2.50
311 Larris Grander#{Raburn TP .75 2.00
312 Wilson Kensing#{Cave TP .40 1.00
313 H.Gim Taveras#{Buch TP .40 1.00
314 Gotay Bass#{Blanco TP .40 1.00
315 Hanrahan Aybar#{Braz TP .60 1.50
316 Krynzel Hendr#{Hart TP .40 1.00
317 Miller Kubel#{Durbin TP .40 1.00
318 Izturis Cordero#{Watson TP .40 1.00
319 Diaz Baldiris#{Lydon TP .40 1.00
320 Sierra Navarro#{Henn TP .40 1.00
321 Swish Blant#{D.Johnson TP .60 1.50
322 Howard Floyd#{Bucktrot TP .75 2.00
323 Doumit Burnett#{Bradley TP .40 1.00
324 Germ Tucker#{Guzman TP .40 1.00
325 Aardsma Knoedler#{Simon TP .40 1.00
326 Lopez Rivera#{Baek TP .40 1.00
327 Molina Rust#{Wainwright TP 4.00 10.00
328 Cantu Kazmir#{Upton TP 1.00 2.50
329 Gonzalez Nivar#{Bourg TP .75 2.00
330 Adams McGow#{Chacin TP .40 1.00
331 Alfonso Soriano AW .60 1.50
332 Albert Pujols AW 1.25 3.00
333 David Ortiz AW 1.00 2.50
334 Manny Ramirez AW 1.00 2.50
335 Jason Bay AW .40 1.00
336 Bobby Crosby AW .40 1.00
337 Roger Clemens AW 1.25 3.00
338 Johan Santana AW .60 1.50
339 Jim Thome AW .60 1.50
340 Vladimir Guerrero AW .60 1.50
341 David Ortiz PS 1.00 2.50
342 Alex Rodriguez PS 1.25 3.00
343 Albert Pujols PS 1.25 3.00
344 Carlos Beltran PS .60 1.50
345 Johnny Damon PS .60 1.50
346 Scott Rolen PS .60 1.50
347 Larry Walker PS .60 1.50
348 Curt Schilling PS .60 1.50
349 Pedro Martinez PS .60 1.50
350 David Ortiz PS 1.00 2.50
423 Mark Teixeira Not issued in packs
501 Miguel Cabrera Not issued in packs

2005 Fleer Tradition Gray Backs

*GRAY BACK 1-300: 1.25X TO 3X BASIC
*GRAY BACK 301-330: .5X TO 1.2X BASIC
*GRAY BACK 331-350: .6X TO 1.5X BASIC
STATED ODDS 1:2 HOBBY, 1:2 RETAIL

2005 Fleer Tradition Gray Backs Gold Letter

*GOLD LTR: 6X TO 15X BASIC
STATED ODDS 1:96 HOBBY, 1:288 RETAIL
STATED APPROX. PRINT RUN 185 SETS
PRINT RUN INFO PROVIDED BY FLEER
CARDS ARE NOT SERIAL-NUMBERED

2005 Fleer Tradition Club 3000/500/300

STATED ODDS 1:360 HOBBY, 1:480 RETAIL
STATED APPROX. PRINT RUN 175 SETS
PRINT RUN INFO PROVIDED BY FLEER
1 Ernie Banks 500 6.00 15.00
2 Stan Musial 3000 10.00 25.00
3 Steve Carlton 3000 4.00 10.00
4 Greg Maddux 300 8.00 20.00
5 Dave Winfield 3000 4.00 10.00
6 Rafael Palmeiro 500 4.00 10.00
7 Rickey Henderson 3000 6.00 15.00
8 Roger Clemens 3000 8.00 20.00
9 Don Sutton 300 2.50 6.00
10 George Brett 3000 12.00 30.00
11 Reggie Jackson 500 4.00 10.00
12 Wade Boggs 3000 4.00 10.00
13 Bob Gibson 3000 4.00 10.00
14 Eddie Murray 3000 4.00 10.00
15 Tom Seaver 3000 4.00 10.00
16 Willie McCovey 500 4.00 10.00
17 Rod Carew 3000 4.00 10.00
18 Fergie Jenkins 300 4.00 10.00
19 Phil Niekro 300 4.00 10.00
20 Frank Robinson 500 4.00 10.00

2005 Fleer Tradition Cooperstown Tribute

STATED ODDS 1:72 HOBBY
RANDOM INSERTS IN RETAIL PACKS
*GOLD: .4X TO 1X BASIC
GOLD ODDS 1:24 RETAIL
1 Mike Schmidt/1995 2.50 6.00
2 Al Kaline/1980 1.50 4.00
3 Yogi Berra/1972 1.50 4.00
4 Robin Yount/1999 1.50 4.00
5 Joe Morgan/1990 1.00 2.50
6 Willie Stargell/1988 1.00 2.50
7 Harmon Killebrew/1984 1.50 4.00
8 Nolan Ryan/1999 5.00 12.00
9 Carlton Fisk/2000 1.00 2.50
10 Johnny Bench/1989 1.50 4.00

2005 Fleer Tradition Cooperstown Tribute Jersey

STATED ODDS 1:200 H, 1:1250 R
STATED APPROX. PRINT RUN 400 SETS
STATED SP PRINT RUN 20 COPIES PER
PRINT RUN INFO PROVIDED BY FLEER
NO SP PRICING DUE TO SCARCITY
PATCH RANDOM IN HOB/RET PACKS
PATCH PRINT RUN 10 SERIAL #'d SETS
NO PATCH PRICING DUE TO SCARCITY
AK Al Kaline 10.00 25.00
CF Carlton Fisk 6.00 15.00
HK Harmon Killebrew 6.00 15.00
JB Johnny Bench 6.00 15.00
MS Mike Schmidt 6.00 15.00
NR Nolan Ryan 12.00 30.00
RY Robin Yount 6.00 15.00
WS Willie Stargell 6.00 15.00

2005 Fleer Tradition Diamond Tributes

COMPLETE SET (25) 10.00 25.00
STATED ODDS 1:6 H, 1:8 R
1 Albert Pujols 1.25 3.00
2 Alex Rodriguez 1.25 3.00
3 Ken Griffey Jr. 2.00 5.00
4 Sammy Sosa 1.00 2.50
5 Chipper Jones 1.00 2.50
6 Johan Santana .60 1.50
7 Roger Clemens 1.25 3.00
8 Pedro Martinez .60 1.50
9 Jim Thome .60 1.50
10 Greg Maddux 1.25 3.00
11 Alfonso Soriano .60 1.50
12 Derek Jeter 2.50 6.00
13 Randy Johnson 1.00 2.50
14 Miguel Cabrera 1.00 2.50
15 Adrian Beltre 1.00 2.50
16 Ivan Rodriguez .60 1.50
17 Manny Ramirez 1.00 2.50
18 Mark Teixeira .60 1.50
19 Adam Dunn .60 1.50
20 Scott Rolen .60 1.50
21 Mike Piazza 1.00 2.50
22 J.D. Drew .40 1.00
23 Hideki Matsui 1.50 4.00
24 Nomar Garciaparra .60 1.50
25 Kaz Matsui .40 1.00

2005 Fleer Tradition Diamond Tributes Game Used

STATED ODDS 1:30 H, 1:625 R
SP PRINT RUNS PROVIDED BY FLEER
SP'S ARE NOT SERIAL-NUMBERED
NO SP PRICING DUE TO SCARCITY
AB Adrian Beltre Bat 3.00 8.00
AP Albert Pujols Bat 6.00 15.00
AS Alfonso Soriano Bat 3.00 8.00
CJ Chipper Jones Bat 4.00 10.00
GM Greg Maddux Jsy 4.00 10.00
HM Hideki Matsui Bat 6.00 15.00
JD J.D. Drew Bat 3.00 8.00
JS Johan Santana Jsy 4.00 10.00
JT Jim Thome Bat 4.00 10.00
KM Kaz Matsui Bat 3.00 8.00
MP Mike Piazza Bat 4.00 10.00
MR Manny Ramirez Bat 4.00 10.00
MT Mark Teixeira Bat 4.00 10.00
NG Nomar Garciaparra Bat 4.00 10.00
PM Pedro Martinez Jsy 4.00 10.00
RC Roger Clemens Jsy 4.00 10.00
RJ Randy Johnson Jsy 4.00 10.00
SS Sammy Sosa Bat 4.00 10.00

2005 Fleer Tradition Diamond Tributes Patch

*PATCH: 1X TO 2.5X BASIC DT JSY
RANDOM INSERTS IN HOB/RET PACKS
STATED PRINT RUN 50 SERIAL #'d SETS
IR Ivan Rodriguez 10.00 25.00
MC Miguel Cabrera 10.00 25.00
SR Scott Rolen 10.00 25.00

2005 Fleer Tradition Diamond Tributes Dual Patch

STATED PRINT RUN 25 SERIAL #'d SETS
NO PRICING DUE TO SCARCITY

2005 Fleer Tradition Standouts

COMPLETE SET (15) 8.00 20.00
STATED ODDS 1:18 H, 1:24 R
1 Albert Pujols 1.25 3.00
2 Ichiro Suzuki 1.25 3.00
3 Derek Jeter 2.50 6.00
4 Randy Johnson 1.00 2.50
5 Greg Maddux 1.25 3.00
6 Hideki Matsui 1.50 4.00
7 Mike Piazza 1.00 2.50
8 Vladimir Guerrero .60 1.50
9 Sammy Sosa 1.00 2.50
10 Jim Thome .60 1.50
11 Chipper Jones 1.00 2.50
12 Alex Rodriguez 1.25 3.00
13 Roger Clemens 1.25 3.00
14 Nomar Garciaparra .60 1.50
15 Lance Berkman .60 1.50

2005 Fleer Tradition Standouts Jersey

STATED ODDS 1:65 H, 1:950 R
*PATCH: 1X TO 2.5X BASIC
PATCH RANDOM IN HOB/RET PACKS
PATCH PRINT RUN 50 SERIAL #'d SETS
AP Albert Pujols 6.00 15.00
CJ Chipper Jones 4.00 10.00
GM Greg Maddux 4.00 10.00
HM Hideki Matsui 8.00 20.00
JT Jim Thome 4.00 10.00
LB Lance Berkman 3.00 8.00
MP Mike Piazza 4.00 10.00
RC Roger Clemens 4.00 10.00
RJ Randy Johnson 4.00 10.00
SS Sammy Sosa 4.00 10.00
VG Vladimir Guerrero 4.00 10.00

2006 Fleer Tradition

COMPLETE SET (200) 12.50 30.00
COMMON CARD (1-200) .12 .30
COMMON RC (1-200) .20 .50
OVERALL PLATE ODDS 1:288 HOBBY
PLATE PRINT RUN 1 SET PER COLOR
BLACK-CYAN-MAGENTA-YELLOW ISSUED
NO PLATE PRICING DUE TO SCARCITY
EXQUISITE EXCH ODDS 1:864 HOBBY
EXQUISITE EXCH DEADLINE 07/27/07
1 Andruw Jones .12 .30
2 Chipper Jones .30 .75
3 John Smoltz .30 .75
4 Tim Hudson .20 .50
5 Joey Devine RC .20 .50
6 Chuck James (RC) .20 .50
7 Alay Soler RC .20 .50
8 Conor Jackson (RC) .30 .75
9 Luis Gonzalez .12 .30
10 Brandon Webb .20 .50
11 Chad Tracy .12 .30
12 Orlando Hudson .12 .30
13 Shawn Green .12 .30
14 Vladimir Guerrero .20 .50
15 Bartolo Colon .12 .30
16 Chone Figgins .12 .30
17 Garret Anderson .12 .30
18 Francisco Rodriguez .20 .50
19 Casey Kotchman .12 .30
20 Lance Berkman .20 .50
21 Craig Biggio .20 .50
22 Andy Pettitte .20 .50
23 Morgan Ensberg .12 .30
24 Brad Lidge .12 .30
25 Jered Weaver (RC) .60 1.50
26 Roy Oswalt .20 .50
27 Eric Chavez .12 .30
28 Rich Harden .12 .30
29 Cole Hamels (RC) .60 1.50
30 Huston Street .12 .30
31 Bobby Crosby .12 .30
32 Nick Swisher .20 .50
33 Vernon Wells .12 .30
34 Roy Halladay .20 .50
35 A.J. Burnett .12 .30
36 Troy Glaus .12 .30
37 B.J. Ryan .12 .30
38 Bengie Molina .12 .30
39 Alex Rios .12 .30
40 Prince Fielder (RC) 1.00 2.50
41 Jose Capellan (RC) .20 .50
42 Rickie Weeks .12 .30
43 Ben Sheets .12 .30
44 Carlos Lee .12 .30
45 J.J. Hardy .12 .30
46 Albert Pujols .40 1.00
47 Skip Schumaker (RC) .20 .50
48 Adam Wainwright (RC) .30 .75
49 Jim Edmonds .20 .50
50 Scott Rolen .20 .50
51 Chris Carpenter .20 .50
52 David Eckstein .12 .30
53 Derrek Lee .12 .30
54 Jon Lester RC .75 2.00
55 Mark Prior .20 .50
56 Aramis Ramirez .12 .30
57 Juan Pierre .12 .30
58 Greg Maddux .40 1.00
59 Michael Barrett .12 .30
60 Carl Crawford .20 .50
61 Scott Kazmir .20 .50
62 Jorge Cantu .12 .30
63 Jonny Gomes .12 .30
64 Julio Lugo .12 .30
65 Aubrey Huff .12 .30
66 Jeff Kent .12 .30
67 Nomar Garciaparra .20 .50
68 Rafael Furcal .12 .30
69 Tim Hamulack (RC) .20 .50
70 Chad Billingsley (RC) .30 .75
71 Hong-Chih Kuo (RC) .50 1.25
72 J.D. Drew .12 .30
73 Moises Alou .12 .30
74 Randy Winn .12 .30
75 Jason Schmidt .12 .30
76 Jeremy Accardo RC .20 .50
77 Matt Cain (RC) 1.25 3.00
78 Joel Zumaya (RC) .50 1.25
79 Travis Hafner .12 .30
80 Victor Martinez .20 .50
81 Grady Sizemore .20 .50
82 C.C. Sabathia .20 .50
83 Jhonny Peralta .12 .30
84 Jason Michaels .12 .30
85 Jeremy Sowers (RC) .20 .50
86 Ichiro Suzuki .40 1.00
87 Richie Sexson .12 .30
88 Adrian Beltre .30 .75
89 Felix Hernandez .20 .50
90 Kenji Johjima RC .50 1.25
91 Jeff Harris RC .20 .50
92 Taylor Buchholz (RC) .20 .50
93 Miguel Cabrera .30 .75
94 Dontrelle Willis .12 .30
95 Jeremy Hermida (RC) .20 .50
96 Mike Jacobs (RC) .20 .50
97 Josh Johnson (RC) .50 1.25
98 Hanley Ramirez (RC) .30 .75
99 Josh Willingham (RC) .30 .75
100 Dan Uggla (RC) .30 .75
101 David Wright .25 .60
102 Jose Reyes .20 .50
103 Pedro Martinez .20 .50
104 Carlos Beltran .20 .50
105 Carlos Delgado .12 .30
106 Billy Wagner .12 .30
107 Lastings Milledge (RC) .20 .50
108 Alfonso Soriano .20 .50
109 Jose Vidro .12 .30
110 Livan Hernandez .12 .30
111 Matt Kemp (RC) .50 1.25
112 Brandon Watson (RC) .20 .50
113 Ryan Zimmerman (RC) .60 1.50
114 Miguel Tejada .20 .50
115 Ramon Hernandez .12 .30
116 Brian Roberts .12 .30
117 Melvin Mora .12 .30
118 Erik Bedard .12 .30
119 Jay Gibbons .12 .30
120 Aaron Rakers (RC) .20 .50
121 Jake Peavy .12 .30
122 Brian Giles .12 .30
123 Khalil Greene .12 .30
124 Trevor Hoffman .20 .50
125 Josh Barfield (RC) .20 .50
126 Ben Johnson (RC) .20 .50
127 Ryan Howard .25 .60
128 Bobby Abreu .12 .30
129 Chase Utley .20 .50
130 Pat Burrell .12 .30
131 Jimmy Rollins .20 .50
132 Brett Myers .12 .30
133 Mike Thompson RC .20 .50
134 Jason Bay .12 .30
135 Oliver Perez .12 .30
136 Matt Capps (RC) .20 .50
137 Paul Maholm (RC) .20 .50
138 Nate McLouth (RC) .20 .50
139 John Van Benschoten (RC) .20 .50
140 Mark Teixeira .20 .50
141 Michael Young .12 .30
142 Hank Blalock .12 .30
143 Kevin Millwood .12 .30
144 Laynce Nix .12 .30
145 Francisco Cordero .12 .30
146 Ian Kinsler (RC) .60 1.50
147 David Ortiz .30 .75
148 Manny Ramirez .30 .75
149 Jason Varitek .30 .75
150 Curt Schilling .20 .50
151 Josh Beckett .12 .30
152 Coco Crisp .12 .30
153 Jonathan Papelbon (RC) 1.00 2.50
154 Ken Griffey Jr. .60 1.50
155 Adam Dunn .20 .50
156 Felipe Lopez .12 .30
157 Bronson Arroyo .12 .30
158 Ryan Freel .12 .30
159 Chris Denorfia (RC) .20 .50
160 Todd Helton .20 .50
161 Garrett Atkins .12 .30
162 Matt Holliday .30 .75
163 Clint Barmes .12 .30
164 Kendry Morales (RC) .50 1.25
165 Ryan Shealy (RC) .20 .50
166 Josh Wilson (RC) .20 .50
167 Reggie Sanders .12 .30
168 Angel Berroa .12 .30
169 Mike Sweeney .12 .30
170 Mark Grudzielanek .12 .30
171 Jeremy Affeldt .12 .30
172 Steve Stemle RC .20 .50
173 Justin Verlander (RC) 1.50 4.00
174 Ivan Rodriguez .20 .50
175 Chris Shelton .12 .30
176 Jeremy Bonderman .12 .30
177 Magglio Ordonez .20 .50
178 Carlos Guillen .12 .30
179 Placido Polanco .12 .30
180 Johan Santana .20 .50
181 Torii Hunter .12 .30
182 Joe Nathan .12 .30
183 Joe Mauer .20 .50
184 Dave Gassner (RC) .20 .50
185 Jason Kubel (RC) .20 .50
186 Francisco Liriano (RC) .50 1.25
187 Jim Thome .20 .50
188 Paul Konerko .20 .50
189 Scott Podsednik .12 .30
190 Tadahito Iguchi .12 .30
191 A.J. Pierzynski .12 .30
192 Jose Contreras .12 .30
193 Brian Anderson (RC) .20 .50
194 Hideki Matsui .30 .75
195 Wil Nieves (RC) .20 .50
196 Alex Rodriguez .40 1.00
197 Gary Sheffield .12 .30
198 Randy Johnson .30 .75
199 Johnny Damon .20 .50
200 Derek Jeter .75 2.00
NNO Exquisite Redemption

2006 Fleer Tradition Black and White

*B/W 1-200: 2.5X TO 6X BASIC
*B/W 1-200: 1.25X TO 3X BASIC RC
STATED ODDS 1:9 HOBBY, 1:36 RETAIL

2006 Fleer Tradition Sepia

*SEPIA 1-200: 1X TO 2.5X BASIC
*SEPIA 1-200: .5X TO 1.2X BASIC RC
STATED ODDS 1:3 HOBBY, 1:18 RETAIL

2006 Fleer Tradition 1934 Goudey Greats

STATED ODDS 1:36 HOBBY
OVERALL PLATE ODDS 1:288 HOBBY
PLATE PRINT RUN 1 SET PER COLOR
BLACK-CYAN-MAGENTA-YELLOW ISSUED
NO PLATE PRICING DUE TO SCARCITY
GG1 Andruw Jones 2.00 5.00
GG2 Chipper Jones 5.00 12.00
GG3 John Smoltz 5.00 12.00
GG4 Tim Hudson 3.00 8.00
GG5 Conor Jackson 3.00 8.00
GG6 Luis Gonzalez 2.00 5.00
GG7 Brandon Webb 3.00 8.00
GG8 Vladimir Guerrero 3.00 8.00
GG9 Bartolo Colon 2.00 5.00
GG10 Lance Berkman 3.00 8.00
GG11 Craig Biggio 3.00 8.00
GG12 Andy Pettitte 3.00 8.00
GG13 Morgan Ensberg 2.00 5.00
GG14 Roy Oswalt 3.00 8.00
GG15 Eric Chavez 2.00 5.00
GG16 Rich Harden 2.00 5.00
GG17 Huston Street 2.00 5.00
GG18 Vernon Wells 2.00 5.00
GG19 Roy Halladay 3.00 8.00
GG20 Troy Glaus 2.00 5.00
GG21 Prince Fielder 10.00 25.00
GG22 Rickie Weeks 2.00 5.00
GG23 Ben Sheets 2.00 5.00
GG24 Carlos Lee 2.00 5.00
GG25 Albert Pujols 6.00 15.00
GG26 Jim Edmonds 3.00 8.00
GG27 Scott Rolen 3.00 8.00
GG28 Chris Carpenter 3.00 8.00
GG29 Derrek Lee 2.00 5.00
GG30 Mark Prior 3.00 8.00
GG31 Greg Maddux 6.00 15.00
GG32 Carl Crawford 3.00 8.00
GG33 Scott Kazmir 3.00 8.00
GG34 Jorge Cantu 2.00 5.00
GG35 Jeff Kent 2.00 5.00
GG36 Nomar Garciaparra 3.00 8.00
GG37 J.D. Drew 2.00 5.00
GG38 Randy Winn 2.00 5.00
GG39 Jason Schmidt 2.00 5.00
GG40 Travis Hafner 2.00 5.00

GG41 Victor Martinez 3.00 8.00
GG42 Grady Sizemore 3.00 8.00
GG43 Jhonny Peralta 2.00 5.00
GG44 Ichiro Suzuki 6.00 15.00
GG45 Richie Sexson 2.00 5.00
GG46 Felix Hernandez 3.00 8.00
GG47 Kenji Johjima 5.00 12.00
GG48 Miguel Cabrera 5.00 12.00
GG49 Dontrelle Willis 2.00 5.00
GG50 Josh Willingham 3.00 8.00
GG51 David Wright 4.00 10.00
GG52 Jose Reyes 3.00 8.00
GG53 Pedro Martinez 3.00 8.00
GG54 Carlos Beltran 3.00 8.00
GG55 Alfonso Soriano 3.00 8.00
GG56 Ryan Zimmerman 6.00 15.00
GG57 Miguel Tejada 3.00 8.00
GG58 Brian Roberts 2.00 5.00
GG59 Jake Peavy 2.00 5.00
GG60 Brian Giles 2.00 5.00
GG61 Khalil Greene 2.00 5.00
GG62 Ryan Howard 4.00 10.00
GG63 Bobby Abreu 2.00 5.00
GG64 Chase Utley 3.00 8.00
GG65 Jimmy Rollins 3.00 8.00
GG66 Jason Bay 2.00 5.00
GG67 Mark Teixeira 3.00 8.00
GG68 Michael Young 2.00 5.00
GG69 Hank Blalock 2.00 5.00
GG70 David Ortiz 5.00 12.00
GG71 Manny Ramirez 5.00 12.00
GG72 Curt Schilling 3.00 8.00
GG73 Josh Beckett 2.00 5.00
GG74 Jonathan Papelbon 10.00 25.00
GG75 Ken Griffey Jr. 10.00 25.00
GG76 Adam Dunn 3.00 8.00
GG77 Todd Helton 3.00 8.00
GG78 Garrett Atkins 2.00 5.00
GG79 Matt Holliday 5.00 12.00
GG80 Reggie Sanders 2.00 5.00
GG81 Justin Verlander 15.00 40.00
GG82 Ivan Rodriguez 3.00 8.00
GG83 Chris Shelton 2.00 5.00
GG84 Jeremy Bonderman 2.00 5.00
GG85 Magglio Ordonez 3.00 8.00
GG86 Johan Santana 3.00 8.00
GG87 Torii Hunter 2.00 5.00
GG88 Joe Nathan 2.00 5.00
GG89 Joe Mauer 3.00 8.00
GG90 Francisco Liriano 5.00 12.00
GG91 Jim Thome 3.00 8.00
GG92 Paul Konerko 3.00 8.00
GG93 Scott Podsednik 2.00 5.00
GG94 Tadahito Iguchi 2.00 5.00
GG95 A.J. Pierzynski 2.00 5.00
GG96 Hideki Matsui 5.00 12.00
GG97 Alex Rodriguez 6.00 15.00
GG98 Gary Sheffield 2.00 5.00
GG99 Derek Jeter 12.00 30.00
GG100 Jason Giambi 2.00 5.00

2006 Fleer Tradition Blue Chip Prospects

COMPLETE SET (25) 12.50 30.00
STATED ODDS 1:6 HOBBY, 1:18 RETAIL
OVERALL PLATE ODDS 1:288 HOBBY
PLATE PRINT RUN 1 SET PER COLOR
BLACK-CYAN-MAGENTA-YELLOW ISSUED
NO PLATE PRICING DUE TO SCARCITY
BC1 Ryan Zimmerman 1.25 3.00
BC2 Conor Jackson .60 1.50
BC3 Jonathan Papelbon 2.00 5.00
BC4 Justin Verlander 3.00 8.00
BC5 Jeremy Hermida .40 1.00
BC6 Josh Willingham .60 1.50
BC7 Hanley Ramirez .60 1.50
BC8 Prince Fielder 2.00 5.00
BC9 Francisco Liriano 1.00 2.50
BC10 Lastings Milledge .40 1.00
BC11 Jon Lester 1.50 4.00
BC12 Matt Cain 2.50 6.00
BC13 Adam Wainwright .60 1.50
BC14 Chuck James .40 1.00
BC15 Kenji Johjima 1.00 2.50
BC16 Josh Johnson 1.00 2.50
BC17 Jason Kubel .40 1.00
BC18 Brian Anderson .40 1.00
BC19 Cole Hamels 1.25 3.00
BC20 Mike Jacobs .40 1.00
BC21 Jered Weaver 1.25 3.00
BC22 Kendry Morales 1.00 2.50
BC23 Alay Soler .40 1.00
BC24 Chris Denorfia .40 1.00
BC25 Chad Billingsley .60 1.50

2006 Fleer Tradition Diamond Tribute

COMPLETE SET (25) 12.50 30.00
STATED ODDS 1:9 HOBBY, 1:36 RETAIL
OVERALL PLATE ODDS 1:288 HOBBY
PLATE PRINT RUN 1 SET PER COLOR
BLACK-CYAN-MAGENTA-YELLOW ISSUED
NO PLATE PRICING DUE TO SCARCITY
DT1 Derek Jeter 2.50 6.00
DT2 Ken Griffey Jr. 2.00 5.00
DT3 Vladimir Guerrero .60 1.50
DT4 Albert Pujols 1.25 3.00
DT5 Derrek Lee .40 1.00
DT6 David Ortiz 1.00 2.50
DT7 Miguel Tejada .60 1.50
DT8 Jim Thome .60 1.50
DT9 Travis Hafner .40 1.00
DT10 Grady Sizemore .60 1.50
DT11 Chris Shelton .40 1.00
DT12 Dontrelle Willis .40 1.00
DT13 Craig Biggio .60 1.50
DT14 Roy Oswalt .60 1.50
DT15 Prince Fielder 2.00 5.00
DT16 David Wright .75 2.00
DT17 Jose Reyes .60 1.50
DT18 Hideki Matsui 1.00 2.50
DT19 Rich Harden .40 1.00
DT20 Bobby Abreu .40 1.00
DT21 Jason Bay .40 1.00
DT22 Jake Peavy .40 1.00
DT23 Felix Hernandez .60 1.50
DT24 Carl Crawford .60 1.50
DT25 Vernon Wells .40 1.00

2006 Fleer Tradition Grass Roots

COMPLETE SET (25) 12.50 30.00
STATED ODDS 1:6 HOBBY, 1:36 RETAIL
OVERALL PLATE ODDS 1:288 HOBBY
PLATE PRINT RUN 1 SET PER COLOR
BLACK-CYAN-MAGENTA-YELLOW ISSUED
NO PLATE PRICING DUE TO SCARCITY
GR1 Ken Griffey Jr. 2.00 5.00
GR2 Albert Pujols 1.25 3.00
GR3 Derek Jeter 2.50 6.00
GR4 Derrek Lee .40 1.00
GR5 Vladimir Guerrero .60 1.50
GR6 Andruw Jones .40 1.00
GR7 Manny Ramirez 1.00 2.50
GR8 Johan Santana .60 1.50
GR9 Victor Martinez .60 1.50
GR10 Todd Helton .60 1.50
GR11 Ivan Rodriguez .60 1.50
GR12 Miguel Cabrera 1.00 2.50
GR13 Lance Berkman .60 1.50
GR14 Bartolo Colon .40 1.00
GR15 Jeff Kent .40 1.00
GR16 Carlos Lee .40 1.00
GR17 Torii Hunter .40 1.00
GR18 Carlos Beltran .60 1.50
GR19 Alex Rodriguez 1.25 3.00
GR20 Randy Johnson 1.00 2.50
GR21 Eric Chavez .40 1.00
GR22 Ryan Howard .75 2.00
GR23 Ichiro Suzuki 1.25 3.00
GR24 Chris Carpenter .60 1.50
GR25 Mark Teixeira .60 1.50

2006 Fleer Tradition Ken Griffey Jr. 1989 Autograph Buyback

RANDOM INSERT IN HOBBY PACKS
STATED PRINT RUN 99 CARDS
CARD IS NOT SERIAL-NUMBERED
PRINT RUN PROVIDED BY UPPER DECK
NO PRICING DUE TO SCARCITY

2006 Fleer Tradition Signature Tradition

STATED ODDS 1:1269 HOBBY, 1:3456 RETAIL
SP INFO PROVIDED BY UPPER DECK
NO PRICING DUE TO SCARCITY
OVERALL PLATE ODDS: 1:288 HOBBY
PLATE PRINT RUN 1 SET PER COLOR
BLACK-CYAN-MAGENTA-YELLOW-ISSUED
PLATES DO NOT FEATURE AUTOS
NO PLATE PRICING DUE TO SCARCITY

2006 Fleer Tradition Traditional Threads

STATED ODDS 1:41 HOBBY, 1:108 RETAIL
SP INFO PROVIDED BY UPPER DECK
OVERALL PLATE ODDS: 1:288 HOBBY
PLATE PRINT RUN 1 SET PER COLOR
BLACK-CYAN-MAGENTA-YELLOW-ISSUED
PLATES DO NOT FEATURE MATERIAL
NO PLATE PRICING DUE TO SCARCITY
AP Albert Pujols Jsy 8.00 20.00
AR Aramis Ramirez Jsy 3.00 8.00
AS Alfonso Soriano Jsy 3.00 8.00
BA Jason Bay Jsy 3.00 8.00
BG Brian Giles Jsy 3.00 8.00
BR Brian Roberts Jsy 3.00 8.00
BS Ben Sheets Jsy 3.00 8.00
CF Chone Figgins Jsy 3.00 8.00
CK Casey Kotchman Jsy SP 4.00 10.00
CL Carlos Lee Jsy 3.00 8.00
CZ Carlos Zambrano Jsy SP 4.00 10.00
DJ Derek Jeter Pants 8.00 20.00
DL Derrek Lee Jsy 3.00 8.00
DO David Ortiz Jsy 4.00 10.00
EB Erik Bedard Jsy 3.00 8.00
FH Felix Hernandez Jsy 4.00 10.00
GJ Geoff Jenkins Jsy 3.00 8.00
GM Greg Maddux Jsy 4.00 10.00
GR Khalil Greene Jsy 4.00 10.00
HB Hank Blalock Jsy 3.00 8.00
JB Josh Barfield Jsy 3.00 8.00
JD Johnny Damon Jsy 4.00 10.00
JH Jeremy Hermida Jsy 4.00 10.00
JL Javy Lopez Jsy 3.00 8.00
JP Jake Peavy Jsy 3.00 8.00
JV Jose Vidro Jsy 3.00 8.00
KG Ken Griffey Jr. Jsy 6.00 15.00
LH Livan Hernandez Jsy 3.00 8.00
MG Marcus Giles Jsy 3.00 8.00
MM Melvin Mora Jsy 3.00 8.00
MT Miguel Tejada Pants 3.00 8.00
MY Michael Young Jsy 3.00 8.00
OV Omar Vizquel Jsy SP 4.00 10.00
PF Prince Fielder Jsy 4.00 10.00
RO Roy Oswalt Jsy 3.00 8.00
RW Rickie Weeks Jsy 3.00 8.00
RZ Ryan Zimmerman Jsy 6.00 15.00
SC Sean Casey Jsy 3.00 8.00
TE Mark Teixeira Jsy 4.00 10.00
VG Vladimir Guerrero Jsy 4.00 10.00
ZD Zach Duke Jsy 3.00 8.00

2006 Fleer Tradition Triple Crown Contenders

COMPLETE SET (15) 10.00 25.00
STATED ODDS 1:9 HOBBY, 1:36 RETAIL
OVERALL PLATE ODDS 1:288 HOBBY
PLATE PRINT RUN 1 SET PER COLOR
BLACK-CYAN-MAGENTA-YELLOW ISSUED
NO PLATE PRICING DUE TO SCARCITY
TC1 Albert Pujols 1.25 3.00
TC2 Derrek Lee .40 1.00
TC3 Manny Ramirez 1.00 2.50
TC4 David Ortiz 1.00 2.50
TC5 Mark Teixeira .60 1.50
TC6 Alex Rodriguez 1.25 3.00
TC7 Andruw Jones .40 1.00
TC8 Todd Helton .60 1.50
TC9 Vladimir Guerrero .60 1.50
TC10 Miguel Cabrera 1.00 2.50
TC11 Hideki Matsui 1.00 2.50
TC12 Travis Hafner .40 1.00
TC13 David Wright .75 2.00
TC14 Ken Griffey Jr. 2.00 5.00
TC15 Jason Bay .40 1.00

2001 Fleer Triple Crown

COMPLETE SET (300) 12.50 30.00
COMMON CARD (1-300) .10 .30
COMMON CARD (301-310) 1.50 4.00
301-310 DIST.IN FLEER PLAT.RC HOB/RET
301-310 PRINT RUN 2999 SERIAL #'d SETS
1 Derek Jeter .75 2.00
2 Vladimir Guerrero .30 .75
3 Henry Rodriguez .10 .30
4 Jason Giambi .10 .30
5 Nomar Garciaparra .50 1.25
6 Jeff Kent .10 .30
7 Garret Anderson .10 .30
8 Todd Helton .20 .50
9 Barry Bonds .75 2.00
10 Preston Wilson .10 .30
11 Troy Glaus .10 .30
12 Geoff Jenkins .10 .30
13 Jim Edmonds .10 .30
14 Bobby Higginson .10 .30
15 Mark Quinn .10 .30
16 Barry Larkin .20 .50
17 Richie Sexson .10 .30
18 Fernando Tatis .10 .30
19 John VanderWal .10 .30
20 Darin Erstad .10 .30
21 Shawn Green .10 .30
22 Scott Rolen .20 .50
23 Tony Batista .10 .30
24 Phil Nevin .10 .30
25 Tim Salmon .20 .50
26 Gary Sheffield .10 .30
27 Ben Grieve .10 .30
28 Jermaine Dye .10 .30
29 Andres Galarraga .10 .30
30 Adrian Beltre .10 .30
31 Rafael Palmeiro .20 .50
32 J.T. Snow .10 .30
33 Edgardo Alfonzo .10 .30
34 Paul Konerko .10 .30
35 Jim Thome .20 .50
36 Andruw Jones .10 .30
37 Mike Sweeney .10 .30
38 Jose Cruz Jr. .10 .30
39 David Ortiz .30 .75
40 Pat Burrell .10 .30
41 Chipper Jones .30 .75
42 Jeff Bagwell .20 .50
43 Raul Mondesi .10 .30
44 Rondell White .10 .30
45 Edgar Martinez .20 .50
46 Cal Ripken 1.00 2.50
47 Moises Alou .10 .30
48 Shannon Stewart .10 .30
49 Tino Martinez .20 .50
50 Jason Kendall .10 .30
51 Richard Hidalgo .10 .30
52 Albert Belle .10 .30
53 Jay Payton .10 .30
54 Cliff Floyd .10 .30
55 Rusty Greer .10 .30
56 Matt Williams .10 .30
57 Sammy Sosa .30 .75
58 Carl Everett .10 .30
59 Carlos Delgado .10 .30
60 Jeremy Giambi .10 .30
61 Jose Canseco .20 .50
62 David Segui .10 .30
63 Jose Vidro .10 .30
64 Matt Stairs .10 .30
65 Travis Fryman .10 .30
66 Ken Griffey Jr. .60 1.50
67 Mike Piazza .50 1.25
68 Mark McGwire .75 2.00
69 Craig Biggio .20 .50
70 Eric Chavez .10 .30
71 Mo Vaughn .10 .30
72 Matt Lawton .10 .30
73 Miguel Tejada .10 .30
74 Brian Giles .10 .30
75 Sean Casey .10 .30
76 Robin Ventura .10 .30
77 Ivan Rodriguez .20 .50
78 Dean Palmer .10 .30
79 Frank Thomas .30 .75
80 Bernie Williams .20 .50
81 Juan Encarnacion .10 .30
82 John Olerud .10 .30
83 Rich Aurilia .10 .30
84 Juan Gonzalez .10 .30
85 Ray Durham .10 .30
86 Steve Finley .10 .30
87 Ken Caminiti .10 .30
88 Roberto Alomar .20 .50
89 Jeromy Burnitz .10 .30
90 J.D. Drew .10 .30
91 Lance Berkman .10 .30
92 Gabe Kapler .10 .30
93 Larry Walker .10 .30
94 Alex Rodriguez .40 1.00
95 Jeffrey Hammonds .10 .30
96 Magglio Ordonez .10 .30
97 David Justice .10 .30
98 Eric Karros .10 .30
99 Manny Ramirez .20 .50
100 Paul O'Neill .20 .50
101 Ron Gant .10 .30
102 Erubiel Durazo .10 .30
103 Jason Varitek .30 .75
104 Chan Ho Park .10 .30
105 Corey Koskie .10 .30
106 Jeff Conine .10 .30
107 Kevin Tapani .10 .30
108 Mike Lowell .10 .30
109 Tim Hudson .10 .30
110 Bobby Abreu .10 .30
111 Bret Boone .10 .30
112 David Wells .10 .30
113 Brian Jordan .10 .30
114 Mitch Meluskey .10 .30
115 Terrence Long .10 .30
116 Matt Clement .10 .30
117 Fernando Vina .10 .30
118 Luis Alicea .10 .30
119 Jay Bell .10 .30
120 Mark Grace .20 .50
121 Carlos Febles .10 .30
122 Mark Redman .10 .30
123 Kevin Jordan .10 .30
124 Pat Meares .10 .30
125 Mark McLemore .10 .30
126 Chris Singleton .10 .30
127 Trot Nixon .10 .30
128 Carlos Beltran .10 .30
129 Lee Stevens .10 .30
130 Kris Benson .10 .30
131 Jay Buhner .10 .30
132 Greg Vaughn .10 .30
133 Eric Young .10 .30
134 Tony Womack .10 .30
135 Roger Cedeno .10 .30
136 Travis Lee .10 .30
137 Marvin Benard .10 .30
138 Aaron Sele .10 .30
139 Rick Ankiel .10 .30
140 Ruben Mateo .10 .30
141 Randy Johnson .30 .75
142 Jason Tyner .10 .30
143 Mike Redmond .10 .30
144 Ron Coomer .10 .30
145 Scott Elarton .10 .30
146 Javy Lopez .10 .30
147 Carlos Lee .10 .30
148 Tony Clark .10 .30
149 Roger Clemens .60 1.50
150 Mike Lieberthal .10 .30
151 Shawn Estes .10 .30
152 Vinny Castilla .10 .30
153 Alex Gonzalez .10 .30
154 Troy Percival .10 .30
155 Pokey Reese .10 .30
156 Todd Hollandsworth .10 .30
157 Marquis Grissom .10 .30
158 Greg Maddux .50 1.25
159 Dante Bichette .10 .30
160 Hideo Nomo .30 .75
161 Jacque Jones .10 .30
162 Kevin Young .10 .30
163 B.J. Surhoff .10 .30
164 Eddie Taubensee .10 .30
165 Neifi Perez .10 .30
166 Orlando Hernandez .10 .30
167 Francisco Cordova .10 .30
168 Miguel Cairo .10 .30
169 Rafael Furcal .10 .30
170 Sandy Alomar Jr. .10 .30
171 Jeff Cirillo .10 .30
172 A.J. Pierzynski .10 .30
173 Fred McGriff .20 .50
174 Mike Mussina .20 .50
175 Aaron Boone .10 .30
176 Nick Johnson .10 .30
177 Kent Bottenfield .10 .30
178 Felipe Crespo .10 .30
179 Ryan Minor .10 .30
180 Charles Johnson .10 .30
181 Damion Easley .10 .30
182 Michael Barrett .10 .30
183 Doug Glanville .10 .30
184 Ben Davis .10 .30
185 Rickey Henderson .30 .75
186 Edgard Clemente .10 .30
187 Dmitri Young .10 .30
188 Tom Goodwin .10 .30
189 Mike Hampton .10 .30
190 Gerald Williams .10 .30
191 Omar Vizquel .20 .50
192 Ben Petrick .10 .30
193 Brad Radke .10 .30
194 Russ Davis .10 .30
195 Milton Bradley .10 .30
196 John Parrish .10 .30
197 Todd Hundley .10 .30
198 Carl Pavano .10 .30
199 Bruce Chen .10 .30
200 Royce Clayton .10 .30
201 Homer Bush .10 .30
202 Mark Grudzielanek .10 .30
203 Mike Lansing .10 .30
204 Daryle Ward .10 .30
205 Jeff D'Amico .10 .30
206 Ray Lankford .10 .30
207 Curt Schilling .10 .30
208 Pedro Martinez .20 .50
209 Johnny Damon .20 .50
210 Al Leiter .10 .30
211 Ruben Rivera .10 .30
212 Kazuhiro Sasaki .10 .30
213 Will Clark .20 .50
214 Rick Helling .10 .30
215 Adam Piatt .10 .30
216 Joe Girardi .10 .30
217 A.J. Burnett .10 .30
218 Mike Bordick .10 .30
219 Mike Cameron .10 .30
220 Tony Gwynn .40 1.00
221 Delvi Cruz .10 .30
222 Bubba Trammell .10 .30
223 Scott Erickson .10 .30
224 Kerry Wood .10 .30
225 Derrek Lee .20 .50
226 Peter Bergeron .10 .30
227 Chris Gomez .10 .30
228 Al Martin .10 .30
229 Brady Anderson .10 .30
230 Ramon Martinez .10 .30
231 Darryl Kile .10 .30
232 Devon White .10 .30
233 Charlie Hayes .10 .30
234 Aramis Ramirez .10 .30
235 Mike Lamb .10 .30
236 Tom Glavine .20 .50
237 Troy O'Leary .10 .30
238 Joe Randa .10 .30
239 Dustin Hermanson .10 .30
240 Adam Kennedy .10 .30
241 Jose Valentin .10 .30
242 Derek Bell .10 .30
243 Mark Kotsay .10 .30
244 Ron Belliard .10 .30
245 Warren Morris .10 .30
246 Ozzie Guillen .10 .30
247 Andy Ashby .10 .30
248 Jose Offerman .10 .30
249 Kevin Brown .10 .30
250 Jorge Posada .20 .50
251 Alex Cabrera .10 .30
252 Chan Perry .10 .30
253 Augie Ojeda .10 .30
254 Santiago Perez .10 .30
255 Grant Roberts .10 .30
256 Dusty Allen .10 .30
257 Elvis Pena .10 .30
258 Matt Kinney .10 .30
259 Timo Perez .10 .30
260 Adam Eaton .10 .30
261 Geraldo Guzman .10 .30
262 Damian Rolls .10 .30
263 Alfonso Soriano .20 .50
264 Corey Patterson .10 .30
265 Juan Alvarez .10 .30
266 Shawn Gilbert .10 .30
267 Adam Bernero .10 .30
268 Ben Weber .10 .30
269 Tike Redman .10 .30
270 Willie Morales .10 .30
271 Tomas De la Rosa .10 .30
272 Rodney Lindsey .10 .30
273 Carlos Casimiro .10 .30
274 Jim Mann .10 .30
275 Pasqual Coco .10 .30
276 Julio Zuleta .10 .30
277 Damon Minor .10 .30
278 Jose Ortiz .10 .30
279 Eric Munson .10 .30
280 Andy Thompson .10 .30
281 Aubrey Huff .10 .30
282 Chris Richard .10 .30
283 Ross Gload .10 .30
284 Travis Dawkins .10 .30
285 Tim Drew .10 .30
286 Barry Zito .20 .50
287 Andy Tracy .10 .30
288 Julio Lugo .10 .30
289 Greg LaRocca .10 .30
290 Keith McDonald .10 .30
291 J.C. Romero .10 .30
292 Adam Melhuse .10 .30
293 Ryan Kohlmeier .10 .30
294 John Bale .10 .30
295 Eric Cammack .10 .30
296 Morgan Burkhart .10 .30
297 Kory DeHaan .10 .30
298 Mike Mahoney .10 .30
299 Hector Ortiz .10 .30
300 Talmadge Nunnari .10 .30
301 Elpidio Guzman/2999 RC 1.50 4.00
302 Drew Henson/2999 RC 2.00 5.00
303 Bud Smith/2999 RC 1.50 4.00
304 Carlos Valderrama/2999 RC 1.50 4.00
305 Tsuyoshi Shinjo/2999 RC 2.00 5.00
306 Ichiro Suzuki/2999 RC 15.00 40.00
307 Jackson Melian/2999 RC 1.50 4.00
308 Morgan Ensberg/2999 RC 2.00 5.00
309 Albert Pujols/2999 RC 20.00 50.00
310 Johnny Estrada/2999 RC 2.00 5.00

2001 Fleer Triple Crown Blue

*PRINT RUN b/wn 36-50: 15X TO 40X
*PRINT RUN b/wn 26-35: 20X TO 50X
*PRINT RUN b/wn 21-25: 25X TO 60X
*PRINT RUN b/wn 16-20: 30X TO 80X
PRINT RUNS BASED ON 2000 HR's
PRINT RUN b/wn 1-15 TOO SCARCE TO PRICE

2001 Fleer Triple Crown Green

*PRINT RUN b/wn 121-150: 6X TO 15X
*PRINT RUN b/wn 81-120: 8X TO 20X
*PRINT RUN b/wn 66-80: 10X TO 25X
*PRINT RUN b/wn 51-65: 12.5X TO 30X
*PRINT RUN b/wn 36-50: 15X TO 40X
PRINT RUNS BASED ON 2000 RBI's

2001 Fleer Triple Crown Purple

*STARS: 2.5X TO 6X BASIC CARDS

2001 Fleer Triple Crown Red

*STARS: 4X TO 10X BASIC CARDS
PRINT RUNS BASED ON 2000 BAT AVG.
PRINT RUNS: 227 TO 372 OF EACH CARD

2001 Fleer Triple Crown Crowning Achievements

COMPLETE SET (15) 20.00 40.00
STATED ODDS 1:9 HOB, 1:12 RET
1 Troy Glaus .50 1.25
2 Mark McGwire 2.00 5.00
3 Larkin Galarraga/Biggio .50 1.25
4 Ken Griffey Jr. 1.50 4.00
5 Rafael Palmeiro .50 1.25
6 Alex Rodriguez 1.00 2.50
7 Roger Clemens 1.50 4.00
8 Mike Piazza 1.25 3.00
9 Cal Ripken 2.50 6.00
10 Randy Johnson .75 2.00
11 Jeff Bagwell .50 1.25
12 Sammy Sosa .75 2.00
13 Greg Maddux 1.25 3.00
14 Barry Bonds 2.00 5.00
15 Fred McGriff .50 1.25

2001 Fleer Triple Crown Crowns of Gold Memorabilia

1 Rick Ankiel Jsy 4.00 10.00
2 Steve Carlton Jsy 4.00 10.00
3 Roger Clemens Jsy 10.00 25.00
4 Carlos Delgado Bat 4.00 10.00
5 Darin Erstad Bat 4.00 10.00
6 Jimmie Foxx Bat 20.00 50.00
7 Todd Helton Bat 6.00 15.00
8 Randy Johnson Jsy 6.00 15.00
9 Frank Robinson Bat 6.00 15.00
10 Gary Sheffield Jsy 4.00 10.00
11 Frank Thomas Bat 6.00 15.00
12 Ted Williams Bat 20.00 50.00

2001 Fleer Triple Crown Crowns of Gold Memorabilia Autographs

STATED PRINT RUNS B/WN 9-98 COPIES PER
1 Steve Carlton Jsy/72 20.00 50.00
2 Roger Clemens Jsy/98 40.00 80.00
3 Frank Robinson Bat/66 40.00 80.00

2001 Fleer Triple Crown Future Threats

COMPLETE SET (15) 15.00 30.00
STATED ODDS 1:7 HOB, 1:10 RET
1 Derek Jeter 1.50 4.00
2 Alex Rodriguez .75 2.00
3 Ordon/Green/Jones .40 1.00
4 Larry Walker .40 1.00
5 Vladimir Guerrero .60 1.50
6 Nomar Garciaparra 1.00 2.50
7 Ken Griffey Jr. 1.25 3.00
8 Barry Bonds 1.50 4.00
9 Chipper Jones .60 1.50
10 Todd Helton .40 1.00
11 Ivan Rodriguez .40 1.00
12 Jeff Bagwell .40 1.00
13 Frank Thomas .60 1.50
14 Carlos Delgado .40 1.00
15 Mike Piazza 1.00 2.50

2001 Fleer Triple Crown Glamour Boys

COMPLETE SET (15) 50.00 100.00
STATED ODDS 1:24 HOB, 1:20 RET
1 Derek Jeter 4.00 10.00
2 Vladimir Guerrero 1.50 4.00
3 Rolen/Bagwell/Williams 1.50 4.00
4 Sammy Sosa 1.50 4.00
5 Ken Griffey Jr. 3.00 8.00
6 Mark McGwire 4.00 10.00
7 Ivan Rodriguez 1.50 4.00
8 Mike Piazza 2.50 6.00
9 Nomar Garciaparra 2.50 6.00
10 Cal Ripken 5.00 12.00
11 Tony Gwynn 2.00 5.00
12 Barry Bonds 4.00 10.00
13 Randy Johnson 1.50 4.00
14 Alex Rodriguez 2.00 5.00
15 Pedro Martinez 1.50 4.00

2002 Fleer Triple Crown

COMPLETE SET (270) 15.00 40.00
1 Mo Vaughn .10 .30
2 Derek Jeter .75 2.00
3 Ken Griffey Jr. .60 1.50
4 Charles Johnson .10 .30
5 Geoff Jenkins .10 .30
6 Chuck Knoblauch .10 .30
7 Jason Kendall .10 .30
8 Jim Edmonds .10 .30
9 David Eckstein .10 .30
10 Carl Everett .10 .30
11 Barry Larkin .20 .50
12 Cliff Floyd .10 .30
13 Ben Sheets .10 .30
14 Jeff Conine .10 .30
15 Brian Giles .10 .30
16 Darryl Kile .10 .30
17 Troy Glaus .10 .30
18 Trot Nixon .10 .30
19 Jim Thome .20 .50
20 Preston Wilson .10 .30
21 Roger Clemens .60 1.50
22 Chad Hermansen .10 .30
23 Matt Morris .10 .30
24 Shawn Wooten .10 .30
25 Manny Ramirez .20 .50
26 Roberto Alomar .20 .50
27 Josh Beckett .10 .30
28 Jose Hernandez .10 .30
29 Mike Mussina .20 .50
30 Jack Wilson .10 .30
31 Bud Smith .10 .30
32 Garret Anderson .10 .30
33 Pedro Martinez .20 .50
34 Travis Fryman .10 .30
35 Jeff Bagwell .20 .50
36 Doug Mientkiewicz .10 .30
37 Andy Pettitte .20 .50
38 Ryan Klesko .10 .30
39 Edgar Renteria .10 .30
40 Mariano Rivera .30 .75
41 Darin Erstad .10 .30
42 Hideo Nomo .30 .75
43 Ellis Burks .10 .30
44 Craig Biggio .20 .50
45 Corey Koskie .10 .30
46 Jason Varitek .30 .75
47 Xavier Nady .10 .30
48 Aubrey Huff .10 .30
49 Tim Salmon .20 .50
50 Nomar Garciaparra .50 1.25
51 Juan Gonzalez .10 .30
52 Moises Alou .10 .30
53 A.J. Pierzynski .10 .30
54 Bernie Williams .20 .50
55 Phil Nevin .10 .30
56 Ben Grieve .10 .30
57 Mark Grace .20 .50
58 Mike Lansing .10 .30
59 Kenny Lofton .10 .30
60 Lance Berkman .10 .30
61 David Ortiz .30 .75
62 Jason Giambi .10 .30
63 Mark Kotsay .10 .30
64 Greg Vaughn .10 .30
65 Junior Spivey .10 .30
66 Fred McGriff .20 .50
67 C.C. Sabathia .10 .30
68 Richard Hidalgo .10 .30
69 Torii Hunter .10 .30
70 Jason Hart .10 .30
71 Bubba Trammell .10 .30
72 Jace Brewer .10 .30
73 Matt Williams .10 .30
74 Matt Stairs .10 .30
75 Omar Vizquel .20 .50
76 Daryle Ward .10 .30
77 Joe Mays .10 .30
78 Eric Chavez .10 .30
79 Andres Galarraga .10 .30
80 Rafael Palmeiro .20 .50
81 Steve Finley .10 .30
82 Eric Young .10 .30
83 Todd Helton .20 .50
84 Roy Oswalt .10 .30
85 Eric Milton .10 .30
86 Ramon Hernandez .10 .30
87 Jeff Kent .10 .30
88 Ivan Rodriguez .20 .50
89 Luis Gonzalez .10 .30
90 Corey Patterson .10 .30
91 Jose Ortiz .10 .30
92 Mike Sweeney .10 .30
93 Cristian Guzman .10 .30
94 Johnny Damon .20 .50
95 Barry Bonds .75 2.00
96 Rusty Greer .10 .30
97 Reggie Sanders .10 .30
98 Sammy Sosa .30 .75
99 Jeff Cirillo .10 .30
100 Carlos Febles .10 .30
101 Jose Vidro .10 .30
102 Jermaine Dye .10 .30
103 Rich Aurilia .10 .30
104 Gabe Kapler .10 .30
105 Randy Johnson .30 .75
106 Rondell White .10 .30
107 Ben Petrick .10 .30
108 Joe Randa .10 .30
109 Fernando Tatis .10 .30
110 Tim Hudson .10 .30
111 John Olerud .10 .30
112 Alex Rodriguez .40 1.00
113 Curt Schilling .10 .30
114 Kerry Wood .10 .30
115 Alex Ochoa .10 .30
116 Carlos Beltran .10 .30
117 Vladimir Guerrero .30 .75
118 Mark Mulder .10 .30
119 Bret Boone .10 .30
120 Carlos Delgado .10 .30
121 Marcus Giles .10 .30
122 Paul Konerko .10 .30
123 Juan Pierre .10 .30
124 Mark Quinn .10 .30
125 Edgardo Alfonzo .10 .30
126 Barry Zito .10 .30
127 Dan Wilson .10 .30
128 Jose Cruz Jr. .10 .30
129 Chipper Jones .30 .75
130 Ray Durham .10 .30
131 Larry Walker .10 .30
132 Neifi Perez .10 .30
133 Robin Ventura .10 .30
134 Miguel Tejada .10 .30
135 Edgar Martinez .20 .50
136 Raul Mondesi .10 .30
137 Javy Lopez .10 .30
138 Jose Canseco .20 .50
139 Mike Hampton .10 .30
140 Eric Karros .10 .30
141 Mike Piazza .50 1.25
142 Travis Lee .10 .30
143 Ichiro Suzuki .60 1.50
144 Shannon Stewart .10 .30
145 Andruw Jones .20 .50
146 Frank Thomas .30 .75
147 Tony Clark .10 .30
148 Adrian Beltre .10 .30
149 Matt Lawton .10 .30
150 Marlon Anderson .10 .30
151 Freddy Garcia .10 .30
152 Brian Jordan .10 .30
153 Carlos Lee .10 .30
154 Eric Munson .10 .30
155 Paul LoDuca .10 .30
156 Jay Payton .10 .30
157 Scott Rolen .20 .50
158 Jamie Moyer .10 .30
159 Tom Glavine .20 .50
160 Magglio Ordonez .10 .30
161 Brandon Inge .10 .30
162 Shawn Green .10 .30
163 Tsuyoshi Shinjo .10 .30
164 Mike Lieberthal .10 .30
165 Kazuhiro Sasaki .10 .30
166 Greg Maddux .50 1.25
167 Chris Singleton .10 .30
168 Juan Encarnacion .10 .30
169 Gary Sheffield .10 .30
170 Nick Johnson .10 .30
171 Bob Abreu .10 .30
172 Aaron Boone .10 .30
173 Rafael Furcal .10 .30
174 Mark Buehrle .10 .30
175 Bobby Higginson .10 .30
176 Kevin Brown .10 .30
177 Tino Martinez .20 .50

178 Pat Burrell .10 .30
179 Fernando Vina .10 .30
180 Jay Gibbons .10 .30
181 Jose Valentin .10 .30
182 Derrek Lee .20 .50
183 Richie Sexson .10 .30
184 Alfonso Soriano .10 .30
185 Jimmy Rollins .10 .30
186 Albert Pujols .60 1.50
187 Brady Anderson .10 .30
188 Sean Casey .10 .30
189 Luis Castillo .10 .30
190 Jeromy Burnitz .10 .30
191 Jorge Posada .20 .50
192 Kevin Young .10 .30
193 Eli Marrero .10 .30
194 Shea Hillenbrand .10 .30
195 Adam Dunn .10 .30
196 Mike Lowell .10 .30
197 Jeffrey Hammonds .10 .30
198 David Justice .10 .30
199 Aramis Ramirez .10 .30
200 J.D. Drew .10 .30
201 Pedro Santana FS .08 .25
202 Endy Chavez FS .08 .25
203 Donnie Bridges FS .08 .25
204 Travis Phelps FS .08 .25
205 Drew Henson FS .08 .25
206 Angel Berroa FS .08 .25
207 George Perez FS .08 .25
208 Billy Sylvester FS .08 .25
209 Juan Cruz FS .08 .25
210 Horacio Ramirez FS .08 .25
211 J.J. Davis FS .08 .25
212 Cody Ransom FS .08 .25
213 Mark Teixeira FS .60 1.50
214 Nate Frese FS .08 .25
215 Brian Rogers FS .08 .25
216 Dewon Brazelton FS .08 .25
217 Carlos Hernandez FS .08 .25
218 Juan Rivera FS .08 .25
219 Luis Lopez FS .08 .25
220 Benito Baez FS .08 .25
221 Bill Ortega FS .08 .25
222 Dustan Mohr FS .08 .25
223 Corky Miller FS .08 .25
224 Tyler Walker FS .08 .25
225 Rick Bauer FS .08 .25
226 Mark Prior FS .60 1.50
227 Rafael Soriano FS .08 .25
228 Greg Miller FS .08 .25
229 Dave Williams FS .08 .25
230 Bert Snow FS .08 .25
231 Barry Bonds SB .40 1.00
232 Rickey Henderson SB .30 .75
233 Alex Rodriguez SB .25 .60
234 Luis Gonzalez SB .10 .30
235 Derek Jeter SB .40 1.00
236 Bud Smith SB .10 .30
237 Sammy Sosa SB .20 .50
238 Jeff Bagwell SB .10 .30
239 Jim Thome SB .10 .30
240 Hideo Nomo SB .20 .50
241 Greg Maddux SB .30 .75
242 Ken Griffey Jr. SB .40 1.00
243 C.Schilling/R.Johnson SB .30 .75
244 Arizona Diamondbacks SB .30 .75
245 Ichiro Suzuki SB .30 .75
246 Albert Pujols SB .30 .75
247 Ichiro Suzuki SB .30 .75
248 Barry Bonds SB .40 1.00
249 Roger Clemens SB .30 .75
250 Randy Johnson SB .20 .50
251 Todd Helton PS .10 .30
252 Rafael Palmeiro PS .10 .30
253 Mike Piazza PS .30 .75
254 Alex Rodriguez PS .25 .60
255 Manny Ramirez PS .20 .50
256 Ken Griffey Jr. PS .40 1.00
257 Jason Giambi PS .10 .30
258 Chipper Jones PS .20 .50
259 Larry Walker PS .10 .30
260 Sammy Sosa PS .20 .50
261 Vladimir Guerrero PS .20 .50
262 Nomar Garciaparra PS .30 .75
263 Randy Johnson PS .20 .50
264 Roger Clemens PS .30 .75
265 Ichiro Suzuki PS .30 .75
266 Barry Bonds PS .40 1.00
267 Paul LoDuca PS .10 .30
268 Albert Pujols PS .30 .75
269 Derek Jeter PS .40 1.00
270 Adam Dunn PS .10 .30
NNO Derek Jeter Promo 1.25 3.00

2002 Fleer Triple Crown Batting Average Parallel

*BATTING AVG: 4X TO 10X BASIC CARDS
RANDOM INSERTS IN PACKS
PRINT RUNS BASED ON 2001 BTG.AVG.
PRINT RUNS: 221-350 OF EACH CARD
SEE BECKETT.COM FOR EXACT PRINT RUNS
150-CARD SKIP-NUMBERED SET
CARDS FEATURE GREEN FOIL

2002 Fleer Triple Crown Home Run Parallel

*PRINT RUN b/wn 66-80: 10X TO 25X
*PRINT RUN b/wn 51-65: 12.5X TO 30X
*PRINT RUN b/wn 36-50: 15X TO 40X
*PRINT RUN b/wn 26-35: 20X TO 50X
*PRINT RUN b/wn 21-25: 25X TO 60X
*PRINT RUN b/wn 16-20: 30X TO 80X
RANDOM INSERTS IN PACKS
PRINT RUNS BASED ON 2001 HR TOTALS
SEE BECKETT.COM FOR EXACT PRINT RUNS
PRINT RUN b/wn 1-15 TOO SCARCE TO PRICE
150-CARD SKIP-NUMBERED SET
CARDS FEATURE RED FOIL

2002 Fleer Triple Crown RBI Parallel

*PRINT RUN b/wn 151-200: 5X TO 12X
*PRINT RUN b/wn 121-150: 6X TO 15X
*PRINT RUN b/wn 81-120: 8X TO 20X
*PRINT RUN b/wn 66-80: 10X TO 25X
*PRINT RUN b/wn 51-65: 12.5X TO 30X
*PRINT RUN b/wn 36-50: 15X TO 40X
*PRINT RUN b/wn 26-35: 20X TO 50X
*PRINT RUN b/wn 21-25: 25X TO 60X
*PRINT RUN b/wn 16-20: 30X TO 80X
RANDOM INSERTS IN PACKS
PRINT RUNS BASED ON 2001 RBI STATS
SEE BECKETT.COM FOR EXACT PRINT RUNS
150-CARD SKIP-NUMBERED SET
CARDS FEATURE BLUE FOIL

2002 Fleer Triple Crown Diamond Immortality

COMPLETE SET (10) 15.00 40.00
STATED ODDS 1:12 HOBBY, 1:20 RETAIL
1 Derek Jeter 2.50 6.00
2 Barry Bonds 2.50 6.00
3 Rickey Henderson 1.50 4.00
4 Roger Clemens 2.00 5.00
5 Alex Rodriguez 1.25 3.00
6 Albert Pujols 2.00 5.00
7 Nomar Garciaparra 1.50 4.00
8 Ichiro Suzuki 2.00 5.00
9 Chipper Jones 1.50 4.00
10 Ken Griffey Jr. 2.00 5.00

2002 Fleer Triple Crown Diamond Immortality Game Used

STATED ODDS 1:129
SP'S ARE NOT SERIAL-NUMBERED
SP PRINT RUN INFO PROVIDED BY FLEER
*MULTI-COLOR PATCH: .75X TO 2X BASIC
1 Barry Bonds Pants 10.00 25.00
2 Roger Clemens Jsy 12.50 30.00
3 Nomar Garciaparra Jsy SP/150 15.00 40.00
4 Rickey Henderson Bat 6.00 15.00
5 Derek Jeter Bat 12.50 30.00
6 Chipper Jones Bat 6.00 15.00
7 Albert Pujols Jsy 12.50 30.00
8 Alex Rodriguez Jsy SP/400 10.00 25.00

2002 Fleer Triple Crown Home Run Kings

COMPLETE SET (25) 75.00 150.00
STATED ODDS 1:24 HOBBY, 1:36 RETAIL
1 Ted Williams 5.00 12.00
2 Todd Helton 2.00 5.00
3 Eddie Murray 3.00 8.00
4 Jeff Bagwell 2.00 5.00
5 Babe Ruth 8.00 20.00
6 Eddie Mathews 3.00 8.00
7 Alex Rodriguez 3.00 8.00
8 Juan Gonzalez 2.00 5.00
9 Chipper Jones 2.50 6.00
10 Luis Gonzalez 2.00 5.00
11 Johnny Bench 3.00 8.00
12 Frank Thomas 2.50 6.00
13 Ernie Banks 3.00 8.00
14 Jimmie Foxx 3.00 8.00
15 Ken Griffey Jr. 5.00 12.00
16 Rafael Palmeiro 2.00 5.00
17 Sammy Sosa 2.50 6.00
18 Reggie Jackson 2.00 5.00
19 Barry Bonds 6.00 15.00
20 Willie McCovey 2.00 5.00
21 Manny Ramirez 2.00 5.00
22 Larry Walker 2.00 5.00
23 Jason Giambi 2.00 5.00
24 Mike Piazza 4.00 10.00
25 Jose Canseco 2.00 5.00

2002 Fleer Triple Crown Home Run Kings Autographs

RANDOM INSERTS IN PACKS
PRINT RUNS BASED ON TOP HR SEASON
ALL ARE EXCHANGE CARDS
NO PRICING DUE TO SCARCITY
2 Barry Bonds/73 100.00 250.00
3 Alex Rodriguez/52 60.00 120.00

2002 Fleer Triple Crown Home Run Kings Game Used

*JERSEYS w/PATCH: .75X TO 2X HI COLUMN
STATED ODDS 1:155
SP PRINT RUNS PROVIDED BY FLEER
SP'S ARE NOT SERIAL-NUMBERED
NO PRICING ON QTY OF 40 OR LESS
1 Jeff Bagwell Jsy 6.00 15.00
3 Barry Bonds Jsy 10.00 25.00
4 Jimmie Foxx Bat 10.00 25.00
5 Jason Giambi Jsy 6.00 15.00
6 Reggie Jackson Bat 6.00 15.00
7 Eddie Mathews Bat 6.00 15.00
8 Eddie Murray Bat 6.00 15.00
9 Rafael Palmeiro Bat 6.00 15.00
10 Mike Piazza Jsy 6.00 15.00
12 Todd Helton Bat 6.00 15.00
13 Alex Rodriguez Bat 6.00 15.00
15 Larry Walker Bat 6.00 15.00
16 Ted Williams Jsy 20.00 50.00

2002 Fleer Triple Crown RBI Kings

COMPLETE SET (15) 100.00 200.00
STATED ODDS 1:144 HOBBY, 1:288 RETAIL
1 Sammy Sosa 5.00 12.00
2 Todd Helton 4.00 10.00
3 Albert Pujols 10.00 25.00
4 Manny Ramirez 4.00 10.00
5 Luis Gonzalez 4.00 10.00
6 Shawn Green 4.00 10.00
7 Barry Bonds 12.50 30.00
8 Ken Griffey Jr. 10.00 25.00
9 Alex Rodriguez 8.00 20.00
10 Jason Giambi 4.00 10.00
11 Jeff Bagwell 4.00 10.00
12 Vladimir Guerrero 5.00 12.00
13 Juan Gonzalez 4.00 10.00
14 Chipper Jones 5.00 12.00
15 Mike Piazza 8.00 20.00

2002 Fleer Triple Crown RBI Kings Game Used

STATED ODDS 1:70
SP PRINT RUNS PROVIDED BY FLEER
SP'S ARE NOT SERIAL-NUMBERED
1 Jeff Bagwell Jsy 6.00 15.00
2 Barry Bonds Pants 10.00 25.00
3 Jason Giambi Jsy 4.00 10.00
4 Luis Gonzalez Bat 4.00 10.00
5 Juan Gonzalez Bat 4.00 10.00
6 Shawn Green Jsy 4.00 10.00
7 Todd Helton Jsy 6.00 15.00
8 Mike Piazza Jsy 10.00 25.00
10 Manny Ramirez Bat 6.00 15.00
11 Alex Rodriguez Shoe SP/500 10.00 25.00

2002 Fleer Triple Crown Season Crowns

COMPLETE SET (10) 15.00 40.00
STATED ODDS 1:12 HOBBY, 1:20 RETAIL
1 Bonds/Sosa/L.Gonz 2.50 6.00
2 Walker/Nomar/Helton 1.00 2.50
3 Sosa/Helton/Manny 1.00 2.50
4 Pedro/Jeter/Ripken 3.00 8.00
5 Canseco/Bonds/A.Rod 2.00 5.00
6 Bonds/Kent/Chipper 2.00 5.00
7 Ichiro/Giambi/I.Rod 2.00 5.00
8 Schilling/Glavine/Pedro 1.00 2.50
9 Randy/Pedro/Maddux 1.50 4.00
10 Randy/Schilling/Smoltz 1.00 2.50

2002 Fleer Triple Crown Season Crowns Autographs

RANDOM INSERTS IN PACKS
STATED PRINT RUNS LISTED BELOW
SCBB Barry Bonds/77 100.00 175.00
SCDJ Derek Jeter/160 300.00 600.00

2002 Fleer Triple Crown Season Crowns Game Used

STATED ODDS 1:90
PRINT RUN B/WN 250-400 OF EACH CARD
SP PRINT RUNS PROVIDED BY FLEER
SP'S ARE NOT SERIAL-NUMBERED
FIRST LISTED PLAYER IS MEMORABILIA
1A Barry Bonds HR Jsy 12.50 30.00
1B Sammy Sosa HR Base 6.00 15.00
2A Larry Walker BA Bat 4.00 10.00
2B Nomar Garciaparra BA Jsy 10.00 25.00
2C Todd Helton BA Jsy 6.00 15.00
3A Sammy Sosa RBI Base 6.00 15.00
3B Todd Helton RBI Jsy 6.00 15.00
3C Manny Ramirez RBI Jsy 6.00 15.00
4A Pedro Martinez AS Jsy 6.00 15.00
4B Derek Jeter AS Pants 12.50 30.00
4C Cal Ripken AS Bat SP/75 12.50 30.00
5A Jose Canseco 40/40 Jsy 12.50 30.00
5B Barry Bonds 40/40 Jsy 12.50 30.00
5C Alex Rodriguez 40/40 Jsy 10.00 25.00
6A Barry Bonds MVP Jsy 12.50 30.00
6B Jeff Kent MVP Jsy 4.00 10.00
7A Ichiro Suzuki MVP Base 12.50 30.00
7B Jason Giambi MVP Jsy 4.00 10.00
7C Ivan Rodriguez MVP Jsy 6.00 15.00
8A Curt Schilling Wins Jsy 4.00 10.00
8B Tom Glavine Wins Jsy 6.00 15.00
8C Pedro Martinez Wins Jsy 6.00 15.00
9A Randy Johnson ERA Jsy 6.00 15.00
9B Pedro Martinez ERA Jsy 6.00 15.00
9C Greg Maddux ERA Jsy 6.00 15.00
10A Randy Johnson K's Jsy 6.00 15.00
10B Curt Schilling K's Jsy 4.00 10.00
10C John Smoltz K's Jsy 6.00 15.00

2002 Fleer Triple Crown Season Crowns Triple Swatch

RANDOM INSERTS IN PACKS
STATED PRINT RUN 100 SERIAL #'d SETS
1 Bonds/Sosa/L.Gonz 20.00 50.00
2 Walker/Nomar/Helton 20.00 50.00
3 Sosa/Helton/Manny 20.00 50.00
6 Bonds/Kent/Chipper 20.00 50.00
7 Ichiro/Giambi/I.Rod 50.00 100.00
8 Schilling/Glavine/Pedro 20.00 50.00
9 Randy/Pedro/Maddux 20.00 50.00
10 Randy/Schilling/Smoltz 20.00 50.00

2001 Fleer White Rose

COMPLETE SET (38) 60.00 150.00
1 Cal Ripken 4.00 10.00
2 Nomar Garciaparra 2.00 5.00
3 Pedro Martinez 2.00 5.00
4 Troy Glaus 1.50 4.00
5 Frank Thomas 1.50 4.00
6 Roberto Alomar 1.25 3.00
7 Jim Thome 1.25 3.00
8 Bobby Higginson .80 2.00
9 Jermaine Dye .40 1.00
10 Jeromy Burnitz .80 2.00
11 Matt Lawton .40 1.00
12 Derek Jeter 4.00 10.00
13 Roger Clemens 2.40 6.00
14 Bernie Williams 1.25 3.00
15 Jason Giambi 1.00 2.50
16 Kazuhiro Sasaki 1.00 2.50
17 Edgar Martinez 1.00 2.50
18 Alex Rodriguez 2.00 5.00
19 Ivan Rodriguez 2.00 5.00
20 Carlos Delgado 2.00 5.00
21 Chipper Jones 2.40 6.00
22 Sammy Sosa 2.00 5.00
23 Ken Griffey 3.00 8.00
24 Jeff Bagwell 2.00 5.00
25 Shawn Green 2.00 5.00
26 Vladimir Guerrero 2.00 5.00
27 Mike Piazza 2.40 6.00
28 Edgardo Alfonzo .80 2.00
29 Pat Burrell .80 2.00
30 Jason Kendall .80 2.00
31 Mark McGwire 2.50 6.00
32 Jim Edmonds .80 2.00
33 Tony Gwynn 2.40 6.00
34 Barry Bonds 2.40 6.00
35 Todd Helton 2.00 5.00
36 Preston Wilson .80 2.00
37 Randy Johnson 2.00 5.00
38 Fred McGriff 1.00 2.50

1916 Fleischmann Bread D381

This 103-card set was produced by Fleischmann Breads in 1916. These unnumbered cards are arranged here for convenience in alphabetical order; cards with tabs intact are worth 50 percent more than the prices listed below. The cards measure approximately 2 3/4" by 5 1/2" (with tab) or 2 3/4" by 4 13/16" (without tab). There is also a similar set issued by Ferguson Bread which is harder to find and is distinguished by having the photo caption written on only one line rather than two as with the Fleischmann cards.

COMPLETE SET 5000.00 10000.00
1 Babe Adams 300.00 600.00
2 Grover Alexander 1250.00 2500.00
3 Walt E. Alexander 250.00 500.00
4 Frank Allen 250.00 500.00
5 Fred Anderson 250.00 500.00
6 Dave Bancroft 500.00 1000.00
7 Jack Barry 250.00 500.00
8 Beals Becker 250.00 500.00
9 Beals Becker 250.00 500.00
Copyright logo more prevalent
10 Eddie Burns 250.00 500.00
11 George J. Burns 250.00 500.00
12 Bobby Byrne 250.00 500.00
13 Ray B. Caldwell 250.00 500.00
14 James Callahan P/MG 250.00 500.00
15 William Carrigan MG 250.00 500.00
16 Larry Cheney 250.00 500.00
17 Tom Clarke 250.00 500.00
Photo goes to waist
18 Tom Clark 250.00 500.00
Photo shows his pants
19 Ty Cobb 10000.00 20000.00
20 Ray W. Collins 250.00 500.00
21 Ray Collins 250.00 500.00
Copyright logo more prominent
22 Jack Coombs 400.00 800.00
23 A. Wilbur Cooper 250.00 500.00
24 George Cutshaw 250.00 500.00
25 Jake Daubert 300.00 600.00
26 Wheezer Dell 250.00 500.00
27 Bill Donovan 250.00 500.00
28 Larry Doyle 300.00 600.00
29 R.J. Egan 250.00 500.00
30 Johnny Evers 750.00 1500.00
31 Ray Fisher 250.00 500.00
32 Harry Gardner (Sic) 250.00 500.00
33 Joe Gedeon 250.00 500.00
34 Larry Gilbert 250.00 500.00
35 Frank Gilhooley 250.00 500.00
36 Hank Gowdy 300.00 600.00
37 Sylvanus Gregg 250.00 500.00
38 Tom Griffith 250.00 500.00
39 Heinie Groh 300.00 600.00
40 Robert Harmon 250.00 500.00
41 Roy A. Hartzell 250.00 500.00
42 Claude Hendricks 250.00 500.00
43 Olaf Hendriksen 250.00 500.00
44 Buck Herzog P 250.00 500.00
MG
45 Hugh High 250.00 500.00
46 Dick Hoblitzell 250.00 500.00
47 Herb H. Hunter 250.00 500.00
48 Harold Janvrin 250.00 500.00
49 Hugh Jennings MG 500.00 1000.00
50 John Johnston 250.00 500.00
51 Erving Kantlehner 250.00 500.00
52 Bennie Kauff 300.00 600.00
53 Ray H. Keating 250.00 500.00
54 Wade Killefer 250.00 500.00
55 Elmer Knetzer 250.00 500.00
56 Brad W. Kocher 250.00 500.00
57 Ed Konetchy 250.00 500.00
58 Fred Lauderus (Sic) 250.00 500.00
59 Dutch Leonard 300.00 600.00
60 Duffy Lewis 300.00 600.00
61 E.H.(Slim) Love 250.00 500.00
62 Albert L. Mamaux 250.00 500.00
63 Rabbit Maranville 500.00 1000.00
64 Rube Marquard 500.00 1000.00
65 Christy Mathewson 2500.00 5000.00
66 Bill McKechnie 500.00 1000.00
67 Chief Meyer (Sic) 300.00 600.00
68 Otto Miller 250.00 500.00
69 Fred Mollwitz 250.00 500.00
70 Herbie Moran 250.00 500.00
71 Mike Mowrey 250.00 500.00
72 Dan Murphy 250.00 500.00
73 Art Nehf 300.00 600.00
74 Rube Oldring 250.00 500.00
75 Oliver O'Mara 250.00 500.00
76 Dode Paskert 250.00 500.00
77 D.C.Pat Ragan 250.00 500.00
78 Wm.A. Rariden 250.00 500.00
79 Davis Robertson 250.00 500.00
80 Wm. Rodgers 250.00 500.00
81 Edw.F.Rousch (Sic) 750.00 1500.00
82 Nap Rucker 300.00 600.00
83 Dick Rudolph 250.00 500.00
84 Walter Schang 300.00 600.00
85 A.J.(Rube) Schauer 250.00 500.00
86 Pete Schneider 250.00 500.00
87 Ferd M. Schupp 250.00 500.00
88 Ernie Shore 300.00 600.00
89 Red Smith 250.00 500.00
90 Fred Snodgrass 300.00 600.00
91 Tris Speaker 1250.00 2500.00
92 George Stallings MG 250.00 500.00
93 Casey Stengel/Sic, Stengle 2500.00 5000.00
94 Sailor Stroud 250.00 500.00
95 Amos Strunk 250.00 500.00
96 Chas.(Jeff) Tesreau 250.00 500.00
97 Chester D. Thomas 250.00 500.00
98 Chester D. Thomas 250.00 500.00
Copyright logo more prominent
99 Fred Toney 250.00 500.00
100 Walter Tragresser 250.00 500.00
101 Honus Wagner 2500.00 5000.00
102 Carl Weilman 250.00 500.00
103 Zack Wheat 500.00 1000.00
104 George Whitted 250.00 500.00
105 Arthur Wilson 250.00 500.00
106 Ivy Wingo 250.00 500.00
107 Joe Wood 400.00 800.00

2003 Flipp Sports Booklets

COMPLETE SET 12.50 30.00
1 Garrett Anderson .40 1.00
2 Lance Berkman .60 1.50
3 Barry Bonds 1.50 4.00
4 Nomar Garciaparra .60 1.50
5 Jason Giambi .40 1.00
6 Troy Glaus .40 1.00
7 Luis Gonzalez .40 1.00
8 Torii Hunter .40 1.00
9 Derek Jeter 2.50 6.00
10 Mike Piazza 1.00 2.50
11 Albert Pujols 1.25 3.00
12 Manny Ramirez 1.00 2.50
13 Alex Rodriguez 1.25 3.00
14 Curt Schilling 1.00 2.50
Randy Johnson
15 Alfonso Soriano .60 1.50
16 Sammy Sosa 1.00 2.50
17 Sammy Sosa 1.00 2.50
Jason Giambi
18 Ichiro Suzuki 1.25 3.00
19 Mike Sweeney .40 1.00
20 Miguel Tejada .60 1.50

1987 Red Foley Sticker Book

The 1987 Red Foley's Best Baseball Book Ever was published by Simon and Schuster and measures 8 1/2" by 11. The book includes 130 stickers, puzzles, quizzes, how-to's, and other trivia features. The stickers appear on four insert pages in the middle of the album. Each sticker measures 1 3/8" by 1 7/8" and displays a glossy color player photo bordered in white. The stickers are to be pasted in the appropriate slots next to a trivia question about the player. The stickers are numbered on the front and checklisted below accordingly.

COMPLETE SET (130) 5.00 12.00
1 Julio Franco .02 .10
2 Willie Randolph .02 .10
3 Jesse Barfield .01 .05
4 Mike Witt .01 .05
5 Orel Hershiser .02 .10
6 Dwight Gooden .08 .25
7 Dan Quisenberry .01 .05
8 Vince Coleman .01 .05
9 Rich Gossage .02 .10
10 Kirk Gibson .02 .10
11 Joaquin Andujar .01 .05
12 David Concepcion .02 .10
13 Andre Dawson .20 .50
14 Tippy Martinez .01 .05
15 Bob James .01 .05
16 Ryne Sandberg .30 .75
17 Bob Knepper .01 .05
18 Bob Stanley .01 .05
19 Jim Presley .01 .05
20 Greg Gross .01 .05
21 Bob Horner .01 .05
22 Paul Molitor .30 .75
23 Kirby Puckett .30 .75
24 Scott Garrelts .01 .05
25 Tony Pena .01 .05
26 Charlie Hough .01 .05
27 Joe Carter .08 .25
28 Dave Winfield .30 .75
29 Tony Fernandez .01 .05
30 Bobby Grich .02 .10
31 Mike Marshall .01 .05
32 Keith Hernandez .02 .10
33 Dennis Leonard .01 .05
34 John Tudor .01 .05
35 Kevin McReynolds .01 .05
36 Lance Parrish .02 .10
37 Carney Lansford .02 .10
38 Buddy Bell .02 .10
39 Tim Raines .02 .10
40 Mike Boddicker .01 .05
41 Carlton Fisk .20 .50
42 Lee Smith .08 .25
43 Glenn Davis .01 .05
44 Jim Rice .02 .10
45 Mark Langston .01 .05
46 Mike Schmidt .40 1.00
47 Dale Murphy .20 .50
48 Cecil Cooper .02 .10
49 Kent Hrbek .02 .10
50 Will Clark .40 1.00
51 Johnny Ray .01 .05
52 Darrell Porter .01 .05
53 Brook Jacoby .01 .05
54 Ron Guidry .02 .10
55 Lloyd Moseby .01 .05
56 Donnie Moore .01 .05
57 Fernando Valenzuela .02 .10
58 Darryl Strawberry .02 .10
59 Hal McRae .02 .10
60 Tommy Herr .01 .05
61 Steve Garvey .08 .25
62 Alan Trammell .08 .25
63 Jose Canseco .30 .75
64 Pete Rose .40 1.00
65 Jeff Reardon .02 .10
66 Eddie Murray .30 .75
67 Ozzie Guillen .02 .10
68 Jody Davis .01 .05
69 Bill Doran .01 .05
70 Roger Clemens .60 1.50
71 Alvin Davis .01 .05
72 Von Hayes .01 .05
73 Zane Smith .01 .05
74 Ted Higuera .01 .05
75 Tom Brunansky .01 .05
76 Chili Davis .08 .25
77 R.J. Reynolds .01 .05
78 Oddibe McDowell .01 .05
79 Brett Butler .02 .10
80 Rickey Henderson .40 1.25
81 Dave Stieb .01 .05
82 Wally Joyner .20 .50
83 Pedro Guerrero .01 .05
84 Jesse Orosco .01 .05
85 Steve Balboni .01 .05
86 Willie McGee .02 .10
87 Graig Nettles .02 .10
88 Lou Whitaker .02 .10
89 Jay Howell .01 .05
90 Dave Parker .02 .10
91 Hubie Brooks .01 .05
92 Rick Dempsey .01 .05
93 Neil Allen .01 .05
94 Shawon Dunston .01 .05
95 Jose Cruz .02 .10
96 Wade Boggs .30 .75
97 Danny Tartabull .01 .05
98 Steve Bedrosian .01 .05
99 Ken Oberkfell .01 .05
100 Ben Oglivie .01 .05
101 Bert Blyleven .02 .10
102 Jeff Leonard .01 .05
103 Rick Rhoden .01 .05
104 Larry Parrish .01 .05
105 Tony Bernazard .01 .05
106 Don Mattingly .60 1.50
107 Willie Upshaw .01 .05
108 Reggie Jackson .30 .75
109 Bill Madlock .02 .10
110 Gary Carter .30 .75
111 George Brett .50 1.25
112 Ozzie Smith .30 .75
113 Tony Gwynn .60 1.50
114 Jack Morris .02 .10
115 Dave Kingman .02 .10
116 John Franco .02 .10
117 Tim Wallach .01 .05
118 Cal Ripken 1.25 3.00
119 Harold Baines .02 .10
120 Leon Durham .01 .05
121 Nolan Ryan 1.25 3.00
122 Dennis(Oil Can) Boyd .01 .05
123 Matt Young .01 .05
124 Shane Rawley .01 .05
125 Bruce Sutter .02 .10
126 Robin Yount .30 .75
127 Frank Viola .01 .05
128 Vida Blue .02 .10
129 Rick Reuschel .02 .10
130 Pete Incaviglia .02 .10

1988 Red Foley Sticker Book

The 1988 Red Foley's Best Baseball Book Ever was published by Simon and Schuster and measures 8 1/2" by 11. The book includes 130 stickers (representing 104 players and 26 teams), puzzles, quizzes, how-to's, and other trivia features. The stickers appear on four insert pages in the middle of the album. Each sticker measures 1 3/8" by 1 7/8" and displays a glossy color player photo bordered in white. The stickers are to be pasted in the appropriate slots next to a trivia question about the player. The stickers are numbered on the front and present the players in alphabetical order.

COMPLETE SET (130) 3.00 8.00
1 Mike Aldrete .01 .05
2 Alan Ashby .01 .05
3 Harold Baines .02 .10
4 Floyd Bannister .01 .05
5 Buddy Bell .02 .10
6 George Bell .01 .05
7 Barry Bonds .75 2.00
8 Scott Bradley .01 .05
9 Bob Brower .01 .05
10 Ellis Burks .20 .50
11 Casey Candaele .01 .05
12 Jack Clark .02 .10
13 Roger Clemens .60 1.50
14 Kal Daniels .01 .05
15 Eric Davis .02 .10
16 Mike Davis .01 .05
17 Andre Dawson .08 .25
18 Rob Deer .01 .05
19 Brian Downing .01 .05
20 Doug Drabek .01 .05
21 Dwight Evans .02 .10
22 Sid Fernandez .01 .05
23 Carlton Fisk .15 .40
24 Scott Fletcher .01 .05
25 Julio Franco .02 .10
26 Gary Gaetti .02 .10
27 Ken Gerhart .01 .05
28 Ken Griffey .02 .10
29 Pedro Guerrero .01 .05
30 Billy Hatcher .01 .05
31 Mike Heath .01 .05
32 Neal Heaton .01 .05
33 Tom Henke .01 .05
34 Larry Herndon .01 .05
35 Brian Holton .01 .05
36 Glenn Hubbard .01 .05
37 Bruce Hurst .01 .05
38 Bo Jackson .15 .40
39 Michael Jackson .01 .05
40 Howard Johnson .01 .05
41 Wally Joyner .02 .10
42 Jimmy Key .01 .05
43 Ray Knight .01 .05
44 John Kruk .02 .10
45 Mike Krukow .01 .05
46 Mark Langston .01 .05
47 Gene Larkin .01 .05
48 Jeff Leonard .01 .05
49 Bill Long .01 .05
50 Fred Lynn .01 .05
51 Dave Magadan .01 .05
52 Joe Magrane .01 .05
53 Don Mattingly .60 1.50
54 Fred McGriff .20 .50
55 Mark McGwire .75 2.00
56 Kevin McReynolds .01 .05
57 Dave Meads .01 .05
58 Keith Moreland .01 .05
59 Dale Murphy .08 .25
60 Juan Nieves .01 .05
61 Paul Noce .01 .05
62 Matt Nokes .01 .05
63 Pete O'Brien .01 .05
64 Paul O'Neill .05 .15
65 Lance Parrish .01 .05
66 Larry Parrish .01 .05
67 Tony Pena .01 .05
68 Terry Pendleton .02 .10
69 Ken Phelps .01 .05
70 Dan Plesac .01 .05
71 Luis Polonia .01 .05
72 Kirby Puckett .20 .50
73 Jeff Reardon .01 .05
74 Rick Rhoden .01 .05
75 Dave Righetti .01 .05
76 Cal Ripken 1.25 3.00
77 Bret Saberhagen .01 .05
78 Benito Santiago .02 .10
79 Mike Schmidt .40 1.00
80 Dick Schofield .01 .05
81 Mike Scott .01 .05
82 John Smiley .02 .10
83 Cory Snyder .01 .05
84 Franklin Stubbs .01 .05
85 B.J. Surhoff .02 .10
86 Rick Sutcliffe .01 .05
87 Pat Tabler .01 .05
88 Danny Tartabull .01 .05
89 Garry Templeton .01 .05
90 Walt Terrell .01 .05
91 Andre Thornton .01 .05
92 Andy Van Slyke .02 .10
93 Ozzie Virgil .01 .05
94 Tim Wallach .01 .05
95 Gary Ward .01 .05
96 Mark Wasinger .01 .05
97 Mitch Webster .01 .05
98 Bob Welch .01 .05
99 Devon White .02 .10
100 Frank White .02 .10
101 Ed Whitson .01 .05
102 Bill Wilkinson .01 .05
103 Glenn Wilson .01 .05
104 Curt Young .01 .05
105 Atlanta Braves .01 .05
106 Philadelphia Phillies .01 .05
107 San Diego Padres .01 .05
108 San Francisco Giants .01 .05
109 Baltimore Orioles .01 .05
110 Detroit Tigers .01 .05
111 Pittsburgh Pirates .01 .05
112 Kansas City Royals .01 .05
113 Houston Astros .01 .05
114 Cleveland Indians .01 .05
115 Milwaukee Brewers .01 .05
116 St. Louis Cardinals .01 .05
117 Chicago White Sox .01 .05
118 Toronto Blue Jays .01 .05
119 Boston Red Sox .01 .05
120 Oakland A's .01 .05
121 Chicago Cubs .01 .05
122 Seattle Mariners .01 .05
123 Texas Rangers .01 .05
124 Los Angeles Dodgers .01 .05
125 New York Yankees .01 .05
126 New York Mets .01 .05
127 Minnesota Twins .01 .05
128 Montreal Expos .01 .05
129 California Angels .01 .05
130 Cincinnati Reds .01 .05

1989 Red Foley Sticker Book

The 1989 Red Foley's Best Baseball Book Ever was published by Simon and Schuster and measures 8 1/2" by 11. The book includes 130 stickers, puzzles, quizzes, how-to's, and other trivia features. The stickers appear on four insert pages in the middle of the album. Each sticker measures 1 3/8" by 1 7/8" and displays a glossy color player photo bordered in white. The stickers are to be pasted in the appropriate slots next to a trivia question about the player. The stickers are numbered on the front and present the players in alphabetical order.

COMPLETE SET (130) 6.00 15.00
1 Doyle Alexander .01 .05
2 Luis Alicea .01 .05
3 Roberto Alomar .40 1.00
4 Alan Ashby .01 .05
5 Floyd Bannister .01 .05
6 Jesse Barfield .01 .05
7 George Bell .01 .05
8 Wade Boggs .20 .50
9 Barry Bonds .60 1.50
10 Bobby Bonilla .02 .10
11 Chris Bosio .01 .05
12 George Brett .50 1.25
13 Hubie Brooks .01 .05
14 Tom Brunansky .01 .05
15 Tim Burke .01 .05
16 Ivan Calderon .01 .05
17 Tom Candiotti .01 .05
18 Jose Canseco .15 .40
19 Gary Carter .20 .50
20 Joe Carter .05 .15
21 Jack Clark .01 .05
22 Will Clark .20 .50
23 Roger Clemens .60 1.50
24 David Cone .15 .40
25 Ed Correa .01 .05
26 Kal Daniels .01 .05
27 Alvin Davis .01 .05
28 Chili Davis .02 .10
29 Eric Davis .02 .10
30 Glenn Davis .01 .05
31 Jody Davis .01 .05
32 Mark Davis .01 .05
33 Andre Dawson .08 .25
34 Rob Deer .01 .05
35 Jose DeLeon .01 .05
36 Bo Diaz .01 .05
37 Bill Doran .01 .05
38 Shawon Dunston .01 .05
39 Dennis Eckersley .20 .50
40 Dwight Evans .02 .10
41 Tony Fernandez .02 .10
42 Brian Fisher .01 .05
43 Carlton Fisk .20 .50
44 Mike Flanagan .01 .05
45 John Franco .02 .10
46 Gary Gaetti .02 .10
47 Andres Galarraga .08 .25
48 Scott Garrelts .01 .05
49 Kirk Gibson .02 .10
50 Dan Gladden .01 .05
51 Dwight Gooden .02 .10
52 Pedro Guerrero .01 .05
53 Ozzie Guillen .02 .10
54 Tony Gwynn .50 1.25
55 Mel Hall .01 .05
56 Von Hayes .01 .05
57 Keith Hernandez .02 .10
58 Orel Hershiser .02 .10
59 Ted Higuera .01 .05
60 Charlie Hough .01 .05

61 Jack Howell .01 .05
62 Kent Hrbek .02 .10
63 Pete Incaviglia .01 .05
64 Bo Jackson .08 .25
65 Brook Jacoby .01 .05
66 Chris James .01 .05
67 Lance Johnson .01 .05
68 Wally Joyner .02 .10
69 Jack Kruk .02 .10
70 Mike LaCoss .01 .05
71 Mark Langston .01 .05
72 Carney Lansford .02 .10
73 Barry Larkin .20 .50
74 Mike LaValliere .01 .05
75 Jose Lind .01 .05
76 Fred Lynn .01 .05
77 Greg Maddux .75 2.00
78 Candy Maldonado .01 .05
79 Don Mattingly .60 1.50
80 Mark McGwire .75 2.00
81 Paul Molitor .20 .50
82 Jack Morris .02 .10
83 Lloyd Moseby .01 .05
84 Dale Murphy .08 .25
85 Eddie Murray .20 .50
86 Matt Nokes .01 .05
87 Pete O'Brien .01 .05
88 Rafael Palmeiro .15 .40
89 Melido Perez .01 .05
90 Gerald Perry .01 .05
91 Tim Raines .02 .10
92 Willie Randolph .02 .10
93 Johnny Ray .01 .05
94 Jeff Reardon .02 .10
95 Jody Reed .01 .05
96 Harold Reynolds .02 .10
97 Dave Righetti .02 .10
98 Billy Ripken .01 .05
99 Cal Ripken Jr. 1.25 3.00
100 Nolan Ryan 1.25 3.00
101 Juan Samuel .01 .05
102 Benito Santiago .02 .10
103 Steve Sax .01 .05
104 Mike Schmidt .40 1.00
105 Rick Schu .01 .05
106 Mike Scott .01 .05
107 Kevin Seitzer .01 .05
108 Ruben Sierra .02 .10
109 Lee Smith .02 .10
110 Ozzie Smith .25 .60
111 Zane Smith .01 .05
112 Dave Stewart .02 .10
113 Darryl Strawberry .02 .10
114 Bruce Sutter .01 .05
115 Bill Swift .01 .05
116 Greg Swindell .01 .05
117 Frank Tanana .01 .05
118 Danny Tartabull .01 .05
119 Milt Thompson .01 .05
120 Robby Thompson .01 .05
121 Alan Trammell .05 .15
122 John Tudor .01 .05
123 Fernando Valenzuela .02 .10
124 Dave Valle .01 .05
125 Frank Viola .01 .05
126 Ozzie Virgil .01 .05
127 Tim Wallach .01 .05
128 Dave Winfield .15 .40
129 Mike Witt .01 .05
130 Robin Yount .20 .50

1990 Red Foley Sticker Book

The 1990 Red Foley's Best Baseball Book Ever was published by Simon and Schuster and measures 8 1/2" by 11. The book includes 130 stickers (104 players and 26 teams), puzzles, quizzes, how-to's, player-team matchups, and other trivia features. The stickers appear on four insert pages in the middle of the album. Each sticker measures 1 3/8" X 1 7/8" and displays a glossy color player photo bordered in white. The stickers are to be pasted in the appropriate slots next to a trivia question about the player. The stickers are numbered on the front and present the players in alphabetical order.

COMPLETE SET (130) 6.00 15.00
1 Allan Anderson .01 .05
2 Scott Bailes .01 .05
3 Jeff Ballard .01 .05
4 Jesse Barfield .01 .05
5 Bert Blyleven .02 .10
6 Wade Boggs .30 .75
7 Barry Bonds .60 1.50
8 Chris Bosio .01 .05
9 George Brett .50 1.25
10 Tim Burke .01 .05
11 Ellis Burks .05 .15
12 Brett Butler .02 .10
13 Ivan Calderon .01 .05
14 Jose Canseco .20 .50
15 Joe Carter .02 .10
16 Jack Clark .02 .10
17 Will Clark .20 .50
18 Roger Clemens .60 1.50
19 Vince Coleman .01 .05
20 Eric Davis .02 .10
21 Glenn Davis .01 .05
22 Mark Davis .01 .05
23 Andre Dawson .08 .25
24 Rob Deer .01 .05
25 Jose DeLeon .01 .05
26 Jim Deshaies .01 .05
27 Doug Drabek .01 .05
28 Lenny Dykstra .02 .10
29 Dennis Eckersley .20 .50
30 Steve Farr .01 .05
31 Tony Fernandez .01 .05
32 Carlton Fisk .20 .50
33 John Franco .02 .10
34 Julio Franco .02 .10
35 Andres Galarraga .08 .25
36 Tom Glavine .08 .25
37 Dwight Gooden .02 .10
38 Mark Grace .20 .50
39 Mike Greenwell .01 .05
40 Ken Griffey Jr. 1.25 3.00
41 Kelly Gruber .01 .05
42 Pedro Guerrero .01 .05
43 Tony Gwynn .50 1.25
44 Bryan Harvey .01 .05
45 Von Hayes .01 .05
46 Willie Hernandez .01 .05
47 Tommy Herr .01 .05
48 Orel Hershiser .02 .10
49 Jay Howell .01 .05
50 Kent Hrbek .02 .10
51 Bo Jackson .08 .25
52 Steve Jeltz .01 .05
53 Jimmy Key .01 .05
54 Ron Kittle .01 .05
55 Mark Langston .01 .05
56 Carney Lansford .02 .10
57 Barry Larkin .15 .40
58 Jeffrey Leonard .01 .05
59 Don Mattingly .60 1.50
60 Fred McGriff .08 .25
61 Mark McGwire .75 2.00
62 Kevin McReynolds .01 .05
63 Randy Myers .02 .10
64 Kevin Mitchell .01 .05
65 Paul Molitor .20 .50
66 Mike Morgan .01 .05
67 Dale Murphy .08 .25
68 Eddie Murray .20 .50
69 Matt Nokes .01 .05
70 Gregg Olson .01 .05
71 Paul O'Neill .05 .15
72 Rafael Palmeiro .30 .75
73 Lance Parrish .01 .05
74 Dan Plesac .01 .05
75 Kirby Puckett .20 .50
76 Jeff Reardon .02 .10
77 Rick Reuschel .01 .05
78 Cal Ripken 1.25 3.00
79 Dave Righetti .01 .05
80 Jeff Russell .01 .05
81 Nolan Ryan 1.25 3.00
82 Benito Santiago .02 .10
83 Steve Sax .01 .05
84 Mike Schooler .01 .05
85 Mike Scott .01 .05
86 Kevin Seitzer .01 .05
87 Dave Smith .01 .05
88 Lonnie Smith .01 .05
89 Ozzie Smith .30 .75
90 John Smoltz .08 .25
91 Cory Snyder .01 .05
92 Darryl Strawberry .02 .10
93 Greg Swindell .01 .05
94 Mickey Tettleton .02 .10
95 Bobby Thigpen .01 .05
96 Alan Trammell .05 .15
97 Dave Valle .01 .05
98 Andy Van Slyke .02 .10
99 Tim Wallach .01 .05
100 Jerome Walton .01 .05
101 Lou Whitaker .02 .10
102 Devon White .01 .05
103 Mitch Williams .01 .05
104 Glenn Wilson .01 .05
105 Cleveland Indians .01 .05
106 Texas Rangers .01 .05
107 Cincinnati Reds .01 .05
108 Baltimore Orioles .01 .05
109 Boston Red Sox .01 .05
110 Chicago White Sox .01 .05
111 Los Angeles Dodgers .01 .05
112 Detroit Tigers .01 .05
113 Seattle Mariners .01 .05
114 Toronto Blue Jays .01 .05
115 Montreal Expos .01 .05
116 Pittsburgh Pirates .01 .05
117 Houston Astros .01 .05
118 St. Louis Cardinals .01 .05
119 San Diego Padres .01 .05
120 California Angels .01 .05
121 New York Yankees .01 .05
122 Chicago Cubs .01 .05
123 Milwaukee Brewers .01 .05
124 Minnesota Twins .01 .05
125 San Francisco Giants .01 .05
126 Kansas City Royals .01 .05
127 Oakland A's .01 .05
128 New York Mets .01 .05
129 Philadelphia Phillies .01 .05
130 Atlanta Braves .01 .05

1991 Red Foley Stickers

The 1991 Red Foley's Best Baseball Book Ever was published by Simon and Schuster and measures 8 1/2" by 11. The 95-page book includes 130 stickers, puzzles, quizzes, how-to's, player-team matchups, and other trivia features. The stickers appear on four insert pages in the middle of the album. Each sticker measures 1 3/8" by 1 7/8" and displays a glossy color player photo bordered in white. The stickers are to be pasted in the appropriate slots throughout the sticker album. Stickers 113-130 feature All-Stars. The stickers are numbered on the front and checklisted below accordingly.

COMPLETE SET (130) 8.00 20.00
1 Jim Abbott .02 .10
2 Rick Aguilera .02 .10
3 Roberto Alomar .15 .40
4 Rob Dibble .02 .10
5 Wally Backman .01 .05
6 Harold Baines .02 .10
7 Steve Bedrosian .01 .05
8 Craig Biggio .08 .25
9 Wade Boggs .40 1.00
10 Bobby Bonilla .01 .05
11 George Brett .60 1.50
12 Greg Brock .01 .05
13 Hubie Brooks .01 .05
14 Tom Brunansky .01 .05
15 Tim Burke .01 .05
16 Tom Candiotti .01 .05
17 Jose Canseco .40 1.00
18 Jack Clark .02 .10
19 Will Clark .30 .75
20 Roger Clemens .75 2.00
21 Vince Coleman .01 .05
22 Kal Daniels .01 .05
23 Glenn Davis .01 .05
24 Mark Davis .01 .05
25 Andre Dawson .15 .40
26 Rob Deer .01 .05
27 Delino DeShields .02 .10
28 Doug Drabek .01 .05
29 Shawon Dunston .01 .05
30 Len Dykstra .02 .10
31 Dennis Eckersley .20 .50
32 Kevin Elster .01 .05
33 Tony Fernandez .02 .10
34 Cecil Fielder .02 .10
35 Chuck Finley .02 .10
36 Carlton Fisk .25 .60
37 Greg Gagne .01 .05
38 Ron Gant .02 .10
39 Tom Glavine .15 .40
40 Dwight Gooden .02 .10
41 Ken Griffey Jr. 1.50 4.00
42 Kelly Gruber .01 .05
43 Pedro Guerrero .01 .05
44 Ozzie Guillen .02 .10
45 Pete Harnisch .01 .05
46 Billy Hatcher .01 .05
47 Von Hayes .01 .05
48 Rickey Henderson .40 1.00
49 Mike Henneman .01 .05
50 Kent Hrbek .02 .10
51 Pete Incaviglia .01 .05
52 Howard Johnson .01 .05
53 Randy Johnson .60 1.50
54 Doug Jones .01 .05
55 Ricky Jordan .01 .05
56 Wally Joyner .02 .10
57 Roberto Kelly .01 .05
58 Barry Larkin .15 .40
59 Craig Lefferts .01 .05
60 Candy Maldonado .01 .05
61 Don Mattingly .75 2.00
62 Oddibe McDowell .01 .05
63 Roger McDowell .01 .05
64 Willie McGee .02 .10
65 Fred McGriff .08 .25
66 Kevin Mitchell .01 .05
67 Mike Morgan .01 .05
68 Eddie Murray .20 .50
69 Gregg Olson .01 .05
70 Joe Orsulak .01 .05
71 Dan Petry .01 .05
72 Dan Plesac .01 .05
73 Jim Presley .01 .05
74 Kirby Puckett .20 .50
75 Tim Raines .02 .10
76 Jeff Reardon .02 .10
77 Dave Righetti .01 .05
78 Cal Ripken 1.50 4.00
79 Nolan Ryan 1.50 4.00
80 Bret Saberhagen .02 .10
81 Chris Sabo .01 .05
82 Ryne Sandberg .20 .50
83 Benito Santiago .02 .10
84 Steve Sax .01 .05
85 Mike Schooler .01 .05
86 Mike Scott .01 .05
87 Ruben Sierra .02 .10
88 Cory Snyder .01 .05
89 Dave Stieb .02 .10
90 Dave Stewart .02 .10
91 Kurt Stillwell .01 .05
92 Bobby Thigpen .01 .05
93 Alan Trammell .08 .25
94 John Tudor .01 .05
95 Dave Valle .01 .05
96 Andy Van Slyke .02 .10
97 Robin Ventura .15 .40
98 Frank Viola .01 .05
99 Tim Wallach .01 .05
100 Matt Williams .08 .25
101 Mitch Williams .01 .05
102 Dave Winfield .30 .75
103 Eric Yelding .01 .05
104 Robin Yount .30 .75
105 Steve Avery .01 .05
106 Travis Fryman .15 .40
107 Juan Gonzalez .30 .75
108 Todd Hundley .15 .40
109 Ben McDonald .01 .05
110 Jose Offerman .01 .05
111 Frank Thomas .30 .75
112 Bernie Williams .15 .40
113 Sandy Alomar Jr. AS .02 .10
114 Jack Armstrong AS .01 .05
115 Wade Boggs AS .30 .75
116 Jose Canseco AS .20 .50
117 Will Clark AS .15 .40
118 Andre Dawson AS .15 .40
119 Len Dykstra AS .02 .10
120 Ken Griffey Jr. AS 1.50 4.00
121 Rickey Henderson AS .40 1.00
122 Mark McGwire AS 1.00 2.50
123 Kevin Mitchell AS .01 .05
124 Cal Ripken AS 1.50 4.00
125 Chris Sabo AS .01 .05
126 Ryne Sandberg AS .30 .75
127 Steve Sax AS .01 .05
128 Mike Scioscia AS .02 .10
129 Ozzie Smith AS .40 1.00
130 Bob Welch AS .01 .05

1992 Red Foley Stickers

The 1992 Red Foley's Best Baseball Book Ever was published by Simon and Schuster and measures 8 1/2" by 11. The book includes 130 stickers, puzzles, quizzes, how-to's, player-team matchups, and other trivia features. The stickers appear on four insert pages in the middle of the album. Each sticker measures 1 3/8" by 1 7/8" and displays a glossy color player photo bordered in white. The stickers were to be pasted in the appropriate slots throughout the sticker album. Stickers 105-130 feature All-Stars.

COMPLETE SET (130) 8.00 20.00
1 Jim Abbott .02 .10
2 Roberto Alomar .08 .25
3 Sandy Alomar Jr. .02 .10
4 Eric Anthony .01 .05
5 Kevin Appier .02 .10
6 Jack Armstrong .01 .05
7 Steve Avery .01 .05
8 Carlos Baerga .01 .05
9 Scott Bankhead .01 .05
10 George Bell .01 .05
11 Albert Belle .02 .10
12 Andy Benes .01 .05
13 Craig Biggio .05 .15
14 Wade Boggs .30 .75
15 Barry Bonds .60 1.50
16 Bob Bonilla .01 .05
17 Sid Bream .01 .05
18 George Brett .60 1.50
19 Hubie Brooks .01 .05
20 Ellis Burks .02 .10
21 Brett Butler .02 .10
22 Jose Canseco .20 .50
23 Joe Carter .02 .10
24 Jack Clark .02 .10
25 Will Clark .08 .25
26 Roger Clemens .60 1.50
27 Vince Coleman .01 .05
28 Eric Davis .02 .10
29 Glenn Davis .01 .05
30 Andre Dawson .05 .15
31 Rob Deer .01 .05
32 Delino Deshields .02 .10
33 Lenny Dykstra .02 .10
34 Scott Erickson .01 .05
35 Cecil Fielder .02 .10
36 Carlton Fisk .20 .50
37 Travis Fryman .02 .10
38 Greg Gagne .01 .05
39 Juan Gonzalez .20 .50
40 Tommy Greene .01 .05
41 Ken Griffey Jr. 1.00 2.50
42 Marquis Grissom .02 .10
43 Kelly Gruber .01 .05
44 Tony Gwynn .40 1.00
45 Dave Henderson .01 .05
46 Rickey Henderson .40 1.00
47 Orel Hershiser .01 .05
48 Kent Hrbek .02 .10
49 Howard Johnson .01 .05
50 Felix Jose .01 .05
51 Wally Joyner .02 .10
52 Dave Justice .08 .25
53 Roberto Kelly .01 .05
54 Ray Lankford .05 .15
55 Barry Larkin .08 .25
56 Mark Lewis .01 .05
57 Kevin Maas .01 .05
58 Greg Maddux .75 2.00
59 Dave Martinez .01 .05
60 Edgar Martinez .05 .15
61 Don Mattingly .60 1.50
62 Ben McDonald .01 .05
63 Jack McDowell .01 .05
64 Willie McGee .02 .10
65 Fred McGriff .05 .15
66 Brian McRae .01 .05
67 Mark McGwire .75 2.00
68 Kevin Mitchell .02 .10
69 Terry Mulholland .01 .05
70 Dale Murphy .08 .25
71 Eddie Murray .08 .25
72 John Olerud .05 .15
73 Rafael Palmeiro .20 .50
74 Terry Pendleton .01 .05
75 Luis Polonia .01 .05
76 Mark Portugal .01 .05
77 Kirby Puckett .15 .40
78 Tim Raines .02 .10
79 Harold Reynolds .02 .10
80 Billy Ripken .01 .05
81 Cal Ripken Jr. 1.25 3.00
82 Nolan Ryan 1.25 3.00
83 Chris Sabo .01 .05
84 Ryne Sandberg .30 .75
85 Benito Santiago .02 .10
86 Kevin Seitzer .01 .05
87 Gary Sheffield .20 .50
88 Ruben Sierra .02 .10
89 John Smiley .01 .05
90 Ozzie Smith .30 .75
91 Darryl Strawberry .02 .10
92 B.J. Surhoff .02 .10
93 Frank Thomas .20 .50
94 Alan Trammell .05 .15
95 Andy Van Slyke .01 .05
96 Greg Vaughn .02 .10
97 Frank Viola .01 .05
98 Tim Wallach .01 .05
99 Matt Williams .05 .15
100 Dave Winfield .20 .50
101 Mike Witt .01 .05
102 Eric Yelding .01 .05
103 Robin Yount .20 .50
104 Todd Zeile .01 .05
105 Roberto Alomar .15 .40
106 Sandy Alomar Jr. .02 .10
107 Wade Boggs .30 .75
108 Bobby Bonilla .02 .10
109 Ivan Calderon .01 .05
110 Will Clark .08 .25
111 Andre Dawson .05 .15
112 Cecil Fielder .02 .10
113 Carlton Fisk .20 .50
114 Tom Glavine .08 .25
115 Ken Griffey Jr. 1.25 3.00
116 Tony Gwynn .60 1.50
117 Dave Henderson .01 .05
118 Rickey Henderson .40 1.00
119 Felix Jose .01 .05
120 Jimmy Key .01 .05
121 Tony LaRussa .01 .05
122 Jack Morris .02 .10
123 Lou Piniella .02 .10
124 Cal Ripken Jr. 1.25 3.00
125 Chris Sabo .01 .05
126 Juan Samuel .01 .05
127 Ryne Sandberg .30 .75
128 Benito Santiago .02 .10
129 Ozzie Smith .40 1.00
130 Danny Tartabull .01 .05

1993 Red Foley Stickers

The 1993 Red Foley's Best Baseball Book Ever was published by Simon and Schuster and measures 8 1/2" by 11". The book includes 130 stickers, puzzles, quizzes, how-to's, player-team matchups, and other trivia features. The stickers appear on four insert pages in the middle of the album. Each sticker measures 1 3/8" by 1 7/8" and displays a color player photo. The stickers were to be pasted in the appropriate slots throughout the sticker album. Stickers 105-130 feature All-Stars.

COMPLETE SET (130) 6.00 15.00
1 Jim Abbott .02 .10
2 Roberto Alomar .08 .25
3 Sandy Alomar .02 .10
4 Steve Avery .01 .05
5 Jeff Bagwell .40 1.00
6 Harold Baines .02 .10
7 Bret Barberie .01 .05
8 Derek Bell .01 .05
9 Jay Bell .01 .05
10 Albert Belle .02 .10
11 Andy Benes .01 .05
12 Craig Biggio .08 .25
13 Wade Boggs .25 .60
14 Barry Bonds .75 2.00
15 Bobby Bonilla .01 .05
16 Jose Canseco .30 .75
17 Joe Carter .02 .10
18 Wes Chamberlain .01 .05
19 Will Clark .08 .25
20 Roger Clemens .75 2.00
21 Milt Cuyler .01 .05
22 Eric Davis .02 .10
23 Delino Deshields .01 .05
24 Rob Dibble .01 .05
25 Doug Drabek .01 .05
26 Shawon Dunston .01 .05
27 Lenny Dykstra .02 .10
28 Scott Erickson .01 .05
29 Cecil Fielder .02 .10
30 Steve Finley .02 .10
31 Tom Glavine .08 .25
32 Dwight Gooden .02 .10
33 Mark Grace .05 .15
34 Ken Griffey Jr. 1.50 4.00
35 Marquis Grissom .01 .05
36 Kelly Gruber .01 .05
37 Mark Gubicza .01 .05
38 Tony Gwynn .75 2.00
39 Mel Hall .01 .05
40 Pete Harnisch .01 .05
41 Brian Harper .01 .05
42 Bryan Harvey .01 .05
43 Rickey Henderson .40 1.00
44 Orel Hershiser .02 .10
45 Gregg Jefferies .01 .05
46 Howard Johnson .01 .05
47 Felix Jose .01 .05
48 Wally Joyner .02 .10
49 Dave Justice .08 .25
50 Roberto Kelly .01 .05
51 Chuck Knoblauch .08 .25
52 John Kruk .02 .10
53 Barry Larkin .08 .25
54 Kenny Lofton .08 .25
55 Greg Maddux 1.00 2.50
56 Dennis Martinez .02 .10
57 Edgar Martinez .05 .15
58 Tino Martinez .08 .25
59 Don Mattingly .75 2.00
60 Jack McDowell .01 .05
61 Willie McGee .02 .10
62 Fred McGriff .05 .15
63 Mark McGwire 1.00 2.50
64 Brian McRae .01 .05
65 Randy Milligan .01 .05
66 Kevin Mitchell .02 .10
67 Paul Molitor .08 .25
68 Dale Murphy .05 .15
69 Mike Mussina .20 .50
70 Charles Nagy .01 .05
71 Gregg Olson .01 .05
72 Rafael Palmeiro .15 .40
73 Dean Palmer .02 .10
74 Phil Plantier .01 .05
75 Luis Polonia .01 .05
76 Kirby Puckett .30 .75
77 Tim Raines .02 .10
78 Cal Ripken Jr. 1.50 4.00
79 Bip Roberts .01 .05
80 Ivan Rodriguez .40 1.00
81 Nolan Ryan 1.50 4.00
82 Bret Saberhagen .02 .10
83 Ryne Sandberg .25 .60
84 Deion Sanders .05 .15
85 Reggie Sanders .01 .05
86 Benito Santiago .02 .10
87 Mike Scioscia .02 .10
88 Lee Smith .02 .10
89 Ozzie Smith .40 1.00
90 Lee Stevens .01 .05
91 Darryl Strawberry .02 .10
92 B.J. Surhoff .02 .10
93 Danny Tartabull .01 .05
94 Mickey Tettleton .01 .05
95 Frank Thomas .40 1.00
96 Robby Thompson .01 .05
97 Alan Trammell .05 .15
98 Greg Vaughn .02 .10
99 Mo Vaughn .02 .10
100 Andy Van Slyke .01 .05
101 Robin Ventura .05 .15
102 Matt Williams .05 .15
103 Robin Yount .20 .50
104 Todd Zeile .02 .10
105 Roberto Alomar .08 .25
106 Sandy Alomar .02 .10
107 Barry Bonds .75 2.00
108 Kevin Brown .05 .15
109 Joe Carter .02 .10
110 Will Clark .08 .25
111 Bobby Cox .01 .05
112 Dennis Eckersley .20 .50
113 Tony Fernandez .02 .10
114 Tom Glavine .08 .25
115 Ken Griffey Jr. 1.50 4.00
116 Tony Gwynn .75 2.00
117 Tom Kelly .01 .05
118 John Kruk .02 .10
119 Fred McGriff .05 .15
120 Mark McGwire 1.00 2.50
121 Kirby Puckett .15 .40
122 Cal Ripken Jr. 1.50 4.00
123 Bip Roberts .01 .05
124 Ivan Rodriguez .40 1.00
125 Gary Sheffield .20 .50
126 Ruben Sierra .02 .10
127 Ozzie Smith .40 1.00
128 Andy Van Slyke .01 .05
129 Robin Ventura .05 .15
130 Larry Walker .02 .10

1994 Red Foley's Magazine Inserts

Bound into Red Foley's 1994 Best Baseball Book Ever, these four nine-card perforated sheets feature two-player Team Leaders cards (1-28) and single-player Superstar cards (29-36). If separated from their perforated sheets, the cards would measure the standard size. All the cards feature white-bordered color player action shots on their fronts. Each Team Leaders card has the two players' photos stacked vertically, with their names appearing to the right, and the team name and subset title appearing to the left. A colored stripe also appears on each side of the player photos. The back carries, with one stacked upon the other, each player's name, team, position, biography, and career highlights. The Superstars cards have each player's name appearing above the photo and the subset title appearing below, both accompanied by colored stripes. The back is highlighted by red stars at the top and bottom, and carries the player's name, team, position, biography, and career highlights. The cards are unnumbered and checklisted below in alphabetical order, within each subset. The two-player Team Leaders cards are listed in the order of the players on the top halves of the cards.

COMPLETE SET (36) 8.00 20.00
1 Roberto Alomar / John Olerud .08 .25
2 Jeff Bagwell / Doug Drabek .40 1.00
3 Jay Bell / Andy Van Slyke .08 .25
4 Albert Belle / Carlos Baerga .20 .50
5 Andy Benes / Tony Gwynn .40 1.00
6 Bobby Bonilla / Dwight Gooden .08 .25
7 Jay Buhner / Randy Johnson .20 .50
8 Jose Canseco / Kevin Brown .40 1.00
9 Will Clark / Matt Williams .30 .75
10 Cecil Fielder / Mike Henneman .20 .50
11 Mark Grace / Randy Myers .20 .50
12 Charlie Hayes / Andres Galarraga .08 .25
13 John Kruk / Tommy Greene .08 .25
14 Ray Lankford / Ozzie Smith .40 1.00
15 Barry Larkin / Reggie Sanders .20 .50
16 Greg Maddux / Tom Glavine .40 1.00
17 Don Mattingly / Jim Abbott .30 .75
18 Mark McGwire / Dennis Eckersley .40 1.00
19 Brian McRae / David Cone .08 .25
20 Mike Piazza / Orel Hershiser .40 1.00
21 Kirby Puckett / Rick Aguilera .40 1.00
22 Cal Ripken / Mike Mussina .75 2.00
23 Tim Salmon / Mark Langston .08 .25
24 Gary Sheffield / Bryan Harvey .40 1.00
25 Frank Thomas / Jack McDowell .75 2.00
26 Mo Vaughn / Frank Viola .20 .50
27 Larry Walker / Marquis Grissom .20 .50
28 Robin Yount / Cal Eldred .20 .50
29 Barry Bonds 1.00 2.50
30 Joe Carter .20 .50
31 Roger Clemens 1.00 2.50
32 Juan Gonzalez .50 1.25
33 Ken Griffey Jr. 1.50 4.00
34 Fred McGriff .30 .75
35 Jose Rijo .08 .25
36 Ryne Sandberg 1.00 2.50

1995 Red Foley

The cards measure standard size. The cards have no numbers so we grouped both single player in alphabetical order and multi-player cards in alphabetical team order.

COMPLETE SET (36) 8.00 20.00
1 Barry Bonds .75 2.00
2 Joe Carter .20 .50
3 Roger Clemens .75 2.00
4 Juan Gonzalez .40 1.00
5 Ken Griffey, Jr. 1.25 3.00
6 Fred McGriff .30 .75
7 Cal Ripken Jr. 1.50 4.00
8 Frank Thomas .50 1.25
9 David Justice / Greg Maddux .40 1.00
10 Rafael Palmiero / Mike Mussina .20 .50
11 Mo Vaughn / Aaron Sele .20 .50
12 Tim Salmon / Chuck Finley .20 .50
13 Mark Grace / Randy Myers .20 .50
14 Robin Ventura / Wilson Alvarez .08 .25
15 Barry Larkin / Jose Rijo .08 .25
16 Albert Belle / Carlos Baerga .30 .75
17 Andres Galarraga / Dante Bichette .08 .25
18 Cecil Fielder / Travis Fryman .20 .50
19 Gary Sheffield / Benito Santiago .40 1.00
20 Jeff Bagwell / Craig Biggio .30 .75
21 Brian McRae / David Cone .08 .25
22 Mike Piazza / Orel Hershiser .40 1.00
23 Cal Eldred / Dave Nilsson .08 .25
24 Kirby Puckett / Rick Aguilera .20 .50
25 Larry Walker / Ken Hill .20 .50
26 Barry Bonilla / Bret Saberhagen .08 .25
27 Don Mattingly / Jimmy Key .40 1.00
28 Mark McGwire / Dennis Eckersley .30 .75
29 John Kruk / Lenny Dykstra .08 .25
30 Andy Van Slyke / Al Martin .08 .25
31 Gregg Jefferies / Ozzie Smith .20 .50
32 Tony Gwynn / Andy Benes .40 1.00
33 Matt Williams / Rod Beck .30 .75
34 Jay Buhner / Randy Johnson .40 1.00
35 Jose Canseco / Will Clark .40 1.00
36 Roberto Alomar / John Olerud .08 .25

1996 Red Foley

These 2" by 2 3/4" cards were issued on two pages of 16 cards each. The fronts have a photo as well as the player's identification. The backs have player information and a brief biography.

COMPLETE SET (32) 10.00 25.00
1 Moises Alou .20 .50
2 Bill Pulsipher .08 .25
3 Paul O'Neill .20 .50
4 Mark McGwire 1.50 4.00
5 Len Dykstra .20 .50
6 Jay Bell .08 .25
7 Ozzie Smith .60 1.50
8 Tony Gwynn .75 2.00
9 Barry Bonds .75 2.00
10 Ken Griffey jr. 1.25 3.00
11 Ivan Rodriguez .50 1.25
12 Roberto Alomar .40 1.00
13 Kenny Rogers .20 .50
14 Eddie Murray .50 1.25
15 Cal Ripken Jr. 1.50 4.00
16 Rickey Henderson .60 1.50
17 Greg Maddux 1.25 3.00
18 Rafael Palmeiro .40 1.00
19 Mo Vaughn .20 .50
20 Tim Salmon .40 1.00
21 Sammy Sosa .60 1.50
22 Frank Thomas .50 1.25
23 Barry Larkin .40 1.00
24 Carlos Baerga .08 .25
25 Larry Walker .40 1.00
26 Cecil Fielder .20 .50
27 Jeff Conine .20 .50
28 Craig Biggio .30 .75
29 Wally Joyner .20 .50
30 Mike Piazza 1.25 3.00
31 Kevin Seitzer .08 .25
32 Kirby Puckett .50 1.25

1988 Foot Locker Slam Fest

This nine-card set was produced by Foot Locker to commemorate the "Foot Locker Slam Fest" slam dunk contest, televised on ESPN on May 17, 1988. The cards were given out in May at participating Foot Locker stores to customers. Between May 18 and July 31, customers could turn in the winner's card (Mike Conley) and receive a free pair of Wilson athletic shoes and 50 percent off any purchase at Foot Locker. These standard size cards (2 1/2" by 3 1/2") feature color posed shots of the participants, who were professional athletes from sports other than basketball. The pictures have magenta and blue borders on a white card face. A colored banner with the words "Foot Locker" overlays the top of the picture. A line drawing of a referee overlays the lower left corner of the picture. The backs are printed in blue on white and promote the slam dunk contest and an in-store contest. The cards are unnumbered and checklisted below in alphabetical order.

COMPLETE SET (9) 12.00 30.00
9 Devon White BB 1.25 3.00

1989 Foot Locker Slam Fest

This ten-card standard-size set was produced by Foot Locker and Nike to commemorate the "Foot Locker Slam Fest" slam dunk contest, which was televised during halftimes of NBC college basketball games through March 12, 1989. The cards were wrapped in cellophane and issued with one stick of gum. They were given out at participating Foot Locker stores upon request with a purchase. The cards feature color posed shots of the participants, who were professional athletes from sports other than basketball. A banner with the words "Foot Locker" traverses the top of the card face. The cards are unnumbered and checklisted below in alphabetical order.

COMPLETE SET (10) 3.20 8.00
3 Vince Coleman BB .20 .50

1991 Foot Locker Slam Fest

This 30-card standard-size set was issued by Foot Locker in three ten-card series to commemorate the "Foot Locker Slam Fest" dunk contest televised during halftimes of NBC college basketball games through March 10, 1991. Each set contained two Domino's Pizza coupons and a 5.00 discount coupon on any purchase of 50.00 or more at Foot Locker. The set was released in substantial quantity after the promotional coupons expired. The fronts feature both posed and action photos enclosed in an arch like double red borders. The card top carries a blue border with "Foot Locker" in blue print on a white background. Beneath the photo appears "Limited Edition" and the player's name. The backs present career highlights, card series, and numbers placed within an arch of double red borders. The player's name and team name appear in black lettering at the bottom. The cards are numbered on the back; the card numbering below adds the number 10 to each card number in the second series and 20 to each card number in the third series.

COMPLETE SET (30) 2.00 5.00
1-Jan Ken Griffey Jr. BB .75 2.00
2-Jan Delino DeShields BB .04 .10
3-Jan Barry Bonds BB .30 .75
4-Jan Jack Armstrong BB .02 .05
5-Jan Dave Justice BB .16 .40
6-Jan Deion Sanders BB FB .30 .75
7-Jan Michael Dean Perry FB .02 .05
3-Feb Bobby Jones BK .02 .05
2-Mar Bo Jackson BB FB .10 .25

1991 Foul Ball

This 36-card boxed set was produced by Eclipse Enterprises and its topic is well summarized by the blurb on the box, "Baseball's Greatest Scandals, Scoundrels and Screw-ups". The cards measure the standard size and feature Gary Cohen as writer and William Cone as artist. The fronts feature color art with white borders, while the backs have extended captions on the situation portrayed by the card.

COMMON PLAYER (1-36) 4.00 10.00
1 Foul Ball .20 .50
2 The Black Sox Scandal .40 1.00
3 The Big Cocaine Bust .08 .25
4 The Death of a Team .08 .25
5 Pete Rose .40 1.00
Bets on Baseball
6 Denny McLain .08 .25
Takes a Fall
7 Ty Cobb .40 1.00
Clobbers a Fan
8 Juan Marichal .20 .50
Johnny Roseboro
9 Phil Douglas .08 .25
Kenesaw M. Landis
John McGraw
10 Beer Night at the Park .08 .25
11 Disco Demolition Night .08 .25
12 Al Campanis .08 .25
Strikes Out
13 Lenny Randle .08 .25
Frank Lucchesi
14 George Steinbrenner .20 .50
Boss George Buys It
15 The Last Stolen Base .08 .25
16 Luis Polonia .08 .25
Scores Twice
17 Charlie Finley .08 .25
Sells Out
18 Dave Pallone .08 .25
An Ump's Double Life
19 Norm Cash .08 .25
The Bat Man Tells All
20 Gaylord Perry .30 .75
A Professional Spitter
21 Dock Ellis .08 .25
Delivers A Message
22 A Major League Trade .08 .25
23 Ray Kroc .08 .25
Grabs the Mike
24 Ted Turner .08 .25
Makes the Team
25 Graig Nettles .20 .50
Bounces Out
26 The Pine Tar Game .08 .25
27 Dave Winfield .40 1.00
Gets the Bird
28 Pascual Perez .08 .25
Goes Astray
29 Dave Stewart .08 .25
Gets Tricked
30 Wade Boggs .40 1.00
Margo Adams
31 Two Yankee Relievers .08 .25
32 Reggie Jackson .40 1.00
Bar Mania
33 Kiteman Grounds Out .08 .25
34 Eddie Gaedel .40 1.00
Short Career
35 The Flying Fan .08 .25
36 Jim Bouton .20 .50
Ball Four

1887 Four Base Hits N-Unc.

The fourteen known baseball cards inscribed "Four Base Hits" were catalogued in the N690 classification for two reasons: they are identical in size and format to N690-1, and two players, Mays and Roseman, have the same pictures in both sets. Although it is known that the Charles Gross Company "farmed out" some of its insert designs to other companies, "Four Base Hits" will retain this catalog number until new evidence places them elsewhere. As far as is known, the Mickey Welch card is currently unique.

COMPLETE SET 100000.00 200000.00
1 Tom Dailey (sic, Daly) 12500.00 25000.00
2 John Clarkson 50000.00 100000.00
3 Pat Deasley 12500.00 25000.00
4 Buck Ewing 50000.00 100000.00
5 Pete Gillespie 12500.00 25000.00
6 Frank Hankinson 12500.00 25000.00
7 Mike King Kelly 60000.00 120000.00
8 Al Mays 12500.00 25000.00
9 James Mutrie 12500.00 25000.00
10 James (Chief) Roseman 12500.00 25000.00
11 Marty Sullivan 12500.00 25000.00
12 George Van Haltren 12500.00 25000.00
13 John Mont. Ward 50000.00 100000.00
14 Mickey Welch 50000.00 100000.00

1996 Four Queens Chips

These cards, which cover several different series, were issued by the four queens casino in Las Vegas. These chips have the same player photo on each side and were issued in five dollar demoniations. They cover several different sets, so we have sequenced them in alphabetical order by theme.

COMPLETE SET 25.00 60.00
1 Vida Blue 2.50 6.00
A's
2 John Odom 2.00 5.00
A's
3 Dick Williams MG 2.00 5.00
A's
4 Hank Bauer 2.50 6.00
Don Larsen's Perfect Game`
5 Andy Carey 2.00 5.00
Don Larsen's Perfect Game
6 Don Larsen 2.50 6.00
Perfect Game
7 Don Larsen 2.50 6.00
With other players
Perfect Game
8 Gil McDougald 2.50 6.00
Don Larsen's perfect game
9 Enos Slaughter 4.00 10.00
Don Larsen's perfect game
10 Hank Bauer 2.50 6.00
Yankees
11 Irv Noren 2.00 5.00
Yankees
12 Bill Skowron 2.50 6.00
Yankees

1980 Franchise Babe Ruth

This 80-card set measures the standard size and was manufactured by the Franchise of Bel Air, Maryland. The cards present the life of Babe Ruth and include his activities both on and off the field. The fronts have black and white photos framed by white borders. The set, which had an original print run of 1,000 sets was originally issued in complete set form and available for $8 directly from the manufacturer at the time of the issue

COMPLETE SET (80) 10.00 25.00
COMMON PLAYER (1-80) .75 1.50

1983 Franchise Brooks Robinson

Produced by The Franchise, this 40-card standard-size set captures moments from the life and career of Brooks Robinson, the Baltimore Orioles' all-time great third baseman. On a white card face, the fronts display either posed or action black-and-white photos enclosed by an orange border stripe. Some of the front photos are horizontally oriented while others are vertically oriented. Superimposed on each card is an orange "Hall of Fame" icon. Between two orange stripes, the horizontally oriented backs feature text providing information relating to the front photo. The cards are numbered on the back in a baseball glove icon in the upper left corner.

COMPLETE SET (40) 3.00 8.00
COMMON PLAYER (1-40) .10 .25
1 Brooks Robinson .25 .60
Title Card
7 Brooks Robinson .15 .40
Ron Hansen
Marv Breeding
Jim Ge
8 Brooks Robinson .15 .40
Walt Dropo
Celebration time
9 Brooks Robinson .25 .60
Yogi Berra
Instinctive baserunne
10 Brooks Robinson .08 .25
Connie Robinson
Wedding Day
11 Brooks Robinson .08 .25
Eddie Robinson
First business pa
12 Brooks Robinson .25 .60
Luis Aparicio
Jerry Adair
Jim G
13 Brooks Robinson .25 .60
Al Kaline
Two Baltimore heroes
16 Brooks Robinson .15 .40
Bobby Richardson
Tony Kubek
Ups
17 Brooks Robinson .15 .40
Tom Tresh
Tag out at third
18 Brooks Robinson .15 .40
Jerry Adair
Norm Siebern
Gettin
19 Brooks Robinson .25 .60
Carl Yastrzemski
Two future MVPs
20 Brooks Robinson .30 .75
Rocky Marciano
The original Rock
21 Brooks Robinson .25 .60
Hank Bauer
Bauer's gloveman
22 Brooks Robinson .25 .60
Luis Aparicio
Dave Johnson
Boog
23 Brooks Robinson .25 .60
Boog Powell
Curt Blefary
Frank
24 Brooks Robinson .25 .60
Hank Bauer
Frank Robinson
All-S
25 Brooks Robinson .25 .60
Frank Robinson
Lethal lumber
26 Brooks Robinson .25 .60
Mark Belanger
Dave Johnson
Boog
27 Brooks Robinson .15 .40
Tony Oliva
Respect for Oliva
28 Brooks Robinson .25 .60
Harmon Killebrew
Out of Harm's w
29 Brooks Robinson .15 .40
Frank Lane SCOUT
Master trader
33 Brooks Robinson .25 .60
Willie Stargell
Rappin' with Wil
36 Brooks Robinson .15 .40
Lee May
Respect for teammate
37 Brooks Robinson .15 .40
Doug DeCinces
Touch of Class
39 Brooks Robinson .15 .40
Thurman Munson
Honored by Yankee
40 Brooks Robinson .25 .60
Harmon Killebrew
Two greats at t

1960 Free Press Hot Stove League Manager

Issued as inserts in the Detroit Free Press, these clippings measure approximately 5 1/2" by 6". These were issued and featured various highlights of what a manager decision was at a key part of a game. Please note that this checklist is basically complete (we still need to id card number 17) and that last addition would be greatly appreciated.

COMPLETE SET 50.00 100.00
1 Duke Snider 6.00 15.00
2 Eddie Sawyer MG 1.00 2.50
3 Elmer Valo 1.25 3.00
4 Joe Gordon MG 1.25 3.00
5 Don Blasingame 1.00 2.50
6 Paul Richards MG 1.00 2.50
7 Billy Consolo 1.00 2.50
8 Leo Kiely 1.00 2.50
9 Dave Philley 1.00 2.50
10 George Strickland MG 1.00 2.50
11 Felipe Alou 3.00 8.00
12 Al Lopez MG 2.00 5.00
13 Yogi Berra 6.00 15.00
14 Don McMahon 1.00 2.50
15 Johnny Temple 1.00 2.50
16 Solly Hemus MG 1.00 2.50
18 Bill Rigney MG 1.00 2.50
19 Bob Cerv 1.00 2.50
20 Walt Alston MG 2.00 5.00
21 Nellie Fox 3.00 8.00
22 Danny Murtaugh MG 1.00 2.50
23 Orlando Cepeda 3.00 8.00
24 George Altman 1.00 2.50

1992 French's

The 1992 French's Special Edition Combo Series consists of 18 two-player cards and a title/checklist card. The cards measure the standard size. Each card features one player from the American League and one player from the National League. The cards were licensed by the MLBPA and produced by MSA (Michael Schechter Associates). Collectors could obtain the title/checklist card and three free player cards through an on-pack promotion by purchasing a 16 oz. size of French's Classic Yellow Mustard (the cards were enclosed in a plastic hangtag). Alternatively, collectors could collect all 18 player cards in the series by sending in 3.00 plus 75 cents for postage and handling along with one quality seal from the 16 oz. size of French's Classic Yellow Mustard. The released production figures were 43,000 18-card sets and 4,800,000 three-card hangtags.

COMPLETE SET (19) 3.00 8.00
1 Chuck Knoblauch .40 1.00
Jeff Bagwell
2 Roger Clemens .30 .75
Tom Glavine
3 Julio Franco .08 .25
Terry Pendleton
4 Jose Canseco .20 .50
Howard Johnson
5 Scott Erickson .08 .25
John Smiley
6 Bryan Harvey .08 .25
Lee Smith
7 Kirby Puckett .30 .75
Barry Bonds
8 Robin Ventura .30 .75
Matt Williams
9 Tony Pena .08 .25
Tom Pagnozzi
10 Sandy Alomar Jr. .20 .50
Benito Santiago
11 Don Mattingly .40 1.00
Will Clark
12 Roberto Alomar .40 1.00
Ryne Sandberg
13 Cal Ripken 1.00 2.50
Ozzie Smith
14 Wade Boggs .20 .50
Chris Sabo
15 Ken Griffey Jr. 1.00 2.50
Dave Justice
16 Joe Carter .40 1.00
Tony Gwynn
17 Rickey Henderson .40 1.00
Darryl Strawberry
18 Jack Morris .08 .25
Steve Avery
NNO Title .08 .25
Checklist Card

1977-83 Fritsch One Year Winners

This 118-card standard-size set honors players who played roughly a season or less and were thus forgotten in baseball lore. The set was issued as three parts of one series. Cards 1-18 were issued in 1977 and feature black and white player photos, bordered in white and green. Cards 19-54 were issued in 1979 and have color player photos with white borders. Cards 55-118 were issued in 1983 and have colored photois with blue and white borders. The extended caption and Major League statistical record on the horizontally oriented backs are banded above and below by red stripes. The cards are numbered on the back in a baseball diamond in the upper left corner.

COMPLETE SET (118) 12.50 30.00
1 Eddie Gaedel .60 1.50
2 Chuck Connors .30 .75
3 Joe Brovia .10 .25
4 Ross Grimsley Sr. .10 .25
5 Bob Thorpe .10 .25
6 Pete Gray .30 .75
7 Cy Buker .10 .25
8 Ted Fritsch Sr. .15 .40
9 Ron Necciai .15 .40
10 Nino Escalera .10 .25
11 Bobo Holloman .15 .40
12 Tony Roig .10 .25
13 Paul Pettit .15 .40
14 Paul Schramka .10 .25
15 Hal Trosky Jr. .15 .40
16 Floyd Wooldridge .10 .25
17 Jim Westlake .10 .25
18 Leon Brinkopf .10 .25
19 Daryl Robertson .10 .25
20 Gerry Shoen .10 .25
21 Jim Brenneman .10 .25
22 Pat House .10 .25
23 Ken Poulsen .10 .25
24 Arlo Brunsberg .10 .25
25 Jay Hankins .10 .25
26 Chuck Nieson .10 .25
27 Dick Joyce .10 .25
28 Jim Ellis .10 .25
29 John Duffie .10 .25
30 Vern Holtgrave .10 .25
31 Bill Bethea .10 .25
32 Joe Moock .10 .25
33 John Hoffman .10 .25
34 Jorge Rubio .10 .25
35 Fred Rath .10 .25
36 Jess Hickman .10 .25
37 Tom Fisher .10 .25
38 Dick Scott .10 .25
39 Jim Hibbs .10 .25
40 Paul Gilliford .10 .25
41 Bob Botz .10 .25
42 Jack Kubiszyn .10 .25
43 Rich Rusteck .10 .25
44 Roy Gleason .10 .25
45 Glenn Vaughan .10 .25
46 Bill Graham .40 1.00
47 Dennis Musgraves .10 .25
48 Ron Henry .10 .25
49 Mike Jurewicz .10 .25
50 Pidge Browne .15 .40
51 Ron Keller .10 .25
52 Doug Gallagher .10 .25
53 Dave Thies .10 .25
54 Don Eaddy .10 .25
55 Don Prince .10 .25
56 Tom Granly .10 .25
57 Roy Heiser .10 .25
58 Hank Izquierdo .10 .25
59 Rex Johnston .10 .25
60 Jack Damaska .10 .25
61 John Flavin .10 .25
62 John Glenn .10 .25
63 Stan Johnson .10 .25
64 Don Choate .10 .25
65 Bill Kern .10 .25
66 Dick Luebke .10 .25
67 Glen Clark .10 .25
68 Lamar Jacobs .10 .25
69 Rick Herrscher .15 .40
70 Jim McManus .10 .25
71 Len Church .10 .25
72 Moose Stubing .10 .25
73 Cal Emery .10 .25
74 Lee Gregory .10 .25
75 Mike Page .10 .25
76 Benny Valenzuela .10 .25
77 John Papa .10 .25
78 Jim Stump .10 .25
79 Brian McCall .10 .25
80 Al Kenders .10 .25
81 Corky Withrow .10 .25
82 Verle Tiefenthaler .10 .25
83 Dave Wissman .10 .25
84 Tom Fletcher .10 .25
85 Dale Willis .10 .25
86 Larry Foster .10 .25
87 Johnnie Seale .10 .25
88 Jim Lekew .10 .25
89 Charlie Shoemaker .10 .25
90 Don Arlich .10 .25
91 George Gerberman .10 .25
92 John Preqenger .10 .25
93 Merlin Nippert .10 .25
94 Steve Demeter .10 .25
95 John Paciorek .15 .40
96 Larry Loughlin .10 .25
97 Alan Brice .10 .25
98 Chet Boak .10 .25
99 Alan Koch .10 .25
100 Danny Thomas .10 .25
101 Elder White .10 .25
102 Jim Snyder .10 .25
103 Ted Schreiber .10 .25
104 Evans Killeen .10 .25
105 Ray Daviault .10 .25
106 Larry Foss .10 .25
107 Wayne Graham .10 .25
108 Santiago Rosario .10 .25
109 Bob Sprout .10 .25
110 Tom Hughes .10 .25
111 Em Lindbeck .10 .25
112 Ray Blemker .10 .25
113 Shaun Fitzmaurice .10 .25
114 Ron Stillwell .10 .25
115 Carl Thomas .10 .25
116 Mike DeGerick .10 .25
117 Jay Dahl .10 .25
118 Al Lary .10 .25

1988 Fritsch Baseball Card Museum

This set was issued to commemorate the opening of Larry Fritsch's Baseball Card Museum in Cooperstown, New York. This set features reprints of some of the hobby's most expensive cards.

COMPLETE SET (8) 2.50 6.00
1 Honus Wagner 1.00 2.50
T206
2 Joe Doyle .20 .50
T206
With and without
NAT'L on front
3 Ty Cobb 1.00 2.50
T205
4 Joe Jackson 1.00 2.50
Cracker Jack
5 Eddie Plank .40 1.00
T206
6 1909 T206 Sherry Magee/(With spellings .20
.50
Magie and
7 Jim Thorpe .60 1.50
Colgan's Chips
8 Baseball Card Museum .08 .25
Advertisement

1991 Front Row Ken Griffey Jr.

This 15-card standard-size set is composed of the ten-card insert set plus a five-card promo set. The ten-card insert set features different action shots of Ken Griffey Jr. An official certificate of authenticity included with the set gives the set serial number and production run ("X of 25,000"). These cards were randomly inserted into 1992 Front Row Baseball Draft Pick wax boxes. Except for a baseball icon on their backs marked with the word "Promo," the promo cards are identical with the first five cards in the insert set. The Promo cards in the checklist below have been numbered with a P suffix in order to avoid confusion. According to Front Row, 25,000 sets were produced. All these cards can be distinguished from the regular issue by their backs, which are gold-foil stamped with the "Front Row Collector's Club Charter Member" seal.

COMPLETE SET (15) 6.00 15.00
COMMON CARD (1-10) .40 1.00
COMMON PROMO (1P-5P) .40 1.00

1992 Front Row Aaron

This five-card standard-size set features Hall of Famer Hank Aaron. Each set includes an official certificate of authenticity that gives the production run (25,000) and the set serial number. Aaron autographed the first card in 5,000 sets that were initially offered exclusively to Front Row Collector's Club Members. Cards 1-4 carry color player photos on the fronts, while card No. 5 has a black and white photo.

COMPLETE SET (5) 2.00 5.00
COMMON CARD .40 1.00
1AU Hank Aaron AU 30.00 60.00

1992 Front Row ATG Holograms

These three standard-size hologram cards commemorate an outstanding season of three of baseball's all-time greats. The production run was 100,000 for each card. The cards are unnumbered and checklisted below in alphabetical order.

COMPLETE SET (3) 2.00 5.00
1 Hank Aaron .75 2.00
2 Roy Campanella .50 1.25
3 Tom Seaver .75 2.00

1992 Front Row Banks

This five-card standard-size set features Hall of Famer Ernie Banks. Each set includes an official certificate of authenticity that gives the production run (25,000) and the set serial number. Banks autographed the first card in 5,000 sets that were initially offered exclusively to Front Row Collector's Club Members. Cards 1-4 carry color player photos on the fronts, while card No. 5 has a black and white photo.

COMPLETE SET (5) 1.50 4.00
COMMON PLAYER (1-5) .40 1.00
1AU Ernie Banks AU 10.00 25.00

1992 Front Row Berra

This five-card standard-size set features Hall of Famer Yogi Berra. Each set includes an official certificate of authenticity that gives the production run (25,000) and the set serial number. Berra autographed the first card in 5,000 sets that were initially offered exclusively to Front Row Collector's Club Members. Card Nos. 1 and 3 carry color player photos on the fronts, while card Nos. 2, 4 and 5 have black and white photos.

COMPLETE SET (5) 1.50 4.00
COMMON PLAYER (1-5) .40 1.00
1AU Yogi Berra AU 20.00 50.00

1992 Front Row Brooks Robinson

This five-card standard-size set features Hall of Famer Brooks Robinson. Each set includes an official certificate of authenticity that gives the production run (25,000) and the set serial number. Robinson autographed the first card in 5,000 sets that were initially offered exclusively to Front Row Collector's Club Members.

COMPLETE SET (5) 1.50 4.00
COMMON PLAYER (1-5) .40 1.00
1AU Brooks Robinson 12.00 30.00
Autograph

1992 Front Row Buck Leonard

This five-card standard-size set features Hall of Famer Buck Leonard. Each set includes an official certificate of authenticity that gives the production run (25,000) and the set serial number. Leonard autographed the first card in 5,000 sets that were initially offered exclusively to Front Row Collector's Club Members.

COMPLETE SET (5) 1.50 4.00
COMMON PLAYER (1-5) .40 1.00
1AU Buck Leonard AU 12.50 30.00

1992 Front Row Dandridge

This five-card standard-size set features Hall of Famer Ray Dandridge. Each set includes an official certificate of authenticity, giving the production run (25,000) and the set serial number. Dandridge autographed the first card in 5,000 sets that were initially offered exclusively to Front Row Collector's Club Members.

COMPLETE SET (5) 1.50 4.00
COMMON PLAYER (1-5) .40 1.00
1AU Ray Dandridge AU 10.00 25.00

1992 Front Row Ford

This five-card standard-size set features Hall of Famer Whitey Ford. Each set includes an official certificate of authenticity that gives the production run (25,000) and the set serial number. Ford autographed the first card in 5,000 sets that were initially offered exclusively to Front Row Collector's Club Members.

COMPLETE SET (5) 1.50 4.00
COMMON PLAYER (1-5) .40 1.00
1AU Whitey Ford AU 8.00 20.00

1992 Front Row Griffey Club House

This ten-card standard-size set features full-bleed color player photos on the front. The only text on the front appears in a black square at the lower right corner, which reads "Club House Series, Ken Griffey Jr." According to Front Row, 25,000 sets were produced.

COMPLETE SET (10) 4.00 10.00
COMMON PLAYER (1-10) .40 1.00

1992 Front Row Griffey Gold

This three-card standard-size set features color player photos on the fronts bordered by 23K gold dust stamping. Each set was accompanied by a certificate of authenticity carrying the production run (20,000) and the set serial number. Front Row issued 5,000 uncut strips of the three-card set.

COMPLETE SET (3) 6.00 15.00
COMMON PLAYER (1-3) 2.00 5.00

1992 Front Row Griffey Holograms

This three-card hologram standard-size set features three-dimensional shots of Ken Griffey Jr. Each set includes an official certificate of authenticity giving the set serial number and production run (50,000). All Seattle Mariner logos have been airbrushed off the cards as they were not licensed by the league or team.

COMPLETE SET (3) 2.50 6.00
COMMON PLAYER (1-3) .80 2.00

1992 Front Row Griffey Jr. Oversized Card

This oversized promo card measures approximately 7 1/2" X 10 1/2" and features a color action shot of Griffey at bat. The card is unnumbered.

NNO Ken Griffey Jr. 1.50 4.00

1992 Front Row Irvin

This five-card standard-size set features Hall of Famer Monte Irvin. Each set includes an official certificate of authenticity, giving the production run (25,000) and the set serial number. Irvin autographed the first card in 5,000 sets that were initially offered exclusively to Front Row Collector's Club Members. The fronts feature either black and white (cards 1-2) or color player photos (cards 3-5).

COMPLETE SET (5) 1.50 4.00
COMMON PLAYER (1-5) .40 1.00
1AU Monte Irvin AU 8.00 20.00

1992 Front Row Seaver

This five card set feature highlights in the career of Hall of Fame pitcher Tom Seaver. Like most of the 1992 Front Row sets, this standard-size set was issued in a quantity of 25,000 sets with 4,000 of card number 1 being autographed.

COMPLETE SET (5) 1.50 4.00
COMMON CARD (1-5) .40 1.00
1AU Tom Seaver AU 25.00 60.00

1992 Front Row Stargell

This five-card standard-size set features Hall of Famer Willie Stargell. Each set includes an official certificate of authenticity, giving the production run (25,000) and the set serial number. Stargell autographed the first card in 5,000 sets that were initially offered exclusively to Front Row Collector's Club Members.

COMPLETE SET (5) 1.50 4.00
COMMON PLAYER (1-5) .40 1.00
1AU Willie Stargell AU 8.00 20.00

1992 Front Row Thomas

This seven-card, standard-size set features on the front color player photos bordered in white. Each set includes an official certificate of authenticity that gives the production run (30,000) and the set serial number. Thomas autographed the first card in 4,000 sets that were initially offered exclusively to Front Row Collector's Club Members.

COMPLETE SET (7) 2.50 6.00
COMMON PLAYER (1-7) .40 1.00
1AU Frank Thomas AU 15.00 40.00
4EO Frank Thomas
Front Row Exclusive Offer on Back

1992 Front Row Thomas Gold

This three-card, standard-size set features color player photos on the fronts bordered by 23K gold dust stamping. Each set was accompanied by a certificate of authenticity carrying the production run (20,000) and the set serial number. Five thousand uncut strips of the three-card set were also produced.

COMPLETE SET (3) 6.00 15.00
COMMON PLAYER (1-3) 2.00 5.00

1992 Front Row Tyler Green

This seven card standard-size set was among the many individual player sets issued by Front Row. Each set features highlights of Travis Green's early baseball career and includes an Official Certificate of Authenticity

COMMON PLAYER (1-7) .60 1.50
COMMON PLAYER (1-7) .10 .25

1993 Front Row Brock

The five standard-size cards comprising this set feature borderless color photos that have the Cardinals name and logo airbrushed from Brock's uniform. The set comes with a certificate of authenticity that carries the serial number out of 5,000 sets produced.

COMPLETE SET (5) 1.50 4.00
COMMON PLAYER (1-5) .40 1.00

1993 Front Row Campanella

The five standard-size cards comprising this set feature borderless color photos that have the Dodgers name and logo airbrushed from Campanella's uniform. The set comes with a certificate of authenticity that carries the serial number out of 5,000 sets produced.

COMPLETE SET (5) 2.00 5.00
COMMON PLAYER (1-5) .40 1.00

1993 Front Row Fingers

Front Row issued this five-card standard-size set as part of "The Gold Collection" line. Just 5,000 sets were produced.

COMPLETE SET (5) 1.50 4.00
COMMON PLAYER (1-5) .40 1.00

1993 Front Row Griffey Jr. Gold Collection

This ten-card standard-size set features borderless color action shots on its fronts.

COMPLETE SET (10) 4.00 10.00
COMMON PLAYER (1-10) .40 1.00

1993 Front Row Palmer

This five-card Front Row Premium standard-size set spotlights former Baltimore Orioles' pitcher Jim Palmer. Two thousand of these sets carry an authentic autograph, which appears on the first card.

COMPLETE SET (5) 1.50 4.00
COMMON PLAYER (1-5) .40 1.00

1993 Fun Pack

This 225-card standard-size single series set was issued by Upper Deck and targeted primarily at youngsters. Cards were distributed exclusively in hobby and retail foil fin-wrapped packs. Topical subsets featured are Stars of Tomorrow (1-9), Hot Shots (10-21), Kid Stars (22-27), Upper Deck Heroes (28-36), All-Star Advice (210-215), All-Star Fold Outs (216-220), and Checklists (221-225) and randomly numbered Glow Stars. Card numbers 37-209 are arranged alphabetically according to team names, with each team subset beginning with a Glow Star card. There are no key Rookie Cards in this set.The Hot Shot subset cards were only available in retail packs or through a as a mail-in redemption promotion available in hobby packs.

COMPLETE SET (225) 25.00 60.00
HOT SHOTS ONLY IN MAGENTA PACKS
HOT SHOTS DISTRIBUTED W/TRADE CARDS
TRADE CARDS ONLY IN GREEN PACKS
1 Wil Cordero SOT .05 .15
2 Brent Gates .05 .15
3 Benji Gil .05 .15
4 Phil Hiatt .05 .15
5 David McCarty .05 .15
6 Mike Piazza 1.25 3.00
7 Tim Salmon .20 .50
8 J.T.Snow RC .20 .50
9 Kevin Young .05 .15
10 Roberto Alomar HS .20 .50
11 Barry Bonds HS .75 2.00
12 Jose Canseco HS .20 .50
13 Will Clark HS .20 .50
14 Roger Clemens HS .60 1.50
15 Juan Gonzalez HS .05 .15
16 Ken Griffey Jr. HS .60 1.50
17 Mark McGwire HS .75 2.00
18 Nolan Ryan HS 1.00 2.50
19 Ryne Sandberg HS .50 1.25
20 Gary Sheffield HS .10 .30
21 Frank Thomas HS .30 .75
22 Roberto Alomar KS .10 .30
23 Roger Clemens KS .30 .75
24 Ken Griffey Jr. KS .40 1.00
25 Gary Sheffield KS .05 .15
26 Nolan Ryan KS .50 1.25
27 Frank Thomas KS .20 .50
28 Reggie Jackson HERO .10 .30
29 Roger Clemens HERO .30 .75
30 Ken Griffey Jr. HERO .40 1.00
31 Bo Jackson HERO .10 .30
32 Cal Ripken HERO .50 1.25
33 Nolan Ryan HERO .50 1.25
34 Deion Sanders HERO .10 .30
35 Ozzie Smith HERO .30 .75
36 Frank Thomas HERO .20 .50
37 Tim Salmon GS .10 .30
38 Chili Davis .10 .30
39 Chuck Finley .10 .30
40 Mark Langston .05 .15
41 Luis Polonia .05 .15
42 Jeff Bagwell GS .10 .30
43 Jeff Bagwell .20 .50
44 Craig Biggio .20 .50
45 Ken Caminiti .10 .30
46 Doug Drabek .05 .15
47 Steve Finley .10 .30
48 Mark McGwire GS .40 1.00
49 Dennis Eckersley .10 .30
50 Rickey Henderson .30 .75
51 Mark McGwire .75 2.00
52 Ruben Sierra .10 .30
53 Terry Steinbach .05 .15
54 Roberto Alomar GS .10 .30
55 Roberto Alomar .20 .50
56 Joe Carter .10 .30
57 Juan Guzman .05 .15
58 Paul Molitor .10 .30
59 Jack Morris .10 .30
60 John Olerud .10 .30
61 Tom Glavine GS .10 .30
62 Steve Avery .05 .15
63 Tom Glavine .20 .50
64 David Justice .10 .30
65 Greg Maddux .50 1.25
66 Terry Pendleton .10 .30
67 Deion Sanders .20 .50
68 John Smoltz .20 .50
69 Robin Yount GS .30 .75
70 Cal Eldred .05 .15
71 Pat Listach .05 .15
72 Greg Vaughn .05 .15
73 Robin Yount .50 1.25
74 Ozzie Smith GS .30 .75
75 Gregg Jefferies .05 .15
76 Ray Lankford .10 .30
77 Lee Smith .10 .30
78 Ozzie Smith .50 1.25
79 Bob Tewksbury .05 .15
80 Ryne Sandberg GS .30 .75
81 Mark Grace .20 .50
82 Mike Morgan .05 .15
83 Randy Myers .10 .30
84 Ryne Sandberg .50 1.25
85 Sammy Sosa .30 .75

86 Eric Karros GS .05 .15
87 Brett Butler .10 .30
88 Orel Hershiser .10 .30
89 Eric Karros .10 .30
90 Ramon Martinez .05 .15
91 Jose Offerman .05 .15
92 Darryl Strawberry .10 .30
93 Marquis Grissom GS .05 .15
94 Delino DeShields .05 .15
95 Marquis Grissom .10 .30
96 Ken Hill .05 .15
97 Dennis Martinez .10 .30
98 Larry Walker .10 .30
99 Barry Bonds GS .40 1.00
100 Barry Bonds .75 2.00
101 Will Clark .20 .50
102 Bill Swift .05 .15
103 Robby Thompson .05 .15
104 Matt Williams .10 .30
105 Carlos Baerga GS .05 .15
106 Sandy Alomar Jr. .05 .15
107 Carlos Baerga .05 .15
108 Albert Belle .10 .30
109 Kenny Lofton .10 .30
110 Charles Nagy .05 .15
111 Ken Griffey Jr. GS .40 1.00
112 Jay Buhner .10 .30
113 Dave Fleming .05 .15
114 Ken Griffey Jr. .60 1.50
115 Randy Johnson .30 .75
116 Edgar Martinez .20 .50
117 Benito Santiago GS .05 .15
118 Bret Barberie .05 .15
119 Jeff Conine .10 .30
120 Brian Harvey .05 .15
121 Benito Santiago .10 .30
122 Walt Weiss .05 .15
123 Dwight Gooden GS .05 .15
124 Bobby Bonilla .10 .30
125 Vince Coleman .05 .15
126 Dwight Gooden .10 .30
127 Howard Johnson .05 .15
128 Eddie Murray .30 .75
129 Bret Saberhagen .10 .30
130 Cal Ripken GS .50 1.25
131 Brady Anderson .10 .30
132 Mike Devereaux .05 .15
133 Ben McDonald .05 .15
134 Mike Mussina .20 .50
135 Cal Ripken 1.00 2.50
136 Fred McGriff GS .10 .30
137 Andy Benes .05 .15
138 Tony Gwynn .40 1.00
139 Fred McGriff .20 .50
140 Phil Plantier .05 .15
141 Gary Sheffield .10 .30
142 Darren Daulton GS .05 .15
143 Darren Daulton .10 .30
144 Len Dykstra .10 .30
145 Dave Hollins .05 .15
146 John Kruk .10 .30
147 Mitch Williams .05 .15
148 Andy Van Slyke GS .10 .30
149 Jay Bell .10 .30
150 Zane Smith .05 .15
151 Andy Van Slyke .20 .50
152 Tim Wakefield .30 .75
153 Juan Gonzalez GS .05 .15
154 Kevin Brown .10 .30
155 Jose Canseco .20 .50
156 Juan Gonzalez .10 .30
157 Rafael Palmeiro .20 .50
158 Dean Palmer .10 .30
159 Ivan Rodriguez .20 .50
160 Nolan Ryan 1.00 2.50
161 Roger Clemens GS .30 .75
162 Roger Clemens .60 1.50
163 Andre Dawson .10 .30
164 Mike Greenwell .05 .15
165 Tony Pena .05 .15
166 Frank Viola .10 .30
167 Barry Larkin GS .10 .30
168 Rob Dibble .10 .30
169 Roberto Kelly .05 .15
170 Barry Larkin .20 .50
171 Kevin Mitchell .05 .15
172 Bip Roberts .05 .15
173 Andres Galarraga GS .05 .15
174 Dante Bichette .10 .30
175 Jerald Clark .05 .15
176 Andres Galarraga .10 .30
177 Charlie Hayes .05 .15
178 David Nied .05 .15
179 David Cone GS .05 .15
180 Kevin Appier .10 .30
181 George Brett .75 2.00
182 David Cone .10 .30
183 Felix Jose .05 .15
184 Wally Joyner .10 .30
185 Cecil Fielder GS .05 .15
186 Cecil Fielder .10 .30
187 Travis Fryman .10 .30
188 Tony Phillips .05 .15
189 Mickey Tettleton .05 .15
190 Lou Whitaker .10 .30
191 Kirby Puckett GS .20 .50
192 Scott Erickson .05 .15
193 Chuck Knoblauch .10 .30
194 Shane Mack .05 .15
195 Kirby Puckett .30 .75
196 Dave Winfield .10 .30
197 Frank Thomas GS .20 .50
198 George Bell .05 .15
199 Bo Jackson .30 .75
200 Jack McDowell .05 .15
201 Tim Raines .10 .30
202 Frank Thomas .30 .75
203 Robin Ventura .10 .30
204 Jim Abbott GS .10 .30
205 Jim Abbott .20 .50
206 Wade Boggs .20 .50
207 Jimmy Key .10 .30
208 Don Mattingly .75 2.00
209 Danny Tartabull .05 .15
210 Brett Butler ASA .05 .15
211 Tony Gwynn ASA .20 .50
212 Rickey Henderson ASA .20 .50
213 Ramon Martinez ASA .05 .15
214 Nolan Ryan ASA .50 1.25
215 Ozzie Smith ASA .30 .75
216 Marquis Grissom FOLD .05 .15
217 Dean Palmer FOLD .05 .15
218 Cal Ripken FOLD .50 1.25
219 Deion Sanders FOLD .10 .30
220 Darryl Strawberry FOLD .05 .15
221 David McCarty CL .05 .15
222 Barry Bonds CL .40 1.00
223 Juan Gonzalez CL .05 .15
224 Ken Griffey Jr. CL .40 1.00
225 Frank Thomas CL .20 .50
NNO Hot Shots Card Punched .05 .15
NNO Hot Shots Card Expired .05 .15

1993 Fun Pack All-Stars

COMPLETE SET (9) 6.00 15.00
STATED ODDS 1:5
AS1 F.Thomas .40 1.00
McGriff
AS2 I.Rodriguez .25 .60
D.Daulton
AS3 M.McGwire 1.25 3.00
W.Clark
AS4 R.Alomar 1.00 2.50
R.Sandberg
AS5 R.Ventura .20 .50
T.Pendleton
AS6 C.Ripken 1.50 4.00
O.Smith
AS7 J.Gonzalez 1.25 3.00
B.Bonds
AS8 K.Griffey Jr. 1.00 2.50
M.Grissom
AS9 K.Puckett .60 1.50
T.Gwynn

1993 Fun Pack Mascots

COMPLETE SET (5) 1.00 2.50
RANDOM INSERTS IN PACKS
1 Phillie Phanatic .40 1.00
2 Pirate Parrot .20 .50
3 Fredbird .20 .50
4 BJ Birdie .20 .50
5 Youppi .20 .50

1994 Fun Pack

Issued by Upper Deck for the second straight year, the Fun Pack set consists of 240 cards. The following subsets are included in this set: Stars of Tomorrow (1-9), Standouts (175-192), Pro-Files (193-198), Headline Stars (199-207), What's the Call (208-216), Foldouts (217-225) and Fun Cards (226-234). Some dealers believe the Standout subset may be short printed. One of Michael Jordan's baseball Rookie Cards is in this set.
COMPLETE SET (240) 30.00 80.00
PRODUCED BY UPPER DECK
1 Manny Ramirez .50 1.25
2 Cliff Floyd .20 .50
3 Rondell White .20 .50
4 Carlos Delgado .30 .75
5 Chipper Jones .50 1.25
6 Javier Lopez .20 .50
7 Ryan Klesko .20 .50
8 Steve Karsay .08 .25
9 Rich Becker .08 .25
10 Gary Sheffield .08 .25
11 Jeffrey Hammonds .08 .25
12 Roberto Alomar .30 .75
13 Brent Gates .08 .25
14 Andres Galarraga .20 .50
15 Tim Salmon .30 .75
16 Dwight Gooden .20 .50
17 Mark Grace .30 .75
18 Andy Van Slyke .30 .75
19 Juan Gonzalez .20 .50
20 Mickey Tettleton .08 .25
21 Roger Clemens 1.00 2.50
22 Will Clark .30 .75
23 David Justice .20 .50
24 Ken Griffey Jr. 1.00 2.50
25 Barry Bonds 1.25 3.00
26 Bill Swift .08 .25
27 Fred McGriff .30 .75
28 Randy Myers .08 .25
29 Joe Carter .20 .50
30 Nigel Wilson .08 .25
31 Mike Piazza .75 2.00
32 Dave Winfield .20 .50
33 Steve Avery .08 .25
34 Kirby Puckett .50 1.25
35 Frank Thomas .50 1.25
36 Aaron Sele .08 .25
37 Ricky Gutierrez .08 .25
38 Curt Schilling .20 .50
39 Mike Greenwell .08 .25
40 Andy Benes .08 .25
41 Kevin Brown .20 .50
42 Mo Vaughn .20 .50
43 Dennis Eckersley .20 .50
44 Ken Hill .08 .25
45 Cecil Fielder .20 .50
46 Bobby Jones .08 .25
47 Tom Glavine .30 .75
48 Wally Joyner .20 .50
49 Ellis Burks .20 .50
50 Jason Bere .08 .25
51 Randy Johnson .50 1.25
52 Darryl Kile .20 .50
53 Jeff Montgomery .08 .25
54 Alex Fernandez .08 .25
55 Kevin Appier .20 .50
56 Brian McRae .08 .25
57 John Wetteland .20 .50
58 Bob Tewksbury .08 .25
59 Todd Van Poppel .08 .25
60 Ryne Sandberg 1.00 2.50
61 Bret Barberie .08 .25
62 Phil Plantier .08 .25
63 Chris Hoiles .08 .25
64 Tony Phillips .08 .25
65 Salomon Torres .08 .25
66 Juan Guzman .08 .25
67 Paul O'Neill .30 .75
68 Dante Bichette .20 .50
69 Lenny Dykstra .20 .50
70 Ivan Rodriguez .30 .75
71 Dean Palmer .20 .50
72 Brett Butler .20 .50
73 Rick Aguilera .20 .50
74 Robby Thompson .08 .25
75 Jim Abbott .30 .75
76 Al Martin .08 .25
77 Roberto Hernandez .08 .25
78 Jay Buhner .20 .50
79 Devon White .20 .50
80 Travis Fryman .20 .50
81 Jeromy Burnitz .20 .50
82 John Burkett .08 .25
83 Orlando Merced .08 .25
84 Jose Rijo .08 .25
85 Eddie Murray .50 1.25
86 Howard Johnson .08 .25
87 Chuck Carr .08 .25
88 Pedro Martinez .50 1.25
89 Charlie Hayes .08 .25
90 Matt Williams .20 .50
91 Steve Finley .20 .50
92 Pat Listach .08 .25
93 Sandy Alomar Jr. .08 .25
94 Delino DeShields .08 .25
95 Rod Beck .08 .25
96 Todd Zeile UER .20 .50
Card misnumbered 97
97 Duane Ward UER .08 .25
Card misnumbered 98
98 Darryl Hamilton .08 .25
99 John Olerud .20 .50
100 Andre Dawson .20 .50
101 Ozzie Smith .75 2.00
102 Rick Wilkins .08 .25
103 Alan Trammell .20 .50
104 Jeff Blauser .08 .25
105 Bret Boone .20 .50
106 J.T. Snow .20 .50
107 Kenny Lofton .20 .50
108 Cal Ripken Jr. 1.50 4.00
109 Carlos Baerga .08 .25
110 Bip Roberts .08 .25
111 Barry Larkin .30 .75
112 Mark Langston .08 .25
113 Ozzie Guillen .20 .50
114 Chad Curtis .08 .25
115 Dave Hollins .08 .25
116 Reggie Sanders .20 .50
117 Jeff Conine .20 .50
118 Mark Whiten .08 .25
119 Tony Gwynn .60 1.50
120 John Kruk .20 .50
121 Eduardo Perez .08 .25
122 Walt Weiss .08 .25
123 Don Mattingly 1.25 3.00
124 Rickey Henderson .50 1.25
125 Mark McGwire 1.25 3.00
126 Wade Boggs .30 .75
127 Bobby Bonilla .08 .25
128 Jeff King .08 .25
129 Jack McDowell .08 .25
130 Albert Belle .20 .50
131 Greg Maddux .75 2.00
132 Dennis Martinez .20 .50
133 Jose Canseco .30 .75
134 Bryan Harvey .08 .25
135 Dave Fleming .08 .25
136 Larry Walker .20 .50
137 Ken Caminiti .20 .50
138 Doug Drabek .08 .25
139 Alex Gonzalez .08 .25
140 Darren Daulton .20 .50
141 Ruben Sierra .20 .50
142 Kirk Rueter .08 .25
143 Raul Mondesi .20 .50
144 Greg Vaughn .08 .25
145 Danny Tartabull .08 .25
146 Eric Karros .20 .50
147 Chuck Knoblauch .20 .50
148 Mike Mussina .30 .75
149 Brady Anderson .20 .50
150 Paul Molitor .20 .50
151 Bo Jackson .50 1.25
152 Jeff Bagwell .30 .75
153 Gregg Jefferies UER .08 .25
Name spelled Greg on front
154 Rafael Palmeiro .30 .75
155 Orel Hershiser .20 .50
156 Derek Bell .08 .25
157 Jeff Kent .30 .75
158 Craig Biggio .30 .75
159 Marquis Grissom .20 .50
160 Matt Mieske .08 .25
161 Jay Bell .20 .50
162 Sammy Sosa .50 1.25
163 Robin Ventura .20 .50
164 Deion Sanders .30 .75
165 Jimmy Key .20 .50
166 Cal Eldred .08 .25
167 David McCarty .08 .25
168 Carlos Garcia .08 .25
169 Willie Greene .08 .25
170 Michael Jordan RC 4.00 10.00
171 Roberto Mejia .08 .25
172 Phil Hiatt UER .08 .25
Card misnumbered 72
173 Marc Newfield .08 .25
174 Kevin Stocker .08 .25
175 Randy Johnson STA .50 1.25
176 Ivan Rodriguez STA .20 .50
177 Frank Thomas STA .50 1.25
178 Roberto Alomar STA .30 .75
179 Travis Fryman STA .20 .50
180 Cal Ripken Jr. STA 1.50 4.00
181 Juan Gonzalez STA .08 .25
182 Ken Griffey Jr. STA 1.00 2.50
183 Albert Belle STA .20 .50
184 Greg Maddux STA .75 2.00
185 Mike Piazza STA .75 2.00
186 Fred McGriff STA .30 .75
187 Robby Thompson STA .08 .25
188 Matt Williams STA .20 .50
189 Jeff Blauser STA .08 .25
190 Barry Bonds STA 1.25 3.00
191 Lenny Dykstra STA .20 .50
192 David Justice STA .08 .25
193 Ken Griffey Jr. PF .60 1.50
194 Barry Bonds PF .60 1.50
195 Frank Thomas PF .30 .75
196 Juan Gonzalez PF .08 .25
197 Randy Johnson PF .30 .75
198 Chuck Carr PF .08 .25
199 B.Bonds HES/J.Gonzalez 1.25 3.00
200 Griffey Jr. HES/D.Mattingly 1.50 4.00
201 Roberto Alomar HES .30 .75
Carlos Baerga
202 Dave Winfield HES .50 1.25
Robin Yount
203 M.Piazza HES/T.Salmon .75 2.00
204 Albert Belle HES .50 1.25
Frank Thomas
205 Cliff Floyd HES .20 .50
Rondell White
206 K.Puckett HES/T.Gwynn .60 1.50
207 R.Clemens HES/G.Maddux 1.00 2.50
208 Mike Piazza WC .50 1.25
209 J.Canseco WC Off Head .30 .75
210 Frank Thomas WC .30 .75
211 Roberto Alomar WC .20 .50
212 Barry Bonds WC .60 1.50
213 Rickey Henderson WC .30 .75
214 John Kruk WC .08 .25
215 Juan Gonzalez WC .08 .25
216 Ken Griffey Jr. WC .60 1.50
217 Roberto Alomar FOLD SP .60 1.50
218 Craig Biggio FOLD .20 .50
219 Cal Ripken Jr. FOLD .75 2.00
220 Mike Piazza FOLD .50 1.25
221 Brent Gates FOLD .08 .25
222 Walt Weiss FOLD .08 .25
223 Bobby Bonilla FOLD .08 .25
224 Ken Griffey Jr. FOLD .60 1.50
225 Barry Bonds FOLD .60 1.50
226 Barry Bonds FUN .60 1.50
227 Joe Carter FUN .08 .25
228 Mike Greenwell FUN .08 .25
229 Ken Griffey Jr. FUN .60 1.50
230 John Kruk FUN .08 .25
231 Mike Piazza FUN .50 1.25
232 Kirby Puckett FUN .50 1.25
233 John Smoltz FUN .20 .50
234 Rick Wilkins FUN .08 .25
235 Ken Griffey Jr. CL .60 1.50
236 Frank Thomas CL .20 .50
237 Barry Bonds CL .60 1.50
238 Mike Piazza CL .50 1.25
239 Tim Salmon CL .20 .50
240 Juan Gonzalez CL .08 .25
P172 Ken Griffey Jr. Promo 1.50 4.00

1994 Fun Pack Scratch Offs

1 American League .08 .25
2 Atlanta Braves .08 .25
3 Baltimore Orioles .08 .25
4 Boston Red Sox .08 .25
5 California Angels .08 .25
6 Chicago Cubs .08 .25
7 Chicago White Sox .08 .25
8 Cincinnati Reds .08 .25
9 Cleveland Indians .08 .25
10 Colorado Rockies .08 .25
11 Detroit Tigers .08 .25
12 Florida Marlins .08 .25
13 Houston Astros .08 .25
14 Kansas City Royals .08 .25
15 Los Angeles Dodgers .08 .25
16 Milwaukee Brewers .08 .25
17 Minnesota Twins .08 .25
18 Montreal Expos .08 .25
19 National League .08 .25
20 New York Mets .08 .25
21 New York Yankees .08 .25
22 Oakland Athletics .08 .25
23 Philadelphia Phillies .08 .25
24 Pittsburgh Pirates .08 .25
25 San Diego Padres .08 .25
26 San Francisco Giants .08 .25
27 Seattle Mariners .08 .25
28 St. Louis Cardinals .08 .25
29 Texas Rangers .08 .25
30 Toronto Blue Jays .08 .25

1976 Funky Facts

This 40-card standard-size set is subtitled "The Wierd [sic] World of Baseball". A paper insert included with the set carries a checklist on its back. Inside a white outer border and a color inner border, the fronts feature colorful cartoon drawings. A trivia question appears above each picture in a pale yellow bar. Each back shows five trivia questions and their answers. The first question repeats the question found on card fronts.
COMPLETE SET 4.00 10.00
COMMON CARD .10 .25

1963 Gad Fun Cards

This set of 1963 Fun Cards were issued by a sports illustrator by the name of Gad from Minneapolis, Minnesota. The cards are printed on cardboard stock paper. The borderless fronts have black and white line drawings. A fun sport's fact or player career statistic is depicted in the drawing. The backs of the first six cards display numbers used to play the game explained on card number 6. The other backs carry a cartoon with a joke or riddle. Copyright information is listed on the lower portion of the card.
COMPLETE SET (84) 37.50 75.00
1 Babe Ruth 4.00 8.00
2 Lost Baseballs Fact .25 .50
3 Baseball Slang .25 .50
Fireman
4 Baseball Hurling Fact .25 .50
5 Lou Gehrig 2.50 5.00
6 Number Game Directions .25 .50
7 Baseball Fact .25 .50
Consecutive Home Runs
8 Old Hoss Radbourne .50 1.00
10 Joe Nuxhall .38 .75
11 Ty Cobb 2.50 5.00
12 Baseball Slang .25 .50
Jake
13 Pop Schriver .25 .50
14 Boston Red Sox .25 .50
15 John Taylor .25 .50
16 Cincinnati Red Stockings .25 .50
17 Runs Scored in a Game .25 .50
18 Baseball Slang .25 .50
Duster
19 1908 Baseball Fact .25 .50
20 Evar Swanson .25 .50
21 1929 World Series Pinch Hitters .25 .50
22 Rogers Hornsby .75 1.50
23 Highlanders .25 .50
24 Baseball Slang .25 .50
Strawberry
25 Lew Flick .25 .50
26 Cy Young 1.50 3.00
27 Jim Konstanty .25 .50
28 Carl Weilman .25 .50
29 Warren Rosar .25 .50
30 Baseball Slang .25 .50
Rabbit Ears
31 Graham McNamee .25 .50
32 Ty Cobb 2.50 5.00
Batting Record
33 Joe DiMaggio 2.50 5.00
34 Babe Ruth 4.00 8.00
Earnings
35 Baseball Slang .25 .50
Chinese Homer
36 Ed Delahanty .38 .75
37 1912 Detroit Tiger Team Strike .25 .50
38 Bobo Holloman .25 .50
39 Walter Johnson 1.50 3.00
40 Sam Crawford .50 1.00
41 Lifetime Record .25 .50
Stolen Bases
42 Baseball Slang .25 .50
Showboat
43 Lou Gehrig/23 Bases-loaded Homers 2.50 5.00
44 Yankee Stadium .25 .50
45 Nick Altrock .50 1.00
46 Moses Walker .50 1.00
Welday Walker
47 Joseph Borden .25 .50
48 Baseball Slang .25 .50
Around the Horn
49 Hugh Duffy .50 1.00
50 Longest Game .25 .50
Baseball History
51 Jim Scott .25 .50
52 Longest Homer in 1919 .25 .50
53 Record .25 .50
Runs Scored in One Inning
54 Baseball Slang .25 .50
Jockey
55 Umpires in 1871 .25 .50
57 Eddie Collins .50 1.00
58 Milwaukee Braves .25 .50
59 Bill Wambsganss .25 .50
60 Baseball Slang .25 .50
Annie Oakley
61 Bob Feller .50 1.00
62 Wally Pipp .25 .50
63 Shortest World Series Game .25 .50
64 Chicago White Sox .25 .50
65 Cleveland Indians .25 .50
66 Baseball Slang .25 .50
Baltimore Chop
67 14 Pitchers Used in One Game .25 .50

1888 G and B Chewing Gum Co E223

These cards measure approximately 1" by 2 1/8" and primarily feature players from the National League. This is one of the few nineteenth century issues which are not tobacco related. The set was issued by the G and B Chewing Gum Co and is the first set baseball issue released by a gum or candy company. The cards are unnumbered and we have sequenced them in alphabetical order. If more than one pose is known, we have put the number of said poses next to the player's name. The complete set price only includes one of each variation. Portraits are worth approximately 1.5X times the value of the drawings. Some cards were recently discovered and added to this checklist so any further additions are appreciated.
COMPLETE SET 250000.00 500000.00
1 Cap Anson 15000.00 30000.00
2 Lady Baldwin (3) 5000.00 10000.00
3 Sam Barkley 5000.00 10000.00
4 Steve Brady 5000.00 10000.00
5 Bill Brown (2) 5000.00 10000.00
6 Dan Brouthers 5000.00 10000.00
7 Charlie Buffington 5000.00 10000.00
8 Oyster Burns 6000.00 12000.00
9 Bob Caruthers 5000.00 10000.00
10 John Clarkson 10000.00 20000.00
11 Pop Smith 5000.00 10000.00
12 John Coleman 5000.00 10000.00
13 Charles Comiskey 15000.00 30000.00
14 Roger Connor (2) 10000.00 20000.00
15 Ed Daily 5000.00 10000.00
16 Pat Deasley 5000.00 10000.00
17 Jim Donahue 5000.00 10000.00
18 Pat Dorgan 5000.00 10000.00
19 Dude Esterbrook 5000.00 10000.00
20 Buck Ewing 10000.00 20000.00
21 Charlie Ferguson 6000.00 12000.00
22 Frank Flint 6000.00 12000.00
23 Charles Getzein 5000.00 10000.00
24 Jack Glasscock 5000.00 10000.00
25 Kid Gleason 7500.00 15000.00
26 Frank Hankinson 5000.00 10000.00
27 Ned Hanlon 10000.00 20000.00
28 Pete Hotaling 5000.00 10000.00
29 Richard Johnston 5000.00 10000.00
30 Tim Keefe (3) 10000.00 20000.00
31 Mike Kelly (2) 20000.00 40000.00
32 August Krock 5000.00 10000.00
33 Connie Mack 20000.00 40000.00
34 Kid Madden 5000.00 10000.00
35 George Miller 5000.00 10000.00
36 John Morrill 5000.00 10000.00
37 Henry Porter 6000.00 12000.00
38 James Mutrie MG 5000.00 10000.00
39 Sam Nicoll 5000.00 10000.00
40 Tip O'Neill 6000.00 12000.00
41 Jim O'Rourke 15000.00 30000.00
42 Fred Pfeffer 5000.00 10000.00
43 Al Reach 25000.00 50000.00
44 Danny Richardson (2) 5000.00 10000.00
45 Yank Robinson 5000.00 10000.00
46 Chief Roseman 5000.00 10000.00
47 Jimmy Ryan (2) 7500.00 15000.00
48 William J. Sowders 5000.00 10000.00
49 Albert G. Spalding 60000.00 120000.00
50 Martin J. Sullivan 5000.00 10000.00
51 Billy Sunday (2) 15000.00 30000.00
52 Ezra Sutton 5000.00 10000.00
53 Mike Tiernan (2) 5000.00 10000.00
54 Sam Thompson 15000.00 30000.00
55 Lawrence Twitchell 5000.00 10000.00
56 George Van Haltren 5000.00 10000.00
57 John Montgomery Ward 15000.00 30000.00
58 Curt Welch 6000.00 12000.00
59 Mickey Welch (2) 15000.00 30000.00
60 Grasshopper Whitney 5000.00 10000.00
61 Pete Wood 5000.00 10000.00

1993 Gahan Wilson Monster Baseball

Produced by Mirage Publishing. This mini-set was issued in a standard wrapper, and features illustrations of monsters playing on various fictitious baseball teams. The backs have statistics for the players and biographical information. Read about such players as Eddy Gein of the Serials, and Spikes Lugosi of the Suckers. The cards are unnumbered. Artwork by Gahan Wilson.
COMPLETE SET (10) 5.00 12.00
COMMON PLAYER (1-10) .60 1.50

1976 Galasso Baseball's Great Hall of Fame

These 32 cards feature players considered among the all time greats. This was the first of many collector issue sets released by Renato Galasso Inc. Many of these sets were released as premiums with orders to RGI. This set is sequenced in alphabetical order.
COMPLETE SET 10.00 25.00
1 Luke Appling .20 .50
2 Ernie Banks .40 1.00
3 Yogi Berra .40 1.00
4 Roy Campanella .40 1.00
5 Roberto Clemente 1.25 3.00
6 Alvin Dark .10 .25
7 Joe DiMaggio 1.25 3.00
8 Bob Feller .30 .75
9 Whitey Ford .30 .75
10 Jimmy Foxx .40 1.00
(Jimmie)
11 Lou Gehrig 1.25 3.00
12 Charlie Gehringer .20 .50
13 Henry Greenberg .20 .50
14 Gabby Hartnett .20 .50
15 Carl Hubbell .30 .75
16 Al Kaline .30 .75
17 Mickey Mantle 1.50 4.00
18 Willie Mays .75 2.00
19 Johnny Mize .20 .50
20 Stan Musial .60 1.50
21 Mel Ott .20 .50
22 Satchell Paige .60 1.50
23 Robin Roberts .30 .75
25 Babe Ruth 1.50 4.00
26 Duke Snider .40 1.00
27 Warren Spahn .30 .75
28 Tris Speaker .30 .75
29 Honus Wagner .40 1.00
30 Ted Williams 1.25 3.00
31 Rudy York .10 .25
32 Cy Young .40 1.00

1977-84 Galasso Glossy Greats

This 270-card standard-size set was issued by Renata Galasso Inc. (a hobby card dealer) and originally offered as a free bonus when ordering hand-collated Topps sets. The set may be subdivided into six series with 45 cards per series, with one series being issued per year as follows: TCMA printed the first four series and Renata Galasso Inc. the last two. The fronts display black and white player photos bordered in white. The player's name, position and team for which he played appear in the bottom white border. The backs are white, printed in red and blue ink and carry a career summary and an advertisement for Renata Galasso Inc. The backs have a red baseball in each of the upper corners with the card number in the left one.
COMPLETE SET (270) 60.00 120.00
1 Joe DiMaggio 1.25 3.00
2 Ralph Kiner .15 .40
3 Don Larsen .12 .30
4 Robin Roberts .15 .40
5 Roy Campanella .30 .75
6 Smoky Burgess .08 .20
7 Mickey Mantle 1.25 3.00
8 Willie Mays .75 2.00
9 George Kell .15 .40
10 Ted Williams 1.00 2.50
11 Carl Furillo .12 .30
12 Bob Feller .15 .40
13 Casey Stengel .30 .75
14 Richie Ashburn .15 .40
15 Gil Hodges .15 .40
16 Stan Musial .75 2.00
17 Don Newcombe .12 .30
18 Jackie Jensen .12 .30
19 Lou Boudreau .15 .40
20 Jackie Robinson .75 2.00
21 Billy Goodman .08 .20
22 Satchel Paige .40 1.00
23 Hoyt Wilhelm .15 .40
24 Duke Snider .30 .75
25 Whitey Ford .40 1.00
26 Monte Irvin .15 .40
27 Hank Sauer .08 .20
28 Sal Maglie .08 .20
29 Ernie Banks .30 .75
30 Billy Pierce .08 .20
31 Pee Wee Reese .30 .75
32 Al Lopez .15 .40
33 Allie Reynolds .08 .20
34 Eddie Mathews .15 .40
35 Al Rosen .08 .20
36 Early Wynn .15 .40
37 Phil Rizzuto .15 .40
38 Warren Spahn .15 .40
39 Bobby Thomson .12 .30
40 Enos Slaughter .15 .40
41 Roberto Clemente 1.00 2.50
42 Luis Aparicio .15 .40
43 Roy Sievers .08 .20
44 Hank Aaron .75 2.00
45 Mickey Vernon .08 .20
46 Lou Gehrig 1.25 3.00
47 Lefty O'Doul .08 .20
48 Chuck Klein .15 .40
49 Paul Waner .15 .40
50 Mel Ott .15 .40
51 Riggs Stephenson .08 .20
52 Dizzy Dean .15 .40
53 Frank Frisch .15 .40
54 Red Ruffing .15 .40
55 Lefty Grove .15 .40
56 Heinie Manush .15 .40
57 Jimmie Foxx .30 .75
58 Al Simmons .15 .40
59 Charlie Root .08 .20
60 Goose Goslin .15 .40
61 Mickey Cochrane .15 .40
62 Gabby Hartnett .15 .40
63 Joe Medwick .15 .40
64 Ernie Lombardi .15 .40
65 Joe Cronin .15 .40
66 Pepper Martin .08 .20
67 Jim Bottomley .15 .40
68 Bill Dickey .30 .75
69 Babe Ruth 1.50 4.00
70 Joe McCarthy MG .12 .30
71 Doc Cramer .08 .20
72 KiKi Cuyler .15 .40
73 Johnny Vander Meer .12 .30
74 Paul Derringer .08 .20
75 Fred Fitzsimmons .08 .20
76 Lefty Gomez .15 .40
77 Arky Vaughan .15 .40
78 Stan Hack .08 .20
79 Earl Averill .15 .40
80 Luke Appling .15 .40
81 Mel Harder .08 .20
82 Hank Greenberg .15 .40
83 Schoolboy Rowe .08 .20
84 Billy Herman .15 .40
85 Gabby Street .08 .20
86 Lloyd Waner .15 .40
87 Jocko Conlon .12 .30
88 Carl Hubbell .30 .75
89 Checklist 1 .08 .20
90 Checklist 2 .08 .20
91 Babe Ruth 1.50 4.00
92 Rogers Hornsby .15 .40
93 Edd Roush .15 .40
94 George Sisler .15 .40
95 Harry Heilmann .15 .40
96 Tris Speaker .30 .75
97 Burleigh Grimes .15 .40
98 John McGraw .30 .75
99 Eppa Rixey .15 .40
100 Ty Cobb 1.25 3.00
101 Zack Wheat .15 .40
102 Pie Traynor .30 .75
103 Max Carey .15 .40
104 Dazzy Vance .15 .40
105 Walter Johnson .40 1.00
106 Herb Pennock .15 .40
107 Joe Sewell .15 .40
108 Sam Rice .15 .40
109 Earle Combs .15 .40
110 Ted Lyons .15 .40
111 Eddie Collins .30 .75
112 Bill Terry .15 .40
113 Hack Wilson .15 .40
114 Rabbit Maranville .15 .40
115 Charlie Grimm .08 .20
116 Tony Lazzeri .15 .40
117 Waite Hoyt .15 .40
118 Stan Coveleski .15 .40
119 George Kelly .15 .40
120 Jimmie Dykes .08 .20
121 Red Faber .15 .40
122 Dave Bancroft .15 .40
123 Judge Landis COMM .12 .30
124 Branch Rickey .12 .30
125 Jesse Haines .15 .40
126 Carl Mays .08 .20
127 Fred Lindstrom .15 .40
128 Miller Huggins .15 .40
129 Sad Sam Jones .08 .20
130 Joe Judge .08 .20
131 Ross Youngs .15 .40
132 Bucky Harris .15 .40
133 Bob Meusel .12 .30
134 Billy Evans .12 .30
135 Checklist 3 .08 .20
136 Ty Cobb 1.25 3.00
137 Nap Lajoie .15 .40
138 Tris Speaker .15 .40
139 Heinie Groh .08 .20
140 Sam Crawford .15 .40
141 Clyde Milan .08 .20
142 Chief Bender .15 .40
143 Big Ed Walsh .15 .40
144 Walter Johnson .30 .75
145 Connie Mack MG .15 .40
146 Hal Chase .12 .30
147 Hugh Duffy .15 .40
148 Honus Wagner .30 .75
149 Tom Connolly UMP .12 .30
150 Clark Griffith .12 .30
151 Zack Wheat .15 .40
152 Christy Mathewson .30 .75
153 Grover Cleveland .30 .75
Alexander
154 Joe Jackson .60 1.50
155 Home Run Baker .15 .40
156 Ed Plank .15 .40
157 Larry Doyle .08 .20
158 Rube Marquard .15 .40
159 John Evers .15 .40
160 Joe Tinker .15 .40
161 Frank Chance .15 .40
162 Wilbert Robinson MG .12 .30
163 Roger Peckinpaugh .08 .20
164 Fred Clarke .15 .40
165 Babe Ruth 1.50 4.00
166 Wilbur Cooper .08 .20
167 Germany Schaefer .08 .20

168 Addie Joss .15 .40
169 Cy Young .15 .40
170 Ban Johnson PRES .12 .30
171 Joe Judge .08 .20
172 Harry Hooper .15 .40
173 Bill Klem UMP .12 .30
174 Ed Barrow MG .12 .30
175 Ed Cicotte .12 .30
176 Hughie Jennings MG .12 .30
177 Ray Schalk .15 .40
178 Nick Altrock .12 .30
179 Roger Bresnahan MG .15 .40
180 Checklist 4 .08 .20
The 100&000 Infield
Stuffy McInnis/
181 Lou Gehrig 1.25 3.00
182 Eddie Collins .15 .40
183 Art Fletcher CO .08 .20
184 Jimmie Foxx .15 .40
185 Lefty Gomez .15 .40
186 Oral Hildebrand .08 .20
187 General Crowder .08 .20
188 Bill Dickey .15 .40
189 Wes Ferrell .08 .20
190 Al Simmons .15 .40
191 Tony Lazzeri .15 .40
192 Sam West .08 .20
193 Babe Ruth 1.50 4.00
194 Connie Mack MG .15 .40
195 Lefty Grove .15 .40
196 Eddie Rommel .08 .20
197 Ben Chapman .08 .20
198 Joe Cronin .15 .40
199 Rick Ferrell .15 .40
200 Charlie Gehringer .15 .40
201 Jimmy Dykes .08 .20
202 Earl Averill .15 .40
203 Pepper Martin .08 .20
204 Bill Terry .15 .40
205 Pie Traynor .15 .40
206 Gabby Hartnett .15 .40
207 Frank Frisch .15 .40
208 Carl Hubbell .15 .40
209 Paul Waner .15 .40
210 Woody English .08 .20
211 Bill Hallahan .08 .20
212 Dick Bartell .08 .20
213 Bill McKechnie CO .12 .30
214 Max Carey CO .15 .40
215 John McGraw MG .15 .40
216 Jimmie Wilson .08 .20
217 Chick Hafey .15 .40
218 Chuck Klein .15 .40
219 Lefty O'Doul .08 .20
220 Wally Berger .08 .20
221 Hal Schumacher .08 .20
222 Lon Warneke .08 .20
223 Tony Cuccinello .08 .20
224 Americal League .08 .20
Team Photo
225 National League .08 .20
Team Photo
226 Roger Maris .30 .75
227 Babe Ruth 1.50 4.00
228 Jackie Robinson .75 2.00
229 Pete Gray .15 .40
230 Ted Williams 1.00 2.50
231 Hank Aaron .75 2.00
232 Mickey Mantle 1.25 3.00
233 Gil Hodges .30 .75
234 Walter Johnson .15 .40
235 Joe DiMaggio 1.25 3.00
236 Lou Gehrig 1.25 3.00
237 Stan Musial .75 2.00
238 Mickey Cochrane .15 .40
239 Denny McLain .08 .20
240 Carl Hubbell .15 .40
241 Harvey Haddix .08 .20
242 Christy Mathewson .15 .40
243 Johnny Vander Meer .08 .20
244 Sandy Koufax .30 .75
245 Willie Mays .75 2.00
246 Don Drysdale .15 .40
247 Bobby Richardson .08 .20
248 Hoyt Wilhelm .15 .40
249 Yankee Stadium .08 .20
250 Bill Terry .15 .40
251 Roy Campanella .30 .75
252 Roberto Clemente 1.00 2.50
253 Casey Stengel .15 .40
254 Ernie Banks .30 .75
255 Bobby Thomson .12 .30
256 Mel Ott .15 .40
257 Tony Oliva .08 .20
258 Satchel Paige .40 1.00
259 Joe Jackson .60 1.50
260 Nap Lajoie .15 .40
261 Bill Mazeroski .12 .30
262 Bill Wambsganss .08 .20
263 Willie McCovey .15 .40
264 Warren Spahn .15 .40
265 Lefty Gomez .15 .40
266 Dazzy Vance .15 .40
267 Sam Crawford .15 .40
268 Tris Speaker .15 .40
269 Lou Brock .30 .75
270 Cy Young .15 .40

1983 Galasso '33 Goudey Reprint

This set was issued by Renata Galasso Inc to honor the 50th anniversary of the original Goudey set. These cards have a glossy feel which are very dissimiliar to the original as well as being clearly marked on the back as reprints. The words "Renata Galasso" reprint are marked between the Goudey Gum Co and Boston near the back bottom.

COMPLETE SET (240) 15.00 40.00
1 Benny Bengough .20 .50
2 Dazzy Vance .20 .50
3 Hugh Critz .10 .25
4 Heinie Schuble .10 .25
5 Babe Herman .10 .25
6 Jimmy Dykes .10 .25
7 Ted Lyons .15 .40
8 Roy Johnson .10 .25
9 Dave Harris .10 .25
10 Glenn Myatt .10 .25
11 Billy Rogell .10 .25
12 George Pipgras .10 .25
13 Lafayette Thompson .10 .25
14 Henry Johnson .10 .25
15 Victor Sorrell .10 .25
16 George Blaeholder .10 .25
17 Watson Clark .10 .25
18 Muddy Ruel .10 .25
19 Bill Dickey .60 1.50
20 Bill Terry .20 .50
21 Phil Collins .10 .25
22 Pie Traynor .20 .50
23 Kiki Cuyler .20 .50
24 Horace Ford .10 .25
25 Paul Waner .20 .50
26 Chalmer Cissell .10 .25
27 George Connally .10 .25
28 Dick Bartell .10 .25
29 Jimmie Foxx 1.00 2.50
30 Frank Hogan .10 .25
31 Tony Lazzeri .75 2.00
32 Bud Clancy .10 .25
33 Ralph Kress .10 .25
34 Bob O'Farrell .10 .25
35 Al Simmons .60 1.50
36 Tommy Thevenow .10 .25
37 Jimmy Wilson .10 .25
38 Fred Brickell .10 .25
39 Mark Koenig .10 .25
40 Taylor Douthit .10 .25
41 Gus Mancuso .10 .25
42 Eddie Collins .15 .40
43 Lew Fonseca .10 .25
44 Jim Bottomley .15 .40
45 Larry Benton .10 .25
46 Ethan Allen .10 .25
47 Heinie Manush .20 .50
48 Marty McManus .10 .25
49 Frankie Frisch .60 1.50
50 Ed Brandt .10 .25
51 Charlie Grimm .10 .25
52 Andy Cohen .10 .25
53 Babe Ruth 1.50 4.00
54 Ray Kremer .10 .25
55 Pat Malone .10 .25
56 Red Ruffing .20 .50
57 Earl Clark .10 .25
58 Lefty O'Doul .12 .30
59 Bing Miller .10 .25
60 Waite Hoyt .12 .30
61 Max Bishop .10 .25
62 Pepper Martin .12 .30
63 Joe Cronin .15 .40
64 Burleigh Grimes .20 .50
65 Milt Gaston .10 .25
66 George Grantham .10 .25
67 Guy Bush .10 .25
68 Horace Lisenbee .10 .25
69 Randy Moore .10 .25
70 Floyd (Pete) Scott .10 .25
71 Robert J. Burke .10 .25
72 Owen Carroll .10 .25
73 Jesse Haines .12 .30
74 Eppa Rixey .15 .40
75 Willie Kamm .10 .25
76 Mickey Cochrane .75 2.00
77 Adam Comorosky .10 .25
78 Jack Quinn .10 .25
79 Red Faber .12 .30
80 Clyde Manion .10 .25
81 Sam Jones .10 .25
82 Dib Williams .10 .25
83 Pete Jablonowski .10 .25
84 Glenn Spencer .10 .25
85 Heinie Sand .10 .25
86 Phil Todt .10 .25
87 Frank O'Rourke .10 .25
88 Russell Rollings .10 .25
89 Tris Speaker .60 1.50
90 Jess Petty .10 .25
91 Tom Zachary .10 .25
92 Lou Gehrig 1.25 3.00
93 John Welch .10 .25
94 Bill Walker .10 .25
95 Alvin Crowder .10 .25
96 Willis Hudlin .10 .25
97 Joe Morrissey .10 .25
98 Wally Berger .10 .25
99 Tony Cuccinello .10 .25
100 George Uhle .10 .25
101 Richard Coffman .10 .25
102 Travis Jackson .15 .40
103 Earle Combs .12 .30
104 Fred Marberry .10 .25
105 Bernie Friberg .10 .25
106 Napoleon Lajoie 1.00 2.50
107 Heinie Manush .12 .30
108 Joe Kuhel .10 .25
109 Joe Cronin .60 1.50
110 Goose Goslin .20 .50
111 Monte Weaver .10 .25
112 Fred Schulte .10 .25
113 Oswald Bluege .10 .25
114 Luke Sewell .10 .25
115 Cliff Heathcote .10 .25
116 Eddie Morgan .10 .25
117 Rabbit Maranville .12 .30
118 Val Picinich .10 .25
119 Rogers Hornsby .75 2.00
120 Carl Reynolds .10 .25
121 Walter Stewart .10 .25
122 Alvin Crowder .10 .25
123 Jack Russell .10 .25
124 Earl Whitehill .10 .25
125 Bill Terry .20 .50
126 Joe Moore .10 .25
127 Mel Ott .75 2.00
128 Chuck Klein .20 .50
129 Hal Schumacher PIT .10 .25
130 Fred Fitzsimmons .10 .25
131 Fred Frankhouse .10 .25
132 Jim Elliott .10 .25
133 Fred Lindstrom .12 .30
134 Sam Rice .20 .50
135 Woody English .10 .25
136 Flint Rhem .10 .25
137 Fred(Red) Lucas .10 .25
138 Herb Pennock .20 .50
139 Ben Cantwell .10 .25
140 Bump Hadley .10 .25
141 Ray Benge .10 .25
142 Paul Richards .10 .25
143 Glenn Wright .10 .25
144 Babe Ruth 1.50 4.00
145 Rube Walberg .10 .25
146 Walter Stewart PIT .10 .25
147 Leo Durocher .20 .50
148 Eddie Farrell .10 .25
149 Babe Ruth 1.50 4.00
150 Ray Kolp .10 .25
151 Jake Flowers .10 .25
152 Zack Taylor .10 .25
153 Buddy Myer .10 .25
154 Jimmie Foxx 1.00 2.50
155 Joe Judge .10 .25
156 Danny MacFayden .10 .25
157 Sam Byrd .10 .25
158 Moe Berg .75 2.00
159 Oswald Bluege .10 .25
160 Lou Gehrig 1.25 3.00
161 Al Spohrer .10 .25
162 Leo Mangum .10 .25
163 Luke Sewell .10 .25
164 Lloyd Waner .20 .50
165 Joe Sewell .12 .30
166 Sam West .10 .25
167 Jack Russell .10 .25
168 Goose Goslin .20 .50
169 Al Thomas .10 .25
170 Harry McCurdy .10 .25
171 Charlie Jamieson .10 .25
172 Billy Hargrave .10 .25
173 Roscoe Holm .10 .25
174 Warren(Curly) Ogden .10 .25
175 Dan Howley MG .10 .25
176 John Ogden .10 .25
177 Walter French .10 .25
178 Jackie Warner .10 .25
179 Fred Leach .10 .25
180 Eddie Moore .10 .25
181 Babe Ruth 1.50 4.00
182 Andy High .10 .25
183 Rube Walberg .10 .25
184 Charley Berry .10 .25
185 Bob Smith .10 .25
186 John Schulte .10 .25
187 Heinie Manush .15 .40
188 Rogers Hornsby .75 2.00
189 Joe Cronin .20 .50
190 Fred Schulte .10 .25
191 Ben Chapman .10 .25
192 Walter Brown .10 .25
193 Lynford Lary .10 .25
194 Earl Averill .20 .50
195 Evar Swanson .10 .25
196 Leroy Mahaffey .10 .25
197 Rick Ferrell .12 .30
198 Jack Burns .10 .25
199 Tom Bridges .10 .25
200 Bill Hallahan .10 .25
201 Ernie Orsatti .10 .25
202 Gabby Hartnett .20 .50
203 Lon Warneke .10 .25
204 Riggs Stephenson .10 .25
205 Heinie Meine .10 .25
206 Gus Suhr .10 .25
207 Mel Ott .75 2.00
208 Bernie James .10 .25
209 Adolfo Luque .10 .25
210 Virgil Davis .10 .25
211 Hack Wilson .75 2.00
212 Billy Urbanski .10 .25
213 Earl Adams .10 .25
214 John Kerr .10 .25
215 Russ Van Atta .10 .25
216 Lefty Gomez .60 1.50
217 Frank Crosetti .15 .40
218 Wes Ferrell .10 .25
219 Mule Haas .10 .25
220 Lefty Grove .75 2.00
221 Dale Alexander .10 .25
222 Charley Gehringer .75 2.00
223 Dizzy Dean 1.00 2.50
224 Frank Demaree .10 .25
225 Bill Jurges .10 .25
226 Charley Root .10 .25
227 Billy Herman .15 .40
228 Tony Piet .10 .25
229 Arky Vaughan .15 .40
230 Carl Hubbell .75 2.00
231 Joe Moore FIELD .10 .25
232 Lefty O'Doul .12 .30
233 Johnny Vergez .10 .25
234 Carl Hubbell .75 2.00
235 Fred Fitzsimmons .10 .25
236 George Davis .10 .25
237 Gus Mancuso .10 .25
238 Hugh Critz .10 .25
239 Leroy Parmelee .10 .25
240 Hal Schumacher .12 .30

1984 Galasso Baseball Collector Series

COMPLETE SET (20) 5.00 12.00
1 Roberto Clemente 1.25 3.00
2 Duke Snider .30 .75
3 Sandy Koufax 1.00 2.50
4 Carl Hubbell .30 .75
5 Ty Cobb .75 2.00
6 Willie Mays 1.00 2.50
7 Jackie Robinson .50 1.25
8 Joe DiMaggio 1.00 2.50
9 Stan Musial .75 2.00
10 Pie Traynor .30 .75
11 Yogi Berra .50 1.25
12 Babe Ruth 1.25 3.00
13 Brooks Robinson .30 .75
14 Walter Johnson .50 1.25
15 Ted Williams 1.00 2.50
16 Bill Dickey .20 .50
17 Lou Gehrig 1.00 2.50
18 Hank Aaron 1.00 2.50
19 Eddie Mathews .50 1.25
20 Mickey Mantle 1.50 4.00

1984 Galasso Hall of Famers Ron Lewis

These 45 deckle edge cards measure approximately 2 3/4" by 5". The full bleed fronts have pictures of Ron Lewis oil paintings. The backs have vital statistics, a brief biography and career stats. The checklist card back says the set is numbered out of 10,000 and gives the set number. This set only covers Hall of Famers from 1936 through 1946.

COMPLETE SET (45) 10.00 25.00
1 Ty Cobb 1.25 3.00
2 Babe Ruth 1.50 4.00
3 Walter Johnson .60 1.50
4 Christy Mathewson .60 1.50
5 Honus Wagner .60 1.50
6 Nap Lajoie .50 1.25
7 Tris Speaker .50 1.25
8 Cy Young .60 1.50
9 Morgan Bulkeley .30 .75
10 Ban Johnson .30 .75
11 John McGraw .30 .75
12 Connie Mack .30 .75
13 George Wright .30 .75
14 Grover Alexander .60 1.50
15 Alexander Cartwright .30 .75
16 Henry Chadwick .30 .75
17 Eddie Collins .50 1.25
18 Lou Gehrig 1.25 3.00
19 Willie Keeler .30 .75
20 George Sisler .30 .75
21 Cap Anson .30 .75
22 Charles Comiskey .30 .75
23 Candy Cummings .30 .75
24 Buck Ewing .30 .75
25 Charlie Radbourne .30 .75
26 A.G. Spalding .30 .75
27 Rogers Hornsby .60 1.50
28 Judge Landis .30 .75
29 Roger Bresnahan .30 .75
30 Dan Brouthers .30 .75
31 Fred Clarke .30 .75
32 Jimmy Collins .30 .75
33 Ed Delahanty .30 .75
34 Hugh Duffy .30 .75
35 Hughie Jennings .30 .75
36 Mike King Kelly .30 .75
37 Jim O'Rouke .30 .75
38 Wilbert Robinson .30 .75
39 Jesse Burkett .30 .75
40 Frank Chance .30 .50
41 Jack Chesbro .30 .75
42 Johnny Evers .30 .75
43 Joe Tinker .30 .75
44 Eddie Plank .30 .75
45 Galasso Hall of Fame CL .30 .75

1984 Galasso Reggie Jackson

Produced by Renata Galasso, this 30-card standard-size set features color action player photos with turquoise borders. The player's first name appears in yellow script at the lower left corner. A small black-and-white cut-out photo of Jackson batting appears in the lower right corner. The horizontal backs are white and carry a pale blue box that contains career highlights. The same cut-out batting photo appears to the left of the box. The backs of card numbers 22-30 join to form a three-by-three card puzzle showing various baseball cards of Jackson against the background of his number 44 pinstriped jersey. A mini version of this set was also made.

COMPLETE SET (30) 6.00 15.00
COMMON PLAYER (1-30) .20 .50
*MINI SET: 2X VALUE
1B Reggie Jackson AU/(Stat Card) 15.00 40.00

1985-86 Galasso Gooden

Issued over two years, this standard-size set features then young sensation Dwight Gooden at the beginning of his career. The 1985 cards have blue borders, while the 1986 cards have yellow borders. These cards were issued by Renata Galasso, Inc. who were then among the largest baseball card dealers.

COMPLETE SET 6.00 15.00
COMMON CARD .10 .25
16 Dwight Gooden .30 .75
Hank Aaron

1986 Galasso Mattingly

This 30 card standard-size set was issued by Renata Galasso, Inc. and featured Yankee slugger Don Mattingly. Cards numbered 1-21 feature front photos and the backs have questions/answers. The last nine cards in the set form a puzzle back.

COMPLETE SET (30) 6.00 15.00
COMMON CARD .30 .75

1981 Garvey Gafline

This one-card microfiche set features a small portrait of the Los Angeles Dodgers player, Steve Garvey, printed with his biographical information and career statistics on GAFLINE 08 film.

1 Steve Garvey 8.00 20.00

1920 Gassler's American Maid Bread D381-1

These cards measure approximately 2" by 3". The cards have a photo on most of the card with the player's name and position on the bottom.The back has an advertisment for Gassler's Bread. The cards are unnumbered and we have sequenced them alphabetically by team which are also sequenced alphabetically.

COMPLETE SET 750.00 1500.00
1 Kid Gleason MG 150.00 300.00
2 Harry Hooper 200.00 400.00
3 Dick Kerr 150.00 300.00
4 Amos Strunk 100.00 200.00
5 George Burns 100.00 200.00
6 W. L. Gardner 100.00 200.00
7 Rip Collins 100.00 200.00
8 Wm. Fewster 100.00 200.00
9 Harry Harper 100.00 200.00
10 Waite Hoyt 200.00 400.00
11 Miller Huggins MG 200.00 400.00
12 M.J. McNally 100.00 200.00
13 Bob Meusel 150.00 300.00
14 Walter Pipp 125.00 250.00
15 Jack Quinn 100.00 200.00
16 Robert Roth 100.00 200.00
17 Wally Schang 125.00 250.00
18 Aaron Ward 100.00 200.00
19 Wm. Jacobson 100.00 200.00
20 Clyde Milan 125.00 250.00
21 Walter Holke 100.00 200.00
22 P. J. Kilduff 100.00 200.00
23 Zach Wheat 200.00 400.00
24 Charles Deal 100.00 200.00
25 Charles Hollacher 100.00 200.00
26 Zeb Terry 100.00 200.00
27 Geo. J. Burns 100.00 200.00
28 Cecil Causey 100.00 200.00
29 Hugh Jennings MG 200.00 400.00
30 Arthur Nehf 125.00 250.00
31 John Rawlings 100.00 200.00
32 Bill Ryan 100.00 200.00
33 Pat Shea 100.00 200.00
34 Earl Smith 100.00 200.00
35 Frank Snyder 100.00 200.00
36 Jeff Pfeffer 100.00 200.00
37 Ty Cobb 1250.00 2500.00

1911-14 General Baking D304

These cards, which measure 1 3/4" by 2 1/2" feature drawings of leading players. Many of the players in this set were members of the 1911 pennant winners, leading one to believe that this set was issued sometime the next summer. Various other bread manufacturers also produced this set, most noticeably Brunner's Bread and Butter Krust. Other companies that issued these cards include Weber Bakery and Martens Bakery.

COMPLETE SET (25) 3000.00 6000.00
1 J. Frank Baker 750.00 1500.00
2 Jack Barry 500.00 1000.00
3 George Bell 500.00 1000.00
4 Charles Bender 750.00 1500.00
5 Frank Chance 1000.00 2000.00
6 Hal Chase 1000.00 2000.00
7 Ty Cobb 3000.00 6000.00
8 Eddie Collins 2000.00 4000.00
9 Otis Crandall 500.00 1000.00
10 Sam Crawford 1000.00 2000.00
11 John Evers 1000.00 2000.00
12 Arthur Fletcher 500.00 1000.00
13 Charles Herzog 500.00 1000.00
14 Billy Kelly 500.00 1000.00
15 Napoleon Lajoie 1500.00 3000.00
16 Rube Marquard 1000.00 2000.00
17 Christy Mathewson 2500.00 5000.00
18 Fred Merkle 500.00 1000.00
19 Chief Meyers 500.00 1000.00
20 Marty O'Toole 500.00 1000.00
21 Nap Rucker 500.00 1000.00
22 Arthur Shafer 500.00 1000.00
23 Fred Tenney 500.00 1000.00
24 Honus Wagner 3000.00 6000.00
25 Cy Young 2500.00 5000.00

1985 General Mills Stickers

Found in boxes of Cheerios and Honey Nut Cheerios in Canada, each General Mills sticker card features two stickers, with a National League player on the left and an American League player on the right. Each sticker pair measures approximately 3 3/4" by 2 3/8" while each individual player sticker measures 1 7/8" by 2 3/8". On a white background, the fronts feature color player portraits, with the player's name in a yellow bar under the photo. The National League player's team and position (in French and English) appear in a red bar under the photo, while the American League player's team and position (also in French and English) appear in a blue bar. The players' cap team logos have been airbrushed. The General Mills logo is printed inside a triangle in the upper left corner of each sticker. The backs are blank. The set features one player per team. The pairs are valued at the sum of the individual player values. Some players are featured with more than one partner, e.g. Gary Carter is found with either Tom Brunansky or Dave Stieb and Steve Garvey is found with either George Bell or Jim Rice. The stickers are unnumbered and checklisted below in alphabetical order by National Leaguers (1-12) and American Leaguers (13-26). The number of the sticker that each player is paired with is as follows: 1/15, 1/23, 2/16, 3/13, 3/22, 4/21, 5/26, 6/19, 7/24, 8/18, 9/14, 10/25, 11/17 and 12/20.

COMPLETE SET (26) 8.00 20.00
1 Gary Carter DP .75 2.00
2 Andre Dawson .40 1.00
3 Steve Garvey DP .20 .50
4 Jeff Leonard .08 .25
5 Dale Murphy .40 1.00
6 Terry Puhl .08 .25
7 Johnny Ray .08 .25
8 Ryne Sandberg 1.50 4.00
9 Mike Schmidt 1.00 2.50
10 Ozzie Smith .60 1.50
11 Mario Soto .08 .25
12 Fernando Valenzuela .20 .50
13 Buddy Bell .20 .50
14 George Brett 1.25 3.00
15 Tom Brunansky .08 .25
16 Alvin Davis .20 .50
17 Carlton Fisk .60 1.50
18 Mike Hargrove .20 .50
19 Reggie Jackson .75 2.00
20 Dwayne Murphy .08 .25
21 Eddie Murray .60 1.50
22 Jim Rice .20 .50
23 Dave Stieb .08 .25
24 Lou Whitaker .30 .75
25 Dave Winfield .60 1.50
26 Robin Yount .60 1.50

1986 General Mills Booklets

Printed on thin glossy stock, each of these six booklets measures approximately 15" by 3 13/16" when unfolded; each single player (and the complete booklet when folded) measures approximately 2 9/16" by 3 13/16". Each booklet features ten color player head shots, five on each side. The players' cap logos have been airbrushed. The sixth (non-player) panel is an entry for a contest to win a day with your favorite player at spring training in 1987. The player's statistics in English and French appear under each photo. The title card carries the booklet number in the top right corner. The set is sometimes referred to as the "Cheerios" set as it was inserted inside Cheerios cereal boxes; Cheerios is a product of General Mills. Booklets still in the original clear cellophane protective wrapping are worth an additional ten percent over the prices listed below.

COMPLETE SET (60) 100.00 200.00
1A Wade Boggs 4.00 10.00
1B Kirk Gibson 1.50 4.00
1C Rickey Henderson 6.00 15.00
1D Don Mattingly 12.00 25.00
1E Jack Morris 1.50 4.00
1F Lance Parrish .75 2.00
1G Jim Rice 1.50 4.00
1H Dave Righetti .75 2.00
1I Cal Ripken 20.00 50.00
1J Lou Whitaker 2.50 6.00
2A Harold Baines 1.50 4.00
2B Phil Bradley .75 2.00
2C George Brett 10.00 25.00
2D Carlton Fisk 4.00 10.00
2E Ozzie Guillen 3.00 8.00
2F Kent Hrbek 1.50 4.00
2G Reggie Jackson 5.00 12.00
2H Dan Quisenberry .75 2.00
2I Bret Saberhagen 1.50 4.00
2J Frank White .75 2.00
3A Jesse Barfield .75 2.00
3B George Bell .75 2.00
3C Bill Caudill .75 2.00
3D Tony Fernandez .75 2.00
3E Damaso Garcia .75 2.00
3F Lloyd Moseby .75 2.00
3G Rance Mulliniks .75 2.00
3H Dave Stieb 1.50 4.00
3I Willie Upshaw .75 2.00
3J Ernie Whitt .75 2.00
4A Gary Carter 4.00 10.00
4B Jack Clark .75 2.00
4C George Foster .75 2.00
4D Dwight Gooden 2.50 6.00
4E Gary Matthews .75 2.00
4F Willie McGee 1.50 4.00
4G Ryne Sandberg 8.00 20.00
4H Mike Schmidt 5.00 12.00
4I Lee Smith 1.50 4.00
4J Ozzie Smith 8.00 20.00
5A David Concepcion 1.50 4.00
5B Pedro Guerrero .75 2.00
5C Terry Kennedy .75 2.00
5D Dale Murphy 3.00 8.00
5E Graig Nettles 1.50 4.00
5F Dave Parker 1.50 4.00
5G Tony Perez 4.00 10.00
5H Steve Sax .75 2.00
5I Bruce Sutter 4.00 10.00
5J Fernando Valenzuela 1.50 4.00
6A Hubie Brooks .75 2.00
6B Andre Dawson 4.00 10.00
6C Mike Fitzgerald .75 2.00
6D Vance Law .75 2.00
6E Tim Raines 1.50 4.00
6F Jeff Reardon .75 2.00
6G Bryn Smith .75 2.00
6H Jason Thompson .75 2.00
6I Tim Wallach .75 2.00
6J Mitch Webster .75 2.00

1987 General Mills Booklets

Printed on thin glossy stock, each of these six booklets measures approximately 15" by 3 3/4" when unfolded; each single player (and the complete booklet when folded) measures approximately 2 9/16" by 3 3/4". Each booklet features ten color player head shots, five on each side from a respective grouping (each division and both Canadian teams). The sixth (non-player) panel is an entry for a contest to win a day with your favorite player at Spring Training in 1988. The players' cap logos have been airbrushed. Player statistics in English and French appear under each photo. The title card carries the booklet number in the top right corner. The set is sometimes referred to as the "Cheerios" set as it was inserted inside Cheerios cereal boxes; Cheerios is a product of General Mills. Booklets still in the original clear cellophane protective wrapping are worth an additional ten percent over the prices listed below.

COMPLETE SET (60) 8.00 20.00
1A Jesse Barfield .08 .25
1B George Bell .08 .25
1C Tony Fernandez .20 .50
1D Kelly Gruber .08 .25
1E Tom Henke .08 .25
1F Jimmy Key .30 .75
1G Lloyd Moseby .08 .25
1H Dave Stieb .08 .25
1I Willie Upshaw .08 .25
1J Ernie Whitt .08 .25
2A Wade Boggs .40 1.25
2B Roger Clemens .60 1.50
2C Kirk Gibson .20 .50
2D Rickey Henderson .60 1.50
2E Don Mattingly 1.25 3.00
2F Jack Morris .20 .50
2G Eddie Murray .50 1.25
2H Pat Tabler .08 .25
2I Dave Winfield .40 1.25
2J Robin Yount .40 1.25
3A Phil Bradley .08 .25
3B George Brett .75 2.00
3C Jose Canseco .60 1.50
3D Carlton Fisk .50 1.25
3E Reggie Jackson .50 1.25
3F Wally Joyner .40 1.00
3G Kirk McCaskill .08 .25
3H Larry Parrish .08 .25
3I Kirby Puckett .60 1.50
3J Dan Quisenberry .08 .25
4A Hubie Brooks .08 .25
4B Mike Fitzgerald .08 .25
4C Andres Galarraga .30 .75
4D Vance Law .08 .25
4E Andy McGaffigan .08 .25
4F Bryn Smith .08 .25
4G Jason Thompson .08 .25
4H Tim Wallach .08 .25
4I Mitch Webster .08 .25
4J Floyd Youmans .08 .25
5A Gary Carter .50 1.25
5B Dwight Gooden .30 .75
5C Keith Hernandez .20 .50
5D Willie McGee .20 .50
5E Tim Raines .20 .50
5F R.J. Reynolds .08 .25
5G Ryne Sandberg .60 1.50
5H Mike Schmidt .50 1.25
5I Ozzie Smith .75 2.00
5J Darryl Strawberry .20 .50
6A Kevin Bass .08 .25
6B Eric Davis .30 .75
6C Bill Doran .08 .25
6D Pedro Guerrero .08 .25
6E Tony Gwynn 1.00 2.50
6F Dale Murphy .40 1.00
6G Dave Parker .20 .50
6H Steve Sax .08 .25
6I Mike Scott .08 .25
6J Fernando Valenzuela .20 .50

1956 Gentry Magazine Ty Cobb

NNO Ty Cobb 40.00 100.00

1933 George C. Miller R300

The cards in this 32-card set measure 2 1/2" by 3". This set of soft tone color baseball cards issued in 1933 by the George C. Miller Company consists of 16 players from each league. The bottom portion of the reverse contained a premium offer and many cards are found with this section cut off. Cards without the coupon are considered fair to good condition at best. The Andrews card (with coupon intact) is considered extremely scarce in relation to all other common players. Very few copies are known of the Andrews with the coupon attached.

COMPLETE SET (32) 60000.00 120000.00
1 Dale Alexander 1500.00 3000.00
2 Ivy Andrews 10000.00 20000.00
3 Earl Averill 2500.00 5000.00
4 Dick Bartell 1500.00 3000.00
5 Wally Berger 1500.00 3000.00
6 Jim Bottomley 2500.00 5000.00
7 Joe Cronin 2500.00 5000.00
8 Dizzy Dean 3000.00 6000.00
9 Bill Dickey 3000.00 6000.00
10 Jimmy Dykes 1500.00 3000.00
11 Wes Ferrell 2000.00 4000.00
12 Jimmy Foxx 3000.00 6000.00
(Jimmie)
13 Frank Frisch 2500.00 5000.00
14 Charlie Gehringer 2500.00 5000.00
15 Goose Goslin 2500.00 5000.00
16 Charlie Grimm 1500.00 3000.00
17 Lefty Grove 3000.00 6000.00
18 Chick Hafey 2000.00 4000.00
19 Ray Hayworth 1500.00 3000.00
20 Chuck Klein 2500.00 5000.00
21 Rabbit Maranville 2500.00 5000.00
22 Oscar Melillo 1500.00 3000.00
23 Lefty O'Doul 2000.00 4000.00
24 Mel Ott 3000.00 6000.00
25 Carl Reynolds 1500.00 3000.00
26 Red Ruffing 2500.00 5000.00
27 Al Simmons 2500.00 5000.00
28 Joe Stripp 1500.00 3000.00
29 Bill Terry 2500.00 5000.00
30 Lloyd Waner 2500.00 5000.00
31 Paul Waner 2500.00 5000.00
32 Lon Warneke 1500.00 3000.00

1972 Gera Postcard

This postcard was given away at what was supposed to be lady umpire Bernice Gera's first game. As the only game she actually umpired in was one day later, this card features several factual errors. The postcard features a photo of Gera on top and then the basic information about the game she umpired in. Gera only umpired in one game before concluding her professional career.

1 Bernice Gera 4.00 10.00

1886 Giants Old Judge N167

These cards measure approximately 1 1/2" by 2 1/2". All the players portrayed are members of the New York National team which became the Giants. Though their existance has not been confirmed, it was rumored that the Deasley and Mutrie cards may exist. We have sequenced this set in alphabetical order.

COMPLETE SET 150000.00 300000.00
1 Roger Connor 25000.00 50000.00
2 Larry Corcoran 7500.00 15000.00
3 Tom Deasley
4 Mike Dorgan 7500.00 15000.00
5 Dude Esterbrook 7500.00 15000.00
6 Buck Ewing 25000.00 50000.00
7 Joe Gerhardt 7500.00 15000.00
8 Pete Gillespie 7500.00 15000.00
9 Tim Keefe 25000.00 50000.00
10 Jim Mutrie MG
11 James O'Rourke 25000.00 50000.00
12 Danny Richardson 7500.00 15000.00
13 John M. Ward 25000.00 50000.00
14 Mickey Welsh (sic) 25000.00 50000.00

1886 Giants J.Wood Studio Cabinets

These blank-backed cabinets, which measure 4 1/8" by 6 1/2" were issued by the J.Wood Photo Studios. These images are the same images later used in the Old Judge N167 Giants set. Since these cabinets are unnumbered, we have sequenced them in alphabetical order. Listed prices reference raw VG condition.

1 Roger Connor 2500.00 4000.00
2 Larry Corcoran 1500.00 2500.00
3 Pat Deasley 1500.00 2500.00
4 Mike Dorgan 1500.00 2500.00
5 Dude Esterbrook 1500.00 2500.00
6 Buck Ewing 2500.00 4000.00
7 Joe Gerhardt 1500.00 2500.00
8 Pete Gillespie 1500.00 2500.00
9 Tim Keefe 2500.00 4000.00
10 Jim Mutrie MG 1500.00 2500.00
11 Jim O'Rourke 2500.00 4000.00
12 Danny Richardson 1500.00 2500.00
13 John Ward 2500.00 4000.00
14 Mickey Welch 1500.00 2500.00
15 New York Giants Team (No Caps) 1500.00 2500.00
16 New York Giants Team (with Caps) 3000.00 5000.00

1906 Giants Ullman's Art Frame Series

These cards, issued the year after the Giants won their first World Series, show an action view of the player or players inside a brown or green border made to resemble a picture frame. At the bottom is a gold area made to look like an identification tag for a picture containing a description of the scene and players identified. There are probably more cards in this set so additions to the checklist are appreciated. Other postcards, on non-sports related subjects were directly available from the company in 1906 and thus it is therefore possible for these to have been readily available from the company in direct sale format.

COMPLETE SET (3)	1500.00	3000.00
1 Red Ames	400.00	800.00
2 Mike Donlin	500.00	1000.00
3 George Ferguson	300.00	600.00
4 Matty Fitzgerald	300.00	600.00
5 Bill Gilbert	300.00	600.00
6 Christy Mathewson	1250.00	2500.00
7 Harry Mathewson	300.00	600.00
8 Dan McGann	300.00	600.00
9 Joe McGinnity	600.00	1200.00
10 John McGraw MG	600.00	1200.00
11 Sammy Strang Frank Bowerman	300.00	600.00
12 Hooks Wiltse	300.00	600.00

1909 Giants Derby Cigar

These 12 blank-backed cards measure 1 3/4" by 2 3/4" and were assumed to be issued by the Derby Cigar Co. They feature members of the New York Giants and the players photo is in an oval design in the middle with the name and position at the bottom

COMPLETE SET (12)	6000.00	12000.00
1 Josh Devore	1250.00	2500.00
2 Larry Doyle	1500.00	3000.00
3 Art Fletcher	1250.00	2500.00
4 Buck Herzog	1250.00	2500.00
5 Rube Marquard	2500.00	5000.00
6 Christy Mathewson	4000.00	8000.00
7 John McGraw MG	3000.00	6000.00
8 Fred Merkle	1500.00	3000.00
9 Chief Meyers	1500.00	3000.00
10 Red Murray	1250.00	2500.00
11 Fred Snodgrass	1500.00	3000.00
12 Hooks Wiltse	1250.00	2500.00

1913 Giants Evening Sun

This group of 21 newspaper supplements, which measured 12" by 9" were produced to honor the pennant winning 1913 New York Giants. The artist who drew these sketches was Lawrence Semon, who also produced postcards featuring many of these players. Since these are unnumbered, we have sequenced this set in alphabetical order.

COMPLETE SET		
1 George Burns	250.00	500.00
2 Doc Crandall	125.00	250.00
3 Al Demaree	125.00	250.00
4 Art Fletcher	125.00	250.00
5 Art Fromme	125.00	250.00
6 Grover Hartley	125.00	250.00
7 Buck Herzog	150.00	300.00
8 Rube Marquard	250.00	500.00
9 Christy Mathewson	500.00	1000.00
10 Moose McCormick	125.00	250.00
11 John McGraw MG	250.00	500.00
12 Fred Merkle	125.00	250.00
13 Chief Meyers	150.00	300.00
14 Red Murray	125.00	250.00
15 Wilbert Robinson CO	200.00	400.00
16 Art Shafer	125.00	250.00
17 Fred Snodgrass	150.00	300.00
18 Jeff Tesreau	125.00	250.00
19 Jim Thorpe	1500.00	3000.00
20 Hooks Wiltse	125.00	250.00
21 Art Wilson	125.00	250.00

1932 Giants Schedule

This set of the 1932 New York Giants was issued in a postcard format with a black and white action photo on the front. Player information is printed in the wide bottom margin. The back displays the team's schedule. It has been alleged that the Hubbell was counterfeited. However, many dealers believe an inordinate amount of the Hubbell's were printed and a warehouse find made them appear to be too clean to be more than 60 years old. It seems like the Hubbell commonly seen in the marketplace is just a double print and has been noted as such. Some other dealers believe the common Hubbell variety is a proof issue. In addition, cards of Clarence Mitchell and Hall of Famer Fred Lindstrom were recently discovered.

COMPLETE SET	2500.00	5000.00
COMMON DP		
1 Ethan Allen	75.00	150.00
2 Herman Bell	75.00	150.00
3 Hugh Critz	75.00	150.00
4 Fred Fitzsimmons	150.00	300.00
5 Chick Fullis	75.00	150.00
6 Sam Gibson	75.00	150.00
7 Fran Healy Sic, Healey	75.00	150.00
8 Frank Hogan	75.00	150.00
9 Carl Hubbell DP	75.00	150.00
10 Carl Hubbell	400.00	800.00
11 Travis Jackson	200.00	400.00
12 Len Koenecke	75.00	150.00
13 Sam Leslie	75.00	150.00
14 Fred Lindstrom	200.00	400.00
15 Dolph Luque	125.00	250.00
16 Clarence Mitchell	75.00	150.00
17 Jim Mooney	75.00	150.00
18 Bob O'Farrell	125.00	250.00
19 Mel Ott	400.00	800.00
20 Roy Parmelee	75.00	150.00
21 Bill Terry	300.00	600.00
22 Johnny Vergez	75.00	150.00
23 Bill Walker	75.00	150.00

1948 Giants Team Issue

This 26-card set, which measures 6 1/2" by 9" features black-and-white photos of the New York Giants with white borders and was issued by Harry M. Stevens, Inc. A facsimile autograph is printed across the front. The backs are blank. The cards are unnumbered and checklisted below in alphabetical order. Mel Ott was originally issued with this set but was pulled after being let go in midseason. He was replaced by Leo Durocher as manager. As far as can be determined there is an even number of Ott and Durocher cards issued. The set is considered complete with either the Ott or the Durocher card.

COMPLETE SET (26)	75.00	150.00
1 Jack Conway	2.50	5.00
2 Walker Cooper	3.00	6.00
3 Leo Durocher MG	12.50	25.00
4 Sid Gordon	2.50	5.00
5 Andy Hansen	2.50	5.00
6 Clint Hartung	2.50	5.00
7 Larry Jansen	4.00	8.00
8 Sheldon Jones	2.50	5.00
9 Monte Kennedy	2.50	5.00
10 Buddy Kerr	2.50	5.00
11 Dave Koslo	2.50	5.00
12 Thornton Lee	2.50	5.00
13 Mickey Livingston	2.50	5.00
14 Whitey Lockman	4.00	8.00
15 Jack Lohrke	2.50	5.00
16 Willard Marshall	2.50	5.00
17 Johnnie McCarthy	2.50	5.00
18 Earl McGowan	2.50	5.00
19 Johnny Mize	7.50	15.00
20 Bobo Newsom	4.00	8.00
21 Met Ott MG	12.50	25.00
22 Ray Poat	2.50	5.00
23 Bobbie Rhawn	2.50	5.00
24 Bill Rigney	4.00	8.00
25 Bob Thomson	5.00	10.00
26 Ken Trinkle	2.50	5.00
27 Wes Westrum	3.00	6.00

1949 Giants Team Issue

This 25-card set features black-and-white photos of the New York Giants with white borders and was issued by Harry M. Stevens, Inc. A facsimile autograph is printed across the front. The backs are blank. The cards are unnumbered and checklisted below in alphabetical order.

COMPLETE SET (25)	75.00	150.00
1 Hank Behrman	2.50	5.00
2 Walker Cooper	2.50	5.00
3 Leo Durocher MG	10.00	20.00
4 Fred Fitzsimmons CO	2.50	5.00
5 Frank Frisch CO	7.50	15.00
6 Augie Galan	2.50	5.00
7 Sid Gordon	2.50	5.00
8 Bert Haas	2.50	5.00
9 Andy Hansen	2.50	5.00
10 Clint Hartung	2.50	5.00
11 Bob Hofman	2.50	5.00
12 Larry Jansen	4.00	8.00
13 Sheldon Jones	2.50	5.00
14 Monte Kennedy	2.50	5.00
15 Buddy Kerr	2.50	5.00
16 Dave Koslo	2.50	5.00
17 Mickey Livingston	2.50	5.00
18 Whitey Lockman	4.00	8.00
19 Willard Marshall	2.50	5.00
20 Johnny Mize	7.50	15.00
21 Don Mueller	2.50	5.00
22 Ray Poat	2.50	5.00
23 Bobbie Rhawn	2.50	5.00
24 Bill Rigney	4.00	8.00
25 Bob Thomson	5.00	10.00

1954 Giants Jacobellis

These black and white photos, which were issued as Grandstand Magazine premiums, measure approximately 8 1/4" by 10" feature members of the 1954 New York Giants. The fronts feature the players photo, his name and on the bottom a small note that the photo was taken by Bill Jacobellis. Since these photos are unnumbered, we have sequenced them in alphabetical order.

COMPLETE SET	60.00	120.00
1 John Antonelli	6.00	12.00
2 Al Dark	6.00	12.00
3 Ruben Gomez	5.00	10.00
4 Whitey Lockman	6.00	12.00
5 Willie Mays	25.00	50.00
6 Don Mueller	5.00	10.00
7 Dusty Rhodes	5.00	10.00
8 New York Giants	10.00	20.00

1955 Giants Golden Stamps

This 32-stamp set features color photos of the New York Giants and measures approximately 2" by 2 5/8". The stamps are designed to be placed in a 32-page album which measures approximately 8 3/8" by 10 15/16". The album contains black-and-white drawings of players with statistics and life stories. The stamps are unnumbered and listed below according to where they fall in the album.

COMPLETE SET (32)	100.00	200.00
1 1954 Giants Team	6.00	12.00
2 Leo Durocher MG	10.00	20.00
3 Johnny Antonelli	1.25	2.50
4 Sal Maglie	2.00	4.00
5 Ruben Gomez	1.25	2.50
6 Hoyt Wilhelm	6.00	12.00
7 Marv Grissom	1.25	2.50
8 Jim Hearn	1.25	2.50
9 Paul Giel	1.25	2.50
10 Al Corwin	1.25	2.50
11 George Spencer	1.25	2.50
12 Don Liddle	1.25	2.50
13 Windy McCall	1.25	2.50
14 Al Worthington	1.25	2.50
15 Wes Westrum	1.25	2.50
16 Whitey Lockman	1.50	3.00
17 Dave Williams	1.25	2.50
18 Hank Thompson	2.00	4.00
19 Alvin Dark	2.00	4.00
20 Monte Irvin	6.00	12.00
21 Willie Mays	30.00	60.00
22 Don Mueller	1.25	2.50
23 Dusty Rhodes	1.25	2.50
24 Ray Katt	1.25	2.50
25 Joe Amalfitano	1.25	2.50
26 Billy Gardner	1.25	2.50
27 Foster Castleman	1.25	2.50
28 Bobby Hoffman	1.25	2.50
29 Bill Taylor	1.25	2.50
30 Manager and Coaches	2.00	4.00
31 Bobby Weinstein BB	1.25	2.50
32 Polo Grounds	10.00	20.00
XX Album	2.50	5.00

1956 Giants Jay Publishing

This 12-card set of the New York Giants measures approximately 5 1/8" by 7". The fronts feature black-and-white posed player photos with the player's and team name printed below in the white border. These cards were packaged 12 to a packet and originally sold for 25 cents by mail. The backs are blank. The cards are unnumbered and checklisted below in alphabetical order.

COMPLETE SET (12)	30.00	60.00
1 Johnny Antonelli	2.00	4.00
2 Al Dark	2.50	5.00
3 Ruben Gomez	1.50	3.00
4 Monte Irvin	3.00	6.00
5 Whitey Lockman	2.50	5.00
6 Sal Maglie	2.50	5.00
7 Willie Mays	10.00	20.00
8 Don Mueller	1.50	3.00
9 Bill Rigney	2.00	4.00
10 Hank Thompson	2.00	4.00
11 Wes Westrum	1.50	3.00
12 Dave Williams	1.50	3.00

1957 Giants Jay Publishing

This 12-card set of the New York Giants measures approximately 5" by 7". The fronts feature black-and-white posed player photos with the player's and team name printed below in the white border. These cards were packaged 12 to a packet and originally sold for 25 cents by mail. The backs are blank. The cards are unnumbered and checklisted below in alphabetical order. A pre-Rookie Card of Bill White (precedes his Rookie Card by 2 years) is featured in this set.

COMPLETE SET (12)	30.00	60.00
1 Johnny Antonelli	2.50	5.00
2 Jackie Brandt	1.50	3.00
3 Eddie Bressoud	1.50	3.00
4 Ruben Gomez	1.50	3.00
5 Willie Mays	10.00	20.00
6 Don Mueller	1.50	3.00
7 Bill Rigney	2.00	4.00
8 Bill Sarni	1.50	3.00
9 Red Schoendienst	3.00	6.00
10 Daryl Spencer	1.50	3.00
11 Bill White	3.00	6.00
12 Allan Worthington	1.50	3.00

1958 Giants Jay Publishing

This 12-card set of the San Francisco Giants measures approximately 5" by 7" and features black-and-white player photos in a white border. These cards were packaged 12 to a packet. The backs are blank. The cards are unnumbered and checklisted below in alphabetical order.

COMPLETE SET (12)	25.00	50.00
1 John Antonelli	2.00	4.00
2 Curt Barclay	1.50	3.00
3 Paul Giel	1.50	3.00
4 Ruben Gomez	1.50	3.00
5 Willie Kirkland	1.50	3.00
6 Whitey Lockman	2.00	4.00
7 Willie Mays	10.00	20.00
8 Danny O'Connell	1.50	3.00
9 Hank Sauer	2.00	4.00
10 Bob Schmidt	1.50	3.00
11 Daryl Spencer	1.50	3.00
12 Al Worthington	1.50	3.00

1958 Giants S.F. Call-Bulletin

The cards in this 25-card set measure approximately 2" by 4". The 1958 San Francisco Call-Bulletin set of unnumbered cards features black print on orange paper. These cards were given away as inserts in the San Francisco Call-Bulletin newspaper. The backs of the cards list the Giants home schedule and a radio station ad. The cards are entitled "Giant Payoff" and feature San Francisco Giant players only. The bottom part of the card (tab) could be detached as a ticket stub; hence, cards with the tab intact are worth approximately double the prices listed below. The catalog designation for this set is M126. The Tom Bowers card was issued in very short supply; also Bressoud, Jablonski, and Kirkland are tougher to find than the others; all of these tougher cards are indicated as SP's in our checklist.

COMPLETE SET (25)	700.00	1400.00
COMMON CARD (1-25)	5.00	10.00
COMMON SP	60.00	120.00
1 John Antonelli	6.00	12.00
2 Curt Barclay	5.00	10.00
3 Tom Bowers SP	325.00	600.00
4 Ed Bressoud SP	60.00	120.00
5 Orlando Cepeda	25.00	50.00
6 Ray Crone	5.00	10.00
7 Jim Davenport	6.00	12.00
8 Paul Giel	10.00	20.00
9 Ruben Gomez	5.00	10.00
10 Marv Grissom	5.00	10.00
11 Ray Jablonski SP	60.00	120.00
12 Willie Kirkland SP	75.00	150.00
13 Whitey Lockman	6.00	12.00
14 Willie Mays	125.00	250.00
15 Mike McCormick	6.00	12.00
16 Stu Miller	6.00	12.00
17 Ray Monzant	5.00	10.00
18 Danny O'Connell	5.00	10.00
19 Bill Rigney MG	5.00	10.00
20 Hank Sauer	6.00	12.00
21 Bob Schmidt	5.00	10.00
22 Daryl Spencer	5.00	10.00
23 Valmy Thomas	5.00	10.00
24 Bobby Thomson	10.00	20.00
25 Al Worthington	5.00	10.00

1958-61 Giants Falstaff Beer Team Photos

This four-card set features color photos of the 1958, 1959, 1960, and 1961 San Francisco Giants teams. Each card measures approximately 6 1/4" by 9" and displays the Falstaff logo on the front. The backs carry a team promotional message.

COMPLETE SET (4)	60.00	120.00
COMMON CARD (1-4)	12.50	25.00
1 1958 Giants Team Photo	25.00	50.00
2 1959 Giants Team Photo	20.00	40.00

1959 Giants Jay Publishing

This 12-card set of the San Francisco Giants measures approximately 5" by 7" and features black-and-white player photos in a white border. These cards were packaged 12 to a packet and originally sold for 25 cents. The backs are blank. The cards are unnumbered and checklisted below in alphabetical order.

COMPLETE SET	20.00	50.00
1 Jackie Brandt	1.25	3.00
2 Orlando Cepeda	3.00	8.00
3 Jim Davenport	1.25	3.00
4 Sam Jones	1.25	3.00
5 Willie Kirkland	1.25	3.00
6 Hobie Landrith	1.25	3.00
7 Willie Mays	8.00	20.00
8 Stu Miller	1.25	3.00
9 Jack Sanford	1.25	3.00
10 Hank Sauer	1.50	4.00
11 Bob Schmidt	1.25	3.00
12 Daryl Spencer	1.25	3.00

1960 Giants Jay Publishing

This 12-card set of the San Francisco Giants measures approximately 5" by 7" and features black-and-white player photos in a white border. These cards were packaged 12 to a packet. The backs are blank. The cards are unnumbered and checklisted below in alphabetical order. Willie McCovey is featured in his Rookie Card year.

COMPLETE SET (12)	30.00	60.00
1 John Antonelli	1.00	2.50
2 Don Blasingame	1.00	2.50
3 Eddie Bressoud	1.00	2.50
4 Orlando Cepeda	2.50	6.00
5 Jim Davenport	1.00	2.50
6 Sam Jones	1.00	2.50
7 Willie Kirkland	1.00	2.50
8 Willie Mays	8.00	20.00
9 Willie McCovey	5.00	12.00
10 Mike McCormick	1.00	2.50
11 Jack Sanford	1.00	2.50
12 Bob Schmidt	1.00	2.50

1961 Giants Jay Publishing

This 12-card set of the San Francisco Giants measures approximately 5" by 7". The fronts feature black-and-white posed player photos with the player's and team name printed below in the white border. These cards were packaged 12 in a packet. The backs are blank. The cards are unnumbered and checklisted below in alphabetical order. Juan Marichal is featured in his Rookie Card year.

COMPLETE SET (12)	12.50	25.00
1 Felipe Alou	1.00	2.50
2 Don Blasingame	.60	1.50
3 Orlando Cepeda	1.50	4.00
4 Alvin Dark MG	.75	2.00
5 Jim Davenport	.75	2.00
6 Sam Jones	.60	1.50
7 Harvey Kuenn	.75	2.00
8 Juan Marichal	4.00	10.00
9 Willie Mays	5.00	12.00
10 Mike McCormick	.60	1.50
11 Stu Miller	.60	1.50
12 Bob Schmidt	.60	1.50

1962 Giants Jay Publishing

This 12-card set of the San Francisco Giants measures approximately 5" by 7". The fronts feature black-and-white posed player photos with the player's and team name printed below in the white border. These cards were packaged 12 in a packet. The backs are blank. The cards are unnumbered and checklisted below in alphabetical order.

COMPLETE SET (12)	30.00	60.00
1 Felipe Alou	1.50	4.00
2 Ed Bailey	1.00	2.50
3 Orlando Cepeda	3.00	8.00
4 Jim Davenport	1.25	3.00
5 Tom Haller	1.00	2.50
6 Chuck Hiller	1.00	2.50
7 Harvey Kuenn	1.25	3.00
8 Juan Marichal	4.00	10.00
9 Willie Mays	8.00	20.00
10 Mike McCormick	1.25	3.00
11 Stu Miller	1.00	2.50
12 Billy Pierce	1.50	4.00

1962 Giants Photo Album

Issued by the San Fransisco News Cal-Bulletin, these photos feature biographical information, a player portrait and a biography of the featured player. Each of these pages were part of a special photo album commemorating the opening of what would be pennant winning season for the 1962 Giants. Since these photos are unnumbered, we have sequenced them in the order they appeared in the photo album. Gaylord Perry appears in this set in his Rookie Card year.

COMPLETE SET	100.00	200.00
1 Al Dark MG	2.50	6.00
2 Mike McCormick	2.50	6.00
3 Stu Miller	2.00	5.00
4 Jack Sanford	2.00	5.00
5 Juan Marichal	8.00	20.00
6 Bob Bolin	2.00	5.00
7 Jim Duffalo	2.00	5.00
8 Don Larsen	3.00	8.00
9 Billy O'Dell	2.00	5.00
10 Billy Pierce	3.00	8.00
11 Dick LeMay	2.00	5.00
12 Gaylord Perry	10.00	25.00
13 Ed Bailey	2.00	5.00
14 Tom Haller	2.00	5.00
15 Joe Pignatano	2.00	5.00
16 Orlando Cepeda	6.00	15.00
17 Chuck Hiller	2.00	5.00
18 Jose Pagan	2.00	5.00
19 Jim Davenport	2.00	5.00
20 Felipe Alou	4.00	10.00
21 Willie Mays	15.00	40.00
22 Harvey Kuenn	2.50	6.00
23 Willie McCovey	8.00	20.00
24 Ernie Bowman	2.00	5.00
25 Dick Phillips	2.00	5.00
26 Manny Mota	4.00	10.00

1963 Giants Jay Publishing

This 12 card set of the San Francisco Giants measures approximately 5" by 7". The fronts feature black-and-white posed player photos with the player's and team name printed below in the white border. These cards were packaged 12 in a packet. The backs are blank. The cards are unnumbered and checklisted below in alphabetical order.

COMPLETE SET (12)	30.00	60.00
1 Felipe Alou	1.50	4.00
2 Orlando Cepeda	3.00	8.00
3 Alvin Dark MG	1.25	3.00
4 Jim Davenport	1.25	3.00
5 Tom Haller	1.00	2.50
6 Chuck Hiller	1.00	2.50
7 Willie Mays	8.00	20.00
8 Willie McCovey	4.00	10.00
9 Billy O'Dell	1.00	2.50
10 Jose Pagan	1.00	2.50
11 Billy Pierce	1.50	4.00
12 Jack Sanford	1.00	2.50

1964 Giants Jay Publishing

This 12-card set of the San Francisco Giants measures approximately 5" X 7". The fronts feature black-and-white posed player photos with the player's and team name printed below in the white border. These cards were packaged 12 to a packet and originally sold for 25 cents. The backs are blank. The cards are unnumbered and checklisted below in alphabetical order.

COMPLETE SET (12)	20.00	50.00
1 Orlando Cepeda	3.00	8.00
2 Del Crandall	1.00	2.50
3 Alvin Dark MG	1.00	2.50
4 Jim Davenport	.75	2.00
5 Tom Haller	.75	2.00
6 Juan Marichal	4.00	10.00
7 Willie Mays	8.00	20.00
8 Willie McCovey	4.00	10.00
9 Billy O'Dell	.75	2.00
10 Jose Pagan	.75	2.00
11 Jack Sanford	.75	2.00
12 Bob Shaw	.75	2.00

1965 Giants Jay Publishing

This 12-card set of the San Francisco Giants measures approximately 5" by 7". The fronts feature black-and-white posed player photos with the player's and team name printed below in the white border. These cards were packaged 12 to a packet. The backs are blank. The cards are unnumbered and checklisted below in alphabetical order.

COMPLETE SET (12)	30.00	60.00
1 Jesus Alou	1.00	2.50
2 Matty Alou	1.25	3.00
3 Orlando Cepeda	2.50	6.00
4 Jim Davenport	.75	2.00
5 Herman Franks MG	.75	2.00
6 Tom Haller	.75	2.00
7 Bob Hendley	.75	2.00
8 Juan Marichal	4.00	10.00
9 Willie Mays	8.00	20.00
10 Willie McCovey	4.00	10.00
11 Jose Pagan	.75	2.00
12 Gaylord Perry	2.00	5.00

1965 Giants Team Issue

These photos, which measure approximately 5" by 7" feature members of the 1965 San Francisco Giants. The color photos take up most of the cards with the player being identified on the bottom. The backs are blank and we have sequenced them in alphabetical order.

COMPLETE SET (10)	15.00	40.00
1 Jim Davenport	.75	2.00
2 Herman Franks MG	.75	2.00
3 Tom Haller	.75	2.00
4 Jim Ray Hart	.75	2.00
5 Juan Marichal	2.50	6.00
6 Willie Mays	15.00	40.00
7 Willie McCovey	2.50	6.00
8 Lindy McDaniel	.75	2.00
9 Gaylord Perry	2.00	5.00
10 Team Photo	1.50	4.00

1970 Giants

This 12-card set is approximately 4 1/2" X 7", with the player's name and "Giants" printed on front. Cards were printed in black and white on pebbled white stock with a blank back.

COMPLETE SET (12)	12.50	30.00
1 Bobby Bonds	2.00	5.00
2 Dick Dietz	.60	1.50
3 Charles Fox MG	.60	1.50
4 Ken Henderson	.60	1.50
5 Ron Hunt	1.25	3.00
6 Hal Lanier	.75	2.00
7 Frank Linzy	.60	1.50
8 Juan Marichal	2.00	5.00
9 Willie Mays	4.00	10.00
10 Willie McCovey	2.00	5.00
11 Gaylord Perry	2.00	5.00
12 Frank Reberger	.60	1.50

1970 Giants Chevrolet Bonds

This one-card set measures approximately 3" by 5 3/4" with the top half of the card containing a black-and-white photo of Giants outfielder, Bobby Bonds. The bottom white margin was where the collector could have the player sign his Giants autograph card which was issued by Chevrolet and Nor-Cal Leasing Co. The back is blank.

1 Bobby Bonds	4.00	10.00

1971 Giants Ticketron

The 1971 Ticketron San Francisco Giants set is a ten-card set featuring members of the division-winning 1971 San Francisco Giants. The set measures approximately 3 7/8" by 6" and features an attractive full-color photo framed by white borders on the front along with a facsimile autograph. The back contains an ad for Ticketron as well as the 1971 Giants home schedule. These unnumbered cards are listed in alphabetical order for convenience.

COMPLETE SET (10)	50.00	100.00
1 Bobby Bonds	4.00	10.00
2 Dick Dietz	1.25	3.00
3 Charles Fox MG	1.25	3.00
4 Tito Fuentes	1.25	3.00
5 Ken Henderson	2.00	5.00
6 Juan Marichal	6.00	15.00
7 Willie Mays	20.00	50.00
8 Willie McCovey	6.00	15.00
9 Don McMahon	1.25	3.00
10 Gaylord Perry	6.00	15.00

1972-76 Giants Team Issue

This 18-card set features black-and-white photos of the San Francisco Giants. The cards are unnumbered and checklisted below in alphabetical order.

COMPLETE SET (18)	20.00	50.00
1 Bobby Bonds	2.50	6.00
2 Ron Bryant	1.00	2.50
3 Don Carrithers	1.00	2.50
4 Pete Falcone	1.00	2.50
5 Charlie Fox CO	1.00	2.50
6 Alan Gallagher	1.00	2.50
7 Russ Gibson	1.00	2.50
8 Ed Goodson	1.00	2.50
9 Ed Halicki	1.00	2.50
10 Jim Howarth	1.00	2.50
11 Dave Kingman	2.00	5.00
12 Garry Maddox	2.00	5.00
13 Juan Marichal	2.50	6.00
14 Willie McCovey	2.50	6.00
15 Mike Phillips	1.00	2.50
16 Bill Rigney MG	1.00	2.50
17 Chris Speier	1.00	2.50
18 Jim Willoughby	1.00	2.50

1973 Giants TCMA 1886

This set features the New York National League Team of 1886. Since these cards are not numbered, we have sequenced them in alphabetical order.

COMPLETE SET	6.00	15.00
1 Roger Connor	.75	2.00
2 Larry Corcoran	.20	.50
3 Tom Deasley	.20	.50
4 Mike Dorgan	.20	.50
5 Dude Esterbrook	.20	.50
6 Buck Ewing	.75	2.00
7 Joe Gerhardt	.20	.50
8 Peter Gillespie	.20	.50
9 Tim Keefe	.75	2.00
10 Jim Mutrie	.30	.75
11 Jim O'Rourke	.75	2.00
12 Daniel Richardson	.20	.50
13 John M. Ward	.75	2.00
14 Mickey Welch	.75	2.00
15 Bat Boy	.20	.50

1974 Giants 1937 TCMA

This 36-card set measures 2 5/8" by 3 3/8". The cards feature orange and black photos on orange card stock. The cards are unnumbered and have been checklisted alphabetically. Reportedly, Dick Bartell objected to being in the set and more than half of the sets originally produced were destroyed.

COMPLETE SET (36)	15.00	40.00
1 Tom Baker	.60	1.50
2 Dick Bartell	.60	1.50
3 Wally Berger	.60	1.50
4 Don Brennan	.60	1.50
5 Walter Brown	.60	1.50
6 Clydell Castleman	.60	1.50
7 Lou Chiozza	.60	1.50
8 Dick Coffman	.60	1.50
9 Harry Danning	.60	1.50
10 George Davis	.60	1.50
11 Charlie English	.60	1.50
12 Fred Fitzsimmons	.60	1.50
13 Frank Gabler	.60	1.50
14 Harry Gumbert	.60	1.50
15 Mickey Haslin	.60	1.50
16 Carl Hubbell	1.00	2.50
17 Travis Jackson	.60	1.50
18 Mark Koenig	.60	1.50
19 Hank Leiber	.60	1.50
20 Sam Leslie	.60	1.50
21 Bill Lohrman	.60	1.50
22 Eddie Mayo	.60	1.50
23 Johnny McCarthy	.60	1.50
24 Cliff Melton	.60	1.50
25 Jo Jo Moore	.60	1.50
26 Mel Ott	1.50	4.00
27 Jimmy Ripple	.60	1.50
28 Hal Schumacher	.60	1.50
29 Al Smith	.60	1.50
30 Roy Spencer	.60	1.50
31 Bill Terry	.60	1.50
32 Hy Vandenberg	.60	1.50
33 Phil Weintraub	.60	1.50
34 Burgess Whitehead	.60	1.50
35 Babe Young	.60	1.50
36 Title Card	.60	1.50

1975 Giants

Most of the cards in this 12-card set measure approximately 3" by 5 1/2"; a few measure slightly smaller at 3" by 5". The fronts feature black-and-white portraits of members of the 1975 Giants team. The pictures are 2 1/2" by 3" and rest on a white card face accented only by the player's name printed in black below the photo and a facsimile autograph in the lower white margin. The backs are blank. The cards are unnumbered and checklisted below in alphabetical order.

COMPLETE SET (12)	4.00	10.00
1 Mike Caldwell	.50	1.25
2 Pete Falcone	.40	1.00
3 Marc Hill	.40	1.00
4 Gary Matthews	.60	1.50
5 Randy Moffitt	.40	1.00
6 Willie Montanez	.40	1.00
7 Steve Ontiveros	.40	1.00
8 Dave Rader	.40	1.00
9 Derrel Thomas	.40	1.00
10 Gary Thomasson	.40	1.00
11 Wes Westrum MG	.40	1.00
12 Charles Williams	.40	1.00

1975 Giants All-Time TCMA

This 13-card set features black-and-white photos with white borders of all-time New York Giants great players. The cards are unnumbered and checklisted below in alphabetical order.

COMPLETE SET (13)	5.00	12.00
1 Alvin Dark	.20	.50
2 Frankie Frisch	.40	1.00
3 Carl Hubbell	.60	1.50
4 Fred Lindstrom	.30	.75
5 Christy Mathewson	.60	1.50
6 Willie Mays	1.25	3.00
7 John McGraw MG	.30	.75
8 Mel Ott Name in black ink	.60	1.50
9 Mel Ott Name in red ink	.60	1.50
10 Bill Terry	.40	1.00
11 Bobby Thomson	.30	.75
12 Wes Westrum	.20	.50
13 Hoyt Wilhelm	.40	1.00

1975 Giants 1951 TCMA

This 34-card set features the 1951 New York Giants Team. The fronts display black-and-white player photos while the backs carry player statistics. The set includes two jumbo cards which measure approximately 3 1/2" by 5". The cards are unnumbered and checklisted below in alphabetical order with the jumbo cards listed last.

COMPLETE SET (34)	12.50	30.00
1 George Bamberger	.20	.50
2 Roger Bowman	.20	.50
3 Al Corwin	.20	.50
4 Al Dark	.60	1.50
5 Allen Gettel	.20	.50
6 Clint Hartung	.20	.50
7 Jim Hearn	.20	.50
8 Monte Irvin	.75	2.00
9 Larry Jansen	.40	1.00
10 Sheldon Jones	.20	.50
11 John Spider Jorgensen	.20	.50
12 Monte Kennedy	.20	.50
13 Alex Konikowski	.20	.50
14 Dave Koslo	.20	.50
15 Jack Kramer	.20	.50
16 Carroll Whitey Lockman	.40	1.00
17 Jack Lucky Lohrke	.20	.50
18 Sal Maglie	.60	1.50
19 Jack Maguire	.20	.50
20 Willie Mays	4.00	10.00
21 Don Mueller	.40	1.00
22 Ray Noble	.20	.50
23 Earl Rapp	.20	.50
24 Bill Rigney	.20	.50
25 George Spencer	.20	.50
26 Eddie Stanky	.40	1.00
27 Bobby Thomson	.75	2.00
28 Hank Thompson	.20	.50
29 Wes Westrum	.40	1.00
30 Davey Williams	.20	.50
31 Artie Wilson	.20	.50
32 Sal Yvars	.20	.50
33 Herman Franks CO/	.60	1.50
34 Leo Durocher MG Willie Mays	2.00	5.00

1975 Giants Team Issue

This 18-card set of the 1975 San Francisco Giants features player portraits in white borders. The cards are unnumbered and checklisted below in alphabetical order.

COMPLETE SET (18)	3.00	8.00
1 Jim Barr	.20	.50
2 Tom Bradley	.20	.50
3 Mike Caldwell	.20	.50
4 John D'Acquisto	.20	.50
5 Pete Falcone	.20	.50
6 Marc Hill	.20	.50
7 Von Joshua	.20	.50
8 Gary Matthews	.40	1.00
9 Randy Moffitt	.20	.50
10 John Motefussco	.20	.50
11 Willie Montanez	.20	.50
12 Bobby Murcer	.30	.75
13 Steve Ontiveros	.20	.50
14 Dave Radar	.20	.50
15 Chris Speier	.20	.50
16 Derrel Thomas	.20	.50
17 Wes Westrum MG	.20	.50
18 Charles Williams	.20	.50

1976 Giants Postcards

This 24-card set of the San Francisco Giants features player photos on postcard-size cards. The cards are unnumbered and checklisted below in alphabetical order.

COMPLETE SET (24)	4.00	10.00
1 Glenn Adams	.20	.50
2 Chris Arnold	.20	.50
3 Jim Barr	.20	.50
4 Mike Caldwell	.20	.50
5 John D'Acquisto	.20	.50
6 Rob Dressler	.20	.50
7 Ed Halicki	.20	.50
8 Dave Heaverlo	.20	.50
9 Larry Herndon	.20	.50
10 Marc Hill	.20	.50
11 Gary Lavelle	.20	.50
12 Gary Matthews	.40	1.00
13 Randy Moffitt	.20	.50
14 John Montefusco	.20	.50
15 Bobby Murcer	.30	.75
16 Steve Ontiveros	.20	.50
17 Dave Rader	.20	.50
18 Ken Reitz	.20	.50
19 Bill Rigney MG	.20	.50
20 Mike Sadek	.20	.50
21 Chris Speier	.20	.50
22 Derrel Thomas	.20	.50
23 Gary Thomasson	.20	.50
24 Charles Williams	.20	.50

1977 Giants

This 25-card set measures 3 1/2" by 5" and features black-and-white close-up player photos. The pictures are framed by an orange border and set on a black card face. The player's name, position and team name appear below the picture. The backs are blank. The cards are unnumbered and checklisted below in alphabetical order.

COMPLETE SET (25)	8.00	20.00
1 Joe Altobelli MG	.30	.75
2 Jim Barr	.30	.75
3 Jack Clark	.75	2.00
4 Terry Cornutt	.30	.75
5 Rob Dressler	.30	.75
6 Darrell Evans	.60	1.50
7 Frank Funk INS	.30	.75
8 Ed Halicki	.30	.75
9 Tom Haller CO	.40	1.00
10 Marc Hill	.30	.75
11 Skip James	.30	.75
12 Bob Knepper	.30	.75
13 Gary Lavelle	.30	.75
14 Bill Madlock	.60	1.50
15 Willie McCovey	1.25	3.00
16 Randy Moffitt	.30	.75
17 John Montefusco	.40	1.00
18 Marty Perez	.30	.75
19 Frank Riccelli	.30	.75
20 Mike Sadek	.30	.75
21 Hank Sauer INS	.40	1.00
22 Chris Speier	.40	1.00

23 Gary Thomasson .30 .75
24 Tommy Toms .30 .75
25 Bobby Winkles CO .30 .75

1977 Giants Team Issue

This 25-card set of the 1977 San Francisco Giants features player portraits in white borders. The cards are unnumbered and checklisted below in alphabetical order.

COMPLETE SET (25) 5.00 12.00
1 Gary Alexander .20 .50
2 Joe Altobelli MG .20 .50
3 Rob Andrews .20 .50
4 Jim Barr .20 .50
5 Jack Clark 1.25 3.00
6 Terry Cornutt .20 .50
7 Randy Elliott .20 .50
8 Darrell Evans .40 1.00
9 Tim Foli .20 .50
10 Ed Halicki .20 .50
11 Vic Harris .20 .50
12 Dave Heaverlo .20 .50
13 Marc Hill .20 .50
14 Bob Knepper .20 .50
15 Gary Lavelle .20 .50
16 Johnnie LeMaster .20 .50
17 Bill Madlock .30 .75
18 Lynn McGlothen .20 .50
19 Randy Moffitt .20 .50
20 John Montefusco .20 .50
21 Mike Sadek .20 .50
22 Darrel Thomas .20 .50
23 Gary Thomasson .20 .50
24 Terry Whitfield .20 .50
25 Charlie Williams .20 .50

1978 Giants Team Issue

This 25-card set of the 1978 San Francisco Giants features player portraits in white borders. The cards are unnumbered and checklisted below in alphabetical order.

COMPLETE SET (25) 5.00 12.00
1 Joe Altobelli MG .20 .50
2 Rob Andrews .20 .50
3 Jim Barr .20 .50
4 Vida Blue .40 1.00
5 Jack Clark .60 1.50
6 John Curtis .20 .50
7 Darrell Evans .30 .75
8 Ed Halicki .20 .50
9 Vic Harris .20 .50
10 Tom Heintzelman .20 .50
11 Larry Herndon .20 .50
12 Marc Hill .20 .50
13 Mike Ivie .20 .50
14 Skip James .20 .50
15 Bob Knepper .20 .50
16 Gary Lavelle .20 .50
17 Johnnie LeMaster .20 .50
18 Bill Madlock .40 1.00
19 Randy Moffitt .20 .50
20 John Montefusco .20 .50
21 Willie McCovey 1.00 2.50
22 Lynn McGlothen .20 .50
23 Mike Sadek .20 .50
24 Terry Whitfield .20 .50
25 Charlie Williams .20 .50

1979 Giants Police

The cards in this 30-card set measure approximately 2 5/8" by 4 1/8". The 1979 Police Giants set features cards numbered by the player's uniform number. This full color set features the player's photo, the Giants' logo, and the player's name, number and position on the front of the cards. A facsimile autograph in an attractive blue ink is also contained on the front. The backs, printed in orange and black, feature Tips from the Giants, the Giants' and sponsoring radio station, KNBR, logos and a line listing the Giants, KNBR, and the San Francisco Police Department as sponsors of the set. The 15 cards which are shown with an asterisk below were available only from the Police. The other 15 cards were given away at the ballpark on June 17, 1979. These cards look very similar to the Giants police set issued in 1980, the following year. Both sets credit Dennis Desprois photographically on each card but this (1979) set seems to have a fuzzier focus on the pictures. The sets can be distinguished on the front since this set's cards have a number sign before the player's uniform number. Also on the card backs the KNBR logo is usually left justified for the cards in the 1979 set whereas the 1980 set has the KNBR logo centered on the card back.

COMPLETE SET (30) 8.00 20.00
1 Dave Bristol MG .20 .50
2 Marc Hill .20 .50
3 Mike Sadek * .20 .50
5 Tom Haller .20 .50
6 Joe Altobelli CO * .30 .75
8 Larry Shepard CO * .30 .75
9 Heity Cruz .20 .50
10 Johnnie LeMaster .20 .50
12 Jim Davenport CO .30 .75
14 Vida Blue .40 1.00
15 Mike Ivie .20 .50
16 Roger Metzger .20 .50
17 Randy Moffitt .20 .50
18 Bill Madlock .40 1.00
21 Rob Andrews * .20 .50
22 Jack Clark * .60 1.50
25 Dave Roberts .20 .50
26 John Montefusco .30 .75
28 Ed Halicki * .20 .50
30 John Tamargo .20 .50
31 Larry Herndon .20 .50
36 Bill North * .20 .50
39 Bob Knepper * .30 .75
40 John Curtis * .20 .50
41 Darrell Evans * .60 1.50
43 Tom Griffin * .20 .50
44 Willie McCovey * 1.50 4.00
45 Terry Whitfield * .20 .50
46 Gary Lavelle * .20 .50
49 Max Venable * .20 .50

1979 Giants Team Issue

Originally sold by the Giants for 20 cents each, these cards featured members of the 1979 San Francisco Giants. More cards may be known so any additions are appreciated, these cards are not numbered so we have sequenced them in alphabetical order.

COMPLETE SET 4.00 10.00
1 Rob Andrews .20 .50
2 Vida Blue .30 .75
3 Jack Clark .40 1.00
4 Tom Griffin .20 .50
5 Ed Halicki .20 .50
6 Marc Hill .20 .50
7 Mike Ivie .20 .50
8 Willie McCovey 1.00 2.50
9 Roger Metzger .20 .50
10 Greg Minton .20 .50
11 John Montefusco .20 .50
12 Phil Nastu .20 .50
13 Bill North .20 .50
14 Mike Sadek .20 .50
15 Max Venable .20 .50

1980 Giants Eureka Federal Savings

This eight-card set of the San Francisco Giants measures approximately 9 1/2" by 12" and features art work by Todd Alan Gold. Each card displays three color drawings of the same player, two action and one portrait. The backs are blank. These complimentary cards were available at all Eureka Federal Savings branches. The cards are unnumbered and checklisted below in alphabetical order.

COMPLETE SET (8) 4.00 10.00
1 Al Holland .40 1.00
2 Gary Lavelle .40 1.00
3 Johnnie LeMaster .40 1.00
4 Milt May .40 1.00
5 Willie McCovey 2.00 5.00
6 John Montefusco .40 1.00
7 Bill North .40 1.00
8 Rennie Stennett .40 1.00

1980 Giants Greats TCMA

This 12-card standard-size set features some great Giants from both New York and San Francisco. The fronts have red borders with the player's photo inside. The player's name is printed on the bottom. The back carries a biography.

COMPLETE SET (12) 3.00 8.00
1 Willie Mays 1.00 2.50
2 Wes Westrum .08 .25
3 Carl Hubbell .40 1.00
4 Hoyt Wilhelm .20 .50
5 Bobby Thomson .20 .50
6 Frankie Frisch .30 .75
7 Bill Terry .30 .75
8 Alvin Dark .20 .50
9 Mel Ott .50 1.25
10 Christy Mathewson .50 1.25
11 Fred Lindstrom .20 .50
12 John McGraw MG .30 .75

1980 Giants Police

The cards in this 31-card set measure approximately 2 5/8" by 4 1/8". The 1980 Police San Francisco Giants set features cards numbered by the player's uniform number. This full color set features the player's photo, the Giants' logo, and the player's name, number and position on the front of the cards. A facsimile autograph in an attractive blue ink is also contained on the front. The backs, printed in orange and black, feature Tips from the Giants, the Giants' and sponsoring radio station, KNBR, logos and a line listing the Giants, KNBR, and the San Francisco Police Department as sponsors of the set. The sets were given away at the ballpark on May 31, 1980.

COMPLETE SET (31) 6.00 15.00
1 Dave Bristol MG .20 .50
2 Marc Hill .20 .50
3 Mike Sadek .20 .50
5 Jim Lefebvre CO .20 .50
6 Rennie Stennett .20 .50
7 Milt May .20 .50
8 Vern Benson CO .20 .50
9 Jim Wohlford .20 .50
10 Johnnie LeMaster .20 .50
12 Jim Davenport CO .20 .50
14 Vida Blue .30 .75
15 Mike Ivie .20 .50
16 Roger Metzger .20 .50
17 Randy Moffitt .20 .50
19 Al Holland .20 .50
20 Joe Strain .20 .50
22 Jack Clark .40 1.00
26 John Montefusco .20 .50
28 Ed Halicki .20 .50
31 Larry Herndon .20 .50
32 Ed Whitson .20 .50
36 Bill North .20 .50
38 Greg Minton .20 .50
39 Bob Knepper .20 .50
41 Darrell Evans .40 1.00
42 John Van Ornum .20 .50
43 Tom Griffin .20 .50
44 Willie McCovey 1.25 3.00
45 Terry Whitfield .20 .50
46 Gary Lavelle .20 .50
47 Don McMahon CO .20 .50

1980 Giants Team Issue

This 30-card set of the 1980 San Francisco Giants features player portraits in white borders. The cards are unnumbered and checklisted below in alphabetical order.

COMPLETE SET (30) 8.00 20.00
1 Dave Bristol .20 .50
2 Vida Blue .40 1.00
3 Bill Bordley .20 .50
4 Jack Clark .40 1.00
5 Darrell Evans .40 1.00
6 Tom Griffin .20 .50
7 Ed Halicki .20 .50
8 Larry Herndon .20 .50
9 Marc Hill .20 .50
10 Al Holland .20 .50
11 Mike Ivie .20 .50
12 Bob Knepper .20 .50
13 Gary Lavelle .20 .50
14 Johnnie LeMaster .20 .50
15 Dennis Littlejohn .20 .50
16 Milt May .20 .50
17 Roger Metzger .20 .50
18 Willie McCovey 1.50 4.00
19 Greg Minton .20 .50
20 Randy Moffitt .20 .50
21 John Montefusco .20 .50
22 Rich Murray .20 .50
23 Bill North .20 .50
24 Allen Ripley .20 .50
25 Mike Sadek .20 .50
26 Rennie Stennett .20 .50
27 Joe Strain .20 .50
28 Terry Whitfield .20 .50
29 Ed Whitson .20 .50
30 Jim Wohlford .20 .50

1981 Giants 1962 TCMA

This 36-card set was printed in 1981 by TCMA and features black-and-white photos of the 1962 San Francisco Giants team in orange borders. The backs carry player information.

COMPLETE SET (36) 6.00 15.00
1 Alvin Dark MG .20 .50
2 Whitey Lockman CO .20 .50
3 Larry Jansen CO .08 .25
4 Wes Westrum CO .08 .25
5 Ed Bailey .08 .25
6 Tom Haller .08 .25
7 Harvey Kuenn .20 .50
8 Willie Mays 2.00 5.00
9 Felipe Alou .30 .75
10 Orlando Cepeda .40 1.00
11 Chuck Hiller .08 .25
12 Jose Pagan .08 .25
13 Jim Davenport .08 .25
14 Willie McCovey .40 1.00
15 Matty Alou .20 .50
16 Manny Mota .20 .50
17 Ernie Bowman .08 .25
18 Carl Boles .08 .25
19 John Orsino .08 .25
20 Joe Pignatano .08 .25
21 Gaylord Perry .40 1.00
22 Jim Duffalo .08 .25
23 Dick LeMay .08 .25
24 Bob Garibaldi .08 .25
25 Bobby Bolin .08 .25
26 Don Larsen .20 .50
27 Mike McCormick .08 .25
28 Stu Miller .08 .25
29 Jack Sanford .08 .25
30 Billy O'Dell .08 .25
31 Juan Marichal 1.00 2.50
32 Billy Pierce .30 .75
33 Dick Phillips .08 .25
34 Cap Peterson .08 .25
35 Bob Nieman .08 .25
36 Luis Olmo .08 .25

1981 Giants Team Issue

This 22-card set of the 1981 San Francisco Giants features player photos. The cards are unnumbered and checklisted below in alphabetical order.

COMPLETE SET (22) 5.00 12.00
1 Doyle Alexander .20 .50
2 Dave Bergman .20 .50
3 Vida Blue .40 1.00
4 Fred Breining .20 .50
5 Enos Cabell .20 .50
6 Tom Griffin .20 .50
7 Al Holland .20 .50
8 Gary Lavelle .20 .50
9 Jerry Martin .20 .50
10 Milt May .20 .50
11 Randy Moffit .20 .50
12 Joe Morgan 1.25 3.00
13 Bill North .20 .50
14 Joe Pettini .20 .50
15 Allen Ripley .20 .50
16 Frank Robinson MG .60 1.50
17 Mike Sadek .20 .50
18 Billy Smith .20 .50
19 Rennie Stennett .20 .50
20 Max Venable .20 .50
21 Ed Whitson .20 .50
22 Jim Wohlford .20 .50

1982 Giants 25th Anniversary Team Issue

This 31-card set features photos of the 1982 San Francisco Giants. The cards are unnumbered and checklisted below in alphabetical order.

COMPLETE SET (31) 8.00 20.00
1 Jim Barr .20 .50
2 Dave Bergman .20 .50
3 Fred Breining .20 .50
4 Bob Brenly .60 1.50
5 Jack Clark .40 1.00
6 Jim Davenport CO .20 .50
7 Chili Davis 1.25 3.00
8 Darrell Evans .40 1.00
9 Alan Fowlkes .20 .50
10 Rich Gale .20 .50
11 Atlee Hammaker .20 .50
12 Al Holland .20 .50
13 Duane Kuiper .20 .50
14 Bill Laskey .20 .50
15 Johnnie LeMaster .20 .50
16 Gary Lavelle .20 .50
17 Jeff Leonard .20 .50
18 Renie Martin .20 .50
19 Don McMahon CO .20 .50
20 Greg Minton .20 .50
21 Joe Morgan 1.00 2.50
22 Tom O'Malley .20 .50
23 Milt May .20 .50
24 Willie McCovey 1.00 2.50
25 John Von Ornum .20 .50
26 Frank Robinson MG .75 2.00
27 Reggie Smith .30 .75
28 Guy Sularz .20 .50
29 Champ Summers .20 .50
30 Max Venable .20 .50
31 Jim Wohlford .20 .50

1983 Giants Mother's

The cards in this 20-card set measure the standard size. For the first time in 30 years, Mother's Cookies issued a baseball card set. The full color set, produced by hobbyist Barry Colla, features San Francisco Giants players only. Fifteen cards were issued at the Houston Astros vs. San Francisco Giants game of August 7, 1983. Five of the cards were redeemable by sending in a coupon. The five additional cards received from redemption of the coupon were not guaranteed to be the five needed to complete the set. The fronts feature the player's photo, his name, and the Giants' logo, while the backs feature player biographies and the Mother's Cookies logo. The backs also contain a space in which to obtain the player's autograph.

COMPLETE SET (20) 5.00 12.00
1 Frank Robinson MG 1.00 2.50
2 Jack Clark .60 1.50
3 Chili Davis .75 2.00
4 Johnnie LeMaster .20 .50
5 Greg Minton .20 .50
6 Bob Brenly .60 1.50
7 Fred Breining .20 .50
8 Jeff Leonard .20 .50
9 Darrell Evans .60 1.50
10 Tom O'Malley .20 .50
11 Duane Kuiper .20 .50
12 Mike Krukow .20 .50
13 Atlee Hammaker .20 .50
14 Gary Lavelle .20 .50
15 Bill Laskey .20 .50
16 Max Venable .20 .50
17 Joel Youngblood .20 .50
18 Dave Bergman .20 .50
19 Mike Vail .20 .50
20 Andy McGaffigan .20 .50

1983 Giants Postcards

This 27-card set measuring approximately 3 1/2 by 5 1/2 features borderless glossy color photos of the San Francisco Giants. The backs display a postcard format. The cards are unnumbered and checklisted below in alphabetical order.

COMPLETE SET (27) 6.00 15.00
1 Jim Barr .20 .50
2 Dave Bergman .20 .50
3 Fred Breining .20 .50
4 Bob Brenly .40 1.00
5 Mark Calvert .20 .50
6 Mike Chris .20 .50
7 Jack Clark .40 1.00
8 Coaches Card .20 .50
Tom McCraw;|Herm Starrette
Danny Oz
9 Chili Davis .60 1.50
10 Darrell Evans .30 .75
11 Atlee Hammaker .20 .50
12 Mike Krukow .20 .50
13 Duane Kuiper .20 .50
14 Bill Laskey .20 .50
15 Gary Lavelle .20 .50
16 Johnnie LeMaster .20 .50
17 Jeff Leonard .20 .50
18 Renie Martin .20 .50
19 Milt May .20 .50
20 Andy McGaffigan .20 .50
21 Greg Minton .20 .50
22 Tom O'Malley .20 .50
23 Joe Pettini .20 .50
24 Frank Robinson MG .60 1.50
25 Champ Summers .20 .50
26 Max Venable .20 .50
27 Joel Youngblood .20 .50

1984 Giants Mother's

The cards in this 28-card set measure the standard-size. In 1984, the Los Angeles based Mother's Cookies Co. issued five sets of cards featuring players from major league teams. The San Francisco Giants set features previous Giant All-Star selections depicted by drawings. Similar to their 1952 and 1953 issues, the cards have rounded corners. The backs of the cards contain the Mother's Cookies logo. The cards were distributed in partial sets to fans at the respective stadiums of the teams involved. Whereas 20 cards were given to each patron, a redemption card, redeemable for eight more cards was included. Unfortunately, the eight cards received by redeeming the coupon were not necessarily the eight needed to complete a set. Hobbyist Barry Colla was involved in the production of these sets.

COMPLETE SET (28) 6.00 15.00
1 Willie Mays 2.00 5.00
2 Willie McCovey 1.00 2.50
3 Juan Marichal .75 2.00
4 Gaylord Perry .60 1.50
5 Tom Haller .08 .25
6 Jim Davenport .08 .25
7 Jack Clark .30 .75
8 Greg Minton .08 .25
9 Atlee Hammaker .08 .25
10 Gary Lavelle .08 .25
11 Orlando Cepeda .40 1.00
12 Bobby Bonds .30 .75
13 John Antonelli .08 .25
14 Bob Schmidt UER/(Photo actually .08 .25
Wes Westrum)
15 Sam Jones .08 .25
16 Mike McCormick .08 .25
17 Ed Bailey .08 .25
18 Stu Miller .20 .50
19 Felipe Alou .40 1.00
20 Jim Ray Hart .08 .25
21 Dick Dietz .08 .25
22 Chris Speier .08 .25
23 Bobby Murcer .40 1.00
24 John Montefusco .08 .25
25 Vida Blue .30 .75
26 Ed Whitson .08 .25
27 Darrell Evans .30 .75
28 Giants Checklist Card .20 .50
All-Star Game Logo

1984 Giants Postcards

This 31-card set features glossy posed color player photos of the San Francisco Giants and measures approximately 3 7/16" by 5 1/2". The backs have a postcard format. The cards are unnumbered and checklisted below in alphabetical order.

COMPLETE SET (31) 3.00 8.00
1 Dusty Baker .30 .75
2 Bob Brenly .20 .50
3 Don Buford CO .08 .25
4 Jack Clark .30 .75
5 Chili Davis .40 1.00
6 Mark Davis .08 .25
7 Atlee Hammaker .08 .25
8 Mike Krukow .08 .25
9 Duane Kuiper .08 .25
10 Bill Laskey .08 .25
11 Gary Lavelle .08 .25
12 Johnnie LeMaster .08 .25
13 Jeff Leonard .08 .25
14 Randy Lerch .08 .25
15 Renie Martin .08 .25
16 Tom McCraw CO .08 .25
17 Greg Minton .08 .25
18 Fran Mullins .08 .25
19 Steve Nicosia .08 .25
20 Al Oliver .30 .75
21 Danny Ozark CO .08 .25
22 John Rabb .08 .25
23 Gene Richards .08 .25
24 Frank Robinson MG .40 1.00
25 Jeff Robinson .08 .25
26 Herm Starrette CO .08 .25
27 Scott Thompson .08 .25
28 Manny Trillo .08 .25
29 John Van Ornum .08 .25
30 Frank Williams .08 .25
31 Joel Youngblood .08 .25

1985 Giants Mother's

The cards in this 28-card set measure the standard size. In 1985, the Los Angeles based Mother's Cookies Co. again issued five sets of cards featuring players from major league teams. The San Francisco Giants set features current players depicted by photos on cards with rounded corners. The backs of the cards contain the Mother's Cookies logo. Cards were passed out at the stadium on June 30.

COMPLETE SET (28) 3.00 8.00
1 Jim Davenport MG .08 .25
2 Chili Davis .40 1.00
3 Dan Gladden .20 .50
4 Jeff Leonard .08 .25
5 Manny Trillo .08 .25
6 Atlee Hammaker .08 .25
7 Bob Brenly .08 .25
8 Greg Minton .08 .25
9 Bill Laskey .08 .25
10 Vida Blue .30 .75
11 Mike Krukow .08 .25
12 Frank Williams .08 .25
13 Jose Uribe .08 .25
14 Johnnie LeMaster .08 .25
15 Scot Thompson .08 .25
16 Dave LaPoint .08 .25
17 David Green .08 .25
18 Chris Brown .08 .25
19 Joel Youngblood .08 .25
20 Mark Davis .20 .50
21 Jim Gott .08 .25
22 Doug Gwosdz .08 .25
23 Scott Garrelts .08 .25
24 Gary Rajsich .08 .25
25 Rob Deer .20 .50
26 Brad Wellman .08 .25
27 Giants' Coaches .08 .25
Rocky Bridges
Chuck Hiller
Tom
28 Giants' Checklist .08 .25
Candlestick Park

1985 Giants Postcards

This 31-card set features glossy color player photos of the San Francisco Giants and measures approximately 3 1/2" by 5 1/2". The backs have a postcard format with the player's name printed in the upper left. The cards are unnumbered and checklisted below in alphabetical order.

COMPLETE SET (31) 3.00 8.00
1 Vida Blue .20 .50
2 Bob Brenly .08 .25
3 Rocky Bridges CO .08 .25
4 Chris Brown .08 .25
5 Jim Davenport MG .08 .25
6 Chili Davis .40 1.00
7 Mark Davis .08 .25
8 Rob Deer .20 .50
9 Scott Garrelts .08 .25
10 Dan Gladden .20 .50
11 Jim Gott .08 .25
12 David Green .08 .25
13 Doug Gwosdz .08 .25
14 Atlee Hammaker .08 .25
15 Chuck Hiller CO .08 .25
16 Mike Krukow .08 .25
17 Dave LaPoint .08 .25
18 Bill Laskey .08 .25
19 Johnnie LeMaster .08 .25
20 Jeff Leonard .08 .25
21 Tom McCraw CO .08 .25
22 Bob Miller CO .08 .25
23 Greg Minton .08 .25
24 Jack Mull CO .08 .25
25 Gary Rajsich .08 .25
26 Scot Thompson .08 .25
27 Manny Trillo .08 .25
28 Jose Uribe .08 .25
29 Brad Wellman .08 .25
30 Frank Williams .08 .25
31 Joel Youngblood .08 .25

1986 Giants Mother's

This set consists of 28 full-color, rounded-corner cards each measuring the standard size. Starter sets (only 20 cards but also including a certificate for eight more cards) were given out at the ballpark and collectors were encouraged to trade to fill in the rest of their set. Cards were originally given out at Candlestick Park on July 13th. A rookie year card of Will Clark is in this set.

COMPLETE SET (28) 6.00 15.00
1 Roger Craig MG .20 .50
2 Chili Davis .40 1.00
3 Dan Gladden .20 .50
4 Jeff Leonard .08 .25
5 Bob Brenly .08 .25
6 Atlee Hammaker .08 .25
7 Will Clark 4.00 10.00
8 Greg Minton .08 .25
9 Candy Maldonado .08 .25
10 Vida Blue .30 .75
11 Mike Krukow .08 .25
12 Bob Melvin .20 .50
13 Jose Uribe .08 .25
14 Dan Driessen .08 .25
15 Jeff D. Robinson .08 .25
16 Robby Thompson .30 .75
17 Mike LaCoss .08 .25
18 Chris Brown .08 .25
19 Scott Garrelts .08 .25
20 Mark Davis .20 .50
21 Jim Gott .08 .25
22 Brad Wellman .08 .25
23 Roger Mason .08 .25
24 Bill Laskey .08 .25
25 Brad Gulden .08 .25
26 Joel Youngblood .08 .25
27 Juan Berenguer .08 .25
28 Checklist Card .08 .25
Bob Lillis CO
Gordy MacKenzie CO#

1986 Giants Postcards

This 30-card set of the San Francisco Giants features color player photos printed on postcard-size cards. The cards are unnumbered and checklisted below in alphabetical order. A rookie year card of Will Clark is in this set.

COMPLETE SET (30) 8.00 20.00
1 Mike Aldrete .20 .50
2 Juan Berenguer .20 .50
3 Vida Blue .30 .75
4 Bob Brenly .20 .50
5 Chris Brown .20 .50
6 Will Clark 2.00 5.00
7 Roger Craig MG .30 .75
8 Chili Davis .40 1.00
9 Mark Davis .20 .50
10 Bill Fahey CO .20 .50
11 Scott Garrelts .20 .50
12 Dan Gladden .20 .50
13 Jim Gott .20 .50
14 Atlee Hammaker .20 .50
15 Mike Krukow .20 .50
16 Bill Laskey .20 .50
17 Jeffrey Leonard .20 .50
18 Bob Lillis CO .20 .50
19 Candy Maldonado .20 .50
20 Roger Mason .20 .50
21 Willie Mays .75 2.00
Willie McCovey
22 Gordon MacKenzie CO .20 .50
23 Bob Melvin .30 .75
24 Greg Minton .20 .50
25 Jose Morales CO .20 .50
26 Jeff Robinson .20 .50
27 Norm Sherry CO .20 .50
28 Rob Thompson .40 1.00
29 Jose Uribe .20 .50
30 Brad Wellman .20 .50

1987 Giants Mother's

This set consists of 28 full-color, rounded-corner cards each measuring the standard size. Starter sets (only 20 cards but also including a certificate for eight more cards) were given out at the ballpark and collectors were encouraged to trade to fill in the rest of their set. Cards were originally given out at Candlestick Park on June 27th during a game against the Astros. Photos were taken by Dennis Desprois. The sets were reportedly given out free to the first 25,000 paid admissions at the game. There is an early Matt Williams card in this set.

COMPLETE SET (28) 8.00 20.00
1 Roger Craig MG .20 .50
2 Will Clark 2.00 5.00
3 Chili Davis .40 1.00
4 Bob Brenly .08 .25
5 Chris Brown .08 .25
6 Mike Krukow .08 .25
7 Candy Maldonado .08 .25
8 Jeffrey Leonard .08 .25
9 Greg Minton .08 .25
10 Robby Thompson .20 .50
11 Scott Garrelts .08 .25
12 Bob Melvin .20 .50
13 Jose Uribe .08 .25
14 Mark Davis .20 .50
15 Eddie Milner .08 .25
16 Harry Spilman .08 .25
17 Kelly Downs .08 .25
18 Chris Speier .08 .25
19 Jim Gott .08 .25
20 Joel Youngblood .08 .25
21 Mike LaCoss .08 .25
22 Matt Williams 4.00 10.00
23 Roger Mason .08 .25
24 Mike Aldrete .08 .25
25 Jeff D. Robinson .08 .25
26 Mark Grant .08 .25
27 Giants' Coaches .08 .25
Don Zimmer
Bob Lillis
Jose Mora
28 Checklist Card .08 .25
Candlestick Park

1987 Giants Postcards

This 36-card set of the San Francisco Giants features color player photos printed on postcard-size cards. The cards are unnumbered and checklisted below in alphabetical order. A rookie year card of Matt Williams is in this set.

COMPLETE SET (36) 10.00 25.00
1 Mike Aldrete .20 .50
2 Randy Bockus .20 .50
3 Bob Brenly .20 .50
4 Chris Brown .20 .50
5 Will Clark 1.25 3.00
6 Keith Comstock .20 .50
7 Roger Craig MG .30 .75
8 Chili Davis .40 1.00
9 Mark Davis .20 .50
10 Kelly Downs .20 .50
11 Bill Fahey CO .20 .50
12 Scott Garrelts .20 .50
13 Jim Gott .20 .50
14 Atlee Hammaker .20 .50
15 Mike Krukow .20 .50
16 Mike LaCoss .20 .50
17 Jeffrey Leonard .20 .50
18 Bob Lillis CO .20 .50
19 Gordy MacKenzie CO .20 .50
20 Candy Maldonado .20 .50
21 Willie Mays 1.25 3.00
22 Willie McCovey .75 2.00
23 Bob Melvin .30 .75
24 Eddie Milner .20 .50
25 Jose Morales CO .20 .50
26 Jon Perlman .20 .50
27 Jeff Robinson .20 .50
28 Norm Sherry CO .20 .50
29 Chris Speier .20 .50
30 Harry Spilman .20 .50
31 Robby Thompson .30 .75
32 Jose Uribe .20 .50
33 Mark Wasinger .20 .50
34 Matt Williams 2.50 6.00
35 Joel Youngblood .20 .50
36 Don Zimmer CO .30 .75

1988 Giants Mother's

This set consists of 28 full-color, rounded-corner cards each measuring the standard size. Starter sets (only 20 cards but also including a certificate for eight more cards) were given out at the ballpark and collectors were encouraged to trade to fill in the rest of their set. Cards were originally given out at Candlestick Park on July 30th during a game. Photos were taken by Dennis Desprois. The sets were reportedly given out free to the first 35,000 paid admissions at the game.

COMPLETE SET (28) 4.00 10.00
1 Roger Craig MG .20 .50
2 Will Clark 1.25 3.00
3 Kevin Mitchell .30 .75
4 Bob Brenly .08 .25
5 Mike Aldrete .08 .25
6 Mike Krukow .08 .25
7 Candy Maldonado .08 .25
8 Jeffrey Leonard .08 .25
9 Dave Dravecky .30 .75
10 Robby Thompson .08 .25
11 Scott Garrelts .08 .25
12 Bob Melvin .20 .50
13 Jose Uribe .08 .25
14 Brett Butler .40 1.00
15 Rick Reuschel .20 .50
16 Harry Spilman .08 .25
17 Kelly Downs .08 .25
18 Chris Speier .08 .25
19 Atlee Hammaker .08 .25
20 Joel Youngblood .08 .25
21 Mike LaCoss .08 .25
22 Don Robinson .08 .25
23 Mark Wasinger .08 .25
24 Craig Lefferts .08 .25
25 Phil Garner .20 .50
26 Joe Price .08 .25
27 Giants' Coaches .20 .50
Dusty Baker
Bill Fahey
Bob Lill
28 Checklist Card .08 .25
Giants NL Champs Logo

1988 Giants Postcards

This 35-card set of the San Francisco Giants features color player photos printed on postcard-size cards. The cards are unnumbered and checklisted below in alphabetical order.

COMPLETE SET (35) 8.00 20.00
1 Mike Aldrete .20 .50
2 Dusty Baker CO .30 .75
3 Bob Brenly .20 .50
4 Brett Butler .40 1.00
5 Candlestick Park .20 .50
6 Will Clark .60 1.50
7 Roger Craig MG .30 .75
8 Kelly Downs .20 .50
9 Dave Dravecky .20 .50
10 Bill Fahey CO .20 .50
11 Scott Garrelts .20 .50
12 Atlee Hammaker .20 .50
13 Mike Krukow .20 .50
14 Mike LaCoss .20 .50
15 Craig Lefferts .20 .50
16 Jeffrey Leonard .20 .50
17 Bob Lillis CO .20 .50
18 Gordy MacKenzie CO .20 .50
19 Candy Maldonado .20 .50
20 Willie Mays 1.25 3.00
21 Willie McCovey .75 2.00
22 Bob Melvin .30 .75
23 Kevin Mitchell .30 .75
24 Jose Morales CO .20 .50
25 Joe Price .20 .50
26 Rick Reuschel .30 .75
27 Don Robinson .20 .50
28 Norm Sherry CO .20 .50
29 Chris Speier .20 .50
30 Harry Spilman .20 .50
31 Robby Thompson .20 .50
32 Jose Uribe .20 .50
33 Mark Wasinger .20 .50
34 Joel Youngblood .20 .50
35 1987 NL West Champions .30 .75

1989 Giants Mother's

The 1989 Mother's Cookies San Francisco Giants set contains 28 standard-size cards with rounded corners. The fronts have borderless color photos, and the horizontally oriented backs have biographical information. Starter sets containing 20 of these cards were given away at a Giants home game during the 1989 season.

COMPLETE SET (28) 5.00 12.00
1 Roger Craig MG .20 .50
2 Will Clark 1.00 2.50
3 Kevin Mitchell .30 .75
4 Kelly Downs .08 .25
5 Brett Butler .40 1.00
6 Mike Krukow .08 .25
7 Candy Maldonado .08 .25
8 Terry Kennedy .08 .25
9 Dave Dravecky .30 .75
10 Robby Thompson .08 .25

11 Scott Garrelts .08 .25
12 Matt Williams 2.00 5.00
13 Jose Uribe .08 .25
14 Tracy Jones .08 .25
15 Rick Reuschel .20 .50
16 Ernest Riles .08 .25
17 Jeff Brantley .20 .50
18 Chris Speier .08 .25
19 Atlee Hammaker .08 .25
20 Ed Jurak .08 .25
21 Mike LaCoss .08 .25
22 Don Robinson .08 .25
23 Kirt Manwaring .08 .25
24 Craig Lefferts .08 .25
25 Donell Nixon .08 .25
26 Joe Price .08 .25
27 Rich Gossage .30 .75
28 Checklist Card .20 .50
Bill Fahey CO
Dusty Baker CO
Bob

1990 Giants Mother's

The 1990 Mother's Cookies San Francisco Giants set features cards with rounded corners measuring the standard size. The cards have full-color fronts and biographical information with no stats on the back. The Giants cards were given away at the July 29th game to the first 25,000 children 14 and under. They were distributed in 20-card random packets at the game and eight more at the redemption booths. However, both groups of cards were random and there was no guarantee of getting a complete set in the cards. The promotional idea was that the only way one could finish the set was to trade for them. The redemption certificates were to be used at the Labor Day San Francisco card show. In addition to this the Mother's A's cards were also redeemable at that show.

COMPLETE SET (28) 5.00 12.00
1 Roger Craig MG .20 .50
2 Will Clark 1.25 3.00
3 Gary Carter .50 1.25
4 Kelly Downs .08 .25
5 Kevin Mitchell .30 .75
6 Steve Bedrosian .20 .50
7 Brett Butler .40 1.00
8 Rick Reuschel .20 .50
9 Matt Williams .60 1.50
10 Robby Thompson .08 .25
11 Mike LaCoss .10 .25
12 Terry Kennedy .10 .25
13 Atlee Hammaker .08 .25
14 Rick Leach .08 .25
15 Ernest Riles .08 .25
16 Scott Garrelts .08 .25
17 Jose Uribe .08 .25
18 Greg Litton .08 .25
19 Dave Anderson .08 .25
20 Don Robinson .08 .25
21 Ernie Camacho .08 .25
22 Bill Bathe .08 .25
23 Randy O'Neal .08 .25
24 Kevin Bass .08 .25
25 Jeff Brantley .20 .50
26 John Burkett .08 .25
27 Giants Coaches .20 .50
Dusty Baker
Bob Lillis
Bill Fahe
28 Checklist Card .08 .25

1990 Giants Smokey

This set measures 5" by 7". These cards all contain a safety message. These cards are unnumbered so we have checklisted them below in alphabetical order.

COMPLETE SET (21) 5.00 12.00
1 Dusty Baker CO .30 .75
2 Steve Bedrosian .30 .75
3 Gary Carter .40 1.00
4 Will Clark 1.25 3.00
5 Roger Craig MG .20 .50
6 Kelly Downs .20 .50
7 Bill Fahey CO .20 .50
8 Scott Garrelts .20 .50
9 Atlee Hanmaker .20 .50
10 Terry Kennedy .20 .50
11 Wendell Kim CO .20 .50
12 Mike LaCoss .20 .50
13 Bob Lillis CO .20 .50
14 Greg Litton .20 .50
15 Kevin Mitchell .30 .75
16 Earnest Riles .20 .50
17 Don Robinson .20 .50
18 Norm Sherry CO .20 .50
19 Robby Thompson .20 .50
20 Jose Uribe .20 .50
21 Matt Williams .60 1.50

1991 Giants Mother's

The 1991 Mother's Cookies San Francisco Giants set contains 28 cards with rounded corners measuring the standard size.

COMPLETE SET (28) 4.00 10.00
1 Roger Craig MG .20 .50
2 Will Clark 1.00 2.50
3 Steve Decker .08 .25
4 Kelly Downs .08 .25
5 Kevin Mitchell .20 .50
6 Willie McGee .20 .50
7 Bud Black .08 .25
8 Dave Righetti .20 .50
9 Matt Williams .50 1.25
10 Robby Thompson .08 .25
11 Mike LaCoss .08 .25
12 Terry Kennedy .08 .25
13 Mark Leonard .08 .25
14 Rick Reuschel .20 .50
15 Mike Felder .08 .25
16 Scott Garrelts .08 .25
17 Jose Uribe .08 .25
18 Greg Litton .08 .25
19 Dave Anderson .08 .25
20 Don Robinson .08 .25
21 Mike Kingery .08 .25
22 Trevor Wilson .08 .25
23 Kirt Manwaring .08 .25
24 Kevin Bass .08 .25
25 Jeff Brantley .08 .25
26 John Burkett .08 .25
27 Giant's Coaches .20 .50
Dusty Baker
Bill Fahey
Wendell
28 Checklist Card .08 .25
Mark Letendre TR
Greg Lynn TR

1991 Giants Pacific Gas and Electric

These cards were issued on six-card sheets; after perforation they measure approximately 2 1/2" by 3 1/2". One sheet was inserted in each of the first five 1991 San Francisco Giants Magazines, which were published by Woodford. The front design has color action player photos, with gray borders on a white card face. Toward the bottom of the picture are the words "San Francisco Giants," two bats, and a red banner with player information. The horizontally oriented backs are printed in black on white and include biography, Major League statistics, and various PGE (Pacific Gas and Electric) advertisements. The cards are numbered on the back in the upper right corner.

COMPLETE SET (30) 8.00 20.00
1 Kevin Mitchell .30 .75
2 Robby Thompson .20 .50
3 John Burkett .20 .50
4 Kelly Downs .20 .50
5 Terry Kennedy .20 .50
6 Roger Craig MG .30 .75
7 Jeff Brantley .30 .75
8 Greg Litton .20 .50
9 Trevor Wilson .20 .50
10 Kevin Bass .20 .50
11 Matt Williams 1.25 3.00
12 Jose Uribe .20 .50
13 Steve Decker .20 .50
14 Will Clark 2.50 6.00
15 Dave Righetti .30 .75
16 Mike Kingery .20 .50
17 Mike LaCoss .20 .50
18 Dave Anderson .20 .50
19 Bud Black .20 .50
20 Mike Benjamin .20 .50
21 Don Robinson .20 .50
22 Mark Leonard .20 .50
23 Willie McGee .30 .75
24 Francisco Oliveras .20 .50
25 Kirt Manwaring .20 .50
26 Rick Parker .20 .50
27 Mike Remlinger .20 .50
28 Mike Felder .20 .50
29 Scott Garrelts .20 .50
30 Tony Perezchica .20 .50

1991 Giants Postcards

These postcards measures approximately 4" by 6" and features color player action shots on its orange and brown bordered fronts. Many of these postcards were signed in response to fans writing in for autograph requests. The postcards are unnumbered and checklisted below in alphabetical order.

COMPLETE SET (2) .75 2.00
1 Terry Kennedy .40 1.00
2 Francisco Oliveras .40 1.00

1991 Giants S.F. Examiner

The sixteen 6" by 9" giant-sized cards in this set were issued on orange cardboard sheets measuring approximately 8 1/2" by 11" and designed for storage in a three-ring binder. The cards are unnumbered and checklisted below in alphabetical order.

COMPLETE SET (16) 8.00 20.00
1 Kevin Bass .40 1.00
2 Mike Benjamin .40 1.00
3 Bud Black .40 1.00
4 Jeff Brantley .60 1.50
5 John Burkett .40 1.00
6 Will Clark 2.00 5.00
7 Steve Decker .40 1.00
8 Scott Garrelts .40 1.00
9 Mike LaCoss .40 1.00
10 Willie McGee .60 1.50
11 Kevin Mitchell .60 1.50
12 Dave Righetti .60 1.50
13 Don Robinson .40 1.00
14 Robby Thompson .40 1.00
15 Jose Uribe .40 1.00
16 Matt Williams 1.25 3.00

1992 Giants AT and T Team Postcards

These poscards feature team photos of the first 35 years of the San Francisco Giants. These postcards are sequenced in year order.

COMPLETE SET (35) 12.50 30.00
COMMON PLAYER (1-35) .40 1.00
1 1958 Team Photo .75 2.00
5 1962 Team Photo .60 1.50
32 1989 Team Photo .60 1.50

1992 Giants Fan Fair Fun Bucks

These "promotional buck" featured various San Francisco Giants. They are unnumbered so we have sequenced them in alphabetical order.

COMPLETE SET 3.00 8.00
1 Dusty Baker .40 1.00
2 Orlando Cepeda 1.00 2.50
3 Willie Mays 2.00 5.00

1992 Giants Mother's

The set was sponsored by Mother's Cookies and features full-bleed color player photos of the San Francisco Giants. The 28 cards in this set have rounded corners and measure the standard size. The backs, printed in purple and red, have biographical information. The set included two coupons: one featured a mail-in offer to obtain a trading card collectors album for 3.95, while the second featured a mail-in offer to obtain an additional eight trading cards.

COMPLETE SET (28) 4.00 10.00
1 Roger Craig MG .20 .50
2 Will Clark 1.00 2.50
3 Bill Swift .08 .25
4 Royce Clayton .20 .50
5 John Burkett .08 .25
6 Willie McGee .20 .50
7 Bud Black .08 .25
8 Dave Righetti .20 .50
9 Matt Williams .60 1.50
10 Robby Thompson .08 .25
11 Darren Lewis .08 .25
12 Mike Jackson .20 .50
13 Mark Leonard .08 .25
14 Rod Beck .60 1.50
15 Mike Felder .08 .25
16 Bryan Hickerson .08 .25
17 Jose Uribe .08 .25
18 Greg Litton .08 .25
19 Cory Snyder .08 .25
20 Jim McNamara .08 .25
21 Kelly Downs .08 .25
22 Trevor Wilson .08 .25
23 Kirt Manwaring .08 .25
24 Kevin Bass .08 .25
25 Jeff Brantley .20 .50
26 Dave Burba .08 .25
27 Chris James .08 .25
28 Checklist Card .20 .50
Carlos Alfonso CO
Dusty Baker CO

1992 Giants Pacific Gas and Electric

This 36-card set was sponsored by Pacific Gas and Electric and was issued in six-card perforated sheets. Each card measures approximately 2 3/4" by 3 3/4" and features on its front a brown-bordered color player action photo set off by a simulated wood picture frame. The cards are unnumbered and checklisted below in alphabetical order.

COMPLETE SET (36) 10.00 25.00
1 Carlos Alfonso CO .20 .50
2 Dusty Baker CO .40 1.00
3 Kevin Bass .20 .50
4 Rod Beck .60 1.50
5 Mike Benjamin .20 .50
6 Bud Black .20 .50
7 Jeff Brantley .30 .75
8 Bob Brenly CO .20 .50
9 Dave Burba .20 .50
10 John Burkett .20 .50
11 Will Clark 1.50 4.00
12 Will Clark AS .75 2.00
13 Royce Clayton .20 .50
14 Roger Craig MG .30 .75
15 Kelly Downs .20 .50
16 Mike Felder .20 .50
17 Scott Garrelts .20 .50
18 Gil Heredia .20 .50
19 Bryan Hickerson .20 .50
20 Mike Jackson .30 .75
21 Chris James .20 .50
22 Wendell Kim CO .20 .50
23 Mark Leonard(At bat) .20 .50
24 Mark Leonard(Dropping bat) .20 .50
25 Darren Lewis .20 .50
26 Bob Lillis CO .20 .50
27 Kirt Manwaring .20 .50
28 Willie McGee .30 .75
29 Jim McNamara .20 .50
30 Dave Righetti .30 .75
31 Cory Snyder .20 .50
32 Bill Swift .20 .50
33 Robby Thompson .20 .50
34 Jose Uribe .20 .50
35 Matt Williams .75 2.00
36 Trevor Wilson .20 .50

1993 Giants Mother's

The 1993 Mother's Cookies Giants set consists of 28 standard-size cards with rounded corners.

COMPLETE SET (28) 6.00 15.00
1 Dusty Baker MG .20 .50
2 Will Clark 1.25 3.00
3 Matt Williams .60 1.50
4 Barry Bonds 2.50 6.00
5 Bill Swift .08 .25
6 Royce Clayton .08 .25
7 John Burkett .08 .25
8 Willie McGee .20 .50
9 Kirt Manwaring .08 .25
10 Dave Righetti .20 .50
11 Todd Benzinger .08 .25
12 Rod Beck .40 1.00
13 Darren Lewis .08 .25
14 Robby Thompson .08 .25
15 Mark Carreon .08 .25
16 Dave Martinez .08 .25
17 Jeff Brantley .20 .50
18 Dave Burba .08 .25
19 Mike Benjamin .08 .25
20 Mike Jackson .08 .25
21 Craig Colbert .08 .25
22 Bud Black .08 .25
23 Trevor Wilson .08 .25
24 Kevin Rogers .08 .25
25 Jeff Reed .08 .25
26 Bryan Hickerson .08 .25
27 Gino Minutelli .08 .25
28 Checklist .20 .50
Coaches
Dick Pole
Bobby Bonds
Denny S

1993 Giants Postcards

These postcards measure 4" by 6". The fronts feature black-and-white posed and action player shots. The backs are typical postcard back. The cards are unnumbered and checklisted below in alphabetical order.

COMPLETE SET (35) 8.00 20.00
1 Dusty Baker MG .30 .75
2 Rod Beck .60 1.50
3 Mike Benjamin .20 .50
4 Todd Benzinger .20 .50
5 Buddy Black .20 .50
6 Barry Bonds(Catching the ball) 2.50 6.00
7 Barry Bonds(Running) 2.50 6.00
8 Bobby Bonds CO .30 .75
9 Jeff Brantley .30 .75
10 Bob Brenly CO .20 .50
11 Dave Burba .20 .50
12 John Burkett .20 .50
13 Mark Carreon .20 .50
14 Will Clark(Batting) 1.25 3.00
15 Will Clark(Running) 1.25 3.00
16 Royce Clayton .20 .50
17 Bryan Hickerson .20 .50
18 Craig Colbert .20 .50
19 Mike Jackson .30 .75
20 Wendell Kim CO .20 .50
21 Darren Lewis .20 .50
22 Bob Lillis CO .20 .50
23 Kirt Manwaring .20 .50
24 Dave Martinez .20 .50
25 Willie McGee .30 .75
26 Luis Mercedes .20 .50
27 Dick Pole CO .20 .50
28 Jeff Reed .20 .50
29 Dave Righetti .30 .75
30 Kevin Rogers .20 .50
31 Bill Swift .20 .50
32 Robby Thompson .20 .50
33 Matt Williams .60 1.50
34 Trevor Wilson .20 .50
35 Team Photo .30 .75

1993 Giants Stadium Club

This 30-card standard-size set features the 1993 San Francisco Giants. The set was issued in hobby (plastic box) and retail (blister) form. The Barry Bonds card says 24K gold on the front. All the Bonds cards were printed that way so there is no extra value to these cards.

COMP. FACT SET (30) 1.50 4.00
1 Barry Bonds .75 2.00
2 Dave Righetti .08 .25
3 Matt Williams .30 .75
4 Royce Clayton .02 .10
5 Salomon Torres .02 .10
6 Kirt Manwaring .02 .10
7 J.R. Phillips .02 .10
8 Kevin Rogers .02 .10
9 Will Clark .40 1.00
10 John Burkett .02 .10
11 Willie McGee .08 .25
12 Rod Beck .08 .25
13 Jeff Reed .02 .10
14 Jeff Brantley .08 .25
15 Steve Hosey .02 .10
16 Chris Hancock .02 .10
17 Adell Davenport .02 .10
18 Mike Jackson .08 .25
19 Dave Martinez .02 .10
20 Bill Swift .02 .10
21 Steve Scarsone .02 .10
22 Trevor Wilson .02 .10
23 Mark Carreon .02 .10
24 Bud Black .02 .10
25 Darren Lewis .02 .10
26 Dan Carlson .02 .10
27 Craig Colbert .02 .10
28 Greg Brummett .02 .10
29 Bryan Hickerson .02 .10
30 Robby Thompson .02 .10

1994 Giants AMC

Sponsored by AMC Theatres, these 24 blank-backed cards measure approximately 4 1/4" by 11" and feature white-bordered black-and-white player action photos. Some of the cards carry facsimile autographs across their photos. According to reports at the time, the cards came both with and without facsimile autographs.

COMPLETE SET (24) 10.00 25.00
1 Dusty Baker MG .60 1.50
2 Rod Beck .75 2.00
3 Mike Benjamin .40 1.00
4 Todd Benzinger .40 1.00
5 Barry Bonds 4.00 10.00
6 John Burkett .40 1.00
7 Mark Carreon .40 1.00
8 Royce Clayton .40 1.00
9 Steve Frey .40 1.00
10 Mike Jackson .60 1.50
11 Darren Lewis .40 1.00
12 Kirt Manwaring .40 1.00
13 Dave Martinez .40 1.00
14 Willie McGee .60 1.50
15 Rich Monteleone .40 1.00
16 John Patterson .40 1.00
17 Mark Portugal .40 1.00
18 Jeff Reed .40 1.00
19 Kevin Rogers .40 1.00
20 Steve Scarsone .40 1.00
21 Bill Swift .40 1.00
22 Robby Thompson .40 1.00
23 Salomon Torres .40 1.00
24 Matt Williams 1.00 2.50

1994 Giants KTVU-TV

This nine-card set features color player photos of the San Francisco Giants. The cards are unnumbered and checklisted below in alphabetical order.

COMPLETE SET (9) 5.00 12.00
1 Dusty Baker MG .60 1.50
2 Rod Beck .75 2.00
3 Barry Bonds 2.50 6.00
4 Bobby Bonds CO .60 1.50
5 John Burkett .40 1.00
6 Billy Swift .40 1.00
7 Robby Thompson .40 1.00
8 Matt Williams 1.00 2.50
9 Title Card .40 1.00

1994 Giants Mother's

The 1994 Mother's Cookies Giants set consists of 28 standard-size cards with rounded corners.

COMPLETE SET (28) 4.00 10.00
1 Dusty Baker MG .20 .50
2 Robby Thompson .08 .25
3 Barry Bonds 2.00 5.00
4 Royce Clayton .08 .25
5 John Burkett .08 .25
6 Bill Swift .08 .25
7 Matt Williams .40 1.00
8 Rod Beck .30 .75
9 Steve Scarsone .08 .25
10 Mark Portugal .08 .25
11 John Patterson .08 .25
12 Darren Lewis .08 .25
13 Kirt Manwaring .08 .25
14 Salomon Torres .08 .25
15 Willie McGee .20 .50
16 Dave Martinez .08 .25
17 Darryl Strawberry .20 .50
18 Steve Frey .08 .25
19 Rich Monteleone .08 .25
20 Todd Benzinger .08 .25
21 Jeff Reed .08 .25
22 Mike Benjamin .08 .25
23 Mike Jackson .08 .25
24 Pat Gomez .08 .25
25 Dave Burba .08 .25
26 Bryan Hickerson .08 .25
27 Mark Carreon .08 .25
28 Checklist .20 .50
Coaches
Bobby Bonds
Bob Lillis
Wendel

1994 Giants S.F. Chronicle

These three pins came attached to cards of the featured players. The brass pins carry the player's names in black lettering, except for card No. 3, which carries the player's names on their "uniforms." The cards measure approximately 2 1/2" by 5 1/8" and feature on their fronts borderless color player photos framed by a thin white line. The cards and pins are unnumbered and checklisted below in alphabetical order.

COMPLETE SET (3) 3.00 8.00
1 Dusty Baker MG .75 2.00
2 Barry Bonds 2.00 5.00
3 Bill Swift .40 1.00
John Burkett

1994 Giants Target Bottle Caps

Measuring approximately 1 5/8" in diameter, these bottle caps were issued as a perforated board measuring approximately 4 3/8"" by 8". Each sheet has four rows of two caps each. The fronts feature a color player portrait. The backs carry the player's name and number. The bottle caps are unnumbered and checklisted below in alphabetical order.

COMPLETE SET 4.00 10.00
1 Dusty Baker MG .20 .50
2 Rod Beck .20 .50
3 Mike Benjamin .08 .25
4 Todd Benzinger .08 .25
5 Barry Bonds 1.50 4.00
6 Dave Burba .08 .25
7 John Burkett .08 .25
8 Mark Carreon .08 .25
9 Royce Clayton .08 .25
10 Steve Frey .08 .25
11 Bryan Hickerson .08 .25
12 Mike Jackson .20 .50
13 Darren Lewis .08 .25
14 Kirt Manwaring .08 .25
15 Dave Martinez .08 .25
16 Willie McGee .20 .50
17 Tony Menendez .08 .25
18 Rich Montelone .08 .25
19 John Patterson .08 .25
20 Mark Portugal .08 .25
21 Jeff Reed .08 .25
22 Kevin Rogers .08 .25
23 Steve Scarsone .08 .25
24 Bill Swift .08 .25
25 Robby Thompson .08 .25
26 Salomon Torres .08 .25
27 Matt Williams .40 1.00
28 Title Cap .08 .25
29 BB Logo .08 .25

1994 Giants Team Issue

These nine blank-backed photo sheets measure 8" by 10" and feature on their black-and gold-bordered fronts with black-and-white player photos of award-winning Giants. The sheets are unnumbered and checklisted below in alphabetical order.

COMPLETE SET (9) 5.00 12.00
1 Dusty Baker MG(Wearing sunglasses) .60 1.50
2 Dusty Baker MG(Waving cap) .60 1.50
3 Barry Bonds(Dropping bat) 1.50 4.00
4 Barry Bonds(Running) 1.50 4.00
5 Barry Bonds .75 2.00
Robby Thompson
Matt Williams
6 Barry Bonds .75 2.00
Kirt Manwaring
Robby Thompson
Matt
7 John Burkett .40 1.00
Bill Swift
8 Darren Lewis .40 1.00
9 The 1993 Giants 1.25 3.00
Matt Williams
Will Clark
Barry

1994 Giants U.S. Playing Cards

These 56 playing standard-size cards have rounded corners, and feature color posed and action player photos on their white-bordered fronts. The player's name and position appear near the bottom. The white and black backs carry the logos for the Giants, baseball's 125th Anniversary, MLBPA, and Bicycle Sports Collection. The set is checklisted below in playing card order by suits and assigned numbers to aces (1), jacks (11), queens (12), and kings (13).

COMPLETE SET (56) 1.50 4.00
1C Matt Williams .15 .40
1D Bill Swift .01 .05
1H Robby Thompson .01 .05
1S Barry Bonds .40 1.00
2C John Patterson .01 .05
2D Luis Mercedes .01 .05
2H Paul Faries .01 .05
2S Salomon Torres .01 .05
3C Steve Hosey .01 .05
3D Mike Benjamin .01 .05
3H Trevor Wilson .01 .05
3S Kevin Rogers .01 .05
4C Jeff Reed .01 .05
4D Mark Carreon .01 .05
4H Steve Scarsone .01 .05
4S Todd Benzinger .01 .05
5C Mike Jackson .02 .10
5D Dave Burba .01 .05
5H Bryan Hickerson .01 .05
5S Dave Martinez .01 .05
6C Kirt Manwaring .01 .05
6D John Burkett .01 .05
6H Rod Beck .05 .15
6S Darren Lewis .01 .05
7C Royce Clayton .01 .05
7D Matt Williams .15 .40
7H Barry Bonds .40 1.00
7S Willie McGee .02 .10
8C Robby Thompson .01 .05
8D Salomon Torres .01 .05
8H John Patterson .01 .05
8S Bill Swift .01 .05
9C Luis Mercedes .01 .05
9D Kevin Rogers .01 .05
9H J.R. Phillips .01 .05
9S Paul Faries .01 .05
10C Mike Benjamin .01 .05
10D Todd Benzinger .01 .05
10H Jeff Reed .01 .05
10S Trevor Wilson .01 .05
11C Mark Carreon .01 .05
11D Dave Martinez .01 .05
11H Mike Jackson .02 .10
11S Steve Scarsone .01 .05
12C Dave Burba .01 .05
12D Darren Lewis .01 .05
12H Kirt Manwaring .01 .05
12S Bryan Hickerson .01 .05
13C John Burkett .01 .05
13D Willie McGee .02 .10
13H Royce Clayton .01 .05
13S Rod Beck .05 .15
NNO Featured Players .01 .05

1995 Giants Mother's

This 1995 Mother's Cookies San Francisco Giants set consists of 28 standard-size cards with rounded corners.

COMPLETE SET (28) 4.00 10.00
1 Dusty Baker MG .20 .50
2 Robby Thompson .08 .25
3 Barry Bonds 1.50 4.00
4 Royce Clayton .08 .25
5 Glenallen Hill .08 .25
6 Terry Mulholland .08 .25
7 Matt Williams .40 1.00
8 Mark Portugal .08 .25
9 John Patterson .08 .25
10 Rod Beck .30 .75
11 Mark Leiter .08 .25
12 Kirt Manwaring .08 .25
13 Steve Scarsone .08 .25
14 Darren Lewis .08 .25
15 Tom Lampkin .08 .25
16 William Vanlandingham .08 .25
17 Joe Rosselli .08 .25
18 Chris Hook .08 .25
19 Mark Dewey .08 .25
20 J.R. Phillips .08 .25
21 Jeff Reed .08 .25
22 Pat Gomez .08 .25
23 Mike Benjamin .08 .25
24 Trevor Wilson .08 .25
25 Dave Burba .08 .25
26 Jose Bautista .08 .25
27 Mark Carreon .08 .25
28 Coaches .20 .50
Checklist
Dick Pole
Bobby Bonds
Wendell

1996 Giants Mother's

This 28-card set consists of borderless posed color player portraits in stadium settings.

COMPLETE SET (28) 3.00 8.00
1 Dusty Baker MG .20 .50
2 Barry Bonds 1.50 4.00
3 Rod Beck .20 .50
4 Matt Williams .40 1.00
5 Robby Thompson .08 .25
6 Glenallen Hill .08 .25
7 Kirt Manwaring .08 .25
8 Mark Carreon .08 .25
9 Osvaldo Fernandez .08 .25
10 J.R. Phillips .08 .25
11 Shawon Dunston .08 .25
12 Mark Leiter .08 .25
13 William Vanlandingham .08 .25
14 Stan Javier .08 .25
15 Allen Watson .08 .25
16 Mel Hall .08 .25
17 Doug Creek .08 .25
18 Steve Scarsone .08 .25
19 Mark Dewey .08 .25
20 Mark Gardner .08 .25
21 David McCarty .08 .25
22 Tom Lampkin .08 .25
23 Jeff Juden .08 .25
24 Steve Decker .08 .25
25 Rich DeLucia .08 .25
26 Kim Batiste .08 .25
27 Steve Bourgeois .08 .25
28 Coaches Card CL .08 .25
Bob Lillis
Dick Pole
Bobby Bond

1998 Giants Mother's

This 28-card set of the San Francisco Giants sponsored by Mother's Cookies consists of posed color player photos with rounded corners. The backs carry biographical information and the sponsor's logo on a lavender background in red and purple print. A blank slot for the player's autograph rounds out the back.

COMPLETE SET (28) 4.00 10.00
1 Dusty Baker MG .20 .50
2 Barry Bonds 1.25 3.00
3 Shawn Estes .08 .25
4 Jeff Kent .40 1.00
5 Orel Hershiser .20 .50
6 Brian Johnson .08 .25
7 J.T. Snow .30 .75
8 Bill Mueller .40 1.00
9 Kirk Rueter .08 .25
10 Darryl Hamilton .08 .25
11 Rich Aurilia .08 .25
12 Mark Gardner .08 .25
13 Stan Javier .08 .25
14 Robb Nen .30 .75
15 Rich Rodriguez .08 .25
16 Brent Mayne .08 .25
17 Julian Tavarez .08 .25
18 Rey Sanchez .08 .25
19 Chris Jones .08 .25
20 Charlie Hayes .08 .25
21 Danny Darwin .08 .25
22 Jim Poole .08 .25
23 Marvin Benard .08 .25
24 Steve Reed .08 .25
25 Alex Diaz .08 .25
26 John Johnstone .08 .25
27 Jon Miller ANN .20 .50
Ted Robinson
ANNDuane Kuiper ANN
28 Coaches Card CL .08 .25
Carlos Alfonso
Gene Clines
Sonn

1999 Giants Keebler

This 28-card standard-size was issued by Keebler Cookies and is in the tradition of the Mothers Cookies sets. They were issued in 28 card packs with 20 of the cards being different and eight cards of the same to be used as trade bait. The borderless fronts have player portraits along with the players name and a 3Com final season logo on the bottom. The easy to read backs have biographical information about the players.

COMPLETE SET (28) 4.00 10.00
1 Dusty Baker MG .20 .50
2 Barry Bonds 1.25 3.00
3 Jeff Kent .40 1.00
4 Robb Nen .30 .75
5 Bill Mueller .30 .75
6 Russ Ortiz .08 .25
7 Ellis Burks .30 .75
8 Marvin Benard .08 .25
9 Kirk Rueter .08 .25
10 J.T.Snow .30 .75
11 Stan Javier .08 .25
12 Chris Brock .08 .25
13 Charlie Hayes .08 .25
14 Joe Nathan .08 .25
15 Rich Rodriguez .08 .25
16 Brent Mayne .08 .25
17 Shawn Estes .08 .25
18 Rich Aurilia .20 .50
19 Mark Gardner .08 .25
20 Scott Servais .08 .25
21 John Johnstone .08 .25
22 Felix Rodriguez .08 .25
23 Armando Rios .08 .25
24 Alan Embree .08 .25
25 F.P. Santangelo .08 .25
26 Jerry Spradlin .08 .25
27 Lon Simmons ANN .08 .25
28 Carlos Alfonso CO .08 .25
Gene Clines CO
Sonny Jackson C

1999 Giants Postcards

These postcards measure 2 13/16" by 5 1/2" and have blank backs. The cards have two different Giants logos but both styles have the Giants logo on the top with the player photo and uniform number underneath and the Pacific Bell logo on the bottom. We have sequenced these cards in alphabetical order. There is no difference in pricing for either type of Giants logo.

COMPLETE SET 6.00 15.00
1 Rich Aurilia .30 .75
2 Dusty Baker MG .30 .75
3 Marvin Benard .20 .50
4 Barry Bonds 1.25 3.00
5 Chris Brock .20 .50
6 Ellis Burks .40 1.00
7 Alan Embree .20 .50
8 Shawn Estes .20 .50
9 Mark Gardner .20 .50
10 Charlie Hayes .20 .50
11 Stan Javier .20 .50
12 Jeff Kent .75 2.00
13 Ramon E.Martinez .20 .50
14 Brent Mayne .20 .50
15 Bill Mueller .40 1.00
Looking Up
16 Bill Mueller .40 1.00
Fielding
17 Joe Nathan .20 .50
18 Robb Nen .40 1.00
19 Russ Ortiz .40 1.00
20 Rich Rodriguez .20 .50
21 Kirk Rueter .20 .50
22 F.P. Santangelo .20 .50
23 J.T. Snow .30 .75
24 Scott Servais .20 .50

2000 Giants Bonds Pac-Bell

1 Barry Bonds 2.00 5.00

2000 Giants Keebler

COMPLETE SET (28) 4.00 10.00
1 Dusty Baker MG .20 .50
2 Barry Bonds 1.20 3.00
3 Jeff Kent .60 1.50
4 Robb Nen .30 .75
5 J.T. Snow .30 .75
6 Russ Ortiz .20 .50
7 Ellis Burks .30 .75
8 Bill Mueller .40 1.00
9 Shawn Estes .10 .25
10 Marvin Benard .10 .25
11 Kirk Rueter .10 .25
12 Bobby Estalella .10 .25
13 Livan Hernandez .30 .75
14 Rich Aurilia .20 .50
15 Alan Embree .10 .25
16 Armando Rios .10 .25
17 Felix Rodriguez .10 .25
18 Doug Mirabelli .10 .25
19 John Johnstone .10 .25
20 Russ Davis .10 .25
21 Joe Nathan .40 1.00
22 Aaron Fultz .10 .25
23 Felipe Crespo .10 .25
24 Mark Gardner .10 .25
25 Ramon E. Martinez .10 .25
26 Calvin Murray .10 .25
27 Carlos Alfonso CO .10 .25

Sonny Jackson CO
Gene Clines C
28 Checklist .10 .25
Willie Mays Plaza Shown

2001 Giants Keebler

COMPLETE SET 4.80 12.00
1 Dusty Baker MG .20 .50
2 Jeff Kent .50 1.25
3 Barry Bonds 1.20 3.00
4 Robb Nen .30 .75
5 J.T. Snow .20 .50
6 Russ Ortiz .20 .50
7 Rich Aurilia .20 .50
8 Benito Santiago .20 .50
9 Shawn Estes .10 .25
10 Marvin Benard .10 .25
11 Kirk Rueter .10 .25
12 Calvin Murray .10 .25
13 Livan Hernandez .30 .75
14 Eric Davis .20 .50
15 Aaron Fultz .10 .25
16 Armando Rios .10 .25
17 Felix Rodriguez .10 .25
18 Shawon Dunston .10 .25
19 Mark Gardner .10 .25
20 Ramon Martinez .10 .25
21 Pedro Feliz .20 .50
22 Chad Zerbe .10 .25
23 Felipe Crespo .10 .25
24 Tim Worrell .10 .25
25 Edwards Guzman .10 .25
26 Ryan Vogelsong .10 .25
27 Brian Boehringer .10 .25
28 Carlos Alfonso CO .10 .25
Gene Clines CO
Sonny Jackson C

2002 Giants Coke Topps

COMPLETE SET 50.00 120.00
COMMON CARD 2.50 6.00
COMMON CARDS SP
1 Jeff Kent 8.00 20.00
2 Rich Aurilia 5.00 12.00
3 J.T. Snow 2.50 6.00
4 Marvin Benard 2.50 6.00
5 Pedro Feliz 2.50 6.00
6 Shawon Dunston SP 4.00 10.00
7 Robb Nen SP 8.00 20.00
8 Felix Rodriguez 2.50 6.00
9 Russ Ortiz 5.00 12.00
10 Kirk Rueter 4.00 10.00
11 Livan Hernandez 4.00 10.00
12 Barry Bonds 10.00 25.00

2002 Giants Keebler

COMPLETE SET 4.00 10.00
1 Dusty Baker MG .30 .75
2 Barry Bonds 1.25 3.00
3 Jeff Kent .50 1.25
4 Robb Nen .30 .75
5 J.T. Snow .08 .25
6 Russ Ortiz .20 .50
7 Rich Aurilia .20 .50
8 Marvin Benard .08 .25
9 Kirk Rueter .20 .50
10 Benito Santiago .20 .50
11 Jason Schmidt .40 1.00
12 Reggie Sanders .08 .25
13 Livan Hernandez .30 .75
14 Tsuyoshi Shinjo .20 .50
15 Aaron Fultz .08 .25
16 Ramon Martinez .08 .25
17 Felix Rodriguez .08 .25
18 Shawon Dunston .08 .25
19 Tim Worrell .08 .25
20 David Bell .08 .25
21 Pedro Feliz .20 .50
22 Chad Zerbe .08 .25
23 Damon Minor .08 .25
24 Yorvit Torrealba .08 .25
25 Jay Witasick .08 .25
26 Ryan Jensen .08 .25
27 Jason Christiansen .08 .25
28 Carlos Alfonso CO .08 .25
Gene Clines CO
Sonny Jackson C

2003 Giants Chevron

1 Robb Nen 1.25 3.00
Lou Seal

2006 Giants Topps

COMPLETE SET (14) 3.00 8.00
SFG1 Barry Bonds .50 1.25
SFG2 Moises Alou .12 .30
SFG3 Steve Finley .12 .30
SFG4 Jason Schmidt .12 .30
SFG5 Mike Matheny .12 .30
SFG6 Lance Niekro .12 .30
SFG7 Ray Durham .12 .30
SFG8 Omar Vizquel .20 .50
SFG9 Pedro Feliz .12 .30
SFG10 Randy Winn .12 .30
SFG11 Matt Morris .12 .30
SFG12 Armando Benitez .12 .30
SFG13 Matt Cain .75 2.00
SFG14 Noah Lowry .12 .30

2007 Giants Topps

COMPLETE SET (14) 3.00 8.00
SFG1 Barry Zito .20 .50
SFG2 Pedro Feliz .12 .30
SFG3 Randy Winn .12 .30
SFG4 Ray Durham .12 .30
SFG5 Rich Aurilia .12 .30
SFG6 Armando Benitez .12 .30
SFG7 Bengie Molina .12 .30
SFG8 Noah Lowry .12 .30
SFG9 Dave Roberts .20 .50
SFG10 Matt Cain .20 .50
SFG11 Eliezer Alfonzo .12 .30
SFG12 Matt Morris .12 .30
SFG13 Ryan Klesko .12 .30
SFG14 Omar Vizquel .20 .50

2008 Giants Topps

COMPLETE SET (14) 3.00 8.00
SFG1 Tim Lincecum .20 .50
SFG2 Barry Zito .20 .50
SFG3 Aaron Rowand .12 .30
SFG4 Ray Durham .12 .30
SFG5 Noah Lowry .12 .30
SFG6 Matt Cain .20 .50
SFG7 Bengie Molina .12 .30
SFG8 Omar Vizquel .20 .50
SFG9 Dave Roberts .20 .50
SFG10 Rajai Davis .12 .30
SFG11 Kevin Frandsen .12 .30
SFG12 Rich Aurilia .12 .30
SFG13 Randy Winn .12 .30
SFG14 Brad Hennessey .12 .30

2009 Giants Topps

SFG1 Tim Lincecum .25 .60
SFG2 Aaron Rowand .15 .40
SFG3 Matt Cain .25 .60
SFG4 Bengie Molina .15 .40
SFG5 Barry Zito .25 .60
SFG6 Fred Lewis .15 .40
SFG7 Jonathan Sanchez .15 .40
SFG8 Pablo Sandoval .30 .75
SFG9 Randy Johnson .40 1.00
SFG10 Edgar Renteria .15 .40
SFG11 Brian Wilson .40 1.00
SFG12 Nate Schierholtz .15 .40
SFG13 Randy Winn .15 .40
SFG14 John Bowker .15 .40
SFG15 AT&T Park .15 .40

2009 Giants Topps Emerald

COMPLETE SET (31) 8.00 20.00
1 Tim Lincecum .60 1.50
2 Steve Holm .40 1.00
3 Bengie Molina .40 1.00
4 Joe Martinez .40 1.00
5 Alex Hinshaw .40 1.00
6 Randy Johnson 1.00 2.50
7 Andres Torres .40 1.00
8 Eugenio Velez .40 1.00
9 Jeremy Affeldt .40 1.00
10 Brandon Medders .40 1.00
11 Bob Howry .40 1.00
12 Pablo Sandoval .75 2.00
13 Emmanuel Burriss .40 1.00
14 Matt Cain .60 1.50
15 Edgar Renteria .40 1.00
16 Nate Schierholtz .40 1.00
17 Barry Zito .60 1.50
18 Aaron Rowand .40 1.00
19 Travis Ishikawa .40 1.00
20 Justin Miller .40 1.00
21 Randy Winn .40 1.00
22 Rich Aurilia .40 1.00
23 Juan Uribe .40 1.00
24 Merkin Valdez .40 1.00
25 Jonathan Sanchez .40 1.00
26 Brian Wilson 1.00 2.50
27 Fred Lewis .40 1.00
28 Bruce Bochy MG .60 1.50
29 Dave Righetti .40 1.00
Ron Wotus
30 Mark Gardner .40 1.00
Bill Hayes
31 Tim Flannery .40 1.00
Roberto Kelly
Carney Lansford

2010 Giants Topps

SFG1 Tim Lincecum .25 .60
SFG2 Jonathan Sanchez .15 .40
SFG3 Pablo Sandoval .25 .60
SFG4 Barry Zito .25 .60
SFG5 Juan Uribe .15 .40
SFG6 Bengie Molina .15 .40
SFG7 Madison Bumgarner 1.50 4.00
SFG8 Edgar Renteria .15 .40
SFG9 Aubrey Huff .15 .40
SFG10 Mark DeRosa .15 .40
SFG11 Freddy Sanchez .15 .40
SFG12 Buster Posey 1.25 3.00
SFG13 Brian Wilson .40 1.00
SFG14 Fred Lewis .15 .40
SFG15 Matt Cain .25 .60
SFG16 Travis Ishikawa .15 .40
SFG17 Nate Schierholtz .15 .40

2010 Giants Topps Emerald

COMPLETE SET (32) 20.00 50.00
1 Buster Posey 12.50 30.00
2 Jeremy Affeldt .40 1.00
3 Matt Cain .60 1.50
4 Waldis Joaquin .40 1.00
5 Tim Lincecum .60 1.50
6 Brandon Medders .40 1.00
7 Guillermo Mota .40 1.00
8 Sergio Romo 6.00 15.00
9 Dan Runzler .60 1.50
10 Jonathan Sanchez .40 1.00
11 Todd Wellemeyer .40 1.00
12 Brian Wilson 1.00 2.50
13 Barry Zito .60 1.50
14 John Bowker .40 1.00
15 Mark DeRosa .40 1.00
16 Matt Downs .40 1.00
17 Aubrey Huff .40 1.00
18 Travis Ishikawa .40 1.00
19 Bengie Molina .40 1.00
20 Edgar Renteria .40 1.00
21 Aaron Rowand .40 1.00
22 Freddy Sanchez .40 1.00
23 Pablo Sandoval .60 1.50
24 Nate Schierholtz .40 1.00
25 Andres Torres .40 1.00
26 Juan Uribe .40 1.00
27 Eugenio Velez .40 1.00
28 Eli Whiteside .40 1.00
29 Bruce Bochy MG .60 1.50
30 Hensley Meulens .40 1.00
Tim Flannery
Roberto Kelly
31 Dave Righetti .40 1.00
Ron Wotus
32 Mark Gardner .40 1.00
Bill Hayes

2010 Giants Topps World Series Champions

COMPLETE SET (27) 6.00 15.00
COMMON CARD .20 .50
SFG1 Tim Lincecum .30 .75
SFG2 Andres Torres .20 .50
SFG3 Cody Ross .20 .50
SFG4 Pablo Sandoval .30 .75
SFG5 Juan Uribe .20 .50
SFG6 Freddy Sanchez .20 .50
SFG7 Aubrey Huff .20 .50
SFG8 Buster Posey 1.50 4.00
SFG9 Pat Burrell .20 .50
SFG10 Matt Cain .30 .75
SFG11 Jonathan Sanchez .20 .50
SFG12 Madison Bumgarner 2.00 5.00
SFG13 Brian Wilson .50 1.25
SFG14 Jeremy Affeldt .20 .50
SFG15 Aaron Rowand .20 .50
SFG16 Nate Schierholtz .20 .50
SFG17 Mike Fontenot .20 .50
SFG18 Travis Ishikawa .20 .50
SFG19 Sergio Romo 3.00 8.00
SFG20 Ramon Ramirez .20 .50
SFG21 Javier Lopez .20 .50
SFG22 Edgar Renteria .20 .50
SFG23 NLDS Highlight .20 .50
SFG24 NLCS Highlight .20 .50
SFG25 WS Highlight .20 .50
SFG26 Winning the WS .20 .50
SFG27 Bruce Bochy MG .30 .75

2011 Giants Topps

SFG1 Buster Posey .50 1.25
SFG2 Tim Lincecum .25 .60
SFG3 Aubrey Huff .15 .40
SFG4 Matt Cain .25 .60
SFG5 Pat Burrell .15 .40
SFG6 Madison Bumgarner .30 .75
SFG7 Miguel Tejada .25 .60
SFG8 Cody Ross .15 .40
SFG9 Aaron Rowand .15 .40
SFG10 Freddy Sanchez .15 .40
SFG11 Jonathan Sanchez .15 .40
SFG12 Pablo Sandoval .25 .60
SFG13 Barry Zito .25 .60
SFG14 Andres Torres .15 .40
SFG15 Mark DeRosa .15 .40
SFG16 Brian Wilson .40 1.00
SFG17 ATT Park .15 .40

2011 Giants Topps Emerald

COMPLETE SET (32) 8.00 20.00
SFG1 Tim Lincecum .60 1.50
SFG2 Madison Bumgarner .75 2.00
SFG3 Matt Cain .60 1.50
SFG4 Santiago Casilla .40 1.00
SFG5 Jeremy Affeldt .40 1.00
SFG6 Javier Lopez .40 1.00
SFG7 Guillermo Mota .40 1.00
SFG8 Ramon Ramirez .40 1.00
SFG9 Sergio Romo .60 1.50
SFG10 Jonathan Sanchez .40 1.00
SFG11 Ryan Vogelsong .40 1.00
SFG12 Brian Wilson 1.00 2.50
SFG13 Barry Zito .60 1.50
SFG14 Buster Posey 1.25 3.00
SFG15 Eli Whiteside .40 1.00
SFG16 Emmanuel Burriss .40 1.00
SFG17 Brandon Crawford .60 1.50
SFG18 Mark DeRosa .40 1.00
SFG19 Mike Fontenot .40 1.00
SFG20 Pablo Sandoval .60 1.50
SFG21 Aubrey Huff .40 1.00
SFG22 Freddy Sanchez .40 1.00
SFG23 Miguel Tejada .60 1.50
SFG24 Pat Burrell .40 1.00
SFG25 Cody Ross .40 1.00
SFG26 Aaron Rowand .40 1.00
SFG27 Nate Schierholtz .40 1.00
SFG28 Andres Torres .40 1.00
SFG29 Bruce Bochy .60 1.50
SFG30 Dave Righetti .60 1.50
Ron Wotus
SFG31 Mark Gardner .40 1.00
Bill Hayes
SFG32 Tim Flannery .40 1.00
Roberto Kelly
Hensley Meulens

2012 Giants Topps

SF1 Tim Lincecum .30 .75
SF2 Brandon Belt .30 .75
SF3 Melky Cabrera .25 .60
SF4 Matt Cain .30 .75
SF5 Angel Pagan .25 .60
SF6 Ryan Vogelsong .25 .60
SF7 Mike Fontenot .15 .40
SF8 Aubrey Huff .25 .60
SF9 Freddy Sanchez .40 1.00
SF10 Madison Bumgarner .30 .75
SF11 Barry Zito .30 .75
SF12 Pablo Sandoval .30 .75
SF13 Buster Posey .50 1.25
SF14 Brian Wilson .40 1.00
SF15 Nate Schierholtz .25 .60
SF16 Brandon Crawford .25 .60
SF17 AT&T Park .15 .40

2012 Giants Topps Emerald

COMPLETE SET (32) 8.00 20.00
SF1 Jeremy Affeldt .60 1.50
SF2 Madison Bumgarner .75 2.00
SF3 Matt Cain .75 2.00
SF4 Santiago Casilla .60 1.50
SF5 Steve Edlefsen .40 1.00
SF6 Clay Hensley .60 1.50
SF7 Tim Lincecum .75 2.00
SF8 Javier Lopez .60 1.50
SF9 Guillermo Mota .40 1.00
SF10 Sergio Romo .75 2.00
SF11 Ryan Vogelsong .60 1.50
SF12 Brian Wilson 1.00 2.50
SF13 Barry Zito .75 2.00
SF14 Buster Posey 1.25 3.00
SF15 Hector Sanchez 1.00 2.50
SF16 Joaquin Arias .40 1.00
SF17 Brandon Belt .75 2.00
SF18 Emmanuel Burriss .40 1.00
SF19 Brandon Crawford .60 1.50
SF20 Brett Pill 1.00 2.50
SF21 Pablo Sandoval .75 2.00
SF22 Aubrey Huff .60 1.50
SF23 Ryan Theriot 2.00 5.00
SF24 Gregor Blanco .40 1.00
SF25 Melky Cabrera .60 1.50
SF26 Angel Pagan .60 1.50
SF27 Freddy Sanchez 1.00 2.50
SF28 Nate Schierholtz .60 1.50
SF29 Bruce Bochy .60 1.50
SF30 Dave Righetti .40 1.00
Ron Wotus
SF31 Mark Gardner .40 1.00
Bill Hayes
SF32 Tim Flannery .40 1.00
Roberto Kelly
Hensley Meulens

2013 Giants Topps

COMPLETE SET (17) 3.00 8.00
SFG1 Buster Posey .30 .75
SFG2 Matt Cain .20 .50
SFG3 Pablo Sandoval .20 .50
SFG4 Madison Bumgarner .20 .50
SFG5 Ryan Vogelsong .25 .60
SFG6 Tim Lincecum .30 .75
SFG7 Barry Zito .20 .50
SFG8 Brandon Belt .20 .50
SFG9 Brandon Crawford .20 .50
SFG10 Marco Scutaro .20 .50
SFG11 Sergio Romo .25 .60
SFG12 Gregor Blanco .20 .50
SFG13 Angel Pagan .15 .40
SFG14 Hunter Pence .30 .75
SFG15 Santiago Casilla .15 .40
SFG16 Jeremy Affeldt .15 .40
SFG17 AT&T Park .15 .40

2014 Giants Topps

COMPLETE SET (17) 3.00 8.00
SFG1 Buster Posey .30 .75
SFG2 Matt Cain .20 .50
SFG3 Pablo Sandoval .20 .50
SFG4 Madison Bumgarner .20 .50
SFG5 Angel Pagan .15 .40
SFG6 Tim Lincecum .20 .50
SFG7 Tim Hudson .20 .50
SFG8 Brandon Belt .20 .50
SFG9 Brandon Crawford .20 .50
SFG10 Marco Scutaro .20 .50
SFG11 Sergio Romo .20 .50
SFG12 Gregor Blanco .15 .40
SFG13 Ryan Vogelsong .15 .40
SFG14 Hunter Pence .20 .50
SFG15 Michael Morse .15 .40
SFG16 Jeremy Affeldt .15 .40
SFG17 AT&T Park .15 .40

2015 Giants Topps

COMPLETE SET (17) 3.00 8.00
SFG1 Madison Bumgarner .20 .50
SFG2 Brandon Belt .20 .50
SFG3 Joaquin Arias .15 .40
SFG4 Matt Cain .20 .50
SFG5 Santiago Casilla .15 .40
SFG6 Travis Ishikawa .15 .40
SFG7 Brandon Crawford .20 .50
SFG8 Joe Panik .20 .50
SFG9 Tim Hudson .20 .50
SFG10 Tim Lincecum .20 .50
SFG11 Hunter Pence .20 .50
SFG12 Buster Posey .30 .75
SFG13 Casey McGehee .15 .40
SFG14 Yusmeiro Petit .15 .40
SFG15 Andrew Susac .15 .40
SFG16 Angel Pagan .15 .40
SFG17 Gregor Blanco .15 .40

2016 Giants Topps

COMPLETE SET (17) 3.00 8.00
SFG1 Buster Posey .30 .75
SFG2 Brandon Belt .20 .50
SFG3 Joe Panik .20 .50
SFG4 Brandon Crawford .20 .50
SFG5 Matt Duffy .15 .40
SFG6 Jeff Samardzija .15 .40
SFG7 Angel Pagan .15 .40
SFG8 Hunter Pence .20 .50
SFG9 Madison Bumgarner .20 .50
SFG10 Matt Cain .20 .50
SFG11 Kelby Tomlinson .15 .40
SFG12 Chris Heston .15 .40
SFG13 Jake Peavy .15 .40
SFG14 Santiago Casilla .15 .40
SFG15 Johnny Cueto .20 .50
SFG16 Hunter Strickland .15 .40
SFG17 Denard Span .15 .40

2017 Giants Topps

COMPLETE SET (17) 3.00 8.00
SF1 Buster Posey .30 .75
SF2 Hunter Pence .20 .50
SF3 Madison Bumgarner .20 .50
SF4 Jeff Samardzija .15 .40
SF5 Mac Williamson .15 .40
SF6 Jarrett Parker .15 .40
SF7 Mark Melancon .15 .40
SF8 Brandon Belt .20 .50
SF9 Matt Moore .20 .50
SF10 Brandon Crawford .20 .50
SF11 Hunter Pence .20 .50
SF12 Johnny Cueto .20 .50
SF13 Eduardo Nunez .15 .40
SF14 Denard Span .15 .40
SF15 Hunter Strickland .15 .40
SF16 Joe Panik .20 .50
SF17 Trevor Brown .15 .40

2018 Giants Topps

COMPLETE SET (17) 2.00 5.00
SG1 Buster Posey .30 .75
SG2 Hunter Strickland .15 .40
SG3 Ty Blach .15 .40
SG4 Brandon Belt .20 .50
SG5 Johnny Cueto .20 .50
SG6 Jeff Samardzija .15 .40
SG7 Hunter Pence .20 .50
SG8 Evan Longoria .20 .50
SG9 Jarrett Parker .15 .40
SG10 Joe Panik .20 .50
SG11 Brandon Crawford .20 .50
SG12 Cory Gearrin .15 .40
SG13 Pablo Sandoval .20 .50
SG14 Mark Melancon .15 .40
SG15 Chris Stratton .15 .40
SG16 Sam Dyson .15 .40
SG17 Gorkys Hernandez .15 .40

2019 Giants Topps

COMPLETE SET (17) 2.00 5.00
SG1 Buster Posey .30 .75
SG2 Evan Longoria .20 .50
SG3 Joe Panik .20 .50
SG4 Johnny Cueto .20 .50
SG5 Jeff Samardzija .15 .40
SG6 Brandon Crawford .20 .50
SG7 Brandon Belt .20 .50
SG8 Steven Duggar .20 .50
SG9 Chris Shaw .15 .40
SG10 Austin Slater .15 .40
SG11 Andrew Suarez .15 .40
SG12 Chris Stratton .15 .40
SG13 Will Smith .15 .40
SG14 Mark Melancon .15 .40
SG15 Sam Dyson .15 .40
SG16 Alen Hanson .20 .50
SG17 Reyes Moronta .15 .40

2020 Giants Topps

SF1 Buster Posey .30 .75
SF2 Shaun Anderson .15 .40
SF3 Chris Shaw .15 .40
SF4 Jeff Samardzija .15 .40
SF5 Brandon Belt .20 .50
SF6 Jaylin Davis .25 .60
SF7 Mike Yastrzemski .40 1.00
SF8 Mauricio Dubon .20 .50
SF9 Brandon Crawford .20 .50
SF10 Evan Longoria .20 .50
SF11 Johnny Cueto .20 .50
SF12 Alex Dickerson .15 .40
SF13 Steven Duggar .15 .40
SF14 Tyler Beede .15 .40
SF15 Austin Slater .15 .40
SF16 Dereck Rodriguez .15 .40
SF17 Logan Webb .25 .60

2017 Giants Topps National Baseball Card Day

COMPLETE SET (10) 5.00 12.00
SFG1 Brandon Belt .75 2.00
SFG2 Brandon Crawford .75 2.00
SFG3 Johnny Cueto .75 2.00
SFG4 Mark Melancon .60 1.50
SFG5 Matt Moore .75 2.00
SFG6 Joe Panik .75 2.00
SFG7 Hunter Pence .75 2.00
SFG8 Buster Posey 1.25 3.00
SFG9 Jeff Samardzija .60 1.50
SFG10 1997 San Francisco Giants .60 1.50

2013 Giants Topps Chevron

COMPLETE SET (32) 8.00 20.00
SF1 Jeremy Affeldt .40 1.00
SF2 Madison Bumgarner .50 1.25
SF3 Matt Cain .50 1.25
SF4 Santiago Casilla .40 1.00
SF5 Chad Gaudin .40 1.00
SF6 Cole Gillespie .25 .60
SF7 George Kontos .40 1.00
SF8 Tim Lincecum .50 1.25
SF9 Javier Lopez .50 1.25
SF10 Jean Machi .40 1.00
SF11 Jose Mijares .40 1.00
SF12 Nick Noonan .50 1.25
SF13 Sergio Romo .40 1.00
SF14 Ryan Vogelsong .40 1.00
SF15 Barry Zito .50 1.25
SF16 Buster Posey .75 2.00
SF17 Hector Sanchez .40 1.00
SF18 Tony Abreu .25 .60
SF19 Joaquin Arias .40 1.00
SF20 Brandon Belt .50 1.25
SF21 Brandon Crawford .50 1.25
SF22 Pablo Sandoval .50 1.25
SF23 Marco Scutaro .75 2.00
SF24 Gregor Blanco .40 1.00
SF25 Angel Pagan .40 1.00
SF26 Hunter Pence .75 2.00
SF27 Andres Torres .60 1.50
SF28 Bruce Bochy .50 1.25
SF29 Dave Righetti .40 1.00
Ron Wotus
SF30 Mark Gardner .25 .60
Bill Hayes
SF31 Tim Flannery .40 1.00
Roberto Kelly
Hensley Meulens
NNO Baseball and Science .40 1.00

1981 Bob Gibson Omaha Hall of Fame

This one card black and white card set, which measures 6" by 8" was issued to attendees of the program which was used to celebrate Bob Gibson's induction into the Omaha Hall of Fame.

1 Bob Gibson 4.00 10.00

1942 Gillette Razor Label

This label was produced by the Gillette Razor company and honors the 1941 American League and National League Champions. The narrow cardboard label measures 4 3/8" by 1 3/8". The left side has two player photos printed in blue ink, the upper head shot is of "Lefty Gomez of the New York Yankees, and below is Johnny Mize of St. Louis Cardinals. The right side also carries two player head shots in blue ink of Bucky Walters of the Cincinnati Reds, and Red Rolfe of the New York Yankees. The middle portion is printed in red, blue, and yellow and has a navy blue pennant for the American League and a red pennant for the National League. The Gillette logo is printed where the two pennants intersect.

2000-01 Gold Collectibles 23K Game Used

1 Hank Aaron Bat 12.00 30.00
Numbered to 1000
2 Barry Bonds Bat 12.00 30.00
Numbered to 100
3 Roberto Clemente Bat 16.00 40.00
Numbered to 1000
4 Tony Gwynn Bat 12.00 30.00
Numbered to 1000
5 Mark McGwire Bat 12.00 30.00
Numbered to 1000
6 Cal Ripken Jr Bat 16.00 40.00
Numbered to 1000
7 Nolan Ryan Bat 16.00 40.00
Numbered to 1000
8 Ted Williams Bat 16.00 40.00
Numbered to 1000
9 Barry Bonds Bat 12.00 30.00
Numbered to 750
10 Ken Griffey Jr. Bat 15.00 40.00
Follow-Through, Numbered to 750
11 Ken Griffey Jr. Bat 15.00 40.00
Swinging, Numbered to 750
12 Tony Gwynn Bat 8.00 20.00
Numbered to 750
13 Cal Ripken Jr Bat 20.00 50.00
Numbered to 750
14 Alex Rodriguez Bat 8.00 20.00
Numbered to 750
15 Frank Thomas Bat 8.00 20.00
Numbered to 750
16 Bernie Williams Bat 8.00 20.00
Numbered to 750
17 Ted Williams Bat 16.00 40.00
Numbered to 750
18 Barry Bonds Bat 16.00 40.00
Single Season Homer run King
19 Derek Jeter/1996 Rookie of the Year 20.00 50.00
20 Subway Series 20.00 50.00
Bat Pieces from Derek Jeter
and Mike Piazza, Numbered to 2000

1934 Gold Medal Flour R313A

The 1934 Gold Medal Flour series was believed to have been issued to commemorate the World Series of 1934 which featured the Detroit Tigers and the St. Louis Cardinals as well as some other stars of the early 1930's. Each card measures approximately 3 1/4" by 5 3/8". The cards are blank backed and unnumbered. Some cards have recently been discovered, which were not cards of either Tigers or Cardinals. Therefore, even more additions are possible so any additions to this checklist are appreciated

COMPLETE SET 500.00 1000.00
1 Earl Averill 150.00 300.00
2 George Blaeholder 75.00 150.00
3 Tommy Bridges 15.00 30.00
4 Irving Burns 75.00 150.00
5 Bruce Campbell 75.00 150.00
6 Tex Carleton 15.00 30.00
7 Mickey Cochrane 30.00 60.00
8 Dizzy Dean 100.00 200.00
9 Paul Dean 25.00 50.00
10 George Earnshaw
11 Frank Frisch 30.00 60.00
12 Goose Goslin 30.00 60.00
13 Odell Hale 75.00 150.00
14 William Hallahan 15.00 30.00
15 Mel Harder 100.00 200.00
17 Chuck Klein
18 Jack Knott 75.00 150.00
19 Fred Marberry 15.00 30.00
20 Pepper Martin 25.00 50.00
21 Joe Medwick 30.00 60.00
22 William Rogell 15.00 30.00
23 Al Simmons
24 Hal Trosky 75.00 150.00
25 Joe Vosmik 75.00 150.00
26 Bill Walker 15.00 30.00
27 Jo-Jo White 15.00 30.00

1969 Globe Imports

These very thin paper-stock blank-backed cards, which measure approximately 1 5/8" by 2 1/4" and feature the playing card ID in both the upper left and lower right corner with a player photo in the middle. Since these were designed as playing card type elements we have sequenced our checklist with A meaning 1, through King at 13.

COMPLETE SET 12.50 30.00
C1 Richie Allen .40 1.00
C2 Reggie Smith .30 .75
C3 Jerry Koosman .30 .75
C4 Tony Oliva .40 1.00
C5 Bud Harrelson .20 .50
C6 Rick Reichardt .10 .25
C7 Billy Williams .60 1.50
C8 Pete Rose 4.00 10.00
C9 Jim Maloney .10 .25
C10 Tim McCarver .40 1.00
C11 Max Alvis .10 .25
C12 Ron Swoboda .20 .50
C13 Johnny Callison .10 .25
D1 Bob Gibson 1.00 2.50
D2 Paul Casanova .10 .25
D3 Juan Marichal 1.00 2.50
D4 Jim Fregosi .20 .50
D5 Earl Wilson .10 .25
D6 Tony Horton .10 .25
D7 Harmon Killebrew 1.00 2.50
D8 Tom Seaver 2.50 6.00
D9 Curt Flood .40 1.00
D10 Frank Robinson 1.50 4.00
D11 Bob Aspromonte .10 .25
D12 Lou Brock 1.00 2.50
D13 Jim Lonborg .20 .50
H1 Willie Mays 2.50 6.00
H2 Chris Short .10 .25
H3 Tony Conigliaro .30 .75
H4 Bill Freehan .20 .50
H5 Willie McCovey 1.25 3.00
H6 Joel Horlen .10 .25
H7 Ernie Banks 1.50 4.00
H8 Jim Wynn .20 .50
H9 Brooks Robinson 1.00 2.50
H10 Orlando Cepeda 1.00 2.50
H11 Al Kaline 1.00 2.50
H12 Gene Alley .10 .25
H13 Rusty Staub .30 .75
S1a Ken Harrelson .20 .50
S1b Mickey Mantle 15.00 40.00
S2 Denny McLain .20 .50
S3 Rick Monday .10 .25
S4 Richie Allen .40 1.00
S5 Mel Stottlemyre .20 .50
S6 Tommy John .30 .75
S7 Don Mincher .10 .25
S8 Chico Cardenas .10 .25
S9 Willie Davis .20 .50
S10 Bert Campaneris .20 .50
S11 Ron Santo .40 1.00
S12 Al Ferrara .10 .25
S13 Clete Boyer .10 .25

1961 Golden Press

The cards in this 33-card set measure 2 1/2" by 3 1/2". The 1961 Golden Press set of full color cards features members of Baseball's Hall of Fame. The cards came in a booklet with perforations for punching the cards out of the book. The catalog designation for this set is W524. The price for the full book intact is double the complete set price listed. Some collectors believe that the three cards which appear on the cover are more difficult to obtain in high-graded third party professional graded condition than the other cards in this set.

COMPLETE SET (33) 100.00 250.00
1 Mel Ott 2.50 6.00
2 Grover C. Alexander 2.00 5.00
3 Babe Ruth 30.00 60.00
4 Hank Greenberg 2.00 5.00
5 Bill Terry 1.25 3.00
6 Carl Hubbell 1.25 3.00
7 Rogers Hornsby 2.50 6.00
8 Dizzy Dean 4.00 10.00
9 Joe DiMaggio 20.00 50.00
10 Charlie Gehringer .60 1.50
11 Gabby Hartnett .60 1.50
12 Mickey Cochrane 1.25 3.00
13 George Sisler .60 1.50
14 Joe Cronin .60 1.50
15 Pie Traynor .60 1.50
16 Lou Gehrig 20.00 50.00
17 Lefty Grove 2.00 5.00
18 Chief Bender .60 1.50
19 Frankie Frisch .60 1.50
20 Al Simmons .60 1.50
21 Home Run Baker .60 1.50
22 Jimmy Foxx 2.50 6.00
(Jimmie)
23 John McGraw .60 1.50
24 Christy Mathewson 4.00 10.00
25 Ty Cobb 20.00 50.00
26 Dazzy Vance .60 1.50
27 Bill Dickey 1.25 3.00
28 Eddie Collins 1.25 3.00
29 Walter Johnson 5.00 12.00
30 Tris Speaker 2.00 5.00
31 Nap Lajoie 2.00 5.00
32 Honus Wagner 4.00 10.00
33 Cy Young 2.50 6.00
XX Album 3.00 8.00

1990 Good Humor Ice Cream Big League Sticks

This 26-piece set of ice cream sticks are shaped like baseball bats.They carry facsimile autographs and are individually numbered and are in alphabetical order.

COMPLETE SET (26) 15.00 40.00
1 Jim Abbott .20 .50
2 George Bell .08 .25
3 Wade Boggs .60 1.50
4 Bobby Bonilla .08 .25
5 Jose Canseco .60 1.50
6 Will Clark .60 1.50
7 Eric Davis .20 .50
8 Carlton Fisk .60 1.50
9 Kirk Gibson .20 .50
10 Dwight Gooden .20 .50
11 Ken Griffey Jr. 2.50 6.00
12 Von Hayes .08 .25
13 Don Mattingly 1.50 4.00
14 Gregg Olson .08 .25
15 Kirby Puckett 1.00 2.50
16 Tim Raines .20 .50
17 Nolan Ryan 3.00 8.00
18 Bret Saberhagen .08 .25
19 Ryne Sandberg 1.50 4.00
20 Benito Santiago .20 .50
21 Mike Scott .08 .25
22 Lonnie Smith .08 .25
23 Ozzie Smith 1.50 4.00
24 Cory Snyder .08 .25
25 Alan Trammell .30 .75
26 Robin Yount .60 1.50
XX Album 4.00 10.00

1888 Goodwin Champions N162

This 50-card set issued by Goodwin was one of the major competitors to the N28 and N29 sets marketed by Allen and Ginter. It contains individuals representing 18 sports, with eight baseball players pictured. Each color card is backlisted and bears advertising for "Old Judge" and "Gypsy Queen" cigarettes on the front. The set was released to the public in 1888 and an album (catalog: A36) is associated with it as a premium issue.

1 Ed Andrews (Baseball) 350.00 700.00
2 Cap Anson (Baseball) 1750.00 3500.00
3 Dan Brouthers (Baseball) 700.00 1400.00
4 Bob Caruthers (Baseball) 400.00 750.00
5 Fred Dunlap (Baseball) 350.00 700.00
6 Jack Glasscock (Baseball) 400.00 750.00
7 Tim Keefe (Baseball) 700.00 1400.00
8 King Kelly (Baseball) 1250.00 2500.00

1933 Goudey

The cards in this 240-card set measure approximately 2 3/8" by 2 7/8". The 1933 Goudey set, was that company's first baseball issue. The four Babe Ruth and two Lou Gehrig cards in the set are extremely popular with collectors. Card number 106, Napoleon Lajoie, was not printed in 1933, and was circulated to a limited number of collectors in 1934 upon request (it was printed along with the 1934 Goudey cards). An album was offered to house the 1933 set. Several minor leaguers are depicted. Card number 1 (Bengough) is very rarely found in mint condition; in fact, as a general rule all the first series cards are more difficult to find in Mint condition. Players with more than one card are also sometimes differentiated below by their pose: BAT (Batting), FIELD (Fielding), PIT (Pitching), THROW (Throwing). One of the Babe Ruth cards was double printed (DP) apparently in place of the Lajoie and hence is easier to obtain than the others. Due to the scarcity of the Lajoie card, the set is considered complete at 239 cards and is priced as such below. One copy of card number 106 as Leo Durocher is known to exist. The card was apparently cut from a proof sheet and is the only known copy to exist. A large window display poster which measured 5 3/8" by 11 1/4" was sent to stores and used the same Babe Ruth photo as in the Goudey Premium set. The gum used was approximately the same dimension as the actual card. At the factory each piece was scored twice so it could be snapped into three pieces. The gum had a spearmint flavor and according to collectors who remember chewing said gum, the flavor did not last very long.

COMPLETE SET (239)	75000.00	200000.00
COMMON CARD (1-52)	30.00	80.00
COMMON (41/43/53-240)	50.00	120.00
WRAPPER (1-CENT, BAT.)	40.00	100.00
WRAPPER (1-CENT, AD)	50.00	120.00
1 Benny Bengough RC	750.00	2000.00
2 Dazzy Vance RC	400.00	1000.00
3 Hugh Critz BAT RC	60.00	150.00
4 Heinie Schuble RC	60.00	150.00
5 Babe Herman RC	125.00	300.00
6 Jimmy Dykes RC	75.00	200.00
7 Ted Lyons RC	150.00	400.00
8 Roy Johnson RC	40.00	100.00
9 Dave Harris RC	50.00	120.00
10 Glenn Myatt RC	100.00	250.00
11 Billy Rogell RC	60.00	150.00
12 George Pipgras RC	100.00	250.00
13 Fresco Thompson RC	75.00	200.00
14 Henry Johnson RC	60.00	150.00
15 Victor Sorrell RC	50.00	120.00
16 George Blaeholder RC	60.00	150.00
17 Watson Clark RC	50.00	120.00
18 Muddy Ruel RC	50.00	120.00
19 Bill Dickey RC	500.00	1200.00
20 Bill Terry THROW RC	150.00	400.00
21 Phil Collins RC	60.00	150.00
22 Pie Traynor RC	300.00	800.00
23 Kiki Cuyler RC	200.00	500.00
24 Horace Ford RC	75.00	200.00
25 Paul Waner RC	400.00	1000.00
26 Bill Cissell RC	40.00	100.00
27 George Connally RC	60.00	150.00
28 Dick Bartell RC	50.00	120.00
29 Jimmie Foxx RC	1000.00	2500.00
30 Frank Hogan RC	50.00	120.00
31 Tony Lazzeri RC	400.00	1000.00
32 Bud Clancy RC	60.00	150.00
33 Ralph Kress RC	40.00	100.00
34 Bob O'Farrell RC	60.00	150.00
35 Al Simmons RC	200.00	500.00
36 Tommy Thevenow RC	40.00	100.00
37 Jimmy Wilson RC	50.00	120.00
38 Fred Brickell RC	60.00	150.00
39 Mark Koenig RC	60.00	150.00
40 Taylor Douthit RC	50.00	120.00
41 Gus Mancuso CATCH	50.00	120.00
42 Eddie Collins RC	150.00	400.00
43 Lew Fonseca RC	60.00	150.00
44 Jim Bottomley RC	150.00	400.00
45 Larry Benton RC	50.00	120.00
46 Ethan Allen RC	60.00	150.00
47 Heinie Manush BAT RC	125.00	300.00
48 Marty McManus RC	60.00	150.00
49 Frankie Frisch RC	300.00	800.00
50 Ed Brandt RC	40.00	100.00
51 Charlie Grimm RC	60.00	150.00
52 Andy Cohen RC	40.00	100.00
53 Babe Ruth RC	25000.00	60000.00
54 Ray Kremer RC	30.00	80.00
55 Pat Malone RC	40.00	100.00
56 Red Ruffing RC	200.00	500.00
57 Earl Clark RC	30.00	80.00
58 Lefty O'Doul RC	60.00	150.00
59 Bing Miller RC	60.00	150.00
60 Waite Hoyt RC	150.00	400.00
61 Max Bishop RC	50.00	120.00
62 Pepper Martin RC	60.00	150.00
63 Joe Cronin BAT RC	125.00	300.00
64 Burleigh Grimes RC	150.00	400.00
65 Milt Gaston RC	40.00	100.00
66 George Grantham RC	30.00	80.00
67 Guy Bush RC	50.00	120.00
68 Horace Lisenbee RC	30.00	80.00
69 Randy Moore RC	40.00	100.00
70 Floyd (Pete) Scott RC	40.00	100.00
71 Robert J. Burke RC	40.00	100.00
72 Owen Carroll RC	40.00	100.00
73 Jesse Haines RC	150.00	400.00
74 Eppa Rixey RC	150.00	400.00
75 Willie Kamm RC	40.00	100.00
76 Mickey Cochrane RC	250.00	600.00
77 Adam Comorosky RC	50.00	120.00
78 Jack Quinn RC	40.00	100.00
79 Red Faber RC	125.00	300.00
80 Clyde Manion RC	40.00	100.00
81 Sam Jones RC	40.00	100.00
82 Dib Williams RC	30.00	80.00
83 Pete Jablonowski RC	40.00	100.00
84 Glenn Spencer RC	50.00	120.00
85 Heinie Sand RC	50.00	120.00
86 Phil Todt RC	50.00	120.00
87 Frank O'Rourke RC	40.00	100.00
88 Russell Rollings RC	30.00	80.00
89 Tris Speaker RET	300.00	800.00
90 Jess Petty RC	60.00	150.00
91 Tom Zachary RC	30.00	80.00
92 Lou Gehrig RC	6000.00	15000.00
93 John Welch RC	60.00	150.00
94 Bill Walker RC	50.00	120.00
95 Alvin Crowder RC	50.00	120.00
96 Willis Hudlin RC	40.00	100.00
97 Joe Morrissey RC	30.00	80.00
98 Wally Berger RC	50.00	120.00
99 Tony Cuccinello RC	30.00	80.00
100 George Uhle RC	60.00	150.00
101 Richard Coffman RC	40.00	100.00
102 Travis Jackson RC	150.00	400.00
103 Earle Combs RC	150.00	400.00
104 Fred Marberry RC	75.00	200.00
105 Bernie Friberg RC	40.00	100.00
106 Napoleon Lajoie SP	25000.00	60000.00
107 Heinie Manush RC	100.00	250.00
108 Joe Kuhel RC	60.00	150.00
109 Joe Cronin RC	75.00	200.00
110 Goose Goslin RC	75.00	200.00
111 Monte Weaver RC	50.00	120.00
112 Fred Schulte RC	40.00	100.00
113 Oswald Bluege POR RC	50.00	120.00
114 Luke Sewell FIELD RC	50.00	120.00
115 Cliff Heathcote RC	60.00	150.00
116 Eddie Morgan RC	40.00	100.00
117 Rabbit Maranville RC	150.00	400.00
118 Val Picinich RC	75.00	200.00
119 Rogers Hornsby Field RC	400.00	1000.00
120 Carl Reynolds RC	50.00	120.00
121 Walter Stewart RC	30.00	80.00
122 Alvin Crowder RC	40.00	100.00
123 Jack Russell RC	40.00	100.00
124 Earl Whitehill RC	50.00	120.00
125 Bill Terry RC	100.00	250.00
126 Joe Moore BAT RC	50.00	120.00
127 Mel Ott RC	600.00	1500.00
128 Chuck Klein RC	150.00	400.00
129 Hal Schumacher PIT RC	60.00	150.00
130 Fred Fitzsimmons POR RC	40.00	100.00
131 Fred Frankhouse RC	60.00	150.00
132 Jim Elliott RC	50.00	120.00
133 Fred Lindstrom RC	150.00	400.00
134 Sam Rice RC	150.00	400.00
135 Woody English RC	40.00	100.00
136 Flint Rhem RC	50.00	120.00
137 Red Lucas RC	50.00	120.00
138 Herb Pennock RC	200.00	500.00
139 Ben Cantwell RC	40.00	100.00
140 Bump Hadley RC	60.00	150.00
141 Ray Benge RC	40.00	100.00
142 Paul Richards RC	30.00	80.00
143 Glenn Wright RC	60.00	150.00
144 Babe Ruth Bat DP RC	15000.00	40000.00
145 Rube Walberg RC	40.00	100.00
146 Walter Stewart PIT RC	40.00	100.00
147 Leo Durocher RC	100.00	250.00
148 Eddie Farrell RC	40.00	100.00
149 Babe Ruth RC	15000.00	40000.00
150 Ray Kolp RC	50.00	120.00
151 Jake Flowers RC	50.00	120.00
152 Zack Taylor RC	40.00	100.00
153 Buddy Myer RC	40.00	100.00
154 Jimmie Foxx RC	1000.00	2500.00
155 Joe Judge RC	75.00	200.00
156 Danny MacFayden RC	50.00	120.00
157 Sam Byrd RC	50.00	120.00
158 Moe Berg RC	400.00	1000.00
159 Oswald Bluege FIELD RC	40.00	100.00
160 Lou Gehrig RC	8000.00	20000.00
161 Al Spohrer RC	60.00	150.00
162 Leo Mangum RC	75.00	200.00
163 Luke Sewell POR RC	40.00	100.00
164 Lloyd Waner RC	400.00	1000.00
165 Joe Sewell RC	100.00	250.00
166 Sam West RC	60.00	150.00
167 Jack Russell RC	40.00	100.00
168 Goose Goslin RC	125.00	300.00
169 Al Thomas RC	30.00	80.00
170 Harry McCurdy RC	40.00	100.00
171 Charlie Jamieson RC	50.00	120.00
172 Billy Hargrave RC	30.00	60.00
173 Roscoe Holm RC	50.00	120.00
174 Warren (Curly) Ogden RC	40.00	100.00
175 Dan Howley MG RC	60.00	150.00
176 John Ogden RC	50.00	120.00
177 Walter French RC	50.00	120.00
178 Jackie Warner RC	40.00	100.00
179 Fred Leach RC	30.00	60.00
180 Eddie Moore RC	40.00	100.00
181 Babe Ruth RC	20000.00	50000.00
182 Andy High RC	60.00	150.00
183 Rube Walberg RC	30.00	80.00
184 Charley Berry RC	60.00	150.00
185 Bob Smith RC	50.00	120.00
186 John Schulte RC	50.00	120.00
187 Heinie Manush RC	75.00	200.00
188 Rogers Hornsby RC	250.00	600.00
189 Joe Cronin RC	100.00	250.00
190 Fred Schulte RC	30.00	80.00
191 Ben Chapman RC	40.00	100.00
192 Walter Brown RC	40.00	100.00
193 Lynford Lary RC	50.00	120.00
194 Earl Averill RC	150.00	400.00
195 Evar Swanson RC	40.00	100.00
196 Leroy Mahaffey RC	50.00	120.00
197 Rick Ferrell RC	200.00	500.00
198 Jack Burns RC	40.00	100.00
199 Tom Bridges RC	60.00	150.00
200 Bill Hallahan RC	60.00	150.00
201 Ernie Orsatti RC	60.00	150.00
202 Gabby Hartnett RC	125.00	300.00
203 Lon Warneke RC	30.00	80.00
204 Riggs Stephenson RC	40.00	100.00
205 Heinie Meine RC	50.00	120.00
206 Gus Suhr RC	30.00	80.00
207 Mel Ott Bat RC	250.00	600.00
208 Bernie James RC	50.00	120.00
209 Adolfo Luque RC	30.00	80.00
210 Spud Davis RC	40.00	100.00
211 Hack Wilson RC	500.00	1200.00
212 Billy Urbanski RC	60.00	150.00
213 Earl Adams RC	50.00	120.00
214 John Kerr RC	40.00	100.00
215 Russ Van Atta RC	40.00	100.00
216 Lefty Gomez RC	200.00	500.00
217 Frank Crosetti RC	100.00	250.00
218 Wes Ferrell RC	60.00	150.00
219 Mule Haas UER RC	60.00	150.00
220 Lefty Grove RC	500.00	1200.00
221 Dale Alexander RC	40.00	100.00
222 Charley Gehringer RC	300.00	800.00
223 Dizzy Dean RC	750.00	2000.00
224 Frank Demaree RC	50.00	120.00
225 Bill Jurges RC	40.00	100.00
226 Charley Root RC	125.00	300.00
227 Billy Herman RC	200.00	500.00
228 Tony Piet RC	30.00	80.00
229 Arky Vaughan RC	150.00	400.00
230 Carl Hubbell PIT RC	200.00	500.00
231 Joe Moore FIELD RC	40.00	100.00
232 Lefty O'Doul RC	100.00	250.00
233 Johnny Vergez RC	50.00	120.00
234 Carl Hubbell RC	250.00	600.00
235 Fred Fitzsimmons PIT RC	40.00	100.00
236 George Davis RC	50.00	120.00
237 Gus Mancuso FIELD RC	60.00	150.00
238 Hugh Critz FIELD RC	40.00	100.00
239 Leroy Parmelee RC	40.00	100.00
240 Hal Schumacher RC	50.00	120.00

1933 World Wide Gum V353

The cards in this 94-card set measure approximately 2 3/8" by 2 7/8". World Wide Gum, the Canadian subsidiary of Goudey issued this set of numbered color cards in 1933. Cards 1 to 52 contain obverses identical to the American issue, but cards 53 to 94 have a slightly different order. The fronts feature white-bordered color player drawings. The words "Big League Chewing Gum" are printed in white lettering within a red stripe near the bottom. The green ink backs are found printed in English only, or in French and English (the latter are slightly harder to find and are valued at a 25 percent premium over the prices listed below). The catalog designation for this set is V353.

COMPLETE SET (94)	12000.00	20000.00
1 Benny Bengough	350.00	600.00
2 Dazzy Vance	75.00	120.00
3 Hugh Critz	35.00	60.00
4 Heinie Schulbe	35.00	60.00
5 Babe Herman	60.00	100.00
6 Jimmy Dykes	50.00	80.00
7 Ted Lyons	75.00	120.00
8 Roy Johnson	35.00	60.00
9 Dave Harris	35.00	60.00
10 Glenn Myatt	35.00	60.00
11 Billy Rogell	35.00	60.00
12 George Pipgras	50.00	80.00
13 Lafayette Thompson	35.00	60.00
14 Henry Johnson	35.00	60.00
15 Victor Sorrell	35.00	60.00
16 George Blaeholder	35.00	60.00
17 Watson Clark	35.00	60.00
18 Muddy Ruel	35.00	60.00
19 Bill Dickey	250.00	400.00
20 Bill Terry	125.00	200.00
21 Phil Collins	35.00	60.00
22 Pie Traynor	75.00	120.00
23 Kiki Cuyler	75.00	120.00
24 Horace Ford	35.00	60.00
25 Paul Waner	75.00	120.00
26 Chalmer Cissell	35.00	60.00
27 George Connally	35.00	60.00
28 Dick Bartell	50.00	80.00
29 Jimmy Foxx (Jimmie)	300.00	500.00
30 Frank Hogan	35.00	60.00
31 Tony Lazzeri	125.00	200.00
32 Bud Clancy	35.00	60.00
33 Ralph Kress	35.00	60.00
34 Bob O'Farrell	50.00	80.00
35 Al Simmons	125.00	200.00
36 Tommy Thevenow	35.00	60.00
37 Jimmy Wilson	50.00	80.00
38 Fred Bickell	35.00	60.00
39 Mark Koenig	50.00	80.00
40 Taylor Douthit	35.00	60.00
41 Gus Mancuso	35.00	60.00
42 Eddie Collins	75.00	120.00
43 Lew Fonseca	50.00	80.00
44 Jim Bottomley	75.00	120.00
45 Larry Benton	35.00	60.00
46 Ethan Allen	50.00	80.00
47 Heinie Manush	75.00	120.00
48 Marty McManus	35.00	60.00
49 Frank Frisch	75.00	120.00
50 Ed Brandt	35.00	60.00
51 Charlie Grimm	50.00	80.00
52 Andy Cohen	35.00	60.00
53 Jack Quinn	50.00	80.00
54 Urban Faber	75.00	120.00
55 Lou Gehrig	2500.00	5000.00
56 John Welch	35.00	60.00
57 Bill Walker	35.00	60.00
58 Lefty O'Doul	60.00	100.00
59 Bing Miller	50.00	80.00
60 Waite Hoyt	75.00	120.00
61 Max Bishop	50.00	80.00
62 Pepper Martin	60.00	100.00
63 Joe Cronin	75.00	120.00
64 Burleigh Grimes	75.00	120.00
65 Milt Gaston	35.00	60.00
66 George Grantham	35.00	60.00
67 Guy Bush	35.00	60.00
68 Willie Kamm	35.00	60.00
69 Mickey Cochrane	125.00	200.00
70 Adam Comorosky	35.00	60.00
71 Alvin Crowder	35.00	60.00
72 Willis Hudlin	35.00	60.00
73 Eddie Farrell	35.00	60.00
74 Leo Durocher	125.00	200.00
75 Walter Stewart	35.00	60.00
76 George Walberg	35.00	60.00
77 Glenn Wright	50.00	80.00
78 Buddy Myer	50.00	80.00
79 James(Zack) Taylor	35.00	60.00
80 George H.(Babe)Ruth	4000.00	8000.00
81 D'Arcy(Jake) Flowers	35.00	60.00
82 Ray Kolp	35.00	60.00
83 Oswald Bluege	35.00	60.00
84 Moe Berg	175.00	300.00
85 Jimmy Foxx (Jimmie)	300.00	500.00
86 Sam Byrd	35.00	60.00
87 Danny MacFayden	35.00	60.00
88 Joe Judge	50.00	80.00
89 Joe Sewell	75.00	120.00
90 Lloyd Waner	75.00	120.00
91 Luke Sewell	50.00	80.00
92 Leo Mangum	35.00	60.00
93 George H.(Babe)Ruth	3000.00	5000.00
94 Al Spohrer	50.00	80.00

1934 Goudey

The cards in this 96-card color set measure approximately 2 3/8" by 2 7/8". Cards 1-48 are considered to be the easiest to find (although card number 1, Foxx, is very scarce in mint condition) while 73-96 are much more difficult to find. Cards of this 1934 Goudey series are slightly less abundant than cards of the 1933 Goudey set. Of the 96 cards, 84 contain a "Lou Gehrig Says" line on the front in a blue design, while 12 of the high series (80-91) contain a "Chuck Klein Says" line in a red design. These Chuck Klein cards are indicated in the checklist below by CK and are in fact the 12 National Leaguers in the high series.

COMPLETE SET (96)	12000.00	30000.00
COMMON CARD (1-48)	20.00	50.00
COMMON CARD (49-72)	30.00	80.00
COMMON CARD (73-96)	50.00	120.00
WRAPPER (1-CENT, WHT.)	75.00	100.00
WRAPPER (1-CENT, CLR.)	75.00	100.00
1 Jimmie Foxx	1000.00	2500.00
2 Mickey Cochrane	200.00	500.00
3 Charlie Grimm	25.00	60.00
4 Woody English	25.00	60.00
5 Ed Brandt	30.00	80.00
6 Dizzy Dean	500.00	1200.00
7 Leo Durocher	150.00	400.00
8 Tony Piet	25.00	60.00
9 Ben Chapman	50.00	120.00
10 Chuck Klein	100.00	250.00
11 Paul Waner	75.00	200.00
12 Carl Hubbell	150.00	400.00
13 Frankie Frisch	125.00	300.00
14 Willie Kamm	30.00	80.00
15 Alvin Crowder	30.00	80.00
16 Joe Kuhel	25.00	60.00
17 Hugh Critz	30.00	80.00
18 Heinie Manush	75.00	200.00
19 Lefty Grove	400.00	1000.00
20 Frank Hogan	25.00	60.00
21 Bill Terry	125.00	300.00
22 Arky Vaughan	75.00	200.00
23 Charley Gehringer	125.00	300.00
24 Ray Benge	30.00	80.00
25 Roger Cramer RC	25.00	60.00
26 Gerald Walker RC	25.00	60.00
27 Luke Appling RC	125.00	300.00
28 Ed Coleman RC	25.00	60.00
29 Larry French RC	25.00	60.00
30 Julius Solters RC	25.00	60.00
31 Buck Jordan RC	25.00	60.00
32 Blondy Ryan RC	25.00	60.00
33 Don Hurst RC	25.00	60.00
34 Chick Hafey RC	75.00	200.00
35 Ernie Lombardi RC	100.00	250.00
36 Walter Betts RC	30.00	80.00
37 Lou Gehrig	8000.00	20000.00
38 Oral Hildebrand RC	30.00	80.00
39 Fred Walker RC	30.00	80.00
40 John Stone	30.00	80.00
41 George Earnshaw RC	30.00	80.00
42 John Allen RC	25.00	60.00
43 Dick Porter RC	30.00	80.00
44 Tom Bridges	25.00	60.00
45 Oscar Melillo RC	40.00	100.00
46 Joe Stripp RC	30.00	80.00
47 John Frederick RC	30.00	80.00
48 Tex Carleton RC	30.00	80.00
49 Sam Leslie RC	40.00	100.00
50 Walter Beck RC	25.00	60.00
51 Rip Collins RC	30.00	75.00
52 Herman Bell RC	30.00	75.00
53 George Watkins RC	50.00	120.00
54 Wesley Schulmerich RC	30.00	80.00
55 Ed Holley RC	25.00	60.00
56 Mark Koenig	25.00	60.00
57 Bill Swift RC	30.00	75.00
58 Earl Grace RC	25.00	60.00
59 Joe Mowry RC	25.00	60.00
60 Lynn Nelson RC	25.00	60.00
61 Lou Gehrig	5000.00	12000.00
62 Hank Greenberg RC	1250.00	3000.00
63 Minter Hayes RC	30.00	75.00
64 Frank Grube RC	30.00	75.00
65 Cliff Bolton RC	30.00	75.00
66 Mel Harder RC	30.00	80.00
67 Bob Weiland RC	30.00	80.00
68 Bob Johnson RC	40.00	100.00
69 John Marcum RC	25.00	60.00
70 Pete Fox RC	25.00	60.00
71 Lyle Tinning RC	30.00	80.00
72 Arndt Jorgens RC	25.00	60.00
73 Ed Wells RC	50.00	120.00
74 Bob Boken RC	40.00	100.00
75 Bill Werber RC	50.00	120.00
76 Hal Trosky RC	75.00	200.00
77 Joe Vosmik RC	50.00	120.00
78 Pinky Higgins RC	50.00	120.00
79 Eddie Durham RC	50.00	120.00
80 Marty McManus CK	75.00	200.00
81 Bob Brown CK RC	75.00	200.00
82 Bill Hallahan CK	50.00	120.00
83 Jim Mooney CK RC	50.00	120.00
84 Paul Derringer CK RC	60.00	150.00
85 Adam Comorosky CK	60.00	150.00
86 Lloyd Johnson CK RC	40.00	100.00
87 George Darrow CK RC	50.00	120.00
88 Homer Peel CK RC	50.00	120.00
89 Linus Frey CK RC	50.00	120.00
90 KiKi Cuyler CK	250.00	600.00
91 Dolph Camilli CK RC	60.00	150.00
92 Steve Larkin RC	75.00	200.00
93 Fred Ostermueller RC	50.00	120.00
94 Red Rolfe RC	75.00	200.00
95 Myril Hoag RC	60.00	150.00
96 James DeShong RC	150.00	400.00

1934 World Wide Gum V354

The cards in this 96-card set measure approximately 2 3/8" by 2 7/8". The 1934 Canadian Goudey set was issued by World Wide Gum Company. Cards 1 to 48 have the same format as the 1933 American Goudey issue while cards 49 to 96 have the same format as the 1934 American Goudey issue. Cards numbers 49 to 96 all have the "Lou Gehrig Says" endorsement on the front of the cards. No Chuck Klein endorsement exists as it does in the 1934 American issue. The fronts feature white-bordered color player drawings. The words "Big League Chewing Gum" are printed in white lettering within a red stripe near the bottom. The green ink backs are found printed in English only, or in French and English (the latter are slightly harder to find and are valued at a 25 percent premium over the prices listed below). It has been recently speculated that the final 24 cards are printed in far greater quantity than the first 72 cards in the set. The catalog designation for this set is V354.

COMPLETE SET (96)	7800.00	13000.00
1 Rogers Hornsby	350.00	600.00
2 Eddie Morgan	35.00	60.00
3 Val Picinich	35.00	60.00
4 Rabbit Maranville	75.00	120.00
5 Flint Rhem	35.00	60.00
6 Jim Elliott	35.00	60.00
7 Fred(Red) Lucas	35.00	60.00
8 Fred Marberry	35.00	60.00
9 Clifton Heathcote	35.00	60.00
10 Bernie Friberg	35.00	60.00
11 Woody English	35.00	60.00
12 Carl Reynolds	35.00	60.00
13 Ray Benge	35.00	60.00
14 Ben Cantwell	35.00	60.00
15 Bump Hadley	35.00	60.00
16 Herb Pennock	75.00	120.00
17 Fred Lindstrom	75.00	120.00
18 Sam Rice	75.00	120.00
19 Fred Frankhouse	35.00	60.00
20 Fred Fitzsimmons	50.00	80.00
21 Earle Combs	75.00	120.00
22 George Uhle	35.00	60.00
23 Richard Coffman	35.00	60.00
24 Travis Jackson	75.00	120.00
25 Robert J. Burke	35.00	60.00
26 Randy Moore	35.00	60.00
27 Heinie Sand	35.00	60.00
28 George (Babe) Ruth	3000.00	5000.00
29 Tris Speaker	175.00	300.00
30 Perce(Pat) Malone	35.00	60.00
31 Sam Jones	50.00	80.00
32 Eppa Rixey	75.00	120.00
33 Floyd (Pete) Scott	35.00	60.00
34 Pete Jablonowski	35.00	60.00
35 Clyde Manion	35.00	60.00
36 Dib Williams	35.00	60.00
37 Glenn Spencer	35.00	60.00
38 Ray Kremer	35.00	60.00
39 Phil Todt	35.00	60.00
40 Russell Rollings	35.00	60.00
41 Earl Clark	35.00	60.00
42 Jess Petty	35.00	60.00
43 Frank O'Rourke	35.00	60.00
44 Jesse Haines	75.00	120.00
45 Horace Lisenbee	35.00	60.00
46 Owen Carroll	35.00	60.00
47 Tom Zachary	50.00	80.00
48 Red Ruffing	75.00	120.00
49 Ray Benge	35.00	60.00
50 Woody English	35.00	60.00
51 Ben Chapman	50.00	80.00
52 Joe Kuhel	35.00	60.00
53 Bill Terry	125.00	200.00
54 Robert(Lefty) Grove	175.00	300.00
55 Dizzy Dean	500.00	800.00
56 Chuck Klein	75.00	120.00
57 Charley Gehringer	125.00	200.00
58 Jimmie Foxx	250.00	400.00
59 Mickey Cochrane	125.00	200.00
60 Willie Kamm	35.00	60.00
61 Charlie Grimm	60.00	100.00
62 Ed Brandt	35.00	60.00
63 Tony Piet	35.00	60.00
64 Frank Frisch	75.00	120.00
65 Alvin Crowder	35.00	60.00
66 Frank Hogan	35.00	60.00
67 Paul Waner	75.00	120.00
68 Heinie Manush	75.00	120.00
69 Leo Durocher	75.00	120.00
70 Arky Vaughan	75.00	120.00
71 Carl Hubbell	125.00	200.00
72 Hugh Critz	35.00	60.00
73 John(Blondy) Ryan	35.00	60.00
74 Doc Cramer	50.00	80.00
75 Baxter Jordan	35.00	60.00
76 Ed Coleman	35.00	60.00
77 Julius(Moose) Solters	35.00	60.00
78 Chick Hafey	75.00	120.00
79 Larry French	35.00	60.00
80 Frank(Don) Hurst	35.00	60.00
81 Gerald Walker	35.00	60.00
82 Ernie Lombardi	75.00	120.00
83 Walter(Huck) Betts	35.00	60.00
84 Luke Appling	75.00	120.00
85 John Frederick	35.00	60.00
86 Fred(Dixie) Walker	60.00	100.00
87 Tom Bridges	50.00	80.00
88 Dick Porter	35.00	60.00
89 John Stone	35.00	60.00
90 James(Tex) Carleton	35.00	60.00
91 Joe Stripp	35.00	60.00
92 Lou Gehrig	2500.00	4000.00
93 George Earnshaw	50.00	80.00
94 Oscar Melillo	35.00	60.00
95 Oral Hildebrand	35.00	60.00
96 John Allen	50.00	80.00

1934 Goudey Card Album

These rare 1934 Goudey American and National League Card albums were issued one per box of Big League Gum or could be had by redeeming 50 Big League wrappers to the Goudey Gum Company. The American League album is red and the National League album is blue. Each has 10 spaces allocated for each of the teams in their respective leagues and for their All-Star teams. Each team has its own biography printed in the album.

COMPLETE SET (2)	500.00	1000.00
1 American League/(red)	250.00	500.00
2 National League/(blue)	250.00	500.00

1934 Goudey Premiums R309-1

The most ambitious premium issue of the Goudey Gum Company was the R309-1 set of 1934. Printed on heavy cardboard, the black and white picture was embellished with a gold and frame-like border and a back stand. Each of these thick cards measures approximately 5 1/2" by 8 15/16". The Babe Ruth card seems to be more common than the other cards in this short set. The Ruth card was available as a redemption for 50 wrappers sent to Goudey.

COMPLETE SET (4)	750.00	1200.00
1 A.L. All-Stars of 1933	200.00	400.00
2 N.L. All-Stars of 1933	200.00	400.00
3 World Champ 1933 Giants	250.00	500.00
4 Babe Ruth	500.00	1000.00

1935 Goudey Premiums R309-2

The 16 cards in the R309-2 Goudey Premium set are unnumbered, glossy black and white photos on thin paper stock. Teams (1-3) and individual players (4-16) are featured in this relatively scarce premium set from 1935. The ballplayer is identified by his name rendered in longhand in the "wide pen" style of later Goudey issues. This written name is not a facsimile autograph. Each card measures approximately 5 1/2" by 9".

COMPLETE SET (16)	900.00	1500.00
COMMON TEAM (1-3)	50.00	80.00
COMMON PLAYER (4-16)	50.00	80.00
1 Boston Red Sox	75.00	150.00
2 Cleveland Indians	75.00	150.00
3 Washington Senators	75.00	150.00
4 Elden Auker	75.00	150.00
5 Johnny Babich	75.00	150.00
6 Dick Bartell	75.00	150.00
7 Lester R. Bell	75.00	150.00
8 Wally Berger	100.00	200.00
9 Mickey Cochrane	200.00	400.00
10 Fox Goslin Walker	125.00	250.00
11 Lefty Gomez	150.00	300.00
12 Hank Greenberg	200.00	400.00
13 Oscar Melillo	75.00	150.00
14 Mel Ott	200.00	400.00
15 Schoolboy Rowe	75.00	150.00
16 Vito Tamulis	75.00	150.00

1935 Goudey 4-in-1

The cards in this confusing 36-card set (the number of different front pictures) measure approximately 2 3/8" by 2 7/8". The 1935 Goudey set is sometimes called the Goudey Puzzle set, or the Goudey 4-in-1n set. There are 36 different card fronts but 114 different front/back combinations. Our checklist details all 114 cards, grouped together by the 36 different card front combinations. The player combinations are listed alphabetically by reading the player names in clockwise order starting from the top left corner. The card backs can be arranged to form one of nine different puzzles picturing either a player or a team and each back specifically details both the puzzle (or "picture" as it states on the actual card backs) it belongs too using numbers 1-9 and the specific piece it is within the puzzle (using letters A-M). The following is the list of the puzzle back pictures: 1) Detroit Tigers; 2) Chuck Klein; 3) Frankie Frisch; 4) Mickey Cochrane; 5) Joe Cronin; 6) Jimmy Foxx; 7) Al Simmons; 8) Cleveland Indians; and 9) Washington Senators. The first seven puzzles were actually created in two separate combinations of card fronts; thus the Chuck Klein puzzle (catalogued as "Picture 2" on the card backs) is actually available in two different groups of six card fronts - one group of which has been verified as a short print. The SP cards have all been tagged in our checklist. Finally, a limited number of cards feature blue borders (rather than the standard red borders). Though they're not short-printed, we've tagged the cards for referential purposes.

COMPLETE SET (114)	8000.00	13500.00
COMMON CARDS (1-9)	30.00	50.00
COMMON CARDS (11-17)	45.00	80.00
WRAPPER (1-CENT, WHITE)	150.00	200.00
2-Jan Berry/Burk/Kres/Vance 2C SP	60.00	100.00
4-Jan Berry/Burk/Kres/Vance 4C	35.00	60.00
7-Jan Berry/Burk/Kres/Vance 7C	35.00	60.00
8-Feb Burns/Hems/Grub/Weil 8C	30.00	50.00
9-Feb Burns/Hems/Grub/Weil 9C	30.00	50.00
8-Mar Campbell/Mey/Good/Kamp 8D	30.00	50.00
9-Mar Campbell/Mey/Good/Kamp 9D	30.00	50.00
1-Apr Cochrane/Gehringer/Brid/Rog 1D	60.00	120.00
2-Apr Cochrane/Gehringer/Brid/Rog 2D	70.00	120.00
6-Apr Cochrane/Gehringer Brid/Rog 6D SP	90.00	150.00
7-Apr Cochrane/Gehringer Brid/Rog 7D SP	90.00	150.00
2-May Critz/Bartell/Ott/Manc 2A SP	90.00	150.00
4-May Critz/Bartell/Ott/Manc 4A	60.00	100.00
7-May Critz/Bartell/Ott/Manc 7A	60.00	100.00
1-Jun Cronin/Reyn/Bish/Ciss 1G SP	60.00	100.00
3-Jun Cronin/Reyn/Bish/Ciss 3E SP	60.00	100.00
5-Jun Cronin/Reyn/Bish/Ciss 5E SP	60.00	100.00
6-Jun Cronin/Reyn/Bish/Ciss 6E	35.00	60.00
8-Jul DeShong/Allen/Rolfe/Walk 8E	30.00	50.00
9-Jul DeShong/Allen/Rolfe/Walk 9E	30.00	50.00
1-Aug Earn/Dyk/Sew/Appling 1I	35.00	60.00
2-Aug Earn/Dyk/Sew/Appling 2F	35.00	60.00
6-Aug Earn/Dyk/Sew/Appling 6F SP	60.00	100.00
7-Aug Earn/Dyk/Sew/Appling 7F SP	60.00	100.00
8-Sep Fox/Greenberg/Walk/Rowe 8F	60.00	100.00
9-Sep Fox/Greenberg/Walk/Rowe 9F	60.00	100.00
1-Oct Frisch/Dean/Ors/Carl 1A	90.00	150.00
2-Oct Frisch/Dean/Ors/Carl 2A	90.00	150.00
6-Oct Frisch/Dean/Ors/Carl 6A SP	150.00	250.00
7-Oct Frisch/Dean/Ors/Carl 7A SP	150.00	250.00
1-Nov Grimes/Klein/Cuyler/Eng 1F	60.00	100.00
3-Nov Grimes/Klein/Cuyler/Eng 3D	60.00	100.00
4-Nov Grimes/Klein/Cuyler/Eng 4D SP	90.00	150.00
5-Nov Grimes/Klein/Cuyler/Eng 5D SP	90.00	150.00
8-Dec Hayes/Lyons/Haas/Bon 8B	35.00	60.00
9-Dec Hayes/Lyons/Haas/Bon 9B	35.00	60.00
13-8 Herman/Suhr/Padd/Blant 8K	35.00	60.00
13-9 Herman/Suhr/Padd/Blant 9K	35.00	60.00
14-1 Hudlin/Myatt/Com/Bottomley 1K SP	60.00	100.00
14-3 Hudlin/Myatt/Com/Bottomley 3B SP	60.00	100.00
14-5 Hudlin/Myatt/Com/Bottomley 5B	35.00	60.00
14-6 Hudlin/Myatt/Com/Bottomley 6B	35.00	60.00
15-8 Johnson/Cole/Marc/Cramer 8J	30.00	50.00
15-9 Johnson/Cole/Marc/Cramer 9J	30.00	50.00
16-1 Kamm/Hild/Averill/Tro 1L	35.00	60.00
16-2 Kamm/Hild/Averill/Tro 2E	35.00	60.00
16-6 Kamm/Hild/Averill/Tro 6E SP	60.00	100.00
16-7 Kamm/Hild/Averill/Tro 7E SP	60.00	100.00
17-8 Koenig/Fitz/Benge/Zach 8A	30.00	50.00
17-8 Koenig/Fitz/Benge/Zach 8M	30.00	50.00
18-8 Kuhel/White/Myer/Stone 8H	30.00	50.00
18-9 Kuhel/White/Myer/Stone 9H	30.00	50.00
19-1 Leslie/Frey/Stripp/Clark 1G	30.00	50.00
19-3 Leslie/Frey/Stripp/Clark 3E	30.00	50.00
19-4 Leslie/Frey/Stripp/Clark 4E SP	45.00	80.00
19-5 Leslie/Frey/Stripp/Clark 5E	30.00	50.00
20-1 Mahaffey/Foxx/Will/Hig 1B	70.00	120.00
20-2 Mahaffey/Foxx/Will/Hig 2B	70.00	120.00
20-6 Mahaffey/Foxx/Will/Hig 6B SP	90.00	150.00
20-7 Mahaffey/Foxx/Will/Hig 7B SP	125.00	200.00
21-1 Manush/Lary/Weav/Had 1C	35.00	60.00
21-2 Manush/Lary/Weav/Had 2C	35.00	60.00
21-6 Manush/Lary/Weav/Had 6C SP	60.00	100.00
21-7 Manush/Lary/Weav/Had 7C SP	60.00	100.00
22-2 Martin/O'Far/Byrd/Mac 2F SP	45.00	80.00
22-4 Martin/O'Far/Byrd/Mac 4F	30.00	50.00
22-7 Martin/O'Far/Byrd/Mac 7F	30.00	50.00
23-2 Moore/Hogan/Frank/Bran 2E SP	45.00	80.00
23-4 Moore/Hogan/Frank/Bran 4E	30.00	50.00
23-7 Moore/Hogan/Frank/Bran 7E	30.00	50.00
24-1 Piet/Com/Bottomley/Adam 1H	35.00	60.00
24-3 Piet/Com/Bottomley/Adam 3F	35.00	60.00
24-4 Piet/Com/Bottomley/Adam 4F SP	60.00	100.00
24-5 Piet/Com/Bottomley/Adam 5F SP	60.00	100.00
25-1 Ruel/Simmons/Kam Cochrane 1J SP	90.00	150.00
25-3 Ruel/Simmons/Kam Cochrane 3A SP	90.00	150.00
25-5 Ruel/Simmons/Kam/Cochrane 5A	60.00	100.00
25-6 Ruel/Simmons/Kam/Cochrane 6A	60.00	100.00
26-2 Ruff/Mal/Lazzeri/Dickey 2D SP	150.00	250.00
26-4 Ruff/Mal/Lazzeri/Dickey 4D	90.00	150.00
26-7 Ruff/Mal/Lazzeri/Dickey 7D	90.00	150.00
27-1 Ruth/McM/Bran/Maranville 1J	1500.00	2500.00
27-3 Ruth/McM/Bran/Maranville 3A	1000.00	2000.00
27-4 Ruth/McM/Bran Maranville 4A SP	1500.00	2500.00
27-5 Ruth/McM/Bran Maranville 5A SP	1000.00	1500.00
28-1 Schuble/Marb/Goslin/Crow 1H SP	60.00	100.00
28-3 Schuble/Marb/Goslin/Crow 3F SP	60.00	100.00
28-5 Schuble/Marb/Goslin/Crow 5F	35.00	60.00
28-6 Schuble/Marb/Goslin/Crow 6F	35.00	60.00
29-8 Spohrer/Rhem/Cant/Bent 8L	30.00	50.00
29-9 Spohrer/Rhem/Cant/Bent 9L	30.00	50.00
30-1 Terry/Schu/Man/Jackson 1K	60.00	100.00
30-3 Terry/Schu/Man/Jackson 3B	60.00	100.00
30-4 Terry/Schu/Man/Jackson 4B SP	90.00	150.00
30-5 Terry/Schu/Man/Jackson 5B SP	90.00	150.00
31-2 Traynor/Luc/Thev/Wright 2B SP	60.00	100.00
31-4 Traynor/Luc/Thev/Wright 4B	35.00	60.00
31-7 Traynor/Luc/Thev/Wright 7B	35.00	60.00
32-8 Vosmik/Knick/Hard/Stew 8I	30.00	50.00
32-9 Vosmik/Knick/Hard/Stew 9I	30.00	50.00
33-1 Waner/Bush/Hoyt/Waner 1E	60.00	100.00
33-3 Waner/Bush/Hoyt/Waner 3C	60.00	100.00
33-4 Waner/Bush/Hoyt/Waner 4C SP	90.00	150.00
33-5 Waner/Bush/Hoyt/Waner 5C	60.00	100.00
34-8 Werber/Ferrell/Ferrell/Ost 8G	35.00	60.00
34-9 Werber/Ferrell/Ferrell/Ost 9G	35.00	60.00
35-1 West/Melillo/Blae/Coff 1F SP	45.00	80.00
35-3 West/Melillo/Blae/Coff 3D SP	45.00	80.00
35-5 West/Melillo/Blae/Coff 5D	30.00	50.00
35-6 West/Melillo/Blae/Coff 6D	30.00	50.00
36-1 Wilson/Allen/Jonnard/Brick 1E SP	45.00	80.00
36-3 Wilson/Allen/Jonnard/Brick 3C SP	45.00	80.00
36-5 Wilson/Allen/Jonnard/Brick 5C SP	45.00	80.00
36-6 Wilson/Allen/Jonnard/Brick 6C	30.00	50.00

1936 Goudey Black and White

The cards in this 25-card black and white set measure approximately 2 3/8" by 2 7/8". In contrast to the color artwork of its previous sets, the 1936 Goudey set contained a simple black and white player photograph. A facsimile autograph appeared within the picture area. Each card was issued with a number of different "game situation" backs, and there may be as many as 200 different front/back combinations. This unnumbered set is checklisted and numbered below in alphabetical order for convenience. The cards were issued in penny packs which came 100 to a box.

COMPLETE SET (25)	500.00	1200.00
WRAPPER (1-CENT)	150.00	200.00
1 Wally Berger	25.00	60.00
2 Zeke Bonura	15.00	40.00
3 Frenchy Bordagaray XRC	15.00	40.00
4 Bill Brubaker XRC	20.00	50.00
5 Dolph Camilli	15.00	40.00
6 Clyde Castleman XRC	15.00	40.00
7 Mickey Cochrane	60.00	150.00
8 Joe Coscarart XRC	15.00	40.00
9 Frank Crosetti	40.00	100.00
10 Kiki Cuyler	25.00	60.00
11 Paul Derringer	15.00	40.00
12 Jimmy Dykes	15.00	40.00
13 Rick Ferrell	30.00	80.00
14 Lefty Gomez	60.00	150.00
15 Hank Greenberg	150.00	400.00
16 Bucky Harris XRC	25.00	60.00
17 Rollie Hemsley	15.00	40.00
18 Pinky Higgins	15.00	40.00
19 Oral Hildebrand	15.00	40.00
20 Chuck Klein	60.00	150.00
21 Pepper Martin	25.00	60.00
22 Bobo Newsom XRC	15.00	40.00
23 Joe Vosmik	15.00	40.00
24 Paul Waner	60.00	150.00
25 Bill Werber	15.00	40.00

1936 Goudey Wide Pen Premiums R314

Each card measures approximately 3 1/4" by 5 1/2". These black and white unnumbered cards could be obtained directly from a retail outlet rather than through the mail only. Four types of this card exist. Type A contains cards, mainly individual players, with "Litho USA" in the bottom border. Type B does not have the "Litho USA" marking and comes both with and without a border. Type C cards are American players on creamy paper stock with medium thickness signatures and no "Litho USA" markings. Type D consists of Canadian players from Montreal (M) or Toronto (T) on creamy stock paper with non-glossy photos.

COMPLETE SET (208)	5000.00	10000.00
COMMON CARD (A1-A119)	10.00	20.00
COMMON CARD (B1-B25)	25.00	50.00
COMMON CARD (C1-C25)	25.00	50.00
COMMON CARD (D1-D39)	40.00	80.00
A1 Ethan Allen	15.00	30.00
A2 Earl Averill	25.00	50.00
A3 Dick Bartell	12.50	25.00
A4 Dick Bartell	15.00	30.00
A5 Wally Berger	15.00	30.00
A6 Geo. Blaeholder	12.50	25.00
A7 Cy Blanton	12.50	25.00
A8 Cliff Bolton	12.50	25.00
A9 Stan Bordagaray	12.50	25.00
A10 Tommy Bridges	15.00	30.00
A11 Bill Brubaker	12.50	25.00
A12 Sam Byrd	12.50	25.00
A13 Dolph Camilli	15.00	30.00
A14 Clydell Castleman/(throwing)	12.50	25.00
A15 Clydell Castleman	12.50	25.00
A16 Phil Cavarretta	20.00	40.00
A17 Mickey Cochrane	40.00	80.00
A18 Earle Combs	25.00	50.00
A19 Joe Coscarart	12.50	25.00
A20 Joe Cronin	25.00	50.00
A21 Frank Crosetti	25.00	50.00
A22 Tony Cuccinello	12.50	25.00

A23 KiKi Cuyler 25.00 50.00
A24 Curt Davis 12.50 25.00
A25 Virgil Davis 12.50 25.00
A26 Paul Derringer 15.00 30.00
A27 Bill Dickey 25.00 50.00
A28 Jimmy Dykes kneeling 15.00 30.00
A29 Rick Ferrell 25.00 50.00
A30 Wes Ferrell 20.00 40.00
A31 Lou Finney 12.50 25.00
A32 Ervin Pete Fox 12.50 25.00
A33 Tony Freitas 12.50 25.00
A34 Lonnie Frey 12.50 25.00
A35 Frankie Frisch 40.00 80.00
A36 Augie Galan 12.50 25.00
A37 Charley Gehringer 40.00 80.00
A38 Charlie Gelbert 12.50 25.00
A39 Lefty Gomez 40.00 80.00
A40 Goose Goslin 25.00 50.00
A41 Earl Grace 12.50 25.00
A42 Hank Greenberg 50.00 100.00
A43 Mule Haas 12.50 25.00
A44 Odell Hale 12.50 25.00
A45 Bill Hallahan 12.50 25.00
A46 Mel Harder 15.00 30.00
A47 Bucky Harris 25.00 50.00
A48 Gabby Hartnett 25.00 50.00
A49 Ray Hayworth 12.50 25.00
A50 Rollie Hemsley 12.50 25.00
A51 Babe Herman 20.00 40.00
A52 Frank Higgins 12.50 25.00
A53 Oral Hildebrand 12.50 25.00
A54 Myril Hoag 12.50 25.00
A55 Waite Hoyt 25.00 50.00
A56 Woody Jensen 12.50 25.00
A57 Bob Johnson 15.00 30.00
A58 Buck Jordan 12.50 25.00
A59 Alex Kampouris 12.50 25.00
A60 Chuck Klein 25.00 50.00
A61 Joe Kuhel 12.50 25.00
A62 Lyn Lary 12.50 25.00
A63 Cookie Lavagetto 15.00 30.00
A64 Sam Leslie 12.50 25.00
A65 Fred Lindstrom 25.00 50.00
A66 Ernie Lombardi 25.00 50.00
A67 Al Lopez 25.00 50.00
A68 Dan MacFayden 12.50 25.00
A69 John Marcum 12.50 25.00
A70 Pepper Martin 20.00 40.00
A71 Eric McNair 12.50 25.00
A72 Joe Medwick 25.00 50.00
A73 Gene Moore 12.50 25.00
A74 Randy Moore 12.50 25.00
A75 Terry Moore 15.00 30.00
A76 Edward Moriarty 12.50 25.00
A77 Wally Moses 12.50 25.00
A78 Buddy Myer 12.50 25.00
A79 Buck Newsom 15.00 30.00
A80 Fred Ostermueller 12.50 25.00
A81 Marvin Owen 12.50 25.00
A82 Tommy Padden 12.50 25.00
A83 Ray Pepper 12.50 25.00
A84 Tony Piet 12.50 25.00
A85 Rabbit Pytlak 12.50 25.00
A86 Rip Radcliff 12.50 25.00
A87 Bobby Reis 12.50 25.00
A88 Lew Riggs 12.50 25.00
A89 Bill Rogell 12.50 25.00
A90 Red Rolfe 15.00 30.00
A91 Schoolboy Rowe 15.00 30.00
A92 Al Schacht 20.00 40.00
A93 Luke Sewell 15.00 30.00
A94 Al Simmons 40.00 80.00
A95 John Stone 12.50 25.00
A96 Gus Suhr 12.50 25.00
A97 Joe Sullivan 12.50 25.00
A98 Bill Swift 12.50 25.00
A99 Vito Tamulis 12.50 25.00
A100 Dan Taylor 12.50 25.00
A101 Cecil Travis 12.50 25.00
A102 Hal Trosky 15.00 30.00
A103 Bill Urbanski 12.50 25.00
A104 Russ Van Atta 12.50 25.00
A105 Arky Vaughan 25.00 50.00
A106 Gerald Walker 12.50 25.00
A107 Bucky Walters 20.00 40.00
A108 Lloyd Waner 25.00 50.00
A109 Paul Waner 25.00 50.00
A110 Lon Warneke 12.50 25.00
A111 Rabbit Warstler 12.50 25.00
A112 Bill Werber 12.50 25.00
A113 Jo-Jo White 12.50 25.00
A114 Burgess Whitehead 12.50 25.00
A115 John Whitehead 12.50 25.00
A116 Whitlow Wyatt 12.50 25.00
A117 J.DiMaggio McCarthy 200.00 400.00
A118 W.Ferrell R.Ferrell 25.00 50.00
A119 F.Pytlak S.O'Neill 12.50 25.00
B1 Mel Almada 25.00 50.00
B2 Luke Appling 50.00 100.00
B3 Henry Bonura 25.00 50.00
B4 B. Chapman B. Werber 25.00 50.00
B5 Herman Clifton 25.00 50.00
B6 Roger Doc Cramer 30.00 60.00
B7 Joe Cronin 50.00 100.00
B8 Jimmy Dykes 30.00 60.00
B9 Ervin Pete Fox 25.00 50.00
B10 Jimmie Foxx 125.00 250.00
B11 Hank Greenberg 50.00 100.00
B12 Oral Hildebrand 25.00 50.00
B13 Alex Hooks 25.00 50.00
B14 Willis Hudlin 25.00 50.00
B15 Bill Knickerbocker 25.00 50.00
B16 Heinie Manush 40.00 80.00
B17 Steve O'Neill 25.00 50.00
B18 Marvin Owen 25.00 50.00
B19 Al Simmons 50.00 100.00
B20 Lem Moose Solters 25.00 50.00
B21 Hal Trosky (batting) 30.00 60.00
B22 Joe Vosmik 25.00 50.00
B23 Joe Vosmik(batting) 25.00 50.00
B24 Joe Vosmik(fielding) 25.00 50.00
B25 Earl Whitehill 25.00 50.00
C1 Luke Appling batting 50.00 100.00
C2 Earl Averill 50.00 100.00
C3 Cy Blanton 25.00 50.00
C4 Zeke Bonura batting 25.00 50.00
C5 Tom Bridges 25.00 50.00
C6 Joe DiMaggio 800.00 1500.00
C7 Bobby Doerr 50.00 100.00
C8 Jimmy Dykes 25.00 50.00
C9 Bob Feller 150.00 300.00
C10 Elbie Fletcher 25.00 50.00
C11 Pete Fox (batting) 25.00 50.00
C12 Gus Galan batting 25.00 50.00
C13 Charley Gehringer 50.00 100.00
C14 Hank Greenberg 100.00 200.00
C15 Mel Harder 40.00 80.00
C16 Gabby Hartnett 50.00 100.00
C17 Pinky Higgins 25.00 50.00
C18 Carl Hubbell 100.00 200.00
C19 Wally Moses batting 25.00 50.00
C20 Lou Newsom 30.00 60.00
C21 Schoolboy Rowe throwing 30.00 60.00
C22 Julius Solters 25.00 50.00
C23 Hal Trosky 30.00 60.00
C24 Joe Vosmik kneeling 25.00 50.00
C25 Johnnie Whitehead throwing 25.00 50.00
D1 Buddy Bates M 40.00 80.00
D2 Del Bissonette M 40.00 80.00
D3 Lincoln Blakely T 40.00 80.00
D4 Isaac J. Boone T 40.00 80.00
D5 John H. Burnett T 40.00 80.00
D6 Leon Chagnon M 40.00 80.00
D7 Gus Dugas M 40.00 80.00
D8 Henry N. Erickson 40.00 80.00
D9 Art Funk T 40.00 80.00
D10 George Granger M 40.00 80.00
D11 Thomas G. Heath 40.00 80.00
D12 Phil Hensich M 40.00 80.00
D13 LeRoy Hermann T 40.00 80.00
D14 Henry Johnson M 40.00 80.00
D15 Hal King M 40.00 80.00
D16 Charles S. Lucas T 40.00 80.00
D17 Edward S. Miller T 40.00 80.00
D18 Jake F. Mooty T 40.00 80.00
D19 Guy Moreau 40.00 80.00
D20 George Murray T 40.00 80.00
D21 Glenn Myatt M 40.00 80.00
D22 Lauri Myllykangas M 40.00 80.00
D23 Franci J. Nicholas T 40.00 80.00
D24 Bill O'Brien 40.00 80.00
D25 Thomas Oliver T 40.00 80.00
D26 James Pattison T 40.00 80.00
D27 Crip Polli M 40.00 80.00
D28 Harlin Pool T 40.00 80.00
D29 Walter Purcey T 40.00 80.00
D30 Bill Rhiel M 40.00 80.00
D31 Ben Sankey M 40.00 80.00
D32 Leslie Scarsella T 40.00 80.00
D33 Bob Seeds M 40.00 80.00
D34 Frank Shaughnessy M 40.00 80.00
D35 Harry Smythe M 40.00 80.00
D36 Ben Tate M 40.00 80.00
D37 Fresco Thompson M 50.00 100.00
D38 Charles Wilson M 40.00 80.00
D39 Francis Wistert T 40.00 80.00

1937 Goudey Knot Hole R325

The cards in this 24-card set measure approximately 2 3/8" by 2 7/8". The 1937 "Knot Hole League Game" was another of the many innovative marketing ideas of the Goudey Gum Company. Advertised as a series of 100 game cards promising "exciting" baseball action, the set actually was limited to the 24 cards listed below.

COMPLETE SET (24) 90.00 150.00
COMMON PLAYER (1-24) 5.00 8.00

1937 Goudey Thum Movies R342

These numbered booklets are the same dimensions (2" by 3") as the R326 Flip Movies except that these are twice the thickness as they comprise both parts within a single cover. They were produced by Goudey Gum. The desirability of the set is decreased by the fact that the outside of the Thum Movie booklet does not show any picture of the player; this is in contrast to the R326 Flip Movie style which shows an inset photo of the player on the cover.

COMPLETE SET (13) 850.00 1400.00
1 John Irving Burns 50.00 80.00
2 Joe Vosmik 50.00 80.00
3 Mel Ott 90.00 150.00
4 Joe DiMaggio 250.00 400.00
5 Wally Moses 50.00 80.00
6 Van Lingle Mungo 50.00 80.00
7 Luke Appling 90.00 150.00
8 Bob Feller 90.00 150.00
9 Paul Derringer 50.00 80.00
10 Paul Waner 90.00 150.00
11 Joe Medwick 90.00 150.00
12 James Emory Foxx 90.00 150.00
13 Wally Berger 60.00 100.00

1937 Goudey Flip Movies R326

The 26 "Flip Movies" which comprise this set are a miniature version (2" by 3") of the popular penny arcade features of the period. Each movie comes in two parts, clearly labeled, and there are several cover colors as well as incorrect photos known to exist.

COMPLETE SET (13) 750.00 1250.00
1A John Irving Burns Poles Two Bagger 25.00 50.00
1B John Irving Burns Poles Two Bagger 25.00 50.00
2A Joe Vosmik Triples 25.00 50.00
2B Joe Vosmik Triples 25.00 50.00
3A Mel Ott Puts It Over The Fence 50.00 100.00
3B Mel Ott Puts It Over The Fence 50.00 100.00
4A Joe DiMaggio Socks A Sizzling Long Drive 150.00 300.00
4B Joe DiMaggio Socks A Sizzling Long Drive 150.00 300.00
5A Wally Moses Leans Against A Fast Ball 25.00 50.00
5B Wally Moses Leans Against A Fast Ball 25.00 50.00
6A Van Lingle Mungo Tosses Fire-Ball 25.00 50.00
6B Van Lingle Mungo Tosses Fire-Ball 25.00 50.00
7A Luke Appling Gets Set For Double Play 50.00 100.00
7B Luke Appling Gets Set For Double Play 50.00 100.00
8A Bob Feller Puts His Hop On A Fast One 50.00 100.00
8B Bob Feller/(Puts His Hop On A Fast One) 50.00 100.00
9A Paul Derringer Demonstrates Sharp Curve 25.00 50.00
9B Paul Derringer Demonstrates Sharp Curve 25.00 50.00
10A Paul Waner Big Poison Smacks A Triple 50.00 100.00
10B Paul Waner Big Poison Smacks A Triple 50.00 100.00
11A Joe Medwick Bats Hard Grounder 50.00 100.00
11B Joe Medwick Bats Hard Grounder 50.00 100.00
12A James Emory Foxx Smacks A Homer 50.00 100.00
12B James Emory Foxx Smacks A Homer 50.00 100.00
13A Wally Berger Puts One In The Bleachers 30.00 60.00
13B Wally Berger Puts One In The Bleachers 30.00 60.00

1938 Goudey Heads-Up

The cards in this 48-card set measure approximately 2 3/8" by 2 7/8". The 1938 Goudey set is commonly referred to as the Heads-Up set. These very popular but difficult to obtain cards came in two series of the same 24 players. The first series, numbers 241-264, is distinguished from the second series, numbers 265-288, in that the second contains etched cartoons and comments surrounding the player picture. Although the set starts with number 241, it is not a continuation of the 1933 Goudey set, but a separate set in its own right.

COMPLETE SET (48) 9000.00 15000.00
COMMON CARD (241-264) 60.00 100.00
COMMON CARD (265-288) 60.00 100.00
WRAPPER (1-CENT, 6-FIG.) 700.00 800.00
241 Charley Gehringer 175.00 300.00
242 Pete Fox 60.00 100.00
243 Joe Kuhel 60.00 100.00
244 Frank Demaree 60.00 100.00
245 Frank Pytlak XRC 60.00 100.00
246 Ernie Lombardi 100.00 175.00
247 Joe Vosmik 60.00 100.00
248 Dick Bartell 60.00 100.00
249 Jimmie Foxx 300.00 600.00
250 Joe DiMaggio XRC 2500.00 5000.00
251 Bump Hadley 60.00 100.00
252 Zeke Bonura 60.00 100.00
253 Hank Greenberg 250.00 400.00
254 Van Lingle Mungo 75.00 125.00
255 Moose Solters 60.00 100.00
256 Vernon Kennedy XRC 60.00 100.00
257 Al Lopez 125.00 200.00
258 Bobby Doerr XRC 150.00 250.00
259 Billy Werber 60.00 100.00
260 Rudy York XRC 75.00 125.00
261 Rip Radcliff XRC 60.00 100.00
262 Joe Medwick 150.00 250.00
263 Marvin Owen 60.00 100.00
264 Bob Feller XRC 800.00 1500.00
265 Charley Gehringer 175.00 300.00
266 Pete Fox 60.00 100.00
267 Joe Kuhel 60.00 100.00
268 Frank Demaree 60.00 100.00
269 Frank Pytlak XRC 60.00 100.00
270 Ernie Lombardi 250.00 500.00
271 Joe Vosmik 60.00 100.00
272 Dick Bartell 60.00 100.00
273 Jimmie Foxx 400.00 800.00
274 Joe DiMaggio XRC 2500.00 5000.00
275 Bump Hadley 60.00 100.00
276 Zeke Bonura 60.00 100.00
277 Hank Greenberg 250.00 400.00
278 Van Lingle Mungo 75.00 125.00
279 Moose Solters 60.00 100.00
280 Vernon Kennedy XRC 60.00 100.00
281 Al Lopez 150.00 250.00
282 Bobby Doerr XRC 150.00 250.00
283 Billy Werber 60.00 100.00
284 Rudy York XRC 75.00 125.00
285 Rip Radcliff XRC 60.00 100.00
286 Joe Medwick 150.00 250.00
287 Marvin Owen 60.00 100.00
288 Bob Feller XRC 800.00 1500.00

1939 Goudey Premiums R303A

This series of 48 paper premiums were issued in 1939 by the Goudey Company. Each premium photo measures approximately 4" by 6 3/16". This set carries the name Diamond Stars Gum on the reverse, although the National Chicle Company who produced the Diamond Stars baseball cards is in no way connected with this set. The backs contain instructions on various baseball disciplines. The color of the set is brown, not the more reddish color of sepia normally listed for this set.

COMPLETE SET (48) 2000.00 4000.00
1 Luke Appling 40.00 80.00
2 Earl Averill 40.00 80.00
3 Wally Berger 30.00 60.00
4 Darrell Blanton 25.00 50.00
5 Zeke Bonura 25.00 50.00
6 Mace Brown 25.00 50.00
7 George Case 25.00 50.00
8 Ben Chapman 25.00 50.00
9 Joe Cronin 40.00 80.00
10 Frank Crosetti 30.00 60.00
11 Paul Derringer 30.00 60.00
12 Bill Dickey 50.00 100.00
13 Joe DiMaggio 300.00 600.00
14 Bob Feller 100.00 200.00
15 Jimmie Foxx 75.00 150.00
16 Charley Gehringer 50.00 100.00
17 Lefty Gomez 50.00 100.00
18 Ival Goodman 30.00 60.00
19 Joe Gordon 30.00 60.00
20 Hank Greenberg 60.00 120.00
21 Buddy Hassett 25.00 50.00
22 Jeff Heath 25.00 50.00
23 Tommy Henrich 40.00 80.00
24 Billy Herman 40.00 80.00
25 Frank Higgins 25.00 50.00
26 Fred Hutchinson 30.00 60.00
27 Bob Johnson 25.00 50.00
28 Ken Keltner 25.00 50.00
29 Mike Kreevich 25.00 50.00
30 Ernie Lombardi 40.00 80.00
31 Gus Mancuso 25.00 50.00
32 Eric McNair 25.00 50.00
33 Van Mungo 30.00 60.00
34 Buck Newsom 30.00 60.00
35 Mel Ott 50.00 100.00
36 Marvin Owen 25.00 50.00
37 Frankie Pytlak 25.00 50.00
38 Woody Rich 25.00 50.00
39 Charlie Root 25.00 50.00
40 Al Simmons 40.00 80.00
41 Jim Tabor 25.00 50.00
42 Cecil Travis 25.00 50.00
43 Hal Trosky 30.00 60.00
44 Arky Vaughan 40.00 80.00
45 Joe Vosmik 25.00 50.00
46 Lon Warneke 25.00 50.00
47 Ted Williams 300.00 600.00
48 Rudy York 30.00 60.00

1939 Goudey Premiums R303B

This set of 24 paper photos is slightly larger than its counterpart R303A and was also issued in 1939. Each premium photo measures approximately 4 3/4" by 7 5/16". The photos of R303A series are the same ones depicted on these cards, and the reverses contain "How to" instructions and the Diamond Stars Gum name. The photos are the same as R303A. This set comes in two distinct colors, black and sepia.

COMPLETE SET (24) 1000.00 2000.00
1 Luke Appling 40.00 80.00
2 George Case 25.00 50.00
3 Ben Chapman 25.00 50.00
4 Joe Cronin 40.00 80.00
5 Bill Dickey 50.00 100.00
6 Joe DiMaggio 350.00 700.00
7 Bob Feller 125.00 250.00
8 Jimmie Foxx 100.00 200.00
9 Lefty Gomez 50.00 100.00
10 Ival Goodman 25.00 50.00
11 Joe Gordon 30.00 60.00
12 Hank Greenberg 75.00 150.00
13 Jeff Heath 25.00 50.00
14 Billy Herman 40.00 80.00
15 Frank Higgins 25.00 50.00
16 Ken Keltner 25.00 50.00
17 Mike Kreevich 25.00 50.00
18 Ernie Lombardi 40.00 80.00
19 Gus Mancuso 25.00 50.00
20 Mel Ott 75.00 150.00
21 Al Simmons 40.00 80.00
22 Arky Vaughan 40.00 80.00
23 Joe Vosmik 25.00 50.00
24 Rudy York 30.00 60.00

1941 Goudey

The cards in this 33-card set measure 2 3/8" by 2 7/8". The 1941 Series of blank backed baseball cards was the last baseball issue marketed by Goudey before the war closed the door on that company for good. Each black and white player photo comes with four color backgrounds (blue, green, red, or yellow). Cards without numbers are probably miscut. Cards 21-25 are especially scarce in relation to the rest of the set. In fact the eight hardest to find cards in the set are, in order, 22, 24, 23, 25, 21, 27, 29 and 32.

COMPLETE SET (33) 1200.00 2000.00
COMMON PLAYER (1-33) 15.00 30.00
COMMON SP
WRAPPER (1-CENT) 150.00 200.00
1 Hugh Mulcahy 15.00 30.00
2 Harland Clift XRC 15.00 30.00
3 Louis Chiozza 15.00 30.00
4 Buddy Rosar XRC 15.00 30.00
5 George McQuinn 15.00 30.00
6 George Dickman 15.00 30.00
7 Wayne Ambler 15.00 30.00
8 Bob Muncrief XRC 15.00 30.00
9 Bill Dietrich XRC 15.00 30.00
10 Taft Wright 15.00 30.00
11 Don Heffner 15.00 30.00
12 Fritz Ostermueller 15.00 30.00
13 Frank Hayes 15.00 30.00
14 John Kramer XRC 15.00 30.00
15 Dario Lodigiani XRC 15.00 30.00
16 George Case 15.00 30.00
17 Vito Tamulis 15.00 30.00
18 Whitlow Wyatt 20.00 40.00
19 Bill Posedel 15.00 30.00
20 Carl Hubbell 50.00 80.00
21 Harold Warstler SP 60.00 120.00
22 Joe Sullivan SP XRC 175.00 300.00
23 Norman Young SP 100.00 200.00
24 Stanley Andrews SP XRC 125.00 250.00
25 Morris Arnovich SP 60.00 120.00
26 Elbert Fletcher 15.00 30.00
27 Bill Crouch XRC 40.00 60.00
28 Al Todd XRC 15.00 30.00
29 Debs Garms 30.00 50.00
30 Jim Tobin 15.00 30.00
31 Chester Ross XRC 15.00 30.00
32 George Coffman 20.00 40.00
33 Mel Ott 75.00 125.00

1990 Grace W/R

Produced and distributed by W/R Associates in care of Baseball Cards-N-More (Louisville, KY), the sheet has an 5 1/8" by 7" oversized color portrait of Grace in its center, surrounded on three sides by standard-size cards that trace Grace's career. The cards are unnumbered and checklisted below in chronological order.

COMPLETE SET (9) 1.50 4.00
COMMON PLAYER (1-9) .20 .50
9 Mark Grace/(Oversized card/5 1/8 by 7).40 1.00

2000 Grace Illinois Lottery

1 Mark Grace .75 2.00

1978 Grand Slam

Issued by Renata Galasso, Inc., these 200 cards, which measure 2 1/4" by 3 1/4" features some of the leading figures in baseball history. All the players in this set were alive at time of issue and many collectors wrote to these players to get autographs.

COMPLETE SET (200) 60.00 120.00
1 Leo Durocher .60 1.50
2 Bob Lemon .60 1.50
3 Earl Averill .60 1.50
4 Dale Alexander .10 .25
5 Hank Greenberg .75 2.00
6 Waite Hoyt .60 1.50
7 Al Lopez .60 1.50
8 Lloyd Waner .40 1.00
9 Bob Feller 1.25 3.00
10 Guy Bush .10 .25
11 Stan Hack .20 .50
12 Zeke Bonura .10 .25
13 Wally Moses .10 .25
14 Fred Fitzsimmons .10 .25
15 Johnny Vander Meer .20 .50
16 Riggs Stephenson .20 .50
17 Bucky Walters .40 1.00
18 Charlie Grimm .40 1.00
19 Phil Cavaretta .30 .75
20 Wally Berger .20 .50
21 Joe Sewell .40 1.00
22 Edd Roush .40 1.00
23 Johnny Mize .60 1.50
24 Bill Dickey .75 2.00
25 Lou Boudreau .60 1.50
26 Bill Terry 1.25 3.00
27 Willie Kamm .10 .25
28 Charlie Gehringer .75 2.00
29 Stanley Coveleskie .60 1.50
30 Larry French .10 .25
31 George Kelly .30 .75
32 Terry Moore .20 .50
33 Billy Herman .40 1.00
34 Babe Herman .30 .75
35 Carl Hubbell 1.25 3.00
36 Buck Leonard 1.25 3.00
37 Gus Suhr .10 .25
38 Burleigh Grimes .40 1.00
39 Lew Fonseca .10 .25
40 Travis Jackson .30 .75
41 Enos Slaughter .60 1.50
42 Fred Lindstrom .30 .75
43 Rick Ferrell .30 .75
44 Cookie Lavagetto .10 .25
45 Stan Musial 2.50 6.00
46 Hal Trosky .10 .25
47 Hal Newhouser .40 1.00
48 Paul Dean .10 .25
49 George Halas 1.25 3.00
50 Jocko Conlan .40 1.00
51 Joe DiMaggio 5.00 12.00
52 Bobby Doerr .60 1.50
53 Carl Reynolds .10 .25
54 Pete Reiser .30 .75
55 Frank McCormick .10 .25
56 Mel Harder .20 .50
57 George Uhle .10 .25
58 Doc Cramer .10 .25
59 Taylor Douthit .10 .25
60 Cecil Travis .10 .25
61 James Cool Papa Bell 1.25 3.00
62 Charlie Keller .30 .75
63 Bill Hallahan .10 .25
64 Debs Garms .10 .25
65 Rube Marquard .40 1.00
66 Rube Walberg .10 .25
67 Augie Galan .20 .50
68 George Pipgras .10 .25
69 Hal Schumacher .10 .25
70 Dolf Camilli .20 .50
71 Paul Richards .10 .25
72 Judy Johnson 1.25 3.00
73 Frank Crosetti .30 .75
74 Peanuts Lowery .10 .25
75 Walter Alston .30 .75
76 Dutch Leonard .10 .25
77 Barney McCosky .10 .25
78 Joe Dobson .10 .25
79 George Kell .60 1.50
80 Ted Lyons .40 1.00
81 Johnny Pesky .20 .50
82 Hank Borowy .10 .25
83 Ewell Blackwell .10 .25
84 Pee Wee Reese 1.25 3.00
85 Monte Irvin .75 2.00
86 Joe Moore .10 .25
87 Joe Wood .40 1.00
88 Babe Dahlgren .10 .25
89 Bibb Falk .10 .25
90 Ed Lopat .30 .75
91 Rip Sewell .10 .25
92 Marty Marion .20 .50
93 Taft Wright .10 .25
94 Allie Reynolds .30 .75
95 Harry Walker .20 .50
96 Tex Hughson .10 .25
97 George Selkirk .10 .25
98 Dom DiMaggio .40 1.00
99 Walker Cooper .10 .25
100 Phil Rizzuto 1.25 3.00
101 Robin Roberts 1.25 3.00
102 Joe Adcock .30 .75
103 Hank Bauer .30 .75
104 Frank Baumholtz .10 .25
105 Ray Boone .10 .25
106 Smoky Burgess .10 .25
107 Walt Dropo .10 .25
108 Alvin Dark .20 .50
109 Carl Erskine .20 .50
110 Dick Donovan .10 .25
111 Dee Fondy .10 .25
112 Mike Garcia .10 .25
113 Bob Friend .10 .25
114 Ned Garver .10 .25
115 Billy Goodman .10 .25
116 Larry Jansen .10 .25
117 Jackie Jensen .20 .50
118 John Antonelli .10 .25
119 Ted Kluszewski .40 1.00
120 Harvey Kuenn .20 .50
121 Clem Labine .10 .25
122 Red Schoendienst .40 1.00
123 Don Larsen .30 .75
124 Vern Law .20 .50
125 Charlie Maxwell .10 .25
126 Wally Moon .10 .25
127 Bob Nieman .10 .25
128 Don Newcombe .20 .50
129 Wally Post .10 .25
130 Johnny Podres .20 .50
131 Vic Raschi .20 .50
132 Dusty Rhodes .10 .25
133 Jim Rivera .10 .25
134 Pete Runnels .10 .25
135 Hank Sauer .20 .50
136 Roy Sievers .20 .50
137 Bobby Shantz .20 .50
138 Curt Simmons .10 .25
139 Bob Skinner .10 .25
140 Bill Skowron .30 .75
141 Warren Spahn .75 2.00
142 Gerry Staley .10 .25
143 Frank Thomas .20 .50
144 Bobby Thomson .30 .75
145 Bob Turley .10 .25
146 Vic Wertz .10 .25
147 Bill Virdon .10 .25
148 Gene Woodling .10 .25
149 Eddie Yost .10 .25
150 Sandy Koufax 2.50 6.00
151 Lefty Gomez .75 2.00
152 Al Rosen .40 1.00
153 Vince DiMaggio .20 .50
154 Bill Nicholson .10 .25
155 Mark Koenig .10 .25
156 Max Lanier .10 .25
157 Ken Keltner .10 .25
158 Whit Wyatt .10 .25
159 Marv Owen .10 .25
160 Red Lucas .10 .25
161 Babe Phelps .10 .25
162 Pete Donohue .10 .25
163 Johnny Cooney .10 .25
164 Glenn Wright .10 .25
165 Willis Hudlin .10 .25
166 Tony Cuccinello .10 .25
167 Bill Bevens .10 .25
168 Dave Ferriss .10 .25
169 Whitey Kurowski .10 .25
170 Buddy Hassett .10 .25
171 Ossie Bluege .10 .25
172 Hoot Evers .10 .25
173 Thornton Lee .10 .25
174 Spud Davis .10 .25
175 Bob Shawkey .30 .75
176 Smead Jolley .10 .25
177 Andy High .10 .25
178 George McQuinn .10 .25
179 Mickey Vernon .20 .50
180 Birdie Tebbetts .10 .25
181 Jack Kramer .10 .25
182 Don Kolloway .10 .25
183 Claude Passeau .10 .25
184 Frank Shea .10 .25
185 Bob O'Farrell .10 .25
186 Bob Johnson .10 .25
187 Ival Goodman .10 .25
188 Mike Kreevich .10 .25
189 Joe Stripp .10 .25
190 Mickey Owen .10 .25
191 Hughie Critz .10 .25
192 Ethan Allen .10 .25
193 Billy Rogell .10 .25
194 Joe Kuhel .10 .25
195 Dale Mitchell .20 .50
196 Eldon Auker .10 .25
197 Johnny Beazley .10 .25
198 Spud Chandler .20 .50
199 Ralph Branca .20 .50
200 Joe Cronin .75 2.00

1975-76 Great Plains Greats

This 42-card set measures approximately 2 1/2" by 3 3/4". The set was issued by the Great Plains Sports Collectors Association in conjunction with their annual show. The first series cards have the photos surrounded by a green border while the second series cards have an orange border. The Lloyd Waner card with a green border is an extra addition to the first series. The card is only available as a single when cut from an uncut sheet. Since it was not issued with the regular set, we are calling it a Short Print. Waner was never distributed since he did not sign a release form. The 1st series was available directly from the producer at time of issue for $4.25. The 2nd series was available from the producer at time of issue for $2.25. 2,000 1st series sets were printed.

COMPLETE SET (42) 10.00 25.00
MINOR STARS .20 .50
COMMON SP
1 Bob Feller .40 1.00
2 Carl Hubbell .40 1.00
3 Jocko Conlan .20 .50
4 Hal Trosky .10 .25
5 Allie Reynolds .10 .25
6 Burleigh Grimes .30 .75
7 Jake Beckley .20 .50
8 Al Simmons .40 1.00
9 Paul Waner .40 1.00
10 Chief Bender .30 .75
11 Fred Clarke .20 .50
12 Jim Bottomley .10 .25
13 Dave Bancroft .20 .50
14 Bing Miller .10 .25
15 Walter Johnson .75 2.00
16 Grover Alexander .75 2.00
17 Bob Johnson .10 .25
18 Roger Maris .40 1.00
19 Ken Keltner .10 .25
20 Red Faber .20 .50
21 Cool Papa Bell .40 1.00
22 Yogi Berra .40 1.00
23 Fred Lindstrom .20 .50
24 Ray Schalk .20 .50
25A Lloyd Waner SP
26 John Hopp .10 .25
27 Mel Harder .10 .25
28 Dutch Leonard .10 .25
29 Bob O'Farrell .10 .25
30 Cap Anson .30 .75
31 Dazzy Vance .20 .50
32 Red Schoendienst .20 .50
33 George Pipgras .10 .25
34 Harvey Kuenn .10 .25
35 Red Ruffing .20 .50
36 Roy Sievers .10 .25
37 Ken Boyer .20 .50
38 Al Smith .10 .25
39 Casey Stengel .40 1.00
40 Bob Gibson .30 .75
41 Mickey Mantle 1.50 4.00
42 Denny McLain .20 .50

2000 Greats of the Game

COMPLETE SET (107) 15.00 40.00
1 Mickey Mantle 2.00 5.00
2 Gil Hodges .40 1.00
3 Monte Irvin .40 1.00
4 Satchel Paige .60 1.50
5 Roy Campanella .60 1.50
6 Richie Ashburn .40 1.00
7 Roger Maris .60 1.50
8 Ozzie Smith .75 2.00
9 Reggie Jackson .40 1.00
10 Eddie Mathews .60 1.50
11 Dave Righetti .25 .60
12 Dave Winfield .40 1.00
13 Lou Whitaker .25 .60
14 Phil Garner .25 .60
15 Ron Cey .25 .60
16 Brooks Robinson .40 1.00
17 Bruce Sutter .40 1.00
18 Dave Parker .25 .60
19 Johnny Bench .60 1.50
20 Fernando Valenzuela .25 .60
21 George Brett 1.25 3.00
22 Paul Molitor .60 1.50
23 Hoyt Wilhelm .40 1.00
24 Luis Aparicio .40 1.00
25 Frank White .25 .60
26 Herb Score .25 .60
27 Kirk Gibson .25 .60
28 Mike Schmidt 1.00 2.50
29 Don Baylor .25 .60
30 Joe Pepitone .25 .60
31 Hal McRae .25 .60
32 Lee Smith .25 .60
33 Nolan Ryan 2.00 5.00
34 Bill Mazeroski .40 1.00
35 Bobby Doerr .40 1.00
36 Duke Snider .40 1.00
37 Dick Groat .25 .60
38 Larry Doby .40 1.00
39 Kirby Puckett .60 1.50
40 Steve Carlton .40 1.00
41 Dennis Eckersley .40 1.00
42 Jim Bunning .40 1.00
43 Ron Guidry .25 .60
44 Alan Trammell .40 1.00
45 Bob Feller .40 1.00
46 Dave Concepcion .25 .60
47 Dwight Evans .25 .60
48 Enos Slaughter .40 1.00
49 Tom Seaver .40 1.00
50 Tony Oliva .25 .60
51 Mel Stottlemyre .25 .60
52 Tommy John .25 .60
53 Willie McCovey .40 1.00
54 Red Schoendienst .40 1.00
55 Gorman Thomas .25 .60
56 Ralph Kiner .40 1.00
57 Robin Yount .60 1.50
58 Andre Dawson .40 1.00
59 Al Kaline .60 1.50
60 Dom DiMaggio .25 .60
61 Juan Marichal .40 1.00
62 Jack Morris .40 1.00
63 Warren Spahn .40 1.00
64 Preacher Roe .25 .60
65 Darrell Evans .25 .60
66 Jim Kaat .25 .60
67 Rocky Colavito .40 1.00
68 Bob Gibson .40 1.00
69 Whitey Ford .40 1.00
70 Moose Skowron .25 .60
71 Boog Powell .25 .60
72 Al Lopez .25 .60
73 Lou Brock .40 1.00
74 Mickey Lolich .25 .60
75 Rod Carew .40 1.00
76 Bob Lemon .25 .60
77 Frank Howard .25 .60
78 Phil Rizzuto .40 1.00
79 Carl Yastrzemski 1.00 2.50
80 Rico Carty .25 .60
81 Jim Kaat .25 .60
82 Bert Blyleven .40 1.00
83 George Kell .40 1.00
84 Jim Palmer .40 1.00
85 Maury Wills .25 .60
86 Jim Rice .40 1.00
87 Joe Carter .25 .60
88 Clete Boyer .25 .60

89 Yogi Berra .60 1.50
90 Cecil Cooper .25 .60
91 Davey Johnson .25 .60
92 Lou Boudreau .40 1.00
93 Orlando Cepeda .40 1.00
94 Tommy Henrich .25 .60
95 Hank Bauer .25 .60
96 Don Larsen .25 .60
97 Vida Blue .25 .60
98 Ben Oglivie .25 .60
99 Don Mattingly 1.25 3.00
100 Dale Murphy .60 1.50
101 Ferguson Jenkins .40 1.00
102 Bobby Bonds .25 .60
103 Dick Allen .25 .60
104 Stan Musial 1.00 2.50
105 Gaylord Perry .40 1.00
106 Willie Randolph .25 .60
107 Willie Stargell .40 1.00
P33 Nolan Ryan Promo .60 1.50
NNO Checklist .12 .30

2000 Greats of the Game Autographs

STATED ODDS 1:6
SP INFO CONFIRMED BY FLEER
JETER EXCH.AVAIL VIA '04 MAIL-IN
JETER EXCH PRINT RUN 150 CARDS
JETER EXCH IS NOT SERIAL #'d
JETER PRINT RUN PROVIDED BY FLEER
1 Luis Aparicio 8.00 20.00
2 Hank Bauer 6.00 15.00
3 Don Baylor 5.00 12.00
4 Johnny Bench SP 60.00 150.00
5A Yogi Berra SP 50.00 120.00
Black Ink
5B Yogi Berra SP
Blue Ink
6 Vida Blue 6.00 15.00
7 Bert Blyleven 10.00 25.00
8 Bobby Bonds 8.00 20.00
9 Lou Boudreau 30.00 80.00
10 Jim Bouton 6.00 15.00
11 Clete Boyer 6.00 15.00
12 George Brett SP 150.00 300.00
13 Lou Brock 25.00 60.00
14 Jim Bunning 10.00 25.00
15 Rod Carew 30.00 80.00
16 Steve Carlton 12.00 30.00
17 Joe Carter SP 40.00 80.00
18 Orlando Cepeda 10.00 25.00
19 Ron Cey 6.00 15.00
20 Rocky Colavito 25.00 60.00
21A Dave Concepcion 6.00 15.00
21B Dave Concepcion Red Ink 20.00 50.00
22 Cecil Cooper 6.00 15.00
23 Andre Dawson 6.00 15.00
24 Dom DiMaggio 20.00 50.00
25 Bobby Doerr 8.00 20.00
26 Darrell Evans 6.00 15.00
27 Bob Feller 12.00 30.00
28 Whitey Ford SP 75.00 200.00
29 Phil Garner 6.00 15.00
30 Bob Gibson 20.00 50.00
31 Kirk Gibson 20.00 50.00
32 Dick Groat 6.00 15.00
33 Ron Guidry 6.00 15.00
34 Tommy Henrich SP 60.00 150.00
35 Frank Howard 6.00 15.00
36 Reggie Jackson SP 60.00 150.00
37 Ferguson Jenkins 10.00 25.00
38 Derek Jeter Mail-In/150 * 600.00 1200.00
39 Tommy John 6.00 15.00
40 Davey Johnson 6.00 15.00
41 Jim Kaat 6.00 15.00
42 Al Kaline 15.00 40.00
43 George Kell 6.00 15.00
44 Ralph Kiner 12.00 30.00
45 Don Larsen 10.00 25.00
46 Mickey Lolich 6.00 15.00
47 Juan Marichal 10.00 25.00
48 Eddie Mathews 30.00 80.00
49 Don Mattingly SP 75.00 200.00
50 Bill Mazeroski 12.50 30.00
51 Willie McCovey SP 60.00 120.00
52 Hal McRae 6.00 15.00
53 Paul Molitor 20.00 50.00
54 Jack Morris 10.00 25.00
55 Dale Murphy 10.00 25.00
56 Stan Musial SP 50.00 120.00
57 Ben Oglivie 6.00 15.00
58 Tony Oliva 6.00 15.00
59 Jim Palmer SP 75.00 200.00
60 Dave Parker 6.00 15.00
61 Joe Pepitone 6.00 15.00
62 Gaylord Perry 8.00 20.00
63 Boog Powell 6.00 15.00
64 Kirby Puckett SP 300.00 600.00
65 Willie Randolph 10.00 25.00
66 Jim Rice 8.00 20.00
67 Dave Righetti 6.00 15.00
68 Phil Rizzuto SP 75.00 200.00
69 Brooks Robinson 15.00 40.00
70 Preacher Roe 6.00 15.00
71 Nolan Ryan 75.00 200.00
72 Mike Schmidt SP 200.00 500.00
73 Red Schoendienst 15.00 40.00
74 Herb Score 6.00 15.00
75 Herb Score ROY '55 10.00 25.00
76 Tom Seaver 40.00 100.00
77 Moose Skowron 8.00 20.00
78 Enos Slaughter 15.00 40.00
79 Lee Smith 10.00 25.00
80 Ozzie Smith SP 75.00 150.00
81 Duke Snider SP 75.00 200.00
82 Warren Spahn SP 75.00 200.00
83 Willie Stargell 25.00 60.00
84 Bruce Sutter 6.00 15.00
85 Gorman Thomas 6.00 15.00
86 Alan Trammell 8.00 20.00
87 Frank White 6.00 15.00
88 Hoyt Wilhelm 10.00 25.00
89 Maury Wills 6.00 15.00
90 Dave Winfield SP 150.00 400.00
91 Carl Yastrzemski 30.00 80.00
92 Robin Yount SP 150.00 300.00

2000 Greats of the Game Autographs Memorable Moments

PRINT RUNS B/WN 55-99 COPIES PER
1 Ron Guidry 75.00 200.00
CY 78
2 Nolan Ryan 30.00 80.00
HOF 99
3 Herb Score 125.00 200.00
ROY 55
4 Tom Seaver 200.00 500.00
CY 69

2000 Greats of the Game Retrospection

COMPLETE SET (15) 10.00 25.00
STATED ODDS 1:6
1 Rod Carew .60 1.50
2 Stan Musial 1.50 4.00
3 Nolan Ryan 3.00 8.00
4 Tom Seaver .60 1.50
5 Brooks Robinson .60 1.50
6 Al Kaline 1.00 2.50
7 Mike Schmidt 1.50 4.00
8 Thurman Munson 1.00 2.50
9 Steve Carlton .40 1.00
10 Roger Maris 1.00 2.50
11 Duke Snider .60 1.50
12 Yogi Berra 1.00 2.50
13 Carl Yastrzemski 1.50 4.00
14 Reggie Jackson .60 1.50
15 Johnny Bench 1.00 2.50

2000 Greats of the Game Yankees Clippings

STATED ODDS 1:48
YC1 Mickey Mantle Pants 50.00 120.00
YC2 Ron Guidry 12.00 30.00
YC3 Don Larsen 12.00 30.00
YC4 Elston Howard 20.00 50.00
YC5 Mel Stottlemyre 8.00 20.00
YC6 Don Mattingly 20.00 50.00
YC7 Reggie Jackson 12.00 30.00
YC8 Tommy John 10.00 25.00
YC9 Dave Winfield 10.00 25.00
YC10 Willie Randolph 12.00 30.00
YC10A Willie Randolph Grey 6.00 15.00
YC11 Tommy Henrich 6.00 15.00
YC12 Billy Martin 15.00 40.00
YC13 Dave Righetti 12.00 30.00
YC14 Joe Pepitone 10.00 25.00
YC15 Thurman Munson 50.00 120.00

2001 Greats of the Game Promo Sheets

COMPLETE SET (6) 9.00 18.00
1 Ankiel 1.50 3.00
Bagwell
Bonds
Burrell
Clemens
Delgado
2 Drew 1.50 3.00
Edmonds
Erstad
Galarraga
Garciaparra
Giambi
3 Glaus 1.50 4.00
Alomar
Griffey Jr.
Guerrero
Gwynn
Helton
4 Jeter 1.50 3.00
Johnson
C.Jones
A.Jones
Maddux
Martinez
5 McGwire 1.00 2.50
Ordonez
Piazza
Ramirez
Ripken
Rodriguez
6 Rodriguez 1.50 3.00
Kent
Sheffield
Sosa
Thomas
Williams

2001 Greats of the Game

COMPLETE SET (137) 20.00 50.00
1 Roberto Clemente 2.50 6.00
2 George Anderson .40 1.00
3 Babe Ruth 3.00 8.00
4 Paul Molitor .40 1.00
5 Don Larsen .40 1.00
6 Cy Young 1.00 2.50
7 Billy Martin .60 1.50
8 Lou Brock .60 1.50
9 Fred Lynn .40 1.00
10 Johnny VanderMeer .40 1.00
11 Harmon Killebrew 1.00 2.50
12 Dave Winfield .40 1.00
13 Orlando Cepeda .40 1.00
14 Johnny Mize .60 1.50
15 Walter Johnson 1.00 2.50
16 Roy Campanella 1.00 2.50
17 Monte Irvin .60 1.50
18 Mookie Wilson .40 1.00
19 Elston Howard .60 1.50
20 Walter Alston .40 1.00
21 Rollie Fingers .40 1.00
22 Brooks Robinson .60 1.50
23 Hank Greenberg 1.00 2.50
24 Maury Wills .40 1.00
25 Rich Gossage .40 1.00
26 Leon Day .40 1.00
27 Jimmie Foxx 1.00 2.50
28 Alan Trammell .40 1.00
29 Dennis Martinez .40 1.00
30 Don Drysdale .60 1.50
31 Bob Feller .40 1.00
32 Jackie Robinson 1.00 2.50
33 Whitey Ford .60 1.50
34 Enos Slaughter .40 1.00
35 Rod Carew .60 1.50
36 Eddie Mathews 1.00 2.50
37 Ron Cey .40 1.00
38 Thurman Munson 1.00 2.50
39 Henry Kimbro .40 1.00
40 Ty Cobb 1.50 4.00
41 Rocky Colavito 1.00 2.50
42 Satchel Paige 1.00 2.50
43 Andre Dawson .40 1.00
44 Phil Rizzuto 1.00 2.50
45 Roger Maris 1.00 2.50
46 Bobby Bonds .40 1.00
47 Joe Carter .40 1.00
48 Christy Mathewson 1.00 2.50
49 Tony Lazzeri .40 1.00
50 Gil Hodges 1.00 2.50
51 Ray Dandridge .40 1.00
52 Gaylord Perry .40 1.00
53 Ernie Banks 1.00 2.50
54 Lou Gehrig 2.00 5.00
55 George Kell .40 1.00
56 Wes Parker .40 1.00
57 Sam Jethroe .40 1.00
58 Joe Morgan .40 1.00
59 Steve Garvey .40 1.00
60 Joe Torre .60 1.50
61 Roger Craig .40 1.00
62 Warren Spahn .60 1.50
63 Willie McCovey .40 1.00
64 Cool Papa Bell .40 1.00
65 Frank Robinson .60 1.50
66 Richie Allen .40 1.00
67 Bucky Dent .40 1.00
68 George Foster .40 1.00
69 Hoyt Wilhelm .40 1.00
70 Phil Niekro .40 1.00
71 Buck Leonard .40 1.00
72 Preacher Roe .40 1.00
73 Yogi Berra 1.00 2.50
74 Joe Black .40 1.00
75 Nolan Ryan 2.50 6.00
76 Pop Lloyd .40 1.00
77 Lester Lockett .40 1.00
78 Paul Blair .40 1.00
79 Ryne Sandberg 1.50 4.00
80 Bill Perkins .40 1.00
81 Frank Howard .40 1.00
82 Hack Wilson .60 1.50
83 Robin Yount 1.00 2.50
84 Harry Heilmann .40 1.00
85 Mike Schmidt 2.00 5.00
86 Vida Blue .40 1.00
87 George Brett 2.00 5.00
88 Juan Marichal .40 1.00
89 Tom Seaver .60 1.50
90 Bill Skowron .40 1.00
91 Don Mattingly 2.00 5.00
92 Jim Bunning .60 1.50
93 Eddie Murray 1.00 2.50
94 Tommy Lasorda .40 1.00
95 Pee Wee Reese 1.00 2.50
96 Bill Dickey .60 1.50
97 Ozzie Smith 1.50 4.00
98 Dale Murphy .60 1.50
99 Artie Wilson .40 1.00
100 Bill Terry .40 1.00
101 Jim Hunter .60 1.50
102 Don Sutton .40 1.00
103 Luis Aparicio .40 1.00
104 Reggie Jackson .60 1.50
105 Ted Radcliffe .40 1.00
106 Carl Erskine .40 1.00
107 Johnny Bench 1.00 2.50
108 Carl Furillo .40 1.00
109 Stan Musial 1.50 4.00
110 Carlton Fisk .60 1.50
111 Rube Foster .40 1.00
112 Tony Oliva .40 1.00
113 Hank Bauer .40 1.00
114 Jim Rice .40 1.00
115 Willie Mays 2.00 5.00
116 Ralph Kiner .40 1.00
117 Al Kaline 1.00 2.50
118 Billy Williams .40 1.00
119 Buck O'Neil .40 1.00
120 Tony Perez .40 1.00
121 Dave Parker .40 1.00
122 Kirk Gibson .40 1.00
123 Lou Piniella .40 1.00
124 Ted Williams 2.00 5.00
125 Steve Carlton .40 1.00
126 Dizzy Dean 1.00 2.50
127 Willie Stargell .60 1.50
128 Joe Niekro .40 1.00
129 Lloyd Waner .60 1.50
130 Wade Boggs .60 1.50
131 Wilmer Fields .40 1.00
132 Bill Mazeroski .60 1.50
133 Duke Snider .60 1.50
134 Joe Williams .40 1.00
135 Bob Gibson .60 1.50
136 Jim Palmer .40 1.00
137 Oscar Charleston .40 1.00

2001 Greats of the Game Autographs

STATED ODDS 1:8 HOB, 1:20 RET
SP PRINT RUNS PROVIDED BY FLEER
SP'S ARE NOT SERIAL-NUMBERED
1 Richie Allen 12.00 30.00
2 Sparky Anderson 6.00 15.00
3 Luis Aparicio 10.00 25.00
4 Ernie Banks SP/250 60.00 150.00
5 Hank Bauer 6.00 15.00
6 Johnny Bench SP/400 20.00 50.00
7 Yogi Berra SP/500 40.00 100.00
8 Joe Black 10.00 25.00
9 Paul Blair 8.00 20.00
9A Paul Blair Double-Signed 6.00 15.00
10 Vida Blue 6.00 15.00
11 Wade Boggs 25.00 60.00
12 Bobby Bonds 6.00 15.00
13 George Brett SP/247 125.00 250.00
14 Lou Brock SP/500 15.00 40.00
15 Jim Bunning 10.00 25.00
16 Rod Carew 30.00 80.00
17 Steve Carlton 15.00 40.00
18 Joe Carter 8.00 20.00
19 Orlando Cepeda 12.00 30.00
20 Ron Cey 6.00 15.00
21 Rocky Colavito 30.00 80.00
22 Roger Craig 6.00 15.00
23 Andre Dawson 8.00 20.00
24 Bucky Dent 6.00 15.00
25 Larry Doby 30.00 80.00
26 Carl Erskine 6.00 15.00
27 Bob Feller 10.00 25.00
28 Wilmer Fields 12.00 30.00
29 Rollie Fingers 6.00 15.00
30 Carlton Fisk 12.00 30.00
31 Whitey Ford 25.00 60.00
32 George Foster 6.00 15.00
33 Steve Garvey SP/400 15.00 40.00
34 Bob Gibson 20.00 50.00
35 Kirk Gibson 20.00 50.00
36 Rich Gossage 6.00 15.00
37 Frank Howard 6.00 15.00
38 Monte Irvin 6.00 15.00
39 Reggie Jackson SP/400 50.00 120.00
40 Sam Jethroe 6.00 15.00
41 Al Kaline 20.00 50.00
42 George Kell 6.00 15.00
43 Harmon Killebrew 15.00 40.00
44 Ralph Kiner 10.00 25.00
45 Don Larsen 12.00 30.00
46 Tommy Lasorda SP/400 75.00 200.00
47 Lester Lockett 8.00 20.00
48 Fred Lynn 10.00 25.00
49 Juan Marichal 12.00 30.00
50 Dennis Martinez 6.00 15.00
51 Don Mattingly 30.00 80.00
52 Willie Mays SP/100 300.00 600.00
53 Bill Mazeroski UER 12.00 30.00
54 Willie McCovey 25.00 60.00
55 Paul Molitor 10.00 25.00
56 Joe Morgan 40.00 100.00
57 Dale Murphy 15.00 40.00
58 Eddie Murray SP/140 150.00 400.00
59 Stan Musial SP/525 60.00 150.00
60 Joe Niekro 6.00 15.00
61 Phil Niekro 15.00 40.00
62 Tony Oliva 10.00 25.00
63 Buck O'Neil 10.00 25.00
64 Jim Palmer SP/600 12.00 30.00
65 Dave Parker 10.00 25.00
66 Tony Perez 20.00 50.00
67 Gaylord Perry 6.00 15.00
68 Lou Piniella 8.00 20.00
69 Ted Radcliffe 15.00 40.00
70 Jim Rice 6.00 15.00
71 Phil Rizzuto SP/425 25.00 60.00
72 Brooks Robinson 12.00 30.00
73 Frank Robinson 25.00 60.00
74 Preacher Roe 6.00 15.00
75 Nolan Ryan SP/650 60.00 150.00
76 Ryne Sandberg 30.00 80.00
77 Mike Schmidt SP/213 100.00 250.00
78 Tom Seaver 30.00 80.00
79 Bill Skowron 8.00 20.00
80 Enos Slaughter 8.00 20.00
81 Ozzie Smith 25.00 60.00
82 Duke Snider SP/600 20.00 50.00
83 Warren Spahn 20.00 50.00
84 Willie Stargell NO AU 10.00 25.00
85 Don Sutton 12.00 30.00
86 Joe Torre SP/500 50.00 120.00
87 Alan Trammell 6.00 15.00
88 Hoyt Wilhelm 15.00 40.00
89 Billy Williams 8.00 20.00
90 Maury Wills 10.00 25.00
91 Artie Wilson 10.00 25.00
92 Mookie Wilson 6.00 15.00
93 Dave Winfield SP/370 20.00 50.00
94 Robin Yount SP/400 75.00 200.00

2001 Greats of the Game Dodger Blues

STATED ODDS 1:36 HOBBY
LESS THAN 200 OF EACH SP PRODUCED
SP INFO PROVIDED BY FLEER
1 Walter Alston Jsy 10.00 25.00
2 Walter Alston Uni 10.00 25.00
3 Roy Campanella Bat SP 25.00 60.00
4 Roger Craig Jsy 10.00 25.00
5 Don Drysdale Jsy 10.00 25.00
6 Carl Furillo Jsy 10.00 25.00
7 Steve Garvey Jsy 10.00 25.00
8 Gil Hodges Uni 10.00 25.00
9 Wes Parker Bat 10.00 25.00
10 Wes Parker Jsy 10.00 25.00
11 Pee Wee Reese Jsy 10.00 25.00
12 Jackie Robinson Uni SP 125.00 250.00
13 Preacher Roe Jsy 10.00 25.00
14 Duke Snider Bat SP 60.00 120.00
15 Don Sutton Jsy 10.00 25.00

2001 Greats of the Game Feel the Game Classics

STATED ODDS 1:72 HOB, 1:400 RET
SP PRINT RUNS PROVIDED BY FLEER
SP'S ARE NOT SERIAL-NUMBERED
1 Luis Aparicio Bat SP/200 * 10.00 25.00
2 George Brett Jsy SP/300 * 20.00 50.00
3 Lou Brock Jsy 10.00 25.00
4 Orlando Cepeda Bat SP/300 * 10.00 25.00
5 Whitey Ford Jsy 6.00 15.00
6 Hank Greenberg Bat SP/300 * 10.00 25.00
7 Elston Howard Bat SP/300 * 10.00 25.00
8 Jim Hunter Jsy 6.00 15.00
9 Harmon Killebrew Bat 10.00 25.00
10 Roger Maris Bat 10.00 25.00
11 Eddie Mathews Bat 5.00 12.00
12 Willie McCovey Bat SP/200 * 10.00 25.00
13 Johnny Mize Bat 3.00 8.00
14 Paul Molitor Jsy 5.00 12.00
15 Jim Palmer Jsy 3.00 8.00
16 Tony Perez Bat 3.00 8.00
17 B.Robinson Bat SP/144 * 15.00 40.00
18 Babe Ruth Bat SP/250 * 60.00 120.00
19 Mike Schmidt Jsy 8.00 20.00
20 Tom Seaver Jsy 3.00 8.00
21 Enos Slaughter Bat SP/300 * 10.00 25.00
22 Willie Stargell Jsy 3.00 8.00
23 Hack Wilson Bat 12.00 30.00
24 Harry Heilmann Bat 10.00 25.00

2001 Greats of the Game Retrospection

COMPLETE SET (10) 10.00 25.00
STATED ODDS 1:6 HOB/RET
1 Babe Ruth 2.50 6.00
2 Stan Musial 1.50 4.00
3 Jimmie Foxx 1.00 2.50
4 Roberto Clemente 2.50 6.00
5 Ted Williams 2.00 5.00
6 Mike Schmidt 1.50 4.00
7 Cy Young 1.00 2.50
8 Satchel Paige 1.00 2.50
9 Hank Greenberg 1.00 2.50
10 Jim Bunning .75 2.00

2002 Greats of the Game

COMPLETE SET (100) 15.00 40.00
1 Cal Ripken 3.00 8.00
2 Paul Molitor .40 1.00
3 Roberto Clemente 2.50 6.00
4 Cy Young 1.00 2.50
5 Tris Speaker 1.00 2.50
6 Lou Brock .60 1.50
7 Fred Lynn .40 1.00
8 Harmon Killebrew 1.00 2.50
9 Ted Williams 2.00 5.00
10 Dave Winfield .40 1.00
11 Orlando Cepeda .40 1.00
12 Johnny Mize .60 1.50
13 Walter Johnson 1.00 2.50
14 Roy Campanella 1.00 2.50
15 George Sisler .40 1.00
16 Bo Jackson 1.00 2.50
17 Rollie Fingers .40 1.00
18 Brooks Robinson .60 1.50
19 Billy Williams .40 1.00
20 Maury Wills .40 1.00
21 Jimmie Foxx 1.00 2.50
22 Alan Trammell .40 1.00
23 Rogers Hornsby 1.00 2.50
24 Don Drysdale .60 1.50
25 Bob Feller .40 1.00
26 Jackie Robinson 1.00 2.50
27 Whitey Ford .60 1.50
28 Enos Slaughter .40 1.00
29 Rod Carew .60 1.50
30 Eddie Mathews 1.00 2.50
31 Ron Cey .40 1.00
32 Thurman Munson 1.00 2.50
33 Ty Cobb 1.50 4.00
34 Rocky Colavito 1.00 2.50
35 Satchel Paige 1.00 2.50
36 Andre Dawson .40 1.00
37 Phil Rizzuto 1.00 2.50
38 Roger Maris 1.00 2.50
39 Earl Weaver .40 1.00
40 Joe Carter .40 1.00
41 Christy Mathewson 1.00 2.50
42 Tony Lazzeri .40 1.00
43 Gil Hodges 1.00 2.50
44 Gaylord Perry .40 1.00
45 Steve Carlton .40 1.00
46 George Kell .40 1.00
47 Mickey Cochrane .60 1.50
48 Joe Morgan .40 1.00
49 Steve Garvey .40 1.00
50 Bob Gibson .60 1.50
51 Lefty Grove .60 1.50
52 Warren Spahn .60 1.50
53 Willie McCovey .40 1.00
54 Frank Robinson .60 1.50
55 Rich Gossage .40 1.00
56 Hank Bauer .40 1.00
57 Hoyt Wilhelm .40 1.00
58 Mel Ott 1.00 2.50
59 Preacher Roe .40 1.00
60 Yogi Berra 1.00 2.50
61 Nolan Ryan 2.50 6.00
62 Dizzy Dean 1.00 2.50
63 Ryne Sandberg 1.50 4.00
64 Frank Howard .40 1.00
65 Hack Wilson .60 1.50
66 Robin Yount 1.00 2.50
67 Al Kaline 1.00 2.50
68 Mike Schmidt 2.00 5.00
69 Vida Blue .40 1.00
70 George Brett 2.00 5.00
71 Sparky Anderson .40 1.00
72 Tom Seaver .60 1.50
73 Bill Skowron .40 1.00
74 Don Mattingly 2.00 5.00
75 Carl Yastrzemski 1.50 4.00
76 Eddie Murray 1.00 2.50
77 Jim Palmer .40 1.00
78 Bill Dickey .60 1.50
79 Ozzie Smith 1.50 4.00
80 Dale Murphy .60 1.50
81 Nap Lajoie 1.00 2.50
82 Jim Hunter .60 1.50
83 Duke Snider .60 1.50
84 Luis Aparicio .40 1.00
85 Reggie Jackson .60 1.50
86 Honus Wagner 1.25 3.00
87 Johnny Bench 1.00 2.50
88 Stan Musial 1.50 4.00
89 Carlton Fisk .60 1.50
90 Tony Oliva .40 1.00
91 Wade Boggs .60 1.50
92 Jim Rice .40 1.00
93 Bill Mazeroski .60 1.50
94 Ralph Kiner .40 1.00
95 Tony Perez .40 1.00
96 Kirby Puckett 1.00 2.50
97 Bobby Bonds .40 1.00
98 Bill Terry .40 1.00
99 Juan Marichal .40 1.00
100 Hank Greenberg 1.00 2.50

2002 Greats of the Game Autographs

STATED ODD 1:24
SP PRINT RUNS PROVIDED BY FLEER
AD Andre Dawson 6.00 15.00
AK Al Kaline 12.00 30.00
AT Alan Trammell 8.00 20.00
BB Bobby Bonds 6.00 15.00
BF Bob Feller 8.00 20.00
BG Bob Gibson SP/200 12.50 30.00
BM Bill Mazeroski SP/200 12.50 30.00
BR Brooks Robinson 10.00 25.00
BS Bill Skowron 6.00 15.00
BW Billy Williams 6.00 15.00
CE Ron Cey 6.00 15.00
CF Carlton Fisk SP/100 20.00 40.00
CO Rocky Colavito 15.00 40.00
CR Cal Ripken SP/100 125.00 200.00
CY Carl Yastrzemski SP/200 40.00 80.00
DM Don Mattingly SP/300 50.00 100.00
DP Dave Parker 6.00 15.00
DS Duke Snider 10.00 25.00
DW Dave Winfield SP/250 12.50 30.00
EM Eddie Murray SP/250 40.00 80.00
ES Enos Slaughter 10.00 25.00
FH Frank Howard 6.00 15.00
FL Fred Lynn 6.00 15.00
FR Frank Robinson SP/250 15.00 40.00
GB George Brett SP/150 75.00 150.00
GK George Kell 6.00 15.00
GP Gaylord Perry 6.00 15.00
HB Hank Bauer 6.00 15.00
HK Harmon Killebrew 15.00 40.00
HW Hoyt Wilhelm 8.00 20.00
JB Johnny Bench 30.00 60.00
JC Joe Carter 8.00 20.00
JM Juan Marichal 10.00 25.00
JM Joe Morgan 12.00 30.00
JP Jim Palmer 6.00 15.00
JR Jim Rice 6.00 15.00
KP Kirby Puckett SP/250 150.00 300.00
LA Luis Aparicio 8.00 20.00
LB Lou Brock SP/250 12.00 30.00
MS Mike Schmidt SP/150 40.00 80.00
MU Dale Murphy 6.00 15.00
MW Maury Wills 6.00 15.00
NR Nolan Ryan SP/150 60.00 120.00
OC Orlando Cepeda 10.00 25.00
OS Ozzie Smith SP/300 15.00 40.00
PB Paul Blair 6.00 10.00
PM Paul Molitor 12.00 30.00
PR Phil Rizzuto SP/300 30.00 60.00
PR Preacher Roe 6.00 15.00
RC Rod Carew SP/250 20.00 50.00
RF Rollie Fingers 6.00 15.00
RG Rich Gossage 10.00 25.00
RJ Reggie Jackson SP/150 30.00 60.00
RK Ralph Kiner SP/250 10.00 25.00
RS Ryne Sandberg SP/200 20.00 50.00
RY Robin Yount SP/250 30.00 60.00
SA Sparky Anderson 12.00 30.00
SC Steve Carlton 10.00 25.00
SG Steve Garvey 6.00 15.00
SM Stan Musial SP/200 60.00 120.00
TO Tony Oliva 8.00 20.00
TP Tony Perez 10.00 25.00
TS Tom Seaver SP/150 30.00 80.00
VB Vida Blue 6.00 15.00
WB Wade Boggs 15.00 40.00
WF Whitey Ford 15.00 40.00
WM Willie McCovey 20.00 50.00
WS Warren Spahn 15.00 40.00
YB Yogi Berra 30.00 80.00

2002 Greats of the Game Dueling Duos

COMPLETE SET (29) 75.00 150.00
STATED ODDS 1:6
1 J.Bench 1.50 4.00
C.Fisk
2 R.Campanella 2.00 5.00
Y.Berra
3 S.Musial 2.50 6.00
T.Williams
4 C.Yastrzemski 2.00 5.00
R.Jackson
5 B.Ruth 4.00 10.00
J.Foxx
6 K.Puckett 2.50 6.00
D.Mattingly
7 S.Carlton 3.00 8.00
N.Ryan
8 W.Boggs 3.00 8.00
D.Mattingly
9 B.Robinson 1.50 4.00
R.Maris
10 P.Molitor 3.00 8.00
D.Mattingly
11 S.Anderson 1.25 3.00
E.Weaver
12 B.Gibson 1.25 3.00
D.Snider
13 Y.Berra 2.00 5.00
G.Hodges
14 J.Morgan 2.50 6.00
R.Sandberg
15 T.Perez 2.00 5.00
C.Yastrzemski
16 J.Foxx 1.50 4.00
B.Dickey
17 R.Kiner 1.25 3.00
D.Snider
18 N.Fox 1.25 3.00
R.Colavito
19 W.McCovey 1.50 4.00
J.Bench
20 D.Snider 1.25 3.00
E.Mathews
21 R.Jackson 1.25 3.00
J.Rice
22 E.Murray 1.50 4.00
J.Rice
23 P.Molitor 1.25 3.00
D.Winfield
24 R.Yount 1.50 4.00
D.Winfield
25 E.Slaughter 1.25 3.00
T.Kluszewski
26 W.Boggs 3.00 8.00
G.Brett
27 G.Brett 3.00 8.00
M.Schmidt
28 G.Brett 3.00 8.00
E.Murray
29 G.Brett 5.00 12.00
C.Ripken

2002 Greats of the Game Dueling Duos Game Used Single

STATED ODDS 1:24
SP PRINT RUNS PROVIDED BY FLEER
BD1 Bill Dickey Bat 8.00 20.00
BG1 Bob Gibson Jsy SP/200 8.00 20.00
BR1 Brooks Robinson Bat 8.00 20.00
CF1 Carlton Fisk Bat 8.00 20.00
CR1 Cal Ripken Bat 15.00 40.00
CY1 Carl Yastrzemski Bat 12.50 30.00
CY2 Carl Yastrzemski Bat 12.50 30.00
DM1 Don Mattingly Bat 8.00 20.00
DM2 Don Mattingly Bat 8.00 20.00
DM3 Don Mattingly Bat 8.00 20.00
DS1 Duke Snider Bat SP/200 8.00 20.00
DS2 Duke Snider Bat 8.00 20.00
DS3 Duke Snider Bat 8.00 20.00
DW1 Dave Winfield Bat 6.00 15.00
DW2 Dave Winfield Bat 6.00 15.00
EM1 Eddie Mathews Bat 8.00 20.00
EM1 Eddie Murray Bat 8.00 20.00
EM2 Eddie Murray Bat 8.00 20.00
ES1 Enos Slaughter Bat 6.00 15.00
EW1 Earl Weaver Pants SP/400 6.00 15.00
GB1 George Brett Bat 8.00 20.00
GB2 George Brett Bat 8.00 20.00
GB3 George Brett Bat 10.00 25.00
GH1 Gil Hodges Bat 8.00 20.00
JB1 Johnny Bench Bat 8.00 20.00
JB2 Johnny Bench Bat 8.00 20.00
JF2 Jimmie Foxx Bat SP/400 12.50 30.00
JM1 Joe Morgan Bat 6.00 15.00
JR1 Jim Rice Bat 6.00 15.00
JR2 Jim Rice Bat 8.00 20.00
KP1 Kirby Puckett Bat 8.00 20.00
NF1 Nellie Fox Bat 8.00 20.00
PM1 Paul Molitor Bat 6.00 15.00
PM2 Paul Molitor Bat 6.00 15.00
RC1 Rocky Colavito Bat 8.00 20.00
RJ1 Reggie Jackson Bat 8.00 20.00
RJ2 Reggie Jackson Bat 8.00 20.00
RK1 Ralph Kiner Bat 8.00 20.00
RM1 Roger Maris Pants 10.00 25.00
RS1 Ryne Sandberg Bat 10.00 25.00
RY1 Robin Yount Bat 8.00 20.00
SA1 Sparky Anderson Pants SP/400 6.00 15.00
TK1 Ted Kluszewski Bat 8.00 20.00
TP1 Tony Perez Bat 6.00 15.00
WB1 Wade Boggs Bat 8.00 20.00
WB2 Wade Boggs Bat 8.00 20.00
WM1 Willie McCovey Bat 8.00 20.00
YB1 Yogi Berra Bat 8.00 20.00
YB2 Yogi Berra Bat 8.00 20.00
YB3 Yogi Berra Fld Glv 12.50 30.00

2002 Greats of the Game Through the Years Level 1

STATED ODDS 1:24
SP PRINT RUNS PROVIDED BY FLEER
LEVEL 1 FEATURE HOME JSY
NNO CARDS LISTED ALPHABETICALLY
1 Johnny Bench Pants 8.00 20.00
2 Vida Blue 6.00 15.00
3 Wade Boggs 6.00 15.00
4 George Brett 10.00 25.00
5 Carlton Fisk Hitting 6.00 15.00
6 Carlton Fisk Fielding 6.00 15.00
7 Bo Jackson Royals 8.00 20.00
8 Bo Jackson White Sox 8.00 20.00
9 Reggie Jackson A's 6.00 15.00
10 Reggie Jackson Angels 6.00 15.00
11 Ted Kluszewski 6.00 15.00
12 Don Mattingly 10.00 25.00
13 Willie McCovey 6.00 15.00
14 Paul Molitor Blue Jays 6.00 15.00
15 Paul Molitor Brewers 6.00 15.00
16 Eddie Murray 8.00 20.00
17 Jim Palmer 6.00 15.00
18 Tony Perez 6.00 15.00
19 Jim Rice Red Sox Home 6.00 15.00
20 Jim Rice Red Sox Road 6.00 15.00
21 Cal Ripken Orioles Hitting 10.00 25.00
22 Cal Ripken Orioles Fielding 10.00 25.00
23 Brooks Robinson Bat 6.00 15.00
24 Frank Robinson 6.00 15.00
25 Jack Robinson Pants SP/200 12.50 30.00
26 Nolan Ryan 10.00 25.00
27 Hoyt Wilhelm 6.00 15.00
28 Ted Williams SP/350 30.00 60.00
29 Dave Winfield 6.00 15.00
30 Carl Yastrzemski 10.00 25.00
31 Robin Yount 8.00 20.00

2002 Greats of the Game Through the Years Level 1 Patch

RANDOM INSERTS IN PACKS
STATED PRINT RUN 100 SERIAL #'d SETS
NNO CARDS LISTED ALPHABETICALLY
1 Johnny Bench 20.00 50.00
2 Wade Boggs 15.00 40.00
3 George Brett 40.00 80.00
4 Carlton Fisk Hitting 15.00 40.00
5 Carlton Fisk Fielding 15.00 40.00
6 Bo Jackson Royals 20.00 50.00
7 Bo Jackson White Sox 20.00 50.00
8 Reggie Jackson A's 15.00 40.00
9 Reggie Jackson Angels 15.00 40.00
10 Ted Kluszewski 15.00 40.00
11 Don Mattingly 40.00 80.00
12 Willie McCovey 15.00 40.00
13 Paul Molitor Blue Jays 30.00 60.00
14 Paul Molitor Brewers 30.00 60.00
15 Eddie Murray 20.00 50.00
16 Jim Palmer 15.00 40.00
17 Tony Perez 15.00 40.00
18 Jim Rice Red Sox 15.00 40.00
19 Jim Rice Red Sox 15.00 40.00
20 Cal Ripken Hitting 50.00 100.00
21 Cal Ripken Fielding 50.00 100.00
22 Frank Robinson 15.00 40.00
23 Nolan Ryan 40.00 80.00
24 Ted Williams 60.00 120.00
25 Dave Winfield 15.00 40.00
26 Carl Yastrzemski 40.00 80.00
27 Robin Yount 20.00 50.00

2002 Greats of the Game Through the Years Level 2

STATED PRINT RUN 100 SERIAL #'d SETS
LEVEL 2 FEATURE HOME & AWAY JSY
NNO CARDS LISTED ALPHABETICALLY
1 Johnny Bench 10.00 25.00
2 Wade Boggs 8.00 20.00
3 George Brett 15.00 40.00
4 Carlton Fisk White Sox 8.00 20.00
5 Bo Jackson Royals 10.00 25.00
6 Bo Jackson White Sox 10.00 25.00
7 Reggie Jackson A's 8.00 20.00

8 Ted Kluszewski 8.00 20.00
9 Don Mattingly 15.00 40.00
10 Willie McCovey 8.00 20.00
11 Paul Molitor Brewers 8.00 20.00
12 Eddie Murray 10.00 25.00
13 Jim Palmer 8.00 20.00
14 Jim Rice Home 8.00 20.00
15 Jim Rice Road 8.00 20.00
16 Cal Ripken Hitting 20.00 50.00
17 Cal Ripken Fielding 20.00 50.00
18 Nolan Ryan 10.00 25.00
19 Ted Williams 30.00 60.00
20 Dave Winfield 8.00 20.00
21 Carl Yastrzemski 10.00 25.00
22 Robin Yount 10.00 25.00

2004 Greats of the Game

COMPLETE SERIES 1 (80) 15.00 40.00
COMPLETE SERIES 2 (65) 10.00 25.00
COMMON CARD (1-145) .20 .50
1 Lou Gehrig 1.00 2.50
2 Ty Cobb .75 2.00
3 Dizzy Dean .30 .75
4 Jimmie Foxx .50 1.25
5 Hank Greenberg .50 1.25
6 Babe Ruth 1.25 3.00
7 Honus Wagner .50 1.25
8 Mickey Cochrane .30 .75
9 Pepper Martin .20 .50
10 Charlie Gehringer .20 .50
11 Carl Hubbell .30 .75
12 Bill Terry .20 .50
13 Mel Ott .50 1.25
14 Bill Dickey .20 .50
15 Ted Williams 1.00 2.50
16 Roger Maris Yanks .50 1.25
17 Thurman Munson .50 1.25
18 Phil Rizzuto .30 .75
19 Stan Musial .75 2.00
20 Duke Snider Brooklyn .30 .75
21 Reggie Jackson Yanks .30 .75
22 Don Mattingly 1.00 2.50
23 Vida Blue .20 .50
24 Harmon Killebrew .50 1.25
25 Lou Brock .30 .75
26 Al Kaline .50 1.25
27 Dave Parker .20 .50
28 Nolan Ryan Astros 1.50 4.00
29 Jim Rice .30 .75
30 Paul Molitor Brewers .50 1.25
31 Dwight Evans .20 .50
32 Brooks Robinson .30 .75
33 Jose Canseco .30 .75
34 Alan Trammell .30 .75
35 Johnny Bench .50 1.25
36 Carlton Fisk R.Sox .30 .75
37 Jim Palmer .30 .75
38 George Brett 1.00 2.50
39 Mike Schmidt .75 2.00
40 Tony Perez .30 .75
41 Paul Blair .20 .50
42 Fred Lynn .20 .50
43 Carl Yastrzemski .50 1.25
44 Steve Carlton Phils .30 .75
45 Dennis Eckersley .30 .75
46 Tom Seaver Mets .30 .75
47 Juan Marichal .30 .75
48 Tony Gwynn .50 1.25
49 Moose Skowron .20 .50
50 Bob Gibson .30 .75
51 Luis Tiant .20 .50
52 Eddie Murray O's .30 .75
53 Frank Robinson Reds .30 .75
54 Rocky Colavito .30 .75
55 Bobby Shantz .20 .50
56 Ernie Banks .50 1.25
57 Rod Carew Angels .30 .75
58 Gorman Thomas .20 .50
59 Bernie Carbo .20 .50
60 Joe Rudi .20 .50
61 Graig Nettles .20 .50
62 Ron Guidry .20 .50
63 Whitey Ford .30 .75
64 George Kell .30 .75
65 Cal Ripken 1.50 4.00
66 Willie McCovey .30 .75
67 Bo Jackson .50 1.25
68 Kirby Puckett .50 1.25
69 Ted Kluszewski .30 .75
70 Johnny Podres .20 .50
71 Davey Lopes .20 .50
72 Chris Short .20 .50
73 Jeff Torborg .20 .50
74 Bill Freehan .20 .50
75 Frank Tanana .20 .50
76 Jack Morris .30 .75
77 Rick Dempsey .20 .50
78 Yogi Berra .50 1.25
79 Tim McCarver .20 .50
80 Rusty Staub .20 .50
81 Tony Lazzeri .30 .75
82 Al Rosen .20 .50
83 Willie McGee .20 .50
84 Preacher Roe .20 .50
85 Dave Kingman .20 .50
86 Luis Aparicio .30 .75
87 John Kruk .20 .50
88 Bing Miller .20 .50
89 Joe Charboneau .20 .50
90 Mark Fidrych .20 .50
91 Catfish Hunter .30 .75
92 Nap Lajoie .50 1.25
93 Eddie Murray Indians .30 .75
94 Johnny Pesky .20 .50
95 Tom Seaver Reds .30 .75
96 Frank Robinson O's .30 .75
97 Enos Slaughter .30 .75
98 Cecil Travis .20 .50
99 Robin Yount .50 1.25
100 Don Zimmer .20 .50
101 Babe Herman .20 .50
102 Ron Santo .30 .75
103 Willie Stargell .30 .75
104 Paul Molitor Jays .50 1.25
105 Jimmy Piersall .20 .50
106 Johnny Sain .20 .50
107 Joe Pepitone .20 .50
108 Ryne Sandberg 1.00 2.50
109 Jim Thorpe .50 1.25
110 Steve Garvey .20 .50
111 Ray Knight .20 .50
112 Fernando Valenzuela .20 .50
113 Will Clark .30 .75
114 Tony Kubek .20 .50
115 Jim Bouton .20 .50
116 Jerry Koosman .20 .50
117 Steve Carlton Cards .30 .75
118 Richie Ashburn .30 .75
119 Roberto Clemente 1.25 3.00
120 Paul O'Neill .30 .75
121 Reggie Jackson Angels .30 .75
122 Andre Dawson .30 .75
123 Hoyt Wilhelm .30 .75
124 Dale Murphy .50 1.25
125 Dwight Gooden .20 .50
126 Roger Maris Cards .50 1.25
127 Bill Mazeroski .30 .75
128 Don Newcombe .20 .50
129 Robin Roberts .30 .75
130 Duke Snider LA .30 .75
131 Eddie Mathews .50 1.25
132 Wade Boggs .30 .75
133 Rollie Fingers .30 .75
134 Frankie Frisch .30 .75
135 Billy Williams .30 .75
136 Rod Carew Twins .30 .75
137 Dom DiMaggio .20 .50
138 Orel Hershiser .20 .50
139 Gary Carter .30 .75
140 Keith Hernandez .20 .50
141 Bob Lemon .30 .75
142 Nolan Ryan Angels 1.50 4.00
143 Ozzie Smith .60 1.50
144 Rick Sutcliffe .20 .50
145 Carlton Fisk W.Sox .30 .75

2004 Greats of the Game Blue

*1-80 POST-WAR: 1.25X TO 3X
*1-80 PRE-WAR: 1X TO 2.5X
*81-145 POST-WAR p/r 81-96: 4X TO 10X
*81-145 POST-WAR p/r 51-80: 4X TO 10X
*81-145 POST-WAR p/r 36-50: 5X TO 12X
*81-145 PRE-WAR p/r 36-50: 4X TO 10X
*81-145 PRE-WAR p/r 26-35: 5X TO 12X
*81-145 PRE-WAR p/r 18-25: 6X TO 15X
1-80 SER.1 ODDS 1:7.5 H, 1:24 R
81-145 SER.2 ODDS 1:60 H, 1:110 R
1-80 PRINT RUN 500 SERIAL #'d SETS
81-145 PRINT RUN B/WN 1-96 COPIES PER
81-145 NO PRICING ON QTY OF 1

2004 Greats of the Game Autographs

OVERALL SER.1 AU ODDS 1:5 H, 1:960 R
OVERALL SER.2 AU ODDS 1:7.5 H, 1:960 R
GROUP A PRINT RUN 125-150 SETS
GROUP B PRINT RUN 175-250 SETS
GROUP C1 PRINT RUN 275-300 SETS
A-C CARDS ARE NOT SERIAL-NUMBERED
PRINT RUN INFO PROVIDED BY FLEER
EXCHANGE DEADLINE INDEFINITE
AD Andre Dawson C2 6.00 15.00
AK Al Kaline D1 20.00 50.00
AR Al Rosen E2 6.00 15.00
AT Alan Trammell F1 10.00 25.00
BC Bernie Carbo G1 6.00 15.00
BF Bill Freehan G1 6.00 15.00
BG Bob Gibson F1 20.00 50.00
BJ Bo Jackson C1 20.00 50.00
BM Bill Mazeroski C2 10.00 25.00
BR Brooks Robinson F1 10.00 25.00
BS Bobby Shantz G1 6.00 15.00
BW Billy Williams C2 8.00 20.00
CF1 Carlton Fisk R.Sox D1 10.00 25.00
CF2 Carlton Fisk W.Sox D2 10.00 25.00
CR Cal Ripken A1 30.00 80.00
CY Carl Yastrzemski D1 30.00 60.00
DC David Cone B2 6.00 15.00
DD Dom DiMaggio B2 20.00 50.00
DE Dennis Eckersley B1 10.00 25.00
DEV Dwight Evans F1 6.00 15.00
DG Dwight Gooden B2 6.00 15.00
DK Dave Kingman E2 10.00 25.00
DL Davey Lopes G1 6.00 15.00
DM Don Mattingly A1 40.00 80.00
DMC Denny McLain G1 6.00 15.00
DMU Dale Murphy C2 10.00 25.00
DN Don Newcombe C2 10.00 25.00
DP Dave Parker G1 6.00 15.00
DS1 D.Snider Brooklyn D1 20.00 50.00
DS2 Duke Snider LA B2 20.00 50.00
DZ Don Zimmer C2 6.00 15.00
EB Ernie Banks A1 30.00 60.00
EM Eddie Murray B1 20.00 50.00
FL Fred Lynn F1 6.00 15.00
FR1 Frank Robinson Reds E1 12.00 30.00
FR2 Frank Robinson O's C2 12.00 30.00
FT Frank Tanana G1 6.00 15.00
GB George Brett A1 50.00 100.00
GC Gary Carter B2 10.00 25.00
GK George Kell F1 6.00 15.00
GN Graig Nettles G1 6.00 15.00
GT Gorman Thomas G1 6.00 15.00
HK Harmon Killebrew F1 10.00 25.00
JB Johnny Bench D1 20.00 50.00
JBO Jim Bouton D2 6.00 15.00
JC Jose Canseco D1 4.00 10.00
JCH Joe Charboneau E2 6.00 15.00
JK Jerry Koosman E2 6.00 15.00
JKR John Kruk B2 6.00 15.00
JM Juan Marichal F1 8.00 20.00
JMO Jack Morris F1 6.00 15.00
JP Jim Palmer F1 10.00 25.00
JPI Jimmy Piersall D2 6.00 15.00
JPO Johnny Podres G1 6.00 15.00
JPP Joe Pepitone E2 6.00 15.00
JPS Johnny Pesky E2 6.00 15.00
JR Jim Rice F1 10.00 25.00
JRU Joe Rudi G1 6.00 15.00
JT Jeff Torborg G1 6.00 15.00
KH Keith Hernandez D2 6.00 15.00
KP Kirby Puckett A1 100.00 200.00
LA Luis Aparicio E2 10.00 25.00
LB Lou Brock F1 20.00 50.00
LT Luis Tiant G1 6.00 15.00
MM Marty Marion G1 6.00 15.00
MS Mike Schmidt B1 30.00 60.00
MSK Moose Skowron G1 6.00 15.00
NR1 Nolan Ryan Astros A1 60.00 120.00
NR2 Nolan Ryan Angels B2 60.00 120.00
OH Orel Hershiser A2 15.00 40.00
OS Ozzie Smith B2 20.00 50.00
PB Paul Blair G1 6.00 15.00
PM1 Paul Molitor Brewers B1 10.00 25.00
PO Paul O'Neill B2 15.00 40.00
PRO Preacher Roe B2 10.00 25.00
RCO Rocky Colavito D1 15.00 40.00
RC1 Rod Carew Angels D1 10.00 25.00
RD Rick Dempsey A1 10.00 25.00
RF Rollie Fingers D2 6.00 15.00
RG Ron Guidry F1 8.00 20.00
RJ1 R.Jackson Yanks A1 20.00 50.00
RJ2 R.Jackson Angels B2 6.00 15.00
RK Ray Knight E2 6.00 15.00
RR Robin Roberts E2 8.00 20.00
RS Ryne Sandberg B2 30.00 60.00
RST Rusty Staub G1 6.00 15.00
RST Ron Santo D2 12.00 30.00
SC1 Steve Carlton Phils D1 8.00 20.00
SC2 Steve Carlton Cards D2 8.00 20.00
SG Steve Garvey D2 6.00 15.00
SM Stan Musial A1 40.00 80.00
TG Tony Gwynn E1 20.00 50.00
TK Tony Kubek C2 10.00 25.00
TM Tim McCarver F1 8.00 20.00
TP Tony Perez F1 8.00 20.00
TS1 Tom Seaver Mets A1 30.00 80.00
VB Vida Blue G1 6.00 15.00
WC Will Clark B2 8.00 20.00
WF Whitey Ford D1 15.00 40.00
WM Willie McCovey E1 15.00 40.00
WMG Willie McGee D2 12.00 30.00
YB Yogi Berra B1 20.00 50.00

2004 Greats of the Game Announcing Greats

SER.2 STATED ODDS 1:12 RETAIL
1 H.Kalas/M.Schmidt 1.50 4.00
2 V.Scully/S.Garvey 1.00 2.50
3 H.Caray/R.Sandberg 2.00 5.00
4 N.Martin/C.Fisk .60 1.50
5 E.Harwell/K.Gibson .60 1.50
6 K.Harrelson/C.Yastrzemski 1.00 2.50
7 P.Rizzuto/D.Mattingly 2.00 5.00
8 M.Allen/Y.Berra 1.00 2.50
9 J.Miller/C.Ripken 3.00 8.00
10 M.Brennaman/J.Bench 1.00 2.50

2004 Greats of the Game Announcing Greats Autograph Dual

OVERALL SER.2 AU ODDS 1:7.5 HOBBY
OVERALL SER.2 AU-GU ODDS 1:24 RETAIL
PRINT RUNS B/WN 1-50 COPIES PER
NO PRICING ON QTY OF 8 OR LESS
EXCHANGE DEADLINE INDEFINITE
HKMS H.Kalas/M.Schmidt/25 100.00 200.00

2004 Greats of the Game Battery Mates

RANDOM INSERTS IN SER.1 PACKS
PRINT RUNS B/WN 1934-1979 COPIES PER
1 S.Carlton .60 1.50
T.McCarver/1972
2 D.Drysdale 1.00 2.50
R.Campy/1957
3 T.Seaver 1.00 2.50
J.Bench/1979
4 W.Ford 1.00 2.50
Y.Berra/1956
5 R.Guidry 1.00 2.50
T.Munson/1978
6 N.Ryan 3.00 8.00
J.Torborg/1973
7 D.McLain .40 1.00
B.Freehan/1968
8 L.Gomez .40 1.00
B.Dickey/1934
9 J.Palmer .60 1.50
R.Dempsey/1977
10 L.Tiant .60 1.50
C.Fisk/1973

2004 Greats of the Game Battery Mates Autograph

OVERALL SER.1 AU ODDS 1:5 H, 1:960 R
PRINT RUNS B/WN 56-79 COPIES PER
AUTO IS ONLY FOR 1ST PLAYER LISTED
JPRD J.Palmer w 8.00 20.00
Dempsey/77
NRJT J.Torborg w 6.00 15.00
Ryan/73
RGTM R.Guidry w 10.00 25.00
Munson/78
SCTM S.Carlton w 8.00 20.00
McCarver/72
TSJB J.Bench w 25.00 60.00
Seaver/79
WFYB W.Ford w 20.00 50.00
Berra/56

2004 Greats of the Game Battery Mates Autograph Dual

OVERALL SER.1 AU ODDS 1:5 H, 1:960 R
STATED PRINT RUN 10 SERIAL #'d SETS
NO PRICING DUE TO SCARCITY

2004 Greats of the Game Comparison Cuts

OVERALL SER.1 AU ODDS 1:5 H, 1:960 R
STATED PRINT RUN 1 SERIAL #'d SET
NO PRICING DUE TO SCARCITY

2004 Greats of the Game Etched in Time Cuts

OVERALL SER.1 AU ODDS 1:5 H, 1:960 R
OVERALL SER.2 AU ODDS 1:7.5 HOBBY
OVERALL SER.2 AU-GU ODDS 1:24 RETAIL
PRINT RUNS B/WN 1-95 COPIES PER
NO PRICING ON QTY OF 10 OR LESS
BH Babe Herman S2/35 75.00 150.00
CS Chris Short S2/30 100.00 200.00
DC Dolph Camilli S2/40 100.00 200.00
EA Ethan Allen S2/75 20.00 50.00
EAV Earl Averill S2/50 40.00 80.00
ER Edd Roush S2/95 20.00 50.00
HK Harvey Kuenn S2/32 60.00 120.00
LA Luke Appling S2/23 60.00 120.00
PR Pete Runnels S2/35 60.00 120.00
RF Rick Ferrell S2/50 60.00 120.00
SM Sal Maglie S2/40 60.00 120.00
WC Walker Cooper S2/20 60.00 120.00

2004 Greats of the Game Forever

OVERALL SER.2 ODDS 1:5 HOB, 1:12 RET
PRINT RUNS B/WN 1909-1984 COPIES PER
1 Fernando Valenzuela/1980 .60 1.50
2 Steve Garvey/1969 .60 1.50
3 Zach Wheat/1909 1.00 2.50
4 Orel Hershiser/1983 .60 1.50
5 Duke Snider/1947 1.00 2.50
6 Jim Rice/1974 1.00 2.50
7 Carlton Fisk/1969 1.00 2.50
8 Wade Boggs/1982 1.00 2.50
9 Ted Williams/1939 3.00 8.00
10 Carl Yastrzemski/1961 1.50 4.00
11 Dom DiMaggio/1940 .60 1.50
12 Ron Santo/1960 1.00 2.50
13 Billy Williams/1959 1.00 2.50
14 Ryne Sandberg/1981 3.00 8.00
15 Ernie Banks/1953 1.50 4.00
16 Gabby Hartnett/1922 .60 1.50
17 Hack Wilson/1923 1.00 2.50
18 Dwight Gooden/1984 .60 1.50
19 Ray Knight/1974 .60 1.50
20 Tom Seaver/1967 1.00 2.50
21 Nolan Ryan/1966 5.00 12.00
22 Keith Hernandez/1974 .60 1.50
23 Darryl Strawberry/1983 .60 1.50
24 Bob Gibson/1959 1.00 2.50
25 Pepper Martin/1928 .60 1.50
26 Stan Musial/1941 2.50 6.00
27 Frankie Frisch/1919 1.00 2.50
28 Steve Carlton/1965 1.00 2.50
29 Ozzie Smith/1978 2.00 5.00

2004 Greats of the Game Forever Game Jersey

SER.2 STATED ODDS 1:24 RETAIL
SP INFO PROVIDED BY FLEER
NO SP PRICING DUE TO SCARCITY
EXCHANGE DEADLINE INDEFINITE
BG Bob Gibson 6.00 15.00
BW Billy Williams 4.00 10.00
CF Carlton Fisk 6.00 15.00
DD Dom DiMaggio 10.00 25.00
DG Dwight Gooden 4.00 10.00
DS Darryl Strawberry 4.00 10.00
OH Orel Hershiser 4.00 10.00
OS Ozzie Smith 6.00 15.00
SC Steve Carlton 4.00 10.00
SM Stan Musial 10.00 25.00
TW Ted Williams 12.50 30.00
WB Wade Boggs 6.00 15.00

2004 Greats of the Game Forever Game Jersey Logo

STATED PRINT RUN 149 SERIAL #'d SETS
*JSY NBR: .5X TO 1.2X JSY LOGO
JSY NBR PRINT RUN 99 SERIAL #'d SETS
SER.2 GU ODDS 1:15 HOBBY
EXCHANGE DEADLINE INDEFINITE
BG Bob Gibson 6.00 15.00
BW Billy Williams 4.00 10.00
CF Carlton Fisk 6.00 15.00
CY Carl Yastrzemski 8.00 20.00
DD Dom DiMaggio 10.00 25.00
DG Dwight Gooden 4.00 10.00
DS Darryl Strawberry 4.00 10.00
EB Ernie Banks 10.00 25.00
JR Jim Rice 4.00 10.00
NR Nolan Ryan 30.00 60.00
OH Orel Hershiser 4.00 10.00
OS Ozzie Smith 6.00 15.00
RK Ray Knight 4.00 10.00
RS Ryne Sandberg 6.00 15.00
SM Stan Musial 10.00 25.00
TW Ted Williams 30.00 60.00
WB Wade Boggs 6.00 15.00

2004 Greats of the Game Forever Game Patch Logo

STATED PRINT RUN 49 SERIAL #'d SETS
NUMBER PRINT RUN 25 SERIAL #'d SETS
NO NUMBER PRICING DUE TO SCARCITY
SER.2 GU ODDS 1:15 HOBBY
EXCHANGE DEADLINE INDEFINITE
BG Bob Gibson 10.00 25.00
CF Carlton Fisk 10.00 25.00
CY Carl Yastrzemski 20.00 50.00
DG Dwight Gooden 6.00 15.00
DS Darryl Strawberry 6.00 15.00
EB Ernie Banks 15.00 40.00
JR Jim Rice 10.00 25.00
OS Ozzie Smith 20.00 50.00
RS Ryne Sandberg 10.00 25.00
TW Ted Williams 60.00 120.00
WB Wade Boggs 10.00 25.00

2004 Greats of the Game Forever Game Patch Dual Logo

STATED PRINT RUN 19 SERIAL #'d SETS
DUAL NBR PRINT RUN 5 SERIAL #'d SETS
OVERALL SER.2 GU ODDS 1:15 HOBBY
EXCHANGE DEADLINE INDEFINITE
NO PRICING DUE TO SCARCITY

2004 Greats of the Game Glory of Their Time

RANDOM INSERTS IN SER.1 PACKS
PRINT RUNS B/WN 1911-1997 COPIES PER
1 Harmon Killebrew/1961 1.25 3.00
2 Johnny Bench/1974 1.25 3.00
3 George Brett/1980 2.50 6.00
4 Tony Gwynn/1987 1.25 3.00
5 Paul Molitor/1987 1.25 3.00
6 Don Mattingly/1986 2.50 6.00
7 Reggie Jackson/1980 .75 2.00
8 Carlton Fisk/1985 .75 2.00
9 Cal Ripken/1983 4.00 10.00
10 Brooks Robinson/1964 .75 2.00
11 Eddie Murray/1980 .75 2.00
12 Moose Skowron/1960 .50 1.25
13 Lou Brock/1974 .75 2.00
14 Don Drysdale/1962 .75 2.00
15 Tony Gwynn/1997 1.25 3.00
16 Mike Schmidt/1980 2.00 5.00
17 Carl Yastrzemski/1967 1.25 3.00
18 Babe Ruth/1927 3.00 8.00
19 Nolan Ryan/1989 4.00 10.00
20 Yogi Berra/1950 1.25 3.00
21 Al Kaline/1955 1.25 3.00
22 Ty Cobb/1911 2.00 5.00
23 Duke Snider/1955 .75 2.00
24 Stan Musial/1948 2.00 5.00
25 Jose Canseco/1988 .75 2.00
26 Rocky Colavito/1958 .75 2.00
27 Dave Winfield/1979 .75 2.00
28 Nolan Ryan/1982 4.00 10.00
29 Thurman Munson/1977 1.25 3.00
30 Jackie Robinson/1949 1.25 3.00
31 Kirby Puckett/1988 1.25 3.00
32 Ted Kluszewski/1954 .75 2.00
33 Warren Spahn/1953 .75 2.00
34 Willie McCovey/1969 .75 2.00
35 Phil Rizzuto/1950 .75 2.00

2004 Greats of the Game Glory of Their Time Game Used

STATED PRINT RUN 250 SERIAL #'d SETS
*GOLD: .4X TO 1X BASIC
GOLD STATED ODDS 1:24 RETAIL
OVERALL SER.1 GU ODDS 1:30 H, 1:24 R
AK Al Kaline Pants 6.00 15.00
BR Brooks Robinson Jsy 6.00 15.00
CF1 Carlton Fisk Jsy 6.00 15.00
CF2 Carlton Fisk Bat 6.00 15.00
CR Cal Ripken Jsy 10.00 25.00
CY Carl Yastrzemski Jsy 8.00 20.00
DD Don Drysdale Jsy 6.00 15.00
DM Don Mattingly Pants 8.00 20.00
DW Dave Winfield Jsy 4.00 10.00
EM Eddie Murray Jsy 6.00 15.00
GB George Brett Jsy 8.00 20.00
HK Harmon Killebrew Bat 6.00 15.00
JB Johnny Bench Jsy 6.00 15.00
JC1 Jose Canseco Jsy 6.00 15.00
JC2 Jose Canseco Bat 6.00 15.00
KP Kirby Puckett Bat 6.00 15.00
LB Lou Brock Jsy 6.00 15.00
MS Mike Schmidt Jsy 8.00 20.00
MS Moose Skowron Pants 4.00 10.00
NR1 Nolan Ryan Jsy 10.00 25.00
NR2 Nolan Ryan Bat 10.00 25.00
PM Paul Molitor Jsy 4.00 10.00
PR Phil Rizzuto Bat 6.00 15.00
RC Rocky Colavito Bat 12.50 30.00
RJ Reggie Jackson Pants 6.00 15.00
TG1 Tony Gwynn White Jsy 6.00 15.00
TG2 Tony Gwynn Grey Jsy 6.00 15.00
TK Ted Kluszewski Pants 6.00 15.00
TM Thurman Munson Pants 10.00 25.00
WM Willie McCovey Pants 6.00 15.00
WS Warren Spahn Jsy 6.00 15.00
YB Yogi Berra Pants 6.00 15.00

2004 Greats of the Game Personality Cuts

OVERALL SER.1 AU ODDS 1:5 H, 1:960 R
OVERALL SER.2 AU ODDS 1:7.5 HOBBY
OVERALL SER.2 AU-GU ODDS 1:24 RETAIL
PRINT RUNS B/WN 1-2 COPIES PER
NO PRICING DUE TO SCARCITY

2004 Greats of the Game Yankees Clippings

SER.2 STATED ODDS 1:45 HOBBY
SP PRINT RUNS PROVIDED BY FLEER
SP'S ARE NOT SERIAL-NUMBERED
EXCHANGE DEADLINE INDEFINITE
BS Bill Skowron 12.00 30.00
DM Don Mattingly 12.50 30.00
PO Paul O'Neill 10.00 25.00
RJ Reggie Jackson 10.00 25.00
WB Wade Boggs 8.00 20.00
YB Yogi Berra 10.00 25.00

2004 Greats of the Game Yankees Clippings Autograph

OVERALL SER.2 AU ODDS 1:7.5 HOBBY
PRINT RUNS B/WN 3-26 COPIES PER
NO PRICING DUE TO SCARCITY
EXCHANGE DEADLINE INDEFINITE

2006 Greats of the Game

COMPLETE SET (100) 20.00 50.00
COMMON CARD (1-100) .30 .75
ONE PLATE PER FOIL PLATE PACK
PLATE PACKS ISSUED TO DEALERS
PLATE PRINT RUN 1 SET PER COLOR
BLACK-CYAN-MAGENTA-YELLOW ISSUED
NO PLATE PRICING DUE TO SCARCITY
1 Al Kaline .75 2.00
2 Alan Trammell .50 1.25
3 Andre Dawson .50 1.25
4 Barry Larkin .50 1.25
5 Bill Buckner .30 .75
6 Bill Freehan .30 .75
7 Bill Madlock .30 .75
8 Bill Mazeroski .50 1.25
9 Billy Williams .50 1.25
10 Bo Jackson .75 2.00
11 Bob Feller .50 1.25
12 Bob Gibson .50 1.25
13 Bobby Doerr .30 .75
14 Bobby Murcer .30 .75
15 Boog Powell .30 .75
16 Brooks Robinson .50 1.25
17 Bruce Sutter .30 .75
18 Bucky Dent .30 .75
19 Cal Ripken 2.50 6.00
20 Rico Petrocelli .30 .75
21 Carlton Fisk .50 1.25
22 Chris Chambliss .30 .75
23 Dave Concepcion .30 .75
24 Dave Parker .30 .75
25 Dave Winfield .50 1.25
26 David Cone .30 .75
27 Denny McLain .30 .75
28 Don Mattingly 1.50 4.00
29 Don Newcombe .30 .75
30 Don Sutton .30 .75
31 Dusty Baker .30 .75
32 Dwight Evans .30 .75
33 Eric Davis .30 .75
34 Ernie Banks .75 2.00
35 Fergie Jenkins .50 1.25
36 Frank Robinson .50 1.25
37 Fred Lynn .30 .75
38 Fred McGriff .50 1.25
39 Andre Thornton .30 .75
40 Garry Maddox .30 .75
41 Gary Matthews .30 .75
42 Gaylord Perry .50 1.25
43 George Foster .30 .75
44 George Kell .50 1.25
45 Graig Nettles .30 .75
46 Greg Luzinski .30 .75
47 Harmon Killebrew .75 2.00
48 Jack Clark .30 .75
49 Jack Morris .50 1.25
50 Jim Palmer .50 1.25
51 Jim Rice .50 1.25
52 Joe Morgan .50 1.25
53 John Kruk .30 .75
54 Johnny Bench .75 2.00
55 Jose Canseco .50 1.25
56 Kirby Puckett .75 2.00
57 Kirk Gibson .30 .75
58 Lee Mazzilli .30 .75
59 Lou Brock .50 1.25
60 Lou Piniella .30 .75
61 Luis Aparicio .50 1.25
62 Luis Tiant .30 .75
63 Mark Fidrych .30 .75
64 Mark Grace .50 1.25
65 Maury Wills .30 .75
66 Mike Schmidt 1.25 3.00
67 Nolan Ryan 2.50 6.00
68 Ozzie Smith 1.00 2.50
69 Paul Molitor .75 2.00
70 Paul O'Neill .50 1.25
71 Phil Niekro .50 1.25
72 Ralph Kiner .50 1.25
73 Randy Hundley .30 .75
74 Red Schoendienst .50 1.25
75 Reggie Jackson .50 1.25
76 Robin Yount .75 2.00
77 Rod Carew .50 1.25
78 Rollie Fingers .50 1.25
79 Ron Cey .30 .75
80 Ron Guidry .30 .75
81 Ron Santo .50 1.25
82 Rusty Staub .30 .75
83 Ryne Sandberg 1.50 4.00
84 Sparky Lyle .30 .75
85 Stan Musial 1.25 3.00
86 Steve Carlton .50 1.25
87 Steve Garvey .30 .75
88 Steve Sax .30 .75
89 Tommy Herr .30 .75
90 Tim McCarver .30 .75
91 Tim Raines .50 1.25
92 Tom Seaver .50 1.25
93 Tony Gwynn .75 2.00
94 Tony Perez .50 1.25
95 Wade Boggs .50 1.25
96 Whitey Ford .50 1.25
97 Will Clark .50 1.25
98 Willie Horton .30 .75
99 Willie McCovey .50 1.25
100 Yogi Berra .75 2.00

2006 Greats of the Game Copper

*COPPER: 1.5X TO 4X BASIC
STATED ODDS 1:15 H
STATED PRINT RUN 299 SERIAL #'d SETS

2006 Greats of the Game Pewter

*PEWTER: 1X TO 2.5X BASIC
STATED ODDS 1:5 H, 1:15 R

2006 Greats of the Game Autographs

STATED ODDS 1:15 H, 1:15 R
TIER 1 QTY B/WN 50-90 COPIES PER
TIER 2 QTY B/WN 100-150 COPIES PER
TIER 3 QTY B/WN 151-300 COPIES PER
TIER 4 QTY B/WN 301-600 COPIES PER
CARDS ARE NOT SERIAL-NUMBERED
PRINT RUN INFO PROVIDED BY UD
SOME CARDS CARRY AU INSCRIPTIONS
AU INSCRIPTIONS NOT INTENDED FOR SET
AU INSCRIPTIONS DETAILED BELOW
PARENTHESES PERCENTAGE OF PRINT RUN
1 Al Kaline T3 15.00 40.00
2 Alan Trammell T3 8.00 20.00
3 Andre Dawson T3 8.00 20.00
4 Barry Larkin T3 10.00 25.00
5 Bill Buckner T3 8.00 20.00
6 Bill Freehan T4 10.00 25.00
7a Bill Madlock T4 (35) 4.00 10.00
7b B.Madlock Maddog T4 (65) 5.00 12.00
8 Bill Mazeroski T2 12.00 30.00
9 Billy Williams T3 8.00 20.00
10 Bo Jackson T2 30.00 60.00
11 Bob Feller T2 8.00 20.00
12 Bob Gibson T2 12.00 30.00
13 Bobby Doerr T3 6.00 15.00
14 Bobby Murcer T3 15.00 40.00
15 Boog Powell T4 4.00 10.00
16 Brooks Robinson T3 12.00 30.00
17 Bruce Sutter T3 8.00 20.00
18 Bucky Dent T3 5.00 12.00
19 Cal Ripken T1/50 * 30.00 60.00
20 Rico Petrocelli T4 6.00 15.00
21 Carlton Fisk T2 12.00 30.00
22 Chris Chambliss T3 5.00 12.00
23 Dave Concepcion T3 10.00 25.00
24 Dave Parker T2 10.00 25.00
25 Dave Winfield T2 12.00 30.00
26 David Cone T3 10.00 25.00
27 Denny McLain T3 10.00 25.00
28 Don Mattingly T2 30.00 60.00
29 Don Newcombe T4 6.00 15.00
30 Don Sutton T3 8.00 20.00
31 Dusty Baker T1/75 * 8.00 20.00
32a Dwight Evans T3 (90) 12.00 30.00
33 Eric Davis T4 8.00 20.00
34 Ernie Banks T2 15.00 40.00
35 Fergie Jenkins T2 5.00 12.00
36 Frank Robinson T2 20.00 50.00
37 Fred Lynn T3 5.00 12.00
38 Fred McGriff T3 10.00 25.00
39 A.Thornton Thunder T4 4.00 10.00
40 Garry Maddox T2 6.00 15.00
41 G.Matthews Sarge T4 12.00 30.00
42 Gaylord Perry T3 6.00 15.00
43 George Foster T3 4.00 10.00
44 George Kell T3 6.00 15.00
45 Graig Nettles T3 6.00 15.00
46 Greg Luzinski T2 6.00 15.00
47 Harmon Killebrew T2 20.00 50.00
48a Jack Clark T4 (50) 5.00 12.00
48b J.Clark Ripper T4 (50) 5.00 12.00
49 Jack Morris T3 8.00 20.00
50 Jim Palmer T3 6.00 15.00
51 Jim Rice T3 10.00 25.00
52 Joe Morgan T2 10.00 25.00
53 John Kruk T3 5.00 12.00
54 Johnny Bench T2 20.00 50.00
56 Kirby Puckett T2 100.00 250.00
57 Kirk Gibson T2 8.00 20.00
58 Lee Mazzilli T3 4.00 10.00
59 Lou Brock T2 15.00 40.00
60 Lou Piniella T3 6.00 15.00
61 Luis Aparicio T3 6.00 15.00
62 Luis Tiant T3 4.00 10.00
63 Mark Fidrych T2 20.00 50.00
64 Mark Grace T3 5.00 12.00
65 Maury Wills T3 6.00 15.00
66 Mike Schmidt T2 15.00 40.00
67 Nolan Ryan T1/50 * 100.00 200.00
68 Ozzie Smith T2 15.00 40.00
69 Paul Molitor T3 12.00 30.00
70 Paul O'Neill T3 4.00 10.00
71 Phil Niekro T3 8.00 20.00
72 Ralph Kiner T2 6.00 15.00
73 Randy Hundley T4 4.00 10.00
74 Red Schoendienst T3 10.00 25.00
75 Reggie Jackson T2 15.00 40.00
76 Robin Yount T2 30.00 80.00
77 Rod Carew T3 15.00 40.00
78 Rollie Fingers T3 4.00 10.00
79 Ron Cey T3 4.00 10.00
80a Ron Guidry T3 (50) 8.00 20.00
80b R.Guidry Gator T3 (50) 8.00 20.00
81 Ron Santo T3 15.00 40.00
82a Rusty Staub T3 (20) 10.00 25.00
82b R.Staub Orange T3 (80) 10.00 25.00
83 Ryne Sandberg T1/90 * 30.00 60.00
84 Sparky Lyle T3 4.00 10.00
85 Stan Musial T2 30.00 60.00
86 Steve Carlton T3 15.00 40.00
87 Steve Garvey T2 5.00 12.00
88 Steve Sax T4 5.00 12.00
89 T.Herr T-Bird T4 6.00 15.00
90 Tim McCarver T3 10.00 25.00
91a Tim Raines T3 (50) 6.00 15.00
91b T.Raines Rock T3 (50) 8.00 20.00
92 Tom Seaver T2 15.00 40.00
93 Tony Gwynn T2 12.00 30.00
94 Tony Perez T3 20.00 50.00
95 Wade Boggs T2 20.00 50.00
96 Whitey Ford T2 20.00 50.00
97a Will Clark T2 (60) 15.00 40.00
97b W.Clark Thrill T2 (40) 30.00 80.00
98 Willie Horton T4 6.00 15.00
99 Willie McCovey T1/75 * 25.00 60.00
100 Yogi Berra T2 25.00 60.00

2006 Greats of the Game Autographics

STATED ODDS 1:180 H, 1:960 R
PRINT RUNS B/WN 10-99 COPIES PER
CARDS ARE NOT SERIAL-NUMBERED
PRINT RUN INFO PROVIDED BY UD
NO PRICING ON QTY OF 25 OR LESS
ONE PLATE PER FOIL PLATE PACK
PLATE PACKS ISSUED TO DEALERS
PLATE PRINT RUN 1 SET PER COLOR
BLACK-CYAN-MAGENTA-YELLOW ISSUED
PLATES DO NOT FEATURE AUTOS
NO PLATE PRICING DUE TO SCARCITY
AD Andre Dawson/99 * 10.00 25.00
AK Al Kaline/50 * 30.00 80.00
BL Barry Larkin/50 * 20.00 50.00
BM Bobby Murcer/99 * 20.00 50.00
BR Brooks Robinson/50 * 15.00 40.00
BS Bruce Sutter/50 * 15.00 40.00
BW Billy Williams/50 * 15.00 40.00
DN Don Newcombe/99 * 10.00 25.00
DP Dave Parker/99 * 15.00 40.00
FM Fred McGriff/99 * 15.00 40.00
GF G.Foster Destroyer/50 * 10.00 25.00
JP Jim Palmer/99 * 15.00 40.00
JR Jim Rice/99 * 10.00 25.00
MG Mark Grace/50 * 15.00 40.00
MW Maury Wills/99 * 10.00 25.00
PM Paul Molitor/50 * 15.00 40.00
PN Phil Niekro/50 * 10.00 25.00
RG Ron Guidry/99 * 10.00 25.00
RS Ron Santo/99 * 15.00 40.00
SC Steve Carlton/50 * 15.00 40.00
SG Steve Garvey/50 * 12.00 30.00
SU Don Sutton/50 * 10.00 25.00
TP Tony Perez/99 * 10.00 25.00

2006 Greats of the Game Bat Barrel Auto Greats

OVERALL AUTO ODDS 2:15 H, 2:15 R
PRINT RUNS B/WN 1-5 COPIES PER
NO PRICING DUE TO SCARCITY
ONE PLATE PER FOIL PLATE PACK
PLATE PACKS ISSUED TO DEALERS
PLATE PRINT RUN 1 SET PER COLOR

BLACK-CYAN-MAGENTA-YELLOW ISSUED
PLATES DO NOT FEATURE AUTOS OR GU
NO PLATE PRICING DUE TO SCARCITY

2006 Greats of the Game Cardinals Greats

COMPLETE SET (10) 10.00 25.00
OVERALL INSERTS ONE PER PACK
ONE PLATE PER FOIL PLATE PACK
PLATE PACKS ISSUED TO DEALERS
PLATE PRINT RUN 1 SET PER COLOR
BLACK-CYAN-MAGENTA-YELLOW ISSUED
NO PLATE PRICING DUE TO SCARCITY
BG Bob Gibson 1.25 3.00
DD Dizzy Dean 1.25 3.00
LB Lou Brock 1.25 3.00
OS Ozzie Smith 2.50 6.00
RH Rogers Hornsby 1.25 3.00
RS Red Schoendienst 1.25 3.00
SC Steve Carlton 1.25 3.00
SM Stan Musial 3.00 8.00
TH Tommy Herr .75 2.00
TM Tim McCarver .75 2.00

2006 Greats of the Game Cardinals Greats Memorabilia

OVERALL GAME-USED ODDS 2:15 H, 1:15 R
SP PRINT RUN INFO PROVIDED BY UD
SP's ARE NOT SERIAL-NUMBERED
BG Bob Gibson Pants 4.00 10.00
DD Dizzy Dean Jsy SP/99 * 30.00 60.00
LB Lou Brock Pants 4.00 10.00
OS Ozzie Smith Bat 6.00 15.00
RH Rogers Hornsby Bat 12.50 30.00
RS Red Schoendienst Bat 3.00 8.00
SC Steve Carlton Bat 3.00 8.00
SM Stan Musial Bat 6.00 15.00
TH Tommy Herr Bat 3.00 8.00
TM Tim McCarver Pants 3.00 8.00

2006 Greats of the Game Cardinals Greats Autograph

STATED PRINT RUN 30 SERIAL #'d SETS
*AUTO MEM: .4X TO 1X AUTO
AUTO MEM PRINT RUN 30 SERIAL #'d SETS
OVERALL AUTO ODDS 2:15 H, 2:15 R
BG Bob Gibson 20.00 50.00
LB Lou Brock 10.00 25.00
OS Ozzie Smith 30.00 60.00
RS Red Schoendienst 15.00 40.00
SC Steve Carlton 15.00 40.00
SM Stan Musial 25.00 60.00
TH Tommy Herr 10.00 25.00
TM Tim McCarver 10.00 25.00

2006 Greats of the Game Cubs Greats

COMPLETE SET (10) 10.00 25.00
OVERALL INSERTS ONE PER PACK
ONE PLATE PER FOIL PLATE PACK
PLATE PACKS ISSUED TO DEALERS
PLATE PRINT RUN 1 SET PER COLOR
BLACK-CYAN-MAGENTA-YELLOW ISSUED
NO PLATE PRICING DUE TO SCARCITY
AD Andre Dawson 1.25 3.00
BS Bruce Sutter 1.25 3.00
BW Billy Williams 1.25 3.00
EB Ernie Banks 2.00 5.00
FJ Fergie Jenkins 1.25 3.00
GM Gary Matthews .75 2.00
MG Mark Grace 1.25 3.00
RH Randy Hundley .75 2.00
RS Ron Santo 1.25 3.00
SA Ryne Sandberg 4.00 10.00

2006 Greats of the Game Cubs Greats Memorabilia

OVERALL GAME-USED ODDS 2:15 H, 1:15 R
AD Andre Dawson Bat 3.00 8.00
BS Bruce Sutter Pants 3.00 8.00
BW Billy Williams Jsy 3.00 8.00
EB Ernie Banks Pants 6.00 15.00
FJ Fergie Jenkins Jsy 3.00 8.00
GM Gary Matthews Bat 3.00 8.00
MG Mark Grace Bat 4.00 10.00
RS Ron Santo Bat 8.00 20.00
SA Ryne Sandberg Bat 6.00 15.00

2006 Greats of the Game Cubs Greats Autograph

STATED PRINT RUN 30 SERIAL #'d SETS
*AUTO MEM: .4X TO 1X AUTO
AUTO MEM PRINT RUN 30 SERIAL #'d SETS
OVERALL AUTO ODDS 2:15 H, 2:15 R
AD Andre Dawson 15.00 40.00
BS Bruce Sutter 15.00 40.00
BW Billy Williams 15.00 40.00
EB Ernie Banks 50.00 100.00
FJ Fergie Jenkins 10.00 25.00
GM Gary Matthews 10.00 25.00
MG Mark Grace 20.00 50.00
RS Ron Santo 30.00 60.00
SA Ryne Sandberg 30.00 60.00

2006 Greats of the Game Decade Greats

COMPLETE SET (30) 30.00 60.00
OVERALL INSERTS ONE PER PACK
ONE PLATE PER FOIL PLATE PACK
PLATE PACKS ISSUED TO DEALERS
PLATE PRINT RUN 1 SET PER COLOR
BLACK-CYAN-MAGENTA-YELLOW ISSUED
NO PLATE PRICING DUE TO SCARCITY
BF Bob Feller 1.25 3.00
BI Bill Madlock .75 2.00
BJ Bo Jackson 2.00 5.00
BM Bill Mazeroski 1.25 3.00
BR Brooks Robinson 1.25 3.00
CC Chris Chambliss .75 2.00
CR Cal Ripken 6.00 15.00
DP Dave Parker .75 2.00
EA Earl Averill .75 2.00
EM Eddie Mathews 2.00 5.00
JC Jack Clark .75 2.00
JK John Kruk .75 2.00
JM Johnny Mize 1.25 3.00
KP Kirby Puckett 2.00 5.00
MC Mickey Cochrane 1.25 3.00
MO Mel Ott .75 2.00
MS Mike Schmidt 3.00 8.00
NR Nolan Ryan 6.00 15.00
PM Paul Molitor 2.00 5.00
PT Pie Traynor 1.25 3.00
RC Roberto Clemente 5.00 12.00
RO Rod Carew 1.25 3.00
RY Robin Yount 2.00 5.00
SC Steve Carlton 1.25 3.00
TG Tony Gwynn 2.00 5.00
TR Tim Raines 1.25 3.00
TS Tom Seaver 1.25 3.00
WC Will Clark 1.25 3.00
WM Willie McCovey 1.25 3.00
WS Willie Stargell 1.25 3.00

2006 Greats of the Game Decade Greats Memorabilia

OVERALL GAME-USED ODDS 2:15 H, 1:15 R
SP PRINT RUNS B/WN 50-99 COPIES PER
SP PRINT RUN INFO PROVIDED BY UD
SP's ARE NOT SERIAL-NUMBERED
BF Bob Feller Pants 4.00 10.00
BI Bill Madlock Bat 3.00 8.00
BJ Bo Jackson Bat 6.00 15.00
BM Bill Mazeroski Bat 4.00 10.00
BR Brooks Robinson Bat 4.00 10.00
CC Chris Chambliss Bat 3.00 8.00
CR Cal Ripken Pants 8.00 20.00
DP Dave Parker Pants 3.00 8.00
EA Earl Averill Bat 8.00 20.00
EM Eddie Mathews Pants 6.00 15.00
JC Jack Clark Bat 3.00 8.00
JK John Kruk Bat 3.00 8.00
JM Johnny Mize Pants 4.00 10.00
KP Kirby Puckett Bat 6.00 15.00
MC M.Cochrane Bat SP/50 * 40.00 80.00
MO Mel Ott Bat SP/99 * 20.00 50.00
MS Mike Schmidt Bat 4.00 10.00
NR Nolan Ryan Jsy 6.00 15.00
PM Paul Molitor Bat 3.00 8.00
RC Roberto Clemente Jsy 20.00 50.00
RO Rod Carew Pants 4.00 10.00
RY Robin Yount Bat 4.00 10.00
SC Steve Carlton Bat 3.00 8.00
TG Tony Gwynn Pants 4.00 10.00
TR Tim Raines Jsy 3.00 8.00
TS Tom Seaver Jsy 4.00 10.00
WC Will Clark Jsy 4.00 10.00
WM Willie McCovey Bat 4.00 10.00
WS Willie Stargell Bat 4.00 10.00

2006 Greats of the Game Decade Greats Autograph

STATED PRINT RUN 30 SERIAL #'d SETS
*AUTO MEM: .4X TO 1X AUTO
AUTO MEM PRINT RUN 30 SERIAL #'d SETS
OVERALL AUTO ODDS 2:15 H, 2:15 R
BF Bob Feller 20.00 50.00
BI Bill Madlock 20.00 50.00
BJ Bo Jackson 40.00 80.00
BM Bill Mazeroski 10.00 25.00
BR Brooks Robinson 20.00 50.00
CC Chris Chambliss 15.00 40.00
CR Cal Ripken 50.00 120.00
DP Dave Parker 20.00 50.00
JC Jack Clark 10.00 25.00
JK John Kruk 15.00 40.00
KP Kirby Puckett 50.00 100.00
MS Mike Schmidt 50.00 120.00
NR Nolan Ryan 60.00 120.00
PM Paul Molitor 20.00 50.00
RO Rod Carew 20.00 50.00
RY Robin Yount 30.00 60.00
SC Steve Carlton 15.00 40.00
TG Tony Gwynn 30.00 60.00
TR Tim Raines 10.00 25.00
TS Tom Seaver 30.00 80.00
WC Will Clark 30.00 80.00
WM Willie McCovey 20.00 50.00

2006 Greats of the Game Dodger Greats

COMPLETE SET (10) 10.00 25.00
OVERALL INSERTS ONE PER PACK
ONE PLATE PER FOIL PLATE PACK
PLATE PACKS ISSUED TO DEALERS
PLATE PRINT RUN 1 SET PER COLOR
BLACK-CYAN-MAGENTA-YELLOW ISSUED
NO PLATE PRICING DUE TO SCARCITY
CA Roy Campanella 2.00 5.00
DB Dusty Baker .75 2.00
DD Don Drysdale 1.25 3.00
DS Don Sutton .75 2.00
JR Jackie Robinson 2.00 5.00
MW Maury Wills .75 2.00
PR Pee Wee Reese 1.25 3.00
RC Ron Cey .75 2.00
SG Steve Garvey .75 2.00
SS Steve Sax .75 2.00

2006 Greats of the Game Dodger Greats Memorabilia

OVERALL GAME-USED ODDS 2:15 H, 1:15 R
SP PRINT RUNS B/WN 25-199 COPIES PER
SP PRINT RUN INFO PROVIDED BY UD
SP's ARE NOT SERIAL-NUMBERED
NO PRICING ON QTY OF 30 OR LESS
DB Dusty Baker Jsy 3.00 8.00
DD Don Drysdale Jsy SP/69 * 8.00 20.00
JR Jackie Robinson Bat SP/199 * 20.00 50.00
MW Maury Wills Bat 3.00 8.00
PR Pee Wee Reese Jsy 4.00 10.00
RC Ron Cey Jsy 3.00 8.00
SG Steve Garvey Jsy 3.00 8.00
SS Steve Sax Jsy 3.00 8.00

2006 Greats of the Game Dodger Greats Autograph

STATED PRINT RUN 30 SERIAL #'d SETS
*AUTO MEM: .4X TO 1X AUTO
AUTO MEM PRINT RUN 30 SERIAL #'d SETS
OVERALL AUTO ODDS 2:15 H, 2:15 R
DB Dusty Baker 20.00 50.00
DS Don Sutton 15.00 40.00
MW Maury Wills 10.00 25.00
RC Ron Cey 20.00 50.00
SG Steve Garvey 20.00 50.00
SS Steve Sax 10.00 25.00

2006 Greats of the Game Nickname Greats

OVERALL INSERTS ONE PER PACK
ONE PLATE PER FOIL PLATE PACK
PLATE PACKS ISSUED TO DEALERS
PLATE PRINT RUN 1 SET PER COLOR
BLACK-CYAN-MAGENTA-YELLOW ISSUED
NO PLATE PRICING DUE TO SCARCITY
AG Andres Galarraga 2.00 5.00
AH Al Hrabosky 1.25 3.00
AT Andre Thornton 1.25 3.00
BE Steve Bedrosian 1.25 3.00
BF Bob Feller 2.00 5.00
BH Burt Hooton 1.25 3.00
BL Bill Lee 1.25 3.00
BM Bill Madlock 1.25 3.00
CF Carlton Fisk 2.00 5.00
CH Joe Charboneau 1.25 3.00
DB Don Baylor 1.25 3.00
DD Darren Daulton 1.25 3.00
DE Dwight Evans 1.25 3.00
DF Dan Ford 1.25 3.00
DM Don Mattingly 6.00 15.00
DP Dave Parker 1.25 3.00
DR Dave Righetti 1.25 3.00
EV Ellis Valentine 1.25 3.00
FR Frank Robinson 2.00 5.00
FS Fred Stanley 1.25 3.00
GF George Foster 1.25 3.00
GH Glenn Hubbard 1.25 3.00
GM Garry Maddox 1.25 3.00
GS George Scott 1.25 3.00
HE Tommy Herr 1.25 3.00
HJ Howard Johnson 1.25 3.00
JB Jim Bouton 1.25 3.00
JC Jack Clark 1.25 3.00
JJ Jay Johnstone 1.25 3.00
JM John Montefusco 1.25 3.00
JP Joe Pepitone 1.25 3.00
JS John Shelby 1.25 3.00
JW Jimmy Wynn 1.25 3.00
KH Ken Harrelson 1.25 3.00
LA Luis Aparicio 2.00 5.00
LM Lee Mazzilli 1.25 3.00
LP Lou Piniella 1.25 3.00
MA Gary Matthews 1.25 3.00
MF Mark Fidrych 1.25 3.00
MH Mike Hargrove 1.25 3.00
ML Mike Lavalliere 1.25 3.00
MR Mickey Rivers 1.25 3.00
MW Mitch Williams 1.25 3.00
MZ Dennis Martinez 1.25 3.00
RA Doug Rader 1.25 3.00
RB Rick Burleson 1.25 3.00
RC Ron Cey 1.25 3.00
RG Ron Guidry 1.25 3.00
RR Rick Reuschel 1.25 3.00
RS Rusty Staub 1.25 3.00
SB Steve Balboni 1.25 3.00
SF Sid Fernandez 1.25 3.00
SL Sparky Lyle 1.25 3.00
SM Sam McDowell 1.25 3.00
ST Steve Trout 1.25 3.00
TB Tom Brunansky 1.25 3.00
TH Tom Henke 1.25 3.00
TR Tim Raines 2.00 5.00
WC Will Clark 2.00 5.00
WM Willie McCovey 2.00 5.00

2006 Greats of the Game Nickname Greats Autographs

OVERALL AUTO ODDS 2:15 H, 2:15 R
TIER 1 QTY B/WN 29-50 COPIES PER
TIER 2 QTY 100 COPIES PER
TIER 3 QTY B/WN 175-250 COPIES PER
TIER 4 QTY B/WN 251-400 COPIES PER
TIER 5 QTY B/WN 401-650 COPIES PER
CARDS ARE NOT SERIAL-NUMBERED
PRINT RUN INFO PROVIDED BY UD
AU INSCRIPTIONS INTENDED FOR ALL CARDS
NOT ALL CARDS CARRY AU INSCRIPTIONS
AU INSCRIPTIONS ARE DETAILED BELOW
PARENTHESES PERCENTAGE OF PRINT RUN
NO MCCOVEY PRICING DUE TO SCARCITY
EXCHANGE DEADLINE 04/10/09
AH A.Hrabosky Hungarian T5 6.00 15.00
AT1 Andre Thornton T5 (90) 4.00 10.00
AT2 A.Thornton Thunder T5 (10) 6.00 15.00
BE S.Bedrosian Bedrock T5 8.00 20.00
BF B.Feller Rapid T2/100 * 20.00 50.00
BH B.Hooton Happy T5 4.00 10.00
BL B.Lee Spaceman T5 8.00 20.00
BM Bill Madlock T4 4.00 10.00
CF Carlton Fisk T1/50 * 20.00 50.00
CH J.Charboneau Super Joe T5 6.00 15.00
DD D.Daulton Dutch T5 5.00 12.00
DE Dwight Evans T2/100 * 10.00 25.00
DF D.Ford Disco Dan T5 6.00 15.00
DP D.Parker Cobra T2/100 * 20.00 50.00
DR D.Righetti Rags T5 4.00 10.00
EV E.Valentine Bubba T5 4.00 10.00
FR Frank Robinson T1/50 * 30.00 60.00
FS F.Stanley Chicken T5 6.00 15.00
GF1 George Foster T3 (50) 4.00 10.00
GF2 G.Foster Destroyer T3 (50) 10.00 25.00
GH G.Hubbard Bam Bam T5 6.00 15.00
GM G.Maddox Secretary T5 8.00 20.00
GS G.Scott Boomer T5 6.00 15.00
HE Tommy Herr T5 8.00 20.00
HJ H.Johnson Hojo T3 6.00 15.00
JB J.Bouton Bulldog T3 10.00 25.00
JC Jack Clark T4 6.00 15.00
JJ J.Johnstone Moon T5 6.00 15.00
JM J.Montefusco Count T5 4.00 10.00
JP J.Pepitone Pepi T5 4.00 10.00
JS J.Shelby T-Bone T5 4.00 10.00
JW J.Wynn Toy Cannon T5 6.00 15.00
LM L.Mazzilli Stallion T5 6.00 15.00
LP L.Piniella Sweet T2/100 * 20.00 50.00
MA G.Matthews Sarge T5 4.00 10.00
MF M.Fidrych Bird T4 12.50 30.00
MF M.Hargrove Delay T5 6.00 15.00
ML M.Lavalliere Spanky T5 4.00 10.00
MR M.Rivers Quick T3 8.00 20.00
MW M.Williams Wild Thing T5 4.00 10.00
RA D.Rader Rooster T5 6.00 15.00
RB R.Burleson Rooster T5 6.00 15.00
RG Ron Guidry T3 8.00 20.00
RR R.Reuschel Daddy T5 4.00 10.00
RS Rusty Staub T3 15.00 40.00
SB S.Balboni Bye Bye T5 6.00 15.00
SF S.Fernandez El Sid T5 4.00 10.00
SL S.Lyle Count T4 6.00 15.00
SM S.McDowell Sudden T5 6.00 15.00
ST1 Steve Trout T5 (20) 6.00 15.00
ST2 S.Trout Rainbow T5 (80) 8.00 20.00
TB T.Brunansky Bruno T5 4.00 10.00
TH T.Henke Terminator T5 6.00 15.00
TR Tim Raines T3 6.00 15.00
WC Will Clark T2/100 * 20.00 50.00

2006 Greats of the Game Red Sox Greats

COMPLETE SET (10) 10.00 25.00
OVERALL INSERTS ONE PER PACK
ONE PLATE PER FOIL PLATE PACK
PLATE PACKS ISSUED TO DEALERS
PLATE PRINT RUN 1 SET PER COLOR
BLACK-CYAN-MAGENTA-YELLOW ISSUED
NO PLATE PRICING DUE TO SCARCITY
BD Bobby Doerr .75 2.00
CF Carlton Fisk 1.25 3.00
DE Dwight Evans .75 2.00
FL Fred Lynn .75 2.00
JF Jimmie Foxx 2.00 5.00
JR Jim Rice 1.25 3.00
LT Luis Tiant .75 2.00
RP Rico Petrocelli .75 2.00
TW Ted Williams 4.00 10.00
WB Wade Boggs 1.25 3.00

2006 Greats of the Game Red Sox Greats Memorabilia

OVERALL GAME-USED ODDS 2:15 H, 1:15 R
SP PRINT RUNS B/WN 25-199 COPIES PER
SP PRINT RUN INFO PROVIDED BY UD
SP's ARE NOT SERIAL-NUMBERED
BD Bobby Doerr Bat 3.00 8.00
CF Carlton Fisk Pants 4.00 10.00
DE Dwight Evans Jsy 4.00 10.00
FL Fred Lynn Pants 3.00 8.00
JF Jimmie Foxx Bat SP/99 * 15.00 40.00
JR Jim Rice Bat 3.00 8.00
LT Luis Tiant Jsy 3.00 8.00
RP Rico Petrocelli Pants 3.00 8.00
TW Ted Williams Jsy SP/199 * 12.50 30.00
WB Wade Boggs Pants 4.00 10.00

2006 Greats of the Game Red Sox Greats Autograph

STATED PRINT RUN 30 SERIAL #'d SETS
*AUTO MEM: .4X TO 1X AUTO
AUTO MEM PRINT RUN 30 SERIAL #'d SETS
OVERALL AUTO ODDS 2:15 H, 2:15 R
BD Bobby Doerr 10.00 25.00
CF Carlton Fisk 20.00 50.00
DE Dwight Evans 30.00 60.00
FL Fred Lynn 10.00 25.00
JR Jim Rice 10.00 25.00
LT Luis Tiant 10.00 25.00
RP Rico Petrocelli 10.00 25.00
WB Wade Boggs 15.00 40.00

2006 Greats of the Game Reds Greats

COMPLETE SET (10) 10.00 25.00
OVERALL INSERTS ONE PER PACK
ONE PLATE PER FOIL PLATE PACK
PLATE PACKS ISSUED TO DEALERS
PLATE PRINT RUN 1 SET PER COLOR
BLACK-CYAN-MAGENTA-YELLOW ISSUED
NO PLATE PRICING DUE TO SCARCITY
BL Barry Larkin 1.25 3.00
DC Dave Concepcion .75 2.00
ED Eric Davis .75 2.00
FR Frank Robinson 1.25 3.00
GF George Foster .75 2.00
JB Johnny Bench 2.00 5.00
JM Joe Morgan 1.25 3.00
KG Ken Griffey Sr. .75 2.00
TP Tony Perez 1.25 3.00
TS Tom Seaver 1.25 3.00

2006 Greats of the Game Reds Greats Memorabilia

OVERALL GAME-USED ODDS 2:15 H, 1:15 R
BL Barry Larkin Pants 4.00 10.00
DC Dave Concepcion Bat 3.00 8.00
ED Eric Davis Jsy 3.00 8.00
FR Frank Robinson Bat 4.00 10.00
GF George Foster Bat 3.00 8.00
JB Johnny Bench Bat 6.00 15.00
JM Joe Morgan Bat 3.00 8.00
KG Ken Griffey Sr. Pants 3.00 8.00
TP Tony Perez Bat 3.00 8.00
TS Tom Seaver Bat 4.00 10.00

2006 Greats of the Game Reds Greats Autograph

STATED PRINT RUN 30 SERIAL #'d SETS
*AUTO MEM: .4X TO 1X AUTO
AUTO MEM PRINT RUN 30 SERIAL #'d SETS
OVERALL AUTO ODDS 2:15 H, 2:15 R
BL Barry Larkin 30.00 60.00
DC Dave Concepcion 15.00 40.00
ED Eric Davis 20.00 50.00
FR Frank Robinson 30.00 60.00
GF G.Foster Destroyer 10.00 25.00
JB Johnny Bench 30.00 60.00
JM Joe Morgan 15.00 40.00
KG Ken Griffey Sr. 15.00 40.00
TP Tony Perez 15.00 40.00
TS Tom Seaver 30.00 80.00

2006 Greats of the Game Tigers Greats

COMPLETE SET (10) 10.00 25.00
OVERALL INSERTS ONE PER PACK
ONE PLATE PER FOIL PLATE PACK
PLATE PACKS ISSUED TO DEALERS
PLATE PRINT RUN 1 SET PER COLOR
BLACK-CYAN-MAGENTA-YELLOW ISSUED
NO PLATE PRICING DUE TO SCARCITY
AK Al Kaline 2.00 5.00
AT Alan Trammell 1.25 3.00
BF Bill Freehan .75 2.00
DM Denny McLain .75 2.00
GK George Kell 1.25 3.00
JM Jack Morris 1.25 3.00
KG Kirk Gibson .75 2.00
MF Mark Fidrych .75 2.00
TC Ty Cobb 3.00 8.00
WH Willie Horton .75 2.00

2006 Greats of the Game Tigers Greats Memorabilia

OVERALL GAME-USED ODDS 2:15 H, 1:15 R
SP PRINT RUNS 99 COPIES PER
SP PRINT RUN INFO PROVIDED BY UD
SP's ARE NOT SERIAL NUMBERED
AK Al Kaline Bat 4.00 10.00
AT Alan Trammell Bat 3.00 8.00
BF Bill Freehan Bat 3.00 8.00
GK George Kell Bat 4.00 10.00
JM Jack Morris Jsy 3.00 8.00
KG Kirk Gibson Jsy 4.00 10.00
MF Mark Fidrych Jsy 3.00 8.00
TC Ty Cobb Bat SP/99 * 30.00 60.00
WH Willie Horton Bat SP/99 * 4.00 10.00

2006 Greats of the Game Tigers Greats Autograph

STATED PRINT RUN 30 SERIAL #'d SETS
*AUTO MEM: .4X TO 1X AUTO
AUTO MEM PRINT RUN 30 SERIAL #'d SETS
OVERALL AUTO ODDS 2:15 H, 2:15 R
AK Al Kaline 30.00 80.00
AT Alan Trammell 15.00 40.00
BF Bill Freehan 15.00 40.00
DM Denny McLain 10.00 25.00
GK George Kell 30.00 80.00
JM Jack Morris 10.00 25.00
KG Kirk Gibson 20.00 50.00
MF Mark Fidrych 20.00 50.00
WH Willie Horton 10.00 25.00

2006 Greats of the Game Yankee Clippings

COMPLETE SET (10) 12.50 30.00
OVERALL INSERTS ONE PER PACK
ONE PLATE PER FOIL PLATE PACK
PLATE PACKS ISSUED TO DEALERS
PLATE PRINT RUN 1 SET PER COLOR
BLACK-CYAN-MAGENTA-YELLOW ISSUED
NO PLATE PRICING DUE TO SCARCITY
BM Bobby Murcer .75 2.00
BR Babe Ruth 5.00 12.00
DM Don Mattingly 4.00 10.00
GN Graig Nettles .75 2.00
JD Joe DiMaggio 4.00 10.00
RG Ron Guidry .75 2.00
RJ Reggie Jackson 1.25 3.00
TM Thurman Munson 2.00 5.00
WF Whitey Ford 1.25 3.00
YB Yogi Berra 2.00 5.00

2006 Greats of the Game Yankee Clippings Memorabilia

OVERALL GAME-USED ODDS 2:15 H, 1:15 R
SP PRINT RUNS B/WN 25-199 COPIES PER
SP PRINT RUN INFO PROVIDED BY UD
SP's ARE NOT SERIAL-NUMBERED
NO SP PRICING ON QTY OF 30 OR LESS
BM Bobby Murcer Bat 4.00 10.00
DM Don Mattingly Bat 6.00 15.00
GN Graig Nettles Bat 3.00 8.00
JD Joe DiMaggio Pants SP/99 * 20.00 50.00
RG Ron Guidry Jsy 4.00 10.00
RJ Reggie Jackson Jsy 4.00 10.00
TM Thurman Munson Pants 8.00 20.00
WF Whitey Ford Pants 6.00 15.00
YB Yogi Berra Bat SP/199 * 8.00 20.00

2006 Greats of the Game Yankee Clippings Autograph

STATED PRINT RUN 30 SERIAL #'d SETS
*AUTO MEM: .4X TO 1X AUTO
AUTO MEM PRINT RUN 30 SERIAL #'d SETS
OVERALL AUTO ODDS 2:15 H, 2:15 R
BM Bobby Murcer 25.00 60.00
DM Don Mattingly 50.00 100.00
GN Graig Nettles 15.00 40.00
RG Ron Guidry 30.00 60.00
RJ Reggie Jackson 30.00 60.00
WF Whitey Ford 40.00 80.00
YB Yogi Berra 40.00 100.00

1988 Grenada Baseball Stamps

These stamps, featuring active major league stars as well as great retired players were issued by the Island of Grenada. Grenada, had previously gained recognition earlier in the decade as an island which had been invaded by U.S. forces. The stamps have both a posed and action shot along with the value of the stamp on the front. As the stamps are meant to be used postally, the backs are blank except for gum which can be attached to envelopes.

COMPLETE SET (81) 10.00 25.00
1 Johnny Bench .20 .50
2 Dave Stieb .01 .05
3 Reggie Jackson .20 .50
4 Harold Baines .02 .10
5 Wade Boggs .08 .25
6 Pete O'Brien .01 .05
7 Stan Musial .40 1.00
8 Wally Joyner .02 .10
9 Grover C. Alexander .08 .25
10 Jose Cruz .02 .10
11 AL Logo .01 .05
12 Al Kaline .08 .25
13 Chuck Klein .02 .10
14 Don Mattingly .40 1.00
15 Mike Witt .01 .05
16 Mark Langston .01 .05
17 Hubie Brooks .01 .05
18 Harmon Killebrew .15 .40
19 Jackie Robinson .75 2.00
20 Dwight Gooden .02 .10
21 Brooks Robinson .15 .40
22 Nolan Ryan .75 2.00
23 Mike Schmidt .25 .60
24 Gary Gaetti .02 .10
25 Nellie Fox .05 .15
26 Tony Gwynn .30 1.00
27 Dizzy Dean .15 .40
28 Luis Aparicio .08 .25
29 Paul Molitor .15 .40
30 Lou Gehrig .75 2.00
31 Jeffrey Leonard .01 .05
32 Eric Davis .02 .10
33 Pete Incaviglia .01 .05
34 Steve Rogers .01 .05
35 Ozzie Smith .15 .40
36 Randy Jones .01 .05
37 Gary Carter .15 .40
38 Hank Aaron .60 1.50
39 Gaylord Perry .08 .25
40 Ty Cobb .60 1.50
41 Andre Dawson .05 .15
42 Charlie Hough .02 .10
43 Kirby Puckett .20 .50
44 Robin Yount .08 .25
45 Don Drysdale .15 .40
46 Mickey Mantle .75 2.00
47 Roger Clemens .30 1.00
48 Rod Carew .15 .40
49 Ryne Sandberg .30 .75
50 Mike Scott .01 .05
51 Tim Raines .02 .10
52 Willie Mays .40 1.00
53 Bret Saberhagen .01 .05
54 Honus Wagner .30 .75
55 George Brett .30 .75
56 Joe Carter .02 .10
57 Frank Robinson .15 .40
58 Mel Ott .15 .40
59 Benito Santiago .02 .10
60 Teddy Higuera .01 .05
61 Lloyd Moseby .01 .05
62 Bobby Bonilla .02 .10
63 Warren Spahn .15 .40
64 Ernie Banks .20 .50
65 NL Logo .01 .05
66 Julio Franco .02 .10
67 Jack Morris .02 .10
68 Fernando Valenzuela .02 .10
69 Lefty Grove .15 .40
70 Ted Williams .75 2.00
71 Darryl Strawberry .02 .10
72 Dale Murphy .05 .15
73 Roberto Clemente .75 2.00
74 Cal Ripken Jr. .75 2.00
75 Bob Feller .15 .40
76 George Bell .01 .05
77 Mark McGwire .40 1.00
78 Alvin Davis .01 .05
79 Pete Rose .30 .75
80 Dan Quisenberry .01 .05
81 Babe Ruth .75 2.00

1974 Greyhound Heroes of Base Paths

Beginning in 1965, the Greyhound Award for Stolen Bases was given to the champions in each league and the second-place finishers. The 1974 Heroes of the Base Paths pamphlet unfolds to reveal five 4" by 9" panels. The first panel is the title page and features on the back a picture of Joe Black holding the trophy. The second and third panels have on the fronts the history of the award and major league statistics pertaining to stolen bases, while the backs have an essay on the art of base stealing. Finally, the fourth and fifth panels display six player cards; after perforation, the cards measure 4" by 3". Cards 1-4 feature the AL and NL winners and the runner-ups for each league, in that order. The player cards display a black and white head shot of the player on the left half, with player information and number of stolen bases on the right half. The backs have statistics. Both sides of the cards are framed by thin brown border stripes. Cards 5-6 display black and white player photos of past winners in the AL and NL, respectively. The cards are unnumbered.

COMPLETE SET (6) 5.00 12.00
1 Bill North .50 1.25
2 Lou Brock 1.50 4.00
3 Rod Carew 1.50 4.00
4 Davey Lopes .60 1.50
5 American League .50 1.25
Dagoberto Campaneris
Tommy Harpe
6 National League .60 1.50
Lou Brock
Maury Wills
Bobby Tol

1975 Greyhound Heroes of Base Paths

The Greyhound Award for Stolen Bases was given to the champions in each league and the second-place finishers. The 1975 Heroes of the Base Paths pamphlet unfolds to reveal five 4" by 9" panels. The first panel is the title page and features on the back a picture of Maury Wills holding the trophy. The second and third panels have on the fronts the history of the award and major league statistics pertaining to stolen bases, while backs have an essay on the art of base stealing. The fourth and fifth panels display six player cards; after perforation, cards measure approximately 4" by 3". Cards 1-4 feature the AL and NL winners and the runner-ups for each league, in that order. The player cards display a black and white head shot of the player on the left half, with player information and number of stolen bases on the right half. The backs have statistics. Both sides of the cards are framed by thin powder blue border stripes. Cards 5-6 display black and white player photos of Billy North and Davey Lopes. The cards are unnumbered.

COMPLETE SET (6) 4.00 10.00
1 Mickey Rivers .20 .50
2 Davey Lopes .30 .75
3 Claudell Washington .20 .50
4 Joe Morgan 1.00 2.50
5 Billy North .20 .50
6 Davey Lopes .30 .75

1976 Greyhound Heroes of Base Paths

The Greyhound Award for Stolen Bases was given to the champions in each league and the second-place finishers. The 1976 Heroes of the Base Paths pamphlet unfolds to reveal five 4" by 9" panels. The first panel is the title page and features on the back a picture of Maury Wills holding the trophy. The second and third panels have on the fronts the history of the award and major league statistics pertaining to stolen bases& while the backs have an essay on the art of base stealing. The fourth and fifth panels display six player cards; after perforation, cards measure approximately 4" by 3". Cards 1-4 feature the AL and NL winners and the runner-ups for each league, in that order. The player cards display a black and white head shot of the player on the left half, with player information and number of stolen bases on the right half. The backs have statistics. Both sides of the cards are framed by thin powder reddish-brown stripes. Cards 5-6 display black and white player photos of Billy North and Davey Lopes. The cards are unnumbered.

COMPLETE SET (6) 1.50 4.00
1 Bill North .20 .50
2 Davey Lopes .30 .75
3 Ron LeFlore .20 .50
4 Joe Morgan .75 2.00
5 Billy North .20 .50
6 Davey Lopes .30 .75

1992 Griffey Arena Kid Comic Holograms

Released in September 1992, this five-card hologram standard-size set was produced by Arena Holograms. The production run was reported to be 1,700 individually numbered cases and premium gold edition cards were randomly inserted throughout. The gold versions are valued at five times the values listed below. Each foil pack contained one card in a card protector and each protector had a different color border (1-clear, 2-black, 3-red, 4-white and 5-blue).

COMMON PLAYER (1-5) 2.00 5.00
COMMON PLAYER (1-5) .40 1.00

1991 Griffey Card Guard Promo

These standard-size cards were used as advertisements for Card Guard. The front has a color photo of Ken Griffey Jr. dressed in a tuxedo and holding a baseball card protected by Card Guard. His autograph is inscribed across the picture in gold ink. The back has an advertisement for Card Guard, highlighting its special features. There are two different angles used for Griffey's photo and we have notated each of those in our checklist

COMPLETE SET .75 2.00
COMMON PLAYER .40 1.00

1994 Griffey Dairy Queen

The 1994 Dairy Queen Ken Griffey Jr. set consists of ten standard-size cards. The cards were distributed in five-card packs at the restaurants, with the gold cards randomly inserted. The fronts feature color action shots of Griffey with the set title's logo appearing in the upper left corner of the picture. Ken Griffey's name is printed below the photo in gold block lettering beside the Dairy Queen logo. The photo is bordered in gold on some sets, and in green on others. The production run on the green-border sets was 90,000, while that of the gold-bordered sets was 10,000. The gold versions are valued at double the values listed below. Except for card number 2, the backs are in a horizontal format, with a posed or action photo on the left side. According to the information on the back, Ken Griffey Jr. personally authorized the set.

COMPLETE SET (10) 4.00 10.00
COMMON CARD (1-10) .50 1.25

1996 Griffey Nike

This one-card set was issued in conjunction with Nike's presendential ad campaign for Ken Griffey. The front features a black-and-white image over a white background with red printing and a top and bottom blue border containing white stars and the Nike symbol. The back displays player information.

1 Ken Griffey 1.00 2.50

1994 Griffey Nintendo

This standard-size card was inserted in packages of Nintendo's video game, Ken Griffey Jr. Presents: Major League Baseball. The front features a borderless color photo of Griffey at bat. His name, team name, and position appear in white lettering within purple and blue bars near the top. His facsimile autograph in silver ink appears vertically on the left. The horizontal back features on the left side a rear view of Griffey at bat, and on the right, his 1993 season highlights. His biography and 1993 statistics are shown within a yellow stripe across the bottom. The single card is unnumbered.

1 Ken Griffey Jr. 1.50 4.00

1996 Griffey Nintendo

This standard-size card was inserted in packages of Nintendo's video game, Ken Griffey Jr. Presents: Major League Baseball. The cardback features Griffey's 1995 season stats and highlights. The single card is unnumbered.

1 Ken Griffey Jr. 2.00 5.00

1977 Burleigh Grimes Daniels

This 16-card set features black-and-white photos with blue borders of different aspects in the life of Hall of Famer and last legal spitball pitcher Burleigh Grimes. Card number 12 comes with or without an autograph. Sets were available from the producer upon release for $3.49 or in uncut sheet form for $6.49.

COMPLETE SET (16) 15.00 40.00
1 Burleigh Grimes .75 2.00
Dodger Manager 1937-38
2 Burleigh Grimes .75 2.00
Lord Burleigh
3 Burleigh Grimes .75 2.00
Clarence Mitchell
Last Spitballe
4 Burleigh Grimes .75 2.00
Rogers Hornsby
John McGraw
Edd
5 Burleigh Grimes .75 2.00
Zack Wheat
Winning Combination
6 Burleigh Grimes .75 2.00
World Champion
7 Burleigh Grimes .75 2.00
Old Stubblebeard
8 Burleigh Grimes .75 2.00
Joe McCarthy MG
9 Burleigh Grimes .75 2.00
Dazzy Vance
Van Mungo
Watson Cl
10 Burleigh Grimes .75 2.00
Babe Ruth
11 Burleigh Grimes .75 2.00
Babe Ruth
Leo Durocher
Dodger S
12 Burleigh Grimes .75 2.00
Chief Bender
12A Burleigh Grimes AU 8.00 20.00
Chief Bender
13 Burleigh Grimes .75 2.00
Robin Roberts
Number 270
14 Burleigh Grimes .75 2.00
The Origin
15 Burleigh Grimes .75 2.00

Red Faber
Luke Appling
Heinie M
16 Burleigh Grimes .75 2.00
Lord Burleigh 1977

1982 GS Gallery All-Time Greats

This 24-card set measure 2 1/2" by 3". Issued by long time dealer G.S. Gallery, these cards have full color pictures or drawings on the front. The backs have vital statistics and lifetime totals.

COMPLETE SET (24) 6.00 15.00
1 Stan Musial .75 2.00
2 Alvin Dark .08 .25
3 Harry Walker .08 .25
4 Dom DiMaggio .20 .50
5 Carl Furillo .20 .50
6 Joe DiMaggio 1.25 3.00
7 Joe Adcock .08 .25
8 Lou Boudreau .30 .75
9 Ted Williams 1.25 3.00
10 Phil Rizzuto .40 1.00
11 Pee Wee Reese .40 1.00
12 James Dykes .08 .25
13 Nellie Fox .30 .75
14 George Kell .30 .75
15 Ralph Kiner .30 .75
16 Roger Maris .40 1.00
17 Ted Kluszewski .20 .50
18 Wally Moon .08 .25
19 Hank Sauer .08 .25
20 Bob Thomson .20 .50
21 Mel Parnell .08 .25
22 Ewell Blackwell .08 .25
23 Richie Ashburn .40 1.00
24 Jackie Robinson 1.00 2.50

1973 Hall of Fame Picture Pack

This 20-card set issued in a special envelope measures approximately 5" by 6 3/4" and features black-and-white photos of players who are in the Baseball Hall of Fame in Cooperstown, New York. Player information and statistics are printed on the front in the bottom margin. The backs are blank. The cards are unnumbered and checklisted below in alphabetical order. These sets were also issued in a 4 7/8" by 7 1/2" format and an easy way to tell the difference is that the "shorter" photos have career statistical information while the "longer" photos have just career batting average (for players) and length of major league service.

COMPLETE SET (20) 15.00 40.00
1 Yogi Berra 1.00 2.50
2 Roy Campanella 1.00 2.50
3 Ty Cobb 1.25 3.00
4 Joe Cronin .40 1.00
5 Dizzy Dean .75 2.00
6 Joe DiMaggio 1.50 4.00
7 Bob Feller .40 1.00
8 Lou Gehrig 1.50 4.00
9 Rogers Hornsby .60 1.50
10 Sandy Koufax 1.00 2.50
11 Christy Mathewson .60 1.50
12 Stan Musial 1.00 2.50
13 Satchel Paige .60 1.50
14 Jackie Robinson 1.25 3.00
15 Babe Ruth 2.00 5.00
16 Warren Spahn .40 1.00
17 Casey Stengel .40 1.00
18 Honus Wagner .75 2.00
19 Ted Williams 1.25 3.00
20 Cy Young .60 1.50

1981-89 Hall of Fame Plaque Metal

These standard-size blank-backed cards, made of metal, duplicates the Hall of Fame plaques of these baseball immortals. These cards were issued in a continuing series from 1981 through 1989. Each series, until the final series, had an initial cost of $19 for the series. We are sequencing this set in the order that the HOF used for each series.

COMPLETE SET (204) 600.00 1200.00
1 Cool Papa Bell 5.00 12.00
2 Ty Cobb 15.00 40.00
3 Eddie Collins 10.00 25.00
4 Kenesaw Landis 4.00 10.00
5 Christy Mathewson 10.00 25.00
6 Willie Mays 12.50 30.00
7 Babe Ruth 20.00 50.00
8 Casey Stengel 8.00 20.00
9 Ted Williams 15.00 40.00
10 Jocko Conlan 4.00 10.00
11 Morgan Bulkeley 4.00 10.00
12 Cy Young 10.00 25.00
13 Satchel Paige 12.50 30.00
14 Mordecai Brown 8.00 20.00
15 Joe Cronin 6.00 15.00
16 Bob Feller 8.00 20.00
17 Jackie Robinson 15.00 40.00
18 Duke Snider 10.00 25.00
19 Connie Mack 8.00 20.00
20 Alexander Cartwright 4.00 10.00
21 Cap Anson 8.00 20.00
22 Josh Gibson 12.50 30.00
23 Stan Musial 12.50 30.00
24 Addie Joss 4.00 10.00
25 Paul Waner 5.00 12.00
26 Judy Johnson 6.00 15.00
27 Carl Hubbell 8.00 20.00
28 Bill Klem 4.00 10.00
29 Ford Frick 4.00 10.00
30 Ed Delahanty 5.00 12.00
31 John Henry Lloyd 8.00 20.00
32 Rogers Hornsby 12.50 30.00
33 Bill Terry 6.00 15.00
34 Lefty Gomez 5.00 12.00
35 Mel Ott 8.00 20.00
36 Roy Campanella 8.00 20.00
37 Al Lopez 4.00 10.00
38 Branch Rickey 4.00 10.00
39 Buck Ewing 4.00 10.00
40 Buck Leonard 6.00 15.00
41 Lefty Grove 10.00 25.00
42 Heinie Manush 5.00 12.00
43 Lloyd Waner 4.00 10.00
44 Bill Dickey 6.00 15.00
45 Al Kaline 8.00 20.00
46 Ban Johnson 4.00 10.00
47 King Kelly 5.00 12.00
48 Frank Chance 8.00 20.00
49 George Sisler 6.00 15.00
50 Rabbit Maranville 4.00 10.00
51 Jim Bottomley 4.00 10.00
52 Frankie Frisch 5.00 12.00
53 Monte Irvin 5.00 12.00
54 Hank Greenberg 8.00 20.00
55 Miller Huggins 4.00 10.00
56 Tom Connolly 4.00 10.00
57 Joe Tinker 8.00 20.00
58 George Kelly 4.00 10.00
59 Zack Wheat 5.00 12.00
60 Jimmie Foxx 12.50 30.00
61 Fred Lindstrom 4.00 10.00
62 Oscar Charleston 5.00 12.00
63 Yogi Berra 10.00 25.00
64 Ed Barrow 4.00 10.00
65 Candy Cummings 4.00 10.00
66 Johnny Evers 8.00 20.00
67 Dave Bancroft 4.00 10.00
68 Max Carey 5.00 12.00
69 Lou Gehrig 15.00 40.00
70 Pie Traynor 8.00 20.00
71 Martin Dihigo 6.00 15.00
72 Sandy Koufax 12.50 30.00
73 George Wright 4.00 10.00
74 Bill McKechnie 4.00 10.00
75 Dan Brouthers 5.00 12.00
76 Nap Lajoie 10.00 25.00
77 Hugh Duffy 5.00 12.00
78 Edd Roush 5.00 12.00
79 Roger Bresnahan 4.00 10.00
80 Billy Herman 4.00 10.00
81 Ernie Banks 10.00 25.00
82 Will Harridge 4.00 10.00
83 Roger Connor 4.00 10.00
84 Honus Wagner 12.50 30.00
85 Elmer Flick
86 Tris Speaker
87 Joe Sewell
88 Luke Appling
89 Hack Wilson
90 Roberto Clemente
91 Tom Yawkey
92 Wilbert Robinson
93 John Montgomery Ward
94 Bobby Wallace
95 Willie Keeler
96 Harry Hooper
97 Chick Hafey
98 Lou Boudreau
99 Robin Roberts
100 Henry Chadwick
101 Jim O'Rourke
102 Jake Beckley
103 Ed Walsh
104 Eddie Plank
105 Goose Goslin
106 Ross Youngs
107 Red Ruffing
108 Ralph Kiner
109 John McGraw
110 Cal Hubbard
111 Billy Hamilton
112 Jimmy Collins
113 Stan Coveleski
114 Walter Johnson
115 Jesse Haines
116 Chief Bender
117 Bob Lemon
118 Al Simmons
119 Jesse Burkett
120 Pud Galvin
121 Warren Spahn
122 Jack Chesbro
123 Ray Schalk
124 Charles Comiskey
125 Johnny Mize
126 Albert Spalding
127 Burleigh Grimes
128 Gabby Hartnett
129 Bucky Harris
130 John Clarkson
131 Clark Griffith
132 Early Wynn
133 Joe McGinnity
134 Bob Gibson
135 Grover C. Alexander
136 Larry MacPhail
137 Rube Marquard
138 Red Faber
139 Chuck Klein
140 Rube Foster
141 Earl Combs
142 Tim Keefe
143 Rube Waddell
144 Whitey Ford
145 Herb Pennock
146 Fred Clarke
147 Earl Averill
148 Dizzy Dean
149 Harry Wright
150 Old Hoss Radbourne
151 Sam Crawford
152 Warren Giles
153 Eddie Mathews
154 Amos Rusie
155 Billy Evans
156 Joe Kelley
157 Sam Thompson
158 Eppa Rixey
159 Joe McCarthy
160 Kiki Cuyler
161 Joe Medwick
162 Mickey Mantle
163 Mickey Welch
164 Home Run Baker
165 Dazzy Vance
166 Charlie Gehringer
167 Mickey Cochrane
168 Happy Chandler
169 Travis Jackson
170 Ted Lyons
171 Joe DiMaggio
172 Hank Aaron
173 Harry Heilmann
174 Waite Hoyt
175 Hugh Jennings
176 Tommy McCarthy
177 Kid Nichols
178 Sam Rice
179 Frank Robinson
180 George Weiss
181 Walt Alston
182 George Kell
183 Juan Marichal
184 Brooks Robinson
185 Luis Aparicio
186 Don Drysdale
187 Rick Ferrell
188 Harmon Killebrew
189 Pee Wee Reese
190 Lou Brock
191 Enos Slaughter
192 Arky Vaughan
193 Hoyt Wilhelm
194 Bobby Doerr
195 Ernie Lombardi
196 Willie McCovey
197 Ray Dandridge
198 Catfish Hunter
199 Billy Williams
200 Willie Stargell
201 Al Barlick
202 Johnny Bench
203 Red Schoendienst
204 Carl Yastrzemski

1978 Hall of Fame Plaque Postcards Dexter

This 54-card set was produced by Dexter Press and measures approximately 3 1/2" by 5 1/2". The fronts feature a facsimile Cooperstown National Baseball Hall of Fame player's plaque. The backs display a postcard format. The cards are unnumbered and checklisted below in alphabetical order.

COMPLETE SET (53) 40.00 80.00
1 Grover Alexander .60 1.50
2 Lou Boudreau .20 .50
3 Roy Campanella .40 1.00
5 Roberto Clemente 2.00 5.00
6 Ty Cobb 3.00 8.00
7 Stan Coveleskie .20 .50
8 Sam Crawford .20 .50
9 Martin Dihigo .20 .50
10 Joe DiMaggio 3.00 8.00
11 Billy Evans .20 .50
12 Johnny Evers .20 .50
13 Red Faber .20 .50
14 Elmer Flick .20 .50
15 Ford Frick .20 .50
16 Frankie Frisch .20 .50
17 Pud Galvin .20 .50
18 Lou Gehrig 3.00 8.00
19 Warren Giles .20 .50
20 Will Harridge .20 .50
21 Harry Heilmann .20 .50
22 Harry Hooper .20 .50
23 Waite Hoyt .20 .50
24 Miller Huggins .20 .50
25 Judy Johnson .20 .50
26 Addie Joss .20 .50
27 Tim Keefe .20 .50
28 Willie Keeler .20 .50
29 George Kelly .20 .50
30 Sandy Koufax 1.25 3.00
31 Nap Lajoie .20 .50
32 Pop Lloyd .20 .50
33 Connie Mack .75 2.00
34 Larry MacPhail .20 .50
35 Mickey Mantle 3.00 8.00
36 Heinie Manush .20 .50
37 Eddie Mathews .75 2.00
38 Willie Mays 2.00 5.00
39 Ducky Medwick .20 .50
40 Stan Musial 1.25 3.00
41 Herb Pennock .20 .50
42 Edd Roush .20 .50
43 Amos Rusie .20 .50
44 Babe Ruth 4.00 10.00
45 Ray Schalk .20 .50
46 Al Simmons .20 .50
47 Albert Spalding .20 .50
48 Joe Tinker .40 1.00
49 Harold Traynor .20 .50
50A Dazzy Vance .20 .50
67557-D code on back
51 Lloyd Waner .20 .50
52 Ted Williams 3.00 8.00
53 Hack Wilson .20 .50
54 Ross Youngs .20 .50

1996-03 Hallmark Ornament Cards

These cards were issued as a bonus for purchasing an Hallmark Ornament. These cards all have the Hallmark logo in the upper right. The back has a brief biography of the featured player.

1 Hank Aaron 1996 2.50 6.00
2 Nolan Ryan 1996 4.00 10.00
3 Cal Ripken Jr. 1997 4.00 10.00
4 Mark McGwire 2000 2.50 6.00
5 Sammy Sosa 2001 2.00 5.00
6 Jason Giambi 2003 1.00 2.50

1978 Halsey Hall Recalls

This 21-card set measures 2 1/2" by 3 3/4". The players featured were all local Minneapolis-St. Paul heroes whose exploits were remembered by local legend Halsey Hall. These sets were available upon issue from the producer for $3.50. The set was produced by Olde Cards Inc.

COMPLETE SET (21) 15.00 40.00
1 Halsey Hall .60 1.50
2 Ray Dandridge 1.25 3.00
3 Bruno Haas .30 .75
4 Fabian Gaffke .30 .75
5 George Stumpf .30 .75
6 Roy Campanella 3.00 8.00
7 Babe Barna .30 .75
8 Tom Sheehan .30 .75
9 Ray Moore .30 .75
10 Ted Williams 8.00 20.00
11 Harley Davidson .30 .75
12 Jack Cassini .30 .75
13 Pea Ridge Day .30 .75
14 Oscar Roettger .30 .75
15 Buzz Arlett .30 .75
16 Joe Hauser .30 .75
17 Rube Benton .30 .75
18 Dave Barnhill .30 .75
19 Hoyt Wilhelm 1.25 3.00
20 Willie Mays 4.00 10.00
21 Nicollet Park CL .30 .75
26 Ray Moore .30 .75

1998 Hamburger Helper

This eight-card standard-size set features color action player photos that appeared on cards which could be cut off the back of the boxes of different variations of Betty Crocker's Hamburger Helper. The backs carry player information and career statistics. There is a premium for a complete box.

COMPLETE SET (8) 8.00 20.00
1 Mark McGwire 1.50 4.00
2 Rafael Palmeiro .75 2.00
3 Tino Martinez .40 1.00
4 Barry Bonds 1.50 4.00
5 Larry Walker .40 1.00
6 Juan Gonzalez .40 1.00
7 Mike Piazza 2.00 5.00
8 Frank Thomas 1.00 2.50

1912 Hassan Triple Folders T202

The cards in this 132-card set measure approximately 2 1/4" by 5 1/4". The 1912 T202 Hassan Triple Folder issue is perhaps the most ingenious baseball card ever issued. The two end cards of each panel are full color, T205-like individual cards whereas the black and white center panel pictures an action photo or portrait. The end cards can be folded across the center panel and stored in this manner. Seventy-six different center panels are known to exist; however, many of the center panels contain more than one combination of end cards. The center panel titles are listed below in alphabetical order while the different combinations of end cards are listed below each center panel as they appear left to right on the front of the card. A total of 132 different card fronts exist. The set price below includes all panel and player combinations listed in the checklist. Back color variations (red or black) also exist. The Birmingham's Home Run card is difficult to obtain as are other cards whose center panel exists with but one combination of end cards. The Devlin with Mathewson end panels on numbers 29A and 74C picture Devlin as a Giant. Devlin is pictured as a Rustler on 29B and 74D. Listed pricing references cards in raw "EX" condition.

COMPLETE SET (132) 20000.00 35000.00
1 A Close (Wallace/LaPorte) 150.00 250.00
2 A Close (Wallace/Pelty) 150.00 250.00
3 A Desperate (O'Leary/Cobb) 900.00 1500.00
4 A Great (Barger/Bergen) 125.00 200.00
5 A Great (Rucker/Bergen) 125.00 200.00
6 A Wide (Mullin/Stanage) 125.00 200.00
7 Ambrose (Blair/Quinn) 125.00 200.00
8 Baker Gets (Collins/Baker) 250.00 400.00
9 Birmingham Gets (Johnson/Street) 350.00 600.00
10 Birmingham's HR (Birmingham/Turner) 150.00 250.00
11 Bush Just (Moran/Magee) 125.00 200.00
12 Carrigan (Gaspar/McLean) 125.00 200.00
13 Carrigan (Wagner/Carrigan) 125.00 200.00
14 Catching (Oakes/Bresnahan) 150.00 250.00
15 Caught (Bresnahan/Harmon) 150.00 250.00
16 Chance (Chance/Foxen) 150.00 250.00
17 Chance (McIntire/Archer) 125.00 200.00
18 Chance (Overall/Archer) 125.00 200.00
19 Chance (Rowan/Archer) 125.00 200.00
20 Chance (Shean/Chance) 150.00 250.00
21 Chase Dives (Chase/Wolter) 125.00 200.00
22 Chase Dives (Gibson/Clarke) 150.00 250.00
23 Chase Dives (Phillippe/Gibson) 125.00 200.00
24 Chase Gets (Egan/Mitchell) 125.00 200.00
25 Chase Gets (Wolter/Chase) 125.00 200.00
26 Chase Guard (Chase/Wolter) 125.00 200.00
27 Chase Guard (Gibson/Clarke) 125.00 200.00
28 Chase Guard (Leifield/Gibson) 125.00 200.00
29 Chase Ready (Paskert/Magee) 125.00 200.00
30 Chase Safe (Barry/Baker) 300.00 500.00
31 Chief (Bender/Thomas) 150.00 250.00
32 Clarke Hikes (Bridwell/Kling) 125.00 200.00
33 Close First (Ball/Stovall) 125.00 200.00
34 Close Plate (Payne/White) 125.00 200.00
35 Close Plate (Walsh/Payne) 150.00 250.00
36 Close Third (Carrigan/Wagner) 125.00 200.00
37 Close Third (Wood/Speaker) 300.00 500.00
38 Collins (Byrne/Clarke) 150.00 250.00
39 Collins (Collins/Baker) 250.00 400.00
40 Collins (Collins/Murphy) 150.00 250.00
41 Crawford (Stanage/Summers) 125.00 200.00
42 Cree Rolls (Daubert/Hummel) 125.00 200.00
43 Davy Jones (Delahanty/Jones) 125.00 200.00
44 Devlin (Devlin G/Mathewson) 500.00 800.00
45 Devlin (Devlin R/Mathewson) 500.00 800.00
46 Devlin (Fletcher/Mathewson) 350.00 600.00
47 Devlin (Meyers/Mathewson) 300.00 500.00
48 Donlin (Camnitz/Gibson) 125.00 200.00
49 Donlin (Dooin/Magee) 125.00 200.00
50 Donlin (Doyle/Merkle) 125.00 200.00
51 Donlin (Gibson/Phillippe) 125.00 200.00
52 Donlin (Leach/Wilson) 125.00 200.00
53 Dooin (Dooin/Doolan) 125.00 200.00
54 Dooin (Dooin/Lobert) 125.00 200.00
55 Dooin (Dooin/Titus) 125.00 200.00
56 Easy (Doyle/Merkle) 125.00 200.00
57 Elberfeld Beats (Elberfeld/Milan) 125.00 200.00
58 Elberfeld Gets (Elberfeld/Milan) 125.00 200.00
59 Engle (Speaker/Engle) 175.00 300.00
60 Evers (Archer/Evers) 150.00 250.00
61 Evers (Archer/Overall) 125.00 200.00
62 Evers (Archer/Reulbach) 125.00 200.00
63 Evers (Chance/Evers) 250.00 400.00
64 Evers (Tinker/Chance) 500.00 800.00
65 Fast Work (O'Leary/Cobb) 900.00 1500.00
66 Ford (Ford/Sweeney) 125.00 200.00
67 Ford (Ford/Vaughn) 125.00 200.00
68 Good Play (Moriarty/Cobb) 900.00 1500.00
69 Grant (Grant/Hoblitzell) 125.00 200.00
70 Hal Chase (McConnell/McIntyre) 125.00 200.00
71 Hal Chase (McLean/Suggs) 125.00 200.00
72 Harry Lord (Lennox/Tinker) 150.00 250.00
73 Hartsel Strikes (Gray/Groom) 125.00 200.00
74 Hartzell (Dahlen/Scanlan) 125.00 200.00
75 Held (Lord/Tannehill) 125.00 200.00
76 Jake Stahl (Cicotte/Stahl) 125.00 200.00
77 Jim Delahanty (Delahanty/Jones) 125.00 200.00
78 Just Before (Ames/Meyers) 125.00 200.00
79 Just Before (Becker/Devore) 125.00 200.00
80 Just Before (Bresnahan/McGraw) 250.00 400.00
81 Just Before (Crandall/Meyers) 125.00 200.00
82 Just Before (Fletcher/Mathewson) 350.00 600.00
83 Just Before (Marquard/Meyers) 150.00 250.00
84 Just Before (McGraw/Jennings) 250.00 400.00
85 Just Before (Meyers/Mathewson) 300.00 500.00
86 Just Before (Meyers/Wiltse) 125.00 200.00
87 Just Before (Murray/Snodgrass) 125.00 200.00
88 Knight (Knight/Johnson) 350.00 600.00
89 Lobert Almost (Bridwell/Kling) 125.00 200.00
90 Lobert Almost (Kling/Steinfeldt) 125.00 200.00
91 Lobert Almost (Kling/Young) 350.00 600.00
92 Lobert Almost (Mattern/Kling) 125.00 200.00
93 Lobert Gets (Dooin/Tenney) 125.00 200.00
94 Lobert Catches (Lord/L.Tannehill) 125.00 200.00
95 McConnell (Needham/Richie) 125.00 200.00
96 McIntyre (McConnell/McIntyre) 125.00 200.00
97 Moriarty (Stanage/Willett) 125.00 200.00
98 Nearly (Bates/Bescher) 125.00 200.00
99 Oldring (Lord/Oldring) 125.00 200.00
100 Schaefer On (McBride/Milan) 125.00 200.00
101 Schaefer Steals (McBride/Griffith) 125.00 200.00
102 Scoring (Lord/Oldring) 125.00 200.00
103 Scrambling (Barger/B.Bergen) 125.00 200.00
104 Scrambling (Chase/Wolter) 125.00 200.00
105 Speaker Almost (Miller/Clarke) 150.00 250.00
106 Speaker Round (Wood/Speaker) 350.00 600.00
107 Speaker Scores (Speaker/Engle) 300.00 500.00
108 Stahl Safe (Austin/Stovall) 125.00 200.00
109 Stone (Schulte/Sheckard) 125.00 200.00
110 Sullivan (Evans/Huggins) 150.00 250.00
111 Sullivan (Gray/Groom) 125.00 200.00
112 Sweeney (Ford/Sweeney) 125.00 200.00
113 Sweeney (Ford/Vaughn) 125.00 200.00
114 Tenney (Latham/Raymond) 125.00 200.00
115 The Athletic (Barry/Baker) 175.00 300.00
116 The Athletic (Brown/Graham) 150.00 250.00
117 The Athletic (Hauser/Konetchy) 125.00 200.00
118 The Athletic (Krause/Thomas) 125.00 200.00
119 The Pinch (Egan/Hoblitzell) 125.00 200.00
120 The Scissors (Birmingham/Turner) 125.00 200.00
121 Tom Jones (Fromme/McLean) 125.00 200.00
122 Tom Jones (Gaspar/McLean) 125.00 200.00
123 Too Late (Ames/Meyers) 125.00 200.00
124 Too Late (Crandall/Meyers) 125.00 200.00
125 Too Late (Devlin G/Mathewson) 700.00 1200.00
126 Too Late (Devlin R/Mathewson) 900.00 1500.00
127 Too Late (Marquard/Meyers) 250.00 400.00
128 Too Late (Meyers/Wiltse) 125.00 200.00
129 Ty Cobb Steals (Jennings/Cobb) 1200.00 2000.00
130 Ty Cobb Steals (Moriarty/Cobb) 1200.00 2000.00
131 Ty Cobb Steals (Stovall/Austin) 600.00 1000.00
132 Wheat Strikes (Dahlen/Wheat) 150.00 250.00

1911 Helmar Stamps

Each stamp measures 1 1/8" by 1 3/8". The stamps are very thin and have an ornate, bright colorful border surrounding the black-and-white photo of the player. There are many differnet border color combinations. There is no identification of issuer to be found anywhere on the stamp. Since the stamps are unnumbered, they are listed below alphabetically within team: Boston Red Sox (1-5), Chicago White Sox (6-20), Cleveland Indians (21-26), Detroit Tigers (27-38), New York Yankees (39-51), Philadelphia A's (52-59), St. Louis Browns (60-66), Washington Senators (67-76), Boston Bees NL (77-81), Brooklyn Dodgers (82-89), Chicago Cubs (90-108), Cincinnati Reds (109-119), New York Giants (120-139), Philadelphia Phillies (140-152), Pittsburgh Pirates (153-166), and St. Louis Cardinals (166-177).

COMPLETE SET (178) 5000.00 10000.00
1 Bill Carrigan 25.00 50.00
2 Ed Cicotte 75.00 150.00
3 Hack Engle 25.00 50.00
4 Tris Speaker 50.00 100.00
5 Heine Wagner 25.00 50.00
6 Bruno Block 25.00 50.00
7 Ping Bodie 25.00 50.00
8 Nixey Callahan 25.00 50.00
9 Shano Collins 25.00 50.00
10 Patsy Dougherty 25.00 50.00
11 Bristol Lord 25.00 50.00
12 Ambrose McConnell 25.00 50.00
13 Matthew McIntyre 25.00 50.00
14 Freddy Parent 25.00 50.00
15 Jim Scott 25.00 50.00
16 William Sullivan 25.00 50.00
17 Lee Ford Tannehill 25.00 50.00
18 Ed Walsh 50.00 100.00
19 Guy White 25.00 50.00
20 Irving Young 100.00 200.00
21 Neal Ball 25.00 50.00
22 Dode Birmingham 25.00 50.00
23 George Davis 50.00 100.00
24 Napoleon Lajoie 100.00 200.00
25 Paddy Livingston 25.00 50.00
26 Terry Turner 25.00 50.00
27 Donie Bush 25.00 50.00
28 Ty Cobb 250.00 500.00
29 Sam Crawford 50.00 100.00
30 Jim Delahanty 25.00 50.00
31 Patsy Donovan 25.00 50.00
32 Hughie Jennings 50.00 100.00
33 Davy Jones 25.00 50.00
34 George Moriarity 25.00 50.00
35 George Mullin 30.00 60.00
36 Boss Schmidt 25.00 50.00
37 Oscar Strange 25.00 50.00
38 Robert Willett 25.00 50.00
39 Lew Brockett 25.00 50.00
40 Hal Chase 50.00 100.00
41 Birdie Cree 25.00 50.00
42 Ray Fisher 25.00 50.00
43 Russ Ford 25.00 50.00
44 Earl Gardner 25.00 50.00
45 Jack Quinn 30.00 60.00
46 Gabby Street 25.00 50.00
47 Ed Sweeney 25.00 50.00
48 James(Hippo) Vaughn 30.00 60.00
49 John Warhop 25.00 50.00
50 Harry Wolter 25.00 50.00
51 Harry Wolverton 25.00 50.00
52 Frank Baker 50.00 100.00
53 Jack Barry 25.00 50.00
54 Chief Bender 50.00 100.00
55 Eddie Collins 50.00 100.00
56 Harry Krause 25.00 50.00
57 Danny Murphy 25.00 50.00
58 Rube Oldring 25.00 50.00
59 Ira Thomas 25.00 50.00
60 Jimmy Austin 25.00 50.00
61 Joe Lake 25.00 50.00
62 Frank LaPorte 25.00 50.00
63 Barney Pelty 25.00 50.00
64 John Powell 25.00 50.00
65 George Stovall 25.00 50.00
66 Bobby Wallace 50.00 100.00
67 Wid Conroy 25.00 50.00
68 Dolly Gray 25.00 50.00
69 Clark Griffith 50.00 100.00
70 Bob Groom 25.00 50.00
71 Tom Hughes 25.00 50.00
72 Walter Johnson 100.00 200.00
73 John Knight 25.00 50.00
74 George McBride 25.00 50.00
75 Clyde Milan 30.00 60.00
76 Germany Schaefer 25.00 50.00
77 Al Bridwell 25.00 50.00
78 Hank Gowdy 25.00 50.00
79 Johnny Kling 25.00 50.00
80 Al Mattern 25.00 50.00
81 Ed Sweeney 25.00 50.00
82 Cy Barger 25.00 50.00
83 George Bell 25.00 50.00
84 Bill Dahlen 25.00 50.00
85 Jake Daubert 40.00 80.00
86 Tex Erwin 25.00 50.00
87 John Hummel 25.00 50.00
88 Nap Rucker 40.00 80.00
89 Zach Wheat 50.00 100.00
90 Jimmy Archer 25.00 50.00
91 Mordecai Brown 50.00 100.00
92 Frank Chance 50.00 100.00
93 Leonard(King) Cole 25.00 50.00
94 Johnny Evers 50.00 100.00
95 George(Peaches) Graham 25.00 50.00
96 Solly Hoffman 25.00 50.00
97 Ed Lennox 25.00 50.00
98 Harry McIntire 25.00 50.00
99 Tom Needham 25.00 50.00
100 Ed Reulbach 25.00 50.00
101 Lewis Richie 25.00 50.00
102 Richter 25.00 50.00
103 John Rowan 25.00 50.00
104 Frank Schulte 25.00 50.00
105 Dave Shean 25.00 50.00
106 Jimmy Sheckard 25.00 50.00
107 Joe Tinker 50.00 100.00
108 Fred Toney 25.00 50.00
109 Johnny Bates 25.00 50.00
110 Bob Bescher 25.00 50.00
111 Ed Burns 25.00 50.00
112 Fred Clarke 50.00 100.00
113 Art Fromme 25.00 50.00
114 Harry Gaspar 25.00 50.00
115 Ed Grant 25.00 50.00
116 Doc Hoblitzell 25.00 50.00
117 Larry McLean 25.00 50.00
118 Clarence Mitchell 25.00 50.00
119 George Suggs 25.00 50.00
120 Red Ames 25.00 50.00
121 Beals Becker 25.00 50.00
122 Doc Crandall 25.00 50.00
123 Art Devlin 25.00 50.00
124 Josh Devore 25.00 50.00
125 Larry Doyle 30.00 60.00
126 Louis Drucke 25.00 50.00
127 Arthur Fletcher 25.00 50.00
128 Grover Hartley 25.00 50.00
129 Buck Herzog 30.00 60.00
130 Rube Marquard 50.00 100.00
131 Christy Mathewson 100.00 200.00
132 John McGraw 50.00 100.00
133 Fred Merkle 30.00 60.00
134 John(Chief) Meyers 30.00 60.00
135 Red Murray 25.00 50.00
136 Shafer 25.00 50.00
137 Fred Snodgrass 30.00 60.00
138 John(Chief) Wilson 30.00 60.00
139 Hooks Wiltse 25.00 50.00
140 Zinn Beck 25.00 50.00
141 Red Dooin 25.00 50.00
142 Mickey Doolan 25.00 50.00
143 Tom Downey 25.00 50.00
144 Otto Knabe 25.00 50.00
145 Hans Lobert 25.00 50.00
146 Fred Luderus 25.00 50.00
147 Sherry Magee 40.00 80.00
148 Earl Moore 25.00 50.00
149 Pat Moran 25.00 50.00
150 Dode Paskert 25.00 50.00
151 William(Doc) Scanlan 25.00 50.00
152 John Titus 25.00 50.00
153 Bert Adams 25.00 50.00
154 Bobby Byrne 25.00 50.00
155 Howard Camnitz 25.00 50.00
156 Max Carey 50.00 100.00
157 Fred Clarke 50.00 100.00
158 Mike Donlin 30.00 60.00
159 John Ferry 25.00 50.00
160 George Gibson 25.00 50.00
161 Thomas Leach 25.00 50.00
162 Albert(Lefty) Leifield 25.00 50.00
163 Roy(Doc) Miller 25.00 50.00
164 Martin O'Toole 25.00 50.00
165 Michael Simon 25.00 50.00
166 John(Chief) Wilson 30.00 60.00
167 John Bliss 25.00 50.00
168 Roger Bresnahan 50.00 100.00
169 Louis Evans 25.00 50.00
170 Robert Harmon 25.00 50.00
171 Arnold Hauser 25.00 50.00
172 Miller Huggins 50.00 100.00
173 Ed Konetchy 25.00 50.00
174 Mike Mowrey 25.00 50.00
175 Ennis(Rebel) Oakes 25.00 50.00
176 Edward Phelps 25.00 50.00
177 Slim Sallee 25.00 50.00
178 Bill Steele 25.00 50.00

1989 Hershiser Socko

The 1989 Socko Orel Hershiser set contains seven unnumbered standard-size cards. The fronts are blue, green and yellow, and feature full color photos of Hershiser with the Dodger logos airbrushed out. The backs are white and include "Tips from Orel." The cards were distributed as a promotional set through Socko beverages.

COMPLETE SET (7) 2.50 6.00
COMMON PLAYER (1-7) .40 1.00

2012 Heritage Auctions National Convention

COMPLETE SET (4) 12.50 30.00
STATED PRINT RUN 1500 SER.#'d SETS
1 Connie Mack 4.00 10.00
2 Honus Wagner 8.00 20.00
3 Ty Cobb 6.00 15.00
4 Cy Young 4.00 10.00

1962 H.F. Gardner Sports Stars PC768

This colorful 1960's set feature people of color stars only. The reverses can be identified by the line "Color by H.F. Gardner" at the lower left. A short biography of the subject player(s) is present on the reverse.

COMPLETE SET (5) 50.00 100.00
1 Hank Aaron 25.00 50.00
Tommy Aaron
2 Billy Bruton 2.50 5.00
3 Lee Maye 2.50 5.00
4 Billy Williams 10.00 20.00

1992 High 5

This 130-decal set features five players each from the 26 Major League Baseball teams. The collector could also purchase a stadium display board to display all the decals. The decals measure the standard size. The fronts are actually reusable stickers and display color action player photos. The color of the inner border varies from card to card , while the outermost border is on all cards. The pictures are accented above and on the right by a thin color stripe. The "High 5" logo and team logo appear in the upper left and lower right corners respectively. The decals are checklisted below alphabetically within and according to teams. Stickers from expansion teams Colorado Rockies and Florida Marlins were promised for 1993. However, no 1993 set was ever issued.

COMPLETE SET (130) 30.00 80.00
1 Mike Devereaux .08 .25
2 Ben McDonald .08 .25
3 Gregg Olson .08 .25
4 Joe Orsulak .08 .25
5 Cal Ripken 2.00 5.00
6 Wade Boggs .50 1.25
7 Roger Clemens 1.00 2.50
8 Phil Plantier .08 .25
9 Jeff Reardon .20 .50
10 Mo Vaughn .30 .75
11 Jim Abbott .20 .50
12 Chuck Finley .08 .25
13 Brian Harvey .08 .25
14 Mark Langston .08 .25
15 Dave Winfield .50 1.25
16 Carlton Fisk .50 1.25
17 Jack McDowell .20 .50
18 Bobby Thigpen .08 .25
19 Frank Thomas .60 1.50
20 Robin Ventura .30 .75
21 Steve Avery .08 .25
22 Ron Gant .20 .50
23 Tom Glavine .50 1.25
24 Dave Justice .40 1.00
25 Terry Pendleton .08 .25
26 George Bell .08 .25
27 Andre Dawson .40 1.00
28 Mark Grace .40 1.00
29 Greg Maddux 1.25 3.00
30 Ryne Sandberg 1.00 2.50
31 Eric Davis .20 .50
32 Barry Larkin .40 1.00
33 Hal Morris .08 .25
34 Jose Rijo .08 .25
35 Chris Sabo .08 .25
36 Jeff Bagwell .75 2.00
37 Craig Biggio .40 1.00
38 Ken Caminiti .30 .75
39 Luis Gonzalez .40 1.00
40 Pete Harnisch .08 .25
41 Sandy Alomar Jr. .20 .50
42 Carlos Baerga .08 .25
43 Albert Belle .20 .50
44 Alex Cole .08 .25
45 Charles Nagy .08 .25
46 Cecil Fielder .20 .50
47 Travis Fryman .20 .50
48 Tony Phillips .08 .25
49 Alan Trammell .30 .75
50 Lou Whitaker .20 .50
51 Brett Butler .20 .50
52 Lenny Harris .08 .25
53 Ramon Martinez .08 .25
54 Eddie Murray .50 1.25
55 Darryl Strawberry .20 .50
56 Ivan Calderon .08 .25
57 Delino DeShields .20 .50
58 Marquis Grissom .08 .25
59 Dennis Martinez .20 .50
60 Larry Walker .30 .75
61 George Brett 1.00 2.50
62 Jim Eisenreich .08 .25
63 Brian McRae .08 .25
64 Jeff Montgomery .08 .25
65 Bret Saberhagen .08 .25
66 Chris Bosio .08 .25
67 Paul Molitor .50 1.25
68 B.J. Surhoff .20 .50
69 Greg Vaughn .20 .50
70 Robin Yount .50 1.25
71 David Cone .30 .75
72 Dwight Gooden .20 .50
73 Gregg Jefferies .08 .25
74 Howard Johnson .08 .25
75 Kevin McReynolds .08 .25

76 Wes Chamberlain .08 .25
77 Len Dykstra .20 .50
78 John Kruk .20 .50
79 Terry Mulholland .08 .25
80 Mitch Williams .08 .25
81 Rick Aguilera .20 .50
82 Scott Erickson .08 .25
83 Kent Hrbek .08 .25
84 Kirby Puckett .60 1.50
85 Kevin Tapani .08 .25
86 Mel Hall .08 .25
87 Roberto Kelly .08 .25
88 Kevin Maas .08 .25
89 Don Mattingly 1.00 2.50
90 Steve Sax .08 .25
91 Barry Bonds 1.00 2.50
92 Doug Drabek .08 .25
93 John Smiley .08 .25
94 Zane Smith .08 .25
95 Andy Van Slyke .08 .25
96 Felix Jose .08 .25
97 Ray Lankford .20 .50
98 Lee Smith .20 .50
99 Ozzie Smith 1.00 2.50
100 Todd Zeile .20 .50
101 Harold Baines .30 .75
102 Jose Canseco .50 1.25
103 Dennis Eckersley .50 1.25
104 Dave Henderson .08 .25
105 Rickey Henderson .60 1.50
106 Jay Buhner .20 .50
107 Ken Griffey Jr. 1.25 3.00
108 Randy Johnson .60 1.50
109 Edgar Martinez .30 .75
110 Harold Reynolds .20 .50
111 Julio Franco .20 .50
112 Juan Gonzalez .40 1.00
113 Rafael Palmeiro .40 1.00
114 Nolan Ryan 2.00 5.00
115 Ruben Sierra .20 .50
116 Roberto Alomar .40 1.00
117 Joe Carter .20 .50
118 Kelly Gruber .08 .25
119 John Olerud .30 .75
120 Devon White .08 .25
121 Tony Fernandez .20 .50
122 Tony Gwynn 1.00 2.50
123 Bruce Hurst .08 .25
124 Fred McGriff .30 .75
125 Benito Santiago .20 .50
126 Will Clark .50 1.25
127 Willie McGee .20 .50
128 Kevin Mitchell .08 .25
129 Robby Thompson .08 .25
130 Matt Williams .30 .75
NNO Ken Griffey Jr. PROMO 2.00 5.00

1992 High 5 Superstars

This 36-decal set features some of baseball's greatest players. Six different assortments, each featuring five player decals and one High 5 nonplayer decal, were issued (AL infielders, outfielders and pitchers as well as NL infielders, outfielders and pitchers). The decals measure the standard size. The fronts are actually reusable stickers and display color action player photos. The color of the inner border varies from decal to decal, (gradated blue, black or green) while the outermost border is white on all decals. The backs of six decals combine to form six separate 5" by 7" color close-up photos of players featured on the fronts (Clark, Griffey Jr., Justice, Ryan, Strawberry and Thomas). Each of these composite pictures includes one High 5 Superstar nonplayer decal. The decals are unnumbered and checklisted below in alphabetical order.

COMPLETE SET (36) 15.00 40.00
1 Steve Avery .08 .25
2 Jeff Bagwell .60 1.50
3 Wade Boggs .50 1.25
4 Barry Bonds 1.00 2.50
5 Jose Canseco .50 1.25
6 Joe Carter .20 .50
7 Will Clark .50 1.25
8 Roger Clemens 1.00 2.50
9 Dennis Eckersley .50 1.25
10 Scott Erickson .08 .25
11 Cecil Fielder .20 .50
12 Julio Franco .20 .50
13 Tom Glavine .50 1.25
14 Juan Gonzalez .50 1.25
15 Dwight Gooden .20 .50
16 Ron Gant .08 .25
17 Ken Griffey Jr. 1.25 3.00
18 Tony Gwynn 1.00 2.50
19 Rickey Henderson .60 1.50
20 Howard Johnson .08 .25
21 Dave Justice .40 1.00
22 Mark Langston .08 .25
23 Ramon Martinez .20 .50
24 Cal Ripken 2.00 5.00
25 Nolan Ryan 2.00 5.00
26 Ryne Sandberg 1.00 2.50
27 John Smiley .08 .25
28 Darryl Strawberry .20 .50
29 Frank Thomas .60 1.50
30 Matt Williams .30 .75
31 High 5 Superstar (Part of Will Clark 5x7 Portrait) .20 .50
32 High 5 Superstar (Part of Ken Griffey Jr. 5x7 Portrait) 1.25 3.00
33 High 5 Superstar (Part of David Justice 5x7 Portrait) .08 .25
34 High 5 Superstar (Part of Nolan Ryan 5x7 Portrait) 1.00 2.50
35 High 5 Superstar (Part of Darryl Strawberry 5x7 Portrait) .08 .25
36 High 5 Superstar (Part of Frank Thomas 5x7 Portrait) .40 1.00

1996-98 Highland Mint Mini Mint-Cards

These mini Mint-Cards are not replicas but feature Highland Mint's own design. They are one-quarter scale of regular Mint-Cards. The high relief on the fronts is four times greater than that used on regular Mint-Cards. The backs display text and statistics. Each card is individually-numbered, includes a certificate of authenticity, and is packaged in a leather display box. Mini Mint-Cards were issued as a matching set with the cards displayed side by side. Both cards carry the same serial number. The mintage is given below with reference to gold-plated on silver, silver, and bronze quantities. The suggested retail price was $300.00 for the gold, $150.00 for the silver, and $65.00 for the bronze.

1 K.Griffey Jr. F.Thomas G/500 100.00 250.00
2 K.Griffey Jr. F.Thomas S/1000 60.00 150.00
3 K.Griffey Jr. F.Thomas B/5000 25.00 60.00
4 R.Johnson N.Ryan G/375 240.00 200.00
5 R.Johnson N.Ryan S/500 50.00 100.00
7 R.Johnson N.Ryan B/2500 20.00 50.00
9 G.Maddux C.Young G/375 240.00 200.00
11 G.Maddux C.Young S/500 50.00 100.00
13 G.Maddux C.Young B/2500 20.00 50.00
15 M.Piazza R.Campanella S/500 50.00 100.00
17 M.Piazza R.Campanella B/2500 20.00 50.00
19 C.Ripken L.Gehrig G/375 325.00 300.00
21 C.Ripken L.Gehrig S/500 75.00 150.00
23 C.Ripken L.Gehrig B/2500 50.00 80.00

1994-98 Highland Mint Mint-Cards Pinnacle/UD

These Highland Mint cards are metal replicas of already issued Pinnacle and Upper Deck cards. All these standard size replicas contain 4.25 ounces of metal. Both the silver and gold version feature 4.25 Troy Ounces of .999 silver with the gold being gold plated as well. Suggested retail was initially $50 for bronze and $235 for silver. Each includes a certificate of authenticity, and is packaged in a numbered album and a three-piece Lucite display. They are checklisted below alphabetically; the final mintage figures for each card are also listed.

1 Jeff Bagwell 92 S/750 150.00 200.00
2 Jeff Bagwell 92 B/2500 20.00 50.00
3 Michael Jordan 94 G/500 200.00 400.00
4 Michael Jordan 94 S/1000 175.00 300.00
5 Michael Jordan 94 B/5000 20.00 50.00
6 Greg Maddux 92 S/750 150.00 200.00
7 Greg Maddux 92 B/2500 20.00 50.00
8 Mickey Mantle 92 G/500 200.00 400.00
9 Mickey Mantle 92 S/1000 175.00 300.00
10 Mickey Mantle 92 B/5000 20.00 50.00
11 Nolan Ryan 92 G/500 200.00 400.00
12 Nolan Ryan 92 S/1000 150.00 225.00
13 Nolan Ryan 92 B/5000 20.00 50.00

1992-94 Highland Mint Mint-Cards Topps

These metal cards, from the Highland Mint, measure the standard size and are reproductions of Topps baseball cards. Each mint-card bears a serial number on its bottom edge and both the silver and gold versions were produced with 4.25 Troy Ounces of .999 silver. The gold version was also plated in 24K gold. These cards were originally available only in hobby stores, and were packaged in a lucite display holder within an album. Each card comes with a sequentially numbered Certificate of Authenticity. When the Highland Mint/Topps relationship was ended in 1994, the remaining unsold stock was destroyed; the final available mintage according to Highland Mint is listed below. The cards are checklisted below alphabetically.

1 Roberto Alomar 88 S/214 150.00 200.00
2 Roberto Alomar 88 B/928 12.50 30.00
3 Ernie Banks 54 S/437 150.00 200.00
4 Ernie Banks 54 B/920 12.50 30.00
5 Johnny Bench 69 S/500 150.00 200.00
6 Johnny Bench 69 B/1384 12.50 30.00
7 Barry Bonds 86 S/596 150.00 200.00
8 Barry Bonds 86 B/2677 12.50 30.00
9 George Brett 75 S/999 150.00 200.00
10 George Brett 75 B/3560 35.00 50.00
11 Will Clark 86 S/150 150.00 250.00
12 Will Clark 86 B/1044 12.50 30.00
13 Roger Clemens 85 S/432 150.00 200.00
14 Roger Clemens 85 B/1789 12.50 30.00
15 Juan Gonzalez 90 S/365 150.00 200.00
16 Juan Gonzalez 90 B/1899 12.50 30.00
17 Ken Griffey Jr. 92 G/500 200.00 500.00
18 Ken Griffey Jr. 92 S/1000 100.00 250.00
19 Ken Griffey Jr. 92 B/5000 25.00 60.00
20 David Justice 90 S/265 150.00 200.00
21 David Justice 90 B/1396 12.50 30.00
22 Don Mattingly 84 S/414 150.00 200.00
23 Don Mattingly 84 B/1550 35.00 50.00
24 Paul Molitor 79 S/260 150.00 200.00
25 Paul Molitor 79 B/639 35.00 50.00
26 Mike Piazza 93 G/374 250.00 400.00
27 Mike Piazza 93 S/750 150.00 200.00
28 Mike Piazza 93 B/2500 20.00 40.00
29 Kirby Puckett 85 S/359 150.00 200.00
30 Kirby Puckett 85 B/1723 20.00 40.00
31 Cal Ripken 92 S/1000 150.00 250.00
32 Cal Ripken 92 B/4065 90.00 80.00
33 Cal Ripken 92 B/5000
34 Brooks Robinson 57 S/796 150.00 200.00
35 Brooks Robinson 57 B/2043 12.50 30.00
36 Nolan Ryan 92 S/999 250.00 400.00
37 Nolan Ryan 92 B/5000 60.00 120.00
38 Tim Salmon 93 S/264 150.00 200.00
39 Tim Salmon 93 B/768 12.50 30.00
40 Ryne Sandberg 92 S/430 150.00 200.00
41 Ryne Sandberg 92 B/1932 20.00 40.00
42 Deion Sanders 89 S/187 150.00 200.00
43 Deion Sanders 89 B/668 12.50 30.00
44 Mike Schmidt 74 S/500 150.00 200.00
45 Mike Schmidt 74 B/1641 12.50 30.00
46 Ozzie Smith 79 S/211 150.00 200.00
47 Ozzie Smith 79 B/1088 35.00 50.00
48 Frank Thomas 92 G/500 250.00 400.00
49 Frank Thomas 92 S/1000 150.00 250.00
50 Frank Thomas 92 B/5000 35.00 50.00
51 Dave Winfield 74 S/266 150.00 200.00
52 Dave Winfield 74 B/1216 12.50 30.00
53 Carl Yastrzemski 60 S/500 150.00 200.00
54 Carl Yastrzemski 60 B/1072 12.50 30.00
55 Robin Yount 75 S/349 150.00 200.00
56 Robin Yount 75 B/1564 12.50 30.00

1999 Hillshire Farms Home Run Heroes Autographs

Available through a wrapper redemption offer from Hillshire Meats, these four standard-size cards feature autographs of retired Hall of Famers. The black-bordered photos have the player photo along with the "Hilshire Farms" logo and the players name on the bottom. The back has biographical information, career stats and a blurb. These cards came with an certificate of authenticity. Since these cards are unnumbered, we have sequenced them in alphabetical order.

COMPLETE SET 20.00 50.00
1 Ernie Banks 12.00 30.00
2 Harmon Killebrew 6.00 15.00
3 Frank Robinson 6.00 15.00
4 Willie Stargell 10.00 25.00

1958 Hires Root Beer

The cards in this 66-card set measure approximately 2 5/16" by 3 1/2" or 2 5/16" by 7" with tabs. The 1958 Hires Root Beer set of numbered, colored cards was issued with detachable coupons as inserts with Hires Root Beer cartons. Cards with the coupon still intact are worth 2.5 times the prices listed below. The card front picture is surrounded by a wood grain effect which makes it look like the player is seen through a knot hole. The numbering of this set is rather strange in that it begins with 10 and skips 69.

COMPLETE SET (66) 1000.00 2000.00
10 Richie Ashburn 60.00 120.00
11 Chico Carrasquel 12.50 25.00
12 Dave Philley 12.50 25.00
13 Don Newcombe 15.00 30.00
14 Wally Post 12.50 25.00
15 Rip Repulski 12.50 25.00
16 Chico Fernandez 12.50 25.00
17 Larry Doby 30.00 60.00
18 Hector Brown 12.50 25.00
19 Danny O'Connell 12.50 25.00
20 Granny Hamner 12.50 25.00
21 Dick Groat 15.00 30.00
22 Ray Narleski 12.50 25.00
23 Pee Wee Reese 60.00 120.00
24 Bob Friend 12.50 25.00
25 Willie Mays 200.00 400.00
26 Bob Nieman 12.50 25.00
27 Frank Thomas 15.00 30.00
28 Curt Simmons 15.00 30.00
29 Stan Lopata 12.50 25.00
30 Bob Skinner 12.50 25.00
31 Ron Kline 12.50 25.00
32 Willie Miranda 12.50 25.00
33 Bobby Avila 12.50 25.00
34 Clem Labine 15.00 30.00
35 Ray Jablonski 12.50 25.00
36 Bill Mazeroski 40.00 80.00
37 Billy Gardner 12.50 25.00
38 Pete Runnels 12.50 25.00
39 Jack Sanford 12.50 25.00
40 Dave Sisler 12.50 25.00
41 Don Zimmer 15.00 30.00
42 Johnny Podres 15.00 30.00
43 Dick Farrell 12.50 25.00
44 Hank Aaron 200.00 400.00
45 Bill Virdon 12.50 25.00
46 Bobby Thomson 15.00 30.00
47 Willard Nixon 12.50 25.00
48 Billy Loes 12.50 25.00
49 Hank Sauer 15.00 30.00
50 Johnny Antonelli 15.00 30.00
51 Daryl Spencer 12.50 25.00
52 Ken Lehman 12.50 25.00
53 Sammy White 12.50 25.00
54 Charley Neal 12.50 25.00
55 Don Drysdale 60.00 120.00
56 Jackie Jensen 25.00 50.00
57 Ray Katt 12.50 25.00
58 Frank Sullivan 12.50 25.00
59 Roy Face 15.00 30.00
60 Willie Jones 12.50 25.00
61 Duke Snider 60.00 120.00
62 Whitey Lockman 12.50 25.00
63 Gino Cimoli 12.50 25.00
64 Marv Grissom 12.50 25.00
65 Gene Baker 12.50 25.00
66 George Zuverink 12.50 25.00
67 Ted Kluszewski 25.00 50.00
68 Jim Busby 12.50 25.00
69 Not Issued
70 Curt Barclay 12.50 25.00
71 Hank Foiles 12.50 25.00
72 Gene Stephens 12.50 25.00
73 Al Worthington 12.50 25.00
74 Al Walker 12.50 25.00
75 Bob Boyd 12.50 25.00
76 Al Pilarcik 12.50 25.00

1958 Hires Root Beer Test

The cards in this eight-card test set measure approximately 2 5/16" by 3 1/2" or 2 5/16" by 7" with tabs. The 1958 Hires Root Beer test set features unnumbered, color cards. The card front photos are shown on a yellow or orange back ground instead of the wood grain background used in the Hires regular set. The cards contain a detachable coupon just as the regular Hires issue does. Cards were test marketed on a very limited basis in a few cities. Cards with the coupon still intact are especially tough to find and are worth triple the prices in the checklist below. The checklist below is ordered alphabetically.

COMPLETE SET (8) 750.00 1500.00
1 Johnny Antonelli 100.00 200.00
2 Jim Busby 75.00 150.00
3 Chico Fernandez 75.00 150.00
4 Bob Friend 100.00 200.00
5 Vern Law 100.00 200.00
6 Stan Lopata 75.00 150.00
7 Willie Mays 500.00 1000.00
8 Al Pilarcik 75.00 150.00

1992 Hit The Books Bookmarks

These bookmarks were produced of leading major leaguers. The purpose was to increase interest in reading and visiting local libraries. These bookmarks are unnumbered and we have sequenced them in alphabetical order.

COMPLETE SET (36) 20.00 50.00
1 Jim Abbott .50 1.25
2 Sandy Alomar .50 1.25
3 Jay Bell .40 1.00
4 Craig Biggio .75 2.00
5 Mike Boddicker .40 1.00
6 Bobby Bonilla .40 1.00
7 George Brett 1.50 4.00
8 Brett Butler .50 1.25
9 Joe Carter .50 1.25
10 Will Clark .75 2.00
11 Colorado Rockies .40 1.00
12 Andre Dawson .60 1.50
13 Cecil Fielder .50 1.25
14 Florida Marlins .40 1.00
15 Ozzie Guillen .50 1.25
16 Tony Gwynn 1.50 4.00
17 Howard Johnson .40 1.00
18 Dave Justice .75 2.00
19 Mark Langston .40 1.00
20 Barry Larkin .75 2.00
21 Don Mattingly 1.50 4.00
22 Ben McDonald .40 1.00
23 Paul Molitor 1.00 2.50
24 Dale Murphy .60 1.50
25 Tony Pena .40 1.00
26 Kirby Puckett 1.50 4.00
27 Harold Reynolds .50 1.25
28 Cal Ripken 3.00 8.00
29 Chris Sabo .40 1.00
30 Ryne Sandberg 1.50 4.00
31 Mike Scioscia .50 1.25
32 Ruben Sierra .50 1.25
33 Ozzie Smith 1.50 4.00
34 Dave Stewart .40 1.00
35 Andy Van Slyke .40 1.00
36 Tim Wallach .40 1.00

1989 HOF Sticker Book

Lou Gehrig, 1b

These stickers honor members of the baseball Hall of Fame. They are numbered in order of position played: First Base (1-9), Second Base (10-13), Shortstop (14-21), Third Base (22-26), Outfield (27-53), Catcher (54-58), Pitcher (59-84), Manager (85-89) and Builders (90-100).

COMPLETE SET (100) 10.00 25.00
1 Lou Gehrig .75 2.00
2 Bill Terry .30 .75
3 Johnny Mize .20 .50
4 Willie McCovey .20 .50
5 Cap Anson .30 .75
6 Ernie Banks .30 .75
7 Dan Brouthers .08 .25
8 George Kelly .08 .25
9 Roger Connor .08 .25
10 Nap Lajoie .30 .75
11 Bobby Doerr .08 .25
12 Jackie Robinson .75 2.00
13 Frankie Frisch .20 .50
14 Honus Wagner .30 .75
15 George Wright .08 .25
16 Hughie Jennings .08 .25
17 Rabbit Maranville .08 .25
18 Luis Aparicio .20 .50
19 Joe Cronin .20 .50
20 Dave Bancroft .08 .25
21 Arky Vaughan .08 .25
22 Joe Sewell .08 .25
23 Jimmy Collins .08 .25
24 George Kell .08 .25
25 Eddie Mathews .20 .50
26 Ray Dandridge .08 .25
27 Willie Stargell .20 .50
28 Ted Williams .75 2.00
29 Billy Williams .20 .50
30 Stan Musial .60 1.50
31 Ed Delahanty .08 .25
32 Monte Irvin .08 .25
33 Jesse Burkett .08 .25
34 Chick Hafey .08 .25
35 Joe Kelley .08 .25
36 Heinie Manush .08 .25
37 Ty Cobb .60 1.50
38 Max Carey .08 .25
39 Joe DiMaggio .75 2.00
40 Mickey Mantle .75 2.00
41 Tris Speaker .30 .75
42 Lloyd Waner .08 .25
43 Billy Hamilton .08 .25
44 Hank Aaron .60 1.50
45 Paul Waner .20 .50
46 Roberto Clemente .75 2.00
47 Babe Ruth .75 2.00
48 Chuck Klein .08 .25
49 Mel Ott .20 .50
50 Sam Crawford .08 .25
51 Willie Keeler .08 .25
52 Harry Hooper .08 .25
53 Elmer Flick .08 .25
54 Roy Campanella .30 .75
55 Roger Bresnahan .08 .25
56 Mickey Cochrane .20 .50
57 Buck Ewing .08 .25
58 Ernie Lombardi .08 .25
59 Cy Young .30 .75
60 Mordecai Brown .08 .25
61 Red Faber .08 .25
62 Bob Feller .30 .75
63 Martin Dihigo .08 .25
64 Candy Cummings .08 .25
65 Christy Mathewson .30 .75
66 Rube Marquard .08 .25
67 Herb Pennock .08 .25
68 Bob Lemon .08 .25
69 Eppa Rixey .08 .25
70 Whitey Ford .30 .75
71 Waite Hoyt .08 .25
72 Grover Alexander .30 .75
73 Dazzy Vance .08 .25
74 Lefty Grove .20 .50
75 Carl Hubbell .20 .50
76 Lefty Gomez .08 .25
77 Ed Walsh .08 .25
78 Eddie Plank .08 .25
79 Sandy Koufax .30 .75
80 Pud Galvin .08 .25
81 Hoyt Wilhelm .08 .25
82 Catfish Hunter .08 .25
83 Red Ruffing .08 .25
84 Warren Spahn .20 .50
85 Connie Mack .08 .25
86 Wilbert Robinson .02 .10
87 Joe McCarthy .02 .10
88 Bill McKechnie .02 .10
89 John McGraw .20 .50
90 Alexander Cartwright .02 .10
91 Branch Rickey .02 .10
92 Warren Giles .02 .10
93 Tom Yawkey .02 .10
94 Ed Barrow .02 .10
95 Kenesaw Landis .02 .10
96 Ban Johnson .02 .10
97 Happy Chandler .02 .10
98 Jocko Conlan .02 .10
99 Cal Hubbard .02 .10
100 Billy Evans .02 .10

1990 HOF Sticker Book

Unlike the previous year when all the people pictured were in the Hall of Fame, this year's version features a mix of players in the Hall or players who participated in special events. These stickers are sequenced in chronological order.

COMPLETE SET (100) 10.00 25.00
1 George Bradley .07 .20
2 Old Hoss Radbourn .15 .40
3 Guy Hecker .07 .20
4 Tim Keefe .15 .40
5 Curt Welch .07 .20
6 George Gore .07 .20
7 Tip O'Neill .07 .20
8 Hugh Duffy .15 .40
9 Cap Anson .30 .75
10 Christy Mathewson .30 .75
11 Joe McGinnity .15 .40
12 Ed Reulbach .07 .20
13 Jack Taylor .07 .20
14 Cy Young .30 .75
15 Ernie Shore .07 .20
16 Smokey Joe Wood .07 .20
17 Fred Toney (Hippo Vaughn .07 .20
18 Chief Wilson .07 .20
19 Ty Cobb .60 1.50
20 Fielder Jones .07 .20
21 George Stallings MG .07 .20
22 Leon Cadore Joe Oeschger .07 .20
23 George Sisler .25 .60
24 Bill Wambsganss .07 .20
25 Babe Ruth 1.00 2.50
26 Jim Bottomley .15 .40
27 Rogers Hornsby .30 .75
28 Walter Johnson .30 .75
29 Hack Wilson .15 .40
30 Wes Ferrell .07 .20
31 Lefty Grove .25 .60
32 Carl Hubbell .25 .60
33 Joe Sewell .07 .20
34 Johnny Frederick .07 .20
35 Rudy York .07 .20
36 Johnny Vander Meer .07 .20
37 Pinky Higgins .07 .20
38 Lou Gehrig .75 2.00
39 Joe DiMaggio .75 2.00
40 Ted Williams .75 2.00
41 Jim Tobin .07 .20
42 Hal Newhouser .15 .40
43 Cookie Lavagetto .07 .20
44 Jim Konstanty .07 .20
45 Connie Mack MG .25 .60
46 Bobby Thomson .07 .20
47 Bobo Holloman .07 .20
48 Gene Stephens .07 .20
49 Mickey Mantle .75 2.00
50 Joe Adcock .07 .20
51 Stan Musial .60 1.50
52 Al Kaline .25 .60
53 Dale Long .07 .20
54 Don Larsen .07 .20
55 Dave Philley .07 .20
56 Vic Power .07 .20
57 Harvey Haddix .07 .20
58 Roy Face .07 .20
59 Larry Sherry .07 .20
60 Casey Stengel MG .25 .60
61 Bobby Richardson .07 .20
62 Bill Mazeroski .15 .40
63 Roger Maris .07 .20
64 Bill Fischer .07 .20
65 Willie Mays .60 1.50
66 Maury Wills .07 .20
67 Bert Campaneris .07 .20
68 Warren Spahn .25 .60
69 Sandy Koufax .30 .75
70 Tony Cloninger .07 .20
71 Carl Yastrzemski .30 .75
72 Denny McLain .07 .20
73 Don Drysdale .25 .60
74 Bob Gibson .25 .60
75 Frank Howard .07 .20
76 Tom Seaver .30 .75
77 Nolan Ryan .75 2.00
78 Steve Carlton .30 .75
79 Mike Marshall .07 .20
80 Nate Colbert .07 .20
81 Hank Aaron .60 1.50
82 Rennie Stennett .07 .20
83 Fred Lynn .07 .20
84 Pete Rose .30 .75
85 Pedro Guerrero .07 .20
86 Lou Brock .25 .60
87 Rickey Henderson .25 .60
88 Reggie Jackson .30 .75
89 Bob Horner .07 .20
90 Don Mattingly .30 .75
91 Mark McGwire .75 2.00
92 Benito Santiago .07 .20
93 George Brett .60 1.50
94 Mike Schmidt .30 .75
95 Jose Canseco .25 .60
96 Andre Dawson .15 .40
97 Ron Guidry .07 .20
98 Dwight Gooden .15 .40
99 Orel Hershiser .15 .40
100 Vince Coleman .07 .20

1959 Home Run Derby

Though commonly referenced as a 1959 release, this 20-card set was most likely produced in 1960 by American Motors to publicize a 1959 television program. Though the show was filmed in the 1959 off-season, it appears that the set was released in early 1960 based on the fact that Rocky Colavito was traded to the Tigers in April, 1960 and his card in the set lists him with the Tigers while showing him in an Indians uniform. The cards are black and white and blank backed. The cards measure approximately 3 1/8" by 5 1/4". The cards are unnumbered and are ordered alphabetically below for convenience. During 1988, the 19 player cards in this set were publicly reprinted.

COMPLETE SET (20) 3000.00 6000.00
1 Hank Aaron 300.00 600.00
2 Bob Allison 60.00 150.00
3 Ernie Banks 150.00 300.00
4 Ken Boyer 60.00 150.00
5 Bob Cerv 50.00 120.00
6 Rocky Colavito 150.00 300.00
7 Gil Hodges 150.00 300.00
8 Jackie Jensen 60.00 150.00
9 Al Kaline 200.00 400.00
10 Harmon Killebrew 250.00 500.00
11 Jim Lemon 50.00 120.00
12 Mickey Mantle 1000.00 2000.00
13 Eddie Mathews 200.00 400.00
14 Willie Mays 400.00 800.00
15 Wally Post 50.00 120.00
16 Frank Robinson 250.00 500.00
17 Mark Scott ANN 50.00 120.00
18 Duke Snider 200.00 400.00
19 Dick Stuart 60.00 150.00
20 Gus Triandos 50.00 120.00

1999 Home Run Heroes

COMPLETE SET (16) 25.00 60.00
RANDOM IN ALL LICENSEES RETAIL PACKS
1 Mark McGwire Fleer 2.50 6.00
2 Sammy Sosa SI .75 2.00
3 Mike Piazza Circa 1.50 4.00
4 Nomar Garciaparra Circa 1.50 4.00
5 Mark McGwire UD 2.50 6.00
6 Sammy Sosa UD .75 2.00
7 Ken Griffey Jr. UD 2.00 5.00
8 Frank Thomas UD .75 2.00
9 Mark McGwire Topps Chr 2.50 6.00
10 Sammy Sosa Topps Chr .75 2.00
11 Alex Rodriguez Topps Chr 1.50 4.00
12 Vladimir Guerrero Topps Chr .75 2.00
13 Mark McGwire Pacific 2.50 6.00
14 Sammy Sosa Pacific .75 2.00
15 Juan Gonzalez Pacific .75 2.00
16 Manny Ramirez Pacific .75 2.00

1991 Homers Cookies Classics

This nine-card standards-size set was sponsored by Legend Food Products in honor of Hall of Famers in baseball history. One free card was randomly inserted in each box of Homers Baseball Cookies. The cards have vintage sepia-toned player photos, with bronze borders on a white card face. The player's name appears in a bronze stripe overlaying the bottom edge of the picture. In black print on white, the back presents lifetime statistics, career highlights, and a checklist for the set.

COMPLETE SET (9) 2.50 6.00
1 Babe Ruth .60 1.50
2 Satchel Paige .30 .75
3 Lefty Gomez .20 .50
4 Ty Cobb .30 .75
5 Cy Young .25 .60
6 Bob Feller .25 .60
7 Roberto Clemente .40 1.00
8 Dizzy Dean .25 .60
9 Lou Gehrig .40 1.00

2013 Hometown Heroes

COMPLETE SET w/o SPs(260) 20.00 50.00
1 Kerry Wood .15 .40
2 Craig Biggio .20 .50
3 Andrew McCutchen .25 .60
4 Jose Rijo .15 .40
5 Jim Abbott .15 .40
6 Pat Burrell .15 .40
7 Billy Butler .15 .40
8 David Eckstein .15 .40
9 Hunter Pence .20 .50
10 Fred Lynn .15 .40
11 Vince Coleman .15 .40
12 Dustin Pedroia .25 .60
13 Jim Rice .20 .50
14 Yasiel Puig RC 1.00 2.50
15 Ryan Howard .20 .50
16 Dennis Eckersley .20 .50
17 Bill Buckner .15 .40
18 Mark Grace .20 .50
19 Robin Yount .25 .60
20 Frank White .15 .40
21 Nomar Garciaparra .20 .50
22 Joe Carter .15 .40
23 Rick Aguilera .15 .40
24 Matt Williams .15 .40
25 Johnny Damon .20 .50
26 Andre Dawson .20 .50
27 Elvis Andrus .20 .50
28 Ozzie Smith .30 .75
29 Joe Mauer .20 .50
30 Paul Molitor .25 .60
31 John Tudor .15 .40
32 John Franco .15 .40
33 Cole Hamels .20 .50
34 Paul O'Neill .20 .50
35 Frank Robinson .20 .50
36 Tim Lincecum .20 .50
37 Willie Horton .15 .40
38 Teddy Higuera .15 .40
39 Jurickson Profar RC .30 .75
40 Ben McDonald .15 .40
41 Greg Gagne .15 .40
42 Jorge Posada .20 .50
43 Jack Morris .15 .40
44 Lee Mazzilli .15 .40
45 Chipper Jones .25 .60
46 Keith Moreland .15 .40
47 Denny McLain .15 .40
48 Ian Kinsler .20 .50
49 Orel Hershiser .15 .40
50 Rickey Henderson .25 .60
51 Dan Gladden .15 .40
52 Curt Schilling .20 .50
53 Juan Samuel .15 .40
54 Matt Kemp .20 .50
55 Roberto Alomar .20 .50
56 Adam Wainwright .20 .50
57 Dale Murphy .25 .60
58 Buddy Bell .15 .40
59 Wil Myers .25 .60
60 Steve Avery .15 .40
61 Willie Wilson .15 .40
62 Justin Verlander .25 .60
63 Ron Cey .15 .40
64 Frank Thomas .25 .60
65 Tino Martinez .20 .50
66 Cleon Jones .15 .40
67 Ron Gant .15 .40
68 Mike Scott .15 .40
69 David Freese .15 .40
70 Tony Pena .15 .40
71 Pat Tabler .15 .40
72 Ichiro .30 .75
73 Tony Gwynn .25 .60
74 Jack McDowell .15 .40
75 Pete Rose .50 1.25
76 Kent Hrbek .15 .40
77 Bobby Witt .15 .40
78 Cal Ripken Jr. .75 2.00
79 Alex Rodriguez .30 .75
80 Wade Boggs .20 .50
81 Matt Harvey .20 .50
82 Fernando Valenzuela .15 .40
83 Jim Palmer .20 .50
84 Jose Altuve .20 .50
85 Yadier Molina .30 .75
86 Ernie Banks .25 .60
87 Mike Krukow .15 .40
88 Mickey Lolich .15 .40
89 Joe Charboneau .15 .40
90 John Kruk .15 .40
91 Bucky Dent .15 .40
92 Derek Jeter .60 1.50
93 Rick Dempsey .15 .40
94 Ryne Sandberg .50 1.25
95 Jerome Walton .15 .40

96 David Price .20 .50
97 Andy Van Slyke .15 .40
98 Jon Jay .15 .40
99 Eric Hosmer .20 .50
100 Felix Hernandez .20 .50
101 Ozzie Guillen .15 .40
102 Max Scherzer .25 .60
103 Dan Petry .15 .40
104 Ruben Sierra .15 .40
105 Brandon Phillips .15 .40
106 Kevin Mitchell .15 .40
107 Jody Davis .15 .40
108 Mark Mulder .15 .40
109 Gorman Thomas .15 .40
110 Dwayne Murphy .15 .40
111 Mike Zunino RC .40 1.00
112 Jeff Conine .15 .40
113 Ron Darling .15 .40
114 Chase Utley .20 .50
115 Matt Cain .20 .50
116 Shawn Green .15 .40
117 Dusty Baker .15 .40
118 Terry Pendleton .15 .40
119 Mike Boddicker .15 .40
120 Nolan Ryan .75 2.00
121 Mariano Rivera .30 .75
122 Tom Seaver .20 .50
123 Ellis Burks .15 .40
124 Lenny Dykstra .15 .40
125 Bob Brenly .15 .40
126 Tony Fernandez .15 .40
127 Will Clark .20 .50
128 Dylan Bundy RC .60 1.50
129 Jack Clark .15 .40
130 Alex Gordon .20 .50
131 Johnny Ray .15 .40
132 Chase Headley .15 .40
133 Jordan Zimmermann .20 .50
134 Greg Maddux .30 .75
135 Evan Gattis RC .50 1.25
136 Alex Rodriguez .30 .75
137 Gerrit Cole RC 1.50 4.00
138 Bob Gibson .20 .50
139 George Brett .50 1.25
140 Ryan Zimmerman .20 .50
141 Gary Gaetti .15 .40
142 Shelby Miller RC .60 1.50
143 Jeff Bagwell .20 .50
144 Roger Clemens .30 .75
145 Mike Schmidt .40 1.00
146 David Murphy .15 .40
147 Harold Reynolds .15 .40
148 Shawon Dunston .15 .40
149 Joey Votto .25 .60
150 Bobby Thigpen .15 .40
151 Barry Larkin .20 .50
152 Andres Galarraga .20 .50
153 Mookie Wilson .15 .40
154 Dave Stieb .15 .40
155 Darryl Strawberry .15 .40
156 Evan Longoria .20 .50
157 Jason Varitek .25 .60
158 Roy Halladay .20 .50
159 Asdrubal Cabrera .20 .50
160 Tom Brunansky .15 .40
161 Mike Greenwell .15 .40
162 Lou Brock .20 .50
163 Rick Monday .15 .40
164 Alan Trammell .20 .50
165 Josh Reddick .15 .40
166 Gio Gonzalez .20 .50
167 Lance Parrish .15 .40
168 Buster Posey .30 .75
169 Bill Madlock .15 .40
170 Kris Medlen .20 .50
171 Andre Thornton .15 .40
172 Mickey Tettleton .15 .40
173 Pablo Sandoval .20 .50
174 Rob Dibble .15 .40
175 Bill Buckner .15 .40
176 Ken Griffey Jr. .50 1.25
177 Zack Wheeler RC .50 1.25
178 Brooks Robinson .20 .50
179 Carlos Gonzalez .20 .50
180 Pedro Martinez .20 .50
181 Gary Pettis .15 .40
182 Jesse Barfield .15 .40
183 Tino Martinez .20 .50
184 Oscar Gamble .15 .40
185 Ben Sheets .15 .40
186 Tim Salmon .15 .40
187 Stephen Strasburg .25 .60
188 Chris Perez .15 .40
189 David Ortiz .25 .60
190 Bernie Williams .20 .50
191 Randy Johnson .25 .60
192 Tommy Lasorda .20 .50
193 Dave Stewart .15 .40
194 Skip Schumaker .15 .40
195 Manny Machado RC 1.50 4.00
196 Garry Templeton .15 .40
197 Glenn Davis .15 .40
198 Tony La Russa .20 .50
199 Adam Jones .20 .50
200 Reggie Jackson .20 .50
201 Bo Jackson .25 .60
202 Reggie Jackson .20 .50
203 Andy Pettitte .20 .50
204 Giancarlo Stanton .25 .60
205 Troy Tulowitzki .25 .60
206 Huston Street .15 .40
207 Larry Bowa .15 .40
208 Mark Lemke .15 .40
209 Jason Heyward .20 .50
210 Lance Berkman .20 .50
211 Robin Ventura .15 .40
212 Wally Joyner .15 .40
213 Bryce Harper .40 1.00
214 Frank Viola .15 .40
215 Kevin Youkilis .15 .40
216 Kevin Seitzer .15 .40
217 Juan Pierre .15 .40
218 Bob Horner .15 .40
219 Todd Helton .20 .50
220 Yovani Gallardo .15 .40
221 Fred McGriff .20 .50
222 David Wright .20 .50
223 Steve Finley .15 .40
224 Mike Trout 2.00 5.00
225 Jake Peavy .15 .40
226 Kevin Gausman RC .75 2.00
227 Mike Hargrove .15 .40
228 Jim Sundberg .15 .40
229 Dwight Gooden .15 .40
230 Goose Gossage .20 .50
231 Luis Gonzalez .15 .40
232 Davey Lopes .15 .40
233 Matt Moore .20 .50
234 Mike Mussina .20 .50
235 Rusty Greer .15 .40
236 Gary Sheffield .15 .40
237 Jose Bautista .20 .50
238 Eric Davis .15 .40
239 Tom Browning .15 .40
240 Joe Girardi .20 .50
241 Carlton Fisk .20 .50
242 Albert Pujols .30 .75
243 Mark Grace .20 .50
244 Justin Morneau .20 .50
245 Garrett Jones .15 .40
246 Jay Buhner .15 .40
247 Ben Zobrist .20 .50
248 Vinny Castilla .15 .40
249 Jean Segura .20 .50
250 Harold Baines .20 .50
251 Hyun-Jin Ryu RC .60 1.50
252 Willie McGee .15 .40
253 Clayton Kershaw .40 1.00
254 Edwin Encarnacion .25 .60
255 Paul Konerko .20 .50
256 Dickie Thon .15 .40
257 Marc Rzepczynski .15 .40
258 Fergie Jenkins .20 .50
259 Jeff Montgomery .15 .40
260 Miguel Cabrera .25 .60
261 Yasiel Puig SP 3.00 8.00
262 Jurickson Profar SP 1.00 2.50
263 Wil Myers SP 1.25 3.00
264 Mike Zunino SP 1.25 3.00
265 Dylan Bundy SP 2.00 5.00
266 Evan Gattis SP 1.50 4.00
267 Gerrit Cole SP 5.00 12.00
268 Zack Wheeler SP 1.50 4.00
269 Manny Machado SP 5.00 12.00
270 Shelby Miller SP 2.00 5.00
271 Mark Grace SP 1.00 2.50
272 Fred McGriff SP 1.00 2.50
273 Frank Robinson SP 1.00 2.50
274 Curt Schilling SP 1.00 2.50
275 Greg Maddux SP 1.50 4.00
276 Carlton Fisk SP 1.00 2.50
277 John Franco SP .75 2.00
278 Roberto Alomar SP 1.00 2.50
279 Ellis Burks SP .75 2.00
280 Prince Fielder SP 1.00 2.50
281 Nolan Ryan SP 4.00 10.00
282 James Shields SP .75 2.00
283 Bo Jackson SP 1.25 3.00
284 Dave Stewart SP .75 2.00
285 Josh Beckett SP .75 2.00
286 CC Sabathia SP 1.00 2.50
287 Jack Morris SP 1.00 2.50
288 Dave Kingman SP .75 2.00
289 Wade Boggs SP 1.00 2.50
290 Rickey Henderson SP 1.25 3.00
291 Pete Rose SP 2.50 6.00
292 Neil Walker SP .75 2.00
293 Steve Garvey SP .75 2.00
294 Matt Williams SP .75 2.00
295 Randy Johnson SP 1.25 3.00
296 Lee Smith SP .75 2.00
297 James Loney SP 1.00 2.50
298 Will Clark SP 1.00 2.50
299 Paul Molitor SP 1.25 3.00
300 Andre Dawson SP 1.00 2.50

2013 Hometown Heroes States

*STATE VET: 1.5X TO 4X BASIC
*STATE RC: 1X TO 2.5X BASIC RC
*STATE SP: .4X TO 1X BASIC SP

2013 Hometown Heroes Zip Code

*ZIP VET: 2.5X TO 6X BASIC
*ZIP RC: 1.5X TO 4X BASIC RC
*ZIP SP: .5X TO 1.2X BASIC SP

2013 Hometown Heroes Calling the Shots

1 Don Mattingly 2.00 5.00
2 Joe Girardi .75 2.00
3 Joe Torre .60 1.50
4 Lou Piniella .40 1.00
5 Tommy Lasorda .75 2.00
6 Kirk Gibson .40 1.00
7 Whitey Herzog .40 1.00
8 Terry Francona .60 1.50
9 Ozzie Guillen .60 1.50
10 Tony La Russa .75 2.00
11 Tony La Russa .75 2.00
12 Robin Ventura .60 1.50

2013 Hometown Heroes Calling the Shots Black

*BLACK: 1X TO 2.5X BASIC

2013 Hometown Heroes Calling the Shots Gold

*GOLD: .75X TO 2X BASIC
1 Don Mattingly 12.00 30.00

2013 Hometown Heroes City Hall

1 Frank Viola .60 1.50
2 Jim Sundberg .60 1.50
3 Randy Johnson 1.00 2.50
4 Jim Rice .75 2.00
5 Juan Samuel .60 1.50
6 John Franco .60 1.50
7 Jose Rijo .60 1.50
8 Rick Dempsey .60 1.50
9 Dale Murphy 1.00 2.50
10 Willie Wilson .60 1.50
11 Andres Galarraga .60 1.50
12 Tony Gwynn 1.00 2.50
13 Nolan Ryan 3.00 8.00
14 Kent Hrbek .60 1.50
15 Andre Thornton .60 1.50

2013 Hometown Heroes City Hall Black

*BLACK: 1X TO 2.5X BASIC

2013 Hometown Heroes City Hall Gold

*GOLD: .75X TO 2X BASIC

2013 Hometown Heroes City Hall Signatures

EXCHANGE DEADLINE 4/2/2015
1 Gary Gaetti 4.00 10.00
2 Tony Fernandez 4.00 10.00
3 Kent Hrbek 4.00 10.00
5 John Kruk 6.00 15.00
6 Mookie Wilson 4.00 10.00
7 Eric Davis 6.00 15.00
8 Mike Boddicker 4.00 10.00
9 Andre Thornton 4.00 10.00
10 Craig Biggio 12.00 30.00

2013 Hometown Heroes Curtain Call

1 Luis Gonzalez .60 1.50
2 Joe Carter .60 1.50
3 Kerry Wood .60 1.50
4 Josh Hamilton .75 2.00
5 Shawn Green .60 1.50
6 Justin Verlander 1.00 2.50
7 Nolan Ryan 3.00 8.00
8 Rickey Henderson 1.00 2.50
9 Pete Rose 2.00 5.00
10 Kirk Gibson .40 1.00
11 Derek Jeter 2.50 6.00
12 David Freese .60 1.50
13 Ryne Sandberg 2.00 5.00
14 Reggie Jackson .75 2.00
15 Cal Ripken Jr. 3.00 8.00

2013 Hometown Heroes Curtain Call Black

*BLACK: 1X TO 2.5X BASIC

2013 Hometown Heroes Curtain Call Gold

*GOLD: .75X TO 2X BASIC

2013 Hometown Heroes Defining Moments

1 Mike Piazza 1.00 2.50
2 Derek Jeter 2.50 6.00
3 Stephen Strasburg 1.00 2.50
4 Mike Trout 8.00 20.00
5 Ernie Banks 1.00 2.50
6 Ken Griffey Jr. 2.00 5.00
7 Dwight Gooden .60 1.50
8 Andre Dawson .75 2.00
9 Cal Ripken Jr. 3.00 8.00
10 Edgar Martinez .60 1.50
11 Ichiro 1.25 3.00
12 Curt Schilling .75 2.00
13 David Freese .60 1.50
14 Mookie Wilson .60 1.50
15 Yu Darvish 1.00 2.50
16 Bryce Harper 1.50 4.00
17 Matt Harvey .75 2.00
18 David Ortiz 1.00 2.50
19 Brandon Phillips .60 1.50
20 Troy Tulowitzki 1.00 2.50

2013 Hometown Heroes Defining Moments Black

*BLACK: 1X TO 2.5X BASIC

2013 Hometown Heroes Defining Moments Gold

*GOLD: .75X TO 2X BASIC

2013 Hometown Heroes Face of the Franchise Signatures

EXCHANGE DEADLINE 4/2/2015
1 Joe Mauer
2 Ernie Banks 20.00 50.00
3 Ozzie Smith
4 Nolan Ryan
5 David Wright
6 Frank Thomas 20.00 50.00
7 Alan Trammell 15.00 40.00
8 George Brett
9 Evan Longoria 12.50 30.00
10 Troy Tulowitzki

2013 Hometown Heroes Homegrown Heroes

1 Cal Ripken Jr. 3.00 8.00
2 Joe Mauer .75 2.00
3 Derek Jeter 2.50 6.00
4 Jorge Posada .75 2.00
5 Mariano Rivera 1.25 3.00
6 Al Kaline 1.00 2.50
7 Alan Trammell .75 2.00
8 Bernie Williams .75 2.00
9 Craig Biggio .75 2.00
10 Frank White .60 1.50
11 George Brett 2.00 5.00
12 Jim Palmer .75 2.00
13 Stan Musial 1.50 4.00
14 Tony Gwynn 1.00 2.50
15 Todd Helton .75 2.00
16 Chipper Jones 1.00 2.50
17 Mike Schmidt 1.50 4.00
18 Robin Yount 1.00 2.50

2013 Hometown Heroes Homegrown Heroes Black

*BLACK: 1X TO 2.5X BASIC

2013 Hometown Heroes Homegrown Heroes Gold

*GOLD: .75X TO 2X BASIC

2013 Hometown Heroes Hometown Signatures

EXCHANGE DEADLINE 4/2/2015
HRJS Juan Samuel 4.00 10.00
HSAG Andres Galarraga 10.00 25.00
HSAV Andy Van Slyke 6.00 15.00
HSBB Bill Buckner 5.00 12.00
HSBE Buddy Bell 4.00 10.00
HSBS Ben Sheets 4.00 10.00
HSBT Bobby Thigpen 4.00 10.00
HSCR Jose Cruz 4.00 10.00
HSCS Curt Schilling
HSDA Darryl Strawberry 4.00 10.00
HSDB Dylan Bundy 10.00 25.00
HSDE David Eckstein 4.00 10.00
HSDL Davey Lopes 4.00 10.00
HSDM David Murphy 4.00 10.00
HSDS Dave Stewart 4.00 10.00
HSDS Dave Stieb 6.00 15.00
HSDT Dickie Thon 4.00 10.00
HSDW Dwayne Murphy 6.00 15.00
HSDY Lenny Dykstra 4.00 10.00
HSEB Ellis Burks 4.00 10.00
HSEV Evan Gattis 4.00 10.00
HSFW Frank White 4.00 10.00
HSGA Garry Templeton 4.00 10.00
HSGD Glenn Davis 4.00 10.00
HSGG Greg Gagne 4.00 10.00
HSGP Gary Pettis 4.00 10.00
HSGT Gorman Thomas 4.00 10.00
HSHB Harold Baines 8.00 20.00
HSHR Harold Reynolds 4.00 10.00
HSJA Jack Clark 5.00 12.00
HSJB Jesse Barfield 4.00 10.00
HSJB Jay Buhner 4.00 10.00
HSJD Jody Davis 4.00 10.00
HSJE Jeff Conine 4.00 10.00
HSJM Jeff Montgomery 4.00 10.00
HSJO Joe Charboneau 6.00 15.00
HSJP Jorge Posada 10.00 25.00
HSJP Jurickson Profar 4.00 10.00
HSJR Johnny Ray 4.00 10.00
HSJT John Tudor 4.00 10.00
HSJW Jerome Walton 4.00 10.00
HSKG Kevin Gausman 4.00 10.00
HSKH Kent Hrbek 4.00 10.00
HSKM Keith Moreland 4.00 10.00
HSKM Kevin Mitchell 4.00 10.00
HSKS Kevin Seitzer 5.00 12.00
HSLB Larry Bowa 4.00 10.00
HSLD Leon Durham 4.00 10.00
HSLM Lee Mazzilli 4.00 10.00
HSLP Lou Piniella 4.00 10.00
HSLP Lance Parrish 6.00 15.00
HSMG Mike Greenwell 4.00 10.00
HSMG Mark Grace 4.00 10.00
HSMH Mike Hargrove 4.00 10.00
HSMK Mike Krukow 4.00 10.00
HSML Mark Lemke 4.00 10.00
HSMM Mike Mussina 40.00 80.00
HSMM Manny Machado 20.00 50.00
HSMS Mike Scott 4.00 10.00
HSMT Mickey Tettleton 5.00 12.00
HSMW Matt Williams 4.00 10.00
HSMZ Mike Zunino 4.00 10.00
HSOG Oscar Gamble 4.00 10.00
HSOZ Ozzie Guillen 4.00 10.00
HSPL Paul Lo Duca 4.00 10.00
HSPO Paul O'Neill
HSPT Pat Tabler 4.00 10.00
HSRD Rob Deer 6.00 15.00
HSRD Ron Darling 4.00 10.00
HSRI Jose Rijo 8.00 20.00
HSRI Rick Dempsey 4.00 10.00
HSRO Rob Dibble 4.00 10.00
HSRS Ruben Sierra 4.00 10.00
HSSA Steve Avery 8.00 20.00
HSSD Shawon Dunston 4.00 10.00
HSSG Steve Garvey 6.00 15.00
HSSM Shelby Miller
HSSU Jim Sundberg 5.00 12.00
HSSY Steve Yeager 4.00 10.00
HSTB Tom Brunansky 4.00 10.00
HSTE Terry Pendleton 4.00 10.00
HSTL Tony La Russa 5.00 12.00
HSTO Tom Browning 6.00 15.00
HSTP Tony Pena
HSTS Tim Salmon 6.00 15.00
HSVC Vinny Castilla 4.00 10.00
HSVC Vince Coleman 4.00 10.00
HSWC Will Clark 15.00 40.00
HSWL Wil Myers 6.00 15.00
HSWM Willie McGee 15.00 40.00
HSWW Willie Wilson 4.00 10.00
HSZA Zoilo Almonte 20.00 50.00

2013 Hometown Heroes Left Their Marks Autographs

EXCHANGE DEADLINE 4/2/2015
1 Rick Monday 4.00 10.00
2 Kerry Wood 4.00 10.00
3 Curt Schilling
4 Ozzie Smith
5 John Franco 4.00 10.00
6 Luis Gonzalez 4.00 10.00
7 Roger Clemens
8 Nolan Ryan 50.00 100.00
9 Bucky Dent 4.00 10.00
10 Bob Horner 4.00 10.00

2013 Hometown Heroes Nicknames

1 Ryne Sandberg 2.00 5.00
2 Dwight Gooden .60 1.50
3 Dave Parker .60 1.50
4 Ken Griffey Jr. 2.00 5.00
5 Mike Trout 8.00 20.00
6 Felix Hernandez .75 2.00
7 Ron Cey .60 1.50
8 Nolan Ryan 3.00 8.00
9 Orel Hershiser .60 1.50
10 Lance Berkman .75 2.00
11 Roger Clemens 1.25 3.00
12 Andre Dawson .75 2.00
13 Fernando Valenzuela .60 1.50
14 Jose Bautista .75 2.00
15 Michael Morse .60 1.50
16 Shane Victorino .75 2.00
17 Ozzie Smith 1.25 3.00
18 Roy Halladay .75 2.00
19 Derek Jeter 2.50 6.00
20 Rickey Henderson 1.00 2.50

2013 Hometown Heroes Nicknames Black

*BLACK: 1X TO 2.5X BASIC
4 Ken Griffey Jr. 8.00 20.00

2013 Hometown Heroes Nicknames Gold

*GOLD: .75X TO 2X BASIC

2013 Hometown Heroes Rivalry

1 Johnny Damon .75 2.00
2 Wade Boggs .75 2.00
3 Roger Clemens 1.25 3.00
4 Dave Kingman .60 1.50
5 Yogi Berra 1.00 2.50
6 Dwight Gooden .60 1.50
7 Lee Mazzilli .60 1.50
8 Gary Sheffield .60 1.50
9 Darryl Strawberry .60 1.50
10 Steve Stone .60 1.50
11 Andy Van Slyke .60 1.50
12 Lou Brock .75 2.00
13 Leon Durham .60 1.50
14 Lee Smith .60 1.50
15 Dusty Baker .60 1.50
16 Robin Ventura .60 1.50
17 Orel Hershiser .60 1.50
18 Lenny Dykstra .60 1.50
19 Tommy John .60 1.50
20 Don Sutton .60 1.50

2013 Hometown Heroes Rivalry Black

*BLACK: 1X TO 2.5X BASIC

2013 Hometown Heroes Rivalry Gold

*GOLD: .75X TO 2X BASIC

2013 Hometown Heroes Scripted Legacy

EXCHANGE DEADLINE 4/2/2015
1 Cal Ripken Jr. 75.00 150.00
2 Ryne Sandberg
3 Barry Larkin 12.00 30.00
4 George Brett 60.00 120.00
5 Paul Molitor
6 Tom Seaver
7 Reggie Jackson
8 Rickey Henderson 50.00 120.00
9 Mike Schmidt
10 Tony Gwynn

2013 Hometown Heroes Signed by the Enemy

EXCHANGE DEADLINE 4/2/2015
1 Johnny Damon
2 Lou Brock
3 Lenny Dykstra 4.00 10.00
4 Dave Kingman 4.00 10.00
5 Josh Hamilton 20.00 50.00
6 Wade Boggs
8 Bruce Sutter 8.00 20.00
9 Roger Clemens

2013 Hometown Heroes Sport Discs

1 Stephen Strasburg 2.00 5.00
2 Mike Trout 15.00 40.00
3 Bryce Harper 3.00 8.00
4 Yu Darvish 2.00 5.00
5 Justin Verlander 2.00 5.00
6 Derek Jeter 5.00 12.00
7 Mariano Rivera 2.50 6.00
8 Robinson Cano 1.50 4.00
9 Albert Pujols 2.50 6.00
10 Troy Tulowitzki 2.00 5.00
11 Evan Longoria 1.50 4.00
12 Matt Harvey 1.50 4.00
13 Matt Kemp 1.50 4.00
14 Justin Upton 1.50 4.00
15 Buster Posey 2.50 6.00
16 David Wright 1.50 4.00
17 Andrew McCutchen 2.00 5.00
18 Joe Mauer 1.50 4.00
19 Clayton Kershaw 3.00 8.00
20 Jean Segura 1.50 4.00
21 Jose Bautista 1.50 4.00
22 Prince Fielder 1.50 4.00
23 Miguel Cabrera 2.00 5.00
24 Brandon Phillips 1.25 3.00
25 Dustin Pedroia 2.00 5.00
26 Shelby Miller 3.00 8.00
27 Carlos Gonzalez 1.50 4.00
28 Albert Pujols 2.50 6.00
29 Ichiro 2.50 6.00
30 Alex Rodriguez 2.50 6.00
31 Randy Johnson 2.00 5.00
32 Chipper Jones 2.00 5.00
33 Cal Ripken Jr. 6.00 15.00
34 Roger Clemens 2.50 6.00
35 Jason Varitek 2.00 5.00
36 Ryne Sandberg 4.00 10.00
37 Kerry Wood 1.25 3.00
38 Frank Thomas 2.00 5.00
39 Denny McLain 1.25 3.00
40 Craig Biggio 1.50 4.00
41 Bo Jackson 2.00 5.00
42 Jim Abbott 1.25 3.00
43 Bill Buckner 1.25 3.00
44 Tommy Lasorda 1.50 4.00
45 Jurickson Profar 1.50 4.00
46 Dave Kingman 1.25 3.00
47 Don Mattingly 4.00 10.00
48 Paul O'Neill 1.50 4.00
49 Rickey Henderson 2.00 5.00
50 Manny Machado 8.00 20.00
51 John Kruk 1.25 3.00
52 Tony Gwynn 2.00 5.00
53 Will Clark 1.50 4.00
54 Yasiel Puig 6.00 15.00
55 Ken Griffey Jr. 4.00 10.00
56 Lou Brock 1.50 4.00
57 Wil Myers 2.00 5.00
58 Nolan Ryan 6.00 15.00
59 Robin Ventura 1.25 3.00
60 Hyun-Jin Ryu 3.00 8.00

1947 Homogenized Bond

The cards in this 48-card set measure approximately 2 1/4" by 3 1/2". The 1947 W571/D305 Homogenized Bread are sets of unnumbered cards containing 44 baseball players and four boxers. The W571 set exists in two styles. Style one is identical to the D305 set except for the back printing while style two has perforated edges and movie stars depicted on the backs. The second style of W571 cards contains only 13 cards. The four boxers in the checklist below are indicated by BOX. The checklist below is ordered alphabetically. There are 24 cards in the set which were definitely produced in greater supply. These 24 (marked by DP below) are quite a bit more common than the other 24 cards in the set.

COMPLETE SET 500.00 1000.00
1 Rex Barney 6.00 12.00
2 Yogi Berra 100.00 200.00
3 Ewell Blackwell DP 1.00 2.00
4 Lou Boudreau DP 2.50 5.00
5 Ralph Branca 6.00 12.00
6 Harry Brecheen DP 1.00 2.00
9 Dom DiMaggio 7.50 15.00
10 Joe DiMaggio 125.00 250.00
11 Bobby Doerr DP 2.50 5.00
12 Bruce Edwards 6.00 12.00
13 Bob Elliott DP 1.00 2.00
14 Del Ennis DP 1.00 2.00
15 Bob Feller DP 6.00 12.00
16 Carl Furillo 10.00 20.00
17 Joe Gordon DP 1.00 2.00
18 Sid Gordon 6.00 12.00
19 Joe Hatten 6.00 12.00
20 Gil Hodges 40.00 80.00
21 Tommy Holmes DP 1.00 2.00
22 Larry Jansen 6.00 12.00
23 Sheldon Jones 6.00 12.00
24 Edwin Joost 6.00 12.00
25 Charlie Keller 7.50 15.00
26 Ken Keltner DP 1.00 2.00
27 Buddy Kerr 6.00 12.00
28 Ralph Kiner DP 4.00 8.00
30 John Lindell 6.00 12.00
31 Whitey Lockman 6.00 12.00
33 Willard Marshall 6.00 12.00
34 Johnny Mize DP 4.00 8.00
35 Stan Musial DP 25.00 50.00
36 Andy Pafko DP 1.00 2.00
37 Johnny Pesky DP 1.00 2.00
38 Pee Wee Reese 30.00 60.00
39 Phil Rizzuto DP 6.00 12.00
40 Aaron Robinson DP 1.00 2.00
41 Jackie Robinson DP 40.00 80.00
42 John Sain DP 2.50 5.00
43 Enos Slaughter DP 4.00 8.00
44 Vern Stephens DP 1.00 2.00
45 Birdie Tebbetts 6.00 12.00
46 Bobby Thomson 7.50 15.00
47 Johnny VanderMeer 7.50 15.00
48 Ted Williams DP 25.00 50.00

1927 Honey Boy Ice Cream

These 21 cards, which measure approximately 1 5/8" by 2 /38" feature a mix of major and minor league players.Honey Boy was a Canadian product. Some collectors refer to this set as the "Purity" set since that was the specific brand that these cards were inserted in. The first half of this set is dedicated to Canadian players while the second half is devoted to major leaguers. The cards were redeemable for a "brick" of Honey Boy Ice Cream. When all 21 cards were accumulated and sent in, the cards were then given a punch hole and returned to the lucky collector along with the brick.

COMPLETE SET (21) 7000.00 14000.00
COMMON MINORS (1-9) 150.00 300.00
COMMON MAJORS (10-21) 400.00 800.00
1 Steamer Maxwell Arenas 150.00 300.00
2 Cecil Brown Dominion Express 150.00 300.00
3 Carson McVey Transcona 150.00 300.00
4 Sam Perlman Tigers 150.00 300.00
5 Snake Siddle Arenas 150.00 300.00
6 Eddie Cass Columbus 150.00 300.00
7 Jimmy Bradley Columbus 150.00 300.00
8 Gordon Caslake Dominion Express 150.00 300.00
9 Ward McVey Tigers 150.00 300.00
10 Tris Speaker 750.00 1500.00
11 George Sisler 750.00 1500.00
12 Emil Meusel 400.00 800.00
13 Edd Roush 600.00 1200.00
14 Babe Ruth 1500.00 3000.00
15 Harry Heilmann 600.00 1200.00
16 Heinie Groh 400.00 800.00
17 Eddie Collins 750.00 1500.00
18 Grover Alexander 750.00 1500.00
19 Dave Bancroft 600.00 1200.00
20 Frank Frisch 750.00 1500.00
21 George Burns 400.00 800.00

2017 Honus Bonus Fantasy Baseball

PRINTING PLATES RANDOMLY INSERTED
PLATE PRINT RUN 1 SET PER COLOR
BLACK-CYAN-MAGENTA-YELLOW ISSUED
NO PLATE PRICING DUE TO SCARCITY
1 Kyle Schwarber .40 1.00
2 Chris Archer .25 .60
3 Mallex Smith .25 .60
4 Gary Sanchez .40 1.00
5 Nolan Arenado .60 1.50
6 Bryce Harper .60 1.50
7 Jose Abreu .40 1.00
8 Clayton Kershaw .60 1.50
9 Angel Pagan .25 .60
10 Steve Cishek .25 .60
11 Yasmani Grandal .25 .60
12 Tony Watson .25 .60
13 Scott Schebler .30 .75
14 Zach Duke .25 .60
15 Aledmys Diaz .30 .75
16 Johnny Cueto .30 .75
17 Domingo Santana .30 .75
18 Adonis Garcia .25 .60
19 Fernando Rodney .25 .60
20 Yoenis Cespedes .40 1.00
21 Huston Street .25 .60
22 Leonys Martin .25 .60
23 Mike Fiers .25 .60
24 Ben Zobrist .30 .75
25 Lucas Giolito .30 .75
26 Michael Bourn .25 .60
27 Patrick Corbin .30 .75
28 Alex Dickerson .25 .60
29 Justin Bour .30 .75
30 Sandy Leon .25 .60
31 Justin Upton .30 .75
32 Derek Law .25 .60
33 Khris Davis .40 1.00
34 Michael Pineda .25 .60
35 Jake Smolinski .25 .60
36 Trevor Story .40 1.00
37 Archie Bradley .25 .60
38 Josh Bell .60 1.50
39 Tim Adleman .25 .60
40 Ian Desmond .25 .60
41 Ryan Dull .25 .60
42 Wilson Ramos .25 .60
43 Joey Rickard .25 .60
44 Luis Cessa .25 .60
45 Chase Utley .30 .75
46 Adeiny Hechavarria .25 .60
47 Max Scherzer .40 1.00
48 Lorenzo Cain .25 .60
49 Jason Castro .25 .60
50 Michael Fulmer .25 .60
51 Norichika Aoki .25 .60
52 Ryon Healy .30 .75
53 Vince Velasquez .25 .60
54 Billy Hamilton .30 .75
55 Robinson Cano .30 .75
56 Marcus Semien .40 1.00
57 James Shields .25 .60
58 Matt Holliday .40 1.00
59 Scott Kazmir .25 .60
60 Daniel Descalso .25 .60
61 Wade Davis .25 .60
62 Billy Butler .25 .60
63 Zach Britton .30 .75
64 Roman Quinn .25 .60
65 Jason Grilli .25 .60
66 Tucker Barnhart .25 .60
67 David Wright .30 .75
68 Albert Almora Jr. .25 .60
69 Devin Mesoraco .25 .60
70 Aaron Sanchez .30 .75
71 Rougned Odor .30 .75
72 Kendall Graveman .25 .60
73 Jacoby Ellsbury .30 .75
74 Tyler Thornburg .25 .60
75 Daniel Murphy .30 .75
76 Neftali Feliz .25 .60
77 Tim Anderson .40 1.00
78 Tanner Roark .25 .60
79 Greg Bird .30 .75
80 Ken Giles .25 .60
81 Hernan Perez .25 .60
82 Deolis Guerra .25 .60
83 Eddie Rosario .30 .75
84 Omar Narvaez .30 .75
85 Brett Gardner .30 .75
86 Jose Reyes .30 .75
87 Johnny Giavotella .25 .60
88 Ben Revere .25 .60
89 Manny Machado .40 1.00
90 Brandon Nimmo .30 .75
91 Brian Dozier .40 1.00
92 Buster Posey .50 1.25
93 Asdrubal Cabrera .30 .75
94 Hyun Soo Kim .30 .75
95 Eduardo Escobar .25 .60
96 Rafael Ortega .25 .60
97 Jeurys Familia .30 .75
98 Jose Peraza .30 .75
99 Bryan Shaw .25 .60
100 Paul Goldschmidt .40 1.00
101 Robbie Ross, Jr. .25 .60
102 Kole Calhoun .25 .60
103 Chris Sale .40 1.00
104 Jorge Soler .40 1.00
105 Rob Refsnyder .25 .60
106 Sergio Romo .25 .60
107 Tyler Naquin .40 1.00
108 Luis Severino .30 .75
109 Danny Espinosa .25 .60
110 Jefry Marte .25 .60
111 Kevin Pillar .25 .60
112 Evan Gattis .25 .60
113 Carlos Gomez .25 .60
114 Kolten Wong .30 .75
115 Ender Inciarte .25 .60
116 Nick Tropeano .25 .60
117 Jonathan Villar .25 .60
118 Julio Teheran .30 .75
119 Kris Bryant .50 1.25
120 Andrew McCutchen .40 1.00
121 Francisco Rodriguez .30 .75
122 Orlando Arcia .40 1.00
123 Kevin Gausman .40 1.00
124 Adam Duvall .30 .75
125 Adrian Beltre .40 1.00
126 Arodys Vizcaino .25 .60
127 Brian McCann .30 .75
128 Adam Wainwright .30 .75
129 Ryan Schimpf .25 .60
130 Danny Salazar .30 .75
131 Mike Zunino .25 .60
132 Julio Urias .40 1.00
133 Eugenio Suarez .30 .75
134 Steven Wright .25 .60
135 Mike Moustakas .30 .75
136 Carlos Gonzalez .30 .75
137 Pedro Baez .25 .60
138 Michael Conforto .30 .75
139 Matt Moore .30 .75
140 Scooter Gennett .30 .75
141 Kevin Kiermaier .30 .75
142 Yoan Moncada .75 2.00
143 Jay Bruce .30 .75
144 Yangervis Solarte .25 .60
145 Miguel Sano .30 .75
146 Jett Bandy .25 .60
147 Chad Bettis .25 .60
148 Cameron Maybin .25 .60
149 Erasmo Ramirez .25 .60
150 Javier Baez .50 1.25
151 Jordan Zimmermann .30 .75
152 Jorge Polanco .30 .75
153 Russell Martin .25 .60
154 Hector Santiago .25 .60
155 Charlie Blackmon .40 1.00
156 Francisco Lindor .40 1.00
157 Danny Valencia .30 .75
158 Chris Carter .25 .60
159 Adam Frazier .25 .60
160 Mauricio Cabrera .25 .60

161 Nomar Mazara .25 .60
162 Mike Leake .25 .60
163 Maikel Franco .30 .75
164 Andrelton Simmons .25 .60
165 Michael Lorenzen .25 .60
166 Corey Seager .40 1.00
167 Trevor Plouffe .25 .60
168 Collin McHugh .25 .60
169 Nick Markakis .30 .75
170 Sean Manaea .25 .60
171 Adrian Gonzalez .30 .75
172 Ichiro .50 1.25
173 Brian Ellington .25 .60
174 Yonder Alonso .25 .60
175 Joey Gallo .30 .75
176 Byron Buxton .40 1.00
177 Jhonny Peralta .25 .60
178 Adam Conley .25 .60
179 Matt Duffy .25 .60
180 Carson Fulmer .25 .60
181 Alex Bregman 1.25 3.00
182 Brett Lawrie .30 .75
183 Marco Estrada .25 .60
184 Addison Russell .40 1.00
185 Gerardo Parra .25 .60
186 Dallas Keuchel .30 .75
187 Jackie Bradley Jr. .40 1.00
188 Junior Guerra .25 .60
189 Carlos Correa .40 1.00
190 Rubby De La Rosa .25 .60
191 Carlos Santana .30 .75
192 Anthony DeSclafani .25 .60
193 Stephen Piscotty .30 .75
194 Mike Foltynewicz .25 .60
195 Ian Kinsler .30 .75
196 Carlos Carrasco .25 .60
197 Howie Kendrick .25 .60
198 Jameson Taillon .30 .75
199 Jayson Werth .30 .75
200 Rick Porcello .30 .75
201 Jose Altuve .30 .75
202 Ryan Zimmerman .30 .75
203 Jerad Eickhoff .25 .60
204 Freddie Freeman .50 1.25
205 Danny Duffy .25 .60
206 Devon Travis .25 .60
207 Jake Diekman .25 .60
208 Manuel Margot .25 .60
209 Jose De Leon .25 .60
210 Jason Kipnis .30 .75
211 Brad Brach .25 .60
212 Lucas Duda .30 .75
213 Hisashi Iwakuma .30 .75
214 A. J. Pollock .25 .60
215 Tony Cingrani .30 .75
216 Jace Peterson .25 .60
217 Dan Straily .25 .60
218 Justin Smoak .25 .60
219 DJ LeMahieu .40 1.00
220 Zack Cozart .25 .60
221 Jeff Samardzija .25 .60
222 J.D. Martinez .40 1.00
223 Melky Cabrera .25 .60
224 Hector Neris .25 .60
225 Robbie Grossman .25 .60
226 Andrew Cashner .25 .60
227 Jonathan Lucroy .30 .75
228 Josh Harrison .25 .60
229 Seung Hwan Oh .50 1.25
230 Raul Mondesi .30 .75
231 Will Harris .25 .60
232 Matt Adams .25 .60
233 Roberto Osuna .25 .60
234 Justin Morneau .30 .75
235 Dylan Bundy .30 .75
236 Yasmany Tomas .25 .60
237 Noah Syndergaard .30 .75
238 J.T. Realmuto .40 1.00
239 Clay Buchholz .25 .60
240 Mark Trumbo .25 .60
241 Jimmy Nelson .25 .60
242 Francisco Cervelli .25 .60
243 Colby Lewis .25 .60
244 David Dahl .30 .75
245 David Robertson .25 .60
246 Anthony Rendon .40 1.00
247 Wei-Yin Chen .25 .60
248 Hanley Ramirez .30 .75
249 Taijuan Walker .25 .60
250 Brandon Drury .25 .60
251 Alex Colome .25 .60
252 Adam Eaton .40 1.00
253 Luis Perdomo .25 .60
254 Jedd Gyorko .25 .60
255 Pedro Alvarez .25 .60
256 J.A. Happ .30 .75
257 Ryan Braun .30 .75
258 Tyler Anderson .25 .60
259 Elvis Andrus .30 .75
260 Jose Berrios .30 .75
261 Ryan Howard .30 .75
262 Kevin Siegrist .25 .60
263 Starlin Castro .25 .60
264 Edinson Volquez .25 .60
265 Xander Bogaerts .40 1.00
266 Randall Delgado .25 .60
267 Rajai Davis .25 .60
268 Jeremy Hellickson .25 .60
269 Justin Turner .40 1.00
270 Jose Iglesias .30 .75
271 Jon Lester .30 .75
272 Randal Grichuk .25 .60
273 Jake Barrett .25 .60
274 Jorge Alfaro .30 .75
275 Zach Davies .25 .60
276 Cesar Hernandez .25 .60
277 Cole Hamels .30 .75
278 Luis Valbuena .25 .60
279 Aroldis Chapman .40 1.00
280 Yasiel Puig .40 1.00
281 Dee Gordon .25 .60
282 Jacob deGrom .75 2.00
283 Stephen Vogt .30 .75
284 CC Sabathia .30 .75
285 Dexter Fowler .30 .75
286 Tony Barnette .25 .60
287 Jonathan Schoop .25 .60
288 Tyler Chatwood .25 .60
289 Cheslor Cuthbert .25 .60
290 Marcell Ozuna .40 1.00
291 Stephen Strasburg .40 1.00
292 Jon Jay .25 .60
293 Nelson Cruz .40 1.00
294 Luke Gregerson .25 .60
295 Chris Davis .25 .60
296 Ivan Nova .30 .75
297 Yulieski Gurriel .40 1.00
298 Brock Holt .25 .60
299 Chris Owings .25 .60
300 Denard Span .25 .60
301 Derek Norris .25 .60
302 Mike Napoli .25 .60
303 Welington Castillo .25 .60
304 Jason Hammel .30 .75
305 Steven Moya .25 .60
306 Kenley Jansen .30 .75
307 Seth Smith .25 .60
308 Zack Greinke .40 1.00
309 Edwin Encarnacion .40 1.00
310 Justin Wilson .25 .60
311 Austin Jackson .25 .60
312 Bartolo Colon .25 .60
313 Joey Votto .40 1.00
314 Masahiro Tanaka .30 .75
315 Jarrod Dyson .25 .60
316 Tony Wolters .25 .60
317 Martin Prado .25 .60
318 David Price .30 .75
319 Brad Miller .30 .75
320 Mike Trout 2.00 5.00
321 Jake Arrieta .30 .75
322 Travis Jankowski .25 .60
323 Robbie Ray .25 .60
324 Salvador Perez .30 .75
325 Matt Shoemaker .30 .75
326 Jed Lowrie .25 .60
327 Cam Bedrosian .25 .60
328 Miguel Montero .25 .60
329 Miguel Gonzalez .25 .60
330 Steven Souza .30 .75
331 Brad Hand .25 .60
332 David Freese .25 .60
333 Sam Dyson .25 .60
334 Victor Martinez .30 .75
335 Gerrit Cole .40 1.00
336 Trea Turner .30 .75
337 Ryan Pressly .25 .60
338 C. J. Cron .25 .60
339 Freddy Galvis .25 .60
340 Jung Ho Kang .25 .60
341 Tyler Flowers .25 .60
342 Brandon Moss .25 .60
343 Cameron Rupp .25 .60
344 Brandon Maurer .25 .60
345 Jose Bautista .30 .75
346 Ricky Nolasco .25 .60
347 Luis Sardinas .25 .60
348 Anthony Rizzo .50 1.25
349 Josh Reddick .25 .60
350 Jake Lamb .30 .75
351 Marcus Stroman .30 .75
352 Jeremy Hazelbaker .30 .75
353 Dellin Betances .30 .75
354 Jason Heyward .30 .75
355 Yu Darvish .40 1.00
356 Evan Longoria .30 .75
357 Nathan Eovaldi .30 .75
358 Troy Tulowitzki .40 1.00
359 Yordano Ventura SP 12.00 30.00
360 Willson Contreras .40 1.00
361 David Phelps .25 .60
362 George Springer .30 .75
363 Steven Matz .25 .60
364 Chris Young .25 .60
365 Carlos Rodon .40 1.00
366 Jean Segura .30 .75
367 Mike Clevinger .30 .75
368 Andrew Benintendi .75 2.00
369 Jake Odorizzi .25 .60
370 Chase Headley .25 .60
371 Chris Tillman .25 .60
372 Colby Rasmus .30 .75
373 Travis Shaw .25 .60
374 Pedro Strop .25 .60
375 Alex Gordon .30 .75
376 JaCoby Jones .30 .75
377 Aaron Nola .30 .75
378 Matt Kemp .30 .75
379 John Lackey .30 .75
380 Raimel Tapia .30 .75
381 Colin Rea .25 .60
382 Matt Carpenter .40 1.00
383 Trevor Bauer .50 1.25
384 Miguel Cabrera .40 1.00
385 Albert Pujols .50 1.25
386 Dansby Swanson .60 1.50
387 Jose Quintana .25 .60
388 Carlos Beltran .30 .75
389 Ryan Madson .25 .60
390 Gregory Polanco .30 .75
391 Blake Snell .30 .75
392 Josh Donaldson .30 .75
393 Corey Kluber .30 .75
394 Logan Forsythe .25 .60
395 Addison Reed .25 .60
396 Joe Mauer .30 .75
397 Giancarlo Stanton .40 1.00
398 Craig Kimbrel .30 .75
399 Keon Broxton .25 .60
400 Raisel Iglesias .30 .75
401 Dae-Ho Lee .40 1.00
402 Brandon Guyer .25 .60
403 Dustin Pedroia .40 1.00
404 Nick Castellanos .40 1.00
405 Joc Pederson .30 .75
406 Todd Frazier .25 .60
407 Lonnie Chisenhall .25 .60
408 Brandon Finnegan .25 .60
409 Kyle Seager .25 .60
410 Brandon Phillips .25 .60
411 Ross Stripling .25 .60
412 Hunter Pence .30 .75
413 Zach Eflin .25 .60
414 Yunel Escobar .25 .60
415 Kenta Maeda .30 .75
416 Avisail Garcia .30 .75
417 Mychal Givens .25 .60
418 Aaron Judge 3.00 8.00
419 Jaime Garcia .25 .60
420 Nick Hundley .25 .60
421 Brandon Kintzler .25 .60
422 Kendrys Morales .25 .60
423 Drew Pomeranz .30 .75
424 Odubel Herrera .30 .75
425 Matt Harvey .30 .75
426 Hunter Renfroe .30 .75
427 A. J. Ramos .25 .60
428 Corey Dickerson .25 .60
429 Mat Latos .30 .75
430 Didi Gregorius .30 .75
431 Mark Melancon .25 .60
432 Mitch Moreland .25 .60
433 Felix Hernandez .30 .75
434 Curtis Granderson .30 .75
435 Justin Verlander .40 1.00
436 Christian Yelich .50 1.25
437 Jake Thompson .25 .60
438 Starling Marte .30 .75
439 Blake Treinen .40 1.00
440 J.J. Hardy .25 .60
441 Matt Bowman .25 .60
442 Michael Saunders .30 .75
443 Boone Logan .25 .60
444 Franklin Gutierrez .25 .60
445 Carlos Martinez .30 .75
446 Neil Walker .25 .60
447 Sonny Gray .30 .75
448 Mookie Betts .75 2.00
449 Nate Jones .25 .60
450 Melvin Upton Jr. .30 .75
451 Taylor Rogers .40 1.00
452 Alcides Escobar .30 .75
453 Shae Simmons .25 .60
454 Travis d'Arnaud .30 .75
455 Jeanmar Gomez .25 .60
456 Adam Jones .30 .75
457 Felipe Rivero .30 .75
458 Brandon Belt .30 .75
459 Edwin Diaz .30 .75
460 Joe Panik .30 .75
461 Cody Allen .25 .60
462 Wilmer Flores .30 .75
463 Sean Doolittle .25 .60
464 Mark Reynolds .25 .60
465 Madison Bumgarner .30 .75
466 Tommy Joseph .40 1.00
467 Kelvin Herrera .25 .60
468 Ketel Marte .30 .75
469 James Paxton .30 .75
470 Paulo Orlando .25 .60
471 Rich Hill .25 .60
472 Jordy Mercer .25 .60
473 Hector Rondon .25 .60
474 Martin Maldonado .25 .60
475 Santiago Casilla .25 .60
476 Marwin Gonzalez .25 .60
477 Josh Tomlin .25 .60
478 Yadier Molina .50 1.25
479 Gio Gonzalez .30 .75
480 Brandon Crawford .30 .75
481 Christian Friedrich .25 .60
482 Eric Hosmer .30 .75
483 Kyle Hendricks .40 1.00
484 James McCann .30 .75
485 Ervin Santana .25 .60
486 Conor Gillaspie .30 .75
487 Jon Gray .25 .60
488 Max Kepler .30 .75
489 Hunter Strickland .25 .60
490 Tyler Austin .30 .75
491 Chase Anderson .25 .60
492 Austin Romine .25 .60
493 Ian Kennedy .25 .60
494 Jose Ramirez .30 .75
495 Wil Myers .30 .75
496 Jim Johnson .25 .60
497 Matt Wieters .40 1.00
498 Kyle Barraclough .25 .60
499 Kurt Suzuki .25 .60
500 Andrew Miller .30 .75

2017 Honus Bonus Fantasy Baseball Silver Foil

*SILVER FOIL: .5X TO 1.2X BASIC
RANDOM INSERTS IN PACKS

2017 Honus Bonus Fantasy Baseball Career Milestones

EACH CARD SERIAL #'d 1/1
PRINT RUNS B/WN 3-3030 COPIES PER
TOTAL PRINT RUNS LISTED BELOW
NO PRICING ON QTY 16 OR LESS
1 Adam Wainwright W/134* 2.50 6.00
2 Adrian Beltre HR/445* 2.50 6.00
3 Adrian Beltre H/2942* 2.00 5.00
4 Adrian Gonzalez HR/308* 2.00 5.00
5 Albert Pujols HR/591* 3.00 8.00
6 Albert Pujols H/2825* 2.50 6.00
7 Alex Bregman HR/8*
8 Alex Gordon HR/151* 2.50 6.00
9 Andrew McCutchen HR/175* 3.00 8.00
10 Andrew Miller SV/49* 4.00 10.00
11 Anthony Rizzo HR/134* 4.00 10.00
12 Aroldis Chapman SV/182* 3.00 8.00
13 Bartlolo Colon W/233* 2.00 5.00
14 Ben Zobrist HR/145* 2.50 6.00
15 Brandon Crawford HR/59* 3.00 8.00
16 Brian Dozier HR/117* 3.00 8.00
17 Bryce Harper HR/121* 5.00 12.00
18 Bryce Harper RBI/254* 5.00 12.00
19 Buster Posey HR/116* 4.00 10.00
20 Carlos Beltran HR/421* 2.00 5.00
21 Carlos Correa HR/42* 5.00 12.00
22 Carlos Gonzalez HR/201* 2.50 6.00
23 CC Sabathia W/223* 2.50 6.00
24 Chase Utley HR/250* 2.50 6.00
25 Chris Archer W/41* 3.00 8.00
26 Chris Davis HR/241* 2.00 5.00
27 Chris Sale W/74* 4.00 10.00
28 Christian Yelich HR/41* 6.00 15.00
29 Clayton Kershaw W/126* 5.00 12.00
30 Cole Hamels W/136* 2.50 6.00
31 Corey Kluber W/58* 3.00 8.00
32 Corey Seager HR/30* 5.00 12.00
33 Craig Kimbrel SV/256* 2.50 6.00
34 Curtis Granderson HR/293* 2.00 5.00
35 Daniel Murphy HR/87* 3.00 8.00
36 Dansby Swanson HR/3*
37 David Price W/121* 2.50 6.00
38 David Wright HR/242* 2.50 6.00
39 Dustin Pedrioa HR/133* 3.00 8.00
40 Edwin Encarnacion HR/310* 2.50 6.00
41 Eric Hosmer HR/102* 2.50 6.00
42 Evan Longoria HR/241* 2.50 6.00
43 Felix Hernandez W/154* 2.50 6.00
44 Francisco Lindor HR/27* 5.00 12.00
45 Francisco Rodriguez SV/430* 2.00 5.00
46 Freddie Freeman HR/138* 4.00 10.00
47 Gary Sanchez HR/20* 6.00 15.00
48 Giancarlo Stanton HR/208* 3.00 8.00
49 Hanley Ramirez HR/240* 2.50 6.00
50 Hunter Pence HR/207* 2.50 6.00
51 Ian Kinsler HR/212* 2.50 6.00
52 Ichiro HR/114* 4.00 10.00
53 Ichiro H/3030* 2.50 6.00
54 Jake Arrieta W/74* 3.00 8.00
55 Jake Lamb HR/39* 4.00 10.00
56 Jason Kipnis HR/76* 3.00 8.00
57 Jay Bruce HR/241* 2.50 6.00
58 Jayson Werth HR/219* 2.50 6.00
59 Joc Pederson HR/51* 3.00 8.00
60 Joe Mauer HR/130* 2.50 6.00
61 Joey Votto HR/221* 3.00 8.00
62 Jon Lester W/146* 2.50 6.00
63 Jose Abreu HR/91* 4.00 10.00
64 Jose Altuve HR/60* 3.00 8.00
65 Jose Bautista HR/308* 2.00 5.00
66 Josh Donaldson HR/141* 2.50 6.00
67 Justin Upton HR/221* 2.50 6.00
68 Justin Verlander W/173* 3.00 8.00
69 Kris Bryant HR/65* 5.00 12.00
70 Kyle Hendricks W/31* 5.00 12.00
71 Kyle Schwarber HR/16*
72 Kyle Seager HR/126* 2.00 5.00
73 Lorenzo Cain HR/42* 3.00 8.00
74 Madison Bumgarner W/100* 2.50 6.00
75 Maikel Franco HR/39* 4.00 10.00
76 Manny Machado HR/105* 3.00 8.00
77 Mark Trumbo HR/178* 2.00 5.00
78 Masahiro Tanaka W/39* 4.00 10.00
79 Matt Harvey W/29* 4.00 10.00
80 Matt Holliday HR/295* 2.50 6.00
81 Matt Kemp HR/240* 2.50 6.00
82 Max Scherzer W/125* 3.00 8.00
83 Miguel Cabrera HR/446* 2.50 6.00
84 Miguel Cabrera RBI/1180* 2.00 5.00
85 Mike Napoli HR/238* 2.00 5.00
86 Mike Trout HR/168* 15.00 40.00
87 Mike Trout RBI/384* 12.00 30.00
88 Mookie Betts HR/54* 8.00 20.00
89 Nelson Cruz HR/284* 2.50 6.00
90 Noah Syndergaard W/23* 5.00 12.00
91 Nolan Arenado HR/111* 5.00 12.00
92 Paul Goldschmidt HR/140* 3.00 8.00
93 Robinson Cano HR/278* 2.00 5.00
94 Ryan Braun HR/285* 2.00 5.00
95 Ryan Howard HR/382* 2.00 5.00
96 Ryan Zimmerman HR/215* 2.50 6.00
97 Stephen Strasburg W/69* 4.00 10.00
98 Tommy Joseph HR/21* 6.00 15.00
99 Trevor Story HR/27* 5.00 12.00
100 Troy Tulowitski HR/217* 3.00 8.00
101 Victor Martinez HR/227* 2.50 6.00
102 Wil Myers HR/55* 3.00 8.00
103 Xander Bogaerts HR/41* 5.00 12.00
104 Yadier Molina HR/108* 4.00 10.00
105 Yoenis Cespedes HR/137* 3.00 8.00
106 Yu Darvish W/46* 5.00 12.00
107 Zach Britton SV/120* 2.50 6.00
108 Zack Greinke W/155* 3.00 8.00

1905-10 Carl Horner Cabinets

These portraits, which measure an approximate 5 1/2" by 7" feature photographs which were also used in the W600 set or later in the T206 set. These are rarely seen in the secondary market and since several cards were discovered recently, it is believed that there should be many additions to this checklists. Since these are unnumbered, we have sequenced them in alphabetical order.

COMPLETE SET 30000.00 60000.00
1 Doug Altizer
2 Nick Altrock 1000.00 2000.00
3 Frank Arrelanes 1000.00 2000.00
4 Harry Barton 1000.00 2000.00
5 Jake Beckley 2000.00 4000.00
6 Heinie Berger
7 Frank Bowerman
8 Dave Brain
9 Bill Bradley
10 Kitty Bransfield
11 Roger Bresnahan 2000.00 4000.00
12 Ray Collins
13 Jack Cronin
14 Bill Dahlen 1000.00 2000.00
15 Don Daub 1000.00 2000.00
16 Frank Delahanty
17 Red Dooin
18 Pat Donahue
19 Mickey Doolan
20 Fred Dunlap
21 Kid Elberfeld 1000.00 2000.00
22 Rube Ellis 1000.00 2000.00
23 Dave Foutz MG 1000.00 2000.00
24 Billy Gilbert 1000.00 2000.00
25 Danny Green 1000.00 2000.00
26 John Grim 1000.00 2000.00
27 Mike Griffin 1000.00 2000.00
28 Otto Hess 1000.00 2000.00
29 Tom Jones
30 Addie Joss 2500.00 5000.00
31 Brickyard Kennedy 1000.00 2000.00
32 Red Kleinow
33 Harry Krause
34 Rube Kroh 1000.00 2000.00
35 Nap Lajoie
36 Tommy Leach
37 Lefty Leifeld
38 Bris Lord
39 Sherry Magee
40 George McBride
41 Dan McGann
42 Joe McGinnity 2000.00 4000.00
43 Deacon McGuire
44 Sam Mertes
45 Joe Mulvey 1000.00 2000.00
46 Danny Murphy
47 Harry Niles 1000.00 2000.00
48 Fred Odwell
49 Boss Schmidt
50 Tris Speaker
51 George Stovall 1000.00 2000.00
52 Sammy Strang
53 Bill Sweeney
54 John Taylor OWN
55 Fred Tenney
56 Joe Tinker 2500.00 5000.00
57 Kirby White
58 Vic Willis 2000.00 4000.00
59 Hooks Wiltse 1000.00 2000.00
60 Art Wilson
61 Joe Wood
62 Cy Young 5000.00 10000.00

1975 Hostess

The cards in this 150-card set measure approximately 2 1/4" by 3 1/4" individually or 3 1/4" by 7 1/4" as panels of three. The 1975 Hostess set was issued in panels of three cards each on the backs of family-size packages of Hostess cakes. Card number 125, Bill Madlock, was listed correctly as an infielder and incorrectly as a pitcher. Number 11, Burt Hooton, and number 89, Doug Rader, are spelled two different ways. Some panels are more difficult to find than others as they were issued only on the backs of less popular Hostess products. These scarcer cards are shown with SP in the checklist. Although complete panel prices are not explicitly listed, they would generally have a value of 20-30 percent greater than the sum of the values of the individual players on that panel. One of the more interesting cards in the set is that of Robin Yount; Hostess issued one of the few Yount cards available in 1975, his rookie year for cards. An album to hold these cards was issued. The albums were originally intended to be given out in grocery stores. However, most seemingly were distributed through Hostess stores.

COMPLETE INDIV.SET (150) 100.00 200.00
COMMON CARD (1-150) .15 .40
COMMON SP .25 .60
1 Bob Tolan .15 .40
2 Cookie Rojas .15 .40
3 Darrell Evans .25 .60
4 Sal Bando .25 .60
5 Joe Morgan 1.25 3.00
6 Mickey Lolich .25 .60
7 Don Sutton 1.25 3.00
8 Bill Melton .15 .40
9 Tim Foli .15 .40
10 Joe Lahoud .15 .40
11A Burt Hooton ERR .30 .75
Misspelled Bert
Hooten on card
11B Burt Hooton COR .30 .75
12 Paul Blair .15 .40
13 Jim Barr .15 .40
14 Toby Harrah .15 .40
15 John Milner .15 .40
16 Ken Holtzman .15 .40
17 Cesar Cedeno .15 .40
18 Dwight Evans .50 1.25
19 Willie McCovey 1.00 2.50
20 Tony Oliva .50 1.25
21 Manny Sanguillen .15 .40
22 Mickey Rivers .15 .40
23 Lou Brock 1.25 3.00
24 Graig Nettles UER .50 1.25
Craig on front
25 Jim Wynn .15 .40
26 George Scott .15 .40
27 Greg Luzinski .30 .75
28 Bert Campaneris .25 .60
29 Pete Rose 3.00 8.00
30 Buddy Bell .30 .75
31 Gary Matthews .25 .60
32 Freddie Patek .15 .40
33 Mike Lum .15 .40
34 Ellie Rodriguez .15 .40
35 Milt May UER .15 .40
Photo actually
Lee May
36 Willie Horton .25 .60
37 Dave Winfield 6.00 15.00
38 Tom Grieve .15 .40
39 Barry Foote .15 .40
40 Joe Rudi .15 .40
41 Bake McBride .15 .40
42 Mike Cuellar .15 .40
43 Garry Maddox .15 .40
44 Carlos May .15 .40
45 Bud Harrelson .15 .40
46 Dave Chalk .15 .40
47 Dave Concepcion .50 1.25
48 Carl Yastrzemski 1.50 4.00
49 Steve Garvey .75 2.00
50 Amos Otis .15 .40
51 Rick Reuschel .15 .40
52 Rollie Fingers 1.00 2.50
53 Bob Watson .25 .60
54 John Ellis .15 .40
55 Bob Bailey .15 .40
56 Rod Carew 1.50 4.00
57 Rich Hebner .15 .40
58 Nolan Ryan 12.50 30.00
59 Reggie Smith .25 .60
60 Joe Coleman .15 .40
61 Ron Cey .25 .60
62 Darrell Porter .25 .60
63 Steve Carlton 1.50 4.00
64 Gene Tenace .15 .40
65 Jose Cardenal .15 .40
66 Bill Lee .15 .40
67 Dave Lopes .25 .60
68 Wilbur Wood .15 .40
69 Steve Renko .15 .40
70 Joe Torre .50 1.25
71 Ted Sizemore .15 .40
72 Bobby Grich .25 .60
73 Chris Speier .15 .40
74 Bert Blyleven .30 .75
75 Tom Seaver 3.00 8.00
76 Nate Colbert .15 .40
77 Don Kessinger .15 .40
78 George Medich .15 .40
79 Andy Messersmith SP .25 .60
80 Robin Yount SP 12.50 30.00
81 Al Oliver SP .30 .75
82 Bill Singer SP .25 .60
83 Johnny Bench SP 4.00 10.00
84 Gaylord Perry SP 1.25 3.00
85 Dave Kingman SP .60 1.50
86 Ed Herrmann SP .25 .60
87 Ralph Garr SP .25 .60
88 Reggie Jackson SP 4.00 10.00
89A Doug Rader ERR SP .50 1.25
Misspelled Radar
89B Doug Rader COR SP 2.00 5.00
90 Elliott Maddox SP .25 .60
91 Bill Russell SP .50 1.25
92 John Mayberry SP .25 .60
93 Dave Cash SP .25 .60
94 Jeff Burroughs SP .25 .60
95 Ted Simmons SP .60 1.50
96 Joe Decker SP .25 .60
97 Bill Buckner SP .50 1.25
98 Bobby Darwin SP .25 .60
99 Phil Niekro SP 1.25 3.00
100 Jim Sundberg .15 .40
101 Greg Gross .15 .40
102 Luis Tiant .30 .75
103 Glenn Beckert .15 .40
104 Hal McRae .25 .60
105 Mike Jorgensen .15 .40
106 Mike Hargrove .50 1.25
107 Don Gullett .25 .60
108 Tito Fuentes .15 .40
109 John Grubb .15 .40
110 Jim Kaat .30 .75
111 Felix Millan .15 .40
112 Don Money .15 .40
113 Rick Monday .15 .40
114 Dick Bosman .15 .40
115 Roger Metzger .15 .40
116 Fergie Jenkins 1.00 2.50
117 Dusty Baker .30 .75
118 Billy Champion SP .25 .60
119 Bob Gibson SP 1.50 4.00
120 Bill Freehan SP .30 .75
121 Cesar Geronimo .15 .40
122 Jorge Orta .15 .40
123 Cleon Jones .15 .40
124 Steve Busby .15 .40
125A Bill Madlock ERR .50 1.25
Pitcher
125B Bill Madlock COR .50 1.25
Infielder
126 Jim Palmer 1.25 3.00
127 Tony Perez .75 2.00
128 Larry Hisle .15 .40
129 Rusty Staub .30 .75
130 Hank Aaron SP 6.00 15.00
131 Rennie Stennett SP .25 .60
132 Rico Petrocelli SP .30 .75
133 Mike Schmidt 6.00 15.00
134 Sparky Lyle .30 .75
135 Willie Stargell 1.00 2.50
136 Ken Henderson .15 .40
137 Willie Montanez .15 .40
138 Thurman Munson 1.00 2.50
139 Richie Zisk .15 .40
140 George Hendrick UER .15 .40
named spelled Hendricks
141 Bobby Murcer .25 .60
142 Lee May UER .15 .40
name in all CAPS on back
143 Carlton Fisk 3.00 8.00
144 Brooks Robinson 1.50 4.00
145 Bobby Bonds .50 1.25
146 Gary Sutherland .15 .40
147 Oscar Gamble .15 .40
148 Jim Hunter 1.25 3.00
149 Tug McGraw .30 .75
150 Dave McNally .25 .60
NNO Album 2.50 6.00

1975 Hostess Twinkie

The cards in this 60-card set measure approximately 2 1/4" by 3 1/4". The 1975 Hostess Twinkie set was issued on a limited basis in the far western part of the country. The set contains the same numbers as the regular set to number 36; however, the set is skip numbered after number 36. The cards were issued as the backs for 25-cent Twinkies packs. The fronts are indistinguishable from the regular Hostess cards; however the card backs are different in that the Twinkie cards have a thick black bar in the middle of the reverse. The cards are frequently found with product stains. One of the more interesting cards in the set is that of Robin Yount; Hostess issued one of the few Yount cards available in 1975, his rookie year for cards.

COMPLETE SET (60) 75.00 150.00
1 Bob Tolan .40 1.00
2 Cookie Rojas .40 1.00
3 Darrell Evans .60 1.50
4 Sal Bando .60 1.50
5 Joe Morgan 2.50 6.00
6 Mickey Lolich .75 2.00
7 Don Sutton 2.00 5.00
8 Bill Melton .40 1.00
9 Tim Foli .40 1.00
10 Joe Lahoud .40 1.00
11 Burt Hooton UER/(Misspelled Bert .40 1.00
Hooten on card)
12 Paul Blair .40 1.00
13 Jim Barr .40 1.00
14 Toby Harrah .40 1.00
15 John Milner .40 1.00
16 Ken Holtzman .40 1.00
17 Cesar Cedeno .60 1.50
18 Dwight Evans 1.00 2.50
19 Willie McCovey 2.00 5.00
20 Tony Oliva .75 2.00
21 Manny Sanguillen .40 1.00
22 Mickey Rivers .40 1.00
23 Lou Brock 2.50 6.00
24 Graig Nettles UER/(Craig on front) 1.00 2.50
25 Jim Wynn .60 1.50
26 George Scott .40 1.00
27 Greg Luzinski .60 1.50
28 Bert Campaneris .60 1.50
29 Pete Rose 6.00 15.00
30 Buddy Bell .75 2.00
31 Gary Matthews .60 1.50
32 Freddie Patek .40 1.00
33 Mike Lum .40 1.00
34 Ellie Rodriguez .40 1.00
35 Milt May UER/(Lee May picture) .40 1.00
36 Willie Horton .60 1.50
40 Joe Rudi .60 1.50
43 Garry Maddox .40 1.00
46 Dave Chalk .40 1.00
49 Steve Garvey 1.50 4.00
52 Rollie Fingers 2.00 5.00
58 Nolan Ryan 20.00 50.00
61 Ron Cey .75 2.00
64 Gene Tenace .40 1.00
65 Jose Cardenal .40 1.00
67 Dave Lopes .75 2.00
68 Wilbur Wood .40 1.00
73 Chris Speier .40 1.00
77 Don Kessinger .40 1.00
79 Andy Messersmith .40 1.00
80 Robin Yount 12.50 40.00
82 Bill Singer .40 1.00
103 Glenn Beckert .40 1.00
110 Jim Kaat .75 2.00
112 Don Money .60 1.50
113 Rick Monday .60 1.50
122 Jorge Orta .40 1.00
125 Bill Madlock .75 2.00
130 Hank Aaron 8.00 20.00
136 Ken Henderson .40 1.00
XX Checklist 10.00 25.00

1976 Hostess

The cards in this 150-card set measure approximately 2 1/4" by 3 1/4" individually or 3 1/4" by 7 1/4" as panels of three. The 1976 Hostess set contains full-color, numbered cards issued in panels of three cards each on family-size packages of Hostess cakes. Scarcer panels (those only found on less popular Hostess products) are listed in the checklist below with SP. Complete panels of three have a value 20-30 percent more than the sum of the individual cards on the panel. Nine additional numbers (151-159) were apparently planned but never actually issued. These exist as proof cards and are quite scarce, e.g., 151 Ferguson Jenkins (even though he already appears in the set as card number 138), 152 Mike Cuellar, 153 Tom Murphy, 154 Al Cowens, 155 Barry Foote, 156 Steve Carlton, 157 Richie Zisk, 158 Ken Holtzman, and 159 Cliff Johnson. One of the more interesting cards in the set is that of Dennis Eckersley; Hostess issued one of the few Eckersley cards available in 1976, his rookie year for cards. An album to hold these cards were issued. Many of these cards were issued with brown printing on the back, those cards are valued the same as the black printed cards.

COMPLETE INDIV.SET (150) 150.00 300.00
COMMON CARD (1-150) .20 .50
COMMON SP .30 .75
1 Fred Lynn .60 1.50
2 Joe Morgan 1.50 4.00
3 Phil Niekro 1.50 4.00
4 Gaylord Perry 1.25 3.00
5 Bob Watson .30 .75
6 Bill Freehan .30 .75
7 Lou Brock 1.50 4.00
8 Al Fitzmorris .20 .50
9 Rennie Stennett .20 .50
10 Tony Oliva .60 1.50
11 Robin Yount 8.00 20.00
12 Rick Manning .20 .50
13 Bobby Grich .30 .75
14 Terry Forster .20 .50
15 Dave Kingman .40 1.00
16 Thurman Munson 1.25 3.00
17 Rick Reuschel .20 .50
18 Bobby Bonds .60 1.50
19 Steve Garvey 1.00 2.50
20 Vida Blue .30 .75
21 Dave Rader .20 .50
22 Johnny Bench 3.00 8.00
23 Luis Tiant .30 .75
24 Darrell Evans .30 .75
25 Larry Dierker .20 .50
26 Willie Horton .30 .75
27 John Ellis .20 .50
28 Al Cowens .20 .50
29 Jerry Reuss .20 .50
30 Reggie Smith .30 .75
31 Bobby Darwin SP .30 .75
32 Fritz Peterson SP .30 .75
33 Rod Carew SP 4.00 10.00
34 Carlos May SP .30 .75
35 Tom Seaver SP 6.00 15.00
36 Brooks Robinson SP 4.00 10.00
37 Jose Cardenal .20 .50
38 Ron Blomberg .20 .50
39 Leroy Stanton .20 .50
40 Dave Cash .20 .50
41 John Montefusco .20 .50
42 Bob Tolan .20 .50
43 Carl Morton .20 .50
44 Rick Burleson .20 .50
45 Don Gullett .20 .50
46 Vern Ruhle .20 .50
47 Cesar Cedeno .30 .75
48 Toby Harrah .20 .50
49 Willie Stargell 1.25 3.00
50 Al Hrabosky .20 .50
51 Amos Otis .20 .50
52 Bud Harrelson .20 .50
53 Jim Hughes .20 .50
54 George Scott .20 .50
55 Mike Vail SP .30 .75
56 Jim Palmer SP 2.50 6.00
57 Jorge Orta SP .30 .75
58 Chris Chambliss SP .40 1.00
59 Dave Chalk SP .30 .75
60 Ray Burris SP .30 .75

61 Bert Campaneris SP .40 1.00
62 Gary Carter SP 6.00 15.00
63 Ron Cey SP .60 1.50
64 Carlton Fisk SP 6.00 15.00
65 Marty Perez SP .30 .75
66 Pete Rose SP 8.00 20.00
67 Roger Metzger SP .30 .75
68 Jim Sundberg SP .30 .75
69 Ron LeFlore SP .30 .75
70 Ted Sizemore SP .30 .75
71 Steve Busby SP .30 .75
72 Manny Sanguillen SP .30 .75
73 Larry Hisle SP .30 .75
74 Pete Broberg SP .30 .75
75 Boog Powell SP .75 2.00
76 Ken Singleton SP .40 1.00
77 Goose Gossage SP .75 2.00
78 Jerry Grote SP .30 .75
79 Nolan Ryan SP 20.00 50.00
80 Rick Monday SP .40 1.00
81 Graig Nettles SP .75 2.00
82 Chris Speier .20 .50
83 Dave Winfield 5.00 12.00
84 Mike Schmidt 6.00 15.00
85 Buzz Capra .20 .50
86 Tony Perez 1.00 2.50
87 Dwight Evans .60 1.50
88 Mike Hargrove .30 .75
89 Joe Coleman .20 .50
90 Greg Gross .20 .50
91 John Mayberry .20 .50
92 John Candelaria .30 .75
93 Bake McBride .20 .50
94 Hank Aaron 6.00 15.00
95 Buddy Bell .30 .75
96 Steve Braun .20 .50
97 Jon Matlack .20 .50
98 Lee May .20 .50
99 Wilbur Wood .20 .50
100 Bill Madlock .30 .75
101 Frank Tanana .30 .75
102 Mickey Rivers .20 .50
103 Mike Ivie .20 .50
104 Rollie Fingers 1.25 3.00
105 Dave Lopes .30 .75
106 George Foster .40 1.00
107 Denny Doyle .20 .50
108 Earl Williams .20 .50
109 Tom Veryzer .20 .50
110 J.R. Richard .20 .50
111 Jeff Burroughs .20 .50
112 Al Oliver .30 .75
113 Ted Simmons .40 1.00
114 George Brett 12.50 40.00
115 Frank Duffy .20 .50
116 Bert Blyleven .40 1.00
117 Darrell Porter .20 .50
118 Don Baylor .40 1.00
119 Bucky Dent .30 .75
120 Felix Millan .20 .50
121 Mike Cuellar .20 .50
122 Gene Tenace .20 .50
123 Bobby Murcer .30 .75
124 Willie McCovey 1.25 3.00
125 Greg Luzinski .30 .75
126 Larry Parrish .20 .50
127 Jim Rice .75 2.00
128 Dave Concepcion .40 1.00
129 Jim Wynn .20 .50
130 Tom Grieve .20 .50
131 Mike Cosgrove .20 .50
132 Dan Meyer .20 .50
133 Dave Parker .75 2.00
134 Don Kessinger .20 .50
135 Hal McRae .30 .75
136 Don Money .20 .50
137 Dennis Eckersley 8.00 20.00
138 Fergie Jenkins 1.25 3.00
139 Mike Torrez .20 .50
140 Jerry Morales .20 .50
141 Jim Hunter 1.25 3.00
142 Gary Matthews .20 .50
143 Randy Jones .20 .50
144 Mike Jorgensen .20 .50
145 Larry Bowa .30 .75
146 Reggie Jackson 4.00 10.00
147 Steve Yeager .20 .50
148 Dave May .20 .50
149 Carl Yastrzemski 2.50 6.00
150 Cesar Geronimo .20 .50
XX Album 3.00 8.00

1976 Hostess Twinkie

The cards in this 60-card set measure approximately 2 1/4" by 3 1/4". The 1976 Hostess Twinkies set contains the first 60 cards of the 1976 Hostess set. These cards were issued as backs on 25-cent Twinkie packages as in the 1975 Twinkies set. The fronts are indistinguishable from the regular Hostess cards; however the card backs are different in that the Twinkie cards have a thick black bar in the middle of the reverse. The cards are frequently found with product stains.

COMPLETE SET (60) 60.00 120.00
1 Fred Lynn 1.00 2.50
2 Joe Morgan 2.50 6.00
3 Phil Niekro 2.00 5.00
4 Gaylord Perry 2.00 5.00
5 Bob Watson .60 1.50
6 Bill Freehan .60 1.50
7 Lou Brock 2.00 5.00
8 Al Fitzmorris .40 1.00
9 Rennie Stennett .40 1.00
10 Tony Oliva 1.00 2.50
11 Robin Yount 6.00 15.00
12 Rick Manning .40 1.00
13 Bobby Grich .60 1.50
14 Terry Forster .40 1.00
15 Dave Kingman 1.00 2.50
16 Thurman Munson 2.50 6.00
17 Rick Reuschel .60 1.50
18 Bobby Bonds 1.00 2.50
19 Steve Garvey 2.50 6.00
20 Vida Blue .75 2.00
21 Dave Rader .40 1.00
22 Johnny Bench 4.00 10.00
23 Luis Tiant .60 1.50
24 Darrell Evans .60 1.50
25 Larry Dierker .40 1.00
26 Willie Horton .60 1.50
27 John Ellis .40 1.00
28 Al Cowens .40 1.00
29 Jerry Reuss .60 1.50
30 Reggie Smith .60 1.50
31 Bobby Darwin .40 1.00
32 Fritz Peterson .40 1.00
33 Rod Carew 2.50 6.00
34 Carlos May .40 1.00
35 Tom Seaver 4.00 10.00
36 Brooks Robinson 2.50 6.00
37 Jose Cardenal .40 1.00
38 Ron Blomberg .40 1.00
39 Leroy Stanton .40 1.00
40 Dave Cash .40 1.00
41 John Montefusco .40 1.00
42 Bob Tolan .40 1.00
43 Carl Morton .40 1.00
44 Rick Burleson .60 1.50
45 Don Gullett .60 1.50
46 Vern Ruhle .40 1.00
47 Cesar Cedeno .60 1.50
48 Toby Harrah .60 1.50
49 Willie Stargell 2.00 5.00
50 Al Hrabosky .60 1.50
51 Amos Otis .60 1.50
52 Bud Harrelson .60 1.50
53 Jim Hughes .60 1.50
54 George Scott .60 1.50
55 Mike Vail .60 1.50
56 Jim Palmer 2.00 5.00
57 Jorge Orta .40 1.00
58 Chris Chambliss .75 2.00
59 Dave Chalk .40 1.00
60 Ray Burris .40 1.00

1977 Hostess

The cards in this 150-card set measure approximately 2 1/4" by 3 1/4" individually or 3 1/4" by 7 1/4" as panels of three. The 1977 Hostess set contains full-color, numbered cards issued in panels of three cards each with Hostess family-size cake products. Scarcer cards are listed in the checklist below with SP. Although complete panel prices are not explicitly listed below, they would generally have a value 20-30 percent greater than the sum of the individual players on the panel. There were ten additional cards proofed, but not produced or distributed; they are 151 Ed Kranepool, 152 Ross Grimsley, 153 Ken Brett, 154 Rowland Office, 155 Rick Wise, 156 Paul Splittorff, 157 Gerald Augustine, 158 Ken Forsch, 159 Jerry Reuss (Reuss is also number 119 in the set), and 160 Nelson Briles. An album to hold these cards were issued.

COMPLETE INDIV.SET (150) 125.00 250.00
COMMON CARD (1-150) .20 .50
COMMON SP .30 .75
1 Jim Palmer 1.50 4.00
2 Joe Morgan 1.50 4.00
3 Reggie Jackson 4.00 10.00
4 Carl Yastrzemski 2.50 6.00
5 Thurman Munson 1.25 3.00
6 Johnny Bench 3.00 8.00
7 Tom Seaver 3.00 8.00
8 Pete Rose 4.00 10.00
9 Rod Carew 1.50 4.00
10 Luis Tiant .30 .75
11 Phil Garner .30 .75
12 Sixto Lezcano .20 .50
13 Mike Torrez .20 .50
14 Dave Lopes .30 .75
15 Doug DeCinces .20 .50
16 Jim Spencer .20 .50
17 Hal McRae .30 .75
18 Mike Hargrove .30 .75
19 Willie Montanez SP .30 .75
20 Roger Metzger SP .30 .75
21 Dwight Evans SP .75 2.00
22 Steve Rogers SP .30 .75
23 Jim Rice SP 1.00 2.50
24 Pete Falcone SP .30 .75
25 Greg Luzinski SP .60 1.50
26 Randy Jones SP .30 .75
27 Willie Stargell SP 2.00 5.00
28 John Hiller SP .30 .75
29 Bobby Murcer SP .75 2.00
30 Rick Monday SP .40 1.00
31 John Montefusco SP .30 .75
32 Lou Brock SP 2.00 5.00
33 Bill North SP .30 .75
34 Robin Yount SP 10.00 25.00
35 Steve Garvey SP 2.00 5.00
36 George Brett SP 12.50 35.00
37 Toby Harrah SP .30 .75
38 Jerry Royster SP .30 .75
39 Bob Watson SP .40 1.00
40 George Foster .30 .75
41 Gary Carter 1.50 4.00
42 John Denny .20 .50
43 Mike Schmidt 5.00 12.00
44 Dave Winfield 4.00 10.00
45 Al Oliver .30 .75
46 Mark Fidrych 1.25 3.00
47 Larry Herndon .20 .50
48 Dave Goltz .20 .50
49 Jerry Morales .20 .50
50 Ron LeFlore .20 .50
51 Fred Lynn .30 .75
52 Vida Blue .30 .75
53 Rick Manning .20 .50
54 Bill Buckner .30 .75
55 Lee May .30 .75
56 John Mayberry .20 .50
57 Darrel Chaney .20 .50
58 Cesar Cedeno .30 .75
59 Ken Griffey .40 1.00
60 Dave Kingman .40 1.00
61 Ted Simmons .40 1.00
62 Larry Bowa .30 .75
63 Frank Tanana .30 .75
64 Jason Thompson .20 .50
65 Ken Brett .20 .50
66 Roy Smalley .20 .50
67 Ray Burris .20 .50
68 Rick Burleson .20 .50
69 Buddy Bell .30 .75
70 Don Sutton 1.50 4.00
71 Mark Belanger .20 .50
72 Dennis Leonard .20 .50
73 Gaylord Perry 1.25 3.00
74 Dick Ruthven .20 .50
75 Jose Cruz .30 .75
76 Cesar Geronimo .20 .50
77 Jerry Koosman .30 .75
78 Garry Templeton .20 .50
79 Jim Hunter 1.25 3.00
80 John Candelaria .20 .50
81 Nolan Ryan 12.50 40.00
82 Rusty Staub .30 .75
83 Jim Barr .20 .50
84 Butch Wynegar .30 .75
85 Jose Cardenal .20 .50
86 Claudell Washington .20 .50
87 Bill Travers .20 .50
88 Rick Waits .20 .50
89 Ron Cey .30 .75
90 Al Bumbry .20 .50
91 Bucky Dent .30 .75
92 Amos Otis .20 .50
93 Tom Grieve .20 .50
94 Enos Cabell .20 .50
95 Dave Concepcion .40 1.00
96 Felix Millan .20 .50
97 Bake McBride .20 .50
98 Chris Chambliss .30 .75
99 Butch Metzger .20 .50
100 Rennie Stennett .20 .50
101 Dave Roberts .20 .50
102 Lyman Bostock .30 .75
103 Rick Reuschel .20 .50
104 Carlton Fisk 4.00 10.00
105 Jim Slaton .20 .50
106 Dennis Eckersley 3.00 8.00
107 Ken Singleton .20 .50
108 Ralph Garr .20 .50
109 Freddie Patek SP .30 .75
110 Jim Sundberg SP .30 .75
111 Phil Niekro SP 2.00 5.00
112 J.R. Richard SP .30 .75
113 Gary Nolan SP .30 .75
114 Jon Matlack SP .30 .75
115 Keith Hernandez SP .75 2.00
116 Graig Nettles SP .60 1.50
117 Steve Carlton SP 3.00 8.00
118 Bill Madlock SP .60 1.50
119 Jerry Reuss SP .40 1.00
120 Aurelio Rodriguez SP .30 .75
121 Dan Ford SP .30 .75
122 Ray Fosse SP .30 .75
123 George Hendrick SP .30 .75
124 Alan Ashby .20 .50
125 Joe Lis .20 .50
126 Sal Bando .20 .50
127 Richie Zisk .20 .50
128 Rich Gossage .60 1.50
129 Don Baylor .30 .75
130 Dave McKay .20 .50
131 Bob Grich .30 .75
132 Dave Pagan .20 .50
133 Dave Cash .20 .50
134 Steve Braun .20 .50
135 Dan Meyer .20 .50
136 Bill Stein .20 .50
137 Rollie Fingers 1.25 3.00
138 Brian Downing .20 .50
139 Bill Singer .20 .50
140 Doyle Alexander .20 .50
141 Gene Tenace .20 .50
142 Gary Matthews .20 .50
143 Don Gullett .20 .50
144 Wayne Garland .20 .50
145 Pete Broberg .20 .50
146 Joe Rudi .20 .50
147 Glenn Abbott .20 .50
148 George Scott .20 .50
149 Bert Campaneris .20 .50
150 Andy Messersmith .20 .50
XX Album 3.00 8.00

1977 Hostess Twinkie

COMPLETE SET (150) 175.00 350.00
1 Jim Palmer 2.50 6.00
2 Joe Morgan 2.50 6.00
3 Reggie Jackson 6.00 15.00
4 Carl Yastrzemski 4.00 10.00
5 Thurman Munson 2.00 5.00
6 Johnny Bench 5.00 12.00
7 Tom Seaver 5.00 12.00
8 Pete Rose 6.00 15.00
9 Rod Carew 2.50 6.00
10 Luis Tiant .50 1.25
11 Phil Garner .50 1.25
12 Sixto Lezcano .30 .75
13 Mike Torrez .30 .75
14 Dave Lopes .50 1.25
15 Doug DeCinces .30 .75
16 Jim Spencer .30 .75
17 Hal McRae .50 1.25
18 Mike Hargrove .50 1.25
19 Willie Montanez .50 1.25
20 Roger Metzger .50 1.25
21 Dwight Evans 1.25 3.00
22 Steve Rogers .50 1.25
23 Jim Rice 1.50 4.00
24 Pete Falcone .50 1.25
25 Greg Luzinski 1.00 2.50
26 Randy Jones .50 1.25
27 Willie Stargell 3.00 8.00
28 John Hiller .50 1.25
29 Bobby Murcer 1.25 3.00
30 Rick Monday .60 1.50
31 John Montefusco .50 1.25
32 Lou Brock 3.00 8.00
33 Bill North .50 1.25
34 Robin Yount 15.00 40.00
35 Steve Garvey 3.00 8.00
36 George Brett 20.00 50.00
37 Toby Harrah .50 1.25
38 Jerry Royster .50 1.25
39 Bob Watson .60 1.50
40 George Foster .50 1.25
41 Gary Carter 2.50 6.00
42 John Denny .30 .75
43 Mike Schmidt 8.00 20.00
44 Dave Winfield 6.00 15.00
45 Al Oliver .50 1.25
46 Mark Fidrych 2.00 5.00
47 Larry Herndon .30 .75
48 Dave Goltz .30 .75
49 Jerry Morales .30 .75
50 Ron LeFlore .30 .75
51 Fred Lynn .50 1.25
52 Vida Blue .50 1.25
53 Rick Manning .30 .75
54 Bill Buckner .50 1.25
55 Lee May .50 1.25
56 John Mayberry .30 .75
57 Darrel Chaney .30 .75
58 Cesar Cedeno .50 1.25
59 Ken Griffey .60 1.50
60 Dave Kingman .60 1.50
61 Ted Simmons .60 1.50
62 Larry Bowa .50 1.25
63 Frank Tanana .50 1.25
64 Jason Thompson .30 .75
65 Ken Brett .30 .75
66 Roy Smalley .30 .75
67 Ray Burris .30 .75
68 Rick Burleson .30 .75
69 Buddy Bell .50 1.25
70 Don Sutton 2.50 6.00
71 Mark Belanger .30 .75
72 Dennis Leonard .30 .75
73 Gaylord Perry 2.00 5.00
74 Dick Ruthven .30 .75
75 Jose Cruz .50 1.25
76 Cesar Geronimo .30 .75
77 Jerry Koosman .50 1.25
78 Garry Templeton .30 .75
79 Jim Hunter 2.00 5.00
80 John Candelaria .30 .75
81 Nolan Ryan 20.00 50.00
82 Rusty Staub .50 1.25
83 Jim Barr .30 .75
84 Butch Wynegar .50 1.25
85 Jose Cardenal .30 .75
86 Claudell Washington .30 .75
87 Bill Travers .30 .75
88 Rick Waits .30 .75
89 Ron Cey .50 1.25
90 Al Bumbry .30 .75
91 Bucky Dent .50 1.25
92 Amos Otis .30 .75
93 Tom Grieve .30 .75
94 Enos Cabell .30 .75
95 Dave Concepcion .60 1.50
96 Felix Millan .30 .75
97 Bake McBride .30 .75
98 Chris Chambliss .50 1.25
99 Butch Metzger .30 .75
100 Rennie Stennett .30 .75
101 Dave Roberts .30 .75
102 Lyman Bostock .50 1.25
103 Rick Reuschel .30 .75
104 Carlton Fisk 6.00 15.00
105 Jim Slaton .30 .75
106 Dennis Eckersley 5.00 12.00
107 Ken Singleton .30 .75
108 Ralph Garr .30 .75
109 Freddie Patek .50 1.25
110 Jim Sundberg .50 1.25
111 Phil Niekro 3.00 8.00
112 J.R. Richard .50 1.25
113 Gary Nolan .50 1.25
114 Jon Matlack .50 1.25
115 Keith Hernandez 1.25 3.00
116 Graig Nettles 1.00 2.50
117 Steve Carlton 5.00 12.00
118 Bill Madlock 1.00 2.50
119 Jerry Reuss .60 1.50
120 Aurelio Rodriguez .50 1.25
121 Dan Ford .50 1.25
122 Ray Fosse .50 1.25
123 George Hendrick .50 1.25
124 Alan Ashby .30 .75
125 Joe Lis .30 .75
126 Sal Bando .30 .75
127 Richie Zisk .30 .75
128 Rich Gossage 1.00 2.50
129 Don Baylor .50 1.25
130 Dave McKay .30 .75
131 Bob Grich .50 1.25
132 Dave Pagan .30 .75
133 Dave Cash .30 .75
134 Steve Braun .30 .75
135 Dan Meyer .30 .75
136 Bill Stein .30 .75
137 Rollie Fingers 2.00 5.00
138 Brian Downing .30 .75
139 Bill Singer .30 .75
140 Doyle Alexander .30 .75
141 Gene Tenace .30 .75
142 Gary Matthews .30 .75
143 Don Gullett .30 .75
144 Wayne Garland .30 .75
145 Pete Broberg .30 .75
146 Joe Rudi .30 .75
147 Glenn Abbott .30 .75
148 George Scott .30 .75
149 Bert Campaneris .30 .75
150 Andy Messersmith .30 .75

1978 Hostess

The cards in this 150-card set measure approximately 2 1/4" by 3 1/4" individually or 3 1/4" by 7 1/4" as panels of three. The 1978 Hostess set contains full-color, numbered cards issued in panels of three cards each on family packages of Hostess cake products. Scarcer cards are listed in the checklist with SP. The 1978 Hostess panels are considered by some collectors to be somewhat more difficult to obtain than Hostess panels of other years. Although complete panel prices are not explicitly listed below, they would generally have a value 20-25 percent greater than the sum of the individual players on the panel. There is additional interest in Eddie Murray number 31, since this card corresponds to his rookie year in cards. An album to hold all these cards were issued. There was an album issued for these cards. It is priced below.

COMPLETE INDIV.SET (150) 125.00 250.00
COMMON CARD (1-150) .20 .50
COMMON SP .30 .75
1 Butch Hobson .20 .50
2 George Foster .30 .75
3 Bob Forsch .20 .50
4 Tony Perez .60 1.50
5 Bruce Sutter .60 1.50
6 Hal McRae .30 .75
7 Tommy John .60 1.50
8 Greg Luzinski .30 .75
9 Enos Cabell .20 .50
10 Doug DeCinces .20 .50
11 Willie Stargell 1.25 3.00
12 Ed Halicki .20 .50
13 Larry Hisle .20 .50
14 Jim Slaton .20 .50
15 Buddy Bell .30 .75
16 Earl Williams .20 .50
17 Glenn Abbott .20 .50
18 Dan Ford .20 .50
19 Gary Matthews .20 .50
20 Eric Soderholm .20 .50
21 Bump Wills .20 .50
22 Keith Hernandez .60 1.50
23 Dave Cash .20 .50
24 George Scott .20 .50
25 Ron Guidry .60 1.50
26 Dave Kingman .40 1.00
27 George Brett 10.00 25.00
28 Bob Watson SP .40 1.00
29 Bob Boone SP .60 1.50
30 Reggie Smith SP .40 1.00
31 Eddie Murray SP 12.50 40.00
32 Gary Lavelle SP .30 .75
33 Rennie Stennett SP .30 .75
34 Duane Kuiper SP .30 .75
35 Sixto Lezcano SP .30 .75
36 Dave Rozema SP .30 .75
37 Butch Wynegar SP .30 .75
38 Mitchell Page SP .30 .75
39 Bill Stein SP .30 .75
40 Elliott Maddox .20 .50
41 Mike Hargrove .30 .75
42 Bobby Bonds .60 1.50
43 Garry Templeton .20 .50
44 Johnny Bench 3.00 8.00
45 Jim Rice .75 2.00
46 Bill Buckner .30 .75
47 Reggie Jackson 3.00 8.00
48 Freddie Patek .20 .50
49 Steve Carlton 1.50 4.00
50 Cesar Cedeno .30 .75
51 Steve Yeager .20 .50
52 Phil Garner .30 .75
53 Lee May .30 .75
54 Darrell Evans .30 .75
55 Steve Kemp .20 .50
56 Dusty Baker .30 .75
57 Ray Fosse .20 .50
58 Manny Sanguillen .20 .50
59 Tom Johnson .20 .50
60 Lee Stanton .20 .50
61 Jeff Burroughs .20 .50
62 Bobby Grich .30 .75
63 Dave Winfield 3.00 8.00
64 Dan Driessen .20 .50
65 Ted Simmons .40 1.00
66 Jerry Remy .20 .50
67 Al Cowens .20 .50
68 Sparky Lyle .30 .75
69 Manny Trillo .20 .50
70 Don Sutton 1.25 3.00
71 Larry Bowa .30 .75
72 Jose Cruz .30 .75
73 Willie McCovey 1.25 3.00
74 Bert Blyleven .40 1.00
75 Ken Singleton .20 .50
76 Bill North .20 .50
77 Jason Thompson .20 .50
78 Dennis Eckersley 2.00 5.00
79 Jim Sundberg .20 .50
80 Jerry Koosman .30 .75
81 Bruce Bochte .20 .50
82 George Hendrick .20 .50
83 Nolan Ryan 12.50 40.00
84 Roy Howell .20 .50
85 Butch Metzger .20 .50
86 Doc Medich .20 .50
87 Joe Morgan 1.50 4.00
88 Dennis Leonard .20 .50
89 Willie Randolph .40 1.00
90 Bobby Murcer .30 .75
91 Rick Manning .20 .50
92 J.R. Richard .20 .50
93 Ron Cey .30 .75
94 Sal Bando .20 .50
95 Ron LeFlore .20 .50
96 Dave Goltz .20 .50
97 Dan Meyer .20 .50
98 Chris Chambliss .30 .75
99 Biff Pocoroba .20 .50
100 Oscar Gamble .20 .50
101 Frank Tanana .30 .75
102 Len Randle .20 .50
103 Tommy Hutton .20 .50
104 John Candelaria .20 .50
105 Jorge Orta .20 .50
106 Ken Reitz .20 .50
107 Bill Campbell .20 .50
108 Dave Concepcion .40 1.00
109 Joe Ferguson .20 .50
110 Mickey Rivers .30 .75
111 Paul Splittorff .20 .50
112 Dave Lopes .20 .50
113 Mike Schmidt 4.00 10.00
114 Joe Rudi .20 .50
115 Milt May .20 .50
116 Jim Palmer 1.50 4.00
117 Bill Madlock .30 .75
118 Roy Smalley .20 .50
119 Cecil Cooper .30 .75
120 Rick Langford .20 .50
121 Ruppert Jones .20 .50
122 Phil Niekro 1.25 3.00
123 Toby Harrah .20 .50
124 Chet Lemon .20 .50
125 Gene Tenace .20 .50
126 Steve Henderson .20 .50
127 Mike Torrez .20 .50
128 Pete Rose 4.00 10.00
129 John Denny .20 .50
130 Darrell Porter .20 .50
131 Rick Reuschel .20 .50
132 Graig Nettles .40 1.00
133 Garry Maddox .20 .50
134 Mike Flanagan .20 .50
135 Dave Parker .60 1.50
136 Terry Whitfield .20 .50
137 Wayne Garland .20 .50
138 Robin Yount 6.00 15.00
139 Gaylord Perry 1.25 3.00
140 Rod Carew 1.50 4.00
141 Wayne Gross .20 .50
142 Barry Bonnell .20 .50
143 Willie Montanez .20 .50
144 Rollie Fingers 1.25 3.00
145 Lyman Bostock .30 .75
146 Gary Carter 1.25 3.00
147 Ron Blomberg .20 .50
148 Bob Bailor .20 .50
149 Tom Seaver 2.50 6.00
150 Thurman Munson 1.25 3.00
XX Album 3.00 8.00

1979 Hostess

The cards in this 150-card set measure approximately 2 1/4" by 3 1/4" individually or 3 1/4" by 7 1/4" as panels of three. The 1979 Hostess set contains full color, numbered cards issued in panels of three cards each on the backs of family sized Hostess cake products. Scarcer cards are listed in the checklist below with SP. Although complete panel prices are not explicitly listed below they would generally have a value 20-25 percent greater than the sum of the individual players on the panel. The collectors who don't consider 1978 to be the most difficult Hostess to acquire, believe that 1979's are the toughest to get. The shelf life on the 1979's seemed to be slightly shorter than other years.There is additional interest in Ozzie Smith (102) since this card corresponds to his rookie year in cards. An album to hold these cards were issued.

COMPLETE INDIV.SET (150) 200.00 400.00
COMMON CARD (1-150) .20 .50
COMMON SP .30 .75
1 John Denny .30 .75
2 Jim Rice 1.00 2.50
3 Doug Bair .30 .75
4 Darrell Porter .30 .75
5 Ross Grimsley .30 .75
6 Bobby Murcer .50 1.25
7 Lee Mazzilli .50 1.25
8 Steve Garvey .75 2.00
9 Mike Schmidt 6.00 15.00
10 Terry Whitfield .30 .75
11 Jim Palmer 2.50 6.00
12 Omar Moreno .30 .75
13 Duane Kuiper .30 .75
14 Mike Caldwell .30 .75
15 Steve Kemp .30 .75
16 Dave Goltz .30 .75
17 Mitchell Page .30 .75
18 Bill Stein .30 .75
19 Gene Tenace .30 .75
20 Jeff Burroughs .30 .75
21 Francisco Barrios .30 .75
22 Mike Torrez .30 .75
23 Ken Reitz .30 .75
24 Gary Carter 2.00 5.00
25 Al Hrabosky .30 .75
26 Thurman Munson 2.00 5.00
27 Bill Buckner .50 1.25
28 Ron Cey SP .60 1.50
29 J.R. Richard SP .60 1.50
30 Greg Luzinski SP .60 1.50
31 Ed Ott SP .50 1.25
32 Dennis Martinez SP 2.00 5.00
33 Darrell Evans SP .60 1.50
34 Ron LeFlore .30 .75
35 Rick Waits .30 .75
36 Cecil Cooper .50 1.25
37 Leon Roberts .30 .75
38 Rod Carew 2.50 6.00
39 John Henry Johnson .30 .75
40 Chet Lemon .30 .75
41 Craig Swan .30 .75
42 Gary Matthews .30 .75
43 Lamar Johnson .30 .75
44 Ted Simmons .50 1.25
45 Ken Griffey .50 1.25
46 Fred Patek .30 .75
47 Frank Tanana .50 1.25
48 Goose Gossage .60 1.50
49 Burt Hooton .30 .75
50 Ellis Valentine .30 .75
51 Ken Forsch .30 .75
52 Bob Knepper .30 .75
53 Dave Parker 1.00 2.50
54 Doug DeCinces .30 .75
55 Robin Yount 6.00 15.00
56 Rusty Staub .50 1.25
57 Gary Alexander .30 .75
58 Julio Cruz .30 .75
59 Matt Keough .30 .75
60 Roy Smalley .30 .75
61 Joe Morgan 2.50 6.00
62 Phil Niekro 2.00 5.00
63 Don Baylor .50 1.25
64 Dwight Evans .60 1.50
65 Tom Seaver 4.00 10.00
66 George Hendrick .30 .75
67 Rick Reuschel .30 .75
68 George Brett 10.00 25.00
69 Lou Piniella .50 1.25
70 Enos Cabell .30 .75
71 Steve Carlton 2.50 6.00
72 Reggie Smith .50 1.25
73 Rick Dempsey SP .60 1.50
74 Vida Blue SP 1.00 2.50
75 Phil Garner SP .60 1.50
76 Rick Manning SP .50 1.25
77 Mark Fidrych SP 1.50 4.00
78 Mario Guerrero SP .50 1.25
79 Bob Stinson SP .50 1.25
80 Al Oliver SP 1.00 2.50
81 Doug Flynn SP .50 1.25
82 John Mayberry .30 .75
83 Gaylord Perry 2.00 5.00
84 Joe Rudi .30 .75
85 Dave Concepcion .60 1.50
86 John Candelaria .30 .75
87 Pete Vuckovich .30 .75
88 Ivan DeJesus .30 .75
89 Ron Guidry .60 1.50
90 Hal McRae .50 1.25
91 Cesar Cedeno .30 .75
92 Don Sutton 2.00 5.00
93 Andre Thornton .30 .75
94 Roger Erickson .30 .75
95 Larry Hisle .30 .75
96 Jason Thompson .30 .75
97 Jim Sundberg .30 .75
98 Bob Horner .50 1.25
99 Ruppert Jones .30 .75
100 Willie Montanez .30 .75
101 Nolan Ryan 20.00 50.00
102 Ozzie Smith 20.00 50.00
103 Eric Soderholm .30 .75
104 Willie Stargell 2.00 5.00
105A Bob Bailor ERR/(Reverse negative).50 1.25
105B Bob Bailor COR 1.00 2.50
106 Carlton Fisk 5.00 12.00
107 George Foster .50 1.25
108 Keith Hernandez 1.00 2.50
109 Dennis Leonard .30 .75
110 Graig Nettles .60 1.50
111 Jose Cruz .50 1.25
112 Bobby Grich .50 1.25
113 Bob Boone .50 1.25
114 Dave Lopes .30 .75
115 Eddie Murray 10.00 25.00
116 Jack Clark .60 1.50
117 Lou Whitaker 2.50 6.00
118 Miguel Dilone .30 .75
119 Sal Bando .30 .75
120 Reggie Jackson 6.00 15.00
121 Dale Murphy 5.00 12.00
122 Jon Matlack .30 .75
123 Bruce Bochte .30 .75
124 John Stearns .30 .75
125 Dave Winfield 5.00 12.00
126 Jorge Orta .30 .75
127 Garry Templeton .30 .75
128 Johnny Bench 4.00 10.00
129 Butch Hobson .30 .75
130 Bruce Sutter .50 1.25
131 Bucky Dent .50 1.25
132 Amos Otis .30 .75
133 Bert Blyleven .60 1.50
134 Larry Bowa .50 1.25
135 Ken Singleton .30 .75
136 Sixto Lezcano .30 .75
137 Roy Howell .30 .75
138 Bill Madlock .50 1.25
139 Dave Revering .30 .75
140 Richie Zisk .30 .75
141 Butch Wynegar .30 .75
142 Alan Ashby .30 .75
143 Sparky Lyle .50 1.25
144 Pete Rose 6.00 15.00
145 Dennis Eckersley 1.50 4.00
146 Dave Kingman .60 1.50
147 Buddy Bell .50 1.25
148 Mike Hargrove .50 1.25
149 Jerry Koosman .50 1.25
150 Toby Harrah .30 .75
XX Album 5.00 12.00

1987 Hostess Stickers

This set of 30 small, full-color stickers was produced in Canada by Hostess Potato Chips and distributed in bags of potato chips. Each sticker was loosely wrapped in cellophane (to protect against potato chip stains) and measures approximately 1 3/8" by 1 3/4" with rounded corners. The backs of the stickers contain the player's name, team and position in English as well as in French. They are numbered on the front in the lower left corner. The first six cards are Blue Jays and Expos; the rest of the set consists of one player per American team.

COMPLETE SET (30) 15.00 40.00
1 Jesse Barfield .20 .50
2 Ernie Whitt .20 .50
3 George Bell .20 .50
4 Hubie Brooks .20 .50
5 Tim Wallach .20 .50
6 Floyd Youmans .20 .50
7 Dale Murphy .60 1.50
8 Ryne Sandberg 2.00 5.00
9 Eric Davis .40 1.00
10 Mike Scott .20 .50
11 Fernando Valenzuela .30 .75
12 Gary Carter .75 2.00
13 Mike Schmidt 1.00 2.50
14 Tony Pena .30 .75
15 Ozzie Smith 2.00 5.00
16 Tony Gwynn 2.00 5.00
17 Mike Krukow .20 .50
18 Eddie Murray 1.25 3.00
19 Wade Boggs .75 2.00
20 Wally Joyner .60 1.50
21 Harold Baines .30 .75
22 Brook Jacoby .20 .50
23 Lou Whitaker .30 .75
24 George Brett 2.00 5.00
25 Robin Yount .75 2.00
26 Kirby Puckett 1.25 3.00
27 Don Mattingly 2.00 5.00
28 Jose Canseco 1.00 2.50
29 Phil Bradley .20 .50
30 Pete O'Brien .20 .50

1993 Hostess

These standard-size cards were free with the purchase of packages of Hostess Baseballs, a new snack food. The frosted yellow cakes have creamy filling and were decorated with red icing to resemble the stitching of a baseball. Each two-cake snack pack contained one three-card pack and cost 85 cents, while each eight-cake family pack contained two packs and cost 2.99. The cards were issued in two series (1-16 and 17-32), the first being available nationally beginning on April 12 and the second series beginning mid-season. A

checklist was included on the back of each family pack.
COMPLETE SET (32) 2.50 6.00
1 Andy Van Slyke .02 .10
2 Ryne Sandberg .20 .50
3 Bobby Bonilla .02 .10
4 John Kruk .07 .20
5 Ray Lankford .07 .20
6 Gary Sheffield .20 .50
7 Darryl Strawberry .07 .20
8 Barry Larkin .15 .40
9 Terry Pendleton .04 .10
10 Jose Canseco .20 .50
11 Dennis Eckersley .20 .50
12 Brian McRae .02 .10
13 Frank Thomas .20 .50
14 Roberto Alomar .15 .40
15 Carlos Baerga .02 .10
16 Cecil Fielder .07 .20
17 Will Clark .15 .40
18 Andres Galarraga .15 .40
19 Jeff Bagwell .15 .40
20 Brett Butler .07 .20
21 Benito Santiago .07 .20
22 Tom Glavine .15 .40
23 Rickey Henderson .20 .50
24 Wally Joyner .07 .20
25 Ken Griffey Jr. .50 1.25
26 Cal Ripken .60 1.50
27 Roger Clemens .30 .75
28 Don Mattingly .30 .75
29 Kirby Puckett .20 .50
30 Larry Walker .07 .20
31 Jack McDowell .02 .10
32 Pat Listach .02 .10

2002 Hot Prospects

COMP.SET w/o SP's (80) 12.50 30.00
COMMON CARD (1-80) .20 .50
COMMON CARD (81-105) 3.00 8.00
81-105 PRINT RUN 1000 SERIAL #'d SETS
COMMON CARD (106-125) 2.00 5.00
106-125 PRINT RUN 1500 SERIAL #'d SETS
81-125 RANDOM INSERTS IN PACKS
1 Derek Jeter 1.25 3.00
2 Garret Anderson .20 .50
3 Scott Rolen .30 .75
4 Bret Boone .20 .50
5 Lance Berkman .20 .50
6 Andruw Jones .30 .75
7 Ivan Rodriguez .30 .75
8 Bernie Williams .30 .75
9 Cristian Guzman .20 .50
10 Mo Vaughn .20 .50
11 Troy Glaus .20 .50
12 Tim Salmon .30 .75
13 Jason Giambi .20 .50
14 Cliff Floyd .20 .50
15 Tim Hudson .20 .50
16 Curt Schilling .20 .50
17 Sammy Sosa .50 1.25
18 Alex Rodriguez .60 1.50
19 Chuck Knoblauch .20 .50
20 Jason Kendall .20 .50
21 Ben Sheets .20 .50
22 Nomar Garciaparra .75 2.00
23 Ryan Klesko .20 .50
24 Greg Vaughn .20 .50
25 Rafael Palmeiro .30 .75
26 Miguel Tejada .20 .50
27 Shea Hillenbrand .20 .50
28 Jim Thome .30 .75
29 Randy Johnson .50 1.25
30 Barry Larkin .30 .75
31 Paul LoDuca .20 .50
32 Pedro Martinez .30 .75
33 Luis Gonzalez .20 .50
34 Carlos Delgado .20 .50
35 Richie Sexson .20 .50
36 Albert Pujols 1.00 2.50
37 Bobby Abreu .20 .50
38 Gary Sheffield .20 .50
39 Magglio Ordonez .20 .50
40 Eric Chavez .20 .50
41 Jeff Bagwell .30 .75
42 Doug Mientkiewicz .20 .50
43 Moises Alou .20 .50
44 Todd Helton .30 .75
45 Ichiro Suzuki 1.00 2.50
46 Jose Cruz Jr. .20 .50
47 Freddy Garcia .20 .50
48 Tino Martinez .30 .75
49 Roger Clemens 1.00 2.50
50 Greg Maddux .75 2.00
51 Mike Piazza .75 2.00
52 Roberto Alomar .30 .75
53 Adam Dunn .20 .50
54 Kerry Wood .20 .50
55 Edgar Martinez .30 .75
56 Ken Griffey Jr. 1.00 2.50
57 Juan Gonzalez .20 .50
58 Pat Burrell .20 .50
59 Corey Koskie .20 .50
60 Jose Vidro .20 .50
61 Ben Grieve .20 .50
62 Barry Bonds 1.25 3.00
63 Raul Mondesi .20 .50
64 Jimmy Rollins .20 .50
65 Mike Sweeney .20 .50
66 Josh Beckett .20 .50
67 Chipper Jones .50 1.25
68 Jeff Kent .20 .50
69 Tony Batista .20 .50
70 Phil Nevin .20 .50
71 Brian Jordan .20 .50
72 Rich Aurilia .20 .50
73 Brian Giles .20 .50
74 Frank Thomas .50 1.25
75 Larry Walker .20 .50
76 Shawn Green .20 .50
77 Manny Ramirez .30 .75
78 Craig Biggio .30 .75
79 Vladimir Guerrero .50 1.25
80 Jeromy Burnitz .20 .50
81 Mark Teixeira FS Pants 4.00 10.00
82 Corey Thurman FS Pants RC 3.00 8.00
83 Mark Prior FS Bat 4.00 10.00
84 Marlon Byrd FS Pants 3.00 8.00
85 Austin Kearns FS Pants 3.00 8.00
86 Satoru Komiyama FS Jsy RC 3.00 8.00
87 So Taguchi FS Bat RC 4.00 10.00
88 Jorge Padilla FS Pants RC 3.00 8.00
89 Rene Reyes FS Pants RC 3.00 8.00
90 Jorge Nunez FS Pants RC 3.00 8.00
91 Ron Calloway FS Pants RC 3.00 8.00
92 Kazuhisa Ishii FS Jsy RC 4.00 10.00
93 Dewon Brazelton FS Pants 3.00 8.00
94 Angel Berroa FS Pants 3.00 8.00
95 Felix Escalona FS Pants RC 3.00 8.00
96 Sean Burroughs FS Bat 3.00 8.00
97 Brandon Duckworth FS Pants 3.00 8.00
98 Hank Blalock FS Pants 4.00 10.00
99 Eric Hinske FS Pants 3.00 8.00
100 Carlos Pena FS Jsy 3.00 8.00
101 Morgan Ensberg FS Pants 3.00 8.00
102 Ryan Ludwick FS Pants 3.00 8.00
103 Chris Snelling FS Pants RC 3.00 8.00
104 Jason Lane FS Pants 3.00 8.00
105 Drew Henson FS Bat 3.00 8.00
106 Bobby Kielty HP 2.00 5.00
107 Earl Snyder HP RC 2.00 5.00
108 Nate Field HP RC 2.00 5.00
109 Juan Diaz HP 2.00 5.00
110 Ryan Anderson HP 2.00 5.00
111 Esteban German HP 2.00 5.00
112 Takahito Nomura HP RC 2.00 5.00
113 David Kelton HP 2.00 5.00
114 Steve Kent HP RC 2.00 5.00
115 Colby Lewis HP 2.00 5.00
116 Jason Simontacchi HP RC 2.00 5.00
117 Rodrigo Rosario HP RC 2.00 5.00
118 Ben Howard HP RC 2.00 5.00
119 Hansel Izquierdo HP RC 2.00 5.00
120 John Ennis HP RC 2.00 5.00
121 Anderson Machado HP RC 2.00 5.00
122 Luis Ugueto HP RC 2.00 5.00
123 Anastacio Martinez HP RC 2.00 5.00
124 Reed Johnson HP RC 3.00 8.00
125 Juan Cruz HP 2.00 5.00

2002 Hot Prospects Future Swatch Autographs

RANDOM INSERTS IN PACKS
STATED PRINT RUN 100 SERIAL #'d SETS
ALL WERE EXCHANGE CARDS
83 Mark Prior FS Bat 10.00 25.00
87 So Taguchi FS Bat 10.00 25.00
89 Rene Reyes FS Pants 6.00 15.00
105 Drew Henson FS Bat 6.00 15.00

2002 Hot Prospects Co-Stars

COMPLETE SET (15) 20.00 50.00
STATED ODDS 1:6 HOBBY
1 B.Bonds 2.50 6.00
A.Rodriguez
2 D.Jeter 2.50 6.00
N.Garciaparra
3 A.Jones 1.25 3.00
C.Jones
4 J.Gonzalez .75 2.00
J.Thome
5 P.Martinez 1.25 3.00
R.Johnson
6 A.Dunn .75 2.00
P.Burrell
7 F.Thomas 1.25 3.00
M.Ramirez
8 J.Bagwell .75 2.00
L.Berkman
9 S.Taguchi .75 2.00
K.Ishii
10 J.Rollins .75 2.00
M.Tejada
11 M.Ensberg .75 2.00
C.Pena
12 A.Dunn .75 2.00
A.Kearns
13 V.Guerrero 1.25 3.00
S.Rolen
14 D.Henson .75 2.00
X.Nady
15 M.Piazza 2.00 5.00
I.Rodriguez

2002 Hot Prospects Inside Barry Bonds Memorabilia

RANDOM INSERTS IN PACKS
STATED PRINT RUNS LISTED BELOW
1 B.Bonds Home Pants/1000 6.00 15.00
2 B.Bonds Away Pants/900 6.00 15.00
3 B.Bonds Away Jsy/800 6.00 15.00
4 B.Bonds Bat/700 6.00 15.00
5 B.Bonds Base/600 6.00 15.00
6 B.Bonds Cleats/500 6.00 15.00
7 B.Bonds Btg Glv/400 6.00 15.00
8 B.Bonds Cap/300 6.00 15.00

2002 Hot Prospects Jerseygraphs

STATED ODDS 1:186 HOBBY
SP PRINT RUNS PROVIDED BY FLEER
SP'S ARE NOT SERIAL-NUMBERED
JAB Adrian Beltre SP/169 10.00 25.00
JBB Barry Bonds SP/65 60.00 120.00
JCJ Chipper Jones SP/100 50.00 100.00
JDE David Espinosa 6.00 15.00
JDH Drew Henson 10.00 25.00
JDJ Derek Jeter SP/108 125.00 250.00
JDS Dane Sardinha 6.00 15.00
JGM Kazuhisa Ishii SP/40 20.00 50.00
JST So Taguchi SP/100 6.00 15.00

2002 Hot Prospects MLB Hot Materials

STATED ODDS 1:9 HOBBY
SP PRINT RUNS PROVIDED BY FLEER
SP'S ARE NOT SERIAL-NUMBERED
AD2 Adam Dunn Jsy 2.50 6.00
AR Alex Rodriguez Jsy 5.00 12.00
BB Bret Boone Bat 1.50 4.00
BB2 Barry Bonds Pants 6.00 15.00
BD Brandon Duckworth Pants 1.50 4.00
BG Brian Giles Pants 1.50 4.00
BW Bernie Williams Jsy 2.50 6.00
CD Carlos Delgado Jsy 1.50 4.00
CG Cristian Guzman Bat SP/261 1.50 4.00
CP Carlos Pena Jsy SP/120 2.50 6.00
CP2 Corey Patterson Jsy 1.50 4.00
CS Curt Schilling Jsy 2.50 6.00
FG Freddy Garcia Jsy 1.50 4.00
FT Frank Thomas Jsy 4.00 10.00
GK Gabe Kapler Jsy 1.50 4.00
GM Greg Maddux Jsy 6.00 15.00
GS Gary Sheffield Bat 1.50 4.00
IR Ivan Rodriguez Jsy 2.50 6.00
JB Josh Beckett Jsy 1.50 4.00
JB2 Jeff Bagwell Jsy SP/108 6.00 15.00
JG Juan Gonzalez Jsy 1.50 4.00
JT Jim Thome Bat 2.50 6.00
JU Juan Uribe Bat 1.50 4.00
KI Kazuhisa Ishii Jsy SP/70 2.50 6.00
LB Lance Berkman Jsy 2.50 6.00
MM Mark Mulder Jsy 1.50 4.00
MO Moises Alou Bat 1.50 4.00
MO Magglio Ordonez Jsy 2.50 6.00
MP Mike Piazza Jsy 4.00 10.00
MS Mike Sweeney Jsy 1.50 4.00
NJ Nick Johnson Jsy 1.50 4.00
PL Paul LoDuca Jsy 1.50 4.00
PM Pedro Martinez Jsy 2.50 6.00
RF Rafael Furcal Jsy 1.50 4.00
RO Roy Oswalt Jsy 2.50 6.00
RP Rafael Palmeiro Jsy 2.50 6.00
SB Sean Burroughs Bat SP/350 1.50 4.00
SG Shawn Green Jsy 1.50 4.00
ST So Taguchi Bat 2.50 6.00
TA Tony Armas Jr. Jsy 1.50 4.00
TH Todd Helton Jsy 2.50 6.00
TH Torii Hunter Bat 1.50 4.00
TM Tino Martinez Bat 2.50 6.00
VW Vernon Wells Bat 1.50 4.00

2002 Hot Prospects MLB Hot Tandems

RANDOM INSERTS IN PACKS
STATED PRINT RUN 100 SERIAL #'d SETS
ADCP Dunn Jsy/Patterson Jsy 4.00 10.00
ADLB Dunn Jsy/Berkman Jsy 4.00 10.00
ARIR A.Rod Jsy/I.Rod Jsy 20.00 50.00
BBDJ Bonds Pants/Jeter Jsy 20.00 50.00
BBFG Boone Bat/Garcia Jsy 2.50 6.00
BBKI Bonds Pants/Ishii Jsy 12.00 30.00
BBTH Boone Bat/Hunter Bat 2.50 6.00
BDJB D'worth Pants/Beckett Jsy 2.50 6.00
BDRO D'worth Pants/Oswalt Jsy 4.00 10.00
BWJP B.Will Jsy/Posada Bat 4.00 10.00
BWNJ B.Will Jsy/N.Johnson Jsy 4.00 10.00
CDVW Delgado Jsy/V.Wells Bat 2.50 6.00
CGTH Guzman Bat/Hunter Bat 2.50 6.00
CPCP C.Pena Jsy/Patterson Jsy 4.00 10.00
CPNJ C.Pena Jsy/N.John Jsy 4.00 10.00
CSGM Schill Jsy/Maddux Jsy 10.00 25.00
CSPM Schilling Jsy/Pedro Jsy 4.00 10.00
FTMO Thomas Jsy/Magglio Jsy 6.00 15.00
GKJG Kapler Jsy/Gonzalez Jsy 2.50 6.00
GKRP Kapler Jsy/Palmeiro Jsy 4.00 10.00
GMPM Maddux Jsy/Pedro Jsy 10.00 25.00
GSRF Sheffield Bat/Furcal Jsy 2.50 6.00
HBAK Blalock Pnts/Kearns Pnts 2.50 6.00
HBMT Blalock Pants/Teix Pants 4.00 10.00
JBLB Bagwell Jsy/Berkman Jsy 4.00 10.00
JBMP Bagwell Jsy/Piazza Jsy 6.00 15.00
JBRO Beckett Jsy/Oswalt Jsy 4.00 10.00
JGRP J.Gonz Jsy/Palmeiro Jsy 4.00 10.00
JPMP Posada Bat/Piazza Jsy 10.00 25.00
JTSG Thome Bat/Green Jsy 4.00 10.00
JUCG Uribe Bat/Guzman Bat 2.50 6.00
JUMT Uribe Bat/Tejada Jsy 4.00 10.00
KIDJ Ishii Jsy/Jeter Jsy 15.00 40.00
KIMP Ishii Jsy/Prior Bat 4.00 10.00
KISK Ishii Jsy/Komiyama Jsy 4.00 10.00
KIST Ishii Jsy/Taguchi Bat 4.00 10.00
MAMO Alou Bat/Magglio Jsy 4.00 10.00
MBAK Byrd Pants/Kearns Pants 2.50 6.00
MBJP Byrd Pants/Padilla Pants 2.50 6.00
MMMT Mulder Jsy/Tejada Jsy 4.00 10.00
MSTH Sweeney Jsy/Helton Jsy 4.00 10.00
PLSG LoDuca Jsy/Green Jsy 2.50 6.00
SBDH Burroughs Bat/Henson Bat 2.50 6.00
TAFG Armas Jsy/F.Garcia Jsy 2.50 6.00
TMTH T.Mart Bat/Helton Jsy 4.00 10.00

2002 Hot Prospects We're Number One

COMPLETE SET (10) 20.00 50.00
STATED ODDS 1:15 HOBBY
AR Alex Rodriguez 2.50 6.00
BB Barry Bonds 5.00 12.00
CJ Chipper Jones 1.50 4.00
DJ Derek Jeter 5.00 12.00
JD J.D. Drew 1.00 2.50
KG Ken Griffey Jr. 4.00 10.00
MR Manny Ramirez 1.00 2.50
NG Nomar Garciaparra 3.00 8.00
RC Roger Clemens 4.00 10.00
TH Todd Helton 1.00 2.50

2002 Hot Prospects We're Number One Autographs

RANDOM INSERTS IN PACKS
STATED PRINT RUNS LISTED BELOW
BB Barry Bonds/85 100.00 175.00
DJ Derek Jeter/92 75.00 150.00

2002 Hot Prospects We're Number One Memorabilia

STATED ODDS 1:25 HOBBY
SP INFO PROVIDED BY FLEER
GRIFFEY SP IS 1/2 QTY OF OTHER CARDS
AR Alex Rodriguez Jsy 6.00 15.00
BB Barry Bonds Jsy 10.00 25.00
CJ Chipper Jones Jsy 6.00 15.00
DJ Derek Jeter Jsy 10.00 25.00
JD J.D. Drew Jsy 6.00 15.00
KG Ken Griffey Jr. Base SP 8.00 20.00
MR Manny Ramirez Jsy 6.00 15.00
NG Nomar Garciaparra Jsy 8.00 20.00
TH Todd Helton Jsy 6.00 15.00

2003 Hot Prospects

COMP.LO SET w/o SP's (80) 12.50 30.00
COMMON CARD (1-80) .20 .50
FS BAT/JSY PRINT RUN 1250 #'d SETS
CUT AU MINORS 3.00 8.00
CUT AU PRINT RUN 500 SERIAL #'d SETS
GG AU PRINT RUN 400 SERIAL #'d SETS
81-119 RANDOM INSERTS IN PACKS
ONE CUT AU OR GG AU PER HOBBY BOX
COMMON CARD (120-127) 3.00 8.00
120-127 RANDOM IN FLEER R/G PACKS
120-127 PRINT RUN 250 SERIAL #'d SETS
CARDS 88/96/106 AND 108 DO NOT EXIST
1 Derek Jeter 1.25 3.00
2 Ryan Klesko .20 .50
3 Troy Glaus .20 .50
4 Jeff Kent .20 .50
5 Frank Thomas .50 1.25
6 Gary Sheffield .20 .50
7 Jim Edmonds .30 .75
8 Pat Burrell .20 .50
9 Jacque Jones .20 .50
10 Jason Jennings .20 .50
11 Pedro Martinez .30 .75
12 Rafael Palmeiro .30 .75
13 Jason Kendall .20 .50
14 Tom Glavine .30 .75
15 Josh Beckett .20 .50
16 Luis Gonzalez .20 .50
17 Edgar Martinez .30 .75
18 Miguel Tejada .30 .75
19 Fred McGriff .30 .75
20 Adam Dunn .30 .75
21 Lance Berkman .30 .75
22 Magglio Ordonez .30 .75
23 Darin Erstad .20 .50
24 Rich Aurilia .20 .50
25 Mike Piazza .50 1.25
26 Shawn Green .20 .50
27 Larry Walker .30 .75
28 Manny Ramirez .50 1.25
29 Juan Gonzalez .20 .50
30 Eric Chavez .20 .50
31 Torii Hunter .20 .50
32 A.J. Burnett .20 .50
33 Sammy Sosa .50 1.25
34 Eric Hinske .20 .50
35 Brian Giles .20 .50
36 Mike Sweeney .20 .50
37 Sean Casey .20 .50
38 Chipper Jones .50 1.25
39 Scott Rolen .30 .75
40 Jason Giambi .20 .50
41 Mo Vaughn .20 .50
42 Roy Oswalt .30 .75
43 Paul Konerko .30 .75
44 Tim Salmon .20 .50
45 Edgardo Alfonzo .20 .50
46 Jermaine Dye .20 .50
47 Ben Sheets .20 .50
48 Todd Helton .30 .75
49 Greg Maddux .60 1.50
50 Albert Pujols .60 1.50
51 Jim Thome .30 .75
52 Vladimir Guerrero .30 .75
53 Ivan Rodriguez .30 .75
54 Nomar Garciaparra .30 .75
55 Alex Rodriguez .60 1.50
56 Alfonso Soriano .30 .75
57 Kazuhisa Ishii .20 .50
58 Austin Kearns .20 .50
59 Curt Schilling .30 .75
60 Bret Boone .20 .50
61 Mark Prior .30 .75
62 Garret Anderson .20 .50
63 Barry Bonds .75 2.00
64 Roger Clemens .60 1.50
65 Jeff Bagwell .30 .75
66 Omar Vizquel .30 .75
67 Jay Gibbons .20 .50
68 Aubrey Huff .20 .50
69 Bobby Abreu .20 .50
70 Richie Sexson .20 .50
71 Bobby Higginson .20 .50
72 Kerry Wood .20 .50
73 Carlos Delgado .20 .50
74 Sean Burroughs .20 .50
75 Jose Vidro .20 .50
76 Ken Griffey Jr. 1.00 2.50
77 Randy Johnson .50 1.25
78 Ichiro Suzuki .60 1.50
79 Barry Zito .30 .75
80 Carlos Beltran .30 .75
81 Joe Borchard FS Jsy 2.00 5.00
82 Mark Teixeira FS Bat 3.00 8.00
83 Brandon Webb FS Jsy RC 6.00 15.00
84 Shane Victorino Pants AU RC 8.00 20.00
85 Hee Seop Choi FS Jsy 2.00 5.00
86 Hank Blalock FS Bat 2.00 5.00
87 Brett Myers FS Jsy 2.00 5.00
89 Jesse Foppert FS Jsy 2.00 5.00
90 Lyle Overbay FS Jsy 2.00 5.00
91 Brian Stokes Pants AU RC 4.00 10.00
92 Josh Hall Bat AU RC 4.00 10.00
93 Chris Waters Pants AU RC 3.00 8.00
94 Lew Ford Pants AU RC 3.00 8.00
95 Ian Ferguson AU RC 3.00 8.00
97 Josh Stewart AU RC 3.00 8.00
98 Pete LaForest AU RC 3.00 8.00
99 J.Contreras Jsy AU/300 RC 8.00 20.00
100 Termel Sledge AU RC 3.00 8.00
101 Guillermo Quiroz AU RC 3.00 8.00
102 Alejandro Machado AU RC 3.00 8.00
103 Nook Logan Pants AU RC 6.00 15.00
104 Rob Hammock Pants AU RC 4.00 10.00
105 Hideki Matsui FS Base RC 5.00 12.00
107 Rocco Baldelli FS Jsy 2.00 5.00
109 T.Wellemeyer Pants AU RC 4.00 10.00
110 Mike Hessman Pants AU RC 4.00 10.00
111 J.Bonderman Pants AU RC 20.00 50.00
112 Craig Brazell Pants AU RC 4.00 10.00
113 Franc Rosario Pants AU RC 4.00 10.00
114 Jeff Duncan Pants AU RC 4.00 10.00
115 Dan Cabrera Pants AU RC 4.00 10.00
116 Dontrelle Willis Pants AU 8.00 20.00
117 Cory Stewart AU RC 3.00 8.00
118 Tim Olson Pants AU RC 4.00 10.00
119 C.Wang Pants AU/500 RC 40.00 100.00
120 Josh Willingham Pants RC 5.00 12.00
121 Rickie Weeks Bat RC 5.00 12.00
122 Prentice Redman Pants RC 3.00 8.00
123 Mike Ryan Pants RC 3.00 8.00
124 Oscar Villarreal Pants RC 3.00 8.00
125 Ryan Wagner Pants RC 2.00 5.00
126 Bo Hart Pants RC 2.00 5.00
127 Edwin Jackson Pants RC 3.00 8.00

2003 Hot Prospects Class Of

COMPLETE SET (10) 5.00 12.00
STATED ODDS 1:15
1 B.Zito .60 1.50
J.Beckett
2 P.Burrell .40 1.00
J.Drew
3 M.Prior .60 1.50
M.Teixeira
4 A.Kearns .40 1.00
S.Burroughs
5 T.Glaus .60 1.50
L.Berkman
6 D.Erstad .60 1.50
T.Helton
7 M.Ramirez 1.00 2.50
S.Green
8 M.Morris .40 1.00
K.Wood
9 N.Garciaparra .60 1.50
P.Konerko
10 A.Rodriguez 1.25 3.00
T.Hunter

2003 Hot Prospects Class Of Game Used

RANDOM INSERTS IN PACKS
STATED PRINT RUN 375 SERIAL #'d SETS
AKSB Kearns Jsy/Burroughs Jsy 4.00 10.00
ARTH A.Rod Jsy/Torii Jsy 8.00 20.00
BZJB Zito Jsy/Beckett Jsy 4.00 10.00
DETH Erstad Jsy/Helton Jsy 6.00 15.00
MMKW Morris Jsy/Wood Jsy 4.00 10.00
MPMT Prior Jsy/Teixeira Bat 6.00 15.00
MRSG Manny Jsy/S.Green Jsy 6.00 15.00
NGPK Nomar Jsy/Konerko Jsy 6.00 15.00
PBJD Burrell Jsy/Drew Jsy 4.00 10.00
TGLB Glaus Jsy/Berkman Jsy 4.00 10.00

2003 Hot Prospects Cream of the Crop

COMPLETE SET (15) 12.50 30.00
STATED ODDS 1:5
1 Barry Bonds 1.50 4.00
2 Derek Jeter 2.50 6.00
3 Ichiro Suzuki 1.25 3.00
4 Nomar Garciaparra .60 1.50
5 Roger Clemens 1.25 3.00
6 Alex Rodriguez 1.25 3.00
7 Greg Maddux 1.25 3.00
8 Mike Piazza 1.00 2.50
9 Sammy Sosa 1.00 2.50
10 Jason Giambi .40 1.00
11 Hideki Matsui 2.00 5.00
12 Albert Pujols 1.25 3.00
13 Vladimir Guerrero .60 1.50
14 Jim Thome .60 1.50
15 Pedro Martinez .60 1.50

2003 Hot Prospects MLB Hot Materials

STATED PRINT RUN 499 SERIAL #'d SETS
*RED HOT: .75X TO 2X BASIC
RED HOT PRINT RUN 50 SERIAL #'d SETS
AD Adam Dunn Jsy 3.00 8.00
AR Alex Rodriguez Jsy 6.00 15.00
AS Alfonso Soriano Jsy 3.00 8.00
BA Tom Glavine Jsy 4.00 10.00
CD Carlos Delgado Jsy 3.00 8.00
CJ Chipper Jones Jsy 4.00 10.00
DJ Derek Jeter Jsy 10.00 25.00
GM Greg Maddux Jsy 4.00 10.00
HC Hee Seop Choi Jsy 3.00 8.00
JB Josh Beckett Jsy 3.00 8.00
JG Jason Giambi Jsy 3.00 8.00
JT Jim Thome Jsy 4.00 10.00
LB Lance Berkman Bat 3.00 8.00
LO Lyle Overbay Jsy 3.00 8.00
MPI Mike Piazza Jsy 4.00 10.00
MPR Mark Prior Jsy 4.00 10.00
MR Manny Ramirez Jsy 4.00 10.00
MS Mike Sweeney Jsy 3.00 8.00
MTJ Miguel Tejada Jsy 3.00 8.00
MTX Mark Teixeira Bat 4.00 10.00
NG Nomar Garciaparra Jsy 6.00 15.00
PB Pat Burrell Jsy 3.00 8.00
RJ Randy Johnson Jsy 4.00 10.00
RP Rafael Palmeiro Jsy 4.00 10.00
SG Shawn Green Jsy 3.00 8.00
SS Sammy Sosa Jsy 4.00 10.00
TG Troy Glaus Jsy 3.00 8.00
THE Todd Helton Jsy 4.00 10.00
THU Torii Hunter Jsy 3.00 8.00
VG Vladimir Guerrero Jsy 4.00 10.00

2003 Hot Prospects MLB Hot Tandems

STATED PRINT RUN 100 SERIAL #'d SETS
RED HOT PRINT RUN 10 SERIAL #'d SETS
NO RED HOT PRICING DUE TO SCARCITY
ARMT A.Rod Jsy/Tejada Jsy 10.00 25.00
CJDJ Chipper Jsy/Jeter Jsy 15.00 40.00
DJMT Jeter Jsy/Tejada Jsy 15.00 40.00
DJNG Jeter Jsy/Nomar Jsy 15.00 40.00
HCLO Choi Jsy/Overbay Jsy 4.00 10.00
JBGM Beckett Jsy/Maddux Jsy 8.00 20.00
JGTG Giambi Jsy/Glaus Jsy 4.00 10.00
JTJG Thome Jsy/Giambi Jsy 6.00 15.00
LBAD Berkman Bat/Dunn Jsy 4.00 10.00
LORJ Overbay Jsy/Randy Jsy 6.00 15.00
MPCJ Piazza Jsy/Chipper Jsy 8.00 20.00
MPDJ Piazza Jsy/Jeter Jsy 15.00 40.00
MPJB Prior Jsy/Beckett Jsy 6.00 15.00
MPSS Prior Jsy/Sosa Jsy 6.00 15.00
MTAR Teixeira Bat/A.Rod Jsy 10.00 25.00
NGMT Nomar Jsy/Tejada Jsy 10.00 25.00
PBJT Burrell Jsy/Thome Jsy 6.00 15.00
RJGM Randy Jsy/Maddux Jsy 8.00 20.00
RPAD Palmeiro Jsy/Dunn Jsy 4.00 10.00
RPMT Palmeiro Jsy/Teixeira Bat 6.00 15.00
SSPB Sosa Jsy/Burrell Jsy 6.00 15.00
TGSG Glaus Jsy/S.Green Jsy 4.00 10.00
THAD Torii Jsy/Berkman Bat 4.00 10.00
THVG Torii Jsy/Guerrero Jsy 6.00 15.00
VGSG Guerrero Jsy/S.Green Jsy 6.00 15.00

2003 Hot Prospects MLB Hot Triple Patch

RANDOM INSERTS IN PACKS
STATED PRINT RUN 50 SERIAL #'d SETS
BGJ Berkman/Glaus/Chipper 30.00 60.00
BTB Burrell/Thome/Berkman 20.00 50.00
DJB Dunn/Randy/Beckett 15.00 40.00
GGJ Guerrero/Glaus/Chipper 30.00 60.00
GRT Giambi/A.Rod/Tejada 30.00 60.00
GSP Garciaparra/Sosa/Piazza 30.00 60.00
GTD Giambi/Tejada/Dunn 15.00 40.00
HSG Torii/Sosa/Guerrero 30.00 60.00
JGR Jeter/Nomar/A.Rod 60.00 120.00
JHP Jeter/Torii/Prior 50.00 100.00
JSG Randy/Soriano/S.Green 30.00 60.00
PBM Prior/Beckett/Maddux 20.00 50.00
PBT Piazza/Burrell/Thome 30.00 60.00
PCT Palmeiro/Choi/Teixeira 20.00 50.00
SMG Soriano/Maddux/S.Green 40.00 80.00

2003 Hot Prospects PlayerGraphs

STATED PRINT RUN 400 SERIAL #'d SETS
*RED HOT: .6X TO 1.5X BASIC
RED HOT PRINT RUN 100 SERIAL #'d SETS
AH Aubrey Huff 6.00 15.00
BM Brett Myers 6.00 15.00
CZ Carlos Zambrano 10.00 25.00
FR Francisco Rodriguez 10.00 25.00
HB Hank Blalock 6.00 15.00
JR Jose Reyes 6.00 15.00
MP Mark Prior 6.00 15.00
MT Mark Teixiera 6.00 15.00
RO Roy Oswalt 6.00 15.00
VW Vernon Wells 6.00 15.00
XN Xavier Nady 6.00 15.00

2004 Hot Prospects Draft

COMP.SET w/o RC's (60) 6.00 15.00
COMMON CARD (1-60) .20 .50
COMMON (61-70/112-113) .75 2.00
61-70/112-113 ODDS 1:15 H, 1:120 R
61-70/112-113 PRINT RUN 1000 #'d SETS
COMMON (71-110/114-120) 3.00 8.00
71-111/114-120 ODDS 1:9 H, 1:990 R
71-111/114-120 PRINT RUN 299 #'d SETS
EXCHANGE DEADLINE INDEFINITE
1 Miguel Tejada .30 .75
2 Jose Vidro .20 .50
3 Hideki Matsui .75 2.00
4 Roger Clemens .60 1.50
5 Craig Wilson .20 .50
6 Bobby Crosby .20 .50
7 Pat Burrell .20 .50
8 Mike Sweeney .20 .50
9 Craig Biggio .30 .75
10 Scott Rolen .30 .75
11 Roy Halladay .30 .75
12 Lyle Overbay .20 .50
13 Rocco Baldelli .20 .50
14 Mike Piazza .50 1.25
15 Rafael Palmeiro .30 .75
16 Hank Blalock .20 .50
17 Sammy Sosa .50 1.25
18 Dontrelle Willis .20 .50
19 Alfonso Soriano .30 .75
20 Gary Sheffield .20 .50
21 Jim Thome .30 .75
22 Ivan Rodriguez .30 .75
23 Adam Dunn .30 .75
24 Kerry Wood .20 .50
25 Khalil Greene .30 .75
26 Richie Sexson .20 .50
27 Nomar Garciaparra .30 .75
28 Andruw Jones .20 .50
29 Tom Glavine .30 .75
30 Carlos Beltran .30 .75
31 Chipper Jones .50 1.25
32 Jeff Bagwell .30 .75
33 Tim Hudson .30 .75
34 Alex Rodriguez .60 1.50
35 Omar Vizquel .30 .75
36 Albert Pujols .60 1.50
37 Frank Thomas .50 1.25
38 Ben Sheets .20 .50
39 Jason Schmidt .20 .50
40 Miguel Cabrera .50 1.25
41 Carlos Delgado .20 .50
42 Ichiro Suzuki .60 1.50
43 Curt Schilling .30 .75
44 Todd Helton .30 .75
45 Ken Griffey Jr. 1.00 2.50
46 Mark Prior .30 .75
47 Vladimir Guerrero .30 .75
48 Pedro Martinez .30 .75
49 Manny Ramirez .50 1.25
50 Joe Mauer .40 1.00
51 Jorge Posada .30 .75
52 Troy Glaus .20 .50
53 Randy Johnson .50 1.25
54 Adrian Beltre .50 1.25
55 Eric Gagne .20 .50
56 Josh Beckett .20 .50
57 Jason Giambi .20 .50
58 Barry Zito .30 .75
59 Lance Berkman .30 .75
60 Derek Jeter 1.25 3.00
61 Kaz Matsui HP RC 1.25 3.00
62 Jason Bartlett HP RC 2.50 6.00
63 John Gall HP RC .75 2.00
64 Chris Saenz HP RC .75 2.00
65 Merkin Valdez HP RC .75 2.00
66 Akinori Otsuka HP RC .75 2.00
67 Joey Gathright HP RC .75 2.00
68 Brad Halsey HP RC .75 2.00
69 David Aardsma HP RC .75 2.00
70 Scott Kazmir HP RC 4.00 10.00
71 Matt Bush AU RC 6.00 15.00
72 John Bowker AU RC 3.00 8.00
73 Mike Ferris AU RC 3.00 8.00
75 Scott Elbert AU RC 6.00 15.00
76 Josh Fields AU RC 3.00 8.00
77 Bill Bray AU RC 3.00 8.00
78 Greg Golson AU RC 12.50 30.00
79 Neil Walker AU RC 4.00 10.00
80 Philip Hughes AU RC 8.00 20.00
81 Chris Nelson AU RC 3.00 8.00
82 Mark Rogers AU RC 3.00 8.00
83 Trevor Plouffe AU RC 6.00 15.00
85 Thomas Diamond AU RC 3.00 8.00
86 B.J. Szymanski AU RC 3.00 8.00
87 Richie Robnett AU RC 3.00 8.00
88 Seth Smith AU RC 3.00 8.00
89 Kyle Waldrop AU RC 3.00 8.00
90 Curtis Thigpen AU RC 3.00 8.00
92 Blake DeWitt AU RC 12.50 30.00
93 Taylor Tankersley AU RC 3.00 8.00
94 Zach Jackson AU RC 3.00 8.00
95 Justin Orenduff AU RC 3.00 8.00
96 Tyler Lumsden AU RC 3.00 8.00
97 Danny Putnam AU RC 3.00 8.00
98 Jon Poterson AU RC 3.00 8.00
99 Matt Fox AU RC 1.25 3.00
100 Gio Gonzalez AU RC 6.00 15.00
101 Huston Street AU RC 3.00 8.00
102 Jay Rainville AU RC 6.00 15.00
103 Matt Durkin AU RC 3.00 8.00
104 Brett Smith AU RC 3.00 8.00
105 Justin Hoyman AU RC 3.00 8.00
106 Erick San Pedro AU RC 3.00 8.00
107 Jeff Marquez AU RC 3.00 8.00
108 Hunter Pence AU RC 6.00 15.00
109 Dustin Pedroia AU RC 30.00 80.00
110 Kurt Suzuki AU RC 5.00 12.00
111 Billy Buckner AU RC 3.00 8.00
115 Homer Bailey AU RC 6.00 15.00
116 David Purcey AU RC 3.00 8.00
117 Jeremy Sowers AU RC 3.00 8.00
119 Eric Hurley AU RC 3.00 8.00
120 Grant Johnson AU RC 3.00 8.00

2004 Hot Prospects Draft Die Cuts

*DIE CUT p/r 47-64: .5X TO 1.2X BASIC
*DIE CUT p/r 92: .4X TO 1X BASIC
ONE PER RED FOIL BONUS PACK
RED PACKS ISSUED TO DISTRIBUTORS
PRINT RUNS B/WN 15-92 COPIES PER
NO PRICING ON QTY OFF 3 OR LESS
CARDS ARE NOT SERIAL-NUMBERED
PRINT RUN INFO PROVIDED BY FLEER
SEE BECKETT.COM FOR ALL PRINT RUNS
71 Matt Bush AU/59 * 8.00 20.00
75 Scott Elbert AU/51 * 10.00 25.00
76 Josh Fields AU/50 * 6.00 15.00
78 Greg Golson AU/50 * 15.00 40.00
80 Philip Hughes AU/47 * 15.00 40.00
81 Chris Nelson AU/62 * 20.00 50.00
82 Mark Rogers AU/59 * 15.00 40.00
83 Trevor Plouffe AU/58 * 12.50 30.00
85 Thomas Diamond AU/58 * 20.00 50.00
87 Richie Robnett AU/61 * 12.50 30.00
89 Kyle Waldrop AU/62 * 12.50 30.00
92 Blake DeWitt AU/64 * 40.00 80.00
93 Taylor Tankersley AU/63 * 8.00 20.00
94 Zach Jackson AU/61 * 8.00 20.00
96 Tyler Lumsden AU/59 * 8.00 20.00
97 Danny Putnam AU/61 * 8.00 20.00
98 Jon Poterson AU/58 * 8.00 20.00
99 Matt Fox AU/61 * 1.50 4.00
100 Gio Gonzalez AU/60 * 15.00 40.00
101 Huston Street AU/27 * 6.00 15.00
105 Justin Hoyman AU/62 * 8.00 20.00
110 Kurt Suzuki AU/92 * 10.00 25.00
115 Homer Bailey AU/48 * 8.00 20.00
116 David Purcey AU/61 * 6.00 15.00
117 Jeremy Sowers AU/61 * 30.00 60.00
119 Eric Hurley AU/61 * 12.50 30.00

2004 Hot Prospects Draft Red Hot

*RED 1-60: 2.5X TO 6X BASIC
*RED 61-70: 1X TO 2.5X BASIC
1-70 PRINT RUN 150 SERIAL #'d SETS
71-120 PRINT RUN 25 SERIAL #'d SETS
71-120 NO PRICING DUE TO SCARCITY
OVERALL PARALLEL ODDS 1:15 H, 1:120 R
CARDS 112 AND 113 DO NOT EXIST
EXCHANGE DEADLINE INDEFINITE

2004 Hot Prospects Draft White Hot

OVERALL PARALLEL ODDS 1:15 H, 1:120 R
STATED PRINT RUN 1 SERIAL #'d SET
NO PRICING DUE TO SCARCITY
CARDS 112 AND 113 DO NOT EXIST
EXCHANGE DEADLINE INDEFINITE

2004 Hot Prospects Draft Alumni Ink

STATED PRINT RUN 15 SERIAL #'d SETS
RED HOT PRINT RUN 5 SERIAL #'d SETS
WHITE HOT PRINT RUN 1 SERIAL #'d SET
OVERALL AU-GU ODDS 1:12 H, 1:24 R
NO PRICING DUE TO SCARCITY
EXCHANGE DEADLINE INDEFINITE

2004 Hot Prospects Draft Double Team Jersey

STATED PRINT RUN 100 SERIAL #'d SETS
*RED HOT: .6X TO 1.5X BASIC
RED HOT PRINT RUN 25 SERIAL #'d SETS
WHITE HOT PRINT RUN 1 SERIAL #'d SET
NO WHITE HOT PRICING DUE TO SCARCITY
*PATCH: 1X TO 2.5X BASIC
PATCH PRINT RUN 50 SERIAL #'d SETS
PATCH RED HOT PRINT RUN 10 #'d SETS
NO PATCH RED HOT PRICING AVAILABLE
PATCH WHITE HOT PRINT RUN 1 #'d SET
NO PATCH WHITE HOT PRICING AVAILABLE
OVERALL AU-GU ODDS 1:12 H, 1:24 R
AS Alfonso Soriano Rgr-Yanks 4.00 10.00
CB Carlos Beltran Astros-Royals 4.00 10.00
EM Eddie Murray Mets-O's 10.00 25.00
GM Greg Maddux Braves-Cubs 8.00 20.00
HN Hideo Nomo Dgr-Sox 6.00 15.00
IR I.Rodriguez Marlins-Tigers 6.00 15.00
JG Jason Giambi A's-Yanks 4.00 10.00
MP Mike Piazza Dgr-Mets 8.00 20.00
MR Manny Ramirez Indians-Sox 6.00 15.00
MT Miguel Tejada A's-O's 4.00 10.00
NR Nolan Ryan Astros-Rgr 15.00 40.00
PM Pedro Martinez Expos-Sox 6.00 15.00
RCA Rod Carew Angels-Twins 10.00 25.00
RCL Roger Clemens Astros-Sox 8.00 20.00
RH R.Henderson A's-Padres 10.00 25.00
RJ Reggie Jackson A's-Yanks 10.00 25.00

SR Scott Rolen Cards-Phils 6.00 15.00
TG Tom Glavine Braves-Mets 6.00 15.00
VG Vlad Guerrero Angels-Expos 6.00 15.00

2004 Hot Prospects Draft Double Team Autograph Patch Red Hot

STATED PRINT RUN 22 SERIAL #'d SETS
WHITE HOT PRINT RUN 1 SERIAL #'d SET
NO WHITE HOT PRICING DUE TO SCARCITY
OVERALL AU-GU ODDS 1:12 H, 1:24 R
IR I.Rodriguez Marlins-Tigers 50.00 100.00
MP Mike Piazza Dgr-Mets 100.00 200.00
MR Manny Ramirez Indians-Sox 60.00 120.00
RJ Reggie Jackson A's-Yanks 50.00 100.00
SR Scott Rolen Cards-Phils 40.00 80.00
VG Vlad Guerrero Angels-Expos 50.00 100.00

2004 Hot Prospects Draft MLB Hot Materials

STATED PRINT RUN 325 SERIAL #'d SETS
*RED HOT: .75X TO 2X BASIC
RED HOT PRINT RUN 50 SERIAL #'d SETS
WHITE HOT PRINT RUN 1 SERIAL #'d SET
NO WHITE HOT PRICING DUE TO SCARCITY
OVERALL AU-GU ODDS 1:12 H, 1:24 R
AD Adam Dunn Jsy 2.00 5.00
AJ Andruw Jones Jsy 3.00 8.00
APE Andy Pettitte Jsy 3.00 8.00
APU Albert Pujols Jsy 6.00 15.00
AS Alfonso Soriano Jsy 2.00 5.00
CD Carlos Delgado Jsy 2.00 5.00
CJ Chipper Jones Jsy 3.00 8.00
CS Curt Schilling Jsy 3.00 8.00
DW Dontrelle Willis Jsy 3.00 8.00
EG Eric Gagne Jsy 2.00 5.00
FT Frank Thomas Jsy 3.00 8.00
HB Hank Blalock Jsy 2.00 5.00
HM Hideki Matsui Jsy 8.00 20.00
HN Hideo Nomo Jsy 3.00 8.00
IR Ivan Rodriguez Jsy 3.00 8.00
JB Jeff Bagwell Jsy 3.00 8.00
JD J.D. Drew Jsy 2.00 5.00
JE Jim Edmonds Jsy 2.00 5.00
JM Joe Mauer Jsy 3.00 8.00
JP Jorge Posada Jsy 3.00 8.00
JS Jason Schmidt Jsy 2.00 5.00
JT Jim Thome Jsy 3.00 8.00
KM Kaz Matsui Jsy 3.00 8.00
KW Kerry Wood Jsy 2.00 5.00
LB Lance Berkman Jsy 2.00 5.00
LO Lyle Overbay Jsy 2.00 5.00
MC Miguel Cabrera Jsy 3.00 8.00
MM Mike Mussina Jsy 3.00 8.00
MPI Mike Piazza Jsy 4.00 10.00
MPR Mark Prior Jsy 3.00 8.00
MR Manny Ramirez Jsy 3.00 8.00
MTJ Miguel Tejada Jsy 2.00 5.00
MTX Mark Teixeira Jsy 3.00 8.00
RC Roger Clemens Jsy 4.00 10.00
RJ Randy Johnson Jsy 3.00 8.00
SS Sammy Sosa Jsy 3.00 8.00
THE Todd Helton Jsy 3.00 8.00
THN Torii Hunter Jsy 2.00 5.00
THU Tim Hudson Jsy 2.00 5.00
VG Vladimir Guerrero Jsy 3.00 8.00

2004 Hot Prospects Draft Past Present Future Autograph

STATED PRINT RUN 33 SERIAL #'d SETS
RED HOT PRINT RUN 3 SERIAL #'d SETS
NO RED HOT PRICING DUE TO SCARCITY
WHITE HOT PRINT RUN 1 SERIAL #'d SET
NO WHITE HOT PRICING DUE TO SCARCITY
OVERALL AU-GU ODDS 1:12 H, 1:24 R
EXCHANGE DEADLINE INDEFINITE
BDB Bench/Dunn/Bailey 75.00 150.00
BMH Berra/Mussina/Hughes 75.00 200.00
BRP Buckner/Manny/Pedroia 50.00 120.00
CTG Carlton/Thome/Golson 50.00 100.00
FMF Fisk/Meaux/Fields 10.00 25.00
GNE K.Gibson/Nomo/Elbert 200.00 350.00
KWW Kiner/J.Wilson/N.Walker 40.00 80.00
RYD Ryan/M.Young/Diamond 125.00 200.00
WPD Mookie/Piazza/Durkin 75.00 150.00

2004 Hot Prospects Draft Rewind

STATED ODDS 1:5
1 Joe Mauer .75 2.00
2 Derek Jeter 2.50 6.00
3 Chipper Jones 1.00 2.50
4 Greg Maddux 1.25 3.00
5 Alex Rodriguez 1.25 3.00
6 Nomar Garciaparra .60 1.50
7 Curt Schilling .60 1.50
8 Kerry Wood .40 1.00
9 Troy Glaus .40 1.00
10 Pat Burrell .40 1.00
11 Mark Mulder .40 1.00
12 Josh Beckett .40 1.00
13 Barry Zito .60 1.50
14 Mark Prior .60 1.50
15 Rickie Weeks .40 1.00
16 Khalil Greene .60 1.50
17 Ken Griffey Jr. 2.00 5.00
18 Gary Sheffield .40 1.00
19 Todd Helton .60 1.50
20 Barry Larkin .60 1.50
21 Kevin Brown .40 1.00
22 Frank Thomas 1.00 2.50
23 Manny Ramirez 1.00 2.50
24 Roger Clemens 1.25 3.00
25 Lance Berkman .60 1.50
26 Randy Johnson 1.00 2.50
27 Jason Giambi .40 1.00
28 Ben Sheets .40 1.00
29 Scott Rolen .60 1.50
30 Tom Glavine .60 1.50

2004 Hot Prospects Draft Rewind Jersey

PRINT RUNS B/WN 101-158 COPIES PER
RED HOT PRINT RUN 10 SERIAL #'d SETS
NO RED HOT PRICING DUE TO SCARCITY
WHITE HOT PRINT RUN 1 SERIAL #'d SET
NO WHITE HOT PRICING DUE TO SCARCITY
*PATCH p/r 68: .6X TO 1.5X BASIC
*PATCH p/r 41-57: .6X TO 1.5X BASIC
*PATCH p/r 20-29: .75X TO 2X BASIC
*PATCH p/r 16-19: 1X TO 2.5X BASIC
PATCH PRINT RUNS B/WN 10-68 PER
NO PATCH PRICING ON QTY OF 14 OR LESS
PATCH RED HOT PRINT RUN 5 #'d SETS
NO PATCH RED HOT PRICING AVAILABLE
PATCH WHITE HOT PRINT RUN 1 #'d SET
NO PATCH WHITE HOT PRICING AVAILABLE
OVERALL AU-GU ODDS 1:12 H, 1:24 R
BL Barry Larkin/104 4.00 10.00
BS Ben Sheets/110 3.00 8.00
BZ Barry Zito/109 3.00 8.00
CJ Chipper Jones/101 4.00 10.00
CK Casey Kotchman/113 6.00 15.00
CS Curt Schilling/139 4.00 10.00
EC Eric Chavez/110 3.00 8.00
FT Frank Thomas/107 4.00 10.00
GM Greg Maddux/131 6.00 15.00
GS Gary Sheffield/106 3.00 8.00
JB Josh Beckett/102 3.00 8.00
JG Jason Giambi/158 3.00 8.00
JM Joe Mauer/101 4.00 10.00
KB Kevin Brown/104 3.00 8.00
KG Khalil Greene/113 4.00 10.00
KW Kerry Wood/104 3.00 8.00
LB Lance Berkman/116 3.00 8.00
MM Mark Mulder/102 3.00 8.00
MP Mark Prior/102 4.00 10.00
MR Manny Ramirez/113 4.00 10.00
PB Pat Burrell/101 3.00 8.00
RB Rocco Baldelli/119 3.00 8.00
RC Roger Clemens/119 6.00 15.00
RJ Randy Johnson/136 4.00 10.00
RW Rickie Weeks/102 3.00 8.00
SR Scott Rolen/146 4.00 10.00
TG Troy Glaus/103 3.00 8.00
TG Tom Glavine/147 4.00 10.00
TH Todd Helton/108 4.00 10.00
ZG Zack Greinke/106 3.00 8.00

2004 Hot Prospects Draft Tandems

STATED ODDS 1:15 H/R
1 M.Prior 1.25 3.00
G.Maddux
2 J.Thome .60 1.50
P.Burrell
3 K.Griffey Jr. 2.00 5.00
A.Dunn
4 M.Piazza 1.00 2.50
T.Glavine
5 A.Rodriguez 2.50 6.00
D.Jeter
6 R.Clemens 1.25 3.00
A.Pettitte
7 J.Giambi 1.50 4.00
H.Matsui
8 A.Soriano .60 1.50
H.Blalock
9 M.Ramirez 1.00 2.50
D.Ortiz
10 M.Cabrera 1.00 2.50
D.Willis
11 H.Matsui 1.50 4.00
I.Suzuki
12 A.Pujols 1.25 3.00
S.Rolen
13 P.Martinez .60 1.50
C.Schilling
14 S.Sosa 1.00 2.50
N.Garciaparra
15 K.Matsui 2.50 6.00
D.Jeter

1990 Hottest 50 Players Stickers

Issued by Publications International, this sticker album measures 8 1/4" by 10 7/8" and includes 50 giant player stickers and 6 bonus stadium stickers. The oversized stickers measure 4 1/8 by 5 1/2" and feature glossy color action player photos inside a white border. The NL players stickers have a red stripe at the top and a blue stripe at the bottom, while the AL Rookies stickers have a blue stripe at the top and a red stripe at the bottom. The 32-page sticker album has slots for two stickers per page and presents career summary, biography, and statistics out to the side. The stickers are unnumbered and checklisted below in alphabetical order.

COMPLETE SET (56) 15.00 40.00
1 George Bell .08 .25
2 Wade Boggs 1.00 2.50
3 Bobby Bonilla .08 .25
4 Jose Canseco .75 2.00
5 Joe Carter .20 .50
6 Will Clark .75 2.00
7 Roger Clemens 2.00 5.00
8 Alvin Davis .08 .25
9 Eric Davis .20 .50
10 Glenn Davis .08 .25
11 Mark Davis .08 .25
12 Carlton Fisk 1.00 2.50
13 John Franco .20 .50
14 Gary Gaetti .08 .25
15 Andres Galarraga .40 1.00
16 Dwight Gooden .20 .50
17 Mark Grace .40 1.00
18 Pedro Guerrero .08 .25
19 Tony Gwynn 2.00 5.00
20 Rickey Henderson 1.25 3.00
21 Orel Hershiser .20 .50
22 Bo Jackson .40 1.00
23 Ricky Jordan .08 .25
24 Wally Joyner .20 .50
25 Don Mattingly 2.00 5.00
26 Fred McGriff .30 .75
27 Kevin Mitchell .08 .25
28 Paul Molitor .60 1.50
29 Dale Murphy .40 1.00
30 Eddie Murray .60 1.50
31 Kirby Puckett 1.25 3.00
32 Tim Raines .20 .50
33 Harold Reynolds .20 .50
34 Cal Ripken Jr. 4.00 10.00
35 Nolan Ryan 4.00 10.00
36 Bret Saberhagen .20 .50
37 Ryne Sandberg 2.00 5.00
38 Steve Sax .08 .25
39 Mike Scott .08 .25
40 Ruben Sierra .20 .50
41 Ozzie Smith 2.00 5.00
42 John Smoltz .40 1.00
43 Darryl Strawberry .20 .50
44 Greg Swindell .08 .25
45 Mickey Tettleton .20 .50
46 Alan Trammell .30 .75
47 Andy Van Slyke .20 .50
48 Lou Whitaker .20 .50
49 Devon White .08 .25
50 Robin Yount 1.00 2.50
51 Dodger Stadium .08 .25
52 Jack Murphy Stadium .08 .25
53 Shea Stadium .08 .25
54 Three Rivers Stadium .08 .25
55 Tiger Stadium .08 .25
56 Yankee Stadium .08 .25

1990 Hottest 50 Rookies Stickers

Issued by Publications International, this sticker album measures 8 1/4" by 10 7/8" and includes 50 giant rookie stickers and 6 bonus stadium stickers. The oversized stickers measure 4 1/8 by 5 1/2" and feature glossy color action player photos inside a white border. The NL Rookie stickers have a red stripe at the top and a blue stripe at the bottom, while the AL Rookie stickers have a blue stripe at the top and a red stripe at the bottom. The 32-page sticker album has slots for two stickers per page and presents career summary, biography, and statistics out to the side. The stickers are unnumbered and checklisted below in alphabetical order.

COMPLETE SET (56) 12.50 30.00
1 Jim Abbott .20 .50
2 Sandy Alomar Jr. .20 .50
3 Kent Anderson .08 .25
4 Eric Anthony .08 .25
5 Jeff Ballard .08 .25
6 Albert Belle .20 .50
7 Andy Benes .08 .25
8 Lance Blankenship .08 .25
9 Jeff Brantley .20 .50
10 Cris Carpenter .08 .25
11 Mark Carreon .08 .25
12 Dennis Cook .08 .25
13 Scott Coolbaugh .08 .25
14 Luis de los Santos .08 .25
15 Junior Felix .08 .25
16 Mark Gardner .08 .25
17 German Gonzalez .08 .25
18 Tom Gordon .30 .75
19 Ken Griffey Jr. 3.00 8.00
20 Marquis Grissom .30 .75
21 Charlie Hayes .08 .25
22 Gregg Jefferies .08 .25
23 Randy Johnson 2.00 5.00
24 Felix Jose .08 .25
25 Jeff King .08 .25
26 Randy Kramer .08 .25
27 Derek Lilliquist .08 .25
28 Greg Litton .08 .25
29 Kelly Mann .08 .25
30 Ramon Martinez .20 .50
31 Luis Medina .08 .25
32 Hal Morris .08 .25
33 Joe Oliver .08 .25
34 Gregg Olson .20 .50
35 Dean Palmer .40 1.00
36 Carlos Quintana .08 .25
37 Kevin Ritz .08 .25
38 Deion Sanders 1.00 2.50
39 Scott Scudder .08 .25
40 Steve Searcy .08 .25
41 Gary Sheffield 1.25 3.00
42 Dwight Smith .08 .25
43 Sammy Sosa 2.50 6.00
44 Greg Vaughn .20 .50
45 Robin Ventura .40 1.00
46 Jerome Walton .08 .25
47 Dave West .08 .25
48 John Wetteland .40 1.00
49 Eric Yelding .08 .25
50 Todd Zeile .20 .50
51 Dodger Stadium .08 .25
52 Jack Murphy Stadium .08 .25
53 Shea Stadium .08 .25
54 Three Rivers Stadium .08 .25
55 Tiger Stadium .08 .25
56 Yankee Stadium .08 .25

1976 Houston Post Dierker

This one-card set was distributed by the Houston Post and honors Larry Dierker's no hitter.

COMPLETE SET (1) 2.00 5.00
1 Larry Dierker 2.00 5.00

1988 Houston Show

This 20-card set measures approximately 2 1/4" by 3 1/4". On a white card face, the fronts feature black-and-white player photos accented by a purple picture frame. A white star appears at each corner of the frame, and a row of purple stars edges the pictures on the left and right sides. The backs carry the player's name, the card number, a career summary, and "1988 TTC, Houston TX 77035" as a tagline.

COMPLETE SET (20) 12.50 30.00
1 Brooks Robinson .75 2.00
2 Hank Aaron 3.00 8.00
3 Gaylord Perry .40 1.00
4 Stan Musial 2.50 6.00
5 Willie Mays 3.00 8.00
6 Ernie Banks 1.25 3.00
7 Rod Carew .75 2.00
8 Duke Snider .75 2.00
9 Mickey Mantle 6.00 15.00
10 Lou Brock .75 2.00
11 Yogi Berra .75 2.00
12 Nolan Ryan 5.00 12.00
13 Roger Clemens 1.50 4.00
14 Jose Cruz .20 .50
15 Gerald Young .08 .25
16 Enos Slaughter .40 1.00
17 Glenn Davis .08 .25
18 J.R. Richard .08 .25
19 Fergie Jenkins .40 1.00
20 Pete Incaviglia .08 .25

1979 Elston Howard Sausage

This one-card set features a small black-and-white head photo of Elston Howard of the New York Yankees on a black card with white printing. The white back displays information about the player. Some of the cards were personally autographed. The card was used as a business card advertising Elston Howard's Sausage, a division of Piedmont Provision Co.

1 Elston Howard 4.00 10.00

1953-59 Howard Photo Service PC751

The Howard Photo Service late 1950's postcard set was, until recently, thought to contain only the Bob Turley card. However, the recently discovered cards indicates that additional cards may be found in the future. These black and white postcards were issued in New York.

COMPLETE SET (5) 40.00 80.00
1 Ned Garver 5.00 10.00
2 Billy Hitchcock 5.00 10.00
3 Dave Madison 5.00 10.00
4 Willie Mays 20.00 40.00
5 Bob Turley 7.50 15.00

1997 Howard University Robinson

This one-card set measures approximately 4 1/4" by 6" and features a black-and-white action photo of Jackie Robinson. The back displays information about some important events in the history of African Americans in athletics.

1 Jackie Robinson 1.25 3.00

1993 Hoyle

One of these nine cards was inserted in specially marked Hoyle Official Playing Card decks. The back of the card box contains a checklist for all nine cards and an opening at the bottom, where the name of the player whose card is inserted in the pack appears. The cards measure the standard size and have rounded corners. On a grey background, the fronts feature black-and-white action player photos with black and white borders. The player's name appears in a white bar under the photo, while a facsimile autograph printed on the lower portion of the photo. The backs carry a player biography and stats. The cards are unnumbered and checklisted below in alphabetical order.

COMPLETE SET (9) 4.00 10.00
1 Ty Cobb .75 2.00
2 Dizzy Dean .40 1.00
3 Lou Gehrig .75 2.00
4 Walter Johnson .50 1.25
5 Satchel Paige .50 1.25
6 Babe Ruth .75 2.00
7 Casey Stengel .40 1.00
8 Honus Wagner .50 1.25
9 Cy Young .50 1.25

1993 Humpty Dumpty Canadian

This 51-card set measures approximately 1 7/16" by 1 15/16" and was issued by Humpty Dumpty. The full-bleed color action photos have the player's team logo in one of the upper corners. The back carries the player's name, position, biography and statistics in both French and English. The Humpty Dumpty logo appears at the top over a navy blue border. The cards are numbered on the back.

COMPLETE SET (51) 15.00 40.00
1 Cal Ripken 2.00 5.00
2 Mike Mussina .40 1.00
3 Roger Clemens 1.00 2.50
4 Chuck Finley .20 .50
5 Sandy Alomar Jr. .20 .50
6 Frank Thomas .50 1.25
7 Robin Ventura .30 .75
8 Cecil Fielder .20 .50
9 George Brett 1.00 2.50
10 Cal Eldred .08 .25
11 Kirby Puckett .60 1.50
12 Dave Winfield .50 1.25
13 Jim Abbott .08 .25
14 Rickey Henderson .60 1.50
15 Ken Griffey Jr. 1.25 3.00
16 Nolan Ryan 2.00 5.00
17 Ivan Rodriguez .50 1.25
18 Paul Molitor .50 1.25
19 John Olerud .30 .75
20 Joe Carter .20 .50
21 Jack Morris .20 .50
22 Roberto Alomar .40 1.00
23 Pat Borders .08 .25
24 Devon White .08 .25
25 Juan Guzman .08 .25
26 Steve Avery .08 .25
27 John Smoltz .30 .75
28 Mark Grace .40 1.00
29 Jose Rijo .08 .25
30 David Nied .08 .25
31 Benito Santiago .20 .50
32 Jeff Bagwell .60 1.50
33 Tim Wallach .08 .25
34 Eric Karros .20 .50
35 Delino DeShields .08 .25
36 Wilfredo Cordero .08 .25
37 Marquis Grissom .20 .50
38 Ken Hill .08 .25
39 Moises Alou .20 .50
40 Chris Nabholz .08 .25
41 Dennis Martinez .20 .50
42 Larry Walker .30 .75
43 Bobby Bonilla .08 .25
44 Len Dykstra .20 .50
45 Tim Wakefield .40 1.00
46 Andy Van Slyke .08 .25
47 Tony Gwynn 1.00 2.50
48 Fred McGriff .30 .75
49 Barry Bonds 1.00 2.50
50 Ozzie Smith 1.00 2.50
51 Checklist 1-51 .08 .25
xx Album 2.00 5.00

1987 Hygrade All-Time Greats

This set features some of baseball's all-time greats. The fronts carry a color player photo in a green border. A small gold oval in the lower left indicates the player's playing years. The backs display player information and why the player is one of the all-time greats. It is believed that these cards were actually issued at a couple different times, therefore cropping differences may exist for all players. In addition, it appears as if some of these cropping differences came as the players had to have any semblence of a major league logo removed from the fronts. The cards are unnumbered and checklisted below in alphabetical order.

COMPLETE SET (109) 12.50 30.00
1 Hank Aaron .40 1.00
2 Joe Adcock .02 .10
3 Grover Alexander .20 .50
4 Dick Allen .02 .10
5 Luis Aparicio .08 .25
6 Luke Appling .02 .10
7 Richie Ashburn .08 .25
8A Ernie Banks .20 .50
8B Ernie Banks .20 .50
No Logo
9 Hank Bauer .02 .10
10 Johnny Bench .30 .75
11 Yogi Berra .20 .50
12 Lou Boudreau .08 .25
13 Lou Brock .08 .25
14 Three Finger Brown .02 .10
15 Jim Bunning .08 .25
16 Roy Campanella .20 .50
17 Rod Carew .30 .75
18 Orlando Cepeda .08 .25
19 Roberto Clemente .40 1.00
20A Ty Cobb .40 1.00
20A Ty Cobb .40 1.00
Card has Orange Borders
21 Mickey Cochrane .08 .25
22 Rocky Colavito .20 .50
23 Eddie Collins .08 .25
24 Sam Crawford .08 .25
25 Joe Cronin .02 .10
26 Bill Dickey .08 .25
27 Joe DiMaggio .40 1.00
28 Larry Doby .08 .25
29 Don Drysdale .30 .75
29 Ralph Kiner .02 .10
30 Leo Durocher .08 .25
31 Carl Erskine .02 .10
32 Bob Feller .08 .25
33 Curt Flood .02 .10
34 Whitey Ford .20 .50
35 Jimmie Foxx .20 .50
36 Frankie Frisch .02 .10
37 Carl Furillo .02 .10
38A Lou Gehrig
38B Lou Gehrig .40 1.00
Card has Orange Borders
39 Charlie Gehringer .02 .10
40 Bob Gibson .20 .50
41 Hank Greenberg .20 .50
42 Lefty Grove .08 .25
43 Gabby Hartnett .02 .10
44 Gil Hodges .08 .25
45 Rogers Hornsby .20 .50
46 Carl Hubbell .20 .50
47 Catfish Hunter .20 .50
48 Monte Irvin .08 .25
49 Fergie Jenkins .08 .25
50 Walter Johnson .30 .75
51A Jim Kaat .02 .10
Chi White Sox
51B Jim Kaat .08 .25
St. Louis
52 Al Kaline .30 .75
53 George Kell .08 .25
55 Ted Kluszewski .08 .25
56 Don Larsen .02 .10
57 Bob Lemon .08 .25
58 Ernie Lombardi .08 .25
59 Eddie Lopat .02 .10
60 Mickey Mantle .60 1.50
61 Juan Marichal .20 .50
62 Roger Maris .08 .25
63 Billy Martin .08 .25
64 Eddie Mathews .30 .75
65 Christy Mathewson .02 .10
66 Willie Mays .40 1.00
67 Bill Mazeroski .08 .25
68 Joe Morgan .30 .75
69 Thurman Munson .40 1.00
70 Stan Musial .20 .50
71 Tony Oliva .08 .25
72 Mel Ott .02 .10
73 Jim Palmer .20 .50
74 Gaylord Perry .08 .25
75 Boog Powell .08 .25
76 Pee Wee Reese .40 1.00
77 Robin Roberts .08 .25
78 Brooks Robinson .20 .50
79 Frank Robinson .20 .50
80A Jackie Robinson .40 1.00
80B Jackie Robinson
Card has Orange Borders
81A Babe Ruth .60 1.50
81B Babe Ruth .60 1.50
Card has Orange Boders
82 Tom Seaver .40 1.00
83 Bobby Shantz .08 .25
84 Al Simmons .02 .10
85 George Sisler .02 .10
86 Enos Slaughter .08 .25
87 Duke Snider .40 1.00
88 Duke Snider .20 .50
89 Warren Spahn .20 .50
90 Tris Speaker .02 .10
91 Willie Stargell .30 .75
92 Bill Terry .02 .10
93 Bobby Thomson .08 .25
94 Pie Traynor .08 .25
95 Ed Walsh .02 .10
96 Paul Waner .08 .25
97 Hoyt Wilhelm .08 .25
98 Billy Williams .08 .25
99 Ted Williams .40 1.00
100 Maury Wills .02 .10
101 Early Wynn .08 .25
102 Carl Yastrzemski .20 .50
103 Ross Youngs .02 .10

1996 Illinois Lottery

This five-card set consists of legendary Chicago Cubs and White Sox players and also included St. Louis Cardinals player, Red Schoendeinst. The cards are actually real Illinois scratch-off lottery ticket stubs and can be found scratched or unscratched. The cards are unnumbered and checklisted below in alphabetical order.

COMPLETE SET (5) 2.00 5.00
1 Ernie Banks .75 2.00
2 Carlton Fisk .75 2.00
3 Minnie Minoso .40 1.00
4 Red Schoendeinst .50 1.25
5 Billy Williams .60 1.50

2014 Immaculate Collection

1-100 PRINT RUN 99 SER.#'d SETS
101-127/154 PRINT RUN 49 SER.#'d SETS
128-152/155 PRINT RUN 99 SER.#'d SETS
EXCHANGE DEADLINE 3/3/2016
1 Mike Trout 10.00 25.00
2 Derek Jeter 10.00 25.00
3 Albert Pujols 2.50 6.00
4 Ichiro Suzuki 3.00 8.00
5 Clayton Kershaw 3.00 8.00
6 David Ortiz 2.00 5.00
7 Miguel Cabrera 2.00 5.00
8 Buster Posey 6.00 15.00
9 Joe Mauer 1.50 4.00
10 Jose Fernandez 2.00 5.00
11 Bryce Harper 3.00 8.00
12 Andrew McCutchen 2.00 5.00
13 Yu Darvish 2.00 5.00
14 Manny Machado 2.00 5.00
15 David Wright 1.50 4.00
16 Robinson Cano 1.50 4.00
17 Yadier Molina 2.50 6.00
18 Dustin Pedroia 2.00 5.00
19 Evan Longoria 1.50 4.00
20 Stephen Strasburg 2.00 5.00
21 Freddie Freeman 2.50 6.00
22 Paul Goldschmidt 2.00 5.00
23 Giancarlo Stanton 2.00 5.00
24 Matt Kemp 1.50 4.00
25 Yoenis Cespedes 2.00 5.00
26 Joey Votto 2.00 5.00
27 Chris Sale 2.00 5.00
28 Josh Hamilton 1.50 4.00
29 Ryan Braun 1.50 4.00
30 Jacoby Ellsbury 1.50 4.00
31 Matt Harvey 1.50 4.00
32 Wil Myers 1.25 3.00
33 Yasiel Puig 2.00 5.00
34 Ryan Howard 1.50 4.00
35 Jason Heyward 1.50 4.00
36 Troy Tulowitzki 2.00 5.00
37 Justin Verlander 2.00 5.00
38 Pedro Alvarez 1.25 3.00
39 Michael Wacha 1.50 4.00
40 Gerrit Cole 2.00 5.00
41 Matt Holliday 2.00 5.00
42 Jose Bautista 1.50 4.00
43 Adrian Gonzalez 1.50 4.00
44 Jimmy Rollins 1.50 4.00
45 Paul Konerko 1.50 4.00
46 Mark Trumbo 1.25 3.00
47 Shelby Miller 1.50 4.00
48 Zack Wheeler 1.50 4.00
49 Josh Donaldson 1.50 4.00
50 Jean Segura 1.50 4.00
51 Prince Fielder 1.50 4.00
52 Alex Rodriguez 2.50 6.00
53 Eric Hosmer 1.50 4.00
54 Adrian Beltre 2.00 5.00
55 Jose Reyes 1.50 4.00
56 Madison Bumgarner 5.00 12.00
57 Max Scherzer 2.00 5.00
58 Chris Davis 1.25 3.00
59 Adam Wainwright 1.50 4.00
60 Carlos Beltran 1.50 4.00
61 Adam Jones 1.50 4.00
62 Cliff Lee 1.50 4.00
63 David Price 1.50 4.00
64 Sonny Gray 1.50 4.00
65 Tyler Skaggs 1.25 3.00
66 Pablo Sandoval 1.50 4.00
67 Felix Hernandez 1.50 4.00
68 Hyun-Jin Ryu 1.50 4.00
69 Jose Altuve 1.50 4.00
70 Alex Gordon 1.50 4.00
71 Edwin Encarnacion 2.00 5.00
72 Alex Wood 1.25 3.00
73 Salvador Perez 1.50 4.00
74 Zack Greinke 2.00 5.00
75 Matt Carpenter 2.00 5.00
76 Chase Utley 1.50 4.00
77 Justin Upton 1.50 4.00
78 Shin-Soo Choo 1.50 4.00
79 Anthony Rendon 2.00 5.00
80 Mike Napoli 1.25 3.00
81 Starling Marte 1.50 4.00
82 Carlos Gonzalez 1.50 4.00
83 Craig Kimbrel 1.50 4.00
84 Hanley Ramirez 1.50 4.00
85 Andrelton Simmons 1.25 3.00
86 Hisashi Iwakuma 1.50 4.00
87 Brian McCann 1.50 4.00
88 Cole Hamels 1.50 4.00
89 Carlos Santana 1.50 4.00
90 Everth Cabrera 1.25 3.00
91 Aramis Ramirez 1.25 3.00
92 Brandon Phillips 1.25 3.00
93 Matt Adams 1.25 3.00
94 Mariano Rivera 2.50 6.00
95 Frank Thomas 2.00 5.00
96 Ken Griffey Jr. 6.00 15.00
97 Cal Ripken Jr. 5.00 12.00
98 George Brett 6.00 15.00
99 Nolan Ryan 6.00 15.00
100 Pete Rose 6.00 15.00
101 Kolten Wong JSY AU/49 10.00 25.00
104 Juan Centeno JSY AU/49 RC 3.00 8.00
105 Enny Romero JSY AU/49 3.00 8.00
106 Josmil Pinto JSY AU/49 RC 3.00 8.00
107 G.Polanco JSY AU/49 RC 5.00 12.00
108 Cameron Rupp JSY AU/49 RC 3.00 8.00
109 Ryan Goins JSY AU/49 RC 4.00 10.00
110 Abraham Almonte JSY AU/49 RC 3.00 8.00
111 Billy Hamilton JSY AU/49 RC 6.00 15.00
113 Oscar Taveras JSY AU/49 6.00 15.00
114 Jimmy Nelson JSY AU/49 RC 3.00 8.00
115 Jose Ramirez JSY AU/49 RC 15.00 40.00
116 Marcus Semien JSY AU/49 RC 15.00 40.00
117 Matt Davidson JSY AU/49 4.00 10.00
118 Matt Shoemaker JSY AU/49 5.00 12.00
119 Michael Choice JSY AU/49 3.00 8.00
120 Reymond Fuentes JSY AU/49 RC 3.00 8.00
121 Taijuan Walker JSY AU/49 3.00 8.00
122 Yordano Ventura JSY AU/49 12.00 30.00
123 Chad Bettis JSY AU/49 3.00 8.00
124 Matt den Dekker JSY AU/49 6.00 15.00
125 J.R. Murphy JSY AU/49 3.00 8.00
126 Xander Bogaerts JSY AU/49 15.00 40.00
127 N.Castellanos JSY AU/49 RC 8.00 20.00
128 Masahiro Tanaka JSY/99 RC 8.00 20.00
129 Taijuan Walker AU/99 RC 8.00 20.00
130 Jose Abreu AU/99 RC 20.00 50.00
131 Xander Bogaerts AU/99 RC 15.00 40.00
132 Kolten Wong AU/99 RC 4.00 10.00
133 Matt den Dekker AU/99 RC 4.00 10.00
134 Michael Choice AU/99 RC 3.00 8.00
135 Jimmy Nelson AU/99 RC 3.00 8.00
136 Matt Davidson AU/99 RC 4.00 10.00
137 J.R. Murphy AU/80 RC 3.00 8.00
140 Yordano Ventura AU/99 RC 8.00 20.00
141 Tanner Roark AU/99 RC 3.00 8.00
143 James Paxton AU/99 RC 10.00 25.00
144 Matt Shoemaker AU/99 RC 3.00 8.00
145 Enny Romero AU/99 RC 3.00 8.00
146 Kris Johnson AU/99 RC 3.00 8.00
147 Stolmy Pimentel AU/99 RC 3.00 8.00
148 Chad Bettis AU/99 RC 3.00 8.00
149 Ehire Adrianza AU/99 RC 3.00 8.00
150 G.Springer AU/99 RC 20.00 50.00
151 Chris Owings AU/99 RC
152 O.Taveras AU/99 RC EXCH 4.00 10.00
154 Jose Abreu JSY AU/49 25.00 60.00
155 Jose Abreu JSY/99 RC 15.00 40.00

2014 Immaculate Collection Accolades Materials

RANDOM INSERTS IN PACKS
PRINT RUNS B/WN 5-99 COPIES PER
NO PRICING ON QTY 10 OR LESS
1 Honus Wagner/20 50.00 120.00
3 Joe Jackson/79 50.00 120.00
5 Ty Cobb/99 25.00 60.00
6 Pee Wee Reese/99 5.00 12.00
7 Burleigh Grimes/20 40.00 100.00
8 Jimmie Foxx/99 10.00 25.00
9 Mel Ott/49 15.00 40.00
10 Rogers Hornsby/99 20.00 50.00
11 Tris Speaker/99 12.00 30.00
12 Gil Hodges/99 5.00 12.00
13 Lou Gehrig/99 40.00 100.00
14 Jackie Robinson/99 20.00 50.00
15 Leo Durocher/49 10.00 25.00
16 Joe DiMaggio/49 30.00 80.00
17 Nolan Ryan/99 10.00 25.00
18 Greg Maddux/49 8.00 20.00
19 Lou Brock/99 5.00 12.00
20 Cal Ripken Jr./99 8.00 20.00
21 Reggie Jackson/99 5.00 12.00
22 Mike Schmidt/49 10.00 25.00
23 Rod Carew/25 8.00 20.00
24 Willie McCovey/49 5.00 12.00
25 Tony Gwynn/99 6.00 15.00

2014 Immaculate Collection Accolades Materials Prime

*PRIME: 1X TO 2.5X BASIC
RANDOM INSERTS IN PACKS
PRINT RUNS B/WN 1-25 COPIES PER
NO PRICING ON QTY 10 OR LESS

2014 Immaculate Collection All-Star Autographs

RANDOM INSERTS IN PACKS
PRINT RUNS B/WN 15-99 COPIES PER
EXCHANGE DEADLINE 3/3/2016
5 Adam Jones/25 12.00 30.00
6 Max Scherzer/25 15.00 40.00
7 David Wright/25 15.00 40.00
8 Matt Harvey/25 EXCH 30.00 80.00
9 Salvador Perez/99 EXCH 15.00 40.00
11 Carlos Gomez/99 6.00 15.00
12 Freddie Freeman/49 12.00 30.00
13 Jose Fernandez/49 EXCH 12.00 30.00
15 Chris Sale/25 10.00 25.00

2014 Immaculate Collection Clubhouse Material

RANDOM INSERTS IN PACKS
PRINT RUNS B/WN 15-99 COPIES PER
NO PRICING ON QTY 15 OR LESS
1 Jim Palmer/49 6.00 15.00
2 Alex Rodriguez/25 10.00 25.00
3 Tony Gwynn/99 4.00 10.00
4 Jose Bautista/49 3.00 8.00
5 Ken Griffey Jr./25 30.00 80.00
6 Alan Trammell/99 5.00 12.00
7 Josh Hamilton/49 3.00 8.00
9 Kirby Puckett/20 20.00 50.00
10 Rickey Henderson/99 4.00 10.00
11 Pete Rose/49 8.00 20.00
12 Miguel Cabrera/49 4.00 10.00
13 Justin Verlander/49 4.00 10.00
14 Nick Swisher/99 3.00 8.00
15 A.J. Burnett/25 2.50 6.00
17 Yu Darvish/25 10.00 25.00
18 Evan Longoria/25 3.00 8.00
19 Tony Gwynn/99 4.00 10.00
20 Prince Fielder/99 3.00 8.00
21 Robinson Cano/25 3.00 8.00
22 CC Sabathia/49 3.00 8.00
23 Derek Jeter/25 12.00 30.00
24 Mike Schmidt/49 6.00 15.00
25 Victor Martinez/25 5.00 12.00
28 Drew Smyly/99 2.50 6.00
29 Albert Pujols/99 5.00 12.00
30 Yasiel Puig/99 6.00 15.00

2014 Immaculate Collection Clubhouse Signatures

RANDOM INSERTS IN PACKS
PRINT RUNS B/WN 15-99 COPIES PER
NO PRICING ON QTY 15 OR LESS
EXCHANGE DEADLINE 3/3/2016
1 Matt Carpenter/25 15.00 40.00
4 Chris Davis/25 6.00 15.00

6 Evan Gattis/99 4.00 10.00
10 Mark Grace/25 10.00 25.00
11 Norichika Aoki/99 6.00 15.00
12 Reymond Fuentes/99 4.00 10.00
14 Justin Upton/25 8.00 20.00
15 R.A. Dickey/25 8.00 20.00
16 Roy Halladay/25 15.00 40.00
17 Hisashi Iwakuma/99 6.00 15.00
18 Josh Donaldson/99 12.00 30.00
19 Miguel Sano/99 12.00 30.00
20 Darryl Strawberry/25 12.00 30.00
21 Shelby Miller/99 5.00 12.00
22 Shane Victorino/49 5.00 12.00
23 David Freese/25 4.00 10.00
24 Rafael Palmeiro/25 8.00 20.00
25 Adrian Beltre/25 6.00 15.00
27 George Springer/99 10.00 25.00
28 Dan Petry/99 4.00 10.00
29 Garry Templeton/99 4.00 10.00
30 Glenn Hubbard/99 4.00 10.00
31 Mark Langston/99 4.00 10.00
32 Shawon Dunston/99 4.00 10.00
33 Ellis Burks/99 4.00 10.00
34 Jose Abreu/99 25.00 60.00
35 Michael Wacha/49 10.00 25.00
36 Billy Hamilton/99 5.00 12.00
37 J.R. Murphy/99 4.00 10.00
38 Michael Choice/99 4.00 10.00
40 Eric Hosmer/25 10.00 25.00
41 Xander Bogaerts/75 15.00 40.00
42 Gerrit Cole/25 6.00 15.00
43 John Kruk/25 8.00 20.00
44 Taijuan Walker/99 4.00 10.00
45 Oscar Taveras/99 8.00 20.00
46 Carlos Gonzalez/25 8.00 20.00
47 Darin Ruf/99 5.00 12.00
48 Gregory Polanco/99 4.00 10.00
49 Raul Ibanez/49 5.00 12.00
50 Paul Konerko/49 12.00 30.00
51 Matt den Dekker/99 5.00 12.00
52 Andre Thornton/99 4.00 10.00
53 Jose Fernandez/25 12.00 30.00
54 Victor Martinez/25 15.00 40.00
55 Frank White/99 4.00 10.00
57 Bret Saberhagen/99 4.00 10.00
58 Jay Bruce/49 10.00 25.00
59 Zack Wheeler/49 5.00 12.00
60 Gary Gaetti/99 4.00 10.00

2014 Immaculate Collection Derek Jeter Tribute All-Star

RANDOM INSERTS IN PACKS
STATED PRINT RUN 14 SER.#'d SETS
1 Derek Jeter 10.00 25.00
2 Derek Jeter 10.00 25.00
3 Derek Jeter 10.00 25.00
4 Derek Jeter 10.00 25.00
5 Derek Jeter 10.00 25.00
6 Derek Jeter 10.00 25.00
7 Derek Jeter 10.00 25.00
8 Derek Jeter 10.00 25.00
9 Derek Jeter 10.00 25.00
10 Derek Jeter 10.00 25.00
11 Derek Jeter 10.00 25.00
12 Derek Jeter 10.00 25.00
13 Derek Jeter 10.00 25.00
14 Derek Jeter 10.00 25.00

2014 Immaculate Collection Derek Jeter Tribute All-Star Jersey Number

*JSY NUM: 1.5X TO 4X BASIC
RANDOM INSERTS IN PACKS
STATED PRINT RUN 2 SER.#'d SETS

2014 Immaculate Collection Diamond Fabric

RANDOM INSERTS IN PACKS
PRINT RUNS B/WN 45-99 COPIES PER
1 Austin Jackson/99 2.50 6.00
2 Andrew McCutchen/99 20.00 50.00
3 Stephen Strasburg/49 4.00 10.00
4 Eric Hosmer/99 3.00 8.00
5 Yoenis Cespedes/49 4.00 10.00
6 Dustin Pedroia/99 4.00 10.00
7 Adrian Beltre/99 4.00 10.00
8 Edwin Encarnacion/99 4.00 10.00
9 Madison Bumgarner/99 3.00 8.00
10 Rick Porcello/99 3.00 8.00
11 Matt Kemp/49 3.00 8.00
12 Manny Machado/49 4.00 10.00
13 Nick Swisher/99 3.00 8.00
14 Bryce Harper/49 10.00 25.00
15 Wil Myers/49 2.50 6.00

2014 Immaculate Collection Immaculate Autograph Materials

RANDOM INSERTS IN PACKS
PRINT RUNS B/WN 10-99 COPIES PER
NO PRICING ON QTY 10
EXCHANGE DEADLINE 3/3/2016
1 Stephen Strasburg/99 12.00 30.00
2 Troy Tulowitzki/99 10.00 25.00
3 Evan Longoria/99 6.00 15.00
4 Brandon Phillips/49 4.00 10.00
5 David Wright/99 12.00 30.00
6 Alan Trammell/49 10.00 25.00
7 Darryl Strawberry/99 8.00 20.00
8 Craig Biggio/49 15.00 40.00
9 Mark Grace/99 6.00 15.00
10 Evan Gattis/49 4.00 10.00
11 Fred McGriff/49 8.00 20.00
12 Edgar Martinez/49 5.00 12.00
13 Miguel Cabrera/49 40.00 100.00
14 Wade Boggs/49 15.00 40.00
15 Bo Jackson/49 30.00 80.00
16 Gary Sheffield/49 4.00 10.00
17 Barry Larkin/49 20.00 50.00
18 Joe Girardi/49 10.00 25.00
19 Jose Canseco/49 15.00 40.00
20 Tom Glavine/49 12.00 30.00
21 David Justice/49 10.00 25.00
22 Ken Griffey Jr./25 125.00 250.00
23 Will Clark/25 20.00 50.00
24 Pat Corbin/99 5.00 12.00
26 Ellis Burks/25 10.00 25.00
27 Luis Gonzalez/25 6.00 15.00
28 Nomar Garciaparra/49 15.00 40.00
29 Mike Trout/49 125.00 250.00
30 Clayton Kershaw/49 40.00 100.00
31 Wil Myers/99 4.00 10.00
32 Dennis Eckersley/49 8.00 20.00
33 Jose Fernandez/49 10.00 25.00
34 Gerrit Cole/99 8.00 20.00
35 Yoenis Cespedes/49 8.00 20.00
36 Mike Schmidt/25 20.00 50.00
37 Michael Morse/49 4.00 10.00
38 Shane Victorino/99 5.00 12.00
39 Shelby Miller/99 5.00 12.00
40 Nolan Ryan/20 40.00 100.00
41 Frank Thomas/25 40.00 100.00
42 Jay Bruce/99 8.00 20.00
43 Rafael Palmeiro/49 5.00 12.00
44 Adam Jones/99 8.00 20.00
45 Carlos Gonzalez/99 5.00 12.00
46 Eric Hosmer/99 10.00 25.00
47 Adrian Beltre/49 12.00 30.00

2014 Immaculate Collection Immaculate Autograph Materials Prime

*PRIME: .6X TO 1.5X BASIC
RANDOM INSERTS IN PACKS
PRINT RUNS B/WN 1-20 COPIES PER
NO PRICING ON QTY 15 OR LESS
EXCHANGE DEADLINE 3/3/2016
6 Alan Trammell/20 25.00 60.00

2014 Immaculate Collection Immaculate Autographs

RANDOM INSERTS IN PACKS
PRINT RUNS B/WN 15-99 COPIES PER
NO PRICING ON QTY 15
EXCHANGE DEADLINE 3/3/2016
1 Stephen Strasburg/25 15.00 40.00
2 Josh Donaldson/99 8.00 20.00
3 Carlos Gomez/99 6.00 15.00
4 Matt Carpenter/49 10.00 25.00
5 Jeff Bagwell/25 20.00 50.00
6 Shane Victorino/25 4.00 10.00
7 Matt Harvey/25 25.00 60.00
8 Brian McCann/25 8.00 20.00
9 David Freese/25 3.00 8.00
10 Evan Gattis/49 3.00 8.00
11 Victor Martinez/49 12.00 30.00
12 Shelby Miller/49 4.00 10.00
13 Paul Konerko/49 6.00 15.00
14 Pablo Sandoval/25 8.00 20.00
15 Paul Molitor/25 12.00 30.00
18 Joe Girardi/49 6.00 15.00
19 Robinson Cano/25 15.00 40.00
20 Wil Myers/25 15.00 40.00
21 Wally Joyner/49 3.00 8.00
22 Roy Halladay/25 15.00 40.00
23 Prince Fielder/25 8.00 20.00
24 David Wright/25 15.00 40.00
25 Dustin Pedroia/25 25.00 60.00
30 Bo Jackson/25 50.00 120.00
34 Brooks Robinson/25 15.00 40.00
35 Willie McCovey/25 20.00 50.00
36 Rickey Henderson/25 25.00 60.00
39 Giancarlo Stanton/25 25.00 60.00
42 Eric Davis/99 8.00 20.00
43 Joe Carter/25 10.00 25.00
45 Andres Galarraga/99 8.00 20.00
46 Bob Dernier/99 3.00 8.00
47 Starling Marte/99 10.00 25.00
48 Zoilo Almonte/99 4.00 10.00
49 Michael Wacha/25 12.00 30.00
50 Jarrod Parker/49 3.00 8.00
51 Junior Lake/99 3.00 8.00
53 Chris Sale/49 10.00 25.00
54 Kerry Wood/49 6.00 15.00
55 Adrian Gonzalez/25 10.00 25.00
56 Manny Machado/49 15.00 40.00
57 Bret Saberhagen/99 3.00 8.00
58 Jean Segura EXCH 4.00 10.00
59 Joe Mauer/25 15.00 40.00
60 Jose Canseco/49 6.00 15.00
61 Jay Bruce/49 6.00 15.00
62 Patrick Corbin/99 4.00 10.00
64 Carlos Martinez/99 4.00 10.00
65 Ivan Nova/99 4.00 10.00
66 Adam Eaton/99 3.00 8.00
67 Adam Jones/25 8.00 20.00
68 Gerardo Parra/99 3.00 8.00
69 Freddie Freeman/49 8.00 20.00
70 Gerrit Cole/49 8.00 20.00
71 Jose Fernandez/49 10.00 25.00
72 Justin Upton/25 4.00 10.00
73 Norichika Aoki/99 12.00 30.00
74 Wilin Rosario/99 3.00 8.00
75 Salvador Perez/99 8.00 20.00
76 Jered Weaver/25 10.00 25.00
77 Fred McGriff/25 12.00 30.00
78 Alan Trammell/25 10.00 25.00
79 Andre Thornton/99 3.00 8.00
80 Carlos Gonzalez/25 6.00 15.00
84 Max Scherzer/25 15.00 40.00
85 Raul Ibanez/49 4.00 10.00
86 Steve Finley/25 3.00 8.00
88 Bobby Witt/99 3.00 8.00
89 Zack Wheeler/49 6.00 15.00
90 Tony Pena/99 3.00 8.00
91 Yoenis Cespedes/25 6.00 15.00
92 Mookie Wilson/99 8.00 20.00
94 Ellis Burks/99 3.00 8.00
95 Anthony Rizzo/49 20.00 50.00
96 Brandon Barnes/99 3.00 8.00
97 Clayton Kershaw/25 40.00 100.00
98 Felix Hernandez/25 20.00 50.00
99 R.A. Dickey/25 6.00 15.00
100 Alex Wood/99 3.00 8.00

2014 Immaculate Collection Immaculate Dual Players Memorabilia

RANDOM INSERTS IN PACKS
PRINT RUNS B/WN 10-49 COPIES PER
NO PRICING ON QTY 10
1 D.Mattingly/K.Griffey Jr./49 6.00 15.00
2 E.Gattis/H.Pence/49 4.00 10.00
3 M.McGwire/R.Palmeiro/49 10.00 25.00
4 R.Howard/A.Beltre/49 5.00 12.00
5 A.Pujols/M.McGwire/49 10.00 25.00
7 E.Encarnacion/J.Bautista/49 5.00 12.00
8 D.Ortiz/D.Pedroia/49 8.00 20.00
9 G.Cole/H.Ryu/25 5.00 12.00
10 E.Gattis/M.Zunino/25 5.00 12.00
11 Z.Wheeler/T.Skaggs/25 4.00 10.00
12 T.Cobb/H.Wagner/20 100.00 200.00
13 L.Gehrig/P.Reese/49 50.00 120.00
14 M.Ott/R.Hornsby/25 40.00 100.00

2014 Immaculate Collection Immaculate Dual Players Memorabilia Prime

*PRIME: .75X TO 2X BASIC
RANDOM INSERTS IN PACKS
PRINT RUNS B/WN 1-25 COPIES PER
NO PRICING ON QTY 15 OR LESS

2014 Immaculate Collection Immaculate Duals Memorabilia

RANDOM INSERTS IN PACKS
PRINT RUNS B/WN 25-99 COPIES PER
1 Giancarlo Stanton/99 4.00 10.00
2 Matt Cain/49 3.00 8.00
3 Evan Longoria/99 3.00 8.00
4 Aroldis Chapman/99 4.00 10.00
5 Devin Mesoraco/99 2.50 6.00
6 Yoenis Cespedes/25 4.00 10.00
7 Matt Kemp/49 3.00 8.00
8 Miguel Cabrera/99 4.00 10.00
9 Torii Hunter/99 2.50 6.00
10 Neftali Feliz/99 2.50 6.00
11 Will Middlebrooks/49 2.50 6.00
12 Drew Smyly/99 2.50 6.00
13 Tyler Skaggs/25 2.50 6.00
14 Brett Lawrie/49 3.00 8.00
15 Jacoby Ellsbury/99 3.00 8.00

2014 Immaculate Collection Immaculate Duals Memorabilia Prime

*PRIME: .75X TO 2X BASIC
RANDOM INSERTS IN PACKS
PRINT RUNS B/WN 10-49 COPIES PER
NO PRICING ON QTY 10

2014 Immaculate Collection Immaculate Heroes Autographs

RANDOM INSERTS IN PACKS
PRINT RUNS B/WN 15-75 COPIES PER
NO PRICING ON QTY 15
EXCHANGE DEADLINE 3/3/2016
2 Nolan Ryan/25 90.00 150.00
3 Mariano Rivera/25 75.00 200.00
4 Gaylord Perry/25 6.00 15.00
5 Jeff Bagwell/49 15.00 40.00
6 Shane Victorino/49 5.00 12.00
7 Tim Wakefield/49 10.00 25.00
8 Andy Pettitte/25 15.00 40.00
9 David Freese/25 4.00 10.00
10 Tom Glavine/49 15.00 40.00
11 Victor Martinez/49 12.00 30.00
13 Paul Konerko/75 12.00 30.00
14 Pablo Sandoval/25 12.00 30.00
18 Joe Girardi/49 6.00 15.00
20 Wil Myers/25 8.00 20.00
21 Wally Joyner/75 4.00 10.00

2014 Immaculate Collection Immaculate Heroes Materials

RANDOM INSERTS IN PACKS
PRINT RUNS B/WN 10-99 COPIES PER
NO PRICING ON QTY 15 OR LESS
1 Frank Thomas/49 6.00 15.00
2 Nolan Ryan/49 20.00 50.00
3 Roy Halladay/20 5.00 12.00
4 Tom Glavine/49 5.00 12.00
6 Mark McGwire/49 10.00 25.00
7 Roger Clemens/49 6.00 15.00
8 Andy Pettitte/49 5.00 12.00
9 Tommy Lasorda/49 5.00 12.00
10 Nomar Garciaparra/49 5.00 12.00
11 Rollie Fingers/49 6.00 15.00
12 Mariano Rivera/25 10.00 25.00
13 Don Mattingly/49 10.00 25.00
14 Fred McGriff/20 5.00 12.00
15 Ryne Sandberg/49 8.00 20.00
16 Goose Gossage/49 5.00 12.00
17 Lenny Dykstra/49 4.00 10.00
18 Michael Young/49 4.00 10.00
19 Carlton Fisk/20 10.00 25.00
20 Todd Helton/49 5.00 12.00
21 Tony Perez/20 15.00 40.00
23 Harold Baines/49 5.00 12.00
24 Andre Dawson/49 5.00 12.00
26 Bo Jackson/49 10.00 25.00
27 Bob Horner/49 4.00 10.00
29 Tim Hudson/49 5.00 12.00
30 Derek Jeter/99 10.00 25.00

2014 Immaculate Collection Immaculate Heroes Materials Prime

*PRIME: .75X TO 2X BASIC
RANDOM INSERTS IN PACKS
PRINT RUNS B/WN 2-25 COPIES PER
NO PRICING ON QTY 15 OR LESS
5 Alan Trammell/25 10.00 25.00
25 Bert Blyleven/25 10.00 25.00

2014 Immaculate Collection Immaculate Hitters Memorabilia

RANDOM INSERTS IN PACKS
PRINT RUNS B/WN 10-99 COPIES PER
NO PRICING ON QTY 10
1 Brandon Phillips/49 2.50 6.00
2 Jay Bruce/99 3.00 8.00
3 Adam Jones/79 3.00 8.00
4 Paul Goldschmidt/49 4.00 10.00
5 Yoenis Cespedes/49 4.00 10.00
6 Chris Davis/99 2.50 6.00
7 Alfonso Soriano/99 3.00 8.00
8 Chase Utley/79 3.00 8.00
9 Carlos Gonzalez/79 3.00 8.00
10 Miguel Cabrera/99 4.00 10.00
11 Dustin Pedroia/79 4.00 10.00
12 Evan Longoria/99 3.00 8.00
13 David Wright/49 3.00 8.00
14 Jacoby Ellsbury/79 3.00 8.00
15 Bryce Harper/49 6.00 15.00
16 Prince Fielder/79 3.00 8.00
17 Nick Swisher/79 3.00 8.00
18 Eric Hosmer/25 3.00 8.00
19 Adrian Beltre/49 4.00 10.00
20 Jean Segura/99 3.00 8.00
21 Evan Gattis/49 2.50 6.00
22 Mike Napoli/79 2.50 6.00
24 Pablo Sandoval/49 8.00 20.00
25 Mark Teixeira/79 3.00 8.00

2014 Immaculate Collection Immaculate Hitters Memorabilia Prime

*PRIME: .75X TO 2X BASIC
RANDOM INSERTS IN PACKS
PRINT RUNS B/WN 5-25 COPIES PER
NO PRICING ON QTY 15 OR LESS

2014 Immaculate Collection Immaculate Ink

RANDOM INSERTS IN PACKS
PRINT RUNS B/WN 15-99 COPIES PER
NO PRICING ON QTY 15 OR LESS
EXCHANGE DEADLINE 3/3/2016
1 Jim Palmer/25 10.00 25.00
2 Jorge Posada/25 10.00 25.00
3 Craig Biggio/25 12.00 30.00
4 Mark Grace/25 10.00 25.00
5 Jose Canseco/49 10.00 25.00
6 Rafael Palmeiro/25 12.00 30.00
9 Gaylord Perry/49 10.00 25.00
11 Roy Halladay/20 12.00 30.00
12 Pablo Sandoval/49 5.00 12.00
13 Freddie Freeman/99 6.00 15.00
14 Giancarlo Stanton/25 20.00 50.00
18 Jay Bruce/99 6.00 15.00
20 Adam Jones/25 5.00 12.00
22 Carlos Gomez/99 6.00 15.00
23 Jose Fernandez/49 40.00 100.00
24 Oscar Taveras/99 10.00 25.00
25 Shelby Miller/99 5.00 12.00
26 Wil Myers/25 4.00 10.00
27 David Wright/25 10.00 25.00
28 Dustin Pedroia/25 20.00 50.00
34 Paul Konerko/49 12.00 30.00
35 Jay Buhner/99 10.00 25.00
36 Edgar Martinez/49 8.00 20.00
38 Felix Hernandez/25 15.00 40.00
39 Matt Harvey/25 20.00 50.00
41 Darryl Strawberry/25 10.00 25.00
43 Clayton Kershaw/25 30.00 80.00
44 Chris Sale/25 6.00 15.00
46 Manny Machado/25 20.00 50.00
47 Jered Weaver/25 10.00 25.00
48 Harold Baines/79 6.00 15.00
49 Steve Garvey/49 12.00 30.00
50 Al Kaline/25 25.00 50.00
51 Carlos Gonzalez/25 8.00 20.00
52 Eric Hosmer/25 20.00 50.00
56 Brian McCann/25 5.00 12.00
57 Carlos Correa/99 60.00 150.00
58 Javier Baez/99 10.00 25.00
59 Jameson Taillon/99 5.00 12.00
60 Archie Bradley/99 4.00 10.00

2014 Immaculate Collection Immaculate Pitchers Memorabilia

RANDOM INSERTS IN PACKS
PRINT RUNS B/WN 49-99 COPIES PER
1 Justin Verlander/79 4.00 10.00
2 Felix Hernandez/49 3.00 8.00
3 Max Scherzer/99 4.00 10.00
4 Gerrit Cole/49 4.00 10.00
5 Hisashi Iwakuma/79 3.00 8.00
6 Stephen Strasburg/49 4.00 10.00
7 Aroldis Chapman/99 4.00 10.00
8 Dillon Gee/99 2.50 6.00
9 Madison Bumgarner/49 6.00 15.00
10 Pat Corbin/79 3.00 8.00
11 Cliff Lee/49 3.00 8.00
12 Johan Santana/49 3.00 8.00
13 Hyun-Jin Ryu/49 3.00 8.00
14 Yovani Gallardo/99 2.50 6.00
15 Jon Lester/79 3.00 8.00

2014 Immaculate Collection Immaculate Pitchers Memorabilia Prime

*PRIME: .75X TO 2X BASIC
RANDOM INSERTS IN PACKS
PRINT RUNS B/WN 10-25 COPIES PER
NO PRICING ON QTY 15 OR LESS

2014 Immaculate Collection Immaculate Quad Players Memorabilia

RANDOM INSERTS IN PACKS
PRINT RUNS B/WN 25-49 COPIES PER
1 Mchd/Frnndz/Myrs/Puig/25 15.00 40.00
2 Rpkn/Thms/Grffy/Pzz/49 25.00 60.00
3 Sndbrg/Brtt/Schmdt/Hndrsn/49 20.00 50.00
4 Brock/Rose/Jackson/Carew/25 20.00 50.00
5 Ortiz/Pujols/Jeter/Ichiro/49 30.00 80.00

2014 Immaculate Collection Immaculate Quads Memorabilia

RANDOM INSERTS IN PACKS
STATED PRINT RUN 25 SER.#'d SETS
1 Adam Dunn 10.00 25.00
2 Jose Reyes 10.00 25.00
3 Nelson Cruz 5.00 12.00
4 Curtis Granderson 4.00 10.00
5 Troy Tulowitzki 5.00 12.00

2014 Immaculate Collection Immaculate Singles Memorabilia

RANDOM INSERTS IN PACKS
PRINT RUNS B/WN 25-99 COPIES PER
1 Jay Bruce/99 3.00 8.00
2 Adrian Gonzalez/99 3.00 8.00
3 Logan Morrison/99 2.50 6.00
4 Josh Hamilton/99 3.00 8.00
5 Justin Upton/99 3.00 8.00
6 Shelby Miller/99 3.00 8.00
7 Carl Crawford/99 3.00 8.00
8 David Freese/99 2.50 6.00
9 Matt Kemp/99 3.00 8.00
10 Mark Teixeira/99 3.00 8.00
11 B.J. Upton/99 3.00 8.00
12 Michael Bourn/99 2.50 6.00
13 Starlin Castro/99 3.00 8.00
14 Ryan Braun/99 3.00 8.00
15 Nelson Cruz/99 4.00 10.00
16 Mike Napoli/99 2.50 6.00
17 Pablo Sandoval/99 3.00 8.00
18 Matt Holliday/99 4.00 10.00
19 Ryan Howard/99 3.00 8.00
20 Neftali Feliz/99 2.50 6.00
21 Bryce Harper/99 6.00 15.00
22 Stephen Strasburg/99 4.00 10.00
23 Prince Fielder/99 3.00 8.00
24 Felix Hernandez/99 3.00 8.00
25 Tom Seaver/25 10.00 25.00
26 Reggie Jackson/99 3.00 8.00
27 George Brett/99 10.00 25.00
28 Pete Rose/99 10.00 25.00
29 Cal Ripken Jr./99 12.00 30.00
30 Taijuan Walker/99 2.50 6.00
31 Travis d'Arnaud/99 3.00 8.00
32 Kolten Wong/99 5.00 12.00
33 Yordano Ventura/99 3.00 8.00
34 Nick Castellanos/49 8.00 20.00
35 Michael Choice/99 2.50 6.00
36 Cameron Rupp/99 2.50 6.00
37 J.R. Murphy/99 2.50 6.00
38 Ryan Goins/99 3.00 8.00
39 Wilmer Flores/99 3.00 8.00
40 Reymond Fuentes/99 2.50 6.00

2014 Immaculate Collection Immaculate Singles Memorabilia Prime

*PRIME: .6X TO 1.5X BASIC
RANDOM INSERTS IN PACKS
PRINT RUNS B/WN 1-99 COPIES PER
NO PRICING ON QTY 15 OR LESS

2014 Immaculate Collection Immaculate Swatches

RANDOM INSERTS IN PACKS
PRINT RUNS B/WN 15-99 COPIES PER
NO PRICING ON QTY 15
2 Justin Verlander/99 4.00 10.00
3 Alex Rodriguez/99 6.00 15.00
4 Mark Teixeira/99 3.00 8.00
5 Bryce Harper/49 6.00 15.00
6 Mike Trout/49 10.00 25.00
7 Manny Machado/49 4.00 10.00
8 Jose Fernandez/49 4.00 10.00
9 Wil Myers/99 2.50 6.00
10 Stephen Strasburg/99 4.00 10.00
11 Miguel Cabrera/99 5.00 12.00
12 Prince Fielder/99 3.00 8.00
13 Matt Harvey/99 3.00 8.00
14 Robinson Cano/99 3.00 8.00
15 Jay Bruce/99 3.00 8.00
16 Ichiro Suzuki/49 10.00 25.00
17 Brandon Phillips/99 2.50 6.00
18 Paul Goldschmidt/99 4.00 10.00
19 Matt Cain/99 3.00 8.00
20 Yoenis Cespedes/99 4.00 10.00
21 Derek Jeter/99 10.00 25.00
22 Albert Pujols/99 5.00 12.00
23 Chris Davis/99 2.50 6.00
24 Troy Tulowitzki/99 4.00 10.00
25 Evan Longoria/99 3.00 8.00
26 Andrew McCutchen/99 8.00 20.00
27 Josh Hamilton/99 3.00 8.00
28 Jose Bautista/99 3.00 8.00
29 Adam Jones/99 3.00 8.00
30 David Ortiz/99 4.00 10.00
31 Dustin Pedroia/99 4.00 10.00
32 Carlos Gonzalez/99 3.00 8.00
33 Adrian Beltre/99 4.00 10.00
34 Edwin Encarnacion/99 4.00 10.00
35 Ryan Howard/99 3.00 8.00
36 Shin-Soo Choo/99 3.00 8.00
37 Max Scherzer/99 4.00 10.00
38 Joey Votto/99 4.00 10.00
39 David Wright/99 3.00 8.00
40 Carlos Beltran/99 3.00 8.00
41 Cliff Lee/99 3.00 8.00
42 Buster Posey/99 6.00 15.00
43 CC Sabathia/99 3.00 8.00
44 Pete Rose/49 8.00 20.00
45 Darryl Strawberry/99 2.50 6.00
46 Kirby Puckett/99 4.00 10.00
47 Tom Glavine/99 3.00 8.00
48 Craig Biggio/49 3.00 8.00
49 Jeff Bagwell/99 3.00 8.00
50 Jose Canseco/25 6.00 15.00
51 Joe Girardi/99 3.00 8.00
52 Paul Molitor/99 4.00 10.00
53 Bernie Williams/49 3.00 8.00
54 Ozzie Smith/99 3.00 8.00
55 George Brett/49 8.00 20.00
56 Bo Jackson/99 10.00 25.00
57 Ryne Sandberg/25 10.00 25.00
58 Rickey Henderson/99 5.00 12.00
59 Tony Gwynn/99 4.00 10.00
60 Chipper Jones/99 4.00 10.00
61 Frank Thomas/25 12.00 30.00
62 Cal Ripken Jr./99 8.00 20.00
63 Nolan Ryan/99 12.00 30.00
64 Roberto Alomar/99 3.00 8.00
65 Ken Griffey Jr./49 12.00 30.00
66 Kolten Wong/99 3.00 8.00
67 Travis d'Arnaud/99 3.00 8.00
68 Wilmer Flores/99 3.00 8.00
69 Juan Centeno/99 2.50 6.00
70 Enny Romero/99 2.50 6.00
71 Josmil Pinto/99 2.50 6.00
72 Kris Johnson/99 2.50 6.00
73 Cameron Rupp/99 2.50 6.00
74 Ryan Goins/99 3.00 8.00
75 Abraham Almonte/99 2.50 6.00
76 Billy Hamilton/99 4.00 10.00
77 Charlie Leesman/99 2.50 6.00
78 David Holmberg/99 2.50 6.00
79 Jimmy Nelson/99 2.50 6.00
80 Jose Ramirez/99 20.00 50.00
81 Marcus Semien/99 12.00 30.00
82 Matt Davidson/99 3.00 8.00
83 Matt Shoemaker/99 4.00 10.00
84 Michael Choice/99 2.50 6.00
85 Reymond Fuentes/99 2.50 6.00
86 Taijuan Walker/99 2.50 6.00
87 Yordano Ventura/99 3.00 8.00
88 Nick Castellanos/99 4.00 10.00
89 Byron Buxton/99 6.00 15.00
90 Oscar Taveras/99 10.00 25.00
91 Xander Bogaerts/99 5.00 12.00
92 Chad Bettis/99 2.50 6.00
93 Matt den Dekker/99 2.50 6.00
94 J.R. Murphy/99 2.50 6.00
95 Masahiro Tanaka/99 12.00 30.00

2014 Immaculate Collection Immaculate Swatches Premium

*PREMIUM: 2X TO 5X BASIC
RANDOM INSERTS IN PACKS
PRINT RUNS B/WN 1-20 COPIES PER
NO PRICING ON QTY 15 OR LESS

2014 Immaculate Collection Immaculate Swatches Prime

*PRIME: .75X TO 2X BASIC
RANDOM INSERTS IN PACKS
PRINT RUNS B/WN 1-99 COPIES PER
NO PRICING ON QTY 15 OR LESS
1 Yasiel Puig/25 8.00 20.00
5 Bryce Harper/25 20.00 50.00
63 Nolan Ryan/25 30.00 80.00
95 Masahiro Tanaka/25 40.00 100.00

2014 Immaculate Collection Immaculate Trios Memorabilia

RANDOM INSERTS IN PACKS
PRINT RUNS B/WN 25-49 COPIES PER
1 Josh Hamilton/49 4.00 10.00
2 Tim Hudson/49 4.00 10.00
3 Johnny Cueto/49 4.00 10.00
4 Nick Markakis/49 4.00 10.00
5 Jeff Samardzija/49 3.00 8.00
6 Christian Yelich/49 6.00 15.00
7 Hisashi Iwakuma/25 6.00 15.00
8 Wellington Castillo/49 3.00 8.00
9 Alex Avila/49 3.00 8.00
10 Jason Heyward/49 4.00 10.00

2014 Immaculate Collection Immaculate Trios Players Memorabilia

RANDOM INSERTS IN PACKS
PRINT RUNS B/WN 25-79 COPIES PER
1 Votl/Cbrra/McCtchn/49 15.00 40.00
2 Sbha/Lee/Schrzr/79 8.00 20.00
3 Psy/Hmltn/Cbrr/49 6.00 15.00
4 Myrs/Hrpr/Trout/49 20.00 50.00
5 Dvis/Gldschmdt/Cbrra/79 6.00 15.00
6 Phillips/Gonzalez/Goldschmidt/49 5.00 12.00
7 Jones/Hunter/Cano/79 4.00 10.00
8 Bltrn/Pjls/Ortz/79 6.00 15.00
9 Cnsco/Rdrguz/Smo/49 10.00 25.00
10 Mrry/Brks/Schmdt/25 15.00 40.00

2014 Immaculate Collection Premium Material

RANDOM INSERTS IN PACKS
PRINT RUNS B/WN 25-99 COPIES PER
1 Alex Rodriguez/49 10.00 25.00
2 Adam Jones/49 4.00 10.00
3 Julio Teheran/25 4.00 10.00
4 Jose Fernandez/49 5.00 12.00
5 Michael Morse/49 3.00 8.00
6 Matt Harvey/79 4.00 10.00
7 Jose Bautista/25 8.00 20.00
8 Adam Eaton/49 3.00 8.00
9 Hisashi Iwakuma/49 4.00 10.00
10 Albert Pujols/25 6.00 15.00
11 Torii Hunter/79 3.00 8.00
12 Derek Jeter/79 30.00 60.00
13 Yasiel Puig/99 5.00 12.00
14 Anthony Rizzo/79 5.00 12.00
15 Justin Upton/49 4.00 10.00
16 Jacoby Ellsbury/49 4.00 10.00
17 Prince Fielder/49 4.00 10.00
18 Aramis Ramirez/49 3.00 8.00
19 David Wright/49 4.00 10.00
20 Pat Corbin/49 3.00 8.00
21 Justin Verlander/79 5.00 12.00
22 Yovani Gallardo/79 3.00 8.00
23 Miguel Cabrera/49 5.00 12.00
24 Xander Bogaerts/99 8.00 20.00
25 Jon Lester/49 4.00 10.00
26 Jeff Samardzija/99 3.00 8.00
27 Chase Utley/49 4.00 10.00
28 Drew Smyly/79 3.00 8.00
29 Pete Rose/25 12.00 30.00
30 Mike Piazza/49 5.00 12.00
31 Dennis Eckersley/79 5.00 12.00
32 Wilmer Flores/99 4.00 10.00
33 Cameron Rupp/99 3.00 8.00
34 Jose Ramirez/99 25.00 60.00
35 Reymond Fuentes/99 3.00 8.00
36 Yordano Ventura/99 4.00 10.00
37 Michael Choice/99 3.00 8.00
38 Travis d'Arnaud/99 4.00 10.00
39 Billy Hamilton/99 4.00 10.00
40 Taijuan Walker/99 3.00 8.00
41 Kolten Wong/49 6.00 15.00

2014 Immaculate Collection Rookie Autographs Materials Prime

*PRIME: .6X TO 1.5X BASIC
RANDOM INSERTS IN PACKS
PRINT RUNS B/WN 10-99 COPIES PER
NO PRICING ON QTY 10
EXCHANGE DEADLINE 3/3/2016
155 Jose Abreu JSY/25 100.00 250.00

2014 Immaculate Collection The Greatest Materials

RANDOM INSERTS IN PACKS
PRINT RUNS B/WN 10-49 COPIES PER
NO PRICING ON QTY 10 OR LESS
1 Mark McGwire/49 12.00 30.00
2 Pete Rose/49 12.00 30.00
3 George Brett/49 15.00 40.00
4 Mike Schmidt/25 10.00 25.00
5 Nolan Ryan/25 30.00 80.00
6 Reggie Jackson/49 6.00 15.00
7 Lou Brock/49 6.00 15.00
9 Robin Yount/49 8.00 20.00
10 Ozzie Smith/49 8.00 20.00
11 Jim Rice/49 6.00 15.00
12 Dale Murphy/49 8.00 20.00
13 Eddie Murray/49 6.00 15.00
14 Gaylord Perry/49 6.00 15.00
15 Carlton Fisk/25 10.00 25.00
16 Mike Piazza/49 10.00 25.00
17 Paul Molitor/49 6.00 15.00
18 Dennis Eckersley/49 6.00 15.00
19 Wade Boggs/49 6.00 15.00
20 Orlando Cepeda/25 8.00 20.00
22 Carl Yastrzemski/49 8.00 20.00
23 John Smoltz/49 8.00 20.00
24 Will Clark/49 6.00 15.00
25 Rod Carew/25 6.00 15.00
26 Gil Hodges/49 10.00 25.00
27 Ty Cobb/49 25.00 60.00
28 Lou Gehrig/49 40.00 100.00
29 Pee Wee Reese/49 10.00 25.00
30 Joe DiMaggio/49 30.00 80.00

2014 Immaculate Collection The Greatest Materials Prime

*PRIME: .6X TO 1.5X BASIC
RANDOM INSERTS IN PACKS
PRINT RUNS B/WN 1-25 COPIES PER
NO PRICING ON QTY 15 OR LESS

2014 Immaculate Collection The Greatest Signatures

RANDOM INSERTS IN PACKS
STATED PRINT RUN 20 SER.#'d SETS
EXCHANGE DEADLINE 3/3/2016
1 Ken Griffey Jr. 75.00 150.00
2 Cal Ripken Jr. 30.00 80.00
3 George Brett 50.00 120.00
4 Bo Jackson 40.00 100.00
5 Mariano Rivera 60.00 150.00
6 Ryne Sandberg 30.00 80.00
7 Nolan Ryan 50.00 125.00
8 Brooks Robinson 12.00 30.00
9 Willie McCovey 12.00 30.00
10 Rickey Henderson 30.00 80.00
11 Bob Gibson EXCH 12.00 30.00
12 Tony Gwynn 15.00 40.00
13 Johnny Bench 15.00 40.00
14 Chipper Jones 50.00 120.00
15 Frank Thomas 30.00 80.00

2015 Immaculate Collection

1-100 PRINT RUN 99 SER.#'d SETS
JSY AU PRINT RUN 99 SER.#'d SETS
AU PRINT RUNS B/WN 49-99 COPIES PER
EXCHANGE DEADLINE 2/26/2017
1 Mike Trout 8.00 20.00
2 Clayton Kershaw 2.50 6.00
3 Babe Ruth 4.00 10.00
4 Jose Abreu 1.50 4.00
5 Ichiro Suzuki 2.00 5.00
6 Giancarlo Stanton 1.50 4.00
7 Jose Bautista 1.25 3.00
8 David Wright 1.25 3.00
9 Bryce Harper 2.50 6.00
10 Robinson Cano 1.25 3.00
11 David Price 1.25 3.00
12 Miguel Cabrera 1.50 4.00
13 Troy Tulowitzki 1.50 4.00
14 Evan Longoria 1.25 3.00
15 Stephen Strasburg 1.50 4.00
16 Masahiro Tanaka 1.25 3.00
17 Yasiel Puig 1.50 4.00
18 Buster Posey 2.00 5.00
19 Madison Bumgarner 1.25 3.00
20 Felix Hernandez 1.25 3.00
21 Albert Pujols 2.00 5.00
22 Ryan Howard 1.25 3.00
23 Adam Jones 1.25 3.00
24 Yu Darvish 1.50 4.00
25 Alex Rodriguez 2.00 5.00
26 Chase Utley 1.25 3.00
27 Chris Davis 1.00 2.50
28 Yadier Molina 2.00 5.00
29 Alex Gordon 1.25 3.00
30 David Ortiz 1.50 4.00
31 Joey Votto 1.50 4.00
32 Matt Kemp 1.25 3.00
33 Carlos Gonzalez 1.25 3.00
34 Ryan Braun 1.25 3.00
35 Adrian Beltre 1.50 4.00
36 Wil Myers 1.25 3.00
37 Andrew McCutchen 1.50 4.00
38 Salvador Perez 1.25 3.00
39 Adam Wainwright 1.25 3.00
40 Eric Hosmer 1.25 3.00
41 Nelson Cruz 1.50 4.00
42 Chris Sale 1.50 4.00
43 Corey Kluber 1.25 3.00
44 Jacob deGrom 3.00 8.00
45 Matt Harvey 1.25 3.00
46 Yoenis Cespedes 1.25 3.00
47 Freddie Freeman 2.00 5.00
48 Jose Fernandez 1.50 4.00
49 Justin Verlander 1.50 4.00
50 Paul Goldschmidt 1.50 4.00
51 Wei-Yin Chen 1.00 2.50
52 Jose Altuve 1.50 4.00
53 Torii Hunter 1.00 2.50
54 Max Scherzer 1.50 4.00
55 Jon Lester 1.25 3.00
56 Anthony Rizzo 2.00 5.00
57 Sonny Gray 1.25 3.00
58 Victor Martinez 1.25 3.00
59 Yordano Ventura 1.25 3.00
60 Kennys Vargas 1.00 2.50
61 Joe Mauer 1.25 3.00
62 Zack Greinke 1.50 4.00
63 Hunter Pence 1.25 3.00
64 Johnny Cueto 1.25 3.00
65 Jered Weaver 1.25 3.00
66 James Shields 1.00 2.50
67 Chris Carter 1.00 2.50
68 Michael Brantley 1.25 3.00
69 Carlos Gomez 1.00 2.50
70 Josh Donaldson 1.25 3.00
71 Jonathan Lucroy 1.25 3.00
72 Josh Harrison 1.00 2.50
73 Edwin Encarnacion 1.50 4.00
74 Todd Frazier 1.00 2.50
75 Justin Upton 1.25 3.00
76 Jordan Zimmermann 1.25 3.00
77 Kyle Seager 1.00 2.50
78 Adrian Gonzalez 1.25 3.00
79 Matt Carpenter 1.50 4.00
80 Anthony Rendon 1.50 4.00
81 Manny Machado 1.50 4.00
82 Hanley Ramirez 1.25 3.00
83 Dustin Pedroia 1.50 4.00
84 Jason Heyward 1.25 3.00
85 CC Sabathia 1.25 3.00
86 Nolan Arenado 2.50 6.00
87 Mookie Betts 3.00 8.00
88 Taijuan Walker 1.00 2.50
89 Julio Teheran 1.25 3.00

90 Gregory Polanco 1.25 3.00
91 Kirby Puckett 1.50 4.00
92 Bo Jackson 1.50 4.00
93 Pete Rose 3.00 8.00
94 Nolan Ryan 5.00 12.00
95 Ken Griffey Jr. 3.00 8.00
96 Stan Musial 2.50 6.00
97 Ty Cobb 2.50 6.00
98 Lou Gehrig 3.00 8.00
99 Roberto Clemente 4.00 10.00
100 Babe Ruth 4.00 10.00
101 Archie Bradley JSY AU/49 RC 4.00 10.00
102 Rusney Castillo JSY AU/49 RC 5.00 12.00
103 Yasmany Tomas JSY AU/49 RC 5.00 12.00
104 Matt Barnes JSY AU/49 RC 4.00 10.00
105 Brandon Finnegan JSY AU/49 RC 4.00 10.00
106 Kris Bryant JSY AU/49 100.00 200.00
107 Kendall Graveman JSY AU/49 RC 4.00 10.00
108 Yorman Rodriguez JSY AU/49 RC 4.00 10.00
109 Gary Brown JSY AU/49 RC 4.00 10.00
110 R.J. Alvarez JSY AU/49 RC 4.00 10.00
111 Jorge Soler JSY AU/49 10.00 25.00
112 Maikel Franco JSY AU/49 RC 5.00 12.00
113 Addison Russell JSY AU/49 RC 15.00 40.00
114 Lane Adams JSY AU/49 RC 4.00 10.00
115 Joc Pederson JSY AU/49 RC 15.00 40.00
116 Steven Moya JSY AU/49 RC 5.00 12.00
117 Cory Spangenberg JSY AU/49 RC 4.00 10.00
118 Francisco Lindor JSY AU/49 RC 20.00 50.00
119 Raisel Iglesias JSY AU/49 RC 5.00 12.00
120 Ryan Rua JSY AU/49 RC 4.00 10.00
121 Dilson Herrera JSY AU/49 RC 5.00 12.00
122 Edwin Escobar JSY AU/49 RC 4.00 10.00
123 Javier Baez JSY AU/49 RC 20.00 50.00
124 Matt Szczur JSY AU/49 RC 5.00 12.00
125 Jake Lamb JSY AU/49 RC 10.00 25.00
126 Michael Taylor JSY AU/49 RC 4.00 10.00
127 Rymer Liriano JSY AU/49 RC 4.00 10.00
128 Trevor May JSY AU/49 RC 4.00 10.00
129 Joey Gallo JSY AU/25 12.00 30.00
130 Carlos Correa JSY AU/49 30.00 80.00
131 Devon Travis AU/99 RC 3.00 8.00
132 Daniel Norris AU/99 RC 3.00 8.00
133 Odubel Herrera AU/99 RC 15.00 40.00
134 Odubel Herrera AU/99 RC 15.00 40.00
135 Roberto Osuna AU/99 RC 3.00 8.00
136 Daniel Muno AU/99 RC 3.00 8.00
137 James McCann AU/99 RC 10.00 25.00
138 Matt Clark AU/99 RC 3.00 8.00
139 Dalton Pompey AU/99 RC 6.00 15.00
140 Terrance Gore AU/99 RC 3.00 8.00
141 Jorge Soler AU/99 RC 3.00 8.00
142 Buck Farmer AU/99 RC 3.00 8.00
143 Mike Foltynewicz AU/99 RC 3.00 8.00
144 Anthony Ranaudo AU/99 RC 3.00 8.00
145 Miguel Castro AU/99 RC 3.00 8.00
147 Christian Walker AU/99 RC 6.00 15.00
148 Kris Bryant AU/99 RC 60.00 150.00
149 A.J. Cole AU/99 RC 3.00 8.00
150 Blake Swihart AU/99 RC 4.00 10.00
151 Dalier Hinojosa AU/99 RC 3.00 8.00
152 Austin Hedges AU/99 RC 3.00 8.00
153 Noah Syndergaard AU/99 RC 6.00 15.00
154 Lance McCullers AU/99 RC 6.00 15.00
155 Carlos Rodon AU/99 RC 8.00 20.00
156 Joey Gallo AU/49 RC 12.00 30.00
157 Jung-Ho Kang AU/99 RC 15.00 40.00
158 Carlos Correa AU/99 RC 30.00 80.00
159 Kevin Plawecki AU/99 RC 3.00 8.00

2015 Immaculate Collection Blue

*BLUE 132-159: .5X TO 1.2X BASIC
RANDOM INSERTS IN PACKS
1-100 PRINT RUN 10 SER.#'d SETS
132-159 PRINT RUNS B/WN 25-49 COPIES PER
NO 1-100 PRICING DUE TO SCARCITY
EXCHANGE DEADLINE 2/26/2017

2015 Immaculate Collection Red

*RED: .6X TO 1.5X BASIC
RANDOM INSERTS IN PACKS
STATED PRINT RUN 25 SER.#'d SETS
1 Mike Trout 15.00 40.00
91 Kirby Puckett 30.00 80.00
92 Bo Jackson 10.00 25.00
94 Nolan Ryan 15.00 40.00
95 Ken Griffey Jr. 15.00 40.00
99 Roberto Clemente 10.00 25.00

2015 Immaculate Collection Accolades Materials

RANDOM INSERTS IN PACKS
STATED PRINT RUN B/WN 5-99 COPIES PER
NO PRICING ON QTY 10 OR LESS
2 Lou Gehrig/25 50.00 120.00
3 Ty Cobb/15 30.00 80.00
5 Herb Pennock/20 8.00 20.00
6 Don Drysdale/99 3.00 8.00
7 Bob Feller/99 5.00 12.00
8 Harmon Killebrew/25 4.00 10.00
9 Luke Appling/49 5.00 12.00
10 Bill Dickey/25 5.00 12.00
11 Ken Boyer/20 4.00 10.00
12 Charlie Gehringer/15 12.00 30.00
13 Joe Cronin/25 5.00 12.00
14 Stan Musial/25 6.00 15.00
15 Ted Williams/25 20.00 50.00
17 Miller Huggins/25 5.00 12.00
19 Frankie Frisch/15 10.00 25.00
21 Gabby Hartnett/49 8.00 20.00
22 Gil McDougald/49 5.00 12.00
23 Lou Gehrig/25 50.00 120.00
25 Eddie Mathews/99 5.00 12.00

2015 Immaculate Collection All-Star Autographs

RANDOM INSERTS IN PACKS
PRINT RUNS B/WN 15-99 COPIES PER
EXCHANGE DEADLINE 2/26/2017
1 Paul Goldschmidt/15 15.00 40.00
2 Troy Tulowitzki/15 10.00 25.00
3 Jonathan Lucroy/15 8.00 20.00
4 Josh Donaldson/15 30.00 80.00
5 Jose Abreu/99 20.00 50.00
6 Yadier Molina/15 60.00 150.00
7 Yoenis Cespedes/15 5.00 12.00
8 Anthony Rizzo/15 20.00 50.00
9 Todd Frazier/15 15.00 40.00
10 Chris Sale/15 15.00 40.00

2015 Immaculate Collection Collegiate Autographs Materials

RANDOM INSERTS IN PACKS
PRINT RUNS B/WN 49-99 COPIES PER
EXCHANGE DEADLINE 2/26/2017
*PRIME/25: .75X TO 2X BASIC
1 Deven Marrero/99 4.00 10.00
2 Christian Walker/99 8.00 20.00
3 Andy Wilkins/99 4.00 10.00
4 Tyler Naquin/99 6.00 15.00
5 Luke Weaver/99 6.00 15.00
6 Michael Conforto/49 20.00 50.00
7 Peter O'Brien/99 6.00 15.00
8 Robert Refsnyder/99 5.00 12.00

2015 Immaculate Collection Collegiate Ink

RANDOM INSERTS IN PACKS
PRINT RUNS B/WN 25-79 COPIES PER
EXCHANGE DEADLINE 2/26/2017
12 James McCann/49 8.00 20.00
13 Andy Wilkins/79 6.00 15.00
14 Anthony Ranaudo/49 4.00 10.00
15 Kendall Graveman/49 4.00 10.00
16 Christian Walker/79 8.00 20.00
17 Brandon Finnegan/49 4.00 10.00
19 Jake Lamb/79 6.00 15.00
20 George Springer/25 8.00 20.00
21 Trea Turner/25 15.00 40.00
22 Carlos Rodon/25 10.00 25.00
38 Kyle Schwarber/49 30.00 80.00
39 Matt Szczur/79 5.00 12.00
40 Stephen Piscotty/79 5.00 12.00

2015 Immaculate Collection Collegiate Ink Red

*RED INK: .5X TO 1.2X BASIC
RANDOM INSERTS IN PACKS
PRINT RUNS B/WN 15-25 COPIES PER
EXCHANGE DEADLINE 2/26/2017
11 Fred Lynn/25 5.00 12.00
23 Stephen Strasburg/15 20.00 50.00
24 Troy Tulowitzki/15 12.00 30.00
25 Evan Longoria/15 10.00 25.00
26 Ryan Braun/15 8.00 20.00
27 Max Scherzer/15 25.00 60.00
28 Alex Gordon/15 20.00 50.00
29 Kyle Seager/15 10.00 25.00
30 Garrett Richards/15 10.00 25.00
31 Sonny Gray/15 15.00 40.00
32 Josh Donaldson/15 25.00 60.00
33 Dallas Keuchel/15 6.00 15.00
34 Dustin Pedroia/15 15.00 40.00
35 Charlie Blackmon/15 8.00 20.00
36 Jake Arrieta/15 30.00 80.00
37 Pedro Alvarez/15 10.00 25.00

2015 Immaculate Collection Collegiate Materials

RANDOM INSERTS IN PACKS
STATED PRINT RUN B/WN 25-99 COPIES PER
*JUMBO/25-99: .4X TO 1X BASIC
*PRIME/25: .5X TO 1.2X BASIC
1 Deven Marrero/99 2.50 6.00
2 Christian Walker/99 5.00 12.00
3 Andy Wilkins/25 2.50 6.00
4 Tyler Naquin/99 4.00 10.00
5 Luke Weaver/99 4.00 10.00
6 Michael Conforto/49 6.00 15.00
7 Peter O'Brien/99 4.00 10.00
8 Robert Refsnyder/99 3.00 8.00

2015 Immaculate Collection Diamond Signatures

RANDOM INSERTS IN PACKS
PRINT RUNS B/WN 10-99 COPIES PER
NO PRICING ON QTY 10
EXCHANGE DEADLINE 2/26/2017
1 Jose Abreu/99 15.00 40.00
2 Jose Altuve/49 20.00 50.00
3 Kris Bryant/25 75.00 200.00
4 Rusney Castillo/25 5.00 12.00
5 Yasmany Tomas/25 15.00 40.00
6 Jung-Ho Kang/99 25.00 60.00
7 Felix Hernandez/25 15.00 40.00
8 David Ortiz/15 30.00 80.00
10 Salvador Perez/48 20.00 50.00

2015 Immaculate Collection Diamond Signatures Holo Gold

*HOLO GOLD: .5X TO 1.2X BASIC
RANDOM INSERTS IN PACKS
PRINT RUN B/WN 10-25 COPIES PER
NO PRICING ON QTY 10
EXCHANGE DEADLINE 2/26/2017
9 Adam Jones/15 20.00 50.00

2015 Immaculate Collection Immaculate Autograph Dual Materials

RANDOM INSERTS IN PACKS
PRINT RUNS B/WN 10-25 COPIES PER
NO PRICING ON QTY 10
EXCHANGE DEADLINE 2/26/2017
2 Jose Canseco/25 15.00 40.00
3 Byron Buxton/25 15.00 40.00
4 Andre Dawson/25 10.00 25.00
5 Adam Jones/15 8.00 20.00
6 Taijuan Walker/25 5.00 12.00
7 Yordano Ventura/25 10.00 25.00
8 Jose Abreu/25 12.00 30.00
9 Yoan Moncada/25 50.00 120.00
12 George Springer/25 6.00 15.00
14 Evan Gattis/25 5.00 12.00
15 Tom Glavine/25 12.00 30.00
16 Troy Tulowitzki/25 12.00 30.00
17 Evan Longoria/25 8.00 20.00
18 Jim Rice/25 10.00 25.00
19 Dave Winfield/15 15.00 40.00
20 Jameson Taillon/20 6.00 15.00
21 Billy Butler/20 5.00 12.00
22 Dallas Keuchel/20 12.00 30.00
23 Danny Santana/20 5.00 12.00
24 David Wright/20 15.00 40.00
25 Kyle Seager/20 10.00 25.00
26 Michael Brantley/20 10.00 25.00
27 Robinson Cano/20 10.00 25.00
28 Yadier Molina/20 40.00 100.00
29 Jacob deGrom/20 40.00 100.00
30 Kennys Vargas/20 5.00 12.00

2015 Immaculate Collection Immaculate Autograph Jumbo Materials

RANDOM INSERTS IN PACKS
PRINT RUNS B/WN 15-25 COPIES PER
EXCHANGE DEADLINE 2/26/2017
1 Joe Panik/25 6.00 15.00
2 Eric Hosmer/15 15.00 40.00
3 Dale Murphy/15 20.00 50.00
4 Devin Mesoraco/25 5.00 12.00
5 Matt Adams/25 5.00 12.00
6 Paul Goldschmidt/15 12.00 30.00
7 Starling Marte/25 10.00 25.00
8 Francisco Lindor/25 15.00 40.00
9 Josh Harrison/25 8.00 20.00
10 Yoan Moncada/25 40.00 100.00
11 Kennys Vargas/25 5.00 12.00
12 Chris Sale/25 10.00 25.00
13 Josh Donaldson/25 12.00 30.00
14 Freddie Freeman/25 8.00 20.00
15 Sonny Gray/25 6.00 15.00
16 Anthony Rendon/25 10.00 25.00
17 Kyle Schwarber/25 40.00 100.00
18 Evan Gattis/25 5.00 12.00
19 Joe Mauer/15 10.00 25.00
20 Matt Szczur/25 6.00 15.00
21 Yasmany Tomas/25 10.00 25.00
22 Gary Brown/25 5.00 12.00
23 Rusney Castillo/25 6.00 15.00
24 Kris Bryant/25 100.00 200.00
25 Addison Russell/25 20.00 50.00
26 Archie Bradley/25 5.00 12.00
27 Michael Taylor/25 10.00 25.00
28 Javier Baez/25 10.00 25.00
29 Maikel Franco/25 6.00 15.00
30 Jorge Soler/25 10.00 25.00

2015 Immaculate Collection Immaculate Autograph Materials

RANDOM INSERTS IN PACKS
PRINT RUNS B/WN 5-25 COPIES PER
NO PRICING ON QTY 10 OR LESS
EXCHANGE DEADLINE 2/26/2017
1 Vladimir Guerrero/15 10.00 25.00
6 Jose Fernandez/25 30.00 80.00
7 Evan Gattis/25 5.00 12.00
8 Mike Napoli/25 5.00 12.00
9 Sonny Gray/25 6.00 15.00
10 Byron Buxton/25 15.00 40.00
11 Adrian Beltre/15 10.00 25.00
12 Jameson Taillon/25 6.00 15.00
13 Salvador Perez/25 12.00 30.00
14 Anthony Rendon/25 10.00 25.00
15 Troy Tulowitzki/15 10.00 25.00
16 Evan Longoria/15 10.00 25.00
18 David Ortiz/15 30.00 80.00
19 Yoenis Cespedes/15 10.00 25.00
20 Eric Hosmer/15 15.00 40.00
21 Jose Altuve/15 25.00 60.00
22 Justin Upton/15 6.00 15.00
23 Andy Pettitte/15 20.00 50.00
24 Wei-Chung Wang/20 5.00 12.00
25 Tim Raines/20 6.00 15.00
26 Max Scherzer/20 15.00 40.00
27 Jose Abreu/20 12.00 30.00
28 Manny Machado/20 25.00 60.00
29 Pablo Sandoval/20 10.00 25.00
31 Adrian Gonzalez/20 6.00 15.00
32 Adam Jones/20 10.00 25.00
33 Freddie Freeman/20 10.00 25.00
34 Dustin Pedroia/20 12.00 30.00
36 Don Sutton/20 6.00 15.00
37 Edwin Encarnacion/20 8.00 20.00
38 Josh Donaldson/20 12.00 30.00
39 Paul Molitor/20 10.00 25.00
40 Andre Dawson/20 10.00 25.00
41 Yoan Moncada/20 50.00 120.00

2015 Immaculate Collection Immaculate Autograph Quad Materials

RANDOM INSERTS IN PACKS
PRINT RUNS B/WN 10-20 COPIES PER
NO PRICING ON QTY 15 OR LESS
EXCHANGE DEADLINE 2/26/2017
4 Kennys Vargas/20 8.00 20.00

2015 Immaculate Collection Immaculate Dual Autograph Materials

RANDOM INSERTS IN PACKS
PRINT RUNS B/WN 5-20 COPIES PER
NO PRICING ON QTY 10 OR LESS
EXCHANGE DEADLINE 2/26/2017
1 D.Ortiz/K.Vargas/20 25.00 60.00

2015 Immaculate Collection Immaculate Dual Players Memorabilia

RANDOM INSERTS IN PACKS
STATED PRINT RUN B/WN 15-99 COPIES PER
*PRIME/15-25: .6X TO 1.5X BASIC
1 Chance/Cobb/15 40.00 100.00
2 Ruth/Gehrig/20 150.00 250.00
3 P.Molitor/R.Carew/99 4.00 10.00
4 A.Bradley/Y.Tomas/99 3.00 8.00
5 Russell/Lindor/99 5.00 12.00
6 Thomas/Griffey Jr./99 10.00 25.00
7 Cabrera/Martinez/99 4.00 10.00
8 Rodriguez/Griffey Jr./99 10.00 25.00
9 Puig/Pederson/25 10.00 25.00
10 Fernandez/Stanton/49 4.00 10.00
11 K.Vargas/D.Ortiz/99 4.00 10.00
12 J.Abreu/R.Castillo/49 4.00 10.00
13 M.Tanaka/Y.Darvish/49 4.00 10.00
14 P.Martinez/V.Guerrero/99 3.00 8.00
15 Martinez/Clemens/49 8.00 20.00
16 McCutchen/Stanton/49 4.00 10.00
17 Canseco/McGwire/15 40.00 100.00
18 Harper/Strasburg/49 6.00 15.00
19 Taillon/Glasnow/99 5.00 12.00
20 Soler/Bryant/99 12.00 30.00

2015 Immaculate Collection Immaculate Duals Memorabilia

RANDOM INSERTS IN PACKS
STATED PRINT RUN B/WN 49-99 COPIES PER
1 Kris Bryant/99 12.00 30.00
2 Adrian Beltre/49 4.00 10.00
3 Aramis Ramirez/99 2.50 6.00
4 Brian McCann/99 3.00 8.00
5 Don Mattingly/99 8.00 20.00
6 Jeff Bagwell/99 3.00 8.00
7 Jose Bautista/99 3.00 8.00
8 Matt Carpenter/49 4.00 10.00
9 Billy Butler/99 2.50 6.00
10 Mookie Betts/49 5.00 12.00
11 Salvador Perez/99 3.00 8.00
12 Yasmany Tomas/99 3.00 8.00
13 Christian Yelich/99 5.00 12.00
14 Mike Napoli/49 2.50 6.00
15 Johnny Bench/49 10.00 25.00
16 Bo Jackson/49 8.00 20.00
17 Andy Pettitte/49 3.00 8.00
18 Yu Darvish/49 4.00 10.00
19 Ken Griffey Jr./49 12.00 30.00
20 Rickey Henderson/49 8.00 20.00

2015 Immaculate Collection Immaculate Equipment

RANDOM INSERTS IN PACKS
STATED PRINT RUN B/WN 10-49 COPIES PER
NO PRICING ON QTY 10
1 Lou Gehrig/15 200.00 400.00
3 Kirby Puckett/15 60.00 150.00
4 Rod Carew/25 6.00 15.00
5 Kris Bryant/49 25.00 60.00
6 Barry Bonds/49 8.00 20.00
7 Ken Griffey Jr./20 20.00 50.00
8 Tony Gwynn/25 15.00 40.00
9 Vladimir Guerrero/49 5.00 12.00
10 Javier Baez/20 8.00 20.00
11 Miguel Sano/20 8.00 20.00
12 Francisco Lindor/49 10.00 25.00
13 Kyle Schwarber/20 10.00 25.00
14 Michael Taylor/20 2.50 6.00
15 Yasmany Tomas/49 3.00 8.00
16 Byron Buxton/49 6.00 15.00
17 Addison Russell/49 10.00 25.00
18 Jose Bautista/15 5.00 12.00
19 Rickey Henderson/20 15.00 40.00
20 Albert Pujols/20 10.00 25.00

2015 Immaculate Collection Immaculate Heroes Materials

RANDOM INSERTS IN PACKS
STATED PRINT RUN B/WN 15-99 COPIES PER
1 Babe Ruth/15 200.00 400.00
2 Roberto Clemente/15 40.00 100.00
3 Wade Boggs/99 3.00 8.00
4 George Brett/49 8.00 20.00
5 Ozzie Smith/79 5.00 12.00
6 Bo Jackson/49 6.00 15.00
7 Barry Bonds/99 6.00 15.00
8 Red Schoendienst/99 3.00 8.00
9 Cal Ripken/99 6.00 15.00
10 Vladimir Guerrero/99 3.00 8.00
11 Mike Schmidt/49 5.00 12.00
12 Fred Lynn/99 2.50 6.00
13 Pete Rose/49 6.00 15.00
14 Greg Maddux/99 5.00 12.00
15 Robin Yount/25 10.00 25.00
16 Tony Gwynn/99 4.00 10.00
17 Reggie Jackson/79 3.00 8.00
18 Mark McGwire/99 5.00 12.00
19 Dave Winfield/99 3.00 8.00
20 Harmon Killebrew/49 4.00 10.00

2015 Immaculate Collection Immaculate Hitters Materials

RANDOM INSERTS IN PACKS
STATED PRINT RUN B/WN 15-99 COPIES PER
1 Pete Rose/25 12.00 30.00
2 Tony Gwynn/49 4.00 10.00
3 Adrian Gonzalez/49 3.00 8.00
4 Freddie Freeman/25 5.00 12.00
5 Nelson Cruz/49 3.00 8.00
6 Adrian Beltre/49 4.00 10.00
7 Giancarlo Stanton/25 4.00 10.00
8 Mike Trout/15 15.00 40.00
9 Jose Altuve/49 3.00 8.00
10 Kris Bryant/99 15.00 40.00
11 Jose Abreu/49 4.00 10.00
12 Miguel Cabrera/25 6.00 15.00
13 Corey Seager/99 5.00 12.00
14 Adam Jones/49 3.00 8.00
15 Robinson Cano/49 3.00 8.00
16 Josh Donaldson/99 3.00 8.00
17 Andrew McCutchen/20 8.00 20.00
18 Paul Goldschmidt/99 3.00 8.00
19 Evan Longoria/99 3.00 8.00
20 Jacoby Ellsbury/49 3.00 8.00

2015 Immaculate Collection Immaculate Ink

RANDOM INSERTS IN PACKS
PRINT RUNS B/WN 10-99 COPIES PER
NO PRICING ON QTY 10 OR LESS
EXCHANGE DEADLINE 2/26/2017
*HOLOGLD/15-25: .5X TO 1.2X BASIC
1 Jose Abreu/99 8.00 20.00
4 Charlie Blackmon/49 6.00 15.00
5 Anthony Rizzo/25 20.00 50.00
6 Andres Galarraga/25 10.00 25.00
7 Paul Goldschmidt/25 8.00 20.00
8 Josh Donaldson/25 20.00 50.00
9 Troy Tulowitzki/25 10.00 25.00
10 Evan Longoria/25 10.00 25.00
11 Roberto Alomar/25 12.00 30.00
12 Corey Kluber/49 5.00 12.00
15 Starling Marte/49 10.00 25.00
16 Justin Upton/25 10.00 25.00
19 Luis Severino/49 20.00 50.00
20 Kyle Seager/49 4.00 10.00
21 Miguel Sano/49 10.00 25.00
22 Jose Altuve/49 20.00 50.00
24 Frank Howard/49 4.00 10.00
27 Tim Raines/49 6.00 15.00
29 Rusney Castillo/25 5.00 12.00
32 Salvador Perez/49 12.00 30.00
33 Orlando Cepeda/25 20.00 50.00
35 Matt Adams/49 5.00 12.00
36 Mookie Betts/49 50.00 120.00
38 Kris Bryant/49 75.00 200.00
39 Wei-Yin Chen/25 30.00 80.00
42 Noah Syndergaard/49 20.00 50.00
43 Gregory Polanco/49 5.00 12.00
44 Yordano Ventura/49 8.00 20.00
45 Anthony Rendon/49 8.00 20.00
46 Victor Martinez/25 12.00 30.00
48 Sonny Gray/25 5.00 12.00
49 Chris Davis/15 10.00 25.00
51 Dennis Eckersley/25 6.00 15.00
52 Paul Molitor/25 6.00 15.00
53 Brooks Robinson/15 15.00 40.00
54 Bert Blyleven/25 10.00 25.00
56 Tony La Russa/25 10.00 25.00
57 Willie Horton/49 4.00 10.00
58 Dave Kingman/49 4.00 10.00
59 Kennys Vargas/49 4.00 10.00
60 Andre Thornton/49 4.00 10.00

2015 Immaculate Collection Immaculate Jumbo

RANDOM INSERTS IN PACKS
STATED PRINT RUN B/WN 5-99 COPIES PER
NO PRICING ON QTY 10 OR LESS
1 Kendall Graveman/49 2.50 6.00
2 Yasmany Tomas/49 3.00 8.00
3 Matt Barnes/49 2.50 6.00
4 Brandon Finnegan/49 2.50 6.00
5 Raisel Iglesias/49 3.00 8.00
6 Aaron Judge/49 30.00 80.00
7 Yorman Rodriguez/49 2.50 6.00
8 Tony Gwynn/25 12.00 30.00
9 Luis Severino/49 3.00 8.00
10 Maikel Franco/49 3.00 8.00
11 Michael Conforto/49 6.00 15.00
12 Daniel Carbonell/49 3.00 8.00
13 Daniel Robertson/49 2.50 6.00
14 Steven Moya/49 2.50 6.00
15 Cory Spangenberg/49 2.50 6.00
16 Andy Wilkins/49 2.50 6.00
17 Stephen Piscotty/25 8.00 20.00
18 Ryan Rua/49 2.50 6.00
19 Dilson Herrera/49 2.50 6.00
20 Edwin Escobar/49 2.50 6.00
21 D.J. Peterson/49 2.50 6.00
22 Matt Szczur/49 3.00 8.00
23 Peter O'Brien/49 4.00 10.00
24 Michael Taylor/49 2.50 6.00
25 Tyler Beede/49 2.50 6.00
26 Trevor May/49 2.50 6.00
27 Alex Rodriguez/20 8.00 20.00
28 Javier Baez/49 20.00 50.00
29 Christian Walker/49 5.00 12.00
30 Addison Russell/49 6.00 15.00
31 Corey Seager/49 8.00 20.00
32 Kris Bryant/49 20.00 50.00
33 Archie Bradley/49 2.50 6.00
34 Yoan Moncada/49 10.00 25.00
35 Kyle Zimmer/49 2.50 6.00
36 Willy Adames/49 4.00 10.00
37 Deven Marrero/49 2.50 6.00
38 Byron Buxton/49 12.00 30.00
39 Luis Encarnacion/49 2.50 6.00
40 Francisco Lindor/49 20.00 50.00
41 Kennys Vargas/49 2.50 6.00
42 Kyle Schwarber/49 8.00 20.00
43 Miguel Sano/49 5.00 12.00
45 Robert Refsnyder/49 3.00 8.00
46 Trea Turner/49 15.00 40.00
47 Tyler Glasnow/49 10.00 25.00
48 Manuel Margot/49 2.50 6.00
49 Jameson Taillon/49 2.50 6.00
50 R.J. Alvarez/49 2.50 6.00
53 Prince Fielder/49 2.50 6.00
55 Eric Hosmer/20 3.00 8.00
57 Rymer Liriano/49 2.50 6.00
59 Hanley Ramirez/49 2.50 6.00
61 Adrian Gonzalez/15 3.00 8.00
62 Mark McGwire/20 12.00 30.00
66 Barry Bonds/20 20.00 50.00
67 Justin Upton/49 3.00 8.00
69 Yu Darvish/20 4.00 10.00
70 Lane Adams/49 2.50 6.00
71 Carlos Beltran/49 2.50 6.00
73 Aramis Ramirez/49 2.50 6.00
74 Billy Butler/49 2.50 6.00
77 Matt Harvey/20 10.00 25.00
79 Brian McCann/49 3.00 8.00
82 Carlos Gonzalez/15 3.00 8.00
83 Luke Appling/20 10.00 25.00
84 Johnny Cueto/20 3.00 8.00
86 Mark Trumbo/49 2.50 6.00
87 Yadier Molina/20 10.00 25.00
88 Nelson Cruz/20 4.00 10.00
90 Pablo Sandoval/25 3.00 8.00
93 Mike Trout/20 15.00 40.00
95 Felix Hernandez/15 3.00 8.00
96 Clayton Kershaw/15 10.00 25.00
97 Adam Jones/15 3.00 8.00

2015 Immaculate Collection Immaculate Pitchers Materials

SEMISTARS 3.00 8.00
RANDOM INSERTS IN PACKS
STATED PRINT RUN B/WN 20-99 COPIES PER
1 Johnny Cueto/99 3.00 8.00
2 Clayton Kershaw/25 6.00 15.00
3 Yu Darvish/49 4.00 10.00
4 Masahiro Tanaka/25 3.00 8.00
5 Chris Sale/25 4.00 10.00
6 Jose Fernandez/20 4.00 10.00
7 Jon Lester/99 3.00 8.00
8 Madison Bumgarner/49 3.00 8.00
9 Nolan Ryan/49 8.00 20.00
10 Roger Clemens/99 3.00 8.00
11 Max Scherzer/99 3.00 8.00
12 Sonny Gray/99 3.00 8.00
13 Matt Harvey/99 3.00 8.00
14 Felix Hernandez/25 3.00 8.00
15 Archie Bradley/99 2.50 6.00
16 Jeff Samardzija/99 2.50 6.00
17 John Smoltz/49 4.00 10.00

2015 Immaculate Collection Immaculate Quad Players Memorabilia

RANDOM INSERTS IN PACKS
STATED PRINT RUN B/WN 10-99 COPIES PER
NO PRICING ON QTY 10
1 Ghrg/Clmnte/Wllms/Msl/49 125.00 250.00
2 Pnnck/Appling/Dcky/Byr/25 20.00 50.00
3 Ghrngr/Chnce/Cobb/Crnn/20 60.00 150.00
5 Fllr/Drysdle/Sttn/Unkns/99 10.00 25.00
6 Brynt/Rssll/Baez/Schwrbr/99 40.00 100.00
7 Rssll/Bxtn/Lndr/Brnt/99 25.00 60.00
8 Uhra/Tnka/Drvsh/Szki/49 15.00 40.00
9 Tms/Abru/Cstllo/Puig/99 4.00 10.00
10 Pnce/Bmgrnr/Sndvl/Blt/99 10.00 25.00
11 Tiant/Crw/Ryn/Jcksn/49 20.00 50.00
12 Trre/Rse/Rbnsn/Cpda/99 12.00 30.00
13 McCtchn/Krshw/Trt/Stntn/49 20.00 50.00
14 Hndrsn/Hndrsn/Hndrsn/Hndrsn/49 15.00 40.00
15 Bggo/Smltz/Mrtnz/Jhnsn/99 12.00 30.00

2015 Immaculate Collection Immaculate Quads Memorabilia

RANDOM INSERTS IN PACKS
STATED PRINT RUN 99 SER.#'d SETS
1 Byron Buxton 6.00 15.00
2 Kennys Vargas 2.50 6.00
3 Kris Bryant 25.00 60.00
4 Addison Russell 8.00 20.00
5 Javier Baez 20.00 50.00
6 Corey Seager 6.00 15.00
7 Francisco Lindor 20.00 50.00
8 Kyle Schwarber 10.00 25.00
9 Yasmany Tomas 3.00 8.00
10 Archie Bradley 2.50 6.00
11 Miguel Sano 5.00 12.00
12 Raisel Iglesias 3.00 8.00
13 Maikel Franco 3.00 8.00
14 Michael Taylor 2.50 6.00
15 Michael Conforto 6.00 15.00

2015 Immaculate Collection Immaculate Swatches

RANDOM INSERTS IN PACKS
STATED PRINT RUN B/WN 15-99 COPIES PER
*PRIME/15-99: .5X TO 1.2X BASIC
1 Miguel Cabrera/79 4.00 10.00
2 Felix Hernandez/25 4.00 10.00
3 Andrew McCutchen/49 4.00 10.00
4 Clayton Kershaw/25 6.00 15.00
5 Mike Trout/49 20.00 50.00
6 Jose Abreu/25 4.00 10.00
7 Yu Darvish/99 4.00 10.00
8 Yasiel Puig/99 4.00 10.00
9 Giancarlo Stanton/49 4.00 10.00
10 Troy Tulowitzki/25 4.00 10.00
11 Yadier Molina/49 5.00 12.00
12 Alex Gordon/25 3.00 8.00
13 Robinson Cano/99 3.00 8.00
14 Bryce Harper/25 6.00 15.00
15 Prince Fielder/99 3.00 8.00
16 Anthony Rendon/25 4.00 10.00
17 Johnny Cueto/99 3.00 8.00
18 Ichiro Suzuki/25 5.00 12.00
19 Jose Bautista/49 3.00 8.00
20 Hyun-Jin Ryu/99 3.00 8.00
21 Cliff Lee/99 3.00 8.00
22 Max Scherzer/99 4.00 10.00
23 Carlos Gomez/49 2.50 6.00
24 Buster Posey/49 5.00 12.00
25 Paul Goldschmidt/49 4.00 10.00
26 Stephen Strasburg/49 4.00 10.00
27 Anthony Rizzo/49 5.00 12.00
28 Masahiro Tanaka/25 3.00 8.00
29 Billy Hamilton/99 3.00 8.00
30 Adrian Beltre/49 4.00 10.00
31 Jose Altuve/99 3.00 8.00
32 Madison Bumgarner/99 3.00 8.00
33 Hanley Ramirez/99 3.00 8.00
34 Adrian Gonzalez/99 3.00 8.00
35 Kris Bryant/99 12.00 30.00
36 Kendall Graveman/99 2.50 6.00
37 Yasmany Tomas/99 3.00 8.00
38 Matt Barnes/99 2.50 6.00
39 Brandon Finnegan/99 2.50 6.00
40 Raisel Iglesias/99 3.00 8.00
41 Aaron Judge/99 20.00 50.00
42 Yorman Rodriguez/99 2.50 6.00
43 Gary Brown/25 2.50 6.00
44 Luis Severino/99 3.00 8.00
45 Maikel Franco/99 3.00 8.00
46 Michael Conforto/99 4.00 15.00
47 Daniel Carbonell/99 3.00 8.00
48 Daniel Robertson/99 2.50 6.00
49 Steven Moya/99 2.50 6.00
50 Cory Spangenberg/99 2.50 6.00
51 Andy Wilkins/99 2.50 6.00
52 Stephen Piscotty/99 3.00 8.00
53 Ryan Rua/99 2.50 6.00
54 Dilson Herrera/99 2.50 6.00
55 Edwin Escobar/99 2.50 6.00
56 D.J. Peterson/99 2.50 6.00
57 Matt Szczur/99 3.00 8.00
58 Peter O'Brien/99 4.00 10.00
59 Michael Taylor/99 2.50 6.00
60 Tyler Beede/99 2.50 6.00
61 Trevor May/99 2.50 6.00
62 Jake Lamb/25 4.00 10.00
63 Javier Baez/99 20.00 50.00
64 Christian Walker/99 5.00 12.00
65 Jorge Soler/99 4.00 10.00
66 Addison Russell/99 5.00 12.00
67 Corey Seager/99 6.00 15.00
68 Archie Bradley/99 2.50 6.00
69 Yoan Moncada/99 6.00 15.00
70 Kyle Zimmer/99 2.50 6.00
71 Willy Adames/99 4.00 10.00
72 Deven Marrero/99 2.50 6.00
73 Byron Buxton/99 12.00 30.00
74 Luis Encarnacion/99 2.50 6.00
75 Francisco Lindor/99 20.00 50.00
76 Kennys Vargas/99 2.50 6.00
77 Kyle Schwarber/99 8.00 20.00
78 Miguel Sano/99 3.00 8.00
80 Robert Refsnyder/99 3.00 8.00
81 Trea Turner/99 8.00 20.00
82 Tyler Glasnow/99 8.00 20.00
83 Manuel Margot/99 2.50 6.00
84 Jameson Taillon/99 3.00 8.00
85 Bo Jackson/49 6.00 15.00
86 Ken Griffey Jr./99 8.00 20.00
87 George Brett/49 8.00 20.00
88 Barry Bonds/99 6.00 15.00
89 Frank Thomas/49 4.00 10.00
90 Craig Biggio/49 3.00 8.00
91 Cal Ripken/99 6.00 15.00
92 Nolan Ryan/99 6.00 15.00
93 Roberto Alomar/25 6.00 15.00
94 Pete Rose/99 8.00 20.00
95 Rickey Henderson/49 6.00 15.00
96 Ryne Sandberg/49 5.00 12.00
97 Mark McGwire/99 5.00 12.00
98 Pedro Martinez/79 3.00 8.00
99 Babe Ruth/15 150.00 300.00
100 Stan Musial/25 10.00 25.00
101 Roberto Clemente/15 40.00 100.00
102 Lou Gehrig/20 60.00 150.00
104 Herb Pennock/49 5.00 12.00
105 Don Drysdale/79 5.00 12.00
106 Bob Feller/49 4.00 10.00
107 Harmon Killebrew/49 5.00 12.00
108 Luke Appling/25 5.00 12.00
111 Charlie Gehringer/25 10.00 25.00
113 Ted Williams/99 25.00 60.00
115 Gabby Hartnett/99 6.00 15.00
116 Gil McDougald/49 6.00 15.00
117 Gary Carter/49 3.00 8.00
118 Kirby Puckett/79 8.00 20.00
119 Tony Gwynn/99 4.00 10.00

2015 Immaculate Collection Immaculate Trios Memorabilia

RANDOM INSERTS IN PACKS
STATED PRINT RUN 99 SER.#'d SETS
1 Byron Buxton 12.00 30.00
2 Kris Bryant 20.00 50.00
3 Yasmany Tomas 3.00 8.00
4 Archie Bradley 2.50 6.00
5 Kennys Vargas 2.50 6.00
6 Michael Taylor 2.50 6.00
7 Addison Russell 5.00 12.00
8 Cory Spangenberg 2.50 6.00
9 Maikel Franco 3.00 8.00
10 Lane Adams 2.50 6.00
11 Yorman Rodriguez 2.50 6.00
12 Steven Moya 3.00 8.00
13 Trevor May 2.50 6.00
14 R.J. Alvarez 2.50 6.00
15 Francisco Lindor 20.00 50.00

2015 Immaculate Collection Immaculate Trios Players Memorabilia

RANDOM INSERTS IN PACKS
STATED PRINT RUN B/WN 25-99 COPIES PER
1 Kllbrw/Clmnte/Msl/49 25.00 60.00
2 Ruth/Gehrig/Cobb/25 400.00 600.00
3 Applng/Ghrngr/Crnn/49 12.00 30.00
4 Marichal/Hunter/Drysdale/25 3.00 8.00
5 Rssll/Baez/Brynt/99 15.00 30.00
6 Szki/Tnka/Drvsh/25 12.00 30.00
7 Abru/Csttlo/Puig/49 4.00 10.00
8 Beltre/Ortiz/Cano/99 4.00 10.00
9 Lynn/Rice/Fisk/49 10.00 25.00
10 Rssll/Sgr/Lndr/99 6.00 15.00
11 Spngnbrg/Trnr/Baez/99 20.00 50.00
12 Jdge/Svrno/Rfsndr/99 20.00 50.00
13 Escobar/Margot/Marrero/99 2.50 6.00
14 Peterson/Franco/Sano/49 3.00 8.00
15 Soler/Iglesias/Tomas/99 4.00 10.00

2015 Immaculate Collection Multisport Autographs

RANDOM INSERTS IN PACKS
PRINT RUNS B/WN 5-25 COPIES PER
NO PRICING ON QTY 10 OR LESS
EXCHANGE DEADLINE 2/26/2017
1 Andrew Wiggins/15 150.00 250.00
2 Jabari Parker/15 100.00 200.00
5 Dante Exum/25 12.00 30.00
9 Kevin White/25 12.00 30.00
10 DeVante Parker/25 12.00 30.00

2015 Immaculate Collection Recollection Collection Autographs

RANDOM INSERTS IN PACKS
PRINT RUNS B/WN 1-99 COPIES PER
NO PRICING ON QTY 10 OR LESS
EXCHANGE DEADLINE 2/26/2017
1 Bill Buckner/99 5.00 12.00
2 Billy Hamilton/99 5.00 12.00
3 Bob Horner/99 4.00 10.00
7 Chris Owings/99 4.00 10.00
11 Fergie Jenkins/25 10.00 25.00
15 Jean Segura/98 5.00 12.00
19 Jean Segura/99 5.00 12.00
20 Jean Segura/99 5.00 12.00
24 Jonathan Schoop/99 4.00 10.00
28 Marcus Semien/99 6.00 15.00
32 Michael Young/25 8.00 20.00
36 Travis d'Arnaud/99 8.00 20.00

2015 Immaculate Collection Shadowbox Material Signatures

RANDOM INSERTS IN PACKS
PRINT RUNS B/WN 10-99 COPIES PER
NO PRICING ON QTY 10
EXCHANGE DEADLINE 2/26/2017
1 Robinson Cano/15 15.00 40.00
2 Jose Abreu/99 30.00 80.00
3 Todd Frazier/49 5.00 12.00
4 Byron Buxton/49 12.00 30.00
6 Adrian Gonzalez/25 8.00 20.00
7 Adrian Beltre/25 20.00 50.00
8 Devin Mesoraco/49 5.00 12.00
9 Jason Heyward/49 8.00 20.00
10 Jorge Soler/49 8.00 20.00
11 Kris Bryant/49 75.00 200.00
12 Felix Hernandez/25 20.00 50.00
13 Chris Sale/49 10.00 25.00
14 Victor Martinez/49 8.00 20.00
15 David Wright/15 10.00 25.00
16 Dustin Pedroia/15 20.00 50.00
17 Edwin Encarnacion/49 8.00 20.00
18 Eric Hosmer/49 15.00 40.00
19 Josh Donaldson/25 15.00 40.00
20 Manny Machado/25 25.00 60.00
21 Evan Longoria/25 10.00 25.00

2015 Immaculate Collection Shadowbox Signatures

RANDOM INSERTS IN PACKS
PRINT RUNS B/WN 7-99 COPIES PER
NO PRICING ON QTY 10 OR LESS
EXCHANGE DEADLINE 2/26/2017
*HOLOGLD/15-25: .5X TO 1.2X BASIC
2 Rusney Castillo/49 5.00 12.00
3 Yasmany Tomas/49 15.00 40.00
4 Matt Barnes/49 4.00 10.00
5 Brandon Finnegan/49 4.00 10.00
6 Daniel Norris/49 4.00 10.00
7 Kendall Graveman/49 4.00 10.00
8 Yorman Rodriguez/79 4.00 10.00
9 Gary Brown/49 4.00 10.00

10 R.J. Alvarez/78 4.00 10.00
11 Dalton Pompey/49 5.00 12.00
12 Maikel Franco/49 10.00 25.00
13 James McCann/49 10.00 25.00
14 Lane Adams/79 4.00 10.00
15 Joc Pederson/49 15.00 40.00
16 Steven Moya/49 5.00 12.00
17 Cory Spangenberg/49 4.00 10.00
18 Andy Wilkins/79 4.00 10.00
19 Terrance Gore/79 4.00 10.00
20 Ryan Rua/79 4.00 10.00
21 Dilson Herrera/79 5.00 12.00
22 Edwin Escobar/79 4.00 10.00
23 Jorge Soler/49 6.00 15.00
24 Matt Szczur/49 5.00 12.00
25 Buck Farmer/49 4.00 10.00
26 Michael Taylor/49 4.00 10.00
27 Rymer Liriano/49 4.00 10.00
28 Trevor May/49 4.00 10.00
29 Jake Lamb/49 6.00 15.00
30 Javier Baez/49 8.00 20.00
31 Mike Foltynewicz/49 4.00 10.00
32 Kennys Vargas/49 4.00 10.00
33 Anthony Ranaudo/49 4.00 10.00
34 Jung-Ho Kang/49 20.00 50.00
35 Jose Abreu/99 30.00 80.00
36 Jason Heyward/25 10.00 25.00
37 Edwin Encarnacion/25 6.00 15.00
38 Jacob deGrom/25 40.00 100.00
39 David Ortiz/15 30.00 80.00
40 Carlos Rodon/25 10.00 25.00
41 Tyler Glasnow/49 10.00 25.00
42 Anthony Rendon/49 8.00 20.00
43 Corey Seager/49 25.00 60.00
44 Max Scherzer/25 20.00 50.00
45 Omar Vizquel/49 8.00 20.00
46 Francisco Lindor/49 30.00 80.00
47 Addison Russell/48 20.00 50.00
48 Chris Sale/49 10.00 25.00
49 Freddie Freeman/25 8.00 20.00
50 Dustin Pedroia/25 15.00 40.00
51 David Wright/25 10.00 25.00
52 Kris Bryant/25 75.00 200.00
53 Wei-Yin Chen/25 30.00 80.00
54 Adam Jones/25 6.00 15.00
55 Jose Fernandez/25 12.00 30.00
56 Manny Machado/25 20.00 50.00
57 Pablo Sandoval/25 6.00 15.00
59 Josh Harrison/99 6.00 15.00
60 Evan Gattis/49 4.00 10.00
61 Matt Adams/49 4.00 10.00
62 Michael Brantley/25 5.00 12.00
63 Ryan Braun/25 6.00 15.00
64 Corey Kluber/25 6.00 15.00

2015 Immaculate Collection The Greatest Materials

RANDOM INSERTS IN PACKS
STATED PRINT RUN B/WN 5-99 COPIES PER
NO PRICING ON QTY 5
3 Barry Bonds/99 5.00 12.00
4 Duke Snider/99 5.00 12.00
5 Tony Perez/15 3.00 8.00
6 Joe Morgan/15 3.00 8.00
7 Rod Carew/49 3.00 8.00
8 Mark McGwire/49 6.00 15.00
9 Roberto Alomar/25 3.00 8.00
10 Mariano Rivera/20 5.00 12.00
11 Ryne Sandberg/20 8.00 20.00
12 Tommy Lasorda/99 3.00 8.00
13 Bob Feller/49 6.00 15.00
14 Goose Gossage/49 3.00 8.00
15 Rollie Fingers/49 3.00 8.00

2016 Immaculate Collection

1-100 PRINT RUN 99 SER.#'d SETS
JSY AU PRINT RUN 99 SER.#'d SETS
EXCHANGE DEADLINE 2/17/2018
1 Babe Ruth 4.00 10.00
2 Bill Dickey 1.00 2.50
3 Charlie Gehringer 1.00 2.50
4 Frank Chance 1.25 3.00
5 George Case 1.00 2.50
6 George Kelly 1.00 2.50
7 Gil Hodges 1.25 3.00
8 Honus Wagner 1.50 4.00
9 Jimmie Foxx 1.50 4.00
10 Joe Jackson 2.00 5.00
11 Leo Durocher 1.00 2.50
12 Lou Gehrig 3.00 8.00
13 Mel Ott 1.50 4.00
14 Miller Huggins 1.00 2.50
15 Nap Lajoie 1.50 4.00
16 Pee Wee Reese 1.25 3.00
17 Roger Maris 1.50 4.00
18 Rogers Hornsby 1.25 3.00
19 Stan Musial 2.50 6.00
20 Ted Kluszewski 1.25 3.00
21 Tommy Henrich 1.00 2.50
22 Ty Cobb 2.50 6.00
23 Mike Trout 8.00 20.00
24 Bryce Harper 2.50 6.00
25 Carlos Correa 1.50 4.00
26 Josh Donaldson 1.25 3.00
27 Andrew McCutchen 1.50 4.00
28 Ichiro Suzuki 2.00 5.00
29 Clayton Kershaw 2.50 6.00
30 Jake Arrieta 1.25 3.00
31 Dallas Keuchel 1.25 3.00
32 Jose Bautista 1.25 3.00
33 Joey Votto 1.50 4.00
34 Kris Bryant 6.00 15.00
35 Zack Greinke 1.50 4.00
36 Anthony Rizzo 2.00 5.00
37 Paul Goldschmidt 1.50 4.00
38 Chris Davis 1.00 2.50
39 Adrian Beltre 1.50 4.00
40 Albert Pujols 2.00 5.00
41 Buster Posey 2.00 5.00
42 David Wright 1.25 3.00
43 Jacob deGrom 3.00 8.00
44 Jose Abreu 1.50 4.00
45 Xander Bogaerts 1.50 4.00
46 Joc Pederson 1.25 3.00
47 Sonny Gray 1.25 3.00
48 Todd Frazier 1.00 2.50
49 Yadier Molina 2.00 5.00
50 Noah Syndergaard 1.25 3.00
51 Felix Hernandez 1.25 3.00
52 Chris Sale 1.50 4.00
53 David Price 1.25 3.00
54 Francisco Lindor 1.50 4.00
55 Alex Gordon 1.25 3.00
56 Brandon Crawford 1.25 3.00
57 Miguel Cabrera 1.50 4.00
58 A.J. Pollock 1.00 2.50
59 Jose Altuve 1.25 3.00
60 Troy Tulowitzki 1.50 4.00
61 Lorenzo Cain 1.00 2.50
62 Robinson Cano 1.25 3.00
63 Jonathan Lucroy 1.25 3.00
64 Matt Carpenter 1.50 4.00
65 Madison Bumgarner 1.25 3.00
66 Adam Wainwright 1.25 3.00
67 Nelson Cruz 1.50 4.00
68 Pete Rose 3.00 8.00
69 Nolan Arenado 2.50 6.00
70 Manny Machado 1.50 4.00
71 Yoenis Cespedes 1.50 4.00
72 Giancarlo Stanton 1.50 4.00
73 Max Scherzer 1.50 4.00
74 Gerrit Cole 1.50 4.00
75 Corey Kluber 1.25 3.00
76 George Springer 1.25 3.00
77 Mookie Betts 3.00 8.00
78 Charlie Blackmon 1.50 4.00
79 Maikel Franco 1.25 3.00
80 Wil Myers 1.25 3.00
81 Brian McCann 1.25 3.00
82 Salvador Perez 1.25 3.00
83 Alex Rodriguez 2.00 5.00
84 David Ortiz 1.50 4.00
85 Prince Fielder 1.25 3.00
86 Adrian Gonzalez 1.25 3.00
87 Eric Hosmer 1.25 3.00
88 Jason Kipnis 1.25 3.00
89 Michael Brantley 1.25 3.00
90 Anthony Rendon 1.50 4.00
91 Evan Longoria 1.25 3.00
92 Carlos Gonzalez 1.25 3.00
93 Jung-Ho Kang 1.00 2.50
94 J.D. Martinez 1.50 4.00
95 Adam Eaton 1.00 2.50
96 Starling Marte 1.25 3.00
97 Hunter Pence 1.25 3.00
98 Joe Panik 1.25 3.00
99 Yu Darvish 1.50 4.00
100 Matt Harvey 1.25 3.00
101 Brian Ellington JSY AU RC 4.00 10.00
103 Elias Diaz JSY AU RC 4.00 10.00
104 Carl Edwards Jr. JSY AU RC 6.00 15.00
105 Corey Seager JSY AU RC 40.00 100.00
106 Tyler Duffey JSY AU RC 4.00 10.00
108 Frankie Montas JSY AU RC 5.00 12.00
109 Jonathan Gray JSY AU RC 4.00 10.00
110 Jorge Lopez JSY AU RC 4.00 10.00
111 Jose Peraza JSY AU RC 6.00 15.00
112 John Lamb JSY AU RC 4.00 10.00
113 Kelby Tomlinson JSY AU RC 6.00 15.00
114 Travis Jankowski JSY AU RC 4.00 10.00
115 Ketel Marte JSY AU RC 8.00 20.00
116 Kyle Schwarber JSY AU RC 12.00 30.00
117 Luis Severino JSY AU RC 10.00 25.00
118 Mac Williamson JSY AU RC 5.00 12.00
119 Max Kepler JSY AU RC 6.00 15.00
120 Michael Conforto JSY AU RC EXCH 20.00 50.00
121 Michael Reed JSY AU RC 4.00 10.00
122 Miguel Sano JSY AU RC 10.00 25.00
123 Peter O'Brien JSY AU RC 4.00 10.00
124 Raul Mondesi JSY AU RC 8.00 20.00
125 Trevor Story JSY AU RC 10.00 25.00
126 Rob Refsnyder JSY AU RC 5.00 12.00
127 Stephen Piscotty JSY AU RC 6.00 15.00
128 Tom Murphy JSY AU RC 4.00 10.00
129 Trayce Thompson JSY AU RC 6.00 15.00
130 Trea Turner JSY AU RC 12.00 30.00
131 Alex Dickerson JSY AU RC 4.00 10.00
132 Brian Johnson JSY AU RC 4.00 10.00
133 Colin Rea JSY AU RC 4.00 10.00
134 Daniel Alvarez JSY AU RC 4.00 10.00
135 Jerad Eickhoff JSY AU RC 6.00 15.00
136 Kyle Waldrop JSY AU RC 5.00 12.00
137 Luke Jackson JSY AU RC 4.00 10.00
138 Pedro Severino JSY AU RC 4.00 10.00
139 Socrates Brito JSY AU RC 4.00 10.00
140 Zack Godley JSY AU RC 6.00 15.00

2016 Immaculate Collection Red

*RED 1-100: .6X TO 1.5X BASIC
*RED JSY AU/49: .5X TO 1.2X BASIC p/r 99
*RED JSY AU/25: .6X TO 1.5X BASIC p/r 99
RANDOM INSERTS IN PACKS
1-100 PRINT RUN 25 SER.#'d SETS
101-140 PRINT RUNS B/WN 25-49 COPIES PER
EXCHANGE DEADLINE 2/17/2018
102 Brandon Drury JSY AU/49 EXCH 8.00 20.00
107 Greg Bird JSY AU/49 6.00 15.00

2016 Immaculate Collection Diamond Inscriptions

RANDOM INSERTS IN PACKS
PRINT RUNS B/WN 25-99 COPIES PER
*RED/25: .5X TO 1.2X p/r 99
*RED/25: .4X TO 1X p/r 25
EXCHANGE DEADLINE 2/17/2018
1 Aaron Nola/25 12.00 30.00
2 Alex Dickerson/25 4.00 10.00
3 Byung-ho Park/25 12.00 30.00
4 Carl Edwards Jr./25 5.00 12.00
5 Colin Rea/25 4.00 10.00
6 Corey Seager/25 40.00 100.00
8 Jerad Eickhoff/25 12.00 30.00
10 Ketel Marte/25 8.00 20.00
11 Kyle Schwarber/25 10.00 25.00
12 Kyle Waldrop/25 5.00 12.00
14 Mac Williamson/25 4.00 10.00
15 Michael Reed/25 4.00 10.00
16 Miguel Sano/25 12.00 30.00
17 Raul Mondesi/25 8.00 20.00
18 Socrates Brito/25
19 Stephen Piscotty/25 6.00 15.00
20 Tom Murphy/25 4.00 10.00
21 Jose Abreu/99 10.00 25.00
22 Starling Marte/99 10.00 25.00
23 Joe Panik/99 4.00 10.00
24 Omar Vizquel/99 4.00 10.00
25 Kris Bryant/99 40.00 100.00
26 Josh Donaldson/99 12.00 30.00
27 Manny Machado/99 20.00 50.00
28 Fernando Rodney/99 3.00 8.00
29 Billy Burns/99 3.00 8.00
30 Yasmany Tomas/25 4.00 10.00
31 James McCann/25 5.00 12.00
32 Jorge Soler/25 6.00 15.00
33 Daniel Norris/25 4.00 10.00
34 Brandon Finnegan/25 10.00 25.00
35 Maikel Franco/25
36 Eddie Rosario/25 5.00 12.00
37 Odubel Herrera/25
38 Kevin Plawecki/25 4.00 10.00
39 Carlos Rodon/25 6.00 15.00
40 Steven Matz/25 6.00 15.00
41 Joc Pederson/99 8.00 20.00
42 Andres Galarraga/99 6.00 15.00
43 Byron Buxton/25
44 Devon Travis/25 4.00 10.00
45 Dilson Herrera/25
46 Adrian Gonzalez/99 5.00 12.00
47 Albert Pujols/25 50.00 120.00
48 Jason Heyward/25 12.00 30.00
49 Jose Altuve/99
50 Kolten Wong/99 4.00 10.00
51 Lorenzo Cain/99
52 Edgar Martinez/99 15.00 40.00
53 Robinson Cano/99 10.00 25.00
54 Xander Bogaerts/99 20.00 50.00
55 Yadier Molina/99 25.00 60.00

2016 Immaculate Collection Dual Diamond Inscriptions

RANDOM INSERTS IN PACKS
PRINT RUNS B/WN 25-99 COPIES PER
EXCHANGE DEADLINE 2/17/2018
*RED/25: .5X TO 1.2X BASIC
1 Bryant/Schwarber/49
2 Fisk/Rice/49 25.00 60.00
4 Keuchel/Arrieta/49
5 dGrm/Syndrgrd/49 60.00 150.00
6 Griffey Jr./Piazza/49 125.00 300.00
7 Park/Sano/99 10.00 25.00
9 Henderson/Brock/25 50.00 120.00

2016 Immaculate Collection Dugout Collection Ink

RANDOM INSERTS IN PACKS
PRINT RUNS B/WN 15-25 COPIES PER
NO PRICING ON QTY 15
EXCHANGE DEADLINE 2/17/2018
1 Julio Urias/25 10.00 25.00
2 Willson Contreras/25
3 Yoan Moncada/25 10.00 25.00
4 Clint Frazier/25 10.00 25.00
5 Trevor Story/25 15.00 40.00
6 Mike Gerber/25 4.00 10.00
7 A.J. Reed/25 4.00 10.00
8 Orlando Arcia/25 10.00 25.00
9 Aaron Judge/25 60.00 150.00
10 Javier Guerra/25 4.00 10.00
11 Brandon Nimmo/25 6.00 15.00
13 Lucas Giolito/25 6.00 15.00
14 Aaron Blair/25 4.00 10.00
15 Rafael Devers/25 30.00 80.00
16 Lewis Brinson/25 6.00 15.00
17 Jose Berrios/25
18 Jorge Mateo/25 5.00 12.00

2016 Immaculate Collection Hitters Ink

RANDOM INSERTS IN PACKS
PRINT RUNS B/WN 10-25 COPIES PER
NO PRICING ON QTY 15 OR LESS
EXCHANGE DEADLINE 2/17/2018
1 Ken Griffey Jr./25 75.00 200.00
2 Mike Piazza/25 25.00 60.00
3 Josh Donaldson/25 12.00 30.00
5 Jose Abreu/25 8.00 20.00
6 Frank Thomas/25 25.00 60.00
7 Reggie Jackson/25 15.00 40.00
8 Mark McGwire/25 40.00 100.00
9 Barry Bonds/25 60.00 150.00
11 Jose Bautista/25 12.00 30.00
13 Paul Goldschmidt/25 15.00 40.00
14 David Ortiz/25 30.00 80.00
15 George Brett/25 40.00 100.00
16 Johnny Bench/25 20.00 50.00
18 Roberto Alomar/25 12.00 30.00
19 Edgar Martinez/25 5.00 12.00
20 Paul Molitor/25 6.00 15.00
21 Craig Biggio/25 12.00 30.00
22 Vladimir Guerrero/25 8.00 20.00
23 Chipper Jones/25 40.00 100.00
24 Rod Carew/25 10.00 25.00
25 Pete Rose/25 20.00 50.00

2016 Immaculate Collection Immaculate Autograph Dual Materials

RANDOM INSERTS IN PACKS
PRINT RUNS B/WN 10-49 COPIES PER
NO PRICING ON QTY 15 OR LESS
EXCHANGE DEADLINE 2/17/2018
*RED/25: .5X TO 1.2X BASIC
1 Josh Donaldson/25 15.00 40.00
2 Clayton Kershaw/25 40.00 100.00
3 Carlos Gomez/25 6.00 15.00
4 Jose Abreu/25 10.00 25.00
5 Anthony Rizzo/25
6 David Price/25 10.00 25.00
8 Edwin Encarnacion/25 10.00 25.00
9 Freddie Freeman/25 8.00 20.00
10 Michael Brantley/25 4.00 10.00
11 Todd Frazier/25
12 Matt Carpenter/49 5.00 12.00
13 Xander Bogaerts/49 15.00 40.00
15 Billy Hamilton/20
16 Lorenzo Cain/49
17 Brandon Phillips/49 10.00 25.00
18 Kyle Seager/25 3.00 8.00
19 Brett Gardner/25 4.00 10.00
20 Mookie Betts/25 30.00 80.00
22 Brandon Belt/25 4.00 10.00
25 Eric Hosmer/25 10.00 25.00

2016 Immaculate Collection Immaculate Autograph Materials

RANDOM INSERTS IN PACKS
PRINT RUNS B/WN 15-99 COPIES PER
NO PRICING ON QTY 15 OR LESS
EXCHANGE DEADLINE 2/17/2018
*RED/25: .5X TO 1.2X BASIC
1 Kris Bryant/49 40.00 100.00
2 David Wright/25 15.00 40.00
3 Don Mattingly/25 30.00 80.00
5 David Ortiz/25 25.00 60.00
6 Todd Helton/25 8.00 20.00
7 Edgar Martinez/99 6.00 15.00
8 Prince Fielder/25 6.00 15.00
14 Brian McCann/25 4.00 10.00
16 Gerrit Cole/49 5.00 12.00
17 Joe Mauer/25 10.00 25.00
18 Wil Myers/25 4.00 10.00
19 Frank Thomas/49 25.00 60.00
20 Anthony Rendon/49 6.00 15.00
21 Pete Rose/25 25.00 60.00
22 Evan Longoria/25 6.00 15.00
23 Troy Tulowitzki/25
25 Bob Gibson/25 12.00 30.00
26 Matt Carpenter/49 5.00 12.00
27 Clayton Kershaw/25 40.00 100.00
28 Max Scherzer/25 25.00 60.00
29 Jose Canseco/25 15.00 40.00
30 Will Clark/25 20.00 50.00

2016 Immaculate Collection Immaculate Autograph Quad Materials

RANDOM INSERTS IN PACKS
PRINT RUNS B/WN 25-49 COPIES PER
EXCHANGE DEADLINE 2/17/2018
*RED/25: .5X TO 1.2X BASIC
1 Barry Bonds/25 100.00 250.00
2 Mark McGwire/25 60.00 150.00
3 Joe Mauer/49 10.00 25.00
4 Joe Panik/49 8.00 20.00
5 Rusney Castillo/25 3.00 8.00
6 Edgar Martinez/49 6.00 15.00
7 Dale Murphy/49 8.00 20.00
8 Will Clark/49 20.00 50.00
9 Ron Guidry/49 20.00 50.00
10 Maikel Franco/49 8.00 20.00
11 Jose Peraza/25 12.00 30.00
12 Lucas Giolito/25 5.00 12.00
13 Aaron Blair/25 5.00 12.00
14 Yoan Moncada/25 40.00 100.00
15 Dansby Swanson/25 15.00 40.00
16 Steven Matz/25 8.00 20.00
17 Alex Bregman/25 20.00 50.00
18 Blake Snell/25 4.00 10.00
19 Alex Reyes/25
20 Rafael Devers/25 30.00 80.00

2016 Immaculate Collection Immaculate Autograph Triple Materials

RANDOM INSERTS IN PACKS
STATED PRINT RUN 25 SER.#'d SETS
EXCHANGE DEADLINE 2/17/2018
1 Evan Longoria 6.00 15.00
2 Evan Gattis
3 Jose Canseco 15.00 40.00
4 Frank Thomas 25.00 60.00
5 David Wright 15.00 40.00
6 Manny Machado 30.00 80.00
7 Prince Fielder 6.00 15.00
8 Kris Bryant 60.00 150.00
9 Kyle Schwarber 15.00 40.00
10 Corey Seager
11 Miguel Sano 12.00 30.00
12 Ketel Marte 6.00 15.00
13 Trea Turner 20.00 50.00
14 Max Kepler 12.00 30.00
15 Tom Murphy 3.00 8.00
16 Tyler White 3.00 8.00
17 Byung-ho Park EXCH 12.00 30.00
18 Aaron Nola 6.00 15.00
19 Henry Owens
20 Stephen Piscotty 10.00 25.00

2016 Immaculate Collection Immaculate Autographs

RANDOM INSERTS IN PACKS
PRINT RUNS B/WN 10-49 COPIES PER
NO PRICING ON QTY 10
*RED/25: .5X TO 1.2X p/r 49
*RED/25: .4X TO 1X p/r 25
EXCHANGE DEADLINE 2/17/2018
2 Yoenis Cespedes/25 12.00 30.00
3 Adam Eaton/49 3.00 8.00
4 Kevin Pillar/49 6.00 15.00
5 Michael Wacha/25 6.00 15.00
7 Max Scherzer/25 20.00 50.00
8 Jered Weaver/25 5.00 12.00
9 R.A. Dickey/25 5.00 12.00
10 Shane Victorino/25 5.00 12.00
11 Wil Myers/25 5.00 12.00
12 Jonathan Lucroy/49 6.00 15.00
13 Fernando Rodney/25 4.00 10.00
14 Norichika Aoki/49 3.00 8.00
15 Jean Segura/49 4.00 10.00

2016 Immaculate Collection Immaculate Dual Players Memorabilia

RANDOM INSERTS IN PACKS
PRINT RUNS B/WN 5-99 COPIES PER
NO PRICING ON QTY 15 OR LESS
*RED/25: .5X TO 1.2X BASIC
10 Correa/Bryant/99 6.00 15.00
11 Harper/Dnldsn/99 8.00 20.00
12 D.Keuchel/J.Arrieta/49 4.00 10.00
13 J.Bautista/J.Donaldson/49 4.00 10.00
14 Syndrgrd/dGrm/99 6.00 15.00
15 Gordon/Perez/49 6.00 15.00
16 Ripken/Brett/49 15.00 40.00
17 Posey/Trout/99 10.00 25.00
18 N.Cruz/C.Davis/49 5.00 12.00
19 Altuve/Bogaerts/99 10.00 25.00
20 Schrzr/Krshw/99 6.00 15.00

2016 Immaculate Collection Immaculate Duals Memorabilia

RANDOM INSERTS IN PACKS
PRINT RUNS B/WN 5-99 COPIES PER
NO PRICING ON QTY 5
*RED/25: .5X TO 1.2X BASIC
1 Kyle Schwarber/99 6.00 15.00
2 Ichiro Suzuki/25 5.00 12.00
3 Adam Jones/20 6.00 15.00
4 Adrian Gonzalez/99 3.00 8.00
5 Albert Pujols/99 5.00 12.00
6 Yadier Molina/99 6.00 15.00
7 Andrew McCutchen/99 6.00 15.00
8 Jung-Ho Kang/99 5.00 12.00
9 Jose Altuve/99 5.00 12.00
10 David Price/99 3.00 8.00
11 Anthony Rizzo/99 5.00 12.00
12 Miguel Sano/99 4.00 10.00
13 Corey Seager/99 25.00 60.00
14 David Ortiz/25 6.00 15.00
15 Mookie Betts/49 8.00 20.00
16 Freddie Freeman/49 5.00 12.00
17 Yu Darvish/25 6.00 15.00
18 Frank Thomas/49 4.00 10.00
19 George Brett/99 8.00 20.00

2016 Immaculate Collection Immaculate Heroes Autographs

RANDOM INSERTS IN PACKS
PRINT RUNS B/WN 15-99 COPIES PER
NO PRICING ON QTY 15
*RED/25: .5X TO 1.2X p/r 49-99
*RED/25: .4X TO 1X p/r 25
EXCHANGE DEADLINE 2/17/2018
1 Andre Dawson/99 10.00 25.00
2 Paul Molitor/49 10.00 25.00
3 Roberto Alomar/49 4.00 10.00
4 Will Clark/49 12.00 30.00
5 Dave Winfield/25 10.00 25.00
6 Ron Guidry/25 6.00 15.00
7 Craig Biggio/25 12.00 30.00
8 Bert Blyleven/25 8.00 20.00
9 Bo Jackson/25 40.00 100.00
10 Bob Gibson/49 20.00 50.00
11 Brooks Robinson/25 15.00 40.00
12 Jim Rice/25 5.00 12.00
13 John Smoltz/25 15.00 40.00
14 Juan Gonzalez/25 10.00 25.00
15 Ken Griffey Jr./25
16 Mike Schmidt/25 25.00 60.00
17 Ozzie Smith/25 20.00 50.00
18 Phil Niekro/25
19 Rollie Fingers/25 10.00 25.00
20 Mariano Rivera/25 40.00 100.00
21 Tom Glavine/25 12.00 30.00
24 Ryne Sandberg/25 20.00 50.00

2016 Immaculate Collection Immaculate Initiations Jumbo Materials

RANDOM INSERTS IN PACKS
PRINT RUNS B/WN 15-99 COPIES PER
NO PRICING ON QTY 15 OR LESS
1 Kris Bryant/99 5.00 12.00
2 Francisco Lindor/99 4.00 10.00
3 Javier Baez/99 5.00 12.00
4 Addison Russell/99 4.00 10.00
5 Yasmany Tomas/99 2.50 6.00
6 Maikel Franco/99 3.00 8.00
7 Carlos Correa/25 5.00 12.00
8 Jacob deGrom/99 8.00 20.00
9 Kolten Wong/99 3.00 8.00
10 Nolan Arenado/99 6.00 15.00
12 Mike Trout/25 15.00 40.00
13 Manny Machado/99 4.00 10.00
14 Sonny Gray/49 3.00 8.00
15 Jose Fernandez/25 4.00 10.00
16 Gerrit Cole/99 4.00 10.00
17 Kyle Schwarber/99 5.00 12.00
18 Corey Seager/99 8.00 20.00
19 Masahiro Tanaka/49 3.00 8.00
20 Yasiel Puig/25 4.00 10.00
22 Aaron Nola/49 5.00 12.00
23 Miguel Sano/99 4.00 10.00
24 Mookie Betts/25 8.00 20.00
25 Chris Heston/25 2.50 6.00
26 Dallas Keuchel/99 3.00 8.00
27 Noah Syndergaard/49 4.00 10.00
28 Yordano Ventura/99 3.00 8.00
29 Taijuan Walker/99 2.50 6.00
30 Michael Conforto/99 3.00 8.00
31 Stephen Piscotty/99 4.00 10.00
32 Trea Turner/99 5.00 12.00
33 Raul Mondesi/99 5.00 12.00
34 Byron Buxton/99 4.00 10.00
35 George Springer/99 3.00 8.00
36 Joc Pederson/25 3.00 8.00
37 Xander Bogaerts/25 4.00 10.00
38 Rougned Odor/99 3.00 8.00
39 Steven Matz/25 2.50 6.00
40 Joe Panik/49 3.00 8.00

2016 Immaculate Collection Immaculate Ink

RANDOM INSERTS IN PACKS
PRINT RUNS B/WN 25-49 COPIES PER
*RED/25: .5X TO 1.2X p/r 49
*RED/25: .4X TO 1X p/r 25
EXCHANGE DEADLINE 2/17/2018
1 Kris Bryant/49 60.00 150.00
2 Rusney Castillo/25 3.00 8.00
3 Jonathan Lucroy/49 4.00 10.00
4 Jung-Ho Kang/25 10.00 25.00
5 Sonny Gray/49 8.00 20.00
6 Yasmany Tomas/25 4.00 10.00
7 Adrian Gonzalez/25 6.00 15.00
8 Chris Sale/25 6.00 15.00
9 Corey Kluber/25 10.00 25.00
10 Dallas Keuchel/25 10.00 25.00
11 David Ortiz/25 30.00 80.00
12 Joc Pederson/25 10.00 25.00
13 Jose Altuve/25 10.00 25.00
14 Jose Fernandez/25 25.00 60.00
15 Max Scherzer/25 20.00 50.00
16 Robinson Cano/25 12.00 30.00
17 Yadier Molina/25 30.00 80.00
18 Adam Jones/25 10.00 25.00
19 Wei-Yin Chen/25 40.00 100.00
23 Evan Gattis/25
24 Paul Goldschmidt/25 12.00 30.00
25 Michael Brantley/25 5.00 12.00

2016 Immaculate Collection Immaculate Jumbo Material Autographs

RANDOM INSERTS IN PACKS
PRINT RUNS B/WN 10-25 COPIES PER
NO PRICING ON QTY 10
EXCHANGE DEADLINE 2/17/2018
1 Chipper Jones/25 30.00 80.00
2 Robin Ventura/25 10.00 25.00
3 Joe Girardi/25 8.00 20.00
4 Brandon Belt/25 5.00 12.00
6 Matt Adams/25
7 Yordano Ventura/25
8 Cal Ripken/25 50.00 120.00
9 Frank Thomas/25 40.00 100.00
10 Jose Abreu/25 15.00 40.00
11 Dennis Eckersley/25 8.00 20.00
13 Josh Donaldson/25 15.00 40.00
14 Carl Edwards Jr./25 6.00 15.00
15 Socrates Brito/25
16 Colin Rea/25 4.00 10.00
17 Kyle Waldrop/25 6.00 15.00
18 Alex Dickerson/25
19 Jerad Eickhoff/25 6.00 15.00
20 Luke Jackson/25

2016 Immaculate Collection Immaculate Jumbo Materials

RANDOM INSERTS IN PACKS
PRINT RUNS B/WN 1-99 COPIES PER
NO PRICING ON QTY 15 OR LESS
1 Aaron Nola/25 5.00 12.00
2 Brandon Drury/99 4.00 10.00
3 Byung-ho Park/49 3.00 8.00
4 Carl Edwards Jr./99 3.00 8.00
5 Corey Seager/99 8.00 20.00
6 Frankie Montas/99 3.00 8.00
7 Greg Bird/99 3.00 8.00
8 Henry Owens/25 3.00 8.00
9 Jonathan Gray/99 2.50 6.00
10 Jorge Lopez/99 2.50 6.00
11 Jose Peraza/99 3.00 8.00
12 Kaleb Cowart/99 2.50 6.00
13 Kelby Tomlinson/99 2.50 6.00
15 Ketel Marte/99 5.00 12.00
16 Kyle Schwarber/99 5.00 12.00
17 Luis Severino/99 3.00 8.00
18 Mac Williamson/99 2.50 6.00
19 Max Kepler/99 4.00 10.00
20 Michael Conforto/99 3.00 8.00
21 Michael Reed/99 2.50 6.00
22 Miguel Sano/99 4.00 10.00
23 Peter O'Brien/99 2.50 6.00
24 Raul Mondesi/99 5.00 12.00
25 Richie Shaffer/99 2.50 6.00
26 Rob Refsnyder/99 2.50 6.00
27 Stephen Piscotty/99 4.00 10.00
28 Tom Murphy/99 2.50 6.00
29 Trayce Thompson/99 4.00 10.00
30 Trea Turner/99 8.00 20.00
31 Zack Godley/99 2.50 6.00
32 Socrates Brito/99 2.50 6.00
33 Daniel Alvarez/99 2.50 6.00
34 Brian Johnson/99 2.50 6.00
35 John Lamb/99 2.50 6.00
36 Kyle Waldrop/99 3.00 8.00
37 Brian Ellington/99 2.50 6.00
39 Tyler Duffey/99 3.00 8.00
40 Elias Diaz/99 2.50 6.00
41 Jerad Eickhoff/99 4.00 10.00
42 Travis Jankowski/99 2.50 6.00
43 Colin Rea/99 2.50 6.00
44 Alex Dickerson/99 2.50 6.00
45 Luke Jackson/99 2.50 6.00
46 Pedro Severino/99 2.50 6.00
47 Yoan Moncada/99 6.00 15.00
48 Yoan Lopez/99 2.50 6.00
49 Clint Frazier/99 10.00 25.00
50 Lucas Giolito/99 4.00 10.00
51 Aaron Judge/99 25.00 60.00
52 A.J. Reed/99 2.50 6.00
53 Orlando Arcia/99 3.00 8.00
54 Willson Contreras/99 6.00 15.00
55 Nomar Mazara/99 4.00 10.00
56 Blake Snell/99 3.00 8.00
57 Sean Manaea/99 2.50 6.00
58 Matt Olson/99 5.00 121.00
59 Jose Berrios/99 4.00 10.00
60 Byron Buxton/99 2.50 6.00
61 Mallex Smith/99 2.50 6.00
63 Alex Reyes/99 3.00 8.00
64 Tyler Naquin/99 4.00 10.00
65 Trevor Story/99 12.00 30.00
66 Aaron Blair/99 2.50 6.00
67 J.P. Crawford/25 2.50 6.00
68 Tyler Glasnow/99 10.00 25.00
69 Lewis Brinson/25 4.00 10.00
70 Kris Bryant/99 5.00 12.00
71 Francisco Lindor/99 5.00 12.00
72 Maikel Franco/99 3.00 8.00
76 Vladimir Guerrero/25 6.00 15.00
77 Don Mattingly/25 15.00 40.00
78 Josh Hamilton/99 3.00 8.00
79 Addison Russell/99 4.00 10.00
80 Barry Bonds/25 12.00 30.00
82 Ken Griffey Jr./49 15.00 40.00
83 Mike Piazza/99 4.00 10.00
85 Jim Rice/25 8.00 20.00
87 Mark McGwire/25 10.00 25.00
88 Albert Pujols/25 6.00 15.00
89 Miguel Cabrera/99 4.00 10.00
90 Mike Trout/25 15.00 40.00
91 Yu Darvish/25 4.00 10.00
92 Sonny Gray/99 3.00 8.00
94 Kirby Puckett/25 50.00 120.00
95 Tyler Beede/99 3.00 8.00
96 Luis Encarnacion/99 2.50 6.00
97 Matt Moore/99 3.00 8.00
98 Matt Wieters/25 4.00 10.00
99 Manny Machado/25 6.00 15.00
100 Brian Dozier/25 3.00 8.00

2016 Immaculate Collection Immaculate Marks

RANDOM INSERTS IN PACKS
PRINT RUNS B/WN 25-99 COPIES PER
*RED/25: .5X TO 1.2X p/r 49
*RED/25: .4X TO 1X p/r 25
EXCHANGE DEADLINE 2/17/2018
1 Chipper Jones/49 20.00 50.00
2 Barry Bonds/25 60.00 150.00
3 Don Mattingly/49 20.00 50.00
4 Brooks Robinson/49 12.00 30.00
5 Al Kaline/49 15.00 40.00
6 Bruce Sutter/49 6.00 15.00
7 Wade Boggs/49 20.00 50.00
8 Ryne Sandberg/49 15.00 40.00
9 Dave Winfield/49 8.00 20.00
10 Tom Glavine/49 10.00 25.00
11 Rickey Henderson/49 25.00 60.00
12 Dale Murphy/49 6.00 15.00
14 Whitey Herzog/49
15 Cal Ripken/49 25.00 60.00
16 Roberto Alomar/49 10.00 25.00
17 Rollie Fingers/49 5.00 12.00
18 Fergie Jenkins/99 10.00 25.00
19 Roger Clemens/49 20.00 50.00
20 Billy Williams/99 8.00 20.00
21 John Smoltz/49 10.00 25.00
22 Mike Piazza/49 40.00 100.00
23 Reggie Jackson/49 20.00 50.00
24 Andre Dawson/49 4.00 10.00
25 Will Clark/49 10.00 25.00

2016 Immaculate Collection Immaculate Quad Players Memorabilia

RANDOM INSERTS IN PACKS
PRINT RUNS B/WN 15-99 COPIES PER
NO PRICING ON QTY 15
*RED/25: .5X TO 1.2X BASIC
1 Case/Brck/Cobb/Hndrsn/25 40.00 100.00
5 dGrm/Crra/Abreu/Brnt/49 10.00 25.00
6 Brtt/Grffy Jr./Rpkn/Thms/25 50.00 120.00
8 Fisk/Rdrgz/Bnch/Pzza/49 20.00 50.00
9 Ryan/Clmns/Bllvn/Crltn/49 20.00 50.00
10 Rose/Bnch/Schmdt/Jcksn/49 25.00 60.00
11 Park/Sgr/Mda/Schwrbr/99 6.00 15.00
12 Trnr/Stry/Sano/Psctty/99 15.00 40.00
13 Owns/Svrno/Nola/Gray/99 6.00 15.00
14 Marte/Rfsndr/Stry/Prza/99 15.00 40.00
15 Hrpr/Psy/Sntn/Trt/25 20.00 50.00

2016 Immaculate Collection Immaculate Quads Memorabilia

RANDOM INSERTS IN PACKS
PRINT RUNS B/WN 25-99 COPIES PER
*RED/25: .5X TO 1.2X BASIC
1 Yoan Moncada/99 10.00 25.00
2 Lucas Giolito/99 4.00 10.00
3 Jose Peraza/99 3.00 8.00
4 Willson Contreras/99 8.00 20.00
5 Dansby Swanson/25 8.00 20.00
6 Kyle Schwarber/99 6.00 15.00
7 Corey Seager/99 25.00 60.00
8 Aaron Nola/25 5.00 12.00
9 Miguel Sano/99 4.00 10.00
10 Kenta Maeda/25 5.00 12.00
11 Byung-ho Park/99 3.00 8.00
12 Trea Turner/99 8.00 20.00
13 Stephen Piscotty/99 4.00 10.00
14 Raul Mondesi/99 5.00 12.00
15 Henry Owens/99 3.00 8.00

2016 Immaculate Collection Immaculate Standard Materials

RANDOM INSERTS IN PACKS
PRINT RUNS B/WN 10-99 COPIES PER
NO PRICING ON QTY 15 OR LESS
*RED/49: .5X TO 1.2X BASIC p/r 99
*RED/25: .6X TO 1.5X BASIC p/r 99
1 Cal Ripken/49 12.00 30.00
2 Mark McGwire/49 10.00 25.00
3 Don Mattingly/49 8.00 20.00
4 Barry Bonds/49 8.00 20.00
5 Joe Torre/49 6.00 15.00
6 Kris Bryant/99 5.00 12.00
7 Frank Robinson/49 8.00 20.00
8 A.J. Reed/99 2.50 6.00
9 Vladimir Guerrero/49 6.00 15.00
10 Gregory Polanco/99 3.00 8.00
12 Steve Carlton/99 3.00 8.00
13 Jameson Taillon/99 6.00 15.00
14 Archie Bradley/99 2.50 6.00
15 Yasmany Tomas/99 2.50 6.00
16 Javier Baez/99 5.00 12.00
17 Hanley Ramirez/99 3.00 8.00
18 Taijuan Walker/99 3.00 8.00
19 Francisco Lindor/99 4.00 10.00
20 Maikel Franco/99 3.00 8.00
21 Addison Russell/99 4.00 10.00
23 Michael Taylor/99 2.50 6.00
24 Jimmy Wynn/99 6.00 15.00
25 Mike Piazza/99 4.00 10.00
26 Fergie Jenkins/49 10.00 25.00
28 Tyler Glasnow/99 10.00 25.00
29 Tyler Beede/99 3.00 8.00
30 Brett Phillips/99 2.50 6.00
31 Yordano Ventura/99 3.00 8.00
32 Wei-Chieh Huang/99 2.50 6.00
34 Ron Guidry/49 3.00 8.00
35 Matt Olson/99 5.00 12.00
37 Carlos Beltran/99 3.00 8.00
38 Evan Gattis/49 2.50 6.00
39 Curtis Granderson/99 3.00 8.00
40 Max Scherzer/49 4.00 10.00
41 Prince Fielder/99 3.00 8.00
46 Mark Trumbo/49 2.50 6.00
49 Lucas Giolito/99 4.00 10.00
50 Josh Hamilton/99 3.00 8.00
51 Nelson Cruz/99 4.00 10.00
52 Jake Arrieta/20 5.00 12.00
55 Wil Myers/49 3.00 8.00
59 Aroldis Chapman/20 4.00 10.00
62 Jose Reyes/49 3.00 8.00
63 Pablo Sandoval/49 3.00 8.00
65 Nick Swisher/49 3.00 8.00
70 Jon Lester/49 3.00 8.00
73 Jimmy Rollins/49 3.00 8.00
74 Johnny Cueto/20 3.00 8.00
75 Hanley Ramirez/49 3.00 8.00
80 David Freese/20 2.50 6.00
84 Daniel Murphy/49 3.00 8.00
85 Dexter Fowler/49 3.00 8.00
87 Dansby Swanson/99 6.00 15.00
88 Billy Butler/49 2.50 6.00
89 Nick Markakis/25 3.00 8.00
90 Russell Martin/49 2.50 6.00
96 Byron Buxton/99 4.00 10.00
97 Rickey Henderson/25 12.00 30.00

2016 Immaculate Collection Immaculate Swatches

RANDOM INSERTS IN PACKS
PRINT RUNS B/WN 5-99 COPIES PER
NO PRICING ON QTY 15 OR LESS
*PRIME/49: .5X TO 1.2X BASIC p/r 99
*PRIME/25: .6X TO 1.5X BASIC p/r 99
4 Gil Hodges/25 10.00 25.00
5 Leo Durocher/99 2.50 6.00

8 Pee Wee Reese/25 3.00 8.00
11 Stan Musial/25
12 Tommy Henrich/99 2.50 6.00
14 Kenta Maeda/99 5.00 12.00
15 Ketel Marte/99 5.00 12.00
16 Kyle Schwarber/99 5.00 12.00
17 Luis Severino/99 3.00 8.00
18 Mac Williamson/99 2.50 6.00
19 Max Kepler/99 4.00 10.00
20 Michael Conforto/99 3.00 8.00
21 Michael Reed/99 2.50 6.00
22 Miguel Sano/99 4.00 10.00
23 Peter O'Brien/99 2.50 6.00
24 Raul Mondesi/99 5.00 12.00
25 Richie Shaffer/99 2.50 6.00
26 Rob Refsnyder/99 3.00 8.00
27 Stephen Piscotty/99 4.00 10.00
28 Tom Murphy/99 2.50 6.00
29 Trayce Thompson/99 4.00 10.00
30 Trea Turner/99 5.00 12.00
31 Zack Godley/99 2.50 6.00
32 Socrates Brito/99 2.50 6.00
33 Dariel Alvarez/99 2.50 6.00
34 Brian Johnson/99 2.50 6.00
35 John Lamb/99 2.50 6.00
36 Kyle Waldrop/99 3.00 8.00
37 Brian Ellington/99 2.50 6.00
38 Zach Davies/25 3.00 8.00
39 Tyler Duffey/99 2.50 6.00
40 Elias Diaz/99 2.50 6.00
41 Jerad Eickhoff/99 4.00 10.00
42 Travis Jankowski/99 2.50 6.00
43 Colin Rea/99 2.50 6.00
44 Alex Dickerson/99 2.50 6.00
45 Luke Jackson/99 2.50 6.00
46 Pedro Severino/99 2.50 6.00
47 Aaron Nola/49 5.00 12.00
48 Brandon Drury/99 4.00 10.00
49 Byung-ho Park/99 3.00 8.00
50 Carl Edwards Jr./99 3.00 8.00
51 Corey Seager/99 8.00 20.00
52 Frankie Montas/99 3.00 8.00
53 Greg Bird/99 3.00 8.00
54 Henry Owens/99 3.00 8.00
55 Jonathan Gray/99 2.50 6.00
56 Jorge Lopez/99 2.50 6.00
57 Jose Peraza/99 3.00 8.00
58 Kaleb Cowart/49 2.50 6.00
59 Kelby Tomlinson/99 2.50 6.00
60 Mike Trout/25 20.00 50.00
61 Josh Donaldson/99 3.00 8.00
62 Bryce Harper/49 6.00 15.00
63 Clayton Kershaw/99 5.00 12.00
64 Buster Posey/99 5.00 12.00
65 Dallas Keuchel/99 3.00 8.00
66 Carlos Correa/99 4.00 10.00
67 Kris Bryant/99 8.00 20.00
68 Nelson Cruz/99 4.00 10.00
69 Carlos Gonzalez/99 3.00 8.00
70 Albert Pujols/99 5.00 12.00
71 Edwin Encarnacion/99 4.00 10.00
72 David Ortiz/99 4.00 10.00
73 Anthony Rizzo/99 5.00 12.00
74 Alex Rodriguez/99 5.00 12.00
75 Joe Mauer/99 3.00 8.00
76 Joey Votto/99 4.00 10.00
77 Ryan Howard/99 3.00 8.00
78 Ryan Braun/99 3.00 8.00
79 Kyle Seager/99 2.50 6.00
80 Jake Arrieta/99 3.00 8.00
81 Gerrit Cole/99 4.00 10.00
82 David Price/99 3.00 8.00
83 Adam Wainwright/99 3.00 8.00
84 Sonny Gray/99 3.00 8.00
85 Chris Sale/99 4.00 10.00
86 Chris Archer/20 2.50 6.00
87 Jacob deGrom/99 8.00 20.00
88 Johnny Bench/99 4.00 10.00
89 Barry Bonds/99 5.00 12.00
90 Nolan Ryan/49 15.00 40.00
91 Rickey Henderson/99 5.00 12.00
92 Mark McGwire/99 6.00 15.00
93 Ken Griffey Jr./99 8.00 20.00
94 Mike Piazza/99 4.00 10.00
95 Trevor Story/99 12.00 30.00
96 Reggie Jackson/99 5.00 12.00
97 Eddie Murray/25 8.00 20.00
98 Bert Blyleven/99 3.00 8.00
99 Ernie Banks/99 8.00 20.00

2016 Immaculate Collection Immaculate Trio Players Memorabilia

RANDOM INSERTS IN PACKS
PRINT RUNS B/WN 15-99 COPIES PER
NO PRICING ON QTY 15
*RED/25: .5X TO 1.2X BASIC
1 Brtt/Rpkn/Grffy/49 20.00 50.00
2 Bggo/Ryan/Clmns/99 15.00 40.00
3 Schwrbr/Sgr/Sano/99 6.00 15.00
6 Hdgs/Drchr/Reese/49 12.00 30.00
7 Svrno/Bird/Rfsndr/99 4.00 10.00
8 Park/Sano/Kplr/99 5.00 12.00
10 Encrncn/Btsta/Dnldsn/49 8.00 20.00
11 Crra/Spingr/Altve/99 10.00 25.00
12 Grdn/Prz/Hsmr/49 6.00 15.00
13 Gnzlz/Pdrsn/Puig/49 8.00 20.00
14 Gnzlz/Arndo/Stry/49 15.00 40.00
15 Rzzo/Brynt/Schwrbr/99 15.00 40.00

2016 Immaculate Collection Immaculate Trios Memorabilia

RANDOM INSERTS IN PACKS
PRINT RUNS B/WN 25-99 COPIES PER
*RED/25: .5X TO 1.2X BASIC
1 Kyle Schwarber/49 6.00 15.00
2 Corey Seager/49 25.00 60.00
3 Miguel Sano/49 4.00 10.00
4 Trea Turner/49 8.00 20.00
5 Stephen Piscotty/49 4.00 10.00
6 Jonathan Gray/49 2.50 6.00
7 Byung-ho Park/99 3.00 8.00
8 Kenta Maeda/25 5.00 12.00
9 Aaron Nola/25 5.00 12.00
10 Jose Peraza/49 3.00 8.00
11 Raul Mondesi/25 5.00 12.00
12 Rob Refsnyder/25 3.00 8.00
13 Ketel Marte/49 5.00 12.00
14 Luis Severino/49 3.00 8.00
15 Henry Owens/25 3.00 8.00

2016 Immaculate Collection Jersey Numbers

RANDOM INSERTS IN PACKS
PRINT RUNS B/WN 1-60 COPIES PER
NO PRICING ON QTY 19 OR LESS
1 Mike Trout/27 20.00 50.00
4 Bryce Harper/34 8.00 20.00
5 Clayton Kershaw/22 8.00 20.00
6 Miguel Cabrera/24 5.00 12.00
7 Josh Donaldson/20 4.00 10.00
8 Adrian Beltre/29 5.00 12.00
9 Chris Sale/49 5.00 12.00
10 Madison Bumgarner/40 4.00 10.00
11 Nelson Cruz/23 5.00 12.00
13 David Ortiz/34 5.00 12.00
15 Anthony Rizzo/44 6.00 15.00
17 Buster Posey/28 6.00 15.00
18 Giancarlo Stanton/27 5.00 12.00
20 Paul Goldschmidt/44 5.00 12.00
21 Andrew McCutchen/22 10.00 25.00
23 Dallas Keuchel/60 4.00 10.00
24 Justin Verlander/35 5.00 12.00
25 Nolan Arenado/28 8.00 20.00

2016 Immaculate Collection Past and Present Autographs

RANDOM INSERTS IN PACKS
PRINT RUNS B/WN 25-99 COPIES PER
EXCHANGE DEADLINE 2/17/2018
1 Josh Donaldson/99 12.00 30.00
2 Anthony Rizzo/99 12.00 30.00
3 David Price/25 20.00 50.00
4 Jake Arrieta/49
5 Jason Heyward/49 12.00 30.00
6 Albert Pujols/25 50.00 120.00
8 Don Mattingly/25 25.00 60.00
10 Paul Molitor/49 10.00 25.00

2016 Immaculate Collection Past and Present Autographs Red

*RED/25: .5X TO 1.2X p/r 99
*RED/25: .4X TO 1X p/r 25
RANDOM INSERTS IN PACKS
PRINT RUNS B/WN 10-25 COPIES PER
NO PRICING ON QTY 10
EXCHANGE DEADLINE 2/17/2018
7 Daniel Murphy/25 20.00 50.00

2016 Immaculate Collection Rookie Autographs

RANDOM INSERTS IN PACKS
STATED PRINT RUN 49 SER.#'d SETS
*RED/25: .5X TO 1.2X BASIC
EXCHANGE DEADLINE 2/17/2018
1 Aaron Nola 10.00 25.00
2 Alex Dickerson 3.00 8.00
3 Brian Johnson 3.00 8.00
4 Byung-ho Park 6.00 15.00
5 Carl Edwards Jr. 4.00 10.00
6 Colin Rea 3.00 8.00
7 Corey Seager 25.00 60.00
8 Dariel Alvarez 3.00 8.00
9 Henry Owens 4.00 10.00
10 Jerad Eickhoff 10.00 25.00
11 Jorge Lopez 3.00 8.00
12 Jose Peraza 5.00 12.00
13 Ross Stripling 3.00 8.00
14 Ketel Marte 6.00 15.00
15 Kyle Schwarber 12.00 30.00
16 Kyle Waldrop 4.00 10.00
17 Luis Severino 4.00 10.00
18 Luke Jackson 3.00 8.00
19 Mac Williamson 3.00 8.00
20 Max Kepler 5.00 12.00
21 Michael Reed 3.00 8.00
22 Miguel Sano 10.00 25.00
23 Pedro Severino 3.00 8.00
24 Raul Mondesi 6.00 15.00
25 Socrates Brito 3.00 8.00
26 Stephen Piscotty 8.00 20.00
27 Tom Murphy 3.00 8.00
28 Trea Turner 12.00 30.00
29 Tyler Duffey 3.00 8.00
30 Zack Godley 3.00 8.00
31 Robert Stephenson 3.00 8.00
32 Mallex Smith 3.00 8.00

2016 Immaculate Collection Rookie Premium Patch Autographs

RANDOM INSERTS IN PACKS
PRINT RUNS B/WN 10-25 COPIES PER
NO PRICING ON QTY 10
EXCHANGE DEADLINE 2/17/2018
1 Brian Ellington/25 5.00 12.00
3 Elias Diaz/25 5.00 12.00
4 Carl Edwards Jr./25 6.00 15.00
5 Corey Seager/25 EXCH 40.00 100.00
6 Tyler Duffey/25 5.00 12.00
8 Frankie Montas/25 6.00 15.00
9 Jonathan Gray/25 5.00 12.00
10 Jorge Lopez/25 5.00 12.00
11 Jose Peraza/25 10.00 25.00
13 Kelby Tomlinson/25 6.00 15.00
14 Travis Jankowski/25 10.00 25.00
15 Ketel Marte/25 10.00 25.00
16 Kyle Schwarber/25
17 Luis Severino/25 10.00 25.00
18 Mac Williamson/25 12.00 30.00
19 Max Kepler/25 30.00 80.00
20 Michael Conforto/25 EXCH 20.00 50.00
21 Michael Reed/25 5.00 12.00
22 Miguel Sano/25 12.00 30.00
23 Peter O'Brien/25
25 Trevor Story/25 30.00 80.00
27 Stephen Piscotty/25 15.00 40.00
28 Tom Murphy/25 5.00 12.00
29 Trayce Thompson/25 6.00 15.00
30 Trea Turner/25 20.00 50.00

2016 Immaculate Collection USA Jersey Signatures

RANDOM INSERTS IN PACKS
STATED PRINT RUN 25 SER.#'d SETS
EXCHANGE DEADLINE 2/17/2018
1 Buster Posey
2 Kris Bryant 60.00 150.00
3 Alex Bregman 20.00 50.00
4 Gerrit Cole 6.00 15.00
5 George Springer 12.00 30.00
6 Michael Conforto EXCH 25.00 60.00
7 Michael Wacha 5.00 12.00
8 Sonny Gray 5.00 12.00
9 Trea Turner 25.00 60.00
10 Carlos Rodon 6.00 15.00

2017 Immaculate Collection

1-100 PRINT RUN 99 SER.#'d SETS
JSY AU PRINT RUN 99 SER.#'d SETS
EXCHANGE DEADLINE 2/16/2019
1 Babe Ruth 4.00 10.00
2 Bill Dickey 1.00 2.50
3 Billy Martin 1.25 3.00
4 George Kelly 1.00 2.50
5 Harry Hooper 1.00 2.50
6 Honus Wagner 1.50 4.00
7 Mickey Mantle 5.00 12.00
8 Joe DiMaggio 3.00 8.00
9 Kiki Cuyler 1.25 3.00
10 Lefty Gomez 1.00 2.50
11 Lloyd Waner 1.25 3.00
12 Luke Appling 1.25 3.00
13 Max Carey 1.00 2.50
14 Joe Cronin 1.00 2.50
15 Nellie Fox 1.25 3.00
16 Paul Waner 1.25 3.00
17 Roberto Clemente 8.00 20.00
18 Roger Maris 1.50 4.00
19 Stan Musial 2.50 6.00
20 Ted Lyons 1.00 2.50
21 Ted Williams 4.00 10.00
22 Tommy Henrich 1.00 2.50
23 Ernie Banks 3.00 8.00
24 Herb Pennock 1.25 3.00
25 Jackie Robinson 1.50 4.00
26 Leo Durocher 1.00 2.50
27 Lou Gehrig 3.00 8.00
28 Pee Wee Reese 1.25 3.00
29 Paul Goldschmidt 1.50 4.00
30 A.J. Pollock 1.00 2.50
31 Jean Segura 1.25 3.00
32 Freddie Freeman 2.00 5.00
33 Manny Machado 1.50 4.00
34 Mookie Betts 3.00 8.00
35 Xander Bogaerts 1.50 4.00
36 Chris Sale 1.50 4.00
37 Jackie Bradley Jr. 1.50 4.00
38 David Price 1.25 3.00
39 Rick Porcello 1.25 3.00
40 Kris Bryant 2.00 5.00
41 Anthony Rizzo 2.00 5.00
42 Jon Lester 1.25 3.00
43 Addison Russell 1.50 4.00
44 Jake Arrieta 1.25 3.00
45 Kyle Schwarber 1.50 4.00
46 Joey Votto 1.50 4.00
47 Francisco Lindor 1.50 4.00
48 Corey Kluber 1.25 3.00
49 Edwin Encarnacion 1.50 4.00
50 Carlos Santana 1.25 3.00
51 Jose Ramirez 1.25 3.00
52 Nolan Arenado 2.50 6.00
53 Charlie Blackmon 1.50 4.00
54 Trevor Story 1.50 4.00
55 Miguel Cabrera 1.50 4.00
56 Ian Kinsler 1.25 3.00
57 Justin Verlander 1.50 4.00
58 Michael Fulmer 1.00 2.50
59 Jose Altuve 1.25 3.00
60 Carlos Correa 1.50 4.00
61 Eric Hosmer 1.25 3.00
62 Salvador Perez 1.25 3.00
63 Mike Trout 6.00 15.00
64 Albert Pujols 2.00 5.00
65 Corey Seager 1.50 4.00
66 Clayton Kershaw 2.50 6.00
67 Justin Turner 1.50 4.00
68 Giancarlo Stanton 1.50 4.00
69 Christian Yelich 2.00 5.00
70 Ichiro 2.00 5.00
71 Ryan Braun 1.25 3.00
72 Jonathan Villar 1.00 2.50
73 Brian Dozier 1.50 4.00
74 Noah Syndergaard 1.25 3.00
75 Yoenis Cespedes 1.50 4.00
76 Masahiro Tanaka 1.25 3.00
77 Gary Sanchez 1.50 4.00
78 Andrew McCutchen 3.00 8.00
79 Starling Marte 1.25 3.00
80 Madison Bumgarner 1.25 3.00
81 Buster Posey 2.00 5.00
82 Robinson Cano 1.25 3.00
83 Felix Hernandez 1.25 3.00
84 Nelson Cruz 1.50 4.00
85 Matt Carpenter 1.50 4.00
86 Yadier Molina 2.50 6.00
87 Evan Longoria 1.25 3.00
88 Adrian Beltre 1.50 4.00
89 Josh Donaldson 1.25 3.00
90 Jose Bautista 1.25 3.00
91 J.A. Happ 1.25 3.00
92 Bryce Harper 5.00 12.00
93 Max Scherzer 1.50 4.00
94 Daniel Murphy 1.25 3.00
95 Trea Turner 1.25 3.00
96 George Brett 6.00 15.00
97 Cal Ripken 8.00 20.00
98 Kirby Puckett 8.00 20.00
99 Ken Griffey Jr. 3.00 8.00
100 Nolan Ryan 6.00 15.00
101 Yoan Moncada JSY AU RC 15.00 40.00
102 Bnntndi JSY AU RC 25.00 60.00
103 Swnsn JSY AU RC EXCH 15.00 40.00
104 Alex Bregman JSY AU RC 25.00 60.00
105 David Dahl JSY AU RC 6.00 15.00
106 Tyler Glasnow JSY AU RC 12.00 30.00
107 Josh Bell JSY AU RC 12.00 30.00
108 Alex Reyes JSY AU RC 5.00 12.00
109 Orlando Arcia JSY AU RC 8.00 20.00
110 Jose De Leon JSY AU RC 4.00 10.00
111 Joe Musgrove JSY AU RC 30.00 80.00
112 Manuel Margot JSY AU RC 4.00 10.00
113 Aaron Judge JSY AU RC 100.00 250.00
114 David Paulino JSY AU RC 5.00 12.00
115 Reynaldo Lopez JSY AU RC 4.00 10.00
116 Jeff Hoffman JSY AU RC EXCH 4.00 10.00
117 Braden Shipley JSY AU RC 4.00 10.00
118 Hunter Renfroe JSY AU RC 5.00 12.00
119 Jorge Alfaro JSY AU RC 8.00 20.00
120 Carson Fulmer JSY AU RC 4.00 10.00
121 Luke Weaver JSY AU RC 5.00 12.00
122 Raimel Tapia JSY AU RC 5.00 12.00
123 Adalberto Mejia JSY AU RC EXCH 6.00 15.00
124 Gavin Cecchini JSY AU RC EXCH 6.00 15.00
125 Jacoby Jones JSY AU RC 5.00 12.00
126 Yohander Mendez JSY AU RC 4.00 10.00
127 Chad Pinder JSY AU RC 5.00 12.00
128 Carson Kelly JSY AU RC 5.00 12.00
129 Trey Mancini JSY AU RC 8.00 20.00
130 Teoscar Hernandez JSY AU RC 15.00 40.00
131 Ryon Healy JSY AU RC 6.00 15.00
132 Erik Gonzalez JSY AU RC 4.00 10.00
133 Roman Quinn JSY AU RC 5.00 12.00
134 Matt Olson JSY AU RC 10.00 25.00
135 Jharel Cotton JSY AU RC 6.00 15.00
136 Jake Thompson JSY AU RC EXCH 5.00 12.00
137 Renato Nunez JSY AU RC 5.00 12.00
138 Jose Rondon JSY AU RC 4.00 10.00

2017 Immaculate Collection Gold

*GOLD JSY AU: .5X TO 1.2X BASIC
RANDOM INSERTS IN PACKS
1-100 PRINT RUN 5 SER.#'d SETS
101-138 PRINT RUNS 49 SER.#'d SETS
NO 1-100 PRICING DUE TO SCARCITY
EXCHANGE DEADLINE 2/16/2019

2017 Immaculate Collection Red

*RED: .6X TO 1.5X BASIC
RANDOM INSERTS IN PACKS
STATED PRINT RUN 25 SER.#'d SETS
EXCHANGE DEADLINE 2/16/2019
7 Mickey Mantle 12.00 30.00
17 Roberto Clemente 30.00 80.00
27 Lou Gehrig 10.00 25.00
41 Anthony Rizzo 8.00 20.00
77 Gary Sanchez 12.00 30.00
81 Buster Posey 10.00 25.00
98 Kirby Puckett 20.00 50.00
99 Ken Griffey Jr. 10.00 25.00

2017 Immaculate Collection Immaculate Autographs

RANDOM INSERTS IN PACKS
PRINT RUNS B/WN 10-99 COPIES PER
NO PRICING ON QTY 16 OR LESS
EXCHANGE DEADLINE 2/16/2019
*BLUE/25: .5X TO 1.2X p/r 49-99
3 Carlton Fisk/25 10.00 25.00
4 Darryl Strawberry/25 10.00 25.00
6 George Springer/49 6.00 15.00
8 Jeff Bagwell/25 20.00 50.00
9 Jose Abreu/25 8.00 20.00
11 Ozzie Smith/25 20.00 50.00
13 Mark Prior/99 4.00 10.00
14 Roberto Alomar/25 10.00 25.00
15 Tom Glavine/25 10.00 25.00
16 Wade Boggs/49 15.00 40.00
17 Tyler Naquin/25 5.00 12.00
19 Bob Gibson/25 15.00 40.00
20 Jose Altuve/25 25.00 60.00
21 Jason Kipnis/25 5.00 12.00
24 Jose Canseco/99 10.00 25.00

2017 Immaculate Collection Immaculate Bats Autographs

RANDOM INSERTS IN PACKS
PRINT RUNS B/WN 5-99 COPIES PER
NO PRICING ON QTY 5
EXCHANGE DEADLINE 2/16/2019
1 Yoan Moncada/99 20.00 50.00
4 Dansby Swanson/99 15.00 40.00
5 Josh Bell/99 20.00 50.00
6 Trey Mancini/99 12.00 30.00
7 Aaron Judge/99 100.00 250.00
8 Jacoby Jones/99 6.00 15.00
9 David Dahl/99 6.00 15.00
11 Nolan Arenado/25 30.00 80.00
12 Paul Goldschmidt/25 25.00 60.00
14 Josh Donaldson/25 15.00 40.00
15 Jackie Bradley Jr./25 12.00 30.00
16 Jose Altuve/25 40.00 100.00

2017 Immaculate Collection Immaculate Carbon Material Signatures

RANDOM INSERTS IN PACKS
PRINT RUNS B/WN 5-49 COPIES PER
NO PRICING ON QTY 5
EXCHANGE DEADLINE 2/16/2019
3 Jackie Bradley Jr./25 12.00 30.00
4 Trea Turner/25 15.00 40.00
5 Corey Seager/25 20.00 50.00
6 Starling Marte/25 25.00 60.00
8 Gary Sanchez/25 40.00 100.00
9 Eric Hosmer/25 12.00 30.00
10 Jose Altuve/25
11 Andrew Benintendi/49 30.00 80.00
12 Yoan Moncada/49 20.00 50.00
13 Alex Bregman/49 15.00 40.00
14 Dansby Swanson/49 15.00 40.00
15 Josh Bell/49 12.00 30.00
16 David Dahl/49 6.00 15.00
17 Hunter Renfroe/49 8.00 20.00
18 Aaron Judge/49
19 Trey Mancini/49 20.00 50.00
20 Ryon Healy/49 8.00 20.00
21 Orlando Arcia/49 8.00 20.00
22 Jacoby Jones/49 5.00 12.00
23 Manuel Margot/49 4.00 10.00
24 Nomar Mazara/25 5.00 12.00
26 Tyler Naquin/25 8.00 20.00
27 Stephen Piscotty/25 15.00 40.00

2017 Immaculate Collection Immaculate Carbon Signatures

RANDOM INSERTS IN PACKS
PRINT RUNS B/WN 5-99 COPIES PER
NO PRICING ON QTY 15 OR LESS
EXCHANGE DEADLINE 2/16/2019
*BLUE/25: .5X TO 1.2X p/r 49-99
3 Jackie Bradley Jr./49 12.00 30.00
6 Trea Turner/25 8.00 20.00
7 Corey Seager/25 25.00 60.00
9 Vladimir Guerrero Jr./25 200.00 500.00
10 Andre Dawson/25 15.00 40.00
11 Starling Marte/25 8.00 20.00
13 Gary Sanchez/49 25.00 60.00
14 Nomar Mazara/25 8.00 20.00
15 Eric Hosmer/25 10.00 25.00
16 Frank Thomas/25 20.00 50.00
18 Tyler Naquin/25 5.00 12.00
19 J.P. Crawford/99 10.00 25.00
21 Stephen Piscotty/25 5.00 12.00
25 Cody Bellinger/25 40.00 100.00
26 Jose Abreu/25 10.00 25.00

2017 Immaculate Collection Immaculate Dual Autographs

RANDOM INSERTS IN PACKS
PRINT RUNS B/WN 10-25 COPIES PER
NO PRICING ON QTY 10
EXCHANGE DEADLINE 2/16/2019
*BLUE/25:.5X TO 1.2X BASIC
1 Dawson/Sandberg 60.00 150.00
2 Bagwell/Biggio 50.00 120.00
3 Rodriguez/Bench 50.00 125.00
5 Benintendi/Moncada 30.00 80.00
6 Ortiz/Francona 75.00 200.00
7 Swanson/Bregman 25.00 60.00
8 Seager/Seager 15.00 40.00
9 Griffey Jr./Martinez 75.00 200.00
12 Molitor/Yount 30.00 80.00
13 Strawberry/Gooden 30.00 80.00
14 Thomas/Sandberg 60.00 150.00

2017 Immaculate Collection Immaculate Dual Material Autographs

RANDOM INSERTS IN PACKS
PRINT RUNS B/W 15-99 COPIES PER
NO PRICING ON QTY 15
EXCHANGE DEADLINE 2/16/2019
*BLUE/25: .5X TO 1.2X p/r 49-99
1 Alan Trammell/49 12.00 30.00
2 Bo Jackson/25 40.00 100.00
3 Darryl Strawberry/25 15.00 40.00
4 Dwight Gooden/25 12.00 30.00
5 David Price/25 6.00 15.00
7 Nelson Cruz/24 12.00 30.00
8 Luis Severino/25 15.00 40.00
10 Kyle Schwarber/25 15.00 40.00
11 Trea Turner/25 6.00 15.00
12 Corey Seager/99 20.00 50.00
13 Jose Abreu/25 10.00 25.00
14 Matt Adams/25 5.00 12.00
15 Mike Napoli/25 15.00 40.00
16 Max Scherzer/25 40.00 100.00
17 Cody Bellinger/49 40.00 100.00
18 Yasmany Tomas/25 5.00 12.00
19 Adrian Gonzalez/25 10.00 25.00
20 Jackie Bradley Jr./25 12.00 30.00
21 Kyle Seager/25 5.00 12.00
22 Xander Bogaerts/25 15.00 40.00
23 Jose Altuve/25 20.00 50.00
24 Lorenzo Cain/25 10.00 25.00
25 Ian Happ/99 8.00 20.00

2017 Immaculate Collection Immaculate Dual Players Memorabilia

RANDOM INSERTS IN PACKS
PRINT RUNS B/WN 5-99 COPIES PER
NO PRICING ON QTY 15 OR LESS
*BLUE/25: .6X TO 1.5X BASIC
3 Robinson/Reese/25 20.00 50.00
4 Banks/Cuyler/25 10.00 25.00
5 Fox/Lyons/25 20.00 50.00
8 Carey/Waner/25 15.00 40.00
9 Robinson/Clemente/25 50.00 120.00
10 Maris/Henrich/99 10.00 25.00
11 Bryant/Trout/99 20.00 50.00
12 Wee Reese/Seager/99 4.00 10.00
13 Maris/Mantle/25 60.00 150.00
15 Murphy/Altuve/99 3.00 8.00
16 Beltre/Arenado/99 6.00 15.00
17 Killebrew/Puckett/99 12.00 30.00
18 Ichiro/Rodriguez/49 8.00 20.00
19 Betts/Bogaerts/99 8.00 20.00
20 Pujols/Trout/99 20.00 50.00

2017 Immaculate Collection Immaculate Duals Memorabilia

RANDOM INSERTS IN PACKS
PRINT RUNS B/WN 25-99 COPIES PER
*PRIME/25: .6X TO 1.5X BASIC
1 Kris Bryant/49 8.00 20.00
2 Mike Trout/25 25.00 60.00
3 Buster Posey/99 5.00 12.00
4 Carlos Correa/99 4.00 10.00
5 Frank Thomas/99 6.00 15.00
6 Yu Darvish/25 4.00 10.00
7 Giancarlo Stanton/99 6.00 15.00
8 Yadier Molina/99 5.00 12.00
9 Francisco Lindor/99 4.00 10.00
10 Javier Baez/99 5.00 12.00
11 Alex Gordon/99 5.00 12.00
12 Jose Abreu/99 4.00 10.00
13 Chris Davis/99 2.50 6.00
14 Justin Verlander/99 4.00 10.00
15 Rick Porcello/99 3.00 8.00
16 Daniel Murphy/99 3.00 8.00
17 Charlie Blackmon/99 4.00 10.00
18 Mookie Betts/99 8.00 20.00
19 Robinson Cano/99 3.00 8.00
20 Jake Arrieta/25 3.00 8.00

2017 Immaculate Collection Immaculate Home Plate Signatures

RANDOM INSERTS IN PACKS
PRINT RUNS B/WN 25-99 COPIES PER
EXCHANGE DEADLINE 2/16/2019
*BLUE/25: .5X TO 1.2X p/r 99
1 Alex Reyes/99 4.00 10.00
2 Carson Fulmer/99 3.00 8.00
3 Jose De Leon/99 3.00 8.00
4 Tyler Glasnow/99 5.00 12.00
5 Reynaldo Lopez/99 3.00 8.00
6 Luke Weaver/99 5.00 12.00
7 Jake Thompson/99 3.00 8.00
8 Yadier Molina/25 30.00 80.00
9 Marcus Stroman/25 5.00 12.00
10 Yasmany Tomas/25 4.00 10.00
11 Joe Panik/25 10.00 25.00
12 Justin Turner/25 12.00 30.00
13 Charlie Blackmon/25 12.00 30.00
14 Corey Kluber/25 8.00 20.00
15 Anthony Rizzo/25 50.00 120.00

2017 Immaculate Collection Immaculate Jumbo Materials

RANDOM INSERTS IN PACKS
PRINT RUNS B/WN 1-99 COPIES PER
NO PRICING ON QTY 15 OR LESS
1 Yoan Moncada/99 5.00 12.00
2 Andrew Benintendi/99 6.00 15.00
3 Dansby Swanson/99 5.00 12.00
4 Alex Bregman/99 5.00 12.00
5 David Dahl/99 3.00 8.00
6 Tyler Glasnow/99 10.00 25.00
7 Mickey Mantle/20 150.00 300.00
8 Alex Reyes/99 3.00 8.00
9 Orlando Arcia/99 4.00 10.00
10 Jose De Leon/99 2.50 6.00
11 Joe Musgrove/99 5.00 12.00
12 Manuel Margot/99 2.50 6.00
13 Aaron Judge/99 30.00 80.00
14 David Paulino/99 3.00 8.00
15 Reynaldo Lopez/99 2.50 6.00
16 Jeff Hoffman/99 2.50 6.00
17 Braden Shipley/99 2.50 6.00
18 Hunter Renfroe/99 3.00 8.00
19 Jorge Alfaro/99 3.00 8.00
20 Carson Fulmer/99 2.50 6.00
21 Luke Weaver/99 3.00 8.00
22 Raimel Tapia/99 3.00 8.00
23 Adalberto Mejia/99 2.50 6.00
24 Gavin Cecchini/99 2.50 6.00
25 Jacoby Jones/99 3.00 8.00
26 Yohander Mendez/99 2.50 6.00
27 Chad Pinder/99 2.50 6.00
28 Carson Kelly/99 3.00 8.00
29 Trey Mancini/99 6.00 15.00
30 Teoscar Hernandez/99 10.00 25.00
31 Ryon Healy/99 3.00 8.00
32 Erik Gonzalez/99 2.50 6.00
33 Roman Quinn/99 2.50 6.00
34 Matt Olson/99 5.00 12.00
35 Jharel Cotton/99 2.50 6.00
36 Jake Thompson/99 2.50 6.00
37 Renato Nunez/99 5.00 12.00
38 Jose Rondon/99 2.50 6.00
39 Clayton Kershaw/25 12.00 30.00
40 Goose Gossage/25 3.00 8.00
41 Buster Posey/25 5.00 12.00
42 Brandon Phillips/99 2.50 6.00
43 Adam Duvall/99 3.00 8.00
44 Kyle Schwarber/99 4.00 10.00
45 Corey Seager/99 4.00 10.00
46 Johnny Cueto/25 3.00 8.00
47 Hanley Ramirez/25 3.00 8.00
48 Marcell Ozuna/49 4.00 10.00
49 Ken Griffey Jr./25 12.00 30.00
50 Cody Bellinger/99 12.00 30.00
52 Troy Tulowitzki/25 4.00 10.00
53 Gary Sanchez/49 12.00 30.00
54 Lorenzo Cain/49 2.50 6.00
55 Addison Russell/49 4.00 10.00
56 Kris Bryant/49 6.00 15.00
57 Francisco Lindor/49 4.00 10.00
58 Noah Syndergaard/49 3.00 8.00
65 Paul Molitor/20 12.00 30.00
67 Ryne Sandberg/25 12.00 30.00
69 Stephen Piscotty/99 3.00 8.00
70 Edwin Encarnacion/20 4.00 10.00
71 Greg Maddux/25 15.00 40.00
72 Ivan Rodriguez/25 6.00 15.00
73 Byron Buxton/99 4.00 10.00
74 Willson Contreras/99 4.00 10.00
75 Rickey Henderson/25 12.00 30.00
76 Tony Gwynn/25 20.00 50.00
77 Miguel Sano/99 3.00 8.00
78 A.J. Reed/99 2.50 6.00
79 David Wright/99 3.00 8.00
81 Don Mattingly/25 12.00 30.00
85 Vladimir Guerrero/25 10.00 25.00
87 Bert Blyleven/25 5.00 12.00
88 David Price/25 3.00 8.00
89 Tim Tebow/99 13.00 30.00
92 Jason Heyward/25 3.00 8.00
95 Kirby Puckett/20 25.00 60.00
98 Pete Rose/25 20.00 50.00
99 Rickey Henderson/25 12.00 30.00
100 Yoenis Cespedes/25 4.00 10.00

2017 Immaculate Collection Immaculate Legends Memorabilia

RANDOM INSERTS IN PACKS
PRINT RUNS B/WN 5-99 COPIES PER
NO PRICING ON QTY 15 OR LESS
3 George Kelly/25 12.00 30.00
6 Joe Cronin/25 8.00 20.00
8 Kiki Cuyler/25 12.00 30.00
11 Luke Appling/99 5.00 12.00
12 Max Carey/25 20.00 50.00
17 Stan Musial/25 12.00 30.00
20 Ernie Banks/25 8.00 20.00
21 Herb Pennock/25 8.00 20.00
23 Leo Durocher/99 4.00 10.00
25 Pee Wee Reese/25 12.00 30.00
26 Bob Feller/99 5.00 12.00
27 Duke Snider/99 5.00 12.00
28 Al Kaline/49 6.00 15.00
29 Harmon Killebrew/25 8.00 20.00
30 Bobby Doerr/49 5.00 12.00
32 Eddie Mathews/25 6.00 15.00
34 Rick Ferrell/25 8.00 20.00

2017 Immaculate Collection Immaculate Material

RANDOM INSERTS IN PACKS
PRINT RUNS B/WN 5-99 COPIES PER
NO PRICING ON QTY 15 OR LESS
*GOLD/25-49: .6X TO 1.5X BASIC
1 Yoan Moncada/99 5.00 12.00
2 Andrew Benintendi/99 8.00 20.00
3 Dansby Swanson/99 6.00 15.00
4 Alex Bregman/99 6.00 15.00
5 David Dahl/99 3.00 8.00
6 Tyler Glasnow/99 10.00 25.00
8 Alex Reyes/99 3.00 8.00
9 Orlando Arcia/99 4.00 10.00
10 Jose De Leon/99 2.50 6.00
11 Joe Musgrove/99 5.00 12.00
12 Manuel Margot/99 2.50 6.00
13 Aaron Judge/99 25.00 60.00
14 David Paulino/99 3.00 8.00
15 Josh Bell/49 6.00 15.00
16 Reynaldo Lopez/99 2.50 6.00
17 Jeff Hoffman/99 2.50 6.00
18 Braden Shipley/99 2.50 6.00
19 Hunter Renfroe/99 3.00 8.00
20 Jorge Alfaro/99 3.00 8.00
21 Carson Fulmer/99 2.50 6.00
22 Luke Weaver/99 3.00 8.00
23 Raimel Tapia/99 3.00 8.00
24 Adalberto Mejia/99 2.50 6.00
25 Gavin Cecchini/99 2.50 6.00
26 Jacoby Jones/99 3.00 8.00
27 Yohander Mendez/99 2.50 6.00
28 Chad Pinder/99 2.50 6.00
29 Carson Kelly/99 3.00 8.00
30 Trey Mancini/99 5.00 12.00
31 Teoscar Hernandez/99 10.00 25.00
32 Ryon Healy/99 3.00 8.00
33 Erik Gonzalez/99 2.50 6.00
34 Roman Quinn/99 2.50 6.00
35 Matt Olson/99 5.00 12.00
36 Jharel Cotton/99 2.50 6.00
37 Jake Thompson/99 2.50 6.00
38 Renato Nunez/99 5.00 12.00
39 Jose Rondon/99 2.50 6.00
40 Miguel Sano/99 3.00 8.00
41 George Springer/99 3.00 8.00
42 Javier Baez/99 5.00 12.00
43 Kyle Schwarber/99 4.00 10.00
44 Stephen Piscotty/99 3.00 8.00
45 A.J. Reed/99 2.50 6.00
46 Blake Snell/99 3.00 8.00
47 Brandon Nimmo/99 3.00 8.00
48 Byron Buxton/99 4.00 10.00
49 Greg Bird/99 3.00 8.00
50 Jacob deGrom/99 8.00 20.00
51 Jose Peraza/99 3.00 8.00
52 Ketel Marte/99 3.00 8.00
53 Lucas Giolito/99 3.00 8.00
54 Luis Severino/99 3.00 8.00
55 Raul A. Mondesi/99 3.00 8.00
56 Tim Anderson/99 4.00 10.00
57 Kevin Kiermaier/99 3.00 8.00
58 Tom Murphy/99 2.50 6.00
59 Willson Contreras/99 4.00 10.00
60 Kris Bryant/99 5.00 12.00
61 Roger Maris/25 30.00 80.00
65 Stan Musial/99 15.00 40.00
66 Jose Bautista/99 3.00 8.00
67 Rougned Odor/99 3.00 8.00
68 Victor Martinez/99 3.00 8.00
69 Brandon Phillips/99 2.50 6.00
70 Jay Bruce/99 3.00 8.00
72 Mike Piazza/99 8.00 20.00
73 Bo Jackson/99 12.00 30.00
74 Cole Hamels/99 3.00 8.00
75 Kenta Maeda/99 3.00 8.00
76 Giancarlo Stanton/49 10.00 25.00
77 Elvis Andrus/99 3.00 8.00
78 Don Mattingly/99 12.00 30.00
79 Jorge Posada/99 4.00 10.00
80 Matt Carpenter/99 4.00 10.00
81 Andrew McCutchen/99 4.00 10.00
82 Bryce Harper/49 6.00 15.00
83 Mike Trout/25 30.00 80.00
84 Adam Wainwright/99 3.00 8.00
85 Johnny Cueto/99 3.00 8.00
86 Ian Kinsler/99 3.00 8.00
87 Joey Votto/99 4.00 10.00
88 Yu Darvish/25 4.00 10.00
89 Tim Tebow/99 12.00 30.00
91 Vladimir Guerrero/99 6.00 15.00
92 Jeff Bagwell/99 5.00 12.00
93 Adrian Gonzalez/99 3.00 8.00
94 Maikel Franco/49 5.00 12.00
95 Trevor Story/99 4.00 10.00
96 Michael Taylor/99 2.50 6.00
97 Cal Ripken/99 25.00 60.00
98 Chipper Jones/99 8.00 20.00
100 Reggie Jackson/99 6.00 15.00

2017 Immaculate Collection Immaculate Material Signatures

RANDOM INSERTS IN PACKS
PRINT RUNS B/W 5-99 COPIES PER
NO PRICING ON QTY 15 OR LESS
EXCHANGE DEADLINE 2/16/2019
*BLUE/25: .5X TO 1.2X p/r 49-99
3 Jason Kipnis/49 6.00 15.00
4 Noah Syndergaard/25 12.00 30.00
5 Jacob deGrom/25 25.00 60.00
6 Jim Rice/25 8.00 20.00
7 Steve Finley/49 4.00 10.00
9 Francisco Lindor/99 15.00 40.00
10 Kyle Seager/25 5.00 12.00
11 Dennis Eckersley/25 10.00 25.00
12 Javier Baez/25 20.00 50.00
14 Trea Turner/99 10.00 25.00
16 Corey Seager/49 20.00 50.00
17 Yadier Molina/25 30.00 80.00
18 Joe Panik/25 8.00 20.00
20 Stephen Piscotty/25 6.00 15.00
22 Eric Hosmer/25 15.00 40.00
23 Corey Kluber/25 10.00 25.00
24 Jose Altuve/25 25.00 60.00
26 Dwight Gooden/49 6.00 15.00
27 Chipper Jones/25 40.00 100.00
28 Paul Goldschmidt/25 12.00 30.00
31 Nolan Arenado/25

2017 Immaculate Collection Immaculate Parchment Signatures

RANDOM INSERTS IN PACKS
PRINT RUNS B/WN 7-35 COPIES PER
NO PRICING ON QTY 15 OR LESS
EXCHANGE DEADLINE 2/16/2019
2 Pete Rose/25
3 Goose Gossage/35 12.00 30.00
4 Whitey Ford/25 30.00 80.00
5 Luis Aparicio/20 15.00 40.00

2017 Immaculate Collection Immaculate Quad Autograph Materials Rookie

RANDOM INSERTS IN PACKS
PRINT RUNS B/W 49-99 COPIES PER
EXCHANGE DEADLINE 2/16/2019
*GOLD/49: .4X TO 1X p/r 49-99
*GOLD/25: .5X TO 1.2X p/r 49-99

1 Yoan Moncada/99 15.00 40.00
2 Andrew Benintendi/99 40.00 100.00
3 Dansby Swanson/99 15.00 40.00
4 Alex Bregman/99 20.00 50.00
5 David Dahl/99 5.00 12.00
6 Tyler Glasnow/99 6.00 15.00
7 Josh Bell/99 15.00 40.00
8 Alex Reyes/99 8.00 20.00
9 Orlando Arcia/99 6.00 15.00
10 Jose De Leon/99 4.00 10.00
11 Manuel Margot/99 4.00 10.00
12 Aaron Judge/99 100.00 250.00
14 Hunter Renfroe/99 5.00 12.00
15 Jorge Alfaro/99 5.00 12.00

2017 Immaculate Collection Immaculate Quad Material Autographs

RANDOM INSERTS IN PACKS
PRINT RUNS B/WN 5-25 COPIES PER
NO PRICING ON QTY 15 OR LESS
EXCHANGE DEADLINE 2/16/2019
3 Phil Niekro/25 12.00 30.00
7 Andre Dawson/25 15.00 40.00
8 Bob Feller/25 25.00 60.00
11 Dennis Eckersley/25 8.00 20.00
12 David Ortiz/25 40.00 100.00
14 Jeff Bagwell/25 20.00 50.00
16 Roberto Alomar/25 20.00 50.00
17 Cody Bellinger/25 75.00 200.00
18 Al Kaline/25 30.00 80.00
19 Bobby Doerr/25 25.00 60.00

2017 Immaculate Collection Immaculate Quad Players Memorabilia

RANDOM INSERTS IN PACKS
PRINT RUNS B/WN 5-99 COPIES PER
NO PRICING ON QTY 10 OR LESS
*BLUE/20-25: .6X TO 1.5X BASIC
1 Brtt/Grffy/Rpkn/Thms/49 30.00 80.00
2 Hrpr/Psy/Trt/Brynt/99 30.00 80.00
6 Crrn/Bnks/Drchr/Rse/25 20.00 50.00
8 Mncda/Brgmn/Bnntndi/Swnsn/99 10.00 25.00
9 Jdge/Rnfoe/Dahl/Bell/99 12.00 30.00
10 Josh Donaldson 10.00 25.00
Adrian Beltre
Manny Machado
Nolan Arenado/49
11 Cbrra/McCtchn/Vtto/Altve/99 6.00 15.00
12 Fllr/Clmns/Gbsn/Ryan/49 20.00 50.00
13 Crtr/Rdrgz/Bnch/Pzza/49 10.00 25.00
14 Jmnz/Mtn/Rbls/Grrro/99 10.00 25.00
15 Pujols/Ichiro/25 20.00 50.00

2017 Immaculate Collection Immaculate Quads

RANDOM INSERTS IN PACKS
PRINT RUNS B/WN 3-99 COPIES PER
NO PRICING ON QTY 10 OR LESS
*BLUE/25: .6X TO 1.5X BASIC
1 Mike Trout/25 20.00 50.00
4 Clayton Kershaw/99 6.00 15.00
11 Tony Gwynn/99 6.00 15.00
12 Francisco Lindor/99 4.00 10.00
13 Kris Bryant/49 5.00 12.00
14 Yoan Moncada/99 6.00 15.00

2017 Immaculate Collection Immaculate Rookie Carbon Signatures

RANDOM INSERTS IN PACKS
STATED PRINT RUN 49 SER.#'d SETS
EXCHANGE DEADLINE 2/16/2019
1 Andrew Benintendi 30.00 80.00
2 Yoan Moncada 15.00 40.00
3 Alex Bregman 12.00 30.00
4 Dansby Swanson 10.00 25.00
5 Josh Bell 12.00 30.00
6 David Dahl 8.00 20.00
7 Hunter Renfroe 6.00 15.00
8 Aaron Judge 100.00 250.00
9 Trey Mancini 6.00 15.00
10 Ryon Healy 4.00 10.00
11 Orlando Arcia 6.00 15.00
12 Jacoby Jones 8.00 20.00
13 Manuel Margot 3.00 8.00

2017 Immaculate Collection Immaculate Signatures

RANDOM INSERTS IN PACKS
PRINT RUNS B/WN 5-99 COPIES PER
NO PRICING ON QTY 15 OR LESS
EXCHANGE DEADLINE 2/16/2019
*BLUE/25: .5X TO 1.2X p/r 49-99
1 Eloy Jimenez/99 20.00 50.00
3 Nolan Arenado/25 25.00 60.00
4 Yadier Molina/25 30.00 80.00
6 Corey Seager/49 10.00 25.00
9 Gary Sanchez/99 15.00 40.00
10 Francisco Lindor/99 12.00 30.00
11 Justin Turner/99 10.00 25.00
12 Chris Sale/99 8.00 20.00
13 Josh Donaldson/25 10.00 25.00
14 Corey Kluber/25 8.00 20.00
15 Charlie Blackmon/49 10.00 25.00
18 Terry Francona/25 12.00 30.00
19 Roy Oswalt/25 5.00 12.00
20 Edgar Renteria/49 5.00 12.00
23 Andres Galarraga/99 5.00 12.00
24 Cole Hamels/25 6.00 15.00
25 Jason Giambi/49 5.00 12.00
26 Rafael Palmeiro/25 5.00 12.00
27 Jose Canseco/49 10.00 25.00
31 Willie McGee/99 8.00 20.00
32 Tom Glavine/25 10.00 25.00
33 Craig Biggio/49 10.00 25.00
35 Frank Howard/99 3.00 8.00
36 Paul Goldschmidt/25 15.00 40.00
39 Billy Wagner/99 3.00 8.00
43 Boog Powell/49 5.00 12.00
44 Bo Jackson/25 6.00 15.00
47 Ken Griffey Sr./99 4.00 10.00
49 Mark Grace/25 10.00 25.00

2017 Immaculate Collection Immaculate Signatures Patches Rookie

RANDOM INSERTS IN PACKS
PRINT RUNS B/W 49-99 COPIES PER
EXCHANGE DEADLINE 2/16/2019
*GOLD/49: .4X TO 1X p/r 49-99
*GOLD/25: .5X TO 1.2X p/r 49-99
1 Yoan Moncada/99 15.00 40.00
2 Andrew Benintendi/99 40.00 100.00
3 Dansby Swanson/99 15.00 40.00
4 Alex Bregman/49 20.00 50.00
5 David Dahl/99 5.00 12.00
6 Tyler Glasnow/99 6.00 15.00
7 Josh Bell/49 15.00 40.00
8 Alex Reyes/99 6.00 15.00
9 Orlando Arcia/99 6.00 15.00
10 Jose De Leon/99 4.00 10.00
11 Joe Musgrove/99 30.00 80.00
12 Manuel Margot/99 4.00 10.00
13 Aaron Judge/49 100.00 250.00
14 David Paulino/99 5.00 12.00
15 Reynaldo Lopez/99 4.00 10.00
17 Hunter Renfroe/99 5.00 12.00
18 Jorge Alfaro/99 8.00 20.00
19 Carson Fulmer/99 4.00 10.00
20 Luke Weaver/99 8.00 20.00
22 Jacoby Jones/99 5.00 12.00
23 Yohander Mendez/99 4.00 10.00
24 Carson Kelly/99 5.00 12.00
25 Ryon Healy/99 8.00 20.00
26 Erik Gonzalez/99 4.00 10.00
27 Roman Quinn/99 6.00 15.00
28 Teoscar Hernandez/99 6.00 15.00
29 Raimel Tapia/99 5.00 12.00
30 Matt Olson/99 8.00 20.00

2017 Immaculate Collection Immaculate Swatches

RANDOM INSERTS IN PACKS
PRINT RUNS B/WN 5-99 COPIES PER
NO PRICING ON QTY 15 OR LESS
*PRIME/25-49: .6X TO 1.5X BASIC
3 Billy Martin/99 3.00 8.00
4 George Kelly/25 10.00 25.00
9 Kiki Cuyler/25 10.00 25.00
12 Luke Appling/49 5.00 12.00
13 Max Carey/25 15.00 40.00
14 Joe Cronin/25 6.00 15.00
15 Nellie Fox/49 12.00 30.00
18 Roger Maris/49 10.00 25.00
19 Stan Musial/25 6.00 15.00
20 Ted Lyons/25 10.00 25.00
22 Tommy Henrich/99 2.50 6.00
23 Ernie Banks/25 12.00 30.00
24 Herb Pennock/25 5.00 12.00
25 Jackie Robinson/25 25.00 60.00
26 Leo Durocher/49 2.50 6.00
28 Pee Wee Reese/25 5.00 12.00
29 Yoan Moncada/99 5.00 12.00
30 Andrew Benintendi/99 5.00 12.00
31 Dansby Swanson/99 5.00 12.00
32 Alex Bregman/99 5.00 12.00
33 David Dahl/99 3.00 8.00
34 Tyler Glasnow/99 10.00 25.00
35 Josh Bell/99 6.00 15.00
36 Alex Reyes/99 3.00 8.00
37 Orlando Arcia/99 4.00 10.00
38 Jose De Leon/99 2.50 6.00
39 Joe Musgrove/99 5.00 12.00
40 Manuel Margot/99 2.50 6.00
41 Aaron Judge/99 12.00 30.00
42 David Paulino/99 3.00 8.00
43 Reynaldo Lopez/99 2.50 6.00
44 Jeff Hoffman/99 2.50 6.00
45 Braden Shipley/99 2.50 6.00
46 Hunter Renfroe/99 3.00 8.00
47 Jorge Alfaro/99 3.00 8.00
48 Carson Fulmer/99 2.50 6.00
49 Luke Weaver/99 3.00 8.00
50 Raimel Tapia/99 3.00 8.00
51 Adalberto Mejia/99 2.50 6.00
52 Gavin Cecchini/99 2.50 6.00
53 Jacoby Jones/99 3.00 8.00
54 Yohander Mendez/99 2.50 6.00
55 Chad Pinder/99 2.50 6.00
56 Carson Kelly/99 3.00 8.00
57 Trey Mancini/99 5.00 12.00
58 Teoscar Hernandez/99 10.00 25.00
59 Ryon Healy/99 3.00 8.00
60 Erik Gonzalez/99 2.50 6.00
61 Roman Quinn/99 3.00 8.00
62 Matt Olson/99 5.00 12.00
63 Jharel Cotton/99 2.50 6.00
64 Jake Thompson/99 2.50 6.00
65 Renato Nunez/99 5.00 12.00
66 Jose Rondon/99 2.50 6.00
67 Brendan Rodgers/99 3.00 8.00
68 Kevin Maitan/99 5.00 12.00
69 Victor Robles/99 6.00 15.00
70 Cody Bellinger/99 8.00 20.00
71 Gleyber Torres/99 5.00 12.00
72 Jake Arrieta/25 3.00 8.00
73 Brandon Crawford/99 3.00 8.00
74 Alex Gordon/99 3.00 8.00
75 Eric Hosmer/99 3.00 8.00
76 Adam Duvall/99 3.00 8.00
77 Buster Posey/99 5.00 12.00
78 Yoenis Cespedes/99 4.00 10.00
79 Rick Porcello/99 3.00 8.00
80 Mookie Betts/99 8.00 20.00
81 Cole Hamels/99 3.00 8.00
82 Salvador Perez/99 3.00 8.00
83 Joey Votto/99 4.00 10.00
84 Josh Donaldson/99 3.00 8.00
85 Kris Bryant/99 8.00 20.00
87 Clayton Kershaw/49 6.00 15.00
88 Yadier Molina/99 5.00 12.00
89 Tim Tebow/99 10.00 25.00
90 Corey Seager/99 4.00 10.00
91 Kenta Maeda/99 3.00 8.00
92 Carlos Gonzalez/99 3.00 8.00
93 Josh Tomlin/99 2.50 6.00
94 Felix Hernandez/99 3.00 8.00
95 Jackie Bradley Jr./99 4.00 10.00
96 Manny Machado/99 4.00 10.00
97 Ken Griffey Jr./49 6.00 15.00
98 George Brett/99 8.00 20.00
99 Cal Ripken/99 8.00 20.00
100 Kirby Puckett/99 6.00 15.00

2017 Immaculate Collection Immaculate Trio Players Memorabilia

RANDOM INSERTS IN PACKS
PRINT RUNS B/WN 5-99 COPIES PER
NO PRICING ON QTY 5
*BLUE/25: .6X TO 1.5X BASIC
1 Benintendi/Swanson/Moncada/99 8.00 20.00
2 Judge/Bregman/Dahl/99 12.00 30.00
3 Jones/Bell/Renfroe/99 6.00 15.00
4 Reyes/Fulmer/Glasnow/99 10.00 25.00
5 Trout/Posey/Bryant/49 15.00 40.00
6 Dawson/Sandberg/Banks/99 12.00 30.00
8 Arrieta/Kershaw/Price/25 6.00 15.00
9 Mauer/Sano/Dozier/25 4.00 10.00
10 Thomas/Abreu/Moncada/99 8.00 20.00
11 Benintendi/Pedroia/Ortiz/99 8.00 20.00
12 Jones/Swnsn/Frman/99 6.00 15.00
13 Helton/Pujols/Delgado/99 5.00 12.00
14 Ripken/Brett/Griffey Jr./25 30.00 80.00

2017 Immaculate Collection Immaculate Trios Memorabilia

RANDOM INSERTS IN PACKS
PRINT RUNS B/WN 7-99 COPIES PER
NO PRICING ON QTY 7
*BLUE/25: .6X TO 1.5X BASIC
1 Mike Napoli/99 2.50 6.00
2 Kris Bryant/49 8.00 20.00
3 Eric Hosmer/99 3.00 8.00
4 Troy Tulowitzki/99 4.00 10.00
5 Adam Duvall/99 5.00 12.00
6 Mike Trout/49 20.00 50.00
8 Madison Bumgarner/99 3.00 8.00
9 Jose Bautista/99 3.00 8.00
10 Cole Hamels/99 3.00 8.00
11 Jacob deGrom/99 8.00 20.00
12 Jean Segura/49 3.00 8.00
13 Dustin Pedroia/99 6.00 15.00
14 Trea Turner/99 3.00 8.00
15 Joey Votto/99 6.00 15.00

2017 Immaculate Collection Immaculate Triple Material Autographs

RANDOM INSERTS IN PACKS
PRINT RUNS B/WN 10-99 COPIES PER
NO PRICING ON QTY 10
EXCHANGE DEADLINE 2/16/2019
1 Trea Turner/25 15.00 40.00
2 Joe Panik/25 12.00 30.00
3 Yadier Molina/25 40.00 100.00
4 Freddie Freeman/25
6 Cody Bellinger/25 50.00 120.00
7 Kyle Schwarber/25 15.00 40.00
8 Stephen Piscotty/25 8.00 20.00
9 Gary Sanchez/99 15.00 40.00
10 Ian Happ/99 12.00 30.00
11 Marcus Stroman/25
12 Xander Bogaerts/25 20.00 50.00
13 Justin Turner/25
14 Charlie Blackmon/49 10.00 25.00
15 Corey Kluber/25 8.00 20.00
16 Chris Sale/99 15.00 40.00
18 Anthony Rizzo/25 20.00 50.00
19 Noah Syndergaard/25 12.00 30.00
20 Jason Kipnis/25 10.00 25.00

2017 Immaculate Collection Immaculate Triple Material Autographs Blue

*BLUE/25: .5X TO 1.2X p/r 49-99
RANDOM INSERTS IN PACKS
PRINT RUNS B/WN 5-25 COPIES PER
NO PRICING ON QTY 10 OR LESS
EXCHANGE DEADLINE 2/16/2019
9 Gary Sanchez/25 25.00 60.00

2017 Immaculate Collection Immaculate Triple Signatures

RANDOM INSERTS IN PACKS
PRINT RUNS B/WN 10-25 COPIES PER
NO PRICING ON QTY 10
EXCHANGE DEADLINE 2/16/2019
1 Bnntndi/Swnsn/Mncda 60.00 150.00
2 Bnntndi/Rice/Brdly Jr. 60.00 150.00
3 Rdgrs/Hltn/Arndo 60.00 150.00
4 Dnldsn/Mchdo/Bltre 40.00 100.00
5 Dzr/Pdra/Altve 40.00 100.00
6 Rssll/Rzzo/Baez 50.00 120.00
7 Klbr/Lndr/Rmrz 75.00 200.00

2017 Immaculate Collection Immaculate Tweed Weave Signatures

RANDOM INSERTS IN PACKS
PRINT RUNS B/WN 10-99 COPIES PER
NO PRICING ON QTY 15 OR LESS
EXCHANGE DEADLINE 2/16/2019
*BLUE/25: .5X TO 1.2X p/r 49-99
2 Nelson Cruz/99 6.00 15.00
3 Don Sutton/49 4.00 10.00
4 Goose Gossage/49 10.00 25.00
5 Nomar Mazara/49 6.00 15.00
6 Addison Russell/49 10.00 25.00
8 Paul Molitor/25 12.00 30.00
9 Freddie Freeman/25 12.00 30.00
10 Gerrit Cole/25 8.00 20.00
11 Orlando Cepeda/25 20.00 50.00
13 Yoan Moncada/25 20.00 50.00
16 George Springer/25 8.00 20.00
17 Brooks Robinson/25 12.00 30.00
18 Edgar Renteria/25 6.00 15.00
19 Phil Niekro/25 8.00 20.00
20 Yasmany Tomas/25 4.00 10.00
22 Will Clark/25 12.00 30.00
24 Bob Gibson/25 15.00 40.00
25 Edwin Encarnacion/20 20.00 50.00
26 Manny Machado/20 20.00 50.00
27 Yoenis Cespedes/20 10.00 25.00
36 Cody Bellinger/99 60.00 150.00
37 Aaron Judge/25 125.00 300.00

2017 Immaculate Collection Rookie Autograph Premium Patch

RANDOM INSERTS IN PACKS
STATED PRINT RUN 25 SER.#'d SETS
EXCHANGE DEADLINE 2/16/2019
1 Yoan Moncada 25.00 60.00
2 Andrew Benintendi 50.00 120.00
3 Dansby Swanson EXCH 20.00 50.00
4 Alex Bregman 25.00 60.00
5 David Dahl 8.00 20.00
6 Tyler Glasnow 30.00 80.00
8 Alex Reyes 15.00 40.00
9 Orlando Arcia 20.00 50.00
10 Jose De Leon 6.00 15.00
11 Manuel Margot 6.00 15.00
12 Aaron Judge 150.00 400.00
14 Hunter Renfroe 10.00 25.00
15 Jorge Alfaro 15.00 40.00
16 Carson Fulmer 10.00 25.00
17 Ryon Healy 15.00 40.00

2017 Immaculate Collection Shadowbox Materials

RANDOM INSERTS IN PACKS
PRINT RUNS B/WN 1-25 COPIES PER
NO PRICING ON QTY 15 OR LESS
3 Ichiro/25 20.00 50.00
5 Buster Posey/25 15.00 40.00
6 Manny Machado/25 15.00 40.00
7 Mickey Mantle/25 60.00 120.00
13 Corey Seager/25 10.00 25.00
14 Kyle Schwarber/25 5.00 12.00
15 Miguel Sano/25 10.00 25.00
16 Mike Napoli/25 6.00 15.00
25 Miguel Cabrera/25 5.00 12.00
26 Alex Gordon/25 4.00 10.00
27 Felix Hernandez/25 4.00 10.00
28 Robinson Cano/25 4.00 10.00
29 Dallas Keuchel/25 4.00 10.00
30 Jackie Bradley Jr./25 12.00 30.00
31 Yoenis Cespedes/25 10.00 25.00
32 Salvador Perez/25 4.00 10.00
33 Adrian Gonzalez/25 4.00 10.00
34 Matt Carpenter/25 5.00 12.00
37 Kyle Seager/25 3.00 8.00
38 Rollie Fingers/25 10.00 25.00
40 Barry Larkin/25 10.00 25.00
41 Gary Carter/25 15.00 40.00
48 Todd Frazier/25 3.00 8.00
53 Javier Baez/25 6.00 15.00
54 Addison Russell/25 5.00 12.00
55 Adam Duvall/25 15.00 40.00
56 Billy Hamilton/25 4.00 10.00
57 Brandon Crawford/25 12.00 30.00
62 George Springer/25 4.00 10.00

2018 Immaculate Collection

48-147 PRINT RUN 99 SER.#'d SETS
EXCHANGE DEADLINE 2/1/2020
1 Anthony Banda/99 JSY AU RC 3.00 8.00
2 Luiz Gohara/99 JSY AU RC 3.00 8.00
3 Max Fried/99 JSY AU RC 12.00 30.00
4 O.Albies/99 JSY AU RC 12.00 30.00
5 Lucas Sims/99 JSY AU RC 3.00 8.00
6 A.Hays/99 JSY AU RC 10.00 25.00
7 Chance Sisco/99 JSY AU RC 4.00 10.00
8 Anthony Santander/99 JSY AU RC 3.00 8.00
9 Victor Caratini/99 JSY AU RC 4.00 10.00
10 Nicky Delmonico/99 JSY AU RC 3.00 8.00
11 Tyler Mahle/99 JSY AU RC 4.00 10.00
12 F.Mejia/99 JSY AU RC 6.00 15.00
13 G.Allen/99 JSY AU RC 8.00 20.00
14 R.McMahon/99 JSY AU RC 8.00 20.00
15 J.D. Davis/99 JSY AU RC 4.00 10.00
16 Cameron Gallagher/99 JSY AU RC 3.00 8.00
18 A.Verdugo/49 JSY AU RC 10.00 25.00
19 Kyle Farmer/99 JSY AU RC 3.00 8.00
20 B.Anderson/99 JSY AU RC 12.00 30.00
21 Dillon Peters/99 JSY AU RC 3.00 8.00
22 Brandon Woodruff/99 JSY AU RC 10.00 25.00
23 M.Garver/99 JSY AU RC 3.00 8.00
24 Zack Granite/99 JSY AU RC 3.00 8.00
25 Felix Jorge/99 JSY AU RC 3.00 8.00
26 Tomas Nido/99 JSY AU RC 3.00 8.00
27 R.Hoskins/99 JSY AU RC 25.00 60.00
28 Chris Flexen/99 JSY AU RC 3.00 8.00
29 A.Rosario/99 JSY AU RC 4.00 10.00
30 C.Frazier/99 JSY AU RC 6.00 15.00
31 M.Andujar/99 JSY AU RC 20.00 50.00
32 Tyler Wade/99 JSY AU RC 4.00 10.00
33 Dustin Fowler/99 JSY AU RC 3.00 8.00
34 Paul Blackburn/99 JSY AU RC 3.00 8.00
35 J.P. Crawford/99 JSY AU RC 5.00 12.00
36 Nick Williams/99 JSY AU RC 4.00 10.00
37 S.Ohtani/99 JSY AU RC 250.00 400.00
38 Thyago Vieira/99 JSY AU RC 3.00 8.00
39 Reyes Moronta/99 JSY AU RC 3.00 8.00
40 J.Flaherty/99 JSY AU RC 12.00 30.00
41 H.Bader/99 JSY AU RC 5.00 12.00
42 Willie Calhoun/99 JSY AU RC 5.00 12.00
43 Richard Urena/99 JSY AU RC 3.00 8.00
44 V.Robles/99 JSY AU RC 6.00 15.00
45 Erick Fedde/99 JSY AU RC 3.00 8.00
46 Andrew Stevenson/99 JSY AU RC 3.00 8.00
47 R.Devers/99 JSY AU RC 12.00 30.00
48 Mike Trout 5.00 12.00
49 Miguel Cabrera 1.00 2.50
50 Clayton Kershaw 1.50 4.00
51 Buster Posey 1.25 3.00
52 Jose Altuve .75 2.00
53 Aaron Judge 2.50 6.00
54 Adrian Beltre 1.00 2.50
55 Yadier Molina 1.25 3.00
56 Giancarlo Stanton 1.00 2.50
57 Cody Bellinger 2.00 5.00
58 Nolan Arenado 1.50 4.00
59 Paul Goldschmidt 1.00 2.50
60 Max Scherzer 1.00 2.50
61 Corey Kluber .75 2.00
62 Gary Sanchez 1.00 2.50
63 Andrew McCutchen 1.00 2.50
64 Francisco Lindor 1.00 2.50
65 Marcell Ozuna 1.00 2.50
66 Corey Seager 1.00 2.50
67 Eric Hosmer .75 2.00
68 George Springer .75 2.00
69 Charlie Blackmon 1.00 2.50
70 Chris Sale 1.00 2.50
71 Noah Syndergaard .75 2.00
72 Madison Bumgarner .75 2.00
73 Jose Ramirez .75 2.00
74 Josh Donaldson .75 2.00
75 Trea Turner .75 2.00
76 Mookie Betts 2.00 5.00
77 Yu Darvish 1.00 2.50
78 Luis Severino .75 2.00
79 Robinson Cano .75 2.00
80 Miguel Sano .75 2.00
81 Bryce Harper 1.50 4.00
82 Joey Votto 1.00 2.50
83 Justin Turner 1.00 2.50
84 Albert Pujols 1.25 3.00
85 Xander Bogaerts 1.00 2.50
86 Kris Bryant 1.25 3.00
87 Anthony Rizzo 1.25 3.00
88 Daniel Murphy .75 2.00
89 Carlos Correa 1.00 2.50
90 Salvador Perez .75 2.00
91 Byron Buxton 1.00 2.50
92 Didi Gregorius .75 2.00
93 J.D. Martinez 1.00 2.50
94 Yoan Moncada 1.00 2.50
95 Joey Gallo .75 2.00
96 Andrew Benintendi 1.00 2.50
97 Dansby Swanson 1.00 2.50
98 Freddie Freeman 1.25 3.00
99 Jose Abreu 1.00 2.50
100 Dee Gordon .60 1.50
101 Nelson Cruz 1.00 2.50
102 Khris Davis 1.00 2.50
103 Ernie Banks 1.00 2.50
104 Lou Gehrig 2.00 5.00
105 Joe Jackson 1.25 3.00
106 Babe Ruth 2.00 5.00
107 Honus Wagner 1.00 2.50
108 Joe DiMaggio 2.00 5.00
109 Mickey Mantle 3.00 8.00
110 Roberto Clemente 6.00 15.00
111 Roger Maris 1.00 2.50
112 Stan Musial 1.50 4.00
113 Ted Williams 2.00 5.00
114 Jackie Robinson 1.00 2.50
115 Babe Ruth 2.00 5.00
116 Ken Griffey Jr. 2.50 6.00
117 Nolan Ryan 4.00 10.00
118 Masahiro Tanaka .75 2.00
119 Ender Inciarte .60 1.50
120 DJ LeMahieu 1.00 2.50
121 Manny Machado 1.00 2.50
122 Nomar Mazara .60 1.50
123 Jonathan Schoop .60 1.50
124 Mitch Haniger .75 2.00
125 Matt Chapman 1.00 2.50
126 Hunter Renfroe .60 1.50
127 Nick Castellanos 1.00 2.50
128 Christian Yelich 1.25 3.00
129 A.J. Pollock .60 1.50
130 Matt Olson 1.00 2.50
131 Manuel Margot .60 1.50
132 Josh Bell .75 2.00
133 Paul DeJong 1.00 2.50
134 Trey Mancini .75 2.00
135 Addison Russell .75 2.00
136 Lewis Brinson .60 1.50
137 Bradley Zimmer .60 1.50
138 Jose Berrios .75 2.00
139 Dallas Keuchel .75 2.00
140 Corey Dickerson .60 1.50
141 Ian Happ .75 2.00
142 David Dahl .60 1.50
143 Lance McCullers .60 1.50
144 Gerrit Cole 1.00 2.50
145 Michael Conforto .75 2.00
146 Odubel Herrera .75 2.00
147 Kevin Kiermaier .75 2.00

2018 Immaculate Collection Gold

*GOLD JSY AU: .4X TO 1X BASIC
RANDOM INSERTS IN PACKS
PRINT RUNS B/WN 5-49 COPIES PER
NO PRICING ON QTY 5
EXCHANGE DEADLINE 2/1/2020
17 Walker Buehler JSY AU/49 12.00 30.00
30 Clint Frazier JSY AU/25 6.00 15.00

2018 Immaculate Collection Red

*RED: 1X TO 2.5X BASIC
RANDOM INSERTS IN PACKS
STATED PRINT RUN 25 SER.#'d SETS

2018 Immaculate Collection Dugout Collection Autographs

RANDOM INSERTS IN PACKS
PRINT RUNS B/WN 5-99 COPIES PER
NO PRICING ON QTY 15 OR LESS
EXCHANGE DEADLINE 2/1/2020
*BLUE/25: .6X TO 1.5X p/r 99
*BLUE/25: .5X TO 1.2X p/r 49
*BLUE/25: .4X TO 1X p/r 25
1 Clint Frazier/99 8.00 20.00
4 Victor Robles/99 15.00 40.00
5 Jim Rice/99 4.00 10.00
6 Stephen Piscotty/99 4.00 10.00
8 David Ortiz/25 20.00 50.00
9 Nick Williams/99 3.00 8.00
10 Josh Bell/99 3.00 8.00
11 Erick Fedde/99 2.50 6.00
12 Luiz Gohara/99 2.50 6.00
13 Mitch Keller/99 3.00 8.00
14 Andrew Stevenson/99 2.50 6.00
15 Kyle Lewis/99 5.00 12.00
16 Kyle Tucker/99 6.00 15.00
17 Justus Sheffield/99 8.00 20.00
18 Leody Taveras/99 4.00 10.00
19 Carson Fulmer/99 2.50 6.00
20 Max Fried/99 10.00 25.00
26 Carlos Correa/99 15.00 40.00
27 Robin Yount/99 12.00 30.00
28 Tyler Glasnow/99 4.00 10.00
34 Xander Bogaerts/20 15.00 40.00
37 Keith Hernandez/20 10.00 25.00
41 Rickey Henderson/25 20.00 50.00
52 Ted Simmons/49 20.00 50.00
53 Anthony Rizzo/49 15.00 40.00

2018 Immaculate Collection Immaculate Autographs

RANDOM INSERTS IN PACKS
PRINT RUNS B/WN 5-99 COPIES PER
NO PRICING ON QTY 15 OR LESS
EXCHANGE DEADLINE 2/1/2020
*BLUE/25: .6X TO 1.5X p/r 70-99
*BLUE/25: .5X TO 1.2X p/r 49
*BLUE/25: .4X TO 1X p/r 25
3 Carlos Martinez/70 3.00 8.00
4 Darryl Strawberry/70 5.00 12.00
6 George Springer/99 8.00 20.00
7 Gerrit Cole/25 8.00 20.00
8 Joey Gallo/25 8.00 20.00
9 Jose Abreu/25 8.00 20.00
10 Manny Machado/49 12.00 50.00
12 Nelson Cruz/25 6.00 15.00
14 Trea Turner/25 10.00 25.00
20 Adam Jones/25 6.00 15.00
21 Addison Russell/25 5.00 12.00
23 Byron Buxton/25 6.00 15.00
24 Evan Gattis/99 3.00 8.00

2018 Immaculate Collection Immaculate Carbon Material Signatures

RANDOM INSERTS IN PACKS
PRINT RUNS B/WN 5-25 COPIES PER
NO PRICING ON QTY 15 OR LESS
EXCHANGE DEADLINE 2/1/2020
3 Andres Galarraga/25 6.00 15.00
4 Andrew Benintendi/25 8.00 20.00
15 Juan Gonzalez/25 8.00 20.00
19 Starling Marte/25 6.00 15.00

2018 Immaculate Collection Immaculate Carbon Signatures

RANDOM INSERTS IN PACKS
PRINT RUNS B/WN 5-99 COPIES PER
NO PRICING ON QTY 15 OR LESS
EXCHANGE DEADLINE 2/1/2020
*BLUE/25: .6X TO 1.5X p/r 99
*BLUE/25: .5X TO 1.2X p/r 49
*BLUE/25: .4X TO 1X p/r 20-25
3 Andres Galarraga/49 5.00 12.00
4 Andrew Benintendi/25 25.00 60.00
6 Cody Bellinger/20
7 Jose Abreu/20 8.00 20.00
8 Darryl Strawberry/49 6.00 15.00
10 Edwin Encarnacion/25 8.00 20.00
12 Eric Thames/49 4.00 10.00
13 Gary Sanchez/20 20.00 50.00
17 Jim Rice/25 6.00 15.00
18 Jonathan Lucroy/25 5.00 12.00
19 Juan Gonzalez/99 5.00 12.00
21 Nomar Mazara/20 4.00 10.00
25 Starling Marte/25 5.00 12.00
26 Barry Larkin/20 15.00 40.00
27 Trey Mancini/49 4.00 10.00
28 Xander Bogaerts/25 15.00 40.00
29 Fernando Tatis Jr./49 40.00 100.00
30 Bo Bichette/49 15.00 40.00

2018 Immaculate Collection Immaculate Dual Autographs

RANDOM INSERTS IN PACKS
PRINT RUNS B/WN 7-49 COPIES PER
NO PRICING ON QTY 7
EXCHANGE DEADLINE 2/1/2020
*GOLD/25: .5X TO 1.2X p/r 49
1 Williams/Hoskins/49 30.00 80.00
2 Sims/Albies/49 15.00 40.00
3 Hays/Sisco/49 20.00 50.00
5 Frazier/Andujar/49 60.00 150.00
6 Rosario/Crawford/49 8.00 20.00
7 Mejia/Caratini/49 4.00 10.00
8 Albies/Robles/49 30.00 80.00
9 Frazier/Hoskins/49 25.00 60.00
11 Jimenez/Robert/49 100.00 250.00
12 Springer/Altuve/25 25.00 60.00
IDACJ Bellinger/Turner/25 25.00 60.00

2018 Immaculate Collection Immaculate Dual Material Autographs

RANDOM INSERTS IN PACKS
PRINT RUNS B/WN 10-99 COPIES PER
NO PRICING ON QTY 15 OR LESS
EXCHANGE DEADLINE 2/1/2020
*BLUE/25: .6X TO 1.5X p/r 49-99
*BLUE/25: .4X TO 1X p/r 20-25
148 Scott Kingery/99 10.00 25.00
149 Ronald Guzman/99 3.00 8.00
150 Christian Villanueva/99 6.00 15.00
151 Ronald Acuna Jr./99 75.00 200.00
152 Gleyber Torres/99 30.00 80.00
DMAAG Adrian Gonzalez/25 6.00 15.00
DMABB Byron Buxton/25 8.00 20.00
DMACC Carlos Correa/49 20.00 50.00
DMACS Chris Sale/25 12.00 30.00
DMAHP Hunter Pence/25 10.00 25.00
DMAJA Jose Abreu/20 10.00 25.00
DMAJT Justin Turner/25 15.00 40.00
DMAJV Jonathan Villar/99 3.00 8.00
DMANM Nomar Mazara/25 5.00 12.00
DMAOC Orlando Cepeda/25 12.00 30.00
DMASM Starling Marte/49 4.00 10.00

2018 Immaculate Collection Immaculate Jumbo

RANDOM INSERTS IN PACKS
PRINT RUNS B/WN 4-99 COPIES PER
NO PRICING ON QTY 15 OR LESS
1 Anthony Banda/99 2.00 5.00
2 Luiz Gohara/99 2.00 5.00
3 Max Fried/99 8.00 20.00
4 Ozzie Albies/99 5.00 12.00
5 Lucas Sims/99 2.00 5.00
6 Austin Hays/99 3.00 8.00
7 Chance Sisco/99 2.50 6.00
8 Anthony Santander/99 2.00 5.00
9 Victor Caratini/99 2.50 6.00
10 Nicky Delmonico/99 2.00 5.00
11 Tyler Mahle/99 2.50 6.00
12 Francisco Mejia/99 2.50 6.00
13 Greg Allen/99 2.00 5.00
14 Ryan McMahon/99 5.00 12.00
15 J.D. Davis/99 2.50 6.00
16 Cameron Gallagher/99 2.00 5.00
17 Walker Buehler/99 4.00 10.00
18 Alex Verdugo/99 3.00 8.00
19 Kyle Farmer/99 2.00 5.00
20 Brian Anderson/99 2.50 6.00
21 Dillon Peters/99 2.00 5.00
22 Brandon Woodruff/99 6.00 15.00
23 Mitch Garver/99 2.00 5.00
24 Zack Granite/99 2.00 5.00
25 Felix Jorge/99 2.00 5.00
26 Tomas Nido/99 2.00 5.00
27 Rhys Hoskins/99 6.00 15.00
28 Chris Flexen/99 2.00 5.00
29 Amed Rosario/99 2.50 6.00
30 Clint Frazier/99 4.00 10.00
31 Miguel Andujar/99 6.00 15.00
32 Tyler Wade/99 2.50 6.00
33 Dustin Fowler/99 2.00 5.00
34 Paul Blackburn/99 2.00 5.00
35 J.P. Crawford/99 2.00 5.00
36 Nick Williams/99 2.50 6.00
37 Shohei Ohtani/99 12.00 30.00
38 Thyago Vieira/99 2.00 5.00
39 Reyes Moronta/99 2.00 5.00
40 Jack Flaherty/99 4.00 10.00
41 Harrison Bader/99 3.00 8.00
42 Willie Calhoun/99 3.00 8.00
43 Richard Urena/99 2.00 5.00
44 Victor Robles/99 4.00 10.00
45 Erick Fedde/99 2.00 5.00
46 Andrew Stevenson/99 2.00 5.00
47 Rafael Devers/99 6.00 15.00
48 Shohei Ohtani/99 12.00 30.00
50 Vladimir Guerrero Jr./99 12.00 30.00
51 Brendan Rodgers/99 2.50 6.00
52 Gleyber Torres/99 8.00 20.00
53 Eloy Jimenez/99 6.00 15.00
54 Lazaro Armenteros/99 4.00 10.00
55 Kevin Maitan/99 2.50 6.00
63 Eric Thames/25 4.00 10.00
64 Stephen Piscotty/99 2.00 5.00
69 Corey Seager/99 3.00 8.00
70 Miguel Sano/99 2.50 6.00
71 Andrew Benintendi/99 3.00 8.00
72 Francisco Lindor/20 8.00 20.00
73 Franklin Barreto/99 2.00 5.00
74 Lewis Brinson/99 2.00 5.00
75 Michael Kopech/99 8.00 20.00
77 Aaron Judge/99 10.00 25.00
78 Nick Senzel/99 5.00 12.00
82 Ronald Acuna Jr./99 12.00 30.00
98 Bo Bichette/99 8.00 20.00
99 Fernando Tatis Jr./99 20.00 50.00
100 Juan Soto/99 15.00 40.00

2018 Immaculate Collection Immaculate Jumbo Bats

RANDOM INSERTS IN PACKS
PRINT RUNS B/WN 5-99 COPIES PER
NO PRICING ON QTY 10 OR LESS
*RED/25: .6X TO 1.5X p/r 99
*RED/25: .5X TO 1.2X p/r 49
*RED/25: .4X TO 1X p/r 25
1 Adrian Beltre/49 4.00 10.00
2 Albert Pujols/25 8.00 20.00
3 Anthony Rizzo/99 4.00 10.00
5 Barry Larkin/49 3.00 8.00
6 Shohei Ohtani/49 15.00 40.00
7 Carlos Correa/49 4.00 10.00
8 Carlos Delgado/25 3.00 8.00
9 Eddie Murray/49 6.00 15.00
10 Evan Longoria/25 4.00 10.00
11 Gary Sheffield/25 8.00 20.00
13 Giancarlo Stanton/25 10.00 25.00
14 Ivan Rodriguez/49 3.00 8.00
15 Joe Torre/25 10.00 25.00
16 Joey Votto/25 6.00 15.00
17 Jose Canseco/49 8.00 20.00
18 Jose Ramirez/49 3.00 8.00
20 Omar Vizquel/49 3.00 8.00
21 Rafael Palmeiro/49 3.00 8.00
22 Roberto Alomar/49 8.00 20.00
23 Robin Yount/25 10.00 25.00
25 Yasiel Puig/49 4.00 10.00

2018 Immaculate Collection Immaculate Legend Relics

RANDOM INSERTS IN PACKS
PRINT RUNS B/WN 5-49 COPIES PER
NO PRICING ON QTY 15 OR LESS
*RED/25: .5X TO 1.2X p/r 49
*RED/25: .4X TO 1X p/r 25
3 Billy Martin/49 20.00 50.00
4 Ernie Banks/49 6.00 15.00
7 Herb Pennock/25 10.00 25.00
9 Jackie Robinson/25 20.00 50.00
10 Joe Cronin/25 8.00 20.00
13 Kiki Cuyler/25 4.00 10.00
16 Lloyd Waner/25 5.00 12.00
18 Luke Appling/25 4.00 10.00
19 Max Carey/25 8.00 20.00
20 Mickey Mantle/25 60.00 150.00
22 Paul Waner/25 6.00 15.00
23 Pee Wee Reese/25 10.00 25.00
26 Stan Musial/25 8.00 20.00
29 Tommy Henrich/49 2.50 6.00

2018 Immaculate Collection Immaculate Material Signatures

RANDOM INSERTS IN PACKS
PRINT RUNS B/WN 10-99 COPIES PER
NO PRICING ON QTY 15 OR LESS
EXCHANGE DEADLINE 2/1/2020
1 Jose Abreu/25 10.00 25.00
2 Josh Donaldson/25 10.00 25.00
3 Aaron Judge/49 60.00 150.00
6 Freddie Freeman/25 12.00 30.00
7 Jim Rice/25 12.00 30.00
8 Cody Bellinger/35 25.00 60.00
9 Manny Machado/25 15.00 40.00
11 Wil Myers/25 6.00 15.00
12 Matt Olson/99 4.00 10.00
13 Salvador Perez/25 12.00 30.00
15 Trevor Story/49 5.00 12.00
16 Starling Marte/49 4.00 10.00
17 Nolan Arenado/25 25.00 60.00
18 Marcell Ozuna/35 8.00 20.00
20 Justin Turner/49 10.00 25.00
21 Juan Gonzalez/99 5.00 12.00
23 Andrew Benintendi/25 8.00 20.00
24 Trey Mancini/49 4.00 10.00
25 Gary Sheffield/20 12.00 30.00
26 Gary Sanchez/25 15.00 40.00
28 Cole Hamels/35 8.00 20.00
29 Yoenis Cespedes/25 12.00 30.00
30 Don Mattingly/25 30.00 80.00
31 Barry Larkin/25 6.00 15.00
32 Jeff Bagwell/20 6.00 15.00
33 Bo Jackson/25 40.00 100.00
34 Adrian Beltre/35 15.00 40.00
35 Luis Robert/99 20.00 50.00
36 Carlos Gonzalez/25 6.00 15.00
37 Dustin Pedroia/25 12.00 30.00
38 Noah Syndergaard/25
39 Alan Trammell/25 20.00 50.00
43 Andy Pettitte/25 12.00 30.00
44 Bernie Williams/25 12.00 30.00
45 Byron Buxton/35 6.00 15.00
48 Dwight Gooden/25 12.00 30.00

49 Hunter Pence/35 8.00 20.00
50 Joe Panik/49 4.00 10.00
51 Kyle Seager/49 3.00 8.00
52 Marcus Stroman/49 6.00 15.00
53 Mike Napoli/49 3.00 8.00

2018 Immaculate Collection Immaculate Material Signatures Gold

*GOLD/49: .4X TO 1X p/r 49-99
*GOLD/20-25: .4X TO 1X p/r 20-25
*GOLD/20-25: .5X TO 1.2X p/r 35
*GOLD/20-25: .6X TO 1.5X p/r 49-99
RANDOM INSERTS IN PACKS
PRINT RUNS B/WN 5-49 COPIES PER
NO PRICING ON QTY 15 OR LESS
EXCHANGE DEADLINE 2/1/2020
46 Corey Seager/20 15.00 40.00

2018 Immaculate Collection Immaculate Parchment Signatures

RANDOM INSERTS IN PACKS
PRINT RUNS B/WN 5-99 COPIES PER
NO PRICING ON QTY 15 OR LESS
EXCHANGE DEADLINE 2/1/2020
*BLUE/25: .6X TO 1.5X p/r 79-99
*BLUE/25: .5X TO 1.2X p/r 35-49
*BLUE/25: .4X TO 1X p/r 20-25
3 Carlos Gonzalez/79 3.00 8.00
5 Charles Johnson/99 2.50 6.00
6 Darrell Evans/99 2.50 6.00
8 Dwight Gooden/24 10.00 25.00
10 Gaylord Perry/35 6.00 15.00
11 Ian Kinsler/25 5.00 12.00
12 Jeff Bagwell/25 5.00 12.00
15 Fernando Tatis Jr./99 40.00 100.00
16 Keith Hernandez/49 8.00 20.00
17 Lee Smith/99 5.00 12.00
18 Kyle Tucker/99 6.00 15.00
19 Luis Tiant/79 6.00 15.00
22 Salvador Perez/25 10.00 25.00
23 Tony Oliva/25 15.00 40.00
24 Forrest Whitley/99 6.00 15.00
25 Yoenis Cespedes/20 6.00 15.00

2018 Immaculate Collection Immaculate Quad Material Autographs

RANDOM INSERTS IN PACKS
PRINT RUNS B/WN 5-99 COPIES PER
NO PRICING ON QTY 10 OR LESS
EXCHANGE DEADLINE 2/1/2020
*BLUE/25: .6X TO 1.5X p/r 49-99
*BLUE/25: .4X TO 1X p/r 20-25
2 Victor Robles/25 15.00 40.00
3 Chance Sisco/99 4.00 10.00
4 Michael Kopech/49 15.00 40.00
7 Brendan Rodgers/49 8.00 20.00
9 Mitch Keller/99 8.00 20.00
11 Estevan Florial/99 25.00 60.00
12 Ryan McMahon/49 6.00 15.00
13 Alex Verdugo/99 6.00 15.00
15 Paul Molitor/25 10.00 25.00
18 Nick Williams/99 4.00 10.00
19 Tyler Wade/99 4.00 10.00
20 Cody Bellinger/20 30.00 80.00

2018 Immaculate Collection Immaculate Rookie Bat Autographs

RANDOM INSERTS IN PACKS
PRINT RUNS B/WN 10-99 COPIES PER
NO PRICING ON QTY 10
EXCHANGE DEADLINE 2/1/2020
2 Amed Rosario/99 8.00 20.00
3 Andrew Stevenson/99 2.50 6.00
4 Austin Hays/99 4.00 10.00
6 Chance Sisco/99 4.00 10.00
7 Clint Frazier/25 12.00 30.00
8 Dustin Fowler/99 2.50 6.00
9 Francisco Mejia/37 4.00 10.00
12 Max Fried/99 10.00 25.00
14 Mitch Garver/99 2.50 6.00
16 Nicky Delmonico/99 2.50 6.00
18 Rafael Devers/49 10.00 25.00
19 Rhys Hoskins/25 30.00 80.00
20 Ryan McMahon/99 6.00 15.00
22 Victor Caratini/99 3.00 8.00
23 Victor Robles/47 12.00 30.00
24 Willie Calhoun/99 4.00 10.00
25 Zack Granite/99 2.50 6.00

2018 Immaculate Collection Immaculate Rookie Bat Autographs Red

*RED/49: .5X TO 1.2X p/r 99
*RED/49: .4X TO 1X p/r 37-49
*RED/25: .6X TO 1.5X p/r 99
*RED/25: .5X TO 1.2X p/r 37-49
RANDOM INSERTS IN PACKS
PRINT RUNS B/WN 5-49 COPIES PER
NO PRICING ON QTY 15 OR LESS
EXCHANGE DEADLINE 2/1/2020
15 Nick Williams/49 4.00 10.00

2018 Immaculate Collection Immaculate Rookie Carbon Signatures

RANDOM INSERTS IN PACKS
PRINT RUNS B/WN 5-99 COPIES PER
NO PRICING ON QTY 15 OR LESS
EXCHANGE DEADLINE 2/1/2020
*BLUE/25: .6X TO 1.5X p/r 99
*BLUE/25: .5X TO 1.2X p/r 35-49
*BLUE/25: .4X TO 1X p/r 25
1 Ozzie Albies/99 15.00 40.00
2 Austin Hays/99 4.00 10.00
3 Chance Sisco/99 4.00 10.00
4 Rafael Devers/46 10.00 25.00
5 Victor Caratini/99 3.00 8.00
6 Nicky Delmonico/99 2.50 6.00
7 Francisco Mejia/35 4.00 10.00
8 Ryan McMahon/99 6.00 15.00
10 Alex Verdugo/99 6.00 15.00
11 Mitch Garver/99 2.50 6.00
12 Amed Rosario/49 5.00 12.00
13 Clint Frazier/25 12.00 30.00
14 Dustin Fowler/99 2.50 6.00
17 Rhys Hoskins/25 30.00 80.00
19 Willie Calhoun/99 4.00 10.00
20 Victor Robles/35 12.00 30.00

2018 Immaculate Collection Immaculate Signatures

RANDOM INSERTS IN PACKS
PRINT RUNS B/WN 10-99 COPIES PER
NO PRICING ON QTY 15 OR LESS
EXCHANGE DEADLINE 2/1/2020
*GOLD/49: .5X TO 1.2X p/r 99
*GOLD/25: .5X TO 1.2X p/r 49
1 Willie McGee/99 6.00 15.00
3 Gary Sheffield/25 4.00 10.00
4 Shohei Ohtani/99 125.00 300.00
5 Buddy Bell/99 4.00 10.00
6 Lee Smith/99 5.00 12.00
9 Fred Lynn/25 6.00 15.00
10 Don Sutton/49 4.00 10.00
12 Joe Carter/25 5.00 12.00
14 Terry Francona/49 10.00 25.00
15 Darryl Strawberry/49 6.00 15.00
18 Chris Sale/25 15.00 40.00
19 Charles Johnson/99 2.50 6.00
20 Paul Goldschmidt/25 10.00 25.00
21 Jose Abreu/25 8.00 20.00
24 Eric Thames/99 3.00 8.00

2018 Immaculate Collection Immaculate Swatches

RANDOM INSERTS IN PACKS
PRINT RUNS B/WN 10-99 COPIES PER
NO PRICING ON QTY 10 OR LESS
1 Anthony Banda/99 2.00 5.00
2 Luiz Gohara/99 2.00 5.00
3 Max Fried/99 8.00 20.00
4 Ozzie Albies/99 5.00 12.00
5 Lucas Sims/99 2.00 5.00
6 Austin Hays/99 3.00 8.00
7 Chance Sisco/99 2.50 6.00
8 Anthony Santander/99 2.00 5.00
9 Victor Caratini/99 2.50 6.00
10 Nicky Delmonico/99 2.00 5.00
11 Tyler Mahle/99 2.50 6.00
12 Francisco Mejia/99 2.50 6.00
13 Greg Allen/99 2.00 5.00
14 Ryan McMahon/99 5.00 12.00
15 J.D. Davis/99 2.50 6.00
16 Cameron Gallagher/99 2.00 5.00
17 Walker Buehler/99 4.00 10.00
18 Alex Verdugo/99 3.00 8.00
19 Kyle Farmer/99 2.00 5.00
20 Brian Anderson/99 2.50 6.00
21 Dillon Peters/99 2.00 5.00
22 Brandon Woodruff/99 6.00 15.00
23 Mitch Garver/99 2.00 5.00
24 Zack Granite/99 2.00 5.00
25 Felix Jorge/99 2.00 5.00
26 Tomas Nido/99 2.00 5.00
27 Rhys Hoskins/99 6.00 15.00
28 Chris Flexen/99 2.00 5.00
29 Amed Rosario/99 2.50 6.00
30 Clint Frazier/99 4.00 10.00
31 Miguel Andujar/99 6.00 15.00
32 Tyler Wade/99 2.50 6.00
33 Dustin Fowler/99 2.00 5.00
34 Paul Blackburn/99 2.00 5.00
35 J.P. Crawford/99 2.00 5.00
36 Nick Williams/99 2.50 6.00
37 Shohei Ohtani/99 12.00 30.00
38 Thyago Vieira/99 2.00 5.00
39 Reyes Moronta/99 2.00 5.00
40 Jack Flaherty/99 4.00 10.00
41 Harrison Bader/99 3.00 8.00
42 Willie Calhoun/99 3.00 8.00
43 Richard Urena/99 2.00 5.00
44 Victor Robles/99 4.00 10.00
45 Erick Fedde/99 2.00 5.00
46 Andrew Stevenson/99 2.00 5.00
47 Rafael Devers/99 6.00 15.00
48 Kris Bryant/25 6.00 15.00
49 Bryce Harper/25 6.00 15.00
50 Mike Trout/25 10.00 25.00
51 Salvador Perez/99 2.50 6.00
52 Marcell Ozuna/99 3.00 8.00
53 Evan Longoria/99 2.50 6.00
55 J.D. Martinez/25 5.00 12.00
56 Miguel Cabrera/49 4.00 10.00
57 Adrian Beltre/49 4.00 10.00
58 Jose Altuve/49 3.00 8.00
59 Ronald Acuna Jr./99 12.00 30.00
60 Gleyber Torres/99 8.00 20.00
61 David Price/49 3.00 8.00
62 Noah Syndergaard/49 3.00 8.00
63 Yu Darvish/25 5.00 12.00
64 Vladimir Guerrero Jr./99 12.00 30.00
65 Jason Kipnis/25 4.00 10.00
66 Kirby Puckett/49 8.00 20.00
67 Anthony Rendon/49 4.00 10.00
68 Whit Merrifield/99 3.00 8.00
69 Buster Posey/49 5.00 12.00
70 Todd Frazier/99 2.00 5.00
71 Corey Seager/99 3.00 8.00
72 Andrew Benintendi/99 3.00 8.00
73 Jonathan Schoop/49 2.50 6.00
74 Manny Machado/49 4.00 10.00
76 Dustin Pedroia/49 4.00 10.00
77 Luis Severino/99 2.50 6.00
78 Mariano Rivera/99 4.00 10.00
79 Bernie Williams/99 2.50 6.00
80 Bo Jackson/49 8.00 20.00
81 David Ortiz/49 4.00 10.00
82 Eddie Murray/49 6.00 15.00
83 Frank Howard/49 5.00 12.00
84 George Brett/25 10.00 25.00
85 Greg Maddux/49 5.00 12.00
86 Keith Hernandez/25 3.00 8.00
87 Barry Larkin/49 3.00 8.00
88 Aaron Judge/99 10.00 25.00
89 Shohei Ohtani/99 12.00 30.00
90 Trea Turner/99 2.50 6.00
91 Gary Sanchez/99 3.00 8.00
92 Paul Goldschmidt/25 5.00 12.00
93 Ken Griffey Jr./25 10.00 25.00
94 Cal Ripken/25 12.00 30.00
95 Nolan Ryan/25 15.00 40.00
96 Joe Mauer/25 4.00 10.00

2018 Immaculate Collection Immaculate Swatches Jersey Number

*JSY NUM/20-25: .6X TO 1.5X p/r 99
*JSY NUM/20-25: .5X TO 1.2X p/r 49
*JSY NUM/20-25: .4X TO 1X p/r 25
RANDOM INSERTS IN PACKS
PRINT RUNS B/WN 1-25 COPIES PER
NO PRICING ON QTY 10 OR LESS
54 Jake Arrieta/25 4.00 10.00

2018 Immaculate Collection Immaculate Triple Material Autographs

RANDOM INSERTS IN PACKS
PRINT RUNS B/WN 5-99 COPIES PER
NO PRICING ON QTY 15 OR LESS
EXCHANGE DEADLINE 2/1/2020
*BLUE/25: .6X TO 1.5X p/r 49-99
*BLUE/25: .4X TO 1X p/r 25
2 Vladimir Guerrero Jr./25 200.00 500.00
4 Lou Brock/25 12.00 30.00
6 Don Sutton/25 10.00 25.00
12 Goose Gossage/25 5.00 12.00
14 Clint Frazier/25 15.00 40.00
15 Rhys Hoskins/25 30.00 80.00
16 Ozzie Albies/49 30.00 80.00
17 Rafael Devers/25 20.00 50.00
20 Miguel Andujar/99 40.00 100.00

2018 Immaculate Collection Immaculate Triple Signatures

RANDOM INSERTS IN PACKS
PRINT RUNS B/WN 3-25 COPIES PER
NO PRICING ON QTY 15 OR LESS
EXCHANGE DEADLINE 2/1/2020
5 Torres/Jimenez/Acuna/25 200.00 400.00
6 Tatis/Vlad Jr./Senzel/25 200.00 500.00
8 Tucker/Bichette/Rodgers/25 40.00 100.00

2018 Immaculate Collection Immaculate Tweed Weave Signatures

RANDOM INSERTS IN PACKS
PRINT RUNS B/WN 5-99 COPIES PER
NO PRICING ON QTY 15 OR LESS
EXCHANGE DEADLINE 2/1/2020
*BLUE/25: .6X TO 1.5X p/r 99
4 Andres Galarraga/99 4.00 10.00
6 Boog Powell/25 10.00 25.00
9 Dave Concepcion/40 20.00 50.00
15 Jose Abreu/20 8.00 20.00
16 Juan Gonzalez/70 5.00 12.00
22 Nomar Mazara/25 4.00 10.00
23 Omar Vizquel/20 6.00 15.00

2018 Immaculate Collection Rookie Debut Signatures

RANDOM INSERTS IN PACKS
PRINT RUNS B/WN 5-99 COPIES PER
NO PRICING ON QTY 6 OR LESS
EXCHANGE DEADLINE 2/1/2020
*JSY NUM/50-77: .4X TO 1X p/r 99
*JSY NUM/50-77: .3X TO .8X p/r 49
*JSY NUM/50-77: .25X TO .6X p/r 25
*JSY NUM/30-48: .5X TO 1.2X p/r 99
*JSY NUM/30-48: .4X TO 1X p/r 49
*JSY NUM/30-48: .3X TO .8X p/r 25
*JSY NUM/23-28: .6X TO 1.5X p/r 99
*JSY NUM/23-28: .5X TO 1.2X p/r 49
*JSY NUM/23-25: .4X TO 1X p/r 25
1 Anthony Banda/99 2.50 6.00
2 Luiz Gohara/99 2.50 6.00
3 Max Fried/99 10.00 25.00
4 Ozzie Albies/49 20.00 50.00
5 Lucas Sims/99 2.50 6.00
6 Austin Hays/99 4.00 10.00
7 Chance Sisco/99 4.00 10.00
8 Anthony Santander/99 2.50 6.00
9 Victor Caratini/99 3.00 8.00
10 Nicky Delmonico/99 2.50 6.00
11 Tyler Mahle/99 3.00 8.00
12 Francisco Mejia/99 3.00 8.00
13 Greg Allen/99 5.00 12.00
14 Ryan McMahon/99 6.00 15.00
15 J.D. Davis/99 3.00 8.00
16 Cameron Gallagher/99 2.50 6.00
17 Walker Buehler/99 12.00 30.00
18 Alex Verdugo/99 6.00 15.00
20 Brian Anderson/99 3.00 8.00
21 Dillon Peters/99 2.50 6.00
22 Brandon Woodruff/99 8.00 20.00
23 Mitch Garver/99 2.50 6.00
24 Zack Granite/99 2.50 6.00
25 Felix Jorge/99 2.50 6.00
26 Tomas Nido/99 2.50 6.00
27 Rhys Hoskins/99 25.00 60.00
28 Chris Flexen/99 2.50 6.00
29 Amed Rosario/25 12.00 30.00
30 Clint Frazier/99 6.00 15.00
31 Miguel Andujar/99 15.00 40.00
32 Tyler Wade/99 3.00 8.00
33 Dustin Fowler/99 2.50 6.00
34 Paul Blackburn/99 2.50 6.00
35 J.P. Crawford/25 4.00 10.00
36 Nick Williams/99 3.00 8.00
38 Thyago Vieira/99 2.50 6.00
39 Reyes Moronta/99 2.50 6.00
40 Jack Flaherty/99 10.00 25.00
41 Harrison Bader/99 4.00 10.00
42 Willie Calhoun/99 4.00 10.00
43 Richard Urena/99 2.50 6.00
44 Victor Robles/99 12.00 30.00
45 Erick Fedde/99 2.50 6.00
46 Andrew Stevenson/99 2.50 6.00
47 Rafael Devers/25 12.00 30.00

2018 Immaculate Collection Rookie Dual Material Autographs

RANDOM INSERTS IN PACKS
PRINT RUNS B/WN 49-99 COPIES PER
EXCHANGE DEADLINE 2/1/2020
*GOLD/49: .4X TO 1X BASIC
1 Max Fried/99 12.00 30.00
2 Ozzie Albies/99 20.00 50.00
3 Lucas Sims/99 3.00 8.00
4 Austin Hays/99 5.00 12.00
5 Chance Sisco/99 4.00 10.00
6 Victor Caratini/99 4.00 10.00
7 Nicky Delmonico/99 3.00 8.00
8 Francisco Mejia/99 6.00 15.00
9 Greg Allen/99 3.00 8.00
10 Ryan McMahon/99 6.00 15.00
11 Shohei Ohtani/49 200.00 400.00
12 Walker Buehler/99 15.00 40.00
13 Alex Verdugo/99 10.00 25.00
14 Kyle Farmer/99 3.00 8.00
15 Zack Granite/99 3.00 8.00
16 Jack Flaherty/99 12.00 30.00
17 Chris Flexen/99 3.00 8.00
18 Amed Rosario/99 4.00 10.00
19 Clint Frazier/99 10.00 25.00
20 Miguel Andujar/99 40.00 100.00
21 Tyler Wade/99 4.00 10.00
22 J.P. Crawford/99 3.00 8.00
23 Nick Williams/99 4.00 10.00
25 Harrison Bader/99 5.00 12.00
26 Willie Calhoun/99 5.00 12.00
27 Richard Urena/99 3.00 8.00
28 Victor Robles/99 10.00 25.00
29 Erick Fedde/99 3.00 8.00
30 Rafael Devers/99 12.00 30.00

2018 Immaculate Collection Rookie Premium Patch Autographs

RANDOM INSERTS IN PACKS
PRINT RUNS B/WN 10-25 COPIES PER
NO PRICING ON QTY 15 OR LESS
EXCHANGE DEADLINE 2/1/2020
1 Ozzie Albies/25 30.00 80.00
2 Chance Sisco/25 10.00 25.00
3 Francisco Mejia/25 12.00 30.00
5 Shohei Ohtani/25 150.00 400.00
6 Jack Flaherty/25 20.00 50.00
7 Amed Rosario/25 20.00 50.00
10 J.P. Crawford/25 5.00 12.00
12 Rhys Hoskins/25 50.00 120.00
13 Willie Calhoun/25 8.00 20.00
14 Victor Robles/25 40.00 100.00
15 Rafael Devers/25 20.00 50.00

2018 Immaculate Collection Rookie Quad Material Autographs

RANDOM INSERTS IN PACKS
PRINT RUNS B/WN 49-99 COPIES PER
EXCHANGE DEADLINE 2/1/2020
*GOLD/49: .4X TO 1X BASIC
1 Ozzie Albies/99 20.00 50.00
2 Chance Sisco/99 4.00 10.00
3 Francisco Mejia/99 6.00 15.00
4 Alex Verdugo/99 6.00 15.00
5 Shohei Ohtani/49 200.00 400.00
6 Jack Flaherty/99 12.00 30.00
7 Amed Rosario/99 4.00 10.00
8 Clint Frazier/99 10.00 25.00
9 Miguel Andujar/99 40.00 100.00
10 J.P. Crawford/99 3.00 8.00
11 Nick Williams/99 4.00 10.00
12 Rhys Hoskins/99 20.00 50.00
13 Willie Calhoun/99 5.00 12.00
14 Victor Robles/99 10.00 25.00
15 Rafael Devers/99 12.00 30.00

2018 Immaculate Collection Shadowbox Dual Materials

RANDOM INSERTS IN PACKS
PRINT RUNS B/WN 5-99 COPIES PER
NO PRICING ON QTY 15 OR LESS
3 Marcell Ozuna/49 4.00 10.00
6 Jose Altuve/49 4.00 10.00
7 Aaron Judge/25 15.00 40.00
8 Max Scherzer/25 10.00 25.00
9 Charlie Blackmon/25 5.00 12.00
15 Ichiro/20 12.00 30.00
16 Shohei Ohtani/99 12.00 30.00
17 Edwin Encarnacion/49 4.00 10.00
18 Nelson Cruz/49 4.00 10.00
20 Giancarlo Stanton/99 6.00 15.00
23 Miguel Cabrera/49 4.00 10.00
26 Francisco Lindor/25 8.00 20.00
29 Jose Ramirez/49 3.00 8.00
30 Marcus Stroman/49 3.00 8.00
31 Buster Posey/25 6.00 15.00
33 Gary Sanchez/25 5.00 12.00
34 Stan Musial/25 8.00 20.00
35 Roger Maris/25 20.00 50.00
36 Mickey Mantle/49 30.00 80.00
37 Ernie Banks/49 6.00 15.00
38 Andrew Benintendi/25 5.00 12.00
41 Trea Turner/25 4.00 10.00
43 Madison Bumgarner/49 3.00 8.00
46 Rickey Henderson/25 25.00 60.00
47 Rod Carew/25 8.00 20.00
48 Tom Glavine/49 5.00 12.00

2018 Immaculate Collection Shadowbox Dual Materials Jumbo

RANDOM INSERTS IN PACKS
PRINT RUNS B/WN 1-99 COPIES PER
NO PRICING ON QTY 15 OR LESS
1 Jeff Bagwell/25 4.00 10.00
2 Shohei Ohtani/99 12.00 30.00
3 Ivan Rodriguez/25 4.00 10.00
5 Frank Thomas/25 8.00 20.00
7 Eddie Murray/25 8.00 20.00
8 Don Mattingly/49 10.00 25.00
9 Juan Gonzalez/25 10.00 25.00
11 Rafael Devers/25 10.00 25.00
12 Amed Rosario/99 2.50 6.00
13 Shohei Ohtani/99 12.00 30.00
14 Rhys Hoskins/99 6.00 15.00
15 Clint Frazier/99 4.00 10.00
16 Victor Robles/99 4.00 10.00
19 Mike Piazza/25 8.00 20.00
20 Nolan Ryan/25 15.00 40.00
21 Orel Hershiser/25 12.00 30.00
22 Ryne Sandberg/25 12.00 30.00
23 Buster Posey/25 6.00 15.00
24 Aaron Judge/99 10.00 25.00
25 Nomar Mazara/99 2.00 5.00
26 Salvador Perez/99 2.50 6.00
27 Mickey Mantle/25 60.00 150.00
28 Clayton Kershaw/25 8.00 20.00
29 Ronald Acuna Jr./99 12.00 30.00
30 Vladimir Guerrero Jr./99 12.00 30.00
31 Nick Senzel/99 5.00 12.00
32 Eloy Jimenez/99 6.00 15.00
34 Ted Williams/25 75.00 200.00
40 Robinson Cano/25 4.00 10.00
41 Evan Longoria/49 3.00 8.00
42 Noah Syndergaard/25 4.00 10.00
43 Barry Larkin/25 4.00 10.00
45 Lee Smith/25 3.00 8.00

2019 Immaculate Collection

RANDOM INSERTS IN PACKS
NO PRICING QTY 3
1-50 PRINT RUN B/TW 20-99 COPIES PER
51-150 PRINT RUN B/TW 3-99 COPIES PER
EXCHANGE DEADLINE 2/21/2021
1 Cedric Mullins JSY AU/99 RC 10.00 25.00
2 Enyel De Los Santos JSY AU/99 RC 3.00 8.00
3 Daniel Ponce de Leon JSY AU/99 RC 5.00 12.00
4 Jonathan Davis JSY AU/99 RC 4.00 10.00
5 Kevin Newman JSY AU/99 RC 5.00 12.00
6 Sean Reid-Foley JSY AU/99 RC 3.00 8.00
7 Garrett Hampson JSY AU/99 RC 5.00 12.00
8 Brad Keller JSY AU/99 RC 3.00 8.00
9 Chris Shaw JSY AU/99 RC 3.00 8.00
10 Kevin Kramer JSY AU/99 RC 4.00 10.00
11 Myles Straw JSY AU/99 RC 5.00 12.00
12 Ryan O'Hearn JSY AU/99 RC 3.00 8.00
13 Michael Kopech JSY AU/99 RC 10.00 25.00
14 Jake Cave JSY AU/99 RC 4.00 10.00
15 Corbin Burnes JSY AU/99 RC 10.00 25.00
16 Luis Urias JSY AU/99 RC 5.00 12.00
17 Justus Sheffield JSY AU/99 RC 5.00 12.00
18 Kyle Wright JSY AU/99 RC 5.00 12.00
19 Christin Stewart JSY AU/99 RC 4.00 10.00
20 Vladimir Guerrero Jr. JSY AU/99 RC 50.00 120.00
21 Touki Toussaint JSY AU/99 RC 4.00 10.00
22 Jake Bauers JSY AU/99 RC 5.00 12.00
23 Chance Adams JSY AU/99 RC 3.00 8.00
24 Stephen Gonsalves JSY AU/99 RC 3.00 8.00
25 Caleb Ferguson JSY AU/99 RC 4.00 10.00
26 Danny Jansen JSY AU/99 RC 3.00 8.00
27 Dennis Santana JSY AU/99 RC 3.00 8.00
28 Kyle Tucker JSY AU/99 RC 15.00 40.00
29 Rowdy Tellez JSY AU/99 RC 5.00 12.00
30 Jonathan Loaisiga JSY AU/49 RC 5.00 12.00
31 Eloy Jimenez JSY AU/99 RC 20.00 50.00
32 Cionel Perez JSY AU/99 RC 3.00 8.00
33 Steven Duggar JSY AU/99 RC 4.00 10.00
34 Taylor Ward JSY AU/99 RC 3.00 8.00
35 Jacob Nix JSY AU/99 RC 4.00 10.00
36 Patrick Wisdom JSY AU/99 RC 3.00 8.00
37 Dakota Hudson JSY AU/99 RC 4.00 10.00
38 Fernando Tatis Jr. JSY AU/99 RC 75.00 200.00
39 Framber Valdez JSY AU/99 RC 3.00 8.00
40 Bryse Wilson JSY AU/99 RC 4.00 10.00
41 Luis Ortiz JSY AU/99 RC 3.00 8.00
42 Ramon Laureano JSY AU/99 RC 8.00 20.00
43 Reese McGuire JSY AU/99 RC 5.00 12.00
44 Ryan Borucki JSY AU/99 RC 3.00 8.00
45 Jeff McNeil JSY AU/99 RC 8.00 20.00
46 Kolby Allard JSY AU/99 RC 5.00 12.00
47 David Fletcher JSY AU/99 RC 10.00 25.00
48 Nick Senzel JSY AU/20 RC 15.00 40.00
49 Brandon Lowe JSY AU/99 RC 8.00 20.00
50 Josh James JSY AU/99 RC 5.00 12.00
51 Mike Trout JSY/99 20.00 50.00
52 Kris Bryant JSY/99 4.00 10.00
53 Bryce Harper JSY/99 5.00 12.00
54 Jose Altuve JSY/99 2.50 6.00
55 Christian Yelich JSY/99 4.00 10.00
56 Mookie Betts JSY/99 6.00 15.00
57 Clayton Kershaw JSY/99 5.00 12.00
58 Joey Gallo JSY/99 2.50 6.00
59 Ronald Acuna Jr. JSY/99 8.00 20.00
60 Gleyber Torres JSY/99 5.00 12.00
61 Juan Soto JSY/99 10.00 25.00
62 Walker Buehler JSY/99 4.00 10.00
63 Joey Votto JSY/99 3.00 8.00
64 Nolan Arenado JSY/99 5.00 12.00
65 Whit Merrifield JSY/99 3.00 8.00
66 Brian Anderson JSY/99 2.00 5.00
67 Jacob deGrom JSY/99 6.00 15.00
68 Khris Davis JSY/25 5.00 12.00
69 Starling Marte JSY/99 2.50 6.00
70 Buster Posey JSY/99 4.00 10.00
71 Blake Snell JSY/49 3.00 8.00
72 Jose Berrios JSY/99 2.50 6.00
73 Albert Pujols JSY/99 4.00 10.00
74 Miguel Cabrera JSY/99 3.00 8.00
75 Jose Abreu JSY/99 3.00 8.00
76 David Peralta JSY/99 2.00 5.00
77 Jose Ramirez JSY/99 2.50 6.00
78 Felix Hernandez JSY/99 2.50 6.00
79 Trey Mancini JSY/99 2.50 6.00
80 Yadier Molina JSY/99 4.00 10.00
81 Marcus Stroman JSY/99 2.50 6.00
82 Manny Machado JSY/99 3.00 8.00
83 Max Scherzer JSY/99 3.00 8.00
84 Anthony Rizzo JSY/99 4.00 10.00
85 Shohei Ohtani JSY/99 5.00 12.00
86 Miguel Andujar JSY/99 3.00 8.00
87 Aaron Judge JSY/99 8.00 20.00
88 Javier Baez JSY/99 4.00 10.00
89 Giancarlo Stanton JSY/99 3.00 8.00
90 Freddie Freeman JSY/99 4.00 10.00
91 Carlos Correa JSY/99 3.00 8.00
92 Andrew Benintendi JSY/99 3.00 8.00
93 Cody Bellinger JSY/99 6.00 15.00
94 George Springer JSY/99 2.50 6.00
95 Maikel Franco JSY/99 2.50 6.00
96 Justin Turner JSY/49 4.00 10.00
97 Corey Kluber JSY/99 2.50 6.00
98 Scooter Gennett JSY/99 2.50 6.00
99 Alex Bregman JSY/99 3.00 8.00
100 Francisco Lindor JSY/49 4.00 10.00
102 Josh Hader JSY/99 2.50 6.00
103 Noah Syndergaard JSY/99 2.50 6.00
104 Jameson Taillon JSY/99 2.50 6.00
105 Brandon Crawford JSY/99 2.50 6.00
106 Willson Contreras JSY/99 2.50 6.00
107 Charlie Blackmon JSY/99 3.00 8.00
108 Mitch Haniger JSY/99 2.50 6.00
109 Ozzie Albies JSY/99 3.00 8.00
110 Chris Sale JSY/99 3.00 8.00
111 Justin Verlander JSY/99 3.00 8.00
112 Patrick Corbin JSY/99 2.50 6.00
113 Matt Carpenter JSY/99 3.00 8.00
114 Xander Bogaerts JSY/99 3.00 8.00
115 Trevor Story JSY/62 3.00 8.00
116 Miguel Sano JSY/99 2.50 6.00
117 Matt Olson JSY/99 3.00 8.00
118 Rhys Hoskins JSY/99 4.00 10.00
119 Teoscar Hernandez JSY/99 3.00 8.00
120 Victor Robles JSY/99 4.00 10.00
121 Yoan Moncada JSY/99 3.00 8.00
122 Edwin Encarnacion JSY/99 3.00 8.00
123 Robinson Cano JSY/99 2.50 6.00
124 Nelson Cruz JSY/99 3.00 8.00
125 Marcell Ozuna JSY/99 3.00 8.00
126 Paul Goldschmidt JSY/99 3.00 8.00
127 Jordan Hicks JSY/99 2.50 6.00
128 Edwin Diaz JSY/99 2.50 6.00
129 Stephen Strasburg JSY/99 3.00 8.00
130 Gerrit Cole JSY/99 3.00 8.00
131 Luis Severino JSY/99 2.50 6.00
132 Gary Sanchez JSY/99 3.00 8.00
133 Jon Lester JSY/99 2.50 6.00
134 Rick Porcello JSY/99 2.50 6.00
135 David Price JSY/99 2.50 6.00
136 Ichiro JSY/99 4.00 10.00
137 Joc Pederson JSY/99 2.50 6.00
138 Ryan Braun JSY/99 2.50 6.00
139 Adalberto Mondesi JSY/99 2.50 6.00
140 Amed Rosario JSY/99 2.50 6.00
141 Kyle Schwarber JSY/99 3.00 8.00
142 Trea Turner JSY/99 2.50 6.00
143 Andrew McCutchen JSY/49 4.00 10.00
144 David Dahl JSY/99 2.00 5.00
145 Yasiel Puig JSY/99 3.00 8.00
146 Nicholas Castellanos JSY/99 3.00 8.00
147 Eugenio Suarez JSY/99 2.50 6.00
148 Hunter Renfroe JSY/99 2.00 5.00
149 Michael Conforto JSY/99 2.50 6.00
150 Daniel Murphy JSY/60 2.50 6.00

2019 Immaculate Collection Batting Stance Memorabilia Autographs

RANDOM INSERTS IN PACKS
STATED PRINT RUN 25 SER.#'d SETS
EXCHANGE DEADLINE 2/21/2021
1 Jake Bauers 8.00 20.00
2 Kyle Tucker 12.00 30.00
3 Ryan O'Hearn 5.00 12.00
4 Jeff McNeil 12.00 30.00
5 Jake Cave 6.00 15.00
6 Kevin Kramer 6.00 15.00
7 Cedric Mullins 15.00 40.00
8 Garrett Hampson 8.00 20.00
9 Christin Stewart 6.00 15.00
10 Kevin Newman 8.00 20.00
11 Chris Shaw 5.00 12.00
12 David Fletcher 15.00 40.00
13 Ramon Laureano 12.00 30.00
15 Brandon Lowe 12.00 30.00
16 Taylor Ward 5.00 12.00
17 Rowdy Tellez 8.00 20.00
18 Myles Straw 8.00 20.00
20 Danny Jansen 5.00 12.00

2019 Immaculate Collection Clutch Dual Memorabilia Autographs

RANDOM INSERTS IN PACKS
PRINT RUNS B/WN 4-49 COPIES PER
NO PRICING QTY 15 OR LESS
EXCHANGE DEADLINE 2/21/2021
*RED/25: .5X TO 1.2X p/r 49
3 Cody Bellinger/25 60.00 150.00
4 Marcus Stroman/49 5.00 12.00
5 Trevor Story/25 8.00 20.00
16 Gary Sanchez/25 15.00 40.00
17 Goose Gossage/25 6.00 15.00
19 Matt Carpenter/34 8.00 20.00

2019 Immaculate Collection Clutch Rookies Dual Memorabilia Autographs

RANDOM INSERTS IN PACKS
PRINT RUNS B/WN 25-49 COPIES PER
EXCHANGE DEADLINE 2/21/2021
1 Jake Bauers/25 8.00 20.00
2 Kyle Tucker/49 10.00 25.00
3 Ryan O'Hearn/49 4.00 10.00
4 Myles Straw/25 8.00 20.00
5 Garrett Hampson/25 8.00 20.00
6 Jake Cave/25 6.00 15.00
7 Yusei Kikuchi/49 6.00 15.00
8 Michael Kopech/49 12.00 30.00
9 Luis Urias/49 6.00 15.00
10 Jacob Nix/25 6.00 15.00
11 Cedric Mullins/25 15.00 40.00
12 Brandon Lowe/49 10.00 25.00
13 Rowdy Tellez/49 6.00 15.00
14 Vladimir Guerrero Jr./49 60.00 150.00
15 Fernando Tatis Jr./49 75.00 200.00

2019 Immaculate Collection Complete Quad Memorabilia Autographs

RANDOM INSERTS IN PACKS
STATED PRINT RUN 25 SER.#'d SETS
EXCHANGE DEADLINE 2/21/2021
1 Rhys Hoskins 15.00 40.00
2 Aaron Judge 50.00 120.00
3 Vladimir Guerrero Jr. 60.00 150.00
4 Dansby Swanson 8.00 20.00
5 David Dahl 5.00 12.00
6 Victor Robles 15.00 40.00
7 Alex Reyes 6.00 15.00
8 Josh Bell 6.00 15.00
9 Francisco Mejia 6.00 15.00
10 Walker Buehler 10.00 25.00

2019 Immaculate Collection Cowhide Memorabilia Autographs

RANDOM INSERTS IN PACKS
PRINT RUNS B/WN 5-25 COPIES PER
NO PRICING QTY 15 OR LESS
EXCHANGE DEADLINE 2/21/2021
1 Orlando Arcia/25 5.00 12.00
4 J.P. Crawford/25 5.00 12.00
5 Alex Reyes/25 6.00 15.00
6 Jake Bauers/25 8.00 20.00
7 Fergie Jenkins/20 15.00 40.00
9 Kerry Wood/25 12.00 30.00
14 Pete Alonso/25 60.00 150.00
16 Luis Severino/25 6.00 15.00
17 Michael Taylor/25 5.00 12.00
20 Nolan Ryan/25 50.00 120.00

2019 Immaculate Collection Dual Material Autographs

RANDOM INSERTS IN PACKS
PRINT RUNS B/WN 20-99 COPIES PER
EXCHANGE DEADLINE 2/21/2021
*GOLD/49: .5X TO 1.2X p/r 99
*GOLD/20-25: .5X TO 1.2X p/r 49
*GOLD/20-25: .4X TO 1X p/r 25
1 Cody Bellinger/49 50.00 120.00
2 Aaron Judge/25 60.00 150.00
3 Shohei Ohtani/25 75.00 200.00
4 Pedro Martinez/25 6.00 15.00
5 Frank Robinson/25 20.00 50.00
7 Steve Garvey/49 12.00 30.00
8 Larry Walker/25 25.00 60.00
9 Dale Murphy/49 15.00 40.00
10 Whit Merrifield/99 5.00 12.00
11 Trea Turner/49 5.00 12.00
14 Ken Griffey Jr./20 75.00 200.00
16 Ronald Acuna Jr./49 75.00 200.00
17 Jason Giambi/49 4.00 10.00
18 Miguel Andujar/49 6.00 15.00
19 Jose Abreu/25 8.00 20.00
20 Mitch Haniger/49 5.00 12.00

2019 Immaculate Collection Dugout Collection Dual Memorabilia Autographs

RANDOM INSERTS IN PACKS
PRINT RUNS B/WN 10-25 COPIES PER
NO PRICING QTY 15 OR LESS
EXCHANGE DEADLINE 2/21/2021
1 Stephen Gonsalves/25 5.00 12.00
2 Jonathan Loaisiga/25 6.00 15.00
3 Ramon Laureano/20 12.00 30.00
4 Kevin Kramer/25 6.00 15.00
5 Danny Jansen/25 5.00 12.00
6 Luis Urias/25 8.00 20.00
7 Steven Duggar/25 6.00 15.00
8 Jonathan Davis/25 6.00 15.00
9 Dakota Hudson/25 6.00 15.00
10 Patrick Wisdom/20 5.00 12.00
11 Kevin Newman/25 8.00 20.00
12 Reese McGuire/25 8.00 20.00
13 Justus Sheffield/25 8.00 20.00
14 Michael Kopech/25 15.00 40.00
15 Ryan Borucki/25 5.00 12.00
16 Sean Reid-Foley/25 5.00 12.00
17 Cionel Perez/25 5.00 12.00
18 Kyle Tucker/25 12.00 30.00
19 Caleb Ferguson/25 6.00 15.00
20 Carlos Correa/25 20.00 50.00
21 Edgar Martinez/25 10.00 25.00
23 Ivan Rodriguez/25 15.00 40.00
24 Yusei Kikuchi/25 8.00 20.00
25 Victor Robles/20 10.00 25.00
26 Ryan McMahon/25 8.00 20.00
27 Rhys Hoskins/25 10.00 25.00
28 Harrison Bader/25 6.00 15.00
29 David Dahl/25 5.00 12.00
30 Clint Frazier/25 6.00 15.00
31 Chance Sisco/25 5.00 12.00
32 Alex Reyes/20 6.00 15.00
33 Carson Fulmer/25 5.00 12.00
34 Dustin Fowler/25 5.00 12.00
35 Vladimir Guerrero Jr./20 60.00 150.00
36 Eloy Jimenez/25 20.00 50.00
37 Fernando Tatis Jr./25 60.00 150.00
38 Willie Calhoun/25 5.00 12.00
39 Zack Granite/20 5.00 12.00
40 Rowdy Tellez/25 8.00 20.00

2019 Immaculate Collection Extra Bases Triple Memorabilia Autographs

RANDOM INSERTS IN PACKS
PRINT RUNS B/WN 7-25 COPIES PER
NO PRICING QTY 15 OR LESS
EXCHANGE DEADLINE 2/21/2021
1 Jose Abreu/25 6.00 15.00
2 Miguel Andujar/25 8.00 20.00
3 Xander Bogaerts/25 25.00 60.00
4 Whit Merrifield/25 8.00 20.00
6 Rhys Hoskins/25 10.00 25.00
7 Nolan Arenado/49 25.00 60.00
8 Freddie Freeman/25 10.00 25.00
9 Pete Rose/25 15.00 40.00
10 Craig Biggio/25 15.00 40.00
13 Jose Ramirez/25 6.00 15.00
14 Matt Carpenter/25 8.00 20.00
15 Edgar Martinez/25 6.00 15.00
16 Jim Rice/25 6.00 15.00
18 Francisco Lindor/25 8.00 20.00
19 Juan Gonzalez/25 12.00 30.00
20 Vladimir Guerrero/25 12.00 30.00

2019 Immaculate Collection Hats Off Memorabilia Autographs

RANDOM INSERTS IN PACKS
PRINT RUNS B/WN 10-25 COPIES PER
NO PRICING QTY 15 OR LESS
EXCHANGE DEADLINE 2/21/2021
1 Carson Fulmer/25 5.00 12.00
2 Brendan Rodgers/25 8.00 20.00
3 Lewis Brinson/25 5.00 12.00
4 Yandy Diaz/25 6.00 15.00
5 Sean Newcomb/25 5.00 12.00
6 Lazaro Armenteros/25 6.00 15.00
7 Vladimir Guerrero Jr./25 30.00 80.00
8 Adrian Beltre/25 8.00 20.00
10 Craig Biggio/25 6.00 15.00
11 Robin Yount/25 8.00 20.00
15 Luis Severino/25 6.00 15.00
17 Estevan Florial/25 8.00 20.00
18 Luis Robert/25 60.00 150.00
19 Jo Adell/25 EXCH 25.00 60.00
20 Victor Victor Mesa/25 10.00 25.00

2019 Immaculate Collection Immaculate Doubles Memorabilia Autographs

RANDOM INSERTS IN PACKS
STATED PRINT RUN 99 SER.#'d SETS
EXCHANGE DEADLINE 2/21/2021
*GOLD: .5X TO 1.2X
1 Cedric Mullins 10.00 25.00
2 Enyel De Los Santos 3.00 8.00
3 Daniel Ponce de Leon 5.00 12.00
4 Jonathan Davis 4.00 10.00
5 Kevin Newman 5.00 12.00
6 Sean Reid-Foley 3.00 8.00
7 Garrett Hampson 5.00 12.00
8 Brad Keller 3.00 8.00

9 Chris Shaw 3.00 8.00
10 Kevin Kramer 4.00 10.00
11 Myles Straw 5.00 12.00
12 Ryan O'Hearn 3.00 8.00
13 Michael Kopech 10.00 25.00
14 Jake Cave 4.00 10.00
15 Corbin Burnes 10.00 25.00
16 Luis Urias 5.00 12.00
17 Justus Sheffield 5.00 12.00
18 Kyle Wright 5.00 12.00
19 Christin Stewart 4.00 10.00
20 Vladimir Guerrero Jr. 40.00 100.00
21 Touki Toussaint 4.00 10.00
22 Jake Bauers 5.00 12.00
23 Chance Adams 3.00 8.00
24 Stephen Gonsalves 3.00 8.00
25 Caleb Ferguson 4.00 10.00
26 Danny Jansen 3.00 8.00
27 Dennis Santana 3.00 8.00
28 Kyle Tucker 8.00 20.00
29 Rowdy Tellez 5.00 12.00
30 Jonathan Loaisiga 4.00 10.00
31 Eloy Jimenez 12.00 30.00
32 Cionel Perez 3.00 8.00
33 Steven Duggar 4.00 10.00
34 Taylor Ward 3.00 8.00
35 Jacob Nix 4.00 10.00
36 Patrick Wisdom 3.00 8.00
37 Dakota Hudson 4.00 10.00
38 Fernando Tatis Jr. 50.00 120.00
39 Framber Valdez 3.00 8.00
40 Bryse Wilson 4.00 10.00
41 Luis Ortiz 3.00 8.00
42 Ramon Laureano 8.00 20.00
43 Reese McGuire 5.00 12.00
44 Ryan Borucki 3.00 8.00
45 Jeff McNeil 8.00 20.00
46 Kolby Allard 5.00 12.00
47 David Fletcher 10.00 25.00
49 Brandon Lowe 8.00 20.00
50 Josh James 5.00 12.00

2019 Immaculate Collection Immaculate Duals Memorabilia

1 Mike Trout 15.00 40.00
2 Jose Altuve 2.50 6.00
3 Mookie Betts 8.00 20.00
4 Christian Yelich 4.00 10.00
5 Clayton Kershaw 5.00 12.00
6 Ronald Acuna Jr. 8.00 20.00
7 Nolan Arenado 5.00 12.00
8 Alex Bregman 3.00 8.00
9 Jose Ramirez 2.50 6.00
10 Freddie Freeman 4.00 10.00
11 Miguel Cabrera 3.00 8.00
12 Andrew Benintendi 3.00 8.00
13 Kris Bryant 6.00 15.00
14 Javier Baez 4.00 10.00
15 Aaron Judge 8.00 20.00
16 Shohei Ohtani 5.00 12.00
17 Max Scherzer 3.00 8.00
18 Jacob deGrom 6.00 15.00
19 Blake Snell 2.50 6.00
20 Chris Sale 3.00 8.00
21 Bryce Harper 5.00 12.00
22 Manny Machado 3.00 8.00
23 Juan Soto 10.00 25.00
24 Cody Bellinger 8.00 20.00
25 Gleyber Torres 6.00 15.00

2019 Immaculate Collection Immaculate Fives Memorabilia Autographs

RANDOM INSERTS IN PACKS
STATED PRINT RUN 99 SER.#'d SETS
EXCHANGE DEADLINE 2/21/2021
*GOLD: .5X TO 1.5X
1 Cedric Mullins 10.00 25.00
2 Brad Keller 3.00 8.00
3 Ryan O'Hearn 3.00 8.00
4 Michael Kopech 10.00 25.00
5 Corbin Burnes 10.00 25.00
6 Luis Urias 5.00 12.00
7 Justus Sheffield 5.00 12.00
8 Christin Stewart 4.00 10.00
9 Vladimir Guerrero Jr. 50.00 120.00
10 Jake Bauers 5.00 12.00
11 Danny Jansen 3.00 8.00
12 Kyle Tucker 8.00 20.00
13 Eloy Jimenez 12.00 30.00
14 Steven Duggar 4.00 10.00
15 Dakota Hudson 4.00 10.00
16 Fernando Tatis Jr. 60.00 150.00
17 Ramon Laureano 8.00 20.00
18 Jeff McNeil 8.00 20.00
19 David Fletcher 10.00 25.00
20 Nick Senzel 20.00 50.00

2019 Immaculate Collection Immaculate Jumbo

RANDOM INSERTS IN PACKS
PRINT RUNS B/WN 3-49 COPIES PER
NO PRICING QTY 15 OR LESS
1 Cedric Mullins/49 4.00 10.00
2 Enyel De Los Santos/49 2.00 5.00
3 Daniel Ponce de Leon/49 3.00 8.00
4 Jonathan Davis/49 2.50 6.00
5 Kevin Newman/49 3.00 8.00
6 Sean Reid-Foley/49 2.00 5.00
7 Garrett Hampson/49 3.00 8.00
8 Brad Keller/49 2.00 5.00
9 Chris Shaw/49 2.00 5.00
10 Kevin Kramer/49 2.50 6.00
11 Myles Straw/49 3.00 8.00
12 Ryan O'Hearn/49 2.00 5.00
13 Michael Kopech/49 6.00 15.00
14 Jake Cave/49 2.50 6.00
15 Corbin Burnes/49 5.00 12.00
16 Luis Urias/49 3.00 8.00
17 Justus Sheffield/49 3.00 8.00
18 Kyle Wright/49 3.00 8.00
19 Christin Stewart/49 2.50 6.00
20 Vladimir Guerrero Jr./49 12.00 30.00
21 Touki Toussaint/49 2.50 6.00
22 Jake Bauers/49 3.00 8.00
23 Chance Adams/49 2.00 5.00
24 Stephen Gonsalves/49 2.00 5.00
25 Caleb Ferguson/49 2.50 6.00
26 Danny Jansen/49 2.00 5.00
27 Dennis Santana/49 2.00 5.00
28 Kyle Tucker/49 5.00 12.00
29 Rowdy Tellez/49 3.00 8.00
30 Jonathan Loaisiga/49 2.50 6.00
31 Eloy Jimenez/49 8.00 20.00
32 Cionel Perez/49 2.00 5.00
33 Steven Duggar/49 2.50 6.00
34 Taylor Ward/49 2.00 5.00
35 Jacob Nix/49 2.50 6.00
36 Patrick Wisdom/49 2.00 5.00
37 Dakota Hudson/49 2.50 6.00
38 Fernando Tatis Jr./49 30.00 80.00
39 Framber Valdez/49 2.00 5.00
40 Bryse Wilson/49 2.50 6.00
41 Luis Ortiz/49 2.00 5.00
42 Ramon Laureano/49 4.00 10.00
43 Reese McGuire/49 3.00 8.00
44 Ryan Borucki/49 2.00 5.00
45 Jeff McNeil/49 5.00 12.00
46 Kolby Allard/49 3.00 8.00
47 David Fletcher/49 6.00 15.00
48 Nick Senzel/49 6.00 15.00
49 Brandon Lowe/49 3.00 8.00
50 Josh James/49 3.00 8.00
51 Wander Franco/49 40.00 100.00
52 Brendan McKay/49 3.00 8.00
53 Bo Bichette/49 20.00 50.00
54 Royce Lewis/49 4.00 10.00
56 Jo Adell/49 8.00 20.00
57 Estevan Florial/49 3.00 8.00
62 Gil Hodges/25 4.00 10.00
66 Adalberto Mondesi/49 2.50 6.00
67 Aaron Judge/49 15.00 40.00
68 Shohei Ohtani/49 12.00 30.00
69 Corey Seager/49 3.00 8.00
70 Rhys Hoskins/49 8.00 20.00
71 Rafael Devers/49 4.00 10.00
72 Eric Thames/49 2.00 5.00
76 Mike Piazza/31 5.00 12.00
77 Paul Molitor/49 3.00 8.00
79 Willie Stargell/49 2.50 6.00
80 Adrian Beltre/49 3.00 8.00
82 Ronald Acuna Jr./49 15.00 40.00
84 Don Mattingly/23 10.00 25.00
85 Mookie Betts/25 10.00 25.00
87 Tony Gwynn/49 15.00 40.00
88 Vladimir Guerrero/49 2.50 6.00
89 Carlos Correa/25 12.00 30.00
90 George Brett/25 10.00 25.00
91 Roberto Alomar/25 4.00 10.00
92 Gleyber Torres/49 6.00 15.00
93 Tyler O'Neill/49 2.50 6.00
94 Forrest Whitley/49 3.00 8.00
95 Victor Victor Mesa/49 4.00 10.00
96 Victor Mesa Jr./49 4.00 10.00
97 Yusei Kikuchi/49 3.00 8.00
98 Jesus Sanchez/49 3.00 8.00

2019 Immaculate Collection Immaculate Quads Memorabilia

RANDOM INSERTS IN PACKS
PRINT RUNS B/WN 5-49 COPIES PER
NO PRICING QTY 15 OR LESS
*RED/25: .6X TO 1.5X p/r 49
1 Matt Chapman/49 3.00 8.00
2 Ozzie Albies/49 3.00 8.00
3 Corbin Burnes/49 5.00 12.00
7 Mickey Mantle/49 25.00 60.00
9 Juan Soto/49 10.00 25.00
10 Corey Ray/49 2.00 5.00
11 Joey Gallo/49 2.50 6.00
12 Christian Yelich/49 8.00 20.00
13 Giancarlo Stanton/49 3.00 8.00
14 Jesus Aguilar/49 2.50 6.00
15 Bryce Harper/49 15.00 40.00
16 Eugenio Suarez/49 2.50 6.00
17 Miguel Andujar/49 3.00 8.00
18 Shohei Ohtani/49 12.00 30.00
19 Salvador Perez/49 2.50 6.00
20 Paul Goldschmidt/49 3.00 8.00
21 Corey Kluber/49 2.50 6.00
22 Jose Berrios/49 2.50 6.00
23 Edwin Diaz/49 2.50 6.00
24 Adalberto Mondesi/49 2.50 6.00
25 Gary Sanchez/49 3.00 8.00

2019 Immaculate Collection Immaculate Swatches

RANDOM INSERTS IN PACKS
STATED PRINT RUN 49 SER.#'d SETS
*BSBLLS: .6X TO 1.5X
1 Cedric Mullins 4.00 10.00
2 Enyel De Los Santos 2.00 5.00
3 Daniel Ponce de Leon 3.00 8.00
4 Jonathan Davis 2.50 6.00
5 Kevin Newman 3.00 8.00
6 Sean Reid-Foley 2.00 5.00
7 Garrett Hampson 3.00 8.00
8 Brad Keller 2.00 5.00
9 Chris Shaw 2.00 5.00
10 Kevin Kramer 2.50 6.00
11 Myles Straw 3.00 8.00
12 Ryan O'Hearn 2.00 5.00
13 Michael Kopech 6.00 15.00
14 Jake Cave 2.50 6.00
15 Corbin Burnes 5.00 12.00
16 Luis Urias 3.00 8.00
17 Justus Sheffield 3.00 8.00
18 Kyle Wright 3.00 8.00
19 Christin Stewart 2.50 6.00
20 Vladimir Guerrero Jr. 12.00 30.00
21 Touki Toussaint 2.50 6.00
22 Jake Bauers 3.00 8.00
23 Chance Adams 2.00 5.00
24 Stephen Gonsalves 2.00 5.00
25 Caleb Ferguson 2.50 6.00
26 Danny Jansen 2.00 5.00
27 Dennis Santana 2.00 5.00
28 Kyle Tucker 5.00 12.00
29 Rowdy Tellez 3.00 8.00
30 Jonathan Loaisiga 2.50 6.00
31 Eloy Jimenez 8.00 20.00
32 Cionel Perez 2.00 5.00
33 Steven Duggar 2.50 6.00
34 Taylor Ward 2.00 5.00
35 Jacob Nix 2.50 6.00
36 Patrick Wisdom 2.00 5.00
37 Dakota Hudson 2.50 6.00
38 Fernando Tatis Jr. 30.00 80.00
39 Framber Valdez 2.00 5.00
40 Bryse Wilson 2.50 6.00
41 Luis Ortiz 2.00 5.00
42 Ramon Laureano 4.00 10.00
43 Reese McGuire 3.00 8.00
44 Ryan Borucki 2.00 5.00
45 Jeff McNeil 5.00 12.00
46 Kolby Allard 3.00 8.00
47 David Fletcher 6.00 15.00
48 Nick Senzel 6.00 15.00
49 Brandon Lowe 3.00 8.00
50 Josh James 3.00 8.00
51 Jonathan Villar 2.00 5.00
52 Ketel Marte 2.50 6.00
53 Aaron Judge 8.00 20.00
54 Shohei Ohtani 5.00 12.00
55 Dee Gordon 2.00 5.00
56 Kevin Kiermaier 2.50 6.00
57 Charlie Blackmon 3.00 8.00
58 Brett Gardner 4.00 10.00
59 Marcus Semien 3.00 8.00
60 Kris Bryant 4.00 10.00
61 Francisco Lindor 3.00 8.00
62 Tim Anderson 3.00 8.00
63 Eric Hosmer 2.50 6.00
64 Starling Marte 2.50 6.00
65 George Springer 2.50 6.00
66 Jose Altuve 2.50 6.00
67 Lorenzo Cain 2.00 5.00
68 Francisco Mejia 2.50 6.00
69 Harrison Bader 2.50 6.00
70 Victor Robles 4.00 10.00
71 Willy Adames 2.00 5.00
72 Austin Meadows 3.00 8.00
73 Walker Buehler 4.00 10.00
74 Amed Rosario 2.50 6.00
75 Mike Trout 15.00 40.00

2019 Immaculate Collection Immaculate Triples Memorabilia

RANDOM INSERTS IN PACKS
PRINT RUNS B/WN 20-49 COPIES PER
*RED/25: .6X TO 1.5X p/r 49
1 Ken Griffey Jr./49 15.00 40.00
2 Vladimir Guerrero Jr./49 12.00 30.00
3 Fernando Tatis Jr./49 30.00 80.00
4 Eloy Jimenez/49 8.00 20.00
5 Jesus Luzardo/49 3.00 8.00
6 David Ortiz/49 6.00 15.00
7 Dale Murphy/49 3.00 8.00
8 Larry Walker/49 2.50 6.00
9 Mike Trout/49 20.00 50.00
10 Yusei Kikuchi/49 3.00 8.00
11 Randy Johnson/49 5.00 12.00
12 Dave Concepcion/20 3.00 8.00
13 Mike Mussina/49 2.50 6.00
14 Jose Abreu/49 3.00 8.00
15 John Smoltz/49 3.00 8.00
16 Pedro Martinez/49 2.50 6.00
17 Craig Biggio/49 2.50 6.00
18 Frank Robinson/49 10.00 25.00
19 Kyle Tucker/49 5.00 12.00
20 Mitch Haniger/49 2.50 6.00
21 Roberto Alomar/49 2.50 6.00
22 Mike Piazza/49 3.00 8.00
23 Michael Kopech/49 6.00 15.00
24 Cal Ripken/49 10.00 25.00
25 Luis Severino/49 2.50 6.00

2019 Immaculate Collection Jackets Autographs

RANDOM INSERTS IN PACKS
PRINT RUNS B/WN 20-49 COPIES PER
EXCHANGE DEADLINE 2/21/2021
1 Don Mattingly/25 25.00 60.00
2 Alex Reyes/25 6.00 15.00
3 Joe Morgan/20 6.00 15.00
4 Vladimir Guerrero/25 20.00 50.00
5 Amed Rosario/25 6.00 15.00
6 Chance Sisco/25 5.00 12.00
7 Dansby Swanson/25 8.00 20.00
8 David Dahl/25 5.00 12.00
9 Dustin Fowler/25 5.00 12.00
10 Harrison Bader/25 6.00 15.00
11 Walker Buehler/49 8.00 20.00
12 Willie Calhoun/25 5.00 12.00
13 Yoan Moncada/25 8.00 20.00
14 Carson Fulmer/25 5.00 12.00
15 Clint Frazier/49 8.00 20.00
16 Framber Valdez/25 5.00 12.00
17 Touki Toussaint/25 6.00 15.00
18 Luis Ortiz/25 5.00 12.00
19 Myles Straw/25 8.00 20.00
20 Taylor Ward/25 5.00 12.00

2019 Immaculate Collection Jumbo Jersey Autographs

RANDOM INSERTS IN PACKS
PRINT RUNS B/WN 5-25 COPIES PER
NO PRICING QTY 15 OR LESS
EXCHANGE DEADLINE 2/21/2021
1 Andrew Stevenson/25 5.00 12.00
2 Brandon Nimmo/25 6.00 15.00
3 Brandon Woodruff/25 8.00 20.00
7 Jackie Bradley Jr./25 8.00 20.00
10 Marcell Ozuna/25 8.00 20.00
11 Nelson Cruz/25 10.00 25.00
25 Scooter Gennett/25 6.00 15.00
32 Kerry Wood/25 8.00 20.00
38 Michael Chavis/25 8.00 20.00

2019 Immaculate Collection Legends Dual Materials

RANDOM INSERTS IN PACKS
PRINT RUNS B/WN 10-49 COPIES PER
NO PRICING QTY 15 OR LESS
*RED/25: .6X TO 1.5X p/r 49
3 Mickey Mantle/49 25.00 60.00
5 Yogi Berra/25 5.00 12.00
6 Ted Williams/25 25.00 60.00
7 Bob Turley/49 2.00 5.00
8 Reggie Jackson/49 2.50 6.00
9 Harmon Killebrew/25 5.00 12.00
10 Billy Williams/49 2.50 6.00
11 Orlando Cepeda/25 4.00 10.00
12 Tony Gwynn/49 8.00 20.00
13 Rod Carew/49 2.50 6.00
14 Nolan Ryan/49 10.00 25.00
15 Johnny Bench/49 10.00 25.00
16 Willie McCovey/49 8.00 20.00
17 Bobby Doerr/49 2.50 6.00
18 Larry Doby/49 2.50 6.00
19 Pete Rose/49 15.00 40.00
20 Mariano Rivera/49 4.00 10.00
21 Frank Robinson/49 8.00 20.00
22 George Brett/49 10.00 25.00
23 Bill Mazeroski/49 2.50 6.00
24 Cal Ripken/49 15.00 40.00
25 Ichiro/49 8.00 20.00

2019 Immaculate Collection Legends Materials

RANDOM INSERTS IN PACKS
PRINT RUNS B/WN 7-49 COPIES PER
NO PRICING QTY 15 OR LESS
*RED/25: .6X TO 1.5X
2 Billy Martin/49 2.50 6.00
3 Casey Stengel/49 2.50 6.00
4 Don Drysdale/49 2.50 6.00
5 Edd Roush/49 2.50 6.00
6 Gil Hodges/49 2.50 6.00
7 Herb Pennock/49 2.50 6.00
8 Leo Durocher/49 2.00 5.00
9 Mickey Mantle/49 25.00 60.00
12 Ted Williams/49 15.00 40.00
13 Yogi Berra/49 3.00 8.00
14 Richie Ashburn/49 2.50 6.00
15 Dom DiMaggio/49 2.00 5.00
16 Bob Lemon/49 2.50 6.00
17 Ralph Kiner/49 2.50 6.00
18 Duke Snider/49 2.50 6.00
19 Al Kaline/49 3.00 8.00
20 Nolan Ryan/49 10.00 25.00
21 Rod Carew/49 2.50 6.00
22 Al Simmons/25 4.00 10.00
23 Bob Meusel/49 2.00 5.00
25 Whitey Ford/49 2.50 6.00

2019 Immaculate Collection Matinee Dual Memorabilia Autographs

RANDOM INSERTS IN PACKS
PRINT RUNS B/WN 10-35 COPIES PER
NO PRICING QTY 15 OR LESS
EXCHANGE DEADLINE 2/21/2021
*RED/25: .4X TO 1X
1 Aaron Judge/20 50.00 120.00
2 Nomar Mazara/35 4.00 10.00
6 Barry Larkin/20 20.00 50.00
7 Amed Rosario/20 6.00 15.00
8 Rhys Hoskins/35 12.00 30.00
9 Adrian Beltre/20 8.00 20.00
10 Manny Machado/25 25.00 60.00

2019 Immaculate Collection Moments Memorabilia Autographs

RANDOM INSERTS IN PACKS
PRINT RUNS B/WN 5-25 COPIES PER
NO PRICING QTY 15 OR LESS
EXCHANGE DEADLINE 2/21/2021
6 Juan Marichal/25 15.00 40.00
7 Don Mattingly/25 25.00 60.00
13 John Smoltz/25 8.00 20.00
15 Vladimir Guerrero/25 10.00 25.00
16 Larry Walker/25 25.00 60.00
17 Carlton Fisk/25 15.00 40.00
19 Tommy Lasorda/25 25.00 60.00
20 Dave Winfield/25 12.00 30.00

2019 Immaculate Collection Old English Memorabilia Autographs

RANDOM INSERTS IN PACKS
PRINT RUNS B/WN 3-49 COPIES PER
NO PRICING QTY 17 OR LESS
EXCHANGE DEADLINE 2/21/2021
*RED/20-25: .5X TO 1.2X p/r 34-49
1 Andrew Benintendi/49 15.00 40.00
2 Miguel Andujar/49 10.00 25.00
3 Alex Verdugo/49 8.00 20.00
4 Harrison Bader/49 5.00 12.00
5 Rhys Hoskins/49 15.00 40.00
6 Shohei Ohtani/35 75.00 200.00
8 Josh Donaldson/34 15.00 40.00
9 Clint Frazier/49 5.00 12.00
12 Marcell Ozuna/49 10.00 25.00
13 Kyle Schwarber/17 8.00 20.00
15 Orlando Arcia/49 6.00 15.00
19 Shohei Ohtani/35 75.00 200.00

2019 Immaculate Collection Past and Present Dual Memorabilia Autographs

RANDOM INSERTS IN PACKS
PRINT RUNS B/WN 5-25 COPIES PER
NO PRICING QTY 15 OR LESS
EXCHANGE DEADLINE 2/21/2021
3 Eloy Jimenez/25 25.00 60.00
5 Justus Sheffield/25 10.00 25.00

2019 Immaculate Collection Premium Memorabilia Autographs

RANDOM INSERTS IN PACKS
PRINT RUNS B/WN 25-49 COPIES PER
EXCHANGE DEADLINE 2/21/2021
1 Joey Lucchesi/25 5.00 12.00
2 Francisco Mejia/25 6.00 15.00
3 Austin Riley/49 20.00 50.00
4 Bo Bichette/49 50.00 120.00
5 Ryan McMahon/25 8.00 20.00
6 Brian Anderson/49 4.00 10.00
7 Pete Alonso/25 100.00 250.00
8 Clint Frazier/25 10.00 25.00
9 Adalberto Mondesi/49 5.00 12.00
10 German Marquez/25 5.00 12.00
11 Brandon Woodruff/25 8.00 20.00
12 Lewis Brinson/25 5.00 12.00
13 Jose Berrios/49 5.00 12.00
14 Sean Manaea/25 5.00 12.00
15 Max Fried/25 8.00 20.00

2019 Immaculate Collection Prospect Patch Autographs

RANDOM INSERTS IN PACKS
PRINT RUNS B/WN 20-99 COPIES PER
EXCHANGE DEADLINE 2/21/2021
*GOLD/49: .5X TO 1.2X p/r 99
*GOLD/25: .5X TO 1.2X p/r 49
*GOLD/25: .4X TO 1X p/r 20-30
1 Corey Ray/30 5.00 12.00
3 Jon Duplantier/49 4.00 10.00
6 Mitch Keller/20 6.00 15.00
7 Ke'Bryan Hayes/25 15.00 40.00
8 Leody Taveras/49 6.00 15.00
10 Wander Franco/99 60.00 150.00
11 Sean Murphy/25 6.00 15.00
12 Ian Anderson/49 12.00 30.00
13 Austin Riley/20 25.00 60.00
14 Adbert Alzolay/49 4.00 10.00
15 Kyle Lewis/49 30.00 80.00
16 Julio Pablo Martinez/49 4.00 10.00
17 Khalil Lee/30 5.00 12.00
18 Bo Bichette/25 75.00 200.00
19 Forrest Whitley/25 8.00 20.00
20 Brent Honeywell/49 5.00 12.00

2019 Immaculate Collection Pure Memorabilia Autographs

RANDOM INSERTS IN PACKS
PRINT RUNS B/WN 10-49 COPIES PER
NO PRICING QTY 15 OR LESS
EXCHANGE DEADLINE 2/21/2021
1 Carlos Martinez/25 6.00 15.00
2 Forrest Whitley/25 8.00 20.00
3 Joey Votto/25 8.00 20.00
4 Ken Griffey Sr./25 5.00 12.00
5 Alan Trammell/25 20.00 50.00
6 Pete Alonso/49 50.00 120.00
7 Rafael Devers/25 15.00 40.00
8 Reggie Jackson/25 15.00 40.00
9 Ronald Acuna Jr./49 50.00 120.00
10 Sean Manaea/25 5.00 12.00
11 Trey Mancini/25 6.00 15.00
13 Keston Hiura/49 15.00 40.00
14 Fernando Tatis Jr./49 50.00 120.00
15 Vladimir Guerrero Jr./25 40.00 100.00

2019 Immaculate Collection Rookie Debut Dual Memorabilia Autographs

RANDOM INSERTS IN PACKS
PRINT RUNS B/WN 10-25 COPIES PER
NO PRICING QTY 15 OR LESS
EXCHANGE DEADLINE 2/21/2021
1 Ranger Suarez/25 5.00 12.00
2 Justin Williams/25 5.00 12.00
6 Victor Reyes/25 8.00 20.00
7 Jon Duplantier/25 5.00 12.00
10 Nick Margevicius/25 5.00 12.00
11 Kyle Zimmer/25 5.00 12.00
12 Jake Cave/25 6.00 15.00
13 Josh James/25 8.00 20.00
16 Jake Bauers/25 8.00 20.00
17 Corbin Burnes/25 15.00 40.00
18 Christin Stewart/25 6.00 15.00
22 Chance Adams/25 5.00 12.00
23 Touki Toussaint/25 6.00 15.00
24 Luis Urias/25 8.00 20.00
26 Ryan O'Hearn/25 5.00 12.00
27 Jonathan Loaisiga/25 6.00 15.00
28 Caleb Ferguson/25 6.00 15.00
29 Chris Paddack/25 15.00 40.00

2019 Immaculate Collection Rookie Matinee Dual Memorabilia Autographs

RANDOM INSERTS IN PACKS
PRINT RUNS B/WN 25-49 COPIES PER
EXCHANGE DEADLINE 2/21/2021
1 Jake Bauers/49 6.00 15.00
2 Reese McGuire/25 8.00 20.00
3 Luis Urias/49 6.00 15.00
4 Kyle Tucker/49 12.00 30.00
5 Cedric Mullins/25 15.00 40.00
6 Christin Stewart/49 5.00 12.00
7 Vladimir Guerrero Jr./49 60.00 150.00
8 Danny Jansen/49 4.00 10.00
9 Kevin Newman/25 8.00 20.00
10 Fernando Tatis Jr./49 75.00 200.00
11 Rowdy Tellez/49 6.00 15.00
12 Ryan O'Hearn/49 4.00 10.00
13 Steven Duggar/25 6.00 15.00
14 Brandon Lowe/49 10.00 25.00
15 David Fletcher/49 12.00 30.00
16 Jake Cave/25 6.00 15.00
17 Kevin Kramer/25 6.00 15.00
18 Myles Straw/25 8.00 20.00
19 Taylor Ward/25 5.00 12.00
20 Garrett Hampson/25 8.00 20.00

2019 Immaculate Collection Signatures

RANDOM INSERTS IN PACKS
PRINT RUNS B/WN 7-99 COPIES PER
NO PRICING QTY 15 OR LESS
EXCHANGE DEADLINE 2/21/2021
*GOLD/49: .5X TO 1.2X p/r 99
*GOLD/25: .5X TO 1.2X p/r 49
2 Cesar Hernandez/99 2.50 6.00
3 Whit Merrifield/99 8.00 20.00
4 David Ross/25 15.00 40.00
5 Mike Mussina/49 4.00 10.00
7 Pete Rose/25 20.00 50.00
8 Ted Simmons/49 20.00 50.00
9 Xander Bogaerts/49 12.00 30.00
10 Adrian Gonzalez/25 5.00 12.00
11 Alex Wood/99 2.50 6.00
12 Carlton Fisk/25 15.00 40.00
13 Fergie Jenkins/49 4.00 10.00
14 Carlos Martinez/49 4.00 10.00
15 Jose Berrios/49 4.00 10.00
17 Nomar Mazara/49 8.00 20.00
18 Tim Wakefield/49 8.00 20.00
21 Charlie Blackmon/49 8.00 20.00
22 Darryl Strawberry/49 3.00 8.00
23 Jose Ramirez/49 4.00 10.00
25 Omar Vizquel/49 6.00 15.00
26 Yadier Molina/25 8.00 20.00
27 Dale Murphy/49 10.00 25.00
30 Trea Turner/49 8.00 20.00
32 Francisco Lindor/25 12.00 30.00
33 Steve Garvey/49 12.00 30.00
34 Keith Hernandez/49 10.00 25.00
35 Rafael Devers/49 10.00 25.00
36 Rhys Hoskins/49 10.00 25.00
38 Jason Giambi/25 4.00 10.00
39 Kevin Mitchell/49 12.00 30.00
40 Ozzie Albies/49 12.00 30.00

2019 Immaculate Collection Team Heroes Dual Memorabilia Autographs

RANDOM INSERTS IN PACKS
PRINT RUNS B/WN 10-49 COPIES PER
NO PRICING QTY 15 OR LESS
EXCHANGE DEADLINE 2/21/2021
2 Scooter Gennett/20 6.00 15.00
3 Freddie Freeman/25 15.00 40.00
5 Nolan Arenado/20 25.00 60.00
6 Max Muncy/25 6.00 15.00
7 Eddie Rosario/20 6.00 15.00
8 Luis Severino/20 6.00 15.00
9 Jacob deGrom/25 20.00 50.00
10 George Springer/25 15.00 40.00
11 Anthony Rizzo/20 12.00 30.00
12 Mitch Haniger/49 5.00 12.00
13 Matt Olson/25 10.00 25.00
14 Jose Ramirez/25 6.00 15.00
15 Chris Sale/25 8.00 20.00

2019 Immaculate Collection Winter Collection Triple Memorabilia Autographs

RANDOM INSERTS IN PACKS
STATED PRINT RUN 25 SER.#'d SETS
EXCHANGE DEADLINE 2/21/2021
1 Bryse Wilson 6.00 15.00
2 Kolby Allard 8.00 20.00
3 Cedric Mullins 10.00 25.00
4 Jake Bauers 8.00 20.00
5 Garrett Hampson 8.00 20.00
6 Christin Stewart 6.00 15.00
7 Josh James 8.00 20.00
8 Brad Keller 5.00 12.00
9 Ryan O'Hearn 5.00 12.00
10 David Fletcher 15.00 40.00
11 Dennis Santana 5.00 12.00
12 Corbin Burnes 15.00 40.00
13 Jake Cave 6.00 15.00
14 Jeff McNeil 12.00 30.00
15 Chance Adams 5.00 12.00
16 Enyel De Los Santos 5.00 12.00
17 Jacob Nix 6.00 15.00
18 Chris Shaw 5.00 12.00
19 Daniel Ponce de Leon 8.00 20.00
20 Brandon Lowe 12.00 30.00

2020 Immaculate Collection

RANDOM INSERTS IN PACKS
NO PRICING QTY 15 OR LESS
1-100 PRINT RUN B/TW 10-99 COPIES PER
101-161 STATED PRINT RUN 99 SER.#'d SETS
1 Max Fried JSY/99 3.00 8.00
2 Yogi Berra JSY/25 10.00 25.00
3 Michael Brantley JSY/99 2.50 6.00
4 Vladimir Guerrero Jr. JSY/99 8.00 20.00
5 Juan Soto JSY/99 6.00 15.00
6 Cody Bellinger JSY/99 6.00 15.00
7 Mickey Mantle JSY/49 20.00 50.00
8 Freddie Freeman JSY/99 6.00 15.00
9 Josh Donaldson JSY/99 2.50 6.00
10 Bryce Harper JSY/99 10.00 25.00
11 Josh Bell JSY/99 2.50 6.00
12 Aaron Nola JSY/49 3.00 8.00
13 Ronald Acuna Jr. JSY/99 10.00 25.00
14 Ted Williams JSY/49 20.00 50.00
15 Rafael Devers JSY/99 6.00 15.00
16 Jim Thome JSY/99 2.50 6.00
17 Leo Durocher JSY/99 2.00 5.00
18 Andrew Benintendi JSY/99 3.00 8.00
19 Herb Pennock JSY/49 8.00 20.00
20 Nelson Cruz JSY/99 3.00 8.00
21 Giancarlo Stanton JSY/99 3.00 8.00
22 Anthony Rizzo JSY/99 4.00 10.00
23 Justin Verlander JSY/99 3.00 8.00
24 Rhys Hoskins JSY/99 4.00 10.00
26 Pete Alonso JSY/49 10.00 25.00
27 Alex Bregman JSY/99 3.00 8.00
28 Max Scherzer JSY/25 5.00 12.00
29 Chris Sale JSY/99 3.00 8.00
30 Yoan Moncada JSY/99 3.00 8.00
31 Edd Roush JSY/25 12.00 30.00
32 Shohei Ohtani JSY/99 6.00 15.00
33 Tim Anderson JSY/99 3.00 8.00
34 Roy Campanella JSY/49 6.00 15.00
35 Stephen Strasburg JSY/99 3.00 8.00
36 Jeff Bagwell JSY/99 5.00 12.00
37 Josh Hader JSY/99 2.50 6.00
38 Matt Chapman JSY/99 3.00 8.00
39 Albert Pujols JSY/99 4.00 10.00
41 Mookie Betts JSY/99 8.00 20.00
42 Noah Syndergaard JSY/99 2.50 6.00
44 Matt Olson JSY/99 3.00 8.00
45 Jonathan Villar JSY/49 2.50 6.00
47 Jack Flaherty JSY/99 3.00 8.00
49 Tony Lazzeri JSY/25 12.00 30.00
50 Alan Trammell JSY/99 8.00 20.00
51 Jose Altuve JSY/99 2.50 6.00
53 Eloy Jimenez JSY/99 4.00 10.00
54 Tim Raines JSY/99 2.50 6.00
55 Charlie Blackmon JSY/25 5.00 12.00
56 Chris Paddack JSY/99 3.00 8.00
57 Keston Hiura JSY/99 4.00 10.00
59 Joey Gallo JSY/99 3.00 8.00
60 Nolan Arenado JSY/99 5.00 12.00
61 Mike Trout JSY/99 40.00 100.00
62 Jacob deGrom JSY/49 8.00 20.00
63 Adalberto Mondesi JSY/99 2.50 6.00
64 Walker Buehler JSY/99 4.00 10.00
65 Gary Sanchez JSY/99 3.00 8.00
66 Ozzie Albies JSY/99 3.00 8.00
67 Aaron Judge JSY/99 8.00 20.00
68 Starling Marte JSY/99 2.50 6.00
69 Roberto Clemente JSY/49 30.00 80.00
70 Ron Santo JSY/49 10.00 25.00
71 Marcell Ozuna JSY/99 3.00 8.00
72 Fernando Tatis Jr. JSY/99 8.00 20.00
73 George Springer JSY/99 2.50 6.00
74 Kris Bryant JSY/99 4.00 10.00
75 Trea Turner JSY/99 2.50 6.00
76 Christian Yelich JSY/49 5.00 12.00
77 Ken Boyer JSY/25 6.00 15.00
78 Whit Merrifield JSY/99 3.00 8.00
79 Trevor Story JSY/99 3.00 8.00
80 George Brett JSY/49 12.00 30.00
81 Jose Berrios JSY/99 2.50 6.00
82 Trey Mancini JSY/99 3.00 8.00
83 Gil Hodges JSY/49 5.00 12.00
84 Jose Ramirez JSY/99 2.50 6.00
85 Eddie Rosario JSY/99 2.50 6.00
86 Paul Goldschmidt JSY/99 3.00 8.00
87 Clayton Kershaw JSY/99 5.00 12.00
88 Manny Machado JSY/99 3.00 8.00
89 Gleyber Torres JSY/99 6.00 15.00
90 Stan Musial JSY/49 10.00 25.00
91 Xander Bogaerts JSY/99 3.00 8.00
92 Craig Biggio JSY/99 2.50 6.00
93 Blake Snell JSY/49 3.00 8.00
94 Gerrit Cole JSY/99 5.00 12.00
95 Frank Chance JSY/25 6.00 15.00
96 Javier Baez JSY/99 4.00 10.00
97 Jorge Soler JSY/99 3.00 8.00
98 Austin Meadows JSY/99 3.00 8.00
99 Ramon Laureano JSY/99 2.50 6.00
100 J.D. Martinez JSY/99 3.00 8.00
101 Matt Thaiss JSY AU/99 RC 4.00 10.00
102 Jonathan Hernandez JSY AU/99 RC 3.00 8.00
103 Deivy Grullon JSY AU/99 RC 3.00 8.00
104 Jordan Yamamoto JSY AU/99 RC 3.00 8.00
105 Edwin Rios JSY AU/99 RC 8.00 20.00
106 Lewis Thorpe JSY AU/99 RC 3.00 8.00
107 Nick Solak JSY AU/99 RC 10.00 25.00
108 Zac Gallen JSY AU/99 RC 8.00 20.00
109 Jake Fraley JSY AU/99 RC 4.00 10.00
110 Tyrone Taylor JSY AU/99 RC 3.00 8.00
111 A.J. Puk JSY AU/99 RC 12.00 30.00
112 Patrick Sandoval JSY AU/99 RC 5.00 12.00
113 Randy Arozarena JSY AU/99 RC 40.00 100.00
114 Domingo Leyba JSY AU/99 RC 4.00 10.00
115 Dylan Cease JSY AU/99 RC 5.00 12.00
116 Anthony Kay JSY AU/99 RC 3.00 8.00
117 Gavin Lux JSY AU/99 RC 30.00 80.00
118 Michael King JSY AU/99 RC 5.00 12.00
119 Joe Palumbo JSY AU/99 RC 3.00 8.00
120 Jake Rogers JSY AU/99 RC 3.00 8.00
121 Danny Mendick JSY AU/99 RC 4.00 10.00
122 Sean Murphy JSY AU/99 RC 5.00 12.00
123 Isan Diaz JSY AU/99 RC 5.00 12.00
124 Bobby Bradley JSY AU/99 RC 3.00 8.00
126 Bo Bichette JSY AU/99 RC 40.00 100.00
127 Dustin May JSY AU/99 RC 20.00 50.00
128 Andres Munoz JSY AU/99 RC 5.00 12.00
129 Josh Rojas JSY AU/99 RC 3.00 8.00
130 Kyle Lewis JSY AU/99 RC 25.00 60.00
131 Logan Webb JSY AU/99 RC 5.00 12.00
132 Brusdar Graterol JSY AU/99 RC 5.00 12.00
133 Bryan Abreu JSY AU/99 RC 3.00 8.00
134 Aristides Aquino JSY AU/99 RC 15.00 40.00
135 Tony Gonsolin JSY AU/99 RC 12.00 30.00
136 Sheldon Neuse JSY AU/99 RC 4.00 10.00
137 Brendan McKay JSY AU/99 RC 5.00 12.00
138 Logan Allen JSY AU/99 RC 3.00 8.00
139 Zack Collins JSY AU/99 RC 10.00 25.00
140 Abraham Toro JSY AU/99 RC 4.00 10.00
141 Adbert Alzolay JSY AU/99 RC 6.00 15.00
142 Donnie Walton JSY AU/99 RC 6.00 15.00
143 Jesus Luzardo JSY AU/99 RC 6.00 15.00
144 Aaron Civale JSY AU/99 RC 6.00 15.00
145 Nico Hoerner JSY AU/99 RC 15.00 40.00
146 Michel Baez JSY AU/99 RC 3.00 8.00
147 Justin Dunn JSY AU/99 RC 10.00 25.00
148 Mauricio Dubon JSY AU/99 RC 4.00 10.00
149 T.J. Zeuch JSY AU/99 RC 3.00 8.00
150 Sam Hilliard JSY AU/99 RC 5.00 12.00
151 Rico Garcia JSY AU/99 RC 5.00 12.00
152 Willi Castro JSY AU/99 RC 10.00 25.00
153 Tres Barrera JSY AU/99 RC 6.00 15.00
154 Yordan Alvarez JSY AU/99 RC 25.00 60.00
155 Ronald Bolanos JSY AU/99 RC 3.00 8.00
156 Jaylin Davis JSY AU/99 RC 5.00 12.00
157 Trent Grisham JSY AU/99 RC 25.00 60.00
158 Adrian Morejon JSY AU/99 RC 3.00 8.00
159 Travis Demeritte JSY AU/99 RC 5.00 12.00
160 Brock Burke JSY AU/99 RC 3.00 8.00
161 Yonathan Daza JSY AU/99 RC 4.00 10.00

2020 Immaculate Collection Red

*RED 1-100/49: .5X TO 1.2X
*RED 1-100/25: .6X TO 1.5X
*RED 101-161/49: .6X TO 1.2X
RANDOM INSERTS IN PACKS
PRINT RUNS B/WN 10-49 COPIES PER
NO PRICING QTY 15 OR LESS
7 Mickey Mantle JSY/25 30.00 80.00
14 Ted Williams JSY/25 30.00 80.00
83 Gil Hodges JSY/25 10.00 25.00
90 Stan Musial JSY/25 20.00 50.00
130 Kyle Lewis JSY AU/49 40.00 100.00

2020 Immaculate Collection Batting Stance Memorabilia Autographs

RANDOM INSERTS IN PACKS
PRINT RUNS B/WN 10-25 COPIES PER
NO PRICING QTY 15 OR LESS
EXCHANGE DEADLINE 2/21/2022
4 Deivy Grullon/25 5.00 12.00
6 Randy Arozarena/25 60.00 150.00
7 Nick Solak/25 10.00 25.00
8 Sheldon Neuse/25 6.00 15.00
9 Jaylin Davis/25 8.00 20.00
10 Mauricio Dubon/25 6.00 15.00
12 Jake Fraley/25 6.00 15.00
14 Bo Bichette/25 60.00 150.00
15 Isan Diaz/25 8.00 20.00
16 Sean Murphy/25 8.00 20.00

2020 Immaculate Collection Clearly Clutch Rookies Dual Memorabilia Autographs

RANDOM INSERTS IN PACKS
STATED PRINT RUN 25 SER.#'d SETS
EXCHANGE DEADLINE 2/21/2022
1 Bobby Bradley 3.00 8.00
2 Travis Demeritte 5.00 12.00
3 Nick Solak 6.00 15.00
4 Yonathan Daza 4.00 10.00
5 Zack Collins 4.00 10.00
6 Jake Rogers 3.00 8.00
7 Sean Murphy 5.00 12.00
8 Aristides Aquino 8.00 20.00
9 Sam Hilliard 5.00 12.00
10 Yordan Alvarez 25.00 60.00
12 Kyle Lewis 25.00 60.00
13 Randy Arozarena 40.00 100.00
14 Nico Hoerner 15.00 40.00
15 Willi Castro 5.00 12.00
16 Gavin Lux 15.00 40.00
17 Mauricio Dubon 4.00 10.00
18 Bo Bichette 40.00 100.00
19 Isan Diaz 5.00 12.00
20 Yu Chang 5.00 12.00

2020 Immaculate Collection Clutch Dual Memorabilia Autographs

RANDOM INSERTS IN PACKS
PRINT RUNS B/WN 10-49 COPIES PER
NO PRICING QTY 15 OR LESS
*BLUE/25: .5X TO 1.2X p/r 49
1 Aaron Judge/25 60.00 150.00
2 Billy Williams/15
3 Alex Rodriguez/15
4 Roberto Alomar/24 15.00 40.00
5 Gerrit Cole/15
6 Ryan Braun/15
7 Dallas Keuchel/10
8 Robinson Cano/10
9 Dennis Eckersley/15
10 Rickey Henderson/25 50.00 120.00
11 Dylan Carlson/49 15.00 40.00
12 Reggie Jackson/15
13 Evan Longoria/15
14 Orlando Cepeda/10
15 Fergie Jenkins/49 6.00 15.00
16 Nelson Cruz/22 8.00 20.00
17 Jim Palmer/14
18 Marcell Ozuna/15
19 Jorge Soler/49 6.00 15.00
20 Josh Donaldson/26 12.00 30.00

2020 Immaculate Collection Clutch Rookies Dual Memorabilia Autographs

RANDOM INSERTS IN PACKS
STATED PRINT RUN 49 SER.#'d SETS
EXCHANGE DEADLINE 2/21/2022
*BLUE/25: .5X TO 1.2X
1 Bobby Bradley 4.00 10.00
2 Travis Demeritte 6.00 15.00
3 Nick Solak 6.00 15.00
4 Yonathan Daza 5.00 12.00
5 Zack Collins 6.00 15.00
6 Jake Rogers 4.00 10.00
7 Sean Murphy 6.00 15.00
8 Aristides Aquino 10.00 25.00
9 Sam Hilliard 6.00 15.00
10 Yordan Alvarez 30.00 80.00
12 Kyle Lewis 30.00 80.00
13 Randy Arozarena 50.00 120.00
14 Nico Hoerner 20.00 50.00
15 Willi Castro 6.00 15.00
16 Gavin Lux 20.00 50.00
17 Mauricio Dubon 5.00 12.00
18 Bo Bichette 50.00 120.00
19 Isan Diaz 6.00 15.00
20 Yu Chang 6.00 15.00

2020 Immaculate Collection Debut Jumbo Material Autographs

RANDOM INSERTS IN PACKS
STATED PRINT RUN 99 SER.#'d SETS
EXCHANGE DEADLINE 2/21/2022
*HOLO GOLD/50-73: .4X TO 1X
*HOLO GOLD/39-49: .5X TO 1.2X
*HOLO GOLD/19-31: .6X TO 1.5X
*RED/35-49: .5X TO 1.2X
*HOLO SLVR/25: .6X TO 1.5X
1 Adbert Alzolay 4.00 10.00
2 Tres Barrera 6.00 15.00
3 Andres Munoz 5.00 12.00
4 Tyrone Taylor 3.00 8.00
5 Danny Mendick 4.00 10.00
6 Lewis Thorpe 3.00 8.00
7 Deivy Grullon 3.00 8.00
8 Travis Demeritte 5.00 12.00
9 Domingo Leyba 4.00 10.00
10 T.J. Zeuch 3.00 8.00
11 Donnie Walton 8.00 20.00
12 Ronald Bolanos 3.00 8.00
13 Edwin Rios 8.00 20.00
14 Rico Garcia 5.00 12.00
15 Jaylin Davis 5.00 12.00
16 Randy Arozarena 40.00 100.00
17 Jonathan Hernandez 3.00 8.00
18 Josh Rojas 3.00 8.00
19 Patrick Sandoval 5.00 12.00

2020 Immaculate Collection Debut Moments Memorabilia Autographs

RANDOM INSERTS IN PACKS
STATED PRINT RUN 49 SER.#'d SETS
EXCHANGE DEADLINE 2/21/2022
*BLUE/25: .5X TO 1.2X
1 Matt Thaiss 5.00 12.00
2 Jonathan Hernandez 4.00 10.00
3 Edwin Rios 10.00 25.00
4 Nick Solak 8.00 20.00
5 Jake Fraley 5.00 12.00
6 A.J. Puk 6.00 15.00
7 Randy Arozarena 50.00 120.00
8 Dylan Cease 6.00 15.00
9 Gavin Lux 20.00 50.00
10 Joe Palumbo 4.00 10.00
11 Danny Mendick 5.00 12.00
12 Isan Diaz 10.00 25.00
13 Yu Chang 6.00 15.00
14 Dustin May 25.00 60.00
15 Josh Rojas 4.00 10.00
16 Logan Webb 6.00 15.00
17 Bryan Abreu 4.00 10.00
18 Tony Gonsolin 8.00 20.00
19 Brendan McKay 6.00 15.00
20 Zack Collins 5.00 12.00
21 Adbert Alzolay 5.00 12.00
22 Jesus Luzardo 8.00 20.00
23 Nico Hoerner 20.00 50.00
24 Justin Dunn 5.00 12.00
25 T.J. Zeuch 4.00 10.00
26 Rico Garcia 6.00 15.00
27 Tres Barrera 8.00 20.00
28 Ronald Bolanos 4.00 10.00
30 Travis Demeritte 6.00 15.00
31 Yonathan Daza 5.00 12.00
32 Brock Burke 4.00 10.00
33 Adrian Morejon 4.00 10.00
34 Jaylin Davis 6.00 15.00
35 Yordan Alvarez 30.00 80.00
36 Willi Castro 6.00 15.00
37 Sam Hilliard 6.00 15.00
38 Mauricio Dubon 5.00 12.00
39 Michel Baez 4.00 10.00
40 Aaron Civale 8.00 20.00
41 Donnie Walton 10.00 25.00
42 Abraham Toro 5.00 12.00
43 Logan Allen 4.00 10.00
44 Sheldon Neuse 5.00 12.00
45 Aristides Aquino 10.00 25.00
46 Brusdar Graterol 6.00 15.00
47 Kyle Lewis 30.00 80.00
48 Andres Munoz 6.00 15.00
49 Bo Bichette 50.00 120.00
50 Bobby Bradley 4.00 10.00
51 Sean Murphy 6.00 15.00
52 Jake Rogers 4.00 10.00
53 Michael King 6.00 15.00
54 Anthony Kay 4.00 10.00
55 Domingo Leyba 5.00 12.00
56 Patrick Sandoval 6.00 15.00
57 Tyrone Taylor 4.00 10.00
58 Zac Gallen 10.00 25.00
59 Deivy Grullon 4.00 10.00
60 Jordan Yamamoto 10.00 25.00

2020 Immaculate Collection Debut Moments Memorabilia Leather Autographs

RANDOM INSERTS IN PACKS
STATED PRINT RUN 99 SER.#'d SETS
EXCHANGE DEADLINE 2/21/2022
*BROWN/49: .5X TO 1.2X
1 Matt Thaiss 4.00 10.00
2 Jonathan Hernandez 3.00 8.00
3 Edwin Rios 8.00 20.00
4 Nick Solak 6.00 15.00
5 Jake Fraley 4.00 10.00
6 A.J. Puk 5.00 12.00
7 Randy Arozarena 40.00 100.00
8 Dylan Cease 5.00 12.00
9 Gavin Lux 15.00 40.00
10 Joe Palumbo 3.00 8.00
11 Danny Mendick 4.00 10.00
12 Isan Diaz 5.00 12.00
13 Yu Chang 5.00 12.00
15 Josh Rojas 3.00 8.00
16 Logan Webb 5.00 12.00
17 Bryan Abreu 3.00 8.00
18 Tony Gonsolin 12.00 30.00
19 Brendan McKay 5.00 12.00
20 Zack Collins 4.00 10.00
21 Adbert Alzolay 10.00 25.00
22 Jesus Luzardo 6.00 15.00
23 Nico Hoerner 15.00 40.00
24 Justin Dunn 4.00 10.00
25 T.J. Zeuch 3.00 8.00
26 Rico Garcia 5.00 12.00
27 Tres Barrera 6.00 15.00
28 Ronald Bolanos 3.00 8.00
30 Travis Demeritte 5.00 12.00
31 Yonathan Daza 4.00 10.00
32 Brock Burke 3.00 8.00
33 Adrian Morejon 3.00 8.00
34 Jaylin Davis 5.00 12.00
35 Yordan Alvarez 25.00 60.00
36 Willi Castro 5.00 12.00
37 Sam Hilliard 5.00 12.00
38 Mauricio Dubon 4.00 10.00
39 Michel Baez 3.00 8.00
40 Aaron Civale 6.00 15.00
41 Donnie Walton 8.00 20.00
42 Abraham Toro 4.00 10.00
43 Logan Allen 3.00 8.00
44 Sheldon Neuse 4.00 10.00
45 Aristides Aquino 8.00 20.00
46 Brusdar Graterol 5.00 12.00
47 Kyle Lewis 25.00 60.00
48 Andres Munoz 5.00 12.00
49 Bo Bichette 40.00 100.00
50 Bobby Bradley 3.00 8.00
51 Sean Murphy 5.00 12.00
52 Jake Rogers 6.00 15.00
53 Michael King 5.00 12.00
54 Anthony Kay 3.00 8.00
55 Domingo Leyba 4.00 10.00
56 Patrick Sandoval 5.00 12.00
57 Tyrone Taylor 3.00 8.00
58 Zac Gallen 8.00 20.00
59 Deivy Grullon 3.00 8.00
60 Jordan Yamamoto 3.00 8.00

2020 Immaculate Collection Dugout Collection Dual Memorabilia Autographs

RANDOM INSERTS IN PACKS
STATED PRINT RUN 25 SER.#'d SETS
EXCHANGE DEADLINE 2/21/2022
1 Bobby Bradley 5.00 12.00
2 Domingo Leyba 6.00 15.00
6 Jake Fraley 6.00 15.00
8 Rico Garcia 8.00 20.00
9 Jonathan Hernandez 5.00 12.00
10 Justin Dunn 6.00 15.00
11 Matt Thaiss 6.00 15.00
12 Tony Gonsolin 20.00 50.00
13 Yonathan Daza 6.00 15.00
14 Jordan Yamamoto 5.00 12.00
18 T.J. Zeuch 5.00 12.00
19 Anthony Kay 5.00 12.00
20 Adrian Morejon 5.00 12.00

2020 Immaculate Collection Extra Bases Triple Memorabilia Autographs

RANDOM INSERTS IN PACKS
PRINT RUNS B/WN 10-25 COPIES PER
NO PRICING QTY 15 OR LESS
EXCHANGE DEADLINE 2/21/2022
1 Brandon Lowe/25 12.00 30.00
2 Dakota Hudson/25 15.00 40.00
3 Victor Mesa Jr./25 12.00 30.00
4 Evan White/25 12.00 30.00
5 Kyle Tucker/25 20.00 50.00
6 Kevin Newman/25 10.00 25.00
7 Ryan Mountcastle/25 25.00 60.00
8 Jonathan Loaisiga/25 6.00 15.00
9 Estevan Florial/25 20.00 50.00
10 Mike Soroka/25 30.00 80.00
11 Ryan O'Hearn/25 8.00 20.00
12 Jordan Hicks/25 6.00 15.00
13 Garrett Hampson/25 5.00 12.00
14 Cavan Biggio/25 20.00 50.00
15 Daniel Ponce de Leon/25 8.00 20.00
16 Christin Stewart/25 5.00 12.00
17 Ian Anderson/25 25.00 60.00
18 David Fletcher/25 12.00 30.00
19 Josh James/25 5.00 12.00
20 Alex Reyes/25 6.00 15.00
21 Vladimir Guerrero Jr./25 25.00 60.00
22 Michael Chavis/25 15.00 40.00
23 Alex Kirilloff/25 20.00 50.00
24 Yadier Molina/25 40.00 100.00
25 Austin Riley/25 10.00 25.00
28 Dylan Carlson/25 20.00 50.00
29 Andy Pettitte/25 12.00 30.00

2020 Immaculate Collection Flannel Sigs

RANDOM INSERTS IN PACKS
STATED PRINT RUN 25 SER.#'d SETS
EXCHANGE DEADLINE 2/21/2022
1 Adbert Alzolay 6.00 15.00
2 Nico Hoerner 25.00 60.00
3 Willi Castro 8.00 20.00
4 Brusdar Graterol 8.00 20.00
6 Deivi Garcia 40.00 100.00
7 Estevan Florial 20.00 50.00
8 Jasson Dominguez EXCH 125.00 300.00
9 Michael King 8.00 20.00
10 Adonis Medina 8.00 20.00
12 Deivy Grullon 5.00 12.00
13 Johan Rojas 10.00 25.00

2020 Immaculate Collection Hats Off Memorabilia Autographs

RANDOM INSERTS IN PACKS
PRINT RUNS B/WN 10-25 COPIES PER
NO PRICING QTY 15 OR LESS
EXCHANGE DEADLINE 2/21/2022
4 Joey Bart/25 25.00 60.00
11 Casey Mize/25 25.00 60.00

2020 Immaculate Collection Ichiro Tribute

RANDOM INSERTS IN PACKS
STATED PRINT RUN 51 SER.#'d SETS
1 Ichiro 8.00 20.00

2020 Immaculate Collection Immaculate Duals Memorabilia

RANDOM INSERTS IN PACKS
PRINT RUNS B/WN 10-49 COPIES PER
NO PRICING QTY 15 OR LESS
1 Tim Anderson/49 4.00 10.00
2 Rafael Devers/49 5.00 12.00
3 Mike Trout/49 20.00 50.00
4 Nelson Cruz/49 4.00 10.00
5 Alex Bregman/49 4.00 10.00
6 George Springer/49 3.00 8.00
7 Jose Abreu/49 4.00 10.00
8 Greg Maddux/49 5.00 12.00
9 Lou Brock/49 8.00 20.00
10 Ozzie Smith/49 5.00 12.00
11 Richie Ashburn/10
12 Bert Blyleven/49 3.00 8.00
13 Fergie Jenkins/49 3.00 8.00
14 Brooks Robinson/10
15 Craig Biggio/49 3.00 8.00
16 Pete Alonso/49 10.00 25.00
17 Ronald Acuna Jr./49 8.00 20.00
18 Juan Soto/49 8.00 20.00
19 Christian Yelich/49 5.00 12.00
20 Nolan Arenado/49 6.00 15.00
21 Cody Bellinger/49 8.00 20.00
22 Keston Hiura/49 5.00 12.00
23 Vladimir Guerrero Jr./49 6.00 15.00
24 Gleyber Torres/49 8.00 20.00
25 Joey Votto/49 4.00 10.00
26 Buster Posey/49 5.00 12.00
27 Jose Ramirez/49 3.00 8.00
28 Starling Marte/49 3.00 8.00
29 Marcell Ozuna/49 4.00 10.00
30 Chris Paddack/49 4.00 10.00
32 Xander Bogaerts/49 4.00 10.00
33 Brandon Lowe/49 3.00 8.00
34 Larry Walker/49 3.00 8.00
35 Mookie Betts/49 10.00 25.00

2020 Immaculate Collection Immaculate Duals Memorabilia Blue

*RED/25: .5X TO 1.2X p/r 49
RANDOM INSERTS IN PACKS
PRINT RUNS B/WN 5-25 COPIES PER
NO PRICING QTY 15 OR LESS
9 Lou Brock/25 12.00 30.00
32 Xander Bogaerts/20 10.00 25.00

2020 Immaculate Collection Immaculate Signatures

RANDOM INSERTS IN PACKS
PRINT RUNS B/WN 10-99 COPIES PER
NO PRICING QTY 15 OR LESS
EXCHANGE DEADLINE 2/21/2022
*HOLO SLVR/25: .6X TO 1.5X p/r 99
7 Aaron Judge/25 60.00 150.00
8 Yoshitomo Tsutsugo/99 10.00 25.00
9 Dale Murphy/49 15.00 40.00
10 Eloy Jimenez/49 10.00 25.00
11 Andre Dawson/25 12.00 30.00
12 Fernando Tatis Jr./99 60.00 150.00
13 Frank Thomas/49 25.00 60.00
14 J.D. Martinez/49 10.00 25.00
16 Kenny Lofton/49 8.00 20.00
17 Matt Chapman/25 10.00 25.00
19 Pete Alonso/99 30.00 80.00
21 Reggie Jackson/25 EXCH 15.00 40.00
22 Ronald Acuna Jr./49 50.00 120.00
23 Wade Boggs/25 15.00 40.00
24 Tony Perez/25 25.00 60.00
25 Trevor Hoffman/25 5.00 12.00
27 Pete Rose/25 50.00 120.00
28 Elroy Face/25 8.00 20.00
30 Matt Carpenter/25 15.00 40.00
31 Mark Grace/25 12.00 30.00
32 Jose Ramirez/25 15.00 40.00
33 Jose Canseco/49 10.00 25.00
34 John Smoltz/25 12.00 30.00
35 Gleyber Torres/49 30.00 80.00
37 Adrian Beltre/25 20.00 50.00
38 Alan Trammell/49 15.00 40.00
39 Austin Riley/49 6.00 15.00
40 Clayton Kershaw/25 60.00 150.00

2020 Immaculate Collection Immaculate Signatures Red

*RED/49: .5X TO 1.2X p/r 99
*RED/25: .5X TO 1.2X p/r 49
RANDOM INSERTS IN PACKS
PRINT RUNS B/WN 5-49 COPIES PER
NO PRICING QTY 15 OR LESS
EXCHANGE DEADLINE 2/21/2022
38 Alan Trammell/25 30.00 80.00

2020 Immaculate Collection Immaculate Triples Memorabilia

RANDOM INSERTS IN PACKS
PRINT RUNS B/WN 25-49 COPIES PER
1 Wade Boggs/49 5.00 12.00
2 Vladimir Guerrero/49 3.00 8.00
3 Robin Yount/49 10.00 25.00
4 Willie McCovey/25 4.00 10.00
5 Jeff Bagwell/49 6.00 15.00
6 Dakota Hudson/49 3.00 8.00
7 Mike Soroka/49 4.00 10.00
8 Jeff McNeil/49 3.00 8.00
9 Josh Hader/49 3.00 8.00
10 Eloy Jimenez/49 5.00 12.00
11 Fernando Tatis Jr./49 10.00 25.00
12 Anthony Rizzo/49 5.00 12.00
13 John Smoltz/49 4.00 10.00
14 Clayton Kershaw/49 6.00 15.00
15 Alex Rodriguez/49 8.00 20.00
16 Jose Altuve/49 3.00 8.00
17 Brian Anderson/49 2.50 6.00
18 Josh Bell/49 3.00 8.00
19 Freddie Freeman/49 5.00 12.00
20 Nathaniel Lowe /49 6.00 15.00
21 Luis Arraez/49 5.00 12.00
22 Brendan Rodgers/49 4.00 10.00
23 Gary Carter/25 4.00 10.00
24 Reggie Jackson/49 8.00 20.00
25 Ken Griffey Jr./49 20.00 50.00

2020 Immaculate Collection Immaculate Triples Memorabilia Blue

*RED/25: .5X TO 1.2X p/r 49
RANDOM INSERTS IN PACKS
PRINT RUNS B/WN 10-25 COPIES PER
NO PRICING QTY 15 OR LESS
1 Wade Boggs/25 12.00 30.00
3 Robin Yount/25 15.00 40.00

2020 Immaculate Collection Jackets Autographs

RANDOM INSERTS IN PACKS
PRINT RUNS B/WN 5-25 COPIES PER
NO PRICING QTY 15 OR LESS
EXCHANGE DEADLINE 2/21/2022
6 Steve Garvey/25 40.00 100.00
8 Anthony Kay/25 5.00 12.00
12 Nathaniel Lowe /25 12.00 30.00
15 Ryne Sandberg/25 25.00 60.00
16 Aristides Aquino/25 15.00 40.00
17 Nico Hoerner/25 25.00 60.00
18 Zac Gallen/25 12.00 30.00
19 Dylan Cease/25 8.00 20.00
20 Jesus Luzardo/25 10.00 25.00
21 Kyle Lewis/25 60.00 150.00
22 Logan Allen/25 5.00 12.00
23 Trent Grisham/25 20.00 50.00

2020 Immaculate Collection Jumbo

RANDOM INSERTS IN PACKS
PRINT RUNS B/WN 5-49 COPIES PER
NO PRICING QTY 15 OR LESS
1 Jasson Dominguez/49 40.00 100.00
2 Matt Thaiss/49 3.00 8.00
3 Triston McKenzie/49 5.00 12.00
4 Logan Allen/49 2.50 6.00
5 Michel Baez/49 2.50 6.00
6 Yu Chang/49 6.00 15.00
7 Tony Gonsolin/49 10.00 25.00
8 Danny Mendick/49 3.00 8.00
9 Domingo Leyba/49 3.00 8.00
10 Dustin Pedroia/25 5.00 12.00
11 Pete Alonso/25 12.00 30.00
12 Ke'Bryan Hayes/49 12.00 30.00
13 Justin Dunn/49 3.00 8.00
14 Nico Hoerner/49 10.00 25.00
15 Kyle Lewis/49 6.00 15.00
16 Lewis Thorpe/49 2.50 6.00
17 Ken Griffey Jr./25 25.00 60.00
18 Mark McGwire/25 12.00 30.00
19 Tony Lazzeri/5
20 Nick Solak/49 10.00 25.00
21 Abraham Toro/49 3.00 8.00
22 Aristides Aquino/49 6.00 15.00
23 Patrick Sandoval/49 4.00 10.00
24 Kirby Puckett/10
25 Wander Franco/49 8.00 20.00
26 Bobby Bradley/49 2.50 6.00
27 Sean Murphy/49 4.00 10.00
28 Alex Rodriguez/25 6.00 15.00
29 Adrian Morejon/49 2.50 6.00
30 Logan Webb/49 4.00 10.00
31 Jonathan Hernandez/49 2.50 6.00
32 Dwight Gooden/15
33 Yonathan Daza/49 3.00 8.00
34 Tres Barrera/49 5.00 12.00
35 Yordan Alvarez/49 5.00 12.00
36 A.J. Puk/49 4.00 10.00
37 Rico Garcia/49 4.00 10.00
38 Sheldon Neuse/49 3.00 8.00
39 Gavin Lux/49 6.00 15.00
40 Jesus Sanchez/49 4.00 10.00
41 Donnie Walton/49 6.00 15.00
42 Dylan Carlson/49 10.00 25.00
43 Jake Rogers/49 2.50 6.00
44 Ron Santo/10
45 Josh Rojas/49 2.50 6.00
46 Adbert Alzolay/49 3.00 8.00
47 Dustin May/49 8.00 20.00
48 Aaron Civale/49 5.00 12.00
49 Travis Demeritte/49 4.00 10.00
50 Brendan McKay/49 4.00 10.00
51 Zack Collins/49 3.00 8.00
52 Casey Mize/49 8.00 20.00
53 Willie McCovey/49 3.00 8.00
54 Dylan Cease/49 4.00 10.00
55 Herb Pennock/10
56 Bobby Dalbec/49 15.00 40.00
58 Starlin Castro/49 2.50 6.00
59 Luis Robert/49 20.00 50.00
60 Randy Johnson/49 4.00 10.00
61 Trent Grisham/49 10.00 25.00
62 Tyrone Taylor/49 2.50 6.00
63 Ronald Acuna Jr./49 8.00 20.00
64 Leo Durocher/15
65 Jordan Yamamoto /49 2.50 6.00
66 Randy Arozarena/49 8.00 20.00
67 Jo Adell/49 10.00 25.00
68 Mickey Mantle/7
69 Luis Aparicio/5
70 Bryan Abreu/49 2.50 6.00
71 Zac Gallen/49 6.00 15.00
72 Vladimir Guerrero Jr./49 6.00 15.00
73 Jim Thome/5
74 Deivy Grullon/49 2.50 6.00
75 Ted Williams/15
76 Ketel Marte/49 3.00 8.00
77 Jaylin Davis/49 4.00 10.00
78 Ken Boyer/5
79 Anthony Kay/49 2.50 6.00
80 Andres Munoz/49 4.00 10.00
81 T.J. Zeuch/49 2.50 6.00
82 Jake Fraley/49 3.00 8.00
83 Edwin Rios/49 6.00 15.00
84 Bo Bichette/49 20.00 50.00
85 Alex Kirilloff/49 5.00 12.00
86 Nate Pearson/49 8.00 20.00
87 Ronald Bolanos/49 2.50 6.00
89 Brock Burke/49 2.50 6.00
90 Sixto Sanchez/49 8.00 20.00
91 Jesus Luzardo/49 5.00 12.00
92 Sam Hilliard/49 4.00 10.00
93 Taylor Trammell/25 5.00 12.00
94 Isan Diaz/49 4.00 10.00
95 Albert Pujols/25 15.00 40.00
96 Mauricio Dubon/49 3.00 8.00
97 Brusdar Graterol/49 4.00 10.00
98 Joe Palumbo/49 2.50 6.00
99 Willi Castro/49 4.00 10.00
100 Michael King/49 8.00 20.00

2020 Immaculate Collection Legends Dual Materials

RANDOM INSERTS IN PACKS
PRINT RUNS B/WN 10-49 COPIES PER
NO PRICING QTY 15 OR LESS
1 Edd Roush/10
2 Frank Chance/25 12.00 30.00
3 Herb Pennock/10
4 Leo Durocher/49 2.50 6.00
5 Mickey Mantle/49 20.00 50.00
6 Luis Aparicio/49 6.00 15.00
7 Randy Johnson/49 4.00 10.00
8 Alex Rodriguez/49 5.00 12.00
9 Albert Pujols/49 5.00 12.00
10 Pete Rose/49 10.00 25.00

2020 Immaculate Collection Legends Dual Materials Blue

*RED/25: .5X TO 1.2X p/r 49
RANDOM INSERTS IN PACKS
PRINT RUNS B/WN 5-25 COPIES PER
NO PRICING QTY 15 OR LESS
7 Randy Johnson/25 15.00 40.00
10 Pete Rose/25 15.00 40.00

2020 Immaculate Collection Legends Material

RANDOM INSERTS IN PACKS
PRINT RUNS B/WN 7-49 COPIES PER
NO PRICING QTY 15 OR LESS
1 Billy Martin/10
2 Casey Stengel/10
3 Don Drysdale/10
4 Gil Hodges/49 5.00 12.00
5 Joe Jackson/15
6 Roy Campanella/49 6.00 15.00
7 Tony Lazzeri/25 12.00 30.00
8 Babe Ruth/7
9 Joe DiMaggio/10
10 Joe Sewell/10
11 Ken Boyer/25 6.00 15.00
12 Roberto Clemente/25 40.00 100.00
13 Ron Santo/49 10.00 25.00
14 Stan Musial/49 10.00 25.00
15 Ted Williams/49 20.00 50.00
16 Yogi Berra/10
17 Tony Gwynn/49 4.00 10.00
18 Tim Raines/49 3.00 8.00
19 Cal Ripken/49 12.00 30.00
20 Jim Thome/49 3.00 8.00
21 Harold Baines/49 6.00 15.00
22 Frank Thomas/49 4.00 10.00
23 Johnny Bench/49 6.00 15.00
24 Willie McCovey/49 3.00 8.00
25 Trevor Hoffman/49 3.00 8.00
26 Tom Glavine/49 3.00 8.00
27 Greg Maddux/49 8.00 20.00
28 George Brett/49 12.00 30.00
29 Chipper Jones/49 4.00 10.00
30 Rickey Henderson/49 4.00 10.00

2020 Immaculate Collection Legends Material Blue

*RED/25: .5X TO 1.2X p/r 49
RANDOM INSERTS IN PACKS
PRINT RUNS B/WN 5-25 COPIES PER
NO PRICING QTY 15 OR LESS
4 Gil Hodges/25 10.00 25.00
15 Ted Williams/25 30.00 80.00
23 Johnny Bench/25 15.00 40.00

2020 Immaculate Collection Materials

RANDOM INSERTS IN PACKS
PRINT RUNS B/WN 25-49 COPIES PER
1 Jacob deGrom/49 8.00 20.00
2 Craig Biggio/49 3.00 8.00
3 Eddie Murray/49 3.00 8.00
4 James Paxton/49 3.00 8.00
5 Daniel Murphy/49 3.00 8.00
6 Adrian Beltre/49 4.00 10.00
7 Alex Rodriguez/49 5.00 12.00
8 Adam Wainwright/49 3.00 8.00
9 Amed Rosario/49 3.00 8.00
10 Chris Paddack/49 4.00 10.00
11 Marcell Ozuna/49 4.00 10.00
12 Freddie Freeman/49 5.00 12.00
13 Miguel Sano/49 3.00 8.00
14 J.D. Davis/49 2.50 6.00
15 Sean Manaea/49 2.50 6.00
16 Enos Slaughter/25 8.00 20.00
17 A.J. Puk/49 4.00 10.00
18 Tim Anderson/49 4.00 10.00
19 Wander Franco/49 8.00 20.00
20 Joe Morgan/49 3.00 8.00
21 Keston Hiura/49 5.00 12.00
22 Lucas Giolito/49 3.00 8.00
23 Kyle Seager/49 2.50 6.00
24 Kevin Newman/49 4.00 10.00
25 Isan Diaz/49 4.00 10.00
26 Chris Davis/49 2.50 6.00
27 Bryce Harper/49 6.00 15.00
28 Ken Griffey Jr./49 20.00 50.00
29 Alex Verdugo/49 3.00 8.00
30 Cody Bellinger/49 8.00 20.00
31 Josh Hader/49 3.00 8.00
32 Mike Trout/27 25.00 60.00
33 Willy Adames/49 2.50 6.00
34 Craig Kimbrel/49 3.00 8.00
35 Yordan Alvarez/49 5.00 12.00
36 Forrest Whitley/49 4.00 10.00
37 Gary Carter/49 3.00 8.00
38 Catfish Hunter/49 3.00 8.00
39 Nelson Cruz/49 4.00 10.00
40 Joey Votto/49 4.00 10.00
41 Andrew McCutchen/49 4.00 10.00
42 Zack Wheeler/49 3.00 8.00
43 Brandon Lowe/49 3.00 8.00
44 Rickey Henderson/49 4.00 10.00
45 Anthony Santander/49 2.50 6.00
46 Aaron Nola/49 3.00 8.00
47 Roberto Alomar/49 3.00 8.00
48 Gavin Lux/49 6.00 15.00
49 Adalberto Mondesi/49 3.00 8.00
50 Masahiro Tanaka/49 4.00 10.00
51 Kirby Puckett/49 15.00 40.00
52 CC Sabathia/49 3.00 8.00
53 George Springer/49 3.00 8.00
54 Johnny Cueto/49 3.00 8.00
55 Brendan McKay/49 4.00 10.00

2020 Immaculate Collection Matinee Dual Memorabilia Autographs

RANDOM INSERTS IN PACKS
PRINT RUNS B/WN 10-49 COPIES PER
NO PRICING QTY 15 OR LESS
*BLUE/2.-25: .5X TO 1.2X p/r 49
1 Ian Desmond/49 4.00 10.00
2 Josh Donaldson/49 10.00 25.00
3 Clint Frazier/49 12.00 30.00
4 Stephen Gonsalves/49 4.00 10.00
5 Shohei Ohtani/24 60.00 150.00
6 Xander Bogaerts/31 8.00 20.00
7 Barry Larkin/29 20.00 50.00
8 Gary Sanchez/25 8.00 20.00
9 Edwin Encarnacion/28 8.00 20.00
10 Jonathan Lucroy/23 6.00 15.00
11 Cedric Mullins/17 6.00 15.00
12 Garrett Hampson/17 5.00 12.00
13 Jake Cave/21 6.00 15.00
14 Kevin Kramer/14
15 Kevin Newman/14
16 Byron Buxton/18 8.00 20.00
17 Andres Galarraga/14
18 Fernando Tatis Jr./10

2020 Immaculate Collection Mike Trout MVP

RANDOM INSERTS IN PACKS
STATED PRINT RUN 27 SER.#'d SETS
1 Mike Trout 50.00 120.00

2020 Immaculate Collection Moments Memorabilia Autographs

RANDOM INSERTS IN PACKS
PRINT RUNS B/WN 15-20 COPIES PER
NO PRICING QTY 15 OR LESS
EXCHANGE DEADLINE 2/21/2022
13 Jose Canseco/20 20.00 50.00

2020 Immaculate Collection Monochrome Memorabilia Autographs

RANDOM INSERTS IN PACKS
STATED PRINT RUN 49 SER.#'d SETS
EXCHANGE DEADLINE 2/21/2022
*BLUE/25: .5X TO 1.2X
1 Matt Thaiss 5.00 12.00
2 Jonathan Hernandez 4.00 10.00
3 Edwin Rios 10.00 25.00
4 Nick Solak 8.00 20.00
5 Jake Fraley 8.00 20.00
6 A.J. Puk 6.00 15.00
7 Randy Arozarena 50.00 120.00
8 Dylan Cease 6.00 15.00
9 Gavin Lux 20.00 50.00
10 Joe Palumbo 4.00 10.00
11 Danny Mendick 5.00 12.00
12 Isan Diaz 6.00 15.00
13 Yu Chang 6.00 15.00
14 Dustin May 20.00 50.00
15 Josh Rojas 4.00 10.00
16 Logan Webb 6.00 15.00
17 Bryan Abreu 4.00 10.00
18 Tony Gonsolin 15.00 40.00
19 Brendan McKay 6.00 15.00
20 Zack Collins 5.00 12.00
21 Adbert Alzolay 5.00 12.00
22 Jesus Luzardo 8.00 20.00
23 Nico Hoerner 20.00 50.00
24 Justin Dunn 5.00 12.00
25 T.J. Zeuch 4.00 10.00
26 Rico Garcia 6.00 15.00
27 Tres Barrera 8.00 20.00
28 Ronald Bolanos 4.00 10.00
30 Travis Demeritte 6.00 15.00
31 Yonathan Daza 5.00 12.00
32 Brock Burke 4.00 10.00
33 Adrian Morejon 4.00 10.00
34 Jaylin Davis 6.00 15.00
35 Yordan Alvarez 30.00 80.00
36 Willi Castro 10.00 25.00
37 Sam Hilliard 6.00 15.00
38 Mauricio Dubon 5.00 12.00
39 Michel Baez 4.00 10.00
40 Aaron Civale 8.00 20.00
41 Donnie Walton 10.00 25.00
42 Abraham Toro 5.00 12.00
43 Logan Allen 4.00 10.00
44 Sheldon Neuse 5.00 12.00
45 Aristides Aquino 10.00 25.00
46 Brusdar Graterol 6.00 15.00
47 Kyle Lewis 30.00 80.00
48 Andres Munoz 6.00 15.00
49 Bo Bichette 50.00 120.00
50 Bobby Bradley 4.00 10.00
51 Sean Murphy 6.00 15.00
52 Jake Rogers 4.00 10.00
53 Michael King 6.00 15.00
54 Anthony Kay 4.00 10.00
55 Domingo Leyba 5.00 12.00
56 Patrick Sandoval 6.00 15.00
57 Tyrone Taylor 4.00 10.00
58 Zac Gallen 10.00 25.00
59 Lewis Thorpe 4.00 10.00
60 Jordan Yamamoto 4.00 10.00

2020 Immaculate Collection Monuments

RANDOM INSERTS IN PACKS
PRINT RUNS B/WN 15-25 COPIES PER
NO PRICING QTY 15 OR LESS
1 DMagio/Mntle/Brra/Ruth/25 250.00 600.00
2 Clmnte/Musl/Jcksn/Wllms/25 100.00 250.00
4 Ryn/Jhnson/Clmens/Seavr/20 75.00 200.00
5 Snders/Tebw/Jckson/Wilsn/25 75.00 200.00
6 Bichette/Robert/Alvarez/Lux/25 75.00 200.00
7 Rtschmn/Domnguz/Adll/Frnco/25 75.00 200.00
8 deGrm/Snll/Vrlndr/Schrzr/25 20.00 50.00
9 Trout/Bellngr/Btts/Ylch/25 75.00 200.00
11 Chipper/Ichiro/Pujols/ARod/25 50.00 120.00
12 Cabrra/Posy/Trout/Beltre/25 30.00 80.00
13 Brett/Hendrsn/CRJ/Mttngly/25 40.00 100.00
14 Bnch/Strgell/Torre/Jcksn/25 25.00 60.00
15 Ryan/Ford/Gibsn/Seavr/25 30.00 80.00
16 Sndbrg/Robnsn/Smith/Hrnndz/25 40.00 100.00
17 Rose/Perez/Morgan/Bench/25 30.00 80.00
18 Sparky/Weaver/Torre/Lasorda/25 50.00 120.00
19 Snto/Wllms/Maddx/Sndbrg/25 25.00 60.00
20 Alnso/Acna/Ohtni/Alvarz/25 60.00 150.00

2020 Immaculate Collection Premium Memorabilia Autographs

RANDOM INSERTS IN PACKS
PRINT RUNS B/WN 10-25 COPIES PER
NO PRICING QTY 15 OR LESS
EXCHANGE DEADLINE 2/21/2022
4 J.D. Davis/25 5.00 12.00
6 Tristen Lutz/25 6.00 15.00
9 Chris Paddack/25 8.00 20.00
16 Brandon Lowe/25 12.00 30.00
19 Jeff McNeil/25 10.00 25.00

2020 Immaculate Collection Premium Patch Autographs

RANDOM INSERTS IN PACKS
STATED PRINT RUN 25 SER.#'d SETS
EXCHANGE DEADLINE 2/21/2022
1 Yordan Alvarez 75.00 200.00
2 Bo Bichette 60.00 150.00
3 Gavin Lux 25.00 60.00
4 Aristides Aquino 20.00 50.00
5 Kyle Lewis 60.00 150.00
7 Brusdar Graterol 8.00 20.00
8 Jesus Luzardo 25.00 60.00
9 Brendan McKay 8.00 20.00
10 A.J. Puk 8.00 20.00
11 Nico Hoerner 40.00 100.00
12 Dylan Cease 8.00 20.00
13 Dustin May 25.00 60.00
14 Zac Gallen 12.00 30.00
15 Trent Grisham 20.00 50.00
16 Sean Murphy 8.00 20.00
17 Justin Dunn 10.00 25.00
18 Mauricio Dubon 6.00 15.00
19 Willi Castro 8.00 20.00
20 Yonathan Daza 6.00 15.00

2020 Immaculate Collection Prospect Patch Autographs

RANDOM INSERTS IN PACKS
PRINT RUNS B/WN 23-99 COPIES PER
EXCHANGE DEADLINE 2/21/2022
*HOLO GOLD/45: .4X TO 1X p/r 45
*HOLO GOLD/17-26: .6X TO 1.5X p/r 99
*HOLO GOLD/17-26: .5X TO 1.2X p/r 49
1 Adley Rutschman/23 30.00 80.00
2 Bobby Witt Jr./49 40.00 100.00
3 CJ Abrams/49 12.00 30.00
6 Andrew Vaughn/25 40.00 100.00
9 Wander Franco/49 EXCH 60.00 150.00
10 Ryan Mountcastle/49 20.00 50.00
12 Sixto Sanchez/49 12.00 30.00
13 Jo Adell/99 25.00 60.00
17 Alec Bohm/49 40.00 100.00
18 Alex Kirilloff/49 15.00 40.00
19 Forrest Whitley/99 6.00 15.00

2020 Immaculate Collection Prospect Patch Autographs Red

*RED/25: .6X TO 1.5X p/r 99
RANDOM INSERTS IN PACKS
PRINT RUNS B/WN 15-25 COPIES PER
NO PRICING QTY 15 OR LESS
EXCHANGE DEADLINE 2/21/2022
4 Jasson Dominguez/25 125.00 300.00
14 Luis Robert/25 150.00 400.00

2020 Immaculate Collection Rookie Dual Memorabilia Signatures

RANDOM INSERTS IN PACKS
STATED PRINT RUN 49 SER.#'d SETS
EXCHANGE DEADLINE 2/21/2022
*RED/25: .5X TO 1.2X
1 Matt Thaiss 5.00 12.00
2 Yordan Alvarez 30.00 80.00
3 Adrian Morejon 6.00 15.00
4 Jordan Yamamoto 4.00 10.00
5 Trent Grisham 15.00 40.00
6 Michel Baez 4.00 10.00
7 Sam Hilliard 6.00 15.00
8 Zac Gallen 10.00 25.00

9 Jake Fraley 5.00 12.00
10 Willi Castro 6.00 15.00
11 A.J. Puk 6.00 15.00
12 Brock Burke 4.00 10.00
13 Jesus Luzardo 8.00 20.00
14 Justin Dunn 5.00 12.00
15 Dylan Cease 6.00 15.00
16 Anthony Kay 4.00 10.00
17 Gavin Lux 20.00 50.00
18 Michael King 6.00 15.00
19 Joe Palumbo 4.00 10.00
20 Jake Rogers 4.00 10.00
21 Mauricio Dubon 5.00 12.00
22 Sean Murphy 6.00 15.00
24 Bobby Bradley 4.00 10.00
26 Bo Bichette 50.00 120.00
27 Dustin May 25.00 60.00
28 Aaron Civale 8.00 20.00
29 Nico Hoerner 20.00 50.00
30 Kyle Lewis 30.00 80.00
31 Logan Webb 6.00 15.00
32 Brusdar Graterol 6.00 15.00
33 Bryan Abreu 4.00 10.00
34 Aristides Aquino 10.00 25.00
35 Tony Gonsolin 15.00 40.00
36 Sheldon Neuse 5.00 12.00
37 Brendan McKay 6.00 15.00
38 Logan Allen 4.00 10.00
39 Zack Collins 5.00 12.00
40 Abraham Toro 5.00 12.00

2020 Immaculate Collection Rookie Patch Autographs Holo Gold

*HOLO GOLD/50-85: .4X TO 1X
*HOLO GOLD/30-49: .5X TO 1.2X
*HOLO GOLD/19-23: .6X TO 1.5X
RANDOM INSERTS IN PACKS
PRINT RUNS B/WN 1-85 COPIES PER
NO PRICING QTY 15 OR LESS
EXCHANGE DEADLINE 2/21/2022
130 Kyle Lewis/30 50.00 120.00
134 Aristides Aquino/44 25.00 60.00

2020 Immaculate Collection Rookie Patch Autographs Holo Silver

*HOLO SLVR/25: .6X TO 1.5X
RANDOM INSERTS IN PACKS
STATED PRINT RUN 25 SER.#'d SETS
EXCHANGE DEADLINE 2/21/2022
130 Kyle Lewis 50.00 120.00
134 Aristides Aquino 30.00 80.00
154 Yordan Alvarez 50.00 120.00

2020 Immaculate Collection Rookie Reserve Memorabilia

RANDOM INSERTS IN PACKS
PRINT RUNS B/WN 10-25 COPIES PER
NO PRICING QTY 15 OR LESS
1 Luis Robert/25 60.00 150.00
2 Yordan Alvarez/25 40.00 100.00
3 Aristides Aquino/25 20.00 50.00
6 Brendan McKay/25 5.00 12.00
7 Dustin May/25 12.00 30.00
8 Nico Hoerner/25 20.00 50.00
10 Jesus Luzardo/25 10.00 25.00
11 A.J. Puk/25 5.00 12.00
12 Sean Murphy/25 10.00 25.00
13 Dylan Cease/25 10.00 25.00
14 Kwang-Hyun Kim/25 75.00 200.00
15 Shun Yamaguchi/25 12.00 30.00
16 Trent Grisham/25 12.00 30.00
17 Kyle Lewis/25 30.00 80.00
18 Adbert Alzolay/25 12.00 30.00
19 Zac Gallen/25 8.00 20.00
20 Isan Diaz/25 15.00 40.00

2020 Immaculate Collection Team Heroes Dual Memorabilia Autographs

RANDOM INSERTS IN PACKS
PRINT RUNS B/WN 5-25 COPIES PER
NO PRICING QTY 15 OR LESS
EXCHANGE DEADLINE 2/21/2022
1 Harold Baines/25 10.00 25.00
8 Kerry Wood/25 15.00 40.00
15 Jose Canseco/20 15.00 40.00
16 Andres Galarraga/25 12.00 30.00

2020 Immaculate Collection Winter Collection Triple Memorabilia Autographs

RANDOM INSERTS IN PACKS
STATED PRINT RUN 25 SER.#'d SETS
EXCHANGE DEADLINE 2/21/2022
1 Yordan Alvarez 40.00 100.00
2 Luis Robert EXCH 150.00 400.00
3 Casey Mize 25.00 60.00
4 Bobby Witt Jr. 50.00 120.00
5 Joey Bart 25.00 60.00
6 Dylan Carlson 20.00 50.00
7 Alec Bohm 40.00 100.00
8 Jasson Dominguez 125.00 300.00
9 Andres Gimenez 12.00 30.00
10 Brady Singer 12.00 30.00
14 Travis Demeritte 8.00 20.00
15 Logan Webb 8.00 20.00
16 Zack Collins 6.00 15.00
17 Deivy Grullon 5.00 12.00
18 Bryan Abreu 5.00 12.00
19 Aaron Civale 10.00 25.00
20 Adbert Alzolay 6.00 15.00

2020 Immaculate Collection Yordan Alvarez Rookie of the Year

RANDOM INSERTS IN PACKS
STATED PRINT RUN 44 SER.#'d SETS
1 Yordan Alvarez 10.00 25.00

2000 Impact

COMPLETE SET (200) 6.00 15.00
COMMON CARD (1-200) .08 .20
1 Cal Ripken .60 1.50
2 Jose Canseco .12 .30
3 Manny Ramirez .20 .50
4 Bernie Williams .12 .30
5 Troy Glaus .07 .20
6 Jeff Bagwell .12 .30
7 Corey Koskie .07 .20
8 Barry Larkin .12 .30
9 Mark Quinn .07 .20
10 Russ Ortiz .07 .20
11 Tim Salmon .07 .20
12 Preston Wilson .07 .20
13 Mo Vaughn .07 .20
14 Ray Lankford .07 .20
15 Sterling Hitchcock .07 .20
16 Al Leiter .07 .20
17 Jim Morris .20 .50
18 Freddy Garcia .07 .20
19 Adrian Beltre .20 .50
20 Eric Chavez .07 .20
21 Robinson Cancel .07 .20
22 Edgar Renteria .07 .20
23 John Jaha .07 .20
24 Chuck Finley .07 .20
25 Andres Galarraga .12 .30
26 Paul Byrd .07 .20
27 John Halama .07 .20
28 Eric Karros .07 .20
29 Mike Piazza .20 .50
30 Ryan Rupe .07 .20
31 Frank Thomas .20 .50
32 Randy Velarde .07 .20
33 Bobby Abreu .07 .20
34 Randy Johnson .20 .50
35 Matt Williams .07 .20
36 Tony Gwynn .20 .50
37 Dean Palmer .07 .20
38 Aaron Sele .07 .20
39 Rondell White .07 .20
40 Erubiel Durazo .07 .20
41 Curt Schilling .12 .30
42 Kip Wells .07 .20
43 Craig Biggio .12 .30
44 Tom Glavine .12 .30
45 Trevor Hoffman .12 .30
46 Greg Vaughn .07 .20
47 Edgar Martinez .12 .30
48 Maggiio Ordonez .12 .30
49 Mark Mulder .07 .20
50 John Rocker .07 .20
51 Kenny Rogers .07 .20
52 Gary Sheffield .07 .20
53 Brian Simmons .07 .20
54 Tony Womack .07 .20
55 Ken Caminiti .07 .20
56 Jeff Cirillo .07 .20
57 Ray Durham .07 .20
58 Mike Lieberthal .07 .20
59 Ruben Mateo .07 .20
60 Mike Cameron .07 .20
61 Rusty Greer .07 .20
62 Alex Rodriguez .25 .60
63 Robin Ventura .07 .20
64 Pokey Reese .07 .20
65 Jose Lima .07 .20
66 Neifi Perez .07 .20
67 Rafael Palmeiro .12 .30
68 Scott Rolen .12 .30
69 Mike Hampton .07 .20
70 Sammy Sosa .20 .50
71 Mike Stanley .07 .20
72 Dan Wilson .07 .20
73 Kerry Wood .07 .20
74 Mike Mussina .12 .30
75 Masato Yoshii .07 .20
76 Peter Bergeron .07 .20
77 Carlos Delgado .07 .20
78 Juan Encarnacion .07 .20
79 Nomar Garciaparra .12 .30
80 Jason Kendall .07 .20
81 Pedro Martinez .12 .30
82 Darin Erstad .07 .20
83 Larry Walker .12 .30
84 Rick Ankiel .12 .30
85 Scott Erickson .07 .20
86 Roger Clemens .25 .60
87 Matt Lawton .07 .20
88 Jon Lieber .07 .20
89 Shane Reynolds .07 .20
90 Ivan Rodriguez .12 .30
91 Pat Burrell .07 .20
92 Kent Bottenfield .07 .20
93 David Cone .07 .20
94 Mark Grace .12 .30
95 Paul Konerko .07 .20
96 Eric Milton .07 .20
97 Lee Stevens .07 .20
98 B.J. Surhoff .07 .20
99 Billy Wagner .07 .20
100 Ken Griffey Jr. .40 1.00
101 Randy Wolf .07 .20
102 Henry Rodriguez .07 .20
103 Carlos Beltran .12 .30
104 Rich Aurilia .07 .20
105 Chipper Jones .20 .50
106 Homer Bush .07 .20
107 Johnny Damon .12 .30
108 J.D. Drew .07 .20
109 Orlando Hernandez .07 .20
110 Brad Radke .07 .20
111 Wilton Veras .07 .20
112 Dmitri Young .07 .20
113 Jermaine Dye .07 .20
114 Kris Benson .07 .20
115 Derek Jeter .50 1.25
116 Cole Liniak .07 .20
117 Jim Thome .12 .30
118 Pedro Astacio .07 .20
119 Carlos Febles .07 .20
120 Darryl Kile .07 .20
121 Alfonso Soriano .20 .50
122 Michael Barrett .07 .20
123 Ellis Burks .07 .20
124 Chad Hermansen .07 .20
125 Trot Nixon .07 .20
126 Bobby Higginson .07 .20
127 Rick Helling .07 .20
128 Chris Carpenter .12 .30
129 Vinny Castilla .07 .20
130 Brian Giles .07 .20
131 Todd Helton .12 .30
132 Jason Varitek .20 .50
133 Rob Ducey .07 .20
134 Octavio Dotel .07 .20
135 Adam Kennedy .07 .20
136 Jeff Kent .07 .20
137 Aaron Boone .07 .20
138 Todd Walker .07 .20
139 Jeromy Burnitz .07 .20
140 Roberto Hernandez .07 .20
141 Matt LeCroy .07 .20
142 Ugueth Urbina .07 .20
143 David Wells .07 .20
144 Luis Gonzalez .07 .20
145 Andruw Jones .07 .20
146 Juan Gonzalez .07 .20
147 Moises Alou .07 .20
148 Michael Tejera .07 .20
149 Brian Jordan .07 .20
150 Mark McGwire .30 .75
151 Shawn Green .07 .20
152 Jay Bell .07 .20
153 Fred McGriff .12 .30
154 Rey Ordonez .07 .20
155 Matt Stairs .07 .20
156 A.J. Burnett .07 .20
157 Omar Vizquel .12 .30
158 Damion Easley .07 .20
159 Dante Bichette .07 .20
160 Javy Lopez .07 .20
161 Fernando Seguignol .07 .20
162 Richie Sexson .07 .20
163 Vladimir Guerrero .12 .30
164 Kevin Young .07 .20
165 Josh Beckett .15 .40
166 Albert Belle .07 .20
167 Cliff Floyd .07 .20
168 Gabe Kapler .07 .20
169 Nick Johnson .07 .20
170 Raul Mondesi .07 .20
171 Warren Morris .07 .20
172 Kenny Lofton .07 .20
173 Reggie Sanders .07 .20
174 Mike Sweeney .07 .20
175 Robert Fick .07 .20
176 Barry Bonds .30 .75
177 Luis Castillo .07 .20
178 Roger Cedeno .07 .20
179 Jim Edmonds .07 .20
180 Geoff Jenkins .07 .20
181 Adam Piatt .07 .20
182 Phil Nevin .07 .20
183 Roberto Alomar .12 .30
184 Kevin Brown .07 .20
185 D.T. Cromer .07 .20
186 Jason Giambi .07 .20
187 Fernando Tatis .07 .20
188 Brady Anderson .07 .20
189 Tony Clark .07 .20
190 Alex Fernandez .07 .20
191 Matt Blank .07 .20
192 Greg Maddux .25 .60
193 Kevin Millwood .07 .20
194 Jason Schmidt .07 .20
195 Shannon Stewart .07 .20
196 Rolando Arrojo .07 .20
197 Darren Dreifort .07 .20
198 Ben Grieve .07 .20
199 Bartolo Colon .07 .20
200 Sean Casey .07 .20

2000 Impact Genuine Coverage Batting Gloves

1 Bob Abreu 6.00 15.00
2 Glen Barker 6.00 15.00
3 Barry Bonds 40.00 80.00
4 Jose Cruz Jr. 6.00 15.00
5 Ben Davis 6.00 15.00
6 Jason Giambi 6.00 15.00
7 Trevor Hoffman 6.00 15.00
8 Jacque Jones 6.00 15.00
9 Jason LaRue 6.00 15.00
10 Matt Lawton 6.00 15.00
11 Carlos Lee 6.00 15.00
12 Cole Liniak 6.00 15.00
13 Joe Nathan 6.00 15.00
14 Magglio Ordonez 6.00 15.00
15 Rafael Palmeiro 10.00 25.00
16 Alex Rodriguez 30.00 60.00
17 Shannon Stewart 6.00 15.00
18 Mike Sweeney 6.00 15.00

2000 Impact Mighty Fine in '99

COMPLETE SET (40) 6.00 15.00
1 Clay Bellinger .12 .30
2 Scott Brosius .12 .30
3 Roger Clemens .40 1.00
4 David Cone .12 .30
5 Chad Curtis .12 .30
6 Chili Davis .12 .30
7 Joe Girardi .20 .50
8 Jason Grimsley .12 .30
9 Orlando Hernandez .12 .30
10 Hideki Irabu .12 .30
11 Derek Jeter .75 2.00
12 Chuck Knoblauch .12 .30
13 Ricky Ledee .12 .30
14 Jim Leyritz .12 .30
15 Tino Martinez .12 .30
16 Ramiro Mendoza .12 .30
17 Jeff Nelson .12 .30
18 Paul O'Neill .20 .50
19 Andy Pettitte .20 .50
20 Jorge Posada .20 .50
21 Mariano Rivera .40 1.00
22 Luis Sojo .12 .30
23 Mike Stanton .12 .30
24 Allen Watson .12 .30
25 Bernie Williams .20 .50
26 Chipper Jones .30 .75
27 Ivan Rodriguez .20 .50
28 Randy Johnson .30 .75
29 Pedro Martinez .20 .50
30 Scott Williamson .12 .30
31 Carlos Beltran .20 .50
32 Mark McGwire .50 1.25
33 Ken Griffey Jr. .60 1.50
34 Robin Ventura .12 .30
35 Tony Gwynn .30 .75
36 Wade Boggs .20 .50
37 Cal Ripken 1.00 2.50
38 Jose Canseco .20 .50
39 Alex Rodriguez .40 1.00
40 Fernando Tatis .12 .30

2000 Impact Point of Impact

COMPLETE SET (10) 12.50 30.00
PI1 Ken Griffey Jr. 2.00 5.00
PI2 Mark McGwire 1.50 4.00
PI3 Sammy Sosa 1.00 2.50
PI4 Jeff Bagwell .60 1.50
PI5 Derek Jeter 2.50 6.00
PI6 Chipper Jones 1.00 2.50
PI7 Nomar Garciaparra .60 1.50
PI8 Cal Ripken 3.00 8.00
PI9 Barry Bonds 1.50 4.00
PI10 Alex Rodriguez 1.25 3.00

2000 Impact Tattoos

COMPLETE SET (30) 4.00 10.00
STATED ODDS 1:4
1 Anaheim Angels .20 .50
2 Arizona Diamondbacks .20 .50
3 Atlanta Braves .20 .50
4 Baltimore Orioles .20 .50
5 Boston Red Sox .20 .50
6 Chicago Cubs .20 .50
7 Chicago White Sox .20 .50
8 Cincinnati Reds .20 .50
9 Cleveland Indians .20 .50
10 Colorado Rockies .20 .50
11 Detroit Tigers .20 .50
12 Florida Marlins .20 .50
13 Houston Astros .20 .50
14 Kansas City Royals .20 .50
15 Los Angeles Dodgers .20 .50
16 Milwaukee Brewers .20 .50
17 Minnesota Twins .20 .50
18 Montreal Expos .20 .50
19 New York Mets .20 .50
20 New York Yankees .20 .50
21 Oakland Athletics .20 .50
22 Philadelphia Phillies .20 .50
23 Pittsburgh Pirates .20 .50
24 San Diego Padres .20 .50
25 San Francisco Giants .20 .50
26 Seattle Mariners .20 .50
27 St. Louis Cardinals .20 .50
28 Tampa Bay Devil Rays .20 .50
29 Texas Rangers .20 .50
30 Toronto Blue Jays .20 .50

2011 In The Game Canadiana Red

BLUE/50: .75X TO 2X BASIC RED
UNPRICED ONYX ANNOUNCED RUN 5
ANNOUNCED PRINT RUN 180 SETS
27 Ferguson Jenkins .75 2.00
54 Larry Walker .60 1.50
89 Terry Puhl .60 1.50

2011 In The Game Canadiana Authentic Patch Silver

ANNOUNCED PRINT RUN 30
AP5 Ferguson Jenkins 10.00 20.00
AP7 Larry Walker 10.00 20.00
AP14 Terry Puhl 10.00 20.00

2011 In The Game Canadiana Autographs

OVERALL AUTO/MEM ODDS THREE PER BOX
AFJ1 Ferguson Jenkins 10.00 20.00
AFJ2 Ferguson Jenkins 10.00 20.00
ALW1 Larry Walker 15.00 30.00
ALW2 Larry Walker 15.00 30.00
ATP1 Terry Puhl 6.00 15.00
ATP2 Terry Puhl 6.00 15.00

2011 In The Game Canadiana Autographs Blue

*BLUE: .75X TO 1.5X BLACK AUTOS
OVERALL AUTO ODDS ONE PER BOX

2011 In The Game Canadiana Double Memorabilia Silver

ANNOUNCED PRINT RUN 90
DM7 T.Puhl/L.Walker 10.00 20.00
DM14 F.Jenkins/T.Puhl 10.00 20.00

2011 In The Game Canadiana Mega Memorabilia Silver

MM4 Ferguson Jenkins L 7.50 15.00
MM5 Ferguson Jenkins L 7.50 15.00
MM7 Larry Walker L 7.50 15.00
MM14 Terry Puhl L 7.50 15.00

1905 Indians Souvenir Postcard Shop of Cleveland PC785

These distinguished looking black and white cards measures 3 1/4" by 5 1/2" and is similar to PC 782 in appearance and it was also issued in 1905. The Souvenir Postcard Shop of Cleveland identification appears on the front of the card. The backs are devoid of company identification.

COMPLETE SET 1750.00 3500.00
1 Harry Bay 400.00 800.00
2 Harry Bemis 400.00 800.00
3 Bill Bernhard 400.00 800.00
4 Bill Bradley 400.00 800.00
5 Fred Buelow 400.00 800.00
6 Chuck Carr 400.00 800.00
7 Frank Donahue 400.00 800.00
8 Elmer Flick 750.00 1500.00
9 Otto Hess 400.00 800.00
10 Jay Jackson 400.00 800.00
11 Addie Joss 750.00 1500.00
12 Nick Kahl 400.00 800.00
13 Nap Lajoie 1500.00 3000.00
14 Earl Moore 400.00 800.00
15 Robert Rhoads 400.00 800.00
16 George Stovall 600.00 1200.00
17 Terry Turner 600.00 1200.00
18 Ernest Vinson 400.00 800.00

1913-14 Indians Postcards

These seven postcards were issued over the 1913-14 time period. We are gathering them together since they seem to be team issued to promote appearences by both opposing players and to honor the Indians star players of that time.

COMPLETE SET (7) 1000.00 2000.00
1 Joe Birmingham 50.00 100.00
2 Ray Chapman 150.00 300.00
3 Joe Jackson 750.00 1500.00
4 Doc Johnston 50.00 100.00
5 Willie Mitchell 50.00 100.00
6 I.Olson 50.00 100.00
G.Stovall
7 Heinie Zimmerman 50.00 100.00

1947 Indians Team Issue

These 26 photos measure 6" by 8 1/2". They have player photos and a facsimile autograph. All of this is framed by white borders. The backs are blank and we have sequenced these photos in alphabetical order.

COMPLETE SET (26) 60.00 120.00
1 Don Black 2.00 4.00
2 Eddie Bockman 2.00 4.00
3 Lou Boudreau P 5.00 10.00
MG
4 Jack Conway 2.00 4.00
5 Larry Doby 5.00 10.00
6 Hank Edwards 2.00 4.00
7 Red Embree 2.00 4.00
8 Bob Feller 7.50 15.00
9 Les Fleming 2.00 4.00
10-Jan Allen Gettel 2.00 4.00
11-Jan Joe Gordon 4.00 8.00
12-Jan Steve Gromek 2.00 4.00
13-Jan Mel Harder 3.00 6.00
14-Jan Jim Hegan 2.50 5.00
15-Jan Ken Keltner 2.50 5.00
16-Jan Ed Klieman 2.00 4.00
17-Jan Bob Lemon 5.00 10.00
18-Jan Al Lopez 5.00 10.00
19-Jan George Catfish Metkovich 2.00 4.00
20-Jan Dale Mitchell 2.50 5.00
21-Jan Hal Peck 2.00 4.00
22-Jan Eddie Robinson 2.00 4.00
23-Jan Hank Ruszkowksi 2.00 4.00
24-Jan Pat Seerey 2.00 4.00
25-Jan Bryan Stephens 2.00 4.00
26-Jan Les Willis 2.00 4.00

1947 Indians Van Patrick PC-761

This set of 26 black and white postcards was issued in 1947 and features only Cleveland Indians. The cards were obtained by writing to Van Patrick, then the Cleveland announcer. The backs of the postcards features the name of the player on the front in a short note from Van Patrick. Two cards of Bob Feller exist; they are noted in the listings below. According to advanced postcard collectors, it is possible that other members of the 47 Indians have cards as well but they have yet to be discovered.

COMPLETE SET 500.00 1000.00
1-Jan Don Black 15.00 30.00
2-Jan Eddie Bockman 15.00 30.00
3-Jan Lou Boudreau P 30.00 60.00
MG
4-Jan Jack Conway 15.00 30.00
5-Jan Hank Edwards 15.00 30.00
6-Jan Red Embree 15.00 30.00
7A Bob Feller 40.00 80.00
Pitching, abode wall
7B Bob Feller 40.00 80.00
Pitching, Leg up, fuzzy card back
8-Jan Les Fleming 15.00 30.00
9-Jan Al Gettel 15.00 30.00
10-Jan Joe Gordon 25.00 50.00
11-Jan Steve Gromek 15.00 30.00
12-Jan Mel Harder 25.00 50.00
13-Jan Jim Hegan 20.00 40.00
14-Jan Ken Keltner 20.00 40.00
15-Jan Eddie Klieman 15.00 30.00
16-Jan Bob Lemon 30.00 60.00
17-Jan Al Lopez 30.00 60.00
18-Jan George Metkovich 15.00 30.00
19-Jan Dale Mitchell 15.00 30.00
20-Jan Hal Peck 15.00 30.00
21 Eddie Robinson 15.00 30.00
22 Hank Ruszowski 15.00 30.00
23 Pat Seerey 15.00 30.00
24 Bryan Stephens 15.00 30.00
25 Les Willis 15.00 30.00

1948 Indians Team Issue

This set commemorates the members of the World Champion 1948 Cleveland Indians. The black and white photos measure approximately 6 1/2" by 9" and are blank backed. We have arranged this checklist in alphabetical order.

COMPLETE SET (31) 100.00 200.00
1 Gene Bearden 2.50 5.00
2 Johnny Berardino 6.00 12.00
3 Don Black 2.00 4.00
4 Lou Boudreau 6.00 12.00
5 Russ Christopher 2.00 4.00
6 Allie Clark 2.00 4.00
7 Larry Doby 7.50 15.00
8 Hank Edwards 2.00 4.00
9-Jan Bob Feller 7.50 15.00
10-Jan Joe Gordon 3.00 6.00
11-Jan Hank Greenberg GM 10.00 20.00
In Uniform
12-Jan Hank Greenberg GM 7.50 15.00
In Street Clothes
13-Jan Steve Gromek 2.00 4.00
14-Jan Mel Harder 3.00 6.00
15-Jan Jim Hegan 2.50 5.00
16-Jan Walt Judnich 2.00 4.00
17-Jan Ken Keltner 2.50 5.00
18-Jan Bob Kennedy 2.50 5.00
19-Jan Ed Klieman 2.00 4.00
20-Jan Bob Lemon 4.00 8.00
21-Jan Bill McKechnie CO 4.00 8.00
22-Jan Dale Mitchell 2.50 5.00
23-Jan Bob Muncrief 2.00 4.00
24-Jan Satchel Paige 10.00 20.00
25-Jan Hal Peck 2.00 4.00
26-Jan Eddie Robinson 2.00 4.00
27-Jan Muddy Ruel CO 2.00 4.00
28-Jan Joe Tipton 2.00 4.00
29-Jan Thurman Tucker 2.00 4.00
30-Jan Bill Veeck OWN 4.00 8.00
31-Jan Sam Zoldak 2.00 4.00

1949 Indians Sun

These "self-developing" photos feature members of the 1949 Cleveland Indians. These photos were issued in groups of four negatives and five pieces of photo paper for 25 cents per envelope. Since these photos are unnumbered, we have sequenced them in alphabetical order.

COMPLETE SET (20) 400.00 800.00
1-Jan Gene Bearden 12.50 25.00
2-Jan Al Benton 12.50 25.00
3-Jan Ray Boone 12.50 25.00
4-Jan Lou Boudreau 30.00 60.00
5-Jan Allie Clark 12.50 25.00
6-Jan Larry Doby 30.00 60.00
7-Jan Bob Feller 50.00 100.00
8-Jan Mike Garcia 15.00 30.00
9-Jan Joe Gordon 25.00 50.00
10-Jan Steve Gromek 12.50 25.00
11-Jan Jim Hegan 12.50 25.00
12-Jan Ken Keltner 15.00 30.00
13-Jan Bob Kennedy 12.50 25.00
14-Jan Bob Lemon 30.00 60.00
15-Jan Dale Mitchell 15.00 30.00
16 Hal Peck 12.50 25.00
17 Satchel Paige 75.00 150.00
18 Thurman Tucker 12.50 25.00
19 Mickey Vernon 20.00 40.00
20 Early Wynn 30.00 60.00

1949 Indians Team Issue Action Photos

These 30 photos measure approximatley 6 1/2" by 9". They feature members of the 1949 Cleveland Indians in action poses. The black and white photos are framed by white borders. The backs are blank and we have sequenced this set in alphabetical order. This set was available from the Cleveland Indians for 50 cents at time of issue.

COMPLETE SET (30) 100.00 200.00
1 Bob Avila 2.50 5.00
2 Al Benton 2.00 4.00
3 Gene Bearden 2.00 4.00
4 John Berardino 3.00 6.00
5 Ray Boone 2.50 5.00
6 Lou Boudreau 7.50 15.00
7 Allie Clark 2.00 4.00
8 Larry Doby 7.50 15.00
9 Bob Feller 7.50 15.00
10 Mike Garcia 2.50 5.00
11 Joe Gordon 3.00 6.00
12 Hank Greenberg GM 7.50 15.00
13 Steve Gromek 2.00 4.00
14 Jim Hegan 2.50 5.00
15 Ken Keltner 2.50 5.00
16 Bob Kennedy 2.00 4.00
17 Bob Lemon 6.00 12.00
18 Dale Mitchell 2.50 5.00
19 Satchel Paige 10.00 20.00
20 Frank Papish 2.00 4.00
21 Hal Peck 2.00 4.00
22 Al Rosen 4.00 8.00
23 Mike Tresh 2.00 4.00
24 Thurman Tucker 2.00 4.00
25 Bill Veeck OWN 4.00 8.00
26 Mickey Vernon 3.00 6.00
27 Early Wynn 6.00 12.00
28 Sam Zoldak 2.00 4.00
29 Indians Coaches 2.50 5.00
George Susce
Muddy Ruel
Bill Mc
30 Cleveland Stadium 5.00 10.00

1950 Indians Num Num

This issue features members of the 1950 Cleveland Indians. The black and white photos measure 6 1/2" by 9". Complete sets were sent out by Num Num in special envelopes. Some backs feature a redemption offer for other photos. We have checklisted the set alphabetically.

COMPLETE SET (23) 800.00 1600.00
1 Bob Avila 40.00 80.00
2 Gene Bearden 30.00 60.00
3 Al Benton 30.00 60.00
4 Ray Boone 40.00 80.00
5 Lou Boudreau 60.00 120.00
6 Allie Clark 30.00 60.00
7 Larry Doby 60.00 120.00
8 Luke Easter 50.00 100.00
9 Bob Feller 125.00 250.00
10 Mike Garcia 40.00 80.00
11 Joe Gordon 100.00 200.00
12 Steve Gromek 30.00 60.00
13 Jim Hegan 40.00 80.00
14 Bob Kennedy 40.00 80.00
15 Bob Lemon 60.00 120.00
16 Dale Mitchell 40.00 80.00
17 Ray Murray 30.00 60.00
18 Chick Pierietti 30.00 60.00
19 Al Rosen 50.00 100.00
20 Mike Tresh 30.00 60.00
21 Thurman Tucker 30.00 60.00
22 Early Wynn 60.00 210.00
23 Sam Zoldak 30.00 60.00

1950 Indians Team Issue

These 26 black and white photos measure approximately 6 1/2" by 9". They feature members of the Cleveland Indians. The photos are surrounded by a white border and have facsimile autogrpahs. The photos are unnumbered and we have sequenced them in alphabetical order.

COMPLETE SET (27) 75.00 150.00
1 Bob Avila 2.50 5.00
2 Gene Bearden 2.00 4.00
3 Al Benton 2.00 4.00
4 Ray Boone 2.50 5.00
5 Lou Boudreau P 6.00 12.00
MG
6 Allie Clark 2.00 4.00
7 Larry Doby 10.00 20.00
8 Luke Easter 3.00 6.00
9 Bob Feller 10.00 20.00
10 Jess Flores 2.00 4.00
11 Mike Garcia 2.50 5.00
12 Joe Gordon 3.00 6.00
13 Hank Greenberg GM 12.50 25.00
14 Steve Gromek 2.00 4.00
15 Jim Hegan 2.50 5.00
16 Bob Kennedy 2.50 5.00
17 Bob Lemon 6.00 12.00
18 Dale Mitchell 2.50 5.00
19 Ray Murray 2.00 4.00
20 Chick Pieretti 2.00 4.00
21 Al Rosen 3.00 6.00
22 Dick Rozek 2.00 4.00
23 Ellis Ryan OWN 2.00 4.00
24 Thurman Tucker 2.00 4.00
25 Early Wynn 7.50 15.00
26 Sam Zoldak 2.00 4.00
27 Cleveland Stadium 12.50 25.00

1951 Indians Hage's

This seven-card set of the Cleveland Indians was issued by Hage's Ice Cream and features green-and-brown tinted player photos printed on black-backed cards. The cards are unnumbered and checklisted below in alphabetical order.

COMPLETE SET (7) 750.00 1500.00
1 Ray Boone 125.00 250.00
2 Allie Clark 100.00 200.00
3 Luke Easter 125.00 250.00
4 Jesse Flores 100.00 200.00
5 Al Olsen 100.00 200.00
6 Al Rosen 200.00 400.00
7 George Zuverink 100.00 200.00

1951 Indians Team Issue

These 6 1/2" by 9" photos were issued by the Cleveland Indians and featured members of the 1951 Indians. The black and white photos are surrounded by a white border and have fascimile autographs. The photos are unnumbered and we have sequenced them in alphabetical order. This list may be incomplete and any additions are welcome.

COMPLETE SET 100.00 200.00
1 Bobby Avila 3.00 6.00
2 Johnny Beardino 4.00 8.00
3 Lou Boudreau 5.00 10.00
Batting
4 Lou Boudreau 5.00 10.00
Throwing
5 Ray Boone 2.50 5.00
6 Lou Brissie 2.50 5.00
7 Allie Clark 2.50 5.00
8 Merrill Combs 2.50 5.00
9 Bob Chakales 2.50 5.00
10 Sam Chapman 2.50 5.00
11 Larry Doby 5.00 10.00
12 Luke Easter 2.50 5.00
13 Red Fahr 2.50 5.00
14 Bob Feller 6.00 12.00
15 Jess Flores 2.50 5.00
16 Mike Garcia 3.00 6.00
17 Joe Gordon 4.00 8.00
18 Steve Gromek 2.50 5.00
19 Jim Hegan 3.00 6.00
20 Bob Kennedy 3.00 6.00
21 Bob Lemon 5.00 10.00
Facing Straight Ahead
22 Bob Lemon 5.00 10.00
Facing Left
23 Dale Mitchell 3.00 6.00
24 Ray Murray 2.50 5.00
25 Al Rosen 4.00 8.00
26 Dick Rozek 2.50 5.00
27 Harry Simpson 2.50 5.00
28 Snuffy Stirnweiss 2.50 5.00
29 Thurman Tucker 2.50 5.00
30 Mickey Vernon 3.00 6.00
31 Early Wynn 5.00 10.00
32 Sam Zoldak 2.50 5.00

1952 Indians Num Num

The cards in this 20-card set measure approximately 3 1/2" by 4 1/2". The 1952 Num Num Potato Chips issue features black and white, numbered cards of the Cleveland Indians. Cards came with and without coupons (tabs). The cards were issued without coupons directly by the Cleveland baseball club. When the complete set was obtained the tabs were cut off and exchanged for an autographed baseball. Card Number 16, Kennedy, is rather scarce. Cards with the tabs still intact are worth approximately double the values listed below. The catalog designation for this set is F337-2.

COMPLETE SET (20) 1750.00 3500.00
COMMON CARD (1-20) 50.00 100.00
COMMON SP 750.00 1500.00
1 Lou Brissie 150.00 300.00
2 Jim Hegan 60.00 120.00
3 Birdie Tebbetts 60.00 120.00
4 Bob Lemon 100.00 200.00
5 Bob Feller 250.00 500.00
6 Early Wynn 100.00 200.00
7 Mike Garcia 60.00 120.00
8 Steve Gromek 50.00 100.00
9 Bob Chakales 50.00 100.00
10 Al Rosen 75.00 150.00
11 Dick Rozek 50.00 100.00
12 Luke Easter 60.00 120.00
13 Ray Boone 60.00 120.00
14 Bobby Avila 60.00 120.00
15 Dale Mitchell 60.00 120.00
16 Bob Kennedy SP 750.00 1500.00
17 Harry Simpson 50.00 100.00
18 Larry Doby 100.00 200.00
19 Sam Jones 60.00 120.00
20 Al Lopez MG 100.00 200.00

1953 Indians Team Issue

These photos which measure approximately 6" by 9" feature members of the 1953 Indians. The black and white photos are produced with a glossy paper and have fascimile autographs. Since these cards are unnumbered, we have sequenced them in alphabetical order.

COMPLETE SET 50.00 100.00
1 Al Aber 2.50 5.00
2 Bob Avila 3.00 6.00
3 Ray Boone 2.50 5.00
4 Larry Doby 5.00 10.00

5 Luke Easter 2.50 5.00
6 Bob Feller 6.00 12.00
7 Mike Garcia 3.00 6.00
8 Bill Glynn 2.50 5.00
9 Jim Hegan 2.50 5.00
10 Bob Hooper 2.50 5.00
11 Dave Hoskins 2.50 5.00
12 Bob Kennedy 2.50 5.00
13 Bob Lemon 5.00 10.00
14 Jim Lemon 2.50 5.00
15 Al Lopez MG 5.00 10.00
16 Dale Mitchell 2.50 5.00
17 Al Rosen 4.00 8.00
18 Harry Simpson 2.50 5.00
19 George Strickland 2.50 5.00
20 Early Wynn 5.00 10.00

1954 Indians Team Issue

These photos, which measure approximately 6" by 8 3/4" feature members of the American League champions Cleveland Indians. These photos are similar to the 1953 Indians in style but are slightly smaller and are printed on heavier paper. Since these are unnumbered, we have sequenced them in alphabetical order.

COMPLETE SET 75.00 150.00
1 Bob Avila 2.50 5.00
2 Sam Dente 2.50 5.00
3 Larry Doby 5.00 10.00
4 Bob Feller 6.00 12.00
5 Mike Garcia 3.00 6.00
6 Bill Glynn 2.50 5.00
7 Jim Hegan 2.50 5.00
8 Bob Hooper 2.50 5.00
9 Dave Hoskins 2.50 5.00
10 Art Houtteman 2.50 5.00
11 Bob Lemon 5.00 10.00
12 Al Lopez MG 5.00 10.00
13 Hank Majeski 2.50 5.00
14 Dale Mitchell 2.50 5.00
15 Don Mossi 4.00 8.00
16 Hal Naragon 2.50 5.00
17 Ray Narleski 3.00 6.00
18 Hal Newhouser 5.00 10.00
19 Dave Philley 2.50 5.00
20 Dave Pope 2.50 5.00
21 Rudy Regalado 2.50 5.00
22 Al Rosen 4.00 8.00
23 Al Smith 2.50 5.00
24 George Strickland 2.50 5.00
25 Vic Wertz 2.50 5.00
26 Wally Westlake 2.50 5.00
27 Early Wynn 5.00 10.00

1955 Indians Team Issue

These cards which measure approximately 6" by 8 3/4" feature members of the 1955 Indians. Most of these cards have fascimile autographs printed on them except for Foiles, Kiner, Score and Wertz. This checklist comes from a set purchased directly from the Indians in July, 1955 so there might have been additions both before and after these were issued. Since these cards are unnumbered, we have sequenced them in alphabetical order.

COMPLETE SET 60.00 120.00
1 Bob Avila 3.00 6.00
2 Sam Dente 2.50 5.00
3 Larry Doby 5.00 10.00
4 Bob Feller 6.00 12.00
5 Hank Foiles 2.50 5.00
6 Mike Garcia 3.00 6.00
7 Jim Hegan 2.50 5.00
8 Art Houtteman 2.50 5.00
9 Ralph Kiner 5.00 10.00
10 Bob Lemon 5.00 10.00
11 Dale Mitchell 2.50 5.00
12 Don Mossi 3.00 6.00
13 Hal Naragon 2.50 5.00
14 Ray Narleski 2.50 5.00
15 Dave Philley 2.50 5.00
16 Al Rosen 4.00 8.00
17 Herb Score 5.00 10.00
18 Al Smith 2.50 5.00
19 George Strickland 2.50 5.00
20 Vic Wertz 2.50 5.00
21 Wally Westlake 2.50 5.00
22 Early Wynn 5.00 10.00

1955 Indians Golden Stamps

This 32-stamp set features color photos of the Cleveland Indians and measures approximately 2" by 2 5/8". The stamps are designed to be placed in a 32-page album which measures approximately 8 3/8" by 10 15/16". The album contains black-and-white drawings of players with statistics and life stories. The stamps are unnumbered and listed below according to where they fall in the album.

COMPLETE SET (32) 75.00 150.00
1 Al Lopez MG 2.50 5.00
2 Bob Lemon 6.00 12.00
3 Early Wynn 6.00 12.00
4 Mike Garcia 1.50 3.00
5 Bob Feller 10.00 20.00
6 Art Houtteman 1.25 2.50
7 Herb Score 2.50 5.00
8 Don Mossi 2.00 4.00
9 Ray Narleski 1.25 2.50
10 Jim Hegan 1.50 3.00
11 Vic Wertz 1.25 2.50
12 Bobby Avila 1.25 2.50
13 George Strickland 1.25 2.50
14 Al Rosen 2.00 4.00
15 Larry Doby 6.00 12.00
16 Ralph Kiner 2.50 5.00
17 Al Smith 1.25 2.50
18 Wally Westlake 1.25 2.50
19 Hal Naragon 1.25 2.50
20 Hank Foiles 1.25 2.50
21 Hank Majeski 1.25 2.50
22 Bill Wight 1.25 2.50
23 Sam Dente 1.25 2.50
24 Dave Pope 1.25 2.50
25 Dave Philley 1.25 2.50
26 Dale Mitchell 1.50 3.00
27 Hank Greenberg GM 10.00 20.00
28 Mel Harder CO 1.50 3.00
29 Ralph Kress CO 1.25 2.50
30 Tony Cuccinello CO 1.25 2.50
31 Bill Lobe CO 1.25 2.50
32 Cleveland Stadium 5.00 10.00
XX Album 2.50 5.00

1955-56 Indians Carling Black Label

This ten-card, approximately 8 1/2" by 12", set was issued by Carling Beer and celebrated members of the (then) perennial contending Cleveland Indians. These cards feature a black and white photo with the printed name of the player inserted in the photo. Underneath the photo is a joint advertisement for Carling Black Label Beer and The Cleveland Indians. The set looks like it could be easily replicated and may indeed have been reprinted. The checklist for this unnumbered set is ordered alphabetically.

COMPLETE SET (10) 60.00 120.00
1 Bob Feller 15.00 30.00
2 Mike Garcia 5.00 10.00
3 Jim Hegan 5.00 10.00
4 Art Houtteman 4.00 8.00
5 Ralph Kiner 7.50 15.00
6 Bob Lemon 7.50 15.00
7 Al Rosen 6.00 12.00
8 Herb Score 7.50 15.00
9 Al Smith 4.00 8.00
10 George Strickland 4.00 8.00
11 Early Wynn 7.50 15.00

1956 Indians Team Issue

These cards, which measure approximately 6" by 9" feature members of the 1956 Cleveland Indians. Similar to the 1955 set and many of the photos were also repeats from the 1955 set. This set was produced early in the season so additions to this checklist is appreciated. These cards are not numbered, so we have sequenced them in alphabetical order. Rocky Colavito appears in this set before his Rookie Card year.

COMPLETE SET 60.00 120.00
1 Earl Averill 2.50 5.00
2 Bob Avila 3.00 6.00
3 Rocky Colavito 7.50 20.00
4 Bob Feller 6.00 12.00
5 Mike Garcia 3.00 6.00
6 Jim Hegan 2.50 5.00
7 Art Houtteman 2.50 5.00
8 Bob Lemon 5.00 10.00
9 Al Lopez MG 5.00 10.00
10 Sam Mele 2.50 5.00
11 Dale Mitchell 2.50 5.00
12 Don Mossi 3.00 6.00
13 Ray Narleski 2.50 5.00
14 Rudy Regalado 2.50 5.00
15 Al Rosen 4.00 8.00
16 Al Smith 2.50 5.00
17 George Strickland 2.50 5.00
18 Gene Woodling 2.50 5.00
19 Early Wynn 5.00 10.00

1956 Indians Team Issue Mail

Unlike the other 1956 Indians Team Issue, this set was available to mail order customers. These cards, which measure approximately 6 1/2" by 9" are slightly thinner in card stock than the other Indian team issue. Rocky Colavito appears in this photo set a year before his Topps Rookie Card was issued.

COMPLETE SET 75.00 150.00
1 Earl Averill 2.50 5.00
2 Bob Avila 3.00 6.00
3 Jim Busby 2.50 5.00
4 Chico Carrasquel 2.50 5.00
5 Rocky Colavito 15.00 30.00
6 Bud Daley 2.50 5.00
7 Bob Feller 6.00 12.00
8 Mike Garcia 3.00 6.00
9 Mel Harder CO 2.50 5.00
Bill Lobe CO
Tony Cuccinello CO
R
10 Jim Hegan 2.50 5.00
11 Kenny Kuhn 2.50 5.00
12 Bob Lemon 5.00 10.00
13 Al Lopez MG 5.00 10.00
14 Sam Mele 2.50 5.00
15 Dale Mitchell 2.50 5.00
16 Don Mossi 3.00 6.00
17 Hal Naragon 2.50 5.00
18 Ray Narleski 2.50 5.00
19 Al Rosen 4.00 8.00
20 Herb Score 4.00 8.00
21 Al Smith 2.50 5.00
22 George Strickland 2.50 5.00
23 Vic Wertz 2.50 5.00
24 Gene Woodling 2.50 5.00
25 Early Wynn 5.00 10.00

1957 Indians Sohio

The 1957 Sohio Cleveland Indians set consists of 18 perforated photos; originally issued in strips of three cards, which after perforation measure approximately 5" by 7". These black and white cards were issued with facsimile autographs on the front which were designed to be pasted into a special photo album issued by SOHIO (Standard Oil of Ohio). The set features one of the earliest Roger Maris cards which even predates his 1958 Topps rookie card. In addition, the Rocky Colavito card is popular as well as 1957 was Rocky's rookie year for cards. These unnumbered cards are listed below in alphabetical order for convenience. It has been alleged that counterfeits of this set have been recently produced.

COMPLETE SET (18) 125.00 250.00
1 Bob Avila 3.00 6.00
2 Jim Busby 2.00 4.00
3 Chico Carrasquel 2.00 4.00
4 Rocky Colavito 40.00 80.00
5 Mike Garcia 3.00 6.00
6 Jim Hegan 2.00 4.00
7 Bob Lemon 15.00 30.00
8 Roger Maris 60.00 120.00
9 Don Mossi 3.00 6.00
10 Ray Narleski 2.00 4.00
11 Russ Nixon 2.00 4.00
12 Herb Score 4.00 8.00
13 Al Smith 2.00 4.00
14 George Strickland 2.00 4.00
15 Bob Usher 2.00 4.00
16 Vic Wertz 3.00 6.00
17 Gene Woodling 3.00 6.00
18 Early Wynn 15.00 30.00

1957 Indians Team Issue

This 29-card set of the Cleveland Indians features black-and-white player photos measuring approximately 6 1/2" by 9". The backs are blank. The cards are unnumbered and checklisted below in alphabetical order. An very early card of Roger Maris is in this set.

COMPLETE SET (29) 50.00 100.00
1 Joe Altobelli 1.50 3.00
2 Bob Avila 2.00 4.00
3 Alfonso Carrasquel 1.50 3.00
4 Rocky Colavito 10.00 20.00
5 Bud Daley 1.50 3.00
6 Kerby Farrell MG 1.50 3.00
7 Mike Garcia 1.50 3.00
8 Mel Harder CO 2.00 4.00
Red Kress CO
Kerby Farrell CO
Eddie Stanky CO
9 Jim Hegan 1.50 3.00
10 Art Houtteman 1.50 3.00
11 Kenny Kuhn 1.50 3.00
12 Bob Lemon 5.00 10.00
13 Roger Maris 12.50 25.00
14 Don Mossi 2.00 4.00
15 Hal Naragon 1.50 3.00
16 Ray Narleski 1.50 3.00
17 Russ Nixon 1.50 3.00
18 Stan Pitula 1.50 3.00
19 Lawrence Raines 1.50 3.00
20 Herb Score 2.50 5.00
21 Al Smith 1.50 3.00
22 George Strickland 1.50 3.00
23 Dick Tomanek 1.50 3.00
24 Bob Usher 1.50 3.00
25 Preston Ward 1.50 3.00
26 Vic Wertz 2.00 4.00
27 Dick Williams 2.50 5.00
28 Gene Woodling 2.00 4.00
29 Early Wynn 5.00 10.00

1958 Indians Team Issue

This 30-card set of the Cleveland Indians features black-and-white player photos measuring approximately 6 1/2" by 9" with white borders and facsimile autographs. The backs are blank. The first 24 cards were issued in May. The last five cards were found in the August set with several of the other players dropped. The set could be obtained by mail for 50 cents from the club.

COMPLETE SET (30) 75.00 150.00
1 Bob Avila 2.00 4.00
2 Bobby Bragan MG 1.50 3.00
3 Dick Brown 1.50 3.00
4 Alfonso(Chico) Carrasquel 1.50 3.00
5 Rocky Colavito 10.00 20.00
6 Larry Doby 5.00 10.00
7 Mike Garcia 2.00 4.00
8 Gary Geiger 1.50 3.00
9 Jim Grant 1.50 3.00
10 Bill Harrell 1.50 3.00
11 Red Kress CO 2.00 4.00
Bobby Bragan MG
Eddie Stanky CO
Me
12 Roger Maris 10.00 20.00
13 Cal McLish 1.50 3.00
14 Minnie Minoso 3.00 6.00
15 Bill Moran 1.50 3.00
16 Don Mossi 2.00 4.00
17 Ray Narleski 1.50 3.00
18 Russ Nixon 1.50 3.00
19 J.W. Porter 1.50 3.00
20 Herb Score 2.50 5.00
21 Dick Tomanek 1.50 3.00
22 Mickey Vernon 2.00 4.00
23 Preston Ward 1.50 3.00
24 Hoyt Wilhelm 5.00 10.00
25 Gary Bell 1.50 3.00
26 Rocky Colavito 7.50 15.00
27 Woodie Held 2.00 4.00
28 Bill Hunter 1.50 3.00
29 Don Mossi 2.00 4.00
30 Vic Power 3.00 6.00

1959 Indians

This set features black-and-white photos of the 1959 Cleveland Indians and measures approximately 6 1/2" by 9". Some of the photos have a facsimile autograph identifying the player while others have the player's name printed in a small bar in a bottom corner. The backs are blank. The cards are unnumbered and checklisted below in alphabetical order.

COMPLETE SET (26) 40.00 80.00
1 Gary Bell 1.50 3.00
2 Jim Bolger 1.50 3.00
3 Dick Brodowski 1.50 3.00
4 Al Cicotte 1.50 3.00
5 Rocky Colavito 5.00 10.00
6 Don Ferrarese 1.50 3.00
7 Tito Francona 2.00 4.00
8 Mike Garcia 2.00 4.00
9 Joe Gordon MG 2.50 5.00
10 Jim Grant 1.50 3.00
11 Mel Harder CO 2.00 4.00
12 Carroll Hardy 1.50 3.00
13 Woodie Held 1.50 3.00
14 Frank Lane GM 1.50 3.00
15 Billy Martin 5.00 10.00
16 Cal McLish 1.50 3.00
17 Minnie Minoso 3.00 6.00
18 Hal Naragon 1.50 3.00
19 Russ Nixon 1.50 3.00
20 Jim Perry 2.00 4.00
21 Jim Piersall 2.50 5.00
22 Vic Power 2.00 4.00
23 Herb Score 2.50 5.00
24 George Strickland 1.50 3.00
25 Mickey Vernon 2.00 4.00
26 Ray Webster 1.50 3.00

1960 Indians Jay Publishing

This 12-card set of the Cleveland Indians measures approximately 5" by 7". The fronts feature black-and-white posed player photos with the player's and team name printed below in the white border. These cards were packaged 12 to a packet and originally sold for 25 cents. The backs are blank. The cards are unnumbered and checklisted below in alphabetical order.

COMPLETE SET (12) 20.00 40.00
1 Tito Francona 2.50 6.00
2 Jim Grant 2.00 5.00
3 Woody Held 2.00 5.00
4 Harvey Kuenn 2.50 6.00
5 Barry Latman 2.00 5.00
6 Russ Nixon 2.00 5.00
7 Bubba Phillips 2.00 5.00
8 Jimmy Piersall 3.00 8.00
9 Vic Power 2.50 6.00
10 John Romano 2.00 5.00
11 George Strickland 2.00 5.00
12 John Temple 2.00 5.00

1961 Indians Team Issue

These black-backed photos, which measure approximately 6" by 9" feature members of the 1961 Cleveland Indians. These photos are unnumbered and are sequenced in alphabetical order.

COMPLETE SET 15.00 40.00
1 John Antonelli 1.00 2.50
2 Gary Bell .75 2.00
3 Mike de la Hoz .75 2.00
4 Jimmie Dykes MG 1.00 2.50
5 Tito Francona .75 2.00
6 Jim Grant 1.00 2.50
7 Wynn Hawkins .75 2.00
8 Woodie Held .75 2.00
9 Willie Kirkland .75 2.00
10 Barry Latman .75 2.00
11 Bobby Locke .75 2.00
12 Jim Perry 1.25 3.00
13 Bubba Phillips .75 2.00
14 Jim Piersall 1.50 4.00
15 Vic Power .75 2.00
16 John Romano .75 2.00
17 Dick Stigman .75 2.00
18 John Temple .75 2.00
19 Indians Coaches 1.25 3.00
20 Municipal Stadium .75 2.00

1962 Indians Jay Publishing

This 12-card set of the Cleveland Indians measures approximately 5" by 7". The fronts feature black-and-white posed player photos with the player's and team name printed below in the white border. These cards were packaged 12 to a packet. The backs are blank. The cards are unnumbered and checklisted below in alphabetical order.

COMPLETE SET (12) 20.00 40.00
1 Gary Bell 2.00 5.00
2 Dick Donovan 2.00 5.00
3 Tito Francona 2.50 6.00
4 Jim Grant 2.50 6.00
5 Woody Held 2.50 6.00
6 Willie Kirkland 2.00 5.00
7 Barry Latman 2.00 5.00
8 Mel McGaha MG 2.00 5.00
9 Bob Nieman 2.00 5.00
10 Bubba Phillips 2.00 5.00
11 Pedro Ramos 2.00 5.00
12 John Romano 2.00 5.00

1963 Indians Jay Publishing

This 12-card set of the Cleveland Indians measures approximately 5" by 7". The fronts feature black-and-white posed player photos with the player's and team name printed below in the white border. These cards were packaged 12 to a packet. The backs are blank. The cards are unnumbered and checklisted below in alphabetical order.

COMPLETE SET (12) 25.00 50.00
1 Joe Adcock 3.00 8.00
2 Gary Bell 2.00 5.00
3 Vic Davalillo 2.00 5.00
4 Mike De La Hoz 2.00 5.00
5 Dick Donovan 2.00 5.00
6 Tito Francona 2.50 6.00
7 Jim Grant 2.50 6.00
8 Woody Held 2.00 5.00
9 Willie Kirkland 2.00 5.00
10 Barry Latman 2.00 5.00
11 John Romano 2.00 5.00
12 Birdie Tebbetts MG 2.50 6.00

1964 Indians Jay Publishing

This 12-card set of the Cleveland Indians measures approximately 5" by 7". The fronts feature black-and-white posed player photos with the player's and team name printed below in the white border. These cards were packaged 12 to a packet. The backs are blank. The cards are unnumbered and checklisted below in alphabetical order.

COMPLETE SET (12) 10.00 25.00
1 Max Alvis 1.00 2.50
2 Joe Azcue .75 2.00
3 Vic Davalillo .75 2.00
4 Dick Donovan .75 2.00
5 Tito Francona 1.00 2.50
6 Jim Grant 1.00 2.50
7 Woody Held .75 2.00
8 Jack Kralick .75 2.00
9 Pedro Ramos .75 2.00
10 John Romano .75 2.00
11 Al Smith .75 2.00
12 Birdie Tebbetts MG 1.00 2.50

1965 Indians Jay Publishing

This 12-card set of the Cleveland Indians measures approximately 5" by 7". The fronts feature black-and-white posed player photos with the player's and team name printed below in the white border. These cards were packaged 12 to a packet. The backs are blank. The cards are unnumbered and checklisted below in alphabetical order. Luis Tiant appears in his Rookie Card season.

COMPLETE SET (12) 25.00 50.00
1 Max Alvis 2.00 5.00
2 Gary Bell 2.00 5.00
3 Larry Brown 2.00 5.00
4 Rocky Colavito 4.00 10.00
5 Dick Donovan 2.00 5.00
6 Chuck Hinton 2.00 5.00
7 Jack Kralick 2.00 5.00
8 Sam McDowell 3.00 8.00
9 Birdie Tebbetts MG 2.00 5.00
10 Ralph Terry 2.50 6.00
11 Luis Tiant 4.00 10.00
12 Leon Wagner 2.00 5.00

1966 Indians Photos

These photos, which measure 8" by 10" feature members of the 1966 Cleveland Indians. Since these photos are unnumbered, we have sequenced them in alphabetical order.

COMPLETE SET 10.00 25.00
1 Max Alvis 1.25 3.00
2 Joe Azcue 1.25 3.00
3 Gary Bell 1.25 3.00
4 Larry Brown 1.25 3.00
5 Rocky Colavito 2.00 5.00
6 Del Crandall 1.25 3.00
7 Vic Davalillo 1.25 3.00
8 Steve Hargan 1.25 3.00
9 Chuck Hinton 1.25 3.00
10 Dick Howser 1.25 3.00
11 Pedro Gonzalez 1.25 3.00
12 Tom Kelly 1.25 3.00
13 Jack Kralick 1.25 3.00
14 Jim Landis 1.25 3.00
15 Sam McDowell 2.00 5.00
16 Chico Salmon 1.25 3.00
17 Sonny Siebert 1.25 3.00
18 Duke Sims 1.25 3.00
19 Birdie Tebbetts MG 1.50 4.00
Early Wynn CO
George Strickla
20 Luis Tiant 2.50 6.00
21 Leon Wagner 1.25 3.00
22 Fred Whitfield 1.25 3.00

1966 Indians Team Issue

This 12-card set of the Cleveland Indians measures approximately 4 7/8" by 7 1/8" and features black-and-white player photos in a white border. These cards were packaged 12 to a packet and originally sold for 25 cents. The backs are blank. The cards are unnumbered and checklisted below in alphabetical order.

COMPLETE SET (12) 12.50 30.00
1 Max Alvis .75 2.00
2 Joe Azcue .75 2.00
3 Rocky Colavito 1.50 4.00
4 Vic Davalillo 1.00 2.50
5 Chuck Hinton .75 2.00
6 Dick Howser 1.00 2.50
7 Jack Kralick .75 2.00
8 Sam McDowell 1.25 3.00
9 Don McMahon .75 2.00
10 Birdie Tebbetts MG .75 2.00
11 Luis Tiant 1.50 4.00
12 Leon Wagner .75 2.00

1970 Indians

This 12-card set of the Cleveland Indians measures approximately 4 1/4" by 7" and features white-bordered black-and-white player photos. The player's name and team are printed in the wide top margin. The backs are blank. The cards are unnumbered and checklisted below in alphabetical order.

COMPLETE SET (12) 8.00 20.00
1 Buddy Bradford .60 1.50
2 Larry Brown .60 1.50
3 Alvin Dark .75 2.00
4 Ray Fosse .75 2.00
5 Steve Hargan .60 1.50
6 Ken Harrelson 1.00 2.50
7 Dennis Higgins .60 1.50
8 Sam McDowell 1.00 2.50
9 Graig Nettles 1.25 3.00
10 Vada Pinson 1.25 3.00
11 Ken Suarez .60 1.50
12 Ted Uhlaender .60 1.50

1971 Indians

These 12 cards featuring members of the Cleveland Indians measure approximately 7" by 8 3/4" with the fronts having white-bordered color player photos. The player's name and team is printed in black in the white margin below the picture. The backs are blank. The cards are unnumbered and checklisted below in alphabetical order.

COMPLETE SET (12) 8.00 20.00
1 Buddy Bradford .60 1.50
2 Alvin Dark MG 1.00 2.50
3 Steve Dunning .60 1.50
4 Ray Fosse .75 2.00
5 Steve Hargan .60 1.50
6 Ken Harrelson 1.00 2.50
7 Chuck Hinton .60 1.50
8 Ray Lamb .60 1.50
9 Sam McDowell 1.25 3.00
10 Vada Pinson 1.25 3.00
11 Ken Suarez .60 1.50
12 Ted Uhlaender .60 1.50

1972 Indians Brown Derby Poster

Issued through the Brown Derby restaurant chain, these posters measured 22" by 27" and featured members of the 1972 Cleveland Indians. They were apparently issued each Sunday, but incomplete information is known as to which players were actually produced for this set or whether all 16 players which were supposed to be issued were issued. Since these cards are not numbered, we have sequenced them in alphabetical order. Obviously, more information on this set would be greatly appreciated.

COMPLETE SET 15.00 40.00
1 Chris Chambliss 3.00 8.00
2 Ray Fosse 2.00 5.00
3 Roy Foster 2.00 5.00
4 Graig Nettles 3.00 8.00
5 Gaylord Perry 5.00 12.00
6 Dick Tidrow 2.00 5.00
7 Del Unser 2.00 5.00

1973 Indians Team Issue

This set features color photos of the 1973 Cleveland Indians printed on postcard-size cards with postcard backs. The cards are unnumbered and checklisted below in alphabetical order. Four of the cards had numbers on them, and these numbers are listed after the player's names. These cards were published by Cleveland Sports Pro Enterprises and the photos were taken by Axel Studios. A collector could order these postcards, as they were issued in 25-card sets and evolved during the year from the producer for $3 per set.

COMPLETE SET 12.50 30.00
1 Dwain Anderson 332 .40 1.00
2 Ken Aspromonte MG .40 1.00
3 Fred Beene 322 .40 1.00
4 Buddy Bell 1.00 2.50
5 Dick Bosman .40 1.00
6 Jack Brohamer .40 1.00
7 Leo Cardenas .40 1.00
8 Chris Chambliss .75 2.00
9 Frank Duffy .40 1.00
10 Dave Duncan .40 1.00
11 John Ellis .40 1.00
12 Ed Farmer .40 1.00
13 Oscar Gamble .60 1.50
14 George Hendrick .60 1.50
15 Tom Hilgendorf .40 1.00
16 Jerry Johnson .40 1.00
17 Ray Lamb .40 1.00
18 Ron Lolich .40 1.00
19 John Lowenstein .40 1.00
20 Joe Lutz CO 1.00
21 Steve Mingori .40 1.00
22 Tony Pacheco CO 327 .40 1.00
23 Gaylord Perry 1.50 4.00
24 Tom Ragland .40 1.00
25 Warren Spahn CO 1.50 4.00
26 Charlie Spikes .40 1.00
27 Brent Strom .40 1.00
28 Dick Tidrow .40 1.00
29 Rosendo Rusty Torres 342 .40 1.00
30 Rusty Torres .40 1.00
Back says Leo Cardenas
31 Milt Wilcox .40 1.00
32 Walt Williams .40 1.00

1974 Indians Team Issue

These postcards feature players who made their debut with the Indians in 1974. Many of the 1973 players also appeared in 1974 but they are not listed here. Since these cards are not numbered, we have sequenced them in alphabetical order.

COMPLETE SET 8.00 20.00
1 Luis Alvarado .40 1.00
2 Dwain Anderson .40 1.00
3 Steve Arlin .40 1.00
4 Alan Ashby .40 1.00
5 Fred Beene .40 1.00
6 Ossie Blanco .40 1.00
7 Clay Bryant .40 1.00
8 Tom Buskey .40 1.00
9 Ed Crosby .40 1.00
10 Larry Doby CO 1.00 2.50
11 Bruce Ellingsen .40 1.00
12 Bob Johnson .40 1.00
13 Steve Kline .40 1.00
14 Leron Lee .40 1.00
15 Joe Lis .40 1.00
16 Tony Pacheco CO .40 1.00
17 Jim Perry .60 1.50
18 Fritz Peterson .40 1.00
19 Ken Sanders .40 1.00

1975 Indians 1954 TCMA

The 39-card set of the 1954 Cleveland Indians features black-and-white player photos in white borders. The backs carry player statistics for 1954. The cards are unnumbered and checklisted below in alphabetical order with cards 37, 38, and 39 being jumbo cards.

COMPLETE SET (39) 12.50 30.00
1 Bobby Avila .40 1.00
2 Bob Chakales .20 .50
3 Tony Cuccinello .20 .50
4 Sam Dente .20 .50
5 Larry Doby 1.25 3.00
6 Luke Easter .20 .50
7 Bob Feller 2.00 5.00
8 Mike Garcia .20 .50
9 Joe Ginsberg .20 .50
10 Billy Glynn .20 .50
11 Mickey Grasso .20 .50
12 Mel Harder .40 1.00
13 Jim Hegan .40 1.00
14 Bob Hooper .20 .50
15 Dave Hoskins .20 .50
16 Art Houtteman .20 .50
17 Bob Kennedy .20 .50
18 Bob Lemon .75 2.00
19 Al Lopez .60 1.50
20 Hank Majeski .20 .50
21 Dale Mitchell .40 1.00
22 Don Mossi .60 1.50
23 Hal Naragon .20 .50
24 Ray Narleski .20 .50
25 Rocky Nelson .20 .50
26 Hal Newhouser .75 2.00
27 Dave Philley .20 .50
28 Dave Pope .20 .50
29 Rudy Regaldo .20 .50
30 Al Rosen .75 2.00
31 Jose Santiago .20 .50
32 Al Smith .20 .50
33 George Strickland .20 .50
34 Vic Wertz .20 .50
35 Wally Westlake .20 .50
36 Early Wynn 1.25 3.00
37 Dave Pope .40 1.00
Dave Philley
Larry Doby
Al Smith
38 Bill Lobe .40 1.00
Tony Cuccinello
Red Kress
Mel Harder#
39 Wynn .75 2.00
Lem
Hoop
Hout
Sant
Narl
Garc
Newh
Lopez

1975 Indians JB Robinson

This seven-card set was issued by JB Robinson Jewelers and features 8 1/2" by 8 1/2" color photos of the Cleveland Indians. The cards are unnumbered and checklisted below in alphabetical order.

COMPLETE SET (7) 5.00 12.00
1 Buddy Bell 1.00 2.50
2 Jack Brohamer .40 1.00
3 Rico Carty .75 2.00
4 Frank Duffy .40 1.00
5 Oscar Gamble .60 1.50
6 Boog Powell 1.00 2.50
7 Frank Robinson MG 1.00 2.50

1975 Indians Postcards

This 25-card set of the Cleveland Indians features player photos on postcard-size cards. The cards are unnumbered and checklisted below in alphabetical order.

COMPLETE SET (25) 5.00 12.00
1 Alan Ashby .30 .75
2 Fred Beene .20 .50
3 Buddy Bell .60 1.50
4 Ken Berry .20 .50
5 Dick Bosman .20 .50
6 Jack Brohamer .20 .50
7 Tom Buskey .20 .50
8 Rico Carty .30 .75
9 Ed Crosby .20 .50
10 Frank Duffy .20 .50
11 John Ellis .20 .50
12 Oscar Gamble .30 .75
13 George Hendrick .30 .75
14 Don Hood .20 .50
15 Jim Kern .20 .50
16 Dave LaRoche .20 .50
17 Leron Lee .20 .50
18 John Lowenstein .20 .50
19 Gaylord Perry .75 2.00
20 Jim Perry .30 .75
21 Fritz Peterson .20 .50
22 John Boog Powell .60 1.50
23 Frank Robinson P .75 2.00
MG
24 Charlie Spikes .20 .50
25 Coaching Staff .20 .50

1976 Indians Team Issue

This nine-card set of the Cleveland Indians features color player photos printed on postcard-size cards. The cards are unnumbered and checklisted below in alphabetical order.

COMPLETE SET (9) 3.00 8.00
1 Larvell Banks .20 .50
2 Tom Buskey .20 .50
3 Dennis Eckersley 2.00 5.00
4 Ray Fosse .20 .50
5 Don Hood .20 .50
6 Dave LaRoche .20 .50
7 Boog Powell .60 1.50
8 Ron Pruitt .20 .50
9 Stan Thomas .20 .50

1977 Indians 1920 TCMA

Jim Bagby P

This 22-card set commemorates the 1920 World Champion Cleveland Indians. The fronts feature black-and-white player photos, while the backs display player statistics. One jumbo card measuring approximately 3 3/4" by 5" carries a story about the 1920 Cleveland Indians Team. The cards are unnumbered and checklisted below in alphabetical order with the jumbo card listed as number 22.

COMPLETE SET (22) 8.00 20.00
1 Jim Bagby .40 1.00
2 George Burns .20 .50
3 Ray Caldwell .20 .50
4 Ray Chapman .60 1.50
5 Stan Coleleski .75 2.00
6 Joe Evans .20 .50
7 Larry Gardner .20 .50
8 Jack Graney .20 .50
9 Charlie Jamieson .20 .50
10 Wheeler Doc Johnston .20 .50
11 Harry Lunte .20 .50
12 John Duster Mails .20 .50
13 Guy Morton .20 .50
14 Les Nunamaker .20 .50
15 Steve O'Neill .40 1.00
16 Joe Sewell .75 2.00
17 Elmer Smith .20 .50
18 Tris Speaker P 2.00 5.00
MG
19 George Uhle .20 .50
20 Bill Wambsganss .60 1.50
21 Joe Wood .60 1.50
22 World Series Foes .75 2.00
Wilbert Robinson
Tris Speaker

1977 Indians Team Issue

This 25-card set features black-and-white, glossy photos of the Cleveland Indians printed on postcard-size cards. Jim Bibby's card (number 1) is the only color photo. The cards are unnumbered and checklisted below in alphabetical order.

COMPLETE SET (25) 6.00 15.00
1 Jim Bibby .40 1.00
2 Larvell Blanks .20 .50
3 Bruce Bochte .20 .50
4 Tom Buskey .20 .50
5 Rico Carty .30 .75
6 Rocky Colavito CO .60 1.50
7 Pat Dobson .20 .50
8 Frank Duffy .20 .50
9 Dennis Eckersley 1.25 3.00
10 Al Fitzmorris .20 .50
11 Ray Fosse .20 .50
12 Fred Kendall .20 .50
13 Jim Kern .20 .50
14 Dave LaRoche .20 .50
15 John Lowenstein .20 .50
16 Rick Manning .20 .50
17 Bill Melton .20 .50
18 Sid Monge .20 .50
19 Jim Norris .20 .50
20 Joe Nossek CO .20 .50
21 Ron Pruitt .20 .50
22 Frank Robinson MG .60 1.50
23 Andre Thornton .40 1.00
24 Jeff Torborg CO .20 .50
25 Rick Waits .20 .50

1978 Indians Team Issue
This 31-card set of the Cleveland Indians features black-and-white photos on postcard-size cards. The cards are unnumbered and checklisted below in alphabetical order.
COMPLETE SET (31) 5.00 12.00
1 Buddy Bell .40 1.00
2 Larvell Blanks .20 .50
3 Wayne Cage .20 .50
4 David Clyde .20 .50
5 Rocky Colavito CO .60 1.50
6 Ted Cox .20 .50
7 Paul Dade .20 .50
8 Bo Diaz .20 .50
9 Dave Duncan CO .20 .50
10 Al Fitzmorris .20 .50
11 Wayne Garland .20 .50
12 Johnny Grubb .20 .50
13 Harvey Haddix CO .20 .50
14 Ron Hassey .20 .50
15 Don Hood .20 .50
16 Willie Horton .30 .75
17 Jim Kern .20 .50
18 Dennis Kinney .20 .50
19 Duane Kuiper .20 .50
20 Rick Manning .20 .50
21 Sid Monge .20 .50
22 Jim Norris .20 .50
23 Joe Nossek CO .20 .50
24 Mike Paxton .20 .50
25 Ron Pruitt .20 .50
26 Horace Speed .20 .50
27 Andre Thornton .40 1.00
28 Jeff Torborg MG .20 .50
29 Tom Veryzer .20 .50
30 Rick Waits .20 .50
31 Rick Wise .20 .50

1979 Indians Team Issue
These cards are similar to the other Indians team issues around this period. These cards are black and white with a light paper stock. These cards are unnumbered so we have sequenced them in alphabetical order.
COMPLETE SET 6.00 15.00
1 Gary Alexander .20 .50
2 Del Alston .20 .50
3 Larry Anderson .20 .50
4 Len Barker .20 .50
5 Bobby Bonds .40 1.00
6 Wayne Cage .20 .50
7 David Clyde .20 .50
8 Ted Cox .20 .50
9 Victor Cruz .20 .50
10 Paul Dade .20 .50
11 Bo Diaz .20 .50
12 Dave Duncan .20 .50
13 Dave Garcia MG .20 .50
14 Wayne Garland .20 .50
15 Mike Hargrove .30 .75
16 Toby Harrah .30 .75
17 Chuck Hartenstein .20 .50
18 Don Hood .20 .50
19 Cliff Johnson .20 .50
20 Duane Kuiper .20 .50
21 Rick Manning .20 .50
22 Sid Monge .20 .50
23 Joe Nossek .20 .50
24 Mike Paxton .20 .50
25 Paul Reuschel .20 .50
26 Ron Pruitt .20 .50
27 Dave Rosello .20 .50
28 Horace Speed .20 .50
29 Dan Spillner .20 .50
30 Andre Thornton .30 .75
31 Jeff Torborg MG .20 .50
32 Tom Veryzer .20 .50
33 Rick Waits .20 .50
34 Eric Wilkins .20 .50
35 Rick Wise .20 .50

1980 Indians Team Issue
This 31-card set of the Cleveland Indians features black-and-white player photos printed on postcard-size cards. The cards are unnumbered and checklisted below in alphabetical order. The postcards numbered from 32 through 38 were late additions as the Indians made player moves during the season
COMPLETE SET (31) 6.00 15.00
1 Gary Alexander .20 .50
2 Del Alston .20 .50
3 Len Barker .20 .50
5 Victor Cruz .20 .50
6 John Denny .20 .50
6 Joe Charboneau .60 1.50
7 Bo Diaz .20 .50
8 Dave Duncan CO .20 .50
9 Jerry Dybzinski .20 .50
10 Dave Garcia MG .20 .50
11 Wayne Garland .20 .50
12 Mike Hargrove .40 1.00
13 Toby Harrah .30 .75
14 Ron Hassey .20 .50
15 Cliff Johnson .20 .50
16 Duane Kuiper .20 .50
17 Rick Manning .20 .50
18 Tom McCraw CO .20 .50
19 Sid Monge .20 .50
20 Andres Mora .20 .50
21 Joe Nossek CO .20 .50
22 Jorge Orta .20 .50
23 Bob Owchinko .20 .50
24 Ron Pruitt .20 .50
25 Dave Rosello .20 .50
26 Dennis Sommers CO .20 .50
27 Dan Spillner .20 .50
28 Mike Stanton .20 .50
29 Andre Thornton .30 .75
30 Tom Veryzer .20 .50
31 Rick Waits .20 .50
32 Baseball Bug .20 .50
33 Alan Bannister .20 .50
34 Jack Brohamer .20 .50
35 Miguel Dilone .20 .50
36 Gary Gray .20 .50
37 Ross Grimsley .20 .50
38 Sandy Withol .20 .50

1982 Indians
This 36-card set measures approximately 3 1/2" by 5 1/2" and feature black and white player portraits in a white border with the player's name, position and team name in the bottom margin. The backs are blank. The cards are unnumbered and checklisted below in alphabetical order. This issue features members of the 1982 Cleveland Indians.
COMPLETE SET (36) 6.00 15.00
1 Bud Anderson .20 .50
2 Chris Bando .20 .50
3 Alan Bannister .20 .50
4 Len Barker .20 .50
5 Bert Blyleven .40 1.00
6 John Bohnet .20 .50
7 Carmelo Castillo .20 .50
8 Joe Charboneau .30 .75
9 Rodney Craig .20 .50
10 John Denny .20 .50
11 Miguel Dilone .20 .50
12 Jerry Dybzinski .20 .50
13 Dave Garcia MG .20 .50
14 Gordy Glaser .20 .50
15 Ed Glynn .20 .50
16 Johnny Goryl CO .20 .50
17 Mike Hargrove .40 1.00
18 Toby Harrah .30 .75
19 Ron Hassey .20 .50
20 Von Hayes .30 .75
21 Neal Heaton .20 .50
22 Dennis Lewallyn .20 .50
23 Rick Manning .20 .50
24 Bake McBride .20 .50
25 Tommy McCraw CO .20 .50
26 Bill Nahorodny .20 .50
27 Karl Pagel .20 .50
28 Jack Perconte .20 .50
29 Mel Queen CO .20 .50
30 Dennis Sommers CO .20 .50
31 Lary Sorensen .20 .50
32 Dan Spillner .20 .50
33 Rick Sutcliffe .40 1.00
34 Andre Thornton .30 .75
35 Rick Waits .20 .50
36 Eddie Whitson .20 .50

1982 Indians Burger King
The cards in this 12-card set measure approximately 3" by 5". Tips From The Dugout is the series title of this set issued on a one card per week basis by the Burger King chain in the Cleveland area. Each card contains a black and white photo of manager Dave Garcia or coaches Goryl, McCraw, Queen and Sommers, under whom appears a paragraph explaining some aspect of inside baseball. The photo and "Tip" are set upon a large yellow area surrounded by green borders. The cards are not numbered and are blank-backed. The logos of Burger King and WUAB-TV appear at the base of the card.
COMPLETE SET (12) 5.00 12.00
1A Dave Garcia MG .40 1.00
Be in the Game
1B Dave Garcia MG .40 1.00
Sportsmanship
2A Johnny Goryl CO .40 1.00
Rounding bases
2B Johnny Goryl CO .40 1.00
Third base running
3A Tom McCraw CO .40 1.00
Follow through
3B Tom McCraw CO .40 1.00
Selecting a bat
3C Tom McCraw CO .40 1.00
Watch the ball
4A Mel Queen CO .40 1.00
Master one pitch
4B Mel Queen CO .40 1.00
Warm up
5A Dennis Sommers CO .40 1.00
Get down on a ground ball
5B Dennis Sommers CO .40 1.00
Protect your fingers
5C Dennis Sommers CO .40 1.00
Tagging first base

1982 Indians Wheaties
The cards in this 30-card set measure approximately 2 13/16" by 4 1/8". This set of Cleveland Indians baseball players was co-produced by the Indians baseball club and Wheaties, whose respective logos appear on the front of every card. The cards were given away in groups of 10 as a promotion during games on May 30 (1-10), June 19 (11-20) and July 16, 1982 (21-30). The manager (MG), four coaches (CO), and 25 players are featured in a simple format of a color picture, player name and position. The cards are not numbered and the backs contain a Wheaties ad. The set was later sold at the Cleveland Indians gift shop. The cards are ordered below alphabetically within groups of ten as they were issued.
COMPLETE SET (30) 6.00 15.00
1 Bert Blyleven .40 1.00
2 Joe Charboneau .30 .75
3 Jerry Dybzinski .20 .50
4 Dave Garcia MG .20 .50
5 Toby Harrah .30 .75
6 Ron Hassey .20 .50
7 Dennis Lewallyn .20 .50
8 Rick Manning .20 .50
9 Tommy McCraw CO .20 .50
10 Rick Waits .20 .50
11 Chris Bando .20 .50
12 Len Barker .30 .75
13 Tom Brennan .20 .50
14 Rodney Craig .20 .50
15 Mike Fischlin .20 .50
16 Johnny Goryl CO .20 .50
17 Mel Queen CO .20 .50
18 Lary Sorensen .20 .50
19 Andre Thornton .40 1.00
20 Eddie Whitson .20 .50
21 Alan Bannister .20 .50
22 John Denny .20 .50
23 Miguel Dilone .20 .50
24 Mike Hargrove .40 1.00
25 Von Hayes .40 1.00
26 Bake McBride .20 .50
27 Jack Perconte .20 .50
28 Dennis Sommers CO .20 .50
29 Dan Spillner .20 .50
30 Rick Sutcliffe .40 1.00

1983 Indians Postcards
These postcards feature members of the 1983 Cleveland Indians. They are unnumbered and we have sequenced them in alphabetical order.
COMPLETE SET 4.00 10.00
1 Bud Anderson .08 .25
2 Jay Baller .08 .25
3 Chris Bando .08 .25
4 Alan Bannister .08 .25
5 Len Barker .08 .25
6 Bert Blyleven .30 .75
7 Carmelo Castillo .08 .25
8 Wil Culmer .08 .25
9 Miguel Dilone .08 .25
10 Jerry Dybzinski .08 .25
11 Jim Essian .08 .25
12 Juan Eichelberger .08 .25
13 Mike Ferraro MG .08 .25
14 Mike Fischlin .08 .25
15 Julio Franco .75 2.00
16 Ed Glynn .08 .25
17 Mike Hargrove .30 .75
18 Toby Harrah .20 .50
19 Ron Hassey .08 .25
20 Neal Heaton .08 .25
21 Rick Manning .08 .25
22 Bake McBride .08 .25
23 Don McMahon CO .08 .25
24 Ed Napoleon CO .08 .25
25 Karl Pagel .08 .25
26 Jack Perconte .08 .25
27 Broderick Perkins .08 .25
28 Jerry Reed .08 .25
29 Kevin Rhomberg .08 .25
30 Ramon Romero .08 .25
31 Dennis Sommers CO .08 .25
32 Lary Sorensen .08 .25
33 Dan Spillner .08 .25
34 Rick Sutcliffe .20 .50
35 Andre Thornton .30 .75
36 Manny Trillo .20 .50
37 Otto Velez .08 .25
38 George Vukovich .08 .25
39 Rick Waits .08 .25

1983 Indians Wheaties
The cards in this 32-card set measure approximately 2 13/16" by 4 1/8". The full color set of 1983 Wheaties Indians is quite similar to the Wheaties set of 1982. The backs, however, are significantly different. They contain complete career playing records of the players. The complete sets were given away at the ball park on May 15, 1983. The set was later made available at the Indians Gift Shop. The manager (MG) and several coaches (CO) are included in the set. The cards below are ordered alphabetically by the subject's name.
COMPLETE SET (32) 4.00 10.00
1 Bud Anderson .08 .25
2 Jay Baller .08 .25
3 Chris Bando .08 .25
4 Alan Bannister .08 .25
5 Len Barker .20 .50
6 Bert Blyleven .40 1.00
7 Wil Culmer .08 .25
8 Miguel Dilone .08 .25
9 Juan Eichelberger .08 .25
10 Jim Essian .08 .25
11 Mike Ferraro MG .08 .25
12 Mike Fischlin .08 .25
13 Julio Franco .60 1.50
14 Ed Glynn .08 .25
15 Johnny Goryl CO .08 .25
16 Mike Hargrove .30 .75
17 Toby Harrah .20 .50
18 Ron Hassey .08 .25
19 Neal Heaton .08 .25
20 Rick Manning .08 .25
21 Bake McBride .08 .25
22 Don McMahon CO .08 .25
23 Ed Napoleon CO .08 .25
24 Broderick Perkins .08 .25
25 Dennis Sommers CO .08 .25
26 Lary Sorensen .08 .25
27 Dan Spillner .08 .25
28 Rick Sutcliffe .40 1.00
29 Andre Thornton .30 .75
30 Manny Trillo .20 .50
31 George Vukovich .08 .25
32 Rick Waits .08 .25

1984 Indians
This 33-card set of the Cleveland Indians measures approximately 3 1/2" by 5 1/2" and features black-and-white player portraits in a white border. The player's name, position, and team are printed in the wide bottom margin. The backs are blank. The cards are unnumbered and checklisted below in alphabetical order.
COMPLETE SET (33) 4.00 10.00
1 Luis Aponte .08 .25
2 Chris Bando .08 .25
3 Rick Behenna .08 .25
4 Tony Bernazard .08 .25
5 Bert Blyleven .40 1.00
6 Bobby Bonds CO .30 .75
7 Brett Butler .60 1.50
8 Ernie Camacho .08 .25
9 Carmelo Castillo .08 .25
10 Pat Corrales MG .08 .25
11 Jamie Easterly .08 .25
12 Mike Fischlin .08 .25
13 Julio Franco .60 1.50
14 George Frazier .08 .25
15 Johnny Goryl CO .08 .25
16 Mike Hargrove .30 .75
17 Ron Hassey .08 .25
18 Neal Heaton .08 .25
19 Brook Jacoby .20 .50
20 Mike Jeffcoat .08 .25
21 Don McMahon CO .08 .25
22 Ed Napoleon CO .08 .25
23 Otis Nixon .40 1.00
24 Broderick Perkins .08 .25
25 Kevin Rhomberg .08 .25
26 Dan Spillner .08 .25
27 Dennis Sommers .08 .25
28 Rick Sutcliffe .20 .50
29 Pat Tabler .20 .50
30 Andre Thornton .30 .75
31 George Vukovich .08 .25
32 Tom Waddell .08 .25
33 Jerry Willard .08 .25

1984 Indians Wheaties
The cards in this 29-card set measure approximately 2 13/16" by 4 1/8". For the third straight year, Wheaties distributed a set of Cleveland Indians baseball cards. These over-sized cards were passed out at a Baseball Card Day at the Cleveland Stadium. Similar in appearance to the cards of the past two years, both the Indians and the Wheaties logos appear on the obverse, along with the name, team and position. Cards are numbered on the back by the player's uniform number.
COMPLETE SET (29) 4.00 10.00
2 Brett Butler .40 1.00
4 Tony Bernazard .08 .25
8 Carmelo Castillo .08 .25
10 Pat Tabler .08 .25
13 Ernie Camacho .08 .25
14 Julio Franco .40 1.00
15 Broderick Perkins .08 .25
16 Jerry Willard .08 .25
18 Pat Corrales MG .08 .25
21 Mike Hargrove .30 .75
22 Mike Fischlin .08 .25
23 Chris Bando .08 .25
24 George Vukovich .08 .25
26 Brook Jacoby .20 .50
27 Steve Farr .20 .50
28 Bert Blyleven .40 1.00
29 Andre Thornton .30 .75
30 Joe Carter 2.00 5.00
31 Steve Comer .08 .25
33 Roy Smith .08 .25
34 Mel Hall .20 .50
36 Jamie Easterly .08 .25
37 Don Schulze .08 .25
38 Luis Aponte .08 .25
44 Neal Heaton .08 .25
46 Mike Jeffcoat .08 .25
54 Tom Waddell .08 .25
NNO Indians Coaches .20 .50
John Goryl
Dennis Sommers
Ed Na
NNO Tom-E-Hawk (Mascot) .08 .25

1985 Indians
This 36-card set of the Cleveland Indians measures approximately 3 1/2" by 5 1/2" and features white-bordered, black-and-white player photos. The player's name, position and team are printed in the wide bottom margin. The backs are blank. The cards are unnumbered and checklisted below in alphabetical order.
COMPLETE SET (36) 4.00 10.00
1 Chris Bando .08 .25
2 Rick Behenna .08 .25
3 Butch Benton .08 .25
4 Tony Bernazard .08 .25
5 Bert Blyleven .40 1.00
6 Bobby Bonds CO .20 .50
7 Brett Butler .40 1.00
8 Ernie Camacho .08 .25
9 Joe Carter 1.00 2.50
10 Carmen Castillo .08 .25
11 Pat Corrales MG .08 .25
12 Jamie Easterly .08 .25
13 Mike Fischlin .08 .25
14 Julio Franco .40 1.00
15 John Goryl CO .08 .25
16 Mel Hall .08 .25
17 Mike Hargrove .30 .75
18 Neal Heaton .08 .25
19 Brook Jacoby .08 .25
20 Mike Jeffcoat .08 .25
21 Don McMahon CO .08 .25
22 Ed Napoleon CO .08 .25
23 Otis Nixon .40 1.00
24 Geno Petralli .08 .25
25 Ramon Romero .08 .25
26 Vern Ruhle .08 .25
27 Don Schulze .08 .25
28 Jim Siwy .08 .25
29 Roy Smith .08 .25
30 Dennis Sommers .08 .25
31 Pat Tabler .08 .25
32 Andre Thornton .30 .75
33 Dave Von Ohlen .08 .25
34 George Vukovich .08 .25
35 Tom Waddell .08 .25
36 Jerry Willard .08 .25

1985 Indians Polaroid
This 32-card set features cards (each measuring approximately 2 13/16" by 4 1/8") of the Cleveland Indians. The cards are unnumbered except for uniform number, as they are listed below. The set was also sponsored by J.C. Penney and was distributed at the stadium to fans in attendance on Baseball Card Day.
COMPLETE SET (32) 8.00 20.00
2 Brett Butler .40 1.00
4 Tony Bernazard .20 .50
8 Carmen Castillo .20 .50
10 Pat Tabler .20 .50
12 Benny Ayala .20 .50
13 Ernie Camacho .20 .50
14 Julio Franco .60 1.50
16 Jerry Willard .20 .50
18 Pat Corrales MG .20 .50
20 Otis Nixon .60 1.50
21 Mike Hargrove .40 1.00
22 Mike Fischlin .20 .50
23 Chris Bando .20 .50
24 George Vukovich .20 .50
26 Brook Jacoby .30 .75
27 Mel Hall .30 .75
28 Bert Blyleven .40 1.00
29 Andre Thornton .40 1.00
30 Joe Carter 2.50 6.00
32 Rick Behenna .20 .50
33 Roy Smith .20 .50
35 Jerry Reed .20 .50
36 Jamie Easterly .20 .50
38 Dave Von Ohlen .20 .50
41 Rich Thompson .20 .50
43 Bryan Clark .20 .50
44 Neal Heaton .20 .50
48 Vern Ruhle .20 .50
49 Jeff Barkley .20 .50
50 Ramon Romero .20 .50
54 Tom Waddell .20 .50
NNO Coaching Staff .30 .75
Bobby Bonds
John Goryl
Don McMah

1986 Indians Greats TCMA
This 12-card standard-size set features some of the best all-time Cleveland Indians. The cards feature the player photo, his name and position on the front. The backs have vital statistics, a biography and career totals.
COMPLETE SET (12) 2.50 6.00
1 Hal Trosky .08 .25
2 Nap Lajoie .40 1.00
3 Lou Boudreau .30 .75
4 Al Rosen .08 .25
5 Joe Jackson .75 2.00
6 Tris Speaker .40 1.00
7 Larry Doby .30 .75
8 Jim Hegan .08 .25
9 Cy Young .40 1.00
10 Sam McDowell .08 .25
11 Ray Narleski .08 .25
12 Al Lopez .20 .50

1986 Indians Oh Henry
This 30-card set features Cleveland Indians and was distributed at the stadium to fans in attendance on Baseball Card Day. The cards were printed in one folded sheet which was perforated for easy separation into individual cards. The cards have white borders with a blue frame around each photo. The card backs include detailed career year-by-year statistics. The individual cards measure approximately 2 1/4" by 3 1/8" and have full-color fronts.
COMPLETE SET (30) 6.00 15.00
2 Brett Butler .60 1.50
4 Tony Bernazard .08 .25
6 Andy Allanson .08 .25
7 Pat Corrales MG .08 .25
8 Carmen Castillo .08 .25
10 Pat Tabler .08 .25
13 Ernie Camacho .08 .25
14 Julio Franco .40 1.00
15 Dan Rohn .08 .25
18 Ken Schrom .08 .25
20 Otis Nixon .40 1.00
22 Fran Mullins .08 .25
23 Chris Bando .08 .25
24 Ed Williams .08 .25
26 Brook Jacoby .20 .50
27 Mel Hall .08 .25
29 Andre Thornton .40 1.00
30 Joe Carter 2.00 5.00
35 Phil Niekro 1.00 2.50
36 Jamie Easterly .08 .25
37 Don Schulze .08 .25
42 Rick Yett .08 .25
43 Scott Bailes .08 .25
44 Neal Heaton .08 .25
46 Jim Kern .08 .25
48 Dickie Noles .08 .25
49 Tom Candiotti .40 1.00
53 Reggie Ritter .08 .25
54 Tom Waddell .08 .25
NNO Coaching Staff .20 .50
Jack Aker
Bobby Bonds
Doc Edward

1986 Indians Team Issue
This 52-card set measures approximately 3 1/2" by 5 1/2" and features black-and-white player portraits in a white border with the player's name, position, and team name in the bottom margin. The backs are black. The set is large as players changed during the season, and their cards were added to the set. The cards are unnumbered and checklisted below in alphabetical order.
COMPLETE SET (52) 6.00 15.00
1 Jack Aker CO .08 .25
2 Andy Allanson .08 .25
3 Scott Bailes .08 .25
4 Chris Bando .08 .25
5 Jay Bell .60 1.50
6 Tony Bernazard .08 .25
7 Bobby Bonds .20 .50
8 Bernardo Brito .08 .25
9 Kevin Buckley .08 .25
10 John Butcher .08 .25
11 Brett Butler .20 .50
12 Ernie Camacho .08 .25
13 Tom Candiotti .20 .50
14 Joe Carter .60 1.50
15 Carmen Castillo .08 .25
16 Dave Clark .08 .25
17 Pat Corrales MG .08 .25
18 Keith Creel .08 .25
19 Jamie Easterly .08 .25
20 Doc Edwards CO .08 .25
21 Julio Franco .40 1.00
22 Vic Garcia .08 .25
23 Johnny Goryl CO .08 .25
24 Mel Hall .08 .25
25 Neal Heaton .08 .25
26 Brook Jacoby .08 .25
27 Jim Kern .08 .25
28 Fran Mullins .08 .25
29 Phil Niekro .60 1.50
30 Otis Nixon .40 1.00
31 Junior Noboa .08 .25
32 Dickie Noles .08 .25
33 Bryan Oelkers .08 .25
34 Craig Pippin .08 .25
35 Reggie Ritter .08 .25
36 Scott Roberts .08 .25
37 Dan Rohn .08 .25
38 Jose Roman .08 .25
39 Miguel Roman .08 .25
40 Ken Schrom .08 .25
41 Don Schulze .08 .25
42 Cory Snyder .20 .50
43 Dain Syverson .08 .25
44 Pat Tabler .08 .25
45 Andre Thornton .30 .75
46 Tom Waddell .08 .25
47 Curt Wardle .08 .25
48 Randy Washington .08 .25
49 Jim Weaver .08 .25
50 Ed Williams .08 .25
51 Jim Wilson .08 .25
52 Rich Yett .08 .25

1987 Indians Gatorade
Gatorade sponsored this perforated set of 30 full-color cards of the Cleveland Indians. The cards measure approximately 2 1/8" by 3" (or 3 1/8") and feature the Gatorade logo prominently on the fronts of the cards. The cards were distributed as a tri-folded sheet (each part approximately 9 5/8" by 11 3/16") on April 25th at the stadium during the game against the Yankees. The large team photo is approximately 11 3/16" by 9 5/8". Card backs for the individual players contain year-by-year stats for that player. The cards are referenced and listed below by uniform number.
COMPLETE SET (30) 4.00 10.00
2 Brett Butler .40 1.00
4 Tony Bernazard .08 .25
6 Andy Allanson .08 .25
7 Pat Corrales MG .08 .25
8 Carmen Castillo .08 .25
10 Pat Tabler .08 .25
11 Jamie Easterly .08 .25
12 Dave Clark .08 .25
13 Ernie Camacho .08 .25
14 Julio Franco .40 1.00
17 Junior Noboa .08 .25
18 Ken Schrom .08 .25
20 Otis Nixon .20 .50
21 Greg Swindell .20 .50
22 Frank Wills .08 .25
23 Chris Bando .08 .25
24 Rick Dempsey .20 .50
26 Brook Jacoby .08 .25
27 Mel Hall .08 .25
28 Cory Snyder .20 .50
29 Andre Thornton .30 .75
30 Joe Carter 1.50 4.00
35 Phil Niekro .75 2.00
36 Ed VandeBerg .08 .25
42 Rich Yett .08 .25
43 Scott Bailes .08 .25
46 Doug Jones .30 .75
49 Tom Candiotti .30 .75
54 Tom Waddell .08 .25
NNO Indians MG .20 .50
Coaches
Bobby Bonds
John Goryl
Pat C
NNO Team Photo/(Large size) 1.25 3.00

1988 Indians Gatorade
This set was distributed as 30 perforated player cards attached to a large team photo of the Cleveland Indians. The cards measure approximately 2 1/4" by 3". Card backs are oriented either horizontally or vertically. Card backs are printed in red, blue, and black on white card stock. Card backs contain a facsimile autograph of the player. Cards are not arranged on the sheet in any order. The cards are unnumbered except for uniform number, which is given on the front and back of each card. The cards are referenced and listed below by uniform number. The Gatorade logo is on the front of every card in the lower right corner.
COMPLETE SET (30) 3.00 8.00
2 Tom Spencer CO .08 .25
6 Andy Allanson .08 .25
7 Luis Isaac CO .08 .25
8 Carmen Castillo .08 .25
9 Charlie Manuel CO .08 .25
10 Pat Tabler .08 .25
11 Doug Jones .20 .50
14 Julio Franco .40 1.00
15 Ron Washington .08 .25
16 Jay Bell .75 2.00
17 Bill Laskey .08 .25
20 Willie Upshaw .08 .25
21 Greg Swindell .08 .25
23 Chris Bando .08 .25
25 Dave Clark .08 .25
26 Brook Jacoby .08 .25
27 Mel Hall .08 .25
28 Cory Snyder .08 .25
30 Joe Carter 1.25 3.00
31 Dan Schatzeder .08 .25
32 Doc Edwards MG .08 .25
33 Ron Kittle .08 .25
35 Mark Wiley CO .08 .25
42 Rich Yett .08 .25
43 Scott Bailes .08 .25
45 John Goryl CO .08 .25
47 Jeff Kaiser .08 .25
49 Tom Candiotti .20 .50
50 Jeff Dedmon .08 .25
52 John Farrell .08 .25
NNO Team Photo/(Large size) 1.00 2.50

1988 Indians Team Issue
This 40-card set of the Cleveland Indians features black-and-white player photos printed on postcard-size cards. The cards are unnumbered and checklisted below in alphabetical order
COMPLETE SET (40) 8.00 20.00
1 Darrel Akerfelds .20 .50
2 Andy Allanson .20 .50
3 Scott Bailes .20 .50
4 Chris Bando .20 .50
5 Jay Bell .40 1.00
6 Bud Black .20 .50
7 Tom Candiotti .30 .75
8 Joe Carter .60 1.50
9 Carmen Castillo .20 .50
10 Dave Clark .20 .50
11 Doc Edwards MG .20 .50
12 John Farrell .20 .50
13 Julio Franco .60 1.50
14 Terry Francona .30 .75
15 Don Gordon .20 .50
16 Johnny Goryl CO .20 .50
17 Mel Hall .20 .50
18 Brad Havens .20 .50
19 Tommy Hinzo .20 .50
20 Luis Isaac CO .20 .50
21 Brook Jacoby .20 .50
22 Doug Jones .30 .75
23 Ron Kittle .20 .50
24 Bill Laskey .20 .50
25 Don Lovell .20 .50
26 Charlie Manuel .20 .50
27 Jon Perlman .20 .50
28 Domingo Ramos .20 .50
29 Rick Rodriguez .20 .50
30 Dan Schatzeder .20 .50
31 Charlie Scott .20 .50
32 Cory Snyder .30 .75
33 Tom Spencer CO .20 .50
34 Greg Swindell .30 .75
35 Pat Tabler .20 .50
36 Willie Upshaw .20 .50
37 Ron Washington .20 .50
38 Mark Wiley CO .20 .50
39 Eddie Williams .20 .50
40 Rich Yett .20 .50

1989 Indians Team Issue
This 28-card set was available in the giftshop and was given away at the ballpark on May 13. The cards measure 2 7/8" by 4 1/4" and are printed on thin card stock. On a white card face, the fronts feature color player photos with a white inner border and red outer border. "The Tribe" logo is printed in the upper left corner, while player information is printed in the lower border. The backs carry the same design in red, while seasonal and career statistics and facsimile autograph are in blue. The cards are unnumbered and checklisted below in alphabetical order.
COMPLETE SET (28) 3.00 8.00
1 Luis Aguayo .08 .25
2 Andy Allanson .08 .25
3 Keith Atherton .08 .25
4 Scott Bailes .08 .25
5 Bud Black .08 .25
6 Jerry Browne .08 .25
7 Tom Candiotti .08 .25
8 Joe Carter 1.00 2.50
9 Dave Clark .08 .25
10 Doc Edwards MG .08 .25
11 John Farrell .08 .25
12 Felix Fermin .08 .25
13 Brad Havens .08 .25
14 Brook Jacoby .08 .25
15 Doug Jones .20 .50
16 Pat Keedy .08 .25
17 Brad Komminsk .08 .25
18 Oddibe McDowell .08 .25
19 Luis Medina .08 .25
20 Rod Nichols .08 .25
21 Pete O'Brien .08 .25
22 Jesse Orosco .20 .50
23 Joe Skalski .08 .25
24 Joel Skinner .08 .25
25 Cory Snyder .08 .25
26 Greg Swindell .08 .25
27 Rich Yett .08 .25
28 Coaches Card .08 .25
Jim Davenport
Luis Isaac
Charlie M

1990 Indians Team Issue
This 46-card set was available in the Indians giftshop for sale. The cards are unnumbered and we have checklisted them below in alphabetical order.
COMPLETE SET (46) 15.00 40.00
1 Beau Allred .40 1.00
2 Sandy Alomar Jr. 1.50 4.00
3 Carlos Baerga 1.50 4.00
4 Kevin Bearse .40 1.00
5 Joey Belle 3.00 8.00
6 Bud Black .40 1.00
7 Tom Brookens .40 1.00
8 Jerry Browne .40 1.00
9 Tom Candiotti .40 1.00
10 Colin Charland .40 1.00
11 Rich Dauer CO .40 1.00
12 John Farrell .40 1.00
13 Felix Fermin .40 1.00
14 Cecilio Guante .40 1.00
15 Mike Hargrove CO .75 2.00
16 Keith Hernandez .75 2.00
17 Luis Isaac CO .40 1.00
18 Brook Jacoby .40 1.00
19 Dion James .40 1.00
20 Chris James .40 1.00
21 Doug Jones .75 2.00
22 Carl Keliipuleoli .40 1.00
23 Tom Lampkin .40 1.00
24 Tom Magrann .40 1.00
25 Candy Maldonado .40 1.00
26 Jeff Manto .40 1.00
27 John McNamara MG .40 1.00
28 Jose Morales CO .40 1.00
29 Rod Nichols .40 1.00
30 Al Nipper .40 1.00
31 Steve Olin .40 1.00
32 Jesse Orosco .75 2.00
33 Doug Robertson .40 1.00
34 Rudy Seanez .40 1.00
35 Jeff Shaw 1.00 2.50
36 Doug Sisk .40 1.00
37 Joe Skalski .40 1.00
38 Joel Skinner .40 1.00
39 Cory Snyder .40 1.00
40 Greg Swindell .40 1.00
41 Sergio Valdez .40 1.00
42 Mike Walker .40 1.00
43 Mitch Webster .40 1.00
44 Kevin Wickander .40 1.00
45 Mark Wiley CO .40 1.00
46 Billy Williams CO 1.00 2.50

1991 Indians Fan Club/McDonald's
This 30-card set was sponsored by McDonald's and Channel 43 (WUAB). The cards are printed on thin card stock and measure approximately 2 7/8" by 4 1/4". The cards are unnumbered and checklisted below in alphabetical order.
COMPLETE SET (30) 6.00 15.00
1 Beau Allred .20 .50
2 Sandy Alomar .30 .75
3 Carlos Baerga .30 .75
4 Albert Belle .60 1.50
5 Jerry Browne .20 .50
6 Tom Candiotti .30 .75
7 Alex Cole .20 .50

8 Bruce Egloff .20 .50
9 Jose Escobar .20 .50
10 Felix Fermin .20 .50
11 Brook Jacoby .20 .50
12 John Farrell .20 .50
13 Shawn Hillegas .20 .50
14 Mike Huff .20 .50
15 Chris James .20 .50
16 Doug Jones .30 .75
17 Eric King .20 .50
18 Jeff Manto .20 .50
19 John McNamara MG .20 .50
20 Charles Nagy .30 .75
21 Rod Nichols .20 .50
22 Steve Olin .20 .50
23 Jesse Orosco .30 .75
24 Dave Otto .20 .50
25 Joel Skinner .20 .50
26 Greg Swindell .20 .50
27 Mike Walker .20 .50
28 Turner Ward .20 .50
29 Mitch Webster .20 .50
30 Coaches Card .30 .75
Billy Williams
Jose Morales
Rich D

1992 Indians Fan Club/McDonald's

This 30-card set was sponsored by McDonald's and WUAB Channel 43. The cards are printed on thin card stock and measure approximately 2 7/8" by 4 1/4". The cards are unnumbered and checklisted below in alphabetical order. The set was also produced as a team issue set which is distinguished by the Chief Wahoo mascot logo replacing the McDonald's logo and the removal of the WUAB references. The value for either set is identical.

COMPLETE SET (30) 8.00 20.00
1 Sandy Alomar Jr. .30 .75
2 Jack Armstrong .20 .50
3 Brad Arnsberg .20 .50
4 Carlos Baerga .30 .75
5 Eric Bell .20 .50
6 Albert Belle .60 1.50
7 Alex Cole .20 .50
8 Dennis Cook .20 .50
9 Felix Fermin .20 .50
10 Mike Hargrove MG .30 .75
11 Glenallen Hill .20 .50
12 Thomas Howard .20 .50
13 Brook Jacoby .20 .50
14 Reggie Jefferson .20 .50
15 Mark Lewis .20 .50
16 Derek Lilliquist .20 .50
17 Kenny Lofton .75 2.00
18 Charles Nagy .20 .50
19 Rod Nichols .20 .50
20 Steve Olin .20 .50
21 Junior Ortiz .20 .50
22 Dave Otto .20 .50
23 Tony Perezchica .20 .50
24 Ted Power .20 .50
25 Scott Scudder .20 .50
26 Joel Skinner .20 .50
27 Paul Sorrento .30 .75
28 Jim Thome 1.50 4.00
29 Mark Whiten .20 .50
30 Coaches Card .20 .50
Jeff Newman
Rick Adair
Ken Bolek/

1993 Indians WUAB-TV

This 34-card team-issued set was available in the Indians giftshop. The WUAB Channel 43 logo appears on only one card, that of Slider, the Tribe's mascot. The cards are unnumbered and checklisted below in alphabetical order. A McDonalds version is produced with two extra cards. The two extra cards are in the version not available at the ball park.

COMPLETE SET (34) 5.00 12.00
1 Sandy Alomar Jr. .20 .50
2 Carlos Baerga .20 .50
3 Albert Belle .40 1.00
4 Mike Bielecki .08 .25
5 Mike Christopher .08 .25
6 Mark Clark .08 .25
7 Dennis Cook .08 .25
8 Alvaro Espinoza .08 .25
9 Felix Fermin .08 .25
10 Mike Hargrove MG .08 .25
11 Glenallen Hill .08 .25
12 Thomas Howard .08 .25
13 Reggie Jefferson .08 .25
14 Wayne Kirby .08 .25
15 Tom Kramer .08 .25
16 Mark Lewis .08 .25
17 Derek Lilliquist .08 .25
18 Kenny Lofton .60 1.50
19 Carlos Martinez .08 .25
20 Jose Mesa .20 .50
21 Jeff Mutis .08 .25
22 Charles Nagy .08 .25
23 Bob Ojeda .08 .25
24 Junior Ortiz .08 .25
25 Eric Plunk .08 .25
26 Ted Power .08 .25
27 Scott Scudder .08 .25
28 Joel Skinner .08 .25
29 Paul Sorrento .08 .25
30 Jim Thome .75 2.00
31 Jeff Treadway .08 .25
32 Kevin Wickander .08 .25
33 The Coaching Staff .08 .25
Rick Adair
Ken Bolke
Dom Chi
34 Slider (Mascot) .08 .25
and Liz (WUAB)
35 Ronald McDonald .08 .25
Mascot
36 Fan Club Welcome .08 .25

1996 Indians Fleer

This 20-card standard-size set was issued by Fleer as a test to see how regional team issues would sell. These cards are different from the regular 1996 Fleer issues as the 10-card packs feature the Indians logo. The cards have silver-foil and are issued with UV coating and they are numbered "X" of 20. The set is sequenced in alphabetical order.

COMPLETE SET (20) 1.50 4.00
1 Sandy Alomar Jr. .07 .20
2 Paul Assenmacher .02 .10
3 Carlos Baerga .07 .20
4 Albert Belle .07 .20
5 Orel Hershiser .07 .20
6 Kenny Lofton .10 .30
7 Dennis Martinez .07 .20
8 Jose Mesa .07 .20
9 Eddie Murray .30 .75
10 Charles Nagy .02 .10
11 Tony Pena .02 .10
12 Herb Perry .02 .10
13 Eric Plunk .02 .10
14 Jim Poole .02 .10
15 Manny Ramirez .30 .75
16 Julian Tavarez .02 .10
17 Jim Thome .30 .75
18 Omar Vizquel .20 .50
19 Indians Logo .02 .10
20 Indians CL .02 .10

1996 Indians Upper Deck

This one card standard-size set features the Indians logo on the front and commemorates their achievement in wining the 1948 World Championship. The back describes the history of the logo of the vintage Indians from that Bill Veeck/Lou Boudreau era. It was available in the Cleveland area as a stand alone card.

1 Cleveland Indians Logo 2.00 5.00

1997 Indians Score

This 15-card set of the Cleveland Indians was issued in five-card packs with a suggested retail price of $1.30 each. The fronts feature color player photos with special team specific color foil stamping. The backs carry player information. Only 100 cases were made for each team. Platinum parallel cards were inserted at a rate of 1:6, Premier parallel cards at a rate of 1:31. A card of Brian Giles in his Rookie Card year is a featured card in this set.

COMPLETE SET (15) 2.50 6.00
*PLATINUM: 5X BASIC CARDS
*PREMIER: 20X BASIC CARDS
1 Albert Belle .15 .40
2 Jack McDowell .08 .25
3 Jim Thome .40 1.00
4 Dennis Martinez .15 .40
5 Julio Franco .25 .60
6 Omar Vizquel .30 .75
7 Kenny Lofton .15 .40
8 Manny Ramirez .40 1.00
9 Sandy Alomar Jr. .15 .40
10 Charles Nagy .08 .25
11 Kevin Seitzer .08 .25
12 Mark Carreon .08 .25
13 Jeff Kent .30 .75
14 Danny Graves .15 .40
15 Brian Giles .75 2.00

1997 Indians Score Update

This 15 card set, which is similar in design to the 1997 Score Indians set features some changes from the earlier Indians set. The cards were issued in seven card packs with a suggested retail price of $1.30. An added feature of these packs was that passes to All-Star fanfest were randomly included in the packs. A parallel Tribe collection card was included one every six packs. Brian Giles appears in his Rookie Card season.

COMPLETE SET (15) 2.00 5.00
*TRIBE COLLECTION: 5X BASIC CARDS
1 Matt Williams .25 .60
2 Jack McDowell .08 .25
3 Jim Thome .40 1.00
4 Chad Ogea .08 .25
5 Julio Franco .25 .60
6 Omar Vizquel .30 .75
7 Kenny Lofton .15 .40
8 Manny Ramirez .40 1.00
9 Sandy Alomar Jr .15 .40
10 Charles Nagy .08 .25
11 Kevin Seitzer .08 .25
12 Orel Hershiser .15 .40
13 Paul Assenmacher .08 .25
14 Eric Plunk .08 .25
15 Brian Giles .75 2.00

1998 Indians Score

This 15-card set was issued in special retail packs and features color photos of the Cleveland Indians team. The backs carry player information. A special platinum parallel set was also issued and randomly inserted in packs.

COMPLETE SET (15) 2.50 6.00
*PLATINUM: 5X BASIC CARDS
1 Jack McDowell .08 .25
2 Jim Thome .50 1.25
3 Brian Anderson .08 .25
4 Sandy Alomar Jr. .20 .50
5 Omar Vizquel .40 1.00
6 Brian Giles .40 1.00
7 Charles Nagy .08 .25
8 Mike Jackson .08 .25
9 David Justice .40 1.00
10 Jeff Juden .08 .25
11 Matt Williams .30 .75
12 Marquis Grissom .20 .50
13 Tony Fernandez .20 .50
14 Bartolo Colon .40 1.00
15 Jaret Wright .20 .50

2000 Indians Team Issue

COMPLETE SET 8.00 20.00
1 Jacobs Field .20 .50
2 Roberto Alomar .60 1.50
3 Sandy Alomar Jr. .30 .75
4 Dave Burba .20 .50
5 Bartolo Colon .60 1.50
6 Einar Diaz .20 .50
7 Chuck Finley .30 .75
8 Travis Fryman .30 .75
9 David Justice .40 1.00
10 Steve Karsay .20 .50
11 Charles Nagy .20 .50
12 Manny Ramirez .80 2.00
13 Richie Sexson .60 1.50
14 Paul Shuey .20 .50
15 Jim Thome .80 2.00
16 Omar Vizquel .60 1.50
17 Jaret Wright .30 .75
18 Jacob Cruz .20 .50
19 Scott Kamienicki .20 .50
20 Kenny Lofton .40 1.00
21 Tom Martin .20 .50
22 Alex Ramirez .20 .50
23 Steve Reed .20 .50
24 Ricardo Rincon .20 .50
25 Dave Riske .20 .50
26 Enrique Wilson .20 .50
27 Bobby Witt .20 .50
28 Charlie Manuel MG .20 .50
29 Luis Isaac CO .20 .50
30 Clarence Jones CO .20 .50
31 Grady Little CO .20 .50
32 Dick Pole CO .20 .50
33 Jim Riggleman CO .20 .50
34 Ted Uhlaender CO .20 .50
35 Dan Williams CO .20 .50

2001 Indians Postcards

COMPLETE SET (37) 4.80 12.00
1 Roberto Alomar .40 1.00
2 Russ Branyan .20 .50
3 Dave Burba .10 .25
4 Ellis Burks .20 .50
5 Bartolo Colon .40 1.00
6 Einar Diaz .10 .25
7 Chuck Finley .20 .50
8 Travis Fryman .20 .50
9 Juan Gonzalez .40 1.00
10 Steve Karsay .10 .25
11 Kenny Lofton .20 .50
12 Charles Nagy .10 .25
13 Jim Thome .60 1.50
14 Omar Vizquel .40 1.00
15 Bob Wickman .20 .50
16 Jaret Wright .20 .50
17 Jolbert Cabrera .10 .25
18 Wil Cordero .10 .25
19 Marty Cordova .10 .25
20 Jacob Cruz .10 .25
21 Tim Drew .10 .25
22 John McDonald .10 .25
23 Steve Reed .10 .25
24 Ricardo Rincon .10 .25
25 C.C. Sabathia .40 1.00
26 Paul Shuey .10 .25
27 Justin Speier .10 .25
28 Eddie Taubensee .10 .25
29 Steve Woodard .10 .25
30 Charlie Manuel MG .10 .25
31 Luis Isaac CO .10 .25
32 Clarence Jones CO .10 .25
33 Grady Little CO .10 .25
34 Dick Pole CO .10 .25
35 Joel Skinner CO .10 .25
36 Ted Uhlaender CO .10 .25
37 Dan Williams CO .10 .25

2003 Indians Postcards

COMPLETE SET 10.00 20.00
33 Brady Anderson .30 .75
34 Brian Anderson .20 .50
35 Danny Baez .40 1.00
36 Josh Bard .20 .50
37 Milton Bradley .40 1.00
38 Ellis Burks .30 .75
39 Karim Garcia .20 .50
40 Travis Hafner .60 1.50
41 Matt Lawton .20 .50
42 John McDonald .20 .50
43 Brandon Phillips .30 .75
44 C.C. Sabathia .60 1.50
45 Omar Vizquel .60 1.50
46 Jason Bere .20 .50
47 Casey Blake .40 1.00
48 Ben Broussard .20 .50
49 Jason Davis .20 .50
50 Ricky Gutierrez .20 .50
51 Tim Laker .20 .50
52 Cliff Lee .30 .75
53 Terry Mulholland .20 .50
54 David Riske .20 .50
55 Ricardo Rodriguez .20 .50
56 Carl Sadler .20 .50
57 Jose Santiago .20 .50
58 Bill Selby .20 .50
59 Shane Spencer .20 .50
60 Billy Traber .20 .50
61 Eric Wedge MG .20 .50
62 Jake Westbrook .30 .75
63 Bob Wickman .30 .75
64 Mark Wohlers .20 .50
65 Buddy Bell CO .20 .50
66 Jeff Datz CO .20 .50
67 Luis Isaac CO .20 .50
68 Dave Keller CO .20 .50
69 Eddie Murray CO .60 1.50
70 Joel Skinner CO .20 .50
71 Dan Williams CO .20 .50
72 Carl Willis CO .20 .50

2004 Indians Gravity Games Upper Deck

COMPLETE SET 5.00 10.00
1 C.C. Sabathia .60 1.50
2 Travis Hafner .75 2.00
3 Casey Blake .40 1.00
4 Matt Lawton .20 .50
5 Jason Davis .20 .50
6 Ben Broussard .30 .75
7 Omar Vizquel .60 1.50
8 Cliff Lee .30 .75
9 Ronnie Belliard .30 .75
10 Jody Gerut .20 .50
11 Victor Martinez .75 2.00
12 Coco Crisp .60 1.50

2004 Indians Team Issue

COMPLETE SET
1 Buddy Bell CO .20 .50
2 Ronnie Belliard .30 .75
3 Rafael Betancourt .20 .50
4 Casey Blake .40 1.00
5 Ben Broussard .30 .75
6 Coco Crisp .60 1.50
7 Jeff D'Amico .20 .50
8 Jeff Datz .20 .50
9 Jason Davis .20 .50
10 Chad Durbin .20 .50
11 Alex Escobar .20 .50
12 Jody Gerut .20 .50
13 Travis Hafner .75 2.00
14 Luis Isaac .20 .50
15 Jose Jimenez .20 .50
16 Tim Laker .20 .50
17 Matt Lawton .20 .50
18 Cliff Lee .30 .75
19 Victor Martinez .75 2.00
20 John McDonald .20 .50
21 Lou Merloni .20 .50
22 Eddie Murray CO .60 1.50
23 Dave Riske .20 .50
24 C.C. Sabathia .60 1.50
25 Joel Skinner CO .20 .50
26 Jason Stanford .20 .50
27 Scott Stewart .20 .50
28 Omar Vizquel .60 1.50
29 Eric Wedge MG .20 .50
30 Jake Westbrook .30 .75
31 Dan Williams .20 .50
32 Carl Willis .20 .50

2006 Indians Topps

COMPLETE SET (14) 3.00 8.00
CLE1 C.C. Sabathia .20 .50
CLE2 Cliff Lee .20 .50
CLE3 Travis Hafner .12 .30
CLE4 Victor Martinez .20 .50
CLE5 Casey Blake .12 .30
CLE6 Ronnie Belliard .12 .30
CLE7 Grady Sizemore .20 .50
CLE8 Jhonny Peralta .12 .30
CLE9 Aaron Boone .12 .30
CLE10 Ben Broussard .12 .30
CLE11 Jake Westbrook .12 .30
CLE12 Coco Crisp .12 .30
CLE13 Bob Wickman .12 .30
CLE14 Paul Byrd .12 .30

2007 Indians Topps

COMPLETE SET (14) 3.00 8.00
CLE1 Grady Sizemore .20 .50
CLE2 Jeremy Sowers .12 .30
CLE3 Jake Westbrook .12 .30
CLE4 Josh Barfield .12 .30
CLE5 Casey Blake .12 .30
CLE6 Jhonny Peralta .12 .30
CLE7 Trot Nixon .12 .30
CLE8 C.C. Sabathia .20 .50
CLE9 Joe Borowski .12 .30
CLE10 Andy Marte .12 .30
CLE11 David Dellucci .12 .30
CLE12 Cliff Lee .20 .50
CLE13 Shin-Soo Choo .20 .50
CLE14 Travis Hafner .12 .30

2008 Indians Topps

COMPLETE SET (14) 3.00 8.00
CLE1 Grady Sizemore .20 .50
CLE2 Fausto Carmona .12 .30
CLE3 Asdrubal Cabrera .20 .50
CLE4 Jake Westbrook .12 .30
CLE5 Casey Blake .12 .30
CLE6 Jhonny Peralta .12 .30
CLE7 Ryan Garko .12 .30
CLE8 C.C. Sabathia .20 .50
CLE9 Joe Borowski .12 .30
CLE10 Franklin Gutierrez .12 .30
CLE11 Rafael Betancourt .12 .30
CLE12 Victor Martinez .20 .50
CLE13 Paul Byrd .12 .30
CLE14 Travis Hafner .12 .30

2009 Indians Topps

CLE1 Grady Sizemore .25 .60
CLE2 Cliff Lee .25 .60
CLE3 Victor Martinez .25 .60
CLE4 Fausto Carmona .15 .40
CLE5 Jhonny Peralta .15 .40
CLE6 David Dellucci .15 .40
CLE7 Travis Hafner .15 .40
CLE8 Kelly Shoppach .15 .40
CLE9 Jake Westbrook .15 .40
CLE10 Ben Francisco .15 .40
CLE11 Mark DeRosa .25 .60
CLE12 Asdrubal Cabrera .25 .60
CLE13 Ryan Garko .15 .40
CLE14 Shin-Soo Choo .25 .60
CLE15 Kerry Wood .15 .40

2010 Indians Topps

CLE1 Grady Sizemore .25 .60
CLE2 Asdrubal Cabrera .25 .60
CLE3 Michael Brantley .25 .60
CLE4 Matt LaPorta .15 .40
CLE5 Kerry Wood .15 .40
CLE6 Chris Perez .15 .40
CLE7 Carlos Carrasco .40 1.00
CLE8 Shin-Soo Choo .25 .60
CLE9 Jhonny Peralta .15 .40
CLE10 Fausto Carmona .15 .40
CLE11 Travis Hafner .15 .40
CLE12 Aaron Laffey .15 .40
CLE13 Jake Westbrook .15 .40
CLE14 Trevor Crowe .15 .40
CLE15 Justin Masterson .15 .40
CLE16 Luis Valbuena .15 .40
CLE17 David Huff .15 .40

2011 Indians Topps

CLE1 Carlos Santana .40 1.00
CLE2 Shin-Soo Choo .25 .60
CLE3 Travis Hafner .15 .40
CLE4 Michael Brantley .15 .40
CLE5 Fausto Carmona .15 .40
CLE6 Mitch Talbot .15 .40
CLE7 Carlos Carrasco .25 .60
CLE8 Matt LaPorta .15 .40
CLE9 Justin Masterson .15 .40
CLE10 Chris Perez .15 .40
CLE11 Asdrubal Cabrera .25 .60
CLE12 Trevor Crowe .15 .40
CLE13 Jayson Nix .15 .40
CLE14 Jason Donald .15 .40
CLE15 Grady Sizemore .25 .60
CLE16 Tony Sipp .15 .40
CLE17 Joe Smith .15 .40

2012 Indians Topps

CLE1 Carlos Santana .30 .75
CLE2 Lonnie Chisenhall .25 .60
CLE3 Shin-Soo Choo .30 .75
CLE4 Travis Hafner .25 .60
CLE5 Jason Kipnis .30 .75
CLE6 Ubaldo Jimenez .25 .60
CLE7 Michael Brantley .25 .60
CLE8 Jason Donald .25 .60
CLE9 Vinnie Pestano .25 .60
CLE10 Josh Tomlin .25 .60
CLE11 Matt Laporta .25 .60
CLE12 Asdrubal Cabrera .30 .75
CLE13 Grady Sizemore .30 .75
CLE14 Justin Masterson .25 .60
CLE15 Derek Lowe .25 .60
CLE16 Chris Perez .25 .60
CLE17 Progressive Field .15 .40

2013 Indians Topps

COMPLETE SET (17) 3.00 8.00
CLE1 Asdrubal Cabrera .20 .50
CLE2 Chris Perez .25 .60
CLE3 Drew Stubbs .25 .60
CLE4 Carlos Santana .20 .50
CLE5 Jason Kipnis .30 .75
CLE6 Justin Masterson .25 .60
CLE7 Ubaldo Jimenez .25 .60
CLE8 Brett Myers .15 .40
CLE9 Mark Reynolds .25 .60
CLE10 Michael Brantley .15 .40
CLE11 Lonnie Chisenhall .15 .40
CLE12 Vinnie Pestano .25 .60
CLE13 Mike Aviles .15 .40
CLE14 Nick Swisher .30 .75
CLE15 Trevor Bauer .30 .75
CLE16 Zach McAllister .25 .60
CLE17 Progressive Field .15 .40

2014 Indians Topps

COMPLETE SET (17) 3.00 8.00
CLE1 Jason Kipnis .20 .50
CLE2 David Murphy .15 .40
CLE3 Corey Kluber .20 .50
CLE4 Carlos Santana .20 .50
CLE5 Asdrubal Cabrera .20 .50
CLE6 Justin Masterson .15 .40
CLE7 Michael Bourn .15 .40
CLE8 Yan Gomes .15 .40
CLE9 Danny Salazar .20 .50
CLE10 Michael Brantley .20 .50
CLE11 Lonnie Chisenhall .15 .40
CLE12 John Axford .15 .40
CLE13 Mike Aviles .15 .40
CLE14 Nick Swisher .20 .50
CLE15 Trevor Bauer .30 .75
CLE16 Zach McAllister .15 .40
CLE17 Progressive Field .15 .40

2015 Indians Topps

COMPLETE SET (17) 3.00 8.00
CI1 Corey Kluber .20 .50
CI2 Trevor Bauer .30 .75
CI3 Michael Bourn .15 .40
CI4 Lonnie Chisenhall .15 .40
CI5 Cody Allen .15 .40
CI6 David Murphy .15 .40
CI7 Carlos Santana .20 .50
CI8 Jason Kipnis .20 .50
CI9 Yan Gomes .15 .40
CI10 Jose Ramirez .20 .50
CI11 Michael Brantley .20 .50
CI12 Brandon Moss .15 .40
CI13 Nick Swisher .20 .50
CI14 Ryan Raburn .15 .40
CI15 Carlos Carrasco .15 .40
CI16 Danny Salazar .20 .50
CI17 Mike Aviles .15 .40

2016 Indians Topps

COMPLETE SET (17) 3.00 8.00
CLE1 Francisco Lindor .25 .60
CLE2 Corey Kluber .20 .50
CLE3 Yan Gomes .15 .40
CLE4 Carlos Santana .20 .50
CLE5 Jason Kipnis .20 .50
CLE6 Giovanny Urshela .25 .60
CLE7 Michael Brantley .20 .50
CLE8 Abraham Almonte .15 .40
CLE9 Lonnie Chisenhall .15 .40
CLE10 Mike Napoli .15 .40
CLE11 Carlos Carrasco .15 .40
CLE12 Danny Salazar .20 .50
CLE13 Rajai Davis .15 .40
CLE14 Cody Allen .15 .40
CLE15 Trevor Bauer .30 .75
CLE16 Zach McAllister .15 .40
CLE17 Josh Tomlin .15 .40

2017 Indians Topps

COMPLETE SET (17) 3.00 8.00
CLE1 Francisco Lindor .25 .60
CLE2 Josh Tomlin .15 .40
CLE3 Danny Salazar .20 .50
CLE4 Trevor Bauer .30 .75
CLE5 Jose Ramirez .20 .50
CLE6 Roberto Perez .15 .40
CLE7 Lonnie Chisenhall .15 .40
CLE8 Yan Gomes .25 .60
CLE9 Corey Kluber .20 .50
CLE10 Cody Allen .15 .40
CLE11 Coco Crisp .15 .40
CLE12 Andrew Miller .20 .50
CLE13 Jason Kipnis .20 .50
CLE14 Michael Brantley .20 .50
CLE15 Tyler Naquin .25 .60
CLE16 Carlos Carrasco .15 .40
CLE17 Carlos Santana .20 .50

2018 Indians Topps

COMPLETE SET (17) 2.50 6.00
CI1 Jose Ramirez .20 .50
CI2 Francisco Lindor .25 .60
CI3 Andrew Miller .20 .50
CI4 Jason Kipnis .20 .50
CI5 Carlos Carrasco .15 .40
CI6 Josh Tomlin .15 .40
CI7 Yan Gomes .25 .60
CI8 Danny Salazar .20 .50
CI9 Mike Clevinger .20 .50
CI10 Roberto Perez .15 .40
CI11 Brandon Guyer .15 .40
CI12 Corey Kluber .20 .50
CI13 Cody Allen .15 .40
CI14 Edwin Encarnacion .25 .60
CI15 Michael Brantley .20 .50
CI16 Trevor Bauer .30 .75
CI17 Bradley Zimmer .15 .40

2019 Indians Topps

COMPLETE SET (17) 2.50 6.00
CI1 Francisco Lindor .25 .60
CI2 Corey Kluber .20 .50
CI3 Jose Ramirez .20 .50
CI4 Greg Allen .20 .50
CI5 Jason Kipnis .20 .50
CI6 Leonys Martin .15 .40
CI7 Tyler Naquin .20 .50
CI8 Carlos Carrasco .15 .40
CI9 Trevor Bauer .30 .75
CI10 Mike Clevinger .20 .50
CI11 Shane Bieber .25 .60
CI12 Adam Plutko .15 .40
CI13 Danny Salazar .20 .50
CI14 Carlos Santana .20 .50
CI15 Brad Hand .15 .40
CI16 Jordan Luplow .15 .40
CI17 Jake Bauers .25 .60

2020 Indians Topps

CLE1 Francisco Lindor .25 .60
CLE2 Jose Ramirez .20 .50
CLE3 Mike Clevinger .20 .50
CLE4 Shane Bieber .25 .60
CLE5 Carlos Santana .20 .50
CLE6 Delino DeShields .15 .40
CLE7 Oscar Mercado .25 .60
CLE8 Brad Hand .15 .40
CLE9 Tyler Naquin .20 .50
CLE10 Zach Plesac .25 .60
CLE11 Nick Wittgren .25 .60
CLE12 Franmil Reyes .15 .40
CLE13 Jordan Luplow .15 .40
CLE14 Aaron Civale .30 .75
CLE15 Jake Bauers .20 .50
CLE16 Roberto Perez .15 .40
CLE17 Carlos Carrasco .15 .40

2017 Indians Topps National Baseball Card Day

COMPLETE SET (10) 5.00 12.00
CLE1 Francisco Lindor 1.00 2.50
CLE2 Carlos Santana .75 2.00
CLE3 Corey Kluber .75 2.00
CLE4 Carlos Carrasco .60 1.50
CLE5 Jose Ramirez .75 2.00
CLE6 Edwin Encarnacion 1.00 2.50
CLE7 Cody Allen .60 1.50
CLE8 Andrew Miller .75 2.00
CLE9 Jason Kipnis .75 2.00
CLE10 Jim Thome .75 2.00

1997 Infinity HOF Fantasy Camp

These standard-size cards are from a 1997 Hall Of Fame Fantasy Camp, and was sponsored by INFINITI. They were giveaways at the camp to the particiapants.

COMPLETE SET 8.00 20.00
1 Harmon Killebrew 4.00 10.00
2 Brooks Robinson 4.00 10.00

1980 Italian American Sports Hall of Fame

These exhibit-sized cards were issued to commemorate the first inductees into the Italian American Sports Hall of Fame. The fronts have sepia toned photos of the athlete as well as their name and identification in the lower left column. The bottom right of the card is dedicated to the "Unity" logo. The back is a standard postcard back. Since these cards are unnumbered we have sequenced them in alphabetical order.

COMPLETE SET 5.00 10.00
2 Phil Cavarretta .40 1.00
3 Joe DiMaggio 2.00 5.00
5 Vince Lombardi .75 2.00

2014 ITG Past Present Future Autographs

PPFAB1 Aaron Blair 3.00 8.00
PPFAB2 Aaron Blair 3.00 8.00
PPFAB3 Aaron Blair 3.00 8.00
PPFAB4 Aaron Blair 3.00 8.00
PPFAJ1 Aaron Judge 50.00 120.00
PPFAJ2 Aaron Judge 50.00 120.00
PPFAJ3 Aaron Judge 50.00 120.00
PPFAJ4 Aaron Judge 50.00 120.00
PPFBG1 Bob Gibson
PPFBG2 Bob Gibson
PPFBM1 Billy McKinney 3.00 8.00
PPFBM2 Billy McKinney 3.00 8.00
PPFBM3 Billy McKinney 3.00 8.00
PPFBM4 Billy McKinney 3.00 6.00
PPFBN1 Brandon Nimmo 3.00 8.00
PPFBN2 Brandon Nimmo 3.00 8.00
PPFBS1 Blake Swihart 5.00 12.00
PPFBS2 Blake Swihart 5.00 12.00
PPFBS3 Blake Swihart 5.00 12.00
PPFBS4 Blake Swihart 5.00 12.00
PPFCH1 Courtney Hawkins 3.00 8.00
PPFCH2 Courtney Hawkins 3.00 8.00
PPFCH3 Courtney Hawkins 3.00 8.00
PPFCH4 Courtney Hawkins 3.00 8.00
PPFDD1 D.J. Davis 3.00 8.00
PPFDD2 D.J. Davis 3.00 8.00
PPFDD3 D.J. Davis 3.00 8.00
PPFDD4 D.J. Davis 3.00 8.00
PPFDG1 Doc Gooden 4.00 10.00
PPFDG2 Doc Gooden 4.00 10.00
PPFDH1 Danny Hultzen 3.00 8.00
PPFDH2 Danny Hultzen 3.00 8.00
PPFDH3 Danny Hultzen 3.00 8.00
PPFDH4 Danny Hultzen 3.00 8.00
PPFDO1 David Ortiz 15.00 40.00
PPFDO2 David Ortiz 15.00 40.00
PPFDS1 Don Sutton 3.00 8.00
PPFDS2 Don Sutton 3.00 8.00
PPFFT1 Frank Thomas 40.00 80.00
PPFFT2 Frank Thomas 40.00 80.00
PPFGG1 Goose Gossage 6.00 15.00
PPFGG2 Goose Gossage 6.00 15.00
PPFGS1 George Springer 10.00 25.00
PPFGS2 George Springer 10.00 25.00
PPFHH1 Hunter Harvey 3.00 8.00
PPFHH2 Hunter Harvey 3.00 8.00
PPFHH3 Hunter Harvey 3.00 8.00
PPFHH4 Hunter Harvey 3.00 8.00
PPFJB1 Jed Bradley 3.00 8.00
PPFJB2 Jed Bradley 3.00 8.00
PPFJB3 Jed Bradley 3.00 8.00
PPFJB4 Jed Bradley 3.00 8.00
PPFJBE1 Johnny Bench 20.00 50.00
PPFJBE2 Johnny Bench 20.00 50.00
PPFJC1 Jonathan Crawford 3.00 8.00
PPFJC2 Jonathan Crawford 3.00 8.00
PPFJC3 Jonathan Crawford 3.00 8.00
PPFJC4 Jonathan Crawford 3.00 8.00
PPFJG1 Joey Gallo 5.00 12.00
PPFJG2 Joey Gallo 5.00 12.00
PPFJG3 Joey Gallo 5.00 12.00
PPFJG4 Joey Gallo 5.00 12.00
PPFJM1 Joe Morgan 6.00 15.00
PPFJM2 Joe Morgan 6.00 15.00
PPFJP1 Jorge Polanco 3.00 8.00
PPFJP2 Jorge Polanco 3.00 8.00
PPFJP3 Jorge Polanco 3.00 8.00
PPFJP4 Jorge Polanco 3.00 8.00
PPFJPA1 Jim Palmer 6.00 15.00
PPFJPA2 Jim Palmer 6.00 15.00
PPFJR1 Jim Rice 6.00 15.00
PPFJR2 Jim Rice 6.00 15.00
PPFKC1 Kaleb Cowart
PPFKC2 Kaleb Cowart
PPFKG1 Kevin Gausman 5.00 12.00
PPFKG2 Kevin Gausman 5.00 12.00
PPFKG3 Kevin Gausman 5.00 12.00
PPFKG4 Kevin Gausman 5.00 12.00
PPFKW1 Keenyn Walker 3.00 8.00
PPFKW2 Keenyn Walker 3.00 8.00
PPFKW3 Keenyn Walker 3.00 8.00
PPFKW4 Keenyn Walker 3.00 8.00
PPFKZ1 Kyle Zimmer 3.00 8.00
PPFKZ2 Kyle Zimmer 3.00 8.00
PPFLB1 Lewis Brinson 3.00 8.00
PPFLB2 Lewis Brinson 3.00 8.00
PPFLG1 Lucas Giolito 3.00 8.00
PPFLG2 Lucas Giolito 3.00 8.00
PPFLG3 Lucas Giolito 3.00 8.00
PPFLG4 Lucas Giolito 3.00 8.00
PPFMB1 Matt Barnes 3.00 8.00
PPFMB2 Matt Barnes 3.00 8.00
PPFMF1 Max Fried 3.00 8.00
PPFMF2 Max Fried 3.00 8.00
PPFMF3 Max Fried 3.00 8.00
PPFMF4 Max Fried 3.00 8.00
PPFMR1 Mariano Rivera 60.00 120.00
PPFMR2 Mariano Rivera 60.00 120.00
PPFMS1 Marcus Stroman 3.00 8.00
PPFMS2 Marcus Stroman 3.00 8.00
PPFMS3 Marcus Stroman 3.00 8.00
PPFMS4 Marcus Stroman 3.00 8.00
PPFMSA1 Miguel Sano 8.00 20.00
PPFMSA2 Miguel Sano 8.00 20.00
PPFNS1 Noah Syndergaard 5.00 12.00
PPFNS2 Noah Syndergaard 5.00 12.00
PPFNS3 Noah Syndergaard 5.00 12.00
PPFNS4 Noah Syndergaard 5.00 12.00
PPFOC1 Orlando Cepeda 8.00 20.00
PPFOC2 Orlando Cepeda 8.00 20.00
PPFOS1 Ozzie Smith 20.00 50.00
PPFOS2 Ozzie Smith 20.00 50.00
PPFPM1 Paul Molitor 8.00 20.00
PPFPM2 Paul Molitor 8.00 20.00
PPFPMA1 Pedro Martinez 20.00 50.00
PPFPMA2 Pedro Martinez 20.00 50.00
PPFPR1 Pete Rose 20.00 50.00
PPFPR2 Pete Rose 20.00 50.00
PPFRC1 Rod Carew 8.00 20.00
PPFRC2 Rod Carew 8.00 20.00
PPFRH1 Rickey Henderson 40.00 80.00
PPFRH2 Rickey Henderson 40.00 80.00
PPFRJ1 Reggie Jackson 20.00 50.00
PPFRJ2 Reggie Jackson 20.00 50.00
PPFRY1 Robin Yount 30.00 60.00
PPFRY2 Robin Yount 30.00 60.00
PPFSG1 Scooter Gennett 4.00 10.00
PPFSG2 Scooter Gennett 4.00 10.00
PPFSG3 Scooter Gennett 4.00 10.00
PPFTA1 Tyler Anderson
PPFTA2 Tyler Anderson
PPFTA3 Tyler Anderson
PPFTA4 Tyler Anderson
PPFTG1 Taylor Guerrieri 2.50 6.00
PPFTG2 Taylor Guerrieri 2.50 6.00
PPFTG3 Taylor Guerrieri 2.50 6.00
PPFTGW1 Tony Gwynn 12.00 30.00
PPFTGW2 Tony Gwynn 12.00 30.00
PPFTP1 Tony Perez 12.00 30.00
PPFTP2 Tony Perez 12.00 30.00
PPFWB1 Wade Boggs 12.00 30.00
PPFWB2 Wade Boggs 12.00 30.00
PPFWW1 Walker Weickel 3.00 8.00
PPFWW2 Walker Weickel 3.00 8.00
PPFWW3 Walker Weickel 3.00 8.00
PPFWW4 Walker Weickel 3.00 8.00
PPFBSU1 Bruce Sutter 6.00 15.00
PPFBSU2 Bruce Sutter 6.00 15.00
PPFJCR1 J.P. Crawford 3.00 8.00
PPFJCR2 J.P. Crawford 3.00 8.00
PPFJCR3 J.P. Crawford 3.00 8.00
PPFJCR4 J.P. Crawford 3.00 8.00
PPFJGR1 Jonathan Gray 5.00 12.00
PPFJGR2 Jonathan Gray 5.00 12.00
PPFJGR3 Jonathan Gray 5.00 12.00
PPFJGR4 Jonathan Gray 5.00 12.00
PPFCRJR1 Cal Ripken Jr. 40.00 80.00
PPFCRJR2 Cal Ripken Jr. 40.00 80.00

1910 J.H. Dockman All-Star Baseball E-Unc.

Produced by J.H. Dockman and Son, this unattractive issue is actually the sides of a candy package. The package measures approximately 1 7/8" by 3 3/8" and is 3/4" thick. Each package features two players, crudely drawn, one on each side. The words "All Star Baseball Package" appear on the side of the package and at the top of each player panel. The other side panel displays the words, "Candy and Gift." The end panel indicates a serial number, Dockman's name and reference to the Food and Drugs Act of 1906. A complete box is worth four times the individual value.

COMPLETE SET (16) 2500.00 5000.00
1 Henry Beckendorf 175.00 350.00
2 Roger Bresnahan 300.00 600.00
3 Al Burch 175.00 350.00
4 Frank Chance 350.00 700.00
5 Wid Conroy 175.00 350.00
6 Jack Coombs 250.00 500.00
7 George Gibson 175.00 350.00
8 Doc Hoblitzel 175.00 350.00
9 Johnny Kling 175.00 350.00
10 Frank LaPorte 175.00 350.00
11 Connie Mack 600.00 1200.00
12 Christy Mathewson 900.00 1800.00
13 Matthew McIntyre 175.00 350.00
14 Jimmy Sheckard 175.00 350.00
15 Al Schweitzer 175.00 350.00
16 Harry Wolter 175.00 350.00

1950-54 J.J.K. Copyart Photographers

This set measures 3 1/2" by 5 1/2" and features New York Giants, Boston Braves, Philadelphia Phillies and one Brooklyn Dodger. The postcards are black and white glossy photos with no company identification on the back.

COMPLETE SET (24) 150.00 300.00
1 Johnny Antonelli (2) 5.00 10.00
2 Sam Calderone 4.00 8.00
3 Del Crandall 5.00 10.00
4 Del Ennis 4.00 8.00
5 Jim Hearn (2) 4.00 8.00
6 Tommy Holmes 5.00 10.00
7 Larry Jansen 5.00 10.00
8 Whitey Lockman (2) 4.00 8.00
9 Williard Marhsall 4.00 8.00
10 Eddie Mathews 15.00 30.00
11 Don Mueller 4.00 8.00
12 Danny O'Connell 4.00 8.00
13 Bill Rigney 5.00 10.00
14 Robin Roberts 12.50 25.00
15 Jackie Robinson 40.00 80.00
16 Hank Sauer 5.00 10.00
17 Red Schoendienst 12.50 25.00
18 Curt Simmons 5.00 10.00
19 Sibby Sisti 4.00 8.00
20 Eddie Stanky 7.50 15.00
Boston Braves
21 Eddie Stanly 7.50 15.00
New York Giants
22 Wes Westrum 4.00 8.00
23 Hoyt Wilhelm 12.50 25.00
24 Al Worthington 4.00 8.00

2001 Joe Jackson Ebay

COMPLETE SET 6.00 15.00
COMMON CARD 2.00 5.00

1969 Reggie Jackson Regiment

This one card set was issued during the early days of Reggie Jackson's career. It was issued as a ballpark promotion during his sensational first half of the 1969 season in which he hit 37 homers.

1 Reggie Jackson 40.00 80.00

1981 Reggie Jackson Accel

This three-card standard-size set features baseball great Reggie Jackson in front of some of his prize automobiles. The fronts feature Jackson posed with the cars. The backs have details about the cars. According ro reports at the time, approximately 7,000 sets were printed.

COMPLETE SET (3) 8.00 20.00
COMMON CARD (1-3) 3.20 8.00

1997 Reggie Jackson Viking

This one card was issued by Viking Computer Memory as part of their commemorative card series to honor people who were used as spokespersons for them. This particular card features a pose of Reggie Jackson in his airbrushed Yankee uniform on the front and the back has a writeup about reggie along with a posed shot and an action shot. There might be more cards Viking did so any additions to this checklist are appreciated

2 Reggie Jackson 4.00 10.00

1956 Jay Publishing World Series Pack

This 50-card set of the 1956 World Series Participants measure approximately 5 1/8" by 7". The fronts feature black-and-white posed player photos with the player's and team name printed below in the white border. The backs are blank. The cards are unnumbered and checklisted below in alphabetical order.

COMPLETE SET (50) 150.00 300.00
1 Walt Alston MG 3.00 6.00
2 Sandy Amoros 2.00 4.00
3 Hank Bauer 2.50 5.00
4 Joe Becker CO 1.50 3.00
5 Yogi Berra 5.00 10.00
6 Don Bessent 1.50 3.00
7 Tommy Byrne 1.50 3.00
8 Roy Campanella 5.00 10.00
9 Andy Carey 2.00 4.00
10 Bob Cerv 2.00 4.00
11 Jerry Coleman 2.50 5.00
12 Joe Collins 2.00 4.00
13 Roger Craig 2.00 4.00
14 Frank Crosetti CO 2.00 4.00
15 Bill Dickey CO 3.00 6.00
16 Don Drysdale 10.00 20.00
17 Carl Erskine 3.00 6.00
18 Chico Fernandez 1.50 3.00
19 Whitey Ford 7.50 15.00
20 Carl Furillo 3.00 6.00
21 Jim Gilliam 2.50 5.00
22 Bob Grim 1.50 3.00
23 Billy Herman CO 3.00 6.00
24 Gil Hodges 5.00 10.00
25 Elston Howard 4.00 8.00
26 Billy Hunter 1.50 3.00
27 Randy Jackson 1.50 3.00
28 Sandy Koufax 10.00 20.00
29 Johnny Kucks 1.50 3.00
30 Clem Labine 1.50 3.00
31 Don Larsen 3.00 6.00
32 Sal Maglie 3.00 6.00
33 Mickey Mantle 12.50 25.00
34 Billy Martin 4.00 8.00
35 Gil McDougald 3.00 6.00
36 Tom Morgan 1.50 3.00
37 Don Newcombe 2.50 5.00
38 Jake Pitler CO 1.50 3.00
39 Johnny Podres 2.50 5.00
40 Pee Wee Reese 5.00 10.00
41 Ed Roebuck 1.50 3.00
42 Jackie Robinson 10.00 20.00
43 Charlie Silvera 1.50 3.00
44 Bill Skowron 3.00 6.00
45 Duke Snider 7.50 15.00
46 Casey Stengel MG 4.00 8.00
47 Tom Sturdivant 1.50 3.00
48 Jim Turner CO 1.50 3.00
49 Bob Turley 1.50 3.00
50 Rube Walker 1.50 3.00

1959 Jay Publishing All-Stars

The 23 blank-backed photos comprising the 1958 Jay Publishing All-Stars set measure 5" by 7" and feature white-bordered black-and-white posed player shots. The player's name appears in black lettering within the bottom white margin. The pictures are unnumbered and checklisted below in alphabetical order.

COMPLETE SET (23) 50.00 150.00
1 Henry Aaron 10.00 20.00
2 Luis Aparicio 4.00 8.00
3 Bob Cerv .75 2.00
4 Delmar Crandall .75 2.00
5 Whitey Ford 4.00 8.00
6 Nelson Fox 4.00 8.00
7 Bob Friend .75 2.00
8 Fred Haney MG .75 2.00
9 Jack Jensen 1.50 3.00
10 Frank Malzone .75 2.00
11 Mickey Mantle 20.00 40.00
12 Willie Mays 20.00
Bill White in Background
12 Bill Mazeroski 2.50 6.00
13 Roy McMillan .75 2.00
14 Stan Musial 7.50 15.00
15 Bill Pierce .75 2.00
16 Robin Roberts 4.00 8.00
17 Bob Skinner .75 2.00
18 Bill Skowron 1.50 3.00
19 Warren Spahn 4.00 8.00
20 Casey Stengel MG 4.00 8.00
21 Frank Thomas .75 2.00
22 Gus Triandos .75 2.00
23 Bob Turley .75 2.00

1958 Jay Publishing All-Time Greats

This 10-card set features glossy black-and-white photos of Baseball's all-time great players. The backs are blank. The cards are unnumbered and checklisted below in alphabetical order.

COMPLETE SET (10) 35.00 70.00
1 Ty Cobb 7.50 15.00
2 Joe DiMaggio 7.50 15.00
3 Lou Gehrig 7.50 15.00
4 Rogers Hornsby 2.50 5.00
Spelled Roger
5 Carl Hubbell 1.00 2.00
6 Connie Mack 1.00 2.00
7 Christy Mathewson 2.00 4.00
8 Johnny Mize 1.00 2.00
9 Babe Ruth 10.00 20.00
10 Casey Stengel 2.00 4.00

1958 Jay Publishing Sluggers

This 10-card set features glossy black-and-white photos of some of Baseball's great hitters. The backs are blank. The cards are unnumbered and checklisted below in alphabetical order.

COMPLETE SET (10) 50.00 100.00
1 Hank Aaron 7.50 15.00
2 Larry Berra 4.00 8.00
3 Nelson Fox 2.50 5.00
4 Al Kaline 3.00 6.00
5 Mickey Mantle 12.50 25.00
6 Ed Mathews 3.00 6.00
7 Willie Mays 7.50 15.00
8 Stan Musial 5.00 10.00
9 Duke Snider 4.00 8.00
10 Ted Williams 10.00 20.00

1962 Jello

The cards in this 200-card (only 197 were ever issued) set measure 2 1/2" by 3 3/8". The 1962 Jello set has the same checklist as the Post Cereal set of the same year, but is considered by some to be a test issue. The cards are grouped numerically by team. For example: New York Yankees (1-13), Detroit (14-26), Baltimore (27-36), Cleveland (37-45), Chicago White Sox (46-55), Boston (56-64), Washington (65-73), Los Angeles Angels (74-82), Minnesota (83-91), Kansas City (92-100), Los Angeles Dodgers (101-115), Cincinnati (116-130), San Francisco (131-144), Milwaukee (145-157), St. Louis (158-168), Pittsburgh (169-181), Chicago Cubs (182-191), and Philadelphia (192-200). Although the players and numbers are identical in both sets, the Jello series has its own list of scarce and difficult cards. Numbers 29, 82 and 176 were never issued. A Jello card is easily distinguished from its counterpart in Post by the absence of the Post logo. The catalog designation for this set is F229-1.

COMPLETE SET (197) 2500.00 5000.00
1 Bill Skowron 10.00 25.00
2 Bobby Richardson 225.00 450.00
3 Cletis Boyer 5.00 12.00
4 Tony Kubek 8.00 20.00
5 Mickey Mantle 500.00 1000.00
6 Roger Maris 100.00 200.00
7 Yogi Berra 60.00 120.00
8 Elston Howard 5.00 12.00
9 Whitey Ford 40.00 80.00
10 Ralph Terry 4.00 10.00
11 John Blanchard 4.00 10.00
12 Luis Arroyo 4.00 10.00
13 Bill Stafford 6.00 15.00
14 Norm Cash 5.00 12.00
15 Jake Wood 2.50 6.00
16 Steve Boros 2.50 6.00
17 Chico Fernandez 2.50 6.00
18 Bill Bruton 2.50 6.00
19 Ken Aspromonte 2.50 6.00
20 Al Kaline 30.00 60.00
21 Dick Brown 2.50 6.00
22 Frank Lary 2.50 6.00
23 Don Mossi 4.00 10.00
24 Phil Regan 2.50 6.00
25 Charley Maxwell 2.50 6.00
26 Jim Bunning 12.50 30.00
27 Jim Gentile 4.00 10.00
28 Marv Breeding 2.50 6.00
29 Not issued
30 Ron Hansen 2.50 6.00
31 Jackie Brandt 10.00 25.00
32 Dick Williams 5.00 12.00
33 Gus Triandos 2.50 6.00
34 Milt Pappas 2.50 6.00
35 Hoyt Wilhelm 20.00 50.00
36 Chuck Estrada 2.50 6.00
37 Vic Power 2.50 6.00
38 Johnny Temple 2.50 6.00
39 Bubba Phillips 10.00 25.00
40 Tito Francona 2.50 6.00
41 Willie Kirkland 2.50 6.00
42 John Romano 2.50 6.00
43 Jim Perry 4.00 10.00
44 Woodie Held 2.50 6.00
45 Chuck Essegian 2.50 6.00
46 Roy Sievers 2.50 6.00
47 Nellie Fox 15.00 40.00
48 Al Smith 2.50 6.00
49 Luis Aparicio 15.00 40.00
50 Jim Landis 2.50 6.00
51 Minnie Minoso 10.00 25.00
52 Andy Carey 10.00 25.00
53 Sherman Lollar 2.50 6.00
54 Billy Pierce 4.00 10.00
55 Early Wynn 12.50 30.00
56 Chuck Schilling 10.00 25.00
57 Pete Runnels 4.00 10.00
58 Frank Malzone 4.00 10.00
59 Don Buddin 4.00 10.00
60 Gary Geiger 10.00 25.00
61 Carl Yastrzemski 150.00 300.00
62 Jackie Jensen 12.50 30.00
63 Jim Pagliaroni 10.00 25.00
64 Don Schwall 4.00 10.00
65 Dale Long 4.00 10.00
66 Chuck Cottier 4.00 10.00
67 Billy Klaus 10.00 25.00
68 Coot Veal 4.00 10.00
69 Marty Keough 15.00 40.00
70 Willie Tasby 15.00 40.00
71 Gene Woodling 4.00 10.00
72 Gene Green 15.00 40.00
73 Dick Donovan 4.00 10.00
74 Steve Bilko 4.00 10.00
75 Rocky Bridges 10.00 25.00
76 Eddie Yost 6.00 15.00
77 Leon Wagner 5.00 12.00
78 Albie Pearson 4.00 10.00
79 Ken Hunt 6.00 15.00
80 Earl Averill 15.00 40.00
81 Ryne Duren 5.00 12.00
82 Not issued
83 Bob Allison 4.00 10.00
84 Billy Martin 12.50 30.00
85 Harmon Killebrew 20.00 50.00
86 Zoilo Versalles 4.00 10.00
87 Lenny Green 12.50 30.00
88 Bill Tuttle 2.50 6.00
89 Jim Lemon 2.50 6.00
90 Earl Battey 10.00 25.00
91 Camilo Pascual 2.50 6.00
92 Norm Siebern 4.00 10.00
93 Jerry Lumpe 4.00 10.00
94 Dick Howser 5.00 12.00
95 Gene Stephens 15.00 40.00
96 Leo Posada 5.00 12.00
97 Joe Pignatano 4.00 10.00
98 Jim Archer 4.00 10.00
99 Haywood Sullivan 10.00 25.00
100 Art Ditmar 4.00 10.00
101 Gil Hodges 20.00 50.00
102 Charlie Neal 4.00 10.00
103 Daryl Spencer 4.00 10.00
104 Maury Wills 12.50 30.00
105 Tommy Davis 6.00 15.00
106 Willie Davis 6.00 15.00
107 Johnny Roseboro 15.00 40.00
108 John Podres 6.00 15.00
109 Sandy Koufax 60.00 120.00
110 Don Drysdale 30.00 60.00
111 Larry Sherry 10.00 25.00
112 Jim Gilliam 12.50 30.00
113 Norm Larker 15.00 40.00
114 Duke Snider 40.00 80.00
115 Stan Williams 10.00 25.00
116 Gordy Coleman 40.00 80.00
117 Don Blasingame 10.00 25.00
118 Gene Freese 15.00 40.00
119 Ed Kasko 15.00 40.00
120 Gus Bell 12.50 30.00
121 Vada Pinson 6.00 15.00
122 Frank Robinson 15.00 40.00
123 Bob Purkey 4.00 10.00
124 Joey Jay 4.00 10.00
125 Jim Brosnan 4.00 10.00
126 Jim O'Toole 4.00 10.00
127 Jerry Lynch 4.00 10.00
128 Wally Post 4.00 10.00
129 Ken Hunt 4.00 10.00
130 Jerry Zimmerman 4.00 10.00
131 Willie McCovey 30.00 60.00
132 Jose Pagan 12.50 30.00
133 Felipe Alou 6.00 15.00
134 Jim Davenport 5.00 12.00
135 Harvey Kuenn 6.00 15.00
136 Orlando Cepeda 12.50 30.00
137 Ed Bailey 4.00 10.00
138 Sam Jones 4.00 10.00
139 Mike McCormick 4.00 10.00
140 Juan Marichal 40.00 80.00
141 Jack Sanford 4.00 10.00
142 Willie Mays 125.00 250.00
143 Stu Miller 30.00 60.00
144 Joe Amalfitano 4.00 10.00
145 Joe Adcock 4.00 10.00
146 Frank Bolling 2.50 6.00
147 Eddie Mathews 20.00 50.00
148 Roy McMillan 2.50 6.00
149 Hank Aaron 100.00 200.00
150 Gino Cimoli 10.00 25.00
151 Frank Thomas 4.00 10.00
152 Joe Torre 8.00 20.00
153 Lew Burdette 5.00 12.00
154 Bob Buhl 2.50 6.00
155 Carlton Willey 2.50 6.00
156 Lee Maye 10.00 25.00
157 Al Spangler 15.00 40.00
158 Bill White 30.00 60.00
159 Ken Boyer 10.00 25.00
160 Joe Cunningham 4.00 10.00
161 Carl Warwick 4.00 10.00
162 Carl Sawatski 2.50 6.00
163 Lindy McDaniel 2.50 6.00
164 Ernie Broglio 4.00 10.00
165 Larry Jackson 2.50 6.00
166 Curt Flood 12.50 30.00
167 Curt Simmons 12.50 30.00
168 Alex Grammas 10.00 25.00
169 Dick Stuart 2.50 6.00
170 Bill Mazeroski 12.50 30.00
171 Don Hoak 4.00 10.00
172 Dick Groat 5.00 12.00
173 Roberto Clemente 150.00 300.00
174 Bob Skinner 10.00 25.00
175 Bill Virdon 12.50 30.00
176 Not issued
177 Roy Face 5.00 12.00
178 Bob Friend 2.50 6.00
179 Vern Law 12.50 30.00
180 Harvey Haddix 15.00 40.00
181 Hal Smith 10.00 25.00
182 Ed Bouchee 10.00 25.00
183 Don Zimmer 5.00 12.00
184 Ron Santo 8.00 20.00
185 Andre Rodgers 2.50 6.00
186 Richie Ashburn 15.00 40.00
187 George Altman 2.50 6.00
188 Ernie Banks 15.00 40.00
189 Sam Taylor 2.50 6.00
190 Don Elston 2.50 6.00
191 Jerry Kindall 8.00 20.00
192 Pancho Herrera 2.50 6.00
193 Tony Taylor 4.00 10.00
194 Ruben Amaro 8.00 20.00
195 Don Demeter 2.50 6.00
196 Bobby Gene Smith 2.50 6.00
197 Clay Dalrymple 2.50 6.00
198 Robin Roberts 12.50 30.00
199 Art Mahaffey 2.50 6.00
200 John Buzhardt 2.50 6.00

1963 Jello

The cards in this 200-card set measure 2 1/2" by 3 3/8". The 1963 Jello set contains the same players and numbers as the Post Cereal set of the same year. The players are grouped by team with American Leaguers comprising 1-100 and National Leaguers 101-200. The ordering of teams is as follows: Minnesota (1-11), New York Yankees (12-23), Los Angeles Angels (24-34), Chicago White Sox (35-45), Detroit (46-56), Baltimore (57-66), Cleveland (67-76), Boston (77-84), Kansas City (85-92), Washington (93-100), San Francisco (101-112), Los Angeles Dodgers (113-124), Cincinnati (125-136), Pittsburgh (137-147), Milwaukee (148-157), St. Louis (158-168), Chicago Cubs (169-176), Philadelphia (177-184), Houston (185-192) and New York Mets (193-200). As in 1962, the Jello series has its own list of scarcities (many resulting from an unpopular package size). Since the Post Cereal logo was removed from the 1963 cereal set, Jello cards are primarily distinguishable by (1) smaller card size and (2) smaller print. The catalog designation is F229-2.

COMPLETE SET (200) 1500.00 3000.00
1 Vic Power 1.50 4.00
2 Bernie Allen 8.00 20.00
3 Zoilo Versalles 10.00 25.00
4 Rich Rollins 1.50 4.00
5 Harmon Killebrew 6.00 15.00
6 Lenny Green 10.00 25.00
7 Bob Allison 2.50 6.00
8 Earl Battey 6.00 15.00
9 Camilo Pascual 2.50 6.00
10 Jim Kaat 20.00 50.00
11 Jack Kralick 1.50 4.00
12 Bill Skowron 10.00 25.00
13 Bobby Richardson 3.00 8.00
14 Cletis Boyer 2.50 6.00
15 Mickey Mantle 125.00 250.00
16 Roger Maris 50.00 100.00
17 Yogi Berra 12.50 30.00
18 Elston Howard 20.00 50.00
19 Whitey Ford 8.00 20.00
20 Ralph Terry 1.50 4.00
21 John Blanchard 6.00 15.00
22 Bill Stafford 8.00 20.00
23 Tom Tresh 4.00 10.00
24 Steve Bilko 1.50 4.00
25 Bill Moran 1.50 4.00
26 Joe Koppe 1.50 4.00
27 Felix Torres 1.50 4.00
28 Leon Wagner 1.50 4.00
29 Albie Pearson 1.50 4.00
30 Lee Thomas 1.50 4.00
31 Bob Rodgers 8.00 20.00
32 Dean Chance 3.00 8.00
33 Ken McBride 8.00 20.00
34 George Thomas 8.00 20.00
35 Joe Cunningham 8.00 20.00
36 Nellie Fox 4.00 10.00
37 Luis Aparicio 4.00 10.00
38 Al Smith 2.50 6.00
39 Floyd Robinson 1.50 4.00
40 Jim Landis 1.50 4.00
41 Charlie Maxwell 1.50 4.00
42 Sherman Lollar 2.50 6.00
43 Early Wynn 4.00 10.00
44 Juan Pizarro 8.00 20.00
45 Ray Herbert 10.00 25.00
46 Norm Cash 3.00 8.00
47 Steve Boros 12.50 30.00
48 Dick McAuliffe 3.00 8.00
49 Bill Bruton 8.00 20.00
50 Rocky Colavito 4.00 10.00
51 Al Kaline 6.00 15.00
52 Dick Brown 8.00 20.00
53 Jim Bunning 4.00 10.00
54 Hank Aguirre 1.50 4.00
55 Frank Lary 8.00 20.00
56 Don Mossi 10.00 25.00
57 Jim Gentile 3.00 8.00
58 Jackie Brandt 2.50 6.00
59 Brooks Robinson 6.00 15.00
60 Ron Hansen 1.50 4.00
61 Jerry Adair 15.00 40.00
62 Boog Powell 3.00 8.00
63 Russ Snyder 10.00 25.00
64 Steve Barber 2.50 6.00
65 Milt Pappas 8.00 20.00
66 Robin Roberts 5.00 12.00
67 Tito Francona 1.50 4.00
68 Jerry Kindall 8.00 20.00
69 Woody Held 1.50 4.00
70 Bubba Phillips 1.50 4.00
71 Chuck Essegian 1.50 4.00
72 Willie Kirkland 8.00 20.00
73 Al Luplow 1.50 4.00
74 Ty Cline 15.00 40.00
75 Dick Donovan 1.50 4.00
76 John Romano 1.50 4.00
77 Pete Runnels 3.00 8.00
78 Ed Bressoud 8.00 20.00
79 Frank Malzone 2.50 6.00
80 Carl Yastrzemski 40.00 80.00
81 Gary Geiger 2.50 6.00
82 Lou Clinton 8.00 20.00
83 Earl Wilson 2.50 6.00
84 Bill Monbouquette 1.50 4.00
85 Norm Siebern 1.50 4.00
86 Jerry Lumpe 1.50 4.00
87 Manny Jimenez 1.50 4.00
88 Gino Cimoli 2.50 6.00
89 Ed Charles 15.00 40.00
90 Ed Rakow 2.50 6.00
91 Bobby Del Greco 15.00 40.00
92 Haywood Sullivan 8.00 20.00
93 Chuck Hinton 1.50 4.00
94 Ken Retzer 8.00 20.00
95 Harry Bright 8.00 20.00
96 Bob Johnson 2.50 6.00
97 Dave Stenhouse 6.00 15.00
98 Chuck Cottier 2.50 6.00
99 Tom Cheney 2.50 6.00
100 Claude Osteen 10.00 25.00
101 Orlando Cepeda 4.00 10.00
102 Chuck Hiller 6.00 15.00
103 Jose Pagan 8.00 20.00
104 Jim Davenport 1.50 4.00
105 Harvey Kuenn 2.50 6.00
106 Willie Mays 50.00 100.00
107 Felipe Alou 3.00 8.00
108 Tom Haller 2.50 6.00
109 Juan Marichal 4.00 10.00
110 Jack Sanford 1.50 4.00
111 Bill O'Dell 1.50 4.00
112 Willie McCovey 60.00 120.00
113 Lee Walls 8.00 20.00
114 Jim Gilliam 12.50 30.00
115 Maury Wills 3.00 8.00
116 Ron Fairly 2.50 6.00
117 Tommy Davis 2.50 6.00
118 Duke Snider 5.00 12.00
119 Willie Davis 2.50 6.00
120 John Roseboro 1.50 4.00
121 Sandy Koufax 15.00 40.00
122 Stan Williams 1.50 4.00
123 Don Drysdale 4.00 10.00
124 Daryl Spencer 1.50 4.00
125 Gordy Coleman 2.50 6.00
126 Don Blasingame 8.00 20.00
127 Leo Cardenas 1.50 4.00
128 Eddie Kasko 8.00 20.00
129 Jerry Lynch 1.50 4.00
130 Vada Pinson 4.00 10.00
131 Frank Robinson 5.00 12.00
132 Johnny Edwards 8.00 20.00
133 Joey Jay 1.50 4.00
134 Bob Purkey 1.50 4.00
135 Marty Keough 15.00 40.00
136 Jim O'Toole 8.00 20.00
137 Dick Stuart 1.50 4.00
138 Bill Mazeroski 4.00 10.00
139 Dick Groat 2.50 6.00
140 Don Hoak 1.50 4.00
141 Bob Skinner 1.50 4.00
142 Bill Virdon 2.50 6.00
143 Roberto Clemente 60.00 120.00
144 Smoky Burgess 3.00 8.00
145 Bob Friend 1.50 4.00
146 Al McBean 10.00 25.00
147 Roy Face 2.50 6.00
148 Joe Adcock 2.50 6.00
149 Frank Bolling 1.50 4.00
150 Roy McMillan 2.50 6.00
151 Eddie Mathews 6.00 15.00
152 Hank Aaron 50.00 100.00
153 Del Crandall 10.00 25.00
154 Bob Shaw 2.50 6.00
155 Lew Burdette 2.50 6.00
156 Joe Torre 20.00 50.00
157 Tony Cloninger 15.00 40.00
158 Bill White 4.00 10.00
159 Julian Javier 8.00 20.00
160 Ken Boyer 4.00 10.00
161 Julio Gotay 10.00 25.00
162 Curt Flood 2.50 6.00
163 Charlie James 20.00 50.00
164 Gene Oliver 10.00 25.00
165 Ernie Broglio 1.50 4.00
166 Bob Gibson 50.00 100.00
167 Lindy McDaniel 8.00 20.00
168 Ray Washburn 2.50 6.00
169 Ernie Banks 6.00 15.00
170 Ron Santo 3.00 8.00
171 George Altman 1.50 4.00
172 Billy Williams 40.00 80.00
173 Andre Rodgers 10.00 25.00
174 Ken Hubbs 3.00 8.00
175 Don Landrum 8.00 20.00
176 Dick Bertell 8.00 20.00
177 Roy Sievers 2.50 6.00
178 Tony Taylor 10.00 25.00
179 Johnny Callison 2.50 6.00
180 Don Demeter 1.50 4.00
181 Tony Gonzalez 8.00 20.00
182 Wes Covington 8.00 20.00
183 Art Mahaffey 1.50 4.00
184 Clay Dalrymple 2.50 6.00
185 Al Spangler 1.50 4.00
186 Roman Mejias 1.50 4.00
187 Bob Aspromonte 12.50 30.00
188 Norm Larker 1.50 4.00
189 Johnny Temple 1.50 4.00
190 Carl Warwick 8.00 20.00
191 Bob Lillis 8.00 20.00
192 Dick Farrell 15.00 40.00
193 Gil Hodges 5.00 12.00
194 Marv Throneberry 2.50 6.00
195 Charlie Neal 10.00 25.00
196 Frank Thomas 2.50 6.00
197 Richie Ashburn 4.00 10.00
198 Felix Mantilla 8.00 20.00
199 Rod Kanehl 8.00 20.00
200 Roger Craig 12.50 30.00

1963 Jewish Sports Champions

The 16 cards in this set, measuring roughly 2 2/3" x 3", are cut out of an "Activity Funbook" entitled Jewish Sports Champions. The set pays tribute to famous Jewish athletes from baseball, football, bull fighting to chess. The cards have a green border with a yellow background and a player close-up illustration. Cards that are still attached carry a premium over those that have been cut-out. The cards are unnumbered and listed below in alphabetical order with an assigned sport prefix (BB-baseball, BK- basketball, BX- boxing, FB- football, OT- other).

COMPLETE SET (16) 100.00 200.00
BB1 Hank Greenberg BB 10.00 20.00
BB2 Johnny Kling BB 5.00 10.00
BB3 Sandy Koufax BB 20.00 40.00

1973 Jewish Sports Champions

The 16 cards in this set, measuring roughly 2 2/3" x 3", are cut out of a sequel to the 1968 Activity Funbook. This time, the cards come from a funbook entitled "More Jewish Sports Champions". There are two variations to each card that are valued equally. One has a pink border with a yellow background and blue ink on the player close-up illustration. The other has a blue background and black ink on the player illustration. Cards that are still attached carry a premium over those that have been cut-out. The cards are unnumbered and listed below in alphabetical order.

COMPLETE SET (16) 65.00 125.00
12 Al (Flip) Rosen BB 6.00 12.00

2003 Jewish Major Leaguers

COMPLETE SET 60.00 100.00
*GOLD CARDS: 1.5X TO 4X BASIC CARDS
GOLD CARDS: 500 SERIAL #D SETS
*SILVER CARDS: .75X TO 2X BASIC CARDS
SILVER CARDS: 1500 SERIAL #'D SETS
1 Sandy Koufax 6.00 15.00
2 Harry Danning .60 1.50
3 Hank Greenberg 4.00 10.00
4 Andy Cohen .40 1.00
5 Al Rosen 1.00 2.50
6 Buddy Myer .60 1.50
7 Sid Gordon .60 1.50
8 Shawn Green 3.00 8.00
9 Morrie Arnovich .40 1.00
10 Lipman Pike .40 1.00
11 Nate Berkenstock .40 1.00
12 Jacob Pike .40 1.00
13 Jake Goodman .40 1.00
14 Ike Samuls .40 1.00
15 Leo Fishel .40 1.00
16 Bill Cristall .40 1.00
17 Harry Kane .40 1.00
18 Barney Pelty .40 1.00
19 Moxie Manuel .40 1.00
20 Phil Cooney .40 1.00
21 Guy Zinn .40 1.00
22 Ed Mensor .40 1.00
23 Erskine Mayer .40 1.00
24 Henry Bostick .40 1.00
25 Sam Mayer .40 1.00
26 Sammy Bohne .40 1.00
27 Jake Pitler .40 1.00
28 Bob Berman .40 1.00
29 Eddie Corey .40 1.00
30 Jesse Baker .40 1.00
31 Al Schacht .75 2.00
32 Sam Fishburn .40 1.00
33 Reuben Ewing .40 1.00
34 Heinie Scheer .40 1.00
35 Lou Rosenberg .40 1.00
36 Moe Berg 2.00 5.00
37 Joe Bennett .40 1.00
38 Moses Solomon .40 1.00
39 Happy Foreman .40 1.00
40 Si Rosenthal .40 1.00
41 Ike Danning .40 1.00
42 Jonah Goldman .40 1.00
43 Ed Wineapple .40 1.00
44 Jimmie Reese .60 1.50
45 Harry Rosenberg .40 1.00
46 Jim Levey .40 1.00
47 Alta Cohen .40 1.00
48 Max Rosenfeld .40 1.00
49 Lou Brower .40 1.00
50 Izzy Goldstein .40 1.00
51 Milt Galatzer .40 1.00
52 Phil Weintraub .40 1.00
53 Cy Malis .40 1.00
54 Syd Cohen .40 1.00
55 Fred Sington .40 1.00
56 Harry Eisenstat .40 1.00
57 Chick Starr .40 1.00
58 Goody Rosen .40 1.00
59 Harry Chozen .40 1.00
60 Eddie Feinberg .40 1.00
61 Sam Nahem .40 1.00
62 Dick Conger .40 1.00
63 Murray Franklin .40 1.00
64 Harry Feldman .40 1.00
65 Harry Shuman .40 1.00
66 Eddie Turchin .40 1.00
67 Cy Block .40 1.00
68 Hal Schacker .40 1.00
69 Mike Schemer .40 1.00
70 Herb Karpel .40 1.00
71 Bud Swartz .40 1.00
72 Mickey Rutner .40 1.00
73 Marv Rotblatt .40 1.00
74 Joe Ginsberg .40 1.00
75 Cal Abrams .40 1.00
76 Saul Rogovin .40 1.00
77 Sid Schacht .40 1.00
78 Lou Limmer .40 1.00
79 Duke Markell .40 1.00
80 Al Richter .40 1.00
81 Al Federoff .40 1.00
82 Herb Gorman .40 1.00
83 Moe Savransky .40 1.00
84 Hy Cohen .40 1.00
85 Al Silvera .40 1.00
86 Barry Latman .40 1.00
87 Ed Mayer .40 1.00
88 Larry Sherry .40 1.00
89 Don Taussig .40 1.00
90 Norm Sherry .40 1.00
91 Randy Cardinal .40 1.00
92 Alan Koch .40 1.00
93 Larry Yellen .40 1.00
94 Steve Hertz .40 1.00
95 Art Shamsky .40 1.00
96 Richie Scheinblum .40 1.00
97 Greg Goossen .40 1.00
98 Norm Miller .40 1.00
99 Ken Holtzman .40 1.00
100 Mike Epstein .40 1.00
101 Ron Blomberg .40 1.00
102 Lloyd Allen .40 1.00
103 Dave Roberts .40 1.00
104 Elliott Maddox .40 1.00
105 Steve Stone .60 1.50
106 Steve Yeager .40 1.00
107 Skip Jutze .40 1.00
108 Dick Sharon .40 1.00
109 Jeff Newman .40 1.00
110 Ross Baumgarten .40 1.00
111 Jeff Stember .40 1.00
112 Steve Ratzer .40 1.00
113 Bob Tufts .40 1.00
114 Larry Rothschild .40 1.00
115 Mark Gilbert .40 1.00
116 Steve Rosenberg .40 1.00
117 Roger Samuels .40 1.00
118 Steve Wapnick .40 1.00
119 Scott Radinsky .40 1.00
120 Ruben Amaro Jr. .40 1.00
121 Wayne Rosenthal .40 1.00
122 Eddie Zosky .40 1.00
123 Jesse Levis .40 1.00
124 Brad Ausmus .40 1.00
125 Eric Helfand .40 1.00
126 Mike Lieberthal .40 1.00
127 Andy Lorraine .40 1.00
128 Brian Kowitz .40 1.00
129 Brian Bark .40 1.00
130 Mike Milchin .40 1.00
131 Al Levine .40 1.00
132 Micah Franklin .40 1.00
133 Mike Saipe .40 1.00
134 Keith Glauber .40 1.00
135 Gabe Kapler .40 1.00
136 Scott Schoeneweis .40 1.00
137 David Newhan .60 1.50
138 Jason Marquis .40 1.00
139 Frank Charles .40 1.00
140 Tony Cogan .40 1.00
141 Justin Wayne .40 1.00
142 Matt Ford .40 1.00
143 Header Card .40 1.00
144 Information Card .40 1.00
145 Leader Card .40 1.00
146 Leader Card .40 1.00
147 Checklist Card .40 1.00
148 Checklist Card .40 1.00
149 George Brace .40 1.00

2006 Jewish Major Leaguers Update

COMP.FACT SET
1 Cover Card .40 1.00
2 Roster Card .40 1.00
3 Roster Card .40 1.00
4 Roster Card .40 1.00
5 Offensive Leaders .40 1.00
6 Pitching Leaders .40 1.00
7 Shawn Green .75 2.00
8 Brad Ausmus .40 1.00
9 Mike Lieberthal .40 1.00
10 Al Levine .40 1.00
11 Scott Schoeneweis .40 1.00
12 Jason Marquis .40 1.00
13 Gabe Kapler .40 1.00
14 John Grabow .40 1.00
15 Kevin Youkilis .40 1.00
16 Adam Stern .40 1.00
17 Craig Breslow .40 1.00
18 Adam Greenberg .40 1.00
19 Scott Feldman .40 1.00
20 Aaron Rifkin .40 1.00
Scott Schneider
Tony Schrager
Jeff Pickler
21 Jacob Livingston .40 1.00
22 Jacob Atz .40 1.00
23 Lefty Weinert .40 1.00
24 Lou Boudreau 1.25 3.00
25 Bob Davis .40 1.00
26 Jose Bautista .40 1.00
27 Sam Nahem MEM .40 1.00
28 Thelma Eisen .40 1.00
29 Anita Foss .40 1.00

Card	Low	High
30 Blanche Schachter	.40	1.00
31 Margaret Wigiser UER		
32 Cy Block MEM	.40	1.00
33 Harry Danning MEM	.40	1.00
34 Lipman Pike	.40	1.00
35 Abe Yager	.40	1.00
36 Barney Dreyfuss OWN	.40	1.00
37 Dolly Stark UMP	.40	1.00
38 Hank Greenberg P	1.25	3.00
GM		
39 Allen Roth STAT	.40	1.00
40 Mel Allen ANN	1.00	2.50
41 Ron Blomberg	.50	1.25
42 Richie Scheinblum	.40	1.00
43 Bud Selig COMM	.75	2.00
44 Israel National Team	.40	1.00
45 Marvin Miller	.75	2.00
Don Fehr		
46 Moe Berg	.75	2.00
Heinie Scheer		
47 Saul Rogovin	.40	1.00
Joe Ginsberg		
Lou Limmer		
48 Mike Epstein	.40	1.00
Ron Blomberg		
Ken Holtzman		
Bob Tufts		
Larry Yellen		
Elliott Maddox		
Richie Scheinblum		
Norm Sherry		
49 Sid Gordon	.40	1.00
Goody Rosen		
Morrie Arnovich		
Mike Schemer		
Harry Feldman		
50 Al Schacht	.75	2.00
Max Patkin		
51 Mickey Rutner	.40	1.00
Lou Limmer		
52 Jake Levy	.40	1.00
Hal Saltzman		
53 Solomon Israel	.40	1.00
54 Marty Abramowitz	.40	1.00
55 Gabe Kapler	.40	1.00
Adam Stern		
Kevin Youkilis		

1991 Jimmy Dean

Michael Schechter Associates (MSA) produced this 25-card standard-size set on behalf of Jimmy Dean Sausage. Since these player photos were not expressly licensed by Major League Baseball, the team logos have been airbrushed out. During the promotion, uncut sheets were offered by the company through a mail-in offer involving Jimmy Dean proofs of purchase.

Card	Low	High
COMPLETE SET (25)	5.00	12.00
1 Will Clark	.20	.50
2 Ken Griffey Jr.	.60	1.50
3 Dale Murphy	.15	.40
4 Barry Bonds	.40	1.00
5 Darryl Strawberry	.07	.20
6 Ryne Sandberg	.30	.75
7 Gary Sheffield	.20	.50
8 Sandy Alomar Jr.	.07	.20
9 Frank Thomas	.20	.50
10 Barry Larkin	.15	.40
11 Kirby Puckett	.20	.50
12 George Brett	.40	1.00
13 Kevin Mitchell	.02	.10
14 Dave Justice	.15	.40
15 Cal Ripken	.75	2.00
16 Craig Biggio	.10	.30
17 Rickey Henderson	.25	.60
18 Roger Clemens	.40	1.00
19 Jose Canseco	.20	.50
20 Ozzie Smith	.40	1.00
21 Cecil Fielder	.07	.20
22 Dave Winfield	.20	.50
23 Kevin Maas	.02	.10
24 Nolan Ryan	.75	2.00
25 Dwight Gooden	.07	.20

1992 Jimmy Dean

Michael Schechter Associates (MSA) produced this 18-card standard-size set for Jimmy Dean. In a cello pack, three free cards were included in any Jimmy Dean Sandwich, Flapsticks, or Links/Patties Breakfast Sausage.

Card	Low	High
COMPLETE SET (18)	3.00	8.00
1 Jim Abbott	.07	.20
2 Barry Bonds	.40	1.00
3 Jeff Bagwell	.30	.75
4 Frank Thomas	.20	.50
5 Steve Avery	.02	.10
6 Chris Sabo	.02	.10
7 Will Clark	.20	.50
8 Don Mattingly	.40	1.00
9 Darryl Strawberry	.07	.20
10 Roger Clemens	.40	1.00
11 Ken Griffey Jr.	.60	1.50
12 Chuck Knoblauch	.15	.40
13 Tony Gwynn	.40	1.00
14 Juan Gonzalez	.15	.40
15 Cecil Fielder	.07	.20
16 Bobby Bonilla	.02	.10
17 Wes Chamberlain	.02	.10
18 Ryne Sandberg	.40	1.00

1992 Jimmy Dean Living Legends

This six-card standard-size set was produced by MSA (Michael Schechter Associates) and features future candidates for the Hall of Fame. Collectors could obtain the complete set through a mail-in offer detailed on packages of Jimmy Dean Breakfast Sausage or Smoked Sausage. While supplies lasted, the sets could be obtained by sending in three UPC proofs of purchase from Jimmy Dean Sausage plus 1.00 for shipping and handling. Reportedly 105,000 sets were printed.

Card	Low	High
COMPLETE SET (6)	6.00	15.00
1 George Brett	1.00	2.50
2 Carlton Fisk	.60	1.50
3 Ozzie Smith	.60	1.50
4 Robin Yount	.60	1.50
5 Cal Ripken	2.00	5.00
6 Nolan Ryan	2.00	5.00

1992 Jimmy Dean Rookie Stars

The players in this nine-card standard-size set were chosen based on actual 1992 first-half performance. Three free cards were included in specially marked packages of Jimmy Dean Sausage, Chicken Biscuits, Steak Biscuits, and MiniBurgers. Oversized 7" by 9 3/4" versions of the cards, featuring a Rookie Star front on one side and a Living Legend front on the other, were placed at point of purchase for promotional purchases.

Card	Low	High
COMPLETE SET (9)	1.50	4.00
1 Andy Stankiewicz	.05	.15
2 Pat Listach	.05	.15
3 Brian Jordan	.40	1.00
4 Eric Karros	.30	.75
5 Reggie Sanders	.05	.15
6 Dave Fleming	.05	.15
7 Donovan Osborne	.05	.15
8 Kenny Lofton	.60	1.50
9 Moises Alou	.30	.75

1993 Jimmy Dean

Produced by MSA (Michael Schechter Associates) for Jimmy Dean, these 28 cards measure the standard size. Eighteen cards were distributed in packs of three inside certain packages of Jimmy Dean products. The remaining ten cards were a special issue subset that could only be obtained through redemption of UPC symbols from Jimmy Dean Roll Sausage.

Card	Low	High
COMPLETE SET (28)	4.00	10.00
1 Frank Thomas	.40	1.00
2 Barry Larkin	.30	.75
3 Cal Ripken	1.25	3.00
4 Andy Van Slyke	.08	.25
5 Darren Daulton	.15	.40
6 Don Mattingly	.60	1.50
7 Roger Clemens	.60	1.50
8 Juan Gonzalez	.30	.75
9 Mark Langston	.08	.25
10 Barry Bonds	.60	1.50
11 Ken Griffey Jr.	1.00	2.50
12 Cecil Fielder	.15	.40
13 Kirby Puckett	.40	1.00
14 Tom Glavine	.25	.60
15 George Brett	.60	1.50
16 Nolan Ryan	1.25	3.00
17 Eddie Murray	.40	1.00
18 Gary Sheffield	.40	1.00
19 Doug Drabek	.08	.25
20 Ray Lankford	.15	.40
21 Benito Santiago	.15	.40
22 Mark McGwire	.60	1.50
23 Kenny Lofton	.40	1.00
24 Eric Karros	.25	.60
25 Ryne Sandberg	.50	1.25
26 Charlie Hayes	.08	.25
27 Mike Mussina	.30	.75
28 Pat Listach	.08	.25

1993 Jimmy Dean Rookies

This nine-card standard-size set displays a cutout photo of the player superimposed on a gray studio background. The cards are numbered in alphabetical order.

Card	Low	High
COMPLETE SET (9)	2.00	5.00
1 Rich Amaral	.02	.10
2 Vinny Castilla	.15	.40
3 Jeff Conine	.02	.10
4 Brent Gates	.02	.10
5 Wayne Kirby	.02	.10
6 Mike Lansing	.07	.20
7 David Nied	.02	.10
8 Mike Piazza	1.25	3.00
9 Tim Salmon	.60	1.50

1995 Jimmy Dean All-Time Greats

This six-card standard-size set was cosponsored by Jimmy Dean Foods and the Major League Baseball Players Alumni Association. The cards were individually cello wrapped and inserted inside packages, and an accompanying paper insert featured coupons and a mail-in offer. (The mail-in offer was also found on boxes of Jimmy Dean Breakfast foods.) For two proofs-of-purchase plus $7.00, the collector received one autographed card featuring Billy Williams, Al Kaline, or Jim "Catfish" Hunter. Expiring December 31, 1995, the offer was limited to 12 baseball cards per original order form. The cards are checklisted below in alphabetical order.

Card	Low	High
COMPLETE SET (6)	2.00	5.00
1 Rod Carew	.40	1.00
2 Jim Catfish Hunter	.40	1.00
3 Al Kaline	.40	1.00
4 Mike Schmidt	.75	2.00
5 Billy Williams	.40	1.00
6 Carl Yastrzemski	.60	1.50
NNO Catfish Hunter AU	10.00	25.00
NNO Billy Williams AU	6.00	15.00
NNO Al Kaline AU	8.00	20.00

1997 Jimmy Dean

This two-card set was distributed through Jimmy Dean Products and could be obtained by sending in $12.95 and two UPCs from these products. The cards in this limited editionset were issued as certified autographs, though unsigned versions of the cards have appeared on the secondary market. The fronts feature black-and-white action player photos in a gold margin with a thin white inside border and green diamonds at the corners. The backs carry player information and career statistics. The cards are unnumbered and checklisted below in alphabetical order.

Card	Low	High
COMPLETE SET (2)	12.50	30.00
NNO Yogi Berra AU	15.00	40.00
NNO Yogi Berra	2.00	5.00
NNO Brooks Robinson	2.00	5.00
NNO Brooks Robinson AU	12.00	30.00

1959 Jimmy Fund Membership Card

This one card "set" is presumed to be issued in 1959 and features a photo of the Jimmy Fund building on the front. The back contains a "photo" of Ted Williams along with a statement thanking the member for their support of the Jimmy Fund.

Card	Low	High
1 Jimmy Fund Building	4.00	8.00

1976 Jimmy Fund

These oversize cards were issued in 1976 and featured members of the Baseball Hall of Fame. These cards are rarely seen and have black and white photos on the front with the players names and their Jimmy Fund affiliation on the bottom. As far as is known, the only players issued are in the Hall of Fame. As the cards are blank backed and unnumbered we have sequenced them in alphabetical order. There may be additions to this checklist so any additional information is appreciated.

Card	Low	High
COMPLETE SET	300.00	600.00
1 Cool Papa Bell	20.00	50.00
2 Jocko Conlan UER	20.00	50.00
Spelled Conlin		
3 Stan Coveleskie	20.00	50.00
4 Charlie Gehringer	30.00	60.00
5 Hank Greenberg	40.00	80.00
6 Burleigh Grimes	20.00	50.00
7 Waite Hoyt	20.00	50.00
8 Monte Irvin	30.00	60.00
9 George Kelly	20.00	50.00
10 Sandy Koufax	75.00	150.00
11 Fred Lindstrom	20.00	50.00

1994-96 John Deere

Over a three year period, the John Deere tractor company used professional athletes to promote their products and included cards of these athletes in their set. These five cards were issued in 1994 (Ryan and Novacek), 1995 (Jackson and Petty) and 1996 (Larry Bird). For our cataloguing purposes we are sequencing these cards in alphabetical order. Larry Bird signed some cards for this promotion but these cards are so thinly traded that no pricing is available

Card	Low	High
COMPLETE SET (5)	15.00	40.00
2 Reggie Jackson	3.00	8.00
5 Nolan Ryan	6.00	15.00

1991 Walter Johnson Postcard

This one card postcard set, distributed by the Coffeyville Historical Society, features all time great Walter Johnson. The front is a picture of the Walter Johnson Mural and was commissioned by the Coffeyville Historical Society.

Card	Low	High
1 Walter Johnson	1.25	3.00

1976 Jerry Jonas Promotion Cards

These eight cards were issued by Jerry Jonas Promotions as part of an attempt to secure a major league liscense. These cards were presented at the World Series meetings in 1975. These cards, featuring all time greats, were in the format of the regular 1975 Topps issue. The set is also sometimes found as an uncut sheet of all eight players. According to published reports no more than 100 sets of these were printed.

Card	Low	High
COMPLETE SET	300.00	600.00
1 Sandy Koufax	50.00	100.00
2 Mel Ott	30.00	60.00
3 Willie Mays	75.00	150.00
4 Stan Musial	50.00	100.00
5 Rogers Hornsby	20.00	50.00
6 Honus Wagner	40.00	80.00
7 Grover Alexander	40.00	80.00
8 Robin Roberts	30.00	60.00

1997 Chipper Jones Police

This one-card set features a color photo of the Atlanta Braves player, Chipper Jones, with a member of the Covington Police Department. The back displays information about both pictured men and a Safety Message.

Card	Low	High
1 Chipper Jones	1.25	3.00
Wayne Digby		

1911 Jones, Keyser and Arras Cabinets

These 4 3/4" by 7 1/4" cabinets were issued in 1911 from this New York City based company. The fronts feature a player photo with the image number on the bottom of the photo and the players name on the bottom of the card. There may be more cabinets in this set so any additional information is appreciated.

Card	Low	High
COMPLETE SET	5000.00	12000.00
301 Russ Ford	400.00	800.00
303 Jack Warhop	400.00	800.00
304 Bill Dahlen MG	400.00	800.00
306 Zack Wheat	750.00	1500.00
307 Al Bridwell	400.00	800.00
308 Red Murray	400.00	800.00
310 Fred Snodgrass	500.00	1000.00
311 Red Ames	400.00	800.00
312 Fred Merkle	600.00	1200.00
313 Art Devlin	400.00	800.00
314 Hooks Wiltse	400.00	800.00
315 Josh Devore	400.00	800.00
316 Eddie Collins	1250.00	2500.00
317 Ed Reulbach	400.00	800.00
318 Jimmy Sheckard	400.00	800.00
320 Wildfire Schulte	500.00	1000.00
321 Solly Hofman	400.00	800.00
322 Bill Bergen	400.00	800.00
323 George Bell	400.00	800.00
325 Fred Clarke MG	750.00	1500.00
326 Clark Griffith MG	750.00	1500.00
327 Roger Bresnahan	750.00	1500.00
328 Fred Tenney	400.00	800.00
329 Harry Lord	400.00	800.00
331 Walter Johnson	2000.00	4000.00
332 Nap Lajoie	1500.00	3000.00
333 Joe Tinker	1250.00	2500.00
334 Mordecai Brown	750.00	1500.00
336 Jimmy Archer	400.00	800.00
340 Hal Chase	600.00	1200.00
341 Larry Doyle	500.00	1000.00
342 Chief Meyers	500.00	1000.00
343 Christy Mathewson	2000.00	4000.00
344 Bugs Raymond	400.00	800.00
345 John McGraw MG	1500.00	3000.00
346 Honus Wagner	2000.00	4000.00
347 Ty Cobb	3000.00	6000.00
348 Johnnie Evers	1250.00	2500.00
349 Frank Chance	1250.00	2500.00

1886-88 Joseph Hall Cabinets

In 1888, Joseph Hall produced a 14-card set of cabinets. The cabinet cards feature major league team photos. The horiztontal cabinets measure 6 1/2" by 4 1/4". The cards have says Joseph Hall directly under the team photo.

Card	Low	High
COMPLETE SET	40000.00	80000.00
1 Baltimore, 1888	4000.00	8000.00
2 Boston, 1888	6000.00	12000.00
3 Brooklyn, 1888	4000.00	8000.00
4 Chicago, 1888	6000.00	12000.00
5 Cincinnati, 1888	4000.00	8000.00
6 Cleveland, 1888	4000.00	8000.00
7 Detroit, 1888	5000.00	10000.00
8 Indianapolis, 1888	4000.00	8000.00
9 Kansas City, 1888	4000.00	8000.00
10 Louisville, 1888	4000.00	8000.00
11 New York, 1888	4000.00	8000.00
12 Athletic, 1888	5000.00	10000.00
13 St. Louis, 1888	4000.00	8000.00
14 Washington, 1888	4000.00	8000.00

1910 Ju Ju Drums E286

These round "cards" have a diameter measure of 1 7/16". They were issued by Ju Ju Drums gum. The set can be dated to 1910 by the inclusion of Elmer Zacher who had his only major league season that year. These cards are unnumbered and we have sequenced them in alphabetical order.

Card	Low	High
COMPLETE SET (43)	7500.00	15000.00
1 Eddie Ainsmith	250.00	500.00
2 Jimmy Austin	250.00	500.00
3 Chief Bender	500.00	1000.00
4 Bruno Block	250.00	500.00
5 Jimmy Burke	250.00	500.00
6 Donie Bush	250.00	500.00
7 Frank Chance	600.00	1200.00
8 Harry Cheek	250.00	500.00
9 Eddie Cicotte	500.00	1000.00
10 Ty Cobb	3000.00	6000.00
11 King Cole	250.00	500.00
12 Jack Coombs	500.00	1000.00
13 Bill Dahlen	250.00	500.00
14 Bert Daniels	250.00	500.00
15 George Davis	500.00	1000.00
16 Larry Doyle	300.00	600.00
17 Rube Ellis	250.00	500.00
18 George Ferguson	250.00	500.00
19 Russ Ford	250.00	500.00
20 Robert Harmon	250.00	500.00
21 Robert Hyatt	250.00	500.00
22 William Killefer	250.00	500.00
23 Arthur Krueger	250.00	500.00
24 Thomas Leach	300.00	600.00
25 Christy Mathewson	1500.00	3000.00
26 John McGraw	750.00	1500.00
27 Deacon McGuire	250.00	500.00
28 Chief Meyers	300.00	600.00
29 Roy Miller	250.00	500.00
30 George Mullin	300.00	600.00
31 Tom Needham	250.00	500.00
32 Rube Oldring	250.00	500.00
33 Barney Pelty	250.00	500.00
34 Ed Reulbach	300.00	600.00
35 John Rowan	250.00	500.00
36 David Shean	250.00	500.00
37 Tris Speaker	1000.00	2000.00
38 Ed Sweeney	250.00	500.00
39 Jimmy Walsh	250.00	500.00
40 Honus Wagner	1500.00	3000.00
41 Doc White	250.00	500.00
42 Ralph Works	250.00	500.00
43 Elmer Zacher	250.00	500.00

1893 Just So

These 14 cards measure 2 1/2" by 3 7/8" and feature members of the Cleveland Spiders. So far, these cards have been checklisted but others may exist. We have sequenced these cards in alphabetical order. The earliest known Cy Young card is in this set.

Card	Low	High
COMPLETE SET (13)	200000.00	400000.00
1 Frank Boyd	15000.00	30000.00
2 Jesse Burkett	30000.00	60000.00
3 Cupid Childs	15000.00	30000.00
4 John Clarkson	30000.00	60000.00
5 George Cuppy	15000.00	30000.00
6 George Davies	30000.00	60000.00
7 Charlie Hastings	15000.00	30000.00
8 Ed McKean	15000.00	30000.00
9 Jack O'Connor	15000.00	30000.00
10 Patsy Tebeau	20000.00	40000.00
11 Jake Virtue	15000.00	30000.00
12 Tom Williams	15000.00	30000.00
13 Cy Young	50000.00	100000.00
14 Chief Zimmer	15000.00	30000.00

1982 K-Mart

The cards in this 44-card set measure the standard size. This set was mass produced by Topps for K-Mart's 20th Anniversary Celebration and distributed in a custom box. The set features Topps cards of National and American League MVP's from 1962 through 1981. The backs highlight individual MVP winning performances. The dual National League MVP winners of 1979 and special cards commemorating the accomplishments of Drysdale (scoreless consecutive innings pitched streak), Aaron (home run record), and Rose (National League most hits lifetime record) round out the set. The 1975 Fred Lynn card is an original construction from the multi-player "Rookie Outfielders" card of Lynn of 1975. The Maury Wills card number 2, similarly, was created after the fact as Maury was not originally included in the 1962 Topps set. Topps had solved the same problem in essentially the same way in their 1975 set on card number 200.

Card	Low	High
COMPLETE SET (44)	.75	2.00
1 Mickey Mantle: 62AL	.30	.75
2 Maury Wills: 62NL	.02	.10
3 Elston Howard: 63AL	.01	.05
4 Sandy Koufax: 63NL	.08	.25
5 Brooks Robinson: 64AL	.02	.10
6 Ken Boyer: 64NL	.01	.05
7 Zoilo Versalles: 65AL	.01	.05
8 Willie Mays: 65NL	.20	.50
9 Frank Robinson: 66AL	.02	.10
10 Bob Clemente: 66NL	.20	.50
11 Carl Yastrzemski: 67AL	.02	.10
12 Orlando Cepeda: 67NL	.01	.05
13 Denny McLain: 68AL	.01	.05
14 Bob Gibson: 68NL	.02	.10
15 Harmon Killebrew: 69AL	.02	.10
16 Willie McCovey: 69NL	.02	.10
17 Boog Powell: 70AL	.01	.05
18 Johnny Bench: 70NL	.02	.10
19 Vida Blue: 71AL	.01	.05
20 Joe Torre: 71NL	.01	.05
21 Rich Allen: 72AL	.01	.05
22 Johnny Bench: 72NL	.02	.10
23 Reggie Jackson: 73AL	.05	.15
24 Pete Rose: 73NL	.08	.25
25 Jeff Burroughs: 74AL	.01	.05
26 Steve Garvey: 74NL	.01	.05
27 Fred Lynn: 75AL	.02	.10
28 Joe Morgan: 75NL	.02	.10
29 Thurman Munson: 76AL	.01	.05
30 Joe Morgan: 76NL	.02	.10
31 Rod Carew: 77AL	.02	.10
32 George Foster: 77NL	.01	.05
33 Jim Rice: 78AL	.02	.10
34 Dave Parker: 78NL	.02	.10
35 Don Baylor: 79AL	.01	.05
36 Keith Hernandez: 79NL	.01	.05
37 Willie Stargell: 79NL	.02	.10
38 George Brett: 80AL	.15	.40
39 Mike Schmidt: 80NL	.05	.15
40 Rollie Fingers: 81AL	.02	.10
41 Mike Schmidt: 81NL	.05	.15
42 Don Drysdale '68 HL		
(Scoreless innings)	.02	.10
43 Hank Aaron '74 HL/(Home run record)	.20	.50
44 Pete Rose '81 HL/(NL most hits)	.05	.15

1987 K-Mart

Topps produced this 33-card boxed standard-size set for K-Mart. The set celebrates K-Mart's 25th anniversary and is subtitled, "Stars of the Decades." Card fronts feature a color photo of the player oriented diagonally. Card backs provide statistics for the player's best decade. The set numbering is arranged alphabetically within decade groups: 1960s (1-11), 1970s (12-22), and 1980s (23-33).

Card	Low	High
COMPLETE SET (33)	1.50	4.00
1 Hank Aaron	.30	.75
2 Roberto Clemente	.40	1.00
3 Bob Gibson	.05	.15
4 Harmon Killebrew	.05	.15
5 Mickey Mantle	.75	2.00
6 Juan Marichal	.05	.15
7 Roger Maris	.08	.25
8 Willie Mays	.30	.75
9 Brooks Robinson	.05	.15
10 Frank Robinson	.05	.15
11 Carl Yastrzemski	.05	.15
12 Johnny Bench	.08	.25
13 Lou Brock	.08	.25
14 Rod Carew	.08	.25
15 Steve Carlton	.08	.25
16 Reggie Jackson	.15	.40
17 Jim Palmer	.08	.25
18 Jim Rice	.02	.10
19 Pete Rose	.20	.50
20 Nolan Ryan	.75	2.00
21 Tom Seaver	.15	.40
22 Willie Stargell	.08	.25
23 Wade Boggs	.15	.40
24 George Brett	.30	.75
25 Gary Carter	.10	.30
26 Dwight Gooden	.05	.15
27 Rickey Henderson	.15	.40
28 Don Mattingly	.30	.75
29 Dale Murphy	.08	.25
30 Eddie Murray	.10	.30
31 Mike Schmidt	.20	.50
32 Darryl Strawberry	.02	.10
33 Fernando Valenzuela	.02	.10

1988 K-Mart

Topps produced this 33-card standard-sized boxed set exclusively for K-Mart. The set is subtitled, "Memorable Moments." Card fronts feature a color photo of the player with the K-Mart logo in lower right corner. Card backs provide details for that player's "memorable moment." The set is packaged in a bright yellow and green box with a checklist on the back panel of the box. The cards in the set were numbered by K-Mart essentially in alphabetical order.

Card	Low	High
COMPLETE SET (33)	1.50	4.00
1 George Bell	.01	.05
2 Wade Boggs	.15	.40
3 George Brett	.30	.75
4 Jose Canseco	.20	.50
5 Jack Clark	.02	.10
6 Will Clark	.20	.50
7 Roger Clemens	.30	.75
8 Vince Coleman	.01	.05
9 Andre Dawson	.07	.20
10 Dwight Gooden	.02	.10
11 Pedro Guerrero	.01	.05
12 Tony Gwynn	.40	1.00
13 Rickey Henderson	.25	.60
14 Keith Hernandez	.02	.10
15 Don Mattingly	.40	1.00
16 Mark McGwire	.40	1.00
17 Paul Molitor	.20	.50
18 Dale Murphy	.07	.20
19 Tim Raines	.02	.10
20 Dave Righetti	.01	.05
21 Cal Ripken	.75	2.00
22 Pete Rose	.20	.50
23 Nolan Ryan	.75	2.00
24 Benito Santiago	.02	.10
25 Mike Schmidt	.20	.50
26 Mike Scott	.01	.05
27 Kevin Seitzer	.02	.10
28 Ozzie Smith	.40	1.00
29 Darryl Strawberry	.02	.10
30 Rick Sutcliffe	.01	.05
31 Fernando Valenzuela	.02	.10
32 Todd Worrell	.01	.05
33 Robin Yount	.15	.40

1989 K-Mart

The 1989 K-Mart Dream Team set contains 33 standard-size glossy cards. The fronts are blue. The cards were distributed as a boxed set through K-Mart stores. The set features 11 major league rookies of 1988 plus 11 "American League Rookies of the '80s" and 11 "National League Rookies of the '80s". The complete subject list for the set is provided on the back panel of the custom box.

Card	Low	High
COMPLETE SET (33)	1.25	3.00
1 Mark Grace	.30	.75
2 Ron Gant	.02	.10
3 Chris Sabo	.01	.05
4 Walt Weiss	.01	.05
5 Jay Buhner	.07	.20
6 Cecil Espy	.01	.05
7 Dave Gallagher	.01	.05
8 Damon Berryhill	.01	.05
9 Tim Belcher	.01	.05
10 Paul Gibson	.01	.05
11 Gregg Jefferies	.01	.05
12 Don Mattingly	.30	.75
13 Harold Reynolds	.02	.10
14 Wade Boggs	.15	.40
15 Cal Ripken	.60	1.50
16 Kirby Puckett	.20	.50
17 George Bell	.01	.05
18 Jose Canseco	.20	.50
19 Terry Steinbach	.01	.05
20 Roger Clemens	.30	.75
21 Mark Langston	.01	.05
22 Harold Baines	.02	.10
23 Will Clark	.15	.40
24 Ryne Sandberg	.25	.60
25 Tim Wallach	.01	.05
26 Shawon Dunston	.01	.05
27 Tim Raines	.02	.10
28 Darryl Strawberry	.02	.10
29 Tony Gwynn	.30	.75
30 Tony Pena	.02	.10
31 Dwight Gooden	.02	.10
32 Fernando Valenzuela	.02	.10
33 Pedro Guerrero	.01	.05

1990 K-Mart

The 1990 K-Mart Superstars set is a 33-card, standard-size set issued for the K-Mart chain by the Topps Company. This set was issued with a piece of gum in the custom set box.

Card	Low	High
COMPLETE SET (33)	2.00	5.00
1 Will Clark	.15	.40
2 Ryne Sandberg	.30	.75
3 Howard Johnson	.01	.05
4 Ozzie Smith	.30	.75
5 Tony Gwynn	.40	1.00
6 Kevin Mitchell	.01	.05
7 Jerome Walton	.01	.05
8 Craig Biggio	.20	.50
9 Mike Scott	.01	.05
10 Dwight Gooden	.02	.10
11 Sid Fernandez	.01	.05
12 Joe Magrane	.01	.05
13 Jay Howell	.01	.05
14 Mark Davis	.01	.05
15 Pedro Guerrero	.01	.05
16 Glenn Davis	.01	.05
17 Don Mattingly	.40	1.00
18 Julio Franco	.02	.10
19 Wade Boggs	.15	.40
20 Cal Ripken	.75	2.00
21 Jose Canseco	.15	.40
22 Kirby Puckett	.25	.60
23 Rickey Henderson	.25	.60
24 Mickey Tettleton	.02	.10
25 Nolan Ryan	.75	2.00
26 Bret Saberhagen	.02	.10
27 Jeff Ballard	.01	.05
28 Chuck Finley	.02	.10
29 Dennis Eckersley	.15	.40
30 Dan Plesac	.01	.05
31 Fred McGriff	.07	.20
32 Mark McGwire	.40	1.00
33 Tony LaRussa MG and	.02	.10
Roger Craig MG		

1955 Kahn's

The cards in this six-card set measure 3 1/4" X 4". The 1955 Kahn's Wieners set received very limited distribution. The cards were supposedly given away at an amusement park. The set portrays the players in street clothes rather than in uniform and hence are sometimes referred to as "street clothes" Kahn's. All Kahn's sets from 1955 through 1963 are black and white and contain a 1/2" tab. Cards with the tab still intact are worth approximately 50 percent more than cards without the tab. Cards feature a facsimile autograph of the player on the front. Cards are blank-backed. Only Cincinnati Redlegs players are featured.

Card	Low	High
COMPLETE SET (6)	3400.00	6800.00
1 Gus Bell	750.00	1500.00
2 Ted Kluszewski	1250.00	2500.00
3 Roy McMillan	600.00	1200.00
4 Joe Nuxhall	750.00	1500.00
5 Wally Post	600.00	1200.00
6 Johnny Temple	600.00	1200.00

1956 Kahn's

The cards in this 15-card set measure 3 1/4" X 4". The 1956 Kahn's set was the first set to be issued with Kahn's meat products. The cards are blank backed. The set is distinguished by the old style, short sleeve shirts on the players and the existence of backgounds (Kahn's cards of later years utilize a blank background). Cards which have the tab still intact are worth approximately 50 percent more than cards without the tab. Only Cincinnati Redlegs players are featured. The cards are listed and numbered below in alphabetical order by the subject's name. This set contains a very early Frank Robinson card.

Card	Low	High
COMPLETE SET (15)	1000.00	1600.00
1 Ed Bailey	50.00	80.00
2 Gus Bell	55.00	100.00
3 Joe Black	60.00	120.00
4 Smoky Burgess	55.00	100.00
5 Art Fowler	50.00	80.00
6 Herschel Freeman	50.00	80.00
7 Ray Jablonski	50.00	80.00
8 John Klippstein	50.00	80.00
9 Ted Kluszewski	120.00	200.00
10 Brooks Lawrence	55.00	100.00
11 Roy McMillan	55.00	100.00
12 Joe Nuxhall	55.00	100.00
13 Wally Post	55.00	100.00
14 Frank Robinson	300.00	500.00
15 Johnny Temple	55.00	100.00

1957 Kahn's

The cards in this 29-card set measure 3 1/4" by 4". The 1957 Kahn's Wieners set contains black and white, blank backed, unnumbered cards. The set features only the Cincinnati Redlegs and Pittsburgh Pirates. The cards feature a light background. Each card features a facsimile autograph of the player on the front. The Groat card exists with a "Richard Groat" autograph and also exists with the printed name "Dick Groat" on the card. The set price inlcudes both Groats. The catalog designation is F155-3. The cards are listed and numbered below in alphabetical order by the subject's name. A Bill Mazeroski card was printed during this, his Rookie Card season.

Card	Low	High
COMPLETE SET (29)	1800.00	3000.00
1 Tom Acker	35.00	60.00
2 Ed Bailey	35.00	60.00
3 Gus Bell	50.00	80.00
4 Smoky Burgess	50.00	80.00
5 Roberto Clemente	600.00	1000.00
6 George Crowe	35.00	60.00
7 Roy Face	60.00	100.00
8 Herschel Freeman	35.00	60.00
9 Bob Friend	50.00	80.00
10 Dick Groat	60.00	100.00
11 Richard Groat	100.00	200.00
12 Don Gross	35.00	60.00
13 Warren Hacker	35.00	60.00
14 Don Hoak	50.00	80.00
15 Hal Jeffcoat	35.00	60.00
16 Ron Kline	35.00	60.00
17 John Klippstein	35.00	60.00
18 Ted Kluszewski	100.00	200.00
19 Brooks Lawrence	50.00	80.00
20 Dale Long	35.00	60.00
21 Bill Mazeroski	150.00	250.00
22 Roy McMillan	50.00	80.00
23 Joe Nuxhall	35.00	60.00
24 Wally Post	50.00	80.00
25 Frank Robinson	250.00	400.00
26 John Temple	50.00	80.00
27 Frank Thomas	35.00	60.00
28 Bob Thurman	35.00	60.00
29 Lee Walls	35.00	60.00

1958 Kahn's

The cards in this 29-card set measure approximately 3 1/4" X 4". The 1958 Kahn's Wieners set of unnumbered, black and white cards features Cincinnati Redlegs, Philadelphia Phillies and Pittsburgh Pirates. The backs present a story for each player entitled "My Greatest Thrill in Baseball". A method of distinguishing 1958 Kahn's from 1959 Kahn's is that the word Wieners is found on the front of the 1958 but not on the front of the 1959 cards. Cards of Wally Post, Charlie Rabe and Frank Thomas are somewhat more difficult to find and are designated SP in the our checklist. The cards are listed and numbered below in alphabetical order by the subject's name.

Card	Low	High
COMPLETE SET (29)	2000.00	3200.00
COMMON PLAYER (1-29)	30.00	50.00
COMMON SP	150.00	300.00
1 Ed Bailey	30.00	50.00
2 Gene Baker	30.00	50.00
3 Gus Bell	35.00	60.00
4 Smoky Burgess	35.00	60.00
5 Roberto Clemente	300.00	600.00
6 George Crowe	35.00	60.00
7 Roy Face	50.00	80.00
8 Hank Foiles	30.00	50.00
9 Dee Fondy	30.00	50.00
10 Bob Friend	35.00	60.00
11 Dick Groat	50.00	80.00
12 Harvey Haddix	35.00	60.00
13 Don Hoak	30.00	50.00
14 Hal Jeffcoat	30.00	50.00
15 Ron Kline	30.00	50.00
16 Ted Kluszewski	75.00	125.00
17 Vernon Law	35.00	60.00
18 Brooks Lawrence	35.00	60.00
19 Bill Mazeroski	75.00	125.00
20 Roy McMillan	35.00	60.00
21 Joe Nuxhall	35.00	60.00
22 Wally Post SP	175.00	350.00
23 John Powers	30.00	50.00
24 Bob Purkey	30.00	50.00
25 Charlie Rabe SP	150.00	300.00
26 Frank Robinson	150.00	250.00
27 Bob Skinner	30.00	50.00
28 Johnny Temple	35.00	60.00
29 Frank Thomas SP	175.00	350.00

1959 Kahn's

The cards in this 38-card set measure approximately 3 1/4" X 4". The 1959 Kahn's set features members of the Cincinnati Reds, Cleveland Indians and Pittsburgh Pirates. Backs feature stories entitled "The Toughest Play I have to Make," or "The Toughest Batter I Have To Face." The Brodowski card is very scarce while Haddix, Held and McLish are considered quite difficult to obtain; these scarcities are designated SP in the checklist below. The cards are listed and numbered below in alphabetical order by the subject's name.

Card	Low	High
COMPLETE SET (38)	2500.00	4500.00
COMMON PLAYER (1-38)	30.00	50.00
COMMON SP	200.00	400.00
1 Ed Bailey	30.00	50.00
2 Gary Bell	30.00	50.00
3 Gus Bell	35.00	60.00
4 Dick Brodowski SP	300.00	600.00
5 Smoky Burgess	35.00	60.00
6 Roberto Clemente	300.00	600.00
7 Rocky Colavito	75.00	125.00
8 Roy Face	50.00	80.00
9 Bob Friend	35.00	60.00
10 Joe Gordon MG	35.00	60.00
11 Jim Grant	35.00	60.00
12 Dick Groat	50.00	80.00
13 Harvey Haddix SP/(Blank back)	200.00	400.00
14 Woodie Held SP	200.00	400.00
15 Don Hoak	30.00	50.00
16 Ron Kline	30.00	50.00
17 Ted Kluszewski	75.00	125.00
18 Vernon Law	35.00	60.00
19 Jerry Lynch	30.00	50.00
20 Billy Martin	75.00	125.00
21 Bill Mazeroski	75.00	125.00
22 Cal McLish SP	200.00	400.00
23 Roy McMillan	30.00	50.00
24 Minnie Minoso	60.00	100.00
25 Russ Nixon	30.00	50.00
26 Joe Nuxhall	35.00	60.00
27 Jim Perry	50.00	80.00
28 Vada Pinson	60.00	100.00

29 Vic Power 30.00 50.00
30 Bob Purkey 30.00 50.00
31 Frank Robinson 120.00 200.00
32 Herb Score 50.00 80.00
33 Bob Skinner 30.00 50.00
34 George Strickland 30.00 50.00
35 Dick Stuart 35.00 60.00
36 Johnny Temple 30.00 50.00
37 Frank Thomas 35.00 60.00
38 George Witt 30.00 50.00

1960 Kahn's

The cards in this 42-card set measure 3 1/4" X 4". The 1960 Kahn's set features players of the Chicago Cubs, Chicago White Sox, Cincinnati Redlegs, Cleveland Indians, Pittsburgh Pirates and St. Louis Cardinals. The backs give vital player information and records through the 1959 season. Kline appears with either St. Louis or Pittsburgh. The set price includes both Kline's. The Harvey Kuenn card in this set appears with a blank back and is scarce. The cards are listed and numbered below in alphabetical order by the subject's name.

COMPLETE SET (43) 1000.00 2000.00
1 Ed Bailey 10.00 25.00
2 Gary Bell 10.00 25.00
3 Gus Bell 12.50 30.00
4 Smoky Burgess 12.50 30.00
5 Gino Cimoli 10.00 25.00
6 Roberto Clemente 250.00 500.00
7 Roy Face 12.50 30.00
8 Tito Francona 10.00 25.00
9 Bob Friend 12.50 30.00
10 Jim Grant 12.50 30.00
11 Dick Groat 15.00 40.00
12 Harvey Haddix 12.50 30.00
13 Woodie Held 10.00 25.00
14 Bill Henry 10.00 25.00
15 Don Hoak 10.00 25.00
16 Jay Hook 10.00 25.00
17 Eddie Kasko 10.00 25.00
18A Ron Kline/(Pittsburgh) 20.00 50.00
18B Ron Kline/(St. Louis) 20.00 50.00
19 Ted Kluszewski 30.00 60.00
20 Harvey Kuenn SP/(Blank back) 200.00 400.00
21 Vernon Law 12.50 30.00
22 Brooks Lawrence 12.50 30.00
23 Jerry Lynch 10.00 25.00
24 Billy Martin 30.00 60.00
25 Bill Mazeroski 30.00 60.00
26 Cal McLish 10.00 25.00
27 Roy McMillan 10.00 25.00
28 Don Newcombe 15.00 40.00
29 Russ Nixon 10.00 25.00
30 Joe Nuxhall 12.50 30.00
31 Jim O'Toole 10.00 25.00
32 Jim Perry 12.50 30.00
33 Vada Pinson 20.00 50.00
34 Vic Power 10.00 25.00
35 Bob Purkey 10.00 25.00
36 Frank Robinson 75.00 150.00
37 Herb Score 12.50 30.00
38 Bob Skinner 10.00 25.00
39 Dick Stuart 12.50 30.00
40 Johnny Temple 12.50 30.00
41 Frank Thomas 12.50 30.00
42 Lee Walls 10.00 25.00

1961 Kahn's

The cards in this 43-card set measure approximately 3 1/4" X 4". The 1961 Kahn's Wieners set of black and white, unnumbered cards features members of the Cincinnati Reds, Cleveland Indians and Pittsburgh Pirates. This year was the first year Kahn's made complete sets available to the public; hence they are more available, especially in the better condition grades than the Kahn's of the previous years. The backs give vital player information and year by year career statistics through 1960. The catalog designation is F155-7. The cards are listed and numbered below in alphabetical order by the subject's name.

COMPLETE SET (43) 500.00 1000.00
1 John Antonelli 5.00 12.00
2 Ed Bailey 5.00 12.00
3 Gary Bell 5.00 12.00
4 Gus Bell 6.00 15.00
5 Jim Brosnan 6.00 15.00
6 Smoky Burgess 6.00 15.00
7 Gino Cimoli 5.00 12.00
8 Roberto Clemente 200.00 400.00
9 Gordie Coleman 5.00 12.00
10 Jimmy Dykes MG 6.00 15.00
11 Roy Face 6.00 15.00
12 Tito Francona 5.00 12.00
13 Gene Freese 5.00 12.00
14 Bob Friend 6.00 15.00
15 Jim Grant 6.00 15.00
16 Dick Groat 6.00 15.00
17 Harvey Haddix 6.00 15.00
18 Woodie Held 5.00 12.00
19 Don Hoak 5.00 12.00
20 Jay Hook 5.00 12.00
21 Joey Jay 5.00 12.00
22 Eddie Kasko 5.00 12.00
23 Willie Kirkland 5.00 12.00
24 Vernon Law 6.00 15.00
25 Jerry Lynch 5.00 12.00
26 Jim Maloney 8.00 20.00
27 Bill Mazeroski 15.00 40.00
28 Wilmer Mizell 6.00 15.00
29 Rocky Nelson 5.00 12.00
30 Jim O'Toole 5.00 12.00
31 Jim Perry 6.00 15.00
32 Bubba Phillips 5.00 12.00
33 Vada Pinson 12.50 30.00
34 Wally Post 5.00 12.00
35 Vic Power 5.00 12.00
36 Bob Purkey 5.00 12.00
37 Frank Robinson 50.00 100.00
38 John Romano 5.00 12.00
39 Dick Schofield 5.00 12.00
40 Bob Skinner 5.00 12.00
41 Hal Smith 5.00 12.00
42 Dick Stuart 6.00 15.00
43 Johnny Temple 5.00 12.00

1962 Kahn's

The cards in this 38-card set measure approximately 3 1/4" X 4". The 1962 Kahn's Wieners set of black and white, unnumbered cards features Cincinnati, Cleveland, Minnesota and Pittsburgh players. Card numbers 1 Bell, 33 Power and 34 Purkey exist in two different forms; these variations are listed in the checklist below. The backs of the cards contain career information. The catalog designation is F155-8. The set price below includes the set with all variation cards. The cards are listed and numbered below in alphabetical order by the subject's name.

COMPLETE SET (41) 1000.00 2000.00
1A Gary Bell/(With fat man) 100.00 200.00
1B Gary Bell/(No fat man) 40.00 80.00
2 Jim Brosnan 10.00 25.00
3 Smoky Burgess 10.00 25.00
4 Chico Cardenas 10.00 25.00
5 Roberto Clemente 300.00 600.00
6 Ty Cline 8.00 20.00
7 Gordon Coleman 10.00 25.00
8 Dick Donovan 8.00 20.00
9 John Edwards 8.00 20.00
10 Tito Francona 8.00 20.00
11 Gene Freese 8.00 20.00
12 Bob Friend 10.00 25.00
13 Joe Gibbon 60.00 120.00
14 Jim Grant 12.50 25.00
15 Dick Groat 12.50 30.00
16 Harvey Haddix 10.00 25.00
17 Woodie Held 8.00 20.00
18 Bill Henry 8.00 20.00
19 Don Hoak 8.00 20.00
20 Ken Hunt 8.00 20.00
21 Joey Jay 8.00 20.00
22 Eddie Kasko 8.00 20.00
23 Willie Kirkland 8.00 20.00
24 Barry Latman 8.00 20.00
25 Jerry Lynch 8.00 20.00
26 Jim Maloney 12.50 30.00
27 Bill Mazeroski 15.00 40.00
28 Jim O'Toole 8.00 20.00
29 Jim Perry 10.00 25.00
30 Bubba Phillips 8.00 20.00
31 Vada Pinson 12.50 30.00
32 Wally Post 8.00 20.00
33A Vic Power (Indians) 40.00 80.00
33B Vic Power (Twins) 100.00 200.00
34A Bob Purkey/(With autograph) 40.00 80.00
34B Bob Purkey/(No autograph) 100.00 200.00
35 Frank Robinson 100.00 200.00
36 John Romano 8.00 20.00
37 Dick Stuart 10.00 25.00
38 Bill Virdon 12.50 30.00

1963 Kahn's

The cards in this 30-card set measure approximately 3 1/4" X 4". The 1963 Kahn's Wieners set of black and white, unnumbered cards features players from Cincinnati, Cleveland, St. Louis, Pittsburgh and the New York Yankees. The cards feature a white border around the picture of the players. The backs contain career information. The catalog designation for this set is F155-10. The cards are listed and numbered below in alphabetical order by the subject's name.

COMPLETE SET (30) 1000.00 2000.00
1 Bob Bailey 12.50 30.00
2 Don Blasingame 12.50 30.00
3 Clete Boyer 20.00 50.00
4 Smoky Burgess 15.00 40.00
5 Chico Cardenas 15.00 40.00
6 Roberto Clemente 400.00 800.00
7 Donn Clendenon 15.00 40.00
8 Gordon Coleman 15.00 40.00
9 John Edwards 12.50 30.00
10 Gene Freese 12.50 30.00
11 Bob Friend 15.00 40.00
12 Joe Gibbon 12.50 30.00
13 Dick Groat 20.00 50.00
14 Harvey Haddix 15.00 40.00
15 Elston Howard 40.00 80.00
16 Joey Jay 12.50 30.00
17 Eddie Kasko 12.50 30.00
18 Tony Kubek 50.00 100.00
19 Jerry Lynch 12.50 30.00
20 Jim Maloney 20.00 50.00
21 Bill Mazeroski 50.00 100.00
22 Joe Nuxhall 15.00 40.00
23 Jim O'Toole 12.50 30.00
24 Vada Pinson 30.00 60.00
25 Bob Purkey 12.50 30.00
26 Bobby Richardson 50.00 100.00
27 Frank Robinson 150.00 300.00
28 Bill Stafford 12.50 30.00
29 Ralph Terry 15.00 40.00
30 Bill Virdon 15.00 40.00

1964 Kahn's

The cards in this 31-card set measure 3" X 3 1/2". The 1964 Kahn's set marks the beginning of the full color cards and the elimination of the tabs which existed on previous Kahn's cards. The set of unnumbered cards contains player information through the 1963 season on the backs. The set features Cincinnati, Cleveland and Pittsburgh players. The cards are listed and numbered below in alphabetical order by the subject's name. An early card of Pete Rose highlights this set.

COMPLETE SET (31) 600.00 1200.00
1 Max Alvis 5.00 12.00
2 Bob Bailey 5.00 12.00
3 Chico Cardenas 6.00 15.00
4 Roberto Clemente 200.00 400.00
5 Donn Clendenon 6.00 15.00
6 Vic Davalillo 5.00 12.00
7 Dick Donovan 5.00 12.00
8 John Edwards 5.00 12.00
9 Bob Friend 6.00 15.00
10 Jim Grant 6.00 15.00
11 Tommy Harper 6.00 15.00
12 Woodie Held 6.00 15.00
13 Joey Jay 5.00 12.00
14 Jack Kralick 5.00 12.00
15 Jerry Lynch 5.00 12.00
16 Jim Maloney 6.00 15.00
17 Bill Mazeroski 12.50 30.00
18 Alvin McBean 5.00 12.00
19 Joe Nuxhall 6.00 15.00
20 Jim Pagliaroni . 5.00 12.00
21 Vada Pinson 10.00 25.00
22 Bob Purkey 5.00 12.00
23 Pedro Ramos 5.00 12.00
24 Frank Robinson 60.00 120.00
25 John Romano 5.00 12.00
26 Pete Rose 250.00 500.00
27 John Tsitouris 5.00 12.00
28 Bob Veale 6.00 15.00
29 Bill Virdon 6.00 15.00
30 Leon Wagner 5.00 12.00
31 Fred Whitfield 5.00 12.00

1965 Kahn's

The cards in this 45-card set measure 3" X 3 1/2". The 1965 Kahn's set contains full-color, unnumbered cards. The set features Cincinnati, Cleveland, Pittsburgh and Milwaukee players. Backs contain statistical information through the 1964 season. The cards are listed and numbered below in alphabetical order by the subject's name.

COMPLETE SET (45) 1250.00 2500.00
1 Henry Aaron 200.00 400.00
2 Max Alvis 12.50 30.00
3 Joe Azcue 10.00 25.00
4 Bob Bailey 10.00 25.00
5 Frank Bolling 10.00 25.00
6 Chico Cardenas 12.50 30.00
7 Rico Carty 15.00 40.00
8 Donn Clendenon 12.50 30.00
9 Tony Cloninger 12.50 30.00
10 Gordon Coleman 10.00 25.00
11 Vic Davalillo 10.00 25.00
12 John Edwards 10.00 25.00
13 Sammy Ellis 10.00 25.00
14 Bob Friend 12.50 30.00
15 Tommy Harper 10.00 25.00
16 Chuck Hinton 12.50 30.00
17 Dick Howser 12.50 30.00
18 Joey Jay 10.00 25.00
19 Deron Johnson 12.50 30.00
20 Jack Kralick 10.00 25.00
21 Denver LeMaster 10.00 25.00
22 Jerry Lynch 10.00 25.00
23 Jim Maloney 15.00 40.00
24 Lee Maye 10.00 25.00
25 Bill Mazeroski 30.00 60.00
26 Alvin McBean 10.00 25.00
27 Bill McCool 10.00 25.00
28 Sam McDowell 15.00 40.00
29 Don McMahon 10.00 25.00
30 Denis Menke 10.00 25.00
31 Joe Nuxhall 12.50 30.00
32 Gene Oliver 10.00 25.00
33 Jim O'Toole 10.00 25.00
34 Jim Pagliaroni 10.00 25.00
35 Vada Pinson 20.00 50.00
36 Frank Robinson 125.00 250.00
37 Pete Rose 250.00 500.00
38 Willie Stargell 125.00 250.00
39 Ralph Terry 12.50 30.00
40 Luis Tiant 20.00 50.00
41 Joe Torre 30.00 60.00
42 John Tsitouris 10.00 25.00
43 Bob Veale 12.50 30.00
44 Bill Virdon 12.50 30.00
45 Leon Wagner 10.00 25.00

1966 Kahn's

The cards in this 32-card set measure 2 13/16" X 4". 1966 Kahn's full-color, unnumbered set features players from Atlanta, Cincinnati, Cleveland and Pittsburgh. The set is identified by yellow and white vertical stripes and the name Kahn's written in red across a red rose at the top. The cards contain a 1 5/16" ad in the form of a tab. Cards with the ad (tab) are worth twice as much as cards without the ad. (double the prices below) The cards are listed and numbered below in alphabetical order by the subject's name.

COMPLETE SET (32) 400.00 800.00
1 Henry Aaron/(Portrait& no wind- 75.00 150.00
breaker under je
2 Felipe Alou: Braves/(Full pose& batting 10.00 25.00
screen i
3 Max Alvis: Indians
(Kneeling& full pose& 5.00 12.00
with ba
4 Bob Bailey 5.00 12.00
5 Wade Blasingame 5.00 12.00
6 Frank Bolling 5.00 12.00
7 Chico Cardenas: Reds 6.00 15.00
Fielding
feet at base
8 Roberto Clemente 100.00 200.00
9 Tony Cloninger: 6.00 15.00
Braves (Pitching&
foulpole in
b
10 Vic Davalillo 5.00 12.00
11 John Edwards: Reds 5.00 12.00
Catching
12 Sam Ellis: Reds 5.00 12.00
White hat
13 Pedro Gonzalez 5.00 12.00
14 Tommy Harper: Reds 6.00 15.00
Arm cocked
15 Deron Johnson: Reds/(Batting with batting 6.00
15.00
cage i
16 Mack Jones 5.00 12.00
17 Denver Lemaster 5.00 12.00
18 Jim Maloney: Reds 6.00 15.00
Pitching white hat
19 Bill Mazeroski: 12.50 30.00
Pirates
Throwing
20 Bill McCool: Reds 5.00 12.00
White hat
21 Sam McDowell: Indians 6.00 15.00
Kneeling
22 Denis Menke: Braves/(White windbreaker 5.00
12.00
under jer
23 Joe Nuxhall 6.00 15.00
24 Jim Pagliaroni: 5.00 12.00
Pirates
Catching
25 Milt Pappas 6.00 15.00
26 Vada Pinson: Reds/(Fielding 10.00 25.00
ball on ground
27 Pete Rose: Reds 75.00 150.00
With glove
28 Sonny Siebert: 6.00 15.00
Indians (Pitching&
signature at f
29 Willie Stargell: 30.00 60.00
Pirates (Batting&
clouds in sky
30 Joe Torre: Braves 12.50 30.00
Catching with
hand on mask
31 Bob Veale: Pirates 6.00 15.00
Hands at knee
with glasses
32 Fred Whitfield 5.00 12.00

1967 Kahn's

The cards in this 41-player set measure 2 13/16" X 4". The 1967 Kahn's set of full-color, unnumbered cards is almost identical in style to the 1966 issue. Different meat products had different background colors (yellow and white stripes, red and white stripes, etc.). The set features players from Atlanta, Cincinnati, Cleveland, New York Mets and Pittsburgh. Cards with the ads (see 1966 set) are worth twice as much as cards without the ad, i.e., double the prices below. The complete set price below includes all variations. The cards are listed and numbered below in alphabetical order by the subject's name. Examples have been seen in which the top borders have a very small indentation.

COMPLETE SET (51) 800.00 1600.00
1A Henry Aaron: Braves/(Swinging pose& 125.00
250.00
batting glov
1B Henry Aaron: Braves 150.00 300.00
Swinging pose,
batting glove, ball,
and hat on ground;
Cut Along Dotted Lines
printed on lower tab
2 Gene Alley: Pirates 10.00 25.00
Portrait
3 Felipe Alou: Braves 15.00 40.00
Full pose, bat
on shoulder
4A Matty Alou: Pirates 10.00 25.00
(Portrait with bat/Matio
4B Matty Alou: Pirates
(Portrait with bat/Matio 12.50 30.00
5 Max Alvis: Indians 8.00 20.00
Fielding, hands
on knees
6A Ken Boyer 12.50 30.00
Batting righthanded;
autograph at waist
6B Ken Boyer 15.00 40.00
Batting righthanded;
autograph at shoulders;
Cut Along Dotted Lines
printed on lower tab
7 Chico Cardenas: Reds 10.00 25.00
Fielding
hand on knee
8 Rico Carty 10.00 25.00
9 Tony Cloninger: Braves 10.00 25.00
Pitching, no foul-
pole in background
10 Tommy Davis 10.00 25.00
11 John Edwards: Reds 8.00 20.00
Kneeling with bat
12A Sam Ellis: Reds 8.00 20.00
All red hat
12B Sam Ellis: Reds 10.00 25.00
All red hat;
Cut Along Dotted Lines
printed on lower tab
13 Jack Fisher 8.00 20.00
14 Steve Hargan: Indians 8.00 20.00
Pitching, no clouds
blue sky
15 Tommy Harper: Reds 10.00 25.00
Fielding, glove on
ground
16A Tommy Helms 10.00 25.00
Batting righthanded;
top of bat visible
16B Tommy Helms 12.50 30.00
Batting righthanded;
bat chopped above hat;
Cut Along Dotted Lines
printed on lower tab
17 Deron Johnson: Reds 10.00 25.00
Batting, blue sky
18 Ken Johnson 8.00 20.00
19 Cleon Jones 10.00 25.00
20A Ed Kranepool 10.00 25.00
Ready for throw;
yellow stripes
20B Ed Kranepool 10.00 25.00
Ready for throw;
red stripes
21A Jim Maloney: Reds 10.00 25.00
Pitching, red hat,
follow thru delivery;
yellow stripes
21B Jim Maloney: Reds 12.50 30.00
Pitching, red hat,
follow thru delivery;
red stripes
22 Lee May: Reds 10.00 25.00
Hands on knee
23A Bill Mazeroski: 20.00 50.00
Pirates Portrait;
autograph below waist
23B Bill Mazeroski: 30.00 60.00
Pirates Portrait;
autograph above waist;
Cut Along Dotted Lines
printed on lower tab
24 Bill McCool: Reds Red 8.00 20.00
hat, left hand out
25 Sam McDowell: Indians 12.50 30.00
Pitching, left hand
under glove
26 Denis Menke: Braves 8.00 20.00
Blue sleeves
27 Jim Pagliaroni: 8.00 20.00
Pirates Catching
no chest protector
28 Don Pavletich 8.00 20.00
29 Tony Perez: Reds 50.00 100.00
Throwing
30 Vada Pinson: Reds 15.00 40.00
Ready to throw
31 Dennis Ribant 8.00 20.00
32 Pete Rose: Reds 125.00 250.00
Batting
33 Art Shamsky: Reds 8.00 20.00
34 Bob Shaw 8.00 20.00
35 Sonny Siebert: 8.00 20.00
Indians Pitching
signature at knees
36 Willie Stargell: 50.00 100.00
Pirates Batting
no clouds
37A Joe Torre: Braves 15.00 40.00
Catching, mask
on ground
37B Joe Torre: Braves 30.00 60.00
Catching, mask
on ground;
Cut Along Dotted Lines
printed on lower tab
38 Bob Veale: Pirates 8.00 20.00
Portrait, hands
not shown
39 Leon Wagner: Indians 8.00 20.00
Fielding
40A Fred Whitfield 8.00 20.00
Batting lefthanded
40B Fred Whitfield 8.00 20.00
Batting lefthanded;
Cut Along Dotted Lines
printed on lower tab
41 Woody Woodward 8.00 20.00

1968 Kahn's

The cards in this 50-piece set contain two different sizes. The smaller of the two sizes, which contains 12 cards, is 2 13/16" X 3 1/4" with the ad tab and 2 13/16" X 1 7/8" without the ad tab. The larger size, which contains 38 cards, measures 2 13/16" X 3 7/8" with the ad tab and 2 13/16" X 2 11/16" without the ad tab. The 1968 Kahn's set of full-color, blank backed, unnumbered cards features players from Atlanta, Chicago Cubs, Chicago White Sox, Cincinnati, Cleveland, Detroit, New York Mets and Pittsburgh. In the set of 12, listed with the letter A in the checklist, Maloney exists with either yellow or yellow and green stripes at the top of the card. The large set of 38, listed with a letter B in the checklist, contains five cards which exist in two variations. The variations in this large set have either yellow or red stripes at the top of the cards, with Maloney being an exception. Maloney has either a yellow stripe or a Blue Mountain ad at the top. Cards with the ad tabs (see other Kahn's sets) are worth twice as much as cards without the ad, i.e., double the prices below. The cards are listed and numbered below in alphabetical order (within each subset) by the subject's name. The set features a card of Johnny Bench in his Rookie Card year.

COMPLETE SET (50) 1100.00 2200.00
A1 Hank Aaron 75.00 150.00
A2 Gene Alley 15.00 40.00
A3 Max Alvis 12.50 30.00
A4 Clete Boyer 20.00 50.00
A5 Chico Cardenas 15.00 40.00
A6 Bill Freehan 20.00 50.00
A7 Jim Maloney 2 20.00 50.00
A8 Lee May 20.00 50.00
A9 Bill Mazeroski 50.00 100.00
A10 Vada Pinson 30.00 60.00
A11 Joe Torre 40.00 80.00
A12 Bob Veale 15.00 40.00
B1 Hank Aaron: Braves 75.00 150.00
Full pose
batting
bat cocked
B2 Tommy Agee 15.00 40.00
B3 Gene Alley: Pirates 12.50 30.00
Fielding, full pose
B4 Felipe Alou 30.00 60.00
Full pose
batting, swinging
player in background
B5 Matty Alou: Pirates 15.00 40.00
Portrait with bat
Matio Alou 2
B6 Max Alvis 12.50 30.00
Fielding
glove on ground
B7 Gerry Arrigo: Reds 12.50 30.00
Pitching
followthru delivery
B8 John Bench 200.00 400.00
B9 Clete Boyer 20.00 50.00
B10 Larry Brown 12.50 30.00
B11 Leo Cardenas: Reds 15.00 40.00
Leaping in the air
B12 Bill Freehan 20.00 50.00
B13 Steve Hargan: 12.50 30.00
Indians
Pitching
clouds in background
B14 Joel Horlen 12.50 30.00
White Sox
Portrait
B15 Tony Horton: Indians 20.00 50.00
Portrait
signed Anthony
B16 Willie Horton 20.00 50.00
B17 Fergie Jenkins 60.00 120.00
B18 Deron Johnson: 15.00 40.00
Braves
B19 Mack Jones: Reds 12.50 30.00
B20 Bob Lee 12.50 30.00
B21 Jim Maloney: Reds 20.00 50.00
Red hat
pitching hands up 2
B22 Lee May: Reds 15.00 40.00
Batting
B23 Bill Mazeroski: 50.00 100.00
Pirates
Fielding
hands in front
of body
B24 Dick McAuliffe 12.50 30.00
B25 Bill McCool 12.50 30.00
Red hat
left hand down
B26 Sam McDowell: 20.00 50.00
Indians
Pitching
left hand over glove 2
B27 Tony Perez 50.00 100.00
Fielding ball in glove 2
B28 Gary Peters 12.50 30.00
White Sox
Portrait
B29 Vada Pinson: Reds 20.00 50.00
Batting
B30 Chico Ruiz 12.50 30.00
B31 Ron Santo: Cubs 50.00 100.00
Batting
follow thru 2
B32 Art Shamsky: Mets 12.50 30.00
B33 Luis Tiant: Indians 30.00 60.00
Hands over head
B34 Joe Torre: Braves 40.00 80.00
Batting
B35 Bob Veale: Pirates 12.50 30.00
Hands chest high
B36 Leon Wagner: Indians 12.50 30.00
Batting
B37 Billy Williams: Cubs 60.00 120.00
Bat behind back
B38 Earl Wilson 12.50 30.00

1969 Kahn's

The cards in this 25-piece set contain two different sizes. The three small cards (see 1968 description) measure 2 13/16" X 3 1/4" and the 22 large cards (see 1968 description) measure 2 13/16" X 3 15/16". The 1969 Kahn's Wieners set of full-color, unnumbered cards features players from Atlanta, Chicago Cubs, Chicago White Sox, Cincinnati, Cleveland, Pittsburgh and St. Louis. The small cards have the letter A in the checklist while the large cards have the letter B in the checklist. Four of the larger cards exist in two variations (red or yellow color stripes at the top of the card). These variations are identified in the checklist below. Cards with the ad tabs (see other Kahn's sets) are worth twice as much as cards without the ad, i.e., double the prices below. The cards are listed and numbered below in alphabetical order (within each subset) by the subject's name.

COMPLETE SET (25) 650.00 1300.00
A1 Hank Aaron 150.00 300.00
Portrait
A2 Jim Maloney 15.00 40.00
Pitching
hands at side
A3 Tony Perez 50.00 100.00
Glove on
B1 Hank Aaron 150.00 300.00
B2 Matty Alou 15.00 40.00
Batting
B3 Max Alvis/69 patch 12.50 30.00
B4 Gerry Arrigo 12.50 30.00
Leg up
B5 Steve Blass 15.00 40.00
B6 Clay Carroll 12.50 30.00
B7 Tony Cloninger: Reds 12.50 30.00
B8 George Culver 12.50 30.00
B9 Joel Horlen 15.00 40.00
Pitching
B10 Tony Horton 20.00 50.00
Batting
B11 Alex Johnson 15.00 40.00
B12 Jim Maloney 15.00 40.00
B13 Lee May 15.00 40.00
Foot on bag (2)
B14 Bill Mazeroski 50.00 100.00
Hands on knees (2)
B15 Sam McDowell 15.00 40.00
Leg up (2)
B16 Tony Perez 60.00 120.00
B17 Gary Peters 12.50 30.00
Pitching
B18 Ron Santo 40.00 80.00
Emblem (2)
B19 Luis Tiant 30.00 60.00
Glove at knee
B20 Joe Torre: Cardinals 40.00 80.00
B21 Bob Veale 15.00 40.00
Hands at knees
no glasses
B22 Billy Williams 60.00 120.00
Bat behind head

1985 Kahn's Commemorative Coins

Issued in conjunction with Hillshire Farms, this three card and coin set features all-time leading hitters Carl Yastrzemski and Pete Rose. The cards measure 3 3/4" by 5 1/2" and give highlights of each player's career. The coin is attached to the card is titled "Cooperstown Collection".

COMPLETE SET (3) 6.00 15.00
1 Johnny Bench 3.00 8.00
2 Pete Rose 4.00 10.00
3 Carl Yastrzemski 2.00 5.00

1989 Kahn's Cooperstown

The 1989 Kahn's Cooperstown set contains 11 standard-size cards. This set is sometimes referenced as Hillshire Farms or Kahn's Cooperstown Collection. All players included in the set are members (for the most part they are recent inductees) of the Hall of Fame. The pictures are actually paintings and are surrounded by gold borders. The fronts resemble plaques and also have facsimile autographs. The cards were available from the company via a send-in offer. A set of cards was available in return for three proofs of purchase (and $1 postage and handling) from Hillshire Farms. The last card in the set is actually a coupon card for Kahn's products; this card is not even considered part of the set by some collectors. A related promotion offered two coin cards (coins laminated on cards) featuring Johnny Bench and Carl Yastrzemski. Coin cards are 5 1/2" X 3 3/4" and are blank backed.

COMPLETE SET (12) 4.00 10.00
1 Cool Papa Bell .30 .75
2 Johnny Bench .60 1.50
3 Lou Brock .40 1.00
4 Whitey Ford .40 1.00
5 Bob Gibson .40 1.00
6 Billy Herman .30 .75
7 Harmon Killebrew .40 1.00
8 Eddie Mathews .40 1.00
9 Brooks Robinson .60 1.50
10 Willie Stargell .60 1.50
11 Carl Yastrzemski .60 1.50
12 Coupon Card .08 .25

1887 Kalamazoo Bats N690-1

The Charles Gross Company of Philadelphia marketed this series of baseball players in 1887 in packages of tobacco with the intriguing name Kalamazoo Bats. This name involved a two-fold meaning since the word "bat" also referred to a wad of tobacco. There are 61 sepia photographs of baseball players known; most cards are blank backed although some are found with a list of premiums printed on the reverse. A Tom McLaughlin card was found recently, so this checklist may not be complete and all additions are appreciated. There is only one card known of both the Tom Poorman and the Wilbert Robinson/Fred Mann combo so we are not pricing those cards due to market scarcity. Cards with advertising backs are valued at 1.5X the prices listed in our data base.

COMMON PHILADELPHIA 750.00 1500.00
COMMON N.Y. GIANTS 4000.00 8000.00
COMMON METS 4000.00 8000.00
1 George Andrews: Phila. 4000.00 8000.00
2 Charlie Bastian 4000.00 8000.00
Denny Lyons:
Philadelphia
3 Louis Bierbauer: 4000.00 8000.00
Athletics
4 Louis Bierbauer 4000.00 8000.00
Gallagher:
Athletics
5 Charlie Buffington: 4000.00 8000.00
Philadelphia
6 Dan Casey: Phila. 4000.00 8000.00
7 Jack Clements: Phila. 4000.00 8000.00
8 Roger Connor: New York 40000.00 80000.00
9 Larry Corcoran: 7500.00 15000.00
New York
10 Ed Cushman 12500.00 25000.00
11 Pat Deasley 7500.00 15000.00
12 Jim Devlin: Phila. 4000.00 8000.00
13 Jim Donahue: Mets 12500.00 25000.00
14 Mike Dorgan: New York 7500.00 15000.00
15 Dude Esterbrooke (sic): 12500.00 25000.00
Mets
16 Buck Ewing 40000.00 80000.00
New York
17 Sid Farrar: Phila. 5000.00 10000.00
18 Charlie Ferguson 4000.00 8000.00
Philadelphia
19 Jim Fogarty: Phila. 4000.00 8000.00
20 Jim Fogarty 4000.00 8000.00
James McGuire:
Philadelphia
21 Elmer E. Foster: Mets 12500.00 25000.00
22 Gibson: Philadelphia 4000.00 8000.00
23 Pete Gillespie: 7500.00 15000.00
New York
24 Tom Gunning: Phila. 4000.00 8000.00
25 Art Irwin: Phila. 4000.00 8000.00
26 Irwin (Capt.) and Maul: 4000.00 8000.00
Philadelphia
27 Tim Keefe 12500.00 25000.00
28 Ted Larkin: Athletics 4000.00 8000.00
29 Jack Lynch: Mets 12500.00 25000.00
30 Denny Lyons: Phila. 4000.00 8000.00
31 Denny Lyons 4000.00 8000.00
Billy Taylor:
Philadelphia
32 Fred Mann: Athletics 4000.00 8000.00
33 Charlie Mason MG 4000.00 8000.00
34 Bobby Mathews: 4000.00 8000.00
Athletics
35 Al Maul: Philadelphia 4000.00 8000.00
36 Al Mays: Mets 12500.00 25000.00
37 Jim McGarr 4000.00 8000.00
38 James McGuire (one hand 4000.00 8000.00
at chin throwing):
Phila
39 James McGuire (both 4000.00 8000.00
hands at chin catch-
ing): P
40 Tom McLaughlin 10000.00 20000.00
Mets
41 Jocko Milligan 4000.00 8000.00
Henry Larkin:
Athletics
42 Joe Mulvey: Phila. 4000.00 8000.00
43 Jack Nelson: Mets 12500.00 25000.00
44 Jim O'Rourke: New York 40000.00 80000.00
45 Dave Orr: Mets 12500.00 25000.00
46 Tom Poorman 4000.00 8000.00
47 Danny Richardson 7500.00 15000.00
New York
48 Wilbert Robinson: 7500.00 15000.00
Athletics
49 Wilbert Robinson 4000.00 8000.00
Fred Mann: Athletics
50 James(Chief)Roseman: 12500.00 25000.00
Mets
51 Harry Stowe (sic& 6000.00 12000.00
Stovey) (hands at
hips standin
52 Harry Stowe (sic& 6000.00 12000.00
Stovey)(hands raised
catching)
53 Harry Stowe (sic) 7500.00 15000.00
Jocko Milligan
Athletics
54 George Townsend: 4000.00 8000.00
Athletics
55 George Townsend 4000.00 8000.00
Jocko Milligan
Athletics
56 John M. Ward 40000.00 80000.00
57 Mickey Welch 40000.00 80000.00
58 Gus Weyhing 4000.00 8000.00
59 George Wood: Phila. 4000.00 8000.00
60 Harry Wright: 10000.00 20000.00
Phila.-Mgr.
61 New York 4000.00 8000.00
Players Composite

1887 Kalamazoo Teams N690-2

Like the cards of set N690-1, the team cards of this set are sepia photographs and are blank-backed. There are only six teams known at the present time, and the cards themselves are slightly larger than those of the individual ballplayers in N690-1. They also appear to have been issued in 1887. There are only two copies known of the Pittsburg card and one copy of the Althletic and Philadelphia cards and we are not pricing

those card due to market scarcity.
COMPLETE SET (6) 10000.00 40000.00
1 Athletics Club 7500.00 15000.00
2 Baltimore B.B.C. 20000.00 40000.00
3 Boston B.B.C. 10000.00 20000.00
4 Detroit B.B.C. 15000.00 30000.00
5 Philadelphia B.B.C. 10000.00 20000.00
6 Pittsburg B.B.C. 20000.00 40000.00

1974 Kaline Sun-Glo Pop

Sun-Glo Pop issued this card attached to a bottle of pop. The bright green card has a black and white portrait of Al Kaline (not in uniform) with his name printed in black script lettering below followed by the words "drinks Sun-Glo pop". The back is blank.
1 Al Kaline 4.00 10.00

1910 Kallis and Dane

These two 6 1/2" by 5 1/2" blank backed cards were produced by Kallis and Dane printers and featured pictures and highlights from the 1910 World Series. Any additions to the checklist as well as comments are greatly appreciated.
COMPLETE SET 200.00 400.00
1 Johnny Evers 150.00 300.00
Stealing Home
Harry Steinfeldt at b
2 Paddy Livingston 50.00 100.00
Cutting off a Run
Connie Mack M

1985 KAS Discs

This set was apparently a test issue for the next year's more mass-produced set. Although this set is rarely seen in the secondary market, a few dealers in the mid 1980's got a small supply of this set. Typical of MSA sets all the team insignias are air-brushed out. This set was also issued in a proof square form and those cards are valued at twice the listed prices.
COMPLETE SET 100.00 200.00
1 Steve Carlton 6.00 15.00
2 Jack Clark 2.00 5.00
3 Rich Gossage 3.00 8.00
4 Tony Gwynn 12.50 30.00
5 Keith Hernandez 3.00 8.00
6 Bob Horner 2.00 5.00
7 Kent Hrbek 2.00 5.00
8 Willie McGee 2.50 6.00
9 Dan Quisenberry 2.00 5.00
10 Cal Ripken 20.00 50.00
11 Ryne Sandberg 10.00 25.00
12 Mike Schmidt 8.00 20.00
13 Tom Seaver 8.00 20.00
14 Ozzie Smith 10.00 25.00
15 Rick Sutcliffe 2.00 5.00
16 Bruce Sutter 5.00 12.00
17 Alan Trammell 3.00 8.00
18 Fernando Valenzuela 2.50 6.00
19 Willie Wilson 2.00 5.00
20 Dave Winfield 6.00 15.00

1928 Kashin Publications R315

This listing is actually an amalgamation of different issued sets. The cards all measure 3 1/4" by 5 1/4" and are all blank-backed. Cissell, Clancy, Hendrick, Jolley and Traynor were all issued in a sepia toned version which are both made of thicker stock than the regular photos and are considerably more difficult to acquire than the other cards in the set,
COMPLETE SET (88) 2500.00 5000.00
COMMON PLAYER A/B 10.00 20.00
COMMON PLAYER C/D 12.50 25.00
A1 Earl Averill 50.00 100.00
A2 Benny Bengough 20.00 40.00
A3 Laurence Benton 20.00 40.00
A4 Max Bishop 20.00 40.00
A5 Jim Bottomley 50.00 100.00
A6 Freddy Fitzsimmons 20.00 40.00
A7 Jimmie Foxx 200.00 400.00
A8 Johnny Fredericks 20.00 40.00
A9 Frank Frisch 75.00 150.00
A10 Lou Gehrig 400.00 800.00
A11 Goose Goslin 50.00 100.00
A12 Burleigh Grimes 50.00 100.00
A13 Lefty Grove 125.00 250.00
A14 Mule Haas 20.00 40.00
A15 Babe Herman 25.00 50.00
A16 Rogers Hornsby 200.00 400.00
A17 Carl Hubbell 75.00 150.00
A18 Travis Jackson 40.00 80.00
A19 Chuck Klein 75.00 150.00
A20 Mark Koenig 20.00 40.00
A21 Tony Lazzeri 40.00 80.00
A22 Fred Leach 20.00 40.00
A23 Fred Lindstrom 40.00 80.00
A24 Fred Marberry 20.00 40.00
A25 Bing Miller 20.00 40.00
A26 Lefty O'Doul 30.00 60.00
A27 Bob O'Farrell 20.00 40.00
A28 Herb Pennock 50.00 100.00
A29 George Pipgras 20.00 40.00
A30 Andrew Reese 20.00 40.00
A31 Babe Ruth 500.00 1000.00
A32 Bob Shawkey 25.00 50.00
A33 Al Simmons 50.00 100.00
A34 Riggs Stephenson 30.00 60.00
A35 Bill Terry 75.00 150.00
A36 Pie Traynor 100.00 200.00
A37 Dazzy Vance 50.00 100.00
A38 Paul Waner 50.00 100.00
A39 Hack Wilson 75.00 150.00
A40 Tom Zachary 20.00 40.00
B1 Earl Averill 50.00 100.00
B2 Benny Bengough 20.00 40.00
B3 Laurence Benton 20.00 40.00
B4 Max Bishop 20.00 40.00
B5 Jim Bottomley 50.00 100.00
B6 Freddy Fitzsimmons 20.00 40.00
B7 Jimmie Foxx 150.00 300.00
B8 Johnny Fredericks 20.00 40.00
B9 Frank Frisch 125.00 250.00
B10 Lou Gehrig 400.00 800.00
B11 Goose Goslin 50.00 100.00
B12 Burleigh Grimes 50.00 100.00
B13 Lefty Grove 125.00 250.00
B14 Mule Haas 20.00 40.00
B15 Babe Herman 25.00 50.00
B16 Rogers Hornsby 200.00 400.00
B17 Carl Hubbell 100.00 200.00
B18 Travis Jackson 50.00 100.00
B19 Chuck Klein 75.00 150.00
B20 Mark Koenig 20.00 40.00
B21 Tony Lazzeri 40.00 80.00
B22 Fred Leach 20.00 40.00
B23 Fred Lindstrom 50.00 100.00
B24 Fred Marberry 20.00 40.00
B25 Bing Miller 20.00 40.00
B26 Lefty O'Doul 30.00 60.00
B27 Bob O'Farrell 20.00 40.00
B28 Herb Pennock 50.00 100.00
B29 George Pipgras 20.00 40.00
B30 Andrew Reese 20.00 40.00
B31 Babe Ruth 500.00 1000.00
B32 Bob Shawkey 20.00 40.00
B33 Al Simmons 50.00 100.00
B34 Riggs Stephenson 30.00 60.00
B35 Bill Terry 100.00 200.00
B36 Pie Traynor 75.00 150.00
B37 Dazzy Vance 50.00 100.00
B38 Paul Waner 50.00 100.00
B39 Hack Wilson 75.00 150.00
B40 Tom Zachary 20.00 40.00
C1 Bill Cissell 25.00 50.00
C2 Harvey Hendricks 25.00 50.00
C3 Smead Jolley 25.00 50.00
C4 Carl Reynolds 25.00 50.00
C5 Art Shires 25.00 50.00
D1 Bill Cissell 25.00 50.00
D2 Bud Clancy 25.00 50.00
D3 Smead Jolley 25.00 50.00

1929 Kashin Publications R316

The 1929 R316 Portraits and Action Baseball set features 101 unnumbered, blank backed, black and white cards each measuring 3 1/2" by 4 1/2". The name of the player is written in script at the bottom of the card. The Hadley, Haines, Siebold and Todt cards are considered scarce. The Babe Ruth card seems to be one of the more plentiful cards in the set. These cards were issued in 25 count boxes which had the checklist printed on the reverse. There were four different boxes issued: Orange, Blue, Coral and Canary and Babe Ruth is the only player included in all four of these boxes. This set was issued by Kashin Publications.
COMPLETE SET (101) 2250.00 4500.00
1 Ethan N. Allen 15.00 30.00
2 Dale Alexander 15.00 30.00
3 Larry Benton 15.00 30.00
4 Moe Berg 30.00 60.00
5 Max Bishop 15.00 30.00
6 Del Bissonette 15.00 30.00
7 Lucerne A. Blue 15.00 30.00
8 Jim Bottomley 25.00 50.00
9 Guy T. Bush 15.00 30.00
10 Harold G. Carlson 15.00 30.00
11 Owen Carroll 15.00 30.00
12 Chalmers W. Cissell 15.00 30.00
13 Earle Combs 25.00 50.00
14 Hugh M. Critz 15.00 30.00
15 H.J. DeBerry 15.00 30.00
16 Pete Donohue 15.00 30.00
17 Taylor Douthit 15.00 30.00
18 Chuck Dressen 20.00 40.00
19 Jimmy Dykes 20.00 40.00
20 Howard Ehmke 15.00 30.00
21 Woody English 15.00 30.00
22 Urban Faber 25.00 50.00
23 Fred Fitzsimmons 20.00 40.00
24 Lewis A. Fonseca 15.00 30.00
25 Horace H. Ford 15.00 30.00
26 Jimmie Foxx 40.00 80.00
27 Frankie Frisch 30.00 60.00
28 Lou Gehrig 200.00 400.00
29 Charley Gehringer 30.00 60.00
30 Goose Goslin 25.00 50.00
31 George Grantham 15.00 30.00
32 Burleigh Grimes 25.00 50.00
33 Lefty Grove 30.00 60.00
34 Bump Hadley 100.00 200.00
35 Chick Hafey 25.00 50.00
36 Jesse Haines 125.00 250.00
37 Harvey Hendrick 15.00 30.00
38 Babe Herman 20.00 40.00
39 Andy High 15.00 30.00
40 Urban J. Hodapp 15.00 30.00
41 Frank Hogan 15.00 30.00
42 Rogers Hornsby 40.00 80.00
43 Waite Hoyt 25.00 50.00
44 Willis Hudlin 15.00 30.00
45 Frank O. Hurst 15.00 30.00
46 Charlie Jamieson 15.00 30.00
47 Roy C. Johnson 15.00 30.00
48 Percy Jones 15.00 30.00
49 Sam Jones 20.00 40.00
50 Joseph Judge 15.00 30.00
51 Willie Kamm 15.00 30.00
52 Chuck Klein 25.00 50.00
53 Mark Koenig 15.00 30.00
54 Ralph Kress 15.00 30.00
55 Fred M. Leach 15.00 30.00
56 Fred Lindstrom 25.00 50.00
57 Ad Liska 15.00 30.00
58 Fred Lucas 15.00 30.00
59 Fred Maguire 15.00 30.00
60 Perce L. Malone 15.00 30.00
61 Heinie Manush 25.00 50.00
62 Rabbit Maranville 25.00 50.00
63 Douglas McWeeney 15.00 30.00
64 Oscar Melillo 15.00 30.00
65 Bing Miller 15.00 30.00
66 Lefty O'Doul 20.00 40.00
67 Mel Ott 40.00 80.00
68 Herb Pennock 25.00 50.00
69 William W. Regan 15.00 30.00
70 Harry F. Rice 15.00 30.00
71 Sam Rice 25.00 50.00
72 Lance Richbourg 15.00 30.00
73 Eddie Rommel 15.00 30.00
74 Chas. H. Root 15.00 30.00
75 Ed Roush 25.00 50.00
76 Harold Ruel 15.00 30.00
77 Red Ruffing 25.00 50.00
78 Jack Russell 15.00 30.00
79 Babe Ruth QP 200.00 400.00
80 Fred Schulte 15.00 30.00
81 Joe Sewell 25.00 50.00
82 Luke Sewell 20.00 40.00
83 Art Shires 15.00 30.00
84 Henry Seibold 100.00 200.00
85 Al Simmons 25.00 50.00
86 Bob Smith 15.00 30.00
87 Riggs Stephenson 20.00 40.00
88 Bill Terry 30.00 60.00
89 Alphonse Thomas 15.00 30.00
90 Lafayette Thompson 15.00 30.00
91 Phil Todt 100.00 200.00
92 Pie Traynor 25.00 50.00
93 Dazzy Vance 25.00 50.00
94 Lloyd Waner 25.00 50.00
95 Paul Waner 25.00 50.00
96 Jimmy Welsh 15.00 30.00
97 Earl Whitehill 15.00 30.00
98 A.C. Whitney 15.00 30.00
99 Claude Willoughby 15.00 30.00
100 Hack Wilson 30.00 60.00
101 Tom Zachary 15.00 30.00

1986 Kay-Bee

This 33-card, standard-sized set was produced by Topps but manufactured in Northern Ireland. This boxed set retailed in Kay-Bee stores for $1.99; the checklist was listed on the back of the box. The set is subtitled "Young Superstars of Baseball" and does indeed feature many young players. The cards are numbered on the back; the set card numbering is in alphabetical order by player's name.
COMP. FACT SET (33) 1.50 4.00
1 Rick Aguilera .05 .15
2 Chris Brown .01 .05
3 Tom Browning .01 .05
4 Tom Brunansky .01 .05
5 Vince Coleman .05 .15
6 Ron Darling .01 .05
7 Alvin Davis .01 .05
8 Mariano Duncan .05 .15
9 Shawon Dunston .02 .10
10 Sid Fernandez .01 .05
11 Tony Fernandez .01 .05
12 Brian Fisher .01 .05
13 John Franco .07 .20
14 Julio Franco .07 .20
15 Dwight Gooden .07 .20
16 Ozzie Guillen .20 .50
17 Tony Gwynn .40 1.00
18 Jimmy Key .07 .20
19 Don Mattingly .40 1.00
20 Oddibe McDowell .01 .05
21 Roger McDowell .02 .10
22 Dan Pasqua .01 .05
23 Terry Pendleton .02 .10
24 Jim Presley .01 .05
25 Kirby Puckett .30 .75
26 Earnie Riles .01 .05
27 Bret Saberhagen .07 .20
28 Mark Salas .01 .05
29 Juan Samuel .01 .05
30 Jeff Stone .01 .05
31 Darryl Strawberry .02 .10
32 Andy Van Slyke .02 .10
33 Frank Viola .05 .15

1987 Kay-Bee

This small 33-card boxed standard-size set was produced by Topps for Kay-Bee Toy Stores. The set is subtitled "Super Stars of Baseball" and has full-color fronts. The card backs are printed in blue and black on white card stock. The checklist for the set is printed on the back panel of the yellow box. The set card numbering is alphabetical by player's name.
COMP. FACT SET (33) 1.50 4.00
1 Harold Baines .02 .10
2 Jesse Barfield .01 .05
3 Don Baylor .02 .10
4 Wade Boggs .15 .40
5 George Brett .30 .75
6 Hubie Brooks .01 .05
7 Jose Canseco .20 .50
8 Gary Carter .20 .50
9 Joe Carter .07 .20
10 Roger Clemens .40 1.00
11 Vince Coleman .01 .05
12 Glenn Davis .01 .05
13 Dwight Gooden .05 .15
14 Pedro Guerrero .01 .05
15 Tony Gwynn .40 1.00
16 Rickey Henderson .30 .75
17 Keith Hernandez .05 .15
18 Wally Joyner .07 .20
19 Don Mattingly .40 1.00
20 Jack Morris .02 .10
21 Dale Murphy .07 .20
22 Eddie Murray .15 .40
23 Dave Parker .02 .10
24 Kirby Puckett .30 .75
25 Tim Raines .02 .10
26 Jim Rice .02 .10
27 Dave Righetti .01 .05
28 Ryne Sandberg .30 .75
29 Mike Schmidt .20 .50
30 Mike Scott .01 .05
31 Darryl Strawberry .02 .10
32 Fernando Valenzuela .02 .10
33 Dave Winfield .15 .40

1988 Kay-Bee

This small 33-card boxed standard-size set was produced by Topps for Kay-Bee Toy Stores. The set is subtitled "Superstars of Baseball" and have full-color fronts. The card backs are printed in blue and green on white card stock. The checklist for the set is printed on the back panel of the box. The set card numbering is alphabetical by player's name.
COMP. FACT SET (33) 2.00 5.00
1 George Bell .01 .05
2 Wade Boggs .20 .50
3 Jose Canseco .20 .50
4 Joe Carter .07 .20
5 Jack Clark .02 .10
6 Alvin Davis .01 .05
7 Eric Davis .02 .10
8 Andre Dawson .07 .20
9 Darrell Evans .02 .10
10 Dwight Evans .02 .10
11 Gary Gaetti .02 .10
12 Pedro Guerrero .01 .05
13 Tony Gwynn .40 1.00
14 Howard Johnson .01 .05
15 Wally Joyner .05 .15
16 Don Mattingly .40 1.00
17 Willie McGee .02 .10
18 Mark McGwire .40 1.00
19 Paul Molitor .20 .50
20 Dale Murphy .07 .20
21 Dave Parker .02 .10
22 Lance Parrish .01 .05
23 Kirby Puckett .25 .60
24 Tim Raines .02 .10
25 Cal Ripken .75 2.00
26 Juan Samuel .01 .05
27 Mike Schmidt .20 .50
28 Ruben Sierra .02 .10
29 Darryl Strawberry .02 .10
30 Danny Tartabull .01 .05
31 Alan Trammell .05 .15
32 Tim Wallach .01 .05
33 Dave Winfield .15 .40

1989 Kay-Bee

The 1989 Kay-Bee set contains 33 standard-size glossy cards. The fronts have magenta and yellow borders. The horizontally oriented backs are brown and yellow. The cards were distributed as boxed sets through Kay-Bee toy stores. The set card numbering is alphabetical by player's name.
COMP. FACT SET (33) 2.00 5.00
1 Wade Boggs .10 .30
2 George Brett .30 .75
3 Jose Canseco .20 .50
4 Gary Carter .20 .50
5 Jack Clark .01 .05
6 Will Clark .15 .40
7 Roger Clemens .30 .75
8 Eric Davis .02 .10
9 Andre Dawson .08 .25
10 Dwight Evans .02 .10
11 Carlton Fisk .15 .40
12 Andres Galarraga .10 .30
13 Kirk Gibson .02 .10
14 Dwight Gooden .02 .10
15 Mike Greenwell .01 .05
16 Pedro Guerrero .01 .05
17 Tony Gwynn .40 1.00
18 Rickey Henderson .15 .40
19 Orel Hershiser .02 .10
20 Don Mattingly .30 .75
21 Mark McGwire .40 1.00
22 Dale Murphy .08 .25
23 Eddie Murray .10 .30
24 Kirby Puckett .25 .60
25 Tim Raines .02 .10
26 Ryne Sandberg .25 .60
27 Mike Schmidt .15 .40
28 Ozzie Smith .30 .75
29 Darryl Strawberry .02 .10
30 Alan Trammell .05 .15
31 Frank Viola .01 .05
32 Dave Winfield .10 .30
33 Robin Yount .15 .40

1990 Kay-Bee

The 1990 Kay-Bee Kings of Baseball set is a standard-size 33-card set sequenced alphabetically that Topps produced for the Kay-Bee toy store chain. A solid red border inside a purple white striped box is the major design feature of this set. The set card numbering is alphabetical by player's name.
COMP. FACT SET (33) 2.50 6.00
1 Doyle Alexander .01 .05
2 Bert Blyleven .02 .10
3 Wade Boggs .20 .50
4 George Brett .40 1.00
5 John Candelaria .01 .05
6 Gary Carter .15 .40
7 Vince Coleman .01 .05
8 Andre Dawson .07 .20
9 Dennis Eckersley .15 .40
10 Darrell Evans .02 .10
11 Dwight Evans .02 .10
12 Carlton Fisk .15 .40
13 Ken Griffey Sr. .01 .05
14 Tony Gwynn .40 1.00
15 Rickey Henderson .25 .60
16 Keith Hernandez .02 .10
17 Charlie Hough .01 .05
18 Don Mattingly .40 1.00
19 Jack Morris .02 .10
20 Dale Murphy .07 .20
21 Eddie Murray .15 .40
22 Dave Parker .02 .10
23 Kirby Puckett .30 .75
24 Tim Raines .02 .10
25 Rick Reuschel .01 .05
26 Jerry Reuss .01 .05
27 Jim Rice .02 .10
28 Nolan Ryan .75 2.00
29 Ozzie Smith .40 1.00
30 Frank Tanana .01 .05
31 Willie Wilson .01 .05
32 Dave Winfield .20 .50
33 Robin Yount .20 .50

1937 Kellogg's Pep Stamps

Kellogg's distributed these multi-sport stamps inside specially marked Pep brand cereal boxes in 1937. They were originally issued in four-stamp blocks along with an instructional type tab at the top. The tab contained the sheet number. We've noted the sheet number after each athlete's name below. Note that six athletes appear on two sheets, thereby making those six double prints. There were 24-different sheets produced. We've catalogued the unnumbered stamps below in single loose form according to sport (AR- auto racing, AV- aviation, BB- baseball, BX- boxing, FB- football, GO- golf, HO- horses, SW- swimming, TN- tennis). Stamps can often be found intact in blocks of four along with the tab. Complete blocks of stamps are valued at roughly 50 percent more than the total value of the four individual stamps as priced below. An album was also produced to house the set.
COMPLETE SET (90) 1000.00 2000.00
BB1 Luke Appling 7 12.50 25.00
BB2 Mordecai Brown 22 12.50 25.00
BB3 Leo Durocher 3 12.50 25.00
BB4 Johnny Evers 17 12.50 25.00
BB5 Rick Ferrell 16 10.00 20.00
BB6 Lew Fonseca 15 5.00 10.00
BB7 Gabby Hartnett 5 12.50 25.00
BB8 Billy Herman 6 12.50 25.00
BB9 Walter Johnson 13 25.00 50.00
BB10 Ducky Medwick 1 12.50 25.00
BB11 Buddy Myer 19 5.00 10.00
BB12 George Selkirk 12 5.00 10.00
BB13 Tris Speaker 20/23 12.50 25.00
BB14 Bill Terry 11 12.50 25.00
BB15 Joe Tinker 21 12.50 25.00
BB16 Arky Vaughan 8 12.50 25.00
BB17 Paul Waner 9 12.50 25.00
BB18 Sam West 18 5.00 10.00

1948 Kellogg's All Wheat Sport Tips Series 1

13 Baseball: Placing Hits 3.00 8.00
14 Baseball: Hook Slide 3.00 8.00

1948 Kellogg's All Wheat Sport Tips Series 2

7 Baseball: Batting Trick 3.00 8.00
15 Baseball: Fly Ball 3.00 8.00
18 Baseball: Head Position 3.00 8.00
20 Baseball: Infield Stance 3.00 8.00
21 Baseball: Base Running 3.00 8.00

1948 Kellogg's Pep

These small cards measure approximately 1 7/16" by 1 5/8". The card front presents a black and white head-and-shoulders shot of the player, with a white border. The back has the player's name and a brief description of his accomplishments. The cards are unnumbered, but have been assigned numbers below using a sport (BB- baseball, FB- football, BK- basketball, OT- other) prefix. Other Movie Star Kellogg's Pep cards exist, but they are not listed below. The catalog designation for this set is F273-19. An album was also produced to house the set.
COMPLETE SET (20) 700.00 1400.00
BB1 Phil Cavarretta 15.00 30.00
BB2 Orval Grove 10.00 20.00
BB3 Mike Tresh 10.00 20.00
BB4 Paul(Dizzy) Trout 15.00 30.00
BB5 Dick Wakefield 10.00 20.00

1970 Kellogg's

The cards in this 75-card set measure approximately 2 1/4" by 3 1/2". The 1970 Kellogg's set was Kellogg's first venture into the baseball card producing field. The design incorporates a brilliant color photo of the player set against an indistinct background, which is then covered with a layer of plastic to simulate a 3-D look. Some veteran card dealers consider cards 16-30 to be in shorter supply than the other cards in the set. The cards were individually inserted one per specially marked boxes of Kellogg's cereal. Cards still found with the wrapper intact are valued 50 percent greater than the values listed below. Kellogg's also distributed six-card packs which were available when collectors bought two card team patches. These packs, are still occassionally seen in the hobby and have a current value of $35.
COMPLETE SET (75) 150.00 300.00
1 Ed Kranepool .60 1.50
2 Pete Rose 8.00 20.00
3 Cleon Jones .60 1.50
4 Willie McCovey 3.00 8.00
5 Mel Stottlemyre .60 1.50
6 Frank Howard .60 1.50
7 Tom Seaver 8.00 20.00
8 Don Sutton 2.50 6.00
9 Jim Wynn .60 1.50
10 Jim Maloney .40 1.00
11 Tommie Agee .60 1.50
12 Willie Mays 10.00 25.00
13 Juan Marichal 2.50 6.00
14 Dave McNally .60 1.50
15 Frank Robinson 4.00 10.00
16 Carlos May .40 1.00
17 Bill Singer .40 1.00
18 Rick Reichardt .40 1.00
19 Boog Powell .75 2.00
20 Gaylord Perry 3.00 8.00
21 Brooks Robinson 6.00 15.00
22 Luis Aparicio 2.50 6.00
23 Joel Horlen .40 1.00
24 Mike Epstein .40 1.00
25 Tom Haller .40 1.00
26 Willie Crawford .40 1.00
27 Roberto Clemente 12.50 40.00
28 Matty Alou .40 1.00
29 Willie Stargell 4.00 10.00
30 Tim Cullen .40 1.00
31 Randy Hundley .40 1.00
32 Reggie Jackson 10.00 25.00
33 Rich Allen 1.00 2.50
34 Tim McCarver .75 2.00
35 Ray Culp .40 1.00
36 Jim Fregosi .40 1.00
37 Billy Williams 2.50 6.00
38 Johnny Odom .40 1.00
39 Bert Campaneris .60 1.50
40 Ernie Banks 5.00 12.00
41 Chris Short .40 1.00
42 Ron Santo .75 2.00
43 Glenn Beckert .60 1.50
44 Lou Brock 3.00 8.00
45 Larry Hisle .40 1.00
46 Reggie Smith .60 1.50
47 Rod Carew 4.00 10.00
48 Curt Flood .60 1.50
49 Jim Lonborg .40 1.00
50 Sam McDowell .60 1.50
51 Sal Bando .60 1.50
52 Al Kaline 5.00 12.00
53 Gary Nolan .40 1.00
54 Rico Petrocelli .60 1.50
55 Ollie Brown .40 1.00
56 Luis Tiant .60 1.50
57 Bill Freehan .60 1.50
58 Johnny Bench 10.00 25.00
59 Joe Pepitone .60 1.50
60 Bobby Murcer .60 1.50
61 Harmon Killebrew 4.00 10.00
62 Don Wilson .40 1.00
63 Tony Oliva 1.00 2.50
64 Jim Perry .40 1.00
65 Mickey Lolich .60 1.50
66 Jose Laboy .40 1.00
67 Dean Chance .40 1.00
68 Ken Harrelson .60 1.50
69 Willie Horton .60 1.50
70 Wally Bunker .40 1.00
71A Bob Gibson ERR
(1959 innings/pitched is blank) 3.00 8.00
71B Bob Gibson COR
(1959 innings is 76) 3.00 8.00
72 Joe Morgan 2.50 6.00
73 Denny McLain .60 1.50
74 Tommy Harper .40 1.00
75 Don Mincher .40 1.00

1971 Kellogg's

The cards in this 75-card set measure approximately 2 1/4" by 3 1/2". The 1971 set of 3-D cards marketed by the Kellogg Company is the scarcest of all that company's issues. It was distributed as single cards, one in each package of cereal, without the usual complete set mail-in offer. In addition, card dealers were unable to obtain this set in quantity, as they have in other years. All the cards are available with and without the year 1970 before XOGRAPH on the back in the lower left corner; the version without carries a slight premium for most numbers. Prices listed below are for the more common variety with the year 1970. Cards still found with the wrapper intact are valued 50 percent greater than the values listed below.
COMP.MASTER SET (92) 750.00 1500.00
COMPLETE SET (75) 600.00 1200.00
1A Wayne Simpson 119 SO 5.00 12.00
1B Wayne Simpson 120 SO 5.00 12.00
2 Tom Seaver 20.00 50.00
3A Jim Perry 2238 IP 5.00 12.00
3B Jim Perry 2239 IP 5.00 12.00
4A Bob Robertson 94 RBI 5.00 12.00
4B Bob Robertson 95 RBI 5.00 12.00
5 Roberto Clemente 40.00 80.00
6A Gaylord Perry 2014 IP 10.00 25.00
6B Gaylord Perry 2015 IP 10.00 25.00
7A Felipe Alou Oakland NL 5.00 12.00
7B Felipe Alou Oakland AL 5.00 12.00
8 Denis Menke 5.00 12.00
9A Don Kessinger No 1970 Date 5.00 12.00
9B Don Kessinger Dated 1970, 849 Hits 5.00 12.00
9C Don Kessinger Dated 1970, 850 Hits 5.00 12.00
10 Willie Mays 30.00 60.00
11 Jim Hickman 5.00 12.00
12 Tony Oliva 8.00 20.00
13 Manny Sanguillen 5.00 12.00
14A Frank Howard Washington NL 5.00 12.00
14B Frank Howard Washington AL 5.00 12.00
15 Frank Robinson 12.50 30.00
16 Willie Davis 5.00 12.00
17 Lou Brock 12.50 30.00
18 Cesar Tovar 5.00 12.00
19 Luis Aparicio 10.00 25.00
20 Boog Powell 6.00 15.00
21A Dick Selma 584 SO 5.00 12.00
21B Dick Selma 587 SO 5.00 12.00
22 Danny Walton 5.00 12.00
23 Carl Morton 5.00 12.00
24A Sonny Siebert 1054 SO 5.00 12.00
24B Sonny Siebert 1055 SO 5.00 12.00
25 Jim Merritt 5.00 12.00
26A Jose Cardenal 828 Hits 5.00 12.00
26B Jose Cardenal 829 Hits 5.00 12.00
27 Don Mincher 5.00 12.00
28A Clyde Wright No 1970
Date, Angels Logo 6.00 15.00
28B Clyde Wright No 1970
Date, California Logo 6.00 15.00
28C Clyde Wright Dated
1970, California Logo 5.00 12.00
29 Les Cain 5.00 12.00
30 Danny Cater 5.00 12.00
31 Don Sutton 10.00 25.00
32 Chuck Dobson 5.00 12.00
33 Willie McCovey 12.50 30.00
34 Mike Epstein 5.00 12.00
35A Paul Blair 386 Runs 5.00 12.00
35B Paul Blair 385 Runs 5.00 12.00
36A Gary Nolan No 1970 Date 5.00 12.00
36B Gary Nolan Dated 1970, 577 SO 5.00 12.00
36C Gary Nolan Dated 1970, 581 SO 5.00 12.00
37 Sam McDowell 5.00 12.00
38 Amos Otis 5.00 12.00
39A Ray Fosse 69 RBI 5.00 12.00
39B Ray Fosse 70 RBI 5.00 12.00
40 Mel Stottlemyre 5.00 12.00
41 Clarence Gaston 5.00 12.00
42 Dick Dietz 5.00 12.00
43 Roy White 5.00 12.00
44 Al Kaline 12.50 40.00
45 Carlos May 5.00 12.00
46A Tommie Agee 313 RBI 5.00 12.00
46B Tommie Agee 314 RBI 5.00 12.00
47 Tommy Harper 5.00 12.00
48 Larry Dierker 5.00 12.00
49 Mike Cuellar 5.00 12.00
50 Ernie Banks 12.50 40.00
51 Bob Gibson 12.50 30.00
52 Reggie Smith 5.00 12.00
53A Matty Alou 273 RBI 5.00 12.00
53B Matty Alou 274 RBI 5.00 12.00
54A Alex Johnson No 1970
Date, Angels Logo 6.00 15.00
54B Alex Johnson No 1970
Date, California Logo 6.00 15.00
54C Alex Johnson Dated
1970, California Logo 5.00 12.00
55 Harmon Killebrew 12.50 30.00
56 Bill Grabarkewitz 5.00 12.00
57 Richie Allen 6.00 15.00
58 Tony Perez 10.00 25.00
59A Dave McNally 1065 SO 5.00 12.00
59B Dave McNally 1067 SO 5.00 12.00
60A Jim Palmer 564 SO 12.50 30.00
60B Jim Palmer 567 SO 12.50 30.00
61 Billy Williams 10.00 25.00
62 Joe Torre 8.00 20.00
63A Jim Northrup 2773 AB 5.00 12.00
63B Jim Northrup 2772 AB 5.00 12.00
64A Jim Fregosi No 1970
Date, Angels Logo 6.00 15.00
64B Jim Fregosi No 1970
Date, California Logo 6.00 15.00
64C Jim Fregosi Dated
1970, California Logo, 1326 Hits 5.00 12.00
64D Jim Fregosi Dated
1970, California Logo, 1327 Hits 5.00 12.00
65 Pete Rose 20.00 50.00
66A Bud Harrelson No 1970 Date 5.00 12.00
66B Bud Harrelson Dated 1970, 112 RBI 5.00 12.00
66C Bud Harrelson Dated 1970, 113 RBI 5.00 12.00
67 Tony Taylor 5.00 12.00
68 Willie Stargell 10.00 25.00
69 Tony Horton 6.00 15.00
70A Claude Osteen No 1970 Date,
Card Number Missing 6.00 15.00
70B Claude Osteen No
1970 Date, Number 70 on Back 6.00 15.00
70C Claude Osteen Dated
1970, Number 70 on Back 5.00 12.00
71 Glenn Beckert 5.00 12.00
72 Nate Colbert 5.00 12.00
73A Rick Monday No 1970 Date 5.00 12.00
73B Rick Monday Dated 1970 1705 AB 5.00 12.00
73C Rick Monday Dated 1970 1704 AB 5.00 12.00
74A Tommy John 444 BB 6.00 15.00
74B Tommy John 443 BB 6.00 15.00
75 Chris Short 5.00 12.00

1972 Kellogg's

The cards in this 54-card set measure approximately 2 1/8" by 3 1/4". The dimensions of the cards in the 1972 Kellogg's set were reduced in comparison to those of the 1971 series. In addition, the length of the set was set at 54 cards rather than the 75 of the previous year. The cards of this Kellogg's set are characterized by the diagonal bands found on the obverse. Cards still found with the wrapper intact are valued 50 percent greater than the values listed below.
COMP.MASTER SET (75) 100.00 200.00
COMPLETE SET (54) 60.00 120.00
1A Tom Seaver ERA 2.85 8.00 20.00
1B Tom Seaver ERA 2.81 4.00 10.00
2 Amos Otis .40 1.00
3A Willie Davis Runs 842 .75 2.00
3B Willie Davis Runs 841 .40 1.00
4 Wilbur Wood .40 1.00
5 Bill Parsons .40 1.00
6 Pete Rose 6.00 15.00
7A Willie McCovey HR 360 3.00 8.00
7B Willie McCovey HR 370 1.50 4.00
8 Ferguson Jenkins 1.50 4.00
9A Vida Blue ERA 2.35 .75 2.00
9B Vida Blue ERA 2.31 .40 1.00
10 Joe Torre .75 2.00
11 Merv Rettenmund .40 1.00
12 Bill Melton .40 1.00
13A Jim Palmer Games 170 4.00 10.00
13B Jim Palmer Games 168 2.00 5.00
14 Doug Rader .40 1.00
15A Dave Roberts League Leader .75 2.00
15B Dave Roberts NL Leader .40 1.00
16 Bobby Murcer .60 1.50
17 Wes Parker .40 1.00
18A Joe Coleman BB 294 .75 2.00
18B Joe Coleman BB 393 .40 1.00
19 Manny Sanguillen .40 1.00
20 Reggie Jackson 4.00 10.00
21 Ralph Garr .40 1.00
22 Jim Hunter 1.50 4.00
23 Rick Wise .40 1.00
24 Glenn Beckert .40 1.00
25 Tony Oliva 1.00 2.50
26A Bob Gibson SO 2577 3.00 8.00
26B Bob Gibson SO 2578 1.50 4.00
27A Mike Cuellar ERA 3.80 .75 2.00
27B Mike Cuellar ERA 3.08 .40 1.00
28 Chris Speier .40 1.00
29A Dave McNally ERA 3.18 .75 2.00
29B Dave McNally ERA 3.15 .40 1.00
30 Leo Cardenas .40 1.00
31A Bill Freehan Runs 497 .75 2.00
31B Bill Freehan Runs 500 .40 1.00
32A Bud Harrelson Hits 634 .75 2.00
32B Bud Harrelson Hits 624 .40 1.00
33A Sam McDowell Less than 200 .75 2.00
33B Sam McDowell Less than 225 .40 1.00
34A Claude Osteen ERA 3.25 .75 2.00
34B Claude Osteen ERA 3.51 .40 1.00
35 Reggie Smith .60 1.50
36 Sonny Siebert .40 1.00
37 Lee May .60 1.50
38 Mickey Lolich .60 1.50
39A Cookie Rojas 2B 149 .75 2.00
39B Cookie Rojas 2B 150 .40 1.00
40A Dick Drago Royals .75 2.00
40B Dick Drago Royals .40 1.00
41 Nate Colbert .40 1.00
42 Andy Messersmith .40 1.00
43A Dave Johnson Avg .262 .75 2.00
43B Dave Johnson Avg .264 .60 1.50
44 Steve Blass .40 1.00
45 Bob Robertson .40 1.00
46A Billy Williams Missed Only 1 2.50 6.00
46B Billy Williams Phrase Omitted 1.50 4.00
47 Juan Marichal 1.50 4.00
48 Lou Brock 1.50 4.00
49 Roberto Clemente 8.00 20.00
50 Mel Stottlemyre .40 1.00
51 Don Wilson .40 1.00
52A Sal Bando RBI 355 .75 2.00
52B Sal Bando RBI 356 .40 1.00
53A Willie Stargell 2B 197 3.00 8.00
53B Willie Stargell 2B 196 1.50 4.00
54A Willie Mays RBI 1855 10.00 25.00
54B Willie Mays RBI 1856 5.00 12.00

1972 Kellogg's ATG

The cards in this 15-card set measure 2 1/4" by 3 1/2". The 1972 All-Time Greats 3-D set was issued with Kellogg's Danish Go Rounds. The set contains two different cards of Babe Ruth. The set is a reissue of a 1970 set issued by Rold Gold Pretzels to commemorate baseball's first 100 years. The Rold Gold cards are copyrighted 1970 on the reverse and are valued at approximately double the prices listed below.
COMPLETE SET (15) 30.00 60.00
1 Walter Johnson 1.00 2.50

2 Rogers Hornsby .60 1.50
3 John McGraw .60 1.50
4 Mickey Cochrane .60 1.50
5 George Sisler .60 1.50
6 Babe Ruth 4.00 10.00
7 Lefty Grove .60 1.50
8 Pie Traynor .40 1.00
9 Honus Wagner 1.00 2.50
10 Eddie Collins .40 1.00
11 Tris Speaker .60 1.50
12 Cy Young 1.00 2.50
13 Lou Gehrig 3.00 8.00
14 Babe Ruth 4.00 10.00
15 Ty Cobb 3.00 8.00

1973 Kellogg's

The cards in this 54-card set measure approximately 2 1/4" by 3 1/2". The 1973 Kellogg's set is the only non-3D set produced by the Kellogg Company. Apparently Kellogg's decided to have the cards produced through Visual Panographics rather than by Xograph, as in the other years. The complete set could be obtained from the company through a box-top redemption procedure. The card size is slightly larger than the previous year. According to published reports at the time, the redemption for this set cost either $1.50 and one Raisin Bran box top or $1.25 and two Raisin Bran box tops.

COMPLETE SET (54) 40.00 80.00
1 Amos Otis .30 .75
2 Ellie Rodriguez .20 .50
3 Mickey Lolich .30 .75
4 Tony Oliva .60 1.50
5 Don Sutton 1.25 3.00
6 Pete Rose 5.00 12.00
7 Steve Carlton 2.00 5.00
8 Bobby Bonds .60 1.50
9 Wilbur Wood .20 .50
10 Billy Williams 1.50 4.00
11 Steve Blass .20 .50
12 Jon Matlack .20 .50
13 Cesar Cedeno .30 .75
14 Bob Gibson 1.50 4.00
15 Sparky Lyle .40 1.00
16 Nolan Ryan 10.00 25.00
17 Jim Palmer 2.00 5.00
18 Ray Fosse .20 .50
19 Bobby Murcer .30 .75
20 Jim Hunter 1.25 3.00
21 Tug McGraw .20 .50
22 Reggie Jackson 4.00 10.00
23 Bill Stoneman .20 .50
24 Lou Piniella .40 1.00
25 Willie Stargell 2.00 5.00
26 Dick Allen .60 1.50
27 Carlton Fisk 5.00 12.00
28 Ferguson Jenkins 1.50 4.00
29 Phil Niekro 1.50 4.00
30 Gary Nolan .20 .50
31 Joe Torre .60 1.50
32 Bobby Tolan .20 .50
33 Nate Colbert .20 .50
34 Joe Morgan 1.50 4.00
35 Bert Blyleven .40 1.00
36 Joe Rudi .30 .75
37 Ralph Garr .20 .50
38 Gaylord Perry 1.50 4.00
39 Bobby Grich .30 .75
40 Lou Brock 1.50 4.00
41 Pete Broberg .20 .50
42 Manny Sanguillen .20 .50
43 Willie Davis .30 .75
44 Dave Kingman .60 1.50
45 Carlos May .20 .50
46 Tom Seaver 4.00 10.00
47 Mike Cuellar .20 .50
48 Joe Coleman .20 .50
49 Claude Osteen .20 .50
50 Steve Kline .20 .50
51 Rod Carew 2.00 5.00
52 Al Kaline 2.50 6.00
53 Larry Dierker .20 .50
54 Ron Santo .40 1.00

1974 Kellogg's

The cards in this 54-card set measure 2 1/8" by 3 1/4". In 1974 the Kellogg's set returned to its 3-D format; it also returned to the smaller-size card. Complete sets could be obtained from the company through a box-top offer. The cards are numbered on the back. Cards still found with the wrapper intact are valued 25 percent greater than the values listed below.

COMPLETE SET (54) 50.00 100.00
1 Bob Gibson 1.25 3.00
2 Rick Monday .20 .50
3 Joe Coleman .20 .50
4 Bert Campaneris .30 .75
5 Carlton Fisk 2.50 6.00
6 Jim Palmer 1.25 3.00
7A Ron Santo Cubs 2.50 6.00
7B Ron Santo White Sox .30 .75
8 Nolan Ryan 8.00 20.00
9 Greg Luzinski .30 .75
10A Buddy Bell 134 Runs .30 .75
10B Buddy Bell 135 Runs
11 Bob Watson .30 .75
12 Bill Singer .20 .50
13 Dave May .20 .50
14 Jim Brewer .20 .50
15 Manny Sanguillen .20 .50
16 Jeff Burroughs .30 .75
17 Amos Otis .20 .50
18 Ed Goodson .20 .50
19 Nate Colbert .20 .50
20 Reggie Jackson 4.00 10.00
21 Ted Simmons .40 1.00
22 Bobby Murcer .30 .75
23 Willie Horton .30 .75
24 Orlando Cepeda 1.25 3.00
25 Ron Hunt .20 .50
26 Wayne Twitchell .20 .50
27 Ron Fairly .20 .50
28 Johnny Bench 2.50 6.00
29 John Mayberry .20 .50
30 Rod Carew 1.50 4.00
31 Ken Holtzman .20 .50
32 Billy Williams 1.25 3.00
33 Dick Allen .60 1.50
34A Wilbur Wood K 198 1.25 3.00
34B Wilbur Wood K 199 .20 .50
35 Danny Thompson .20 .50
36 Joe Morgan 1.25 3.00
37 Willie Stargell 1.25 3.00
38 Pete Rose 4.00 10.00
39 Bobby Bonds .60 1.50
40 Chris Speier .20 .50
41 Sparky Lyle .30 .75
42 Cookie Rojas .20 .50
43 Tommy Davis .20 .50
44 Jim Hunter 1.25 3.00
45 Willie Davis .20 .50
46 Bert Blyleven .30 .75
47 Pat Kelly .20 .50
48 Ken Singleton .20 .50
49 Manny Mota .30 .75
50 Dave Johnson .40 1.00
51 Sal Bando .30 .75
52 Tom Seaver 4.00 10.00
53 Felix Millan .20 .50
54 Ron Blomberg .20 .50

1975 Kellogg's

The cards in this 57-card set measure approximately 2 1/8" by 3 1/4". The 1975 Kellogg's 3-D set could be obtained card by card in cereal boxes or as a set from a box-top offer from the company. Card number 44, Jim Hunter, exists with the A's emblem or the Yankees emblem on the back of the card. Cards still found with the wrapper intact are valued 25 percent greater than the values listed below. This set was available from Kellogg's for 2 box tops and a $2 charge.

COMPLETE SET (57) 200.00 400.00
1 Roy White 6.00 15.00
2 Ross Grimsley 2.50 6.00
3 Reggie Smith 2.50 6.00
4A Bob Grich 1973 Work 2.50 6.00
4B Bob Grich Because 2.50 6.00
5 Greg Gross 2.50 6.00
6 Bob Watson 2.50 6.00
7 Johnny Bench 12.50 30.00
8 Jeff Burroughs 2.50 6.00
9 Elliott Maddox 2.50 6.00
10 Jon Matlack 2.50 6.00
11 Pete Rose 15.00 40.00
12 Lee Stanton 2.50 6.00
13 Bake McBride 2.50 6.00
14 Jorge Orta 2.50 6.00
15 Al Oliver 2.50 6.00
16 John Briggs 2.50 6.00
17 Steve Garvey 3.00 8.00
18 Brooks Robinson 8.00 20.00
19 John Hiller 2.50 6.00
20 Lynn McGlothen 2.50 6.00
21 Cleon Jones 2.50 6.00
22 Fergie Jenkins 3.00 8.00
23 Bill North 2.50 6.00
24 Steve Busby 2.50 6.00
25 Richie Zisk 2.50 6.00
26 Nolan Ryan 30.00 60.00
27 Joe Morgan 4.00 10.00
28 Joe Rudi 2.50 6.00
29 Jose Cardenal 2.50 6.00
30 Andy Messersmith 2.50 6.00
31 Willie Montanez 2.50 6.00
32 Bill Buckner 2.50 6.00
33 Rod Carew 4.00 10.00
34 Lou Piniella 2.50 6.00
35 Ralph Garr 2.50 6.00
36 Mike Marshall 2.50 6.00
37 Garry Maddox 2.50 6.00
38 Dwight Evans 3.00 8.00
39 Lou Brock 4.00 10.00
40 Ken Singleton 2.50 6.00
41 Steve Braun 2.50 6.00
42 Rich Allen 5.00 12.00
43 John Grubb 2.50 6.00
44A Jim Hunter A's Logo 5.00 12.00
44B Jim Hunter Yankees Logo 3.00 8.00
45 Gaylord Perry 3.00 8.00
46 George Hendrick 2.50 6.00
47 Sparky Lyle 2.50 6.00
48 Dave Cash 2.50 6.00
49 Luis Tiant 2.50 6.00
50 Cesar Geronimo 2.50 6.00
51 Carl Yastrzemski 8.00 20.00
52 Ken Brett 2.50 6.00
53 Hal McRae 2.50 6.00
54 Reggie Jackson 8.00 20.00
55 Rollie Fingers 4.00 10.00
56 Mike Schmidt 8.00 20.00
57 Richie Hebner 5.00 12.00

1976 Kellogg's

The cards in this 57-card set measure approximately 2 1/8" by 3 1/4". The 1976 Kellogg's 3-D set could be obtained card by card in cereal boxes or as a set from the company for box-tops. Card numbers 1-3 (marked in the checklist below with SP) were apparently printed apart from the other 54 and are in shorter supply. Cards still found with the wrapper intact are valued 25 percent greater than the values listed below.

COMP.MASTER SET (68) 75.00 150.00
COMPLETE SET (57) 40.00 80.00
COMMON CARD (4-57) .20 .50
SHORT PRINT COMMONS 4.00 10.00
1 Steve Hargan SP 4.00 10.00
2 Claudell Washington SP 4.00 10.00
3 Don Gullett SP 4.00 10.00
4 Randy Jones .20 .50
5 Jim Hunter 1.25 3.00
6A Clay Carroll/(Team logo Cincinn- 1.25 3.00
ati Reds on bac
6B Clay Carroll/(Team logo Chicago .40 1.00
White Sox on bac
7 Joe Rudi .20 .50
8 Reggie Jackson 2.50 6.00
9 Felix Millan .20 .50
10 Jim Rice 1.25 3.00
11 Bert Blyleven .30 .75
12 Ken Singleton .20 .50
13 Don Sutton 1.00 2.50
14 Joe Morgan 1.25 3.00
15 Dave Parker .75 2.00
16 Dave Cash .20 .50
17 Ron LeFlore .20 .50
18 Greg Luzinski .30 .75
19 Dennis Eckersley 6.00 15.00
20 Bill Madlock .20 .50
21 George Scott .20 .50
22 Willie Stargell 1.25 3.00
23 Al Hrabosky .20 .50
24 Carl Yastrzemski 2.50 6.00
25A Jim Kaat 1.25 3.00
Team logo
Chicago White Sox on back
25B Jim Kaat/(Team logo Phila- .60 1.50
delphia Phillies
on
26 Marty Perez .20 .50
27 Bob Watson .30 .75
28 Eric Soderholm .20 .50
29 Bill Lee .20 .50
30A Frank Tanana ERR/1975 ERA 2.63 .40 1.00
30B Frank Tanana COR/1975 ERA 2.62 .30 .75
31 Fred Lynn .40 1.00
32A Tom Seaver ERR/(1967 Pct. 552 with 3.00 8.00
no decimal po
32B Tom Seaver COR/1967 Pct. .552 3.00 8.00
33 Steve Busby .20 .50
34 Gary Carter 1.50 4.00
35 Rick Wise .20 .50
36 Johnny Bench 2.50 6.00
37 Jim Palmer 1.25 3.00
38 Bobby Murcer .30 .75
39 Von Joshua .20 .50
40 Lou Brock 1.50 4.00
41A Mickey Rivers/(Missing line in .75 2.00
bio about Yankees
41B Mickey Rivers .30 .75
Bio has Yankees obtained ...
42 Manny Sanguillen .20 .50
43 Jerry Reuss .20 .50
44 Ken Griffey .40 1.00
45A Jorge Orta ERR .30 .75
Lifetime AB 1615
45B Jorge Orta COR .30 .75
Lifetime AB 1616
46 John Mayberry .20 .50
47A Vida Blue .30 .75
Bio struck out more batters
47B Vida Blue .30 .75
Bio pitched more innings
48 Rod Carew 1.50 4.00
49A Jon Matlack ERR/1975 ER 87 .30 .75
49B Jon Matlack COR/1975 ER 86 .30 .75
50 Boog Powell .40 1.00
51A Mike Hargrove ERR .40 1.00
Lifetime AB 935
51B Mike Hargrove COR .40 1.00
Lifetime AB 934
52A Paul Lindblad ERR/1975 ERA 2.43 .30 .75
52B Paul Lindblad COR/1975 ERA 2.72 .30 .75
53 Thurman Munson 1.50 4.00
54 Steve Garvey 1.00 2.50
55 Pete Rose 5.00 12.00
56A Greg Gross ERR .30 .75
Lifetime games 334
56B Greg Gross COR .30 .75
Lifetime games 302
57 Ted Simmons .40 1.00

1977 Kellogg's

The cards in this 57-card set measure approximately 2 1/8" by 3 1/4". The 1977 Kellogg's series of 3-D baseball player cards could be obtained card by card from cereal boxes or by sending in box-tops and money. Each player's picture appears in miniature form on the reverse, an idea begun in 1971 and replaced in subsequent years by the use of a picture of the Kellogg's mascot. Cards still found with the wrapper intact are valued 25 percent greater than the values listed below.

COMPLETE SET (57) 40.00 80.00
1 George Foster .30 .75
2 Bert Campaneris .20 .50
3 Fergie Jenkins 1.25 3.00
4 Dock Ellis .20 .50
5 John Montefusco .20 .50
6 George Brett 8.00 20.00
7 John Candelaria .20 .50
8 Fred Norman .20 .50
9 Bill Travers .20 .50
10 Hal McRae .30 .75
11 Doug Rau .20 .50
12 Greg Luzinski .30 .75
13 Ralph Garr .20 .50
14 Steve Garvey .75 2.00
15 Rick Manning .20 .50
16A Lyman Bostock ERR Ellis Photo 1.25 3.00
16B Lyman Bostock COR .30 .75
17 Randy Jones .20 .50
18A Ron Cey 48 HR .30 .75
18B Ron Cey 58 HR .30 .75
19 Dave Parker .60 1.50
20 Pete Rose 3.00 8.00
21A Wayne Garland No Trade .20 .50
21B Wayne Garland Trade .60 1.50
22 Bill North .20 .50
23 Thurman Munson 1.25 3.00
24 Tom Poquette .20 .50
25 Ron LeFlore .20 .50
26 Mark Fidrych 2.00 5.00
27 Sixto Lezcano .20 .50
28 Dave Winfield 3.00 8.00
29 Jerry Koosman .30 .75
30 Mike Hargrove .30 .75
31 Willie Montanez .20 .50
32 Don Stanhouse .20 .50
33 Jay Johnstone .20 .50
34 Bake McBride .20 .50
35 Dave Kingman .60 1.50
36 Fred Patek .20 .50
37 Garry Maddox .20 .50
38A Ken Reitz No Trade .20 .50
38B Ken Reitz Trade .60 1.50
39 Bobby Grich .30 .75
40 Cesar Geronimo .20 .50
41 Jim Lonborg .20 .50
42 Ed Figueroa .20 .50
43 Bill Madlock .30 .75
44 Jerry Remy .20 .50
45 Frank Tanana .30 .75
46 Al Oliver .30 .75
47 Charlie Hough .30 .75
48 Lou Piniella .30 .75
49 Ken Griffey .60 1.50
50 Jose Cruz .30 .75
51 Rollie Fingers 1.25 3.00
52 Chris Chambliss .30 .75
53 Rod Carew 2.00 5.00
54 Andy Messersmith .20 .50
55 Mickey Rivers .30 .75
56 Butch Wynegar .20 .50
57 Steve Carlton 2.00 5.00

1978 Kellogg's

The cards in this 57-card set measure 2 1/8" by 3 1/4". This 1978 3-D Kellogg's series marks the first year in which Tony the Tiger appears on the reverse of each card next to the team and MLB logos. Once again the set could be obtained as individually wrapped cards in cereal boxes or as a set via a mail-in offer. The key card in the set is Eddie Murray, as it was one of Murray's few card issues in 1978, the year of his Topps Rookie Card. Cards still found with the wrapper intact are valued 25 percent greater than the values listed below.

COMPLETE SET (57) 30.00 60.00
1 Steve Carlton 1.25 3.00
2 Bucky Dent .30 .75
3 Mike Schmidt 2.50 6.00
4 Ken Griffey .40 1.00
5 Al Cowens .20 .50
6 George Brett 6.00 15.00
7 Lou Brock 1.25 3.00
8 Goose Gossage .40 1.00
9 Tom Johnson .20 .50
10 George Foster .30 .75
11 Dave Winfield 1.50 4.00
12 Dan Meyer .20 .50
13 Chris Chambliss .30 .75
14 Paul Dade .20 .50
15 Jeff Burroughs .20 .50
16 Jose Cruz .30 .75
17 Mickey Rivers .30 .75
18 John Candelaria .20 .50
19 Ellis Valentine .20 .50
20 Hal McRae .20 .50
21 Dave Rozema .20 .50
22 Lenny Randle .20 .50
23 Willie McCovey 1.25 3.00
24 Ron Cey .30 .75
25 Eddie Murray 8.00 20.00
26 Larry Bowa .30 .75
27 Tom Seaver 2.00 5.00
28 Garry Maddox .20 .50
29 Rod Carew 1.50 4.00
30 Thurman Munson 1.00 2.50
31 Garry Templeton .30 .75
32 Eric Soderholm .20 .50
33 Greg Luzinski .30 .75
34 Reggie Smith .30 .75
35 Dave Goltz .20 .50
36 Tommy John .40 1.00
37 Ralph Garr .20 .50
38 Alan Bannister .20 .50
39 Bob Bailor .20 .50
40 Reggie Jackson 1.50 4.00
41 Cecil Cooper .30 .75
42 Burt Hooton .20 .50
43 Sparky Lyle .30 .75
44 Steve Ontiveros .20 .50
45 Rick Reuschel .20 .50
46 Lyman Bostock .30 .75
47 Mitchell Page .20 .50
48 Bruce Sutter .40 1.00
49 Jim Rice .60 1.50
50 Ken Forsch .20 .50
51 Nolan Ryan 6.00 15.00
52 Dave Parker .40 1.00
53 Bert Blyleven .30 .75
54 Frank Tanana .30 .75
55 Ken Singleton .20 .50
56 Mike Hargrove .30 .75
57 Don Sutton 1.00 2.50

1979 Kellogg's

The cards in this 60-card set measure approximately 1 15/16" by 3 1/4". The 1979 edition of Kellogg's 3-D baseball cards have a 3/16" reduced width from the previous year; a nicely designed curved panel above the picture gives this set a distinctive appearance. The set contains the largest number of cards issued in a Kellogg's set since the 1971 series. Three different press runs produced numerous variations in this set. The first two printings were included in cereal boxes, while the third printing was for the complete set mail-in offer. Forty-seven cards have three variations, while thirteen cards (4, 6, 9, 15, 19, 20, 30, 33, 41, 43, 45, 51, and 54) are unchanged from the second and third printings. The three printings may be distinguished by the placement of the registered symbol by Tony the Tiger and by team logos. In the third printing, four cards (16, 18, 22, 44) show the "P" team logo (no registered symbol), and card numbers 56 and 57 omit the registered symbol by Tony. Cards still found with the wrapper intact are valued 25 percent greater than the values listed below. The set was available from Kellogg's for two boxtops and $2 and the offer was available until April 30, 1980.

COMPLETE SET (60) 15.00 40.00
1 Bruce Sutter .75 2.00
2 Ted Simmons .20 .50
3 Ross Grimsley .10 .25
4 Wayne Nordhagen .10 .25
5A Jim Palmer Pct. .649 1.25 3.00
5B Jim Palmer
Pct. .650
6 John Henry Johnson .10 .25
7 Jason Thompson .10 .25
8 Pat Zachry .10 .25
9 Dennis Eckersley 1.25 3.00
10A Paul Splittorff IP 1665 .10 .25
10B Paul Splittorff
IP 1666
11A Ron Guidry Hits 397 .30 .75
11B Ron Guidry
Hits 396
12 Jeff Burroughs .10 .25
13 Rod Carew 1.25 3.00
14A Buddy Bell .60 1.50
No Trade
14B Buddy Bell Trade .20 .50
15 Jim Rice .40 1.00
16 Garry Maddox .10 .25
17 Willie McCovey .75 2.00
18 Steve Carlton 1.25 3.00
19A J.R. Richard Stats 1972 .10 .25
19B J.R. Richard Stats 1971
20 Paul Molitor 2.50 6.00
21A Dave Parker Avg. 281 .30 .75
21B Dave Parker
Avg. 318
22A Pete Rose 2.00 5.00
1978 3B 3
22B Pete Rose 1978 3B 33
23A Vida Blue Runs 819 .20 .50
23B Vida Blue
Runs 818
24 Richie Zisk .10 .25
25A Darrell Porter 2B 101 .10 .25
25B Darrell Porter
2B 111
26A Dan Driessen .10 .25
Games 742
26B Dan Driessen Games 642
27A Geoff Zahn Minnesota .10 .25
27B Geoff Zahn Minnesota
28 Phil Niekro .75 2.00
29 Tom Seaver 1.50 4.00
30 Fred Lynn .20 .50
31 Bill Bonham .10 .25
32 George Foster .20 .50
33A Terry Puhl His Lively .10 .25
33B Terry Puhl Terry Stole
34A John Candelaria Age 24 .10 .25
34B John Candelaria
Age 25
35 Bob Knepper .10 .25
36 Fred Patek .10 .25
37 Chris Chambliss .20 .50
38A Bob Forsch 1977 Games 86 .10 .25
38B Bob Forsch
1977 Games 35
39A Ken Griffey 1978 AB 674 .20 .50
39B Ken Griffey
1978 AB 614
40 Jack Clark .20 .50
41A Dwight Evans 1978 Hits 13 .20 .50
41B Dwight Evans
1978 Hits 123
42 Lee Mazzilli .10 .25
43 Mario Guerrero .10 .25
44 Larry Bowa .20 .50
45A Carl Yastrzemski AB 9930 1.50 4.00
45B Carl Yastrzemski
AB 9929
46A Reggie Jackson 1978 Games 162 1.50 4.00
46B Reggie Jackson
1978 Games 139
47 Rick Reuschel .10 .25
48A Mike Flanagan 1976 SO 57 .20 .50
48B Mike Flanagan
1976 SO 56
49A Gaylord Perry .75 2.00
1973 Hits 315
49B Gaylord Perry 1973 Hits 325
50 George Brett 4.00 10.00
51A Craig Reynolds He Spent .10 .25
51B Craig Reynolds In Those
52 Dave Lopes .20 .50
53A Bill Almon 2B 31 .10 .25
53B Bill Almon
2B 41
54 Roy Howell .10 .25
55 Frank Tanana .10 .25
56A Doug Rau 1978 Pct. .577 .10 .25
56B Doug Rau
1978 Pct. .625
57A Rick Monday .10 .25
1976 Runs 107
57B Rick Monday 1976 Runs 197
58 Jon Matlack .10 .25
59A Ron Jackson His Best .10 .25
59B Ron Jackson The Twins
60 Jim Sundberg .10 .25

1980 Kellogg's

The cards in this 60-card set measure approximately 1 7/8" by 3 1/4". The 1980 Kellogg's 3-D set is quite similar to, but smaller (narrower) than, the other recent Kellogg's issues. Sets could be obtained card by card from cereal boxes or as a set from a box-top offer from the company. Cards still found with the wrapper intact are valued 25 percent greater than the values listed below.

COMPLETE SET (60) 15.00 40.00
1 Ross Grimsley .08 .25
2 Mike Schmidt 1.50 4.00
3 Mike Flanagan .08 .25
4 Ron Guidry .20 .50
5 Bert Blyleven .20 .50
6 Dave Kingman .30 .75
7 Jeff Newman .08 .25
8 Steve Rogers .08 .25
9 George Brett 3.00 8.00
10 Bruce Sutter .60 1.50
11 Gorman Thomas .08 .25
12 Darrell Porter .08 .25
13 Roy Smalley .08 .25
14 Steve Carlton .75 2.00
15 Jim Palmer .75 2.00
16 Bob Bailor .08 .25
17 Jason Thompson .08 .25
18 Graig Nettles .20 .50
19 Ron Cey .20 .50
20 Nolan Ryan 3.00 8.00
21 Ellis Valentine .08 .25
22 Larry Hisle .08 .25
23 Dave Parker .30 .75
24 Eddie Murray 1.50 4.00
25 Willie Stargell .75 2.00
26 Reggie Jackson 1.50 4.00
27 Carl Yastrzemski 1.25 3.00
28 Andre Thornton .08 .25
29 Dave Lopes .20 .50
30 Ken Singleton .08 .25
31 Steve Garvey .40 1.00
32 Dave Winfield .75 2.00
33 Steve Kemp .08 .25
34 Claudell Washington .08 .25
35 Pete Rose 1.50 4.00
36 Cesar Cedeno .08 .25
37 John Stearns .08 .25
38 Lee Mazzilli .08 .25
39 Larry Bowa .20 .50
40 Fred Lynn .20 .50
41 Carlton Fisk 1.50 4.00
42 Vida Blue .20 .50
43 Keith Hernandez .20 .50
44 Jim Rice .40 1.00
45 Ted Simmons .20 .50
46 Chet Lemon .08 .25
47 Ferguson Jenkins .75 2.00
48 Gary Matthews .20 .50
49 Tom Seaver 1.50 4.00
50 George Foster .20 .50
51 Phil Niekro .75 2.00
52 Johnny Bench 1.25 3.00
53 Buddy Bell .20 .50
54 Lance Parrish .20 .50
55 Joaquin Andujar .08 .25
56 Don Baylor .30 .75
57 Jack Clark .20 .50
58 J.R. Richard .08 .25
59 Bruce Bochte .08 .25
60 Rod Carew 1.25 3.00

1981 Kellogg's

The cards in this 66-card set measure 2 1/2" by 3 1/2". The 1981 Kellogg's set witnessed an increase in both the size of the card and the size of the set. For the first time, cards were not packed in cereal packages but available only by mail-in procedure. The offer for the card set was advertised on boxes of Kellogg's Corn Flakes. The complete set could be ordered for $3.50 plus two proofs of purchase. The cards were printed on a different stock than in previous years, presumably to prevent the cracking problem which has plagued all Kellogg's 3-D issues. At the end of the promotion, the remainder of the sets not distributed (to cereal-eaters), were "sold" into the organized hobby, thus creating a situation where the set is relatively plentiful compared to other years of Kellogg's. Cards from this set may be found without the laminated finish that creates the 3D effect.

COMPLETE SET (66) 12.50 30.00
1 George Foster .07 .20
2 Jim Palmer .40 1.00
3 Reggie Jackson .60 1.50
4 Al Oliver .07 .20
5 Mike Schmidt .75 2.00
6 Nolan Ryan 1.50 4.00
7 Bucky Dent .07 .20
8 George Brett 1.50 4.00
9 Jim Rice .10 .30
10 Steve Garvey .20 .50
11 Willie Stargell .30 .75
12 Phil Niekro .40 1.00
13 Dave Parker .10 .30
14 Cesar Cedeno .02 .10
15 Don Baylor .07 .20
16 J.R. Richard .02 .10
17 Tony Perez .30 .75
18 Eddie Murray .75 2.00
19 Chet Lemon .02 .10
20 Ben Oglivie .02 .10
21 Dave Winfield .60 1.50
22 Joe Morgan .30 .75
23 Vida Blue .07 .20
24 Willie Wilson .02 .10
25 Steve Henderson .02 .10
26 Rod Carew .40 1.00
27 Garry Templeton .02 .10
28 Dave Concepcion .07 .20
29 Dave Lopes .07 .20
30 Ken Landreaux .02 .10
31 Keith Hernandez .07 .20
32 Cecil Cooper .07 .20
33 Rickey Henderson 1.50 4.00
34 Frank White .07 .20
35 George Hendrick .02 .10
36 Reggie Smith .07 .20
37 Tug McGraw .07 .20
38 Tom Seaver .60 1.50
39 Ken Singleton .02 .10
40 Fred Lynn .07 .20
41 Rich Gossage .10 .30
42 Terry Puhl .02 .10
43 Larry Bowa .02 .10
44 Phil Garner .07 .20
45 Ron Guidry .07 .20
46 Lee Mazzilli .02 .10
47 Dave Kingman .10 .30
48 Carl Yastrzemski .40 1.00
49 Rick Burleson .02 .10
50 Steve Carlton .40 1.00
51 Alan Trammell .30 .75
52 Tommy John .10 .30
53 Paul Molitor .75 2.00
54 Joe Charboneau .20 .50
55 Rick Langford .02 .10
56 Bruce Sutter .40 1.00
57 Robin Yount .60 1.50
58 Steve Stone .02 .10
59 Larry Gura .02 .10
60 Mike Flanagan .02 .10
61 Bob Horner .02 .10
62 Bruce Bochte .02 .10
63 Pete Rose .75 2.00
64 Buddy Bell .07 .20
65 Johnny Bench .60 1.50
66 Mike Hargrove .07 .20

1982 Kellogg's

The cards in this 64-card set measure 2 1/8" by 3 1/4". The 1982 version of 3-D cards prepared for the Kellogg Company by Visual Panographics, Inc., is not only smaller in physical dimensions from the 1981 series (which was standard card size at 2 1/2" by 3 1/2") but is also two cards shorter in length (64 in '82 and 66 in '81). In addition, while retaining the policy of not inserting single cards into cereal packages and offering the sets through box-top mail-ins only, the Kellogg Company accepted box tops from four types of cereals, as opposed to only one type the previous year. Each card features a color 3-D ballplayer picture with a vertical line of white stars on each side set upon a blue background. The player's name and the word Kellogg's are printed in red on the obverse, and the card number is found on the bottom right of the reverse. Every card in the set has a statistical procedural error that was never corrected. All seasonal averages were added up and then divided by the number of seasons played.

COMPLETE SET (64) 12.50 30.00
1 Richie Zisk .02 .10
2 Bill Buckner .07 .20
3 George Brett 1.50 4.00
4 Rickey Henderson 1.25 3.00
5 Jack Morris .10 .30
6 Ozzie Smith 1.25 3.00
7 Rollie Fingers .30 .75
8 Tom Seaver .60 1.50
9 Fernando Valuenzuela .20 .50
10 Hubie Brooks .02 .10
11 Nolan Ryan 1.50 4.00
12 Dave Winfield .40 1.00
13 Bob Horner .02 .10
14 Reggie Jackson .60 1.50
15 Burt Hooton .02 .10
16 Mike Schmidt .75 2.00
17 Bruce Sutter .30 .75
18 Pete Rose .75 2.00
19 Dave Kingman .10 .30
20 Neil Allen .02 .10
21 Don Sutton .30 .75
22 Dave Concepcion .07 .20
23 Keith Hernandez .07 .20
24 Gary Carter .30 .75
25 Carlton Fisk .60 1.50
26 Ron Guidry .07 .20
27 Steve Carlton .40 1.00
28 Robin Yount .60 1.50
29 John Castino .02 .10
30 Johnny Bench .40 1.00
31 Bob Knepper .02 .10
32 Rich Gossage .07 .20
33 Buddy Bell .07 .20
34 Art Howe .02 .10
35 Tony Armas .02 .10
36 Phil Niekro .30 .75
37 Len Barker .02 .10
38 Bob Grich .07 .20
39 Steve Kemp .02 .10
40 Kirk Gibson .20 .50
41 Carney Lansford .02 .10
42 Jim Palmer .40 1.00
43 Carl Yastrzemski .40 1.00
44 Rick Burleson .02 .10
45 Dwight Evans .07 .20
46 Ron Cey .07 .20
47 Steve Garvey .20 .50
48 Dave Parker .10 .30
49 Mike Easler .02 .10
50 Dusty Baker .07 .20
51 Rod Carew .40 1.00
52 Chris Chambliss .07 .20
53 Tim Raines .20 .50
54 Chet Lemon .02 .10
55 Bill Madlock .07 .20
56 George Foster .07 .20
57 Dwayne Murphy .02 .10
58 Ken Singleton .02 .10
59 Mike Norris .02 .10
60 Cecil Cooper .07 .20
61 Al Oliver .07 .20
62 Willie Wilson .02 .10
63 Vida Blue .07 .20
64 Eddie Murray .75 2.00

1983 Kellogg's

The cards in this 60-card set measure approximately 1 7/8" by 3 1/4". For the 14th year in a row and final year, the Kellogg Company issued a card set of Major League players. The set of 3-D cards contains the photo, player's autograph, Kellogg's logo, and name and position of the player on the front of the card. The backs feature the player's team logo, career statistics, player biography, and a narrative on the player's career. Every card in the set has a statistical procedural error that was never corrected. All seasonal averages were added up and then divided by the number of seasons played.

COMPLETE SET (60) 12.50 30.00
1 Rod Carew .40 1.00
2 Rollie Fingers .30 .75
3 Reggie Jackson .60 1.50
4 George Brett 1.25 3.00
5 Hal McRae .07 .20
6 Pete Rose .60 1.50
7 Fernando Valenzuela .10 .30
8 Rickey Henderson .75 2.00
9 Carl Yastrzemski .40 1.00
10 Rich Gossage .07 .20
11 Eddie Murray .60 1.50
12 Buddy Bell .07 .20
13 Jim Rice .10 .30
14 Robin Yount .40 1.00
15 Dave Winfield .40 1.00
16 Harold Baines .30 .75
17 Garry Templeton .02 .10
18 Bill Madlock .07 .20
19 Pete Vuckovich .02 .10
20 Pedro Guerrero .07 .20
21 Ozzie Smith .75 2.00
22 George Foster .07 .20
23 Willie Wilson .02 .10
24 Johnny Ray .02 .10
25 George Hendrick .02 .10
26 Andre Thornton .02 .10
27 Leon Durham .02 .10
28 Cecil Cooper .07 .20
29 Don Baylor .07 .20
30 Lonnie Smith .02 .10
31 Nolan Ryan 1.25 3.00
32 Dan Quisenberry .07 .20
33 Len Barker .02 .10
34 Neil Allen .02 .10
35 Jack Morris .07 .20
36 Dave Stieb .02 .10
37 Bruce Sutter .30 .75
38 Jim Sundberg .02 .10
39 Jim Palmer .40 1.00
40 Lance Parrish .07 .20

41 Floyd Bannister .02 .10
42 Larry Gura .02 .10
43 Britt Burns .02 .10
44 Toby Harrah .02 .10
45 Steve Carlton .40 1.00
46 Greg Minton .02 .10
47 Gorman Thomas .02 .10
48 Jack Clark .07 .20
49 Keith Hernandez .07 .20
50 Greg Luzinski .07 .20
51 Fred Lynn .07 .20
52 Dale Murphy .30 .75
53 Kent Hrbek .07 .20
54 Bob Horner .02 .10
55 Gary Carter .25 .60
56 Carlton Fisk .40 1.00
57 Dave Concepcion .07 .20
58 Mike Schmidt .60 1.50
59 Bill Buckner .07 .20
60 Bob Grich .07 .20

1991 Kellogg's 3D

Sportflics/Optigraphics produced this 15-card set for Kellogg's, and the cards measure approximately 2 1/2" by 3 5/16". The fronts have a three-dimensional image that alternates between a posed or action color shot and a head and shoulders close-up. The card face is aqua blue, with white stripes (that turn pink) and white borders. In red and dark blue print, the horizontally oriented backs have a facial drawing of the player on the left half, and career summary on the right half. The cards are numbered on the back. The cards were inserted in specially marked boxes (18 oz. and 24 oz. only) of Kellogg's Corn Flakes. In addition, the complete set and a blue display rack were available through a mail-in offer for 4.95 and two UPC symbols.

COMPLETE SET (15) 6.00 15.00
1 Gaylord Perry .30 .75
2 Hank Aaron .60 1.50
3 Willie Mays .60 1.50
4 Ernie Banks .60 1.50
5 Bob Gibson .30 .75
6 Harmon Killebrew .30 .75
7 Rollie Fingers .30 .75
8 Steve Carlton .40 1.00
9 Billy Williams .30 .75
10 Lou Brock .40 1.00
11 Yogi Berra .60 1.50
12 Warren Spahn .40 1.00
13 Boog Powell .20 .50
14 Don Baylor .20 .50
15 Ralph Kiner .30 .75

1991 Kellogg's Legends English

This is a parallel to the 1991 Kelloggs Legends Spanish set. Unlike the Spanish test, these cards are totally in English.

1991 Kellogg's Legends Spanish

This 11-card "Hispanic Legends of Baseball" set was sponsored by Kellogg's and celebrates ten Hispanic greats from Major League Baseball. The cards were inserted in boxes of Kellogg's Corn Flakes, Frosted Flakes, and Fruit Loops in selected geographic areas. The cards measure the standard size. The fronts feature color player photos bordered in white. The pictures are accented above and on the left by red, orange, and yellow border stripes. The set name appears on a home plate icon at the upper left corner, while the player's name appears in a white bar that cuts across the picture. On the bilingual (Spanish and English) backs, the biographical and statistical information are vertically oriented on the left portion, while a black and white head shot and player profile fill out the remainder of the back. The cards are unnumbered and checklisted below in alphabetical order. This set also comes saying "Kellogs Legends of Baseball" in English on the front with an English only back.

COMPLETE SET (11) 6.00 15.00
1 Bert Campaneris .30 .75
2 Rod Carew 1.25 3.00
3 Rico Carty .30 .75
4 Cesar Cedeno .30 .75
5 Orlando Cepeda .60 1.50
6 Roberto Clemente 5.00 12.00
7 Mike Cuellar .30 .75
8 Ed Figueroa .20 .50
9 Minnie Minoso .60 1.50
10 Manny Sanguillen .20 .50
NNO Title Card .20 .50

1991 Kellogg's Stand Ups

This set was sponsored by Kellogg's in honor of six retired baseball stars as part of a promotion entitled "Baseball Greats." Six different stars are featured on the backs of (specially marked 7 oz. and 12 oz.) Kellogg's Corn Flakes boxes. Since there were two different size boxes, there are two sizes of each card, the larger is approximately 9 1/4" by 6" coming from the 12 oz. box. The color action portraits can be cut out and stood up for display, and career highlights appear to the right of the stand up. The boxes are unnumbered and checklisted below in alphabetical order. All six of these players were also included in the 15-card Kellogg's 3D Baseball Greats set. The complete set price below includes either the small or the large package cards but not both.

COMPLETE SET (6) 4.00 10.00
1 Hank Aaron 1.50 4.00
2 Ernie Banks 1.25 3.00
3 Yogi Berra 1.25 3.00
4 Lou Brock .75 2.00
5 Steve Carlton .75 2.00
6 Bob Gibson 1.00 2.50

1992 Kellogg's All-Stars

This ten-card standard-size set was produced by Optigraphics Corp. (Grand Prairie, TX) for Kellogg's and features retired baseball stars. One card was protected by a cello pack and inserted into Kellogg's cereal boxes. In the U.S., the cards were inserted in boxes of Corn Flakes, while in Canada they were inserted in Frosted Flakes and some other cereals. The complete set and a baseball display board to hold the collection were available through a mail-in offer for 4.75 and two UPC symbols from the side panel of Corn Flakes boxes (in Canada, for 7.99 and three tokens; one token was found on the side panel of each cereal box). The front of the "Double Action" cards have a three-dimensional image that alternates between two action shots and gives the impression of a batter or pitcher in motion. The pictures are bordered in red, white, and blue. The backs carry a black and white close-up photo, summary of the player's career (teams and years he played for them), awards, and career highlights. The Canadian Frosted Flakes cards are valued at two times the values listed below. The box back pictures both images of the Seaver card. While these pictures resemble the actual card, they are not standard-size or even rectangulary shaped.

COMPLETE SET (10) 2.50 6.00
1 Willie Stargell .30 .75
2 Tony Perez .20 .50
3 Jim Palmer .40 1.00
4 Rod Carew .40 1.00
5 Tom Seaver .60 1.50
6 Phil Niekro .30 .75
7 Bill Madlock .08 .25
8 Jim Rice .20 .50
9 Dan Quisenberry .08 .25
10 Mike Schmidt .75 2.00

1994 Kellogg's Clemente

Protected by a clear plastic cello pack, these three standard-size cards were inserted into Kellogg's Corn Flakes cereal boxes in Puerto Rico, one card per box. The 18-ounce boxes commemorate the 20th anniversary of Clemente's 3,000th hit, the foundation of the Ciudad Deportiva Roberto Clemente, and his unexpected death. The fronts feature color action player photos bordered in white. The pictures are accented by green, blue and red stripes. The player's name and number are printed inside a yellow bar on the bottom of the photo. The team logo appears in the upper right corner, while the set name appears on a home plate icon at the upper left corner. On the backs, the biographical and statistical information are vertically oriented on the left portion, while a black-and-white head shot and player profile fill out the remainder. All text is in Spanish.

COMPLETE SET (3) 60.00 150.00
COMMON CARD (1-3) 20.00 50.00

1988 Kenner Starting Lineup Unissued

These ten standard-size cards were supposed to be included (along with the accompanying statues) in the 1988 Kenner release. Most of these players were traded either after production of the cards or were released by the teams they were then playing for. Please keep us informed of any other interesting Kenner cards which may never have made the market. These cards are not numbered so we have sequenced them in alphabetical order

COMPLETE SET (9) 60.00 120.00
1 Phil Bradley 4.00 10.00
2 Chili Davis 6.00 15.00
3 Mike Davis 4.00 10.00
4 Richard Dotson 4.00 10.00
5 Kirk Gibson 10.00 25.00
6 Goose Gossage 8.00 20.00
7 Ray Knight 4.00 10.00
8 Lee Smith 6.00 15.00
9 Bob Welch 4.00 10.00
10 Glenn Wilson 4.00 10.00

1997 Kenner Starting Lineup Collector's Club Cards

1 Nolan Ryan 4.00 10.00
Jacksonville Suns

1977 Jim Rowe 4-in-1 Exhibits

COMPLETE SET (16) 20.00 50.00
1 Luke Appling 2.00 5.00
Ted Lyons
Red Ruffing
Red Faber
2 Jim Bottomley 2.00 5.00
Earle Combs
George Sisler
Rogers Hornsby
3 Dizzy Dean 3.00 8.00
Stan Musial
Jesse Haines
Frank Frisch
4 Joe DiMaggio 3.00 8.00
Lefty Gomez
Lou Gehrig
Bill Dickey
5 Bob Feller 2.00 5.00
Lou Boudreau
Earl Averill
Bob Lemon
6 Jimmie Foxx 2.00 5.00
Grover Alexander
Robin Roberts
Eppa Rixey
7 Hank Greenberg 3.00 8.00
Charlie Gehringer
Ty Cobb
Goose Goslin
8 Chick Hafey 2.00 5.00
Edd Roush
Bill McKechnie
George Kelly
9 Freddy Lindstom 2.00 5.00
Billy Herman
Kiki Kyler
Gabby Hartnett
10 Heinie Manush 2.00 5.00
Walter Johnson
Bucky Harris
Sam Rice
11 Joe Medwick 2.00 5.00
Max Carey
Dazzy Vance
Burleigh Grimes
12 Mel Ott 2.00 5.00
Carl Hubbell
Dave Bancroft
Bill Terry
13 Al Simmons 2.00 5.00
Lefty Grove
Mickey Cochrane
Eddie Collins
14 Warren Spahn 2.00 5.00
Al Lopez
Casey Stengel
Rabbit Marrinville
15 Pie Traynor 3.00 8.00
Lloyd Waner
Honus Wagner
Paul Waner
16 Ted Williams 4.00 10.00
Herb Pennock
Babe Ruth
Joe Cronin

1987 Kentucky Bluegrass State Games

This 24-card set of standard size cards was co-sponsored by Coca-Cola and Valvoline, and their company logos appear on the bottom of the card face. The card sets were originally given out by the Kentucky county sheriff's departments and the Kentucky Highway Patrol. Reportedly about 350 sets were given to the approximately 120 counties in the state of Kentucky. One card per week was given out from May 25 to October 19, 1987. Once all 22 of the numbered cards were collected, they could be turned in to a local sheriff's department for prizes. The front features a color action player photo, on a blue card face with a white outer border. The player's name and the "Champions Against Drugs" insignia appear below the picture. The back has a anti-drug or alcohol tip on a gray background, with white border. The set commemorates Kentucky's hosting of the 1987 Bluegrass State Games and was endorsed by Governor Martha Layne Collins in Kentucky's Champions Against Drugs Crusade for Youth. The set features stars from a variety of sports as well as public figures. The two cards in the set numbered "SC" for special card were not distributed with the regular cards; they were produced in smaller quantities than the 22 numbered cards. The set features the first card of NBA superstar David Robinson. Reportedly the Robinson cards were distributed at the March 1987 Kentucky Boy's State High School Tournament in Rupp Arena, when David Robinson was in attendance.

COMPLETE SET (24) 25.00 60.00
5 Doug Flynn B .30 .75
13 Pee Wee Reese B 1.60 4.00
22 A.B. Happy Chandler B .40 1.00

1987 Key Food Discs

This set is a parallel to the 1987 MSA Iced Tea Discs. They say Key Food on the front and are valued the same as the regular discs.

COMPLETE SET (20) 3.00 8.00
1 Darryl Strawberry .07 .20
2 Roger Clemens .50 1.25
3 Ron Darling .02 .10
4 Keith Hernandez .07 .20
5 Tony Pena .02 .10
6 Don Mattingly .50 1.25
7 Eric Davis .07 .20
8 Gary Carter .30 .75
9 Dave Winfield .30 .75
10 Wally Joyner .20 .50
11 Mike Schmidt .30 .75
12 Robby Thompson .02 .10
13 Wade Boggs .30 .75
14 Cal Ripken 1.00 2.50
15 Dale Murphy .20 .50
16 Tony Gwynn .75 2.00
17 Jose Canseco .30 .75
18 Rickey Henderson .30 1.00
19 Lance Parrish .02 .10
20 Dave Righetti .02 .10

1988 Key Food Discs

For the second year, Key Foods was one of the title sponsors of the MSA Iced Tea Discs. The words Key Foods are on the front. They are valued the same as the regular discs.

COMPLETE SET (20) 4.00 10.00
1 Wade Boggs .60 1.00
2 Ellis Burks .30 .75
3 Don Mattingly .75 2.00
4 Mark McGwire .75 2.00
5 Matt Nokes .02 .10
6 Kirby Puckett .50 1.25
7 Billy Ripken .02 .10
8 Kevin Seitzer .02 .10
9 Roger Clemens .75 2.00
10 Will Clark .30 .75
11 Vince Coleman .02 .10
12 Eric Davis .08 .25
13 Dave Magadan .02 .10
14 Dale Murphy .20 .50
15 Benito Santiago .08 .25
16 Mike Schmidt .40 1.00
17 Darryl Strawberry .08 .25
18 Steve Bedrosian .02 .10
19 Dwight Gooden .08 .25
20 Fernando Valenzuela .08 .25

1989 Key Food Discs

For the third year, the MSA Iced Tea Discs were also issued by the Key Foods brand. These discs, parallel to the MSA Iced Tea discs are valued the same as those discs.

COMPLETE SET (20) 15.00 40.00
1 Don Mattingly 2.50 6.00
2 Dave Cone .40 1.00
(David)
3 Mark McGwire 2.50 6.00
4 Will Clark 1.00 2.50
5 Darryl Strawberry .60 1.50
6 Dwight Gooden .60 1.50
7 Wade Boggs 1.25 3.00
8 Roger Clemens 2.50 6.00
9 Benito Santiago .60 1.50
10 Orel Hershiser .60 1.50
11 Eric Davis .60 1.50
12 Kirby Puckett 2.00 5.00
13 Dave Winfield 1.50 4.00
14 Andre Dawson 1.00 2.50
15 Steve Bedrosian .40 1.00
16 Cal Ripken 5.00 12.00
17 Andy Van Slyke .40 1.00
18 Jose Canseco 1.25 3.00
19 Jose Oquendo .40 1.00
20 Dale Murphy .75 2.00

1983 KG Glossy

Despite being similar to the 1983 Topps Glossy mail-away set and it is possible that these cards were issued as a test for that set. It is believed that these cards were issued by KG. Since the cards are unnumbered, we have sequenced them in alphabetical order. It is believed that these cards were printed and test released in Michigan. Any further information on this issue is appreciated.

COMPLETE SET 12.50 30.00
1 Wade Boggs 2.50 6.00
2 George Brett 1.00 2.50
3 Rod Carew .60 1.50
4 Steve Carlton .60 1.50
5 Gary Carter .40 1.25
6 Steve Garvey .40 1.00
Dodgers
7 Steve Garvey .40 1.00
Padres
8 Reggie Jackson .60 1.50
9 Ron Kittle .20 .50
10 Bill Madlock .20 .50
11 Dale Murphy .40 1.00
12 Eddie Murray .50 1.25
13 Jim Palmer .50 1.25
14 Lance Parrish .20 .50
15 Cal Ripken 2.00 5.00
16 Pete Rose .75 2.00
17 Steve Sax .20 .50
18 Mike Schmidt .50 1.25
19 Tom Seaver .60 1.50
20 Fernando Valenzuela .40 1.00
21 Dave Winfield .50 1.25
22 Carl Yastrzemski .50 1.25
23 Robin Yount .50 1.25
24 George Brett 2.00 5.00
25 Dale Murphy 1.00 2.50
26 Pete Rose 2.00 5.00

1888 Kimball's N184

This set of 50 color pictures of contemporary athletes was Kimball's answer to the sets produced by Allen and Ginter (N28 and N29) and Goodwin (N162). Issued in 1888, the cards are backlisted but are not numbered. The cards are listed below in alphabetical order without regard to sport. There are four baseball players in the set. An album (catalog: A42) was offered as a premium in exchange for coupons found in the tobacco packages. The baseball players are noted in the checklist below by BB after their name; boxers are noted by BOX.

COMPLETE SET (50) 7000.00
6 E.A.(Ernie) Burch BB 350.00 700.00
10 Dell Darling BB 350.00 700.00
19 Hardie Henderson BB 350.00 700.00
33 James O'Neil BB UER# 400.00 800.00

1988 King B Discs

In 1988 King-B Quality Meat Products (Beef Jerky) introduced a set of 24 discs produced in conjunction with the Major League Baseball Players Association and Mike Schechter Associates. A single disc was inserted inside each specially marked package. The discs are numbered on the back and have a medium blue border on the front. Discs are approximately 2 3/8" in diameter. The disc backs contain very sparse personal or statistical information about the player and are printed in blue on white stock.

COMPLETE SET (24) 30.00 60.00
1 Mike Schmidt 1.50 4.00
2 Dale Murphy 1.00 2.50
3 Kirby Puckett 1.50 4.00
4 Ozzie Smith 3.00 8.00
5 Tony Gwynn 4.00 10.00
6 Mark McGwire 3.00 8.00
7 George Brett 4.00 10.00
8 Darryl Strawberry .60 1.50
9 Wally Joyner .60 1.50
10 Cory Snyder .40 1.00
11 Barry Bonds 5.00 12.00
12 Darrell Evans .60 1.50
13 Mike Scott .40 1.00
14 Andre Dawson 1.00 2.50
15 Don Mattingly 3.00 8.00
16 Candy Maldonado .40 1.00
17 Alvin Davis .40 1.00
18 Carlton Fisk 1.50 4.00
19 Fernando Valenzuela .60 1.50
20 Roger Clemens 3.00 8.00
21 Larry Parrish .40 1.00
22 Eric Davis .60 1.50
23 Paul Molitor 1.50 4.00
24 Cal Ripken 6.00 15.00

1989 King B Discs

The 1989 King-B Disc set contains 24 discs, each measuring approximately 2 3/4" in diameter. The set was prepared by MSA; there are no team logos featured on the disc. The year and lifetime statistics are featured for each player on the back of the disc. The discs were issued one per small cannister of Beef Jerky. It has been estimated that five million discs were produced for this set.

COMPLETE SET (24) 12.50 30.00
1 Kirk Gibson .20 .50
2 Eddie Murray .75 2.00
3 Wade Boggs .60 1.50
4 Mark McGwire 2.00 5.00
5 Ryne Sandberg 1.25 3.00
6 Ozzie Guillen .20 .50
7 Chris Sabo .08 .25
8 Joe Carter .30 .75
9 Alan Trammell .30 .75
10 Nolan Ryan 5.00 12.00
11 Bo Jackson .75 2.00
12 Orel Hershiser .20 .50
13 Robin Yount 1.25 3.00
14 Frank Viola .08 .25
15 Darryl Strawberry .20 .50
16 Dave Winfield 1.25 3.00
17 Jose Canseco 1.25 3.00
18 Von Hayes .08 .25
19 Andy Van Slyke .20 .50
20 Pedro Guerrero .08 .25
21 Tony Gwynn 2.50 6.00
22 Will Clark .75 2.00
23 Danny Jackson .08 .25
24 Pete Incaviglia .08 .25

1990 King B Discs

The 1990 King-B Disc set contains 24 discs, each measuring approximately 2 3/4" inches in diameter. The set was prepared by MSA; there are no team logos featured on the disc. The discs were issued one per small cannister of Beef Jerky.

COMPLETE SET (24) 12.50 30.00
1 Mike Scott .08 .25
2 Kevin Mitchell .08 .25
3 Tony Gwynn 2.00 5.00
4 Ozzie Smith 1.50 4.00
5 Kirk Gibson .20 .50
6 Tim Raines .20 .50
7 Von Hayes .08 .25
8 Bobby Bonilla .08 .25
9 Wade Boggs .75 2.00
10 Chris Sabo .08 .25
11 Dale Murphy .40 1.00
12 Cory Snyder .08 .25
13 Fred McGriff .60 1.50
14 Don Mattingly 2.00 5.00
15 Jerome Walton .08 .25
16 Ken Griffey Jr. 4.00 10.00
17 Bo Jackson .20 .50
18 Robin Yount 1.00 2.50
19 Rickey Henderson 1.00 2.50
20 Jim Abbott .30 .75
21 Kirby Puckett .60 1.50
22 Nolan Ryan 4.00 10.00
23 Gregg Olson .08 .25
24 Lou Whitaker .20 .50

1991 King B Discs

This was the fourth season that MSA issued discs as inserts in King-B meat products. These discs, which measure approximately 2 3/4" in diameter, feature leading major leaguers.

COMPLETE SET (24) 8.00 20.00
1 Willie McGee .20 .50
2 Kevin Seitzer .08 .25
3 Kevin Maas .08 .25
4 Ben McDonald .08 .25
5 Rickey Henderson 1.00 2.50
6 Ken Griffey Jr. 2.50 6.00
7 John Olerud .30 .75
8 Dwight Gooden .20 .50
9 Ruben Sierra .20 .50
10 Luis Polonia .08 .25
11 Wade Boggs .75 2.00
12 Ramon Martinez .08 .25
13 Craig Biggio .60 1.50
14 Cecil Fielder .20 .50
15 Will Clark .60 1.50
16 Matt Williams .40 1.00
17 Sandy Alomar Jr. .20 .50
18 Dave Justice .40 1.00
19 Ryne Sandberg 1.25 3.00
20 Benito Santiago .08 .25
21 Barry Bonds 2.00 5.00
22 Carlton Fisk .60 1.50
23 Kirby Puckett .75 2.00
24 Jose Rijo .08 .25

1992 King B Discs

These discs, which measure approximately 2 3/4" in diameter, feature top major league stars. These discs, inserted in beef jerky containers, were issued in conjunction with Michael Schecter Associates.

COMPLETE SET (24) 5.00 12.00
1 Terry Pendleton .02 .10
2 Chris Sabo .02 .10
3 Frank Thomas .30 .75
4 Todd Zeile .07 .20
5 Bobby Bonilla .02 .10
6 Howard Johnson .02 .10
7 Nolan Ryan 1.25 3.00
8 Ken Griffey Jr. .75 2.00
9 Roger Clemens .60 1.50
10 Tony Gwynn .60 1.50
11 Steve Avery .02 .10
12 Cal Ripken 1.25 3.00
13 Danny Tartabull .02 .10
14 Paul Molitor .30 .75
15 Willie McGee .07 .20
16 Wade Boggs .40 1.00
17 Cecil Fielder .07 .20
18 Jack Morris .07 .20
19 Ryne Sandberg .50 1.25
20 Kirby Puckett .40 1.00
21 Craig Biggio .15 .40
22 Harold Baines .10 .30
23 Scott Erickson .02 .10
24 Joe Carter .07 .20

1993 King B Discs

These discs marked the sixth consecutive season that Michael Schecter Associates in conjunction with King-B meat products produced a 24 disc set. This set measure approximately 2 3/4" in diameter and features major league stars.

COMPLETE SET (24) 3.00 8.00
1 Barry Bonds .40 1.00
2 Ken Griffey Jr. .50 1.25
3 Cal Ripken .75 2.00
4 Frank Thomas .20 .50
5 Steve Avery .02 .10
6 Benito Santiago .07 .20
7 Luis Polonia .02 .10
8 Jose Rijo .02 .10
9 George Brett .40 1.00
10 Darren Daulton .07 .20
11 Cecil Fielder .07 .20
12 Ozzie Smith .30 .75
13 Joe Carter .07 .20
14 Dwight Gooden .07 .20
15 Tom Henke .02 .10
16 Brett Butler .07 .20
17 Nolan Ryan .75 2.00
18 Sandy Alomar .07 .20
19 Tom Glavine .20 .50
20 Rafael Palmeiro .15 .40
21 Roger Clemens .40 1.00
22 Ryne Sandberg .30 .75
23 Doug Drabek .02 .10
24 Chuck Knoblauch .15 .40

1994 King B Discs

The 1994 King-B set contains 24 round cards each measuring approximately 2 7/8" in diameter.

COMPLETE SET (24) 2.00 5.00
1 Fred McGriff .10 .30
2 Paul Molitor .25 .60
3 Jack McDowell .02 .10
4 Darren Daulton .07 .20
5 Wade Boggs .20 .50
6 Ken Griffey Jr. .60 1.50
7 Tim Salmon .15 .40
8 Dennis Eckersley .25 .60
9 Albert Belle .07 .20
10 Travis Fryman .07 .20
11 Chris Hoiles .02 .10
12 Kirby Puckett .25 .60
13 John Olerud .10 .30
14 Frank Thomas .20 .50
15 Lenny Dykstra .07 .20
16 Andres Galarraga .15 .40
17 Barry Larkin .15 .40
18 Greg Maddux .40 1.00
19 Mike Piazza .40 1.00
20 Roberto Alomar .15 .40
21 Robin Ventura .15 .40
22 Ryne Sandberg .30 .75
23 Andy Van Slyke .07 .20
24 Barry Bonds .40 1.00

1995 King B Discs

This was the eighth year that King-B, in conjunction with MSA enterprises, issued discs. The players featured are among the best in baseball. The backs have season and career stats as well as vital statistics.

COMPLETE SET (24) 8.00 20.00
1 Roberto Alomar .20 .50
2 Jeff Bagwell .50 1.25
3 Wade Boggs .50 1.25
4 Barry Bonds 1.00 2.50
5 Joe Carter .07 .20
6 Mariano Duncan .02 .10
7 Len Dykstra .07 .20
8 Andres Galarraga .20 .50
9 Matt Williams .10 .30
10 Raul Mondesi .07 .20
11 Ken Griffey Jr. 1.50 4.00
12 Gregg Jefferies .02 .10
13 Fred McGriff .10 .30
14 Paul Molitor .40 1.00
15 Dave Justice .20 .50
16 Mike Piazza 1.25 3.00
17 Kirby Puckett .50 1.25
18 Cal Ripken 2.00 5.00
19 Ivan Rodriguez .40 1.00
20 Ozzie Smith .60 1.50
21 Gary Sheffield .40 1.00
22 Frank Thomas .30 .75
23 Greg Maddux 1.25 3.00
24 Jimmy Key .07 .20

1996 King B Discs

The 1996 King-B set consists of 24 round cards measuring approximately 2 7/8" in diameter. The fronts feature a color player photo with airbrushed unitorms. The year 1996 is on the left side, while the player's name and 9th annual Collectors edition appears on the bottom. The back has vital statistics, season and career statistics.

COMPLETE SET (24) 8.00 20.00
1 Roger Clemens 1.00 2.50
2 Mo Vaughn .08 .25
3 Dante Bichette .08 .25
4 Jeff Bagwell .50 1.25
5 Randy Johnson .50 1.25
6 Ken Griffey Jr. 1.25 3.00
7 Kirby Puckett .40 1.00
8 Orel Hershiser .08 .25
9 Albert Belle .08 .25
10 Tony Gwynn 1.00 2.50
11 Tom Glavine .30 .75
12 Jim Abbott .08 .25
13 Andres Galarraga .30 .75
14 Frank Thomas .30 .75
15 Barry Larkin .30 .75
16 Mike Piazza 1.25 3.00
17 Matt Williams .20 .50
18 Greg Maddux 1.25 3.00
19 Hideo Nomo 1.00 2.50
20 Roberto Alomar .30 .75
21 Ivan Rodriguez .40 1.00
22 Cal Ripken 2.00 5.00
23 Barry Bonds 1.00 2.50
24 Mark McGwire .75 2.00

1997 King B Discs

This 28-card set of rounded cards measures approximately 2 5/16" in diameter. The fronts feature color action player images on a black-and-gold marblized background. The backs carry player information and career statistics on a black-and-white player photo background. This set marks the 10th Anniversary of the King-B Discs.

COMPLETE SET (28) 8.00 20.00
1 Brady Anderson .15 .40
2 Barry Bonds 1.00 2.50
3 Travis Fryman .15 .40
4 Rey Ordonez .07 .20
5 Kenny Lofton .25 .60
6 Mark McGwire .75 2.00
7 Jeff Bagwell .50 1.25
8 Roger Clemens 1.00 2.50
9 Juan Gonzalez .40 1.00
10 Mike Piazza

3 8884470102.00

1997 King B Discs

11 Tim Salmon .30 .75
12 Jeff Montgomery .07 .20
13 Joe Carter .15 .40
14 David Cone .30 .75
15 Frank Thomas .40 1.00
16 Mickey Morandini .07 .20
17 Ray Lankford .15 .40
18 Pedro Martinez .50 1.25
19 Tom Glavine .40 1.00
20 Chuck Knoblauch .30 .75
21 Dan Wilson .07 .20
22 Gary Sheffield .50 1.25
23 Dante Bichette .07 .20
24 Al Martin .07 .20
25 Barry Larkin .30 .75
26 Ryne Sandberg .60 1.50
27 Steve Finley .15 .40
28 Matt Mieske .07 .20

1998 King B Discs

These 28 discs were issued in 1998 with King-B and honored some of the leading players in baseball. For the first time, this set was issued in conjuction with Pacific Trading Cards.

COMPLETE SET 6.00 15.00
1 Brady Anderson .07 .20
2 Barry Bonds 1.00 2.50
3 Tony Clark .02 .10
4 Rey Ordonez .02 .10
5 Travis Fryman .07 .20
6 Jason Giambi .07 .20
7 Jeff Bagwell .50 1.25
8 Tim Naehring .04 .10
9 Juan Gonzalez .20 .50
10 Mike Piazza 1.25 3.00
11 Tim Salmon .20 .50
12 Jeff Montgomery .02 .10
13 Tom Glavine .20 .50
14 Chuck Knoblauch .07 .20
15 Dan Wilson .02 .10
16 Gary Sheffield .40 1.00
17 Dante Bichette .02 .10
18 Al Martin .02 .10
19 Roger Clemens 1.00 2.50
20 David Cone .20 .50
21 Frank Thomas .40 1.00
22 Mike Lieberthal .07 .20
23 Ray Lankford .07 .20
24 Rondell White .07 .20
25 Barry Larkin .20 .50
26 Matt Mieske .02 .10
27 Steve Finley .07 .20
28 Fernando Vina .02 .10

1999 King B Discs

For the 12th consecutive year, King-B issued discs with their products. This set features some of the leading players in Baseball. This set was issued in conjunction with Pacific Trading Cards and features a color photo on the front and a black and white player photo on the back.

COMPLETE SET 8.00 20.00
1 Brady Anderson .07 .20
2 Barry Bonds 1.00 2.50
3 Scott Rolen .30 .75
4 Tony Clark .02 .10
5 Jeff Bagwell .50 1.25
6 Roberto Alomar .25 .60
7 Mark Kotsay .02 .10
8 Juan Gonzalez .25 .60
9 Tim Salmon .07 .20
10 Tom Glavine .30 .75
11 Frank Thomas .50 1.25
12 Dan Wilson .02 .10
13 Dante Bichette .02 .10
14 Mickey Morandini .02 .10
15 Fred McGriff .15 .40
16 Andy Benes .02 .10
17 Al Martin .02 .10
17 Jeff Montgomery .02 .10
18 Pedro Martinez .50 1.25
19 Barry Larkin .25 .60
20 Carlos Delgado .50 1.25
21 Mike Myers .02 .10
22 Ray Lankford .07 .20
23 Brad Radke .02 .10
25 Raul Mondesi .07 .20
26 Ugueth Urbina .02 .10
27 Derek Jeter 2.00 5.00
28 Ben Grieve .02 .10
29 Mike Piazza 1.00 2.50
30 Wally Joyner .02 .10

2000 King B Discs

COMPLETE SET (30) 8.00 20.00
1 Nomar Garciaparra .80 2.00
2 Larry Walker .30 .60
3 Manny Ramirez 1.25
4 Carlos Beltran .30 .75
5 Mark McGwire .75 2.00
6 Jeromy Burnitz .10 .20
7 Carlos Delgado .50 1.25
8 Tom Glavine .75
9 Shawn Green .30 .60
10 Mark Kotsay .04 .10
11 Warren Morris .04 .10
12 Fred McGriff .20 .40
13 Brady Anderson .04 .10
14 Jeff Bagwell .50 1.25
15 Tony Clark .04 .10
16 Ben Grieve .04 .10
17 Vladimir Guerrero .60 1.50
18 Tony Gwynn 1.00 2.50
19 Derek Jeter 2.00 5.00
20 Barry Larkin .30 .60
21 Rafael Palmeiro .25 .60
22 Mike Piazza 1.20 3.00
23 Brad Radke .04 .10
24 Scott Rolen .20 .40
25 Tim Salmon .10 .20
26 Frank Thomas .80 1.25
27 Mark Grace .30 .60
28 Jeff Kent .30 .60
29 Dan Wilson .04 .10
30 Jay Bell .04 .10

2001 King B Discs

COMPLETE SET (30) 8.00 20.00
1 Brady Anderson .10 .20
2 Jeff Bagwell .50 1.25
3 Jay Bell .04 .10
4 Carlos Beltran .30 .75
5 Jeromy Burnitz .10 .20
6 Tony Clark .04 .10
7 Carlos Delgado .50 1.25
8 Nomar Garciaparra .80 2.00
9 Tom Glavine .30 .75
10 Mark Grace .30 .60

Card	Low	High
11 Shawn Green	.30	.60
12 Ben Grieve	.10	.20
13 Vladimir Guerrero	.50	1.25
14 Tony Gwynn	1.00	2.50
15 Barry Larkin	.30	.60
16 Derek Jeter	2.00	5.00
17 Jeff Kent	.30	.60
18 Mark Kotsay	.04	.10
19 Fred McGriff	.20	.40
20 Mark McGwire	.75	2.00
21 Warren Morris	.04	.10
22 Rafael Palmeiro	.25	.60
23 Mike Piazza	1.00	2.50
24 Brad Radke	.10	.20
25 Manny Ramirez	.50	1.25
26 Scott Rolen	.30	.75
27 Tim Salmon	.10	.20
28 Frank Thomas	.60	1.25
29 Larry Walker	.30	.60
30 Dan Wilson	.04	.10

2002 King B Discs

Card	Low	High
COMPLETE SET (28)	8.00	20.00
1 Randy Johnson	.50	1.25
2 Curt Schilling	.40	1.00
3 Chipper Jones	.60	1.50
4 Greg Maddux	.75	2.00
5 John Burkett	.07	.20
6 Manny Ramirez	.40	1.00
7 Barry Larkin	.25	.60
8 Roberto Alomar	.30	.75
9 Chuck Finley	.20	.40
10 Jim Thome	.40	1.00
11 Juan Gonzalez	.25	.60
12 Larry Walker	.30	.75
13 Charles Johnson	.07	.20
14 Moises Alou	.20	.40
15 Gary Sheffield	.40	1.00
16 Chan Ho Park	.07	.20
17 Vladimir Guerrero	.50	1.25
18 Roger Clemens	.75	2.00
19 Mariano Rivera	.30	.75
20 Jason Giambi	.25	.60
21 Rich Aurilia	.07	.20
22 Jeff Kent	.25	.60
23 Edgar Martinez	.25	.60
24 Kazuhiro Sasaki	.20	.40
25 Bret Boone	.20	.40
26 John Olerud	.20	.40
27 Greg Vaughn	.20	.40
28 Ivan Rodriguez	.50	1.25

1985 Kitty Clover Discs

Very similar to the KAS test set, there was a Kitty Clover test set as well. The player selection is the same as the KAS test set. According to informed sources, 2000 sets were produced of this issue. The team insignias are all air-brushed out. Square corner proof versions exist and are double the prices listed below.

Card	Low	High
COMPLETE SET	25.00	60.00
1 Steve Carlton	2.50	6.00
2 Jack Clark	.75	2.00
3 Rich Gossage	.75	2.00
4 Tony Gwynn	5.00	12.00
5 Keith Hernandez	1.25	3.00
6 Bob Horner	.75	2.00
7 Kent Hrbek	.75	2.00
8 Willie McGee	1.25	3.00
9 Dan Quisenberry	.75	2.00
10 Cal Ripken	10.00	25.00
11 Ryne Sandberg	5.00	12.00
12 Mike Schmidt	4.00	10.00
13 Tom Seaver	4.00	10.00
14 Ozzie Smith	5.00	12.00
15 Rick Sutcliffe	.75	2.00
16 Bruce Sutter	2.00	5.00
17 Alan Trammell	2.00	5.00
18 Fernando Valenzuela	1.25	3.00
19 Willie Wilson	.75	2.00
20 Dave Winfield	2.50	6.00

1962 Kluszewski Charcoal Steak House

This one card postcard set features former Cincinnati Reds slugger Ted Kluszewski. The front features a photo of Klu wearing an Los Angeles Angels cap while the back features information about the Charcoal Steak House. Please note that the date of this card is noted by the cap that big Klu is wearing.

Card	Low	High
1 Ted Kluszewski	12.50	30.00

1992 Kodak Celebration Denver

Issued by Kodak to promote the Kodak Celebration of Baseball Fan Fair in Denver, August 14-16, 1992, this four-card standard-size set (plus one free admission coupon card) features Major League Baseball Players Alumni who were scheduled to appear at the show. Aside from the Jenkins card, which features a color painting of him, the fronts carry white-bordered color player action photos. The cards are unnumbered and checklisted below in alphabetical order.

Card	Low	High
COMPLETE SET (5)	5.00	12.00
1 Orlando Cepeda	1.00	2.50
2 Ferguson Jenkins Art	1.50	4.00
3 Graig Nettles	.75	2.00
4 Brooks Robinson	2.00	5.00
5 Admission Coupon Card	.40	1.00

1999 Kodak Cooperstown Collection

These six photos were produced by Kodak and featured leading players in history. These "moving" photos of which there are two on each card along with a portrait shot were issued in a specialty box. In addition, the materials you needed for a stand so the card so be displayed better were included in the box. The backs are blank. As the items are unnumbered we have sequenced them in alphabetical order.

Card	Low	High
COMPLETE SET (6)	25.00	60.00
1 Hank Aaron	4.00	10.00
2 Lou Gehrig	5.00	12.00
3 Reggie Jackson	4.00	10.00
4 Mickey Mantle	6.00	15.00
5 Jackie Robinson	5.00	12.00
6 Babe Ruth	6.00	15.00

1998 Kodak Mantle

Card	Low	High
1 Mickey Mantle 500 HR Oversized	4.00	10.00

2000 Kodak Motion Cards

Card	Low	High
COMPLETE SET (6)	24.00	60.00
1 Ken Griffey Jr.	4.80	12.00
2 Mark McGwire	4.00	10.00
3 Sammy Sosa	3.00	8.00
4 Derek Jeter	6.00	15.00
5 Mike Piazza	4.80	12.00
6 Alex Rodriguez	4.80	12.00

1985 Kondritz Trading Cards Vince Coleman

This 20 standard-size set was issued to honor Cardinal star rookie Vince Coleman who established an major league record for rookie steals.

Card	Low	High
COMPLETE SET (20)	3.00	8.00
COMMON CARD (1-20)	.20	.50

1986 Kondritz Trading Cards Ozzie Smith

This 20-card standard-size set was issued by Kondritz trading card to commemorate the career of Ozzie Smith. These 20 cards are all red bordered and say Ozzie Smith on the top with the nickname "Oz" in a white circle in the top right corner. The backs have various descriptions about his career.

Card	Low	High
COMPLETE SET (20)	8.00	20.00
COMMON CARD (1-20)	.30	.75
XX Ozzie Smith Sample		

1921 Koester Bread D383

Issued in conjunction with the first all New York World Series, these cards feature members of the Giants and Yankees. The cards measure approximately 2" by 3 1/2" and are unnumbered. Therefore, we have sequenced them in alphabetical order by team. The following players are not known in the E121 issue: Ferguson, Mitchell, O'Leary, Barnes, Berry, Brown, Burkett, Cunningham and Stengel. These players sell at a premium over the other regular cards in this set.

Card	Low	High
COMPLETE SET	1500.00	3000.00
1 Dave Bancroft	100.00	200.00
2 Jesse Barnes	50.00	100.00
3 Joe Berry	50.00	100.00
4 Eddie Brown	50.00	100.00
5 Jesse Burkett	100.00	200.00
6 George Burns	50.00	100.00
7 Red Causey	50.00	100.00
8 Bill Cunningham	50.00	100.00
9 Phil Douglas	50.00	100.00
10 Frank Frisch	100.00	200.00
11 Alex Gaston	50.00	100.00
12 Mike Gonzalez	50.00	100.00
13 Hugh Jennings CO	100.00	200.00
14 George Kelly	100.00	200.00
15 John McGraw MG	100.00	200.00
16 Irish Meusel	50.00	100.00
17 Art Nehf	75.00	150.00
18 Johnny Rawlings	50.00	100.00
19 Rosy Ryan	50.00	100.00
20 Slim Sallee	50.00	100.00
21 Pat Shea	50.00	100.00
22 Earl Smith	50.00	100.00
23 Frank Snyder	50.00	100.00
24 Casey Stengel	150.00	300.00
25 Fred Toney	50.00	100.00
26 Ross Youngs	100.00	200.00
27 Frank Baker	100.00	200.00
28 Ping Bodie	60.00	120.00
29 Rip Collins	50.00	100.00
30 Al DeVormer	50.00	100.00
31 Alex Ferguson	50.00	100.00
32 Chick Fewster	50.00	100.00
33 Harry Harper	50.00	100.00
34 Chicken Hawks	50.00	100.00
35 Fred Hofmann	50.00	100.00
36 Waite Hoyt	100.00	200.00
37 Miller Huggins MG	100.00	200.00
38 Carl Mays	75.00	150.00
39 Mike McNally	50.00	100.00
40 Bob Meusel	75.00	150.00
41 Elmer Miller	50.00	100.00
42 Johnny Mitchell	50.00	100.00
43 Charlie O'Leary CO	50.00	100.00
44 Roger Peckinpaugh	75.00	150.00
45 Bill Piercy	50.00	100.00
46 Jack Quinn	75.00	150.00
47 Tom Rogers	50.00	100.00
48 Braggo Roth	50.00	100.00
49 Babe Ruth	500.00	1000.00
50 Wally Schang	75.00	150.00
51 Bob Shawkey	75.00	150.00
52 Aaron Ward	50.00	100.00

1987 Kraft Foods

Specially marked boxes of 1987 Kraft Macaroni featured a pair of cards. The individual cards measure approximately 2 1/4" by 3 1/2" and are printed in color. The player's team insignia are airbrushed out as the set was only licensed by the Major League Baseball Players Association. The cards are blank backed and are numbered in the lower right corner of the card. The set is subtitled "Home Plate Heroes." The cards on the box provide a dotted blue line as a guide for accurately cutting the cards from the box. There were many different two-card panels. Panel prices are based on the sum of the individual player's values making up that particular panel.

Card	Low	High
COMPLETE SET (48)	10.00	25.00
1 Eddie Murray	.40	1.00
2 Dale Murphy	.30	.75
3 Cal Ripken	1.50	4.00
4 Mike Scott	.02	.10
5 Jim Rice	.08	.25
6 Jody Davis	.02	.10
7 Wade Boggs	.50	1.25
8 Ryne Sandberg	.75	2.00
9 Wally Joyner	.30	.75
10 Eric Davis	.20	.50
11 Ozzie Guillen	.08	.25
12 Tony Pena	.02	.10
13 Harold Baines	.20	.50
14 Johnny Ray	.02	.10
15 Joe Carter	.30	.75
16 Ozzie Smith	.75	2.00
17 Cory Snyder	.02	.10
18 Vince Coleman	.02	.10
19 Kirk Gibson	.08	.25
20 Steve Garvey	.20	.50
21 George Brett	1.00	2.50
22 John Tudor	.02	.10
23 Robin Yount	.40	1.00
24 Von Hayes	.02	.10
25 Kent Hrbek	.08	.25
26 Darryl Strawberry	.08	.25
27 Kirby Puckett	.60	1.50
28 Ron Darling	.02	.10
29 Don Mattingly	.75	2.00
30 Mike Schmidt	.40	1.00
31 Rickey Henderson	.60	1.50
32 Fernando Valenzuela	.08	.25
33 Dave Winfield	.40	1.00
34 Pete Rose	.60	1.50
35 Jose Canseco	.60	1.50
36 Glenn Davis	.02	.10
37 Alvin Davis	.02	.10
38 Steve Sax	.02	.10
39 Pete Incaviglia	.08	.25
40 Jeff Reardon	.08	.25
41 Jesse Barfield	.02	.10
42 Hubie Brooks	.02	.10
43 George Bell	.02	.10
44 Tony Gwynn	.75	2.00
45 Roger Clemens	1.25	3.00
46 Chili Davis	.20	.50
47 Mike Witt	.02	.10
48 Nolan Ryan	1.50	4.00

1993 Kraft

The Kraft Singles Superstars '93 Collector's series consists of 30 pop-up cards. One card was inserted in each specially marked 12-oz., 16-oz., and 3-lb. Kraft Singles package until June. Boxed sets of all the cards could be purchased through a mail-in form enclosed with each card for 1.75 plus proof-of-purchase points from Kraft Singles packages. Also a collector's album could be purchased for 4.75 plus 36 proof-of-purchase points. The standard-size cards feature a color action photo of the player in a batting stance, and these pictures are bordered by either blue (1-15) on American League cards or green (16-30) on National League cards. The cards are numbered on the front at the lower left corner following alphabetical order by league.

Card	Low	High
COMPLETE SET (30)	8.00	20.00
1 Jim Abbott	.20	.50
2 Roberto Alomar	.40	1.00
3 Sandy Alomar	.20	.50
4 George Brett	1.50	4.00
5 Roger Clemens	1.50	4.00
6 Dennis Eckersley	.60	1.50
7 Cecil Fielder	.20	.50
8 Ken Griffey Jr.	2.00	5.00
9 Don Mattingly	1.50	4.00
10 Mark McGwire	1.50	4.00
11 Kirby Puckett	.75	2.00
12 Cal Ripken	3.00	8.00
13 Nolan Ryan	3.00	8.00
14 Robin Ventura	.40	1.00
15 Robin Yount	.50	1.25
16 Bobby Bonilla	.08	.25
17 Ken Caminiti	.30	.75
18 Will Clark	.50	1.25
19 Darren Daulton	.20	.50
20 Doug Drabek	.08	.25
21 Delino DeShields	.08	.25
22 Tom Glavine	.60	1.50
23 Tony Gwynn	1.50	4.00
24 Orel Hershiser	.20	.50
25 Barry Larkin	.40	1.00
26 Terry Pendleton	.08	.25
27 Ryne Sandberg	.75	2.00
28 Gary Sheffield	.50	1.25
29 Lee Smith	.20	.50
30 Andy Van Slyke	.08	.25

1994 Kraft

The 1994 Kraft Singles Superstars set consists of 30 pop-up cards measuring approximately 2 1/2" by 3 3/8" and features "The Single Best Day" of 15 players from the American (1-15) and National (16-30) Leagues. One card was inserted in each specially marked 16-oz. and 3-lb. Kraft Singles package available in April and May. On-pack and in-store point-of-purchase mail-in offers enabled consumers to order a boxed American and/or National League 15-card set for $1.95 plus proof-of-purchase for each set. The cards are numbered on the back at the upper right, following alphabetical order by league.

Card	Low	High
COMPLETE SET (30)	8.00	20.00
1 Carlos Baerga	.20	.50
2 Dennis Eckersley	.50	1.25
3 Cecil Fielder	.20	.50
4 Juan Gonzalez	.40	1.00
5 Ken Griffey Jr.	1.25	3.00
6 Mark Langston	.08	.25
7 Brian McRae	.08	.25
8 Paul Molitor	.40	1.00
9 Kirby Puckett	1.00	2.50
10 Cal Ripken	2.00	5.00
11 Danny Tartabull	.08	.25
12 Frank Thomas	.50	1.25
13 Greg Vaughn	.08	.25
14 Mo Vaughn	.20	.50
15 Dave Winfield	.50	1.25
16 Jeff Bagwell	.50	1.25
17 Barry Bonds	1.00	2.50
18 Bobby Bonilla	.08	.25
19 Delino DeShields	.08	.25
20 Lenny Dykstra	.20	.50
21 Andres Galarraga	.40	1.00
22 Tom Glavine	.40	1.00
23 Mark Grace	.40	1.00
24 Tony Gwynn	1.00	2.50
25 David Justice	.40	1.00
26 Barry Larkin	.40	1.00
27 Mike Piazza	1.25	3.00
28 Gary Sheffield	.50	1.25
29 Ozzie Smith	.75	2.00
30 Andy Van Slyke	.08	.25

1995 Kraft

Consisting of 30 standard-size cards, the 1995 Kraft Singles Superstars Pop-up Action cards were included in specially-marked 12-ounce and 16-ounce packages of Kraft singles. One card was inserted in each package. The set could also be obtained through the mail by filling out the mail-in order form and sending in 36 Kraft Singles purchase points and $1.95 for each 15-card League set. The cards are arranged in alphabetical order within American (1-15) and National (16-30) Leagues.

Card	Low	High
COMPLETE SET (30)	10.00	25.00
1 Roberto Alomar	.40	1.00
2 Joe Carter	.20	.50
3 Cecil Fielder	.20	.50
4 Juan Gonzalez	.30	.75
5 Ken Griffey Jr.	1.50	4.00
6 Jimmy Key	.20	.50
7 Chuck Knoblauch	.40	1.00
8 Kenny Lofton	.40	1.00
9 Mike Mussina	.40	1.00
10 Paul O'Neill	.20	.50
11 Kirby Puckett	.75	2.00
12 Cal Ripken	2.00	5.00
13 Ivan Rodriguez	.50	1.25
14 Frank Thomas	.50	1.25
15 Mo Vaughn	.20	.50
16 Moises Alou	.20	.50
17 Jeff Bagwell	.50	1.25
18 Barry Bonds	1.00	2.50
19 Jeff Conine	.20	.50
20 Len Dykstra	.20	.50
21 Andres Galarraga	.40	1.00
22 Tony Gwynn	1.00	2.50
23 Gregg Jefferies	.08	.25
24 Barry Larkin	.40	1.00
25 Greg Maddux	1.25	3.00
26 Mike Piazza	1.25	3.00
27 Bret Saberhagen	.20	.50
28 Ozzie Smith	.75	2.00
29 Sammy Sosa	.75	2.00
30 Matt Williams	.30	.75

1992 L and K Decals

This 30-card set was distributed by Moore Sports Ltd. of New York and features color player head photos inside a large star printed as decals. The set was issued on uncut sheets which could be cut and used on various items such as mugs, mini-plates, glasses, etc. The back decal contains player statistics. Supposedly there were only 50 sheets produced with extra backs for some of the players and missing backs for others. The decals are unnumbered and checklisted below in alphabetical order.

Card	Low	High
COMPLETE SET (30)	250.00	500.00
1 Wade Boggs	6.00	15.00
2 Barry Bonds	12.50	30.00
3 George Brett	12.50	30.00
4 Will Clark	6.00	15.00
5 Jose Canseco	6.00	15.00
6 Roger Clemens	12.50	30.00
7 David Cone	3.00	8.00
8 Andre Dawson	5.00	12.00
9 Rob Dibble	2.50	6.00
10 Lenny Dykstra	3.00	8.00
11 Cecil Fielder	3.00	8.00
12 Julio Franco	3.00	8.00
13 Doc Gooden	3.00	8.00
14 Ken Griffey Jr.	20.00	50.00
15 Ken Griffey Sr.	2.50	6.00
16 Tony Gwynn	12.50	30.00
17 Rickey Henderson	8.00	20.00
18 Orel Hershiser	3.00	8.00
19 Howard Johnson	2.50	6.00
20 Dave Justice	5.00	12.00
21 Don Mattingly	12.50	30.00
22 Fred McGriff	4.00	10.00
23 Cal Ripken	25.00	60.00
24 Nolan Ryan	25.00	60.00
25 Ryan Sandberg	6.00	15.00
26 Steve Sax	2.50	6.00
27 Ozzie Smith	12.50	30.00
28 Darryl Strawberry	3.00	8.00
29 Frank Viola	2.50	6.00
30 Dave Winfield	6.00	15.00

1911 L1 Leathers

This highly prized set of baseball player pictures on a piece of leather shaped to resemble the hide of a small animal was issued during the 1911 time period. Each "leather" measures 10" by 12". While the pictures are those of the T3 Turkey Red card premium set, only the most popular players of the time are depicted. The cards are numbered at the bottom part of the leather away from the central image.

Card	Low	High
111 Rube Marquard	1750.00	3500.00
112 Marty O'Toole	1250.00	2500.00
113 Rube Benton	1250.00	2500.00
114 Grover C. Alexander	2500.00	5000.00
115 Russ Ford	1250.00	2500.00
116 John McGraw MG	2250.00	4500.00
117 Nap Rucker	1500.00	3000.00
118 Mike Mitchell	1250.00	2500.00
119 Chief Bender	2250.00	4500.00
120 Frank Baker	2250.00	4500.00
121 Napoleon Lajoie	2250.00	4500.00
122 Joe Tinker	2250.00	4500.00
123 Sherry Magee	1500.00	3000.00
124 Howie Camnitz	1250.00	2500.00
125 Eddie Collins	2250.00	4500.00
126 Red Dooin	1250.00	2500.00
127 Ty Cobb	10000.00	20000.00
128 Hugh Jennings MG	1750.00	3500.00
129 Roger Bresnahan	1750.00	3500.00
130 Jake Stahl	1250.00	2500.00
131 Tris Speaker	2250.00	4500.00
132 Ed Walsh	1750.00	3500.00
133 Christy Mathewson	5000.00	10000.00
134 Johnny Evers	2250.00	4500.00
135 Walter Johnson	6000.00	12000.00

1913 Lajoie Game

These cards were issued as part of a game of a baseball game. Each card in that game featured a photo of Napoleon Lajoie. Due to their distribution, these cards are farily common for vintage cards and show up in the secondary market with some frequency.

Card	Low	High
1 Nap Lajoie	10.00	25.00

1996-97 Las Vegas Club Chips

These two chips were issued by the Las Veagas Club and featured various baseball legends on them. They were issued in $10 demonations.

Card	Low	High
COMPLETE SET	15.00	40.00
1 Bob Feller Issued in 1996	4.00	10.00
2 Dizzy Dean/1997	4.00	10.00
3 Lou Gehrig Bath Ruth/1997	6.00	15.00

1967 Laughlin World Series

This set of 64 cards was apparently a limited test issue by sports artist R.G. Laughlin for the World Series set concept that was mass marketed by Fleer two and three years later. The cards are slightly oversized, (2 3/4" by 3 1/2") and are black and white on the front and red and white on the back. All the years are represented except for 1904 when no World Series was played. In the list below, the winning series team is listed first. According to an ad placed by Mr. Laughlin, only 300 of these sets were produced. Although these cards have a 1967 copyright; it is believed they were not released until 1968.

Card	Low	High
COMPLETE SET (64)	150.00	300.00
1 1903 Red Sox Pirates Deacon Phillippe	1.00	2.50
2 1905 Giants A's/(Christy Mathewson)	1.50	4.00
3 1906 White Sox Cubs	1.00	2.50
4 1907 Cubs Tigers	1.00	2.50
5 1908 Cubs Tigers Joe Tinker Johnny Evers Frank Chance	2.00	5.00
6 1909 Pirates Tigers/(Honus Wagner Ty Cobb)	2.00	5.00
7 1910 A's Cubs	1.00	2.50
8 1911 A's Giants John McGraw MG	1.50	4.00
9 1912 Red Sox Giants	1.00	2.50
10 1913 A's Giants	1.00	2.50
11 1914 Braves A's	1.00	2.50
12 1915 Red Sox Phillies/(Babe Ruth)	4.00	10.00
13 1916 Red Sox Dodgers/(Babe Ruth)	4.00	10.00
14 1917 White Sox Giants	1.00	2.50
15 1918 Red Sox Cubs	1.00	2.50
16 1919 Reds White Sox	2.00	5.00
17 1920 Indians Dodgers Bill Wambsganss	1.00	2.50
18 1921 Giants Yankees/(Waite Hoyt)	1.25	3.00
19 1922 Giants Yankees Frank Frisch Heinie Groh	1.25	3.00
20 1923 Yankees Giants/(Babe Ruth)	4.00	10.00
21 1924 Senators Giants	1.00	2.50
22 1925 Pirates Senators/(Walter Johnson)	2.00	5.00
23 1926 Cardinals Yankees Grover C. Alexander Tony Lazzeri	1.50	4.00
24 1927 Yankees Pirates	1.25	3.00
25 1928 Yankees Cardinals Babe Ruth Lou Gehrig	4.00	10.00
26 1929 A's Cubs	1.00	2.50
27 1930 A's Cardinals	1.00	2.50
28 1931 Cardinals A's/(Pepper Martin)	1.25	3.00
29 1932 Yankees Cubs/(Babe Ruth)	4.00	10.00
30 1933 Giants Senators/(Mel Ott)	1.50	4.00
31 1934 Cardinals Tigers Dizzy Dean Paul Dean	2.00	5.00
32 1935 Tigers Cubs	1.00	2.50
33 1936 Yankees Giants	1.00	2.50
34 1937 Yankees Giants/(Carl Hubbell)	1.25	3.00
35 1938 Yankees Cubs	1.00	2.50
36 1939 Yankees Reds/(Joe DiMaggio)	2.00	5.00
37 1940 Reds Tigers	1.00	2.50
38 1941 Yankees Dodgers/(Mickey Owen)	1.25	3.00
39 1942 Cardinals Yankees	1.00	2.50
40 1943 Yankees Cardinals Joe McCarthy MG	1.25	3.00
41 1944 Cardinals Browns	1.00	2.50
42 1945 Tigers Cubs/(Hank Greenberg)	1.50	4.00
43 1946 Cardinals Red Sox/(Enos Slaughter)	1.50	4.00
44 1947 Yankees Dodgers/(Al Gionfriddo)	1.25	3.00
45 1948 Indians Braves/(Bob Feller)	1.50	4.00
46 1949 Yankees Dodgers Allie Reynolds Preacher Roe	1.25	3.00
47 1950 Yankees Phillies	1.00	2.50
48 1951 Yankees Giants	1.00	2.50
49 1952 Yankees Dodgers Johnny Mize Duke Snider	1.50	4.00
50 1953 Yankees Dodgers Casey Stengel MG	1.50	4.00
51 1954 Giants Indians/(Dusty Rhodes)	1.00	2.50
52 1955 Dodgers Yankees/(Johnny Podres)	1.25	3.00
53 1956 Yankees Dodgers/(Don Larsen)	1.25	3.00
54 1957 Braves Yankees/(Lew Burdette)	1.00	2.50
55 1958 Yankees Braves/(Hank Bauer)	1.00	2.50
56 1959 Dodgers Wh.Sox/(Larry Sherry)	1.00	2.50
57 1960 Pirates Yankees	1.25	3.00
58 1961 Yankees Reds/(Whitey Ford)	1.50	4.00
59 1962 Yankees Giants	1.00	2.50
60 1963 Dodgers Yankees/(Sandy Koufax)	12.50	30.00
61 1964 Cardinals Yankees/(Mickey Mantle)	40.00	80.00
62 1965 Dodgers Twins Sandy Koufax	1.50	4.00
63 1966 Orioles Dodgers	1.00	2.50
64 1967 Cardinals Red Sox/(Bob Gibson)	1.50	4.00

1972 Laughlin Great Feats

This 51 card-set is printed on white card stock. Sports artist R.G. Laughlin is copyrighted only on the unnumbered title card but not on each card. The obverses are line drawings in black and white inside a red border. The cards measure 2 9/16" by 3 9/16". The set features "Great Feats" from baseball's past. The cards are blank backed and hence are numbered and captioned on the front. There is a variation set with a blue border and colored in flesh tones in the players pictured; this variation is a little more attractive and hence is valued a little higher. The blue-bordered variation set has larger type in the captions; in fact, the type has been reset and there are some minor wording differences. The blue-bordered set is also 1/16" wider. These sets were originally available from the artist for $3.25.

Card	Low	High
COMPLETE SET (51)	20.00	50.00
1 Joe DiMaggio	2.00	5.00
2 Walter Johnson	.60	1.50
3 Rudy York	.20	.50
4 Sandy Koufax	.60	1.50
5 George Sisler	.30	.75
6 Iron Man McGinnity	.30	.75
7 Johnny VanderMeer	.20	.50
8 Lou Gehrig	2.00	5.00
9 Max Carey	.30	.75
10 Ed Delahanty	.30	.75
11 Pinky Higgins	.20	.50
12 Jack Chesbro	.30	.75
13 Jim Bottomley	.30	.75
14 Rube Marquard	.30	.75
15 Rogers Hornsby	.40	1.00
16 Lefty Grove	.40	1.00
17 Johnny Mize	.30	.75
18 Lefty Gomez	.30	.75
19 Jimmie Foxx	.40	1.00
20 Casey Stengel	.40	1.00
21 Dazzy Vance	.30	.75
22 Jerry Lynch	.20	.50
23 Hughie Jennings	.30	.75
24 Stan Musial	.75	2.00
25 Christy Mathewson	.60	1.50
26 Roy Face	.20	.50
27 Hack Wilson	.30	.75
28 Smoky Burgess	.20	.50
29 Cy Young	.60	1.50
30 Wilbert Robinson	.30	.75
31 Wee Willie Keeler	.30	.75
32 Babe Ruth	2.00	5.00
33 Mickey Mantle	2.50	6.00
34 Hub Leonard	.20	.50
35 Ty Cobb	1.50	4.00
36 Carl Hubbell	.30	.75
37 Joe Oeschger and Leon Cadore	.20	.50
38 Don Drysdale	.30	.75
39 Fred Toney and Hippo Vaughn	.20	.50
40 Joe Sewell	.30	.75
41 Grover C. Alexander	.40	1.00
42 Joe Adcock	.20	.50
43 Eddie Collins	.40	1.00
44 Bob Feller	.60	1.50
45 Don Larsen	.20	.50
46 Dave Philley	.20	.50
47 Bill Fischer	.20	.50
48 Dale Long	.20	.50
49 Bill Wambsganss	.20	.50
50 Roger Maris	.60	1.50
NNO Title Card	.40	1.00

1973 Laughlin Stand-Ups

These "stand-ups" which measure approximately 7" by 11" were created by noted sports artist Robert Laughlin. The fronts feature drawings of a mix of then current superstars and retired greats while the back is signed Bob Laughlin. Since these are unnumbered, we have sequenced them in alphabetical order. It is believed this checklist is incomplete so any additions are appreciated.

Card	Low	High
COMPLETE SET	1000.00	2000.00
1 Hank Aaron	100.00	200.00
2 Johnny Bench	60.00	120.00
3 Roberto Clemente	100.00	200.00
4 Joe DiMaggio	125.00	250.00
5 Lou Gehrig	125.00	250.00
6 Gil Hodges	50.00	100.00
7 Sandy Koufax	125.00	250.00
8 Mickey Mantle	125.00	250.00
9 Babe Ruth	150.00	300.00
10 Ted Williams	125.00	250.00

1974 Laughlin All-Star Games

This 40-card set is printed on white card stock. Sports artist R.G. Laughlin is copyrighted at the bottom of the reverse of each card. The obverses are line drawings primarily in red, light blue, black and white inside a white border. The cards measure approximately 2 11/16" by 3 3/8". The set features memorable moments from each year's All-Star Game. The cards are numbered on the back according to the last two digits of the year and captioned on the front. The backs are printed in blue on white stock. There is no card No. 45 in the set as there was no All-Star Game played in 1945 because of World War II. This set was available from Bob Laughlin for $3.50.

Card	Low	High
COMPLETE SET (40)	60.00	120.00
33 Babe Ruth Homer	4.00	10.00
34 Carl Hubbell Fans Five	.75	2.00
35 Jimmie Foxx Smashes Homer	.75	2.00
36 Dizzy Dean Fogs 'Em	.75	2.00
37 Ducky Medwick Four Hits	.60	1.50
38 John VanderMeer No-Hit	.60	1.50
39 Joe DiMaggio Homers	2.50	6.00
40 Max West's/3-Run Shot	.40	1.00
41 Arky Vaughan Busts Two	.60	1.50
42 Rudy York/2-Run Smash	.40	1.00
43 Bobby Doerr/3-Run Blast	.60	1.50
44 Phil Cavarretta Reaches	.40	1.00
46 Ted Williams Field Day	2.50	6.00
47 Johnny Mize Plants One	.60	1.50
48 Vic Raschi Pitches	.40	1.00
49 Jackie Robinson Scores	2.00	5.00
50 Red Schoendienst Breaks	.60	1.50
51 Ralph Kiner Homers	.60	1.50
52 Hank Sauer Shot	.40	1.00
53 Enos Slaughter Hustles	.60	1.50
54 Al Rosen Hits	.40	1.00
55 Stan Musial Homer	1.25	3.00
56 Ken Boyer Super	.40	1.00
57 Al Kaline Hits	.75	2.00
58 Nellie Fox Gets Two	.60	1.50
59 Frank Robinson Perfect	.75	2.00
60 Willie Mays/3-for-4	2.00	5.00
61 Jim Bunning Hitless	.60	1.50
62 Roberto Clemente Perfect	2.50	6.00
63 Dick Radatz Monster Strikeouts	.40	1.00
64 John Callison Homer	.40	1.00
65 Willie Stargell Big Day	.60	1.50
66 Brooks Robinson Hits	.75	2.00
67 Fergie Jenkins Fans Six	.60	1.50
68 Tom Seaver Terrific	1.25	3.00
69 Willie McCovey Belts Two	.60	1.50
70 Carl Yatrzemski Four Hits	.75	2.00
71 Reggie Jackson Unloads	1.25	3.00
72 Henry Aaron Hammers	2.00	5.00
73 Bobby Bonds Perfect	.60	1.50

1974 Laughlin Old Time Black Stars

This 36-card set is printed on flat (non-glossy) white card stock. Sports artist R.G. Laughlin's work is evident but there are no copyright notices or any mention of him anywhere on any of the cards in this set. The obverses are line drawings in tan and brown. The cards measure approximately 2 5/8" by 3 1/2". The set features outstanding black players form the past. The backs are printed in brown on white stock. These sets were available from Bob Laughlin for $3.

Card	Low	High
COMPLETE SET (36)	150.00	400.00
1 Smokey Joe Williams	5.00	12.00
2 Rap Dixon	3.00	8.00
3 Oliver Marcelle	3.00	8.00
4 Bingo DeMoss	4.00	10.00
5 Willie Foster	4.00	10.00
6 John Beckwith	3.00	8.00
7 Floyd(Jelly) Gardner	3.00	8.00
8 Josh Gibson	10.00	25.00
9 Jose Mendez	3.00	8.00
10 Pete Hill	6.00	15.00
11 Buck Leonard	6.00	15.00
12 Jud Wilson	3.00	8.00
13 Willie Wells	5.00	12.00
14 Jimmie Lyons	3.00	8.00
15 Satchel Paige	10.00	25.00
16 Louis Santop	3.00	8.00

17 Frank Grant 3.00 8.00
18 Christobel Torrienti 4.00 10.00
19 Bullet Rogan 4.00 10.00
20 Dave Malarcher 4.00 10.00
21 Spot Poles 3.00 8.00
22 Home Run Johnson 3.00 8.00
23 Charlie Grant 3.00 8.00
24 Cool Papa Bell 6.00 15.00
25 Cannonball Dick Redding 3.00 8.00
26 Ray Dandridge 5.00 12.00
27 Biz Mackey 5.00 12.00
28 Fats Jenkins 3.00 8.00
29 Martin Dihigo 6.00 15.00
30 Mule Suttles 3.00 8.00
31 Bill Monroe 3.00 8.00
32 Dan McClellan 3.00 8.00
33 John Henry Lloyd 6.00 15.00
34 Oscar Charleston 6.00 15.00
35 Andrew(Rube) Foster 6.00 15.00
36 William(Judy) Johnson 6.00 15.00

1974 Laughlin Sportslang

This 41-card set is printed on white card stock. Sports artist R.G. Laughlin 1974 is copyrighted at the bottom of every reverse. The obverses are drawings in red and blue on a white enamel card stock. The cards measure approximately 2 3/4" by 3 3/8". The set actually features the slang of several sports, not just baseball. The cards are numbered on the back and captioned on the front. The card back also provides an explanation of the slang term pictured on the card front.

COMPLETE SET (41) 50.00 100.00
COMMON PLAYER (1-41) .60 1.50

1975 Laughlin Batty Baseball

This-25 card set is printed on white card stock. Sports artist R.G. Laughlin 1975 is copyrighted on the title card. The obverses are line drawings primarily in orange, black and white. The cards measure 2 9/16" X 3 7/16". The set features a card for each team with a depiction of a fractured nickname for the team. The cards are numbered on the front. The backs are blank on white stock.

COMPLETE SET (25) 60.00 120.00
COMMON PLAYER (1-24) 2.00 5.00

1976 Laughlin Diamond Jubilee

This 32-card set is printed on non-glossy white card stock. Sports artist R.Laughlin 1976 is copyrighted at the bottom of the reverse of each card. The obverses are line drawings primarily in red, blue, black and white inside a red border. The cards measure approximately 2 13/16" by 3 15/16". The set features memorable moments voted by the media and fans in each major league city. The cards are numbered on the back and captioned on the front and the back. The backs are printed in dark blue on white stock. The set was available from the artist for $3.50.

COMPLETE SET (32) 75.00 150.00
1 Nolan Ryan 30.00 60.00
2 Ernie Banks 1.25 3.00
3 Mickey Lolich .40 1.00
4 Sandy Koufax 2.50 6.00
5 Frank Robinson 1.25 3.00
6 Bill Mazeroski .50 1.50
7 Jim Hunter .50 1.50
8 Hank Aaron 4.00 10.00
9 Carl Yastrzemski 1.25 3.00
10 Jim Bunning .50 1.50
11 Brooks Robinson 1.25 3.00
12 John VanderMeer .50 1.50
13 Harmon Killebrew 1.25 3.00
14 Lou Brock 1.25 3.00
15 Steve Busby .40 1.00
16 Nate Colbert .40 1.00
17 Don Larsen .50 1.50
18 Willie Mays 2.50 6.00
19 David Clyde .40 1.00
20 Mack Jones .40 1.00
21 Mike Hegan .40 1.00
22 Jerry Koosman .40 1.00
23 Early Wynn .50 1.50
24 Nellie Fox .50 1.50
25 Joe DiMaggio 5.00 12.00
26 Jackie Robinson 3.00 8.00
27 Ted Williams 5.00 12.00
28 Lou Gehrig 5.00 12.00
29 Bobby Thomson .50 1.50
30 Roger Maris 1.25 3.00
31 Harvey Haddix .40 1.00
32 Babe Ruth 6.00 15.00

1976 Laughlin Indianapolis Clowns

This 42-card set was issued to commemorate the Indianapolis Clowns, a black team that began touring in 1929 and played many games for charity. The cards measure 2 5/8" by 4 1/4". The front design has blackand-white player photos inside a white frame against a light blue card face. The team name is printed in red and white above the picture. In red courier-style print on white, the backs present extended captions. The cards are numbered on the front.

COMPLETE SET (42) 40.00 80.00
1 Ed Hamman 1.25 3.00
Ed the Clown
2 Dero Austin .75 2.00
3 James Williams .75 2.00
Nickname Natureboy
4 Sam Brison .75 2.00
Nickname Birmingham
5 Richard King .75 2.00
Nickname King Tut
6 Syd Pollock .75 2.00
Founder
7 Nataniel(Lefty) Small .75 2.00
8 Grant Greene .75 2.00
Nickname Double Duty
9 Nancy Miller .75 2.00
Lady umpire
10 Billy Vaughn .75 2.00
11 Sam Brison .75 2.00
Putout for Sam
12 Ed Hamman 1.25 3.00
13 Dero Austin .75 2.00
Home delivery
14 Steve(Nub) Anderson .75 2.00
15 Joe Cherry .75 2.00
16 Reece(Goose) Tatum 3.00 8.00
17 James Williams .75 2.00
Natureboy
18 Byron Purnell .75 2.00
19 Bat boy .75 2.00
20 Spec BeBop .75 2.00
21 Satchel Paige 4.00 10.00
22 Prince Jo Henry .75 2.00
23 Ed Hamman .75 2.00
Syd Pollock
24 Paul Casanova 1.25 3.00
25 Steve(Nub) Anderson .75 2.00
Nub singles
26 Comiskey Park 1.25 3.00
27 Toni Stone 2.00 5.00
Second basewoman
28 Dero Austin .75 2.00
Small target
29 Sam Brison and .75 2.00
Natureboy Williams
Calling Dr. Ki
30 Oscar Charleston 2.00 5.00
31 Richard King .75 2.00
King Tut
32 Ed Hamman .75 2.00
Joe Cherry
Hal King
Ed and prospects
33 In style .75 2.00
Team bus
34 Hank Aaron 4.00 10.00
35 The Great Yogi 2.00 5.00
36 W.H.(Chauff) Wilson .75 2.00
37 Sam Brison 1.25 3.00
Sonny Jackson
Doin' their thing
38 Billy Vaughn .75 2.00
The hard way
39 James Williams/1B the easy way .75 2.00
40 Ed Hamman 2.00 5.00
Casey Stengel
Casey and Ed
xx Title Card .75 2.00
xx Baseball Laff Book .75 2.00

1977 Laughlin Erorrs

This set of 39 blank-backed cards is printed on white card stock and measures 2 5/8" by 3 3/4". Sports artist R.G. Laughlin has created illustrations for actual errors made on baseball cards over the years, a sampling of the hundreds of mistakes that found their way into print. The illustrations are bordered in green with "Erorrs" (incorrect spelling intentional) in wide white script at the top of the cards. Each card lists the year, card make and number depicted in the line drawing. The cards are unnumbered and checklisted below in chronological order. This set was available from the artist for $3 at the time of issue.

COMPLETE SET (39) 75.00 150.00
COMMON PLAYER (1-39) 2.00 5.00

1978 Laughlin Long Ago Black Stars

This set of 36 cards is printed on non-glossy white card stock. Sports artist R.G. Laughlin's work is evident and the reverse of each card indicates copyright by R.G. Laughlin 1978. The obverses are line drawings in light and dark green. The cards measure 2 5/8" by 3 1/2". The set features outstanding black players form the past. The cards are numbered on the back. The backs are printed in black on white stock. This is not a reissue of the similar Laughlin set from 1974 Old Time Black Stars but is actually in effect a second series with all new players and was available from Mr. Laughlin at time of issue for $3.75.

COMPLETE SET (36) 60.00 120.00
1 Ted Trent 1.50 4.00
2 Larry Brown 1.25 3.00
3 Newt Allen 2.50 6.00
4 Norman Stearns 1.25 3.00
5 Leon Day 4.00 10.00
6 Dick Lundy 1.25 3.00
7 Bruce Petway 1.50 4.00
8 Bill Drake 1.25 3.00
9 Chaney White 1.25 3.00
10 Webster McDonald 1.25 3.00
11 Tommy Butts 1.25 3.00
12 Ben Taylor 1.25 3.00
13 James(Joe) Greene 1.25 3.00
14 Dick Seay 1.25 3.00
15 Sammy Hughes 1.25 3.00
16 Ted Page 3.00 8.00
17 Willie Cornelius 1.25 3.00
18 Pat Patterson 1.25 3.00
19 Frank Wickware 1.25 3.00
20 Albert Haywood 1.25 3.00
21 Bill Holland 1.25 3.00
22 Sol White 1.25 3.00
23 Chet Brewer 2.50 6.00
24 Crush Holloway 1.25 3.00
25 George Johnson 1.25 3.00
26 George Scales 1.25 3.00
27 Dave Brown 1.25 3.00
28 John Donaldson 1.25 3.00
29 William Johnson 3.00 8.00
30 Bill Yancey 2.50 6.00
31 Sam Bankhead 1.50 4.00
32 Leroy Matlock 1.25 3.00
33 Quincy Troupe 1.50 4.00
34 Hilton Smith 4.00 10.00
35 Jim Crutchfield 1.50 4.00
36 Ted Radcliffe 2.50 6.00

1980 Laughlin 300/400/500

This square (approximately 3 1/4" square) set of 30 players features members of the 300/400/500 club, namely 300 pitching wins, batting .400 or better, or hitting 500 homers since 1900. Cards are blank backed but are numbered on the front. The cards feature the artwork of R.G. Laughlin for the player's body connected to an out of proportion head shot stock photo. This creates an effect faintly reminiscent of the Goudey Heads Up cards.

COMPLETE SET (30) 10.00 25.00
1 Title Card .30 .75
2 Babe Ruth 2.00 5.00
3 Walter Johnson .60 1.50
4 Ty Cobb .75 2.00
5 Christy Mathewson .75 2.00
6 Ted Williams 1.50 4.00
7 Bill Terry .30 .75
8 Grover C. Alexander .40 1.00
9 Napoleon Lajoie .40 1.00
10 Willie Mays .75 2.00
11 Cy Young .60 1.50
12 Mel Ott .40 1.00
13 Joe Jackson .75 2.00
14 Harmon Killebrew .40 1.00
15 Warren Spahn .40 1.00
16 Hank Aaron 1.25 3.00
17 Rogers Hornsby .75 2.00
18 Mickey Mantle 2.00 5.00
19 Lefty Grove .50 1.00
20 Ted Williams .75 2.00
21 Jimmie Foxx .60 1.50
22 Eddie Plank .30 .75
23 Frank Robinson .40 1.00
24 George Sisler .30 .75
25 Eddie Mathews .40 1.00
26 Early Wynn .30 .75
27 Ernie Banks .60 1.50
28 Harry Heilmann .30 .75
29 Lou Gehrig 1.25 3.00
30 Willie McCovey .40 1.00

1980 Laughlin Famous Feats

This set of 40 standard-size cards is printed on white card stock. Sports artist R.G. Laughlin 1980 is copyrighted at the bottom of every obverse. The obverses are line drawings primarily in many colors. The set is subtitled "Second Series" of Famous Feats. The cards are numbered on the front. The backs are blank on white stock.

COMPLETE SET (40) 8.00 20.00
1 Honus Wagner .40 1.00
2 Herb Pennock .20 .50
3 Al Simmons .20 .50
4 Hack Wilson .20 .50
5 Dizzy Dean .30 .75
6 Chuck Klein .20 .50
7 Nellie Fox .20 .50
8 Lefty Grove .30 .75
9 George Sisler .20 .50
10 Lou Gehrig .75 2.00
11 Rube Waddell .20 .50
12 Max Carey .20 .50
13 Thurman Munson .30 .75
14 Mel Ott .30 .75
15 Doc White .08 .25
16 Babe Ruth 1.00 2.50
17 Schoolboy Rowe .08 .25
18 Jackie Robinson .60 1.50
19 Joe Medwick .20 .50
20 Casey Stengel .40 1.00
21 Roberto Clemente .75 2.00
22 Christy Mathewson .40 1.00
23 Jimmie Foxx .30 .75
24 Joe Jackson .60 1.50
25 Walter Johnson .40 1.00
26 Tony Lazzeri .20 .50
27 Hugh Casey .08 .25
28 Ty Cobb .75 2.00
29 Stuffy McInnis .08 .25
30 Cy Young .30 .75
31 Lefty O'Doul .08 .25
32 Eddie Collins .20 .50
33 Joe McCarthy .20 .50
34 Ed Walsh .20 .50
35 George Burns .08 .25
36 Walt Dropo .08 .25
37 Connie Mack .30 .75
38 Babe Adams .08 .25
39 Rogers Hornsby .30 .75
40 Grover C. Alexander .30 .75

1914 Lawrence Semon Postcards

These seven postcards were produced by photographer Lawrence Semon. These postcards feature a large photo of the player using most of the space of the card with the players name and some information on the bottom. Six additions to this checklist were discovered in recent years -- so there might be more and additions to this checklist are welcome.

COMPLETE SET 2000.00 4000.00
1 George Burns 100.00 200.00
2 Frank Chance 200.00 400.00
3 Ty Cobb 600.00 1200.00
4 Walter Johnson 400.00 800.00
5 Connie Mack MG 300.00 600.00
6 Rube Marquard 200.00 400.00
7 John McGraw MG 300.00 600.00

1949 Leaf

The cards in this 98-card set measure 2 3/8" by 2 7/8". The 1949 Leaf set was the first post-war baseball series issued in color. This effort was not entirely successful due to a lack of refinement which resulted in many color variations and cards out of register. In addition, the set was skip numbered from 1-168, with 49 of the 98 cards printed in limited quantities (marked with SP in the checklist). Cards 102 and 136 have variations, and cards are sometimes found with overprinted, incorrect or blank backs. Some cards were produced with a 1948 copyright date but overwhelming evidence seemed to indicate that this set was not actually released until early in 1949. An album to hold these cards was available as a premium. The album could only be obtained by sending in five wrappers and 25 cents. Since so few albums appear on the secondary market, no value is attached to them. Notable Rookie Cards in this set include Stan Musial, Satchel Paige, and Jackie Robinson. A proof card of Hal Newhouser; with a different photo and back biography recently surfaced. So far; there is only one known copy of this card.

COMPLETE SET (98) 25000.00 40000.00
COMMON CARD (1-168) 15.00 25.00
COMMON SP's 200.00 300.00
WRAPPER (1-CENT) 120.00 160.00
1 Joe DiMaggio 1000.00 2000.00
3 Babe Ruth 2000.00 4000.00
4 Stan Musial 1500.00 3000.00
5 Virgil Trucks SP RC 250.00 400.00
8 S.Paige SP RC 9000.00 15000.00
10 Dizzy Trout 25.00 40.00
11 Phil Rizzuto 150.00 300.00
13 Cass Michaels SP RC 200.00 300.00
14 Billy Johnson 25.00 40.00
17 Frank Overmire RC 15.00 25.00
19 Johnny Wyrostek SP 200.00 300.00
20 Hank Sauer SP 250.00 400.00
22 Al Evans RC 15.00 25.00
26 Sam Chapman 25.00 40.00
27 Mickey Harris RC 15.00 25.00
28 Jim Hegan RC 25.00 40.00
29 Elmer Valo RC 25.00 40.00
30 Billy Goodman SP RC 250.00 400.00
31 Lou Brissie RC 15.00 25.00
32 Warren Spahn 400.00 800.00
33 Peanuts Lowrey SP RC 200.00 300.00
36 Al Zarilla SP 200.00 300.00
38 Ted Kluszewski RC 125.00 200.00
39 Ewell Blackwell 35.00 60.00
42A Kent Peterson RC 15.00 25.00
42B Kent Peterson Red Cap
43 Ed Stevens SP RC 200.00 300.00
45 Ken Keltner SP RC 200.00 300.00
46 Johnny Mize 60.00 100.00
47 George Vico RC 15.00 25.00
48 Johnny Schmitz SP RC 200.00 300.00
49 Del Ennis RC 35.00 60.00
50 Dick Wakefield RC 15.00 25.00
51 Alvin Dark SP RC 300.00 500.00
53 Johnny VanderMeer 60.00 100.00
54 Bobby Adams SP RC 200.00 300.00
55 Tommy Henrich SP 300.00 500.00
56 Larry Jansen 25.00 40.00
57 Bob McCall RC 15.00 25.00
59 Luke Appling 60.00 100.00
61 Jake Early RC 15.00 25.00
62 Eddie Joost SP 200.00 300.00
63 Barney McCosky SP 200.00 300.00
65 Bob Elliott UER 60.00 100.00
66 Orval Grove SP RC 200.00 300.00
68 Eddie Miller SP 200.00 300.00
70 Honus Wagner 250.00 500.00
72 Hank Edwards RC 15.00 25.00
73 Pat Seerey RC 15.00 25.00
75 Dom DiMaggio SP 350.00 600.00
76 Ted Williams 800.00 1500.00
77 Roy Smalley RC 15.00 25.00
78 Hoot Evers SP RC 200.00 300.00
79 Jackie Robinson RC 6000.00 12000.00
81 Whitey Kurowski SP RC 200.00 300.00
82 Johnny Lindell 25.00 40.00
83 Bobby Doerr 60.00 100.00
84 Sid Hudson 15.00 25.00
85 Dave Philley SP RC 250.00 400.00
86 Ralph Weigel RC 15.00 25.00
88 Frank Gustine SP RC 200.00 300.00
91 Ralph Kiner 125.00 250.00
93 Bob Feller SP 1400.00 2000.00
95 Snuffy Stirnweiss 25.00 40.00
97 Marty Marion 35.00 60.00
98 Hal Newhouser SP RC 350.00 600.00
98A Hal Newhouser Proof
102A G.Hermansk ERR 150.00 250.00
102B Gene Hermanski COR RC 25.00 40.00
104 Eddie Stewart SP RC 200.00 300.00
106 Lou Boudreau MG RC 60.00 100.00
108 Matt Batts SP RC 200.00 300.00
111 Jerry Priddy RC 15.00 25.00
113 Dutch Leonard SP 200.00 300.00
117 Joe Gordon RC 25.00 40.00
120 George Kell SP RC 350.00 600.00
121 Johnny Pesky SP RC 250.00 400.00
123 Cliff Fannin SP RC 200.00 300.00
125 Andy Pafko RC 15.00 25.00
127 Enos Slaughter SP 500.00 800.00
128 Buddy Rosar 15.00 25.00
129 Kirby Higbe SP 200.00 300.00
131 Sid Gordon SP 200.00 300.00
133 Tommy Holmes SP RC 300.00 500.00
136A C.Aberson Full Slv RC 15.00 25.00
136B C.Aberson Short Slv 150.00 250.00
137 Harry Walker SP RC 250.00 400.00
138 Larry Doby SP RC 400.00 700.00
139 Johnny Hopp RC 15.00 25.00
142 D.Murtaugh SP RC 250.00 400.00
143 Dick Sisler SP RC 200.00 300.00
144 Bob Dillinger SP RC 200.00 300.00
146 Pete Reiser SP 300.00 500.00
149 Hank Majeski SP RC 200.00 300.00
153 Floyd Baker SP RC 200.00 300.00
158 H.Brecheen SP RC 250.00 400.00
159 Mizell Platt RC 15.00 25.00
160 Bob Scheffing SP RC 200.00 300.00
161 V.Stephens SP RC 250.00 400.00
163 F.Hutchinson SP RC 250.00 400.00
165 Dale Mitchell SP RC 250.00 400.00
168 Phil Cavarretta SP RC 300.00 500.00
NNO Album

1949 Leaf Premiums

This set of eight large, blank-backed premiums is rather scarce. They were issued as premiums with the 1949 Leaf Gum set. The catalog designation is R401-4. The set is subtitled "Baseball's Immortals" and there is no reference anywhere on the premium to Leaf, the issuing company. These large photos measure approximately 5 1/2" x 7 3/16" and are printed on thin paper.

COMPLETE SET (8) 2500.00 5000.00
1 Grover C. Alexander 200.00 400.00
2 Mickey Cochrane 200.00 400.00
3 Lou Gehrig 500.00 1000.00
4 Walter Johnson 300.00 600.00
5 Christy Mathewson 300.00 600.00
6 John McGraw 200.00 400.00
7 Babe Ruth 750.00 1500.00
8 Ed Walsh 150.00 300.00

1960 Leaf

The cards in this 144-card set measure the standard size. The 1960 Leaf set was issued in a regular gum package style but with a marble instead of gum. This set was issued in five card nickel packs which came 24 to a box. The series was a joint production by Sports Novelties, Inc., and Leaf, two Chicago-based companies. Cards 73-144 are more difficult to find than the lower numbers. Photo variations exist (probably proof cards) for the eight cards listed with an asterisk and there is a well-known error card, number 25 showing Brooks Lawrence (in a Reds uniform) with Jim Grant's name on front, and Grant's biography and record on back. The corrected version with Grant's photo is the more difficult variety. The only notable Rookie Card in this set is Dallas Green. The complete set price below includes both versions of Jim Grant.

COMPLETE SET (144) 1000.00 2000.00
COMMON CARD (1-72) 1.25 3.00
COMMON CARD (73-144) 12.50 30.00
WRAPPER (5-CENT) 20.00 50.00
1 Luis Aparicio * 10.00 25.00
2 Woody Held 1.25 3.00
3 Frank Lary 1.50 4.00
4 Camilo Pascual 2.00 5.00
5 Pancho Herrera 1.25 3.00
6 Felipe Alou 3.00 8.00
7 Benjamin Daniels 1.25 3.00
8 Roger Craig 2.00 5.00
9 Eddie Kasko 1.25 3.00
10 Bob Grim 1.50 4.00
11 Jim Busby 1.50 4.00
12 Ken Boyer* 3.00 8.00
13 Bob Boyd 1.25 3.00
14 Sam Jones 1.50 4.00
15 Larry Jackson 1.50 4.00
16 Roy Face 1.50 4.00
17 Walt Moryn * 1.25 3.00
18 Jim Gilliam 2.00 5.00
19 Don Newcombe 2.00 5.00
20 Glen Hobbie 1.25 3.00
21 Pedro Ramos 1.50 4.00
22 Ryne Duren 1.25 3.00
23 Joey Jay * 1.50 4.00
24 Lou Berberet 1.25 3.00
25A Jim Grant ERR 6.00 15.00
25B Jim Grant COR 10.00 25.00
26 Tom Borland RC 1.25 3.00
27 Brooks Robinson 25.00 60.00
28 Jerry Adair RC 1.25 3.00
29 Ron Jackson 1.25 3.00
30 George Strickland 1.25 3.00
31 Rocky Bridges 1.25 3.00
32 Bill Tuttle 1.50 4.00
33 Ken Hunt RC 1.25 3.00
34 Hal Griggs 1.25 3.00
35 Jim Coates * 1.25 3.00
36 Brooks Lawrence 1.25 3.00
37 Duke Snider 15.00 40.00
38 Al Spangler RC 1.25 3.00
39 Jim Owens 1.25 3.00
40 Bill Virdon 2.00 5.00
41 Ernie Broglio 1.25 3.00
42 Andre Rodgers 1.25 3.00
43 Julio Becquer 1.50 4.00
44 Tony Taylor 1.50 4.00
45 Jerry Lynch 1.50 4.00
46 Clete Boyer 3.00 8.00
47 Jerry Lumpe 1.25 3.00
48 Charlie Maxwell 1.50 4.00
49 Jim Perry 1.50 4.00
50 Danny McDevitt 1.25 3.00
51 Juan Pizarro 1.25 3.00
52 Dallas Green RC 3.00 8.00
53 Bob Friend 1.50 4.00
54 Jack Sanford 1.50 4.00
55 Jim Rivera 1.25 3.00
56 Ted Wills RC 1.25 3.00
57 Milt Pappas 1.50 4.00
58A Hal Smith * 1.25 3.00
58B Hal Smith
Blacked out team
58C Hal Smith 75.00 200.00
No team on back
59 Bobby Avila 1.25 3.00
60 Clem Labine 2.00 5.00
61 Norman Rehm RC * 1.25 3.00
62 John Gabler RC 1.50 4.00
63 John Tsitouris RC 1.25 3.00
64 Dave Sisler 1.25 3.00
65 Vic Power 1.50 4.00
66 Earl Battey 1.25 3.00
67 Bob Purkey 1.25 3.00
68 Moe Drabowsky 1.50 4.00
69 Hoyt Wilhelm 6.00 15.00
70 Humberto Robinson 1.25 3.00
71 Whitey Herzog 3.00 8.00
72 Dick Donovan * 1.25 3.00
73 Gordon Jones 12.50 30.00
74 Joe Hicks RC 12.50 30.00
75 Ray Culp RC 15.00 40.00
76 Dick Drott 12.50 30.00
77 Bob Duliba RC 12.50 30.00
78 Art Ditmar 12.50 30.00
79 Steve Korcheck 12.50 30.00
80 Henry Mason RC 12.50 30.00
81 Harry Simpson 12.50 30.00
82 Gene Green 12.50 30.00
83 Bob Shaw 12.50 30.00
84 Howard Reed 12.50 30.00
85 Dick Stigman 12.50 30.00
86 Rip Repulski 12.50 30.00
87 Seth Morehead 12.50 30.00
88 Camilo Carreon RC 12.50 30.00
89 Johnny Blanchard 15.00 40.00
90 Billy Hoeft 12.50 30.00
91 Fred Hopke RC 12.50 30.00
92 Joe Martin RC 12.50 30.00
93 Wally Shannon RC 12.50 30.00
94 Hal R. 15.00 40.00
Hal W. Smith
95 Al Schroll 12.50 30.00
96 John Kucks 12.50 30.00
97 Tom Morgan 12.50 30.00
98 Willie Jones 12.50 30.00
99 Marshall Renfroe RC 12.50 30.00
100 Willie Tasby 12.50 30.00
101 Irv Noren 12.50 30.00
102 Russ Snyder RC 12.50 30.00
103 Bob Turley 15.00 40.00
104 Jim Woods RC 12.50 30.00
105 Ronnie Kline 12.50 30.00
106 Steve Bilko 12.50 30.00
107 Elmer Valo 12.50 30.00
108 Tom McAvoy RC 12.50 30.00
109 Stan Williams 12.50 30.00
110 Earl Averill Jr. 12.50 30.00
111 Lee Walls 12.50 30.00
112 Paul Richards MG 12.50 30.00
113 Ed Sadowski 12.50 30.00
114 Stover McIlwain RC 12.50 30.00
115 Chuck Tanner UER 15.00 40.00
116 Lou Klimchock RC 12.50 30.00
117 Neil Chrisley 12.50 30.00
118 Johnny Callison 20.00 50.00
119 Hal Smith 12.50 30.00
120 Carl Sawatski 12.50 30.00
121 Frank Leja 12.50 30.00
122 Earl Torgeson 12.50 30.00
123 Art Schult 12.50 30.00
124 Jim Brosnan 12.50 30.00
125 Sparky Anderson 30.00 60.00
126 Joe Pignatano 12.50 30.00
127 Rocky Nelson 12.50 30.00
128 Orlando Cepeda 40.00 80.00
129 Daryl Spencer 12.50 30.00
130 Ralph Lumenti 12.50 30.00
131 Sam Taylor 12.50 30.00
132 Harry Brecheen CO 15.00 40.00
133 Johnny Groth 12.50 30.00
134 Wayne Terwilliger 12.50 30.00
135 Kent Hadley 12.50 30.00
136 Faye Throneberry 12.50 30.00
137 Jack Meyer 12.50 30.00
138 Chuck Cottier RC 12.50 30.00
139 Joe DeMaestri 12.50 30.00
140 Gene Freese 12.50 30.00
141 Curt Flood 20.00 50.00
142 Gino Cimoli 12.50 30.00
143 Clay Dalrymple RC 12.50 30.00
144 Jim Bunning 40.00 80.00

1985 Leaf/Donruss

This standard-size set of cards was produced in an effort to establish a Canadian baseball card market much as Topps' affiliate O-Pee-Chee had done. The Donruss Company in conjunction with its new parent Leaf Company issued this set to the Canadian market. The set was later released in the United States through hobby dealer channels. The cards were issued in wax packs. A piece of a large Lou Gehrig puzzle was inserted in each pack. Aside from card number differences the cards are essentially the same as the Donruss U.S. regular issue of the cards of the same players; however the backs are in both French and English. Two cards, Dick Perez artwork of Tim Raines (252) and Dave Stieb (251), are called Canadian Greats (CG) and are not contained in the Donruss U.S. set. As in most Canadian sets, the players featured are heavily biased towards Canadian teams and those American teams closest to the Canadian border. Diamond Kings (numbers 1-26 denoted DK) and Rated Rookies (number 27 denoted RR) are included just as in the American set. Those players selected for and included as Diamond Kings do not have a regular card in the set. The player cards are numbered on the back. The checklist cards (listed at the end of the list below) are numbered one, two and three (but are not given a traditional card number); the Diamond Kings checklist card is unnumbered; and the Lou Gehrig puzzle card is mistakenly numbered 635. Key cards in this set include Roger Clemens and Dwight Gooden in their Rookie Card year.

COMPLETE SET (264) 20.00 50.00
1 Ryne Sandberg DK .75 2.00
2 Doug DeCinces DK .01 .05
3 Richard Dotson DK .01 .05
4 Bert Blyleven DK .02 .10
5 Lou Whitaker DK .05 .15
6 Dan Quisenberry DK .01 .05
7 Don Mattingly DK 1.25 3.00
8 Carney Lansford DK .01 .05
9 Frank Tanana DK .01 .05
10 Willie Upshaw DK .01 .05
11 Claudell Washington DK .01 .05
12 Mike Marshall DK .01 .05
13 Joaquin Andujar DK .01 .05
14 Cal Ripken DK 1.50 4.00
15 Jim Rice DK .07 .20
16 Don Sutton DK .20 .50
17 Frank Viola DK .02 .10
18 Alvin Davis DK .01 .05
19 Mario Soto DK .01 .05
20 Jose Cruz DK .02 .10
21 Charlie Lea DK .01 .05
22 Jesse Orosco DK .02 .10
23 Juan Samuel DK .01 .05
24 Tony Pena DK .01 .05
25 Tony Gwynn DK 2.00 5.00
26 Bob Brenly DK .01 .05
27 Steve Kiefer RR .01 .05
28 Joe Morgan .30 .75
29 Luis Leal .01 .05
30 Dan Gladden .02 .10
31 Shane Rawley .01 .05
32 Mark Clear .01 .05
33 Terry Kennedy .01 .05
34 Hal McRae .02 .10
35 Mickey Rivers .01 .05
36 Tom Brunansky .01 .05
37 LaMarr Hoyt .01 .05
38 Orel Hershiser RC .60 1.50
39 Chris Bando .01 .05
40 Lee Lacy .01 .05
41 Lance Parrish .02 .10
42 George Foster .02 .10
43 Kevin McReynolds .01 .05
44 Robin Yount .30 .75
45 Craig McMurtry .01 .05
46 Mike Witt .01 .05
47 Gary Redus .01 .05
48 Dennis Rasmussen .01 .05
49 Gary Woods .01 .05
50 Phil Bradley .02 .10
51 Steve Bedrosian .01 .05
52 Duane Walker .01 .05
53 Geoff Zahn .01 .05
54 Dave Stieb .01 .05
55 Pascual Perez .01 .05
56 Mark Langston RC .07 .20
57 Bob Dernier .01 .05
58 Joe Cowley .01 .05
59 Dan Schatzeder .01 .05
60 Ozzie Smith .75 2.00
61 Bob Knepper .01 .05
62 Keith Hernandez .02 .10
63 Rick Rhoden .01 .05
64 Alejandro Pena .01 .05
65 Damaso Garcia .01 .05
66 Chili Davis .02 .10
67 Al Oliver .02 .10
68 Alan Wiggins .01 .05
69 Darryl Motley .01 .05
70 Gary Ward .01 .05
71 John Butcher .01 .05
72 Scott McGregor .01 .05
73 Bruce Hurst .01 .05
74 Dwayne Murphy .01 .05
75 Greg Luzinski .02 .10
76 Pat Tabler .01 .05
77 Chet Lemon .01 .05
78 Jim Sundberg .01 .05
79 Wally Backman .01 .05
80 Terry Puhl .01 .05
81 Storm Davis .01 .05
82 Jim Wohlford .01 .05
83 Willie Randolph .02 .10
84 Ron Cey .02 .10
85 Jim Beattie .02 .10
86 Rafael Ramirez .01 .05
87 Cesar Cedeno .02 .10
88 Bobby Grich .02 .10
89 Jason Thompson .01 .05
90 Steve Sax .01 .05
91 Tony Fernandez .07 .20
92 Jeff Leonard .01 .05
93 Von Hayes .01 .05
94 Steve Garvey .07 .20
95 Steve Balboni .01 .05
96 Larry Parrish .01 .05
97 Tim Teufel .01 .05
98 Sammy Stewart .01 .05
99 Roger Clemens RC 8.00 20.00
100 Steve Kemp .01 .05
101 Tom Seaver .40 1.00
102 Andre Thornton .01 .05
103 Kirk Gibson .05 .15
104 Ted Simmons .02 .10
105 David Palmer .01 .05
106 Roy Lee Jackson .01 .05
107 Kirby Puckett RC 5.00 12.00
108 Charlie Hough .02 .10
109 Mike Boddicker .01 .05
110 Willie Wilson .01 .05
111 Tim Lollar .01 .05
112 Tony Armas .01 .05
113 Steve Carlton .30 .75
114 Gary Lavelle .01 .05
115 Cliff Johnson .01 .05
116 Ray Burris .01 .05
117 Rudy Law .01 .05
118 Mike Scioscia .05 .15
119 Kent Tekulve UER/(Telukve on back).02 .10
120 George Vukovich .01 .05
121 Barbaro Garbey .01 .05
122 Mookie Wilson .02 .10
123 Ben Oglivie .01 .05
124 Jerry Mumphrey .01 .05
125 Willie McGee .02 .10
126 Jeff Reardon .02 .10
127 Dave Winfield .40 1.00
128 Lee Smith .05 .15
129 Ken Phelps .01 .05
130 Rick Camp .01 .05
131 Dave Concepcion .02 .10
132 Rod Carew .30 .75
133 Andre Dawson .07 .20
134 Doyle Alexander .01 .05
135 Miguel Dilone .01 .05
136 Jim Gott .01 .05
137 Eric Show .01 .05
138 Phil Niekro .07 .20
139 Rick Sutcliffe .01 .05
140 Dave Winfield .60 1.50
Don Mattingly
Two for the Title
141 Ken Oberkfell .01 .05
142 Jack Morris .02 .10
143 Lloyd Moseby .01 .05
144 Pete Rose .50 1.25
145 Gary Gaetti .02 .10
146 Don Baylor .02 .10
147 Bobby Meacham .01 .05
148 Frank White .02 .10
149 Mark Thurmond .01 .05
150 Dwight Evans .02 .10
151 Al Holland .01 .05
152 Joel Youngblood .01 .05
153 Rance Mulliniks .01 .05
154 Bill Caudill .01 .05
155 Carlton Fisk .40 1.00
156 Rick Honeycutt .01 .05
157 John Candelaria .01 .05
158 Alan Trammell .05 .15
159 Darryl Strawberry .07 .20
160 Aurelio Lopez .01 .05
161 Enos Cabell .01 .05
162 Dion James .01 .05
163 Bruce Sutter .20 .50
164 Razor Shines .01 .05
165 Butch Wynegar .01 .05
166 Rich Bordi .01 .05
167 Spike Owen .01 .05
168 Chris Chambliss .01 .05
169 Dave Parker .02 .10
170 Reggie Jackson .30 .75
171 Bryn Smith .01 .05
172 Dave Collins .01 .05
173 Dave Engle .01 .05
174 Buddy Bell .01 .05
175 Mike Flanagan .01 .05
176 George Brett 1.00 2.50
177 Graig Nettles .02 .10
178 Jerry Koosman .01 .05
179 Wade Boggs .60 1.50
180 Jody Davis .01 .05
181 Ernie Whitt .01 .05
182 Dave Kingman .02 .10
183 Vance Law .01 .05
184 Fernando Valenzuela .02 .10
185 Bill Madlock .01 .05
186 Brett Butler .02 .10
187 Doug Sisk .01 .05
188 Dan Petry .01 .05
189 Joe Niekro .01 .05
190 Rollie Fingers .20 .50
191 David Green .01 .05
192 Steve Rogers .01 .05
193 Ken Griffey .02 .10
194 Scott Sanderson .01 .05
195 Barry Bonnell .01 .05
196 Bruce Benedict .01 .05
197 Keith Moreland .01 .05
198 Fred Lynn .02 .10
199 Tim Wallach .01 .05
200 Kent Hrbek .02 .10
201 Pete O'Brien .01 .05

202 Bud Black .01 .05
203 Eddie Murray .60 1.50
204 Goose Gossage .02 .10
205 Mike Schmidt .50 1.25
206 Mike Easler .01 .05
207 Jack Clark .02 .10
208 Rickey Henderson .40 1.25
209 Jesse Barfield .01 .05
210 Ron Kittle .01 .05
211 Pedro Guerrero .01 .05
212 Johnny Ray .01 .05
213 Julio Franco .02 .10
214 Hubie Brooks .01 .05
215 Darrell Evans .02 .10
216 Nolan Ryan 2.00 5.00
217 Jim Gantner .01 .05
218 Tim Raines .02 .10
219 Dave Righetti .01 .05
220 Gary Matthews .01 .05
221 Jack Perconte .01 .05
222 Dale Murphy .07 .20
223 Brian Downing .01 .05
224 Mickey Hatcher .01 .05
225 Lonnie Smith .01 .05
226 Jorge Orta .01 .05
227 Milt Wilcox .01 .05
228 John Denny .01 .05
229 Marty Barrett .01 .05
230 Alfredo Griffin .01 .05
231 Harold Baines .05 .15
232 Bill Russell .01 .05
233 Marvell Wynne .01 .05
234 Dwight Gooden RC .60 1.50
235 Willie Hernandez .01 .05
236 Bill Gullickson .01 .05
237 Ron Guidry .02 .10
238 Leon Durham .01 .05
239 Al Cowens .01 .05
240 Bob Horner .01 .05
241 Gary Carter .30 .75
242 Glenn Hubbard .01 .05
243 Steve Trout .01 .05
244 Jay Howell .01 .05
245 Terry Francona .02 .10
246 Cecil Cooper .02 .10
247 Larry McWilliams .01 .05
248 George Bell .01 .05
249 Larry Herndon .01 .05
250 Ozzie Virgil .01 .05
251 Dave Stieb CG .02 .10
252 Tim Raines CG .07 .20
253 Ricky Horton .01 .05
254 Bill Buckner .02 .10
255 Dan Driessen .01 .05
256 Ron Darling .01 .05
257 Doug Flynn .01 .05
258 Darrell Porter .01 .05
259 George Hendrick .01 .05
260 Checklist DK 1-26/(Unnumbered) .01 .05
261 Checklist 27-106/(Unnumbered) .01 .05
262 Checklist 107-178/(Unnumbered) .01 .05
263 Checklist 179-259/(Unnumbered) .01 .05
635 Lou Gehrig .07 .20
Puzzle Card UER/(Misnumbered)

1986 Leaf/Donruss

This 264-card standard-size set was issued with a puzzle of Hank Aaron. Except for the numbering, the company logo and the bilingual backs, the cards are essentially the same as the Donruss U.S. regular issue cards of the same players. On a light blue background, the horizontal backs carry player biography, statistics and career hightlights in French and English. Two cards, Dick Perez artwork of Jesse Barfield (254) and Jeff Reardon (214), are called Canadian Greats (CG) and are not contained in the Donruss U.S. set. Diamond Kings (numbers 1-26, denoted DK) and Rated Rookies (numbers 27-29, denoted RR) are included just as in the American set. The cards are numbered on the back. As in most Canadian sets, the players featured are heavily biased toward Canadian teams and those American teams closest to the Canadian border. Those players selected for and included as Diamond Kings do not have a regular card in the set. The checklist cards (listed at the end of the list below) are numbered one, two and three (but are not given a traditional card number); the Diamond Kings checklist card is also unnumbered. Two key cards in this set are Andres Galarraga and Fred McGriff, who are Rookie Cards in the 1986 Donruss set.

COMPLETE SET (264) 8.00 20.00
1 Kirk Gibson DK .07 .20
2 Goose Gossage DK .05 .15
3 Willie McGee DK .02 .10
4 George Bell DK .01 .05
5 Tony Armas DK .01 .05
6 Chili Davis DK .02 .10
7 Cecil Cooper DK .02 .10
8 Mike Boddicker DK .01 .05
9 Davey Lopes DK .01 .05
10 Bill Doran DK .01 .05
11 Bret Saberhagen DK .02 .10
12 Brett Butler DK .02 .10
13 Harold Baines DK .05 .15
14 Mike Davis DK .01 .05
15 Tony Perez DK .15 .40
16 Willie Randolph DK .02 .10
17 Bob Boone DK .02 .10
18 Orel Hershiser DK .05 .15
19 Johnny Ray DK .01 .05
20 Gary Ward DK .01 .05
21 Rick Mahler DK .01 .05
22 Phil Bradley DK .01 .05
23 Jerry Koosman DK .02 .10
24 Tom Brunansky DK .01 .05
25 Andre Dawson DK .07 .20
26 Dwight Gooden DK .07 .20
27 Andres Galarraga RR RC 2.00 5.00
28 Fred McGriff RR RC 2.00 5.00
29 Dave Shipanoff RR .01 .05
30 Danny Jackson .01 .05
31 Robin Yount .15 .40
32 Mike Fitzgerald .01 .05
33 Lou Whitaker .02 .10
34 Alfredo Griffin .01 .05
35 Oil Can Boyd .01 .05
36 Ron Guidry .02 .10
37 Rickey Henderson .30 .75
38 Jack Morris .02 .10
39 Brian Downing .01 .05
40 Mike Marshall .01 .05
41 Tony Gwynn .60 1.50
42 George Brett .60 1.50
43 Jim Gantner .01 .05
44 Hubie Brooks .01 .05
45 Tony Fernandez .02 .10
46 Oddibe McDowell .01 .05
47 Ozzie Smith .50 1.25
48 Ken Griffey .02 .10
49 Jose Cruz .02 .10
50 Mariano Duncan .02 .10
51 Mike Schmidt .30 .75
52 Pat Tabler .01 .05
53 Pete Rose .30 .75
54 Frank White .02 .10
55 Carney Lansford .01 .05
56 Steve Garvey .07 .20
57 Vance Law .01 .05
58 Tony Pena .01 .05
59 Wayne Tolleson .01 .05
60 Dale Murphy .07 .20
61 LaMarr Hoyt .01 .05
62 Ryne Sandberg .40 1.00
63 Gary Carter .30 .75
64 Lee Smith .05 .15
65 Alvin Davis .01 .05
66 Edwin Nunez .01 .05
67 Kent Hrbek .02 .10
68 Dave Stieb .02 .10
69 Kirby Puckett .60 1.50
70 Paul Molitor .30 .75
71 Glenn Hubbard .01 .05
72 Lloyd Moseby .01 .05
73 Mike Smithson .01 .05
74 Jeff Leonard .01 .05
75 Danny Darwin .01 .05
76 Kevin McReynolds .01 .05
77 Bill Buckner .02 .10
78 Ron Oester .01 .05
79 Tommy Herr .01 .05
80 Mike Pagliarulo .01 .05
81 Ron Romanick .01 .05
82 Brook Jacoby .01 .05
83 Eddie Murray .40 1.00
84 Gary Pettis .01 .05
85 Chet Lemon .01 .05
86 Toby Harrah .01 .05
87 Mike Scioscia .05 .15
88 Bert Blyleven .02 .10
89 Dave Righetti .01 .05
90 Bob Knepper .01 .05
91 Fernando Valenzuela .02 .10
92 Dave Dravecky .02 .10
93 Julio Franco .02 .10
94 Keith Moreland .01 .05
95 Darryl Motley .01 .05
96 Jack Clark .02 .10
97 Tim Wallach .01 .05
98 Steve Balboni .01 .05
99 Storm Davis .01 .05
100 Jay Howell .01 .05
101 Alan Trammell .05 .15
102 Willie Hernandez .01 .05
103 Don Mattingly .60 1.50
104 Lee Lacy .01 .05
105 Pedro Guerrero .01 .05
106 Willie Wilson .01 .05
107 Craig Reynolds .01 .05
108 Tim Raines .02 .10
109 Shane Rawley .01 .05
110 Larry Parrish .01 .05
111 Eric Show .01 .05
112 Mike Witt .01 .05
113 Dennis Eckersley .30 .75
114 Mike Moore .01 .05
115 Vince Coleman .02 .10
116 Damaso Garcia .01 .05
117 Steve Carlton .20 .50
118 Floyd Bannister .01 .05
119 Mario Soto .01 .05
120 Fred Lynn .02 .10
121 Bob Horner .01 .05
122 Rick Sutcliffe .01 .05
123 Walt Terrell .01 .05
124 Keith Hernandez .02 .10
125 Dave Winfield .30 .75
126 Frank Viola .02 .10
127 Dwight Evans .02 .10
128 Willie Upshaw .01 .05
129 Andre Thornton .01 .05
130 Donnie Moore .01 .05
131 Darryl Strawberry .02 .10
132 Nolan Ryan 1.00 2.50
133 Garry Templeton .01 .05
134 John Tudor .01 .05
135 Dave Parker .02 .10
136 Larry McWilliams .01 .05
137 Terry Pendleton .02 .10
138 Terry Puhl .01 .05
139 Bob Dernier .01 .05
140 Ozzie Guillen RC* .07 .20
141 Jim Clancy .01 .05
142 Cal Ripken 1.00 2.50
143 Mickey Hatcher .01 .05
144 Dan Petry .01 .05
145 Rich Gedman .01 .05
146 Jim Rice .02 .10
147 Butch Wynegar .01 .05
148 Donnie Hill .01 .05
149 Jim Sundberg .01 .05
150 Joe Hesketh .01 .05
151 Chris Codiroli .01 .05
152 Charlie Hough .02 .10
153 Herm Winningham .01 .05
154 Dave Rozema .01 .05
155 Don Slaught .01 .05
156 Juan Beniquez .01 .05
157 Ted Higuera .01 .05
158 Andy Hawkins .01 .05
159 Don Robinson .01 .05
160 Glenn Wilson .01 .05
161 Earnest Riles .01 .05
162 Nick Esasky .01 .05
163 Carlton Fisk .20 .50
164 Claudell Washington .01 .05
165 Scott McGregor .01 .05
166 Nate Snell .01 .05
167 Ted Simmons .02 .10
168 Wade Boggs .25 .60
169 Marty Barrett .01 .05
170 Bud Black .01 .05
171 Charlie Leibrandt .01 .05
172 Charlie Lea .01 .05
173 Reggie Jackson .25 .60
174 Bryn Smith .01 .05
175 Glenn Davis .01 .05
176 Von Hayes .01 .05
177 Danny Cox .01 .05
178 Sammy Khalifa .01 .05
179 Tom Browning .01 .05
180 Scott Garrelts .01 .05
181 Shawon Dunston .02 .10
182 Doyle Alexander .01 .05
183 Jim Presley .01 .05
184 Al Cowens .01 .05
185 Mark Salas .01 .05
186 Tom Niedenfuer .01 .05
187 Dave Henderson .01 .05
188 Lonnie Smith .01 .05
189 Bruce Bochte .01 .05
190 Leon Durham .01 .05
191 Terry Francona .05 .15
192 Bruce Sutter .20 .50
193 Steve Crawford .01 .05
194 Bob Brenly .01 .05
195 Dan Pasqua .01 .05
196 Juan Samuel .01 .05
197 Floyd Rayford .01 .05
198 Tim Burke .01 .05
199 Ben Oglivie .01 .05
200 Don Carman .01 .05
201 Lance Parrish .02 .10
202 Terry Forster .01 .05
203 Neal Heaton .01 .05
204 Ivan Calderon RC .02 .10
205 Jorge Orta .01 .05
206 Tom Henke .01 .05
207 Rick Reuschel .02 .10
208 Dan Quisenberry .02 .10
209 Pete Rose HL .50 1.25
Ty-Breaking
210 Floyd Youmans .01 .05
211 Tom Filer .01 .05
212 R.J. Reynolds .01 .05
213 Gorman Thomas .01 .05
214 Jeff Reardon CG .02 .10
215 Chris Brown .01 .05
216 Rick Aguilera RC .05 .15
217 Ernie Whitt .01 .05
218 Joe Orsulak .01 .05
219 Jimmy Key .05 .15
220 Atlee Hammaker .01 .05
221 Ron Darling .01 .05
222 Zane Smith .01 .05
223 Bob Welch .01 .05
224 Reid Nichols .01 .05
225 Vince Coleman .02 .10
Willie McGee
Fleet Feet
226 Mark Gubicza .01 .05
227 Tim Birtsas .01 .05
228 Mike Hargrove .02 .10
229 Randy St. Claire .01 .05
230 Larry Herndon .01 .05
231 Dusty Baker .02 .10
232 Mookie Wilson .02 .10
233 Jeff Lahti .01 .05
234 Tom Seaver .30 .75
235 Mike Scott .01 .05
236 Don Sutton .20 .50
237 Roy Smalley .01 .05
238 Bill Madlock .02 .10
239 Charlie Hudson .01 .05
Charles on both sides
240 John Franco .07 .20
241 Frank Tanana .02 .10
242 Sid Fernandez .01 .05
243 Phil Niekro .07 .20
Joe Niekro
Knuckle Brothers
244 Dennis Lamp .01 .05
245 Gene Nelson .01 .05
246 Terry Harper .01 .05
247 Vida Blue .02 .10
248 Roger McDowell RC .07 .20
249 Tony Bernazard .01 .05
250 Cliff Johnson .01 .05
251 Hal McRae .01 .05
252 Garth Iorg .01 .05
253 Mitch Webster .01 .05
254 Jesse Barfield CG .02 .10
255 Dan Driessen .01 .05
256 Mike Brown .01 .05
Pirates OF
257 Ron Kittle .01 .05
258 Bo Diaz .01 .05
259 Hank Aaron Puzzle Card .07 .20
260 Pete Rose .50 1.25
King Of Kings
261 Checklist DK 1-26 .01 .05
Unnumbered
262 Checklist 27-106 .01 .05
Unnumbered
263 Checklist 107-186 .01 .05
Unnumbered
264 Checklist 187-260 .01 .05
Unnumbered

1987 Leaf/Donruss

This 264-card standard-size set was issued with a puzzle of Roberto Clemente. Except for the numbering, the company logo and the bilingual backs, the cards are essentially the same as the Donruss U.S. regular issue cards of the same players. On a golden background, the horizontal backs carry player biography, statistics and career hightlights in French and English. Two cards, Dick Perez artwork of Floyd Youmans (65) and Mark Eichhorn (173), are called Canadian Greats (CG) and are not contained in the Donruss U.S. set. Diamond Kings (numbers 1-26, denoted DK) and Rated Rookies (numbers 28-47, denoted RR) are included just as in the American set. The players featured in this set are heavily biased toward Canadian teams and those American teams closest to the Canadian border. Players appearing in their Rookie Card year include Will Clark, Wally Joyner and Greg Maddux. There is also a early Mark McGwire card in this set.

COMPLETE SET (264) 20.00 50.00
1 Wally Joyner DK .07 .20
2 Roger Clemens DK .30 1.00
3 Dale Murphy DK .07 .20
4 Darryl Strawberry DK .02 .10
5 Ozzie Smith DK .20 .50
6 Jose Canseco DK .25 .60
7 Charlie Hough DK .01 .05
8 Brook Jacoby DK .01 .05
9 Fred Lynn DK .02 .10
10 Rick Rhoden DK .01 .05
11 Chris Brown DK .01 .05
12 Von Hayes DK .01 .05
13 Jack Morris DK .02 .10
14 Kevin McReynolds DK .01 .05
15 George Brett DK .25 .60
16 Ted Higuera DK .01 .05
17 Hubie Brooks DK .01 .05
18 Mike Scott DK .01 .05
19 Kirby Puckett DK .20 .50
20 Dave Winfield DK .15 .40
21 Lloyd Moseby DK .01 .05
22 Eric Davis DK .05 .15
23 Jim Presley DK .01 .05
24 Keith Moreland DK .01 .05
25 Greg Walker DK .01 .05
26 Steve Sax DK .01 .05
27 DK Checklist 1-26 .01 .05
28 B.J. Surhoff RR RC .20 .50
29 Randy Myers RR RC .07 .20
30 Ken Gerhart RR .01 .05
31 Benito Santiago RR .05 .15
32 Greg Swindell RR RC .02 .10
33 Mike Birkbeck RR .01 .05
34 Terry Steinbach RR RC .07 .20
35 Bo Jackson RR RC .75 2.00
36 Greg Maddux RR RC 4.00 10.00
37 Jim Lindeman RR .01 .05
38 Devon White RR RC .10 .30
39 Eric Bell RR .01 .05
40 Will Fraser RR .01 .05
41 Jerry Browne RR .01 .05
42 Chris James RR .01 .05
43 Rafael Palmeiro RR RC 1.50 4.00
44 Pat Dodson RR .01 .05
45 Duane Ward RR .02 .10
46 Mark McGwire RR 3.00 8.00
47 Bruce Fields RR .01 .05
48 Jody Davis .01 .05
49 Roger McDowell .01 .05
50 Jose Guzman .01 .05
51 Oddibe McDowell .01 .05
52 Harold Baines .05 .15
53 Dave Righetti .01 .05
54 Moose Haas .01 .05
55 Mark Langston .01 .05
56 Kirby Puckett .40 1.00
57 Dwight Evans .02 .10
58 Willie Randolph .02 .10
59 Wally Backman .01 .05
60 Bryn Smith .01 .05
61 Tim Wallach .01 .05
62 Joe Hesketh .01 .05
63 Garry Templeton .01 .05
64 Robby Thompson .02 .10
65 Floyd Youmans CG .02 .10
66 Ernest Riles .01 .05
67 Robin Yount .20 .50
68 Darryl Strawberry .02 .10
69 Ernie Whitt .01 .05
70 Dave Winfield .20 .50
71 Paul Molitor .20 .50
72 Dave Stieb .02 .10
73 Tom Henke .01 .05
74 Frank Viola .01 .05
75 Scott Garrelts .01 .05
76 Mike Boddicker .01 .05
77 Keith Moreland .01 .05
78 Lou Whitaker .02 .10
79 Dave Parker .02 .10
80 Lee Smith .05 .15
81 Tom Candiotti .01 .05
82 Greg A. Harris .01 .05
83 Fred Lynn .02 .10
84 Dwight Gooden .02 .10
85 Ron Darling .01 .05
86 Mike Krukow .01 .05
87 Spike Owen .01 .05
88 Len Dykstra .05 .15
89 Rick Aguilera .02 .10
90 Jim Clancy .01 .05
91 Joe Johnson .01 .05
92 Damaso Garcia .01 .05
93 Sid Fernandez .01 .05
94 Bob Ojeda .01 .05
95 Ted Higuera .01 .05
96 George Brett .40 1.00
97 Willie Wilson .02 .10
98 Cal Ripken 1.00 2.50
99 Kent Hrbek .02 .10
100 Bert Blyleven .02 .10
101 Ron Guidry .02 .10
102 Andy Allanson .01 .05
103 Dave Henderson .01 .05
104 Kirk Gibson .02 .10
105 Lloyd Moseby .01 .05
106 Tony Fernandez .02 .10
107 Lance Parrish .02 .10
108 Ozzie Smith .30 .75
109 Gary Carter .25 .60
110 Eddie Murray .25 .60
111 Mike Witt .01 .05
112 Bobby Witt .01 .05
113 Willie McGee .02 .10
114 Steve Garvey .05 .15
115 Glenn Davis .01 .05
116 Jose Cruz .02 .10
117 Ozzie Guillen .02 .10
118 Alvin Davis .01 .05
119 Jose Rijo .01 .05
120 Bill Madlock .02 .10
121 Tommy Herr .01 .05
122 Mike Schmidt .30 .75
123 Mike Scioscia .05 .15
124 Terry Pendleton .02 .10
125 Leon Durham .01 .05
126 Alan Trammell .05 .15
127 Jesse Barfield .01 .05
128 Shawon Dunston .01 .05
129 Pete Rose .30 .75
130 Von Hayes .01 .05
131 Julio Franco .02 .10
132 Juan Samuel .01 .05
133 Joe Carter .07 .20
134 Brook Jacoby .01 .05
135 Jack Morris .02 .10
136 Bob Horner .01 .05
137 Calvin Schiraldi .01 .05
138 Tom Browning .01 .05
139 Shane Rawley .01 .05
140 Mario Soto .01 .05
141 Dale Murphy .07 .20
142 Hubie Brooks .01 .05
143 Jeff Reardon .02 .10
144 Will Clark RC .75 2.00
145 Ed Correa .01 .05
146 Glenn Wilson .01 .05
147 Johnny Ray .01 .05
148 Fernando Valenzuela .02 .10
149 Tim Raines .02 .10
150 Don Mattingly .50 1.25
151 Jose Canseco .30 .75
152 Gary Pettis .01 .05
153 Don Sutton .20 .50
154 Jim Presley .01 .05
155 Checklist 28-105 .01 .05
156 Dale Sveum .01 .05
157 Cory Snyder .01 .05
158 Jeff Sellers .01 .05
159 Denny Walling .01 .05
160 Danny Cox .01 .05
161 Bob Forsch .01 .05
162 Joaquin Andujar .01 .05
163 Roberto Clemente .07 .20
Puzzle Card
164 Paul Assenmacher RC .02 .10
165 Marty Barrett .01 .05
166 Ray Knight .01 .05
167 Rafael Santana .01 .05
168 Bruce Ruffin .01 .05
169 Buddy Bell .02 .10
170 Kevin Mitchell RC .08 .25
171 Ken Oberkfell .01 .05
172 Gene Garber .01 .05
173 Mark Eichhorn CG .02 .10
174 Don Carman .01 .05
175 Jesse Orosco .02 .10
176 Mookie Wilson .02 .10
177 Gary Ward .01 .05
178 John Franco .02 .10
179 Eric Davis .05 .15
180 Walt Terrell .01 .05
181 Phil Niekro .15 .40
182 Pat Tabler .01 .05
183 Brett Butler .02 .10
184 George Bell .01 .05
185 Pete Incaviglia RC .05 .15
186 Pete O'Brien .01 .05
187 Jimmy Key .05 .15
188 Frank White .02 .10
189 Mike Pagliarulo .01 .05
190 Roger Clemens .50 1.25
191 Rickey Henderson .30 .75
192 Mike Easler .01 .05
193 Wade Boggs .20 .50
194 Vince Coleman .01 .05
195 Charlie Kerfeld .01 .05
196 Dickie Thon .01 .05
197 Bill Doran .01 .05
198 Alfredo Griffin .01 .05
199 Carlton Fisk .15 .40
200 Phil Bradley .01 .05
201 Reggie Jackson .30 .75
202 Bob Boone .02 .10
203 Steve Sax .01 .05
204 Tom Niedenfuer .01 .05
205 Tim Burke .01 .05
206 Floyd Youmans .01 .05
207 Jay Tibbs .01 .05
208 Chili Davis .05 .15
209 Larry Parrish .01 .05
210 John Cerutti .01 .05
211 Kevin Bass .01 .05
212 Andre Dawson .07 .20
213 Bob Sebra .01 .05
214 Kevin McReynolds .01 .05
215 Jim Morrison .01 .05
216 Candy Maldonado .01 .05
217 John Kruk .07 .20
218 Todd Worrell .02 .10
219 Barry Bonds 8.00 20.00
220 Andy McGaffigan .01 .05
221 Andres Galarraga .15 .40
222 Mike Fitzgerald .01 .05
223 Kirk McCaskill .01 .05
224 Dave Smith .01 .05
225 Ruben Sierra RC .40 1.00
226 Scott Fletcher .01 .05
227 Chet Lemon .01 .05
228 Dan Petry .01 .05
229 Mark Eichhorn .01 .05
230 Cecil Cooper .02 .10
231 Willie Upshaw .01 .05
232 Don Baylor .02 .10
233 Keith Hernandez .02 .10
234 Ryne Sandberg .30 .75
235 Tony Gwynn .50 1.25
236 Chris Brown .01 .05
237 Pedro Guerrero .01 .05
238 Mark Gubicza .01 .05
239 Sid Bream .01 .05
240 Joe Cowley .01 .05
241 Bill Buckner .02 .10
242 John Candelaria .01 .05
243 Scott McGregor .01 .05
244 Tom Brunansky .01 .05
245 Gary Gaetti .02 .10
246 Orel Hershiser .02 .10
247 Jim Rice .02 .10
248 Oil Can Boyd .01 .05
249 Bob Knepper .01 .05
250 Danny Tartabull .01 .05
251 John Cangelosi .01 .05
252 Wally Joyner RC .20 .50
253 Bruce Hurst .01 .05
254 Rich Gedman .01 .05
255 Jim Deshaies .01 .05
256 Tony Pena .01 .05
257 Nolan Ryan 1.00 2.50
258 Mike Scott .01 .05
259 Checklist 106-183 .01 .05
260 Dennis Rasmussen .01 .05
261 Bret Saberhagen .02 .10
262 Steve Balboni .01 .05
263 Tom Seaver .15 .40
264 Checklist 184-264 .01 .05

1987 Leaf Special Olympics

This set is also known as the Candy City team as that is the logo which appears on the front of the card. This set was issued for the proceeds of the set to go to the Special Olympics. The set was in the style of the 1983 Donruss Hall of Fame Heroes set and the only additions were generic cards about various sports. The cards are standard size. These cards were issued in special three card packs which contained two baseball players and one special olympics card. A collector could receive the entire 18 card set by mailing $1 as a donation.

COMPLETE SET (18) 6.00 15.00
COMMON PLAYER (H1-H12) .10 .25
COMMON PLAYER (S1 S6) .04 .10
H1 Mickey Mantle 2.00 5.00
H2 Yogi Berra .30 .75
H3 Roy Campanella .30 .75
H4 Stan Musial .75 2.00
H5 Ted Williams 1.00 2.50
H6 Duke Snider .30 .75
H7 Hank Aaron .75 2.00
H8 Pee Wee Reese .30 .75
H9 Brooks Robinson .20 .50
H10 Al Kaline .20 .50
H11 Willie McCovey .08 .25
H12 Cool Papa Bell .08 .25
S1 Basketball .10 .30
S2 Softball .20 .50
S3 Track And Field .20 .50
S4 Soccer .07 .20
S5 Gymnastics .20 .50
S6 VII International .20 .50
Summer Games

1988 Leaf/Donruss

This 264-card standard-size set was issued with a puzzle of Stan Musial. Except for the numbering, the company logo and the bilingual backs, the cards are essentially the same as the Donruss U.S. regular issue cards of the same players. On a light blue background, the horizontal backs carry player biography, statistics, and career hightlights in French and English. Two cards, Dick Perez artwork of George Bell (213) and Tim Wallach (255), are called Canadian Greats (CG) and are not contained in the Donruss U.S. set. Diamond Kings (numbers 1-26, denoted DK) and Rated Rookies (numbers 28-47, denoted RR) are included just as in the American set. There are also bonus cards of the the two Canadian teams' MVP's, George Bell and Tim Raines, as in the Donruss American set. The players featured are heavily biased toward Canadian teams and those American teams closest to the Canadian border. Players appearing in their Rookie Card year include Roberto Alomar and Mark Grace.

COMPLETE SET (264) 6.00 15.00
1 Mark McGwire DK .40 1.00
2 Tim Raines DK .02 .10
3 Benito Santiago DK .02 .10
4 Alan Trammell DK .05 .15
5 Danny Tartabull DK .01 .05
6 Ron Darling DK .01 .05
7 Paul Molitor DK .20 .50
8 Devon White DK .01 .05
9 Andre Dawson DK .07 .20
10 Julio Franco DK .02 .10
11 Scott Fletcher DK .01 .05
12 Tony Fernandez DK .02 .10
13 Shane Rawley DK .01 .05
14 Kal Daniels DK .01 .05
15 Jack Clark DK .02 .10
16 Dwight Evans DK .02 .10
17 Tommy John DK .02 .10
18 Andy Van Slyke DK .02 .10
19 Gary Gaetti DK .02 .10
20 Mark Langston DK .01 .05
21 Will Clark DK .15 .40
22 Glenn Hubbard DK .01 .05
23 Billy Hatcher DK .01 .05
24 Bob Welch DK .01 .05
25 Ivan Calderon DK .01 .05
26 Cal Ripken DK .60 1.50
27 DK Checklist 1-26 .01 .05
28 Mackey Sasser RR RC .01 .05
29 Jeff Treadway RR .01 .05
30 Mike Campbell RR RC .01 .05
31 Lance Johnson RR RC .05 .15
32 Nelson Liriano RR RC .01 .05
33 Shawn Abner RR .01 .05
34 Roberto Alomar RR RC .60 1.50
35 Shawn Hillegas RR RC .01 .05
36 Joey Meyer RR .01 .05
37 Kevin Elster RR .01 .05
38 Jose Lind RR RC .01 .05
39 Kirt Manwaring RR RC .01 .05
40 Mark Grace RR RC .60 1.50
41 Jody Reed RR RC .01 .05
42 John Farrell RR .01 .05
43 Al Leiter RR RC .15 .40
44 Gary Thurman RR RC .01 .05
45 Vicente Palacios RR RC .01 .05
46 Eddie Williams RR .01 .05
47 Jack McDowell RR RC .07 .20
48 Dwight Gooden .02 .10
49 Mike Witt .01 .05
50 Wally Joyner .05 .15
51 Brook Jacoby .01 .05
52 Bert Blyleven .02 .10
53 Ted Higuera .01 .05
54 Mike Scott .01 .05
55 Jose Guzman .01 .05
56 Roger Clemens .30 .75
57 Dave Righetti .01 .05
58 Benito Santiago .02 .10
59 Ozzie Guillen .02 .10
60 Matt Nokes .01 .05
61 Fernando Valenzuela .02 .10
62 Orel Hershiser .02 .10
63 Sid Fernandez .01 .05
64 Ozzie Virgil .01 .05
65 Wade Boggs .20 .50
66 Floyd Youmans .01 .05
67 Jimmy Key .02 .10
68 Bret Saberhagen .02 .10
69 Jody Davis .01 .05
70 Shawon Dunston .01 .05
71 Julio Franco .05 .15
72 Danny Cox .01 .05
73 Jim Clancy .01 .05
74 Mark Eichhorn .01 .05
75 Scott Bradley .01 .05
76 Charlie Leibrandt .01 .05
77 Nolan Ryan .60 1.50
78 Ron Darling .01 .05
79 John Franco .02 .10
80 Dave Stieb .01 .05
81 Mike Fitzgerald .01 .05
82 Steve Bedrosian .01 .05
83 Dale Murphy .07 .20
84 Tim Burke .01 .05
85 Jack Morris .02 .10
86 Greg Walker .01 .05
87 Kevin Mitchell .02 .10
88 Doug Drabek .01 .05
89 Charlie Hough .02 .10
90 Tony Gwynn .30 .75
91 Rick Sutcliffe .01 .05
92 Shane Rawley .01 .05
93 George Brett .25 .60
94 Frank Viola .01 .05
95 Tony Pena .01 .05
96 Jim Deshaies .01 .05
97 Mike Scioscia .02 .10
98 Rick Rhoden .01 .05
99 Terry Kennedy .01 .05
100 Cal Ripken .60 1.50
101 Pedro Guerrero .01 .05
102 Andy Van Slyke .02 .10
103 Willie McGee .02 .10
104 Mike Kingery .01 .05
105 Kevin Seitzer .01 .05
106 Robin Yount .15 .40
107 Tracy Jones .01 .05
108 Dave Magadan .01 .05
109 Mel Hall .01 .05
110 Billy Hatcher .01 .05
111 Todd Benzinger .01 .05
112 Mike LaValliere .01 .05
113 Barry Bonds .30 .75
114 Tim Raines .02 .10
115 Ozzie Smith .20 .50
116 Dave Winfield .20 .50
117 Keith Hernandez .02 .10
118 Jeffrey Leonard .01 .05
119 Larry Parrish .01 .05
120 Robby Thompson .01 .05
121 Andres Galarraga .07 .20
122 Mickey Hatcher .01 .05
123 Mark Langston .01 .05
124 Mike Schmidt .25 .60
125 Cory Snyder .01 .05
126 Andre Dawson .07 .20
127 Devon White .01 .05
128 Vince Coleman .01 .05
129 Bryn Smith .01 .05
130 Lance Parrish .01 .05
131 Willie Upshaw .01 .05
132 Pete O'Brien .01 .05
133 Tony Fernandez .02 .10
134 Billy Ripken .02 .10
135 Len Dykstra .02 .10
136 Kirk Gibson .02 .10
137 Kevin Bass .01 .05
138 Jose Canseco .20 .50
139 Kent Hrbek .02 .10
140 Lloyd Moseby .01 .05
141 Marty Barrett .01 .05
142 Carmelo Martinez .01 .05
143 Tom Foley .01 .05
144 Kirby Puckett .20 .50
145 Rickey Henderson .25 .60
146 Juan Samuel .01 .05
147 Pete Incaviglia .01 .05
148 Greg Brock .01 .05
149 Eric Davis .02 .10
150 Kal Daniels .01 .05
151 Bob Boone .02 .10
152 John Cerutti .01 .05
153 Mike Greenwell .01 .05
154 Oddibe McDowell .01 .05
155 Scott Fletcher .01 .05
156 Gary Carter .20 .50
157 Harold Baines .02 .10
158 Greg Swindell .01 .05
159 Mark McLemore .02 .10
160 Keith Moreland .01 .05
161 Jim Gantner .01 .05
162 Willie Randolph .02 .10
163 Fred Lynn .01 .05
164 B.J. Surhoff .02 .10
165 Ken Griffey .02 .10
166 Chet Lemon .01 .05
167 Alan Trammell .05 .15
168 Paul Molitor .20 .50
169 Lou Whitaker .02 .10
170 Will Clark .15 .40
171 Dwight Evans .02 .10
172 Eddie Murray .20 .50
173 Darrell Evans .02 .10
174 Ellis Burks RC .15 .40
175 Ivan Calderon .01 .05
176 John Kruk .02 .10
177 Don Mattingly .30 .75
178 Dick Schofield .01 .05
179 Bruce Hurst .01 .05

180 Ron Guidry .02 .10
181 Jack Clark .02 .10
182 Franklin Stubbs .01 .05
183 Bill Doran .01 .05
184 Joe Carter .07 .20
185 Steve Sax .01 .05
186 Glenn Davis .01 .05
187 Bo Jackson .20 .50
188 Bobby Bonilla .01 .05
189 Willie Wilson .01 .05
190 Danny Tartabull .01 .05
191 Bo Diaz .01 .05
192 Buddy Bell .02 .10
193 Tim Wallach .01 .05
194 Mark McGwire .40 1.00
195 Carney Lansford .02 .10
196 Alvin Davis .01 .05
197 Von Hayes .01 .05
198 Mitch Webster .01 .05
199 Casey Candaele .01 .05
200 Gary Gaetti .02 .10
201 Tommy Herr .01 .05
202 Wally Backman .01 .05
203 Brian Downing .01 .05
204 Rance Mulliniks .01 .05
205 Craig Reynolds .01 .05
206 Ruben Sierra .02 .10
207 Ryne Sandberg .25 .60
208 Carlton Fisk .20 .50
209 Checklist 28-107 .01 .05
210 Gerald Young .01 .05
211 Tim Raines MVP/(Bonus card pose) .05 .15
212 John Tudor .01 .05
213 George Bell CG .02 .10
214 George Bell MVP/(Bonus card pose) .02 .10
215 Jim Rice .02 .10
216 Gerald Perry .01 .05
217 Dave Stewart .02 .10
218 Jose Uribe .01 .05
219 Rick Reuschel .02 .10
220 Darryl Strawberry .02 .10
221 Chris Brown .01 .05
222 Ted Simmons .02 .10
223 Lee Mazzilli .01 .05
224 Denny Walling .01 .05
225 Jesse Barfield .01 .05
226 Barry Larkin .20 .50
227 Harold Reynolds .02 .10
228 Kevin McReynolds .01 .05
229 Todd Worrell .02 .10
230 Tommy John .02 .10
231 Rick Aguilera .02 .10
232 Bill Madlock .02 .10
233 Roy Smalley .01 .05
234 Jeff Musselman .01 .05
235 Mike Dunne .01 .05
236 Jerry Browne .01 .05
237 Sam Horn RC .02 .10
238 Howard Johnson .01 .05
239 Candy Maldonado .01 .05
240 Nick Esasky .01 .05
241 Geno Petralli .01 .05
242 Herm Winningham .01 .05
243 Roger McDowell .01 .05
244 Brian Fisher .01 .05
245 John Marzano .01 .05
246 Terry Pendleton .02 .10
247 Rick Leach .01 .05
248 Pascual Perez .01 .05
249 Mookie Wilson .02 .10
250 Ernie Whitt .01 .05
251 Ron Kittle .01 .05
252 Oil Can Boyd .01 .05
253 Jim Gott .01 .05
254 George Bell .01 .05
255 Tim Wallach CG .02 .10
256 Luis Polonia .01 .05
257 Hubie Brooks .01 .05
258 Mickey Brantley .01 .05
259 Gregg Jefferies RC .02 .10
260 Johnny Ray .01 .05
261 Checklist 108-187 .01 .05
262 Dennis Martinez .02 .10
263 Stan Musial Puzzle Card .07 .20
264 Checklist 188-264 .01 .05

1990 Leaf Previews

The 1990 Leaf Previews set contains standard-size cards which were mailed to dealers to announce the 1990 version of Donruss' second major set of the year marketed as an upscale alternative under their Leaf name. This 12-card set was presented in the same style as the other Leaf cards were done in except that "Special Preview" was imprinted in white on the back. The cards were released in two series of 264 and the first series was not released until mid-season.

COMPLETE SET (12) 250.00 500.00
1 Steve Sax 6.00 15.00
2 Joe Carter 10.00 25.00
3 Dennis Eckersley 15.00 40.00
4 Ken Griffey Jr. 125.00 300.00
5 Barry Larkin 20.00 50.00
6 Mark Langston 6.00 15.00
7 Eric Anthony 6.00 15.00
8 Robin Ventura 20.00 50.00
9 Greg Vaughn 10.00 25.00
10 Bobby Bonilla 6.00 15.00
11 Gary Gaetti 10.00 25.00
12 Ozzie Smith 15.00 40.00

1990 Leaf

The 1990 Leaf set was the first premium set introduced by Donruss and represents one of the more significant products issued in the 1990's. The cards were issued in 15-card foil wrapped packs and were not available in factory sets. Each pack also contained one three-piece puzzle panel of a 63-piece Yogi Berra "Donruss Hall of Fame Diamond King" puzzle. This set, which was produced on high quality paper stock, was issued in two separate series of 264 standard-size cards each. The second series was issued approximately six weeks after the release of the first series. The cards feature full-color photos on both the front and back. Rookie Cards in the set include David Justice, John Olerud, Sammy Sosa, Frank Thomas and Larry Walker.

COMPLETE SET (528) 20.00 50.00
COMPLETE SERIES 1 (264) 12.50 30.00
COMPLETE SERIES 2 (264) 6.00 15.00
BEWARE THOMAS COUNTERFEIT
COMP. BERRA PUZZLE .40 1.00
1 Introductory Card .15 .40
2 Mike Henneman .15 .40
3 Steve Bedrosian .15 .40
4 Mike Scott .15 .40
5 Allan Anderson .15 .40
6 Rick Sutcliffe .25 .60
7 Gregg Olson .25 .60
8 Kevin Elster .15 .40
9 Pete O'Brien .15 .40
10 Carlton Fisk .40 1.00
11 Joe Magrane .15 .40
12 Roger Clemens 1.50 4.00
13 Tom Glavine .40 1.00
14 Tom Gordon .25 .60
15 Todd Benzinger .15 .40
16 Hubie Brooks .15 .40
17 Roberto Kelly .15 .40
18 Barry Larkin .40 1.00
19 Mike Boddicker .15 .40
20 Roger McDowell .15 .40
21 Nolan Ryan 2.00 5.00
22 John Farrell .15 .40
23 Bruce Hurst .15 .40
24 Wally Joyner .25 .60
25 Greg Maddux 2.00 5.00
26 Chris Bosio .15 .40
27 John Cerutti .15 .40
28 Tim Burke .15 .40
29 Dennis Eckersley .25 .60
30 Glenn Davis .15 .40
31 Jim Abbott .40 1.00
32 Mike LaValliere .15 .40
33 Andres Thomas .15 .40
34 Lou Whitaker .25 .60
35 Alvin Davis .15 .40
36 Melido Perez .15 .40
37 Craig Biggio .60 1.50
38 Rick Aguilera .25 .60
39 Pete Harnisch .15 .40
40 David Cone .25 .60
41 Scott Garrelts .15 .40
42 Jay Howell .15 .40
43 Eric King .15 .40
44 Pedro Guerrero .15 .40
45 Mike Bielecki .15 .40
46 Bob Boone .25 .60
47 Kevin Brown .25 .60
48 Jerry Browne .15 .40
49 Mike Scioscia .15 .40
50 Chuck Cary .15 .40
51 Wade Boggs .40 1.00
52 Von Hayes .15 .40
53 Tony Fernandez .15 .40
54 Dennis Martinez .25 .60
55 Tom Candiotti .15 .40
56 Andy Benes .25 .60
57 Rob Dibble .25 .60
58 Chuck Crim .15 .40
59 John Smoltz .60 1.50
60 Mike Heath .15 .40
61 Kevin Gross .15 .40
62 Mark McGwire 1.50 4.00
63 Bert Blyleven .25 .60
64 Bob Walk .15 .40
65 Mickey Tettleton .15 .40
66 Sid Fernandez .15 .40
67 Terry Kennedy .15 .40
68 Fernando Valenzuela .25 .60
69 Don Mattingly 1.50 4.00
70 Paul O'Neill .40 1.00
71 Robin Yount 1.00 2.50
72 Bret Saberhagen .25 .60
73 Geno Petralli .15 .40
74 Brook Jacoby .15 .40
75 Roberto Alomar .40 1.00
76 Devon White .25 .60
77 Jose Lind .15 .40
78 Pat Combs .15 .40
79 Dave Stieb .25 .60
80 Tim Wallach .15 .40
81 Dave Stewart .25 .60
82 Eric Anthony RC .15 .40
83 Randy Bush .15 .40
84 Rickey Henderson CL .25 .60
85 Jaime Navarro .15 .40
86 Tommy Gregg .15 .40
87 Frank Tanana .15 .40
88 Omar Vizquel .60 1.50
89 Ivan Calderon .15 .40
90 Vince Coleman .15 .40
91 Barry Bonds 2.00 5.00
92 Randy Milligan .15 .40
93 Frank Viola .15 .40
94 Matt Williams .25 .60
95 Alfredo Griffin .15 .40
96 Steve Sax .15 .40
97 Gary Gaetti .25 .60
98 Ryne Sandberg 1.25 3.00
99 Danny Tartabull .15 .40
100 Rafael Palmeiro .40 1.00
101 Jesse Orosco .15 .40
102 Garry Templeton .15 .40
103 Frank DiPino .15 .40
104 Tony Pena .15 .40
105 Dickie Thon .15 .40
106 Kelly Gruber .15 .40
107 Marquis Grissom RC .75 2.00
108 Jose Canseco .40 1.00
109 Mike Blowers RC .15 .40
110 Tom Browning .15 .40
111 Greg Vaughn .15 .40
112 Oddibe McDowell .15 .40
113 Gary Ward .15 .40
114 Jay Buhner .25 .60
115 Eric Show .15 .40
116 Bryan Harvey .15 .40
117 Andy Van Slyke .40 1.00
118 Jeff Ballard .15 .40
119 Barry Lyons .15 .40
120 Kevin Mitchell .15 .40
121 Mike Gallego .15 .40
122 Dave Smith .15 .40
123 Kirby Puckett .60 1.50
124 Jerome Walton .15 .40
125 Bo Jackson .60 1.50
126 Harold Baines .25 .60
127 Scott Bankhead .15 .40
128 Ozzie Guillen .25 .60
129 Jose Oquendo UER .15 .40
League misspelled as Legue
130 John Dopson .15 .40
131 Charlie Hayes .15 .40
132 Fred McGriff .60 1.50
133 Chet Lemon .15 .40
134 Gary Carter .25 .60
135 Rafael Ramirez .15 .40
136 Shane Mack .15 .40
137 Mark Grace .40 1.00
138 Phil Bradley .15 .40
139 Dwight Gooden .25 .60
140 Harold Reynolds .25 .60
141 Scott Fletcher .15 .40
142 Ozzie Smith 1.00 2.50
143 Mike Greenwell .15 .40
144 Pete Smith .15 .40
145 Mark Gubicza .15 .40
146 Chris Sabo .15 .40
147 Ramon Martinez .15 .40
148 Tim Leary .15 .40
149 Randy Myers .25 .60
150 Jody Reed .15 .40
151 Bruce Ruffin .15 .40
152 Jeff Russell .15 .40
153 Doug Jones .15 .40
154 Tony Gwynn .75 2.00
155 Mark Langston .15 .40
156 Mitch Williams .15 .40
157 Gary Sheffield .60 1.50
158 Tom Henke .15 .40
159 Oil Can Boyd .15 .40
160 Rickey Henderson .60 1.50
161 Bill Doran .15 .40
162 Chuck Finley .25 .60
163 Jeff King .15 .40
164 Nick Esasky .15 .40
165 Cecil Fielder .25 .60
166 Dave Valle .15 .40
167 Robin Ventura .60 1.50
168 Jim Deshaies .15 .40
169 Juan Berenguer .15 .40
170 Craig Worthington .15 .40
171 Gregg Jefferies .25 .60
172 Will Clark .40 1.00
173 Kirk Gibson .25 .60
174 Checklist 89-176 .25 .60
Carlton Fisk
175 Bobby Thigpen .15 .40
176 John Tudor .15 .40
177 Andre Dawson .25 .60
178 George Brett 1.50 4.00
179 Steve Buechele .15 .40
180 Albert Belle .60 1.50
181 Eddie Murray .60 1.50
182 Bob Geren .15 .40
183 Rob Murphy .15 .40
184 Tom Herr .15 .40
185 George Bell .15 .40
186 Spike Owen .15 .40
187 Cory Snyder .15 .40
188 Fred Lynn .15 .40
189 Eric Davis .25 .60
190 Dave Parker .25 .60
191 Jeff Blauser .15 .40
192 Matt Nokes .15 .40
193 Delino DeShields RC .40 1.00
194 Scott Sanderson .15 .40
195 Lance Parrish .15 .40
196 Bobby Bonilla .25 .60
197 Cal Ripken 2.00 5.00
198 Kevin McReynolds .15 .40
199 Robby Thompson .15 .40
200 Tim Belcher .15 .40
201 Jesse Barfield .15 .40
202 Mariano Duncan .15 .40
203 Bill Spiers .15 .40
204 Frank White .25 .60
205 Julio Franco .25 .60
206 Greg Swindell .15 .40
207 Benito Santiago .25 .60
208 Johnny Ray .15 .40
209 Gary Redus .15 .40
210 Jeff Parrett .15 .40
211 Jimmy Key .25 .60
212 Tim Raines .25 .60
213 Carney Lansford .25 .60
214 Gerald Young .15 .40
215 Gene Larkin .15 .40
216 Dan Plesac .15 .40
217 Lonnie Smith .15 .40
218 Alan Trammell .25 .60
219 Jeffrey Leonard .15 .40
220 Sammy Sosa RC 3.00 8.00
221 Todd Zeile .25 .60
222 Bill Landrum .15 .40
223 Mike Devereaux .15 .40
224 Mike Marshall .15 .40
225 Jose Uribe .15 .40
226 Juan Samuel .15 .40
227 Mel Hall .15 .40
228 Kent Hrbek .25 .60
229 Shawon Dunston .15 .40
230 Kevin Seitzer .15 .40
231 Pete Incaviglia .15 .40
232 Sandy Alomar Jr. .25 .60
233 Bip Roberts .15 .40
234 Scott Terry .15 .40
235 Dwight Evans .40 1.00
236 Ricky Jordan .15 .40
237 John Olerud RC 1.25 3.00
238 Zane Smith .15 .40
239 Walt Weiss .15 .40
240 Alvaro Espinoza .15 .40
241 Billy Hatcher .15 .40
242 Paul Molitor .25 .60
243 Dale Murphy .40 1.00
244 Dave Bergman .15 .40
245 Ken Griffey Jr. 5.00 12.00
246 Ed Whitson .15 .40
247 Kirk McCaskill .15 .40
248 Jay Bell .25 .60
249 Ben McDonald RC .40 1.00
250 Darryl Strawberry .25 .60
251 Brett Butler .25 .60
252 Terry Steinbach .15 .40
253 Ken Caminiti .25 .60
254 Dan Gladden .15 .40
255 Dwight Smith .15 .40
256 Kurt Stillwell .15 .40
257 Ruben Sierra .25 .60
258 Mike Schooler .15 .40
259 Lance Johnson .15 .40
260 Terry Pendleton .25 .60
261 Ellis Burks .40 1.00
262 Len Dykstra .25 .60
263 Mookie Wilson .25 .60
264 Nolan Ryan CL UER .60 1.50
265 Nolan Ryan SPEC 1.00 2.50
266 Brian DuBois RC .15 .40
267 Don Robinson .15 .40
268 Glenn Wilson .15 .40
269 Kevin Tapani RC .40 1.00
270 Marvell Wynne .15 .40
271 Bill Ripken .15 .40
272 Howard Johnson .15 .40
273 Brian Holman .15 .40
274 Dan Pasqua .15 .40
275 Ken Dayley .15 .40
276 Jeff Reardon .25 .60
277 Jim Presley .15 .40
278 Jim Eisenreich .15 .40
279 Danny Jackson .15 .40
280 Orel Hershiser .25 .60
281 Andy Hawkins .15 .40
282 Jose Rijo .15 .40
283 Luis Rivera .15 .40
284 John Kruk .25 .60
285 Jeff Huson RC .15 .40
286 Joel Skinner .15 .40
287 Jack Clark .25 .60
288 Chili Davis .25 .60
289 Joe Girardi .40 1.00
290 B.J. Surhoff .25 .60
291 Luis Sojo RC .15 .40
292 Tom Foley .15 .40
293 Mike Moore .15 .40
294 Ken Oberkfell .15 .40
295 Luis Polonia .15 .40
296 Doug Drabek .15 .40
297 David Justice RC 1.25 3.00
298 Paul Gibson .15 .40
299 Edgar Martinez .40 1.00
300 Frank Thomas RC 12.00 30.00
301 Eric Yelding RC .15 .40
302 Greg Gagne .15 .40
303 Brad Komminsk .15 .40
304 Ron Darling .15 .40
305 Kevin Bass .15 .40
306 Jeff Hamilton .15 .40
307 Ron Karkovice .15 .40
308 M.Thompson UER Lankford .40 1.00
309 Mike Harkey .15 .40
310 Mel Stottlemyre Jr. .15 .40
311 Kenny Rogers .25 .60
312 Mitch Webster .15 .40
313 Kal Daniels .15 .40
314 Matt Nokes .15 .40
315 Dennis Lamp .15 .40
316 Ken Howell .15 .40
317 Glenallen Hill .15 .40
318 Dave Martinez .15 .40
319 Chris James .15 .40
320 Mike Pagliarulo .15 .40
321 Hal Morris .15 .40
322 Rob Deer .15 .40
323 Greg Olson C RC .15 .40
324 Tony Phillips .15 .40
325 Larry Walker RC 3.00 8.00
326 Ron Hassey .15 .40
327 Jack Howell .15 .40
328 John Smiley .15 .40
329 Steve Finley .25 .60
330 Dave Magadan .15 .40
331 Greg Litton .15 .40
332 Mickey Hatcher .15 .40
333 Lee Guetterman .15 .40
334 Norm Charlton .15 .40
335 Edgar Diaz RC .15 .40
336 Willie Wilson .15 .40
337 Bobby Witt .15 .40
338 Candy Maldonado .15 .40
339 Craig Lefferts .15 .40
340 Dante Bichette .25 .60
341 Wally Backman .15 .40
342 Dennis Cook .15 .40
343 Pat Borders .15 .40
344 Wallace Johnson .15 .40
345 Willie Randolph .25 .60
346 Danny Darwin .15 .40
347 Al Newman .15 .40
348 Mark Knudson .15 .40
349 Joe Boever .15 .40
350 Larry Sheets .15 .40
351 Mike Jackson .15 .40
352 Wayne Edwards RC .15 .40
353 Bernard Gilkey RC .40 1.00
354 Don Slaught .15 .40
355 Joe Orsulak .15 .40
356 John Franco .25 .60
357 Jeff Brantley .15 .40
358 Mike Morgan .15 .40
359 Deion Sanders .60 1.50
360 Terry Leach .15 .40
361 Les Lancaster .15 .40
362 Storm Davis .15 .40
363 Scott Coolbaugh RC .15 .40
364 Checklist 265-352 .40 1.00
Ozzie Smith
365 Cecilio Guante .15 .40
366 Joey Cora .25 .60
367 Willie McGee .25 .60
368 Jerry Reed .15 .40
369 Darren Daulton .25 .60
370 Manny Lee .15 .40
371 Mark Gardner RC .15 .40
372 Rick Honeycutt .15 .40
373 Steve Balboni .15 .40
374 Jack Armstrong .15 .40
375 Charlie O'Brien .15 .40
376 Ron Gant .25 .60
377 Lloyd Moseby .15 .40
378 Gene Harris .15 .40
379 Joe Carter .25 .60
380 Scott Bailes .15 .40
381 R.J. Reynolds .15 .40
382 Bob Melvin .15 .40
383 Tim Teufel .15 .40
384 John Burkett .15 .40
385 Felix Jose .15 .40
386 Larry Andersen .15 .40
387 David West .15 .40
388 Luis Salazar .15 .40
389 Mike Macfarlane .15 .40
390 Charlie Hough .25 .60
391 Greg Briley .15 .40
392 Donn Pall .15 .40
393 Bryn Smith .15 .40
394 Carlos Quintana .15 .40
395 Steve Lake .15 .40
396 Mark Whiten RC .40 1.00
397 Edwin Nunez .15 .40
398 Rick Parker RC .15 .40
399 Mark Portugal .15 .40
400 Roy Smith .15 .40
401 Hector Villanueva RC .15 .40
402 Bob Milacki .15 .40
403 Alejandro Pena .15 .40
404 Scott Bradley .15 .40
405 Ron Kittle .15 .40
406 Bob Tewksbury .15 .40
407 Wes Gardner .15 .40
408 Ernie Whitt .15 .40
409 Terry Shumpert RC .15 .40
410 Tim Layana RC .15 .40
411 Chris Gwynn .15 .40
412 Jeff D. Robinson .15 .40
413 Scott Scudder .15 .40
414 Kevin Romine .15 .40
415 Jose DeJesus .15 .40
416 Mike Jeffcoat .15 .40
417 Rudy Seanez RC .15 .40
418 Mike Dunne .15 .40
419 Dick Schofield .15 .40
420 Steve Wilson .15 .40
421 Bill Krueger .15 .40
422 Junior Felix .15 .40
423 Drew Hall .15 .40
424 Curt Young .15 .40
425 Franklin Stubbs .15 .40
426 Dave Winfield .25 .60
427 Rick Reed RC .40 1.00
428 Charlie Leibrandt .15 .40
429 Jeff M. Robinson .15 .40
430 Erik Hanson .15 .40
431 Barry Jones .15 .40
432 Alex Trevino .15 .40
433 John Moses .15 .40
434 Dave Wayne Johnson RC .15 .40
435 Mackey Sasser .15 .40
436 Rick Leach .15 .40
437 Lenny Harris .15 .40
438 Carlos Martinez .15 .40
439 Rex Hudler .15 .40
440 Domingo Ramos .15 .40
441 Gerald Perry .15 .40
442 Jeff Russell .15 .40
443 Carlos Baerga RC .40 1.00
444 Will Clark CL .25 .60
445 Stan Javier .15 .40
446 Kevin Maas RC .40 1.00
447 Tom Brunansky .15 .40
448 Carmelo Martinez .15 .40
449 Willie Blair RC .15 .40
450 Andres Galarraga .25 .60
451 Bud Black .15 .40
452 Greg W. Harris .15 .40
453 Joe Oliver .15 .40
454 Greg Brock .15 .40
455 Jeff Treadway .15 .40
456 Lance McCullers .15 .40
457 Dave Schmidt .15 .40
458 Todd Burns .15 .40
459 Max Venable .15 .40
460 Neal Heaton .15 .40
461 Mark Williamson .15 .40
462 Keith Miller .15 .40
463 Mike LaCoss .15 .40
464 Jose Offerman RC .40 1.00
465 Jim Leyritz RC .75 2.00
466 Glenn Braggs .15 .40
467 Ron Robinson .15 .40
468 Mark Davis .15 .40
469 Gary Pettis .15 .40
470 Keith Hernandez .25 .60
471 Dennis Rasmussen .15 .40
472 Mark Eichhorn .15 .40
473 Ted Power .15 .40
474 Terry Mulholland .15 .40
475 Todd Stottlemyre .25 .60
476 Jerry Goff RC .15 .40
477 Gene Nelson .15 .40
478 Rich Gedman .15 .40
479 Brian Harper .15 .40
480 Mike Felder .15 .40
481 Steve Avery .15 .40
482 Jack Morris .25 .60
483 Randy Johnson 1.25 3.00
484 Scott Radinsky RC .15 .40
485 Jose DeLeon .15 .40
486 Stan Belinda RC .15 .40
487 Brian Holton .15 .40
488 Mark Carreon .15 .40
489 Trevor Wilson .15 .40
490 Mike Sharperson .15 .40
491 Alan Mills RC .15 .40
492 John Candelaria .15 .40
493 Paul Assenmacher .15 .40
494 Steve Crawford .15 .40
495 Brad Arnsberg .15 .40
496 Sergio Valdez RC .15 .40
497 Mark Parent .15 .40
498 Tom Pagnozzi .15 .40
499 Greg A. Harris .15 .40
500 Randy Ready .15 .40
501 Duane Ward .15 .40
502 Nelson Santovenia .15 .40
503 Joe Klink RC .15 .40
504 Eric Plunk .15 .40
505 Jeff Reed .15 .40
506 Ted Higuera .15 .40
507 Joe Hesketh .15 .40
508 Dan Petry .15 .40
509 Matt Young .15 .40
510 Jerald Clark .15 .40
511 John Orton RC .15 .40
512 Scott Ruskin RC .15 .40
513 Chris Hoiles RC .40 1.00
514 Daryl Boston .15 .40
515 Francisco Oliveras .15 .40
516 Ozzie Canseco .15 .40
517 Xavier Hernandez RC .15 .40
518 Fred Manrique .15 .40
519 Shawn Boskie RC .15 .40
520 Jeff Montgomery .25 .60
521 Jack Daugherty RC .15 .40
522 Keith Comstock .15 .40
523 Greg Hibbard RC .15 .40
524 Lee Smith .25 .60
525 Dana Kiecker RC .15 .40
526 Darrel Akerfelds .15 .40
527 Greg Myers .15 .40
528 Ryne Sandberg CL .60 1.50

1991 Leaf Previews

COMPLETE SET (26) 12.00 30.00
FOUR PER DONRUSS HOBBY FACT.SET
1 David Justice .40 1.00
2 Ryne Sandberg 1.50 4.00
3 Barry Larkin .60 1.50
4 Craig Biggio .60 1.50
5 Ramon Martinez .20 .50
6 Tim Wallach .20 .50
7 Dwight Gooden .40 1.00
8 Len Dykstra .40 1.00
9 Barry Bonds 3.00 8.00
10 Ray Lankford .40 1.00
11 Tony Gwynn 1.25 3.00
12 Will Clark .60 1.50
13 Leo Gomez .20 .50
14 Wade Boggs .60 1.50
15 Chuck Finley UER .40 1.00
16 Carlton Fisk .60 1.50
17 Sandy Alomar Jr. .20 .50
18 Cecil Fielder .40 1.00
19 Bo Jackson .40 1.00
20 Paul Molitor .40 1.00
21 Kirby Puckett 1.00 2.50
22 Don Mattingly 2.50 6.00
23 Rickey Henderson 1.00 2.50
24 Tino Martinez .40 1.00
25 Nolan Ryan 4.00 10.00
26 Dave Stieb .20 .50

1991 Leaf

This 528-card standard size set was issued by Donruss in two separate series of 264 cards. Cards were exclusively issued in foil packs. The front design has color action player photos, with white and silver borders. A thicker stock was used for these (then) premium level cards. Production for the 1991 set was greatly increased due to the huge demand for the benchmark 1990 Leaf set. However, the 1991 cards were met with modest enthusiasm due to a weak selection of Rookie Cards and superior competition from brands like 1991 Stadium Club.

COMPLETE SET (528) 6.00 15.00
COMPLETE SERIES 1 (264) 2.00 5.00
COMPLETE SERIES 2 (264) 4.00 10.00
COMP. KILLEBREW PUZZLE .50 1.00
1 The Leaf Card .02 .10
2 Kurt Stillwell .02 .10
3 Bobby Witt .02 .10
4 Tony Phillips .02 .10
5 Scott Garrelts .02 .10
6 Greg Swindell .02 .10
7 Billy Ripken .02 .10
8 Dave Martinez .02 .10
9 Kelly Gruber .02 .10
10 Juan Samuel .02 .10
11 Brian Holman .02 .10
12 Craig Biggio .10 .30
13 Lonnie Smith .02 .10
14 Ron Robinson .02 .10
15 Mike LaValliere .02 .10
16 Mark Davis .02 .10
17 Jack Daugherty .02 .10
18 Mike Henneman .02 .10
19 Mike Greenwell .02 .10
20 Dave Magadan .02 .10
21 Mark Williamson .02 .10
22 Marquis Grissom .07 .20
23 Pat Borders .02 .10
24 Mike Scioscia .02 .10
25 Shawon Dunston .02 .10
26 Randy Bush .02 .10
27 John Smoltz .10 .30
28 Chuck Crim .02 .10
29 Don Slaught .02 .10
30 Mike Macfarlane .02 .10
31 Wally Joyner .07 .20
32 Pat Combs .02 .10
33 Tony Pena .02 .10
34 Howard Johnson .02 .10
35 Leo Gomez .02 .10
36 Spike Owen .02 .10
37 Eric Davis .07 .20
38 Roberto Kelly .02 .10
39 Jerome Walton .02 .10
40 Shane Mack .02 .10
41 Kent Mercker .02 .10
42 B.J. Surhoff .07 .20
43 Jerry Browne .02 .10
44 Lee Smith .07 .20
45 Chuck Finley .07 .20
46 Terry Mulholland .02 .10
47 Tom Bolton .02 .10
48 Tom Herr .02 .10
49 Jim Deshaies .02 .10
50 Walt Weiss .02 .10
51 Hal Morris .02 .10
52 Lee Guetterman .02 .10
53 Paul Assenmacher .02 .10
54 Brian Harper .02 .10
55 Paul Gibson .02 .10
56 John Burkett .02 .10
57 Doug Jones .02 .10
58 Jose Oquendo .02 .10
59 Dick Schofield .02 .10
60 Dickie Thon .02 .10
61 Ramon Martinez .02 .10
62 Jay Buhner .07 .20
63 Mark Portugal .02 .10
64 Bob Welch .02 .10
65 Chris Sabo .02 .10
66 Chuck Cary .02 .10
67 Mark Langston .02 .10
68 Joe Boever .02 .10
69 Jody Reed .02 .10
70 Alejandro Pena .02 .10
71 Jeff King .02 .10
72 Tom Pagnozzi .02 .10
73 Joe Oliver .02 .10
74 Mike Witt .02 .10
75 Hector Villanueva .02 .10
76 Dan Gladden .02 .10
77 David Justice .07 .20
78 Mike Gallego .02 .10
79 Tom Candiotti .02 .10
80 Ozzie Smith .30 .75
81 Luis Polonia .02 .10
82 Randy Ready .02 .10
83 Greg A. Harris .02 .10
84 David Justice CL .02 .10
85 Kevin Mitchell .02 .10
86 Mark McLemore .02 .10
87 Terry Steinbach .02 .10
88 Tom Browning .02 .10
89 Matt Nokes .02 .10
90 Mike Harkey .02 .10
91 Omar Vizquel .10 .30
92 Dave Bergman .02 .10
93 Matt Williams .07 .20
94 Steve Olin .02 .10
95 Craig Wilson RC .02 .10
96 Dave Stieb .02 .10
97 Ruben Sierra .07 .20
98 Jay Howell .02 .10
99 Scott Bradley .02 .10
100 Eric Yelding .02 .10
101 Rickey Henderson .20 .50
102 Jeff Reed .02 .10
103 Jimmy Key .07 .20
104 Terry Shumpert .02 .10
105 Kenny Rogers .07 .20
106 Cecil Fielder .07 .20
107 Robby Thompson .02 .10
108 Alex Cole .02 .10
109 Randy Milligan .02 .10
110 Andres Galarraga .07 .20
111 Bill Spiers .02 .10
112 Kal Daniels .02 .10
113 Henry Cotto .02 .10
114 Casey Candaele .02 .10
115 Jeff Blauser .02 .10
116 Robin Yount .30 .75
117 Ben McDonald .02 .10
118 Bret Saberhagen .07 .20
119 Juan Gonzalez .20 .50
120 Lou Whitaker .07 .20
121 Ellis Burks .07 .20
122 Charlie O'Brien .02 .10
123 John Smiley .02 .10
124 Tim Burke .02 .10
125 John Olerud .07 .20
126 Eddie Murray .20 .50
127 Greg Maddux .30 .75
128 Kevin Tapani .02 .10
129 Ron Gant .07 .20
130 Jay Bell .07 .20
131 Chris Hoiles .02 .10
132 Tom Gordon .02 .10
133 Kevin Seitzer .02 .10
134 Jeff Huson .02 .10
135 Jerry Don Gleaton .02 .10
136 Jeff Brantley UER .02 .10
Photo actually Rick Leach on
137 Felix Fermin .02 .10
138 Mike Devereaux .02 .10
139 Delino DeShields .07 .20
140 David Wells .07 .20
141 Tim Crews .02 .10
142 Erik Hanson .02 .10
143 Mark Davidson .02 .10
144 Tommy Gregg .02 .10
145 Jim Gantner .02 .10
146 Jose Lind .02 .10
147 Danny Tartabull .02 .10
148 Geno Petralli .02 .10
149 Travis Fryman .07 .20
150 Tim Naehring .02 .10
151 Kevin McReynolds .02 .10
152 Joe Orsulak .02 .10
153 Steve Frey .02 .10
154 Duane Ward .02 .10
155 Stan Javier .02 .10
156 Damon Berryhill .02 .10
157 Gene Larkin .02 .10
158 Greg Olson .02 .10
159 Mark Knudson .02 .10
160 Carmelo Martinez .02 .10
161 Storm Davis .02 .10
162 Jim Abbott .10 .30
163 Len Dykstra .07 .20
164 Tom Brunansky .02 .10
165 Dwight Gooden .07 .20
166 Jose Mesa .02 .10
167 Oil Can Boyd .02 .10

168 Barry Larkin .10 .30
169 Scott Sanderson .02 .10
170 Mark Grace .10 .30
171 Mark Guthrie .02 .10
172 Tom Glavine .10 .30
173 Gary Sheffield .07 .20
174 Roger Clemens CL .30 .75
175 Chris James .02 .10
176 Milt Thompson .02 .10
177 Donnie Hill .02 .10
178 Wes Chamberlain RC .02 .10
179 John Marzano .02 .10
180 Frank Viola .07 .20
181 Eric Anthony .02 .10
182 Jose Canseco .10 .30
183 Scott Scudder .02 .10
184 Dave Eiland .02 .10
185 Luis Salazar .02 .10
186 Pedro Munoz RC .02 .10
187 Steve Searcy .02 .10
188 Don Robinson .02 .10
189 Sandy Alomar Jr. .02 .10
190 Jose DeLeon .02 .10
191 John Orton .02 .10
192 Darren Daulton .07 .20
193 Mike Morgan .02 .10
194 Greg Briley .02 .10
195 Karl Rhodes .02 .10
196 Harold Baines .07 .20
197 Bill Doran .02 .10
198 Alvaro Espinoza .02 .10
199 Kirk McCaskill .02 .10
200 Jose DeJesus .02 .10
201 Jack Clark .07 .20
202 Daryl Boston .02 .10
203 Randy Tomlin RC .02 .10
204 Pedro Guerrero .07 .20
205 Billy Hatcher .02 .10
206 Tim Leary .02 .10
207 Ryne Sandberg .30 .75
208 Kirby Puckett .20 .50
209 Charlie Leibrandt .02 .10
210 Rick Honeycutt .02 .10
211 Joel Skinner .02 .10
212 Rex Hudler .02 .10
213 Bryan Harvey .02 .10
214 Charlie Hayes .02 .10
215 Matt Young .02 .10
216 Terry Kennedy .02 .10
217 Carl Nichols .02 .10
218 Mike Moore .02 .10
219 Paul O'Neill .10 .30
220 Steve Sax .02 .10
221 Shawn Boskie .02 .10
222 Rich DeLucia RC .02 .10
223 Lloyd Moseby .02 .10
224 Mike Kingery .02 .10
225 Carlos Baerga .02 .10
226 Bryn Smith .02 .10
227 Todd Stottlemyre .02 .10
228 Julio Franco .07 .20
229 Jim Gott .02 .10
230 Mike Schooler .02 .10
231 Steve Finley .07 .20
232 Dave Henderson .02 .10
233 Luis Quinones .02 .10
234 Mark Whiten .02 .10
235 Brian McRae RC .07 .20
236 Rich Gossage .07 .20
237 Rob Deer .02 .10
238 Will Clark .10 .30
239 Albert Belle .07 .20
240 Bob Melvin .02 .10
241 Larry Walker .20 .50
242 Dante Bichette .07 .20
243 Orel Hershiser .07 .20
244 Pete O'Brien .02 .10
245 Pete Harnisch .02 .10
246 Jeff Treadway .02 .10
247 Julio Machado .02 .10
248 Dave Johnson .02 .10
249 Kirk Gibson .07 .20
250 Kevin Brown .07 .20
251 Milt Cuyler .02 .10
252 Jeff Reardon .07 .20
253 David Cone .07 .20
254 Gary Redus .02 .10
255 Junior Noboa .02 .10
256 Greg Myers .02 .10
257 Dennis Cook .02 .10
258 Joe Girardi .02 .10
259 Allan Anderson .02 .10
260 Paul Marak RC .02 .10
261 Barry Bonds .60 1.50
262 Juan Bell .02 .10
263 Russ Morman .02 .10
264 George Brett CL .20 .50
265 Jerald Clark .02 .10
266 Dwight Evans .10 .30
267 Roberto Alomar .10 .30
268 Danny Jackson .02 .10
269 Brian Downing .02 .10
270 John Cerutti .02 .10
271 Robin Ventura .07 .20
272 Gerald Perry .02 .10
273 Wade Boggs .10 .30
274 Dennis Martinez .07 .20
275 Andy Benes .02 .10
276 Tony Fossas .02 .10
277 Franklin Stubbs .02 .10
278 John Kruk .07 .20
279 Kevin Gross .02 .10
280 Von Hayes .02 .10
281 Frank Thomas .20 .50
282 Rob Dibble .07 .20
283 Mel Hall .02 .10
284 Rick Mahler .02 .10
285 Dennis Eckersley .07 .20
286 Bernard Gilkey .02 .10
287 Dan Plesac .02 .10
288 Jason Grimsley .02 .10
289 Mark Lewis .02 .10
290 Tony Gwynn .25 .60
291 Jeff Russell .02 .10
292 Curt Schilling .20 .50
293 Pascual Perez .02 .10
294 Jack Morris .07 .20
295 Hubie Brooks .02 .10
296 Alex Fernandez .02 .10
297 Harold Reynolds .07 .20
298 Craig Worthington .02 .10
299 Willie Wilson .02 .10
300 Mike Maddux .02 .10
301 Dave Righetti .07 .20
302 Paul Molitor .07 .20
303 Gary Gaetti .07 .20
304 Terry Pendleton .07 .20
305 Kevin Elster .02 .10
306 Scott Fletcher .02 .10
307 Jeff Robinson .02 .10
308 Jesse Barfield .02 .10
309 Mike LaCoss .02 .10
310 Andy Van Slyke .10 .30
311 Glenallen Hill .02 .10
312 Bud Black .02 .10
313 Kent Hrbek .07 .20
314 Tim Teufel .02 .10
315 Tony Fernandez .02 .10
316 Beau Allred .02 .10
317 Curtis Wilkerson .02 .10
318 Bill Sampen .02 .10
319 Randy Johnson .25 .60
320 Mike Heath .02 .10
321 Sammy Sosa .20 .50
322 Mickey Tettleton .02 .10
323 Jose Vizcaino .02 .10
324 John Candelaria .02 .10
325 Dave Howard RC .02 .10
326 Jose Rijo .02 .10
327 Todd Zeile .02 .10
328 Gene Nelson .02 .10
329 Dwayne Henry .02 .10
330 Mike Boddicker .02 .10
331 Ozzie Guillen .07 .20
332 Sam Horn .02 .10
333 Wally Whitehurst .02 .10
334 Dave Parker .07 .20
335 George Brett .50 1.25
336 Bobby Thigpen .02 .10
337 Ed Whitson .02 .10
338 Ivan Calderon .02 .10
339 Mike Pagliarulo .02 .10
340 Jack McDowell .02 .10
341 Dana Kiecker .02 .10
342 Fred McGriff .10 .30
343 Mark Lee RC .02 .10
344 Alfredo Griffin .02 .10
345 Scott Bankhead .02 .10
346 Darrin Jackson .02 .10
347 Rafael Palmeiro .10 .30
348 Steve Farr .02 .10
349 Hensley Meulens .02 .10
350 Danny Cox .02 .10
351 Alan Trammell .07 .20
352 Edwin Nunez .02 .10
353 Joe Carter .07 .20
354 Eric Show .02 .10
355 Vance Law .02 .10
356 Jeff Gray RC .02 .10
357 Bobby Bonilla .07 .20
358 Ernest Riles .02 .10
359 Ron Hassey .02 .10
360 Willie McGee .07 .20
361 Mackey Sasser .02 .10
362 Glenn Braggs .02 .10
363 Mario Diaz .02 .10
364 Barry Bonds CL .40 1.00
365 Kevin Bass .02 .10
366 Pete Incaviglia .02 .10
367 Luis Sojo UER .02 .10
1989 stats inter-
spersed with 19
368 Lance Parrish .07 .20
369 Mark Leonard RC .02 .10
370 Heathcliff Slocumb RC .07 .20
371 Jimmy Jones .02 .10
372 Ken Griffey Jr. .50 1.25
373 Chris Hammond FLC .02 .10
374 Chili Davis .07 .20
375 Joey Cora .02 .10
376 Ken Hill .02 .10
377 Darryl Strawberry .07 .20
378 Ron Darling .02 .10
379 Sid Bream .02 .10
380 Bill Swift .02 .10
381 Shawn Abner .02 .10
382 Eric King .02 .10
383 Mickey Morandini .02 .10
384 Carlton Fisk .10 .30
385 Steve Lake .02 .10
386 Mike Jeffcoat .02 .10
387 Darren Holmes RC .07 .20
388 Tim Wallach .02 .10
389 George Bell .02 .10
390 Craig Lefferts .02 .10
391 Ernie Whitt .02 .10
392 Felix Jose .02 .10
393 Kevin Maas .02 .10
394 Devon White .07 .20
395 Otis Nixon .02 .10
396 Chuck Knoblauch .07 .20
397 Scott Coolbaugh .02 .10
398 Glenn Davis .02 .10
399 Manny Lee .02 .10
400 Andre Dawson .07 .20
401 Scott Chiamparino .02 .10
402 Bill Gullickson .02 .10
403 Lance Johnson .02 .10
404 Juan Agosto .02 .10
405 Danny Darwin .02 .10
406 Barry Jones .02 .10
407 Larry Andersen .02 .10
408 Luis Rivera .02 .10
409 Jaime Navarro .02 .10
410 Roger McDowell .02 .10
411 Brett Butler .07 .20
412 Dale Murphy .10 .30
413 Tim Raines UER .07 .20
414 Norm Charlton .02 .10
415 Greg Cadaret .02 .10
416 Chris Nabholz .02 .10
417 Dave Stewart .07 .20
418 Rich Gedman .02 .10
419 Willie Randolph .07 .20
420 Mitch Williams .02 .10
421 Brook Jacoby .02 .10
422 Greg W. Harris .02 .10
423 Nolan Ryan .75 2.00
424 Dave Rohde .02 .10
425 Don Mattingly .50 1.25
426 Greg Gagne .02 .10
427 Vince Coleman .02 .10
428 Dan Pasqua .02 .10
429 Alvin Davis .02 .10
430 Cal Ripken .60 1.50
431 Jamie Quirk .02 .10
432 Benito Santiago .07 .20
433 Jose Uribe .02 .10
434 Candy Maldonado .02 .10
435 Junior Felix .02 .10
436 Deion Sanders .10 .30
437 John Franco .07 .20
438 Greg Hibbard .02 .10
439 Floyd Bannister .02 .10
440 Steve Howe .02 .10
441 Steve Decker RC .02 .10
442 Vicente Palacios .02 .10
443 Pat Tabler .02 .10
444 Checklist 357-448 .02 .10
Darryl Strawberry
445 Mike Felder .02 .10
446 Al Newman .02 .10
447 Chris Donnels RC .02 .10
448 Rich Rodriguez RC .02 .10
449 Turner Ward RC .07 .20
450 Bob Walk .02 .10
451 Gilberto Reyes .02 .10
452 Mike Jackson .02 .10
453 Rafael Belliard .02 .10
454 Wayne Edwards .02 .10
455 Andy Allanson .02 .10
456 Dave Smith .02 .10
457 Gary Carter .07 .20
458 Warren Cromartie .02 .10
459 Jack Armstrong .02 .10
460 Bob Tewksbury .02 .10
461 Joe Klink .02 .10
462 Xavier Hernandez .02 .10
463 Scott Radinsky .02 .10
464 Jeff Robinson .02 .10
465 Gregg Jefferies .02 .10
466 Denny Neagle RC .20 .50
467 Carmelo Martinez .02 .10
468 Donn Pall .02 .10
469 Bruce Hurst .02 .10
470 Eric Bullock .02 .10
471 Rick Aguilera .07 .20
472 Charlie Hough .07 .20
473 Carlos Quintana .02 .10
474 Marty Barrett .02 .10
475 Kevin D. Brown .02 .10
476 Bobby Ojeda .02 .10
477 Edgar Martinez .10 .30
478 Bip Roberts .02 .10
479 Mike Flanagan .02 .10
480 John Habyan .02 .10
481 Larry Casian RC .02 .10
482 Wally Backman .02 .10
483 Doug Dascenzo .02 .10
484 Rick Dempsey .02 .10
485 Ed Sprague .02 .10
486 Steve Chitren RC .02 .10
487 Mark McGwire .60 1.50
488 Roger Clemens .60 1.50
489 Orlando Merced RC .02 .10
490 Rene Gonzales .02 .10
491 Mike Stanton .02 .10
492 Al Osuna RC .02 .10
493 Rick Cerone .02 .10
494 Mariano Duncan .02 .10
495 Zane Smith .02 .10
496 John Morris .02 .10
497 Frank Tanana .02 .10
498 Junior Ortiz .02 .10
499 Dave Winfield .07 .20
500 Gary Varsho .02 .10
501 Chico Walker .02 .10
502 Ken Caminiti .07 .20
503 Ken Griffey Sr. .07 .20
504 Randy Myers .02 .10
505 Steve Bedrosian .02 .10
506 Cory Snyder .02 .10
507 Cris Carpenter .02 .10
508 Tim Belcher .02 .10
509 Jeff Hamilton .02 .10
510 Steve Avery .02 .10
511 Dave Valle .02 .10
512 Tom Lampkin .02 .10
513 Shawn Hillegas .02 .10
514 Reggie Jefferson .02 .10
515 Ron Karkovice .02 .10
516 Doug Drabek .02 .10
517 Tom Henke .02 .10
518 Chris Bosio .02 .10
519 Gregg Olson .02 .10
520 Bob Scanlan RC .02 .10
521 Alonzo Powell RC .02 .10
522 Jeff Ballard .02 .10
523 Ray Lankford .07 .20
524 Tommy Greene .02 .10
525 Mike Timlin RC .07 .20
526 Juan Berenguer .02 .10
527 Scott Erickson .02 .10
528 Checklist 449-528 .02 .10
and BC13-BC26
Sandy Alomar Jr.

1991 Leaf Gold Rookies

COMPLETE SET (26) 6.00 15.00
RANDOM INSERTS IN BOTH SERIES
*265-276 ERR: 4X TO 10X BASIC GR
265-276 ERR RANDOM IN EARLY PACKS
BC1 Scott Leius .40 1.00
BC2 Luis Gonzalez .60 1.50
BC3 Wil Cordero .40 1.00
BC4 Gary Scott .40 1.00
BC5 Willie Banks .40 1.00
BC6 Arthur Rhodes .40 1.00
BC7 Mo Vaughn .40 1.00
BC8 Henry Rodriguez .40 1.00
BC9 Todd Van Poppel .40 1.00
BC10 Reggie Sanders .60 1.50
BC11 Rico Brogna .40 1.00
BC12 Mike Mussina 2.00 5.00
BC13 Kirk Dressendorfer .40 1.00
BC14 Jeff Bagwell 1.50 4.00
BC15 Pete Schourek .40 1.00
BC16 Wade Taylor .40 1.00
BC17 Pat Kelly .40 1.00
BC18 Tim Costo .40 1.00
BC19 Roger Salkeld .40 1.00
BC20 Andujar Cedeno .40 1.00
BC21 Ryan Klesko .60 1.50
BC22 Mike Huff .40 1.00
BC23 Anthony Young .40 1.00
BC24 Eddie Zosky .40 1.00
BC25 Nolan Ryan DP .75 2.00
BC26 Rickey Henderson DP .60 1.50

1992 Leaf Preview

COMPLETE SET (26) 15.00 40.00
COMMON CARD (1-26) .10 .20
FOUR PER DONRUSS HOBBY FACTORY SET
1 Steve Avery .07 .20
2 Ryne Sandberg 1.00 2.50
3 Chris Sabo .07 .20
4 Jeff Bagwell .60 1.50
5 Darryl Strawberry .25 .60
6 Bret Barberie .07 .20
7 Howard Johnson .07 .20
8 John Kruk .25 .60
9 Andy Van Slyke .40 1.00
10 Felix Jose .07 .20
11 Fred McGriff .40 1.00
12 Will Clark .40 1.00
13 Cal Ripken 2.00 5.00
14 Phil Plantier .07 .20
15 Lee Stevens .07 .20
16 Frank Thomas .60 1.50
17 Mark Whiten .07 .20
18 Cecil Fielder .25 .60
19 George Brett 1.50 4.00
20 Robin Yount 1.00 2.50
21 Scott Erickson .07 .20
22 Don Mattingly 1.50 4.00
23 Jose Canseco .40 1.00
24 Ken Griffey Jr. 1.25 3.00
25 Nolan Ryan 2.50 6.00
26 Joe Carter .25 .60

1992 Leaf Gold Previews

COMPLETE SET (33) 15.00 40.00
1 Steve Avery .40 1.00
2 Ryne Sandberg 2.00 5.00
3 Chris Sabo .40 1.00
4 Jeff Bagwell 2.00 5.00
5 Darryl Strawberry .60 1.50
6 Bret Barberie .40 1.00
7 Howard Johnson .40 1.00
8 John Kruk .60 1.50
9 Andy Van Slyke .60 1.50
10 Felix Jose .40 1.00
11 Fred McGriff .75 2.00
12 Will Clark 1.50 4.00
13 Cal Ripken 8.00 20.00
14 Phil Plantier .40 1.00
15 Lee Stevens .40 1.00
16 Frank Thomas 1.50 4.00
17 Mark Whiten .40 1.00
18 Cecil Fielder .60 1.50
19 George Brett 4.00 10.00
20 Robin Yount 1.50 4.00
21 Scott Erickson .40 1.00
22 Don Mattingly 4.00 10.00
23 Jose Canseco 1.50 4.00
24 Ken Griffey Jr. 5.00 12.00
25 Nolan Ryan 8.00 20.00
26 Joe Carter .60 1.50
27 Deion Sanders 1.25 3.00
28 Dean Palmer .60 1.50
29 Andy Benes .60 1.50
30 Gary DiSarcina .40 1.00
31 Chris Hoiles .40 1.00
32 Mark McGwire 4.00 10.00
33 Reggie Sanders .75 2.00

1992 Leaf

The 1992 Leaf set consists of 528 cards, issued in two separate 264-card series. Cards were distributed in first and second series 15-card foil packs. Each pack contained a selection of basic cards and one black gold parallel card. The basic card fronts feature color action player photos on a silver card face. The player's name appears in a black bar edged at the bottom by a thin red stripe. The team logo overlaps the bar at the right corner. Rookie Cards in this set include Brian Jordan and Jeff Kent.

COMPLETE SET (528) 6.00 15.00
COMPLETE SERIES 1 (264) 2.00 5.00
COMPLETE SERIES 2 (264) 4.00 10.00
1 Jim Abbott .08 .25
2 Cal Eldred .01 .05
3 Bud Black .01 .05
4 Dave Howard .01 .05
5 Luis Sojo .01 .05
6 Gary Scott .01 .05
7 Joe Oliver .01 .05
8 Chris Gardner .01 .05
9 Sandy Alomar Jr. .01 .05
10 Greg W. Harris .01 .05
11 Doug Drabek .01 .05
12 Darryl Hamilton .01 .05
13 Mike Mussina .15 .40
14 Kevin Tapani .01 .05
15 Ron Gant .05 .15
16 Mark McGwire .40 1.00
17 Robin Ventura .05 .15
18 Pedro Guerrero .05 .15
19 Roger Clemens .30 .75
20 Steve Farr .01 .05
21 Frank Tanana .01 .05
22 Joe Hesketh .01 .05
23 Erik Hanson .01 .05
24 Greg Cadaret .01 .05
25 Rex Hudler .01 .05
26 Mark Grace .08 .25
27 Kelly Gruber .01 .05
28 Jeff Bagwell .15 .40
29 Darryl Strawberry .05 .15
30 Dave Smith .01 .05
31 Kevin Appier .05 .15
32 Steve Chitren .01 .05
33 Kevin Gross .01 .05
34 Rick Aguilera .05 .15
35 Juan Guzman .01 .05
36 Joe Orsulak .01 .05
37 Tim Raines .05 .15
38 Harold Reynolds .05 .15
39 Charlie Hough .05 .15
40 Tony Phillips .01 .05
41 Nolan Ryan .60 1.50
42 Vince Coleman .01 .05
43 Andy Van Slyke .08 .25
44 Tim Burke .01 .05
45 Luis Polonia .01 .05
46 Tom Browning .01 .05
47 Willie McGee .05 .15
48 Gary DiSarcina .01 .05
49 Mark Lewis .01 .05
50 Phil Plantier .01 .05
51 Doug Dascenzo .01 .05
52 Cal Ripken .50 1.25
53 Pedro Munoz .01 .05
54 Carlos Hernandez .01 .05
55 Jerald Clark .01 .05
56 Jeff Brantley .01 .05
57 Don Mattingly .40 1.00
58 Roger McDowell .01 .05
59 Steve Avery .01 .05
60 John Olerud .05 .15
61 Bill Gullickson .01 .05
62 Juan Gonzalez .08 .25
63 Felix Jose .01 .05
64 Robin Yount .25 .60
65 Greg Briley .01 .05
66 Steve Finley .05 .15
67 Frank Thomas CL .08 .25
68 Tom Gordon .01 .05
69 Rob Dibble .05 .15
70 Glenallen Hill .01 .05
71 Calvin Jones .01 .05
72 Joe Girardi .01 .05
73 Barry Larkin .08 .25
74 Andy Benes .01 .05
75 Milt Cuyler .01 .05
76 Kevin Bass .01 .05
77 Pete Harnisch .01 .05
78 Wilson Alvarez .01 .05
79 Mike Devereaux .01 .05
80 Doug Henry RC .02 .10
81 Orel Hershiser .05 .15
82 Shane Mack .01 .05
83 Mike Macfarlane .01 .05
84 Thomas Howard .01 .05
85 Alex Fernandez .01 .05
86 Reggie Jefferson .01 .05
87 Leo Gomez .01 .05
88 Mel Hall .01 .05
89 Mike Greenwell .01 .05
90 Jeff Russell .01 .05
91 Steve Buechele .01 .05
92 David Cone .05 .15
93 Kevin Reimer .01 .05
94 Mark Lemke .01 .05
95 Bob Tewksbury .01 .05
96 Zane Smith .01 .05
97 Mark Eichhorn .01 .05
98 Kirby Puckett .15 .40
99 Paul O'Neill .08 .25
100 Dennis Eckersley .05 .15
101 Duane Ward .01 .05
102 Matt Nokes .01 .05
103 Mo Vaughn .05 .15
104 Pat Kelly .01 .05
105 Ron Karkovice .01 .05
106 Bill Spiers .01 .05
107 Gary Gaetti .05 .15
108 Mackey Sasser .01 .05
109 Robby Thompson .01 .05
110 Marvin Freeman .01 .05
111 Jimmy Key .05 .15
112 Dwight Gooden .05 .15
113 Charlie Leibrandt .01 .05
114 Devon White .05 .15
115 Charles Nagy .01 .05
116 Rickey Henderson .15 .40
117 Paul Assenmacher .01 .05
118 Junior Felix .01 .05
119 Julio Franco .05 .15
120 Norm Charlton .01 .05
121 Scott Servais .01 .05
122 Gerald Perry .01 .05
123 Brian McRae .01 .05
124 Don Slaught .01 .05
125 Juan Samuel .01 .05
126 Harold Baines .05 .15
127 Scott Livingstone .01 .05
128 Jay Buhner .05 .15
129 Darrin Jackson .01 .05
130 Luis Mercedes .01 .05
131 Brian Harper .01 .05
132 Howard Johnson .01 .05
133 Nolan Ryan CL .15 .40
134 Dante Bichette .05 .15
135 Dave Righetti .05 .15
136 Jeff Montgomery .01 .05
137 Joe Grahe .01 .05
138 Delino DeShields .01 .05
139 Jose Rijo .01 .05
140 Ken Caminiti .05 .15
141 Steve Olin .01 .05
142 Kurt Stillwell .01 .05
143 Jay Bell .05 .15
144 Jaime Navarro .01 .05
145 Ben McDonald .01 .05
146 Greg Gagne .01 .05
147 Jeff Blauser .01 .05
148 Carney Lansford .05 .15
149 Ozzie Guillen .05 .15
150 Milt Thompson .01 .05
151 Jeff Reardon .05 .15
152 Scott Sanderson .01 .05
153 Cecil Fielder .05 .15
154 Greg A. Harris .01 .05
155 Rich DeLucia .01 .05
156 Roberto Kelly .01 .05
157 Bryn Smith .01 .05
158 Chuck McElroy .01 .05
159 Tom Henke .01 .05
160 Luis Gonzalez .05 .15
161 Steve Wilson .01 .05
162 Shawn Boskie .01 .05
163 Mark Davis .01 .05
164 Mike Moore .01 .05
165 Mike Scioscia .01 .05
166 Scott Erickson .01 .05
167 Todd Stottlemyre .01 .05
168 Alvin Davis .01 .05
169 Greg Hibbard .01 .05
170 David Valle .01 .05
171 Dave Winfield .05 .15
172 Alan Trammell .05 .15
173 Kenny Rogers .05 .15
174 John Franco .05 .15
175 Jose Lind .01 .05
176 Pete Schourek .01 .05
177 Von Hayes .01 .05
178 Chris Hammond .01 .05
179 John Burkett .01 .05
180 Dickie Thon .01 .05
181 Joel Skinner .01 .05
182 Scott Cooper .01 .05
183 Andre Dawson .05 .15
184 Billy Ripken .01 .05
185 Kevin Mitchell .01 .05
186 Brett Butler .05 .15
187 Tony Fernandez .01 .05
188 Cory Snyder .01 .05
189 John Habyan .01 .05
190 Dennis Martinez .05 .15
191 John Smoltz .08 .25
192 Greg Myers .01 .05
193 Rob Deer .01 .05
194 Ivan Rodriguez .15 .40
195 Ray Lankford .05 .15
196 Bill Wegman .01 .05
197 Edgar Martinez .08 .25
198 Darryl Kile .05 .15
199 Cal Ripken CL .15 .40
200 Brent Mayne .01 .05
201 Larry Walker .08 .25
202 Carlos Baerga .01 .05
203 Russ Swan .01 .05
204 Mike Morgan .01 .05
205 Hal Morris .01 .05
206 Tony Gwynn .20 .50
207 Mark Leiter .01 .05
208 Kirt Manwaring .01 .05
209 Al Osuna .01 .05
210 Bobby Thigpen .01 .05
211 Chris Hoiles .01 .05
212 B.J. Surhoff .05 .15
213 Lenny Harris .01 .05
214 Scott Leius .01 .05
215 Gregg Jefferies .01 .05
216 Bruce Hurst .01 .05
217 Steve Sax .01 .05
218 Dave Otto .01 .05
219 Sam Horn .01 .05
220 Charlie Hayes .01 .05
221 Frank Viola .05 .15
222 Jose Guzman .01 .05
223 Gary Redus .01 .05
224 Dave Gallagher .01 .05
225 Dean Palmer .05 .15
226 Greg Olson .01 .05
227 Jose DeLeon .01 .05
228 Mike LaValliere .01 .05
229 Mark Langston .01 .05
230 Chuck Knoblauch .05 .15
231 Bill Doran .01 .05
232 Dave Henderson .01 .05
233 Roberto Alomar .08 .25
234 Scott Fletcher .01 .05
235 Tim Naehring .01 .05
236 Mike Gallego .01 .05
237 Lance Johnson .01 .05
238 Paul Molitor .05 .15
239 Dan Gladden .01 .05
240 Willie Randolph .05 .15
241 Will Clark .08 .25
242 Sid Bream .01 .05
243 Derek Bell .05 .15
244 Bill Pecota .01 .05
245 Terry Pendleton .05 .15
246 Randy Ready .01 .05
247 Jack Armstrong .01 .05
248 Todd Van Poppel .01 .05
249 Shawon Dunston .01 .05
250 Bobby Rose .01 .05
251 Jeff Huson .01 .05
252 Bip Roberts .01 .05
253 Doug Jones .01 .05
254 Lee Smith .05 .15
255 George Brett .40 1.00
256 Randy Tomlin .01 .05
257 Todd Benzinger .01 .05
258 Dave Stewart .05 .15
259 Mark Carreon .01 .05
260 Pete O'Brien .01 .05
261 Tim Teufel .01 .05
262 Bob Milacki .01 .05
263 Mark Guthrie .01 .05
264 Darrin Fletcher .01 .05
265 Omar Vizquel .08 .25
266 Chris Bosio .01 .05
267 Jose Canseco .08 .25
268 Mike Boddicker .01 .05
269 Lance Parrish .05 .15
270 Jose Vizcaino .01 .05
271 Chris Sabo .01 .05
272 Royce Clayton .01 .05
273 Marquis Grissom .05 .15
274 Fred McGriff .08 .25
275 Barry Bonds .60 1.50
276 Greg Vaughn .01 .05
277 Gregg Olson .01 .05
278 Dave Hollins .01 .05
279 Tom Glavine .08 .25
280 Bryan Hickerson .01 .05
281 Scott Radinsky .01 .05
282 Omar Olivares .01 .05
283 Ivan Calderon .01 .05
284 Kevin Maas .01 .05
285 Mickey Tettleton .01 .05
286 Wade Boggs .08 .25
287 Stan Belinda .01 .05
288 Bret Barberie .01 .05
289 Jose Oquendo .01 .05
290 Frank Castillo .01 .05
291 Dave Stieb .01 .05
292 Tommy Greene .01 .05
293 Eric Karros .05 .15
294 Greg Maddux .25 .60
295 Jim Eisenreich .01 .05
296 Rafael Palmeiro .08 .25
297 Ramon Martinez .01 .05
298 Tim Wallach .01 .05
299 Jim Thome .15 .40
300 Chito Martinez .01 .05
301 Mitch Williams .01 .05
302 Randy Johnson .15 .40
303 Carlton Fisk .08 .25
304 Travis Fryman .05 .15
305 Bobby Witt .01 .05
306 Dave Magadan .01 .05
307 Alex Cole .01 .05
308 Bobby Bonilla .05 .15
309 Bryan Harvey .01 .05
310 Rafael Belliard .01 .05
311 Mariano Duncan .01 .05
312 Chuck Crim .01 .05
313 John Kruk .05 .15
314 Ellis Burks .05 .15
315 Craig Biggio .08 .25
316 Glenn Davis .01 .05
317 Ryne Sandberg .25 .60
318 Mike Sharperson .01 .05
319 Rich Rodriguez .01 .05
320 Lee Guetterman .01 .05
321 Benito Santiago .05 .15
322 Jose Offerman .01 .05
323 Tony Pena .01 .05
324 Pat Borders .01 .05
325 Mike Henneman .01 .05
326 Kevin Brown .05 .15
327 Chris Nabholz .01 .05
328 Franklin Stubbs .01 .05
329 Tino Martinez .08 .25
330 Mickey Morandini .01 .05
331 Ryne Sandberg CL .15 .40
332 Mark Gubicza .01 .05
333 Bill Landrum .01 .05
334 Mark Whiten .01 .05
335 Darren Daulton .05 .15
336 Rick Wilkins .01 .05
337 Brian Jordan RC .20 .50
338 Kevin Ward .01 .05
339 Ruben Amaro .01 .05
340 Trevor Wilson .01 .05
341 Andujar Cedeno .01 .05
342 Michael Huff .01 .05
343 Brady Anderson .05 .15
344 Craig Grebeck .01 .05
345 Bob Ojeda .01 .05
346 Mike Pagliarulo .01 .05
347 Terry Shumpert .01 .05
348 Dann Bilardello .01 .05
349 Frank Thomas .15 .40
350 Albert Belle .05 .15
351 Jose Mesa .01 .05
352 Rich Monteleone .01 .05
353 Bob Walk .01 .05
354 Monty Fariss .01 .05
355 Luis Rivera .01 .05
356 Anthony Young .01 .05
357 Geno Petralli .01 .05
358 Otis Nixon .01 .05
359 Tom Pagnozzi .01 .05
360 Reggie Sanders .05 .15
361 Lee Stevens .01 .05
362 Kent Hrbek .05 .15
363 Orlando Merced .01 .05
364 Mike Bordick .01 .05
365 Dion James UER/(Blue Jays logo .01 .05
on card back)
366 Jack Clark .05 .15
367 Mike Stanley .01 .05
368 Randy Velarde .01 .05
369 Dan Pasqua .01 .05
370 Pat Listach RC .08 .25
371 Mike Fitzgerald .01 .05
372 Tom Foley .01 .05
373 Matt Williams .05 .15
374 Brian Hunter .01 .05
375 Joe Carter .05 .15
376 Bret Saberhagen .05 .15
377 Mike Stanton .01 .05
378 Hubie Brooks .01 .05
379 Eric Bell .01 .05
380 Walt Weiss .01 .05
381 Danny Jackson .01 .05
382 Manuel Lee .01 .05
383 Ruben Sierra .05 .15
384 Greg Swindell .01 .05
385 Ryan Bowen .01 .05
386 Kevin Ritz .01 .05
387 Curtis Wilkerson .01 .05
388 Gary Varsho .01 .05
389 Dave Hansen .01 .05
390 Bob Welch .01 .05
391 Lou Whitaker .05 .15
392 Ken Griffey Jr. .30 .75
393 Mike Maddux .01 .05
394 Arthur Rhodes .01 .05
395 Chili Davis .05 .15
396 Eddie Murray .15 .40
397 Robin Yount CL .08 .25
398 Dave Cochrane .01 .05
399 Kevin Seitzer .01 .05
400 Ozzie Smith .25 .60
401 Paul Sorrento .01 .05
402 Les Lancaster .01 .05
403 Junior Noboa .01 .05
404 David Justice .05 .15
405 Andy Ashby .01 .05
406 Danny Tartabull .01 .05
407 Bill Swift .01 .05
408 Craig Lefferts .01 .05
409 Tom Candiotti .01 .05
410 Lance Blankenship .01 .05
411 Jeff Tackett .01 .05
412 Sammy Sosa .15 .40
413 Jody Reed .01 .05
414 Bruce Ruffin .01 .05
415 Gene Larkin .01 .05
416 John Vander Wal RC .08 .25
417 Tim Belcher .01 .05
418 Steve Frey .01 .05
419 Dick Schofield .01 .05
420 Jeff King .01 .05
421 Kim Batiste .01 .05
422 Jack McDowell .01 .05
423 Damon Berryhill .01 .05

424 Gary Wayne .01 .05
425 Jack Morris .05 .15
426 Moises Alou .05 .15
427 Mark McLemore .01 .05
428 Juan Guerrero .01 .05
429 Scott Scudder .01 .05
430 Eric Davis .05 .15
431 Joe Slusarski .01 .05
432 Todd Zeile .01 .05
433 Dwayne Henry .01 .05
434 Cliff Brantley .01 .05
435 Butch Henry RC .02 .10
436 Todd Worrell .01 .05
437 Bob Scanlan .01 .05
438 Wally Joyner .05 .15
439 John Flaherty RC .01 .05
440 Brian Downing .01 .05
441 Darren Lewis .01 .05
442 Gary Carter .05 .15
443 Wally Ritchie .01 .05
444 Chris Jones .01 .05
445 Jeff Kent RC 1.00 2.50
446 Gary Sheffield .05 .15
447 Ron Darling .01 .05
448 Deion Sanders .08 .25
449 Andres Galarraga .05 .15
450 Chuck Finley .05 .15
451 Derek Lilliquist .01 .05
452 Carl Willis .01 .05
453 Wes Chamberlain .01 .05
454 Roger Mason .01 .05
455 Spike Owen .01 .05
456 Thomas Howard .01 .05
457 Dave Martinez .01 .05
458 Pete Incaviglia .01 .05
459 Keith A. Miller .01 .05
460 Mike Fetters .01 .05
461 Paul Gibson .01 .05
462 George Bell .01 .05
463 Bobby Bonilla CL .01 .05
464 Terry Mulholland .01 .05
465 Storm Davis .01 .05
466 Gary Pettis .01 .05
467 Randy Bush .01 .05
468 Ken Hill .01 .05
469 Rheal Cormier .01 .05
470 Andy Stankiewicz .01 .05
471 Dave Burba .01 .05
472 Henry Cotto .01 .05
473 Dale Sveum .01 .05
474 Rich Gossage .05 .15
475 William Suero .01 .05
476 Doug Strange .01 .05
477 Bill Krueger .01 .05
478 John Wetteland .05 .15
479 Melido Perez .01 .05
480 Lonnie Smith .01 .05
481 Mike Jackson .01 .05
482 Mike Gardiner .01 .05
483 David Wells .05 .15
484 Barry Jones .01 .05
485 Scott Bankhead .01 .05
486 Terry Leach .01 .05
487 Vince Horsman .01 .05
488 Dave Eiland .01 .05
489 Alejandro Pena .01 .05
490 Julio Valera .01 .05
491 Joe Boever .01 .05
492 Paul Miller RC .01 .05
493 Archi Cianfrocco RC .02 .10
494 Dave Fleming .01 .05
495 Kyle Abbott .01 .05
496 Chad Kreuter .01 .05
497 Chris James .01 .05
498 Donnie Hill .01 .05
499 Jacob Brumfield .01 .05
500 Ricky Bones .01 .05
501 Terry Steinbach .01 .05
502 Bernard Gilkey .01 .05
503 Dennis Cook .01 .05
504 Len Dykstra .05 .15
505 Mike Bielecki .01 .05
506 Bob Kipper .01 .05
507 Jose Melendez .01 .05
508 Rick Sutcliffe .05 .15
509 Ken Patterson .01 .05
510 Andy Allanson .01 .05
511 Al Newman .01 .05
512 Mark Gardner .01 .05
513 Jeff Schaefer .01 .05
514 Jim McNamara .01 .05
515 Peter Hoy .01 .05
516 Curt Schilling .08 .25
517 Kirk McCaskill .01 .05
518 Chris Gwynn .01 .05
519 Sid Fernandez .01 .05
520 Jeff Parrett .01 .05
521 Scott Ruskin .01 .05
522 Kevin McReynolds .01 .05
523 Rick Cerone .01 .05
524 Jesse Orosco .01 .05
525 Troy Afenir .01 .05
526 John Smiley .01 .05
527 Dale Murphy .08 .25
528 Leaf Set Card .01 .05

1992 Leaf Black Gold

COMPLETE SET (528) 25.00 60.00
COMPLETE SERIES 1 (264) 8.00 20.00
COMPLETE SERIES 2 (264) 15.00 40.00
*STARS: 1.5X TO 4X BASIC CARDS
*ROOKIES: 1X TO 2.5X BASIC CARDS
ONE PER PACK

1992 Leaf Gold Rookies

COMPLETE SET (24) 6.00 15.00
COMPLETE SERIES 1 (12) 4.00 10.00
COMPLETE SERIES 2 (12) 2.00 5.00
COMMON CARD (BC1-BC24) .40 1.00
RANDOM INSERTS IN BOTH SERIES
BC1 Chad Curtis .40 1.00
BC2 Brent Gates .40 1.00
BC3 Pedro Martinez 3.00 8.00
BC4 Kenny Lofton .60 1.50
BC5 Turk Wendell .40 1.00
BC6 Mark Hutton .40 1.00
BC7 Todd Hundley .40 1.00
BC8 Matt Stairs .40 1.00
BC9 Eddie Taubensee .40 1.00
BC10 David Nied .40 1.00
BC11 Salomon Torres .40 1.00
BC12 Bret Boone .60 1.50
BC13 Johnny Ruffin .40 1.00
BC14 Ed Martel .40 1.00
BC15 Rick Trlicek .40 1.00
BC16 Raul Mondesi .40 1.00
BC17 Pat Mahomes .40 1.00
BC18 Dan Wilson .40 1.00
BC19 Donovan Osborne .40 1.00
BC20 Dave Silvestri .40 1.00
BC21 Gary DiSarcina .40 1.00
BC22 Denny Neagle .40 1.00
BC23 Steve Hosey .40 1.00
BC24 John Doherty .40 1.00

1993 Leaf

The 1993 Leaf baseball set consists of three series of 220, 220, and 110 standard-size cards, respectively. Cards were distributed in 14-card foil packs, jumbo packs and magazine packs. Rookie Cards in this set include J.T. Snow. White Sox slugger (and at that time, Leaf Representative) Frank Thomas signed 3,500 cards, which were randomly seeded into packs. In addition, a special card commemorating Dave Winfield's 3,000 hit was also seeded into packs. Both cards are listed at the end of our checklist but are not considered part of the 550-card basic set.

COMPLETE SET (550) 15.00 40.00
COMPLETE SERIES 1 (220) 6.00 15.00
COMPLETE SERIES 2 (220) 6.00 15.00
COMPLETE UPDATE (110) 2.00 5.00
COMMON RC .05 .15
WINFIELD 3K RANDOM INSERT IN PACKS
THOMAS AU RANDOM INSERT IN PACKS
1 Ben McDonald .05 .15
2 Sid Fernandez .05 .15
3 Juan Guzman .05 .15
4 Curt Schilling .10 .30
5 Ivan Rodriguez .20 .50
6 Don Slaught .05 .15
7 Terry Steinbach .05 .15
8 Todd Zeile .05 .15
9 Andy Stankiewicz .05 .15
10 Tim Teufel .05 .15
11 Marvin Freeman .05 .15
12 Jim Austin .05 .15
13 Bob Scanlan .05 .15
14 Rusty Meacham .05 .15
15 Casey Candaele .05 .15
16 Travis Fryman .10 .30
17 Jose Offerman .05 .15
18 Albert Belle .10 .30
19 John Vander Wal .05 .15
20 Dan Pasqua .05 .15
21 Frank Viola .10 .30
22 Terry Mulholland .05 .15
23 Gregg Olson .05 .15
24 Randy Tomlin .05 .15
25 Todd Stottlemyre .05 .15
26 Jose Oquendo .05 .15
27 Julio Franco .10 .30
28 Tony Gwynn .40 1.00
29 Ruben Sierra .10 .30
30 Robby Thompson .05 .15
31 Jim Bullinger .05 .15
32 Rick Aguilera .05 .15
33 Scott Servais .05 .15
34 Cal Eldred .05 .15
35 Mike Piazza 1.25 3.00
36 Brent Mayne .05 .15
37 Wil Cordero .05 .15
38 Milt Cuyler .05 .15
39 Howard Johnson .05 .15
40 Kenny Lofton .10 .30
41 Alex Fernandez .05 .15
42 Denny Neagle .10 .30
43 Tony Pena .05 .15
44 Bob Tewksbury .05 .15
45 Glenn Davis .05 .15
46 Fred McGriff .20 .50
47 John Olerud .10 .30
48 Steve Hosey .05 .15
49 Rafael Palmeiro .20 .50
50 David Justice .10 .30
51 Pete Harnisch .05 .15
52 Sam Militello .05 .15
53 Orel Hershiser .10 .30
54 Pat Mahomes .05 .15
55 Greg Colbrunn .05 .15
56 Greg Vaughn .05 .15
57 Vince Coleman .05 .15
58 Brian McRae .05 .15
59 Len Dykstra .10 .30
60 Dan Gladden .05 .15
61 Ted Power .05 .15
62 Donovan Osborne .05 .15
63 Ron Karkovice .05 .15
64 Frank Seminara .05 .15
65 Bob Zupcic .05 .15
66 Kirt Manwaring .05 .15
67 Mike Devereaux .05 .15
68 Mark Lemke .05 .15
69 Devon White .10 .30
70 Sammy Sosa .30 .75
71 Pedro Astacio .05 .15
72 Dennis Eckersley .10 .30
73 Chris Nabholz .05 .15
74 Melido Perez .05 .15
75 Todd Hundley .05 .15
76 Kent Hrbek .10 .30
77 Mickey Morandini .05 .15
78 Tim McIntosh .05 .15
79 Andy Van Slyke .20 .50
80 Kevin McReynolds .05 .15
81 Mike Henneman .05 .15
82 Greg W. Harris .05 .15
83 Sandy Alomar Jr. .05 .15
84 Mike Jackson .05 .15
85 Ozzie Guillen .10 .30
86 Jeff Blauser .05 .15
87 John Valentin .05 .15
88 Rey Sanchez .05 .15
89 Rick Sutcliffe .10 .30
90 Luis Gonzalez .10 .30
91 Jeff Fassero .05 .15
92 Kenny Rogers .10 .30
93 Bret Saberhagen .10 .30
94 Bob Welch .05 .15
95 Darren Daulton .10 .30
96 Mike Gallego .05 .15
97 Orlando Merced .05 .15
98 Chuck Knoblauch .10 .30
99 Bernard Gilkey .05 .15
100 Billy Ashley .05 .15
101 Kevin Appier .10 .30
102 Jeff Brantley .05 .15
103 Bill Gullickson .05 .15
104 John Smoltz .20 .50
105 Paul Sorrento .05 .15
106 Steve Buechele .05 .15
107 Steve Sax .05 .15
108 Andujar Cedeno .05 .15
109 Billy Hatcher .05 .15
110 Checklist .05 .15
111 Alan Mills .05 .15
112 John Franco .10 .30
113 Jack Morris .10 .30
114 Mitch Williams .05 .15
115 Nolan Ryan 1.25 3.00
116 Jay Bell .10 .30
117 Mike Bordick .05 .15
118 Geronimo Pena .05 .15
119 Danny Tartabull .05 .15
120 Checklist .05 .15
121 Steve Avery .05 .15
122 Ricky Bones .05 .15
123 Mike Morgan .05 .15
124 Jeff Montgomery .05 .15
125 Jeff Bagwell .20 .50
126 Tony Phillips .05 .15
127 Lenny Harris .05 .15
128 Glenallen Hill .05 .15
129 Marquis Grissom .10 .30
130 Gerald Williams UER/(Bernie Williams .05
.15
picture and
131 Greg A. Harris .05 .15
132 Tommy Greene .05 .15
133 Chris Hoiles .05 .15
134 Bob Walk .05 .15
135 Duane Ward .05 .15
136 Tom Pagnozzi .05 .15
137 Jeff Huson .05 .15
138 Kurt Stillwell .05 .15
139 Dave Henderson .05 .15
140 Darrin Jackson .05 .15
141 Frank Castillo .05 .15
142 Scott Erickson .05 .15
143 Darryl Kile .10 .30
144 Bill Wegman .05 .15
145 Steve Wilson .05 .15
146 George Brett .75 2.00
147 Moises Alou .10 .30
148 Lou Whitaker .10 .30
149 Chico Walker .05 .15
150 Jerry Browne .05 .15
151 Kirk McCaskill .05 .15
152 Zane Smith .05 .15
153 Matt Young .05 .15
154 Lee Smith .10 .30
155 Leo Gomez .05 .15
156 Dan Walters .05 .15
157 Pat Borders .05 .15
158 Matt Williams .10 .30
159 Dean Palmer .10 .30
160 John Patterson .05 .15
161 Doug Jones .05 .15
162 John Habyan .05 .15
163 Pedro Martinez .60 1.50
164 Carl Willis .05 .15
165 Darrin Fletcher .05 .15
166 B.J. Surhoff .10 .30
167 Eddie Murray .30 .75
168 Keith Miller .05 .15
169 Ricky Jordan .05 .15
170 Juan Gonzalez .10 .30
171 Charles Nagy .05 .15
172 Mark Clark .05 .15
173 Bobby Thigpen .05 .15
174 Tim Scott .05 .15
175 Scott Cooper .05 .15
176 Royce Clayton .05 .15
177 Brady Anderson .10 .30
178 Sid Bream .05 .15
179 Derek Bell .05 .15
180 Otis Nixon .05 .15
181 Kevin Gross .05 .15
182 Ron Darling .05 .15
183 John Wetteland .10 .30
184 Mike Stanley .05 .15
185 Jeff Kent .30 .75
186 Brian Harper .05 .15
187 Mariano Duncan .05 .15
188 Robin Yount .50 1.25
189 Al Martin .05 .15
190 Eddie Zosky .05 .15
191 Mike Munoz .05 .15
192 Andy Benes .05 .15
193 Dennis Cook .05 .15
194 Bill Swift .05 .15
195 Frank Thomas .30 .75
195A Frank Thomas .50 1.25
Franklin visible on batting glove
196 Damon Berryhill .05 .15
197 Mike Greenwell .05 .15
198 Mark Grace .20 .50
199 Darryl Hamilton .05 .15
200 Derrick May .05 .15
201 Ken Hill .05 .15
202 Kevin Brown .10 .30
203 Dwight Gooden .10 .30
204 Bobby Witt .05 .15
205 Juan Bell .05 .15
206 Kevin Maas .05 .15
207 Jeff King .05 .15
208 Scott Leius .05 .15
209 Rheal Cormier .05 .15
210 Darryl Strawberry .10 .30
211 Tom Gordon .05 .15
212 Bud Black .05 .15
213 Mickey Tettleton .05 .15
214 Pete Smith .05 .15
215 Felix Fermin .05 .15
216 Rick Wilkins .05 .15
217 George Bell .05 .15
218 Eric Anthony .05 .15
219 Pedro Munoz .05 .15
220 Albert Bell CL .10 .30
221 Lance Blankenship .05 .15
222 Deion Sanders .20 .50
223 Craig Biggio .20 .50
224 Ryne Sandberg .50 1.25
225 Ron Gant .10 .30
226 Tom Brunansky .05 .15
227 Chad Curtis .05 .15
228 Joe Carter .10 .30
229 Brian Jordan .10 .30
230 Brett Butler .10 .30
231 Frank Bolick .05 .15
232 Rod Beck .05 .15
233 Carlos Baerga .05 .15
234 Eric Karros .10 .30
235 Jack Armstrong .05 .15
236 Bobby Bonilla .10 .30
237 Don Mattingly .75 2.00
238 Jeff Gardner .05 .15
239 Dave Hollins .05 .15
240 Steve Cooke .05 .15
241 Jose Canseco .20 .50
242 Ivan Calderon .05 .15
243 Tim Belcher .05 .15
244 Freddie Benavides .05 .15
245 Roberto Alomar .20 .50
246 Rob Deer .05 .15
247 Will Clark .20 .50
248 Mike Felder .05 .15
249 Harold Baines .10 .30
250 David Cone .10 .30
251 Mark Guthrie .05 .15
252 Ellis Burks .10 .30
253 Jim Abbott .20 .50
254 Chili Davis .10 .30
255 Chris Bosio .05 .15
256 Bret Barberie .05 .15
257 Hal Morris .05 .15
258 Dante Bichette .10 .30
259 Storm Davis .05 .15
260 Gary DiSarcina .05 .15
261 Ken Caminiti .10 .30
262 Paul Molitor .10 .30
263 Joe Oliver .05 .15
264 Pat Listach .05 .15
265 Gregg Jefferies .05 .15
266 Jose Guzman .05 .15
267 Eric Davis .10 .30
268 Delino DeShields .05 .15
269 Barry Bonds .75 2.00
270 Mike Bielecki .05 .15
271 Jay Buhner .10 .30
272 Scott Pose RC .05 .15
273 Tony Fernandez .05 .15
274 Chito Martinez .05 .15
275 Phil Plantier .05 .15
276 Pete Incaviglia .05 .15
277 Carlos Garcia .05 .15
278 Tom Henke .05 .15
279 Roger Clemens .60 1.50
280 Rob Dibble .10 .30
281 Daryl Boston .05 .15
282 Greg Gagne .05 .15
283 Cecil Fielder .10 .30
284 Carlton Fisk .20 .50
285 Wade Boggs .20 .50
286 Damion Easley .05 .15
287 Norm Charlton .05 .15
288 Jeff Conine .10 .30
289 Roberto Kelly .05 .15
290 Jerald Clark .05 .15
291 Rickey Henderson .30 .75
292 Chuck Finley .10 .30
293 Doug Drabek .05 .15
294 Dave Stewart .10 .30
295 Tom Glavine .20 .50
296 Jaime Navarro .05 .15
297 Ray Lankford .10 .30
298 Greg Hibbard .05 .15
299 Jody Reed .05 .15
300 Dennis Martinez .10 .30
301 Dave Martinez .05 .15
302 Reggie Jefferson .05 .15
303 John Cummings RC .05 .15
304 Orestes Destrade .05 .15
305 Mike Maddux .05 .15
306 David Segui .05 .15
307 Gary Sheffield .10 .30
308 Danny Jackson .05 .15
309 Craig Lefferts .05 .15
310 Andre Dawson .10 .30
311 Barry Larkin .20 .50
312 Alex Cole .05 .15
313 Mark Gardner .05 .15
314 Kirk Gibson .10 .30
315 Shane Mack .05 .15
316 Bo Jackson .30 .75
317 Jimmy Key .10 .30
318 Greg Myers .05 .15
319 Ken Griffey Jr. .60 1.50
320 Monty Fariss .05 .15
321 Kevin Mitchell .05 .15
322 Andres Galarraga .10 .30
323 Mark McGwire .75 2.00
324 Mark Langston .05 .15
325 Steve Finley .10 .30
326 Greg Maddux .50 1.25
327 Dave Nilsson .05 .15
328 Ozzie Smith .50 1.25
329 Candy Maldonado .05 .15
330 Checklist .05 .15
331 Tim Pugh RC .05 .15
332 Joe Girardi .05 .15
333 Junior Felix .05 .15
334 Greg Swindell .05 .15
335 Ramon Martinez .05 .15
336 Sean Berry .05 .15
337 Joe Orsulak .05 .15
338 Wes Chamberlain .05 .15
339 Stan Belinda .05 .15
340 Checklist UER/(306 Luis Mercedes) .05 .15
341 Bruce Hurst .05 .15
342 John Burkett .05 .15
343 Mike Mussina .20 .50
344 Scott Fletcher .05 .15
345 Rene Gonzales .05 .15
346 Roberto Hernandez .05 .15
347 Carlos Martinez .05 .15
348 Bill Krueger .05 .15
349 Felix Jose .05 .15
350 John Jaha .05 .15
351 Willie Banks .05 .15
352 Matt Nokes .05 .15
353 Kevin Seitzer .05 .15
354 Erik Hanson .05 .15
355 David Hulse RC .05 .15
356 Domingo Martinez RC .05 .15
357 Greg Olson .05 .15
358 Randy Myers .05 .15
359 Tom Browning .05 .15
360 Charlie Hayes .05 .15
361 Bryan Harvey .05 .15
362 Eddie Taubensee .05 .15
363 Tim Wallach .05 .15
364 Mel Rojas .05 .15
365 Frank Tanana .05 .15
366 John Kruk .10 .30
367 Tim Laker RC .05 .15
368 Rich Rodriguez .05 .15
369 Darren Lewis .05 .15
370 Harold Reynolds .10 .30
371 Jose Melendez .05 .15
372 Joe Grahe .05 .15
373 Lance Johnson .05 .15
374 Jose Mesa .05 .15
375 Scott Livingstone .05 .15
376 Wally Joyner .10 .30
377 Kevin Reimer .05 .15
378 Kirby Puckett .30 .75
379 Paul O'Neill .20 .50
380 Randy Johnson .30 .75
381 Manuel Lee .05 .15
382 Dick Schofield .05 .15
383 Darren Holmes .05 .15
384 Charlie Hough .10 .30
385 John Orton .05 .15
386 Edgar Martinez .20 .50
387 Terry Pendleton .10 .30
388 Dan Plesac .05 .15
389 Jeff Reardon .10 .30
390 David Nied .05 .15
391 Dave Magadan .05 .15
392 Larry Walker .10 .30
393 Ben Rivera .05 .15
394 Lonnie Smith .05 .15
395 Craig Shipley .05 .15
396 Willie McGee .10 .30
397 Arthur Rhodes .05 .15
398 Mike Stanton .05 .15
399 Luis Polonia .05 .15
400 Jack McDowell .05 .15
401 Mike Moore .05 .15
402 Jose Lind .05 .15
403 Bill Spiers .05 .15
404 Kevin Tapani .05 .15
405 Spike Owen .05 .15
406 Tino Martinez .20 .50
407 Charlie Leibrandt .05 .15
408 Ed Sprague .05 .15
409 Bryn Smith .05 .15
410 Benito Santiago .10 .30
411 Jose Rijo .05 .15
412 Pete O'Brien .05 .15
413 Willie Wilson .05 .15
414 Bip Roberts .05 .15
415 Eric Young .05 .15
416 Walt Weiss .05 .15
417 Milt Thompson .05 .15
418 Chris Sabo .05 .15
419 Scott Sanderson .05 .15
420 Tim Raines .10 .30
421 Alan Trammell .10 .30
422 Mike Macfarlane .05 .15
423 Dave Winfield .10 .30
424 Bob Wickman .05 .15
425 David Valle .05 .15
426 Gary Redus .05 .15
427 Turner Ward .05 .15
428 Reggie Sanders .10 .30
429 Todd Worrell .05 .15
430 Julio Valera .05 .15
431 Cal Ripken 1.00 2.50
432 Mo Vaughn .10 .30
433 John Smiley .05 .15
434 Omar Vizquel .20 .50
435 Billy Ripken .05 .15
436 Cory Snyder .05 .15
437 Carlos Quintana .05 .15
438 Omar Olivares .05 .15
439 Robin Ventura .10 .30
440 Checklist .05 .15
441 Kevin Higgins .05 .15
442 Carlos Hernandez .05 .15
443 Dan Peltier .05 .15
444 Derek Lilliquist .05 .15
445 Tim Salmon .20 .50
446 Sherman Obando RC .05 .15
447 Pat Kelly .05 .15
448 Todd Van Poppel .05 .15
449 Mark Whiten .05 .15
450 Checklist .05 .15
451 Pat Meares RC .15 .40
452 Tony Tarasco RC .05 .15
453 Chris Gwynn .05 .15
454 Armando Reynoso .05 .15
455 Danny Darwin .05 .15
456 Willie Greene .05 .15
457 Mike Blowers .05 .15
458 Kevin Roberson RC .05 .15
459 Graeme Lloyd RC .15 .40
460 David West .05 .15
461 Joey Cora .05 .15
462 Alex Arias .05 .15
463 Chad Kreuter .05 .15
464 Mike Lansing RC .15 .40
465 Mike Timlin .05 .15
466 Paul Wagner .05 .15
467 Mark Portugal .05 .15
468 Jim Leyritz .05 .15
469 Ryan Klesko .10 .30
470 Mario Diaz .05 .15
471 Guillermo Velasquez .05 .15
472 Fernando Valenzuela .10 .30
473 Raul Mondesi .10 .30
474 Mike Pagliarulo .05 .15
475 Chris Hammond .05 .15
476 Torey Lovullo .05 .15
477 Trevor Wilson .05 .15
478 Marcos Armas RC .05 .15
479 Dave Gallagher .05 .15
480 Jeff Treadway .05 .15
481 Jeff Branson .05 .15
482 Dickie Thon .05 .15
483 Eduardo Perez .05 .15
484 David Wells .10 .30
485 Brian Williams .05 .15
486 Domingo Cedeno RC .05 .15
487 Tom Candiotti .05 .15
488 Steve Frey .05 .15
489 Greg McMichael RC .05 .15
490 Marc Newfield .05 .15
491 Larry Andersen .05 .15
492 Damon Buford .05 .15
493 Ricky Gutierrez .05 .15
494 Jeff Russell .05 .15
495 Vinny Castilla .30 .75
496 Wilson Alvarez .05 .15
497 Scott Bullett .05 .15
498 Larry Casian .05 .15
499 Jose Vizcaino .05 .15
500 J.T.Snow RC .25 .60
501 Bryan Hickerson .05 .15
502 Jeremy Hernandez .05 .15
503 Jeromy Burnitz .10 .30
504 Steve Farr .05 .15
505 Jayhawk Owens RC .05 .15
506 Craig Paquette .05 .15
507 Jim Eisenreich .05 .15
508 Matt Whiteside RC .05 .15
509 Luis Aquino .05 .15
510 Mike LaValliere .05 .15
511 Jim Gott .05 .15
512 Mark McLemore .05 .15
513 Randy Milligan .05 .15
514 Gary Gaetti .10 .30
515 Lou Frazier RC .05 .15
516 Rich Amaral .05 .15
517 Gene Harris .05 .15
518 Aaron Sele .10 .30
519 Mark Wohlers .05 .15
520 Scott Kamieniecki .05 .15
521 Kent Mercker .05 .15
522 Jim Deshaies .05 .15
523 Kevin Stocker .05 .15
524 Jason Bere .05 .15
525 Tim Bogar RC .05 .15
526 Brad Pennington .05 .15
527 Curt Leskanic RC .15 .40
528 Wayne Kirby .05 .15
529 Tim Costo .05 .15
530 Doug Henry .05 .15
531 Trevor Hoffman .30 .75
532 Kelly Gruber .05 .15
533 Mike Harkey .05 .15
534 John Doherty .05 .15
535 Erik Pappas .05 .15
536 Brent Gates .05 .15
537 Roger McDowell .05 .15
538 Chris Haney .05 .15
539 Blas Minor .05 .15
540 Pat Hentgen .05 .15
541 Chuck Carr .05 .15
542 Doug Strange .05 .15
543 Xavier Hernandez .05 .15
544 Paul Quantrill .05 .15
545 Anthony Young .05 .15
546 Bret Boone .10 .30
547 Dwight Smith .05 .15
548 Bobby Munoz .05 .15
549 Russ Springer .05 .15
550 Roger Pavlik .05 .15
DW Dave Winfield 3000 Hits .40 1.00
FT Frank Thomas AU/3500 30.00 80.00

1993 Leaf Fasttrack

COMPLETE SET (20) 25.00 60.00
COMPLETE SERIES 1 (10) 15.00 40.00
COMPLETE SERIES 2 (10) 12.50 30.00
RANDOM INSERTS IN RETAIL PACKS
1 Frank Thomas 4.00 10.00
2 Tim Wakefield .75 2.00
3 Kenny Lofton 1.50 4.00
4 Mike Mussina 2.50 6.00
5 Juan Gonzalez 1.50 4.00
6 Chuck Knoblauch 1.50 4.00
7 Eric Karros 1.50 4.00
8 Ray Lankford 1.50 4.00
9 Juan Guzman .75 2.00
10 Pat Listach .75 2.00
11 Carlos Baerga .75 2.00
12 Felix Jose .75 2.00
13 Steve Avery .75 2.00
14 Robin Ventura 1.50 4.00
15 Ivan Rodriguez 2.50 6.00
16 Cal Eldred .75 2.00
17 Jeff Bagwell 2.50 6.00
18 David Justice 1.50 4.00
19 Travis Fryman 1.50 4.00
20 Marquis Grissom 1.50 4.00

1993 Leaf Gold All-Stars

COMPLETE REG.SET (20) 15.00 40.00
COMPLETE UPDATE SET (10) 5.00 12.00
R1-R20 ONE PER JUMBO PACK
U1-U10 INSERTS IN UPDATE PACKS
R1 I.Rodriguez .30 .75
D.Daulton
R2 D.Mattingly 1.25 3.00
F.McGriff
R3 J.Bagwell .30 .75
C.Fielder
R4 R.Sandberg .75 2.00
C.Baerga
R5 C.Knoblauch .20 .50
D.DeShields
R6 R.Ventura .20 .50
T.Pendleton
R7 K.Griffey Jr. 1.00 2.50
A.Van Slyke
R8 J.Carter .20 .50
D.Justice
R9 T.Gwynn .60 1.50
J.Canseco
R10 D.Eckersley .20 .50
R.Dibble
R11 M.McGwire 1.25 3.00
W.Clark
R12 F.Thomas .50 1.25
M.Grace
R13 R.Alomar .30 .75
C.Biggio
R14 C.Ripken 1.50 4.00
B.Larkin
R15 E.Martinez .30 .75
G.Sheffield
R16 J.Gonzalez 1.25 3.00
B.Bonds
R17 K.Puckett .50 1.25
M.Grissom
R18 J.Abbott .30 .75
T.Glavine
R19 N.Ryan 2.00 5.00
G.Maddux
R20 R.Clemens 1.00 2.50
D.Drabek
U1 M.Langston .08 .25
T.Mulholland
U2 I.Rodriguez .30 .75
D.Daulton
U3 John Olerud .20 .50
J.Kruk
U4 R.Sandberg .75 2.00
R.Alomar
U5 Wade Boggs .30 .75
G.Sheffield
U6 C.Ripken 1.50 4.00
B.Larkin
U7 K.Puckett .50 1.25
B.Bonds
U8 K.Griffey Jr. 1.00 2.50
M.Grissom
U9 J.Carter .20 .50
D.Justice
U10 Paul Molitor .30 .75
M.Grace

1993 Leaf Gold Rookies

COMPLETE REG.SET (20) 12.50 30.00
COMPLETE UPDATE SET (5) 8.00 20.00
R1-R20 INSERTS IN HOBBY FOIL PACKS
U1-U5 INSERTS IN UPDATE PACKS
*JUMBOS:2X BASIC GOLD ROOKIES
JUMBOS DIST.IN RETAIL PACKS
R1 Kevin Young .75 2.00
R2 Wil Cordero .40 1.00
R3 Mark Kiefer .40 1.00
R4 Gerald Williams .40 1.00
R5 Brandon Wilson .40 1.00
R6 Greg Gohr .40 1.00
R7 Ryan Thompson .40 1.00
R8 Tim Wakefield 2.00 5.00
R9 Troy Neel .40 1.00
R10 Tim Salmon 1.25 3.00
R11 Kevin Rogers .40 1.00
R12 Rod Bolton .40 1.00
R13 Ken Ryan .40 1.00
R14 Phil Hiatt .40 1.00
R15 Rene Arocha .75 2.00
R16 Nigel Wilson .40 1.00
R17 J.T. Snow 1.25 3.00
R18 Benji Gil .40 1.00
R19 Chipper Jones 2.00 5.00
R20 Darrell Sherman .40 1.00
U1 Allen Watson .40 1.00
U2 Jeffrey Hammonds .40 1.00
U3 David McCarty .40 1.00
U4 Mike Piazza 3.00 8.00
U5 Roberto Mejia .40 1.00

1993 Leaf Heading for the Hall

COMPLETE SET (10) 12.50 30.00
COMPLETE SERIES 1 (5) 8.00 20.00
COMPLETE SERIES 2 (5) 4.00 10.00
RANDOM INSERTS IN PACKS
1 Nolan Ryan 5.00 12.00
2 Tony Gwynn 1.50 4.00
3 Robin Yount 2.00 5.00
4 Eddie Murray 1.25 3.00
5 Cal Ripken 4.00 10.00
6 Roger Clemens 2.50 6.00
7 George Brett 3.00 8.00
8 Ryne Sandberg 2.00 5.00
9 Kirby Puckett 1.25 3.00
10 Ozzie Smith 2.00 5.00

1993 Leaf Special Edition

This two card set, which measured 5" by 7" was issued by Donruss/Leaf and featured two of the hottest players in baseball at that time. Each of these cards were serial numbered to 10,000 on the back.

COMPLETE SET 3.00 6.00
1 Frank Thomas 1.00 2.50
2 Barry Bonds 2.00 5.00

1993 Leaf Thomas

COMPLETE SET (10) 10.00 25.00
COMMON THOMAS (1-10) 1.25 3.00
RANDOM INSERTS IN BOTH SERIES PACKS
*JUMBOS: .6X TO 1.5X BASIC THOMAS
ONE JUMBO CARD PER UPDATE BOX
JUMBO PRINT RUN 7500 SERIAL #'d SETS

1994 Leaf Promos

COMPLETE SET (9) 6.00 15.00
1 Roberto Alomar .40 1.00
2 Darren Daulton .20 .50
3 Ken Griffey Jr. 1.25 3.00
4 David Justice .30 .75
5 Don Mattingly 1.00 2.50
6 Mike Piazza 1.25 3.00
7 Cal Ripken 2.00 5.00
8 Ryne Sandberg .60 1.50
9 Frank Thomas .50 1.25

1994 Leaf

The 1994 Leaf baseball set consists of two series of 220 standard-size cards for a total of 440. Randomly seeded "Super Packs" contained complete insert sets. Cards featuring players from the Texas Rangers, Cleveland Indians, Milwaukee Brewers and Houston Astros were held out of the first series in order to have up-to-date photography in each team's new uniforms. A limited number of players from the San Francisco Giants are featured in the first series because of minor modifications to the team's uniforms. Randomly inserted in hobby packs at a rate of one in 36 was a stamped version of Frank Thomas' 1990 Leaf rookie card.

COMPLETE SET (440) 10.00 25.00
COMPLETE SERIES 1 (220) 5.00 12.00
COMPLETE SERIES 2 (220) 5.00 12.00
THOMAS ANN. STATED ODDS 1:36
SUPER PACKS CONTAIN FULL INSERT SETS
1 Cal Ripken 1.00 2.50
2 Tony Tarasco .05 .15
3 Joe Girardi .05 .15
4 Bernie Williams .20 .50
5 Chad Kreuter .05 .15
6 Troy Neel .05 .15
7 Tom Pagnozzi .05 .15
8 Kirk Rueter .05 .15
9 Chris Bosio .05 .15
10 Dwight Gooden .10 .30
11 Mariano Duncan .05 .15
12 Jay Bell .10 .30
13 Lance Johnson .05 .15
14 Richie Lewis .05 .15
15 Dave Martinez .05 .15
16 Orel Hershiser .10 .30
17 Rob Butler .05 .15
18 Glenallen Hill .05 .15
19 Chad Curtis .05 .15
20 Mike Stanton .05 .15
21 Tim Wallach .05 .15
22 Milt Thompson .05 .15
23 Kevin Young .05 .15
24 John Smiley .05 .15
25 Jeff Montgomery .05 .15
26 Robin Ventura .10 .30
27 Scott Lydy .05 .15
28 Todd Stottlemyre .05 .15
29 Mark Whiten .05 .15
30 Robby Thompson .05 .15
31 Bobby Bonilla .10 .30
32 Andy Ashby .05 .15
33 Greg Myers .05 .15
34 Billy Hatcher .05 .15
35 Brad Holman .05 .15
36 Mark McLemore .05 .15
37 Scott Sanders .05 .15
38 Jim Abbott .20 .50
39 David Wells .10 .30
40 Roberto Kelly .05 .15
41 Jeff Conine .10 .30
42 Sean Berry .05 .15
43 Mark Grace .20 .50
44 Eric Young .05 .15
45 Rick Aguilera .05 .15
46 Chipper Jones .30 .75
47 Mel Rojas .05 .15
48 Ryan Thompson .05 .15
49 Al Martin .05 .15
50 Cecil Fielder .10 .30
51 Pat Kelly .05 .15
52 Kevin Tapani .05 .15
53 Tim Costo .05 .15
54 Dave Hollins .05 .15
55 Kirt Manwaring .05 .15
56 Gregg Jefferies .05 .15
57 Ron Darling .05 .15
58 Bill Haselman .05 .15
59 Phil Plantier .05 .15
60 Frank Viola .10 .30
61 Todd Zeile .05 .15
62 Bret Barberie .05 .15
63 Roberto Mejia .05 .15
64 Chuck Knoblauch .10 .30
65 Jose Lind .05 .15
66 Brady Anderson .10 .30
67 Ruben Sierra .10 .30
68 Jose Vizcaino .05 .15
69 Joe Grahe .05 .15
70 Kevin Appier .10 .30
71 Wilson Alvarez .05 .15
72 Tom Candiotti .05 .15
73 John Burkett .05 .15
74 Anthony Young .05 .15
75 Scott Cooper .05 .15
76 Nigel Wilson .05 .15
77 John Valentin .05 .15
78 David McCarty .05 .15
79 Archi Cianfrocco .05 .15
80 Lou Whitaker .10 .30
81 Dante Bichette .10 .30
82 Mark Dewey .05 .15
83 Danny Jackson .05 .15
84 Harold Baines .10 .30
85 Todd Benzinger .05 .15
86 Damion Easley .05 .15
87 Danny Cox .05 .15
88 Jose Bautista .05 .15
89 Mike Lansing .05 .15
90 Phil Hiatt .05 .15
91 Tim Pugh .05 .15
92 Tino Martinez .20 .50
93 Raul Mondesi .10 .30
94 Greg Maddux .50 1.25
95 Al Leiter .10 .30
96 Benito Santiago .10 .30
97 Lenny Dykstra .10 .30
98 Sammy Sosa .30 .75
99 Tim Bogar .05 .15
100 Checklist .05 .15
101 Deion Sanders .20 .50
102 Bobby Witt .05 .15
103 Wil Cordero .05 .15
104 Rich Amaral .05 .15
105 Mike Mussina .20 .50
106 Reggie Sanders .10 .30
107 Ozzie Guillen .10 .30
108 Paul O'Neill .20 .50
109 Tim Salmon .20 .50
110 Rheal Cormier .05 .15
111 Billy Ashley .05 .15
112 Jeff Kent .20 .50
113 Derek Bell .05 .15
114 Danny Darwin .05 .15
115 Chip Hale .05 .15
116 Tim Raines .10 .30
117 Ed Sprague .05 .15
118 Darrin Fletcher .05 .15
119 Darren Holmes .05 .15
120 Alan Trammell .10 .30
121 Don Mattingly .75 2.00
122 Greg Gagne .05 .15
123 Jose Offerman .05 .15
124 Joe Orsulak .05 .15
125 Jack McDowell .05 .15
126 Barry Larkin .20 .50
127 Ben McDonald .05 .15
128 Mike Bordick .05 .15
129 Devon White .10 .30
130 Mike Perez .05 .15
131 Jay Buhner .10 .30
132 Phil Leftwich RC .05 .15
133 Tommy Greene .05 .15
134 Charlie Hayes .05 .15
135 Don Slaught .05 .15
136 Mike Gallego .05 .15
137 Dave Winfield .10 .30
138 Steve Avery .05 .15
139 Derrick May .05 .15
140 Bryan Harvey .05 .15
141 Wally Joyner .10 .30
142 Andre Dawson .10 .30
143 Andy Benes .05 .15
144 John Franco .10 .30
145 Jeff King .05 .15
146 Joe Oliver .05 .15
147 Bill Gullickson .05 .15
148 Armando Reynoso .05 .15
149 Dave Fleming .05 .15
150 Checklist .05 .15
151 Todd Van Poppel .05 .15
152 Bernard Gilkey .05 .15
153 Kevin Gross .05 .15
154 Mike Devereaux .05 .15
155 Tim Wakefield .20 .50
156 Andres Galarraga .10 .30
157 Pat Meares .05 .15
158 Jim Leyritz .05 .15
159 Mike Macfarlane .05 .15
160 Tony Phillips .05 .15
161 Brent Gates .05 .15
162 Mark Langston .05 .15
163 Allen Watson .05 .15
164 Randy Johnson .30 .75
165 Doug Brocail .05 .15
166 Rob Dibble .10 .30
167 Roberto Hernandez .05 .15
168 Felix Jose .05 .15
169 Steve Cooke .05 .15
170 Darren Daulton .10 .30
171 Eric Karros .10 .30
172 Geronimo Pena .05 .15
173 Gary DiSarcina .05 .15
174 Marquis Grissom .10 .30
175 Joey Cora .05 .15
176 Jim Eisenreich .05 .15
177 Brad Pennington .05 .15
178 Terry Steinbach .05 .15
179 Pat Borders .05 .15
180 Steve Buechele .05 .15
181 Jeff Fassero .05 .15
182 Mike Greenwell .05 .15
183 Mike Henneman .05 .15
184 Ron Karkovice .05 .15
185 Pat Hentgen .05 .15
186 Jose Guzman .05 .15
187 Brett Butler .10 .30
188 Charlie Hough .10 .30
189 Terry Pendleton .10 .30
190 Melido Perez .05 .15
191 Orestes Destrade .05 .15
192 Mike Morgan .05 .15
193 Joe Carter .10 .30
194 Jeff Blauser .05 .15
195 Chris Hoiles .05 .15
196 Ricky Gutierrez .05 .15
197 Mike Moore .05 .15
198 Carl Willis .05 .15
199 Aaron Sele .05 .15
200 Checklist .05 .15
201 Tim Naehring .05 .15
202 Scott Livingstone .05 .15
203 Luis Alicea .05 .15
204 Torey Lovullo .05 .15
205 Jim Gott .05 .15
206 Bob Wickman .05 .15
207 Greg McMichael .05 .15
208 Scott Brosius .10 .30
209 Chris Gwynn .05 .15
210 Steve Sax .05 .15
211 Dick Schofield .05 .15
212 Robb Nen .10 .30
213 Ben Rivera .05 .15
214 Vinny Castilla .10 .30
215 Jamie Moyer .10 .30
216 Wally Whitehurst .05 .15
217 Frank Castillo .05 .15
218 Mike Blowers .05 .15
219 Tim Scott .05 .15
220 Paul Wagner .05 .15
221 Jeff Bagwell .20 .50
222 Ricky Bones .05 .15
223 Sandy Alomar Jr. .05 .15
224 Rod Beck .05 .15
225 Roberto Alomar .20 .50
226 Jack Armstrong .05 .15
227 Scott Erickson .05 .15
228 Rene Arocha .05 .15
229 Eric Anthony .05 .15
230 Jeromy Burnitz .10 .30
231 Kevin Brown .10 .30
232 Tim Belcher .05 .15
233 Bret Boone .10 .30
234 Dennis Eckersley .10 .30
235 Tom Glavine .20 .50
236 Craig Biggio .20 .50
237 Pedro Astacio .05 .15
238 Ryan Bowen .05 .15
239 Brad Ausmus .20 .50
240 Vince Coleman .05 .15
241 Jason Bere .05 .15
242 Ellis Burks .10 .30
243 Wes Chamberlain .05 .15
244 Ken Caminiti .10 .30
245 Willie Banks .05 .15
246 Sid Fernandez .05 .15
247 Carlos Baerga .05 .15
248 Carlos Garcia .05 .15
249 Jose Canseco .20 .50
250 Alex Diaz .05 .15
251 Albert Belle .10 .30
252 Moises Alou .10 .30
253 Bobby Ayala .05 .15
254 Tony Gwynn .40 1.00
255 Roger Clemens .60 1.50
256 Eric Davis .10 .30
257 Wade Boggs .20 .50
258 Chili Davis .10 .30
259 Rickey Henderson .30 .75
260 Andujar Cedeno .05 .15
261 Cris Carpenter .05 .15
262 Juan Guzman .05 .15
263 David Justice .10 .30
264 Barry Bonds .75 2.00
265 Pete Incaviglia .05 .15
266 Tony Fernandez .05 .15
267 Cal Eldred .05 .15
268 Alex Fernandez .05 .15
269 Kent Hrbek .10 .30
270 Steve Farr .05 .15
271 Doug Drabek .05 .15
272 Brian Jordan .10 .30
273 Xavier Hernandez .05 .15
274 David Cone .10 .30
275 Brian Hunter .05 .15
276 Mike Harkey .05 .15
277 Delino DeShields .05 .15
278 David Hulse .05 .15
279 Mickey Tettleton .05 .15
280 Kevin McReynolds .05 .15
281 Darryl Hamilton .05 .15
282 Ken Hill .05 .15
283 Wayne Kirby .05 .15
284 Chris Hammond .05 .15
285 Mo Vaughn .10 .30
286 Ryan Klesko .10 .30
287 Rick Wilkins .05 .15
288 Bill Swift .05 .15
289 Rafael Palmeiro .20 .50
290 Brian Harper .05 .15
291 Chris Turner .05 .15
292 Luis Gonzalez .10 .30
293 Kenny Rogers .10 .30
294 Kirby Puckett .30 .75
295 Mike Stanley .05 .15
296 Carlos Reyes RC .05 .15
297 Charles Nagy .05 .15
298 Reggie Jefferson .05 .15
299 Bip Roberts .05 .15
300 Darrin Jackson .05 .15
301 Mike Jackson .05 .15
302 Dave Nilsson .05 .15
303 Ramon Martinez .05 .15
304 Bobby Jones .05 .15
305 Johnny Ruffin .05 .15
306 Brian McRae .05 .15
307 Bo Jackson .30 .75
308 Dave Stewart .10 .30
309 John Smoltz .20 .50
310 Dennis Martinez .10 .30
311 Dean Palmer .10 .30
312 David Nied .05 .15
313 Eddie Murray .30 .75
314 Darryl Kile .10 .30
315 Rick Sutcliffe .10 .30
316 Shawon Dunston .05 .15
317 John Jaha .05 .15
318 Salomon Torres .05 .15
319 Gary Sheffield .10 .30
320 Curt Schilling .10 .30
321 Greg Vaughn .05 .15
322 Jay Howell .05 .15
323 Todd Hundley .05 .15
324 Chris Sabo .05 .15
325 Stan Javier .05 .15
326 Willie Greene .05 .15
327 Hipolito Pichardo .05 .15
328 Doug Strange .05 .15
329 Dan Wilson .05 .15
330 Checklist .05 .15
331 Omar Vizquel .20 .50
332 Scott Servais .05 .15
333 Bob Tewksbury .05 .15
334 Matt Williams .10 .30
335 Tom Foley .05 .15
336 Jeff Russell .05 .15
337 Scott Leius .05 .15
338 Ivan Rodriguez .20 .50
339 Kevin Seitzer .05 .15
340 Jose Rijo .05 .15
341 Eduardo Perez .05 .15
342 Kirk Gibson .10 .30
343 Randy Milligan .05 .15
344 Edgar Martinez .20 .50
345 Fred McGriff .20 .50
346 Kurt Abbott RC .05 .15
347 John Kruk .10 .30
348 Mike Felder .05 .15
349 Dave Staton .05 .15
350 Kenny Lofton .10 .30
351 Graeme Lloyd .05 .15
352 David Segui .05 .15
353 Danny Tartabull .05 .15
354 Bob Welch .05 .15
355 Duane Ward .05 .15
356 Karl Rhodes .05 .15
357 Lee Smith .10 .30
358 Chris James .05 .15
359 Walt Weiss .05 .15
360 Pedro Munoz .05 .15
361 Paul Sorrento .05 .15
362 Todd Worrell .05 .15
363 Bob Hamelin .05 .15
364 Julio Franco .10 .30
365 Roberto Petagine .05 .15
366 Willie McGee .10 .30
367 Pedro Martinez .30 .75
368 Ken Griffey Jr. .60 1.50
369 B.J. Surhoff .10 .30
370 Kevin Mitchell .05 .15
371 John Doherty .05 .15
372 Manuel Lee .05 .15
373 Terry Mulholland .05 .15
374 Zane Smith .05 .15
375 Otis Nixon .05 .15
376 Jody Reed .05 .15
377 Doug Jones .05 .15
378 John Olerud .10 .30
379 Greg Swindell .05 .15
380 Checklist .05 .15
381 Royce Clayton .05 .15
382 Jim Thome .20 .50
383 Steve Finley .10 .30
384 Ray Lankford .10 .30
385 Henry Rodriguez .05 .15
386 Dave Magadan .05 .15
387 Gary Redus .05 .15
388 Orlando Merced .05 .15
389 Tom Gordon .05 .15
390 Luis Polonia .05 .15
391 Mark McGwire .75 2.00
392 Mark Lemke .05 .15
393 Doug Henry .05 .15
394 Chuck Finley .10 .30
395 Paul Molitor .10 .30
396 Randy Myers .05 .15
397 Larry Walker .10 .30
398 Pete Harnisch .05 .15
399 Darren Lewis .05 .15
400 Frank Thomas .30 .75
401 Jack Morris .10 .30
402 Greg Hibbard .05 .15
403 Jeffrey Hammonds .05 .15
404 Will Clark .20 .50
405 Travis Fryman .10 .30
406 Scott Sanderson .05 .15
407 Gene Harris .05 .15
408 Chuck Carr .05 .15
409 Ozzie Smith .50 1.25
410 Kent Mercker .05 .15
411 Andy Van Slyke .20 .50
412 Jimmy Key .10 .30
413 Pat Mahomes .05 .15
414 John Wetteland .10 .30
415 Todd Jones .05 .15
416 Greg Harris .05 .15
417 Kevin Stocker .05 .15
418 Juan Gonzalez .10 .30
419 Pete Smith .05 .15
420 Pat Listach .05 .15
421 Trevor Hoffman .20 .50
422 Scott Fletcher .05 .15
423 Mark Lewis .05 .15
424 Mickey Morandini .05 .15
425 Ryne Sandberg .50 1.25
426 Erik Hanson .05 .15
427 Gary Gaetti .10 .30
428 Harold Reynolds .10 .30
429 Mark Portugal .05 .15
430 David Valle .05 .15
431 Mitch Williams .05 .15
432 Howard Johnson .05 .15
433 Hal Morris .05 .15
434 Tom Henke .05 .15
435 Shane Mack .05 .15
436 Mike Piazza .60 1.50
437 Bret Saberhagen .10 .30
438 Jose Mesa .05 .15
439 Jaime Navarro .05 .15
440 Checklist .05 .15
A300 F.Thomas 90L 5th Ann. .75 2.00

1994 Leaf Clean-Up Crew

COMPLETE SET (12) 12.50 30.00
COMPLETE SERIES 1 (6) 4.00 10.00
COMPLETE SERIES 2 (6) 8.00 20.00
STATED ODDS 1:12 MAG-JUMBOS
1 Larry Walker 1.25 3.00
2 Andres Galarraga 1.25 3.00
3 Dave Hollins .60 1.50
4 Bobby Bonilla 1.25 3.00
5 Cecil Fielder 1.25 3.00
6 Danny Tartabull .60 1.50
7 Juan Gonzalez 1.25 3.00
8 Joe Carter 1.25 3.00
9 Fred McGriff 2.00 5.00
10 Matt Williams 1.25 3.00
11 Albert Belle 1.25 3.00
12 Harold Baines 1.25 3.00

1994 Leaf Gamers

COMPLETE SET (12) 20.00 50.00
COMPLETE SERIES 1 (6) 10.00 25.00
COMPLETE SERIES 2 (6) 10.00 25.00
STATED ODDS 1:8 JUMBO
1 Ken Griffey Jr. 5.00 12.00
2 Lenny Dykstra 1.00 2.50
3 Juan Gonzalez 1.00 2.50
4 Don Mattingly 6.00 15.00
5 David Justice 1.00 2.50
6 Mark Grace 1.50 4.00
7 Frank Thomas 2.50 6.00
8 Barry Bonds 6.00 15.00
9 Kirby Puckett 2.50 6.00
10 Will Clark 1.50 4.00
11 John Kruk 1.00 2.50
12 Mike Piazza 5.00 12.00

1994 Leaf Gold Rookies

COMPLETE SET (20) 6.00 15.00
COMPLETE SERIES 1 (10) 4.00 10.00
COMPLETE SERIES 2 (10) 2.00 5.00
STATED ODDS 1:18 SER.1, 1:12 SER.2
1 Javier Lopez .60 1.50
2 Rondell White .60 1.50
3 Butch Huskey .40 1.00
4 Midre Cummings .40 1.00
5 Scott Ruffcorn .40 1.00
6 Manny Ramirez 1.50 4.00
7 Danny Bautista .40 1.00
8 Russ Davis .40 1.00
9 Steve Karsay .40 1.00
10 Carlos Delgado 1.00 2.50
11 Bob Hamelin .40 1.00
12 Marcus Moore .40 1.00
13 Miguel Jimenez .40 1.00
14 Matt Walbeck .40 1.00
15 James Mouton .40 1.00
16 Rich Becker .40 1.00
17 Brian Anderson .60 1.50
18 Cliff Floyd .60 1.50
19 Steve Trachsel .40 1.00
20 Hector Carrasco .40 1.00

1994 Leaf Gold Stars

COMPLETE SET (15) 20.00 50.00
COMPLETE SERIES 1 (8) 10.00 25.00
COMPLETE SERIES 2 (7) 10.00 25.00
SER.1 STAT.ODDS 1:90H/R, 1:288J, 1:240M
STATED PRINT RUN 10,000 SERIAL #'d SETS
1 Roberto Alomar 1.50 4.00
2 Barry Bonds 6.00 15.00
3 David Justice 1.00 2.50
4 Ken Griffey Jr. 12.00 30.00
5 Lenny Dykstra 1.00 2.50
6 Don Mattingly 6.00 15.00
7 Andres Galarraga 1.00 2.50
8 Greg Maddux 4.00 10.00
9 Carlos Baerga .50 1.25
10 Paul Molitor 1.00 2.50
11 Frank Thomas 2.50 6.00
12 John Olerud 1.00 2.50
13 Juan Gonzalez 1.00 2.50
14 Fred McGriff 1.50 4.00
15 Jack McDowell .50 1.25

1994 Leaf MVP Contenders

COMPLETE SET (30) 75.00 150.00
SER.2 STAT.ODDS 1:36H/R, 1:90J, 1:90MAG
STATED PRINT RUN 10,000 SETS
*GOLD: SAME PRICE AS BASIC MVPS
ONE GOLD SET PER A12 OR N2 VIA MAIL
GOLD SET STATED PRINT RUN 5000 SETS
ONE THOMAS J400 PER A12 OR N2 VIA MAIL
THOMAS J400 PRINT RUN 20,000 CARDS
A1 Albert Belle 1.25 3.00
A2 Jose Canseco 2.00 5.00
A3 Joe Carter 1.25 3.00
A4 Will Clark 2.00 5.00
A5 Cecil Fielder 1.25 3.00
A6 Juan Gonzalez 1.25 3.00
A7 Ken Griffey Jr. 6.00 15.00
A8 Paul Molitor 1.25 3.00
A9 Rafael Palmeiro 2.00 5.00
A10 Kirby Puckett 3.00 8.00
A11 Cal Ripken Jr. 10.00 25.00
A12 Frank Thomas W 2.50 6.00
A13 Mo Vaughn 1.25 3.00
A14 Carlos Baerga .60 1.50
A15 AL Bonus Card .60 1.50
N1 Gary Sheffield 1.25 3.00
N2 Jeff Bagwell W 2.00 5.00
N3 Dante Bichette 1.25 3.00
N4 Barry Bonds 8.00 20.00
N5 Darren Daulton 1.25 3.00
N6 Andres Galarraga 1.25 3.00
N7 Gregg Jefferies .60 1.50
N8 David Justice 1.25 3.00
N9 Ray Lankford 1.25 3.00
N10 Fred McGriff 2.00 5.00
N11 Barry Larkin 2.00 5.00
N12 Mike Piazza 6.00 15.00
N13 Deion Sanders 2.00 5.00
N14 Matt Williams 1.25 3.00
N15 NL Bonus Card .60 1.50
J400 Frank Thomas Jumbo 2.50 6.00

1994 Leaf Power Brokers

COMPLETE SET (10) 8.00 20.00
SER.2 STATED ODDS 1:12 HOB/RET
1 Frank Thomas .75 2.00
2 David Justice .30 .75
3 Barry Bonds 2.00 5.00
4 Juan Gonzalez .30 .75
5 Ken Griffey Jr. 1.50 4.00
6 Mike Piazza 1.50 4.00
7 Cecil Fielder .30 .75
8 Fred McGriff .50 1.25
9 Joe Carter .30 .75
10 Albert Belle .30 .75

1994 Leaf Slideshow

COMPLETE SET (10) 12.00 30.00
COMPLETE SERIES 1 (5) 6.00 15.00
COMPLETE SERIES 2 (5) 6.00 15.00
STATED ODDS 1:54H/R, 1:36J, 1:36M
1 Frank Thomas 2.00 5.00
2 Mike Piazza 4.00 10.00
3 Darren Daulton .75 2.00
4 Ryne Sandberg 3.00 8.00
5 Roberto Alomar 1.25 3.00
6 Barry Bonds 5.00 12.00
7 Juan Gonzalez .75 2.00
8 Tim Salmon 1.25 3.00
9 Ken Griffey Jr. 4.00 10.00
10 David Justice .75 2.00

1994 Leaf Statistical Standouts

COMPLETE SET (10) 6.00 15.00
SER.1 STATED ODDS 1:12 HOB/RET
1 Frank Thomas .50 1.25
2 Barry Bonds 1.25 3.00
3 Juan Gonzalez .20 .50
4 Mike Piazza 1.00 2.50
5 Greg Maddux .75 2.00
6 Ken Griffey Jr. 1.00 2.50
7 Joe Carter .20 .50
8 Dave Winfield .20 .50
9 Tony Gwynn .60 1.50
10 Cal Ripken 1.50 4.00

1995 Leaf Promos

COMPLETE SET (9) 6.00 15.00
1 Jeff Bagwell .60 1.50
2 Wade Boggs .60 1.50
3 Joe Carter .30 .75
4 Greg Maddux 1.25 3.00
5 Raul Mondesi .30 .75
6 Kirby Puckett 1.00 2.50
7 Cal Ripken 2.00 5.00
8 Frank Thomas .50 1.25
9 Matt Williams .40 1.00

1995 Leaf

The 1995 Leaf set was issued in two series of 200 standard-size cards for a total of 400. Full-bleed fronts contain diamond-shaped player hologram in the upper left. The team name is done in silver foil up the left side. Peculiar backs contain two photos, the card number within a stamp or seal like emblem in the upper right and '94 and career stats graph toward bottom left. Hideo Nomo is the only key Rookie Card in this set.

COMPLETE SET (400) 15.00 40.00
COMPLETE SERIES 1 (200) 6.00 15.00
COMPLETE SERIES 2 (200) 10.00 25.00
1 Frank Thomas .30 .75
2 Carlos Garcia .05 .15
3 Todd Hundley .05 .15
4 Damion Easley .05 .15
5 Roberto Mejia .05 .15
6 John Mabry .05 .15
7 Aaron Sele .05 .15
8 Kenny Lofton .10 .30
9 John Doherty .05 .15
10 Joe Carter .10 .30
11 Mike Lansing .05 .15
12 John Valentin .05 .15
13 Ismael Valdes .05 .15
14 Dave McCarty .05 .15
15 Melvin Nieves .05 .15
16 Bobby Jones .05 .15
17 Trevor Hoffman .10 .30
18 John Smoltz .20 .50
19 Leo Gomez .05 .15
20 Roger Pavlik .05 .15
21 Dean Palmer .10 .30
22 Rickey Henderson .30 .75
23 Eddie Taubensee .05 .15
24 Damon Buford .05 .15
25 Mark Wohlers .05 .15
26 Jim Edmonds .20 .50
27 Wilson Alvarez .05 .15
28 Matt Williams .10 .30
29 Jeff Montgomery .05 .15
30 Shawon Dunston .05 .15
31 Tom Pagnozzi .05 .15
32 Jose Lind .05 .15
33 Royce Clayton .05 .15
34 Cal Eldred .05 .15
35 Chris Gomez .05 .15
36 Henry Rodriguez .05 .15
37 Dave Fleming .05 .15
38 Jon Lieber .05 .15
39 Scott Servais .05 .15
40 Wade Boggs .20 .50
41 John Olerud .10 .30
42 Eddie Williams .05 .15
43 Paul Sorrento .05 .15
44 Ron Karkovice .05 .15
45 Kevin Foster .05 .15
46 Miguel Jimenez .05 .15
47 Reggie Sanders .10 .30
48 Rondell White .10 .30
49 Scott Leius .05 .15
50 Jose Valentin .05 .15
51 Wm. VanLandingham .05 .15
52 Denny Hocking .05 .15
53 Jeff Fassero .05 .15
54 Chris Hoiles .05 .15
55 Walt Weiss .05 .15
56 Geronimo Berroa .05 .15
57 Rich Rowland .05 .15
58 Dave Weathers .05 .15
59 Sterling Hitchcock .05 .15
60 Raul Mondesi .10 .30
61 Rusty Greer .10 .30
62 David Justice .10 .30
63 Cecil Fielder .10 .30
64 Brian Jordan .10 .30
65 Mike Lieberthal .10 .30
66 Rick Aguilera .05 .15
67 Chuck Finley .10 .30
68 Andy Ashby .05 .15
69 Alex Fernandez .05 .15
70 Ed Sprague .05 .15
71 Steve Buechele .05 .15
72 Willie Greene .05 .15
73 Dave Nilsson .05 .15
74 Bret Saberhagen .10 .30
75 Jimmy Key .10 .30
76 Darren Lewis .05 .15
77 Steve Cooke .05 .15
78 Kirk Gibson .10 .30
79 Ray Lankford .10 .30
80 Paul O'Neill .20 .50
81 Mike Bordick .05 .15
82 Wes Chamberlain .05 .15
83 Rico Brogna .05 .15
84 Kevin Appier .10 .30
85 Juan Guzman .05 .15
86 Kevin Seitzer .05 .15
87 Mickey Morandini .05 .15
88 Pedro Martinez .20 .50
89 Matt Mieske .05 .15
90 Tino Martinez .20 .50
91 Paul Shuey .05 .15
92 Bip Roberts .05 .15
93 Chili Davis .10 .30
94 Deion Sanders .20 .50
95 Darrell Whitmore .05 .15
96 Joe Orsulak .05 .15
97 Bret Boone .10 .30
98 Kent Mercker .05 .15
99 Scott Livingstone .05 .15
100 Brady Anderson .10 .30
101 James Mouton .05 .15
102 Jose Rijo .05 .15
103 Bobby Munoz .05 .15
104 Ramon Martinez .05 .15
105 Bernie Williams .20 .50
106 Troy Neel .05 .15
107 Ivan Rodriguez .20 .50
108 Salomon Torres .05 .15
109 Johnny Ruffin .05 .15
110 Darryl Kile .10 .30
111 Bobby Ayala .05 .15
112 Ron Darling .05 .15
113 Jose Lima .05 .15
114 Joey Hamilton .05 .15
115 Greg Maddux .50 1.25
116 Greg Colbrunn .05 .15
117 Ozzie Guillen .10 .30
118 Brian Anderson .05 .15
119 Jeff Bagwell .20 .50
120 Pat Listach .05 .15
121 Sandy Alomar Jr. .05 .15
122 Jose Vizcaino .05 .15
123 Rick Helling .05 .15
124 Allen Watson .05 .15
125 Pedro Munoz .05 .15
126 Craig Biggio .20 .50
127 Kevin Stocker .05 .15
128 Wil Cordero .05 .15
129 Rafael Palmeiro .20 .50
130 Gar Finnvold .05 .15
131 Darren Hall .05 .15
132 Heathcliff Slocumb .05 .15
133 Darrin Fletcher .05 .15
134 Cal Ripken 1.00 2.50
135 Dante Bichette .10 .30
136 Don Slaught .05 .15
137 Pedro Astacio .05 .15
138 Ryan Thompson .05 .15
139 Greg Gohr .05 .15
140 Javier Lopez .10 .30
141 Lenny Dykstra .10 .30
142 Pat Rapp .05 .15
143 Mark Kiefer .05 .15
144 Greg Gagne .05 .15
145 Eduardo Perez .05 .15
146 Felix Fermin .05 .15
147 Jeff Frye .05 .15
148 Terry Steinbach .05 .15
149 Jim Eisenreich .05 .15
150 Brad Ausmus .10 .30
151 Randy Myers .05 .15
152 Rick White .05 .15
153 Mark Portugal .05 .15
154 Delino DeShields .05 .15
155 Scott Cooper .05 .15
156 Pat Hentgen .05 .15
157 Mark Gubicza .05 .15
158 Carlos Baerga .05 .15
159 Joe Girardi .05 .15
160 Rey Sanchez .05 .15
161 Todd Jones .05 .15
162 Luis Polonia .05 .15
163 Steve Trachsel .05 .15
164 Roberto Hernandez .05 .15
165 John Patterson .05 .15
166 Rene Arocha .05 .15
167 Will Clark .20 .50
168 Jim Leyritz .05 .15
169 Todd Van Poppel .05 .15
170 Robb Nen .10 .30
171 Midre Cummings .05 .15
172 Jay Buhner .10 .30
173 Kevin Tapani .05 .15
174 Mark Lemke .05 .15
175 Marcus Moore .05 .15
176 Wayne Kirby .05 .15
177 Rich Amaral .05 .15
178 Lou Whitaker .10 .30
179 Jay Bell .10 .30
180 Rick Wilkins .05 .15
181 Paul Molitor .10 .30
182 Gary Sheffield .10 .30
183 Kirby Puckett .30 .75
184 Cliff Floyd .10 .30
185 Darren Oliver .05 .15
186 Tim Naehring .05 .15
187 John Hudek .05 .15
188 Eric Young .05 .15
189 Roger Salkeld .05 .15
190 Kirt Manwaring .05 .15
191 Kurt Abbott .05 .15
192 David Nied .05 .15
193 Todd Zeile .05 .15
194 Wally Joyner .10 .30
195 Dennis Martinez .10 .30
196 Billy Ashley .05 .15
197 Ben McDonald .05 .15
198 Bob Hamelin .05 .15
199 Chris Turner .05 .15
200 Lance Johnson .05 .15
201 Willie Banks .05 .15
202 Juan Gonzalez .10 .30
203 Scott Sanders .05 .15
204 Scott Brosius .10 .30
205 Curt Schilling .10 .30
206 Alex Gonzalez .05 .15
207 Travis Fryman .10 .30
208 Tim Raines .10 .30
209 Steve Avery .05 .15
210 Hal Morris .05 .15
211 Ken Griffey Jr. .60 1.50
212 Ozzie Smith .50 1.25
213 Chuck Carr .05 .15
214 Ryan Klesko .10 .30
215 Robin Ventura .10 .30
216 Luis Gonzalez .10 .30
217 Ken Ryan .05 .15
218 Mike Piazza .50 1.25
219 Matt Walbeck .05 .15
220 Jeff Kent .10 .30
221 Orlando Miller .05 .15
222 Kenny Rogers .10 .30
223 J.T. Snow .10 .30
224 Alan Trammell .10 .30
225 John Franco .10 .30
226 Gerald Williams .05 .15
227 Andy Benes .05 .15
228 Dan Wilson .05 .15
229 Dave Hollins .05 .15
230 Vinny Castilla .10 .30
231 Devon White .10 .30
232 Fred McGriff .20 .50
233 Quilvio Veras .05 .15
234 Tom Candiotti .05 .15
235 Jason Bere .05 .15
236 Mark Langston .05 .15
237 Mel Rojas .05 .15
238 Chuck Knoblauch .10 .30
239 Bernard Gilkey .05 .15

240 Mark McGwire .75 2.00
241 Kirk Rueter .05 .15
242 Pat Kelly .05 .15
243 Ruben Sierra .10 .30
244 Randy Johnson .30 .75
245 Shane Reynolds .05 .15
246 Danny Tartabull .05 .15
247 Darryl Hamilton .05 .15
248 Danny Bautista .05 .15
249 Tom Gordon .05 .15
250 Tom Glavine .20 .50
251 Orlando Merced .05 .15
252 Eric Karros .10 .30
253 Benji Gil .05 .15
254 Sean Bergman .05 .15
255 Roger Clemens .60 1.50
256 Roberto Alomar .20 .50
257 Benito Santiago .10 .30
258 Robby Thompson .05 .15
259 Marvin Freeman .05 .15
260 Jose Offerman .05 .15
261 Greg Vaughn .05 .15
262 David Segui .05 .15
263 Geronimo Pena .05 .15
264 Tim Salmon .20 .50
265 Eddie Murray .30 .75
266 Mariano Duncan .05 .15
267 Hideo Nomo RC .75 2.00
268 Derek Bell .05 .15
269 Mo Vaughn .10 .30
270 Jeff King .05 .15
271 Edgar Martinez .20 .50
272 Sammy Sosa .30 .75
273 Scott Ruffcorn .05 .15
274 Darren Daulton .10 .30
275 John Jaha .05 .15
276 Andres Galarraga .10 .30
277 Mark Grace .20 .50
278 Mike Moore .05 .15
279 Barry Bonds .75 2.00
280 Manny Ramirez .20 .50
281 Ellis Burks .10 .30
282 Greg Swindell .05 .15
283 Barry Larkin .20 .50
284 Albert Belle .10 .30
285 Shawn Green .10 .30
286 John Roper .05 .15
287 Scott Erickson .05 .15
288 Moises Alou .10 .30
289 Mike Blowers .05 .15
290 Brent Gates .05 .15
291 Sean Berry .05 .15
292 Mike Stanley .05 .15
293 Jeff Conine .10 .30
294 Tim Wallach .05 .15
295 Bobby Bonilla .10 .30
296 Bruce Ruffin .05 .15
297 Chad Curtis .05 .15
298 Mike Greenwell .05 .15
299 Tony Gwynn .40 1.00
300 Russ Davis .05 .15
301 Danny Jackson .05 .15
302 Pete Harnisch .05 .15
303 Don Mattingly .75 2.00
304 Rheal Cormier .05 .15
305 Larry Walker .10 .30
306 Hector Carrasco .05 .15
307 Jason Jacome .05 .15
308 Phil Plantier .05 .15
309 Harold Baines .10 .30
310 Mitch Williams .05 .15
311 Charles Nagy .05 .15
312 Ken Caminiti .10 .30
313 Alex Rodriguez .75 2.00
314 Chris Sabo .05 .15
315 Gary Gaetti .10 .30
316 Andre Dawson .10 .30
317 Mark Clark .05 .15
318 Vince Coleman .05 .15
319 Brad Clontz .05 .15
320 Steve Finley .10 .30
321 Doug Drabek .05 .15
322 Mark McLemore .05 .15
323 Stan Javier .05 .15
324 Ron Gant .10 .30
325 Charlie Hayes .05 .15
326 Carlos Delgado .10 .30
327 Ricky Bottalico .05 .15
328 Rod Beck .05 .15
329 Mark Acre .05 .15
330 Chris Bosio .05 .15
331 Tony Phillips .05 .15
332 Garret Anderson .10 .30
333 Pat Meares .05 .15
334 Todd Worrell .05 .15
335 Marquis Grissom .10 .30
336 Brent Mayne .05 .15
337 Lee Tinsley .05 .15
338 Terry Pendleton .10 .30
339 David Cone .10 .30
340 Tony Fernandez .05 .15
341 Jim Bullinger .05 .15
342 Armando Benitez .05 .15
343 John Smiley .05 .15
344 Dan Miceli .05 .15
345 Charles Johnson .10 .30
346 Lee Smith .10 .30
347 Brian McRae .05 .15
348 Jim Thome .20 .50
349 Jose Oliva .05 .15
350 Terry Mulholland .05 .15
351 Tom Henke .05 .15
352 Dennis Eckersley .10 .30
353 Sid Fernandez .05 .15
354 Paul Wagner .05 .15
355 John Dettmer .05 .15
356 John Wetteland .10 .30
357 John Burkett .05 .15
358 Marty Cordova .05 .15
359 Norm Charlton .05 .15
360 Mike Devereaux .05 .15
361 Alex Cole .05 .15
362 Brett Butler .10 .30
363 Mickey Tettleton .05 .15
364 Al Martin .05 .15
365 Tony Tarasco .05 .15
366 Pat Mahomes .05 .15
367 Gary DiSarcina .05 .15
368 Bill Swift .05 .15
369 Chipper Jones .30 .75
370 Orel Hershiser .10 .30
371 Kevin Gross .05 .15
372 Dave Winfield .10 .30
373 Andujar Cedeno .05 .15
374 Jim Abbott .20 .50
375 Glenallen Hill .05 .15
376 Otis Nixon .05 .15
377 Roberto Kelly .05 .15
378 Chris Hammond .05 .15
379 Mike Macfarlane .05 .15
380 J.R. Phillips .05 .15
381 Luis Alicea .05 .15
382 Bret Barberie .05 .15
383 Tom Goodwin .05 .15
384 Mark Whiten .05 .15
385 Jeffrey Hammonds .05 .15
386 Omar Vizquel .20 .50
387 Mike Mussina .20 .50
388 Ricky Bones .05 .15
389 Steve Ontiveros .05 .15
390 Jeff Blauser .05 .15
391 Jose Canseco .20 .50
392 Bob Tewksbury .05 .15
393 Jacob Brumfield .05 .15
394 Doug Jones .05 .15
395 Ken Hill .05 .15
396 Pat Borders .05 .15
397 Carl Everett .10 .30
398 Gregg Jefferies .05 .15
399 Jack McDowell .05 .15
400 Denny Neagle .10 .30
NNO Frank Thomas
Jumbo/10,000
NNO Barry Bonds
Jumbo/10,000

1995 Leaf 300 Club

COMPLETE SET (18) 20.00 50.00
COMPLETE SERIES 1 (9) 10.00 25.00
COMPLETE SERIES 2 (9) 10.00 25.00
STATED ODDS 1:12 RETAIL/MINI
1 Frank Thomas 1.50 4.00
2 Paul Molitor 1.50 4.00
3 Mike Piazza 1.50 4.00
4 Moises Alou .60 1.50
5 Mike Greenwell
6 Will Clark .60 1.50
7 Hal Morris .60 1.50
8 Edgar Martinez 1.00 2.50
9 Carlos Baerga .60 1.50
10 Ken Griffey Jr. 3.00 8.00
11 Wade Boggs 1.00 2.50
12 Jeff Bagwell 1.00 2.50
13 Tony Gwynn 1.50 4.00
14 John Kruk .60 1.50
15 Don Mattingly 3.00 8.00
16 Mark Grace 1.00 2.50
17 Kirby Puckett 1.50 4.00
18 Kenny Lofton .60 1.50

1995 Leaf Checklists

COMPLETE SET (8) 2.00 5.00
COMPLETE SERIES 1 (4) .60 1.50
COMPLETE SERIES 2 (4) 1.25 3.00
RANDOM INSERTS IN BOTH SERIES PACKS
1 Bob Hamelin UER .05 .15
2 David Cone .10 .30
3 Frank Thomas .30 .75
4 Paul O'Neill .20 .50
5 Raul Mondesi .10 .30
6 Greg Maddux .50 1.25
7 Tony Gwynn .40 1.00
8 Jeff Bagwell .20 .50

1995 Leaf Cornerstones

COMPLETE SET (6) 3.00 8.00
SER.1 STATED ODDS 1:18 HOB/RET
1 F.Thomas .60 1.50
R.Ventura
2 C.Fielder .25 .60
T.Fryman
3 D.Mattingly 1.50 4.00
W.Boggs
4 J.Bagwell .40 1.00
K.Caminiti
5 W.Clark .40 1.00
D.Palmer
6 J.R.Phillips .25 .60
M.Williams

1995 Leaf Gold Rookies

COMPLETE SET (16) 3.00 8.00
SER.1 STATED ODDS 1:2 HOB/RET
1 Alex Rodriguez 1.25 3.00
2 Garret Anderson .20 .50
3 Shawn Green .20 .50
4 Armando Benitez .08 .25
5 Darren Dreifort .08 .25
6 Orlando Miller .08 .25
7 Jose Oliva .08 .25
8 Ricky Bottalico .08 .25
9 Charles Johnson .20 .50
10 Brian L.Hunter .20 .50
11 Ray McDavid .08 .25
12 Chan Ho Park .08 .25
13 Mike Kelly .08 .25
14 Cory Bailey .08 .25
15 Alex Gonzalez .08 .25
16 Andrew Lorraine .08 .25

1995 Leaf Gold Stars

COMPLETE SET (14) 25.00 60.00
COMPLETE SERIES 1 (8) 12.00 30.00
COMPLETE SERIES 2 (6) 12.00 30.00
STATED ODDS 1:110 HOB/RET
STATED PRINT RUN 10,000 SERIAL #'d SETS
1 Jeff Bagwell 2.50 6.00
2 Albert Belle 1.50 4.00
3 Tony Gwynn 4.00 10.00
4 Ken Griffey Jr. 8.00 20.00
5 Barry Bonds 6.00 15.00
6 Don Mattingly 8.00 20.00
7 Raul Mondesi 1.50 4.00
8 Joe Carter 1.50 4.00
9 Greg Maddux 6.00 15.00
10 Frank Thomas 4.00 10.00
11 Mike Piazza 4.00 10.00
12 Jose Canseco 2.50 6.00
13 Kirby Puckett 4.00 10.00
14 Matt Williams 1.50 4.00

1995 Leaf Great Gloves

COMPLETE SET (16) 4.00 10.00
SER.2 STATED ODDS 1:2
1 Jeff Bagwell .20 .50
2 Roberto Alomar .20 .50
3 Barry Bonds .75 2.00
4 Wade Boggs .20 .50
5 Andres Galarraga .10 .30
6 Ken Griffey Jr. .60 1.50
7 Marquis Grissom .10 .30
8 Kenny Lofton .10 .30
9 Barry Larkin .20 .50
10 Don Mattingly .75 2.00
11 Greg Maddux .50 1.25
12 Kirby Puckett .30 .75
13 Ozzie Smith .50 1.25
14 Cal Ripken 1.00 2.50
15 Matt Williams .10 .30
16 Ivan Rodriguez .20 .50

1995 Leaf Heading for the Hall

COMPLETE SET (8) 12.50 30.00
SER.2 STATED ODDS 1:75 HOBBY
STATED PRINT RUN 5000 SERIAL #'d SETS
1 Frank Thomas 1.50 4.00
2 Ken Griffey Jr. 3.00 8.00
3 Jeff Bagwell 1.00 2.50
4 Barry Bonds 2.50 6.00
5 Kirby Puckett 1.50 4.00
6 Cal Ripken 5.00 12.00
7 Tony Gwynn 1.50 4.00
8 Paul Molitor 1.50 4.00

1995 Leaf Opening Day

COMPLETE SET (8) 4.00 10.00
1 Frank Thomas .25 .60
2 Jeff Bagwell .30 .75
3 Barry Bonds .60 1.50
4 Ken Griffey Jr. 1.00 2.50
5 Mike Piazza .75 2.00
6 Cal Ripken 1.25 3.00
7 Jose Canseco .25 .60
8 Larry Walker .15 .40

1995 Leaf Slideshow

COMPLETE SET (16) 12.50 30.00
COMPLETE SERIES 1 (8) 6.00 15.00
COMPLETE SERIES 2 (8) 6.00 15.00
STATED ODDS 1:30 HOB, 1:36 RET
SER.1 HAVE SUFFIX A/SER.2 HAVE SUFFIX B
1A Raul Mondesi .40 1.00
2A Frank Thomas 1.00 2.50
3A Fred McGriff .60 1.50
4A Cal Ripken 3.00 8.00
5A Jeff Bagwell .60 1.50
6A Will Clark .40 1.00
7A Matt Williams .40 1.00
8A Ken Griffey Jr. 2.00 5.00

1995 Leaf Statistical Standouts Promos

COMPLETE SET 10.00 25.00
1 Joe Carter .30 .75
2 Ken Griffey Jr. 2.50 6.00
3 Don Mattingly 1.50 4.00
4 Fred McGriff .40 1.00
5 Paul Molitor 1.00 2.50
6 Kirby Puckett 1.25 3.00
7 Cal Ripken 3.00 8.00
8 Frank Thomas .75 2.00
9 Matt Williams .50 1.25

1995 Leaf Statistical Standouts

COMPLETE SET (9) 30.00 60.00
SER.1 STATED ODDS 1:70 HOBBY
1 Joe Carter 1.00 2.50
2 Ken Griffey Jr. 20.00 50.00
3 Don Mattingly 5.00 12.00
4 Fred McGriff 1.50 4.00
5 Paul Molitor 2.50 6.00
6 Kirby Puckett 2.50 6.00
7 Cal Ripken 8.00 20.00
8 Frank Thomas 2.50 6.00
9 Matt Williams 1.00 2.50

1995 Leaf Thomas

COMPLETE SET (6) 4.00 10.00
COMMON CARD (1-6) .75 2.00
SER.2 STATED ODDS 1:18

1995 Leaf Thomas Akklaim

This one-card set features a borderless action photo of Frank Thomas with a small head photo in the upper left inside a baseball diamond frame. The front displays the words "Big Hurt" in big block silver foil lettering. The back shows player information and career statistics on a player picture background.
1 Frank Thomas 2.00 5.00

1996 Leaf

The 1996 Leaf set was issued in one series totalling 220 cards. The fronts feature color action player photos with silver foil printing and lines forming a border on the left and bottom. The backs display another player photo with 1995 season and career statistics. Card number 210 is a checklist for the insert sets and cards number 211-220 feature rookies. The fronts of these 10 cards are different in design from the first 200 with a color action player cut-out over a green-shadow background of the same picture and gold lettering.
COMPLETE SET (220) 8.00 20.00
1 John Smoltz .20 .50
2 Dennis Eckersley .10 .30
3 Delino DeShields .10 .30
4 Cliff Floyd .10 .30
5 Chuck Finley .10 .30
6 Cecil Fielder .10 .30
7 Tim Naehring .10 .30
8 Carlos Perez .10 .30
9 Brad Ausmus .10 .30
10 Matt Lawton RC .15 .40
11 Alan Trammell .10 .30
12 Steve Finley .10 .30
13 Paul O'Neill .20 .50
14 Gary Sheffield .10 .30
15 Mark McGwire .75 2.00
16 Bernie Williams .20 .50
17 Jeff Montgomery .10 .30
18 Chan Ho Park .10 .30
19 Greg Vaughn .10 .30
20 Jeff Kent .10 .30
21 Cal Ripken 1.00 2.50
22 Charles Johnson .10 .30
23 Eric Karros .10 .30
24 Alex Rodriguez .60 1.50
25 Chris Snopek .10 .30
26 Jason Isringhausen .10 .30
27 Chili Davis .10 .30
28 Chipper Jones .30 .75
29 Bret Saberhagen .10 .30
30 Tony Clark .10 .30
31 Marty Cordova .10 .30
32 Dwayne Hosey .10 .30
33 Fred McGriff .20 .50
34 Deion Sanders .20 .50
35 Orlando Merced .10 .30
36 Brady Anderson .10 .30
37 Ray Lankford .10 .30
38 Manny Ramirez .20 .50
39 Alex Fernandez .10 .30
40 Greg Colbrunn .10 .30
41 Ken Griffey Jr. .60 1.50
42 Mickey Morandini .10 .30
43 Chuck Knoblauch .10 .30
44 Quinton McCracken .10 .30
45 Tim Salmon .20 .50
46 Jose Mesa .10 .30
47 Marquis Grissom .10 .30
48 Maddux .10 .30
Johnson CL
49 Raul Mondesi .10 .30
50 Mark Grudzielanek .10 .30
51 Ray Durham .10 .30
52 Matt Williams .10 .30
53 Bob Hamelin .10 .30
54 Lenny Dykstra .10 .30
55 Jeff King .10 .30
56 LaTroy Hawkins .10 .30
57 Terry Pendleton .10 .30
58 Kevin Stocker .10 .30
59 Ozzie Timmons .10 .30
60 David Justice .10 .30
61 Ricky Bottalico .10 .30
62 Andy Ashby .10 .30
63 Larry Walker .10 .30
64 Jose Canseco .20 .50
65 Bret Boone .10 .30
66 Shawn Green .10 .30
67 Chad Curtis .10 .30
68 Travis Fryman .10 .30
69 Roger Clemens .60 1.50
70 David Bell .10 .30
71 Rusty Greer .10 .30
72 Bob Higginson .10 .30
73 Joey Hamilton .10 .30
74 Kevin Seitzer .10 .30
75 Julian Tavarez .10 .30
76 Troy Percival .10 .30
77 Kirby Puckett .30 .75
78 Barry Bonds .75 2.00
79 Michael Tucker .10 .30
80 Paul Molitor .10 .30
81 Carlos Garcia .10 .30
82 Johnny Damon .20 .50
83 Mike Hampton .10 .30
84 Ariel Prieto .10 .30
85 Tony Tarasco .10 .30
86 Pete Schourek .10 .30
87 Tom Glavine .20 .50
88 Rondell White .10 .30
89 Jim Edmonds .10 .30
90 Robby Thompson .10 .30
91 Wade Boggs .20 .50
92 Pedro Martinez .20 .50
93 Gregg Jefferies .10 .30
94 Albert Belle .10 .30
95 Benji Gil .10 .30
96 Denny Neagle .10 .30
97 Mark Langston .10 .30
98 Sandy Alomar Jr. .10 .30
99 Tony Gwynn .40 1.00
100 Todd Hundley .10 .30
101 Dante Bichette .10 .30
102 Eddie Murray .30 .75
103 Lyle Mouton .10 .30
104 John Jaha .10 .30
105 Larkin .10 .30
Vaughn CL
106 Jon Nunnally .10 .30
107 Juan Gonzalez .10 .30
108 Kevin Appier .10 .30
109 Brian McRae .10 .30
110 Lee Smith .10 .30
111 Tim Wakefield .10 .30
112 Sammy Sosa .30 .75
113 Jay Buhner .10 .30
114 Garret Anderson .10 .30
115 Edgar Martinez .20 .50
116 Edgardo Alfonzo .10 .30
117 Billy Ashley .10 .30
118 Joe Carter .10 .30
119 Javy Lopez .10 .30
120 Bobby Bonilla .10 .30
121 Ken Caminiti .10 .30
122 Barry Larkin .20 .50
123 Shannon Stewart .10 .30
124 Orel Hershiser .10 .30
125 Jeff Conine .10 .30
126 Mark Grace .20 .50
127 Kenny Lofton .10 .30
128 Luis Gonzalez .10 .30
129 Rico Brogna .10 .30
130 Mo Vaughn .10 .30
131 Brad Radke .10 .30
132 Jose Herrera .10 .30
133 Rick Aguilera .10 .30
134 Gary DiSarcina .10 .30
135 Andres Galarraga .10 .30
136 Carl Everett .10 .30
137 Steve Avery .10 .30
138 Vinny Castilla .10 .30
139 Dennis Martinez .10 .30
140 John Wetteland .10 .30
141 Alex Gonzalez .10 .30
142 Brian Jordan .10 .30
143 Todd Hollandsworth .10 .30
144 Terrell Wade .10 .30
145 Wilson Alvarez .10 .30
146 Reggie Sanders .10 .30
147 Will Clark .20 .50
148 Hideo Nomo .30 .75
149 J.T.Snow .10 .30
150 Frank Thomas .30 .75
151 Ivan Rodriguez .20 .50
152 Jay Bell .10 .30
153 Nomo .10 .30
Cordova CL
154 David Cone .10 .30
155 Roberto Alomar .20 .50
156 Carlos Delgado .10 .30
157 Carlos Baerga .10 .30
158 Geronimo Berroa .10 .30
159 Joe Vitiello .10 .30
160 Terry Steinbach .10 .30
161 Doug Drabek .10 .30
162 David Segui .10 .30
163 Ozzie Smith .50 1.25
164 Kurt Abbott .10 .30
165 Randy Johnson .30 .75
166 John Valentin .10 .30
167 Mickey Tettleton .10 .30
168 Ruben Sierra .10 .30
169 Jim Thome .20 .50
170 Mike Greenwell .10 .30
171 Quilvio Veras .10 .30
172 Robin Ventura .10 .30
173 Bill Pulsipher .10 .30
174 Rafael Palmeiro .20 .50
175 Hal Morris .10 .30
176 Ryan Klesko .10 .30
177 Eric Young .10 .30
178 Shane Andrews .10 .30
179 Brian L.Hunter .10 .30
180 Brett Butler .10 .30
181 John Olerud .10 .30
182 Moises Alou .10 .30
183 Glenallen Hill .10 .30
184 Ismael Valdes .10 .30
185 Andy Pettitte .20 .50
186 Yamil Benitez .10 .30
187 Jason Bere .10 .30
188 Dean Palmer .10 .30
189 Jimmy Haynes .10 .30
190 Trevor Hoffman .10 .30
191 Mike Mussina .20 .50
192 Greg Maddux .50 1.25
193 Ozzie Guillen .10 .30
194 Pat Listach .10 .30
195 Derek Bell .10 .30
196 Darren Daulton .10 .30
197 John Mabry .10 .30
198 Ramon Martinez .10 .30
199 Jeff Bagwell .20 .50
200 Mike Piazza .50 1.25
201 Al Martin .10 .30
202 Aaron Sele .10 .30
203 Ed Sprague .10 .30
204 Rod Beck .10 .30
205 Gwynn .10 .30
Martinez CL
206 Mike Lansing .10 .30
207 Craig Biggio .20 .50
208 Jeffrey Hammonds .10 .30
209 Dave Nilsson .10 .30
210 Bichette .10 .30
Belle CL
211 Derek Jeter .75 2.00
212 Alan Benes .10 .30
213 Jason Schmidt .20 .50
214 Alex Ochoa .10 .30
215 Ruben Rivera .10 .30
216 Roger Cedeno .10 .30
217 Jeff Suppan .10 .30
218 Billy Wagner .10 .30
219 Mark Loretta .10 .30
220 Karim Garcia .10 .30

1996 Leaf Bronze Press Proofs

*STARS: 4X TO 10X BASIC CARDS
*ROOKIES: 2.5X TO 6X BASIC CARDS
ONE BRZ, GLD OR SLV PROOF PER 10 PACKS
STATED PRINT RUN 2000 SETS

1996 Leaf Gold Press Proofs

*STARS: 12.5X TO 30X BASIC CARDS
*ROOKIES: 8X TO 20X BASIC CARDS
ONE BRZ, GLD OR SLV PROOF PER 10 PACKS
STATED PRINT RUN 500 SETS

1996 Leaf Silver Press Proofs

*STARS: 8X TO 20X BASIC CARDS
*ROOKIES: 5X TO 12X BASIC CARDS
ONE BRZ, GLD OR SLV PROOF PER 10 PACKS
STATED PRINT RUN 1000 SETS

1996 Leaf All-Star Game MVP Contenders

COMPLETE SET (20) 15.00 40.00
FIRST 5000 CARDS RECEIVED OF AS GAME
MVP REDEEMABLE BY MAIL FOR GOLD SET
RANDOM INSERTS IN PACKS
ONE GOLD SET PER PIAZZA VIA MAIL
GOLD STATED PRINT RUN 5000 SETS
1 Frank Thomas .60 1.50
2 Mike Piazza W 1.50 4.00
3 Sammy Sosa .60 1.50
4 Cal Ripken 2.00 5.00
5 Jeff Bagwell .40 1.00
6 Reggie Sanders .25 .60
7 Mo Vaughn .25 .60
8 Tony Gwynn .75 2.00
9 Dante Bichette .25 .60
10 Tim Salmon .40 1.00
11 Chipper Jones .60 1.50
12 Kenny Lofton .25 .60
13 Manny Ramirez .40 1.00
14 Barry Bonds 1.50 4.00
15 Raul Mondesi .25 .60
16 Kirby Puckett .60 1.50
17 Albert Belle .25 .60
18 Ken Griffey Jr. 1.25 3.00
19 Greg Maddux 1.00 2.50
20 Bonus Card .25 .60

1996 Leaf Gold Stars

COMPLETE SET (15) 20.00 50.00
STATED ODDS 1:190
STATED PRINT RUN 2500 SERIAL #'d SETS
1 Frank Thomas 6.00 15.00
2 Dante Bichette .60 1.50
3 Sammy Sosa 1.50 4.00
4 Ken Griffey Jr. 3.00 8.00
5 Mike Piazza 1.50 4.00
6 Tim Salmon .60 1.50
7 Hideo Nomo 1.50 4.00
8 Cal Ripken 5.00 12.00
9 Chipper Jones 1.50 4.00
10 Albert Belle .60 1.50
11 Tony Gwynn 1.50 4.00
12 Mo Vaughn .60 1.50
13 Barry Larkin 1.00 2.50
14 Manny Ramirez 1.00 2.50
15 Greg Maddux 2.50 6.00

1996 Leaf Hats Off

COMPLETE SET (8) 15.00 40.00
STATED ODDS 1:72 RETAIL
STATED PRINT RUN 5000 SERIAL #'d SETS
1 Cal Ripken 6.00 15.00
2 Barry Larkin 1.25 3.00
3 Frank Thomas 2.00 5.00
4 Mo Vaughn .75 2.00
5 Ken Griffey Jr. 4.00 10.00
6 Hideo Nomo 2.00 5.00
7 Albert Belle .75 2.00
8 Greg Maddux 3.00 8.00

1996 Leaf Picture Perfect Promos

COMPLETE SET (12) 30.00 80.00
1 Frank Thomas 1.50 4.00
2 Cal Ripken 8.00 20.00
3 Greg Maddux 5.00 12.00
4 Manny Ramirez 2.00 5.00
5 Chipper Jones 4.00 10.00
6 Tony Gwynn 4.00 10.00
7 Ken Griffey Jr. 5.00 12.00
8 Albert Belle .40 1.00
9 Jeff Bagwell 2.00 5.00
10 Mike Piazza 5.00 12.00
11 Mo Vaughn .40 1.00
12 Barry Bonds 4.00 10.00

1996 Leaf Picture Perfect

COMPLETE SET (12) 12.00 30.00
CARDS 1-6 STATED ODDS 1:140 HOBBY
CARDS 7-12 RANDOM INS.IN RET.PACKS
STATED PRINT RUN 5000 SERIAL #'d SETS
1 Frank Thomas 1.50 4.00
2 Cal Ripken 5.00 12.00
3 Greg Maddux 2.50 6.00
4 Manny Ramirez 1.00 2.50
5 Chipper Jones 1.50 4.00
6 Tony Gwynn 1.50 4.00
7 Ken Griffey Jr. 3.00 8.00
8 Albert Belle .60 1.50
9 Jeff Bagwell 1.00 2.50
10 Mike Piazza 1.50 4.00
11 Mo Vaughn .60 1.50
12 Barry Bonds 2.50 6.00

1996 Leaf Statistical Standouts

COMPLETE SET (8) 15.00 40.00
STATED ODDS 1:210 HOBBY
STATED PRINT RUN 2500 SERIAL #'d SETS
1 Cal Ripken 8.00 20.00
2 Tony Gwynn 2.50 6.00
3 Frank Thomas 2.50 6.00
4 Ken Griffey Jr. 5.00 12.00
5 Hideo Nomo 2.50 6.00
6 Greg Maddux 4.00 10.00
7 Albert Belle 1.00 2.50
8 Chipper Jones 2.50 6.00

1996 Leaf Thomas Greatest Hits

COMPLETE SET (8) 30.00 80.00
COMMON CARD (1-7) 5.00 12.00
COMMON EXCHANGE (8) 6.00 15.00
CARDS 1-4 STATED ODDS 1:210 HOBBY
CARDS 5-7 STATED ODDS 1:210 RETAIL
CARD 8 WAS AVAIL.VIA MAIL-IN OFFER
STATED PRINT RUN 5000 SETS

1996 Leaf Total Bases Promos

COMPLETE SET (12) 12.50 30.00
1 Frank Thomas .75 2.00
2 Albert Belle .30 .75
3 Rafael Palmeiro .60 1.50
4 Barry Bonds 1.50 4.00
5 Kirby Puckett 1.25 3.00
6 Joe Carter .30 .75
7 Paul Molitor 1.00 2.50
8 Fred McGriff .40 1.00
9 Ken Griffey Jr. 2.00 5.00
10 Carlos Baerga .20 .50
11 Juan Gonzalez .75 2.00
12 Cal Ripken 3.00 8.00

1996 Leaf Total Bases

COMPLETE SET (12) 40.00 100.00
STATED ODDS 1:72 HOBBY
STATED PRINT RUN 5000 SERIAL #'d SETS
1 Frank Thomas 3.00 8.00
2 Albert Belle 1.25 3.00
3 Rafael Palmeiro 2.00 5.00
4 Barry Bonds 8.00 20.00
5 Kirby Puckett 3.00 8.00
6 Joe Carter 1.25 3.00
7 Paul Molitor 1.25 3.00
8 Fred McGriff 2.00 5.00
9 Ken Griffey Jr. 10.00 25.00
10 Carlos Baerga 1.25 3.00
11 Juan Gonzalez 1.25 3.00
12 Cal Ripken 10.00 25.00

1997 Leaf

The 400-card Leaf set was issued in two separate 200-card series. 10-card packs carried a suggested retail of $2.99. Each card features color action player photos with foil enhancement. The backs carry another player photo and season and career statistics. The set contains the following subsets: Legacy (188-197/348-367), Checklists (198-200/398-400) and Gamers (368-397). Rookie Cards in this set include Jose Cruz Jr., Brian Giles and Hideki Irabu. In a tie in with the 50th anniversary of Jackie Robinson's major league debut, Donruss/Leaf also issued some collectible items. They made 42 all-leather jackets (issued to match Robinson's uniform number). There were also 311 leather jackets produced (to match Robinson's career batting average). 1,500 lithographs were also produced of which Rachel Robinson (Jackie's widow) signed 500 of them.
COMPLETE SET (400) 15.00 40.00
COMPLETE SERIES 1 (200) 8.00 20.00
COMPLETE SERIES 2 (200) 8.00 20.00
SUBSET CARDS HALF VALUE OF BASE CARDS
J.ROBINSON REPRINT RANDOM IN PACKS
1 Wade Boggs .20 .50
2 Brian McRae .10 .30
3 Jeff D'Amico .10 .30
4 George Arias .10 .30
5 Billy Wagner .10 .30
6 Ray Lankford .10 .30
7 Will Clark .20 .50
8 Edgar Renteria .10 .30
9 Alex Ochoa .10 .30
10 Roberto Hernandez .10 .30
11 Joe Carter .10 .30
12 Gregg Jefferies .10 .30
13 Mark Grace .20 .50
14 Roberto Alomar .20 .50
15 Joe Randa .10 .30
16 Alex Rodriguez .50 1.25
17 Tony Gwynn .40 1.00
18 Steve Gibralter .10 .30
19 Scott Stahoviak .10 .30
20 Matt Williams .10 .30
21 Quinton McCracken .10 .30
22 Ugueth Urbina .10 .30
23 Jermaine Allensworth .10 .30
24 Paul Molitor .10 .30
25 Carlos Delgado .10 .30
26 Bob Abreu .20 .50
27 John Jaha .10 .30
28 Rusty Greer .10 .30
29 Kimera Bartee .10 .30
30 Ruben Rivera .10 .30
31 Jason Kendall .10 .30
32 Lance Johnson .10 .30
33 Robin Ventura .10 .30
34 Kevin Appier .10 .30
35 John Mabry .10 .30
36 Ricky Otero .10 .30
37 Mike Lansing .10 .30
38 Mark McGwire .75 2.00
39 Tim Naehring .10 .30
40 Tom Glavine .20 .50
41 Rey Ordonez .10 .30
42 Tony Clark .10 .30
43 Rafael Palmeiro .20 .50
44 Pedro Martinez .20 .50
45 Keith Lockhart .10 .30
46 Dan Wilson .10 .30
47 John Wetteland .10 .30
48 Chan Ho Park .10 .30
49 Gary Sheffield .10 .30
50 Shawn Estes .10 .30
51 Royce Clayton .10 .30
52 Jaime Navarro .10 .30
53 Raul Casanova .10 .30
54 Jeff Bagwell .20 .50
55 Barry Larkin .20 .50
56 Charles Nagy .10 .30
57 Ken Caminiti .10 .30
58 Todd Hollandsworth .10 .30
59 Pat Hentgen .10 .30
60 Jose Valentin .10 .30
61 Frank Rodriguez .10 .30
62 Mickey Tettleton .10 .30
63 Marty Cordova .10 .30
64 Cecil Fielder .10 .30
65 Barry Bonds .75 2.00
66 Scott Servais .10 .30
67 Ernie Young .10 .30
68 Wilson Alvarez .10 .30
69 Mike Grace .10 .30
70 Shane Reynolds .10 .30
71 Henry Rodriguez .10 .30
72 Eric Karros .10 .30
73 Mark Langston .10 .30
74 Scott Karl .10 .30
75 Trevor Hoffman .10 .30
76 Orel Hershiser .10 .30
77 John Smoltz .20 .50
78 Raul Mondesi .10 .30
79 Jeff Brantley .10 .30
80 Donne Wall .10 .30
81 Joey Cora .10 .30
82 Mel Rojas .10 .30
83 Chad Mottola .10 .30
84 Omar Vizquel .20 .50
85 Greg Maddux .50 1.25
86 Jamey Wright .10 .30
87 Chuck Finley .10 .30
88 Brady Anderson .10 .30
89 Alex Gonzalez .10 .30
90 Andy Benes .10 .30
91 Reggie Jefferson .10 .30
92 Paul O'Neill .20 .50
93 Javier Lopez .10 .30
94 Mark Grudzielanek .10 .30
95 Marc Newfield .10 .30
96 Kevin Ritz .10 .30
97 Fred McGriff .20 .50
98 Dwight Gooden .10 .30
99 Hideo Nomo .30 .75
100 Steve Finley .10 .30
101 Juan Gonzalez .10 .30
102 Jay Buhner .10 .30
103 Paul Wilson .10 .30
104 Alan Benes .10 .30
105 Manny Ramirez .20 .50
106 Kevin Elster .10 .30
107 Frank Thomas .30 .75
108 Orlando Miller .10 .30
109 Ramon Martinez .10 .30
110 Kenny Lofton .10 .30
111 Bernie Williams .20 .50
112 Robby Thompson .10 .30
113 Bernard Gilkey .10 .30
114 Ray Durham .10 .30
115 Jeff Cirillo .10 .30

116 Brian Jordan .10 .30
117 Rich Becker .10 .30
118 Al Leiter .10 .30
119 Mark Johnson .10 .30
120 Ellis Burks .10 .30
121 Sammy Sosa .30 .75
122 Willie Greene .10 .30
123 Michael Tucker .10 .30
124 Eddie Murray .30 .75
125 Joey Hamilton .10 .30
126 Antonio Osuna .10 .30
127 Bobby Higginson .10 .30
128 Tomas Perez .10 .30
129 Tim Salmon .20 .50
130 Mark Wohlers .10 .30
131 Charles Johnson .10 .30
132 Randy Johnson .30 .75
133 Brooks Kieschnick .10 .30
134 Al Martin .10 .30
135 Dante Bichette .10 .30
136 Andy Pettitte .20 .50
137 Jason Giambi .10 .30
138 James Baldwin .10 .30
139 Ben McDonald .10 .30
140 Shawn Green .10 .30
141 Geronimo Berroa .10 .30
142 Jose Offerman .10 .30
143 Curtis Pride .10 .30
144 Terrell Wade .10 .30
145 Ismael Valdes .10 .30
146 Mike Mussina .20 .50
147 Mariano Rivera .30 .75
148 Ken Hill .10 .30
149 Darin Erstad .10 .30
150 Jay Bell .10 .30
151 Mo Vaughn .10 .30
152 Ozzie Smith .50 1.25
153 Jose Mesa .10 .30
154 Osvaldo Fernandez .10 .30
155 Vinny Castilla .10 .30
156 Jason Isringhausen .10 .30
157 B.J. Surhoff .10 .30
158 Robert Perez .10 .30
159 Ron Coomer .10 .30
160 Darren Oliver .10 .30
161 Mike Mohler .10 .30
162 Russ Davis .10 .30
163 Bret Boone .10 .30
164 Ricky Bottalico .10 .30
165 Derek Jeter .75 2.00
166 Orlando Merced .10 .30
167 John Valentin .10 .30
168 Andruw Jones .20 .50
169 Angel Echevarria .10 .30
170 Todd Walker .10 .30
171 Desi Relaford .10 .30
172 Trey Beamon .10 .30
173 Brian Giles RC .60 1.50
174 Scott Rolen .20 .50
175 Shannon Stewart .10 .30
176 Dmitri Young .10 .30
177 Justin Thompson .10 .30
178 Trot Nixon .10 .30
179 Josh Booty .10 .30
180 Robin Jennings .10 .30
181 Marvin Benard .10 .30
182 Luis Castillo .10 .30
183 Wendell Magee .10 .30
184 Vladimir Guerrero .30 .75
185 Nomar Garciaparra .50 1.25
186 Ryan Hancock .10 .30
187 Mike Cameron .10 .30
188 Cal Ripken LG .50 1.25
189 Chipper Jones LG .20 .50
190 Albert Belle LG .10 .30
191 Mike Piazza LG .30 .75
192 Chuck Knoblauch LG .10 .30
193 Ken Griffey Jr. LG .40 1.00
194 Ivan Rodriguez LG .10 .30
195 Jose Canseco LG .10 .30
196 Ryne Sandberg LG .30 .75
197 Jim Thome LG .10 .30
198 Andy Pettitte CL .10 .30
199 Andruw Jones CL .10 .30
200 Derek Jeter CL .40 1.00
201 Chipper Jones .30 .75
202 Albert Belle .10 .30
203 Mike Piazza .50 1.25
204 Ken Griffey Jr. .60 1.50
205 Ryne Sandberg .50 1.25
206 Jose Canseco .20 .50
207 Chili Davis .10 .30
208 Roger Clemens .60 1.50
209 Deion Sanders .20 .50
210 Darryl Hamilton .10 .30
211 Jermaine Dye .10 .30
212 Matt Williams .10 .30
213 Kevin Elster .10 .30
214 John Wetteland .10 .30
215 Garret Anderson .10 .30
216 Kevin Brown .10 .30
217 Matt Lawton .10 .30
218 Cal Ripken 1.00 2.50
219 Moises Alou .10 .30
220 Chuck Knoblauch .10 .30
221 Ivan Rodriguez .20 .50
222 Travis Fryman .10 .30
223 Jim Thome .20 .50
224 Eddie Murray .30 .75
225 Eric Young .10 .30
226 Ron Gant .10 .30
227 Tony Phillips .10 .30
228 Reggie Sanders .10 .30
229 Johnny Damon .20 .50
230 Bill Pulsipher .10 .30
231 Jim Edmonds .10 .30
232 Melvin Nieves .10 .30
233 Ryan Klesko .10 .30
234 David Cone .10 .30
235 Derek Bell .10 .30
236 Julio Franco .10 .30
237 Juan Guzman .10 .30
238 Larry Walker .10 .30
239 Delino DeShields .10 .30
240 Troy Percival .10 .30
241 Andres Galarraga .10 .30
242 Rondell White .10 .30
243 John Burkett .10 .30
244 J.T. Snow .10 .30
245 Alex Fernandez .10 .30
246 Edgar Martinez .20 .50
247 Craig Biggio .20 .50
248 Todd Hundley .10 .30
249 Jimmy Key .10 .30
250 Cliff Floyd .10 .30
251 Jeff Conine .10 .30
252 Curt Schilling .10 .30
253 Jeff King .10 .30
254 Tino Martinez .20 .50
255 Carlos Baerga .10 .30
256 Jeff Fassero .10 .30
257 Dean Palmer .10 .30
258 Robb Nen .10 .30
259 Sandy Alomar Jr. .10 .30
260 Carlos Perez .10 .30
261 Rickey Henderson .30 .75
262 Bobby Bonilla .10 .30
263 Darren Daulton .10 .30
264 Jim Leyritz .10 .30
265 Dennis Martinez .10 .30
266 Butch Huskey .10 .30
267 Joe Vitiello .10 .30
268 Steve Trachsel .10 .30
269 Glenallen Hill .10 .30
270 Terry Steinbach .10 .30
271 Mark McLemore .10 .30
272 Devon White .10 .30
273 Jeff Kent .10 .30
274 Tim Raines .10 .30
275 Carlos Garcia .10 .30
276 Hal Morris .10 .30
277 Gary Gaetti .10 .30
278 John Olerud .10 .30
279 Wally Joyner .10 .30
280 Brian Hunter .10 .30
281 Steve Karsay .10 .30
282 Denny Neagle .10 .30
283 Jose Herrera .10 .30
284 Todd Stottlemyre .10 .30
285 Bip Roberts .10 .30
286 Kevin Seitzer .10 .30
287 Benji Gil .10 .30
288 Dennis Eckersley .10 .30
289 Brad Ausmus .10 .30
290 Otis Nixon .10 .30
291 Darryl Strawberry .10 .30
292 Marquis Grissom .10 .30
293 Darryl Kile .10 .30
294 Quilvio Veras .10 .30
295 Tom Goodwin .10 .30
296 Benito Santiago .10 .30
297 Mike Bordick .10 .30
298 Roberto Kelly .10 .30
299 David Justice .10 .30
300 Carl Everett .10 .30
301 Mark Whiten .10 .30
302 Aaron Sele .10 .30
303 Darren Dreifort .10 .30
304 Bobby Jones .10 .30
305 Fernando Vina .10 .30
306 Ed Sprague .10 .30
307 Andy Ashby .10 .30
308 Tony Fernandez .10 .30
309 Roger Pavlik .10 .30
310 Mark Clark .10 .30
311 Mariano Duncan .10 .30
312 Tyler Houston .10 .30
313 Eric Davis .10 .30
314 Greg Vaughn .10 .30
315 David Segui .10 .30
316 Dave Nilsson .10 .30
317 F.P. Santangelo .10 .30
318 Wilton Guerrero .10 .30
319 Jose Guillen .10 .30
320 Kevin Orie .10 .30
321 Derrek Lee .20 .50
322 Bubba Trammell RC .15 .40
323 Pokey Reese .10 .30
324 Hideki Irabu RC .15 .40
325 Scott Spiezio .10 .30
326 Bartolo Colon .10 .30
327 Damon Mashore .10 .30
328 Ryan McGuire .10 .30
329 Chris Carpenter .10 .30
330 Jose Cruz Jr. RC .15 .40
331 Todd Greene .10 .30
332 Brian Moehler RC .10 .30
333 Mike Sweeney .10 .30
334 Neifi Perez .10 .30
335 Matt Morris .10 .30
336 Marvin Benard .10 .30
337 Karim Garcia .10 .30
338 Jason Dickson .10 .30
339 Brant Brown .10 .30
340 Jeff Suppan .10 .30
341 Deivi Cruz RC .15 .40
342 Antone Williamson .10 .30
343 Curtis Goodwin .10 .30
344 Brooks Kieschnick .10 .30
345 Tony Womack RC .15 .40
346 Rudy Pemberton .10 .30
347 Todd Dunwoody .10 .30
348 Frank Thomas LG .20 .50
349 Andruw Jones LG .10 .30
350 Alex Rodriguez LG .30 .75
351 Greg Maddux LG .30 .75
352 Jeff Bagwell LG .10 .30
353 Juan Gonzalez LG .10 .30
354 Barry Bonds LG .40 1.00
355 Mark McGwire LG .40 1.00
356 Tony Gwynn LG .20 .50
357 Gary Sheffield LG .10 .30
358 Derek Jeter LG .40 1.00
359 Manny Ramirez LG .10 .30
360 Hideo Nomo LG .10 .30
361 Sammy Sosa LG .20 .50
362 Paul Molitor LG .10 .30
363 Kenny Lofton LG .10 .30
364 Eddie Murray LG .20 .50
365 Barry Larkin LG .10 .30
366 Roger Clemens LG .30 .75
367 John Smoltz LG .10 .30
368 Alex Rodriguez GM .30 .75
369 Frank Thomas GM .20 .50
370 Cal Ripken GM .50 1.25
371 Ken Griffey Jr. GM .40 1.00
372 Greg Maddux GM .30 .75
373 Mike Piazza GM .30 .75
374 Chipper Jones GM .20 .50
375 Albert Belle GM .10 .30
376 Chuck Knoblauch GM .10 .30
377 Brady Anderson GM .10 .30
378 David Justice GM .10 .30
379 Randy Johnson GM .20 .50
380 Wade Boggs GM .10 .30
381 Kevin Brown GM .10 .30
382 Tom Glavine GM .10 .30
383 Raul Mondesi GM .10 .30
384 Ivan Rodriguez GM .10 .30
385 Larry Walker GM .10 .30
386 Bernie Williams GM .10 .30
387 Rusty Greer GM .10 .30
388 Rafael Palmeiro GM .10 .30
389 Matt Williams GM .10 .30
390 Eric Young GM .10 .30
391 Fred McGriff GM .10 .30
392 Ken Caminiti GM .10 .30
393 Roberto Alomar GM .10 .30
394 Brian Jordan GM .10 .30
395 Mark Grace GM .10 .30
396 Jim Edmonds GM .10 .30
397 Deion Sanders GM .10 .30
398 Vladimir Guerrero CL .20 .50
399 Darin Erstad CL .10 .30
400 Nomar Garciaparra CL .30 .75
NNO Jackie Robinson 6.00 15.00
RC Reprint

1997 Leaf Fractal Matrix

*BRONZE: 1.25X TO 3X BASIC CARDS
*SILVER: 2X TO 5X BASIC CARDS
*SILVER ROOKIES: .6X TO 1.5X BASIC
*GOLD Y/Z: 3X TO 8X BASIC CARDS
*GOLD X: 6X TO 15X BASIC CARDS
*GOLD X RC's: 2X TO 5X BASIC CARDS
RANDOM INSERTS IN PACKS
SEE WEBSITE FOR AXIS SCHEMATIC

1997 Leaf Fractal Matrix Die Cuts

*X-AXIS: 2X TO 5X BASIC CARDS
*X-AXIS ROOKIES: 1.25X TO 3X BASIC
*Y-AXIS: 3X TO 8X BASIC CARDS
*Y-AXIS ROOKIES: .75X TO 2X BASIC
*Z-AXIS: 2.5X TO 6X BASIC CARDS
RANDOM INSERTS IN PACKS
SEE WEBSITE FOR AXIS SCHEMATIC

1997 Leaf Banner Season

COMPLETE SET (15) 20.00 50.00
1 Jeff Bagwell 1.50 4.00
2 Ken Griffey Jr. 8.00 20.00
3 Juan Gonzalez 1.00 2.50
4 Frank Thomas 2.50 6.00
5 Alex Rodriguez 3.00 8.00
6 Kenny Lofton 1.00 2.50
7 Chuck Knoblauch 1.00 2.50
8 Mo Vaughn 1.00 2.50
9 Chipper Jones 2.50 6.00
10 Ken Caminiti 1.00 2.50
11 Craig Biggio 1.50 4.00
12 John Smoltz 1.50 4.00
13 Pat Hentgen 1.00 2.50
14 Derek Jeter 6.00 15.00
15 Todd Hollandsworth 1.00 2.50

1997 Leaf Dress for Success

COMPLETE SET (18) 15.00 40.00
RANDOM INS.IN SER.1 RETAIL PACKS
STATED PRINT RUN 3500 SERIAL #'d SETS
1 Greg Maddux 2.00 5.00
2 Cal Ripken 4.00 10.00
3 Albert Belle .50 1.25
4 Frank Thomas 1.25 3.00
5 Dante Bichette .50 1.25
6 Gary Sheffield .50 1.25
7 Jeff Bagwell .75 2.00
8 Mike Piazza 1.25 3.00
9 Mark McGwire 2.00 5.00
10 Ken Caminiti .50 1.25
11 Alex Rodriguez 1.50 4.00
12 Ken Griffey Jr. 2.50 6.00
13 Juan Gonzalez .50 1.25
14 Brian Jordan .50 1.25
15 Mo Vaughn .50 1.25
16 Ivan Rodriguez .75 2.00
17 Andruw Jones .50 1.25
18 Chipper Jones 1.25 3.00

1997 Leaf Get-A-Grip

COMPLETE SET (16) 12.00 30.00
RANDOM INS.IN SER.1 HOBBY PACKS
STATED PRINT RUN 3500 SERIAL #'d SETS
1 K.Griffey Jr. 2.00 5.00
G.Maddux
2 F.Thomas 1.00 2.50
J.Smoltz
3 M.Piazza 1.00 2.50
A.Pettitte
4 C.Jones 1.00 2.50
R.Johnson
5 A.Rodriguez 1.25 3.00
T.Glavine
6 J.Bagwell .60 1.50
P.Hentgen
7 J.Gonzalez .40 1.00
K.Brown
8 B.Bonds 1.50 4.00
M.Mussina
9 H.Nomo .60 1.50
A.Belle
10 A.Jones .40 1.00
T.Percival
11 R.Clemens 1.25 3.00
B.Jordan
12 I.Rodriguez .60 1.50
P.Wilson
13 M.Vaughn .40 1.00
A.Benes
14 D.Jeter 2.50 6.00
A.Leiter
15 C.Ripken 3.00 8.00
B.Pulsipher
16 M.Rivera 1.25 3.00
K.Caminiti

1997 Leaf Gold Stars

RANDOM INSERTS IN SER.2 PACKS
STATED PRINT RUN 2500 SERIAL #'d SETS
1 Frank Thomas 1.50 4.00
2 Alex Rodriguez 2.00 5.00
3 Ken Griffey Jr. 3.00 8.00
4 Andruw Jones .60 1.50
5 Chipper Jones 1.50 4.00
6 Jeff Bagwell 1.00 2.50
7 Derek Jeter 4.00 10.00
8 Deion Sanders 1.00 2.50
9 Ivan Rodriguez 1.00 2.50
10 Juan Gonzalez .60 1.50
11 Greg Maddux 2.50 6.00
12 Andy Pettitte 1.00 2.50
13 Roger Clemens 2.00 5.00
14 Hideo Nomo 1.00 2.50
15 Tony Gwynn 1.50 4.00
16 Barry Bonds 2.50 6.00
17 Kenny Lofton .60 1.50
18 Paul Molitor 1.50 4.00
19 Jim Thome 1.00 2.50
20 Albert Belle .60 1.50
21 Cal Ripken 5.00 12.00
22 Mark McGwire 2.50 6.00
23 Barry Larkin 1.00 2.50
24 Mike Piazza 1.50 4.00
25 Darin Erstad .60 1.50
26 Chuck Knoblauch .60 1.50
27 Vladimir Guerrero 1.00 2.50
28 Tony Clark .60 1.50
29 Scott Rolen 1.00 2.50
30 Nomar Garciaparra 1.00 2.50
31 Eric Young .60 1.50
32 Ryne Sandberg 2.50 6.00
33 Roberto Alomar 1.00 2.50
34 Eddie Murray 1.00 2.50
35 Rafael Palmeiro .60 1.50
36 Jose Guillen .60 1.50

1997 Leaf Knot-Hole Gang Samples

COMPLETE SET (12) 15.00 40.00
1 Chuck Knoblauch .40 1.00
2 Ken Griffey Jr. 2.00 5.00
3 Frank Thomas .75 2.00
4 Tony Gwynn 1.50 4.00
5 Mike Piazza 2.50 6.00
6 Jeff Bagwell .75 2.00
7 Rusty Greer .40 1.00
8 Cal Ripken 3.00 8.00
9 Chipper Jones 1.50 4.00
10 Ryan Klesko .30 .75
11 Barry Larkin .60 1.50
12 Paul Molitor 1.00 2.50

1997 Leaf Knot-Hole Gang

COMPLETE SET (12) 20.00 50.00
1 Chuck Knoblauch .60 1.50
2 Ken Griffey Jr. 10.00 25.00
3 Frank Thomas 1.50 4.00
4 Tony Gwynn 2.00 5.00
5 Mike Piazza 2.50 6.00
6 Jeff Bagwell 1.00 2.50
7 Rusty Greer .60 1.50
8 Cal Ripken 5.00 12.00
9 Chipper Jones 1.50 4.00
10 Ryan Klesko .60 1.50
11 Barry Larkin 1.00 2.50
12 Paul Molitor .60 1.50

1997 Leaf Leagues of the Nation

RANDOM INSERTS IN SER.2 PACKS
STATED PRINT RUN 2500 SERIAL #'d SETS
1 J.Gonzalez 2.50 6.00
B.Bonds
2 C.Ripken 5.00 12.00
C.Jones
3 M.McGwire 2.50 6.00
K.Caminiti
4 D.Jeter 4.00 10.00
K.Lofton
5 M.Piazza 1.50 4.00
I.Rodriguez
6 K.Griffey Jr. 3.00 8.00
L.Walker
7 S.Sosa 1.50 4.00
F.Thomas
8 P.Molitor 1.50 4.00
B.Larkin
9 A.Belle 1.00 2.50
D.Sanders
10 J.Bagwell 1.00 2.50
M.Williams
11 M.Vaughn .60 1.50
G.Sheffield
12 A.Rodriguez 2.00 5.00
T.Gwynn
13 S.Rolen 1.00 2.50
T.Martinez
14 D.Erstad .60 1.50
W.Guerrero
15 V.Guerrero 1.00 2.50
T.Clark

1997 Leaf Statistical Standouts

RANDOM INSERTS IN SER.1 PACKS
STATED PRINT RUN 1000 SERIAL #'d SETS
1 Albert Belle 2.00 5.00
2 Juan Gonzalez 2.00 5.00
3 Ken Griffey Jr. 40.00 100.00
4 Alex Rodriguez 6.00 15.00
5 Frank Thomas 5.00 12.00
6 Chipper Jones 5.00 12.00
7 Greg Maddux 8.00 20.00
8 Mike Piazza 5.00 12.00
9 Cal Ripken 15.00 40.00
10 Mark McGwire 8.00 20.00
11 Barry Bonds 8.00 20.00
12 Derek Jeter 12.00 30.00
13 Ken Caminiti 2.00 5.00
14 John Smoltz 3.00 8.00
15 Paul Molitor 5.00 12.00

1997 Leaf Thomas Collection

RANDOM INSERTS IN SER.2 PACKS
STATED PRINT RUN 100 SETS
1 F.Thomas Game Hat 125.00 250.00
2 F.Thomas Home Jersey 125.00 250.00
3 F.Thomas Batting Glove 125.00 250.00
4 F.Thomas Bat 125.00 250.00
5 F.Thomas Sweatband 125.00 250.00
6 F.Thomas Away Jersey 125.00 250.00

1997 Leaf Warning Track

COMPLETE SET (18) 15.00 40.00
1 Ken Griffey Jr. 4.00 10.00
2 Albert Belle .75 2.00
3 Barry Bonds 3.00 8.00
4 Andruw Jones .75 2.00
5 Kenny Lofton .75 2.00
6 Tony Gwynn 2.00 5.00
7 Manny Ramirez 1.25 3.00
8 Rusty Greer .75 2.00
9 Bernie Williams 1.25 3.00
10 Gary Sheffield .75 2.00
11 Juan Gonzalez .75 2.00
12 Raul Mondesi .75 2.00
13 Brady Anderson .75 2.00
14 Rondell White .75 2.00
15 Sammy Sosa 1.25 3.00
16 Deion Sanders 1.25 3.00
17 Dave Justice .75 2.00
18 Jim Edmonds .75 2.00

1997 Leaf Thomas Info

This card was put into the front of every 12 card Leaf Blister pack. The front has an action photo of Thomas while the back explains more about the 97 Leaf Product. The card is a stand alone and not inserted in the unopened part of the pack. The blister pack retailed for $2.99.

1 Frank Thomas .75 2.00

1997 Leaf Thomas Leukemia

This four-card set was produced by Donruss for the Frank Thomas Charitable Foundation. The cards feature borderless color photos of Frank Thomas, who lost a sister to Leukemia, with other people who have some connection to the illness. The back of card number 1 displays a portrait of a Leukemia victim. All proceeds from the sale of the set went to the Foundation. The cards could be ordered by mail from Big Heart Charity Card for $20 each. Only 2500 of each card was produced and are sequentially numbered.

COMPLETE SET (4) 40.00 100.00
COMMON CARD (1-4) 10.00 25.00
1 Frank Thomas 12.50 30.00
Rod Carew
Michelle Carew(on back)

1998 Leaf

The 1998 Leaf set was issued in one series totalling 200 cards. The 10-card packs carried a suggested retail price of $2.99. The set contains the topical subsets: Curtain Calls (148-157), Gold Leaf Stars (158-177), and Gold Leaf Rookies (178-197). All three subsets are short-printed in relation to cards from 1-147 and 201. Those short prints represent one of the early efforts by a manufacturer to incorportate short-print subsets cards into a basic issue set. The product went live in mid-March, 1998. Card number 42 does not exist as Leaf retired the number in honor of Jackie Robinson.

COMPLETE SET (200) 25.00 60.00
COMP.SET w/o SP's (147) 6.00 15.00
COMMON CARD (1-201) .10 .30
COMMON SP (148-197) .60 1.50
CARDS 148-197 ARE SHORTPRINTED
CARD NUMBER 42 DOES NOT EXIST
1 Rusty Greer .10 .30
2 Tino Martinez .20 .50
3 Bobby Bonilla .10 .30
4 Jason Giambi .10 .30
5 Matt Morris .10 .30
6 Craig Counsell .10 .30
7 Reggie Jefferson .10 .30
8 Brian Rose .10 .30
9 Ruben Rivera .10 .30
10 Shawn Estes .10 .30
11 Tony Gwynn .40 1.00
12 Jeff Abbott .10 .30
13 Jose Cruz Jr. .10 .30
14 Francisco Cordova .10 .30
15 Ryan Klesko .10 .30
16 Tim Salmon .20 .50
17 Brett Tomko .10 .30
18 Matt Williams .10 .30
19 Joe Carter .10 .30
20 Harold Baines .10 .30
21 Gary Sheffield .10 .30
22 Charles Johnson .10 .30
23 Aaron Boone .10 .30
24 Eddie Murray .30 .75
25 Matt Stairs .10 .30
26 David Cone .10 .30
27 Jon Nunnally .10 .30
28 Chris Stynes .10 .30
29 Enrique Wilson .10 .30
30 Randy Johnson .30 .75
31 Garret Anderson .10 .30
32 Manny Ramirez .20 .50
33 Jeff Suppan .10 .30
34 Rickey Henderson .30 .75
35 Scott Spiezio .10 .30
36 Rondell White .10 .30
37 Todd Greene .10 .30
38 Delino DeShields .10 .30
39 Kevin Brown .20 .50
40 Chili Davis .10 .30
41 Jimmy Key .10 .30
43 Mike Mussina .20 .50
44 Joe Randa .10 .30
45 Chan Ho Park .10 .30
46 Brad Radke .10 .30
47 Geronimo Berroa .10 .30
48 Wade Boggs .20 .50
49 Kevin Appier .10 .30
50 Moises Alou .10 .30
51 David Justice .10 .30
52 Ivan Rodriguez .20 .50
53 J.T. Snow .10 .30
54 Brian Giles .10 .30
55 Will Clark .20 .50
56 Justin Thompson .10 .30
57 Javier Lopez .10 .30
58 Hideki Irabu .10 .30
59 Mark Grudzielanek .10 .30
60 Abraham Nunez .10 .30
61 Todd Hollandsworth .10 .30
62 Jay Bell .10 .30
63 Nomar Garciaparra .50 1.25
64 Vinny Castilla .10 .30
65 Lou Collier .10 .30
66 Kevin Orie .10 .30
67 John Valentin .10 .30
68 Robin Ventura .10 .30
69 Denny Neagle .10 .30
70 Tony Womack .10 .30
71 Dennis Reyes .10 .30
72 Wally Joyner .10 .30
73 Kevin Brown .20 .50
74 Ray Durham .10 .30
75 Mike Cameron .10 .30
76 Dante Bichette .10 .30
77 Jose Guillen .10 .30
78 Carlos Delgado .10 .30
79 Paul Molitor .10 .30
80 Jason Kendall .10 .30
81 Mark Bellhorn .10 .30
82 Damian Jackson .10 .30
83 Bill Mueller .10 .30
84 Kevin Young .10 .30
85 Curt Schilling .10 .30
86 Jeffrey Hammonds .10 .30
87 Sandy Alomar Jr. .10 .30
88 Bartolo Colon .10 .30
89 Wilton Guerrero .10 .30
90 Bernie Williams .20 .50
91 Deion Sanders .20 .50
92 Mike Piazza .50 1.25
93 Butch Huskey .10 .30
94 Edgardo Alfonzo .10 .30
95 Alan Benes .10 .30
96 Craig Biggio .20 .50
97 Mark Grace .20 .50
98 Shawn Green .10 .30
99 Derrek Lee .20 .50
100 Ken Griffey Jr. .60 1.50
101 Tim Raines .10 .30
102 Pokey Reese .10 .30
103 Lee Stevens .10 .30
104 Shannon Stewart .10 .30
105 John Smoltz .20 .50
106 Frank Thomas .30 .75
107 Jeff Fassero .10 .30
108 Jay Buhner .10 .30
109 Jose Canseco .20 .50
110 Omar Vizquel .20 .50
111 Travis Fryman .10 .30
112 Dave Nilsson .10 .30
113 John Olerud .10 .30
114 Larry Walker .10 .30
115 Jim Edmonds .10 .30
116 Bobby Higginson .10 .30
117 Todd Hundley .10 .30
118 Paul O'Neill .20 .50
119 Bip Roberts .10 .30
120 Ismael Valdes .10 .30
121 Pedro Martinez .20 .50
122 Jeff Cirillo .10 .30
123 Andy Benes .10 .30
124 Bobby Jones .10 .30
125 Brian Hunter .10 .30
126 Darryl Kile .10 .30
127 Pat Hentgen .10 .30
128 Marquis Grissom .10 .30
129 Eric Davis .10 .30
130 Chipper Jones .30 .75
131 Edgar Martinez .20 .50
132 Andy Pettitte .20 .50
133 Cal Ripken 1.00 2.50
134 Scott Rolen .20 .50
135 Ron Coomer .10 .30
136 Luis Castillo .10 .30
137 Fred McGriff .20 .50
138 Neifi Perez .10 .30
139 Eric Karros .10 .30
140 Alex Fernandez .10 .30
141 Jason Dickson .10 .30
142 Lance Johnson .10 .30
143 Ray Lankford .10 .30
144 Sammy Sosa .30 .75
145 Eric Young .10 .30
146 Bubba Trammell .10 .30
147 Todd Walker .10 .30
148 Mo Vaughn CC .60 1.50
149 Jeff Bagwell CC 1.00 2.50
150 Kenny Lofton CC .60 1.50
151 Raul Mondesi CC .60 1.50
152 Mike Piazza CC 2.50 6.00
153 Chipper Jones CC 1.50 4.00
154 Larry Walker CC .60 1.50
155 Greg Maddux CC 2.50 6.00
156 Ken Griffey Jr. CC 3.00 8.00
157 Frank Thomas CC 1.50 4.00
158 Darin Erstad GLS .60 1.50
159 Roberto Alomar GLS 1.00 2.50
160 Albert Belle GLS .60 1.50
161 Jim Thome GLS 1.00 2.50
162 Tony Clark GLS .60 1.50
163 Chuck Knoblauch GLS .60 1.50
164 Derek Jeter GLS 4.00 10.00
165 Alex Rodriguez GLS 2.50 6.00
166 Tony Gwynn GLS 2.00 5.00
167 Roger Clemens GLS 3.00 8.00
168 Barry Larkin GLS 1.00 2.50
169 Andres Galarraga GLS .60 1.50
170 Vladimir Guerrero GLS 1.50 4.00
171 Mark McGwire GLS 4.00 10.00
172 Barry Bonds GLS 4.00 10.00
173 Juan Gonzalez GLS .60 1.50
174 Andruw Jones GLS 1.00 2.50
175 Paul Molitor GLS .60 1.50
176 Hideo Nomo GLS 1.50 4.00
177 Cal Ripken GLS 5.00 12.00
178 Brad Fullmer GLR .60 1.50
179 Jaret Wright GLR .60 1.50
180 Bobby Estalella GLR .60 1.50
181 Ben Grieve GLR .60 1.50
182 Paul Konerko GLR .60 1.50
183 David Ortiz GLR 2.00 5.00
184 Todd Helton GLR 1.00 2.50
185 Juan Encarnacion GLR .60 1.50
186 Miguel Tejada GLR 1.50 4.00
187 Jacob Cruz GLR .60 1.50
188 Mark Kotsay GLR .60 1.50
189 Fernando Tatis GLR .60 1.50
190 Ricky Ledee GLR .60 1.50
191 Richard Hidalgo GLR .60 1.50
192 Richie Sexson GLR .60 1.50
193 Luis Ordaz GLR .60 1.50
194 Eli Marrero GLR .60 1.50
195 Livan Hernandez GLR .60 1.50
196 Homer Bush GLR .60 1.50
197 Raul Ibanez GLR .60 1.50
198 Nomar Garciaparra CL .30 .75
199 Scott Rolen CL .10 .30
200 Jose Cruz Jr. CL .10 .30
201 Al Martin .10 .30

1998 Leaf Fractal Diamond Axis

*STARS 1-147/198-201: 15X TO 40X BASIC
*SP STARS 148-197: 3X TO 8X BASIC SP'S
*SP YG.STARS 148-197: 2.5X TO 6X BASE SP'S
*CURTAIN CALLS: X TO X HI
RANDOM INSERTS IN PACKS
STATED PRINT RUN 50 SERIAL #'d SETS
CARD NUMBER 42 DOES NOT EXIST

1998 Leaf Fractal Matrix

*BRONZE 1-147/198-201: 1.5X TO 4X BASIC
*BRONZE 148-197: .3X TO .8X BASIC
BRONZE X STATED PRINT RUN 1600 SETS
BRONZE Y STATED PRINT RUN 1800 SETS
BRONZE Z STATED PRINT RUN 1900 SETS
*SILVER 1-147/198-201: 3X TO 8X BASIC
*SILVER: 148-197: .6X TO 1.5X BASIC
SILVER X STATED PRINT RUN 600 SETS
SILVER Y STATED PRINT RUN 800 SETS
SILVER Z STATED PRINT RUN 900 SETS
*GOLD 1-147/198-201: 5X TO 12X BASIC
*GOLD: 148-197: 1X TO 2.5X BASIC
GOLD X STATED PRINT RUN 100 SETS
GOLD Y STATED PRINT RUN 300 SETS
GOLD Z STATED PRINT RUN 400 SETS
RANDOM INSERTS IN PACKS
CARD NUMBER 42 DOES NOT EXIST

1998 Leaf Fractal Matrix Die Cuts

*X-AXIS 1-147/198-201: 5X TO 12X BASIC
*X-AXIS 148-197: 1X TO 2.5X BASIC
X-AXIS STATED PRINT RUN 400 SETS
*Y-AXIS 1-147/198-201: 8X TO 20X BASIC
*Y-AXIS 148-197: 1.5X TO 4X BASIC
Y-AXIS STATED PRINT RUN 200 SETS
*Z-AXIS 1-147/198-201: 12.5X TO 30X BASIC
*Z-AXIS 148-197: 2.5X TO 6X BASIC
Z-AXIS STATED PRINT RUN 100 SETS
RANDOM INSERTS IN PACKS
CARD NUMBER 42 DOES NOT EXIST
SEE WEBSITE FOR AXIS SCHEMATIC

1998 Leaf Crusade Green

PLEASE SEE 1998 DONRUSS CRUSADE

1998 Leaf Heading for the Hall Samples

COMPLETE SET (20) 30.00 80.00
1 Roberto Alomar .60 1.50
2 Jeff Bagwell .75 2.00
3 Albert Belle .30 .75
4 Wade Boggs 1.50 4.00
5 Barry Bonds 2.00 5.00
6 Roger Clemens 2.00 5.00
7 Juan Gonzalez .60 1.50
8 Ken Griffey Jr. 2.50 6.00
9 Tony Gwynn 2.00 5.00
10 Barry Larkin .60 1.50
11 Kenny Lofton .40 1.00
12 Greg Maddux 2.50 6.00
13 Mark McGwire 2.50 6.00
14 Paul Molitor 1.00 2.50
15 Eddie Murray .60 1.50
16 Mike Piazza 3.00 8.00
17 Cal Ripken 4.00 10.00
18 Ivan Rodriguez 1.25 3.00
19 Ryne Sandberg 1.50 4.00
20 Frank Thomas 1.00 2.50

1998 Leaf Heading for the Hall

COMPLETE SET (20) 20.00 50.00
RANDOM INSERTS IN PACKS
STATED PRINT RUN 3500 SERIAL #'d SETS
1 Roberto Alomar 1.00 2.50
2 Jeff Bagwell 1.00 2.50
3 Albert Belle .60 1.50
4 Wade Boggs 1.00 2.50
5 Barry Bonds 2.50 6.00
6 Roger Clemens 2.00 5.00
7 Juan Gonzalez .60 1.50
8 Ken Griffey Jr. 3.00 8.00
9 Tony Gwynn 1.50 4.00
10 Barry Larkin 1.00 2.50
11 Kenny Lofton .60 1.50
12 Greg Maddux 2.00 5.00
13 Mark McGwire 2.50 6.00
14 Paul Molitor 1.50 4.00
15 Eddie Murray 1.00 2.50
16 Mike Piazza 1.50 4.00
17 Cal Ripken 5.00 12.00
18 Ivan Rodriguez 1.00 2.50
19 Ryne Sandberg 2.50 6.00
20 Frank Thomas 1.50 4.00

1998 Leaf State Representatives

COMPLETE SET (30) 15.00 40.00
RANDOM INSERTS IN PACKS
STATED PRINT RUN 5000 SERIAL #'d SETS
1 Ken Griffey Jr. 2.00 5.00
2 Frank Thomas 1.00 2.50
3 Alex Rodriguez 1.25 3.00
4 Cal Ripken 3.00 8.00
5 Chipper Jones 1.00 2.50
6 Andruw Jones .40 1.00
7 Scott Rolen .60 1.50
8 Nomar Garciaparra .60 1.50
9 Tim Salmon .40 1.00
10 Manny Ramirez 1.00 2.50
11 Jose Cruz Jr. .40 1.00
12 Vladimir Guerrero .60 1.50

13 Tino Martinez .40 1.00
14 Larry Walker .60 1.50
15 Mo Vaughn .40 1.00
16 Jim Thome .60 1.50
17 Tony Clark .40 1.00
18 Derek Jeter 2.50 6.00
19 Juan Gonzalez .40 1.00
20 Jeff Bagwell .60 1.50
21 Ivan Rodriguez .60 1.50
22 Mark McGwire 1.50 4.00
23 David Justice .40 1.00
24 Chuck Knoblauch .40 1.00
25 Andy Pettitte .60 1.50
26 Raul Mondesi .40 1.00
27 Randy Johnson 1.00 2.50
28 Greg Maddux 1.25 3.00
29 Bernie Williams .60 1.50
30 Rusty Greer .40 1.00

1998 Leaf Statistical Standouts

COMPLETE SET (24) 30.00 80.00
STATED PRINT RUN 2250 SERIAL #'d SETS
*DIE CUTS: 1.5X TO 4X BASIC STAT.STAND
DIE CUT PRINT RUN 250 SERIAL #'d SETS
RANDOM INSERTS IN PACKS
1 Frank Thomas 1.25 3.00
2 Ken Griffey Jr. 2.50 6.00
3 Alex Rodriguez 1.50 4.00
4 Mike Piazza 1.25 3.00
5 Greg Maddux 1.50 4.00
6 Cal Ripken 4.00 10.00
7 Chipper Jones 1.25 3.00
8 Juan Gonzalez .50 1.25
9 Jeff Bagwell .75 2.00
10 Mark McGwire 2.00 5.00
11 Tony Gwynn 1.25 3.00
12 Mo Vaughn .50 1.25
13 Nomar Garciaparra .75 2.00
14 Jose Cruz Jr. .50 1.25
15 Vladimir Guerrero .75 2.00
16 Scott Rolen .75 2.00
17 Andy Pettitte .75 2.00
18 Randy Johnson 1.25 3.00
19 Larry Walker .75 2.00
20 Kenny Lofton .50 1.25
21 Tony Clark .50 1.25
22 David Justice .50 1.25
23 Derek Jeter 3.00 8.00
24 Barry Bonds 2.00 5.00

2002 Leaf Samples

*SAMPLES: X TO X BASIC

2002 Leaf

COMP.SET w/o SP's (149) 10.00 25.00
COMMON (1-41/43-150) .10 .30
COMMON CARD (151-200) 1.50 4.00
151-200 STATED ODDS 1:6 HOBBY/RETAIL
201-202 PRINT RUN PROVIDED BY DONRUSS
201-202 ARE NOT SERIAL-NUMBERED
CARD NUMBER 42 DOES NOT EXIST
1 Tim Salmon .20 .50
2 Troy Glaus .10 .30
3 Curt Schilling .10 .30
4 Luis Gonzalez .10 .30
5 Mark Grace .20 .50
6 Matt Williams .10 .30
7 Randy Johnson .30 .75
8 Tom Glavine .20 .50
9 Brady Anderson .10 .30
10 Hideo Nomo .30 .75
11 Pedro Martinez .20 .50
12 Corey Patterson .10 .30
13 Paul Konerko .10 .30
14 Jon Lieber .10 .30
15 Carlos Lee .10 .30
16 Magglio Ordonez .10 .30
17 Adam Dunn .10 .30
18 Ken Griffey Jr. .60 1.50
19 C.C. Sabathia .10 .30
20 Jim Thome .20 .50
21 Juan Gonzalez .10 .30
22 Kenny Lofton .10 .30
23 Juan Encarnacion .10 .30
24 Tony Clark .10 .30
25 A.J. Burnett .10 .30
26 Josh Beckett .10 .30
27 Lance Berkman .10 .30
28 Eric Karros .10 .30
29 Shawn Green .10 .30
30 Brad Radke .10 .30
31 Joe Mays .10 .30
32 Javier Vazquez .10 .30
33 Alfonso Soriano .10 .30
34 Jorge Posada .20 .50
35 Eric Chavez .10 .30
36 Mark Mulder .10 .30
37 Miguel Tejada .10 .30
38 Tim Hudson .10 .30
39 Bob Abreu .10 .30
40 Pat Burrell .10 .30
41 Ryan Klesko .10 .30
43 John Olerud .10 .30
44 Ellis Burks .10 .30
45 Mike Cameron .10 .30
46 Jim Edmonds .10 .30
47 Ben Grieve .10 .30
48 Carlos Pena .10 .30
49 Alex Rodriguez .40 1.00
50 Raul Mondesi .10 .30
51 Billy Koch .10 .30
52 Manny Ramirez .20 .50
53 Darin Erstad .10 .30
54 Troy Percival .10 .30
55 Andruw Jones .20 .50
56 Chipper Jones .30 .75
57 David Segui .10 .30
58 Chris Stynes .10 .30
59 Trot Nixon .10 .30
60 Sammy Sosa .30 .75
61 Kerry Wood .10 .30
62 Frank Thomas .30 .75
63 Barry Larkin .20 .50
64 Bartolo Colon .10 .30
65 Kazuhiro Sasaki .10 .30
66 Roberto Alomar .20 .50
67 Mike Hampton .10 .30
68 Roger Cedeno .10 .30
69 Cliff Floyd .10 .30
70 Mike Lowell .10 .30
71 Billy Wagner .10 .30
72 Craig Biggio .20 .50
73 Jeff Bagwell .20 .50
74 Carlos Beltran .10 .30
75 Mark Quinn .10 .30
76 Mike Sweeney .10 .30
77 Gary Sheffield .10 .30
78 Kevin Brown .10 .30
79 Paul LoDuca .10 .30
80 Ben Sheets .10 .30
81 Jeromy Burnitz .10 .30
82 Richie Sexson .10 .30
83 Corey Koskie .10 .30
84 Eric Milton .10 .30
85 Jose Vidro .10 .30
86 Mike Piazza .50 1.25
87 Robin Ventura .10 .30
88 Andy Pettitte .20 .50
89 Mike Mussina .20 .50
90 Orlando Hernandez .10 .30
91 Roger Clemens .60 1.50
92 Barry Zito .10 .30
93 Jermaine Dye .10 .30
94 Jimmy Rollins .10 .30
95 Jason Kendall .10 .30
96 Rickey Henderson .30 .75
97 Andres Galarraga .10 .30
98 Bret Boone .10 .30
99 Freddy Garcia .10 .30
100 J.D. Drew .10 .30
101 Jose Cruz Jr. .10 .30
102 Greg Maddux .50 1.25
103 Javy Lopez .10 .30
104 Nomar Garciaparra .50 1.25
105 Fred McGriff .20 .50
106 Keith Foulke .10 .30
107 Ray Durham .10 .30
108 Sean Casey .10 .30
109 Todd Walker .10 .30
110 Omar Vizquel .20 .50
111 Travis Fryman .10 .30
112 Larry Walker .10 .30
113 Todd Helton .20 .50
114 Bobby Higginson .10 .30
115 Charles Johnson .10 .30
116 Moises Alou .10 .30
117 Richard Hidalgo .10 .30
118 Roy Oswalt .10 .30
119 Neifi Perez .10 .30
120 Adrian Beltre .10 .30
121 Chan Ho Park .10 .30
122 Geoff Jenkins .10 .30
123 Doug Mientkiewicz .10 .30
124 Torii Hunter .10 .30
125 Vladimir Guerrero .30 .75
126 Matt Lawton .10 .30
127 Tsuyoshi Shinjo .10 .30
128 Bernie Williams .20 .50
129 Derek Jeter .75 2.00
130 Mariano Rivera .30 .75
131 Tino Martinez .20 .50
132 Jason Giambi .10 .30
133 Scott Rolen .20 .50
134 Brian Giles .10 .30
135 Phil Nevin .10 .30
136 Trevor Hoffman .10 .30
137 Barry Bonds .75 2.00
138 Jeff Kent .10 .30
139 Shannon Stewart .10 .30
140 Shawn Estes .10 .30
141 Edgar Martinez .20 .50
142 Ichiro Suzuki .60 1.50
143 Albert Pujols .60 1.50
144 Bud Smith .10 .30
145 Matt Morris .10 .30
146 Frank Catalanotto .10 .30
147 Gabe Kapler .10 .30
148 Ivan Rodriguez .20 .50
149 Rafael Palmeiro .20 .50
150 Carlos Delgado .10 .30
151 Marlon Byrd ROO 1.50 4.00
152 Alex Herrera ROO 1.50 4.00
153 Brandon Backe ROO RC 2.00 5.00
154 Jorge De La Rosa ROO RC 1.50 4.00
155 Corky Miller ROO 1.50 4.00
156 Dennis Tankersley ROO 1.50 4.00
157 Kyle Kane ROO RC 1.50 4.00
158 Justin Duchscherer ROO 1.50 4.00
159 Brian Mallette ROO RC 1.50 4.00
160 Eric Hinske ROO 1.50 4.00
161 Jason Lane ROO 1.50 4.00
162 Hee Seop Choi ROO 1.50 4.00
163 Juan Cruz ROO 1.50 4.00
164 Rodrigo Rosario ROO RC 1.50 4.00
165 Matt Guerrier ROO 1.50 4.00
166 Anderson Machado ROO RC 1.50 4.00
167 Geronimo Gil ROO 1.50 4.00
168 Dewon Brazelton ROO 1.50 4.00
169 Mark Prior ROO 2.00 5.00
170 Bill Hall ROO 1.50 4.00
171 Jorge Padilla ROO RC 1.50 4.00
172 Josh Pearce ROO 1.50 4.00
173 Allan Simpson ROO RC 1.50 4.00
174 Doug Devore ROO RC 1.50 4.00
175 Luis Garcia ROO 1.50 4.00
176 Angel Berroa ROO 1.50 4.00
177 Steve Bechler ROO RC 1.50 4.00
178 Antonio Perez ROO 1.50 4.00
179 Mark Teixeira ROO 3.00 8.00
180 Mark Ellis ROO 1.50 4.00
181 Michael Cuddyer ROO 1.50 4.00
182 Michael Rivera ROO 1.50 4.00
183 Raul Chavez ROO RC 1.50 4.00
184 Juan Pena ROO 1.50 4.00
185 Austin Kearns ROO 1.50 4.00
186 Ryan Ludwick ROO 1.50 4.00
187 Ed Rogers ROO 1.50 4.00
188 Wilson Betemit ROO 1.50 4.00
189 Nick Neugebauer ROO 1.50 4.00
190 Tom Shearn ROO RC 1.50 4.00
191 Eric Cyr ROO 1.50 4.00
192 Victor Martinez ROO 3.00 8.00
193 Brandon Berger ROO 1.50 4.00
194 Erik Bedard ROO 1.50 4.00
195 Franklyn German ROO RC 1.50 4.00
196 Joe Thurston ROO 1.50 4.00
197 John Buck ROO 1.50 4.00
198 Jeff Deardorff ROO 1.50 4.00
199 Ryan Jamison ROO 1.50 4.00
200 Alfredo Amezaga ROO 1.50 4.00
201 So Taguchi ROO/500 RC * 6.00 15.00
202 Kazuhisa Ishii ROO/250 RC * 10.00 25.00

2002 Leaf Autographs

RANDOM INSERTS IN PACKS
STATED PRINT RUNS LISTED BELOW
201 So Taguchi/50 20.00 50.00

2002 Leaf Lineage

*LINEAGE: 3X TO 8X BASIC CARDS
STATED ODDS 1:12 HOBBY
CARDS 1-50 ARE 1999 REPLICAS
CARDS 51-100 ARE 2000 REPLICAS
CARDS 101-150 ARE 2001 REPLICAS
CARD NUMBER 42 DOES NOT EXIST

2002 Leaf Lineage Century

*CENTURY: 8X TO 20X BASIC CARDS
RANDOM INSERTS IN HOBBY PACKS
STATED PRINT RUN 100 SERIAL #'d SETS
CARDS 1-50 ARE 1999 REPLICAS
CARDS 51-100 ARE 2000 REPLICAS
CARDS 101-150 ARE 2001 REPLICAS
CARD NUMBER 42 DOES NOT EXIST

2002 Leaf Press Proofs Blue

*BLUE: 6X TO 15X BASIC CARDS
STATED ODDS 1:24 RETAIL
CARD NUMBER 42 DOES NOT EXIST

2002 Leaf Press Proofs Platinum

*PLATINUM: 30X TO 80X BASIC CARDS
RANDOM IN HOBBY/RETAIL PACKS
1-150/201 PRINT RUN 25 SERIAL #'d SETS
CARD 202 PRINT RUN 10 SERIAL #'d COPIES
CARD NUMBER 42 DOES NOT EXIST
201-202 NOT PRICED DUE TO SCARCITY

2002 Leaf Press Proofs Red

*RED 1-150: 3X TO 8X BASIC CARDS
1-150 STATED ODDS 1:12 RETAIL
201-202 RANDOM INSERTS IN RETAIL PACKS
CARD 201 PRINT RUN 500 SERIAL #'d COPIES
CARD 202 PRINT RUN 250 SERIAL #'d COPIES
CARD NUMBER 42 DOES NOT EXIST
201 So Taguchi/500 6.00 15.00
202 Kazuhisa Ishii/250 10.00 25.00

2002 Leaf Burn and Turn

COMPLETE SET (10) 40.00 100.00
STATED ODDS 1:96 HOBBY, 1:120 RETAIL
1 F.Vina 3.00 8.00
E.Renteria
2 A.Rodriguez 5.00 12.00
M.Young
3 D.Jeter 10.00 25.00
A.Soriano
4 C.Guillen 3.00 8.00
B.Boone
5 J.Vidro 3.00 8.00
O.Cabrera
6 B.Larkin 3.00 8.00
T.Walker
7 C.Febles 3.00 8.00
N.Perez
8 J.Kent 3.00 8.00
R.Aurilia
9 C.Biggio 3.00 8.00
J.Lugo
10 M.Tejada 3.00 8.00
M.Ellis

2002 Leaf Clean Up Crew

COMPLETE SET (15) 100.00 200.00
STATED ODDS 1:192 HOBBY, 1:240 RETAIL
1 Barry Bonds 12.50 30.00
2 Sammy Sosa 5.00 12.00
3 Luis Gonzalez 4.00 10.00
4 Richie Sexson 4.00 10.00
5 Jim Thome 4.00 10.00
6 Chipper Jones 5.00 12.00
7 Alex Rodriguez 6.00 15.00
8 Troy Glaus 4.00 10.00
9 Rafael Palmeiro 4.00 10.00
10 Lance Berkman 4.00 10.00
11 Mike Piazza 8.00 20.00
12 Jason Giambi 4.00 10.00
13 Todd Helton 4.00 10.00
14 Shawn Green 4.00 10.00
15 Carlos Delgado 4.00 10.00

2002 Leaf Clubhouse Signatures Bronze

PRINT RUNS B/WN 25-300 COPIES PER
NO PRICING ON QTY OF 25 OR LESS
1 Adam Dunn/200 5.00 12.00
2 Alan Trammell/75 10.00 25.00
5 Aramis Ramirez/250 6.00 15.00
6 Austin Kearns/300 4.00 10.00
7 Barry Zito/100 12.50 30.00
8 Billy Williams/150 6.00 15.00
9 Bob Feller/250 6.00 15.00
10 Bud Smith/200 4.00 10.00
14 Jason Lane/250 6.00 15.00
15 Jermaine Dye/125 8.00 20.00
16 Joe Crede/200 6.00 15.00
17 Joe Mays/200 4.00 10.00
18 Johnny Estrada/250 4.00 10.00
19 Mark Ellis/300 4.00 10.00
21 Marlon Byrd/200 4.00 10.00
23 Paul LoDuca/300 6.00 15.00
25 Robert Fick/300 4.00 10.00
26 Ron Santo/300 12.50 30.00
27 Roy Oswalt/300 6.00 15.00
29 Steve Garvey/200 6.00 15.00
30 Terrence Long/250 4.00 10.00
31 Tim Redding/300 4.00 10.00
32 Wilson Betemit/150 4.00 10.00
33 Xavier Nady/200 4.00 10.00

2002 Leaf Clubhouse Signatures Silver

RANDOM INSERTS IN HOBBY/RETAIL
PRINT RUNS B/WN 25-100 COPIES
NO PRICING ON QTY OF 25 OR LESS
1 Adam Dunn/75 6.00 15.00
3 Aramis Ramirez/100 8.00 20.00
4 Austin Kearns/100 6.00 15.00
5 Barry Zito/100 12.50 30.00
6 Billy Williams/100 8.00 20.00
7 Bob Feller/100 15.00 40.00
8 Bud Smith/100 6.00 15.00
10 Edgar Martinez/100 15.00 40.00
11 Eric Chavez/100 8.00 20.00
12 Jason Lane/100 8.00 20.00
13 Jermaine Dye/100 8.00 20.00
14 Joe Crede/50 8.00 20.00
15 Joe Mays/50 6.00 15.00
16 Johnny Estrada/100 6.00 15.00
17 Javier Vazquez/100 8.00 20.00
18 Mark Ellis/100 6.00 15.00
19 Mark Mulder/100 8.00 20.00
20 Marlon Byrd/100 6.00 15.00
21 Miguel Tejada/100 12.50 30.00
25 Rich Aurilia/100 6.00 15.00
26 Robert Fick/100 6.00 15.00
28 Ron Santo/100 15.00 40.00
29 Roy Oswalt/100 8.00 20.00
31 Steve Garvey/100 8.00 20.00
32 Terrence Long/100 6.00 15.00
33 Tim Redding/100 6.00 15.00
36 Wilson Betemit/100 6.00 15.00
37 Xavier Nady/100 6.00 15.00

2002 Leaf Future 500 Club

COMPLETE SET (10) 40.00 80.00
STATED ODDS 1:64 HOBBY, 1:103 RETAIL
1 Sammy Sosa 2.50 6.00
2 Mike Piazza 4.00 10.00
3 Alex Rodriguez 3.00 8.00
4 Chipper Jones 2.50 6.00
5 Jeff Bagwell 2.00 5.00
6 Carlos Delgado 2.00 5.00
7 Shawn Green 2.00 5.00
8 Ken Griffey Jr. 5.00 12.00
9 Rafael Palmeiro 2.00 5.00
10 Vladimir Guerrero 2.50 6.00

2002 Leaf Game Collection

STATED ODDS 1:62 RETAIL
CARDS ARE NOT SERIAL NUMBERED
SP PRINT RUNS PROVIDED BY DONRUSS
NO PRICING ON QTY OF 25 OR LESS
ABB Adrian Beltre Bat 4.00 10.00
AGB Andres Galarraga Bat 4.00 10.00
AJB Andruw Jones Bat SP/300 10.00 25.00
BGB Brian Giles Bat 4.00 10.00
BHB Bobby Higginson Bat 4.00 10.00
CBB Carlos Beltran Bat 4.00 10.00
CBIB Craig Biggio Bat 6.00 15.00
CFB Carlton Fisk Bat 6.00 15.00
CKB Chuck Knoblauch Bat 4.00 10.00
EMB Eddie Murray Bat SP/250 10.00 25.00
GJP Geoff Jenkins Pants 4.00 10.00
JEB Juan Encarnacion Bat 4.00 10.00
JGB Juan Gonzalez Bat 4.00 10.00
KLB Kenny Lofton Bat 4.00 10.00
MGB Mark Grace Bat SP/200 10.00 25.00
MOB Magglio Ordonez Bat SP/150 6.00 15.00
RAB Roberto Alomar Bat 6.00 15.00
RDB Ray Durham Bat 4.00 10.00
RGB Rusty Greer Bat 4.00 10.00
RPB Rafael Palmeiro Bat 6.00 15.00
RVB Robin Ventura Bat 4.00 10.00
SCB Sean Casey Bat 4.00 10.00
SRB Scott Rolen Bat SP/250 10.00 25.00
TCB Tony Clark Bat 4.00 10.00
THB Todd Helton Bat 6.00 15.00
TNB Trot Nixon Bat 4.00 10.00
WBB Wade Boggs Bat 6.00 15.00

2002 Leaf Gold Rookies

COMPLETE SET (10) 25.00 50.00
STATED ODDS 1:24 HOBBY/RETAIL
1 Josh Beckett 1.50 4.00
2 Marlon Byrd 1.50 4.00
3 Dennis Tankersley 1.50 4.00
4 Jason Lane 1.50 4.00
5 Dewon Brazelton 1.50 4.00
6 Mark Prior 1.50 4.00
7 Bill Hall 1.50 4.00
8 Angel Berroa 1.50 4.00
9 Mark Teixeira 2.50 6.00
10 John Buck 1.50 4.00

2002 Leaf Heading for the Hall

COMPLETE SET (10) 40.00 80.00
STATED ODDS 1:64 HOBBY, 1:240 RETAIL
1 Greg Maddux 4.00 10.00
2 Ozzie Smith 4.00 10.00
3 Andre Dawson 2.00 5.00
4 Dennis Eckersley 2.00 5.00
5 Roberto Alomar 2.00 5.00
6 Cal Ripken 8.00 20.00
7 Roger Clemens 5.00 12.00
8 Tony Gwynn 3.00 8.00
9 Alex Rodriguez 3.00 8.00
10 Jeff Bagwell 2.00 5.00

2002 Leaf League of Nations

COMPLETE SET (10) 30.00 60.00
STATED ODDS 1:60 HOBBY/RETAIL
1 Ichiro Suzuki 5.00 12.00
2 Tsuyoshi Shinjo 2.00 5.00
3 Chan Ho Park 2.00 5.00
4 Larry Walker 2.00 5.00
5 Andruw Jones 2.00 5.00
6 Hideo Nomo 5.00 12.00
7 Byung-Hyun Kim 2.00 5.00
8 Sun-Woo Kim 2.00 5.00
9 Orlando Hernandez 2.00 5.00
10 Luke Prokopec 2.00 5.00

2002 Leaf Rookie Reprints

COMPLETE SET (6) 25.00 50.00
RANDOM INSERTS IN HOBBY/RETAIL
STATED PRINT RUNS LISTED BELOW
1 Roger Clemens/1985 6.00 15.00
2 Kirby Puckett/1985 3.00 8.00
3 Andres Galarraga/1986 2.00 5.00
4 Fred McGriff/1986 2.00 5.00
5 Sammy Sosa/1990 3.00 8.00
6 Frank Thomas/1990 3.00 8.00

2002 Leaf Shirt Off My Back

STATED ODDS 1:29 HOBBY
CARDS ARE NOT SERIAL-NUMBERED
SP PRINT RUNS PROVIDED BY DONRUSS
*MULTI-COLOR PATCH 1.25X TO 3X HI
NO PRICING ON QTY OF 25 OR LESS
AB A.J. Burnett 4.00 10.00
AK Al Kaline SP/100 15.00 40.00
AP Andy Pettitte SP/50 20.00 50.00
AR Alex Rodriguez SP/150 15.00 40.00
BL Barry Larkin 6.00 15.00
BR Brad Radke 4.00 10.00
CB Carlos Beltran 4.00 10.00
CD Carlos Delgado 4.00 10.00
CF Cliff Floyd 4.00 10.00
CHP Chan Ho Park SP/100 10.00 25.00
CJ Chipper Jones SP/100 15.00 40.00
CL Carlos Lee 4.00 10.00
CR Cal Ripken SP/50 75.00 150.00
CS Curt Schilling SP/150 10.00 25.00
DE Darin Erstad SP/100 10.00 25.00
DM Don Mattingly SP/100 30.00 60.00
DW Dave Winfield SP/150 10.00 25.00
EK Eric Karros 12.50 30.00
EM Edgar Martinez SP/150 15.00 40.00
FG Freddy Garcia SP/100 10.00 25.00
GB George Brett SP/100 20.00 50.00
GM Greg Maddux SP/100 15.00 40.00
HN Hideo Nomo SP/100 15.00 40.00
JB Jeff Bagwell SP/100 15.00 40.00
JBU Jeromy Burnitz 4.00 10.00
JL Javy Lopez 4.00 10.00
JO John Olerud 4.00 10.00
JS John Smoltz 6.00 15.00
KB Kevin Brown SP/100 10.00 25.00
KM Kevin Millwood 4.00 10.00
KP Kirby Puckett SP/100 15.00 40.00
KS Kazuhiro Sasaki SP/100 10.00 25.00
LB Lance Berkman SP/300 10.00 25.00
LG Luis Gonzalez 4.00 10.00
LW Larry Walker SP/50 12.50 30.00
MB Michael Barrett 4.00 10.00
MBU Mark Buehrle 4.00 10.00
MH Mike Hampton 4.00 10.00
MO Magglio Ordonez 4.00 10.00
MP Mike Piazza SP/150 15.00 40.00
MR Manny Ramirez SP/100 15.00 40.00
MS Mike Sweeney 4.00 10.00
MT Miguel Tejada 4.00 10.00
MW Matt Williams 4.00 10.00
PM Pedro Martinez SP/100 15.00 40.00
RA Roberto Alomar SP/250 6.00 15.00
RD Ryan Dempster 4.00 10.00
RJ Randy Johnson SP/100 15.00 40.00
RP Rafael Palmeiro 6.00 15.00
RS Richie Sexson 4.00 10.00
SR Scott Rolen SP/250 15.00 40.00
TG Tony Gwynn SP/100 15.00 40.00
TG Tom Glavine 6.00 15.00
TGL Troy Glaus SP/275 10.00 25.00
TH Todd Helton 6.00 15.00
TH Tim Hudson 4.00 10.00
TP Troy Percival 4.00 10.00
TS Tsuyoshi Shinjo SP/100 10.00 25.00

2003 Leaf Samples

*SAMPLES: 1.5X TO 4X BASIC CARDS

2003 Leaf

COMP.LO SET (320) 15.00 40.00
COMP.UPDATE SET (9) 3.00 8.00
COMMON CARD (1-270) .12 .30
COMMON CARD (271-320) .15 .40
COMMON CARD (321-329) .20 .50
321-329 ISSUED IN DLP R/T PACKS
HIGGINSON AND PENA ARE BOTH CARD 41
CARD 42 DOES NOT EXIST
1 Brad Fullmer .12 .30
2 Darin Erstad .12 .30
3 David Eckstein .12 .30
4 Garret Anderson .12 .30
5 Jarrod Washburn .12 .30
6 Kevin Appier .12 .30
7 Tim Salmon .12 .30
8 Troy Glaus .12 .30
9 Troy Percival .12 .30
10 Buddy Groom .12 .30
11 Jay Gibbons .12 .30
12 Jeff Conine .12 .30
13 Marty Cordova .12 .30
14 Melvin Mora .12 .30
15 Rodrigo Lopez .12 .30
16 Tony Batista .12 .30
17 Jorge Julio .12 .30
18 Cliff Floyd .12 .30
19 Derek Lowe .12 .30
20 Jason Varitek .30 .75
21 Johnny Damon .20 .50
22 Manny Ramirez .30 .75
23 Nomar Garciaparra .20 .50
24 Pedro Martinez .20 .50
25 Rickey Henderson .30 .75
26 Shea Hillenbrand .12 .30
27 Trot Nixon .12 .30
28 Carlos Lee .12 .30
29 Frank Thomas .30 .75
30 Jose Valentin .12 .30
31 Magglio Ordonez .20 .50
32 Mark Buehrle .20 .50
33 Paul Konerko .20 .50
34 C.C. Sabathia .20 .50
35 Danys Baez .12 .30
36 Ellis Burks .12 .30
37 Jim Thome .20 .50
38 Omar Vizquel .20 .50
39 Ricky Gutierrez .12 .30
40 Travis Fryman .12 .30
41A Bobby Higginson .12 .30
41B Carlos Pena .20 .50
43 Juan Acevedo .12 .30
44 Mark Redman .12 .30
45 Randall Simon .12 .30
46 Robert Fick .12 .30
47 Steve Sparks .12 .30
48 Carlos Beltran .20 .50
49 Joe Randa .12 .30
50 Michael Tucker .12 .30
51 Mike Sweeney .12 .30
52 Paul Byrd .12 .30
53 Raul Ibanez .20 .50
54 Runelvys Hernandez .12 .30
55 A.J. Pierzynski .12 .30
56 Brad Radke .12 .30
57 Corey Koskie .12 .30
58 Cristian Guzman .12 .30
59 David Ortiz .30 .75
60 Doug Mientkiewicz .12 .30
61 Dustan Mohr .12 .30
62 Eddie Guardado .12 .30
63 Jacque Jones .12 .30
64 Torii Hunter .12 .30
65 Alfonso Soriano .20 .50
66 Andy Pettitte .20 .50
67 Bernie Williams .20 .50
68 David Wells .12 .30
69 Derek Jeter .75 2.00
70 Jason Giambi .12 .30
71 Jeff Weaver .12 .30
72 Jorge Posada .20 .50
73 Mike Mussina .20 .50
74 Nick Johnson .12 .30
75 Raul Mondesi .12 .30
76 Robin Ventura .12 .30
77 Roger Clemens .40 1.00
78 Barry Zito .20 .50
79 Billy Koch .12 .30
80 David Justice .12 .30
81 Eric Chavez .12 .30
82 Jermaine Dye .12 .30
83 Mark Mulder .12 .30
84 Miguel Tejada .20 .50
85 Ray Durham .12 .30
86 Scott Hatteberg .12 .30
87 Ted Lilly .12 .30
88 Tim Hudson .20 .50
89 Bret Boone .12 .30
90 Carlos Guillen .12 .30
91 Chris Snelling .12 .30
92 Dan Wilson .12 .30
93 Edgar Martinez .20 .50
94 Freddy Garcia .12 .30
95 Ichiro Suzuki .40 1.00
96 Jamie Moyer .12 .30
97 Joel Pineiro .12 .30
98 John Olerud .12 .30
99 Mark McLemore .12 .30
100 Mike Cameron .12 .30
101 Kazuhiro Sasaki .12 .30
102 Aubrey Huff .12 .30
103 Ben Grieve .12 .30
104 Joe Kennedy .12 .30
105 Paul Wilson .12 .30
106 Randy Winn .12 .30
107 Steve Cox .12 .30
108 Alex Rodriguez .40 1.00
109 Chan Ho Park .20 .50
110 Hank Blalock .12 .30
111 Herbert Perry .12 .30
112 Ivan Rodriguez .20 .50
113 Juan Gonzalez .12 .30
114 Kenny Rogers .12 .30
115 Kevin Mench .12 .30
116 Rafael Palmeiro .20 .50
117 Carlos Delgado .12 .30
118 Eric Hinske .12 .30
119 Jose Cruz .12 .30
120 Josh Phelps .12 .30
121 Roy Halladay .20 .50
122 Shannon Stewart .12 .30
123 Vernon Wells .12 .30
124 Curt Schilling .20 .50
125 Junior Spivey .12 .30
126 Luis Gonzalez .12 .30
127 Mark Grace .20 .50
128 Randy Johnson .30 .75
129 Steve Finley .12 .30
130 Tony Womack .12 .30
131 Andruw Jones .12 .30
132 Chipper Jones .30 .75
133 Gary Sheffield .12 .30
134 Greg Maddux .40 1.00
135 John Smoltz .30 .75
136 Kevin Millwood .12 .30
137 Rafael Furcal .12 .30
138 Tom Glavine .20 .50
139 Alex Gonzalez .12 .30
140 Corey Patterson .12 .30
141 Fred McGriff .20 .50
142 Jon Lieber .12 .30
143 Kerry Wood .12 .30
144 Mark Prior .20 .50
145 Matt Clement .12 .30
146 Moises Alou .12 .30
147 Sammy Sosa .30 .75
148 Aaron Boone .12 .30
149 Adam Dunn .20 .50
150 Austin Kearns .12 .30
151 Barry Larkin .20 .50
152 Danny Graves .12 .30
153 Elmer Dessens .12 .30
154 Ken Griffey Jr. .60 1.50
155 Sean Casey .12 .30
156 Todd Walker .12 .30
157 Gabe Kapler .12 .30
158 Jason Jennings .12 .30
159 Jay Payton .12 .30
160 Larry Walker .20 .50
161 Mike Hampton .12 .30
162 Todd Helton .20 .50
163 Todd Zeile .12 .30
164 A.J. Burnett .12 .30
165 Derrek Lee .12 .30
166 Josh Beckett .12 .30
167 Juan Encarnacion .12 .30
168 Luis Castillo .12 .30
169 Mike Lowell .12 .30
170 Preston Wilson .12 .30
171 Billy Wagner .12 .30
172 Craig Biggio .20 .50
173 Daryle Ward .12 .30
174 Jeff Bagwell .20 .50
175 Lance Berkman .20 .50
176 Octavio Dotel .12 .30
177 Richard Hidalgo .12 .30
178 Roy Oswalt .20 .50
179 Adrian Beltre .30 .75
180 Eric Gagne .12 .30
181 Eric Karros .12 .30
182 Hideo Nomo .30 .75
183 Kazuhisa Ishii .12 .30
184 Kevin Brown .12 .30
185 Mark Grudzielanek .12 .30
186 Odalis Perez .12 .30
187 Paul Lo Duca .12 .30
188 Shawn Green .12 .30
189 Alex Sanchez .12 .30
190 Ben Sheets .12 .30
191 Jeffrey Hammonds .12 .30
192 Jose Hernandez .12 .30
193 Takahito Nomura .12 .30
194 Richie Sexson .12 .30
195 Andres Galarraga .20 .50
196 Bartolo Colon .12 .30
197 Brad Wilkerson .12 .30
198 Javier Vazquez .12 .30
199 Jose Vidro .12 .30
200 Michael Barrett .12 .30
201 Tomo Ohka .12 .30
202 Vladimir Guerrero .20 .50
203 Al Leiter .12 .30
204 Armando Benitez .12 .30
205 Edgardo Alfonzo .12 .30
206 Mike Piazza .30 .75
207 Mo Vaughn .12 .30
208 Pedro Astacio .12 .30
209 Roberto Alomar .20 .50
210 Roger Cedeno .12 .30
211 Timo Perez .12 .30
212 Bobby Abreu .12 .30
213 Jimmy Rollins .20 .50
214 Mike Lieberthal .12 .30
215 Pat Burrell .12 .30
216 Randy Wolf .12 .30
217 Travis Lee .12 .30
218 Vicente Padilla .12 .30
219 Aramis Ramirez .12 .30
220 Brian Giles .12 .30
221 Craig Wilson .12 .30
222 Jason Kendall .12 .30
223 Josh Fogg .12 .30
224 Kevin Young .12 .30
225 Kip Wells .12 .30
226 Mike Williams .12 .30
227 Brett Tomko .12 .30
228 Brian Lawrence .12 .30
229 Mark Kotsay .12 .30
230 Oliver Perez .12 .30
231 Phil Nevin .12 .30
232 Ryan Klesko .12 .30
233 Sean Burroughs .12 .30
234 Trevor Hoffman .20 .50
235 Barry Bonds .50 1.25
236 Benito Santiago .12 .30
237 Jeff Kent .12 .30
238 Kirk Rueter .12 .30
239 Livan Hernandez .12 .30
240 Kenny Lofton .12 .30
241 Rich Aurilia .12 .30
242 Russ Ortiz .12 .30
243 Albert Pujols .40 1.00
244 Edgar Renteria .12 .30
245 J.D. Drew .12 .30
246 Jason Isringhausen .12 .30
247 Jim Edmonds .20 .50
248 Matt Morris .12 .30
249 Tino Martinez .12 .30
250 Scott Rolen .20 .50
251 Curt Schilling PT .20 .50
252 Ivan Rodriguez PT .20 .50
253 Mike Piazza PT .30 .75
254 Sammy Sosa PT .30 .75
255 Matt Williams PT .12 .30
256 Frank Thomas PT .30 .75
257 Barry Bonds PT .50 1.25
258 Roger Clemens PT .40 1.00
259 Rickey Henderson PT .30 .75
260 Ken Griffey Jr. PT .60 1.50
261 Greg Maddux PT .40 1.00
262 Randy Johnson PT .30 .75
263 Jeff Bagwell PT .20 .50
264 Roberto Alomar PT .20 .50
265 Tom Glavine PT .20 .50
266 Juan Gonzalez PT .12 .30
267 Mark Grace PT .20 .50
268 Mike Mussina PT .20 .50
269 Ryan Klesko PT .12 .30
270 Fred McGriff PT .20 .50
271 Joe Borchard ROO .15 .40
272 Chris Snelling ROO .15 .40
273 Brian Tallet ROO .15 .40
274 Cliff Lee ROO 1.00 2.50
275 Freddy Sanchez ROO .15 .40
276 Chone Figgins ROO .15 .40
277 Kevin Cash ROO .15 .40
278 Josh Bard ROO .15 .40
279 Jeriome Robertson ROO .15 .40
280 Jeremy Hill ROO .15 .40
281 Shane Nance ROO .15 .40
282 Jeff Baker ROO .15 .40
283 Trey Hodges ROO .15 .40
284 Eric Eckenstahler ROO .15 .40
285 Jim Rushford ROO .15 .40
286 Carlos Rivera ROO .15 .40
287 Josh Bonifay ROO .15 .40
288 Garrett Atkins ROO .15 .40
289 Nic Jackson ROO .15 .40
290 Corwin Malone ROO .15 .40
291 Jimmy Gobble ROO .15 .40
292 Josh Wilson ROO .15 .40
293 Clint Barmes ROO RC .40 1.00
294 Jon Adkins ROO .15 .40
295 Tim Kalita ROO .15 .40
296 Nelson Castro ROO .15 .40
297 Colin Young ROO .15 .40
298 Adrian Burnside ROO .15 .40
299 Luis Martinez ROO .15 .40
300 Termel Sledge ROO RC .15 .40
301 Todd Donovan ROO .15 .40
302 Jeremy Ward ROO .15 .40
303 Wilson Valdez ROO .15 .40
304 Jose Contreras ROO RC .40 1.00
305 Marshall McDougall ROO .15 .40
306 Mitch Wylie ROO .15 .40
307 Ron Calloway ROO .15 .40
308 Jose Valverde ROO .15 .40
309 Jason Davis ROO .15 .40
310 Scotty Layfield ROO .15 .40
311 Matt Thornton ROO .15 .40
312 Adam Walker ROO .15 .40
313 Gustavo Chacin ROO .15 .40
314 Ron Chiavacci ROO .15 .40
315 Wilbert Nieves ROO .15 .40
316 Cliff Bartosh ROO .15 .40
317 Mike Gonzalez ROO .15 .40
318 Jeremy Guthrie ROO .15 .40
319 Eric Junge ROO .15 .40
320 Ben Kozlowski ROO .15 .40
321 Hideki Matsui ROO RC 1.00 2.50
322 Ramon Nivar ROO RC .20 .50

323 Adam Loewen ROO RC .20 .50
324 Brandon Webb ROO RC .60 1.50
325 Chien-Ming Wang ROO RC .75 2.00
326 Delmon Young ROO RC 1.25 3.00
327 Ryan Wagner ROO RC .20 .50
328 Dan Haren ROO RC 1.00 2.50
329 Rickie Weeks ROO RC .60 1.50

2003 Leaf Autographs

CARD 304 RANDOM INSERT IN PACKS
322-329 RANDOM IN DLP R/T PACKS
PRINT RUNS B/WN 10-100 COPIES PER
NO PRICING ON QTY OF 25 OR LESS
304 Jose Contreras ROO/100 12.50 30.00
322 Ramon Nivar ROO/100 4.00 10.00
323 Adam Loewen ROO/100 6.00 15.00
324 Brandon Webb ROO/100 10.00 25.00
325 C.Wang ROO/50 75.00 150.00
327 Ryan Wagner ROO/100 4.00 10.00
328 Dan Haren ROO/100 6.00 15.00

2003 Leaf Press Proofs Blue

*BLUE 1-250: 6X TO 15X BASIC
*BLUE 251-270: 6X TO 15X BASIC
*BLUE 271-320: 5X TO 12X BASIC
*BLUE 271-320: 5X TO 12X BASIC RC's
*BLUE 321-329: 4X TO 10X BASIC
1-320 RANDOM INSERTS IN PACKS
321-329 RANDOM IN DLP R/T PACKS
STATED PRINT RUN 50 SERIAL #'d SETS

2003 Leaf Press Proofs Red

*RED 1-250: 2.5X TO 6X BASIC
*RED 251-270: 2.5X TO 6X BASIC
*RED 271-320: 2X TO 5X BASIC
*RED 271-320: 2X TO 5X BASIC RC's
*RED 321-329: 2.5X TO 6X BASIC RC's
1-320 STATED ODDS 1:12 HOBBY/RETAIL
321-329 RANDOM IN DLP R/T PACKS
321-329 PRINT RUN 100 SERIAL #'d SETS

2003 Leaf 60

STATED ODDS 1:8 HOBBY/RETAIL
*FOIL: 2.5X TO 6X BASIC CARDS
FOIL RANDOM INSERTS IN PACKS
FOIL PRINT RUN 60 SERIAL #'d SETS
1 Troy Glaus .40 1.00
2 Curt Schilling .60 1.50
3 Randy Johnson 1.00 2.50
4 Andruw Jones .40 1.00
5 Chipper Jones 1.00 2.50
6 Greg Maddux 1.25 3.00
7 Tom Glavine .60 1.50
8 Manny Ramirez 1.00 2.50
9 Nomar Garciaparra .60 1.50
10 Pedro Martinez .60 1.50
11 Rickey Henderson 1.00 2.50
12 Sammy Sosa 1.00 2.50
13 Frank Thomas 1.00 2.50
14 Magglio Ordonez .60 1.50
15 Mark Buehrle .60 1.50
16 Adam Dunn .60 1.50
17 Ken Griffey Jr. 2.00 5.00
18 Jim Thome .60 1.50
19 Omar Vizquel .60 1.50
20 Larry Walker .60 1.50
21 Todd Helton .60 1.50
22 Lance Berkman .60 1.50
23 Roy Oswalt .60 1.50
24 Mike Sweeney .40 1.00
25 Hideo Nomo 1.00 2.50
26 Kazuhisa Ishii .40 1.00
27 Shawn Green .40 1.00
28 Torii Hunter .40 1.00
29 Vladimir Guerrero .60 1.50
30 Mike Piazza 1.00 2.50
31 Alfonso Soriano .60 1.50
32 Bernie Williams .60 1.50
33 Derek Jeter 2.50 6.00
34 Jason Giambi .40 1.00
35 Roger Clemens 1.25 3.00
36 Barry Zito .60 1.50
37 Miguel Tejada .60 1.50
38 Pat Burrell .40 1.00
39 Ryan Klesko .40 1.00
40 Barry Bonds 1.50 4.00
41 Jeff Kent .40 1.00
42 Ichiro Suzuki 1.25 3.00
43 John Olerud .40 1.00
44 Albert Pujols 1.25 3.00
45 Jim Edmonds .60 1.50
46 Scott Rolen .60 1.50
47 Alex Rodriguez 1.25 3.00
48 Ivan Rodriguez .60 1.50
49 Rafael Palmeiro .60 1.50
50 Roy Halladay .60 1.50

2003 Leaf Certified Samples

STATED ODDS 1:23 HOBBY/RETAIL
*MIRROR RED: 1.5X TO 4X BASIC
MIRROR RED PRINT RUN 150 #'d SETS
*MIRROR BLUE: 1X TO 2.5X BASIC
MIRROR BLUE PRINT RUN 75 #'d SETS
MIRROR GOLD PRINT RUN 25 #'d SETS
MIRROR GOLD TOO SCARCE TO PRICE
1 Derek Jeter 2.50 6.00
2 Greg Maddux 1.25 3.00
3 Mike Piazza 1.00 2.50
4 Barry Bonds 1.50 4.00
5 Lance Berkman .60 1.50
6 Alex Rodriguez 1.25 3.00
7 Alfonso Soriano .60 1.50
8 Ichiro Suzuki 1.25 3.00
9 Sammy Sosa 1.00 2.50
10 Vladimir Guerrero .60 1.50
11 Albert Pujols 1.25 3.00
12 Pedro Martinez .60 1.50
13 Randy Johnson 1.00 2.50
14 Nomar Garciaparra .60 1.50
15 Barry Zito .60 1.50

2003 Leaf Clean Up Crew

STATED ODDS 1:49 HOBBY/RETAIL
1 A.Rod 1.25 3.00
Palmeiro
I.Rod
2 Nomar 1.00 2.50
Manny
Floyd
3 Giambi .60 1.50
Bernie
Posada
4 Aurillia 1.50 4.00
Kent
Bonds
5 Walker .60 1.50
Helton
Payton
6 Berkman .60 1.50
Bagwell
Ward
7 Rolen 1.25 3.00
Pujols
Edmonds
8 Sheffield 1.00 2.50
Chipper
Andruw
9 Tejada .60 1.50
Chavez
Dye
10 Sosa 1.00 2.50
Alou
McGriff

2003 Leaf Clean Up Crew Materials

RANDOM INSERTS IN PACKS
STATED PRINT RUN 50 SERIAL #'d SETS
SEE BECKETT.COM FOR GAME USED INFO
1 A.Rod/Palmeiro/I.Rod 15.00 40.00
2 Nomar/Manny/Floyd 15.00 40.00
3 Giambi/Bernie/Posada 15.00 40.00
4 Aurilia/Kent/Bonds 30.00 60.00
5 Walker/Helton/Payton 15.00 40.00
6 Berkman/Bagwell/Ward 15.00 40.00
7 Rolen/Pujols/Edmonds 30.00 60.00
8 Sheffield/Chipper/Andruw 15.00 40.00
9 Tejada/Chavez/Dye 10.00 25.00
10 Sosa/Alou/McGriff 15.00 40.00

2003 Leaf Clubhouse Signatures Bronze

SP INFO PROVIDED BY DONRUSS
SP'S ARE NOT SERIAL-NUMBERED
NO PRICING ON QTY OF 25 OR LESS
1 Edwin Almonte 3.00 8.00
2 Franklin Nunez 3.00 8.00
3 Josh Bard 3.00 8.00
4 J.C. Romero 3.00 8.00
5 Omar Infante 4.00 10.00
7 Andre Dawson SP/50 10.00 25.00
8 Brian Tallet SP/100 4.00 10.00
9 Bobby Doerr SP/100 6.00 15.00
10 Chris Snelling SP/100 4.00 10.00
11 Corey Patterson SP/100 4.00 10.00
12 Doc Gooden SP/100 6.00 15.00
13 Eric Hinske 3.00 8.00
14 Jeff Baker SP/100 4.00 10.00
15 Jack Morris SP/100 6.00 15.00
17 Torii Hunter SP/75 10.00 25.00
18 Kevin Mench 4.00 10.00
21 Angel Berroa SP/100 4.00 10.00
22 Brian Lawrence 3.00 8.00
23 Drew Henson SP/50 6.00 15.00
24 Jhonny Peralta 6.00 15.00
25 Magglio Ordonez SP/50 10.00 25.00

2003 Leaf Clubhouse Signatures Silver

STATED PRINT RUN 100 SERIAL #'d SETS
1 Edwin Almonte 3.00 8.00
2 Franklin Nunez 3.00 8.00
3 Josh Bard 3.00 8.00
4 J.C. Romero 3.00 8.00
5 Omar Infante 6.00 15.00
8 Brian Tallet 3.00 8.00
9 Bobby Doerr 6.00 15.00
10 Chris Snelling 3.00 8.00
12 Doc Gooden 6.00 15.00
13 Eric Hinske 3.00 8.00
14 Jeff Baker 3.00 8.00
15 Jack Morris 6.00 15.00
17 Torii Hunter 4.00 10.00
18 Kevin Mench 4.00 10.00
21 Angel Berroa 3.00 8.00
22 Brian Lawrence 3.00 8.00
23 Drew Henson 3.00 8.00
24 Jhonny Peralta 6.00 15.00
25 Magglio Ordonez 6.00 15.00

2003 Leaf Game Collection

STATED PRINT RUN 150 SERIAL #'d SETS
1 Miguel Tejada Hat 4.00 10.00
2 Shannon Stewart Hat 4.00 10.00
3 Mike Schmidt Jacket 20.00 50.00
4 Nolan Ryan Jacket 12.00 30.00
5 Rafael Palmeiro Fld Glv 10.00 25.00
6 Andruw Jones Shoe 6.00 15.00
7 Bernie Williams Shoe 6.00 15.00
8 Ivan Rodriguez Shoe 6.00 15.00
9 Lance Berkman Shoe 4.00 10.00
10 Magglio Ordonez Shoe 4.00 10.00
11 Roy Oswalt Fld Glv 6.00 15.00
12 Andy Pettitte Shoe 6.00 15.00
13 Vladimir Guerrero Fld Glv 15.00 40.00
14 Jason Jennings Fld Glv 6.00 15.00
15 Mike Sweeney Shoe 4.00 10.00
16 Joe Borchard Shoe 4.00 10.00
17 Mark Prior Shoe 6.00 15.00
18 Gary Carter Jacket 4.00 10.00
19 Austin Kearns Fld Glv 6.00 15.00
20 Ryan Klesko Fld Glv 6.00 15.00

2003 Leaf Gold Rookies

STATED ODDS 1:24 HOBBY/RETAIL
MIRROR GOLD PRINT RUN 25 #'d SETS
MIRROR GOLD TOO SCARCE TO PRICE
1 Joe Borchard .40 1.00
2 Chone Figgins .40 1.00
3 Alexis Gomez .40 1.00
4 Chris Snelling .40 1.00
5 Cliff Lee 2.50 6.00
6 Victor Martinez .60 1.50
7 Hee Seop Choi .40 1.00
8 Michael Restovich .40 1.00
9 Anderson Machado .40 1.00
10 Drew Henson .40 1.00

2003 Leaf Hard Hats

COMPLETE SET (12) 6.00 15.00
STATED ODDS 1:13 HOBBY/RETAIL
1 Alex Rodriguez 1.25 3.00
2 Bernie Williams .60 1.50
3 Ivan Rodriguez .60 1.50
4 Jeff Bagwell .60 1.50
5 Rafael Furcal .40 1.00
6 Rafael Palmeiro .60 1.50
7 Tony Gwynn 1.00 2.50
8 Vladimir Guerrero .60 1.50
9 Adrian Beltre 1.00 2.50
10 Shawn Green .40 1.00
11 Andruw Jones .40 1.00
12 George Brett 2.00 5.00

2003 Leaf Hard Hats Batting Helmets

RANDOM INSERTS IN PACKS
STATED PRINT RUN 100 SERIAL #'d SETS
1 Alex Rodriguez 30.00 60.00
2 Bernie Williams 15.00 40.00
3 Ivan Rodriguez 15.00 40.00
4 Jeff Bagwell 15.00 40.00
5 Rafael Furcal 10.00 25.00
6 Rafael Palmeiro 15.00 40.00
7 Tony Gwynn 20.00 50.00
8 Vladimir Guerrero 15.00 40.00
9 Adrian Beltre 10.00 25.00
10 Shawn Green 10.00 25.00
11 Andruw Jones 15.00 40.00
12 George Brett 60.00 120.00

2003 Leaf Home/Away

STATED ODDS 1:34 HOBBY/RETAIL
1A Andruw Jones A .40 1.00
1H Andruw Jones H .40 1.00
2A Cal Ripken A 3.00 8.00
2H Cal Ripken H 3.00 8.00
3A Edgar Martinez A .60 1.50
3H Edgar Martinez H .60 1.50
4A Jim Thome A .60 1.50
4H Jim Thome H .60 1.50
5A Larry Walker A .60 1.50
5H Larry Walker H .60 1.50
6A Nomar Garciaparra A .60 1.50
6H Nomar Garciaparra H .60 1.50
7A Mark Prior A .60 1.50
7H Mark Prior H .60 1.50
8A Mike Piazza A 1.00 2.50
8H Mike Piazza H 1.00 2.50
9A Vladimir Guerrero A .60 1.50
9H Vladimir Guerrero H .60 1.50
10A Chipper Jones A 1.00 2.50
10H Chipper Jones H 1.00 2.50

2003 Leaf Home/Away Materials

RANDOM INSERTS IN PACKS
STATED PRINT RUN 250 SERIAL #'d SETS
1A Andruw Jones A 6.00 15.00
1H Andruw Jones H 6.00 15.00
2A Cal Ripken A 15.00 40.00
2H Cal Ripken H 15.00 40.00
3A Edgar Martinez A 6.00 15.00
3H Edgar Martinez H 6.00 15.00
4A Jim Thome A 6.00 15.00
4H Jim Thome H 6.00 15.00
5A Larry Walker A 4.00 10.00
5H Larry Walker H 4.00 10.00
6A Nomar Garciaparra A 8.00 20.00
6H Nomar Garciaparra H 8.00 20.00
7A Mark Prior A 6.00 15.00
7H Mark Prior H 6.00 15.00
8A Mike Piazza A 8.00 20.00
8H Mike Piazza H 8.00 20.00
9A Vladimir Guerrero A 6.00 15.00
9H Vladimir Guerrero H 6.00 15.00
10A Chipper Jones A 6.00 15.00
10H Chipper Jones H 6.00 15.00

2003 Leaf Maple and Ash

RANDOM INSERTS IN PACKS
STATED PRINT RUN 400 SERIAL #'d SETS
1 Jorge Posada 3.00 8.00
2 Mike Piazza 5.00 12.00
3 Alex Rodriguez 6.00 15.00
4 Jeff Bagwell 3.00 8.00
5 Joe Borchard 2.00 5.00
6 Miguel Tejada 3.00 8.00
7 Adam Dunn 3.00 8.00
8 Jim Thome 3.00 8.00
9 Lance Berkman 3.00 8.00
10 Torii Hunter 2.00 5.00
11 Carlos Delgado 2.00 5.00
12 Reggie Jackson 3.00 8.00
13 Juan Gonzalez 2.00 5.00
14 Vladimir Guerrero 3.00 8.00
15 Richie Sexson 2.00 5.00

2003 Leaf Number Off My Back

STATED PRINT RUN 50 SERIAL #'d SETS
1 Carlos Delgado 10.00 25.00
2 Don Mattingly 30.00 80.00
3 Todd Helton 15.00 40.00
4 Vernon Wells 10.00 25.00
5 Bernie Williams 15.00 40.00
6 Luis Gonzalez 10.00 25.00
7 Kerry Wood 10.00 25.00
8 Eric Chavez 10.00 25.00
9 Shawn Green 10.00 25.00
10 Roy Oswalt 10.00 25.00
11 Nomar Garciaparra 10.00 25.00
12 Robin Yount 25.00 60.00
13 Troy Glaus 10.00 25.00
14 C.C. Sabathia 10.00 25.00
15 Alex Rodriguez 25.00 60.00
16 Mark Mulder 10.00 25.00
17 Will Clark 15.00 40.00
18 Alfonso Soriano 10.00 25.00
19 Andy Pettitte 15.00 40.00
20 Curt Schilling 10.00 25.00

2003 Leaf Shirt Off My Back

STATED PRINT RUN 500 SERIAL #'d SETS
1 Carlos Delgado 3.00 8.00
2 Don Mattingly 10.00 25.00
3 Todd Helton 4.00 10.00
4 Vernon Wells 3.00 8.00
5 Bernie Williams 4.00 10.00
6 Luis Gonzalez 3.00 8.00
7 Kerry Wood 3.00 8.00
8 Eric Chavez 3.00 8.00
9 Shawn Green 3.00 8.00
10 Roy Oswalt 3.00 8.00
11 Nomar Garciaparra 6.00 15.00
12 Robin Yount 6.00 15.00
13 Troy Glaus 3.00 8.00
14 C.C. Sabathia 3.00 8.00
15 Alex Rodriguez 4.00 10.00
16 Mark Mulder 3.00 8.00
17 Will Clark 6.00 15.00
18 Alfonso Soriano 3.00 8.00
19 Andy Pettitte 4.00 10.00
20 Curt Schilling 3.00 8.00

2003 Leaf Slick Leather

STATED ODDS 1:21 HOBBY/RETAIL
1 Omar Vizquel .60 1.50
2 Roberto Alomar .60 1.50
3 Ivan Rodriguez .60 1.50
4 Greg Maddux 1.25 3.00
5 Scott Rolen .60 1.50
6 Todd Helton .60 1.50
7 Andruw Jones .40 1.00
8 Jim Edmonds .60 1.50
9 Barry Bonds 1.50 4.00
10 Eric Chavez .40 1.00
11 Ichiro Suzuki 1.25 3.00
12 Mike Mussina .60 1.50
13 John Olerud .40 1.00
14 Torii Hunter .40 1.00
15 Larry Walker .60 1.50

2004 Leaf

COMPLETE SET (301) 50.00 100.00
COMP.SET w/o SP's (200) 10.00 25.00
COMMON CARD (1-201) .12 .30
COMMON CARD (202-251) .40 1.00
COMMON CARD (252-301) .40 1.00
202-301 RANDOM INSERTS IN PACKS
CARD 42 DOES NOT EXIST
1 Darin Erstad .12 .30
2 Garret Anderson .12 .30
3 Jarrod Washburn .12 .30
4 Kevin Appier .12 .30
5 Tim Salmon .12 .30
6 Troy Glaus .12 .30
7 Troy Percival .12 .30
8 Jason Johnson .12 .30
9 Jay Gibbons .12 .30
10 Melvin Mora .12 .30
11 Sidney Ponson .12 .30
12 Tony Batista .12 .30
13 Derek Lowe .12 .30
14 Robert Person .12 .30
15 Manny Ramirez .30 .75
16 Nomar Garciaparra .20 .50
17 Pedro Martinez .20 .50
18 Jorge De La Rosa .12 .30
19 Bartolo Colon .12 .30
20 Carlos Lee .12 .30
21 Esteban Loaiza .12 .30
22 Frank Thomas .30 .75
23 Joe Crede .12 .30
24 Magglio Ordonez .20 .50
25 Ryan Ludwick .12 .30
26 Luis Garcia .12 .30
27 Brandon Phillips .12 .30
28 C.C Sabathia .20 .50
29 Jhonny Peralta .12 .30
30 Josh Bard .12 .30
31 Omar Vizquel .20 .50
32 Fernando Rodney .12 .30
33 Mike Maroth .12 .30
34 Bobby Higginson .12 .30
35 Omar Infante .12 .30
36 Dmitri Young .12 .30
37 Eric Munson .12 .30
38 Jeremy Bonderman .12 .30
39 Carlos Beltran .20 .50
40 Jeremy Affeldt .12 .30
41 Dee Brown .12 .30
43 Mike Sweeney .12 .30
44 Brent Abernathy .12 .30
45 Runelvys Hernandez .12 .30
46 A.J. Pierzynski .12 .30
47 Corey Koskie .12 .30
48 Cristian Guzman .12 .30
49 Jacque Jones .12 .30
50 Kenny Rogers .12 .30
51 J.C. Romero .12 .30
52 Torii Hunter .12 .30
53 Alfonso Soriano .20 .50
54 Bernie Williams .20 .50
55 David Wells .12 .30
56 Derek Jeter .75 2.00
57 Hideki Matsui .50 1.25
58 Jason Giambi .12 .30
59 Jorge Posada .20 .50
60 Jose Contreras .12 .30
61 Mike Mussina .20 .50
62 Nick Johnson .12 .30
63 Roger Clemens .40 1.00
64 Barry Zito .20 .50
65 Justin Duchscherer .12 .30
66 Eric Chavez .12 .30
67 Erubial Durazo .12 .30
68 Miguel Tejada .20 .50
69 Mark Mulder .12 .30
70 Terrence Long .12 .30
71 Tim Hudson .20 .50
72 Bret Boone .12 .30
73 Dan Wilson .12 .30
74 Edgar Martinez .20 .50
75 Freddy Garcia .12 .30
76 Rafael Soriano .12 .30
77 Ichiro Suzuki .40 1.00
78 Jamie Moyer .12 .30
79 John Olerud .12 .30
80 Kazuhiro Sasaki .12 .30
81 Aubrey Huff .12 .30
82 Carl Crawford .20 .50
83 Joe Kennedy .12 .30
84 Rocco Baldelli .12 .30
85 Toby Hall .12 .30
86 Alex Rodriguez .40 1.00
87 Kevin Mench .12 .30
88 Hank Blalock .12 .30
89 Juan Gonzalez .12 .30
90 Mark Teixeira .20 .50
91 Rafael Palmeiro .20 .50
92 Carlos Delgado .12 .30
93 Eric Hinske .12 .30
94 Josh Phelps .12 .30
95 Brian Bowles .12 .30
96 Roy Halladay .20 .50
97 Shannon Stewart .12 .30
98 Vernon Wells .12 .30
99 Curt Schilling .20 .50
100 Junior Spivey .12 .30
101 Luis Gonzalez .12 .30
102 Lyle Overbay .12 .30
103 Mark Grace .20 .50
104 Randy Johnson .30 .75
105 Shea Hillenbrand .12 .30
106 Andruw Jones .12 .30
107 Chipper Jones .30 .75
108 Gary Sheffield .12 .30
109 Greg Maddux .40 1.00
110 Javy Lopez .12 .30
111 John Smoltz .30 .75
112 Marcus Giles .12 .30
113 Rafael Furcal .12 .30
114 Corey Patterson .12 .30
115 Juan Cruz .12 .30
116 Kerry Wood .12 .30
117 Mark Prior .20 .50
118 Moises Alou .12 .30
119 Sammy Sosa .30 .75
120 Aaron Boone .12 .30
121 Adam Dunn .20 .50
122 Austin Kearns .12 .30
123 Barry Larkin .20 .50
124 Ken Griffey Jr. .60 1.50
125 Brian Reith .12 .30
126 Wily Mo Pena .12 .30
127 Jason Jennings .12 .30
128 Jay Payton .12 .30
129 Larry Walker .20 .50
130 Preston Wilson .12 .30
131 Todd Helton .20 .50
132 Dontrelle Willis .12 .30
133 Ivan Rodriguez .20 .50
134 Josh Beckett .12 .30
135 Juan Encarnacion .12 .30
136 Mike Lowell .12 .30
137 Craig Biggio .20 .50
138 Jeff Bagwell .20 .50
139 Jeff Kent .12 .30
140 Lance Berkman .20 .50
141 Richard Hidalgo .12 .30
142 Roy Oswalt .20 .50
143 Eric Gagne .12 .30
144 Fred McGriff .12 .30
145 Hideo Nomo .30 .75
146 Kazuhisa Ishii .12 .30
147 Kevin Brown .12 .30
148 Paul Lo Duca .12 .30
149 Shawn Green .12 .30
150 Ben Sheets .12 .30
151 Geoff Jenkins .12 .30
152 Rey Sanchez .12 .30
153 Richie Sexson .12 .30
154 Wes Helms .12 .30
155 Shane Nance .12 .30
156 Fernando Tatis .12 .30
157 Javier Vazquez .12 .30
158 Jose Vidro .12 .30
159 Orlando Cabrera .12 .30
160 Henry Mateo .12 .30
161 Vladimir Guerrero .20 .50
162 Zach Day .12 .30
163 Edwin Almonte .12 .30
164 Al Leiter .12 .30
165 Cliff Floyd .12 .30
166 Jae Weong Seo .12 .30
167 Mike Piazza .30 .75
168 Roberto Alomar .20 .50
169 Tom Glavine .20 .50
170 Bobby Abreu .12 .30
171 Brandon Duckworth .12 .30
172 Jim Thome .20 .50
173 Kevin Millwood .12 .30
174 Pat Burrell .12 .30
175 Aramis Ramirez .12 .30
176 Jack Wilson .12 .30
177 Brian Giles .12 .30
178 Jason Kendall .12 .30
179 Kenny Lofton .12 .30
180 Kip Wells .12 .30
181 Kris Benson .12 .30
182 Albert Pujols .40 1.00
183 J.D. Drew .12 .30
184 Jim Edmonds .20 .50
185 Matt Morris .12 .30
186 Scott Rolen .20 .50
187 Woody Williams .12 .30
188 Cliff Bartosh .12 .30
189 Brian Lawrence .12 .30
190 Ryan Klesko .12 .30
191 Sean Burroughs .12 .30
192 Xavier Nady .12 .30
193 Dennis Tankersley .12 .30
194 Donaldo Mendez .12 .30
195 Barry Bonds .50 1.25
196 Benito Santiago .12 .30
197 Edgardo Alfonzo .12 .30
198 Cody Ransom .12 .30
199 Jason Schmidt .12 .30
200 Rich Aurilia .12 .30
201 Ken Harvey .12 .30
202 Adam Loewen ROO .40 1.00
203 Alfredo Gonzalez ROO .40 1.00
204 Arnie Munoz ROO .40 1.00
205 Andrew Brown ROO .40 1.00
206 Josh Hall ROO .40 1.00
207 Josh Stewart PROS .40 1.00
208 Clint Barmes PROS .60 1.50
209 Brandon Webb PROS .40 1.00
210 Chien-Ming Wang PROS 1.50 4.00
211 Edgar Gonzalez PROS .40 1.00
212 Alejandro Machado PROS .40 1.00
213 Jeremy Griffiths PROS .40 1.00
214 Craig Brazell PROS .40 1.00
215 Daniel Cabrera PROS .40 1.00
216 Fernando Cabrera PROS .40 1.00
217 Termel Sledge PROS .40 1.00
218 Rob Hammock PROS .40 1.00
219 Francisco Rosario PROS .40 1.00
220 Francisco Cruceta PROS .40 1.00
221 Rett Johnson PROS .40 1.00
222 Guillermo Quiroz PROS .40 1.00
223 Hong-Chih Kuo PROS .40 1.00
224 Ian Ferguson PROS .40 1.00
225 Tim Olson PROS .40 1.00
226 Todd Wellemeyer PROS .40 1.00
227 Rich Fischer PROS .40 1.00
228 Phil Seibel PROS .40 1.00
229 Joe Valentine PROS .40 1.00
230 Matt Kata PROS .40 1.00
231 Michael Hessman PROS .40 1.00
232 Michel Hernandez PROS .40 1.00
233 Doug Waechter PROS .40 1.00
234 Prentice Redman PROS .40 1.00
235 Nook Logan PROS .40 1.00
236 Oscar Villarreal PROS .40 1.00
237 Pete LaForest PROS .40 1.00
238 Matt Bruback PROS .40 1.00
239 Josh Willingham PROS .60 1.50
240 Greg Aquino PROS .40 1.00
241 Lew Ford PROS .40 1.00
242 Jeff Duncan PROS .40 1.00
243 Chris Waters PROS .40 1.00
244 Miguel Ojeda PROS .40 1.00
245 Rosman Garcia PROS .40 1.00
246 Felix Sanchez PROS .40 1.00
247 Jon Leicester PROS .40 1.00
248 Roger Deago PROS .40 1.00
249 Mike Ryan PROS .40 1.00
250 Chris Capuano PROS .40 1.00
251 Matt White PROS .40 1.00
252 Bernie Williams PTT .60 1.50
253 Mark Grace PTT .60 1.50
254 Chipper Jones PTT 1.00 2.50
255 Greg Maddux PTT 1.25 3.00
256 Sammy Sosa PTT 1.00 2.50
257 Mike Mussina PTT .60 1.50
258 Tim Salmon PTT .40 1.00
259 Barry Larkin PTT .60 1.50
260 Randy Johnson PTT 1.00 2.50
261 Jeff Bagwell PTT .60 1.50
262 Roberto Alomar PTT .60 1.50
263 Tom Glavine PTT .60 1.50
264 Roger Clemens PTT 1.25 3.00
265 Barry Bonds PTT 1.50 4.00
266 Ivan Rodriguez PTT .60 1.50
267 Pedro Martinez PTT .60 1.50
268 Ken Griffey Jr. PTT 2.00 5.00
269 Jim Thome PTT .60 1.50
270 Frank Thomas PTT 1.00 2.50
271 Mike Piazza PTT 1.00 2.50
272 Troy Glaus TC .40 1.00
273 Melvin Mora TC .40 1.00
274 Nomar Garciaparra TC .60 1.50
275 Magglio Ordonez TC .60 1.50
276 Omar Vizquel TC .60 1.50
277 Dmitri Young TC .40 1.00
278 Mike Sweeney TC .40 1.00
279 Torii Hunter TC .40 1.00
280 Derek Jeter TC 2.50 6.00
281 Barry Zito TC .60 1.50
282 Ichiro Suzuki TC 1.25 3.00
283 Rocco Baldelli TC .40 1.00
284 Alex Rodriguez TC 1.25 3.00
285 Carlos Delgado TC .40 1.00
286 Randy Johnson TC 1.00 2.50
287 Greg Maddux TC 1.25 3.00
288 Sammy Sosa TC 1.00 2.50
289 Ken Griffey Jr. TC 2.00 5.00
290 Todd Helton TC .60 1.50
291 Ivan Rodriguez TC .60 1.50
292 Jeff Bagwell TC .60 1.50
293 Hideo Nomo TC 1.00 2.50
294 Richie Sexson TC .40 1.00
295 Vladimir Guerrero TC .60 1.50
296 Mike Piazza TC 1.00 2.50
297 Jim Thome TC .60 1.50
298 Jason Kendall TC .40 1.00
299 Albert Pujols TC 1.25 3.00
300 Ryan Klesko TC .40 1.00
301 Barry Bonds TC 1.50 4.00

2004 Leaf Second Edition

*2ND ED 1-201: .4X TO 1X BASIC
*2ND ED 202-301: .4X TO 1X BASIC
ISSUED IN SECOND EDITION PACKS
CARD 42 DOES NOT EXIST

2004 Leaf Autographs

RANDOM INSERTS IN PACKS
SP INFO PROVIDED BY DONRUSS
SP'S ARE NOT SERIAL-NUMBERED
14 Robert Person 4.00 10.00
18 Jorge De La Rosa 4.00 10.00
25 Ryan Ludwick 12.50 30.00
26 Luis Garcia 4.00 10.00
29 Jhonny Peralta 6.00 15.00
30 Josh Bard 4.00 10.00
32 Fernando Rodney 4.00 10.00
33 Mike Maroth 4.00 10.00
35 Omar Infante 4.00 10.00
41 Dee Brown 4.00 10.00
44 Brent Abernathy SP 6.00 15.00
51 J.C. Romero 4.00 10.00
65 Justin Duchscherer 6.00 15.00
70 Terrence Long SP 6.00 15.00
76 Rafael Soriano 6.00 15.00
85 Toby Hall SP 6.00 15.00
87 Kevin Mench 6.00 15.00
95 Brian Bowles 4.00 10.00
115 Juan Cruz 4.00 10.00
125 Brian Reith 4.00 10.00
126 Wily Mo Pena 6.00 15.00
127 Jason Jennings 4.00 10.00
155 Shane Nance 4.00 10.00
160 Henry Mateo SP 6.00 15.00
163 Edwin Almonte 4.00 10.00
171 Brandon Duckworth 4.00 10.00
176 Jack Wilson 6.00 15.00
180 Kip Wells 4.00 10.00
188 Cliff Bartosh 4.00 10.00
189 Brian Lawrence 4.00 10.00
193 Dennis Tankersley 4.00 10.00
194 Donaldo Mendez 4.00 10.00
198 Cody Ransom SP 6.00 15.00
247 Jon Leicester PROS SP 6.00 15.00

2004 Leaf Autographs Second Edition

*2ND ED: .4X TO 1X BASIC
*2ND ED: .4X TO 1X BASIC SP
RANDOM INSERTS IN PACKS
25 Ryan Ludwick 10.00 25.00
37 Eric Munson 4.00 10.00
150 Ben Sheets 10.00 25.00

2004 Leaf Press Proofs Blue

*BLUE 1-201: 4X TO 10X BASIC
*BLUE 202-251: 1.25X TO 3X BASIC
*BLUE 252-301: 1.25X TO 3X BASIC
RANDOM INSERTS IN PACKS
STATED PRINT RUN 100 SERIAL #'d SETS

2004 Leaf Press Proofs Red

*RED 1-201: 2X TO 5X BASIC
*RED 202-251: .6X TO 1.5X BASIC
*RED 252-301: .6X TO 1.5X BASIC
STATED ODDS 1:8

2004 Leaf Press Proofs Silver

*SILVER 1-201: 6X TO 15X BASIC
*SILVER 202-251: 2X TO 5X BASIC
*SILVER 252-301: 2X TO 5X BASIC
RANDOM INSERTS IN PACKS
STATED PRINT RUN 50 SERIAL #'d SETS

2004 Leaf Clean Up Crew

STATED ODDS 1:49
*2ND ED: .4X TO 1X BASIC
2ND ED.ODDS 1:72 2ND ED.PACKS
1 Sosa 1.00 2.50
Alou
Choi
2 Giambi 1.50 4.00
Soriano
Matsui
3 V.Wells .40 1.00
Delgado
Phelps
4 A.Rod 1.25 3.00
J.Gonz
Blalock
5 Sheffield 1.00 2.50
Chipper
Andruw
6 Griffey Jr. 2.00 5.00
Kearns
Boone
7 Pujols 1.25 3.00
Edmonds
Rolen
8 Bagwell .60 1.50
Berkman
Kent
9 Helton .60 1.50
P.Wilson
Walker
10 Tejada .60 1.50
Durazo
Chavez

2004 Leaf Clean Up Crew Materials

RANDOM INSERTS IN PACKS
STATED PRINT RUN 50 SERIAL #'d SETS
2ND ED.RANDOM IN 2ND ED.PACKS
2ND ED.PRINT RUNS 5 SERIAL #'d SETS
NO 2ND ED.PRICING DUE TO SCARCITY
1 Sosa/Alou/Choi 15.00 40.00
2 Giambi/Soriano/Matsui 30.00 60.00
3 V.Wells/Delgado/Phelps 10.00 25.00
4 A.Rod/J.Gonz/Blalock 15.00 40.00
5 Sheffield/Chipper/Andruw 15.00 40.00
6 Griffey Jr./Kearns/Boone 15.00 40.00
7 Pujols/Edmonds/Rolen 20.00 50.00
8 Bagwell/Berkman/Kent 15.00 40.00
9 Helton/P.Wilson/Walker 15.00 40.00
10 Tejada/Durazo/Chavez 10.00 25.00

2004 Leaf Cornerstones

STATED ODDS 1:78
*2ND ED: .4X TO 1X BASIC
2ND ED.ODDS 1:90 2ND ED.PACKS
1 A.Rodriguez 2.00 5.00
H.Blalock
2 K.Wood 1.00 2.50
M.Prior
3 R.Clemens 2.00 5.00
A.Soriano
4 N.Garciaparra 1.50 4.00
M.Ramirez
5 A.Kearns 1.00 2.50
A.Dunn
6 T.Glavine 1.50 4.00
M.Piazza
7 A.Jones 1.50 4.00
C.Jones
8 A.Pujols 2.00 5.00
S.Rolen
9 C.Schilling 1.50 4.00
R.Johnson
10 H.Nomo 1.50 4.00
K.Ishii

2004 Leaf Cornerstones Materials

RANDOM INSERTS IN PACKS
STATED PRINT RUN 50 SERIAL #'d SETS
2ND ED.RANDOM IN 2ND ED.PACKS
2ND ED.PRINT RUN 10 SERIAL #'d SETS
NO 2ND ED.PRICING DUE TO SCARCITY
1 A.Rod Bat/Blalock Bat 6.00 15.00
2 K.Wood Jsy/Prior Jsy 3.00 8.00
3 Clemens Jsy/Soriano Bat 6.00 15.00
4 Nomar Bat/Manny Jsy 5.00 12.00
5 Kearns Bat/Dunn Jsy 3.00 8.00
6 Glavine Jsy/Piazza Bat 5.00 12.00
7 Andruw Bat/Chipper Jsy 5.00 12.00
8 Pujols Bat/Rolen Bat 6.00 15.00
9 Schilling Jsy/R.Johnson Jsy 5.00 12.00
10 Nomo Jsy/Ishii Jsy 5.00 12.00

2004 Leaf Exhibits 1947-66 Made by Donruss-Playoff Print

STATED PRINT RUN 66 SERIAL #'d SETS
*1921 ACTIVE: .75X TO 2X
*1921 RETIRED: .75X TO 2X

1921 PRINT RUN 21 #'d SETS
*1921 AML ACTIVE: .75X TO 2X
*1921 AML RETIRED: .75X TO 2X
1921 AML PRINT RUN 21 #'d SETS
*1925 L ACTIVE: .75X TO 2X
*1925 L RETIRED: .75X TO 2X
1925 L PRINT RUN 25 #'d SETS
*1925 R ACTIVE: .75X TO 2X
*1925 R RETIRED: .75X TO 2X
1925 R PRINT RUN25 #'d SETS
*1926 B ACTIVE: .75X TO 2X
*1926 B RETIRED: .75X TO 2X
1926 B PRINT RUN 26 #'d SETS
*1926 BDP ACTIVE: .75X TO 2X
*1926 BDP RETIRED: .75X TO 2X
1926 BDP PRINT RUN 26 #'d SETS
*1926 U ACTIVE: .75X TO 2X
*1926 U RETIRED: .75X TO 2X
1926 U PRINT RUN 26 #'d SETS
*1926 UDP ACTIVE: .75X TO 2X
*1926 UDP RETIRED: .75X TO 2X
1926 UDP PRINT RUN 26 #'d SETS
*1927 ACTIVE: .75X TO 2X
*1927 RETIRED: .75X TO 2X
1927 PRINT RUN 27 #'d SETS
*1927 DP ACTIVE: .75X TO 2X
*1927 DP RETIRED: .75X TO 2X
1927 DP PRINT RUN 27 #'d SETS
*1939-46 BOLL: .5X TO 1.2X
1939-46 BOLL PRINT RUN 46 #'d SETS
*1939-46 BOLR: .5X TO 1.2X
1939-46 BOLR PRINT RUN 46 #'d SETS
*1939-46 BWL: .5X TO 1.2X
1939-46 BWL PRINT RUN 46 #'d SETS
*1939-46 BWR: .5X TO 1.2X
1939-46 BWR PRINT RUN 46 #'d SETS
*1939-46 CL: .5X TO 1.2X
1939-46 CL PRINT RUN 46 #'d SETS
*1939-46 CR: .5X TO 1.2X
1939-46 CR PRINT RUN 46 #'d SETS
*1939-46 CYL: .5X TO 1.2X
1939-46 CYL PRINT RUN 46 #'d SETS
*1939-46 CYR: .5X TO 1.2X
1939-46 CYR PRINT RUN 46 #'d SETS
*1939-46 SL: .5X TO 1.2X
1939-46 SL PRINT RUN 46 #'d SETS
*1939-46 SR: .5X TO 1.2X
1939-46 SR PRINT RUN 46 #'d SETS
*1939-46 SYL: .5X TO 1.2X
1939-46 SYL PRINT RUN 46 #'d SETS
*1939-46 SYR: .5X TO 1.2X
1939-46 SYR PRINT RUN 46 #'d SETS
*1939-46 TYL: .5X TO 1.2X
1939-46 TYL PRINT RUN 46 #'d SETS
*1939-46 TYR: .5X TO 1.2X
1939-46 TYR PRINT RUN 46 #'d SETS
*1939-46 VBWL: .5X TO 1.2X
1939-46 VBWL PRINT RUN 46 #'d SETS
*1939-46 VBWR: .5X TO 1.2X
1939-46 VBWR PRINT RUN 46 #'d SETS
*1939-46 VTYL: .5X TO 1.2X
1939-46 VTYL PRINT RUN 46 #'d SETS
*1939-46 VTYR: .5X TO-1.2X
1939-46 VTYR PRINT RUN 46 #'d SETS
*1939-46 YTL: .5X TO 1.2X
1939-46 YTL PRINT RUN 46 #'d SETS
*1939-46 YTR: .5X TO 1.2X
1939-46 YTR PRINT RUN 46 #'d SETS
*1947-66 DP SIG: .4X TO 1X
1947-66 DP SIG PRINT RUN 66 #'d SETS
*1947-66 MPRI: .4X TO 1X
1947-66 MPRI PRINT RUN 66 #'d SETS
*1947-66 MSIG: .4X TO 1X
1947-66 MSIG PRINT RUN 66 #'d SETS
*1947-66 PDPPRI: .4X TO 1X
1947-66 PDPPRI PRINT RUN 66 #'d SETS
*1947-66 PDPSIG: .4X TO 1X
1947-66 PDPSIG PRINT RUN 66 #'d SETS
*1947-66 PPRI: .4X TO 1X
1947-66 PPRI PRINT RUN 66 #'d SETS
*1947-66 PSIG: .4X TO 1X
1947-66 PSIG PRINT RUN 66 #'d SETS
*1962-63 NSNL: .4X TO 1X
1962-63 NSNL PRINT RUN 63 #'d SETS
*1962-63 NSNR: .4X TO 1X
1962-63 NSNR PRINT RUN 63 #'d SETS
*1962-63 SBNL: .4X TO 1X
1962-63 SBNL PRINT RUN 63 #'d SETS
*1962-63 SBNR: .4X TO 1X
1962-63 SBNR PRINT RUN 63 #'d SETS
*1962-63 SRNL: .4X TO 1X
1962-63 SRNL PRINT RUN 63 #'d SETS
*1962-63 SRNR: .4X TO 1X
1962-63 SRNR PRINT RUN 63 #'d SETS
*ALL 2ND ED: .4X TO 1X
SEE CARD BACKS FOR ABBREV.LEGEND
1 Adam Dunn 1.00 2.50
2 Albert Pujols 2.00 5.00
3 Alex Rodriguez 2.00 5.00
4 Alfonso Soriano 1.00 2.50
5 Andruw Jones .60 1.50
6 Barry Bonds 2.50 6.00
7 Barry Larkin 1.00 2.50
8 Barry Zito 1.00 2.50
9 Cal Ripken 5.00 12.00
10 Chipper Jones 1.50 4.00
11 Dale Murphy 1.50 4.00
12 Derek Jeter 4.00 10.00
13 Don Mattingly 3.00 8.00
14 Ernie Banks 1.50 4.00
15 Frank Thomas 1.50 4.00
16 George Brett 3.00 8.00
17 Greg Maddux 2.00 5.00
18 Hank Blalock .60 1.50
19 Hideo Nomo 1.50 4.00
20 Ichiro Suzuki 2.00 5.00
21 Jason Giambi .60 1.50
22 Jim Thome 1.00 2.50
23 Juan Gonzalez .60 1.50
24 Ken Griffey Jr. 3.00 8.00
25 Kirby Puckett 1.50 4.00
26 Mark Prior 1.00 2.50
27 Mike Mussina 1.00 2.50
28 Mike Piazza 1.50 4.00
29 Mike Schmidt 2.50 6.00
30 Nolan Ryan Angels 5.00 12.00
31 Nolan Ryan Astros 5.00 12.00
32 Nolan Ryan Rangers 5.00 12.00
33 Nomar Garciaparra 1.00 2.50
34 Ozzie Smith 2.00 5.00
35 Pedro Martinez 1.00 2.50
36 Randy Johnson 1.50 4.00
37 Reggie Jackson Yanks 1.00 2.50
38 Reggie Jackson A's 1.00 2.50
39 Rickey Henderson 1.50 4.00
40 Roberto Alomar 1.00 2.50
41 Roberto Clemente 4.00 10.00
42 Rod Carew 1.00 2.50
43 Roger Clemens 2.00 5.00
44 Sammy Sosa 1.50 4.00
45 Stan Musial 2.50 6.00
46 Tom Glavine 1.00 2.50
47 Tom Seaver 1.00 2.50
48 Tony Gwynn 1.50 4.00
49 Vladimir Guerrero 1.00 2.50
50 Yogi Berra 1.50 4.00

2004 Leaf Gamers

STATED ODDS 1:19
*QUANTUM: 1X TO 2.5X BASIC
QUANTUM RANDOM INSERTS IN PACKS
QUANTUM PRINT RUN 100 #'d SETS
*2ND ED: .4X TO 1X BASIC
2ND ED.ODDS 1:22 2ND ED.PACKS
2ND ED.QUAN.RANDOM IN 2ND.ED PACKS
2ND ED.QUANTUM PRINT RUN 10 #'d SETS
NO 2ND ED.QUAN.PRICE DUE TO SCARCITY
1 Albert Pujols 1.25 3.00
2 Alex Rodriguez 1.25 3.00
3 Alfonso Soriano .60 1.50
4 Barry Bonds 1.50 4.00
5 Barry Zito .60 1.50
6 Chipper Jones 1.00 2.50
7 Derek Jeter 2.50 6.00
8 Greg Maddux 1.25 3.00
9 Ichiro Suzuki 1.25 3.00
10 Jason Giambi .40 1.00
11 Jeff Bagwell .60 1.50
12 Ken Griffey Jr. 2.00 5.00
13 Manny Ramirez 1.00 2.50
14 Mark Prior .60 1.50
15 Mike Piazza 1.00 2.50
16 Nomar Garciaparra .60 1.50
17 Pedro Martinez .60 1.50
18 Randy Johnson 1.00 2.50
19 Roger Clemens 1.25 3.00
20 Sammy Sosa 1.00 2.50

2004 Leaf Gold Rookies

STATED ODDS 1:23
MIRROR RANDOM INSERTS IN PACKS
MIRROR PRINT RUN 25 SERIAL #'d SETS
NO MIRROR PRICING DUE TO SCARCITY
*2ND ED: .4X TO 1X BASIC
2ND ED.ODDS 1:24 2ND ED.PACKS
2ND ED.MIRR.RANDOM IN 2ND ED.PACKS
2ND ED.MIRROR PRINT RUN 5 #'d SETS
NO 2ND ED.MIRR.PRICE DUE TO SCARCITY
1 Adam Loewen .40 1.00
2 Rickie Weeks .40 1.00
3 Khalil Greene .60 1.50
4 Chad Tracy .40 1.00
5 Alexis Rios .40 1.00
6 Craig Brazell .40 1.00
7 Clint Barmes .60 1.50
8 Pete LaForest .40 1.00
9 Alfredo Gonzalez .40 1.00
10 Arnie Munoz .40 1.00

2004 Leaf Home/Away

STATED ODDS 1:35
*2ND ED: .4X TO 1X BASIC
2ND ED.ODDS 1:35 2ND ED.PACKS
1A Greg Maddux A 2.00 5.00
1H Greg Maddux H 2.00 5.00
2A Sammy Sosa A 1.50 4.00
2H Sammy Sosa H 1.50 4.00
3A Alex Rodriguez A 2.00 5.00
3H Alex Rodriguez H 2.00 5.00
4A Albert Pujols A 2.00 5.00
4H Albert Pujols H 2.00 5.00
5A Jason Giambi A .60 1.50
5H Jason Giambi H .60 1.50
6A Chipper Jones A 1.50 4.00
6H Chipper Jones H 1.50 4.00
7A Vladimir Guerrero A 1.00 2.50
7H Vladimir Guerrero H 1.00 2.50
8A Mike Piazza A 1.50 4.00
8H Mike Piazza H 1.50 4.00
9A Nomar Garciaparra A 1.00 2.50
9H Nomar Garciaparra H 1.00 2.50
10A Austin Kearns A .60 1.50
10H Austin Kearns H .60 1.50

2004 Leaf Home/Away Jerseys

STATED ODDS 1:119
*PRIME: 1.25X TO 3X BASIC
PRIME RANDOM INSERTS IN PACKS
PRIME PRINT RUN 50 #'d SETS
*2ND ED: .4X TO 1X BASIC
2ND ED.RANDOM IN 2ND.ED PACKS
2ND ED.PRIME RANDOM IN 2ND ED.PACKS
2ND ED.PRIME PRINT RUN 5 #'d SETS
NO 2ND ED.PRIME PRICE DUE SCARCITY
1A Greg Maddux A 4.00 10.00
1H Greg Maddux H 4.00 10.00
2A Sammy Sosa A 3.00 8.00
2H Sammy Sosa H 3.00 8.00
3A Alex Rodriguez A 4.00 10.00
3H Alex Rodriguez H 4.00 10.00
4A Albert Pujols A 6.00 15.00
4H Albert Pujols H 6.00 15.00
5A Jason Giambi A 2.00 5.00
5H Jason Giambi H 2.00 5.00
6A Chipper Jones A 3.00 8.00
6H Chipper Jones H 3.00 8.00
7A Vladimir Guerrero A 3.00 8.00
7H Vladimir Guerrero H 3.00 8.00
8A Mike Piazza A 4.00 10.00
8H Mike Piazza H 4.00 10.00
9A Nomar Garciaparra A 4.00 10.00
9H Nomar Garciaparra H 4.00 10.00
10A Austin Kearns A 2.00 5.00
10H Austin Kearns H 2.00 5.00

2004 Leaf Limited Previews

STATED PRINT RUN 999 SERIAL #'d SETS
*GOLD: 1.25X TO 3X BASIC
GOLD PRINT RUN 50 SERIAL #'d SETS
*SILVER: .75X TO 2X BASIC
SILVER PRINT RUN 100 SERIAL #'d SETS
RANDOM INSERTS IN PACKS
1 Derek Jeter 3.00 8.00
2 Barry Zito .75 2.00
3 Ichiro Suzuki 1.50 4.00
4 Pedro Martinez .75 2.00
5 Alfonso Soriano .75 2.00
6 Alex Rodriguez 1.50 4.00
7 Greg Maddux 1.50 4.00
8 Mike Piazza 1.25 3.00
9 Mark Prior .75 2.00
10 Albert Pujols 1.50 4.00
11 Sammy Sosa 1.25 3.00
12 Ken Griffey Jr. 2.50 6.00
13 Nomar Garciaparra .75 2.00
14 Randy Johnson 1.25 3.00
15 Jason Giambi .50 1.25
16 Barry Bonds 2.00 5.00
17 Manny Ramirez 1.25 3.00
18 Chipper Jones 1.25 3.00
19 Jeff Bagwell .75 2.00
20 Roger Clemens 1.50 4.00

2004 Leaf MVP Winners

STATED ODDS 1:11
*GOLD: .6X TO 1.5X BASIC
GOLD RANDOM INSERTS IN PACKS
GOLD PRINT RUN 500 SERIAL #'d SETS
*2ND ED: .4X TO 1X BASIC
2ND ED.ODDS 1:12 2ND ED.PACKS
2ND ED.GOLD RANDOM IN 2ND ED.PACKS
2ND ED.GOLD PRINT RUN 25 #'d SETS
NO 2ND ED.GOLD PRICE DUE TO SCARCITY
1 Stan Musial 1.50 4.00
2 Ernie Banks 1.00 2.50
3 Roberto Clemente 2.50 6.00
4 George Brett 2.00 5.00
5 Mike Schmidt 1.50 4.00
6 Cal Ripken 83 3.00 8.00
7 Dale Murphy 1.00 2.50
8 Ryne Sandberg 2.00 5.00
9 Don Mattingly 2.00 5.00
10 Roger Clemens 1.25 3.00
11 Rickey Henderson 1.00 2.50
12 Cal Ripken 91 3.00 8.00
13 Barry Bonds 92 1.50 4.00
14 Barry Bonds 93 1.50 4.00
15 Frank Thomas 1.00 2.50
16 Ken Griffey Jr. 2.00 5.00
17 Sammy Sosa 1.00 2.50
18 Chipper Jones 1.00 2.50
19 Jason Giambi .40 1.00
20 Ichiro Suzuki 1.25 3.00

2004 Leaf Picture Perfect

STATED ODDS 1:37
*2ND ED: .4X TO 1X BASIC
2ND ED.ODDS 1:45 2ND ED.PACKS
1 Albert Pujols 2.00 5.00
2 Alex Rodriguez 2.00 5.00
3 Alfonso Soriano 1.00 2.50
4 Austin Kearns .60 1.50
5 Carlos Delgado .60 1.50
6 Chipper Jones 1.50 4.00
7 Hank Blalock .60 1.50
8 Jason Giambi .60 1.50
9 Jeff Bagwell 1.00 2.50
10 Jim Thome 1.00 2.50
11 Manny Ramirez 1.50 4.00
12 Mike Piazza 1.50 4.00
13 Nomar Garciaparra 1.00 2.50
14 Sammy Sosa 1.50 4.00
15 Todd Helton 1.00 2.50

2004 Leaf Picture Perfect Bats

STATED ODDS 1:437
*2ND ED: .4X TO 1X BASIC
2ND ED.RANDOM IN 2ND ED.PACKS
1 Albert Pujols 6.00 15.00
2 Alex Rodriguez 4.00 10.00
3 Alfonso Soriano 2.00 5.00
4 Austin Kearns 2.00 5.00
5 Carlos Delgado 2.00 5.00
6 Chipper Jones 3.00 8.00
7 Hank Blalock 2.00 5.00
8 Jason Giambi 2.00 5.00
9 Jeff Bagwell 3.00 8.00
10 Jim Thome 3.00 8.00
11 Manny Ramirez 3.00 8.00
12 Mike Piazza 4.00 10.00
13 Nomar Garciaparra 4.00 10.00
14 Sammy Sosa 3.00 8.00
15 Todd Helton 3.00 8.00

2004 Leaf Players Collection Jersey Green

*LEAF GREEN: .4X TO 1X PRESTIGE
*LEAF PLAT: 1X TO 2.5X PRESTIGE
PLATINUM PRINT RUN 25 SERIAL #'d SETS
RANDOM INSERTS IN PACKS

2004 Leaf Recollection Autographs

RANDOM INSERTS IN PACKS
PRINT RUNS B/WN 1-31 COPIES PER
NO PRICING ON QTY OF 25 OR LESS
ALL CARDS ARE 1990 LEAF BUYBACKS
3 Jesse Barfield 90/29 12.50 30.00
15 Charlie Hough 90/31 8.00 20.00

2004 Leaf Shirt Off My Back

STATED ODDS 1:47
*2ND ED: .4X TO 1X BASIC
2ND ED.RANDOM IN 2ND ED.PACKS
1 Shawn Green 2.00 5.00
2 Andruw Jones 3.00 8.00
3 Ivan Rodriguez 3.00 8.00
4 Hideo Nomo 3.00 8.00
5 Don Mattingly 6.00 15.00
6 Mark Prior 3.00 8.00
7 Alfonso Soriano 2.00 5.00
8 Richie Sexson 2.00 5.00
9 Vernon Wells 2.00 5.00
10 Nomar Garciaparra 4.00 10.00
11 Jason Giambi 2.00 5.00
12 Austin Kearns 2.00 5.00
13 Chipper Jones 3.00 8.00
14 Rickey Henderson 3.00 8.00
15 Alex Rodriguez 4.00 10.00
16 Garret Anderson 2.00 5.00
17 Vladimir Guerrero 3.00 8.00
18 Sammy Sosa 3.00 8.00
19 Mike Piazza 4.00 10.00
20 David Wells 2.00 5.00
21 Scott Rolen 3.00 8.00
22 Adam Dunn 2.00 5.00
23 Carlos Delgado 2.00 5.00
24 Greg Maddux 4.00 10.00
25 Hank Blalock 2.00 5.00

2004 Leaf Shirt Off My Back Jersey Number Patch

RANDOM INSERTS IN PACKS
STATED PRINT RUN 50 SERIAL #'d SETS
BLALOCK PRINT RUN 32 SERIAL #'d CARDS
SOSA PRINT RUN 42 SERIAL #'d CARDS
2ND ED.RANDOM IN 2ND.ED PACKS
2ND ED.PRINT RUN SERIAL 5 #'d SETS
NO 2ND ED.PRICING DUE TO SCARCITY
1 Shawn Green 6.00 15.00
2 Andruw Jones 10.00 25.00
3 Ivan Rodriguez 10.00 25.00
4 Hideo Nomo 10.00 25.00
5 Don Mattingly 15.00 40.00
6 Mark Prior 10.00 25.00
7 Alfonso Soriano 6.00 15.00
8 Richie Sexson 6.00 15.00
9 Vernon Wells 6.00 15.00
10 Nomar Garciaparra 12.50 30.00
11 Jason Giambi 6.00 15.00
12 Austin Kearns 6.00 15.00
13 Chipper Jones 10.00 25.00
14 Rickey Henderson 10.00 25.00
15 Alex Rodriguez 12.50 30.00
16 Garret Anderson 6.00 15.00
17 Vladimir Guerrero 10.00 25.00
18 Sammy Sosa/42 10.00 25.00
19 Mike Piazza 12.50 30.00
20 David Wells 6.00 15.00
21 Scott Rolen 10.00 25.00
22 Adam Dunn 6.00 15.00
23 Carlos Delgado 6.00 15.00
24 Greg Maddux 12.50 30.00
25 Hank Blalock/32 6.00 15.00

2004 Leaf Shirt Off My Back Team Logo Patch

RANDOM INSERTS IN PACKS
PRINT RUNS B/WN 7-75 COPIES PER
NO PRICING ON QTY OF 25 OR LESS
2ND ED.PRINT RUN 5 SERIAL #'d SETS
NO 2ND ED.PRICING DUE TO SCARCITY
1 Shawn Green/41 6.00 15.00
2 Andruw Jones/75 10.00 25.00
3 Ivan Rodriguez/75 10.00 25.00
4 Hideo Nomo/74 12.50 30.00
6 Mark Prior/46 10.00 25.00
7 Alfonso Soriano/28 8.00 20.00
8 Richie Sexson/38 6.00 15.00
9 Vernon Wells/74 6.00 15.00
10 Nomar Garciaparra/75 12.50 30.00
11 Jason Giambi/26 8.00 20.00
12 Austin Kearns/32 8.00 20.00
13 Chipper Jones/75 10.00 25.00
14 Rickey Henderson/40 10.00 25.00
15 Alex Rodriguez/75 12.50 30.00
16 Garret Anderson/71 6.00 15.00
17 Vladimir Guerrero/55 10.00 25.00
18 Sammy Sosa/39 10.00 25.00
19 Mike Piazza/75 12.50 30.00
20 David Wells/74 6.00 15.00
21 Scott Rolen/29 12.50 30.00
22 Adam Dunn/32 8.00 20.00
23 Carlos Delgado/56 6.00 15.00
24 Greg Maddux/75 12.50 30.00
25 Hank Blalock/62 6.00 15.00

2004 Leaf Sunday Dress

STATED ODDS 1:17
*2ND ED: .4X TO 1X BASIC
2ND ED.ODDS 1:20 2ND ED.PACKS
1 Frank Thomas 1.00 2.50
2 Barry Zito .60 1.50
3 Mike Piazza 1.00 2.50
4 Mark Prior .60 1.50
5 Jeff Bagwell .60 1.50
6 Roy Oswalt .60 1.50
7 Todd Helton .60 1.50
8 Magglio Ordonez .60 1.50
9 Alex Rodriguez 1.25 3.00
10 Manny Ramirez 1.00 2.50

2004 Leaf Sunday Dress Jerseys

STATED ODDS 1:119
*PRIME: .75X TO 2X BASIC
PRIME RANDOM INSERTS IN PACKS
PRIME PRINT RUN 100 SERIAL #'d SETS
*2ND ED: .4X TO 1X BASIC
2ND ED.RANDOM IN 2ND ED.PACKS
2ND ED.PRIME RANDOM IN 2ND ED.PACKS
2ND ED.PRIME PRINT RUN 15 #'d SETS
NO 2ND ED.PRIME PRICE DUE SCARCITY
1 Frank Thomas 3.00 8.00
2 Barry Zito 2.00 5.00
3 Mike Piazza 4.00 10.00
4 Mark Prior 3.00 8.00
5 Jeff Bagwell 3.00 8.00
6 Roy Oswalt 2.00 5.00
7 Todd Helton 3.00 8.00
8 Magglio Ordonez 2.00 5.00
9 Alex Rodriguez 4.00 10.00
10 Manny Ramirez 3.00 8.00

2005 Leaf

COMPLETE SET (300) 50.00 120.00
COMP.SETw/o SP's (200) 10.00 25.00
COMMON CARD (1-200) .10 .30
COMMON CARD (201-250) .60 1.50
201-250 STATED ODDS 1:3
COMMON CARD (251-300) .30 .75
251-270 STATED ODDS 1:6
271-300 STATED ODDS 1:4
1 Bartolo Colon .12 .30
2 Casey Kotchman .12 .30
3 Chone Figgins .12 .30
4 Darin Erstad .12 .30
5 Francisco Rodriguez .20 .50
6 Garret Anderson .12 .30
7 Jarrod Washburn .12 .30
8 Troy Glaus .12 .30
9 Vladimir Guerrero .20 .50
10 Brandon Webb .20 .50
11 Casey Fossum .12 .30
12 Luis Gonzalez .12 .30
13 Randy Johnson .30 .75
14 Richie Sexson .12 .30
15 Andruw Jones .12 .30
16 Chipper Jones .30 .75
17 J.D. Drew .12 .30
18 John Smoltz .30 .75
19 Johnny Estrada .12 .30
20 Marcus Giles .12 .30
21 Rafael Furcal .12 .30
22 Russ Ortiz .12 .30
23 Javy Lopez .12 .30
24 Jay Gibbons .12 .30
25 Melvin Mora .12 .30
26 Miguel Tejada .20 .50
27 Rafael Palmeiro .20 .50
28 Sidney Ponson .12 .30
29 Bill Mueller .12 .30
30 Curt Schilling .20 .50
31 David Ortiz .30 .75
32 Doug Mientkiewicz .12 .30
33 Jason Varitek .30 .75
34 Johnny Damon .20 .50
35 Manny Ramirez .30 .75
36 Pedro Martinez .20 .50
37 Trot Nixon .12 .30
38 Aramis Ramirez .12 .30
39 Corey Patterson .12 .30
40 Derrek Lee .12 .30
41 Greg Maddux .40 1.00
42 Kerry Wood .12 .30
43 Mark Prior .20 .50
44 Moises Alou .12 .30
45 Nomar Garciaparra .20 .50
46 Sammy Sosa .30 .75
47 Carlos Lee .12 .30
48 Kip Wells .12 .30
49 Magglio Ordonez .20 .50
50 Mark Buehrle .20 .50
51 Paul Konerko .20 .50
52 Roberto Alomar .20 .50
53 Adam Dunn .20 .50
54 Austin Kearns .12 .30
55 Barry Larkin .20 .50
56 Danny Graves .12 .30
57 Ken Griffey Jr. .60 1.50
58 Sean Casey .12 .30
59 C.C. Sabathia .20 .50
60 Cliff Lee .20 .50
61 Jody Gerut .12 .30
62 Omar Vizquel .20 .50
63 Travis Hafner .12 .30
64 Victor Martinez .20 .50
65 Charles Johnson .12 .30
66 Jason Jennings .12 .30
67 Jeromy Burnitz .12 .30
68 Preston Wilson .12 .30
69 Todd Helton .20 .50
70 Bobby Higginson .12 .30
71 Dmitri Young .12 .30
72 Eric Munson .12 .30
73 Ivan Rodriguez .20 .50
74 Jeremy Bonderman .12 .30
75 Rondell White .12 .30
76 A.J. Burnett .12 .30
77 Carl Pavano .12 .30
78 Dontrelle Willis .12 .30
79 Hee Seop Choi .12 .30
80 Josh Beckett .12 .30
81 Juan Pierre .12 .30
82 Miguel Cabrera .30 .75
83 Mike Lowell .12 .30
84 Paul Lo Duca .12 .30
85 Andy Pettitte .20 .50
86 Carlos Beltran .20 .50
87 Craig Biggio .20 .50
88 Jeff Bagwell .20 .50
89 Jeff Kent .12 .30
90 Lance Berkman .20 .50
91 Roger Clemens .40 1.00
92 Roy Oswalt .20 .50
93 Andres Blanco .12 .30
94 Jeremy Affeldt .12 .30
95 Juan Gonzalez .12 .30
96 Ken Harvey .12 .30
97 Mike Sweeney .12 .30
98 Zack Greinke .40 1.00
99 Adrian Beltre .30 .75
100 Brad Penny .12 .30
101 Eric Gagne .12 .30
102 Kazuhisa Ishii .12 .30
103 Milton Bradley .12 .30
104 Shawn Green .12 .30
105 Steve Finley .12 .30
106 Ben Sheets .12 .30
107 Bill Hall .12 .30
108 Danny Kolb .12 .30
109 Geoff Jenkins .12 .30
110 Junior Spivey .12 .30
111 Lyle Overbay .12 .30
112 Scott Podsednik .12 .30
113 A.J. Pierzynski .12 .30
114 Brad Radke .12 .30
115 Corey Koskie .12 .30
116 Jacque Jones .12 .30
117 Joe Mauer .25 .60
118 Joe Nathan .12 .30
119 Shannon Stewart .12 .30
120 Torii Hunter .12 .30
121 Brad Wilkerson .12 .30
122 Jeff Fassero .12 .30
123 Jose Vidro .12 .30
124 Livan Hernandez .12 .30
125 Nick Johnson .12 .30
126 Al Leiter .12 .30
127 Jose Reyes .20 .50
128 Kazuo Matsui .12 .30
129 Mike Cameron .12 .30
130 Mike Piazza .30 .75
131 Richard Hidalgo .12 .30
132 Tom Glavine .20 .50
133 Alex Rodriguez .40 1.00
134 Bernie Williams .20 .50
135 Derek Jeter .75 2.00
136 Gary Sheffield .12 .30
137 Jason Giambi .12 .30
138 Javier Vazquez .12 .30
139 Jorge Posada .20 .50
140 Kevin Brown .12 .30
141 Mariano Rivera .40 1.00
142 Mike Mussina .20 .50
143 Barry Zito .20 .50
144 Bobby Crosby .12 .30
145 Eric Chavez .12 .30
146 Erubiel Durazo .12 .30
147 Jermaine Dye .12 .30
148 Mark Mulder .12 .30
149 Tim Hudson .20 .50
150 Bobby Abreu .12 .30
151 Eric Milton .12 .30
152 Jim Thome .20 .50
153 Kevin Millwood .12 .30
154 Mike Lieberthal .12 .30
155 Pat Burrell .12 .30
156 Randy Wolf .12 .30
157 Craig Wilson .12 .30
158 Jack Wilson .12 .30
159 Jason Bay .12 .30
160 Jason Kendall .12 .30
161 Kris Benson .12 .30
162 Brian Giles .12 .30
163 Jake Peavy .12 .30
164 Jay Payton .12 .30
165 Khalil Greene .12 .30
166 Mark Loretta .12 .30
167 Ryan Klesko .12 .30
168 Sean Burroughs .12 .30
169 David Aardsma .12 .30
170 Edgardo Alfonzo .12 .30
171 Jason Schmidt .12 .30
172 Merkin Valdez .12 .30
173 Ray Durham .12 .30
174 Bret Boone .12 .30
175 Dan Wilson .12 .30
176 Ichiro Suzuki .40 1.00
177 Jamie Moyer .12 .30
178 Rich Aurilia .12 .30
179 Albert Pujols .40 1.00
180 Edgar Renteria .12 .30
181 Jason Isringhausen .12 .30
182 Jeff Suppan .12 .30
183 Jim Edmonds .20 .50
184 Scott Rolen .20 .50
185 Woody Williams .12 .30
186 Aubrey Huff .12 .30
187 Carl Crawford .20 .50
188 Dewon Brazelton .12 .30
189 Jose Cruz Jr. .12 .30
190 Rocco Baldelli .12 .30
191 Alfonso Soriano .20 .50
192 Hank Blalock .12 .30
193 Kenny Rogers .12 .30
194 Laynce Nix .12 .30
195 Mark Teixeira .20 .50
196 Michael Young .12 .30
197 Alexis Rios .12 .30
198 Carlos Delgado .12 .30
199 Roy Halladay .20 .50
200 Vernon Wells .12 .30
201 Josh Kroeger PROS .60 1.50
202 Angel Guzman PROS .60 1.50
203 Brad Halsey PROS .60 1.50
204 Bucky Jacobsen PROS .60 1.50
205 Carlos Hines PROS .60 1.50
206 Carlos Vasquez PROS .60 1.50
207 Billy Traber PROS .60 1.50
208 Bubba Crosby PROS .60 1.50
209 Chris Oxspring PROS .60 1.50
210 Chris Shelton PROS .60 1.50
211 Colby Miller PROS .60 1.50
212 Dave Crouthers PROS .60 1.50
213 Dennis Sarfate PROS .60 1.50
214 Don Kelly PROS .60 1.50
215 Edwardo Sierra PROS .60 1.50
216 Edwin Moreno PROS .60 1.50
217 Fernando Nieve PROS .60 1.50
218 Freddy Guzman PROS .60 1.50
219 Greg Dobbs PROS .60 1.50
220 Hector Gimenez PROS .60 1.50
221 Andy Green PROS .60 1.50
222 Jason Bartlett PROS .60 1.50
223 Jerry Gil PROS .60 1.50
224 Jesse Crain PROS .60 1.50
225 Joey Gathright PROS .60 1.50
226 John Gall PROS .60 1.50
227 Jorge Sequea PROS .60 1.50
228 Jorge Vasquez PROS .60 1.50
229 Josh Labandeira PROS .60 1.50
230 Justin Leone PROS .60 1.50
231 Lance Cormier PROS .60 1.50
232 Lincoln Holdzkom PROS .60 1.50
233 Miguel Olivo PROS .60 1.50
234 Mike Rouse PROS .60 1.50
235 Onil Joseph PROS .60 1.50
236 Phil Stockman PROS .60 1.50
237 Ramon Ramirez PROS .60 1.50
238 Robb Quinlan PROS .60 1.50
239 Roberto Novoa PROS .60 1.50
240 Ronald Belisario PROS .60 1.50
241 Ronny Cedeno PROS .60 1.50
242 Ruddy Yan PROS .60 1.50
243 Ryan Meaux PROS .60 1.50
244 Ryan Wing PROS .60 1.50
245 Scott Proctor PROS .60 1.50
246 Sean Henn PROS .60 1.50
247 Tim Bausher PROS .60 1.50
248 Tim Bittner PROS .60 1.50
249 William Bergolla PROS .60 1.50
250 Yadier Molina PROS 6.00 15.00
251 Bernie Williams PTT .50 1.25
252 Craig Biggio PTT .50 1.25
253 Chipper Jones PTT .75 2.00
254 Greg Maddux PTT 1.00 2.50
255 Sammy Sosa PTT .75 2.00
256 Mike Mussina PTT .50 1.25
257 Tim Salmon PTT .30 .75
258 Barry Larkin PTT .50 1.25
259 Randy Johnson PTT .75 2.00
260 Jeff Bagwell PTT .50 1.25
261 Roberto Alomar PTT .50 1.25
262 Tom Glavine PTT .50 1.25
263 Roger Clemens PTT 1.00 2.50
264 Alex Rodriguez PTT 1.00 2.50
265 Ivan Rodriguez PTT .50 1.25
266 Pedro Martinez PTT .50 1.25
267 Ken Griffey Jr. PTT 1.50 4.00
268 Jim Thome PTT .50 1.25
269 Frank Thomas PTT .75 2.00
270 Mike Piazza PTT .75 2.00
271 Garret Anderson TC .30 .75
272 Luis Gonzalez TC .30 .75
273 John Smoltz TC .75 2.00
274 Rafael Palmeiro TC .50 1.25
275 Curt Schilling TC .50 1.25
276 Mark Prior TC .50 1.25
277 Magglio Ordonez TC .50 1.25
278 Adam Dunn TC .50 1.25
279 Travis Hafner TC .30 .75
280 Jeromy Burnitz TC .30 .75
281 Carlos Guillen TC .30 .75
282 Dontrelle Willis TC .30 .75
283 Carlos Beltran TC .50 1.25
284 Zack Greinke TC 1.00 2.50
285 Adrian Beltre TC .75 2.00
286 Ben Sheets TC .30 .75
287 Johan Santana TC .50 1.25
288 Livan Hernandez TC .30 .75
289 Kazuo Matsui TC .30 .75
290 Derek Jeter TC 2.00 5.00
291 Tim Hudson TC .50 1.25
292 Eric Milton TC .30 .75
293 Jason Kendall TC .30 .75
294 Jake Peavy TC .30 .75
295 Ray Durham TC .30 .75
296 Ichiro Suzuki TC 1.00 2.50
297 Scott Rolen TC .50 1.25
298 Carl Crawford TC .50 1.25
299 Hank Blalock TC .30 .75
300 Roy Halladay TC .50 1.25

2005 Leaf Black

*BLACK 1-200: 1X TO 2.5X BASIC
*BLACK 201-250: .4X TO 1X BASIC
*BLACK 251-300: .5X TO 1.2X BASIC
ONE PER RETAIL PACK

2005 Leaf Green

*GREEN 1-200: 1.5X TO 4X BASIC
*GREEN 201-250: .4X TO 1X BASIC
*GREEN 251-300: .6X TO 1.5X BASIC
ONE PER RETAIL BLASTER PACK

2005 Leaf Orange

*ORANGE 1-200: 1.5X TO 4X BASIC
*ORANGE 201-250: .4X TO 1X BASIC
*ORANGE 251-300: .6X TO 1.5X BASIC
ONE PER RETAIL BLISTER PACK

2005 Leaf Press Proofs Blue

*BLUE 1-200: 5X TO 12X BASIC
*BLUE 201-250: .75X TO 2X BASIC
*BLUE 251-300: 2X TO 5X BASIC
RANDOM INSERTS IN PACKS
STATED PRINT RUN 75 SERIAL #'d SETS

2005 Leaf Press Proofs Gold

*GOLD 1-200: 10X TO 25X BASIC
*GOLD 201-250: 1.5X TO 4X BASIC
*GOLD 251-300: 4X TO 10X BASIC
RANDOM INSERTS IN PACKS
STATED PRINT RUN 25 SERIAL #'d SETS

2005 Leaf Press Proofs Red

*RED 1-200: 2X TO 5X BASIC
*RED 201-250: .4X TO 1X BASIC
*RED 251-300: .75X TO 2X BASIC
STATED ODDS 1:8

2005 Leaf Autographs

RANDOM INSERTS IN PACKS
SP INFO BASED ON BECKETT RESEARCH
201 Josh Kroeger PROS 4.00 10.00
202 Angel Guzman PROS 4.00 10.00
203 Brad Halsey PROS 4.00 10.00
204 Bucky Jacobsen PROS 4.00 10.00
205 Carlos Hines PROS 4.00 10.00
207 Billy Traber PROS 4.00 10.00
208 Bubba Crosby PROS 4.00 10.00
210 Chris Shelton PROS 6.00 15.00
211 Colby Miller PROS 4.00 10.00
212 Dave Crouthers PROS 4.00 10.00
217 Fernando Nieve PROS 4.00 10.00
220 Hector Gimenez PROS 4.00 10.00
221 Andy Green PROS 4.00 10.00
222 Jason Bartlett PROS 4.00 10.00
228 Jorge Vasquez PROS 4.00 10.00
232 Lincoln Holdzkom PROS 4.00 10.00
233 Miguel Olivo PROS 4.00 10.00
234 Mike Rouse PROS 4.00 10.00
236 Phil Stockman PROS 4.00 10.00
237 Ramon Ramirez PROS 4.00 10.00
242 Ruddy Yan PROS 4.00 10.00
245 Scott Proctor PROS 4.00 10.00
247 Tim Bausher PROS 4.00 10.00
249 William Bergolla PROS 4.00 10.00

2005 Leaf Autographs Red

PRINT RUNS B/WN 50-100 COPIES PER
BLUE PRINT RUNS B/WN 15-25 PER
NO BLUE PRICING DUE TO SCARCITY
GOLD PRINT RUNS B/WN 9-10 PER
NO GOLD PRICING DUE TO SCARCITY
RANDOM INSERTS IN PACKS
3 Chone Figgins/100 4.00 10.00
19 Johnny Estrada/100 4.00 10.00
24 Jay Gibbons/100 4.00 10.00
47 Carlos Lee/100 6.00 15.00
56 Danny Graves/100 4.00 10.00
60 Cliff Lee/100 12.50 30.00
63 Travis Hafner/50 8.00 20.00
74 Jeremy Bonderman/100 6.00 15.00
94 Jeremy Affeldt/100 4.00 10.00
96 Ken Harvey/100 4.00 10.00
103 Milton Bradley/100 6.00 15.00
111 Lyle Overbay/50 5.00 12.00
118 Joe Nathan/100 10.00 25.00
144 Bobby Crosby/100 6.00 15.00
154 Mike Lieberthal/50 8.00 20.00
157 Craig Wilson/50 5.00 12.00

158 Jack Wilson/100 6.00 15.00
163 Jake Peavy/50 8.00 20.00
172 Merkin Valdez/100 4.00 10.00
182 Jeff Suppan/100 6.00 15.00
187 Carl Crawford/50 8.00 20.00
188 Dewon Brazelton/50 5.00 12.00
194 Laynce Nix/100 4.00 10.00
201 Josh Kroeger PROS/100 4.00 10.00
202 Angel Guzman PROS/100 4.00 10.00
203 Brad Halsey PROS/100 4.00 10.00
204 Bucky Jacobsen PROS/100 4.00 10.00
205 Carlos Hines PROS/100 4.00 10.00
207 Billy Traber PROS/100 4.00 10.00
208 Bubba Crosby PROS/100 4.00 10.00
210 Chris Shelton PROS/100 10.00 25.00
211 Colby Miller PROS/100 4.00 10.00
212 Dave Crouthers PROS/100 4.00 10.00
217 Fernando Nieve PROS/100 4.00 10.00
218 Freddy Guzman PROS/100 4.00 10.00
220 Hector Gimenez PROS/100 4.00 10.00
221 Andy Green PROS/100 4.00 10.00
222 Jason Bartlett PROS/100 4.00 10.00
224 Jesse Crain PROS/100 6.00 15.00
227 Jorge Sequea PROS/84 4.00 10.00
228 Jorge Vasquez PROS/100 4.00 10.00
233 Miguel Olivo PROS/100 4.00 10.00
234 Mike Rouse PROS/100 4.00 10.00
236 Phil Stockman PROS/100 4.00 10.00
237 Ramon Ramirez PROS/100 4.00 10.00
238 Robb Quinlan PROS/100 4.00 10.00
241 Ronny Cedeno PROS/65 10.00 25.00
242 Ruddy Yan PROS/100 4.00 10.00
243 Ryan Meaux PROS/93 4.00 10.00
247 Tim Bausher PROS/100 4.00 10.00
249 William Bergolla PROS/100 4.00 10.00
250 Yadier Molina PROS/100 100.00 250.00

2005 Leaf 4 Star Staffs

STATED ODDS 1:48
*DIE CUT: .6X TO 1.5X BASIC
DIE CUT RANDOM INSERTS IN PACKS
DIE CUT PRINT RUN 250 SERIAL #'d SETS
1 Glav 2.00 5.00
Madd
Smoltz
Millwood
2 Beckett .60 1.50
Burn
Willis
Pavano
3 Clemens 2.00 5.00
Muss
Wells
Pett
4 Prior 2.00 5.00
Maddux
Wood
Zamb
5 Clemens 2.00 5.00
Pett
Muss
Rivera
6 Pedro 1.00 2.50
Schill
Lowe
Wake
7 Mulder 1.00 2.50
Zito
Huds
Harden
8 Randy 1.50 4.00
Schilling
Webb
Kim
9 Ryan 5.00 12.00
Brown
Moyer
Rogers
10 Woody 2.00 5.00
Clemens
Halla
Esc
11 Clemens 2.00 5.00
Pett
Oswalt
Miller
12 Zito 1.00 2.50
Mulder
Hudson
Koch
13 Nomo 1.50 4.00
Brown
Ishii
Gagne
14 Glav 2.00 5.00
Smoltz
Madd
Schmidt
15 Nomo 1.50 4.00
Pedro
Lowe
Wake

2005 Leaf Alternate Threads

STATED ODDS 1:18
*HOLO: .75X TO 2X BASIC
HOLO RANDOM INSERTS IN PACKS
HOLO PRINT RUN 150 SERIAL #'d SETS
*HOLO DC: 1.5X TO 4X BASIC
HOLO DC RANDOM INSERTS IN PACKS
HOLO DC PRINT RUN 50 SERIAL #'d SETS
1 Adam Dunn .60 1.50
2 C.C. Sabathia .60 1.50
3 Curt Schilling .60 1.50
4 Dontrelle Willis .40 1.00
5 Greg Maddux 1.25 3.00
6 Hank Blalock .40 1.00
7 Ichiro Suzuki 1.25 3.00
8 Jeff Bagwell .60 1.50
9 Ken Griffey Jr. 2.00 5.00
10 Ken Harvey .40 1.00
11 Magglio Ordonez .60 1.50
12 Mark Mulder .40 1.00
13 Mark Teixeira .60 1.50
14 Michael Young .40 1.00
15 Miguel Tejada .60 1.50
16 Mike Piazza 1.00 2.50
17 Pedro Martinez .60 1.50
18 Randy Johnson 1.00 2.50
19 Roger Clemens 1.25 3.00
20 Sammy Sosa 1.00 2.50
21 Tim Hudson .60 1.50
22 Todd Helton .60 1.50
23 Torii Hunter .40 1.00
24 Travis Hafner .40 1.00
25 Vernon Wells .40 1.00

2005 Leaf Certified Materials Preview

STATED ODDS 1:21
*BLUE: 1.25X TO 3X BASIC
BLUE RANDOM INSERTS IN PACKS
BLUE PRINT RUN 100 SERIAL #'d SETS
*GOLD: 3X TO 8X BASIC
GOLD RANDOM INSERTS IN PACKS
GOLD PRINT RUN 25 SERIAL #'d SETS
*RED: 1X TO 2.5X BASIC
RED RANDOM INSERTS IN PACKS
RED PRINT RUN 200 SERIAL #'d SETS
1 Albert Pujols 1.25 3.00
2 Alex Rodriguez 1.25 3.00
3 Alfonso Soriano .60 1.50
4 Curt Schilling .60 1.50
5 Derek Jeter 2.50 6.00
6 Greg Maddux 1.25 3.00
7 Ichiro Suzuki 1.25 3.00
8 Jim Thome .60 1.50
9 Ken Griffey Jr. 2.00 5.00
10 Manny Ramirez 1.00 2.50
11 Mark Prior .60 1.50
12 Randy Johnson 1.00 2.50
13 Roger Clemens 1.25 3.00
14 Sammy Sosa 1.00 2.50
15 Vladimir Guerrero .60 1.50

2005 Leaf Clean Up Crew

STATED ODDS 1:49
*DIE CUT: .6X TO 1.5X BASIC
DIE CUT RANDOM INSERTS IN PACKS
DIE CUT PRINT RUN 250 SERIAL #'d SETS
1 Pujols 1.25 3.00
Edmonds
Rolen
2 Mora .60 1.50
Tejada
Palmeiro
3 Soriano .60 1.50
Young
Blalock
4 Sheffield 1.50 4.00
A.Rod
Matsui
5 Alou 1.00 2.50
Sosa
Garciaparra
6 Lo Duca 1.00 2.50
Lowell
Cabrera
7 Beltran .60 1.50
Berkman
Bagwell
8 Konerko 1.00 2.50
Ordonez
Thomas
9 Casey 2.00 5.00
Griffey Jr.
Dunn
10 Guerrero .60 1.50
Anderson
Glaus
11 Morgan 1.00 2.50
Bench
Perez
12 K.Hern .60 1.50
Strawberry
Carter
13 Rice 1.25 3.00
Yastrzemski
Evans
14 Sandberg 2.00 5.00
Dawson
Grace
15 Ripken 3.00 8.00
Murray
Palmeiro

2005 Leaf Cornerstones

STATED ODDS 1:37
1 A.Pujols 1.25 3.00
S.Rolen
2 H.Matsui 1.50 4.00
J.Posada
3 S.Sosa 1.00 2.50
N.Garciaparra
4 M.Ramirez 1.00 2.50
D.Ortiz
5 M.Cabrera 1.00 2.50
M.Lowell
6 H.Blalock .60 1.50
M.Teixeira
7 C.Jones 1.00 2.50
J.Drew
8 C.Biggio .60 1.50
J.Bagwell
9 M.Piazza 1.00 2.50
K.Matsui
10 S.Green 1.00 2.50
A.Beltre
11 J.Thome .60 1.50
B.Abreu
12 M.Schmidt 1.50 4.00
S.Carlton
13 C.Ripken 3.00 8.00
E.Murray
14 C.Yastrzemski 1.25 3.00
D.Evans
15 J.Bench 1.00 2.50
J.Morgan
16 D.Murphy 1.00 2.50
P.Niekro
17 A.Trammell .60 1.50
K.Gibson
18 J.Canseco 1.00 2.50
R.Henderson
19 P.Molitor 1.00 2.50
R.Yount
20 G.Brett 2.00 5.00
B.Jackson

2005 Leaf Cornerstones Bats

RANDOM INSERTS IN PACKS
1 A.Pujols/S.Rolen 10.00 25.00
2 H.Matsui/J.Posada 15.00 40.00
3 S.Sosa/N.Garciaparra 6.00 15.00
4 M.Ramirez/D.Ortiz 10.00 25.00
5 M.Cabrera/M.Lowell 6.00 15.00
6 H.Blalock/M.Teixeira 6.00 15.00
7 C.Jones/J.Drew 6.00 15.00
8 C.Biggio/J.Bagwell 6.00 15.00
9 M.Piazza/K.Matsui 6.00 15.00
10 S.Green/A.Beltre 4.00 10.00

2005 Leaf Cornerstones Jerseys

STATED PRINT RUN 250 SERIAL #'d SETS
*PRIME p/r 50: 1X TO 2.5X BASIC
*PRIME p/r 25: 1.25X TO 3X BASIC
PRIME PRINT RUN B/WN 25-50 PER
RANDOM INSERTS IN PACKS
1 A.Pujols/S.Rolen 10.00 25.00
2 H.Matsui/J.Posada 15.00 40.00
4 M.Ramirez/D.Ortiz 10.00 25.00
5 M.Cabrera/M.Lowell 6.00 15.00
6 H.Blalock/M.Teixeira 6.00 15.00
8 C.Biggio/J.Bagwell 6.00 15.00
9 M.Piazza/K.Matsui 6.00 15.00
10 S.Green/A.Beltre 4.00 10.00

2005 Leaf Cy Young Winners

STATED ODDS 1:31
*GOLD: .6X TO 1.5X BASIC
GOLD RANDOM INSERTS IN PACKS
GOLD PRINT RUN 350 SERIAL #'d SETS
*GOLD DC: 1X TO 2.5X BASIC
GOLD DC RANDOM INSERTS IN PACKS
GOLD DC PRINT RUN 100 SERIAL #'d SETS
1 Warren Spahn .60 1.50
2 Whitey Ford .60 1.50
3 Bob Gibson .60 1.50
4 Tom Seaver .60 1.50
5 Steve Carlton .60 1.50
6 Jim Palmer .60 1.50
7 Rollie Fingers .60 1.50
8 Dwight Gooden .40 1.00
9 Roger Clemens 1.25 3.00
10 Orel Hershiser .40 1.00
11 Greg Maddux 1.25 3.00
12 Dennis Eckersley .60 1.50
13 Randy Johnson 1.00 2.50
14 Pedro Martinez .60 1.50
15 Eric Gagne .40 1.00

2005 Leaf Fans of the Game

STATED ODDS 1:24
1 Sean Astin .75 2.00
2 Tony Danza .75 2.00
3 Taye Diggs .75 2.00

2005 Leaf Fans of the Game Autographs

RANDOM INSERTS IN PACKS
SP PRINT RUNS PROVIDED BY DONRUSS
SP'S ARE NOT SERIAL-NUMBERED
1 Sean Astin 12.50 30.00
2 Tony Danza SP/50 150.00 250.00
3 Taye Diggs 4.00 10.00

2005 Leaf Game Collection

STATED ODDS 1:118
SP INFO BASED ON BECKETT RESEARCH
1 Cal Ripken Bat 15.00 40.00
2 Carl Crawford Jsy 3.00 8.00
3 Dale Murphy Bat SP 8.00 20.00
4 Don Mattingly Bat SP 10.00 25.00
5 George Brett Jsy SP 10.00 25.00
6 Victor Martinez Bat SP 4.00 10.00
7 Sean Casey Bat 3.00 8.00
8 Torii Hunter Bat 3.00 8.00
9 Magglio Ordonez Bat 3.00 8.00
10 Lance Berkman Bat 3.00 8.00
11 Mike Schmidt Bat SP 10.00 25.00
12 Nolan Ryan Jkt SP 15.00 40.00
13 Paul Lo Duca Bat 3.00 8.00
14 Preston Wilson Bat 3.00 8.00
15 Rod Carew Jkt SP 8.00 20.00
16 Reggie Jackson Bat SP 8.00 20.00
17 Ivan Rodriguez Bat 4.00 10.00
18 L.Walker Cards Bat 4.00 10.00
19 Miguel Tejada Bat SP 4.00 10.00
20 Vladimir Guerrero Bat SP 6.00 15.00

2005 Leaf Game Collection Autograph

RANDOM INSERTS IN PACKS
PRINT RUNS B/WN 5-200 COPIES PER
NO PRICING ON QTY OF 25 OR LESS
2 Carl Crawford Jsy/200 6.00 15.00
6 Victor Martinez Bat/200 6.00 15.00
7 Sean Casey Bat/200 6.00 15.00
8 Torii Hunter Bat/50 12.50 30.00
13 Paul Lo Duca Bat/100 6.00 15.00

2005 Leaf Gamers

STATED ODDS 1:13
*QUANTUM: 1.25X TO 3X BASIC
QUANTUM RANDOM INSERTS IN PACKS
QUANTUM PRINT RUN 175 SER.#'d SETS
*QUANTUM DC: 2.5X TO 6X BASIC
QUANTUM DC RANDOM INSERTS IN PACKS
QUANTUM DC PRINT RUN 50 SER.#'d SETS
1 Albert Pujols 1.25 3.00
2 Alex Rodriguez 1.25 3.00
3 Alfonso Soriano .60 1.50
4 Chipper Jones 1.00 2.50
5 Derek Jeter 2.50 6.00
6 Greg Maddux 1.25 3.00
7 Ichiro Suzuki 1.25 3.00
8 Jim Thome .60 1.50
9 Ken Griffey Jr. 2.00 5.00
10 Lance Berkman .60 1.50
11 Miguel Tejada .60 1.50
12 Mike Piazza 1.00 2.50
13 Roger Clemens 1.25 3.00
14 Scott Rolen .60 1.50
15 Vladimir Guerrero .60 1.50

2005 Leaf Gold Rookies

STATED ODDS 1:24
*MIRROR: 2X TO 5X BASIC
MIRROR RANDOM INSERTS IN PACKS
MIRROR PRINT RUN 25 SERIAL #'d SETS
1 Dennis Sarfate .40 1.00
2 Don Kelly .40 1.00
3 Eddy Rodriguez .40 1.00
4 Edwin Moreno .40 1.00
5 Greg Dobbs .40 1.00
6 Josh Labandeira .40 1.00
7 Kevin Cave .40 1.00
8 Mariano Gomez .40 1.00
9 Ronald Belisario .40 1.00
10 Ruddy Yan .40 1.00

2005 Leaf Gold Rookies Autograph

SP INFO BASED ON BECKETT RESEARCH
MIRROR PRINT RUN 25 SERIAL #'d SETS
NO MIRROR PRICING DUE TO SCARCITY
RANDOM INSERTS IN PACKS
2 Don Kelly 4.00 10.00
5 Greg Dobbs 4.00 10.00
9 Ronald Belisario 4.00 10.00
10 Ruddy Yan 4.00 10.00

2005 Leaf Gold Stars

STATED ODDS 1:27
*MIRROR: 2.5X TO 6X BASIC
MIRROR RANDOM INSERTS IN PACKS
MIRROR PRINT RUN 25 SERIAL #'d SETS
1 Albert Pujols 1.25 3.00
2 Ichiro Suzuki 1.25 3.00
3 Derek Jeter 2.50 6.00
4 Alex Rodriguez 1.25 3.00
5 Scott Rolen .60 1.50
6 Randy Johnson 1.00 2.50
7 Roger Clemens 1.25 3.00
8 Greg Maddux 1.25 3.00
9 Alfonso Soriano .60 1.50
10 Mark Mulder .40 1.00
11 Sammy Sosa 1.00 2.50
12 Mike Piazza 1.00 2.50
13 Rafael Palmeiro .60 1.50
14 Ivan Rodriguez .60 1.50
15 Miguel Cabrera 1.00 2.50
16 Stan Musial 1.50 4.00
17 Nolan Ryan 3.00 8.00
18 Don Mattingly 2.00 5.00
19 George Brett 2.00 5.00
20 Cal Ripken 3.00 8.00

2005 Leaf Home/Road

STATED ODDS 1:22
HOME AND ROAD VALUED EQUALLY
1H Albert Pujols H 1.25 3.00
1R Albert Pujols R 1.25 3.00
2H Alfonso Soriano H .60 1.50
2R Alfonso Soriano R .60 1.50
3H Carlos Beltran H .60 1.50
3R Carlos Beltran R .60 1.50
4H Chipper Jones H 1.00 2.50
4R Chipper Jones R 1.00 2.50
5H Frank Thomas H 1.00 2.50
5R Frank Thomas R 1.00 2.50
6H Hank Blalock H .40 1.00
6R Hank Blalock R .40 1.00
7H Ivan Rodriguez H .60 1.50
7R Ivan Rodriguez R .60 1.50
8H Manny Ramirez H 1.00 2.50
8R Manny Ramirez R 1.00 2.50
9H Mark Prior H .60 1.50
9R Mark Prior R .60 1.50
10H Miguel Cabrera H 1.00 2.50
10R Miguel Cabrera R 1.00 2.50
11H Miguel Tejada H .60 1.50
11R Miguel Tejada R .60 1.50
12H Mike Piazza H 1.00 2.50
12R Mike Piazza R 1.00 2.50
13H Roger Clemens H 1.25 3.00
13R Roger Clemens R 1.25 3.00
14H Todd Helton H .60 1.50
14R Todd Helton R .60 1.50
15H Vladimir Guerrero H .60 1.50
15R Vladimir Guerrero R .60 1.50

2005 Leaf Home/Road Jersey

RANDOM INSERTS IN PACKS
SP INFO BASED ON BECKETT RESEARCH
1H Albert Pujols H 8.00 20.00
1R Albert Pujols R 8.00 20.00
2H Alfonso Soriano H 3.00 8.00
3H Carlos Beltran H 3.00 8.00
3R Carlos Beltran R 3.00 8.00
4R Chipper Jones R 4.00 10.00
5H Frank Thomas H 4.00 10.00
5R Frank Thomas R 4.00 10.00
6H Hank Blalock H 3.00 8.00
7H Ivan Rodriguez H 4.00 10.00
7R Ivan Rodriguez R 4.00 10.00
8R Manny Ramirez R 4.00 10.00
9H Mark Prior H 4.00 10.00
11H Miguel Tejada H 3.00 8.00
11R Miguel Tejada R 3.00 8.00
12H Mike Piazza H 4.00 10.00
13H Roger Clemens H 6.00 15.00
13R Roger Clemens R 6.00 15.00
14H Todd Helton H 4.00 10.00
14R Todd Helton R 4.00 10.00
15H Vladimir Guerrero H 4.00 10.00

2005 Leaf Home/Road Jersey Prime

*PRIME: 1X TO 2.5X BASIC
RANDOM INSERTS IN PACKS
STATED PRINT RUN 50 SERIAL #'d SETS
4H Chipper Jones H 10.00 25.00
6R Hank Blalock R 8.00 20.00
8H Manny Ramirez H 10.00 25.00
9R Mark Prior R 10.00 25.00
10H Miguel Cabrera H 10.00 25.00
10R Miguel Cabrera R 10.00 25.00
12R Mike Piazza R 10.00 25.00
15R Vladimir Guerrero R 10.00 25.00

2005 Leaf Patch Off My Back

*PATCH: 1X TO 2.5X SHIRT OFF BACK
*PATCH: .6X TO 1.5X SHIRT OFF BACK SP
RANDOM INSERTS IN PACKS
STATED PRINT RUN 50 SERIAL #'d SETS
2 Aubrey Huff 6.00 15.00
3 Austin Kearns 6.00 15.00
24 Mariano Rivera 10.00 25.00

2005 Leaf Patch Off My Back Autograph

RANDOM INSERTS IN PACKS
PRINT RUNS B/WN 10-75 COPIES PER
NO PRICING ON QTY OF 25 OR LESS
2 Aubrey Huff/50 15.00 40.00
4 Bobby Crosby/75 15.00 40.00
5 C.C. Sabathia/75 15.00 40.00
7 David Ortiz/50 40.00 80.00
8 Dewon Brazelton/75 10.00 25.00
14 Jack Wilson/75 15.00 40.00
16 Jay Gibbons/50 10.00 25.00
18 Jody Gerut/75 10.00 25.00
20 Johan Santana/50 15.00 40.00
22 Jose Vidro/75 10.00 25.00
26 Michael Young/75 15.00 40.00

2005 Leaf Picture Perfect

STATED ODDS 1:20
*DIE CUT: 1.25X TO 3X BASIC
DIE CUT RANDOM INSERTS IN PACKS
DIE CUT PRINT RUN 100 SERIAL #'d SETS
1 Albert Pujols 1.25 3.00
2 Alex Rodriguez 1.25 3.00
3 Alfonso Soriano .60 1.50
4 Derek Jeter 2.50 6.00
5 Greg Maddux 1.25 3.00
6 Hideki Matsui 1.50 4.00
7 Ichiro Suzuki 1.25 3.00
8 Ivan Rodriguez .60 1.50
9 Jim Thome .60 1.50
10 Mark Mulder .40 1.00
11 Mark Prior .60 1.50
12 Miguel Tejada .60 1.50
13 Mike Mussina .60 1.50
14 Mike Piazza 1.00 2.50
15 Nomar Garciaparra .60 1.50
16 Randy Johnson 1.00 2.50
17 Roger Clemens 1.25 3.00
18 Sammy Sosa 1.00 2.50
19 Scott Rolen .60 1.50
20 Vladimir Guerrero .60 1.50

2005 Leaf Recollection Autographs

RANDOM INSERTS IN PACKS
PRINT RUNS B/WN 1-29 COPIES PER
NO PRICING DUE TO SCARCITY

2005 Leaf Shirt Off My Back

STATED ODDS 1:48
SP INFO BASED ON BECKETT RESEARCH
1 Adam Dunn SP 4.00 10.00
4 Bobby Crosby SP 4.00 10.00
5 C.C. Sabathia SP 4.00 10.00
7 David Ortiz SP 6.00 15.00
8 Dewon Brazelton 3.00 8.00
9 Edgar Martinez 4.00 10.00
10 Frankie Francisco 3.00 8.00
11 Garret Anderson 3.00 8.00
12 Hideki Matsui SP 10.00 25.00
13 Hideo Nomo 4.00 10.00
14 Jack Wilson 3.00 8.00
15 Javy Lopez SP 4.00 10.00
16 Jay Gibbons SP 4.00 10.00
18 Jody Gerut SP 4.00 10.00
19 Joey Gathright 3.00 8.00
20 Johan Santana 4.00 10.00
21 Jose Reyes 3.00 8.00
22 Jose Vidro 3.00 8.00
23 Lance Berkman SP 4.00 10.00
25 Mark Teixeira 4.00 10.00
26 Michael Young SP 4.00 10.00
27 Mike Cameron 3.00 8.00
28 Mike Sweeney 3.00 8.00
29 Omar Vizquel SP 6.00 15.00
30 Preston Wilson SP 4.00 10.00
31 Rocco Baldelli SP 4.00 10.00
32 Scott Rolen SP 6.00 15.00
33 Sean Burroughs SP 4.00 10.00
34 Sean Casey 3.00 8.00
35 Tim Hudson 3.00 8.00
36 Torii Hunter 3.00 8.00
37 Trevor Hoffman 3.00 8.00
38 Troy Glaus 3.00 8.00
39 Vernon Wells 3.00 8.00
40 Victor Martinez SP 4.00 10.00

2005 Leaf Sportscasters 70 Green Batting-Ball

STATED PRINT RUN 70 SERIAL #'d SETS
*PARALLEL #'d OF 50-65: .4X TO 1X
*PARALLEL #'d OF 40-45: .5X TO 1.2X
*PARALLEL #'d OF 30-35: .6X TO 1.5X
*PARALLEL #'d OF 20-25: .75X TO 2X
*PARALLEL #'d OF 15: 1X TO 2.5X
PARALLELS #'d FROM 5-65 COPIES PER
NO PRICING ON QTY OF 10 OR LESS
OVERALL SPORTSCASTER ODDS 1:4
1 Adam Dunn 1.00 2.50
2 Al Kaline 1.50 4.00
3 Albert Pujols 2.00 5.00
4 Alex Rodriguez 2.00 5.00
5 Alfonso Soriano 1.00 2.50
6 Bob Gibson 1.00 2.50
7 Cal Ripken 5.00 12.00
8 Carl Yastrzemski 2.00 5.00
9 Dale Murphy 1.50 4.00
10 Derek Jeter 4.00 10.00
11 Don Mattingly 3.00 8.00
12 Duke Snider 1.00 2.50
13 Eric Gagne .60 1.50
14 Ernie Banks 1.50 4.00
15 Frank Robinson 1.00 2.50
16 George Brett 3.00 8.00
17 Greg Maddux 2.00 5.00
18 Harmon Killebrew 1.50 4.00
19 Ichiro Suzuki 2.00 5.00
20 Ivan Rodriguez 1.00 2.50
21 Jim Edmonds 1.00 2.50
22 Jim Palmer 1.00 2.50
23 Jim Thome 1.00 2.50
24 Johnny Bench 1.50 4.00
25 Ken Griffey Jr. 3.00 8.00
26 Larry Walker 1.00 2.50
27 Mark Mulder .60 1.50
28 Mark Prior 1.00 2.50
29 Miguel Tejada 1.00 2.50
30 Mike Mussina 1.00 2.50
31 Mike Piazza 1.50 4.00
32 Mike Schmidt 2.50 6.00
33 Nolan Ryan 5.00 12.00
34 Nomar Garciaparra 1.00 2.50
35 Pedro Martinez 1.00 2.50
36 Rafael Palmeiro 1.00 2.50
37 Randy Johnson 1.50 4.00
38 Reggie Jackson 1.00 2.50
39 Rickey Henderson 1.50 4.00
40 Roberto Clemente 4.00 10.00
41 Rod Carew 1.00 2.50
42 Roger Clemens 2.00 5.00
43 Ryne Sandberg 3.00 8.00
44 Sammy Sosa 1.50 4.00
45 Stan Musial 2.50 6.00
46 Steve Carlton 1.00 2.50
47 Tony Gwynn 2.00 5.00
48 Vladimir Guerrero 1.00 2.50
49 Warren Spahn 1.00 2.50
50 Willie McCovey 1.00 2.50

2015 Leaf 25th Metal Autographs Silver

OVERALL FOUR AUTOS PER BOX
ANNCD PRINT RUNS B/WN 12-94 COPIES PER
NO PRICING ON QTY 14 OR LESS
EXCHANGE DEADLINE 12/31/2018
BAAB1 Alex Bregman/91* 10.00 25.00
BAAB2 Andrew Benintendi/90* 25.00 60.00
BAAR1 Ashe Russell/89* 6.00 15.00
BABB1 Byron Buxton/90* 10.00 25.00
BABR1 Brendan Rodgers/89* 10.00 25.00
BABR2 Brooks Robinson/54* 10.00 25.00
BABS1 Bruce Sutter/17* 5.00 12.00
BACF2 Carson Fulmer/90* 10.00 25.00
BACR1 Cornelius Randolph/90* 6.00 15.00
BACRJ Cal Ripken Jr. 25.00 60.00
BADM1 Don Mattingly/16* 20.00 50.00
BADS1 Dansby Swanson/90* 20.00 50.00
BADT1 Dillon Tate/82* 6.00 15.00
BAFT1 Frank Thomas EXCH 25.00 60.00
BAGW1 Garrett Whitley/90* 4.00 10.00
BAIH1 Ian Happ/88* 8.00 20.00
BAJB1 Johnny Bench/56* 15.00 40.00
BAJD1 Jose De Leon/90* 4.00 10.00
BAJK1 James Kaprielian/88* 5.00 12.00
BAJM1 Jorge Mateo/90* 8.00 20.00
BAJN1 Josh Naylor/88* 3.00 8.00
BAJP1 Jim Palmer/52* 8.00 20.00
BAJS2 John Smoltz/16* 10.00 25.00
BAJU1 Julio Urias/41* 10.00 25.00
BAKA1 Kolby Allard/91* 6.00 15.00
BAKN1 Kevin Newman/89* 6.00 15.00
BAKS1 Kyle Schwarber/41* 10.00 25.00
BAKT1 Kyle Tucker/89* 15.00 40.00
BAMM1 Manuel Margot/89* 5.00 12.00
BAPB1 Phil Bickford/94* 2.50 6.00
BAPM1 Pedro Martinez/16* 15.00 40.00
BAPR2 Pete Rose/79* 10.00 25.00
BARD1 Rafael Devers/81* 8.00 20.00
BARJ1 Reggie Jackson/56* 15.00 40.00
BARY1 Robin Yount/57* 20.00 50.00
BASM1 Steve Matz/92* 12.00 30.00
BATC1 Trent Clark/91* 2.50 6.00
BATG1 Tom Glavine/52* 10.00 25.00
BATJ1 Tyler Jay/89* 2.50 6.00
BATS1 Tyler Stephenson/88* 6.00 15.00
BAWB1 Wade Boggs/62* 12.00 30.00
BAYA1 Yadier Alvares/81* 4.00 10.00
BAYM1 Yoan Moncada/83* 20.00 50.00

2015 Leaf 25th Metal Autographs Blue

*BLUE: .5X TO 1.2X BASIC
OVERALL FOUR AUTOS PER BOX
PRINT RUNS B/WN 15-25 COPIES PER
NO PRICING ON QTY 15
EXCHANGE DEADLINE 12/31/2018
BACF1 Carlton Fisk/25 12.00 30.00
BAKGJ Ken Griffey Jr./25 60.00 150.00

2015 Leaf 25th Buyback Autographs Silver

OVERALL FOUR AUTOS PER BOX
PRINT RUNS B/WN 8-40 COPIES PER
NO PRICING ON QTY 8
EXCHANGE DEADLINE 12/31/2018
1 Nolan Ryan/35 40.00 100.00
No Hit King
2 Nolan Ryan/39 40.00 100.00
3 Von Hayes/40 5.00 12.00
4 Dave Magadan/40 5.00 12.00
5 Pete Incaviglia/40 5.00 12.00
6 Mookie Wilson/40 5.00 12.00
7 Jim Leyritz/39 5.00 12.00
8 Sid Fernandez/40 6.00 15.00
9 Mitch Williams/39 5.00 12.00
10 Willie McGee/40 10.00 25.00
11 Tom Herr/40 12.00 30.00
12 Bob Boone/40 5.00 12.00
13 Mike Lavalliere/40 5.00 12.00
14 Robin Yount/40 20.00 50.00
15 Dwight Smith/40 5.00 12.00
16 Greg Maddux/38 30.00 80.00
17 Mark Grace/40 15.00 40.00
18 Tom Glavine/19 25.00 60.00
20 Don Mattingly/40 30.00 80.00
21 Juan Samuel/40 5.00 12.00
22 Keith Hernandez/40 8.00 20.00
23 Ozzie Smith/39 20.00 50.00
24 Wade Boggs/40 20.00 50.00
25 Lonnie Smith/40 6.00 15.00
26 Carlos Baerga/38 10.00 25.00
27 Dave Winfield/40 15.00 40.00
28 Roberto Alomar/40 15.00 40.00
29 Jerome Walton/40 5.00 12.00
30 Lee Smith/40 5.00 12.00
31 Andy Van Slyke/40 12.00 30.00
32 Dennis Eckersley/39 10.00 25.00
33 Dwight Gooden/40 10.00 25.00
34 Lance Parrish/40 10.00 25.00
35 Rickey Henderson/40 40.00 100.00
36 Bo Jackson/40 30.00 80.00
37 Tim Raines/40 8.00 20.00
38 Kirk Gibson/40 10.00 25.00
39 Fred Lynn/40 5.00 12.00
40 Craig Biggio/39 20.00 50.00
41 Paul Molitor/40 15.00 40.00
42 Jose Canseco/37 15.00 40.00
43 Mike Pagliarulo/40 5.00 12.00
44 Darryl Strawberry/40 10.00 25.00
45 Frank Thomas/40 150.00 250.00

2015 Leaf 25th Clear Acetate Autographs Blue

*BLUE: .5X TO 1.2X BASIC
OVERALL FOUR AUTOS PER BOX
STATED PRINT RUN 25 SER.#'d SETS
EXCHANGE DEADLINE 12/31/2018
CF1 Carlton Fisk 12.00 30.00
JW1 Jameis Winston 10.00 25.00
KGJ Ken Griffey Jr. 90.00 150.00

2015 Leaf 25th Clear Acetate Autographs Gray

OVERALL FOUR AUTOS PER BOX
ANNCD PRINT RUNS B/WN 5-56 COPIES PER
NO PRICING ON QTY 13 OR LESS
EXCHANGE DEADLINE 12/31/2018
AB1 Alex Bregman/56* 15.00 40.00
BR1 Brendan Rodgers/55* 10.00 25.00
BR2 Brooks Robinson/51* 10.00 25.00
BS1 Bruce Sutter/32* 5.00 12.00
CF2 Carson Fulmer/55* 8.00 20.00
CRJ Cal Ripken Jr. 25.00 60.00
DM1 Don Mattingly/16* 30.00 80.00
DS1 Dansby Swanson/55* 20.00 50.00
FT1 Frank Thomas EXCH 20.00 50.00
JB1 Johnny Bench/51* 15.00 40.00
JP1 Jim Palmer/52* 4.00 10.00
JS2 John Smoltz/16* 10.00 25.00
JU1 Julio Urias/36* 10.00 25.00
KT1 Kyle Tucker/56* 6.00 15.00
PM1 Pedro Martinez/16* 20.00 50.00
PR2 Pete Rose/51* 15.00 40.00
RD1 Rafael Devers/32* 8.00 20.00
RJ1 Reggie Jackson/50* 12.00 30.00
RY1 Robin Yount/51* 15.00 40.00
SM1 Steve Matz/55* 10.00 25.00
TG1 Tom Glavine/50* 8.00 20.00
WB1 Wade Boggs/45* 12.00 30.00
YM1 Yoan Moncada/56* 15.00 40.00

2015 Leaf 25th Pure Glass Autographs Blue

*BLUE: .5X TO 1.2X BASIC
OVERALL FOUR AUTOS PER BOX
PRINT RUNS B/WN 10-25 COPIES PER
NO PRICING ON QTY 10
EXCHANGE DEADLINE 12/31/2018
CF1 Carlton Fisk/25 12.00 30.00
KGJ Ken Griffey Jr./25 90.00 150.00

2015 Leaf 25th Pure Glass Autographs Charcoal

OVERALL FOUR AUTOS PER BOX
ANNCD PRINT RUNS B/WN 13-79 COPIES PER
NO PRICING ON QTY 13 OR LESS
EXCHANGE DEADLINE 12/31/2018
AB1 Alex Bregman/78* 8.00 20.00
AJ1 Aaron Judge/55* 75.00 200.00
BR1 Brendan Rodgers/79* 10.00 25.00
BR2 Brooks Robinson/49* 10.00 25.00
BS1 Bruce Sutter/35* 5.00 12.00
CRJ Cal Ripken Jr. EXCH 25.00 60.00
DC1 Daz Cameron/78* 6.00 15.00
DM1 Don Mattingly/25* 30.00 80.00
DS1 Dansby Swanson/73* 20.00 50.00
DT1 Dillon Tate/79* 3.00 8.00
FT1 Frank Thomas/51* 20.00 50.00
JB1 Johnny Bench/49* 15.00 40.00
JD1 Jose De Leon/49* 4.00 10.00
JP1 Jim Palmer/51* 10.00 25.00
JS2 John Smoltz/25* 10.00 25.00
JU1 Julio Urias/44* 10.00 25.00
JW1 Jameis Winston/31*
PM1 Pedro Martinez/25* 20.00 50.00
PR2 Pete Rose/49* 12.00 30.00
RJ1 Reggie Jackson/48* 15.00 40.00
RY1 Robin Yount/49* 15.00 40.00
TG1 Tom Glavine/51* 10.00 25.00
WB1 Wade Boggs/49* 12.00 30.00
YM1 Yoan Moncada/77* 15.00 40.00

2012 Best of Baseball Preview Autographs

BBP1 Pete Rose 10.00 25.00

2012 Leaf Best of Baseball Autographs

I1 Ichiro Suzuki 150.00 300.00
AD1 Andre Dawson 6.00 15.00
AK1 Al Kaline 12.00 30.00
BS1 Bruce Sutter 4.00 10.00
BW1 Billy Williams 6.00 15.00
DS1 Don Sutton 4.00 10.00
FT1 Frank Thomas 15.00 40.00
JB1 Jim Bunning 8.00 20.00
JP1 Jim Palmer 5.00 12.00
JR1 Jim Rice 5.00 12.00
LB1 Lou Brock 8.00 20.00
OC1 Orlando Cepeda 5.00 12.00
PG1 Pat Gillick 10.00 25.00
PR1 Pete Rose 10.00 25.00
TG1 Tony Gwynn 20.00 50.00
WC1 Will Clark 8.00 20.00
WH1 Whitey Herzog 10.00 25.00
WF1` Whitey Ford 15.00 40.00

2013 Leaf Best of Baseball

STATED PRINT RUN 25 SER.#'d SETS
BAA1 Albert Almora 3.00 8.00
BAA2 Austin Aune 2.00 5.00
BAM1 Alfredo Marte 1.50 4.00
BAR1 Addison Russell 2.50 6.00
BAW1 Alex Wood 2.00 5.00
BBB2 Barrett Barnes 1.50 4.00
BBJ1 Brian Johnson 1.00 2.50
BCC1 Carlos Correa 20.00 50.00
BCH1 Courtney Hawkins 1.50 4.00
BCK1 Carson Kelly 2.00 5.00
BCRJ Cal Ripken Jr. 20.00 50.00
BCS1 Corey Seager 8.00 20.00
BCY1 Christian Yelich 12.00 30.00
BDC1 Daniel Corcino 1.50 4.00
BDD1 David Dahl 2.00 5.00
BDJD D.J. Davis 2.00 5.00

BDS1 Don Sutton 1.50 4.00
BEH1 Elier Hernandez 1.50 4.00
BFL1 Francisco Lindor 12.00 30.00
BFT1 Frank Thomas 2.50 6.00
BGC1 Gavin Cecchini 2.00 5.00
BGP2 Gaylord Perry 2.00 5.00
BJA1 Jesus Aguilar 4.00 10.00
BJB1 Jim Bunning 2.00 5.00
BJB2 Javier Baez 6.00 15.00
BJB3 Jorge Bonifacio 2.00 5.00
BJB4 Johnny Bench 2.50 6.00
BJC1 Jamie Callahan 1.50 4.00
BJC2 Jose Canseco 12.00 30.00
BJG1 Joey Gallo 5.00 12.00
BJM2 Joe Morgan 2.00 5.00
BJOB J.O. Berrios 2.50 6.00
BJP1 James Paxton 2.00 5.00
BJP2 Jim Palmer 2.00 5.00
BJS1 Jorge Soler 3.00 8.00
BJS2 John Smoltz 2.50 6.00
BJV1 Jesmuel Valentin 1.50 4.00
BJW1 Jesse Winker 2.50 6.00
BKB1 Keon Barnum 1.50 4.00
BKP1 Kevin Plawecki 1.50 4.00
BLA1 Luis Aparicio 2.00 5.00
BLB2 Lewis Brinson 2.00 5.00
BMB1 Mitch Brown 1.50 4.00
BMG1 Mitchell Gueller 1.50 4.00
BMN1 Mitch Nay 1.50 4.00
BMO1 Matt Olson 8.00 20.00
BMO2 Marcell Ozuna 4.00 10.00
BMW2 Michael Wacha 5.00 12.00
BMZ1 Mike Zunino 2.50 6.00
BNM1 Nomar Mazara 3.00 8.00
BNR1 Nolan Ryan 8.00 20.00
BOA1 Oswaldo Arcia 1.50 4.00
BOS1 Ozzie Smith 3.00 8.00
BPC1 Phillips Castillo 1.50 4.00
BPM1 Paul Molitor 2.50 6.00
BPR1 Pete Rose 10.00 25.00
BRJ1 Randy Johnson 2.50 6.00
BRO1 Rougned Odor 4.00 10.00
BRR1 Rio Ruiz 1.50 4.00
BSC1 Steve Carlton 2.00 5.00
BSH1 Slade Heathcott 1.50 4.00
BST1 Stryker Trahan 1.50 4.00
BSW1 Shane Watson 1.00 2.50
BTA1 Tyler Austin 2.50 6.00
BTH1 Ty Hensley 2.00 5.00
BTR1 Tanner Rahier 2.00 5.00
BTS1 Tom Seaver 2.00 5.00
BTZL Tzu-Wei Lin 2.00 5.00
BWM1 Wyatt Mathisen 1.50 4.00
BXB1 Xander Bogaerts 5.00 12.00
BYB1 Yogi Berra 2.50 6.00
BYLW Yao-Lin Wang 1.50 4.00
BYP1 Yasiel Puig 30.00 80.00

2013 Leaf Best of Baseball Autographs

BAA1 Albert Almora 8.00 20.00
BAA2 Austin Aune
BAM1 Alfredo Marte
BAR1 Addison Russell
BAW1 Alex Wood 4.00 10.00
BBB2 Barrett Barnes
BBJ1 Brian Johnson 3.00 8.00
BCC1 Carlos Correa 15.00 40.00
BCH1 Courtney Hawkins
BCK1 Carson Kelly 3.00 8.00
BCRJ Cal Ripken Jr. 30.00 60.00
BCS1 Corey Seager
BCY1 Christian Yelich
BDC1 Daniel Corcino
BDD1 David Dahl 4.00 10.00
BDJD D.J. Davis
BDS1 Don Sutton
BEH1 Elier Hernandez 3.00 8.00
BFL1 Francisco Lindor 3.00 8.00
BFT1 Frank Thomas 15.00 40.00
BGC1 Gavin Cecchini
BGP2 Gaylord Perry
BJA1 Jesus Aguilar 5.00 12.00
BJB1 Jim Bunning 3.00 8.00
BJB2 Javier Baez 12.50 30.00
BJB3 Jorge Bonifacio
BJB4 Johnny Bench 15.00 40.00
BJC1 Jamie Callahan 3.00 8.00
BJC2 Jose Canseco 20.00 50.00
BJG1 Joey Gallo 12.00 30.00
BJM2 Joe Morgan 8.00 20.00
BJOB J.O. Berrios 6.00 15.00
BJP1 James Paxton
BJP2 Jim Palmer 5.00 12.00
BJS1 Jorge Soler 10.00 25.00
BJS2 John Smoltz
BJV1 Jesmuel Valentin
BJW1 Jesse Winker
BKB1 Keon Barnum 4.00 10.00
BKP1 Kevin Plawecki
BLA1 Luis Aparicio 6.00 15.00
BLB2 Lewis Brinson 3.00 8.00
BMB1 Mitch Brown 4.00 10.00
BMG1 Mitchell Gueller
BMN1 Mitch Nay 3.00 8.00
BMO1 Matt Olson 6.00 15.00
BMO2 Marcell Ozuna 3.00 8.00
BMW2 Michael Wacha 10.00 25.00
BMZ1 Mike Zunino 5.00 12.00
BNM1 Nomar Mazara
BNR1 Nolan Ryan 50.00 100.00
BOA1 Oswaldo Arcia
BOS1 Ozzie Smith 30.00 60.00
BPC1 Phillips Castillo 3.00 8.00
BPM1 Paul Molitor 8.00 20.00
BPR1 Pete Rose 12.50 30.00
BRJ1 Randy Johnson
BRO1 Rougned Odor 3.00 8.00
BRR1 Rio Ruiz 3.00 8.00
BSC1 Steve Carlton
BSH1 Slade Heathcott 4.00 10.00
BST1 Stryker Trahan 3.00 8.00
BSW1 Shane Watson
BTA1 Tyler Austin 3.00 8.00
BTH1 Ty Hensley 3.00 8.00
BTR1 Tanner Rahier
BTS1 Tom Seaver
BTZL Tzu-Wei Lin 3.00 8.00
BWM1 Wyatt Mathisen
BXB1 Xander Bogaerts 15.00 40.00
BYB1 Yogi Berra
BYLW Yao-Lin Wang 4.00 10.00
BYP1 Yasiel Puig

2015 Leaf Best of Baseball

PRINTING PLATES RANDOMLY INSERTED
PLATE PRINT RUN 1 SET PER COLOR
BLACK-CYAN-MAGENTA-YELLOW ISSUED
NO PLATE PRICING DUE TO SCARCITY
YM01 Yoan Moncada 2.00 5.00
YM02 Yoan Moncada 2.00 5.00
YM03 Yoan Moncada 2.00 5.00
YM04 Yoan Moncada 2.00 5.00
YM05 Yoan Moncada 2.00 5.00
YM06 Yoan Moncada 2.00 5.00
YM07 Yoan Moncada 2.00 5.00
YM08 Yoan Moncada 2.00 5.00
YM09 Yoan Moncada 2.00 5.00

2015 Leaf Best of Baseball Gold

*GOLD: .6X TO 1.5X BASIC
RANDOM INSERTS IN PACKS
STATED PRINT RUN 25 SER.#'d SETS

2015 Leaf Best of Baseball Red

*RED: .75X TO 2X BASIC
RANDOM INSERTS IN PACKS
STATED PRINT RUN 10 SER.#'d SETS

2015 Leaf Best of Baseball Silver Spectrum

*SILVER SPEC: 1X TO 2.5X BASIC
RANDOM INSERTS IN PACKS
STATED PRINT RUN 5 SER.#'d SETS

2015 Leaf Best of Baseball Autographs

RANDOM INSERTS IN PACKS
*GOLD/25: .5X TO 1.2X BASIC
*RED/10: .6X TO 1.5X BASIC
*SLVR SPEC/5: .75X TO 2X BASIC
PRINTING PLATES RANDOMLY INSERTED
PLATE PRINT RUN 1 SET PER COLOR
BLACK-CYAN-MAGENTA-YELLOW ISSUED
NO PLATE PRICING DUE TO SCARCITY
YM01 Yoan Moncada 12.00 30.00
YM02 Yoan Moncada 12.00 30.00
YM03 Yoan Moncada 12.00 30.00
YM04 Yoan Moncada 12.00 30.00
YM05 Yoan Moncada 12.00 30.00
YM06 Yoan Moncada 12.00 30.00
YM07 Yoan Moncada 12.00 30.00
YM08 Yoan Moncada 12.00 30.00
YM09 Yoan Moncada 12.00 30.00

2017 Leaf Best of Baseball

1 A.J. Puk 2.00 5.00
2 Al Kaline 2.00 5.00
3 Alex Rodriguez 2.50 6.00
4 Blake Rutherford 2.00 5.00
5 Cal Ripken Jr. 6.00 15.00
6 Don Mattingly 4.00 10.00
7 Frank Thomas 2.00 5.00
8 Ian Anderson 4.00 10.00
9 Jason Groome 2.50 6.00
10 Johnny Bench 2.00 5.00
11 Ken Griffey Jr. 4.00 10.00
12 Mariano Rivera 2.50 6.00
13 Nick Senzel 4.00 10.00
14 Nolan Ryan 6.00 15.00
15 Omar Vizquel 1.50 4.00
16 Pete Rose 4.00 10.00
17 Reggie Jackson 1.50 4.00
18 Rickey Henderson 2.00 5.00
19 Riley Pint 1.25 3.00
20 Stan Musial 3.00 8.00
21 Tim Tebow 10.00 25.00

2017 Leaf Best of Baseball Blue

*BLUE: .5X TO 1.2X BASIC
STATED PRINT RUN 35 SER.#'d SETS

2017 Leaf Best of Baseball Purple

*PURPLE: .6X TO 1.5X BASIC
STATED PRINT RUN 25 SER.#'d SETS

2018 Leaf Best of Baseball

BB01 Alex Rodriguez .50 1.25
BB02 Alexander Cartwright .30 .75
BB03 Cal Ripken Jr. 1.25 3.00
BB04 Charlie Sheen .25 .60
BB05 Estevan Florial .40 1.00
BB06 Frank Thomas .40 1.00
BB07 Greg Maddux .50 1.25
BB08 Ichiro .50 1.25
BB09 Jesus Sanchez .40 1.00
BB10 Jonathan India 1.50 4.00
BB11 Jose Canseco .30 .75
BB12 Ken Griffey Jr. .75 2.00
BB13 Luis Urias .50 1.25
BB14 Nolan Ryan 1.25 3.00
BB15 Reggie Jackson .30 .75
BB16 Ronald Acuna 8.00 20.00
BB17 Shohei Ohtani 6.00 15.00
BB18 Shohei Ohtani 6.00 15.00

2016 Leaf Babe Ruth Collection

COMPLETE SET (80) 6.00 15.00
1 Babe Ruth .25 .60
2 Babe Ruth .25 .60
3 Babe Ruth .25 .60
4 Babe Ruth .25 .60
5 Babe Ruth .25 .60
6 Babe Ruth .25 .60
7 Babe Ruth .25 .60
8 Babe Ruth .25 .60
9 Babe Ruth .25 .60
10 Babe Ruth .25 .60
11 Babe Ruth .25 .60
12 Babe Ruth .25 .60
13 Babe Ruth .25 .60
14 Babe Ruth .25 .60
15 Babe Ruth .25 .60
16 Babe Ruth .25 .60
17 Babe Ruth .25 .60
18 Babe Ruth .25 .60
19 Babe Ruth .25 .60
20 Babe Ruth .25 .60
21 Babe Ruth .25 .60
22 Babe Ruth .25 .60
23 Babe Ruth .25 .60
24 Babe Ruth .25 .60
25 Babe Ruth .25 .60
26 Babe Ruth .25 .60
27 Babe Ruth .25 .60
28 Babe Ruth .25 .60
29 Babe Ruth .25 .60
30 Babe Ruth .25 .60
31 Babe Ruth .25 .60
32 Babe Ruth .25 .60
33 Babe Ruth .25 .60
34 Babe Ruth .25 .60
35 Babe Ruth .25 .60
36 Babe Ruth .25 .60
37 Babe Ruth .25 .60
38 Babe Ruth .25 .60
39 Babe Ruth .25 .60
40 Babe Ruth .25 .60
41 Babe Ruth .25 .60
42 Babe Ruth .25 .60
43 Babe Ruth .25 .60
44 Babe Ruth .25 .60
45 Babe Ruth .25 .60
46 Babe Ruth .25 .60
47 Babe Ruth .25 .60
48 Babe Ruth .25 .60
49 Babe Ruth .25 .60
50 Babe Ruth .25 .60
51 Babe Ruth .25 .60
52 Babe Ruth .25 .60
53 Babe Ruth .25 .60
54 Babe Ruth .25 .60
55 Babe Ruth .25 .60
56 Babe Ruth .25 .60
57 Babe Ruth .25 .60
58 Babe Ruth .25 .60
59 Babe Ruth .25 .60
60 Babe Ruth .25 .60
61 Babe Ruth .25 .60
62 Babe Ruth .25 .60
63 Babe Ruth .25 .60
64 Babe Ruth .25 .60
65 Babe Ruth .25 .60
66 Babe Ruth .25 .60
67 Babe Ruth .25 .60
68 Babe Ruth .25 .60
69 Babe Ruth .25 .60
70 Babe Ruth .25 .60
71 Babe Ruth .25 .60
72 Babe Ruth .25 .60
73 Babe Ruth .25 .60
74 Babe Ruth .25 .60
75 Babe Ruth .25 .60
76 Babe Ruth .25 .60
77 Babe Ruth .25 .60
78 Babe Ruth .25 .60
79 Babe Ruth .25 .60
80 Babe Ruth .25 .60

2016 Leaf Babe Ruth Collection Boston Bat Silver

RANDOMLY INSERTED IN PACKS
*GOLD/1: .75X TO 2X BASIC
STATED PRINT RUN 3 SER.#'d SETS

2016 Leaf Babe Ruth Collection Career Achievements

COMPLETE SET (10) 2.00 5.00
RANDOMLY INSERTS IN PACKS

2016 Leaf Babe Ruth Collection New York Bat Silver

RANDOMLY INSERTED IN PACKS
*GOLD/1: .75X TO 2X BASIC
STATED PRINT RUN 3 SER.#'d SETS

2016 Leaf Babe Ruth Collection Quotables

COMPLETE SET (10) 2.00 5.00
RANDOMLY INSERTS IN PACKS

2016 Leaf Babe Ruth Collection Yankee Stadium Seat Silver

RANDOMLY INSERTED IN PACKS
*GOLD/5: .6X TO 1.5X BASIC

2017 Leaf Babe Ruth Immortal Collection

COMMON CARD 4.00 10.00
STATED PRINT RUN 50 SER.#'d SETS

2017 Leaf Babe Ruth Immortal Collection Gold Spectrum

*GOLD SPECTRUM: .75X TO 2X BASIC
STATED PRINT RUN 10 SER,#'d SETS

2017 Leaf Babe Ruth Immortal Collection Purple Spectrum

*PURPLE SPECTRUM: 4X TO 10X BASIC
STATED PRINT RUN 1 SER,#'d SET

2017 Leaf Babe Ruth Immortal Collection Red Spectrum

*RED SPECTRUM: .6X TO 1.5X BASIC
STATED PRINT RUN 20 SER,#'d SETS

2017 Leaf Babe Ruth Immortal Collection Boston Bat

COMMON CARD 30.00 80.00
STATED PRINT RUN 20 SER.#'d SETS
*RED SPEC/10: .5X TO 1.2X BASIC
*GOLD SPEC/5: .6X TO 1.5X BASIC
*PURPLE SPEC/1: 1.2X TO 3X BASIC

2017 Leaf Babe Ruth Immortal Collection New York Bat

COMMON CARD 30.00 80.00
STATED PRINT RUN 20 SER.#'d SETS
*RED SPEC/10: .5X TO 1.2X BASIC
*GOLD SPEC/5: .6X TO 1.5X BASIC
*PURPLE SPEC/1: 2X TO 5X BASIC

2017 Leaf Babe Ruth Immortal Collection Yankee Stadium Seat

COMMON CARD 12.00 30.00
STATED PRINT RUN 50 SER.#'d SETS
*RED SPEC/20: .4X TO 1X BASIC
*GOLD SPEC/10: .4 TO 1X BASIC
*PURPLE SPEC/1: 2.5X TO 6X BASIC

2005 Leaf Century

COMPLETE SET (200) 30.00 60.00
COMMON ACTIVE .20 .50
COMMON RET .20 .50
1 Brian Roberts .20 .50
2 Derek Jeter 1.25 3.00
3 Harmon Killebrew .50 1.25
4 Angel Berroa .20 .50
5 George Brett 1.00 2.50
6 Stan Musial .75 2.00
7 Ivan Rodriguez .30 .75
8 Cal Ripken 1.50 4.00
9 Hank Blalock .20 .50
10 Miguel Tejada .30 .75
11 Barry Larkin .30 .75
12 Alfonso Soriano .30 .75
13 Alex Rodriguez .60 1.50
14 Paul Konerko .30 .75
15 Jim Edmonds .30 .75
16 Garret Anderson .20 .50
17 Todd Helton .30 .75
18 Moises Alou .20 .50
19 Tony Gwynn .60 1.50
20 Mike Schmidt .75 2.00
21 Sammy Sosa .50 1.25
22 Roger Clemens .60 1.50
23 Tony Perez .30 .75
24 Manny Ramirez .50 1.25
25 Jim Thome .30 .75
26 Chase Utley .30 .75
27 Scott Rolen .30 .75
28 Austin Kearns .20 .50
29 John Smoltz .50 1.25
30 Ken Griffey Jr. 1.00 2.50
31 Mike Piazza .50 1.25
32 Steve Carlton .30 .75
33 Larry Walker .30 .75
34 Nolan Ryan 1.50 4.00
35 Mike Mussina .30 .75
36 Joe Nathan .20 .50
37 Kenny Rogers .20 .50
38 Eric Gagne .20 .50
39 Brett Myers .20 .50
40 Rich Harden .20 .50
41 Victor Martinez .30 .75
42 Mariano Rivera .60 1.50
43 Dennis Eckersley .30 .75
44 Roy Oswalt .30 .75
45 Pedro Martinez .30 .75
46 Jason Bay .20 .50
47 Tom Glavine .30 .75
48 Torii Hunter .20 .50
49 Larry Bigbie .20 .50
50 Nomar Garciaparra .30 .75
51 Ichiro Suzuki .60 1.50
52 C.C. Sabathia .30 .75
53 Bobby Abreu .20 .50
54 Doug Mientkiewicz .20 .50
55 Hideki Matsui .75 2.00
56 Mark Buehrle .30 .75
57 Johan Santana .30 .75
58 Johnny Damon .30 .75
59 Edgar Martinez .30 .75
60 Preston Wilson .20 .50
61 Livan Hernandez .20 .50
62 Eric Chavez .20 .50
63 Lyle Overbay .20 .50
64 Jason Schmidt .20 .50
65 Cliff Lee .30 .75
66 Shingo Takatsu .20 .50
67 Jeff Bagwell .30 .75
68 Danny Graves .20 .50
69 Kip Wells .20 .50
70 Steve Finley .20 .50
71 Lew Ford .20 .50
72 Chone Figgins .20 .50
73 Delmon Young .50 1.25
74 Esteban Loaiza .20 .50
75 Barry Zito .30 .75
76 Carlos Delgado .20 .50
77 Joe Mauer .40 1.00
78 Ryan Wagner .20 .50
79 John Lackey .30 .75
80 Adrian Beltre .50 1.25
81 Vernon Wells .20 .50
82 Sean Burroughs .20 .50
83 Francisco Cordero .20 .50
84 Carlos Guillen .20 .50
85 Eric Byrnes .20 .50
86 Jose Reyes .30 .75
87 Rocco Baldelli .20 .50
88 Josh Beckett .20 .50
89 Casey Kotchman .20 .50
90 Scott Podsednik .20 .50
91 Mike Sweeney .20 .50
92 Khalil Greene .20 .50
93 Trot Nixon .20 .50
94 Chad Cordero .20 .50
95 Derek Lowe .20 .50
96 Jason Giambi .20 .50
97 Jose Guillen .20 .50
98 Craig Biggio .30 .75
99 Pat Burrell .20 .50
100 Kazuo Matsui .20 .50
101 Rafael Furcal .20 .50
102 Jack Wilson .20 .50
103 Edgar Renteria .20 .50
104 Carlos Beltran .30 .75
105 Albert Pujols .60 1.50
106 Melvin Mora .20 .50
107 J.D. Drew .20 .50
108 Andre Dawson .30 .75
109 Jody Gerut .20 .50
110 Michael Young .20 .50
111 Gary Sheffield .20 .50
112 Wade Boggs .30 .75
113 Carl Crawford .30 .75
114 Paul Lo Duca .20 .50
115 Tim Hudson .30 .75
116 Aramis Ramirez .20 .50
117 Lance Berkman .30 .75
118 Javy Lopez .20 .50
119 Robin Yount .50 1.25
120 Mark Mulder .20 .50
121 Sean Casey .20 .50
122 Will Clark .30 .75
123 Don Mattingly 1.00 2.50
124 Miguel Cabrera .50 1.25
125 Rafael Palmeiro .30 .75
126 David Ortiz .50 1.25
127 Vladimir Guerrero .30 .75
128 Ken Harvey .20 .50
129 Rod Carew .30 .75
130 Magglio Ordonez .30 .75
131 Greg Maddux .60 1.50
132 Roy Halladay .30 .75
133 Javier Vazquez .20 .50
134 Kerry Wood .20 .50
135 Frank Thomas .50 1.25
136 Tom Gordon .20 .50
137 Jake Peavy .20 .50
138 Curt Schilling .30 .75
139 Dewon Brazelton .20 .50
140 Jae Weong Seo .20 .50
141 Danny Kolb .20 .50
142 Jeff Kent .20 .50
143 Juan Encarnacion .20 .50
144 Adam Dunn .30 .75
145 Carlos Lee .20 .50
146 Matt Clement .20 .50
147 Guillermo Mota .20 .50
148 Travis Hafner .20 .50
149 Brad Wilkerson .20 .50
150 Eric Milton .20 .50
151 Randy Johnson .50 1.25
152 Joe Crede .20 .50
153 Mark Kotsay .20 .50
154 Jason Varitek .50 1.25
155 David Wright .40 1.00
156 Brad Penny .20 .50
157 Francisco Rodriguez .30 .75
158 Gary Carter .30 .75
159 Adrian Gonzalez .40 1.00
160 Derrek Lee .20 .50
161 Mark Prior .30 .75
162 Carlos Zambrano .30 .75
163 Bobby Crosby .20 .50
164 Jermaine Dye .20 .50
165 Kris Benson .20 .50
166 Dontrelle Willis .20 .50
167 Dallas McPherson .20 .50
168 Johnny Estrada .20 .50
169 Milton Bradley .20 .50
170 Shannon Stewart .20 .50
171 Ben Sheets .20 .50
172 Richard Hidalgo .20 .50
173 Laynce Nix .20 .50
174 B.J. Upton .30 .75
175 Craig Wilson .20 .50
176 Hideo Nomo .50 1.25
177 Troy Glaus .20 .50
178 Akinori Otsuka .20 .50
179 Rickie Weeks .20 .50
180 Mike Lowell .20 .50
181 Marcus Giles .20 .50
182 Randy Wolf .20 .50
183 A.J. Burnett .20 .50
184 Aubrey Huff .20 .50
185 Billy Ripken .20 .50
186 Octavio Dotel .20 .50
187 Kazuhisa Ishii .20 .50
188 Mark Teixeira .30 .75
189 Todd Walker .20 .50
190 Dale Murphy .50 1.25
191 Alexis Rios .20 .50
192 Reggie Sanders .20 .50
193 Orlando Cabrera .20 .50
194 Shawn Green .20 .50
195 Andy Pettitte .30 .75
196 Chipper Jones .50 1.25
197 Jose Vidro .20 .50
198 Jacque Jones .20 .50
199 Brian Giles .20 .50
200 Andruw Jones .20 .50

2005 Leaf Century Post Marks Gold

*GOLD ACTIVE: 3X TO 8X BASIC
*GOLD RETIRED: 2.5X TO 6X BASIC
OVERALL INSERT ODDS 1:3
STATED PRINT RUN 50 SERIAL #'d SETS

2005 Leaf Century Post Marks Platinum

OVERALL INSERT ODDS 1:3
STATED PRINT RUN 1 SERIAL #'d SET
NO PRICING DUE TO SCARCITY

2005 Leaf Century Post Marks Silver

*SILVER ACTIVE: 2.5X TO 6X BASIC
*SILVER RETIRED: 2X TO 5X BASIC
OVERALL INSERT ODDS 1:3
STATED PRINT RUN 100 SERIAL #'d SETS

2005 Leaf Century Material Bat

*BAT p/r 250: .4X TO 1X POS p/r 250
*BAT p/r 250: .3X TO .8X POS p/r 100
*BAT p/r 100: .5X TO 1.2X POS p/r 250
*BAT p/r 100: .4X TO 1X POS p/r 100
*BAT p/r 50: .75X TO 2X POS p/r 250
*BAT p/r 50: .6X TO 1.5X POS p/r 100
*BAT p/r 25: 1.25X TO 3X POS p/r 250
OVERALL INSERT ODDS 1:3
PRINT RUNS B/WN 5-250 COPIES PER
NO PRICING ON QTY OF 5
18 Moises Alou/50 3.00 8.00
50 Nomar Garciaparra/100 4.00 10.00
54 Doug Mientkiewicz/50 3.00 8.00
58 Johnny Damon/100 3.00 8.00
73 Delmon Young/100 3.00 8.00
107 J.D. Drew/100 2.00 5.00
114 Paul Lo Duca/100 2.00 5.00
143 Juan Encarnacion/50 3.00 8.00
149 Brad Wilkerson/100 2.00 5.00
152 Joe Crede/50 2.00 5.00
156 Brad Penny/50 3.00 8.00
160 Derrek Lee/250 3.00 8.00
172 Richard Hidalgo/50 3.00 8.00
174 B.J. Upton/50 5.00 12.00
179 Rickie Weeks/25 3.00 8.00
191 Alexis Rios/50 3.00 8.00
193 Orlando Cabrera/50 3.00 8.00
199 Brian Giles/250 2.00 5.00

2005 Leaf Century Material Fabric Number

*NBR p/r 75: .5X TO 1.2X POS p/r 250
*NBR p/r 36-65: .75X TO 2X POS p/r 250
*NBR p/r 36-65: .6X TO 1.5X POS p/r 100
*NBR p/r 20-35: 1.25X TO 3X POS p/r 250
*NBR p/r 20-35: 1X TO 2.5X POS p/r 100
*NBR p/r 20-35: .4X TO 1X POS p/r 25
*NBR p/r 15-19: 1.5X TO 4X POS p/r 250
*NBR p/r 15-19: 1.25X TO 3X POS p/r 100
OVERALL INSERT ODDS 1:3
PRINT RUNS B/WN 1-75 COPIES PER
NO PRICING ON QTY OF 14 OR LESS

2005 Leaf Century Material Fabric Position

PRINT RUNS B/WN 1-250 COPIES PER
NO PRICING ON QTY OF 5 OR LESS
PRIME PRINT RUN 1 SERIAL #'d SET
NO PRIME PRICING DUE TO SCARCITY
OVERALL INSERT ODDS 1:3
1 Brian Roberts Jsy/250 2.00 5.00
3 Harmon Killebrew Jsy/250 6.00 15.00
4 Angel Berroa Jsy/250 2.00 5.00
5 George Brett Jsy/250 8.00 20.00
6 Stan Musial Pants/100 8.00 20.00
7 Ivan Rodriguez Jsy/250 3.00 8.00
8 Cal Ripken Jkt/250 10.00 25.00
9 Hank Blalock Jsy/250 2.00 5.00
10 Miguel Tejada Jsy/250 2.00 5.00
11 Barry Larkin Jsy/100 3.00 8.00
12 Alfonso Soriano Jsy/250 2.00 5.00
14 Paul Konerko Jsy/250 2.00 5.00
15 Jim Edmonds Jsy/250 2.00 5.00
16 Garret Anderson Jsy/250 2.00 5.00
17 Todd Helton Jsy/250 3.00 8.00
19 Tony Gwynn Jsy/250 6.00 15.00
20 Mike Schmidt Jsy/250 8.00 20.00
21 Sammy Sosa Jsy/250 3.00 8.00
22 Roger Clemens Jsy/250 5.00 12.00
23 Tony Perez Jsy/250 3.00 8.00
24 Manny Ramirez Jsy/250 3.00 8.00
25 Jim Thome Jsy/250 3.00 8.00
27 Scott Rolen Jsy/250 3.00 8.00
28 Austin Kearns Jsy/250 2.00 5.00
29 John Smoltz Jsy/250 3.00 8.00
31 Mike Piazza Jsy/250 3.00 8.00
32 Steve Carlton Pants/250 3.00 8.00
34 Nolan Ryan Jsy/250 10.00 25.00
35 Mike Mussina Jsy/250 3.00 8.00
39 Brett Myers Jsy/250 2.00 5.00
41 Victor Martinez Jsy/250 2.00 5.00
42 Mariano Rivera Jsy/250 3.00 8.00
43 Dennis Eckersley Jsy/250 3.00 8.00
44 Roy Oswalt Jsy/250 2.00 5.00
45 Pedro Martinez Jsy/250 3.00 8.00
46 Jason Bay Jsy/250 2.00 5.00
47 Tom Glavine Jsy/250 3.00 8.00
48 Torii Hunter Jsy/250 2.00 5.00
49 Larry Bigbie Jsy/250 2.00 5.00
52 C.C. Sabathia Jsy/250 2.00 5.00
53 Bobby Abreu Jsy/250 2.00 5.00
55 Hideki Matsui Jsy/250 8.00 20.00
56 Mark Buehrle Jsy/250 2.00 5.00
57 Johan Santana Jsy/250 3.00 8.00
59 Edgar Martinez Jsy/250 3.00 8.00
60 Preston Wilson Jsy/250 2.00 5.00
61 Livan Hernandez Jsy/250 2.00 5.00
62 Eric Chavez Jsy/250 2.00 5.00
63 Lyle Overbay Jsy/250 2.00 5.00
65 Cliff Lee Jsy/250 2.00 5.00
67 Jeff Bagwell Jsy/250 3.00 8.00
71 Lew Ford Jsy/250 2.00 5.00
72 Chone Figgins Jsy/250 2.00 5.00
75 Barry Zito Jsy/250 2.00 5.00
76 Carlos Delgado Jsy/250 2.00 5.00
78 Ryan Wagner Jsy/250 2.00 5.00
80 Adrian Beltre Jsy/250 2.00 5.00
81 Vernon Wells Jsy/250 2.00 5.00
82 Sean Burroughs Jsy/250 2.00 5.00
83 Francisco Cordero Jsy/250 2.00 5.00
85 Eric Byrnes Jsy/25 5.00 12.00
86 Jose Reyes Jsy/250 2.00 5.00
87 Rocco Baldelli Jsy/250 2.00 5.00
88 Josh Beckett Jsy/250 2.00 5.00
90 Scott Podsednik Jsy/250 2.00 5.00
91 Mike Sweeney Jsy/250 2.00 5.00
93 Trot Nixon Jsy/250 2.00 5.00
96 Jason Giambi Jsy/250 2.00 5.00
98 Craig Biggio Jsy/250 3.00 8.00
99 Pat Burrell Jsy/250 2.00 5.00
100 Kazuo Matsui Jsy/250 2.00 5.00
101 Rafael Furcal Jsy/250 2.00 5.00
102 Jack Wilson Jsy/250 2.00 5.00
103 Edgar Renteria Jsy/250 2.00 5.00
104 Carlos Beltran Jsy/250 2.00 5.00
105 Albert Pujols Jsy/250 6.00 15.00
106 Melvin Mora Jsy/100 2.00 5.00
108 Andre Dawson Jsy/250 3.00 8.00
109 Jody Gerut Jsy/250 2.00 5.00
110 Michael Young Jsy/250 2.00 5.00
111 Gary Sheffield Jsy/250 2.00 5.00
112 Wade Boggs Jsy/100 5.00 12.00
113 Carl Crawford Jsy/250 2.00 5.00
115 Tim Hudson Jsy/250 2.00 5.00
116 Aramis Ramirez Jsy/250 2.00 5.00
117 Lance Berkman Jsy/250 2.00 5.00
118 Javy Lopez Jsy/250 2.00 5.00
119 Robin Yount Jsy/250 4.00 10.00
120 Mark Mulder Jsy/250 2.00 5.00
121 Sean Casey Jsy/250 2.00 5.00
122 Will Clark Jsy/250 4.00 10.00
123 Don Mattingly Pants/250 8.00 20.00
124 Miguel Cabrera Jsy/250 3.00 8.00
125 Rafael Palmeiro Jsy/250 3.00 8.00
126 David Ortiz Jsy/250 3.00 8.00
127 Vladimir Guerrero Jsy/250 3.00 8.00
128 Ken Harvey Jsy/250 2.00 5.00
129 Rod Carew Jsy/250 4.00 10.00
130 Magglio Ordonez Jsy/250 2.00 5.00
131 Greg Maddux Jsy/250 5.00 12.00
132 Roy Halladay Jsy/250 2.00 5.00
134 Kerry Wood Jsy/250 2.00 5.00
135 Frank Thomas Jsy/250 3.00 8.00
138 Curt Schilling Jsy/250 3.00 8.00
139 Dewon Brazelton Jsy/100 2.00 5.00
140 Jae Weong Seo Jsy/100 2.00 5.00
141 Danny Kolb Jsy/250 2.00 5.00
142 Jeff Kent Jsy/100 2.00 5.00
144 Adam Dunn Jsy/250 2.00 5.00
145 Carlos Lee Jsy/250 2.00 5.00
146 Matt Clement Jsy/250 2.00 5.00
148 Travis Hafner Jsy/250 2.00 5.00
151 Randy Johnson Pants/250 3.00 8.00
154 Jason Varitek Jsy/100 4.00 10.00
157 Fran Rodriguez Jsy/100 2.00 5.00
158 Gary Carter Jsy/250 3.00 8.00
161 Mark Prior Jsy/250 3.00 8.00
162 Carlos Zambrano Jsy/100 2.00 5.00
163 Bobby Crosby Jsy/250 2.00 5.00
164 Jermaine Dye Jsy/100 2.00 5.00
166 Dontrelle Willis Jsy/250 2.00 5.00
168 Johnny Estrada Jsy/100 2.00 5.00
170 Shannon Stewart Jsy/100 2.00 5.00
171 Ben Sheets Jsy/250 2.00 5.00
173 Laynce Nix Jsy/100 2.00 5.00
175 Craig Wilson Jsy/100 2.00 5.00
176 Hideo Nomo Jsy/250 3.00 8.00
177 Troy Glaus Jsy/250 2.00 5.00
180 Mike Lowell Jsy/250 2.00 5.00
183 A.J. Burnett Jsy/100 2.00 5.00
184 Aubrey Huff Jsy/250 2.00 5.00
187 Kazuhisa Ishii Jsy/250 2.00 5.00
188 Mark Teixeira Jsy/250 3.00 8.00
190 Dale Murphy Jsy/250 4.00 10.00
194 Shawn Green Jsy/250 2.00 5.00
195 Andy Pettitte Jsy/250 3.00 8.00
196 Chipper Jones Jsy/250 3.00 8.00
197 Jose Vidro Jsy/100 2.00 5.00
198 Jacque Jones Jsy/250 2.00 5.00
200 Andruw Jones Jsy/250 3.00 8.00

2005 Leaf Century Signature Post Marks Gold

*GOLD p/r 50: .6X TO 1.5X SILV p/r 250
*GOLD p/r 50: .5X TO 1.2X SILV p/r 100
*GOLD p/r 25: .75X TO 2X SILV p/r 250
*GOLD p/r 25: .6X TO 1.5X SILV p/r 100
*GOLD p/r 25: .5X TO 1.2X SILV p/r 50
OVERALL INSERT ODDS 1:3
PRINT RUNS B/WN 1-50 COPIES PER
NO PRICING ON QTY OF 10 OR LESS

2005 Leaf Century Signature Post Marks Platinum

OVERALL INSERT ODDS 1:3
STATED PRINT RUN 1 SERIAL #'d SET
NO PRICING DUE TO SCARCITY

2005 Leaf Century Signature Post Marks Silver

OVERALL INSERT ODDS 1:3
PRINT RUNS B/WN 1-250 COPIES PER
NO PRICING ON QTY OF 10 OR LESS
1 Brian Roberts/250 6.00 15.00
4 Angel Berroa/25 6.00 15.00
36 Joe Nathan/250 10.00 25.00
39 Brett Myers/250 6.00 15.00
40 Rich Harden/100 6.00 15.00
49 Larry Bigbie/250 6.00 15.00
52 C.C. Sabathia/25 10.00 25.00
56 Mark Buehrle/50 15.00 40.00
61 Livan Hernandez/100 8.00 20.00
63 Lyle Overbay/100 4.00 10.00
65 Cliff Lee/250 6.00 15.00
68 Danny Graves/100 4.00 10.00
71 Lew Ford/100 4.00 10.00
72 Chone Figgins/250 6.00 15.00
74 Esteban Loaiza/250 6.00 15.00
78 Ryan Wagner/250 4.00 10.00
79 John Lackey/250 6.00 15.00
82 Sean Burroughs/25 6.00 15.00
83 Francisco Cordero/100 6.00 15.00
85 Eric Byrnes/100 4.00 10.00
89 Casey Kotchman/250 6.00 15.00
90 Scott Podsednik/100 10.00 25.00
93 Trot Nixon/25 10.00 25.00
94 Chad Cordero/250 6.00 15.00
97 Jose Guillen/100 6.00 15.00
102 Jack Wilson/100 6.00 15.00
106 Melvin Mora/100 6.00 15.00
108 Andre Dawson/25 10.00 25.00
109 Jody Gerut/250 4.00 10.00
116 Aramis Ramirez/25 10.00 25.00
128 Ken Harvey/250 4.00 10.00
136 Tom Gordon/250 6.00 15.00
137 Jake Peavy/100 10.00 25.00
139 Dewon Brazelton/250 4.00 10.00
140 Jae Weong Seo/100 6.00 15.00
141 Danny Kolb/250 4.00 10.00
145 Carlos Lee/100 6.00 15.00
147 Guillermo Mota/250 4.00 10.00
148 Travis Hafner/100 6.00 15.00
155 David Wright/25 40.00 80.00
156 Brad Penny/250 4.00 10.00
157 Francisco Rodriguez/100 10.00 25.00
159 Adrian Gonzalez/250 10.00 25.00
160 Derrek Lee/25 15.00 40.00
162 Carlos Zambrano/25 10.00 25.00
163 Bobby Crosby/100 6.00 15.00
164 Jermaine Dye/250 6.00 15.00
168 Johnny Estrada/200 4.00 10.00
169 Milton Bradley/100 6.00 15.00
170 Shannon Stewart/50 8.00 20.00
173 Laynce Nix/250 4.00 10.00
175 Craig Wilson/100 4.00 10.00
181 Marcus Giles/25 10.00 25.00
182 Randy Wolf/250 4.00 10.00
184 Aubrey Huff/100 6.00 15.00
185 Billy Ripken/250 4.00 10.00
186 Octavio Dotel/250 6.00 15.00
189 Todd Walker/100 6.00 15.00
191 Alexis Rios/200 6.00 15.00
193 Orlando Cabrera/25 10.00 25.00
197 Jose Vidro/25 10.00 25.00
198 Jacque Jones/100 6.00 15.00

2005 Leaf Century Air Mail Bat

OVERALL INSERT ODDS 1:3
PRINT RUNS B/WN 50-250 COPIES PER
1 Babe Ruth/50 100.00 200.00
2 Frank Robinson/250 3.00 8.00
3 Harmon Killebrew/100 8.00 20.00

4 Sammy Sosa/100 4.00 10.00
5 Reggie Jackson/250 4.00 10.00
6 Mike Schmidt/100 10.00 25.00
7 Rafael Palmeiro/100 3.00 8.00
8 Ted Williams/50 60.00 120.00
9 Willie McCovey/250 4.00 10.00
10 Ernie Banks/100 6.00 15.00

2005 Leaf Century Air Mail Bat Signature

OVERALL INSERT ODDS 1:3
PRINT RUNS B/WN 1-25 COPIES PER
NO PRICING ON QTY OF 5 OR LESS
2 Frank Robinson/25 20.00 50.00
3 Harmon Killebrew/25 50.00 100.00
9 Willie McCovey/25 20.00 50.00

2005 Leaf Century Pennant Patches

OVERALL INSERT ODDS 1:3
PRINT RUNS B/WN 5-25 COPIES PER
NO PRICING ON QTY OF 10 OR LESS
1 Ozzie Smith/25 20.00 50.00
2 Keith Hernandez/25 10.00 25.00
3 Rickey Henderson/25 20.00 50.00
4 Paul Molitor/25 10.00 25.00
5 George Brett/25 30.00 60.00
6 Steve Garvey/25 10.00 25.00
7 Randy Johnson/25 12.50 30.00
8 Cal Ripken/25 30.00 60.00
9 Darryl Strawberry/25 10.00 25.00
10 Chipper Jones/25 15.00 40.00
11 Steve Carlton/25 10.00 25.00
12 Orel Hershiser/25 10.00 25.00
13 Carlton Fisk/25 12.50 30.00
14 Dave Parker/25 10.00 25.00
15 Rollie Fingers/25 10.00 25.00
16 Dwight Gooden/25 10.00 25.00
18 Dontrelle Willis/25 6.00 15.00
19 Dave Righetti/25 10.00 25.00

2005 Leaf Century Pennant Patches Signature

OVERALL INSERT ODDS 1:3
PRINT RUNS B/WN 5-25 COPIES PER
NO PRICING ON QTY OF 10 OR LESS
2 Keith Hernandez/25 20.00 50.00
6 Steve Garvey/25 20.00 50.00
9 Darryl Strawberry/25 20.00 50.00
11 Steve Carlton/25 20.00 50.00
15 Rollie Fingers/25 20.00 50.00
16 Dwight Gooden/25 20.00 50.00

2005 Leaf Century Shirts

OVERALL INSERT ODDS 1:3
PRINT RUNS B/WN 25-100 COPIES PER
1 Rod Carew/100 5.00 12.00
2 Red Schoendienst/50 4.00 10.00
3 Harmon Killebrew/50 10.00 25.00
4 Joe Cronin/50 20.00 50.00
5 Early Wynn/50 4.00 10.00
6 Gaylord Perry/100 3.00 8.00
7 Willie McCovey/100 5.00 12.00
8 Carl Yastrzemski/100 10.00 25.00
9 Reggie Jackson/100 5.00 12.00
10 Duke Snider/50 6.00 15.00
11 Luis Aparicio/100 3.00 8.00
12 Bob Gibson/50 6.00 15.00
13 Maury Wills/50 4.00 10.00
14 Ernie Banks/50 12.00 30.00
15 Enos Slaughter/100 8.00 20.00
16 Whitey Ford/100 6.00 15.00
17 Warren Spahn/100 8.00 20.00
18 Roger Maris/100 10.00 25.00
19 Hal Newhouser/100 6.00 15.00
20 Marty Marion/25 6.00 15.00

2005 Leaf Century Shirts Signature

PRINT RUNS B/WN 1-50 COPIES PER
NO PRICING ON QTY OF 10 OR LESS
PRIME PRINT RUN 1 SERIAL #'d SET
NO PRIME PRICING DUE TO SCARCITY
OVERALL INSERT ODDS 1:3
2 Red Schoendienst/25 12.50 30.00
6 Gaylord Perry/50 10.00 25.00
7 Willie McCovey/50 15.00 40.00
11 Luis Aparicio/50 10.00 25.00
13 Maury Wills/50 10.00 25.00

2005 Leaf Century Stamps Material Centennial

*CTL p/r 39: .5X TO 1.2X USA p/r 72-100
*CTL p/r 39: .4X TO 1X USA p/r 44-48
*CTL p/r 39: .3X TO .8X USA p/r 20-28
*CTL p/r 21: .4X TO 1X USA p/r 20-28
*CTL p/r 16: .4X TO 1X USA p/r 16
OVERALL INSERT ODDS 1:3
PRINT RUNS B/WN 1-39 COPIES PER
NO PRICING ON QTY OF 11 OR LESS
COOP.STAMP ON 1ST #'d COPY PER CARD
3 Babe Ruth Jsy/39 250.00 400.00
8 Ted Williams Jsy/39 30.00 60.00
12 Dave Concepcion Jsy/39 8.00 20.00
23 Roger Maris Jsy/39 40.00 80.00
60 Lou Boudreau Jsy/39 12.50 30.00
61 Alan Trammell Bat/39 8.00 20.00
69 Michael Young Jsy/39 8.00 20.00

2005 Leaf Century Stamps Material Legendary Fields

*LGD FLD p/r 34: .6X TO 1.5X USA p/r 72-100
*LGD FLD p/r 34: .5X TO 1.2X USA p/r 44-48
*LGD FLD p/r 34: .4X TO 1X USA p/r 20-28
*LGD FLD p/r 34: .3X TO .8X USA p/r 16
*LGD FLD p/r 21: .4X TO 1X USA p/r 20-28
OVERALL INSERT ODDS 1:3
PRINT RUNS B/WN 1-34 COPIES PER
NO PRICING ON QTY OF 11 OR LESS
COOP.STAMP ON 1ST #'d COPY PER CARD
12 Dave Concepcion Jsy/34 10.00 25.00
23 Roger Maris Jsy/34 40.00 80.00
61 Alan Trammell Bat/34 10.00 25.00
74 Kirk Gibson Jsy/34 30.00 60.00

2005 Leaf Century Stamps Material Legendary Players 20

*LGD PLY p/r 21: .4X TO 1X USA p/r 21
OVERALL INSERT ODDS 1:3
PRINT RUNS B/WN 19-21 COPIES PER
20-CENT STAMP FEATURED
COOP.STAMP ON 1ST #'d COPY PER CARD
3 Babe Ruth Jsy/19 300.00 500.00

2005 Leaf Century Stamps Material Legendary Players 33

*LGD PLY p/r 21: .4X TO 1X USA p/r 21
OVERALL INSERT ODDS 1:3
PRINT RUNS B/WN 19-21 COPIES PER
33-CENT STAMP FEATURED
COOP.STAMP ON 1ST #'d COPY PER CARD
3 Babe Ruth Jsy/19 300.00 500.00

2005 Leaf Century Stamps Material Olympic

*OLY p/r 92: .4X TO 1X USA p/r 72-100
*OLY p/r 92: .3X TO .8X USA p/r 44-48
*OLY p/r 92: .25X TO .6X USA p/r 20-28
*OLY p/r 44-48: .5X TO 1.2X USA p/r 72-100
*OLY p/r 44-48: .4X TO 1X USA p/r 44-48
*OLY p/r 20-30: .6X TO 1.5X USA p/r 72-100
*OLY p/r 20-30: .4X TO 1X USA p/r 20-28
*OLY p/r 16: .4X TO 1X USA p/r 16
OVERALL INSERT ODDS 1:3
PRINT RUNS B/WN 1-92 COPIES PER
NO PRICING ON QTY OF 13 OR LESS
COOP.STAMP ON 1ST #'d COPY PER CARD
60 Lou Boudreau Jsy/92 10.00 25.00
61 Alan Trammell Bat/92 6.00 15.00

2005 Leaf Century Stamps Material Pro Ball

*PRO p/r 69: .4X TO 1X USA p/r 72-100
*PRO p/r 69: .3X TO .8X USA p/r 44-48
*PRO p/r 69: .25X TO .6X USA p/r 20-28
*PRO p/r 45-48: .5X TO 1.2X USA p/r 72-100
*PRO p/r 45-48: .4X TO 1X USA p/r 44-48
*PRO p/r 20-27: .6X TO 1.5X USA p/r 72-100
*PRO p/r 20-27: .4X TO 1X USA p/r 20-28
*PRO p/r 16: .4X TO 1X USA p/r 16
OVERALL INSERT ODDS 1:3
COOP.STAMP ON 1ST #'d COPY PER CARD
60 Lou Boudreau Jsy/69 10.00 25.00
61 Alan Trammell Bat/69 6.00 15.00

2005 Leaf Century Stamps Material USA Flag

OVERALL INSERT ODDS 1:3
PRINT RUNS B/WN 1-100 COPIES PER
NO PRICING ON QTY OF 13 OR LESS
COOP.STAMP ON 1ST #'d COPY PER CARD
1 Pee Wee Reese Bat/100 8.00 20.00
4 George Brett Jsy/100 15.00 40.00
5 Stan Musial Bat/100 12.50 30.00
6 Bob Feller Pants/100 8.00 20.00
7 Cal Ripken Pants/100 40.00 80.00
11 Dwight Evans Jsy/24 12.50 30.00
13 Ernie Banks Jsy/100 10.00 25.00
14 Pedro Martinez Jsy/45 10.00 25.00
15 Whitey Ford Jsy/16 15.00 40.00
16 Scott Rolen Jsy/27 12.50 30.00
17 Tony Gwynn Jsy/100 12.50 30.00
18 Mike Schmidt Jsy/100 20.00 50.00
19 Roberto Clemente Hat/21 75.00 150.00
20 Roger Clemens Jsy/100 10.00 25.00
21 Don Mattingly Jsy/100 15.00 40.00
22 Tony Perez Bat/100 6.00 15.00
24 Billy Williams Jsy/100 6.00 15.00
25 Juan Marichal Pants/100 6.00 15.00
26 Hank Blalock Jsy/100 6.00 15.00
27 Maury Wills Jsy/100 6.00 15.00
28 Fergie Jenkins Pants/100 6.00 15.00
29 Steve Carlton Jsy/100 6.00 15.00
30 Dale Murphy Jsy/100 8.00 20.00
31 Kerry Wood Jsy/100 6.00 15.00
32 Gaylord Perry Jsy/100 6.00 15.00
33 Fred Lynn Jsy/100 6.00 15.00
34 Tom Seaver Bat/100 8.00 20.00
36 Reggie Jackson Pants/44 10.00 25.00
37 Bob Gibson Jsy/100 8.00 20.00
38 Jack Morris Jsy/100 6.00 15.00
39 Torii Hunter Jsy/48 8.00 20.00
40 Andre Dawson Jsy/100 6.00 15.00
41 Dave Righetti Jsy/100 6.00 15.00
42 Hideki Matsui Pants/100 20.00 50.00
43 Lou Brock Jkt/100 8.00 20.00
44 Yogi Berra Bat/100 10.00 25.00
45 Frankie Frisch Jkt/100 10.00 25.00
46 Sean Casey Jsy/100 6.00 15.00
47 Sammy Sosa Jsy/100 10.00 25.00
48 Ralph Kiner Bat/100 10.00 25.00
49 Hoyt Wilhelm Jsy/100 6.00 15.00
50 Jim Rice Jsy/100 6.00 15.00
51 Duke Snider Pants/100 10.00 25.00
52 Harold Baines Jsy/100 6.00 15.00
53 Willie Stargell Jsy/100 8.00 20.00
54 Johnny Bench Pants/100 10.00 25.00
55 Carlton Fisk Jsy/72 8.00 20.00
56 Jim Palmer Jsy/100 6.00 15.00
57 Bobby Doerr Jsy/100 6.00 15.00
58 Mark Prior Jsy/100 8.00 20.00
62 Al Kaline Bat/100 10.00 25.00
63 Warren Spahn Pants/100 10.00 25.00
64 Bert Blyleven Jsy/28 10.00 25.00
65 Miguel Cabrera Jsy/24 12.50 30.00
66 Luis Tiant Jsy/23 10.00 25.00
67 Harmon Killebrew Jsy/100 15.00 40.00
68 Richie Ashburn Pants/100 10.00 25.00
70 Tony Oliva Jsy/100 6.00 15.00
71 Mark Mulder Jsy/20 10.00 25.00
72 Nolan Ryan Jsy/100 12.50 30.00
73 Willie McCovey Jsy/44 10.00 25.00
74 Kirk Gibson Jsy/100 6.00 15.00
75 Carl Yastrzemski Pants/100 12.50 30.00

2005 Leaf Century Stamps Signature Centennial

*CTL p/r 39-59: .5X TO 1.2X USA p/r 100
*CTL p/r 39-59: .4X TO 1X USA p/r 48-49
*CTL p/r 39-59: .3X TO .8X USA p/r 20-27
*CTL p/r 39-59: .25X TO .6X USA p/r 19
*CTL p/r 20-27: .4X TO 1X USA p/r 20-27
OVERALL INSERT ODDS 1:3
PRINT RUNS B/WN 1-59 COPIES PER
NO PRICING ON QTY OF 10 OR LESS
COOP.STAMP ON 1ST #'d COPY PER CARD
11 Dwight Evans/39 20.00 50.00
15 Whitey Ford/27 20.00 50.00

2005 Leaf Century Stamps Signature Olympic

*OLY p/r 91-92: .4X TO 1X USA p/r 100
*OLY p/r 91-92: .25X TO .6X USA p/r 20-27
*OLY p/r 48: .4X TO 1X USA p/r 48-49
*OLY p/r 20-27: .4X TO 1X USA p/r 20-27
*OLY p/r 19: .4X TO 1X USA p/r 19
OVERALL INSERT ODDS 1:3
PRINT RUNS B/WN 1-34 COPIES PER
NO PRICING ON QTY OF 10 OR LESS
COOP.STAMP ON 1ST #'d COPY PER CARD
50 Jim Rice/92 10.00 25.00

2005 Leaf Century Stamps Signature Pro Ball

*PRO p/r 69: .4X TO 1X USA p/r 100
*PRO p/r 69: .25X TO .6X USA p/r 20-27
*PRO p/r 47-49: .5X TO 1.2X USA p/r 100
*PRO p/r 47-49: .4X TO 1X USA p/r 48-49
*PRO p/r 20-28: .6X TO 1.5X USA p/r 100
*PRO p/r 20-28: .4X TO 1X USA p/r 20-27
*PRO p/r 19: .4X TO 1X USA p/r 19
OVERALL INSERT ODDS 1:3
PRINT RUNS B/WN 1-69 COPIES PER
NO PRICING ON QTY OF 14 OR LESS
COOP.STAMP ON 1ST #'d COPY PER CARD

2005 Leaf Century Stamps Signature USA Flag

OVERALL INSERT ODDS 1:3
PRINT RUNS B/WN 1-100 COPIES PER
NO PRICING ON QTY OF 14 OR LESS
COOP.STAMP ON 1ST #'d COPY PER CARD
2 Red Schoendienst/100 10.00 25.00
6 Bob Feller/100 12.50 30.00
11 Dwight Evans/24 20.00 50.00
22 Tony Perez/24 20.00 50.00
24 Billy Williams/26 15.00 40.00
25 Juan Marichal/27 15.00 40.00
27 Maury Wills/100 10.00 25.00
28 Fergie Jenkins/100 10.00 25.00
29 Steve Carlton/100 10.00 25.00
30 Dale Murphy/100 12.50 30.00
32 Gaylord Perry/100 10.00 25.00
33 Fred Lynn/100 10.00 25.00
35 Ron Guidry/49 15.00 40.00
38 Jack Morris/100 8.00 20.00
39 Torii Hunter/48 10.00 25.00
40 Andre Dawson/100 10.00 25.00
41 Dave Righetti/19 15.00 40.00
43 Lou Brock/20 20.00 50.00
46 Sean Casey/21 15.00 40.00
48 Ralph Kiner/100 10.00 25.00
51 Duke Snider/25 20.00 50.00
52 Harold Baines/100 10.00 25.00
56 Jim Palmer/22 20.00 50.00
57 Bobby Doerr/100 10.00 25.00
59 Monte Irvin/100 10.00 25.00
61 Alan Trammell/100 12.50 30.00
62 Al Kaline/100 20.00 50.00
64 Bert Blyleven/100 10.00 25.00
65 Miguel Cabrera/24 30.00 60.00
66 Luis Tiant/100 8.00 20.00
70 Tony Oliva/100 10.00 25.00
71 Mark Mulder/20 15.00 40.00

2005 Leaf Century Stamps Signature Material Centennial

*M.CTL p/r 39: .6X TO 1.5X USA p/r 100
*M.CTL p/r 39: .4X TO 1X USA p/r 20-27
*M.CTL p/r 20-24: .5X TO 1.2X USA p/r 20-27
*M.CTL p/r 19: .5X TO 1.2X USA p/r 19
OVERALL INSERT ODDS 1:3
COOP.STAMP ON 1ST #'d COPY PER CARD
37 Bob Gibson Jsy/39 20.00 50.00
50 Jim Rice Jsy/39 15.00 40.00
67 Harmon Killebrew Jsy/39 40.00 80.00
74 Kirk Gibson Jsy/39 15.00 40.00

2005 Leaf Century Stamps Signature Material Legendary Fields

*M.LGD FLDp/r23-34: .75X TO 2X USA p/r100
*M.LGD FLDp/r23-34:.5X TO 1.2XUSAp/r20-27
*M.LGD FLD p/r 23-34: .4X TO 1X USA p/r 19
OVERALL INSERT ODDS 1:3
PRINT RUNS B/WN 1-34 COPIES PER
NO PRICING ON QTY OF 6 OR LESS
COOP.STAMP ON 1ST #'d COPY PER CARD
50 Jim Rice Jsy/33 20.00 50.00
74 Kirk Gibson Jsy/23 20.00 50.00

2005 Leaf Century Stamps Signature Material Olympic

*M.OLY p/r 20-29: .75X TO 2X USA p/r 100
*M.OLY p/r 20-29: .5X TO 1.2X USA p/r 20-27
*M.OLY p/r 19: .5X TO 1.2X USA p/r 19
OVERALL INSERT ODDS 1:3
PRINT RUNS B/WN 1-29 COPIES PER
NO PRICING ON QTY OF 14 OR LESS
COOP.STAMP ON 1ST #'d COPY PER CARD
15 Whitey Ford Jsy/16 40.00 80.00
37 Bob Gibson Jsy/29 15.00 40.00
74 Kirk Gibson Jsy/23 20.00 50.00

2005 Leaf Century Stamps Signature Material Pro Ball

*M.PRO p/r 69: .5X TO 1.2X USA p/r 100
*M.PRO p/r 45-48: .6X TO 1.5X USA p/r 100
*M.PRO p/r 20-27: .75X TO 2X USA p/r 100
*M.PRO p/r 20-27: .5X TO 1.2X USA p/r 20-27
*M.PRO p/r 19: .5X TO 1.2X USA p/r 19
OVERALL INSERT ODDS 1:3
PRINT RUNS B/WN 1-69 COPIES PER
NO PRICING ON QTY OF 14 OR LESS
COOP.STAMP ON 1ST #'d COPY PER CARD
37 Bob Gibson Jsy/45 20.00 50.00
74 Kirk Gibson Jsy/23 20.00 50.00

2005 Leaf Century Stamps Signature Material Prime USA Flag

OVERALL INSERT ODDS 1:3
PRINT RUNS B/WN 1-10 COPIES PER
NO PRICING DUE TO SCARCITY
COOP.STAMP ON 1ST #'d COPY PER CARD

2005 Leaf Century Timeline Threads Jersey Number

*NBR p/r 36-65: .6X TO 1.5X POS p/r 66-125
*NBR p/r 20-35: 1X TO 2.5X POS p/r 66-125
*NBR p/r 20-35: .6X TO 1.5X POS p/r 36-65
*NBR p/r 15-19: 1.25X TO 3X POS p/r 66-125
*NBR p/r 15-19: .75X TO 2X POS p/r 36-65
OVERALL INSERT ODDS 1:3
PRINT RUNS B/WN 1-51 COPIES PER
NO PRICING ON QTY OF 14 OR LESS
40 Sandy Koufax Jsy/32 75.00 150.00

2005 Leaf Century Timeline Threads Position

PRINT RUNS B/WN 26-103 COPIES PER
PRIME PRINT RUN 1 SERIAL #'d SET
NO PRIME PRICING DUE TO SCARCITY
OVERALL INSERT ODDS 1:3
1 Bobby Doerr Jsy/39 4.00 10.00
2 Burleigh Grimes Pants/26 30.00 60.00
3 Babe Ruth Pants/30 150.00 250.00
4 Joe Cronin Pants/38 10.00 25.00
5 Johnny Bench Pants/71 6.00 15.00
6 Orlando Cepeda Pants/62 4.00 10.00
7 Ivan Rodriguez Jsy/103 3.00 8.00
8 Cal Ripken Jsy/98 10.00 25.00
9 Tony Perez Jsy/78 3.00 8.00
10 Andre Dawson Jsy/86 3.00 8.00
11 Tommy John Jsy/86 3.00 8.00
12 Alfonso Soriano Jsy/102 2.00 5.00
13 Ozzie Smith Jsy/78 10.00 25.00
14 Ernie Banks Jsy/70 6.00 15.00
15 Carlton Fisk Jsy/80 5.00 12.00
16 Bo Jackson Jsy/89 6.00 15.00
17 Bert Blyleven Jsy/83 3.00 8.00
18 Darryl Strawberry Jsy/88 3.00 8.00
19 Bob Feller Pants/36 6.00 15.00
20 Lou Brock Jsy/74 5.00 12.00
21 Sammy Sosa Jsy/103 4.00 10.00
22 Roger Clemens Jsy/101 6.00 15.00
23 Don Mattingly Jsy/94 10.00 25.00
24 Rickey Henderson Jsy/83 6.00 15.00
25 Albert Pujols Jsy/103 8.00 20.00
26 Wade Boggs Jsy/87 5.00 12.00
27 Joe Morgan Jsy/82 3.00 8.00
28 Gary Carter Jsy/86 3.00 8.00
29 Catfish Hunter Jsy/78 5.00 12.00
30 Maury Wills Jsy/65 4.00 10.00
31 Hoyt Wilhelm Jsy/68 3.00 8.00
32 Matt Williams Jsy/95 3.00 8.00
33 Eddie Murray Pants/88 8.00 20.00
34 Nolan Ryan Pants/90 12.50 30.00
35 Phil Niekro Jsy/80 3.00 8.00
36 Paul Molitor Jsy/96 3.00 8.00
37 Dale Murphy Jsy/83 5.00 12.00
38 Curt Schilling Jsy/99 3.00 8.00
39 Fred Lynn Jsy/75 3.00 8.00
40 Sandy Koufax Jsy/64 75.00 150.00
41 Don Sutton Jsy/76 3.00 8.00
42 Randy Johnson Jsy/98 4.00 10.00
43 Dennis Eckersley Jsy/97 3.00 8.00
44 Frank Thomas Jsy/94 4.00 10.00
45 Mike Mussina Jsy/100 3.00 8.00
46 Greg Maddux Jsy/96 6.00 15.00
47 Jim Palmer Pants/76 3.00 8.00
48 Harmon Killebrew Jsy/62 10.00 25.00
49 Mike Piazza Jsy/99 4.00 10.00
50 Billy Martin Jsy/83 5.00 12.00

2005 Leaf Century Timeline Threads Signature Position

*SIG NBR: .4X TO 1X SIG POS
PRINT RUNS B/WN 1-19 COPIES PER
NO PRICING ON QTY OF 14 OR LESS
PRIME PRINT RUN 1 SERIAL #'d SET
NO PRIME PRICING DUE TO SCARCITY
OVERALL INSERT ODDS 1:3
1 Bobby Doerr Jsy/19 15.00 40.00
6 Orlando Cepeda Pants/19 15.00 40.00
9 Tony Perez Jsy/19 15.00 40.00
11 Tommy John Jsy/19 15.00 40.00
13 Ozzie Smith Jsy/19 40.00 80.00
16 Bo Jackson Jsy/16 60.00 120.00
17 Bert Blyleven Jsy/19 15.00 40.00
18 Darryl Strawberry Jsy/18 15.00 40.00
19 Bob Feller Pants/19 30.00 60.00
20 Lou Brock Jsy/19 30.00 60.00
23 Don Mattingly Jsy/19 60.00 120.00
30 Maury Wills Jsy/19 15.00 40.00
31 Hoyt Wilhelm Jsy/19 30.00 60.00
34 Nolan Ryan Pants/19 75.00 150.00
35 Phil Niekro Jsy/19 15.00 40.00
39 Fred Lynn Jsy/19 15.00 40.00
41 Don Sutton Jsy/19 15.00 40.00
43 Dennis Eckersley Jsy/19 15.00 40.00
47 Jim Palmer Pants/19 30.00 60.00

2004 Leaf Certified Cuts

COMP.SET w/o SP's (200) 20.00 50.00
COMMON CARD (1-200) .30 .75
COMMON CARD (201-221) .60 1.50
COMMON CARD (222-250) .60 1.50
201-250 RANDOM INSERTS IN PACKS
201-250 PRNT RUN 599 SERIAL #'d SETS
COMMON CARD (251-300) .75 2.00
251-300 RANDOM INSERTS IN PACKS
251-300 PRINT RUN 499 SERIAL #'d SETS
COMMON AU p/r 299-499 3.00 8.00
COMMON AU p/r 199 4.00 10.00
OVERALL AU ODDS THREE PER BOX
AUTO PRINT RUNS B/WN 99-499 #'d PER
*OTSUKA JAPANESE SIG: .75X TO 2X HI
1 Vladimir Guerrero .50 1.25
2 Garret Anderson .30 .75
3 John Lackey .50 1.25
4 Bartolo Colon .30 .75
5 Troy Glaus .30 .75
6 Tim Salmon .30 .75
7 Shea Hillenbrand .30 .75
8 Brandon Webb .30 .75
9 Roberto Alomar .50 1.25
10 Randy Johnson .75 2.00
11 Alex Cintron .30 .75
12 Richie Sexson .30 .75
13 Luis Gonzalez .30 .75
14 Adam LaRoche .30 .75
15 Rafael Furcal .30 .75
16 Chipper Jones .75 2.00
17 Marcus Giles .30 .75
18 Andruw Jones .30 .75
19 Russ Ortiz .30 .75
20 Rafael Palmeiro .50 1.25
21 Melvin Mora .30 .75
22 Luis Matos .30 .75
23 Jay Gibbons .30 .75
24 Adam Loewen .30 .75
25 Larry Bigbie .30 .75
26 Rodrigo Lopez .30 .75
27 Javy Lopez .30 .75
28 Miguel Tejada .50 1.25
29 Trot Nixon .30 .75
30 Curt Schilling .50 1.25
31 Jason Varitek .75 2.00
32 Manny Ramirez .75 2.00
33 Keith Foulke Sox .30 .75
34 Derek Lowe .30 .75
35 Pedro Martinez .50 1.25
36 Nomar Garciaparra .50 1.25
37 Bill Mueller .30 .75
38 Johnny Damon .50 1.25
39 David Ortiz .75 2.00
40 Mark Prior .50 1.25
41 Kerry Wood .30 .75
42 Sammy Sosa .75 2.00
43 Derrek Lee .30 .75
44 Greg Maddux 1.00 2.50
45 Aramis Ramirez .30 .75
46 Matt Clement .30 .75
47 Carlos Zambrano .50 1.25
48 Todd Walker .30 .75
49 Moises Alou .30 .75
50 Corey Patterson .30 .75
51 Frank Thomas .75 2.00
52 Magglio Ordonez .50 1.25
53 Carlos Lee .30 .75
54 Mark Buehrle .50 1.25
55 Esteban Loaiza .30 .75
56 Joe Crede .30 .75
57 Paul Konerko .50 1.25
58 Adam Dunn .50 1.25
59 Austin Kearns .30 .75
60 Barry Larkin .50 1.25
61 Ryan Wagner .30 .75
62 Danny Graves .30 .75
63 Sean Casey .30 .75
64 Ken Griffey Jr. 1.50 4.00
65 Jody Gerut .30 .75
66 Cliff Lee .50 1.25
67 Victor Martinez .50 1.25
68 C.C. Sabathia .50 1.25
69 Omar Vizquel .50 1.25
70 Travis Hafner .30 .75
71 Todd Helton .50 1.25
72 Preston Wilson .30 .75
73 Jeromy Burnitz .30 .75
74 Larry Walker .50 1.25
75 Ivan Rodriguez .50 1.25
76 Rondell White .30 .75
77 Miguel Cabrera .75 2.00
78 Luis Castillo .30 .75
79 Josh Beckett .30 .75
80 Mike Lowell .30 .75
81 Dontrelle Willis .30 .75
82 Brad Penny .30 .75
83 Hee Seop Choi .30 .75
84 Juan Pierre .30 .75
85 Andy Pettitte .50 1.25
86 Jeff Bagwell .50 1.25
87 Roy Oswalt .50 1.25
88 Lance Berkman .50 1.25
89 Morgan Ensberg .30 .75
90 Craig Biggio .50 1.25
91 Octavio Dotel .30 .75
92 Wade Miller .30 .75
93 Jeff Kent .30 .75
94 Richard Hidalgo .30 .75
95 Roger Clemens 1.00 2.50
96 Carlos Beltran .50 1.25
97 Angel Berroa .30 .75
98 Jeremy Affeldt .30 .75
99 Juan Gonzalez .30 .75
100 Mike Sweeney .30 .75
101 Kazuhisa Ishii .30 .75
102 Shawn Green .30 .75
103 Milton Bradley .30 .75
104 Paul Lo Duca .30 .75
105 Hideo Nomo .75 2.00
106 Eric Gagne .30 .75
107 Adrian Beltre .75 2.00
108 Scott Podsednik .30 .75
109 Rickie Weeks .30 .75
110 Ben Sheets .30 .75
111 Geoff Jenkins .30 .75
112 Jacque Jones .30 .75
113 Johan Santana .50 1.25
114 Shannon Stewart .30 .75
115 Corey Koskie .30 .75
116 Lew Ford .30 .75
117 Torii Hunter .30 .75
118 Chad Cordero .30 .75
119 Orlando Cabrera .30 .75
120 Jose Vidro .30 .75
121 Nick Johnson .30 .75
122 Brad Wilkerson .30 .75
123 Mike Piazza .75 2.00
124 Jae Weong Seo .30 .75
125 Jose Reyes .50 1.25
126 Tom Glavine .50 1.25
127 Jorge Posada .50 1.25
128 Gary Sheffield .30 .75
129 Bernie Williams .50 1.25
130 Mike Mussina .50 1.25
131 Mariano Rivera 1.00 2.50
132 Bubba Crosby .30 .75
133 Kevin Brown .30 .75
134 Javier Vazquez .30 .75
135 Jason Giambi .30 .75
136 Derek Jeter 2.00 5.00
137 Alex Rodriguez 1.00 2.50
138 Hideki Matsui 1.25 3.00
139 Mark Mulder .30 .75
140 Jermaine Dye .30 .75
141 Tim Hudson .50 1.25
142 Barry Zito .50 1.25
143 Eric Chavez .30 .75
144 Bobby Crosby .30 .75
145 Eric Byrnes .30 .75
146 Marlon Byrd .30 .75
147 Billy Wagner .30 .75
148 Mike Lieberthal .30 .75
149 Jimmy Rollins .50 1.25
150 Jim Thome .50 1.25
151 Bobby Abreu .30 .75
152 Pat Burrell .30 .75
153 Jose Castillo .30 .75
154 Craig Wilson .30 .75
155 Jason Bay .50 1.25
156 Jason Kendall .30 .75
157 Raul Mondesi .30 .75
158 Jay Payton .30 .75
159 Trevor Hoffman .50 1.25
160 Jake Peavy .30 .75
161 Sean Burroughs .30 .75
162 Phil Nevin .30 .75
163 Brian Giles .30 .75
164 Ryan Klesko .30 .75
165 Todd Linden .30 .75
166 Jerome Williams .30 .75
167 Jason Schmidt .30 .75
168 Ray Durham .30 .75
169 Marquis Grissom .30 .75
170 Shigetoshi Hasegawa .30 .75
171 Edgar Martinez .50 1.25
172 Freddy Garcia .30 .75
173 Bret Boone .30 .75
174 Raul Ibanez .50 1.25
175 Ichiro Suzuki 1.00 2.50
176 Randy Winn .30 .75
177 Scott Rolen .50 1.25
178 Jim Edmonds .50 1.25
179 Albert Pujols 1.00 2.50
180 Matt Morris .30 .75
181 Edgar Renteria .30 .75
182 Aubrey Huff .30 .75
183 Delmon Young .50 1.25
184 Dewon Brazelton .30 .75
185 Rocco Baldelli .30 .75
186 Carl Crawford .50 1.25
187 Mark Teixeira .50 1.25
188 Hank Blalock .30 .75
189 Michael Young .30 .75
190 Laynce Nix .30 .75
191 Alfonso Soriano .50 1.25
192 Kevin Mench .30 .75
193 Adrian Gonzalez .60 1.50
194 Alexis Rios .30 .75
195 Roy Halladay .50 1.25
196 Vernon Wells .30 .75
197 Carlos Delgado .30 .75
198 Bill Hall .30 .75
199 Jose Guillen .30 .75
200 Jeremy Bonderman .30 .75
201 Roger Clemens Yanks SP 2.00 5.00
202 Alex Rodriguez Rgr SP 2.00 5.00
203 Greg Maddux Braves SP 2.00 5.00
204 Miguel Tejada A's SP 1.00 2.50
205 Alfonso Soriano Yanks SP 1.00 2.50
206 Andy Pettitte Yanks SP 1.00 2.50
207 Curt Schilling D'backs SP 1.00 2.50
208 Gary Sheffield Braves SP .60 1.50
209 Ivan Rodriguez Marlins SP 1.00 2.50
210 Jim Thome Indians SP 1.00 2.50
211 Mike Mussina O's SP 1.00 2.50
212 Mike Piazza Dodgers SP 1.50 4.00
213 Randy Johnson M's SP 1.50 4.00
214 Roger Clemens Sox SP 2.00 5.00
215 Sammy Sosa Sox SP 1.50 4.00
216 Alex Rodriguez M's SP 2.00 5.00
217 Randy Johnson Astros SP 1.50 4.00
218 Vladimir Guerrero Expos SP 1.00 2.50
219 Rafael Palmeiro Rgr SP 1.00 2.50
220 Manny Ramirez Indians SP 1.50 4.00
221 Mike Piazza Marlins SP 1.50 4.00
222 Cal Ripken LGD 5.00 12.00
223 Ted Williams LGD 3.00 8.00
224 Duke Snider LGD 1.00 2.50
225 Ernie Banks LGD 1.50 4.00
226 Ryne Sandberg LGD 3.00 8.00
227 Mark Grace LGD 1.00 2.50
228 Andre Dawson LGD 1.00 2.50
229 Bob Feller LGD 1.00 2.50
230 Ty Cobb LGD 2.50 6.00
231 George Brett LGD 3.00 8.00
232 Bo Jackson LGD 1.50 4.00
233 Robin Yount LGD 1.50 4.00
234 Harmon Killebrew LGD 1.50 4.00
235 Gary Carter LGD 1.00 2.50
236 Don Mattingly LGD 3.00 8.00
237 Phil Rizzuto LGD 1.00 2.50
238 Babe Ruth LGD 4.00 10.00
239 Lou Gehrig LGD 3.00 8.00
240 Reggie Jackson LGD 1.00 2.50
241 Rickey Henderson LGD 1.50 4.00
242 Mike Schmidt LGD 2.50 6.00
243 Roberto Clemente LGD 4.00 10.00
244 Tony Gwynn LGD 1.50 4.00
245 Will Clark LGD 1.00 2.50
246 Lou Brock LGD 1.00 2.50
247 Bob Gibson LGD 1.00 2.50
248 Stan Musial LGD 2.50 6.00
249 Nolan Ryan LGD 5.00 12.00
250 Dale Murphy LGD 1.50 4.00
251 A.Baldiris ROO AU/499 RC 3.00 8.00
252 A.Otsuka ROO AU/99 RC 8.00 20.00
253 A.Blanco ROO AU/499 RC 3.00 8.00
254 A.Chavez ROO AU/499 RC 3.00 8.00
255 C.Hines ROO AU/199 RC 4.00 10.00
256 C.Vasquez ROO AU/499 RC 4.00 10.00
257 Casey Daigle ROO/499 RC .75 2.00
258 C.Oxspring ROO AU/499 RC 3.00 8.00
259 C.Miller ROO AU/499 RC 3.00 8.00
260 D.Crouthers ROO AU/199 RC 4.00 10.00
261 D.Kelly ROO AU/499 RC 3.00 8.00
262 E.Rodriguez ROO AU/499 RC 4.00 10.00
263 E.Sierra ROO AU/299 RC 4.00 10.00
264 E.Moreno ROO AU/499 RC 4.00 10.00
265 F.Nieve ROO AU/499 RC 3.00 8.00
266 F.Guzman ROO AU/499 RC 3.00 8.00
267 G.Dobbs ROO AU/499 RC 3.00 8.00
268 B.Halsey ROO AU/499 RC 4.00 10.00
269 H.Gimenez ROO AU/499 RC 3.00 8.00
270 I.Ochoa ROO AU/499 RC 3.00 8.00
271 J.Woods ROO AU/499 RC 3.00 8.00
272 J.Brown ROO AU/499 RC 3.00 8.00
273 J.Bartlett ROO AU/499 RC 4.00 10.00
274 J.Szuminski ROO AU/499 RC 3.00 8.00
275 John Gall ROO/499 RC .75 2.00
276 J.Vasquez ROO AU/499 RC 3.00 8.00
277 J.Labandeira ROO AU/499 RC 3.00 8.00
278 J.Hampson ROO AU/499 RC 3.00 8.00
279 Kazuo Matsui ROO/499 RC 1.25 3.00
280 K.Cave ROO AU/499 RC 3.00 8.00
281 L.Cormier ROO AU/499 RC 3.00 8.00
282 L.Holdzkom ROO AU/199 RC 4.00 10.00
283 M.Valdez ROO AU/199 RC 4.00 10.00
284 M.Wuertz ROO AU/499 RC 4.00 10.00
285 M.Johnston ROO AU/499 RC 3.00 8.00
286 M.Rouse ROO AU/329 RC 3.00 8.00
287 O.Joseph ROO AU/499 RC 3.00 8.00
288 P.Stockman ROO AU/499 RC 3.00 8.00
289 R.Novoa ROO AU/499 RC 3.00 8.00
290 R.Belisario ROO AU/499 RC 3.00 8.00
291 R.Cedeno ROO AU/499 RC 6.00 15.00
292 R.Meaux ROO AU/499 RC 3.00 8.00
293 Scott Proctor ROO/499 RC .75 2.00
294 S.Henn ROO AU/199 RC 4.00 10.00
295 S.Camp ROO AU/499 RC 3.00 8.00
296 S.Hill ROO AU/499 RC 3.00 8.00
297 S.Takatsu ROO AU/99 RC 10.00 25.00
298 T.Bittner ROO AU/199 RC 4.00 10.00
299 William Bergolla ROO/499 RC .75 2.00
300 Y.Molina ROO AU/499 RC 100.00 250.00

2004 Leaf Certified Cuts Marble Blue

*BLUE 1-200: 2.5X TO 6X BASIC
*BLUE 201-221: 1.25X TO 3X BASIC
*BLUE 222-250: 1.25X TO 3X BASIC
*BLUE 251-300: .6X TO 1.5X BASIC
COMMON CARD (251-300) 2.00 5.00
SEMISTARS 3.00 8.00
UNLISTED STARS 5.00 12.00
RANDOM INSERTS IN PACKS
STATED PRINT RUN 50 SERIAL #'d SETS
251 Aarom Baldiris ROO 2.00 5.00
252 Akinori Otsuka ROO 2.00 5.00
253 Andres Blanco ROO 2.00 5.00
254 Angel Chavez ROO 2.00 5.00
255 Carlos Hines ROO 2.00 5.00
256 Carlos Vasquez ROO 2.00 5.00
257 Casey Daigle ROO 2.00 5.00
258 Chris Oxspring ROO 2.00 5.00
259 Colby Miller ROO 2.00 5.00
260 Dave Crouthers ROO 2.00 5.00
261 Don Kelly ROO 3.00 8.00
262 Eddy Rodriguez ROO 2.00 5.00
263 Edwardo Sierra ROO 2.00 5.00
264 Edwin Moreno ROO 2.00 5.00
265 Fernando Nieve ROO 2.00 5.00
266 Freddy Guzman ROO 2.00 5.00
267 Greg Dobbs ROO 2.00 5.00
268 Brad Halsey ROO 2.00 5.00
269 Hector Gimenez ROO 2.00 5.00
270 Ivan Ochoa ROO 2.00 5.00
271 Jake Woods ROO 2.00 5.00
272 Jamie Brown ROO 2.00 5.00
273 Jason Bartlett ROO 6.00 15.00
274 Jason Szuminski ROO 2.00 5.00
275 John Gall ROO 2.00 5.00
276 Jorge Vasquez ROO 2.00 5.00
277 Josh Labandeira ROO 2.00 5.00
278 Justin Hampson ROO 2.00 5.00
279 Kazuo Matsui ROO 3.00 8.00
280 Kevin Cave ROO 2.00 5.00
281 Lance Cormier ROO 2.00 5.00
282 Lincoln Holdzkom ROO 2.00 5.00
283 Merkin Valdez ROO 2.00 5.00
284 Michael Wuertz ROO 2.00 5.00
285 Mike Johnston ROO 2.00 5.00
286 Mike Rouse ROO 2.00 5.00
287 Onil Joseph ROO 2.00 5.00
288 Phil Stockman ROO 2.00 5.00
289 Roberto Novoa ROO 2.00 5.00
290 Ronald Belisario ROO 2.00 5.00
291 Ronny Cedeno ROO 2.00 5.00
292 Ryan Meaux ROO 2.00 5.00
293 Scott Proctor ROO 2.00 5.00
294 Sean Henn ROO 2.00 5.00
295 Shawn Camp ROO 2.00 5.00
296 Shawn Hill ROO 2.00 5.00
297 Shingo Takatsu ROO 2.00 5.00
298 Tim Bittner ROO 2.00 5.00
299 William Bergolla ROO 2.00 5.00
300 Yadier Molina ROO 50.00 120.00

2004 Leaf Certified Cuts Marble Gold

*GOLD 1-200: 4X TO 10X BASIC
*GOLD 201-221: 2X TO 5X BASIC
*GOLD 222-250: 2X TO 5X BASIC
RANDOM INSERTS IN PACKS
STATED PRINT RUN 25 SERIAL #'d SETS
251-300 NO PRICING DUE TO SCARCITY

2004 Leaf Certified Cuts Marble Red

*RED 1-200: 1.5X TO 4X BASIC
*RED 201-221: .75X TO 2X BASIC
*RED 222-250: .75X TO 2X BASIC
*RED 251-300: .4X TO 1X BASIC
COMMON CARD (250-300) 1.25 3.00
SEMISTARS 2.00 5.00
UNLISTED STARS 3.00 8.00
RANDOM INSERTS IN PACKS
STATED PRINT RUN 100 SERIAL #'d SETS
251 Aarom Baldiris ROO 1.25 3.00
252 Akinori Otsuka ROO 1.25 3.00
253 Andres Blanco ROO 1.25 3.00
254 Angel Chavez ROO 1.25 3.00
255 Carlos Hines ROO 1.25 3.00
256 Carlos Vasquez ROO 1.25 3.00
257 Casey Daigle ROO 1.25 3.00
258 Chris Oxspring ROO 1.25 3.00
259 Colby Miller ROO 1.25 3.00
260 Dave Crouthers ROO 1.25 3.00
261 Don Kelly ROO 2.00 5.00
262 Eddy Rodriguez ROO 1.25 3.00
263 Edwardo Sierra ROO 1.25 3.00
264 Edwin Moreno ROO 1.25 3.00
265 Fernando Nieve ROO 1.25 3.00
266 Freddy Guzman ROO 1.25 3.00
267 Greg Dobbs ROO 1.25 3.00
268 Brad Halsey ROO 1.25 3.00
269 Hector Gimenez ROO 1.25 3.00
270 Ivan Ochoa ROO 1.25 3.00
271 Jake Woods ROO 1.25 3.00
272 Jamie Brown ROO 1.25 3.00
273 Jason Bartlett ROO 4.00 10.00
274 Jason Szuminski ROO 1.25 3.00
275 John Gall ROO 1.25 3.00
276 Jorge Vasquez ROO 1.25 3.00
277 Josh Labandeira ROO 1.25 3.00
278 Justin Hampson ROO 1.25 3.00
279 Kazuo Matsui ROO 2.00 5.00
280 Kevin Cave ROO 1.25 3.00
281 Lance Cormier ROO 1.25 3.00
282 Lincoln Holdzkom ROO 1.25 3.00
283 Merkin Valdez ROO 1.25 3.00
284 Michael Wuertz ROO 1.25 3.00

285 Mike Johnston ROO 1.25 3.00
286 Mike Rouse ROO 1.25 3.00
287 Onil Joseph ROO 1.25 3.00
288 Phil Stockman ROO 1.25 3.00
289 Roberto Novoa ROO 1.25 3.00
290 Ronald Belisario ROO 1.25 3.00
291 Ronny Cedeno ROO 1.25 3.00
292 Ryan Meaux ROO 1.25 3.00
293 Scott Proctor ROO 1.25 3.00
294 Sean Henn ROO 1.25 3.00
295 Shawn Camp ROO 1.25 3.00
296 Shawn Hill ROO 1.25 3.00
297 Shingo Takatsu ROO 1.25 3.00
298 Tim Bittner ROO 1.25 3.00
299 William Bergolla ROO 1.25 3.00
300 Yadier Molina ROO 50.00 120.00

2004 Leaf Certified Cuts Marble Material Blue Number

*BLUE p/r 66-100: .4X TO 1X RED p/r 66-100
*BLUE p/r 36-65: .6X TO 1.5X RED p/r 66-100
*BLUE p/r 36-65: .25X TO .6X RED p/r 20-35
*BLUE p/r 36-65: .2X TO .5X RED p/r 15-19
*BLUE p/r 20-35: 1X TO 2.5X RED p/r 66-100
*BLUE p/r 20-35: .6X TO 1.5X RED p/r 36-65
*BLUE p/r 20-35: .4X TO 1X RED p/r 20-35
*BLUE p/r 20-35: .3X TO .8X RED p/r 15-19
*BLUE p/r 15-19: 1.25X TO 3X RED p/r 66-100
*BLUE p/r 15-19: .75X TO 2X RED p/r 36-65
*BLUE p/r 15-19: .5X TO 1.2X RED p/r 20-35
*BLUE p/r 15-19: .4X TO 1X RED p/r 15-19
OVERALL GU ODDS ONE PER BOX
PRINT RUNS B/WN 1-75 COPIES PER
NO PRICING ON QTY OF 14 OR LESS

2004 Leaf Certified Cuts Marble Material Red Position

OVERALL GU ODDS ONE PER BOX
PRINT RUNS B/WN 1-100 COPIES PER
NO PRICING ON QTY OF 10 OR LESS
1 Vladimir Guerrero Jsy/100 4.00 10.00
2 Garret Anderson Jsy/100 2.00 5.00
5 Troy Glaus Jsy/75 2.00 5.00
6 Tim Salmon Jsy/75 3.00 8.00
10 Randy Johnson Jsy/100 4.00 10.00
13 Luis Gonzalez Jsy/100 2.00 5.00
15 Rafael Furcal Jsy/100 2.00 5.00
16 Chipper Jones Jsy/100 4.00 10.00
17 Marcus Giles Jsy/100 2.00 5.00
18 Andruw Jones Jsy/100 3.00 8.00
20 Rafael Palmeiro Jsy/100 3.00 8.00
21 Melvin Mora Jsy/50 3.00 8.00
22 Luis Matos Jsy/50 3.00 8.00
23 Jay Gibbons Jsy/100 2.00 5.00
25 Larry Bigbie Jsy/50 3.00 8.00
26 Rodrigo Lopez Jsy/50 3.00 8.00
27 Javy Lopez Jsy/25 5.00 12.00
28 Miguel Tejada Jsy/100 2.00 5.00
30 Curt Schilling Jsy/50 5.00 12.00
31 Jason Varitek Jsy/100 4.00 10.00
32 Manny Ramirez Jsy/100 3.00 8.00
35 Pedro Martinez Jsy/100 3.00 8.00
39 David Ortiz Jsy/100 4.00 10.00
40 Mark Prior Jsy/100 3.00 8.00
41 Kerry Wood Pants/100 2.00 5.00
42 Sammy Sosa Jsy/100 4.00 10.00
44 Greg Maddux Jsy/50 8.00 20.00
45 Aramis Ramirez Jsy/100 2.00 5.00
51 Frank Thomas Jsy/100 4.00 10.00
52 Magglio Ordonez Jsy/100 2.00 5.00
53 Carlos Lee Jsy/100 2.00 5.00
54 Mark Buehrle Jsy/100 2.00 5.00
57 Paul Konerko Jsy/50 3.00 8.00
58 Adam Dunn Jsy/100 2.00 5.00
59 Austin Kearns Jsy/100 2.00 5.00
60 Barry Larkin Jsy/100 2.00 5.00
65 Jody Gerut Jsy/100 2.00 5.00
66 Cliff Lee Jsy/100 2.00 5.00
67 Victor Martinez Jsy/100 2.00 5.00
68 C.C. Sabathia Jsy/100 2.00 5.00
69 Omar Vizquel Jsy/100 3.00 8.00
70 Travis Hafner Jsy/100 2.00 5.00
71 Todd Helton Jsy/100 3.00 8.00
72 Preston Wilson Jsy/100 2.00 5.00
75 Ivan Rodriguez Jsy/50 5.00 12.00
77 Miguel Cabrera Jsy/100 3.00 8.00
79 Josh Beckett Jsy/100 2.00 5.00
81 Dontrelle Willis Jsy/100 3.00 8.00
82 Brad Penny Jsy/100 2.00 5.00
86 Jeff Bagwell Jsy/100 3.00 8.00
87 Roy Oswalt Jsy/100 2.00 5.00
88 Lance Berkman Jsy/100 2.00 5.00
89 Morgan Ensberg Jsy/100 2.00 5.00
90 Craig Biggio Jsy/100 3.00 8.00
93 Jeff Kent Jsy/100 2.00 5.00
94 Richard Hidalgo Pants/100 2.00 5.00
95 Roger Clemens Jsy/25 12.50 30.00
96 Carlos Beltran Jsy/100 2.00 5.00
97 Angel Berroa Pants/100 2.00 5.00
100 Mike Sweeney Jsy/100 2.00 5.00
101 Kazuhisa Ishii Jsy/100 2.00 5.00
102 Shawn Green Jsy/100 2.00 5.00
104 Paul Lo Duca Jsy/100 2.00 5.00
105 Hideo Nomo Jsy/100 4.00 10.00
107 Adrian Beltre Jsy/100 2.00 5.00
110 Ben Sheets Jsy/100 2.00 5.00
111 Geoff Jenkins Jsy/100 2.00 5.00
112 Jacque Jones Jsy/100 2.00 5.00
113 Johan Santana Jsy/100 3.00 8.00
114 Shannon Stewart Jsy/100 2.00 5.00
117 Torii Hunter Jsy/75 2.00 5.00
123 Mike Piazza Jsy/100 5.00 12.00
125 Jose Reyes Jsy/75 2.00 5.00
126 Tom Glavine Jsy/75 3.00 8.00
127 Jorge Posada Jsy/100 3.00 8.00
129 Bernie Williams Jsy/100 3.00 8.00
130 Mike Mussina Jsy/25 8.00 20.00
131 Mariano Rivera Jsy/100 4.00 10.00
138 Hideki Matsui Jsy/100 12.50 30.00
139 Mark Mulder Jsy/100 2.00 5.00
142 Barry Zito Jsy/100 2.00 5.00
143 Eric Chavez Jsy/100 2.00 5.00
146 Marlon Byrd Jsy/100 2.00 5.00
150 Jim Thome Jsy/100 3.00 8.00
151 Bobby Abreu Jsy/100 2.00 5.00
152 Pat Burrell Jsy/100 2.00 5.00
154 Craig Wilson Jsy/100 2.00 5.00
156 Jason Kendall Jsy/100 2.00 5.00
161 Sean Burroughs Jsy/100 2.00 5.00
164 Ryan Klesko Jsy/100 2.00 5.00
166 Jerome Williams Jsy/25 5.00 12.00
171 Edgar Martinez Jsy/100 3.00 8.00
172 Freddy Garcia Jsy/100 2.00 5.00
177 Scott Rolen Jsy/100 3.00 8.00
178 Jim Edmonds Jsy/100 2.00 5.00
179 Albert Pujols Jsy/100 10.00 25.00
180 Matt Morris Jsy/75 2.00 5.00
181 Edgar Renteria Jsy/25 5.00 12.00
182 Aubrey Huff Jsy/100 2.00 5.00
184 Dewon Brazelton Jsy/100 2.00 5.00
185 Rocco Baldelli Jsy/100 2.00 5.00
186 Carl Crawford Jsy/100 2.00 5.00
187 Mark Teixeira Jsy/25 8.00 20.00
188 Hank Blalock Jsy/100 2.00 5.00
191 Alfonso Soriano Jsy/100 2.00 5.00
192 Kevin Mench Jsy/100 2.00 5.00
195 Roy Halladay Jsy/100 2.00 5.00
196 Vernon Wells Jsy/100 2.00 5.00
197 Carlos Delgado Jsy/100 2.00 5.00
200 Jeremy Bonderman Jsy/100 2.00 5.00
201 R.Clemens Yanks Jsy/100 5.00 12.00
202 Alex Rodriguez Rgr Jsy/100 5.00 12.00
203 G.Maddux Braves Jsy/100 5.00 12.00
204 Miguel Tejada A's Jsy/100 2.00 5.00
205 Alf Soriano Yanks Jsy/100 2.00 5.00
206 A.Pettitte Yanks Jsy/100 3.00 8.00
207 C.Schilling D'backs Jsy/100 2.00 5.00
208 G.Sheffield Braves Jsy/50 3.00 8.00
209 I.Rodriguez Marlins Jsy/100 3.00 8.00
210 Jim Thome Indians Jsy/25 8.00 20.00
211 Mike Mussina O's Jsy/50 5.00 12.00
212 M.Piazza Dodgers Jsy/100 5.00 12.00
213 R.Johnson M's Jsy/100 4.00 10.00
214 R.Clemens Sox Jsy/100 5.00 12.00
215 Sammy Sosa Sox Jsy/50 6.00 15.00
216 A.Rodriguez M's Jsy/100 5.00 12.00
217 R.Johnson Astros Jsy/100 4.00 10.00
218 V.Guerrero Expos Jsy/100 4.00 10.00
219 R.Palmeiro Rgr Jsy/100 3.00 8.00
221 M.Piazza Marlins Jsy/100 5.00 12.00
222 Cal Ripken LGD Jsy/50 20.00 50.00
223 Ted Williams LGD Jsy/25 60.00 120.00
225 Ernie Banks LGD Jsy/50 8.00 20.00
226 R.Sandberg LGD Jsy/100 8.00 20.00
227 Mark Grace LGD Jsy/25 10.00 25.00
228 Andre Dawson LGD Jsy/100 3.00 8.00
229 Bob Feller LGD Jsy/25 10.00 25.00
231 George Brett LGD Jsy/100 8.00 20.00
232 Bo Jackson LGD Jsy/100 6.00 15.00
233 Robin Yount LGD Jsy/100 6.00 15.00
234 H.Killebrew LGD Jsy/25 12.50 30.00
235 Gary Carter LGD Jkt/100 3.00 8.00
236 Don Mattingly LGD Jsy/50 12.50 30.00
237 Phil Rizzuto LGD Pants/25 10.00 25.00
238 Babe Ruth LGD Pants/50 125.00 200.00
239 Lou Gehrig LGD Pants/50 40.00 80.00
240 R.Jackson LGD Jsy/100 5.00 12.00
241 R.Henderson LGD Jsy/100 6.00 15.00
242 Mike Schmidt LGD Jsy/50 12.50 30.00
243 R.Clemente LGD Jsy/50 30.00 60.00
244 Tony Gwynn LGD Jsy/100 6.00 15.00
245 Will Clark LGD Jsy/100 5.00 12.00
246 Lou Brock LGD Jsy/25 10.00 25.00
247 Bob Gibson LGD Jsy/25 10.00 25.00
248 Stan Musial LGD Jsy/25 20.00 50.00
249 Nolan Ryan LGD Jsy/50 12.00 30.00
250 Dale Murphy LGD Jsy/100 5.00 12.00

2004 Leaf Certified Cuts Marble Signature Blue

*1-250 p/r 75: .4X TO 1X RED p/r 66-100
*1-250 p/r 50: .5X TO 1.2X RED p/r 66-100
*1-250 p/r 50: .4X TO 1X RED p/r 36-65
*1-250 p/r 50: .3X TO .8X RED p/r 20-35
*1-250 p/r 50: .25X TO .6X RED p/r 15-19
*1-250 p/r 25: .6X TO 1.5X RED p/r 66-100
*1-250 p/r 25: .5X TO 1.2X RED p/r 36-65
*1-250 p/r 25: .4X TO 1X RED p/r 20-35
*251-300 p/r 65-75: .4X TO 1X RED p/r 66-100
OVERALL AU ODDS THREE PER BOX
PRINT RUNS B/WN 1-75 COPIES PER
1-250 NO PRICING ON QTY OF 10 OR LESS
251-300 NO PRICING ON QTY 25 OR LESS
66 Cliff Lee/75 5.00 12.00
265 Fernando Nieve ROO/75 5.00 12.00

2004 Leaf Certified Cuts Marble Signature Gold

*1-250 p/r 25: .6X TO 1.5X RED p/r 66-100
*1-250 p/r 25: .5X TO 1.2X RED p/r 36-65
*1-250 p/r 25: .4X TO 1X RED p/r 20-35
*1-250 p/r 25: .3X TO .8X RED p/r 15-19
OVERALL AU ODDS THREE PER BOX
PRINT RUNS B/WN 1-25 COPIES PER
1-250 NO PRICING ON QTY OF 10 OR LESS
251-300 NO PRICING DUE TO SCARCITY
33 Keith Foulke Sox/25 15.00 40.00
66 Cliff Lee/25 6.00 15.00

2004 Leaf Certified Cuts Marble Signature Red

OVERALL AU ODDS THREE PER BOX
PRINT RUNS B/WN 1-100 COPIES PER
1-250 NO PRICING ON QTY OF 10 OR LESS
251-300 NO PRICING ON QTY 25 OR LESS
2 Garret Anderson/50 8.00 20.00
3 John Lackey/100 6.00 15.00
7 Shea Hillenbrand/100 6.00 15.00
8 Brandon Webb/100 8.00 20.00
11 Alex Cintron/100 4.00 10.00
14 Adam LaRoche/100 4.00 10.00
15 Rafael Furcal/50 8.00 20.00
17 Marcus Giles/50 8.00 20.00
19 Russ Ortiz/100 4.00 10.00
21 Melvin Mora/100 6.00 15.00
22 Luis Matos/100 4.00 10.00
23 Jay Gibbons/100 4.00 10.00
24 Adam Loewen/17 8.00 20.00
25 Larry Bigbie/100 6.00 15.00
26 Rodrigo Lopez/100 4.00 10.00
29 Trot Nixon/50 8.00 20.00
33 Keith Foulke Sox/100 10.00 25.00
39 David Ortiz/50 20.00 50.00
40 Mark Prior/25 12.00 30.00
43 Derrek Lee/50 12.00 30.00
45 Aramis Ramirez/100 6.00 15.00
46 Matt Clement/25 10.00 25.00
47 Carlos Zambrano/100 10.00 25.00
48 Todd Walker/100 4.00 10.00
53 Carlos Lee/100 6.00 15.00
54 Mark Buehrle/50 15.00 40.00
55 Esteban Loaiza/100 4.00 10.00
58 Adam Dunn/25 6.00 15.00
59 Austin Kearns/25 6.00 15.00
63 Sean Casey/25 10.00 25.00
65 Jody Gerut/100 4.00 10.00
66 Cliff Lee/100 4.00 10.00
67 Victor Martinez/100 6.00 15.00
68 C.C. Sabathia/100 10.00 25.00
70 Travis Hafner/100 6.00 15.00
72 Preston Wilson/100 6.00 15.00
77 Miguel Cabrera/50 15.00 40.00
80 Mike Lowell/25 10.00 25.00
82 Brad Penny/100 4.00 10.00
89 Morgan Ensberg/100 6.00 15.00
90 Craig Biggio/25 15.00 40.00
91 Octavio Dotel/100 4.00 10.00
92 Wade Miller/100 4.00 10.00
96 Carlos Beltran/50 8.00 20.00
97 Angel Berroa/50 5.00 12.00
98 Jeremy Affeldt/100 4.00 10.00
103 Milton Bradley/100 6.00 15.00
104 Paul Lo Duca/50 8.00 20.00
108 Scott Podsednik/100 10.00 25.00
109 Rickie Weeks/25 10.00 25.00
112 Jacque Jones/100 6.00 15.00
113 Johan Santana/50 4.00 10.00
114 Shannon Stewart/50 8.00 20.00
116 Lew Ford/100 4.00 10.00
117 Torii Hunter/25 10.00 25.00
118 Chad Cordero/100 6.00 15.00
119 Orlando Cabrera/100 6.00 15.00
120 Jose Vidro/50 5.00 12.00
132 Bubba Crosby/100 4.00 10.00
139 Mark Mulder/25 10.00* 25.00
140 Jermaine Dye/100 6.00 15.00
144 Bobby Crosby/100 6.00 15.00
145 Eric Byrnes/100 4.00 10.00
146 Marlon Byrd/100 4.00 10.00
148 Mike Lieberthal/100 6.00 15.00
153 Jose Castillo/100 4.00 10.00
154 Craig Wilson/100 4.00 10.00
155 Jason Bay/100 6.00 15.00
158 Jay Payton/100 4.00 10.00
161 Sean Burroughs/25 6.00 15.00
165 Todd Linden/100 4.00 10.00
170 Shigetoshi Hasegawa/50 20.00 50.00
171 Edgar Martinez/25 20.00 50.00
174 Raul Ibanez/100 8.00 20.00
177 Scott Rolen/50 12.00 30.00
182 Aubrey Huff/100 6.00 15.00
183 Delmon Young/25 15.00 40.00
184 Dewon Brazelton/100 4.00 10.00
186 Carl Crawford/100 6.00 15.00
187 Mark Teixeira/25 10.00 25.00
188 Hank Blalock/50 8.00 20.00
189 Michael Young/100 6.00 15.00
190 Laynce Nix/100 4.00 10.00
191 Alfonso Soriano/25 15.00 40.00
193 Adrian Gonzalez/100 6.00 15.00
194 Alexis Rios/100 6.00 15.00
196 Vernon Wells/50 8.00 20.00
198 Bill Hall/100 4.00 10.00
199 Jose Guillen/100 6.00 15.00
200 Jeremy Bonderman/100 6.00 15.00
205 Alfonso Soriano Yanks/25 15.00 40.00
222 Cal Ripken LGD/25 100.00 200.00
224 Duke Snider LGD/25 15.00 40.00
228 Andre Dawson LGD/100 10.00 25.00
229 Bob Feller LGD/100 10.00 25.00
235 Gary Carter LGD/25 12.00 30.00
237 Phil Rizzuto LGD/25 15.00 40.00
245 Will Clark LGD/25 12.00 30.00
247 Bob Gibson LGD/25 15.00 40.00
248 Stan Musial LGD/25 30.00 80.00
249 Nolan Ryan LGD/25 75.00 150.00
250 Dale Murphy LGD/50 12.00 30.00
251 Aarom Baldiris ROO/100 4.00 10.00
253 Andres Blanco ROO/100 3.00 8.00
254 Angel Chavez ROO/100 3.00 8.00
255 Carlos Hines ROO/100 3.00 8.00
256 Carlos Vasquez ROO/100 5.00 12.00
258 Chris Oxspring ROO/100 3.00 8.00
259 Colby Miller ROO/100 3.00 8.00
260 Dave Crouthers ROO/50 4.00 10.00
261 Don Kelly ROO/100 3.00 8.00
262 Eddy Rodriguez ROO/100 5.00 12.00
263 Edwardo Sierra ROO/100 5.00 12.00
264 Edwin Moreno ROO/100 5.00 12.00
266 Freddy Guzman ROO/100 3.00 8.00
267 Greg Dobbs ROO/100 3.00 8.00
268 Brad Halsey ROO/100 5.00 12.00
269 Hector Gimenez ROO/100 3.00 8.00
270 Ivan Ochoa ROO/100 3.00 8.00
271 Jake Woods ROO/100 3.00 8.00
272 Jamie Brown ROO/100 3.00 8.00
273 Jason Bartlett ROO/100 5.00 12.00
274 Jason Szuminski ROO/100 3.00 8.00
275 John Gall ROO/100 5.00 12.00
276 Jorge Vasquez ROO/100 3.00 8.00
277 Josh Labandeira ROO/100 3.00 8.00
280 Kevin Cave ROO/100 3.00 8.00
281 Lance Cormier ROO/100 3.00 8.00
283 Merkin Valdez ROO/100 5.00 12.00
284 Michael Wuertz ROO/100 5.00 12.00
285 Mike Johnston ROO/100 3.00 8.00
287 Onil Joseph ROO/100 3.00 8.00
288 Phil Stockman ROO/100 3.00 8.00
289 Roberto Novoa ROO/100 4.00 10.00
291 Ronny Cedeno ROO/100 8.00 20.00
292 Ryan Meaux ROO/100 3.00 8.00
293 Scott Proctor ROO/100 5.00 12.00
295 Shawn Camp ROO/100 3.00 8.00
299 William Bergolla ROO/100 3.00 8.00
300 Yadier Molina ROO/100 150.00 400.00

2004 Leaf Certified Cuts Marble Signature Material Gold Number

*1-221 p/r 35-65: .6X TO 1.5X RED p/r 66-100
*1-221 p/r 35-65: .5X TO 1.2X RED p/r 36-65
*1-221 p/r 35-65: .4X TO 1X RED p/r 20-35
*1-221 p/r 20-35: .75X TO 2X RED p/r 66-100
*1-221 p/r 20-35: .6X TO 1.5X RED p/r 36-65
*1-221 p/r 20-35: .5X TO 1.2X RED p/r 20-35
*1-221 p/r 15-19: 1X TO 2.5X RED p/r 66-100
*1-221 p/r 15-19: .75X TO 2X RED p/r 36-65
*222-250 p/r 36-65: .4X TO 1X RED p/r 20-35
*222-250p/r20-35: .5X TO 1.2X REDp/r20-35
*222-250p/r15-19: 1X TO 2.5X REDp/r66-100
OVERALL AU ODDS THREE PER BOX
PRINT RUNS B/WN 1-57 COPIES PER
NO PRICING ON QTY OF 13 OR LESS
1 Vladimir Guerrero Jsy/27 12.50 30.00
18 Andruw Jones Jsy/25 20.00 50.00
32 Manny Ramirez Jsy/24 40.00 80.00
41 Kerry Wood Pants/34 20.00 50.00
42 Sammy Sosa Jsy/21 50.00 100.00
44 Greg Maddux Jsy/31 60.00 120.00
51 Frank Thomas Jsy/35 30.00 60.00
52 Magglio Ordonez Jsy/30 12.50 30.00
66 Cliff Lee Jsy/34 10.00 25.00
71 Todd Helton Jsy/17 30.00 60.00
81 Dontrelle Willis Jsy/35 8.00 20.00
85 Andy Pettitte Jsy/21 30.00 60.00
88 Lance Berkman Jsy/17 30.00 60.00
101 Kazuhisa Ishii Jsy/17 15.00 40.00
102 Shawn Green Jsy/15 30.00 60.00
123 Mike Piazza Jsy/31 75.00 150.00
124 Jae Weong Seo Jsy/26 12.50 30.00
127 Jorge Posada Jsy/20 75.00 150.00
130 Mike Mussina Jsy/35 20.00 50.00
141 Tim Hudson Jsy/15 30.00 60.00
178 Jim Edmonds Jsy/15 30.00 60.00
195 Roy Halladay Jsy/32 20.00 50.00
227 Mark Grace LGD Jsy/17 30.00 60.00
232 Bo Jackson LGD Jsy/16 75.00 150.00
236 D.Mattingly LGD Jsy/23 50.00 100.00
240 R.Jackson LGD Jsy/44 30.00 60.00
241 R.Henderson LGD Jsy/35 25.00 60.00
242 M.Schmidt LGD Pants/20 50.00 100.00
244 Tony Gwynn LGD Jsy/19 50.00 100.00
246 Lou Brock LGD Jsy/20 20.00 50.00

2004 Leaf Certified Cuts Marble Signature Material Gold Position

*1-221 p/r 50: .6X TO 1.5X RED p/r 66-100
*1-221 p/r 50: .5X TO 1.2X RED p/r 36-65
*1-221 p/r 50: .4X TO 1X RED p/r 20-35
*1-221 p/r 25: .6X TO 1.5X RED p/r 36-65
*1-221 p/r 25: .5X TO 1.2X RED p/r 20-35
*222-250 p/r 50: .6X TO 1.5X RED p/r 66-100
*222-250 p/r 25: .6X TO 1.5X RED p/r 36-65
OVERALL AU ODDS THREE PER BOX
PRINT RUNS B/WN 1-50 COPIES PER
NO PRICING ON QTY OF 10 OR LESS
66 Cliff Lee Jsy/50 10.00 25.00
234 H.Killebrew LGD Jsy/25 50.00 100.00

2004 Leaf Certified Cuts Check Signature Blue

OVERALL AU ODDS THREE PER BOX
PRINT RUNS B/WN 2-60 COPIES PER
NO PRICING ON QTY OF 10 OR LESS
ALL CARDS FEATURE BLUE CHECKS
1 Al Kaline/22 40.00 100.00
2 Andre Dawson/22 12.50 30.00
22 Duke Snider/20 20.00 50.00
31 George Kell/60 10.00 25.00
77 Whitey Ford/16 30.00 60.00

2004 Leaf Certified Cuts Check Signature Green

*GREEN p/r 15-18: .6X TO 1.5X BLUE p/r 60
*GREEN p/r 15-18: .4X TO 1X BLUE p/r 16
OVERALL AU ODDS THREE PER BOX
PRINT RUNS B/WN 1-18 COPIES PER
NO PRICING ON QTY OF 5 OR LESS
ALL BUT RYAN FEATURE GREEN CHECKS
RYAN IS BLUE CHECK W/GREEN HOF LOGO

2004 Leaf Certified Cuts Check Signature Red

*RED p/r 36: .4X TO 1X BLUE p/r 60
*RED p/r 16-17: .5X TO 1.2X BLUE p/r 20
*RED p/r 16-17: .4X TO 1X BLUE p/r 16
OVERALL AU ODDS THREE PER BOX
PRINT RUNS B/WN 3-36 COPIES PER
NO PRICING ON QTY OF 11 OR LESS
ALL BUT RYAN FEATURE RED CHECKS
RYAN IS BLUE CHECK W/RED 34 LOGO

2004 Leaf Certified Cuts Check Signature Material Blue

OVERALL AU ODDS THREE PER BOX
PRINT RUNS B/WN 1-100 COPIES PER
NO PRICING ON QTY OF 6 OR LESS
1 Al Kaline Bat/50 25.00 50.00
2 Andre Dawson Jsy/50 10.00 25.00
4 Bob Gibson Hat/50 15.00 40.00
5 Bobby Doerr Jsy/50 10.00 25.00
6 Brooks Robinson Bat/50 15.00 40.00
7 Cal Ripken White Jsy/25 125.00 250.00
8 Cal Ripken Orange Jsy/25 125.00 250.00
9 Cal Ripken Bat/25 125.00 250.00
10 Cal Ripken Jkt/25 125.00 250.00
13 Carlton Fisk Jkt/35 20.00 50.00
14 Carlton Fisk Jsy/35 20.00 50.00
16 Dale Murphy White Jsy/50 15.00 40.00
17 Dale Murphy Gray Jsy/50 15.00 40.00
18 Don Mattingly White Jsy/25 50.00 100.00
19 Don Mattingly Gray Jsy/25 50.00 100.00
20 Don Mattingly Bat/25 50.00 100.00
21 Don Mattingly Jkt/25 50.00 100.00
22 Duke Snider Pants/100 15.00 40.00
23 Ozzie Smith Padres Jsy/40 20.00 50.00
24 Ozzie Smith Cards Jsy/40 40.00 80.00
25 Ozzie Smith Bat/40 30.00 60.00
26 Frank Robinson Bat/50 15.00 40.00
27 George Brett White Jsy/30 50.00 100.00
28 George Brett Blue Jsy/30 50.00 100.00
29 George Brett Bat/30 50.00 100.00
32 Hal Newhouser Jsy/15 20.00 50.00
33 Harmon Killebrew Shoe/35 50.00 100.00
34 Harmon Killebrew Bat/35 50.00 100.00
38 Kirby Puckett Fld Glv/25 50.00 100.00
39 Kirby Puckett Bat/25 50.00 100.00
40 Lou Boudreau Jsy/15 60.00 120.00
41 Lou Brock Jsy/50 15.00 40.00
43 Luis Aparicio Pants/50 10.00 25.00
44 Mark Grace Fld Glv/50 15.00 40.00
46 Mike Schmidt Fld Glv/25 50.00 100.00
47 Mike Schmidt Jsy/25 50.00 100.00
48 Mike Schmidt Jkt/25 50.00 100.00
49 Mike Schmidt Bat/25 50.00 100.00
50 Nolan Ryan Astros Jkt/30 40.00 80.00
51 Nolan Ryan Rgr Pants/30 40.00 80.00
52 Nolan Ryan Angels Jkt/30 40.00 80.00
53 Paul Molitor Bat/50 15.00 40.00
57 Red Schoendienst Bat/50 10.00 25.00
63 Ron Santo Bat/25 20.00 50.00
65 Ryne Sandberg Jsy/50 20.00 50.00
67 Stan Musial White Jsy/30 50.00 100.00
68 Stan Musial Gray Jsy/30 50.00 100.00
69 Stan Musial Bat/30 50.00 100.00
70 Steve Carlton Pants/25 12.50 30.00
71 Steve Carlton Jsy/25 12.50 30.00
73 Tony Gwynn White Jsy/50 15.00 40.00
74 Tony Gwynn Navy Jsy/50 15.00 40.00
77 Whitey Ford Pants/50 15.00 40.00
78 Will Clark Jsy/50 15.00 40.00
79 Will Clark Bat/50 15.00 40.00

2004 Leaf Certified Cuts Check Signature Material Green

*GREEN p/r 25-33: .6X TO 1.5X BLUE p/r 100
*GREEN p/r 25-33: .5X TO 1.2X BLUE p/r 50
*GREEN p/r 15: .6X TO 1.5X BLUE p/r 50
OVERALL AU ODDS THREE PER BOX
PRINT RUNS B/WN 5-33 COPIES PER
NO PRICING ON QTY OF 10 OR LESS

2004 Leaf Certified Cuts Check Signature Material Red

*RED p/r 50: .5X TO 1.2X BLUE p/r 100
*RED p/r 25: .5X TO 1.2X BLUE p/r 36-65
*RED p/r 25: .4X TO 1X BLUE p/r 20-35
*RED p/r 15: .5X TO 1.2X BLUE p/r 20-35
OVERALL AU ODDS THREE PER BOX
PRINT RUNS B/WN 6-50 COPIES PER
NO PRICING ON QTY OF 14 OR LESS

2004 Leaf Certified Cuts Hall of Fame Souvenirs

RANDOM INSERTS IN PACKS
PRINT RUNS B/WN 75-100 COPIES PER
1 Ernie Banks/84 2.50 6.00
2 Stan Musial/93 4.00 10.00
3 Nolan Ryan/99 8.00 20.00
4 Duke Snider/87 1.50 4.00
5 Bob Feller/94 1.50 4.00
6 George Brett/98 5.00 12.00
7 Robin Yount/78 2.50 6.00
8 Harmon Killebrew/83 2.50 6.00
9 Gary Carter/78 1.50 4.00
10 Phil Rizzuto/75 1.50 4.00
11 Reggie Jackson/94 1.50 4.00
12 Mike Schmidt/97 4.00 10.00
13 Lou Brock/80 1.50 4.00
14 Bob Gibson/84 1.50 4.00
15 Bobby Doerr/75 1.50 4.00
16 Tony Perez/77 1.50 4.00
17 Whitey Ford/78 1.50 4.00
18 Juan Marichal/84 1.50 4.00
19 Monte Irvin/75 1.50 4.00
20 Fergie Jenkins/75 1.50 4.00
21 Ralph Kiner/75 1.50 4.00
22 Eddie Murray/85 1.50 4.00
23 George Kell/75 1.50 4.00
24 Hoyt Wilhelm/84 1.50 4.00
25 Carlton Fisk/80 1.50 4.00
26 Rod Carew/91 1.50 4.00
27 Frank Robinson/89 1.50 4.00
28 Gaylord Perry/77 1.50 4.00
29 Red Schoendienst/75 1.50 4.00
30 Brooks Robinson/92 1.50 4.00
31 Al Kaline/88 2.50 6.00
32 Orlando Cepeda/75 1.50 4.00
33 Steve Carlton/96 1.50 4.00
34 Luis Aparicio/85 1.50 4.00
35 Warren Spahn/83 1.50 4.00
36 Kirby Puckett/82 2.50 6.00
37 Phil Niekro/80 1.50 4.00
38 Jim Bunning/75 1.50 4.00
39 Tom Seaver/99 1.50 4.00
40 Paul Molitor/85 2.50 6.00
41 Johnny Bench/96 2.50 6.00
42 Don Sutton/82 1.50 4.00
43 Robin Roberts/87 1.50 4.00
44 Jim Palmer/93 1.50 4.00
45 Joe Morgan/82 1.50 4.00
46 Roberto Clemente/93 6.00 15.00
47 Lou Gehrig/100 5.00 12.00
48 Babe Ruth/95 6.00 15.00
49 Ty Cobb/98 4.00 10.00
50 Ted Williams/94 5.00 12.00

2004 Leaf Certified Cuts Hall of Fame Souvenirs Material

OVERALL GU ODDS ONE PER BOX
STATED PRINT RUN 25 SERIAL #'d SETS
1 Ernie Banks Jsy 12.50 30.00
2 Stan Musial Jsy 20.00 50.00
3 Nolan Ryan Jsy 30.00 60.00
4 Duke Snider Pants 10.00 25.00
5 Bob Feller Jsy 10.00 25.00
6 George Brett Jsy 20.00 50.00
7 Robin Yount Jsy 12.50 30.00
8 Harmon Killebrew Jsy 12.50 30.00
9 Gary Carter Jkt 6.00 15.00
10 Phil Rizzuto Pants 10.00 25.00
11 Reggie Jackson Jsy 10.00 25.00
12 Mike Schmidt Jsy 20.00 50.00
13 Lou Brock Jsy 10.00 25.00
14 Bob Gibson Jsy 10.00 25.00
15 Bobby Doerr Jsy 6.00 15.00
16 Tony Perez Bat 6.00 15.00
17 Whitey Ford Pants 10.00 25.00
18 Juan Marichal Jsy 6.00 15.00
20 Fergie Jenkins Pants 6.00 15.00
21 Ralph Kiner Bat 10.00 25.00
22 Eddie Murray Jsy 12.50 30.00
24 Hoyt Wilhelm Jsy 6.00 15.00
25 Carlton Fisk Jsy 10.00 25.00
26 Rod Carew Jsy 10.00 25.00
27 Frank Robinson Jsy 6.00 15.00
29 Red Schoendienst Jsy 6.00 15.00
30 Brooks Robinson Bat 10.00 25.00
31 Al Kaline Pants 12.50 30.00
32 Orlando Cepeda Bat 6.00 15.00
33 Steve Carlton Pants 6.00 15.00
34 Luis Aparicio Pants 6.00 15.00
35 Warren Spahn Pants 12.50 30.00
36 Kirby Puckett Jsy 12.50 30.00
37 Phil Niekro Jsy 6.00 15.00
39 Tom Seaver Jsy 10.00 25.00
40 Paul Molitor Bat 6.00 15.00
41 Johnny Bench Jsy 12.50 30.00
42 Don Sutton Jsy 6.00 15.00
43 Robin Roberts Hat 6.00 15.00
44 Jim Palmer Jsy 6.00 15.00
45 Joe Morgan Jsy 6.00 15.00
46 Roberto Clemente Jsy 25.00 60.00
47 Lou Gehrig Pants 75.00 150.00
48 Babe Ruth Pants 150.00 250.00
49 Ty Cobb Pants 25.00 60.00
50 Ted Williams Jsy 60.00 120.00

2004 Leaf Certified Cuts Hall of Fame Souvenirs Signature

OVERALL AU ODDS THREE PER BOX
PRINT RUNS B/WN 5-50 COPIES PER
NO PRICING ON QTY OF 10 OR LESS
3 Nolan Ryan/34 20.00 50.00
4 Duke Snider/50 12.50 30.00
5 Bob Feller/50 8.00 20.00
8 Harmon Killebrew/25 40.00 80.00
9 Gary Carter/50 10.00 25.00
10 Phil Rizzuto/50 12.50 30.00
12 Mike Schmidt/20 40.00 80.00
13 Lou Brock/50 12.50 30.00
14 Bob Gibson/45 12.50 30.00
15 Bobby Doerr/50 8.00 20.00
16 Tony Perez/50 8.00 20.00
17 Whitey Ford/16 30.00 60.00
18 Juan Marichal/50 8.00 20.00
19 Monte Irvin/50 12.50 30.00
20 Fergie Jenkins/50 8.00 20.00
21 Ralph Kiner/50 12.50 30.00
22 Eddie Murray/33 15.00 40.00
23 George Kell/50 12.50 30.00
24 Hoyt Wilhelm/49 12.50 30.00
25 Carlton Fisk/27 15.00 40.00
26 Rod Carew/29 15.00 40.00
28 Gaylord Perry/50 8.00 20.00
29 Red Schoendienst/50 8.00 20.00
30 Brooks Robinson/50 12.50 30.00
31 Al Kaline/50 25.00 50.00
32 Orlando Cepeda/50 8.00 20.00
33 Steve Carlton/50 8.00 20.00
34 Luis Aparicio/50 8.00 20.00
35 Warren Spahn/21 30.00 60.00
36 Kirby Puckett/34 50.00 100.00
37 Phil Niekro/50 8.00 20.00
38 Jim Bunning/50 8.00 20.00
40 Paul Molitor/25 10.00 25.00
42 Don Sutton/50 8.00 20.00
43 Robin Roberts/50 12.50 30.00
44 Jim Palmer/22 10.00 25.00
45 Joe Morgan/25 10.00 25.00

2004 Leaf Certified Cuts Hall of Fame Souvenirs Signature Material

*MTL AU p/r 36-45: .5X TO 1.2X AU p/r 36-50
*MTL AU p/r 20-35: .6X TO 1.5X AU p/r 36-50
*MTL AU p/r 20-35: .5X TO 1.2X AU p/r 20-35
*MTL AU p/r 16-19: .75X TO 2X AU p/r 36-50
*MTL AU p/r 16-19: .6X TO 1.5X AU p/r 20-35
*MTL AU p/r 16-19: .5X TO 1.2X AU p/r 15-19
OVERALL AU ODDS THREE PER BOX
PRINT RUNS B/WN 1-45 COPIES PER
NO PRICING ON QTY OF 11 OR LESS

2004 Leaf Certified Cuts K-Force

1-44 PRINT RUNS B/WN 17-500 #'d PER
45-50 PRINT RUNS B/WN 20-500 #'d PER
1 Nolan Ryan Rgr/500 4.00 10.00
2 Steve Carlton/500 .75 2.00
3 Roger Clemens Astros/500 1.50 4.00
4 Randy Johnson D'backs/500 1.25 3.00
5 Bert Blyleven/500 .75 2.00
6 Tom Seaver Reds/500 .75 2.00
7 Don Sutton/500 .75 2.00
8 Gaylord Perry/500 .75 2.00
9 Phil Niekro/500 .75 2.00
10 Fergie Jenkins/500 .75 2.00
11 Bob Gibson/500 .75 2.00
12 Nolan Ryan Angels/383 4.00 10.00
13 Randy Johnson M's/308 1.25 3.00
14 Bob Feller/348 .75 2.00
15 Curt Schilling Phils/319 .75 2.00
16 Pedro Martinez Sox/313 .75 2.00
17 Dwight Gooden/276 .50 1.25
18 John Smoltz/276 1.25 3.00
19 Curt Schilling D'backs/316 .75 2.00
20 Randy Johnson Astros/329 1.25 3.00
21 Pedro Martinez Expos/305 .75 2.00
22 Roger Clemens Sox/291 1.50 4.00
23 Roger Clemens Jays/292 1.50 4.00
24 Tom Seaver Mets/289 .75 2.00
25 Hal Newhouser/275 .75 2.00
26 Jim Bunning/201 1.00 2.50
27 Robin Roberts/198 1.00 2.50
28 Warren Spahn/191 1.00 2.50
29 Jack Morris/232 1.00 2.50
30 Nolan Ryan Astros/270 4.00 10.00
31 Hideo Nomo/236 1.50 4.00
32 Barry Zito/205 1.00 2.50
33 Mike Mussina/214 1.00 2.50
34 Roy Oswalt/208 1.00 2.50
35 Mark Prior/245 1.00 2.50
36 Kerry Wood/266 .50 1.25
37 Roy Halladay/204 1.00 2.50
38 Esteban Loaiza/207 .60 1.50
39 Whitey Ford/94 1.25 3.00
40 Bob Gibson/17 2.50 6.00
41 Ben Sheets/18 1.50 4.00
42 Hoyt Wilhelm/139 1.00 2.50
43 Satchel Paige/91 2.00 5.00
44 Burleigh Grimes/136 1.00 2.50
45 M.Prior .75 2.00
K.Wood/500
46 N.Ryan 4.00 10.00
R.Clemens/500
47 S.Carlton 1.25 3.00
R.Johnson/500
48 N.Ryan 4.00 10.00
R.Clemens/500
49 N.Ryan 4.00 10.00
S.Carlton/500
50 K.Wood 5.00 12.00
R.Clemens/20

2004 Leaf Certified Cuts K-Force Material

1-44 PRINT RUNS B/WN 2-100 #'d PER
1-44 NO PRICING ON QTY OF 5 OR LESS
45-50 PRINT RUN 50 SERIAL #'d SETS
OVERALL GU ODDS ONE PER BOX
1 Nolan Ryan Rgr Jsy/100 10.00 25.00
2 Steve Carlton Jsy/32 6.00 15.00
3 R.Clemens Astros Jsy/25 12.50 30.00
4 R.Johnson D'backs Jsy/51 6.00 15.00
5 Bert Blyleven Jsy/28 6.00 15.00
6 Tom Seaver Reds Jsy/25 10.00 25.00
8 Gaylord Perry Jsy/36 4.00 10.00
9 Phil Niekro Jsy/35 6.00 15.00
10 Fergie Jenkins Pants/31 6.00 15.00
11 Bob Gibson Jsy/45 6.00 15.00
12 Nolan Ryan Angels Jkt/100 15.00 40.00
13 Randy Johnson M's Jsy/51 6.00 15.00
14 Bob Feller Jsy/25 10.00 25.00
15 Curt Schilling Phils Jsy/25 5.00 12.00
16 Pedro Martinez Sox Jsy/45 5.00 12.00
17 Dwight Gooden Jsy/25 6.00 15.00
18 John Smoltz Jsy/25 8.00 20.00
19 C.Schilling D'backs Jsy/25 5.00 12.00
20 R.Johnson Astros Jsy/51 6.00 15.00
21 P.Martinez Expos Jsy/45 5.00 12.00
22 R.Clemens Sox Jsy/100 5.00 12.00
25 Hal Newhouser Jsy/25 10.00 25.00
28 Warren Spahn Jsy/50 8.00 20.00
29 Jack Morris Jsy/47 4.00 10.00
30 N.Ryan Astros Jkt/100 10.00 25.00
31 Hideo Nomo Jsy/25 10.00 25.00
32 Barry Zito Jsy/25 5.00 12.00
33 Mike Mussina Jsy/25 8.00 20.00
34 Roy Oswalt Jsy/44 3.00 8.00
35 Mark Prior Jsy/50 5.00 12.00
36 Kerry Wood Jsy/34 5.00 12.00
39 Whitey Ford Jsy/50 6.00 15.00
40 Bob Gibson Jsy/50 6.00 15.00
41 Ben Sheets Jsy/25 5.00 12.00
43 Satchel Paige CO Jsy/100 30.00 60.00
44 Burleigh Grimes Pants/100 10.00 25.00
45 Prior Jsy/Wood Pants/50 10.00 25.00
46 Ryan Jsy/Clemens Jsy/50 20.00 50.00
47 Carlton Jsy/Randy Jsy/50 10.00 25.00
48 Ryan Pants/Clemens Jsy/50 20.00 50.00
49 Ryan Jsy/Carlton Pants/50 10.00 25.00
50 Wood Jsy/Clemens Jsy/50 10.00 25.00

2004 Leaf Certified Cuts K-Force Signature

OVERALL AU ODDS THREE PER BOX
PRINT RUNS B/WN 1-50 COPIES PER
NO PRICING ON QTY OF 10 OR LESS
2 Steve Carlton/50 8.00 20.00
5 Bert Blyleven/50 8.00 20.00
7 Don Sutton/50 8.00 20.00
8 Gaylord Perry/50 8.00 20.00
9 Phil Niekro/50 12.50 30.00
10 Fergie Jenkins/50 8.00 20.00
14 Bob Feller/50 12.50 30.00
17 Dwight Gooden/50 8.00 20.00
26 Jim Bunning/50 12.50 30.00
27 Robin Roberts/50 8.00 20.00
29 Jack Morris/50 8.00 20.00
34 Roy Oswalt/50 8.00 20.00
38 Esteban Loaiza/50 5.00 12.00

2004 Leaf Certified Cuts K-Force Signature Material

*A.MTL AU p/r 36-50: .5X TO 1.2X AU p/r 50
*R.MTL AU p/r 36-50: .5X TO 1.2X AU p/r 50
*R.MTL AU p/r 20-35: .6X TO 1.5X AU p/r 50
*R.MTL AU p/r 15-19: .75X TO 2X AU p/r 50
PRINT RUNS B/WN 1-47 COPIES PER
NO PRICING ON QTY OF 5 OR LESS
PRIME PRINT RUN 1 SERIAL #'d SET
NO PRIME PRICING DUE TO SCARCITY
OVERALL AU ODDS THREE PER BOX
1 Nolan Ryan Rgr Jsy/34 40.00 80.00
11 Bob Gibson Jsy/45 15.00 40.00
12 Nolan Ryan Angels Jkt/34 40.00 80.00
28 Warren Spahn Jsy/21 40.00 80.00
30 Nolan Ryan Astros Jkt/34 40.00 80.00
36 Kerry Wood Jsy/34 10.00 25.00
37 Roy Halladay Jsy/32 20.00 50.00
39 Whitey Ford Jsy/16 30.00 60.00
40 Bob Gibson Jsy/45 15.00 40.00

2004 Leaf Certified Cuts Stars

RANDOM INSERTS IN PACKS
STATED PRINT RUN 599 SERIAL #'d SETS
1 Ryne Sandberg 3.00 8.00
2 Mark Prior 1.00 2.50
3 Andre Dawson 1.00 2.50
4 Don Mattingly 3.00 8.00
5 Vladimir Guerrero 1.00 2.50
6 Garret Anderson .60 1.50
7 Dale Murphy 1.50 4.00
8 Cal Ripken 5.00 12.00
9 Mark Grace 1.00 2.50
10 Kerry Wood .60 1.50
11 Frank Thomas 1.50 4.00
12 Magglio Ordonez 1.00 2.50
13 Adam Dunn 1.00 2.50
14 Preston Wilson .60 1.50
15 Bo Jackson 1.50 4.00
16 Carlos Beltran 1.00 2.50
17 Tony Gwynn 1.50 4.00
18 Will Clark 1.00 2.50
19 Edgar Martinez 1.00 2.50
20 Scott Rolen 1.00 2.50
21 Alfonso Soriano 1.00 2.50
22 Randy Johnson 1.50 4.00
23 Chipper Jones 1.50 4.00
24 Andruw Jones .60 1.50
25 Javy Lopez .60 1.50
26 Curt Schilling 1.00 2.50
27 Manny Ramirez 1.50 4.00
28 Sammy Sosa 1.50 4.00
29 Greg Maddux 2.00 5.00
30 Todd Helton 1.00 2.50
31 Jeff Bagwell 1.00 2.50
32 Shawn Green .60 1.50
33 Mike Piazza 1.50 4.00
34 Jorge Posada 1.00 2.50
35 Gary Sheffield .60 1.50
36 Mike Mussina 1.00 2.50
37 Miguel Cabrera 1.50 4.00
38 Rickey Henderson 1.50 4.00
39 Albert Pujols 2.00 5.00
40 Vernon Wells .60 1.50
41 Fred Lynn .60 1.50
42 Alan Trammell 1.00 2.50
43 Lenny Dykstra .60 1.50
44 Dwight Gooden .60 1.50
45 Keith Hernandez .60 1.50

46 Luis Tiant .60 1.50
47 Orel Hershiser .60 1.50
48 George Foster .60 1.50
49 Darryl Strawberry .60 1.50
50 Marty Marion .60 1.50

2004 Leaf Certified Cuts Stars Signature

OVERALL AU ODDS THREE PER BOX
PRINT RUNS B/WN 1-50 COPIES PER
NO PRICING ON QTY OF 10 OR LESS
3 Andre Dawson/50 8.00 20.00
4 Don Mattingly/25 50.00 100.00
6 Garret Anderson/50 8.00 20.00
7 Dale Murphy/50 15.00 40.00
12 Maggio Ordonez/25 8.00 20.00
13 Adam Dunn/25 8.00 20.00
14 Preston Wilson/50 8.00 20.00
16 Carlos Beltran/50 8.00 20.00
18 Will Clark/25 15.00 40.00
19 Edgar Martinez/25 20.00 50.00
20 Scott Rolen/25 8.00 20.00
37 Miguel Cabrera/50 20.00 50.00
40 Vernon Wells/25 10.00 25.00
41 Fred Lynn/50 5.00 12.00
42 Alan Trammell/50 8.00 20.00
43 Lenny Dykstra/50 8.00 20.00
44 Dwight Gooden/50 8.00 20.00
45 Keith Hernandez/50 8.00 20.00
46 Luis Tiant/50 8.00 20.00
47 Orel Hershiser/50 12.50 30.00
48 George Foster/50 5.00 12.00
49 Darryl Strawberry/50 8.00 20.00

2004 Leaf Certified Cuts Stars Signature Jersey

*JSY AU p/r 36-50: .5X TO 1.2X AU p/r 36-50
*JSY AU p/r 36-50: .6X TO 1.5X AU p/r 36-50
*JSY AU p/r 20-35: .6X TO 1.5X AU p/r 36-50
*JSY AU p/r 20-35: .5X TO 1.2X AU p/r 20-35
*JSY AU p/r 15-19: .75X TO 2X AU p/r 36-50
PRINT RUNS B/WN 1-44 COPIES PER
NO PRICING ON QTY OF 12 OR LESS
PRIME PRINT RUN 1 SERIAL #'d SET
NO PRIME PRICING DUE TO SCARCITY
OVERALL AU ODDS THREE PER BOX
1 Ryne Sandberg/23 50.00 100.00
2 Mark Prior/22 15.00 40.00
5 Vladimir Guerrero/27 30.00 60.00
9 Mark Grace/17 20.00 50.00
10 Kerry Wood/34 20.00 50.00
11 Frank Thomas/35 40.00 80.00
15 Bo Jackson/16 75.00 150.00
17 Tony Gwynn/19 50.00 100.00
24 Andruw Jones/25 10.00 25.00
28 Sammy Sosa/21 50.00 100.00
29 Greg Maddux/31 30.00 80.00
30 Todd Helton/17 30.00 60.00
32 Shawn Green/15 30.00 60.00
34 Jorge Posada/20 75.00 150.00
50 Marty Marion/25 12.50 30.00

2001 Leaf Certified Materials

COMP.SET w/o SP's (110) 15.00 40.00
COMMON CARD (1-110) .40 1.00
COMMON FABRIC (111-160) 4.00 10.00
111-160 RANDOM INSERTS IN PACKS
111-160 PRINT RUN 200 SERIAL #'d SETS
1 Alex Rodriguez 1.25 3.00
2 Barry Bonds 2.50 6.00
3 Cal Ripken 3.00 8.00
4 Chipper Jones 1.00 2.50
5 Derek Jeter 2.50 6.00
6 Troy Glaus .40 1.00
7 Frank Thomas 1.00 2.50
8 Greg Maddux 1.50 4.00
9 Ivan Rodriguez .60 1.50
10 Jeff Bagwell .60 1.50
11 Eric Karros .40 1.00
12 Todd Helton .60 1.50
13 Ken Griffey Jr. 2.00 5.00
14 Manny Ramirez Sox .60 1.50
15 Mark McGwire 2.50 6.00
16 Mike Piazza 1.50 4.00
17 Nomar Garciaparra 1.50 4.00
18 Pedro Martinez .60 1.50
19 Randy Johnson 1.00 2.50
20 Rick Ankiel .40 1.00
21 Rickey Henderson 1.00 2.50
22 Roger Clemens 2.00 5.00
23 Sammy Sosa 1.00 2.50
24 Tony Gwynn 1.25 3.00
25 Vladimir Guerrero 1.00 2.50
26 Kazuhiro Sasaki .40 1.00
27 Roberto Alomar .60 1.50
28 Barry Zito .60 1.50
29 Pat Burrell .40 1.00
30 Harold Baines .40 1.00
31 Carlos Delgado .40 1.00
32 J.D. Drew .40 1.00
33 Jim Edmonds .40 1.00
34 Darin Erstad .40 1.00
35 Jason Giambi .40 1.00
36 Tom Glavine .60 1.50
37 Juan Gonzalez .40 1.00
38 Mark Grace .60 1.50
39 Shawn Green .40 1.00
40 Tim Hudson .40 1.00
41 Andruw Jones .60 1.50
42 Jeff Kent .40 1.00
43 Barry Larkin .60 1.50
44 Rafael Furcal .40 1.00
45 Mike Mussina .60 1.50
46 Hideo Nomo 1.00 2.50
47 Rafael Palmeiro .60 1.50
48 Scott Rolen .60 1.50
49 Gary Sheffield .40 1.00
50 Bernie Williams .60 1.50
51 Bob Abreu .40 1.00
52 Edgardo Alfonzo .40 1.00
53 Edgar Martinez .60 1.50
54 Magglio Ordonez .40 1.00
55 Kerry Wood .40 1.00
56 Adrian Beltre .40 1.00
57 Lance Berkman .40 1.00
58 Kevin Brown .40 1.00
59 Sean Casey .40 1.00
60 Eric Chavez .40 1.00
61 Bartolo Colon .40 1.00
62 Johnny Damon .60 1.50
63 Jermaine Dye .40 1.00
64 Juan Encarnacion .40 1.00
65 Carl Everett .40 1.00
66 Brian Giles .40 1.00
67 Mike Hampton .40 1.00
68 Richard Hidalgo .40 1.00
69 Geoff Jenkins .40 1.00
70 Jacque Jones .40 1.00
71 Jason Kendall .40 1.00
72 Ryan Klesko .40 1.00
73 Chan Ho Park .40 1.00
74 Richie Sexson .40 1.00
75 Mike Sweeney .40 1.00
76 Fernando Tatis .40 1.00
77 Miguel Tejada .40 1.00
78 Jose Vidro .40 1.00
79 Larry Walker .40 1.00
80 Preston Wilson .40 1.00
81 Craig Biggio .60 1.50
82 Fred McGriff .60 1.50
83 Jim Thome .60 1.50
84 Garret Anderson .40 1.00
85 Russell Branyan .40 1.00
86 Tony Batista .40 1.00
87 Terrence Long .40 1.00
88 Deion Sanders .60 1.50
89 Rusty Greer .40 1.00
90 Orlando Hernandez .40 1.00
91 Gabe Kapler .40 1.00
92 Paul Konerko .40 1.00
93 Carlos Lee .40 1.00
94 Kenny Lofton .40 1.00
95 Raul Mondesi .40 1.00
96 Jorge Posada .60 1.50
97 Tim Salmon .60 1.50
98 Greg Vaughn .40 1.00
99 Mo Vaughn .40 1.00
100 Omar Vizquel .60 1.50
101 Ray Durham .40 1.00
102 Jeff Cirillo .40 1.00
103 Dean Palmer .40 1.00
104 Ryan Dempster .40 1.00
105 Carlos Beltran .40 1.00
106 Timo Perez .40 1.00
107 Robin Ventura .40 1.00
108 Andy Pettitte .60 1.50
109 Aramis Ramirez .40 1.00
110 Phil Nevin .40 1.00
111 Alex Escobar FF Fld Glv 4.00 10.00
112 Johnny Estrada FF Fld Glv RC 6.00 15.00
113 Pedro Feliz FF Fld Glv 4.00 10.00
114 Nate Frese FF Fld Glv RC 4.00 10.00
115 Joe Kennedy FF Fld Glv RC 6.00 15.00
116 Brandon Larson FF Fld Glv RC 4.00 10.00
117 Alexis Gomez FF Fld Glv RC 4.00 10.00
118 Jason Hart FF 4.00 10.00
119 Jason Michaels FF Fld Glv RC 4.00 10.00
120 Marcus Giles FF Fld Glv 4.00 10.00
121 Christian Parker FF RC 4.00 10.00
122 Jackson Melian FF RC 4.00 10.00
123 Donaldo Mendez FF Spikes RC 4.00 10.00
124 Adrian Hernandez FF RC 4.00 10.00
125 Bud Smith FF RC 4.00 10.00
126 Jose Mieses FF Fld Glv RC 4.00 10.00
127 Roy Oswalt FF Spikes 10.00 25.00
128 Eric Munson FF 4.00 10.00
129 Xavier Nady FF Fld Glv 4.00 10.00
130 Horacio Ramirez FF Fld Glv RC 6.00 15.00
131 Abraham Nunez FF Spikes 4.00 10.00
132 Jose Ortiz FF 4.00 10.00
133 Jeremy Owens FF RC 4.00 10.00
134 Claudio Vargas FF RC 4.00 10.00
135 R.Rodriguez FF Fld Glv RC 4.00 10.00
136 Aubrey Huff FF Jsy 4.00 10.00
137 Ben Sheets FF 6.00 15.00
138 Adam Dunn FF Fld Glv 6.00 15.00
139 Andres Torres FF Fld Glv RC 4.00 10.00
140 Elpidio Guzman FF Fld Glv RC 4.00 10.00
141 Jay Gibbons FF Fld Glv RC 6.00 15.00
142 Wilkin Ruan FF RC 4.00 10.00
143 Tsuyoshi Shinjo FF Base RC 6.00 15.00
144 Alfonso Soriano FF 6.00 15.00
145 Josh Towers FF Fld Glv RC 6.00 15.00
146 Ichiro Suzuki FF Base RC 75.00 200.00
147 Juan Uribe FF RC 6.00 15.00
148 Joe Crede FF Fld Glv 10.00 25.00
149 Carlos Valderrama FF RC 4.00 10.00
150 Matt White FF Fld Glv RC 4.00 10.00
151 Dee Brown FF Jsy 4.00 10.00
152 Juan Cruz FF Spikes RC 4.00 10.00
153 Cory Aldridge FF RC 4.00 10.00
154 Wilmy Caceres FF RC 4.00 10.00
155 Josh Beckett FF 6.00 15.00
156 Wilson Betemit FF Spikes RC 8.00 20.00
157 Corey Patterson FF Pants 4.00 10.00
158 Albert Pujols FF Hat RC 100.00 250.00
159 Rafael Soriano FF Fld Glv RC 4.00 10.00
160 Jack Wilson FF RC 6.00 15.00

2001 Leaf Certified Materials Mirror Gold

*STARS 1-110: 10X TO 25X BASIC CARDS
STATED PRINT RUN 25 SERIAL #'d SETS
111-160 NOT PRICED DUE TO SCARCITY

2001 Leaf Certified Materials Mirror Red

*STARS 1-110: 4X TO 10X BASIC CARDS
STATED PRINT RUN 75 SERIAL #'d SETS
EXCHANGE DEADLINE 11/01/03
111 Alex Escobar FF Fld Glv AU 6.00 15.00
112 Johnny Estrada FF Fld Glv AU 10.00 25.00
113 Pedro Feliz FF Fld Glv AU 6.00 15.00
114 Nate Frese FF Fld Glv AU 6.00 15.00
115 Joe Kennedy FF Fld Glv 6.00 15.00
116 Brandon Larson FF Fld Glv AU 4.00 10.00
117 Alexis Gomez FF Fld Glv AU 4.00 10.00
118 Jason Hart FF AU 6.00 15.00
119 Jason Michaels FF Fld Glv AU 6.00 15.00
120 Marcus Giles FF Fld Glv AU 10.00 25.00
121 Christian Parker FF AU 4.00 10.00
122 Jackson Melian FF 4.00 10.00
123 Donaldo Mendez FF Spikes AU 4.00 10.00
124 Adrian Hernandez FF AU 4.00 10.00
125 Bud Smith FF AU 4.00 10.00
126 Jose Mieses FF Fld Glv AU 6.00 15.00
127 Roy Oswalt FF Spikes AU 20.00 50.00
128 Eric Munson FF 4.00 10.00
129 Xavier Nady FF Fld Glv AU 10.00 25.00
130 Horacio Ramirez FF Fld Glv AU 10.00 25.00
131 Abraham Nunez FF Spikes AU 6.00 15.00
132 Jose Ortiz FF AU 6.00 15.00
133 Jeremy Owens FF AU 6.00 15.00
134 Claudio Vargas FF AU 4.00 10.00
135 Ricardo Rodriguez FF Fld Glv AU 6.00 15.00
136 Aubrey Huff FF Jsy AU 10.00 25.00
137 Ben Sheets FF AU 10.00 25.00
138 Adam Dunn FF Fld Glv AU 15.00 40.00
139 Andres Torres FF Fld Glv AU 4.00 10.00
140 Elpidio Guzman FF Fld Glv AU 4.00 10.00
141 Jay Gibbons FF Fld Glv AU 10.00 25.00
142 Wilkin Ruan FF AU 6.00 15.00
143 Tsuyoshi Shinjo FF Base 6.00 15.00
144 Alfonso Soriano FF AU 10.00 25.00
145 Josh Towers FF Fld Glv AU 10.00 25.00
146 Ichiro Suzuki FF Base 125.00 300.00
147 Juan Uribe FF AU 10.00 25.00
148 Joe Crede FF Fld Glv AU 15.00 40.00
149 Carlos Valderrama FF AU 4.00 10.00
150 Matt White FF Fld Glv AU 6.00 15.00
151 Dee Brown FF Jsy AU 6.00 15.00
152 Juan Cruz FF Spikes AU 6.00 15.00
153 Cory Aldridge FF AU 4.00 10.00
154 Wilmy Caceres FF AU 6.00 15.00
155 Josh Beckett FF AU 15.00 40.00
156 Wilson Betemit FF Spikes AU 12.50 30.00
157 Corey Patterson FF Pants AU 6.00 15.00
158 Albert Pujols FF Hat AU 500.00 1200.00
159 Rafael Soriano FF Fld Glv AU 6.00 15.00
160 Jack Wilson FF AU 10.00 25.00

2001 Leaf Certified Materials Fabric of the Game

SEE BECKETT.COM FOR PRINT RUNS
LESS THAN 100 OF EACH BASE CARD SP
CAREER CARDS ARE SILVER
CAREER CARDS LISTED WITH CR SUFFIX
CENTURY'S FEATURE PATCH SWATCH
CARD 32 NOT INTENDED FOR RELEASE
NO PRICING ON QTY OF 27 OR LESS
1SN Lou Gehrig/184 60.00 120.00
2CR Babe Ruth/136 100.00 200.00
2SN Babe Ruth/60 250.00 400.00
3BA Stan Musial SP 40.00 80.00
3CR Stan Musial/177 20.00 50.00
3SN Stan Musial/39 30.00 60.00
4BA Nolan Ryan 10.00 25.00
4CR Nolan Ryan/61 50.00 100.00
4JN Nolan Ryan/34 60.00 120.00
5CR Roberto Clemente/166 60.00 120.00
5SN Roberto Clemente/29 50.00 100.00
6BA Al Kaline SP 15.00 40.00
6CR Al Kaline/137 15.00 40.00
6SN Al Kaline/29 40.00 80.00
7BA Brooks Robinson 10.00 25.00
7CR Brooks Robinson/68 15.00 40.00
7SN Brooks Robinson/28 40.00 80.00
8BA Mel Ott 12.50 30.00
8CR Mel Ott/72 30.00 60.00
8SN Mel Ott/42 40.00 80.00
9BA Dave Winfield SP 10.00 25.00
9CR Dave Winfield/88 10.00 25.00
9JN Dave Winfield/31 15.00 40.00
9SN Dave Winfield/37 15.00 40.00
10BA Eddie Mathews SP 15.00 40.00
10CR Eddie Mathews/72 8.00 20.00
10JN Eddie Mathews/41 12.50 30.00
10SN Eddie Mathews/47 12.50 30.00
11BA Ernie Banks 10.00 25.00
11CR Ernie Banks/50 15.00 40.00
11SN Ernie Banks/47 12.00 30.00
12BA Frank Robinson SP 15.00 40.00
12CR Frank Robinson/72 15.00 40.00
12SN Frank Robinson/49 25.00 60.00
13BA George Brett SP 20.00 50.00
13CR George Brett/137 20.00 50.00
13SN George Brett/30 20.00 50.00
14BA Hank Aaron SP 60.00 120.00
14CR Hank Aaron/98 40.00 80.00
14JN Hank Aaron/44 40.00 80.00
14SN Hank Aaron/47 40.00 80.00
15BA Harmon Killebrew 10.00 25.00
15SN Harmon Killebrew/49 25.00 60.00
16BA Joe Morgan SP 12.50 30.00
16CR Joe Morgan/96 12.50 30.00
16SN Joe Morgan/27 25.00 60.00
17BA Johnny Bench 10.00 25.00
17CR Johnny Bench/68 15.00 40.00
17SN Johnny Bench/45 25.00 60.00
18BA Kirby Puckett SP 15.00 40.00
18CR Kirby Puckett/134 15.00 40.00
18JN Kirby Puckett AU/34 250.00 500.00
18SN Kirby Puckett/31 40.00 80.00
19BA Mike Schmidt SP 20.00 50.00
19CR Mike Schmidt/59 30.00 60.00
19SN Mike Schmidt/48 40.00 80.00
20BA Phil Rizzuto SP 15.00 40.00
20CR Phil Rizzuto/149 15.00 40.00
21BA Reggie Jackson SP 15.00 40.00
21CR Reggie Jackson/49 25.00 60.00
21JN Reggie Jackson/44 25.00 60.00
21SN Reggie Jackson/47 25.00 60.00
22BA Jim Hunter 10.00 25.00
22CR Jim Hunter/42 15.00 40.00
22JN Jim Hunter/27 20.00 50.00
23BA Rod Carew SP 15.00 40.00
23CR Rod Carew/92 15.00 40.00
23JN Rod Carew/29 40.00 80.00
23SN Rod Carew/100 15.00 40.00
24BA Bob Feller 6.00 15.00
24CR Bob Feller/44 15.00 40.00
24SN Bob Feller/36 15.00 40.00
25BA Lou Brock SP 15.00 40.00
25CR Lou Brock/141 15.00 40.00
26BA Tom Seaver SP 15.00 40.00
26CR Tom Seaver/61 15.00 40.00
26JN Tom Seaver/41 25.00 60.00
27BA Paul Molitor SP 10.00 25.00
27CR Paul Molitor/114 10.00 25.00
27SN Paul Molitor/41 15.00 40.00
28BA Willie McCovey SP 10.00 25.00
28JN Willie McCovey/44 15.00 40.00
28SN Willie McCovey/126 10.00 25.00
29BA Yogi Berra 10.00 25.00
29CR Yogi Berra/49 15.00 40.00
29JN Yogi Berra/35 40.00 80.00
29SN Yogi Berra/30 40.00 80.00
30BA Don Drysdale SP 15.00 40.00
30CR Don Drysdale/49 25.00 60.00
30JN Don Drysdale/53 15.00 40.00
31BA Duke Snider SP 15.00 40.00
31CR Duke Snider/99 15.00 40.00
31SN Duke Snider/43 10.00 25.00
33BA Orlando Cepeda 6.00 15.00
33CR Orlando Cepeda/27 20.00 50.00
33JN Orlando Cepeda/30 20.00 50.00
33SN Orlando Cepeda/46 15.00 40.00
34BA Casey Stengel SP 15.00 40.00
34JN Casey Stengel/37 25.00 60.00
34SN Casey Stengel/103 10.00 25.00
35BA Robin Yount SP 15.00 40.00
35CR Robin Yount/126 15.00 40.00
35SN Robin Yount/29 20.00 50.00
36BA Eddie Murray 10.00 25.00
36CR Eddie Murray/35 40.00 80.00
36SN Eddie Murray/33 40.00 80.00
37BA Jim Palmer 6.00 15.00
37CR Jim Palmer/53 10.00 25.00
38BA Juan Marichal 6.00 15.00
38CR Juan Marichal/52 10.00 25.00
38JN Juan Marichal/27 20.00 50.00
38SN Juan Marichal/26 20.00 50.00
39BA Willie Stargell 10.00 25.00
39CR Willie Stargell/55 15.00 40.00
39SN Willie Stargell/48 25.00 60.00
40BA Ted Williams SP 20.00 50.00
40CR Ted Williams/71 50.00 100.00
40SN Ted Williams/43 75.00 150.00
41BA Cal Ripken 20.00 50.00
41CR Cal Ripken/277 20.00 50.00
41SN Cal Ripken/114 12.50 30.00
42BA Vladimir Guerrero SP 10.00 25.00
42CR Vladimir Guerrero/322 6.00 15.00
42SN Vladimir Guerrero/44 20.00 50.00
43BA Greg Maddux 10.00 25.00
43CR Greg Maddux/240 10.00 25.00
43JN Greg Maddux/31 40.00 80.00
44BA Barry Bonds 12.50 30.00
44CR Barry Bonds/289 10.00 25.00
44SN Barry Bonds/49 50.00 100.00
45BA Pedro Martinez 6.00 15.00
45CR Pedro Martinez/268 6.00 15.00
45JN Pedro Martinez/45 20.00 50.00
46BA Ivan Rodriguez 6.00 15.00
46CR Ivan Rodriguez/304 6.00 15.00
46SN Ivan Rodriguez/35 25.00 60.00
47BA Roger Maris 20.00 50.00
47CR Roger Maris/275 20.00 50.00
47SN Roger Maris/61 50.00 100.00
48BA Randy Johnson 6.00 15.00
48CR Randy Johnson/179 6.00 15.00
48JN Randy Johnson/51 15.00 40.00
49BA Roger Clemens 10.00 25.00
49CR Roger Clemens/260 12.50 30.00
50BA Todd Helton 6.00 15.00
50CR Todd Helton/334 6.00 15.00
50SN Todd Helton/42 20.00 50.00
51BA Tony Gwynn 6.00 15.00
51CR Tony Gwynn/134 15.00 40.00
51SN Tony Gwynn/119 15.00 40.00
52BA Troy Glaus 4.00 10.00
52CR Troy Glaus/256 4.00 10.00
52SN Troy Glaus/47 12.50 30.00
53BA Phil Niekro 6.00 15.00
53CR Phil Niekro/245 6.00 15.00
53JN Phil Niekro/35 20.00 50.00
54BA Don Sutton 6.00 15.00
54CR Don Sutton/178 6.00 15.00
55BA Frank Thomas 6.00 15.00
55CR Frank Thomas/321 6.00 15.00
55JN Frank Thomas/35 12.50 30.00
55SN Frank Thomas/43 20.00 50.00
56BA Jeff Bagwell 6.00 15.00
56CR Jeff Bagwell/305 6.00 15.00
56SN Jeff Bagwell/135 10.00 25.00
57BA Rickey Henderson 6.00 15.00
57CR Rickey Henderson/282 6.00 15.00
57JN Rickey Henderson/35 25.00 60.00
57SN Rickey Henderson/28 40.00 80.00
58BA Darin Erstad SP 6.00 15.00
58CR Darin Erstad/301 4.00 10.00
58SN Darin Erstad/100 6.00 15.00
59BA Andruw Jones 6.00 15.00
59CR Andruw Jones/272 6.00 15.00
59SN Andruw Jones/36 20.00 50.00
60BA Roberto Alomar 6.00 15.00
60CR Roberto Alomar/170 6.00 15.00
60SN Roberto Alomar/120 10.00 25.00
61BA Mike Piazza SP 15.00 40.00
61CR Mike Piazza/328 10.00 25.00
61JN Mike Piazza/31 40.00 80.00
61SN Mike Piazza/40 40.00 80.00
62BA Chipper Jones 6.00 15.00
62CR Chipper Jones/189 6.00 15.00
62SN Chipper Jones/45 20.00 50.00
63BA Shawn Green 4.00 10.00
63CR Shawn Green/143 6.00 15.00
63SN Shawn Green/123 6.00 15.00
64BA Don Mattingly SP 20.00 50.00
64CR Don Mattingly/222 8.00 20.00
64SN Don Mattingly/145 10.00 25.00
65BA Rafael Palmeiro 6.00 15.00
65CR Rafael Palmeiro/296 6.00 15.00
65SN Rafael Palmeiro/47 20.00 50.00
66BA Wade Boggs 10.00 25.00
66CR Wade Boggs/116 15.00 40.00
66JN Wade Boggs/26 40.00 80.00
66SN Wade Boggs/89 15.00 40.00
67BA Hoyt Wilhelm 6.00 15.00
67CR Hoyt Wilhelm/143 10.00 25.00
67JN Hoyt Wilhelm/31 20.00 50.00
67SN Hoyt Wilhelm/27 20.00 50.00
68BA Andre Dawson 6.00 15.00
68CR Andre Dawson/314 6.00 15.00
68SN Andre Dawson/49 15.00 40.00
69BA Ryne Sandberg 15.00 40.00
69CR Ryne Sandberg/282 10.00 25.00
69SN Ryne Sandberg/40 40.00 80.00
70BA Nomar Garciaparra SP 15.00 40.00
70CR Nomar Garciaparra/333 10.00 25.00
70SN Nomar Garciaparra/35 50.00 100.00
71BA Tom Glavine 6.00 15.00
71CR Tom Glavine/208 6.00 15.00
71JN Tom Glavine/47 20.00 50.00
71SN Tom Glavine/247 6.00 15.00
72BA Magglio Ordonez 4.00 10.00
72CR Magglio Ordonez/301 4.00 10.00
72JN Magglio Ordonez/30 15.00 40.00
72SN Magglio Ordonez/126 6.00 15.00
73BA Bernie Williams 6.00 15.00
73CR Bernie Williams/304 6.00 15.00
73JN Bernie Williams/51 15.00 40.00
73SN Bernie Williams/30 25.00 60.00
74BA Jim Edmonds 4.00 10.00
74CR Jim Edmonds/291 6.00 15.00
74SN Jim Edmonds/108 6.00 15.00
75BA Hideo Nomo 20.00 50.00
75CR Hideo Nomo/69 50.00 100.00
76BA Barry Larkin 6.00 15.00
76CR Barry Larkin/300 6.00 15.00
76SN Barry Larkin/33 25.00 60.00
77BA Scott Rolen 6.00 15.00
77CR Scott Rolen/284 6.00 15.00
77SN Scott Rolen/31 25.00 60.00
78BA Miguel Tejada 4.00 10.00
78CR Miguel Tejada/253 4.00 10.00
78SN Miguel Tejada/30 15.00 40.00
79BA Freddy Garcia 4.00 10.00
79CR Freddy Garcia/249 4.00 10.00
79JN Freddy Garcia/34 15.00 40.00
79SN Freddy Garcia/170 4.00 10.00
80BA Edgar Martinez 6.00 15.00
80CR Edgar Martinez/320 6.00 15.00
80SN Edgar Martinez/37 20.00 50.00
81BA Edgardo Alfonzo 4.00 10.00
81CR Edgardo Alfonzo/296 4.00 10.00
81SN Edgardo Alfonzo/108 6.00 15.00
82BA Steve Garvey 6.00 15.00
82CR Steve Garvey/272 6.00 15.00
82SN Steve Garvey/33 20.00 50.00
83BA Larry Walker 4.00 10.00
83CR Larry Walker/311 4.00 10.00
83SN Larry Walker/49 12.50 30.00
84BA A.J. Burnett 4.00 10.00
84CR A.J. Burnett/90 6.00 15.00
84JN A.J. Burnett/43 12.50 30.00
84SN A.J. Burnett/57 10.00 25.00
85BA Richie Sexson 4.00 10.00
85CR Richie Sexson/242 4.00 10.00
85SN Richie Sexson/116 6.00 15.00
86BA Mark Mulder 4.00 10.00
86CR Mark Mulder/88 6.00 15.00
87BA Kerry Wood 4.00 10.00
87JN Kerry Wood/34 15.00 40.00
87SN Kerry Wood/233 4.00 10.00
88BA Sean Casey 4.00 10.00
88CR Sean Casey/312 4.00 10.00
89BA Jermaine Dye SP 6.00 15.00
89CR Jermaine Dye/286 4.00 10.00
89SN Jermaine Dye/118 6.00 15.00
90BA Kevin Brown SP 6.00 15.00
90CR Kevin Brown/170 4.00 10.00
90JN Kevin Brown/27 15.00 40.00
90SN Kevin Brown/257 4.00 10.00
91BA Craig Biggio 6.00 15.00
91CR Craig Biggio/291 6.00 15.00
91SN Craig Biggio/88 10.00 25.00
92BA Mike Sweeney SP 6.00 15.00
92CR Mike Sweeney/302 4.00 10.00
92JN Mike Sweeney/29 15.00 40.00
92SN Mike Sweeney/144 6.00 15.00
93BA Jim Thome 6.00 15.00
93CR Jim Thome/233 6.00 15.00
93SN Jim Thome/40 20.00 50.00
94BA Al Leiter 4.00 10.00
94CR Al Leiter/106 6.00 15.00
94SN Al Leiter/247 4.00 10.00
95BA Barry Zito 6.00 15.00
95CR Barry Zito/272 6.00 15.00
95JN Barry Zito/75 10.00 25.00
95SN Barry Zito/78 10.00 25.00
96BA Rafael Furcal 4.00 10.00
96CR Rafael Furcal/295 4.00 10.00
96SN Rafael Furcal/37 12.50 30.00
97BA J.D. Drew 4.00 10.00
97CR J.D. Drew/276 4.00 10.00
98BA Andres Galarraga 4.00 10.00
98CR Andres Galarraga/291 4.00 10.00
98SN Andres Galarraga/150 4.00 10.00
99BA Kazuhiro Sasaki 4.00 10.00
99CR Kazuhiro Sasaki/266 4.00 10.00
99SN Kazuhiro Sasaki/45 12.50 30.00
100BA Chan Ho Park 4.00 10.00
100CR Chan Ho Park/65 10.00 25.00
100JN Chan Ho Park/61 10.00 25.00
100SN Chan Ho Park/217 4.00 10.00
101BA Eric Milton 4.00 10.00
101CR Eric Milton/28 15.00 40.00
101SN Eric Milton/163 4.00 10.00
102BA Carlos Lee 4.00 10.00
102CR Carlos Lee/297 4.00 10.00
102JN Carlos Lee/45 12.50 30.00
103BA Preston Wilson 4.00 10.00
103CR Preston Wilson/266 4.00 10.00
103JN Preston Wilson/44 12.50 30.00
103SN Preston Wilson/31 15.00 40.00
104BA Adrian Beltre 4.00 10.00
104CR Adrian Beltre/272 4.00 10.00
104JN Adrian Beltre/29 15.00 40.00
104SN Adrian Beltre/85 6.00 15.00
105BA Luis Gonzalez 4.00 10.00
105CR Luis Gonzalez/281 4.00 10.00
105SN Luis Gonzalez/114 6.00 15.00
106BA Kenny Lofton 4.00 10.00
106CR Kenny Lofton/306 4.00 10.00
107BA Shannon Stewart 4.00 10.00
107CR Shannon Stewart/297 4.00 10.00
108BA Javy Lopez 4.00 10.00
108CR Javy Lopez/290 4.00 10.00
108SN Javy Lopez/106 6.00 15.00
109BA Raul Mondesi 4.00 10.00
109CR Raul Mondesi/286 4.00 10.00
109JN Raul Mondesi/43 12.50 30.00
109SN Raul Mondesi/33 15.00 40.00
110BA Mark Grace 8.00 20.00
110CR Mark Grace/308 8.00 20.00
110SN Mark Grace/51 15.00 40.00
111BA Curt Schilling 4.00 10.00
111CR Curt Schilling/110 6.00 15.00
111JN Curt Schilling/38 12.50 30.00
111SN Curt Schilling/235 4.00 10.00
112BA Cliff Floyd 4.00 10.00
112CR Cliff Floyd/275 4.00 10.00
112JN Cliff Floyd/30 15.00 40.00
113BA Moises Alou 4.00 10.00
113CR Moises Alou/303 4.00 10.00
113SN Moises Alou/124 6.00 15.00
114BA Aaron Sele 4.00 10.00
114CR Aaron Sele/92 6.00 15.00
114JN Aaron Sele/30 15.00 40.00
115BA Jose Cruz Jr. 4.00 10.00
115CR Jose Cruz Jr./245 4.00 10.00
115SN Jose Cruz Jr./31 15.00 40.00
116BA John Olerud 4.00 10.00
116CR John Olerud/186 4.00 10.00
116SN John Olerud/107 6.00 15.00
117BA Jose Vidro 4.00 10.00
117CR Jose Vidro/296 4.00 10.00
118BA John Smoltz 6.00 15.00
118CR John Smoltz/335 6.00 15.00
118JN John Smoltz/29 25.00 60.00

2002 Leaf Certified

COMP.SET w/o SP's (150) 30.00 80.00
COMMON CARD (1-150) .40 1.00
COMMON CARD (151-200) 3.00 8.00
151-200 RANDOM INSERTS IN PACKS
151-200 PRINT RUN 500 SERIAL #'d SETS
1 Alex Rodriguez 1.25 3.00
2 Luis Gonzalez .40 1.00
3 Javier Vazquez .40 1.00
4 Juan Uribe .40 1.00
5 Ben Sheets .40 1.00
6 George Brett 2.00 5.00
7 Magglio Ordonez .40 1.00
8 Randy Johnson 1.00 2.50
9 Joe Kennedy .40 1.00
10 Richie Sexson .40 1.00
11 Larry Walker .40 1.00
12 Lance Berkman .40 1.00
13 Jose Cruz Jr. .40 1.00
14 Doug Davis .40 1.00
15 Cliff Floyd .40 1.00
16 Ryan Klesko .40 1.00
17 Troy Glaus .40 1.00
18 Robert Person .40 1.00
19 Bartolo Colon .40 1.00
20 Adam Dunn .40 1.00
21 Kevin Brown .40 1.00
22 John Smoltz .60 1.50
23 Edgar Martinez .60 1.50
24 Eric Karros .40 1.00
25 Tony Gwynn 1.25 3.00
26 Mark Mulder .40 1.00
27 Don Mattingly 2.00 5.00
28 Brandon Duckworth .40 1.00
29 C.C. Sabathia .40 1.00
30 Nomar Garciaparra 1.50 4.00
31 Adam Johnson .40 1.00
32 Miquel Tejada .40 1.00
33 Ryne Sandberg 2.00 5.00
34 Roger Clemens 2.00 5.00
35 Edgardo Alfonzo .40 1.00
36 Jason Jennings .40 1.00
37 Todd Helton .60 1.50
38 Nolan Ryan 2.50 6.00
39 Paul LoDuca .40 1.00
40 Cal Ripken 3.00 8.00
41 Terrence Long .40 1.00
42 Mike Sweeney .40 1.00
43 Carlos Lee .40 1.00
44 Ben Grieve .40 1.00
45 Tony Armas Jr. .40 1.00
46 Joe Mays .40 1.00
47 Jeff Kent .40 1.00
48 Andy Pettitte .60 1.50
49 Kirby Puckett 1.00 2.50
50 Aramis Ramirez .40 1.00
51 Tim Redding .40 1.00
52 Freddy Garcia .40 1.00
53 Javy Lopez .40 1.00
54 Mike Schmidt 2.00 5.00
55 Wade Miller .40 1.00
56 Ramon Ortiz .40 1.00
57 Ray Durham .40 1.00
58 J.D. Drew .40 1.00
59 Bret Boone .40 1.00
60 Mark Buehrle .40 1.00
61 Geoff Jenkins .40 1.00
62 Greg Maddux 1.50 4.00
63 Mark Grace .60 1.50
64 Toby Hall .40 1.00
65 A.J. Burnett .40 1.00
66 Bernie Williams .60 1.50
67 Roy Oswalt .40 1.00
68 Shannon Stewart .40 1.00
69 Barry Zito .40 1.00
70 Juan Pierre .40 1.00
71 Preston Wilson .40 1.00
72 Rafael Furcal .40 1.00
73 Sean Casey .40 1.00
74 John Olerud .40 1.00
75 Paul Konerko .40 1.00
76 Vernon Wells .40 1.00
77 Juan Gonzalez .40 1.00
78 Ellis Burks .40 1.00
79 Jim Edmonds .40 1.00
80 Robert Fick .40 1.00
81 Michael Cuddyer .40 1.00
82 Tim Hudson .40 1.00
83 Phil Nevin .40 1.00
84 Curt Schilling .40 1.00
85 Juan Cruz .40 1.00
86 Jeff Bagwell .60 1.50
87 Raul Mondesi .40 1.00
88 Bud Smith .40 1.00
89 Omar Vizquel .60 1.50
90 Vladimir Guerrero 1.00 2.50
91 Garret Anderson .40 1.00
92 Mike Piazza 1.50 4.00
93 Josh Beckett .40 1.00
94 Carlos Delgado .40 1.00
95 Kazuhiro Sasaki .40 1.00
96 Chipper Jones 1.00 2.50
97 Jacque Jones .40 1.00
98 Pedro Martinez .60 1.50
99 Marcus Giles .40 1.00
100 Craig Biggio .60 1.50
101 Orlando Cabrera .40 1.00
102 Al Leiter .40 1.00
103 Michael Barrett .40 1.00
104 Hideo Nomo 1.00 2.50
105 Mike Mussina .60 1.50
106 Jeremy Giambi .40 1.00
107 Cristian Guzman .40 1.00
108 Frank Thomas 1.00 2.50
109 Carlos Beltran .40 1.00
110 Jorge Posada .60 1.50
111 Roberto Alomar .60 1.50
112 Bob Abreu .40 1.00
113 Robin Ventura .40 1.00
114 Pat Burrell .40 1.00
115 Kenny Lofton .40 1.00
116 Adrian Beltre .40 1.00
117 Gary Sheffield .40 1.00
118 Jermaine Dye .40 1.00
119 Manny Ramirez .60 1.50
120 Brian Giles .40 1.00
121 Tsuyoshi Shinjo .40 1.00
122 Rafael Palmeiro .60 1.50
123 Mo Vaughn .40 1.00
124 Kerry Wood .40 1.00
125 Moises Alou .40 1.00
126 Rickey Henderson 1.00 2.50
127 Corey Patterson .40 1.00
128 Jim Thome .60 1.50
129 Richard Hidalgo .40 1.00
130 Darin Erstad .40 1.00
131 Johnny Damon Sox .60 1.50
132 Juan Encarnacion .40 1.00
133 Scott Rolen .60 1.50
134 Tom Glavine .60 1.50
135 Ivan Rodriguez .60 1.50
136 Jay Gibbons .40 1.00
137 Trot Nixon .40 1.00
138 Nick Neugebauer .40 1.00
139 Barry Larkin .60 1.50
140 Andruw Jones .60 1.50
141 Shawn Green .40 1.00
142 Jose Vidro .40 1.00
143 Derek Jeter 2.50 6.00
144 Ichiro Suzuki 2.00 5.00
145 Ken Griffey Jr. 2.00 5.00
146 Barry Bonds 2.50 6.00
147 Albert Pujols 2.00 5.00
148 Sammy Sosa 1.00 2.50
149 Jason Giambi .40 1.00
150 Alfonso Soriano .40 1.00
151 Drew Henson NG Bat 3.00 8.00
152 Luis Garcia NG Bat 3.00 8.00
153 Geronimo Gil NG Jsy 3.00 8.00
154 Corky Miller NG Jsy 3.00 8.00
155 Mike Rivera NG Bat 3.00 8.00
156 Mark Ellis NG Jsy 3.00 8.00
157 Josh Pearce NG Bat 3.00 8.00
158 Ryan Ludwick NG Bat 3.00 8.00
159 So Taguchi NG Bat RC 4.00 10.00
160 Cody Ransom NG Jsy 3.00 8.00
161 Jeff Deardorff NG Bat 3.00 8.00
162 Franklyn German NG Bat RC 3.00 8.00
163 Ed Rogers NG Jsy 3.00 8.00
164 Eric Cyr NG Jsy 3.00 8.00
165 Victor Alvarez NG Jsy RC 3.00 8.00
166 Victor Martinez NG Jsy 4.00 10.00
167 Brandon Berger NG Jsy 3.00 8.00
168 Juan Diaz NG Jsy 3.00 8.00
169 Kevin Frederick NG Jsy RC 3.00 8.00
170 Earl Snyder NG Bat RC 3.00 8.00
171 Morgan Ensberg NG Bat 3.00 8.00
172 Ryan Jamison NG Jsy 3.00 8.00
173 Rodrigo Rosario NG Jsy RC 3.00 8.00
174 Willie Harris NG Bat 3.00 8.00
175 Ramon Vazquez NG Bat 3.00 8.00
176 Kazuhisa Ishii NG Bat RC 4.00 10.00
177 Hank Blalock NG Jsy 4.00 10.00
178 Mark Prior NG Bat 4.00 10.00
179 Dewon Brazelton NG Jsy 3.00 8.00
180 Doug Devore NG Jsy RC 3.00 8.00
181 Jorge Padilla NG Bat RC 3.00 8.00
182 Mark Teixeira NG Jsy 4.00 10.00
183 Orlando Hudson NG Bat 3.00 8.00
184 John Buck NG Jsy 3.00 8.00
185 Erik Bedard NG Jsy 3.00 8.00
186 Allan Simpson NG Jsy RC 3.00 8.00
187 Travis Hafner NG Jsy 3.00 8.00
188 Jason Lane NG Jsy 3.00 8.00
189 Marlon Byrd NG Jsy 3.00 8.00
190 Joe Thurston NG Jsy 3.00 8.00
191 Brandon Backe NG Jsy RC 4.00 10.00
192 Josh Phelps NG Jsy 3.00 8.00
193 Bill Hall NG Bat 3.00 8.00
194 Chris Snelling NG Bat RC 3.00 8.00
195 Austin Kearns NG Jsy 3.00 8.00
196 Antonio Perez NG Bat 3.00 8.00
197 Angel Berroa NG Bat 3.00 8.00
198 Andy Machado NG Jsy RC 3.00 8.00
199 Alfredo Amezaga NG Jsy 3.00 8.00
200 Eric Hinske NG Bat 3.00 8.00

2002 Leaf Certified Mirror Blue

*MIRROR BLUE 1-150: .6X TO 1.5X MIR.RED
*MIRROR BLUE 151-200: .6X TO 1.5X MIR.RED
STATED PRINT RUN 75 SERIAL #'d SETS

2002 Leaf Certified Mirror Red

STATED PRINT RUN 150 SERIAL #'d SETS
1 Alex Rodriguez Jsy 10.00 25.00
2 Luis Gonzalez Jsy 4.00 10.00
3 Javier Vazquez Jsy 4.00 10.00
4 Juan Uribe Jsy 4.00 10.00
5 Ben Sheets Jsy 4.00 10.00
6 George Brett Jsy 20.00 50.00
7 Magglio Ordonez Jsy 4.00 10.00
8 Randy Johnson Jsy 8.00 20.00
9 Joe Kennedy Jsy 4.00 10.00
10 Richie Sexson Jsy 4.00 10.00
11 Larry Walker Jsy 4.00 10.00
12 Lance Berkman Jsy 4.00 10.00
13 Jose Cruz Jr. Jsy 4.00 10.00
14 Doug Davis Jsy 4.00 10.00
15 Cliff Floyd Jsy 4.00 10.00
16 Ryan Klesko Bat SP/100 4.00 10.00
17 Troy Glaus Jsy 4.00 10.00

18 Robert Person Jsy 4.00 10.00
19 Bartolo Colon Jsy 4.00 10.00
20 Adam Dunn Jsy 4.00 10.00
21 Kevin Brown Jsy 4.00 10.00
22 John Smoltz Jsy 6.00 15.00
23 Edgar Martinez Jsy 6.00 15.00
24 Eric Karros Jsy 4.00 10.00
25 Tony Gwynn Jsy 10.00 25.00
26 Mark Mulder Jsy 4.00 10.00
27 Don Mattingly Jsy 20.00 50.00
28 Brandon Duckworth Jsy 4.00 10.00
29 C.C. Sabathia Jsy 4.00 10.00
30 Nomar Garciaparra Jsy 10.00 25.00
31 Adam Johnson Jsy 4.00 10.00
32 Miguel Tejada Jsy 4.00 10.00
33 Ryne Sandberg Jsy 20.00 50.00
34 Roger Clemens Jsy 15.00 40.00
35 Edgardo Alfonzo Jsy 4.00 10.00
36 Jason Jennings Jsy 4.00 10.00
37 Todd Helton Jsy 6.00 15.00
38 Nolan Ryan Jsy 40.00 80.00
39 Paul LoDuca Jsy 4.00 10.00
40 Cal Ripken Jsy 40.00 80.00
41 Terrence Long Jsy 4.00 10.00
42 Mike Sweeney Jsy 4.00 10.00
43 Carlos Lee Jsy 4.00 10.00
44 Ben Grieve Jsy 4.00 10.00
45 Tony Armas Jr. Jsy 4.00 10.00
46 Joe Mays Jsy 4.00 10.00
47 Jeff Kent Jsy 4.00 10.00
48 Andy Pettitte Jsy 6.00 15.00
49 Kirby Puckett Jsy 8.00 20.00
50 Aramis Ramirez Jsy 4.00 10.00
51 Tim Redding Jsy 4.00 10.00
52 Freddy Garcia Jsy 4.00 10.00
53 Javy Lopez Jsy 4.00 10.00
54 Mike Schmidt Jsy 20.00 50.00
55 Wade Miller Jsy 4.00 10.00
56 Ramon Ortiz Jsy 4.00 10.00
57 Ray Durham Jsy 4.00 10.00
58 J.D. Drew Jsy 4.00 10.00
59 Bret Boone Jsy 4.00 10.00
60 Mark Buehrle Jsy 4.00 10.00
61 Geoff Jenkins Jsy 4.00 10.00
62 Greg Maddux Jsy 10.00 25.00
63 Mark Grace Jsy 6.00 15.00
64 Toby Hall Jsy 4.00 10.00
65 A.J. Burnett Jsy 4.00 10.00
66 Bernie Williams Jsy 6.00 15.00
67 Roy Oswalt Jsy 4.00 10.00
68 Shannon Stewart Jsy 4.00 10.00
69 Barry Zito Jsy 4.00 10.00
70 Juan Pierre Jsy 4.00 10.00
71 Preston Wilson Jsy 4.00 10.00
72 Rafael Furcal Jsy 4.00 10.00
73 Sean Casey Jsy 4.00 10.00
74 John Olerud Jsy 4.00 10.00
75 Paul Konerko Jsy 4.00 10.00
76 Vernon Wells Jsy 4.00 10.00
77 Juan Gonzalez Jsy 4.00 10.00
78 Ellis Burks Jsy 4.00 10.00
79 Jim Edmonds Jsy 4.00 10.00
80 Robert Fick Jsy 4.00 10.00
81 Michael Cuddyer Jsy 4.00 10.00
82 Tim Hudson Jsy 4.00 10.00
83 Phil Nevin Jsy 4.00 10.00
84 Curt Schilling Jsy 4.00 10.00
85 Juan Cruz Jsy 4.00 10.00
86 Jeff Bagwell Jsy 6.00 15.00
87 Raul Mondesi Jsy 4.00 10.00
88 Bud Smith Jsy 4.00 10.00
89 Omar Vizquel Jsy 6.00 15.00
90 Vladimir Guerrero Jsy 8.00 20.00
91 Garret Anderson Jsy 4.00 10.00
92 Mike Piazza Jsy 10.00 25.00
93 Josh Beckett Jsy 4.00 10.00
94 Carlos Delgado Jsy 4.00 10.00
95 Kazuhiro Sasaki Jsy 4.00 10.00
96 Chipper Jones Jsy 8.00 20.00
97 Jacque Jones Jsy 4.00 10.00
98 Pedro Martinez Jsy 6.00 15.00
99 Marcus Giles Jsy 4.00 10.00
100 Craig Biggio Jsy 6.00 15.00
101 Orlando Cabrera Jsy 4.00 10.00
102 Al Leiter Jsy 4.00 10.00
103 Michael Barrett Jsy 4.00 10.00
104 Hideo Nomo Jsy 8.00 20.00
105 Mike Mussina Jsy 6.00 15.00
106 Jeremy Giambi Jsy 4.00 10.00
107 Cristian Guzman Jsy 4.00 10.00
108 Frank Thomas Jsy 8.00 20.00
109 Carlos Beltran Bat 4.00 10.00
110 Jorge Posada Bat 6.00 15.00
111 Roberto Alomar Bat 6.00 15.00
112 Bob Abreu Bat 4.00 10.00
113 Robin Ventura Bat 4.00 10.00
114 Pat Burrell Bat 4.00 10.00
115 Kenny Lofton Bat 4.00 10.00
116 Adrian Beltre Bat 4.00 10.00
117 Gary Sheffield Bat 4.00 10.00
118 Jermaine Dye Bat 4.00 10.00
119 Manny Ramirez Bat 6.00 15.00
120 Brian Giles Bat 4.00 10.00
121 Tsuyoshi Shinjo Bat 4.00 10.00
122 Rafael Palmeiro Bat 6.00 15.00
123 Mo Vaughn Bat 4.00 10.00
124 Kerry Wood Bat 4.00 10.00
125 Moises Alou Bat 4.00 10.00
126 Rickey Henderson Bat 8.00 20.00
127 Corey Patterson Bat 4.00 10.00
128 Jim Thome Bat 6.00 15.00
129 Richard Hidalgo Bat 4.00 10.00
130 Darin Erstad Bat 4.00 10.00
131 Johnny Damon Sox Bat 6.00 15.00
132 Juan Encarnacion Bat 4.00 10.00
133 Scott Rolen Bat 6.00 15.00
134 Tom Glavine Bat 6.00 15.00
135 Ivan Rodriguez Bat 6.00 15.00
136 Jay Gibbons Bat 4.00 10.00
137 Trot Nixon Bat 4.00 10.00
138 Nick Neugebauer Bat 4.00 10.00
139 Barry Larkin Bat 6.00 15.00
140 Andruw Jones Bat 6.00 15.00
141 Shawn Green Bat 4.00 10.00
142 Jose Vidro Jsy 4.00 10.00
143 Derek Jeter Base 12.50 30.00
144 Ichiro Suzuki Base 10.00 25.00
145 Ken Griffey Jr. Base 8.00 20.00
146 Barry Bonds Base 12.50 30.00
147 Albert Pujols Base 8.00 20.00
148 Sammy Sosa Base 8.00 20.00
149 Jason Giambi Base 4.00 10.00
150 Alfonso Soriano Jsy 4.00 10.00
151 Drew Henson NG Bat 3.00 8.00
152 Luis Garcia NG Bat 3.00 8.00
153 Geronimo Gil NG Jsy 3.00 8.00
154 Corky Miller NG Jsy 3.00 8.00
155 Mike Rivera NG Bat 3.00 8.00
156 Mark Ellis NG Jsy 3.00 8.00
157 Josh Pearce NG Bat 3.00 8.00
158 Ryan Ludwick NG Bat 3.00 8.00
159 So Taguchi NG Bat 4.00 10.00
160 Cody Ransom NG Jsy 3.00 8.00
161 Jeff Deardorff NG Bat 3.00 8.00
162 Franklyn German NG Bat 3.00 8.00
163 Ed Rogers NG Jsy 3.00 8.00
164 Eric Cyr NG Jsy 3.00 8.00
165 Victor Alvarez NG Jsy 3.00 8.00
166 Victor Martinez NG Jsy 4.00 10.00
167 Brandon Berger NG Jsy 3.00 8.00
168 Juan Diaz NG Jsy 3.00 8.00
169 Kevin Frederick NG Jsy 3.00 8.00
170 Earl Snyder NG Bat 3.00 8.00
171 Morgan Ensberg NG Bat 3.00 8.00
172 Ryan Jamison NG Jsy 3.00 8.00
173 Rodrigo Rosario NG Jsy 3.00 8.00
174 Willie Harris NG Bat 3.00 8.00
175 Ramon Vazquez NG Bat 3.00 8.00
176 Kazuhisa Ishii NG Bat 4.00 10.00
177 Hank Blalock NG Jsy 4.00 10.00
178 Mark Prior NG Bat 4.00 10.00
179 Dewon Brazelton NG Jsy 3.00 8.00
180 Doug Devore NG Jsy 3.00 8.00
181 Jorge Padilla NG Bat 3.00 8.00
182 Mark Teixeira NG Jsy 4.00 10.00
183 Orlando Hudson NG Bat 3.00 8.00
184 John Buck NG Jsy 3.00 8.00
185 Erik Bedard NG Jsy 3.00 8.00
186 Allan Simpson NG Jsy 3.00 8.00
187 Travis Hafner NG Jsy 3.00 8.00
188 Jason Lane NG Jsy 3.00 8.00
189 Marlon Byrd NG Jsy 3.00 8.00
190 Joe Thurston NG Jsy 3.00 8.00
191 Brandon Backe NG Jsy 4.00 10.00
192 Josh Phelps NG Jsy 3.00 8.00
193 Bill Hall NG Bat 3.00 8.00
194 Chris Snelling NG Bat 3.00 8.00
195 Austin Kearns NG Jsy 3.00 8.00
196 Antonio Perez NG Bat 3.00 8.00
197 Angel Berroa NG Bat 3.00 8.00
198 Anderson Machado NG Jsy 3.00 8.00
199 Alfredo Amezaga NG Jsy 3.00 8.00
200 Eric Hinske NG Bat 3.00 8.00

2002 Leaf Certified All-Certified Team

COMPLETE SET (25) 40.00 100.00
STATED ODDS 1:17
*BLUE: 2X TO 5X BASIC ALL-CERT.TEAM
BLUE PRINT RUN 50 SERIAL #'d SETS
GOLD PRINT RUN 25 SERIAL #'d SETS
NO GOLD PRICING DUE TO SCARCITY
*RED: 1.25X TO 3X BASIC ALL-CERT.TEAM
RED: RANDOM INSERTS IN PACKS
RED PRINT RUN 75 SERIAL #'d SETS
1 Ichiro Suzuki 3.00 8.00
2 Alex Rodriguez 2.00 5.00
3 Sammy Sosa 1.50 4.00
4 Jeff Bagwell 1.25 3.00
5 Greg Maddux 2.50 6.00
6 Todd Helton 1.25 3.00
7 Nomar Garciaparra 2.50 6.00
8 Ken Griffey Jr. 3.00 8.00
9 Roger Clemens 3.00 8.00
10 Adam Dunn 1.25 3.00
11 Chipper Jones 1.50 4.00
12 Hideo Nomo 1.50 4.00
13 Lance Berkman 1.25 3.00
14 Barry Bonds 4.00 10.00
15 Manny Ramirez 1.25 3.00
16 Jason Giambi 1.25 3.00
17 Rickey Henderson 1.50 4.00
18 Randy Johnson 1.50 4.00
19 Derek Jeter 4.00 10.00
20 Kazuhisa Ishii 1.25 3.00
21 Frank Thomas 1.50 4.00
22 Mike Piazza 2.50 6.00
23 Albert Pujols 3.00 8.00
24 Pedro Martinez 1.25 3.00
25 Vladimir Guerrero 1.50 4.00

2002 Leaf Certified Fabric of the Game

STATED PRINT RUNS LISTED BELOW
NO PRICING ON QTY OF 25 OR LESS
1DY Bobby Doerr/37 12.50 30.00
2DY Ozzie Smith/78 15.00 40.00
3DY Pee Wee Reese/40 20.00 50.00
4BA Tommy Lasorda/80 6.00 15.00
4DY Tommy Lasorda/54 10.00 25.00
4PS Tommy Lasorda/50 10.00 25.00
5DY Red Schoendienst/45 12.50 30.00
7DY Harmon Killebrew/54 15.00 40.00
8DY Roger Maris A's/57 20.00 50.00
10DY Mel Ott/26 20.00 50.00
11BA Paul Molitor/100 6.00 15.00
11DY Paul Molitor/78 6.00 15.00
11PS Paul Molitor/50 10.00 25.00
12DY Duke Snider/47 12.50 30.00
13DY Brooks Robinson/55 10.00 25.00
14BA George Brett/40 40.00 80.00
14DY George Brett/73 30.00 60.00
15BA Johnny Bench/80 10.00 25.00
15DY Johnny Bench/67 12.50 30.00
15PS Johnny Bench/50 15.00 40.00
16DY Lou Boudreau/38 12.50 30.00
17DY Stan Musial/41 15.00 40.00
18DY Al Kaline/53 15.00 40.00
19BA Steve Garvey/100 6.00 15.00
19DY Steve Garvey/69 10.00 25.00
19PS Steve Garvey/45 12.50 30.00
20BA Nomar Garciaparra/100 12.50 30.00
20DY Nomar Garciaparra/96 12.50 30.00
20PS Nomar Garciaparra/50 15.00 40.00
21BA Joe Morgan/80 6.00 15.00
21DY Joe Morgan/63 10.00 25.00
21PS Joe Morgan/50 10.00 25.00
22DY Willie Stargell/62 15.00 40.00
23BA Andre Dawson/80 6.00 15.00
23DY Andre Dawson/76 6.00 15.00
23PS Andre Dawson/50 10.00 25.00
24BA Gary Carter/100 6.00 15.00
24DY Gary Carter/74 10.00 25.00
24PS Gary Carter/50 10.00 25.00
25DY Reggie Jackson A's/67 10.00 25.00
27DY Phil Rizzuto/41 10.00 25.00
28DY Luis Aparicio/56 10.00 25.00
29BA Robin Yount/80 10.00 25.00
29DY Robin Yount/74 10.00 25.00
29PS Robin Yount/50 15.00 40.00
30BA Tony Gwynn/100 10.00 25.00
30DY Tony Gwynn/82 10.00 25.00
30PS Tony Gwynn/50 15.00 40.00
31DY Ernie Banks/53 15.00 40.00
32BA Joe Torre/50 15.00 40.00
32DY Joe Torre/60 15.00 40.00
33BA Bo Jackson/100 10.00 25.00
33DY Bo Jackson/86 10.00 25.00
33PS Bo Jackson/35 30.00 60.00
34BA Alfonso Soriano/80 6.00 15.00
34DY Alfonso Soriano/99 6.00 15.00
34PS Alfonso Soriano/50 10.00 25.00
35BA Cal Ripken/80 12.50 30.00
35DY Cal Ripken/81 12.50 30.00
35PS Cal Ripken/50 20.00 50.00
36BA Miguel Tejada/100 6.00 15.00
36DY Miguel Tejada/97 6.00 15.00
36PS Miguel Tejada/50 10.00 25.00
37BA Alex Rodriguez M's/100 10.00 25.00
37DY Alex Rodriguez M's/94 10.00 25.00
37PS Alex Rodriguez M's/50 15.00 40.00
38BA Mike Schmidt/80 20.00 50.00
38DY Mike Schmidt/72 20.00 50.00
38PS Mike Schmidt/50 25.00 60.00
39DY Lou Brock/61 15.00 40.00
40BA Don Sutton/80 6.00 15.00
40DY Don Sutton/66 10.00 25.00
40PS Don Sutton/50 10.00 25.00
41DY Roberto Clemente/55 75.00 150.00
42DY Jim Palmer/65 10.00 25.00
43BA Don Mattingly/40 20.00 50.00
43DY Don Mattingly/82 10.00 25.00
44BA Ryne Sandberg/4040 12.00 30.00
44DY Ryne Sandberg/81 10.00 25.00
45DY Early Wynn/39 12.50 30.00
46BA Mike Piazza Dodgers/100 10.00 25.00
46DY Mike Piazza Dodgers/92 10.00 25.00
46JN Mike Piazza Dodgers/31 20.00 50.00
46PS Mike Piazza Dodgers/50 12.50 30.00
47BA Wade Boggs/100 10.00 25.00
47DY Wade Boggs/82 10.00 25.00
47JN Wade Boggs/26 30.00 60.00
47PS Wade Boggs/45 20.00 50.00
48DY Catfish Hunter/65 15.00 40.00
48JN Catfish Hunter/27 30.00 60.00
49DY Juan Marichal/60 10.00 25.00
49JN Juan Marichal/27 15.00 40.00
50BA Carlton Fisk Red Sox/80 10.00 25.00
50DY Carlton Fisk Red Sox/69 15.00 40.00
50JN Carlton Fisk Red Sox/27 30.00 60.00
50PS Carlton Fisk Red Sox/50 15.00 40.00
51BA Curt Schilling/100 6.00 15.00
51DY Curt Schilling/88 6.00 15.00
51JN Curt Schilling/38 12.50 30.00
51PS Curt Schilling/50 10.00 25.00
52BA Rod Carew Angels/80 10.00 25.00
52DY Rod Carew Angels/67 15.00 40.00
52PS Rod Carew Angels/50 15.00 40.00
52RD Rod Carew Twins/67 10.00 25.00
54BA Joe Carter/100 6.00 15.00
54DY Joe Carter/83 6.00 15.00
54JN Joe Carter/29 15.00 40.00
54PS Joe Carter/50 10.00 25.00
55DY Nolan Ryan Angels/66 12.50 30.00
55PS Nolan Ryan Angels/30 12.50 30.00
56BA Orlando Cepeda/80 6.00 15.00
56DY Orlando Cepeda/58 10.00 25.00
56JN Orlando Cepeda/30 15.00 40.00
56PS Orlando Cepeda/50 10.00 25.00
57BA Dave Winfield/80 6.00 15.00
57DY Dave Winfield/73 10.00 25.00
57JN Dave Winfield/31 15.00 40.00
57PS Dave Winfield/50 10.00 25.00
58BA Hoyt Wilhelm/80 6.00 15.00
58DY Hoyt Wilhelm/52 10.00 25.00
58JN Hoyt Wilhelm/31 15.00 40.00
58PS Hoyt Wilhelm/50 10.00 25.00
59BA Steve Carlton/80 6.00 15.00
59DY Steve Carlton/65 10.00 25.00
59JN Steve Carlton/32 15.00 40.00
59PS Steve Carlton/50 10.00 25.00
60BA Eddie Murray/100 10.00 25.00
60DY Eddie Murray/77 10.00 25.00
60JN Eddie Murray/33 30.00 60.00
60PS Eddie Murray/50 10.00 25.00
61BA Nolan Ryan Rangers/40 15.00 40.00
61DY Nolan Ryan Rangers/66 15.00 40.00
61JN Nolan Ryan Rangers/34 50.00 100.00
62BA Nolan Ryan Astros/40 30.00 60.00
62DY Nolan Ryan Astros/66 40.00 80.00
62JN Nolan Ryan Astros/34 30.00 60.00
63BA Kirby Puckett/40 20.00 50.00
63DY Kirby Puckett/84 15.00 40.00
63JN Kirby Puckett/34 30.00 60.00
64DY Yogi Berra/46 10.00 25.00
64JN Yogi Berra/35 10.00 25.00
65BA Phil Niekro/80 6.00 15.00
65DY Phil Niekro/64 10.00 25.00
65JN Phil Niekro/35 15.00 40.00
65PS Phil Niekro/50 10.00 25.00
66BA Gaylord Perry/80 6.00 15.00
66DY Gaylord Perry/62 10.00 25.00
66JN Gaylord Perry/36 12.50 30.00
66PS Gaylord Perry/50 10.00 25.00
67BA Pedro Martinez Expos/100 10.00 25.00
67DY Pedro Martinez Expos/92 10.00 25.00
67JN Pedro Martinez Expos/45 20.00 50.00
67PS Pedro Martinez Expos/50 10.00 25.00
68BA Alex Rodriguez Rgr/100 10.00 25.00
68DY Alex Rodriguez Rgr/94 10.00 25.00
68PS Alex Rodriguez Rgr/50 15.00 40.00
69BA Dave Parker/100 6.00 15.00
69DY Dave Parker/73 6.00 15.00
69JN Dave Parker/39 12.50 30.00
69PS Dave Parker/50 10.00 25.00
70BA Darin Erstad/100 6.00 15.00
70DY Darin Erstad/96 6.00 15.00
70PS Darin Erstad/50 10.00 25.00
71DY Eddie Mathews/52 10.00 25.00
71JN Eddie Mathews/41 15.00 40.00
72DY Tom Seaver Mets/67 15.00 40.00
72JN Tom Seaver Mets/41 20.00 50.00
73DY Tom Seaver Reds/67 10.00 25.00
73JN Tom Seaver Reds/41 20.00 50.00
74DY Jackie Robinson/47 25.00 60.00
74JN Jackie Robinson/42 25.00 60.00
75BA Randy Johnson M's/80 10.00 25.00
75DY Randy Johnson M's/88 10.00 25.00
75JN Randy Johnson M's/51 15.00 40.00
75PS Randy Johnson M's/50 10.00 25.00
76DY Reg Jackson Yanks/67 15.00 40.00
76JN Reg Jackson Yanks/44 20.00 50.00
77BA Reg Jackson Angels/80 10.00 25.00
77DY Reg Jackson Angels/67 15.00 40.00
77JN Reg Jackson Angels/44 20.00 50.00
77PS Reg Jackson Angels/50 15.00 40.00
78BA Willie McCovey/80 6.00 15.00
78DY Willie McCovey/59 10.00 25.00
78JN Willie McCovey/44 12.50 30.00
78PS Willie McCovey/50 10.00 25.00
79BA Eric Davis/100 6.00 15.00
79DY Eric Davis/84 6.00 15.00
79JN Eric Davis/34 15.00 40.00
79PS Eric Davis/50 10.00 25.00
80BA Carlos Delgado/95 6.00 15.00
80DY Carlos Delgado/93 6.00 15.00
81BA Dale Murphy/100 10.00 25.00
81DY Dale Murphy/76 10.00 25.00
81PS Dale Murphy/50 15.00 40.00
82BA Brian Giles/100 6.00 15.00
82DY Brian Giles/95 6.00 15.00
82PS Brian Giles/50 10.00 25.00
83BA Kazuhiro Sasaki/100 6.00 15.00
83DY Kazuhiro Sasaki/100 6.00 15.00
83PS Kazuhiro Sasaki 50 10.00 25.00
84BA Phil Nevin/100 6.00 15.00
84DY Phil Nevin/95 6.00 15.00
84PS Phil Nevin/50 10.00 25.00
85BA Frank Thomas/80 20.00 50.00
85DY Frank Thomas/90 10.00 25.00
85JN Frank Thomas/35 20.00 50.00
85PS Frank Thomas/50 10.00 25.00
86BA Raul Mondesi/100 6.00 15.00
86DY Raul Mondesi/90 6.00 15.00
86JN Raul Mondesi/43 12.50 30.00
86PS Raul Mondesi/50 10.00 25.00
87DY Don Drysdale/56 15.00 40.00
87JN Don Drysdale/53 15.00 40.00
88BA Gary Sheffield/100 6.00 15.00
88DY Gary Sheffield/88 6.00 15.00
88PS Gary Sheffield/50 10.00 25.00
89BA Andy Pettitte/100 6.00 15.00
89DY Andy Pettitte/95 6.00 15.00
89JN Andy Pettitte/46 20.00 50.00
89PS Andy Pettitte/50 10.00 25.00
90BA Lance Berkman/45 12.50 30.00
90DY Lance Berkman/99 6.00 15.00
91BA Paul Lo Duca/100 6.00 15.00
91DY Paul Lo Duca/98 6.00 15.00
91PS Paul Lo Duca/50 10.00 25.00
92DY Kevin Brown/86 6.00 15.00
92JN Kevin Brown/27 15.00 40.00
93BA Jim Thome/100 10.00 25.00
93DY Jim Thome/91 10.00 25.00
93PS Jim Thome/50 15.00 40.00
94BA Mike Sweeney/100 6.00 15.00
94DY Mike Sweeney/95 6.00 15.00
94JN Mike Sweeney/29 15.00 40.00
94PS Mike Sweeney/50 10.00 25.00
95BA Pedro Martinez R.Sox/100 10.00 25.00
95DY Pedro Martinez R.Sox/92 10.00 25.00
95JN Pedro Martinez R.Sox/45 20.00 50.00
95PS Pedro Martinez R.Sox/45 20.00 50.00
96BA Cliff Floyd/100 6.00 15.00
96DY Cliff Floyd/93 6.00 15.00
96JN Cliff Floyd/30 15.00 40.00
96PS Cliff Floyd/50 10.00 25.00
97BA Larry Walker/100 6.00 15.00
97DY Larry Walker/89 6.00 15.00
97JN Larry Walker/33 15.00 40.00
97PS Larry Walker/50 10.00 25.00
98BA Ivan Rodriguez/80 10.00 25.00
98DY Ivan Rodriguez/91 10.00 25.00
98PS Ivan Rodriguez/50 15.00 40.00
99BA Aramis Ramirez/100 6.00 15.00
99DY Aramis Ramirez/98 6.00 15.00
99PS Aramis Ramirez/50 10.00 25.00
100BA Roberto Alomar/100 10.00 25.00
100DY Roberto Alomar/88 10.00 25.00
100PS Roberto Alomar/50 15.00 40.00
101BA Ben Sheets/100 6.00 15.00
101DY Ben Sheets/101 6.00 15.00
101PS Ben Sheets/50 10.00 25.00
102DY Adam Dunn/101 6.00 15.00
102JN Adam Dunn/39 12.50 30.00
103DY Hideo Nomo/95 15.00 40.00
104BA C.C. Sabathia/50 10.00 25.00
104DY C.C. Sabathia/101 6.00 15.00
104JN C.C. Sabathia/52 10.00 25.00
104PS C.C. Sabathia/50 10.00 25.00
105BA R.Henderson A's/100 15.00 40.00
105DY R.Henderson A's/79 15.00 40.00
105JN R.Henderson A's/30 30.00 60.00
105PS R.Henderson A's/50 15.00 40.00
106BA Carlton Fisk W.Sox/80 10.00 25.00
106DY Carlton Fisk W.Sox/69 15.00 40.00
106JN Carlton Fisk W.Sox/72 15.00 40.00
106PS Carlton Fisk W.Sox/50 15.00 40.00
107BA Chan Ho Park/100 6.00 15.00
107DY Chan Ho Park/94 6.00 15.00
107JN Chan Ho Park/61 10.00 25.00
107PS Chan Ho Park/50 10.00 25.00
108BA Mike Mussina/100 10.00 25.00
108DY Mike Mussina/91 10.00 25.00
108JN Mike Mussina 35 30.00 60.00
108PS Mike Mussina/50 15.00 40.00
109BA Mark Mulder/100 6.00 15.00
109DY Mark Mulder/100 6.00 15.00
109PS Mark Mulder/50 15.00 40.00
110BA Tsuyoshi Shinjo/100 6.00 15.00
110DY Tsuyoshi Shinjo/101 6.00 15.00
110PS Tsuyoshi Shinjo/30 15.00 40.00
111BA Pat Burrell/100 6.00 15.00
111DY Pat Burrell/100 6.00 15.00
111PS Pat Burrell/50 10.00 25.00
112BA Edgar Martinez/100 10.00 25.00
112DY Edgar Martinez/87 10.00 25.00
112PS Edgar Martinez/50 15.00 40.00
113BA Barry Larkin/100 10.00 25.00
113DY Barry Larkin/86 10.00 25.00
113PS Barry Larkin/50 15.00 40.00
114BA Jeff Kent/100 6.00 15.00
114DY Jeff Kent/92 6.00 15.00
114PS Jeff Kent/50 10.00 25.00
115BA Chipper Jones/100 12.00 30.00
115DY Chipper Jones/93 12.00 30.00
115PS Chipper Jones/50 15.00 40.00
116BA Magglio Ordonez/100 6.00 15.00
116DY Magglio Ordonez/97 6.00 15.00
116JN Magglio Ordonez/30 15.00 40.00
116PS Magglio Ordonez/50 10.00 25.00
117BA Jim Edmonds/100 6.00 15.00
117DY Jim Edmonds/93 6.00 15.00
117PS Jim Edmonds/50 10.00 25.00
118BA Andruw Jones/100 10.00 25.00
118DY Andruw Jones/96 10.00 25.00
118PS Andruw Jones/45 20.00 50.00
119BA Jose Canseco/100 12.00 30.00
119DY Jose Canseco/85 12.00 30.00
119PS Jose Canseco/50 15.00 40.00
120BA Manny Ramirez/100 10.00 25.00
120DY Manny Ramirez/93 10.00 25.00
120PS Manny Ramirez/50 15.00 40.00
121BA Sean Casey/100 6.00 15.00
121DY Sean Casey/97 6.00 15.00
121PS Sean Casey/50 10.00 25.00
122BA Bret Boone/100 12.00 30.00
122DY Bret Boone/92 12.00 30.00
122JN Bret Boone/29 15.00 40.00
122PS Bret Boone/50 15.00 40.00
123BA Tim Hudson/100 6.00 15.00
123DY Tim Hudson/99 6.00 15.00
123PS Tim Hudson/50 10.00 25.00
124BA Craig Biggio/100 10.00 25.00
124DY Craig Biggio/88 10.00 25.00
124PS Craig Biggio/50 15.00 40.00
125BA Mike Piazza Mets/100 10.00 25.00
125DY Mike Piazza Mets/92 10.00 25.00
125JN Mike Piazza Mets/31 20.00 50.00
125PS Mike Piazza Mets/50 12.50 30.00
126BA Jack Morris/100 6.00 15.00
126DY Jack Morris/77 6.00 15.00
126JN Jack Morris/47 12.50 30.00
127BA Roy Oswalt/100 10.00 25.00
127DY Roy Oswalt/101 10.00 25.00
127JN Roy Oswalt/39 12.50 30.00
127PS Roy Oswalt/50 12.50 30.00
128BA Shawn Green/100 6.00 15.00
128DY Shawn Green/93 6.00 15.00
128PS Shawn Green/50 10.00 25.00
129BA Carlos Beltran/100 6.00 15.00
129DY Carlos Beltran/98 6.00 15.00
129PS Carlos Beltran/50 10.00 25.00
130BA Todd Helton/100 10.00 25.00
130DY Todd Helton/97 10.00 25.00
130PS Todd Helton/50 15.00 40.00
131BA Barry Zito/75 6.00 15.00
131DY Barry Zito/100 6.00 15.00
131JN Barry Zito/75 6.00 15.00
131PS Barry Zito/30 15.00 40.00
132BA J.D. Drew/100 6.00 15.00
132DY J.D. Drew/98 6.00 15.00
132PS J.D. Drew/50 10.00 25.00
133BA Mark Grace/100 10.00 25.00
133DY Mark Grace 88 10.00 25.00
133PS Mark Grace/50 15.00 40.00
134BA R.Henderson Mets/100 15.00 40.00
134DY R.Henderson Mets/79 15.00 40.00
134PS R.Henderson Mets/50 15.00 40.00
135BA Greg Maddux/100 15.00 40.00
135DY Greg Maddux/86 15.00 40.00
135PS Greg Maddux/50 12.50 30.00
136BA Garret Anderson/100 6.00 15.00
136DY Garret Anderson/94 6.00 15.00
136PS Garret Anderson/50 10.00 25.00
137BA Rafael Palmeiro/100 10.00 25.00
137DY Rafael Palmeiro/86 10.00 25.00
137PS Rafael Palmeiro/50 15.00 40.00
138BA Luis Gonzalez/50 10.00 25.00
138DY Luis Gonzalez/90 6.00 15.00
138PS Luis Gonzalez/45 12.50 30.00
139BA Nick Johnson/100 6.00 15.00
139DY Nick Johnson/101 6.00 15.00
139JN Nick Johnson/26 15.00 40.00
139PS Nick Johnson/50 10.00 25.00
140BA Vladimir Guerrero/80 10.00 25.00
140DY Vladimir Guerrero/96 10.00 25.00
140PS Vladimir Guerrero/50 15.00 40.00
141DY Mark Buehrle/100 6.00 15.00
141JN Mark Buehrle/56 10.00 25.00
142BA Troy Glaus/100 6.00 15.00
142DY Troy Glaus/98 6.00 15.00
142PS Troy Glaus/50 10.00 25.00
143BA Juan Gonzalez/100 6.00 15.00
143DY Juan Gonzalez/89 6.00 15.00
143PS Juan Gonzalez/50 10.00 25.00
144BA Kerry Wood/100 6.00 15.00
144DY Kerry Wood/98 6.00 15.00
144JN Kerry Wood/34 15.00 40.00
144PS Kerry Wood/50 10.00 25.00
145BA Roger Clemens/80 15.00 40.00
145DY Roger Clemens/84 15.00 40.00
145PS Roger Clemens/50 30.00 60.00
146BA Bob Abreu/100 6.00 15.00
146DY Bob Abreu/96 6.00 15.00
146JN Bob Abreu/53 10.00 25.00
146PS Bob Abreu/50 10.00 25.00
147BA Bernie Williams/95 10.00 25.00
147DY Bernie Williams/97 10.00 25.00
147JN Bernie Williams/51 15.00 40.00
148BA Tom Glavine/100 10.00 25.00
148DY Tom Glavine/87 10.00 25.00
148JN Tom Glavine/47 20.00 50.00
148PS Tom Glavine/50 15.00 40.00
149BA Jorge Posada/100 10.00 25.00
149DY Jorge Posada/95 10.00 25.00
149PS Jorge Posada/50 15.00 40.00
150BA R.Johnson D'Backs/80 10.00 25.00
150DY R.Johnson D'Backs/88 10.00 25.00
150JN R.Johnson D'Backs/51 15.00 40.00
150PS R.Johnson D'Backs/50 15.00 40.00

2002 Leaf Certified Skills

COMPLETE SET (20) 50.00 120.00
STATED ODDS 1:17
*BLUE: 1.25X TO 3X BASIC SKILLS
BLUE PRINT RUN 75 SERIAL #'d SETS
GOLD PRINT RUN 25 SERIAL #'d SETS
NO GOLD PRICING DUE TO SCARCITY
*RED: .75X TO 2X BASIC SKILLS
RED: RANDOM INSERTS IN PACKS
RED PRINT RUN 150 SERIAL #'d SETS
1 Barry Bonds 4.00 10.00
2 Greg Maddux 2.50 6.00
3 Rickey Henderson 1.50 4.00
4 Ichiro Suzuki 3.00 8.00
5 Pedro Martinez 1.25 3.00
6 Kazuhisa Ishii 1.25 3.00
7 Alex Rodriguez 2.00 5.00
8 Mike Piazza 2.50 6.00
9 Sammy Sosa 1.50 4.00
10 Derek Jeter 4.00 10.00
11 Albert Pujols 3.00 8.00
12 Roger Clemens 3.00 8.00
13 Mark Prior 1.00 2.50
14 Chipper Jones 1.50 4.00
15 Ken Griffey Jr. 3.00 8.00
16 Frank Thomas 1.50 4.00
17 Randy Johnson 1.50 4.00
18 Vladimir Guerrero 1.50 4.00
19 Nomar Garciaparra 2.50 6.00
20 Jeff Bagwell 1.25 3.00

2003 Leaf Certified Materials

COMP.LO SET w/o SP's (200) 12.50 30.00
COMMON CARD (1-200) .40 1.00
COMMON CARD (201-205) 1.00 2.50
COM (201-219/221-250) 4.00 10.00
201-219/221-250 PRINT RUN 400 #'d SETS
COMMON (251-259) p/r 250 4.00 10.00
COM (220/251-259) p/r 100-150 4.00 10.00
CARD 220 RANDOM IN LCM PACKS
251-259 RANDOM IN DLP R/T PACKS
220/251-259 PRINTS B/WN 100-250 PER
1 Troy Glaus .40 1.00
2 Alfredo Amezaga .40 1.00
3 Garret Anderson .40 1.00
4 Nolan Ryan Angels 3.00 8.00
5 Darin Erstad .40 1.00
6 Junior Spivey .40 1.00
7 Randy Johnson 1.00 2.50
8 Curt Schilling .60 1.50
9 Luis Gonzalez .40 1.00
10 Steve Finley .40 1.00
11 Matt Williams .40 1.00
12 Greg Maddux 1.25 3.00
13 Chipper Jones 1.00 2.50
14 Gary Sheffield .40 1.00
15 Adam LaRoche .40 1.00
16 Andruw Jones .40 1.00
17 Robert Fick .40 1.00
18 John Smoltz 1.00 2.50
19 Javy Lopez .40 1.00
20 Jay Gibbons .40 1.00
21 Geronimo Gil .40 1.00
22 Cal Ripken 3.00 8.00
23 Nomar Garciaparra .60 1.50
24 Pedro Martinez .60 1.50
25 Freddy Sanchez .40 1.00
26 Rickey Henderson 1.00 2.50
27 Manny Ramirez 1.00 2.50
28 Casey Fossum .40 1.00
29 Sammy Sosa 1.00 2.50
30 Kerry Wood .40 1.00
31 Corey Patterson .40 1.00
32 Nic Jackson .40 1.00
33 Mark Prior .60 1.50
34 Juan Cruz .40 1.00
35 Steve Smyth .40 1.00
36 Magglio Ordonez .60 1.50
37 Joe Borchard .40 1.00
38 Frank Thomas 1.00 2.50
39 Mark Buehrle .60 1.50
40 Joe Crede .40 1.00
41 Carlos Lee .40 1.00
42 Paul Konerko .60 1.50
43 Adam Dunn .60 1.50
44 Corky Miller .40 1.00
45 Brandon Larson .40 1.00
46 Ken Griffey Jr. 2.00 5.00
47 Barry Larkin .60 1.50
48 Sean Casey .40 1.00
49 Wily Mo Pena .40 1.00
50 Austin Kearns .40 1.00
51 Victor Martinez .60 1.50
52 Brian Tallet .40 1.00
53 Cliff Lee 2.50 6.00
54 Jeremy Guthrie .40 1.00
55 C.C. Sabathia .60 1.50
56 Ricardo Rodriguez .40 1.00
57 Omar Vizquel .60 1.50
58 Travis Hafner .40 1.00
59 Todd Helton .60 1.50
60 Jason Jennings .40 1.00
61 Jeff Baker .40 1.00
62 Larry Walker .60 1.50
63 Travis Chapman .40 1.00
64 Mike Maroth .40 1.00
65 Josh Beckett .40 1.00
66 Ivan Rodriguez .60 1.50
67 Brad Penny .40 1.00
68 A.J. Burnett .40 1.00
69 Craig Biggio .60 1.50
70 Roy Oswalt .60 1.50
71 Jason Lane .40 1.00
72 Nolan Ryan Astros 3.00 8.00
73 Wade Miller .40 1.00
74 Richard Hidalgo .40 1.00
75 Jeff Bagwell .60 1.50
76 Lance Berkman .60 1.50
77 Rodrigo Rosario .40 1.00
78 Jeff Kent .40 1.00
79 John Buck .40 1.00
80 Angel Berroa .40 1.00
81 Mike Sweeney .40 1.00
82 Mac Suzuki .40 1.00
83 Alexis Gomez .40 1.00
84 Carlos Beltran .60 1.50
85 Runelvys Hernandez .40 1.00
86 Hideo Nomo 1.00 2.50
87 Paul Lo Duca .40 1.00
88 Cesar Izturis .40 1.00
89 Kazuhisa Ishii .40 1.00
90 Shawn Green .40 1.00
91 Joe Thurston .40 1.00
92 Adrian Beltre 1.00 2.50
93 Kevin Brown .40 1.00
94 Richie Sexson .40 1.00
95 Ben Sheets .40 1.00
96 Takahito Nomura .40 1.00
97 Geoff Jenkins .40 1.00
98 Bill Hall .40 1.00
99 Torii Hunter .40 1.00
100 A.J. Pierzynski .40 1.00
101 Michael Cuddyer .40 1.00
102 Jose Morban .40 1.00
103 Brad Radke .40 1.00
104 Jacque Jones .40 1.00
105 Eric Milton .40 1.00
106 Joe Mays .40 1.00
107 Adam Johnson .40 1.00
108 Javier Vazquez .40 1.00
109 Vladimir Guerrero .60 1.50
110 Jose Vidro .40 1.00
111 Michael Barrett .40 1.00
112 Orlando Cabrera .40 1.00
113 Tom Glavine .60 1.50
114 Roberto Alomar .60 1.50
115 Tsuyoshi Shinjo .40 1.00
116 Cliff Floyd .40 1.00
117 Mike Piazza 1.00 2.50
118 Al Leiter .40 1.00
119 Don Mattingly 2.00 5.00
120 Roger Clemens 1.25 3.00
121 Derek Jeter 2.50 6.00
122 Alfonso Soriano .60 1.50
123 Drew Henson .40 1.00
124 Brandon Claussen .40 1.00
125 Christian Parker .40 1.00
126 Jason Giambi .40 1.00
127 Mike Mussina .60 1.50
128 Bernie Williams .60 1.50
129 Jason Anderson .40 1.00
130 Nick Johnson .40 1.00
131 Jorge Posada .60 1.50
132 Andy Pettitte .60 1.50
133 Barry Zito .60 1.50
134 Miguel Tejada .60 1.50
135 Eric Chavez .40 1.00
136 Tim Hudson .60 1.50
137 Mark Mulder .40 1.00
138 Terrence Long .40 1.00
139 Mark Ellis .40 1.00
140 Jim Thome .60 1.50
141 Pat Burrell .40 1.00
142 Marlon Byrd .40 1.00
143 Bobby Abreu .40 1.00
144 Brandon Duckworth .40 1.00
145 Robert Person .40 1.00
146 Anderson Machado .40 1.00
147 Aramis Ramirez .40 1.00
148 Jack Wilson .40 1.00
149 Carlos Rivera .40 1.00
150 Jose Castillo .40 1.00
151 Walter Young .40 1.00
152 Brian Giles .40 1.00
153 Jason Kendall .40 1.00
154 Ryan Klesko .40 1.00
155 Mike Rivera .40 1.00
156 Sean Burroughs .40 1.00
157 Brian Lawrence .40 1.00
158 Xavier Nady .40 1.00
159 Dennis Tankersley .40 1.00
160 Phil Nevin .40 1.00
161 Barry Bonds 1.50 4.00
162 Kenny Lofton .40 1.00
163 Rich Aurilia .40 1.00
164 Ichiro Suzuki 1.25 3.00
165 Edgar Martinez .60 1.50
166 Chris Snelling .40 1.00
167 Rafael Soriano .40 1.00
168 John Olerud .40 1.00
169 Bret Boone .40 1.00
170 Freddy Garcia .40 1.00
171 Aaron Sele .40 1.00
172 Kazuhiro Sasaki .40 1.00
173 Albert Pujols 1.25 3.00
174 Scott Rolen .60 1.50
175 So Taguchi .40 1.00
176 Jim Edmonds .60 1.50
177 Edgar Renteria .40 1.00
178 J.D. Drew .40 1.00
179 Antonio Perez .40 1.00
180 Dewon Brazelton .40 1.00
181 Aubrey Huff .40 1.00
182 Toby Hall .40 1.00
183 Ben Grieve .40 1.00
184 Joe Kennedy .40 1.00
185 Alex Rodriguez 1.25 3.00
186 Rafael Palmeiro .60 1.50
187 Hank Blalock .40 1.00
188 Mark Teixeira .60 1.50
189 Juan Gonzalez .40 1.00
190 Kevin Mench .40 1.00
191 Nolan Ryan Rgr 3.00 8.00
192 Doug Davis .40 1.00
193 Eric Hinske .40 1.00
194 Vinny Chulk .40 1.00
195 Alexis Rios .40 1.00
196 Carlos Delgado .40 1.00
197 Shannon Stewart .40 1.00
198 Josh Phelps .40 1.00
199 Vernon Wells .40 1.00
200 Roy Halladay .60 1.50
201 Babe Ruth RET 6.00 15.00
202 Lou Gehrig RET 5.00 12.00
203 Jackie Robinson RET 2.50 6.00
204 Ty Cobb RET 4.00 10.00
205 Thurman Munson RET 2.50 6.00
206 Prentice Redman NG AU RC 4.00 10.00
207 Craig Brazell NG AU RC 4.00 10.00
208 Nook Logan NG AU RC 6.00 15.00
209 Hong-Chih Kuo NG AU RC 8.00 20.00
210 Matt Kata NG AU RC 4.00 10.00
211 C.Wang NG AU RC 30.00 60.00
212 Alej Machado NG AU RC 4.00 10.00
213 Mike Hessman NG AU RC 4.00 10.00
214 Franc Rosario NG AU RC 4.00 10.00
215 Pedro Liriano NG AU 4.00 10.00
216 J.Bonderman NG AU RC 4.00 10.00
217 Oscar Villarreal NG AU RC 4.00 10.00
218 Arnie Munoz NG AU RC 4.00 10.00
219 Tim Olson NG AU RC 4.00 10.00
220 J.Contreras NG AU/100 RC 15.00 40.00

221 Franc Cruceta NG AU RC 4.00 10.00
222 John Webb NG AU 4.00 10.00
223 Phil Seibel NG AU RC 4.00 10.00
224 Aaron Looper NG AU RC 4.00 10.00
225 Brian Stokes NG AU RC 4.00 10.00
226 Guillermo Quiroz NG AU RC 4.00 10.00
227 Fern Cabrera NG AU RC 4.00 10.00
228 Josh Hall NG AU RC 4.00 10.00
229 Diego Markwell NG AU RC 4.00 10.00
230 Andrew Brown NG AU RC 6.00 15.00
231 Doug Waechter NG AU RC 6.00 15.00
232 Felix Sanchez NG AU RC 4.00 10.00
233 Gerardo Garcia NG AU 4.00 10.00
234 Matt Bruback NG AU RC 4.00 10.00
235 Michel Hernandez NG AU RC 4.00 10.00
236 Rett Johnson NG AU RC 4.00 10.00
237 Ryan Cameron NG AU RC 4.00 10.00
238 Rob Hammock NG AU RC 4.00 10.00
239 Clint Barmes NG AU RC 4.00 10.00
240 Brandon Webb NG AU RC 6.00 15.00
241 Jon Leicester NG AU RC 4.00 10.00
242 Shane Bazzell NG AU RC 4.00 10.00
243 Joe Valentine NG AU RC 4.00 10.00
244 Josh Stewart NG AU RC 4.00 10.00
245 Pete LaForest NG AU RC 4.00 10.00
246 Shane Victorino NG AU RC 4.00 10.00
247 Terrmel Sledge NG AU RC 4.00 10.00
248 Lew Ford NG AU RC 4.00 10.00
249 Todd Wellemeyer NG AU RC 4.00 10.00
250 Hideki Matsui NG RC 6.00 15.00
251 A.Loewen NG AU/250 RC 4.00 10.00
252 Dan Haren NG AU/250 RC 6.00 15.00
253 D.Willis NG AU/150 4.00 10.00
254 Ramon Nivar NG AU/250 RC 4.00 10.00
255 Chad Gaudin NG AU/250 RC 4.00 10.00
256 Kevin Correia NG AU/150 RC 4.00 10.00
257 R.Weeks NG AU/100 RC 10.00 25.00
258 R.Wagner NG AU/250 RC 4.00 10.00
259 Del.Young NG AU/100 RC 15.00 40.00

2003 Leaf Certified Materials Beckett Samples

*SAMPLES: 1.5X TO 4X BASIC
INSERTED IN BECKETT MAGAZINES
1 Troy Glaus 1.50 4.00
2 Alfredo Amezaga 1.50 4.00
3 Garret Anderson 1.50 4.00
4 Nolan Ryan Angels 12.00 30.00
5 Darin Erstad 1.50 4.00
6 Junior Spivey 1.50 4.00
7 Randy Johnson 4.00 10.00
8 Curt Schilling 2.50 6.00
9 Luis Gonzalez 1.50 4.00
10 Steve Finley 1.50 4.00
11 Matt Williams 1.50 4.00
12 Greg Maddux 5.00 12.00
13 Chipper Jones 4.00 10.00
14 Gary Sheffield 1.50 4.00
15 Adam LaRoche 1.50 4.00
16 Andruw Jones 1.50 4.00
17 Robert Fick 1.50 4.00
18 John Smoltz 4.00 10.00
19 Javy Lopez 1.50 4.00
20 Jay Gibbons 1.50 4.00
21 Geronimo Gil 1.50 4.00
22 Cal Ripken 12.00 30.00
23 Nomar Garciaparra 2.50 6.00
24 Pedro Martinez 2.50 6.00
25 Freddy Sanchez 1.50 4.00
26 Rickey Henderson 4.00 10.00
27 Manny Ramirez 4.00 10.00
28 Casey Fossum 1.50 4.00
29 Sammy Sosa 4.00 10.00
30 Kerry Wood 1.50 4.00
31 Corey Patterson 1.50 4.00
32 Nic Jackson 1.50 4.00
33 Mark Prior 2.50 6.00
34 Juan Cruz 1.50 4.00
35 Steve Smyth 1.50 4.00
36 Magglio Ordonez 2.50 6.00
37 Joe Borchard 1.50 4.00
38 Frank Thomas 4.00 10.00
39 Mark Buehrle 2.50 6.00
40 Joe Crede 1.50 4.00
41 Carlos Lee 1.50 4.00
42 Paul Konerko 2.50 6.00
43 Adam Dunn 2.50 6.00
44 Corky Miller 1.50 4.00
45 Brandon Larson 1.50 4.00
46 Ken Griffey Jr. 8.00 20.00
47 Barry Larkin 2.50 6.00
48 Sean Casey 1.50 4.00
49 Wily Mo Pena 1.50 4.00
50 Austin Kearns 1.50 4.00
51 Victor Martinez 2.50 6.00
52 Brian Tallet 1.50 4.00
53 Cliff Lee 10.00 25.00
54 Jeremy Guthrie 1.50 4.00
55 C.C. Sabathia 2.50 6.00
56 Ricardo Rodriguez 1.50 4.00
57 Omar Vizquel 2.50 6.00
58 Travis Hafner 1.50 4.00
59 Todd Helton 2.50 6.00
60 Jason Jennings 1.50 4.00
61 Jeff Baker 1.50 4.00
62 Larry Walker 2.50 6.00
63 Travis Chapman 1.50 4.00
64 Mike Maroth 1.50 4.00
65 Josh Beckett 1.50 4.00
66 Ivan Rodriguez 2.50 6.00
67 Brad Penny 1.50 4.00
68 A.J. Burnett 1.50 4.00
69 Craig Biggio 2.50 6.00
70 Roy Oswalt 2.50 6.00
71 Jason Lane 1.50 4.00
72 Nolan Ryan Astros 12.00 30.00
73 Wade Miller 1.50 4.00
74 Richard Hidalgo 1.50 4.00
75 Jeff Bagwell 2.50 6.00
76 Lance Berkman 2.50 6.00
77 Rodrigo Rosario 1.50 4.00
78 Jeff Kent 1.50 4.00
79 John Buck 1.50 4.00
80 Angel Berroa 1.50 4.00
81 Mike Sweeney 1.50 4.00
82 Mac Suzuki 1.50 4.00
83 Alexis Gomez 1.50 4.00
84 Carlos Beltran 2.50 6.00
85 Runelvys Hernandez 1.50 4.00
86 Hideo Nomo 4.00 10.00
87 Paul Lo Duca 1.50 4.00
88 Cesar Izturis 1.50 4.00
89 Kazuhisa Ishii 1.50 4.00
90 Shawn Green 1.50 4.00
91 Joe Thurston 1.50 4.00
92 Adrian Beltre 4.00 10.00
93 Kevin Brown 1.50 4.00
94 Richie Sexson 1.50 4.00
95 Ben Sheets 1.50 4.00
96 Takahito Nomura 1.50 4.00
97 Geoff Jenkins 1.50 4.00
98 Bill Hall 1.50 4.00
99 Torii Hunter 1.50 4.00
100 A.J. Pierzynski 1.50 4.00
101 Michael Cuddyer 1.50 4.00
102 Jose Morban 1.50 4.00
103 Brad Radke 1.50 4.00
104 Jacque Jones 1.50 4.00
105 Eric Milton 1.50 4.00
106 Joe Mays 1.50 4.00
107 Adam Johnson 1.50 4.00
108 Javier Vazquez 1.50 4.00
109 Vladimir Guerrero 2.50 6.00
110 Jose Vidro 1.50 4.00
111 Michael Barrett 1.50 4.00
112 Orlando Cabrera 1.50 4.00
113 Tom Glavine 2.50 6.00
114 Roberto Alomar 2.50 6.00
115 Tsuyoshi Shinjo 1.50 4.00
116 Cliff Floyd 1.50 4.00
117 Mike Piazza 4.00 10.00
118 Al Leiter 1.50 4.00
119 Don Mattingly 8.00 20.00
120 Roger Clemens 5.00 12.00
121 Derek Jeter 10.00 25.00
122 Alfonso Soriano 2.50 6.00
123 Drew Henson 1.50 4.00
124 Brandon Claussen 1.50 4.00
125 Christian Parker 1.50 4.00
126 Jason Giambi 1.50 4.00
127 Mike Mussina 2.50 6.00
128 Bernie Williams 2.50 6.00
129 Jason Anderson 1.50 4.00
130 Nick Johnson 1.50 4.00
131 Jorge Posada 2.50 6.00
132 Andy Pettitte 2.50 6.00
133 Barry Zito 2.50 6.00
134 Miguel Tejada 2.50 6.00
135 Eric Chavez 1.50 4.00
136 Tim Hudson 2.50 6.00
137 Mark Mulder 1.50 4.00
138 Terrence Long 1.50 4.00
139 Mark Ellis 1.50 4.00
140 Jim Thome 2.50 6.00
141 Pat Burrell 1.50 4.00
142 Marlon Byrd 1.50 4.00
143 Bobby Abreu 1.50 4.00
144 Brandon Duckworth 1.50 4.00
145 Robert Person 1.50 4.00
146 Anderson Machado 1.50 4.00
147 Aramis Ramirez 1.50 4.00
148 Jack Wilson 1.50 4.00
149 Carlos Rivera 1.50 4.00
150 Jose Castillo 1.50 4.00
151 Walter Young 1.50 4.00
152 Brian Giles 1.50 4.00
153 Jason Kendall 1.50 4.00
154 Ryan Klesko 1.50 4.00
155 Mike Rivera 1.50 4.00
156 Sean Burroughs 1.50 4.00
157 Brian Lawrence 1.50 4.00
158 Xavier Nady 1.50 4.00
159 Dennis Tankersley 1.50 4.00
160 Phil Nevin 1.50 4.00
161 Barry Bonds 6.00 15.00
162 Kenny Lofton 1.50 4.00
163 Rich Aurilia 1.50 4.00
164 Ichiro Suzuki 5.00 12.00
165 Edgar Martinez 2.50 6.00
166 Chris Snelling 1.50 4.00
167 Rafael Soriano 1.50 4.00
168 John Olerud 1.50 4.00
169 Bret Boone 1.50 4.00
170 Freddy Garcia 1.50 4.00
171 Aaron Sele 1.50 4.00
172 Kazuhiro Sasaki 1.50 4.00
173 Albert Pujols 5.00 12.00
174 Scott Rolen 2.50 6.00
175 So Taguchi 1.50 4.00
176 Jim Edmonds 2.50 6.00
177 Edgar Renteria 1.50 4.00
178 J.D. Drew 1.50 4.00
179 Antonio Perez 1.50 4.00
180 Dewon Brazelton 1.50 4.00
181 Aubrey Huff 1.50 4.00
182 Toby Hall 1.50 4.00
183 Ben Grieve 1.50 4.00
184 Joe Kennedy 1.50 4.00
185 Alex Rodriguez 5.00 12.00
186 Rafael Palmeiro 2.50 6.00
187 Hank Blalock 1.50 4.00
188 Mark Teixeira 2.50 6.00
189 Juan Gonzalez 1.50 4.00
190 Kevin Mench 1.50 4.00
191 Nolan Ryan Rgr 12.00 30.00
192 Doug Davis 1.50 4.00
193 Eric Hinske 1.50 4.00
194 Vinny Chulk 1.50 4.00
195 Alexis Rios 1.50 4.00
196 Carlos Delgado 1.50 4.00
197 Shannon Stewart 1.50 4.00
198 Josh Phelps 1.50 4.00
199 Vernon Wells 1.50 4.00
200 Roy Halladay 2.50 6.00

2003 Leaf Certified Materials Mirror Blue

*BLUE 1-200: 3X TO 8X BASIC
*BLUE 201-205: 1.25X TO 3X BASIC
COMMON CARD (206-259) 3.00 8.00
MINOR STARS 3.00 8.00
UNLISTED STARS 8.00 20.00
1-250 RANDOM INSERTS IN PACKS
251-259 RANDOM IN DLP R/T PACKS
STATED PRINT RUN 50 SERIAL #'d SETS

2003 Leaf Certified Materials Mirror Blue Autographs

1-250 RANDOM INSERTS IN PACKS
251-259 RANDOM IN DLP R/T PACKS
PRINT RUNS B/WN 5-50 COPIES PER
NO PRICING ON QTY OF 25 OR LESS
2 Alfredo Amezaga/50 6.00 15.00
6 Junior Spivey/50 6.00 15.00
15 Adam LaRoche/50 6.00 15.00
20 Jay Gibbons/50 6.00 15.00
21 Geronimo Gil/50 6.00 15.00
28 Casey Fossum/50 6.00 15.00
32 Nic Jackson/50 6.00 15.00
33 Mark Prior/50 12.50 30.00
34 Juan Cruz/50 6.00 15.00
35 Steve Smyth/50 6.00 15.00
37 Joe Borchard/50 6.00 15.00
39 Mark Buehrle/50 20.00 50.00
40 Joe Crede/30 10.00 25.00
45 Brandon Larson/50 6.00 15.00
49 Wily Mo Pena/50 10.00 25.00
51 Victor Martinez/50 15.00 40.00
52 Brian Tallet/50 6.00 15.00
53 Cliff Lee/50 8.00 20.00
54 Jeremy Guthrie/50 6.00 15.00
56 Ricardo Rodriguez/50 6.00 15.00
60 Jason Jennings/50 6.00 15.00
61 Jeff Baker/50 6.00 15.00
63 Travis Chapman/50 6.00 15.00
64 Mike Maroth/50 6.00 15.00
70 Roy Oswalt/50 10.00 25.00
71 Jason Lane/50 10.00 25.00
73 Wade Miller/50 6.00 15.00
77 Rodrigo Rosario/50 6.00 15.00
80 Angel Berroa/50 6.00 15.00
82 Mac Suzuki/50 10.00 25.00
85 Runelvys Hernandez/50 6.00 15.00
88 Cesar Izturis/50 6.00 15.00
91 Joe Thurston/50 6.00 15.00
98 Bill Hall/30 6.00 15.00
102 Jose Morban/50 6.00 15.00
107 Adam Johnson/50 6.00 15.00
124 Brandon Claussen/50 6.00 15.00
125 Christian Parker/50 6.00 15.00
129 Jason Anderson/50 6.00 15.00
138 Terrence Long/50 6.00 15.00
142 Marlon Byrd/50 6.00 15.00
144 Brandon Duckworth/50 6.00 15.00
145 Robert Person/50 6.00 15.00
146 Anderson Machado/50 6.00 15.00
148 Jack Wilson/50 10.00 25.00
149 Carlos Rivera/50 6.00 15.00
150 Jose Castillo/50 6.00 15.00
151 Walter Young/50 6.00 15.00
155 Mike Rivera/50 6.00 15.00
157 Brian Lawrence/50 6.00 15.00
158 Xavier Nady/50 6.00 15.00
159 Dennis Tankersley/50 6.00 15.00
166 Chris Snelling/50 6.00 15.00
167 Rafael Soriano/50 6.00 15.00
179 Antonio Perez/50 6.00 15.00
180 Dewon Brazelton/50 6.00 15.00
181 Aubrey Huff/50 10.00 25.00
182 Toby Hall/50 6.00 15.00
184 Joe Kennedy/50 6.00 15.00
187 Hank Blalock/50 10.00 25.00
188 Mark Teixeira/50 15.00 40.00
190 Kevin Mench/50 10.00 25.00
193 Eric Hinske/50 6.00 15.00
194 Vinny Chulk/50 6.00 15.00
195 Alexis Rios/50 10.00 25.00
206 Prentice Redman NG/50 6.00 15.00
207 Craig Brazell NG/50 6.00 15.00
208 Nook Logan NG/50 10.00 25.00
209 Hong-Chih Kuo NG/40 10.00 25.00
210 Matt Kata NG/50 6.00 15.00
211 Chien-Ming Wang NG/40 50.00 100.00
212 Alejandro Machado NG/50 6.00 15.00
213 Michael Hessman NG/50 6.00 15.00
214 Francisco Rosario NG/50 6.00 15.00
215 Pedro Liriano NG/50 6.00 15.00
217 Oscar Villarreal NG/50 6.00 15.00
218 Arnie Munoz NG/50 6.00 15.00
219 Tim Olson NG/50 6.00 15.00
221 Francisco Cruceta NG/50 6.00 15.00
222 John Webb NG/50 6.00 15.00
223 Phil Seibel NG/50 6.00 15.00
224 Aaron Looper NG/50 6.00 15.00
225 Brian Stokes NG/50 6.00 15.00
226 Guillermo Quiroz NG/50 6.00 15.00
227 Fernando Cabrera NG/50 6.00 15.00
228 Josh Hall NG/50 6.00 15.00
229 Diegomar Markwell NG/50 6.00 15.00
230 Andrew Brown NG/50 10.00 25.00
231 Doug Waechter NG/50 10.00 25.00
232 Felix Sanchez NG/50 6.00 15.00
233 Gerardo Garcia NG/50 6.00 15.00
234 Matt Bruback NG/50 6.00 15.00
235 Michel Hernandez NG/50 6.00 15.00
236 Rett Johnson NG/50 6.00 15.00
237 Ryan Cameron NG/50 6.00 15.00
238 Rob Hammock NG/50 6.00 15.00
239 Clint Barmes NG/50 12.50 30.00
240 Brandon Webb NG/50 20.00 50.00
241 Jon Leicester NG/50 6.00 15.00
242 Shane Bazzell NG/50 6.00 15.00
243 Joe Valentine NG/50 6.00 15.00
244 Josh Stewart NG/50 6.00 15.00
245 Pete LaForest NG/50 6.00 15.00
246 Shane Victorino NG/50 10.00 25.00
247 Terrmel Sledge NG/50 6.00 15.00
248 Lew Ford NG/50 10.00 25.00
249 Todd Wellemeyer NG/50 6.00 15.00
251 Adam Loewen NG/50 15.00 40.00
252 Dan Haren NG/50 15.00 40.00
254 Ramon Nivar NG/50 6.00 15.00
255 Chad Gaudin NG/50 6.00 15.00
258 Ryan Wagner NG/50 6.00 15.00

2003 Leaf Certified Materials Mirror Blue Materials

PRINT RUNS B/WN 10-100 COPIES PER
NO PRICING ON QTY OF 25 OR FEWER
1 Troy Glaus Jsy/100 4.00 10.00
2 Alfredo Amezaga Jsy/100 4.00 10.00
3 Garret Anderson Bat/100 4.00 10.00
5 Darin Erstad Bat/100 4.00 10.00
6 Junior Spivey Bat/100 4.00 10.00
7 Randy Johnson Jsy/100 6.00 15.00
8 Curt Schilling Jsy/100 4.00 10.00
9 Luis Gonzalez Jsy/100 4.00 10.00
10 Steve Finley Jsy/100 4.00 10.00
11 Matt Williams Jsy/100 4.00 10.00
12 Greg Maddux Jsy/100 10.00 25.00
13 Chipper Jones Jsy/50 10.00 25.00
14 Gary Sheffield Bat/100 4.00 10.00
15 Adam LaRoche Bat/100 4.00 10.00
16 Andruw Jones Jsy/100 6.00 15.00
17 Robert Fick Bat/100 4.00 10.00
18 John Smoltz Jsy/100 6.00 15.00
19 Javy Lopez Jsy/100 4.00 10.00
20 Jay Gibbons Jsy/100 4.00 10.00
21 Geronimo Gil Jsy/100 4.00 10.00
23 Nomar Garciaparra Jsy/100 12.50 30.00
24 Pedro Martinez Jsy/100 6.00 15.00
25 Freddy Sanchez Bat/100 4.00 10.00
26 Rickey Henderson Bat/100 6.00 15.00
27 Manny Ramirez Jsy/100 6.00 15.00
28 Casey Fossum Jsy/100 4.00 10.00
29 Sammy Sosa Jsy/100 6.00 15.00
30 Kerry Wood Jsy/100 4.00 10.00
31 Corey Patterson Bat/100 4.00 10.00
32 Nic Jackson Bat/100 4.00 10.00
33 Mark Prior Jsy/100 6.00 15.00
34 Juan Cruz Jsy/100 4.00 10.00
35 Steve Smyth Jsy/100 4.00 10.00
36 Magglio Ordonez Jsy/100 4.00 10.00
37 Joe Borchard Jsy/100 4.00 10.00
38 Frank Thomas Jsy/100 6.00 15.00
39 Mark Buehrle Jsy/100 4.00 10.00
40 Joe Crede Hat/100 4.00 10.00
41 Carlos Lee Jsy/100 4.00 10.00
42 Paul Konerko Jsy/100 4.00 10.00
43 Adam Dunn Jsy/100 4.00 10.00
45 Brandon Larson Spikes/40 6.00 15.00
46 Ken Griffey Jr. Base/100 15.00 40.00
47 Barry Larkin Jsy/100 6.00 15.00
48 Sean Casey Bat/100 4.00 10.00
49 Wily Mo Pena Bat/100 4.00 10.00
50 Austin Kearns Jsy/100 4.00 10.00
51 Victor Martinez Jsy/100 6.00 15.00
55 C.C. Sabathia Jsy/100 4.00 10.00
56 Ricardo Rodriguez Bat/100 4.00 10.00
57 Omar Vizquel Jsy/100 6.00 15.00
58 Travis Hafner Bat/100 4.00 10.00
59 Todd Helton Jsy/100 6.00 15.00
60 Jason Jennings Jsy/100 4.00 10.00
62 Larry Walker Jsy/100 4.00 10.00
63 Travis Chapman Bat/100 4.00 10.00
64 Mike Maroth Jsy/100 4.00 10.00
65 Josh Beckett Jsy/100 4.00 10.00
66 Ivan Rodriguez Bat/100 6.00 15.00
67 Brad Penny Jsy/100 4.00 10.00
68 A.J. Burnett Jsy/100 4.00 10.00
69 Craig Biggio Jsy/100 6.00 15.00
70 Roy Oswalt Jsy/100 4.00 10.00
71 Jason Lane Jsy/100 4.00 10.00
73 Wade Miller Jsy/100 4.00 10.00
74 Richard Hidalgo Pants/100 4.00 10.00
75 Jeff Bagwell Jsy/100 6.00 15.00
76 Lance Berkman Jsy/100 4.00 10.00
77 Rodrigo Rosario Jsy/100 4.00 10.00
78 Jeff Kent Bat/100 4.00 10.00
79 John Buck Jsy/100 4.00 10.00
80 Angel Berroa Bat/100 4.00 10.00
81 Mike Sweeney Jsy/100 4.00 10.00
84 Carlos Beltran Jsy/100 4.00 10.00
86 Hideo Nomo Jsy/100 15.00 40.00
87 Paul Lo Duca Jsy/100 4.00 10.00
88 Cesar Izturis Pants/100 4.00 10.00
89 Kazuhisa Ishii Jsy/100 4.00 10.00
90 Shawn Green Jsy/100 4.00 10.00
91 Joe Thurston Jsy/100 4.00 10.00
92 Adrian Beltre Bat/100 4.00 10.00
93 Kevin Brown Jsy/100 4.00 10.00
94 Richie Sexson Jsy/100 4.00 10.00
95 Ben Sheets Jsy/100 4.00 10.00
97 Geoff Jenkins Jsy/100 4.00 10.00
98 Bill Hall Bat/100 4.00 10.00
99 Torii Hunter Jsy/100 4.00 10.00
101 Michael Cuddyer Jsy/100 4.00 10.00
102 Jose Morban Bat/100 4.00 10.00
103 Brad Radke Jsy/100 4.00 10.00
104 Jacque Jones Jsy/100 4.00 10.00
105 Eric Milton Jsy/100 4.00 10.00
106 Joe Mays Jsy/100 4.00 10.00
107 Adam Johnson Jsy/100 4.00 10.00
108 Javier Vazquez Jsy/100 4.00 10.00
109 Vladimir Guerrero Jsy/100 6.00 15.00
110 Jose Vidro Jsy/100 4.00 10.00
111 Michael Barrett Jsy/40 6.00 15.00
112 Orlando Cabrera Jsy/100 4.00 10.00
113 Tom Glavine Bat/100 6.00 15.00
114 Roberto Alomar Bat/100 6.00 15.00
115 Tsuyoshi Shinjo Jsy/100 4.00 10.00
116 Cliff Floyd Bat/100 4.00 10.00
117 Mike Piazza Jsy/100 10.00 25.00
118 Al Leiter Jsy/100 4.00 10.00
120 Roger Clemens Jsy/100 12.50 30.00
121 Derek Jeter Base/100 15.00 40.00
122 Alfonso Soriano Jsy/100 4.00 10.00
123 Drew Henson Bat/100 4.00 10.00
124 Brandon Claussen Hat/40 6.00 15.00
125 Christian Parker Pants/100 4.00 10.00
126 Jason Giambi Jsy/100 4.00 10.00
127 Mike Mussina Jsy/40 10.00 25.00
128 Bernie Williams Jsy/100 6.00 15.00
130 Nick Johnson Jsy/100 4.00 10.00
131 Jorge Posada Jsy/100 6.00 15.00
132 Andy Pettitte Jsy/100 6.00 15.00
133 Barry Zito Jsy/100 4.00 10.00
134 Miguel Tejada Jsy/100 4.00 10.00
135 Eric Chavez Jsy/100 4.00 10.00
136 Tim Hudson Jsy/100 4.00 10.00
137 Mark Mulder Jsy/100 4.00 10.00
138 Terrence Long Jsy/100 4.00 10.00
139 Mark Ellis Jsy/100 4.00 10.00
140 Jim Thome Bat/100 6.00 15.00
141 Pat Burrell Bat/100 4.00 10.00
142 Marlon Byrd Jsy/100 4.00 10.00
143 Bobby Abreu Jsy/100 4.00 10.00
144 Brandon Duckworth Jsy/100 4.00 10.00
145 Robert Person Jsy/100 4.00 10.00
146 Anderson Machado Jsy/100 4.00 10.00
147 Aramis Ramirez Jsy/100 4.00 10.00
148 Jack Wilson Bat/100 4.00 10.00
150 Jose Castillo Bat/100 4.00 10.00
151 Walter Young Bat/100 4.00 10.00
152 Brian Giles Bat/100 4.00 10.00
153 Jason Kendall Jsy/100 4.00 10.00
154 Ryan Klesko Jsy/50 6.00 15.00
155 Mike Rivera Bat/100 4.00 10.00
157 Brian Lawrence Bat/100 4.00 10.00
158 Xavier Nady Hat/40 6.00 15.00
159 Dennis Tankersley Jsy/100 4.00 10.00
160 Phil Nevin Jsy/100 4.00 10.00
161 Barry Bonds Base/100 12.50 30.00
162 Kenny Lofton Bat/100 4.00 10.00
163 Rich Aurilia Jsy/100 4.00 10.00
164 Ichiro Suzuki Base/100 15.00 40.00
165 Edgar Martinez Jsy/100 6.00 15.00
166 Chris Snelling Bat/100 4.00 10.00
167 Rafael Soriano Jsy/100 4.00 10.00
168 John Olerud Jsy/100 4.00 10.00
169 Bret Boone Jsy/100 4.00 10.00
170 Freddy Garcia Jsy/100 4.00 10.00
171 Aaron Sele Jsy/100 4.00 10.00
172 Kazuhiro Sasaki Jsy/100 4.00 10.00
173 Albert Pujols Jsy/100 15.00 40.00
174 Scott Rolen Bat/100 6.00 15.00
175 So Taguchi Jsy/100 4.00 10.00
176 Jim Edmonds Jsy/100 4.00 10.00
177 Edgar Renteria Jsy/100 4.00 10.00
178 J.D. Drew Jsy/100 4.00 10.00
179 Antonio Perez Bat/100 4.00 10.00
180 Dewon Brazelton Jsy/100 4.00 10.00
181 Aubrey Huff Jsy/50 6.00 15.00
182 Toby Hall Jsy/100 4.00 10.00
183 Ben Grieve Jsy/100 4.00 10.00
184 Joe Kennedy Jsy/100 4.00 10.00
185 Alex Rodriguez Jsy/100 12.50 30.00
186 Rafael Palmeiro Jsy/100 6.00 15.00
187 Hank Blalock Jsy/100 4.00 10.00
188 Mark Teixeira Jsy/100 6.00 15.00
189 Juan Gonzalez Bat/100 4.00 10.00
190 Kevin Mench Jsy/100 4.00 10.00
192 Doug Davis Jsy/100 4.00 10.00
193 Eric Hinske Jsy/100 4.00 10.00
196 Carlos Delgado Jsy/100 4.00 10.00
197 Shannon Stewart Jsy/100 4.00 10.00
198 Josh Phelps Jsy/100 4.00 10.00
199 Vernon Wells Jsy/100 4.00 10.00
200 Roy Halladay Jsy/100 4.00 10.00

2003 Leaf Certified Materials Mirror Red

*ACTIVE RED 1-200: 2X TO 5X BASIC
*RETIRED RED 1-200: 2X TO 5X BASIC
*RED 201-205: .75X TO 2X BASIC
COMMON CARD (206-259) 2.00 5.00
SEMISTARS 3.00 8.00
UNLISTED STARS 5.00 12.00
1-250 RANDOM INSERTS IN PACKS
251-259 RANDOM IN DLP R/T PACKS
STATED PRINT RUN 100 SERIAL #'d SETS

2003 Leaf Certified Materials Mirror Red Autographs

1-250 RANDOM INSERTS IN PACKS
251-259 RANDOM IN DLP R/T PACKS
PRINT RUNS B/WN 5-100 COPIES PER
NO PRICING ON QTY OF 25 OR LESS
2 Alfredo Amezaga/100 6.00 15.00
15 Adam LaRoche/100 6.00 15.00
20 Jay Gibbons/100 6.00 15.00
25 Freddy Sanchez/100 6.00 15.00
28 Casey Fossum/50 6.00 15.00
32 Nic Jackson/100 6.00 15.00
35 Steve Smyth/94 6.00 15.00
45 Brandon Larson/100 6.00 15.00
49 Wily Mo Pena/100 10.00 25.00
56 Ricardo Rodriguez/100 6.00 15.00
63 Travis Chapman/100 6.00 15.00
64 Mike Maroth/100 6.00 15.00
71 Jason Lane/100 10.00 25.00
77 Rodrigo Rosario/100 6.00 15.00
85 Runelvys Hernandez/100 6.00 15.00
88 Cesar Izturis/100 6.00 15.00
91 Joe Thurston/100 6.00 15.00
98 Bill Hall/100 6.00 15.00
102 Jose Morban/100 6.00 15.00
124 Brandon Claussen/60 6.00 15.00
129 Jason Anderson/100 6.00 15.00
142 Marlon Byrd/100 6.00 15.00
146 Anderson Machado/100 6.00 15.00
149 Carlos Rivera/100 6.00 15.00
150 Jose Castillo/100 6.00 15.00
151 Walter Young/100 6.00 15.00
155 Mike Rivera/100 6.00 15.00
157 Brian Lawrence/100 6.00 15.00
166 Chris Snelling/100 6.00 15.00
190 Kevin Mench/100 10.00 25.00
193 Eric Hinske/100 6.00 15.00
194 Vinny Chulk/100 6.00 15.00
195 Alexis Rios/100 8.00 20.00
206 Prentice Redman NG/100 4.00 10.00
207 Craig Brazell NG/100 4.00 10.00
208 Nook Logan NG/100 6.00 15.00
209 Hong-Chih Kuo NG/50 20.00 50.00
210 Matt Kata NG/100 4.00 10.00
211 Chien-Ming Wang NG/50 50.00 100.00
212 Alejandro Machado NG/100 4.00 10.00
213 Michael Hessman NG/100 4.00 10.00
214 Francisco Rosario NG/100 4.00 10.00
215 Pedro Liriano NG/100 4.00 10.00
217 Oscar Villarreal NG/100 4.00 10.00
218 Arnie Munoz NG/100 4.00 10.00
219 Tim Olson NG/100 4.00 10.00
221 Francisco Cruceta NG/100 4.00 10.00
222 John Webb NG/100 4.00 10.00
223 Phil Seibel NG/100 4.00 10.00
224 Aaron Looper NG/100 4.00 10.00
225 Brian Stokes NG/100 4.00 10.00
226 Guillermo Quiroz NG/100 4.00 10.00
227 Fernando Cabrera NG/100 4.00 10.00
228 Josh Hall NG/100 4.00 10.00
229 Diegomar Markwell NG/100 4.00 10.00
230 Andrew Brown NG/100 6.00 15.00
231 Doug Waechter NG/100 6.00 15.00
232 Felix Sanchez NG/100 4.00 10.00
233 Gerardo Garcia NG/100 4.00 10.00
234 Matt Bruback NG/100 4.00 10.00
235 Michel Hernandez NG/100 4.00 10.00
236 Rett Johnson NG/100 4.00 10.00
237 Ryan Cameron NG/100 4.00 10.00
238 Rob Hammock NG/100 4.00 10.00
239 Clint Barmes NG/100 10.00 25.00
240 Brandon Webb NG/100 10.00 25.00
241 Jon Leicester NG/100 4.00 10.00
242 Shane Bazzell NG/100 4.00 10.00
243 Joe Valentine NG/100 4.00 10.00
244 Josh Stewart NG/100 4.00 10.00
245 Pete LaForest NG/100 4.00 10.00
246 Shane Victorino NG/100 8.00 20.00
247 Terrmel Sledge NG/100 4.00 10.00
248 Lew Ford NG/100 6.00 15.00
249 Todd Wellemeyer NG/100 4.00 10.00
251 Adam Loewen NG/100 6.00 15.00
252 Dan Haren NG/100 6.00 15.00
253 Dontrelle Willis NG/50 5.00 12.00
254 Ramon Nivar NG/100 4.00 10.00
255 Chad Gaudin NG/100 4.00 10.00
256 Kevin Correia NG/100 4.00 10.00
258 Ryan Wagner NG/100 4.00 10.00
259 Delmon Young NG/50 20.00 50.00

2003 Leaf Certified Materials Mirror Red Materials

PRINT RUNS B/WN 15-250 COPIES PER
NO PRICING ON QTY OF 25 OR LESS
1 Troy Glaus Jsy/250 3.00 8.00
2 Alfredo Amezaga Jsy/100 4.00 10.00
3 Garret Anderson Bat/250 3.00 8.00
4 Nolan Ryan Angels Jsy/35 40.00 80.00
5 Darin Erstad Bat/250 3.00 8.00
6 Junior Spivey Bat/250 3.00 8.00
7 Randy Johnson Jsy/250 4.00 10.00
8 Curt Schilling Jsy/250 3.00 8.00
9 Luis Gonzalez Jsy/250 3.00 8.00
10 Steve Finley Jsy/250 3.00 8.00
11 Matt Williams Jsy/100 4.00 10.00
12 Greg Maddux Jsy/250 8.00 20.00
13 Chipper Jones Jsy/250 4.00 10.00
14 Gary Sheffield Bat/125 4.00 10.00
15 Adam LaRoche Bat/250 3.00 8.00
16 Andruw Jones Jsy/250 4.00 10.00
17 Robert Fick Bat/250 3.00 8.00
18 John Smoltz Jsy/250 4.00 10.00
19 Javy Lopez Jsy/250 3.00 8.00
20 Jay Gibbons Jsy/250 3.00 8.00
21 Geronimo Gil Jsy/250 3.00 8.00
22 Cal Ripken Jsy/35 60.00 120.00
23 Nomar Garciaparra Jsy/250 10.00 25.00
24 Pedro Martinez Jsy/250 4.00 10.00
25 Freddy Sanchez Bat/250 3.00 8.00
26 Rickey Henderson Bat/250 4.00 10.00
27 Manny Ramirez Jsy/250 4.00 10.00
28 Casey Fossum Jsy/250 3.00 8.00
29 Sammy Sosa Jsy/250 4.00 10.00
30 Kerry Wood Jsy/250 3.00 8.00
31 Corey Patterson Bat/250 3.00 8.00
32 Nic Jackson Bat/250 3.00 8.00
33 Mark Prior Jsy/250 4.00 10.00
34 Juan Cruz Jsy/250 3.00 8.00
35 Steve Smyth Jsy/250 3.00 8.00
36 Magglio Ordonez Jsy/250 3.00 8.00
37 Joe Borchard Jsy/250 3.00 8.00
38 Frank Thomas Jsy/250 4.00 10.00
39 Mark Buehrle Jsy/250 3.00 8.00
40 Joe Crede Hat/100 4.00 10.00
41 Carlos Lee Jsy/250 3.00 8.00
42 Paul Konerko Jsy/250 3.00 8.00
43 Adam Dunn Jsy/250 3.00 8.00
45 Brandon Larson Spikes/150 3.00 8.00
46 Ken Griffey Jr. Base/250 12.50 30.00
47 Barry Larkin Jsy/250 4.00 10.00
48 Sean Casey Bat/250 3.00 8.00
49 Wily Mo Pena Bat/250 3.00 8.00
50 Austin Kearns Jsy/250 3.00 8.00
51 Victor Martinez Jsy/100 6.00 15.00
55 C.C. Sabathia Jsy/250 3.00 8.00
56 Ricardo Rodriguez Bat/250 3.00 8.00
57 Omar Vizquel Jsy/250 4.00 10.00
58 Travis Hafner Bat/250 3.00 8.00
59 Todd Helton Jsy/250 4.00 10.00
60 Jason Jennings Jsy/250 3.00 8.00
62 Larry Walker Jsy/250 3.00 8.00
63 Travis Chapman Bat/250 3.00 8.00
64 Mike Maroth Jsy/250 3.00 8.00
65 Josh Beckett Jsy/250 3.00 8.00
66 Ivan Rodriguez Bat/250 4.00 10.00
67 Brad Penny Jsy/250 3.00 8.00
68 A.J. Burnett Jsy/250 3.00 8.00
69 Craig Biggio Jsy/250 4.00 10.00
70 Roy Oswalt Jsy/250 3.00 8.00
71 Jason Lane Jsy/250 3.00 8.00
72 Nolan Ryan Astros Jsy/35 40.00 80.00
73 Wade Miller Jsy/250 3.00 8.00
74 Richard Hidalgo Pants/250 3.00 8.00
75 Jeff Bagwell Jsy/250 4.00 10.00
76 Lance Berkman Jsy/250 3.00 8.00
77 Rodrigo Rosario Jsy/250 3.00 8.00
78 Jeff Kent Bat/250 3.00 8.00
79 John Buck Jsy/250 3.00 8.00
80 Angel Berroa Bat/250 4.00 10.00
81 Mike Sweeney Jsy/250 3.00 8.00
84 Carlos Beltran Jsy/250 3.00 8.00
86 Hideo Nomo Jsy/250 12.50 30.00
87 Paul Lo Duca Jsy/250 3.00 8.00
88 Cesar Izturis Pants/250 3.00 8.00
89 Kazuhisa Ishii Jsy/250 3.00 8.00
90 Shawn Green Jsy/250 3.00 8.00
91 Joe Thurston Jsy/250 3.00 8.00
92 Adrian Beltre Bat/250 3.00 8.00
93 Kevin Brown Jsy/250 3.00 8.00
94 Richie Sexson Jsy/250 3.00 8.00
95 Ben Sheets Jsy/250 3.00 8.00
97 Geoff Jenkins Jsy/250 3.00 8.00
98 Bill Hall Bat/250 3.00 8.00
99 Torii Hunter Jsy/250 3.00 8.00
101 Michael Cuddyer Jsy/250 3.00 8.00
102 Jose Morban Bat/250 3.00 8.00
103 Brad Radke Jsy/250 3.00 8.00
104 Jacque Jones Jsy/250 3.00 8.00
105 Eric Milton Jsy/250 3.00 8.00
106 Joe Mays Jsy/250 3.00 8.00
107 Adam Johnson Jsy/250 3.00 8.00
108 Javier Vazquez Jsy/250 3.00 8.00
109 Vladimir Guerrero Jsy/250 4.00 10.00
110 Jose Vidro Jsy/250 3.00 8.00
111 Michael Barrett Jsy/50 6.00 15.00
112 Orlando Cabrera Jsy/250 3.00 8.00
113 Tom Glavine Bat/250 4.00 10.00
114 Roberto Alomar Bat/250 4.00 10.00
115 Tsuyoshi Shinjo Jsy/250 3.00 8.00
116 Cliff Floyd Bat/250 3.00 8.00
117 Mike Piazza Jsy/250 8.00 20.00
118 Al Leiter Jsy/250 3.00 8.00
119 Don Mattingly Jsy/35 40.00 80.00
120 Roger Clemens Jsy/250 10.00 25.00
121 Derek Jeter Base/250 12.50 30.00
122 Alfonso Soriano Jsy/250 3.00 8.00
123 Drew Henson Bat/250 3.00 8.00
124 Brandon Claussen Hat/50 6.00 15.00
125 Christian Parker Pants/250 3.00 8.00
126 Jason Giambi Jsy/250 3.00 8.00
127 Mike Mussina Jsy/250 4.00 10.00
128 Bernie Williams Jsy/250 4.00 10.00
130 Nick Johnson Jsy/250 3.00 8.00
131 Jorge Posada Jsy/250 4.00 10.00
132 Andy Pettitte Jsy/250 4.00 10.00
133 Barry Zito Jsy/250 3.00 8.00
134 Miguel Tejada Jsy/250 3.00 8.00
135 Eric Chavez Jsy/250 3.00 8.00
136 Tim Hudson Jsy/250 3.00 8.00
137 Mark Mulder Jsy/250 3.00 8.00
138 Terrence Long Jsy/250 3.00 8.00
139 Mark Ellis Jsy/250 3.00 8.00
140 Jim Thome Bat/250 4.00 10.00
141 Pat Burrell Bat/250 3.00 8.00
142 Marlon Byrd Jsy/250 3.00 8.00
143 Bobby Abreu Jsy/250 3.00 8.00
144 Brandon Duckworth Jsy/250 3.00 8.00
145 Robert Person Jsy/250 3.00 8.00
146 Anderson Machado Jsy/250 3.00 8.00
147 Aramis Ramirez Jsy/250 3.00 8.00
148 Jack Wilson Bat/250 3.00 8.00
150 Jose Castillo Bat/250 3.00 8.00
151 Walter Young Bat/250 3.00 8.00
152 Brian Giles Bat/250 3.00 8.00
153 Jason Kendall Jsy/250 3.00 8.00
155 Mike Rivera Bat/250 3.00 8.00
157 Brian Lawrence Bat/250 3.00 8.00
158 Xavier Nady Hat/60 6.00 15.00
159 Dennis Tankersley Jsy/250 3.00 8.00
160 Phil Nevin Jsy/250 3.00 8.00
161 Barry Bonds Base/250 10.00 25.00
162 Kenny Lofton Bat/250 3.00 8.00
163 Rich Aurilia Jsy/250 3.00 8.00
164 Ichiro Suzuki Base/250 12.50 30.00
165 Edgar Martinez Jsy/100 6.00 15.00
166 Chris Snelling Bat/250 3.00 8.00
167 Rafael Soriano Jsy/250 3.00 8.00
168 John Olerud Jsy/250 3.00 8.00
169 Bret Boone Jsy/250 3.00 8.00
170 Freddy Garcia Jsy/250 3.00 8.00
171 Aaron Sele Jsy/250 3.00 8.00
172 Kazuhiro Sasaki Jsy/250 3.00 8.00
173 Albert Pujols Jsy/250 12.50 30.00
174 Scott Rolen Bat/250 4.00 10.00
175 So Taguchi Jsy/250 3.00 8.00
176 Jim Edmonds Jsy/250 3.00 8.00
177 Edgar Renteria Jsy/250 3.00 8.00
178 J.D. Drew Jsy/250 3.00 8.00
179 Antonio Perez Bat/250 3.00 8.00
180 Dewon Brazelton Jsy/250 3.00 8.00
181 Aubrey Huff Jsy/50 6.00 15.00
182 Toby Hall Jsy/250 3.00 8.00
183 Ben Grieve Jsy/100 4.00 10.00
184 Joe Kennedy Jsy/250 3.00 8.00
185 Alex Rodriguez Jsy/250 10.00 25.00
186 Rafael Palmeiro Jsy/250 4.00 10.00
187 Hank Blalock Jsy/250 3.00 8.00
188 Mark Teixeira Jsy/250 4.00 10.00
189 Juan Gonzalez Bat/250 3.00 8.00
190 Kevin Mench Jsy/250 3.00 8.00
191 Nolan Ryan Rgr Jsy/35 40.00 80.00
192 Doug Davis Jsy/250 3.00 8.00
193 Eric Hinske Jsy/250 3.00 8.00
196 Carlos Delgado Jsy/250 3.00 8.00
197 Shannon Stewart Jsy/250 3.00 8.00
198 Josh Phelps Jsy/250 3.00 8.00
199 Vernon Wells Jsy/250 3.00 8.00
200 Roy Halladay Jsy/250 3.00 8.00

2003 Leaf Certified Materials Fabric of the Game

PRINT RUNS BETWEEN 1-102 COPIES PER
NO PRICING ON QTY OF 25 OR LESS
1BA Bobby Doerr BA/50 4.00 10.00
1JY Bobby Doerr JY/39 6.00 15.00
1PS Bobby Doerr PS/50 4.00 10.00
2BA Ozzie Smith BA/100 10.00 25.00
2IN Ozzie Smith IN/50 12.50 30.00
2JY Ozzie Smith JY/88 10.00 25.00
2PS Ozzie Smith PS/50 12.50 30.00
3DY Pee Wee Reese DY/32 12.50 30.00
3JY Pee Wee Reese JY/58 6.00 15.00
4BA Jeff Bagwell Pants BA/100 4.00 10.00
4DY Jeff Bagwell Pants DY/65 6.00 15.00
4IN Jeff Bagwell Pants IN/50 6.00 15.00
4JY Jeff Bagwell Pants JY/98 4.00 10.00
4PS Jeff Bagwell Pants PS/50 6.00 15.00
5BA Tommy Lasorda BA/100 4.00 10.00
5DY Tommy Lasorda DY/58 4.00 10.00
5JY Tommy Lasorda JY/84 4.00 10.00
5PS Tommy Lasorda PS/50 4.00 10.00
6JY Red Schoendienst JY/55 4.00 10.00
6PS Red Schoendienst PS/50 4.00 10.00
7BA Harmon Killebrew BA/50 6.00 15.00
7DY Harmon Killebrew DY/61 6.00 15.00
7IN Harmon Killebrew IN/50 6.00 15.00
7JY Harmon Killebrew JY/71 6.00 15.00
7PS Harmon Killebrew PS/50 6.00 15.00
8DY Roger Maris DY/55 15.00 40.00
8JY Roger Maris JY/58 15.00 40.00
8PS Roger Maris PS/50 15.00 40.00
9BA Alex Rodriguez M's BA/100 6.00 15.00
9DY Alex Rodriguez M's DY/77 6.00 15.00
9IN Alex Rodriguez M's IN/50 10.00 25.00
9JY Alex Rodriguez M's JY/99 6.00 15.00
9PS Alex Rodriguez M's PS/50 10.00 25.00
10BA Alex Rodriguez Rgr BA/100 6.00 15.00
10DY Alex Rodriguez Rgr DY/72 10.00 25.00
10IN Alex Rodriguez Rgr IN/50 10.00 25.00
10JY Alex Rodriguez Rgr JY/101 6.00 15.00
10PS Alex Rodriguez Rgr PS/50 10.00 25.00
11BA Dale Murphy BA/50 6.00 15.00
11DY Dale Murphy DY/66 6.00 15.00
11IN Dale Murphy IN/50 6.00 15.00
11JY Dale Murphy JY/85 6.00 15.00
11PS Dale Murphy PS/50 6.00 15.00
12BA Alan Trammell BA/100 4.00 10.00
12IN Alan Trammell IN/50 4.00 10.00
12JY Alan Trammell JY/90 4.00 10.00
12PS Alan Trammell PS/50 4.00 10.00
13JY Babe Ruth Pants JY/30 200.00 350.00
14JY Lou Gehrig JY/38 100.00 200.00
15JY Babe Ruth JY/30 250.00 400.00

16JY Mel Ott JY/46 15.00 40.00
17BA Paul Molitor BA/100 4.00 10.00
17DY Paul Molitor DY/70 4.00 10.00
17IN Paul Molitor IN/50 4.00 10.00
17JY Paul Molitor JY/84 4.00 10.00
17PS Paul Molitor PS/50 4.00 10.00
18DY Duke Snider DY/58 6.00 15.00
18JY Duke Snider JY/62 6.00 15.00
19BA Miguel Tejada BA/50 4.00 10.00
19DY Miguel Tejada DY/68 4.00 10.00
19IN Miguel Tejada IN/50 4.00 10.00
19JY Miguel Tejada JY/99 3.00 8.00
19PS Miguel Tejada PS/50 4.00 10.00
20JY Lou Gehrig Pants JY/38 175.00 350.00
21DY Brooks Robinson DY/54 6.00 15.00
21JY Brooks Robinson JY/66 6.00 15.00
22BA George Brett BA/50 15.00 40.00
22DY George Brett DY/69 15.00 40.00
22IN George Brett IN/50 15.00 40.00
22JY George Brett JY/91 12.50 30.00
22PS George Brett PS/50 15.00 40.00
23BA Johnny Bench BA/50 6.00 15.00
23DY Johnny Bench DY/59 6.00 15.00
23IN Johnny Bench IN/50 6.00 15.00
23JY Johnny Bench JY/81 6.00 15.00
23PS Johnny Bênch PS/50 6.00 15.00
24JY Lou Boudreau JY/48 6.00 15.00
25BA Nomar Garciaparra BA/100 10.00 25.00
25IN Nomar Garciaparra IN/50 10.00 25.00
25JY Nomar Garciaparra JY/100 10.00 25.00
25PS Nomar Garciaparra PS/50 10.00 25.00
26BA Tsuyoshi Shinjo BA/50 4.00 10.00
26DY Tsuyoshi Shinjo DY/62 4.00 10.00
26JY Tsuyoshi Shinjo JY/101 3.00 8.00
27BA Pat Burrell BA/100 3.00 8.00
27DY Pat Burrell DY/46 5.00 12.00
27JY Pat Burrell JY/101 3.00 8.00
28BA Albert Pujols BA/100 10.00 25.00
28IN Albert Pujols IN/50 12.50 30.00
28JY Albert Pujols JY/101 10.00 25.00
28PS Albert Pujols PS/50 12.50 30.00
29JY Stan Musial JY/43 15.00 40.00
30JY Al Kaline JY/64 6.00 15.00
31BA Ivan Rodriguez BA/100 4.00 10.00
31DY Ivan Rodriguez DY/72 6.00 15.00
31IN Ivan Rodriguez IN/50 6.00 15.00
31JY Ivan Rodriguez JY/101 4.00 10.00
31PS Ivan Rodriguez PS/50 6.00 15.00
32BA Craig Biggio BA/100 4.00 10.00
32DY Craig Biggio DY/65 6.00 15.00
32JY Craig Biggio JY/101 4.00 10.00
32PS Craig Biggio PS/50 6.00 15.00
33DY Joe Morgan DY/59 15.00 40.00
33JY Joe Morgan JY/74 4.00 10.00
34BA Willie Stargell BA/50 6.00 15.00
34JY Willie Stargell JY/68 6.00 15.00
34PS Willie Stargell PS/50 6.00 15.00
35BA Andre Dawson BA/100 4.00 10.00
35IN Andre Dawson IN/50 4.00 10.00
35JY Andre Dawson JY/87 4.00 10.00
35PS Andre Dawson PS/50 4.00 10.00
36BA Gary Carter BA/100 4.00 10.00
36DY Gary Carter DY/62 4.00 10.00
36IN Gary Carter IN/50 4.00 10.00
36JY Gary Carter JY/85 4.00 10.00
36PS Gary Carter PS/50 4.00 10.00
37BA Cal Ripken BA/50 10.00 25.00
37DY Cal Ripken DY/54 30.00 60.00
37IN Cal Ripken IN/50 15.00 40.00
37JY Cal Ripken JY/101 10.00 25.00
37PS Cal Ripken PS/50 12.50 30.00
38JY Enos Slaughter JY/53 6.00 15.00
39BA Reggie Jackson A's BA/50 6.00 15.00
39DY Reggie Jackson A's DY/68 6.00 15.00
39JY Reggie Jackson A's JY/75 6.00 15.00
39PS Reggie Jackson A's PS/50 6.00 15.00
40JY Phil Rizzuto JY/47 10.00 25.00
41BA Chipper Jones BA/100 4.00 10.00
41DY Chipper Jones DY/66 6.00 15.00
41IN Chipper Jones IN/50 6.00 15.00
41JY Chipper Jones JY/101 4.00 10.00
41PS Chipper Jones PS/50 6.00 15.00
42BA H.Nomo Dodgers BA/100 4.00 10.00
42DY H.Nomo Dodgers DY/58 6.00 15.00
42IN H.Nomo Dodgers IN/50 6.00 15.00
42JY H.Nomo Dodgers JY/95 4.00 10.00
42PS H.Nomo Dodgers PS/50 6.00 15.00
43JY Luis Aparicio JY/69 4.00 10.00
44BA H.Nomo R.Sox BA/100 4.00 10.00
44IN H.Nomo R.Sox IN/50 6.00 15.00
44JY H.Nomo R.Sox JY/101 4.00 10.00
44PS H.Nomo R.Sox PS/50 6.00 15.00
45BA Edgar Martinez BA/100 4.00 10.00
45DY Edgar Martinez DY/77 4.00 10.00
45JY Edgar Martinez JY/100 4.00 10.00
45PS Edgar Martinez PS/50 6.00 15.00
46BA Barry Larkin BA/100 4.00 10.00
46DY Barry Larkin DY/59 6.00 15.00
46JY Barry Larkin JY/100 4.00 10.00
46PS Barry Larkin PS/50 6.00 15.00
47BA Alfonso Soriano BA/100 3.00 8.00
47IN Alfonso Soriano IN/50 4.00 10.00
47JY Alfonso Soriano JY/102 3.00 8.00
47PS Alfonso Soriano PS/50 4.00 10.00
48BA Wade Boggs Rays BA/100 6.00 15.00
48DY Wade Boggs Rays DY/98 6.00 15.00
48IN Wade Boggs Rays IN/50 6.00 15.00
48JY Wade Boggs Rays JY/99 6.00 15.00
48PS Wade Boggs Rays PS/50 6.00 15.00
49BA Wade Boggs Yanks BA/50 6.00 15.00
49IN Wade Boggs Yanks IN/50 6.00 15.00
49JY Wade Boggs Yanks JY/94 6.00 15.00
49PS Wade Boggs Yanks PS/50 6.00 15.00
50JY Ernie Banks JY/68 6.00 15.00
51BA Joe Torre BA/50 4.00 10.00
51DY Joe Torre DY/66 4.00 10.00
51IN Joe Torre IN/50 4.00 10.00
51JY Joe Torre JY/66 4.00 10.00
51PS Joe Torre PS/50 4.00 10.00
52BA Tim Hudson BA/100 3.00 8.00
52DY Tim Hudson DY/68 4.00 10.00
52JY Tim Hudson JY/101 3.00 8.00
52PS Tim Hudson PS/50 4.00 10.00
53BA Shawn Green BA/100 3.00 8.00
53DY Shawn Green DY/58 4.00 10.00
53JY Shawn Green JY/102 3.00 8.00
53PS Shawn Green PS/50 4.00 10.00
54BA Carlos Beltran BA/100 3.00 8.00
54DY Carlos Beltran DY/69 4.00 10.00
54JY Carlos Beltran JY/101 3.00 8.00
54PS Carlos Beltran PS/50 4.00 10.00
55BA Bo Jackson BA/50 6.00 15.00
55DY Bo Jackson DY/69 6.00 15.00
55JY Bo Jackson JY/90 6.00 15.00
55PS Bo Jackson PS/50 6.00 15.00
56BA Hal Newhouser BA/50 4.00 10.00
56JY Hal Newhouser JY/55 4.00 10.00
56PS Hal Newhouser PS/50 4.00 10.00
57BA Jason Giambi A's BA/100 3.00 8.00
57DY Jason Giambi A's DY/68 4.00 10.00
57IN Jason Giambi A's IN/50 4.00 10.00
57JY Jason Giambi A's JY/101 3.00 8.00
57PS Jason Giambi A's PS/50 4.00 10.00
58BA Lance Berkman BA/100 3.00 8.00
58DY Lance Berkman DY/65 4.00 10.00
58IN Lance Berkman IN/50 4.00 10.00
58JY Lance Berkman JY/102 3.00 8.00
58PS Lance Berkman PS/50 4.00 10.00
59BA Todd Helton BA/100 4.00 10.00
59DY Todd Helton DY/93 4.00 10.00
59JY Todd Helton JY/100 4.00 10.00
59PS Todd Helton PS/50 6.00 15.00
60BA Mark Grace BA/100 4.00 10.00
60JY Mark Grace JY/95 4.00 10.00
60PS Mark Grace PS/50 6.00 15.00
61BA Fred Lynn BA/100 4.00 10.00
61JY Fred Lynn JY/75 4.00 10.00
61PS Fred Lynn PS/50 4.00 10.00
62JY Bob Feller JY/52 6.00 15.00
63BA Robin Yount BA/100 6.00 15.00
63DY Robin Yount DY/70 10.00 25.00
63IN Robin Yount IN/50 6.00 15.00
63JY Robin Yount JY/88 6.00 15.00
63PS Robin Yount PS/50 6.00 15.00
64BA Tony Gwynn BA/100 8.00 20.00
64DY Tony Gwynn DY/69 10.00 25.00
64IN Tony Gwynn IN/50 10.00 25.00
64JY Tony Gwynn JY/99 10.00 25.00
64PS Tony Gwynn PS/50 8.00 20.00
65BA Tony Gwynn Pants BA/100 8.00 20.00
65DY Tony Gwynn Pants DY/69 10.00 25.00
65IN Tony Gwynn Pants IN/50 10.00 25.00
65JY Tony Gwynn Pants JY/99 8.00 20.00
65PS Tony Gwynn Pants PS/50 10.00 25.00
66DY Frank Robinson DY/54 6.00 15.00
66JY Frank Robinson JY/70 6.00 15.00
67BA Mike Schmidt BA/50 15.00 40.00
67DY Mike Schmidt DY/46 15.00 40.00
67IN Mike Schmidt IN/50 15.00 40.00
67JY Mike Schmidt JY/81 12.50 30.00
67PS Mike Schmidt PS/50 15.00 40.00
68JY Lou Brock JY/66 6.00 15.00
69BA Don Sutton BA/50 4.00 10.00
69DY Don Sutton DY/58 4.00 10.00
69JY Don Sutton JY/72 4.00 10.00
70BA Mark Mulder BA/100 3.00 8.00
70DY Mark Mulder DY/68 4.00 10.00
70JY Mark Mulder JY/101 3.00 8.00
70PS Mark Mulder PS/50 4.00 10.00
71BA Luis Gonzalez BA/100 3.00 8.00
71DY Luis Gonzalez DY/98 3.00 8.00
71JY Luis Gonzalez JY/101 3.00 8.00
71PS Luis Gonzalez PS/50 4.00 10.00
72BA Jorge Posada BA/100 4.00 10.00
72JY Jorge Posada JY/101 4.00 10.00
72PS Jorge Posada PS/50 6.00 15.00
73BA Sammy Sosa BA/100 12.50 30.00
73IN Sammy Sosa IN/50 6.00 15.00
73JY Sammy Sosa JY/101 4.00 10.00
73PS Sammy Sosa PS/50 6.00 15.00
74BA Roberto Alomar BA/100 4.00 10.00
74DY Roberto Alomar DY/62 6.00 15.00
74JY Roberto Alomar JY/102 4.00 10.00
74PS Roberto Alomar PS/50 6.00 15.00
75JY Roberto Clemente JY/69 60.00 120.00
76BA Jeff Kent BA/100 3.00 8.00
76DY Jeff Kent DY/58 4.00 10.00
76JY Jeff Kent JY/101 3.00 8.00
76PS Jeff Kent PS/50 4.00 10.00
77DY Sean Casey DY/59 4.00 10.00
77JY Sean Casey JY/100 3.00 8.00
78BA R.Clemens R.Sox BA/50 10.00 25.00
78IN R.Clemens R.Sox IN/50 10.00 25.00
78JY R.Clemens R.Sox JY/95 10.00 25.00
78PS R.Clemens R.Sox PS/50 10.00 25.00
79DY Warren Spahn DY/53 6.00 15.00
79JY Warren Spahn JY/58 6.00 15.00
80BA R.Clemens Yanks BA/100 10.00 25.00
80IN R.Clemens Yanks IN/50 10.00 25.00
80JY R.Clemens Yanks JY/102 10.00 25.00
80PS R.Clemens Yanks PS/50 10.00 25.00
81BA Jim Palmer BA/50 6.00 15.00
81DY Jim Palmer DY/54 6.00 15.00
81JY Jim Palmer JY/69 6.00 15.00
81PS Jim Palmer PS/50 6.00 15.00
82BA Juan Gonzalez BA/50 4.00 10.00
82JY Juan Gonzalez JY/101 3.00 8.00
82PS Juan Gonzalez PS/50 4.00 10.00
83BA Will Clark BA/100 6.00 15.00
83DY Will Clark DY/58 6.00 15.00
83JY Will Clark JY/88 12.50 30.00
83PS Will Clark PS/50 6.00 15.00
84BA Don Mattingly BA/50 12.50 30.00
84IN Don Mattingly IN/50 12.50 30.00
84JY Don Mattingly JY/93 12.50 30.00
84PS Don Mattingly PS/50 12.50 30.00
85BA Ryne Sandberg BA/40 10.00 25.00
85IN Ryne Sandberg IN/50 10.00 25.00
85JY Ryne Sandberg JY/85 10.00 25.00
85PS Ryne Sandberg PS/50 10.00 25.00
86JY Early Wynn JY/55 4.00 10.00
87BA Manny Ramirez BA/50 6.00 15.00
87JY Manny Ramirez JY/102 4.00 10.00
87PS Manny Ramirez PS/50 6.00 15.00
88BA R.Henderson Mets BA/100 6.00 15.00
88DY R.Henderson Mets DY/62 10.00 25.00
88IN R.Henderson Mets IN/50 10.00 25.00
88JY R.Henderson Mets JY/99 6.00 15.00
88PS R.Henderson Mets PS/50 10.00 25.00
89BA R.Henderson Padres BA/100 6.00 15.00
89DY R.Henderson Padres DY/69 10.00 25.00
89JY R.Henderson Padres JY/102 6.00 15.00
89PS R.Henderson Padres PS/50 10.00 25.00
90BA Jason Giambi Yanks BA/100 3.00 8.00
90IN Jason Giambi Yanks IN/50 4.00 10.00
90JY Jason Giambi Yanks JY/102 3.00 8.00
90PS Jason Giambi Yanks PS/50 4.00 10.00
91BA Carlos Delgado BA/100 3.00 8.00
91DY Carlos Delgado DY/77 3.00 8.00
91JY Carlos Delgado JY/100 3.00 8.00
91PS Carlos Delgado PS/50 4.00 10.00
92BA Jim Thome BA/100 4.00 10.00
92JY Jim Thome JY/102 4.00 10.00
92PS Jim Thome PS/50 6.00 15.00
93BA Andruw Jones BA/100 4.00 10.00
93DY Andruw Jones DY/66 6.00 15.00
93JY Andruw Jones JY/101 4.00 10.00
93PS Andruw Jones PS/50 6.00 15.00
94BA Rafael Palmeiro BA/100 4.00 10.00
94DY Rafael Palmeiro DY/72 6.00 15.00
94JY Rafael Palmeiro JY/102 4.00 10.00
94PS Rafael Palmeiro PS/50 6.00 15.00
95BA Troy Glaus BA/100 3.00 8.00
95DY Troy Glaus DY/97 3.00 8.00
95IN Troy Glaus IN/50 4.00 10.00
95JY Troy Glaus JY/100 3.00 8.00
95PS Troy Glaus PS/50 4.00 10.00
96BA Wade Boggs R.Sox BA/100 6.00 15.00
96IN Wade Boggs R.Sox IN/50 6.00 15.00
96JN Wade Boggs R.Sox JN/26 12.50 30.00
96JY Wade Boggs R.Sox JY/86 6.00 15.00
96PS Wade Boggs R.Sox PS/50 6.00 15.00
97BA Catfish Hunter BA/50 6.00 15.00
97DY Catfish Hunter DY/68 6.00 15.00
97JN Catfish Hunter JN/27 12.50 30.00
97JY Catfish Hunter JY/68 6.00 15.00
97PS Catfish Hunter PS/50 6.00 15.00
98BA Juan Marichal BA/50 4.00 10.00
98DY Juan Marichal DY/58 4.00 10.00
98JN Juan Marichal JN/27 8.00 20.00
98JY Juan Marichal JY/67 4.00 10.00
98PS Juan Marichal PS/50 4.00 10.00
99BA Carlton Fisk R.Sox BA/50 6.00 15.00
99JN Carlton Fisk R.Sox JN/27 12.50 30.00
99JY Carlton Fisk R.Sox JY/80 6.00 15.00
99PS Carlton Fisk R.Sox PS/50 6.00 15.00
100BA Vladimir Guerrero BA/100 4.00 10.00
100DY Vladimir Guerrero DY/69 6.00 15.00
100JN Vladimir Guerrero JN/27 10.00 25.00
100JY Vladimir Guerrero JY/101 4.00 10.00
100PS Vladimir Guerrero PS/50 6.00 15.00
101BA Rod Carew Angels BA/50 6.00 15.00
101DY Rod Carew Angels DY/65 6.00 15.00
101JN Rod Carew Angels JN/29 12.50 30.00
101JY Rod Carew Angels JY/85 6.00 15.00
101PS Rod Carew Angels PS/50 6.00 15.00
102BA Rod Carew Twins BA/50 6.00 15.00
102DY Rod Carew Twins DY/61 6.00 15.00
102JN Rod Carew Twins JN/29 12.50 30.00
102JY Rod Carew Twins JY/71 6.00 15.00
102PS Rod Carew Twins PS/50 6.00 15.00
103BA Joe Carter BA/50 4.00 10.00
103DY Joe Carter DY/77 4.00 10.00
103JN Joe Carter JN/29 8.00 20.00
103JY Joe Carter JY/94 4.00 10.00
104BA Mike Sweeney BA/100 6.00 15.00
104DY Mike Sweeney DY/69 8.00 20.00
104JN Mike Sweeney JN/29 12.50 30.00
104JY Mike Sweeney JY/101 6.00 15.00
104PS Mike Sweeney PS/50 8.00 20.00
105DY Nolan Ryan Angels DY/65 15.00 40.00
105JN Nolan Ryan Angels JN/30 20.00 50.00
105JY Nolan Ryan Angels JY/70 12.00 30.00
105PS Nolan Ryan Angels PS/50 15.00 40.00
106BA Orlando Cepeda BA/50 4.00 10.00
106DY Orlando Cepeda DY/58 4.00 10.00
106IN Orlando Cepeda IN/50 4.00 10.00
106JN Orlando Cepeda JN/30 8.00 20.00
106JY Orlando Cepeda JY/65 4.00 10.00
106PS Orlando Cepeda PS/50 4.00 10.00
107BA Magglio Ordonez BA/100 3.00 8.00
107JN Magglio Ordonez JN/30 6.00 15.00
107JY Magglio Ordonez JY/102 3.00 8.00
107PS Magglio Ordonez PS/50 4.00 10.00
108BA Hoyt Wilhelm BA/50 4.00 10.00
108JN Hoyt Wilhelm JN/31 8.00 20.00
108JY Hoyt Wilhelm JY/68 4.00 10.00
108PS Hoyt Wilhelm PS/50 4.00 10.00
109BA Mike Piazza BA/100 6.00 15.00
109DY Mike Piazza DY/62 10.00 25.00
109IN Mike Piazza IN/50 10.00 25.00
109JN Mike Piazza JN/31 15.00 40.00
109JY Mike Piazza JY/100 6.00 15.00
109PS Mike Piazza PS/50 10.00 25.00
110BA Greg Maddux BA/100 6.00 15.00
110DY Greg Maddux DY/66 10.00 25.00
110IN Greg Maddux IN/50 10.00 25.00
110JN Greg Maddux JN/31 15.00 40.00
110JY Greg Maddux JY/102 6.00 15.00
110PS Greg Maddux PS/50 10.00 25.00
111BA Mark Prior BA/100 4.00 10.00
111IN Mark Prior IN/50 6.00 15.00
111JY Mark Prior JY/102 4.00 10.00
111PS Mark Prior PS/50 6.00 15.00
112BA Torii Hunter BA/100 3.00 8.00
112DY Torii Hunter DY/61 4.00 10.00
112IN Torii Hunter IN/50 4.00 10.00
112JN Torii Hunter JN/48 5.00 12.00
112JY Torii Hunter JY/101 3.00 8.00
112PS Torii Hunter PS/50 4.00 10.00
113BA Steve Carlton BA/100 4.00 10.00
113DY Steve Carlton DY/46 6.00 15.00
113IN Steve Carlton IN/50 4.00 10.00
113JN Steve Carlton JN/32 8.00 20.00
113JY Steve Carlton JY/81 4.00 10.00
113PS Steve Carlton PS/50 4.00 10.00
114BA Jose Canseco BA/100 6.00 15.00
114DY Jose Canseco DY/68 6.00 15.00
114IN Jose Canseco IN/50 6.00 15.00
114JN Jose Canseco JN/33 10.00 25.00
114JY Jose Canseco JY/89 6.00 15.00
114PS Jose Canseco PS/50 6.00 15.00
115BA Nolan Ryan Rgr BA/50 12.00 30.00
115DY Nolan Ryan Rgr DY/72 12.00 30.00
115IN Nolan Ryan Rgr IN/50 12.00 30.00
115JN Nolan Ryan Rgr JN/34 12.00 30.00
115JY Nolan Ryan Rgr JY/90 12.00 30.00
115PS Nolan Ryan Rgr PS/50 12.00 30.00
116BA Nolan Ryan Astros BA/50 15.00 40.00
116DY Nolan Ryan Astros DY/65 12.00 30.00
116JN Nolan Ryan Astros JN/34 15.00 40.00
116JY Nolan Ryan Astros JY/84 12.50 30.00
116PS Nolan Ryan Astros PS/50 12.50 30.00
117JY Ty Cobb Pants JY/27 75.00 150.00
118BA Kerry Wood BA/100 3.00 8.00
118JN Kerry Wood JN/34 6.00 15.00
118JY Kerry Wood JY/101 3.00 8.00
118PS Kerry Wood PS/50 4.00 10.00
119BA M.Mussina Yanks BA/50 6.00 15.00
119JN M.Mussina Yanks JN/35 10.00 25.00
119JY M.Mussina Yanks JY/101 4.00 10.00
119PS M.Mussina Yanks PS/50 6.00 15.00
120JN Yogi Berra JN/35 12.50 30.00
120JY Yogi Berra JY/47 10.00 25.00
121JY Thurman Munson JY/79 10.00 25.00
122BA Frank Thomas BA/100 4.00 10.00
122JN Frank Thomas JN/35 10.00 25.00
122JY Frank Thomas JY/94 6.00 15.00
122PS Frank Thomas PS/50 6.00 15.00
123BA R.Henderson A's BA/50 10.00 25.00
123DY R.Henderson A's DY/68 10.00 25.00
123JN R.Henderson A's JN/35 12.00 30.00
123JY R.Henderson A's JY/80 6.00 15.00
123PS R.Henderson A's PS/50 10.00 25.00
124BA M.Muss O's Pants BA/100 4.00 10.00
124DY M.Muss O's Pants DY/54 6.00 15.00
124JN M.Muss O's Pants JN/35 10.00 25.00
124JY M.Muss O's Pants JY/97 4.00 10.00
124PS M.Muss O's Pants PS/50 6.00 15.00
125BA Gaylord Perry BA/100 4.00 10.00
125DY Gaylord Perry DY/77 4.00 10.00
125JN Gaylord Perry JN/36 6.00 15.00
125JY Gaylord Perry JY/82 4.00 10.00
125PS Gaylord Perry PS/50 4.00 10.00
126BA Nick Johnson BA/100 3.00 8.00
126JN Nick Johnson JN/36 5.00 12.00
126JY Nick Johnson JY/102 3.00 8.00
126PS Nick Johnson PS/50 4.00 10.00
127BA Curt Schilling BA/100 3.00 8.00
127DY Curt Schilling DY/98 3.00 8.00
127JN Curt Schilling JN/38 5.00 12.00
127JY Curt Schilling JY/102 3.00 8.00
127PS Curt Schilling PS/50 4.00 10.00
128BA Dave Parker BA/100 4.00 10.00
128JN Dave Parker JN/39 6.00 15.00
128JY Dave Parker JY/80 4.00 10.00
128PS Dave Parker PS/50 4.00 10.00
129DY Eddie Mathews DY/53 6.00 15.00
129JN Eddie Mathews JN/41 10.00 25.00
129JY Eddie Mathews JY/59 6.00 15.00
130DY Tom Seaver Mets DY/62 6.00 15.00
130JN Tom Seaver Mets JN/41 10.00 25.00
130JY Tom Seaver Mets JY/69 6.00 15.00
131DY Tom Seaver Reds DY/59 6.00 15.00
131JN Tom Seaver Reds JN/41 10.00 25.00
131JY Tom Seaver Reds JY/78 6.00 15.00
132JN Jackie Robinson JN/42 15.00 40.00
132JY Jackie Robinson JY/52 40.00 80.00
133BA R.Jackson Angels BA/100 6.00 15.00
133DY R.Jackson Angels DY/65 6.00 15.00
133IN R.Jackson Angels IN/50 6.00 15.00
133JN R.Jackson Angels JN/44 10.00 25.00
133JY R.Jackson Angels JY/80 6.00 15.00
133PS R.Jackson Angels PS/50 6.00 15.00
134BA Willie McCovey BA/100 4.00 10.00
134DY Willie McCovey DY/58 12.50 30.00
134JN Willie McCovey JN/44 6.00 15.00
134JY Willie McCovey JY/77 4.00 10.00
134PS Willie McCovey PS/50 4.00 10.00
135BA Eric Davis BA/100 4.00 10.00
135DY Eric Davis DY/59 4.00 10.00
135JN Eric Davis JN/44 6.00 15.00
135JY Eric Davis JY/89 4.00 10.00
135PS Eric Davis PS/50 4.00 10.00
136BA Adam Dunn BA/100 3.00 8.00
136DY Adam Dunn DY/59 4.00 10.00
136JN Adam Dunn JN/44 5.00 12.00
136JY Adam Dunn JY/102 3.00 8.00
136PS Adam Dunn PS/50 4.00 10.00
137BA Roy Oswalt BA/100 3.00 8.00
137DY Roy Oswalt DY/65 4.00 10.00
137IN Roy Oswalt IN/50 4.00 10.00
137JN Roy Oswalt JN/44 5.00 12.00
137JY Roy Oswalt JY/102 3.00 8.00
137PS Roy Oswalt PS/50 4.00 10.00
138BA P.Martinez Expos BA/50 6.00 15.00
138DY P.Martinez Expos DY/69 6.00 15.00
138JN P.Martinez Expos JN/45 8.00 20.00
138JY P.Martinez Expos JY/95 4.00 10.00
138PS P.Martinez Expos PS/50 6.00 15.00
139BA P.Martinez R.Sox BA/100 4.00 10.00
139IN P.Martinez R.Sox IN/50 6.00 15.00
139JN P.Martinez R.Sox JN/45 8.00 20.00
139JY P.Martinez R.Sox JY/102 4.00 10.00
139PS P.Martinez R.Sox PS/50 6.00 15.00
140BA Andy Pettitte BA/100 4.00 10.00
140JN Andy Pettitte JN/46 8.00 20.00
140JY Andy Pettitte JY/97 4.00 10.00
140PS Andy Pettitte PS/50 6.00 15.00
141BA Jack Morris BA/100 4.00 10.00
141IN Jack Morris IN/50 4.00 10.00
141JN Jack Morris JN/47 6.00 15.00
141JY Jack Morris JY/85 4.00 10.00
141PS Jack Morris PS/50 4.00 10.00
142BA Tom Glavine BA/100 4.00 10.00
142DY Tom Glavine DY/66 6.00 15.00
142JN Tom Glavine JN/47 8.00 20.00
142JY Tom Glavine JY/100 4.00 10.00
142PS Tom Glavine PS/50 6.00 15.00
143BA R.Johnson M's BA/100 4.00 10.00
143DY R.Johnson M's DY/77 4.00 10.00
143IN R.Johnson M's IN/50 6.00 15.00
143JN R.Johnson M's JN/51 6.00 15.00
143JY R.Johnson M's JY/98 4.00 10.00
143PS R.Johnson M's PS/50 6.00 15.00
144BA Bernie Williams BA/100 4.00 10.00
144IN Bernie Williams IN/50 6.00 15.00
144JN Bernie Williams JN/51 6.00 15.00
144JY Bernie Williams JY/100 4.00 10.00
144PS Bernie Williams PS/50 6.00 15.00
145BA R.Johnson D'backs BA/50 6.00 15.00
145DY R.Johnson D'backs DY/98 4.00 10.00
145IN R.Johnson D'backs IN/50 6.00 15.00
145JN R.Johnson D'backs JN/51 6.00 15.00
145JY R.Johnson D'backs JY/102 4.00 10.00
145PS R.Johnson D'backs PS/50 6.00 15.00
146DY Don Drysdale DY/58 6.00 15.00
146JN Don Drysdale JN/53 6.00 15.00
146JY Don Drysdale JY/64 6.00 15.00
147BA Mark Buehrle BA/100 3.00 8.00
147JN Mark Buehrle JN/56 4.00 10.00
147JY Mark Buehrle JY/101 3.00 8.00
147PS Mark Buehrle PS/50 4.00 10.00
148BA Chan Ho Park BA/100 4.00 10.00
148DY Chan Ho Park DY/58 6.00 15.00
148JN Chan Ho Park JN/61 6.00 15.00
148JY Chan Ho Park JY/101 4.00 10.00
148PS Chan Ho Park PS/50 6.00 15.00
149BA Carlton Fisk W.Sox BA/100 6.00 15.00
149IN Carlton Fisk W.Sox IN/50 6.00 15.00
149JN Carlton Fisk W.Sox JN/72 6.00 15.00
149JY Carlton Fisk W.Sox JY/92 6.00 15.00
149PS Carlton Fisk W.Sox PS/50 6.00 15.00
150BA Barry Zito BA/100 3.00 8.00
150DY Barry Zito DY/68 4.00 10.00
150JN Barry Zito JN/75 4.00 10.00
150JY Barry Zito JY/101 3.00 8.00
150PS Barry Zito PS/50 4.00 10.00

2004 Leaf Certified Materials

COMP.SET w/o SP's (200) 15.00 40.00
COMMON CARD (1-200) .25 .60
COMMON CARD (201-211) .60 1.50
201-211 STATED ODDS 1:120
COMMON CARD (212-240) .60 1.50
212-240 PRINT RUN 500 SERIAL #'d SETS
COMMON NO AU (241-300) .60 1.50
NO AU SEMIS 241-300 1.00 2.50
NO AU UNLISTED 241-300 1.50 4.00
241-300 NO AU PRINT RUN 500 #'d PER
COMMON AU p/r 1000 3.00 8.00
COMMON AU p/r 300-500 3.00 8.00
AU MINORS p/r 200-250 4.00 10.00
COMMON AU p/r 100 5.00 12.00
OVERALL AU ODDS 1:10
AU PRINT RUNS B/WN 100-1000 PER
AU PRINT RUN 500 #'d PER UNLESS NOTED
1 A.J. Burnett .25 .60
2 Adam Dunn .40 1.00
3 Adam LaRoche .25 .60
4 Adam Loewen .25 .60
5 Adrian Beltre .60 1.50
6 Al Leiter .25 .60
7 Albert Pujols .75 2.00
8 Alex Rodriguez Yanks .75 2.00
9 Alexis Rios .25 .60
10 Alfonso Soriano Rgr .40 1.00
11 Andruw Jones .25 .60
12 Andy Pettitte .40 1.00
13 Angel Berroa .25 .60
14 Aramis Ramirez .25 .60
15 Aubrey Huff .25 .60
16 Austin Kearns .25 .60
17 Barry Larkin .40 1.00
18 Barry Zito .40 1.00
19 Ben Sheets .25 .60
20 Bernie Williams .40 1.00
21 Bobby Abreu .25 .60
22 Brad Penny .25 .60
23 Brad Wilkerson .25 .60
24 Brandon Webb .25 .60
25 Brendan Harris .25 .60
26 Bret Boone .25 .60
27 Brett Myers .25 .60
28 Bubba Crosby .25 .60
29 Brian Giles .25 .60
30 Chad Cordero .25 .60
31 Bubba Nelson .25 .60
32 Byron Gettis .25 .60
33 C.C. Sabathia .40 1.00
34 Carl Crawford .40 1.00
35 Carl Everett .25 .60
36 Carlos Beltran .40 1.00
37 Carlos Delgado .25 .60
38 Carlos Lee .25 .60
39 Chad Gaudin .25 .60
40 Cliff Lee .40 1.00
41 Chipper Jones .60 1.50
42 Cliff Floyd .25 .60
43 Clint Barmes .40 1.00
44 Corey Patterson .25 .60
45 Craig Biggio .40 1.00
46 Curt Schilling Sox .40 1.00
47 Dan Haren .25 .60
48 Darin Erstad .25 .60
49 David Ortiz .60 1.50
50 Delmon Young .40 1.00
51 Derek Jeter 1.50 4.00
52 Dewon Brazelton .25 .60
53 Dontrelle Willis .25 .60
54 Edgar Martinez .40 1.00
55 Edgar Renteria .25 .60
56 Edwin Almonte .25 .60
57 Edwin Jackson .25 .60
58 Eric Chavez .25 .60
59 Eric Hinske .25 .60
60 Eric Munson .25 .60
61 Erubial Durazo .25 .60
62 Frank Thomas .60 1.50
63 Fred McGriff .25 .60
64 Freddy Garcia .25 .60
65 Garret Anderson .25 .60
66 Garrett Atkins .25 .60
67 Gary Sheffield .25 .60
68 Geoff Jenkins .25 .60
69 Greg Maddux Cubs .75 2.00
70 Hank Blalock .25 .60
71 Hee Seop Choi .25 .60
72 Hideki Matsui 1.00 2.50
73 Hideo Nomo .60 1.50
74 Craig Wilson .25 .60
75 Ichiro Suzuki .75 2.00
76 Ivan Rodriguez Tigers .40 1.00
77 J.D. Drew .25 .60
78 John Lackey .40 1.00
79 Jacque Jones .25 .60
80 Jae Weong Seo .25 .60
81 Jamie Moyer .25 .60
82 Jason Giambi Yanks .25 .60
83 Jason Jennings .25 .60
84 Jason Kendall .25 .60
85 Melvin Mora .25 .60
86 Jason Varitek .60 1.50
87 Javier Vazquez .25 .60
88 Javy Lopez .25 .60
89 Jay Gibbons .25 .60
90 Jay Payton .25 .60
91 Jeff Bagwell .40 1.00
92 Jeff Baker .25 .60
93 Jeff Kent .25 .60
94 Jeremy Bonderman .25 .60
95 Milton Bradley .25 .60
96 Jerome Williams .25 .60
97 Jim Edmonds .40 1.00
98 Jim Thome .40 1.00
99 Jody Gerut .25 .60
100 Joe Borchard .25 .60
101 Joe Crede .25 .60
102 Johan Santana .40 1.00
103 John Olerud .25 .60
104 John Smoltz .60 1.50
105 Johnny Damon .40 1.00
106 Jorge Posada .40 1.00
107 Jose Castillo .25 .60
108 Jose Reyes .40 1.00
109 Jose Vidro .25 .60
110 Josh Beckett .25 .60
111 Josh Phelps .25 .60
112 Juan Encarnacion .25 .60
113 Juan Gonzalez .25 .60
114 Junior Spivey .25 .60
115 Kazuhisa Ishii .25 .60
116 Kenny Lofton .25 .60
117 Kerry Wood .25 .60
118 Kevin Millwood .25 .60
119 Kevin Youkilis .25 .60
120 Lance Berkman .40 1.00
121 Larry Bigbie .25 .60
122 Larry Walker .40 1.00
123 Luis Castillo .25 .60
124 Luis Gonzalez .25 .60
125 Luis Matos .25 .60
126 Lyle Overbay .25 .60
127 Magglio Ordonez .40 1.00
128 Manny Ramirez .60 1.50
129 Marcus Giles .25 .60
130 Mariano Rivera .75 2.00
131 Mark Buehrle .40 1.00
132 Mark Mulder .25 .60
133 Mark Prior .40 1.00
134 Mark Teixeira .40 1.00
135 Marlon Byrd .25 .60
136 Matt Morris .25 .60
137 Miguel Cabrera .60 1.50
138 Mike Lowell .25 .60
139 Mike Mussina .40 1.00
140 Mike Piazza .60 1.50
141 Mike Sweeney .25 .60
142 Morgan Ensberg .25 .60
143 Nick Johnson .25 .60
144 Nomar Garciaparra .40 1.00
145 Omar Vizquel .40 1.00
146 Orlando Cabrera .25 .60
147 Orlando Hudson .25 .60
148 Pat Burrell .25 .60
149 Paul Konerko .40 1.00
150 Paul Lo Duca .25 .60
151 Pedro Martinez .40 1.00
152 Jermaine Dye .25 .60
153 Preston Wilson .25 .60
154 Rafael Furcal .25 .60
155 Rafael Palmeiro O's .40 1.00
156 Randy Johnson .60 1.50
157 Rich Aurilia .25 .60
158 Rich Harden .25 .60
159 Richard Hidalgo .25 .60
160 Richie Sexson .25 .60
161 Rickie Weeks .25 .60
162 Roberto Alomar .40 1.00
163 Rocco Baldelli .25 .60
164 Roger Clemens Astros .75 2.00
165 Roy Halladay .40 1.00
166 Roy Oswalt .40 1.00
167 Ryan Howard .50 1.25
168 Ryan Klesko .25 .60
169 Rodrigo Lopez .25 .60
170 Sammy Sosa .60 1.50
171 Scott Podsednik .25 .60
172 Scott Rolen .40 1.00
173 Sean Burroughs .25 .60
174 Sean Casey .25 .60
175 Shannon Stewart .25 .60
176 Shawn Green .25 .60
177 Shea Hillenbrand .25 .60
178 Shigetoshi Hasegawa .25 .60
179 Steve Finley .25 .60
180 Tim Hudson .40 1.00
181 Todd Helton .40 1.00
182 Tom Glavine .40 1.00
183 Torii Hunter .25 .60
184 Trot Nixon .25 .60
185 Troy Glaus .25 .60
186 Vernon Wells .25 .60
187 Victor Martinez .40 1.00
188 Vladimir Guerrero Angels .40 1.00
189 Wade Miller .25 .60
190 Brandon Larson .25 .60
191 Travis Hafner .25 .60
192 Tim Salmon .25 .60
193 Tim Redding .25 .60
194 Runelvys Hernandez .25 .60
195 Ramon Nivar .25 .60
196 Moises Alou .25 .60
197 Michael Young .25 .60
198 Laynce Nix .25 .60
199 Tino Martinez .40 1.00
200 Randall Simon .25 .60
201 Roger Clemens Yanks SP 2.00 5.00
202 Greg Maddux Braves SP 2.00 5.00
203 Vladimir Guerrero Expos SP 1.00 2.50
204 Miguel Tejada SP 1.00 2.50
205 Kevin Brown SP .60 1.50
206 Jason Giambi A's SP .60 1.50
207 Curt Schilling D'backs SP 1.00 2.50
208 Alex Rodriguez Rgr SP 2.00 5.00
209 Alfonso Soriano Yanks SP 1.00 2.50
210 Ivan Rodriguez Marlins SP 1.00 2.50
211 Rafael Palmeiro Rgr SP 1.00 2.50
212 Gary Carter LGD 1.00 2.50
213 Duke Snider LGD 1.00 2.50
214 Whitey Ford LGD 1.00 2.50
215 Bob Feller LGD 1.00 2.50
216 Reggie Jackson LGD 1.00 2.50
217 Ryne Sandberg LGD 3.00 8.00
218 Dale Murphy LGD 1.50 4.00
219 Tony Gwynn LGD 1.50 4.00
220 Don Mattingly LGD 3.00 8.00
221 Mike Schmidt LGD 2.50 6.00
222 Rickey Henderson LGD 1.50 4.00
223 Cal Ripken LGD 5.00 12.00
224 Nolan Ryan LGD 5.00 12.00
225 George Brett LGD 3.00 8.00
226 Bob Gibson LGD 1.00 2.50
227 Lou Brock LGD 1.00 2.50
228 Andre Dawson LGD 1.00 2.50
229 Rod Carew LGD 1.00 2.50
230 Wade Boggs LGD 1.00 2.50
231 Roberto Clemente LGD 4.00 10.00
232 Roy Campanella LGD 1.50 4.00
233 Babe Ruth LGD 4.00 10.00
234 Lou Gehrig LGD 3.00 8.00
235 Ty Cobb LGD 2.50 6.00
236 Roger Maris LGD 1.50 4.00
237 Satchel Paige LGD 1.50 4.00
238 Ernie Banks LGD 1.50 4.00
239 Ted Williams LGD 3.00 8.00
240 Stan Musial LGD 2.50 6.00
241 Hector Gimenez NG AU RC 3.00 8.00
242 Justin Germano NG AU RC 4.00 10.00
243 Ian Snell NG AU RC 6.00 15.00
244 Graham Koonce NG AU 3.00 8.00
245 Jose Capellan NG AU RC 3.00 8.00
246 Onil Joseph NG AU RC 3.00 8.00
247 S.Takatsu NG AU/200 RC 6.00 15.00
248 Carlos Hines NG AU RC 3.00 8.00
249 Linc Holdzkom NG AU RC 3.00 8.00
250 Mike Gosling NG AU RC 3.00 8.00
251 Eduardo Sierra NG AU RC 4.00 10.00
252 Renyel Pinto NG AU RC 3.00 8.00
253 Merkin Valdez NG AU RC 3.00 8.00
254 Angel Chavez NG AU RC 3.00 8.00
255 I.Ochoa NG AU/1000 RC 3.00 8.00
256 G.Dobbs NG AU/300 RC 3.00 8.00
257 William Bergolla NG AU RC 3.00 8.00
258 Aarom Baldiris NG AU RC 3.00 8.00
259 Kazuo Matsui NG RC 1.00 2.50
260 Carlos Vasquez NG AU RC 4.00 10.00
261 Freddy Guzman NG AU RC 3.00 8.00
262 Aki Otsuka NG AU/200 RC 12.50 30.00
263 M.Gomez NG AU/200 RC 4.00 10.00
264 Nick Regilio NG AU RC 3.00 8.00
265 Jamie Brown NG AU RC 3.00 8.00
266 Shawn Hill NG AU RC 3.00 8.00
267 Roberto Novoa NG AU RC 3.00 8.00
268 Sean Henn NG AU RC 3.00 8.00
269 Ramon Ramirez NG AU RC 3.00 8.00
270 R.Cedeno NG AU/1000 RC 6.00 15.00
271 Ryan Wing NG AU/400 RC 3.00 8.00
272 Ruddy Yan NG AU 3.00 8.00
273 Fernando Nieve NG AU RC 3.00 8.00
274 Rusty Tucker NG AU RC 4.00 10.00
275 Jason Bartlett NG AU RC 4.00 10.00
276 Mike Rouse NG AU RC 3.00 8.00
277 Dennis Sarfate NG AU RC 3.00 8.00
278 Cory Sullivan NG AU RC 3.00 8.00
279 C.Daigle NG AU/250 RC 4.00 10.00
280 C.Shelton NG AU/400 RC 10.00 25.00
281 J. Harper NG AU/400 RC 3.00 8.00
282 Michael Wuertz NG AU RC 4.00 10.00
283 T.Bausher NG AU/400 RC 3.00 8.00
284 Jorge Sequea NG AU RC 3.00 8.00
285 J.Labandeira NG AU/100 RC 5.00 12.00
286 Justin Leone NG AU RC 4.00 10.00
287 Tim Bittner NG AU RC 3.00 8.00
288 Andres Blanco NG AU RC 3.00 8.00
289 K.Cave NG AU/1000 RC 3.00 8.00
290 M.Johnston NG AU/1000 RC 3.00 8.00
291 J.Szuminski NG AU RC 3.00 8.00
292 Shawn Camp NG RC .60 1.50
293 Colby Miller NG AU RC 3.00 8.00
294 Jake Woods NG AU RC 3.00 8.00
295 Ryan Meaux NG AU RC 3.00 8.00
296 Don Kelly NG AU RC 3.00 8.00
297 Edwin Moreno NG AU RC 3.00 8.00
298 Phil Stockman NG AU RC 3.00 8.00
299 Jorge Vasquez NG RC .60 1.50
300 Kaz Tadano NG AU RC 6.00 15.00

2004 Leaf Certified Materials Mirror Blue

*1-200: 2.5X TO 6X BASIC
*201-211: 1.25X TO 3X BASIC
*212-240: 1.25X TO 3X BASIC
RANDOM INSERTS IN PACKS
STATED PRINT RUN 50 SERIAL #'d SETS
COMMON CARD (241-300) 1.50 4.00
241 Hector Gimenez NG 1.50 4.00
242 Justin Germano NG 1.50 4.00
243 Ian Snell NG 1.50 4.00
244 Graham Koonce NG 1.50 4.00
245 Jose Capellan NG 1.50 4.00
246 Onil Joseph NG 1.50 4.00
247 Shingo Takatsu NG 1.50 4.00
248 Carlos Hines NG 1.50 4.00
249 Lincoln Holdzkom NG 1.50 4.00
250 Mike Gosling NG 1.50 4.00
251 Eduardo Sierra NG 1.50 4.00
252 Renyel Pinto NG 1.50 4.00
253 Merkin Valdez NG 1.50 4.00
254 Angel Chavez NG 1.50 4.00
255 Ivan Ochoa NG 1.50 4.00
256 Greg Dobbs NG 1.50 4.00
257 William Bergolla NG 1.50 4.00
258 Aarom Baldiris NG 1.50 4.00
259 Kazuo Matsui NG 2.50 6.00
260 Carlos Vasquez NG 1.50 4.00
261 Freddy Guzman NG 1.50 4.00
262 Akinori Otsuka NG 1.50 4.00
263 Mariano Gomez NG 1.50 4.00
264 Nick Regilio NG 1.50 4.00
265 Jamie Brown NG 1.50 4.00
266 Shawn Hill NG 1.50 4.00
267 Roberto Novoa NG 1.50 4.00
268 Sean Henn NG 1.50 4.00
269 Ramon Ramirez NG 1.50 4.00
270 Ronny Cedeno NG 1.50 4.00
271 Ryan Wing NG 1.50 4.00
272 Ruddy Yan NG 1.50 4.00
273 Fernando Nieve NG 1.50 4.00
274 Rusty Tucker NG 1.50 4.00
275 Jason Bartlett NG 5.00 12.00
276 Mike Rouse NG 1.50 4.00
277 Dennis Sarfate NG 1.50 4.00
278 Cory Sullivan NG 1.50 4.00
279 Casey Daigle NG 1.50 4.00
280 Chris Shelton NG 1.50 4.00
281 Jesse Harper NG 1.50 4.00
282 Michael Wuertz NG 1.50 4.00
283 Tim Bausher NG 1.50 4.00
284 Jorge Sequea NG 1.50 4.00
285 Josh Labandeira NG 1.50 4.00
286 Justin Leone NG 1.50 4.00
287 Tim Bittner NG 1.50 4.00

288 Andres Blanco NG 1.50 4.00
289 Kevin Cave NG 1.50 4.00
290 Mike Johnston NG 1.50 4.00
291 Jason Szuminski NG 1.50 4.00
292 Shawn Camp NG 1.50 4.00
293 Colby Miller NG 1.50 4.00
294 Jake Woods NG 1.50 4.00
295 Ryan Meaux NG 1.50 4.00
296 Don Kelly NG 2.50 6.00
297 Edwin Moreno NG 1.50 4.00
298 Phil Stockman NG 1.50 4.00
299 Jorge Vasquez NG 1.50 4.00
300 Kazuhito Tadano NG 1.50 4.00

2004 Leaf Certified Materials Mirror Gold

*GOLD 1-200: 4X TO 10X BASIC
*GOLD 201-211: 1.5X TO 4X BASIC
*GOLD 212-240: 1.5X TO 4X BASIC
RANDOM INSERTS IN PACKS
STATED PRINT RUN 25 SERIAL #'d SETS
241-300 NO PRICING DUE TO SCARCITY

2004 Leaf Certified Materials Mirror Red

*RED 1-200: 1.5X TO 4X BASIC
*RED 201-211: .75X TO 2X BASIC
*RED 212-240: .75X TO 2X BASIC
RANDOM INSERTS IN PACKS
STATED PRINT RUN 100 SERIAL #'d SETS
COMMON CARD (241-300) 1.00 2.50
241 Hector Gimenez NG 1.00 2.50
242 Justin Germano NG 1.00 2.50
243 Ian Snell NG 1.00 2.50
244 Graham Koonce NG 1.00 2.50
245 Jose Capellan NG 1.00 2.50
246 Onil Joseph NG 1.00 2.50
247 Shingo Takatsu NG 1.00 2.50
248 Carlos Hines NG 1.00 2.50
249 Lincoln Holdzkom NG 1.00 2.50
250 Mike Gosling NG 1.00 2.50
251 Eduardo Sierra NG 1.00 2.50
252 Renyel Pinto NG 1.00 2.50
253 Merkin Valdez NG 1.00 2.50
254 Angel Chavez NG 1.00 2.50
255 Ivan Ochoa NG 1.00 2.50
256 Greg Dobbs NG 1.00 2.50
257 William Bergolla NG 1.00 2.50
258 Aarom Baldiris NG 1.00 2.50
259 Kazuo Matsui NG 1.50 4.00
260 Carlos Vasquez NG 1.00 2.50
261 Freddy Guzman NG 1.00 2.50
262 Akinori Otsuka NG 1.00 2.50
263 Mariano Gomez NG 1.00 2.50
264 Nick Regilio NG 1.00 2.50
265 Jamie Brown NG 1.00 2.50
266 Shawn Hill NG 1.00 2.50
267 Roberto Novoa NG 1.00 2.50
268 Sean Henn NG 1.00 2.50
269 Ramon Ramirez NG 1.00 2.50
270 Ronny Cedeno NG 1.00 2.50
271 Ryan Wing NG 1.00 2.50
272 Ruddy Yan NG 1.00 2.50
273 Fernando Nieve NG 1.00 2.50
274 Rusty Tucker NG 1.00 2.50
275 Jason Bartlett NG 3.00 8.00
276 Mike Rouse NG 1.00 2.50
277 Dennis Sarfate NG 1.00 2.50
278 Cory Sullivan NG 1.00 2.50
279 Casey Daigle NG 1.00 2.50
280 Chris Shelton NG 1.00 2.50
281 Jesse Harper NG 1.00 2.50
282 Michael Wuertz NG 1.00 2.50
283 Tim Bausher NG 1.00 2.50
284 Jorge Sequea NG 1.00 2.50
285 Josh Labandeira NG 1.00 2.50
286 Justin Leone NG 1.00 2.50
287 Tim Bittner NG 1.00 2.50
288 Andres Blanco NG 1.00 2.50
289 Kevin Cave NG 1.00 2.50
290 Mike Johnston NG 1.00 2.50
291 Jason Szuminski NG 1.00 2.50
292 Shawn Camp NG 1.00 2.50
293 Colby Miller NG 1.00 2.50
294 Jake Woods NG 1.00 2.50
295 Ryan Meaux NG 1.00 2.50
296 Don Kelly NG 1.50 4.00
297 Edwin Moreno NG 1.00 2.50
298 Phil Stockman NG 1.00 2.50
299 Jorge Vasquez NG 1.00 2.50
300 Kazuhito Tadano NG 1.00 2.50

2004 Leaf Certified Materials Mirror White

*WHITE 1-200: 1.5X TO 4X BASIC
*WHITE 201-211: .75X TO 2X BASIC
*WHITE 212-240: .75X TO 2X BASIC
RANDOM INSERTS IN PACKS
PRINT RUN 100 SERIAL #'d SETS
COMMON CARD (241-300) 1.00 2.50
241 Hector Gimenez NG 1.00 2.50
242 Justin Germano NG 1.00 2.50
243 Ian Snell NG 1.00 2.50
244 Graham Koonce NG 1.00 2.50
245 Jose Capellan NG 1.00 2.50
246 Onil Joseph NG 1.00 2.50
247 Shingo Takatsu NG 1.00 2.50
248 Carlos Hines NG 1.00 2.50
249 Lincoln Holdzkom NG 1.00 2.50
250 Mike Gosling NG 1.00 2.50
251 Eduardo Sierra NG 1.00 2.50
252 Renyel Pinto NG 1.00 2.50
253 Merkin Valdez NG 1.00 2.50
254 Angel Chavez NG 1.00 2.50
255 Ivan Ochoa NG 1.00 2.50
256 Greg Dobbs NG 1.00 2.50
257 William Bergolla NG 1.00 2.50
258 Aarom Baldiris NG 1.00 2.50
259 Kazuo Matsui NG 1.50 4.00
260 Carlos Vasquez NG 1.00 2.50
261 Freddy Guzman NG 1.00 2.50
262 Akinori Otsuka NG 1.00 2.50
263 Mariano Gomez NG 1.00 2.50
264 Nick Regilio NG 1.00 2.50
265 Jamie Brown NG 1.00 2.50
266 Shawn Hill NG 1.00 2.50
267 Roberto Novoa NG 1.00 2.50
268 Sean Henn NG 1.00 2.50
269 Ramon Ramirez NG 1.00 2.50
270 Ronny Cedeno NG 1.00 2.50
271 Ryan Wing NG 1.00 2.50
272 Ruddy Yan NG 1.00 2.50
273 Fernando Nieve NG 1.00 2.50
274 Rusty Tucker NG 1.00 2.50
275 Jason Bartlett NG 3.00 8.00
276 Mike Rouse NG 1.00 2.50
277 Dennis Sarfate NG 1.00 2.50
278 Cory Sullivan NG 1.00 2.50
279 Casey Daigle NG 1.00 2.50
280 Chris Shelton NG 1.00 2.50
281 Jesse Harper NG 1.00 2.50
282 Michael Wuertz NG 1.00 2.50
283 Tim Bausher NG 1.00 2.50
284 Jorge Sequea NG 1.00 2.50
285 Josh Labandeira NG 1.00 2.50
286 Justin Leone NG 1.00 2.50
287 Tim Bittner NG 1.00 2.50
288 Andres Blanco NG 1.00 2.50
289 Kevin Cave NG 1.00 2.50
290 Mike Johnston NG 1.00 2.50
291 Jason Szuminski NG 1.00 2.50
292 Shawn Camp NG 1.00 2.50
293 Colby Miller NG 1.00 2.50
294 Jake Woods NG 1.00 2.50
295 Ryan Meaux NG 1.00 2.50
296 Don Kelly NG 1.50 4.00
297 Edwin Moreno NG 1.00 2.50
298 Phil Stockman NG 1.00 2.50
299 Jorge Vasquez NG 1.00 2.50
300 Kazuhito Tadano NG 1.00 2.50

2004 Leaf Certified Materials Mirror Autograph Blue

*1-240 p/r 100: .5X TO 1.2X RED p/r 200-250
*1-240 p/r 100: .4X TO 1X RED p/r 100
*1-240 p/r 50: .6X TO 1.5X RED p/r 200-250
*1-240 p/r 50: .5X TO 1.2X RED p/r 100
*1-240 p/r 50: .4X TO 1X RED p/r 50
*1-240 p/r 25: 1X TO 2.5X RED p/r 250
*1-240 p/r 25: .6X TO 1.5X RED p/r 50
*1-240 p/r 25: .4X TO 1X RED p/r 25
*241-300 p/r 100: .5X TO 1.2X REDp/r200-250
*241-300 p/r 100: .4X TO 1X RED p/r 100
*241-300 p/r 50: .4X TO 1X RED p/r 50
OVERALL AU ODDS 1:10
PRINT RUNS B/WN 1-100 COPIES PER
NO PRICING ON QTY OF 10 OR LESS
2 Adam Dunn/47 12.50 30.00
167 Ryan Howard/100 15.00 40.00

2004 Leaf Certified Materials Mirror Autograph Gold

*1-240 p/r 25: 1X TO 2.5X RED p/r 200-250
*1-240 p/r 25: .75X TO 2X RED p/r 100
*1-240 p/r 25: .6X TO 1.5X RED p/r 50
*1-240 p/r 25: .4X TO 1X RED p/r 25
OVERALL AU ODDS 1:10
PRINT RUNS B/WN 1-25 COPIES PER
1-240 NO PRICING ON QTY OF 10 OR LESS
241-300 NO PRICING ON QTY OF 25 OR LESS
167 Ryan Howard/25 50.00 100.00

2004 Leaf Certified Materials Mirror Autograph Red

OVERALL AU ODDS 1:10
PRINT RUNS B/WN 1-250 COPIES PER
NO PRICING ON QTY OF 10 OR LESS
3 Adam LaRoche/250 3.00 8.00
4 Adam Loewen/250 3.00 8.00
7 Albert Pujols/25 75.00 150.00
9 Alexis Rios/250 5.00 12.00
10 Alfonso Soriano Rgr/25 20.00 50.00
11 Andruw Jones/25 20.00 50.00
12 Andy Pettitte/25 20.00 50.00
13 Angel Berroa/100 4.00 10.00
14 Aramis Ramirez/100 6.00 15.00
15 Aubrey Huff/250 5.00 12.00
16 Austin Kearns/200 3.00 8.00
17 Barry Larkin/25 30.00 60.00
22 Brad Penny/25 8.00 20.00
24 Brandon Webb/250 3.00 8.00
25 Brendan Harris/50 5.00 12.00
27 Brett Myers/100 6.00 15.00
28 Bubba Crosby/250 3.00 8.00
30 Chad Cordero/250 5.00 12.00
31 Bubba Nelson/250 3.00 8.00
32 Byron Gettis/250 3.00 8.00
36 Carlos Beltran/100 6.00 15.00
38 Carlos Lee/250 5.00 12.00
39 Chad Gaudin/100 4.00 10.00
40 Cliff Lee/250 8.00 20.00
43 Clint Barmes/100 6.00 15.00
47 Dan Haren/250 3.00 8.00
49 David Ortiz/250 15.00 40.00
50 Delmon Young/50 12.50 30.00
52 Dewon Brazelton/250 3.00 8.00
53 Dontrelle Willis/100 10.00 25.00
56 Edwin Almonte/250 3.00 8.00
57 Edwin Jackson/250 5.00 12.00
58 Eric Chavez/25 12.50 30.00
62 Frank Thomas/50 20.00 50.00
65 Garret Anderson/250 5.00 12.00
67 Gary Sheffield/50 12.50 30.00
70 Hank Blalock/100 6.00 15.00
74 Craig Wilson/250 3.00 8.00
78 John Lackey/250 5.00 12.00
79 Jacque Jones/250 5.00 12.00
80 Jae Weong Seo/100 6.00 15.00
85 Melvin Mora/250 5.00 12.00
86 Jason Varitek/100 15.00 40.00
89 Jay Gibbons/250 3.00 8.00
90 Jay Payton/250 3.00 8.00
91 Jeff Bagwell/50 20.00 50.00
92 Jeff Baker/25 8.00 20.00
96 Jerome Williams/100 4.00 10.00
97 Jim Edmonds/25 12.50 30.00
99 Jody Gerut/250 3.00 8.00
100 Joe Borchard/250 3.00 8.00
101 Joe Crede/50 8.00 20.00
102 Johan Santana/250 6.00 15.00
106 Jorge Posada/25 75.00 150.00
107 Jose Castillo/250 3.00 8.00
109 Jose Vidro/250 3.00 8.00
110 Josh Beckett/25 20.00 50.00
113 Juan Gonzalez/25 12.50 30.00
114 Junior Spivey/25 8.00 20.00
117 Kerry Wood/50 12.50 30.00
119 Kevin Youkilis/250 6.00 15.00
120 Lance Berkman/25 12.50 30.00
121 Larry Bigbie/250 5.00 12.00
123 Luis Castillo/25 8.00 20.00
125 Luis Matos/250 3.00 8.00
127 Magglio Ordonez/250 5.00 12.00
129 Marcus Giles/250 5.00 12.00
131 Mark Buehrle/250 10.00 25.00
132 Mark Mulder/250 5.00 12.00
133 Mark Prior/100 10.00 25.00
134 Mark Teixeira/100 10.00 25.00
135 Marlon Byrd/250 3.00 8.00
137 Miguel Cabrera/250 20.00 50.00
140 Mike Piazza/25 75.00 150.00
142 Morgan Ensberg/250 5.00 12.00
146 Orlando Cabrera/25 12.50 30.00
150 Paul Lo Duca/25 12.50 30.00
152 Jermaine Dye/250 5.00 12.00
153 Preston Wilson/250 5.00 12.00
154 Rafael Furcal/100 6.00 15.00
157 Rich Aurilia/25 8.00 20.00
158 Rich Harden/203 5.00 12.00
165 Roy Halladay/50 8.00 20.00
166 Roy Oswalt/50 8.00 20.00
167 Ryan Howard/100 20.00 50.00
169 Rodrigo Lopez/250 3.00 8.00
170 Sammy Sosa/50 50.00 100.00
171 Scott Podsednik/250 8.00 20.00
172 Scott Rolen/100 10.00 25.00
175 Shannon Stewart/100 6.00 15.00
176 Shawn Green/25 20.00 50.00
177 Shea Hillenbrand/250 5.00 12.00
178 Shigetoshi Hasegawa/250 15.00 40.00
179 Steve Finley/100 6.00 15.00
183 Torii Hunter/250 3.00 8.00
184 Trot Nixon/250 5.00 12.00
187 Victor Martinez/250 5.00 12.00
188 Vlad Guerrero Angels/50 12.00 30.00
190 Brandon Larson/200 3.00 8.00
191 Travis Hafner/250 5.00 12.00
197 Michael Young/250 6.00 15.00
212 Gary Carter LGD/250 10.00 25.00
213 Duke Snider LGD/250 8.00 20.00
214 Whitey Ford LGD/50 20.00 50.00
215 Bob Feller LGD/250 8.00 20.00
216 Reggie Jackson LGD/50 20.00 50.00
217 Ryne Sandberg LGD/50 20.00 50.00
218 Dale Murphy LGD/50 6.00 15.00
219 Tony Gwynn LGD/50 25.00 60.00
220 Don Mattingly LGD/50 20.00 50.00
221 Mike Schmidt LGD/50 20.00 50.00
222 Rickey Henderson LGD/50 40.00 80.00
223 Cal Ripken LGD/50 50.00 100.00
224 Nolan Ryan LGD/50 40.00 80.00
225 George Brett LGD/50 40.00 80.00
226 Bob Gibson LGD/100 10.00 25.00
227 Lou Brock LGD/100 10.00 25.00
228 Andre Dawson LGD/250 5.00 12.00
229 Rod Carew LGD/50 12.50 30.00
230 Wade Boggs LGD/50 12.50 30.00
238 Ernie Banks LGD/50 30.00 60.00
240 Stan Musial LGD/100 20.00 50.00
241 Hector Gimenez NG/200 3.00 8.00
242 Justin Germano NG/100 5.00 12.00
243 Ian Snell NG/100 6.00 15.00
244 Graham Koonce NG/200 3.00 8.00
245 Jose Capellan NG/100 4.00 10.00
246 Onil Joseph NG/200 3.00 8.00
247 Shingo Takatsu NG/50 10.00 25.00
248 Carlos Hines NG/200 3.00 8.00
249 Lincoln Holdzkom NG/100 4.00 10.00
250 Mike Gosling NG/100 4.00 10.00
251 Eduardo Sierra NG/200 4.00 10.00
252 Renyel Pinto NG/100 4.00 10.00
253 Merkin Valdez NG/200 3.00 8.00
254 Angel Chavez NG/200 3.00 8.00
255 Ivan Ochoa NG/200 3.00 8.00
257 William Bergolla NG/200 3.00 8.00
258 Aarom Baldiris NG/100 4.00 10.00
260 Carlos Vasquez NG/200 4.00 10.00
261 Freddy Guzman NG/200 3.00 8.00
262 Akinori Otsuka NG/50 15.00 40.00
264 Nick Regilio NG/200 3.00 8.00
266 Shawn Hill NG/200 3.00 8.00
268 Sean Henn NG/200 3.00 8.00
269 Ramon Ramirez NG/200 3.00 8.00
270 Ronny Cedeno NG/100 6.00 15.00
273 Fernando Nieve NG/200 3.00 8.00
274 Rusty Tucker NG/200 4.00 10.00
275 Jason Bartlett NG/200 4.00 10.00
276 Mike Rouse NG/200 3.00 8.00
277 Dennis Sarfate NG/200 3.00 8.00
278 Cory Sullivan NG/200 3.00 8.00
282 Michael Wuertz NG/200 4.00 10.00
284 Jorge Sequea NG/100 4.00 10.00
287 Tim Bittner NG/250 3.00 8.00
288 Andres Blanco NG/100 4.00 10.00
289 Kevin Cave NG/100 4.00 10.00
290 Mike Johnston NG/100 4.00 10.00
293 Colby Miller NG/100 4.00 10.00
294 Jake Woods NG/100 4.00 10.00
295 Ryan Meaux NG/200 3.00 8.00
296 Don Kelly NG/100 4.00 10.00
297 Edwin Moreno NG/100 4.00 10.00
298 Phil Stockman NG/100 4.00 10.00

2004 Leaf Certified Materials Mirror Autograph White

*1-240 p/r 100: .5X TO 1.2X RED p/r 250
*1-240 p/r 100: .4X TO 1X RED p/r 100
*1-240 p/r 50: .6X TO 1.5X RED p/r 200-250
*1-240 p/r 50: .5X TO 1.2X RED p/r 100
*1-240 p/r 50: .4X TO 1X RED p/r 50
*1-240 p/r 25: 1X TO 2.5X RED p/r 203
*1-240 p/r 25: .75X TO 2X RED p/r 100
*1-240 p/r 25: .6X TO 1.5X RED p/r 50
*1-240 p/r 25: .4X TO 1X RED p/r 25
*241-300 p/r 100: .5X TO 1.2X RED p/r 200
*241-300 p/r 100: .4X TO 1X RED p/r 100
*241-300 p/r 50: .6X TO 1.5X RED p/r 200-250
*241-300 p/r 50: .5X TO 1.2X RED p/r 100
OVERALL AU ODDS 1:10
PRINT RUNS B/WN 1-100 COPIES PER
NO PRICING ON QTY OF 10 OR LESS
2 Adam Dunn/24 20.00 50.00
167 Ryan Howard/25 50.00 100.00

2004 Leaf Certified Materials Mirror Bat Blue

*BLUE p/r 100: .5X TO 1.2X RED p/r 175-250
*BLUE p/r 50: .75X TO 2X RED p/r 150-250
*BLUE p/r 25: 1X TO 2.5X RED p/r 100
RANDOM INSERTS IN PACKS
PRINT RUNS B/WN 25-100 COPIES PER
23 Brad Wilkerson/100 2.00 5.00
58 Eric Chavez/50 3.00 8.00
142 Morgan Ensberg/50 3.00 8.00
151 Pedro Martinez/50 5.00 12.00
156 Randy Johnson/50 6.00 15.00
166 Roy Oswalt/50 3.00 8.00
172 Scott Rolen/50 5.00 12.00
180 Tim Hudson/50 3.00 8.00
182 Tom Glavine/50 5.00 12.00
207 Curt Schilling D'backs/50 3.00 8.00
217 Ryne Sandberg LGD/50 12.50 30.00
218 Dale Murphy LGD/50 6.00 15.00
219 Tony Gwynn LGD/50 10.00 25.00
221 Mike Schmidt LGD/50 12.50 30.00
223 Cal Ripken LGD/50 25.00 60.00
224 Nolan Ryan LGD/50 15.00 40.00
225 George Brett LGD/50 12.50 30.00

2004 Leaf Certified Materials Mirror Bat Gold

*GOLD p/r 25: 1:25X TO 3X RED p/r 150-250
*GOLD p/r 25: 1X TO 2.5X RED p/r 100
RANDOM INSERTS IN PACKS
STATED PRINT RUN 25 SERIAL #'d SETS
207 SCHILLING PRINT RUN 20 COPIES
18 Barry Zito 5.00 12.00
19 Ben Sheets 5.00 12.00
22 Brad Penny 5.00 12.00
23 Brad Wilkerson 5.00 12.00
46 Curt Schilling Sox 8.00 20.00
58 Eric Chavez 5.00 12.00
69 Greg Maddux Cubs 12.50 30.00
142 Morgan Ensberg 5.00 12.00
151 Pedro Martinez 8.00 20.00
156 Randy Johnson 10.00 25.00
166 Roy Oswalt 5.00 12.00
172 Scott Rolen 8.00 20.00
180 Tim Hudson 5.00 12.00
182 Tom Glavine 8.00 20.00
207 Curt Schilling D'backs 5.00 12.00
213 Duke Snider LGD 10.00 25.00
217 Ryne Sandberg LGD 20.00 50.00
218 Dale Murphy LGD 10.00 25.00
219 Tony Gwynn LGD 15.00 40.00
221 Mike Schmidt LGD 20.00 50.00
223 Cal Ripken LGD 40.00 100.00
224 Nolan Ryan LGD 25.00 60.00
225 George Brett LGD 20.00 50.00
231 Roberto Clemente LGD 40.00 100.00
232 Roy Campanella LGD 12.50 30.00
233 Babe Ruth LGD 150.00 250.00
234 Lou Gehrig LGD 75.00 150.00
235 Ty Cobb LGD 60.00 120.00
236 Roger Maris LGD 20.00 50.00
238 Ernie Banks LGD 12.50 30.00
239 Ted Williams LGD 20.00 50.00

2004 Leaf Certified Materials Mirror Bat Red

PRINT RUNS B/WN 100-250 COPIES PER
BLACK PRINT RUN 1 SERIAL #'d SET
NO BLACK PRICING DUE TO SCARCITY
EMERALD PRINT RUN 5 SERIAL #'d SETS
NO EMERALD PRICING DUE TO SCARCITY
2 Adam Dunn/150 2.00 5.00
3 Adam LaRoche/250 2.00 5.00
5 Adrian Beltre/150 2.00 5.00
7 Albert Pujols/150 6.00 15.00
8 Alex Rodriguez Yanks/250 4.00 10.00
9 Alexis Rios/250 2.00 5.00
10 Alfonso Soriano Rgr/150 2.00 5.00
11 Andruw Jones/150 3.00 8.00
12 Andy Pettitte/250 3.00 8.00
13 Angel Berroa/150 2.00 5.00
15 Aubrey Huff/150 2.00 5.00
16 Austin Kearns/150 2.00 5.00
17 Barry Larkin/150 3.00 8.00
20 Bernie Williams/150 3.00 8.00
21 Bobby Abreu/150 2.00 5.00
24 Brandon Webb/150 2.00 5.00
25 Brendan Harris/250 2.00 5.00
26 Bret Boone/150 2.00 5.00
29 Brian Giles/250 2.00 5.00
35 Carl Everett/250 2.00 5.00
36 Carlos Beltran/150 2.00 5.00
37 Carlos Delgado/150 2.00 5.00
38 Carlos Lee/150 2.00 5.00
41 Chipper Jones/150 3.00 8.00
42 Cliff Floyd/250 2.00 5.00
43 Clint Barmes/250 2.00 5.00
44 Corey Patterson/250 2.00 5.00
45 Craig Biggio/150 3.00 8.00
47 Dan Haren/150 2.00 5.00
48 Darin Erstad/150 2.00 5.00
49 David Ortiz/250 3.00 8.00
50 Delmon Young/250 3.00 8.00
51 Derek Jeter/150 8.00 20.00
54 Edgar Martinez/150 3.00 8.00
55 Edgar Renteria/150 2.00 5.00
59 Eric Hinske/150 2.00 5.00
60 Eric Munson/250 2.00 5.00
61 Erubial Durazo/250 2.00 5.00
62 Frank Thomas/150 3.00 8.00
63 Fred McGriff/150 3.00 8.00
65 Garret Anderson/150 2.00 5.00
67 Gary Sheffield/250 2.00 5.00
68 Geoff Jenkins/150 2.00 5.00
70 Hank Blalock/150 2.00 5.00
71 Hee Seop Choi/250 2.00 5.00
73 Hideo Nomo/150 3.00 8.00
76 Ivan Rodriguez Tigers/250 3.00 8.00
77 J.D. Drew/250 2.00 5.00
79 Jacque Jones/150 2.00 5.00
82 Jason Giambi Yanks/150 2.00 5.00
83 Jason Jennings/150 2.00 5.00
86 Jason Varitek/150 3.00 8.00
88 Javy Lopez/250 2.00 5.00
89 Jay Gibbons/150 2.00 5.00
91 Jeff Bagwell/150 3.00 8.00
92 Jeff Baker/250 2.00 5.00
93 Jeff Kent/150 2.00 5.00
97 Jim Edmonds/150 2.00 5.00
98 Jim Thome/150 3.00 8.00
100 Joe Borchard/150 2.00 5.00
101 Joe Crede/250 2.00 5.00
103 John Olerud/150 2.00 5.00
105 Johnny Damon/250 3.00 8.00
106 Jorge Posada/150 3.00 8.00
107 Jose Castillo/250 2.00 5.00
108 Jose Reyes/150 2.00 5.00
109 Jose Vidro/150 2.00 5.00
110 Josh Beckett/150 2.00 5.00
111 Josh Phelps/150 2.00 5.00
112 Juan Encarnacion/250 2.00 5.00
113 Juan Gonzalez/250 2.00 5.00
114 Junior Spivey/250 2.00 5.00
115 Kazuhisa Ishii/150 2.00 5.00
116 Kenny Lofton/250 2.00 5.00
117 Kerry Wood/150 2.00 5.00
119 Kevin Youkilis/250 2.00 5.00
120 Lance Berkman/150 2.00 5.00
122 Larry Walker/150 2.00 5.00
123 Luis Castillo/150 2.00 5.00
124 Luis Gonzalez/150 2.00 5.00
126 Lyle Overbay/250 2.00 5.00
127 Magglio Ordonez/150 2.00 5.00
128 Manny Ramirez/150 3.00 8.00
129 Marcus Giles/250 2.00 5.00
131 Mark Buehrle/150 2.00 5.00
132 Mark Mulder/150 2.00 5.00
133 Mark Prior/150 3.00 8.00
134 Mark Teixeira/150 3.00 8.00
135 Marlon Byrd/150 2.00 5.00
137 Miguel Cabrera/250 3.00 8.00
138 Mike Lowell/150 2.00 5.00
140 Mike Piazza/150 4.00 10.00
141 Mike Sweeney/150 2.00 5.00
143 Nick Johnson/250 2.00 5.00
144 Nomar Garciaparra/150 5.00 12.00
145 Omar Vizquel/150 3.00 8.00
146 Orlando Cabrera/250 2.00 5.00
147 Orlando Hudson/150 2.00 5.00
148 Pat Burrell/150 2.00 5.00
149 Paul Konerko/150 2.00 5.00
150 Paul Lo Duca/150 2.00 5.00
152 Jermaine Dye/250 2.00 5.00
153 Preston Wilson/150 2.00 5.00
154 Rafael Furcal/150 2.00 5.00
155 Rafael Palmeiro O's/150 3.00 8.00
157 Rich Aurilia/250 2.00 5.00
159 Richard Hidalgo/150 2.00 5.00
160 Richie Sexson/250 2.00 5.00
161 Rickie Weeks/250 2.00 5.00
162 Roberto Alomar/250 3.00 8.00
163 Rocco Baldelli/150 2.00 5.00
164 Roger Clemens Astros/250 4.00 10.00
168 Ryan Klesko/150 2.00 5.00
170 Sammy Sosa/150 3.00 8.00
174 Sean Casey/250 2.00 5.00
175 Shannon Stewart/150 2.00 5.00
176 Shawn Green/150 2.00 5.00
181 Todd Helton/150 3.00 8.00
183 Torii Hunter/150 2.00 5.00
184 Trot Nixon/150 2.00 5.00
185 Troy Glaus/150 2.00 5.00
186 Vernon Wells/150 2.00 5.00
187 Victor Martinez/250 2.00 5.00
188 Vladimir Guerrero Angels/250 3.00 8.00
189 Wade Miller/250 2.00 5.00
190 Brandon Larson/175 2.00 5.00
191 Travis Hafner/150 2.00 5.00
192 Tim Salmon/150 3.00 8.00
195 Ramon Nivar/150 2.00 5.00
196 Moises Alou/250 2.00 5.00
197 Michael Young/250 2.00 5.00
198 Laynce Nix/150 2.00 5.00
199 Tino Martinez/250 3.00 8.00
200 Randall Simon/250 2.00 5.00
201 Roger Clemens Yanks/150 4.00 10.00
203 Vladimir Guerrero Expos/150 3.00 8.00
204 Miguel Tejada/150 2.00 5.00
206 Jason Giambi A's/150 2.00 5.00
208 Alex Rodriguez Rgr/150 4.00 10.00
209 Alfonso Soriano Yanks/150 2.00 5.00
210 Ivan Rodriguez Marlins/150 3.00 8.00
211 Rafael Palmeiro Rgr/150 3.00 8.00
212 Gary Carter LGD/150 3.00 8.00
216 Reggie Jackson LGD/150 4.00 10.00
220 Don Mattingly LGD/150 6.00 15.00
222 Rickey Henderson LGD/150 4.00 10.00
227 Lou Brock LGD/150 4.00 10.00
228 Andre Dawson LGD/150 3.00 8.00
229 Rod Carew LGD/150 4.00 10.00
230 Wade Boggs LGD/150 4.00 10.00
240 Stan Musial LGD/100 10.00 25.00

2004 Leaf Certified Materials Mirror Bat White

*WHITE p/r 200: .4X TO 1X RED p/r 250
*WHITE p/r 100: .5X TO 1.2X RED p/r 150
*WHITE p/r 50: .6X TO 1.5X RED p/r 100
RANDOM INSERTS IN PACKS
PRINT RUNS B/WN 25-200 COPIES PER
14 Aramis Ramirez/100 2.00 5.00
23 Brad Wilkerson/200 2.00 5.00
156 Randy Johnson/100 4.00 10.00
166 Roy Oswalt/100 2.00 5.00
180 Tim Hudson/100 2.00 5.00
182 Tom Glavine/100 3.00 8.00
205 Kevin Brown/100 2.00 5.00
218 Dale Murphy LGD/100 5.00 12.00
219 Tony Gwynn LGD/100 6.00 15.00
221 Mike Schmidt LGD/100 8.00 20.00
223 Cal Ripken LGD/100 15.00 40.00
224 Nolan Ryan LGD/100 10.00 25.00
225 George Brett LGD/100 8.00 20.00
231 Roberto Clemente LGD/50 30.00 80.00
232 Roy Campanella LGD/50 8.00 20.00
233 Babe Ruth LGD/25 150.00 250.00
234 Lou Gehrig LGD/25 75.00 150.00
235 Ty Cobb LGD/25 60.00 120.00
236 Roger Maris LGD/25 20.00 50.00
238 Ernie Banks LGD/50 8.00 20.00
239 Ted Williams LGD/25 40.00 100.00

2004 Leaf Certified Materials Mirror Combo Red

2-211 PRINT RUN 250 SERIAL #'d SETS
212-239 PRINT RUNS B/WN 50-250 PER
BLACK PRIME PRINT RUN 1 SERIAL #'d SET
NO BLACK PRIME PRICING AVAILABLE
RANDOM INSERTS IN PACKS
2 Adam Dunn Bat-Jsy 3.00 8.00
5 Adrian Beltre Bat-Jsy 3.00 8.00
7 Albert Pujols Bat-Jsy 10.00 25.00
11 Andruw Jones Bat-Jsy 5.00 12.00
13 Angel Berroa Bat-Pants 3.00 8.00
15 Aubrey Huff Bat-Jsy 3.00 8.00
16 Austin Kearns Bat-Jsy 3.00 8.00
17 Barry Larkin Bat-Jsy 5.00 12.00
18 Barry Zito Bat-Jsy 3.00 8.00
19 Ben Sheets Bat-Jsy 3.00 8.00
20 Bernie Williams Bat-Jsy 5.00 12.00
21 Bobby Abreu Bat-Jsy 3.00 8.00
22 Brad Penny Bat-Jsy 3.00 8.00
24 Brandon Webb Bat-Jsy 3.00 8.00
26 Bret Boone Bat-Jsy 3.00 8.00
36 Carlos Beltran Bat-Jsy 3.00 8.00
37 Carlos Delgado Bat-Jsy 3.00 8.00
38 Carlos Lee Bat-Jsy 3.00 8.00
41 Chipper Jones Bat-Jsy 5.00 12.00
45 Craig Biggio Bat-Pants 5.00 12.00
47 Dan Haren Bat-Jsy 3.00 8.00
51 Derek Jeter Bat-Jsy 10.00 25.00
52 Dewon Brazelton Fld Glv-Jsy 3.00 8.00
54 Edgar Martinez Bat-Jsy 5.00 12.00
55 Edgar Renteria Bat-Jsy 3.00 8.00
58 Eric Chavez Bat-Jsy 3.00 8.00
59 Eric Hinske Bat-Jsy 3.00 8.00
62 Frank Thomas Bat-Jsy 5.00 12.00
63 Fred McGriff Bat-Jsy 5.00 12.00
65 Garret Anderson Bat-Jsy 3.00 8.00
68 Geoff Jenkins Bat-Jsy 3.00 8.00
70 Hank Blalock Bat-Jsy 3.00 8.00
73 Hideo Nomo Bat-Jsy 5.00 12.00
79 Jacque Jones Bat-Jsy 3.00 8.00
82 Jason Giambi Yanks Bat-Jsy 3.00 8.00
83 Jason Jennings Bat-Jsy 3.00 8.00
86 Jason Varitek Bat-Jsy 5.00 12.00
89 Jay Gibbons Bat-Jsy 3.00 8.00
91 Jeff Bagwell Bat-Jsy 5.00 12.00
93 Jeff Kent Bat-Jsy 3.00 8.00
97 Jim Edmonds Bat-Jsy 3.00 8.00
98 Jim Thome Bat-Jsy 5.00 12.00
100 Joe Borchard Bat-Jsy 3.00 8.00
103 John Olerud Bat-Jsy 3.00 8.00
106 Jorge Posada Bat-Jsy 5.00 12.00
108 Jose Reyes Bat-Jsy 3.00 8.00
109 Jose Vidro Bat-Jsy 3.00 8.00
110 Josh Beckett Bat-Jsy 3.00 8.00
111 Josh Phelps Bat-Jsy 3.00 8.00
115 Kazuhisa Ishii Bat-Jsy 3.00 8.00
117 Kerry Wood Bat-Jsy 3.00 8.00
120 Lance Berkman Bat-Jsy 3.00 8.00
122 Larry Walker Bat-Jsy 3.00 8.00
123 Luis Castillo Bat-Jsy 3.00 8.00
124 Luis Gonzalez Bat-Jsy 3.00 8.00
127 Magglio Ordonez Bat-Jsy 3.00 8.00
128 Manny Ramirez Bat-Jsy 5.00 12.00
131 Mark Buehrle Bat-Jsy 3.00 8.00
132 Mark Mulder Bat-Jsy 3.00 8.00
133 Mark Prior Bat-Jsy 5.00 12.00
134 Mark Teixeira Bat-Jsy 5.00 12.00
135 Marlon Byrd Bat-Jsy 3.00 8.00
138 Mike Lowell Bat-Jsy 3.00 8.00
140 Mike Piazza Bat-Jsy 6.00 15.00
141 Mike Sweeney Bat-Jsy 3.00 8.00
142 Morgan Ensberg Bat-Jsy 3.00 8.00
144 Nomar Garciaparra Bat-Jsy 6.00 15.00
145 Omar Vizquel Bat-Jsy 5.00 12.00
147 Orlando Hudson Bat-Jsy 3.00 8.00
148 Pat Burrell Bat-Jsy 3.00 8.00
149 Paul Konerko Bat-Jsy 3.00 8.00
150 Paul Lo Duca Bat-Jsy 3.00 8.00
151 Pedro Martinez Bat-Jsy 5.00 12.00
153 Preston Wilson Bat-Jsy 3.00 8.00
154 Rafael Furcal Bat-Jsy 3.00 8.00
155 Rafael Palmeiro O's Bat-Jsy 5.00 12.00
156 Randy Johnson Bat-Jsy 5.00 12.00
159 Richard Hidalgo Bat-Pants 3.00 8.00
163 Rocco Baldelli Bat-Jsy 3.00 8.00
166 Roy Oswalt Bat-Jsy 3.00 8.00
168 Ryan Klesko Bat-Jsy 3.00 8.00
170 Sammy Sosa Bat-Jsy 5.00 12.00
172 Scott Rolen Bat-Jsy 5.00 12.00
175 Shannon Stewart Bat-Jsy 3.00 8.00
176 Shawn Green Bat-Jsy 3.00 8.00
180 Tim Hudson Bat-Jsy 3.00 8.00
181 Todd Helton Bat-Jsy 5.00 12.00
182 Tom Glavine Bat-Jsy 5.00 12.00
183 Torii Hunter Bat-Jsy 3.00 8.00
184 Trot Nixon Bat-Jsy 3.00 8.00
185 Troy Glaus Bat-Jsy 3.00 8.00
186 Vernon Wells Bat-Jsy 3.00 8.00
191 Travis Hafner Bat-Jsy 3.00 8.00
192 Tim Salmon Bat-Jsy 5.00 12.00
195 Ramon Nivar Bat-Jsy 3.00 8.00
201 R.Clemens Yanks Bat-Jsy 6.00 15.00
203 Vlad Guerrero Expos Bat-Jsy 5.00 12.00
204 Miguel Tejada Bat-Jsy 3.00 8.00
206 Jason Giambi A's Bat-Jsy 3.00 8.00
207 Curt Schilling D'backs Bat-Jsy 3.00 8.00
208 Alex Rodriguez Rgr Bat-Jsy 6.00 15.00
209 Alf Soriano Yanks Bat-Jsy 3.00 8.00
210 Ivan Rod Marlins Bat-Jsy 5.00 12.00
211 Rafael Palmeiro Rgr Bat-Jsy 5.00 12.00
212 G.Carter LGD Bat-Pants/250 4.00 10.00
216 R.Jackson LGD Bat-Jsy/250 6.00 15.00
217 R.Sandberg LGD Bat-Jsy/250 10.00 25.00
218 D.Murphy LGD Bat-Jsy/250 6.00 15.00
219 T.Gwynn LGD Bat-Jsy/250 6.00 15.00
220 D.Mattingly LGD Bat-Jsy/250 10.00 25.00
221 M.Schm LGD Bat-Pants/250 10.00 25.00
222 R.Hend LGD Bat-Jsy/250 6.00 15.00
223 C.Ripken LGD Bat-Jsy/250 12.00 30.00
224 N.Ryan LGD Bat-Jsy/250 10.00 25.00
225 G.Brett LGD Bat-Jsy/250 10.00 25.00
227 L.Brock LGD Bat-Jsy/250 6.00 15.00
228 A.Dawson LGD Bat-Jsy/250 4.00 10.00
229 R.Carew LGD Bat-Jkt/250 6.00 15.00
230 W.Boggs LGD Bat-Jsy/250 6.00 15.00
231 R.Clemente LGD Bat-Jsy/100 60.00 120.00
232 R.Campy LGD Bat-Pants/100 8.00 20.00
233 B.Ruth LGD Bat-Pants/50 125.00 250.00
234 L.Gehrig LGD Bat-Pants/50 100.00 200.00
235 T.Cobb LGD Bat-Pants/50 100.00 200.00
236 R.Maris LGD Bat-Pants/100 20.00 50.00
238 E.Banks LGD Bat-Pants/100 8.00 20.00
239 T.Williams LGD Bat-Jkt/100 50.00 100.00

2004 Leaf Certified Materials Mirror Fabric Blue Position

*1-211 p/r 100: .5X TO 1.2X RED p/r 150-250
1-211 PRINT RUN 100 SERIAL #'d SETS
*212-239 p/r 100: .5X TO 1.2X REDp/r150-250
*212-239 p/r 25: 1X TO 2.5X RED p/r 100
212-239 PRINT RUN 25-100 #'d COPIES PER
24 Brandon Webb Jsy 2.00 5.00
26 Bret Boone Jsy 2.00 5.00
37 Carlos Delgado Jsy 2.00 5.00
52 Dewon Brazelton Jsy 2.00 5.00
65 Garret Anderson Jsy 2.00 5.00
80 Jae Weong Seo Jsy 2.00 5.00
100 Joe Borchard Jsy 2.00 5.00
106 Jorge Posada Jsy 3.00 8.00
127 Magglio Ordonez Jsy 2.00 5.00
128 Manny Ramirez Jsy 3.00 8.00
132 Mark Mulder Jsy 2.00 5.00
134 Mark Teixeira Jsy 3.00 8.00
138 Mike Lowell Jsy 2.00 5.00
149 Paul Konerko Jsy 2.00 5.00
150 Paul Lo Duca Jsy 2.00 5.00
155 Rafael Palmeiro O's Jsy 3.00 8.00
166 Roy Oswalt Jsy 2.00 5.00
183 Torii Hunter Jsy 2.00 5.00
184 Trot Nixon Jsy 2.00 5.00
211 Rafael Palmeiro Rgr Jsy 3.00 8.00
214 W.Ford LGD Jsy/100 5.00 12.00
216 R.Jackson LGD Jsy/100 5.00 12.00
217 R.Sandberg LGD Jsy/100 8.00 20.00
218 D.Murphy LGD Jsy/100 5.00 12.00
219 T.Gwynn LGD Jsy/100 6.00 15.00
220 Don Mattingly LGD Jsy/100 8.00 20.00
221 M.Schmidt LGD Pants/100 8.00 20.00
222 R.Henderson LGD Jsy/100 6.00 15.00
223 Cal Ripken LGD Jsy/100 15.00 40.00
224 Nolan Ryan LGD Jsy/100 10.00 25.00
225 George Brett LGD Jsy/100 8.00 20.00
227 L.Brock LGD Jsy/100 5.00 12.00
228 A.Dawson LGD Jsy/100 3.00 8.00
229 R.Carew LGD Jkt/100 5.00 12.00
230 W.Boggs LGD Jsy/100 5.00 12.00
231 R.Clemente LGD Jsy/25 40.00 100.00
232 R.Campy LGD Pants/25 12.50 30.00
233 Babe Ruth LGD Pants/25 150.00 250.00
234 Lou Gehrig LGD Pants/25 75.00 150.00
235 Ty Cobb LGD Pants/25 60.00 120.00
236 Roger Maris LGD Pants/25 20.00 50.00
238 E.Banks LGD Pants/25 12.50 30.00
239 Ted Williams LGD Jkt/25 40.00 100.00

2004 Leaf Certified Materials Mirror Fabric Gold Number

*1-211 p/r 25: 1.25X TO 3X RED p/r 150-250
1-211 PRINT RUN 25 SERIAL #'d SETS
*212-239 p/r 25: 1.25X TO 3X RED p/r 150-250
212-239 PRINT RUNS B/WN 10-25 #'d PER
212-239 NO PRICING ON QTY OF 10 OR LESS
RANDOM INSERTS IN PACKS
24 Brandon Webb Jsy 5.00 12.00
26 Bret Boone Jsy 5.00 12.00
37 Carlos Delgado Jsy 5.00 12.00
52 Dewon Brazelton Jsy 5.00 12.00
63 Fred McGriff Jsy 8.00 20.00
65 Garret Anderson Jsy 5.00 12.00
80 Jae Weong Seo Jsy 5.00 12.00
100 Joe Borchard Jsy 5.00 12.00
106 Jorge Posada Jsy 8.00 20.00
127 Magglio Ordonez Jsy 5.00 12.00
128 Manny Ramirez Jsy 8.00 20.00
132 Mark Mulder Jsy 5.00 12.00
134 Mark Teixeira Jsy 8.00 20.00
138 Mike Lowell Jsy 5.00 12.00
149 Paul Konerko Jsy 5.00 12.00
150 Paul Lo Duca Jsy 5.00 12.00
155 Rafael Palmeiro O's Jsy 8.00 20.00
166 Roy Oswalt Jsy 5.00 12.00
183 Torii Hunter Jsy 5.00 12.00
184 Trot Nixon Jsy 5.00 12.00
211 Rafael Palmeiro Rgr Jsy 8.00 20.00
214 Whitey Ford LGD Jsy/25 10.00 25.00
215 B.Feller LGD Jsy/25 6.00 15.00
216 R.Jackson LGD Jsy/25 10.00 25.00
217 Ryne Sandberg LGD Jsy/25 20.00 50.00
218 D.Murphy LGD Jsy/25 10.00 25.00
219 Tony Gwynn LGD Jsy/25 15.00 40.00
220 Don Mattingly LGD Jsy/25 20.00 50.00
221 Mike Schmidt LGD Pants/25 20.00 50.00
222 R.Henderson LGD Jsy/25 12.50 30.00
223 Cal Ripken LGD Jsy/25 40.00 100.00
224 Nolan Ryan LGD Jsy/25 25.00 60.00
225 George Brett LGD Jsy/25 20.00 50.00
227 L.Brock LGD Jsy/25 10.00 25.00
228 A.Dawson LGD Jsy/25 6.00 15.00
229 R.Carew LGD Jkt/25 10.00 25.00
230 W.Boggs LGD Jsy/25 10.00 25.00

2004 Leaf Certified Materials Mirror Fabric Red

PRINT RUNS B/WN 100-250 COPIES PER
BLACK AL/NL PRINT RUN 1 SERIAL #'d SET
NO BLK AL/NL PRICING DUE TO SCARCITY
BLACK NUMBER PRINT RUN 1 #'d SET
NO BLACK NBR.PRICING DUE TO SCARCITY
BLACK POSITION PRINT RUN 1 #'d SET
NO BLACK POS.PRICING DUE TO SCARCITY
BLACK PRIME PRINT RUN 1 SERIAL #'d SET
NO BLK PRIME PRICING DUE TO SCARCITY
EMERALD PRINT RUN 1-5 COPIES PER
NO EMERALD PRICING DUE TO SCARCITY
1 A.J. Burnett Jsy/250 2.00 5.00
2 Adam Dunn Jsy/150 2.00 5.00
5 Adrian Beltre Jsy/150 2.00 5.00
6 Al Leiter Jsy/250 2.00 5.00
7 Albert Pujols Jsy/150 6.00 15.00
11 Andruw Jones Jsy/150 3.00 8.00
13 Angel Berroa Pants/150 2.00 5.00
15 Aubrey Huff Jsy/150 2.00 5.00
16 Austin Kearns Jsy/150 2.00 5.00
17 Barry Larkin Jsy/150 3.00 8.00
18 Barry Zito Jsy/150 2.00 5.00
19 Ben Sheets Jsy/150 2.00 5.00
20 Bernie Williams Jsy/150 3.00 8.00

21 Bobby Abreu Jsy/150 2.00 5.00
22 Brad Penny Jsy/150 2.00 5.00
27 Brett Myers Jsy/250 2.00 5.00
33 C.C. Sabathia Jsy/250 2.00 5.00
34 Carl Crawford Jsy/250 2.00 5.00
36 Carlos Beltran Jsy/150 2.00 5.00
38 Carlos Lee Jsy/150 2.00 5.00
39 Chad Gaudin Jsy/250 2.00 5.00
41 Chipper Jones Jsy/150 3.00 8.00
45 Craig Biggio Pants/150 3.00 8.00
47 Dan Haren Jsy/150 2.00 5.00
48 Darin Erstad Jsy/250 2.00 5.00
51 Derek Jeter Jsy/150 8.00 20.00
53 Dontrelle Willis Jsy/250 3.00 8.00
54 Edgar Martinez Jsy/150 3.00 8.00
55 Edgar Renteria Jsy/150 2.00 5.00
58 Eric Chavez Jsy/150 2.00 5.00
59 Eric Hinske Jsy/150 2.00 5.00
62 Frank Thomas Jsy/150 3.00 8.00
64 Freddy Garcia Jsy/250 2.00 5.00
66 Garrett Atkins Jsy/250 2.00 5.00
68 Geoff Jenkins Jsy/150 2.00 5.00
70 Hank Blalock Jsy/150 2.00 5.00
72 Hideki Matsui Base/250 6.00 15.00
73 Hideo Nomo Jsy/150 3.00 8.00
75 Ichiro Suzuki Base/250 6.00 15.00
79 Jacque Jones Jsy/150 2.00 5.00
81 Jamie Moyer Jsy/250 2.00 5.00
82 Jason Giambi Yanks Jsy/150 2.00 5.00
83 Jason Jennings Jsy/150 2.00 5.00
84 Jason Kendall Jsy/250 2.00 5.00
86 Jason Varitek Jsy/150 3.00 8.00
89 Jay Gibbons Jsy/150 2.00 5.00
91 Jeff Bagwell Jsy/150 3.00 8.00
93 Jeff Kent Jsy/150 2.00 5.00
96 Jerome Williams Jsy/250 2.00 5.00
97 Jim Edmonds Jsy/150 2.00 5.00
98 Jim Thome Jsy/150 3.00 8.00
102 Johan Santana Jsy/250 3.00 8.00
103 John Olerud Jsy/150 2.00 5.00
104 John Smoltz Jsy/250 3.00 8.00
108 Jose Reyes Jsy/150 2.00 5.00
109 Jose Vidro Jsy/150 2.00 5.00
110 Josh Beckett Jsy/150 2.00 5.00
111 Josh Phelps Jsy/150 2.00 5.00
115 Kazuhisa Ishii Jsy/150 2.00 5.00
117 Kerry Wood Jsy/150 2.00 5.00
118 Kevin Millwood Jsy/250 2.00 5.00
120 Lance Berkman Jsy/150 2.00 5.00
121 Larry Bigbie Jsy/250 2.00 5.00
122 Larry Walker Jsy/150 2.00 5.00
123 Luis Castillo Jsy/150 2.00 5.00
124 Luis Gonzalez Jsy/150 2.00 5.00
130 Mariano Rivera Jsy/250 3.00 8.00
131 Mark Buehrle Jsy/150 2.00 5.00
133 Mark Prior Jsy/150 3.00 8.00
135 Marlon Byrd Jsy/150 2.00 5.00
136 Matt Morris Jsy/250 2.00 5.00
139 Mike Mussina Jsy/250 3.00 8.00
140 Mike Piazza Jsy/150 4.00 10.00
141 Mike Sweeney Jsy/150 2.00 5.00
142 Morgan Ensberg Jsy/150 2.00 5.00
144 Nomar Garciaparra Jsy/150 5.00 12.00
145 Omar Vizquel Jsy/150 3.00 8.00
147 Orlando Hudson Jsy/150 2.00 5.00
148 Pat Burrell Jsy/150 2.00 5.00
151 Pedro Martinez Jsy/150 3.00 8.00
153 Preston Wilson Jsy/150 2.00 5.00
154 Rafael Furcal Jsy/150 2.00 5.00
156 Randy Johnson Jsy/150 3.00 8.00
158 Rich Harden Jsy/250 2.00 5.00
159 Richard Hidalgo Pants/150 2.00 5.00
163 Rocco Baldelli Jsy/150 2.00 5.00
165 Roy Halladay Jsy/250 2.00 5.00
168 Ryan Klesko Jsy/150 2.00 5.00
170 Sammy Sosa Jsy/150 3.00 8.00
172 Scott Rolen Jsy/150 3.00 8.00
173 Sean Burroughs Jsy/250 2.00 5.00
175 Shannon Stewart Jsy/150 2.00 5.00
176 Shawn Green Jsy/150 2.00 5.00
179 Steve Finley Jsy/250 2.00 5.00
180 Tim Hudson Jsy/150 2.00 5.00
181 Todd Helton Jsy/150 3.00 8.00
182 Tom Glavine Jsy/150 3.00 8.00
185 Troy Glaus Jsy/150 2.00 5.00
186 Vernon Wells Jsy/150 2.00 5.00
191 Travis Hafner Jsy/150 2.00 5.00
192 Tim Salmon Jsy/150 3.00 8.00
193 Tim Redding Jsy/250 2.00 5.00
194 Runelvys Hernandez Jsy/250 2.00 5.00
195 Ramon Nivar Jsy/150 2.00 5.00
201 R.Clemens Yanks Jsy/150 4.00 10.00
202 G.Maddux Braves Jsy/250 5.00 12.00
203 V.Guerrero Expos Jsy/150 3.00 8.00
204 Miguel Tejada Jsy/150 2.00 5.00
205 Kevin Brown Jsy/250 2.00 5.00
206 Jason Giambi A's Jsy/150 2.00 5.00
207 C.Schilling D'backs Jsy/150 2.00 5.00
208 Alex Rodriguez Rgr Jsy/150 4.00 10.00
209 Alf Soriano Yanks Jsy/150 2.00 5.00
210 Ivan Rod Marlins Jsy/150 3.00 8.00
212 Gary Carter LGD Pants/150 3.00 8.00
226 Bob Gibson LGD Jsy/250 4.00 10.00
237 S.Paige LGD CO Jsy/100 25.00 60.00

2004 Leaf Certified Materials Mirror Fabric White

*1-211 p/r 200-215: .4X TO 1X REDp/r150-250
*1-211 p/r 100: .5X TO 1.2X RED p/r 150-250
*1-211 p/r 50: .75X TO 2X RED p/r 250
*212-239 p/r 200: .4X TO 1X RED p/r 150
*212-239 p/r 25: 1.25X TO 3X RED p/r 250
*212-239 p/r 25: 1X TO 2.5X RED p/r 100
212-239 PRINT RUNS B/WN 25-200 #'d PER
RANDOM INSERTS IN PACKS
24 Brandon Webb Pants/200 2.00 5.00
37 Carlos Delgado Jsy/200 2.00 5.00
52 Dewon Brazelton Jsy/200 2.00 5.00
65 Garret Anderson Jsy/200 2.00 5.00
106 Jorge Posada Jsy/200 3.00 8.00
127 Magglio Ordonez Jsy/200 2.00 5.00
128 Manny Ramirez Jsy/200 3.00 8.00
132 Mark Mulder Jsy/200 2.00 5.00
134 Mark Teixeira Jsy/200 3.00 8.00
138 Mike Lowell Jsy/75 2.00 5.00
149 Paul Konerko Jsy/100 2.00 5.00
150 Paul Lo Duca Jsy/200 2.00 5.00
155 Rafael Palmeiro O's Jsy/50 5.00 12.00
166 Roy Oswalt Jsy/100 2.00 5.00
183 Torii Hunter Jsy/200 2.00 5.00
184 Trot Nixon Jsy/50 3.00 8.00
211 Rafael Palmeiro Rgr Jsy/200 3.00 8.00
216 Reggie Jackson LGD Jsy/25 10.00 25.00
217 Ryne Sandberg LGD Jsy/25 20.00 50.00
219 Tony Gwynn LGD Jsy/25 15.00 40.00
220 Don Mattingly LGD Jsy/25 20.00 50.00
221 Mike Schmidt LGD Pants/25 20.00 50.00
222 R.Henderson LGD Jsy/25 12.50 30.00
223 Cal Ripken LGD Jsy/25 40.00 100.00
224 Nolan Ryan LGD Jsy/25 25.00 60.00
225 George Brett LGD Jsy/25 20.00 50.00
227 Lou Brock LGD Jsy/25 10.00 25.00
228 Andre Dawson LGD Jsy/25 6.00 15.00
229 Rod Carew LGD Jkt/25 10.00 25.00
230 Wade Boggs LGD Jsy/25 10.00 25.00
231 R.Clemente LGD Jsy/25 40.00 100.00
232 R.Campy LGD Pants/25 12.50 30.00
233 Babe Ruth LGD Pants/25 150.00 250.00
234 Lou Gehrig LGD Pants/25 -75.00 150.00
235 Ty Cobb LGD Pants/25 60.00 120.00
236 Roger Maris LGD Pants/25 20.00 50.00
238 Ernie Banks LGD Pants/25 12.50 30.00
239 Ted Williams LGD Jkt/25 40.00 100.00

2004 Leaf Certified Materials Fabric of the Game

RANDOM INSERTS IN PACKS
PRINT RUNS B/WN 1-100 COPIES PER
NO PRICING ON QTY OF 10 OR LESS
1 Ozzie Smith Padres Jsy/100 6.00 15.00
2 Al Kaline Pants/100 6.00 15.00
3 Alan Trammell Jsy/100 3.00 8.00
4 Albert Pujols Grey Jsy/100 10.00 25.00
5 Alex Rodriguez M's Jsy/100 5.00 12.00
6 Alex Rodriguez Rgr Jsy/100 5.00 12.00
7 A.Dawson Cubs Jsy/100 3.00 8.00
8 A.Dawson Cubs Pants/100 3.00 8.00
11 Billy Williams Jsy/100 3.00 8.00
12 Bo Jackson Royals Jsy/100 6.00 15.00
13 Bob Feller Jsy/50 6.00 15.00
14 Bob Gibson Jsy/50 6.00 15.00
15 Bobby Doerr Jsy/100 3.00 8.00
16 Brooks Robinson Jsy/25 10.00 25.00
17 Cal Ripken Jsy/100 10.00 25.00
18 Carl Yastrzemski Jsy/100 8.00 20.00
19 Carlton Fisk R.Sox Jsy/100 5.00 12.00
20 Dale Murphy Jsy/100 5.00 12.00
21 D.Strawberry Mets Pants/100 3.00 8.00
22 D.Strawberry Dgr Jsy/100 3.00 8.00
23 Dave Parker Reds Jsy/100 3.00 8.00
24 Dave Parker Pirates Jsy/100 3.00 8.00
25 D.Winfield Yanks Jsy/50 4.00 10.00
26 D.Winfield Padres Jsy/100 3.00 8.00
27 Deion Sanders Jsy/25 10.00 25.00
28 Derek Jeter Jsy/100 10.00 25.00
29 Don Drysdale Jsy/100 6.00 15.00
30 Don Mattingly Jsy/100 8.00 20.00
31 Don Mattingly Jkt/100 8.00 20.00
32 Don Sutton Jsy/100 3.00 8.00
33 Duke Snider Jsy/100 5.00 12.00
34 Dwight Gooden Jsy/100 3.00 8.00
35 Early Wynn Jsy/100 3.00 8.00
36 Eddie Mathews Jsy/50 8.00 20.00
37 Eddie Murray Dgr Jsy/100 5.00 12.00
38 Eddie Murray O's Jsy/100 5.00 12.00
39 Enos Slaughter Jsy/100 6.00 15.00
40 Eric Davis Jsy/50 4.00 10.00
41 Ernie Banks Jsy/100 6.00 15.00
42 Fergie Jenkins Pants/100 3.00 8.00
43 Frank Robinson Jsy/100 3.00 8.00
45 Gary Carter Jsy/100 3.00 8.00
46 Gaylord Perry Jsy/25 6.00 15.00
47 George Brett White Jsy/100 8.00 20.00
48 George Foster Jsy/100 3.00 8.00
49 Hal Newhouser Jsy/100 3.00 8.00
50 Harmon Killebrew Jsy/25 12.50 30.00
51 Harmon Killebrew Pants/25 12.50 30.00
52 Harold Baines Jsy/100 3.00 8.00
53 Hoyt Wilhelm Jsy/50 4.00 10.00
54 Jack Morris Jsy/100 3.00 8.00
56 Catfish Hunter Jsy/100 5.00 12.00
57 Jim Palmer Jsy/100 3.00 8.00
58 Jim Rice Jsy/100 3.00 8.00
59 Joe Carter Jsy/100 3.00 8.00
60 Joe Morgan Reds Jsy/100 3.00 8.00
61 Tommy Lasorda Jsy/100 3.00 8.00
62 Johnny Mize Pants/100 5.00 12.00
63 Johnny Bench Jsy/100 6.00 15.00
64 Jose Canseco Grey Jsy/100 5.00 12.00
65 Juan Marichal Jsy/100 3.00 8.00
66 Kirby Puckett Jsy/100 6.00 15.00
67 Lou Boudreau Jsy/100 3.00 8.00
68 Lou Brock Jsy/100 5.00 12.00
71 Luis Aparicio Jsy/100 3.00 8.00
72 Luis Aparicio Pants/100 3.00 8.00
73 Mariano Rivera Jsy/100 4.00 10.00
74 Mark Grace Cubs Jsy/100 5.00 12.00
75 Mark Prior Jsy/100 3.00 8.00
76 Mel Ott Jsy/25 12.50 30.00
77 Mel Ott Pants/25 20.00 50.00
78 Mike Schmidt Jsy/100 8.00 20.00
79 Mike Schmidt Pants/100 8.00 20.00
80 Mike Schmidt Jkt/100 8.00 20.00
81 Nolan Ryan Angels Jsy/100 10.00 25.00
82 Nolan Ryan Angels Jkt/100 10.00 25.00
83 Nolan Ryan Astros Jsy/100 10.00 25.00
84 Nolan Ryan Astros Jkt/100 10.00 25.00
85 Nolan Ryan Rgr Jsy/100 10.00 25.00
86 Nolan Ryan Rgr Pants/100 20.00 50.00
88 Ozzie Smith Cards Jsy/100 6.00 15.00
89 Paul Molitor Jsy/100 3.00 8.00
90 Pee Wee Reese Jsy/100 5.00 12.00
91 Phil Niekro Jsy/100 3.00 8.00
92 Phil Rizzuto Jsy/100 5.00 12.00
93 Phil Rizzuto Pants/100 5.00 12.00
94 Red Schoendienst Jsy/100 3.00 8.00
95 R.Jackson A's Jkt/100 5.00 12.00
96 R.Jackson Angels Jsy/100 5.00 12.00
97 Richie Ashburn Jsy/100 10.00 25.00
98 R.Henderson Yanks Jsy/50 6.00 15.00
99 Roberto Clemente Jsy/50 30.00 80.00
100 Robin Yount Jsy/100 6.00 15.00
101 R.Carew Angels Jsy/100 5.00 12.00
102 R.Carew Angels Pants/100 5.00 12.00
103 R.Carew Angels Jkt/100 5.00 12.00
104 R.Carew Twins Jsy/100 5.00 12.00
105 R.Clemens Sox Jsy/100 5.00 12.00
106 R.Clemens Yanks Jsy/100 5.00 12.00
107 Roger Maris A's Jsy/100 15.00 40.00
108 Roger Maris A's Pants/100 12.50 30.00
109 Roger Maris Yanks Jsy/100 15.00 40.00
110 Roy Campanella Pants/100 8.00 20.00
111 Ryne Sandberg Jsy/100 8.00 20.00
112 Stan Musial White Jsy/50 12.50 30.00
113 Steve Carlton Phils Jsy/100 3.00 8.00
114 Ted Williams Jsy/100 12.50 30.00
115 Ted Williams Jkt/100 12.50 30.00
116 Thurman Munson Jsy/100 10.00 25.00
117 T.Munson Pants/100 10.00 25.00
118 Tony Gwynn Jsy/100 6.00 15.00
119 Wade Boggs Yanks Jsy/100 5.00 12.00
120 Wade Boggs Sox Jsy/100 5.00 12.00
121 Warren Spahn Jsy/100 6.00 15.00
122 Warren Spahn Pants/100 6.00 15.00
123 Whitey Ford Jsy/100 5.00 12.00
124 Whitey Ford Pants/100 5.00 12.00
125 Will Clark Jsy/100 5.00 12.00
126 Willie McCovey Jsy/100 5.00 12.00
127 W.Stargell Black Jsy/100 5.00 12.00
128 Yogi Berra Jsy/25 12.50 30.00
129 Frankie Frisch Jkt/100 8.00 20.00
130 Marty Marion Jsy/100 3.00 8.00
131 Tommy John Pants/100 3.00 8.00
132 Chipper Jones Jsy/100 4.00 10.00
133 S.Sosa White Jsy/100 4.00 10.00
134 R.Henderson Dgr Jsy/100 4.00 10.00
135 Mike Piazza Dgr Jsy/100 5.00 12.00
136 Mike Piazza Mets Jsy/100 5.00 12.00
137 N.Garciaparra Grey Jsy/100 5.00 12.00
138 Hideo Nomo Dgr Jsy/100 4.00 10.00
139 Hideo Nomo Mets Jsy/50 6.00 15.00
140 R.Johnson M's Jsy/100 4.00 10.00
141 R.Johnson D'backs Jsy/100 4.00 10.00
142 R.Johnson Astros Jsy/100 4.00 10.00
143 J.Giambi Yanks Jsy/100 2.00 5.00
144 Jason Giambi A's Jsy/100 2.00 5.00
145 C.Schilling Phils Jsy/100 2.00 5.00
146 Dennis Eckersley Jsy/100 5.00 12.00
147 Carlton Fisk W.Sox Jkt/100 5.00 12.00
148 Tom Seaver Mets Jsy/25 10.00 25.00
149 Joe Torre Jsy/100 5.00 12.00
150 P.Martinez Sox Jsy/100 3.00 8.00
151 A.Pujols White Jsy/100 10.00 25.00
152 Andre Dawson Sox Jsy/50 4.00 10.00
153 Bert Blyleven Jsy/100 3.00 8.00
154 Bo Jackson Sox Jsy/100 6.00 15.00
155 Cal Ripken Pants/100 15.00 40.00
156 C.Fisk W.Sox Jsy/100 5.00 12.00
157 C.Schill D'backs Jsy/100 2.00 5.00
158 D.Strawberry Yanks Jsy/100 3.00 8.00
159 Dave Concepcion Jsy/100 3.00 8.00
160 Dwight Evans Jsy/100 5.00 12.00
161 Ernie Banks Pants/100 6.00 15.00
163 Gary Carter Pants/100 3.00 8.00
164 Gary Sheffield Jsy/100 2.00 5.00
165 George Brett Blue Jsy/100 8.00 20.00
166 Greg Maddux Jsy/100 5.00 12.00
167 Ivan Rodriguez Jsy/100 3.00 8.00
168 Joe Morgan Giants Jsy/100 3.00 8.00
169 J.Canseco White Jsy/100 5.00 12.00
170 J.Gonzalez Rgr Jsy/100 2.00 5.00
171 J.Gonzalez Indians Jsy/100 2.00 5.00
172 Keith Hernandez Jsy/100 3.00 8.00
173 Ken Boyer Jsy/100 8.00 20.00
174 Kerry Wood Jsy/100 2.00 5.00
175 Lee Smith Jsy/100 3.00 8.00
176 Luis Tiant Jsy/100 3.00 8.00
177 Manny Ramirez Jsy/100 3.00 8.00
178 M.Grace D'backs Jsy/100 5.00 12.00
179 Matt Williams Jsy/100 3.00 8.00
180 Miguel Tejada Jsy/100 2.00 5.00
181 Mike Mussina Jsy/100 3.00 8.00
182 M.Piazza Marlins Jsy/100 5.00 12.00
183 N.Garc White Jsy/100 5.00 12.00
184 P.Martinez Dgr Jsy/100 3.00 8.00
185 Rafael Palmeiro Jsy/100 3.00 8.00
186 R.Jackson Yanks Pants/100 5.00 12.00
187 R.Henderson M's Jsy/100 4.00 10.00
188 R.Hend Mets Pants/100 4.00 10.00
189 R.Henderson A's Jsy/100 4.00 10.00
190 Sammy Sosa Blue Jsy/100 4.00 10.00
191 Satchel Paige CO Jsy/100 25.00 60.00
192 Shawn Green Jsy/100 2.00 5.00
193 Stan Musial Grey Jsy/50 12.50 30.00
194 Steve Carlton Sox Jsy/100 3.00 8.00
195 Steve Garvey Jsy/100 3.00 8.00
196 Tom Seaver Reds Jsy/100 5.00 12.00
197 Tony Gwynn Pants/100 6.00 15.00
198 Vladimir Guerrero Jsy/100 4.00 10.00
199 Wade Boggs Rays Jsy/100 5.00 12.00
200 W.Stargell Grey Jsy/100 5.00 12.00

2004 Leaf Certified Materials Fabric of the Game AL/NL

*AL/NL p/r 100: 4X TO 1X FOTG p/r 100
*AL/NL p/r 50: .6X TO 1.5X FOTG p/r 100
*AL/NL p/r 50: .4X TO 1X FOTG p/r 50
*AL/NL p/r 25: 1X TO 2.5X FOTG p/r 100
*AL/NL p/r 25: .6X TO 1.5X FOTG p/r 50
*AL/NL p/r 25: .4X TO 1X FOTG p/r 25
RANDOM INSERTS IN PACKS
PRINT RUNS B/WN 1-100 #'d COPIES PER
NO PRICING ON QTY OF 10 OR LESS

2004 Leaf Certified Materials Fabric of the Game Jersey Number

*JSY # p/r 72: .4X TO 1X FOTG p/r 100
*JSY # p/r 36-53: .6X TO 1.5X FOTG p/r 100
*JSY # p/r 36-53: .4X TO 1X FOTG p/r 50
*JSY # p/r 36-53: .25X TO .6X FOTG p/r 25
*JSY # p/r 20-35: 1X TO 2.5X FOTG p/r 100
*JSY # p/r 20-35: .6X TO 1.5X FOTG p/r 50
*JSY # p/r 20-35: .4X TO 1X FOTG p/r 25
*JSY # p/r 15-19: 1.25X TO 3X FOTG p/r 100
*JSY # p/r 15-19: .75X TO 2X FOTG p/r 50
RANDOM INSERTS IN PACKS
PRINT RUNS B/WN 1-72 #'d COPIES PER
NO PRICING ON QTY OF 14 OR LESS
44 Fred Lynn Jsy/19 8.00 20.00
55 Jackie Robinson Jsy/42 25.00 60.00

2004 Leaf Certified Materials Fabric of the Game Jersey Year

*JSY YR p/r 66-99: .4X TO 1X FOTG p/r 100
*JSY YR p/r 66-99: .25X TO .6X FOTG p/r 50
*JSY YR p/r 66-99: .15X TO .4X FOTG p/r 25
*JSY YR p/r 38-65: .6X TO 1.5X FOTG p/r 100
*JSY YR p/r 38-65: .4X TO 1X FOTG p/r 50
*JSY YR p/r 38-65: .25X TO .6X FOTG p/r 25
*JSY YR p/r 20-34: 1X TO 2.5X FOTG p/r 100
*JSY YR p/r 19: 1.25X TO 3X FOTG p/r 100
*JSY YR p/r 19: .75X TO 2X FOTG p/r 50
*JSY YR p/r 19: .5X TO 1.2X FOTG p/r 25
RANDOM INSERTS IN PACKS
PRINT RUNS B/WN 1-99 COPIES PER
NO PRICING ON QTY OF 1 CARD
9 Babe Ruth Jsy/25 300.00 500.00
10 Babe Ruth Pants/30 150.00 250.00
44 Fred Lynn Jsy/19 8.00 20.00
55 Jackie Robinson Jsy/19 40.00 100.00
69 Lou Gehrig Jsy/19 175.00 300.00
70 Lou Gehrig Pants/38 100.00 200.00
87 Ty Cobb Pants/25 60.00 120.00

2004 Leaf Certified Materials Fabric of the Game Position

*POS p/r 100: .4X TO 1X FOTG p/r 100
*POS p/r 50: .6X TO 1.5X FOTG p/r 100
*POS p/r 50: .4X TO 1X FOTG p/r 50
*POS p/r 25: 1X TO 2.5X FOTG p/r 100
*POS p/r 25: .6X TO 1.5X FOTG p/r 50
*POS p/r 25: .4X TO 1X FOTG p/r 25
RANDOM INSERTS IN PACKS
PRINT RUNS B/WN 1-100 COPIES PER
NO PRICING ON QTY OF 10 OR LESS

2004 Leaf Certified Materials Fabric of the Game Reward

*RWD p/r 50: .6X TO 1.5X FOTG p/r 100
*RWD p/r 50: .4X TO 1X FOTG p/r 50
*RWD p/r 25: 1X TO 2.5X FOTG p/r 100
*RWD p/r 25: .6X TO 1.5X FOTG p/r 50
*RWD p/r 25: .4X TO 1X FOTG p/r 25
RANDOM INSERTS IN PACKS
PRINT RUNS B/WN 1-50 #'d COPIES PER
NO PRICING ON QTY OF 10 OR LESS
87 Ty Cobb Pants/50 50.00 100.00

2004 Leaf Certified Materials Fabric of the Game Stats

*STAT p/r 66: .4X TO 1X FOTG p/r 100
*STAT p/r 36-57: .6X TO 1.5X FOTG p/r 100
*STAT p/r 36-57: .4X TO 1X FOTG p/r 50
*STAT p/r 36-57: .25X TO .6X FOTG p/r 25
*STAT p/r 20-35: 1X TO 2.5X FOTG p/r 100
*STAT p/r 20-35: .6X TO 1.5X FOTG p/r 50
*STAT p/r 20-35: .4X TO 1X FOTG p/r 25
*STAT p/r 15-19: 1.25X TO 3X FOTG p/r 100
*STAT p/r 15-19: .75X TO 2X FOTG p/r 50
RANDOM INSERTS IN PACKS
PRINT RUNS B/WN 1-66 #'d COPIES PER
NO PRICING ON QTY OF 14 OR LESS
55 Jackie Robinson Jsy/19 40.00 100.00

2004 Leaf Certified Materials Fabric of the Game Autograph AL/NL

RANDOM INSERTS IN PACKS
PRINT RUNS B/WN 1-25 COPIES PER
NO PRICING ON QTY OF 10 OR LESS
15 Bobby Doerr Jsy/25 15.00 40.00

2005 Leaf Certified Materials

COMP.SET w/o SP's (200) 15.00 40.00
COMMON CARD (1-190) .25 .60
COMMON CARD (191-200) .25 .60
COMMON (201-250) p/r 499 1.25 3.00
COMMON AU (201-250) p/r 499 3.00 8.00
COMMON AU (201-250) p/r 299 4.00 10.00
COMMON AU (211) p/r 115 6.00 15.00
201-250 RANDOM INSERTS IN PACKS
201-250 PRINT RUN 499 SERIAL #'d SETS
201-250 T2 PRINT RUN 299 #'d COPIES PER
CARD 211 T3 PRINT RUN 115 #'d COPIES
1 A.J. Burnett .25 .60
2 Adam Dunn .40 1.00
3 Adrian Beltre .60 1.50
4 Bret Boone .25 .60
5 Albert Pujols .75 2.00
6 Alex Rodriguez .75 2.00
7 Alfonso Soriano .40 1.00
8 Andruw Jones .25 .60
9 Andy Pettitte .40 1.00
10 Aramis Ramirez .25 .60
11 Aubrey Huff .25 .60
12 Austin Kearns .25 .60
13 B.J. Upton .40 1.00
14 Brandon Webb .40 1.00
15 Barry Zito .40 1.00
16 Tim Salmon .25 .60
17 Bobby Abreu .25 .60
18 Bobby Crosby .25 .60
19 Brad Penny .25 .60
20 Preston Wilson .25 .60
21 C.C. Sabathia .40 1.00
22 Carl Crawford .40 1.00
23 Keith Foulke .25 .60
24 Carlos Beltran .40 1.00
25 Casey Kotchman .25 .60
26 Chipper Jones .60 1.50
27 Chone Figgins .25 .60
28 Craig Biggio .40 1.00
29 Craig Wilson .25 .60
30 Curt Schilling Sox .40 1.00
31 Danny Kolb .25 .60
32 David Ortiz Sox .60 1.50
33 Orlando Hudson .25 .60
34 David Wright .50 1.25
35 Derek Jeter 1.50 4.00
36 Jake Peavy .25 .60
37 Derrek Lee .25 .60
38 Dontrelle Willis .25 .60
39 Edgar Renteria .25 .60
40 Angel Berroa .25 .60
41 Eric Chavez .25 .60
42 Akinori Otsuka .25 .60
43 Francisco Rodriguez .40 1.00
44 Garret Anderson .25 .60
45 Gary Sheffield .25 .60
46 Greg Maddux Cubs .75 2.00
47 Hideki Matsui 1.00 2.50
48 Hideo Nomo .60 1.50
49 Ichiro Suzuki .75 2.00
50 Ivan Rodriguez Tigers .40 1.00
51 J.D. Drew .25 .60
52 J.T. Snow .25 .60
53 Jack Wilson .25 .60
54 Jamie Moyer .25 .60
55 Jason Bay .25 .60
56 Jason Giambi .25 .60
57 Trot Nixon .25 .60
58 Jason Schmidt .25 .60
59 Jason Varitek .60 1.50
60 Roy Oswalt .40 1.00
61 Javy Lopez .25 .60
62 Eric Byrnes .25 .60
63 Jeff Bagwell .40 1.00
64 Jeff Kent Dgr .25 .60
65 Jeff Suppan .25 .60
66 Jeremy Bonderman .25 .60
67 Jermaine Dye .25 .60
68 Kazuhito Tadano .25 .60
69 Jim Edmonds .40 1.00
70 Jim Thome .40 1.00
71 Johan Santana .40 1.00
72 John Smoltz .60 1.50
73 Johnny Damon .40 1.00
74 Johnny Estrada .25 .60
75 Brett Myers .25 .60
76 Jose Guillen .25 .60
77 Jose Vidro .25 .60
78 Josh Beckett .25 .60
79 Edwin Jackson .25 .60
80 Raul Ibanez .40 1.00
81 Rich Harden .25 .60
82 Justin Morneau .40 1.00
83 Kazuhisa Ishii .25 .60
84 Kazuo Matsui .25 .60
85 Ken Griffey Jr. 1.25 3.00
86 Ken Harvey .25 .60
87 Frank Thomas .60 1.50
88 Kerry Wood .25 .60
89 Wade Miller .25 .60
90 Kevin Millwood .25 .60
91 Jeremy Affeldt .25 .60
92 Francisco Cordero .25 .60
93 Lance Berkman .40 1.00
94 Larry Walker Cards .40 1.00
95 Laynce Nix .25 .60
96 Luis Gonzalez .25 .60
97 Lyle Overbay .25 .60
98 Carlos Zambrano .40 1.00
99 Manny Ramirez .60 1.50
100 Marcus Giles .25 .60
101 Mark Buehrle .40 1.00
102 Mark Loretta .25 .60
103 Mark Mulder .25 .60
104 Mark Prior .40 1.00
105 Mark Teixeira .40 1.00
106 Marlon Byrd .25 .60
107 Rafael Furcal .25 .60
108 Melvin Mora .25 .60
109 Michael Young .25 .60
110 Miguel Cabrera .60 1.50
111 Miguel Tejada O's .40 1.00
112 Mike Lowell .25 .60
113 Mike Mussina .40 1.00
114 Mike Piazza .60 1.50
115 Moises Alou .25 .60
116 Livan Hernandez .25 .60
117 Nomar Garciaparra .40 1.00
118 Omar Vizquel .40 1.00
119 Orlando Cabrera .25 .60
120 Pat Burrell .25 .60
121 Paul Konerko .40 1.00
122 Paul Lo Duca .25 .60
123 Pedro Martinez Mets .40 1.00
124 Rafael Palmeiro O's .40 1.00
125 Randy Johnson .60 1.50
126 Richard Hidalgo .25 .60
127 Richie Sexson .25 .60
128 Magglio Ordonez .40 1.00
129 Roger Clemens Astros .75 2.00
130 Russ Ortiz .25 .60
131 Sammy Sosa Cubs .60 1.50
132 Scott Podsednik .25 .60
133 Scott Rolen .40 1.00
134 Sean Burroughs .25 .60
135 Sean Casey .25 .60
136 Shawn Green D'backs .25 .60
137 Jorge Posada .40 1.00
138 Roy Halladay .40 1.00
139 Steve Finley .25 .60
140 Tim Hudson Braves .40 1.00
141 Todd Helton .40 1.00
142 Tom Glavine Mets .40 1.00
143 Torii Hunter .25 .60
144 Travis Hafner .25 .60
145 Trevor Hoffman .40 1.00
146 Troy Glaus D'backs .25 .60
147 Vernon Wells .25 .60
148 Victor Martinez .40 1.00
149 Vladimir Guerrero Angels .40 1.00
150 Sammy Sosa O's .60 1.50
151 Hank Blalock .25 .60
152 Danny Graves .25 .60
153 Rocco Baldelli .25 .60
154 Carlos Delgado Marlins .25 .60
155 Bubba Nelson .25 .60
156 Kevin Youkilis .25 .60
157 Jacque Jones .25 .60
158 Mike Lieberthal .25 .60
159 Ben Sheets .25 .60
160 Lew Ford .25 .60
161 Ervin Santana .25 .60
162 Jody Gerut .25 .60
163 Nick Johnson .25 .60
164 Brian Roberts .25 .60
165 Joe Nathan .25 .60
166 Mike Sweeney .25 .60
167 Ryan Wagner .25 .60
168 David Dellucci .25 .60
169 Jae Weong Seo .25 .60
170 Tom Gordon .25 .60
171 Carlos Lee .25 .60
172 Octavio Dotel .25 .60
173 Jose Castillo .25 .60
174 Troy Percival .25 .60
175 Carlos Delgado Jays .25 .60
176 Curt Schilling D'backs .40 1.00
177 David Ortiz Twins .60 1.50
178 Greg Maddux Braves .75 2.00
179 Ivan Rodriguez Rgr .40 1.00
180 Jeff Kent Giants .25 .60
181 Larry Walker Rockies .40 1.00
182 Miguel Tejada A's .40 1.00
183 Pedro Martinez Sox .40 1.00
184 Rafael Palmeiro Rgr .40 1.00
185 Roger Clemens Yanks .75 2.00
186 Shawn Green Dgr .25 .60
187 Tim Hudson A's .40 1.00
188 Tom Glavine Braves .40 1.00
189 Troy Glaus Angels .25 .60
190 Vladimir Guerrero Expos .40 1.00
191 Cal Ripken LGD 2.00 5.00
192 Don Mattingly LGD 1.25 3.00
193 George Brett LGD 1.25 3.00
194 Harmon Killebrew LGD .60 1.50
195 Mike Schmidt LGD 1.00 2.50
196 Nolan Ryan LGD 2.00 5.00
197 Stan Musial LGD 1.00 2.50
198 Tony Gwynn LGD .75 2.00
199 Wade Boggs LGD .40 1.00
200 Willie Mays LGD 1.25 3.00
201 A.Concepcion NG AU RC 3.00 8.00
202 Agustin Montero NG AU RC 3.00 8.00
203 Carlos Ruiz NG AU RC 5.00 12.00
204 C.Rogowski NG AU RC 4.00 10.00
205 Chris Resop NG AU RC 4.00 10.00
206 Chris Roberson NG AU RC 3.00 8.00
207 Colter Bean NG RC 1.25 3.00
208 Danny Rueckel NG AU RC 3.00 8.00
209 Dave Gassner NG AU RC 3.00 8.00
210 Devon Lowery NG AU RC 3.00 8.00
211 N.Nakamura NG AU T3 RC 15.00 40.00
212 E.Threets NG AU T2 RC 4.00 10.00
213 Garrett Jones NG AU T2 RC 10.00 25.00
214 Geovany Soto NG AU RC 8.00 20.00
215 J.Gothreaux NG AU T2 RC 4.00 10.00
216 J.Hammel NG AU T2 RC 4.00 10.00
217 Jeff Miller NG AU T2 RC 4.00 10.00
218 Jeff Niemann NG AU T2 RC 6.00 15.00
219 Huston Street NG 1.50 4.00
220 John Hattig NG AU RC 3.00 8.00
221 J.Verlander NG AU T2 RC 15.00 40.00
222 Justin Wechsler NG AU RC 3.00 8.00
223 Luke Scott NG AU RC 10.00 25.00
224 Mark McLemore NG AU RC 3.00 8.00
225 M.Woodyard NG AU T2 RC 4.00 10.00
226 M.Lindstrom NG AU T2 RC 4.00 10.00
227 Miguel Negron NG AU RC 4.00 10.00
228 Mike Morse NG AU RC 6.00 15.00
229 Nate McLouth NG AU RC 4.00 10.00
230 P.Reynoso NG AU T2 RC 4.00 10.00
231 Phil Humber NG AU T2 RC 4.00 10.00
232 Tony Pena NG AU RC 3.00 8.00
233 R.Messenger NG AU RC 3.00 8.00
234 Raul Tablado NG AU RC 3.00 8.00
235 Russ Rohlicek NG AU RC 3.00 8.00
236 Ryan Speier NG AU RC 3.00 8.00
237 Scott Munter NG AU RC 3.00 8.00
238 Sean Thompson NG AU RC 3.00 8.00
239 Sean Tracey NG AU T2 RC 4.00 10.00
240 Marcos Carvajal NG RC 1.25 3.00
241 Travis Bowyer NG AU RC 3.00 8.00
242 Ubaldo Jimenez NG AU RC 4.00 10.00
243 W.Balentien NG AU RC 4.00 10.00
244 Eude Brito NG RC 1.25 3.00
245 Ambiorix Burgos NG RC 1.25 3.00
246 Tadahito Iguchi NG RC 3.00 8.00
247 Dae-Sung Koo NG RC 1.25 3.00
248 Chris Seddon NG RC 1.25 3.00
249 Keiichi Yabu NG AU RC 6.00 15.00
250 Y.Betancourt NG AU RC 12.00 30.00

2005 Leaf Certified Materials Mirror Blue

*1-190: 2.5X TO 6X BASIC
*191-200: 2.5X TO 6X BASIC
COMMON (201-250) 2.50 6.00
SEMIS 201-250 4.00 10.00
UNLISTED 201-250 6.00 15.00
RANDOM INSERTS IN PACKS
STATED PRINT RUN 50 SERIAL #'d SETS
201 Ambiorix Concepcion NG 2.50 6.00
202 Agustin Montero NG 2.50 6.00
203 Carlos Ruiz NG 4.00 10.00
204 Casey Rogowski NG 4.00 10.00
205 Chris Resop NG 2.50 6.00
206 Chris Roberson NG 2.50 6.00
207 Colter Bean NG 2.50 6.00
208 Danny Rueckel NG 2.50 6.00
209 Dave Gassner NG 2.50 6.00
210 Devon Lowery NG 2.50 6.00
211 Norihiro Nakamura NG 2.50 6.00
212 Erick Threets NG 2.50 6.00
213 Garrett Jones NG 4.00 10.00
214 Geovany Soto NG 12.00 30.00
215 Jared Gothreaux NG 2.50 6.00
216 Jason Hammel NG 6.00 15.00
217 Jeff Miller NG 2.50 6.00
218 Jeff Niemann NG 6.00 15.00
219 Huston Street NG 2.50 6.00
220 John Hattig NG 2.50 6.00
222 Justin Wechsler NG 2.50 6.00
223 Luke Scott NG 6.00 15.00
224 Mark McLemore NG 2.50 6.00
225 Mark Woodyard NG 2.50 6.00
226 Matt Lindstrom NG 2.50 6.00
227 Miguel Negron NG 4.00 10.00
228 Mike Morse NG 8.00 20.00
229 Nate McLouth NG 4.00 10.00
230 Paulino Reynoso NG 2.50 6.00
231 Phil Humber NG 6.00 15.00
232 Tony Pena NG 2.50 6.00
233 Randy Messenger NG 2.50 6.00
234 Raul Tablado NG 2.50 6.00
235 Russ Rohlicek NG 2.60 6.00
236 Ryan Speier NG 2.50 6.00
237 Scott Munter NG 2.50 6.00
238 Sean Thompson NG 2.50 6.00
239 Sean Tracey NG 2.50 6.00
240 Marcos Carvajal NG 2.50 6.00
241 Travis Bowyer NG 2.50 6.00
243 Wladimir Balentien NG 4.00 10.00
244 Eude Brito NG 2.50 6.00
245 Ambiorix Burgos NG 2.50 6.00
246 Tadahito Iguchi NG 4.00 10.00
247 Dae-Sung Koo NG 2.50 6.00
248 Chris Seddon NG 2.50 6.00
249 Keiichi Yabu NG 2.50 6.00
250 Yuniesky Betancourt NG 10.00 25.00

2005 Leaf Certified Materials Mirror Gold

*GOLD 1-190: 4X TO 10X BASIC
*GOLD 191-200: 4X TO 10X BASIC
RANDOM INSERTS IN PACKS
STATED PRINT RUN 25 SERIAL #'d SETS
201-250 NO PRICING DUE TO SCARCITY

2005 Leaf Certified Materials Mirror Red

*1-190: 1.5X TO 4X BASIC
*191-200: 1.5X TO 4X BASIC
COMMON (201-250) 1.50 4.00
SEMIS 201-250 2.50 6.00
UNLISTED 201-250 4.00 10.00
RANDOM INSERTS IN PACKS
STATED PRINT RUN 100 SERIAL #'d SETS
201 Ambiorix Concepcion NG 1.50 4.00
202 Agustin Montero NG 1.50 4.00
203 Carlos Ruiz NG 2.50 6.00
204 Casey Rogowski NG 2.50 6.00
205 Chris Resop NG 1.50 4.00
206 Chris Roberson NG 1.50 4.00
207 Colter Bean NG 1.50 4.00
208 Danny Rueckel NG 1.50 4.00
209 Dave Gassner NG 1.50 4.00
210 Devon Lowery NG 1.50 4.00
211 Norihiro Nakamura NG 1.50 4.00
212 Erick Threets NG 1.50 4.00
213 Garrett Jones NG 2.50 6.00
214 Geovany Soto NG 8.00 20.00
215 Jared Gothreaux NG 1.50 4.00
216 Jason Hammel NG 4.00 10.00
217 Jeff Miller NG 1.50 4.00
218 Jeff Niemann NG 4.00 10.00
219 Huston Street NG 1.50 4.00
220 John Hattig NG 1.50 4.00
221 Justin Verlander NG 30.00 80.00
222 Justin Wechsler NG 1.50 4.00
223 Luke Scott NG 4.00 10.00
224 Mark McLemore NG 1.50 4.00
225 Mark Woodyard NG 1.50 4.00
226 Matt Lindstrom NG 1.50 4.00
227 Miguel Negron NG 2.50 6.00
228 Mike Morse NG 5.00 12.00
229 Nate McLouth NG 2.50 6.00
230 Paulino Reynoso NG 1.50 4.00
231 Phil Humber NG 4.00 10.00
232 Tony Pena NG 1.50 4.00
233 Randy Messenger NG 1.50 4.00
234 Raul Tablado NG 1.50 4.00
235 Russ Rohlicek NG 1.50 4.00
236 Ryan Speier NG 1.50 4.00
237 Scott Munter NG 1.50 4.00
238 Sean Thompson NG 1.50 4.00
239 Sean Tracey NG 1.50 4.00
240 Marcos Carvajal NG 1.50 4.00
241 Travis Bowyer NG 1.50 4.00
242 Ubaldo Jimenez NG 6.00 15.00
243 Wladimir Balentien NG 2.50 6.00
244 Eude Brito NG 1.50 4.00
245 Ambiorix Burgos NG 1.50 4.00
246 Tadahito Iguchi NG 2.50 6.00
247 Dae-Sung Koo NG 1.50 4.00
248 Chris Seddon NG 1.50 4.00
249 Keiichi Yabu NG 1.50 4.00
250 Yuniesky Betancourt NG 6.00 15.00

2005 Leaf Certified Materials Mirror White

*1-190: 1.5X TO 4X BASIC
*191-200: 1.5X TO 4X BASIC
COMMON (201-250) 1.50 4.00
SEMIS 201-250 2.50 6.00
UNLISTED 201-250 4.00 10.00
RANDOM INSERTS IN PACKS
201 Ambiorix Concepcion NG 1.50 4.00
202 Agustin Montero NG 1.50 4.00
203 Carlos Ruiz NG 2.50 6.00
204 Casey Rogowski NG 2.50 6.00
205 Chris Resop NG 1.50 4.00
206 Chris Roberson NG 1.50 4.00
207 Colter Bean NG 1.50 4.00
208 Danny Rueckel NG 1.50 4.00
209 Dave Gassner NG 1.50 4.00
210 Devon Lowery NG 1.50 4.00
211 Norihiro Nakamura NG 1.50 4.00
212 Erick Threets NG 1.50 4.00
213 Garrett Jones NG 2.50 6.00
214 Geovany Soto NG 8.00 20.00
215 Jared Gothreaux NG 1.50 4.00
216 Jason Hammel NG 4.00 10.00
217 Jeff Miller NG 1.50 4.00
218 Jeff Niemann NG 4.00 10.00
219 Huston Street NG 1.50 4.00
220 John Hattig NG 1.50 4.00
221 Justin Verlander NG 30.00 80.00
222 Justin Wechsler NG 1.50 4.00
223 Luke Scott NG 4.00 10.00
224 Mark McLemore NG 1.50 4.00
225 Mark Woodyard NG 1.50 4.00
226 Matt Lindstrom NG 1.50 4.00
227 Miguel Negron NG 2.50 6.00
228 Mike Morse NG 5.00 12.00
229 Nate McLouth NG 2.50 6.00
230 Paulino Reynoso NG 1.50 4.00
231 Phil Humber NG 4.00 10.00
232 Tony Pena NG 1.50 4.00
233 Randy Messenger NG 1.50 4.00
234 Raul Tablado NG 1.50 4.00
235 Russ Rohlicek NG 1.50 4.00
236 Ryan Speier NG 1.50 4.00
237 Scott Munter NG 1.50 4.00
238 Sean Thompson NG 1.50 4.00
239 Sean Tracey NG 1.50 4.00
240 Marcos Carvajal NG 1.50 4.00
241 Travis Bowyer NG 1.50 4.00
243 Wladimir Balentien NG 2.50 6.00
244 Eude Brito NG 1.50 4.00
245 Ambiorix Burgos NG 1.50 4.00
246 Tadahito Iguchi NG 2.50 6.00

247 Dae-Sung Koo NG 1.50 4.00
248 Chris Seddon NG 1.50 4.00
249 Keiichi Yabu NG 1.50 4.00
250 Yuniesky Betancourt NG 6.00 15.00

2005 Leaf Certified Materials Mirror Autograph Blue

*1-190 p/r 100: .5X TO 1.2X RED p/r 250
*1-190 p/r 50: .5X TO 1.2X RED p/r 100
*1-190 p/r 25: .5X TO 1.2X RED p/r 50
*1-190 p/r 25: .4X TO 1X RED p/r 25
*201-250 p/r 49: .5X TO 1.2X RED p/r 99
OVERALL AU-GU ODDS 4 PER BOX
PRINT RUNS B/WN 1-100 COPIES PER
1-200 NO PRICING ON 10 OR LESS
201-250 NO PRICING ON 25 OR LESS

2005 Leaf Certified Materials Mirror Autograph Gold

*1-190 p/r 25: .75X TO 2X RED p/r 250
*1-190 p/r 25: .6X TO 1.5X RED p/r 100
*1-190 p/r 25: .5X TO 1.2X RED p/r 50
*1-190 p/r 25: .4X TO 1X RED p/r 25
OVERALL AU-GU ODDS 4 PER BOX
PRINT RUNS B/WN 1-25 COPIES PER
1-200 NO PRICING ON QTY OF 5 OR LESS
201-250 NO PRICING DUE TO SCARCITY
2 Adam Dunn/25 15.00 40.00
11 Aubrey Huff/25 10.00 25.00
12 Austin Kearns/25 6.00 15.00
13 B.J. Upton/25 10.00 25.00
14 Brandon Webb/25 6.00 15.00
19 Brad Penny/25 6.00 15.00
21 C.C. Sabathia/25 10.00 25.00
23 Keith Foulke/25 15.00 40.00
27 Chone Figgins/25 6.00 15.00
29 Craig Wilson/25 6.00 15.00
31 Danny Kolb/25 6.00 15.00
34 David Wright/25 30.00 60.00
36 Jake Peavy/25 15.00 40.00
37 Derrek Lee/25 20.00 50.00
39 Edgar Renteria/25 10.00 25.00
40 Angel Berroa/25 6.00 15.00
41 Eric Chavez/25 10.00 25.00
42 Akinori Otsuka/25 10.00 25.00
43 Francisco Rodriguez/25 15.00 40.00
44 Garret Anderson/25 10.00 25.00
54 Jamie Moyer/25 10.00 25.00
55 Jason Bay/25 10.00 25.00
57 Trot Nixon/25 10.00 25.00
60 Roy Oswalt/25 10.00 25.00
63 Jeff Bagwell/25 30.00 60.00
65 Jeff Suppan/25 10.00 25.00
75 Brett Myers/25 10.00 25.00
76 Jose Guillen/25 10.00 25.00
77 Jose Vidro/25 10.00 25.00
81 Rich Harden/25 10.00 25.00
97 Lyle Overbay/25 10.00 25.00
98 Carlos Zambrano/25 15.00 40.00
101 Mark Buehrle/25 20.00 50.00
102 Mark Loretta/25 6.00 15.00
107 Rafael Furcal/25 10.00 25.00
109 Michael Young/25 10.00 25.00
110 Miguel Cabrera/25 20.00 50.00
116 Livan Hernandez/25 10.00 25.00
118 Omar Vizquel/25 15.00 40.00
119 Orlando Cabrera/25 10.00 25.00
121 Paul Konerko/25 15.00 40.00
128 Magglio Ordonez/25 10.00 25.00
130 Russ Ortiz/25 6.00 15.00
134 Sean Burroughs/25 6.00 15.00
135 Sean Casey/25 10.00 25.00
139 Steve Finley/25 10.00 25.00
143 Torii Hunter/25 10.00 25.00
144 Travis Hafner/25 10.00 25.00
147 Vernon Wells/25 10.00 25.00
152 Danny Graves/25 6.00 15.00
157 Jacque Jones/25 10.00 25.00
158 Mike Lieberthal/25 10.00 25.00
163 Nick Johnson/25 10.00 25.00
170 Tom Gordon/25 6.00 15.00
171 Carlos Lee/25 10.00 25.00
172 Octavio Dotel/25 6.00 15.00
174 Troy Percival/25 10.00 25.00
194 Harmon Killebrew LGD/25 30.00 60.00

2005 Leaf Certified Materials Mirror Autograph Red

OVERALL AU-GU ODDS 4 PER BOX
PRINT RUNS B/WN 1-250 COPIES PER
1-200 NO PRICING ON QTY OF 10 OR LESS
201-250 NO PRICING ON QTY OF 19 OR LESS
16 Tim Salmon/25 15.00 40.00
18 Bobby Crosby/50 8.00 20.00
25 Casey Kotchman/50 8.00 20.00
33 Orlando Hudson/250 3.00 8.00
53 Jack Wilson/50 8.00 20.00
62 Eric Byrnes/50 5.00 12.00
66 Jeremy Bonderman/50 8.00 20.00
67 Jermaine Dye/50 8.00 20.00
68 Kazuhito Tadano/100 6.00 15.00
79 Edwin Jackson/250 6.00 15.00
80 Raul Ibanez/50 10.00 25.00
86 Ken Harvey/250 3.00 8.00
89 Wade Miller/250 3.00 8.00
91 Jeremy Affeldt/250 3.00 8.00
92 Francisco Cordero/25 10.00 25.00
95 Laynce Nix/100 4.00 10.00
106 Marlon Byrd/250 3.00 8.00
155 Bubba Nelson/250 3.00 8.00
156 Kevin Youkilis/50 5.00 12.00
160 Lew Ford/50 5.00 12.00
161 Ervin Santana/250 3.00 8.00
162 Jody Gerut/50 5.00 12.00
164 Brian Roberts/25 10.00 25.00
165 Joe Nathan/50 8.00 20.00
167 Ryan Wagner/50 5.00 12.00
168 David Dellucci/50 12.50 30.00
169 Jae Weong Seo/25 6.00 15.00
173 Jose Castillo/250 3.00 8.00
202 Agustin Montero NG/99 3.00 8.00
211 Norihiro Nakamura NG/99 20.00 50.00
218 Jeff Niemann NG/49 10.00 25.00
221 Justin Verlander NG/50 60.00 120.00
223 Luke Scott NG/99 12.50 30.00
229 Nate McLouth NG/99 8.00 20.00
230 Paulino Reynoso NG/49 4.00 10.00
231 Phil Humber NG/49 12.50 30.00
234 Raul Tablado NG/99 3.00 8.00
239 Sean Tracey NG/49 4.00 10.00
243 Wladimir Balentien NG/99 8.00 20.00

2005 Leaf Certified Materials Mirror Autograph White

*1-190 p/r 50: .6X TO 1.5X RED p/r 250
*1-190 p/r 50: .5X TO 1.2X RED p/r 100
*1-190 p/r 25: .75X TO 2X RED p/r 250
*1-190 p/r 25: .5X TO 1.2X RED p/r 50
*201-250 p/r 49: .5X TO 1.2X RED p/r 99
*201-250 p/r 49: .4X TO 1X RED p/r 49
OVERALL AU-GU ODDS 4 PER BOX
PRINT RUNS B/WN 1-50 COPIES PER
1-200 NO PRICING ON QTY OF 10 OR LESS
201-250 NO PRICING ON QTY OF 15 OR LESS
19 Brad Penny/25 6.00 15.00
81 Rich Harden/50 8.00 20.00
211 Norihiro Nakamura NG/49 30.00 60.00

2005 Leaf Certified Materials Mirror Bat Blue

*BLUEp/r75-100: .5X TO 1.2X REDp/r200-250
*BLUE p/r 75-100: .4X TO 1X RED p/r 100
OVERALL AU-GU ODDS 4 PER BOX
PRINT RUNS B/WN 75-100 COPIES PER
32 David Ortiz Sox/100 3.00 8.00
37 Derrek Lee/100 3.00 8.00
117 Nomar Garciaparra/100 4.00 10.00
144 Travis Hafner/100 2.50 6.00

2005 Leaf Certified Materials Mirror Bat Gold

*GOLD: .75X TO 2X RED p/r 200-250
*GOLD: .6X TO 1.5X RED p/r 100
*GOLD: .5X TO 1.2X RED p/r 50
OVERALL AU-GU ODDS 4 PER BOX
STATED PRINT RUN 25 SERIAL #'d SETS
7 Alfonso Soriano 4.00 10.00
24 Carlos Beltran 4.00 10.00
30 Curt Schilling Sox 5.00 12.00
32 David Ortiz Sox 5.00 12.00
37 Derrek Lee 5.00 12.00
39 Edgar Renteria 4.00 10.00
78 Josh Beckett 4.00 10.00
84 Kazuo Matsui 4.00 10.00
88 Kerry Wood 4.00 10.00
97 Lyle Overbay 4.00 10.00
117 Nomar Garciaparra 6.00 15.00
140 Tim Hudson Braves 4.00 10.00
144 Travis Hafner 4.00 10.00

2005 Leaf Certified Materials Mirror Bat Red

OVERALL AU-GU ODDS 4 PER BOX
PRINT RUNS B/WN 50-250 COPIES PER
2 Adam Dunn/250 2.00 5.00
5 Albert Pujols/250 6.00 15.00
8 Andruw Jones/250 2.50 6.00
11 Aubrey Huff/250 2.00 5.00
13 B.J. Upton/250 2.00 5.00
14 Brandon Webb/100 2.50 6.00
16 Tim Salmon/250 2.50 6.00
25 Casey Kotchman/250 2.00 5.00
26 Chipper Jones/250 3.00 8.00
28 Craig Biggio/50 4.00 10.00
29 Craig Wilson/250 2.00 5.00
34 David Wright/250 4.00 10.00
38 Dontrelle Willis/250 2.00 5.00
44 Garret Anderson/250 2.00 5.00
45 Gary Sheffield/250 2.00 5.00
59 Jason Varitek/250 3.00 8.00
61 Javy Lopez/250 2.00 5.00
63 Jeff Bagwell/250 2.50 6.00
77 Jose Vidro/250 2.00 5.00
93 Lance Berkman/250 2.00 5.00
99 Manny Ramirez/250 2.50 6.00
105 Mark Teixeira/250 2.50 6.00
109 Michael Young/250 2.00 5.00
110 Miguel Cabrera/250 2.50 6.00
111 Miguel Tejada O's/250 2.00 5.00
121 Paul Konerko/250 2.00 5.00
124 Rafael Palmeiro O's/250 2.50 6.00
128 Magglio Ordonez/250 2.00 5.00
136 Shawn Green D'backs/250 2.00 5.00
141 Todd Helton/250 2.50 6.00
142 Tom Glavine Mets/250 2.50 6.00
143 Torii Hunter/200 2.00 5.00
148 Victor Martinez/250 2.00 5.00
149 V.Guerrero Angels/250 3.00 8.00
150 Sammy Sosa O's/250 3.00 8.00
153 Rocco Baldelli/250 2.00 5.00
160 Lew Ford/250 2.00 5.00
166 Mike Sweeney/100 2.50 6.00
184 Rafael Palmeiro Rgr/100 3.00 8.00
188 Tom Glavine Braves/250 2.50 6.00
190 V.Guerrero Expos/250 3.00 8.00

2005 Leaf Certified Materials Mirror Bat White

*WHITE p/r 250: .4X TO 1X RED p/r 200-250
*WHITE p/r 250: .3X TO .8X RED p/r 100
*WHITEp/r75-100: .5XTO1.2X REDp/r200-250
*WHITE p/r 75-100: .3X TO .8X RED p/r 50
*WHITE p/r 50: .5X TO 1.2X RED p/r 100
OVERALL AU-GU ODDS 4 PER BOX
PRINT RUNS B/WN 50-250 COPIES PER

2005 Leaf Certified Materials Mirror Fabric Black HR

OVERALL AU-GU ODDS 4 PER BOX
STATED PRINT RUN 1 SERIAL #'d SET
NO PRICING DUE TO SCARCITY

2005 Leaf Certified Materials Mirror Fabric Black MLB Logo

OVERALL AU-GU ODDS 4 PER BOX
STATED PRINT RUN 1 SERIAL #'d SET
NO PRICING DUE TO SCARCITY

2005 Leaf Certified Materials Mirror Fabric Black Number

OVERALL AU-GU ODDS 4 PER BOX
STATED PRINT RUN 1 SERIAL #'d SET
NO PRICING DUE TO SCARCITY

2005 Leaf Certified Materials Mirror Fabric Black Position

OVERALL AU-GU ODDS 4 PER BOX
STATED PRINT RUN 1 SERIAL #'d SET
NO PRICING DOE TO SCARCITY

2005 Leaf Certified Materials Mirror Fabric Black Prime

OVERALL AU-GU ODDS 4 PER BOX
STATED PRINT RUN 1 SERIAL #'d SET
NO PRICING DUE TO SCARCITY

2005 Leaf Certified Materials Mirror Fabric Blue

*BLUE p/r 100: .5X TO 1.2X RED p/r 225-250
*BLUE p/r 100: .4X TO 1X RED p/r 100
*BLUE p/r 50: .6X TO 1.5X RED p/r 225-250
OVERALL AU-GU ODDS 4 PER BOX
PRINT RUNS B/WN 50-100 COPIES PER
18 Bobby Crosby Jsy/50 3.00 8.00
73 Johnny Damon Jsy/100 3.00 8.00
78 Josh Beckett Jsy/100 2.50 6.00
113 Mike Mussina Jsy/50 4.00 10.00
151 Hank Blalock Jsy/100 2.50 6.00

2005 Leaf Certified Materials Mirror Fabric Emerald

OVERALL AU-GU ODDS 4 PER BOX
STATED PRINT RUN 5 SERIAL #'d SETS
NO PRICING DUE TO SCARCITY

2005 Leaf Certified Materials Mirror Fabric Gold

*GOLD: .75X TO 2X RED p/r 225-250
*GOLD: .6X TO 1.5X RED p/r 100
OVERALL AU-GU ODDS 4 PER BOX
STATED PRINT RUN 25 SERIAL #'d SETS
18 Bobby Crosby Jsy 4.00 10.00
55 Jason Bay Jsy 4.00 10.00
77 Jose Vidro Jsy 4.00 10.00
78 Josh Beckett Jsy 4.00 10.00
105 Mark Teixeira Jsy 5.00 12.00
108 Melvin Mora Jsy 4.00 10.00
151 Hank Blalock Jsy 4.00 10.00

2005 Leaf Certified Materials Mirror Fabric Red

OVERALL AU-GU ODDS 4 PER BOX
PRINT RUNS B/WN 100-250 COPIES PER
2 Adam Dunn Jsy/250 2.00 5.00
5 Albert Pujols Jsy/250 6.00 15.00
7 Alfonso Soriano Jsy/250 2.00 5.00
8 Andruw Jones Jsy/250 2.50 6.00
10 Aramis Ramirez Jsy/250 2.00 5.00
11 Aubrey Huff Jsy/250 2.00 5.00
13 B.J. Upton Jsy/250 2.00 5.00
14 Brandon Webb Pants/100 2.50 6.00
15 Barry Zito Jsy/250 2.00 5.00
17 Bobby Abreu Jsy/250 2.00 5.00
20 Preston Wilson Jsy/250 2.00 5.00
25 Casey Kotchman Jsy/250 2.00 5.00
26 Chipper Jones Jsy/250 3.00 8.00
28 Craig Biggio Jsy/250 2.50 6.00
30 Curt Schilling Sox Jsy/250 2.50 6.00
32 David Ortiz Sox Jsy/250 3.00 8.00
37 Derrek Lee Jsy/250 2.50 6.00
38 Dontrelle Willis Jsy/225 2.00 5.00
41 Eric Chavez Jsy/250 2.00 5.00
43 F.Rodriguez Jsy/250 2.00 5.00
44 Garret Anderson Jsy/250 2.00 5.00
45 Gary Sheffield Jsy/250 2.00 5.00
46 Greg Maddux Cubs Jsy/250 4.00 10.00
47 Hideki Matsui Jsy/250 6.00 15.00
48 Hideo Nomo Jsy/250 3.00 8.00
50 I.Rodriguez Tigers Jsy/250 2.50 6.00
57 Trot Nixon Jsy/250 2.00 5.00
60 Roy Oswalt Jsy/250 2.00 5.00
61 Javy Lopez Jsy/250 2.00 5.00
63 Jeff Bagwell Jsy/250 2.50 6.00
69 Jim Edmonds Jsy/250 2.00 5.00
70 Jim Thome Jsy/250 2.50 6.00
71 Johan Santana Jsy/250 3.00 8.00
82 Justin Morneau Jsy/250 2.00 5.00
84 Kazuo Matsui Jsy/250 2.00 5.00
87 Frank Thomas Jsy/250 3.00 8.00
88 Kerry Wood Jsy/250 2.00 5.00
92 Francisco Cordero Jsy/250 2.00 5.00
93 Lance Berkman Jsy/250 2.00 5.00
94 Larry Walker Cards Jsy/250 2.50 6.00
96 Luis Gonzalez Jsy/250 2.00 5.00
97 Lyle Overbay Jsy/250 2.00 5.00
98 Carlos Zambrano Jsy/250 2.00 5.00
99 Manny Ramirez Jsy/250 2.50 6.00
104 Mark Prior Jsy/250 2.50 6.00
109 Michael Young Jsy/250 2.00 5.00
110 Miguel Cabrera Jsy/250 2.50 6.00
111 Miguel Tejada O's Jsy/250 2.00 5.00
114 Mike Piazza Jsy/250 3.00 8.00
121 Paul Konerko Jsy/250 2.00 5.00
124 R.Palmeiro O's Jsy/250 2.50 6.00
129 R.Clemens Astros Jsy/250 4.00 10.00
131 Sammy Sosa Cubs Jsy/250 3.00 8.00
133 Scott Rolen Jsy/250 2.50 6.00
135 Sean Casey Jsy/250 2.00 5.00
138 Roy Halladay Jsy/250 2.00 5.00
141 Todd Helton Jsy/250 2.50 6.00
144 Travis Hafner Jsy/250 2.00 5.00
147 Vernon Wells Jsy/250 2.00 5.00
148 Victor Martinez Jsy/250 2.00 5.00
149 V.Guerrero Angels Jsy/250 3.00 8.00
153 Rocco Baldelli Jsy/250 2.00 5.00
159 Ben Sheets Jsy/250 2.00 5.00
160 Lew Ford Jsy/250 2.00 5.00
166 Mike Sweeney Jsy/250 2.00 5.00
178 G.Maddux Braves Jsy/250 10.00 25.00
179 I.Rodriguez Rgr Jsy/250 2.50 6.00
183 P.Martinez Sox Jsy/250 2.50 6.00
184 R.Palmeiro Rgr Jsy/250 2.50 6.00
185 R.Clemens Yanks Jsy/250 4.00 10.00
188 T.Glav Braves Jsy/250 2.50 6.00
190 V.Guer Expos Jsy/100 4.00 10.00

2005 Leaf Certified Materials Mirror Fabric White

*WHITEp/r150-250: .4XTO1X REDp/r225-250
*WHITEp/r100: .5X TO 1.2X REDp/r225-250
*WHITE p/r 50: .6X TO 1.5X RED p/r 225-250
*WHITE p/r 25: .75X TO 2X RED p/r 225-250
OVERALL AU-GU ODDS 4 PER BOX
PRINT RUNS B/WN 25-250 COPIES PER
34 David Wright Jsy/100 5.00 12.00
78 Josh Beckett Jsy/250 2.00 5.00
95 Laynce Nix Jsy/100 2.50 6.00
113 Mike Mussina Jsy/100 3.00 8.00
151 Hank Blalock Jsy/100 2.50 6.00

2005 Leaf Certified Materials Cuts Blue

OVERALL AU-GU ODDS 4 PER BOX
PRINT RUNS B/WN 1-80 COPIES PER
NO PRICING ON QTY OF 10 OR LESS
3 Willie Mays/26 100.00 150.00
7 Jim Palmer/50 8.00 20.00
12 Steve Carlton/50 8.00 20.00
15 Maury Wills/80 6.00 15.00
20 Dale Murphy/50 12.50 30.00

2005 Leaf Certified Materials Cuts Green

*GREEN p/r 80: .4X TO 1X BLUE p/r 80
*GREEN p/r 50: .4X TO 1X BLUE p/r 50
OVERALL AU-GU ODDS 4 PER BOX
PRINT RUNS B/WN 3-80 COPIES PER
NO PRICING ON QTY OF 11 OR LESS

2005 Leaf Certified Materials Cuts Red

*RED p/r 60: .5X TO 1.2X BLUE p/r 80
*RED p/r 50: .4X TO 1X BLUE p/r 50
OVERALL AU-GU ODDS 4 PER BOX
PRINT RUNS B/WN 1-60 COPIES PER
NO PRICING ON QTY OF 10 OR LESS

2005 Leaf Certified Materials Cuts Material Blue

OVERALL AU-GU ODDS 4 PER BOX
PRINT RUNS B/WN 4-43 COPIES PER
NO PRICING ON QTY OF 8 OR LESS
2 Hank Aaron Bat/43 200.00 300.00
3 Willie Mays Pants/24 125.00 200.00
4 Sandy Koufax Jsy/32 175.00 300.00
6 Nolan Ryan Jsy/34 60.00 120.00
7 Jim Palmer Hat/22 15.00 40.00
8 Tony Gwynn Pants/19 30.00 60.00
9 Rod Carew Jsy/29 15.00 40.00
10 Ryne Sandberg Jsy/23 40.00 80.00
12 Steve Carlton Pants/32 10.00 25.00
14 Mike Schmidt Jsy/20 40.00 80.00
19 Don Mattingly Jsy/23 50.00 100.00

2005 Leaf Certified Materials Cuts Material Green

*GRN p/r 20-32: .4X TO 1X BLUE p/r 20-34
*GRN p/r 19: .4X TO 1X BLUE p/r 19
OVERALL AU-GU ODDS 4 PER BOX
PRINT RUNS B/WN 4-32 COPIES PER
NO PRICING ON QTY OF 10 OR LESS
3 Willie Mays Pants/24 125.00 200.00

2005 Leaf Certified Materials Cuts Material Red

*RED p/r 20-32: .4X TO 1X BLUE p/r 20-34
*RED p/r 19: .4X TO 1X BLUE p/r 19
OVERALL AU-GU ODDS 4 PER BOX
PRINT RUNS B/WN 4-32 COPIES PER
NO PRICING ON QTY OF 10 OR LESS
3 Willie Mays Pants/24 125.00 200.00

2005 Leaf Certified Materials Fabric of the Game

1-160 PRINT RUNS B/WN 5-100 COPIES PER
161-180 PRINTS B/WN 10-100 COPIES PER
OVERALL AU-GU ODDS 4 PER BOX
NO PRICING ON QTY OF 10 OR LESS
1 Al Oliver Jsy/50 4.00 10.00
2 Alan Trammell Jsy/100 3.00 8.00
3 A.Galarraga Braves Jsy/100 3.00 8.00
4 A.Galarraga Giants Jsy/100 3.00 8.00
6 Babe Ruth Pants/25 175.00 300.00
7 Billy Martin Pants/100 4.00 10.00
8 Billy Williams Jsy/50 4.00 10.00
9 Bo Jackson Sox Jsy/100 6.00 15.00
10 B.Jackson Royals Jsy/100 5.00 12.00
12 Bob Gibson Jsy/25 6.00 15.00
13 Bobby Doerr Pants/50 4.00 10.00
14 Burleigh Grimes Pants/25 30.00 60.00
15 Cal Ripken Jsy/50 15.00 40.00
16 Cal Ripken Jsy/50 15.00 40.00
17 Carl Yastrzemski Pants/50 6.00 15.00
18 Carlton Fisk Jkt/50 5.00 12.00
19 Catfish Hunter Pants/50 4.00 10.00
20 D.Straw Yanks Jsy/25 5.00 12.00
21 D.Straw Dgr Jsy/100 3.00 8.00
22 Dave Concepcion Jsy/50 4.00 10.00
23 Dave Righetti Jsy/50 4.00 10.00
24 Dave Winfield Pants/100 3.00 8.00
25 David Cone Jsy/100 3.00 8.00
26 David Justice Jsy/100 4.00 10.00
27 D.Sanders Yanks Jsy/50 5.00 12.00
28 D.Sanders Reds Jsy/50 5.00 12.00
29 D.Eckersley Cards Jsy/50 4.00 10.00
30 D.Eckersley A's Pants/50 4.00 10.00
31 Don Mattingly Jsy/100 6.00 15.00
32 Don Sutton Astros Jsy/25 5.00 12.00
33 Don Sutton Dgr Jsy/50 4.00 10.00
37 Dwight Gooden Jsy/100 3.00 8.00
38 Eddie Murray Dgr Jsy/25 8.00 20.00
39 Eddie Murray O's Pants/50 6.00 15.00
40 Edgar Martinez Jsy/100 3.00 8.00
41 Ernie Banks Jsy/25 8.00 20.00
42 Fergie Jenkins Jsy/50 4.00 10.00
43 Frankie Frisch Jkt/50 6.00 15.00
44 Fred Lynn Jsy/50 4.00 10.00
45 Fred McGriff Jsy/100 4.00 10.00
46 Gary Carter Mets Jsy/50 4.00 10.00
47 Gary Carter Expos Jsy/50 4.00 10.00
48 Gaylord Perry M's Jsy/50 4.00 10.00
49 G.Perry Giants Jsy/50 4.00 10.00
50 George Brett Jsy/25 10.00 25.00
51 Hal Newhouser Jsy/50 5.00 12.00
54 H.Killebrew Twins Jsy/25 8.00 20.00
55 H.Kill Senators Jsy/50 6.00 15.00
56 Harold Baines Jsy/50 4.00 10.00
57 Hoyt Wilhelm Jsy/100 3.00 8.00
58 Jack Morris Jsy/100 3.00 8.00
59 Jim Thorpe Jsy/25 125.00 200.00
60 Jose Cruz Jsy/100 3.00 8.00
61 Jim Rice Jsy/50 4.00 10.00
62 Joe Cronin Jsy/50 6.00 15.00
63 Joe Cronin Pants/100 5.00 12.00
64 Joe Morgan Jsy/50 4.00 10.00
65 Joe Torre Jsy/50 5.00 12.00
66 John Kruk Jsy/100 4.00 10.00
67 Johnny Bench Jsy/50 6.00 15.00
68 Juan Marichal Pants/100 3.00 8.00
71 Kirk Gibson Jsy/100 3.00 8.00
72 Lee Smith Jsy/100 3.00 8.00
73 Lenny Dykstra Jsy/100 3.00 8.00
74 Lou Boudreau Jsy/25 6.00 15.00
75 Luis Aparicio Jsy/50 4.00 10.00
76 Luis Tiant Pants/100 3.00 8.00
77 Mark Grace Jsy/50 5.00 12.00
78 Hoyt Wilhelm Jsy/100 3.00 8.00
79 M.Williams Giants Jsy/100 4.00 10.00
80 M.Williams D'backs Jsy/50 5.00 12.00
82 Nolan Ryan Astros Jsy/50 8.00 20.00
83 Nolan Ryan Rgr Jsy/15 10.00 25.00
84 Nolan Ryan Mets Jsy/25 8.00 20.00
85 Nolan Ryan Angels Jsy/25 8.00 20.00
86 Orlando Cepeda Pants/50 4.00 10.00
87 Ozzie Smith Pants/25 8.00 20.00
88 P.Molitor Brewers Jsy/50 4.00 10.00
89 Paul Molitor Twins Jsy/50 4.00 10.00
90 P.Molitor Brewers Pants/50 4.00 10.00
91 Phil Niekro Jsy/50 4.00 10.00
92 R.Jack Yanks Pants/100 4.00 10.00
93 R.Jackson A's Jkt/100 4.00 10.00
94 R.Jackson Angels Jsy/50 5.00 12.00
95 Reggie Jackson A's Jsy/50 5.00 12.00
96 R.Henderson Mets Jkt/100 8.00 20.00
97 R.Henderson Dgr Jsy/50 10.00 25.00
98 R.Henderson A's Jsy/50 10.00 25.00
99 R.Henderson M's Jsy/50 10.00 25.00
100 R.Hend Yanks Jsy/50 10.00 25.00
101 R.Hend Padres Pants/50 10.00 25.00
102 R.Ventura Yanks Jsy/100 3.00 8.00
103 R.Ventura Mets Jsy/100 3.00 8.00
104 Robin Yount Jsy/50 6.00 15.00
105 Rod Carew Angels Jsy/100 4.00 10.00
106 Rod Carew Twins Jsy/100 4.00 10.00
107 Roger Maris Pants/50 12.50 30.00
108 Ron Cey Jsy/50 4.00 10.00
109 Ron Guidry Pants/100 3.00 8.00
110 Ryne Sandberg Jsy/50 15.00 40.00
111 Sandy Koufax Jsy/25 75.00 150.00
112 Stan Musial Jsy/25 10.00 25.00
113 Stan Musial Pants/25 10.00 25.00
114 Steve Garvey Jsy/100 3.00 8.00
115 Ted Williams Jkt/50 20.00 50.00
116 Ted Williams Jsy/25 30.00 60.00
117 Tom Seaver Jsy/50 6.00 15.00
118 Tom Seaver Pants/50 5.00 12.00
119 Tommy John Jsy/100 3.00 8.00
120 Tommy John Pants/100 3.00 8.00
121 Tommy Lasorda Jsy/100 4.00 10.00
122 Tony Gwynn Jsy/100 5.00 12.00
123 Tony Gwynn Pants/100 5.00 12.00
124 Tony Perez Jsy/50 4.00 10.00
125 Wade Boggs Jsy/100 4.00 10.00
126 Warren Spahn Jsy/25 6.00 15.00
127 Whitey Ford Jsy/25 6.00 15.00
128 Will Clark Jsy/50 5.00 12.00
129 Willie Mays Pants/50 15.00 40.00
130 Willie McCovey Pants/100 4.00 10.00
131 R.Clemens Astros Jsy/50 6.00 15.00
132 R.Clemens Yanks Jsy/50 6.00 15.00
133 Roger Clemens Sox Jsy/50 6.00 15.00
134 Randy Johnson M's Jsy/50 5.00 12.00
135 R.Johnson Expos Jsy/50 5.00 12.00
136 Cal Ripken Jsy/50 15.00 40.00
137 Don Mattingly Jsy/100 6.00 15.00
138 George Brett Jsy/25 30.00 60.00
139 H.Killebrew Twins Jsy/25 8.00 20.00
140 Mike Schmidt Jsy/50 8.00 20.00
141 Nolan Ryan Angels Jkt/25 12.50 30.00
143 Tony Gwynn Jsy/100 5.00 12.00
144 Wade Boggs Jsy/50 5.00 12.00
145 Willie Mays Jsy/25 20.00 50.00
146 Hideo Nomo Jsy/100 4.00 10.00
147 D.Murphy Braves Jsy/100 4.00 10.00
148 D.Murphy Phils Jsy/100 4.00 10.00
149 Bo Jackson Royals Jsy/50 6.00 15.00
150 D.Straw Dgr Jsy/50 4.00 10.00
151 D.Sanders Yanks Jsy/50 5.00 12.00
152 D.Sanders Yanks Pants/50 5.00 12.00
153 D.Eckersley A's Jsy/50 4.00 10.00
154 Dwight Gooden Jsy/100 3.00 8.00
155 Edgar Martinez Jsy/100 4.00 10.00
156 Lou Brock Jsy/50 5.00 12.00
157 Steve Carlton Pants/50 4.00 10.00
158 Albert Pujols Jsy/50 10.00 25.00
159 Tom Glavine Jsy/100 4.00 10.00
160 Hideki Matsui Pants/50 10.00 25.00
161 B.Ruth P/J.Thorpe J/25 300.00 500.00
162 T.Will JK/S.Musial J/50 30.00 60.00
164 W.Ford J/S.Koufax J/25 75.00 150.00
165 R.Maris P/D.Matt J/25 12.50 30.00
166 N.Ryan J/T.Seaver J/50 15.00 40.00
167 C.Ripken J/G.Brett J/100 12.00 30.00
168 R.Sand J/M.Schmidt J/50 15.00 40.00
169 T.Gwynn J/W.Boggs J/50 8.00 20.00
170 C.Fisk J/J.Bench P/50 8.00 20.00
172 R.Jackson P/D.Straw J/50 6.00 15.00
173 R.Yount J/P.Molitor J/50 8.00 20.00
174 W.Spahn P/J.Marichal J/50 6.00 15.00
175 B.Jackson J/Deion P/100 6.00 15.00
176 T.Gwynn J/R.Hend J/100 10.00 25.00
177 H.Matsui J/J.Edm J/100 10.00 25.00
178 R.Hend P/L.Brock J/100 10.00 25.00
179 R.Clem J/A.Pujols J/100 10.00 25.00
180 H.Nomo J/K.Ishii J/100 6.00 15.00

2005 Leaf Certified Materials Fabric of the Game Jersey Number

*1-160 p/r 72: .3X TO .8X FOTG p/r 50
*1-160 p/r 36-55: .5X TO 1.2X FOTG p/r 100
*1-160 p/r 36-55: .4X TO 1X FOTG p/r 50
*1-160 p/r 36-55: .3X TO .8X FOTG p/r 25
*1-160 p/r 20-35: .6X TO 1.5X FOTG p/r 100
*1-160 p/r 20-35: .5X TO 1.2X FOTG p/r 50
*1-160 p/r 20-35: .4X TO 1X FOTG p/r 25
*1-160 p/r 20-35: .3X TO .8X FOTG p/r 15
*1-160 p/r 15-19: .75X TO 2X FOTG p/r 100
*1-160 p/r 15-19: .6X TO 1.5X FOTG p/r 50
*1-160 p/r 15-19: .5X TO 1.2X FOTG p/r 25
1-160 PRINT RUNS B/WN 1-72 COPIES PER
*161-180 p/r 50: .5X TO 1.2X FOTG p/r 100
*161-180 p/r 50: .4X TO 1X FOTG p/r 50
*161-180 p/r 25: .6X TO 1.5X FOTG p/r 100
*161-180 p/r 25: .5X TO 1.2X FOTG p/r 50
161-180 PRINTS B/WN 3-50 COPIES PER
OVERALL AU-GU ODDS 4 PER BOX
NO PRICING ON QTY OF 14 OR LESS
36 Dwight Evans Jsy/24 6.00 15.00
52 Hank Aaron Atl Jsy/44 20.00 50.00
53 Hank Aaron Mil Jsy/44 20.00 50.00
111 Sandy Koufax Jsy/32 75.00 150.00

2005 Leaf Certified Materials Fabric of the Game Position

*1-160 p/r 100: .4X TO 1X FOTG p/r 100
*1-160 p/r 100: .3X TO .8X FOTG p/r 50
*1-160 p/r 50: .5X TO 1.2X FOTG p/r 100
*1-160 p/r 50: .4X TO 1X FOTG p/r 50
*1-160 p/r 25: .6X TO 1.5X FOTG p/r 100
*1-160 p/r 25: .5X TO 1.2X FOTG p/r 50
*1-160 p/r 25: .4X TO 1X FOTG p/r 25
1-160 PRINT RUNS B/WN 3-100 COPIES PER
*161-180 p/r 100: .4X TO 1X FOTG p/r 100
*161-180 p/r 100: .3X TO .8X FOTG p/r 50
*161-180 p/r 50: .5X TO 1.2X FOTG p/r 100
*161-180 p/r 50: .4X TO 1X FOTG p/r 50
*161-180 p/r 25: .5X TO 1.2X FOTG p/r 50
*161-180 p/r 25: .4X TO 1X FOTG p/r 25
161-180 PRINTS B/WN 5-100 COPIES PER
OVERALL AU-GU ODDS 4 PER BOX
NO PRICING ON QTY OF 10 OR LESS
111 Sandy Koufax Jsy/25 75.00 150.00
161 B.Ruth P/J.Thorpe J/25 300.00 500.00
164 W.Ford J/S.Koufax J/25 75.00 150.00

2005 Leaf Certified Materials Fabric of the Game Reward

*1-160 p/r 50: .5X TO 1.2X FOTG p/r 100
*1-160 p/r 50: .4X TO 1X FOTG p/r 50
*1-160 p/r 50: .3X TO .8X FOTG p/r 25
*1-160 p/r 25: .6X TO 1.5X FOTG p/r 100
*1-160 p/r 25: .5X TO 1.2X FOTG p/r 50
*1-160 p/r 25: .4X TO 1X FOTG p/r 25
1-160 PRINT RUNS B/WN 3-100 COPIES PER
*161-180 p/r 50: .5X TO 1.2X FOTG p/r 100
*161-180 p/r 50: .4X TO 1X FOTG p/r 50
*161-180 p/r 25: .5X TO 1.2X FOTG p/r 50
*161-180 p/r 25: .4X TO 1X FOTG p/r 25
161-180 PRINTS B/WN 10-50 COPIES PER
OVERALL AU-GU ODDS 4 PER BOX
NO PRICING ON QTY OF 10 OR LESS
111 Sandy Koufax Jsy/25 75.00 150.00
161 B.Ruth P/J.Thorpe J/25 300.00 500.00
163 W.Mays J/B.Gibson J/25 20.00 50.00
164 W.Ford J/S.Koufax J/25 40.00 80.00

2005 Leaf Certified Materials Fabric of the Game Stats

*1-160 p/r 75: .4X TO 1X FOTG p/r 100
*1-160 p/r 75: .3X TO .8X FOTG p/r 50
*1-160 p/r 75: .25X TO .6X FOTG p/r 25
*1-160 p/r 50: .5X TO 1.2X FOTG p/r 100
*1-160 p/r 50: .4X TO 1X FOTG p/r 50
*1-160 p/r 25: .6X TO 1.5X FOTG p/r 100
*1-160 p/r 25: .5X TO 1.2X FOTG p/r 50
*1-160 p/r 25: .4X TO 1X FOTG p/r 25
1-160 PRINT RUNS B/WN 3-75 COPIES PER
*161-180 p/r 50: .5X TO 1.2X FOTG p/r 100
*161-180 p/r 50: .4X TO 1X FOTG p/r 50
*161-180 p/r 25: .5X TO 1.2X FOTG p/r 50
*161-180 p/r 25: .4X TO 1X FOTG p/r 25
161-180 PRINTS B/WN 10-50 COPIES PER
OVERALL AU-GU ODDS 4 PER BOX
NO PRICING ON QTY OF 10 OR LESS
111 Sandy Koufax Jsy/25 75.00 150.00
142 Stan Musial Jsy/25 10.00 25.00
161 B.Ruth P/J.Thorpe J/25 300.00 500.00
163 W.Mays J/B.Gibson J/25 20.00 50.00
164 W.Ford J/S.Koufax J/25 75.00 150.00

2005 Leaf Certified Materials Fabric of the Game Prime

*1-160 p/r 25: 1X TO 2.5X FOTG p/r 100
*1-160 p/r 25: .75X TO 2X FOTG p/r 50
*1-160 p/r 25: .6X TO 1.5X FOTG p/r 25
*1-160 p/r 25: .5X TO 1.2X FOTG p/r 15
*1-160 p/r 17-18: .75X TO 2X FOTG p/r 50
*1-160 p/r 17-18: .6X TO 1.5X FOTG p/r 25
1-160 PRINT RUNS B/WN 5-25 COPIES PER
161-180 PRINTS B/WN 3-5 COPIES PER
OVERALL AU-GU ODDS 4 PER BOX
NO PRICING ON QTY OF 13 OR LESS
36 Dwight Evans Jsy/25 10.00 25.00
69 Keith Hernandez Jsy/25 8.00 20.00

2005 Leaf Certified Materials Fabric of the Game Autograph

OVERALL AU-GU ODDS 4 PER BOX
STATED PRINT RUN 1 SERIAL #'d SET
NO PRICING DUE TO SCARCITY

2005 Leaf Certified Materials Fabric of the Game Autograph Jersey Number

OVERALL AU-GU ODDS 4 PER BOX
STATED PRINT RUN 1 SERIAL #'d SET
NO PRICING DUE TO SCARCITY

2005 Leaf Certified Materials Fabric of the Game Autograph Position

OVERALL AU-GU ODDS 4 PER BOX
STATED PRINT RUN 1 SERIAL #'d SET
NO PRICING DUE TO SCARCITY

2005 Leaf Certified Materials Fabric of the Game Autograph Reward

OVERALL AU-GU ODDS 4 PER BOX
STATED PRINT RUN 1 SERIAL #'d SET
NO PRICING DUE TO SCARCITY

2005 Leaf Certified Materials Fabric of the Game Autograph Stats

OVERALL AU-GU ODDS 4 PER BOX
STATED PRINT RUN 1 SERIAL #'d SET
NO PRICING DUE TO SCARCITY

2005 Leaf Certified Materials Fabric of the Game Autograph Prime

OVERALL AU-GU ODDS 4 PER BOX
STATED PRINT RUN 1 SERIAL #'d SET
NO PRICING DUE TO SCARCITY

2005 Leaf Certified Materials Gold Team

STATED ODDS 1:7
*MIRROR: 1.25X TO 3X BASIC
MIRROR RANDOM INSERTS IN PACKS
1 Albert Pujols 1.25 3.00
2 Alex Rodriguez 1.25 3.00
3 Carlos Beltran Astros .60 1.50
4 Chipper Jones 1.00 2.50
5 Curt Schilling .60 1.50
6 Derek Jeter 2.50 6.00
7 Greg Maddux 1.25 3.00
8 Hank Blalock .40 1.00
9 Ichiro Suzuki 1.25 3.00
10 Ivan Rodriguez .60 1.50
11 Jim Thome .60 1.50
12 Ken Griffey Jr. 2.00 5.00
13 Lyle Overbay .40 1.00
14 Manny Ramirez 1.00 2.50
15 Mark Mulder A's .40 1.00
16 Mark Prior .60 1.50
17 Michael Young .40 1.00
18 Miguel Cabrera 1.00 2.50
19 Mike Piazza 1.00 2.50
20 Pedro Martinez .60 1.50
21 Randy Johnson M's 1.00 2.50
22 Roger Clemens 1.25 3.00
23 Sammy Sosa Cubs 1.00 2.50
24 Tim Hudson A's .60 1.50
25 Todd Helton .60 1.50

2005 Leaf Certified Materials Gold Team Autograph

OVERALL AU-GU ODDS 4 PER BOX
PRINT RUNS B/WN 5-10 COPIES PER
NO PRICING DUE TO SCARCITY

2005 Leaf Certified Materials Gold Team Jersey Number

OVERALL AU-GU ODDS 4 PER BOX
PRINT RUNS B/WN 100-250 COPIES PER
1 Albert Pujols/100 8.00 20.00
3 Carlos Beltran Astros/200 2.00 5.00
4 Chipper Jones/100 4.00 10.00
5 Curt Schilling/250 2.50 6.00
7 Greg Maddux/100 5.00 12.00
8 Hank Blalock/250 2.00 5.00
10 Ivan Rodriguez/120 3.00 8.00
11 Jim Thome/250 2.50 6.00
13 Lyle Overbay/250 2.00 5.00
14 Manny Ramirez/250 2.50 6.00
15 Mark Mulder A's/250 2.00 5.00
16 Mark Prior/100 3.00 8.00
17 Michael Young/250 2.00 5.00
18 Miguel Cabrera/100 3.00 8.00
19 Mike Piazza/250 3.00 8.00
20 Pedro Martinez/100 3.00 8.00
21 Randy Johnson M's/250 3.00 8.00
22 Roger Clemens/250 4.00 10.00
23 Sammy Sosa Cubs/250 3.00 8.00
24 Tim Hudson A's/100 2.50 6.00
25 Todd Helton/100 3.00 8.00

2005 Leaf Certified Materials Gold Team Jersey Number Prime

*PRIME p/r 25: 1.25X TO 3X JSY p/r 200-250
*PRIME p/r 25: 1X TO 2.5X JSY p/r 100-120
OVERALL AU-GU ODDS 4 PER BOX
PRINT RUNS B/WN 5-25 COPIES PER
NO PRICING ON QTY OF 10 OR LESS

2005 Leaf Certified Materials Skills

STATED ODDS 1:7
*MIRROR: 1.25X TO 3X BASIC
MIRROR RANDOM INSERTS IN PACKS
1 Andy Pettitte .60 1.50
2 Barry Zito .60 1.50
3 Bobby Crosby .40 1.00
4 Brandon Webb .60 1.50
5 Craig Biggio .60 1.50
6 David Ortiz 1.00 2.50
7 Dontrelle Willis .40 1.00
8 Francisco Rodriguez .60 1.50
9 Gary Sheffield .40 1.00
10 Jack Wilson .40 1.00
11 Jason Bay .40 1.00
12 Jeff Bagwell .60 1.50
13 Jim Edmonds .60 1.50
14 Josh Beckett .40 1.00
15 Kerry Wood .40 1.00
16 Lance Berkman .60 1.50
17 Mark Buehrle .60 1.50
18 Mark Teixeira .60 1.50
19 Miguel Tejada .60 1.50
20 Paul Konerko .60 1.50
21 Scott Rolen .60 1.50
22 Sean Burroughs .40 1.00
23 Vernon Wells .40 1.00
24 Victor Martinez .60 1.50
25 Vladimir Guerrero .60 1.50

2005 Leaf Certified Materials Skills Autograph

OVERALL AU-GU ODDS 4 PER BOX
PRINT RUNS B/WN 5-25 COPIES PER
NO PRICING ON QTY OF 10 OR LESS
3 Bobby Crosby/25 10.00 25.00
11 Jason Bay/25 10.00 25.00

2005 Leaf Certified Materials Skills Jersey Position

OVERALL AU-GU ODDS 4 PER BOX
PRINT RUNS B/WN 100-250 COPIES PER
1 Andy Pettitte/250 2.50 6.00
2 Barry Zito/250 2.00 5.00
3 Bobby Crosby/100 2.50 6.00
4 Brandon Webb Pants/100 2.50 6.00
5 Craig Biggio/250 2.50 6.00
6 David Ortiz/250 2.50 6.00
7 Dontrelle Willis/100 2.50 6.00
8 Francisco Rodriguez/250 2.00 5.00
9 Gary Sheffield/50 3.00 8.00
10 Jack Wilson/50 3.00 8.00
11 Jason Bay/100 2.50 6.00
12 Jeff Bagwell/250 2.50 6.00
13 Jim Edmonds/250 2.00 5.00
14 Josh Beckett/250 2.00 5.00
15 Kerry Wood/50 3.00 8.00
16 Lance Berkman/250 2.00 5.00
17 Mark Buehrle/150 2.00 5.00
19 Miguel Tejada/250 2.00 5.00
20 Paul Konerko/100 2.50 6.00
21 Scott Rolen/100 3.00 8.00
22 Sean Burroughs/100 2.50 6.00
23 Vernon Wells/250 2.00 5.00

24 Victor Martinez/250 2.00 5.00
25 Vladimir Guerrero/250 3.00 8.00

2005 Leaf Certified Materials Skills Jersey Position Prime

*PRIME p/r 25: 1.25X TO 3X JSY p/r 150-250
*PRIME p/r 25: 1X TO 2.5X JSY p/r 100
*PRIME p/r 25: .75X TO 2X JSY p/r 50
OVERALL AU-GU ODDS 4 PER BOX
PRINT RUNS B/WN 5-25 COPIES PER
NO PRICING ON QTY OF 5
18 Mark Teixeira/25 8.00 20.00

2016 Leaf Clear

*BLUE/25: .8X TO 2X BASIC CARDS

1998 Leaf Fractal Foundations

COMPLETE SET (200) 75.00 150.00
STATED PRINT RUN 3,999 SERIAL #'d SETS
CARD NUMBER 42 DOES NOT EXIST
1 Rusty Greer .75 2.00
2 Tino Martinez 1.25 3.00
3 Bobby Bonilla .75 2.00
4 Jason Giambi .75 2.00
5 Matt Morris .75 2.00
6 Craig Counsell .75 2.00
7 Reggie Jefferson .75 2.00
8 Brian Rose .75 2.00
9 Ruben Rivera .75 2.00
10 Shawn Estes .75 2.00
11 Tony Gwynn 2.50 6.00
12 Jeff Abbott .75 2.00
13 Jose Cruz Jr. .75 2.00
14 Francisco Cordova .75 2.00
15 Ryan Klesko .75 2.00
16 Tim Salmon 1.25 3.00
17 Brett Tomko .75 2.00
18 Matt Williams .75 2.00
19 Joe Carter .75 2.00
20 Harold Baines .75 2.00
21 Gary Sheffield .75 2.00
22 Charles Johnson .75 2.00
23 Aaron Boone .75 2.00
24 Eddie Murray 2.00 5.00
25 Matt Stairs .75 2.00
26 David Cone .75 2.00
27 Jon Nunnally .75 2.00
28 Chris Stynes .75 2.00
29 Enrique Wilson .75 2.00
30 Randy Johnson 2.00 5.00
31 Garret Anderson .75 2.00
32 Manny Ramirez 1.25 3.00
33 Jeff Suppan .75 2.00
34 Rickey Henderson 2.00 5.00
35 Scott Spiezio .75 2.00
36 Rondell White .75 2.00
37 Todd Greene .75 2.00
38 Delino DeShields .75 2.00
39 Kevin Brown 1.25 3.00
40 Chili Davis .75 2.00
41 Jimmy Key .75 2.00
43 Mike Mussina 1.25 3.00
44 Joe Randa .75 2.00
45 Chan Ho Park .75 2.00
46 Brad Radke .75 2.00
47 Geronimo Berroa .75 2.00
48 Wade Boggs 1.25 3.00
49 Kevin Appier .75 2.00
50 Moises Alou .75 2.00
51 David Justice .75 2.00
52 Ivan Rodriguez 1.25 3.00
53 J.T. Snow .75 2.00
54 Brian Giles .75 2.00
55 Will Clark 1.25 3.00
56 Justin Thompson .75 2.00
57 Javier Lopez .75 2.00
58 Hideki Irabu .75 2.00
59 Mark Grudzielanek .75 2.00
60 Abraham Nunez .75 2.00
61 Todd Hollandsworth .75 2.00
62 Jay Bell .75 2.00
63 Nomar Garciaparra 3.00 8.00
64 Vinny Castilla .75 2.00
65 Lou Collier .75 2.00
66 Kevin Orie .75 2.00
67 John Valentin .75 2.00
68 Robin Ventura .75 2.00
69 Denny Neagle .75 2.00
70 Tony Womack .75 2.00
71 Dennis Reyes .75 2.00
72 Wally Joyner .75 2.00
73 Kevin Brown 1.25 3.00
74 Ray Durham .75 2.00
75 Mike Cameron .75 2.00
76 Dante Bichette .75 2.00
77 Jose Guillen .75 2.00
78 Carlos Delgado .75 2.00
79 Paul Molitor .75 2.00
80 Jason Kendall .75 2.00
81 Mark Bellhorn .75 2.00
82 Damian Jackson .75 2.00
83 Bill Mueller .75 2.00
84 Kevin Young .75 2.00
85 Curt Schilling .75 2.00
86 Jeffrey Hammonds .75 2.00
87 Sandy Alomar Jr. .75 2.00
88 Bartolo Colon .75 2.00
89 Wilton Guerrero .75 2.00
90 Bernie Williams 1.25 3.00
91 Deion Sanders 1.25 3.00
92 Mike Piazza 3.00 8.00
93 Butch Huskey .75 2.00
94 Edgardo Alfonzo .75 2.00
95 Alan Benes .75 2.00
96 Craig Biggio 1.25 3.00
97 Mark Grace 1.25 3.00
98 Shawn Green .75 2.00
99 Derrek Lee 1.25 3.00
100 Ken Griffey Jr. 4.00 10.00
101 Tim Raines .75 2.00
102 Pokey Reese .75 2.00
103 Lee Stevens .75 2.00
104 Shannon Stewart .75 2.00
105 John Smoltz 1.25 3.00
106 Frank Thomas 2.00 5.00
107 Jeff Fassero .75 2.00
108 Jay Buhner .75 2.00
109 Jose Canseco 1.25 3.00
110 Omar Vizquel 1.25 3.00
111 Travis Fryman .75 2.00
112 Dave Nilsson .75 2.00
113 John Olerud .75 2.00
114 Larry Walker .75 2.00
115 Jim Edmonds .75 2.00
116 Bobby Higginson .75 2.00
117 Todd Hundley .75 2.00
118 Paul O'Neill 1.25 3.00
119 Bip Roberts .75 2.00
120 Ismael Valdes .75 2.00
121 Pedro Martinez 1.25 3.00
122 Jeff Cirillo .75 2.00
123 Andy Benes .75 2.00
124 Bobby Jones .75 2.00
125 Brian Hunter .75 2.00
126 Darryl Kile .75 2.00
127 Pat Hentgen .75 2.00
128 Marquis Grissom .75 2.00
129 Eric Davis .75 2.00
130 Chipper Jones 2.00 5.00
131 Edgar Martinez 1.25 3.00
132 Andy Pettitte 1.25 3.00
133 Cal Ripken 6.00 15.00
134 Scott Rolen 1.25 3.00
135 Ron Coomer .75 2.00
136 Luis Castillo .75 2.00
137 Fred McGriff 1.25 3.00
138 Neifi Perez .75 2.00
139 Eric Karros .75 2.00
140 Alex Fernandez .75 2.00
141 Jason Dickson .75 2.00
142 Lance Johnson .75 2.00
143 Ray Lankford .75 2.00
144 Sammy Sosa 2.00 5.00
145 Eric Young .75 2.00
146 Bubba Trammell .75 2.00
147 Todd Walker .75 2.00
148 Mo Vaughn CC .75 2.00
149 Jeff Bagwell CC 1.25 3.00
150 Kenny Lofton CC .75 2.00
151 Raul Mondesi CC .75 2.00
152 Mike Piazza CC 3.00 8.00
153 Chipper Jones CC 2.00 5.00
154 Larry Walker CC .75 2.00
155 Greg Maddux CC 3.00 8.00
156 Ken Griffey Jr. CC 4.00 10.00
157 Frank Thomas CC 2.00 5.00
158 Darin Erstad GLS .75 2.00
159 Roberto Alomar GLS 1.25 3.00
160 Albert Belle GLS .75 2.00
161 Jim Thome GLS 1.25 3.00
162 Tony Clark GLS .75 2.00
163 Chuck Knoblauch GLS .75 2.00
164 Derek Jeter GLS 5.00 12.00
165 Alex Rodriguez GLS 3.00 8.00
166 Tony Gwynn GLS 2.50 6.00
167 Roger Clemens GLS 4.00 10.00
168 Barry Larkin GLS 1.25 3.00
169 Andres Galarraga GLS .75 2.00
170 Vladimir Guerrero GLS 2.00 5.00
171 Mark McGwire GLS 5.00 12.50
172 Barry Bonds GLS 5.00 12.00
173 Juan Gonzalez GLS .75 2.00
174 Andruw Jones GLS 1.25 3.00
175 Paul Molitor GLS .75 2.00
176 Hideo Nomo GLS 2.00 5.00
177 Cal Ripken GLS 6.00 15.00
178 Brad Fullmer GLR .75 2.00
179 Jaret Wright GLR .75 2.00
180 Bobby Estalella GLR .75 2.00
181 Ben Grieve GLR .75 2.00
182 Paul Konerko GLR .75 2.00
183 David Ortiz GLR 2.50 6.00
184 Todd Helton GLR 1.25 3.00
185 Juan Encarnacion GLR .75 2.00
186 Miguel Tejada GLR 2.00 5.00
187 Jacob Cruz GLR .75 2.00
188 Mark Kotsay GLR .75 2.00
189 Fernando Tatis GLR .75 2.00
190 Ricky Ledee GLR .75 2.00
191 Richard Hidalgo GLR .75 2.00
192 Richie Sexson GLR .75 2.00
193 Luis Ordaz GLR .75 2.00
194 Eli Marrero GLR .75 2.00
195 Livan Hernandez GLR .75 2.00
196 Homer Bush GLR .75 2.00
197 Raul Ibanez GLR .75 2.00
198 Nomar Garciaparra CL 2.00 5.00
199 Scott Rolen CL .75 2.00
200 Jose Cruz Jr. CL .75 2.00
201 Al Martin .75 2.00

1998 Leaf Fractal Materials

*PLASTIC: .25X TO .6X BASIC CARDS
PLASTIC X PRINT RUN 3050 SERIAL #'d SETS
PLASTIC Y PRINT RUN 3150 SERIAL #'d SETS
PLASTIC Z PRINT RUN 3200 SERIAL #'d SETS
*LEATHER: .5X TO 1.25X BASIC CARDS
LEATHER X PRINT RUN 800 SERIAL #'d SETS
LEATHER Y PRINT RUN 900 SERIAL #'d SETS
LEATHER Z PRINT RUN 950 SERIAL #'d SETS
*NYLON: 1X TO 2.5X BASIC CARDS
NYLON X PRINT RUN 300 SERIAL #'d SETS
NYLON Y PRINT RUN 400 SERIAL #'d SETS
NYLON Z PRINT RUN 450 SERIAL #'d SETS
*WOOD Y/Z: 1.25X TO 3X BASIC CARDS
*WOOD X: 6X TO 15X BASIC CARDS
WOOD X PRINT RUN 50 SERIAL #'d SETS
WOOD Y PRINT RUN 150 SERIAL #'d SETS
WOOD Z PRINT RUN 200 SERIAL #'d SETS
CARD NUMBER 42 DOES NOT EXIST

1998 Leaf Fractal Materials Die Cuts

*X-AXIS: 1.25X TO 3X BASIC CARDS
X-AXIS PRINT RUN 200 SERIAL #'d SETS
*Y-AXIS: 2X TO 5X BASIC CARDS
Y-AXIS PRINT RUN 100 SERIAL #'d SETS
*Z-AXIS: 2.5X TO 6X BASIC CARDS
Z-AXIS PRINT RUN 50 SERIAL #'d SETS
RANDOM INSERTS IN PACKS
CARD NUMBER 42 DOES NOT EXIST

1998 Leaf Fractal Materials Z2 Axis

*STARS: 6X TO 15X BASIC FOUNDATION
RANDOM INSERTS IN PACKS
STATED PRINT RUN 20 SERIAL #'d SETS
CARD NUMBER 42 DOES NOT EXIST

1998 Leaf Fractal Materials Samples

COMPLETE SET (50) 250.00 500.00
5 Matt Morris 2.50 6.00
9 Ruben Rivera 1.50 4.00
10 Shawn Estes 1.50 4.00
15 Ryan Klesko 4.00 10.00
17 Brett Tomko 1.50 4.00
22 Charles Johnson 1.50 4.00
33 Jeff Suppan 1.50 4.00
36 Rondell White 2.50 6.00
39 Kevin Brown 2.50 6.00
53 J.T. Snow 2.50 6.00
55 Will Clark 6.00 15.00
58 Hideki Irabu 1.50 4.00
66 Kevin Orie 1.50 4.00
70 Tony Womack 1.50 4.00
71 Dennis Reyes 1.50 4.00
76 Dante Bichette 1.50 4.00
78 Carlos Delgado 6.00 15.00
81 Mark Bellhorn 4.00 10.00
87 Sandy Alomar Jr. 2.50 6.00
89 Wilton Guerrero 1.50 4.00
93 Butch Huskey 1.50 4.00
94 Edgardo Alfonzo 2.50 6.00
95 Alan Benes 1.50 4.00
97 Mark Grace 6.00 15.00
98 Shawn Green 5.00 12.00
99 Derrek Lee 4.00 10.00
105 John Smoltz 5.00 12.00
108 Jay Buhner 2.50 6.00
109 Jose Canseco 6.00 15.00
116 Bobby Higginson 2.50 6.00
117 Todd Hundley 2.50 6.00
136 Luis Castillo 2.50 6.00
137 Fred McGriff 4.00 10.00
138 Neifi Perez 1.50 4.00
146 Bubba Trammell 1.50 4.00
147 Todd Walker 2.50 6.00
158 Darin Erstad 5.00 12.00
160 Albert Belle 2.50 6.00
161 Jim Thome 5.00 12.00
162 Tony Clark 1.50 4.00
163 Chuck Knoblauch 2.50 6.00
167 Roger Clemens 12.50 30.00
170 Vladimir Guerrero 8.00 20.00
171 Mark McGwire 15.00 40.00
172 Barry Bonds 12.50 30.00
176 Hideo Nomo 30.00 80.00
189 Fernando Tatis 1.50 4.00
194 Eli Marrero 1.50 4.00
195 Livan Hernandez 2.50 6.00
201 Al Martin 1.60 4.00

1960 Leaf Full Face

This eight-card set, which measures the standard size, was probably issued as promos to display the general design of the 1960 Leaf Set. These cards feature full facial shots of the featured players. There has been discussion that these cards were samples used to promote the Leaf product as most of the known examples surfaced in the Chicago area where Leaf Gum had their headquarters.

COMPLETE SET (8) 1500.00 3000.00
1 Luis Aparicio 400.00 800.00
12 Ken Boyer 300.00 600.00
17 Walt Moryn 150.00 300.00
23 Joey Jay 150.00 300.00
35 Jim Coates 200.00 400.00
58 Hal Smith 150.00 300.00
61 Vic Rehm 150.00 300.00
72 Dick Donovan 150.00 300.00

2015 Leaf Heroes of Baseball

COMPLETE SET (60) 6.00 15.00
1 Al Kaline .25 .60
2 Albert Pujols .30 .75
3 Andre Dawson .20 .50
4 Bert Blyleven .20 .50
5 Bill Mazeroski .20 .50
6 Billy Williams .20 .50
7 Bob Gibson .20 .50
8 Brooks Robinson .20 .50
9 Bruce Sutter .20 .50
10 Cal Ripken Jr. .75 2.00
11 Carlton Fisk .20 .50
12 Darryl Strawberry .15 .40
13 Dennis Eckersley .20 .50
14 Don Mattingly .50 1.25
15 Don Sutton .20 .50
16 Doug Harvey .15 .40
17 Dwight Gooden .15 .40
18 Earl Weaver .20 .50
19 Eddie Murray .20 .50
20 Ferguson Jenkins .20 .50
21 Frank Robinson .20 .50
22 Frank Thomas .25 .60
23 Gaylord Perry .20 .50
24 Goose Gossage .20 .50
25 Greg Maddux .30 .75
26 Ichiro .30 .75
27 Ivan Rodriguez .20 .50
28 Jim Bunning .20 .50
29 Jim Palmer .20 .50
30 Jim Rice .20 .50
31 Joe Morgan .20 .50
32 John Smoltz .25 .60
33 Johnny Bench .25 .60
34 Jose Canseco .20 .50
35 Lou Brock .20 .50
36 Luis Aparicio .20 .50
37 Mike Piazza .25 .60
38 Orlando Cepeda .20 .50
39 Ozzie Smith .30 .75
40 Paul Molitor .25 .60
41 Pedro Martinez .20 .50
42 Pete Rose .50 1.25
43 Rafael Palmeiro .20 .50
44 Randy Johnson .25 .60
45 Red Schoendienst .20 .50
46 Reggie Jackson .20 .50
47 Rickey Henderson .25 .60
48 Roberto Alomar .20 .50
49 Rod Carew .20 .50
50 Rollie Fingers .20 .50
51 Ryne Sandberg .50 1.25
52 Stan Musial .40 1.00
53 Steve Carlton .20 .50
54 Tommy Lasorda .20 .50
55 Tony Gwynn .25 .60
56 Tony La Russa .20 .50
57 Wade Boggs .20 .50
58 Whitey Ford .20 .50
59 Whitey Herzog .15 .40
60 Will Clark .20 .50

2015 Leaf Heroes of Baseball Musial Autographs

ONE AUTO PER BOX
MASM1 Stan Musial 10.00 25.00
MASM2 Stan Musial 10.00 25.00
MASM3 Stan Musial 10.00 25.00
MASM4 Stan Musial 10.00 25.00
MASM5 Stan Musial 10.00 25.00
MASM6 Stan Musial 10.00 25.00
MASM7 Stan Musial 10.00 25.00
MASM8 Stan Musial 10.00 25.00
MASM9 Stan Musial 10.00 25.00
MASM10 Stan Musial 10.00 25.00
MASM11 Stan Musial 10.00 25.00
MASM12 Stan Musial 10.00 25.00
MASM13 Stan Musial 10.00 25.00
MASM14 Stan Musial 10.00 25.00
MASM15 Stan Musial 10.00 25.00
MASM16 Stan Musial 10.00 25.00
MASM17 Stan Musial 10.00 25.00
MASM18 Stan Musial 10.00 25.00
MASM19 Stan Musial 10.00 25.00
MASM20 Stan Musial 10.00 25.00

2015 Leaf Heroes of Baseball Musial Milestone

COMPLETE SET (20) 8.00 20.00
RANDOM INSERTS IN PACKS
MM01 Stan Musial .60 1.50
MM02 Stan Musial .60 1.50
MM03 Stan Musial .60 1.50
MM04 Stan Musial .60 1.50
MM05 Stan Musial .60 1.50
MM06 Stan Musial .60 1.50
MM07 Stan Musial .60 1.50
MM08 Stan Musial .60 1.50
MM09 Stan Musial .60 1.50
MM10 Stan Musial .60 1.50
MM11 Stan Musial .60 1.50
MM12 Stan Musial .60 1.50
MM13 Stan Musial .60 1.50
MM14 Stan Musial .60 1.50
MM15 Stan Musial .60 1.50
MM16 Stan Musial .60 1.50
MM17 Stan Musial .60 1.50
MM18 Stan Musial .60 1.50
MM19 Stan Musial .60 1.50
MM20 Stan Musial .60 1.50

2013 Leaf Ichiro Immortals Collection

STATED PRINT RUN 51 SER.#'d SETS
1 Ichiro Suzuki 5.00 12.00
2 Ichiro Suzuki 5.00 12.00
3 Ichiro Suzuki 5.00 12.00
4 Ichiro Suzuki 5.00 12.00
5 Ichiro Suzuki 5.00 12.00
6 Ichiro Suzuki 5.00 12.00
7 Ichiro Suzuki 5.00 12.00
8 Ichiro Suzuki 5.00 12.00
9 Ichiro Suzuki 5.00 12.00
10 Ichiro Suzuki 5.00 12.00
11 Ichiro Suzuki 5.00 12.00
12 Ichiro Suzuki 5.00 12.00
13 Ichiro Suzuki 5.00 12.00
14 Ichiro Suzuki 5.00 12.00
15 Ichiro Suzuki 5.00 12.00

2013 Leaf Ichiro Immortals Collection Bronze

*BRONZE: .6X TO 1.5X BASIC
STATED PRINT RUN 20 SER.#'d SETS

2013 Leaf Ichiro Immortals Collection Silver

*SILVER: .75X TO 2X BASIC
STATED PRINT RUN 20 SER.#'d SETS

2013 Leaf Ichiro Immortals Collection Base Set Autographs

STATED PRINT RUN 5 SER.#'d SETS

2013 Leaf Industry Summit Frank Thomas Autograph

FT1 Frank Thomas 10.00 25.00

2012 Leaf Inscriptions

IAD1 Andre Dawson 12.50 30.00
IAK1 Al Kaline 30.00 80.00
IBB1 Bert Blyleven 12.50 30.00
IBR1 Brooks Robinson 15.00 40.00
IBS1 Bruce Sutter 10.00 25.00
ICF1 Carlton Fisk 15.00 40.00
ICR1 Cal Ripken Jr. 100.00 200.00
IDE1 Dennis Eckersley 15.00 40.00
IDM1 Don Mattingly 40.00 80.00
IDS1 Don Sutton 12.50 30.00
IEM1 Eddie Murray 12.50 30.00
IFR1 Frank Robinson 25.00 50.00
IFT1 Frank Thomas 60.00 120.00
IIR1 Ivan Rodriguez 20.00 50.00
IJB1 Johnny Bench 40.00 80.00
IJM1 Joe Morgan 20.00 50.00
IJP1 Jim Palmer 10.00 25.00
IJR1 Jim Rice 25.00 50.00
ILB1 Lou Brock 15.00 40.00
INR1 Nolan Ryan 100.00 200.00
IOC1 Orlando Cepeda 20.00 50.00
IPR1 Pete Rose 30.00 60.00
IRC1 Rod Carew 10.00 25.00
IRH1 Rickey Henderson 40.00 80.00
IRJ1 Reggie Jackson 40.00 80.00
IRS1 Red Schoendienst 10.00 25.00
ISC1 Steve Carlton 25.00 50.00
ITG1 Tony Gwynn 30.00 60.00
ITS1 Tom Seaver 40.00 100.00
IWB1 Wade Boggs 40.00 80.00
IWC1 Will Clark 30.00 60.00
IWF1 Whitey Ford 15.00 40.00

2010 Leaf Joe Jackson

COMPLETE SET (15) 100.00 200.00
COMMON JACKSON (2-14) 2.50 6.00
COMMON JACKSON SP (1/15) 10.00 25.00
1 Joe Jackson 10.00 25.00
2 Joe Jackson 2.50 6.00
3 Joe Jackson 2.50 6.00
4 Joe Jackson 2.50 6.00
5 Joe Jackson 2.50 6.00
6 Joe Jackson 2.50 6.00
7 Joe Jackson 2.50 6.00
8 Joe Jackson 2.50 6.00
9 Joe Jackson 2.50 6.00
10 Joe Jackson 2.50 6.00
11 Joe Jackson 2.50 6.00
12 Joe Jackson 2.50 6.00
13 Joe Jackson 2.50 6.00
14 Joe Jackson 2.50 6.00
15 Joe Jackson 10.00 25.00

2011 Leaf Legends of Sport

STATED PRINT RUN 6-50
NO PRICING ON CARDS #'d TO 12 OR LESS
BA2 Al Kaline/20 30.00 80.00
BA5 Andre Dawson/20 20.00 50.00
BA9 Bert Blyleven/10
BA10 Bill Mazeroski/27 12.00 30.00
BA12 Billy Williams/15 12.00 30.00
BA13 Bob Gibson/20 15.00 40.00
BA15 Brooks Robinson/26 15.00 40.00
BA16 Bruce Sutter/30 12.00 30.00
BA17 Cal Ripken Jr./20 60.00 120.00
BA19 Carl Yastrzemski/15 30.00 60.00
BA20 Carlton Fisk/18 15.00 40.00
BA23 Dennis Eckersley/14 12.00 30.00
BA24 Don Sutton/40 10.00 25.00
BA25 Doug Harvey/40 15.00 40.00
BA26 Earl Weaver/14 10.00 25.00
BA27 Eddie Murray/16 30.00 80.00
BA29 Ferguson Jenkins/20 10.00 25.00
BA30 Frank Robinson/22 20.00 50.00
BA31 Gaylord Perry/36 12.00 30.00
BA32 Goose Gossage/16 12.00 30.00
BA33 Ichiro/10
BA37 Jim Palmer/15 15.00 40.00
BA38 Jim Rice/25 10.00 25.00
BA41 Joe Morgan/14 15.00 40.00
BA42 Johnny Bench/16 20.00 50.00
BA43 Jose Canseco/15 30.00 60.00
BA48 Lou Brock/20 15.00 40.00
BA49 Luis Aparicio/24 15.00 40.00
BA55 Mike Piazza/15 75.00 150.00
BA58 Nolan Ryan/25 60.00 120.00
BA59 Orlando Cepeda/50 10.00 25.00
BA63 Paul Molitor/31 15.00 40.00
BA64 Pete Rose/27 12.00 30.00
BA66 Rafael Palmeiro/23 20.00 50.00
BA67 Red Schoendienst/15 15.00 40.00
BA68 Reggie Jackson/15 20.00 50.00
BA70 Rickey Henderson/23 75.00 150.00
BA71 Roberto Alomar/24 30.00 80.00
BA72 Rod Carew/37 15.00 40.00
BA73 Rollie Fingers/17 10.00 25.00
BA75 Ryne Sandberg/15 40.00 100.00
BA77 Stan Musial/22 75.00 150.00
BA78 Steve Carlton/21 20.00 50.00
BA81 Tom Seaver/17 20.00 50.00
BA82 Tommy Lasorda/34 40.00 100.00
BA84 Tony Gwynn/16 30.00 80.00
BA85 Tony LaRussa/13 12.00 30.00
BA86 Tony Perez/26 15.00 40.00
BA87 Wade Boggs/50 15.00 40.00
BA88 Whitey Ford/31 15.00 40.00
BA89 Whitey Herzog/13 15.00 40.00
BA90 Yogi Berra/15 30.00 80.00
BA92 Willie Mays/14 EXCH 75.00 150.00

2011 Leaf Legends of Sport Award Winners Autographs Bronze

STATED PRINT RUN 10-50
AW4 Billy Williams/15 12.00 30.00
AW6 Carl Yastrzemski/15 30.00 80.00
AW7 Don Sutton/40 10.00 25.00
AW8 Eddie Murray/16 30.00 80.00
AW9 Goose Gossage/16 12.00 30.00
AW10 Ichiro/10
AW12 Jim Palmer/15 15.00 40.00
AW13 Jim Rice/25 20.00 50.00
AW17 Orlando Cepeda/50 10.00 25.00
AW18 Paul Molitor/30 15.00 40.00
AW19 Pete Rose/27 30.00 80.00
AW20 Pete Rose/27 30.00 80.00
AW21 Reggie Jackson/15 20.00 50.00
AW22 Rollie Fingers/16 10.00 25.00
AW25 Tom Seaver/17 20.00 50.00
AW26 Tony LaRussa/13 12.00 30.00
AW27 Whitey Ford/31 15.00 40.00
AW28 Whitey Herzog/17 15.00 40.00

2011 Leaf Legends of Sport Cut Signatures

HA Hank Aaron
RC Roberto Clemente
AB7 Al Barlick 15.00 40.00
BL1 Buck Leonard 15.00 40.00
MI8 Monte Irvin 12.00 30.00
SK4 Sandy Koufax
BL12 Bob Lemon 12.00 30.00
BR11 Babe Ruth

2011 Leaf Legends of Sport Moments of Greatness Autographs Bronze

STATED PRINT RUN 10-50
MG1 Al Kaline/20 30.00 80.00
MG3 Bert Blyleven/10
MG4 Billy Williams/15 12.00 30.00
MG5 Bob Gibson/20 15.00 40.00
MG6 Cal Ripken Jr./20 30.00 60.00
MG8 Dennis Eckersley/14 12.00 30.00
MG9 Earl Weaver/14 10.00 25.00
MG10 Earl Weaver/14 10.00 25.00
MG12 Ferguson Jenkins/19 10.00 25.00
MG13 Ferguson Jenkins/19 10.00 25.00
MG14 Gaylord Perry/35 12.00 30.00
MG15 Goose Gossage/15 12.00 30.00
MG22 Nolan Ryan/24 60.00 120.00
MG23 Orlando Cepeda/50 10.00 25.00
MG26 Pete Rose/26 30.00 80.00
MG27 Rafael Palmeiro/23 20.00 50.00
MG28 Red Schoendienst/15 15.00 40.00
MG30 Tony LaRussa/13 12.00 30.00
MG31 Whitey Herzog/17 15.00 40.00
MG32 Whitey Herzog/16 15.00 40.00
MG33 Mike Piazza/15 75.00 150.00
MG34 Doug Harvey/40 15.00 40.00

2011 Leaf Legends of Sport Numeration Autographs

STATED PRINT RUN 4-30
NO PRICING ON CARDS #'d TO 12 OR LESS
NU1 Al Kaline/6
NU2 Bill Mazeroski/9
NU4 Brooks Robinson/5
NU5 Cal Ripken Jr./8
NU6 Earl Weaver/4
NU8 Frank Robinson/20 20.00 50.00
NU10 Joe Morgan/8
NU13 Orlando Cepeda/30 12.00 30.00
NU14 Paul Molitor/4
NU15 Pete Rose/14 30.00 80.00
NU16 Rafael Palmeiro/25 20.00 50.00
NU17 Rod Carew/29 10.00 25.00
NU18 Stan Musial/6
NU19 Tony LaRussa/10
NU20 Tony Perez/24 15.00 40.00
NU21 Wade Boggs/26 20.00 50.00
NU22 Whitey Herzog/6
NU23 Andre Dawson/10

2011 Leaf Legends of Sport Perennial All-Stars Autographs

STATED PRINT RUN 5-24
NO PRICING ON CARDS #'d TO 13 OR LESS
PE1 Al Kaline/18 30.00 80.00
PE4 Bill Mazeroski/10
PE5 Billy Williams/6
PE6 Bob Gibson/9
PE7 Bruce Sutter/6
PE8 Cal Ripken Jr./19 60.00 120.00
PE9 Carl Yastrzemski/18 30.00 60.00
PE10 Carlton Fisk/11
PE11 Dennis Eckersley/6
PE12 Eddie Murray/8
PE14 Frank Robinson/14 20.00 50.00
PE15 Gaylord Perry/5
PE16 Goose Gossage/9
PE17 Ichiro/10
PE18 Jim Rice/8
PE20 Joe Morgan/10
PE21 Johnny Bench/15 20.00 50.00
PE22 Jose Canseco/6
PE23 Lou Brock/6
PE24 Luis Aparicio/13
PE26 Mike Piazza/12
PE27 Nolan Ryan/8
PE28 Orlando Cepeda/11
PE30 Paul Molitor/10
PE31 Pete Rose/17 30.00 80.00
PE32 Red Schoendienst/10
PE33 Reggie Jackson/19 20.00 50.00
PE35 Roberto Alomar/12
PE36 Rollie Fingers/7
PE37 Ryne Sandberg/10
PE38 Stan Musial/24 30.00 80.00
PE39 Steve Carlton/10
PE40 Tom Seaver/12
PE41 Tony Gwynn/15 30.00 80.00
PE42 Tony Perez/7
PE43 Wade Boggs/12
PE44 Whitey Ford/10

2012 Leaf Legends of Sport

BAAK1 Al Kaline 20.00 50.00
BAAP1 Albert Pujols
BABG1 Bob Gibson 12.00 30.00
BABR2 Brooks Robinson 10.00 25.00
BABS1 Bruce Sutter 6.00 15.00
BACF1 Carlton Fisk 10.00 25.00
BACR1 Cal Ripken Jr. 40.00 80.00
BADM1 Don Mattingly 30.00 60.00
BAEM1 Eddie Murray 20.00 40.00
BAEW1 Earl Weaver 10.00 25.00
BAFR1 Frank Robinson 10.00 25.00
BAFT1 Frank Thomas 40.00 80.00
BAGC1 Gary Carter
BAGM1 Greg Maddux 40.00 80.00
BAGP2 Gaylord Perry 8.00 20.00
BAI1 Ichiro 250.00 400.00
BAIR1 Ivan Rodriguez 12.00 30.00
BAJB2 Johnny Bench 25.00 50.00
BAJB3 Jim Bunning 8.00 20.00
BAJC2 Jose Canseco 25.00 50.00
BAJM2 Joe Morgan 15.00 40.00
BAJP1 Jim Palmer 8.00 20.00
BAJS1 John Smoltz 12.00 30.00
BALA1 Luis Aparicio 8.00 20.00
BALB2 Lou Brock 25.00 50.00
BAOS1 Ozzie Smith 20.00 40.00
BAPG1 Pat Gillick 6.00 15.00
BAPM1 Paul Molitor 10.00 25.00
BAPM2 Pedro Martinez 25.00 50.00
BAPR1 Pete Rose 12.00 30.00
BARC1 Rod Carew 12.00 30.00
BARH1 Rickey Henderson 50.00 100.00
BARJ2 Randy Johnson 25.00 50.00
BARS1 Red Schoendienst 8.00 20.00
BARS2 Ryne Sandberg 25.00 50.00
BASC1 Steve Carlton 10.00 25.00
BATG1 Tony Gwynn 30.00 60.00
BATL1 Tommy Lasorda 30.00 80.00
BAWB1 Wade Boggs 20.00 50.00
BAWF1 Whitey Ford 20.00 50.00
BAWH1 Whitey Herzog 8.00 20.00

2012 Leaf Legends of Sport AKA Autographs

AKAAK1 Al Kaline 12.00 30.00
AKABG1 Bob Gibson 12.00 30.00
AKACF1 Carlton Fisk 10.00 25.00
AKACR1 Cal Ripken Jr. 40.00 80.00
AKACY1 Carl Yastrzemski 30.00 60.00
AKAEB1 Ernie Banks 25.00 50.00
AKAEM1 Eddie Murray 20.00 40.00
AKAFT1 Frank Thomas 30.00 60.00
AKAGC1 Gary Carter
AKAIR1 Ivan Rodriguez 20.00 40.00
AKAJB2 Johnny Bench 25.00 50.00
AKAJP1 Jim Palmer 8.00 20.00
AKALB2 Lou Brock 25.00 50.00
AKANR1 Nolan Ryan 40.00 80.00
AKAOS1 Ozzie Smith 20.00 40.00
AKAPR1 Pete Rose 20.00 40.00
AKARC1 Rod Carew 12.00 30.00
AKARH1 Rickey Henderson 50.00 100.00
AKARJ1 Reggie Jackson 20.00 40.00
AKARJ2 Randy Johnson 25.00 50.00
AKARS2 Ryne Sandberg 25.00 50.00
AKASC1 Steve Carlton 10.00 25.00
AKATP1 Tony Perez 12.00 30.00
AKAWC1 Will Clark 20.00 50.00
AKAWF1 Whitey Ford 12.00 30.00

2012 Leaf Legends of Sport Award Winners Autographs

AWJS1 John Smoltz 25.00 50.00
AWPG1 Pat Gillick 6.00 15.00
AWRS2 Ryne Sandberg 25.00 50.00

2012 Leaf Legends of Sport Numerations Autographs

PRINT RUN 5-45
NAAP1 Albert Pujols/5
NABG1 Bob Gibson/45 12.00 30.00
NADM1 Don Mattingly/23 40.00 80.00
NADS4 Don Sutton/20 8.00 20.00
NAFT1 Frank Thomas/35 40.00 80.00
NAGP2 Gaylord Perry/36 10.00 25.00
NAIR1 Ivan Rodriguez/7
NAJC2 Jose Canseco/33 30.00 60.00
NANR1 Nolan Ryan/34 50.00 100.00
NAPR1 Pete Rose/14
NARH1 Rickey Henderson/35 60.00 120.00
NARJ1 Reggie Jackson/44 25.00 50.00
NARS2 Ryne Sandberg/23 30.00 60.00
NATP1 Tony Perez/24 15.00 40.00
NAWC1 Will Clark/22 25.00 50.00
NAYB1 Yogi Berra/8

2012 Leaf Legends of Sport Perennial All-Stars Autographs

PASPR1 Pete Rose 12.00 30.00

2012 Leaf Legends of Sport Signature Swatches

SSCR1 Cal Ripken Jr. BAT 50.00 100.00
SSFJ1 Ferguson Jenkins HAT 10.00 25.00
SSIS1 Ichiro JSY 300.00 500.00
SSNR1 Nolan Ryan JSY 50.00 100.00
SSOS1 Ozzie Smith JSY 25.00 50.00
SSRC1 Rod Carew JSY 12.00 30.00
SSRJ1 Reggie Jackson
SSTG1 Tony Gwynn JSY 20.00 50.00
SSTL1 Tony LaRussa JSY 10.00 25.00

2012 Leaf Legends of Sport Unsigned Bronze

ANNOUNCED PRINT RUN 70
ONLINE EXCLUSIVE
10 Yasiel Puig 125.00 250.00

2012 Leaf Legends of Sport We Are the Champions Autographs

WCBG1 Bob Gibson 12.00 30.00
WCBS1 Bruce Sutter 6.00 15.00
WCJC2 Jose Canseco 20.00 40.00
WCJP1 Jim Palmer 8.00 20.00
WCPR1 Pete Rose 12.00 30.00
WCRH1 Rickey Henderson 50.00 100.00
WCRJ1 Reggie Jackson 25.00 50.00
WCTL1 Tommy Lasorda 25.00 60.00
WCWB1 Wade Boggs 12.00 30.00
WCWH1 Whitey Herzog 10.00 25.00

1994 Leaf Limited

This 160-card standard-size set was issued exclusively to hobby dealers. The set is organized alphabetically within teams with AL preceding NL.

COMPLETE SET (160) 12.50 30.00
1 Jeffrey Hammonds .20 .50
2 Ben McDonald .20 .50
3 Mike Mussina .60 1.50
4 Rafael Palmeiro .60 1.50
5 Cal Ripken 3.00 8.00
6 Lee Smith .40 1.00
7 Roger Clemens 2.00 5.00
8 Scott Cooper .20 .50
9 Andre Dawson .40 1.00
10 Mike Greenwell .20 .50
11 Aaron Sele .20 .50
12 Mo Vaughn .40 1.00
13 Brian Anderson RC .40 1.00
14 Chad Curtis .20 .50
15 Chili Davis .40 1.00
16 Gary DiSarcina .20 .50
17 Mark Langston .20 .50
18 Tim Salmon .60 1.50
19 Wilson Alvarez .20 .50
20 Jason Bere .20 .50
21 Julio Franco .40 1.00
22 Jack McDowell .20 .50
23 Tim Raines .40 1.00
24 Frank Thomas 1.00 2.50
25 Robin Ventura .40 1.00
26 Carlos Baerga .20 .50
27 Albert Belle .40 1.00
28 Kenny Lofton .40 1.00
29 Eddie Murray 1.00 2.50
30 Manny Ramirez 1.00 2.50
31 Cecil Fielder .40 1.00
32 Travis Fryman .40 1.00
33 Mickey Tettleton .20 .50
34 Alan Trammell .40 1.00
35 Lou Whitaker .40 1.00
36 David Cone .40 1.00
37 Gary Gaetti .40 1.00
38 Greg Gagne .20 .50
39 Bob Hamelin .20 .50
40 Wally Joyner .40 1.00
41 Brian McRae .20 .50
42 Ricky Bones .20 .50
43 Brian Harper .20 .50
44 John Jaha .20 .50
45 Pat Listach .20 .50
46 Dave Nilsson .20 .50
47 Greg Vaughn .20 .50

48 Kent Hrbek .40 1.00
49 Chuck Knoblauch .40 1.00
50 Shane Mack .20 .50
51 Kirby Puckett 1.00 2.50
52 Dave Winfield .40 1.00
53 Jim Abbott .60 1.50
54 Wade Boggs .60 1.50
55 Jimmy Key .40 1.00
56 Don Mattingly 2.50 6.00
57 Paul O'Neill .60 1.50
58 Danny Tartabull .20 .50
59 Dennis Eckersley .40 1.00
60 Rickey Henderson 1.00 2.50
61 Mark McGwire 2.50 6.00
62 Troy Neel .20 .50
63 Ruben Sierra .40 1.00
64 Eric Anthony .20 .50
65 Jay Buhner .40 1.00
66 Ken Griffey Jr. 2.00 5.00
67 Randy Johnson 1.00 2.50
68 Edgar Martinez .60 1.50
69 Tino Martinez .60 1.50
70 Jose Canseco .60 1.50
71 Will Clark .60 1.50
72 Juan Gonzalez .40 1.00
73 Dean Palmer .40 1.00
74 Ivan Rodriguez .60 1.50
75 Roberto Alomar .60 1.50
76 Joe Carter .40 1.00
77 Carlos Delgado .60 1.50
78 Paul Molitor .40 1.00
79 John Olerud .40 1.00
80 Devon White .40 1.00
81 Steve Avery .20 .50
82 Tom Glavine .60 1.50
83 David Justice .40 1.00
84 Roberto Kelly .20 .50
85 Ryan Klesko .40 1.00
86 Javier Lopez .40 1.00
87 Greg Maddux 1.50 4.00
88 Fred McGriff .60 1.50
89 Shawon Dunston .20 .50
90 Mark Grace .60 1.50
91 Derrick May .20 .50
92 Sammy Sosa 1.00 2.50
93 Rick Wilkins .20 .50
94 Bret Boone .40 1.00
95 Barry Larkin .60 1.50
96 Kevin Mitchell .20 .50
97 Hal Morris .20 .50
98 Deion Sanders .60 1.50
99 Reggie Sanders .40 1.00
100 Dante Bichette .40 1.00
101 Ellis Burks .40 1.00
102 Andres Galarraga .40 1.00
103 Joe Girardi .20 .50
104 Charlie Hayes .20 .50
105 Chuck Carr .20 .50
106 Jeff Conine .40 1.00
107 Bryan Harvey .20 .50
108 Benito Santiago .40 1.00
109 Gary Sheffield .40 1.00
110 Jeff Bagwell .60 1.50
111 Craig Biggio .60 1.50
112 Ken Caminiti .40 1.00
113 Andujar Cedeno .20 .50
114 Doug Drabek .20 .50
115 Luis Gonzalez .40 1.00
116 Brett Butler .40 1.00
117 Delino DeShields .20 .50
118 Eric Karros .40 1.00
119 Raul Mondesi .40 1.00
120 Mike Piazza 2.00 5.00
121 Henry Rodriguez .20 .50
122 Tim Wallach .20 .50
123 Moises Alou .40 1.00
124 Cliff Floyd .40 1.00
125 Marquis Grissom .40 1.00
126 Ken Hill .20 .50
127 Larry Walker .40 1.00
128 John Wetteland .40 1.00
129 Bobby Bonilla .40 1.00
130 John Franco .40 1.00
131 Jeff Kent .60 1.50
132 Bret Saberhagen .40 1.00
133 Ryan Thompson .20 .50
134 Darren Daulton .40 1.00
135 Mariano Duncan .20 .50
136 Lenny Dykstra .40 1.00
137 Danny Jackson .20 .50
138 John Kruk .40 1.00
139 Jay Bell .40 1.00
140 Jeff King .20 .50
141 Al Martin .20 .50
142 Orlando Merced .20 .50
143 Andy Van Slyke .60 1.50
144 Bernard Gilkey .20 .50
145 Gregg Jefferies .20 .50
146 Ray Lankford .40 1.00
147 Ozzie Smith 1.50 4.00
148 Mark Whiten .20 .50
149 Todd Zeile .20 .50
150 Derek Bell .20 .50
151 Andy Benes .20 .50
152 Tony Gwynn 1.25 3.00
153 Phil Plantier .20 .50
154 Bip Roberts .20 .50
155 Rod Beck .20 .50
156 Barry Bonds 2.50 6.00
157 John Burkett .20 .50
158 Royce Clayton .20 .50
159 Bill Swift .20 .50
160 Matt Williams .40 1.00

1994 Leaf Limited Gold All-Stars

COMPLETE SET (18) 15.00 40.00
STATED ODDS 1:7
STATED PRINT RUN 10,000 SERIAL #'d SETS
1 Frank Thomas .75 2.00
2 Gregg Jefferies .15 .40
3 Roberto Alomar .50 1.25
4 Mariano Duncan .15 .40
5 Wade Boggs .50 1.25
6 Matt Williams .30 .75
7 Cal Ripken 2.50 6.00
8 Ozzie Smith 1.25 3.00
9 Kirby Puckett .75 2.00
10 Barry Bonds 2.00 5.00
11 Ken Griffey Jr. 1.50 4.00
12 Tony Gwynn 1.00 2.50
13 Joe Carter .30 .75
14 David Justice .30 .75
15 Ivan Rodriguez .50 1.25
16 Mike Piazza 1.50 4.00
17 Jimmy Key .30 .75
18 Greg Maddux 1.25 3.00

1994 Leaf Limited Rookies

This 80-card standard-size premium set was issued by Donruss exclusively to hobby dealers. The set showcases top rookies and prospects of 1994. Rookie Cards in this set include Armando Benitez, Rusty Greer and Chan Ho Park.

COMPLETE SET (80) 10.00 25.00
1 Charles Johnson .30 .75
2 Rico Brogna .15 .40
3 Melvin Nieves .15 .40
4 Rich Becker .15 .40
5 Russ Davis .15 .40
6 Matt Mieske .15 .40
7 Paul Shuey .15 .40
8 Hector Carrasco .15 .40
9 J.R. Phillips .15 .40
10 Scott Ruffcorn .15 .40
11 Kurt Abbott RC .15 .40
12 Danny Bautista .15 .40
13 Rick White .15 .40
14 Steve Dunn .15 .40
15 Joe Ausanio .15 .40
16 Salomon Torres .15 .40
17 Ricky Bottalico RC .15 .40
18 Johnny Ruffin .15 .40
19 Kevin Foster RC .15 .40
20 W.VanLandingham RC .15 .40
21 Troy O'Leary .15 .40
22 Mark Acre RC .15 .40
23 Norberto Martin .15 .40
24 Jason Jacome RC .15 .40
25 Steve Trachsel .15 .40
26 Denny Hocking .15 .40
27 Mike Lieberthal .30 .75
28 Gerald Williams .15 .40
29 John Mabry RC .30 .75
30 Greg Blosser .15 .40
31 Carl Everett .30 .75
32 Steve Karsay .15 .40
33 Jose Valentin .15 .40
34 Jon Lieber .30 .75
35 Chris Gomez .15 .40
36 Jesus Tavarez RC .15 .40
37 Tony Longmire .15 .40
38 Luis Lopez .15 .40
39 Matt Walbeck .15 .40
40 Rikkert Faneyte RC .15 .40
41 Shane Reynolds .15 .40
42 Joey Hamilton .15 .40
43 Ismael Valdes RC .30 .75
44 Danny Miceli .15 .40
45 Darren Bragg RC .15 .40
46 Alex Gonzalez .15 .40
47 Rick Helling .15 .40
48 Jose Oliva .15 .40
49 Jim Edmonds .75 2.00
50 Miguel Jimenez .15 .40
51 Tony Eusebio .15 .40
52 Shawn Green .75 2.00
53 Billy Ashley .15 .40
54 Rondell White .30 .75
55 Cory Bailey RC .15 .40
56 Tim Davis .15 .40
57 John Hudek RC .15 .40
58 Darren Hall .15 .40
59 Darren Dreifort .15 .40
60 Mike Kelly .15 .40
61 Marcus Moore .15 .40
62 Garret Anderson .75 2.00
63 Brian L. Hunter .15 .40
64 Mark Smith .15 .40
65 Garey Ingram RC .15 .40
66 Rusty Greer RC .50 1.25
67 Marc Newfield .15 .40
68 Gar Finnvold .15 .40
69 Paul Spoljaric .15 .40
70 Ray McDavid .15 .40
71 Orlando Miller .15 .40
72 Jorge Fabregas .15 .40
73 Ray Holbert .15 .40
74 Armando Benitez RC .30 .75
75 Ernie Young RC .30 .75
76 James Mouton .15 .40
77 Robert Perez RC .15 .40
78 Chan Ho Park RC .50 1.25
79 Roger Salkeld .15 .40
80 Tony Tarasco .15 .40

1994 Leaf Limited Rookies Phenoms

COMPLETE SET (10) 150.00 300.00
STATED ODDS 1:12
STATED PRINT RUN 5000 SERIAL #'d SETS
1 Raul Mondesi 3.00 8.00
2 Bob Hamelin 2.00 5.00
3 Midre Cummings 2.00 5.00
4 Carlos Delgado 4.00 10.00
5 Cliff Floyd 3.00 8.00
6 Jeffrey Hammonds 2.00 5.00
7 Ryan Klesko 3.00 8.00
8 Javier Lopez 3.00 8.00
9 Manny Ramirez 8.00 20.00
10 Alex Rodriguez 40.00 100.00

1995 Leaf Limited

This 192 standard-size card set was issued in two series. Each series contained 96 cards. These cards were issued in six-box cases with 20 packs per box and five cards per pack. Forty-five thousand boxes of each series was produced. Rookie Cards in this set include Bob Higginson and Hideo Nomo.

COMPLETE SET (192) 15.00 40.00
COMPLETE SERIES 1 (96) 8.00 20.00
COMPLETE SERIES 2 (96) 8.00 20.00
1 Frank Thomas .50 1.25
2 Geronimo Berroa .08 .25
3 Tony Phillips .08 .25
4 Roberto Alomar .30 .75
5 Steve Avery .08 .25
6 Darryl Hamilton .08 .25
7 Scott Cooper .08 .25
8 Mark Grace .30 .75
9 Billy Ashley .08 .25
10 Wil Cordero .08 .25
11 Barry Bonds 1.25 3.00
12 Kenny Lofton .20 .50
13 Jay Buhner .20 .50
14 Alex Rodriguez 1.25 3.00
15 Bobby Bonilla .20 .50
16 Brady Anderson .20 .50
17 Ken Caminiti .20 .50
18 Charlie Hayes .08 .25
19 Jay Bell .20 .50
20 Will Clark .30 .75
21 Jose Canseco .30 .75
22 Bret Boone .20 .50
23 Dante Bichette .20 .50
24 Kevin Appier .20 .50
25 Chad Curtis .08 .25
26 Marty Cordova .08 .25
27 Jason Bere .08 .25
28 Jimmy Key .20 .50
29 Rickey Henderson .50 1.25
30 Tim Salmon .30 .75
31 Joe Carter .20 .50
32 Tom Glavine .30 .75
33 Pat Listach .08 .25
34 Brian Jordan .20 .50
35 Brian McRae .08 .25
36 Eric Karros .20 .50
37 Pedro Martinez .30 .75
38 Royce Clayton .08 .25
39 Eddie Murray .50 1.25
40 Randy Johnson .50 1.25
41 Jeff Conine .20 .50
42 Brett Butler .20 .50
43 Jeffrey Hammonds .08 .25
44 Andujar Cedeno .08 .25
45 Dave Hollins .08 .25
46 Jeff King .08 .25
47 Benji Gil .08 .25
48 Roger Clemens 1.00 2.50
49 Barry Larkin .30 .75
50 Joe Girardi .08 .25
51 Bob Hamelin .08 .25
52 Travis Fryman .20 .50
53 Chuck Knoblauch .20 .50
54 Ray Durham .20 .50
55 Don Mattingly 1.25 3.00
56 Ruben Sierra .20 .50
57 J.T. Snow .20 .50
58 Derek Bell .08 .25
59 David Cone .20 .50
60 Marquis Grissom .20 .50
61 Kevin Seitzer .08 .25
62 Ozzie Smith .75 2.00
63 Rick Wilkins .08 .25
64 Hideo Nomo RC 1.25 3.00
65 Tony Tarasco .08 .25
66 Manny Ramirez .30 .75
67 Charles Johnson .20 .50
68 Craig Biggio .30 .75
69 Bobby Jones .08 .25
70 Mike Mussina .30 .75
71 Alex Gonzalez .08 .25
72 Gregg Jefferies .08 .25
73 Rusty Greer .20 .50
74 Mike Greenwell .08 .25
75 Hal Morris .08 .25
76 Paul O'Neill .30 .75
77 Luis Gonzalez .20 .50
78 Chipper Jones .50 1.25
79 Mike Piazza .75 2.00
80 Rondell White .20 .50
81 Glenallen Hill .08 .25
82 Shawn Green .20 .50
83 Bernie Williams .30 .75
84 Jim Thome .30 .75
85 Terry Pendleton .20 .50
86 Rafael Palmeiro .30 .75
87 Tony Gwynn .60 1.50
88 Mickey Tettleton .08 .25
89 John Valentin .08 .25
90 Deion Sanders .30 .75
91 Larry Walker .20 .50
92 Michael Tucker .08 .25
93 Alan Trammell .20 .50
94 Tim Raines .20 .50
95 David Justice .20 .50
96 Tino Martinez .30 .75
97 Cal Ripken 1.50 4.00
98 Deion Sanders .30 .75
99 Darren Daulton .20 .50
100 Paul Molitor .20 .50
101 Randy Myers .08 .25
102 Wally Joyner .20 .50
103 Carlos Perez RC .20 .50
104 Brian L.Hunter .08 .25
105 Wade Boggs .30 .75
106 Bob Higginson RC .30 .75
107 Jeff Kent .20 .50
108 Jose Offerman .08 .25
109 Dennis Eckersley .20 .50
110 Dave Nilsson .08 .25
111 Chuck Finley .20 .50
112 Devon White .20 .50
113 Bip Roberts .08 .25
114 Ramon Martinez .08 .25
115 Greg Maddux .75 2.00
116 Curtis Goodwin .08 .25
117 John Jaha .08 .25
118 Ken Griffey Jr. 1.00 2.50
119 Geronimo Pena .08 .25
120 Shawon Dunston .08 .25
121 Ariel Prieto RC .08 .25
122 Kirby Puckett .50 1.25
123 Carlos Baerga .08 .25
124 Todd Hundley .08 .25
125 Tim Naehring .08 .25
126 Gary Sheffield .20 .50
127 Dean Palmer .20 .50
128 Rondell White .20 .50
129 Greg Gagne .08 .25
130 Jose Rijo .08 .25
131 Ivan Rodriguez .30 .75
132 Jeff Bagwell .30 .75
133 Greg Vaughn .08 .25
134 Chili Davis .20 .50
135 Al Martin .08 .25
136 Kenny Rogers .20 .50
137 Aaron Sele .08 .25
138 Raul Mondesi .20 .50
139 Cecil Fielder .20 .50
140 Tim Wallach .08 .25
141 Andres Galarraga .20 .50
142 Lou Whitaker .20 .50
143 Jack McDowell .08 .25
144 Matt Williams .20 .50
145 Ryan Klesko .20 .50
146 Carlos Garcia .08 .25
147 Albert Belle .20 .50
148 Ryan Thompson .08 .25
149 Roberto Kelly .08 .25
150 Edgar Martinez .30 .75
151 Robby Thompson .08 .25
152 Mo Vaughn .20 .50
153 Todd Zeile .08 .25
154 Harold Baines .20 .50
155 Phil Plantier .08 .25
156 Mike Stanley .08 .25
157 Ed Sprague .08 .25
158 Moises Alou .20 .50
159 Quilvio Veras .08 .25
160 Reggie Sanders .20 .50
161 Delino DeShields .08 .25
162 Rico Brogna .08 .25
163 Greg Colbrunn .08 .25
164 Steve Finley .20 .50
165 Orlando Merced .08 .25
166 Mark McGwire 1.25 3.00
167 Garret Anderson .20 .50
168 Paul Sorrento .08 .25
169 Mark Langston .08 .25
170 Danny Tartabull .08 .25
171 Vinny Castilla .20 .50
172 Javier Lopez .20 .50
173 Bret Saberhagen .20 .50
174 Eddie Williams .08 .25
175 Scott Leius .08 .25
176 Juan Gonzalez .20 .50
177 Gary Gaetti .20 .50
178 Jim Edmonds .30 .75
179 John Olerud .20 .50
180 Lenny Dykstra .20 .50
181 Ray Lankford .20 .50
182 Ron Gant .20 .50
183 Doug Drabek .08 .25
184 Fred McGriff .30 .75
185 Andy Benes .08 .25
186 Kurt Abbott .08 .25
187 Bernard Gilkey .08 .25
188 Sammy Sosa .50 1.25
189 Lee Smith .20 .50
190 Dennis Martinez .20 .50
191 Ozzie Guillen .20 .50
192 Robin Ventura .20 .50

1995 Leaf Limited Gold

COMPLETE SET (24) 10.00 25.00
ONE GOLD PER SERIES ONE PACK
1 Frank Thomas .50 1.25
2 Jeff Bagwell .30 .75
3 Raul Mondesi .20 .50
4 Barry Bonds 1.25 3.00
5 Albert Belle .20 .50
6 Ken Griffey Jr. 1.00 2.50
7 Cal Ripkin UER 1.50 4.00
8 Will Clark .30 .75
9 Jose Canseco .30 .75
10 Larry Walker .20 .50
11 Kirby Puckett .50 1.25
12 Don Mattingly 1.25 3.00
13 Tim Salmon .30 .75
14 Roberto Alomar .30 .75
15 Greg Maddux .75 2.00
16 Mike Piazza .75 2.00
17 Matt Williams .20 .50
18 Kenny Lofton .20 .50
19 Alex Rodriguez UER 1.25 3.00
20 Tony Gwynn .60 1.50
21 Mo Vaughn .20 .50
22 Chipper Jones .50 1.25
23 Manny Ramirez .30 .75
24 Deion Sanders .30 .75

1995 Leaf Limited Bat Patrol

COMPLETE SET (24) 10.00 25.00
ONE PER SERIES 2 PACK
1 Frank Thomas .50 1.25
2 Tony Gwynn .60 1.50
3 Wade Boggs .30 .75
4 Larry Walker .20 .50
5 Ken Griffey Jr. 1.00 2.50
6 Jeff Bagwell .30 .75
7 Manny Ramirez .30 .75
8 Mark Grace .30 .75
9 Kenny Lofton .20 .50
10 Mike Piazza .75 2.00
11 Will Clark .30 .75
12 Mo Vaughn .20 .50
13 Carlos Baerga .08 .25
14 Rafael Palmeiro .30 .75
15 Barry Bonds 1.25 3.00
16 Kirby Puckett .50 1.25
17 Roberto Alomar .30 .75
18 Barry Larkin .30 .75
19 Eddie Murray .50 1.25
20 Tim Salmon .30 .75
21 Don Mattingly 1.25 3.00
22 Fred McGriff .30 .75
23 Albert Belle .20 .50
24 Dante Bichette .20 .50

1995 Leaf Limited Lumberjacks

COMPLETE SET (16) 25.00 60.00
COMPLETE SERIES 1 (8) 12.50 30.00
COMPLETE SERIES 2 (8) 12.50 30.00
STATED ODDS 1:23
STATED PRINT RUN 5000 SERIAL #'d SETS
1 Albert Belle .60 1.50
2 Barry Bonds 2.50 6.00
3 Juan Gonzalez 1.00 2.50
4 Ken Griffey Jr. 3.00 8.00
5 Fred McGriff 1.00 2.50
6 Mike Piazza 1.50 4.00
7 Kirby Puckett 1.50 4.00
8 Mo Vaughn .60 1.50
9 Frank Thomas 1.50 4.00
10 Jeff Bagwell 1.00 2.50
11 Matt Williams .60 1.50
12 Jose Canseco 1.00 2.50
13 Raul Mondesi .60 1.50
14 Manny Ramirez 1.00 2.50
15 Cecil Fielder .60 1.50
16 Cal Ripken 5.00 12.00

1996 Leaf Limited

The 1996 Leaf Limited set was issued exclusively to hobby outlets with a maximum production run of 45,000 boxes. Each box contained two smaller mini-boxes, enabling the dealer to use his imagination in the marketing of this product. The five-card packs carried a suggested retail price of $3.24. Each Master Box was sequentially- numbered via a box topper. If this number matched the 1996 year-ending stats, the collector and the dealer both had a chance to win prizes such as a Frank Thomas game-used bat, autographed batting glove, or a "Two Biggest Weapons" poster. The collector would return the winning box number to the hobby shop, and the dealer would mail it to Donruss with both receiving the same prize. The card fronts displayed color player photos with another photo and player information on the backs.

COMPLETE SET (90) 12.50 30.00
1 Ivan Rodriguez .40 1.00
2 Roger Clemens 1.25 3.00
3 Gary Sheffield .25 .60
4 Tino Martinez .40 1.00
5 Sammy Sosa .60 1.50
6 Reggie Sanders .25 .60
7 Ray Lankford .25 .60
8 Manny Ramirez .40 1.00
9 Jeff Bagwell .40 1.00
10 Greg Maddux 1.00 2.50
11 Ken Griffey Jr. 1.25 3.00
12 Rondell White .25 .60
13 Mike Piazza 1.00 2.50
14 Marc Newfield .25 .60
15 Cal Ripken 2.00 5.00
16 Carlos Delgado .25 .60
17 Tim Salmon .40 1.00
18 Andres Galarraga .25 .60
19 Chuck Knoblauch .25 .60
20 Matt Williams .25 .60
21 Mark McGwire 1.50 4.00
22 Ben McDonald .25 .60
23 Frank Thomas .60 1.50
24 Johnny Damon .40 1.00
25 Gregg Jefferies .25 .60
26 Travis Fryman .25 .60
27 Chipper Jones .60 1.50
28 David Cone .25 .60
29 Kenny Lofton .25 .60
30 Mike Mussina .40 1.00
31 Alex Rodriguez 1.25 3.00
32 Carlos Baerga .25 .60
33 Brian Hunter .25 .60
34 Juan Gonzalez .25 .60
35 Bernie Williams .40 1.00
36 Wally Joyner .25 .60
37 Fred McGriff .40 1.00
38 Randy Johnson .60 1.50
39 Marty Cordova .25 .60
40 Garret Anderson .25 .60
41 Albert Belle .25 .60
42 Edgar Martinez .40 1.00
43 Barry Larkin .40 1.00
44 Paul O'Neill .40 1.00
45 Cecil Fielder .25 .60
46 Rusty Greer .25 .60
47 Mo Vaughn .25 .60
48 Dante Bichette .25 .60
49 Ryan Klesko .25 .60
50 Roberto Alomar .40 1.00
51 Raul Mondesi .25 .60
52 Robin Ventura .25 .60
53 Tony Gwynn .75 2.00
54 Mark Grace .40 1.00
55 Jim Thome .40 1.00
56 Jason Giambi .25 .60
57 Tom Glavine .40 1.00
58 Jim Edmonds .25 .60
59 Pedro Martinez .40 1.00
60 Charles Johnson .25 .60
61 Wade Boggs .40 1.00
62 Orlando Merced .25 .60
63 Craig Biggio .40 1.00
64 Brady Anderson .25 .60
65 Hideo Nomo .60 1.50
66 Ozzie Smith 1.00 2.50
67 Eddie Murray .60 1.50
68 Will Clark .40 1.00
69 Jay Buhner .25 .60
70 Kirby Puckett .60 1.50
71 Barry Bonds 1.50 4.00
72 Ray Durham .25 .60
73 Sterling Hitchcock .25 .60
74 John Smoltz .40 1.00
75 Andre Dawson .25 .60
76 Joe Carter .25 .60
77 Ryne Sandberg 1.00 2.50
78 Rickey Henderson .60 1.50
79 Brian Jordan .25 .60
80 Greg Vaughn .25 .60
81 Andy Pettitte .40 1.00
82 Dean Palmer .25 .60
83 Paul Molitor .25 .60
84 Rafael Palmeiro .40 1.00
85 Henry Rodriguez .25 .60
86 Larry Walker .25 .60
87 Ismael Valdes .25 .60
88 Derek Bell .25 .60
89 J.T. Snow .25 .60
90 Jack McDowell .25 .60

1996 Leaf Limited Gold

*STARS: 2.5X TO 6X BASIC CARDS
STATED ODDS 1:11

1996 Leaf Limited Lumberjacks Samples

COMPLETE SET (10) 30.00 80.00
1 Ken Griffey Jr. 4.00 10.00
2 Sammy Sosa 2.00 5.00
3 Cal Ripken 6.00 15.00
4 Frank Thomas 1.25 3.00
5 Alex Rodriguez 4.00 10.00
6 Mo Vaughn .60 1.50
7 Chipper Jones 3.00 8.00
8 Mike Piazza 4.00 10.00
9 Jeff Bagwell 1.50 4.00
10 Mark McGwire 4.00 10.00

1996 Leaf Limited Lumberjacks

COMPLETE SET (10) 60.00 120.00
STATED PRINT RUN 4500 SERIAL #'d SETS
*BLACK: 1X TO 2.5X BASIC LUMBERJACK
BLACK PRINT RUN 500 SERIAL #'d SETS
RANDOM INSERTS IN PACKS
1 Ken Griffey Jr. 5.00 12.00
2 Sammy Sosa 2.50 6.00
3 Cal Ripken 8.00 20.00
4 Frank Thomas 2.50 6.00
5 Alex Rodriguez 3.00 8.00
6 Mo Vaughn 1.00 2.50
7 Chipper Jones 2.50 6.00
8 Mike Piazza 2.50 6.00
9 Jeff Bagwell 1.50 4.00
10 Mark McGwire 4.00 10.00

1996 Leaf Limited Pennant Craze Promos

Issued to promote the Leaf Limited Pennant Craze insert set, these cards are differentiated from the regular Leaf Limited insert cards as they are numbered 0000/2500 on the back.

COMPLETE SET (10) 15.00 40.00
1 Juan Gonzalez .75 2.00
2 Cal Ripken 4.00 10.00
3 Frank Thomas .75 2.00
4 Ken Griffey Jr. 2.50 6.00
5 Albert Belle .30 .75
6 Greg Maddux 2.50 6.00
7 Paul Molitor 1.00 2.50
8 Alex Rodriguez 2.00 5.00
9 Barry Bonds 2.00 5.00
10 Chipper Jones 2.00 5.00

1996 Leaf Limited Pennant Craze

COMPLETE SET (10) 12.50 30.00
RANDOM INSERTS IN PACKS
STATED PRINT RUN 2500 SERIAL #'d SETS
1 Juan Gonzalez .60 1.50
2 Cal Ripken 5.00 12.00
3 Frank Thomas 1.50 4.00
4 Ken Griffey Jr. 10.00 25.00
5 Albert Belle .60 1.50
6 Greg Maddux 2.50 6.00
7 Paul Molitor 1.50 4.00
8 Alex Rodriguez 2.00 5.00
9 Barry Bonds 2.50 6.00
10 Chipper Jones 1.50 4.00

1996 Leaf Limited Rookies

COMPLETE SET (10) 15.00 40.00
STATED ODDS 1:7
*GOLD: 1X TO 2.5X BASIC ROOKIES
GOLD: RANDOM INSERTS IN PACKS
1 Alex Ochoa .40 1.00
2 Darin Erstad 1.50 4.00
3 Ruben Rivera .40 1.00
4 Derek Jeter 8.00 20.00
5 Jermaine Dye .75 2.00
6 Jason Kendall .75 2.00
7 Mike Grace .40 1.00
8 Andruw Jones 1.25 3.00
9 Rey Ordonez .40 1.00
10 George Arias .40 1.00

2001 Leaf Limited

COMP.SET w/o SP'S (150) 40.00 100.00
COMMON CARD (1-150) .40 1.00
COMMON HAT (326-375) 10.00 25.00
COMMON LUM/500 (151-200) 3.00 8.00
COMMON LUM/250 (151-200) 4.00 10.00
COMMON LUM/100 (151-200) 6.00 15.00
151-200 RANDOM INSERTS IN PACKS
151-200 PRINT RUNS LISTED BELOW
COMMON CARD (201-250) 2.00 5.00
201-250 PRINT RUN 1500 SERIAL #'d SETS
COMMON CARD (251-300) 2.00 5.00
251-300 PRINT RUN 1000 SERIAL #'d SETS
COMMON AUTO (301-325) 4.00 10.00
301-325 PRINT RUN 1000 SERIAL #'d SETS
COMMON BASE (326-375) 6.00 15.00
BASE PRINT RUN 300 SERIAL #'d SETS
COMMON BAT (326-375) 3.00 8.00
BAT PRINT RUN 500-700 SERIAL #'d SETS
HAT PRINT RUN 100 SERIAL #'d SETS
COMMON JSY (326-375) 3.00 8.00
JSY PRINT RUN 500 SERIAL #'d SETS
COMMON PANTS (326-375) 3.00 8.00
PANTS PRINT RUN 650 SERIAL #'d SETS
COMMON SPIKES (326-375) 10.00 25.00
SPIKES PRINT RUN 125 SERIAL #'d SETS
326-375 RANDOM INSERTS IN PACKS
326-375 PRINT RUNS LISTED BELOW
1 Curt Schilling .40 1.00
2 Craig Biggio .60 1.50
3 Brian Giles .40 1.00
4 Scott Brosius .40 1.00
5 Barry Larkin .60 1.50
6 Bartolo Colon .40 1.00
7 John Olerud .40 1.00
8 Cal Ripken 3.00 8.00
9 Moises Alou .40 1.00
10 Barry Zito .60 1.50
11 Ken Griffey Jr. 2.00 5.00
12 Garret Anderson .40 1.00
13 Andy Pettitte .60 1.50
14 Jim Edmonds .40 1.00
15 Tom Glavine .60 1.50
16 Jose Canseco .60 1.50
17 Fred McGriff .60 1.50
18 Robin Ventura .40 1.00
19 Tony Gwynn 1.25 3.00
20 Jeff Cirillo .40 1.00
21 Brad Radke .40 1.00
22 Ellis Burks .40 1.00
23 Scott Rolen .60 1.50
24 Rickey Henderson 1.00 2.50
25 Edgar Martinez .60 1.50
26 Kerry Wood .40 1.00
27 Al Leiter .40 1.00
28 Jose Cruz Jr. .40 1.00
29 Sean Casey .40 1.00
30 Eric Chavez .40 1.00
31 Jarrod Washburn .40 1.00
32 Gary Sheffield .40 1.00
33 Jermaine Dye .40 1.00
34 Bernie Williams .60 1.50
35 Tony Armas Jr. .40 1.00
36 Carlos Beltran .40 1.00
37 Geoff Jenkins .40 1.00
38 Shawn Green .40 1.00
39 Ryan Klesko .40 1.00
40 Richie Sexson .40 1.00
41 Pat Burrell .40 1.00
42 J.D. Drew .40 1.00
43 Larry Walker .40 1.00
44 Andres Galarraga .40 1.00
45 Tino Martinez .60 1.50
46 Rafael Furcal .40 1.00
47 Cristian Guzman .40 1.00
48 Omar Vizquel .60 1.50
49 Bret Boone .40 1.00
50 Wade Miller .40 1.00
51 Eric Milton .40 1.00
52 Gabe Kapler .40 1.00
53 Johnny Damon .60 1.50
54 Shannon Stewart .40 1.00
55 Kenny Lofton .40 1.00
56 Raul Mondesi .40 1.00
57 Jorge Posada .60 1.50
58 Mark Grace .60 1.50
59 Robert Fick .40 1.00
60 Phil Nevin .40 1.00
61 Mike Mussina .60 1.50
62 Joe Mays .40 1.00
63 Todd Helton .60 1.50
64 Tim Hudson .40 1.00
65 Manny Ramirez Sox .60 1.50
66 Sammy Sosa 1.00 2.50
67 Darin Erstad .40 1.00
68 Roberto Alomar .60 1.50
69 Jeff Bagwell .60 1.50
70 Mark McGwire 2.50 6.00
71 Jason Giambi .40 1.00
72 Cliff Floyd .40 1.00
73 Barry Bonds 2.50 6.00
74 Juan Gonzalez .40 1.00
75 Jeremy Giambi .40 1.00
76 Carlos Lee .40 1.00
77 Randy Johnson 1.00 2.50
78 Frank Thomas 1.00 2.50
79 Carlos Delgado .40 1.00
80 Pedro Martinez .60 1.50
81 Rusty Greer .40 1.00
82 Brian Jordan .40 1.00
83 Vladimir Guerrero 1.00 2.50
84 Mike Sweeney .40 1.00
85 Jose Vidro .40 1.00
86 Paul LoDuca .40 1.00
87 Matt Morris .40 1.00
88 Adrian Beltre .40 1.00
89 Aramis Ramirez .40 1.00
90 Derek Jeter 2.50 6.00
91 Rich Aurilia .40 1.00
92 Freddy Garcia .40 1.00
93 Preston Wilson .40 1.00
94 Greg Maddux 1.50 4.00
95 Miguel Tejada .40 1.00
96 Luis Gonzalez .40 1.00
97 Torii Hunter .40 1.00
98 Nomar Garciaparra 1.50 4.00
99 Jamie Moyer .40 1.00
100 Javier Vazquez .40 1.00
101 Ben Grieve .40 1.00
102 Mike Piazza 1.50 4.00
103 Paul O'Neill .60 1.50
104 Terrence Long .40 1.00
105 Charles Johnson .40 1.00
106 Rafael Palmeiro .60 1.50
107 David Cone .40 1.00
108 Alex Rodriguez 1.25 3.00
109 John Burkett .40 1.00
110 Chipper Jones 1.00 2.50
111 Ryan Dempster .40 1.00
112 Bobby Abreu .40 1.00
113 Brad Fullmer .40 1.00
114 Kazuhiro Sasaki .40 1.00
115 Mariano Rivera 1.00 2.50
116 Edgardo Alfonzo .40 1.00
117 Ray Durham .40 1.00
118 Richard Hidalgo .40 1.00
119 Jeff Weaver .40 1.00
120 Paul Konerko .40 1.00
121 Jon Lieber .40 1.00
122 Mike Hampton .40 1.00
123 Mike Cameron .40 1.00
124 Kevin Brown .40 1.00
125 Doug Mientkiewicz .40 1.00
126 Jim Thome .60 1.50
127 Corey Koskie .40 1.00
128 Trot Nixon .40 1.00
129 Darryl Kile .40 1.00
130 Ivan Rodriguez .60 1.50
131 Carl Everett .40 1.00
132 Jeff Kent .40 1.00
133 Rondell White .40 1.00
134 Chan Ho Park .40 1.00
135 Robert Person .40 1.00
136 Troy Glaus .40 1.00
137 Aaron Sele .40 1.00
138 Roger Clemens 2.00 5.00
139 Tony Clark .40 1.00
140 Mark Buehrle .60 1.50
141 David Justice .40 1.00
142 Magglio Ordonez .40 1.00
143 Bobby Higginson .40 1.00
144 Hideo Nomo 1.00 2.50
145 Tim Salmon .60 1.50
146 Mark Mulder .40 1.00
147 Troy Percival .40 1.00
148 Lance Berkman .40 1.00
149 Russ Ortiz .40 1.00
150 Andruw Jones .60 1.50
151 Mike Piazza LUM/500 6.00 15.00

Card	Low	High
152 Manny Ramirez Sox LUM/500	4.00	10.00
153 Bernie Williams LUM/500	4.00	10.00
154 N.Garciaparra LUM/500	6.00	15.00
155 Andres Galarraga LUM/500	3.00	8.00
156 Kenny Lofton LUM/500	3.00	8.00
157 Scott Rolen LUM/250	6.00	15.00
158 Jim Thome LUM/500	4.00	10.00
159 Darin Erstad LUM/500	3.00	8.00
160 Garret Anderson LUM/500	3.00	8.00
161 Andruw Jones LUM/500	4.00	10.00
162 Juan Gonzalez LUM/500	3.00	8.00
163 Rafael Palmeiro LUM/500	4.00	10.00
164 Magglio Ordonez LUM/500	3.00	8.00
165 Jeff Bagwell LUM/250	6.00	15.00
166 Eric Chavez LUM/500	3.00	8.00
167 Brian Giles LUM/500	3.00	8.00
168 Adrian Beltre LUM/500	3.00	8.00
169 Tony Gwynn LUM/500	6.00	15.00
170 Shawn Green LUM/500	3.00	8.00
171 Todd Helton LUM/500	4.00	10.00
172 Troy Glaus LUM/100	6.00	15.00
173 Lance Berkman LUM/500	3.00	8.00
174 Ivan Rodriguez LUM/500	4.00	10.00
175 Sean Casey LUM/500	3.00	8.00
176 Aramis Ramirez LUM/100	6.00	15.00
177 J.D. Drew LUM/500	3.00	8.00
178 Barry Bonds LUM/250	6.00	15.00
179 Barry Larkin LUM/500	4.00	10.00
180 Cal Ripken LUM/500	8.00	20.00
181 Frank Thomas LUM/500	4.00	10.00
182 Craig Biggio LUM/250	6.00	15.00
183 Carlos Lee LUM/500	3.00	8.00
184 Chipper Jones LUM/500	4.00	10.00
185 Miguel Tejada LUM/250	4.00	10.00
186 Jose Vidro LUM/500	3.00	8.00
187 Terrence Long LUM/500	3.00	8.00
188 Moises Alou LUM/500	3.00	8.00
189 Trot Nixon LUM/500	3.00	8.00
190 Shannon Stewart LUM/500	3.00	8.00
191 Ryan Klesko LUM/500	3.00	8.00
192 Carlos Beltran LUM/500	3.00	8.00
193 Vladimir Guerrero LUM/500	4.00	10.00
194 Edgar Martinez LUM/500	4.00	10.00
195 Luis Gonzalez LUM/500	3.00	8.00
196 Richard Hidalgo LUM/500	3.00	8.00
197 Roberto Alomar LUM/500	4.00	10.00
198 Mike Sweeney LUM/100	6.00	15.00
199 Bobby Abreu LUM/250	4.00	10.00
200 Cliff Floyd LUM/500	3.00	8.00
201 Jackson Melian RC	2.00	5.00
202 Jason Jennings	2.00	5.00
203 Toby Hall	2.00	5.00
204 Jason Karnuth RC	2.00	5.00
205 Jason Smith RC	2.00	5.00
206 Mike Maroth RC	3.00	8.00
207 Sean Douglass RC	2.00	5.00
208 Adam Johnson	2.00	5.00
209 Luke Hudson RC	2.00	5.00
210 Nick Maness RC	2.00	5.00
211 Les Walrond RC	2.00	5.00
212 Travis Phelps RC	2.00	5.00
213 Carlos Garcia RC	2.00	5.00
214 Bill Ortega RC	2.00	5.00
215 Gene Altman RC	2.00	5.00
216 Nate Frese RC	2.00	5.00
217 Bob File RC	2.00	5.00
218 Steve Green RC	2.00	5.00
219 Kris Keller RC	2.00	5.00
220 Matt White RC	2.00	5.00
221 Nate Teut RC	2.00	5.00
222 Nick Johnson	2.00	5.00
223 Jeremy Fikac RC	2.00	5.00
224 Abraham Nunez	2.00	5.00
225 Mike Penney RC	2.00	5.00
226 Roy Smith RC	2.00	5.00
227 Tim Christman RC	2.00	5.00
228 Carlos Pena	2.00	5.00
229 Joe Beimel RC	2.00	5.00
230 Mike Koplove RC	2.00	5.00
231 Scott MacRae RC	2.00	5.00
232 Kyle Lohse RC	3.00	8.00
233 Jerrod Riggan RC	2.00	5.00
234 Scott Podsednik RC	6.00	15.00
235 Winston Abreu RC	2.00	5.00
236 Ryan Freel RC	3.00	8.00
237 Ken Vining RC	2.00	5.00
238 Bret Prinz RC	2.00	5.00
239 Paul Phillips RC	2.00	5.00
240 Josh Fogg RC	2.00	5.00
241 Saul Rivera RC	2.00	5.00
242 Esix Snead RC	2.00	5.00
243 John Grabow RC	2.00	5.00
44 Tony Cogan RC	2.00	5.00
45 Pedro Santana RC	2.00	5.00
46 Jack Cust	2.00	5.00
47 Joe Crede	3.00	8.00
48 Juan Moreno RC	2.00	5.00
49 Kevin Joseph RC	2.00	5.00
50 Scott Stewart RC	2.00	5.00
51 Rob Mackowiak RC	3.00	8.00
52 Luis Pineda RC	2.00	5.00
53 Bert Snow RC	2.00	5.00
4 Dustan Mohr RC	2.00	5.00
5 Justin Kaye RC	2.00	5.00
6 Chad Paronto RC	2.00	5.00
7 Nick Punto RC	2.00	5.00
8 Brian Roberts RC	3.00	8.00
9 Eric Hinske RC	3.00	8.00
0 Victor Zambrano RC	3.00	8.00
1 Juan A.Pena RC	2.00	5.00
2 Rick Bauer RC	2.00	5.00
3 Jorge Julio RC	2.00	5.00
4 Craig Monroe RC	3.00	8.00
5 Stubby Clapp RC	2.00	5.00
6 Martin Vargas RC	2.00	5.00
7 Josue Perez RC	2.00	5.00
8 Cody Ransom RC	2.00	5.00
9 Will Ohman RC	2.00	5.00
0 Juan Diaz RC	2.00	5.00
Ramon Vazquez RC	2.00	5.00
Grant Balfour RC	2.00	5.00
Ryan Jensen RC	2.00	5.00
Benito Baez RC	2.00	5.00
Angel Santos RC	2.00	5.00
Brian Reith RC	2.00	5.00
Brandon Lyon RC	2.00	5.00
Erik Hiljus RC	2.00	5.00
Brandon Knight RC	2.00	5.00
Jose Acevedo RC	2.00	5.00
281 Cesar Crespo RC	2.00	5.00
282 Kevin Olsen RC	2.00	5.00
283 Duaner Sanchez RC	2.00	5.00
284 Endy Chavez RC	2.00	5.00
285 Blaine Neal RC	2.00	5.00
286 Brett Jodie RC	2.00	5.00
287 Brad Voyles RC	2.00	5.00
288 Doug Nickle RC	2.00	5.00
289 Junior Spivey RC	3.00	8.00
290 Henry Mateo RC	2.00	5.00
291 Xavier Nady	2.00	5.00
292 Lance Davis RC	2.00	5.00
293 Willie Harris RC	2.00	5.00
294 Mark Lukasiewicz RC	2.00	5.00
295 Ryan Drese RC	3.00	8.00
296 Morgan Ensberg RC	3.00	8.00
297 Jose Mieses RC	2.00	5.00
298 Jason Michaels RC	2.00	5.00
299 Kris Foster RC	2.00	5.00
300 Justin Duchscherer RC	2.00	5.00
301 Elpidio Guzman AU RC	4.00	10.00
302 Cory Aldridge AU RC	4.00	10.00
303 Angel Berroa AU/500 RC	6.00	15.00
304 Travis Hafner AU RC	8.00	20.00
305 Horacio Ramirez AU RC	6.00	15.00
306 Juan Uribe AU RC	10.00	25.00
307 Mark Prior AU/500 RC	5.00	12.00
308 Brandon Larson AU RC	4.00	10.00
309 Nick Neugebauer AU/750	4.00	10.00
310 Zach Day AU/750 RC	4.00	10.00
311 Jeremy Owens AU RC	4.00	10.00
312 Dewon Brazelton AU/500 RC	4.00	10.00
313 Bran Duckworth AU/750 RC	4.00	10.00
314 Adrian Hernandez AU RC	4.00	10.00
315 Mark Teixeira AU/500 RC	6.00	15.00
316 Brian Rogers AU RC	4.00	10.00
317 David Brous AU/750 RC	4.00	10.00
318 Geronimo Gil AU RC	4.00	10.00
319 Erick Almonte AU RC	4.00	10.00
320 Claudio Vargas AU RC	4.00	10.00
321 Wilkin Ruan AU RC	4.00	10.00
322 David Williams AU RC	4.00	10.00
323 Alexis Gomez AU RC	4.00	10.00
324 Mike Rivera AU RC	4.00	10.00
325 Brandon Berger AU RC	4.00	10.00
326 Keith Ginter Bat/125	10.00	25.00
327 Brandon Inge Bat/700	3.00	8.00
328 Brent Abernathy Bat/700	3.00	8.00
329 Billy Sylvester Bat/700 RC	3.00	8.00
330 Bart Miadich Jsy/500 RC	3.00	8.00
331 Tsuy Shinjo Jsy/500 RC	4.00	10.00
332 Eric Valent Spikes/125	10.00	25.00
333 Dee Brown Jsy/500	3.00	8.00
334 Andres Torres Spikes/125 RC	10.00	25.00
335 Timo Perez Bat/700	3.00	8.00
336 Cesar Izturis Pants/650	3.00	8.00
337 Pedro Feliz Spikes/125	10.00	25.00
338 Jason Hart Bat/200	4.00	10.00
339 Greg Miller Bat/700 RC	3.00	8.00
340 Eric Munson Bat/700	3.00	8.00
341 Aubrey Huff Jsy/450	3.00	8.00
342 Wilmy Caceres Bat/700 RC	3.00	8.00
343 Alex Escobar Pants/650	3.00	8.00
344 Brian Lawrence Bat/700 RC	3.00	8.00
345 A Pettyjohn Pants/650 RC	3.00	8.00
346 Donaldo Mendez Bat/700 RC	3.00	8.00
347 C Valderrama Jsy/250 RC	4.00	10.00
348 Christ Parker Pants/650 RC	3.00	8.00
349 Corky Miller Jsy/500 RC	3.00	8.00
350 Michael Cuddyer Jsy/500	3.00	8.00
351 Adam Dunn Bat/500	4.00	10.00
352 Josh Beckett Pants/650	4.00	10.00
353 Juan Cruz Jsy/500 RC	3.00	8.00
354 Ben Sheets Jsy/400	4.00	10.00
355 Roy Oswalt Bat/100	15.00	40.00
356 Raf Soriano Pants/650 RC	3.00	8.00
357 R.Rodriguez Pants/650 RC	3.00	8.00
358 Jimmy Rollins Base/300	6.00	15.00
359 C.C. Sabathia Jsy/500	3.00	8.00
360 Bud Smith Jsy/500 RC	3.00	8.00
361 Jose Ortiz Hat/100	10.00	25.00
362 Marcus Giles Jsy/400	3.00	8.00
363 Jack Wilson Hat/100 RC	20.00	50.00
364 Wilson Betemit Hat/100 RC	10.00	25.00
365 Corey Patterson Pants/650	3.00	8.00
366 J.Gibbons Spikes/125 RC	15.00	40.00
367 Albert Pujols Jsy/250 RC	150.00	400.00
368 Joe Kennedy Hat/100 RC	10.00	25.00
369 Alfonso Soriano Hat/100	15.00	40.00
370 Delvin James Pants/650 RC	3.00	8.00
371 Josh Towers Pants/650 RC	4.00	10.00
372 Jeremy Affeldt Pants/650 RC	3.00	8.00
373 Tim Redding Jsy/500	3.00	8.00
374 I.Suzuki Base/100 RC	300.00	800.00
375 Johnny Estrada Bat/100 RC	10.00	25.00

2003 Leaf Limited

Card	Low	High
COMMON CARD (1-151)	.60	1.50
1-151 PRINT RUN 999 SERIAL #'d SETS		
COMMON CARD (151-170)	.75	2.00
151-170 RANDOM INSERTS IN PACKS		
151-170 PRINT RUN 399 SERIAL #'d SETS		
COMMON AU GU (171-200)	6.00	15.00
AU GU 171-200 PRINT 99 SERIAL #'d SETS		
COMMON GU (174/199)	3.00	8.00
GU 174/199 PRINT RUN 99 SERIAL #'d SETS		
COMMON AU (171-204) p/r 99	6.00	15.00
COMMON AU (171-200) p/r 49	10.00	25.00
AU 171-204 PRINT B/WN 49-99 COPIES PER		
171-200 RANDOM INSERTS IN PACKS		
A EQUALS AWAY UNIFORM IMAGE		
H EQUALS HOME UNIFORM IMAGE		
1 Derek Jeter Btg	4.00	10.00
2 Eric Chavez	.60	1.50
3 Alex Rodriguez Rgr A	2.00	5.00
4 Miguel Tejada Fldg	1.00	2.50
5 Nomar Garciaparra H	1.00	2.50
6 Jeff Bagwell H	1.00	2.50
7 Jim Thome Phils A	1.00	2.50
8 Pat Burrell w/Bat	.60	1.50
9 Albert Pujols H	2.00	5.00
10 Juan Gonzalez Rgr Btg	.60	1.50
11 Shawn Green Jays	.60	1.50
12 Craig Biggio H	1.00	2.50
13 Chipper Jones H	1.50	4.00
14 H.Nomo Dodgers	1.50	4.00
15 Vernon Wells	.60	1.50
16 Gary Sheffield	.60	1.50
17 Barry Larkin	1.00	2.50
18 Josh Beckett White	.60	1.50
19 Edgar Martinez A	1.00	2.50
20 I.Rodriguez Marlins	1.00	2.50
21 Jeff Kent Astros	.60	1.50
22 Roberto Alomar Mets A	1.00	2.50
23 Alfonso Soriano A	1.00	2.50
24 Jim Thome Indians H	1.00	2.50
25 J.Gonzalez Indians Btg	.60	1.50
26 Carlos Beltran	1.00	2.50
27 S.Green Dodgers H	.60	1.50
28 Tim Hudson H	1.00	2.50
29 Deion Sanders	1.00	2.50
30 Rafael Palmeiro O's	1.00	2.50
31 Todd Helton H	1.00	2.50
32 L.Berkman No Socks	1.00	2.50
33 M.Mussina Yanks H	1.00	2.50
34 Kazuhisa Ishii H	.60	1.50
35 Pat Burrell Run	.60	1.50
36 Miguel Tejada Btg	1.00	2.50
37 J.Gonzalez Rgr Stand	.60	1.50
38 Roberto Alomar Mets H	1.00	2.50
39 R.Alom Indians Bunt	1.00	2.50
40 Luis Gonzalez	.60	1.50
41 Jorge Posada	1.00	2.50
42 Mark Mulder Leg	.60	1.50
43 Sammy Sosa H	1.50	4.00
44 Mark Prior H	1.00	2.50
45 R.Clemens Yanks H	2.00	5.00
46 Tom Glavine Mets H	1.00	2.50
47 Mark Teixeira A	1.00	2.50
48 Manny Ramirez H	1.50	4.00
49 Frank Thomas Swing	1.50	4.00
50 Troy Glaus White	.60	1.50
51 Andruw Jones H	.60	1.50
52 J.Giambi Yanks H	.60	1.50
53 Jim Thome Phils H	1.00	2.50
54 Barry Bonds H	2.50	6.00
55 R.Palmeiro Rgr A	1.00	2.50
56 Edgar Martinez H	1.00	2.50
57 Vladimir Guerrero H	1.00	2.50
58 Roberto Alomar O's	1.00	2.50
59 Mike Sweeney	.60	1.50
60 Magglio Ordonez A	1.00	2.50
61 Ken Griffey Jr. Btg	3.00	8.00
62 Craig Biggio A	1.00	2.50
63 Greg Maddux H	2.00	5.00
64 Mike Piazza Mets H	1.50	4.00
65 T.Glavine Braves A	1.00	2.50
66 Kerry Wood H	.60	1.50
67 Frank Thomas Arms	1.50	4.00
68 M.Mussina Yanks A	1.00	2.50
69 Nick Johnson H	.60	1.50
70 Bernie Williams H	1.00	2.50
71 Scott Rolen	1.00	2.50
72 C.Schill D'backs Leg	1.00	2.50
73 Adam Dunn A	1.00	2.50
74 Roy Oswalt A	1.00	2.50
75 P.Martinez Sox H	1.00	2.50
76 Tom Glavine Mets A	1.00	2.50
77 Torii Hunter Swing	.60	1.50
78 Austin Kearns	.60	1.50
79 R.Johnson D'backs A	1.50	4.00
80 Bernie Williams A	1.00	2.50
81 Ichiro Suzuki Btg	2.00	5.00
82 Kerry Wood A	.60	1.50
83 Kazuhisa Ishii A	.60	1.50
84 R.Johnson Astros	1.50	4.00
85 Nick Johnson A	.60	1.50
86 J.Beckett Pinstripe	.60	1.50
87 Curt Schilling Phils	1.00	2.50
88 Mike Mussina O's	1.00	2.50
89 P.Martinez Dodgers	1.00	2.50
90 Barry Zito A	1.00	2.50
91 Jim Edmonds	1.00	2.50
92 R.Henderson Sox	1.50	4.00
93 R.Henderson Padres	1.50	4.00
94 R.Henderson M's	1.50	4.00
95 R.Henderson Mets	1.50	4.00
96 R.Henderson Jays	1.50	4.00
97 R.Johnson M's Arm Up	1.50	4.00
98 Mark Grace	1.00	2.50
99 P.Martinez Expos	1.00	2.50
100 Hee Seop Choi	.60	1.50
101 Ivan Rodriguez Rgr	1.00	2.50
102 Jeff Kent Giants	.60	1.50
103 Hideo Nomo Sox	1.50	4.00
104 Hideo Nomo Mets	1.50	4.00
105 Mike Piazza Dodgers	1.50	4.00
106 T.Glavine Braves H	1.00	2.50
107 R.Alom Indians Swing	1.00	2.50
108 Roger Clemens Sox	2.00	5.00
109 Jason Giambi A's H	.60	1.50
110 Jim Thome Indians A	1.00	2.50
111 Alex Rodriguez M's H	2.00	5.00
112 J.Gonz Indians Hands	.60	1.50
113 Torii Hunter Crouch	.60	1.50
114 Roy Oswalt H	1.00	2.50
115 C.Schill D'backs Throw	1.00	2.50
116 Magglio Ordonez H	1.00	2.50
117 R.Palmeiro Rgr H	1.00	2.50
118 Andruw Jones A	.60	1.50
119 Manny Ramirez A	1.50	4.00
120 Mark Teixeira H	1.00	2.50
121 Mark Mulder Stance	.60	1.50
122 Garret Anderson	.60	1.50
123 Tim Hudson A	1.00	2.50
124 Todd Helton A	1.00	2.50
125 Troy Glaus Pinstripe	.60	1.50
126 Derek Jeter Run	4.00	10.00
127 Barry Bonds A	2.50	6.00
128 Greg Maddux A	2.00	5.00
129 R.Clemens Yanks A	2.00	5.00
130 Nomar Garciaparra A	1.00	2.50
131 Mike Piazza Mets A	1.50	4.00
132 Alex Rodriguez Rgr H	2.00	5.00
133 Ichiro Suzuki Run	2.00	5.00
134 R.Johnson D'backs H	1.50	4.00
135 Sammy Sosa A	1.50	4.00
136 Ken Griffey Jr. Fldg	3.00	8.00
137 Alfonso Soriano H	1.00	2.50
138 J.Giambi Yanks A	.60	1.50
139 Albert Pujols A	2.00	5.00
140 Chipper Jones A	1.50	4.00
141 Adam Dunn H	1.00	2.50
142 P.Martinez Sox A	1.00	2.50
143 Vladimir Guerrero A	1.00	2.50
144 Mark Prior A	1.00	2.50
145 Barry Zito H	1.00	2.50
146 Jeff Bagwell A	1.00	2.50
147 Lance Berkman Socks	1.00	2.50
148 S.Green Dodgers A	.60	1.50
149 Jason Giambi A's A	.60	1.50
150 R.Johnson M's Arm Out	1.50	4.00
151 Alex Rodriguez M's A	2.00	5.00
152 Babe Ruth	5.00	12.00
153 Ty Cobb	3.00	8.00
154 Jackie Robinson	2.00	5.00
155 Lou Gehrig	4.00	10.00
156 Thurman Munson	2.00	5.00
157 Roberto Clemente	5.00	12.00
158 Nolan Ryan Rgr	6.00	15.00
159 Nolan Ryan Angels	6.00	15.00
160 Nolan Ryan Astros	6.00	15.00
161 Cal Ripken	6.00	15.00
162 Don Mattingly	4.00	10.00
163 Stan Musial	3.00	8.00
164 Tony Gwynn	2.00	5.00
165 Yogi Berra	2.00	5.00
166 Johnny Bench	2.00	5.00
167 Mike Schmidt	3.00	8.00
168 George Brett	4.00	10.00
169 Ryne Sandberg	4.00	10.00
170 Ernie Banks	2.00	5.00
171 J.Bonder A PH AU Jsy RC	6.00	15.00
172 J.Contreras A PH AU RC	15.00	40.00
173 C.Wang PH AU RC	40.00	80.00
174 H.Matsui H PH Base RC	10.00	25.00
175 H.Kuo PH AU Bat RC	30.00	60.00
176 B.Webb A PH AU Bat RC	12.50	30.00
177 Rich Fischer PH AU RC	6.00	15.00
178 R.Hammock PH AU Bat RC	6.00	15.00
179 T.Welle Stance PH AU/49 RC	10.00	25.00
180 P.Redman PH AU Bat RC	6.00	15.00
181 Nook Logan PH AU RC	10.00	25.00
182 Craig Brazell PH AU RC	6.00	15.00
183 Tim Olson PH AU Bat RC	6.00	15.00
184 Matt Kata PH AU Bat RC	6.00	15.00
185 Alej Machado PH AU RC	6.00	15.00
186 Mike Hessman PH AU RC	6.00	15.00
187 Oscar Villarreal PH AU RC	6.00	15.00
188 G.Quiroz PH AU Bat RC	6.00	15.00
189 M.Hernandez PH AU RC	6.00	15.00
190 C.Barmes H PH AU Bat RC	10.00	25.00
191 P.LaForest PH AU Bat RC	6.00	15.00
192 Adam Loewen PH AU RC	15.00	40.00
193 T.Sledge PH AU Bat RC	6.00	15.00
194 Lew Ford PH AU Bat RC	10.00	25.00
195 T.Welle Throw PH AU/49 RC	6.00	15.00
196 C.Barmes A PH AU Bat RC	10.00	25.00
197 J.Bonder H PH AU Jsy RC	30.00	60.00
198 B.Webb H PH AU Jsy RC	6.00	15.00
199 H.Matsui A PH Base RC	10.00	25.00
200 J.Contreras H PH AU RC	15.00	40.00
201 Delmon Young PH AU RC	150.00	250.00
202 Rickie Weeks PH AU RC	8.00	20.00
203 Edwin Jackson PH AU RC	6.00	15.00
204 Dan Haren PH AU RC	15.00	40.00

2003 Leaf Limited Gold Spotlight

*GOLD 1-151: 1.25X TO 3X BASIC
*GOLD 152-170: 1X TO 2.5X BASIC
1-170 PRINT RUN 50 SERIAL #'d SETS
171-204 PRINT RUN 25 SERIAL #'d SETS
179/195/202 PRINT RUN 10 SERIAL #'d PER
171-204 NO PRICING DUE TO SCARCITY
1-200 RANDOM INSERTS IN PACKS

2003 Leaf Limited Silver Spotlight

*SILVER 1-151: .75X TO 2X BASIC
*SILVER 152-170: .6X TO 1.5X BASIC
1-170 PRINT RUN 100 SERIAL #'d SETS
*SILVER AU GU 171-200: .5X TO 1.2X
*SILVER GU 174/199: .6X TO 1.5X
*SILVER AU 171-204 p/r 50: .5X TO 1.2X
171-204 PRINT RUN 50 SERIAL #'d SETS
179/195 PRINT 29 SERIAL #'d COPIES PER
CARD 202 PRINT RUN 25 SERIAL #'d COPIES
NO PRICING ON QTY OF 29 OR LESS
1-200 RANDOM INSERTS IN PACKS

Card	Low	High
173 Chien-Ming Wang PH AU	75.00	150.00
174 Hideki Matsui H PH Base	15.00	40.00
190 C.Barmes H PH AU Bat	20.00	40.00
196 C.Barmes A PH AU Bat	20.00	40.00
197 J.Bonderman H PH AU Jsy	40.00	80.00
199 Hideki Matsui A PH Base	15.00	40.00
201 Delmon Young PH AU	175.00	300.00

2003 Leaf Limited Moniker

RANDOM INSERTS IN PACKS
PRINT RUNS B/WN 1-10 COPIES PER
NO PRICING DUE TO SCARCITY

2003 Leaf Limited Moniker Bat

PRINT RUNS B/WN 1-25 COPIES PER
NO PRICING ON QTY OF 10 OR LESS

2003 Leaf Limited Moniker Jersey

PRINT RUNS B/WN 1-25 COPIES PER
NO PRICING ON QTY OF 10 OR LESS

2003 Leaf Limited Moniker Jersey Number

PRINT RUNS B/WN 1-25 COPIES PER
NO PRICING ON QTY OF 10 OR LESS

2003 Leaf Limited Moniker Jersey Position

PRINT RUNS B/WN 1-25 COPIES PER
NO PRICING ON QTY OF 10 OR LESS

2003 Leaf Limited Threads

PRINT RUNS B/WN 5-100 COPIES PER
NO PRICING ON QTY OF 10 OR LESS

Card	Low	High
1 Derek Jeter Btg Base/50	10.00	25.00
2 Eric Chavez/25	6.00	15.00
3 Alex Rodriguez Rgr A/100	6.00	15.00
4 Miguel Tejada Fldg/50	4.00	10.00
5 Nomar Garciaparra H/100	6.00	15.00
6 Jeff Bagwell H/50	6.00	15.00
7 Jim Thome Phils A/50	6.00	15.00
8 Pat Burrell w Bat/25	6.00	15.00
9 Albert Pujols H/100	10.00	25.00
10 Juan Gonzalez Rgr Btg/25	6.00	15.00
11 Shawn Green Jays/25	6.00	15.00
12 Craig Biggio H/25	10.00	25.00
13 Chipper Jones H/50	6.00	15.00
14 H.Nomo Dodgers/100	8.00	20.00
15 Vernon Wells/25	6.00	15.00
16 Gary Sheffield/25	6.00	15.00
17 Barry Larkin/25	10.00	25.00
18 Josh Beckett White/25	6.00	15.00
19 Edgar Martinez A/25	10.00	25.00
20 I.Rodriguez Marlins/25	10.00	25.00
21 Jeff Kent Astros/25	6.00	15.00
22 Roberto Alomar Mets A/25	10.00	25.00
23 Alfonso Soriano A/100	3.00	8.00
24 Jim Thome Indians H/25	10.00	25.00
25 J.Gonzalez Indians Btg/25	6.00	15.00
26 Carlos Beltran/25	6.00	15.00
27 S.Green Dodgers H/50	4.00	10.00
28 Tim Hudson H/25	6.00	15.00
29 Deion Sanders/25	10.00	25.00
30 Rafael Palmeiro O's/25	10.00	25.00
31 Todd Helton H/50	6.00	15.00
32 L.Berkman No Socks/25	6.00	15.00
33 M.Mussina Yanks H/50	6.00	15.00
34 Kazuhisa Ishii H/50	4.00	10.00
35 Pat Burrell Run/25	6.00	15.00
36 Miguel Tejada Btg/50	4.00	10.00
37 J.Gonzalez Rgr Stand/25	6.00	15.00
38 Roberto Alomar Mets H/25	10.00	25.00
39 R.Alom Indians Bunt/25	10.00	25.00
40 Luis Gonzalez/25	6.00	15.00
41 Jorge Posada/50	6.00	15.00
42 Mark Mulder Leg/25	6.00	15.00
43 Sammy Sosa H/100	4.00	10.00
44 Mark Prior H/50	6.00	15.00
45 R.Clemens Yanks H/100	6.00	15.00
46 Tom Glavine Mets H/25	10.00	25.00
47 Mark Teixeira A/25	10.00	25.00
48 Manny Ramirez H/50	6.00	15.00
49 Frank Thomas Swing/25	10.00	25.00
50 Troy Glaus White/50	4.00	10.00
51 Andruw Jones H/50	6.00	15.00
52 J.Giambi Yanks H/100	3.00	8.00
53 Jim Thome Phils H/50	6.00	15.00
54 Barry Bonds H Base/50	12.00	30.00
55 R.Palmeiro Rgr A/25	10.00	25.00
56 Edgar Martinez H/25	10.00	25.00
57 Vladimir Guerrero H/50	6.00	15.00
58 Roberto Alomar O's/25	10.00	25.00
59 Mike Sweeney/25	6.00	15.00
60 Magglio Ordonez A/25	6.00	15.00
62 Craig Biggio A/25	10.00	25.00
63 Greg Maddux H/100	6.00	15.00
64 Mike Piazza Mets H/100	6.00	15.00
65 T.Glavine Braves A/25	10.00	25.00
66 Kerry Wood H/25	6.00	15.00
67 Frank Thomas Arms/25	15.00	40.00
68 M.Mussina Yanks A/50	6.00	15.00
69 Nick Johnson H/25	6.00	15.00
70 Bernie Williams H/50	6.00	15.00
71 Scott Rolen/25	10.00	25.00
72 C.Schill D'backs Leg/25	6.00	15.00
73 Adam Dunn A/50	4.00	10.00
74 Roy Oswalt A/25	6.00	15.00
75 P.Martinez Sox H/50	6.00	15.00
76 Tom Glavine Mets A/25	10.00	25.00
77 Torii Hunter Swing/25	6.00	15.00
78 Austin Kearns/25	6.00	15.00
79 R.Johnson D'backs A/100	4.00	10.00
80 Bernie Williams A/50	6.00	15.00
81 Ichiro Suzuki Btg Base/50	15.00	40.00
82 Kerry Wood A/25	6.00	15.00
83 Kazuhisa Ishii A/50	4.00	10.00
84 R.Johnson Astros/50	6.00	15.00
85 Nick Johnson A/25	6.00	15.00
86 J.Beckett Pinstripe/25	6.00	15.00
87 Curt Schilling Phils/25	6.00	15.00
88 Mike Mussina O's/50	6.00	15.00
89 P.Martinez Dodgers/25	10.00	25.00
90 Barry Zito A/50	4.00	10.00
91 Jim Edmonds/100	3.00	8.00
92 R.Henderson Sox/100	4.00	10.00
93 R.Henderson Padres/50	8.00	20.00
94 R.Henderson M's/50	8.00	20.00
95 R.Henderson Mets/50	8.00	20.00
96 R.Henderson Jays/50	8.00	20.00
97 R.Johnson M's Arm Up/50	6.00	15.00
98 Mark Grace/50	6.00	15.00
99 P.Martinez Expos/25	10.00	25.00
100 Hee Seop Choi/25	6.00	15.00
101 Ivan Rodriguez Rgr/25	10.00	25.00
102 Jeff Kent Giants/25	6.00	15.00
104 Hideo Nomo Mets/50	8.00	20.00
105 Mike Piazza Dodgers/100	6.00	15.00
106 T.Glavine Braves H/25	10.00	25.00
107 R.Alom Indians Swing/25	10.00	25.00
108 Roger Clemens Sox/100	6.00	15.00
109 Jason Giambi A's H/25	6.00	15.00
110 Jim Thome Indians A/25	10.00	25.00
111 Alex Rodriguez M's H/100	6.00	15.00
112 J.Gonz Indians Hands/25	6.00	15.00
113 Torii Hunter Crouch/25	6.00	15.00
114 Roy Oswalt H/25	6.00	15.00
115 C.Schill D'backs Throw/25	6.00	15.00
116 Magglio Ordonez H/25	6.00	15.00
117 R.Palmeiro Rgr H/25	10.00	25.00
118 Andruw Jones A/50	6.00	15.00
119 Manny Ramirez A/50	6.00	15.00
120 Mark Teixeira H/25	10.00	25.00
121 Mark Mulder Stance/25	6.00	15.00
123 Tim Hudson A/25	6.00	15.00
124 Todd Helton A/50	6.00	15.00
125 Troy Glaus Pinstripe/50	4.00	10.00
126 Derek Jeter Run Base/50	15.00	40.00
127 Barry Bonds A Base/50	15.00	40.00
128 Greg Maddux A/100	6.00	15.00
129 R.Clemens Yanks A/100	6.00	15.00
130 Nomar Garciaparra A/100	6.00	15.00
131 Mike Piazza Mets A/100	8.00	20.00
132 Alex Rodriguez Rgr H/100	6.00	15.00
133 Ichiro Suzuki Run Base/50	15.00	40.00
134 R.Johnson D'backs H/100	4.00	10.00
135 Sammy Sosa A/100	4.00	10.00
137 Alfonso Soriano H/100	3.00	8.00
138 J.Giambi Yanks A/100	3.00	8.00
139 Albert Pujols A/100	10.00	25.00
140 Chipper Jones A/25	10.00	25.00
141 Adam Dunn H/50	4.00	10.00
142 P.Martinez Sox A/50	6.00	15.00
143 Vladimir Guerrero A/50	6.00	15.00
144 Mark Prior A/50	6.00	15.00
145 Barry Zito H/50	4.00	10.00
146 Jeff Bagwell A/50	6.00	15.00
147 Lance Berkman Socks/25	6.00	15.00
148 S.Green Dodgers A/25	6.00	15.00
149 Jason Giambi A's A/25	6.00	15.00
150 R.Johnson M's Arm Out/25	10.00	25.00
151 Alex Rodriguez M's A/100	6.00	15.00
153 Ty Cobb Pants/100	40.00	100.00
154 Jackie Robinson/50	30.00	60.00
156 Thurman Munson/100	10.00	25.00
158 Nolan Ryan Rgr/100	10.00	25.00
159 Nolan Ryan Angels/100	12.00	30.00
160 Nolan Ryan Astros/100	12.00	30.00
161 Cal Ripken/100	12.50	30.00
162 Don Mattingly/100	15.00	40.00
163 Stan Musial/100	10.00	25.00
164 Tony Gwynn/100	8.00	20.00
165 Yogi Berra/100	8.00	20.00
166 Johnny Bench/100	8.00	20.00
167 Mike Schmidt/100	15.00	40.00
168 George Brett/100	15.00	40.00
169 Ryne Sandberg/100	10.00	25.00
170 Ernie Banks/50	20.00	50.00

2003 Leaf Limited Threads Double

PRINT RUNS B/WN 5-25 COPIES PER
NO PRICING ON QTY 15 OR LESS

Card	Low	High
3 A.Rod Rgr A Hat-Jsy/25	25.00	60.00
4 M.Tejada Fldg Hat-Jsy/25	10.00	25.00
10 J.Gonz Rgr Btg Hat-Jsy/25	10.00	25.00
12 Craig Biggio H Hat-Jsy/25	15.00	40.00
14 H.Nomo Dgr Jsy-Pants/25	30.00	80.00
15 Vernon Wells Hat-Jsy/25	10.00	25.00
26 Carlos Beltran Hat-Jsy/25	10.00	25.00
28 Tim Hudson H Hat-Jsy/25	10.00	25.00
31 Todd Helton H Hat-Jsy/25	15.00	40.00
32 L.Berk No Socks Hat-Jsy/25	10.00	25.00
34 Kazuhisa Ishii H Hat-Jsy/25	10.00	25.00
37 J.Gonz Rgr Stand Hat-Jsy/25	10.00	25.00
43 Sammy Sosa H Hat-Jsy/25	15.00	40.00
44 Mark Prior H Hat-Jsy/25	15.00	40.00
47 Mark Teixeira A Hat-Jsy/25	15.00	40.00
51 Andruw Jones H Hat-Jsy/25	15.00	40.00
54 Barry Bonds H Ball-Base/25	30.00	80.00
55 R.Palmeiro Rgr A Hat-Jsy/25	15.00	40.00
60 M.Ordonez A Hat-Jsy/25	10.00	25.00
73 Adam Dunn A Hat-Jsy/25	10.00	25.00
75 P.Martinez Sox H Hat-Jsy/25	15.00	40.00
78 Austin Kearns Hat-Jsy/25	10.00	25.00
81 I.Suzuki Btg Ball-Base/25	30.00	80.00
90 Barry Zito A Hat-Jsy/25	10.00	25.00
94 R.Hend M's Hat-Jsy/25	15.00	40.00
101 I.Rodriguez Rgr Hat-Jsy/25	15.00	40.00
109 J.Giambi A's H Hat-Jsy/25	10.00	25.00
116 M.Ordonez H Hat-Jsy/25	10.00	25.00
117 R.Palmeiro Rgr H Hat-Jsy/25	15.00	40.00
118 Andruw Jones A Hat-Jsy/25	15.00	40.00
120 Mark Teixeira H Hat-Jsy/25	15.00	40.00
123 Tim Hudson A Hat-Jsy/25	10.00	25.00
124 Todd Helton A Hat-Jsy/25	10.00	25.00
127 Barry Bonds A Ball-Base/25	30.00	80.00
132 A.Rod Rgr H Hat-Jsy/25	25.00	60.00
133 I.Suzuki Run Ball-Base/25	30.00	80.00
135 Sammy Sosa A Hat-Jsy/25	15.00	40.00
141 Adam Dunn H Hat-Jsy/25	10.00	25.00
142 P.Martinez Sox A Hat-Jsy/25	15.00	40.00
144 Mark Prior A Hat-Jsy/25	15.00	40.00
145 Barry Zito H Hat-Jsy/25	10.00	25.00
146 Jeff Bagwell A Jsy-Pants/25	15.00	40.00
147 L.Berkman Socks Hat-Jsy/25	10.00	25.00
149 J.Giambi A's A Hat-Jsy/25	10.00	25.00
158 N.Ryan Rgr Jsy-Pants/25	50.00	120.00
162 D.Mattingly Btg Glv-Jsy/25	40.00	100.00
164 Tony Gwynn Btg Glv-Jsy/25	25.00	60.00
167 Mike Schmidt Hat-Jsy/25	40.00	100.00
168 George Brett Hat-Jsy/25	40.00	100.00
169 Ryne Sandberg Hat-Jsy/25	50.00	120.00

2003 Leaf Limited Threads Double Prime

PRINT RUNS B/WN 1-10 COPIES PER
NO PRICING DUE TO SCARCITY

2003 Leaf Limited Threads Number

PRINT RUNS B/WN 1-75 COPIES PER
NO PRICING ON QTY OF 19 OR LESS

Card	Low	High
7 Jim Thome Phils A/25	10.00	25.00
18 Josh Beckett White/61	4.00	10.00
24 Jim Thome Indians H/25	10.00	25.00
25 J.Gonzalez Indians Btg/22	10.00	25.00
29 Deion Sanders/21	15.00	40.00
30 Rafael Palmeiro O's/25	10.00	25.00
33 M.Mussina Yanks H/35	10.00	25.00
40 Luis Gonzalez/20	10.00	25.00
41 Jorge Posada/20	15.00	40.00
42 Mark Mulder Leg/20	10.00	25.00
43 Sammy Sosa H/21	15.00	40.00
44 Mark Prior H/22	15.00	40.00
45 R.Clemens Yanks H/22	25.00	60.00
46 Tom Glavine Mets H/47	6.00	15.00
47 Mark Teixeira A/23	15.00	40.00
48 Manny Ramirez H/24	15.00	40.00
49 Frank Thomas Swing/35	10.00	25.00
50 Troy Glaus White/25	6.00	15.00
51 Andruw Jones H/25	10.00	25.00
52 J.Giambi Yanks H/25	6.00	15.00
53 Jim Thome Phils H/25	10.00	25.00
55 R.Palmeiro Rgr A/25	10.00	25.00
57 Vladimir Guerrero H/27	10.00	25.00
59 Mike Sweeney/29	6.00	15.00
60 Magglio Ordonez A/30	6.00	15.00
63 Greg Maddux H/31	15.00	40.00
64 Mike Piazza Mets H/31	15.00	40.00
65 T.Glavine Braves A/47	6.00	15.00
66 Kerry Wood H/52	4.00	10.00
67 Frank Thomas Arms/35	10.00	25.00
68 M.Mussina Yanks A/35	10.00	25.00
69 Nick Johnson H/36	4.00	10.00
70 Bernie Williams H/51	6.00	15.00
71 Scott Rolen/27	10.00	25.00
72 C.Schill D'backs Leg/38	4.00	10.00
73 Adam Dunn A/44	4.00	10.00
74 Roy Oswalt A/44	4.00	10.00
75 P.Martinez Sox H/45	6.00	15.00
76 Tom Glavine Mets A/47	6.00	15.00
77 Torii Hunter Swing/48	4.00	10.00
78 Austin Kearns/28	6.00	15.00
79 R.Johnson D'backs A/51	6.00	15.00
80 Bernie Williams A/51	6.00	15.00
82 Kerry Wood A/34	6.00	15.00
84 R.Johnson Astros/51	6.00	15.00
85 Nick Johnson A/36	4.00	10.00
86 J.Beckett Pinstripe/61	4.00	10.00
87 Curt Schilling Phils/38	4.00	10.00
88 Mike Mussina O's/35	10.00	25.00
89 P.Martinez Dodgers/45	6.00	15.00
90 Barry Zito A/75	4.00	10.00
92 R.Henderson Sox/35	10.00	25.00
93 R.Henderson Padres/24	15.00	40.00
94 R.Henderson M's/35	10.00	25.00
95 R.Henderson Mets/24	15.00	40.00
96 R.Henderson Jays/24	15.00	40.00
97 R.Johnson M's Arm Up/51	6.00	15.00
99 P.Martinez Expos/45	6.00	15.00
102 Jeff Kent Giants/21	10.00	25.00
105 Mike Piazza Dodgers/31	15.00	40.00
106 T.Glavine Braves H/47	6.00	15.00
108 Roger Clemens Sox/21	25.00	60.00
110 Jim Thome Indians A/25	10.00	25.00
112 J.Gonz Indians Hands/22	10.00	25.00
113 Torii Hunter Crouch/48	4.00	10.00
114 Roy Oswalt H/44	4.00	10.00
115 C.Schill D'backs Throw/38	4.00	10.00
116 Magglio Ordonez H/30	6.00	15.00
117 R.Palmeiro Rgr H/25	10.00	25.00
118 Andruw Jones A/25	10.00	25.00
119 Manny Ramirez A/24	15.00	40.00
120 Mark Teixeira H/23	15.00	40.00
121 Mark Mulder Stance/20	10.00	25.00
125 Troy Glaus Pinstripe/25	6.00	15.00
128 Greg Maddux A/31	15.00	40.00
129 R.Clemens Yanks A/22	25.00	60.00
131 Mike Piazza Mets A/31	20.00	50.00
134 R.Johnson D'backs H/51	6.00	15.00
135 Sammy Sosa A/21	15.00	40.00
138 J.Giambi Yanks A/25	6.00	15.00
141 Adam Dunn H/44	4.00	10.00
142 P.Martinez Sox A/45	6.00	15.00
143 Vladimir Guerrero A/27	10.00	25.00
145 Barry Zito H/75	4.00	10.00
150 R.Johnson M's Arm Out/51	6.00	15.00
154 Jackie Robinson/42	30.00	60.00
157 Roberto Clemente/21	60.00	120.00
158 Nolan Ryan Rgr/34	30.00	80.00
159 Nolan Ryan Angels/30	30.00	80.00
160 Nolan Ryan Astros/34	30.00	80.00
162 Don Mattingly/23	25.00	60.00
165 Yogi Berra/42	10.00	25.00
167 Mike Schmidt/20	25.00	60.00
169 Ryne Sandberg/23	30.00	80.00

2003 Leaf Limited Threads Position

2-151 PRINT RUNS 25 SERIAL #'d SETS
152-170 PRINTS B/WN 5-25 COPIES PER
NO PRICING ON QTY OF 10 OR LESS

Card	Low	High
2 Eric Chavez	6.00	15.00
3 Alex Rodriguez Rgr A	15.00	40.00
4 Miguel Tejada Fldg	6.00	15.00
5 Nomar Garciaparra H	15.00	40.00
6 Jeff Bagwell H	10.00	25.00
7 Jim Thome Phils A	10.00	25.00
8 Pat Burrell w Bat	6.00	15.00
9 Albert Pujols H	25.00	60.00
10 Juan Gonzalez Rgr Btg	6.00	15.00
11 Shawn Green Jays	6.00	15.00
12 Craig Biggio H	10.00	25.00
13 Chipper Jones H	10.00	25.00
14 Hideo Nomo Dodgers	20.00	50.00
15 Vernon Wells	6.00	15.00
16 Gary Sheffield	6.00	15.00
17 Barry Larkin	10.00	25.00
18 Josh Beckett White	6.00	15.00
19 Edgar Martinez A	10.00	25.00
20 Ivan Rodriguez Marlins	10.00	25.00
21 Jeff Kent Astros	6.00	15.00
22 Roberto Alomar Mets A	10.00	25.00
23 Alfonso Soriano A	6.00	15.00
24 Jim Thome Indians H	10.00	25.00
25 J.Gonzalez Indians Btg	6.00	15.00
26 Carlos Beltran	6.00	15.00
27 S.Green Dodgers H	6.00	15.00
28 Tim Hudson H	6.00	15.00
29 Deion Sanders	10.00	25.00
30 Rafael Palmeiro O's	10.00	25.00
31 Todd Helton H	10.00	25.00
32 L.Berkman No Socks	6.00	15.00
33 Mike Mussina Yanks H	10.00	25.00
34 Kazuhisa Ishii H	6.00	15.00
35 Pat Burrell Run	6.00	15.00
36 Miguel Tejada Btg	6.00	15.00
37 J.Gonzalez Rgr Stand	6.00	15.00
38 Roberto Alomar Mets H	10.00	25.00
39 R.Alomar Indians Bunt	10.00	25.00
40 Luis Gonzalez	6.00	15.00
41 Jorge Posada	10.00	25.00
42 Mark Mulder Leg	6.00	15.00
43 Sammy Sosa H	10.00	25.00
44 Mark Prior H	10.00	25.00
45 R.Clemens Yanks H	15.00	40.00
46 Tom Glavine Mets H	10.00	25.00
47 Mark Teixeira A	10.00	25.00
48 Manny Ramirez H	10.00	25.00
49 Frank Thomas Swing	10.00	25.00
50 Troy Glaus White	6.00	15.00
51 Andruw Jones H	10.00	25.00
52 Jason Giambi Yanks H	10.00	25.00
53 Jim Thome Phils H	10.00	25.00
55 Rafael Palmeiro Rgr A	10.00	25.00
56 Edgar Martinez H	10.00	25.00
57 Vladimir Guerrero H	10.00	25.00
58 Roberto Alomar O's	10.00	25.00
59 Mike Sweeney	6.00	15.00
60 Magglio Ordonez A	6.00	15.00
62 Craig Biggio A	10.00	25.00
63 Greg Maddux H	15.00	40.00
64 Mike Piazza Mets H	15.00	40.00

65 T.Glavine Braves A 10.00 25.00
66 Kerry Wood H 6.00 15.00
67 Frank Thomas Arms 10.00 25.00
68 Mike Mussina Yanks A 10.00 25.00
69 Nick Johnson H 6.00 15.00
70 Bernie Williams H 10.00 25.00
71 Scott Rolen 10.00 25.00
72 C.Schilling D'backs Leg 6.00 15.00
73 Adam Dunn A 6.00 15.00
74 Roy Oswalt A 6.00 15.00
75 Pedro Martinez Sox H 10.00 25.00
76 Tom Glavine Mets A 10.00 25.00
77 Torii Hunter Swing 6.00 15.00
78 Austin Kearns 6.00 15.00
79 R.Johnson D'backs A 10.00 25.00
80 Bernie Williams A 10.00 25.00
82 Kerry Wood A 6.00 15.00
83 Kazuhisa Ishii A 6.00 15.00
84 Randy Johnson Astros 10.00 25.00
85 Nick Johnson A 6.00 15.00
86 J.Beckett Pinstripe 6.00 15.00
87 Curt Schilling Phils 6.00 15.00
88 Mike Mussina O's 10.00 25.00
89 P.Martinez Dodgers 10.00 25.00
90 Barry Zito A 6.00 15.00
91 Jim Edmonds 6.00 15.00
92 R.Henderson Sox 10.00 25.00
93 R.Henderson Padres 10.00 25.00
94 R.Henderson M's 10.00 25.00
95 R.Henderson Mets 10.00 25.00
96 R.Henderson Jays 10.00 25.00
97 R.Johnson M's Arm Up 10.00 25.00
98 Mark Grace 10.00 25.00
99 Pedro Martinez Expos 10.00 25.00
100 Hee Seop Choi 6.00 15.00
101 Ivan Rodriguez Rgr 10.00 25.00
102 Jeff Kent Giants 6.00 15.00
103 Hideo Nomo Sox 20.00 50.00
104 Hideo Nomo Mets 20.00 50.00
105 Mike Piazza Dodgers 15.00 40.00
106 Tom Glavine Braves H 10.00 25.00
107 R.Alomar Indians Swing 10.00 25.00
108 Roger Clemens Sox 15.00 40.00
109 Jason Giambi A's H 6.00 15.00
110 Jim Thome Indians A 10.00 25.00
111 Alex Rodriguez M's H 15.00 40.00
112 J.Gonz Indians Hands 6.00 15.00
113 Torii Hunter Crouch 6.00 15.00
114 Roy Oswalt H 6.00 15.00
115 C.Schilling D'backs Throw 6.00 15.00
116 Magglio Ordonez H 6.00 15.00
117 Rafael Palmeiro Rgr H 10.00 25.00
118 Andruw Jones A 10.00 25.00
119 Manny Ramirez A 10.00 25.00
120 Mark Teixeira H 10.00 25.00
121 Mark Mulder Stance 6.00 15.00
123 Tim Hudson A 6.00 15.00
124 Todd Helton A 10.00 25.00
125 Troy Glaus Pinstripe 6.00 15.00
128 Greg Maddux A 15.00 40.00
129 Roger Clemens Yanks A 15.00 40.00
130 Nomar Garciaparra A 15.00 40.00
131 Mike Piazza Mets A 20.00 50.00
132 Alex Rodriguez Rgr H 15.00 40.00
134 R.Johnson D'backs H 10.00 25.00
135 Sammy Sosa A 10.00 25.00
137 Alfonso Soriano H 6.00 15.00
138 J.Giambi Yanks A 10.00 25.00
139 Albert Pujols A 25.00 60.00
140 Chipper Jones A 10.00 25.00
141 Adam Dunn H 6.00 15.00
142 Pedro Martinez Sox A 10.00 25.00
143 Vladimir Guerrero A 10.00 25.00
144 Mark Prior A 10.00 25.00
145 Barry Zito H 6.00 15.00
146 Jeff Bagwell A 10.00 25.00
147 Lance Berkman Socks 6.00 15.00
148 S.Green Dodgers A 6.00 15.00
149 Jason Giambi A's A 6.00 15.00
150 R.Johnson M's Arm Out 10.00 25.00
151 Alex Rodriguez M's A 15.00 40.00
153 Ty Cobb Pants 60.00 150.00
156 Thurman Munson 20.00 50.00
158 Nolan Ryan Rgr 30.00 80.00
159 Nolan Ryan Angels 30.00 80.00
160 Nolan Ryan Astros 30.00 80.00
161 Cal Ripken 50.00 120.00
162 Don Mattingly 25.00 60.00
163 Stan Musial 30.00 80.00
164 Tony Gwynn 15.00 40.00
165 Yogi Berra 12.50 30.00
166 Johnny Bench 12.50 30.00
167 Mike Schmidt 25.00 60.00
168 George Brett 25.00 60.00
169 Ryne Sandberg 30.00 80.00

2003 Leaf Limited Threads Prime

2-151 PRINTS 25 #'d PER UNLESS NOTED
152-170 PRINTS B/WN 3-25 COPIES PER
NO PRICING ON QTY OF 10 OR LESS
2 Eric Chavez 10.00 25.00
3 Alex Rodriguez Rgr A 25.00 60.00
4 Miguel Tejada Fldg 10.00 25.00
5 Nomar Garciaparra H 10.00 25.00
6 Jeff Bagwell H 15.00 40.00
7 Jim Thome Phils A/20 20.00 50.00
8 Pat Burrell w/Bat 10.00 25.00
9 Albert Pujols H 40.00 100.00
10 Juan Gonzalez Rgr Btg 10.00 25.00
11 Shawn Green Jays 10.00 25.00
12 Craig Biggio H 15.00 40.00
13 Chipper Jones H 15.00 40.00
14 Hideo Nomo Dodgers 30.00 80.00
15 Vernon Wells 10.00 25.00
16 Gary Sheffield 10.00 25.00
17 Barry Larkin 15.00 40.00
18 Josh Beckett White 10.00 25.00
19 Edgar Martinez A 15.00 40.00
20 Ivan Rodriguez Marlins 15.00 40.00
21 Jeff Kent Astros 10.00 25.00
22 Roberto Alomar Mets A 15.00 40.00
23 Alfonso Soriano A 10.00 25.00
24 Jim Thome Indians H 15.00 40.00
25 J.Gonzalez Indians Btg 10.00 25.00
26 Carlos Beltran 10.00 25.00
27 S.Green Dodgers H 10.00 25.00
28 Tim Hudson H 10.00 25.00
29 Deion Sanders 15.00 40.00
30 Rafael Palmeiro O's 15.00 40.00
31 Todd Helton H 15.00 40.00
32 L.Berkman No Socks 10.00 25.00
33 Mike Mussina Yanks H 15.00 40.00
34 Kazuhisa Ishii H 10.00 25.00
35 Pat Burrell Run 10.00 25.00
36 Miguel Tejada Btg 10.00 25.00
37 J.Gonzalez Rgr Stand 10.00 25.00
38 Roberto Alomar Mets H 15.00 40.00
39 R.Alomar Indians Bunt 15.00 40.00
40 Luis Gonzalez 10.00 25.00
41 Jorge Posada 15.00 40.00
42 Mark Mulder Leg 10.00 25.00
43 Sammy Sosa H 15.00 40.00
44 Mark Prior H 15.00 40.00
45 Roger Clemens Yanks H 25.00 60.00
46 Tom Glavine Mets H 15.00 40.00
47 Mark Teixeira A 15.00 40.00
48 Manny Ramirez H 15.00 40.00
49 Frank Thomas Swing 15.00 40.00
50 Troy Glaus White 10.00 25.00
51 Andruw Jones H 15.00 40.00
52 Jason Giambi Yanks H 10.00 25.00
53 Jim Thome Phils H 15.00 40.00
55 Rafael Palmeiro Rgr A 15.00 40.00
56 Edgar Martinez H 15.00 40.00
57 Vladimir Guerrero H 15.00 40.00
58 Roberto Alomar O's 15.00 40.00
59 Mike Sweeney 10.00 25.00
60 Magglio Ordonez A 10.00 25.00
62 Craig Biggio A 15.00 40.00
63 Greg Maddux H 10.00 25.00
64 Mike Piazza Mets H 10.00 25.00
65 Tom Glavine Braves A 15.00 40.00
66 Kerry Wood H 10.00 25.00
67 Frank Thomas Arms 15.00 40.00
68 Mike Mussina Yanks A 10.00 25.00
69 Nick Johnson H 10.00 25.00
70 Bernie Williams H 15.00 40.00
71 Scott Rolen 15.00 40.00
72 C.Schilling D'backs Leg 10.00 25.00
73 Adam Dunn A 10.00 25.00
74 Roy Oswalt A 10.00 25.00
75 Pedro Martinez Sox H 15.00 40.00
76 Tom Glavine Mets A 15.00 40.00
77 Torii Hunter Swing 10.00 25.00
78 Austin Kearns 10.00 25.00
79 R.Johnson D'backs A 15.00 40.00
80 Bernie Williams A 15.00 40.00
82 Kerry Wood A 10.00 25.00
83 Kazuhisa Ishii A 10.00 25.00
84 Randy Johnson Astros 15.00 40.00
85 Nick Johnson A 10.00 25.00
86 J.Beckett Pinstripe 10.00 25.00
87 Curt Schilling Phils 10.00 25.00
88 Mike Mussina O's 15.00 40.00
89 P.Martinez Dodgers 15.00 40.00
90 Barry Zito A 10.00 25.00
91 Jim Edmonds 10.00 25.00
92 R.Henderson Sox 15.00 40.00
93 R.Henderson Padres 15.00 40.00
94 R.Henderson M's 15.00 40.00
95 R.Henderson Mets 15.00 40.00
96 R.Henderson Jays 15.00 40.00
97 R.Johnson M's Arm Up 15.00 40.00
98 Mark Grace 15.00 40.00
99 Pedro Martinez Expos 15.00 40.00
100 Hee Seop Choi 10.00 25.00
101 Ivan Rodriguez Rgr 15.00 40.00
102 Jeff Kent Giants 10.00 25.00
104 Hideo Nomo Mets 30.00 80.00
105 Mike Piazza Dodgers 25.00 60.00
106 Tom Glavine Braves H 15.00 40.00
107 R.Alomar Indians Swing 15.00 40.00
108 Roger Clemens Sox 25.00 60.00
109 Jason Giambi A's H 10.00 25.00
110 Jim Thome Indians A 15.00 40.00
111 Alex Rodriguez M's H 25.00 60.00
112 J.Gonz Indians Hands 10.00 25.00
113 Torii Hunter Crouch 10.00 25.00
114 Roy Oswalt H 10.00 25.00
115 C.Schilling D'backs Throw 10.00 25.00
116 Magglio Ordonez H 10.00 25.00
117 Rafael Palmeiro Rgr H 15.00 40.00
118 Andruw Jones A 15.00 40.00
119 Manny Ramirez A 15.00 40.00
120 Mark Teixeira H 15.00 40.00
121 Mark Mulder Stance 10.00 25.00
123 Tim Hudson A 10.00 25.00
124 Todd Helton A 15.00 40.00
125 Troy Glaus Pinstripe 10.00 25.00
128 Greg Maddux A 25.00 60.00
129 Roger Clemens Yanks A 25.00 60.00
130 Nomar Garciaparra A 25.00 60.00
131 Mike Piazza Mets A 30.00 80.00
132 Alex Rodriguez Rgr H 25.00 60.00
134 R.Johnson D'backs H 15.00 40.00
135 Sammy Sosa A 15.00 40.00
137 Alfonso Soriano H 10.00 25.00
138 J.Giambi Yanks A 10.00 25.00
139 Albert Pujols A 40.00 100.00
140 Chipper Jones A 15.00 40.00
141 Adam Dunn H 10.00 25.00
142 P.Martinez Sox A 15.00 40.00
143 Vladimir Guerrero A 15.00 40.00
144 Mark Prior A 15.00 40.00
145 Barry Zito H 10.00 25.00
146 Jeff Bagwell A 15.00 40.00
147 Lance Berkman Socks 10.00 25.00
148 S.Green Dodgers A 10.00 25.00
149 Jason Giambi A's A 10.00 25.00
150 R.Johnson M's Arm Out 15.00 40.00
151 Alex Rodriguez M's A 25.00 60.00
153 Ty Cobb Pants 60.00 150.00
156 Thurman Munson 30.00 80.00
158 Nolan Ryan Rgr 50.00 120.00
159 Nolan Ryan Angels 50.00 120.00
160 Nolan Ryan Astros 50.00 120.00
161 Cal Ripken 60.00 150.00
162 Don Mattingly 40.00 100.00
163 Stan Musial 60.00 150.00
164 Tony Gwynn 25.00 60.00
165 Yogi Berra 20.00 50.00
166 Johnny Bench 20.00 50.00
167 Mike Schmidt 40.00 100.00
168 George Brett 40.00 100.00
169 Ryne Sandberg 50.00 120.00

2003 Leaf Limited Timber

RANDOM INSERTS IN PACKS
STATED PRINT RUN 25 SERIAL #'d SETS
CARD 170 PRINT RUN 1 SERIAL #'d CARD
NO 170 PRICING DUE TO SCARCITY
2 Eric Chavez 6.00 15.00
3 Alex Rodriguez Rgr A 15.00 40.00
4 Miguel Tejada Fldg 6.00 15.00
5 Nomar Garciaparra H 15.00 40.00
6 Jeff Bagwell H 10.00 25.00
7 Jim Thome Phils A 10.00 25.00
8 Pat Burrell w
Bat 6.00 15.00
9 Albert Pujols H 25.00 60.00
10 Juan Gonzalez Rgr Btg 6.00 15.00
11 Shawn Green Jays 6.00 15.00
12 Craig Biggio H 10.00 25.00
13 Chipper Jones H 10.00 25.00
14 Hideo Nomo Dodgers 20.00 50.00
15 Vernon Wells 6.00 15.00
16 Gary Sheffield 6.00 15.00
17 Barry Larkin 10.00 25.00
18 Josh Beckett White 6.00 15.00
19 Edgar Martinez A 10.00 25.00
20 Ivan Rodriguez Marlins 10.00 25.00
21 Jeff Kent Astros 6.00 15.00
22 Roberto Alomar Mets A 10.00 25.00
23 Alfonso Soriano A 6.00 15.00
24 Jim Thome Indians H 10.00 25.00
25 J.Gonzalez Indians Btg 6.00 15.00
26 Carlos Beltran 6.00 15.00
27 S.Green Dodgers H 6.00 15.00
28 Tim Hudson H 6.00 15.00
30 Rafael Palmeiro O's 10.00 25.00
31 Todd Helton H 10.00 25.00
32 L.Berkman No Socks 6.00 15.00
33 Mike Mussina Yanks H 10.00 25.00
34 Kazuhisa Ishii H 6.00 15.00
35 Pat Burrell Run 6.00 15.00
36 Miguel Tejada Btg 6.00 15.00
37 J.Gonzalez Rgr Stand 6.00 15.00
38 Roberto Alomar Mets H 10.00 25.00
39 R.Alomar Indians Bunt 10.00 25.00
40 Luis Gonzalez 6.00 15.00
41 Jorge Posada 10.00 25.00
42 Mark Mulder Leg 6.00 15.00
43 Sammy Sosa H 10.00 25.00
44 Mark Prior H 10.00 25.00
45 R.Clemens Yanks H 15.00 40.00
46 Tom Glavine Mets H 10.00 25.00
47 Mark Teixeira A 10.00 25.00
48 Manny Ramirez H 10.00 25.00
49 Frank Thomas Swing 10.00 25.00
50 Troy Glaus White 6.00 15.00
51 Andruw Jones H 10.00 25.00
52 Jason Giambi Yanks H 6.00 15.00
53 Jim Thome Phils H 10.00 25.00
55 Rafael Palmeiro Rgr A 10.00 25.00
56 Edgar Martinez H 10.00 25.00
57 Vladimir Guerrero H 10.00 25.00
58 Roberto Alomar O's 10.00 25.00
59 Mike Sweeney 6.00 15.00
60 Magglio Ordonez A 6.00 15.00
62 Craig Biggio A 10.00 25.00
63 Greg Maddux H 15.00 40.00
64 Mike Piazza Mets H 15.00 40.00
65 T.Glavine Braves A 10.00 25.00
66 Kerry Wood H 6.00 15.00
67 Frank Thomas Arms 10.00 25.00
68 Mike Mussina Yanks A 10.00 25.00
69 Nick Johnson H 6.00 15.00
70 Bernie Williams H 10.00 25.00
71 Scott Rolen 10.00 25.00
72 C.Schilling D'backs Leg 6.00 15.00
73 Adam Dunn A 6.00 15.00
74 Roy Oswalt A 6.00 15.00
75 Pedro Martinez Sox H 10.00 25.00
76 Tom Glavine Mets A 10.00 25.00
77 Torii Hunter Swing 6.00 15.00
78 Austin Kearns 6.00 15.00
79 R.Johnson D'backs A 10.00 25.00
80 Bernie Williams A 10.00 25.00
82 Kerry Wood A 6.00 15.00
83 Kazuhisa Ishii A 6.00 15.00
84 Randy Johnson Astros 10.00 25.00
85 Nick Johnson A 6.00 15.00
86 J.Beckett Pinstripe 6.00 15.00
87 Curt Schilling Phils 6.00 15.00
88 Mike Mussina O's 10.00 25.00
89 P.Martinez Dodgers 10.00 25.00
90 Barry Zito A 6.00 15.00
91 Jim Edmonds 6.00 15.00
92 R.Henderson Sox 10.00 25.00
93 R.Henderson Padres 10.00 25.00
94 R.Henderson M's 10.00 25.00
95 R.Henderson Mets 10.00 25.00
96 R.Henderson Jays 10.00 25.00
97 R.Johnson M's Arm Up 10.00 25.00
98 Mark Grace 10.00 25.00
99 Pedro Martinez Expos 10.00 25.00
101 Ivan Rodriguez Rgr 10.00 25.00
102 Jeff Kent Giants 6.00 15.00
103 Hideo Nomo Sox 20.00 50.00
104 Hideo Nomo Mets 20.00 50.00
105 Mike Piazza Dodgers 15.00 40.00
106 Tom Glavine Braves H 10.00 25.00
107 R.Alomar Indians Swing 10.00 25.00
108 Roger Clemens Sox 15.00 40.00
109 Jason Giambi A's H 6.00 15.00
110 Jim Thome Indians A 10.00 25.00
111 Alex Rodriguez M's H 15.00 40.00
112 J.Gonz Indians Hands 6.00 15.00
113 Torii Hunter Crouch 6.00 15.00
114 Roy Oswalt H 6.00 15.00
115 C.Schilling D'backs Throw 6.00 15.00
116 Magglio Ordonez H 6.00 15.00
117 Rafael Palmeiro Rgr H 10.00 25.00
118 Andruw Jones A 10.00 25.00
119 Manny Ramirez A 10.00 25.00
120 Mark Teixeira H 10.00 25.00
121 Mark Mulder Stance 6.00 15.00
122 Garret Anderson 6.00 15.00
123 Tim Hudson A 6.00 15.00
124 Todd Helton A 10.00 25.00
125 Troy Glaus Pinstripe 6.00 15.00
128 Greg Maddux A 15.00 40.00
129 Roger Clemens Yanks A 15.00 40.00
130 Nomar Garciaparra A 15.00 40.00
131 Mike Piazza Mets A 15.00 40.00
132 Alex Rodriguez Rgr H 15.00 40.00
134 R.Johnson D'backs H 10.00 25.00
135 Sammy Sosa A 10.00 25.00
137 Alfonso Soriano H 6.00 15.00
138 J.Giambi Yanks A 6.00 15.00
139 Albert Pujols A 25.00 60.00
140 Chipper Jones A 10.00 25.00
141 Adam Dunn H 6.00 15.00
142 Pedro Martinez Sox A 10.00 25.00
143 Vladimir Guerrero A 10.00 25.00
144 Mark Prior A 10.00 25.00
145 Barry Zito H 6.00 15.00
146 Jeff Bagwell A 10.00 25.00
147 Lance Berkman Socks 6.00 15.00
148 S.Green Dodgers A 6.00 15.00
149 Jason Giambi A's A 6.00 15.00
150 R.Johnson M's Arm Out 10.00 25.00
151 Alex Rodriguez M's A 15.00 40.00
152 Babe Ruth 125.00 250.00
153 Ty Cobb 60.00 120.00
155 Lou Gehrig 75.00 150.00
156 Thurman Munson 20.00 50.00
157 Roberto Clemente 60.00 120.00
158 Nolan Ryan Rgr 15.00 40.00
159 Nolan Ryan Angels 15.00 40.00
160 Nolan Ryan Astros 15.00 40.00
161 Cal Ripken 50.00 120.00
162 Don Mattingly 25.00 60.00
163 Stan Musial 25.00 60.00
164 Tony Gwynn 15.00 40.00
165 Yogi Berra 12.50 30.00
166 Johnny Bench 12.50 30.00
167 Mike Schmidt 25.00 60.00
168 George Brett 12.00 30.00
169 Ryne Sandberg 30.00 80.00

2003 Leaf Limited TNT

RANDOM INSERTS IN PACKS
PRINT RUNS B/WN 1-25 COPIES PER
NO PRICING ON QTY OF 10 OR LESS
2 Eric Chavez Bat-Jsy 10.00 25.00
3 A.Rod Rgr A Bat-Jsy 20.00 50.00
5 N.Garciaparra H Bat-Jsy 20.00 50.00
6 Jeff Bagwell H Bat-Jsy 15.00 40.00
7 J.Thome Phils A Bat-Jsy 15.00 40.00
8 P.Burrell w
Bat Bat-Jsy 10.00 25.00
9 Albert Pujols H Bat-Jsy 25.00 60.00
10 J.Gonz Rgr Btg Bat-Jsy 10.00 25.00
11 S.Green Jays Bat-Jsy 10.00 25.00
12 Craig Biggio H Bat-Jsy 10.00 25.00
13 C.Jones H Bat-Jsy 15.00 40.00
14 H.Nomo Dodgers Bat-Jsy 20.00 50.00
15 Vernon Wells Bat-Jsy 10.00 25.00
16 G.Sheffield Bat-Jsy 10.00 25.00
17 Barry Larkin Bat-Jsy 15.00 40.00
18 J.Beckett White Bat-Jsy 10.00 25.00
19 E.Martinez A Bat-Jsy 15.00 40.00
20 I.Rodriguez Marlins Bat-Jsy 15.00 40.00
21 Jeff Kent Astros Bat-Jsy 10.00 25.00
22 R.Alomar Mets A Bat-Jsy 15.00 40.00
23 A.Soriano A Bat-Jsy 10.00 25.00
24 J.Thome Indians H Bat-Jsy 15.00 40.00
25 J.Gonz Indians Btg Bat-Jsy 10.00 25.00
26 Carlos Beltran Bat-Jsy 10.00 25.00
27 S.Green Dodgers H Bat-Jsy 10.00 25.00
28 Tim Hudson H Bat-Jsy 10.00 25.00
30 R.Palmeiro O's Bat-Jsy 15.00 40.00
31 Todd Helton H Bat-Jsy 15.00 40.00
32 L.Berk No Socks Bat-Jsy 10.00 25.00
33 M.Mussina Yanks H Bat-Jsy 15.00 40.00
34 Kazuhisa Ishii H Bat-Jsy 10.00 25.00
35 Pat Burrell Run Bat-Jsy 10.00 25.00
37 J.Gonz Rgr Stand Bat-Jsy 10.00 25.00
38 R.Alomar Mets H Bat-Jsy 15.00 40.00
39 R.Alom Indians Bunt Bat-Jsy 15.00 40.00
40 Luis Gonzalez Bat-Jsy 10.00 25.00
41 Jorge Posada Bat-Jsy 15.00 40.00
42 M.Mulder Leg Bat-Jsy 10.00 25.00
43 Sammy Sosa H Bat-Jsy 15.00 40.00
44 Mark Prior H Bat-Jsy 15.00 40.00
45 R.Clemens Yanks H Bat-Jsy 20.00 50.00
46 T.Glavine Mets H Bat-Jsy 15.00 40.00
47 Mark Teixeira A Bat-Jsy 15.00 40.00
48 Manny Ramirez H Bat-Jsy 15.00 40.00
49 F.Thomas Swing Bat-Jsy 15.00 40.00
50 Troy Glaus White Bat-Jsy 10.00 25.00
51 Andruw Jones H Bat-Jsy 15.00 40.00
52 J.Giambi Yanks H Bat-Jsy 10.00 25.00
53 J.Thome Phils H Bat-Jsy 15.00 40.00
55 R.Palmeiro Rgr A Bat-Jsy 15.00 40.00
56 E.Martinez H Bat-Jsy 15.00 40.00
57 V.Guerrero H Bat-Jsy 15.00 40.00
59 Mike Sweeney Bat-Jsy 10.00 25.00
60 M.Ordonez A Bat-Jsy 10.00 25.00
62 Craig Biggio A Bat-Jsy 15.00 40.00
63 Greg Maddux H Bat-Jsy 10.00 25.00
64 M.Piazza Mets H Bat-Jsy 20.00 50.00
65 T.Glavine Braves A Bat-Jsy 15.00 40.00
66 Kerry Wood H Bat-Jsy 10.00 25.00
67 F.Thomas Arms Bat-Jsy 15.00 40.00
68 M.Mussina Yanks A Bat-Jsy 15.00 40.00
69 Nick Johnson H Bat-Jsy 10.00 25.00
70 Bernie Williams H Bat-Jsy 15.00 40.00
71 Scott Rolen Bat-Jsy 15.00 40.00
72 C.Schill D'backs Leg Bat-Jsy 10.00 25.00
73 Adam Dunn A Bat-Jsy 10.00 25.00
74 Roy Oswalt A Bat-Jsy 10.00 25.00
75 P.Martinez Sox H Bat-Jsy 15.00 40.00
76 T.Glavine Mets A Bat-Jsy 15.00 40.00
77 T.Hunter Swing Bat-Jsy 10.00 25.00
78 Austin Kearns Bat-Jsy 10.00 25.00
79 R.John D'backs A Bat-Jsy 15.00 40.00
80 Bernie Williams A Bat-Jsy 15.00 40.00
82 Kerry Wood A Bat-Jsy 10.00 25.00
83 Kazuhisa Ishii A Bat-Jsy 10.00 25.00
84 R.Johnson Astros Bat-Jsy 15.00 40.00
85 Nick Johnson A Bat-Jsy 10.00 25.00
86 J.Beckett Pinstripe Bat-Jsy 10.00 25.00
87 C.Schilling Phils Bat-Jsy 10.00 25.00
88 Mike Mussina O's Bat-Jsy 15.00 40.00
89 P.Martinez Dgr Bat-Jsy 15.00 40.00
90 Barry Zito A Bat-Jsy 10.00 25.00
91 Jim Edmonds Bat-Jsy 10.00 25.00
92 R.Henderson Sox Bat-Jsy 15.00 40.00
93 R.Hend Padres Bat-Jsy 15.00 40.00
94 R.Henderson M's Bat-Jsy 15.00 40.00
95 R.Hend Mets Bat-Jsy 15.00 40.00
96 R.Hend Jays Bat-Jsy 15.00 40.00
97 R.John M's Arm Up Bat-Jsy 15.00 40.00
98 Mark Grace Bat-Jsy 15.00 40.00
99 P.Martinez Expos Bat-Jsy 15.00 40.00
101 I.Rodriguez Rgr Bat-Jsy 15.00 40.00
102 Jeff Kent Giants Bat-Jsy 10.00 25.00
103 Hideo Nomo Sox Bat-Jsy 20.00 50.00
104 Hideo Nomo Mets Bat-Jsy 20.00 50.00
105 M.Piazza Dodgers Bat-Jsy 20.00 50.00
106 T.Glav Braves H Bat-Jsy 15.00 40.00
107 R.Alom Ind Swing Bat-Jsy 15.00 40.00
108 R.Clemens Sox Bat-Jsy 20.00 50.00
109 J.Giambi A's H Bat-Jsy 10.00 25.00
110 J.Thome Indians A Bat-Jsy 15.00 40.00
111 A.Rod M's H Bat-Jsy 20.00 50.00
112 J.Gonz Ind Hands Bat-Jsy 10.00 25.00
113 T.Hunter Crouch Bat-Jsy 10.00 25.00
114 Roy Oswalt H Bat-Jsy 10.00 25.00
115 C.Schill D'b Throw Bat-Jsy 10.00 25.00
116 M.Ordonez H Bat-Jsy 10.00 25.00
117 R.Palmeiro Rgr H Bat-Jsy 15.00 40.00
118 Andruw Jones A Bat-Jsy 15.00 40.00
119 Manny Ramirez A Bat-Jsy 15.00 40.00
120 Mark Teixeira H Bat-Jsy 15.00 40.00
121 M.Mulder Stance Bat-Jsy 10.00 25.00
123 Tim Hudson A Bat-Jsy 10.00 25.00
124 Todd Helton A Bat-Jsy 15.00 40.00
125 T.Glaus Pinstripe Bat-Jsy 10.00 25.00
128 Greg Maddux A Bat-Jsy 20.00 50.00
129 R.Clemens Yanks A Bat-Jsy 20.00 50.00
130 N.Garciaparra A Bat-Jsy 20.00 50.00
131 M.Piazza Mets A Bat-Jsy 10.00 25.00
132 A.Rod Rgr H Bat-Jsy 20.00 50.00
134 R.John D'backs H Bat-Jsy 15.00 40.00
135 Sammy Sosa A Bat-Jsy 15.00 40.00
137 A.Soriano H Bat-Jsy 10.00 25.00
138 J.Giambi Yanks A Bat-Jsy 10.00 25.00
139 Albert Pujols A Bat-Jsy 25.00 60.00
140 Chipper Jones A Bat-Jsy 15.00 40.00
141 Adam Dunn H Bat-Jsy 10.00 25.00
142 P.Martinez Sox A Bat-Jsy 15.00 40.00
143 V.Guerrero A Bat-Jsy 15.00 40.00
144 Mark Prior A Bat-Jsy 15.00 40.00
145 Barry Zito H Bat-Jsy 10.00 25.00
146 Jeff Bagwell A Bat-Jsy 15.00 40.00
147 L.Berkman Socks Bat-Jsy 10.00 25.00
148 S.Green Dgr A Bat-Jsy 10.00 25.00
149 J.Giambi A's A Bat-Jsy 10.00 25.00
150 R.John M's Arm Out Bat-Jsy 15.00 40.00
151 A.Rod M's A Bat-Jsy 20.00 50.00
156 Thurman Munson Bat-Jsy 30.00 80.00
158 Nolan Ryan Rgr Bat-Jsy 15.00 40.00
159 N.Ryan Angels Bat-Jsy 15.00 40.00
160 N.Ryan Astros Bat-Jsy 15.00 40.00
161 Cal Ripken Bat-Jsy 50.00 120.00
162 Don Mattingly Bat-Jsy 30.00 80.00
163 Stan Musial Bat-Jsy 40.00 100.00
164 Tony Gwynn Bat-Jsy 20.00 50.00
165 Yogi Berra Bat-Jsy 25.00 60.00
166 Johnny Bench Bat-Jsy 25.00 60.00
167 Mike Schmidt Bat-Jsy 30.00 80.00
168 George Brett Bat-Jsy 30.00 80.00
169 Ryne Sandberg Bat-Jsy 20.00 50.00

2003 Leaf Limited TNT Prime

*TNT PRIME: .5X TO 1.2X BASIC TNT
PRINT RUNS B/WN 1-25 COPIES PER
NO PRICING ON QTY OF 10 OR LESS

2003 Leaf Limited 7th Inning Stretch Jersey

RANDOM INSERTS IN PACKS
PRINT RUNS B/WN 40-50 COPIES PER
1 Alex Rodriguez 10.00 25.00
3 Sammy Sosa 6.00 15.00
4 Juan Gonzalez 6.00 15.00
5 Albert Pujols 15.00 40.00
6 Chipper Jones 6.00 15.00
7 Alfonso Soriano/40 6.00 15.00
8 Jim Thome 6.00 15.00
9 Mike Piazza 10.00 25.00
10 Rafael Palmeiro 6.00 15.00

2003 Leaf Limited Jersey Numbers

1-54 PRINT RUNS B/WN 5-100 COPIES PER
55-100 PRINT RUNS B/WN 5-25 COPIES PER
NO PRICING ON QTY OF 10 OR LESS
1 Rod Carew Angels/50 10.00 25.00
2 Nolan Ryan Angels/50 20.00 50.00
3 Reggie Jackson Angels/50 10.00 25.00
4 Brooks Robinson/50 10.00 25.00
5 Frank Robinson/25 10.00 25.00
6 Cal Ripken/100 12.50 30.00
7 Carlton Fisk W.Sox/50 10.00 25.00
8 Roger Clemens/100 8.00 20.00
10 Lou Boudreau/50 6.00 15.00
11 Bob Feller/25 10.00 25.00
13 Alan Trammell/50 6.00 15.00
14 Harmon Killebrew/50 15.00 40.00
15 Rod Carew Twins/50 10.00 25.00
16 Kirby Puckett/50 15.00 40.00
19 Yogi Berra/50 15.00 40.00
20 Thurman Munson/50 10.00 25.00
21 Don Mattingly/100 15.00 40.00
25 Alex Rodriguez/100 8.00 20.00
26 Randy Johnson M's/50 6.00 15.00
27 Nolan Ryan Rgr/100 20.00 50.00
28 Dale Murphy/50 10.00 25.00
29 Warren Spahn/50 15.00 40.00
30 Eddie Mathews/50 15.00 40.00
32 Ryne Sandberg/100 10.00 25.00
33 Johnny Bench/50 15.00 40.00
34 Joe Morgan/50 6.00 15.00
35 Randy Johnson Astros/50 6.00 15.00
36 Nolan Ryan Astros/100 12.50 30.00
37 Pee Wee Reese/50 10.00 25.00
38 Duke Snider/50 10.00 25.00
39 Jackie Robinson/25 40.00 100.00
40 Robin Yount/50 15.00 40.00
41 Paul Molitor/50 6.00 15.00
42 Pedro Martinez/50 6.00 15.00
43 Randy Johnson Expos/50 6.00 15.00
44 Tom Seaver/25 15.00 40.00
45 Gary Carter/50 6.00 15.00
46 Mike Schmidt/50 20.00 50.00
47 Steve Carlton/50 6.00 15.00
48 Willie Stargell/50 10.00 25.00
50 Ozzie Smith/50 10.00 25.00
51 Stan Musial/100 15.00 40.00
52 Enos Slaughter/50 15.00 40.00
53 Orlando Cepeda/50 6.00 15.00
54 Willie McCovey/50 6.00 15.00
57 H.Killebrew/R.Carew/25 40.00 100.00
58 H.Killebrew/K.Puckett/25 40.00 100.00
68 Y.Berra/T.Munson/25 30.00 80.00
69 Y.Berra/D.Mattingly/25 40.00 100.00
71 D.Murphy/W.Spahn/25 30.00 80.00
72 D.Murphy/E.Mathews/25 30.00 80.00
73 W.Spahn/E.Mathews/25 25.00 60.00
74 J.Bench/J.Morgan/25 25.00 60.00
75 P.Reese/D.Snider/25 25.00 60.00
78 R.Yount/P.Molitor/25 30.00 80.00
81 O.Smith/S.Musial/25 25.00 60.00
82 S.Musial/E.Slaughter/25 15.00 40.00
83 O.Cepeda/W.McCovey/25 25.00 60.00
84 N.Ryan/R.Jackson/25 40.00 100.00
90 A.Rodriguez/R.Johnson/25 20.00 50.00
91 P.Martinez/R.Johnson/25 20.00 50.00
94 R.Jackson A's-Angels/25 25.00 60.00
95 N.Ryan Angels-Rgr/25 15.00 40.00
96 N.Ryan Rgr-Astros/25 15.00 40.00
97 N.Ryan Astros-Angels/25 15.00 40.00
98 N.Ryan/R.Johnson/25 40.00 100.00
99 C.Ripken/R.Palmeiro/25 60.00 120.00
100 D.Murphy/D.Sanders/25 30.00 80.00

2003 Leaf Limited Jersey Numbers Retired

PRINT RUNS B/WN 1-72 COPIES PER
NO PRICING ON QTY OF 19 OR LESS
1 Rod Carew Angels/29 15.00 40.00
2 Nolan Ryan Angels/30 30.00 80.00
5 Frank Robinson/20 12.50 30.00
7 Carlton Fisk R.Sox/27 15.00 40.00
9 Carlton Fisk W.Sox/72 10.00 25.00
15 Rod Carew Twins/29 15.00 40.00
16 Kirby Puckett/34 20.00 50.00
21 Don Mattingly/23 25.00 60.00
27 Nolan Ryan Rgr/34 30.00 80.00
29 Warren Spahn/21 25.00 60.00
30 Eddie Mathews/41 10.00 25.00
36 Nolan Ryan Astros/34 30.00 80.00
39 Jackie Robinson/42 30.00 80.00
44 Tom Seaver/41 10.00 25.00
46 Mike Schmidt/20 25.00 60.00
47 Steve Carlton/32 10.00 25.00
49 Roberto Clemente/21 60.00 120.00
53 Orlando Cepeda/30 10.00 25.00
54 Willie McCovey/44 6.00 15.00

2003 Leaf Limited Leather

RANDOM INSERTS IN PACKS
PRINT RUNS B/WN 10-25 COPIES PER
NO PRICNG ON QTY OF 10 OR LESS
1 Alex Rodriguez/25 12.50 30.00
2 Chipper Jones/25 15.00 40.00
3 Jimmie Foxx/25 50.00 100.00
4 Kirby Puckett/25 15.00 40.00
5 Mike Schmidt/25 40.00 100.00
6 Roger Clemens/25 25.00 60.00
7 Steve Carlton/25 15.00 40.00
8 Tony Gwynn/25 25.00 60.00
10 Vladimir Guerrero/25 15.00 40.00
11 Adam Dunn/25 15.00 40.00
12 Andruw Jones/25 15.00 40.00
13 Curt Schilling/25 15.00 40.00
14 Randy Johnson/25 15.00 40.00
15 Mark Prior/25 15.00 40.00

2003 Leaf Limited Lineups Bat

PRINT RUNS B/WN 25-50 COPIES PER
ALL ARE DUAL BAT CARDS UNLESS NOTED
CARD NUMBER 3 DOES NOT EXIST
1 P.Molitor/R.Yount/50 15.00 40.00
2 D.Mattingly/B.Williams/50 20.00 50.00
4 Matsui Ball/Jeter Ball/25 40.00 100.00
5 R.Sandberg/A.Dawson/50 20.00 50.00
6 G.Brett/B.Jackson/50 15.00 40.00
7 R.Jackson/J.Canseco/50 15.00 40.00
8 M.Grace/R.Sandberg/50 15.00 40.00
9 R.Henderson/J.Canseco/50 20.00 50.00
10 M.Piazza/H.Nomo/50 15.00 40.00

2003 Leaf Limited Lineups Jersey

RANDOM INSERTS IN PACKS
PRINT RUNS B/WN 5-50 COPIES PER
NO PRICING ON QTY OF 5 OR LESS
ALL ARE DUAL JSY CARDS UNLESS NOTED
1 P.Molitor/R.Yount/50 15.00 40.00
2 D.Mattingly/B.Williams/50 20.00 50.00
3 S.Sosa/H.Seop Choi/50 15.00 40.00
4 Matsui Base/Jeter Base/50 15.00 40.00
5 R.Sandberg/A.Dawson/50 20.00 50.00
6 G.Brett/B.Jackson/50 15.00 40.00
8 M.Grace/R.Sandberg/50 15.00 40.00
10 M.Piazza/H.Nomo/50 15.00 40.00

2003 Leaf Limited Lumberjacks Bat

1-37 PRINT RUNS B/WN 1-25 COPIES PER
38-45 PRINT RUNS B/WN 1-25 COPIES PER
NO PRICING ON QTY OF 15 OR LESS
1 Babe Ruth/25 75.00 150.00
2 Lou Gehrig/25 40.00 80.00
3 Roberto Clemente/25 60.00 120.00
4 Stan Musial/25 25.00 60.00
5 Rogers Hornsby/25 30.00 80.00
6 Don Mattingly/25 25.00 60.00
7 Rickey Henderson/25 10.00 25.00
8 Cal Ripken/25 50.00 120.00
9 Yogi Berra/25 20.00 50.00
10 Reggie Jackson/25 15.00 40.00
11 George Brett/25 25.00 60.00
12 Mel Ott/25 25.00 60.00
13 Roger Maris/25 25.00 60.00
14 Ryne Sandberg/25 30.00 80.00
16 Richie Ashburn/25 15.00 40.00
17 Mike Schmidt/25 12.50 30.00
18 Tony Gwynn/25 15.00 40.00
19 Ty Cobb/25 30.00 80.00
20 Thurman Munson/25 20.00 50.00
21 Jimmie Foxx/25 15.00 40.00
22 Duke Snider/25 15.00 40.00
24 Alex Rodriguez/25 15.00 40.00
25 Nomar Garciaparra/25 15.00 40.00
26 Hideki Matsui Base/25 30.00 80.00
27 Ichiro Suzuki Base/25 25.00 60.00
28 Barry Bonds Base/25 25.00 60.00
29 Mike Piazza/25 15.00 40.00
30 Alfonso Soriano/25 10.00 25.00
31 Al Kaline/25 20.00 50.00
33 Dale Murphy/25 15.00 40.00
35 Willie McCovey/25 10.00 25.00
37 Brooks Robinson/25 15.00 40.00
38 Matsui Base/Ichiro Base/25 60.00 120.00
40 D.Mattingly/L.Gehrig/25 100.00 200.00
41 Y.Berra/T.Munson/25 30.00 80.00
42 M.Schmidt/R.Ashburn/25 40.00 100.00
43 S.Musial/R.Hornsby/25 50.00 100.00
44 D.Mattingly/R.Maris/25 40.00 80.00

2003 Leaf Limited Lumberjacks Bat-Jersey

1-37 PRINT RUNS B/WN 1-25 COPIES PER
38-45 PRINT RUNS B/WN 1-25 COPIES PER
NO PRICING ON QTY OF 15 OR LESS
ALL ARE BAT-JSY COMBOS UNLESS NOTED
4 Stan Musial/25 40.00 100.00
6 Don Mattingly/25 40.00 100.00
8 Cal Ripken/25 60.00 150.00
9 Yogi Berra/25 25.00 60.00
11 George Brett/25 40.00 100.00
13 Roger Maris Bat-Pants/25 60.00 120.00
14 Ryne Sandberg/25 15.00 40.00
15 Eddie Mathews/25 15.00 40.00
17 Mike Schmidt/25 40.00 100.00
18 Tony Gwynn/25 25.00 60.00
20 Thurman Munson/25 30.00 80.00
24 Alex Rodriguez/25 25.00 60.00
25 Nomar Garciaparra/25 25.00 60.00
26 Hideki Matsui Base-Ball/25 50.00 100.00
27 Ichiro Suzuki Base-Ball/25 30.00 80.00
28 Barry Bonds Base-Ball/25 30.00 80.00
29 Mike Piazza/25 25.00 60.00
30 Alfonso Soriano/25 15.00 40.00
33 Dale Murphy/25 20.00 50.00
35 Willie McCovey/25 12.50 30.00
36 Willie Stargell/25 20.00 50.00
37 Brooks Robinson/25 20.00 50.00
38A Matsui Base/Ichiro Ball/25 60.00 120.00
38B Matsui Ball/Ichiro Base/25 60.00 120.00
41A Berra Jsy/Munson Bat/25 30.00 80.00
41B Berra Bat/Munson Jsy/25 30.00 80.00
42 Schmidt Jsy/Ashburn Bat/25 40.00 100.00
43 Musial Jsy/Hornsby Bat/25 50.00 100.00

2003 Leaf Limited Lumberjacks Jersey

1-37 PRINT RUNS B/WN 1-25 COPIES PER
38-45 PRINT RUNS B/WN 1-25 COPIES PER
NO PRICING ON QTY OF 15 OR LESS
4 Stan Musial/25 25.00 60.00
6 Don Mattingly/25 25.00 60.00
8 Cal Ripken/25 50.00 120.00
9 Yogi Berra/25 15.00 40.00
11 George Brett/25 25.00 60.00
12 Mel Ott/25 25.00 60.00
14 Ryne Sandberg/25 30.00 80.00
15 Eddie Mathews/25 15.00 40.00
17 Mike Schmidt/25 25.00 60.00
18 Tony Gwynn/25 15.00 40.00
20 Thurman Munson/25 20.00 50.00
22 Duke Snider/25 12.50 30.00
24 Alex Rodriguez/25 15.00 40.00
25 Nomar Garciaparra/25 15.00 40.00
26 Hideki Matsui Ball/25 30.00 80.00
27 Ichiro Suzuki Ball/25 25.00 60.00
28 Barry Bonds Ball/25 25.00 60.00
29 Mike Piazza/25 15.00 40.00
30 Alfonso Soriano/25 10.00 25.00
32 Harmon Killebrew/25 15.00 40.00
33 Dale Murphy/25 12.50 30.00
34 Orlando Cepeda/25 8.00 20.00
35 Willie McCovey/25 8.00 20.00
36 Willie Stargell/25 12.50 30.00
37 Brooks Robinson/25 12.50 30.00
38 Matsui Ball/Ichiro Ball/25 60.00 120.00
41 Y.Berra/T.Munson/25 20.00 50.00

2003 Leaf Limited Player Threads

RANDOM INSERTS IN PACKS
PRINT RUNS B/WN 5-50 COPIES PER
NO PRICING ON QTY OF 5 OR LESS
1 Roger Clemens/50 10.00 25.00
2 Alex Rodriguez/50 10.00 25.00
3 Pedro Martinez/50 6.00 15.00
4 Randy Johnson/50 6.00 15.00
5 Curt Schilling/50 4.00 10.00
7 Nolan Ryan/50 25.00 60.00
8 Hideo Nomo/50 15.00 40.00
9 Mike Piazza/50 10.00 25.00
11 Rickey Henderson Mets/50 6.00 15.00
12 Ivan Rodriguez/50 6.00 15.00
13 Gary Sheffield/50 4.00 10.00
14 Jeff Kent/50 4.00 10.00
15 Roberto Alomar/50 6.00 15.00
16 Rafael Palmeiro/50 6.00 15.00
17 Juan Gonzalez/50 4.00 10.00
18 Shawn Green/50 4.00 10.00
19 Jason Giambi/50 4.00 10.00
20 Jim Thome/50 6.00 15.00
21 Scott Rolen/50 6.00 15.00
22 Mike Mussina/50 6.00 15.00
23 Tom Glavine/50 6.00 15.00
24 Sammy Sosa/50 6.00 15.00

2003 Leaf Limited Player Threads Double

RANDOM INSERTS IN PACKS
STATED PRINT RUN 50 SERIAL #'d SETS
CARD 6/10 PRINT RUN 5 SERIAL #'d SETS
1 R.Clemens Yanks-Sox 15.00 40.00
2 Alex Rodriguez Rgr-M's 15.00 40.00
3 P.Martinez Sox-Dodgers 10.00 25.00
4 Randy Johnson D'backs-Astros 10.00 25.00
5 C.Schilling D'backs-Phils 6.00 15.00

7 Nolan Ryan Rgr-Astros 12.00 30.00
8 H.Nomo Dodgers-Sox 25.00 60.00
9 M.Piazza Mets-Dodgers 15.00 40.00
11 R.Henderson Mets-M's 10.00 25.00
12 I.Rodriguez Marlins-Rgr 10.00 25.00
13 G.Sheffield Braves-Dodgers 6.00 15.00
14 Jeff Kent Astros-Giants 6.00 15.00
15 R.Alomar Mets-Indians 10.00 25.00
16 Rafael Palmeiro Rgr-O's 10.00 25.00
17 J.Gonzalez Rgr-Indians 6.00 15.00
18 S.Green Dodgers-Jays 6.00 15.00
19 Jason Giambi Yanks-A's 6.00 15.00
20 Jim Thome Phils-Indians 10.00 25.00
21 Scott Rolen Cards-Phils 10.00 25.00
22 Mike Mussina Yanks-O's 10.00 25.00
23 Tom Glavine Mets-Braves 10.00 25.00
24 Sammy Sosa Cubs-Sox 10.00 25.00

2003 Leaf Limited Player Threads Triple

RANDOM INSERTS IN PACKS
STATED PRINT RUN 50 SERIAL #'d SETS
HENDERSON PADRES-SOX-A'S 5 #'d CARDS
NO HENDERSON PADRES-SOX-A'S PRICING
4 R.John D'backs-Astros-M's 15.00 40.00
7 N.Ryan Rgr-Astros-Angels 12.00 30.00
8 H.Nomo Dodgers-Sox-Mets 40.00 100.00
11 R.Henderson Mets-M's-Jays 15.00 40.00
13 G.Sheffield Braves-Dgr-Brew 10.00 25.00
14 J.Kent Astros-Giants-Jays 10.00 25.00
15 R.Alomar Mets-Indians-O's 15.00 40.00

2003 Leaf Limited Team Threads

RANDOM INSERTS IN PACKS
PRINT RUNS B/WN 10-50 COPIES PER
NO PRICING ON QTY OF 10 OR LESS
26 A.Rodriguez/N.Ryan/50 20.00 50.00
27 M.Piazza/H.Nomo/50 15.00 40.00
28 C.Ripken/M.Mussina/50 40.00 100.00
29 H.Nomo/K.Ishii/50 15.00 40.00
30 N.Ryan/R.Johnson/50 20.00 50.00

2003 Leaf Limited Team Trademarks Autographs

RANDOM INSERTS IN PACKS
PRINT RUNS B/WN 5-25 COPIES PER
NO PRICING ON QTY OF 10 OR LESS
1 Alan Trammell/25 20.00 50.00
3 Jim Palmer/25 12.00 30.00
5 Gary Carter/25 20.00 50.00
6 Andre Dawson/25 20.00 50.00
8 Dale Murphy/25 30.00 60.00
10 Bobby Doerr/25 12.00 30.00
11 Brooks Robinson/25 30.00 60.00
12 Eric Davis/25 20.00 50.00
13 Fred Lynn/25 12.00 30.00
15 Jack Morris/25 12.00 30.00
16 Al Kaline/25 20.00 50.00
17 Deion Sanders/25 60.00 120.00
18 Luis Aparicio/25 12.00 30.00
20 Phil Rizzuto/25 30.00 60.00
24 Will Clark/25 60.00 120.00

2003 Leaf Limited Team Trademarks Autographs Jersey

PRINT RUNS B/WN 1-47 COPIES PER
NO PRICING ON QTY OF 24 OR LESS
12 Eric Davis/44 20.00 50.00
15 Jack Morris/47 15.00 40.00
19 Orlando Cepeda/30 20.00 50.00
23 Rod Carew Twins/29 40.00 80.00
25 Willie McCovey/44 30.00 60.00
27 Nolan Ryan Astros/34 75.00 150.00
31 Rod Carew Angels/29 40.00 80.00
32 Nolan Ryan Rgr/34 75.00 150.00
34 Nolan Ryan Angels/30 75.00 150.00
37 Greg Maddux/31 100.00 200.00

2003 Leaf Limited Team Trademarks Threads Number

PRINT RUNS B/WN 1-47 COPIES PER
NO PRICING ON QTY OF 19 OR LESS
3 Jim Palmer/22 12.50 30.00
12 Eric Davis/44 6.00 15.00
15 Jack Morris/47 6.00 15.00
17 Deion Sanders/24 20.00 50.00
19 Orlando Cepeda/30 10.00 25.00
23 Rod Carew Twins/29 15.00 40.00
24 Will Clark/22 40.00 100.00
25 Willie McCovey/44 6.00 15.00
27 Nolan Ryan Astros/34 20.00 50.00
30 Mike Schmidt/20 25.00 60.00
31 Rod Carew Angels/29 15.00 40.00
32 Nolan Ryan Rgr/34 20.00 50.00
34 Nolan Ryan Angels/30 20.00 50.00
36 Roger Clemens/22 25.00 60.00
37 Greg Maddux/31 15.00 40.00

2003 Leaf Limited Team Trademarks Threads Prime

PRINT RUNS B/WN 5-25 COPIES PER
NO PRICING ON QTY OF 10 OR LESS
1 Alan Trammell/25 15.00 40.00
2 Joe Morgan/25 15.00 40.00
3 Jim Palmer/25 15.00 40.00
5 Gary Carter/25 15.00 40.00
6 Andre Dawson/25 15.00 40.00
7 Duke Snider/25 25.00 60.00
8 Dale Murphy/25 25.00 60.00
9 Bo Jackson/25 25.00 60.00
10 Bobby Doerr/20 20.00 50.00
11 Brooks Robinson/25 25.00 60.00
12 Eric Davis/25 15.00 40.00
13 Fred Lynn/25 10.00 25.00
14 Harmon Killebrew/25 30.00 80.00
15 Jack Morris/25 10.00 25.00
17 Deion Sanders/25 25.00 60.00
18 Luis Aparicio/25 15.00 40.00
19 Orlando Cepeda/25 15.00 40.00
22 Robin Yount/25 25.00 60.00
23 Rod Carew Twins/25 25.00 60.00
24 Will Clark/25 50.00 100.00
25 Willie McCovey/25 15.00 40.00
26 Tony Gwynn/25 15.00 40.00
27 Nolan Ryan Astros/25 50.00 100.00
28 Cal Ripken/25 60.00 120.00
29 Stan Musial/25 60.00 120.00
30 Mike Schmidt/25 40.00 100.00
31 Rod Carew Angels/25 25.00 60.00
32 Nolan Ryan Rgr/25 50.00 100.00
33 George Brett/25 40.00 100.00
34 Nolan Ryan Angels/25 50.00 100.00
35 Alex Rodriguez/25 25.00 60.00
36 Roger Clemens/20 30.00 80.00
37 Greg Maddux/25 25.00 60.00
38 Albert Pujols/25 40.00 100.00
39 Alfonso Soriano/25 15.00 40.00
40 Mark Grace/25 25.00 60.00

2004 Leaf Limited

COMMON CARD (1-200/230-250) .60 1.50
1-200/230-250 PRINT RUN 749 #'d SETS
COMMON CARD (201-229) .75 2.00
201-229 PRINT RUN 499 SERIAL #'d SETS
COMMON AUTO (251-275) 5.00 12.00
251-275: OVERALL AU-GU ONE PER PACK
251-275 AUTO PRINT RUN 99 #'d SETS
1 Adam Dunn A 1.00 2.50
2 Adrian Beltre 1.50 4.00
3 Albert Pujols H 2.00 5.00
4 Alex Rodriguez Yanks 2.00 5.00
5 Alfonso Soriano Rgr 1.00 2.50
6 Andruw Jones .60 1.50
7 Andy Pettitte Astros 1.00 2.50
8 Angel Berroa .60 1.50
9 Aramis Ramirez .60 1.50
10 Aubrey Huff .60 1.50
11 Austin Kearns .60 1.50
12 Barry Larkin 1.00 2.50
13 Barry Zito H 1.00 2.50
14 Bartolo Colon .60 1.50
15 Ben Sheets .60 1.50
16 Bernie Williams 1.00 2.50
17 Bobby Abreu .60 1.50
18 Brandon Webb .60 1.50
19 Brian Giles .60 1.50
20 C.C. Sabathia 1.00 2.50
21 Carlos Beltran Royals A 1.00 2.50
22 Carlos Delgado .60 1.50
23 Chipper Jones H 1.50 4.00
24 Craig Biggio 1.00 2.50
25 Curt Schilling Sox 1.00 2.50
26 Darin Erstad .60 1.50
27 Delmon Young 1.00 2.50
28 Derek Jeter 4.00 10.00
29 Derrek Lee .60 1.50
30 Dontrelle Willis .60 1.50
31 Edgar Renteria .60 1.50
32 Eric Chavez .60 1.50
33 Esteban Loaiza .60 1.50
34 Frank Thomas 1.50 4.00
35 Fred McGriff .60 1.50
36 Garret Anderson H .60 1.50
37 Gary Sheffield Yanks .60 1.50
38 Geoff Jenkins .60 1.50
39 Greg Maddux Cubs 2.00 5.00
40 Hank Blalock H .60 1.50
41 Hideki Matsui 2.50 6.00
42 Hideo Nomo Dodgers 1.50 4.00
43 Ichiro Suzuki 2.00 5.00
44 Ivan Rodriguez Tigers 1.00 2.50
45 J.D. Drew .60 1.50
46 Jacque Jones .60 1.50
47 Jae Weong Seo .60 1.50
48 Jake Peavy .60 1.50
49 Jamie Moyer .60 1.50
50 Jason Giambi Yanks .60 1.50
51 Jason Kendall .60 1.50
52 Jason Schmidt .60 1.50
53 Jason Varitek 1.50 4.00
54 Javier Vazquez .60 1.50
55 Javy Lopez .60 1.50
56 Jay Gibbons .60 1.50
57 Jay Payton .60 1.50
58 Jeff Bagwell H 1.00 2.50
59 Jeff Kent .60 1.50
60 Jeremy Bonderman .60 1.50
61 Jermaine Dye .60 1.50
62 Jeromy Burnitz .60 1.50
63 Jim Edmonds 1.00 2.50
64 Jim Thome Phils 1.00 2.50
65 Jimmy Rollins 1.00 2.50
66 Jody Gerut .60 1.50
67 Johan Santana 1.00 2.50
68 John Olerud .60 1.50
69 John Smoltz 1.50 4.00
70 Johnny Damon 1.00 2.50
71 Jorge Posada 1.00 2.50
72 Jose Contreras .60 1.50
73 Jose Reyes 1.00 2.50
74 Jose Vidro .60 1.50
75 Josh Beckett H .60 1.50
76 Juan Gonzalez Royals .60 1.50
77 Juan Pierre .60 1.50
78 Junior Spivey .60 1.50
79 Kazuhisa Ishii .60 1.50
80 Keith Foulke Sox .60 1.50
81 Ken Griffey Jr. Reds 3.00 8.00
82 Ken Harvey .60 1.50
83 Kenny Rogers .60 1.50
84 Kerry Wood .60 1.50
85 Kevin Brown Yanks .60 1.50
86 Kevin Millwood .60 1.50
87 Kip Wells .60 1.50
88 Lance Berkman 1.00 2.50
89 Larry Bigbie .60 1.50
90 Larry Walker 1.00 2.50
91 Laynce Nix .60 1.50
92 Luis Castillo .60 1.50
93 Luis Gonzalez .60 1.50
94 Luis Matos .60 1.50
95 Lyle Overbay .60 1.50
96 Magglio Ordonez H 1.00 2.50
97 Manny Ramirez Sox 1.50 4.00
98 Marcus Giles .60 1.50
99 Mark Buehrle 1.00 2.50
100 Mark Mulder .60 1.50
101 Mark Prior H 1.00 2.50
102 Mark Teixeira 1.00 2.50
103 Marlon Byrd .60 1.50
104 Matt Morris .60 1.50
105 Melvin Mora .60 1.50
106 Michael Young .60 1.50
107 Miguel Cabrera Batting 1.50 4.00
108 Miguel Tejada O's 1.00 2.50
109 Mike Lowell .60 1.50
110 Mike Mussina Yanks 1.00 2.50
111 Mike Piazza Mets 1.50 4.00
112 Mike Sweeney .60 1.50
113 Milton Bradley .60 1.50
114 Moises Alou .60 1.50
115 Morgan Ensberg .60 1.50
116 Nick Johnson .60 1.50
117 Nomar Garciaparra 1.00 2.50
118 Omar Vizquel 1.00 2.50
119 Orlando Cabrera .60 1.50
120 Pat Burrell .60 1.50
121 Paul Konerko 1.00 2.50
122 Paul Lo Duca .60 1.50
123 Pedro Martinez Sox 1.00 2.50
124 Preston Wilson H .60 1.50
125 Rafael Furcal .60 1.50
126 Rafael Palmeiro O's 1.00 2.50
127 Randy Johnson D'backs 1.50 4.00
128 Rich Harden .60 1.50
129 Richard Hidalgo .60 1.50
130 Richie Sexson .60 1.50
131 Rickie Weeks .60 1.50
132 Roberto Alomar 1.00 2.50
133 Robin Ventura .60 1.50
134 Rocco Baldelli .60 1.50
135 Roger Clemens Astros 2.00 5.00
136 Roy Halladay 1.00 2.50
137 Roy Oswalt A 1.00 2.50
138 Russ Ortiz .60 1.50
139 Ryan Klesko .60 1.50
140 Sammy Sosa H 1.50 4.00
141 Scott Podsednik .60 1.50
142 Scott Rolen Cards A 1.00 2.50
143 Sean Burroughs .60 1.50
144 Sean Casey .60 1.50
145 Shannon Stewart .60 1.50
146 Shawn Green Dodgers .60 1.50
147 Shigetoshi Hasegawa .60 1.50
148 Sidney Ponson .60 1.50
149 Steve Finley .60 1.50
150 Tim Hudson 1.00 2.50
151 Tim Salmon .60 1.50
152 Tino Martinez 1.00 2.50
153 Todd Helton H 1.00 2.50
154 Tom Glavine Mets 1.00 2.50
155 Torii Hunter .60 1.50
156 Trot Nixon .60 1.50
157 Troy Glaus .60 1.50
158 Vernon Wells H .60 1.50
159 Victor Martinez A 1.00 2.50
160 Vinny Castilla .60 1.50
161 Vladimir Guerrero Angels 1.00 2.50
162 Alex Rodriguez Rgr 2.00 5.00
163 Alfonso Soriano Yanks 1.00 2.50
164 Andy Pettitte Yanks 1.00 2.50
165 Curt Schilling D'backs 1.00 2.50
166 Gary Sheffield Braves .60 1.50
167 Greg Maddux Braves 2.00 5.00
168 Hideo Nomo Sox 1.50 4.00
169 Ivan Rodriguez Marlins 1.00 2.50
170 Jason Giambi A's .60 1.50
171 Jim Thome Indians 1.00 2.50
172 Juan Gonzalez Rgr .60 1.50
173 Ken Griffey Jr. M's 3.00 8.00
174 Kevin Brown Dodgers .60 1.50
175 Manny Ramirez Indians 1.50 4.00
176 Miguel Tejada A's 1.00 2.50
177 Mike Mussina O's 1.00 2.50
178 Mike Piazza Dodgers 1.50 4.00
179 Pedro Martinez Expos 1.00 2.50
180 Rafael Palmeiro Rgr 1.00 2.50
181 Randy Johnson Astros 1.50 4.00
182 Roger Clemens Sox 2.00 5.00
183 Scott Rolen Phils 1.00 2.50
184 Shawn Green Jays .60 1.50
185 Tom Glavine Braves 1.00 2.50
186 Vladimir Guerrero Expos 1.00 2.50
187 Alex Rodriguez M's 2.00 5.00
188 Mike Piazza Marlins 1.50 4.00
189 Randy Johnson M's 1.50 4.00
190 Roger Clemens Yanks 2.00 5.00
191 Albert Pujols A 2.00 5.00
192 Barry Zito A 1.00 2.50
193 Chipper Jones A 1.50 4.00
194 Garret Anderson A .60 1.50
195 Jeff Bagwell A 1.00 2.50
196 Josh Beckett A .60 1.50
197 Magglio Ordonez A 1.00 2.50
198 Mark Prior A 1.00 2.50
199 Sammy Sosa A 1.50 4.00
200 Todd Helton A 1.00 2.50
201 Andre Dawson RET 1.25 3.00
202 Babe Ruth RET 5.00 12.00
203 Bob Feller RET 1.25 3.00
204 Bob Gibson RET 1.25 3.00
205 Bobby Doerr RET 1.25 3.00
206 Cal Ripken RET 6.00 15.00
207 Dale Murphy RET 2.00 5.00
208 Don Mattingly RET 4.00 10.00
209 Gary Carter RET 1.25 3.00
210 George Brett RET 4.00 10.00
211 Jackie Robinson RET 2.00 5.00
212 Lou Brock RET 1.25 3.00
213 Lou Gehrig RET 4.00 10.00
214 Mark Grace RET 1.25 3.00
215 Maury Wills RET .75 2.00
216 Mike Schmidt RET 3.00 8.00
217 Nolan Ryan RET 6.00 15.00
218 Orel Hershiser RET .75 2.00
219 Paul Molitor RET 2.00 5.00
220 Roberto Clemente RET 5.00 12.00
221 Rod Carew RET 1.25 3.00
222 Roy Campanella RET 2.00 5.00
223 Ryne Sandberg RET 4.00 10.00
224 Stan Musial RET 3.00 8.00
225 Ted Williams RET 4.00 10.00
226 Tony Gwynn RET 2.00 5.00
227 Ty Cobb RET 3.00 8.00
228 Whitey Ford RET 1.25 3.00
229 Yogi Berra RET 2.00 5.00
230 Carlos Beltran Astros H 1.00 2.50
231 David Ortiz H 1.50 4.00
232 David Ortiz A 1.50 4.00
233 Carlos Zambrano 1.00 2.50
234 Carlos Lee .60 1.50
235 Travis Hafner .60 1.50
236 Brad Penny .60 1.50
237 Wade Miller .60 1.50
238 Edgar Martinez 1.00 2.50
239 Carl Crawford 1.00 2.50
240 Roy Oswalt H 1.00 2.50
241 Kazuo Matsui RC 1.00 2.50
242 Carlos Beltran Astros A 1.00 2.50
243 Carlos Beltran Royals H 1.00 2.50
244 Miguel Cabrera Fielding 1.50 4.00
245 Scott Rolen Cards H 1.00 2.50
246 Hank Blalock A .60 1.50
247 Vernon Wells A .60 1.50
248 Adam Dunn H 1.00 2.50
249 Preston Wilson A .60 1.50
250 Victor Martinez H 1.00 2.50
251 Aarom Baldiris PH AU RC 5.00 12.00
252 Akinori Otsuka PH AU RC 10.00 25.00
253 Andres Blanco PH AU RC 5.00 12.00
254 Brad Halsey PH AU RC 5.00 12.00
255 Joey Gathright PH AU RC 5.00 12.00
256 Colby Miller PH AU RC 5.00 12.00
257 Fernando Nieve PH AU RC 5.00 12.00
258 Freddy Guzman PH AU RC 5.00 12.00
259 Hector Gimenez PH AU RC 5.00 12.00
260 Jake Woods PH AU RC 5.00 12.00
261 Jason Bartlett PH AU RC 6.00 15.00
262 John Gall PH AU RC 5.00 12.00
263 Jose Capellan PH AU RC 5.00 12.00
264 Josh Labandeira PH AU RC 5.00 12.00
265 Justin Germano PH AU RC 5.00 12.00
266 Kazuhito Tadano PH AU RC 12.50 30.00
267 Lance Cormier PH AU RC 5.00 12.00
268 Merkin Valdez PH AU RC 5.00 12.00
269 Mike Gosling PH AU RC 5.00 12.00
270 Ramon Ramirez PH AU RC 5.00 12.00
271 Rusty Tucker PH AU RC 5.00 12.00
272 Shawn Hill PH AU RC 5.00 12.00
273 Shingo Takatsu PH AU RC 10.00 25.00
274 William Bergolla PH AU RC 5.00 12.00
275 Yadier Molina PH AU RC 150.00 400.00

2004 Leaf Limited Bronze Spotlight

*BRONZE 1-200/230-250: .75X TO 2X
*BRONZE 201-229: .75X TO 2X
*BRONZE RC'S 1-200/230-250: .75X TO 2X
RANDOM INSERTS IN PACKS
STATED PRINT RUN 100 SERIAL #'d SETS

2004 Leaf Limited Gold Spotlight

*GOLD 1-200/230-250: 2X TO 5X
*GOLD 201-229: 2X TO 5X
RC'S 1-200/230-250: 2X TO 5X
RANDOM INSERTS IN PACKS
STATED PRINT RUN 25 SERIAL #'d SETS

2004 Leaf Limited Silver Spotlight

*SILVER 1-200/230-250: 1.25X TO 3X
*SILVER 201-229: 1.25X TO 3X
*SILVER RC'S 1-200/230-250: 1X TO 2.5X
RANDOM INSERTS IN PACKS
STATED PRINT RUN 50 SERIAL #'d SETS

2004 Leaf Limited Moniker Bronze

OVERALL AU-GU ODDS ONE PER PACK
PRINT RUNS B/WN 1-100 COPIES PER
NO PRICING ON QTY OF 10 OR LESS
1 Adam Dunn A/50 8.00 20.00
3 Albert Pujols H/25 150.00 250.00
5 Alfonso Soriano Rgr/100 10.00 25.00
6 Andruw Jones/50 12.50 30.00
8 Angel Berroa/25 6.00 15.00
11 Austin Kearns/50 5.00 12.00
18 Brandon Webb/21 6.00 15.00
21 Carlos Beltran Royals A/50 8.00 20.00
23 Chipper Jones H/25 30.00 60.00
24 Craig Biggio/25 15.00 40.00
30 Dontrelle Willis/25 15.00 40.00
31 Edgar Renteria/25 10.00 25.00
34 Frank Thomas/50 20.00 50.00
36 Garret Anderson H/50 8.00 20.00
37 Gary Sheffield Yanks/50 12.50 30.00
39 Greg Maddux Cubs/25 50.00 100.00
40 Hank Blalock H/50 8.00 20.00
46 Jacque Jones/25 10.00 25.00
58 Jeff Bagwell H/25 40.00 80.00
71 Jorge Posada/25 75.00 150.00
76 Juan Gonzalez Royals/25 10.00 25.00
79 Kazuhisa Ishii/25 10.00 25.00
84 Kerry Wood/25 15.00 40.00
88 Lance Berkman/50 6.00 15.00
98 Marcus Giles/25 10.00 25.00
100 Mark Mulder/100 6.00 15.00
101 Mark Prior H/50 10.00 25.00
102 Mark Teixeira/50 8.00 20.00
106 Michael Young/50 8.00 20.00
107 Miguel Cabrera Batting/50 30.00 60.00
109 Mike Lowell/25 10.00 25.00
122 Paul Lo Duca/25 10.00 25.00
131 Rickie Weeks/25 10.00 25.00
137 Roy Oswalt A/50 8.00 20.00
140 Sammy Sosa H/25 50.00 100.00
142 Scott Rolen Cards A/25 15.00 40.00
144 Sean Casey/25 10.00 25.00
145 Shannon Stewart/25 10.00 25.00
153 Todd Helton H/25 15.00 40.00
155 Torii Hunter/50 6.00 15.00
156 Trot Nixon/25 10.00 25.00
158 Vernon Wells H/25 10.00 25.00
163 Alfonso Soriano Yanks/100 6.00 15.00
166 Gary Sheffield Braves/50 12.50 30.00
167 Greg Maddux Braves/25 50.00 100.00
172 Juan Gonzalez Rgr/25 10.00 25.00
183 Scott Rolen Phils/25 15.00 40.00
191 Albert Pujols A/25 75.00 150.00
193 Chipper Jones A/25 30.00 60.00
194 Garret Anderson A/50 8.00 20.00
195 Jeff Bagwell A/25 40.00 80.00
198 Mark Prior A/50 10.00 25.00
199 Sammy Sosa A/25 50.00 100.00
200 Todd Helton A/25 15.00 40.00
201 Andre Dawson RET/100 12.50 30.00
203 Bob Feller RET/100 10.00 25.00
204 Bob Gibson RET/100 10.00 25.00
205 Bobby Doerr RET/100 6.00 15.00
206 Cal Ripken RET/25 125.00 200.00
207 Dale Murphy RET/100 6.00 15.00
208 Don Mattingly RET/100 30.00 60.00
209 Gary Carter RET/100 15.00 40.00
210 George Brett RET/25 40.00 80.00
212 Lou Brock RET/100 10.00 25.00
214 Mark Grace RET/100 10.00 25.00
215 Maury Wills RET/100 6.00 15.00
216 Mike Schmidt RET/100 10.00 25.00
217 Nolan Ryan RET/100 50.00 100.00
218 Orel Hershiser RET/25 15.00 40.00
219 Paul Molitor RET/100 6.00 15.00
221 Rod Carew RET/100 10.00 25.00
223 Ryne Sandberg RET/100 20.00 50.00
224 Stan Musial RET/100 50.00 100.00
226 Tony Gwynn RET/100 15.00 40.00
230 Carlos Beltran Astros H/50 8.00 20.00
231 David Ortiz H/50 20.00 50.00
232 David Ortiz A/50 20.00 50.00
233 Carlos Zambrano/25 15.00 40.00
234 Carlos Lee/25 10.00 25.00
238 Edgar Martinez/25 20.00 50.00
240 Roy Oswalt H/50 8.00 20.00
242 Carlos Beltran Astros A/50 8.00 20.00
243 Carlos Beltran Royals H/50 8.00 20.00
244 Miguel Cabrera Fielding/50 20.00 50.00
245 Scott Rolen Cards H/25 15.00 40.00
246 Hank Blalock A/50 8.00 20.00
247 Vernon Wells A/25 10.00 25.00
248 Adam Dunn H/50 8.00 20.00

2004 Leaf Limited Moniker Gold

*1-220/230-250 p/r 25: .6X TO 1.5X p/r 100
*1-220/230-250 p/r 25: .5X TO 1.2X p/r 50
*201-229 p/r 25: .6X TO 1.5X p/r 100
OVERALL AU-GU ODDS ONE PER PACK
PRINT RUNS B/WN 1-25 COPIES PER
NO PRICING ON QTY OF 10 OR LESS

2004 Leaf Limited Moniker Silver

*1-200/230-250 p/r 50: .5X TO 1.2X p/r 100
*1-200/230-250 p/r 25: .5X TO 1.2X p/r 50
*201-229 p/r 50: .5X TO 1.2X p/r 100
OVERALL AU-GU ODDS ONE PER PACK
PRINT RUNS B/WN 1-50 COPIES PER
NO PRICING ON QTY OF 10 OR LESS

2004 Leaf Limited Moniker Bat

*1-200/230-250 p/r 40-50: .5X TO 1.2X Jsy/75
*1-200/230-250p/r40-50: .4X TO 1X Jsy/38-50
*1-200/230-250 p/r 40-50: .3X TO .8X Jsy/25
*1-200/230-250 p/r 25: .5X TO 1.2X Jsy/50
*1-200/230-250 p/r 25: .4X TO 1X Jsy/25
*1-200/230-250 p/r 15: .6X TO 1.5X Jsy/50
*1-200/230-250 p/r 15: .5X TO 1.2X Jsy/25
*201-229 p/r 100: .4X TO 1X Jsy/100
*201-229 p/r 50: .5X TO 1.2X Jsy/100
*201-229 p/r 50: .4X TO 1X Jsy/50
*201-229 p/r 50: .3X TO .8X Jsy/25
*201-229 p/r 25: .5X TO 1.2X Jsy/50
*201-229 p/r 25: .4X TO 1X Jsy/25
OVERALL AU-GU ODDS ONE PER PACK
PRINT RUNS B/WN 1-100 COPIES PER
NO PRICING ON QTY OF 10 OR LESS
27 Delmon Young/50 15.00 40.00
31 Edgar Renteria/25 12.50 30.00
37 Gary Sheffield Yanks/25 20.00 50.00
61 Jermaine Dye/25 12.50 30.00
106 Michael Young/50 10.00 25.00
131 Rickie Weeks/25 12.50 30.00
212 Lou Brock RET/50 15.00 40.00
214 Mark Grace RET/25 20.00 50.00
250 Victor Martinez H/25 12.50 30.00

2004 Leaf Limited Moniker Jersey

OVERALL AU-GU ODDS ONE PER PACK
PRINT RUNS B/WN 1-100 COPIES PER
NO PRICING ON QTY OF 10 OR LESS
1 Adam Dunn A/50 8.00 20.00
5 Alfonso Soriano Rgr/50 10.00 25.00
6 Andruw Jones/25 20.00 50.00
8 Angel Berroa Pants/25 8.00 20.00
9 Aramis Ramirez/25 12.50 30.00
10 Aubrey Huff/25 12.50 30.00
11 Austin Kearns/25 8.00 20.00
15 Ben Sheets/25 12.50 30.00
18 Brandon Webb/25 8.00 20.00
20 C.C. Sabathia/25 12.50 30.00
21 Carlos Beltran Royals A/50 10.00 25.00
23 Chipper Jones H/25 40.00 80.00
24 Craig Biggio/25 12.00 30.00
30 Dontrelle Willis/25 20.00 50.00
32 Eric Chavez/50 10.00 25.00
34 Frank Thomas/25 40.00 80.00
35 Fred McGriff/25 20.00 50.00
36 Garret Anderson H/50 10.00 25.00
40 Hank Blalock H/50 10.00 25.00
46 Jacque Jones/25 12.50 30.00
63 Jim Edmonds/25 20.00 50.00
66 Jody Gerut/25 8.00 20.00
67 Johan Santana/25 20.00 50.00
71 Jorge Posada/25 20.00 50.00
74 Jose Vidro/25 8.00 20.00
84 Kerry Wood/25 10.00 25.00
88 Lance Berkman/25 20.00 50.00
89 Larry Bigbie/25 12.50 30.00
98 Marcus Giles/25 12.50 30.00
99 Mark Buehrle/25 30.00 60.00
100 Mark Mulder/75 8.00 20.00
101 Mark Prior H/50 12.50 30.00
102 Mark Teixeira/25 20.00 50.00
105 Melvin Mora/25 12.50 30.00
107 Miguel Cabrera Batting/38 25.00 60.00
109 Mike Lowell/25 12.50 30.00
115 Morgan Ensberg/25 8.00 20.00
122 Paul Lo Duca/25 12.50 30.00
124 Preston Wilson H/25 12.50 30.00
137 Roy Oswalt A/25 12.50 30.00
142 Scott Rolen Cards A/50 8.00 20.00
143 Sean Burroughs/25 8.00 20.00
144 Sean Casey/25 12.50 30.00
145 Shannon Stewart/25 12.50 30.00
149 Steve Finley/25 12.50 30.00
153 Todd Helton H/25 20.00 50.00
154 Tom Glavine Mets/25 20.00 50.00
155 Torii Hunter/25 12.50 30.00
156 Trot Nixon/25 12.50 30.00
158 Vernon Wells H/50 10.00 25.00
159 Victor Martinez A/50 10.00 25.00
163 Alfonso Soriano Yanks/50 15.00 40.00
166 Gary Sheffield Braves/25 10.00 25.00
172 Juan Gonzalez Rgr/25 12.50 30.00
183 Scott Rolen Phils/50 15.00 40.00
185 Tom Glavine Braves/25 20.00 50.00
193 Chipper Jones A/25 40.00 80.00
194 Garret Anderson A/50 10.00 25.00
198 Mark Prior A/50 12.50 30.00
200 Todd Helton A/25 20.00 50.00
201 Andre Dawson RET/50 10.00 25.00
204 Bob Gibson RET/50 15.00 40.00
205 Bobby Doerr RET/50 12.50 30.00
207 Dale Murphy RET/100 6.00 15.00
208 Don Mattingly RET/50 25.00 60.00
209 Gary Carter RET/100 15.00 40.00
216 Mike Schmidt RET/50 20.00 50.00
217 Nolan Ryan RET/100 50.00 120.00
218 Orel Hershiser RET/50 15.00 40.00
219 Paul Molitor RET/50 10.00 25.00
221 Rod Carew RET/50 15.00 40.00
223 Ryne Sandberg RET/25 20.00 50.00
224 Stan Musial RET/25 60.00 120.00
226 Tony Gwynn RET/100 20.00 50.00
228 Whitey Ford RET Pants/25 20.00 50.00
229 Yogi Berra RET/25 40.00 100.00
230 Carlos Beltran Astros H/50 10.00 25.00
231 David Ortiz H/50 30.00 60.00
232 David Ortiz A/50 30.00 60.00
234 Carlos Lee/50 10.00 25.00
235 Travis Hafner/25 12.50 30.00
236 Brad Penny/25 8.00 20.00
237 Wade Miller/25 8.00 20.00
238 Edgar Martinez/50 12.00 30.00
239 Carl Crawford/25 12.50 30.00
240 Roy Oswalt H/25 12.50 30.00
242 Carlos Beltran Astros A/50 10.00 25.00
243 Carlos Beltran Royals H/50 10.00 25.00
244 Miguel Cabrera Fielding/50 20.00 50.00
245 Scott Rolen Cards H/50 15.00 40.00
246 Hank Blalock A/50 10.00 25.00
247 Vernon Wells A/50 10.00 25.00
248 Adam Dunn H/50 8.00 20.00
249 Preston Wilson A/25 12.50 30.00

2004 Leaf Limited Moniker Jersey Number

*1-200/230-250 p/r 75: .4X TO 1X Jsy/75
*1-200/230-250 p/r 50: .4X TO 1X Jsy/38-50
*1-200/230-250 p/r 25: .5X TO 1.2X Jsy/50
*1-200/230-250 p/r 25: .4X TO 1X Jsy/25
*201-229 p/r 100: .4X TO 1X Jsy/100
*201-229 p/r 50: .4X TO 1X Jsy/50
*201-229 p/r 25: .5X TO 1.2X Jsy/50
*201-229 p/r 25: .4X TO 1X Jsy/25
OVERALL AU-GU ODDS ONE PER PACK
PRINT RUNS B/WN 1-100 COPIES PER
NO PRICING ON QTY OF 10 OR LESS
140 Sammy Sosa H/25 50.00 100.00
199 Sammy Sosa A/25 50.00 100.00

2004 Leaf Limited Threads Jersey

OVERALL AU-GU ODDS ONE PER PACK
PRINT RUNS B/WN 1-100 COPIES PER
NO PRICING ON QTY OF 10 OR LESS
NO RC YR PRICING DUE TO SCARCITY
1 Adam Dunn A/25 5.00 12.00
3 Albert Pujols H/50 10.00 25.00
5 Alfonso Soriano Rgr/25 5.00 12.00
6 Andruw Jones/25 8.00 20.00
11 Austin Kearns/25 5.00 12.00
12 Barry Larkin/25 8.00 20.00
13 Barry Zito H/25 5.00 12.00
16 Bernie Williams/50 5.00 12.00
21 Carlos Beltran Royals A/25 5.00 12.00
22 Carlos Delgado/25 5.00 12.00
23 Chipper Jones H/50 6.00 15.00
24 Craig Biggio/25 8.00 20.00
25 Curt Schilling Sox/25 8.00 20.00
30 Dontrelle Willis/25 8.00 20.00
31 Edgar Renteria/25 5.00 12.00
32 Eric Chavez/25 5.00 12.00
34 Frank Thomas/25 10.00 25.00
36 Garret Anderson H/25 5.00 12.00
39 Greg Maddux Cubs/50 8.00 20.00
40 Hank Blalock H/25 5.00 12.00
41 Hideki Matsui/50 8.00 20.00
42 Hideo Nomo Dodgers/50 6.00 15.00
44 Ivan Rodriguez Tigers/25 8.00 20.00
50 Jason Giambi Yanks/50 3.00 8.00
55 Javy Lopez/25 5.00 12.00
58 Jeff Bagwell H/50 5.00 12.00
59 Jeff Kent/50 3.00 8.00
63 Jim Edmonds/25 5.00 12.00
64 Jim Thome Phils/50 5.00 12.00
69 John Smoltz/25 8.00 20.00
71 Jorge Posada/25 8.00 20.00
75 Josh Beckett H/25 5.00 12.00
76 Juan Gonzalez Royals/25 5.00 12.00
84 Kerry Wood/50 3.00 8.00
88 Lance Berkman/50 3.00 8.00
90 Larry Walker/25 5.00 12.00
93 Luis Gonzalez/25 5.00 12.00
96 Magglio Ordonez H/25 5.00 12.00
97 Manny Ramirez Sox/50 5.00 12.00
100 Mark Mulder/25 5.00 12.00
101 Mark Prior H/50 5.00 12.00
107 Miguel Cabrera Batting/25 8.00 20.00
108 Miguel Tejada O's/25 5.00 12.00
110 Mike Mussina Yanks/50 5.00 12.00
111 Mike Piazza Mets/50 8.00 20.00
112 Mike Sweeney/25 5.00 12.00
123 Pedro Martinez Sox/50 5.00 12.00
126 Rafael Palmeiro O's/25 8.00 20.00
127 Randy Johnson D'backs/25 10.00 25.00
137 Roy Oswalt A/25 5.00 12.00
140 Sammy Sosa H/50 6.00 15.00
142 Scott Rolen Cards A/25 8.00 20.00
146 Shawn Green Dodgers/25 5.00 12.00
150 Tim Hudson/25 5.00 12.00
153 Todd Helton H/50 5.00 12.00
154 Tom Glavine Mets/25 8.00 20.00
155 Torii Hunter/25 5.00 12.00
157 Troy Glaus/25 5.00 12.00
158 Vernon Wells H/25 5.00 12.00
161 Vladimir Guerrero Angels/25 10.00 25.00
162 Alex Rodriguez Rgr/100 5.00 12.00
163 Alfonso Soriano Yanks/50 3.00 8.00
164 Andy Pettitte Yanks/25 8.00 20.00
165 Curt Schilling D'backs/25 5.00 12.00
166 Gary Sheffield Braves/25 5.00 12.00
167 Greg Maddux Braves/50 8.00 20.00
168 Hideo Nomo Sox/25 10.00 25.00
169 Ivan Rodriguez Marlins/50 5.00 12.00
170 Jason Giambi A's/25 5.00 12.00
172 Juan Gonzalez Rgr/25 5.00 12.00
174 Kevin Brown Dodgers/25 5.00 12.00
176 Miguel Tejada A's/25 5.00 12.00
177 Mike Mussina O's/50 5.00 12.00
178 Mike Piazza Dodgers/25 12.50 30.00
179 Pedro Martinez Expos/25 8.00 20.00
180 Rafael Palmeiro Rgr/25 8.00 20.00
181 Randy Johnson Astros/50 6.00 15.00
182 Roger Clemens Sox/100 5.00 12.00
183 Scott Rolen Phils/25 8.00 20.00
184 Shawn Green Jays/25 5.00 12.00
185 Tom Glavine Braves/25 8.00 20.00
186 Vladimir Guerrero Expos/25 10.00 25.00
187 Alex Rodriguez M's/100 5.00 12.00
189 Randy Johnson M's/50 6.00 15.00
190 Roger Clemens Yanks/100 5.00 12.00
191 Albert Pujols A/50 10.00 25.00
192 Barry Zito A/25 5.00 12.00
193 Chipper Jones A/50 6.00 15.00
194 Garret Anderson A/25 5.00 12.00
195 Jeff Bagwell A/50 5.00 12.00
196 Josh Beckett A/25 5.00 12.00
197 Magglio Ordonez A/25 5.00 12.00
198 Mark Prior A/50 5.00 12.00
199 Sammy Sosa A/50 6.00 15.00
200 Todd Helton A/50 5.00 12.00
201 Andre Dawson RET/50 4.00 10.00
202 Babe Ruth RET/25 250.00 400.00
203 Bob Feller RET Pants/25 10.00 25.00
205 Bobby Doerr RET/50 4.00 10.00
206 Cal Ripken RET/100 20.00 50.00
207 Dale Murphy RET/100 5.00 12.00
208 Don Mattingly RET/50 12.50 30.00
209 Gary Carter RET/50 4.00 10.00
210 George Brett RET/100 8.00 20.00
211 J.Robinson RET Jkt/50 20.00 50.00
212 Lou Brock RET/25 10.00 25.00
213 Lou Gehrig RET/25 100.00 175.00
214 Mark Grace RET/25 10.00 25.00
215 Maury Wills RET/50 4.00 10.00
216 Mike Schmidt RET/100 8.00 20.00
217 Nolan Ryan RET/100 12.00 30.00
218 Orel Hershiser RET/25 10.00 25.00
219 Paul Molitor RET/50 4.00 10.00
220 Roberto Clemente RET/25 50.00 100.00
221 Rod Carew RET/100 5.00 12.00
222 R.Campanella RET Pants/50 8.00 20.00
223 Ryne Sandberg RET/50 12.50 30.00
224 Stan Musial RET/25 10.00 25.00
225 Ted Williams RET/50 20.00 50.00
226 Tony Gwynn RET/100 6.00 15.00
227 Ty Cobb RET Pants/100 40.00 80.00
228 Whitey Ford RET Pants/25 10.00 25.00
229 Yogi Berra RET/25 12.50 30.00
230 Carlos Beltran Astros H/25 5.00 12.00
231 David Ortiz H/25 10.00 25.00
232 David Ortiz A/25 10.00 25.00
238 Edgar Martinez/25 8.00 20.00
240 Roy Oswalt H/25 5.00 12.00
242 Carlos Beltran Astros A/25 5.00 12.00
243 Carlos Beltran Royals H/25 5.00 12.00
244 Miguel Cabrera Fielding/25 8.00 20.00
245 Scott Rolen Cards H/25 8.00 20.00
246 Hank Blalock A/25 5.00 12.00
247 Vernon Wells A/25 5.00 12.00
248 Adam Dunn H/25 5.00 12.00

2004 Leaf Limited Threads Jersey Number

*1-200/230-250 p/r 100: .4X TO 1X Thrd/100
*1-200/230-250 p/r 50: .4X TO 1X Thrd/50
*1-200/230-250 p/r 25: .6X TO 1.5X Thrd/50
*1-200/230-250 p/r 25: .4X TO 1X Thrd/25
*201-229 p/r 100: .4X TO 1X Thrd/100
*201-229 p/r 100: .3X TO .8X Thrd/50
*201-229 p/r 50: .4X TO 1X Thrd/50
*201-229 p/r 25: .4X TO 1X Thrd/25
OVERALL AU-GU ODDS ONE PER PACK
PRINT RUNS B/WN 1-100 COPIES PER
NO PRICING ON QTY OF 10 OR LESS

2004 Leaf Limited Timber

*1-200/230-250 p/r 100: .4X TO 1X Thrd/100
*1-200/230-250 p/r 50: .4X TO 1X Thrd/50
*1-200/230-250 p/r 25: 1X TO 2.5X Thrd/100
*1-200/230-250 p/r 25: .6X TO 1.5X Thrd/50
*1-200/230-250 p/r 25: .4X TO 1X Thrd/25
*201-229 p/r 100: .4X TO 1X Thrd/100
*201-229 p/r 100: .25X TO .6X Thrd/50
*201-229 p/r 100: .15X TO .4X Thrd/25
*201-229 p/r 50: .6X TO 1.5X Thrd/100
*201-229 p/r 50: .4X TO 1X Thrd/50
*201-229 p/r 25: 1X TO 2.5X Thrd/100
*201-229 p/r 25: .6X TO 1.5X Thrd/50
*201-229 p/r 25: .4X TO 1X Thrd/25
OVERALL AU-GU ODDS ONE PER PACK
PRINT RUNS B/WN 1-100 COPIES PER
NO PRICING ON QTY OF 10 OR LESS
4 Alex Rodriguez Yanks/100 5.00 12.00
7 Andy Pettitte Astros/25 8.00 20.00
35 Fred McGriff/25 8.00 20.00
37 Gary Sheffield Yanks/25 5.00 12.00
85 Kevin Brown Yanks/25 5.00 12.00
102 Mark Teixeira/25 8.00 20.00
106 Michael Young/25 5.00 12.00
109 Mike Lowell/25 5.00 12.00
116 Nick Johnson/25 5.00 12.00
117 Nomar Garciaparra/25 12.50 30.00
122 Paul Lo Duca/25 5.00 12.00

130 Richie Sexson/25 5.00 12.00
134 Rocco Baldelli/25 5.00 12.00
135 Roger Clemens Astros/25 12.50 30.00
156 Trot Nixon/25 5.00 12.00
171 Jim Thome Indians/25 8.00 20.00
175 Manny Ramirez Indians/25 8.00 20.00
188 Mike Piazza Marlins/25 12.50 30.00
202 Babe Ruth RET/100 75.00 150.00
213 Lou Gehrig RET/100 30.00 60.00
220 Roberto Clemente RET/100 40.00 80.00
225 Ted Williams RET/100 15.00 40.00
238 Edgar Martinez/25 10.00 25.00

2004 Leaf Limited TNT

*1-200/230-250 p/r 100: .5X TO 1.2X Thrd/100
*1-200/230-250 p/r 100: .3X TO .8X Thrd/50
*1-200/230-250 p/r 50: .5X TO 1.2X Thrd/50
*1-200/230-250 p/r 50: .3X TO .8X Thrd/25
*1-200/230-250 p/r 25: .75X TO 2X Thrd/50
*1-200/230-250 p/r 25: .5X TO 1.2X Thrd/25
*201-229 p/r 100: .5X TO 1.2X Thrd/100
*201-229 p/r 100: .3X TO .8X Thrd/50
*201-229 p/r 50: .75X TO 2X Thrd/100
*201-229 p/r 50: .5X TO 1.2X Thrd/50
*201-229 p/r 25: .75X TO 2X Thrd/50
*201-229 p/r 25: .5X TO 1.2X Thrd/25
OVERALL AU-GU ODDS ONE PER PACK
PRINT RUNS B/WN 5-100 COPIES PER
NO PRICING ON QTY OF 10 OR LESS
3 Albert Pujols H Bat-Jsy/100 12.50 30.00
102 Mark Teixeira Bat-Jsy/25 10.00 25.00
109 Mike Lowell Bat-Jsy/25 6.00 15.00

2004 Leaf Limited Cuts

OVERALL AU-GU ODDS ONE PER PACK
PRINT RUNS B/WN 50-100 COPIES PER
CUTS FABRIC IS NOT GAME-USED
1 Nolan Ryan/100 50.00 120.00
2 Bob Gibson/50 20.00 50.00
3 Harmon Killebrew/100 12.00 30.00
4 Duke Snider/100 10.00 25.00
5 George Brett/100 40.00 80.00
6 Stan Musial/100 50.00 100.00
7 Alan Trammell/100 10.00 25.00
8 Cal Ripken/100 30.00 80.00
9 Steve Carlton/50 12.00 30.00
10 Phil Rizzuto/100 15.00 40.00
11 Mark Prior/50 20.00 50.00
12 Will Clark/100 10.00 25.00
13 Lou Brock/100 15.00 40.00
14 Ozzie Smith/100 30.00 60.00
15 Bob Feller/100 15.00 40.00
16 Gary Carter/50 15.00 40.00
17 Al Kaline/100 25.00 50.00
18 Brooks Robinson/100 15.00 40.00
19 Tony Gwynn/100 15.00 40.00
20 Mike Schmidt/100 15.00 40.00
21 Ralph Kiner/50 12.00 30.00
22 Jim Palmer/50 12.00 30.00
23 Don Mattingly/100 30.00 80.00
24 Paul Molitor/50 12.00 30.00
25 Dale Murphy/100 15.00 40.00

2004 Leaf Limited Cuts Gold

*GOLD p/r 45: .4X TO 1X BASIC p/r 50
*GOLD p/r 20-35: .6X TO 1.5X BASIC p/r 100
*GOLD p/r 20-35: .5X TO 1.2X BASIC p/r 50
*GOLD p/r 19: .75X TO 2X BASIC p/r 100
OVERALL AU-GU ODDS ONE PER PACK
PRINT RUNS B/WN 1-45 COPIES PER
NO PRICING ON QTY OF 10 OR LESS
CUTS FABRIC IS NOT GAME-USED

2004 Leaf Limited Legends Material Number

PRINT RUNS B/WN 5-100 COPIES PER
*POSITION: .4X TO 1X NUMBER
POSITION PRINT RUNS B/WN 5-100 PER
OVERALL AU-GU ODDS ONE PER PACK
NO PRICING ON QTY OF 5 OR LESS
1 Al Kaline Pants/50 8.00 20.00
2 Babe Ruth Pants/50 125.00 200.00
3 Bob Feller Jsy/50 6.00 15.00
4 Bob Gibson Jsy/50 6.00 15.00
6 Burleigh Grimes Pants/100 20.00 50.00
7 Carl Yastrzemski Jsy/100 8.00 20.00
8 Harmon Killebrew Jsy/25 12.50 30.00
9 Hoyt Wilhelm Jsy/100 3.00 8.00
10 Johnny Mize Pants/100 5.00 12.00
11 Ernie Banks Pants/50 8.00 20.00
12 Lou Brock Jsy/50 6.00 15.00
13 Luis Aparicio Pants/100 3.00 8.00
14 Pee Wee Reese Jsy/50 6.00 15.00
15 Reggie Jackson Jsy/100 5.00 12.00
16 Red Schoendienst Jsy/50 4.00 10.00
17 Roberto Clemente Jsy/25 50.00 100.00
18 Roger Maris Pants/100 12.50 30.00
19 Stan Musial Jsy/100 10.00 25.00
20 Ted Williams Jsy/50 30.00 80.00
21 Ty Cobb Pants/50 50.00 100.00
22 Warren Spahn Jsy/100 6.00 15.00
23 Whitey Ford Pants/100 5.00 12.00
24 Yogi Berra Jsy/50 8.00 20.00
25 Satchel Paige CO Jsy/100 30.00 60.00

2004 Leaf Limited Legends Material Autographs Number

PRINT RUNS B/WN 5-50 COPIES PER
*POSITION: .4X TO 1X NUMBER
POSITION PRINT RUNS B/WN 5-100 PER
OVERALL AU-GU ODDS ONE PER PACK
NO PRICING ON QTY OF 10 OR LESS
1 Al Kaline Pants/50 20.00 50.00
3 Bob Feller Jsy/50 15.00 40.00
4 Bob Gibson Jsy/50 15.00 40.00
7 Carl Yastrzemski Jsy/25 50.00 100.00
8 Harmon Killebrew Jsy/50 50.00 100.00
9 Hoyt Wilhelm Jsy/25 20.00 50.00
12 Lou Brock Jsy/50 15.00 40.00
13 Luis Aparicio Pants/50 10.00 25.00
15 Reggie Jackson Jsy/50 30.00 60.00
16 Red Schoendienst Jsy/50 15.00 40.00
19 Stan Musial Jsy/50 50.00 100.00
23 Whitey Ford Pants/25 20.00 50.00
24 Yogi Berra Jsy/25 40.00 100.00

2004 Leaf Limited Lumberjacks

1-40 PRINT RUNS B/WN 16-714 PER
41-50 PRINT RUN 500 #'d SETS
RANDOM INSERTS IN PACKS
1 Al Kaline/399 1.50 4.00
2 Albert Pujols/114 3.00 8.00
3 Andre Dawson/438 1.00 2.50
4 Babe Ruth/714 4.00 10.00
5 Bo Jackson/141 2.00 5.00
6 Bobby Doerr/223 1.25 3.00
7 Brooks Robinson/268 1.00 2.50
8 Cal Ripken/431 5.00 12.00
9 Carlton Fisk/376 1.00 2.50
10 Dale Murphy/398 1.50 4.00
11 Darryl Strawberry/335 .60 1.50
12 Don Mattingly/222 4.00 10.00
13 Duke Snider/407 1.00 2.50
14 Eddie Mathews/512 1.50 4.00
15 Eddie Murray/504 1.00 2.50
16 Frank Robinson/586 1.00 2.50
17 Frank Thomas/418 1.50 4.00
18 Gary Carter/324 1.00 2.50
19 George Brett/317 3.00 8.00
20 Harmon Killebrew/573 1.50 4.00
21 Hideki Matsui/16 12.00 30.00
22 Lou Gehrig/493 3.00 8.00
23 Mark Grace/173 1.25 3.00
24 Mike Piazza/358 1.50 4.00
25 Mike Schmidt/548 2.50 6.00
26 Orlando Cepeda/379 1.00 2.50
27 Rafael Palmeiro/528 1.00 2.50
28 Ralph Kiner/369 1.00 2.50
29 Reggie Jackson/563 1.00 2.50
30 Rickey Henderson/297 1.50 4.00
31 Roger Maris/275 1.50 4.00
32 Ryne Sandberg/282 3.00 8.00
33 Sammy Sosa/539 1.50 4.00
34 Scott Rolen/192 1.25 3.00
35 Stan Musial/475 2.50 6.00
36 Ted Williams/521 3.00 8.00
37 Thurman Munson/113 2.50 6.00
38 Vladimir Guerrero/234 1.25 3.00
39 Willie McCovey/521 1.00 2.50
40 Willie Stargell/475 1.00 2.50
41 R.Clemente 4.00 10.00
S.Musial
42 C.Ripken 5.00 12.00
E.Banks
43 B.Ruth 4.00 10.00
L.Gehrig
44 G.Brett 3.00 8.00
M.Schmidt
45 F.Robinson 1.50 4.00
J.Robinson
46 D.Mattingly 3.00 8.00
R.Maris
47 N.Garciaparra 3.00 8.00
T.Williams
48 J.Bench 1.50 4.00
M.Piazza
49 R.Jackson 1.50 4.00
S.Sosa
50 M.Ott 1.50 4.00
W.McCovey

2004 Leaf Limited Lumberjacks Black

*1-40 p/r 66: 1.5X TO 4X LJ p/r 251+
*1-40 p/r 37-61: 1.5X TO 4X LJ p/r 251+
*1-40 p/r 37-61: .75X TO 2X LJ p/r 126-250
*1-40 p/r 37-61: .6X TO 1.5X LJ p/r 66-125
*1-40 p/r 20-35: 2X TO 5X LJ p/r 251+
*1-40 p/r 20-35: 1.5X TO 4X LJ p/r 126-250
*1-40 p/r 20-35: 1.25X TO 3X LJ p/r 66-125
*1-40 p/r 16-17: 2X TO 5X LJ p/r 126-250
*1-40 p/r 16-17: .4X TO 1X LJ p/r 16
1-40 PRINT RUNS B/WN 16-66 COPIES PER
*BLACK 41-50: 1X TO 2.5X LJ 41-50
41-50 PRINT RUN 100 SERIAL #'d SETS

2004 Leaf Limited Lumberjacks Autographs

OVERALL AU-GU ODDS ONE PER PACK
PRINT RUNS B/WN 1-100 COPIES PER
NO PRICING ON QTY OF 10 OR LESS
1 Al Kaline/100 20.00 50.00
3 Andre Dawson/100 6.00 15.00
5 Bo Jackson/25 30.00 60.00
6 Bobby Doerr/100 6.00 15.00
7 Brooks Robinson/100 10.00 25.00
8 Cal Ripken/25 60.00 120.00
9 Carlton Fisk/25 15.00 40.00
10 Dale Murphy/100 10.00 25.00
11 Darryl Strawberry/100 6.00 15.00
12 Don Mattingly/25 40.00 80.00
13 Duke Snider/100 10.00 25.00
16 Frank Robinson/100 10.00 25.00
17 Frank Thomas/50 20.00 50.00
18 Gary Carter/100 12.50 30.00
19 George Brett/25 40.00 80.00
20 Harmon Killebrew/100 10.00 25.00
23 Mark Grace/25 15.00 40.00
25 Mike Schmidt/50 30.00 60.00
28 Ralph Kiner/100 10.00 25.00
29 Reggie Jackson/25 20.00 50.00
30 Rickey Henderson/25 30.00 60.00
32 Ryne Sandberg/25 40.00 80.00
34 Scott Rolen/25 6.00 15.00
35 Stan Musial/50 30.00 60.00
39 Willie McCovey/25 15.00 40.00

2004 Leaf Limited Lumberjacks Autographs Bat

*BAT p/r 100: .5X TO1.2X AU p/r 100
*BAT p/r 50: .6X TO1.5X AU p/r 100
*BAT p/r 50: .5X TO1.2X AU p/r 50
*BAT p/r 25: .75X TO2X AU p/r 100
*BAT p/r 25: .6X TO1.5X AU p/r 50
*BAT p/r 25: .5X TO1.2X AU p/r 25
*BAT p/r 17: .6X TO1.5X AU p/r 25
OVERALL AU-GU ODDS ONE PER PACK
PRINT RUNS B/WN 1-100 COPIES PER
NO PRICING ON QTY OF 10 OR LESS

2004 Leaf Limited Lumberjacks Autographs Jersey

*JSY p/r 100: .5X TO 1.2X AU p/r 100
*JSY p/r 50: .6X TO 1.5X AU p/r 100
*JSY p/r 50: .5X TO 1.2X AU p/r 50
*JSY p/r 50: .4X TO 1X AU p/r 25
*JSY p/r 25: .75X TO 2X AU p/r 100
*JSY p/r 25: .6X TO 1.5X AU p/r 50
*JSY p/r 25: .5X TO 1.2X AU p/r 25
*JSY p/r 17: .6X TO 1.5X AU p/r 25
OVERALL AU-GU ODDS ONE PER PACK
PRINT RUNS B/WN 5-100 COPIES PER
NO PRICING ON QTY OF 10 OR LESS
15 Eddie Murray/25 40.00 80.00
26 Orlando Cepeda Pants/50 10.00 25.00

2004 Leaf Limited Lumberjacks Bat

OVERALL AU-GU ODDS ONE PER PACK
PRINT RUNS B/WN 25-100 COPIES PER
1 Al Kaline/100 6.00 15.00
2 Albert Pujols/100 6.00 15.00
3 Andre Dawson/25 6.00 15.00
4 Babe Ruth/100 60.00 120.00
5 Bo Jackson/50 8.00 20.00
6 Bobby Doerr/25 6.00 15.00
7 Brooks Robinson/100 5.00 12.00
8 Cal Ripken/100 12.50 30.00
9 Carlton Fisk/100 5.00 12.00
10 Dale Murphy/50 6.00 15.00
11 Darryl Strawberry/25 6.00 15.00
12 Don Mattingly/100 8.00 20.00
14 Eddie Mathews/100 6.00 15.00
15 Eddie Murray/100 6.00 15.00
16 Frank Robinson/100 3.00 8.00
17 Frank Thomas/25 10.00 25.00
18 Gary Carter/50 4.00 10.00
19 George Brett/100 8.00 20.00
20 Harmon Killebrew/100 6.00 15.00
21 Hideki Matsui/100 12.50 30.00
22 Lou Gehrig/100 40.00 100.00
23 Mark Grace/25 10.00 25.00
24 Mike Piazza/50 8.00 20.00
25 Mike Schmidt/100 8.00 20.00
26 Orlando Cepeda/50 4.00 10.00
27 Rafael Palmeiro/50 5.00 12.00
28 Ralph Kiner/100 3.00 8.00
29 Reggie Jackson/100 5.00 12.00
30 Rickey Henderson/100 6.00 15.00
31 Roger Maris/100 12.50 30.00
32 Ryne Sandberg/100 8.00 20.00
33 Sammy Sosa/100 4.00 10.00
34 Scott Rolen/25 8.00 20.00
35 Stan Musial/100 10.00 25.00
36 Ted Williams/100 25.00 60.00
37 Thurman Munson/100 10.00 25.00
38 Vladimir Guerrero/25 10.00 25.00
39 Willie McCovey/100 5.00 12.00
40 Willie Stargell/50 6.00 15.00
41 R.Clemente/S.Musial/100 20.00 50.00
42 C.Ripken/E.Banks/50 20.00 50.00
43 B.Ruth/L.Gehrig/25 175.00 300.00
44 G.Brett/M.Schmidt/50 20.00 50.00
46 D.Mattingly/R.Maris/50 20.00 50.00
47 Nomar/T.Williams/100 30.00 80.00
48 J.Bench/M.Piazza/25 15.00 40.00
49 R.Jackson/S.Sosa/50 10.00 25.00
50 M.Ott/W.McCovey/100 10.00 25.00

2004 Leaf Limited Lumberjacks Jersey

*1-40 p/r 100: .4X TO 1X BAT p/r 100
*1-40 p/r 100: .25X TO .6X BAT p/r 50
*1-40 p/r 100: .15X TO .4X BAT p/r 25
*1-40 p/r 50: .6X TO 1.5X BAT p/r 100
*1-40 p/r 50: .4X TO 1X BAT p/r 50
*1-40 p/r 50: .25X TO .6X BAT p/r 25
*1-40 p/r 25: 1X TO 2.5X BAT p/r 100
*1-40 p/r 25: .4X TO 1X BAT p/r 25
*41-50 p/r 100: .25X TO .6X BAT p/r 50
*41-50 p/r 100: .15X TO .4X BAT p/r 25
*41-50 p/r 50: .6X TO 1.5X BAT p/r 100
*41-50 p/r 50: .25X TO .6X BAT p/r 25
*41-50 p/r 25: 1X TO 2.5X BAT p/r 100
*41-50 p/r 25: .4X TO 1X BAT p/r 25
OVERALL AU-GU ODDS ONE PER PACK
PRINT RUNS B/WN 4-100 COPIES PER
NO PRICING ON QTY OF 4 OR LESS

2004 Leaf Limited Lumberjacks Combos

*COMBO p/r 100: .5X TO 1.2X BAT p/r 100
*COMBO p/r 100: .3X TO .8X BAT p/r 50
*COMBO p/r 50: .75X TO 2X BAT p/r 100
*COMBO p/r 50: .5X TO 1.2X BAT p/r 50
*COMBO p/r 50: .3X TO .8X BAT p/r 25
*COMBO p/r 25: 1.25X TO 3X BAT p/r 100
*COMBO p/r 25: .5X TO 1.2X BAT p/r 25
*COMBO p/r 17: .6X TO 1.5X BAT p/r 25
OVERALL AU-GU ODDS ONE PER PACK
PRINT RUNS B/WN 17-100 COPIES PER

2004 Leaf Limited Matching Numbers

PRINT RUNS B/WN 25-100 COPIES PER
PRIME PRINT RUN 1 SERIAL #'d SET
NO PRIME PRICING DUE TO SCARCITY
OVERALL AU-GU ODDS ONE PER PACK
1 Doerr Jsy/Reese Jsy/100 6.00 15.00
2 Gehrig Pants/Ott Jsy/50 60.00 120.00
3 Pujols Jsy/Brett Jsy/100 15.00 40.00
4 Ripken Jsy/Yaz Jsy/100 30.00 60.00
5 Gooden Jsy/Ford Pants/50 8.00 20.00
6 Grace Jsy/Helton Jsy/25 10.00 25.00
7 Yount Jsy/Gwynn Jsy/50 10.00 25.00
8 F.Rob Jsy/Schmidt Jsy/100 6.00 15.00
9 Clemente Jsy/Sosa Jsy/100 30.00 80.00
10 ClemensJsy/SpahnPant/100 12.50 30.00
11 Prior Jsy/Clemens Jsy/50 12.50 30.00
12 Mattingly Jkt/Ryno Jsy/100 10.00 25.00
13 B.Will Jsy/Boggs Jsy/100 6.00 15.00
14 Hunter Jsy/Marichal Jsy/50 6.00 15.00
15 Ferg Pants/Maddux Jsy/50 10.00 25.00
16 Wood Pants/Ryan Jsy/100 15.00 40.00
17 Rickey Jsy/Maris Pants/100 8.00 20.00
18 Willis Jsy/Mussina Jsy/50 8.00 20.00
19 Reggie Jsy/McCov Jsy/100 6.00 15.00
20 Gibson Jsy/Pedro Jsy/50 8.00 20.00
21 Snider Jsy/Molitor Jsy/100 6.00 15.00
22 Bench Jsy/Boudr Jsy/100 8.00 20.00
23 Daws Jsy/Chipper Jsy/100 8.00 20.00
24 Banks Jsy/Boyer Jsy/100 8.00 20.00
25 Manny Jsy/Rickey Jsy/100 8.00 20.00
26 Fisk Jsy/Rolen Jsy/100 6.00 15.00
27 Ryan Jsy/Cepeda Pnt/100 12.50 30.00
28 Hallad Jsy/Carlton Jsy/100 4.00 10.00
29 Mathews Jsy/Seav Jsy/100 8.00 20.00
30 Webb Jsy/Hersh Jsy/100 6.00 15.00

2004 Leaf Limited Player Threads Jersey Number

PRINT RUNS B/WN 10-100 COPIES PER
NO PRICING ON QTY OF 10 OR LESS
PRIME PRINT RUN 1 SERIAL #'d SET
NO PRIME PRICING DUE TO SCARCITY
OVERALL AU-GU ODDS ONE PER PACK
1 Mike Piazza/100 5.00 12.00
3 Nolan Ryan Jkt/100 10.00 25.00
4 Reggie Jackson/100 5.00 12.00
5 Wade Boggs/50 6.00 15.00
6 Steve Carlton Pants/100 3.00 8.00
7 Ivan Rodriguez/25 8.00 20.00
8 Pedro Martinez/50 5.00 12.00
10 R.Hend Mets Pants/100 6.00 15.00
11 Randy Johnson/50 6.00 15.00
12 Curt Schilling/25 8.00 20.00
13 Roger Maris/50 10.00 25.00
14 Sammy Sosa/100 4.00 10.00
15 Gary Carter Pants/50 4.00 10.00
16 Gary Sheffield/25 5.00 12.00
17 Eddie Murray/50 8.00 20.00
18 Hideo Nomo/50 6.00 15.00
19 Rafael Palmeiro/50 5.00 12.00
20 Andre Dawson/50 4.00 10.00

2004 Leaf Limited Player Threads Double

*DBL p/r 100: .6X TO 1.5X PT p/r 100
*DBL p/r 100: .4X TO 1X PT p/r 50
*DBL p/r 100: .25X TO .6X PT p/r 25
*DBL p/r 50: .75X TO 2X PT p/r 100
*DBL p/r 50: .6X TO 1.5X PT p/r 50
*DBL p/r 50: .4X TO 1X PT p/r 25
OVERALL AU-GU ODDS ONE PER PACK
PRINT RUNS B/WN 10-100 COPIES PER
NO PRICING ON QTY OF 10 OR LESS
2 R.Clemens Sox-Yanks/100 10.00 25.00
9 R.Henderson A's-Jays/50 12.50 30.00

2004 Leaf Limited Player Threads Triple

*TRIPLE p/r 50: 1.25X TO 3X PT p/r 100
*TRIPLE p/r 50: .75X TO 2X PT p/r 50
*TRIPLE p/r 25: 1.5X TO 4X PT p/r 100
*TRIPLE p/r 25: 1X TO 2.5X PT p/r 50
*TRIPLE p/r 25: .6X TO 1.5X PT p/r 25
OVERALL AU-GU ODDS ONE PER PACK
PRINT RUNS B/WN 10-50 COPIES PER
NO PRICING ON QTY OF 10 OR LESS
2 R.Clem Astro-Sox-Yank/25 25.00 60.00
13 Maris A's-Cards Bat-Ynk/25 20.00 50.00

2004 Leaf Limited Team Threads Jersey Number

STATED PRINT RUN 100 SERIAL #'d SETS
PRIME PRINT RUN 1 SERIAL #'d SET
NO PRIME PRICING DUE TO SCARCITY
OVERALL AU-GU ODDS ONE PER PACK
ALL ARE DUAL JSY CARDS UNLESS NOTED
1 S.Musial/A.Pujols 12.00 30.00
2 C.Ripken Jkt/M.Mussina 12.00 30.00
3 C.Fisk/R.Clemens 12.00 30.00
4 D.Murphy/C.Jones 8.00 20.00
5 T.Gwynn/D.Winfield 12.00 30.00
6 D.Mattingly/H.Matsui 30.00 60.00
7 L.Boudreau/E.Wynn 8.00 20.00
8 E.Banks/S.Sosa 8.00 20.00
9 N.Ryan Jkt/J.Bagwell 30.00 60.00
10 M.Schmidt/J.Thome 12.00 30.00

2004 Leaf Limited Team Trademarks

STATED PRINT RUN 100 SERIAL #'d SETS
GOLD PRINT RUN 10 SERIAL #'d SETS
NO GOLD PRICING DUE TO SCARCITY
RANDOM INSERTS IN PACKS
1 Bob Gibson 2.50 6.00
2 Cal Ripken 12.00 30.00
3 Carl Yastrzemski 4.00 10.00
4 Dale Murphy 4.00 10.00
5 Gary Carter 2.50 6.00
6 George Brett 8.00 20.00
7 Tom Seaver 2.50 6.00
8 Kerry Wood 1.50 4.00
9 Lou Brock 2.50 6.00
10 Luis Aparicio 2.50 6.00
11 Mike Piazza 4.00 10.00
12 Nolan Ryan Astros 12.00 30.00
13 Nolan Ryan Rgr 12.00 30.00
14 Randy Johnson 4.00 10.00
15 Reggie Jackson 2.50 6.00
16 Rickey Henderson 4.00 10.00
17 Robin Yount 4.00 10.00
18 Rod Carew 2.50 6.00
19 Ryne Sandberg 8.00 20.00
20 Steve Carlton 2.50 6.00
21 Steve Garvey 1.50 4.00
22 Johnny Bench 4.00 10.00
23 Tony Gwynn 4.00 10.00
24 Whitey Ford 2.50 6.00
25 Will Clark 2.50 6.00

2004 Leaf Limited Team Trademarks Autographs

OVERALL AU-GU ODDS ONE PER PACK
PRINT RUNS B/WN 5-100 COPIES PER
NO PRICING ON QTY OF 10 OR LESS
1 Bob Gibson/100 10.00 25.00
2 Cal Ripken/25 125.00 200.00
3 Carl Yastrzemski/25 40.00 80.00
4 Dale Murphy/100 15.00 40.00
5 Gary Carter/100 15.00 40.00
6 George Brett/25 40.00 80.00
7 Tom Seaver/25 30.00 80.00
8 Kerry Wood/25 6.00 15.00
9 Lou Brock/100 10.00 25.00
10 Luis Aparicio/100 8.00 20.00
12 Nolan Ryan Astros/25 60.00 120.00
13 Nolan Ryan Rgr/25 60.00 120.00
15 Reggie Jackson/25 30.00 60.00
17 Robin Yount/50 15.00 40.00
18 Rod Carew/50 12.50 30.00
19 Ryne Sandberg/25 20.00 50.00
20 Steve Carlton/100 6.00 15.00
21 Steve Garvey/50 8.00 20.00
22 Johnny Bench/25 30.00 60.00
23 Tony Gwynn/100 30.00 80.00
24 Whitey Ford/25 15.00 40.00
25 Will Clark/34 20.00 50.00

2004 Leaf Limited Team Trademarks Autographs Jersey Number

*JSY NBR p/r 84-100: .5X TO 1.2X AU p/r 100
*JSY NBR p/r 84-100: .3X TO .8X AU p/r 25-34
*JSY NBR p/r 50: .6X TO 1.5X AU p/r 100
*JSY NBR p/r 50: .5X TO 1.2X AU p/r 50
*JSY NBR p/r 50: .4X TO 1X AU p/r 25-34
*JSY NBR p/r 25: .75X TO 2X AU p/r 100
*JSY NBR p/r 25: .5X TO 1.2X AU p/r 25-34
PRINT RUNS B/WN 5-100 COPIES PER
NO PRICING ON QTY OF 10 OR LESS
PRIME PRINT RUN 1 SERIAL #'d SET
NO PRIME PRICING DUE TO SCARCITY
OVERALL AU-GU ODDS ONE PER PACK

2004 Leaf Limited Team Trademarks Jersey Number

PRINT RUNS B/WN 6-100 COPIES PER
NO PRICING ON QTY OF 6 OR LESS
PRIME PRINT RUN 1 SERIAL #'d SET
NO PRIME PRICING DUE TO SCARCITY
OVERALL AU-GU ODDS ONE PER PACK
1 Bob Gibson/100 5.00 12.00
2 Cal Ripken Pants/100 10.00 25.00
3 Carl Yastrzemski/100 8.00 20.00
4 Dale Murphy/100 5.00 12.00
5 Gary Carter/100 3.00 8.00
6 George Brett/100 8.00 20.00
7 Tom Seaver/100 5.00 12.00
8 Kerry Wood Pants/50 3.00 8.00
9 Lou Brock/100 5.00 12.00
10 Luis Aparicio Pants/100 3.00 8.00
11 Mike Piazza/50 8.00 20.00
12 Nolan Ryan Astros/100 10.00 25.00
13 Nolan Ryan Rgr/100 10.00 25.00
14 Randy Johnson/50 6.00 15.00
15 Reggie Jackson Pants/100 5.00 12.00
16 Rickey Henderson/100 6.00 15.00
17 Robin Yount/100 6.00 15.00
18 Rod Carew Jkt/100 5.00 12.00
19 Ryne Sandberg/100 8.00 20.00
20 Steve Carlton/50 4.00 10.00
22 Johnny Bench/100 6.00 15.00
23 Tony Gwynn/100 6.00 15.00
24 Whitey Ford/100 5.00 12.00
25 Will Clark/50 6.00 15.00

2005 Leaf Limited

COMMON CARD (1-150) 1.00 2.50
1-150 PRINT RUN 699 SERIAL #'d SETS
COMMON CARD (151-168) 1.25 3.00
COMMON CARD (169-175) 1.25 3.00
COMMON CARD (197) 2.00 5.00
151-175/197 PRINT RUN 99 #'d SETS
COM.AU (176-196/198-200) 6.00 15.00
176-196/198-200 PRINT RUN 99 #'d SETS
COM.AU CUT (201-205) 10.00 25.00
201-205 PRINTS B/WN 70-99 COPIES PER
201-205: OVERALL AU ODDS 1:2
201-205 CUTS FABRIC IS NOT GAME-USED
CARD 204 DOES NOT EXIST
1 Roger Clemens H 3.00 8.00
2 Roger Clemens A 3.00 8.00
3 Ichiro Suzuki H 3.00 8.00
4 Ichiro Suzuki A 3.00 8.00
5 Todd Helton H 1.50 4.00
6 Todd Helton A 1.50 4.00
7 Vladimir Guerrero H 1.50 4.00
8 Vladimir Guerrero A 1.50 4.00
9 Miguel Cabrera H 2.50 6.00
10 Miguel Cabrera A 2.50 6.00
11 Albert Pujols H 3.00 8.00
12 Albert Pujols A 3.00 8.00
13 Mark Prior H 1.50 4.00
14 Mark Prior A 1.50 4.00
15 Chipper Jones H 2.50 6.00
16 Chipper Jones A 2.50 6.00
17 Jeff Bagwell H 1.50 4.00
18 Jeff Bagwell A 1.50 4.00
19 Kerry Wood H 1.00 2.50
20 Kerry Wood A 1.00 2.50
21 Gary Sheffield 1.00 2.50
22 Carl Crawford 1.50 4.00
23 Mariano Rivera 3.00 8.00
24 Curt Schilling 1.50 4.00
25 Ben Sheets 1.00 2.50
26 Jimmy Rollins 1.50 4.00
27 Melvin Mora 1.00 2.50
28 Corey Patterson 1.00 2.50
29 Rafael Furcal 1.00 2.50
30 Jim Thome 1.50 4.00
31 Derek Jeter 6.00 15.00
32 Jake Peavy 1.00 2.50
33 Francisco Cordero 1.00 2.50
34 Aramis Ramirez 1.00 2.50
35 Javy Lopez 1.00 2.50
36 Aaron Rowand 1.00 2.50
37 Jason Bay 1.00 2.50
38 Michael Young 1.00 2.50
39 Ivan Rodriguez 1.50 4.00
40 Joe Nathan 1.00 2.50
41 Oliver Perez 1.00 2.50
42 Adam Dunn 1.50 4.00
43 Eric Chavez 1.00 2.50
44 Pedro Martinez 1.50 4.00
45 Roy Oswalt 1.50 4.00
46 Carlos Delgado 1.00 2.50
47 Jeff Kent 1.00 2.50
48 Johnny Damon 1.50 4.00
49 Edgar Renteria 1.00 2.50
50 Mark Buehrle 1.50 4.00
51 Carl Pavano 1.00 2.50
52 J.D. Drew 1.00 2.50
53 Hank Blalock 1.00 2.50
54 Moises Alou 1.00 2.50
55 Brad Radke 1.00 2.50
56 Brad Wilkerson 1.00 2.50
57 Sean Casey 1.00 2.50
58 Mike Lowell 1.00 2.50
59 Octavio Dotel 1.00 2.50
60 Francisco Rodriguez 1.50 4.00
61 Jose Guillen 1.00 2.50
62 Greg Maddux 3.00 8.00
63 A.J. Burnett 1.00 2.50
64 Chris Carpenter 1.50 4.00
65 Jose Reyes 1.50 4.00
66 Travis Hafner 1.00 2.50
67 Rich Harden 1.00 2.50
68 Bret Boone 1.00 2.50
69 Scott Podsednik 1.00 2.50
70 Andruw Jones 1.00 2.50
71 Milton Bradley 1.00 2.50
72 Zack Greinke 3.00 8.00
73 Torii Hunter 1.00 2.50
74 Paul Konerko 1.50 4.00
75 David Wells 1.00 2.50
76 Tim Hudson 1.50 4.00
77 Sammy Sosa 2.50 6.00
78 Jason Varitek 2.50 6.00
79 Lance Berkman 1.50 4.00
80 Justin Morneau 1.50 4.00
81 Troy Glaus 1.00 2.50
82 Jose Vidro 1.00 2.50
83 Joe Mauer 2.00 5.00
84 Josh Beckett 1.00 2.50
85 Craig Biggio 1.50 4.00
86 Luis Gonzalez 1.00 2.50
87 Larry Walker 1.50 4.00
88 Barry Zito 1.50 4.00
89 Jacque Jones 1.00 2.50
90 Lyle Overbay 1.00 2.50
91 Roy Halladay 1.50 4.00
92 Orlando Cabrera 1.00 2.50
93 Magglio Ordonez 1.50 4.00
94 Mike Sweeney 1.00 2.50
95 Rafael Palmeiro 1.50 4.00
96 Brandon Webb 1.50 4.00
97 Preston Wilson 1.00 2.50
98 Shannon Stewart 1.00 2.50
99 Trot Nixon 1.00 2.50
100 Mike Piazza 2.50 6.00
101 Dontrelle Willis 1.00 2.50
102 Ken Griffey Jr. 5.00 12.00
103 Andy Pettitte 1.50 4.00
104 Kazuo Matsui 1.00 2.50
105 Bobby Crosby 1.00 2.50
106 Shawn Green 1.00 2.50
107 Alfonso Soriano 1.50 4.00
108 Carlos Zambrano 1.50 4.00
109 Keith Foulke 1.00 2.50
110 Aubrey Huff 1.00 2.50
111 Adrian Beltre 2.50 6.00
112 Mark Teixeira 1.50 4.00
113 Randy Johnson 2.50 6.00
114 Miguel Tejada 1.50 4.00
115 Alex Rodriguez 3.00 8.00
116 Carlos Beltran 1.50 4.00
117 Bobby Abreu 1.00 2.50
118 Johan Santana 1.50 4.00
119 Manny Ramirez 2.50 6.00
120 Juan Pierre 1.00 2.50
121 Scott Rolen 1.50 4.00
122 Livan Hernandez 1.00 2.50
123 Carlos Lee 1.00 2.50
124 Derrek Lee 1.00 2.50
125 Brian Giles 1.00 2.50
126 Nomar Garciaparra 1.50 4.00
127 John Smoltz 2.50 6.00
128 Jim Edmonds 1.50 4.00
129 Bartolo Colon 1.00 2.50
130 Garret Anderson 1.00 2.50
131 Austin Kearns 1.00 2.50
132 Shingo Takatsu 1.00 2.50
133 Omar Vizquel 1.50 4.00
134 Tom Glavine 1.50 4.00
135 Mark Mulder 1.00 2.50
136 Bernie Williams 1.50 4.00
137 Richie Sexson 1.00 2.50
138 Mike Mussina 1.50 4.00
139 Mark Loretta 1.00 2.50
140 Vernon Wells 1.00 2.50
141 David Wright 2.00 5.00
142 Marcus Giles 1.00 2.50
143 David Ortiz 2.50 6.00
144 Victor Martinez 1.50 4.00
145 Hideki Matsui 4.00 10.00
146 C.C. Sabathia 1.50 4.00
147 Angel Berroa 1.00 2.50
148 Troy Percival 1.00 2.50
149 Paul Lo Duca 1.00 2.50
150 Jorge Posada 1.50 4.00
151 Willie Mays LGD 6.00 15.00
152 Ryne Sandberg LGD 6.00 15.00
153 Rickey Henderson LGD 3.00 8.00
154 Ted Williams LGD 6.00 15.00
155 Roberto Clemente LGD 8.00 20.00
156 George Brett LGD 6.00 15.00
157 Whitey Ford LGD 2.00 5.00
158 Duke Snider LGD 2.00 5.00
159 Don Mattingly LGD 6.00 15.00
160 Bob Gibson LGD 2.00 5.00
161 Hank Aaron LGD 6.00 15.00
162 Al Kaline LGD 3.00 8.00
163 Nolan Ryan LGD 10.00 25.00
164 Stan Musial LGD 5.00 12.00
165 George Kell LGD 2.00 5.00
166 Harmon Killebrew LGD 3.00 8.00
167 Cal Ripken LGD 10.00 25.00
168 Babe Ruth LGD 8.00 20.00
169 Roger Clemens Sox SP 4.00 10.00
170 Curt Schilling D'backs SP 2.00 5.00
171 Rafael Palmeiro Rgr SP 2.00 5.00
172 Randy Johnson M's SP 3.00 8.00
173 Mike Piazza Dgr SP 3.00 8.00
174 Greg Maddux Braves SP 4.00 10.00
175 Sammy Sosa Cubs SP 3.00 8.00
176 Hayden Penn PH AU RC 10.00 25.00
177 A.Concepcion PH AU RC 6.00 15.00
178 Casey Rogowski PH AU RC 8.00 20.00
179 Prince Fielder PH AU RC 20.00 50.00
180 Geovany Soto PH AU RC 12.50 30.00
181 W.Balentien PH AU RC 10.00 25.00
182 Jason Hammel PH AU RC 6.00 15.00
183 Keiichi Yabu PH AU RC 10.00 25.00
184 B.McCarthy PH AU RC 20.00 50.00
185 Ubaldo Jimenez PH AU RC 12.50 30.00
186 Keiichi Yabu PH AU RC 10.00 25.00
187 Miguel Negron PH AU RC 8.00 20.00
188 Mike Morse PH AU RC 6.00 15.00
189 Nate McLouth PH AU RC 10.00 25.00
190 N.Nakamura PH AU RC 15.00 40.00
191 B.McCarthy PH AU RC 20.00 50.00
192 Tony Pena PH AU RC 6.00 15.00
193 A.Concepcion PH AU RC 6.00 15.00
194 Raul Tablado PH AU RC 6.00 15.00
195 Hayden Penn PH AU RC 10.00 25.00
196 Sean Thompson PH AU RC 6.00 15.00
197 Tadahito Iguchi PH RC 3.00 8.00
198 Ubaldo Jimenez PH AU RC 6.00 15.00
199 W.Balentien PH AU RC 6.00 15.00
200 Prince Fielder PH AU RC 6.00 15.00
201 P.Humber PHC AU/99 RC 20.00 50.00
202 J.Niemann PHC AU/95 RC 6.00 15.00
203 J.Verlander PHC AU/70 RC 40.00 80.00
205 Y.Betan PHC AU/99 RC 50.00 80.00

2005 Leaf Limited Bronze Spotlight

*BRZ 1-150: .6X TO 1.5X BASIC
*BRZ 151-168: .4X TO 1X BASIC
*BRZ 169-175: .4X TO 1X BASIC
*BRZ 176-196/298-200: .12X TO .3X BASIC AU
*BRZ 197: .3X TO .8X BASIC
OVERALL INSERT ODDS ONE PER PACK
STATED PRINT RUN 99 SERIAL #'d SETS
179 Prince Fielder PH 6.00 15.00
180 Geovany Soto PH 6.00 15.00
185 Ubaldo Jimenez PH 3.00 8.00
198 Ubaldo Jimenez PH 3.00 8.00
200 Prince Fielder PH 6.00 15.00

2005 Leaf Limited Gold Spotlight

*GOLD 1-150: 1.5X TO 4X BASIC
*GOLD 151-168: 1X TO 2.5X BASIC
*GOLD 169-175: 1X TO 2.5X BASIC
OVERALL INSERT ODDS ONE PER PACK
1-200 PRINT RUN 25 SERIAL #'d SETS
201-205 AU PRINTS B/WN 5-25 COPIES PER
176-205 NO PRICING DUE TO SCARCITY
201-205 CUTS FABRIC IS NOT GAME-USED
CARD 204 DOES NOT EXIST

2005 Leaf Limited Platinum Spotlight

OVERALL INSERT ODDS ONE PER PACK
STATED PRINT RUN 1 SERIAL #'d SET
NO PRICING DUE TO SCARCITY
201-205 CUTS FABRIC IS NOT GAME-USED
CARD 204 DOES NOT EXIST

2005 Leaf Limited Silver Spotlight

*SILV 1-150: .75X TO 2X BASIC
*SILV 151-168: .5X TO 1.2X BASIC
*SILV 169-175: .5X TO 1.2X BASIC
COMMON CARD (176-200) 1.50 4.00
SEMISTARS 176-200 2.50 6.00
UNLISTED STARS 176-200 4.00 10.00
*SILV 176-196/298-200: .15X TO .4X BASE AU
*SILV 197: .4X TO 1X BASIC
OVERALL INSERT ODDS ONE PER PACK
STATED PRINT RUN 50 SERIAL #'d SETS
179 Prince Fielder PH 8.00 20.00
180 Geovany Soto PH 8.00 20.00
186 Keiichi Yabu PH 1.50 4.00
198 Ubaldo Jimenez PH 4.00 10.00
200 Prince Fielder PH 8.00 20.00

2005 Leaf Limited Monikers Bronze

OVERALL AU-GU ODDS ONE PER PACK
PRINT RUNS B/WN 1-100 COPIES PER
1-175 NO PRICING ON QTY OF 12 OR LESS
176-200 NO PRICING ON QTY 20 OR LESS
9 Miguel Cabrera H/100 25.00 60.00
10 Miguel Cabrera A/100 25.00 60.00
13 Mark Prior H/50 10.00 25.00
14 Mark Prior A/50 10.00 25.00
25 Ben Sheets/100 6.00 15.00
27 Melvin Mora/50 8.00 20.00
29 Rafael Furcal/25 10.00 25.00
32 Jake Peavy/50 12.00 30.00
33 Francisco Cordero/25 10.00 25.00
38 Michael Young/25 10.00 25.00
40 Joe Nathan/25 10.00 25.00
43 Eric Chavez/25 10.00 25.00
45 Roy Oswalt/50 8.00 20.00
49 Edgar Renteria/25 10.00 25.00
50 Mark Buehrle/25 20.00 50.00
57 Sean Casey/50 8.00 20.00
59 Octavio Dotel/25 6.00 15.00
60 Francisco Rodriguez/25 15.00 40.00
61 Jose Guillen/25 10.00 25.00
66 Travis Hafner/50 8.00 20.00
67 Rich Harden/50 8.00 20.00
71 Milton Bradley/25 10.00 25.00
73 Torii Hunter/25 10.00 25.00
74 Paul Konerko/50 12.00 30.00
76 Tim Hudson/25 15.00 40.00
80 Justin Morneau/100 6.00 15.00
82 Jose Vidro/25 10.00 25.00
84 Josh Beckett/25 15.00 40.00
85 Craig Biggio/25 15.00 40.00
89 Jacque Jones/50 8.00 20.00
91 Roy Halladay/25 15.00 40.00
93 Magglio Ordonez/100 6.00 15.00
96 Brandon Webb/50 5.00 12.00
97 Preston Wilson/50 8.00 20.00
98 Shannon Stewart/50 8.00 20.00
99 Trot Nixon/50 12.00 30.00
105 Bobby Crosby/40 8.00 20.00
107 Alfonso Soriano/25 10.00 25.00
108 Carlos Zambrano/50 8.00 20.00
109 Keith Foulke/25 15.00 40.00
110 Aubrey Huff/50 8.00 20.00
112 Mark Teixeira/100 6.00 15.00
116 Carlos Beltran/25 10.00 25.00
118 Johan Santana/100 8.00 20.00
121 Scott Rolen/25 15.00 40.00
123 Carlos Lee/50 8.00 20.00
124 Derrek Lee/50 12.00 30.00
130 Garret Anderson/100 6.00 15.00
131 Austin Kearns/100 4.00 10.00
133 Omar Vizquel/50 12.00 30.00
135 Mark Mulder/50 8.00 20.00
139 Mark Loretta/25 6.00 15.00
141 David Wright/50 20.00 50.00
144 Victor Martinez/25 10.00 25.00
151 Willie Mays LGD/25 100.00 175.00
152 Ryne Sandberg LGD/25 30.00 60.00
158 Duke Snider LGD/50 12.00 30.00
159 Don Mattingly LGD/25 30.00 60.00
160 Bob Gibson LGD/50 12.00 30.00
162 Al Kaline LGD/50 12.00 30.00
163 Nolan Ryan LGD/25 50.00 100.00
164 Stan Musial LGD/25 60.00 120.00
165 George Kell LGD/50 12.00 30.00
166 Harmon Killebrew LGD/50 20.00 50.00
167 Cal Ripken LGD/25 50.00 100.00
176 Hayden Penn PH/50 10.00 25.00
177 Ambiorix Concepcion PH/50 6.00 15.00
179 Prince Fielder PH/50 50.00 100.00
181 Wladimir Balentien PH/50 12.00 30.00
182 Jason Hammel PH/50 6.00 15.00
183 Keiichi Yabu PH/50 15.00 40.00

184 Brandon McCarthy PH/50 30.00 60.00
185 Ubaldo Jimenez PH/50 15.00 40.00
186 Keiichi Yabu PH/50 8.00 20.00
187 Miguel Negron PH/50 10.00 25.00
188 Mike Morse PH/50 8.00 20.00
189 Nate McLouth PH/50 15.00 40.00
190 Norihiro Nakamura PH/50 20.00 50.00
191 Brandon McCarthy PH/50 30.00 60.00
192 Tony Pena PH/50 6.00 15.00
193 Ambiorix Concepcion PH/50 6.00 15.00
194 Raul Tablado PH/50 6.00 15.00
195 Hayden Penn PH/50 12.00 30.00
196 Sean Thompson PH/50 6.00 15.00
198 Ubaldo Jimenez PH/50 6.00 15.00
199 Wladimir Balentien PH/50 12.00 30.00
200 Prince Fielder PH/50 50.00 100.00

2005 Leaf Limited Monikers Gold

*1-175 p/r 25: .6X TO 1.5X BRZ p/r 100
*1-175 p/r 25: .5X TO 1.2X BRZ p/r 40-50
*1-175 p/r 25: .4X TO 1X BRZ p/r 25
OVERALL AU-GU ODDS ONE PER PACK
PRINT RUNS B/WN 1-25 COPIES PER
1-175 NO PRICING ON QTY OF 10 OR LESS
176-200 NO PRICING DUE TO SCARCITY
21 Gary Sheffield/25 15.00 40.00
37 Jason Bay/25 10.00 25.00
88 Barry Zito/25 10.00 25.00
90 Lyle Overbay/25 6.00 15.00
151 Willie Mays LGD/25 100.00 175.00
163 Nolan Ryan LGD/25 50.00 100.00
167 Cal Ripken LGD/25 50.00 100.00

2005 Leaf Limited Monikers Silver

*1-175 p/r 50: .5X TO 1.2X BRZ p/r 100
*1-175 p/r 50: .4X TO 1X BRZ p/r 40-50
*1-175 p/r 25: .5X TO 1.2X BRZ p/r 40-50
*1-175 p/r 25: .4X TO 1X BRZ p/r 25
OVERALL AU-GU ODDS ONE PER PACK
PRINT RUNS B/WN 1-50 COPIES PER
1-175 NO PRICING ON QTY OF 10 OR LESS
176-200 NO PRICING DUE TO SCARCITY
151 Willie Mays LGD/25 100.00 175.00
163 Nolan Ryan LGD/25 50.00 100.00
167 Cal Ripken LGD/25 60.00 120.00

2005 Leaf Limited Monikers Material Bat Bronze

*1-175 p/r 100: .5X TO 1.2X BRZ p/r 100
*1-175 p/r 100: .4X TO 1X BRZ p/r 40-50
*1-175 p/r 100: .3X TO .8X BRZ p/r 25
*1-175 p/r 50: .6X TO 1.5X BRZ p/r 100
*1-175 p/r 50: .5X TO 1.2X BRZ p/r 40-50
*1-175 p/r 50: .4X TO 1X BRZ p/r 25
*1-175 p/r 25: .6X TO 1.5X BRZ p/r 40-50
*1-175 p/r 25: .5X TO 1.2X BRZ p/r 25
OVERALL AU-GU ODDS ONE PER PACK
PRINT RUNS B/WN 1-100 COPIES PER
NO PRICING ON QTY OF 10 OR LESS
34 Aramis Ramirez/100 8.00 20.00
37 Jason Bay/100 8.00 20.00
111 Adrian Beltre/25 12.50 30.00
140 Vernon Wells/50 10.00 25.00
143 David Ortiz/50 20.00 50.00
147 Angel Berroa/100 5.00 12.00

2005 Leaf Limited Monikers Material Bat Platinum

OVERALL AU-GU ODDS ONE PER PACK
STATED PRINT RUN 1 SERIAL #'d SET
NO PRICING DUE TO SCARCITY

2005 Leaf Limited Monikers Material Button Gold

PRINT RUNS B/WN 1-5 COPIES PER
PLATINUM PRINT RUN 1 SERIAL #'d SET
OVERALL AU-GU ODDS ONE PER PACK
NO PRICING DUE TO SCARCITY

2005 Leaf Limited Monikers Material Jersey Prime Gold

*1-175 p/r 100: .5X TO 1.2X BRZ p/r 40-50
*1-175 p/r 100: .4X TO 1X BRZ p/r 25
*1-175 p/r 50: .75X TO 2X BRZ p/r 100
*1-175 p/r 50: .6X TO 1.5X BRZ p/r 40-50
*1-175 p/r 50: .5X TO 1.2X BRZ p/r 25
*1-175 p/r 20-30: 1X TO 2.5X BRZ p/r 100
*1-175 p/r 20-30: .75X TO 2X BRZ p/r 40-50
*1-175 p/r 20-30: .6X TO 1.5X BRZ p/r 25
PRINT RUNS B/WN 1-100 COPIES PER
NO PRICING ON QTY OF 10 OR LESS
PLATINUM PRINT RUN 1 SERIAL #'d SET
NO PLATINUM PRICING DUE TO SCARCITY
OVERALL AU-GU ODDS ONE PER PACK
34 Aramis Ramirez/100 10.00 25.00
70 Andruw Jones/50 15.00 40.00
88 Barry Zito/25 15.00 40.00
103 Andy Pettitte/20 30.00 60.00
117 Bobby Abreu/100 10.00 25.00
128 Jim Edmonds/25 30.00 60.00
140 Vernon Wells/50 12.50 30.00
163 Nolan Ryan LGD/25 60.00 120.00
167 Cal Ripken LGD/25 100.00 175.00

2005 Leaf Limited Monikers Material Jersey Number Silver

*1-175 p/r 75: .5X TO 1.2X BRZ p/r 100
*1-175 p/r 75: .4X TO 1X BRZ p/r 40-50
*1-175 p/r 75: .3X TO .8X BRZ p/r 25
*1-175 p/r 50: .6X TO 1.5X BRZ p/r 100
*1-175 p/r 50: .5X TO 1.2X BRZ p/r 40-50
*1-175 p/r 50: .4X TO 1X BRZ p/r 25
*1-175 p/r 24-25: .6X TO 1.5X BRZ p/r 40-50
*1-175 p/r 24-25: .5X TO 1.2X BRZ p/r 25
*1-175 p/r 15: 1X TO 2.5X BRZ p/r 100
PRINT RUNS B/WN 1-75 COPIES PER
NO PRICING ON QTY OF 10 OR LESS
PRIME PLATINUM PRINT RUN 1 #'d SET
NO PRIME PLAT.PRICING DUE TO SCARCITY
OVERALL AU-GU ODDS ONE PER PACK
34 Aramis Ramirez/75 8.00 20.00
70 Andruw Jones/25 20.00 50.00
90 Lyle Overbay/75 5.00 12.00
101 Dontrelle Willis/24 12.50 30.00
117 Bobby Abreu/75 8.00 20.00
128 Jim Edmonds/25 20.00 50.00
140 Vernon Wells/50 10.00 25.00
143 David Ortiz/75 15.00 40.00
163 Nolan Ryan LGD/25 50.00 100.00
167 Cal Ripken LGD/25 60.00 120.00

2005 Leaf Limited Threads Jersey Prime

OVERALL AU-GU ODDS ONE PER PACK
PRINT RUNS B/WN 5-100 COPIES PER
NO PRICING ON QTY OF 5
PRICES ARE FOR 2 COLOR PATCHES
REDUCE 20% FOR 1-COLOR PATCH
ADD 20% FOR 3-4 COLOR PATCH
ADD 50% FOR 5-COLOR+ PATCH
1 Roger Clemens H/25 12.50 30.00
5 Todd Helton H/100 5.00 12.00
6 Todd Helton A/100 5.00 12.00
7 Vladimir Guerrero H/100 6.00 15.00
8 Vladimir Guerrero A Jkt/30 10.00 25.00
9 Miguel Cabrera H/100 5.00 12.00
10 Miguel Cabrera A/100 5.00 12.00
12 Albert Pujols A/50 15.00 40.00
13 Mark Prior H/100 5.00 12.00
14 Mark Prior A/25 8.00 20.00
15 Chipper Jones H/100 6.00 15.00
16 Chipper Jones A/100 6.00 15.00
17 Jeff Bagwell H/100 5.00 12.00
18 Jeff Bagwell A/100 5.00 12.00
19 Kerry Wood H/100 3.00 8.00
22 Carl Crawford/100 3.00 8.00
23 Mariano Rivera/60 8.00 20.00
25 Ben Sheets/100 3.00 8.00
27 Melvin Mora/25 5.00 12.00
28 Corey Patterson/100 3.00 8.00
29 Rafael Furcal/100 3.00 8.00
30 Jim Thome/100 5.00 12.00
34 Aramis Ramirez/50 4.00 10.00
35 Javy Lopez/100 3.00 8.00
38 Michael Young/100 3.00 8.00
39 Ivan Rodriguez/100 5.00 12.00
42 Adam Dunn/100 3.00 8.00
43 Eric Chavez/100 3.00 8.00
45 Roy Oswalt/100 3.00 8.00
48 Johnny Damon/50 6.00 15.00
50 Mark Buehrle/50 4.00 10.00
53 Hank Blalock/100 3.00 8.00
55 Brad Radke/50 4.00 10.00
57 Sean Casey/50 4.00 10.00
58 Mike Lowell/100 3.00 8.00
60 Francisco Rodriguez/100 3.00 8.00
62 Greg Maddux/25 12.50 30.00
63 A.J. Burnett/75 3.00 8.00
66 Travis Hafner/100 3.00 8.00
68 Bret Boone/100 3.00 8.00
70 Andruw Jones/100 5.00 12.00
73 Torii Hunter/100 3.00 8.00
74 Paul Konerko/100 3.00 8.00
79 Lance Berkman/100 3.00 8.00
80 Justin Morneau/100 3.00 8.00
82 Jose Vidro/100 3.00 8.00
84 Josh Beckett/100 3.00 8.00
86 Luis Gonzalez/100 3.00 8.00
88 Barry Zito/100 3.00 8.00
91 Roy Halladay/100 3.00 8.00
94 Mike Sweeney/100 3.00 8.00
95 Rafael Palmeiro/100 5.00 12.00
97 Preston Wilson/100 3.00 8.00
98 Shannon Stewart/50 4.00 10.00
99 Trot Nixon/25 5.00 12.00
100 Mike Piazza/100 6.00 15.00
101 Dontrelle Willis/100 3.00 8.00
103 Andy Pettitte/50 6.00 15.00
104 Kazuo Matsui/100 3.00 8.00
107 Alfonso Soriano/100 3.00 8.00
110 Aubrey Huff/100 3.00 8.00
111 Adrian Beltre/50 4.00 10.00
112 Mark Teixeira/60 6.00 15.00
114 Miguel Tejada/100 3.00 8.00
117 Bobby Abreu/100 3.00 8.00
119 Manny Ramirez/60 6.00 15.00
121 Scott Rolen/100 5.00 12.00
124 Derrek Lee/50 6.00 15.00
127 John Smoltz/100 5.00 12.00
128 Jim Edmonds/100 3.00 8.00
130 Garret Anderson/60 4.00 10.00
131 Austin Kearns/100 3.00 8.00
138 Mike Mussina/50 6.00 15.00
140 Vernon Wells/100 3.00 8.00
141 David Wright/100 12.50 30.00
142 Marcus Giles/100 3.00 8.00
144 Victor Martinez/75 3.00 8.00
145 Hideki Matsui/100 20.00 50.00
146 C.C. Sabathia/100 3.00 8.00
150 Jorge Posada/75 5.00 12.00
152 Ryne Sandberg LGD/50 12.50 30.00
153 Rickey Henderson LGD/25 12.50 30.00
156 George Brett LGD/50 12.50 30.00
159 Don Mattingly LGD/50 12.50 30.00
160 Bob Gibson LGD/25 10.00 25.00
161 Hank Aaron LGD/25 40.00 80.00
163 Nolan Ryan LGD/100 12.50 30.00
167 Cal Ripken LGD/100 15.00 40.00
169 Roger Clemens Sox/50 10.00 25.00
170 Curt Schilling D'backs/100 3.00 8.00
171 Rafael Palmeiro Rgr/100 5.00 12.00
173 Mike Piazza Dgr/100 6.00 15.00
174 Greg Maddux Braves/100 8.00 20.00
175 Sammy Sosa Cubs/100 6.00 15.00

2005 Leaf Limited Threads Jersey Number

*151-168 p/r 50: .3X TO .8X JPR p/r 100
*151-168 p/r 50: .25X TO .6X JPR p/r 50
OVERALL AU-GU ODDS ONE PER PACK
PRINT RUNS B/WN 1-100 COPIES PER
NO PRICING ON QTY OF 10 OR LESS
154 Ted Williams LGD/25 30.00 60.00
157 Whitey Ford LGD/50 5.00 12.00
158 Duke Snider LGD/25 6.00 15.00
164 Stan Musial LGD/25 12.50 30.00
166 Harmon Killebrew LGD/50 6.00 15.00
168 Babe Ruth LGD/25 175.00 300.00

2005 Leaf Limited Threads MLB Logo

OVERALL AU-GU ODDS ONE PER PACK
STATED PRINT RUN 1 SERIAL #'d SET
NO PRICING DUE TO SCARCITY

2005 Leaf Limited TNT

*1-150/169-175p/r50: .4XTO1X JPRp/r75-100
*1-150/169-175p/r50: .3XTO.8X JPRp/r50-60
*1-150/169-175p/r50: .25X TO.6XJPRp/r25-30
*1-150 p/r 25-30: .5X TO 1.2X JPR p/r 75-100
*1-150 p/r 25-30: .3X TO .8X JPR p/r 25-30
*151-168 p/r 50: .4X TO 1X JPR p/r 100
*151-168 p/r 50: .3X TO .8X JPR p/r 50
*151-168 p/r 50: .25X TO .6X JPR p/r 25
*151-168 p/r 25: .3X TO .8X JPR p/r 25
OVERALL AU-GU ODDS ONE PER PACK
PRINT RUNS B/WN 1-50 COPIES PER
NO PRICING ON QTY OF 10 OR LESS
11 Albert Pujols H Bat-Jsy/50 12.50 30.00
143 David Ortiz Bat-Jsy/50 5.00 12.00
151 Willie Mays LGD Bat-Jsy/25 30.00 60.00
154 T.Williams LGD Bat-Jsy/25 50.00 100.00
164 S.Musial LGD Bat-Jsy/25 15.00 40.00
166 H.Killebrew LGD Bat-Jsy/25 10.00 25.00
172 R.Johnson M's Bat-Jsy/25 8.00 20.00

2005 Leaf Limited TNT Prime

*1-150/169-75pr75-100:.4XTO1XJPRpr 75-100
*1-150 p/r 75-100: .3X TO .8X JPR p/r 50-60
*1-150/169-175pr40-60:.5XTO1.2Xpr75-100
*1-150/169-175p/r40-60:.4XTO1XJPRpr50-60
*1-150 p/r 40-60: .3X TO .8X JPR p/r25-30
*1-150 p/r 25: .6X TO 1.5X JPR p/r 75-100
*1-150 p/r 25: .5X TO 1.2X JPR p/r 50-60
*1-150 p/r 25: .4X TO 1X JPR p/r 25-30
*1-150 p/r 15: .6X TO 1.5X JPR p/r 50-60
*151-168 p/r 100: .4X TO 1X JPR p/r 100
*151-168 p/r 50: .5X TO 1.2X JPR p/r 100
*151-168 p/r 50: .4X TO 1X JPR p/r 50
*151-168 p/r 25: .4X TO 1X JPR p/r 25
OVERALL AU-GU ODDS ONE PER PACK
PRINT RUNS B/WN 5-100 COPIES PER
NO PRICING ON QTY OF 10 OR LESS
PRICES ARE FOR 2-COLOR PATCHES
REDUCE 20% FOR 1-COLOR PATCH
ADD 20% FOR 3-4 COLOR PATCH
ADD 50% FOR 5-COLOR+ PATCH

2005 Leaf Limited Cuts Gold

*GOLD p/r 22-30: .6X TO 1.5X SILVER p/r 99
*GOLD p/r 22-30: .4X TO 1X SILVER p/r 20-34
OVERALL AU-GU ODDS ONE PER PACK
PRINT RUNS B/WN 3-30 COPIES PER
NO PRICING ON QTY OF 12 OR LESS
CUTS FABRIC IS NOT GAME-USED
4 Sandy Koufax/30 250.00 400.00
20 Craig Biggio/25 20.00 50.00

2005 Leaf Limited Cuts Silver

PRINT RUNS B/WN 7-99 COPIES PER
NO PRICING ON QTY OF 7
PLATINUM PRINT RUN 1 SERIAL #'d SET
NO PLATINUM PRICING DUE TO SCARCITY
OVERALL AU-GU ODDS ONE PER PACK
CUTS FABRIC IS NOT GAME-USED
1 Orlando Cepeda/30 15.00 40.00
2 Hank Aaron/44 175.00 300.00
3 Willie Mays/24 125.00 200.00
4 Sandy Koufax/32 150.00 300.00
5 Cal Ripken/25 100.00 175.00
6 Nolan Ryan/34 60.00 120.00
7 Jim Palmer/22 10.00 25.00
8 Tony Gwynn/19 30.00 60.00
9 Rod Carew/29 25.00 60.00
10 Ryne Sandberg/23 40.00 80.00
11 Stan Musial/28 40.00 80.00
12 Steve Carlton/32 15.00 40.00
14 Mike Schmidt/20 40.00 80.00
15 Harmon Killebrew/25 40.00 80.00
17 Duke Snider/53 10.00 50.00
18 Don Mattingly/25 25.00 60.00
19 Dale Murphy/25 20.00 50.00
21 Juan Marichal/99 10.00 25.00
22 Greg Maddux/36 100.00 175.00
23 Lou Brock/20 20.00 50.00
24 Paul Molitor/25 15.00 40.00
25 Wade Boggs/26 20.00 50.00
26 Mark Prior/27 15.00 40.00
28 Al Kaline/28 30.00 80.00
29 Minnie Minoso/25 20.00 50.00

2005 Leaf Limited Legends

STATED PRINT RUN 50 SERIAL #'d SETS
FOIL PRINT RUN 10 SERIAL #'d SETS
NO FOIL PRICING DUE TO SCARCITY
OVERALL INSERT ODDS ONE PER PACK
1 Billy Martin 2.00 5.00
2 Bobby Doerr 2.00 5.00
3 Carlton Fisk 2.00 5.00
4 Harmon Killebrew 3.00 8.00
5 Duke Snider 2.00 5.00
6 George Brett 6.00 15.00
7 Johnny Bench 3.00 8.00
8 Lou Boudreau 2.00 5.00
9 Brooks Robinson 2.00 5.00
10 Al Kaline 3.00 8.00
11 Stan Musial 5.00 12.00
12 Burleigh Grimes 2.00 5.00
13 Cal Ripken 10.00 25.00
14 Carl Yastrzemski 4.00 10.00
15 Willie Stargell 2.00 5.00
16 Yogi Berra 3.00 8.00
17 Enos Slaughter 2.00 5.00
18 Phil Rizzuto 2.00 5.00
19 Luis Aparicio 2.00 5.00
20 Ernie Banks 3.00 8.00
21 Hal Newhouser 2.00 5.00
22 Whitey Ford 2.00 5.00
23 Tony Gwynn 4.00 10.00
24 Bob Feller 2.00 5.00
25 Don Sutton 2.00 5.00
26 Lou Brock 2.00 5.00
27 Jim Palmer 2.00 5.00
28 Billy Williams 2.00 5.00
29 Juan Marichal 2.00 5.00
30 Rod Carew 2.00 5.00
31 Catfish Hunter 2.00 5.00
32 Maury Wills 1.25 3.00
33 Joe Cronin 1.25 3.00
34 Fergie Jenkins 2.00 5.00
35 Sandy Koufax 6.00 15.00
36 Steve Carlton 2.00 5.00
37 Eddie Murray 2.00 5.00
38 Roger Maris 3.00 8.00
39 Gaylord Perry 2.00 5.00
40 Bob Gibson 2.00 5.00
41 Tom Seaver 2.00 5.00
42 Dennis Eckersley 2.00 5.00
43 Reggie Jackson 2.00 5.00
44 Willie McCovey 2.00 5.00
45 Willie Mays NY 6.00 15.00
46 Willie Mays SF 6.00 15.00
47 Rickey Henderson M's 3.00 8.00
48 Rickey Henderson Mets 3.00 8.00
49 Nolan Ryan Angels 10.00 25.00
50 Nolan Ryan Mets 10.00 25.00

2005 Leaf Limited Legends Jersey Number

OVERALL AU-GU ODDS ONE PER PACK
PRINT RUNS B/WN 1-50 COPIES PER
NO PRICING ON QTY OF 14 OR LESS
3 Carlton Fisk/50 5.00 12.00
12 Burleigh Grimes Pants/25 40.00 80.00
21 Hal Newhouser/16 5.00 12.00
22 Whitey Ford/16 8.00 20.00
24 Bob Feller Pants/19 8.00 20.00
25 Don Sutton/20 4.00 10.00
26 Lou Brock/20 6.00 15.00
27 Jim Palmer/22 4.00 10.00
28 Billy Williams/26 4.00 10.00
29 Juan Marichal/27 4.00 10.00
30 Rod Carew/29 6.00 15.00
31 Catfish Hunter Pants/29 4.00 10.00
34 Fergie Jenkins/31 4.00 10.00
35 Sandy Koufax/32 75.00 150.00
36 Steve Carlton/32 4.00 10.00
37 Eddie Murray/33 8.00 20.00
39 Gaylord Perry/36 3.00 8.00
40 Bob Gibson/45 5.00 12.00
41 Tom Seaver/41 5.00 12.00
42 Dennis Eckersley/45 3.00 8.00
43 Reggie Jackson Pants/44 5.00 12.00
44 Willie McCovey/44 5.00 12.00
45 Willie Mays NY/24 15.00 40.00
46 Willie Mays SF/24 15.00 40.00
49 Nolan Ryan Angels/30 12.50 30.00
50 Nolan Ryan Mets/30 12.50 30.00

2005 Leaf Limited Legends Jersey Number Prime

*PRIME p/r 25: .75X TO 2X NBR p/r 36-50
*PRIME p/r 25: .6X TO 1.5X NBR p/r 20-33
*PRIME p/r 15: .75X TO 2X NBR p/r 20-33
OVERALL AU-GU ODDS ONE PER PACK
PRINT RUNS B/WN 1-25 COPIES PER
NO PRICING ON QTY OF 10 OR LESS
PRICES ARE FOR 2 COLOR PATCHES
REDUCE 20% FOR 1-COLOR PATCH
ADD 20% FOR 3-4 COLOR PATCH
ADD 50% FOR 5-COLOR+ PATCH
6 George Brett/25 15.00 40.00
7 Johnny Bench/15 15.00 40.00
11 Stan Musial/25 20.00 50.00
13 Cal Ripken/25 30.00 60.00
14 Carl Yastrzemski/25 12.50 30.00
15 Willie Stargell/25 10.00 25.00
20 Ernie Banks/25 15.00 40.00
23 Tony Gwynn/25 12.50 30.00
47 Rickey Henderson M's/25 12.50 30.00
48 Rickey Henderson Mets/25 12.50 30.00

2005 Leaf Limited Legends Signature

OVERALL AU-GU ODDS ONE PER PACK
PRINT RUNS B/WN 2-50 COPIES PER
NO PRICING ON QTY OF 10 OR LESS
2 Bobby Doerr/50 8.00 20.00
4 Harmon Killebrew/50 20.00 50.00
5 Duke Snider/25 15.00 40.00
9 Brooks Robinson/50 12.50 30.00
10 Al Kaline/50 20.00 50.00
18 Phil Rizzuto/50 12.50 30.00
19 Luis Aparicio/50 8.00 20.00
24 Bob Feller/50 8.00 20.00
25 Don Sutton/50 8.00 20.00
26 Lou Brock/50 12.50 30.00
27 Jim Palmer/50 8.00 20.00
28 Billy Williams/25 10.00 25.00
29 Juan Marichal/50 8.00 20.00
30 Rod Carew/25 15.00 40.00
32 Maury Wills/50 8.00 20.00
34 Fergie Jenkins/50 8.00 20.00
36 Steve Carlton/50 8.00 20.00
39 Gaylord Perry/50 5.00 12.00
40 Bob Gibson/25 20.00 50.00
42 Dennis Eckersley/50 8.00 20.00

2005 Leaf Limited Legends Signature Jersey Number

*NBR p/r 20-30: .6X TO 1.5X SIG p/r 50
*NBR p/r 20-30: .5X TO 1.2X SIG p/r 25
*NBR p/r 15-16: .6X TO 1.5X SIG p/r 25
OVERALL AU-GU ODDS ONE PER PACK
PRINT RUNS B/WN 5-30 COPIES PER
NO PRICING ON QTY OF 14 OR LESS
11 Stan Musial/25 60.00 120.00
13 Cal Ripken/25 75.00 150.00
22 Whitey Ford/16 30.00 60.00
23 Tony Gwynn/25 20.00 50.00
39 Gaylord Perry/25 6.00 15.00
42 Dennis Eckersley/25 15.00 40.00
44 Willie McCovey/25 20.00 50.00
45 Willie Mays NY/24 125.00 200.00
46 Willie Mays SF/24 125.00 200.00
49 Nolan Ryan Angels/30 50.00 100.00
50 Nolan Ryan Mets/30 50.00 100.00

2005 Leaf Limited Legends Signature Jersey Number Prime

*PRIME p/r 20-25: .75X TO 2X SIG p/r 50
*PRIME p/r 20-25: .6X TO 1.5X SIG p/r 25
*PRIME p/r 15: 1X TO 2.5X SIG p/r 50
OVERALL AU-GU ODDS ONE PER PACK
PRINT RUNS B/WN 1-25 COPIES PER
NO PRICING ON QTY OF 14 OR LESS
3 Carlton Fisk/15 40.00 80.00
11 Stan Musial/25 60.00 120.00
13 Cal Ripken/25 125.00 200.00
23 Tony Gwynn/25 30.00 60.00
44 Willie McCovey/20 30.00 60.00

2005 Leaf Limited Lettermen

A.BELTRE p/r 20 40.00 80.00
A.BELTRE p/r 10 50.00 100.00
C.BIGGIO p/r 10 150.00 250.00
C.BIGGIO p/r 5 175.00 300.00
C.JONES p/r 5 175.00 300.00
C.RIPKEN p/r 8 300.00 450.00
D.MATTINGLY p/r 10 150.00 250.00
D.MATTINGLY p/r 5 175.00 300.00
D.SNIDER p/r 11 40.00 80.00
D.MURPHY p/r 20 40.00 80.00
M.CABRERA p/r 20 40.00 80.00
M.CABRERA p/r 10 40.00 80.00
M.SCHMIDT p/r 4-5 150.00 250.00
N.RYAN p/r 21 150.00 250.00
P.MOLITOR p/r 10 75.00 150.00
P.MOLITOR p/r 5 125.00 200.00
R.SANDBERG p/r 11 150.00 250.00
S.MUSIAL p/r 6 150.00 250.00
T.GWYNN p/r 21 125.00 200.00
T.GWYNN p/r 10-11 175.00 300.00
OVERALL AU-GU ODDS ONE PER PACK
PRINT RUNS B/WN 4-21 COPIES PER
LETTERMEN FABRIC IS NOT GAME-USED

2005 Leaf Limited Lumberjacks

STATED PRINT RUN 50 SERIAL #'d SETS
FOIL PRINT RUN 10 SERIAL #'d SETS
NO FOIL PRICING DUE TO SCARCITY
OVERALL INSERT ODDS ONE PER PACK
1 Al Kaline 3.00 8.00
2 Albert Pujols 4.00 10.00
3 Andre Dawson 2.00 5.00
4 Babe Ruth 8.00 20.00
5 Cal Ripken 10.00 25.00
6 Chipper Jones 3.00 8.00
7 Dale Murphy 3.00 8.00
8 Dave Winfield 2.00 5.00
9 Don Mattingly 6.00 15.00
10 Duke Snider 2.00 5.00
11 Eddie Murray 2.00 5.00
12 Frank Robinson 2.00 5.00
13 Frank Thomas 3.00 8.00
14 Gary Carter 2.00 5.00
15 Hack Wilson 2.00 5.00
16 Hank Aaron 6.00 15.00
17 Harmon Killebrew 3.00 8.00
18 Joe Morgan 2.00 5.00
19 Johnny Bench 3.00 8.00
20 Kirby Puckett 3.00 8.00
21 Kirk Gibson 1.25 3.00
22 Manny Ramirez 3.00 8.00
23 Mark Grace 2.00 5.00
24 Mike Piazza 3.00 8.00
25 Mike Schmidt 5.00 12.00
26 Orlando Cepeda 2.00 5.00
27 Paul Molitor 3.00 8.00
28 Rafael Palmeiro 2.00 5.00
29 Ralph Kiner 2.00 5.00
30 Reggie Jackson 2.00 5.00
31 Richie Ashburn 2.00 5.00
32 Rickey Henderson 3.00 8.00
33 Robin Yount 3.00 8.00
34 Rod Carew 2.00 5.00
35 Ryne Sandberg 6.00 15.00
36 Stan Musial 5.00 12.00
37 Ted Williams 6.00 15.00
38 Tony Gwynn 4.00 10.00
39 Vladimir Guerrero 2.00 5.00
40 Willie Mays 6.00 15.00
41 E.Banks 3.00 8.00
B.Williams
42 T.Williams 6.00 15.00
J.Cronin
43 G.Brett 6.00 15.00
B.Jackson
44 J.Kruk 2.00 5.00
J.Thome
45 W.Mays 6.00 15.00
J.Thorpe
46 W.Boggs 2.00 5.00
J.Damon
47 M.Williams 2.00 5.00
W.Clark
48 W.Stargell 2.00 5.00
D.Parker
49 I.Suzuki 4.00 10.00
E.Martinez
50 C.Yastrzemski 4.00 10.00
C.Fisk

2005 Leaf Limited Lumberjacks Bat

1-40 PRINT RUNS B/WN 1-50 COPIES PER
41-50 PRINT RUNS B/WN 5-50 COPIES PER
OVERALL AU-GU ODDS ONE PER PACK
NO PRICING ON QTY OF 5 OR LESS
1 Al Kaline/50 6.00 15.00
4 Babe Ruth/25 125.00 200.00
8 Dave Winfield/50 3.00 8.00
11 Eddie Murray/25 10.00 25.00
12 Frank Robinson/50 3.00 8.00
14 Gary Carter/25 5.00 12.00
15 Hack Wilson/50 20.00 50.00
16 Hank Aaron/50 10.00 25.00
18 Joe Morgan/25 5.00 12.00
19 Johnny Bench/50 6.00 15.00
20 Kirby Puckett/50 6.00 15.00
25 Mike Schmidt/50 8.00 20.00
26 Orlando Cepeda/25 5.00 12.00
27 Paul Molitor/50 3.00 8.00
29 Ralph Kiner/25 8.00 20.00
31 Richie Ashburn/25 8.00 20.00
33 Robin Yount/25 10.00 25.00
35 Ryne Sandberg/25 10.00 25.00
36 Stan Musial/50 10.00 25.00
37 Ted Williams/50 20.00 50.00
40 Willie Mays/50 12.50 30.00
43 G.Brett/B.Jackson/50 10.00 25.00
47 M.Williams/W.Clark/50 8.00 20.00
48 W.Stargell/D.Parker/50 8.00 20.00
50 C.Yastrzemski/C.Fisk/50 10.00 25.00

2005 Leaf Limited Lumberjacks Combos

*COMBO p/r 50: .5X TO 1.2X BAT p/r 50
*COMBO p/r 50: .4X TO 1X BAT p/r 25
*COMBO p/r 25: .6X TO 1.5X BAT p/r 50
*COMBO p/r 25: .5X TO 1.2X BAT p/r 25
OVERALL AU-GU ODDS ONE PER PACK
PRINT RUNS B/WN 1-50 COPIES PER
NO PRICING ON QTY OF 10 OR LESS
2 Albert Pujols Bat-Jsy/50 12.50 30.00
4 Babe Ruth Bat-Jsy/25 300.00 500.00
5 Cal Ripken Bat-Jsy/50 15.00 40.00
6 Chipper Jones Bat-Jsy/25 10.00 25.00
7 Dale Murphy Bat-Jsy/50 6.00 15.00
13 Frank Thomas Bat-Jsy/25 10.00 25.00
21 Kirk Gibson Bat-Jsy/50 4.00 10.00
22 Manny Ramirez Bat-Jsy/50 6.00 15.00
23 Mark Grace Bat-Jsy/50 6.00 15.00
24 Mike Piazza Bat-Jsy/50 8.00 20.00

2005 Leaf Limited Lumberjacks Combos Prime

*PRIME p/r 50: .6X TO 1.5X BAT p/r 50
*PRIME p/r 50: .5X TO 1.2X BAT p/r 25
*PRIME p/r 25: .6X TO 1.5X BAT p/r 25
OVERALL AU-GU ODDS ONE PER PACK
PRINT RUNS B/WN 1-50 COPIES PER
NO PRICING ON QTY OF 10 OR LESS
PRICES ARE FOR 2-COLOR PATCHES
REDUCE 20% FOR 1-COLOR PATCH
ADD 20% FOR 3-4 COLOR PATCH
ADD 50% FOR 5-COLOR+ PATCH
2 Albert Pujols Bat-Jsy/50 12.50 30.00
3 Andre Dawson Bat-Jsy/50 4.00 10.00
5 Cal Ripken Bat-Jsy/25 30.00 60.00
6 Chipper Jones Bat-Jsy/50 8.00 20.00
13 Frank Thomas Bat-Jsy/50 8.00 20.00
21 Kirk Gibson Bat-Jsy/50 4.00 10.00
22 Manny Ramirez Bat-Jsy/25 8.00 20.00
24 Mike Piazza Bat-Jsy/50 8.00 20.00
28 Rafael Palmeiro Bat-Jsy/50 6.00 15.00
32 R.Henderson Bat-Jsy/25 10.00 25.00
34 Rod Carew Bat-Jsy/50 6.00 15.00
39 V.Guerrero Bat-Jsy/50 8.00 20.00

2005 Leaf Limited Lumberjacks Jersey

*JSY 1-40 p/r 50: .4X TO 1X BAT p/r 50
*JSY 1-40 p/r 50: .3X TO .8X BAT p/r 25
*JSY 1-40 p/r 25: .5X TO 1.2X BAT p/r 50
*JSY 1-40 p/r 25: .4X TO 1X BAT p/r 25
1-40 PRINT RUNS B/WN 1-50 COPIES PER
*JSY 41-50 p/r 50: .4X TO 1X BAT p/r 50
*JSY 41-50 p/r 25: .5X TO 1.2X BAT p/r 50
41-50 PRINT RUNS B/WN 5-50 COPIES PER
OVERALL AU-GU ODDS ONE PER PACK
NO PRICING ON QTY OF 5 OR LESS
4 Babe Ruth/25 175.00 300.00
10 Duke Snider Pants/50 5.00 12.00
30 Reggie Jackson/50 5.00 12.00
41 E.Banks/B.Williams/25 15.00 40.00
42 T.Williams/J.Cronin/25 30.00 60.00
44 J.Kruk/J.Thome/25 10.00 25.00
45 W.Mays/J.Thorpe/25 125.00 200.00
46 W.Boggs/J.Damon/50 8.00 20.00

2005 Leaf Limited Lumberjacks Jersey Prime

*PRIME 1-40 p/r 50: .5X TO 1.2X BAT p/r 25
*PRIME 1-40 p/r 25: .75X TO 2X BAT p/r 50
*PRIME 1-40 p/r 25: .6X TO 1.5X BAT p/r 25
1-40 PRINT RUNS B/WN 1-50 COPIES PER
41-50 PRINT RUNS B/WN 1-5 COPIES PER
OVERALL AU-GU ODDS ONE PER PACK
NO PRICING ON QTY OF 10 OR LESS
PRICES ARE FOR 2 COLOR PATCHES
REDUCE 20% FOR 1-COLOR PATCH
ADD 20% FOR 3-4 COLOR PATCH
ADD 50% FOR 5-COLOR+ PATCH
2 Albert Pujols/25 20.00 50.00
3 Andre Dawson/50 5.00 12.00
5 Cal Ripken/25 30.00 60.00
6 Chipper Jones/50 10.00 25.00
13 Frank Thomas/50 10.00 25.00
21 Kirk Gibson/50 5.00 12.00
24 Mike Piazza/50 10.00 25.00
28 Rafael Palmeiro/50 8.00 20.00
32 Rickey Henderson/25 12.50 30.00
34 Rod Carew/50 8.00 20.00
38 Tony Gwynn/50 10.00 25.00
39 Vladimir Guerrero/25 10.00 25.00

2005 Leaf Limited Lumberjacks Signature

OVERALL AU-GU ODDS ONE PER PACK
PRINT RUNS B/WN 1-50 COPIES PER
NO PRICING ON QTY OF 10 OR LESS
1 Al Kaline/50 20.00 50.00
3 Andre Dawson/25 10.00 25.00
5 Cal Ripken/21 60.00 120.00
7 Dale Murphy/50 12.00 30.00
9 Don Mattingly/50 20.00 50.00
10 Duke Snider/50 12.00 30.00
12 Frank Robinson/50 8.00 20.00
13 Frank Thomas/25 20.00 50.00
14 Gary Carter/50 15.00 40.00
17 Harmon Killebrew/50 20.00 50.00
18 Joe Morgan/25 10.00 25.00
19 Johnny Bench/50 15.00 40.00
20 Kirby Puckett/25 50.00 100.00
23 Mark Grace/25 15.00 40.00
25 Mike Schmidt/50 20.00 50.00
27 Paul Molitor/50 8.00 20.00
29 Ralph Kiner/50 10.00 25.00
34 Rod Carew/50 12.00 30.00
35 Ryne Sandberg/50 20.00 50.00
36 Stan Musial/50 15.00 40.00
38 Tony Gwynn/50 15.00 40.00
40 Willie Mays/25 100.00 200.00

2005 Leaf Limited Lumberjacks Signature Bat

*BAT p/r 100: .4X TO 1X SIG p/r 50
*BAT p/r 100: .3X TO .8X SIG p/r 21-25
*BAT p/r 50: .5X TO 1.2X SIG p/r 50
*BAT p/r 50: .4X TO 1X SIG p/r 21-25
*BAT p/r 25: .6X TO 1.5X SIG p/r 50
*BAT p/r 25: .5X TO 1.2X SIG p/r 21-25
OVERALL AU-GU ODDS ONE PER PACK
PRINT RUNS B/WN 1-100 COPIES PER
NO PRICING ON QTY OF 10 OR LESS
21 Kirk Gibson/25 12.50 30.00
26 Orlando Cepeda/100 8.00 20.00
33 Robin Yount/25 30.00 60.00

2005 Leaf Limited Lumberjacks Signature Combos

*COMBO p/r 100: .4X TO 1X SIG p/r 50
*COMBO p/r 100: .3X TO .8X SIG p/r 21-25
*COMBO p/r 50: .5X TO 1.2X SIG p/r 50
*COMBO p/r 25: .6X TO 1.5X SIG p/r 50
*COMBO p/r 25: .5X TO 1.2X SIG p/r 21-25
OVERALL AU-GU ODDS ONE PER PACK
PRINT RUNS B/WN 1-100 COPIES PER
NO PRICING ON QTY OF 10 OR LESS

2005 Leaf Limited Lumberjacks Signature Combos Prime

*PRIME p/r 25: .75X TO 2X SIG p/r 50
*PRIME p/r 25: .6X TO 1.5X SIG p/r 21-25
OVERALL AU-GU ODDS ONE PER PACK
PRINT RUNS B/WN 1-25 COPIES PER
NO PRICING ON QTY OF 10 OR LESS
5 Cal Ripken Bat-Jsy/25 125.00 200.00

2005 Leaf Limited Lumberjacks Signature Jersey

*JSY p/r 100: .4X TO 1X SIG p/r 50
*JSY p/r 100: .3X TO .8X SIG p/r 21-25
*JSY p/r 50: .5X TO 1.2X SIG p/r 50
*JSY p/r 25: .6X TO 1.5X SIG p/r 50
*JSY p/r 25: .5X TO 1.2X SIG p/r 21-25
OVERALL AU-GU ODDS ONE PER PACK
PRINT RUNS B/WN 1-100 COPIES PER
NO PRICING ON QTY OF 10 OR LESS
30 Reggie Jackson/25 30.00 60.00
33 Robin Yount/25 30.00 60.00

2005 Leaf Limited Lumberjacks Signature Jersey Prime

*PRIME p/r 25: .75X TO 2X SIG p/r 50
*PRIME p/r 25: .6X TO 1.5X SIG p/r 21-25
OVERALL AU-GU ODDS ONE PER PACK
PRINT RUNS B/WN 1-25 COPIES PER
NO PRICING ON QTY OF 10 OR LESS
5 Cal Ripken/25 125.00 200.00
33 Robin Yount/25 40.00 80.00

2005 Leaf Limited Matching Numbers

PRINT RUNS B/WN 5-50 COPIES PER
NO PRICING ON QTY OF 5
PRIME PRINT RUNS 1-5 COPIES PER
NO PRIME PRICING DUE TO SCARCITY
OVERALL AU-GU ODDS ONE PER PACK
1 T.Williams J/R.Maris J/25 100.00 200.00
2 N.Ryan J/K.Wood J/50 15.00 40.00
3 C.Ripken J/G.Carter J/50 20.00 50.00
4 W.Mays P/R.Hend J/25 40.00 80.00
5 J.Bench P/A.Pujols J/50 15.00 40.00
6 R.Clemens J/W.Clark J/50 15.00 40.00
7 W.McCov J/R.Jack J/25 10.00 25.00
8 R.Sand J/D.Matt J/50 10.00 25.00
9 D.Snider P/J.Cronin P/25 12.50 30.00

2005 Leaf Limited Team Trademarks

STATED PRINT RUN 50 SERIAL #'d SETS
FOIL PRINT RUN 10 SERIAL #'d SETS
NO FOIL PRICING DUE TO SCARCITY
OVERALL INSERT ODDS ONE PER PACK
1 Ryne Sandberg 6.00 15.00
2 George Brett 6.00 15.00
3 Steve Carlton 2.00 5.00
4 Reggie Jackson 2.00 5.00
5 Edgar Martinez 2.00 5.00
6 Barry Larkin 2.00 5.00
7 Ozzie Smith 4.00 10.00
8 Carlton Fisk 2.00 5.00
9 Wade Boggs 2.00 5.00
10 Will Clark 2.00 5.00
11 Nolan Ryan 10.00 25.00
12 Gary Carter 2.00 5.00
13 Don Mattingly 6.00 15.00
14 Willie Stargell 2.00 5.00
15 Don Sutton 2.00 5.00
16 Kirk Gibson 1.25 3.00
17 Kirby Puckett 3.00 8.00
18 Dale Murphy 3.00 8.00
19 Rickey Henderson 3.00 8.00
20 Willie Mays 6.00 15.00
21 Cal Ripken 10.00 25.00
22 Paul Molitor 3.00 8.00
23 Tony Gwynn 4.00 10.00
24 Andre Dawson 2.00 5.00
25 Bob Feller 2.00 5.00
26 Alan Trammell 2.00 5.00
27 Dave Parker 1.25 3.00
28 Dave Righetti 1.25 3.00
29 Dwight Gooden 1.25 3.00
30 Harold Baines 2.00 5.00
31 Jack Morris 2.00 5.00
32 John Kruk 1.25 3.00
33 Lee Smith 1.25 3.00
34 Lenny Dykstra 1.25 3.00
35 Luis Tiant 1.25 3.00
36 Matt Williams 2.00 5.00
37 Ron Guidry 1.25 3.00
38 Tony Oliva 1.25 3.00

2005 Leaf Limited Team Trademarks Jersey Number

*NBR p/r 44-50: .25X TO .6X PRIME p/r 40-50
*NBR p/r 20-32: .3X TO .8X PRIME p/r 40-50
*NBR p/r 20-32: .25X TO .6X PRIME p/r 25-26
OVERALL AU-GU ODDS ONE PER PACK
PRINT RUNS B/WN 1-50 COPIES PER
NO PRICING ON QTY OF 8 OR LESS
1 Ryne Sandberg/23 10.00 25.00
20 Willie Mays/24 15.00 40.00
25 Bob Feller/19 8.00 20.00

2005 Leaf Limited Team Trademarks Jersey Number Prime

OVERALL AU-GU ODDS ONE PER PACK
PRINT RUNS B/WN 1-50 COPIES PER
NO PRICING ON QTY OF 1
PRICES ARE FOR 2 COLOR PATCHES
REDUCE 20% FOR 1-COLOR PATCH
ADD 20% FOR 3-4 COLOR PATCH
ADD 50% FOR 5-COLOR+ PATCH
1 Ryne Sandberg/50 12.50 30.00
2 George Brett/50 12.50 30.00
3 Steve Carlton/50 5.00 12.00
4 Reggie Jackson/50 8.00 20.00
5 Edgar Martinez/50 8.00 20.00
6 Barry Larkin/50 8.00 20.00
7 Ozzie Smith/50 10.00 25.00
8 Carlton Fisk/50 8.00 20.00
9 Wade Boggs/50 8.00 20.00
10 Will Clark/50 8.00 20.00
11 Nolan Ryan/50 12.50 30.00
12 Gary Carter/50 5.00 12.00
13 Don Mattingly/40 12.50 30.00
14 Willie Stargell/50 8.00 20.00
15 Don Sutton/25 6.00 15.00
16 Kirk Gibson/50 5.00 12.00
18 Dale Murphy/50 8.00 20.00
19 Rickey Henderson/50 10.00 25.00
21 Cal Ripken/25 30.00 60.00
23 Tony Gwynn/50 10.00 25.00

24 Andre Dawson/25 6.00 15.00
26 Alan Trammell/25 6.00 15.00
27 Dave Parker/50 5.00 12.00
29 Dwight Gooden/50 5.00 12.00
30 Harold Baines/25 6.00 15.00
31 Jack Morris/47 5.00 12.00
32 John Kruk/25 10.00 25.00
33 Lee Smith/47 5.00 12.00
34 Lenny Dykstra/25 6.00 15.00
38 Tony Oliva/26 6.00 15.00

2005 Leaf Limited Team Trademarks Signature

OVERALL AU-GU ODDS ONE PER PACK
PRINT RUNS B/WN 5-100 COPIES PER
NO PRICING ON QTY OF 5
1 Ryne Sandberg/25 30.00 60.00
3 Steve Carlton/25 10.00 25.00
4 Reggie Jackson/25 20.00 50.00
5 Edgar Martinez/50 12.50 30.00
6 Barry Larkin/50 15.00 40.00
7 Ozzie Smith/50 15.00 40.00
8 Carlton Fisk/50 12.50 30.00
9 Wade Boggs/25 15.00 40.00
10 Will Clark/50 12.50 30.00
11 Nolan Ryan/50 40.00 80.00
12 Gary Carter/50 10.00 25.00
13 Don Mattingly/25 30.00 60.00
15 Don Sutton/100 6.00 15.00
16 Kirk Gibson/50 8.00 20.00
17 Kirby Puckett/25 50.00 100.00
18 Dale Murphy/100 10.00 25.00
20 Willie Mays/25 100.00 175.00
21 Cal Ripken/50 50.00 100.00
22 Paul Molitor/25 10.00 25.00
23 Tony Gwynn/25 20.00 50.00
24 Andre Dawson/100 6.00 15.00
25 Bob Feller/50 8.00 20.00
26 Alan Trammell/25 10.00 25.00
27 Dave Parker/50 8.00 20.00
28 Dave Righetti/25 10.00 25.00
29 Dwight Gooden/50 8.00 20.00
30 Harold Baines/50 8.00 20.00
31 Jack Morris/50 8.00 20.00
32 John Kruk/25 15.00 40.00
33 Lee Smith/50 8.00 20.00
34 Lenny Dykstra/25 10.00 25.00
35 Luis Tiant/50 8.00 20.00
36 Matt Williams/50 12.50 30.00
37 Ron Guidry/25 10.00 25.00
38 Tony Oliva/50 8.00 20.00

2005 Leaf Limited Team Trademarks Signature Jersey Number

*NBR p/r 72: .4X TO 1X SIG p/r 50
*NBR p/r 39-49: .5X TO 1.2X SIG p/r 50
*NBR p/r 39-49: .4X TO 1X SIG p/r 25
*NBR p/r 20-34: .75X TO 2X SIG p/r 100
*NBR p/r 20-34: .6X TO 1.5X SIG p/r 50
*NBR p/r 20-34: .5X TO 1.2X SIG p/r 25
*NBR p/r 16-19: .75X TO 2X SIG p/r 50
*NBR p/r 16-19: .6X TO 1.5X SIG p/r 25
OVERALL AU-GU ODDS ONE PER PACK
PRINT RUNS B/WN 1-72 COPIES PER
NO PRICING ON QTY OF 11 OR LESS
11 Nolan Ryan Pants/34 50.00 100.00
19 Rickey Henderson/24 50.00 100.00
20 Willie Mays/24 125.00 200.00

2005 Leaf Limited Team Trademarks Signature Jersey Number Prime

*PRIME p/r 39-47: .6X TO 1.5X SIG p/r 50
*PRIME p/r 25-29: 1X TO 2.5X SIG p/r 100
*PRIME p/r 25-29: .75X TO 2X SIG p/r 50
*PRIME p/r 25-29: .6X TO 1.5X SIG p/r 25
*PRIME p/r 16: 1X TO 2.5X SIG p/r 50
OVERALL AU-GU ODDS ONE PER PACK
PRINT RUNS B/WN 1-47 COPIES PER
NO PRICING ON QTY OF 10 OR LESS

2016 Leaf Live

COMPLETE SET (10)
COMMON CARD (1-10)
2 Yoan Moncada/209*
9 John Cusack 3.00 8.00
10 Tim Tebow

2020 Leaf Lumber Kings 500 Home Run Club

RANDOM INSERTS IN PACKS
PRINT RUNS B/WN 15-25 COPIES PER
5HC01 Albert Pujols/25 25.00 60.00
5HC02 Alex Rodriguez/25 10.00 25.00
5HC04 Barry Bonds/25 20.00 50.00
5HC05 David Ortiz/25 8.00 20.00
5HC06 Eddie Murray/25 12.00 30.00
5HC07 Frank Robinson/25 10.00 25.00
5HC08 Frank Thomas/25 30.00 80.00
5HC09 Gary Sheffield/25 5.00 12.00
5HC10 Jim Thome/25 6.00 15.00
5HC11 Ken Griffey Jr./25 15.00 40.00
5HC12 Manny Ramirez/25 6.00 15.00
5HC13 Mickey Mantle/15 50.00 120.00
5HC14 Reggie Jackson/25 10.00 25.00
5HC15 Sammy Sosa/25 6.00 15.00
5HC16 Ted Williams/20 30.00 80.00
5HC17 Willie Mays/25 25.00 60.00
5HC18 Willie McCovey/25 10.00 25.00

2020 Leaf Lumber Kings Bat Rack Four

RANDOM INSERTS IN PACKS
PRINT RUNS B/WN 6-25 COPIES PER
NO PRICING ON QTY 6
BR403 Hunter/Maddux
Glavine/Kershaw/25 12.00 30.00
BR405 Rice/Parker/Murray/McCovey/25 10.00 25.00
BR406 Morgan/Fox/Alomar/Carew/17 8.00 20.00
BR407 Ripken Jr./Brett/Boggs
Robinson/25 20.00 50.00
BR408 Mantle/Mays/Griffey
Jr./Puckett/15 50.00 120.00
BR409 Bagwell/Thome/Delgado/Pujols/25 10.00 25.00
BR410 Brett/Gwynn/Carew/Boggs/25 20.00 50.00
BR411 Dawson/Raines
Guerrero/Walker/25 10.00 25.00

2020 Leaf Lumber Kings Bat Rack Three

RANDOM INSERTS IN PACKS
PRINT RUNS B/WN 12-25 COPIES PER
NO PRICING ON QTY 12
BR301 Mays/McCovey/Bonds/15 25.00 60.00
BR302 Puckett/Carew/Molitor/25 12.00 30.00
BR303 Robinson/Murray/Ripken Jr./25 20.00 50.00
BR306 Carew/Gwynn/Boggs/25 20.00 50.00
BR307 McGriff/Thome/Delgado/25 8.00 20.00
BR308 Morgan/Bench/Perez/17 20.00 50.00
BR309 Brock/Raines/Henderson/25 15.00 40.00
BR310 Mays/Mantle/Snider/15 50.00 120.00
BR311 Ortiz/Ramirez/Garciaparra/25 6.00 15.00

2020 Leaf Lumber Kings Dinger Kings

RANDOM INSERTS IN PACKS
PRINT RUNS B/WN 6-25 COPIES PER
NO PRICING ON QTY 9 OR LESS
DK01 Alex Rodriguez/25 10.00 25.00
DK02 Andre Dawson/25 6.00 15.00
DK04 Barry Bonds/25 20.00 50.00
DK05 David Ortiz/25 8.00 20.00
DK06 Frank Robinson/25 10.00 25.00
DK07 Fred McGriff/25 8.00 20.00
DK08 Giancarlo Stanton/25 6.00 15.00
DK09 Jim Rice/25 10.00 25.00
DK10 Jim Thome/25 6.00 15.00
DK11 Johnny Bench/25 12.00 30.00
DK12 Johnny Mize/15 6.00 15.00
DK13 Jose Canseco/25 10.00 25.00
DK14 Ken Griffey Jr./25 15.00 40.00
DK15 Mickey Mantle/15 50.00 120.00
DK16 Reggie Jackson/25 10.00 25.00
DK17 Roger Maris/15 20.00 50.00
DK18 Ryan Howard/25 6.00 15.00
DK19 Sammy Sosa/25 6.00 15.00
DK20 Ted Kluszewski/25 6.00 15.00
DK22 Willie Mays/20 25.00 60.00
DK23 Willie McCovey/25 10.00 25.00

2020 Leaf Lumber Kings Enshrined Eight

RANDOM INSERTS IN PACKS
PRINT RUNS B/WN 6-25 COPIES PER
NO PRICING ON QTY 10
EE02 Carew/Gwynn/Brett/Boggs/Rice/Ripken
Jr./Dawson/Morgan/25 15.00 40.00
EE03 Robinson/Jackson/McCovey
Perez/Robinson/Murray
Rice/Winfield/25 20.00 50.00
EE04 Puckett/Henderson/Raines
Gwynn/Piazza/Bagwell
Alomar/Rodriguez/25 25.00 60.00
EE05 Thome/Bagwell/Griffey
Jr./Thomas/Piazza/Rodriguez
Alomar/Molitor/25 20.00 50.00
EE06 Snider/Brock/Hunter/Rice/Mays
Robinson/Henderson/Molitor/25 20.00 50.00

2020 Leaf Lumber Kings Game Used Lumber

RANDOM INSERTS IN PACKS
PRINT RUNS B/WN 6-25 COPIES PER
NO PRICING ON QTY 12 OR LESS
GUL01 Albert Pujols 8.00 20.00
GUL02 Alex Rodriguez 10.00 25.00
GUL03 Andre Dawson 6.00 15.00
GUL05 Barry Bonds 20.00 50.00
GUL06 Bo Jackson 12.00 30.00
GUL07 Brooks Robinson 10.00 25.00
GUL08 Cal Ripken Jr. 15.00 40.00
GUL09 Carlos Delgado 5.00 12.00
GUL10 Catfish Hunter 6.00 15.00
GUL11 Clayton Kershaw 12.00 30.00
GUL12 Dave Parker 8.00 20.00
GUL13 Dave Winfield 10.00 25.00
GUL14 David Ortiz 8.00 20.00
GUL15 Derek Jeter 25.00 60.00
GUL16 Don Mattingly 25.00 60.00
GUL17 Duke Snider 12.00 30.00
GUL18 Eddie Murray 12.00 30.00
GUL19 Frank Robinson 10.00 25.00
GUL20 Frank Thomas 12.00 30.00
GUL21 Fred McGriff 8.00 20.00
GUL22 Gary Sheffield 5.00 12.00
GUL23 George Brett 20.00 50.00
GUL24 Giancarlo Stanton 6.00 15.00
GUL25 Greg Maddux 10.00 25.00
GUL26 Ichiro Suzuki 20.00 50.00
GUL27 Ivan Rodriguez 5.00 12.00
GUL28 Jason Giambi 5.00 12.00
GUL29 Jeff Bagwell 8.00 20.00
GUL30 Jim Rice 10.00 25.00
GUL31 Jim Thome 6.00 15.00
GUL32 Joe Carter 5.00 12.00
GUL33 Joe Morgan 8.00 20.00
GUL36 Ken Caminiti 5.00 12.00
GUL37 Ken Griffey Jr. 15.00 40.00
GUL38 Kirby Puckett 12.00 30.00
GUL39 Larry Walker 6.00 15.00
GUL40 Lou Brock 6.00 15.00
GUL41 Lou Piniella 5.00 12.00
GUL42 Manny Ramirez 6.00 15.00
GUL44 Mike Piazza 12.00 30.00
GUL45 Mike Trout 20.00 50.00
GUL46 Nellie Fox 10.00 25.00
GUL47 Nomar Garciaparra 6.00 15.00
GUL48 Paul Molitor 10.00 25.00
GUL49 Paul Waner 8.00 20.00
GUL50 Reggie Jackson 10.00 25.00
GUL51 Rickey Henderson 15.00 40.00
GUL52 Roberto Alomar 8.00 20.00
GUL53 Rod Carew 8.00 20.00
GUL54 Roger Maris 20.00 50.00
GUL55 Ron Cey 5.00 12.00
GUL56 Sammy Sosa 6.00 15.00
GUL57 Ted Kluszewski 6.00 15.00
GUL59 Thurman Munson 20.00 50.00
GUL60 Tim Raines 6.00 15.00
GUL61 Tom Glavine 6.00 15.00
GUL62 Tony Gwynn 12.00 30.00
GUL64 Vladimir Guerrero 6.00 15.00
GUL65 Wade Boggs 10.00 25.00
GUL66 Willie Mays 25.00 60.00
GUL67 Willie McCovey 10.00 25.00

2020 Leaf Lumber Kings Home Run Challenge

RANDOM INSERTS IN PACKS
PRINT RUNS B/WN 15-25 COPIES PER
HRC01 M.Mantle/W.Mays/15 40.00 100.00
HRC02 R.Jackson/J.Rice/25 10.00 25.00
HRC03 D.Snider/F.Robinson/25 10.00 25.00
HRC04 R.Maris/T.Kluszewski/25 10.00 25.00
HRC05 K.Griffey Jr./B.Bonds/25 20.00 50.00
HRC06 S.Sosa/F.Thomas/25 10.00 25.00
HRC07 R.Maris/B.Bonds/15 15.00 40.00
HRC08 W.Mays/K.Griffey Jr./15 20.00 50.00
HRC09 D.Snider/W.Mays/15 20.00 50.00

2020 Leaf Lumber Kings Legendary Lumber Lineup

RANDOM INSERTS IN PACKS
PRINT RUNS B/WN 6-25 COPIES PER
NO PRICING ON QTY 6
LLL01 Murray/Morgan/Ripken Jr./Brett/Bench/Griffey
Jr./Maris/Mays/25 20.00 50.00
LLL02 McCovey/Fox/Jeter/Robinson/Rodriguez
Williams/Mantle/Jackson/25 30.00 80.00
LLL03 Thomas/Carew/Rodriguez
Boggs/Piazza/Henderson
Puckett/Robinson/25 25.00 60.00
LLL04 Pujols/Alomar/Jeter/Cey/Bench
Raines/Mays/Suzuki/25 30.00 80.00
LLL05 Bagwell/Fox/Ripken Jr./Brett/Piazza/Williams
Trout/Maris/25 30.00 80.00
LLL06 Perez/Alomar/Rodriguez/Boggs
Piazza/Brock/Snider/Guerrero/25 25.00 60.00
LLL07 Thome/Fox/Jeter/Robinson
Piazza/Rice/Mays/Waner/25 25.00 60.00
LLL08 Mattingly/Morgan/Rodriguez/Ripken
Jr./Rodriguez/Brock/Puckett
Walker/25 20.00 50.00
LLL10 McCovey/Morgan/Jeter/Robinson
Piazza/Williams/Mays/Waner/15 20.00 50.00

2020 Leaf Lumber Kings Lumber Awards

RANDOM INSERTS IN PACKS
PRINT RUNS B/WN 10-25 COPIES PER
NO PRICING ON QTY 10
LA01 Jackson/Brett/Dawson
Rice/Parker/Morgan/25 10.00 25.00
LA02 Carew/McCovey/Thomas/Griffey
Jr./Bench/Robinson/25 20.00 50.00
LA03 Suzuki/Guerrero/Giambi/Rodriguez
Bonds/Rodriguez/25 10.00 25.00
LA05 Kershaw/Stanton/Trout
Pujols/Sosa/Giambi/15 25.00 60.00
LA06 Ripken Jr./Henderson/Mattingly/Dawson
Canseco/Brett/15 20.00 50.00
LA07 Mays/Robinson/Bench/Carew
Murray/McCovey/25 20.00 50.00
LA08 Dawson/Rose/Ripken
Jr./Canseco/Jeter/Bagwell/25 20.00 50.00
LA09 Piazza/Pujols/Howard/Trout
Suzuki/Garciaparra/25 20.00 50.00

2020 Leaf Lumber Kings Rivals

RANDOM INSERTS IN PACKS
PRINT RUNS B/WN 6-25 COPIES PER
NO PRICING ON QTY 6
R01 Snider/Piazza/Cey/Mays
McCovey/Bonds/25 20.00 50.00
R03 Jeter/Jackson/Mattingly/Ramirez
Garciaparra/Boggs/25 20.00 50.00
R04 Dawson/Sosa/Maddux
Pujols/Brock/Mize/25 12.00 30.00
R05 Morgan/Bench/Rose/Cey
Russell/Piazza/25 15.00 40.00
R06 Raines/Dawson/Walker
Alomar/McGriff/Carter/25 10.00 25.00
R07 Brett/Wilson/Jackson
Pujols/Brock/Mize/25 20.00 50.00

2020 Leaf Lumber Kings Signature Sticks

RANDOM INSERTS IN PACKS
PRINT RUNS B/WN 15-30 COPIES PER
*SILVER/15: .4X TO 1X BASIC
SSAD1 Andre Dawson/15 10.00 25.00
SSBJ1 Bo Jackson/19 30.00 80.00
SSCRJ Cal Ripken Jr./30 25.00 60.00
SSEM1 Eddie Murray/15 15.00 40.00
SSFT1 Frank Thomas/19 20.00 50.00
SSGM1 Greg Maddux/25 25.00 60.00
SSJC1 Jose Canseco/30 15.00 40.00
SSJT1 Jim Thome/30 20.00 50.00
SSRC1 Rod Carew/30 15.00 40.00
SSRH1 Rickey Henderson/25 30.00 80.00
SSRJ1 Reggie Jackson/30 20.00 50.00
SSSS1 Sammy Sosa/30 25.00 60.00
SSTG1 Tom Glavine/15 15.00 40.00
SSWB1 Wade Boggs/19 25.00 60.00

2020 Leaf Lumber Kings Signature Sticks Dual

RANDOM INSERTS IN PACKS
PRINT RUNS B/WN 12-15 COPIES PER
NO PRICING ON QTY 12
SS01 C.Ripken Jr./W.Boggs/15 40.00 100.00
SS02 R.Jackson/J.Thome/15 30.00 80.00
SS04 C.Ripken Jr./P.Rose/15 50.00 120.00

2020 Leaf Lumber Kings WAR Room

RANDOM INSERTS IN PACKS
PRINT RUNS B/WN 6-25 COPIES PER
NO PRICING ON QTY 6
WR03 Maddux/Morgan
Pujols/Ripken Jr./25 10.00 25.00
WR04 Boggs/Brett/Griffey Jr./Carew/25 15.00 40.00
WR05 Glavine/Bagwell/Rose/Robinson/25 12.00 30.00
WR06 Molitor/Bench/Jackson/Thomas/25 12.00 30.00
WR07 Thome/Waner/Trout/Jeter/25 25.00 60.00
WR08 Raines/Gwynn/Murray
Rodriguez/25 10.00 25.00
WR09 Alomar/Dawson
McCovey/Winfield/25 10.00 25.00

2012 Leaf Memories Originals

STATED PRINT RUN 99 SER.#'d SETS
PLATE PRINT RUN 1 SET PER COLOR
BLACK-CYAN-MAGENTA-YELLOW ISSUED
NO PLATE PRICING DUE TO SCARCITY
529 Addison Russell 1.25 3.00
530 Albert Almora 2.00 5.00
531 Andrew Heaney 1.00 2.50
532 Byron Buxton 15.00 40.00
533 Carlos Correa 6.00 15.00
534 Courtney Hawkins .75 2.00
535 David Dahl 2.50 6.00
536 Deven Marrero .75 2.00
537 Gavin Cecchini 1.00 2.50
538 Kyle Zimmer 1.00 2.50
539 Max Fried 3.00 8.00
540 Mike Zunino 1.25 3.00
541 Miguel Sano 1.00 2.50
542 Ty Hensley 1.00 2.50
543 Alen Hanson 1.00 2.50
544 Corey Seager 3.00 8.00
545 Jairo Beras .75 2.00
546 Joey Gallo 2.50 6.00
547 Jorge Soler 3.00 8.00
548 Lance McCullers Jr. .75 2.00
549 Lucas Giolito 2.50 6.00
550 Nick Castellanos 2.50 6.00
551 Nomar Mazara 2.00 5.00
552 Yasiel Puig 50.00 100.00
553 Al Kaline 1.25 3.00
554 Albert Pujols 1.50 4.00
555 Bill Mazeroski .75 2.00
556 Bob Gibson .75 2.00
557 Brooks Robinson .75 2.00
558 Ernie Banks 1.25 3.00
559 Gaylord Perry .75 2.00
560 Ichiro Suzuki 1.50 4.00
561 Ivan Rodriguez .75 2.00
562 Jim Bunning .75 2.00
563 Jim Palmer .75 2.00
564 Johnny Bench 1.25 3.00
565 Lou Brock .75 2.00
566 Luis Aparicio .75 2.00
567 Mike Piazza 1.25 3.00
568 Pat Gillick 1.25 3.00
569 Paul Molitor 1.25 3.00
570 Pedro Martinez .75 2.00
571 Pete Rose 2.50 6.00
572 Red Schoendienst .75 2.00
573 Reggie Jackson .75 2.00
574 Rod Carew .75 2.00
575 Tommy Lasorda .75 2.00
576 Tony Perez .75 2.00
577 Whitey Ford .75 2.00

2012 Leaf Memories Originals Autographs

STATED PRINT RUN 25 SER.#'d SETS
PLATE PRINT RUN 1 SET PER COLOR
BLACK-CYAN-MAGENTA-YELLOW ISSUED
NO PLATE PRICING DUE TO SCARCITY
I1 Ichiro Suzuki 250.00 400.00
IR Ivan Rodriguez 30.00 60.00
AA1 Albert Almora 20.00 50.00
AH1 Andrew Heaney 8.00 20.00
AH2 Alen Hanson 20.00 50.00
AK1 Al Kaline 12.00 30.00
AP1 Albert Pujols 90.00 150.00
AR1 Addison Russell 20.00 50.00
BB2 Byron Buxton 50.00 100.00
BG1 Bob Gibson 12.50 30.00
BM1 Bill Mazeroski 10.00 25.00
BR1 Brooks Robinson 20.00 50.00
CC1 Carlos Correa 50.00 100.00
CH1 Courtney Hawkins 20.00 50.00
CS2 Corey Seager 15.00 40.00
DD1 David Dahl 20.00 50.00
DM1 Deven Marrero 10.00 25.00
EB1 Ernie Banks 30.00 60.00
GC1 Gavin Cecchini 10.00 25.00
GP2 Gaylord Perry 8.00 20.00
JB1 Jim Bunning 8.00 20.00
JB2 Johnny Bench 30.00 60.00
JB3 Jairo Beras 15.00 40.00
JG1 Joey Gallo 20.00 50.00
JP1 Jim Palmer 8.00 20.00
JS2 Jorge Soler 30.00 60.00
KZ1 Kyle Zimmer 10.00 25.00
LA1 Luis Aparicio 15.00 40.00
LB1 Lou Brock 10.00 25.00
LG1 Lucas Giolito 12.50 30.00
LM1 Lance McCullers Jr. 12.50 30.00
MF1 Max Fried 10.00 25.00
MP1 Mike Piazza 75.00 150.00
MS3 Miguel Sano 20.00 50.00
MZ1 Mike Zunino 20.00 50.00
NC1 Nick Castellanos 8.00 20.00
NM1 Nomar Mazara 10.00 25.00
PG1 Pat Gillick 8.00 20.00
PM1 Pedro Martinez 30.00 60.00
PM2 Paul Molitor 15.00 40.00
PR1 Pete Rose 12.50 30.00
RC1 Rod Carew 12.50 30.00
RJ1 Reggie Jackson 20.00 50.00
RS1 Red Schoendienst 8.00 20.00
TH1 Ty Hensley 8.00 20.00
TL1 Tommy Lasorda 30.00 80.00
TP1 Tony Perez 10.00 25.00
WF1 Whitey Ford 15.00 40.00
YP1 Yasiel Puig 300.00 600.00

2012 Leaf Memories 90 Leaf Buyback Autographs

PRINT RUNS B/WN 1-72 COPIES PER
NO PRICING ON QTY 11 OR LESS
4 Mike Scott/33 6.00 15.00
10 Carlton Fisk/72 20.00 50.00
20 Roger McDowell/13 8.00 20.00
21 Nolan Ryan/34 100.00 175.00
25 Greg Maddux/31 90.00 150.00
29 Dennis Eckersley/43 12.50 30.00
30 Glenn Davis/27 8.00 20.00
40 David Cone/44 10.00 25.00
51 Wade Boggs/26 20.00 50.00
63 Bert Blyleven/28 10.00 25.00
68 Fernando Valenzuela/34 75.00 150.00
69 Don Mattingly/23 60.00 120.00
71 Robin Yount/19 40.00 80.00
90 Vince Coleman/29 10.00 25.00
98 Ryne Sandberg/23 40.00 80.00
108 Jose Canseco/33 12.00 30.00
132 Fred McGriff/19 30.00 60.00
139 Dwight Gooden/16 40.00 80.00
154 Tony Gwynn/19 40.00 80.00
156 Mitch Williams/28 10.00 25.00
160 Rickey Henderson/24 150.00 250.00
161 Bill Doran/19 10.00 25.00
165 Cecil Fielder/45 15.00 40.00
168 Jim Deshaies/43 5.00 12.00
169 Juan Berenguer/40 5.00 12.00
181 Eddie Murray/33 30.00 60.00
190 Dave Parker/39 10.00 25.00
195 Lance Parrish/13 12.50 30.00
201 Jesse Barfield/29 8.00 20.00
212 Tim Raines/30 12.50 30.00
217 Lonnie Smith/27 10.00 25.00
228 Kent Hrbek/14 15.00 40.00
235 Dwight Evans/24 20.00 50.00
241 Billy Hatcher/28 10.00 25.00
250 Darryl Strawberry/18 20.00 50.00
265 Nolan Ryan/34 60.00 120.00
272 Howard Johnson/20 12.50 30.00
276 Jeff Reardon/41 5.00 12.00
297 David Justice/23 40.00 80.00
300 Frank Thomas/35 250.00 350.00
304 Ron Darling/15 12.50 30.00
305 Kevin Bass/17 15.00 40.00
341 Wally Backman/19 10.00 25.00
345 Willie Randolph/29 8.00 20.00
346 Danny Darwin/44 6.00 15.00
347 Al Newman/26 6.00 15.00
356 John Franco/31 8.00 20.00
360 Terry Leach/30 6.00 15.00
367 Willie McGee/51 12.50 30.00
387 David West/50 8.00 20.00
390 Charlie Hough/47 5.00 12.00
392 Donn Pall/30 5.00 12.00
426 Dave Winfield/31 20.00 50.00
465 Jim Leyritz/12 10.00 25.00
470 Keith Hernandez/17 12.50 30.00
482 Jack Morris/47 10.00 25.00
483 Randy Johnson/51 50.00 100.00

2013 Leaf Memories

COMPLETE SET (38) 20.00 50.00
PLATE PRINT RUN 1 SET PER COLOR
BLACK-CYAN-MAGENTA-YELLOW ISSUED
NO PLATE PRICING DUE TO SCARCITY
AB1 Archie Bradley .50 1.25
AB2 Aaron Blair .50 1.25
AG1 Alexander Guerrero 2.00 5.00
AG2 Alex Gonzalez .75 2.00
AM1 Austin Meadows 1.25 3.00
BB1 Byron Buxton 2.50 6.00
BMK Billy McKinney .60 1.50
CC1 Carlos Correa 6.00 15.00
CF1 Clint Frazier 2.50 6.00
CK1 Corey Knebel .50 1.25
CM1 Colin Moran .60 1.50
DJP D.J. Peterson .50 1.25
EJ1 Eric Jagielo .60 1.50
ER1 Eduardo Rodriguez 1.50 4.00
HD1 Hunter Dozier .50 1.25
HH1 Hunter Harvey .60 1.50
HR1 Hunter Renfroe .75 2.00
JC1 Jonathon Crawford .50 1.25
JG1 Jonathan Gray .60 1.50
JH1 Josh Hader 1.00 2.50
JPC J.P. Crawford .75 2.00
JS1 Jorge Soler 1.00 2.50
KB1 Kris Bryant 3.00 8.00
KC1 Kyle Crick .75 2.00
MA1 Mark Appel .75 2.00
MAG Miguel Alfredo Gonzalez 1.00 2.50
MG1 Marco Gonzales .75 2.00
MS1 Miguel Sano .60 1.50
NC1 Nick Ciuffo .50 1.25
OM1 Oscar Mercado .75 2.00
OT1 Oscar Taveras .60 1.50
RE1 Ryan Eades .50 1.25
RK1 Rob Kaminsky .60 1.50
RM1 Rafael Montero .50 1.25
SM1 Sean Manaea .50 1.25
TB1 Trey Ball .75 2.00
TD1 Travis Demeritte .60 1.50
TW1 Taijuan Walker .60 1.50

2013 Leaf Memories Blue

*BLUE: .75X TO 2X BASIC
STATED PRINT RUN 50 SER.#'d SETS
AG1 Alexander Guerrero 20.00 50.00

2013 Leaf Memories Gold

*GOLD: 1X TO 2.5X BASIC
STATED PRINT RUN 25 SER.#'d SETS
AG1 Alexander Guerrero 20.00 50.00
KB1 Kris Bryant 15.00 40.00

2013 Leaf Memories 1960 Autographs

JA2 Jose Abreu 20.00 50.00

2013 Leaf Memories 1960 Autographs Purple

*BLACK: .75X TO 2X BASIC
STATED PRINT RUN 25 SER.#'d SETS

2013 Leaf Memories 1960 Autographs Sepia

*SEPIA: .6X TO 1.5X BASIC
STATED PRINT RUN 50 SER.#'d SETS

2013 Leaf Memories 1980s Buyback Autographs

PRINT RUNS B/WN 1-44 COPIES PER
NO PRICING ON QTY 10 OR LESS
37 Rickey Henderson 1986/24 50.00 100.00
37 Lamarr Hoyt 1985/31 8.00 20.00
46 Mike Witt 1985/22 15.00 40.00
47 Jack Mcdowell 1988/40 15.00 40.00
48 Dwight Gooden 1986/16 25.00 60.00
56 Roger Clemens 1988/21 30.00 80.00
84 Dwight Gooden 1987/16 25.00 60.00
99 Roger Clemens 1985/21 30.00 80.00
112 Mike Witt 1986/22 15.00 40.00
113 Steve Carlton 1985/32 12.50 30.00
117 Steve Carlton 1986/32 12.50 30.00
132 Rod Carew 1985/29 12.50 30.00
145 Rickey Henderson 1988/24 50.00 100.00
163 Bruce Sutter 1985/42 6.00 15.00
168 Wade Boggs 1986/26 15.00 40.00
173 Reggie Jackson 1986/44 15.00 40.00
190 Roger Clemens 1987/21 30.00 80.00
191 Rickey Henderson 1987/24 50.00 100.00
192 Bruce Sutter 1986/42 6.00 15.00
234 Dwight Gooden 1985/16 25.00 60.00

2013 Leaf Memories 90 Buyback Autographs

PRINT RUNS B/WN 1-55 COPIES PER
NO PRICING ON QTY 13 OR LESS
12 Roger Clemens/21 30.00 80.00
13 Tom Glavine/47 20.00 50.00
44 Pedro Guerrero/28 6.00 15.00
59 John Smoltz/29 20.00 50.00
71 Robin Yount/19 20.00 50.00
72 Bret Saberhagen/18 10.00 25.00
172 Will Clark/22 75.00 150.00
189 Eric Davis/44 12.50 30.00
280 Orel Hershiser/55 15.00 40.00
284 John Kruk/19 10.00 25.00
288 Chili Davis/30 5.00 12.00
405 Ron Kittle/42 4.00 10.00
468 Mark Davis/48 6.00 15.00
474 Terry Mulholland/45 8.00 20.00

2013 Leaf Memories 91 Buyback Autographs

PRINT RUNS B/WN 1-72 COPIES PER
NO PRICING ON QTY 13 OR LESS
27 John Smoltz/29 20.00 50.00
74 Mike Witt/22 15.00 40.00
77 Dave Justice/23 30.00 60.00
101 Rickey Henderson/24 50.00 100.00
116 Robin Yount/19 20.00 50.00
118 Bret Saberhagen/18 10.00 25.00
165 Dwight Gooden/16 15.00 40.00
238 Will Clark/22 40.00 100.00
252 Jeff Reardon/41 4.00 10.00
273 Wade Boggs/26 15.00 40.00
281 Frank Thomas/35 40.00 80.00
319 Randy Johnson/51 40.00 80.00
384 Carlton Fisk/72 10.00 25.00
423 Nolan Ryan/34 40.00 80.00
488 Roger Clemens/21 30.00 80.00

2013 Leaf Memories 92 Buyback Autographs

PRINT RUNS B/WN 1-72 COPIES PER
NO PRICING ON QTY 13 OR LESS
41 Nolan Ryan/34 40.00 80.00
112 Dwight Gooden/16 25.00 60.00
116 Rickey Henderson/24 50.00 100.00
191 John Smoltz/29 20.00 50.00
241 Will Clark/22 40.00 100.00
286 Wade Boggs/26 15.00 40.00
303 Carlton Fisk/72 10.00 25.00
404 David Justice/23 30.00 60.00
349A Frank Thomas/35 40.00 80.00
349B Frank Thomas/35 40.00 80.00

2013 Leaf Memories Autographs

PLATE PRINT RUN 1 SET PER COLOR
BLACK-CYAN-MAGENTA-YELLOW ISSUED
NO PLATE PRICING DUE TO SCARCITY
AB1 Archie Bradley 6.00 15.00
AB2 Aaron Blair 3.00 8.00
AG2 Alex Gonzalez 5.00 12.00
AG3 Angelo Gumbs 3.00 8.00
AJ1 Aaron Judge 100.00 250.00
AM1 Austin Meadows 8.00 20.00
BB1 Byron Buxton 25.00 60.00
BMK Billy McKinney 3.00 8.00
BS1 Braden Shipley 3.00 8.00
CA2 Chris Anderson 4.00 10.00
CB1 Chris Bostick 4.00 10.00
CC1 Carlos Correa 10.00 25.00
CF1 Clint Frazier 15.00 40.00
CK1 Corey Knebel 3.00 8.00
CM1 Colin Moran 5.00 12.00
DJP D.J. Peterson 5.00 12.00
DS1 Dominic Smith 6.00 15.00
DT1 Domingo Tapia 3.00 8.00
EJ Eloy Jimenez 20.00 50.00
EJ1 Eric Jagielo 4.00 10.00
ER1 Eduardo Rodriguez 6.00 15.00
GK1 Gosuke Katoh 6.00 15.00
GP1 Gregory Polanco 5.00 12.00
HD1 Hunter Dozier 4.00 10.00
HH1 Hunter Harvey 5.00 12.00
HR1 Hunter Renfroe 6.00 15.00
HU1 Henry Urrutia 6.00 15.00
IC1 Ian Clarkin 3.00 8.00
JA1 Jorge Alfaro 5.00 12.00
JC1 Jonathon Crawford 3.00 8.00
JG1 Jonathan Gray 8.00 20.00
JH1 Josh Hader 3.00 8.00
JH2 Jason Hursh 3.00 8.00
JPC J.P. Crawford 3.00 8.00
JS1 Jorge Soler 6.00 15.00
KB1 Kris Bryant 60.00 120.00
KC1 Kyle Crick 6.00 15.00
KS1 Kohl Stewart 5.00 12.00
MA1 Mark Appel 6.00 15.00
MA2 Miguel Almonte 4.00 10.00
MAG Miguel Alfredo Gonzalez 6.00 15.00
MF1 Maikel Franco 5.00 12.00
MG1 Marco Gonzales 4.00 10.00
MS1 Miguel Sano 8.00 20.00
NC1 Nick Ciuffo 3.00 8.00
OM1 Oscar Mercado 3.00 8.00
OT1 Oscar Taveras 15.00 40.00
PE1 Phillip Ervin 5.00 12.00
RDP Rafael de Paula 3.00 8.00
RE1 Ryan Eades 3.00 8.00
RK1 Rob Kaminsky 4.00 10.00
RM1 Rafael Montero 5.00 12.00
RMG Reese McGuire 5.00 12.00
SM1 Sean Manaea 5.00 12.00
TA1 Tim Anderson 6.00 15.00
TB1 Trey Ball 5.00 12.00
TD1 Travis Demeritte 3.00 8.00
TG1 Tyler Glasnow 6.00 15.00
TW1 Taijuan Walker 6.00 15.00

2013 Leaf Memories Autographs Blue

*BLUE p/r 50: .5X TO 1.2X BASIC
*BLUE p/r 20: .75X TO 2X BASIC
PRINT RUNS B/WN 20-50 COPIES PER
KB1 Kris Bryant 75.00 150.00

2013 Leaf Memories Autographs Gold

*GOLD: .75X TO 2X BASIC
PRINT RUNS B/WN 10-25 COPIES PER
NO PRICING ON QTY 10
KB1 Kris Bryant 125.00 250.00

2019 Leaf Metal Babe Ruth Collection

COMMON RUTH 1.25 3.00

2019 Leaf Metal Babe Ruth Collection Black

*BLACK: .75X TO 2X BASIC
RANDOM INSERTS IN PACKS
STATED PRINT RUN 15 SER.#'d SETS

2019 Leaf Metal Babe Ruth Collection Blue

*BLUE: .5X TO 1.2X BASIC
RANDOM INSERTS IN PACKS
STATED PRINT RUN 50 SER.#'d SETS

2019 Leaf Metal Babe Ruth Collection Gold

*GOLD: 10X TO 25X BASIC
RANDOM INSERTS IN PACKS
STATED PRINT RUN 1 SER.#'d SETS

2019 Leaf Metal Babe Ruth Collection Gold Circles

*GOLD CIRCLES: 10X TO 25X BASIC
RANDOM INSERTS IN PACKS
STATED PRINT RUN 1 SER.#'d SETS

2019 Leaf Metal Babe Ruth Collection Green

*GREEN: 1X TO 2.5X BASIC
RANDOM INSERTS IN PACKS
STATED PRINT RUN 10 SER.#'d SETS

2019 Leaf Metal Babe Ruth Collection Orange

*ORANGE: 1.2X TO 3X BASIC
RANDOM INSERTS IN PACKS
STATED PRINT RUN 5 SER.#'d SETS

2019 Leaf Metal Babe Ruth Collection Pink

*PINK: .6X TO 1.5X BASIC
RANDOM INSERTS IN PACKS
STATED PRINT RUN 20 SER.#'d SETS

2019 Leaf Metal Babe Ruth Collection Purple

*PURPLE: .6X TO 1.5X BASIC
RANDOM INSERTS IN PACKS
STATED PRINT RUN 25 SER.#'d SETS

2019 Leaf Metal Babe Ruth Collection Red

*RED: 1.2X TO 3X BASIC
RANDOM INSERTS IN PACKS
STATED PRINT RUN 3 SER.#'d SETS

2019 Leaf Metal Babe Ruth Collection Wave

*WAVE: .5X TO 1.2X BASIC
RANDOM INSERTS IN PACKS

2019 Leaf Metal Babe Ruth Collection Wave Black

*WAVE BLACK: 1X TO 2.5X BASIC
RANDOM INSERTS IN PACKS
STATED PRINT RUN 10 SER.#'d SETS

2019 Leaf Metal Babe Ruth Collection Wave Blue

*WAVE BLUE: .6X TO 1.5X BASIC
RANDOM INSERTS IN PACKS
STATED PRINT RUN 25 SER.#'d SETS

2019 Leaf Metal Babe Ruth Collection Wave Gold

*WAVE GOLD: 10X TO 25X BASIC
RANDOM INSERTS IN PACKS
STATED PRINT RUN 1 SER.#'d SETS

2019 Leaf Metal Babe Ruth Collection Wave Green

*WAVE GREEN: 1X TO 2.5X BASIC
RANDOM INSERTS IN PACKS
STATED PRINT RUN 7 SER.#'d SETS

2019 Leaf Metal Babe Ruth Collection Wave Orange

*WAVE ORANGE: 1.2X TO 3X BASIC
RANDOM INSERTS IN PACKS
STATED PRINT RUN 5 SER.#'d SETS

2019 Leaf Metal Babe Ruth Collection Wave Pink

*WAVE PINK: .75X TO 2X BASIC
RANDOM INSERTS IN PACKS
STATED PRINT RUN 15 SER.#'d SETS

2019 Leaf Metal Babe Ruth Collection Wave Purple

*WAVE PURPLE: .6X TO 1.5X BASIC
RANDOM INSERTS IN PACKS
STATED PRINT RUN 20 SER.#'d SETS

2019 Leaf Metal Babe Ruth Collection Wave Red

*WAVE RED: 1.2X TO 3X BASIC
RANDOM INSERTS IN PACKS
STATED PRINT RUN 3 SER.#'d SETS

2019 Leaf Metal Babe Ruth Collection Bats

COMMON RUTH 25.00 60.00
RANDOM INSERTS IN PACKS
STATED PRINT RUN 10 SER.#'d SETS
*BLUE/8: .4X TO 1X BASE
*PRPLE/7: .4X TO 1X BASE
*WAVE/7: .4X TO 1X BASE
*PINK/6: .4X TO 1X BASE
*BLACK/5: .4X TO 1X BASE
*WAVE BLUE/5: .4X TO 1X BASE
*WAVE PRPLE/5: .4X TO 1X BASE
*GRN/4: .4X TO 1X BASE
*WAVE PINK/4: .4X TO 1X BASE
*ORNGE/3: .5X TO 1.2X BASE
*WAVE BLACK/3: .5X TO 1.2X BASE
*WAVE GRN/3: .5X TO 1.2X BASE
*RED/2: .5X TO 1.2X BASE
*WAVE ORNGE/2: .5X TO 1.2X BASE
*WAVE RED/2: .5X TO 1.2X BASE
*GLD/1: 1X TO 2.5X BASE
*GLD CRCLS/1: 1X TO 2.5X BASE
*WAVE GLD/1: 1X TO 2.5X BASE
*2X GLD/1: 1X TO 2.5X BASE
*2X GLD CRCLS/1: 1X TO 2.5X BASE
*2X WAVE GLD/1: 1X TO 2.5X BASE
*4X GLD/1: 2X TO 5X BASE
*4X GLD CRCLS/1: 2X TO 5X BASE
*4X WAVE GLD/1: 2X TO 5X BASE
*3X GLD/1: 1.2X TO 3X BASE
*3X GLD CRCLS/1: 1.2X TO 3X BASE
*3X WAVE GLD/1: 1.2X TO 3X BASE

2019 Leaf Metal Babe Ruth Collection Yankee Stadium Seats

COMMON RUTH		
RANDOM INSERTS IN PACKS		
STATED PRINT RUN 10 SER.#'d SETS		
*BLUE/8: .4X TO 1X BASE		
*PRPLE/7: .4X TO 1X BASE		
*WAVE/7: .4X TO 1X BASE		
*PINK/6: .4X TO 1X BASE		
*BLACK/5: .5X TO 1.2X BASE		
*WAVE BLUE/5: .5X TO 1.2X BASE		
*WAVE PRPLE/5: .5X TO 1.2X BASE		
*GRN/4: .5X TO 1.2X BASE		
*WAVE PINK/4: .5X TO 1.2X BASE		
*ORNGE/3: .6X TO 1.5X BASE		
*WAVE BLACK/3: .6X TO 1.5X BASE		
*WAVE GRN/3: .6X TO 1.5X BASE		
*RED/2: 1X TO 2.5X BASE		
*WAVE ORNGE/2: 1X TO 2.5X BASE		
*WAVE RED/2: 1X TO 2.5X BASE		
*GLD/1: 2X TO 5X BASE		
*GLD CRCLS/1: 2X TO 5X BASE		
*WAVE GLD/1: 2X TO 5X BASE		

2011 Leaf Muhammad Ali Metal Fans of Ali Autographs

FAUM13 Nolan Ryan	40.00	80.00

2011 Leaf Muhammad Ali Fans of Ali Autographs Bronze

OVERALL NON-ALI AUTO ODDS TWO PER PACK		
CARD FAU7 NOT ISSUED		
FAU5 Nolan Ryan	60.00	120.00

2011 Leaf Muhammad Ali Fans of Ali Autographs Gold

STATED PRINT RUN 5 SER. #'d SETS
UNPRICED DUE TO SCARCITY
CARD FAU7 NOT ISSUED

2011 Leaf Muhammad Ali Fans of Ali Autographs Silver

*SILVER: .6X TO 1.2X BRONZE
STATED PRINT RUN 25 SER. #'d SETS
CARD FAU7 NOT ISSUED

2011 Leaf National Pride Promo

IS1 Ichiro Suzuki	4.00	10.00

2012 Leaf National Convention

I1 Ichiro	.50	1.25
AD1 Andre Dawson	.20	.50
AK1 Al Kaline	.30	.75
BG1 Bob Gibson	.20	.50
BM1 Bill Mazeroski	.20	.50
BR1 Brooks Robinson	.20	.50
BS1 Bruce Sutter	.12	.30
BW1 Billy Williams	.20	.50
CF1 Carlton Fisk	.20	.50
CR1 Cal Ripken Jr.	1.25	3.00
DE1 Dennis Eckersley	.12	.30
DH2 Doug Harvey	.12	.30
DM1 Don Mattingly	.60	1.50
DS1 Don Sutton	.12	.30
FJ1 Ferguson Jenkins	.12	.30
FR1 Frank Robinson	.30	.75
FT1 Frank Thomas	.30	.75
GG2 Goose Gossage	.12	.30
GM1 Greg Maddux	.40	1.00
GP2 Gaylord Perry	.12	.30
JB1 Jim Bunning	.12	.30
JB2 Johnny Bench	.30	.75
JC2 Jose Canseco	.20	.50
JM2 Joe Morgan	.12	.30
JP1 Jim Palmer	.12	.30
JR2 Jim Rice	.20	.50
LB1 Lou Brock	.20	.50
NR1 Nolan Ryan	1.00	2.50
OC1 Orlando Cepeda	.12	.30
PM1 Paul Molitor	.30	.75
PM2 Pedro Martinez	.20	.50
PR1 Pete Rose	.60	1.50
RC1 Rod Carew	.20	.50
RF1 Rollie Fingers	.12	.30
RJ1 Reggie Jackson	.20	.50
RS1 Red Schoendienst	.12	.30
RS2 Ryne Sandberg	.60	1.50
SC1 Steve Carlton	.12	.30
TG1 Tony Gwynn	.30	.75
WB1 Wade Boggs	.20	.50
WC1 Will Clark	.20	.50
WF1 Whitey Ford	.20	.50
WH1 Whitey Herzog	.12	.30

2012 Leaf National Convention VIP

COMPLETE SET (5)	5.00	12.00
VIP4 Ichiro	1.25	3.00
VIP5 Dylan Bundy	2.00	5.00

2013 Leaf National Convention VIP

COMPLETE SET (7)	3.00	8.00
NFT1 Frank Thomas	.40	1.00
NPR1 Pete Rose	.50	1.25
NYP1 Yasiel Puig	2.00	5.00

2013 Leaf National Convention Yasiel Puig

NAYP1 Yasiel Puig	4.00	10.00
NAYP2 Yasiel Puig	4.00	10.00
NAYP3 Yasiel Puig	4.00	10.00
NAYP4 Yasiel Puig	4.00	10.00
NAYP5 Yasiel Puig	4.00	10.00
NAYP6 Yasiel Puig	4.00	10.00

2014 Leaf National Convention

COMPLETE SET (10)	4.00	10.00
7 Ichiro Suzuki BB	.40	1.00

2015 Leaf National Convention '90 Leaf Acetate

CRJ Cal Ripken Jr.	2.00	5.00
FT1 Frank Thomas	1.25	3.00
KS1 Kyle Schwarber	2.00	5.00
PR1 Pete Rose	1.25	3.00

2015 Leaf National Convention VIP

COMPLETE SET (11)		
10 Kyle Schwarber	1.25	3.00
11 Yoan Moncada	1.25	3.00

2014 Leaf Peck and Snyder Promos

COMPLETE SET (45)	25.00	60.00
3 Andrew Wiggins BK		
8 Byron Buxton BB		
9 Carlos Correa BB		
10 Carlos Rodon BB		
14•Frank Thomas BB		
17•Greg Maddux BB		
20•Joey Gallo BB		
24•Kris Bryant BB		
25•Kyle Schwarber BB		
42•Tom Glavine BB		
44•Tyler Kolek BB		

2011 Leaf Pete Rose Legacy

COMMON ROSE (2-59)	2.00	5.00
FIVE BASE CARDS PER BOX		
COMMON ROSE SP (1/60)	30.00	80.00
COMMON ROSE REV.NEG SP (1-60)	30.00	80.00
SHORT PRINT ODDS APPX. 1-2 PER CASE		
1 Pete Rose	25.00	60.00
2A Pete Rose	1.50	4.00
2B Pete Rose Rev Neg SP	25.00	60.00
3 Pete Rose	1.50	4.00
4 Pete Rose	1.50	4.00
5 Pete Rose	1.50	4.00
6A Pete Rose	1.50	4.00
6B Pete Rose Rev Neg SP	25.00	60.00
7 Pete Rose	1.50	4.00
8 Pete Rose	1.50	4.00
9 Pete Rose	1.50	4.00
10 Pete Rose	1.50	4.00
11 Pete Rose	1.50	4.00
12 Pete Rose	1.50	4.00
13 Pete Rose	1.50	4.00
14 Pete Rose	1.50	4.00
15 Pete Rose	1.50	4.00
16A Pete Rose	1.50	4.00
16B Pete Rose Rev Neg SP	25.00	60.00
17 Pete Rose	1.50	4.00
18 Pete Rose	1.50	4.00
19 Pete Rose	1.50	4.00
20A Pete Rose	1.50	4.00
20B Pete Rose Rev Neg SP	25.00	60.00
21 Pete Rose	1.50	4.00
22 Pete Rose	1.50	4.00
23A Pete Rose	1.50	4.00
23B Pete Rose Rev Neg SP	25.00	60.00
24 Pete Rose	1.50	4.00
25 Pete Rose	1.50	4.00
26 Pete Rose	1.50	4.00
27A Pete Rose	1.50	4.00
27B Pete Rose Rev Neg SP	25.00	60.00
28 Pete Rose	1.50	4.00
29 Pete Rose	1.50	4.00
30A Pete Rose	1.50	4.00
30B Pete Rose Rev Neg SP	25.00	60.00
31 Pete Rose	1.50	4.00
32A Pete Rose	1.50	4.00
32B Pete Rose Rev Neg SP	25.00	60.00
33 Pete Rose	1.50	4.00
34 Pete Rose	1.50	4.00
35 Pete Rose	1.50	4.00
36 Pete Rose	1.50	4.00
37A Pete Rose	1.50	4.00
37B Pete Rose Rev Neg SP	25.00	60.00
38B Pete Rose Rev Neg SP	25.00	60.00
38A Pete Rose	1.50	4.00
39 Pete Rose	1.50	4.00
40 Pete Rose	1.50	4.00
41 Pete Rose	1.50	4.00
42 Pete Rose	1.50	4.00
43A Pete Rose	1.50	4.00
43B Pete Rose Rev Neg SP	25.00	60.00
44 Pete Rose	1.50	4.00
45 Pete Rose	1.50	4.00
46 Pete Rose	1.50	4.00
47A Pete Rose	1.50	4.00
47B Pete Rose Rev Neg SP	25.00	60.00
48 Pete Rose	1.50	4.00
49 Pete Rose	1.50	4.00
50 Pete Rose	1.50	4.00
51A Pete Rose	1.50	4.00
51B Pete Rose Rev Neg SP	25.00	60.00
52A Pete Rose	1.50	4.00
52B Pete Rose Rev Neg SP	25.00	60.00
53 Pete Rose	1.50	4.00
54A Pete Rose	1.50	4.00
54B Pete Rose Rev Neg SP	25.00	60.00
55 Pete Rose	1.50	4.00
56 Pete Rose	1.50	4.00
57 Pete Rose	1.50	4.00
58 Pete Rose	1.50	4.00
59 Pete Rose	1.50	4.00
60 Pete Rose	25.00	60.00

2011 Leaf Pete Rose Legacy Autographed Bats Red Ink

COMMON ROSE RED INK AUTO	40.00	80.00
OVERALL AUTO ODDS ONE PER BOX		
STATED PRINT RUN 10 SER.#'d SETS		
ALL VERSIONS EQUALLY PRICED		
AB1 Pete Rose	40.00	80.00
AB2 Pete Rose	40.00	80.00
AB3 Pete Rose	40.00	80.00
AB4 Pete Rose	40.00	80.00
AB5 Pete Rose	40.00	80.00
AB6 Pete Rose	40.00	80.00
AB7 Pete Rose	40.00	80.00
AB8 Pete Rose	40.00	80.00
AB9 Pete Rose	40.00	80.00
AB10 Pete Rose	40.00	80.00
AB11 Pete Rose	40.00	80.00
AB12 Pete Rose	40.00	80.00
AB13 Pete Rose	40.00	80.00
AB14 Pete Rose	40.00	80.00
AB15 Pete Rose	40.00	80.00
AB16 Pete Rose	40.00	80.00
AB17 Pete Rose	40.00	80.00
AB18 Pete Rose	40.00	80.00
AB19 Pete Rose	40.00	80.00
AB20 Pete Rose	40.00	80.00
AB21 Pete Rose	40.00	80.00
AB22 Pete Rose	40.00	80.00
AB23 Pete Rose	40.00	80.00
AB24 Pete Rose	40.00	80.00
AB25 Pete Rose	40.00	80.00
AB26 Pete Rose	40.00	80.00
AB27 Pete Rose	40.00	80.00
AB28 Pete Rose	40.00	80.00
AB29 Pete Rose	40.00	80.00
AB30 Pete Rose	40.00	80.00
AB31 Pete Rose	40.00	80.00
AB32 Pete Rose	40.00	80.00
AB33 Pete Rose	40.00	80.00
AB34 Pete Rose	40.00	80.00
AB35 Pete Rose	40.00	80.00
AB36 Pete Rose	40.00	80.00
AB37 Pete Rose	40.00	80.00
AB38 Pete Rose	40.00	80.00
AB39 Pete Rose	40.00	80.00
AB40 Pete Rose	40.00	80.00

2011 Leaf Pete Rose Legacy Autographed Bats Green Ink

COMMON ROSE GREEN INK AUTO	50.00	100.00
OVERALL AUTO ODDS ONE PER BOX		
STATED PRINT RUN 5 SER.#'d SETS		
ALL VERSIONS EQUALLY PRICED		

2011 Leaf Pete Rose Legacy Autographed Bats Pink Ink

COMMON ROSE PINK INK AUTO	150.00	250.00
OVERALL AUTO ODDS ONE PER BOX		
STATED PRINT RUN 1 SER.#'d SET		
ALL VERSIONS EQUALLY PRICED		

2011 Leaf Pete Rose Legacy Autographed Jerseys Red Ink

COMMON ROSE RED INK AUTO	40.00	80.00
OVERALL AUTO ODDS ONE PER BOX		
STATED PRINT RUN 10 SER.#'d SETS		
ALL VERSIONS EQUALLY PRICED		
AJ1 Pete Rose	40.00	80.00
AJ2 Pete Rose	40.00	80.00
AJ3 Pete Rose	40.00	80.00
AJ4 Pete Rose	40.00	80.00
AJ5 Pete Rose	40.00	80.00
AJ6 Pete Rose	40.00	80.00
AJ7 Pete Rose	40.00	80.00
AJ8 Pete Rose	40.00	80.00
AJ9 Pete Rose	40.00	80.00
AJ10 Pete Rose	40.00	80.00
AJ11 Pete Rose	40.00	80.00
AJ12 Pete Rose	40.00	80.00
AJ13 Pete Rose	40.00	80.00
AJ14 Pete Rose	40.00	80.00
AJ15 Pete Rose	40.00	80.00
AJ16 Pete Rose	40.00	80.00
AJ17 Pete Rose	40.00	80.00
AJ18 Pete Rose	40.00	80.00
AJ19 Pete Rose	40.00	80.00
AJ20 Pete Rose	40.00	80.00
AJ21 Pete Rose	40.00	80.00
AJ22 Pete Rose	40.00	80.00
AJ23 Pete Rose	40.00	80.00
AJ24 Pete Rose	40.00	80.00
AJ25 Pete Rose	40.00	80.00
AJ26 Pete Rose	40.00	80.00
AJ27 Pete Rose	40.00	80.00
AJ28 Pete Rose	40.00	80.00
AJ29 Pete Rose	40.00	80.00
AJ30 Pete Rose	40.00	80.00
AJ31 Pete Rose	40.00	80.00
AJ32 Pete Rose	40.00	80.00
AJ33 Pete Rose	40.00	80.00
AJ34 Pete Rose	40.00	80.00
AJ35 Pete Rose	40.00	80.00
AJ36 Pete Rose	40.00	80.00
AJ37 Pete Rose	40.00	80.00
AJ38 Pete Rose	40.00	80.00
AJ39 Pete Rose	40.00	80.00
AJ40 Pete Rose	40.00	80.00

2011 Leaf Pete Rose Legacy Autographed Jerseys Green Ink

COMMON ROSE GREEN INK AUTO	30.00	60.00
OVERALL AUTO ODDS ONE PER BOX		
STATED PRINT RUN 5 SER.#'d SETS		
ALL VERSIONS EQUALLY PRICED		

2011 Leaf Pete Rose Legacy Autographed Jerseys Pink Ink

COMMON ROSE PINK INK AUTO	150.00	250.00
OVERALL AUTO ODDS ONE PER BOX		
STATED PRINT RUN 1 SER.#'d SET		
ALL VERSIONS EQUALLY PRICED		

2011 Leaf Pete Rose Legacy Autographs

COMMON ROSE AUTO	12.50	30.00
OVERALL AUTO ODDS ONE PER BOX		
STATED PRINT RUN 30 SER.#'d SETS		
ALL VERSIONS EQUALLY PRICED		
A1 Pete Rose	12.50	30.00
A2 Pete Rose	12.50	30.00
A3 Pete Rose	12.50	30.00
A4 Pete Rose	12.50	30.00
A5 Pete Rose	12.50	30.00
A6 Pete Rose	12.50	30.00
A7 Pete Rose	12.50	30.00
A8 Pete Rose	12.50	30.00
A9 Pete Rose	12.50	30.00
A10 Pete Rose	12.50	30.00
A11 Pete Rose	12.50	30.00
A12 Pete Rose	12.50	30.00
A13 Pete Rose	12.50	30.00
A14 Pete Rose	12.50	30.00
A15 Pete Rose	12.50	30.00
A16 Pete Rose	12.50	30.00
A17 Pete Rose	12.50	30.00
A18 Pete Rose	12.50	30.00
A19 Pete Rose	12.50	30.00
A20 Pete Rose	12.50	30.00
A21 Pete Rose	12.50	30.00
A22 Pete Rose	12.50	30.00
A23 Pete Rose	12.50	30.00
A24 Pete Rose	12.50	30.00
A25 Pete Rose	12.50	30.00
A26 Pete Rose	12.50	30.00
A27 Pete Rose	12.50	30.00
A28 Pete Rose	12.50	30.00
A29 Pete Rose	12.50	30.00
A30 Pete Rose	12.50	30.00
A31 Pete Rose	12.50	30.00
A32 Pete Rose	12.50	30.00
A33 Pete Rose	12.50	30.00
A34 Pete Rose	12.50	30.00
A35 Pete Rose	12.50	30.00
A36 Pete Rose	12.50	30.00
A37 Pete Rose	12.50	30.00
A38 Pete Rose	12.50	30.00
A39 Pete Rose	12.50	30.00
A40 Pete Rose	12.50	30.00

2011 Leaf Pete Rose Legacy Autographs Green Ink

COMMON ROSE GREEN INK AUTO	30.00	60.00
OVERALL AUTO ODDS ONE PER BOX		
STATED PRINT RUN 5 SER.#'d SETS		
ALL VERSIONS EQUALLY PRICED		

2011 Leaf Pete Rose Legacy Autographs Pink Ink

COMMON ROSE PINK INK AUTO	75.00	150.00
OVERALL AUTO ODDS ONE PER BOX		
STATED PRINT RUN 1 SER.#'d SET		
ALL VERSIONS EQUALLY PRICED		

2011 Leaf Pete Rose Legacy Autographs Red Ink

COMMON ROSE RED INK AUTO	20.00	50.00
OVERALL AUTO ODDS ONE PER BOX		
STATED PRINT RUN 10 SER.#'d SETS		
ALL VERSIONS EQUALLY PRICED		

2011 Leaf Pete Rose Legacy Career Highlights Autographs Red Ink

COMMON ROSE RED INK AUTO	50.00	100.00
OVERALL AUTO ODDS ONE PER BOX		
STATED PRINT RUN 10 SER.#'d SETS		
ALL VERSIONS EQUALLY PRICED		
CHA1 Pete Rose	50.00	100.00
CHA2 Pete Rose	50.00	100.00
CHA3 Pete Rose	50.00	100.00
CHA4 Pete Rose	50.00	100.00
CHA5 Pete Rose	50.00	100.00
CHA6 Pete Rose	50.00	100.00
CHA7 Pete Rose	50.00	100.00
CHA8 Pete Rose	50.00	100.00
CHA9 Pete Rose	50.00	100.00
CHA10 Pete Rose	50.00	100.00
CHA11 Pete Rose	50.00	100.00
CHA12 Pete Rose	50.00	100.00

2011 Leaf Pete Rose Legacy Career Highlights Autographs Green Ink

COMMON ROSE GREEN INK AUTO	50.00	100.00
OVERALL AUTO ODDS ONE PER BOX		
STATED PRINT RUN 5 SER.#'d SETS		
ALL VERSIONS EQUALLY PRICED		

2011 Leaf Pete Rose Legacy Career Highlights Autographs Pink Ink

OVERALL AUTO ODDS ONE PER BOX
STATED PRINT RUN 1 SER.#'d SET
NO PRICING DUE TO SCARCITY

2011 Leaf Pete Rose Legacy Nicknames Autographs Red Ink

OVERALL AUTO ODDS ONE PER BOX
STATED PRINT RUN 10 SER.#'d SETS
NO PRICING DUE TO SCARCITY

2011 Leaf Pete Rose Legacy Nicknames Autographs Green Ink

OVERALL AUTO ODDS ONE PER BOX
STATED PRINT RUN 5 SER.#'d SETS
NO PRICING DUE TO SCARCITY

2011 Leaf Pete Rose Legacy Nicknames Autographs Pink Ink

OVERALL AUTO ODDS ONE PER BOX
STATED PRINT RUN 1 SER.#'d SET
NO PRICING DUE TO SCARCITY

2011 Leaf Pete Rose Legacy Outside the Lines Autographs Red Ink

COMMON ROSE RED INK AUTO	60.00	120.00
OVERALL AUTO ODDS ONE PER BOX		
STATED PRINT RUN 10 SER.#'d SETS		
ALL VERSIONS EQUALLY PRICED		
OTLA1 Pete Rose	60.00	120.00
OTLA2 Pete Rose	60.00	120.00
OTLA3 Pete Rose	60.00	120.00

2011 Leaf Pete Rose Legacy Outside the Lines Autographs Green Ink

OVERALL AUTO ODDS ONE PER BOX
STATED PRINT RUN 5 SER.#'d SETS
NO PRICING DUE TO SCARCITY

2011 Leaf Pete Rose Legacy Outside the Lines Autographs Pink Ink

OVERALL AUTO ODDS ONE PER BOX
STATED PRINT RUN 1 SER.#'d SET
NO PRICING DUE TO SCARCITY

2011 Leaf Pete Rose Legacy Rose-ism Autographs Red Ink

COMMON ROSE RED INK AUTO	50.00	100.00
OVERALL AUTO ODDS ONE PER BOX		
STATED PRINT RUN 10 SER.#'d SETS		
ALL VERSIONS EQUALLY PRICED		
QA1 Pete Rose	50.00	100.00
QA2 Pete Rose	50.00	100.00
QA3 Pete Rose	50.00	100.00
QA4 Pete Rose	50.00	100.00
QA5 Pete Rose	50.00	100.00
QA6 Pete Rose	50.00	100.00
QA7 Pete Rose	50.00	100.00
QA8 Pete Rose	50.00	100.00
QA9 Pete Rose	50.00	100.00
QA10 Pete Rose	50.00	100.00
QA11 Pete Rose	50.00	100.00
QA12 Pete Rose	50.00	100.00
QA13 Pete Rose	50.00	100.00
QA14 Pete Rose	50.00	100.00
QA15 Pete Rose	50.00	100.00

2011 Leaf Pete Rose Legacy Rose-ism Autographs Green Ink

COMMON ROSE GREEN INK AUTO	50.00	100.00
OVERALL AUTO ODDS ONE PER BOX		
STATED PRINT RUN 5 SER.#'d SETS		
ALL VERSIONS EQUALLY PRICED		

2011 Leaf Pete Rose Legacy Rose-ism Autographs Pink Ink

OVERALL AUTO ODDS ONE PER BOX
STATED PRINT RUN 1 SER.#'d SET
NO PRICING DUE TO SCARCITY

2011 Leaf Pete Rose Legacy The Machine Autographs Green Ink

COMMON ROSE GREEN INK AUTO	50.00	100.00
OVERALL AUTO ODDS ONE PER BOX		
STATED PRINT RUN 5 SER.#'d SETS		
ALL VERSIONS EQUALLY PRICED		
TMA1 Pete Rose	50.00	100.00
TMA2 Pete Rose	50.00	100.00
TMA3 Pete Rose	50.00	100.00
TMA4 Pete Rose	50.00	100.00
TMA5 Pete Rose	50.00	100.00
TMA6 Pete Rose	50.00	100.00
TMA7 Pete Rose	50.00	100.00
TMA8 Pete Rose	50.00	100.00

2011 Leaf Pete Rose Legacy The Machine Autographs Pink Ink

OVERALL AUTO ODDS ONE PER BOX
STATED PRINT RUN 1 SER.#'d SET
NO PRICING DUE TO SCARCITY

2012 Leaf Pete Rose The Living Legend

COMPLETE SET (50)	6.00	15.00
COMMON CARD	.20	.50

2012 Leaf Pete Rose The Living Legend Autographs

COMMON CARD	8.00	20.00

1996 Leaf Preferred

The 1996 Leaf Preferred set was issued by Donruss in one series totalling 150 cards. The six-card packs retailed for $3.49 each. Each card was printed on 20-point card stock for extra thickness and durability. The fronts feature a color action player photo and silver foil printing. The backs carry another player photo, player information and statistics. One in every ten packs contained an insert card.

COMPLETE SET (150)	10.00	25.00
1 Ken Griffey Jr.	.60	1.50
2 Rico Brogna	.10	.30
3 Gregg Jefferies	.10	.30
4 Reggie Sanders	.10	.30
5 Manny Ramirez	.20	.50
6 Shawn Green	.10	.30
7 Tino Martinez	.20	.50
8 Jeff Bagwell	.20	.50
9 Marc Newfield	.10	.30
10 Ray Lankford	.10	.30
11 Jay Bell	.10	.30
12 Greg Maddux	.50	1.25
13 Frank Thomas	.30	.75
14 Travis Fryman	.10	.30
15 Mark McGwire	.75	2.00
16 Chuck Knoblauch	.10	.30
17 Sammy Sosa	.30	.75
18 Matt Williams	.10	.30
19 Roger Clemens	.60	1.50
20 Rondell White	.10	.30
21 Ivan Rodriguez	.20	.50
22 Cal Ripken	1.00	2.50
23 Ben McDonald	.10	.30
24 Kenny Lofton	.10	.30
25 Mike Piazza	.50	1.25
26 David Cone	.10	.30
27 Gary Sheffield	.10	.30
28 Tim Salmon	.20	.50
29 Andres Galarraga	.10	.30
30 Johnny Damon	.20	.50
31 Ozzie Smith	.50	1.25
32 Carlos Baerga	.10	.30
33 Raul Mondesi	.10	.30
34 Moises Alou	.10	.30
35 Alex Rodriguez	.60	1.50
36 Mike Mussina	.20	.50
37 Jason Isringhausen	.10	.30
38 Barry Larkin	.20	.50
39 Bernie Williams	.20	.50
40 Chipper Jones	.30	.75
41 Joey Hamilton	.10	.30
42 Charles Johnson	.10	.30
43 Juan Gonzalez	.10	.30
44 Greg Vaughn	.10	.30
45 Robin Ventura	.10	.30
46 Albert Belle	.10	.30
47 Rafael Palmeiro	.20	.50
48 Brian L.Hunter	.10	.30
49 Mo Vaughn	.10	.30
50 Paul O'Neill	.20	.50
51 Mark Grace	.20	.50
52 Randy Johnson	.30	.75
53 Pedro Martinez	.20	.50
54 Marty Cordova	.10	.30
55 Garret Anderson	.10	.30
56 Joe Carter	.10	.30
57 Jim Thome	.20	.50
58 Edgardo Alfonzo	.10	.30
59 Dante Bichette	.10	.30
60 Darryl Hamilton	.10	.30
61 Roberto Alomar	.20	.50
62 Fred McGriff	.20	.50
63 Kirby Puckett	.30	.75
64 Hideo Nomo	.30	.75
65 Alex Fernandez	.10	.30
66 Ryan Klesko	.10	.30
67 Wade Boggs	.20	.50
68 Eddie Murray	.30	.75
69 Eric Karros	.10	.30
70 Jim Edmonds	.10	.30
71 Edgar Martinez	.20	.50
72 Andy Pettitte	.20	.50
73 Mark Grudzielanek	.10	.30
74 Tom Glavine	.20	.50
75 Ken Caminiti	.10	.30
76 Will Clark	.20	.50
77 Craig Biggio	.20	.50
78 Brady Anderson	.10	.30
79 Tony Gwynn	.40	1.00
80 Larry Walker	.10	.30
81 Brian Jordan	.10	.30
82 Lenny Dykstra	.10	.30
83 Butch Huskey	.10	.30
84 Jack McDowell	.10	.30
85 Cecil Fielder	.10	.30
86 Jose Canseco	.20	.50
87 Jason Giambi	.10	.30
88 Rickey Henderson	.30	.75
89 Kevin Seitzer	.10	.30
90 Carlos Delgado	.10	.30
91 Ryne Sandberg	.50	1.25
92 Dwight Gooden	.10	.30
93 Michael Tucker	.10	.30
94 Barry Bonds	.75	2.00
95 Eric Young	.10	.30
96 Dean Palmer	.10	.30
97 Henry Rodriguez	.10	.30
98 John Mabry	.10	.30
99 J.T. Snow	.10	.30
100 Andre Dawson	.10	.30
101 Ismael Valdes	.10	.30
102 Charles Nagy	.10	.30
103 Jay Buhner	.10	.30
104 Derek Bell	.10	.30
105 Paul Molitor	.10	.30
106 Hal Morris	.10	.30
107 Ray Durham	.10	.30
108 Bernard Gilkey	.10	.30
109 John Valentin	.10	.30
110 Melvin Nieves	.10	.30
111 John Smoltz	.20	.50
112 Terrell Wade	.10	.30
113 Chad Mottola	.10	.30
114 Tony Clark	.10	.30
115 John Wasdin	.10	.30
116 Derek Jeter	.75	2.00
117 Rey Ordonez	.10	.30
118 Jason Thompson RC	.10	.30
119 Robin Jennings	.10	.30
120 Rocky Coppinger RC	.10	.30
121 Billy Wagner	.10	.30
122 Steve Gibralter	.10	.30
123 Jermaine Dye	.10	.30
124 Jason Kendall	.10	.30
125 Mike Grace RC	.10	.30
126 Jason Schmidt	.20	.50
127 Paul Wilson	.10	.30
128 Alan Benes	.10	.30
129 Justin Thompson	.10	.30
130 Brooks Kieschnick	.10	.30
131 George Arias	.10	.30
132 Osvaldo Fernandez RC	.10	.30
133 Todd Hollandsworth	.10	.30
134 Eric Owens	.10	.30
135 Chan Ho Park	.10	.30
136 Mark Loretta	.10	.30
137 Ruben Rivera	.10	.30
138 Jeff Suppan	.10	.30
139 Ugueth Urbina	.10	.30
140 LaTroy Hawkins	.10	.30
141 Chris Snopek	.10	.30
142 Edgar Renteria	.10	.30
143 Raul Casanova	.10	.30
144 Jose Herrera	.10	.30
145 Matt Lawton RC	.10	.30
146 Ralph Milliard RC	.10	.30
147 Frank Thomas CL	.20	.50
148 Jeff Bagwell CL	.10	.30
149 Ken Griffey Jr. CL	.40	1.00
150 Mike Piazza CL	.30	.75

1996 Leaf Preferred Press Proofs

*STARS: 12.5X TO 30X BASIC CARDS
*ROOKIES: 8X TO 20X BASIC CARDS
RANDOM INSERTS IN PACKS
STATED PRINT RUN 500 SETS

1996 Leaf Preferred Staremaster

COMPLETE SET (12)	40.00	100.00
RANDOM INSERTS IN PACKS		
STATED PRINT RUN 2500 SERIAL #'d SETS		
1 Chipper Jones	3.00	8.00
2 Alex Rodriguez	4.00	10.00
3 Derek Jeter	8.00	20.00
4 Tony Gwynn	3.00	8.00
5 Frank Thomas	3.00	8.00
6 Ken Griffey Jr.	6.00	15.00
7 Cal Ripken	10.00	25.00
8 Greg Maddux	5.00	12.00
9 Albert Belle	1.25	3.00
10 Barry Bonds	5.00	12.00
11 Jeff Bagwell	2.00	5.00
12 Mike Piazza	3.00	8.00

1996 Leaf Preferred Steel

ONE PER PACK		
*GOLD: 4X TO 10X BASIC STEEL		
GOLD: RANDOM INSERTS IN PACKS		
1 Frank Thomas	1.00	2.50
2 Paul Molitor	.40	1.00
3 Kenny Lofton	.40	1.00
4 Travis Fryman	.40	1.00
5 Jeff Conine	.40	1.00
6 Barry Bonds	2.50	6.00
7 Gregg Jefferies	.40	1.00
8 Alex Rodriguez	2.00	5.00
9 Wade Boggs	.60	1.50
10 David Justice	1.00	2.50
11 Hideo Nomo	1.00	2.50
12 Roberto Alomar	.60	1.50
13 Todd Hollandsworth	.40	1.00
14 Mark McGwire	2.50	6.00
15 Rafael Palmeiro	.60	1.50
16 Will Clark	.60	1.50
17 Cal Ripken	3.00	8.00
18 Derek Bell	.40	1.00
19 Gary Sheffield	.40	1.00
20 Juan Gonzalez	.40	1.00
21 Garret Anderson	.40	1.00
22 Mo Vaughn	.40	1.00
23 Robin Ventura	.40	1.00
24 Carlos Baerga	.40	1.00
25 Tim Salmon	.60	1.50
26 Matt Williams	.40	1.00
27 Fred McGriff	.60	1.50
28 Rondell White	.40	1.00
29 Ray Lankford	.40	1.00
30 Lenny Dykstra	.40	1.00
31 J.T. Snow	.40	1.00
32 Sammy Sosa	1.00	2.50
33 Chipper Jones	1.00	2.50
34 Bobby Bonilla	.40	1.00
35 Paul Wilson	.40	1.00
36 Darren Daulton	.40	1.00
37 Larry Walker	.40	1.00
38 Raul Mondesi	.40	1.00
39 Jeff Bagwell	.60	1.50
40 Derek Jeter	2.50	6.00
41 Kirby Puckett	1.00	2.50
42 Jason Isringhausen	.40	1.00
43 Vinny Castilla	.40	1.00
44 Jim Edmonds	.40	1.00
45 Ron Gant	.40	1.00
46 Carlos Delgado	.40	1.00
47 Jose Canseco	.60	1.50
48 Tony Gwynn	1.25	3.00
49 Mike Mussina	.60	1.50
50 Charles Johnson	.40	1.00
51 Mike Piazza	1.50	4.00
52 Ken Griffey Jr.	2.00	5.00
53 Greg Maddux	1.50	4.00
54 Mark Grace	.60	1.50
55 Ryan Klesko	.40	1.00
56 Dennis Eckersley	.60	1.50
57 Rickey Henderson	1.00	2.50
58 Michael Tucker	.40	1.00
59 Joe Carter	.40	1.00
60 Randy Johnson	1.00	2.50
61 Brian Jordan	.40	1.00
62 Shawn Green	.40	1.00
63 Roger Clemens	2.00	5.00
64 Andres Galarraga	.40	1.00
65 Johnny Damon	.60	1.50
66 Ryne Sandberg	1.50	4.00
67 Alan Benes	.40	1.00
68 Albert Belle	.40	1.00
69 Barry Larkin	.60	1.50
70 Marty Cordova	.40	1.00
71 Dante Bichette	.40	1.00
72 Craig Biggio	.60	1.50
73 Reggie Sanders	.40	1.00
74 Moises Alou	.40	1.00
75 Chuck Knoblauch	.40	1.00
76 Cecil Fielder	.40	1.00
77 Manny Ramirez	.60	1.50

1996 Leaf Preferred Steel Gold Promos

COMPLETE SET (77)	125.00	250.00
1 Frank Thomas	1.25	3.00
2 Paul Molitor	1.50	4.00
3 Kenny Lofton	.75	2.00
4 Travis Fryman	.60	1.50
5 Jeff Conine	.40	1.00
6 Barry Bonds	3.00	8.00
7 Gregg Jefferies	.40	1.00
8 Alex Rodriguez	4.00	10.00
9 Wade Boggs	2.00	5.00
10 David Justice	1.00	2.50
11 Hideo Nomo	3.00	8.00
12 Roberto Alomar	1.00	2.50
13 Todd Hollandsworth	.40	1.00
14 Mark McGwire	4.00	10.00
15 Rafael Palmeiro	1.00	2.50
16 Will Clark	1.00	2.50
17 Cal Ripken	15.00	40.00
18 Derek Bell	.40	1.00
19 Gary Sheffield	1.50	4.00
20 Juan Gonzalez	1.25	3.00
21 Garret Anderson	.60	1.50
22 Mo Vaughn	.60	1.50
23 Robin Ventura	1.00	2.50
24 Carlos Baerga	.40	1.00
25 Tim Salmon	.75	2.00
26 Matt Williams	.75	2.00
27 Fred McGriff	.75	2.00
28 Rondell White	.60	1.50
29 Ray Lankford	.40	1.00
30 Lenny Dykstra	.60	1.50
31 J.T. Snow	.60	1.50
32 Sammy Sosa	2.50	6.00
33 Chipper Jones	3.00	8.00
34 Bobby Bonilla	.40	1.00
35 Paul Wilson	.40	1.00
36 Darren Daulton	.60	1.50
37 Larry Walker	.60	1.50
38 Raul Mondesi	.60	1.50
39 Jeff Bagwell	2.00	5.00
40 Derek Jeter	20.00	50.00
41 Kirby Puckett	2.00	5.00
42 Jason Isringhausen	.75	2.00
43 Vinny Castilla	.60	1.50
44 Jim Edmonds	1.00	2.50
45 Ron Gant	.40	1.00
46 Carlos Delgado	1.25	3.00
47 Jose Canseco	1.25	3.00
48 Tony Gwynn	3.00	8.00
49 Mike Mussina	1.00	2.50
50 Charles Johnson	.40	1.00
51 Mike Piazza	4.00	10.00
52 Ken Griffey Jr.	4.00	10.00
53 Greg Maddux	4.00	10.00
54 Mark Grace	1.00	2.50
55 Ryan Klesko	.60	1.50
56 Dennis Eckersley	1.50	4.00
57 Rickey Henderson	2.50	6.00
58 Michael Tucker	.40	1.00
59 Joe Carter	.60	1.50
60 Randy Johnson	2.50	6.00
61 Brian Jordan	.60	1.50
62 Shawn Green	.75	2.00
63 Roger Clemens	3.00	8.00
64 Andres Galarraga	1.00	2.50
65 Johnny Damon	1.25	3.00
66 Ryne Sandberg	1.50	4.00
67 Alan Benes	.40	1.00
68 Albert Belle	.60	1.50

69 Barry Larkin	1.00	2.50
70 Marty Cordova	.40	1.00
71 Dante Bichette	.60	1.50
72 Craig Biggio	1.00	2.50
73 Reggie Sanders	.60	1.50
74 Moises Alou	.60	1.50
75 Chuck Knoblauch	.60	1.50
76 Cecil Fielder	.60	1.50
77 Manny Ramirez	2.00	5.00

1996 Leaf Preferred Steel Power

COMPLETE SET (8)	12.50	30.00
RANDOM INSERTS IN PACKS		
STATED PRINT RUN 5000 SERIAL #'d SETS		
1 Albert Belle	.75	2.00
2 Mo Vaughn	.75	2.00
3 Ken Griffey Jr.	4.00	10.00
4 Cal Ripken	6.00	15.00
5 Mike Piazza	2.00	5.00
6 Barry Bonds	3.00	8.00
7 Jeff Bagwell	1.25	3.00
8 Frank Thomas	2.00	5.00

2014 Leaf Ripken Legacy Ironman Autographs

*GOLD/20: .5X TO 1.2X BASIC		
*PLATINUM/8: .75X TO 2X BASIC		
IM1 Cal Ripken Jr.	20.00	50.00
IM2 Cal Ripken Jr.	20.00	50.00
IM3 Cal Ripken Jr.	20.00	50.00
IM4 Cal Ripken Jr.	20.00	50.00
IM5 Cal Ripken Jr.	20.00	50.00
IM6 Cal Ripken Jr.	20.00	50.00
IM7 Cal Ripken Jr.	20.00	50.00
IM8 Cal Ripken Jr.	20.00	50.00
IM9 Cal Ripken Jr.	20.00	50.00
IM10 Cal Ripken Jr.	20.00	50.00
IM11 Cal Ripken Jr.	20.00	50.00
IM12 Cal Ripken Jr.	20.00	50.00
IM13 Cal Ripken Jr.	20.00	50.00
IM14 Cal Ripken Jr.	20.00	50.00
IM15 Cal Ripken Jr.	20.00	50.00
IM16 Cal Ripken Jr.	20.00	50.00
IM17 Cal Ripken Jr.	20.00	50.00
IM18 Cal Ripken Jr.	20.00	50.00
IM19 Cal Ripken Jr.	20.00	50.00
IM20 Cal Ripken Jr.	20.00	50.00

2014 Leaf Q Autographs Silver

*GOLD/25: .5X TO 1.2X BASIC		
ACRJ Cal Ripken Jr. EXCH	25.00	60.00
ANR1 Nolan Ryan	30.00	80.00
1-Apr Pete Rose	15.00	40.00
ARH1 Rickey Henderson SP	20.00	50.00
ARJ1 Reggie Jackson	20.00	50.00

2014 Leaf Q Memorabilia Silver

*GOLD/25: .75X TO 2X BASIC		
MI1 Ichiro	15.00	40.00
MI2 Ichiro	15.00	40.00
MI3 Ichiro	15.00	40.00
MAP1 Albert Pujols	8.00	20.00
MRH1 Rickey Henderson	6.00	15.00

2014 Leaf Q Memorabilia Autographs Gold

*GOLD: .6X TO 1.5X BASIC
*GOLD BAT: .4X TO 1X BASIC
*GOLD JKT: .4X TO 1X BASIC
*GOLD SHOE: .4X TO 1X BASIC
RANDOM INSERTS IN PACKS
STATED PRINT RUN 25 SER.#'d SETS
SOME NOT PRICED DUE TO LACK OF INFO

2014 Leaf Q Memorabilia Autographs Silver

AMI1 Ichiro SP	200.00	300.00
AMBR1 Brooks Robinson SP	20.00	50.00
AMCF1 Carlton Fisk	20.00	50.00
AMCR1 Cal Ripken Jr. Bat EXCH	40.00	100.00
AMCR2 Cal Ripken Jr. Jsy EXCH	40.00	100.00
AMDM1 Don Mattingly SP	25.00	60.00
AMDS1 Deion Sanders	25.00	60.00
AMDW2 Dave Winfield SP	20.00	50.00
AMFT1 Frank Thomas	25.00	60.00
AMJB1 Johnny Bench SP	20.00	50.00
AMJC2 Jose Canseco	15.00	40.00
AMNR1 Nolan Ryan	50.00	120.00
AMOS1 Ozzie Smith Bat	20.00	50.00
AMOS2 Ozzie Smith Jsy	20.00	50.00
AMOT1 Oscar Taveras Bat	10.00	25.00
AMOT2 Oscar Taveras Shoes SP	20.00	50.00
AMPR1 Pete Rose Bat SP	20.00	50.00
AMPR2 Pete Rose Jsy	20.00	50.00
AMRA1 Roberto Alomar SP	12.00	30.00
AMRC1 Rod Carew	12.00	30.00
AMRH1 Rickey Henderson Bat SP	20.00	50.00
AMRH2 Rickey Henderson Jsy SP	20.00	50.00
AMRJ1 Reggie Jackson SP	20.00	50.00
AMTLR Tony La Russa	15.00	40.00
AMWB1 Wade Boggs SP	20.00	50.00

2014 Leaf Q Pure Autographs Charcoal

*BLUE/22-25: .5X TO 1.2X BASIC		
PI1 Ichiro SP	150.00	250.00
PBR2 Brooks Robinson	12.00	30.00
PCRJ Cal Ripken Jr. EXCH	30.00	80.00
PFT1 Frank Thomas SP	30.00	80.00
PGM1 Greg Maddux	30.00	80.00
PJB1 Johnny Bench	15.00	40.00
PJC2 Jose Canseco SP	12.00	30.00
PMR1 Mariano Rivera	50.00	120.00
PNR1 Nolan Ryan	40.00	100.00
POS1 Ozzie Smith	20.00	50.00
PPR2 Pete Rose	15.00	40.00
PRH1 Rickey Henderson	20.00	50.00
PRJ1 Reggie Jackson	20.00	50.00
PTG2 Tom Glavine	12.00	30.00
PWB1 Wade Boggs	15.00	40.00

1998 Leaf Rookies and Stars

The 1998 Leaf Rookies and Stars set was issued in one series totalling 339 cards. The nine-card packs retailed for $2.99 each. The product was released very late in the year going live in December, 1998. This late release allowed for the inclusion of several rookies added to the 40 man roster at the end of the 1998 season. The set contains the topical subsets: Power Tools (131-160), Team Line-Up (161-190), and Rookies (191-300). Cards 131-230 were shortprinted, being seeded at a rate of 1:2 packs. In addition, 39 cards were tacked on to the end of the set (301-339) just prior to release. These cards were seeded at noticeably shorter rates (approximately 1:8 packs) than other subsets. Several key Rookie Cards, including J.D. Drew, Troy Glaus, Gabe Kapler and Ruben Mateo appear within this run of "high series" cards. Though not confirmed by the manufacturer, it is believed that card number 317 Ryan Minor was printed in a lesser amount than the other cards in the high series. All card fronts feature full-bleed color action photos. The featured player's name lines the bottom of the card with his jersey number in the lower left corner. This product was originally created by Pinnacle in their final days as a card manufacturer. After Playoff went out of business, Playoff paid for the right to distribute this product and release it late in 1998 as much of the product had already been created. Because of the especially strong selection of Rookie Cards and an large number of shortprints, this set endured to become one of the more popular and notable base brand issues of the late 1990's.

COMPLETE SET (339)	100.00	200.00
COMP.SET w/o SP's (200)	10.00	25.00
COMMON (1-130/231-300)	.10	.30
COMMON CARD (131-190)	.40	1.00
COMMON CARD (191-230)	.75	2.00
COMMON RC (191-230)	.75	2.00
COMMON CARD (301-339)	1.00	2.50
COMMON RC (301-339)	1.00	2.50
SP STATED ODDS 1:2		
SP CL: 131-230/301-339		
1 Andy Pettitte	.20	.50
2 Roberto Alomar	.20	.50
3 Randy Johnson	.30	.75
4 Manny Ramirez	.20	.50
5 Paul Molitor	.10	.30
6 Mike Mussina	.20	.50
7 Jim Thome	.20	.50
8 Tino Martinez	.20	.50
9 Gary Sheffield	.10	.30
10 Chuck Knoblauch	.10	.30
11 Bernie Williams	.20	.50
12 Tim Salmon	.20	.50
13 Sammy Sosa	.30	.75
14 Wade Boggs	.20	.50
15 Andres Galarraga	.10	.30
16 Pedro Martinez	.20	.50
17 David Justice	.10	.30
18 Chan Ho Park	.10	.30
19 Jay Buhner	.10	.30
20 Ryan Klesko	.10	.30
21 Barry Larkin	.20	.50
22 Will Clark	.20	.50
23 Raul Mondesi	.10	.30
24 Rickey Henderson	.30	.75
25 Jim Edmonds	.10	.30
26 Ken Griffey Jr.	.60	1.50
27 Frank Thomas	.30	.75
28 Cal Ripken	1.00	2.50
29 Alex Rodriguez	.50	1.25
30 Mike Piazza	.50	1.25
31 Greg Maddux	.50	1.25
32 Chipper Jones	.30	.75
33 Tony Gwynn	.40	1.00
34 Derek Jeter	.75	2.00
35 Jeff Bagwell	.20	.50
36 Juan Gonzalez	.10	.30
37 Nomar Garciaparra	.50	1.25
38 Andruw Jones	.20	.50
39 Hideo Nomo	.30	.75
40 Roger Clemens	.60	1.50
41 Mark McGwire	.75	2.00
42 Scott Rolen	.20	.50
43 Vladimir Guerrero	.30	.75
44 Barry Bonds	.75	2.00
45 Darin Erstad	.10	.30
46 Albert Belle	.10	.30
47 Kenny Lofton	.10	.30
48 Mo Vaughn	.10	.30
49 Ivan Rodriguez	.20	.50
50 Jose Cruz Jr.	.10	.30
51 Tony Clark	.10	.30
52 Larry Walker	.10	.30
53 Mark Grace	.20	.50
54 Edgar Martinez	.20	.50
55 Fred McGriff	.20	.50
56 Rafael Palmeiro	.20	.50
57 Matt Williams	.10	.30
58 Craig Biggio	.20	.50
59 Ken Caminiti	.10	.30
60 Jose Canseco	.20	.50
61 Brady Anderson	.10	.30
62 Moises Alou	.10	.30
63 Justin Thompson	.10	.30
64 John Smoltz	.20	.50
65 Carlos Delgado	.10	.30
66 J.T. Snow	.10	.30
67 Jason Giambi	.10	.30
68 Garret Anderson	.10	.30
69 Rondell White	.10	.30
70 Eric Karros	.10	.30
71 Javier Lopez	.10	.30
72 Pat Hentgen	.10	.30
73 Dante Bichette	.10	.30
74 Charles Johnson	.10	.30
75 Tom Glavine	.20	.50
76 Rusty Greer	.10	.30
77 Travis Fryman	.10	.30
78 Todd Hundley	.10	.30
79 Ray Lankford	.10	.30
80 Denny Neagle	.10	.30
81 Henry Rodriguez	.10	.30
82 Sandy Alomar Jr.	.10	.30
83 Robin Ventura	.10	.30
84 John Olerud	.10	.30
85 Omar Vizquel	.20	.50
86 Darren Dreifort	.10	.30
87 Kevin Brown	.10	.30
88 Curt Schilling	.10	.30
89 Francisco Cordova	.10	.30
90 Brad Radke	.10	.30
91 David Cone	.10	.30
92 Paul O'Neill	.20	.50
93 Vinny Castilla	.10	.30
94 Marquis Grissom	.10	.30
95 Brian L.Hunter	.10	.30
96 Kevin Appier	.10	.30
97 Bobby Bonilla	.10	.30
98 Eric Young	.10	.30
99 Jason Kendall	.10	.30
100 Shawn Green	.10	.30
101 Edgardo Alfonzo	.10	.30
102 Alan Benes	.10	.30
103 Bobby Higginson	.10	.30
104 Todd Greene	.10	.30
105 Jose Guillen	.10	.30
106 Neifi Perez	.10	.30
107 Edgar Renteria	.10	.30
108 Chris Stynes	.10	.30
109 Todd Walker	.10	.30
110 Brian Jordan	.10	.30
111 Joe Carter	.10	.30
112 Ellis Burks	.10	.30
113 Brett Tomko	.10	.30
114 Mike Cameron	.10	.30
115 Shannon Stewart	.10	.30
116 Kevin Orie	.10	.30
117 Brian Giles	.10	.30
118 Hideki Irabu	.10	.30
119 Delino DeShields	.10	.30
120 David Segui	.10	.30
121 Dustin Hermanson	.10	.30
122 Kevin Young	.10	.30
123 Jay Bell	.10	.30
124 Doug Glanville	.10	.30
125 John Roskos RC	.10	.30
126 Damon Hollins	.10	.30
127 Matt Stairs	.10	.30
128 Cliff Floyd	.10	.30
129 Derek Bell	.10	.30
130 Darryl Strawberry	.10	.30
131 Ken Griffey Jr. PT SP	2.00	5.00
132 Tim Salmon PT SP	.60	1.50
133 Manny Ramirez PT SP	.60	1.50
134 Paul Konerko PT SP	.40	1.00
135 Frank Thomas PT SP	1.00	2.50
136 Todd Helton PT SP	.60	1.50
137 Larry Walker PT SP	.40	1.00
138 Mo Vaughn PT SP	.40	1.00
139 Travis Lee PT SP	.40	1.00
140 Ivan Rodriguez PT SP	.60	1.50
141 Ben Grieve PT SP	.40	1.00
142 Brad Fullmer PT SP	.40	1.00
143 Alex Rodriguez PT SP	1.50	4.00
144 Mike Piazza PT SP	1.50	4.00
145 Greg Maddux PT SP	1.50	4.00
146 Chipper Jones PT SP	1.00	2.50
147 Kenny Lofton PT SP	.40	1.00
148 Albert Belle PT SP	.40	1.00
149 Barry Bonds PT SP	2.50	6.00
150 Vladimir Guerrero PT SP	1.00	2.50
151 Tony Gwynn PT SP	1.25	3.00
152 Derek Jeter PT SP	2.50	6.00
153 Jeff Bagwell PT SP	.60	1.50
154 Juan Gonzalez PT SP	.40	1.00
155 N.Garciaparra PT SP	1.50	4.00
156 Andruw Jones PT SP	.60	1.50
157 Hideo Nomo PT SP	1.00	2.50
158 Roger Clemens PT SP	2.00	5.00
159 Mark McGwire PT SP	2.50	6.00
160 Scott Rolen PT SP	.60	1.50
161 Travis Lee TLU SP	.40	1.00
162 Ben Grieve TLU SP	.40	1.00
163 Jose Guillen TLU SP	.40	1.00
164 Mike Piazza TLU SP	1.50	4.00
165 Kevin Appier TLU SP	.40	1.00
166 Marquis Grissom TLU SP	.40	1.00
167 Rusty Greer TLU SP	.40	1.00
168 Ken Caminiti TLU SP	.40	1.00
169 Craig Biggio TLU SP	.60	1.50
170 Ken Griffey Jr. TLU SP	2.00	5.00
171 Larry Walker TLU SP	.40	1.00
172 Barry Larkin TLU SP	.60	1.50
173 A.Galarraga TLU SP	.40	1.00
174 Wade Boggs TLU SP	.60	1.50
175 Sammy Sosa TLU SP	1.00	2.50
176 Todd Dunwoody TLU SP	.40	1.00
177 Jim Thome TLU SP	.60	1.50
178 Paul Molitor TLU SP	.40	1.00
179 Tony Clark TLU SP	.40	1.00
180 Jose Cruz Jr. TLU SP	.40	1.00
181 Darin Erstad TLU SP	.40	1.00
182 Barry Bonds TLU SP	2.50	6.00
183 Vlad.Guerrero TLU SP	1.00	2.50
184 Scott Rolen TLU SP	.60	1.50
185 Mark McGwire TLU SP	2.50	6.00
186 N.Garciaparra TLU SP	1.50	4.00
187 Gary Sheffield TLU SP	.40	1.00
188 Cal Ripken TLU SP	3.00	8.00
189 Frank Thomas TLU SP	1.00	2.50
190 Andy Pettitte TLU SP	.60	1.50
191 Paul Konerko SP	.75	2.00
192 Todd Helton SP	1.25	3.00
193 Mark Kotsay SP	.75	2.00
194 Brad Fullmer SP	.75	2.00
195 Kevin Millwood SP RC	3.00	8.00
196 David Ortiz SP	5.00	12.00
197 Kerry Wood SP	1.00	2.50
198 Miguel Tejada SP	2.00	5.00
199 Fernando Tatis SP	.75	2.00
200 Jaret Wright SP	.75	2.00
201 Ben Grieve SP	.75	2.00
202 Travis Lee SP	.75	2.00
203 Wes Helms SP	.75	2.00
204 Geoff Jenkins SP	4.00	10.00
205 Russell Branyan SP	.75	2.00
206 Esteban Yan SP RC	1.25	3.00
207 Ben Ford SP RC	.75	2.00
208 Rich Butler SP RC	.75	2.00
209 Ryan Jackson SP RC	.75	2.00
210 A.J. Hinch SP	.75	2.00
211 Magglio Ordonez RC	6.00	15.00
212 Dave Dellucci SP RC	2.00	5.00
213 Billy McMillon SP	.75	2.00
214 Mike Lowell SP RC	4.00	10.00
215 Todd Erdos SP RC	.75	2.00
216 Carlos Mendoza SP RC	.75	2.00
217 Frank Catalanotto SP RC	2.00	5.00
218 Julio Ramirez SP RC	1.25	3.00
219 John Halama SP RC	1.25	3.00
220 Wilson Delgado SP	.75	2.00
221 Mike Judd SP RC	1.25	3.00
222 Rolando Arrojo SP RC	1.25	3.00
223 Jason LaRue SP RC	1.25	3.00
224 Manny Aybar SP RC	1.25	3.00
225 Jorge Velandia SP	.75	2.00
226 Mike Kinkade SP RC	1.25	3.00
227 Carlos Lee SP RC	6.00	15.00
228 Bobby Hughes SP	.75	2.00
229 Ryan Christenson SP RC	.75	2.00
230 Masato Yoshii SP RC	1.25	3.00
231 Richard Hidalgo	.10	.30
232 Rafael Medina	.10	.30
233 Damian Jackson	.10	.30
234 Derek Lowe	.10	.30
235 Mario Valdez	.10	.30
236 Eli Marrero	.10	.30
237 Juan Encarnacion	.10	.30
238 Livan Hernandez	.10	.30
239 Bruce Chen	.10	.30
240 Eric Milton	.10	.30
241 Jason Varitek	.30	.75
242 Scott Elarton	.10	.30
243 Manuel Barrios RC	.10	.30
244 Mike Caruso	.10	.30
245 Tom Evans	.10	.30
246 Pat Cline	.10	.30
247 Matt Clement	.10	.30
248 Karim Garcia	.10	.30
249 Richie Sexson	.10	.30
250 Sidney Ponson	.10	.30
251 Randall Simon	.10	.30
252 Tony Saunders	.10	.30
253 Javier Valentin	.10	.30
254 Danny Clyburn	.10	.30
255 Michael Coleman	.10	.30
256 Hanley Frias RC	.10	.30
257 Miguel Cairo	.10	.30
258 Rob Stanifer RC	.10	.30
259 Lou Collier	.10	.30
260 Abraham Nunez	.10	.30
261 Ricky Ledee	.10	.30
262 Carl Pavano	.10	.30
263 Derrek Lee	.20	.50
264 Jeff Abbott	.10	.30
265 Bob Abreu	.10	.30
266 Bartolo Colon	.10	.30
267 Mike Drumright	.10	.30
268 Daryle Ward	.10	.30
269 Gabe Alvarez	.10	.30
270 Josh Booty	.10	.30
271 Damian Moss	.10	.30
272 Brian Rose	.10	.30
273 Jarrod Washburn	.10	.30
274 Bobby Estalella	.10	.30
275 Enrique Wilson	.10	.30
276 Derrick Gibson	.10	.30
277 Ken Cloude	.10	.30
278 Kevin Witt	.10	.30
279 Donnie Sadler	.10	.30
280 Sean Casey	.10	.30
281 Jacob Cruz	.10	.30
282 Ron Wright	.10	.30
283 Jeremi Gonzalez	.10	.30
284 Desi Relaford	.10	.30
285 Bobby Smith	.10	.30
286 Javier Vazquez	.10	.30
287 Steve Woodard	.10	.30
288 Greg Norton	.10	.30
289 Cliff Politte	.10	.30
290 Felix Heredia	.10	.30
291 Braden Looper	.10	.30
292 Felix Martinez	.10	.30
293 Brian Meadows	.10	.30
294 Edwin Diaz	.10	.30
295 Pat Watkins	.10	.30
296 Marc Pisciotta RC	.10	.30
297 Rick Gorecki	.10	.30
298 DaRond Stovall	.10	.30
299 Andy Larkin	.10	.30
300 Felix Rodriguez	.10	.30
301 Blake Stein SP	1.00	2.50
302 John Rocker SP RC	2.50	6.00
303 Justin Baughman SP RC	1.00	2.50
304 Jesus Sanchez SP RC	1.50	4.00
305 Randy Winn SP	1.00	2.50
306 Lou Merloni SP	1.00	2.50
307 Jim Parque SP RC	1.50	4.00
308 Dennis Reyes SP	1.00	2.50
309 Orlando Hernandez SP RC	4.00	10.00
310 Jason Johnson SP	1.00	2.50
311 Torii Hunter SP	1.00	2.50
312 Mike Piazza Marlins SP	4.00	10.00
313 Mike Frank SP RC	1.00	2.50
314 Troy Glaus SP RC	10.00	25.00
315 Jin Ho Cho SP RC	1.50	4.00
316 Ruben Mateo SP RC	1.00	2.50
317 Ryan Minor SP RC	1.50	4.00
318 Aramis Ramirez SP	1.00	2.50
319 Adrian Beltre SP	4.00	10.00
320 Matt Anderson SP RC	1.00	2.50
321 Gabe Kapler SP RC	2.50	6.00
322 Jeremy Giambi SP RC	1.50	4.00
323 Carlos Beltran SP	3.00	8.00
324 Dermal Brown SP	1.00	2.50
325 Ben Davis SP	1.00	2.50
326 Eric Chavez SP	1.00	2.50
327 Bobby Howry SP RC	1.00	2.50
328 Roy Halladay SP	5.00	12.00
329 George Lombard SP	1.00	2.50
330 Michael Barrett SP	1.00	2.50
331 Fernando Seguignol SP RC	1.00	2.50
332 J.D. Drew SP RC	5.00	12.00
333 Odalis Perez SP RC	4.00	10.00
334 Alex Cora SP RC	2.00	5.00
335 Placido Polanco SP RC	2.00	5.00
336 Armando Rios SP RC	1.50	4.00
337 Sammy Sosa HR SP	2.50	6.00
338 Mark McGwire HR SP	6.00	15.00
339 S.Sosa M.McGwire CL SP	4.00	10.00

1998 Leaf Rookies and Stars Longevity

*STARS 1-130/231-300: 15X TO 40X BASIC		
*RC's 1-130/231-300: 25X TO 50X BASIC		
*STARS 131-190: 3X TO 8X BASIC		
*STARS 191-230: 3X TO 8X BASIC		
*RC's 191-230: 2X TO 4X BASIC		
*STARS 301-339: 2.5X TO 6X BASIC		
*RC's 301-339: 1.5X TO 3X BASIC		
RANDOM INSERTS IN PACKS		
STATED PRINT RUN 50 SERIAL #'d SETS		
211 Magglio Ordonez	25.00	60.00
314 Troy Glaus	125.00	200.00

1998 Leaf Rookies and Stars Longevity Holographic

*SP YOUNG STARS 131-230: X TO X HI
*ROOKIES 1-130/231-300: X TO X HI
RANDOM INSERTS IN PACKS
STATED PRINT RUN 1 SERIAL #'d SET
NO PRICING DUE TO SCARCITY

1998 Leaf Rookies and Stars True Blue

COMPLETE SET (339)	1500.00	3000.00
*STARS 1-130/231-300: 6X TO 15X BASIC		
*ROOKIES 1-130/231-300: 4X TO 10X BASIC		
*STARS 131-190: 1X TO 2.5X BASIC		
*STARS 191-230: 1X TO 2.5X BASIC		
*ROOKIES 191-230: .5X TO 1.2X BASIC		
*STARS 301-339: .75X TO 2X BASIC		
*ROOKIES 301-339: .4X TO 1X BASIC		
RANDOM INSERTS IN PACKS		
STATED PRINT RUN 500 SETS		

1998 Leaf Rookies and Stars Crosstraining

COMPLETE SET (10)	10.00	25.00
RANDOM INSERTS IN PACKS		
STATED PRINT RUN 1000 SERIAL #'d SETS		
1 Kenny Lofton	.75	2.00
2 Ken Griffey Jr.	4.00	10.00
3 Alex Rodriguez	2.50	6.00
4 Greg Maddux	2.50	6.00
5 Barry Bonds	3.00	8.00
6 Ivan Rodriguez	1.25	3.00
7 Chipper Jones	2.00	5.00
8 Jeff Bagwell	1.25	3.00
9 Nomar Garciaparra	1.25	3.00
10 Derek Jeter	5.00	12.00

1998 Leaf Rookies and Stars Crusade Update Green

COMPLETE SET (30)	150.00	300.00
RANDOM INSERTS IN PACKS		
GREEN PRINT RUN 250 SERIAL #'d SETS		
101 Richard Hidalgo	4.00	10.00
102 Paul Konerko	6.00	15.00
103 Miguel Tejada	10.00	25.00
104 Fernando Tatis	4.00	10.00
105 Travis Lee	4.00	10.00
106 Wes Helms	4.00	10.00
107 Rich Butler	4.00	10.00
108 Mark Kotsay	6.00	15.00
109 Eli Marrero	4.00	10.00
110 David Ortiz	12.50	30.00
111 Juan Encarnacion	4.00	10.00
112 Jaret Wright	4.00	10.00
113 Livan Hernandez	6.00	15.00
114 Ron Wright	4.00	10.00
115 Ryan Christenson	4.00	10.00
116 Eric Milton	4.00	10.00
117 Brad Fullmer	4.00	10.00
118 Karim Garcia	4.00	10.00
119 Abraham Nunez	4.00	10.00
120 Ricky Ledee	4.00	10.00
121 Carl Pavano	6.00	15.00
122 Derrek Lee	8.00	20.00
123 A.J. Hinch	4.00	10.00
124 Brian Rose	4.00	10.00
125 Bobby Estalella	4.00	10.00
126 Kevin Millwood	10.00	25.00
127 Kerry Wood	6.00	15.00
128 Sean Casey	6.00	15.00
129 Russell Branyan	4.00	10.00
130 Magglio Ordonez	15.00	40.00

1998 Leaf Rookies and Stars Crusade Update Purple

*PURPLE: .75X TO 2X GREEN
*PURPLE: .75X TO 2X GREEN RC'S
RANDOM INSERTS IN PACKS
STATED PRINT RUN 100 SERIAL #'d SETS

1998 Leaf Rookies and Stars Crusade Update Red

RANDOM INSERTS IN PACKS
STATED PRINT RUN 25 SERIAL #'d SETS
NO PRICING DUE TO SCARCITY

1998 Leaf Rookies and Stars Extreme Measures

COMPLETE SET (10)	60.00	120.00
RANDOM INSERTS IN PACKS		
PRINT RUNS B/WN 280-989 COPIES PER		
1 Ken Griffey Jr./944	8.00	20.00
2 Frank Thomas/653	4.00	10.00
3 Tony Gwynn/628	5.00	12.00
4 Mark McGwire/942	10.00	25.00
5 Larry Walker/280	2.50	6.00
6 Mike Piazza/960	6.00	15.00
7 Roger Clemens/708	8.00	20.00
8 Greg Maddux/980	6.00	15.00
9 Jeff Bagwell/873	2.50	6.00
10 Nomar Garciaparra/989	6.00	15.00

1998 Leaf Rookies and Stars Extreme Measures Die Cuts

RANDOM INSERTS IN PACKS		
PRINT RUNS B/WN 11-720 COPIES PER		
NO PRICING ON 11 OR LESS		
1 Ken Griffey Jr./56	25.00	60.00
2 Frank Thomas/347	6.00	15.00
3 Tony Gwynn/372	6.00	15.00
4 Mark McGwire/58	40.00	80.00
5 Larry Walker/720	4.00	10.00
6 Mike Piazza/40	20.00	50.00
7 Roger Clemens/292	10.00	25.00
8 Greg Maddux/20		
9 Jeff Bagwell/127	8.00	20.00
10 Nomar Garciaparra/11		

1998 Leaf Rookies and Stars Freshman Orientation Samples

COMPLETE SET (20)	15.00	40.00
1 Todd Helton	2.00	5.00
2 Ben Grieve	.40	1.00
3 Travis Lee	.40	1.00
4 Paul Konerko	1.50	4.00
5 Jaret Wright	.40	1.00
6 Livan Hernandez	.75	2.00
7 Brad Fullmer	.40	1.00
8 Carl Pavano	.40	1.00
9 Richard Hidalgo	.40	1.00
10 Miguel Tejada	1.50	4.00
11 Mark Kotsay	.40	1.00
12 David Ortiz	1.50	4.00
13 Juan Encarnacion	.60	1.50
14 Fernando Tatis	.60	1.50
15 Kevin Millwood	2.00	5.00
16 Kerry Wood	1.50	4.00
17 Magglio Ordonez	4.00	10.00
18 Derrek Lee	1.50	4.00
19 Jose Cruz Jr.	.60	1.50
20 A.J. Hinch	.40	1.00

1998 Leaf Rookies and Stars Freshman Orientation

COMPLETE SET (20)	10.00	25.00
RANDOM INSERTS IN PACKS		
STATED PRINT RUN 5000 SERIAL #'d SETS		
1 Todd Helton	.75	2.00
2 Ben Grieve	.40	1.00
3 Travis Lee	.40	1.00
4 Paul Konerko	.60	1.50
5 Jaret Wright	.40	1.00
6 Livan Hernandez	.60	1.50
7 Brad Fullmer	.40	1.00
8 Carl Pavano	.60	1.50
9 Richard Hidalgo	.40	1.00
10 Miguel Tejada	1.25	3.00
11 Mark Kotsay	.60	1.50
12 David Ortiz	1.50	4.00
13 Juan Encarnacion	.40	1.00
14 Fernando Tatis	.40	1.00
15 Kevin Millwood	1.25	3.00
16 Kerry Wood	.60	1.50
17 Magglio Ordonez	1.50	4.00
18 Derrek Lee	.75	2.00
19 Jose Cruz Jr.	.40	1.00
20 A.J. Hinch	.40	1.00

1998 Leaf Rookies and Stars Great American Heroes Samples

COMPLETE SET (20)	30.00	80.00
1 Frank Thomas	1.00	2.50
2 Cal Ripken	4.00	10.00
3 Ken Griffey Jr.	2.50	6.00
4 Alex Rodriguez	2.50	6.00
5 Greg Maddux	2.00	5.00
6 Mike Piazza	2.50	6.00
7 Chipper Jones	2.00	5.00
8 Tony Gwynn	1.50	4.00
9 Jeff Bagwell	1.00	2.50
10 Juan Gonzalez	.75	2.00
11 Hideo Nomo	2.00	5.00
12 Roger Clemens	2.00	5.00
13 Mark McGwire	2.50	6.00
14 Barry Bonds	2.00	5.00
15 Kenny Lofton	.40	1.00
16 Larry Walker	.30	.75
17 Paul Molitor	1.00	2.50
18 Wade Boggs	1.00	2.50
19 Barry Larkin	.60	1.50
20 Andres Galarraga	.40	1.00

1998 Leaf Rookies and Stars Great American Heroes

COMPLETE SET (20)	75.00	150.00
RANDOM INSERTS IN PACKS		
STATED PRINT RUN 2500 SERIAL #'d SETS		
THREE DIFF.PIAZZA VERSIONS EXIST		
PIAZZA PRINT RUNS: 2500 OF EACH		
ALL THREE PIAZZA'S VALUED EQUALLY		
1 Frank Thomas	2.50	6.00
2 Cal Ripken	8.00	20.00
3 Ken Griffey Jr.	5.00	12.00
4 Alex Rodriguez	4.00	10.00
5 Greg Maddux	4.00	10.00
6 Mike Piazza	4.00	10.00
6B Mike Piazza Marlins	4.00	10.00
6C Mike Piazza Mets	4.00	10.00
7 Chipper Jones	2.50	6.00
8 Tony Gwynn	3.00	8.00
9 Jeff Bagwell	1.50	4.00
10 Juan Gonzalez	1.00	2.50
11 Hideo Nomo	2.50	6.00
12 Roger Clemens	5.00	12.00
13 Mark McGwire	6.00	15.00
14 Barry Bonds	6.00	15.00
15 Kenny Lofton	1.00	2.50
16 Larry Walker	1.00	2.50
17 Paul Molitor	1.00	2.50
18 Wade Boggs	1.50	4.00
19 Barry Larkin	1.50	4.00
20 Andres Galarraga	1.00	2.50

1998 Leaf Rookies and Stars Greatest Hits

COMPLETE SET (20)	60.00	120.00
RANDOM INSERTS IN PACKS		
STATED PRINT RUN 2500 SERIAL #'d SETS		
1 Ken Griffey Jr.	5.00	12.00
2 Frank Thomas	2.50	6.00
3 Cal Ripken	8.00	20.00
4 Alex Rodriguez	4.00	10.00
5 Ben Grieve	2.50	6.00
6 Mike Piazza	4.00	10.00
7 Chipper Jones	2.50	6.00
8 Tony Gwynn	3.00	8.00
9 Derek Jeter	6.00	15.00
10 Jeff Bagwell	1.50	4.00
11 Tino Martinez	1.50	4.00
12 Juan Gonzalez	1.00	2.50
13 Nomar Garciaparra	4.00	10.00
14 Mark McGwire	6.00	15.00
15 Scott Rolen	1.50	4.00
16 David Justice	1.00	2.50
17 Darin Erstad	1.00	2.50
18 Mo Vaughn	1.00	2.50
19 Ivan Rodriguez	1.50	4.00
20 Travis Lee	1.50	4.00

1998 Leaf Rookies and Stars Home Run Derby

COMPLETE SET (20)	40.00	100.00
RANDOM INSERTS IN PACKS		
STATED PRINT RUN 2500 SERIAL #'d SETS		
1 Tino Martinez	1.50	4.00
2 Jim Thome	1.50	4.00
3 Larry Walker	1.00	2.50
4 Tony Clark	1.00	2.50
5 Jose Cruz Jr.	1.00	2.50
6 Barry Bonds	6.00	15.00
7 Scott Rolen	1.50	4.00
8 Paul Konerko	1.00	2.50
9 Travis Lee	1.00	2.50
10 Todd Helton	2.50	6.00
11 Mark McGwire	6.00	15.00
12 Andruw Jones	1.50	4.00
13 Nomar Garciaparra	4.00	10.00
14 Juan Gonzalez	1.00	2.50
15 Jeff Bagwell	1.50	4.00
16 Chipper Jones	2.50	6.00
17 Mike Piazza	4.00	10.00
18 Frank Thomas	2.50	6.00
19 Ken Griffey Jr.	5.00	12.00
20 Albert Belle	1.00	2.50

1998 Leaf Rookies and Stars Leaf MVP's

COMPLETE SET (20)	30.00	80.00
RANDOM INSERTS IN PACKS		
STATED PRINT RUN 5000 SERIAL #'d SETS		
*PENNANT ED: 1.5X TO 4X BASIC LEAF MVP		
PENNANT ED.1ST 500 SERIAL #'d SETS		
RANDOM INSERTS IN PACKS		
1 Frank Thomas	1.50	4.00
2 Chuck Knoblauch	.60	1.50
3 Cal Ripken	5.00	12.00
4 Alex Rodriguez	2.50	6.00
5 Ivan Rodriguez	1.00	2.50
6 Albert Belle	.60	1.50
7 Ken Griffey Jr.	3.00	8.00
8 Juan Gonzalez	.60	1.50
9 Roger Clemens	3.00	8.00
10 Mo Vaughn	.60	1.50
11 Jeff Bagwell	1.00	2.50
12 Craig Biggio	1.00	2.50
13 Chipper Jones	1.50	4.00
14 Barry Larkin	1.00	2.50
15 Mike Piazza	2.50	6.00
16 Barry Bonds	4.00	10.00
17 Andruw Jones	1.00	2.50
18 Tony Gwynn	2.00	5.00
19 Greg Maddux	2.50	6.00
20 Mark McGwire	4.00	10.00

1998 Leaf Rookies and Stars Major League Hard Drives Samples

COMPLETE SET (20)	25.00	60.00
1 Jeff Bagwell	1.00	2.50
2 Juan Gonzalez	.75	2.00
3 Nomar Garciaparra	2.50	6.00
4 Ken Griffey Jr.	2.50	6.00
5 Frank Thomas	2.50	6.00
6 Cal Ripken	4.00	10.00
7 Alex Rodriguez	2.50	6.00
8 Mike Piazza	2.50	6.00
9 Chipper Jones	2.00	5.00
10 Tony Gwynn	1.50	4.00
11 Derek Jeter	4.00	10.00
12 Mo Vaughn	.30	.75
13 Ben Grieve	.20	.50
14 Manny Ramirez	1.00	2.50
15 Vladimir Guerrero	1.25	3.00
16 Scott Rolen	.60	1.50
17 Darin Erstad	.60	1.50
18 Kenny Lofton	.40	1.00
19 Brad Fullmer	.20	.50
20 David Justice	.40	1.00

1998 Leaf Rookies and Stars Major League Hard Drives

COMPLETE SET (20)	75.00	150.00
RANDOM INSERTS IN PACKS		
STATED PRINT RUN 2500 SERIAL #'d SETS		
THREE DIFF.PIAZZA VERSIONS EXIST		
PIAZZA PRINT RUNS: 2500 OF EACH		
ALL THREE PIAZZA'S VALUED EQUALLY		
1 Jeff Bagwell	1.50	4.00
2 Juan Gonzalez	1.00	2.50
3 Nomar Garciaparra	4.00	10.00
4 Ken Griffey Jr.	5.00	12.00
5 Frank Thomas	2.50	6.00
6 Cal Ripken	8.00	20.00
7 Alex Rodriguez	4.00	10.00
8 Mike Piazza	4.00	10.00
8B Mike Piazza Marlins	4.00	10.00
8C Mike Piazza Mets	4.00	10.00
9 Chipper Jones	2.50	6.00
10 Tony Gwynn	3.00	8.00
11 Derek Jeter	6.00	15.00
12 Mo Vaughn	1.00	2.50
13 Ben Grieve	2.50	6.00
14 Manny Ramirez	1.50	4.00
15 Vladimir Guerrero	2.50	6.00
16 Scott Rolen	1.50	4.00
17 Darin Erstad	1.00	2.50
18 Kenny Lofton	1.00	2.50
19 Brad Fullmer	1.00	2.50
20 David Justice	1.00	2.50

1998 Leaf Rookies and Stars Standing Ovations Samples

COMPLETE SET (10)	20.00	50.00
1 Barry Bonds	2.00	5.00
2 Mark McGwire	2.00	5.00
3 Ken Griffey Jr.	2.50	6.00
4 Frank Thomas	1.00	2.50
5 Tony Gwynn	1.50	4.00
6 Cal Ripken	4.00	10.00
7 Greg Maddux	2.50	6.00
8 Roger Clemens	2.00	5.00
9 Paul Molitor	1.00	2.50
10 Ivan Rodriguez	1.00	2.50

1998 Leaf Rookies and Stars Standing Ovations

COMPLETE SET (10)	10.00	25.00
RANDOM INSERTS IN PACKS		
STATED PRINT RUN 5000 SERIAL #'d SETS		
1 Barry Bonds	1.50	4.00

2 Mark McGwire 1.50 4.00
3 Ken Griffey Jr. 2.00 5.00
4 Frank Thomas 1.00 2.50
5 Tony Gwynn 1.00 2.50
6 Cal Ripken 3.00 8.00
7 Greg Maddux 1.25 3.00
8 Roger Clemens 1.25 3.00
9 Paul Molitor 1.00 2.50
10 Ivan Rodriguez .60 1.50

1998 Leaf Rookies and Stars Ticket Masters

COMPLETE SET (20) 75.00 150.00
STATED PRINT RUN 2500 SERIAL #'d SETS
*DIE CUTS: 1.25X TO 3X BASIC TICKET
DIE CUTS 1ST 250 SERIAL #'d SETS
RANDOM INSERTS IN PACKS
1 K.Griffey Jr. A.Rodriguez 6.00 15.00
2 F.Thomas A.Belle 3.00 8.00
3 C.Ripken R.Alomar 10.00 25.00
4 G.Maddux C.Jones 5.00 12.00
5 T.Gwynn K.Caminiti 4.00 10.00
6 D.Jeter A.Pettitte 8.00 20.00
7 J.Bagwell C.Biggio 2.00 5.00
8 J.Gonzalez I.Rodriguez 2.00 5.00
9 N.Garciaparra M.Vaughn 5.00 12.00
10 V.Guerrero B.Fullmer 3.00 8.00
11 A.Jones A.Galarraga 2.00 5.00
12 T.Martinez C.Knoblauch 2.00 5.00
13 R.Mondesi P.Konerko 1.25 3.00
14 R.Clemens J.Cruz Jr. 6.00 15.00
15 M.McGwire B.Jordan 8.00 20.00
16 K.Lofton M.Ramirez 2.00 5.00
17 L.Walker T.Helton 1.25 3.00
18 D.Erstad T.Salmon 1.25 3.00
19 T.Lee M.Williams 1.25 3.00
20 B.Grieve J.Giambi 1.25 3.00

2001 Leaf Rookies and Stars Samples

*SINGLES: 1.5X TO 4X BASIC CARDS

2001 Leaf Rookies and Stars

COMP.SET w/o SP'S (100) 8.00 20.00
COMMON CARD (1-100) .10 .30
COMMON CARD (101-200) 1.25 3.00
101-200 STATED ODDS 1:4
COMMON CARD (201-300) 2.00 5.00
201-300 STATED ODDS 1:24
1 Alex Rodriguez .40 1.00
2 Derek Jeter .75 2.00
3 Aramis Ramirez .10 .30
4 Cliff Floyd .10 .30
5 Nomar Garciaparra .50 1.25
6 Craig Biggio .20 .50
7 Ivan Rodriguez .20 .50
8 Cal Ripken 1.00 2.50
9 Fred McGriff .20 .50
10 Chipper Jones .30 .75
11 Roberto Alomar .20 .50
12 Moises Alou .10 .30
13 Freddy Garcia .10 .30
14 Bobby Abreu .10 .30
15 Shawn Green .10 .30
16 Jason Giambi .10 .30
17 Todd Helton .20 .50
18 Robert Fick .10 .30
19 Tony Gwynn .40 1.00
20 Luis Gonzalez .10 .30
21 Sean Casey .10 .30
22 Roger Clemens .60 1.50
23 Brian Giles .10 .30
24 Manny Ramirez Sox .20 .50
25 Barry Bonds .75 2.00
26 Richard Hidalgo .10 .30
27 Vladimir Guerrero .30 .75
28 Kevin Brown .10 .30
29 Mike Sweeney .10 .30
30 Ken Griffey Jr. .60 1.50
31 Mike Piazza .50 1.25
32 Richie Sexson .10 .30
33 Matt Morris .10 .30
34 Jorge Posada .20 .50
35 Eric Chavez .10 .30
36 Mark Buehrle .20 .50
37 Jeff Bagwell .20 .50
38 Curt Schilling .10 .30
39 Bartolo Colon .10 .30
40 Mark Quinn .10 .30
41 Tony Clark .10 .30
42 Brad Radke .10 .30
43 Gary Sheffield .10 .30
44 Doug Mientkiewicz .10 .30
45 Pedro Martinez .20 .50
46 Carlos Lee .10 .30
47 Troy Glaus .10 .30
48 Preston Wilson .10 .30
49 Phil Nevin .10 .30
50 Chan Ho Park .10 .30
51 Randy Johnson .30 .75
52 Jermaine Dye .10 .30
53 Terrence Long .10 .30
54 Joe Mays .10 .30
55 Scott Rolen .20 .50
56 Miguel Tejada .10 .30
57 Jim Thome .20 .50
58 Jose Vidro .10 .30
59 Gabe Kapler .10 .30
60 Darin Erstad .10 .30
61 Jim Edmonds .10 .30
62 Jarrod Washburn .10 .30
63 Tom Glavine .20 .50
64 Adrian Beltre .10 .30
65 Sammy Sosa .30 .75
66 Juan Gonzalez .10 .30
67 Rafael Furcal .10 .30
68 Mike Mussina .20 .50
69 Mark McGwire .75 2.00
70 Ryan Klesko .10 .30
71 Raul Mondesi .10 .30
72 Trot Nixon .10 .30
73 Barry Larkin .20 .50
74 Rafael Palmeiro .20 .50
75 Mark Mulder .10 .30
76 Carlos Delgado .10 .30
77 Mike Hampton .10 .30
78 Carl Everett .10 .30
79 Paul Konerko .10 .30
80 Larry Walker .10 .30
81 Kerry Wood .10 .30
82 Frank Thomas .30 .75
83 Andruw Jones .20 .50
84 Eric Milton .10 .30
85 Ben Grieve .10 .30
86 Carlos Beltran .10 .30
87 Tim Hudson .10 .30
88 Hideo Nomo .30 .75
89 Greg Maddux .50 1.25
90 Edgar Martinez .20 .50
91 Lance Berkman .10 .30
92 Pat Burrell .10 .30
93 Jeff Kent .10 .30
94 Magglio Ordonez .10 .30
95 Cristian Guzman .10 .30
96 Jose Canseco .20 .50
97 J.D. Drew .10 .30
98 Bernie Williams .20 .50
99 Kazuhiro Sasaki .10 .30
100 Rickey Henderson .30 .75
101 Wilson Guzman RC 1.25 3.00
102 Nick Neugebauer 1.25 3.00
103 Lance Davis RC 1.25 3.00
104 Felipe Lopez 1.25 3.00
105 Toby Hall 1.25 3.00
106 Jack Cust 1.25 3.00
107 Jason Karnuth RC 1.25 3.00
108 Bart Miadich RC 1.25 3.00
109 Brian Roberts RC 3.00 8.00
110 Brandon Larson RC 1.25 3.00
111 Sean Douglass RC 1.25 3.00
112 Joe Crede 2.00 5.00
113 Tim Redding 1.25 3.00
114 Adam Johnson 1.25 3.00
115 Marcus Giles 1.25 3.00
116 Jose Ortiz 1.25 3.00
117 Jose Mieses RC 1.25 3.00
118 Nick Maness RC 1.25 3.00
119 Les Walrond RC 1.25 3.00
120 Travis Phelps RC 1.25 3.00
121 Troy Mattes RC 1.25 3.00
122 Carlos Garcia RC 1.25 3.00
123 Bill Ortega RC 1.25 3.00
124 Gene Altman RC 1.25 3.00
125 Nate Frese RC 1.25 3.00
126 Alfonso Soriano 2.00 5.00
127 Jose Nunez RC 1.25 3.00
128 Bob File RC 1.25 3.00
129 Dan Wright 1.25 3.00
130 Nick Johnson 1.25 3.00
131 Brent Abernathy 1.25 3.00
132 Steve Green RC 1.25 3.00
133 Billy Sylvester RC 1.25 3.00
134 Scott MacRae RC 1.25 3.00
135 Kris Keller RC 1.25 3.00
136 Scott Stewart RC 1.25 3.00
137 Henry Mateo RC 1.25 3.00
138 Timo Perez 1.25 3.00
139 Nate Teut RC 1.25 3.00
140 Jason Michaels RC 1.25 3.00
141 Junior Spivey RC 2.00 5.00
142 Carlos Pena 1.25 3.00
143 Wilmy Caceres RC 1.25 3.00
144 David Lundquist 1.25 3.00
145 Jack Wilson RC 2.00 5.00
146 Jeremy Fikac RC 1.25 3.00
147 Alex Escobar 1.25 3.00
148 Abraham Nunez 1.25 3.00
149 Xavier Nady 1.25 3.00
150 Michael Cuddyer 1.25 3.00
151 Greg Miller RC 1.25 3.00
152 Eric Munson 1.25 3.00
153 Aubrey Huff 1.25 3.00
154 Tim Christman RC 1.25 3.00
155 Erick Almonte RC 1.25 3.00
156 Mike Penney RC 1.25 3.00
157 Delvin James RC 1.25 3.00
158 Ben Sheets 2.00 5.00
159 Jason Hart 1.25 3.00
160 Jose Acevedo RC 1.25 3.00
161 Will Ohman RC 1.25 3.00
162 Erik Hiljus RC 1.25 3.00
163 Juan Moreno RC 1.25 3.00
164 Mike Koplove RC 1.25 3.00
165 Pedro Santana RC 1.25 3.00
166 Jimmy Rollins 1.25 3.00
167 Matt White RC 1.25 3.00
168 Cesar Crespo RC 1.25 3.00
169 Carlos Hernandez 1.25 3.00
170 Chris George 1.25 3.00
171 Brad Voyles RC 1.25 3.00
172 Luis Pineda RC 1.25 3.00
173 Carlos Zambrano 2.00 5.00
174 Nate Cornejo 1.25 3.00
175 Jason Smith RC 1.25 3.00
176 Craig Monroe RC 3.00 8.00
177 Cody Ransom RC 1.25 3.00
178 John Grabow RC 1.25 3.00
179 Pedro Feliz 1.25 3.00
180 Jeremy Owens RC 1.25 3.00
181 Kurt Ainsworth 1.25 3.00
182 Luis Lopez 1.25 3.00
183 Stubby Clapp RC 1.25 3.00
184 Ryan Freel RC 3.00 8.00
185 Duaner Sanchez RC 1.25 3.00
186 Jason Jennings 1.25 3.00
187 Kyle Lohse RC 2.00 5.00
188 Jerrod Riggan RC 1.25 3.00
189 Joe Beimel RC 1.25 3.00
190 Nick Punto RC 1.25 3.00
191 Willie Harris RC 1.25 3.00
192 Ryan Jensen RC 1.25 3.00
193 Adam Pettyjohn RC 1.25 3.00
194 Donaldo Mendez RC 1.25 3.00
195 Bret Prinz RC 1.25 3.00
196 Paul Phillips RC 1.25 3.00
197 Brian Lawrence RC 1.25 3.00
198 Cesar Izturis 1.25 3.00
199 Blaine Neal RC 1.25 3.00
200 Josh Fogg RC 2.00 5.00
201 Josh Towers RC 3.00 8.00
202 Tim Spooneybarger RC 2.00 5.00
203 Michael Rivera RC 2.00 5.00
204 Juan Cruz RC 2.00 5.00
205 Albert Pujols RC 60.00 150.00
206 Josh Beckett 3.00 8.00
207 Roy Oswalt 3.00 8.00
208 Elpidio Guzman RC 2.00 5.00
209 Horacio Ramirez RC 3.00 8.00
210 Corey Patterson 2.00 5.00
211 Geronimo Gil RC 2.00 5.00
212 Jay Gibbons RC 3.00 8.00
213 Orlando Woodards RC 2.00 5.00
214 David Espinosa 2.00 5.00
215 Angel Berroa RC 3.00 8.00
216 Brandon Duckworth RC 2.00 5.00
217 Brian Reith RC 2.00 5.00
218 David Brous RC 2.00 5.00
219 Bud Smith RC 2.00 5.00
220 Ramon Vazquez RC 2.00 5.00
221 Mark Teixeira RC 10.00 25.00
222 Justin Atchley RC 2.00 5.00
223 Tony Cogan RC 2.00 5.00
224 Grant Balfour RC 2.00 5.00
225 Ricardo Rodriguez RC 2.00 5.00
226 Brian Rogers RC 2.00 5.00
227 Adam Dunn 3.00 8.00
228 Wilson Betemit RC 3.00 8.00
229 Juan Diaz RC 2.00 5.00
230 Jackson Melian RC 2.00 5.00
231 Claudio Vargas RC 2.00 5.00
232 Wilkin Ruan RC 2.00 5.00
233 Justin Duchscherer RC 2.00 5.00
234 Kevin Olsen RC 2.00 5.00
235 Tony Fiore RC 2.00 5.00
236 Jeremy Affeldt RC 2.00 5.00
237 Mike Maroth RC 2.00 5.00
238 C.C. Sabathia 2.00 5.00
239 Cory Aldridge RC 2.00 5.00
240 Zach Day RC 2.00 5.00
241 Brett Jodie RC 2.00 5.00
242 Winston Abreu RC 2.00 5.00
243 Travis Hafner RC 10.00 25.00
244 Joe Kennedy RC 2.00 5.00
245 Rick Bauer RC 2.00 5.00
246 Mike Young 3.00 8.00
247 Ken Vining RC 2.00 5.00
248 Doug Nickle RC 2.00 5.00
249 Pablo Ozuna 2.00 5.00
250 Dustan Mohr RC 2.00 5.00
251 Ichiro Suzuki RC 15.00 40.00
252 Ryan Drese RC 3.00 8.00
253 Morgan Ensberg RC 3.00 8.00
254 George Perez RC 2.00 5.00
255 Roy Smith RC 2.00 5.00
256 Juan Uribe RC 3.00 8.00
257 Dewon Brazelton RC 2.00 5.00
258 Endy Chavez RC 2.00 5.00
259 Kris Foster RC 2.00 5.00
260 Eric Knott RC 2.00 5.00
261 Corky Miller RC 2.00 5.00
262 Larry Bigbie 2.00 5.00
263 Andres Torres RC 2.00 5.00
264 Adrian Hernandez RC 2.00 5.00
265 Johnny Estrada RC 3.00 8.00
266 David Williams RC 2.00 5.00
267 Steve Lomasney 2.00 5.00
268 Victor Zambrano RC 3.00 8.00
269 Keith Ginter 2.00 5.00
270 Casey Fossum RC 2.00 5.00
271 Josue Perez RC 2.00 5.00
272 Josh Phelps 2.00 5.00
273 Mark Prior RC 10.00 25.00
274 Brandon Berger RC 2.00 5.00
275 Scott Podsednik RC 5.00 12.00
276 Jorge Julio RC 2.00 5.00
277 Esix Snead RC 2.00 5.00
278 Brandon Knight RC 2.00 5.00
279 Saul Rivera RC 2.00 5.00
280 Benito Baez RC 2.00 5.00
281 Rob MacKowiak RC 3.00 8.00
282 Eric Hinske RC 3.00 8.00
283 Juan Rivera 2.00 5.00
284 Kevin Joseph RC 2.00 5.00
285 Juan A. Pena RC 2.00 5.00
286 Brandon Lyon RC 2.00 5.00
287 Adam Everett 2.00 5.00
288 Eric Valent 2.00 5.00
289 Ken Harvey 2.00 5.00
290 Bert Snow RC 2.00 5.00
291 Wily Mo Pena 2.00 5.00
292 Rafael Soriano RC 2.00 5.00
293 Carlos Valderrama RC 2.00 5.00
294 Christian Parker RC 2.00 5.00
295 Tsuyoshi Shinjo RC 3.00 8.00
296 Martin Vargas RC 2.00 5.00
297 Luke Hudson RC 2.00 5.00
298 Dee Brown 2.00 5.00
299 Alexis Gomez RC 2.00 5.00
300 Angel Santos RC 2.00 5.00

2001 Leaf Rookies and Stars Autographs

PRINT RUNS B/WN 50-250 COPIES PER
CARDS ARE NOT SERIAL-NUMBERED
PRINT RUN INFO PROVIDED BY DONRUSS
SKIP-NUMBERED 76-CARD SET
107 Jason Karnuth/250 * 4.00 10.00
110 Brandon Larson/100 * 6.00 15.00
117 Jose Mieses/250 * 4.00 10.00
118 Nick Maness/250 * 4.00 10.00
119 Les Walrond/250 * 4.00 10.00
122 Carlos Garcia/250 * 4.00 10.00
123 Bill Ortega/250 * 4.00 10.00
124 Gene Altman/250 * 4.00 10.00
125 Nate Frese/250 * 4.00 10.00
130 Nick Johnson/100 * 10.00 25.00
133 Billy Sylvester/250 * 4.00 10.00
135 Kris Keller/250 * 4.00 10.00
139 Nate Teut/250 * 4.00 10.00
140 Jason Michaels/250 * 4.00 10.00
143 Wilmy Caceres/250 * 4.00 10.00
145 Jack Wilson/100 * 10.00 25.00
151 Greg Miller/250 * 4.00 10.00
155 Erick Almonte/250 * 4.00 10.00
156 Mike Penney/250 * 4.00 10.00
157 Delvin James/250 * 4.00 10.00
161 Will Ohman/250 * 4.00 10.00
167 Matt White/250 * 4.00 10.00
180 Jeremy Owens/250 * 4.00 10.00
184 Ryan Freel/250 * 10.00 25.00
185 Duaner Sanchez/250 * 4.00 10.00
193 Adam Pettyjohn/100 * 6.00 15.00
194 Donaldo Mendez/100 * 6.00 15.00
196 Paul Phillips/250 * 4.00 10.00
197 Brian Lawrence/100 * 6.00 15.00
199 Blaine Neal/250 * 4.00 10.00
201 Josh Towers/100 * 6.00 15.00
203 Michael Rivera/250 * 4.00 10.00
204 Juan Cruz/100 * 6.00 15.00
207 Roy Oswalt/50 * 30.00 60.00
208 Elpidio Guzman/100 * 6.00 15.00
209 Horacio Ramirez/250 * 6.00 15.00
210 Corey Patterson/50 * 10.00 25.00
211 Geronimo Gil/250 * 4.00 10.00
212 Jay Gibbons/100 * 10.00 25.00
213 Orlando Woodards/250 * 4.00 10.00
215 Angel Berroa/100 * 10.00 25.00
216 Brandon Duckworth/100 * 6.00 15.00
218 David Brous/250 * 4.00 10.00
219 Bud Smith/50 * 10.00 25.00
221 Mark Teixeira/100 * 12.00 30.00
223 Tony Cogan/250 * 4.00 10.00
225 Ricardo Rodriguez/250 * 4.00 10.00
226 Brian Rogers/250 * 4.00 10.00
227 Adam Dunn/50 * 20.00 50.00
228 Wilson Betemit/100 * 15.00 40.00
231 Claudio Vargas/250 * 4.00 10.00
232 Wilkin Ruan/250 * 4.00 10.00
234 Kevin Olsen/250 * 4.00 10.00
236 Jeremy Affeldt/250 * 6.00 15.00
237 Mike Maroth/250 * 6.00 15.00
238 C.C. Sabathia/50 * 10.00 25.00
239 Cory Aldridge/250 * 4.00 10.00
240 Zach Day/250 * 4.00 10.00
243 Travis Hafner/250 * 10.00 25.00
244 Joe Kennedy/100 * 6.00 15.00
254 George Perez/250 * 4.00 10.00
256 Juan Uribe/250 * 6.00 15.00
257 Dewon Brazelton/100 * 6.00 15.00
261 Corky Miller/100 * 6.00 15.00
263 Andres Torres/100 * 6.00 15.00
265 Johnny Estrada/100 * 6.00 15.00
266 David Williams/250 * 4.00 10.00
270 Casey Fossum/250 * 4.00 10.00
273 Mark Prior/100 * 125.00 200.00
274 Brandon Berger/250 * 4.00 10.00
277 Esix Snead/250 * 4.00 10.00
282 Eric Hinske/250 * 6.00 15.00
292 Rafael Soriano/250 * 6.00 15.00
293 Carlos Valderrama/250 * 4.00 10.00
299 Alexis Gomez/250 * 4.00 10.00

2001 Leaf Rookies and Stars Longevity

*LONGEVITY: 1-100: 12.5X TO 30X BASIC
1-100 PRINT RUN 50 SERIAL #'d SETS
101-300 PRINT RUN 25 SERIAL #'d SETS
101-300 NO PRICING DUE TO SCARCITY

2001 Leaf Rookies and Stars Dress for Success

STATED ODDS 1:96
DFS1 Cal Ripken 12.00 30.00
DFS2 Mike Piazza 4.00 10.00
DFS3 Barry Bonds 6.00 15.00
DFS4 Frank Thomas 4.00 10.00
DFS5 Nomar Garciaparra 2.50 6.00
DFS6 Richie Sexson 1.50 4.00
DFS7 Brian Giles 1.50 4.00
DFS8 Todd Helton 2.50 6.00
DFS9 Ivan Rodriguez 2.50 6.00
DFS10 Andruw Jones 2.50 6.00
DFS11 Juan Gonzalez 1.50 4.00
DFS12 Vladimir Guerrero 4.00 10.00
DFS13 Greg Maddux 6.00 15.00
DFS14 Tony Gwynn 4.00 10.00
DFS15 Randy Johnson 4.00 10.00
DFS16 Jeff Bagwell 2.50 6.00
DFS17 Kerry Wood SP 1.50 4.00
DFS18 Roberto Alomar 2.50 6.00
DFS19 Chipper Jones 4.00 10.00
DFS20 Pedro Martinez 2.50 6.00
DFS21 Shawn Green 1.50 4.00
DFS22 Magglio Ordonez 1.50 4.00
DFS23 Darin Erstad SP 1.50 4.00
DFS24 Rafael Palmeiro SP 2.50 6.00
DFS25 Edgar Martinez 2.50 6.00

2001 Leaf Rookies and Stars Dress for Success Prime Cuts

*PRIME CUTS: 1.25X TO 3X BASIC DRESS
STATED PRINT RUN 50 SERIAL #'d SETS
DFS17 Kerry Wood 15.00 40.00
DFS23 Darin Erstad 15.00 40.00
DFS24 Rafael Palmeiro 20.00 50.00

2001 Leaf Rookies and Stars Freshman Orientation

STATED ODDS 1:96
FO2 Josh Towers Pants 6.00 15.00
FO3 Vernon Wells Jsy 4.00 10.00
FO4 Corey Patterson Pants 4.00 10.00
FO6 Ben Sheets Jsy 6.00 15.00
FO7 Pedro Feliz Bat 4.00 10.00
FO8 Keith Ginter Bat 4.00 10.00
FO9 Luis Rivas Bat 4.00 10.00
FO10 Andres Torres Bat 4.00 10.00
FO11 Carlos Valderrama Jsy 4.00 10.00
FO12 Brandon Inge Jsy 4.00 10.00
FO14 Cesar Izturis Bat 4.00 10.00
FO15 Marcus Giles Jsy 4.00 10.00
FO16 Tsuyoshi Shinjo Jsy 6.00 15.00
FO17 Eric Valent Bat 4.00 10.00
FO18 David Espinosa Bat 4.00 10.00
FO19 Aubrey Huff Jsy 4.00 10.00
FO20 Wilmy Caceres Jsy 4.00 10.00
FO21 Bud Smith Jsy 4.00 10.00
FO22 Ricardo Rodriguez Pants 4.00 10.00
FO23 Wes Helms Jsy 4.00 10.00
FO24 Jason Hart Bat 4.00 10.00
FO25 Dee Brown Jsy 4.00 10.00

2001 Leaf Rookies and Stars Freshman Orientation Autographs

STATED PRINT RUN 100 SETS
LESS THAN 100 OF EACH SP PRINTED
PRINT RUNS PROVIDED BY DONRUSS
CARDS ARE NOT SERIAL NUMBERED
FO7 Pedro Feliz Bat 8.00 20.00
FO8 Keith Ginter Bat 8.00 20.00
FO9 Luis Rivas Bat 8.00 20.00
FO10 Andres Torres Bat 8.00 20.00
FO11 Carlos Valderrama Jsy 8.00 20.00
FO13 Jay Gibbons Cap 10.00 25.00
FO14 Cesar Izturis Bat 8.00 20.00
FO15 Marcus Giles Jsy 8.00 20.00
FO17 Eric Valent Bat 8.00 20.00
FO18 David Espinosa Bat 8.00 20.00
FO19 Aubrey Huff Jsy 8.00 20.00
FO20 Wilmy Caceres Jsy 8.00 20.00
FO22 Ricardo Rodriguez Pants 8.00 20.00
FO24 Jason Hart Bat 8.00 20.00
FO25 Dee Brown Jsy 8.00 20.00

2001 Leaf Rookies and Stars Freshman Orientation Class Officers

*CLASS OFFICER: .75X TO 2X BASIC FRESH
STATED PRINT RUN 50 SERIAL #'d SETS
FO1 Adam Dunn Bat 8.00 20.00
FO5 Albert Pujols Bat 125.00 300.00
FO13 Jay Gibbons Cap 8.00 20.00

2001 Leaf Rookies and Stars Great American Treasures

STATED ODDS 1:1120 HOBBY, 1:1152 RETAIL
PRINT RUNS B/WN 25-200 COPIES PER
PRINT RUN INFO PROVIDED BY DONRUSS
CARDS ARE NOT SERIAL-NUMBERED
NO PRICING ON QTY OF 25 DUE TO SCARCITY
GT1 B.Bonds 517 HR Jsy/50 * 125.00 200.00
GT2 M.Ordonez HR Bat/200 * 15.00 40.00
GT6 T.Glavine 96 WS Jsy/100 * 10.00 25.00
GT7 I.Rod 99 MVP Bat/200 * 20.00 50.00
GT11 R.Sandberg 91 AS Bat/200 * 10.00 25.00
GT16 H.Killebrew 570 HR Bat/200 * 10.00 25.00
GT17 M.Ordonez 00 AS Cap/100 * 20.00 50.00
GT18 W.Boggs WS Bat/200 * 10.00 25.00

2001 Leaf Rookies and Stars Players Collection

STATED PRINT RUN 100 SERIAL #'d SETS
QUAD PRINT RUN 25 SERIAL #'d SETS
NO QUAD PRICING DUE TO SCARCITY
PC1 Tony Gwynn Bat SP 10.00 25.00
PC2 Tony Gwynn Jsy 10.00 25.00
PC3 Tony Gwynn Pants 10.00 25.00
PC4 Tony Gwynn Shoe 10.00 25.00
PC6 Cal Ripken White Jsy SP 30.00 60.00
PC7 Cal Ripken Bat SP 30.00 60.00
PC8 Cal Ripken Glove 30.00 60.00
PC9 Cal Ripken Gray Jsy 30.00 60.00
PC11 Barry Bonds Jsy 20.00 50.00
PC12 Barry Bonds Shoe 20.00 50.00
PC13 Barry Bonds Pants 20.00 50.00
PC14 Barry Bonds Bat 20.00 50.00

2001 Leaf Rookies and Stars Slideshow

STATED PRINT RUN 100 SERIAL #'d SETS
VIEW MASTER PRINT RUN 25 #'d SETS
NO V'MASTER PRICING DUE TO SCARCITY
S1 Cal Ripken 20.00 50.00
S2 Chipper Jones SP 10.00 25.00
S3 Jeff Bagwell 10.00 25.00
S4 Larry Walker 6.00 15.00
S5 Greg Maddux SP 10.00 25.00
S6 Ivan Rodriguez 10.00 25.00
S7 Andruw Jones SP 10.00 25.00
S8 Lance Berkman SP 6.00 15.00
S9 Luis Gonzalez SP 6.00 15.00
S10 Tony Gwynn 10.00 25.00
S11 Troy Glaus SP 6.00 15.00
S12 Todd Helton 10.00 25.00
S13 Roberto Alomar 10.00 25.00
S14 Barry Bonds 20.00 50.00
S15 Vladimir Guerrero SP 10.00 25.00
S16 Sean Casey SP 6.00 15.00
S17 Curt Schilling SP 6.00 15.00
S18 Frank Thomas 10.00 25.00
S19 Pedro Martinez 10.00 25.00
S20 Juan Gonzalez 6.00 15.00
S21 Randy Johnson 10.00 25.00
S22 Kerry Wood SP 6.00 15.00
S23 Mike Sweeney 6.00 15.00
S24 Magglio Ordonez 6.00 15.00
S25 Kazuhiro Sasaki 6.00 15.00
S26 Manny Ramirez Sox 10.00 25.00
S27 Roger Clemens 15.00 40.00
S28 Albert Pujols SP 75.00 200.00
S29 Hideo Nomo 10.00 25.00
S30 Miguel Tejada SP 6.00 15.00

2001 Leaf Rookies and Stars Statistical Standouts

STATED ODDS 1:96
*SUPER: 1X TO 2.5X BASIC STAT. STANDOUT
SUPER STATED PRINT RUN 50 SERIAL #'D SETS
SS1 Ichiro Suzuki 20.00 50.00
SS3 Ivan Rodriguez 6.00 15.00
SS4 Jeff Bagwell 6.00 15.00
SS6 Mike Sweeney 4.00 10.00
SS7 Miguel Tejada 4.00 10.00
SS9 Darin Erstad 4.00 10.00
SS10 Alex Rodriguez 10.00 25.00
SS11 Jason Giambi 4.00 10.00
SS12 Cal Ripken 10.00 25.00
SS13 Albert Pujols 12.00 30.00
SS14 Carlos Delgado 4.00 10.00
SS15 Rafael Palmeiro 6.00 15.00
SS16 Lance Berkman 4.00 10.00
SS20 Derek Jeter 15.00 40.00
SS21 Edgar Martinez 6.00 15.00
SS22 Troy Glaus 4.00 10.00
SS23 Magglio Ordonez 4.00 10.00
SS24 Mark McGwire 10.00 25.00
SS25 Manny Ramirez Sox 6.00 15.00

2001 Leaf Rookies and Stars Statistical Standouts Super

*SUPER: 1X TO 2.5X BASIC STAT.STAND
STATED PRINT RUN 50 SERIAL #'d SETS

2001 Leaf Rookies and Stars Triple Threads

STATED PRINT RUN 100 SERIAL #'d SETS
TT1 Pedro/Manny Sox/Nomar 10.00 25.00
TT2 F.Rob/Ripken/B.Rob 30.00 80.00
TT3 Ruth/Gehrig/Berra 350.00 500.00
TT4 Dawson/Sandberg/Banks 10.00 25.00
TT5 Spahn/Aaron/Mathews 30.00 80.00
TT6 Maddux/C.Jones/A.Jones 10.00 25.00
TT7 Ryan/I.Rod/J.Gonz 30.00 80.00
TT8 Berkman/Bagwell/Biggio 10.00 25.00
TT9 Carew/Killebrew/Puckett 30.00 80.00
TT10 L.Gonz/Schilling/R.John 10.00 25.00

2002 Leaf Rookies and Stars Samples

8 David Segui .60 1.50
20 Trot Nixon .60 1.50
45 Chuck Knoblauch .60 1.50
48 Paul Byrd .60 1.50
49 Mac Suzuki .60 1.50
60 Roger Clemens
96 Brent Abernathy .60 1.50
97 Chan Ho Park 1.00 2.50
98 Alex Rodriguez 2.00 5.00
99 Juan Gonzalez .60 1.50
100 Rafael Palmeiro 1.00 2.50

2002 Leaf Rookies and Stars

COMP.SET w/o SP's (300) 15.00 40.00
COMMON CARD (1-300) .10 .30
COMMON SP (1-300) .75 2.00
SP 1-300 ODDS 1:4
SEE BECKETT.COM FOR SP CHECKLIST
COMMON CARD (301-400) .40 1.00
301-400 ODDS 1:2
1 Darin Erstad .10 .30
2 Garret Anderson .10 .30
3 Troy Glaus .10 .30
4 David Eckstein .10 .30
5 Adam Kennedy .10 .30
6 Kevin Appier Angels .10 .30
6A Kevin Appier Mets SP .75 2.00
6B Kevin Appier Royals SP .75 2.00
7 Jarrod Washburn .10 .30
8 David Segui .10 .30
9 Jay Gibbons .10 .30
10 Tony Batista .10 .30
11 Scott Erickson .10 .30
12 Jeff Conine .10 .30
13 Melvin Mora .10 .30
14 Shea Hillenbrand .10 .30
15 Manny Ramirez Red Sox .20 .50
15A Manny Ramirez Indians SP 1.00 2.50
16 Pedro Martinez Red Sox .20 .50
16A Pedro Martinez Dodgers SP 1.00 2.50
16B Pedro Martinez Expos SP 1.00 2.50
17 Nomar Garciaparra .50 1.25
18 Rickey Henderson Red Sox .30 .75
18A Rickey Henderson Angels SP 1.50 4.00
18B Rickey Henderson A's SP 1.50 4.00
18C Rickey Henderson Bl.Jays SP 1.50 4.00
18D Rickey Henderson M's SP 1.50 4.00
18E Rickey Henderson Mets SP 1.50 4.00
18F Rickey Henderson Padres SP 1.50 4.00
18G Rickey Henderson Yanks SP 1.50 4.00
19 Johnny Damon Red Sox .20 .50
19A Johnny Damon A's SP 1.00 2.50
19B Johnny Damon Royals SP 1.00 2.50
20 Trot Nixon .10 .30
21 Derek Lowe .10 .30
22 Jason Varitek .30 .75
23 Tim Wakefield .10 .30
24 Frank Thomas .30 .75
25 Kenny Lofton White Sox .10 .30
25A Kenny Lofton Indians SP .75 2.00
25B Kenny Lofton Giants SP .75 2.00
26 Magglio Ordonez .10 .30
27 Ray Durham .10 .30
28 Mark Buehrle .10 .30
29 Paul Konerko White Sox .10 .30
29A Paul Konerko Dodgers SP .75 2.00
29B Paul Konerko Reds SP .75 2.00
30 Jose Valentin .10 .30
31 C.C. Sabathia .10 .30
32 Ellis Burks Indians .10 .30
32A Ellis Burks Giants SP .75 2.00
32B Ellis Burks Red Sox SP .75 2.00
32C Ellis Burks Rockies SP .75 2.00
33 Omar Vizquel Indians .20 .50
33A Omar Vizquel Mariners SP 1.00 2.50
34 Jim Thome .20 .50
35 Matt Lawton .10 .30
36 Travis Fryman Indians .10 .30
36A Travis Fryman Tigers SP .75 2.00
37 Robert Fick .10 .30
38 Bobby Higginson .10 .30
39 Steve Sparks .10 .30
40 Mike Rivera .10 .30
41 Wendell Magee .10 .30
42 Randall Simon .10 .30
43 Carlos Pena Tigers .10 .30
43A Carlos Pena A's SP .75 2.00
43B Carlos Pena Rangers SP .75 2.00
44 Mike Sweeney .10 .30
45 Chuck Knoblauch .10 .30
46 Carlos Beltran .10 .30
47 Joe Randa .10 .30
48 Paul Byrd .10 .30
49 Mac Suzuki .10 .30
50 Torii Hunter .10 .30
51 Jacque Jones .10 .30
52 David Ortiz .30 .75
53 Corey Koskie .10 .30
54 Brad Radke .10 .30
55 Doug Mientkiewicz .10 .30
56 A.J. Pierzynski .10 .30
57 Dustan Mohr .10 .30
58 Derek Jeter .75 2.00
59 Bernie Williams .20 .50
60 Roger Clemens Yankees .60 1.50
60A Roger Clemens Blue Jays SP 3.00 8.00
60B Roger Clemens Red Sox SP 3.00 8.00
61 Mike Mussina Yankees .20 .50
61A Mike Mussina Orioles SP 1.00 2.50
62 Jorge Posada .20 .50
63 Alfonso Soriano .10 .30
64 Jason Giambi Yankees .10 .30
64A Jason Giambi A's SP .75 2.00
65 Robin Ventura Yankees .10 .30
65A Robin Ventura Mets SP .75 2.00
65B Robin Ventura White Sox SP .75 2.00
66 Andy Pettitte .20 .50
67 David Wells Yankees .10 .30
67A David Wells Blue Jays SP .75 2.00
67B David Wells Tigers SP .75 2.00
68 Nick Johnson .10 .30
69 Jeff Weaver Yankees .10 .30
69A Jeff Weaver Tigers SP .75 2.00
70 Raul Mondesi Yankees .10 .30
70A Raul Mondesi Blue Jays SP .75 2.00
70B Raul Mondesi Dodgers SP .75 2.00
71 Tim Hudson .10 .30
72 Barry Zito .10 .30
73 Mark Mulder .10 .30
74 Miguel Tejada .10 .30
75 Eric Chavez .10 .30
76 Billy Koch A's .10 .30
76A Billy Koch Blue Jays SP .75 2.00
77 Jermaine Dye A's .10 .30
77A Jermaine Dye Royals SP .75 2.00
78 Scott Hatteberg .10 .30
79 Ichiro Suzuki .60 1.50
80 Edgar Martinez .20 .50
81 Mike Cameron Mariners .10 .30
81A Mike Cameron White Sox SP .75 2.00
82 John Olerud Mariners .10 .30
82A John Olerud Blue Jays SP .75 2.00
82B John Olerud Mets SP .75 2.00
83 Bret Boone .10 .30
84 Dan Wilson .10 .30
85 Freddy Garcia .10 .30
86 Jamie Moyer .10 .30
87 Carlos Guillen .10 .30
88 Ruben Sierra .10 .30
89 Kazuhiro Sasaki .10 .30
90 Mark McLemore .10 .30
91 Ben Grieve .10 .30
92 Aubrey Huff .10 .30
93 Steve Cox .10 .30
94 Toby Hall .10 .30
95 Randy Winn .10 .30
96 Brent Abernathy .10 .30
97 Chan Ho Park Rangers .10 .30
97A Chan Ho Park Dodgers SP .75 2.00
98 Alex Rodriguez Rangers .40 1.00
98A Alex Rodriguez Mariners SP 2.00 5.00
99 Juan Gonzalez Rangers .10 .30
99A Juan Gonzalez Indians SP .75 2.00
99B Juan Gonzalez Tigers SP .75 2.00
100 Rafael Palmeiro Rangers .20 .50
100A Rafael Palmeiro Cubs SP 1.00 2.50
100B Rafael Palmeiro Orioles SP 1.00 2.50
101 Ivan Rodriguez .20 .50
102 Rusty Greer .10 .30
103 Kenny Rogers Rangers .10 .30
103A Kenny Rogers A's SP .75 2.00
103B Kenny Rogers Yankees SP .75 2.00
104 Hank Blalock .20 .50
105 Mark Teixeira .30 .75
106 Carlos Delgado .10 .30
107 Shannon Stewart .10 .30
108 Eric Hinske .10 .30
109 Roy Halladay .10 .30
110 Felipe Lopez .10 .30
111 Vernon Wells .10 .30
112 Curt Schilling D'backs .10 .30
112A Curt Schilling Phillies SP .75 2.00
113 Randy Johnson D'backs .30 .75
113A Randy Johnson Astros SP 1.50 4.00
113B Randy Johnson Expos SP 1.50 4.00
113C Randy Johnson Mariners SP 1.50 4.00
114 Luis Gonzalez D'backs .10 .30
114A Luis Gonzalez Astros SP .75 2.00
114B Luis Gonzalez Cubs SP .75 2.00
115 Mark Grace D'backs .20 .50
115A Mark Grace Cubs SP 1.00 2.50
116 Junior Spivey .10 .30
117 Tony Womack .10 .30
118 Matt Williams D'backs .10 .30
118A Matt Williams Giants SP .75 2.00
118B Matt Williams Indians SP .75 2.00
119 Danny Bautista .10 .30
120 Byung-Hyun Kim .10 .30
121 Craig Counsell .10 .30
122 Greg Maddux Braves .50 1.25
122A Greg Maddux Cubs SP 2.50 6.00
123 Tom Glavine .20 .50
124 John Smoltz Braves .20 .50
124A John Smoltz Tigers SP 1.00 2.50
125 Chipper Jones .30 .75
126 Gary Sheffield .10 .30
127 Andruw Jones .20 .50
128 Vinny Castilla .10 .30
129 Damian Moss .10 .30
130 Rafael Furcal .10 .30
131 Kerry Wood .10 .30
132 Fred McGriff Cubs .20 .50
132A Fred McGriff Blue Jays SP 1.00 2.50
132B Fred McGriff Braves SP 1.00 2.50
132C Fred McGriff Devil Rays SP 1.00 2.50
132D Fred McGriff Padres SP 1.00 2.50
133 Sammy Sosa Cubs .30 .75
133A Sammy Sosa Rangers SP 1.50 4.00
133B Sammy Sosa White Sox SP 1.50 4.00
134 Alex Gonzalez .10 .30
135 Corey Patterson .10 .30
136 Moises Alou .10 .30
137 Mark Prior 2.00 5.00
138 Jon Lieber .10 .30
139 Matt Clement .10 .30
140 Ken Griffey Jr. Reds .60 1.50
140A Ken Griffey Jr. Mariners SP 3.00 8.00
141 Barry Larkin .20 .50
142 Adam Dunn .10 .30
143 Sean Casey Reds .10 .30
143A Sean Casey Indians SP .75 2.00
144 Jose Rijo .10 .30
145 Elmer Dessens .10 .30
146 Austin Kearns .10 .30
147 Corky Miller .10 .30
148 Todd Walker Reds .10 .30
148A Todd Walker Rockies SP .75 2.00
149 Chris Reitsma .10 .30

150 Ryan Dempster .10 .30
151 Larry Walker Rockies .10 .30
151A Larry Walker Expos SP .75 2.00
152 Todd Helton .20 .50
153 Juan Uribe .10 .30
154 Juan Pierre .10 .30
155 Mike Hampton .10 .30
156 Todd Zeile .10 .30
157 Josh Beckett .10 .30
158 Mike Lowell Marlins .10 .30
158A Mike Lowell Yankees SP .75 2.00
159 Derrek Lee .20 .50
160 A.J. Burnett .10 .30
161 Luis Castillo .10 .30
162 Tim Raines .10 .30
163 Preston Wilson .10 .30
164 Juan Encarnacion .10 .30
165 Jeff Bagwell .20 .50
166 Craig Biggio .20 .50
167 Lance Berkman .10 .30
168 Wade Miller .10 .30
169 Roy Oswalt .10 .30
170 Richard Hidalgo .10 .30
171 Carlos Hernandez .10 .30
172 Daryle Ward .10 .30
173 Shawn Green Dodgers .10 .30
173A Shawn Green Blue Jays SP .75 2.00
174 Adrian Beltre .10 .30
175 Paul Lo Duca .10 .30
176 Eric Karros .10 .30
177 Kevin Brown .10 .30
178 Hideo Nomo Dodgers .30 .75
178A Hideo Nomo Brewers SP 1.50 4.00
178B Hideo Nomo Mets SP 1.50 4.00
178C Hideo Nomo Red Sox SP 1.50 4.00
178D Hideo Nomo Tigers SP 1.50 4.00
179 Odalis Perez .10 .30
180 Eric Gagne .10 .30
181 Brian Jordan .10 .30
182 Cesar Izturis .10 .30
183 Geoff Jenkins .10 .30
184 Richie Sexson Brewers .10 .30
184A Richie Sexson Indians SP .75 2.00
185 Jose Hernandez .10 .30
186 Ben Sheets .10 .30
187 Ruben Quevedo .10 .30
188 Jeffrey Hammonds .10 .30
189 Alex Sanchez .10 .30
190 Vladimir Guerrero .30 .75
191 Jose Vidro .10 .30
192 Orlando Cabrera .10 .30
193 Michael Barrett .10 .30
194 Javier Vazquez .10 .30
195 Tony Armas Jr. .10 .30
196 Andres Galarraga .10 .30
197 Tomo Ohka .10 .30
198 Bartolo Colon Expos .10 .30
198A Bartolo Colon Indians SP .75 2.00
199 Cliff Floyd Expos .10 .30
199A Cliff Floyd Marlins SP .75 2.00
199B Cliff Floyd Red Sox SP .75 2.00
200 Mike Piazza Mets .50 1.25
200A Mike Piazza Dodgers SP 2.50 6.00
200B Mike Piazza Marlins SP 2.50 6.00
201 Jeromy Burnitz .10 .30
202 Roberto Alomar Mets .20 .50
202A Roberto Alomar Bl.Jays SP 1.00 2.50
202B Roberto Alomar Indians SP 1.00 2.50
202C Roberto Alomar Orioles SP 1.00 2.50
202D Roberto Alomar Padres SP 1.00 2.50
203 Mo Vaughn Mets .10 .30
203A Mo Vaughn Angels SP .75 2.00
203B Mo Vaughn Red Sox SP .75 2.00
204 Al Leiter Mets .10 .30
204A Al Leiter Blue Jays SP .75 2.00
205 Pedro Astacio .10 .30
206 Edgardo Alfonzo .10 .30
207 Armando Benitez .10 .30
208 Scott Rolen .20 .50
209 Pat Burrell .10 .30
210 Bobby Abreu Phillies .10 .30
210A Bobby Abreu Astros SP .75 2.00
211 Mike Lieberthal .10 .30
212 Brandon Duckworth .10 .30
213 Jimmy Rollins .10 .30
214 Jeremy Giambi .10 .30
215 Vicente Padilla .10 .30
216 Travis Lee .10 .30
217 Jason Kendall .10 .30
218 Brian Giles Pirates .10 .30
218A Brian Giles Indians SP .75 2.00
219 Aramis Ramirez .10 .30
220 Pokey Reese .10 .30
221 Kip Wells .10 .30
222 Josh Fogg Pirates .10 .30
222A Josh Fogg White Sox SP .75 2.00
223 Mike Williams .10 .30
224 Ryan Klesko Padres .10 .30
224A Ryan Klesko Braves SP .75 2.00
225 Phil Nevin Padres .10 .30
225A Phil Nevin Tigers SP .75 2.00
226 Brian Lawrence .10 .30
227 Mark Kotsay .10 .30
228 Brett Tomko .10 .30
229 Trevor Hoffman Padres .10 .30
229A Trevor Hoffman Marlins SP .75 2.00
230 Barry Bonds Giants .75 2.00
230A Barry Bonds Pirates SP 4.00 10.00
231 Jeff Kent Giants .10 .30
231A Jeff Kent Blue Jays SP .75 2.00
232 Rich Aurilia .10 .30
233 Tsuyoshi Shinjo Giants .10 .30
233A Tsuyoshi Shinjo Mets SP .75 2.00
234 Benito Santiago Giants .10 .30
234A Benito Santiago Padres SP .75 2.00
235 Kirk Rueter .10 .30
236 Kurt Ainsworth .10 .30
237 Livan Hernandez .10 .30
238 Russ Ortiz .10 .30
239 David Bell .10 .30
240 Jason Schmidt .10 .30
241 Reggie Sanders .10 .30
242 Jim Edmonds Cardinals .10 .30
242A Jim Edmonds Angels SP .75 2.00
243 J.D. Drew .10 .30
244 Albert Pujols .60 1.50
245 Fernando Vina .10 .30
246 Tino Martinez Cardinals .20 .50
246A Tino Martinez Mariners SP 1.00 2.50
246B Tino Martinez Yankees SP 1.00 2.50
247 Edgar Renteria .10 .30
248 Matt Morris .10 .30
249 Woody Williams .10 .30
250 Jason Isringhausen Cards .10 .30
250A Jason Isringhausen A's SP .75 2.00
251 Cal Ripken 82 ROY 1.00 2.50
252 Cal Ripken 83 MVP 1.00 2.50
253 Cal Ripken 91 MVP 1.00 2.50
254 Cal Ripken 91 AS 1.00 2.50
255 Ryne Sandberg 84 MVP .60 1.50
256 Don Mattingly 85 MVP .60 1.50
257 Don Mattingly 85-94 GLV .60 1.50
258 Roger Clemens 01 CY .60 1.50
259 Roger Clemens 87 CY .60 1.50
260 Roger Clemens 91 CY .60 1.50
261 Roger Clemens 97 CY .60 1.50
262 Roger Clemens 98 CY .60 1.50
263 Roger Clemens 86 CY .60 1.50
264 Roger Clemens 86 MVP .60 1.50
265 Rickey Henderson 90 MVP .30 .75
266 Rickey Henderson 81 GLV .30 .75
267 Jose Canseco 88 MVP .20 .50
268 Barry Bonds 01 MVP .75 2.00
269 Barry Bonds 90 MVP .75 2.00
270 Barry Bonds 92 MVP .75 2.00
271 Barry Bonds 93 MVP .75 2.00
272 Jeff Bagwell 94 MVP .10 .30
273 Kirby Puckett 91 ALCS .30 .75
274 Kirby Puckett 93 AS .30 .75
275 Greg Maddux 95 CY .50 1.25
276 Greg Maddux 92 CY .50 1.25
277 Greg Maddux 93 CY .50 1.25
278 Greg Maddux 94 CY .50 1.25
279 Ken Griffey Jr. 97 MVP .60 1.50
280 Mike Piazza 93 ROY .50 1.25
281 Kirby Puckett 86-89 GLV .30 .75
282 Mike Piazza 96 AS .50 1.25
283 Frank Thomas 93 MVP .20 .50
284 Hideo Nomo 95 ROY .20 .50
285 Randy Johnson 01 CY .20 .50
286 Juan Gonzalez 96 MVP .10 .30
287 Derek Jeter 96 ROY .75 2.00
288 Derek Jeter 00 WS .75 2.00
289 Derek Jeter 00 AS .75 2.00
290 Nomar Garciaparra 97 ROY .50 1.25
291 Pedro Martinez 00 CY .20 .50
292 Kerry Wood 98 ROY .10 .30
293 Sammy Sosa 98 MVP .20 .50
294 Chipper Jones 99 MVP .20 .50
295 Ivan Rodriguez 99 MVP .10 .30
296 Ivan Rodriguez 92-01 GLV .10 .30
297 Albert Pujols 01 ROY .60 1.50
298 Ichiro Suzuki 01 ROY .60 1.50
299 Ichiro Suzuki 01 MVP .60 1.50
300 Ichiro Suzuki 01 GLV .60 1.50
301 So Taguchi RS RC .50 1.25
302 Kazuhisa Ishii RS RC .50 1.25
303 Jeremy Lambert RS RC .40 1.00
304 Sean Burroughs RS .40 1.00
305 P.J. Bevis RS RC .40 1.00
306 Jon Rauch RS .40 1.00
307 Scotty Layfield RS RC .40 1.00
308 Miguel Asencio RS RC .40 1.00
309 Franklyn German RS RC .40 1.00
310 Luis Ugueto RS RC .40 1.00
311 Jorge Sosa RS RC .50 1.25
312 Felix Escalona RS RC .40 1.00
313 Jose Valverde RS RC .40 1.00
314 Jeremy Ward RS RC .40 1.00
315 Kevin Gryboski RS RC .40 1.00
316 Francis Beltran RS RC .40 1.00
317 Joe Thurston RS .40 1.00
318 Cliff Lee RS RC 3.00 8.00
319 Takahito Nomura RS RC .40 1.00
320 Bill Hall RS .40 1.00
321 Marlon Byrd RS .40 1.00
322 Andy Shibilo RS RC .40 1.00
323 Edwin Almonte RS RC .40 1.00
324 Brandon Backe RS RC .50 1.25
325 Chone Figgins RS RC .75 2.00
326 Brian Mallette RS RC .40 1.00
327 Rodrigo Rosario RS RC .40 1.00
328 Anderson Machado RS RC .40 1.00
329 Jorge Padilla RS RC .40 1.00
330 Allan Simpson RS RC .40 1.00
331 Doug Devore RS RC .40 1.00
332 Drew Henson RS .40 1.00
333 Raul Chavez RS RC .40 1.00
334 Tom Shearn RS RC .40 1.00
335 Ben Howard RS RC .40 1.00
336 Chris Baker RS RC .40 1.00
337 Travis Hughes RS RC .40 1.00
338 Kevin Mench RS .40 1.00
339 Brian Tallet RS RC .40 1.00
340 Mike Moriarty RS RC .40 1.00
341 Corey Thurman RS RC .40 1.00
342 Terry Pearson RS RC .40 1.00
343 Steve Kent RS RC .40 1.00
344 Satoru Komiyama RS RC .40 1.00
345 Jason Lane RS .40 1.00
346 Freddy Sanchez RS RC 1.25 3.00
347 Brandon Puffer RS RC .40 1.00
348 Clay Condrey RS RC .40 1.00
349 Rene Reyes RS RC .40 1.00
350 Hee Seop Choi RS .40 1.00
351 Rodrigo Lopez RS .40 1.00
352 Colin Young RS RC .40 1.00
353 Jason Simontacchi RS RC .40 1.00
354 Oliver Perez RS RC .75 2.00
355 Kirk Saarloos RS RC .40 1.00
356 Marcus Thames RS .40 1.00
357 Jeff Austin RS RC .40 1.00
358 Justin Kaye RS .40 1.00
359 Julio Mateo RS RC .40 1.00
360 Mike A. Smith RS RC .40 1.00
361 Chris Snelling RS RC .60 1.50
362 Dennis Tankersley RS .40 1.00
363 Runelvys Hernandez RS RC .40 1.00
364 Aaron Cook RS RC .40 1.00
365 Joe Borchard RS .40 1.00
366 Earl Snyder RS RC .40 1.00
367 Shane Nance RS RC .40 1.00
368 Aaron Guiel RS RC .40 1.00
369 Steve Bechler RS RC .40 1.00
370 Tim Kalita RS RC .40 1.00
371 Shawn Sedlacek RS RC .40 1.00
372 Eric Good RS RC .40 1.00
373 Eric Junge RS RC .40 1.00
374 Matt Thornton RS RC .40 1.00
375 Travis Driskill RS RC .40 1.00
376 Mitch Wylie RS RC .40 1.00
377 John Ennis RS RC .40 1.00
378 Reed Johnson RS RC .75 2.00
379 Juan Brito RS RC .40 1.00
380 Ron Calloway RS RC .40 1.00
381 Adrian Burnside RS RC .40 1.00
382 Josh Bard RS RC .40 1.00
383 Matt Childers RS RC .40 1.00
384 Gustavo Chacin RS RC .75 2.00
385 Luis Martinez RS RC .40 1.00
386 Trey Hodges RS RC .40 1.00
387 Hansel Izquierdo RS RC .40 1.00
388 Jeriome Robertson RS RC .40 1.00
389 Victor Alvarez RS RC .40 1.00
390 David Ross RS RC .50 1.25
391 Ron Chiavacci RS .40 1.00
392 Adam Walker RS RC .40 1.00
393 Mike Gonzalez RS RC .40 1.00
394 John Foster RS RC .40 1.00
395 Kyle Kane RS RC .40 1.00
396 Cam Esslinger RS RC .40 1.00
397 Kevin Frederick RS RC .40 1.00
398 Franklin Nunez RS RC .40 1.00
399 Todd Donovan RS RC .40 1.00
400 Kevin Cash RS RC .40 1.00

2002 Leaf Rookies and Stars Great American Signings

PRINT RUNS PROVIDED BY DONRUSS
CARDS ARE NOT SERIAL-NUMBERED
NO PRICING ON QTY OF 25 OR LESS
9 Jay Gibbons/150* 4.00 10.00
40 Mike Rivera/175* 4.00 10.00
49 Mac Suzuki/100* 15.00 40.00
68 Nick Johnson/175* 6.00 15.00
92 Aubrey Huff/175* 6.00 15.00
96 Brent Abernathy/175* 4.00 10.00
108 Eric Hinske/175* 4.00 10.00
146 Austin Kearns/75* 6.00 15.00
169 Roy Oswalt/100* 6.00 15.00
182 Cesar Izturis/175* 4.00 10.00
221 Kip Wells/175* 4.00 10.00
226 Brian Lawrence/175* 4.00 10.00
301 So Taguchi/50* 15.00 40.00
309 Franklyn German/175* 4.00 10.00
310 Luis Ugueto/175* 4.00 10.00
312 Felix Escalona/100* 6.00 15.00
316 Francis Beltran/175* 4.00 10.00
320 Bill Hall/175* 6.00 15.00
324 Brandon Backe/175* 6.00 15.00
327 Rodrigo Rosario/175* 4.00 10.00
328 Anderson Machado/175* 4.00 10.00
329 Jorge Padilla/175* 4.00 10.00
331 Doug Devore/175* 4.00 10.00
332 Drew Henson/50* 6.00 15.00
333 Raul Chavez/175* 4.00 10.00
334 Tom Shearn/175* 4.00 10.00
335 Ben Howard/175* 4.00 10.00
336 Chris Baker/175* 4.00 10.00
337 Travis Hughes/175* 4.00 10.00
341 Corey Thurman/175* 4.00 10.00
344 Satoru Komiyama/75* 10.00 25.00
345 Jason Lane/150* 6.00 15.00
349 Rene Reyes/175* 4.00 10.00
354 Oliver Perez/175* 15.00 40.00
361 Chris Snelling/175* 8.00 20.00
362 Dennis Tankersley/175* 4.00 10.00

2002 Leaf Rookies and Stars Longevity

*LONGEVITY 1-300: 6X TO 15X BASIC
*LONGEVITY 1-300: 1.25X TO 3X BASIC SP'S
*RETIRED STARS 251-300: 12.5X TO 30X
1-300 PRINT RUN 100 SERIAL #'d SETS
301-400 PRINT RUN 25 SERIAL #'d SETS
301-400 NO PRICING DUE TO SCARCITY

2002 Leaf Rookies and Stars BLC Homers

LUIS GONZALEZ (1-3) 10.00 25.00
TODD HELTON (4-11) 15.00 40.00
JIM THOME (12-14) 15.00 40.00
RAFAEL PALMEIRO (15-19) 15.00 40.00
TROY GLAUS (20-22) 10.00 25.00
GARY SHEFFIELD (23-25) 10.00 25.00
MIKE PIAZZA (26-30) 20.00 50.00
STATED PRINT RUN 25 SERIAL #'d SETS

2002 Leaf Rookies and Stars Dress for Success

RANDOM INSERTS IN PACKS
STATED PRINT RUN 250 SERIAL #'d SETS
PRIME CUT RANDOM INSERTS IN PACKS
PRIME CUT PRINT RUN 25 SERIAL #'d SETS
PRIME CUT: NO PRICING DUE TO SCARCITY
1 Mike Piazza Jsy-Jsy 10.00 25.00
2 Cal Ripken Jsy-Jsy 12.00 30.00
3 Carlos Delgado Jsy-Jsy 8.00 20.00
4 Chipper Jones Jsy-Jsy 10.00 25.00
5 Bernie Williams Jsy-Shoe 10.00 25.00
6 Carlos Beltran Jsy-Shoe 8.00 20.00
7 Curt Schilling Jsy-Jsy 8.00 20.00
8 Greg Maddux Jsy-Jsy 10.00 25.00
9 Ivan Rodriguez Jsy-Jsy 10.00 25.00
10 Alex Rodriguez Jsy-Jsy 8.00 20.00
11 Roger Clemens Jsy-Jsy 15.00 40.00
12 Todd Helton Jsy-Jsy 10.00 25.00
13 Jim Edmonds Shoe-Jsy 8.00 20.00
14 Manny Ramirez Jsy-Fld Glv 10.00 25.00
15 Mark Buehrle Jsy-Shoe 8.00 20.00

2002 Leaf Rookies and Stars Freshman Orientation

STATED ODDS 1:142
*CLASS OFFICERS: .6X TO 1.5X BASIC
CLASS OFFICERS PRINT RUN 50 #'d SETS
1 Andres Torres Bat 4.00 10.00
2 Mark Ellis Jsy 4.00 10.00
3 Erik Bedard Bat 4.00 10.00
4 Delvin James Jsy 4.00 10.00
5 Austin Kearns Bat 4.00 10.00
6 Josh Pearce Bat 4.00 10.00
7 Rafael Soriano Jsy 4.00 10.00
8 Jason Lane Bat 4.00 10.00
9 Mark Prior Jsy 4.00 10.00
10 Alfredo Amezaga Bat 4.00 10.00
11 Ryan Ludwick Bat 4.00 10.00
12 So Taguchi Bat 6.00 15.00
13 Duaner Sanchez Bat 4.00 10.00
14 Kazuhisa Ishii Jsy 6.00 15.00
15 Zach Day Pants 4.00 10.00
16 Eric Cyr Bat 4.00 10.00
17 Francis Beltran Jsy 4.00 10.00
18 Joe Borchard Jsy 4.00 10.00
19 Jeremy Affeldt Shoe 4.00 10.00
20 Alexis Gomez Shoe 4.00 10.00

2002 Leaf Rookies and Stars Statistical Standouts

STATED ODDS 1:12
1 Adam Dunn 1.00 2.50
2 Alex Rodriguez 3.00 8.00
3 Andruw Jones 1.50 4.00
4 Brian Giles 1.00 2.50
5 Chipper Jones 2.50 6.00
6 Cliff Floyd 1.00 2.50
7 Craig Biggio 1.50 4.00
8 Frank Thomas 2.50 6.00
9 Fred McGriff 1.50 4.00
10 Garret Anderson 1.00 2.50
11 Greg Maddux 4.00 10.00
12 Luis Gonzalez 1.00 2.50
13 Magglio Ordonez 1.00 2.50
14 Ivan Rodriguez 1.50 4.00
15 Ken Griffey Jr. 5.00 12.00
16 Ichiro Suzuki 5.00 12.00
17 Jason Giambi 1.00 2.50
18 Derek Jeter 6.00 15.00
19 Sammy Sosa 2.50 6.00
20 Albert Pujols 5.00 12.00
21 J.D. Drew 1.00 2.50
22 Jeff Bagwell 1.50 4.00
23 Jim Edmonds 1.00 2.50
24 Jose Vidro 1.00 2.50
25 Juan Encarnacion 1.00 2.50
26 Kerry Wood 1.00 2.50
27 Al Leiter 1.00 2.50
28 Curt Schilling 1.00 2.50
29 Manny Ramirez 1.50 4.00
30 Lance Berkman 1.00 2.50
31 Miguel Tejada 1.00 2.50
32 Mike Piazza 4.00 10.00
33 Nomar Garciaparra 4.00 10.00
34 Omar Vizquel 1.50 4.00
35 Pat Burrell 1.00 2.50
36 Paul Konerko 1.00 2.50
37 Rafael Palmeiro 1.50 4.00
38 Randy Johnson 2.50 6.00
39 Richie Sexson 1.00 2.50
40 Roger Clemens 5.00 12.00
41 Shawn Green 1.00 2.50
42 Todd Helton 1.50 4.00
43 Tom Glavine 1.50 4.00
44 Troy Glaus 1.00 2.50
45 Vladimir Guerrero 2.50 6.00
46 Mike Sweeney 1.00 2.50
47 Alfonso Soriano 1.00 2.50
48 Barry Zito 1.00 2.50
49 John Smoltz 1.50 4.00
50 Ellis Burks 1.00 2.50

2002 Leaf Rookies and Stars Statistical Standouts Materials

STATED ODDS 1:69
SP'S ARE NOT SERIAL-NUMBERED
SP PRINT RUNS PROVIDED BY DONRUSS
SUPER: RANDOM INSERTS IN PACKS
SUPER PRINT RUN 25 SERIAL #'d SETS
SUPER: NO PRICING DUE TO SCARCITY
1 Adam Dunn Bat/200 * 4.00 10.00
2 Alex Rodriguez Bat/200 * 8.00 20.00
3 Andruw Jones Bat/200 * 6.00 15.00
4 Brian Giles Bat 4.00 10.00
5 Chipper Jones Bat/200 * 6.00 15.00
6 Cliff Floyd Jsy 4.00 10.00
7 Craig Biggio Pants 6.00 15.00
8 Frank Thomas Jsy/125 * 6.00 15.00
9 Fred McGriff Bat 6.00 15.00
11 Greg Maddux Jsy/200 * 8.00 20.00
12 Luis Gonzalez Jsy 4.00 10.00
13 Magglio Ordonez Bat/150 * 4.00 10.00
15 Ken Griffey Jr. Base/100 * 10.00 25.00
17 Jason Giambi Base 4.00 10.00
19 Sammy Sosa Base/100 * 6.00 15.00
21 J.D. Drew Bat/150 * 4.00 10.00
23 Jim Edmonds Bat 4.00 10.00
24 Jose Vidro Bat 4.00 10.00
25 Juan Encarnacion Bat 4.00 10.00
26 Kerry Wood Jsy/200 * 4.00 10.00
27 Al Leiter Jsy 4.00 10.00
29 Manny Ramirez Bat/100 * 6.00 15.00
31 Miguel Tejada Jsy 4.00 10.00
32 Mike Piazza Bat/200 * 8.00 20.00
33 Nomar Garciaparra Bat/200 * 10.00 25.00
34 Omar Vizquel Jsy 6.00 15.00
35 Pat Burrell Bat 4.00 10.00
36 Paul Konerko Jsy 4.00 10.00
37 Rafael Palmeiro Bat 6.00 15.00
38 Randy Johnson Jsy/200 * 6.00 15.00
39 Richie Sexson Jsy 4.00 10.00
40 Roger Clemens Jsy/200 * 12.50 30.00
41 Shawn Green Jsy 4.00 10.00
42 Todd Helton Jsy/175 * 6.00 15.00
43 Tom Glavine Jsy/125 * 6.00 15.00
44 Troy Glaus Jsy 4.00 10.00
45 Vladimir Guerrero Jsy 6.00 15.00
46 Mike Sweeney Bat 4.00 10.00
47 Alfonso Soriano Jsy/200 * 4.00 10.00
48 Barry Zito Jsy/100 * 4.00 10.00
50 Ellis Burks Jsy/50 * 4.00 10.00

2002 Leaf Rookies and Stars Triple Threads

RANDOM INSERTS IN PACKS
STATED PRINT RUN 100 SERIAL #'d SETS
1 Reggie/Soriano/Mattingly 50.00 100.00
2 A.Rod/Palmeiro/I.Rod 10.00 25.00
3 Piazza/G.Carter/Rickey 30.00 60.00
4 D.Murphy/A.Jones/C.Jones 12.00 30.00
5 Schmidt/Carlton/Rolen 50.00 100.00
6 Rickey Henderson 12.00 30.00
7 Bench/Morgan/Seaver 30.00 60.00
8 R.Johnson/Pedro/Guerrero 20.00 50.00
9 Ryan/Carew/Glaus 50.00 100.00
10 Brock/Drew/Musial 12.00 30.00

2002 Leaf Rookies and Stars View Masters

RANDOM INSERTS IN PACKS
STATED PRINT RUN 100 SERIAL #'d SETS
SLIDESHOW: RANDOM INSERTS IN PACKS
SLIDESHOW PRINT 25 SERIAL #'d SETS
SLIDESHOW: NO PRICE DUE TO SCARCITY
1 Carlos Delgado 6.00 15.00
2 Todd Helton 10.00 25.00
3 Tony Gwynn 15.00 40.00
4 Bernie Williams 10.00 25.00
5 Luis Gonzalez 6.00 15.00
6 Larry Walker 6.00 15.00
7 Troy Glaus 6.00 15.00
8 Alfonso Soriano 6.00 15.00
9 Curt Schilling 6.00 15.00
10 Chipper Jones 10.00 25.00
11 Vladimir Guerrero 10.00 25.00
12 Adam Dunn 6.00 15.00
13 Rickey Henderson 10.00 25.00
14 Miguel Tejada 6.00 15.00
15 Kazuhisa Ishii 10.00 25.00
16 Greg Maddux 15.00 40.00
17 Pedro Martinez 10.00 25.00
18 Nomar Garciaparra 20.00 50.00
19 Mike Piazza 15.00 40.00
20 Lance Berkman 6.00 15.00

2013 Leaf Rookie Retro Genetic Matrix

COMPLETE SET (25) 50.00 100.00
ONE CARD PER ROOKIE RETRO PACK
GMAR1 Addison Russell 1.50 4.00
GMBB2 Byron Buxton 6.00 15.00
GMCC1 Carlos Correa 4.00 10.00
GMDD1 David Dahl 1.50 4.00
GMJG1 Joey Gallo 2.00 5.00
GMJS1 Jorge Soler 2.00 5.00
GMMZ1 Mike Zunino 1.50 4.00
GMYP1 Yasiel Puig 12.50 30.00

2013 Leaf Rookie Retro Genetic Matrix Green

*GREEN/50: .6X TO 1.5X BASIC CARDS

2013 Leaf Sports Heroes

BABG1 Bob Gibson 10.00 25.00
BABM1 Bill Mazeroski 6.00 15.00
BABR1 Brooks Robinson 10.00 25.00
BABS2 Bruce Sutter/5*
BACF1 Carlton Fisk/13*
BACRJ Cal Ripken Jr. 30.00 60.00
BADE1 Dennis Eckersley 8.00 20.00
BAEB1 Ernie Banks 15.00 40.00
BAEM1 Eddie Murray 12.00 30.00
BAFJ1 Ferguson Jenkins 6.00 15.00
BAFT1 Frank Thomas 20.00 50.00
BAGM1 Greg Maddux/5*
BAI1 Ichiro 150.00 250.00
BAIR1 Ivan Rodriguez 8.00 20.00
BAJB1 Jim Bunning/6*
BAJB2 Johnny Bench 15.00 40.00
BAJC3 Jose Canseco 15.00 40.00
BAJM2 Joe Morgan 10.00 25.00
BAJP2 Jim Palmer 6.00 15.00
BALA1 Luis Aparicio/15* 10.00 25.00
BALB2 Lou Brock 10.00 25.00
BAOC1 Orlando Cepeda 6.00 15.00
BAOS1 Ozzie Smith 12.00 30.00
BAPM1 Paul Molitor 8.00 20.00
BAPR2 Pete Rose 8.00 20.00
BARC1 Rod Carew 8.00 20.00
BARH1 Rickey Henderson 25.00 50.00
BARJ2 Reggie Jackson 12.00 30.00
BARS1 Red Schoendienst/8*
BARS2 Ryne Sandberg 15.00 40.00
BASC1 Steve Carlton/5*
BATG1 Tom Glavine 12.00 30.00
BATL1 Tommy Lasorda/15* 15.00 40.00
BATP1 Tony Perez/5*
BAWB1 Wade Boggs 8.00 20.00
BAWC1 Will Clark 8.00 20.00
BAWF1 Whitey Ford/8*
BAWH1 Whitey Herzog 8.00 20.00

2013 Leaf Sports Heroes Inscriptions Autographs

STATED PRINT RUN 60 SER. #'d SETS
ICJ1 Chipper Jones 60.00 120.00
IFT1 Frank Thomas 40.00 80.00
IJB1 Johnny Bench 25.00 50.00
IOS1 Ozzie Smith 25.00 50.00
IRA1 Roberto Alomar 25.00 50.00
IRJ2 Reggie Jackson 15.00 40.00

2013 Leaf Sports Heroes Inscriptions Autographs Silver

*SILVER: .5X TO 1.2X BASIC CARDS
STATED PRINT RUN 25 SER.#'d SETS

2013 Leaf Sports Heroes Loyalty Autographs

*SILVER/25: .5X TO 1.2X BASIC CARDS
LBG1 Bob Gibson 10.00 25.00
LBM1 Bill Mazeroski/12*
LBR1 Brooks Robinson 12.00 30.00
LCRJ Cal Ripken Jr. 20.00 50.00
LEB1 Ernie Banks 12.00 30.00
LJB2 Johnny Bench 15.00 40.00
LJP2 Jim Palmer 6.00 15.00
LWF1 Whitey Ford/8*

2013 Leaf Sports Heroes Loyalty Autographs Silver

*SILVER: .5X TO 1.2X BASIC CARDS
STATED PRINT RUN 25 SER.#'d SETS

2013 Leaf Sports Heroes Pink Ribbon Inscription Autographs

STATED PRINT RUN 60 SER. #'d SETS
PR1 Pete Rose 25.00 50.00

2013 Leaf Sports Heroes Pink Ribbon Inscription Autographs Silver

*SILVER: .5X TO 1.2X BASIC CARDS
STATED PRINT RUN 25 SER.#'d SETS

2013 Leaf Sports Heroes Team of Dreams Autographs

STATED PRINT RUN 25 SER. #'d SETS
BS Bruce Sutter 8.00 20.00
CF Carlton Fisk 20.00 50.00
DG Dwight Gooden 10.00 25.00
FT Frank Thomas 30.00 60.00
JB Johnny Bench 15.00 40.00
JP Jim Palmer 8.00 20.00
JR Jim Rice 8.00 20.00
OS Ozzie Smith 12.00 30.00
PM Paul Molitor 10.00 25.00
PR Pete Rose 15.00 40.00
RC Rod Carew 8.00 20.00
RH Rickey Henderson 30.00 60.00
RJ Reggie Jackson 15.00 40.00
WB Wade Boggs 12.00 30.00

2013 Leaf Sports Heroes Team of Dreams Corn Stalks

STATED PRINT RUN 25 SER. #'d SETS
ALSO RELEASED IN 2013 LEAF HOLIDAY BONUS PACKS
BS Bruce Sutter 12.00 30.00
CF Carlton Fisk 15.00 40.00
DG Dwight Gooden 12.00 30.00
FT Frank Thomas 20.00 50.00
JB Johnny Bench 20.00 50.00
JP Jim Palmer 15.00 40.00
JR Jim Rice 12.00 30.00
MP Matthew Perry 8.00 20.00
OS Ozzie Smith 12.00 30.00
PM Paul Molitor 15.00 40.00
PR Pete Rose 15.00 40.00
RC Rod Carew 10.00 25.00
RH Rickey Henderson 15.00 40.00
RJ Reggie Jackson 12.00 30.00
RO Randy Owen 10.00 25.00
WB Wade Boggs 15.00 40.00

2016 Leaf Sports Heroes Gold

*GOLD/15-25: .6X TO 1.5X BASIC AU

1996 Leaf Signature

The 1996 Leaf Signature Set was issued by Donruss in two series totalling 150 cards. The four-card packs carried a suggested retail price of $9.99 each. It's interesting to note that the Extended Series was the last of the 1996 releases. In fact, it was released in January, 1997 - so late in the year that it's categorization as a 1996 issue was a bit of a stretch at that time. Production for the Extended Series was only 40 percent that of the regular issue. Extended Series packs actually contained a mix of both series cards, thus the Extended Series cards are somewhat scarcer. Card fronts feature borderless color action player photos with the card name printed in a silver foil emblem. The backs carry player information. Rookie Cards include Darin Erstad. This product was a benchmark release in hobby history due to it's inclusion of one or more autograph cards per pack (explaining it's high suggested retail pack price). The product was highly successful upon release and opened the doors for wide incorporation of autograph cards into a wide array of brands from that point forward.

COMPLETE SET (150) 40.00 100.00
COMPLETE SERIES 1 (100) 25.00 60.00
COMPLETE SERIES 2 (50) 15.00 40.00
COMMON CARD (1-100) .20 .50
COMMON CARD (101-150) .10 .30
1 Mike Piazza .75 2.00
2 Juan Gonzalez .20 .50
3 Greg Maddux .75 2.00
4 Marc Newfield .20 .50
5 Wade Boggs .30 .75
6 Ray Lankford .20 .50
7 Frank Thomas .50 1.25
8 Rico Brogna .20 .50
9 Tim Salmon .30 .75
10 Ken Griffey Jr. 1.00 2.50
11 Manny Ramirez .30 .75
12 Cecil Fielder .20 .50
13 Gregg Jefferies .20 .50
14 Rondell White .20 .50
15 Cal Ripken 1.50 4.00
16 Alex Rodriguez 1.00 2.50
17 Bernie Williams .30 .75
18 Andres Galarraga .20 .50
19 Mike Mussina .30 .75
20 Chuck Knoblauch .20 .50
21 Joe Carter .20 .50
22 Jeff Bagwell .30 .75
23 Mark McGwire 1.25 3.00
24 Sammy Sosa .50 1.25
25 Reggie Sanders .20 .50
26 Chipper Jones .50 1.25
27 Jeff Cirillo .20 .50
28 Roger Clemens 1.00 2.50
29 Craig Biggio .30 .75
30 Gary Sheffield .20 .50
31 Paul O'Neill .30 .75
32 Johnny Damon .30 .75
33 Jason Isringhausen .20 .50
34 Jay Bell .20 .50
35 Henry Rodriguez .20 .50
36 Matt Williams .20 .50
37 Randy Johnson .50 1.25
38 Fred McGriff .30 .75
39 Jason Giambi .20 .50
40 Ivan Rodriguez .30 .75
41 Raul Mondesi .20 .50
42 Barry Larkin .30 .75
43 Ryan Klesko .20 .50
44 Joey Hamilton .20 .50
45 Todd Hundley .20 .50
46 Jim Edmonds .20 .50
47 Dante Bichette .20 .50
48 Roberto Alomar .30 .75
49 Mark Grace .30 .75
50 Brady Anderson .20 .50
51 Hideo Nomo .50 1.25
52 Ozzie Smith .75 2.00
53 Robin Ventura .20 .50
54 Andy Pettitte .30 .75
55 Kenny Lofton .20 .50
56 John Mabry .20 .50
57 Paul Molitor .20 .50
58 Rey Ordonez .20 .50
59 Albert Belle .20 .50
60 Charles Johnson .20 .50
61 Edgar Martinez .30 .75
62 Derek Bell .20 .50
63 Carlos Delgado .20 .50
64 Raul Casanova .20 .50
65 Ismael Valdes .20 .50
66 J.T. Snow .20 .50
67 Derek Jeter 1.25 3.00
68 Jason Kendall .20 .50
69 John Smoltz .30 .75
70 Chad Mottola .20 .50
71 Jim Thome .30 .75
72 Will Clark .30 .75
73 Mo Vaughn .20 .50
74 John Wasdin .20 .50
75 Rafael Palmeiro .30 .75
76 Mark Grudzielanek .20 .50
77 Larry Walker .20 .50
78 Alan Benes .20 .50
79 Michael Tucker .20 .50
80 Billy Wagner .20 .50
81 Paul Wilson .20 .50
82 Greg Vaughn .20 .50
83 Dean Palmer .20 .50
84 Ryne Sandberg .75 2.00
85 Eric Young .20 .50
86 Jay Buhner .20 .50
87 Tony Clark .20 .50
88 Jermaine Dye .20 .50
89 Barry Bonds 1.25 3.00
90 Ugueth Urbina .20 .50
91 Charles Nagy .20 .50
92 Ruben Rivera .20 .50
93 Todd Hollandsworth .20 .50
94 Darin Erstad RC 1.50 4.00
95 Brooks Kieschnick .20 .50
96 Edgar Renteria .20 .50
97 Lenny Dykstra .20 .50
98 Tony Gwynn .60 1.50
99 Kirby Puckett .50 1.25
100 Checklist .20 .50
101 Andruw Jones 1.00 2.50
102 Alex Ochoa .10 .30
103 David Cone .20 .50
104 Rusty Greer .20 .50
105 Jose Canseco .30 .75
106 Ken Caminiti .20 .50
107 Mariano Rivera 1.00 2.50
108 Ron Gant .20 .50
109 Darryl Strawberry .20 .50
110 Vladimir Guerrero 1.25 3.00
111 George Arias .10 .30
112 Jeff Conine .20 .50
113 Bobby Higginson .20 .50
114 Eric Karros .20 .50
115 Brian Hunter .10 .30
116 Eddie Murray .50 1.25
117 Todd Walker .10 .30
118 Chan Ho Park .20 .50
119 John Jaha .10 .30
120 Dave Justice .20 .50
121 Makoto Suzuki .10 .30
122 Scott Rolen .50 1.25
123 Tino Martinez .30 .75
124 Kimera Bartee .10 .30
125 Garret Anderson .20 .50
126 Brian Jordan .20 .50
127 Andre Dawson .20 .50
128 Javier Lopez .20 .50
129 Bill Pulsipher .10 .30
130 Dwight Gooden .20 .50
131 Al Martin .10 .30
132 Terrell Wade .10 .30
133 Steve Gibralter .10 .30
134 Tom Glavine .30 .75
135 Kevin Appier .20 .50
136 Tim Raines .20 .50
137 Curtis Pride .10 .30
138 Todd Greene .10 .30
139 Bobby Bonilla .20 .50
140 Trey Beamon .10 .30
141 Marty Cordova .10 .30
142 Rickey Henderson .50 1.25
143 Ellis Burks .20 .50
144 Dennis Eckersley .20 .50
145 Kevin Brown .20 .50
146 Carlos Baerga .10 .30
147 Brett Butler .20 .50
148 Marquis Grissom .20 .50
149 Karim Garcia .10 .30
150 Frank Thomas CL .30 .75

1996 Leaf Signature Gold Press Proofs

COMPLETE SET (150) 700.00 1100.00
COMPLETE SERIES 1 (100) 400.00 800.00
*SER.1 STARS: 4X TO 10X BASIC CARDS
*SER.1 ROOKIES: 1.25X TO 3X BASIC
*SER.2 STARS: 3X TO 8X BASIC CARDS
STATED ODDS 1:12
67 Derek Jeter 20.00 50.00

1996 Leaf Signature Platinum Press Proofs

*SER.1 STARS: 10X TO 25X BASIC
*SER. 1 ROOKIES: 2.5X TO 6X BASIC
*SER.2 STARS: 8X TO 20X BASIC
RANDOM INSERTS IN EXTENDED PACKS
STATED PRINT RUN 150 SETS
67 Derek Jeter 125.00 250.00

1996 Leaf Signature Autographs

ONE OR MORE BRONZE AUTOS PER PACK
BRONZE NON-SP PRINT RUN 3500 SETS
BRONZE SP PRINT RUN 700 SETS
BRONZE CARDS PRICED BELOW

1 Kurt Abbott 2.00 5.00
2 Juan Acevedo 2.00 5.00
3 Terry Adams 2.00 5.00
4 Manny Alexander 2.00 5.00
5 Roberto Alomar SP 15.00 40.00
6 Moises Alou 4.00 10.00
7 Wilson Alvarez 2.00 5.00
8 Garret Anderson 2.00 5.00
9 Shane Andrews 2.00 5.00
10 Andy Ashby 2.00 5.00
11 Pedro Astacio 2.00 5.00
12 Brad Ausmus 2.00 5.00
13 Bobby Ayala 2.00 5.00
14 Carlos Baerga 4.00 10.00
15 Harold Baines 4.00 10.00
16 Jason Bates 2.00 5.00
17 Allen Battle 2.00 5.00
18 Rich Becker 2.00 5.00
19 David Bell 4.00 10.00
20 Rafael Belliard 4.00 10.00
21 Andy Benes 2.00 5.00
22 Armando Benitez 2.00 5.00
23 Jason Bere 2.00 5.00
24 Geronimo Berroa 2.00 5.00
25 Willie Blair 2.00 5.00
26 Mike Blowers 2.00 5.00
27 Wade Boggs SP 15.00 40.00
28 Ricky Bones 2.00 5.00
29 Mike Bordick 4.00 10.00
30 Toby Borland 2.00 5.00
31 Ricky Bottalico 2.00 5.00
32 Darren Bragg 2.00 5.00
33 Jeff Branson 2.00 5.00
34 Tilson Brito 2.00 5.00
35 Rico Brogna 2.00 5.00
36 Scott Brosius 2.00 5.00
37 Damon Buford 2.00 5.00
38 Mike Busby 2.00 5.00
39 Tom Candiotti 2.00 5.00
40 Frank Castillo 2.00 5.00
41 Andujar Cedeno 2.00 5.00
42 Domingo Cedeno 2.00 5.00
43 Roger Cedeno 2.00 5.00
44 Norm Charlton 2.00 5.00
45 Jeff Cirillo 4.00 10.00
46 Will Clark 10.00 25.00
47 Jeff Conine 2.00 5.00
48 Steve Cooke 2.00 5.00
49 Joey Cora 2.00 5.00
50 Marty Cordova 2.00 5.00
51 Rheal Cormier 2.00 5.00
52 Felipe Crespo 2.00 5.00
53 Chad Curtis 2.00 5.00
54 Johnny Damon 4.00 10.00
55 Russ Davis 8.00 20.00
56 Andre Dawson 6.00 15.00
57 Carlos Delgado 2.50 6.00
58 Doug Drabek 2.00 5.00
59 Darren Dreifort 2.00 5.00
60 Shawon Dunston 2.00 5.00
61 Ray Durham 2.00 5.00
62 Jim Edmonds 5.00 12.00
63 Joey Eischen 2.00 5.00
64 Jim Eisenreich 2.00 5.00
65 Sal Fasano 2.00 5.00
66 Jeff Fassero 2.00 5.00
67 Alex Fernandez 2.00 5.00
68 Darrin Fletcher 2.00 5.00
69 Chad Fonville 2.00 5.00
70 Kevin Foster 2.00 5.00
71 John Franco 4.00 10.00
72 Julio Franco 8.00 20.00
73 Marvin Freeman 2.00 5.00
74 Travis Fryman 5.00 12.00
75 Gary Gaetti 2.00 5.00
76 Carlos Garcia 2.00 5.00
77 Jason Giambi 2.00 5.00
78 Benji Gil 2.00 5.00
79 Greg Gohr 2.00 5.00
80 Chris Gomez 2.00 5.00
81 Leo Gomez 2.00 5.00
82 Tom Goodwin 2.00 5.00
83 Mike Grace 2.00 5.00
84 Mike Greenwell 4.00 10.00
85 Rusty Greer 2.00 5.00
86 Mark Grudzielanek 2.00 5.00
87 Mark Gubicza 2.00 5.00
88 Juan Guzman 2.00 5.00
89 Darryl Hamilton 2.00 5.00
90 Joey Hamilton 2.00 5.00
91 Chris Hammond 2.00 5.00
92 Mike Hampton 4.00 10.00
93 Chris Haney 2.00 5.00
94 Todd Haney 2.00 5.00
95 Erik Hanson 2.00 5.00
96 Pete Harnisch 2.00 5.00
97 LaTroy Hawkins 2.00 5.00
98 Charlie Hayes 2.00 5.00
99 Jimmy Haynes 2.00 5.00
100 Roberto Hernandez 2.00 5.00
101 Bobby Higginson 2.00 5.00
102 Glenallen Hill 2.00 5.00
103 Ken Hill 2.00 5.00
104 Sterling Hitchcock 2.00 5.00
105 Trevor Hoffman 10.00 25.00
106 Dave Hollins 2.00 5.00
107 Dwayne Hosey 2.00 5.00
108 Thomas Howard 2.00 5.00
109 Steve Howe 4.00 10.00
110 John Hudek 2.00 5.00
111 Rex Hudler 2.00 5.00
112 Brian L.Hunter 2.00 5.00
113 Butch Huskey 4.00 10.00
114 Mark Hutton 2.00 5.00
115 Jason Jacome 2.00 5.00
116 John Jaha 2.00 5.00
117 Reggie Jefferson 2.00 5.00
118 Derek Jeter SP 350.00 700.00
119 Bobby Jones 2.00 5.00
120 Todd Jones 2.00 5.00
121 Brian Jordan 2.00 5.00
122 Kevin Jordan 2.00 5.00
123 Jeff Juden 2.00 5.00
124 Ron Karkovice 2.00 5.00
125 Roberto Kelly 2.00 5.00
126 Mark Kiefer 2.00 5.00
127 Brooks Kieschnick 2.00 5.00
128 Jeff King 4.00 10.00
129 Mike Lansing 2.00 5.00
130 Matt Lawton 2.00 5.00
131 Al Leiter 2.00 5.00
132 Mark Leiter 2.00 5.00
133 Curtis Leskanic 4.00 10.00
134 Darren Lewis 2.00 5.00
135 Mark Lewis 2.00 5.00
136 Felipe Lira 2.00 5.00
137 Pat Listach 2.00 5.00
138 Keith Lockhart 2.00 5.00
139 Kenny Lofton SP 12.50 30.00
140 John Mabry 2.00 5.00
141 Mike Macfarlane 2.00 5.00
142 Kirt Manwaring 2.00 5.00
143 Al Martin 2.00 5.00
144 Norberto Martin 2.00 5.00
145 Dennis Martinez 4.00 10.00
146 Pedro Martinez 30.00 80.00
147 Sandy Martinez 2.00 5.00
148 Mike Matheny 2.00 5.00
149 T.J. Mathews 2.00 5.00
150 David McCarty 2.00 5.00
151 Ben McDonald 2.00 5.00
152 Pat Meares 2.00 5.00
153 Orlando Merced 2.00 5.00
154 Jose Mesa 2.00 5.00
155 Matt Mieske 2.00 5.00
156 Orlando Miller 2.00 5.00
157 Mike Mimbs 2.00 5.00
158 Paul Molitor SP 20.00 40.00
159 Raul Mondesi SP 10.00 25.00
160 Jeff Montgomery 2.00 5.00
161 Mickey Morandini 2.00 5.00
162 Lyle Mouton 2.00 5.00
163 James Mouton 2.00 5.00
164 Jamie Moyer 5.00 12.00
165 Rodney Myers 2.00 5.00
166 Denny Neagle 4.00 10.00
167 Robb Nen 4.00 10.00
168 Marc Newfield 2.00 5.00
169 Dave Nilsson 2.00 5.00
170 Otis Nixon * 30.00 60.00
171 Jon Nunnally 2.00 5.00
172 Chad Ogea 2.00 5.00
173 Troy O'Leary 2.00 5.00
174 Rey Ordonez 2.00 5.00
175 Jayhawk Owens 2.00 5.00
176 Tom Pagnozzi 2.00 5.00
177 Dean Palmer 2.00 5.00
178 Roger Pavlik 2.00 5.00
179 Troy Percival 4.00 10.00
180 Carlos Perez 2.00 5.00
181 Robert Perez 2.00 5.00
182 Andy Pettitte 20.00 50.00
183 Phil Plantier 2.00 5.00
184 Mike Potts 2.00 5.00
185 Curtis Pride 2.00 5.00
186 Ariel Prieto 2.00 5.00
187 Bill Pulsipher 2.00 5.00
188 Brad Radke 2.00 5.00
189 Manny Ramirez SP 20.00 50.00
190 Joe Randa 2.00 5.00
191 Pat Rapp 2.00 5.00
192 Bryan Rekar 2.00 5.00
193 Shane Reynolds 2.00 5.00
194 Arthur Rhodes 2.00 5.00
195 Mariano Rivera 75.00 200.00
196 Alex Rodriguez SP 50.00 100.00
197 Frank Rodriguez 2.00 5.00
198 Mel Rojas 2.00 5.00
199 Ken Ryan 2.00 5.00
200 Bret Saberhagen 4.00 10.00
201 Tim Salmon 4.00 10.00
202 Rey Sanchez 2.00 5.00
203 Scott Sanders 2.00 5.00
204 Steve Scarsone 2.00 5.00
205 Curt Schilling 15.00 40.00
206 Jason Schmidt 2.00 5.00
207 David Segui 2.00 5.00
208 Kevin Seitzer 2.00 5.00
209 Scott Servais 2.00 5.00
210 Don Slaught 2.00 5.00
211 Zane Smith 2.00 5.00
212 Paul Sorrento 2.00 5.00
213 Scott Stahoviak 2.00 5.00
214 Mike Stanley 2.00 5.00
215 Terry Steinbach 2.00 5.00
216 Kevin Stocker 2.00 5.00
217 Jeff Suppan 4.00 10.00
218 Bill Swift 2.00 5.00
219 Greg Swindell 2.00 5.00
220 Kevin Tapani 2.00 5.00
221 Danny Tartabull 2.00 5.00
222 Julian Tavarez 2.00 5.00
223 Frank Thomas SP 20.00 50.00
224 Ozzie Timmons 2.00 5.00
225 Michael Tucker 2.00 5.00
226 Ismael Valdes 2.00 5.00
227 Jose Valentin 2.00 5.00
228 Todd Van Poppel 2.00 5.00
229 Mo Vaughn SP 12.00 30.00
230 Quilvio Veras 2.00 5.00
231 Fernando Vina 2.00 5.00
232 Joe Vitiello 2.00 5.00
233 Jose Vizcaino 2.00 5.00
234 Omar Vizquel 8.00 20.00
235 Terrell Wade 2.00 5.00
236 Paul Wagner 2.00 5.00
237 Matt Walbeck 2.00 5.00
238 Jerome Walton 4.00 10.00
239 Turner Ward 2.00 5.00
240 Allen Watson 2.00 5.00
241 David Weathers 2.00 5.00
242 Walt Weiss 3.00 8.00
243 Turk Wendell 2.00 5.00
244 Rondell White 4.00 10.00
245 Brian Williams 2.00 5.00
246 George Williams 2.00 5.00
247 Paul Wilson 2.00 5.00
248 Bobby Witt 2.00 5.00
249 Bob Wolcott 2.00 5.00
250 Eric Young 2.00 5.00
251 Ernie Young 2.00 5.00
252 Greg Zaun 2.00 5.00
NNO F.Thomas Jumbo AU/1500 25.00 60.00
NNO Frank Thomas Fascimile
Auto Sample .75 2.00

1996 Leaf Signature Autographs Gold

*GOLD: .6X TO 1.5X BRONZE CARDS
RANDOM INSERTS IN PACKS
GOLD NON-SP PRINT RUN 500 SETS
GOLD SP PRINT RUN 100 SETS
CARDS ARE UNNUMBERED

146 Pedro Martinez 40.00 100.00
223 Jim Thome SP/514 30.00 80.00

1996 Leaf Signature Autographs Silver

*SILVER: .4X TO 1X BRONZE CARDS
RANDOM INSERTS IN PACKS
SILVER NON-SP PRINT RUN 1000 SETS
SILVER SP PRINT RUN 200 SETS
UNNUMBERED CARDS

118 Derek Jeter SP 800.00 1000.00
223 Jim Thome SP/410 30.00 80.00

1996 Leaf Signature Extended Autographs

TWO OR MORE AUTOGRAPHS PER PACK
NON-SP PRINT RUN 5000 OF EACH CARD
EXCH.DEADLINE: 12/31/98

1 Scott Aldred 2.00 5.00
2 Mike Aldrete 2.00 5.00
3 Rich Amaral 2.00 5.00
4 Alex Arias 2.00 5.00
5 Paul Assenmacher 2.00 5.00
6 Roger Bailey 2.00 5.00
7 Erik Bennett 2.00 5.00
8 Sean Bergman 2.00 5.00
9 Doug Bochtler 2.00 5.00
10 Tim Bogar 2.00 5.00
11 Pat Borders 2.00 5.00
12 Pedro Borbon 2.00 5.00
13 Shawn Boskie 2.00 5.00
14 Rafael Bournigal 2.00 5.00
15 Mark Brandenburg 2.00 5.00
16 John Briscoe 2.00 5.00
17 Jorge Brito 2.00 5.00
18 Doug Brocail 2.00 5.00
19 Jay Buhner SP/1000 8.00 20.00
20 Scott Bullett 2.00 5.00
21 Dave Burba 2.00 5.00
22 Ken Caminiti SP/1000 20.00 50.00
23 John Cangelosi 2.00 5.00
24 Cris Carpenter 2.00 5.00
25 Chuck Carr 2.00 5.00
26 Larry Casian 2.00 5.00
27 Tony Castillo 2.00 5.00
28 Jason Christiansen 2.00 5.00
29 Archi Cianfrocco 2.00 5.00
30 Mark Clark 2.00 5.00
31 Terry Clark 2.00 5.00
32 Roger Clemens SP/1000 30.00 80.00
33 Jim Converse 2.00 5.00
34 Dennis Cook 2.00 5.00
35 Francisco Cordova 2.00 5.00
36 Jim Corsi 2.00 5.00
37 Tim Crabtree 2.00 5.00
38 Doug Creek SP/1950 6.00 15.00
39 John Cummings 2.00 5.00
40 Omar Daal 2.00 5.00
41 Rich DeLucia 2.00 5.00
42 Mark Dewey 2.00 5.00
43 Alex Diaz 2.00 5.00
44 Jermaine Dye SP/2500 6.00 15.00
45 Ken Edenfield 2.00 5.00
46 Mark Eichhorn 2.00 5.00
47 John Ericks 2.00 5.00
48 Darin Erstad 4.00 10.00
49 Alvaro Espinoza 2.00 5.00
50 Jorge Fabregas 2.00 5.00
51 Mike Fetters 2.00 5.00
52 John Flaherty 2.00 5.00
53 Bryce Florie 2.00 5.00
54 Tony Fossas 2.00 5.00
55 Lou Frazier 2.00 5.00
56 Mike Gallego 2.00 5.00
57 Karim Garcia SP/2500 6.00 15.00
58 Jason Giambi 6.00 15.00
59 Ed Giovanola 2.00 5.00
60 Tom Glavine SP/1250 15.00 40.00
61 Juan Gonzalez SP/1000 15.00 40.00
62 Craig Grebeck 2.00 5.00
63 Buddy Groom 2.00 5.00
64 Kevin Gross 2.00 5.00
65 Eddie Guardado 4.00 10.00
66 Mark Guthrie 2.00 5.00
67 Tony Gwynn SP/1000 60.00 150.00
68 Chip Hale 2.00 5.00
69 Darren Hall 2.00 5.00
70 Lee Hancock 2.00 5.00
71 Dave Hansen 2.00 5.00
72 Bryan Harvey 2.00 5.00
73 Bill Haselman 2.00 5.00
74 Mike Henneman 2.00 5.00
75 Doug Henry 2.00 5.00
76 Gil Heredia 2.00 5.00
77 Carlos Hernandez 2.00 5.00
78 Jose Hernandez 2.00 5.00
79 Darren Holmes 2.00 5.00
80 Mark Holzemer 2.00 5.00
81 Rick Honeycutt 2.00 5.00
82 Chris Hook 2.00 5.00
83 Chris Howard 2.00 5.00
84 Jack Howell 2.00 5.00
85 David Hulse 2.00 5.00
86 Edwin Hurtado 2.00 5.00
87 Jeff Huson 2.00 5.00
88 Mike James 2.00 5.00
89 Derek Jeter SP/1000 300.00 800.00
90 Brian Johnson 2.00 5.00
91 Randy Johnson SP/1000 60.00 150.00
92 Mark Johnson 2.00 5.00
93 Andruw Jones SP/2000 6.00 15.00
94 Chris Jones 2.00 5.00
95 Ricky Jordan 2.00 5.00
96 Matt Karchner 2.00 5.00
97 Scott Karl 2.00 5.00
98 Jason Kendall SP/2500 5.00 12.00
99 Brian Keyser 2.00 5.00
100 Mike Kingery 2.00 5.00
101 Wayne Kirby 2.00 5.00
102 Ryan Klesko SP/1000 3.00 8.00
103 Chuck Knoblauch SP/1000 12.00 30.00
104 Chad Kreuter 2.00 5.00
105 Tom Lampkin 2.00 5.00
106 Scott Leius 2.00 5.00
107 Jon Lieber 4.00 10.00
108 Nelson Liriano 2.00 5.00
109 Scott Livingstone 2.00 5.00
110 Graeme Lloyd 2.00 5.00
111 Kenny Lofton SP/1000 15.00 40.00
112 Luis Lopez 2.00 5.00
113 Torey Lovullo 2.00 5.00
114 Greg Maddux SP/500 150.00 300.00
115 Mike Maddux 2.00 5.00
116 Dave Magadan 2.00 5.00
117 Mike Magnante 2.00 5.00
118 Joe Magrane 2.00 5.00
119 Pat Mahomes 2.00 5.00
120 Matt Mantei 2.00 5.00
121 John Marzano 2.00 5.00
122 Terry Mathews 2.00 5.00
123 Chuck McElroy 2.00 5.00
124 Fred McGriff SP/1000 20.00 50.00
125 Mark McLemore 2.00 5.00
126 Greg McMichael 2.00 5.00
127 Blas Minor 2.00 5.00
128 Dave Mlicki 2.00 5.00
129 Mike Mohler 2.00 5.00
130 Paul Molitor SP/1000 12.00 30.00
131 Steve Montgomery 2.00 5.00
132 Mike Mordecai 2.00 5.00
133 Mike Morgan 2.00 5.00
134 Mike Munoz 2.00 5.00
135 Greg Myers 2.00 5.00
136 Jimmy Myers 2.00 5.00
137 Mike Myers 2.00 5.00
138 Bob Natal 2.00 5.00
139 Dan Naulty 2.00 5.00
140 Jeff Nelson 4.00 10.00
141 Warren Newson 2.00 5.00
142 Chris Nichting 2.00 5.00
143 Melvin Nieves 2.00 5.00
144 Charlie O'Brien 2.00 5.00
145 Alex Ochoa 2.00 5.00
146 Omar Olivares 2.00 5.00
147 Joe Oliver 3.00 8.00
148 Lance Painter 2.00 5.00
149 Rafael Palmeiro SP/2000 10.00 25.00
150 Mark Parent 2.00 5.00
151 Steve Parris SP/1800 6.00 15.00
152 Bob Patterson 2.00 5.00
153 Tony Pena 5.00 12.00
154 Eddie Perez 2.00 5.00
155 Yorkis Perez 2.00 5.00
156 Robert Person 2.00 5.00
157 Mark Petkovsek 2.00 5.00
158 Andy Pettitte SP/1000 30.00 60.00
159 J.R. Phillips 2.00 5.00
160 Hipolito Pichardo 2.00 5.00
161 Eric Plunk 2.00 5.00
162 Jimmy Poole 2.00 5.00
163 Kirby Puckett SP/1000 150.00 300.00
164 Paul Quantrill 2.00 5.00
165 Tom Quinlan 2.00 5.00
166 Jeff Reboulet 2.00 5.00
167 Jeff Reed 2.00 5.00
168 Steve Reed 2.00 5.00
169 Carlos Reyes 2.00 5.00
170 Bill Risley 2.00 5.00
171 Kevin Ritz 2.00 5.00
172 Kevin Roberson 2.00 5.00
173 Rich Robertson 2.00 5.00
174 Alex Rodriguez SP/500 75.00 200.00
175 Ivan Rodriguez SP/1250 20.00 50.00
176 Bruce Ruffin 2.00 5.00
177 Juan Samuel 2.00 5.00
178 Tim Scott 2.00 5.00
179 Kevin Sefcik 2.00 5.00
180 Jeff Shaw 2.00 5.00
181 Danny Sheaffer 2.00 5.00
182 Craig Shipley 2.00 5.00
183 Dave Silvestri 2.00 5.00
184 Aaron Small 2.00 5.00
185 John Smoltz SP/1000 30.00 60.00
186 Luis Sojo 2.00 5.00
187 Sammy Sosa SP/1000 40.00 100.00
188 Steve Sparks 2.00 5.00
189 Tim Spehr 2.00 5.00
190 Russ Springer 2.00 5.00
191 Matt Stairs 2.00 5.00
192 Andy Stankiewicz 2.00 5.00
193 Mike Stanton 6.00 12.00
194 Kelly Stinnett 2.00 5.00
195 Doug Strange 2.00 5.00
196 Mark Sweeney 2.00 5.00
197 Jeff Tabaka 2.00 5.00
198 Jesus Tavarez 2.00 5.00
199 Frank Thomas SP/1000 40.00 80.00
200 Larry Thomas 2.00 5.00
201 Mark Thompson 2.00 5.00
202 Mike Timlin 3.00 8.00
203 Steve Trachsel 2.00 5.00
204 Tom Urbani 2.00 5.00
205 Julio Valera 2.00 5.00
206 Dave Valle 2.00 5.00
207 William VanLandingham 2.00 5.00
208 Mo Vaughn SP/1000 8.00 20.00
209 Dave Veres 2.00 5.00
210 Ed Vosberg 2.00 5.00
211 Don Wengert 2.00 5.00
212 Matt Whiteside 2.00 5.00
213 Bob Wickman 4.00 10.00
214 Matt Williams SP/1250 8.00 20.00
215 Mike Williams 2.00 5.00
216 Woody Williams 4.00 10.00
217 Craig Worthington 2.00 5.00
NNO F.Thomas Jumbo AU 25.00 60.00

1996 Leaf Signature Extended Autographs Century Marks

RANDOM INSERTS IN PACKS
STATED PRINT RUN 100 SETS

1 Jay Buhner 30.00 80.00
2 Ken Caminiti 30.00 80.00
3 Roger Clemens 200.00 400.00
4 Jermaine Dye 30.00 60.00
5 Darin Erstad 25.00 60.00
6 Karim Garcia 20.00 50.00
7 Jason Giambi 30.00 60.00
8 Tom Glavine 50.00 120.00
9 Juan Gonzalez 30.00 60.00
10 Tony Gwynn 100.00 200.00
11 Derek Jeter 2000.00 4000.00
12 Randy Johnson 300.00 600.00
13 Andruw Jones 10.00 25.00
14 Jason Kendall 30.00 60.00
15 Ryan Klesko 30.00 60.00
16 Chuck Knoblauch 30.00 60.00
17 Kenny Lofton 30.00 60.00
18 Greg Maddux 300.00 600.00
19 Fred McGriff 60.00 120.00
20 Paul Molitor 50.00 100.00
21 Alex Ochoa 15.00 40.00
22 Rafael Palmeiro 40.00 100.00
23 Andy Pettitte 75.00 150.00
24 Kirby Puckett 100.00 200.00
25 Alex Rodriguez 125.00 300.00
26 Ivan Rodriguez 50.00 100.00
27 John Smoltz 75.00 150.00
28 Sammy Sosa 200.00 500.00
29 Frank Thomas 100.00 200.00
30 Mo Vaughn 30.00 80.00
31 Matt Williams 25.00 60.00

2004 Leather and Lumber

COMP.SET w/o SP's (150) 15.00 40.00
COMMON CARD (1-150) .15 .40
COMMON RETIRED (1-150) .15 .40
COMMON AUTO (151-175) 3.00 8.00
COMMON CARD (151-175) .50 1.25
151-175 RANDOM INSERTS IN PACKS
151-175 PRINT RUN 500 SERIAL #'d SETS

1 Bartolo Colon .15 .40
2 Garret Anderson .15 .40
3 Tim Salmon .15 .40
4 Troy Glaus .15 .40
5 Vladimir Guerrero .25 .60
6 Brandon Webb .15 .40
7 Luis Gonzalez .15 .40
8 Randy Johnson .40 1.00
9 Richie Sexson .15 .40
10 Shea Hillenbrand .15 .40
11 Adam LaRoche .15 .40
12 Andruw Jones .15 .40
13 Chipper Jones .40 1.00
14 Dale Murphy .40 1.00
15 J.D. Drew .15 .40
16 Marcus Giles .15 .40
17 Rafael Furcal .15 .40
18 Cal Ripken 1.25 3.00
19 Javy Lopez .15 .40
20 Jay Gibbons .15 .40
21 Luis Matos .15 .40
22 Miguel Tejada .25 .60
23 Rafael Palmeiro .25 .60
24 Curt Schilling .25 .60
25 Jason Varitek .40 1.00
26 Manny Ramirez .40 1.00
27 Nomar Garciaparra .25 .60
28 Pedro Martinez .25 .60
29 Trot Nixon .15 .40
30 Greg Maddux .50 1.25
31 Kerry Wood .15 .40
32 Mark Prior .25 .60
33 Ryne Sandberg .75 2.00
34 Sammy Sosa .40 1.00
35 Carlos Lee .15 .40
36 Frank Thomas .40 1.00
37 Magglio Ordonez .25 .60
38 Paul Konerko .25 .60
39 Adam Dunn .25 .60
40 Austin Kearns .15 .40
41 Barry Larkin .25 .60
42 Ken Griffey Jr. .75 2.00
43 Ryan Wagner .15 .40
44 C.C. Sabathia .25 .60
45 Jody Gerut .15 .40
46 Omar Vizquel .25 .60
47 Larry Walker .25 .60
48 Preston Wilson .15 .40
49 Todd Helton .25 .60
50 Alan Trammell .25 .60
51 Ivan Rodriguez .25 .60
52 Jeremy Bonderman .15 .40
53 Dontrelle Willis .15 .40
54 Josh Beckett .15 .40
55 Luis Castillo .15 .40
56 Miguel Cabrera .40 1.00
57 Mike Lowell .15 .40
58 Andy Pettitte .25 .60
59 Craig Biggio .25 .60
60 Jeff Bagwell .25 .60
61 Jeff Kent .15 .40
62 Lance Berkman .25 .60
63 Roger Clemens .50 1.25
64 Roy Oswalt .25 .60
65 Angel Berroa .15 .40
66 Carlos Beltran .25 .60
67 George Brett .75 2.00
68 Juan Gonzalez .15 .40
69 Mike Sweeney .15 .40
70 Eric Gagne .15 .40
71 Hideo Nomo .40 1.00
72 Kazuhisa Ishii .15 .40
73 Paul Lo Duca .15 .40
74 Shawn Green .15 .40
75 Geoff Jenkins .15 .40
76 Junior Spivey .15 .40
77 Rickie Weeks .15 .40
78 Robin Yount .40 1.00
79 Scott Podsednik .15 .40
80 Jacque Jones .15 .40
81 Johan Santana .25 .60
82 Shannon Stewart .15 .40
83 Torii Hunter .15 .40
84 Andre Dawson .25 .60
85 Chad Cordero .15 .40
86 Jose Vidro .15 .40
87 Nick Johnson .15 .40
88 Orlando Cabrera .15 .40
89 Gary Carter .25 .60
90 Jae Weong Seo .15 .40
91 Jose Reyes .25 .60
92 Mike Piazza .40 1.00
93 Tom Glavine .25 .60
94 Alex Rodriguez .50 1.25
95 Bernie Williams .25 .60
96 Derek Jeter 1.00 2.50
97 Don Mattingly .75 2.00
98 Gary Sheffield .15 .40
99 Hideki Matsui .60 1.50
100 Jason Giambi .15 .40
101 Jorge Posada .25 .60
102 Mike Mussina .25 .60
103 Barry Zito .25 .60
104 Bobby Crosby .15 .40
105 Eric Chavez .15 .40
106 Jermaine Dye .15 .40
107 Mark Mulder .15 .40
108 Rich Harden .15 .40
109 Rickey Henderson .40 1.00
110 Tim Hudson .25 .60
111 Bobby Abreu .15 .40
112 Brett Myers .15 .40
113 Jim Thome .25 .60
114 Kevin Millwood .15 .40
115 Marlon Byrd .15 .40
116 Mike Schmidt .60 1.50
117 Pat Burrell .15 .40
118 Dave Parker .15 .40
119 Jason Bay .25 .60
120 Jason Kendall .15 .40
121 Brian Giles .15 .40
122 Jay Payton .15 .40
123 Ryan Klesko .15 .40
124 Tony Gwynn .40 1.00
125 Edgardo Alfonzo .15 .40
126 Jason Schmidt .15 .40
127 Jerome Williams .15 .40
128 Bret Boone .15 .40
129 Edgar Martinez .25 .60
130 Ichiro Suzuki .50 1.25
131 Jamie Moyer .15 .40
132 John Olerud .15 .40
133 Albert Pujols .50 1.25
134 Edgar Renteria .15 .40
135 Jim Edmonds .25 .60
136 Matt Morris .15 .40
137 Scott Rolen .25 .60
138 Aubrey Huff .15 .40
139 Carl Crawford .25 .60
140 Delmon Young .25 .60
141 Rocco Baldelli .15 .40
142 Alfonso Soriano .25 .60
143 Hank Blalock .15 .40
144 Mark Teixeira .25 .60
145 Michael Young .15 .40
146 Nolan Ryan 1.25 3.00
147 Carlos Delgado .15 .40
148 Eric Hinske .15 .40
149 Roy Halladay .25 .60
150 Vernon Wells .15 .40
151 Andres Blanco ROO AU RC 3.00 8.00
152 Kevin Cave ROO AU RC 3.00 8.00
153 Ryan Meaux ROO AU RC 3.00 8.00
154 Tim Bausher ROO AU RC 3.00 8.00
155 Jesse Harper ROO AU RC 3.00 8.00
156 Mike Wuertz ROO AU RC 4.00 10.00
157 Colby Miller ROO AU RC 3.00 8.00
158 Don Kelly ROO AU RC 3.00 8.00
159 Edwin Moreno ROO AU RC 4.00 10.00
160 Mike Johnston ROO AU RC 3.00 8.00
161 O.Rodriguez ROO AU RC 3.00 8.00
162 Phil Stockman ROO AU RC 3.00 8.00
163 Yadier Molina ROO RC 50.00 120.00
164 Jorge Vasquez ROO AU RC 3.00 8.00
165 Scott Proctor ROO AU RC 4.00 10.00
166 Jake Woods ROO AU RC 3.00 8.00
167 Aarom Baldiris ROO AU RC 3.00 8.00
168 Jason Bartlett ROO AU RC 4.00 10.00
169 Casey Daigle ROO AU RC 3.00 8.00
170 Dennis Sarfate ROO AU RC 3.00 8.00
171 E.Sierra ROO AU RC 4.00 10.00
172 Merkin Valdez ROO AU RC 3.00 8.00
173 E.Rodriguez ROO AU RC 4.00 10.00
174 Kazuo Matsui ROO RC .75 2.00
175 David Aardsma ROO RC .50 1.25

2004 Leather and Lumber B/W

*B/W: 1X TO 2.5X BASIC
*B/W ROO: .4X TO 1X BASIC ROO
RANDOM INSERTS IN PACKS
STATED PRINT RUN 1000 SERIAL #'d SETS
SKIP-NUMBERED 25-CARD SET
CL: 13-14/18/27/30/32-34/63/67/78/89/92
CL: 94/96-97/99/109/116/124/130/133/142
CL: 146/174

2004 Leather and Lumber Gold

*GOLD 1-150: 8X TO 20X BASIC
*GOLD RETIRED 1-150: 6X TO 15X BASIC
RANDOM INSERTS IN PACKS
STATED PRINT RUN 25 SERIAL #'d SETS
NO PRICING ON 151-175 DUE TO SCARCITY

2004 Leather and Lumber Gold B/W

*GOLD B/W: 8X TO 20X BASIC
*GOLD RETIRED B/W: 6X TO 15X BASIC
RANDOM INSERTS IN PACKS
STATED PRINT RUN 25 SERIAL #'d SETS
NO CARD 174 PRICING DUE TO SCARCITY

2004 Leather and Lumber Silver

*SILVER 1-150: 3X TO 8X BASIC
*SILVER RETIRED 1-150: 3X TO 8X BASIC
RANDOM INSERTS IN PACKS
STATED PRINT RUN 100 SERIAL #'d SETS

151 Andres Blanco ROO 1.25 3.00
152 Kevin Cave ROO 1.25 3.00
153 Ryan Meaux ROO 1.25 3.00
154 Tim Bausher ROO 1.25 3.00
155 Jesse Harper ROO 1.25 3.00
156 Michael Wuertz ROO 1.25 3.00
157 Colby Miller ROO 1.25 3.00
158 Don Kelly ROO 2.00 5.00
159 Edwin Moreno ROO 1.25 3.00
160 Mike Johnston ROO 1.25 3.00
161 Orlando Rodriguez ROO 1.25 3.00
162 Phil Stockman ROO 1.25 3.00
163 Yadier Molina ROO 125.00 300.00
164 Jorge Vasquez ROO 1.25 3.00
165 Scott Proctor ROO 1.25 3.00
166 Jake Woods ROO 1.25 3.00
167 Aarom Baldiris ROO 1.25 3.00
168 Jason Bartlett ROO 4.00 10.00
169 Casey Daigle ROO 1.25 3.00
170 Dennis Sarfate ROO 1.25 3.00
171 Edwardo Sierra ROO 1.25 3.00
172 Merkin Valdez ROO 1.25 3.00
173 Eddy Rodriguez ROO 1.25 3.00
174 Kazuo Matsui ROO 2.00 5.00
175 David Aardsma ROO 1.25 3.00

2004 Leather and Lumber Silver B/W

*SILV.RETIRED B/W 1-150: 3X TO 8X BASIC
*SILV.B/W 174: 1X TO 2.5X BASIC
RANDOM INSERTS IN PACKS
STATED PRINT RUN 100 SERIAL #'d SETS

2004 Leather and Lumber Materials Bat

*BAT p/r 100: .5X TO 1.2X JSY p/r 150-250
*BAT p/r 100: .4X TO 1X JSY p/r 100
*BAT p/r 100: .25X TO .6X JSY p/r 50
*BAT p/r 100: .15X TO .4X JSY p/r 25
*BAT p/r 50: .6X TO 1.5X JSY p/r 100
*BAT p/r 25: 1.25X TO 3X JSY p/r 150-250
OVERALL AU-GU ODDS 1:6 HOBBY
PRINT RUNS B/WN 1-100 COPIES PER
NO PRICING ON QTY OF 10 OR LESS

5 Vladimir Guerrero/100 4.00 10.00
11 Adam LaRoche/100 2.00 5.00
15 J.D. Drew/100 2.00 5.00
24 Curt Schilling/100 3.00 8.00
27 Nomar Garciaparra/100 5.00 12.00
63 Roger Clemens/50 8.00 20.00
68 Juan Gonzalez/100 2.00 5.00
76 Junior Spivey/100 2.00 5.00
77 Rickie Weeks/25 5.00 12.00
87 Nick Johnson/100 2.00 5.00
94 Alex Rodriguez/100 5.00 12.00
98 Gary Sheffield/100 2.00 5.00
121 Brian Giles/100 2.00 5.00
125 Edgardo Alfonzo/100 2.00 5.00
128 Bret Boone/100 2.00 5.00
140 Delmon Young/100 3.00 8.00
142 Alfonso Soriano/100 2.00 5.00
144 Mark Teixeira/100 3.00 8.00
145 Michael Young/100 2.00 5.00

2004 Leather and Lumber Materials Bat B/W

*BAT B/Wp/r100: .5X TO 1.2X JSYp/r150-250
*BAT B/W p/r 100: .4X TO 1X JSY p/r 100
*BAT B/W p/r 100: .25X TO .6X JSY p/r 50
*BAT B/W p/r 50: .4X TO 1X JSY p/r 50
*BAT B/W p/r 25: 1X TO 2.5X JSY p/r 100
OVERALL AU-GU ODDS 1:6 HOBBY
PRINT RUNS B/WN 25-100 COPIES PER

27 Nomar Garciaparra/100 5.00 12.00
63 Roger Clemens/50 8.00 20.00
94 Alex Rodriguez/100 5.00 12.00
142 Alfonso Soriano/100 2.00 5.00
174 Kazuo Matsui ROO/100 6.00 15.00

2004 Leather and Lumber Materials Jersey

OVERALL AU-GU ODDS 1:6 HOBBY
PRINT RUNS B/WN 1-250 COPIES PER
NO PRICING ON QTY OF 10 OR LESS

2 Garret Anderson/50 3.00 8.00
3 Tim Salmon/250 3.00 8.00
4 Troy Glaus/200 2.00 5.00
6 Brandon Webb/100 2.00 5.00
7 Luis Gonzalez/250 2.00 5.00
8 Randy Johnson/100 4.00 10.00
12 Andruw Jones/250 3.00 8.00
13 Chipper Jones/250 3.00 8.00
14 Dale Murphy/250 4.00 10.00
16 Marcus Giles/250 2.00 5.00
17 Rafael Furcal/250 2.00 5.00
18 Cal Ripken/100 15.00 40.00
19 Javy Lopez/150 2.00 5.00
20 Jay Gibbons/250 2.00 5.00
21 Luis Matos/250 2.00 5.00
22 Miguel Tejada/250 2.00 5.00
23 Rafael Palmeiro/250 3.00 8.00
25 Jason Varitek/250 3.00 8.00
26 Manny Ramirez/250 3.00 8.00
28 Pedro Martinez/250 3.00 8.00
29 Trot Nixon/25 5.00 12.00
30 Greg Maddux/100 5.00 12.00
31 Kerry Wood/250 2.00 5.00
32 Mark Prior/250 3.00 8.00
33 Ryne Sandberg/50 15.00 40.00
34 Sammy Sosa/250 3.00 8.00
35 Carlos Lee/250 2.00 5.00
36 Frank Thomas/250 3.00 8.00
37 Magglio Ordonez/250 2.00 5.00
38 Paul Konerko/250 2.00 5.00
39 Adam Dunn/250 2.00 5.00
40 Austin Kearns/250 2.00 5.00
41 Barry Larkin/250 3.00 8.00
44 C.C. Sabathia/250 2.00 5.00
45 Jody Gerut/250 2.00 5.00
46 Omar Vizquel/250 3.00 8.00
47 Larry Walker/250 2.00 5.00
48 Preston Wilson/250 2.00 5.00
49 Todd Helton/250 3.00 8.00
50 Alan Trammell/50 4.00 10.00
51 Ivan Rodriguez/100 3.00 8.00
52 Jeremy Bonderman/150 2.00 5.00
53 Dontrelle Willis/100 3.00 8.00
54 Josh Beckett/250 2.00 5.00
55 Luis Castillo/250 2.00 5.00
56 Miguel Cabrera/50 5.00 12.00
57 Mike Lowell/25 5.00 12.00
58 Andy Pettitte/25 8.00 20.00
59 Craig Biggio/250 3.00 8.00
60 Jeff Bagwell/250 3.00 8.00
61 Jeff Kent/250 2.00 5.00
62 Lance Berkman/250 2.00 5.00
64 Roy Oswalt/250 2.00 5.00
65 Angel Berroa/50 3.00 8.00
66 Carlos Beltran/250 2.00 5.00
67 George Brett/250 6.00 15.00
69 Mike Sweeney/100 2.00 5.00
71 Hideo Nomo/250 3.00 8.00
72 Kazuhisa Ishii/250 2.00 5.00
73 Paul Lo Duca/250 2.00 5.00
74 Shawn Green/250 2.00 5.00
75 Geoff Jenkins/250 2.00 5.00
78 Robin Yount/250 4.00 10.00
80 Jacque Jones/250 2.00 5.00
81 Johan Santana/250 3.00 8.00
82 Shannon Stewart/250 2.00 5.00
83 Torii Hunter/250 2.00 5.00
84 Andre Dawson/50 4.00 10.00

2004 Leather and Lumber Materials Jersey

86 Jose Vidro/100 2.00 5.00
88 Orlando Cabrera/100 2.00 5.00
89 Gary Carter/250 3.00 8.00
90 Jae Weong Seo/100 2.00 5.00
91 Jose Reyes/250 2.00 5.00
92 Mike Piazza/250 4.00 10.00
93 Tom Glavine/250 3.00 8.00
95 Bernie Williams/250 3.00 8.00
96 Derek Jeter/150 8.00 20.00
97 Don Mattingly/250 6.00 15.00
99 Hideki Matsui/250 8.00 20.00
100 Jason Giambi/250 2.00 5.00
101 Jorge Posada/50 5.00 12.00
102 Mike Mussina/100 3.00 8.00
103 Barry Zito/250 2.00 5.00
105 Eric Chavez/100 2.00 5.00
107 Mark Mulder/250 2.00 5.00
108 Rich Harden/50 3.00 8.00
109 Rickey Henderson/100 6.00 15.00
110 Tim Hudson/250 2.00 5.00
111 Bobby Abreu/250 2.00 5.00
112 Brett Myers/250 2.00 5.00
113 Jim Thome/250 3.00 8.00
114 Kevin Millwood/250 2.00 5.00
115 Marlon Byrd/250 2.00 5.00
116 Mike Schmidt/50 10.00 25.00
117 Pat Burrell/250 2.00 5.00
118 Dave Parker/250 3.00 8.00
120 Jason Kendall/50 3.00 8.00
123 Ryan Klesko/250 2.00 5.00
124 Tony Gwynn/100 6.00 15.00
127 Jerome Williams/200 2.00 5.00
129 Edgar Martinez/250 3.00 8.00
131 Jamie Moyer/250 2.00 5.00
132 John Olerud/150 2.00 5.00
133 Albert Pujols/250 6.00 15.00
134 Edgar Renteria/100 2.00 5.00
135 Jim Edmonds/250 2.00 5.00
136 Matt Morris/250 2.00 5.00
137 Scott Rolen/250 3.00 8.00
138 Aubrey Huff/100 2.00 5.00
139 Carl Crawford/250 2.00 5.00
141 Rocco Baldelli/250 2.00 5.00
143 Hank Blalock/250 2.00 5.00
146 Nolan Ryan/100 12.50 30.00
147 Carlos Delgado/250 2.00 5.00
148 Eric Hinske/100 2.00 5.00
149 Roy Halladay/100 2.00 5.00
150 Vernon Wells/250 2.00 5.00

2004 Leather and Lumber Materials Jersey B/W

*JSY B/W p/r 150-250: .4X TO 1X p/r 150-250
*JSY B/W p/r 150-250: .3X TO .8X p/r 100
*JSY B/W p/r 100: .5X TO 1.2X p/r 150-250
*JSY B/W p/r 100: .4X TO 1X p/r 100
*JSY B/W p/r 50: .4X TO 1X p/r 50
OVERALL AU-GU ODDS 1:6 HOBBY
PRINT RUNS B/WN 50-250 COPIES PER
174 Kazuo Matsui ROO/50 8.00 20.00

2004 Leather and Lumber Materials Jersey Prime

*PRIME p/r 25: 1.5X TO 4X p/r 150-250
*PRIME p/r 25: 1.25X TO 3X p/r 100
*PRIME p/r 25: .75X TO 2X p/r 50
*PRIME p/r 25: .5X TO 1.2X p/r 25
OVERALL AU-GU ODDS 1:6 HOBBY
PRIME ISSUED ONLY IN HOBBY PACKS
PRINT RUNS B/WN 1-25 COPIES PER
NO PRICING ON QTY OF 10 OR LESS
128 Bret Boone/25 8.00 20.00
144 Mark Teixeira/25 12.50 30.00

2004 Leather and Lumber Materials Jersey Prime B/W

*PRIME B/W p/r 25: 1.5X TO 4X p/r 150-250
*PRIME B/W p/r 25: 1.25X TO 3X p/r 100
OVERALL AU-GU ODDS 1:6 HOBBY
PRIME ISSUED ONLY IN HOBBY PACKS
PRINT RUNS B/WN 1-25 COPIES PER
NO PRICING ON QTY OF 10 OR LESS
NO CARD 174 PRICING DUE TO SCARCITY

2004 Leather and Lumber Signatures Bronze

OVERALL AU-GU ODDS 1:6 HOBBY
PRINT RUNS B/WN 1-100 COPIES PER
NO PRICING ON QTY OF 10 OR LESS
2 Garret Anderson/25 10.00 25.00
10 Shea Hillenbrand/100 6.00 15.00
11 Adam LaRoche/100 4.00 10.00
14 Dale Murphy/25 15.00 40.00
16 Marcus Giles/50 8.00 20.00
17 Rafael Furcal/25 10.00 25.00
20 Jay Gibbons/100 4.00 10.00
21 Luis Matos/100 4.00 10.00
35 Carlos Lee/100 6.00 15.00
39 Adam Dunn/25 6.00 15.00
44 C.C. Sabathia/100 8.00 20.00
45 Jody Gerut/100 4.00 10.00
48 Preston Wilson/50 8.00 20.00
50 Alan Trammell/50 8.00 20.00
52 Jeremy Bonderman/100 6.00 15.00
56 Miguel Cabrera/50 20.00 50.00
65 Angel Berroa/100 4.00 10.00
66 Carlos Beltran/100 6.00 15.00
79 Scott Podsednik/100 10.00 25.00
80 Jacque Jones/100 6.00 15.00
81 Johan Santana/100 6.00 15.00
82 Shannon Stewart/100 6.00 15.00
83 Torii Hunter/50 8.00 20.00
84 Andre Dawson/100 6.00 15.00
85 Chad Cordero/100 6.00 15.00
86 Jose Vidro/100 4.00 10.00
88 Orlando Cabrera/100 6.00 15.00
104 Bobby Crosby/100 6.00 15.00
106 Jermaine Dye/100 6.00 15.00
108 Rich Harden/50 8.00 20.00
115 Marlon Byrd/25 6.00 15.00
119 Jason Bay/100 6.00 15.00
122 Jay Payton/50 5.00 12.00
138 Aubrey Huff/50 8.00 20.00
139 Carl Crawford/50 8.00 20.00
145 Michael Young/100 8.00 20.00
151 Andres Blanco ROO/50 4.00 10.00
152 Kevin Cave ROO/50 4.00 10.00
153 Ryan Meaux ROO/50 4.00 10.00
154 Tim Bausher ROO/50 4.00 10.00
155 Jesse Harper ROO/50 4.00 10.00
156 Michael Wuertz ROO/50 6.00 15.00
158 Don Kelly ROO/50 4.00 10.00
159 Edwin Moreno ROO/50 6.00 15.00
160 Mike Johnston ROO/50 4.00 10.00
161 Orlando Rodriguez ROO/50 4.00 10.00
164 Jorge Vasquez ROO/50 4.00 10.00
166 Jake Woods ROO/50 4.00 10.00
167 Aarom Baldiris ROO/50 5.00 12.00
170 Dennis Sartate ROO/50 4.00 10.00
173 Eddy Rodriguez ROO/50 6.00 15.00

2004 Leather and Lumber Signatures Bronze B/W

*BRONZE B/W p/r 25: .4X TO 1X p/r 25
OVERALL AU-GU ODDS 1:6 HOBBY
PRINT RUNS B/WN 1-25 COPIES PER
NO PRICING ON QTY OF 10 OR LESS

2004 Leather and Lumber Signatures Gold

*GOLD 1-150 p/r 25: .6X TO 1.5X p/r 100
*GOLD 1-150 p/r 25: .5X TO 1.2X p/r 50
*GOLD 1-150 p/r 25: .4X TO 1X p/r 25
*GOLD 151-175 p/r 50: .4X TO 1X p/r 50
OVERALL AU-GU ODDS 1:6 HOBBY
GOLD SIGS ISSUED ONLY IN HOBBY PACKS
PRINT RUNS B/WN 1-25 COPIES PER
NO PRICING ON QTY OF 10 OR LESS
168 Jason Bartlett ROO/50 6.00 15.00

2004 Leather and Lumber Signatures Gold B/W

*GOLD B/W p/r 25: .4X TO 1X p/r 25
OVERALL AU-GU ODDS 1:6 HOBBY
GOLD SIGS ISSUED ONLY IN HOBBY PACKS
PRINT RUNS B/WN 1-25 COPIES PER
NO PRICING ON QTY OF 10 OR LESS

2004 Leather and Lumber Signatures Silver

*SILV 1-150 p/r 50: .5X TO 1.2X p/r 100
*SILV 1-150 p/r 50: .4X TO 1X p/r 50
*SILV 1-150 p/r 50: .3X TO .8X p/r 25
*SILV 1-150 p/r 25: .4X TO 1X p/r 25
*SILV 151-175 p/r 100: .3X TO .8X p/r 50
OVERALL AU-GU ODDS 1:6 HOBBY
PRINT RUNS B/WN 1-100 COPIES PER
NO PRICING ON QTY OF 14 OR LESS
29 Trot Nixon/25 10.00 25.00
32 Mark Prior/25 12.50 30.00
40 Austin Kearns/25 6.00 15.00
43 Ryan Wagner/50 5.00 12.00
73 Paul Lo Duca/25 10.00 25.00
107 Mark Mulder/25 10.00 25.00
143 Hank Blalock/50 8.00 20.00
150 Vernon Wells/50 8.00 20.00

2004 Leather and Lumber Signatures Silver B/W

*SILV B/W p/r 25: .4X TO 1X p/r 25
OVERALL AU-GU ODDS 1:6 HOBBY
PRINT RUNS B/WN 1-25 COPIES PER
NO PRICING ON QTY OF 10 OR LESS
32 Mark Prior/25 12.50 30.00

2004 Leather and Lumber Fans of the Game

STATED ODDS 1:24
1 John Travolta 2.00 5.00
2 Dennis Haysbert .75 2.00
3 Chris O'Donnell .75 2.00
4 Abby Wambach 2.00 5.00
5 Jules Asner 1.25 3.00

2004 Leather and Lumber Fans of the Game Autographs

OVERALL AU-GU ODDS 1:6 HOBBY
SP PRINT RUNS PROVIDED BY DONRUSS
SP'S ARE NOT SERIAL-NUMBERED
1 John Travolta SP/150 75.00 150.00
2 Dennis Haysbert 12.50 30.00
3 Chris O'Donnell 10.00 25.00
4 Abby Wambach SP/250 20.00 50.00
5 Jules Asner SP/300 10.00 25.00

2004 Leather and Lumber Hall of Fame

RANDOM INSERTS IN PACKS
PRINT RUNS B/WN 1989-2002 COPIES PER
*SILVER: 1.25X TO 3X BASIC
SILVER RANDOM IN HOBBY PACKS
SILVER PRINT RUN 100 SERIAL #'d SETS
1 Carl Yastrzemski/1989 1.00 2.50
2 Carlton Fisk/2000 .60 1.50
3 George Brett/1999 2.00 5.00
4 Johnny Bench/1989 1.00 2.50
5 Mike Schmidt/1995 1.50 4.00
6 Nolan Ryan/1999 3.00 8.00
7 Ozzie Smith/2002 1.25 3.00
8 Robin Yount/1999 1.00 2.50
9 Rod Carew/1991 .60 1.50
10 Tom Seaver/1992 .60 1.50

2004 Leather and Lumber Hall of Fame Materials

OVERALL AU-GU ODDS 1:6 HOBBY
PRINT RUNS B/WN 100-250 COPIES PER
1 Carl Yastrzemski Jsy/250 6.00 15.00
2 Carlton Fisk Jsy/250 4.00 10.00
3 George Brett Jsy/250 6.00 15.00
4 Johnny Bench Jsy/100 6.00 15.00
5 Mike Schmidt Jkt/250 6.00 15.00
6 Nolan Ryan Pants/100 12.50 30.00
7 Ozzie Smith Jsy/100 8.00 20.00
8 Robin Yount Jsy/250 4.00 10.00
9 Rod Carew Jkt/250 4.00 10.00
10 Tom Seaver Jsy/200 4.00 10.00

2004 Leather and Lumber Leather Cuts Glove

PRINT RUNS B/WN 32-224 COPIES PER
BALL PRINT RUNS B/WN 5-10 COPIES PER
NO BALL PRICING DUE TO SCARCITY
*LUMBER: .4X TO 1X BASIC
LUMBER PRINT B/WN 32-224 COPIES PER
OVERALL AU-GU ODDS 1:6 HOBBY
CUTS ISSUED ONLY IN HOBBY PACKS
1 Adam Dunn/192 10.00 25.00
2 Al Kaline/192 12.00 30.00
3 Alfonso Soriano/160 10.00 25.00
4 Andre Dawson/224 6.00 15.00
5 Angel Berroa/224 4.00 10.00
6 Harmon Killebrew/192 15.00 40.00
7 Bob Gibson/96 10.00 25.00
8 Brooks Robinson/192 10.00 25.00
9 Cal Ripken/32 90.00 150.00
10 Dale Murphy/224 10.00 25.00
11 Darryl Strawberry/224 6.00 15.00
12 Delmon Young/192 10.00 25.00
13 Don Mattingly/96 30.00 60.00
14 Duke Snider/96 15.00 40.00
15 Dwight Gooden/224 6.00 15.00
16 Ozzie Smith/96 30.00 60.00
17 Frank Robinson/192 10.00 25.00
18 Garret Anderson/224 6.00 15.00
19 Gary Carter/160 30.00 60.00
20 George Kell/224 8.00 20.00
21 Hank Blalock/224 6.00 15.00
22 Jim Palmer/192 10.00 25.00
23 Kirk Gibson/160 6.00 15.00
24 Lou Brock/192 10.00 25.00
25 Ryne Sandberg/160 30.00 60.00
26 Mark Prior/160 10.00 25.00
27 Miguel Cabrera/224 20.00 50.00
28 Mike Lowell/160 6.00 15.00
29 Nolan Ryan/96 40.00 80.00
30 Luis Aparicio/224 10.00 25.00
31 Paul Molitor/160 6.00 15.00
32 Red Schoendienst/224 10.00 25.00
33 Rickie Weeks/224 6.00 15.00
34 Ron Santo/224 10.00 25.00
35 Roy Oswalt/224 6.00 15.00
36 Stan Musial/96 40.00 80.00
37 Steve Carlton/192 6.00 15.00
38 Tony Gwynn/192 15.00 40.00
39 Vernon Wells/160 6.00 15.00
40 Will Clark/192 10.00 25.00
41 Bob Feller/224 10.00 25.00
42 Bobby Doerr/224 6.00 15.00
44 Ralph Kiner/224 8.00 20.00
45 Torii Hunter/224 6.00 15.00
46 Rollie Fingers/224 6.00 15.00
47 Steve Garvey/224 6.00 15.00
48 Alan Trammell/224 10.00 25.00
49 Maury Wills/224 6.00 15.00
50 Gaylord Perry/224 6.00 15.00

2004 Leather and Lumber Leather in Leather

RANDOM INSERTS IN PACKS
STATED PRINT RUN 2499 SERIAL #'d SETS
*SILVER ACTIVE: 1X TO 2.5X BASIC
*SILVER RETIRED: 1X TO 2.5X BASIC
SILVER RANDOM IN HOBBY PACKS
SILVER PRINT RUN 100 SERIAL #'d SETS
1 Garret Anderson BB .40 1.00
2 Albert Pujols BB 1.25 3.00
3 John Smoltz BB 1.00 2.50
4 Cal Ripken BB 3.00 8.00
5 Ichiro Suzuki BB 1.25 3.00
6 Pedro Martinez BB .60 1.50
7 Shawn Green BB .40 1.00
8 Juan Gonzalez BB .40 1.00
9 Mariano Rivera BB 1.25 3.00
10 Jason Giambi BB .40 1.00
11 Dave Parker BG .40 1.00
12 Dwight Gooden BG .40 1.00
13 Eric Munson BG .40 1.00
14 Frank Thomas BG 1.00 2.50
15 Joe Carter BG .40 1.00
16 Jose Canseco BG .60 1.50
17 Paul O'Neill BG .60 1.50
18 Tony Gwynn BG 1.00 2.50
19 Wade Boggs BG .60 1.50
20 Xavier Nady BG .40 1.00
21 Albert Pujols FG 1.25 3.00
22 Alex Rodriguez FG 1.25 3.00
23 Chipper Jones FG 1.00 2.50
24 Derek Jeter FG 2.50 6.00
25 Jack Wilson FG .40 1.00
26 Lenny Dykstra FG .40 1.00
27 Mark Grace FG .60 1.50
28 Steve Carlton FG .60 1.50
29 Tony Perez FG .60 1.50
30 Vladimir Guerrero FG .60 1.50
31 Bernie Williams SH .60 1.50
32 Eddie Murray SH .60 1.50
33 Frank Robinson SH .60 1.50
34 Greg Maddux SH 1.25 3.00
35 Harmon Killebrew SH 1.00 2.50
36 Manny Ramirez SH 1.00 2.50
37 Mike Piazza SH 1.00 2.50
38 Paul Molitor SH 1.00 2.50
39 Sammy Sosa SH 1.00 2.50
40 Tim Hudson SH .60 1.50

2004 Leather and Lumber Leather in Leather Materials

OVERALL AU-GU ODDS 1:6 HOBBY
L IN L MATERIAL ISSUED ONLY IN HOBBY
PRINT RUNS B/WN 10-50 COPIES PER
NO PRICING ON QTY OF 10 OR LESS
1 Garret Anderson Ball/50 4.00 10.00
2 Albert Pujols Ball/50 15.00 40.00
3 John Smoltz Ball/50 15.00 40.00
4 Cal Ripken Ball/50 40.00 80.00
5 Ichiro Suzuki Ball/50 30.00 60.00
6 Pedro Martinez Ball/50 6.00 15.00
7 Shawn Green Ball/50 4.00 10.00
8 Juan Gonzalez Ball/50 4.00 10.00
9 Mariano Rivera Ball/50 8.00 20.00
10 Jason Giambi Ball/50 4.00 10.00
11 Dave Parker Btg Glv/25 8.00 20.00
12 Dwight Gooden Btg Glv/25 8.00 20.00
13 Eric Munson Btg Glv/50 4.00 10.00
14 Frank Thomas Btg Glv/25 12.50 30.00
15 Joe Carter Btg Glv/50 6.00 15.00
16 Jose Canseco Btg Glv/50 8.00 20.00
17 Paul O'Neill Btg Glv/50 10.00 25.00
18 Tony Gwynn Btg Glv/50 15.00 40.00
19 Wade Boggs Btg Glv/25 12.50 30.00
20 Xavier Nady Btg Glv/50 4.00 10.00
22 Alex Rodriguez Fld Glv/25 15.00 40.00
23 Chipper Jones Fld Glv/25 12.50 30.00
24 Derek Jeter Fld Glv/25 20.00 50.00
25 Jack Wilson Fld Glv/50 4.00 10.00
26 Lenny Dykstra Fld Glv/50 6.00 15.00
27 Mark Grace Fld Glv/50 8.00 20.00
28 Steve Carlton Fld Glv/50 6.00 15.00
29 Tony Perez Fld Glv/25 8.00 20.00
31 Bernie Williams Spikes/50 6.00 15.00
32 Eddie Murray Spikes/50 15.00 40.00
33 Frank Robinson Spikes/50 6.00 15.00
34 Greg Maddux Spikes/25 15.00 40.00
35 Harmon Killebrew Spikes/25 15.00 40.00
36 Manny Ramirez Spikes/50 6.00 15.00
37 Mike Piazza Spikes/25 15.00 40.00
38 Paul Molitor Spikes/25 8.00 20.00
39 Sammy Sosa Spikes/25 12.50 30.00
40 Tim Hudson Spikes/50 4.00 10.00

2004 Leather and Lumber Lumber/Leather Bat-Ball

*BALL p/r 25: .6X TO 1.5X SPIKE p/r 50
*BALL p/r 25: .4X TO 1X SPIKE p/r 25
OVERALL AU-GU ODDS 1:6 HOBBY
L/L BAT COMBOS ISSUED ONLY IN HOBBY
PRINT RUNS B/WN 5-25 COPIES PER
NO PRICING ON QTY OF 10 OR LESS
4 Aubrey Huff/25 6.00 15.00
5 Austin Kearns/25 6.00 15.00
16 Gary Sheffield/25 6.00 15.00
42 Richie Sexson/25 6.00 15.00
47 Tony Gwynn/25 15.00 40.00

2004 Leather and Lumber Lumber/Leather Bat-Btg Glove

*BTG GLV p/r 25: .6X TO 1.5X SPIKE p/r 50
*BTG GLV p/r 25: .4X TO 1X SPIKE p/r 25
OVERALL AU-GU ODDS 1:6 HOBBY
L/L BAT COMBOS ISSUED ONLY IN HOBBY
PRINT RUNS B/WN 1-25 COPIES PER
NO PRICING ON QTY OF 10 OR LESS
4 Aubrey Huff/25 6.00 15.00
16 Gary Sheffield/25 6.00 15.00
28 Kirby Puckett/25 30.00 80.00
42 Richie Sexson/25 6.00 15.00
47 Tony Gwynn/25 15.00 40.00

2004 Leather and Lumber Lumber/Leather Bat-Fld Glove

*FLD.GLV p/r 50: .4X TO 1X SPIKE p/r 50
*FLD.GLV p/r 50: .25X TO .6X SPIKE p/r 25
*FLD.GLV p/r 25: .6X TO 1.5X SPIKE p/r 50
*FLD.GLV p/r 25: .4X TO 1X SPIKE p/r 25
OVERALL AU-GU ODDS 1:6 HOBBY
L/L BAT COMBOS ISSUED ONLY IN HOBBY
PRINT RUNS B/WN 1-50 COPIES PER
NO PRICING ON QTY OF 10 OR LESS
12 Derek Jeter/25 30.00 60.00
16 Gary Sheffield/25 6.00 15.00
28 Kirby Puckett/25 30.00 80.00
45 Ryne Sandberg/25 30.00 60.00
47 Tony Gwynn/25 15.00 40.00

2004 Leather and Lumber Lumber/Leather Bat-Spikes

OVERALL AU-GU ODDS 1:6 HOBBY
L/L BAT COMBOS ISSUED ONLY IN HOBBY
PRINT RUNS B/WN 1-50 COPIES PER
NO PRICING ON QTY OF 10 OR LESS
1 Andruw Jones/25 10.00 25.00
3 Angel Berroa/25 6.00 15.00
6 Barry Zito/25 6.00 15.00
7 Ben Sheets/50 4.00 10.00
8 Brad Penny/50 4.00 10.00
9 Brian Giles/50 4.00 10.00
10 Carlos Lee/50 4.00 10.00
11 Corey Patterson/50 4.00 10.00
13 Don Mattingly/25 20.00 50.00
15 Gary Carter/50 6.00 15.00
17 Ivan Rodriguez/50 6.00 15.00
18 Jack Cust/50 4.00 10.00
19 Jason Jennings/50 4.00 10.00
21 Jim Edmonds/50 4.00 10.00
22 Joe Borchard/50 4.00 10.00
23 Joe Crede/50 4.00 10.00
24 Josh Beckett/25 6.00 15.00
25 Josh Phelps/50 4.00 10.00
26 Juan Pierre/50 4.00 10.00
27 Kenny Lofton/50 4.00 10.00
29 Lance Berkman/25 6.00 15.00
30 Magglio Ordonez/25 6.00 15.00
31 Marcus Giles/50 4.00 10.00
32 Mark Buehrle/50 4.00 10.00
33 Mark Prior/25 10.00 25.00
34 Mark Teixeira/25 10.00 25.00
35 Marlon Byrd/50 4.00 10.00
38 Nick Johnson/25 6.00 15.00
39 Orlando Hudson/50 4.00 10.00
40 Paul Lo Duca/25 6.00 15.00
41 Rafael Palmeiro/25 10.00 25.00
43 Roy Oswalt/25 6.00 15.00
44 Ryan Klesko/50 4.00 10.00
46 Sean Casey/50 4.00 10.00
48 Travis Hafner/50 4.00 10.00
49 Victor Martinez/50 4.00 10.00
50 Wade Miller/50 4.00 10.00

2004 Leather and Lumber Naturals

RANDOM INSERTS IN PACKS
STATED PRINT RUN 2499 SERIAL #'d SETS
*SILVER ACTIVE: 1X TO 2.5X BASIC
*SILVER RETIRED: 1X TO 2.5X BASIC
SILVER RANDOM IN HOBBY PACKS
SILVER PRINT RUN 100 SERIAL #'d SETS
1 Eric Chavez .40 1.00
2 Garret Anderson .40 1.00
3 Lance Berkman .60 1.50
4 Paul Molitor 1.00 2.50
5 Rafael Palmeiro .60 1.50
6 Ralph Kiner .60 1.50
7 Todd Helton .60 1.50
8 Tony Gwynn 1.00 2.50
9 Wade Boggs .60 1.50
10 Will Clark .60 1.50

2004 Leather and Lumber Naturals Bat

OVERALL AU-GU ODDS 1:6 HOBBY
PRINT RUNS B/WN 20-250 COPIES PER
1 Eric Chavez/20 5.00 12.00
2 Garret Anderson/250 2.00 5.00
3 Lance Berkman/250 2.00 5.00
4 Paul Molitor/250 3.00 8.00
5 Rafael Palmeiro/250 3.00 8.00
6 Ralph Kiner/250 4.00 10.00
7 Todd Helton/250 3.00 8.00
8 Tony Gwynn/250 6.00 15.00
9 Wade Boggs/250 4.00 10.00
10 Will Clark/250 4.00 10.00

2004 Leather and Lumber Pennants/Pinstripes

RANDOM INSERTS IN PACKS
STATED PRINT RUN 2499 SERIAL #'d SETS
*GOLD ACTIVE: 1X TO 2.5X BASIC
*GOLD RETIRED: 1X TO 2.5X BASIC
GOLD RANDOM IN HOBBY PACKS
GOLD PRINT RUN 100 SERIAL #'d SETS
1 Reggie Jackson .60 1.50
2 Mike Schmidt 1.50 4.00
3 Steve Carlton .60 1.50
4 Dwight Gooden .40 1.00
5 Darryl Strawberry .40 1.00
6 Roger Clemens 1.25 3.00
7 Curt Schilling .60 1.50
8 Mark Grace .60 1.50
9 Ivan Rodriguez .60 1.50
10 Josh Beckett .40 1.00

2004 Leather and Lumber Pennants/Pinstripes Materials

OVERALL AU-GU ODDS 1:6 HOBBY
PRINT RUNS B/WN 25-250 COPIES PER
1 Reggie Jackson Pants/100 5.00 12.00
2 Mike Schmidt Jsy/25 15.00 40.00
3 Steve Carlton Jsy/100 3.00 8.00
4 Dwight Gooden Jsy/250 3.00 8.00
5 Darryl Strawberry Pants/250 3.00 8.00
6 Roger Clemens Jsy/250 4.00 10.00
7 Curt Schilling Jsy/250 2.00 5.00
8 Mark Grace Jsy/250 4.00 10.00
9 Ivan Rodriguez Jsy/250 3.00 8.00
10 Josh Beckett Jsy/100 2.00 5.00

2004 Leather and Lumber Rivals

RANDOM INSERTS IN PACKS
STATED PRINT RUN 2499 SERIAL #'d SETS
*SILVER ACTIVE: 1X TO 2.5X BASIC
*SILVER RETIRED: 1X TO 2.5X BASIC
SILVER RANDOM IN HOBBY PACKS
SILVER PRINT RUN 100 SERIAL #'d SETS
1 D.Jeter 2.50 6.00
N.Garciaparra
2 M.Prior 1.25 3.00
A.Pujols
3 W.Spahn 1.50 4.00
S.Musial
4 D.Sutton .60 1.50
R.Jackson
5 R.Clemens 1.25 3.00
M.Piazza
6 D.Eckersley .60 1.50
M.Williams
7 K.Wood 1.00 2.50
F.Thomas
8 J.Palmer .60 1.50
W.Stargell
9 T.Seaver 1.50 4.00
M.Schmidt
10 J.Morris 2.00 5.00
G.Brett
11 R.Johnson 1.00 2.50
T.Helton
12 T.John .60 1.50
R.Carew
13 P.Martinez .60 1.50
J.Giambi
14 D.Gooden .60 1.50
W.Boggs
15 B.Gibson 1.00 2.50
E.Banks
16 H.Nomo 1.00 2.50
B.Larkin
17 R.Halladay .60 1.50
V.Guerrero
18 G.Maddux 1.25 3.00
J.Bagwell
19 B.Zito 1.25 3.00
A.Rodriguez
20 S.Carlton .60 1.50
A.Dawson
21 M.Rivera 1.25 3.00
C.Jones
22 T.Glavine 1.00 2.50
M.Ramirez
23 W.Ford 1.00 2.50
H.Killebrew
24 C.Yastrzemski 1.00 2.50
C.Hunter
25 N.Ryan 3.00 8.00
R.Ventura
26 C.Fisk .60 1.50
J.Morgan
27 P.Rizzuto .60 1.50
D.Snider
28 F.Jenkins .60 1.50
L.Brock
29 J.Canseco .60 1.50
W.Clark
30 M.Mussina .60 1.50
J.Beckett
31 R.Henderson 1.00 2.50
I.Rodriguez
32 D.Mattingly 2.00 5.00
E.Murray
33 T.Glaus .40 1.00
E.Chavez
34 R.Sandberg- 2.00 5.00
S.Garvey
35 B.Gibson 1.00 2.50
R.Maris
36 R.Clemens 3.00 8.00
C.Ripken
37 O.Hershiser .40 1.00
D.Strawberry
38 C.Schilling 1.00 2.50
P.Molitor
39 I.Suzuki 1.50 4.00
H.Matsui
40 S.Sosa 1.00 2.50
J.Thome

2004 Leather and Lumber Rivals Materials

OVERALL AU-GU ODDS 1:6 HOBBY
PRINT RUNS B/WN 5-250 COPIES PER
NO PRICING ON QTY OF 10 OR LESS
1 Jeter Jsy/Nomar Bat/250 10.00 25.00
2 Prior Jsy/Pujols Jsy/250 10.00 25.00
3 Spahn Pants/Musial Jsy/100 15.00 40.00
5 Clemens Jsy/Piazza Jsy/250 10.00 25.00
7 Wood Jsy/Thomas Jsy/250 4.00 10.00
8 Palmer Jsy/Stargell Jsy/250 6.00 15.00
9 Seaver Jsy/Schmidt Jsy/250 8.00 20.00
10 Morris Jsy/Brett Jsy/250 6.00 15.00
11 Randy Jsy/Helton Jsy/250 4.00 10.00
12 John Pants/Carew Jkt/250 6.00 15.00
13 Pedro Jsy/Giambi Jsy/250 4.00 10.00
14 Gooden Jsy/Boggs Jsy/250 6.00 15.00
15 Gibson Jsy/Banks Pants/100 10.00 25.00
16 Nomo Jsy/Larkin Jsy/250 6.00 15.00
17 Halladay Jsy/Vladdie Jsy/250 4.00 10.00
18 Maddux Jsy/Bagwell Jsy/250 6.00 15.00
19 Zito Jsy/A.Rod Jsy/250 6.00 15.00
20 Carlton Jsy/Dawson Jsy/250 4.00 10.00
22 Glavine Jsy/Manny Jsy/250 4.00 10.00
23 Ford Pants/Killebrew Jsy/100 15.00 40.00
24 Yaz Jsy/Hunter Jsy/250 10.00 25.00
25 Ryan Pants/Ventura Jsy/250 10.00 25.00
26 Fisk Jsy/Morgan Jsy/250 6.00 15.00
28 Jenkins Pants/Brock Jsy/100 10.00 25.00
29 Canseco Bat/Clark Bat/250 8.00 20.00
30 Mussina Jsy/Beckett Jsy/250 4.00 10.00
31 Rickey Jsy/I.Rod Jsy/250 6.00 15.00
32 Matt Pants/Murray Jsy/250 10.00 25.00
33 Glaus Jsy/Chavez Jsy/250 3.00 8.00
34 Ryno Jsy/Garvey Jsy/250 10.00 25.00
35 Gibson Jsy/Maris Jsy/100 20.00 50.00
36 Clem Jsy/Ripken Pants/250 10.00 25.00
38 Schill Jsy/Molitor Bat/250 4.00 10.00
39 Ichiro Base/Hideki Base/250 20.00 50.00
40 Sosa Jsy/Thome Jsy/250 4.00 10.00

2005 Leather and Lumber

COMP.SET w/o SP's (150) 15.00 40.00
COMMON CARD (1-136) .15 .40
COMMON CARD (137-150) .20 .50
COMMON AUTO (151-175) 4.00 10.00
151-175 PRINT RUN 256 SERIAL #'d SETS
COMMON AUTO (177) 6.00 15.00
177 PRINT RUN 128 SERIAL #'d CARDS
151-175/177: AU-GU ODDS 4 PER BOX
CARD 176 DOES NOT EXIST
1 Adam Dunn .25 .60
2 Adrian Beltre .40 1.00
3 Akinori Otsuka .15 .40
4 Al Leiter .15 .40
5 Albert Pujols .50 1.25
6 Alex Rodriguez .50 1.25
7 Alfonso Soriano .25 .60
8 Andy Pettitte .25 .60
9 Aramis Ramirez .15 .40
10 Aubrey Huff .15 .40
11 Austin Kearns .15 .40
12 Barry Larkin .25 .60
13 Barry Zito .25 .60
14 Bartolo Colon .15 .40
15 Bernie Williams .25 .60
16 Bobby Abreu .15 .40
17 Bobby Crosby .15 .40
18 Brad Penny .15 .40
19 Brian Giles .15 .40
20 C.C. Sabathia .25 .60
21 Carl Crawford .25 .60
22 Carl Pavano .15 .40
23 Carlos Beltran .25 .60
24 Carlos Delgado .15 .40
25 Carlos Lee .15 .40
26 Carlos Zambrano .25 .60
27 Casey Kotchman .15 .40
28 Chipper Jones .40 1.00
29 Chone Figgins .15 .40
30 Craig Biggio .25 .60
31 Craig Monroe .15 .40
32 Cristian Guzman .15 .40
33 Curt Schilling .25 .60
34 Dan Haren .15 .40
35 Darin Erstad .15 .40
36 David Dellucci .15 .40
37 David Ortiz .40 1.00
38 David Wells .15 .40
39 Derek Jeter 1.00 2.50
40 Dontrelle Willis .15 .40
41 Edgar Renteria .15 .40
42 Eric Gagne .15 .40
43 Frank Thomas .40 1.00
44 Garret Anderson .15 .40
45 Gary Sheffield .15 .40
46 Geoff Jenkins .15 .40
47 Greg Maddux .50 1.25
48 Hideo Nomo .40 1.00
49 Ichiro Suzuki .50 1.25
50 Ivan Rodriguez .25 .60
51 J.D. Drew .15 .40
52 Jake Peavy .15 .40
53 Jamie Moyer .15 .40
54 Jason Giambi .15 .40
55 Jason Kendall .15 .40
56 Jason Schmidt .15 .40
57 Jason Varitek .40 1.00
58 Javy Lopez .15 .40
59 Jay Gibbons .15 .40
60 Jeff Bagwell .25 .60
61 Jeff Kent .15 .40
62 Jeremy Bonderman .15 .40
63 Jermaine Dye .15 .40
64 Jim Edmonds .25 .60
65 Jim Thome .25 .60
66 Joe Nathan .15 .40
67 Johan Santana .25 .60
68 John Olerud .15 .40
69 John Smoltz .40 1.00
70 Johnny Damon .25 .60
71 Johnny Estrada .15 .40
72 Jose Reyes .25 .60
73 Jose Vidro .15 .40
74 Josh Beckett .15 .40
75 Juan Pierre .15 .40
76 Junior Spivey .15 .40
77 Justin Morneau .25 .60
78 Kazuhisa Ishii .15 .40
79 Kazuo Matsui .15 .40
80 Ken Griffey Jr. .75 2.00
81 Kerry Wood .15 .40
82 Kevin Brown .15 .40
83 Kevin Millwood .15 .40
84 Khalil Greene .15 .40
85 Lance Berkman .25 .60
86 Larry Walker .25 .60
87 Laynce Nix .15 .40
88 Lyle Overbay .15 .40
89 Magglio Ordonez .25 .60
90 Manny Ramirez .40 1.00
91 Marcus Giles .15 .40
92 Mark Loretta .15 .40
93 Mark Mulder .15 .40
94 Mark Prior .25 .60
95 Mark Teixeira .25 .60
96 Melvin Mora .15 .40
97 Michael Young .15 .40
98 Miguel Tejada .25 .60
99 Mike Lieberthal .15 .40
100 Mike Lowell .15 .40
101 Mike Mussina .25 .60
102 Mike Piazza .40 1.00
103 Milton Bradley .15 .40
104 Moises Alou .15 .40
105 Morgan Ensberg .15 .40
106 Nomar Garciaparra .25 .60
107 Omar Vizquel .25 .60
108 Paul Konerko .25 .60
109 Paul Lo Duca .15 .40
110 Pedro Martinez .25 .60
111 Rafael Furcal .15 .40
112 Rafael Palmeiro .25 .60
113 Randy Johnson .40 1.00
114 Richie Sexson .15 .40
115 Rocco Baldelli .15 .40
116 Roger Clemens .50 1.25
117 Roy Halladay .25 .60
118 Sammy Sosa .40 1.00
119 Scott Podsednik .15 .40
120 Scott Rolen .25 .60
121 Sean Burroughs .15 .40
122 Sean Casey .15 .40
123 Shannon Stewart .15 .40
124 Shawn Green .15 .40
125 Steve Finley .15 .40
126 Tim Hudson .25 .60
127 Tim Salmon .15 .40
128 Todd Helton .25 .60
129 Tom Glavine .25 .60
130 Torii Hunter .15 .40
131 Travis Hafner .15 .40
132 Troy Glaus .15 .40
133 Troy Percival .15 .40
134 Vernon Wells .15 .40
135 Victor Martinez .25 .60
136 Vladimir Guerrero .25 .60
137 Andre Dawson RET .30 .75
138 Brooks Robinson RET .30 .75
139 Cal Ripken RET 1.50 4.00
140 Dale Murphy RET .50 1.25
141 Darryl Strawberry RET .20 .50
142 George Brett RET 1.00 2.50
143 Harmon Killebrew RET .50 1.25
144 Jim Palmer RET .30 .75
145 Lou Brock RET .30 .75
146 Mike Schmidt RET .75 2.00
147 Nolan Ryan RET 1.50 4.00
148 Steve Carlton RET .30 .75
149 Tony Gwynn RET .60 1.50
150 Willie Mays RET 1.00 2.50
151 Agustin Montero AU RC 4.00 10.00
152 Carlos Ruiz AU RC 10.00 25.00
153 Casey Rogowski AU RC 6.00 15.00
154 Chris Resop AU RC 4.00 10.00
155 Chris Roberson AU RC 4.00 10.00
156 Colter Bean AU RC 6.00 15.00
157 Danny Rueckel AU RC 4.00 10.00
158 Dave Gassner AU RC 4.00 10.00
159 Geovany Soto AU RC 30.00 60.00
160 John Hattig AU RC 4.00 10.00
161 Justin Wechsler AU RC 4.00 10.00
162 Luke Scott AU RC 12.50 30.00
163 Mark McLemore AU RC 4.00 10.00
164 Miguel Negron AU RC 6.00 15.00
165 Mike Morse AU RC 8.00 20.00
166 Nate McLouth AU RC 6.00 15.00
167 Phil Humber AU RC 8.00 20.00
168 Randy Messenger AU RC 4.00 10.00
169 Raul Tablado AU RC 4.00 10.00
170 Russ Rohlicek AU RC 4.00 10.00
171 Ryan Speier AU RC 4.00 10.00
172 Scott Munter AU RC 4.00 10.00
173 Sean Thompson AU RC 4.00 10.00
174 Sean Tracey AU RC 4.00 10.00
175 Wladimir Balentien AU RC 6.00 15.00
177 Norihiro Nakamura AU RC 20.00 50.00

2005 Leather and Lumber Gold

*GOLD 1-136: 4X TO 10X BASIC
*GOLD 137-150: 4X TO 10X BASIC
OVERALL INSERT ODDS 1:2
STATED PRINT RUN 50 SERIAL #'d SETS

2005 Leather and Lumber Silver

*SILVER 1-136: 2.5X TO 6X BASIC
*SILVER 137-150: 2.5X TO 6X BASIC
OVERALL INSERT ODDS 1:2
STATED PRINT RUN 100 SERIAL #'d SETS

2005 Leather and Lumber Materials Bat

*1-136 p/r 150-250: .4X TO 1X JSYp/r150-250
*1-136 p/r 150-250: .3X TO .8X JSY p/r 75-100
*1-136 p/r 150-250: .2X TO .5X JSY p/r 25
*1-136 p/r 75-100: .5X TO 1.2X JSYp/r150-250

*1-136 p/r 75-100: .4X TO 1X JSY p/r 75-100
*1-136 p/r 50: .6X TO 1.5X JSY p/r 150-250
*1-136 p/r 25: .75X TO 2X JSY p/r 150-250
*137-150 p/r 100: .5X TO 1.2X JSYp/r150-250
*137-150 p/r 50: .6X TO 1.5X JSY p/r 150-250
*137-150 p/r 50: .4X TO 1X JSY p/r 50
*137-150 p/r 25: .4X TO 1X JSY p/r 25
OVERALL AU-GU ODDS 4 PER HOBBY BOX
PRINT RUNS B/WN 25-250 COPIES PER
1 Adam Dunn/250 2.00 5.00
2 Adrian Beltre/100 2.50 6.00
5 Albert Pujols/250 6.00 15.00
7 Alfonso Soriano/100 2.50 6.00
8 Andy Pettitte/100 3.00 8.00
9 Aramis Ramirez/100 2.50 6.00
10 Aubrey Huff/250 2.00 5.00
11 Austin Kearns/100 2.50 6.00
12 Barry Larkin/200 2.50 6.00
13 Barry Zito/25 4.00 10.00
15 Bernie Williams/250 2.50 6.00
18 Brad Penny/75 2.50 6.00
19 Brian Giles/50 3.00 8.00
23 Carlos Beltran/100 2.50 6.00
24 Carlos Delgado/250 2.00 5.00
25 Carlos Lee/150 2.00 5.00
27 Casey Kotchman/250 2.00 5.00
29 Chone Figgins/250 2.00 5.00
30 Craig Biggio/250 2.50 6.00
31 Craig Monroe/250 2.00 5.00
33 Curt Schilling/100 3.00 8.00
35 Darin Erstad/250 2.00 5.00
37 David Ortiz/250 3.00 8.00
40 Dontrelle Willis/250 2.00 5.00
43 Frank Thomas/50 5.00 12.00
44 Garret Anderson/250 2.00 5.00
46 Geoff Jenkins/50 3.00 8.00
47 Greg Maddux/250 5.00 12.00
51 J.D. Drew/250 2.00 5.00
57 Jason Varitek/100 4.00 10.00
58 Javy Lopez/250 2.00 5.00
59 Jay Gibbons/250 2.00 5.00
60 Jeff Bagwell/250 2.50 6.00
61 Jeff Kent/250 2.00 5.00
68 John Olerud/250 2.00 5.00
72 Jose Reyes/250 2.00 5.00
73 Jose Vidro/250 2.00 5.00
75 Juan Pierre/250 2.00 5.00
81 Kerry Wood/100 2.50 6.00
82 Kevin Brown/100 2.50 6.00
85 Lance Berkman/250 2.00 5.00
87 Laynce Nix/250 2.00 5.00
89 Magglio Ordonez/250 2.00 5.00
90 Manny Ramirez/100 3.00 8.00
94 Mark Prior/100 3.00 8.00
97 Michael Young/250 2.00 5.00
104 Moises Alou/250 2.00 5.00
106 Nomar Garciaparra/100 4.00 10.00
109 Paul Lo Duca/250 2.00 5.00
111 Rafael Furcal/250 2.00 5.00
112 Rafael Palmeiro/250 2.50 6.00
114 Richie Sexson/250 2.00 5.00
115 Rocco Baldelli/250 2.00 5.00
118 Sammy Sosa/100 4.00 10.00
122 Sean Casey/100 2.50 6.00
123 Shannon Stewart/50 3.00 8.00
124 Shawn Green/250 2.00 5.00
126 Tim Hudson/50 3.00 8.00
127 Tim Salmon/250 2.50 6.00
129 Tom Glavine/250 2.50 6.00
130 Torii Hunter/250 2.00 5.00
132 Troy Glaus/250 2.00 5.00
138 Brooks Robinson RET/100 4.00 10.00
139 Cal Ripken RET/50 15.00 40.00
145 Lou Brock RET/100 4.00 10.00
146 Mike Schmidt RET/50 8.00 20.00
147 Nolan Ryan RET/50 12.50 30.00
149 Tony Gwynn RET/100 5.00 12.00
150 Willie Mays RET/25 20.00 50.00

2005 Leather and Lumber Materials Jersey

OVERALL AU-GU ODDS 4 PER HOBBY BOX
PRINT RUNS B/WN 20-250 COPIES PER
1 Adam Dunn/150 2.00 5.00
5 Albert Pujols/250 6.00 15.00
7 Alfonso Soriano/150 2.00 5.00
8 Andy Pettitte/150 2.50 6.00
9 Aramis Ramirez/250 2.00 5.00
10 Aubrey Huff/250 2.00 5.00
12 Barry Larkin/250 2.50 6.00
13 Barry Zito/150 2.00 5.00
15 Bernie Williams/150 2.50 6.00
16 Bobby Abreu/250 2.00 5.00
17 Bobby Crosby/150 2.00 5.00
20 C.C. Sabathia/250 2.00 5.00
21 Carl Crawford/200 2.00 5.00
26 Carlos Zambrano/250 2.00 5.00
27 Casey Kotchman/150 2.00 5.00
28 Chipper Jones/250 3.00 8.00
29 Chone Figgins/200 2.00 5.00
30 Craig Biggio/200 2.50 6.00
33 Curt Schilling/250 2.50 6.00
35 Darin Erstad/150 2.00 5.00
36 David Dellucci/250 2.00 5.00
37 David Ortiz/250 3.00 8.00
40 Dontrelle Willis/250 2.00 5.00
43 Frank Thomas Pants/150 3.00 8.00
44 Garret Anderson/250 2.00 5.00
45 Gary Sheffield/250 2.00 5.00
46 Geoff Jenkins/250 2.00 5.00
47 Greg Maddux/25 10.00 25.00
48 Hideo Nomo/250 3.00 8.00
50 Ivan Rodriguez/150 2.50 6.00
53 Jamie Moyer/50 3.00 8.00
54 Jason Giambi/250 2.00 5.00
57 Jason Varitek/100 4.00 10.00
58 Javy Lopez/150 2.00 5.00
59 Jay Gibbons/75 2.50 6.00
60 Jeff Bagwell/250 2.50 6.00
62 Jeremy Bonderman/150 2.00 5.00
64 Jim Edmonds/250 2.00 5.00
65 Jim Thome/150 2.50 6.00
67 Johan Santana/250 3.00 8.00
69 John Smoltz/250 2.50 6.00
70 Johnny Damon/250 2.50 6.00
71 Johnny Estrada/250 2.00 5.00
72 Jose Reyes/150 2.00 5.00
73 Jose Vidro/150 2.00 5.00
74 Josh Beckett/50 3.00 8.00
76 Junior Spivey/250 2.00 5.00
77 Justin Morneau/250 2.00 5.00
78 Kazuhisa Ishii/250 2.00 5.00
79 Kazuo Matsui/250 2.00 5.00
81 Kerry Wood Pants/150 2.00 5.00
85 Lance Berkman/250 2.00 5.00
86 Larry Walker/250 2.50 6.00
87 Laynce Nix/250 2.00 5.00
88 Lyle Overbay/200 2.00 5.00
90 Manny Ramirez/250 2.50 6.00
91 Marcus Giles/150 2.00 5.00
94 Mark Prior/250 2.50 6.00
95 Mark Teixeira/250 2.50 6.00
96 Melvin Mora/100 2.50 6.00
97 Michael Young/25 4.00 10.00
98 Miguel Tejada/250 2.00 5.00
100 Mike Lowell/250 2.00 5.00
101 Mike Mussina/250 2.50 6.00
102 Mike Piazza/250 3.00 8.00
105 Morgan Ensberg/150 2.00 5.00
108 Paul Konerko/150 2.00 5.00
111 Rafael Furcal/150 2.00 5.00
112 Rafael Palmeiro/150 2.50 6.00
115 Rocco Baldelli/250 2.00 5.00
116 Roger Clemens/150 4.00 10.00
117 Roy Halladay/150 2.00 5.00
119 Scott Podsednik/250 2.00 5.00
120 Scott Rolen/250 2.50 6.00
121 Sean Burroughs/150 2.00 5.00
122 Sean Casey/250 2.00 5.00
123 Shannon Stewart/150 2.00 5.00
128 Todd Helton/250 2.50 6.00
130 Torii Hunter/250 2.00 5.00
131 Travis Hafner/25 4.00 10.00
134 Vernon Wells/250 2.00 5.00
135 Victor Martinez/150 2.00 5.00
136 Vladimir Guerrero/250 3.00 8.00
137 Andre Dawson RET/50 4.00 10.00
139 Cal Ripken RET/250 10.00 25.00
140 Dale Murphy RET/250 3.00 8.00
141 D.Strawberry RET Pants/150 2.50 6.00
143 Harmon Killebrew RET/100 5.00 12.00
144 Jim Palmer RET Pants/20 5.00 12.00
145 Lou Brock RET Jkt/250 3.00 8.00
146 Mike Schmidt RET/50 8.00 20.00
147 Nolan Ryan RET/250 8.00 20.00
148 Steve Carlton RET/25 5.00 12.00
149 Tony Gwynn RET/250 4.00 10.00
150 Willie Mays RET Pants/25 20.00 50.00

2005 Leather and Lumber Materials Jersey Prime

*1-136 p/r 25: 1.25X TO 3X JSY p/r 150-250
*1-136 p/r 25: 1X TO 2.5X JSY p/r 75-100
*1-136 p/r 25: .75X TO 2X JSY p/r 50
*1-136 p/r 15: 1.5X TO 4X JSY p/r 150-250
*137-150 p/r 25: 1.25X TO 3X JSY p/r 150-250
*137-150 p/r 25: .75X TO 2X JSY p/r 50
*137-150 p/r 15: 1.5X TO 4X JSY p/r 150-250
OVERALL AU-GU ODDS 4 PER HOBBY BOX
PRINT RUNS B/WN 1-25 COPIES PER
NO PRICING ON QTY OF 10 OR LESS
11 Austin Kearns/25 6.00 15.00

2005 Leather and Lumber Signatures Gold

PRINT RUNS B/WN 5-100 COPIES PER
PLATINUM PRINT RUN 1 SERIAL #'d SET
NO PLATINUM PRICING DUE TO SCARCITY
OVERALL AU-GU ODDS 4 PER HOBBY BOX
1 Adam Dunn/25 15.00 40.00
2 Adrian Beltre/25 10.00 25.00
3 Akinori Otsuka/50 15.00 40.00
10 Aubrey Huff/50 8.00 20.00
11 Austin Kearns/25 6.00 15.00
17 Bobby Crosby/100 6.00 15.00
18 Brad Penny/100 4.00 10.00
25 Carlos Lee/100 6.00 15.00
26 Carlos Zambrano/100 10.00 25.00
27 Casey Kotchman/100 6.00 15.00
29 Chone Figgins/100 4.00 10.00
31 Craig Monroe/100 4.00 10.00
34 Dan Haren/100 6.00 15.00
36 David Dellucci/100 6.00 15.00
44 Garret Anderson/25 10.00 25.00
52 Jake Peavy/100 10.00 25.00
53 Jamie Moyer/100 6.00 15.00
59 Jay Gibbons/100 4.00 10.00
62 Jeremy Bonderman/100 6.00 15.00
63 Jermaine Dye/100 6.00 15.00
66 Joe Nathan/100 6.00 15.00
71 Johnny Estrada/50 5.00 12.00
73 Jose Vidro/25 10.00 25.00
87 Laynce Nix/100 4.00 10.00
88 Lyle Overbay/100 4.00 10.00
89 Magglio Ordonez/25 10.00 25.00
92 Mark Loretta/100 4.00 10.00
99 Mike Lieberthal/100 6.00 15.00
103 Milton Bradley/100 6.00 15.00
105 Morgan Ensberg/100 6.00 15.00
107 Omar Vizquel/25 15.00 40.00
108 Paul Konerko/25 15.00 40.00
111 Rafael Furcal/50 8.00 20.00
117 Roy Halladay/25 15.00 40.00
119 Scott Podsednik/50 12.50 30.00
121 Sean Burroughs/100 4.00 10.00
122 Sean Casey/25 10.00 25.00
123 Shannon Stewart/100 6.00 15.00
125 Steve Finley/50 8.00 20.00
126 Tim Hudson/25 15.00 40.00
127 Tim Salmon/100 10.00 25.00
130 Torii Hunter/25 10.00 25.00
131 Travis Hafner/100 6.00 15.00
133 Troy Percival/50 8.00 20.00
134 Vernon Wells/25 10.00 25.00
135 Victor Martinez/100 6.00 15.00
137 Andre Dawson RET/100 6.00 15.00
138 Brooks Robinson RET/25 15.00 40.00
140 Dale Murphy RET/50 12.50 30.00
141 Darryl Strawberry RET/100 6.00 15.00
143 Harmon Killebrew RET/50 20.00 50.00
144 Jim Palmer RET/25 10.00 25.00
145 Lou Brock RET/25 15.00 40.00
146 Mike Schmidt RET/25 40.00 80.00
148 Steve Carlton RET/50 8.00 20.00
149 Tony Gwynn RET/25 30.00 60.00

2005 Leather and Lumber Signatures Lumber Cuts

*LUMBER: .4X TO 1X HOBBY LEATHER
RANDOM INSERTS IN RETAIL PACKS
STATED PRINT RUN 256 SERIAL #'d SETS
CARD 166 PRINT RUN 254 #'d COPIES
CARD 177 PRINT RUN 128 #'d COPIES
CARD 176 DOES NOT EXIST
177 Norihiro Nakamura/128 12.00 30.00

2005 Leather and Lumber Big Bang

STATED PRINT RUN 2000 SERIAL #'d SETS
*GOLD ACTIVE: .75X TO 2X BASIC
*GOLD RETIRED: 1X TO 2.5X BASIC
GOLD PRINT RUN 100 SERIAL #'d SETS
PLATINUM PRINT RUN 1 SERIAL #'d SET
NO PLATINUM PRICING DUE TO SCARCITY
*SILVER ACTIVE: .6X TO 1.5X BASIC
*SILVER RETIRED: .75X TO 2X BASIC
SILVER PRINT RUN 200 SERIAL #'d SETS
OVERALL INSERT ODDS 1:2 HOBBY
1 Adam Dunn .60 1.50
2 Adrian Beltre 1.00 2.50
3 Albert Pujols 1.25 3.00
4 Alex Rodriguez 1.25 3.00
5 Chipper Jones 1.00 2.50
6 Dale Murphy 1.00 2.50
7 Darryl Strawberry .40 1.00
8 Dave Parker .40 1.00
9 David Ortiz 1.00 2.50
10 Duke Snider .60 1.50
11 Frank Robinson .60 1.50
12 Gary Sheffield .40 1.00
13 George Foster .40 1.00
14 Harmon Killebrew 1.00 2.50
15 Jim Edmonds .60 1.50
16 Jim Rice .60 1.50
17 Jim Thome .60 1.50
18 Ken Griffey Jr. 2.00 5.00
19 Manny Ramirez 1.00 2.50
20 Matt Williams .40 1.00
21 Mike Piazza 1.00 2.50
22 Mike Schmidt 1.50 4.00
23 Rafael Palmeiro .60 1.50
24 Sammy Sosa 1.00 2.50
25 Ted Williams 2.00 5.00

2005 Leather and Lumber Big Bang Bat

*BAT p/r 250: .4X TO 1X JSY p/r 250
*BAT p/r 250: .3X TO .8X JSY p/r 100
*BAT p/r 100: .5X TO 1.2X JSY p/r 250
*BAT p/r 100: .4X TO 1X JSY p/r 100
*BAT p/r 50: .6X TO 1.5X JSY p/r 250
OVERALL AU-GU ODDS 4 PER HOBBY BOX
11 Frank Robinson/100 3.00 8.00
13 George Foster/250 2.50 6.00

2005 Leather and Lumber Big Bang Combos

*COM p/r 100: .6X TO 1.5X JSY p/r 250
*COM p/r 100: .5X TO 1.2X JSY p/r 100
*COM p/r 50: .75X TO 2X JSY p/r 250
*COM p/r 25: 1X TO 2.5X JSY p/r 250
PRINT RUNS B/WN 25-100 COPIES PER
PRIME PRINT RUN 5 SERIAL #'d SETS
NO PRIME PRICING DUE TO SCARCITY
OVERALL AU-GU ODDS 4 PER HOBBY BOX
2 Adrian Beltre Bat-Jsy/25 5.00 12.00

2005 Leather and Lumber Big Bang Jersey

PRINT RUNS B/WN 25-250 COPIES PER
PRIME PRINT RUN 5 SERIAL #'d SETS
NO PRIME PRICING DUE TO SCARCITY
OVERALL AU-GU ODDS 4 PER HOBBY BOX
1 Adam Dunn/250 2.00 5.00
3 Albert Pujols/250 6.00 15.00
5 Chipper Jones/250 3.00 8.00
6 Dale Murphy/250 3.00 8.00
7 Darryl Strawberry Pants/250 2.50 6.00
8 Dave Parker/250 2.50 6.00
9 David Ortiz/250 2.50 6.00
10 Duke Snider/25 6.00 15.00
12 Gary Sheffield/250 2.00 5.00
14 Harmon Killebrew/100 5.00 12.00
15 Jim Edmonds/250 2.00 5.00
16 Jim Rice Pants/250 2.50 6.00
17 Jim Thome/250 2.50 6.00
19 Manny Ramirez/100 3.00 8.00
20 Matt Williams/250 2.50 6.00
21 Mike Piazza/250 3.00 8.00
22 Mike Schmidt/100 6.00 15.00
23 Rafael Palmeiro Pants/250 2.50 6.00
24 Sammy Sosa/250 3.00 8.00
25 Ted Williams Jkt/250 15.00 40.00

2005 Leather and Lumber Game Ball Signatures

OVERALL AU-GU ODDS 4 PER HOBBY BOX
PRINT RUNS B/WN 1-50 COPIES PER
NO PRICING ON QTY OF 11 OR LESS
1 Ben Grieve/50 6.00 15.00
3 Eli Marrero/24 8.00 20.00
4 Jeff Fassero/24 12.50 30.00
5 Jose Guillen/47 10.00 25.00
7 Mark Grudzielanek/23 12.50 30.00
8 Mike Lowell/23 20.00 50.00
9 Paul Konerko/45 15.00 40.00

2005 Leather and Lumber Great Gloves

STATED PRINT RUN 2000 SERIAL #'d SETS
*GOLD ACTIVE: 1.25X TO 3X BASIC
*GOLD RETIRED: 1.5X TO 4X BASIC
GOLD PRINT RUN 50 SERIAL #'d SETS
PLATINUM PRINT RUN 1 SERIAL #'d SET
NO PLATINUM PRICING DUE TO SCARCITY
*SILVER ACTIVE: .75X TO 2X BASIC
*SILVER RETIRED: 1X TO 2.5X BASIC
SILVER PRINT RUN 100 SERIAL #'d SETS
OVERALL INSERT ODDS 1:2 HOBBY
1 Austin Kearns .40 1.00
2 Gary Carter .60 1.50
3 Ivan Rodriguez .60 1.50
4 Mark Grace .60 1.50
5 Mark Teixeira .60 1.50
6 Mike Schmidt 1.50 4.00
7 Omar Vizquel .60 1.50
8 Scott Rolen .60 1.50
9 Tony Gwynn 1.25 3.00
10 Willie Mays 2.00 5.00

2005 Leather and Lumber Great Gloves Fielding Glove

*FLD GLV p/r 25: .75X TO 2X JSY p/r 50
OVERALL AU-GU ODDS 4 PER HOBBY BOX
STATED PRINT RUN 25 SERIAL #'d SETS
6 Mike Schmidt/25 20.00 50.00

2005 Leather and Lumber Great Gloves Jersey

PRINT RUNS B/WN 25-50 COPIES PER
PRIME PRINT RUN 5 SERIAL #'d SETS
NO PRIME PRICING DUE TO SCARCITY
OVERALL AU-GU ODDS 4 PER HOBBY BOX
1 Austin Kearns/50 3.00 8.00
2 Gary Carter/50 4.00 10.00
3 Ivan Rodriguez/50 4.00 10.00
4 Mark Grace/50 5.00 12.00
5 Mark Teixeira/50 4.00 10.00
6 Mike Schmidt/50 8.00 20.00
7 Omar Vizquel/50 4.00 10.00
8 Scott Rolen/50 4.00 10.00
9 Tony Gwynn/50 6.00 15.00
10 Willie Mays/25 20.00 50.00

2005 Leather and Lumber Hitters Inc.

STATED PRINT RUN 2000 SERIAL #'d SETS
*GOLD ACTIVE: .75X TO 2X BASIC
*GOLD RETIRED: 1X TO 2.5X BASIC
GOLD PRINT RUN 100 SERIAL #'d SETS
PLATINUM PRINT RUN 1 SERIAL #'d SET
NO PLATINUM PRICING DUE TO SCARCITY
*SILVER ACTIVE: .6X TO 1.5X BASIC
*SILVER RETIRED: .75X TO 2X BASIC
SILVER PRINT RUN 200 SERIAL #'d SETS
OVERALL INSERT ODDS 1:2 HOBBY
1 Albert Pujols 1.25 3.00
2 Alfonso Soriano .60 1.50
3 Cal Ripken 3.00 8.00
4 Don Mattingly 2.00 5.00
5 Dwight Evans .60 1.50
6 George Brett 2.00 5.00
7 Hank Blalock .40 1.00
8 Ichiro Suzuki 1.25 3.00
9 Ivan Rodriguez .60 1.50
10 Jack Wilson .40 1.00
11 Keith Hernandez .40 1.00
12 Larry Walker .60 1.50
13 Lou Brock .60 1.50
14 Lyle Overbay .40 1.00
15 Michael Young .40 1.00
16 Paul Molitor 1.00 2.50
17 Rod Carew .60 1.50
18 Sean Casey .40 1.00
19 Steve Garvey .40 1.00
20 Todd Helton .60 1.50
21 Tony Gwynn 1.25 3.00
22 Travis Hafner .40 1.00
23 Ted Williams 2.00 5.00
24 Wade Boggs .60 1.50
25 Willie Mays 2.00 5.00

2005 Leather and Lumber Hitters Inc. Bat

*BAT p/r 100: .4X TO 1X JSY p/r 100
*BAT p/r 100: .3X TO .8X JSY p/r 50
*BAT p/r 50: .5X TO 1.2X JSY p/r 100
*BAT p/r 50: .3X TO .8X JSY p/r 20
*BAT p/r 25: .4X TO 1X JSY p/r 25
OVERALL AU-GU ODDS 4 PER HOBBY BOX
PRINT RUNS B/WN 25-100 COPIES PER
15 Michael Young/100 2.50 6.00

2005 Leather and Lumber Hitters Inc. Jersey

OVERALL AU-GU ODDS 4 PER HOBBY BOX
PRINT RUNS B/WN 20-100 COPIES PER
1 Albert Pujols/100 8.00 20.00
2 Alfonso Soriano/100 2.50 6.00
3 Cal Ripken/100 12.50 30.00
4 Don Mattingly/100 6.00 15.00
5 Dwight Evans/100 4.00 10.00
6 George Brett/20 10.00 25.00
7 Hank Blalock/100 2.50 6.00
9 Ivan Rodriguez/100 3.00 8.00
10 Jack Wilson/100 2.50 6.00
12 Larry Walker/100 3.00 8.00
13 Lou Brock/50 5.00 12.00
14 Lyle Overbay/100 2.50 6.00
16 Paul Molitor/100 3.00 8.00
17 Rod Carew/100 4.00 10.00
18 Sean Casey/100 2.50 6.00
19 Steve Garvey/100 3.00 8.00
20 Todd Helton/100 3.00 8.00
21 Tony Gwynn/100 5.00 12.00
22 Travis Hafner/100 2.50 6.00
23 Ted Williams Jkt/100 20.00 50.00
24 Wade Boggs/100 4.00 10.00
25 Willie Mays/25 20.00 50.00

2005 Leather and Lumber Hitters Inc. Signatures Bat

*BAT p/r 25: .4X TO 1X JSY p/r 25
OVERALL AU-GU ODDS 4 PER HOBBY BOX
PRINT RUNS B/WN 5-25 COPIES PER
NO PRICING ON QTY OF 10 OR LESS
15 Michael Young/25 12.50 30.00

2005 Leather and Lumber Hitters Inc. Signatures Jersey

OVERALL AU-GU ODDS 4 PER HOBBY BOX
PRINT RUNS B/WN 5-25 COPIES PER
NO PRICING ON QTY OF 10 OR LESS
5 Dwight Evans/25 20.00 50.00
7 Hank Blalock/25 12.50 30.00
10 Jack Wilson/25 8.00 20.00
13 Lou Brock/25 20.00 50.00
14 Lyle Overbay/25 8.00 20.00
17 Rod Carew/25 20.00 50.00
18 Sean Casey/25 12.50 30.00
19 Steve Garvey/25 12.50 30.00
22 Travis Hafner/25 12.50 30.00

2005 Leather and Lumber Leather Cuts

PRINT RUNS B/WN 1-128 COPIES PER
NO PRICING ON QTY OF 13 OR LESS
*LUMBER: .4X TO 1X BASIC
LUMBER PRINT RUNS B/WN 1-128 PER
NO LUMBER PRICING ON 13 OR LESS
OVERALL AU-GU ODDS 4 PER HOBBY BOX
2 Andre Dawson/128 6.00 15.00
3 Bert Blyleven/128 6.00 15.00
4 Lee Smith/32 10.00 25.00
5 Billy Williams/64 8.00 20.00
6 Bob Feller/128 10.00 25.00
7 Joe Pepitone/128 10.00 25.00
8 Bobby Doerr/128 6.00 15.00
9 Juan Marichal/112 6.00 15.00
12 Dale Murphy/96 10.00 25.00
13 Darryl Strawberry/128 6.00 15.00
14 Johnny Podres/128 6.00 15.00
15 Dave Righetti/16 12.50 30.00
18 Duke Snider/128 10.00 25.00
19 Dwight Evans/24 15.00 40.00
20 Dwight Gooden/128 6.00 15.00
21 Fergie Jenkins/96 6.00 15.00
23 Fred Lynn/128 6.00 15.00
24 Justin Morneau/128 6.00 15.00
25 Gaylord Perry/128 6.00 15.00
27 George Foster/128 6.00 15.00
28 Harmon Killebrew/64 20.00 50.00
29 Jack Morris/128 6.00 15.00
30 Jim Palmer/128 6.00 15.00
31 Jim Rice/128 6.00 15.00
33 John Kruk/128 10.00 25.00
34 Randy Jones/128 4.00 10.00
35 Keith Hernandez/128 6.00 15.00
36 Lenny Dykstra/128 6.00 15.00
37 Lou Brock/64 12.50 30.00
38 Luis Aparicio/128 6.00 15.00
39 Lyle Overbay/128 4.00 10.00
40 Maury Wills/128 6.00 15.00
41 Earl Weaver/128 6.00 15.00
42 Miguel Cabrera/64 20.00 50.00
44 Monte Irvin/96 6.00 15.00
46 Kent Hrbek/128 6.00 15.00
47 Red Schoendienst/128 6.00 15.00
48 Rich Gossage/128 6.00 15.00
50 Minnie Minoso/128 10.00 25.00
51 Sean Casey/64 8.00 20.00
54 Steve Stone/128 6.00 15.00
55 Tommy John/128 6.00 15.00
57 Victor Martinez/128 6.00 15.00
61 Lee Smith/128 6.00 15.00

2005 Leather and Lumber Leather Cuts Bat

*BAT p/r 96-128: .5X TO 1.2X CUT p/r 96-128
*BAT p/r 96-128: .4X TO 1X CUT p/r 64
*BAT p/r 96-128: .3X TO .8X CUT p/r 24-32
*BAT p/r 40-60: .6X TO 1.5X CUT p/r 96-128
*BAT p/r 40-60: .5X TO 1.2X CUT p/r 64
PRINT RUNS B/WN 6-128 COPIES PER
NO PRICING ON QTY OF 14 OR LESS
*LUMBER: .4X TO 1X LEATHER
LUMBER PRINT RUNS B/WN 6-128 PER
NO LUMBER PRICING ON 14 OR LESS
OVERALL AU-GU ODDS 4 PER HOBBY BOX
1 Al Kaline/58 25.00 50.00
10 Cal Ripken/60 75.00 150.00
22 Frank Robinson/40 10.00 25.00
60 Willie Mays/15 150.00 250.00

2005 Leather and Lumber Leather Cuts Jersey

*JSY p/r 96-128: .5X TO 1.2X CUT p/r 96-128
*JSY p/r 96-128: .3X TO .8X CUT p/r 24-32
*JSY p/r 44-64: .6X TO 1.5X CUT p/r 96-128
*JSY p/r 44-64: .5X TO 1.2X CUT p/r 64
*JSY p/r 44-64: .4X TO 1X CUT p/r 24-32
*JSY p/r 44-64: .3X TO .8X CUT p/r 16
*JSY p/r 32: .75X TO 2X CUT p/r 96-128
*JSY p/r 32: .6X TO 1.5X CUT p/r 64
PRINT RUNS B/WN 6-128 COPIES PER
NO PRICING ON QTY OF 14 OR LESS
*LUMBER: .4X TO 1X LEATHER
LUMBER PRINT RUNS B/WN 6-128 PER
NO LUMBER PRICING ON 14 OR LESS
OVERALL AU-GU ODDS 4 PER HOBBY BOX
10 Cal Ripken/60 75.00 150.00
16 David Cone/120 8.00 20.00
60 Willie Mays/15 150.00 250.00

2005 Leather and Lumber Lumber/Leather

STATED PRINT RUN 2000 SERIAL #'d SETS
*GOLD ACTIVE: 1.25X TO 3X BASIC
*GOLD RETIRED: 1.5X TO 4X BASIC
GOLD PRINT RUN 50 SERIAL #'d SETS
PLATINUM PRINT RUN 1 SERIAL #'d SET
NO PLATINUM PRICING DUE TO SCARCITY
*SILVER ACTIVE: .75X TO 2X BASIC
*SILVER RETIRED: 1X TO 2.5X BASIC
SILVER PRINT RUN 100 SERIAL #'d SETS
OVERALL INSERT ODDS 1:2 HOBBY
1 Albert Pujols 1.25 3.00
2 Alex Rodriguez 1.25 3.00
3 Alfonso Soriano .60 1.50
4 Cal Ripken 3.00 8.00
5 Carlos Lee .40 1.00
6 Derek Jeter 2.50 6.00
7 Don Mattingly 2.00 5.00
8 Ichiro Suzuki 1.25 3.00
9 Ivan Rodriguez .60 1.50
10 Jack Wilson .40 1.00
11 Josh Beckett .40 1.00
12 Ken Griffey Jr. 2.00 5.00
13 Lance Berkman .60 1.50
14 Magglio Ordonez .60 1.50
15 Mark Grace .60 1.50
16 Mark Prior .60 1.50
17 Mark Teixeira .60 1.50
18 Mike Schmidt 1.50 4.00
19 Nolan Ryan 3.00 8.00
20 Nomar Garciaparra .60 1.50
21 Paul Lo Duca .40 1.00
22 Rafael Palmeiro .60 1.50
23 Randy Johnson 1.00 2.50
24 Richie Sexson .40 1.00
25 Rickey Henderson 1.00 2.50
26 Roger Clemens 1.25 3.00
27 Ryan Klesko .40 1.00
28 Stan Musial 1.50 4.00
29 Steve Carlton .60 1.50
30 Tim Hudson .60 1.50
31 Tony Gwynn 1.25 3.00
32 Travis Hafner .40 1.00
33 Victor Martinez .60 1.50
34 Wade Boggs .60 1.50
35 Willie Mays 2.00 5.00

2005 Leather and Lumber Lumber/Leather Bat-Btg Glove

*ACTIVE p/r 25: .4X TO 1X FLD GLV p/r 25
*RET p/r 25: .4X TO 1X FLD GLV p/r 25
OVERALL AU-GU ODDS 4 PER HOBBY BOX
PRINT RUNS B/WN 1-25 COPIES PER
NO PRICING ON QTY OF 10 OR LESS
3 Alfonso Soriano/25 6.00 15.00
7 Don Mattingly/25 20.00 50.00
14 Magglio Ordonez/25 6.00 15.00
25 Rickey Henderson/25 12.50 30.00

2005 Leather and Lumber Lumber/Leather Bat-Fld Glove

OVERALL AU-GU ODDS 4 PER HOBBY BOX
PRINT RUNS B/WN 5-25 COPIES PER
NO PRICING ON QTY OF 10 OR LESS
5 Carlos Lee/25 6.00 15.00
9 Ivan Rodriguez/25 8.00 20.00
10 Jack Wilson/25 6.00 15.00
13 Lance Berkman/25 6.00 15.00
15 Mark Grace/25 10.00 25.00
16 Mark Prior/25 8.00 20.00
18 Mike Schmidt/25 20.00 50.00
21 Paul Lo Duca/25 6.00 15.00
22 Rafael Palmeiro/25 8.00 20.00
24 Richie Sexson/25 6.00 15.00
27 Ryan Klesko/25 6.00 15.00
29 Steve Carlton/25 8.00 20.00
30 Tim Hudson/25 6.00 15.00
31 Tony Gwynn/25 12.50 30.00

2005 Leather and Lumber Lumber/Leather Bat-Spikes

*ACTIVE p/r 25: .4X TO 1X FLD GLV p/r 25
*RETIRED p/r 25: .4X TO 1X FLD GLV p/r 25
OVERALL AU-GU ODDS 4 PER HOBBY BOX
PRINT RUNS B/WN 1-25 COPIES PER
NO PRICING ON QTY OF 10 OR LESS
1 Albert Pujols/25 15.00 40.00
11 Josh Beckett/25 5.00 12.00
14 Magglio Ordonez/25 5.00 12.00
25 Rickey Henderson/25 10.00 25.00

2005 Leather and Lumber Naturals

STATED PRINT RUN 2000 SERIAL #'d SETS
*GOLD ACTIVE: 1.25X TO 3X BASIC
*GOLD RETIRED: 1.5X TO 4X BASIC
GOLD PRINT RUN 50 SERIAL #'d SETS
PLATINUM PRINT RUN 1 SERIAL #'d SET
NO PLATINUM PRICING DUE TO SCARCITY
*SILVER ACTIVE: .75X TO 2X BASIC
*SILVER RETIRED: 1X TO 2.5X BASIC
SILVER PRINT RUN 100 SERIAL #'d SETS
OVERALL INSERT ODDS 1:2 HOBBY
1 Andruw Jones .40 1.00
2 Bernie Williams .60 1.50
3 Brooks Robinson .60 1.50
4 Cal Ripken 3.00 8.00
5 Casey Kotchman .40 1.00
6 Craig Biggio .60 1.50
7 Craig Wilson .40 1.00
8 David Ortiz 1.00 2.50
9 Eddie Murray .60 1.50
10 Javy Lopez .40 1.00
11 Jeff Bagwell .60 1.50
12 Lance Berkman .60 1.50
13 Magglio Ordonez .60 1.50
14 Michael Young .40 1.00
15 Rafael Palmeiro .60 1.50
16 Reggie Jackson .60 1.50
17 Rickey Henderson 1.00 2.50
18 Rocco Baldelli .40 1.00
19 Sammy Sosa 1.00 2.50
20 Shawn Green .40 1.00
21 Ted Williams 2.00 5.00
22 Tony Gwynn 1.25 3.00
23 Wade Boggs .60 1.50
24 Will Clark .60 1.50
25 Willie Mays 2.00 5.00

2005 Leather and Lumber Naturals Bat

*BAT p/r 100: .4X TO 1X JSY p/r 100
*BAT p/r 100: .3X TO .8X JSY p/r 50
*BAT p/r 50: .5X TO 1.2X JSY p/r 100
*BAT p/r 25: .4X TO 1X JSY p/r 25
OVERALL AU-GU ODDS 4 PER HOBBY BOX
PRINT RUNS B/WN 25-100 COPIES PER
3 Brooks Robinson/100 4.00 10.00

2005 Leather and Lumber Naturals Combos

*COM p/r 100: .5X TO 1.2X JSY p/r 100
*COM p/r 50: .6X TO 1.5X JSY p/r 100
*COM p/r 50: .5X TO 1.2X JSY p/r 50
*COM p/r 25: .6X TO 1.5X JSY p/r 50
*COM p/r 25: .5X TO 1.2X JSY p/r 25
PRINT RUNS B/WN 25-100 COPIES PER
PRIME PRINT RUN 5 SERIAL #'d SETS
NO PRIME PRICING DUE TO SCARCITY
OVERALL AU-GU ODDS 4 PER HOBBY BOX
3 Brooks Robinson Bat-Jsy/25 8.00 20.00

2005 Leather and Lumber Naturals Jersey

PRINT RUNS B/WN 25-100 COPIES PER
PRIME PRINT RUN 5 SERIAL #'d SETS
NO PRIME PRICING DUE TO SCARCITY
OVERALL AU-GU ODDS 4 PER HOBBY BOX
1 Andruw Jones/100 3.00 8.00
2 Bernie Williams/100 3.00 8.00
4 Cal Ripken/100 12.50 30.00
5 Casey Kotchman/100 2.50 6.00
6 Craig Biggio/100 3.00 8.00
7 Craig Wilson/100 2.50 6.00
8 David Ortiz/100 3.00 8.00
9 Eddie Murray/100 5.00 12.00
10 Javy Lopez/100 2.50 6.00
11 Jeff Bagwell/100 3.00 8.00
12 Lance Berkman/100 2.50 6.00
13 Magglio Ordonez/50 3.00 8.00
14 Michael Young/50 3.00 8.00
15 Rafael Palmeiro/100 3.00 8.00
16 Reggie Jackson/100 4.00 10.00
17 Rickey Henderson Jkt/100 5.00 12.00
18 Rocco Baldelli/100 2.50 6.00
19 Sammy Sosa/100 4.00 10.00
20 Shawn Green/100 2.50 6.00
21 Ted Williams Jkt/100 20.00 50.00
22 Tony Gwynn/100 5.00 12.00
23 Wade Boggs/100 4.00 10.00
24 Will Clark/50 5.00 12.00
25 Willie Mays/25 20.00 50.00

2005 Leather and Lumber Rivals

STATED PRINT RUN 2000 SERIAL #'d SETS
*GOLD ACTIVE: 1.25X TO 3X BASIC
*GOLD RETIRED: 1.5X TO 4X BASIC
GOLD PRINT RUN 50 SERIAL #'d SETS
PLATINUM PRINT RUN 1 SERIAL #'d SET
NO PLATINUM PRICING DUE TO SCARCITY
*SILVER ACTIVE: .75X TO 2X BASIC
*SILVER RETIRED: 1X TO 2.5X BASIC
SILVER PRINT RUN 100 SERIAL #'d SETS
OVERALL INSERT ODDS 1:2 HOBBY
1 I.Suzuki 1.50 4.00
H.Matsui
2 M.Mulder .60 1.50
V.Guerrero
3 T.Hudson .60 1.50
M.Teixeira
4 R.Clemens 1.25 3.00
A.Pujols
5 G.Maddux 1.25 3.00
J.Bagwell
6 R.Johnson 1.00 2.50
A.Beltre
7 K.Wood .60 1.50
L.Walker
8 M.Mussina 1.00 2.50
M.Ramirez
9 C.Sabathia .60 1.50
T.Hunter
10 J.Beckett 1.00 2.50
C.Jones
11 D.Jeter 2.50 6.00
M.Tejada
12 A.Rodriguez 1.25 3.00
H.Blalock
13 C.Beltran 1.00 2.50
S.Sosa
14 M.Prior .60 1.50
J.Thome
15 M.Cabrera 1.00 2.50
A.Jones
16 J.Santana .60 1.50
M.Ordonez
17 J.Beckett .60 1.50
C.Biggio
18 A.Dunn .60 1.50
S.Green
19 J.Morris .60 1.50
R.Carew
20 J.Palmer 1.00 2.50
P.Molitor
21 M.Schmidt 2.00 5.00
G.Brett
22 C.Ripken 3.00 8.00
D.Mattingly
23 B.Gibson 1.00 2.50
E.Banks
24 E.Murray .60 1.50
B.Blyleven
25 W.Spahn 2.00 5.00
W.Mays

2005 Leather and Lumber Rivals Bat

*BAT p/r 100: .5X TO 1.2X JSY p/r 150-250
*BAT p/r 100: .4X TO 1X JSY p/r 100
*BAT p/r 50: .6X TO 1.5X JSY p/r 150-250
OVERALL AU-GU ODDS 4 PER HOBBY BOX
PRINT RUNS B/WN 50-100 COPIES PER

2005 Leather and Lumber Rivals Jersey

PRINT RUNS B/WN 25-250 COPIES PER
PRIME PRINT RUN 5 SERIAL #'d SETS
NO PRIME PRICING DUE TO SCARCITY
OVERALL AU-GU ODDS 4 PER HOBBY BOX
2 M.Mulder/V.Guerrero/100 5.00 12.00
3 T.Hudson/M.Teixeira/250 3.00 8.00
4 R.Clemens/A.Pujols/100 8.00 20.00
5 G.Maddux/J.Bagwell/250 4.00 10.00
7 K.Wood/L.Walker/250 3.00 8.00
9 C.Sabathia/T.Hunter/150 2.50 6.00
10 J.Beck Pants/C.Jones/150 4.00 10.00
13 C.Beltran/S.Sosa/250 4.00 10.00
14 M.Prior/J.Thome/250 3.00 8.00
15 M.Cabrera/A.Jones/250 3.00 8.00
16 J.Santana/M.Ordonez/100 5.00 12.00
18 A.Dunn/S.Green/100 3.00 8.00
19 J.Morris/R.Carew/250 4.00 10.00
21 M.Schmidt/G.Brett/100 6.00 15.00
22 C.Ripken/D.Mattingly/100 12.00 30.00
23 B.Gibson/E.Banks/50 8.00 20.00
24 E.Murray/B.Blyleven/250 5.00 12.00
25 Spahn Pant/Mays Pant/50 50.00 100.00

1923 Lections

These 2 1/2" by 4" blank-backed horizontal cards are on heavy cardboard stock. The player's picture is on the left side and a game diagram is one the right. It is believed that these cards were issued in the Albany, New York area.Any additional findings to this checklist are appreciated.

COMPLETE SET 7500.00 15000.00
1 Frank Chance 1250.00 2500.00
2 Howard Ehmke 500.00 1000.00
3 Frank Frisch 1250.00 2500.00
4 Rogers Horsnby 2500.00 5000.00
5 Charlie Jamieson 500.00 1000.00
6 Bob Meusel 1000.00 2000.00
7 Irish Meusel 500.00 1000.00
8 Babe Ruth 4250.00 8500.00
9 Charles Schmidt 500.00 1000.00
10 Bob Shawkey 750.00 1500.00

1993 Legendary Foils Promos

COMPLETE SET 1.50 4.00
1 Satchel Paige .75 2.00
2 Honus Wagner .75 2.00

1993-94 Legendary Foils

The Legendary Foils Sport Series is a monthly series featuring baseball Hall of Famers. There are two editions. One is the Gold Edition, limited to 5,000 sets, and the Colored Edition, limited to 95,000 cards per player. The cards measure approximately 3 1/2" by 5" and come in a blue and black custom designed folder. The embossed fronts carry the players portrait and a short career summary. The Gold Edition cards are shiny gold on a matte gold background, while the Color Edition cards have a blue background. The serial number also appears on the front. The backs are silver and carry Legendary Foil logos.

COMPLETE SET 15.00 40.00
1 Roberto Clemente 2.50 6.00
2 Dizzy Dean 1.25 3.00
3 Lou Gehrig 2.50 6.00
4 Rogers Hornsby 1.25 3.00
5 Carl Hubbell 1.25 3.00
6 Walter Johnson 1.25 3.00
7 Tony Lazzeri .75 2.00
8 Satchel Paige 1.50 4.00
9 Babe Ruth 3.00 8.00
10 Casey Stengel 1.25 3.00
11 Pie Traynor 1.25 3.00
12 Honus Wagner 1.25 3.00

1993-94 Legendary Foils Hawaii IX

This Legendary Foils card of Babe Ruth was given out at the Ninth Hawaiian Show. Just 300 cards were produced. It measures approximately 2 5/8" by 3 3/4". On a matte gold background, the embossed front carries the player's portrait inside a circle and a short career summary in shiny gold lettering underneath it. Two bats on each side frame the text, and a baseball appears above each pair of bats. The top of the card is rounded alongside the two baseballs and the top part of the circle. The words "Hawaii IX" is printed on the bottom of the front. The back is silver, carrying the Legendary Foil logo and a production number. Where the serial number appears on regular series cards, this card reads "Hawaii IX."

1 Babe Ruth 2.00 5.00

1996 Liberty Sports

This 21-card set features borderless color action player photos and was produced by Liberty Satellite Sports. The backs carry player information, career statistics, and sponsor logos. It is believed that this set was produced especially for executives and media members at the various Fox satellites around the nation.

COMPLETE SET (21) 100.00 200.00
1 Cal Ripken Jr. 20.00 50.00
2 Paul O'Neill 1.25 3.00
3 Mo Vaughn 1.25 3.00
4 Travis Fryman 1.25 3.00
5 Brian Jordan 1.25 3.00
6 Ken Griffey Jr. 12.50 30.00
7 Craig Biggio 2.00 5.00
8 Chili Davis 1.25 3.00
9 Greg Maddux 12.50 30.00
10 Gary Sheffield 4.00 10.00
11 Frank Thomas 6.00 15.00
12 Barry Larkin 2.00 5.00
13 John Franco 1.25 3.00
14 Albert Belle 1.25 3.00
15 Mark McGwire 10.00 25.00
16 Barry Bonds 10.00 25.00
17 Lenny Dykstra .75 2.00
NNO Mickey Lopez .80 2.00
NNO Title Card .75 2.00
NNO Tim Salmon 2.00 5.00
NNO Matt Williams 1.50 4.00

1992 Lime Rock Griffey Holograms

This three-card standard-size set was produced by Lime Rock and features baseball's "first family," the Griffeys. Included with each set was a serially numbered coupon that entitled the holder to a free issue of Lime Rock's Inside Trader Club Quarterly News. The sets were sold in a box and included a gold-embossed folder for displaying the cards. According to Lime Rock, 250,000 sets and 5,000 strips were produced. Moreover, 2,500 cards were personally autographed and randomly inserted. Members of Lime Rock's Inside Trader Club had the exclusive right to purchase the same cards as a strip. Also, 750 promo sets were produced and distributed at the National Sports Collectors Convention in Atlanta (the promo cards are blank backed). The cards were also produced in a gold version (reportedly 1,000 sets). Each standard-size, full-bleed hologram captures Ken Sr., Ken Jr. and Craig in game action. At the top of each front appear the words "Griffey Baseball" in the background. Also the player's autograph is inscribed across the holograms. On a pastel green background, the backs carry a color close-up photo, career summary and statistics.

COMPLETE SET (3) 2.00 5.00
1 Ken Griffey Sr. .40 1.00
2 Ken Griffey Jr. 2.00 5.00
3 Craig Griffey .20 .50

1992 Lime Rock Griffey Holograms Autographs

This three-card standard-size set was produced by Lime Rock and features baseball's "first family," the Griffeys. 2,500 of these cards were personally autographed and randomly inserted.

COMPLETE SET (3) 100.00 200.00
1 Ken Griffey Sr. 10.00 25.00
2 Ken Griffey Jr. 50.00 120.00
3 Craig Griffey 2.00 5.00

2011 Limited

COMMON CARD (1-30) .40 1.00
STATED PRINT RUN 249 SER.#'d SETS
1 Matt Kemp .75 2.00
2 Colby Rasmus .60 1.50
3 David Price .75 2.00
4 Cliff Lee .60 1.50
5 David Freese .40 1.00
6 Albert Pujols 1.25 3.00
7 Andrew McCutchen 1.00 2.50
8 Clayton Kershaw 1.50 4.00
9 CC Sabathia .60 1.50
10 Miguel Cabrera 1.00 2.50
11 Elvis Andrus .60 1.50
12 Adam Jones .60 1.50
13 David Wright UER .75 2.00
14 Hunter Pence .60 1.50
15 Ian Kennedy .40 1.00
16 Alex Presley RC .60 1.50
17 Jacoby Ellsbury .75 2.00
18 Wilson Ramos .40 1.00
19 Josh Hamilton .60 1.50
20 Prince Fielder .60 1.50
21 Jose Bautista .60 1.50
22 Yovani Gallardo .40 1.00
23 Brett Gardner .60 1.50
24 Ryan Braun .60 1.50
25 Mariano Rivera 1.25 3.00
26 David Ortiz 1.00 2.50
27 Andre Ethier .60 1.50
28 Logan Morrison .40 1.00
29 Todd Helton .60 1.50
30 Bill Bray .40 1.00

2011 Limited OptiChrome

*OPTICHROME: .5X TO 1.2X BASIC
STATED PRINT RUN 199 SER.#'d SETS

2011 Limited Draft Hits

STATED PRINT RUN 249 SER.#'d SETS
1 Josh Bell 2.50 6.00
2 Anthony Rendon 4.00 10.00
3 George Springer 2.50 6.00
4 Dylan Bundy 1.25 3.00
5 Bubba Starling .60 1.50
6 Matt Barnes .60 1.50
7 Andrew Susac .60 1.50
8 Michael Fulmer 1.00 2.50
9 Tyler Collins .40 1.00
10 Trevor Bauer 4.00 10.00
11 Jason Esposito 1.00 2.50
12 Archie Bradley 1.25 3.00
13 Jake Hager .40 1.00
14 Gerrit Cole 4.00 10.00
15 Levi Michael .60 1.50
16 Mikie Mahtook 1.00 2.50
17 Kevin Matthews .40 1.00
18 Trevor Story 6.00 15.00
19 Jacob Anderson 1.25 3.00
20 Sonny Gray 1.00 2.50
21 Austin Hedges .40 1.00
22 Greg Bird .75 2.00
23 Javier Baez 5.00 12.00
24 Brandon Nimmo 2.00 5.00
25 Cory Spangenberg .60 1.50
26 Danny Hultzen 2.00 5.00
27 Joe Ross 1.00 2.50
28 Francisco Lindor 5.00 12.00
29 Robert Stephenson .75 2.00
30 Joe Panik 1.00 2.50

2011 Limited Draft Hits OptiChrome

*OPTICHROME: .5X TO 1.2X BASIC
STATED PRINT RUN 199 SER.#'d SETS

2011 Limited Draft Hits Signatures

PRINT RUNS B/WN 99-299 COPIES PER
EXCHANGE DEADLINE 10/05/2013
1 Josh Bell/149 12.00 30.00
2 Anthony Rendon/199 20.00 50.00
3 George Springer/229 10.00 25.00
4 Dylan Bundy/149 4.00 10.00
5 Bubba Starling/99 10.00 25.00
6 Matt Barnes/148 4.00 10.00
7 Andrew Susac/299 3.00 8.00
8 Michael Fulmer/297 12.00 30.00
9 Tyler Collins/297 3.00 8.00
10 Trevor Bauer/99 10.00 25.00
11 Jason Esposito/299 3.00 8.00
12 Archie Bradley/99 10.00 25.00
13 Jake Hager/295 3.00 8.00
14 Gerrit Cole/99 15.00 40.00
15 Levi Michael/299 3.00 8.00
16 Mikie Mahtook/299 5.00 12.00
17 Kevin Matthews/296 3.00 8.00
18 Trevor Story/299 12.00 30.00
19 Jacob Anderson/299 3.00 8.00
20 Sonny Gray/149 3.00 8.00
21 Austin Hedges/149 4.00 10.00
22 Greg Bird/299 20.00 50.00
23 Javier Baez/149 20.00 50.00
24 Brandon Nimmo/149 4.00 10.00
25 Cory Spangenberg/149 4.00 10.00
26 Danny Hultzen/99 5.00 12.00
27 Joe Ross/299 3.00 8.00
28 Francisco Lindor/149 20.00 50.00
29 Robert Stephenson/299 6.00 15.00
30 Joe Panik/299 8.00 20.00

2011 Limited Gamers Caps

PRINT RUNS B/WN 10-99 COPIES PER
NO PRICING ON QTY LESS THAN 19
1 Dwight Gooden/70 4.00 10.00
2 Hanley Ramirez/99 3.00 8.00
3 Frank Robinson/55 10.00 25.00
4 Reggie Jackson/49 8.00 20.00
5 Buster Posey/75 8.00 20.00
6 Gordon Beckham/99 3.00 8.00
7 Rick Porcello/99 3.00 8.00
8 Ryne Sandberg/44 8.00 20.00
12 Brett Anderson/99 3.00 8.00
14 Jason Kipnis/99 3.00 8.00

2011 Limited Gamers Gloves

PRINT RUNS B/WN 19-299 COPIES PER
NO PRICING ON QTY 19
1 Brett Anderson/105 3.00 8.00
2 Alex Rodriguez/70 10.00 25.00
3 Tony Gwynn/52 6.00 15.00
4 Ryne Sandberg/67 10.00 25.00
5 Mark Teixeira/299 5.00 12.00
7 Steve Carlton/49 10.00 25.00
8 Derek Jeter/299 10.00 25.00
9 Ken Boyer/299 4.00 10.00
10 Jimmie Foxx/49 40.00 80.00
11 Dwight Gooden/44 6.00 15.00
12 Rick Porcello/299 3.00 8.00
14 Dave Winfield/120 6.00 15.00
15 Willie Randolph/299 4.00 10.00

2011 Limited Greats

STATED PRINT RUN 299 SER.#'d SETS
1 Ken Griffey Jr. 5.00 12.00
2 Jim Abbott 1.00 2.50
3 Denny McLain 1.00 2.50
4 Fred Lynn 1.00 2.50
5 Don Mattingly 5.00 12.00
6 Nomar Garciaparra 1.50 4.00
7 Paul O'Neill 1.50 4.00
8 Minnie Minoso 1.00 2.50
9 Vida Blue 1.00 2.50
10 Robin Ventura 1.00 2.50
11 Ron Blomberg 1.00 2.50
12 Lee Smith 1.00 2.50
13 Will Clark 1.50 4.00
14 Pete Rose 12.50 30.00
15 Alan Trammell 1.50 4.00
16 Tino Martinez 1.50 4.00
17 Tim McCarver 1.00 2.50
18 Jim Palmer 1.50 4.00
19 David Justice 1.00 2.50
20 Dave Parker 1.00 2.50
21 Frank Thomas 2.50 6.00
22 Craig Biggio 1.50 4.00
23 Carl Yastrzemski 4.00 10.00
24 Bo Jackson 2.50 6.00
25 Tommy John 1.00 2.50
26 Jim Rice 1.50 4.00
27 Ron LeFlore 1.00 2.50
28 Pete Incaviglia 1.00 2.50
29 Frank Howard 1.00 2.50
30 Rusty Staub 1.00 2.50
31 Edgar Martinez 1.50 4.00
32 Lou Piniella 1.00 2.50
33 Steve Finley 1.00 2.50
34 Darin Erstad 1.00 2.50
35 Reggie Sanders 1.00 2.50
36 J.T. Snow 1.00 2.50
37 Shawn Green 1.00 2.50
38 Devon White 1.00 2.50
39 Royce Clayton 1.00 2.50

2011 Limited Greats Signatures

PRINT RUNS B/WN 5-499 COPIES PER
NO PRICING ON QTY 24 OR LESS
EXCHANGE DEADLINE 10/05/2013
2 Jim Abbott/499 6.00 15.00
3 Denny McLain/499 6.00 15.00
4 Fred Lynn/149 6.00 15.00
7 Paul O'Neill/300 8.00 20.00
8 Minnie Minoso/292 8.00 20.00
9 Vida Blue/499 4.00 10.00
10 Robin Ventura/199 4.00 10.00
11 Ron Blomberg/101 3.00 8.00
12 Lee Smith/250 5.00 12.00
13 Will Clark/30 20.00 50.00
14 Pete Rose/30 15.00 40.00
15 Alan Trammell/499 3.00 8.00
17 Tim McCarver/49 8.00 20.00
18 Jim Palmer/30 12.00 30.00
19 David Justice/299 8.00 20.00
20 Dave Parker/499 4.00 10.00
21 Frank Thomas/33 20.00 50.00
24 Bo Jackson/49 30.00 80.00
25 Tommy John/299 5.00 12.00
26 Jim Rice/181 5.00 12.00
27 Ron LeFlore/499 4.00 10.00
28 Pete Incaviglia/399 3.00 8.00
29 Frank Howard/299 6.00 15.00
30 Rusty Staub/300 4.00 10.00
31 Edgar Martinez/250 6.00 15.00
32 Lou Piniella/100 6.00 15.00
33 Steve Finley/499 3.00 8.00
34 Darin Erstad/199 6.00 15.00
35 Reggie Sanders/499 3.00 8.00
36 J.T. Snow/499 4.00 10.00
37 Shawn Green/399 3.00 8.00
38 Devon White/499 3.00 8.00
39 Royce Clayton/499 3.00 8.00

2011 Limited Hall of Fame Gear

PRINT RUNS B/WN 10-125 COPIES PER
NO PRICING ON QTY 19 OR LESS
PRIME PRINT RUNS B/WN 1-20 COPIES PER
NO PRIME PRICING AVAILABLE
1 Ty Cobb/25 100.00 200.00
2 Nellie Fox/99 12.50 30.00
4 Duke Snider/99 6.00 15.00
6 Paul Molitor/28 4.00 10.00
7 Orlando Cepeda/58 4.00 10.00
8 Nolan Ryan/125 10.00 25.00
9 Phil Niekro/125 4.00 10.00
10 Red Schoendienst/49 6.00 15.00
11 Roberto Alomar/99 5.00 12.00
12 Ryne Sandberg/32 20.00 50.00
13 Juan Marichal/38 4.00 10.00
14 Wade Boggs/43 6.00 15.00
15 Dave Winfield/99 5.00 12.00

2011 Limited Hard Hats

PRINT RUNS B/WN 90-99 COPIES PER
1 Derek Jeter/90 12.50 30.00
2 B.J. Surhoff/99 5.00 12.00
3 Jim Thome/99 10.00 25.00
4 Tony Gwynn/97 8.00 20.00
6 Kirk Gibson/97 12.50 30.00
7 Dwight Gooden/99 10.00 25.00
8 Austin Jackson/93 3.00 8.00
9 Andy Dirks/93 4.00 10.00
10 Alex Avila/93 12.50 30.00

2011 Limited International Flair Signatures

PRINT RUNS B/WN 49-499 COPIES PER
EXCHANGE DEADLINE 10/05/2013
1 Duanel Jones/499 3.00 8.00
2 Ronald Guzman/499 3.00 8.00
3 Danry Vasquez/499 3.00 8.00
4 Leonys Martin/316 4.00 10.00
5 Miguel Cabrera/49 12.00 30.00
6 Mariekson Gregorius/399 5.00 12.00
7 Hernan Perez/499 3.00 8.00
8 Jose Osuna/499 3.00 8.00
9 Adeiny Hechavarria/399 3.00 8.00
10 Jamaine Cotton/499 3.00 8.00

2011 Limited Leather

STATED PRINT RUN 199 SER.#'d SETS
1 Al Kaline 2.50 6.00
2 Brandon Phillips 1.00 2.50
3 Adrian Gonzalez 2.00 5.00
4 Adrian Beltre 2.50 6.00
5 Joe Mauer 2.00 5.00
6 Andre Ethier 1.50 4.00
7 Dale Murphy 2.50 6.00
8 Yadier Molina 3.00 8.00
9 Justin Upton 1.50 4.00
10 Jack Morris 1.50 4.00
11 Cliff Lee 1.50 4.00
12 Ryan Braun 1.50 4.00
13 Elvis Andrus 1.50 4.00
14 Brooks Robinson 1.50 4.00
15 Carl Crawford 1.50 4.00
16 Don Mattingly 10.00 25.00
17 Jimmy Rollins 1.50 4.00
18 Buster Posey 3.00 8.00

2011 Limited Leather Signatures

PRINT RUNS B/WN 10-199 COPIES PER
NO PRICING ON QTY 23 OR LESS
EXCHANGE DEADLINE 10/05/2013
3 Adrian Gonzalez/49 10.00 25.00
6 Andre Ethier/149 4.00 10.00
7 Dale Murphy/25 10.00 25.00
9 Justin Upton/49 10.00 25.00
10 Jack Morris/199 5.00 12.00
12 Ryan Braun/25 8.00 20.00
13 Elvis Andrus/99 8.00 20.00
14 Brooks Robinson/30 10.00 25.00
18 Buster Posey/40 15.00 40.00

2011 Limited Lumberjacks

STATED PRINT RUN 249 SER.#'d SETS
1 Josh Hamilton 1.50 4.00
2 Joe Jackson 3.00 8.00
3 Mike Schmidt 4.00 10.00
4 Robinson Cano 1.50 4.00
5 Ryan Zimmerman 1.50 4.00
6 Joey Votto 2.50 6.00
7 David Freese 1.00 2.50
8 Rickey Henderson 2.50 6.00
9 Jose Bautista 1.50 4.00
10 Adrian Beltre 2.50 6.00

2011 Limited Lumberjacks Bats

PRINT RUNS B/WN 49-299 COPIES PER
1 Josh Hamilton/299 3.00 8.00
2 Joe Jackson/199 50.00 100.00
3 Mike Schmidt/49 4.00 10.00
4 Robinson Cano/299 3.00 8.00
5 Ryan Zimmerman/299 3.00 8.00
6 Joey Votto/299 3.00 8.00
7 David Freese/299 4.00 10.00
8 Rickey Henderson/299 5.00 12.00
10 Adrian Beltre/99 3.00 8.00

2011 Limited Lumberjacks Signatures

PRINT RUNS B/WN 20-149 COPIES PER
NO PRICING ON QTY 20 OR LESS
EXCHANGE DEADLINE 10/05/2013
1 Josh Hamilton/149 15.00 40.00
7 David Freese/99 10.00 25.00
9 Jose Bautista/49 10.00 25.00
10 Adrian Beltre/49 10.00 25.00

2011 Limited Match-Ups

STATED PRINT RUNS 199 SER.#'d SETS
1 A.Presley/A.McCutchen 1.00 2.50
2 G.Cole/J.Bell 4.00 10.00
3 A.Gonzalez/M.Cabrera 1.00 2.50
4 A.Bradley/T.Bauer 4.00 10.00
5 C.Kershaw/R.Braun 1.50 4.00
6 D.Bundy/N.Delmonico 1.25 3.00
7 CC Sabathia/David Ortiz 1.00 2.50
8 A.Rendon/M.Purke 4.00 10.00
9 C.Kershaw/M.Kemp 1.50 4.00
10 Jed Bradley/Taylor Jungmann .60 1.50
11 Al Kaline/Denny McLain 1.00 2.50
12 F.Lindor/U.Jimenez 5.00 12.00
13 Brooks Robinson/Frank Robinson .60 1.50
14 Jose Bautista/Josh Hamilton .60 1.50
15 Edgar Martinez/Felix Hernandez .60 1.50

2011 Limited Match-Ups Signatures

PRINT RUNS B/WN 5-99 COPIES PER
NO PRICING ON QTY 20 OR LESS
EXCHANGE DEADLINE 10/05/2013
1 A.Presley/A.McCutchen/49 12.50 30.00
2 G.Cole/J.Bell/25 25.00 60.00
4 A.Bradley/T.Bauer/25 50.00 100.00
6 D.Bundy/N.Delmonico/99 20.00 50.00
8 A.Rendon/M.Purke/99 12.00 30.00
10 Jed Bradley/Taylor Jungmann/99 8.00 20.00
11 A.Kaline/D.McLain/30 25.00 50.00
12 F.Lindor/U.Jimenez/49 8.00 20.00

2011 Limited Materials

PRINT RUNS B/WN 10-499 COPIES PER
NO PRICING ON QTY 10
1 B.J. Upton/399 3.00 8.00
2 David Wright/280 3.00 8.00
3 CC Sabathia/499 3.00 8.00
4 Curt Flood/249 8.00 20.00
5 Bernie Williams/319 3.00 8.00
6 Todd Helton/499 3.00 8.00
7 Johan Santana/499 3.00 8.00
8 Hanley Ramirez/499 3.00 8.00
9 Clayton Kershaw/377 3.00 8.00
10 Frank Thomas/499 3.00 8.00
11 Harmon Killebrew/199 4.00 10.00
12 Chipper Jones/499 5.00 12.00
13 Jack Morris/330 3.00 8.00
14 Pete Rose/499 8.00 20.00
15 Ichiro Suzuki/499 6.00 15.00
16 Dwight Gooden/149 3.00 8.00
17 David Ortiz/399 3.00 8.00
18 Joe Torre/99 4.00 10.00

2011 Limited Materials Prime

PRINT RUNS B/WN 1-49 COPIES PER
NO PRICING ON QTY 20 OR LESS
1 B.J. Upton/49 3.00 8.00
2 David Wright/49 20.00 50.00
3 CC Sabathia/49 3.00 8.00
5 Bernie Williams/44 6.00 15.00
7 Johan Santana/49 3.00 8.00
8 Hanley Ramirez/49 3.00 8.00
10 Frank Thomas/49 10.00 25.00
14 Pete Rose/49 10.00 25.00

2011 Limited Moniker Bats

PRINT RUNS B/WN 2-199 COPIES PER
NO PRICIN ON QTY 20 OR LESS
EXCHANGE DEADLINE 10/05/2013
6 Drew Stubbs/199 5.00 12.00
7 Hanley Ramirez/25 6.00 15.00
12 Dwight Gooden/62 8.00 20.00
14 Pete Rose/25 50.00 100.00

2011 Limited Moniker Jersey

PRINT RUNS B/WN 10-149 COPIES PER
NO PRICIN ON QTY 15 OR LESS
EXCHANGE DEADLINE 10/05/2013
1 Chipper Jones/25 75.00 150.00
2 Bert Blyleven/30 8.00 20.00
3 Bernie Williams/35 30.00 60.00
4 Red Schoendienst/25 30.00 60.00
5 Vida Blue/149 5.00 12.00
6 Drew Stubbs/149 3.00 8.00
7 Hanley Ramirez/25 5.00 12.00
12 Dwight Gooden/149 6.00 15.00

2011 Limited Prospects

STATED PRINT RUN 249 SER.#'d SETS
1 Michael Choice .60 1.50
2 Jackie Bradley Jr. 1.50 4.00
3 Pratt Maynard 4.00 10.00
4 Blake Swihart .60 1.50
5 Andrew Chafin .40 1.00
6 Pedro Villarreal .40 1.00
7 Jared Hoying .60 1.50
8 Alex Meyer .40 1.00
9 Kolten Wong .60 1.50
10 Alex Santana .60 1.50
11 Shawon Dunston Jr. .40 1.00
12 Dante Bichette Jr. .60 1.50
13 Matt Dean .60 1.50
14 Jon Griffin .40 1.00
15 Lenny Linsky .60 1.50
16 Tommy Shirley .40 1.00
17 Nicky Delmonico .40 1.00
18 Parker Bridwell .60 1.50
19 Albert Cartwright .60 1.50
20 Hernan Perez .60 1.50
21 Justin Boudreaux .40 1.00
22 Miles Head .60 1.50
23 Zack MacPhee .60 1.50
24 Jace Peterson .40 1.00
25 Granden Goetzman .40 1.00
26 Adam Davis .40 1.00
27 Charlie Leesman .40 1.00
28 Barret Loux .40 1.00
29 Adrian Houser .60 1.50
30 Travis Harrison .60 1.50
31 Taylor Jungmann .60 1.50
32 Kyle Parker .60 1.50
33 Jake Dunning .40 1.00
34 Kylin Turnbull .40 1.00
35 Ryan Tatusko .60 1.50
36 Mike Walker .60 1.50
37 Corey Williams .40 1.00
38 Robert Stephenson .75 2.00
39 Kyle Crick 1.00 2.50
40 Chris Reed .60 1.50

2011 Limited Prospects OptiChrome

*OPTICHROME: .5X TO 1.2X BASIC
STATED PRINT RUN 199 SER.#'d SETS

2011 Limited Prospects Signatures

PRINT RUNS B/WN 32-899 COPIES PER
EXCHANGE DEADLINE 10/05/2013
1 Michael Choice/499 3.00 8.00
2 Jackie Bradley Jr./71 12.00 30.00
3 Pratt Maynard/499 2.00 5.00
4 Blake Swihart/210 3.00 8.00
5 Andrew Chafin/750 2.00 5.00
6 Pedro Villarreal/899 2.00 5.00
7 Jared Hoying/899 3.00 8.00
8 Alex Meyer/399 2.00 5.00
9 Kolten Wong/240 3.00 8.00
10 Alex Santana/399 3.00 8.00
11 Shawon Dunston Jr./339 2.00 5.00
12 Dante Bichette Jr./299 3.00 8.00
13 Matt Dean/520 3.00 8.00
14 Jon Griffin/520 2.00 5.00
15 Lenny Linsky/452 3.00 8.00
16 Tommy Shirley/899 2.00 5.00
17 Nicky Delmonico/399 2.00 5.00
18 Parker Bridwell/699 3.00 8.00
19 Albert Cartwright/899 3.00 8.00
20 Hernan Perez/599 3.00 8.00
21 Justin Boudreaux/723 2.00 5.00
22 Miles Head/899 3.00 8.00
23 Zack MacPhee/820 3.00 8.00
24 Jace Peterson/32 2.00 5.00
25 Granden Goetzman/349 2.00 5.00
26 Adam Davis/820 2.00 5.00
27 Charlie Leesman/609 2.00 5.00
28 Barret Loux/599 2.00 5.00
29 Adrian Houser/299 3.00 8.00
30 Travis Harrison/320 3.00 8.00
31 Taylor Jungmann/199 3.00 8.00
32 Kyle Parker/137 3.00 8.00
33 Jake Dunning/899 2.00 5.00
34 Kylin Turnbull/399 2.00 5.00
35 Ryan Tatusko/620 3.00 8.00
36 Mike Walker/899 3.00 8.00
37 Corey Williams/399 2.00 5.00
38 Robert Stephenson/146 4.00 10.00
39 Kyle Crick/90 5.00 12.00
40 Chris Reed/128 3.00 8.00

2011 Limited Rawlings Gold Gloves

STATED PRINT RUN 299 SER.#'d SETS
1 Roberto Alomar 2.00 5.00
2 Dustin Pedroia 3.00 8.00
3 Erick Aybar 1.25 3.00
4 Cal Ripken Jr. 10.00 25.00
5 Ken Griffey Jr. 6.00 15.00
6 Keith Hernandez 1.25 3.00
7 Adrian Gonzalez 2.50 6.00
8 Andre Ethier 2.00 5.00
9 Adam Jones 2.00 5.00
10 Ozzie Smith 10.00 25.00

2011 Limited Signatures

PRINT RUNS B/WN 30-399 COPIES PER
EXCHANGE DEADLINE 10/05/2013
1 Matt Kemp/49 8.00 20.00
2 Colby Rasmus/299 3.00 8.00
4 Cliff Lee/49 6.00 15.00
5 David Freese/149 4.00 10.00
7 Andrew McCutchen/249 20.00 50.00
8 Clayton Kershaw/99 30.00 80.00
9 CC Sabathia/249 8.00 20.00
10 Miguel Cabrera/49 40.00 80.00
11 Elvis Andrus/299 3.00 8.00
12 Adam Jones/399 6.00 15.00
13 D.Wright/49 UER 8.00 20.00
15 Ian Kennedy/199 4.00 10.00
16 Alex Presley/299 4.00 10.00
18 Wilson Ramos/299 3.00 8.00
19 Josh Hamilton/99 3.00 8.00
21 Jose Bautista/49 8.00 20.00
22 Yovani Gallardo/99 4.00 10.00
23 Brett Gardner/399 4.00 10.00
24 Ryan Braun/49 10.00 25.00
25 Mariano Rivera/30 40.00 80.00
26 David Ortiz/49 10.00 25.00
27 Andre Ethier/249 4.00 10.00
28 Logan Morrison/299 3.00 8.00
29 Todd Helton/49 10.00 25.00
30 Bill Bray/396 3.00 8.00

2011 Limited Silver Sluggers

STATED PRINT RUN 249 SER.#'d SETS
1 Adrian Gonzalez 2.00 5.00
2 Robinson Cano 1.50 4.00
3 Hanley Ramirez 1.50 4.00
4 Miguel Cabrera 2.50 6.00
5 Ken Griffey Jr. 5.00 12.00
6 Roberto Alomar 1.50 4.00
7 Justin Upton 1.50 4.00
8 Jose Bautista 1.50 4.00
9 Alex Avila 1.50 4.00
10 Yovani Gallardo 1.00 2.50
11 Josh Hamilton 1.50 4.00
12 Will Clark 1.50 4.00
13 Ryan Braun 1.50 4.00
14 David Ortiz 2.50 6.00
15 Adrian Beltre 2.50 6.00

2011 Limited Silver Sluggers Signatures

PRINT RUNS B/WN 20-49 COPIES PER
NO PRICING ON QTY 20
EXCHANGE DEADLINE 10/05/2013
1 Adrian Gonzalez/25 15.00 40.00
2 Robinson Cano/49 12.00 30.00
3 Hanley Ramirez/25 20.00 50.00
4 Miguel Cabrera/49 20.00 50.00
7 Justin Upton/49 6.00 15.00
8 Jose Bautista/25 10.00 25.00
9 Alex Avila/49 10.00 25.00
11 Josh Hamilton/49 10.00 25.00
12 Will Clark/49 15.00 40.00
13 Ryan Braun/49 10.00 25.00
14 David Ortiz/49 12.50 30.00
15 Adrian Beltre/49 10.00 25.00

2011 Limited USA Baseball National Team

STATED PRINT RUN 199 SER.#'d SETS
1 Mark Appel 2.50 6.00
2 D.J. Baxendale 1.50 4.00
3 Josh Elander 1.00 2.50
4 Chris Elder 1.00 2.50
5 Dominic Ficociello 1.00 2.50
6 Nolan Fontana 1.00 2.50
7 Kevin Gausman 5.00 12.00
8 Brian Johnson 1.00 2.50
9 Branden Kline 1.00 2.50
10 Corey Knebel 1.00 2.50
11 Michael Lorenzen 1.00 2.50
12 David Lyon 1.00 2.50
13 Deven Marrero 2.50 6.00
14 Hoby Milner 1.00 2.50
15 Andrew Mitchell 1.00 2.50
16 Tom Murphy 1.00 2.50
17 Tyler Naquin 2.50 6.00
18 Matt Reynolds 1.50 4.00
19 Brady Rodgers 1.00 2.50
20 Marcus Stroman 2.50 6.00
21 Michael Wacha 3.00 8.00
22 Erich Weiss 1.00 2.50
23 Albert Almora 1.50 4.00
24 Alex Bregman 8.00 20.00
25 Gavin Cecchini 1.50 4.00
26 Troy Conyers 1.00 2.50
27 David Dahl 5.00 12.00
28 Chase De Jong 2.00 5.00
29 Carson Fulmer 2.00 5.00
30 Joey Gallo 5.00 12.00
31 Cole Irvin 1.50 4.00
32 Carson Kelly 1.50 4.00
33 Jeremy Martinez 1.00 2.50
34 Chris Okey 1.00 2.50
35 Nelson Rodriguez 1.50 4.00
36 Addison Russell 3.00 8.00
37 Clate Schmidt 1.00 2.50
38 Nick Travieso 3.00 8.00
39 Hunter Virant 1.00 2.50
40 Walker Weickel 1.00 2.50
41 Mikey White 1.00 2.50
42 Jesse Winker 6.00 15.00
43 Willie Abreu 1.50 4.00
44 Tyler Alamo 1.00 2.50
45 Bryson Brigman 1.00 2.50
46 Nick Ciuffo 1.00 2.50
47 Trevor Clifton 1.00 2.50
48 Zack Collins 1.50 4.00
49 Joe DeMers 1.00 2.50
50 Steven Farinaro 1.00 2.50
51 Jake Jarvis 1.00 2.50
52 Austin Meadows 4.00 10.00
53 Hunter Mercado-Hood 1.00 2.50
54 Dom Nunez 1.00 2.50
55 Arden Pabst 1.00 2.50
56 Christian Pelaez 1.00 2.50
57 Carson Sands 1.00 2.50
58 Jordan Sheffield 1.00 2.50
59 Keegan Thompson 1.00 2.50
60 Touki Toussaint 1.50 4.00
61 Riley Unroe 1.00 2.50
62 Matt Vogel 1.00 2.50

2011 Limited USA Baseball National Teams Prime Patches

PRINT RUNS B/WN 16-25 COPIES PER
NO PRICING ON QTY 24 OR LESS
PRICING BELOW FOR BASIC PATCH CARDS
PREMIUM PATCHES MAY SELL FOR MORE
1 Mark Appel/25 10.00 25.00
2 D.J. Baxendale/25 6.00 15.00
3 Josh Elander/25 4.00 10.00
4 Chris Elder/25 4.00 10.00
5 Dominic Ficociello/25 4.00 10.00
7 Kevin Gausman/25 20.00 50.00
8 Brian Johnson/25 4.00 10.00
9 Branden Kline/25 4.00 10.00
10 Michael Lorenzen/25 4.00 10.00
11 David Lyon/25 4.00 10.00
12 Deven Marrero/25 10.00 25.00
13 Hoby Milner/25 4.00 10.00
14 Andrew Mitchell/25 4.00 10.00
16 Tyler Naquin/25 10.00 25.00
18 Brady Rodgers/25 4.00 10.00
19 Marcus Stroman/25 10.00 25.00
20 Michael Wacha/25 12.00 30.00
25 Troy Conyers/25 4.00 10.00
26 David Dahl/25 20.00 50.00
28 Carson Fulmer/25 8.00 20.00
29 Joey Gallo/25 20.00 50.00
30 Cole Irvin/25 6.00 15.00
31 Carson Kelly/25 6.00 15.00
33 Chris Okey/25 4.00 10.00
34 Nelson Rodriguez/25 6.00 15.00
35 Addison Russell/25 12.00 30.00
36 Clate Schmidt/25 4.00 10.00
37 Nick Travieso/25 12.00 30.00
39 Walker Weickel/25 4.00 10.00
41 Jesse Winker/25 12.00 30.00
43 Tyler Alamo/25 4.00 10.00
45 Nick Ciuffo/25 4.00 10.00
46 Trevor Clifton/25 4.00 10.00
47 Zack Collins/25 6.00 15.00
48 Joe DeMers/25 4.00 10.00
49 Steven Farinaro/25 4.00 10.00
50 Jake Jarvis/25 4.00 10.00
52 Hunter Mercado-Hood/25 4.00 10.00
56 Carson Sands/25 4.00 10.00
57 Jordan Sheffield/25 4.00 10.00
60 Riley Unroe/25 4.00 10.00

2018 Limited

INSERTED IN '18 CHRONICLES PACKS
*SLVR/199: 1X TO 2.5X BASE
*SLVR RC/199: .6X TO 1.5X BASE RC
*GOLD/99: 1.2X TO 3X BASE
*GOLD RC/99: .75X TO 2X BASE RC
1 Aaron Judge .60 1.50
2 Rhys Hoskins RC 1.00 2.50
3 Kris Bryant .30 .75
4 Adrian Beltre .25 .60
5 Cody Bellinger .50 1.25
6 Rafael Devers RC .75 2.00
7 Clint Frazier RC .50 1.25
8 Miguel Andujar RC 1.00 2.50
9 Ronald Acuna Jr. RC 8.00 20.00
10 Nolan Arenado .40 1.00
11 Amed Rosario RC .30 .75
12 Gleyber Torres RC 2.50 6.00
13 Austin Hays RC .40 1.00
14 Manny Machado .25 .60
15 Ozzie Albies RC .75 2.00
16 Mike Trout 1.25 3.00
17 Paul Goldschmidt .25 .60
18 Shohei Ohtani RC 6.00 15.00
19 Bryce Harper .40 1.00
20 Clayton Kershaw .40 1.00

2018 Limited Ruby

*RUBY: 3X TO 8X BASIC
*RUBY RC: 2X TO 5X BASIC RC
INSERTED IN '18 CHRONICLES PACKS
STATED PRINT RUN 25 SER.#'d SETS
16 Mike Trout 15.00 40.00

2019 Limited

RANDOM INSERTS IN PACKS
*GOLD/199: 1.2X TO 3X
*BLUE/99: 1.5X TO 4X
*RED/50: 2X TO 5X
*HOLO SLVR/25: 3X TO 8X
1 Pete Alonso RC 4.00 10.00
2 Eloy Jimenez RC 1.50 4.00
3 Fernando Tatis Jr. RC 2.00 5.00
4 Michael Kopech RC .50 1.25
5 Carter Kieboom RC .25 .60
6 Yusei Kikuchi RC .25 .60
7 Chris Paddack RC .30 .75
8 Mike Trout 1.25 3.00
9 Cole Tucker RC .25 .60
10 Mookie Betts .50 1.25
11 Bryan Reynolds RC .50 1.25
12 Shohei Ohtani .40 1.00
13 Vladimir Guerrero Jr. RC 2.50 6.00
14 Paul DeJong .25 .60
15 Anthony Rizzo .30 .75
16 Darwinzon Hernandez RC .15 .40
17 Brandon Nimmo .20 .50
18 Matt Olson .25 .60
19 Josh Naylor .20 .50
20 Kyle Schwarber .25 .60

2020 Limited

RANDOM INSERTS IN PACKS
1 Shogo Akiyama RC .40 1.00
2 Yordan Alvarez RC 2.50 6.00
3 Bo Bichette RC 3.00 8.00
4 Aristides Aquino RC .60 1.50
5 Gavin Lux RC 1.25 3.00
6 Yoshitomo Tsutsugo RC .60 1.50
7 Brendan McKay RC .40 1.00
8 Luis Robert RC 4.00 10.00
9 Dylan Cease RC .40 1.00
10 Sheldon Neuse RC .30 .75
11 Trent Grisham RC 1.00 2.50
12 Yonathan Daza RC .30 .75
13 Michel Baez RC .25 .60
14 Nico Hoerner RC 1.00 2.50
15 Jesus Luzardo RC .50 1.25
16 Brusdar Graterol RC .40 1.00
17 Nolan Arenado .40 1.00
18 Jacob deGrom .50 1.25
19 Trea Turner .20 .50
20 Alex Bregman .25 .60

2020 Limited Signatures

RANDOM INSERTS IN PACKS
PRINT RUNS B/WN 5-99 COPIES PER
NO PRICING QTY 15 OR LESS
EXCHANGE DEADLINE 3/18/2022
1 Shogo Akiyama/49 6.00 15.00
2 Yordan Alvarez/50 40.00 100.00
3 Bo Bichette/30 30.00 80.00
4 Aristides Aquino/60 8.00 20.00
6 Yoshitomo Tsutsugo/99 10.00 25.00
8 Luis Robert EXCH/99 75.00 200.00
9 Dylan Cease/90 5.00 12.00
10 Sheldon Neuse/97 4.00 10.00
11 Trent Grisham/96 12.00 30.00
12 Yonathan Daza/99 4.00 10.00
13 Michel Baez/99 3.00 8.00
14 Nico Hoerner/99 12.00 30.00
16 Brusdar Graterol/99 5.00 12.00
19 Trea Turner/25

1991 Line Drive

This 50-card standard-size set features notable retired players and managers. The fronts of card numbers 1-42 have color player photos with blue borders on a white card face. Card Nos. 43-50 are similar in design but have sepia-toned photos. The backs of all cards are horizontally-oriented and feature biography, career highlights and lifetime statistics, all inside a red border.

COMPLETE SET (50) 3.00 8.00
1 Don Drysdale .08 .25
2 Joe Torre .08 .25
3 Bob Gibson .08 .25
4 Bobby Richardson .08 .25
5 Ron Santo .08 .25
6 Eric Soderholm .01 .05
7 Yogi Berra .20 .50
8 Steve Garvey .08 .25
9 Steve Carlton .08 .25
10 Toby Harrah .01 .05
11 Luis Tiant .05 .15
12 Earl Weaver MG .08 .25
13 Bill Mazeroski .08 .25
14 Don Baylor .05 .15
15 Lew Burdette .02 .10
16 Jim Lonborg .01 .05
17 Jerry Grote .01 .05
18 Ernie Banks .20 .50
19 Doug DeCinces .02 .10
20 Jimmy Piersall .02 .10
21 Ken Holtzman .01 .05
22 Manny Mota .01 .05
23 Alvin Dark .02 .10
24 Lou Brock .08 .25
25 Ralph Houk .01 .05
26 Graig Nettles .02 .10
27 Bill White .05 .15
28 Billy Williams .08 .25
29 Willie Horton .02 .10
30 Tommie Agee .01 .05
31 Rico Petrocelli .01 .05
32 Julio Cruz .01 .05
33 Robin Roberts .08 .25
34 Dave Johnson .01 .05
35 Wilbur Wood .01 .05
36 Cesar Cedeno .01 .05
37 George Foster .02 .10
38 Thurman Munson .08 .25
39 Roberto Clemente .40 1.00
40 Eddie Mathews .08 .25
41 Harmon Killebrew .08 .25
42 Monte Irvin .08 .25
43 Bob Feller .08 .25
44 Jimmie Foxx .08 .25
45 Walter Johnson .08 .25
46 Casey Stengel .08 .25
47 Satchel Paige .30 .75
48 Ty Cobb .40 1.00
49 Mickey Cochrane .08 .25
50 Dizzy Dean .08 .25

1991 Line Drive Mattingly

This set was issued to commemorate the career of Yankee star Don Mattingly. These standard-size cards feature a photo of Mattingly on the front from various points of his career with information about that part of his career on the back.

COMPLETE SET (20) 2.50 6.00
COMMON CARD (1-20) .20 .50
1 Don Mattingly .20 .50
2 Don Mattingly .20 .50
3 Don Mattingly .20 .50
4 Don Mattingly .20 .50
5 Don Mattingly .20 .50
6 Don Mattingly .20 .50
7 Don Mattingly .20 .50
8 Don Mattingly .20 .50
9 Don Mattingly .20 .50
10 Don Mattingly .20 .50
11 Don Mattingly .20 .50
12 Don Mattingly .20 .50
13 Don Mattingly .20 .50
14 Don Mattingly .20 .50
15 Don Mattingly .20 .50
16 Don Mattingly .20 .50
17 Don Mattingly .20 .50
18 Don Mattingly .20 .50
19 Don Mattingly .20 .50
20 Don Mattingly .20 .50

1991 Line Drive Sandberg

This 20-card standard-size set was sold as part of a boxed Ryne Sandberg Baseball Card Kit that included a personalized collector's album, the Ryne Sandberg Story and a free mail-in offer to receive an 8" X 10" color photo of a top baseball star. The cards feature color action photos, with blue borders on the left half of the card and red on the right half, on a white card face. In blue and red lettering, the player's name appears above the picture. In dark blue lettering and red borders, the back presents assorted information on Sandberg.

COMPLETE SET (20) 4.00 10.00
COMMON PLAYER (1-20) .20 .50

1973-74 Linnett Portraits

Measuring 8 1/2" by 11", these 179 charcoal drawings are facial portraits by noted sports artist Charles Linnett. The player's facsimile autograph is inscribed across the lower right corner. The backs are blank. Three portraits of players from the same team or major stars issued in those groups of three were included in each clear plastic packet. A checklist was also included in each packet, with an offer to order individual player portraits for 50 cents each. Originally, the suggested retail price was 99 cents. In later issues, the price was raised to $1.19. The portraits are unnumbered and listed alphabetically by teams as follows: Atlanta Braves (1-6), Baltimore Orioles (7-13), Boston Red Sox (14-32), California Angels (33-38), Chicago Cubs (39-46), Chicago White Sox (47-53), Cincinnati Reds (54-59), Cleveland Indians (60-67), Detroit Tigers (68-79), Houston Astros (80-86), Kansas City Royals (87-91), Los Angeles Dodgers (92-97), Milwaukee Brewers (98-103), Minnesota Twins (104-109), New York Mets (110-125), New York Yankees (126-136), Oakland A's (137-141), Philadelphia Phillies (142-147), Pittsburgh Pirates (148-153), San Diego Padres (154-156), San Francisco Giants (157-164), St. Louis Cardinals (165-171), and Texas Rangers (172-179). The Mets packages were as follows: Jon Matlack, Felix Millan and Duffy Dyer; Rusty Staub, Jerry Koosman and John Milner; and Wayne Garrett, Cleon Jones and Bud Harrelson.

COMPLETE SET 350.00 700.00
1 Hank Aaron 6.00 15.00
2 Darrell Evans 3.00 8.00
3 Ralph Garr 2.50 6.00
4 Dave Johnson 3.00 8.00
5 Mike Lum 2.00 5.00
6 Carl Morton 2.00 5.00
7 Mark Belanger 2.50 6.00
8 Paul Blair 2.00 5.00
9 Al Bumbry 2.00 5.00
10 Bobby Grich 3.00 8.00
11 Lee May 2.50 6.00
12 Jim Palmer 5.00 12.00
13 Brooks Robinson 6.00 15.00
14 Luis Aparicio 5.00 12.00
15 Bob Bolin 2.00 5.00
16 Danny Cater 2.00 5.00
17 Orlando Cepeda 5.00 12.00
18 John Curtis 2.00 5.00
19 Dwight Evans 4.00 10.00
20 Carlton Fisk 5.00 12.00
21 Doug Griffin 2.00 5.00
22 Mario Guerrero 2.00 5.00
23 Tommy Harper 2.00 5.00
24 John Kennedy 2.00 5.00
25 Bill Lee 3.00 8.00
26 Rick Miller 2.00 5.00
27 Bob Montgomery 2.00 5.00
28 Marty Pattin 2.00 5.00
29 Rico Petrocelli 2.50 6.00
30 Luis Tiant 4.00 10.00
31 Bob Veale 2.00 5.00
32 Carl Yastrzemski 10.00 25.00
33 Bob Oliver 2.00 5.00
34 Frank Robinson 5.00 12.00
35 Nolan Ryan 8.00 20.00
36 Bill Singer 2.00 5.00
37 Lee Stanton 2.00 5.00
38 Bobby Valentine 3.00 8.00
39 Bill Bonham 2.00 5.00
40 Jose Cardenal 2.00 5.00
41 Don Kessinger 2.50 6.00
42 Bob Locker 2.00 5.00
43 Rick Monday 2.50 6.00
44 Ron Santo 4.00 10.00
45 Steve Stone 2.50 6.00
46 Billy Williams 5.00 12.00
47 Dick Allen 4.00 10.00
48 Ed Herrmann 2.00 5.00
49 Eddie Leon 2.00 5.00
50 Bill Melton 2.00 5.00
51 Jorge Orta 2.00 5.00
52 Rick Reichardt 2.00 5.00
53 Wilbur Wood 2.00 5.00
54 Johnny Bench 5.00 12.00
55 Cesar Geronimo 2.00 5.00
56 Don Gullett 2.00 5.00
57 Joe Morgan 5.00 12.00
58 Tony Perez 5.00 12.00
59 Pete Rose 6.00 15.00
60 Buddy Bell 3.00 8.00
61 Chris Chambliss 2.50 6.00
62 John Ellis 2.00 5.00
63 George Hendrick 2.00 5.00
64 Steve Kline 2.00 5.00
65 Gaylord Perry 5.00 12.00
66 Jim Perry 2.50 6.00
67 Charlie Spikes 2.00 5.00
68 Norm Cash 4.00 10.00
69 Bill Freehan 3.00 8.00
70 John Hiller 2.00 5.00
71 Willie Horton 2.50 6.00
72 Al Kaline 5.00 12.00
73 Mickey Lolich 4.00 10.00
74 Dick McAuliffe 2.50 6.00
75 Jim Northrup 2.50 6.00
76 Ben Oglivie 2.00 5.00
77 Aurelio Rodriguez 2.00 5.00
78 Fred Scherman 2.00 5.00
79 Mickey Stanley 2.00 5.00
80 Cesar Cedeno 2.50 6.00
81 Greg Gross 2.00 5.00
82 Roger Metzger 2.00 5.00
83 Jerry Reuss 2.50 6.00
84 Dave Roberts (P) 2.00 5.00
85 Bob Watson 2.50 6.00
86 Don Wilson 2.00 5.00
87 John Mayberry 2.00 5.00
88 Amos Otis 2.00 5.00
89 Fred Patek 2.00 5.00
90 Cookie Rojas 2.00 5.00
91 Paul Splittorff 2.00 5.00
92 Bill Buckner 2.50 6.00
93 Willie Crawford 2.00 5.00
94 Joe Ferguson 2.00 5.00
95 Dave Lopes 2.50 6.00
96 Bill Russell 2.50 6.00
97 Don Sutton 5.00 12.00
98 John Briggs 2.00 5.00
99 Jim Colborn 2.00 5.00
100 Pedro Garcia 2.00 5.00
101 Dave May 2.00 5.00
102 Don Money 2.00 5.00
103 George Scott 2.50 6.00
104 Bert Blyleven 4.00 10.00
105 Steve Braun 2.00 5.00
106 Steve Brye 2.00 5.00
107 Rod Carew 5.00 12.00
108 Bobby Darwin 2.00 5.00
109 Danny Thompson 2.00 5.00
110 Duffy Dyer 2.00 5.00
111 Wayne Garrett 2.00 5.00
112 Bud Harrelson 2.00 5.00
113 Cleon Jones 2.00 5.00
114 Jerry Koosman 2.50 6.00
115 Teddy Martinez 2.00 5.00
116 Jon Matlack 2.00 5.00
117 Jim McAndrew 2.00 5.00
118 Tug McGraw 3.00 8.00
119 Felix Millan 2.00 5.00
120 John Milner 2.00 5.00
121 Harry Parker 2.00 5.00
122 Tom Seaver 6.00 15.00
123 Rusty Staub 4.00 10.00
124 George Stone 2.00 5.00
125 George Theodore 2.00 5.00
126 Bernie Allen 2.00 5.00
127 Felipe Alou 4.00 10.00
128 Matty Alou 3.00 8.00
129 Ron Blomberg 2.00 5.00
130 Sparky Lyle 3.00 8.00
131 Gene Michael 2.00 5.00
132 Thurman Munson 5.00 12.00
133 Bobby Murcer 3.00 8.00
134 Graig Nettles 4.00 10.00
135 Lou Piniella 3.00 8.00
136 Mel Stottlemyre 2.50 6.00
137 Sal Bando 2.50 6.00
138 Bert Campaneris 3.00 8.00
139 Rollie Fingers 5.00 12.00
140 Jim Hunter 5.00 12.00
141 Reggie Jackson 6.00 15.00
142 Bob Boone 3.00 8.00
143 Larry Bowa 2.50 6.00
144 Steve Carlton 5.00 12.00
145 Dave Cash 2.00 5.00
146 Greg Luzinski 3.00 8.00
147 Willie Montanez 2.00 5.00
148 Ken Brett 2.00 5.00
149 Dave Giusti 2.00 5.00
150 Ed Kirkpatrick 2.00 5.00
151 Al Oliver 4.00 10.00
152 Manny Sanguillen 2.50 6.00
153 Willie Stargell 5.00 12.00
154 Nate Colbert 2.00 5.00
155 John Grubb 2.00 5.00
156 Dave Roberts (3B) 2.00 5.00
157 Bobby Bonds 4.00 10.00
158 Ron Bryant 2.00 5.00
159 Dave Kingman 4.00 10.00
160 Garry Maddox 2.00 5.00
161 Gary Matthews 2.50 6.00
162 Willie McCovey 5.00 12.00
163 Sam McDowell 2.50 6.00
164 Chris Speier 2.00 5.00
165 Lou Brock 5.00 12.00
166 Bernie Carbo 2.00 5.00
167 Bob Gibson 5.00 12.00
168 Lynn McGlothen 2.00 5.00
169 Ted Simmons 4.00 10.00
170 Reggie Smith 3.00 8.00
171 Joe Torre 4.00 10.00
172 Jim Bibby 2.00 5.00
173 Jeff Burroughs 2.50 6.00
174 David Clyde 2.00 5.00
175 Jim Fregosi 2.50 6.00
176 Toby Harrah 2.00 5.00
177 Vic Harris 2.00 5.00
178 Ferguson Jenkins 5.00 12.00
179 Dave Nelson 2.00 5.00

1976 Linnett Superstars

The Linnett Superstars set contains 36 oversized cards measuring approximately 4" by 5 5/8". The cards feature black and white facial portraits of the players, with various color borders. In the corners of the portrait appear four different logos: MLB, MLBPA, team and PeeWee's. The backs have a picture and discussion of either great cars of the world or sailing ships. The cards are checklisted below according to teams as follows: Cincinnati Reds, (90-101) Boston Red Sox, (102-113) and Los Angeles Dodgers (114-125).

COMPLETE SET 40.00 80.00
90 Don Gullett .40 1.00
91 Johnny Bench 3.00 8.00
92 Tony Perez 2.00 5.00
93 Mike Lum .40 1.00
94 Ken Griffey .75 2.00
95 George Foster .60 1.50
96 Joe Morgan 2.00 5.00
97 Pete Rose 4.00 10.00
98 Dave Concepcion .75 2.00
99 Cesar Geronimo .40 1.00
100 Dan Driessen .40 1.00
101 Pedro Borbon .40 1.00
102 Carl Yastrzemski 3.00 8.00
103 Fred Lynn .75 2.00
104 Dwight Evans .75 2.00
105 Ferguson Jenkins 2.00 5.00
106 Rico Petrocelli .60 1.50
107 Denny Doyle .40 1.00
108 Luis Tiant .75 2.00
109 Carlton Fisk 2.00 5.00
110 Rick Burleson .60 1.50
111 Bill Lee .60 1.50
112 Rick Wise .40 1.00
113 Jim Rice 1.00 2.50
114 Davey Lopes .60 1.50
115 Steve Garvey .75 2.00
116 Bill Russell .40 1.00
117 Ron Cey .75 2.00
118 Steve Yeager .40 1.00
119 Doug Rau .40 1.00
120 Don Sutton 1.25 3.00
121 Joe Ferguson .40 1.00
122 Mike Marshall .40 1.00
123 Bill Buckner .40 1.00
124 Rick Rhoden .40 1.00
125 Ted Sizemore .40 1.00

1988 Little Sun Black Sox

This 15-card set was produced by Little Sun of Monrovia, California, and recounts the history of the Black Sox scandal of 1919. The fronts feature sepia player portraits with player information and statistics on the back. Only 5,000 of the set were produced.

COMPLETE SET (15) 3.00 8.00
1 Black Sox Scandal .08 .25
2 Chick Gandil .40 1.00
3 Eddie Cicotte .40 1.00
4 Joe Jackson .75 2.00
5 Buck Weaver .40 1.00
6 Swede Risberg .20 .50
7 Happy Felsch .08 .25
8 Lefty Williams .08 .25
9 Fred McMullin .08 .25
10 Eddie Collins .40 1.00
11 Kid Gleason MG .08 .25
12 Charles Comiskey OWN .20 .50
13 Abe Attell .30 .75
14 Arnold Rothstein .08 .25
15 Judge Landis .20 .50
NNO Title Card .08 .25

1990 Little Sun Writers

This 24-card standard-size set honors some of the more influential writers in baseball history, i.e., "major league writers." The cards have yellow and green borders surrounding black and white photos of the writers pictured. The writer's name is given in black lettering below the picture. The backs have brief biographies of the writers along with "Did you know" features usually about writers not in the set.

COMPLETE SET (24) 2.00 5.00
1 Checklist Card .08 .25
2 Henry Chadwick .20 .50
3 Jacob C. Morse .08 .25
4 Francis C. Richter .08 .25
5 Grantland Rice .30 .75
6 Lee Allen .08 .25
7 Joe Reichler .08 .25
8 Red Smith .30 .75
9 Dick Young .20 .50
10 Jim Brosnan .20 .50
11 Charles Einstein .20 .50
12 Lawrence Ritter .30 .75
13 Roger Kahn .30 .75
14 Robert Creamer .20 .50
15 W.P. Kinsella .20 .50
16 Harold Seymour .20 .50
17 Ron Shelton .20 .50
18 Tom Clark .08 .25
19 Mark Harris .20 .50
20 John Holway .20 .50
21 Peter Golenbock .08 .25
22 Jim Bouton .40 1.00
23 John Thorn .20 .50
24 Mike Shannon/(Not the ex-Cardinal .08 .25
player)

1993 Lofton Champs SkyBox

This one-card set was createdto promote Champs Manufacturing. The front has a posed photo of Kenny Lofton on a motorcycle while the back has biographical information about Lofton.

FC2 Kenny Lofton 2.00 5.00

1968 Lolich Macomb Mall

This one card set, which is a photograph which measures 8 1/2" by 11" features Mickey Lolich and was given away to commemorate his appearance at the Macomb Mall in 1968.

1 Mickey Lolich 4.00 10.00

1887 Lone Jack N370

There are rulers and celebrities as well as baseball players in this set of sepia photographs issued by the Lone Jack Cigarette Company of Lynchburg, Va. The ballplayers are all members of the 1886 St. Louis Club which won the World Championship, and the pictures are identical to those found in set N172.

COMPLETE SET 30000.00 60000.00
1 Al Bushong 4000.00 8000.00
2 Arlie Latham 600.00 12000.00
4 Bill (Yank) Robinson 4000.00 8000.00
6 Bob Caruthers 5000.00 10000.00
7 Charles Commiskey(sic) 7500.00 15000.00
8 Chris Von Der Ahe OWN 600.00 12000.00
9 Curt Welsh (sic) 5000.00 10000.00
10 Dave Foutz 4000.00 8000.00
15 Hugh Nicol 4000.00 8000.00
16 James O'Neil (sic) 5000.00 10000.00
23 Nat Hudson 4000.00 8000.00
32 Rudy Kimler (sic) 4000.00 8000.00
36 William Gleason 5000.00 10000.00

1981 Long Beach Press Telegram

This 26-card set was distributed as a cut-out in the Long Beach Press Telegram and measures approximately 6 1/2" by 7 1/4". Each cut-out is really two cards each displaying a black-and-white player photo with player information and statistics printed below each picture.

COMPLETE SET (54) 15.00 40.00
1 Steve Garvey 1.50 4.00
Rod Carew
2 Davey Lopes .60 1.50
Bobby Grich
3A Bill Russell .60 1.50
Rick Burleson
Russell listed as 2nd
3B Bill Russell .40 1.00
Rich Burleson
Russell listed as SS
4 Ron Cey .60 1.50
Butch Hobson
5 Dusty Baker .75 2.00
Don Baylor
6 Ken Landreaux .40 1.00
Fred Lynn
7 Pedro Guerrero .40 1.00
Dan Ford
8 Mike Scioscia .40 1.00
Brian Downing
9 Jerry Reuss .60 1.50
Geoff Zahn
10 Fernando Valenzuela 1.00 2.50
Jesse Jefferson
11 Burt Hooton .40 1.00
Mike Witt
12 Rick Sutcliffe .60 1.50
Ken Forsch
13 Bob Welch .60 1.50
Bill Travers
14 Bobby Castillo .40 1.00
Andy Hassler
15 Steve Howe .60 1.50
Aase
16 Terry Forster .40 1.00
Luis Sanchez
17 Reggie Smith .60 1.50
Juan Beniquez
18A Derrel Thomas .40 1.00
Ed Ott
Ott has a face shot
18B Derrel Thomas .40 1.00
Ed Ott
Ott has an action shot
19 Steve Yeager .75 2.00
Tom Brunansky
20 Rick Monday .40 1.00
Bert Campaneris
21 Joe Ferguson .40 1.00
Fred Patek
22 Burt Hooten .40 1.00
23 Dave Goltz .40 1.00
John D'Acquisto
24 Dave Stewart 1.00 2.50
Steve Renko
25 Pepe Frias .40 1.00
Larry Harlow
26 Tom Lasorda MG 1.00 2.50
Jim Fregosi MG

1886 Lorillard Team Cards

These four cards, which measure approximately 4" by 5" feature composite "head" shots of members of four National League teams. The backs feature schedules for these teams, as well as an advertisement for Lorillard Tobacco. All of these cards are extremely condition sensitive and finding ex-mt examples of these cards is a real challenge.

COMPLETE SET (4) 9000.00 18000.00
1 Chicago NL 4000.00 8000.00
2 Detroit NL 5000.00 10000.00
3 New York NL 6000.00 12000.00
4 Philadelphia NL 3000.00 6000.00

1982-89 Louisville Slugger

This set consists of standard size tags that were attached to Louisville Slugger products. Each card has a hole in its upper left corner. Each card has white borders surrounding the a color player's photo in the middle, with his name circled in blue on top and the "Louisville Slugger" ID on the bottom. The backs have biographical information as well as year by year highlights. The cards are unnumbered and checklisted below in alphabetical order.

COMPLETE SET 4.00 10.00
1 Eric Davis 1.00 2.50
2 Steve Garvey .75 2.00
Dodgers
3 Steve Garvey .75 2.00
Padres
4 Pedro Guerrero .40 1.00
5 Orel Hershiser .60 1.50
6 Ray Knight .40 1.00
7 Fred Lynn .40 1.00
8 Gary Matthews .60 1.50
9 Graig Nettles .60 1.50
Yankees
10 Graig Nettles .60 1.50
Padres
11 Mike Pagliarulo .40 1.00
12 Rick Rhoden .40 1.00
13 Andy Van Slyke .60 1.50
14 Lou Whitaker .60 1.50

1987 M and M's Star Lineup

The Mars Candy Company is the sponsor of this 24-card set of cards. The cards were printed in perforated pairs. The pairs measure approximately 5" by 3 1/2" whereas the individual cards measure the standard 2 1/2" by 3 1/2". The players are shown without team logos. The cards were designed and produced by MSA, Mike Schechter Associates. The cards are numbered on the front and back. The backs show statistics for every year since 1980 even if the player was not even playing during those earlier years. The values below are for individual players; panels intact would be valued at 25 percent more than the sum of the two individual players.

COMPLETE SET (24) 4.00 10.00
COMPLETE IND. SET (24) 2.50 6.00
1 Wally Joyner .15 .40
2 Tony Pena .02 .10
3 Mike Schmidt .25 .60
4 Ryne Sandberg .40 1.00
5 Wade Boggs .20 .50
6 Jack Morris .07 .20
7 Roger Clemens .40 1.00
8 Harold Baines .07 .20
9 Dale Murphy .15 .40
10 Jose Canseco .30 .75
11 Don Mattingly .40 1.00
12 Gary Carter .20 .50
13 Cal Ripken .75 2.00
14 George Brett .40 1.00
15 Kirby Puckett .30 .75
16 Joe Carter .15 .40
17 Mike Witt .02 .10
18 Mike Scott .02 .10
19 Fernando Valenzuela .07 .20
20 Steve Garvey .10 .30
21 Steve Sax .02 .10
22 Nolan Ryan .75 2.00
23 Tony Gwynn .50 1.00
24 Ozzie Smith .40 1.00

1953 MacGregor Staff

This set features black-and-white photos of players on the MacGregor Sporting Goods Advisory Staff. The cards measure approximately 8" by 9 1/8" with facsimile autographs on the fronts and blank backs. The cards are unnumbered and checklisted below in alphabetical order. The checklist may be incomplete.

COMPLETE SET 125.00 250.00
1 Ralph Kiner 40.00 80.00
2 Ted Kluszewski 30.00 60.00
3 Robin Roberts 40.00 80.00
4 Al Schoendienst 30.00 60.00
5 Warren Spahn 40.00 80.00

1960 MacGregor Staff

This 25-card set represents members of the MacGregor Sporting Goods Advisory Staff. Since the cards are unnumbered they ordered below in alphabetical order. The cards are blank backed and measure approximately 3 3/4" by 5". The photos are in black and white. The catalog designation for the set is H801-10. Cards have a facsimile autograph in white lettering on the front. These cards were sent out as complete sets as mailing envelopes have been seen.

COMPLETE SET (25) 300.00 600.00
1 Hank Aaron 60.00 120.00
2 Richie Ashburn 8.00 20.00
3 Gus Bell 5.00 12.00
4 Lou Berberet 4.00 10.00
5 Jerry Casale 4.00 10.00
6 Del Crandall 5.00 12.00
7 Art Ditmar 4.00 10.00
8 Gene Freese 4.00 10.00
9 James Gilliam 6.00 15.00
10 Ted Kluszewski 8.00 20.00
11 Jim Landis 4.00 10.00
12 Al Lopez MG 6.00 15.00
13 Willie Mays 75.00 150.00
14 Bill Mazeroski 8.00 20.00
15 Mike McCormick 5.00 12.00
16 Gil McDougald 6.00 15.00
17 Russ Nixon 4.00 10.00
18 Bill Rigney MG 4.00 10.00
19 Robin Roberts 8.00 20.00
20 Frank Robinson 15.00 40.00
21 John Roseboro 5.00 12.00
22 Red Schoendienst 8.00 20.00
23 Bill Skowron 6.00 15.00
24 Daryl Spencer 4.00 10.00
25 Johnny Temple 4.00 10.00

1965 MacGregor Staff

This ten-card set represents members of the MacGregor Sporting Goods Advisory Staff. Since the cards are unnumbered they are ordered below in alphabetical order. The cards are blank backed and measure approximately 3 9/16" by 5 1/8". The photos are in black and white. The catalog designation for the set is H825-2.

COMPLETE SET (10) 500.00 1000.00
1 Roberto Clemente 250.00 500.00
2 Al Downing 12.50 30.00
3 Johnny Edwards 12.50 30.00
4 Ron Hansen 12.50 30.00
5 Deron Johnson 12.50 30.00
6 Willie Mays 200.00 400.00
7 Tony Oliva 30.00 60.00
8 Claude Osteen 12.50 30.00
9 Bobby Richardson 30.00 60.00
10 Zoilo Versalles 12.50 30.00

1950 Mack 66 Years in the Big Leagues

These four black and white (with a seeming sepia tone) cards were issued in conjuction with the release of Connie Mack's Book "My 66 Years in the Big Leagues". The players featured are Mack's most memorable three personalities. The cards were also shipped in a special promotional envelope to inspire more sales of the book. The cards measure 2 1/4" by 3 1/2" and were printed on thin white stock.

COMPLETE SET (4) 750.00 1500.00
1 Connie Mack 125.00 250.00
2 Christy Mathewson 200.00 400.00
3 Babe Ruth 400.00 800.00
4 Rube Waddell 100.00 200.00

1926 Major League Die-Cuts

Measuring approximately 2 5/8" by 1 1/8" these die-cut cards feature a drawing on the top as well as the player's name, position and team on the bottom. Since these are unnumbered, we have sequenced them in alphabetical order by team. This checklist is incomplete, so all additions are appreciated.

COMPLETE SET 1500.00 3000.00
1 John Bischoff 15.00 30.00
2 Ira Flagstead 15.00 30.00
3 Alex Gaston 15.00 30.00
4 Fred Haney 15.00 30.00
5 Slim Harriss 15.00 30.00
6 Fred Heimach 15.00 30.00
7 Baby Doll Jacobson 15.00 30.00
8 Bill Regan 15.00 30.00
9 Topper Rigney 15.00 30.00
10 Red Ruffing 30.00 60.00
11 Wally Shaner 15.00 30.00
12 Phil Todt 15.00 30.00
13 Hal Wiltse 15.00 30.00
14 Ted Wingfield 15.00 30.00
15 Bill Barrett 15.00 30.00
16 Ted Blankenship 15.00 30.00
17 Wilbur Cooper 15.00 30.00
18 Buck Crouse 15.00 30.00
19 Jim Joe Edwards 15.00 30.00
20 Bibb Falk 15.00 30.00
21 Bill Hunnefield 15.00 30.00
22 Willie Kamm 15.00 30.00
23 Ted Lyons 30.00 60.00
24 John Mostil 15.00 30.00
25 Ray Schalk 30.00 60.00
26 Earl Sheely 15.00 30.00
27 Tommy Thomas 15.00 30.00
28 George Burns 15.00 30.00
29 Charlie Jamieson 15.00 30.00
30 Benn Karr 15.00 30.00
31 Dutch Levsen 15.00 30.00
32 Glenn Myatt 15.00 30.00
33 Joe Sewell 30.00 60.00
34 Joe Shaute 15.00 30.00
35 Sherry Smith 15.00 30.00
36 Tris Speaker 50.00 100.00
37 Freddy Spurgeon 15.00 30.00
38 Homer Summa 15.00 30.00
39 George Uhle 15.00 30.00
40 Max Bishop 15.00 30.00
41 Mickey Cochrane 40.00 80.00
42 Eddie Collins 60.00 120.00
43 Jimmy Dykes 20.00 40.00
44 Howard Ehmke 15.00 30.00
45 Walter French 15.00 30.00
46 Sam Gray 15.00 30.00
47 Lefty Grove 75.00 150.00
48 Joe Hauser 20.00 40.00
49 Bill Lamar 15.00 30.00
50 Cy Perkins 15.00 30.00
51 Ed Rommel 20.00 40.00
52 Al Simmons 50.00 100.00
53 Rube Walberg 15.00 30.00
54 Benny Bengough 15.00 30.00
55 Pat Collins 15.00 30.00
56 Earl Combs 30.00 60.00
57 Joe Dugan 20.00 40.00
58 Lou Gehrig 100.00 200.00
59 Waite Hoyt 30.00 60.00
60 Sam Jones 20.00 40.00
61 Mark Koenig 20.00 40.00
62 Tony Lazzeri 30.00 60.00
63 Bob Meusel 25.00 50.00
64 Herb Pennock 30.00 60.00
65 Babe Ruth 150.00 300.00
66 Urban Shocker 20.00 40.00
67 Myles Thomas 15.00 30.00
68 Dixie Davis 15.00 30.00
69 Cedric Durst 15.00 30.00
70 Milt Gaston 15.00 30.00
71 Wally Gerber 15.00 30.00
72 Joe Giard 15.00 30.00
73 Pinky Hargrave 15.00 30.00
74 Marty McManus 15.00 30.00
75 Oscar Melillo 15.00 30.00
76 Bing Miller 15.00 30.00
77 Harry Rice 15.00 30.00
78 Wally Schang 20.00 40.00
79 George Sisler 40.00 80.00
80 Tom Zachary 15.00 30.00

1995 Major League Players Alumni Autograph

These cards feature an authentic autograph of the player along with an action shot. The "Legends Autograph Collection" logo is on the upper left corner. The back features career history, a brief bio and career statistics. The card also came with a certificate of authenticity from the MLBP Alumni Association.

COMPLETE SET 15.00 40.00
1 Harmon Killebrew 12.50 30.00
2 Brooks Robinson 6.00 15.00
3 Willie Stargell 10.00 25.00
4 Al Kaline 12.00 30.00

1996 Major League Alumni

This one card standard-size set features Hall of Famer Brooks Robinson. The front of the card features Brooks ready to field while the back has information about Robinson's playing career as well as what he done after his career along with a line of complete career statistics.

1 Brooks Robinson 6.00 15.00

1998-01 Major League Dad

Apparently issued over a period of year, these standard-size full-bleed cards feature popular players posing along with their kids. The fronts have the words "Major League Dad". The backs include various player information along with a plea for dads to support their children, no matter what the circumstances.

COMPLETE SET 3.00 8.00
1 Greg Vaughn .75 2.00
2 Wally Joyner .75 2.00
3 Jeff Shaw .60 1.50
4 Tim Salmon 1.25 3.00
5 Chad Kreuter .40 1.00

1989 Major League Movie

These 11 cards measure approximately 2 3/4" by 3 1/2". They were issued to promote the movie "Major League". The cards have color photos surrounded by blue borders. The actor and the role they play are noted on the bottom of the card. Their position on the imaginary Cleveland Indians is mentioned in the upper right corner. The backs are blank. We have sequenced this set in alphabetical order by actor.

COMPLETE SET (11) 75.00 150.00
1 Tom Berenger 6.00 15.00
2 Corbin Bernsen 6.00 15.00
3 James Gammon 6.00 15.00
4 Dennis Haysbert 6.00 15.00
5 Andy Romano 6.00 15.00
6 Chelcie Ross 6.00 15.00
7 Charlie Sheen 10.00 25.00
8 Wesley Snipes 8.00 20.00
9 Steve Yeager 6.00 15.00
10 Key Players 8.00 20.00
Charlie Sheen
Dennis Haysbert
Tom Berenger
11 Team Leaders 6.00 15.00
Andy Romano
James Gannon
Steve Yeager

1992 Manning 1919 Black Sox Reprints

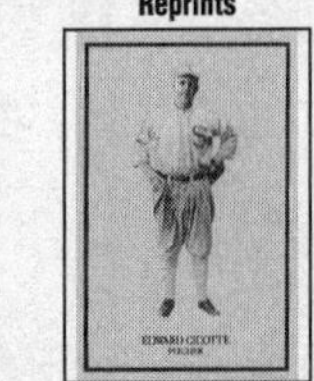

Designed by TNTL Studios, (Toms River, NJ) this 26-card set measures approximately 2" by 3" and features reprinted photos of members of the 1919 White Sox team. The photos are black-and-white cut-outs against white backgrounds. Some of the cards have thin black borders but most do not. The "Shoeless Joe" Jackson card has a red border stripe and a color background that shows grass and sky. The backs of the borderless cards are blank. The backs of the other cards contain player information. The cards are unnumbered and checklisted below in alphabetical order.

COMPLETE SET (26) 2.00 5.00
1 Joe Benz .02 .10
2 Eddie Cicotte .10 .30
3 Eddie Collins .20 .50
4 Shano Collins .02 .10
5 Charles Comiskey OWN .10 .30
6 Dave Danforth .02 .10
7 Red Faber .10 .30
8 Happy Felsch .10 .30
9 Chick Gandil .07 .20
10 Kid Gleason MG .07 .20
11 Joe Jackson .40 1.00
Color background

12 Joe Jackson .40 1.00
13 Joe Jenkins .02 .10
14 Ted Jourdan .02 .10
15 Nemo Leibold .02 .10
16 Bryd Lynn .02 .10
17 Fred McMullen .07 .20
18 Eddie Murphy .02 .10
19 Swede Risberg .07 .20
20 Pants Rowland GM .02 .10
21 Reb Russell .02 .10
22 Ray Schalk .10 .30
23 James Scott .02 .10
24 Buck Weaver .20 .50
25 Lefty Williams .07 .20
26 Mellie Wolfgang .02 .10

1995 Mantle Donor Card

This card was issued almost immediately after Mickey Mantle received a liver tranplant on June 8, 1995. The purpose of this card was to encourage others to donate their organs to donor if it were ever needed. This card was issued by the Mickey Mantle Foundation. This card when in its original state measures 3 1/2" by 7 1/2" but part of the card could be perforated and kept as the organ donor card. That card, which feature a picture of the Mick on the front, measures 3 1/2" by 2 1/2". While we have put a nominal monetary value on this card, we prefer that the card not be traded in the secondary market, rather that it be given to people to fill out and be used if needed.

1 Mickey Mantle .40 1.00

1956 Mantle Holiday Inn Postcard

This one-card set features a borderless color photo of Mickey Mantle in the Dugout Lounge at the Holiday Inn in Joplin, Missouri, which was operated by him. The back displays a postcard format. It is believed that there may be at least four different poses of this postcard Any further information is greatly appreciated.

2004 Mickey Mantle Museum

COMPLETE SET 20.00 50.00
COMMON CARD 2.00 5.00
4 Mickey Mantle 4.00 10.00
Roger Maris
10 Mickey Mantle 2.50 6.00
Mickey Mantle Jr.

1980 Mantle Reserve Life

This one-card set features a painting of Mickey Mantle in various baseball playing action with a facsimile autograph printed in the top right. The set commemorates him as the Director of Public Relations for Reserve Life Insurance Company. The back displays player information and career statistics.

1 Mickey Mantle 5.00 10.00

1997 Mantle 23K

This one card metallic set features Mickey Mantle. The front of the card has a Mantle relief with the words "MVP 1956, 1957 and 1962." The back has a portrait and action relief of Mantle along with his career stats and vital stats. This card is serial numbered to 5000.

1 Mickey Mantle 8.00 20.00

1991 Mantle Video

This one-card set measures approximately 4 1/8" by 6" and features a sepia color photo of Mickey Mantle. The set was produced as an advertisement for a video about him. The back displays information about how the video could be purchased and a small advertisement for Mickey Mantle's Restaurant at the bottom.

1 Mickey Mantle 1.25 3.00

1923 Maple Crispette V117

This 30-card set was produced by Maple Crispette Co. of Montreal around 1923. The cards are black and white and measure approximately 1 3/8" by 2 1/4". The card backs explain a send-in offer for a ball, bat or glove in return for 30 baseball (or hockey) cards collected. The cards are numbered on the front. The Stengel card was undoubtedly the short-printed card in the set that made the send-in offer a very difficult task to fulfill.

COMPLETE SET (30) 6000.00 12000.00
1 J. Barnes 100.00 200.00
2 Pie Traynor 200.00 400.00
3 Ray Schalk 200.00 400.00
4 Eddie Collins 200.00 400.00
5 Lee Fohl MG 100.00 200.00
6 Howard Summa 100.00 200.00
7 Waite Hoyt 200.00 400.00
8 Babe Ruth 5000.00 10000.00
9 Cozy Dolan CO 100.00 200.00
10 Johnny Bassler 100.00 200.00
11 George Dauss 100.00 200.00
12 Joe Sewell 200.00 400.00
13 Syl Johnson 100.00 200.00
14 Ivy Wingo 100.00 200.00
15 Casey Stengel SP 6000.00 12000.00
16 Arnold Statz 100.00 200.00
17 Emil Meusel 100.00 200.00
18 Bill Jacobson 100.00 200.00
19 Jim Bottomley 200.00 400.00
20 Sam Bohne 100.00 200.00
21 Bucky Harris 200.00 400.00
22 Ty Cobb 3000.00 6000.00
23 Roger Peckinpaugh 125.00 250.00
24 Muddy Ruel 100.00 200.00
25 Bill McKechnie 200.00 400.00
26 Riggs Stephenson 125.00 250.00
27 Herb Pennock 200.00 400.00
28 Ed Roush 200.00 400.00
29 Bill Wambsganss 125.00 250.00
30 Walter Johnson 750.00 1500.00

1980 Marchant Exhibits

These 32 exhibit cards, which measure the same as the original issue, was relased in 1980 and made by card dealer Paul Marchant who issued this set to honor various popular players. This set, clearly marked as reprints, are unnumbered and are sequenced in alphabetical order. According to the manufacturer only 5,000 of these sets were produced.

COMPLETE SET 6.00 15.00
1 Johnny Antonelli .02 .10
2 Richie Ashburn .10 .30
3 Earl Averill .07 .20
4 Ernie Banks .10 .30
5 Ewell Blackwell .02 .10
6 Lou Brock .10 .30
7 Dean Chance .02 .10
8 Roger Craig .02 .10
9 Lou Gehrig .40 1.00
10 Gil Hodges .10 .30
11 Jackie Jensen .02 .10
12 Charlie Keller .02 .10
13 George Kell .07 .20
14 Alex Kellner .02 .10
15 Harmon Killebrew .07 .20
16 Dale Long .02 .10
17 Sal Maglie .02 .10
18 Roger Maris .20 .50
19 Willie Mays .30 .75
20 Minnie Minoso .07 .20
21 Stan Musial .20 .50
22 Billy Pierce .02 .10
23 Jim Piersall .02 .10
24 Eddie Plank .07 .20
25 Pete Reiser .02 .10
26 Brooks Robinson .10 .30
27 Pete Runnels .02 .10
28 Herb Score .02 .10
29 Warren Spahn .10 .30
30 Billy Williams .10 .30
31 1948 Indians Team .02 .10
32 1948 Braves Team .02 .10

1980 Marchant Exhibits HOF Blue

Noted long-time dealer Paul Marchant bought out the rights to use the exhibit name in 1980. He then issued this set, which measured the same size as the original exhibits to honor various Hall of Famers. This set was very noticeably marked as a "reprint" so there would be no confusion with the original cards. According to the manufacturer, 10,000 of these sets were produced.

COMPLETE SET 5.00 12.00
1 Grover C. Alexander .07 .20
2 Lou Boudreau .07 .20
3 Roger Bresnahan .02 .10
4 Roy Campanella .10 .30
5 Frank Chance .02 .10
6 Ty Cobb .30 .75
7 Mickey Cochrane .07 .20
8 Dizzy Dean .20 .50
9 Bill Dickey .07 .20
10 Joe DiMaggio .40 1.00
11 Johnny Evers .07 .20
12 Jimmy Foxx .10 .30
(Jimmie)
13 Lefty Gomez .07 .20
14 Hank Greenberg .07 .20
15 Lefty Grove .07 .20
16 Rogers Hornsby .10 .30
17 Carl Hubbell .07 .20
18 Hughie Jennings .02 .10
19 Walter Johnson .20 .50
20 Nap Lajoie .10 .30
21 Bob Lemon .07 .20
22 Mickey Mantle .40 1.00
23 Christy Mathewson .10 .30
24 Mel Ott .07 .20
25 Satchel Paige .20 .50
26 Jackie Robinson .40 1.00
27 Babe Ruth .60 1.50
28 Tris Speaker .10 .30
29 Joe Tinker .07 .20
30 Honus Wagner .10 .30
31 Ted Williams .30 .75
32 Cy Young .10 .30

1977-78 Mariners Postcards

This 23-card set features photos of the 1978 Seattle Mariners printed on 3 1/2" by 3 5/8" black and white postcard-size cards. They either have standard postcard backs or blank backs. The cards are unnumbered and checklisted below in alphabetical order.

COMPLETE SET (23) 4.00 10.00
1 Glenn Abbott .20 .50
Long Hair
2 Glenn Abbott .20 .50
Short Hair
3 Jose Baez .20 .50
4 Bruce Bochte .20 .50
5 Don Bryant CO .20 .50
6 Steve Burke .20 .50
7 Jim Busby CO .20 .50
8 Julio Cruz .20 .50
9 John Hale .20 .50
10 Rick Honeycutt .20 .50
11 Tom House .20 .50
12 Darrell Johnson MG .20 .50
13 Rick Jones .20 .50
14 Ruppert Jones .20 .50
15 Bill Laxton .20 .50
16 Byron McLaughlin .20 .50
17 Dan Meyer .20 .50
18 Larry Milbourne .20 .50
19 Paul Mitchell .20 .50
20 John Montague .20 .50
21 Dave Pagan .20 .50
22 Mike Parrott .20 .50
23 Vada Pinson CO .30 .75
24 Dick Pole .20 .50
25 Shane Rawley .20 .50
26 Craig Reynolds .20 .50
27 Leon Roberts .20 .50
28 Bob Robertson .20 .50
29 Enrique Romo .20 .50
30 Tommy Smith .20 .50
31 Lee Stanton(Smiling .20 .50
32 Lee Stanton .20 .50
Letters on Uniform
33 Bill Stein .20 .50
Mountain Background
34 Bill Stein .20 .50
Fence Background
35 Bob Stinson .20 .50
Fence Background
36 Bob Stinson .20 .50
Hill Background
37 Wes Stock CO .20 .50
38 Fred Thomas .20 .50
39 Jim Todd .20 .50
40 Gary Wheelock .20 .50

1978 Mariners Fred Meyer

These thirteen portraits were issued by Fred Meyer and featured members of the Seattle Mariners. The fronts feature player portraits against a blue background and the backs are blank. We have sequenced this set in alphabetical order. Interestingly a cover sheet was issued for this set and included photos of Darrell Johnson (who was the Mariners first manager) and Dick Pole. Neither Johnson nor Pole was included in the set.

COMPLETE SET (12) 20.00 50.00
1 Glenn Abbott 2.00 5.00
2 Jose Baez 2.00 5.00
3 Bruce Bochte 2.00 5.00
4 Julio Cruz 2.00 5.00
5 John Hale 2.00 5.00
6 Ruppert Jones 2.00 5.00
7 Danny Meyer 2.00 5.00
8 Craig Reynolds 2.00 5.00
9 Enrique Romo 2.00 5.00
10 Lee Stanton 2.00 5.00
11 Bill Stein 2.00 5.00
12 Bob Stinson 2.00 5.00
13 Cover Sheet 4.00 10.00
Bill Stein
Julio Cruz
Danny Meyer/

1979 Mariners Postcards

These 29 postcards, which measure 3 34/" by 5 1/2" feature members of the 1979 Seattle Mariners. The fronts have a player photo, a facsimile signature as well as the "Seattle Mariners" team logo on the bottom. The backs are standard postcard backs. Since these cards are unnumbered, we have sequenced this set in alphabetical order.

COMPLETE SET (29) 6.00 15.00
1 Glenn Abbott .20 .50
2 Floyd Bannister .20 .50
3 Bruce Bochte .20 .50
4 Don Bryant CO .20 .50
5 Larry Cox .20 .50
6 Julio Cruz .20 .50
7 Joe Decker .20 .50
8 Rob Dressler .20 .50
9 John Hale .20 .50
10 Rick Honeycutt .20 .50
11 Willie Horton .30 .75
12 Darrell Johnson MG .20 .50
13 Odell Jones .20 .50
14 Ruppert Jones .20 .50
15 Byron McLaughlin .20 .50
16 Mario Mendoza .20 .50
17 Dan Meyer .20 .50
18 Larry Milbourne .20 .50
19 John Montague .20 .50
20 Tom Paciorek .20 .50
21 Mike Parrott .20 .50
22 Vada Pinson CO .30 .75
23 Shane Rawley .20 .50
24 Leon Roberts .20 .50
25 Joe Simpson .20 .50
26 Bill Stein .20 .50
27 Bob Stinson .20 .50
28 Wes Stock CO .20 .50
29 Bobby Valentine .30 .75

1980 Mariners Postcards

These postcards which measure 3 3/4" by 5 1/2" feature members of the 1980 Seattle Mariners. These are unnumbered so we have sequenced them in alphabetical order. One way to differentiate these postcards from earlier Mariner postcards is that the the words "Baseball Club" were absent from under Mariners on the front. The two late season cards; Wills and Walton, come without a postcard back

COMPLETE SET 5.00 12.00
1 Glenn Abbott .20 .50
2 Jim Anderson .20 .50
3 Floyd Bannister .20 .50
4 Jim Beattie .20 .50
5 Juan Beniquez .20 .50
6 Bruce Bochte .20 .50
7 Don Bryant CO .20 .50
8 Ted Cox .20 .50
9 Rodney Craig .20 .50
10 Julo Cruz .20 .50
11 Rob Dressler .20 .50
12 Dave Heaverlo .20 .50
13 Marc Hill .20 .50
14 Rick Honeycutt .20 .50
15 Willie Horton .30 .75
16 Darrell Johnson MG .20 .50
17 Bill Mazeroski CO .60 1.50
18 Byron McLaughlin .20 .50
19 Mario Mendoza .20 .50
20 Larry Milbourne .20 .50
21 Dan Meyer .20 .50
22 Tom Paciorek .20 .50
23 Mike Parrott .20 .50
24 Vada Pinson CO .30 .75
25 Shane Rawley .20 .50
26 Dave Roberts .20 .50
27 Leon Roberts .20 .50
28 Joe Simpson .20 .50
29 Bill Stein .20 .50
30 Wes Stock CO .20 .50
31 Reggie Walton .20 .50
32 Maury Wills MG .40 1.00

1981 Mariners Police

The cards in this 16-card set measure approximately 2 5/8" by 4 1/8". The full color Seattle Mariners Police set of this year was sponsored by the Washington State Crime Prevention Association, the Kiwanis Club, Coca-Cola and Ernst Home Centers. The fronts feature the player's name, his position, and the Seattle Mariners name in addition to the player's photo. The backs, in red and blue, feature Tips from the Mariners and the logos of the four sponsors of the set. The cards are numbered in the lower left corners of the backs. This set was also produced with blank backs and sticker backs. Blank back sets are valued at 2X the price listed. The sticker back sets are available in very limited quantities and no price is established for those cards.

COMPLETE SET (16) 5.00 12.00
1 Jeff Burroughs .40 1.00
2 Floyd Bannister .20 .50
3 Glenn Abbott .20 .50
4 Jim Anderson .20 .50
5 Danny Meyer .20 .50
6 Dave Edler .20 .50
7 Julio Cruz .20 .50
8 Kenny Clay .20 .50
9 Lenny Randle .20 .50
10 Mike Parrott .20 .50
11 Tom Paciorek .20 .50
12 Jerry Narron .20 .50
13 Richie Zisk .30 .75
14 Maury Wills MG .60 1.50
15 Joe Simpson .20 .50
16 Shane Rawley .20 .50

1981 Mariners Postcards

This 31-card set features black and white photos which measure 3 3/4" by 5 1/2" of the 1981 Seattle Mariners printed on postcard-size cards. The cards are unnumbered and checklisted below in alphabetical order. All Mariners postcards from 1981 to 1984 were issued in the 3 3/4" by 5 1/2" and all have postcard backs.

COMPLETE SET (31) 6.00 15.00
1 Glenn Abbott .20 .50
2 Brian Allard .20 .50
3 Jim Anderson .20 .50
4 Larry Anderson .20 .50
5 Rick Auerbach .20 .50
6 Floyd Bannister .20 .50
7 Bruce Bochte .20 .50
8 Terry Bulling .20 .50
9 Jeff Burroughs .30 .75
10 Bryan Clark .20 .50
11 Kenny Clay .20 .50
12 Julio Cruz .20 .50
13 Tommy Davis CO .30 .75
14 Jerry Don Gleaton .20 .50
15 Dick Drago .20 .50
16 Dave Edler .20 .50
17 Frank Funk CO .20 .50
18 Gary Gray .20 .50
19 Dave Henderson .60 1.50
20 Rene Lachemann CO .20 .50
21 Dan Meyer .20 .50
22 Jerry Narron .20 .50
23 Tom Paciorek .20 .50
24 Mike Parrott .20 .50
25 Jim Presley .60 1.50
26 Lenny Randle .20 .50
27 Shane Rawley .20 .50
28 Cananea Reyes .20 .50
29 Joe Simpson .20 .50
30 Wes Stock CO .20 .50
31 Richie Zisk .20 .50

1982 Mariners Postcards

This 34-card set features 3 3/4" bv 5 1/2" black and white photos of the 1982 Seattle Mariners printed on postcard-size cards. The cards are unnumbered and checklisted below in alphabetical order. There is also a report of a 4" by 5" set issued the same year with blank backs. Any confirmation on these cards are appreciated.

COMPLETE SET (32) 6.00 15.00
1 Glenn Abbott .20 .50
2 Brian Allard .20 .50
3 Larry Anderson .20 .50
4 Floyd Bannister .20 .50
5 Jim Beattie .30 .75
6 Bruce Bochte .20 .50
7 Thad Bosley .20 .50
8 Bobby Brown .20 .50
9 Bud Bulling .20 .50
10 Manny Castillo .20 .50
11 Bill Caudill .20 .50
12 Bryan Clark .20 .50
13 Chuck Cottier CO .20 .50
14 Al Cowens .20 .50
15 Julio Cruz .20 .50
16 Todd Cruz .20 .50
17 Dave Duncan CO .20 .50
18 Jim Essian .20 .50
19 Gary Gray .20 .50
20 Dave Henderson .60 1.50
21 Rene Lachemann MG .20 .50
22 Jim Maler .20 .50
23 Mike Moore .20 .50
24 Gene Nelson .20 .50
25 Gaylord Perry 1.00 2.50
26 Vada Pinson CO .40 1.00
27 Bill Plummer .20 .50
28 Lenny Randle .20 .50
29 Paul Serna .20 .50
30 Joe Simpson .20 .50
31 Mike Stanton .20 .50
32 Steve Stroughter .20 .50
33 Ed Vandeberg .20 .50
34 Richie Zisk .20 .50

1983 Mariners Nalley's

Six members of the 1983 Seattle Mariners are featured in this set. The oversized photos, approximately 8 3/4" by 10 3/4", are in full-color and take up the entire back of potato chip box. Next to the player photo is statistics and a biography. We have arranged the listing of this set in alphabetical order.

COMPLETE SET 8.00 20.00
1 Bill Caudill 1.25 3.00
2 Al Cowens 1.25 3.00
3 Todd Cruz 1.25 3.00
4 Gaylord Perry 2.50 6.00
5 Rick Sweet 1.25 3.00
6 Richie Zisk 1.50 4.00

1984 Mariners Mother's

The cards in this 28-card set measure the standard size. In 1984, The Los Angeles-based Mother's Cookies Co. issued five sets of cards featuring players from major league teams. The Seattle Mariners set features current players depicted by photos. Similar to their 1952 and 1953 issues, the cards have rounded corners. The backs of the cards contain the Mother's Cookies logo. The cards were distributed in partial sets to fans at the respective stadiums of the teams involved. Whereas 20 cards were given to each patron, a redemption card, redeemable for eight more cards was included. Unfortunately, the eight cards received by redeeming the coupon were not necessarily the eight needed to complete a set. Hobbyist Barry Colla was involved in the production of these sets. The key card in the set is Mark Langston, one of his earliest cards issued.

COMPLETE SET (28) 5.00 12.00
1 Del Crandall MG .08 .25
2 Barry Bonnell .08 .25
3 Dave Henderson .20 .50
4 Bob Kearney .08 .25
5 Mike Moore .08 .25
6 Spike Owen .20 .50
7 Gorman Thomas .20 .50
8 Ed VandeBerg .08 .25
9 Matt Young .08 .25
10 Larry Milbourne .08 .25
11 Dave Beard .08 .25
12 Jim Beattie .20 .50
13 Mark Langston 1.25 3.00
14 Orlando Mercado .08 .25
15 Jack Perconte .08 .25
16 Pat Putnam .08 .25
17 Paul Mirabella .08 .25
18 Domingo Ramos .08 .25
19 Al Cowens .08 .25
20 Mike Stanton .08 .25
21 Steve Henderson .08 .25
22 Bob Stoddard .08 .25
23 Alvin Davis .40 1.00
24 Phil Bradley .30 .75
25 Roy Thomas .08 .25
26 Darnell Coles .20 .50
27 Mariners' Coaches .08 .25
Rick Sweet
Frank Funk
Ben Hin
28 Mariners' Checklist .08 .25
Seattle Kingdome

1984 Mariners Postcards

These postcards, which measure approximately 3 3/4" by 5 1/2" have closeup photos on the front with the players name and team logo on the bottom. The back of the cards have a postcard back. Since the cards are unnumbered, we have sequenced them in alphabetical order. Harold Reynolds, later to become a stalwart on ESPN, had a postcard two years before his Rookie Card in this set.

COMPLETE SET 6.00 15.00
1 Jim Beattie .30 .75
2 Barry Bonnell .20 .50
3 Phil Bradley .20 .50
4 Darnell Coles .20 .50
5 Chuck Cottier CO .20 .50
6 Al Cowens .20 .50
7 Del Crandall MG .20 .50
8 Alvin Davis .30 .75
9 Steve Henderson .20 .50
10 Bob Kearney .20 .50
11 Mark Langston .60 1.50
12 Larry Milbourne .20 .50
13 Paul Mirabella .20 .50
14 Mike Moore .20 .50
15 Ricky Nelson .20 .50
16 Spike Owen .20 .50
17 Jack Perconte .20 .50
18 Harold Reynolds .60 1.50
19 Phil Roof .20 .50
20 Mike Stanton .20 .50
21 Bob Stoddard .20 .50
22 Rick Sweet .20 .50
23 Bill Swift .20 .50
24 Gorman Thomas .30 .75
25 Roy Thomas .20 .50
26 Ed Vande Berg .20 .50
27 Matt Young .20 .50

1985 Mariners Mother's

The cards in this 28-card set measure the standard size. In 1985, the Los Angeles based Mother's Cookies Co. again issued five sets of cards featuring players from major league teams. The Seattle Mariners set features current players depicted by photos on cards with rounded corners. The backs of the cards contain the Mother's Cookies logo. Cards were passed out at the stadium on August 10.

COMPLETE SET (28) 3.00 8.00
1 Chuck Cottier MG .08 .25
2 Alvin Davis .30 .75
3 Mark Langston .40 1.00
4 Dave Henderson .20 .50
5 Ed VandeBerg .08 .25
6 Al Cowens .08 .25
7 Spike Owen .08 .25
8 Mike Moore .08 .25
9 Gorman Thomas .20 .50
10 Barry Bonnell .08 .25
11 Jack Perconte .08 .25
12 Domingo Ramos .08 .25
13 Bob Kearney .08 .25
14 Matt Young .08 .25
15 Jim Beattie .20 .50
16 Mike Stanton .08 .25
17 David Valle .08 .25
18 Ken Phelps .08 .25
19 Salome Barojas .08 .25
20 Jim Presley .20 .50
21 Phil Bradley .20 .50
22 Dave Geisel .08 .25
23 Harold Reynolds .60 1.50
24 Ed Nunez .08 .25
25 Mike Morgan .08 .25
26 Ivan Calderon .20 .50
27 Mariners' Coaches .08 .25
Marty Martinez
Jim Mahoney
Ph
28 Checklist Card .08 .25
Seattle Kingdome

1986 Mariners Greats TCMA

This 12-card standard-size set features some of the best players for the Mariners first decade. The front has a player photo, his name as well as his position. The back has vital statistics, a biography and career totals.

COMPLETE SET (12) .75 2.00
1 Pat Putnam .08 .25
2 Larry Milbourne .08 .25
3 Todd Cruz .08 .25
4 Bill Stein .08 .25
5 Leon Roberts .08 .25
6 Leroy Stanton .08 .25
7 Dan Meyer .08 .25
8 Bob Stinson .08 .25
9 Glenn Abbott .08 .25
10 John Montague .08 .25
11 Bryan Clark .08 .25
12 Rene Lachemann MG .08 .25

1986 Mariners Mother's

This set consists of 28 full-color, rounded-corner cards each measuring the standard size. Starter sets (only 20 cards but also including a certificate for eight more cards) were given out at the ballpark and collectors were encouraged to trade to fill in the rest of their set. Cards were originally given out on July 27th at the Seattle Kingdome.

COMPLETE SET (28) 3.00 8.00
1 Dick Williams MG .20 .50
2 Alvin Davis .20 .50
3 Mark Langston .40 1.00
4 Dave Henderson .20 .50
5 Steve Yeager .08 .25
6 Al Cowens .08 .25
7 Jim Presley .08 .25
8 Phil Bradley .08 .25
9 Gorman Thomas .08 .25
10 Barry Bonnell .08 .25
11 Milt Wilcox .08 .25
12 Domingo Ramos .08 .25
13 Paul Mirabella .08 .25
14 Matt Young .08 .25
15 Ivan Calderon .20 .50
16 Bill Swift .08 .25
17 Pete Ladd .08 .25
18 Ken Phelps .08 .25
19 Karl Best .08 .25
20 Spike Owen .08 .25
21 Mike Moore .08 .25
22 Danny Tartabull .40 1.00
23 Bob Kearney .08 .25
24 Edwin Nunez .08 .25
25 Mike Morgan .08 .25
26 Roy Thomas .08 .25
27 Jim Beattie .20 .50
28 Checklist Card .08 .25
Deron Johnson CO
Marty Martinez C

1986 Mariners Pacific Northwest Bell

This 16-card set of the Seattle Mariners measures approximately 3 3/4" by 5 1/2" and features black-and-white player portraits in white borders. The backs carry player information and sponsor logo. The cards are unnumbered and checklisted below in alphabetical order. These same cards were also issued with postcard backs, these cards were primarily used at signing sessions at Mariners home games and to respond to fan email.

COMPLETE SET (16) 6.00 15.00
1 Jim Beattie .50 1.25
2 Karl Best .40 1.00
3 Phil Bradley .40 1.00
4 Alvin Davis .40 1.00
5 Lee Guetterman .40 1.00
6 Mark Huismann .40 1.00
7 Mark Langston .60 1.50
8 Mike Moore .40 1.00
9 Mike Morgan .40 1.00
10 Ken Phelps .40 1.00
11 Harold Reynolds .75 2.00
12 Bill Swift .40 1.00
13 Danny Tartabull .60 1.50
14 Dave Valle .40 1.00
15 Steve Yeager .40 1.00
16 Matt Young .40 1.00

1987 Mariners Mother's

This set consists of 28 full-color, rounded-corner cards each measuring the standard size. Starter sets (only 20 cards but also including a certificate for eight more cards) were given out at the ballpark and collectors were encouraged to trade to fill in the rest of their set. Cards were originally given out on August 9th at the Seattle Kingdome. Photos were taken by Barry Colla. The sets were reportedly given out free to the first 20,000 paid admissions at the game.

COMPLETE SET (28) 3.00 8.00
1 Dick Williams MG .20 .50
2 Alvin Davis .20 .50
3 Mike Moore .08 .25
4 Jim Presley .08 .25
5 Mark Langston .40 1.00
6 Phil Bradley .08 .25
7 Ken Phelps .08 .25
8 Mike Morgan .08 .25
9 David Valle .08 .25
10 Harold Reynolds .30 .75
11 Edwin Nunez .08 .25
12 Bob Kearney .08 .25
13 Scott Bankhead .08 .25
14 Scott Bradley .08 .25
15 Mickey Brantley .08 .25
16 Mark Huismann .08 .25
17 Mike Kingery .20 .50
18 John Moses .08 .25
19 Donell Nixon .08 .25
20 Rey Quinones .08 .25
21 Domingo Ramos .08 .25
22 Jerry Reed .08 .25
23 Rich Renteria .08 .25
24 Rich Monteleone .08 .25
25 Mike Trujillo .08 .25
26 Bill Wilkinson .08 .25
27 John Christensen .08 .25
28 Checklist Card .20 .50
Billy Connors CO
Frank Howard CO#

1988 Mariners Mother's

This set consists of 28 full-color, rounded-corner cards each measuring the standard size. Starter sets (only 20 cards but also including a certificate for eight more cards) were given out at the ballpark and collectors were encouraged to trade to fill in the rest of their set. Cards were originally given out on August 14th at the Seattle Kingdome. Photos were taken by Barry Colla. The sets were reportedly given out free to the first 20,000 paid admissions at the game.

COMPLETE SET (28) 3.00 8.00
1 Dick Williams MG .20 .50
2 Alvin Davis .20 .50
3 Mike Moore .08 .25
4 Jim Presley .08 .25
5 Mark Langston .40 1.00
6 Henry Cotto .08 .25
7 Ken Phelps .08 .25
8 Steve Trout .08 .25
9 David Valle .08 .25
10 Harold Reynolds .30 .75
11 Edwin Nunez .08 .25
12 Glenn Wilson .08 .25
13 Scott Bankhead .08 .25
14 Scott Bradley .08 .25
15 Mickey Brantley .08 .25
16 Bruce Fields .08 .25
17 Mike Kingery .08 .25
18 Mike Campbell .08 .25
19 Mike Jackson .30 .75
20 Rey Quinones .08 .25
21 Mario Diaz .08 .25
22 Jerry Reed .08 .25
23 Rich Renteria .08 .25
24 Julio Solano .08 .25
25 Bill Swift .08 .25
26 Bill Wilkinson .08 .25
27 Howie Bedell CO .08 .25
Billy Connors CO
Frank Howard CO
Bill Plummer CO
Phil Roof CO
Jim Snyder
Ossie Virgil CO
28 Checklist Card .08 .25
Henry Genzale EQMG
Rick Griffin T

1989 Mariners Mother's

COMPLETE SET (28) 8.00 20.00
1 Jim Lefebvre MG .08 .25
2 Alvin Davis .20 .50
3 Ken Griffey Jr. 5.00 12.00
4 Jim Presley .08 .25
5 Mark Langston .30 .75
6 Henry Cotto .08 .25
7 Mickey Brantley .08 .25
8 Jeffrey Leonard .08 .25
9 Dave Valle .08 .25
10 Harold Reynolds .30 .75
11 Edgar Martinez .75 2.00
12 Tom Niedenfuer .08 .25
13 Scott Bankhead .08 .25
14 Scott Bradley .08 .25
15 Omar Vizquel 1.00 2.50
16 Erik Hanson .08 .25
17 Bill Swift .08 .25
18 Mike Campbell .08 .25
19 Mike Jackson .20 .50
20 Rich Renteria .08 .25
21 Mario Diaz .08 .25
22 Jerry Reed .08 .25
23 Darnell Coles .08 .25
24 Steve Trout .08 .25
25 Mike Schooler .08 .25
26 Julio Solano .08 .25
27 Mariners Coaches .08 .25
Mike Paul
Gene Clines
Bill Plu
28 Checklist Card .08 .25
Henry Genzale EQMG
Rick Griffin T

1990 Mariners Mother's

1990 Mother's Cookies Seattle Mariners set contains 28 standard-size cards with the traditional Mother's Cookies rounded corners. The cards have full-color fronts and biographical information with no stats on the back. These Mariners cards were released for the August 5th game and given to the first 25,000 people who passed through the gates. They were distributed in 20-card random packets at the game and eight more at the redemption booths. However, both groups of cards were random and there was no guarantee of getting a complete set in the cards. The promotional idea was that the only way one could finish the set was to trade for them. The redemption for eight more cards were available at the Kingdome Card Show on August 12, 1990.

COMPLETE SET (28) 8.00 20.00
1 Jim Lefebvre MG .08 .25
2 Alvin Davis .20 .50
3 Ken Griffey Jr. 4.00 10.00
4 Jeffrey Leonard .08 .25
5 David Valle .08 .25
6 Harold Reynolds .30 .75
7 Jay Buhner .75 2.00
8 Erik Hanson .08 .25
9 Henry Cotto .08 .25
10 Edgar Martinez .50 1.25
11 Bill Swift .08 .25
12 Omar Vizquel .40 1.00
13 Randy Johnson 1.50 4.00
14 Greg Briley .08 .25
15 Gene Harris .08 .25
16 Matt Young .08 .25
17 Pete O'Brien .08 .25
18 Brent Knackert .08 .25
19 Mike Jackson .20 .50
20 Brian Holman .08 .25
21 Mike Schooler .08 .25
22 Darnell Coles .08 .25
23 Keith Comstock .08 .25
24 Scott Bankhead .08 .25
25 Scott Bradley .08 .25
26 Mike Brumley .08 .25
27 Mariners Coaches .08 .25
Rusty Kuntz
Gene Clines
Bill P
28 Checklist Card .08 .25
Mariners Personnel
Henry Genzale

1991 Mariners Country Hearth

This 30-card standard-size set was sponsored and produced by the Country Hearth Breads and Langendorf Baking Company, and individual cards were inserted unprotected in specially marked loaves of Country Hearth. In addition, the cards (ten at a time) were given away to fans attending the Mariners home game at the Seattle Kingdome on August 17, 1991. According to sources, only 20,000 sets were produced, and all cards were produced in equal quantities. This set is difficult to acquire in near mint or better condition as any card inserted into the bread was not properly protected and have moisture spots on them.

COMPLETE SET (30) 10.00 25.00
1 Jim Lefebvre MG .20 .50
2 Jeff Schaefer .20 .50
3 Harold Reynolds .40 1.00
4 Greg Briley .20 .50
5 Scott Bradley .20 .50
6 Dave Valle .20 .50
7 Edgar Martinez 1.00 2.50
8 Pete O'Brien .20 .50
9 Omar Vizquel .60 1.50
10 Tino Martinez 1.00 2.50
11 Scott Bankhead .20 .50
12 Bill Swift .20 .50
13 Jay Buhner 1.00 2.50
14 Alvin Davis .30 .75
15 Ken Griffey Jr./(Ready to swing) 2.50 6.00
16 Tracy Jones .20 .50
17 Brent Knackert .20 .50
18 Henry Cotto .20 .50
19 Ken Griffey Sr./(Watching ball after hit) .60 1.50
20 Keith Comstock .20 .50
21 Brian Holman .20 .50
22 Russ Swan .20 .50
23 Mike Jackson .30 .75
24 Erik Hanson .20 .50
25 Mike Schooler .20 .50
26 Randy Johnson 1.25 3.00
27 Rich DeLucia .20 .50
28 Ken Griffey Jr. Sr./(Both on same card) 1.25 3.00
29 Mariner Moose Mascot .30 .75
NNO Title Card .60 1.50

1992 Mariners Mother's

The 1992 Mother's Cookies Mariners set contains 28 cards with rounded corners measuring the standard size.

COMPLETE SET (28) 6.00 15.00
1 Bill Plummer MG .08 .25
2 Ken Griffey Jr. 2.00 5.00
3 Harold Reynolds .30 .75
4 Kevin Mitchell .20 .50
5 David Valle .08 .25
6 Jay Buhner .60 1.50
7 Erik Hanson .08 .25
8 Pete O'Brien .08 .25
9 Henry Cotto .08 .25
10 Mike Schooler .08 .25
11 Tino Martinez 1.00 2.50
12 Dennis Powell .08 .25
13 Randy Johnson 1.00 2.50
14 Dave Cochrane .08 .25
15 Greg Briley .08 .25
16 Omar Vizquel .40 1.00
17 Dave Fleming .08 .25
18 Matt Sinatro .08 .25
19 Jeff Nelson .20 .50
20 Edgar Martinez .40 1.00
21 Calvin Jones .08 .25
22 Russ Swan .08 .25
23 Jim Acker .08 .25
24 Jeff Schaefer .08 .25
25 Clay Parker .08 .25
26 Brian Holman .08 .25
27 Coaches .08 .25
Dan Warthen
Russ Nixon
Rusty Kuntz
Mar
28 Checklist .08 .25

1993 Mariners Dairy Queen

Subtitled "Magic Mariner Moments," the four cards comprising this set were issued with metal pins which came attached to cardboard tabs beneath the perforated card bottoms. The cards measure approximately 2 1/2" by 3 7/8" and feature gray-bordered color action player photos on their fronts. The player's name appears in black lettering within a white bar near the bottom of the picture and the Mariners logo rests in the lower left. The player's accomplishment is displayed in a green banner across the top of the photo. The white back is framed by a thin black line and carries the player's name in black lettering above text describing his accomplishment. At the bottom are drawings of the four pins and the week of issue for each card and pin combination. The white metal pins feature the player's name and number in green lettering upon a white jersey. The set's subtitle and the player's accomplishment are carried in red and green banners, respectively, across the top of the pin.

COMPLETE SET (4) 5.00 12.00
1 Randy Johnson 1.50 4.00
2 Edgar Martinez 1.00 2.50
3 Chris Bosio .40 1.00
4 Ken Griffey Jr. 3.00 8.00

1993 Mariners Mother's

The 1993 Mother's Cookies Mariners set consists of 28 standard-size cards with rounded corners.

COMPLETE SET (28) 6.00 15.00
1 Lou Piniella MG .30 .75
2 Dave Fleming .08 .25
3 Pete O'Brien .08 .25
4 Ken Griffey Jr. 2.00 5.00
5 Henry Cotto .08 .25
6 Jay Buhner .60 1.50
7 David Valle .08 .25
8 Dwayne Henry .08 .25
9 Mike Felder .08 .25
10 Norm Charlton .08 .25
11 Edgar Martinez .40 1.00
12 Erik Hanson .08 .25
13 Mike Blowers .08 .25
14 Omar Vizquel .30 .75
15 Randy Johnson 1.00 2.50
16 Russ Swan .08 .25
17 Tino Martinez .60 1.50
18 Rich DeLucia .08 .25
19 Jeff Nelson .20 .50
20 Chris Bosio .08 .25
21 Tim Leary .08 .25
22 Mackey Sasser .08 .25
23 Dennis Powell .08 .25
24 Mike Hampton .50 1.25
25 Fernando Vina .30 .75
26 John Cummings .08 .25
27 Rich Amaral .08 .25
28 Checklist .20 .50
Coaches
Sam Perlozzo
Sam Mejias
Lee E

1993 Mariners Stadium Club

This 30-card standard-size set features the 1993 Seattle Mariners. The set was issued in hobby (plastic box) and retail (blister) form.

COMP.FACT SET (30) 3.00 8.00
1 Ken Griffey Jr. 1.25 3.00
2 Desi Relaford .08 .25
3 Dave Wainhouse .02 .10
4 Rich Amaral .02 .10
5 Brian Deak .02 .10
6 Bret Boone .30 .75
7 Bill Haselman .02 .10
8 Dave Fleming .02 .10
9 Fernando Vina .20 .50
10 Greg Litton .02 .10
11 Mackey Sasser .02 .10
12 Lee Tinsley .02 .10
13 Norm Charlton .02 .10
14 Russ Swan .02 .10
15 Brian Holman .02 .10
16 Randy Johnson .60 1.50
17 Erik Hanson .02 .10
18 Tino Martinez .30 .75
19 Marc Newfield .02 .10
20 Dave Valle .02 .10
21 John Cummings .02 .10
22 Mike Hampton .40 1.00
23 Jay Buhner .20 .50
24 Edgar Martinez .30 .75
25 Omar Vizquel .20 .50
26 Pete O'Brien .02 .10
27 Brian Turang .02 .10
28 Chris Bosio .02 .10
29 Mike Felder .02 .10
30 Shawn Estes .08 .25

1994 Mariners Mother's

The 1994 Mariners Mother's Cookies set consists of 28 standard-size cards with rounded corners. The set includes a coupon with a mail-in offer to obtain a trading card collectors album for 3.95. The set had limited distribution since the original Mother's promotion night was cancelled due to the Kingdome closure and then the baseball strike.

COMPLETE SET (28) 8.00 20.00
1 Lou Piniella MG .30 .75
2 Randy Johnson 1.00 2.50
3 Eric Anthony .08 .25
4 Ken Griffey Jr. 2.50 6.00
5 Felix Fermin .08 .25
6 Jay Buhner .60 1.50
7 Chris Bosio .08 .25
8 Reggie Jefferson .08 .25
9 Greg Hibbard .08 .25
10 Dave Fleming .08 .25
11 Rich Amaral .08 .25
12 Rich Gossage .40 1.00
13 Edgar Martinez .40 1.00
14 Bobby Ayala .08 .25
15 Darren Bragg .08 .25
16 Tino Martinez .60 1.50
17 Mike Blowers .08 .25
18 John Cummings .08 .25
19 Keith Mitchell .08 .25
20 Bill Haselman .08 .25
21 Greg Pirkl .08 .25
22 Mackey Sasser .08 .25
23 Tim Davis .08 .25
24 Dan Wilson .08 .25
25 Jeff Nelson .20 .50
26 Kevin King .08 .25
27 Torey Lovullo .08 .25
28 Checklist .08 .25
Coaches
Sam Perlozzo
Lee Elia
Sammy E

1995 Mariners Mother's

This 1995 Mother's Cookies Seattle Mariners set consists of 28 standard-size cards with rounded corners.

COMPLETE SET (28) 8.00 20.00
1 Lou Piniella MG .30 .75
2 Randy Johnson 1.00 2.50
3 Dave Fleming .08 .25
4 Ken Griffey Jr. 2.00 5.00
5 Edgar Martinez .40 1.00
6 Jay Buhner .40 1.00
7 Alex Rodriguez 3.00 8.00
8 Joey Cora .08 .25
9 Tim Davis .08 .25
10 Mike Blowers .08 .25
11 Chris Bosio .08 .25
12 Dan Wilson .08 .25
13 Rich Amaral .08 .25
14 Bobby Ayala .08 .25
15 Darren Bragg .08 .25
16 Bob Wells .08 .25
17 Doug Strange .08 .25
18 Chad Kreuter .08 .25
19 Rafael Carmona .08 .25
20 Luis Sojo .08 .25
21 Tim Belcher .08 .25
22 Steve Frey .08 .25
23 Tino Martinez .40 1.00
24 Felix Fermin .08 .25
25 Jeff Nelson .20 .50
26 Alex Diaz .08 .25
27 Bill Risley .08 .25
28 Coaches .08 .25
Checklist
Sam Perlozo
Matt Sinatro
Lee

1995 Mariners Pacific

Produced by Pacific, this 50-card boxed standard-size set highlights the events leading up to the Seattle Mariners clinching the American League Western Division Pennant and their playoff run during the Division Series and the American League Championship Series. The set divides into game action shots (1-17) and player (and manager) cards (18-50).

COMPLETE SET (50) 6.00 15.00
1 Ken Griffey Jr. IA .50 1.25
2 Vince Coleman IA .02 .10
3 Luis Sojo IA .02 .10
4 Mariners win the West .15 .40
5 Randy Johnson IA .25 .60
6 Ken Griffey Jr. IA .50 1.25
7 Tino ignites Mariners .15 .40
8 Edgar Martinez IA .08 .25
9 Ken Griffey Jr. IA .50 1.25
10 Thunder in the Kingdome .08 .25
11 Series win ends years of futility .08 .25
12 Bob Wolcott IA .02 .10
13 Jay Buhner IA .08 .25
14 Randy Johnson IA .25 .60
15 Lou Piniella IA .08 .25
16 Joey Cora IA .02 .10
17 Dave Niehaus ANN .25 .60
18 Rich Amaral .02 .10
19 Bobby Ayala .02 .10
20 Tim Belcher .02 .10
21 Andy Benes .02 .10
22 Mike Blowers .02 .10
23 Chris Bosio .02 .10
24 Darren Bragg .02 .10
25 Jay Buhner .25 .60
26 Rafael Carmona .02 .10
27 Norm Charlton .02 .10
28 Vince Coleman .02 .10
29 Joey Cora .02 .10
30 Alex Diaz .02 .10
31 Felix Fermin .02 .10
32 Ken Griffey Jr. 1.00 2.50
33 Lee Guetterman .02 .10
34 Randy Johnson .50 1.25
35 Edgar Martinez .30 .75
36 Tino Martinez .15 .40
37 Jeff Nelson .08 .25
38 Warren Newson .02 .10
39 Greg Pirkl .02 .10
40 Arquimedez Pozo .02 .10
41 Bill Risley .02 .10
42 Alex Rodriguez UER 1.25 3.00
43 Luis Sojo .02 .10
44 Doug Strange .02 .10
45 Salomon Torres .02 .10
46 Bob Wells .02 .10
47 Chris Widger .02 .10
48 Dan Wilson .08 .25
49 Bob Wolcott .02 .10
50 Lou Piniella MG .08 .25

1996 Mariners Mother's

This 28-card set consists of borderless posed color player portraits. The player's and team's names appear in one of the top rounded corners. The backs carry biographical information and the sponsor's logo on a white background in red and purple print. A blank slot for the player's autograph rounds out the back.

COMPLETE SET (28) 6.00 15.00
1 Lou Piniella MG .30 .75
2 Randy Johnson .75 2.00
3 Jay Buhner .40 1.00
4 Ken Griffey Jr. 1.50 4.00
5 Ricky Jordan .08 .25
6 Rich Amaral .08 .25
7 Edgar Martinez .40 1.00
8 Joey Cora .08 .25
9 Alex Rodriguez 1.50 4.00
10 Sterling Hitchcock .08 .25
11 Chris Bosio .08 .25
12 John Marzano .08 .25
13 Bob Wells .08 .25
14 Rafael Carmona .08 .25
15 Dan Wilson .08 .25
16 Norm Charlton .08 .25
17 Paul Sorrento .08 .25
18 Mike Jackson .08 .25
19 Luis Sojo .08 .25
20 Bobby Ayala .08 .25
21 Alex Diaz .08 .25
22 Doug Strange .08 .25
23 Bob Wolcott .08 .25
24 Darren Bragg .08 .25
25 Paul Menhart .08 .25
26 Edwin Hurtado .08 .25
27 Russ Davis .08 .25
28 Coaches Card CL .08 .25
Lee Elia
John McLarren
Steve Sm

1997 Mariners Score

This 15-card set of the Seattle Mariners was issued in five-card packs with a suggested retail price of $1.30 each. The fronts feature color player photos with special team specific color foil stamping. The backs carry player information. Only 100 cases were made for each team. Platinum parallel cards were inserted at a rate of 1:6, Premier parallel cards at a rate of 1:31.

COMPLETE SET (15) 3.00 8.00
*PLATINUM: 4X BASIC CARDS
*PREMIER: 20X BASIC CARDS
1 Chris Bosio .08 .25
2 Edgar Martinez .40 1.00
3 Alex Rodriguez 1.50 4.00
4 Paul Sorrento .08 .25
5 Bob Wells .08 .25
6 Ken Griffey Jr. 1.50 4.00
7 Jay Buhner .40 1.00
8 Dan Wilson .08 .25
9 Randy Johnson .75 2.00
10 Joey Cora .08 .25
11 Mark Whiten .08 .25
12 Rich Amaral .08 .25
13 Raul Ibanez .40 1.00
14 Jamie Moyer .15 .40
15 Mac Suzuki .08 .25

1997 Mariners Upper Deck Pepsi Game

Produced by Upper Deck and sponsored by the Pepsi-Cola Company, this set features borderless color player photos of the Seattle Mariners and was given away at a Mariners game.

COMPLETE SET (21) 6.00 15.00
P1 Joey Cora .08 .25
P2 Ken Griffey Jr. 1.50 4.00
P3 Jay Buhner

0.75 8839580102.00

1997 Mariners Upper Deck Pepsi Game

P4 Alex Rodriguez 1.50 4.00
P5 Norm Charlton .08 .25
P6 Edgar Martinez .40 1.00
P7 Paul Sorrento .08 .25
P8 Randy Johnson .75 2.00
P9 Rich Amaral .08 .25
P10 Russ Davis .08 .25
P11 Greg McCarthy .08 .25
P12 Jamie Moyer .20 .50
P13 Jeff Fassero .08 .25
P14 Scott Sanders .08 .25
P15 Dan Wilson .08 .25
P16 Mike Blowers .08 .25
P17 Bobby Ayala .08 .25
P18 Brent Gates .08 .25
P19 John Marzano .08 .25
P20 Lou Piniella MG .20 .50
NNO Sponsor Card .08 .25
Pepsi-Cola Co.
Coupon

1997 Mariners Upper Deck Pepsi Insert

This 19 card set, issued in 1997 by Upper Deck, was inserted randomly into 12-packs of Pepsi. These cards are differentiated from the set given away at the ballpark by their having a "M" prefix.

COMPLETE SET 20.00 50.00
M1 Joey Cora .75 2.00
M2 Ken Griffey Jr. 4.00 10.00
M3 Jay Buhner 1.50 4.00
M4 Alex Rodriguez 4.00 10.00
M5 Norm Charlton .75 2.00
M6 Edgar Martinez 1.50 4.00
M7 Paul Sorrento .75 2.00
M8 Randy Johnson 2.00 5.00
M9 Rich Amaral .75 2.00
M10 Russ Davis .75 2.00
M11 Bob Wolcott .75 2.00
M12 Jamie Moyer 1.00 2.50
M13 Bob Wells .75 2.00
M14 Mac Suzuki .75 2.00
M15 Dan Wilson .75 2.00
M16 Tim Davis .75 2.00
M17 Bobby Ayala .75 2.00
M18 Salomon Torres .75 2.00
M19 Raul Ibanez 1.25 3.00

1998 Mariners Score

This 15-card set was issued in special retail packs and features color photos of the Seattle Mariners team. The backs carry player information. A special platinum parallel set was also issued and randomly inserted in packs.

COMPLETE SET (15) 3.00 8.00
*PLATINUM: 5X BASIC CARDS
1 Dan Wilson .08 .25
2 Alex Rodriguez 1.25 3.00
3 Jeff Fassero .08 .25
4 Ken Griffey Jr. 1.25 3.00
5 Bobby Ayala .08 .25
6 Jay Buhner .20 .50
7 Mike Timlin .08 .25
8 Edgar Martinez .40 1.00
9 Randy Johnson .60 1.50
10 Joey Cora .08 .25
11 Heathcliff Slocumb .08 .25
12 Russ Davis .08 .25
13 Paul Sorrento .08 .25
14 Rich Amaral .08 .25
15 Jamie Moyer .30 .75

2000 Mariners Getwell Tour

COMPLETE SET 20.00 50.00
1 Paul Abbott .40 1.00
2 David Bell .80 2.00
3 Mike Cameron .80 2.00
4 Norm Charlton .40 1.00
5 Jeff Cirillo .40 1.00
6 Ryan Franklin .40 1.00
7 Charles Gipson .40 1.00
8 Carlos Guillen 1.60 4.00
9 Raul Ibanez 1.20 3.00
10 Stan Javier .40 1.00
11 Tom Lampkin .40 1.00
12 Edgar Martinez 2.00 5.00
13 Mark McLemore .40 1.00
14 Jamie Moyer 1.20 3.00
15 Dave Myers .40 1.00
16 John Olerud 1.20 3.00
17 Jose Paniagua .40 1.00
18 Joel Pineiro 2.00 5.00
19 Arthur Lee Rhodes .40 1.00
20 Rick Rizzs ANN .40 1.00
21 Kazuhiro Sasaki 1.60 4.00
22 Aaron Sele .40 1.00
23 Matt Sinatro .40 1.00
24 Ichiro Suzuki 4.00 10.00
25 Dave Valle ANN .40 1.00

2000 Mariners Keebler

COMPLETE SET (28) 8.00 18.00
1 Lou Piniella MG .20 .50
2 Alex Rodriguez 1.60 4.00
3 Jamie Moyer .30 .75
4 Edgar Martinez .40 1.00
5 Kazuhiro Sasaki 1.25 3.00
6 Jay Buhner .30 .75
7 Rickey Henderson .50 1.50
8 John Olerud .40 1.00
9 Aaron Sele .10 .25
10 Charles Gipson .10 .25
11 Arthur Rhodes .10 .25
12 Dan Wilson .10 .25
13 Jose Mesa .10 .25
14 Mike Cameron .30 .75
15 John Halama .10 .25
16 Mark McLemore .10 .25
17 Brett Tomko .10 .25
18 Tom Lampkin .10 .25
19 Freddy Garcia .40 1.00
20 John Mabry .10 .25
21 Paul Abbott .10 .25
22 Stan Javier .10 .25
23 Gil Meche .10 .25
24 David Bell .20 .50
25 Frankie Rodriguez .10 .25
26 Raul Ibanez .30 .75
27 Jose Paniagua .10 .25
28 L.Bowa .10 .25
J.McLaren
J.Moses
G.Perry
B.Price
M.Sinatro

2001 Mariners FanFest

COMPLETE SET (9) 20.00 50.00
1 Jay Buhner Fleer .60 1.50
2 Ken Griffey Jr. UD 4.00 10.00
3 Randy Johnson Donruss 2.50 6.00
4 Edgar Martinez Topps 1.00 2.50
5 John Olerud Topps .60 1.50
6 Lou Piniella UD .40 1.00
7 Alex Rodriguez Donruss 2.50 6.00
8 Ichiro Suzuki Fleer 8.00 20.00
9 A.Davis .40 1.00
H.Reynolds Krause

2001 Mariners Keebler

COMPLETE SET (28) 12.50 30.00
1 Lou Piniella MG .30 .75
2 Edgar Martinez .60 1.50
3 Mike Cameron .30 .75
4 Jamie Moyer .30 .75
5 Ichiro Suzuki 10.00 25.00
6 Jay Buhner .40 1.00
7 Kazuhiro Sasaki .60 1.50
8 John Olerud .40 1.00
9 Aaron Sele .08 .25
10 Bret Boone .30 .75
11 Arthur Rhodes .08 .25
12 Al Martin .08 .25
13 Jeff Nelson .20 .50
14 Dan Wilson .08 .25
15 John Halama .08 .25
16 Stan Javier .08 .25
17 Brett Tomko .08 .25
18 Carlos Guillen .40 1.00
19 Freddy Garcia .60 1.50
20 David Bell .20 .50
21 Paul Abbott .08 .25
22 Mark McLemore .08 .25
23 Tom Lampkin .08 .25
24 Charles Gipson .08 .25
25 Ryan Franklin .08 .25
26 Anthony Sanders .08 .25
27 Jose Paniagua .08 .25
28 Lee Elia CO .08 .25
John McLaren CO
John Moses CO
Dave Myers CO
Gerald Perry CO
Bryan Price CO
Matt Sinatro Co

2001 Mariners Seattle Post-Intelligencer

COMPLETE SET (8) 12.50 25.00
1 Bret Boone 1.25 3.00
2 Mike Cameron 1.25 3.00
3 Freddy Garcia 1.50 4.00
4 Edgar Martinez 2.00 5.00
5 Jeff Nelson 1.00 2.50
6 John Olerud 1.00 2.50
7 Kazuhiro Sasaki 1.00 2.50
8 Ichiro Suzuki 3.00 8.00

2002 Mariners Franz Upper Deck

COMPLETE SET 3.00 8.00
1 John Olerud .40 1.00
2 Edgar Martinez .60 1.50
3 Ichiro Suzuki .75 2.00
4 Carlos Guillen .40 1.00
5 Jeff Cirillo .08 .25
6 Bret Boone .20 .50
7 Ben Davis .08 .25
8 Ruben Sierra .20 .50
9 Mike Cameron .30 .75
10 Freddy Garcia .60 1.50
11 Kazuhiro Sasaki .40 1.00
12 Jamie Moyer .30 .75
13 Dan Wilson .08 .25
14 Jeff Nelson .20 .50
15 James Baldwin .08 .25
16 Mark McLemore .08 .25

2002 Mariners Knothole

COMPLETE SET 3.00 8.00
1 Paul Abbott .08 .25
2 Alex Arias .08 .25
3 James Baldwin .08 .25
4 Bret Boone .40 1.00
5 Mike Cameron .30 .75
6 Jeff Cirillo .08 .25
7 Ben Davis .08 .25
8 Ryan Franklin .08 .25
9 Freddy Garcia .40 1.00
10 Charles Gipson .08 .25
11 Carlos Guillen .08 .25
12 John Halama .08 .25
13 Shigetoshi Hasegawa .08 .25
14 Edgar Martinez .40 1.00
15 Mark McLemore .20 .50
16 Jamie Moyer .30 .75
17 Jeff Nelson .20 .50
18 John Olerud .40 1.00
19 Joel Pineiro .20 .50
20 Desi Relaford .08 .25
21 Arthur Rhodes .08 .25
22 Kazuhiro Sasaki .20 .50
23 Ruben Sierra .20 .50
24 Ichiro Suzuki .60 1.50
25 Dan Wilson .08 .25
26 Lou Piniella MG .20 .50
27 John McLaren CO .08 .25
John Moses CO
Dave Myers CO
Ger

2003 Mariners Keebler

COMPLETE SET 6.00 12.00
1 Bob Melvin MG .10 .25
2 Ichiro Suzuki .75 2.00
3 Edgar Martinez .60 1.50
4 Jamie Moyer .20 .50
5 Mike Cameron .30 .75
6 Bret Boone .40 1.00
7 Kazuhiro Sasaki .20 .50
8 John Olerud .30 .75
9 Mark McLemore .10 .25
10 Arthur Rhodes .10 .25
11 Randy Winn .30 .75
12 Freddy Garcia .50 1.25
13 Dan Wilson .10 .25
14 Jeff Nelson .20 .50
15 Carlos Guillen .40 1.00
16 Ryan Franklin .10 .25
17 Ben Davis .10 .25
18 Joel Pineiro .10 .25
19 Jeff Cirillo .10 .25
20 Shigetoshi Hasegawa .20 .50
21 Greg Colbrunn .10 .25
22 John Mabry .10 .25
23 Julio Mateo .10 .25
24 Willie Bloomquist .10 .25
25 Gil Meche .10 .25
26 Giovanni Carrara .10 .25
27 Chris Snelling .10 .25
28 Orlando Gomez CO .10 .25
Lamar Johnson CO
Rene Lachemann

2004 Mariners Archway Upper Deck

COMPLETE SET
1 Ichiro Suzuki 1.00 2.50
2 Raul Ibanez .30 .75
3 Randy Winn .30 .75
4 John Olerud .20 .50
5 Bret Boone .20 .50
6 Rich Aurilia .10 .25
7 Scott Spiezio .10 .25
8 Dan Wilson .10 .25
9 Edgar Martinez .60 1.50
10 Freddy Garcia .40 1.00
11 Jamie Moyer .20 .50
12 Joel Pineiro .10 .25
13 Gil Meche .10 .25
14 Ryan Franklin .10 .25
15 Shigetoshi Hasegawa .20 .50
16 Eddie Guardado .20 .50

2004 Mariners Team Issue

COMPLETE SET
1 Willie Bloomquist .20 .50
2 Bret Boone .30 .75
3 Giovanni Carrara .20 .50
4 Shigetoshi Hasegawa .20 .50
5 Edgar Martinez .75 2.00
6 Jamie Moyer .40 1.00
7 Mike Myers .20 .50
8 Jeff Nelson .30 .75
9 John Olerud .30 .75
10 Joel Pineiro .20 .50
11 Scott Spiezio .20 .50
12 Dan Wilson .30 .75
13 Randy Winn .40 1.00
14 Mariners Moose .20 .50
Mascot

2005 Mariners Hispanic Heroes

1 Adrian Beltre .75 2.00
2 Yuniesky Betancourt 1.25 3.00
3 Eddie Guardado .50 1.25
4 Felix Hernandez 2.50 6.00
5 Raul Ibanez .60 1.50
6 Jose Lopez 1.50 4.00
7 Julio Mateo .40 1.00
8 Joel Pineiro .40 1.00
9 Yorvit Torrealba .40 1.00

2006 Mariners Topps

SEA1 Felix Hernandez .20 .50
SEA2 Ichiro Suzuki .40 1.00
SEA3 Adrian Beltre .30 .75
SEA4 Richie Sexson .12 .30
SEA5 Raul Ibanez .20 .50
SEA6 Jeremy Reed .12 .30
SEA7 Jose Lopez .12 .30
SEA8 Joel Pineiro .12 .30
SEA9 Eddie Guardado .12 .30
SEA10 Gil Meche .12 .30
SEA11 Jamie Moyer .12 .30
SEA12 Jarrod Washburn .12 .30
SEA13 Mike Morse .12 .30
SEA14 Kenji Johjima .30 .75

2007 Mariners Topps

COMPLETE SET (14) 3.00 8.00
SEA1 Ichiro Suzuki .40 1.00
SEA2 Jose Lopez .12 .30
SEA3 Kenji Johjima .30 .75
SEA4 Yuniesky Betancourt .12 .30
SEA5 Adrian Beltre .30 .75
SEA6 Ben Broussard .12 .30
SEA7 Felix Hernandez .20 .50
SEA8 J.J. Putz .12 .30
SEA9 Richie Sexson .12 .30
SEA10 Jose Guillen .12 .30
SEA11 Horacio Ramirez .12 .30
SEA12 Jose Vidro .12 .30
SEA13 Jarrod Washburn .12 .30
SEA14 Raul Ibanez .20 .50

2008 Mariners Topps

COMPLETE SET (14) 3.00 8.00
SEA1 Ichiro Suzuki .40 1.00
SEA2 Jose Lopez .12 .30
SEA3 Kenji Johjima .12 .30
SEA4 Yuniesky Betancourt .12 .30
SEA5 Adrian Beltre .30 .75
SEA6 Carlos Silva .12 .30
SEA7 Felix Hernandez .20 .50
SEA8 J.J. Putz .12 .30
SEA9 Richie Sexson .12 .30
SEA10 Adam Jones .20 .50
SEA11 Miguel Batista .12 .30
SEA12 Jose Vidro .12 .30
SEA13 Jarrod Washburn .12 .30
SEA14 Raul Ibanez .20 .50

2009 Mariners Topps

SEA1 Ichiro Suzuki .50 1.25
SEA2 Felix Hernandez .25 .60
SEA3 Jose Lopez .15 .40
SEA4 Brandon Morrow .15 .40
SEA5 Adrian Beltre .40 1.00
SEA6 Matt Tuiasosopo .15 .40
SEA7 Kenji Johjima .25 .60
SEA8 Ken Griffey Jr. .75 2.00
SEA9 Yuniesky Betancourt .15 .40
SEA10 Erik Bedard .15 .40
SEA11 Wladimir Balentien .15 .40
SEA12 Franklin Gutierrez .15 .40
SEA13 Carlos Silva .15 .40
SEA14 Jeff Clement .15 .40
SEA15 Safeco Field .15 .40

2010 Mariners Topps

SEA1 Ken Griffey Jr. .75 2.00
SEA2 Michael Saunders .25 .60
SEA3 Jack Wilson .15 .40
SEA4 Milton Bradley .15 .40
SEA5 Ryan Langerhans .15 .40
SEA6 Josh Bard .15 .40
SEA7 Ichiro Suzuki .50 1.25
SEA8 Casey Kotchman .15 .40
SEA9 Ian Snell .15 .40
SEA10 David Aardsma .15 .40
SEA11 Felix Hernandez .25 .60
SEA12 Jose Lopez .15 .40
SEA13 Franklin Gutierrez .15 .40
SEA14 Ryan Rowland-Smith .15 .40
SEA15 Cliff Lee .25 .60
SEA16 Chone Figgins .15 .40
SEA17 Adam Moore .15 .40

2011 Mariners Topps

SEA1 Ichiro Suzuki .50 1.25
SEA2 Felix Hernandez .25 .60
SEA3 Franklin Gutierrez .15 .40
SEA4 Doug Fister .15 .40
SEA5 Chone Figgins .15 .40
SEA6 Jack Cust .15 .40
SEA7 Milton Bradley .15 .40
SEA8 Erik Bedard .15 .40
SEA9 Brendan Ryan .15 .40
SEA11 Josh Wilson .15 .40
SEA12 Michael Saunders .25 .60
SEA13 Miguel Olivo .15 .40
SEA14 Adam Moore .15 .40
SEA15 Jason Vargas .15 .40
SEA16 Jack Wilson .15 .40
SEA17 Safeco Field .15 .40
SEA 10 Rob Johnson .15 .40

2012 Mariners Topps

SEA1 Dustin Ackley .25 .60
SEA2 Ichiro Suzuki .50 1.25
SEA3 Trayvon Robinson .25 .60
SEA4 Franklin Gutierrez .25 .60
SEA5 Felix Hernandez .30 .75
SEA6 Jason Vargas .25 .60
SEA7 Brandon League .25 .60
SEA8 Brendan Ryan .25 .60
SEA9 Mike Carp .25 .60
SEA10 Miguel Olivo .25 .60
SEA11 Jesus Montero .25 .60
SEA12 Kyle Seager .25 .60
SEA13 Justin Smoak .30 .75
SEA14 Alex Liddi .25 .60
SEA15 Mariner Moose .15 .40
SEA16 The Kingdome .15 .40
SEA17 Safeco Field .15 .40

2013 Mariners Topps

COMPLETE SET (17) 3.00 8.00
SEA1 Felix Hernandez .20 .50
SEA2 Dustin Ackley .15 .40
SEA3 Kyle Seager .25 .60
SEA4 Kendrys Morales .15 .40
SEA5 Hisashi Iwakuma .20 .50
SEA6 Jesus Montero .25 .60
SEA7 Justin Smoak .15 .40
SEA8 Michael Saunders .20 .50
SEA9 Jason Bay .20 .50
SEA10 Franklin Gutierrez .15 .40
SEA11 Casper Wells .25 .60
SEA12 Michael Morse .15 .40
SEA13 Brendan Ryan .15 .40
SEA14 Blake Beavan .15 .40
SEA15 Erasmo Ramirez .15 .40
SEA16 Tom Wilhelmsen .15 .40
SEA17 Safeco Field .15 .40

2014 Mariners Topps

COMPLETE SET (17) 3.00 8.00
SEA1 Felix Hernandez .20 .50
SEA2 Dustin Ackley .15 .40
SEA3 Kyle Seager .15 .40
SEA4 Logan Morrison .15 .40
SEA5 Hisashi Iwakuma .20 .50
SEA6 Brad Miller .20 .50
SEA7 Justin Smoak .15 .40
SEA8 Michael Saunders .20 .50
SEA9 Taijuan Walker .15 .40
SEA10 Mike Zunino .15 .40
SEA11 Nick Franklin .15 .40
SEA12 Robinson Cano .20 .50
SEA13 Franklin Gutierrez .15 .40
SEA14 James Paxton .25 .60
SEA15 Corey Hart .15 .40
SEA16 Erasmo Ramirez .15 .40
SEA17 Safeco Field .15 .40

2015 Mariners Topps
COMPLETE SET (17) 3.00 8.00
SM1 Robinson Cano .20 .50
SM2 Charlie Furbush .15 .40
SM3 Felix Hernandez .20 .50
SM4 Austin Jackson .15 .40
SM5 Dominic Leone .15 .40
SM6 Logan Morrison .15 .40
SM7 Fernando Rodney .15 .40
SM8 Kyle Seager .15 .40
SM9 Chris Young .15 .40
SM10 Mike Zunino .15 .40
SM11 Hisashi Iwakuma .20 .50
SM12 Dustin Ackley .15 .40
SM13 Roenis Elias .15 .40
SM14 Chris Taylor .20 .50
SM15 Justin Ruggiano .15 .40
SM16 Seth Smith .15 .40
SM17 Nelson Cruz .25 .60

2016 Mariners Topps
COMPLETE SET (17) 3.00 8.00
SEA1 Nelson Cruz .25 .60
SEA2 Felix Hernandez .20 .50
SEA3 Chris Iannetta .15 .40
SEA4 Robinson Cano .20 .50
SEA5 Ketel Marte .30 .75
SEA6 Kyle Seager .15 .40
SEA7 Seth Smith .15 .40
SEA8 Hisashi Iwakuma .20 .50
SEA9 Adam Lind .20 .50
SEA10 James Paxton .20 .50
SEA11 Taijuan Walker .15 .40
SEA12 Steve Cishek .15 .40
SEA13 Nori Aoki .15 .40
SEA14 Leonys Martin .15 .40
SEA15 Nate Karns .15 .40
SEA16 Wade Miley .15 .40
SEA17 Franklin Gutierrez .15 .40

2017 Mariners Topps
COMPLETE SET (17) 3.00 8.00
SEA1 Robinson Cano .20 .50
SEA2 Jarrod Dyson .15 .40
SEA3 Shawn O'Malley .15 .40
SEA4 Felix Hernandez .20 .50
SEA5 Hisashi Iwakuma .20 .50
SEA6 Leonys Martin .15 .40
SEA7 Yovani Gallardo .15 .40
SEA8 James Paxton .20 .50
SEA9 Mike Zunino .15 .40
SEA10 Jean Segura .20 .50
SEA11 Mike Freeman .15 .40
SEA12 Edwin Diaz .20 .50
SEA13 Ben Gamel .20 .50
SEA14 Steve Cishek .15 .40
SEA15 Dan Vogelbach .25 .60
SEA16 Nelson Cruz .25 .60
SEA17 Kyle Seager .15 .40

2018 Mariners Topps
COMPLETE SET (17) 2.00 5.00
SM1 Robinson Cano .20 .50
SM2 Taylor Motter .15 .40
SM3 Jean Segura .15 .40
SM4 Marco Gonzalez .15 .40
SM5 Daniel Vogelbach .15 .40
SM6 Guillermo Heredia .15 .40
SM7 Taylor Motter .15 .40
SM8 Hisashi Iwakuma .20 .50
SM9 Edwin Diaz .20 .50
SM10 James Paxton .20 .50
SM11 Felix Hernandez .20 .50
SM12 Mike Zunino .15 .40
SM13 Mitch Haniger .20 .50
SM14 Ben Gamel .20 .50
SM15 Mike Leake .15 .40
SM16 Kyle Seager .15 .40
SM17 Nelson Cruz .25 .60

2019 Mariners Topps
COMPLETE SET (17) 3.00 8.00
SM1 Mitch Haniger .20 .50
SM2 Ryon Healy .15 .40
SM3 Kyle Seager .15 .40
SM4 Jay Bruce .20 .50
SM5 Dee Gordon .15 .40
SM6 Mallex Smith .15 .40
SM7 David Freitas .15 .40
SM8 Sam Tuivailala .15 .40
SM9 Edwin Encarnacion .25 .60
SM10 Marco Gonzales .15 .40
SM11 Wade LeBlanc .15 .40
SM12 Felix Hernandez .20 .50
SM13 Justus Sheffield .25 .60
SM14 Dan Vogelbach .15 .40
SM15 Yusei Kikuchi .25 .60
SM16 J.P. Crawford .15 .40
SM17 Omar Narvaez .20 .50

2020 Mariners Topps
SEA1 Dee Gordon .15 .40
SEA2 Kyle Lewis 1.25 3.00
SEA3 Marco Gonzales .15 .40
SEA4 Yusei Kikuchi .20 .50
SEA5 Kyle Seager .15 .40
SEA6 Austin Nola .25 .60
SEA7 Dan Vogelbach .15 .40
SEA8 Mallex Smith .15 .40
SEA9 Mitch Haniger .20 .50
SEA10 J.P. Crawford .15 .40
SEA11 Tim Lopes .20 .50
SEA12 Dylan Moore .15 .40
SEA13 Justus Sheffield .25 .60
SEA14 Jake Fraley .20 .50
SEA15 Justin Dunn .20 .50
SEA16 Sam Tuivailala .15 .40
SEA17 Reggie McClain .25 .60

2017 Mariners Topps National Baseball Card Day
COMPLETE SET (10) 5.00 12.00
SEA1 Robinson Cano .75 2.00
SEA2 Hisashi Iwakuma .75 2.00
SEA3 Kyle Seager .60 1.50
SEA4 Jean Segura .75 2.00
SEA5 Nelson Cruz 1.00 2.50
SEA6 Felix Hernandez .75 2.00
SEA7 Mitch Haniger 1.00 2.50
SEA8 Edwin Diaz .75 2.00
SEA9 James Paxton .75 2.00
SEA10 Edgar Martinez .75 2.00

1962 Maris Game
These cards, were issued as part of the Roger Maris board game issued in 1962. Since each of the 88 cards in the set feature the same photo, we are only listing one card from the set. Each card is the same value. These cards came from the "Roger Maris Baseball Game" which was produced by Play-Rite.
1 Roger Maris 4.00 10.00

1962 Maris Gehl's
These black and white photos 4" by 5" photos were issued in packages of Gehl's ice-cream and feature cards of then single-season home run king, Roger Maris.
COMPLETE SET (6) 6000.00 9000.00

1987 Marketcom Sports Illustrated
This 20-card white-bordered, multi-sport set measures approximately 3 1/16" by 4 14/16" and features color action photos of players in various sports produced by Marketcom. Cards #1-13 display Baseball players; cards #14-17, Basketball players; cards #18-20, Football players. The backs are blank. The set was issued to promote the Sports Illustrated sticker line. The cards are unnumbered and checklisted below alphabetically within each sport.
COMPLETE SET (20) 60.00 150.00
1 Wade Boggs 3.00 8.00
2 Gary Carter 1.50 4.00
3 Roger Clemens 8.00 20.00
4 Eric Davis 1.25 3.00
5 Andrew Dawson 2.00 5.00
6 Dwight Gooden 1.25 3.00
7 Rickey Henderson 2.00 5.00
8 Don Mattingly 6.00 15.00
9 Dale Murray 1.50 4.00
10 Kirby Puckett 6.00 15.00
11 Ryne Sandberg 6.00 15.00
12 Ozzie Smith 6.00 15.00
13 Darryl Strawberry .75 2.00

1993 Marlins Florida Agriculture
These were given out in eight-card perforated sheets at the Sunshine State Games in Tallahassee in July 1993. The sheet measures approximately 7" by 10" and features two rows of standard-size cards. Also a 8 1/12" by 11" playing-field board was included with the set for use in playing a baseball card game. The fronts feature color photos of the players posing with various fruits and vegetables. The Florida Agriculture Department's Fresh 2-U logo appears in the upper left. The backs carry player information on the upper panel and Florida agricultural statistics on the lower panel.
COMPLETE SET (8) 2.50 6.00
1 Title Card .30 .75
2 Billy the Marlin/(Mascot) .60 1.50
3 Ryan Bowen .30 .75
4 Benito Santiago .40 1.00
5 Richie Lewis .30 .75
6 Bret Barberie .30 .75
7 Rich Renteria .30 .75
8 Jeff Conine .75 2.00

1993 Marlins Stadium Club
This 30-card standard-size set features the 1993 Florida Marlins. The set was issued in hobby (plastic box) and retail (blister) form as well as being distributed in shrinkwrapped cardboard boxes with a manager card pictured on it.
COMPLETE SET (30) 1.50 4.00
1 Nigel Wilson .02 .10
2 Bryan Harvey .02 .10
3 Bob McClure .02 .10
4 Alex Arias .02 .10
5 Walt Weiss .02 .10
6 Charlie Hough .08 .25
7 Scott Chiamparino .02 .10
8 Junior Felix .02 .10
9 Jack Armstrong .02 .10
10 Dave Magadan .02 .10
11 Cris Carpenter .02 .10
12 Benito Santiago .08 .25
13 Jeff Conine .02 .10
14 Jerry Don Gleaton .02 .10
15 Steve Decker .02 .10
16 Ryan Bowen .02 .10
17 Ramon Martinez .02 .10
18 Bret Barberie .02 .10
19 Monty Fariss .02 .10
20 Trevor Hoffman .30 .75
21 Scott Pose .02 .10
22 Mike Myers .02 .10
23 Geronimo Berroa .02 .10
24 Darrell Whitmore .02 .10
25 Chuck Carr .02 .10
26 Dave Weathers .02 .10
27 Matt Turner .02 .10
28 Jose Martinez .02 .10
29 Orestes Destrade .02 .10
30 Carl Everett .08 .25

1993 Marlins Publix
Sponsored by Coca-Cola, this 30-card standard-size inaugural season Marlins set features color player action photos on its fronts. The cards are unnumbered and checklisted below in alphabetical order.
COMPLETE SET (30) 5.00 12.00
1 Luis Aquino .08 .25
2 Alex Arias .08 .25
3 Jack Armstrong .08 .25
4 Bret Barberie .08 .25
5 Ryan Bowen .08 .25
6 Greg Briley .08 .25
7 Chuck Carr .08 .25
8 Jeff Conine .40 1.00
9 Henry Cotto .08 .25
10 Orestes Destrade .08 .25
11 Chris Hammond .08 .25
12 Bryan Harvey .20 .50
13 Charlie Hough .30 .75
14 Joe Klink .08 .25
15 Rene Lachemann MG .08 .25
16 Richie Lewis .08 .25
17 Bob Natal .08 .25
18 Robb Nen .40 1.00
19 Pat Rapp .08 .25
20 Rich Renteria .08 .25
21 Rich Rodriguez .08 .25
22 Benito Santiago .20 .50
23 Gary Sheffield .60 1.50
24 Matt Turner .08 .25
25 Walt Weiss .20 .50
26 Darrell Whitmore .08 .25
27 Nigel Wilson .08 .25
28 Marcel Lachemann CO .20 .50
Vada Pinson CO
Doug Rader CO
29 Billy the Marlin/(Mascot) .20 .50
30 Coupon card .08 .25

1993 Marlins U.S. Playing Cards
This 56-card standard-size set celebrates the 1993 Inaugural Year of the Florida Marlins. Since this set is similar to a playing card set, the set is checklisted below as if it were a playing card deck. In the checklist C means Clubs, D means Diamonds, H means Hearts, S means Spades, and JK means Joker. The cards are checklisted in playing order by suits and numbers are assigned to Aces, (1) Jacks, (11) Queens, (12) and Kings (13). Included in the set are a Marlins' opening day player roster card and a 1993 home schedule card. The jokers, home schedule card and the opening day player roster card are unnumbered and listed at the end of our checklist.
COMPLETE SET (56) 1.50 4.00
1C Walt Weiss .01 .05
1D Dave Magadan .01 .05
1H Benito Santiago .02 .10
1S Alex Arias .01 .05
2C Dave Magadan .01 .05
2D Jack Armstrong .01 .05
2H Walt Weiss .01 .05
2S Benito Santiago .02 .10
3C Cris Carpenter .01 .05
3D Bryan Harvey .01 .05
3H Monty Fariss .01 .05
3S Ryan Bowen .01 .05
4C Dave Magadan .01 .05
4D Richie Lewis .01 .05
4H Chris Hammond .01 .05
4S Steve Decker .01 .05
5C Bob McClure .01 .05
5D Scott Pose .01 .05
5H Joe Klink .01 .05
5S Jeff Conine .10 .30
6C Junior Felix .01 .05
6D Rich Renteria .01 .05
6H Chuck Carr .01 .05
6S Bret Barberie .01 .05
7C Walt Weiss .01 .05
7D Trevor Hoffman .20 .50
7H Alex Arias .01 .05
7S Orestes Destrade .01 .05
8C Steve Decker .01 .05
8D Jim Corsi .01 .05
8H Charlie Hough .02 .10
8S Greg Briley .01 .05
9C Jeff Conine .10 .30
9D Ryan Bowen .01 .05
9H Junior Felix .01 .05
9S Charlie Hough .02 .10
10C Bryan Harvey .01 .05
10D Orestes Destrade .01 .05
10H Jim Corsi .01 .05
10S Rob Natal .01 .05
11C Orestes Destrade .01 .05
11D Bret Barberie .01 .05
11H Jeff Conine .10 .30
11S Jack Armstrong .01 .05
12C Chris Hammond .02 .10
12D Chuck Carr .01 .05
12H Trevor Hoffman .20 .50
12S Junior Felix .01 .05
13C Monty Farris .01 .05
13D Cris Carpenter .01 .05
13H Rich Renteria .01 .05
13S Richie Lewis .01 .05
JKO National League Logo .01 .05
NNO 1993 Home Schedule .01 .05

1993 Marlins Upper Deck
This 27-card set of the Florida Marlins features the same design as the players' 1993 regular Upper Deck cards. The difference is found in the gold foil stamping. The cards are checklisted below according to their corresponding numbers in the regular Upper Deck set.
COMPLETE SET (27) 2.00 5.00
9 Nigel Wilson .02 .10
435 Charles Johnson .25 .60
479 Dave Magadan .02 .10
Orestes Destrade
Bret Barberie
Jef
506 Jose Martinez .02 .10
518 Charlie Hough .08 .25
524 Orestes Destrade .02 .10
528 Dave Magadan .02 .10
533 Walt Weiss .02 .10
552 Bret Barberie .02 .10
590 Chuck Carr .02 .10
631 Alex Arias .02 .10
634 Greg Briley .02 .10
661 Chris Hammond .02 .10
684 Bryan Harvey .08 .25
711 Luis Aquino .02 .10
715 Joe Klink .02 .10
717 Monty Fariss .02 .10
726 Cris Carpenter .02 .10
744 Steve Decker .02 .10
754 Jeff Conine .15 .40
758 Jack Armstrong .02 .10
762 Scott Pose .02 .10
771 Junior Felix .02 .10
773 Trevor Hoffman .25 .60
776 Benito Santiago .08 .25
780 Ryan Bowen .02 .10
825 Nigel Wilson CL .02 .10

1994 Marlins Team Issue
This 17-card blank-backed set of the Florida Marlins measures approximately 3 1/2" by 5" and features black-and-white player portraits with white borders. The cards are unnumbered and checklisted below in alphabetical order.
COMPLETE SET (17) 5.00 12.00
1 Bret Barberie .20 .50
2 Ryan Bowen .20 .50
3 Chuck Carr .20 .50
4 Jeff Conine .60 1.50
5 Chris Hammond .30 .75
6 Bryan Harvey .30 .75
7 Charlie Hough .40 1.00
8 Charles Johnson .20 .50
9 Richie Lewis .20 .50
10 Dave Magadan .20 .50
11 Bob Natal .20 .50
12 Robb Nen .60 1.50
13 Pat Rapp .20 .50
14 Rich Renteria .20 .50
15 Benito Santiago .30 .75
16 Gary Sheffield .75 2.00
17 Darrell Whitmore .20 .50

1997 Marlins Pacific
This 33-card set was produced by Pacific for the Florida Marlins and sponsored by NationsBank. The cards were distributed to 16,000 kids twelve years old and under at the Marlins Kids Opening Day game on June 27, 1996. The fronts feature borderless color action player photos. The backs carry a small player portrait, player information and statistics printed in both Spanish and English.
COMPLETE SET (33) 3.00 8.00
1 Kurt Abbott .08 .25
2 Moises Alou .20 .50
3 Alex Arias .08 .25
4 Bobby Bonilla .20 .50
5 Kevin Brown .40 1.00
6 John Cangelosi .08 .25
7 Luis Castillo .40 1.00
8 Jeff Conine .30 .75
9 Jim Eisenreich .20 .50
10 Alex Fernandez .08 .25
11 Cliff Floyd .40 1.00
12 Rick Helling .08 .25
13 Felix Heredia .08 .25
14 Mark Hutton .08 .25
15 Charles Johnson .08 .25
16 Al Leiter .40 1.00
17 Robb Nen .20 .50
18 Jay Powell .08 .25
19 Pat Rapp .08 .25
20 Edgar Renteria .30 .75
21 Tony Saunders .08 .25
22 Gary Sheffield .60 1.50
23 Devon White .08 .25
24 Gregg Zaun .08 .25
25 Jim Leyland MG
26 Rich Donnelly CO .08 .25
27 Bruce Kimm CO .08 .25
28 Jerry Manuel CO .08 .25
29 Milt May CO .08 .25
30 Larry Rothschild CO .08 .25
31 Tommy Sandt CO .08 .25
32 Billy the Marlin(Mascot) .08 .25
NNO Title Card CL .08 .25

2000 Marlins Kids
COMPLETE SET 6.00 15.00
1 Armando Almanaza .20 .50
2 Antonio Alfonseca .20 .50
3 David Berg .20 .50
4 John Boles MG .20 .50
5 Joe Breeden CO .20 .50
6 A.J. Burnett .60 1.50
7 Luis Castillo .60 1.50
8 Vic Darensbourg .20 .50
9 Ryan Dempster .20 .50
10 Rich Dubee CO .20 .50
11 Alex Fernandez .20 .50
12 Cliff Floyd .60 1.50
13 Alex Gonzalez .20 .50
14 Fredi Gonzalez CO .20 .50
15 Mark Kotsay .20 .50
16 Mike Lowell .30 .75
17 Derrek Lee .75 2.00
18 Braden Looper .30 .75
19 Jack Maloof CO .20 .50
20 Dan Miceli .20 .50
21 Kevin Millar .60 1.50
22 Vladimir Nunez .20 .50
23 Brad Penny .60 1.50
24 Mike Redmond .20 .50
25 Jesus Sanchez .20 .50
26 Preston Wilson .30 .75

2002 Marlins Kids
COMPLETE SET 3.00 8.00
1 Armando Almanza .20 .50
2 Josh Beckett 1.25 3.00
3 A.J. Burnett .40 1.00
4 Luis Castillo .60 1.50
5 Ryan Dempster .20 .50
6 Cliff Floyd .60 1.50
7 Andy Fox .20 .50
8 Charles Johnson .30 .75
9 Derrek Lee .75 2.00
10 Braden Looper .30 .75
11 Mike Lowell .30 .75
12 Kevin Millar .60 1.50
13 Vladimir Nunez .20 .50
14 Eric Owens .20 .50
15 Tim Raines .60 1.50
16 Mike Redmond .20 .50
17 Michael Tejera .20 .50

2003 Marlins Team Issue
COMPLETE SET 7.50 15.00
1 Armando Almanza .20 .50
2 Josh Beckett 1.00 2.50
3 A.J. Burnett .60 1.50
4 Luis Castillo .60 1.50
5 Juan Encarnacion .40 1.00
6 Andy Fox .20 .50
7 Alex Gonzalez .30 .75
8 Todd Hollandsworth .20 .50
9 Derrek Lee .75 2.00
10 Braden Looper .30 .75
11 Mike Lowell .30 .75
12 Jack McKeon MG .20 .50
13 Carl Pavano .40 1.00
14 Brad Penny .60 1.50
15 Juan Pierre .60 1.50
16 Mark Redman .20 .50
17 Mike Redmond .20 .50
18 Ivan Rodriguez .75 2.00
19 Tim Spooneybarger .20 .50
20 Michael Tejera .20 .50

2004 Marlins Team Issue
COMPLETE SET 8.00 20.00
1 Pierre Arsenault BC
2 Josh Beckett .60 1.50
3 Armando Benitez .40 1.00
4 Nate Bump .20 .50
5 A.J. Burnett .60 1.50
6 Luis Castillo .60 1.50
7 Miguel Cabrera .75 2.00
8 Ramon Castro .20 .50
9 Hee Seop Choi .40 1.00
10 Jeff Conine .30 .75
11 Wil Cordero .20 .50
12 Jeff Cox CO .20 .50
13 Doug Davis CO .20 .50
14 Andre Dawson .75 2.00
15 Damion Easley .20 .50
16 Chad Fox .20 .50
17 Alex Gonzalez .20 .50
18 Lenny Harris .20 .50
19 Perry Hill CO .20 .50
20 Mike Lowell .30 .75
21 Jack McKeon MG .20 .50
22 Mike Mordecai .20 .50
23 Abraham Nunez .20 .50
24 Darren Oliver .20 .50
25 Matt Perisho .20 .50
25 Carl Pavano .40 1.00
26 Brad Penny .40 1.00
27 Tony Perez .75 2.00
28 Juan Pierre .60 1.50
29 Mike Redmond .20 .50
30 Bill Robinson CO .20 .50
31 Wayne Rosenthal CO .20 .50
32 Tim Spooneybarger .20 .50
33 Tony Taylor CO .20 .50
34 Justin Wayne .20 .50
35 Dontrelle Willis .60 1.50
36 Billy the Marlin .20 .50
Mascot

2005 Marlins Team Issue
COMPLETE SET
1 Pierre Arsenault COOR .20 .50
2 Chris Aguila .20 .50
3 Antonio Alfonseca .20 .50
4 Josh Beckett .50 1.25
5 Nate Bump .20 .50
6 A.J. Burnett .50 1.25
7 Miguel Cabrera .75 2.00
8 Luis Castillo .50 1.25
9 Jeff Conine .30 .75
10 Jeff Cox CO .20 .50
11 Andre Dawson ASST .60 1.50
12 Carlos Delgado .75 2.00
13 Luis Dorante CO .20 .50
14 Harry Dunlop .20 .50
15 Damion Easley .20 .50
16 Juan Encarnacion .40 1.00
17 Alex Gonzalez .20 .50
18 Lenny Harris .20 .50
19 Perry Hill CO .20 .50
20 Todd Jones .30 .75
21 Al Leiter .30 .75
22 Paul LoDuca .30 .75
23 Mike Lowell .30 .75
24 Jack McKeon MG .20 .50
25 Jim Mecir .20 .50
26 Brian Moehler .20 .50
27 Guillermo Mota .20 .50
28 Tony Perez ASST .60 1.50
29 Matt Perisho .20 .50
30 Juan Pierre .50 1.25
31 John Riedling .20 .50
32 Bill Robinson CO .20 .50
33 Tim Spooneybarger .20 .50
34 Matt Treanor .20 .50
35 Ismael Valdez .20 .50
36 Mark Wiley .20 .50
37 Dontrelle Willis .75 2.00

2006 Marlins Topps
FLA1 Wes Helms .12 .30
FLA2 Robert Andino .12 .30
FLA3 Hanley Ramirez .20 .50
FLA4 Brian Moehler .12 .30
FLA5 Matt Treanor .12 .30
FLA6 Mike Jacobs .12 .30
FLA7 Jeremy Hermida .12 .30
FLA8 Miguel Cabrera .30 .75
FLA9 Dontrelle Willis .12 .30
FLA10 Nate Bump .12 .30
FLA11 Miguel Olivo .12 .30
FLA12 Jason Vargas .12 .30
FLA13 Scott Olsen .12 .30
FLA14 Josh Willingham .20 .50

2007 Marlins Topps
COMPLETE SET (14) 3.00 8.00
FLA1 Miguel Cabrera .30 .75
FLA2 Dan Uggla .12 .30
FLA3 Alfredo Amezaga .12 .30
FLA4 Jeremy Hermida .12 .30
FLA5 Dontrelle Willis .12 .30
FLA6 Mike Jacobs .12 .30
FLA7 Josh Johnson .30 .75
FLA8 Aaron Boone .12 .30
FLA9 Hanley Ramirez .20 .50
FLA10 Miguel Olivo .12 .30
FLA11 Scott Olsen .12 .30
FLA12 Ricky Nolasco .12 .30
FLA13 Josh Willingham .20 .50
FLA14 Anibal Sanchez .12 .30

2008 Marlins Topps
COMPLETE SET (14) 3.00 8.00
FLA1 Hanley Ramirez .20 .50
FLA2 Dan Uggla .12 .30
FLA3 Alfredo Amezaga .12 .30
FLA4 Jeremy Hermida .12 .30
FLA5 Andrew Miller .20 .50
FLA6 Mike Jacobs .12 .30
FLA7 Jose Castillo .12 .30
FLA8 Kevin Gregg .12 .30
FLA9 Cameron Maybin .12 .30
FLA10 Rick VandenHurk .12 .30
FLA11 Scott Olsen .12 .30
FLA12 Cody Ross .12 .30
FLA13 Josh Willingham .20 .50
FLA14 Mike Rabelo .12 .30

2009 Marlins Topps
FLA1 Hanley Ramirez .25 .60
FLA2 Josh Johnson .25 .60
FLA3 Dan Uggla .15 .40
FLA4 Ricky Nolasco .15 .40
FLA5 Jorge Cantu .15 .40
FLA6 Matt Lindstrom .15 .40
FLA7 Chris Volstad .15 .40
FLA8 Alfredo Amezaga .15 .40
FLA9 Gaby Sanchez .25 .60
FLA10 Jeremy Hermida .15 .40
FLA11 Andrew Miller .25 .60
FLA12 Cody Ross .15 .40
FLA13 Cameron Maybin .15 .40
FLA14 John Baker .15 .40
FLA15 Billy The Marlin .15 .40

2010 Marlins Topps
FLA1 Hanley Ramirez .25 .60
FLA2 Gaby Sanchez .15 .40
FLA3 Josh Johnson .25 .60
FLA4 Chris Coghlan .15 .40
FLA5 Ricky Nolasco .15 .40
FLA6 Leo Nunez .15 .40
FLA7 John Baker .15 .40
FLA8 Emilio Bonifacio .15 .40
FLA9 Cameron Maybin .15 .40
FLA10 Jorge Cantu .15 .40
FLA11 Andrew Miller .25 .60
FLA12 Anibal Sanchez .15 .40
FLA13 Chris Volstad .15 .40
FLA14 Cody Ross .15 .40
FLA15 Dan Uggla .15 .40
FLA16 Sean West .15 .40
FLA17 Ronny Paulino .15 .40

2011 Marlins Topps
FLA1 Hanley Ramirez .25 .60
FLA2 Chris Coghlan .15 .40
FLA3 Josh Johnson .25 .60
FLA4 Chris Volstad .15 .40
FLA5 Gaby Sanchez .15 .40
FLA6 Mike Stanton .40 1.00
FLA7 John Baker .15 .40
FLA8 John Buck .15 .40
FLA9 Logan Morrison .15 .40
FLA10 Ricky Nolasco .15 .40
FLA11 Leo Nunez .15 .40
FLA12 Anibal Sanchez .15 .40
FLA13 Omar Infante .15 .40
FLA14 Emilio Bonifacio .15 .40
FLA15 Javier Vazquez .15 .40
FLA16 Wes Helms .15 .40
FLA17 Sun Life Stadium .15 .40

2012 Marlins Topps
MIA1 Jose Reyes .25 .60
MIA2 Logan Morrison .25 .60
MIA3 Anibal Sanchez .25 .60
MIA4 Ricky Nolasco .25 .60
MIA5 Omar Infante .25 .60
MIA6 Hanley Ramirez .30 .75
MIA7 Josh Johnson .30 .75
MIA8 Emilio Bonifacio .25 .60
MIA9 John Buck .25 .60
MIA10 Mark Buehrle .30 .75
MIA11 Heath Bell .25 .60
MIA12 Mike Stanton .40 1.00
MIA13 Gaby Sanchez .30 .75
MIA14 Matt Dominguez .30 .75
MIA15 Carlos Zambrano .30 .75
MIA16 Bryan Petersen .25 .60
MIA17 Marlins Park .15 .40

2013 Marlins Topps
COMPLETE SET (17) 3.00 8.00
MIA1 Giancarlo Stanton .25 .60
MIA2 Juan Pierre .25 .60
MIA3 Justin Ruggiano .25 .60
MIA4 Greg Dobbs .25 .60
MIA5 Adeiny Hechavarria .30 .75
MIA6 Rob Brantly .15 .40
MIA7 Ricky Nolasco .25 .60
MIA8 Logan Morrison .25 .60
MIA9 Donovan Solano .25 .60
MIA10 Steve Cishek .15 .40
MIA11 Jacob Turner .30 .75
MIA12 Henderson Alvarez .15 .40
MIA13 Nate Eovaldi .20 .50
MIA14 Wade LeBlanc .15 .40
MIA15 Placido Polanco .25 .60
MIA16 A.J. Ramos .20 .50
MIA17 Marlins Park .15 .40

2014 Marlins Topps
COMPLETE SET (17) 3.00 8.00
MIA1 Giancarlo Stanton .25 .60
MIA2 Jose Fernandez .25 .60
MIA3 Jake Marisnick .15 .40
MIA4 Garrett Jones .15 .40
MIA5 Adeiny Hechavarria .15 .40
MIA6 Casey McGehee .15 .40
MIA7 Marcell Ozuna .25 .60
MIA8 Ed Lucas .15 .40
MIA9 Donovan Solano .25 .60
MIA10 Steve Cishek .15 .40
MIA11 Jacob Turner .20 .50
MIA12 Henderson Alvarez .15 .40
MIA13 Nathan Eovaldi .20 .50
MIA14 Christian Yelich .30 .75
MIA15 Jarrod Saltalamacchia .15 .40
MIA16 Rafael Furcal .15 .40
MIA17 Marlins Park .15 .40

2015 Marlins Topps
COMPLETE SET (17) 3.00 8.00
MM1 Giancarlo Stanton .25 .60
MM2 Steve Cishek .15 .40
MM3 Justin Bour .25 .60
MM4 Martin Prado .15 .40
MM5 Tom Koehler .15 .40
MM6 Bryan Morris .15 .40
MM7 Jarrod Saltalamacchia .15 .40
MM8 Carter Capps .15 .40
MM9 Christian Yelich .30 .75
MM10 Henderson Alvarez .15 .40
MM11 Adeiny Hechavarria .15 .40
MM12 Marcell Ozuna .25 .60
MM13 Jose Fernandez .25 .60
MM14 Dee Gordon .15 .40
MM15 Donovan Solano .25 .60
MM16 Michael Morse .15 .40
MM17 Mat Latos .20 .50

2016 Marlins Topps
COMPLETE SET (17) 3.00 8.00
CC1 Giancarlo Stanton .25 .60
MM2 J.T. Realmuto .25 .60
MM3 Justin Bour .20 .50
MM4 Dee Gordon .15 .40
MM5 Adeiny Hechavarria .15 .40
MM6 Martin Prado .15 .40
MM7 Christian Yelich .30 .75
MM8 Marcell Ozuna .25 .60
MM9 Ichiro Suzuki .30 .75
MM10 Jose Fernandez .25 .60
MM11 Tom Koehler .15 .40
MM12 A.J. Ramos .15 .40
MM13 Carter Capps .15 .40
MM14 Jarred Cosart .15 .40
MM15 David Phelps .15 .40
MM16 Jeff Mathis .20 .50
FLA17 Wei-Yin Chen .15 .40

2017 Marlins Topps
COMPLETE SET (17) 3.00 8.00
MIA1 Giancarlo Stanton .25 .60
MIA2 Miguel Rojas .15 .40
MIA3 Adam Conley .15 .40
MIA4 Marcell Ozuna .25 .60
MIA5 Adeiny Hechavarria .15 .40
MIA6 Derek Dietrich .20 .50
MIA7 Christian Yelich .30 .75
MIA8 Ichiro .30 .75
MIA9 Justin Bour .20 .50
MIA10 Edinson Volquez .15 .40
MIA11 A.J. Ramos .15 .40
MIA12 Martin Prado .15 .40
MIA13 Dee Gordon .15 .40
MIA14 J.T. Realmuto .25 .60
MIA15 Wei-Yin Chen .15 .40
MIA16 Tom Koehler .15 .40
MIA17 A.J. Ellis .15 .40

2018 Marlins Topps
COMPLETE SET (17) 2.00 5.00
MM1 Justin Bour .15 .40
MM2 Brian Anderson .20 .50
MM3 Wei-Yin Chen .15 .40
MM4 J.T. Realmuto .25 .60
MM5 Miguel Rojas .15 .40
MM6 Martin Prado .15 .40
MM7 Adam Conley .15 .40
MM8 Dillon Peters .15 .40
MM9 Christian Yelich .30 .75
MM10 Braxton Lee .15 .40
MM11 Derek Dietrich .20 .50
MM12 Jose Urena .15 .40
MM13 JT Riddle .15 .40
MM14 Dan Straily .15 .40
MM15 Brad Ziegler .15 .40
MM16 Magneuris Sierra .25 .60
MM17 Junichi Tazawa .15 .40

2019 Marlins Topps
COMPLETE SET (17) 2.00 5.00
MM1 J.T. Realmuto .25 .60
MM2 Brian Anderson .15 .40
MM3 Starlin Castro .15 .40
MM4 Lewis Brinson .15 .40
MM5 J.T. Riddle .15 .40
MM6 Tayron Guerrero .15 .40
MM7 Austin Dean .15 .40
MM8 Peter O'Brien .15 .40
MM9 Jose Urena .15 .40
MM10 Trevor Richards .15 .40
MM11 Sandy Alcantara .15 .40
MM12 Wei-Yin Chen .15 .40
MM13 Miguel Rojas .15 .40
MM14 Adam Conley .15 .40
MM15 Jeff Brigham .15 .40
MM16 Isaac Galloway .15 .40
MM17 Magneuris Sierra .25 .60

2020 Marlins Topps
MIA1 Jesus Aguilar .20 .50
MIA2 Pablo Lopez .15 .40
MIA3 Miguel Rojas .15 .40
MIA4 Isan Diaz .25 .60
MIA5 Marlins Park .15 .40
MIA6 Jorge Alfaro .15 .40
MIA7 Jonathan Villar .15 .40
MIA8 Brian Anderson .15 .40
MIA9 Sandy Alcantara .15 .40
MIA10 Jose Urena .15 .40
MIA11 Caleb Smith .15 .40
MIA12 Jordan Yamamoto .15 .40
MIA13 JT Riddle .15 .40
MIA14 Garrett Cooper .15 .40
MIA15 Harold Ramirez .15 .40
MIA16 Lewis Brinson .15 .40
MIA17 Robert Dugger .15 .40

2017 Marlins Topps National Baseball Card Day
COMPLETE SET (10) 5.00 12.00
MIA1 Christian Yelich 1.25 3.00
MIA2 Marcell Ozuna 1.00 2.50
MIA3 Martin Prado .60 1.50
MIA4 Wei-Yin Chen .60 1.50
MIA5 Giancarlo Stanton 1.00 2.50
MIA6 Ichiro 1.25 3.00
MIA7 Justin Bour .75 2.00
MIA8 A.J. Ramos .60 1.50
MIA9 Adeiny Hechavarria .60 1.50
MIA10 Ivan Rodriguez .75 2.00

2004 Maryland Lottery
COMPLETE SET (50) 20.00 50.00
COMP.SET w/out SP's (45) .10 .25

COMMON CARD (1-45) .20 .50
COMMON SP (46-50) .75 2.00
1 Luis Aparicio .40 1.00
2 Steve Barber .20 .50
3 Don Baylor .40 1.00
4 Mark Belanger .20 .50
5 Mike Boddicker .20 .50
6 Don Buford .20 .50
7 Al Bumbry .20 .50
8 Mike Cuellar .30 .75
9 Rich Dauer .20 .50
10 Storm Davis .20 .50
11 Doug DeCinces .20 .50
12 Pat Dobson .20 .50
13 Moe Drabowsky .20 .50
14 Andy Etchebarren .20 .50
15 Bobby Grich .30 .75
16 George Kell .40 1.00
17 Tito Landrum .20 .50
18 Lee MacPhail GM .30 .75
19 Tippy Martinez .20 .50
20 Scott McGregor .20 .50
21 Dave McNally .30 .75
22 Milt Pappas .30 .75
23 Paul Richards MG .30 .75
24 Gary Roenicke .20 .50
25 Dave Schmidt .20 .50
26 Steve Stone .30 .75
27 Gus Triandos .20 .50
28 Gene Woodling .20 .50
29 Terry Crowley .20 .50
30 Elrod Hendricks .20 .50
31 Municipal Stadium .20 .50
32 Oriole Park .20 .50
33 Rex Barney ANN .30 .75
34 Rick Dempsey .20 .50
35 Mike Flanagan .30 .75
36 Jim Gentile .20 .50
37 Reggie Jackson .75 2.00
38 Frank Robinson .75 2.00
39 Chuck Thompson ANN .20 .50
40 Earl Weaver MG .40 1.00
41 Opening Day 1954 .20 .50
42 Brady Anderson .40 1.00
43 Boog Powell .40 1.00
44 Brooks Robinson .75 2.00
45 Jim Palmer .75 2.00
46 1966 World Series .75 2.00
47 1970 World Series .75 2.00
48 1983 World Series .75 2.00
49 2131 Ironman Breaks Record 4.00 10.00
Scoreboard Picture
50 Babe Ruth 8.00 20.00

1994 Mascot Mania

Given out in Pittsburgh during July 9 through 12, 1994, this 16-card set measures the standard size and features 16 MLB mascots. The cards are unnumbered and checklisted below in alphabetical order.

COMPLETE SET (16) 3.00 8.00
1 Bernie Brewer .20 .50
Milwaukee Brewers
2 Billy the Marlin .20 .50
Florida Marlins
3 BJ Birdy .20 .50
Toronto Blue Jays
4 Bluepper .20 .50
San Diego Padres
5 Dinger .20 .50
Colorado Rockies
6 Fredbird .20 .50
St. Louis Cardinals
7 Homer the Brave .20 .50
Atlanta Braves
8 Mariner Moose .20 .50
Seattle Mariners
9 Orbit .20 .50
Houston Astros
10 Oriole Bird .20 .50
Baltimore Orioles
11 Phillie Phanatic .40 1.00
Philadelphia Phillies
12 Pirate Parrot .20 .50
Pittsburgh Pirates
13 Rally .40 1.00
Atlanta Braves
14 Slider .40 1.00
Cleveland Indians
15 Trunk .20 .50
Oakland Athletics
16 Youppi .20 .50
Montreal Expos

1989 Master Bread Discs

The 1989 Master Bread disc set contains 12 discs each measuring 2 3/4" in diameter. The set was produced by MSA; there are no team logos featured on the disc. The year and lifetime statistics are featured for each player on the back of the disc. The set features only American League players.

COMPLETE SET (12) 8.00 20.00
1 Frank Viola .20 .50
2 Kirby Puckett 1.25 3.00
3 Gary Gaetti .20 .50
4 Alan Trammell .60 1.50
5 Wade Boggs 1.00 2.50
6 Don Mattingly 2.00 5.00
7 Wally Joyner .40 1.00
8 Paul Molitor 1.00 2.50
9 George Brett 2.00 5.00
10 Jose Canseco 1.00 2.50
11 Julio Franco .75 2.00
12 Cal Ripken Jr. 4.00 10.00

1989 Mathewson Bucknell

This one card set, which measures approximately 2 5/8" by 3 1/2" was issued by Bucknell to commemorate the dedication of the stadium there in his honor. The front has a drawing by noted sports artist M. Schact and the back has information about Mathewson's time both at Bucknell and as a major league pitcher.

1 Christy Mathewson .75 2.00

1992 Mattingly's Restaurant

This standard-size card was sold as a fund-raiser at Don Mattingly's restaurant in Evansville, Indiana. The front features Mattingly along with two handicapped youths. The back has vital statistics, career information and some highlights.

1 Don Mattingly 1.25 3.00

1909-17 Max Stein/United States Publishing House PC758

These sepia-colored postcards were issued from the 1909-16 time period. The Marquard and Zimmerman cards have "United States Pub." marked on the back, leading to the theory that perhaps these two cards belong to another postcard set. The backs are quite attractive.

COMPLETE SET (25) 4000.00 8000.00
1 Ping Bodie 75.00 150.00
2 Frank Chance 150.00 300.00
3 Ty Cobb 600.00 1200.00
4 Johnny Evers 125.00 250.00
5 Rube Marquard 125.00 250.00
6 Christy Mathewson 300.00 600.00
7 John McGraw MG 150.00 300.00
8 Chief Meyers 100.00 200.00
9 Marty O'Toole 75.00 150.00
10 Frank Schulte 75.00 150.00
11 Tris Speaker 150.00 300.00
12 Jake Stahl 75.00 150.00
13 Jim Thorpe 400.00 800.00
14 Joe Tinker 150.00 300.00
15 Honus Wagner 300.00 600.00
16 Ed Walsh 150.00 300.00
17 Buck Weaver 200.00 400.00
18 Joe Wood 100.00 200.00
19 Heinie Zimmerman 75.00 150.00
20 Johnny 125.00 250.00
21 Doc Miller 75.00 150.00
22 Boston American Team 150.00 300.00
23 Chicago Cubs 1916 150.00 300.00
24 Cincinnati Reds 1916 150.00 300.00
25 N.Y. National Team 150.00 300.00

1895 Mayo's Cut Plug N300

The Mayo Tobacco Works of Richmond, Va., issued this set of 48 ballplayers about 1895. Some recent speculation has been made that this set was issued beginning in 1894. The cards contain sepia portraits although some pictures appear to be black and white. There are 40 different individuals known in the set; cards 1 to 28 appear in uniform, while the last twelve (29-40) appear in street clothes. Eight of the former also appear with variations in uniform. The player's name appears within the picture area and a "Mayo's Cut Plug" ad is printed in a panel at the base of the card. Similar to the football set issued around the same time, the cards have black blank backs. Due to the fact that N300's are found in off-grade, our pricing references the technical grade of "EX".

COMPLETE SET (48) 75000.00 150000.00
1 Charlie S. Abbey CF:/Washington 600.00 1000.00
2 Cap Anson: Chicago 5000.00 8000.00
3 Jimmy Bannon RF:/Boston 600.00 1000.00
4A Dan Brouthers 1B:/Baltimore 3000.00 5000.00
4B Dan Brouthers 1B:/Louisville 3000.00 5000.00
5 Ed W. Cartwright FB:/Washington 600.00 1000.00
6 Dad Clarkson P:/St. Louis 1500.00 2500.00
7 Tommy W. Corcoran SS/Brooklyn 600.00 1000.00
8 Lave Cross 2B:/Philadelphia 600.00 1000.00
9 William F. Dahlen SS:/Chicago 600.00 1000.00
10 Tom P. Daly 2B:/Brooklyn 600.00 1000.00
11 Ed J. Delehanty LF:/Phila. 3500.00 6000.00
12 Hugh Duffy CF:/Boston 1800.00 3000.00
13A Buck Ewing RF:/Cincinnati 3000.00 5000.00
13B Buck Ewing RF:/Cleveland 3000.00 5000.00
14 Dave Foutz 1B:/Brooklyn 600.00 1000.00
15 Bill Joyce CF:/Brooklyn 600.00 1000.00
16 Charlie Ganzel C:/Boston 600.00 1000.00
17A Jack Glasscock SS:/Louisville 600.00 1000.00
17B Jack Glasscock SS:/Pittsburgh 600.00 1000.00
18 Mike Griffin CF:/Brooklyn 600.00 1000.00
19A George Haddock P:/no team 600.00 1000.00
19B George Haddock P:/Philadelphia 600.00 1000.00
20 Bill W. Hallman 2B:/Phila. 600.00 1000.00
21 Billy Hamilton CF:/Phila. 2500.00 4000.00
22 Wm.(Brickyard) Kennedy
P: Brooklyn 600.00 1000.00
23A Tom F. Kinslow C:/no team 900.00 1200.00
23B Tom F. Kinslow C:/Pitts." 900.00 1200.00
24 Arlie Latham 3B:/Cincinnati 600.00 1000.00
25 Herman Long SS: Boston 600.00 1000.00
26 Tom Lovett P: Boston 600.00 1000.00
27 Link Lowe 2B: Boston 600.00 1000.00
28 Tommy McCarthy LF:/Boston 1800.00 3000.00
29 Yale Murphy SS:/New York 600.00 1000.00
30 Billy Nash 3B: Boston 600.00 1000.00
31 Kid Nicols P: Boston 3500.00 6000.00
32A Fred Pfeffer 2B:/Louisville 600.00 1000.00
32B Fred Pfeffer/(Retired) 600.00 1000.00
33 Wilbert Robinson C:/Baltimore 2500.00 4000.00
34A Amos Rusie P:/New York 2500.00 4000.00
34B Amos Russie (Sic) P:/New York 2500.00 4000.00
35 James Ryan RF:/Chicago 600.00 1000.00
36 Billy Shindle 3B:/Brooklyn 600.00 1000.00
37 George J. Smith SS:/Cinc. 600.00 1000.00
38 Otis H. Stockdale P:/Washington 600.00 1000.00
39 Tommy Tucker 1B:/Boston 600.00 1000.00
40A John Ward 2B:/New York 2500.00 4000.00
40B John Ward (Retired) 2500.00 4000.00

1950-69 J.D. McCarthy PC753

One of the most prolific producers of postward postcards was J.D McCarthy on Michigan. During the 1950's and 1960's, thousands of these black and white postcards were issued. Most of the popular players of that era have been featured on the McCarthy postcards and a checklist is not provided. Some McCarthy postcards are much more difficult to obtain. Among the scarcities known are Jehoise Heard (less than 10 have been proven to exist) and Gus Triandos Orioles portrait card. We are interested in any additions to this currently short list of scarcities.

COMMON PLAYER (1950'S) 5.00 10.00
COMMON PLAYER (1960'S) 2.50 5.00

1998 McGwire Dental

This one card set feature slugger Mark McGwire. The front has a color action shot and the back has advice on how to protect ones teeth.

1 Mark McGwire 2.00 5.00

1998 Mark McGwire Little League

This one-card set features a color action photo of Mark McGwire with a thin yellow and wider green borders. The back displays Safety Tips for Little Leaguers.

1 Mark McGwire 2.00 5.00

1998 McGwire St Louis 62

This one card postcard set, which measures approximately 6" by 4" feature three different poses of Mark McGwire during the at-bat in which he hit his 62nd homer.

1 Mark McGwire .75 2.00

1992 McGwire Police

This 24-card standard-size set was sponsored by the Clovis Police Department, The Oakland A's, and 25 Clovis area businesses. The program raised $9,200 in a four-day period. Both businesses and officers gave out 12 1/2" by 18" posters and cards, and graduating DARE students also received cards. The cards were cut from the poster, but some uncut posters (measuring approximately 20" by 25") with the cards still attached were given away to VIPs and sponsors for framing. The fronts feature color action photos of Mark McGwire on a green card face. The pictures have bright yellow borders, and the upper left corner is cut off to display the City of Clovis insignia. The player's name is printed in bright yellow print at the top. The backs features "Mark's Moments- (various facts about McGwire) and public service messages. The cards are numbered on the back.

COMPLETE SET (24) 12.50 30.00
COMMON PLAYER (1-24) .60 1.50

1992 MCI Ambassadors

Sponsored by MCI, the third annual Ambassadors of Baseball World Tour set consists of 16 cards. The cards were distributed by MCI to military personnel during the world tour of military bases. The standard-size cards feature white-bordered color photos of baseball stars of the past.

COMPLETE SET (16) 30.00 80.00
1 Earl Weaver MG 2.50 6.00
2 Steve Garvey 2.50 6.00
3 Doug Flynn 1.50 4.00
4 Bert Campaneris 2.00 5.00
5 Bill Madlock 2.00 5.00
6 Graig Nettles 2.00 5.00
7 Dave Kingman 2.00 5.00
8 Paul Blair 1.25 3.00
9 Jeff Burroughs 1.25 3.00
10 Rick Waits 1.25 3.00
11 Elias Sosa 1.25 3.00
12 Tug McGraw 2.00 5.00
13 Ferguson Jenkins 4.00 10.00
14 Bob Feller 4.00 10.00
15 Ferguson Jenkins/(Special art card) 2.50 6.00
16 Title card 1.25 3.00

1993 MCI Ambassadors

This 14-card, standard-size set was sponsored by MCI for the 1993 Ambassadors of Baseball World Tour. The cards contain a color portrait or action shot of baseball veterans with an irregular white border.

COMPLETE SET (14) 20.00 50.00
1 Vida Blue 1.50 4.00
2 Paul Blair 1.50 4.00
3 Mudcat Grant 1.50 4.00
4 Phil Niekro 2.50 6.00
5 Bob Feller 2.50 6.00
6 Joe Charboneau 1.50 4.00
7 Joe Rudi 1.50 4.00
8 Catfish Hunter 2.50 6.00
9 Manny Sanguillen 1.50 4.00
10 Harmon Killebrew 2.50 6.00
11 Al Oliver 2.50 6.00
12 Bob Dernier 1.25 3.00
13 Graig Nettles 2.50 6.00
Sparky Lyle
NNO Title Card 1.25 3.00

1994 MCI Ambassadors

The 1994 Ambassadors of Baseball 15-card standard-size set was sponsored by Major League Baseball Players Alumni and MCI. The sets were released at a few select military bases where the retired players appeared in charity games. The front design is the same as the 1993 issue, with the MCI logo at the upper right and the Ambassadors of Baseball World Tour logo at the lower left. The two tribute cards list the names of players who served during World War II.

COMPLETE SET (15) 15.00 40.00
1 Sparky Lyle 1.50 4.00
2 John Stearns .75 2.00
3 Bobby Thomson 2.50 6.00
4 Jimmy Wynn .75 2.00
5 Ferguson Jenkins 2.50 6.00
6 Tug McGraw 1.50 4.00
7 Paul Blair .75 2.00
8 Ron LeFlore .75 2.00
9 Manny Sanguillen .75 2.00
10 Doug Flynn .75 2.00
11 Bill North .75 2.00
S1 Doug Flynn/(Instructing children) .75 2.00
S2 World War II Tribute 1.50 4.00
Card (AL)
S3 World War II Tribute 1.50 4.00
Card (NL)
S4 Manny Sanguillen/(Signing autographs) 1.50 4.00

1995 MCI Ambassadors

This 16-card standard-size set was sponsored by MCI, MLB, and Major League Baseball Players Alumni. Approximately 2,000 sets were produced and distributed at certain U.S. military bases where the retired players appeared in charity games.

COMPLETE SET (16) 15.00 40.00
1 Vida Blue 1.25 3.00
2 Bert Campaneris 1.25 3.00
3 Tug McGraw 1.25 3.00
4 Doug Flynn .75 2.00
5 Paul Blair .75 2.00
6 Harmon Killebrew 2.00 5.00
7 Sparky Lyle 1.25 3.00
8 Steve Garvey 2.00 5.00
9 Bert Blyleven 1.25 3.00
10 Omar Moreno .75 2.00
11 Bill Lee .75 2.00
12 Maury Wills 1.25 3.00
13 Dave Parker 1.25 3.00
14 Luis Aparicio 1.25 3.00
15 Brooks Robinson 2.00 5.00
16 George Foster 1.25 3.00

1991 MDA All-Stars

This 20-card standard-size set was produced by Smith-Kline Beecham for the Muscular Dystrophy Association. It includes 18 All-Star Alumni cards that feature retired baseball All-Stars. A vinyl album designed to house the cards was also issued. Since the set was licensed by the Major League Baseball Players Alumni, all team logos have been airbrushed out.

COMPLETE SET (20) 5.00 12.00
1 Steve Carlton .60 1.50
2 Ted Simmons .20 .50
3 Willie Stargell .40 1.00
4 Bill Mazeroski .30 .75
5 Ron Santo .30 .75
6 Dave Concepcion .20 .50
7 Bobby Bonds .30 .75
8 George Foster .20 .50
9 Billy Williams .40 1.00
10 Whitey Ford .60 1.50
11 Yogi Berra .60 1.50
12 Boog Powell .30 .75
13 Davey Johnson .20 .50
14 Brooks Robinson .60 1.50
15 Jim Fregosi .20 .50
16 Harmon Killebrew .60 1.50
17 Ted Williams 1.50 4.00
18 Al Kaline .60 1.50
NNO MDA Fact Card .60 1.50
Brooks Robinson
Tommy
NNO Title Card .20 .50

1992 MDA MVP

This 20-card limited edition set of alumni MVPs was sponsored by SmithKline Beecham Consumer Brands and was produced for the Muscular Dystrophy Association.

COMPLETE SET (20) 6.00 15.00
1 Yogi Berra 1.00 2.50
2 Dick Groat .20 .50
3 Maury Wills .30 .75
4 Brooks Robinson .60 1.50
5 Orlando Cepeda .40 1.00
6 Harmon Killebrew .60 1.50
7 Boog Powell .40 1.00
8 Vida Blue .30 .75
9 Jeff Burroughs .20 .50
10 George Foster .20 .50
11 Rod Carew .60 1.50
12 Jim Rice .30 .75
13 Don Baylor .30 .75
14 Willie Stargell .60 1.50
15 Rollie Fingers .40 1.00
16 Ray Knight .20 .50
17 History Card .20 .50
18 Trivia Card .20 .50
19 Fact Sheet/(Players Alumni) .20 .50
20 Fact Sheet .40 1.00
Harmon and Drew

1964 Meadow Gold Dairy

Issued as a four-card panel on Meadow Gold milk cartons, these cards feature some of the leading players at the time. Another part of the unopened milk carton features an advertisement for the 1964 Auravision records. When cut from the milk carton and the panels, these cards measure approximately 1 3/4" by 2 1/16". Since these are unnumbered, we have sequenced these in alphabetical order.

COMPLETE SET (4) 250.00 500.00
1 Sandy Koufax 60.00 120.00
2 Mickey Mantle 125.00 250.00
3 Willie Mays 60.00 120.00
4 Bill Mazeroski 30.00 60.00
5 Full Sheet

1986 Meadow Gold Blank Back

This unnumbered set of 16 full-color cards is blank backed. The cards were found (one card per package) on the flap of 1/2 gallon cartons of Meadow Gold "Double Play" ice cream. The cards are attractive but the team logos have been airbrushed away. The cards measure approximately 2 3/8" by 3 1/2." The accent colors used on the front of the cards are light blue and red. The Ripken card is supposedly a little more difficult to find.

COMPLETE SET (16) 20.00 50.00
1 Wade Boggs 1.25 3.00
2 George Brett 2.00 5.00
3 Carlton Fisk 1.25 3.00
4 Steve Garvey .60 1.50
5 Dwight Gooden .60 1.50
6 Pedro Guerrero .40 1.00
7 Reggie Jackson 1.25 3.00
8 Don Mattingly 2.00 5.00
9 Willie McGee .60 1.50
10 Dale Murphy .75 2.00
11 Cal Ripken 3.00 8.00
12 Pete Rose 1.25 3.00
13 Ryne Sandberg 1.50 4.00
14 Mike Schmidt 1.25 3.00
15 Fernando Valenzuela .60 1.50
16 Dave Winfield 1.25 3.00

1986 Meadow Gold Milk

These cards were printed crudely on milk cartons of various sizes of Meadow Gold milk. The cards are approximately 2 1/2" by 3 3/16" and are very similar to the Keller's Butter cards. The same art was used on the Schmidt card which is in both sets. Both Keller's and Meadow Gold are subsidiaries of Beatrice Foods. The set was licensed by Mike Schechter Associates and the Major League Baseball Players' Association. The cards are blank backed and are printed in red and brown on white waxed cardboard. Complete boxes would bring double the values listed below. Since the cards are unnumbered, they are listed below in alphabetical order.

COMPLETE SET 20.00 50.00
1 Wade Boggs 1.50 4.00
2 George Brett 15.00 40.00
3 Steve Carlton 1.50 4.00
4 Dwight Gooden .75 2.00
5 Don Mattingly 2.50 6.00
6 Willie McGee .60 1.50
7 Dale Murphy 1.25 3.00
8 Cal Ripken 5.00 12.00
9 Pete Rose 1.50 4.00
10 Ryne Sandberg 2.50 6.00
11 Mike Schmidt 1.50 4.00
12 Fernando Valenzuela .75 2.00

1986 Meadow Gold Stat Back

Meadow Gold produced three sets in 1986, but this was the only one with printing on the back. This full-color set contains 20 star players. The cards were distributed as two-card panels with Meadow Gold popsicles, fudgesicles and bubblegum coolers. As with the other sets, this one was only licensed by the Major League Players Association and hence the team logos have been artistically removed. The back printing is in red on white card stock. The cards measure approximately 2 9/16" by 3 1/2" and are numbered on the back. Two of the cards were misspelled by Meadow Gold as noted in the checklist below. Intact panels are valued at 50 percent more than the sum of the individual players making up the panel.

COMPLETE SET 20.00 50.00
1 George Brett 2.00 5.00
2 Fernando Valenzuela .30 .75
3 Dwight Gooden .30 .75
4 Dale Murphy .40 1.00
5 Don Mattingly 2.00 5.00
6 Reggie Jackson .75 2.00
7 Dave Winfield .75 2.00
8 Pete Rose .75 2.00
9 Wade Boggs .75 2.00
10 Willie McGee .30 .75
11 Cal Ripken ERR 2.50 6.00
sic, Ripkin
12 Ryne Sandberg 1.50 4.00
13 Carlton Fisk .75 2.00
14 Jim Rice .30 .75
15 Steve Garvey .30 .75
16 Mike Schmidt 1.50 4.00
17 Bruce Sutter .60 1.50
18 Pedro Guerrero .20 .50
19 Rick Sutcliffe ERR .20 .50
sic, Sutcliffe
20 Rich Gossage .30 .75

1911 Mecca Double Folders T201

The cards in this 50-card set measure approximately 2 1/4" by 4 11/16". The 1911 Mecca Double Folder issue contains unnumbered cards. This issue was one of the first to list statistics of players portrayed on the cards. Each card portrays two players, one when the card is folded, another when the card is unfolded. The card of Dougherty and Lord is considered scarce.

COMPLETE SET (50) 4000.00 6000.00
1 Abstein/Butler 90.00 150.00
2 Baker/Downey 90.00 150.00
3 Barrett/McGlyn 90.00 150.00
4 Bender/Oldring 125.00 200.00
5 Brown/Hofman 125.00 200.00
6 Chase/Sweeney 125.00 200.00
7 Cicotte/Thoney 125.00 200.00
8 Clarke/Byrne 125.00 200.00
9 F.Baker/E.Collins 175.00 300.00
10 Crawford/Cobb 1200.00 2000.00
11 Donovan/Stroud 90.00 150.00
12 Downs/Odell 90.00 150.00
13 Doyle/Meyers 90.00 150.00
14 Evers/Chance 250.00 400.00
15 Ford/Johnson 90.00 150.00
16 Foster/Ward 90.00 150.00
17 Gasper/Clarke 90.00 150.00
18 Grant/McLean 90.00 150.00
19 W.Blair/R.Hartzell 90.00 150.00
20 Hickman/Hinchman 90.00 150.00
21 R.Bresnahan/M.Huggins 175.00 300.00
22 Johnson/Street 400.00 700.00
23 Killian/Fitzpatrick 90.00 150.00
24 Kling/Cole 90.00 150.00
25 Lajoie/Falkenberg 250.00 400.00
26 Lake/Wallace 125.00 200.00
27 LaPorte/Stephens 90.00 150.00
28 J.Barry/J.Lapp 90.00 150.00
29 Leach/Gibson 90.00 150.00
30 Leifield/Simon 90.00 150.00
31 Lobert/Moore 90.00 150.00
32 Lord/Dougherty 150.00 250.00
33 Lush/Hauser 90.00 150.00
34 Mattern/Graham 90.00 150.00
35 Mathewson/Bridwell UER 400.00 700.00
36 McBride/Elberfeld 90.00 150.00
37 McCabe/Starr 90.00 150.00
38 McGinnity/McCarty 125.00 200.00
39 Miller/Herzog 90.00 150.00
40 Rucker/Daubert 90.00 150.00
41 Seymour/Dygert 90.00 150.00
42 Speaker/Gardner 250.00 400.00
43 Summers/Jennings 125.00 200.00
44 Thomas/Coombs 90.00 150.00
45 Titus/Dooin 90.00 150.00
46 Turner/Stovall 90.00 150.00
47 Walsh/Payne 125.00 200.00
48 B.Bergen/Z.Wheat 125.00 200.00
49 Wiltse/Merkle 90.00 150.00
50 Woodruff/Williams 90.00 150.00

1992 Megacards Ruth Prototypes

COMPLETE SET (9) 10.00 25.00
COMMON CARD 1.20 3.00

1992 Megacards Ruth

Released by Megacards, the 1992 Babe Ruth Collection consists of 165 standard-size cards, including a card for every year of his career. The cards are very similar to the Conlon sets produced in conjunction with The Sporting News. The cards were sold in both ten-card packs and 22-card blister packs. Complete sets were also available in a commemorative tin. The set is arranged as follows: Babe Ruth (1-4), Year in Review (5-29), World Series (30-39), Place in History (40-70), Career Highlights (71-97), Trivia (98-104), Sultan of SWAT (105-115), The Bambino-The Man (116-142), and Being Remembered (143-163). The set concludes with checklist cards (164-165). The set could also be purchased in a special commemorative tin.

COMPLETE SET (165) 8.00 20.00
COMP.FACT SET (165)
COMMON CARD (1-165) .04 .10
1 Lifetime Pitching .15 .40
Statistics 1916
7 Won 17 of His Last/21 Decisions 1915 .02 .10
9 Defeats .08 .25
Walter Johnson for 6th Time/1917
19 The Best Baseball .25 .60
Team in History 1927
31 Hurls 14 Inning .08 .25
Complete Game Gem 1916
36 Belts 4 Home Runs in .08 .25
Losing Cause 1926
37 Yanks Destroy Bucs in
Four Games 1927
39 Yanks Sweep Cubs/1932 .25 .60
42 Lifetime-2,174 Runs .25 .60
Scored 1928
43 Lifetime-5,793 Total .25 .60
Bases 1942
47 Lifetime-8.5 Home Run .15 .40
Percentage 1934
50 Lifetime-2,211 RBIs .15 .40
51 Lifetime-.342 Batting .25 .60
Average 1928
52 Lifetime-.690 .15 .40
Slugging Average 1934
55 Season-177 Runs .25 .60
Score 1939
57 Season-457 Total .08 .25
Bases 1926
58 Season-119 Extra .08 .25
Base Hits 1947
59 Season-171 Runs .25 .60
Batted In 1934
60 Season-60 Home Runs/1927 .25 .60
62 Season-.847 Slugging .08 .25
Average 1920
70 World Series- .744 .25 .60
Slugging Average 1927
73 Babe Derails .15 .40
Big Train 1942
76 Babe Becomes a Yankee/1920 .08 .25
79 Wins Only Batting .25 .60
Title 1924
80 Babe Hits 3 Home Runs .02 .10
in Series Game:
October 6&
81 Babe and .30 .75
Lou Gehrig
Smack 107 Home Runs
82 The Babe's 60th Home .08 .25
Run: September 30& 1927
86 The Called Shot - .25 .60
The Believers 1932
87 The Called Shot - .08 .25
The Doubters 1948
89 Slams First HR in .25 .60
First AS Game 1933
91 Babe Hits His 700th .08 .25
Home Run 1934
92 Banzai Beibu Russu- .08 .25
The Babe in Japan 1934
94 Inaugurated Into .15 .40
Hall of Fame 1939
95 Faces .08 .25
Walter Johnson
Again
August 23, 1942
96 Babe Ruth Day: .08 .25
27-Apr-47
97 Babe's Farewell 1948 .08 .25
100 Hub Pruett: .08 .25
Babe Buster 1929
102 Never Won a Triple .08 .25
Crown 1926
118 Babe and .02 .10
Brother Matthias
120 Babe's First Wife .08 .25
Helen Ruth
121 Babe's Second Wife .08 .25
Claire Ruth
122 Lou Gehrig .15 .40
Appreciation Day:
July 4, 1939
123 Babe's Friendship .08 .25
with
Herb Pennock 1921
124 The Babe .08 .25
Miller Huggins
125 The Babe .25 .60
Ty Cobb
126 Babe and .15 .40
Walter Johnson 1942
128 Babe's Barnstorming .25 .60
131 Babe's Big Bucks 1927 .08 .25
134 Babe in the Movies .08 .25
140 The Johnny Sylvester .08 .25
Story
141 Moving with the Great/1923 .08 .25
143 Being Remembered by .08 .25
Bill James 1928
144 Being Remembered by .08 .25
Bill James 1929
145 Being Remembered by .08 .25
Bill James 1920
146 Being Remembered by .15 .40
Mel Allen 1923
147 Being Remembered by .15 .40
Mel Allen 1928
148 Being Remembered by .08 .25
Wes Ferrell 1930
149 Being Remembered by .25 .60
George Bush 1948
150 Being Remembered by .25 .60
Ethan Allen 1948
151 Being Remembered by .08 .25
Daughter Dorothy 1926
152 Being Remembered by .08 .25
Daughter Julia 1947
153 Being Remembered by .08 .25
Daughter Julia 1938
154 Being Remembered by .08 .25
Mark Koenig 1927
155 Being Remembered by .08 .25
Donald Honig 1927
156 Being Remembered by .08 .25
Lloyd Waner and
Waite Hoyt 1
157 Being Remembered by .08 .25
Waite Hoyt 1938
158 Being Remembered by .08 .25
Bill Dickey 1938
159 Being Remembered by .08 .25
Bob Meusel 1922
160 Being Remembered by .08 .25
Jim Chapman 1941
161 Being Remembered by .08 .25
Christy Walsh 1926
163 Being Remembered by .08 .25
Grantland Rice 1923

1994 Megacards Ruthian Shots

Produced by Megacards and titled "Ruthian Shots," this five-card standard-size set was given away at card shows when the collector purchased a 1994 Conlon Collection wax box.

COMPLETE SET (5) 4.00 10.00
COMMON CARD (1-5) .80 2.00
1 Babe Ruth 1.25 3.00
Pitcher for the
Boston Red Sox
3 Babe Ruth 1.50 4.00
Lou Gehrig
Fishing
5 Babe Ruth/(In car with Miller 1.00 2.50
Huggins& Yankee MG

1995 Megacards Griffey Jr. Wish List

In this 25-card standard-size set, Ken Griffey Jr. shares his personal thoughts about the game, his dreams for the future and his commitment to terminally ill and underprivileged children. The suggested retail price for each set was $9.99. Just 100,000 sets were produced, with a percentage of all proceeds to benefit the Make-A-Wish Foundation. A sweepstakes card inside each pack entitled the collector to be entered in a chance drawing of 500 autographed collectibles (including 5 jerseys, 10 bats, 60 balls and 425 cards from this set). Also included in each set was one of three Ken Griffey Jr. MegaCaps.

COMP.FACT SET (25) 4.00 10.00
COMMON CARD (1-25) .20 .50
XX Ken Griffey AU 100.00 250.00

1995 Megacards Ruth

This 25-card standard-size set offers classic glimpses and new insights into Babe Ruth. Twenty-one cards are in black-and-white, while four cards feature computer-enhanced color (11-12, 21, 24). The suggested retail price for each set was 9.99. All card fronts carry the Babe Ruth 100th Anniversary logo in gold foil. One hundred thousand sets were produced. Each set included an official entry blank to a sweepstakes featuring the following prizes: 1 Babe Ruth autographed ball, 200 Don Mattingly autographed cards, 200 Ken Griffey Jr. autographed cards and 100 Babe Ruth 165-card sets. Also included in each set was one of three limited edition (34,000) Babe Ruth Megacaps.

COMP.FACT SET (25) 4.00 10.00
COMMON CARD (1-25) .20 .50
3 No Slugger Comes Close .40 1.00
Jimmie Foxx
Babe Ruth
Lo
5 He Knew the Way Home .30 .75
Babe Ruth
Bill Dickey
Ray
6 He Didn't Leave Them .60 1.50
Stranded
Babe Ruth
Lou Geh
9 .342 Plus Power .40 1.00
Lloyd Waner
Babe Ruth
Paul Wane
12 Career Year .75 2.00
Babe Ruth
Lou Gehrig/(Color)
13 Mr. Yankee .60 1.50
Babe Ruth
Don Mattingly
Lou Gehrig
14 Babe and The Kid 1.00 2.50
Babe Ruth
Ken Griffey Jr.
18 The Rewards of .30 .75
Greatness
Babe Ruth
Miller Huggi
21 Babe and Today's Best 1.00 2.50
Babe Ruth
Ken Griffey Jr.#
24 How He Changed the Game .30 .75
Dizzy Dean
Frankie Frisc

1910 Mello Mint E105

The cards in this 50-card set measure 1 1/2" by 2 3/4". The cards were manufactured by the Texas Gum Company. The cards themselves are unnumbered and the fronts are identical to these found in E92. Printed on paper, the backs are horizontally aligned and carry advertising for "Smith's Mello-Mint". The set was issued about 1910. The cards have been alphabetized and numbered in the checklist below. The complete set price includes all variation cards listed in the checklist below.

COMPLETE SET (50) 50000.00 100000.00
1 Jack Barry 600.00 1200.00
2 Harry Bemis 600.00 1200.00
3A Chief Bender/(blue background) 800.00 1600.00
3B Chief Bender/(green background) 800.00 1600.00
4 Bill Bergen 600.00 1200.00
5 Bob Bescher 600.00 1200.00
6 Al Bridwell 600.00 1200.00
7 Doc Casey 600.00 1200.00
8 Frank Chance 600.00 1200.00
9 Hal Chase 750.00 1500.00
10 Ty Cobb 12500.00 25000.00
11 Eddie Collins 1500.00 3000.00
12 Sam Crawford 900.00 1800.00
13 Harry Davis 600.00 1200.00
14 Art Devlin 700.00 1400.00

15 Bill Donovan 600.00 1200.00
16 Red Dooin 600.00 1200.00
17 Mickey Doolan 600.00 1200.00
18 Patsy Dougherty 600.00 1200.00
19A Larry Doyle/batting 700.00 1400.00
19B Larry Doyle/throwing 700.00 1400.00
20 Johnny Evers 1250.00 2500.00
21 George Gibson 600.00 1200.00
22 Topsy Hartsel 600.00 1200.00
23 Fred Jacklitsch 600.00 1200.00
24 Hugh Jennings 900.00 1800.00
25 Red Kleinow 600.00 1200.00
26 Otto Knabe 600.00 1200.00
27 John Knight 600.00 1200.00
28 Nap Lajoie 2250.00 4500.00
29 Hans Lobert 600.00 1200.00
30 Sherry Magee 700.00 1400.00
31 Christy Mathewson 5000.00 10000.00
32 John McGraw MG 1500.00 3000.00
33 Larry McLean 600.00 1200.00
34A Dots Miller/batting 600.00 1200.00
34B Dots Miller/fielding 600.00 1200.00
35 Danny Murphy 600.00 1200.00
36 William O'Hara 600.00 1200.00
37 Germany Schaefer 700.00 1400.00
38 George Schlei 600.00 1200.00
39 Charles Schmidt 600.00 1200.00
40 Johnny Seigle 600.00 1200.00
41 David Shean 600.00 1200.00
42 Frank Smith 600.00 1200.00
43 Joe Tinker 1250.00 2500.00
44A Honus Wagner/batting 10000.00 20000.00
44B Honus Wagner/throwing 10000.00 20000.00
45 Cy Young 2000.00 4000.00
46 Heinie Zimmerman 600.00 1200.00

2004 Merrick Mint

1 Vladimir Guerrero 1.50 4.00
2 Mark Prior 1.50 4.00
3 Albert Pujols 3.00 8.00
4 Alex Rodriguez 3.00 8.00
5 Ichiro Suzuki 3.00 8.00

1996 Metal Universe Promo Sheet

XX Complete Sheet 2.00 5.00
Todd Greene
Jon Nunnally
Brad Ra

1996 Metal Universe

The Metal Universe set (created by Fleer) was issued in one series totalling 250 standard-size cards. The cards were issued in foil-wrapped packs. The theme for the set was based on intermingling fantasy comic book elements with baseball, thus each card features a player set against a wide variety of bizarre backgrounds. The cards are grouped alphabetically within teams below.

COMPLETE SET (250) 15.00 40.00
1 Roberto Alomar .20 .50
2 Brady Anderson .10 .30
3 Bobby Bonilla .10 .30
4 Chris Hoiles .10 .30
5 Ben McDonald .10 .30
6 Mike Mussina .20 .50
7 Randy Myers .10 .30
8 Rafael Palmeiro .20 .50
9 Cal Ripken 1.00 2.50
10 B.J. Surhoff .10 .30
11 Luis Alicea .10 .30
12 Jose Canseco .20 .50
13 Roger Clemens .60 1.50
14 Will Cordero .10 .30
15 Tom Gordon .10 .30
16 Mike Greenwall .10 .30
17 Tim Naehring .10 .30
18 Troy O'Leary .10 .30
19 Mike Stanley .10 .30
20 John Valentin .10 .30
21 Mo Vaughn .10 .30
22 Tim Wakefield .10 .30
23 Garret Anderson .10 .30
24 Chili Davis .10 .30
25 Gary DiSarcina .10 .30
26 Jim Edmonds .10 .30
27 Chuck Finley .10 .30
28 Todd Greene .10 .30
29 Mark Langston .10 .30
30 Troy Percival .10 .30
31 Tony Phillips .10 .30
32 Tim Salmon .20 .50
33 Lee Smith .10 .30
34 J.T. Snow .10 .30
35 Ray Durham .10 .30
36 Alex Fernandez .10 .30
37 Ozzie Guillen .10 .30
38 Roberto Hernandez .10 .30
39 Lyle Mouton .10 .30
40 Frank Thomas .30 .75
41 Robin Ventura .10 .30
42 Sandy Alomar Jr. .10 .30
43 Carlos Baerga .10 .30
44 Albert Belle .10 .30
45 Orel Hershiser .10 .30
46 Kenny Lofton .10 .30
47 Dennis Martinez .10 .30
48 Jack McDowell .10 .30
49 Jose Mesa .10 .30
50 Eddie Murray .30 .75
51 Charles Nagy .10 .30
52 Manny Ramirez .20 .50
53 Julian Tavarez .10 .30
54 Jim Thome .20 .50
55 Omar Vizquel .20 .50
56 Chad Curtis .10 .30
57 Cecil Fielder .10 .30
58 John Flaherty .10 .30
59 Travis Fryman .10 .30
60 Chris Gomez .10 .30
61 Felipe Lira .10 .30
62 Kevin Appier .10 .30
63 Johnny Damon .20 .50
64 Tom Goodwin .10 .30
65 Mark Gubicza .10 .30
66 Jeff Montgomery .10 .30
67 Jon Nunnally .10 .30
68 Ricky Bones .10 .30
69 Jeff Cirillo .10 .30
70 John Jaha .10 .30
71 Dave Nilsson .10 .30
72 Joe Oliver .10 .30
73 Kevin Seitzer .10 .30
74 Greg Vaughn .10 .30
75 Marty Cordova .10 .30
76 Chuck Knoblauch .10 .30
77 Pat Meares .10 .30
78 Paul Molitor .10 .30
79 Pedro Munoz .10 .30
80 Kirby Puckett .30 .75
81 Brad Radke .10 .30
82 Scott Stahoviak .10 .30
83 Matt Walbeck .10 .30
84 Wade Boggs .20 .50
85 David Cone .10 .30
86 Joe Girardi .10 .30
87 Derek Jeter .75 2.00
88 Jim Leyritz .10 .30
89 Tino Martinez .20 .50
90 Don Mattingly .75 2.00
91 Paul O'Neill .20 .50
92 Andy Pettitte .20 .50
93 Tim Raines .10 .30
94 Kenny Rogers .10 .30
95 Ruben Sierra .10 .30
96 John Wetteland .10 .30
97 Bernie Williams .20 .50
98 Geronimo Berroa .10 .30
99 Dennis Eckersley .10 .30
100 Brent Gates .10 .30
101 Mark McGwire .75 2.00
102 Steve Ontiveros .10 .30
103 Terry Steinbach .10 .30
104 Jay Buhner .10 .30
105 Vince Coleman .10 .30
106 Joey Cora .10 .30
107 Ken Griffey Jr. .60 1.50
108 Randy Johnson .30 .75
109 Edgar Martinez .20 .50
110 Alex Rodriguez .60 1.50
111 Paul Sorrento .10 .30
112 Will Clark .20 .50
113 Juan Gonzalez .10 .30
114 Rusty Greer .10 .30
115 Dean Palmer .10 .30
116 Ivan Rodriguez .20 .50
117 Mickey Tettleton .10 .30
118 Joe Carter .10 .30
119 Alex Gonzalez .10 .30
120 Shawn Green .10 .30
121 Erik Hanson .10 .30
122 Pat Hentgen .10 .30
123 Sandy Martinez .10 .30
124 Otis Nixon .10 .30
125 John Olerud .10 .30
126 Steve Avery .10 .30
127 Tom Glavine .20 .50
128 Marquis Grissom .10 .30
129 Chipper Jones .30 .75
130 David Justice .10 .30
131 Ryan Klesko .10 .30
132 Mark Lemke .10 .30
133 Javier Lopez .10 .30
134 Greg Maddux .50 1.25
135 Fred McGriff .20 .50
136 John Smoltz .20 .50
137 Mark Wohlers .10 .30
138 Frank Castillo .10 .30
139 Shawon Dunston .10 .30
140 Luis Gonzalez .10 .30
141 Mark Grace .20 .50
142 Brian McRae .10 .30
143 Jaime Navarro .10 .30
144 Rey Sanchez .10 .30
145 Ryne Sandberg .50 1.25
146 Sammy Sosa .30 .75
147 Bret Boone .10 .30
148 Curtis Goodwin .10 .30
149 Barry Larkin .20 .50
150 Hal Morris .10 .30
151 Reggie Sanders .10 .30
152 Pete Schourek .10 .30
153 John Smiley .10 .30
154 Dante Bichette .10 .30
155 Vinny Castilla .10 .30
156 Andres Galarraga .10 .30
157 Bret Saberhagen .10 .30
158 Bill Swift .10 .30
159 Larry Walker .10 .30
160 Walt Weiss .10 .30
161 Kurt Abbott .10 .30
162 John Burkett .10 .30
163 Greg Colbrunn .10 .30
164 Jeff Conine .10 .30
165 Chris Hammond .10 .30
166 Charles Johnson .10 .30
167 Al Leiter .10 .30
168 Pat Rapp .10 .30
169 Gary Sheffield .10 .30
170 Quilvio Veras .10 .30
171 Devon White .10 .30
172 Jeff Bagwell .20 .50
173 Derek Bell .10 .30
174 Sean Berry .10 .30
175 Craig Biggio .20 .50
176 Doug Drabek .10 .30
177 Tony Eusebio .10 .30
178 Brian L.Hunter .10 .30
179 Orlando Miller .10 .30
180 Shane Reynolds .10 .30
181 Mike Blowers .10 .30
182 Roger Cedeno .10 .30
183 Eric Karros .10 .30
184 Ramon Martinez .10 .30
185 Raul Mondesi .10 .30
186 Hideo Nomo .30 .75
187 Mike Piazza .50 1.25
188 Moises Alou .10 .30
189 Yamil Benitez .10 .30
190 Darrin Fletcher .10 .30
191 Cliff Floyd .10 .30
192 Pedro Martinez .20 .50
193 Carlos Perez .10 .30
194 David Segui .10 .30
195 Tony Tarasco .10 .30
196 Rondell White .10 .30
197 Edgardo Alfonzo .10 .30
198 Rico Brogna .10 .30
199 Carl Everett .10 .30
200 Todd Hundley .10 .30
201 Jason Isringhausen .10 .30
202 Lance Johnson .10 .30
203 Bobby Jones .10 .30
204 Jeff Kent .10 .30
205 Bill Pulsipher .10 .30
206 Jose Vizcaino .10 .30
207 Ricky Bottalico .10 .30
208 Darren Daulton .10 .30
209 Lenny Dykstra .10 .30
210 Jim Eisenreich .10 .30
211 Gregg Jefferies .10 .30
212 Mickey Morandini .10 .30
213 Heathcliff Slocumb .10 .30
214 Jay Bell .10 .30
215 Carlos Garcia .10 .30
216 Jeff King .10 .30
217 Al Martin .10 .30
218 Orlando Merced .10 .30
219 Dan Miceli .10 .30
220 Denny Neagle .10 .30
221 Andy Benes .10 .30
222 Royce Clayton .10 .30
223 Gary Gaetti .10 .30
224 Ron Gant .10 .30
225 Bernard Gilkey .10 .30
226 Brian Jordan .10 .30
227 Ray Lankford .10 .30
228 John Mabry .10 .30
229 Ozzie Smith .50 1.25
230 Todd Stottlemyre .10 .30
231 Andy Ashby .10 .30
232 Brad Ausmus .10 .30
233 Ken Caminiti .10 .30
234 Steve Finley .10 .30
235 Tony Gwynn .40 1.00
236 Joey Hamilton .10 .30
237 Rickey Henderson .30 .75
238 Trevor Hoffman .10 .30
239 Wally Joyner .10 .30
240 Rod Beck .10 .30
241 Barry Bonds .75 2.00
242 Glenallen Hill .10 .30
243 Stan Javier .10 .30
244 Mark Leiter .10 .30
245 Deion Sanders .20 .50
246 William Van Landingham .10 .30
247 Matt Williams .10 .30
248 Checklist .10 .30
249 Checklist .10 .30
250 Checklist .10 .30

1996 Metal Universe Platinum

COMPLETE SET (250) 60.00 120.00
*STARS: 1.25X TO 3X BASIC CARDS
*ROOKIES: 1.25X TO 3X BASIC CARDS
ONE PER PACK

1996 Metal Universe Heavy Metal

COMPLETE SET (10) 10.00 25.00
STATED ODDS 1:8
1 Albert Belle .40 1.00
2 Barry Bonds 2.50 6.00
3 Juan Gonzalez .40 1.00
4 Ken Griffey Jr. 2.00 5.00
5 Mark McGwire 2.50 6.00
6 Mike Piazza 1.50 4.00
7 Sammy Sosa 1.00 2.50
8 Frank Thomas 1.00 2.50
9 Mo Vaughn .40 1.00
10 Matt Williams .40 1.00

1996 Metal Universe Mining For Gold

COMPLETE SET (12) 25.00 60.00
STATED ODDS 1:12 RETAIL
1 Yamil Benitez 1.25 3.00
2 Marty Cordova 1.25 3.00
3 Shawn Green 1.25 3.00
4 Todd Greene 1.25 3.00
5 Brian L.Hunter 1.25 3.00
6 Derek Jeter 8.00 20.00
7 Charles Johnson 1.25 3.00
8 Chipper Jones 3.00 8.00
9 Hideo Nomo 3.00 8.00
10 Alex Ochoa 1.25 3.00
11 Andy Pettitte 2.00 5.00
12 Quilvio Veras 1.25 3.00

1996 Metal Universe Mother Lode

COMPLETE SET (12) 20.00 50.00
STATED ODDS 1:12 HOBBY
1 Barry Bonds 4.00 10.00
2 Jim Edmonds .60 1.50
3 Ken Griffey Jr. 3.00 8.00
4 Kenny Lofton .60 1.50
5 Raul Mondesi .60 1.50
6 Rafael Palmeiro 1.00 2.50
7 Manny Ramirez 1.00 2.50
8 Cal Ripken 5.00 12.00
9 Tim Salmon 1.00 2.50
10 Ryne Sandberg 2.50 6.00
11 Frank Thomas 1.50 4.00
12 Matt Williams .60 1.50

1996 Metal Universe Platinum Portraits

COMPLETE SET (10) 4.00 10.00
STATED ODDS 1:4
1 Garret Anderson .30 .75
2 Marty Cordova .30 .75
3 Jim Edmonds .30 .75
4 Jason Isringhausen .30 .75
5 Chipper Jones .75 2.00
6 Ryan Klesko .30 .75
7 Hideo Nomo .75 2.00
8 Carlos Perez .30 .75
9 Manny Ramirez .50 1.25
10 Rondell White .30 .75

1996 Metal Universe Titanium

COMPLETE SET (10) 30.00 80.00
STATED ODDS 1:24
1 Albert Belle 1.00 2.50
2 Barry Bonds 6.00 15.00
3 Ken Griffey Jr. 5.00 12.00
4 Tony Gwynn 3.00 8.00
5 Greg Maddux 4.00 10.00
6 Mike Piazza 4.00 10.00
7 Cal Ripken 8.00 20.00
8 Frank Thomas 2.50 6.00
9 Mo Vaughn 1.00 2.50
10 Matt Williams 1.00 2.50

1997 Metal Universe

The 1997 Metal Universe set, (produced by Fleer), was issued in one series totalling 250 cards and distributed in eight-card foil packs with a suggested retail price of $2.49. Printed in 100 percent etched foil with UV-coating, the fronts features color photos of star players on full-bleed backgrounds of comic book art with the player's name, team, position and card logo printed near the bottom of the card. The backs carry another player photo and statistics. An Alex Rodriguez promo card was distributed to dealers and hobby media several weekd prior to the product's release.

COMPLETE SET (250) 12.50 30.00
1 Roberto Alomar .20 .50
2 Brady Anderson .10 .30
3 Rocky Coppinger .10 .30
4 Chris Hoiles .10 .30
5 Eddie Murray .30 .75
6 Mike Mussina .20 .50
7 Rafael Palmeiro .20 .50
8 Cal Ripken 1.00 2.50
9 B.J. Surhoff .10 .30
10 Brant Brown .10 .30
11 Mark Grace .20 .50
12 Brian McRae .10 .30
13 Jaime Navarro .10 .30
14 Ryne Sandberg .50 1.25
15 Sammy Sosa .30 .75
16 Amaury Telemaco .10 .30
17 Steve Trachsel .10 .30
18 Darren Bragg .10 .30
19 Jose Canseco .20 .50
20 Roger Clemens .60 1.50
21 Nomar Garciaparra .50 1.25
22 Tom Gordon .10 .30
23 Tim Naehring .10 .30
24 Mike Stanley .10 .30
25 John Valentin .10 .30
26 Mo Vaughn .10 .30
27 Jermaine Dye .10 .30
28 Tom Glavine .20 .50
29 Marquis Grissom .10 .30
30 Andruw Jones .20 .50
31 Chipper Jones .30 .75
32 Ryan Klesko .10 .30
33 Greg Maddux .50 1.25
34 Fred McGriff .20 .50
35 John Smoltz .20 .50
36 Garret Anderson .10 .30
37 George Arias .10 .30
38 Gary DiSarcina .10 .30
39 Jim Edmonds .10 .30
40 Darin Erstad .10 .30
41 Chuck Finley .10 .30
42 Troy Percival .10 .30
43 Tim Salmon .20 .50
44 Bret Boone .10 .30
45 Jeff Brantley .10 .30
46 Eric Davis .10 .30
47 Barry Larkin .20 .50
48 Hal Morris .10 .30
49 Mark Portugal .10 .30
50 Reggie Sanders .10 .30
51 John Smiley .10 .30
52 Wilson Alvarez .10 .30
53 Harold Baines .10 .30
54 James Baldwin .10 .30
55 Albert Belle .10 .30
56 Mike Cameron .10 .30
57 Ray Durham .10 .30
58 Alex Fernandez .10 .30
59 Roberto Hernandez .10 .30
60 Tony Phillips .10 .30
61 Frank Thomas .30 .75
62 Robin Ventura .10 .30
63 Jeff Cirillo .10 .30
64 Jeff D'Amico .10 .30
65 John Jaha .10 .30
66 Scott Karl .10 .30
67 Ben McDonald .10 .30
68 Marc Newfield .10 .30
69 Dave Nilsson .10 .30
70 Jose Valentin .10 .30
71 Dante Bichette .10 .30
72 Ellis Burks .10 .30
73 Vinny Castilla .10 .30
74 Andres Galarraga .10 .30
75 Kevin Ritz .10 .30
76 Larry Walker .10 .30
77 Walt Weiss .10 .30
78 Jamey Wright .10 .30
79 Eric Young .10 .30
80 Julio Franco .10 .30
81 Orel Hershiser .10 .30
82 Kenny Lofton .10 .30
83 Jack McDowell .10 .30
84 Jose Mesa .10 .30
85 Charles Nagy .10 .30
86 Manny Ramirez .20 .50
87 Jim Thome .20 .50
88 Omar Vizquel .20 .50
89 Matt Williams .10 .30
90 Kevin Appier .10 .30
91 Johnny Damon .20 .50
92 Chili Davis .10 .30
93 Tom Goodwin .10 .30
94 Keith Lockhart .10 .30
95 Jeff Montgomery .10 .30
96 Craig Paquette .10 .30
97 Jose Rosado .10 .30
98 Michael Tucker .10 .30
99 Wilton Guerrero .10 .30
100 Todd Hollandsworth .10 .30
101 Eric Karros .10 .30
102 Ramon Martinez .10 .30
103 Raul Mondesi .10 .30
104 Hideo Nomo .30 .75
105 Mike Piazza .50 1.25
106 Ismael Valdes .10 .30
107 Todd Worrell .10 .30
108 Tony Clark .10 .30
109 Travis Fryman .10 .30
110 Bob Higginson .10 .30
111 Mark Lewis .10 .30
112 Melvin Nieves .10 .30
113 Justin Thompson .10 .30
114 Wade Boggs .20 .50
115 David Cone .10 .30
116 Cecil Fielder .10 .30
117 Dwight Gooden .10 .30
118 Derek Jeter .75 2.00
119 Tino Martinez .20 .50
120 Paul O'Neill .20 .50
121 Andy Pettitte .20 .50
122 Mariano Rivera .30 .75
123 Darryl Strawberry .10 .30
124 John Wetteland .10 .30
125 Bernie Williams .20 .50
126 Tony Batista .10 .30
127 Geronimo Berroa .10 .30
128 Scott Brosius .10 .30
129 Jason Giambi .10 .30
130 Jose Herrera .10 .30
131 Mark McGwire .75 2.00
132 John Wasdin .10 .30
133 Bob Abreu .20 .50
134 Jeff Bagwell .20 .50
135 Derek Bell .10 .30
136 Craig Biggio .20 .50
137 Brian Hunter .10 .30
138 Darryl Kile .10 .30
139 Orlando Miller .10 .30
140 Shane Reynolds .10 .30
141 Billy Wagner .10 .30
142 Donne Wall .10 .30
143 Jay Buhner .10 .30
144 Jeff Fassero .10 .30
145 Ken Griffey Jr. .60 1.50
146 Sterling Hitchcock .10 .30
147 Randy Johnson .30 .75
148 Edgar Martinez .20 .50
149 Alex Rodriguez .50 1.25
150 Paul Sorrento .10 .30
151 Dan Wilson .10 .30
152 Moises Alou .10 .30
153 Darrin Fletcher .10 .30
154 Cliff Floyd .10 .30
155 Mark Grudzielanek .10 .30
156 Vladimir Guerrero .30 .75
157 Mike Lansing .10 .30
158 Pedro Martinez .20 .50
159 Henry Rodriguez .10 .30
160 Rondell White .10 .30
161 Will Clark .20 .50
162 Juan Gonzalez .10 .30
163 Rusty Greer .10 .30
164 Ken Hill .10 .30
165 Mark McLemore .10 .30
166 Dean Palmer .10 .30
167 Roger Pavlik .10 .30
168 Ivan Rodriguez .20 .50
169 Mickey Tettleton .10 .30
170 Bobby Bonilla .10 .30
171 Kevin Brown .10 .30
172 Greg Colbrunn .10 .30
173 Jeff Conine .10 .30
174 Jim Eisenreich .10 .30
175 Charles Johnson .10 .30
176 Al Leiter .10 .30
177 Robb Nen .10 .30
178 Edgar Renteria .10 .30
179 Gary Sheffield .10 .30
180 Devon White .10 .30
181 Joe Carter .10 .30
182 Carlos Delgado .10 .30
183 Alex Gonzalez .10 .30
184 Shawn Green .10 .30
185 Juan Guzman .10 .30
186 Pat Hentgen .10 .30
187 Orlando Merced .10 .30
188 John Olerud .10 .30
189 Robert Perez .10 .30
190 Ed Sprague .10 .30
191 Mark Clark .10 .30
192 John Franco .10 .30
193 Bernard Gilkey .10 .30
194 Todd Hundley .10 .30
195 Lance Johnson .10 .30
196 Bobby Jones .10 .30
197 Alex Ochoa .10 .30
198 Rey Ordonez .10 .30
199 Paul Wilson .10 .30
200 Ricky Bottalico .10 .30
201 Gregg Jefferies .10 .30
202 Wendell Magee .10 .30
203 Mickey Morandini .10 .30
204 Ricky Otero .10 .30
205 Scott Rolen .20 .50
206 Benito Santiago .10 .30
207 Curt Schilling .10 .30
208 Rich Becker .10 .30
209 Marty Cordova .10 .30
210 Chuck Knoblauch .10 .30
211 Pat Meares .10 .30
212 Paul Molitor .10 .30
213 Frank Rodriguez .10 .30
214 Terry Steinbach .10 .30
215 Todd Walker .10 .30
216 Andy Ashby .10 .30
217 Ken Caminiti .10 .30
218 Steve Finley .10 .30
219 Tony Gwynn .40 1.00
220 Joey Hamilton .10 .30
221 Rickey Henderson .30 .75
222 Trevor Hoffman .10 .30
223 Wally Joyner .10 .30
224 Scott Sanders .10 .30
225 Fernando Valenzuela .10 .30
226 Greg Vaughn .10 .30
227 Alan Benes .10 .30
228 Andy Benes .10 .30
229 Dennis Eckersley .10 .30
230 Ron Gant .10 .30
231 Brian Jordan .10 .30
232 Ray Lankford .10 .30
233 John Mabry .10 .30
234 Tom Pagnozzi .10 .30
235 Todd Stottlemyre .10 .30
236 Jermaine Allensworth .10 .30
237 Francisco Cordova .10 .30
238 Jason Kendall .10 .30
239 Jeff King .10 .30
240 Al Martin .10 .30
241 Rod Beck .10 .30
242 Barry Bonds .75 2.00
243 Shawn Estes .10 .30
244 Mark Gardner .10 .30
245 Glenallen Hill .10 .30
246 Bill Mueller RC .50 1.25
247 J.T. Snow .10 .30
248 Checklist (1-107) .10 .30
249 Checklist (108-207) .10 .30
250 Checklist (208-250 inserts) .10 .30
P149 Alex Rodriguez Promo .60 1.50

1997 Metal Universe Blast Furnace

COMPLETE SET (12) 10.00 25.00
STATED ODDS 1:48 HOBBY
1 Jeff Bagwell .60 1.50
2 Albert Belle .40 1.00
3 Barry Bonds 1.50 4.00
4 Andres Galarraga .60 1.50
5 Juan Gonzalez .40 1.00
6 Ken Griffey Jr. 2.00 5.00
7 Todd Hundley .40 1.00
8 Mark McGwire 1.50 4.00
9 Mike Piazza 1.00 2.50
10 Alex Rodriguez 1.25 3.00
11 Frank Thomas 1.00 2.50
12 Mo Vaughn .40 1.00

1997 Metal Universe Emerald Autographs

COMPLETE SET (6) 100.00 200.00
ONE CARD VIA MAIL PER EXCH.CARD
*EXCH.CARDS: .1X TO .25X BASIC AUTO
EXCHANGE CARDS: 1:20 BOXES
AU1 Darin Erstad 6.00 15.00
AU2 Todd Hollandsworth 6.00 15.00
AU3 Alex Ochoa 6.00 15.00
AU4 Alex Rodriguez 60.00 120.00
AU5 Scott Rolen 6.00 15.00
AU6 Todd Walker 6.00 15.00

1997 Metal Universe Magnetic Field

COMPLETE SET (10) 10.00 25.00
STATED ODDS 1:12
1 Roberto Alomar .60 1.50
2 Jeff Bagwell .60 1.50
3 Barry Bonds 2.50 6.00
4 Ken Griffey Jr. 2.00 5.00
5 Derek Jeter 2.50 6.00
6 Kenny Lofton .40 1.00
7 Edgar Renteria .40 1.00
8 Cal Ripken 3.00 8.00
9 Alex Rodriguez 1.50 4.00
10 Matt Williams .40 1.00

1997 Metal Universe Mining for Gold

COMPLETE SET (10) 6.00 15.00
STATED ODDS 1:8
1 Bob Abreu .60 1.50
2 Kevin Brown C .40 1.00
3 Nomar Garciaparra 1.50 4.00
4 Vladimir Guerrero 1.00 2.50
5 Wilton Guerrero .40 1.00
6 Andruw Jones .60 1.50
7 Curt Lyons .40 1.00
8 Neifi Perez .40 1.00
9 Scott Rolen .60 1.50
10 Todd Walker .40 1.00

1997 Metal Universe Mother Lode

STATED ODDS 1:288
1 Roberto Alomar 8.00 20.00
2 Jeff Bagwell 8.00 20.00
3 Barry Bonds 20.00 50.00
4 Ken Griffey Jr. 200.00 500.00
5 Andruw Jones 5.00 12.00
6 Chipper Jones 12.00 30.00
7 Kenny Lofton 5.00 12.00
8 Mike Piazza 12.00 30.00
9 Cal Ripken 40.00 100.00
10 Alex Rodriguez 15.00 40.00
11 Frank Thomas 12.00 30.00
12 Matt Williams 5.00 12.00

1997 Metal Universe Platinum Portraits

COMPLETE SET (10) 20.00 50.00
STATED ODDS 1:36
1 James Baldwin 1.25 3.00
2 Jermaine Dye 1.25 3.00
3 Todd Hollandsworth 1.25 3.00
4 Derek Jeter 10.00 25.00
5 Chipper Jones 3.00 8.00
6 Jason Kendall 1.25 3.00
7 Rey Ordonez 1.25 3.00
8 Andy Pettitte 2.00 5.00
9 Edgar Renteria 1.25 3.00
10 Alex Rodriguez 5.00 12.00

1997 Metal Universe Titanium

COMPLETE SET (10) 10.00 25.00
STATED ODDS 1:24 RETAIL
1 Jeff Bagwell .60 1.50
2 Albert Belle .40 1.00
3 Ken Griffey Jr. 2.00 5.00
4 Chipper Jones 1.00 2.50
5 Greg Maddux 1.50 4.00
6 Mark McGwire 1.50 4.00
7 Mike Piazza 1.00 2.50
8 Cal Ripken 3.00 8.00
9 Alex Rodriguez 1.25 3.00
10 Frank Thomas 1.00 2.50

1998 Metal Universe

The 1998 Metal Universe set, produced by Fleer, was issued in one series totalling 220 cards. The fronts feature color player photos with metal etching. The backs carry player information. The set contains the topical subset: Hardball Galaxy (203-217). An Alex Rodriguez promo card was distributed along with all dealer order forms. The card is identical to the regular issue Rodriguez card except for the text "PROMOTIONAL SAMPLE" written diagonally along the card back.

COMPLETE SET (220) 15.00 40.00
1 Jose Cruz Jr. .10 .30
2 Jeff Abbott .10 .30
3 Rafael Palmeiro .20 .50
4 Ivan Rodriguez .20 .50
5 Jaret Wright .10 .30
6 Derek Bell .10 .30
7 Chuck Finley .10 .30
8 Travis Fryman .10 .30
9 Randy Johnson .30 .75
10 Derrek Lee .20 .50
11 Bernie Williams .20 .50
12 Carlos Baerga .10 .30
13 Ricky Bottalico .10 .30
14 Ellis Burks .10 .30
15 Russ Davis .10 .30
16 Nomar Garciaparra .50 1.25
17 Joey Hamilton .10 .30
18 Jason Kendall .10 .30
19 Darryl Kile .10 .30
20 Edgardo Alfonzo .10 .30
21 Moises Alou .10 .30
22 Bobby Bonilla .10 .30
23 Jim Edmonds .10 .30
24 Jose Guillen .10 .30
25 Chuck Knoblauch .10 .30
26 Javy Lopez .10 .30
27 Billy Wagner .10 .30
28 Kevin Appier .10 .30
29 Joe Carter .10 .30
30 Todd Dunwoody .10 .30
31 Gary Gaetti .10 .30
32 Juan Gonzalez .10 .30
33 Jeffrey Hammonds .10 .30
34 Roberto Hernandez .10 .30
35 Dave Nilsson .10 .30
36 Manny Ramirez .20 .50
37 Robin Ventura .10 .30
38 Rondell White .10 .30
39 Vinny Castilla .10 .30
40 Will Clark .20 .50
41 Scott Hatteberg .10 .30
42 Russ Johnson .10 .30
43 Ricky Ledee .10 .30
44 Kenny Lofton .10 .30
45 Paul Molitor .10 .30
46 Justin Thompson .10 .30
47 Craig Biggio .20 .50
48 Damion Easley .10 .30
49 Brad Radke .10 .30
50 Ben Grieve .10 .30
51 Mark Bellhorn .10 .30
52 Henry Blanco .10 .30
53 Mariano Rivera .30 .75
54 Reggie Sanders .10 .30
55 Paul Sorrento .10 .30
56 Terry Steinbach .10 .30
57 Mo Vaughn .10 .30
58 Brady Anderson .10 .30
59 Tom Glavine .20 .50
60 Sammy Sosa .30 .75
61 Larry Walker .10 .30
62 Rod Beck .10 .30
63 Jose Canseco .20 .50
64 Steve Finley .10 .30
65 Pedro Martinez .20 .50
66 John Olerud .10 .30
67 Scott Rolen .20 .50
68 Ismael Valdes .10 .30
69 Andrew Vessel .10 .30
70 Mark Grudzielanek .10 .30
71 Eric Karros .10 .30
72 Jeff Shaw .10 .30
73 Lou Collier .10 .30
74 Edgar Martinez .20 .50
75 Vladimir Guerrero .30 .75
76 Paul Konerko .10 .30
77 Kevin Orie .10 .30
78 Kevin Polcovich .10 .30
79 Brett Tomko .10 .30
80 Jeff Bagwell .20 .50
81 Barry Bonds .75 2.00
82 David Justice .10 .30
83 Hideo Nomo .30 .75
84 Ryne Sandberg .50 1.25
85 Shannon Stewart .10 .30
86 Derek Wallace .10 .30
87 Tony Womack .10 .30
88 Jason Giambi .10 .30
89 Mark Grace .20 .50
90 Pat Hentgen .10 .30
91 Raul Mondesi .10 .30
92 Matt Morris .10 .30
93 Matt Perisho .10 .30
94 Tim Salmon .20 .50
95 Jeremi Gonzalez .10 .30
96 Shawn Green .10 .30
97 Todd Greene .10 .30
98 Ruben Rivera .10 .30
99 Deion Sanders .20 .50
100 Alex Rodriguez .50 1.25
101 Will Cunnane .10 .30
102 Ray Lankford .10 .30
103 Ryan McGuire .10 .30
104 Charles Nagy .10 .30
105 Rey Ordonez .10 .30
106 Mike Piazza .50 1.25
107 Tony Saunders .10 .30
108 Curt Schilling .10 .30
109 Fernando Tatis .10 .30
110 Mark McGwire .75 2.00
111 Dave Dellucci RC .20 .50
112 Garret Anderson .10 .30
113 Shane Bowers RC .10 .30
114 David Cone .10 .30
115 Jeff King .10 .30
116 Matt Williams .10 .30
117 Aaron Boone .10 .30
118 Dennis Eckersley .10 .30
119 Livan Hernandez .10 .30
120 Richard Hidalgo .10 .30

121 Bobby Higginson .10 .30
122 Tino Martinez .20 .50
123 Tim Naehring .10 .30
124 Jose Vidro .10 .30
125 John Wetteland .10 .30
126 Jay Bell .10 .30
127 Albert Belle .10 .30
128 Marty Cordova .10 .30
129 Chili Davis .10 .30
130 Jason Dickson .10 .30
131 Rusty Greer .10 .30
132 Hideki Irabu .10 .30
133 Greg Maddux .50 1.25
134 Billy Taylor .10 .30
135 Jim Thome .20 .50
136 Gerald Williams .10 .30
137 Jeff Cirillo .10 .30
138 Delino DeShields .10 .30
139 Andres Galarraga .10 .30
140 Willie Greene .10 .30
141 John Jaha .10 .30
142 Charles Johnson .10 .30
143 Ryan Klesko .10 .30
144 Paul O'Neill .20 .50
145 Robinson Checo .10 .30
146 Roberto Alomar .20 .50
147 Wilson Alvarez .10 .30
148 Bobby Jones .10 .30
149 Raul Casanova .10 .30
150 Andruw Jones .20 .50
151 Mike Lansing .10 .30
152 Mickey Morandini .10 .30
153 Neifi Perez .10 .30
154 Pokey Reese .10 .30
155 Edgar Renteria .10 .30
156 Eric Young .10 .30
157 Darin Erstad .10 .30
158 Kelvim Escobar .10 .30
159 Carl Everett .10 .30
160 Tom Gordon .10 .30
161 Ken Griffey Jr. .60 1.50
162 Al Martin .10 .30
163 Bubba Trammell .10 .30
164 Carlos Delgado .10 .30
165 Kevin Brown .20 .50
166 Ken Caminiti .10 .30
167 Roger Clemens .60 1.50
168 Ron Gant .10 .30
169 Jeff Kent .10 .30
170 Mike Mussina .20 .50
171 Dean Palmer .10 .30
172 Henry Rodriguez .10 .30
173 Matt Stairs .10 .30
174 Jay Buhner .10 .30
175 Frank Thomas .30 .75
176 Mike Cameron .10 .30
177 Johnny Damon .20 .50
178 Tony Gwynn .40 1.00
179 John Smoltz .20 .50
180 B.J. Surhoff .10 .30
181 Antone Williamson .10 .30
182 Alan Benes .10 .30
183 Jeromy Burnitz .10 .30
184 Tony Clark .10 .30
185 Shawn Estes .10 .30
186 Todd Helton .20 .50
187 Todd Hundley .10 .30
188 Chipper Jones .30 .75
189 Mark Kotsay .10 .30
190 Barry Larkin .20 .50
191 Mike Lieberthal .10 .30
192 Andy Pettitte .20 .50
193 Gary Sheffield .10 .30
194 Jeff Suppan .10 .30
195 Mark Wohlers .10 .30
196 Dante Bichette .10 .30
197 Trevor Hoffman .10 .30
198 J.T. Snow .10 .30
199 Derek Jeter .75 2.00
200 Cal Ripken 1.00 2.50
201 Steve Woodard .10 .30
202 Ray Durham .10 .30
203 Barry Bonds HG .40 1.00
204 Tony Clark HG .10 .30
205 Roger Clemens HG .30 .75
206 Ken Griffey Jr. HG .40 1.00
207 Deion Sanders HG .10 .30
208 Derek Jeter HG .40 1.00
209 Randy Johnson HG .20 .50
210 Brady Anderson HG .10 .30
211 Hideo Nomo HG .20 .50
212 Mike Piazza HG .30 .75
213 Cal Ripken HG .50 1.25
214 Alex Rodriguez HG .30 .75
215 Frank Thomas HG .20 .50
216 Mo Vaughn HG .10 .30
217 Larry Walker HG .10 .30
218 Ken Griffey Jr. CL .40 1.00
219 Alex Rodriguez CL .30 .75
220 Frank Thomas CL .20 .50
P100 Alex Rodriguez Promo .60 1.50

1998 Metal Universe Precious Metal Gems

*STARS: 40X TO 100X BASIC CARDS
*ROOKIES: 40X TO 100X BASIC CARDS
RANDOM INSERTS IN PACKS
STATED PRINT RUN 50 SERIAL #'d SETS

1998 Metal Universe All-Galactic Team

COMPLETE SET (18) 60.00 120.00
STATED ODDS 1:192
1 Ken Griffey Jr. 6.00 15.00
2 Frank Thomas 3.00 8.00
3 Chipper Jones 3.00 8.00
4 Albert Belle 1.25 3.00
5 Juan Gonzalez 1.25 3.00
6 Jeff Bagwell 2.00 5.00
7 Andruw Jones 1.25 3.00
8 Cal Ripken 10.00 25.00
9 Derek Jeter 8.00 20.00
10 Nomar Garciaparra 2.00 5.00
11 Darin Erstad 1.25 3.00
12 Greg Maddux 4.00 10.00
13 Alex Rodriguez 4.00 10.00
14 Mike Piazza 3.00 8.00
15 Vladimir Guerrero 2.00 5.00
16 Jose Cruz Jr. 1.25 3.00
17 Mark McGwire 5.00 12.00
18 Scott Rolen 2.00 5.00

1998 Metal Universe Diamond Heroes

COMPLETE SET (6) 5.00 12.00
STATED ODDS 1:18
1 Ken Griffey Jr. 1.25 3.00
2 Frank Thomas .60 1.50
3 Andruw Jones .40 1.00
4 Alex Rodriguez 1.00 2.50
5 Jose Cruz Jr. .25 .60
6 Cal Ripken 2.00 5.00

1998 Metal Universe Platinum Portraits

COMPLETE SET (12) 75.00 200.00
STATED ODDS 1:360
1 Ken Griffey Jr. 15.00 40.00
2 Frank Thomas 8.00 20.00
3 Chipper Jones 8.00 20.00
4 Jose Cruz Jr. 3.00 8.00
5 Andruw Jones 3.00 8.00
6 Cal Ripken 25.00 60.00
7 Derek Jeter 20.00 50.00
8 Darin Erstad 3.00 8.00
9 Greg Maddux 10.00 25.00
10 Alex Rodriguez 10.00 25.00
11 Mike Piazza 8.00 20.00
12 Vladimir Guerrero 5.00 12.00

1998 Metal Universe Titanium

COMPLETE SET (15) 75.00 150.00
STATED ODDS 1:96 10.00
1 Ken Griffey Jr. 8.00 20.00
2 Frank Thomas 4.00 10.00
3 Chipper Jones 4.00 10.00
4 Jose Cruz Jr. 1.50 4.00
5 Juan Gonzalez 1.50 4.00
6 Scott Rolen 2.50 6.00
7 Andruw Jones 2.50 6.00
8 Cal Ripken 12.50 30.00
9 Derek Jeter 10.00 25.00
10 Nomar Garciaparra 6.00 15.00
11 Darin Erstad 1.50 4.00
12 Greg Maddux 6.00 15.00
13 Alex Rodriguez 6.00 15.00
14 Mike Piazza 6.00 15.00
15 Vladimir Guerrero 4.00 10.00

1998 Metal Universe Universal Language

COMPLETE SET (20) 20.00 50.00
STATED ODDS 1:6
1 Ken Griffey Jr. 1.50 4.00
2 Frank Thomas .75 2.00
3 Chipper Jones .75 2.00
4 Albert Belle .30 .75
5 Juan Gonzalez .30 .75
6 Jeff Bagwell .50 1.25
7 Andruw Jones .50 1.25
8 Cal Ripken 2.50 6.00
9 Derek Jeter 2.00 5.00
10 Nomar Garciaparra 1.25 3.00
11 Darin Erstad .30 .75
12 Greg Maddux 1.25 3.00
13 Alex Rodriguez 1.25 3.00
14 Mike Piazza 1.25 3.00
15 Vladimir Guerrero .75 2.00
16 Jose Cruz Jr. .30 .75
17 Hideo Nomo .75 2.00
18 Kenny Lofton .30 .75
19 Tony Gwynn 1.00 2.50
20 Scott Rolen .50 1.25

1999 Metal Universe Sample Sheet

NNOA A.Belle 10.00 25.00
J.D.Drew AU
D.Jeter
M.Piazza
A.Rod
S.Sosa
NNO A.Belle 2.00 5.00
J.D.Drew
D.Jeter
M.Piazza
A.Rod
S.Sosa

1999 Metal Universe

This 300-card set, produced by Fleer, was distributed in eight-card hobby and retail packs carrying a suggested retail price of $2.69. The product was released in January, 1999. Card fronts feature color action player photos with brushed metal backgrounds in 100 percent etched silver foil and an embossed nameplate with the look of forged steel. The backs carry player information. The set includes the following subsets: Caught on the Fly (233-247), Building Blocks (248-272), and M.L.P.D. (273-300) which features prominent and dominant stars. In an unannounced promotion, thirty-five hand-numbered J.D. Drew Building Blocks subset sample cards were signed by the athlete and randomly seeded into packs. Each of these cards has an embossed authentication seal and the word SAMPLE replaces the card number on back.

COMPLETE SET (300) 20.00 50.00
DREW AU RANDOM INSERT IN PACKS
1 Mark McGwire .75 2.00
2 Jim Edmonds .10 .30
3 Travis Fryman .10 .30
4 Tom Gordon .10 .30
5 Jeff Bagwell .20 .50
6 Rico Brogna .10 .30
7 Tom Evans .10 .30
8 John Franco .10 .30
9 Juan Gonzalez .10 .30
10 Paul Molitor .10 .30
11 Roberto Alomar .20 .50
12 Mike Hampton .10 .30
13 Orel Hershiser .10 .30
14 Todd Stottlemyre .10 .30
15 Robin Ventura .10 .30
16 Todd Walker .10 .30
17 Bernie Williams .20 .50
18 Shawn Estes .10 .30
19 Richie Sexson .10 .30
20 Kevin Millwood .10 .30
21 David Ortiz .30 .75
22 Mariano Rivera .30 .75
23 Ivan Rodriguez .20 .50
24 Mike Sirotka .10 .30
25 David Justice .10 .30
26 Carl Pavano .10 .30
27 Albert Belle .10 .30
28 Will Clark .20 .50
29 Jose Cruz Jr. .10 .30
30 Trevor Hoffman .10 .30
31 Dean Palmer .10 .30
32 Edgar Renteria .10 .30
33 David Segui .10 .30
34 B.J. Surhoff .10 .30
35 Miguel Tejada .10 .30
36 Bob Wickman .10 .30
37 Charles Johnson .10 .30
38 Andruw Jones .20 .50
39 Mike Lieberthal .10 .30
40 Eli Marrero .10 .30
41 Neifi Perez .10 .30
42 Jim Thome .20 .50
43 Barry Bonds .75 2.00
44 Carlos Delgado .10 .30
45 Chuck Finley .10 .30
46 Brian Meadows .10 .30
47 Tony Gwynn .40 1.00
48 Jose Offerman .10 .30
49 Cal Ripken 1.00 2.50
50 Alex Rodriguez .50 1.25
51 Esteban Yan .10 .30
52 Matt Stairs .10 .30
53 Fernando Vina .10 .30
54 Rondell White .10 .30
55 Kerry Wood .10 .30
56 Dmitri Young .10 .30
57 Ken Caminiti .10 .30
58 Alex Gonzalez .10 .30
59 Matt Mantei .10 .30
60 Tino Martinez .20 .50
61 Hal Morris .10 .30
62 Rafael Palmeiro .20 .50
63 Troy Percival .10 .30
64 Bobby Smith .10 .30
65 Ed Sprague .10 .30
66 Brett Tomko .10 .30
67 Steve Trachsel .10 .30
68 Ugueth Urbina .10 .30
69 Jose Valentin .10 .30
70 Kevin Brown .20 .50
71 Shawn Green .10 .30
72 Dustin Hermanson .10 .30
73 Livan Hernandez .10 .30
74 Geoff Jenkins .10 .30
75 Jeff King .10 .30
76 Chuck Knoblauch .10 .30
77 Edgar Martinez .20 .50
78 Fred McGriff .20 .50
79 Mike Mussina .20 .50
80 Dave Nilsson .10 .30
81 Kenny Rogers .10 .30
82 Tim Salmon .20 .50
83 Reggie Sanders .10 .30
84 Wilson Alvarez .10 .30
85 Rod Beck .10 .30
86 Jose Guillen .10 .30
87 Bob Higginson .10 .30
88 Gregg Olson .10 .30
89 Jeff Shaw .10 .30
90 Masato Yoshii .10 .30
91 Todd Helton .20 .50
92 David Dellucci .10 .30
93 Johnny Damon .20 .50
94 Cliff Floyd .10 .30
95 Ken Griffey Jr. .60 1.50
96 Juan Guzman .10 .30
97 Derek Jeter .75 2.00
98 Barry Larkin .20 .50
99 Quinton McCracken .10 .30
100 Sammy Sosa .30 .75
101 Kevin Young .10 .30
102 Jay Bell .10 .30
103 Jay Buhner .10 .30
104 Jeff Conine .10 .30
105 Ryan Jackson .10 .30
106 Sidney Ponson .10 .30
107 Jeromy Burnitz .10 .30
108 Roberto Hernandez .10 .30
109 A.J. Hinch .10 .30
110 Hideki Irabu .10 .30
111 Paul Konerko .10 .30
112 Henry Rodriguez .10 .30
113 Shannon Stewart .10 .30
114 Tony Womack .10 .30
115 Wilton Guerrero .10 .30
116 Andy Benes .10 .30
117 Jeff Cirillo .10 .30
118 Chili Davis .10 .30
119 Eric Davis .10 .30
120 Vladimir Guerrero .30 .75
121 Dennis Reyes .10 .30
122 Rickey Henderson .30 .75
123 Mickey Morandini .10 .30
124 Jason Schmidt .10 .30
125 J.T. Snow .10 .30
126 Justin Thompson .10 .30
127 Billy Wagner .10 .30
128 Armando Benitez .10 .30
129 Sean Casey .10 .30
130 Brad Fullmer .10 .30
131 Ben Grieve .10 .30
132 Robb Nen .10 .30
133 Shane Reynolds .10 .30
134 Todd Zeile .10 .30
135 Brady Anderson .10 .30
136 Aaron Boone .10 .30
137 Orlando Cabrera .10 .30
138 Jason Giambi .10 .30
139 Randy Johnson .30 .75
140 Jeff Kent .10 .30
141 John Wetteland .10 .30
142 Rolando Arrojo .10 .30
143 Scott Brosius .10 .30
144 Mark Grace .20 .50
145 Jason Kendall .10 .30
146 Travis Lee .10 .30
147 Gary Sheffield .10 .30
148 David Cone .10 .30
149 Jose Hernandez .10 .30
150 Todd Jones .10 .30
151 Al Martin .10 .30
152 Ismael Valdes .10 .30
153 Wade Boggs .20 .50
154 Garret Anderson .10 .30
155 Bobby Bonilla .10 .30
156 Darryl Kile .10 .30
157 Ryan Klesko .10 .30
158 Tim Wakefield .10 .30
159 Kenny Lofton .10 .30
160 Jose Canseco .20 .50
161 Doug Glanville .10 .30
162 Todd Hundley .10 .30
163 Brian Jordan .10 .30
164 Steve Finley .10 .30
165 Tom Glavine .20 .50
166 Al Leiter .10 .30
167 Raul Mondesi .10 .30
168 Desi Relaford .10 .30
169 Bret Saberhagen .10 .30
170 Omar Vizquel .20 .50
171 Larry Walker .10 .30
172 Bobby Abreu .10 .30
173 Moises Alou .10 .30
174 Mike Caruso .10 .30
175 Royce Clayton .10 .30
176 Bartolo Colon .10 .30
177 Marty Cordova .10 .30
178 Darin Erstad .10 .30
179 Nomar Garciaparra .50 1.25
180 Andy Ashby .10 .30
181 Dan Wilson .10 .30
182 Larry Sutton .10 .30
183 Tony Clark .10 .30
184 Andres Galarraga .10 .30
185 Ray Durham .10 .30
186 Hideo Nomo .30 .75
187 Steve Woodard .10 .30
188 Scott Rolen .20 .50
189 Mike Stanley .10 .30
190 Jaret Wright .10 .30
191 Vinny Castilla .10 .30
192 Jason Christiansen .10 .30
193 Paul Bako .10 .30
194 Carlos Perez .10 .30
195 Mike Piazza .50 1.25
196 Fernando Tatis .10 .30
197 Mo Vaughn .10 .30
198 Devon White .10 .30
199 Ricky Gutierrez .10 .30
200 Charlie Hayes .10 .30
201 Brad Radke .10 .30
202 Rick Helling .10 .30
203 John Smoltz .20 .50
204 Frank Thomas .30 .75
205 David Wells .10 .30
206 Roger Clemens .60 1.50
207 Mark Grudzielanek .10 .30
208 Chipper Jones .30 .75
209 Ray Lankford .10 .30
210 Pedro Martinez .20 .50
211 Manny Ramirez .20 .50
212 Greg Vaughn .10 .30
213 Craig Biggio .20 .50
214 Rusty Greer .10 .30
215 Greg Maddux .50 1.25
216 Rick Aguilera .10 .30
217 Andy Pettitte .20 .50
218 Dante Bichette .10 .30
219 Damion Easley .10 .30
220 Matt Morris .10 .30
221 John Olerud .10 .30
222 Chan Ho Park .10 .30
223 Curt Schilling .10 .30
224 John Valentin .10 .30
225 Matt Williams .10 .30
226 Ellis Burks .10 .30
227 Tom Goodwin .10 .30
228 Javy Lopez .10 .30
229 Eric Milton .10 .30
230 Paul O'Neill .20 .50
231 Magglio Ordonez .10 .30
232 Derrek Lee .20 .50
233 Ken Griffey Jr. FLY .40 1.00
234 Randy Johnson FLY .20 .50
235 Alex Rodriguez FLY .30 .75
236 Darin Erstad FLY .10 .30
237 Juan Gonzalez FLY .10 .30
238 Derek Jeter FLY .40 1.00
239 Tony Gwynn FLY .20 .50
240 Kerry Wood FLY .10 .30
241 Cal Ripken FLY .50 1.25
242 Sammy Sosa FLY .20 .50
243 Greg Maddux FLY .30 .75
244 Mark McGwire FLY .40 1.00
245 Chipper Jones FLY .20 .50
246 Barry Bonds FLY .40 1.00
247 Ben Grieve FLY .10 .30
248 Ben Davis BB .10 .30
249 Robert Fick BB .10 .30
250 Carlos Guillen BB .10 .30
251 Mike Frank BB .10 .30
252 Ryan Minor BB .10 .30
253 Troy Glaus BB .20 .50
254 Matt Anderson BB .10 .30
255 Josh Booty BB .10 .30
256 Gabe Alvarez BB .10 .30
257 Gabe Kapler BB .10 .30
258 Enrique Wilson BB .10 .30
259 Alex Gonzalez BB .10 .30
260 Preston Wilson BB .10 .30
261 Eric Chavez BB .10 .30
262 Adrian Beltre BB .10 .30
263 Corey Koskie BB .10 .30
264 Robert Machado BB .10 .30
265 Orlando Hernandez BB .10 .30
266 Matt Clement BB .10 .30
267 Luis Ordaz BB .10 .30
268 Jeremy Giambi BB .10 .30
269 J.D. Drew BB .10 .30
270 Cliff Politte BB .10 .30
271 Carlton Loewer BB .10 .30
272 Aramis Ramirez BB .10 .30
273 Ken Griffey Jr. MLPD .40 1.00
274 Randy Johnson MLPD .20 .50
275 Alex Rodriguez MLPD .30 .75
276 Darin Erstad MLPD .10 .30
277 Scott Rolen MLPD .10 .30
278 Juan Gonzalez MLPD .10 .30
279 Jeff Bagwell MLPD .10 .30
280 Mike Piazza MLPD .30 .75
281 Derek Jeter MLPD .40 1.00
282 Travis Lee MLPD .10 .30
283 Tony Gwynn MLPD .20 .50
284 Kerry Wood MLPD .10 .30
285 Albert Belle MLPD .10 .30
286 Sammy Sosa MLPD .20 .50
287 Mo Vaughn MLPD .10 .30
288 Nomar Garciaparra MLPD .30 .75
289 FrankThomas MLPD .20 .50
290 Cal Ripken MLPD .50 1.25
291 Greg Maddux MLPD .30 .75
292 Chipper Jones MLPD .20 .50
293 Ben Grieve MLPD .10 .30
294 Andruw Jones MLPD .10 .30
295 Mark McGwire MLPD .40 1.00
296 Roger Clemens MLPD .30 .75
297 Barry Bonds MLPD .40 1.00
298 Ken Griffey Jr. CL .40 1.00
299 Kerry Wood CL .10 .30
300 Alex Rodriguez CL .30 .75
SAMP J.D. Drew AU/35 15.00 40.00

1999 Metal Universe Precious Metal Gems

*STARS: 20X TO 50X BASIC CARDS
RANDOM INSERTS IN PACKS
STATED PRINT RUN 50 SERIAL #'D SETS

1999 Metal Universe Boyz With The Wood

COMPLETE SET (15) 25.00 60.00
STATED ODDS 1:18
1 Ken Griffey Jr. 2.50 6.00
2 Frank Thomas 1.25 3.00
3 Jeff Bagwell .75 2.00
4 Juan Gonzalez .50 1.25
5 Mark McGwire 3.00 8.00
6 Scott Rolen .75 2.00
7 Travis Lee .50 1.25
8 Tony Gwynn 1.50 4.00
9 Mike Piazza 2.00 5.00
10 Chipper Jones 1.25 3.00
11 Nomar Garciaparra 2.00 5.00
12 Derek Jeter 3.00 8.00
13 Cal Ripken 4.00 10.00
14 Andruw Jones .75 2.00
15 Alex Rodriguez 2.00 5.00

1999 Metal Universe Diamond Soul

COMPLETE SET (15) 30.00 80.00
STATED ODDS 1:72
1 Cal Ripken 8.00 20.00
2 Alex Rodriguez 3.00 8.00
3 Chipper Jones 2.50 6.00
4 Derek Jeter 6.00 15.00
5 Frank Thomas 2.50 6.00
6 Greg Maddux 3.00 8.00
7 Juan Gonzalez 1.00 2.50
8 Ken Griffey Jr. 5.00 12.00
9 Kerry Wood 1.00 2.50
10 Mark McGwire 4.00 10.00
11 Mike Piazza 2.50 6.00
12 Nomar Garciaparra 1.50 4.00
13 Scott Rolen 1.50 4.00
14 Tony Gwynn 2.50 6.00
15 Travis Lee 1.00 2.50

1999 Metal Universe Linchpins

COMPLETE SET (10) 75.00 150.00
STATED ODDS 1:360
1 Mike Piazza 8.00 20.00
2 Mark McGwire 12.00 30.00
3 Kerry Wood 3.00 8.00
4 Ken Griffey Jr. 15.00 40.00
5 Greg Maddux 10.00 25.00
6 Frank Thomas 15.00 40.00
7 Derek Jeter 20.00 50.00
8 Chipper Jones 8.00 20.00
9 Cal Ripken 25.00 60.00
10 Alex Rodriguez 10.00 25.00

1999 Metal Universe Neophytes

COMPLETE SET (15) 4.00 10.00
STATED ODDS 1:6
1 Troy Glaus .50 1.25
2 Travis Lee .30 .75
3 Scott Elarton .30 .75
4 Ricky Ledee .30 .75
5 Richard Hidalgo .30 .75
6 J.D. Drew .30 .75
7 Paul Konerko .30 .75
8 Orlando Hernandez .30 .75
9 Mike Caruso .30 .75
10 Mike Frank .30 .75
11 Miguel Tejada .30 .75
12 Matt Anderson .30 .75
13 Kerry Wood .30 .75
14 Gabe Alvarez .30 .75
15 Adrian Beltre .30 .75

1999 Metal Universe Planet Metal

COMPLETE SET (15) 60.00 120.00
STATED ODDS 1:36
1 Alex Rodriguez 4.00 10.00
2 Andruw Jones 1.50 4.00
3 Cal Ripken 8.00 20.00
4 Chipper Jones 2.50 6.00
5 Darin Erstad 1.00 2.50
6 Derek Jeter 6.00 15.00
7 Frank Thomas 2.50 6.00
8 Travis Lee 1.00 2.50
9 Scott Rolen 1.50 4.00
10 Nomar Garciaparra 4.00 10.00
11 Mike Piazza 4.00 10.00
12 Mark McGwire 6.00 15.00
13 Ken Griffey Jr. 5.00 12.00
14 Juan Gonzalez 1.00 2.50
15 Jeff Bagwell 1.50 4.00

2000 Metal

COMPLETE SET (250) 30.00 60.00
COMP.SET w/o SP's (200) 8.00 20.00
COMMON CARD (1-200) .10 .25
COMMON PROS (201-250) .20 .50
PROSPECTS STATED ODDS 1:2
1 Tony Gwynn .25 .60
2 Derek Jeter .60 1.50
3 Johnny Damon .15 .40
4 Javy Lopez .10 .25
5 Preston Wilson .10 .25
6 Derek Bell .10 .25
7 Richie Sexson .10 .25
8 Vinny Castilla .10 .25
9 Billy Wagner .10 .25
10 Carlos Beltran .15 .40
11 Chris Singleton .10 .25
12 Nomar Garciaparra .15 .40
13 Carlos Febles .10 .25
14 Jason Varitek .25 .60
15 Luis Gonzalez .10 .25
16 Jon Lieber .10 .25
17 Mo Vaughn .10 .25
18 Dave Burba .10 .25
19 Brady Anderson .10 .25
20 Carlos Lee .10 .25
21 Chuck Finley .10 .25
22 Alex Gonzalez .10 .25
23 Matt Williams .10 .25
24 Chipper Jones .25 .60
25 Pokey Reese .10 .25
26 Todd Helton .15 .40
27 Mike Mussina .15 .40
28 Butch Huskey .10 .25
29 Jeff Bagwell .15 .40
30 Juan Encarnacion .10 .25
31 A.J. Burnett .10 .25
32 Micah Bowie .10 .25
33 Brian Jordan .10 .25
34 Scott Erickson .10 .25
35 Sean Casey .10 .25
36 John Smoltz .25 .60
37 Edgard Clemente .10 .25
38 Mike Hampton .10 .25
39 Tom Glavine .15 .40
40 Albert Belle .10 .25
41 Jim Thome .15 .40
42 Jermaine Dye .10 .25
43 Sammy Sosa .25 .60
44 Pedro Martinez .15 .40
45 Paul Konerko .10 .25
46 Damion Easley .10 .25
47 Cal Ripken .75 2.00
48 Jose Lima .10 .25
49 Mike Lowell .10 .25
50 Randy Johnson .25 .60
51 Dean Palmer .10 .25
52 Tim Salmon .10 .25
53 Kevin Millwood .10 .25
54 Mark Grace .15 .40
55 Aaron Boone .10 .25
56 Omar Vizquel .15 .40
57 Moises Alou .10 .25
58 Travis Fryman .10 .25
59 Erubiel Durazo .10 .25
60 Carl Everett .10 .25
61 Charles Johnson .10 .25
62 Trot Nixon .10 .25
63 Andres Galarraga .15 .40
64 Maggio Ordonez .15 .40
65 Pedro Astacio .10 .25
66 Roberto Alomar .15 .40
67 Pete Harnisch .10 .25
68 Scott Williamson .10 .25
69 Alex Fernandez .10 .25
70 Robin Ventura .10 .25
71 Chad Allen .10 .25
72 Darin Erstad .10 .25
73 Ron Coomer .10 .25
74 Ellis Burks .10 .25
75 Kent Bottenfield .10 .25
76 Ken Griffey Jr. .50 1.25
77 Mike Piazza .25 .60
78 Jorge Posada .15 .40
79 Dante Bichette .10 .25
80 Adrian Beltre .25 .60
81 Andruw Jones .10 .25
82 Wilson Alvarez .10 .25
83 Edgardo Alfonzo .10 .25
84 Brian Giles .10 .25
85 Gary Sheffield .10 .25
86 Matt Stairs .10 .25
87 Bret Boone .10 .25
88 Kenny Rogers .10 .25
89 Barry Bonds .40 1.00
90 Scott Rolen .15 .40
91 Edgar Renteria .10 .25
92 Larry Walker .15 .40
93 Roger Cedeno .10 .25
94 Kevin Brown .10 .25
95 Lee Stevens .10 .25
96 Brad Radke .10 .25
97 Andy Pettitte .15 .40
98 Bobby Higginson .10 .25
99 Eric Chavez .10 .25
100 Alex Rodriguez .30 .75
101 Shannon Stewart .10 .25
102 Ryan Rupe .10 .25
103 Freddy Garcia .10 .25
104 John Jaha .10 .25
105 Greg Maddux .30 .75
106 Hideki Irabu .10 .25
107 Rey Ordonez .10 .25
108 Troy O'Leary .10 .25
109 Frank Thomas .25 .60
110 Corey Koskie .10 .25
111 Bernie Williams .15 .40
112 Barry Larkin .15 .40
113 Kevin Appier .10 .25
114 Curt Schilling .15 .40
115 Bartolo Colon .10 .25
116 Edgar Martinez .15 .40
117 Ray Lankford .10 .25
118 Todd Walker .10 .25
119 John Wetteland .10 .25
120 David Nilsson .10 .25
121 Tino Martinez .10 .25
122 Phil Nevin .10 .25
123 Ben Grieve .10 .25
124 Ron Gant .10 .25
125 Jeff Kent .10 .25
126 Rick Helling .10 .25
127 Russ Ortiz .10 .25
128 Troy Glaus .10 .25
129 Chan Ho Park .15 .40
130 Jeromy Burnitz .10 .25
131 Aaron Sele .10 .25
132 Mike Sirotka .10 .25
133 Brad Ausmus .10 .25
134 Jose Rosado .10 .25
135 Mariano Rivera .30 .75
136 Jason Giambi .10 .25
137 Mike Lieberthal .10 .25
138 Chris Carpenter .15 .40
139 Henry Rodriguez .10 .25
140 Mike Sweeney .10 .25
141 Vladimir Guerrero .15 .40
142 Charles Nagy .10 .25
143 Jason Kendall .10 .25
144 Matt Lawton .10 .25
145 Michael Barrett .10 .25
146 David Cone .10 .25
147 Bobby Abreu .10 .25
148 Fernando Tatis .10 .25
149 Jose Canseco .15 .40
150 Craig Biggio .15 .40
151 Matt Mantei .10 .25
152 Jacque Jones .10 .25
153 John Halama .10 .25
154 Trevor Hoffman .15 .40
155 Rondell White .10 .25
156 Reggie Sanders .10 .25
157 Steve Finley .10 .25
158 Roberto Hernandez .10 .25
159 Geoff Jenkins .10 .25
160 Chris Widger .10 .25
161 Orel Hershiser .10 .25
162 Tim Hudson .15 .40
163 Kris Benson .10 .25
164 Kevin Young .10 .25
165 Rafael Palmeiro .15 .40
166 David Wells .10 .25
167 Ben Davis .10 .25
168 Jamie Moyer .10 .25
169 Randy Wolf .10 .25
170 Jeff Cirillo .10 .25
171 Warren Morris .10 .25
172 Billy Koch .10 .25
173 Marquis Grissom .10 .25
174 Geoff Blum .10 .25
175 Octavio Dotel .10 .25
176 Orlando Hernandez .10 .25
177 J.D. Drew .10 .25
178 Carlos Delgado .10 .25
179 Sterling Hitchcock .10 .25
180 Shawn Green .10 .25
181 Tony Clark .10 .25
182 Joe McEwing .10 .25
183 Fred McGriff .15 .40
184 Tony Batista .10 .25
185 Al Leiter .10 .25
186 Roger Clemens .30 .75
187 Al Martin .10 .25
188 Eric Milton .10 .25
189 Bobby Smith .10 .25
190 Rusty Greer .10 .25
191 Shawn Estes .10 .25
192 Ken Caminiti .10 .25
193 Eric Karros .10 .25
194 Manny Ramirez .25 .60
195 Jim Edmonds .10 .25
196 Paul O'Neill .15 .40
197 Rico Brogna .10 .25
198 Ivan Rodriguez .15 .40
199 Doug Glanville .10 .25
200 Mark McGwire .40 1.00
201 Mark Quinn PROS .20 .50
202 Norm Hutchins PROS .20 .50
203 Ramon Ortiz PROS .20 .50
204 Brett Laxton PROS .20 .50
205 Jimmy Anderson PROS .20 .50
206 Calvin Murray PROS .20 .50
207 Wilton Veras PROS .20 .50
208 Chad Hermansen PROS .20 .50
209 Nick Johnson PROS .20 .50
210 Kevin Barker PROS .20 .50
211 Casey Blake PROS .20 .50
212 Chad Meyers PROS .20 .50
213 Kip Wells PROS .20 .50
214 Eric Munson PROS .20 .50
215 Lance Berkman PROS .30 .75
216 Wily Pena PROS .20 .50
217 Gary Matthews Jr. PROS .20 .50
218 Travis Dawkins PROS .20 .50
219 Josh Beckett PROS .40 1.00
220 Tony Armas Jr. PROS .20 .50
221 Alfonso Soriano PROS .50 1.25
222 Pat Burrell PROS .20 .50
223 Danys Baez PROS RC .20 .50
224 Adam Kennedy PROS .20 .50
225 Ruben Mateo PROS .20 .50
226 Vernon Wells PROS .20 .50
227 Brian Cooper PROS .20 .50
228 Jeff DaVanon PROS RC .20 .50
229 Glen Barker PROS .20 .50
230 Robinson Cancel PROS .20 .50
231 D'Angelo Jimenez PROS .20 .50
232 Adam Piatt PROS .20 .50
233 Buddy Carlyle PROS .20 .50
234 Chad Hutchinson PROS .20 .50
235 Matt Riley PROS .20 .50
236 Cole Liniak PROS .20 .50
237 Ben Petrick PROS .20 .50
238 Peter Bergeron PROS .20 .50
239 Cesar King PROS .20 .50
240 Aaron Myette PROS .20 .50
241 Eric Gagne PROS .20 .50
242 Joe Nathan PROS .20 .50
243 Bruce Chen PROS .20 .50
244 Rob Bell PROS .20 .50
245 Juan Sosa PROS RC .20 .50
246 Julio Ramirez PROS .20 .50
247 Wade Miller PROS .20 .50
248 Trace Coquillette PROS RC .20 .50
249 Rob Ramsay PROS .20 .50
250 Rick Ankiel PROS .30 .75
P100 Alex Rodriguez Promo .60 1.50

2000 Metal Emerald

COMPLETE SET (250) 150.00 300.00
*STARS 1-200: 6X TO 15X BASIC
1-200 STATED ODDS 1:4
*PROSPECTS 201-250: .75X TO 2X BASIC
201-250 STATED ODDS 1:8

2000 Metal Base Shredders

STATED ODDS 1:288
1 Roberto Alomar 4.00 10.00
2 Manny Ramirez 4.00 10.00
3 Tony Gwynn 6.00 15.00
4 Ben Davis 3.00 8.00
5 Vladimir Guerrero 4.00 10.00
6 Michael Barrett 3.00 8.00
7 Eric Munson 3.00 8.00
8 Tony Clark 3.00 8.00
9 Ben Grieve 3.00 8.00
10 Miguel Tejada 3.00 8.00
11 Rafael Palmeiro 4.00 10.00
12 Ivan Rodriguez 4.00 10.00
13 Matt Williams 3.00 8.00
14 Erubiel Durazo 3.00 8.00
15 Mo Vaughn 3.00 8.00
16 Troy Glaus 3.00 8.00
17 Larry Walker 3.00 8.00
18 Todd Helton 4.00 10.00

2000 Metal Fusion

COMPLETE SET (15) 8.00 20.00
STATED ODDS 1:4
F1 K.Griffey Jr. 1.25 3.00
A.Rodriguez
F2 M.McGwire 1.00 2.50
R.Ankiel
F3 S.Rolen .40 1.00
C.Schilling
F4 P.Martinez .40 1.00
N.Garciaparra
F5 C.Beltran .40 1.00
C.Febles
F6 S.Sosa .60 1.50
M.Grace
F7 V.Guerrero .40 1.00
U.Urbina
F8 R.Clemens 1.50 4.00
D.Jeter
F9 J.Bagwell .40 1.00
C.Biggio
F10 C.Jones .60 1.50
A.Jones
F11 C.Ripken 2.00 5.00
M.Mussina
F12 M.Ramirez .60 1.50
R.Alomar
F13 S.Casey .40 1.00
B.Larkin
F14 I.Rodriguez .40 1.00
R.Palmeiro
F15 M.Piazza .60 1.50
R.Ventura

2000 Metal Heavy Metal

COMPLETE SET (10) 8.00 20.00
STATED ODDS 1:20
GS1 Sammy Sosa 1.00 2.50
GS2 Mark McGwire 1.50 4.00
GS3 Ken Griffey Jr. 2.00 5.00
GS4 Mike Piazza 1.00 2.50
GS5 Nomar Garciaparra .60 1.50
GS6 Alex Rodriguez 1.25 3.00
GS7 Manny Ramirez 1.00 2.50
GS8 Jeff Bagwell .60 1.50
GS9 Chipper Jones 1.00 2.50
GS10 Vladimir Guerrero .60 1.50

2000 Metal Hit Machines

COMPLETE SET (10) 8.00 20.00
STATED ODDS 1:20
H1 Ken Griffey Jr. 2.00 5.00
H2 Mark McGwire 1.50 4.00
H3 Frank Thomas 1.00 2.50
H4 Tony Gwynn 1.00 2.50
H5 Rafael Palmeiro .60 1.50
H6 Bernie Williams .60 1.50
H7 Derek Jeter 2.50 6.00
H8 Sammy Sosa 1.00 2.50
H9 Mike Piazza 1.00 2.50
H10 Chipper Jones 1.00 2.50

2000 Metal Platinum Portraits

COMPLETE SET (10) 4.00 10.00
STATED ODDS 1:8
PP1 Carlos Beltran .40 1.00
PP2 Vladimir Guerrero .40 1.00
PP3 Manny Ramirez .60 1.50
PP4 Ivan Rodriguez .40 1.00
PP5 Sean Casey .25 .60
PP6 Alex Rodriguez .75 2.00
PP7 Derek Jeter 1.50 4.00
PP8 Nomar Garciaparra .40 1.00
PP9 Vernon Wells .25 .60
PP10 Shawn Green .25 .60

2000 Metal Talent Show

COMPLETE SET (15) 2.00 5.00
STATED ODDS 1:4
TS1 Rick Ankiel .30 .75
TS2 Matt Riley .20 .50
TS3 Chad Hermansen .20 .50
TS4 Ruben Mateo .20 .50
TS5 Eric Munson .20 .50
TS6 Alfonso Soriano .50 1.25
TS7 Wilton Veras .20 .50
TS8 Vernon Wells .20 .50
TS9 Erubiel Durazo .20 .50
TS10 Pat Burrell .20 .50
TS11 Ben Davis .20 .50
TS12 A.J. Burnett .20 .50
TS13 Peter Bergeron .20 .50
TS14 Mark Quinn .20 .50
TS15 Ben Petrick .20 .50

1979 Metallic Creations

These 3" by 5" portrait cards were issued with a 3 1/2" statuette. The cards were drawn by P. Herek and feature a full drawing of the player as well as two action shots In the background. Each player also has a fascimile autograph on the front. The back has career statistics on them. The cards are unnumbered and we have sequenced them in alphabetical order. While the Cedeno, Koufax and Ryan cards are known, there have been extremely few statues spotted of these players, therefore we are calling these cards SP's. The statues and the cards were available for $7.95 upon release. The players listed as SP's were produced late in the run and are available in lesser quantities than the other players listed in our checklist.

COMPLETE SET 200.00 400.00
COMMON CARD 4.00 10.00
COMMON SP 8.00 20.00
1 Hank Aaron 8.00 20.00
2 Rod Carew 5.00 12.00
3 Cesar Cedeno SP 8.00 20.00
4 Ty Cobb 8.00 20.00
5 Steve Garvey 4.00 10.00
6 Lou Gehrig 8.00 20.00
7 Ron Guidry 4.00 10.00
8 Rogers Hornsby 6.00 15.00
9 Walter Johnson 6.00 15.00
10 Ralph Kiner 5.00 12.00
11 Sandy Koufax SP 30.00 60.00
12 Dave Lopes 4.00 10.00
13 Christy Mathewson 5.00 12.00
14 Willie Mays 8.00 20.00
15 Willie McCovey 5.00 12.00
16 Mel Ott 6.00 15.00
17 Babe Ruth 12.50 30.00
18 Nolan Ryan SP 40.00 80.00
19 Tris Speaker 5.00 12.00
20 Honus Wagner 6.00 15.00

1993 Metallic Images

As part of the Cooperstown Collection, this 20-card set came within a special collector tin and had its own individually numbered certificate of authenticity. Production was reportedly limited to 49,900 sets. The metallic cards have rounded corners and edges, measure approximately the standard size, and feature player photos, some action, others posed, reproduced on pinstriped fronts, with the player's team name above the photo. The cards are numbered on the back in alphabetical order except for Blue and Berra. A promo card featuring Willie Mays was issued to dealers.

COMPLETE SET (20) 20.00 50.00
1 Hank Aaron 3.00 8.00
2 Vida Blue .40 1.00
3 Yogi Berra 1.50 4.00
4 Bobby Bonds .75 2.00
5 Lou Brock 1.25 3.00
6 Lew Burdette .40 1.00
7 Rod Carew 1.25 3.00
8 Rocky Colavito .75 2.00
9 George Foster .40 1.00
10 Bob Gibson 1.25 3.00
11 Mickey Lolich .40 1.00
12 Willie Mays 3.00 8.00
13 Johnny Mize 1.25 3.00
14 Don Newcombe .40 1.00
15 Gaylord Perry 1.25 3.00
16 Boog Powell .75 2.00
17 Bill Skowron .40 1.00
18 Warren Spahn 1.25 3.00
19 Willie Stargell 1.25 3.00
20 Luis Tiant .40 1.00
P1 Willie Mays 1.25 3.00
Promo

1994 Metallic Impressions Mantle

Produced by Metallic Impressions, this 10-card standard-size set reproduces in metal the Baseball Heroes cards randomly inserted into 1994 Upper Deck second series packs. The ten cards were issued in an embossed collector's tin with an individually numbered certificate of authenticity. The fronts show photos commemorating key milestones in Mantle's career. The inserted paper backs contain career highlights and a small scrapbook-like photo. 19,950 of these sets were produced.

COMP. FACT SET (10) 12.50 30.00
COMMON CARD (1-10) 1.20 3.00

1997 Pinnacle X-Press Melting Pot Samples

COMPLETE SET (20) 48.00 120.00
STAT.ODDS 1:288 HOB, 1:189 MAST.DECK
1 Jose Guillen .75 2.00
2 Vladimir Guerrero 2.50 6.00
3 Andruw Jones 1.50 4.00
4 Larry Walker .75 2.00
5 Manny Ramirez 2.00 5.00
6 Ken Griffey Jr. 4.00 10.00
7 Alex Rodriguez 5.00 12.00
8 Frank Thomas 2.00 5.00
9 Juan Gonzalez 2.00 5.00
10 Ivan Rodriguez 2.00 5.00
11 Hideo Nomo 3.00 8.00
12 Rafael Palmeiro 1.50 4.00
13 Dave Nilsson .75 2.00
14 Nomar Garciaparra 4.00 10.00
15 Wilton Guerrero .75 2.00
16 Sammy Sosa 3.00 8.00
17 Edgar Renteria .75 2.00
18 Cal Ripken 6.00 15.00
19 Derek Jeter 6.00 15.00
20 Rey Ordonez .75 2.00

1995 Metallic Impressions Ripken

This 10-card metal-on-metal set traces Cal Ripken's career as he was just coming up from the minors to the nights he tied and broke Lou Gehrig's record. The cards are packaged in a collectors tin. Just 29,950 sets were produced and each included a Certificate of Authenticity. The fronts display color photos while the backs present commentary.

COMP. FACT SET (10) 12.50 30.00
COMMON CARD (1-10) 1.20 3.00

1995 Metallic Impressions Ryan

Produced by Metallic Impressions, this 10-card metal set is a retrospect of Nolan Ryan's Hall of Fame career. The cards have embossed fronts and smooth rolled edges. Each set is packaged in a collector's tin and accompanied by an individually numbered certificate of authenticity. The production run was limited to 14,950 sets.

COMP. FACT SET (10) 12.50 30.00

1996 Metallic Impressions Gehrig

Produced by Metallic Impressions, this five-card metal set features sepia photos of Lou Gehrig printed on metal card stock with a commentary on different phases of his career on the backs. The cards have embossed front highlights and smooth rolled edges. Each set is packaged in a collector's tin.

COMP. FACT SET (5) 4.00 10.00
COMMON CARD (1-5) 1.00 2.50

1996 Metallic Impressions Griffey 5

Produced by Metallic Impressions, this five-card metal set is a recap Ken Griffey, Jr. career. The cards have color action player photos on front and smooth rolled edges. Each set is packaged in a collector's tin.

COMP. FACT SET (5) 6.00 15.00
COMMON CARD (1-5) 1.20 3.00

1996 Metallic Impressions Griffey 10

Produced by Metallic Impressions, this 10-card metal set is a retrospect of Ken Griffey, Jr. career. The cards have color action player photos on front and smooth rolled edges. Each set is packaged in a collector's tin and accompanied by an individually numbered certificate of authenticity. The production run was limited to 24,000 sets.

COMP. FACT SET (10) 12.50 30.00
COMMON CARD (1-10) 1.20 3.00

1996 Metallic Impressions Ruth

Produced by Metallic Impressions, this five-card metal set features black-and-white photos of Babe Ruth printed on metal card stock with a commentary on different phases of his career on the backs. The cards have embossed front highlights and smooth rolled edges. Each set is packaged in a collector's tin.

COMP. FACT SET (5) 4.00 10.00
COMMON CARD (1-5) 1.00 2.50

1970 Metropolitan Museum of Art Burdick

This eight-card set consists of West German-made cards from Jefferson Burdick's collection at the Metropolitan Museum of Art. The cards feature black-and-white player photos measuring approximately 2 3/4" by 3 3/4". The cards are unnumbered and checklisted below in alphabetical order.

COMPLETE SET (8) 20.00 50.00
1 Max Bishop 2.00 5.00
R315
2 Lou Gehrig 10.00 25.00
R315
3 Carl Hubbell 6.00 15.00
R315
4 Kores 2.00 5.00
Portland
5 Leard 2.00 5.00
Venice
6 Babe Ruth 12.50 30.00
R315
7 Dazzy Vance 4.00 10.00
R315
8 Zacher 2.00 5.00
Oaks

1962 Mets Jay Publishing

This 12-card set of the original New York Mets measures approximately 5" X 7". The fronts feature black-and-white posed player photos with the player's and team name printed below in the white border. These cards were packaged 12 to a packet. The backs are blank. The cards are unnumbered and checklisted below in alphabetical order. A complete set in the original envelope is valued at fifty percent higher.

COMPLETE SET (12) 30.00 60.00
1 Gus Bell 1.50 4.00
2 Elio Chacon 1.25 3.00
3 Roger Craig 2.00 5.00
4 Gil Hodges 6.00 15.00
5 Jay Hook 1.25 3.00
6 Al Jackson 1.50 4.00
7 Hobie Landrith 1.25 3.00
8 Bob Miller 1.25 3.00
9 Charlie Neal 1.50 4.00
10 Casey Stengel MG 6.00 15.00
11 Frank Thomas 2.00 5.00
12 Don Zimmer 2.50 6.00

1962-65 Mets Requena Photo

These 8" by 10" color photographs feature members of the New York Mets and were taken by known sports photographer Louis Requenna. These photos were taken throughout the early seasons of the Mets. Since these photos are unnumbered, we have sequenced them in alphabetical order.

COMPLETE SET 250.00 500.00
1 George Altman 6.00 15.00
2 Ed Bauta 6.00 15.00
3 Larry Bearnarth 6.00 15.00
4 Yogi Berra CO 15.00 40.00
5 Chris Cannizzaro 6.00 15.00
Portrait
6 Chris Cannizzaro 6.00 15.00
Batting
7 Chris Cannizzaro 6.00 15.00
Kneeling
8 Chris Cannizzaro 6.00 15.00
Squatting
9 Duke Carmel 6.00 15.00
10 Joe Christopher 6.00 15.00
Kneeling
11 Joe Christopher 6.00 15.00
Standing
12 Roger Craig 8.00 20.00
13 Ray Daviault 6.00 15.00
14 John DeMerit 6.00 15.00
15 Don Heffner CO 6.00 15.00
16 Jay Hook 6.00 15.00
17 Ron Hunt 10.00 25.00
Ralph Kiner ANN
18 Ed Kranepool 8.00 20.00
19 Felix Mantilla 6.00 15.00
20 Jim Marshall 6.00 15.00
21 Danny Napoleon 6.00 15.00
22 Charlie Neal 6.00 15.00
23 Jimmy Piersall 8.00 20.00
24 Joe Pignatano 6.00 15.00
25 Duke Snider 12.50 30.00
Full Length Photo
26 Duke Snider 12.50 30.00
Portrait
27 Casey Stengel MG 15.00 40.00
28 Ron Swoboda 8.00 20.00

1963 Mets Jay Publishing

This 12-card set of the New York Mets measures approximately 5" by 7". The fronts feature black-and-white posed player photos with the player's and team name printed below in the white border. These cards were packaged 12 to a packet. The backs are blank. The cards are unnumbered and checklisted below in alphabetical order.

COMPLETE SET (12) 20.00 50.00
1 Larry Burright 1.00 2.50
2 Roger Craig 1.50 4.00
3 Jim Hickman 1.25 3.00
4 Gil Hodges 5.00 12.00
5 Jay Hook 1.25 3.00
6 Al Jackson 1.25 3.00
7 Rod Kanehl 1.25 3.00
8 Charlie Neal 1.25 3.00
9 Duke Snider 5.00 12.00
10 Casey Stengel MG 5.00 12.00
11 Frank Thomas 1.25 3.00
12 Marv Throneberry 1.50 4.00

1964 Mets Jay Publishing

This 12-card set of the New York Mets measures approximately 5" by 7". The fronts feature black and white posed player photos with the player's and team name printed below in the white border. These cards were packaged 12 to an oversized envelope. The backs are blank. The cards are unnumbered and sequenced below in alphabetical order.

COMPLETE SET (12) 15.00 40.00
1 Larry Bearnarth 1.00 2.50
2 Duke Carmel 1.00 2.50
3 Choo Choo Coleman 1.25 3.00
4 Jesse Gonder 1.00 2.50
5 Tim Harkness 1.00 2.50
6 Jim Hickman 1.25 3.00
7 Ron Hunt 1.50 4.00
8 Al Jackson 1.25 3.00
9 Rod Kanehl 1.25 3.00
10 Duke Snider 4.00 10.00
11 Casey Stengel MG 4.00 10.00
12 Carlton Willey 1.00 2.50

1964 Mets Team Issue

This 12-card set of the New York Mets measures approximately 5" by 7". The fronts feature black and white posed player photos. The set was sold at the ballpark or could be obtained through mail order. The backs are blank. The cards are unnumbered and sequenced below in alphabetical order.

COMPLETE SET (12) 12.50 30.00
1 George Altman .75 2.00
2 Larry Bearnarth .75 2.00
3 Jesse Gonder .75 2.00
4 Tim Harkness .75 2.00
5 Jim Hickman .75 2.00
6 Jay Hook .75 2.00
7 Ron Hunt 1.25 3.00
8 Al Jackson .75 2.00
9 Tracy Stallard .75 2.00
10 Casey Stengel MG 3.00 8.00
11 Frank Thomas 1.25 3.00
12 Carl Willey .75 2.00

1965 Mets Jay Publishing

This 12-card set of the New York Mets measures approximately 5" by 7". The fronts feature black and white posed player photos with the player's and team name printed below in the white border. The cards were packaged 12 to an envelope. The backs are blank and are sequenced in alphabetical order.

COMPLETE SET (12) 15.00 40.00
1 Larry Bearnarth .75 2.00
2 Yogi Berra 4.00 10.00
3 Chris Cannizzaro .75 2.00
4 Galen Cisco .75 2.00
5 Jack Fisher .75 2.00
6 Jim Hickman .75 2.00
7 Ron Hunt .75 2.00
8 Al Jackson .75 2.00
9 Ed Kranepool 1.00 2.50
10 Roy McMillan .75 2.00
11 Warren Spahn 3.00 8.00
12 Casey Stengel MG 3.00 8.00

1965 Mets Postcards

This 10-card set were issued by B and E, feature color player photos and measures approximately 3" by 5". The backs display the player's statistical record and the Mets insignia in green. The cards are unnumbered and checklisted below in alphabetical order.

COMPLETE SET (10) 60.00 120.00
1 Yogi Berra 10.00 25.00
2 Joe Christopher 6.00 15.00
3 Jack Fisher 6.00 15.00
4 Ron Hunt 6.00 15.00
5 Al Jackson 6.00 15.00
6 Ed Kranepool 8.00 20.00
7 Roy McMillan 6.00 15.00
8 Warren Spahn 10.00 25.00
9 Casey Stengel MG 10.00 25.00
10 Carl Willey 6.00 15.00

1966 Mets Postcards

This six-card set features color player photos in the same style as the 1965 Mets Postcards set and measures approximately 3" by 5". The backs carry the player's name, Mets insignia, and B and E Advertising in Haledon, NJ as the publisher. There is no reference to the player's statistical record.

COMPLETE SET (6) 40.00 80.00
1 Al Jackson 6.00 15.00
2 Ron Hunt 8.00 20.00
3 Ed Kranepool 6.00 15.00
4 Wes Westrum MG 6.00 15.00
5 Cleon Jones 8.00 20.00
6 Tug McGraw 10.00 25.00

1966 Mets Team Issue

This 12-card set of the New York Mets measures approximately 5" by 7". The fronts feature black and white posed player photos. The set was sold at the ballpark or could be obtained through mail order. The backs are blank. The cards are unnumbered and sequenced below in alphabetical order.

COMPLETE SET (12) 12.50 30.00
1 Yogi Berra CO 3.00 8.00
2 Ken Boyer 2.00 5.00
3 Don Cardwell .75 2.00
4 Tommy Davis 1.25 3.00
5 Jack Fisher .75 2.00
6 Jerry Grote 1.25 3.00
7 Chuck Hiller .75 2.00
8 Cleon Jones 1.25 3.00
9 Ed Kranepool 1.25 3.00
10 Don Shaw .75 2.00
11 Ron Swoboda 1.25 3.00
12 Wes Westrum MG .75 2.00

1967 Mets Postcards

This five-card set features color player photos and measure approximately 3" by 5". The backs carry the player's name printed in black. The cards are unnumbered and checklisted below in alphabetical order. Tom Seaver has a card in his Rookie Card year.

COMPLETE SET (5) 40.00 80.00
1 Tommy Davis 3.00 8.00
2 Jack Fisher 2.00 5.00
3 Jerry Grote 3.00 8.00
4 Ed Kranepool 3.00 8.00
5 Tom Seaver 40.00 80.00

1967 Mets Team Issue

This 12-card set of the New York Mets measures approximately 4 13/16" by 7" and features black-and-white player photos in a white border with blank backs. These cards were originally packaged 12 to a packet. The cards are unnumbered and checklisted below in alphabetical order.

COMPLETE SET (12) 20.00 50.00
1 Yogi Berra CO 6.00 15.00
2 Ken Boyer 3.00 8.00
3 Don Cardwell 1.50 4.00
4 Tommy Davis 2.50 6.00
5 Jack Fisher 1.50 4.00
6 Jerry Grote 2.50 6.00
7 Chuck Hiller 1.50 4.00
8 Cleon Jones 1.50 4.00
9 Ed Kranepool 2.50 6.00
10 Bob Shaw 1.50 4.00
11 Ron Swoboda 2.50 6.00
12 Wes Westrum MG 1.50 4.00

1969 Mets Citgo

These eight 8" by 10" prints were drawn by John Wheeldon. These prints were available at Citgo for a nominal fee after a gasoline fill-up. The fronts feature a large portait pose and a smaller action pose on a colorful background. The backs have the CITGO, MLB and Mets skyline logos, the player's biography and lifetime records. There is also a picture and bio of the artist on the back. The prints are unnumbered and listed in alphabetical order.

COMPLETE SET (8) 30.00 60.00
1 Tommie Agee 2.50 6.00
2 Ken Boswell 2.00 5.00
3 Gary Gentry 2.00 5.00
4 Jerry Grote 2.50 6.00
5 Ed Kranepool 2.50 6.00
6 Jerry Koosman 3.00 8.00
7 Cleon Jones 2.00 5.00
8 Tom Seaver 8.00 20.00

1969 Mets New York Daily News

These 9" by 12" blank-backed charcoal drawings were issued by the Daily News to celebrate the Miracle Mets. An artist named Bruce Stark drew the pictures which were put on white textured paper. Each drawing has a fascimile autograph on the lower left. The blank-backed items are unnumbered and are sequenced in alphabetical order and came in a special folder which featured additional artwork.

COMPLETE SET (20) 60.00 120.00
1 Tommie Agee 2.00 5.00
2 Ken Boswell 1.50 4.00
3 Don Cardwell 1.50 4.00
4 Donn Clendenon 2.00 5.00
5 Wayne Garrett 1.50 4.00
6 Gary Gentry 1.50 4.00
7 Jerry Grote 2.00 5.00
8 Derrel(Bud) Harrelson 3.00 8.00
9 Gil Hodges MG 8.00 20.00
10 Cleon Jones 3.00 8.00
11 Jerry Koosman 3.00 8.00
12 Ed Kranepool 2.00 5.00
13 Jim McAndrew 1.50 4.00
14 Frank(Tug) McGraw 3.00 8.00
15 Nolan Ryan 20.00 50.00
16 Tom Seaver 15.00 40.00
17 Art Shamsky 1.50 4.00
18 Ron Swoboda 2.00 5.00
19 Ron Taylor 1.50 4.00
20 Al Weis 1.50 4.00

1969 Mets Team Issue

This 16-card set of the New York Mets features black and white posed player photos with a facsimile player autograph. The set was sold at the ballpark or could be obtained through mail order. The backs are blank. The cards are unnumbered and sequenced below in alphabetical order.

COMPLETE SET (16) 40.00 80.00
1 Tommie Agee 1.50 4.00
2 Yogi Berra CO 3.00 8.00
3 Ken Boswell 1.50 4.00
4 Ed Charles 1.25 3.00
5 Kevin Collins 1.25 3.00
6 Bud Harrelson 1.50 4.00
7 Gil Hodges MG 2.50 6.00
8 Al Jackson 1.25 3.00
9 Cleon Jones 1.50 4.00
10 Jerry Koosman 2.50 6.00
11 Ed Kranepool 1.50 4.00
12 Nolan Ryan 8.00 20.00
13 Tom Seaver 6.00 15.00
14 Art Shamsky 1.25 3.00
15 Ron Swoboda 1.50 4.00
16 Ron Taylor 1.25 3.00

1969 Mets Team Issue Color

This five-card set of the New York Mets features color player photos measuring approximately 7" by 8 3/4". The backs are blank. The cards are unnumbered and checklisted below in alphabetical order.

COMPLETE SET (5) 15.00 40.00
1 Bud Harrelson 2.00 5.00
2 Jerry Koosman 3.00 8.00
3 Ed Kranepool 2.00 5.00
4 Tom Seaver 8.00 20.00
5 Ron Swoboda 2.00 5.00

1970 Mets Nestle's Quik

These cards, which measure approximately 3" by 5" when cut from the back of Nestle Quik containers feature members of the 1969 Mets in highlghts from different games of the 1969 World Series. This list is incomplete and all additions are appreciated to this checklist.

COMPLETE SET 12.50 30.00
2 Jerry Koosman 5.00 12.00
3 Tommie Agee 4.00 10.00
4 Ron Swoboda 4.00 10.00

1970 Mets Team Issue

This 12-card set of the New York Mets features black-and-white player photos measuring approximately 4 3/4" by 7 1/2". The player's name and team name is printed above the photo. The backs are blank. The set was originally sold at the ballpark or through mail order. The cards are unnumbered and checklisted below in alphabetical order.

COMPLETE SET (12) 12.50 30.00
1 Tommie Agee 1.00 2.50
2 Ken Boswell .75 2.00
3 Donn Clendenon .75 2.00
4 Joe Foy .75 2.00
5 Jerry Grote 1.00 2.50
6 Bud Harrelson .75 2.00
7 Gil Hodges MG 1.50 4.00
8 Cleon Jones 1.00 2.50
9 Jerry Koosman 1.25 3.00
10 Tom Seaver 2.50 6.00
11 Art Shamsky .75 2.00
12 Ron Swoboda 1.00 2.50

1970 Mets Team Issue Color

This five-card set of the New York Mets features color player photos measuring approximately 7" by 8 3/4". The backs are blank. The cards are unnumbered and checklisted below in alphabetical order.

COMPLETE SET (5) 6.00 15.00
1 Bud Harrelson .75 2.00
2 Jerry Koosman 1.25 3.00
3 Ed Kranepool .75 2.00
4 Tom Seaver 2.50 6.00
5 Ron Swoboda .75 2.00

1971 Mets Team Issue

This 20-card set of the New York Mets features black and white posed player photos with a facsimile player autograph and measures approximately 4 7/8" by 6 3/4". The set was originally sold at the ballpark or could be obtained through mail order. The backs are blank. The cards are unnumbered and checklisted below in alphabetical order.

COMPLETE SET (20) 20.00 50.00
1 Tommie Agee .40 1.00
2 Yogi Berra CO 1.25 3.00
3 Donn Clendenon .40 1.00
4 Duffy Dyer .40 1.00
5 Danny Frisella .40 1.00
6 Gary Gentry .40 1.00
7 Jerry Grote .60 1.50
8 Bud Harrelson .60 1.50
9 Gil Hodges MG 1.00 2.50
10 Cleon Jones .60 1.50
11 Jerry Koosman .75 2.00
12 Ed Kranepool .60 1.50
13 Dave Marshall .40 1.00
14 Jim McAndrew .40 1.00
15 Tug McGraw .75 2.00
16 Nolan Ryan 6.00 15.00
17 Tom Seaver 4.00 10.00
18 Art Shamsky .40 1.00
19 Ken Singleton 1.00 2.50
20 Ron Taylor .40 1.00

1971 Mets Team Issue Autographs

This seven-card set of the New York Mets features black-and-white player photos measuring approximately 5 1/4" by 6 1/2" with a blue facsimile autograph printed across the front of the player's jersey. The cards are unnumbered and checklisted below in alphabetical order.

COMPLETE SET (7) 6.00 15.00
1 Tommie Agee 1.25 3.00
2 Danny Frisella .75 2.00
3 Gary Gentry .75 2.00
4 Jim McAndrew .75 2.00
5 Art Shamsky .75 2.00
6 Ken Singleton 1.25 3.00
7 Ron Taylor .75 2.00

1971 Mets Team Issue Color

This set of the New York Mets features color player photos measuring approximately 7" by 8 3/4". Only six players are listed below, all these players are from the "A" set. Since most teams from this period also had a "B" set, it is presumed that there are six other players in this set as well. Cards have blank backs.The cards are unnumbered and checklisted below in alphabetical order.

COMPLETE SET 5.00 12.00
1 Tommie Agee 1.25 3.00
2 Bob Aspromonte .75 2.00
3 Ken Boswell .75 2.00
4 Donn Clendenon .75 2.00
5 Jerry Grote 1.25 3.00
6 Jerry Koosman 1.50 4.00

1972 Mets Team Issue

The 1972 New York Mets Team Issue set was distributed in two different six-photo packs as Set A and Set B. The sets feature player photos measuring approximately 7" by 8 3/4". The cards are unnumbered and checklisted below alphabetically within each set. Set A consists of cards 1-6, and Set B contains cards 7-12.

COMPLETE SET (12) 12.50 30.00
1 Tommie Agee 1.25 3.00
2 Ken Boswell .75 2.00
3 Jerry Grote .75 2.00
4 Cleon Jones .75 2.00
5 Tom Seaver 4.00 10.00
6 Rusty Staub 2.00 5.00
7 Jim Fregosi .75 2.00
8 Wayne Garrett .75 2.00
9 Gary Gentry .75 2.00
10 Bud Harrelson 1.25 3.00
11 Jerry Koosman 1.50 4.00
12 Ed Kranepool 1.25 3.00

1973 Mets Team Issue

This 1973 New York Mets Team set was distributed in two different six-photo packs. The set features color player photos measuring approximately 7" by 8 3/4". The cards are unnumbered and checklisted below alphabetically. No distinction is made in the checklist as to which pack contains each player's photo as there is in the 1972 set.

COMPLETE SET (12) 12.50 30.00
1 Ken Boswell .75 2.00
2 Jim Fregosi 1.00 2.50
3 Jerry Grote 1.00 2.50
4 Bud Harrelson 1.00 2.50
5 Cleon Jones 1.00 2.50
6 Jerry Koosman 1.25 3.00
7 Ed Kranepool 1.00 2.50
8 Willie Mays 3.00 8.00
9 Tug McGraw 1.00 2.50
10 Felix Millan .75 2.00
11 Tom Seaver 2.00 5.00
12 Rusty Staub 1.50 4.00

1974 Mets Dairylea Photo Album

This set was issued in two fold-out strip booklets, each of which measures 8" by 8" in size. The inside front cover contains several small photos; the rest of the bookley contains white bordered portraits. The complete set comes in a white folder. Both the folder and booklets have the Mets logo on the front and the Dairylea trademark on the back. The books and photos are unnumbered and are sequenced the way they came in the booklet. Card numbers 1-13 are from the first book while numbers 14-20 are from the second book. The complete set in booklet form is valued at $45. Individual photos are valued below. Players from George Theodore to Bob Apodaca are all on the inside front cover in the first album. All people listed from Yogi Berra to the end of the set were in the inside front cover of the second booklet.

COMPLETE SET (20) 15.00 40.00
1 George Theodore .60 1.50
2 Ron Hodges .60 1.50
3 George Stone .60 1.50
4 Duffy Dyer .60 1.50
5 Jack Aker .60 1.50
6 Jim Gosger .60 1.50
7 Bob Apodaca .60 1.50
8 Tom Seaver 5.00 12.00
9 Bud Harrelson .75 2.00
10 Ed Kranepool .75 2.00
11 Rusty Staub 1.25 3.00
12 Ray Sadecki .60 1.50
13 Yogi Berra MG 4.00 10.00
Willie Mays CO
14 Ken Boswell .60 1.50
15 Cleon Jones .75 2.00
16 Jerry Grote 1.25 3.00
17 Jerry Koosman 1.25 3.00
18 Wayne Garrett .60 1.50

1974 Mets Japan Ed Broder

This 11-card set of the New York Mets features black-and-white player photos measuring approximately 1 7/8" by 3" and commemorates the 1974 New York Mets Tour of Japan. The backs carry the player's name, team name, tour, and the Mets logo. The cards are unnumbered and checklisted below alphabetically. This set was originally available from Broder for $1.50.

COMPLETE SET (11) 8.00 20.00
1 Yogi Berra MG 1.00 2.50
2 Wayne Garrett .40 1.00
3 Gil Hodges 1.00 2.50
4 Jerry Koosman .75 2.00
5 Ed Kranepool .40 1.00
John Milner
Joe Torre
6 Jon Matlack .40 1.00
7 Felix Millan .40 1.00
8 John Milner .40 1.00
9 Tom Seaver 2.00 5.00
10 George Theodore .40 1.00
11 Joe Torre 1.00 2.50

1975 Mets 1963 Morey

These 3 1/2" by 5 1/2" photos feature members of the 1963 Mets and were issued in color. This set was produced by long time hobbyist Jeffrey Morey.

COMPLETE SET 6.00 15.00
1 Craig Anderson .20 .50
2 Ed Bauta .20 .50
3 Larry Bearnarth .20 .50
4 Chris Cannizzaro .20 .50
5 Duke Carmel .20 .50
6 Chico Fernandez .20 .50
7 Jesse Gonder .20 .50
8 Pumpsie Green .20 .50
9 Tim Harkness .20 .50
10 Solly Hemus CO .20 .50
11 Jim Hickman .20 .50
12 Joe Hicks .20 .50
13 Will Huckle .20 .50
14 Rod Kanehl .20 .50
15 Ed Kranepool .30 .75
16 Joe Christopher .20 .50
17 Marty Kutyna .20 .50
18 Cookie Lavagetto CO .20 .50
19 Al Moran .20 .50
20 Choo Choo Coleman .20 .50
21 Roger Craig .30 .75
22 Steve Dillon .20 .50
23 Grover Powell .20 .50
24 Ted Schreiber .20 .50
25 Norm Sherry .20 .50
26 Dick Smith .20 .50
27 Tracy Stallard .20 .50
28 Casey Stengel MG 1.25 3.00
29 Ernie White CO .20 .50
30 Polo Grounds .40 1.00

1975 Mets SSPC

This 22-card standard-size set of New York Mets features white-bordered posed color player photos on their fronts, which are free of any other markings. The white back carries the player's name in red lettering above his blue-lettered biography and career highlights. The cards are numbered on the back within a circle formed by the player's team name. A similar set of New York Yankees was produced at the same time. The set is dated to 1975 because that year was Dave Kingman's first year as a Met and George Stone's last year.

COMPLETE SET (22) 6.00 15.00
1 John Milner .20 .50
2 Henry Webb .20 .50

3 Tom Hall .20 .50
4 Del Unser .20 .50
5 Wayne Garrett .20 .50
6 Jesus Alou .30 .75
7 Rusty Staub .60 1.50
8 John Stearns .30 .75
9 Dave Kingman .40 1.00
10 Ed Kranepool .30 .75
11 Cleon Jones .30 .75
12 Tom Seaver 3.00 8.00
13 George Stone .20 .50
14 Jerry Koosman .40 1.00
15 Bob Apodaca .20 .50
16 Felix Millan .30 .75
17 Gene Clines .20 .50
18 Mike Phillips .20 .50
19 Yogi Berra MG 1.50 4.00
20 Joe Torre .60 1.50
21 Jon Matlack .40 1.00
22 Ricky Baldwin .20 .50

1976 Mets '63 SSPC

These 18 standard-size cards honored members of the 1963 New York Mets. These cards have color photos covering almost all of the front except for a small white border. The horizontal backs have vital statistics; a biography written as it would have been after the '63 season and career information up to that point. The cards are unnumbered and we have sequenced them in alphabetical order. These cards were inserted in the 1976 Summer edition of Collectors Quarterly.

COMPLETE SET (18) 10.00 25.00
1 Ed Bauta .40 1.00
2 Duke Carmel .40 1.00
3 Joe Christopher .40 1.00
4 Choo Choo Coleman .75 2.00
5 Steve Dillon .40 1.00
6 Jesse Gonder .40 1.00
7 Pumpsie Green .40 1.00
8 Jim Hickman .60 1.50
9 Rod Kanehl .40 1.00
10 Al Moran .40 1.00
11 Grover Powell .40 1.00
12 Ted Schreiber .40 1.00
13 Norm Sherry .40 1.00
14 Dick Smith .40 1.00
15 Duke Snider 2.00 5.00
16 Tracy Stallard .40 1.00
17 Casey Stengel MG 2.00 5.00
18 Ernie White CO .40 1.00

1976 Mets MSA Placemats

This set of four placemats was produced by Creative Dimensions, liscensed by Major League Baseball, and issued by MSA. Each placemat measures 14 1/4" by 11 1/4", has a clear matte finish, and pictures three players, each appearing in a 3" diameter circle. Player statistics and additional artwork complete the placemat. Logos have been airbrushed from the caps as is typical of all MSA products. Placemats are unnumbered and listed below in first player uniform number.

COMPLETE SET (4) 8.00 20.00
1 Bud Harrelson 6.00 15.00
Tom Seaver
Jerry Grote
2 Ed Kranepool 2.50 6.00
Dave Kingman
Joe Torre
3 Bob Apodaca 1.25 3.00
Felix Millan
Del Unser
4 Jerry Koosman 2.00 5.00
Mickey Lolich
Jon Matlack

1977 Mets Dairylea Photo Album

This 27-card set features 8" by 8" player photos and was issued in an album that was given away at the Mets game of April 17th in Shea Stadium. The cards are unnumbered and checklisted below in alphabetical order.

COMPLETE SET (27) 10.00 25.00
1 Luis Alvarado .30 .75
Leo Foster
2 Bob Apodaca .30 .75
3 Rick Baldwin .30 .75
4 Bruce Boisclair .30 .75
5 Nino Espinosa .30 .75
6 Jerry Grote .40 1.00
7 Bud Harrelson .40 1.00
8 Ron Hodges .30 .75
9 Dave Kingman .75 2.00
10 Jerry Koosman .60 1.50
11 Ed Kranepool .30 .75
12 Skip Lockwood .30 .75
13 Joe Frazier MG .30 .75
Joe Pignatano CO
Tom Burgess CO/
14 Jon Matlack .30 .75
15 Lee Mazzilli .75 2.00
16 Felix Millan .30 .75
17 John Milner .30 .75
18 Bob Myrick .30 .75
19 Mike Phillips .30 .75
20 Ray Sadecki .30 .75
21 Tom Seaver 1.50 4.00
22 Roy Staiger .30 .75
23 John Stearns .30 .75
24 Craig Swan .30 .75
25 Jackson Todd .30 .75
26 Joe Torre .75 2.00
27 Mike Vail .30 .75

1978 Mets Dairylea Photo Album

This photo album was distributed at the Mets home game of May 30, 1978. This edition consists of a single booklet, 8" by 8" in size, bound on the left side. Each page contains a white-bordered, unnumbered portrait. They are listed below in the order they appear in the album.

COMPLETE SET (27) 10.00 25.00
1 Joe Torre MG 1.00 2.50
With Coaches
2 Bruce Boisclair .40 1.00
3 Mike Bruhert .40 1.00
4 Mardie Cornejo .40 1.00
5 Nino Espinosa .40 1.00
6 Doug Flynn .40 1.00
7 Tim Foli .40 1.00
8 Tom Grieve .75 2.00
9 Ken Henderson .40 1.00
10 Steve Henderson .40 1.00
11 Ron Hodges .40 1.00
12 Jerry Koosman 1.00 2.50
13 Ed Kranepool .75 2.00
14 Skip Lockwood .40 1.00
15 Elliott Maddox .40 1.00
16 Lee Mazzilli .75 2.00
17 Butch Metzger .40 1.00
18 Willie Montanez .40 1.00
19 Bob Myrick .40 1.00
20 Len Randle .40 1.00
21 Paul Siebert .40 1.00
22 John Stearns .40 1.00
23 Craig Swan .40 1.00
24 Bobby Valentine .75 2.00
25 Joel Youngblood .40 1.00
26 Pat Zachry .40 1.00
27 Bob Apodaca .40 1.00
Sergio Ferrer

1980 Mets Subway Promotional Posters

These six very oversized posters were plastered in the New York Subway trains in early 1980 as a way to hype up the New York Mets, who were then suffering from both bad performance on the field and at Shea Stadium. These posters were in black and white and the backs were back since they were used as advertisments for people riding the trains. Since these are unnumbered, we have sequenced them in alphabetical order.

COMPLETE SET (6) 25.00 60.00
1 Doug Flynn 5.00 10.00
2 Steve Henderson 5.00 10.00
3 Lee Mazzilli 10.00 20.00
4 Craig Swan 5.00 10.00
5 Frank Taveras 5.00 10.00
6 Joel Youngblood 5.00 10.00

1981 Mets Magic Memory

This four card set, which measures 6 7/'" by 4 7/8" features memorable Mets teams and managers. The relevant pictures are on the card front with the backs being brown with white printing, and show statistics. Each card was individually wrapped in cellophane and distributed as a promotion at Mets home games in 1981. The cards are most commonly found with the cellophane intact and are priced accordingly below. The scheduled dates for these giveaways were July 2, July 16, July 23 and August 6. Unfortunately, due to the baseball strike of 1981 the cards were all distributed at later dates in the season. According to information released in 1981, approximately 20,000 of these sets were issued.

COMPLETE SET (4) 12.50 30.00
1 1962 Mets Team Photo 3.00 8.00
2 1969 Mets Team Photo 3.00 8.00
3 1973 Mets Team Photo 3.00 8.00
4 Casey Stengel MG 4.00 10.00
Gil Hodges MG
Yogi Berra MG
Jo

1982 Mets Galasso '62

This 32-card standard-size set features posed black-and-white portraits of the 1962 New York Mets. The fronts are bordered in royal blue with the player's name and position printed in orange on the lower edge. The horizontal backs are printed in blue and orange with player biography, career highlights and statistics. A trivia question appears on the bottom, with the answer printed upside down next to it. These sets were issued with signed Marv Throneberry cards. The original issue price from Renata Galasso was $4.50.

COMPLETE SET (30) 5.00 12.00
1AU Marv Throneberry AU 8.00 20.00
1 Marv Throneberry .40 1.00
2 Richie Ashburn .40 1.00
3 Charlie Neal .20 .50
4 Cliff Cook .20 .50
5 Elio Chacon .60 1.50
6 Chris Cannizzaro .20 .50
7 Jim Hickman .20 .50
8 Rod Kanehl .20 .50
9 Gene Woodling .30 .75
10 Gil Hodges .40 1.00
11 Al Jackson .20 .50
12 Sammy Taylor .20 .50
13 Felix Mantilla .20 .50
14 Ken MacKenzie .20 .50
15 Craig Anderson .20 .50
16 Bob Moorhead .20 .50
17 Joe Christopher .20 .50
18 Bob Miller .20 .50
19 Frank Thomas .30 .75
20 Wilmer Mizell .20 .50
21 Bill Hunter 1.00 2.50
22 Roger Craig .30 .75
23 Jay Hook .20 .50
24 Team Photo .30 .75
25 Choo-Choo Coleman .30 .75
26 Casey Stengel MG .40 1.00
28 Solly Hemus CO .20 .50
29 Rogers Hornsby CO .40 1.00
31 Red Ruffing CO .40 1.00
32 George Weiss GM 1.00 2.50

1982 Mets Photo Album

These photos were perforated on bound edge. Each blank-backed color photo would measure 7 3/4" by 8" if detached. These is a Facsmile autograph in red at lower left; the uniform number in red at upper right. The back album cover carries an ad for Sportschannel. These photos are unnumbered and we have checklisted them below in alphabetical order.

COMPLETE SET (28) 3.00 8.00
1 Neil Allen .08 .25
2 Wally Backman .08 .25
3 Bob Bailor .08 .25
4 George Bamberger MG .08 .25
5 Hubie Brooks .20 .50
6 Pete Falcone .08 .25
7 George Foster .30 .75
8 Ron Gardenhire .40 1.00
9 Tom Hausman .08 .25
10 Ron Hodges .08 .25
11 Mike Howard .08 .25
12 Randy Jones .08 .25
13 Mike Jorgensen .08 .25
14 Dave Kingman .40 1.00
15 Ed Lynch .08 .25
16 Jesse Orosco .20 .50
17 Charlie Puleo .08 .25
18 Gary Rajsich .08 .25
19 Mike Scott .20 .50
20 Rusty Staub .40 1.00
21 John Stearns .08 .25
22 Craig Swan .08 .25
23 Ellis Valentine .08 .25
24 Tom Veryzer .08 .25
25 Mookie Wilson .30 .75
26 Pat Zachry .08 .25
27 Prospects .08 .25
Brian J. Giles
Rick Ownbey
28 Coaches .20 .50
Jim Frey
Bud Harrelson
Frank Howard
Bi

1984 Mets Fan Club

The cards in this eight-player set measure 2 1/2" by 3 1/2". The sheets were produced by Topps for the New York Mets and feature only Mets. The full sheet measures 7 1/2" by 10 1/2". Cards are together on the sheet but are perforated for those collectors who want to separate the individual player cards. The middle (ninth) card is a Mets Fan club membership card which details various promotional days at Shea Stadium on the back. The cards are numbered on the back and printed in orange and blue.

COMPLETE SET (8) 3.00 8.00
1 Dave Johnson MG .30 .75
2 Ron Darling .40 1.00
3 George Foster .40 1.00
4 Keith Hernandez .30 .75
5 Jesse Orosco .30 .75
6 Rusty Staub .60 1.50
7 Darryl Strawberry .75 2.00
8 Mookie Wilson .40 1.00
NNO Membership Card .20 .50

1985 Mets Colla Postcards

This 31-card set features color photos on a postcard format and was mailed in response to fan letters. The backs carry a pre-printed thank you note from the players. Because of legal problems with Barry Colla's licensing agreement, he can no longer sell his postcards making singles difficult to find and these cards are usually found as a set.

COMPLETE SET (31) 5.00 12.00
1 Dave Johnson MG .20 .50
2 Ruben Santana .08 .25
3 Ed Lynch .08 .25
4 Howard Johnson .30 .75
5 Doug Sisk .08 .25
6 Sid Fernandez .30 .75
7 Bruce Berenyi .08 .25
8 Ron Gardenhire .20 .50
9 Brent Gaff .08 .25
10 Roger McDowell .20 .50
11 Ray Knight .08 .25
12 John Christensen .08 .25
13 Danny Heep .08 .25
14 Clint Hurdle .20 .50
15 Mets Coaches .08 .25
16 Bill Latham .08 .25
17 Terry Blocker .08 .25
18 Wally Backman .08 .25
19 Dwight Gooden .75 2.00
20 Ron Darling .30 .75
21 Jesse Orosco .20 .50
22 Darryl Strawberry .30 .75
23 Gary Carter .60 1.50
24 Kevin Chapman .08 .25
25 Keith Hernandez .30 .75
26 George Foster .20 .50
27 Rusty Staub .30 .75
28 Mookie Wilson .30 .75
29 Team Photo .08 .25
30 Ronn Reynolds .08 .25
31 Tom Gorman .08 .25

1985 Mets Fan Club

The cards in this eight-player set measure 2 1/2" by 3 1/2". The sheets were produced by Topps for the New York Mets and feature only Mets players. The full sheet measures approximately 7 1/2" by 10 1/2". Cards are together on the sheet but are perforated for those collectors who want to separate the individual player cards. The middle (ninth) card is a Mets Fan club membership card. The set was available as a membership premium for joining the Junior Mets Fan Club for 4.00. The cards are listed below in alphabetical order for convenience.

COMPLETE SET (8) 3.00 8.00
1 Wally Backman .20 .50
2 Bruce Berenyi .20 .50
3 Gary Carter .75 2.00
4 George Foster .30 .75
5 Dwight Gooden 1.00 2.50
6 Keith Hernandez .40 1.00
7 Doug Sisk .20 .50
8 Darryl Strawberry .40 1.00
NNO Membership Card .20 .50

1985 Mets TCMA

These cards measure 3 1/2" by 5 1/2". The borderless fronts consist of nothing but the photos. The postcard format backs give player identification, vital statistics and previous season stats. The cards are numbered with "NYM85-XX" in the upper right.

COMPLETE SET (40) 6.00 15.00
1 Davey Johnson MG .20 .50
2 Vern Hoscheit CO .08 .25
3 Bill Robinson CO .08 .25
4 Mel Stottlemyre CO .08 .25
5 Bobby Valentine CO .08 .25
6 Bruce Berenyi .08 .25
7 Jeff Bettendorf .08 .25
8 Ron Darling .20 .50
9 Sid Fernandez .20 .50
10 Brent Gaff .08 .25
11 Wes Gardner .08 .25
12 Dwight Gooden .75 2.00
13 Tom Gorman .08 .25
14 Ed Lynch .08 .25
15 Jesse Orosco .20 .50
16 Calvin Schiraldi .08 .25
17 Doug Sisk .08 .25
18 Gary Carter .60 1.50
19 John Gibbons .08 .25
20 Ronn Reynolds .08 .25
21 Wally Backman .08 .25
22 Kelvin Chapman .08 .25
23 Ron Gardenhire .20 .50
24 Keith Hernandez .40 1.00
25 Howard Johnson .30 .75
26 Ray Knight .08 .25
27 Kevin Mitchell .40 1.00
28 Terry Blocker .08 .25
29 Rafael Santana .08 .25
30 Billy Beane .40 1.00
31 John Christensen .08 .25
32 Len Dykstra .75 2.00
33 George Foster .30 .75
34 Danny Heep .08 .25
35 Darryl Strawberry .30 .75
36 Mookie Wilson .30 .75
37 Jeff Bittiger .08 .25
38 Clint Hurdle .20 .50
39 LaSchelle Tarver .08 .25
40 Roger McDowell .20 .50

1986 Mets Colla Postcards

This 26-card set features color photos on a postcard format and was mailed in response to fan letters. The backs carry a pre-printed thank you note from the players.

COMPLETE SET (26) 8.00 20.00
1 Team Photo .40 1.00
2 Dwight Gooden .60 1.50
3 Gary Carter .75 2.00
4 Darryl Strawberry .40 1.00
5 Dave Johnson MG .30 .75
6 Keith Hernandez .60 1.50
7 Mookie Wilson .30 .75
8 Jesse Orosco .30 .75
9 Roger McDowell .30 .75
10 Ray Knight .20 .50
11 Howard Johnson .30 .75
12 George Foster .30 .75
13 Ron Darling .30 .75
14 Rick Aguilera .30 .75
15 Len Dykstra .40 1.00
16 Wally Backman .20 .50
17 Bud Harrelson CO .20 .50
18 Danny Heep .20 .50
19 Bruce Berenyi .20 .50
20 Sid Fernandez .20 .50
21 Tim Corcoran .20 .50
22 Randy Myers .40 1.00
23 Stan Jefferson .20 .50
24 Barry Lyons .20 .50
25 Bob Ojeda .20 .50
26 Tim Teufel .20 .50

1986 Mets Fan Club

The cards in this eight-player set measure 2 1/2" by 3 1/2". The sheets were produced by Topps for the New York Mets and feature only Mets. The full sheet measures approximately 7 1/2" by 10 1/2". Cards are together on the sheet but are perforated for those collectors who want to separate the individual player cards. The middle (ninth) card is a Mets Fan club membership card. The set was available as a membership premium for joining the Junior Mets Fan Club for 5.00. The cards are listed below in alphabetical order for convenience.

COMPLETE SET (8) 3.00 8.00
1 Wally Backman .20 .50
2 Gary Carter .75 2.00
3 Ron Darling .30 .75
4 Dwight Gooden .60 1.50
5 Keith Hernandez .40 1.00
6 Howard Johnson .30 .75
7 Roger McDowell .30 .75
8 Darryl Strawberry .40 1.00
NNO Membership Card .20 .50

1986 Mets Greats TCMA

These 12 standard-size cards feature some of the best Mets from their first 25 seasons. The cards feature black-and-white player photos, his name, and position on the front. The backs have career totals, vital statistics and a biography.

COMPLETE SET (12) 2.00 5.00
1 Ed Kranepool .08 .25
2 Ron Hunt .08 .25
3 Bud Harrelson .08 .25
4 Wayne Garrett .08 .25
5 Cleon Jones .20 .50
6 Tommie Agee .08 .25
7 Rusty Staub .30 .75
8 Jerry Grote .20 .50
9 Gary Gentry .08 .25
10 Jerry Koosman .30 .75
11 Tug McGraw .30 .75
12 Gil Hodges MG .40 1.00

1986 Mets TCMA

These cards measure 3 1/2" by 5 1/2". The borderless fronts consist of nothing but the photos. The postcard format backs give player identification, vital statistics and previous season stats. The cards are numbered with "NYM86-XX" in the upper right.

COMPLETE SET (40) 6.00 15.00
1 Rick Aguilera .40 1.00
2 Bruce Berenyi .08 .25
3 Ron Darling .20 .50
4 Sid Fernandez .20 .50
5 Dwight Gooden .40 1.00
6 Tom Gorman .08 .25
7 Ed Lynch .08 .25
8 Roger McDowell .20 .50
9 Randy Myers .40 1.00
10 Bob Ojeda .08 .25
11 Jesse Orosco .20 .50
12 Doug Sisk .08 .25
13 Gary Carter .60 1.50
14 John Gibbons .30 .75
15 Barry Lyons .08 .25
16 Wally Backman .08 .25
17 Ron Gardenhire .20 .50
18 Keith Hernandez .40 1.00
19 Howard Johnson .20 .50
20 Ray Knight .08 .25
21 Kevin Mitchell .40 1.00
22 Rafael Santana .08 .25
23 Tim Teufel .08 .25
24 Lenny Dykstra .40 1.00
25 George Foster .20 .50
26 Danny Heep .08 .25
27 Mel Stottlemyre CO .08 .25
28 Darryl Strawberry .30 .75
29 Mookie Wilson .30 .75
31 Randy Niemann .08 .25
32 Ed Hearn .08 .25
33 Stan Jefferson .08 .25
34 Bill Robinson CO .08 .25
35 Shawn Abner .08 .25
36 Terry Blocker .08 .25
37 Davey Johnson MG .30 .75
38 Bud Harrelson CO .08 .25
39 Vern Hoscheit CO .08 .25
40 Greg Pavlick CO .08 .25
43 Tim Corcoran .08 .25

1986 Mets World Series Champs

This 30-card limited edition set measures approximately 2 1/2" by 3 5/16" and was distributed by Jim and Dave's Sportcards. The cards were poorly cut and therefore not uniform in size. The set features the 1986 World Series champion Mets team and claims to be bubble gumless cards. This unattractive blue card front displays a head shot drawing of the player with an oval matte effect and an inner white border. There has been some debate about the legitimacy of these cards, as many dealers believe that they should be classified the same as broder cards.

COMPLETE SET (30) 4.00 10.00
1 Keith Hernandez .40 1.00
2 Gary Carter .60 1.50
3 Wally Backman .08 .25
4 Len Dykstra .40 1.00
5 Roger McDowell .30 .75
6 Rick Aguilera .40 1.00
7 Rafael Santana .08 .25
8 Ed Hearn .08 .25
9 Doug Sisk .08 .25
10 Bruce Berenyi .08 .25
11 Darryl Strawberry .30 .75
12 Dwight Gooden .40 1.00
13 Lee Mazzilli .20 .50
14 Danny Heep .08 .25
15 Howard Johnson .20 .50
16 Bob Ojeda .20 .50
17 Rick Anderson .08 .25
18 Kevin Elster .40 1.00
19 Dave Magadan .40 1.00
20 Randy Myers .40 1.00
21 Mookie Wilson .30 .75
22 Ron Darling .20 .50
23 Davey Johnson MG .20 .50
24 Sid Fernandez .20 .50
25 Tim Teufel .08 .25
26 Randy Niemann .08 .25
27 Jesse Orosco .20 .50
28 Kevin Mitchell .40 1.00
29 Ray Knight .08 .25
30 Checklist .08 .25

1987 Mets 1969 TCMA

The Miracle Mets of 1969 are remembered in this standard-size set. Some of the leading players are featured with a photo, identification and position. The backs have a biography and stats from that amazing season.

COMPLETE SET (9) 1.25 3.00
1 Ed Kranepool .20 .50
2 Bud Harrelson .20 .50
3 Cleon Jones .20 .50
Tommie Agee
Ron Swoboda
4 Jerry Koosman .30 .75
5 Gary Gentry .08 .25
6 Tug McGraw .30 .75
7 Ron Taylor .08 .25
8 Jerry Grote .20 .50
9 Ken Boswell .08 .25

1987 Mets Colla Postcards

This 54-card set features color photos on a postcard format and was mailed in response to fan letters. The backs carry a pre-printed thank you note from the players.

COMPLETE SET (54) 12.50 30.00
1 Team Photo .40 1.00
2 Gary Carter .75 2.00
3 Len Dykstra .30 .75
4 Dwight Gooden .40 1.00
5 Howard Johnson .30 .75
6 Lee Mazzilli .30 .75
7 Roger McDowell .20 .50
8 Darryl Strawberry .40 1.00
9 Mookie Wilson .30 .75
10 Wally Backman .20 .50
11 Ron Darling .30 .75
12 Sid Fernandez .30 .75
13 Keith Hernandez .40 1.00
14 Bob Ojeda .20 .50
15 Dave Johnson MG .30 .75
16 Dave Magadan .30 .75
17 Kevin McReynolds .20 .50
18 Randy Myers .40 1.00
19 Jesse Orosco .30 .75
20 Ruben Santana .20 .50
21 Tim Teufel .20 .50
22 Rick Aguilera .30 .75
23 Rick Anderson .20 .50
24 Jose Bautista .20 .50
25 Terry Blocker .20 .50
26 Bob Buchanan .20 .50
27 Tom Burns .20 .50
28 Mark Carreon .20 .50
29 Charlie Corbell .20 .50
30 Reggie Dobie .20 .50
31 Kevin Elster .30 .75
32 John Gibbons .20 .50
33 Brian Givens .20 .50
34 Bud Harrelson CO .20 .50
35 Vein Hoscheit CO .20 .50
36 Clint Hurdle .30 .75
37 Marcus Lawton .20 .50
38 Terry Leach .20 .50
39 Tom McCarthy .20 .50
40 Keith Miller .20 .50
41 Kevin Mitchell .30 .75
42 Greg Olson .20 .50
43 Al Pedrique .20 .50
44 Swam Perlozzo CO .20 .50
45 Bill Robinson CO .20 .50
46 Zolio Sanchez .20 .50
47 Doug Sisk .20 .50
48 Mel Stottlemyre CO .20 .50
49 Gary Walter .20 .50
50 Dave West .20 .50
51 Ralph Kiner ANN .60 1.50
52 Bob Murphy ANN .40 1.00
53 Gary Thorne ANN .20 .50
55 Barry Lyons .20 .50

1987 Mets Fan Club

The cards in this eight-player set measure 2 1/2" by 3 1/2". The sheets were produced by Topps for the New York Mets and feature only Mets. The full sheet measures approximately 7 1/2" by 10 1/2". Cards are together on the sheet but are perforated for those collectors who want to separate the individual player cards. The cards have an outer orange border. The set was available as a membership premium for joining the Junior Mets Fan Club for 6.00. The set and club were also sponsored by Farmland Dairies Milk. The cards are unnumbered on the back although they do contain the player's uniform number on the front.

COMPLETE SET (9) 3.00 8.00
1 Gary Carter .75 2.00
2 Ron Darling .30 .75
3 Len Dykstra .60 1.50
4 Roger McDowell .20 .50
5 Kevin McReynolds .30 .75
6 Bob Ojeda .20 .50
7 Darryl Strawberry .40 1.00
8 Mookie Wilson .40 1.00
9 Mets Team Card/(1986 World Champs).20 .50

1988 Mets Colla Postcards

This 55-card set features color photos on a postcard format and was mailed in response to fan letters. The backs carry a pre-printed thank you note from the players

COMPLETE SET (55) 12.50 30.00
1 Gary Carter .75 2.00
2 Ron Darling .30 .75
3 Len Dykstra .30 .75
4 Dwight Gooden .60 1.50
5 Keith Hernandez .40 1.00
6 Howard Johnson .30 .75
7 Roger McDowell .20 .50
8 Randy Myers .30 .75
9 Darryl Strawberry .40 1.00
10 Tim Teufel .20 .50
11 Mookie Wilson .30 .75
12 Team Photo .40 1.00
13 Rick Aguilera .30 .75
14 Wally Backman .20 .50
15 Mark Carreon .20 .50
16 David Cone .60 1.50
17 Joacquin Contreras .20 .50
18 Andre David .20 .50
19 Reggie Dobie .20 .50
20 Ken Dowell .20 .50
21 Rob Dromerhauser .20 .50
22 Kevin Elster .30 .75
23 Sid Fernandez .30 .75
24 Steve Frey .20 .50
25 Bud Harrelson CO .20 .50
26 Vern Hoscheit CO .20 .50
27 Gregg Jefferies .40 1.00
28 Steve Jelic .20 .50
29 Dave Johnson MG .30 .75
30 Marcus Lawton .20 .50
31 Terry Leach .20 .50
32 Phil Lombardi .20 .50
33 Barry Lyons .20 .50
34 Dave Magadan .20 .50
35 Lee Mazzilli .30 .75
36 Tom McCarthy .20 .50
37 Kevin McReynolds .20 .50
38 Keith Miller .20 .50
39 Randy Milligan .20 .50
40 John Mitchell .20 .50
41 Bob Ojeda .20 .50
42 Greg Pavlick CO .20 .50
43 Sam Perlozzo CO .20 .50
44 Darren Reed .20 .50
45 Bill Robinson CO .20 .50
46 Rich Rodriguez .20 .50
47 Jose Roman .20 .50
48 Jack Savage .20 .50
49 Mel Stottlemyre CO .20 .50
50 Gary Walter .20 .50
51 Todd Welborn .20 .50
52 Dave West .20 .50
53 Bob Murphy ANN .40 1.00
54 Arthur Richman FO .20 .50
55 Gary Thorne ANN .20 .50

1988 Mets Donruss Team Book

The 1988 Donruss Mets Team Book set features 27 cards (three pages with nine cards on each page) plus a large full-page puzzle of Stan Musial. Cards are in full color and are standard size. The set was distributed as a four-page book; although the puzzle page was perforated, the card pages were not. The cover of the "Team Collection" book is primarily bright red. Card fronts are very similar in design to the 1988 Donruss regular issue. The card numbers on the backs are the same for those players that are the same as in the regular Donruss set; the new players pictured are numbered on the back as "NEW." The book is usually sold intact. When cut from the book into individual cards, these cards are distinguishable from the regular 1988 Donruss cards since these have a 1988 copyright on the back whereas the regular issue has a 1987 copyright on the back.

COMPLETE SET (27) 1.25 3.00
37 Kevin Elster RR .08 .25
69 Dwight Gooden .08 .25
76 Ron Darling .02 .10
118 Sid Fernandez .02 .10
199 Gary Carter .30 1.00
241 Wally Backman .02 .10
316 Keith Hernandez .08 .25
323 Dave Magadan .02 .10
364 Len Dykstra .08 .25
439 Darryl Strawberry .20 .50
446 Rick Aguilera .08 .25
562 Keith Miller .02 .10
569 Howard Johnson .08 .25
603 Terry Leach .02 .10
614 Lee Mazzilli .08 .25
617 Kevin McReynolds .02 .10
619 Barry Lyons .02 .10
620 Randy Myers .20 .50
632 Bob Ojeda .02 .10
648 Tim Teufel .02 .10
651 Roger McDowell .02 .10
652 Mookie Wilson .08 .25
653 David Cone .30 .75
657 Gregg Jefferies .08 .25
NEW Jeff Innis .02 .10
NEW Mackey Sasser .02 .10
NEW Gene Walter .02 .10

1988 Mets Fan Club

The cards in this nine-player set measure 2 1/2" by 3 1/2". The sheets were produced by Topps for the New York Mets and feature only Mets. The full sheet measures 7 1/2" by 10 1/2". Cards are together on the sheet but are perforated for those collectors who want to separate the individual player cards. The cards have an outer orange border and an inner dark blue border. The set was available as a membership premium for joining the Junior Mets Fan Club for 6.00. The set and club were also sponsored by Farmland Dairies Milk. The cards are unnumbered on the back although they do contain the player's uniform number on the front.

COMPLETE SET (9) 2.50 6.00
8 Gary Carter .75 2.00
16 Dwight Gooden .40 1.00
17 Keith Hernandez .40 1.00
18 Darryl Strawberry .40 1.00
20 Howard Johnson .30 .75
21 Kevin Elster .20 .50
42 Roger McDowell .20 .50
48 Randy Myers .60 1.50
50 Sid Fernandez .30 .75

1988 Mets Kahn's

These 32-card standard-size sets were issued to the first 48,000 fans at the June 30th game between the New York Mets and the Houston Astros at Shea Stadium. The set includes 30 players, a team card, and a discount coupon card (to be redeemed at the grocery store). The cards are unnumbered except for uniform number and feature full-color photos bordered in blue and orange on the front. The Kahn's logo is printed in red in the corner of the reverse.

COMPLETE SET (32) 5.00 12.00
1 Mookie Wilson .20 .50
2 Mackey Sasser .08 .25
3 Bud Harrelson CO .20 .50
4 Len Dykstra .30 .75
5 Davey Johnson MG .20 .50
6 Wally Backman .08 .25
8 Gary Carter .40 1.25
11 Tim Teufel .08 .25
12 Ron Darling .20 .50
13 Lee Mazzilli .20 .50
15 Rick Aguilera .30 .75
16 Dwight Gooden .40 1.00
17 Keith Hernandez .40 1.00
18 Darryl Strawberry .30 .75
19 Bob Ojeda .08 .25
20 Howard Johnson .30 .75
21 Kevin Elster .20 .50
22 Kevin McReynolds .20 .50
26 Terry Leach .08 .25
28 Bill Robinson CO .08 .25
29 Dave Magadan .20 .50
30 Mel Stottlemyre CO .20 .50
31 Gene Walter .08 .25
33 Barry Lyons .08 .25
34 Sam Perlozzo CO .08 .25
42 Roger McDowell .08 .25
44 David Cone .75 2.00
48 Randy Myers .40 1.00
50 Sid Fernandez .30 .75
52 Greg Pavlick CO .08 .25
NNO Team Photo Card .20 .50
NNO Discount Coupon .08 .25

1989 Mets 1969 Calendar

This 12-card standard size set was issued as an insert in the 1989 Met Calendar. This set features some of the most important people involved in the 1969 Miracle Met season. The cards photos are framed. The sets feature a good mix of portrait and game action photos and the backs have only the stats from 1969 on the back. The set is checklisted alphabetically below.

COMPLETE SET (12) 2.00 5.00
1 Tommie Agee .20 .50
2 Donn Clendenon .20 .50
3 Wayne Garrett .08 .25
4 Jerry Grote .20 .50
5 Bud Harrelson .20 .50
6 Gil Hodges MG .40 1.00
7 Cleon Jones .20 .50
8 Jerry Koosman .40 1.00
9 Ed Kranepool .20 .50
10 Tug McGraw .40 1.00
11 Tom Seaver .75 2.00
12 Ron Swoboda .20 .50

1989 Mets Colla Postcards

This 58-card set features color photos on a postcard format and was mailed in response to fan letters. The backs carry a pre-printed thank you note from the players.

COMPLETE SET (58) 12.50 30.00
1 Mets Team .40 1.00
2 Darryl Strawberry .40 1.00
3 Gary Carter .75 2.00
4 Dave Cone .60 1.50
(David)
5 Ron Darling .30 .75
6 Len Dykstra .30 .75

7 Kevin Elster .20 .50
8 Dwight Gooden .60 1.50
9 Keith Hernandez .30 .75
10 Gregg Jefferies .20 .50
11 Howard Johnson .30 .75
12 Lee Mazzilli .30 .75
13 Kevin McReynolds .20 .50
14 Kevin Miller .20 .50
15 Randy Myers .30 .75
16 Bob Ojeda .20 .50
17 Mackey Sasser .20 .50
18 Tim Teufel .20 .50
19 Mookie Wilson .30 .75
20 Don Aase .20 .50
21 Rick Aguilera .30 .75
22 Blaine Beatty .20 .50
23 Terry Bross .20 .50
24 Kevin Brown .20 .50
25 Mark Carreon .20 .50
26 Rob Dromerhouser .20 .50
27 Tim Drummond .20 .50
28 Sid Fernandez .30 .75
29 Steve Frey .20 .50
30 Wayne Garland CO .20 .50
31 Brian Givens .20 .50
32 Bud Harrelson CO .20 .50
33 Vern Horscheit CO .20 .50
34 Clint Hurdle .30 .75
35 Jeff Innis .20 .50
36 Steve Jelic .20 .50
37 Dave Johnson MG .20 .50
38 Terry Leach .20 .50
39 Dave Liddel .20 .50
40 Phil Lombardi .20 .50
41 Barry Lyons .20 .50
42 Dave Magadan .20 .50
43 Roger McDowell .20 .50
44 John Mitchell .20 .50
45 Bob Murphy ANN .40 1.00
46 Ed Nunez .20 .50
47 Greg Pavlick CO .20 .50
48 Sam Perlozzo .20 .50
49 Darren Reed .20 .50
50 Bill Robinson CO .20 .50
51 Jack Savage .20 .50
52 Craig Shipley .20 .50
53 Bob Sikes .20 .50
54 Mel Stottlemyre CO .30 .75
55 Jeff Tamargo .20 .50
56 Kevin Tapani .60 1.50
57 Dave West .20 .50
58 Wally Whitehurst .20 .50

1989 Mets Fan Club

This set was produced by Topps for the Mets Fan Club as a sheet of nine cards each featuring a member of the New York Mets. The individual cards are standard size; however the set is typically traded as a sheet rather than as individual cards.

COMPLETE SET (9) 2.50 6.00
8 Gary Carter .75 2.00
9 Gregg Jefferies .20 .50
16 Dwight Gooden .40 1.00
18 Darryl Strawberry .40 1.00
22 Kevin McReynolds .30 .75
25 Keith Miller .20 .50
42 Roger McDowell .20 .50
44 David Cone .60 1.50
NNO Mets Team Card/(Eastern Div. Champs) .20 .50

1989 Mets Kahn's

The 1989 Kahn's Mets set contains 36 (32 original and four update) standard-size cards. The fronts have color photos with Mets' colored borders (blue, orange and white). The horizontally oriented backs have career stats. The cards were available from Kahn's by sending three UPC symbols from Kahn's products and a coupon appearing in certain local newspapers. There was also a small late-season update set of Kahn's Mets showing new players who joined the Mets during the season, Jeff Innis, Keith Miller, Jeff Musselman, and Frank Viola. This "Update" subset was distributed at a different Mets Baseball Card Night game than the main set. The main set is referenced alphabetically by subject's name. The update cards are given the prefix "U" in the checklist below.

COMPLETE SET (36) 3.00 8.00
1 Don Aase .02 .10
2 Rick Aguilera .30 .75
3 Mark Carreon .02 .10
4 Gary Carter .30 1.00
5 David Cone .30 .75
6 Ron Darling .08 .25
7 Kevin Elster .02 .10
8 Sid Fernandez .20 .50
9 Dwight Gooden .30 .75
10 Bud Harrelson CO .30 .75
11 Keith Hernandez .30 .75
12 Gregg Jefferies .02 .10
13 Davey Johnson MG .08 .25
14 Howard Johnson .20 .50
15 Barry Lyons .02 .10
16 Dave Magadan .02 .10
17 Lee Mazzilli .08 .25
18 Kevin McReynolds .08 .25
19 Randy Myers .30 .75
20 Bob Ojeda .02 .10
21 Greg Pavlick CO .02 .10
22 Sam Perlozzo CO .02 .10
23 Bill Robinson CO .02 .10
24 Juan Samuel .02 .10
25 Mackey Sasser .02 .10
26 Mel Stottlemyre CO .08 .25
27 Darryl Strawberry .08 .25
28 Tim Teufel .02 .10
29 Dave West .02 .10
30 Mookie Wilson .08 .25
31 Mets Team Photo .08 .25
32 Sponsors Card .02 .10
U1 Jeff Innis .30 .75
U2 Keith Miller .30 .75
U3 Jeff Musselman .30 .75
U4 Frank Viola 1.00

1989 Mets Rini Postcards 1969

This set of 36 postcards measures 3 1/2" by 5 1/2", were limited to 5,000 produced, and showcases the 1969 New York Mets. On a blue background, the horizontal fronts feature color drawings by Susan Rini. The player cards are sequenced in alphabetical order.

COMPLETE SET (36) 6.00 15.00
1 Championship Trophy .08 .25
2 Shea Stadium .08 .25
3 Tommie Agee .30 .75
4 Ken Boswell .08 .25
5 Ed Charles .08 .25
6 Don Cardwell .08 .25
7 Donn Clendenon .08 .25
8 Jack DiLauro .08 .25
9 Duffy Dyer .08 .25
10 Wayne Garrett .08 .25
11 Jerry Grote .40 1.00
12 Rod Gaspar .08 .25
13 Gary Gentry .08 .25
14 Bud Harrelson .40 1.00
15 Gil Hodges MG .75 2.00
16 Cleon Jones .30 .75
17 Ed Kranepool .40 1.00
18 Cal Koonce .08 .25
19 Jerry Koosman .40 1.00
20 Jim McAndrew .08 .25
21 Tug McGraw .40 1.00
22 J.C. Martin .08 .25
23 Bob Pfeil .08 .25
24 Nolan Ryan 2.00 5.00
25 Ron Swoboda .30 .75
26 Tom Seaver 1.25 3.00
27 Art Shamsky .08 .25
28 Ron Taylor .08 .25
29 Al Weis .08 .25
30 Joe Pignatano CO .08 .25
31 Eddie Yost CO .08 .25
32 Ralph Kiner ANN .40 1.00
33 Bob Murphy ANN .30 .75
34 Lindsey Nelson ANN .20 .50
35 Yogi Berra CO .40 1.00
36 Rube Walker CO .08 .25

1990 Mets Colla Postcards

This 53-card set features color photos on a postcard format and was mailed in response to fan letters. The backs carry a pre-printed thank you note from the players.

COMPLETE SET (53) 12.50 30.00
1 Mets Team .40 1.00
2 John Franco .40 1.00
3 Dwight Gooden .60 1.50
4 Howard Johnson .30 .75
5 Gregg Jefferies .20 .50
6 Darryl Strawberry .40 1.00
7 Kevin Elster .20 .50
8 Bud Harrelson CO .20 .50
9 Dave Johnson MG .30 .75
10 Tim Teufel .20 .50
11 Frank Viola .30 .75
12 Dave Cone .60 1.50
(David)
13 Ron Darling .30 .75
14 Sid Fernandez .30 .75
15 Clint Hurdle .30 .75
16 Barry Lyons .20 .50
17 Kevin McReynolds .20 .50
18 Dave Magadan .20 .50
19 Mike Marshall .20 .50
20 Keith Miller .20 .50
21 Jeff Musselman .20 .50
22 Bob Ojeda .20 .50
23 Alejandro Pena .20 .50
24 Mackey Sasser .20 .50
25 Blaine Beatty .20 .50
26 Terry Bross .20 .50
27 Kevin Brown .20 .50
28 Mark Carreon .20 .50
29 Mike Cubbage CO .20 .50
30 Chris Donnells .20 .50
31 Rob Dromerhouser .20 .50
32 Doc Edwards CO .20 .50
33 Vern Hoscheit CO .20 .50
34 Keith Hughes .20 .50
35 Todd Hundley .60 1.50
36 Jeff Innis .20 .50
37 Brent Knackert .20 .50
38 Phil Lombardi .20 .50
39 Julio Machado .20 .50
40 Terry McDaniel .20 .50
41 Orlando Mercado .20 .50
42 Keith Miller .20 .50
43 Tom O'Malley .20 .50
44 Greg Pavlick CO .20 .50
45 Darren Reed .20 .50
46 John Roseboro .20 .50
47 Pete Schourek .30 .75
48 Bob Sikes .20 .50
49 Mel Stottlemyre CO .30 .75
50 Lou Thornton .20 .50
51 Dave Trautwein .20 .50
52 Julio Valera .20 .50
53 Wally Whitehurst .20 .50

1990 Mets Fan Club

The 1990 Mets Fan Club Tropicana set was issued by the New York Mets fan club in association with the Tropicana Juice Company. For the seventh year, the Mets issued a perforated card sheet in conjunction with their fan clubs. This nine-card, standard-size set is skip-numbered and arranged by uniform numbers.

COMPLETE SET (9) 2.50 6.00
9 Gregg Jefferies .20 .50
16 Dwight Gooden .40 1.00
18 Darryl Strawberry .40 1.00
20 Howard Johnson .30 .75
21 Kevin Elster .20 .50
25 Keith Miller .20 .50
29 Frank Viola .40 1.00
44 David Cone .60 1.50
50 Sid Fernandez .30 .75

1990 Mets Hall of Fame

This six-card set was issued by the New York Mets in conjunction with AIWA and the Wiz Home Entertainment Centers. The cards measure approximately 5" by 7" and are in the postcard type format. One set was given away to each fan attending the Mets' home game on September 9, 1990. The fronts feature borderless player photos, while the backs have brief statistics and a sponsor advertisement. The cards are unnumbered and checklisted below by year of induction.

COMPLETE SET 4.00 10.00
1 Casey Stengel MG 1981 1.50 4.00
and Gil Hodges MG 1982
2 Bud Harrelson/1986 .40 1.00
3 Rusty Staub/1986 1.00 2.50
4 Tom Seaver/1988 2.50 6.00
5 Jerry Koosman/1989 .75 2.00
6 Ed Kranepool/1990 .40 1.00

1990 Mets Kahn's

The 1990 Kahn's Mets set was given away as a New York Mets stadium promotion. This standard-size set is skip-numbered by uniform number within the set and features 34 cards and two Kahn's coupon cards. Three players, Thornton, Magadan, and Mercado are wearing different uniform numbers than listed on the front of their cards. In addition to the Shea Stadium promotion, the complete set was also available in specially marked three-packs of Kahn's Wieners.

COMPLETE SET (34) 3.00 8.00
1 Lou Thornton .08 .25
2 Mackey Sasser .08 .25
3 Bud Harrelson CO .20 .50
4 Mike Cubbage CO .08 .25
5 Davey Johnson MG .20 .50
6 Mike Marshall .08 .25
9 Gregg Jefferies .08 .25
10 Dave Magadan .08 .25
11 Tim Teufel .08 .25
13 Jeff Musselman .08 .25
15 Ron Darling .20 .50
16 Dwight Gooden .30 .75
18 Darryl Strawberry .30 .75
19 Bob Ojeda .08 .25
20 Howard Johnson .30 .75
21 Kevin Elster .08 .25
22 Kevin McReynolds .08 .25
25 Keith Miller .08 .25
26 Alejandro Pena .08 .25
27 Tom O'Malley .08 .25
29 Frank Viola .20 .50
30 Mel Stottlemyre CO .20 .50
31 John Franco .40 1.00
32 Doc Edwards CO .08 .25
33 Barry Lyons .08 .25
35 Orlando Mercado .08 .25
40 Jeff Innis .08 .25
44 David Cone .40 1.00
45 Mark Carreon .08 .25
47 Wally Whitehurst .08 .25
48 Julio Machado .08 .25
50 Sid Fernandez .30 .75
52 Greg Pavlick CO .08 .25
NNO Team Photo .20 .50

1990 Mets Topps TV

This Mets team set contains 66 cards measuring the standard size. Cards numbered 1-34 were with the parent club, while cards 35-66 were in the farm system.

COMPLETE FACT. SET (66) 15.00 40.00
1 Dave Johnson MG .20 .50
2 Mike Cubbage CO .08 .25
3 Doc Edwards CO .08 .25
4 Bud Harrelson CO .08 .25
5 Greg Pavlick CO .08 .25
6 Mel Stottlemyre CO .20 .50
7 Blaine Beatty .08 .25
8 David Cone 2.00 5.00
9 Ron Darling .08 .25
10 Sid Fernandez .08 .25
11 John Franco .60 1.50
12 Dwight Gooden 1.50 4.00
13 Jeff Innis .08 .25
14 Julio Machado .08 .25
15 Jeff Musselman .08 .25
16 Bob Ojeda .08 .25
17 Alejandro Pena .08 .25
18 Frank Viola .20 .50
19 Wally Whitehurst .08 .25
20 Barry Lyons .08 .25
21 Orlando Mercado .08 .25
22 Mackey Sasser .08 .25
23 Kevin Elster .08 .25
24 Gregg Jefferies .08 .25
25 Howard Johnson .20 .50
26 Dave Magadan .08 .25
27 Mike Marshall .08 .25
28 Tom O'Malley .08 .25
29 Tim Teufel .08 .25
30 Mark Carreon .08 .25
31 Kevin McReynolds .08 .25
32 Keith Miller .08 .25
33 Darryl Strawberry .75 2.00
34 Lou Thornton .08 .25
35 Shawn Barton .08 .25
36 Tim Bogar .08 .25
37 Terry Bross .08 .25
38 Kevin Brown .08 .25
39 Mike DeButch .08 .25
40 Alex Diaz .08 .25
41 Chris Donnels .08 .25
42 Jeff Gardner .08 .25
43 Denny Gonzalez .08 .25
44 Kenny Graves .08 .25
45 Manny Hernandez .08 .25
46 Keith Hughes .08 .25
47 Todd Hundley 2.50 6.00
48 Chris Jelic .08 .25
49 Dave Liddell .08 .25
50 Terry McDaniel .08 .25
51 Cesar Mejia .08 .25
52 Scott Nielsen .08 .25
53 Dale Plummer .08 .25
54 Darren Reed .08 .25
55 Gil Roca .08 .25
56 Jaime Roseboro .08 .25
57 Roger Samuels .08 .25
58 Zoilo Sanchez .08 .25
59 Pete Schourek .60 1.50
60 Craig Shipley .08 .25
61 Ray Soff .08 .25
62 Steve Swisher MG .08 .25
63 Kelvin Torve .08 .25
64 Dave Trautwein .08 .25
65 Julio Valera .08 .25
66 Alan Zinter .20 .50

1991 Mets Colla Postcards

This 52-card set features color photos on a postcard format and was mailed in response to fan letters. The backs carry a pre-printed thank you note from the players.

COMPLETE SET (52) 10.00 25.00
2 Mets Team .40 1.00
3 John Franco .40 1.00
4 Dwight Gooden .40 1.00
5 Gregg Jefferies .20 .50
6 Dave Magadan .20 .50
7 Daryl Boston .20 .50
8 Vince Coleman .20 .50
9 Bud Harrelson MG .20 .50
10 Tim Teufel .20 .50
11 Frank Viola .30 .75
12 Hubie Brooks .30 .75
13 Mark Carreon .20 .50
14 Dave Cone .60 1.50
(David)
15 Kevin Elster .20 .50
16 Sid Fernandez .30 .75
17 Tommy Herr .20 .50
18 Howard Johnson .30 .75
19 Kevin McReynolds .20 .50
20 Darren Reed .20 .50
21 Mackey Sasser .20 .50
22 Kevin Baez .20 .50
23 Blaine Beatty .20 .50
24 Terry Bross .20 .50
25 Chuck Carr .20 .50
26 Rick Cerone .20 .50
27 Mike Cubbage CO .20 .50
28 Ron Darling .20 .50
29 Chris Donnells .20 .50
30 D.J. Dozier .20 .50
31 Rob Dromerhouser .20 .50
32 Doc Edwards CO .20 .50
33 Eric Hillman .20 .50
34 Todd Hundley .60 1.50
35 Clint Hurdle CO .20 .50
36 Jeff Innis .20 .50
37 John Johnstone .20 .50
38 Terry McDaniel .20 .50
39 Orlando Mercado .20 .50
40 Keith Miller .20 .50
41 Charlie O'Brien .20 .50
42 Greg Pavlick CO .20 .50
43 Alejandro Pena .20 .50
44 Terry Puhl .20 .50
45 Pete Schourek .40 1.00
46 Doug Simons .20 .50
47 Tom Spencer CO .20 .50
48 Mel Stottlemyre CO .20 .50
49 Kevin Torve .20 .50
50 Julio Valera .20 .50
51 Wally Whitehurst .20 .50
52 Anthony Young .20 .50
53 Alan Zinter .20 .50

1991 Mets Kahn's

The 1991 Kahn's Mets set contains 33 cards measuring the standard size. The set is skip-numbered on the card fronts by uniform number and includes two Kahn's coupon cards. The front features color action player photos, on a white and blue pinstripe pattern. The player's name is given in an orange stripe below the picture. In a horizontal format the back presents biographical information, major league statistics, and minor league statistics where appropriate. A complete set was given away to each fan attending the New York Mets game at Shea Stadium on June 17, 1991.

COMPLETE SET (33) 3.00 8.00
1 Vince Coleman .20 .50
2 Mackey Sasser .08 .25
3 Bud Harrelson MG .20 .50
4 Mike Cubbage CO .08 .25
5 Charlie O'Brien .08 .25
7 Hubie Brooks .20 .50
8 Daryl Boston .08 .25
9 Gregg Jefferies .08 .25
10 Dave Magadan .08 .25
11 Tim Teufel .08 .25
13 Rick Cerone .08 .25
15 Ron Darling .20 .50
16 Dwight Gooden .40 1.00
17 David Cone .40 1.00
20 Howard Johnson .30 .75
21 Kevin Elster .08 .25
22 Kevin McReynolds .08 .25
25 Keith Miller .08 .25
26 Alejandro Pena .08 .25
28 Tom Herr .08 .25
29 Frank Viola .20 .50
30 Mel Stottlemyre CO .20 .50
31 John Franco .40 1.00
32 Doc Edwards CO .08 .25
40 Jeff Innis .08 .25
43 Doug Simons .08 .25
45 Mark Carreon .08 .25
47 Wally Whitehurst .08 .25
48 Pete Schourek .30 .75
50 Sid Fernandez .20 .50
51 Tom Spencer CO .08 .25
52 Greg Pavlick CO .08 .25
NNO 1991 New York Mets .20 .50
Team photo

1991 Mets Photo Album Pergament

These 30 blank back photos were issued to honor the 1991 New York Mets. Each color photo has an picture of the player along with their position in the upper right corner. The bottom is devoted to the players name. The backs are blank and the photos are ordered in the way the appear in the perfect bound (the photos are not perforated) album. The back of the album and an multi-page advertisment in the middle is sponsored by Pergament Home Centers.

COMPLETE SET (30) 6.00 15.00
1 Bud Harrelson MG .20 .50
2 Mike Cubbage CO .20 .50
3 Doc Edwards CO .20 .50
4 Greg Pavlick CO .20 .50
5 Tom Spencer CO .20 .50
6 Mel Stottlemyre CO .30 .75
7 Daryl Boston .20 .50
8 Hubie Brooks .20 .50
9 Tim Burke .20 .50
10 Mark Carreon .20 .50
11 Rick Cerone .20 .50
12 Vince Coleman .20 .50
13 David Cone .60 1.50
14 Kevin Elster .20 .50
15 Sid Fernandez .30 .75
16 John Franco .40 1.00
17 Dwight Gooden .30 .75
18 Jeff Innis .20 .50
19 Gregg Jefferies .20 .50
20 Howard Johnson .30 .75
21 Dave Magadan .20 .50
22 Kevin McReynolds .20 .50
23 Keith Miller .20 .50
24 Charlie O'Brien .20 .50
25 Mackey Sasser .20 .50
26 Pete Schourek .30 .75
27 Doug Simons .20 .50
28 Garry Templeton .20 .50
29 Frank Viola .30 .75
30 Wally Whitehurst .20 .50

1991 Mets WIZ

This 450-card commemorative New York Mets set was sponsored by WIZ Home Entertainment Centers and ATT. The set was issued on 30 (approximately) 10" by 9" perforated sheets (15 cards per sheet); after perforation, the cards measure approximately 2" by 3". the cards are numbered on the back and listed in alphabetical order. The set purports to show every player who ever played for the New York Mets. The set was issued in three series to be distributed at three home games during the year, e.g., the first series was issued to all fans attending the Mets home game on May 25, 1991.

1 Don Aase .60 1.50
2 Tommie Agee .60 1.50
3 Rick Aguilera .75 2.00
4 Jack Aker .60 1.50
5 Neil Allen .60 1.50
6 Bill Almon .60 1.50
7 Sandy Alomar Sr. .60 1.50
8 Jesus Alou .60 1.50
9 George Altman .60 1.50
10 Luis Alvarado .60 1.50
11 Craig Anderson .60 1.50
12 Rick Anderson .60 1.50
13 Bob Apodaca .60 1.50
14 Gerry Arrigo .60 1.50
15 Richie Ashburn 2.50 6.00
16 Tucker Ashford .60 1.50
17 Bob Aspromonte .60 1.50
18 Benny Ayala .60 1.50
19 Wally Backman .60 1.50
20 Kevin Baez .60 1.50
21 Bob Bailor .60 1.50
22 Rick Baldwin .60 1.50
23 Billy Baldwin .60 1.50
24 Lute Barnes .60 1.50
25 Ed Bauta .60 1.50
26 Billy Beane .75 2.00
27 Larry Bearnarth .60 1.50
28 Blaine Beatty .60 1.50
29 Jim Beauchamp .60 1.50
30 Gus Bell .60 1.50
31 Dennis Bennett .60 1.50
32 Butch Benton 2.00 5.00
33 Juan Berenguer .60 1.50
34 Bruce Berenyi .60 1.50
35 Dwight Bernard .60 1.50
36 Yogi Berra 2.50 6.00
37 Jim Bethke .60 1.50
38 Mike Bishop 2.00 5.00
39 Terry Blocker .60 1.50
40 Bruce Bochy .60 1.50
41 Bruce Boisclair .60 1.50
42 Dan Boitano .60 1.50
43 Mark Bomback .60 1.50
44 Don Bosch .60 1.50
45 Daryl Boston .60 1.50
46 Ken Boswell .60 1.50
47 Ed Bouchee .60 1.50
48 Larry Bowa .60 1.50
49 Ken Boyer .75 2.00
50 Mark Bradley .60 1.50
51 Eddie Bressoud .60 1.50
52 Hubie Brooks .60 1.50
53 Kevin D. Brown .60 1.50
54 Leon Brown .60 1.50
55 Mike Bruhert .60 1.50
56 Jerry Buchek .60 1.50
57 Larry Burright .60 1.50
58 Ray Burris .60 1.50
59 John Candelaria .60 1.50
60 Chris Cannizzaro .60 1.50
61 Buzz Capra .60 1.50
62 Jose Cardenal .60 1.50
63 Don Cardwell .60 1.50
64 Duke Carmel .60 1.50
65 Chuck Carr .60 1.50
66 Mark Carreon .60 1.50
67 Gary Carter 2.00 5.00
68 Elio Chacon .60 1.50
69 Dean Chance .60 1.50
70 Kelvin Chapman .60 1.50
71 Ed Charles .60 1.50
72 Rich Chiles .60 1.50
73 Harry Chiti .60 1.50
74 John Christensen .60 1.50
75 Joe Christopher .60 1.50
76 Galen Cisco .60 1.50
77 Donn Clendenon .60 1.50
78 Gene Clines .60 1.50
79 Choo Choo Coleman .60 1.50
80 Kevin Collins .60 1.50
81 David Cone 2.00 5.00
82 Bill Connors .60 1.50
83 Cliff Cook .60 1.50
84 Tim Corcoran .60 1.50
85 Mardie Cornejo .60 1.50
86 Billy Cowan .60 1.50
87 Roger Craig .60 1.50
88 Jerry Cram 2.00 5.00
89 Mike Cubbage .60 1.50
90 Ron Darling .60 1.50
91 Ray Daviault .60 1.50
92 Tommy Davis .75 2.00
93 John DeMerit .60 1.50
94 Bill Denehy .60 1.50
95 Jack DiLauro .60 1.50
96 Carlos Diaz .60 1.50
97 Mario Diaz .60 1.50
98 Steve Dillon .60 1.50
99 Sammy Drake .60 1.50
100 Jim Dwyer .60 1.50
101 Duffy Dyer .60 1.50
102 Len Dykstra 1.00 2.50
103 Tom Edens .60 1.50
104 Dave Eilers .60 1.50
105 Larry Elliot .60 1.50
106 Dock Ellis .60 1.50
107 Kevin Elster .75 2.00
108 Nino Espinosa .60 1.50
109 Chuck Estrada .60 1.50
110 Francisco Estrada 6.00 15.00
111 Pete Falcone .60 1.50
112 Sid Fernandez .75 2.00
113 Chico Fernandez .60 1.50
114 Sergio Ferrer .60 1.50
115 Jack Fisher .60 1.50
116 Mike Fitzgerald .60 1.50
117 Shaun Fitzmaurice .60 1.50
118 Gil Flores 2.00 5.00
119 Doug Flynn .60 1.50
120 Tim Foli .60 1.50
121 Rich Folkers .60 1.50
122 Larry Foss .60 1.50
123 George Foster .75 2.00
124 Leo Foster .60 1.50
125 Joe Foy .60 1.50
126 John Franco 1.00 2.50
127 Jim Fregosi .60 1.50
128 Bob Friend .60 1.50
129 Danny Frisella .60 1.50
130 Brent Gaff .60 1.50
131 Bob Gallagher .60 1.50
132 Ron Gardenhire .60 1.50
133 Rob Gardner .60 1.50
134 Wes Gardner .60 1.50
135 Wayne Garrett .60 1.50
136 Rod Gaspar .60 1.50
137 Gary Gentry .60 1.50
138 John Gibbons .60 1.50
139 Bob Gibson .60 1.50
140 Brian Giles .60 1.50
141 Joe Ginsberg .60 1.50
142 Ed Glynn .60 1.50
143 Jesse Gonder .60 1.50
144 Dwight Gooden 2.00 5.00
145 Greg Goossen .60 1.50
146 Tom Gorman .60 1.50
147 Jim Gosger .60 1.50
148 Bill Graham .60 1.50
149 Wayne Graham 1.25 3.00
150 Dallas Green .60 1.50
151 Pumpsie Green .60 1.50
152 Tom Grieve .60 1.50
153 Jerry Grote .60 1.50
154 Joe Grzenda .60 1.50
155 Don Hahn .60 1.50
156 Tom Hall .60 1.50
157 Jack Hamilton .60 1.50
158 Ike Hampton .60 1.50
159 Tim Harkness .60 1.50
160 Bud Harrelson .60 1.50
161 Greg A. Harris .60 1.50
162 Greg Harts 2.00 5.00
163 Andy Hassler .60 1.50
164 Tom Hausman .60 1.50
165 Ed Hearn .60 1.50
166 Richie Hebner .60 1.50
167 Danny Heep .60 1.50
168 Jack Heidemann .60 1.50
169 Bob Heise .60 1.50
170 Ken Henderson .60 1.50
171 Steve Henderson .60 1.50
172 Bob Hendley .60 1.50
173 Phil Hennigan .60 1.50
174 Bill Hepler .60 1.50
175 Ron Herbel .60 1.50
176 Manny Hernandez 2.00 5.00
177 Keith Hernandez 1.00 2.50
178 Tommy Herr .60 1.50
179 Rick Herrscher .60 1.50
180 Jim Hickman .60 1.50
181 Joe Hicks .60 1.50
182 Chuck Hiller .60 1.50
183 Dave Hillman .60 1.50
184 Jerry Hinsley 2.00 5.00
185 Gil Hodges 2.00 5.00
186 Ron Hodges .60 1.50
187 Scott Holman .60 1.50
188 Jay Hook .60 1.50
189 Mike Howard 2.00 5.00
190 Jesse Hudson .60 1.50
191 Keith Hughes .60 1.50
192 Todd Hundley 2.00 5.00
193 Ron Hunt .60 1.50
194 Willard Hunter .60 1.50
195 Clint Hurdle .60 1.50
196 Jeff Innis .60 1.50
197 Al Jackson .60 1.50
198 Roy Lee Jackson .60 1.50
199 Gregg Jefferies .60 1.50
200 Stan Jefferson .60 1.50
201 Chris Jelic .60 1.50
202 Bob D. Johnson .60 1.50
203 Howard Johnson .75 2.00
204 Bob W. Johnson .60 1.50
205 Randy Jones .60 1.50
206 Sherman Jones .60 1.50
207 Cleon Jones .60 1.50
208 Ross Jones .60 1.50
209 Mike Jorgensen .60 1.50
210 Rod Kanehl .60 1.50
211 Dave Kingman 1.00 2.50
212 Bobby Klaus .60 1.50
213 Jay Kleven 2.00 5.00
214 Lou Klimchock .60 1.50
215 Ray Knight .75 2.00
216 Kevin Kobel .60 1.50
217 Gary Kolb .60 1.50
218 Cal Koonce .60 1.50
219 Jerry Koosman .75 2.00
220 Ed Kranepool .75 2.00
221 Gary Kroll .60 1.50
222 Clem Labine .75 2.00
223 Jack Lamabe .60 1.50
224 Hobie Landrith .60 1.50
225 Frank Lary .60 1.50
226 Bill Latham .60 1.50
227 Terry Leach .60 1.50
228 Tim Leary .60 1.50
229 John Lewis .60 1.50
230 David Liddell .60 1.50
231 Phil Linz .60 1.50
232 Ron Locke .60 1.50
233 Skip Lockwood .60 1.50
234 Mickey Lolich .75 2.00
235 Phil Lombardi .60 1.50
236 Al Luplow .60 1.50
237 Ed Lynch .60 1.50
238 Barry Lyons .60 1.50
239 Ken MacKenzie .60 1.50
240 Julio Machado .60 1.50
241 Elliott Maddox .60 1.50
242 Dave Magadan .60 1.50
243 Pepe Mangual .60 1.50
244 Phil Mankowski .60 1.50
245 Felix Mantilla .60 1.50
246 Mike G. Marshall .60 1.50
247 Dave Marshall .60 1.50
248 Jim Marshall .60 1.50
249 Mike A. Marshall .60 1.50
250 J.C. Martin .60 1.50
251 Jerry Martin .60 1.50
252 Teddy Martinez .60 1.50
253 Jon Matlack .60 1.50
254 Jerry May .60 1.50
255 Willie Mays 3.00 8.00
256 Lee Mazzilli .60 1.50
257 Jim McAndrew .60 1.50
258 Bob McClure .60 1.50
259 Roger McDowell .60 1.50
260 Tug McGraw .75 2.00
261 Jeff McKnight .60 1.50
262 Roy McMillan .60 1.50
263 Kevin McReynolds .60 1.50
264 George Medich .60 1.50
265 Orlando Mercado .60 1.50
266 Butch Metzger .60 1.50
267 Felix Millan .60 1.50
268 Bob G. Miller .60 1.50
269 Bob L. Miller .60 1.50
270 Dyar Miller .60 1.50
271 Larry Miller .60 1.50
272 Keith Miller .60 1.50
273 Randy Milligan .60 1.50
274 John Milner .60 1.50
275 John Mitchell .60 1.50
276 Kevin Mitchell .75 2.00
277 Wilmer Mizell .60 1.50
278 Herb Moford .60 1.50
279 Willie Montanez .60 1.50
280 Joe Moock 2.00 5.00
281 Tommy Moore 2.00 5.00
282 Bob Moorhead .60 1.50
283 Jerry Morales .60 1.50
284 Al Moran .60 1.50
285 Jose Moreno .60 1.50
286 Bill Murphy .60 1.50
287 Dale Murray .60 1.50
288 Dennis Musgraves .60 1.50
289 Jeff Musselman .60 1.50
290 Randy Myers 1.00 2.50
291 Bob Myrick .60 1.50
292 Danny Napoleon .60 1.50
293 Charlie Neal .60 1.50
294 Randy Niemann .60 1.50
295 Joe Nolan .60 1.50
296 Dan Norman .60 1.50
297 Ed Nunez .60 1.50
298 Charlie O'Brien .60 1.50
299 Tom O'Malley .60 1.50
300 Bob Ojeda .60 1.50
301 Jose Oquendo .60 1.50
302 Jesse Orosco .75 2.00
303 Junior Ortiz .60 1.50
304 Brian Ostrosser 2.00 5.00
305 Amos Otis .60 1.50
306 Rick Ownbey .60 1.50
307 John Pacella .60 1.50
308 Tom Paciorek .60 1.50
309 Harry Parker .60 1.50
310 Tom Parsons .60 1.50
311 Al Pedrique 2.00 5.00
312 Brock Pemberton 2.00 5.00
313 Alejandro Pena .60 1.50
314 Bobby Pfeil .60 1.50
315 Mike Phillips .60 1.50
316 Jim Piersall .75 2.00
317 Joe Pignatano .60 1.50
318 Grover Powell 2.00 5.00
319 Rich Puig 2.00 5.00
320 Charlie Puleo .60 1.50
321 Gary Rajsich .60 1.50
322 Mario Ramirez 2.00 5.00
323 Lenny Randle .60 1.50
324 Bob Rauch 2.00 5.00
325 Jeff Reardon 1.00 2.50
326 Darren Reed .60 1.50
327 Hal Reniff .60 1.50
328 Ronn Reynolds .60 1.50
329 Tom Reynolds .60 1.50
330 Dennis Ribant .60 1.50
331 Gordie Richardson .60 1.50
332 Dave Roberts .60 1.50
333 Les Rohr .60 1.50
334 Luis Rosado 2.00 5.00
335 Don Rose .60 1.50
336 Don Rowe .60 1.50
337 Dick Rusteck .60 1.50
338 Nolan Ryan 12.00 30.00
339 Ray Sadecki .60 1.50
340 Joe Sambito .60 1.50
341 Amado Samuel 2.00 5.00
342 Juan Samuel .60 1.50
343 Ken Sanders .60 1.50
344 Rafael Santana .60 1.50
345 Mackey Sasser .60 1.50
346 Mac Scarce .60 1.50
347 Jim Schaffer .60 1.50
348 Dan Schatzeder .60 1.50
349 Calvin Schiraldi .60 1.50
350 Al Schmelz 2.00 5.00
351 Dave Schneck 2.00 5.00
352 Ted Schreiber .60 1.50
353 Don Schulze .60 1.50
354 Mike Scott .60 1.50
355 Ray Searage .60 1.50
356 Tom Seaver 3.00 8.00

357 Dick Selma .60 1.50
358 Art Shamsky .60 1.50
359 Bob Shaw .60 1.50
360 Don Shaw .60 1.50
361 Norm Sherry .60 1.50
362 Craig Shipley .60 1.50
363 Bart Shirley .60 1.50
364 Bill Short .60 1.50
365 Paul Siebert .60 1.50
366 Ken Singleton .75 2.00
367 Doug Sisk .60 1.50
368 Bobby Gene Smith .60 1.50
369 Charley Smith .60 1.50
370 Dick Smith .60 1.50
371 Duke Snider 2.50 6.00
372 Warren Spahn 2.50 6.00
373 Larry Stahl .60 1.50
374 Roy Staiger .60 1.50
375 Tracy Stallard .60 1.50
376 Leroy Stanton .60 1.50
377 Rusty Staub .75 2.00
378 John Stearns .60 1.50
379 John Stephenson .60 1.50
380 Randy Sterling .60 1.50
381 George Stone .60 1.50
382 Darryl Strawberry 1.00 2.50
383 John Strohmayer .60 1.50
384 Brent Strom .60 1.50
385 Dick Stuart .60 1.50
386 Tom Sturdivant .60 1.50
387 Bill Sudakis .60 1.50
388 John Sullivan .60 1.50
389 Darrell Sutherland .60 1.50
390 Ron Swoboda .60 1.50
391 Craig Swan .60 1.50
392 Rick Sweet .60 1.50
393 Pat Tabler .60 1.50
394 Kevin Tapani .75 2.00
395 Randy Tate .60 1.50
396 Frank Taveras .60 1.50
397 Chuck Taylor .60 1.50
398 Ron Taylor .60 1.50
399 Bob Taylor .60 1.50
400 Sammy Taylor .60 1.50
401 Walt Terrell .60 1.50
402 Ralph Terry .60 1.50
403 Tim Teufel .60 1.50
404 George Theodore .60 1.50
405 Frank J. Thomas .75 2.00
406 Lou Thornton .60 1.50
407 Marv Throneberry .75 2.00
408 Dick Tidrow .60 1.50
409 Rusty Tillman .60 1.50
410 Jackson Todd .60 1.50
411 Joe Torre 1.00 2.50
412 Mike Torrez .60 1.50
413 Kelvin Torve .60 1.50
414 Alex Trevino .60 1.50
415 Wayne Twitchell .60 1.50
416 Del Unser .60 1.50
417 Mike Vail .60 1.50
418 Bobby Valentine .75 2.00
419 Ellis Valentine .60 1.50
420 Julio Valera .60 1.50
421 Tom Veryzer .60 1.50
422 Frank Viola .75 2.00
423 Bill Wakefield .60 1.50
424 Gene Walter .60 1.50
425 Claudell Washington .60 1.50
426 Hank Webb .60 1.50
427 Al Weis .60 1.50
428 Dave West .60 1.50
429 Wally Whitehurst .60 1.50
430 Carl Willey .60 1.50
431 Nick Willhite .60 1.50
432 Charlie Williams .60 1.50
433 Mookie Wilson .75 2.00
434 Herm Winningham .60 1.50
435 Gene Woodling .60 1.50
436 Billy Wynne 2.00 5.00
437 Joel Youngblood .60 1.50
438 Pat Zachry .60 1.50
439 Don Zimmer .60 1.50
NNO Checklist 1-20 .60 1.50
NNO Checklist 41-60 .60 1.50
NNO Checklist 81-100 .60 1.50
NNO Checklist 121-140 .60 1.50
NNO Checklist 161-180 .60 1.50
NNO Checklist 201-220 .60 1.50
NNO Checklist 241-260 .60 1.50
NNO Checklist 281-300 .60 1.50
NNO Checklist 321-340 .60 1.50
NNO Checklist 361-380 .60 1.50
NNO Checklist 401-420 .60 1.50

1992 Mets Colla Postcards

This 39-card set features color photos on a postcard format and was mailed in response to fan letters. The backs carry a pre-printed thank you note from the players.

COMPLETE SET (39) 10.00 25.00
1 Team Picture .40 1.00
2 Bobby Bonilla .20 .50
3 Dwight Gooden .60 1.50
4 Howard Johnson .30 .75
5 Bret Saberhagen .30 .75
6 David Cone .60 1.50
7 Dave Magadan .30 .75
8 Eddie Murray .75 2.00
9 Willie Randolph .30 .75
10 Tim Burke .20 .50
11 Daryl Boston .20 .50
12 Vince Coleman .20 .50
13 Kevin Elster .20 .50
14 Sid Fernandez .30 .75
15 John Franco .40 1.00
16 Todd Hundley .60 1.50
17 Charlie O'Brien .20 .50
18 Mackey Sasser .20 .50
19 Jeff Torborg MG .20 .50
20 Wally Whitehurst .20 .50
21 Chris Donnels .20 .50
22 DJ Dozier .20 .50
23 Dave Gallagher .20 .50
24 Paul Gibson .20 .50
25 Junior Naboa .20 .50
26 Bill Pecota .20 .50
27 Pete Schourek .20 .50
28 Doug Simons .20 .50
29 Mel Stottlemyre CO .30 .75
30 Julio Valera .20 .50
31 Julian Vasquez .20 .50
32 Anthony Young .20 .50
33 Mike Cubbage CO .20 .50
34 Barry Foote CO .20 .50
35 Clint Hurdle CO .20 .50
36 Dave LaRoche CO .20 .50
37 Tom McCraw CO .20 .50
38 Jerry Stephenson CO .20 .50
40 Jeff Innis .20 .50

1992 Mets Kahn's

The 1992 Kahn's New York Mets set consists of 35 standard-size cards. The set included two manufacturer's coupons (one for 50 cents off Kahn's Beef Franks and another for the same amount off Kahn's Corn Dogs). The cards are skip-numbered by uniform number on the front and checklisted below accordingly.

COMPLETE SET (35) 3.00 8.00
1 Vince Coleman .20 .50
2 Mackey Sasser .08 .25
3 Junior Noboa .08 .25
4 Mike Cubbage CO .08 .25
6 Daryl Boston .08 .25
8 Dave Gallagher .08 .25
9 Todd Hundley .40 1.00
10 Jeff Torborg MG .08 .25
11 Dick Schofield .08 .25
12 Willie Randolph .30 .75
15 Kevin Elster .08 .25
16 Dwight Gooden .40 1.00
17 David Cone .40 1.00
18 Bret Saberhagen .20 .50
19 Anthony Young .08 .25
20 Howard Johnson .30 .75
22 Charlie O'Brien .08 .25
25 Bobby Bonilla .20 .50
26 Barry Foote CO .08 .25
27 Tom McCraw CO .08 .25
28 Dave LaRoche CO .08 .25
29 Dave Magadan .08 .25
30 Mel Stottlemyre CO .20 .50
31 John Franco .40 1.00
32 Bill Pecota .08 .25
33 Eddie Murray .50 1.25
40 Jeff Innis .08 .25
44 Tim Burke .08 .25
45 Paul Gibson .08 .25
47 Wally Whitehurst .08 .25
50 Sid Fernandez .20 .50
51 John Stephenson CO .08 .25
NNO Team Photo .20 .50
NNO Manufacturer's Coupon .08 .25
Kahn's Beef Franks
NNO Manufacturer's Coupon .08 .25
Kahn's Corn Dogs

1992 Mets Modell

Measuring 7 1/2" by 10 1/2", this 9-card perforated sheet was sponsored by Modell's Sporting Goods and distributed as a membership benefit to Team Mets, the junior fan club. If the cards were separated, they would measure the standard size. The cards are unnumbered and checklisted below in alphabetical order.

COMPLETE SET (9) 2.00 5.00
1 Bobby Bonilla .20 .50
2 Vince Coleman .20 .50
3 David Cone .60 1.50
4 Dwight Gooden .60 1.50
5 Todd Hundley .30 .75
6 Howard Johnson .30 .75
7 Eddie Murray .75 2.00
8 Willie Randolph .30 .75
9 Bret Saberhagen .30 .75

1993 Mets Colla Postcards

This 31-card set features color photos on a postcard format and was mailed in response to fan letters. The backs carry a pre-printed thank you note from the players. Because of legal problems with Barry Colla's licensing agreement, he can no longer sell his postcards making singles difficult to find and usually must be purchased as a set.

COMPLETE SET (31) 6.00 15.00
21 Team Photo .40 1.00
22 Bobby Bonilla .30 .75
23 Dwight Gooden .60 1.50
24 Howard Johnson .30 .75
25 Bret Saberhagen .20 .50
26 Tim Bogar .20 .50
27 Vince Coleman .20 .50
28 Mark Dewey .20 .50
29 Mike Draper .20 .50
30 Sid Fernandez .30 .75
31 Tony Fernandez .30 .75
32 John Franco .30 .75
33 Dave Gallagher .20 .50
34 Paul Gibson .20 .50
35 Eric Hillman .20 .50
36 Todd Hundley .30 .75
37 Jeff Innis .20 .50
38 Jeff Kent .60 1.50
39 Mike Maddux .20 .50
40 Jeff McKnight .20 .50
41 Eddie Murray .75 2.00
42 Charlie O'Brien .20 .50
43 Joe Orsulak .20 .50
44 Darren Reed .20 .50
45 Pete Schourek .20 .50
46 Frank Tanana .20 .50
47 Ryan Thompson .20 .50
48 Jeff Torborg CO .20 .50
49 Chico Walker .20 .50
50 Anthony Young .20 .50
110 Dallas Green MG .20 .50

1993 Mets Kahn's

This 29-card set measures the standard size and features white-bordered color player photos on their fronts. The cards are skip-numbered by uniform number on the front and checklisted below accordingly.

COMPLETE SET (29) 3.00 8.00
1 Tony Fernandez .20 .50
6 Joe Orsulak .08 .25
7 Jeff McKnight .08 .25
8 Dave Gallagher .08 .25
9 Todd Hundley .30 .75
11 Vince Coleman .20 .50
12 Jeff Kent .60 1.50
16 Dwight Gooden .40 1.00
18 Bret Saberhagen .20 .50
19 Anthony Young .08 .25
20 Howard Johnson .30 .75
21 Darren Reed .08 .25
22 Charlie O'Brien .08 .25
23 Tim Bogar .08 .25
25 Bobby Bonilla .08 .25
29 Frank Tanana .20 .50
31 John Franco .40 1.00
33 Eddie Murray .60 1.50
34 Chico Walker .08 .25
40 Jeff Innis .08 .25
44 Ryan Thompson .08 .25
47 Mike Draper .08 .25
48 Pete Schourek .20 .50
50 Sid Fernandez .20 .50
51 Mike Maddux .08 .25
NNO Team Photo .20 .50
NNO Title Card .08 .25
NNO Manufacturer's Coupon .08 .25
Kahn's Corn Dogs
NNO Manufacturer's Coupon .08 .25
Kahn's Hot Dogs

1994 Mets '69 Capital Cards Postcard Promos

Licensed by Miracle of 1969 Enterprises, Inc., this boxed set of 32 postcards commemorates the 25th Anniversary of the World Championship season of the 1969 Mets. Capital Cards commissioned renowned sports artist Ron Lewis to create from oil paintings these postcards, which measure 3 1/2" by 5 1/2". Just 25,000 postcard sets were produced, with each having a unique serial number. Also 5,000 individually-numbered uncut sheets were produced. The cards are numbered on the back and the word "PROMO" is stamped across each back.

COMPLETE SET (32) 8.00 20.00
1 Title Card .20 .50
2 Gil Hodges MG .60 1.50
3 Rube Walker CO .20 .50
4 Yogi Berra CO 1.00 2.50
5 Joe Pignatano CO .20 .50
6 Ed Yost CO .20 .50
7 Tommie Agee .30 .75
8 Ken Boswell .20 .50
9 Don Cardwell .20 .50
10 Ed Charles .20 .50
11 Donn Clendenon .30 .75
12 Jack DiLauro .20 .50
13 Duffy Dyer .20 .50
14 Wayne Garrett .20 .50
15 Rod Gasper .20 .50
16 Gary Gentry .20 .50
17 Jerry Grote .30 .75
18 Bud Harrelson .30 .75
19 Cleon Jones .30 .75
20 Cal Koonce .20 .50
21 Jerry Koosman .40 1.00
22 Ed Kranepool .30 .75
23 J.C. Martin .20 .50
24 Jim McAndrew .20 .50
25 Tug McGraw .60 1.50
26 Bob Pfeil .20 .50
27 Nolan Ryan 4.00 10.00
28 Tom Seaver 2.00 5.00
29 Art Shamsky .30 .75
30 Ron Swoboda .30 .75
31 Ron Taylor .20 .50
32 Al Weis .20 .50

1994 Mets '69 Commemorative Sheet

Issued in a 14 1/2" by 11 1/4" blue padded gold-stamped certificate holder, this commemorative sheet featuring 31 perforated caps was released on the 25th anniversary of the 1969 World Champion Mets. Each cap measures 1 5/8" in diameter, and the color player cutouts displayed are the same as those in the Ron Lewis postcard set. The words "1969 Miracle Mets" is gold foil-stamped at the top following the curve; likewise, the player's name is similarly impressed on the front. The backs are blank. The 31 caps are arranged on a sheet that has at its center a special 25th anniversary Mets logo. The enclosed certificate of authenticity carries the sheet serial number and total production figures (25,000). The caps are unnumbered and listed below just as they are in the postcard set, with nonplayers listed first.

COMPLETE SET (31) 6.00 15.00
1 Gil Hodges MG .40 1.00
2 Rube Walker CO .08 .25
3 Yogi Berra CO .40 1.00
4 Joe Pignatano CO .08 .25
5 Ed Yost CO .08 .25
6 Tommie Agee .20 .50
7 Ken Boswell .08 .25
8 Don Cardwell .08 .25
9 Ed Charles .08 .25
10 Donn Clendenon .20 .50
11 Jack DiLauro .08 .25
12 Duffy Dyer .08 .25
13 Wayne Garrett .08 .25
14 Rod Gaspar UER/(Name misspelled Gasper on front) .08 .25
15 Gary Gentry .08 .25
16 Jerry Grote .20 .50
17 Bud Harrelson .20 .50
18 Cleon Jones .20 .50
19 Cal Koonce .08 .25
20 Jerry Koosman .30 .75
21 Ed Kranepool .20 .50
22 J.C. Martin .08 .25
23 Jim McAndrew .08 .25
24 Tug McGraw .40 1.00
25 Bobby Pfeil .08 .25
26 Nolan Ryan 2.00 5.00
27 Tom Seaver 1.00 2.50
28 Art Shamsky .08 .25
29 Ron Swoboda .20 .50
30- Ron Taylor .08 .25
31 Al Weis .08 .25
NNO Uncut Sheet

1994 Mets '69 Spectrum Promos

Issued to herald the commemorative 25th anniversary 1969 Miracle Mets 70-card set, these standard-size promos feature on their fronts white-bordered color photos framed by red lines. The 25th anniversary logo appears in one corner. The blue backs carry player or team season highlights. The "For Promotional Use Only" disclaimer appears within a white ellipse on the back. The cards are numbered on the back with a "P" prefix.

COMPLETE SET (3) 1.25 3.00
P1 Tom Seaver .75 2.00
P2 Jerry Koosman .40 1.00
P3 Met Mania .40 1.00
Oct. 20, 1969/(Parade showing
Seaver

1994 Mets '69 Tribute

This 70-card standard-size boxed set commemorates the 1969 New York Mets championship team. Only 25,000 of these sets were produced and each box contains a Certificate of Authenticity indicating the set number.The fronts feature color and black-and-white posed and action player photos on a white background with a thin red border. In gold foil across the top is printed "The Miracle of '69," "The '69 Countdown," or "World Champions" with the player's name at the bottom in red and blue print. The backs carry the player's name, position, career highlights, and 1969 season statistics.

COMPLETE SET (70) 4.00 10.00
1 Commemorative Card .02 .10
2 1969 Mets Team Photo .08 .25
3 Tom Seaver .60 1.50
4 Jerry Koosman .20 .50
5 Tommie Agee .08 .25
6 Bud Harrelson .08 .25
7 Nolan Ryan 1.25 3.00
8 Jerry Grote .08 .25
9 Ron Swoboda .08 .25
10 Donn Clendenon .08 .25
11 Art Shamsky .08 .25
12 Tug McGraw .30 .75
13 Ed Kranepool .08 .25
14 Cleon Jones .08 .25
15 Ron Taylor .02 .10
16 Gary Gentry .02 .10
17 Ken Boswell .02 .10
18 Ed Charles .02 .10
19 J.C. Martin .02 .10
20 Al Weis .02 .10
21 Jack DiLauro .02 .10
22 Duffy Dyer .02 .10
23 Wayne Garrett .02 .10
24 Jim McAndrew .02 .10
25 Rod Gaspar .02 .10
26 Don Cardwell .02 .10
27 Bobby Pfeil .02 .10
28 Cal Koonce .02 .10
29 Gil Hodges MG .30 .75
30 Yogi Berra CO .30 .75
31 Joe Pignatano CO .02 .10
32 Rube Walker CO .02 .10
33 Eddie Yost CO .02 .10
34 1st Ever Met Game .02 .10
35 Opening Day 1969 .02 .10
36 Ed Kranepool .02 .10
Breaks Homerun Record
37 Jerry Koosman .08 .25
Sets Club Strikeout Record
38 Donn Clendenon .02 .10
Mets Trade for
39 Jerry Koosman/23 Scoreless Innings .08 .25
40 Begin 7 Game Winning Streak .02 .10
41 Vs Division Leading Cubs .02 .10
42 Tom Seaver .30 .75
Near Perfect Game
43 Mets Trail by 3 1/2 Games .02 .10
44 All-Star Break .02 .10
45 All-Star Game .02 .10
46 Mets Sweep Atlanta .02 .10
47 Mets Sweep Padres .02 .10
48 Jerry Koosman .08 .25
Mets Defeat Cubs
Strikes Out 13
49 Defeat Cubs, 1/2 Game Back .02 .10
50 1st Place ! .02 .10
51 9 Game Winning Streak .02 .10
52 Tom Seaver .30 .75
Earns 22nd Victory
53 Steve Carlton .30 .75
Strikes out 19
Mets Win
54 Jerry Koosman .08 .25
Pitches 15th Complete Game
55 Eastern Division Champions .02 .10
56 100th Victory .02 .10
57 Mets Prepare for Braves .02 .10
58 N.L.C.S. Game 1 .02 .10
59 N.L.C.S. Game 2 .02 .10
60 N.L.C.S. Game 3 .02 .10
61 1969 World Series, Game 1 .02 .10
62 1969 World Series, Game 2 .02 .10
63 1969 World Series, Game 3 .02 .10
64 1969 World Series, Game 4 .02 .10
65 1969 World Series, Game 5 .02 .10
66 World Champions .02 .10
67 World Champions .02 .10
68 World Champions .02 .10
69 World Champions .02 .10
NNO Checklist .02 .10

1994 Mets '69 Year Book

Measuring 8 1/4" by 10 7/8", this perforated sheet of nine player cards was inserted inside a reprint of the 1969 Official Year Book issued to celebrate the 25th anniversary of the World Champion Mets. If the cards were separated, they would measure 2 3/4" by 3 1/2". Inside white outer borders, the fronts feature a mix of posed and action color photos framed by an orange-and-purple inner border design. The player's name is printed in the top border, while the team logo and the uniform number are superposed over the picture. On a white background, the backs present statistics for the 1969 season, National League championship series, and the World Series. The cards are unnumbered and are checklisted below in alphabetical order.

COMPLETE SET (9) 1.00 2.50
1 Ed Charles .08 .25
2 Donn Clendenon .20 .50
3 Jerry Grote .20 .50
4 Bud Harrelson .20 .50
5 Cleon Jones .20 .50
6 Jerry Koosman .30 .75
7 Art Shamsky .08 .25
8 Ron Swoboda .20 .50
9 Team Photo .08 .25

1994 Mets Colla Postcards

This 30-card set features color photos on a postcard format and was mailed in response to fan letters. The backs carry a pre-printed thank you note from the players.

COMPLETE SET (30) 8.00 20.00
1 Team Photo .40 1.00
2 Bobby Bonilla .30 .75
3 Dallas Green MG .20 .50
4 Jeff Kent .75 2.00
5 Tim Bogar .20 .50
6 Jeromy Burnitz .60 1.50
7 John Cangelosi .20 .50
8 John Franco .40 1.00
9 Dwight Gooden .40 1.00
10 Bud Harrelson CO .20 .50
11 Eric Hillman .20 .50
12 Todd Hundley .30 .75
13 Jonathon Hurst .20 .50
14 Bobby Jones .20 .50
15 Greg Linton .20 .50
16 Ed Lynch AGM .20 .50
17 Mike Maddux .20 .50
18 Jeff McKnight .20 .50
19 Kevin McReynolds .20 .50
20 Joe Orsulak .20 .50
21 Luis Rivera .20 .50
22 Bret Saberhagen .30 .75
23 David Segui .30 .75
24 Pete Smith .20 .50
25 Kelly Stinnett .20 .50
26 Dave Telgheder .20 .50
27 Ryan Thompson .20 .50
28 Fernando Vina .60 1.50
29 Jose Vizciano .20 .50
30 Mookie Wilson CO .30 .75

1994 Mets Community Relations

This two-card black and white set measures approximately 2 3/4" by 4". These cards were used by these former Mets when visiting hospitals or making other personal experiences.

COMPLETE SET (2) 1.25 3.00
1 Bud Harrelson .40 1.00
2 Mookie Wilson .75 2.00

1994 Mets Team Issue

Consisting of nine cards, this 7 1/2" by 10 1/2" perforated sheet features some past and current Mets. The cards are unnumbered and are checklisted below starting with the upper left and proceeding across and down to the lower right. The cards are also found with PruCare sponsoring on the back. There is no price differential for that set.

COMPLETE SET (9) 2.50 6.00
1 Bobby Bonilla .30 .75
2 Dwight Gooden .40 1.00
3 John Franco .40 1.00
4 Jeff Kent .60 1.50
5 Kevin McReynolds .20 .50
6 Ryan Thompson .20 .50
7 Jeromy Burnitz .40 1.00
8 Bud Harrelson .40 1.00
9 Mookie Wilson .40 1.00

1994 Mets Tribute Sheet '69 Spectrum

This UV-coated sheet measures 8 1/2" by 11" and pays tribute to the 1969 Miracle Mets on their 25th anniversary. Production was limited to 10,000 sheets. The blue front is a photo montage. A large photo in the middle of the sheet depicts the Mets on-field celebration upon winning the 1969 World Series. It is flanked on the right by a team photo and on the left by a shot of the Mets running onto the field to celebrate. A player photo appears in each corner: Jerry Koosman at the upper left, Tom Seaver at the upper right, Ron Swoboda at the lower left and Don Clendenon at the lower right. The 1969 Miracle Mets 25th Anniversary logo lies just below the large middle photo. The back carries a synopsis of the team's accomplishments. There were also an unspecified number of "Promo" versions produced of this sheet.

1 '69 Mets 25th Ann.Sheet 2.00 5.00

1995 Mets Colla Postcards

These cards measure the standard postcard size -- feature a full color glossy borderless photo on the front and a printed message thanking the fan for his/her support on the back

COMPLETE SET (32) 8.00 20.00
1 Mets Team .40 1.00
2 Bobby Bonilla .30 .75
3 John Franco .30 .75
4 Jeff Kent .60 1.50
5 Bret Saberhagen .20 .50
6 Edgardo Alfonzo .60 1.50
7 Tim Bogar .20 .50
8 Rico Brogna .20 .50
9 Brett Butler .30 .75
10 Jerry DiPoto .20 .50
11 Carl Everett .40 1.00
12 Brook Fordyce .20 .50
13 Eric Gunderson .20 .50
14 Pete Harnisch .20 .50
15 Doug Henry .20 .50
16 Todd Hundley .30 .75
17 Jason Jacome .20 .50
18 Bobby Jones .20 .50
19 Kevin Lomon .20 .50
20 Josias Manzanillo .20 .50
21 Blas Minor .20 .50
22 Dave Mlicki .20 .50
23 Kevin Northrup .20 .50
24 Joe Orsulak .20 .50
25 Ricky Otero .20 .50
26 Mike Remlinger .20 .50
27 David Segui .30 .75
28 Bill Spiers .20 .50
29 Kelly Stinnett .20 .50
30 Ryan Thompson .20 .50
31 Jose Vizcaino .20 .50
32 Dallas Green MG .20 .50

1995 Mets Kahn's

This 34-card set was sponsored by Kahn's and was issued with two manufacturer's coupons. The cards are unnumbered and checklisted below in alphabetical order.

COMPLETE SET (34) 2.50 6.00
1 Edgardo Alfonzo .30 .75
2 Jeff Barry .02 .10
3 Tim Bogar .02 .10
4 Bobby Bonilla .08 .25
5 Rico Brogna .02 .10
6 Brett Butler .30 .75
7 Mike Cubbage CO .02 .10
8 Jerry DiPoto .02 .10
9 John Franco .30 .75
10 Dallas Green MG .02 .10
11 Eric Gunderson .02 .10
12 Pete Harnisch .02 .10
13 Doug Henry .02 .10
14 Frank Howard CO .20 .50
15 Todd Hundley .30 .75
16 Jason Isringhausen .30 .75
17 Bobby Jones .02 .10
18 Chris Jones .02 .10
19 Jeff Kent .30 .75
20 Aaron Ledesma .02 .10
21 Tom McCraw CO .02 .10
22 Dave Mlicki .02 .10
23 Blas Minor .02 .10
24 Joe Orsulak .02 .10
25 Ricky Otero .02 .10
26 Greg Pavlick CO .02 .10
27 Bill Pulsipher .02 .10
28 Bret Saberhagen .08 .25
29 Bill Spiers .02 .10
30 Kelly Stinnett .02 .10
31 Steve Swisher CO .02 .10
32 Ryan Thompson .02 .10
33 Jose Vizcaino .02 .10
34 Bobby Wine CO .02 .10

1996 Mets Kahn's

This 34-card set was sponsored by Kahn's and issued with two manufacturer's coupons. The fronts display color player photos set on a black background with the team logo at the bottom and red and gray bars across the top. The backs carry player information and career statistics. The cards are unnumbered and checklisted below in alphabetical order.

COMPLETE SET (34) 5.00 12.00
1 Edgardo Alfonzo .40 1.00
2 Tim Bogar .08 .25
3 Rico Brogna .08 .25
4 Paul Byrd .08 .25
5 Mark Clark .08 .25
6 Mike Cubbage CO .08 .25
7 Jerry Dipoto .08 .25
8 Carl Everett .30 .75
9 John Franco .40 1.00
10 Bernard Gilkey .08 .25
11 Dallas Green MG .08 .25
12 Pete Harnisch .08 .25
13 Doug Henry .08 .25
14 Frank Howard CO .08 .25
15 Todd Hundley .40 1.00
16 Butch Huskey .08 .25
17 Jason Isringhausen .40 1.00
18 Lance Johnson .08 .25
19 Bobby Jones .08 .25
20 Chris Jones .08 .25
21 Brent Mayne .08 .25
22 Tom McCraw CO .08 .25
23 Dave Mlicki .08 .25
24 Alex Ochoa .08 .25
25 Rey Ordonez .08 .25
26 Greg Pavlick CO .08 .25
27 Robert Person .08 .25
28 Bill Pulsipher .08 .25
29 Steve Swisher .08 .25
30 Andy Tomberlin .08 .25
31 Paul Wilson .08 .25
32 Bobby Wine CO .08 .25
NNO Manufacturer's Coupon .08 .25
Kahn's Corn Dogs
NNO Manufacturer's Coupon .08 .25
Kayn's Hot Dogs

1998 Mets Postcards

These 35 color cards measure 3 3/4" by 5 1/4" and feature members of the 1998 Mets. The backs have stats and also the player's uniform number. We have sequenced this set alphabetically.

COMPLETE SET (36) 8.00 20.00
1 Edgardo Alfonzo .60 1.50
2 Bob Apodaca CO .20 .50
3 Carlos Baerga .30 .75
4 Bruce Benedict CO .20 .50
5 Brian Bohanon .20 .50
6 Alberto Castillo .20 .50
7 Dennis Cook .20 .50
8 John Franco .40 1.00
9 Matt Franco .20 .50
10 Bernard Gilkey .20 .50
11 John Hudek .20 .50
12 Todd Hundley .30 .75
13 Butch Huskey .20 .50
14 Bobby Jones .20 .50
15 Al Leiter .40 1.00
16 Luis Lopez .20 .50
17 Greg McMichael .20 .50
18 Brian McRae .20 .50
19 Randy Niemann CO .20 .50
20 Hideo Nomo .60 1.50
21 John Olerud .40 1.00
22 Rey Ordonez .20 .50
23 Mike Piazza 1.25 3.00
24 Rick Reed .20 .50
25 Armando Reynoso .20 .50
26 Tom Robson CO .20 .50
27 Cookie Rojas CO .20 .50
28 Mel Rojas .20 .50
29 Tim Spehr .20 .50
30 Jim Tatum .20 .50
31 Bobby Valentine MG .20 .50
32 Turk Wendell .20 .50
33 Mookie Wilson CO .30 .75
34 Masato Yoshii .40 1.00
35 Mr. Met .20 .50
Mascot

1999 Mets Postcards

These postcards featured members of the 1999 New York Mets. The only numbering on these cards are by uniform numbers so we have sequenced them alphabetically. The photos are all credited to Marc S. Levine. The cards measure 3 3/4" by 5 1/2" and have biographical backs.

COMPLETE SET 6.00 15.00
1 Edgardo Alfonzo .60 1.50
2 Armando Benitez .60 1.50
3 Bobby Bonilla .30 .75
4 Roger Cedeno .30 .75
5 Dennis Cook .20 .50
6 John Franco .30 .75
7 Matt Franco .20 .50
8 Rickey Henderson 1.00 2.50
9 Orel Hershiser .30 .75
10 Bobby Jones .20 .50
11 Al Leiter .40 1.00
12 Luis Lopez .20 .50
13 Greg McMichael .20 .50
14 Brian McRae .20 .50
15 John Olerud .40 1.00
16 Rey Ordonez .20 .50
17 Mike Piazza 1.25 3.00
18 Todd Pratt .20 .50
19 Rick Reed .20 .50
20 Bobby Valentine MG .20 .50
21 Robin Ventura .40 1.00
22 Turk Wendell .20 .50
23 Masato Yoshii .30 .75
24 New York Mets .30 .75

2000 Mets Postcards

COMPLETE SET 12.00 30.00
COMMON SP
1 Kurt Abbott .20 .50
3 Edgardo Alfonzo .80 2.00
4 Derek Bell .20 .50
5 Armando Benitez .80 2.00
6 Dennis Cook .20 .50
7 John Franco .80 2.00
8 Matt Franco .20 .50
9 Darryl Hamilton .20 .50
10 Mike Hampton .60 1.50
11 Rickey Henderson SP 4.00 10.00
12 Bobby Jones .20 .50
13 Al Jackson CO .20 .50
14 Al Leiter .60 1.50
15 Pat Mahomes .20 .50
16 Melvin Mora .80 2.00
17 Jon Nunnally .20 .50
18 Rey Ordonez .20 .50
19 Jay Payton .40 1.00
20 Mike Piazza 2.00 5.00
21 Todd Pratt .20 .50
22 Rick Reed .20 .50
23 Tom Robson CO .20 .50
24 Rich Rodriguez .20 .50
25 Cookie Rojas CO .20 .50
26 Glendon Rusch .20 .50
27 John Stearns CO .20 .50
28 Bobby Valentine MG .20 .50
29 Robin Ventura .60 1.50
30 Turk Wendell .20 .50
31 Mookie Wilson CO .40 1.00
32 Todd Zeile .40 1.00

2000 Mets Star Ledger

COMPLETE SET 20.00 50.00
1 Kurt Abbott .40 1.00
2 Benny Agbayani .80 2.00
3 Edgardo Alfonzo 1.60 4.00
4 Derek Bell .40 1.00
5 Armando Benitez 1.60 4.00
6 Mike Bordick .40 1.00
7 Dennis Cook .40 1.00
8 John Franco 1.60 4.00
9 Matt Franco .40 1.00
10 Darryl Hamilton .40 1.00
11 Mike Hampton 1.20 3.00
12 Lenny Harris .40 1.00
13 Bobby J. Jones .40 1.00
14 Al Leiter 1.20 3.00
15 Pat Mahomes .40 1.00
16 Joe McEwing .40 1.00
17 Jay Payton .80 2.00
18 Timo Perez 1.20 3.00
19 Mike Piazza 4.00 10.00
20 Todd Pratt .40 1.00
21 Rick Reed .40 1.00
22 Glendon Rusch .40 1.00
23 Bubba Trammell .40 1.00
24 Bobby Valentine MG .40 1.00
25 Robin Ventura 1.20 3.00
26 Turk Wendell .40 1.00
27 Rick White .40 1.00
28 Todd Zeile .80 2.00

2001 Mets Team Issue

COMPLETE SET (26) 8.00 20.00
1 Benny Agbayani .30 .75
2 Edgardo Alfonzo .60 1.50
3 Kevin Appier .20 .50
4 Armando Benitez .60 1.50
5 Dave Engle .20 .50
6 Bob Floyd CO .20 .50
7 John Franco .60 1.50
8 Lenny Harris .20 .50
9 Charlie Hough CO .20 .50
10 Al Leiter .40 1.00
11 Joe McEwing .20 .50
12 Randy Niemann CO .20 .50
13 Rey Ordonez .20 .50
14 Jay Payton .30 .75
15 Timo Perez .20 .50
16 Mike Piazza 1.20 3.00
17 Desi Relaford .20 .50
18 Glendon Rusch .20 .50
19 Tsuyoshi Shinjo .60 1.50

20 John Stearns CO .20 .50
21 Jorge Luis Toca .20 .50
22 Steve Trachsel .20 .50
23 Bobby Valentine MG .20 .50
24 Robin Ventura .40 1.00
25 Donne Wall .20 .50
26 Rick White .20 .50
27 Mookie Wilson CO .30 .75
28 Todd Zeile .30 .75

2002 Mets 40th Anniversary Fleer

COMPLETE SET (20) 4.00 10.00
1 Gil Hodges MG .60 1.50
2 Keith Hernandez .40 1.00
3 Edgardo Alfonzo .40 1.00
4 Howard Johnson .20 .50
5 Bud Harrelson .08 .25
6 Mike Piazza .75 2.00
7 Mookie Wilson .20 .50
8 Darryl Strawberry .20 .50
9 Lenny Dykstra .20 .50
10 Tom Seaver 1.25 3.00
11 Jerry Koosman .20 .50
12 Roger McDowell .08 .25
13 John Franco .20 .50
14 Ed Kranepool .08 .25
15 Rusty Staub .30 .75
16 Bob Murphy ANN .20 .50
17 Ralph Kiner ANN .40 1.00
18 New York Mets 1962 Team Photo .20 .50
19 New York Mets 1969 Team Photo .20 .50
20 New York Mets 1986 Team Photo .20 .50

2002 Mets Fleer 9/11

COMPLETE SET 6.00 15.00
1 New York Mets Team Photo .30 .75
2 Al Leiter .40 1.00
3 Mike Piazza 1.25 3.00
4 Al Leiter Wearing Police Cap .40 1.00
5 Mo Vaughn .30 .75
6 Roberto Alomar .60 1.50
7 Edgardo Alfonzo .60 1.50
8 Uniform Patch/9/11/01 .20 .50
9 Rey Ordonez .20 .50
10 Roger Cedeno .20 .50
11 Timo Perez .20 .50
12 Mike Piazza NYPD Helmet 2.00 5.00
13 Jeromy Burnitz .30 .75
14 Bobby Valentine MG .20 .50
15 United States Flag .20 .50

2002 Mets Palm Beach Post

COMPLETE SET 4.00 10.00
1 Edgardo Alfonzo .60 1.50
2 Armando Benitez .60 1.50
3 John Franco .60 1.50
4 Al Leiter .40 1.00
5 Joe McEwing .20 .50
6 Rey Ordonez .20 .50
7 Jay Payton .30 .75
8 Timo Perez .20 .50
9 Mike Piazza 1.25 3.00
10 Bobby Valentine MG .30 .75

2004 Mets Fleer Stadium

COMPLETE SET (8) 2.00 5.00
1 Mike Cameron .20 .50
2 Cliff Floyd .40 1.00
3 Al Leiter .30 .75
4 Kazuo Matsui .50 1.25
5 Mike Piazza .60 1.50
6 Jose Reyes .30 .75
7 Shea Stadium .10 .25
8 Header Card .10 .25

2004 Mets Post Fleer

COMPLETE SET 2.00 5.00
1 Jason Phillips .10 .25
2 Jose Reyes .30 .75
3 Kazuo Matsui .50 1.25
4 Ty Wigginton .10 .25
5 Cliff Floyd .30 .75
6 Mike Cameron .10 .25
7 Karim Garcia .10 .25
8 Mike Piazza .60 1.50
9 Tom Glavine .40 1.00
SP1 Kazuo Matsui 2.00 5.00

2004 Mets Port St Lucie News and Tribune

COMPLETE SET 10.00 25.00
1 Mike Cameron .60 1.50
2 Cliff Floyd 1.00 2.50
3 John Franco .75 2.00
4 Tom Glavine 1.00 2.50
5 Al Leiter .75 2.00
6 Kazuo Matsui 1.25 3.00
7 Joe McEwing .40 1.00
8 Jason Phillips .40 1.00
9 Mike Piazza 1.50 4.00
10 Jose Reyes .75 2.00
11 Jae Weong Seo .60 1.50
12 Steve Trachsel .40 1.00
13 Ty Wigginton .40 1.00
14 Vance Wilson .40 1.00
15 Stadium .40 1.00

2005 Mets Starlight Starbright

COMPLETE SET
1 Manny Acta CO .20 .50
2 Sandy Alomar Sr. CO .20 .50
3 Marlon Anderson .20 .50
4 Manny Aybar .20 .50
5 Heath Bell .20 .50
6 Carlos Beltran .75 2.00
7 Kris Benson .30 .75
8 Miguel Cairo .20 .50
9 Mike Cameron .30 .75
10 Ramon Castro .20 .50
11 Guy Conti CO .20 .50
12 Mike DeJean .20 .50
13 Victor Diaz .40 1.00
14 Rick Down CO .20 .50
15 Cliff Floyd .60 1.50
16 Tom Glavine .60 1.50
17 Aaron Heilman .40 1.00
18 Felix Heredia .20 .50
19 Roberto Hernandez .20 .50
20 Kazuhisa Ishii .20 .50
21 Dae-Sung Koo .20 .50
22 Braden Looper .20 .50
23 Jerry Manuel CO .20 .50
24 Pedro Martinez .75 2.00
25 Kazuo Matsui .60 1.50
26 Doug Mientkiewicz .20 .50
27 Tom Nieto INS .20 .50
28 Rick Peterson CO .20 .50
29 Mike Piazza 1.00 2.50
30 Willie Randolph MG .30 .75
31 Jose Reyes .40 1.00
32 Jae Seo .40 1.00
33 Steve Trachsel .20 .50
34 Eric Valent .20 .50
35 Chris Woodward .20 .50
36 David Wright 1.50 4.00
37 Victor Zambrano .20 .50
38 Header Card .20 .50

2006 Mets Topps

NYM1 David Wright .25 .60
NYM2 Pedro Martinez .20 .50
NYM3 Carlos Beltran .20 .50
NYM4 Jose Reyes .20 .50
NYM5 Cliff Floyd .12 .30
NYM6 Victor Diaz .12 .30
NYM7 Carlos Delgado .12 .30
NYM8 Tom Glavine .20 .50
NYM10 Steve Trachsel .12 .30
NYM11 Billy Wagner .12 .30
NYM12 Paul LoDuca .12 .30
NYM13 Xavier Nady .12 .30
NYM14 Aaron Heilman .12 .30
NYM9A Kris Benson .12 .30
NYM9B Lastings Milledge .12 .30

2006 Mets Topps 1986 Anniversary

COMPLETE SET (5) 1.25 3.00
1 Dwight Gooden .30 .75
2 Davey Johnson MG .30 .75
3 Lee Mazzilli .30 .75
4 Kevin Mitchell .30 .75
5 Darryl Strawberry .30 .75

2007 Mets Topps

COMPLETE SET (14) 3.00 8.00
NYM1 David Wright .25 .60
NYM2 Jose Reyes .20 .50
NYM3 Carlos Beltran .20 .50
NYM4 Jose Valentin .12 .30
NYM5 Shawn Green .12 .30
NYM6 Orlando Hernandez .12 .30
NYM7 Pedro Martinez .20 .50
NYM8 Lastings Milledge .20 .50
NYM9 Billy Wagner .12 .30
NYM10 Paul LoDuca .12 .30
NYM11 Moises Alou .12 .30
NYM12 Carlos Delgado .12 .30
NYM13 Tom Glavine .20 .50
NYM14 Philip Humber .12 .30

2007 Mets Topps Gift Set

COMPLETE SET (55) 8.00 20.00
NYM1 Tom Glavine .25 .60
NYM2 Orlando Hernandez .15 .40
NYM3 John Maine .15 .40
NYM4 Pedro Martinez .25 .60
NYM5 Oliver Perez .15 .40
NYM6 Joe Smith .15 .40
NYM7 Jorge Sosa .15 .40
NYM8 Billy Wagner .15 .40
NYM9 Aaron Heilman .15 .40
NYM10 Ambiorix Burgos .15 .40
NYM11 Philip Humber .15 .40
NYM12 Paul LoDuca .15 .40
NYM13 Carlos Delgado .15 .40
NYM14 Damion Easley .15 .40
NYM15 Julio Franco .15 .40
NYM16 Ruben Gotay .15 .40
NYM17 Jose Reyes .25 .60
NYM18 Jose Valentin .15 .40
NYM19 David Wright .30 .75
NYM20 Carlos Beltran .25 .60
NYM21 Carlos Gomez .30 .75
NYM22 Shawn Green .15 .40
NYM23 Endy Chavez .15 .40
NYM24 Ramon Castro .15 .40
NYM25 Moises Alou .15 .40
NYM26 Willie Randolph MG .15 .40
NYM27 Jerry Manuel CO .15 .40
NYM28 Sandy Alomar Sr. CO .15 .40
NYM29 Howard Johnson CO .15 .40
NYM30 Rick Peterson CO .15 .40
NYM31 Rickey Henderson CO .40 1.00
NYM32 Orlando Hernandez .15 .40
NYM33 Paul Lo Duca .15 .40
NYM34 Carlos Beltran .25 .60
NYM35 Jose Reyes .25 .60
NYM36 David Wright .30 .75
NYM37 Tom Glavine .25 .60
NYM38 Billy Wagner .15 .40
NYM39 Pedro Martinez .25 .60
NYM40 John Maine .15 .40
NYM41 Wright/Delgado/Reyes .30 .75
NYM42 Reyes/Wright .30 .75
NYM43 Gotay/Gomez .30 .75
NYM44 Carlos Beltran .25 .60
NYM45 David Wright .30 .75
NYM46 Jose Reyes .25 .60
NYM47 John Maine .15 .40
NYM48 Carlos Delgado .15 .40
NYM49 Paul LoDuca .15 .40
NYM50 Carlos Gomez .30 .75
NYM51 Tom Glavine .25 .60
NYM52 Jorge Sosa .15 .40
NYM53 Billy Wagner .15 .40
NYM54 Shawn Green .15 .40
NYM55 Mr. Met .15 .40

2008 Mets Topps

COMPLETE SET (14) 3.00 8.00
NYM1 Johan Santana .20 .50
NYM2 Jose Reyes .20 .50
NYM3 Carlos Beltran .20 .50
NYM4 Luis Castillo .12 .30
NYM5 Oliver Perez .12 .30
NYM6 Orlando Hernandez .12 .30
NYM7 Pedro Martinez .20 .50
NYM8 David Wright .20 .50
NYM9 Billy Wagner .12 .30
NYM10 Brian Schneider .12 .30
NYM11 Moises Alou .12 .30
NYM12 Carlos Delgado .12 .30
NYM13 Ryan Church .12 .30
NYM14 John Maine .12 .30

2009 Mets Topps

NYM1 David Wright .30 .75
NYM2 Johan Santana .25 .60
NYM3 Carlos Beltran .25 .60
NYM4 Fernando Tatis .15 .40
NYM5 Jose Reyes .25 .60
NYM6 John Maine .15 .40
NYM7 Ryan Church .15 .40
NYM8 Mike Pelfrey .15 .40
NYM9 Brian Schneider .15 .40
NYM10 J.J. Putz .15 .40
NYM11 Carlos Delgado .15 .40
NYM12 Daniel Murphy .60 1.50
NYM13 Francisco Rodriguez .25 .60
NYM14 Luis Castillo .15 .40
NYM15 Citi Field .15 .40

2010 Mets Topps

NYM1 David Wright .30 .75
NYM2 Jon Niese .15 .40
NYM3 Carlos Delgado .15 .40
NYM4 Luis Castillo .15 .40
NYM5 Jeff Francoeur .25 .60
NYM6 Daniel Murphy .30 .75
NYM7 John Maine .15 .40
NYM8 Fernando Martinez .15 .40
NYM9 Francisco Rodriguez .25 .60
NYM10 Mike Pelfrey .15 .40
NYM11 Angel Pagan .15 .40
NYM12 Jose Reyes .25 .60
NYM13 Johan Santana .25 .60
NYM14 Omir Santos .15 .40
NYM15 Carlos Beltran .25 .60
NYM16 Josh Thole .25 .60
NYM17 Jason Bay .25 .60

2011 Mets Topps

NYM1 David Wright .30 .75
NYM2 Josh Thole .15 .40
NYM3 Ruben Tejada .15 .40
NYM4 Johan Santana .25 .60
NYM5 Jose Reyes .25 .60
NYM6 Dillon Gee .25 .60
NYM7 Mike Pelfrey .15 .40
NYM8 Angel Pagan .15 .40
NYM9 Jon Niese .15 .40
NYM10 R.A. Dickey .25 .60
NYM11 Ike Davis .15 .40
NYM12 Jason Bay .25 .60
NYM13 Jenrry Mejia .15 .40
NYM14 Fernando Martinez .15 .40
NYM15 Carlos Beltran .25 .60
NYM16 Chris Young .15 .40
NYM17 Citi Field .15 .40

2012 Mets Topps

NYM1 David Wright .30 .75
NYM2 Mike Pelfrey .25 .60
NYM3 Jason Bay .30 .75
NYM4 Johan Santana .30 .75
NYM5 Ike Davis .25 .60
NYM6 Andres Torres .25 .60
NYM7 Lucas Duda .30 .75
NYM8 Josh Thole .25 .60
NYM9 Jon Niese .25 .60
NYM10 R.A. Dickey .30 .75
NYM11 Frank Francisco .25 .60
NYM12 Ruben Tejada .25 .60
NYM13 Daniel Murphy .30 .75
NYM14 Dillon Gee .25 .60
NYM15 Bobby Parnell .25 .60
NYM16 Justin Turner .40 1.00
NYM17 Citi Field .15 .40

2013 Mets Topps

COMPLETE SET (17) 3.00 8.00
NYM1 David Wright .20 .50
NYM2 Johan Santana .30 .75
NYM3 John Buck .20 .50
NYM4 Ike Davis .15 .40
NYM5 Daniel Murphy .30 .75
NYM6 Ruben Tejada .15 .40
NYM7 Jordany Valdespin .15 .40
NYM8 Jonathon Niese .25 .60
NYM9 Dillon Gee .25 .60
NYM10 Matt Harvey .30 .75
NYM11 Jenrry Mejia .15 .40
NYM12 Bobby Parnell .15 .40
NYM13 Mike Baxter .15 .40
NYM14 Lucas Duda .30 .75
NYM15 Kirk Nieuwenhuis .15 .40
NYM16 Justin Turner .25 .60
NYM17 Citi Field .15 .40

2014 Mets Topps

COMPLETE SET (17) 3.00 8.00
NYM1 David Wright .20 .50
NYM2 Travis d'Arnaud .20 .50
NYM3 Zack Wheeler .20 .50
NYM4 Ike Davis .15 .40
NYM5 Daniel Murphy .20 .50
NYM6 Ruben Tejada .15 .40
NYM7 Bartolo Colon .15 .40
NYM8 Curtis Granderson .20 .50
NYM9 Dillon Gee .15 .40
NYM10 Matt Harvey .20 .50
NYM11 Jonathon Niese .15 .40
NYM12 Bobby Parnell .15 .40
NYM13 Wilmer Flores .20 .50
NYM14 Lucas Duda .20 .50
NYM15 Juan Lagares .15 .40
NYM16 Chris Young .15 .40
NYM17 Citi Field .15 .40

2015 Mets Topps

COMPLETE SET (17) 3.00 8.00
NYM1 David Wright .20 .50
NYM2 Lucas Duda .20 .50
NYM3 Dillon Gee .15 .40
NYM4 Curtis Granderson .20 .50
NYM5 Jenrry Mejia .15 .40
NYM6 Daniel Murphy .20 .50
NYM7 Matt Harvey .20 .50
NYM8 Zack Wheeler .20 .50
NYM9 Bartolo Colon .15 .40
NYM10 Juan Lagares .15 .40
NYM11 Dilson Herrera .20 .50
NYM12 Jon Niese .15 .40
NYM13 Wilmer Flores .20 .50
NYM14 Bobby Parnell .15 .40
NYM15 Travis d'Arnaud .20 .50
NYM16 Michael Cuddyer .15 .40
NYM17 Jacob deGrom .50 1.25

2016 Mets Topps

COMPLETE SET (17) 3.00 8.00
NYM1 Jacob deGrom .50 1.25
NYM2 Travis d'Arnaud .20 .50
NYM3 Lucas Duda .20 .50
NYM4 Neil Walker .15 .40
NYM5 Wilmer Flores .20 .50
NYM6 David Wright .20 .50
NYM7 Asdrubal Cabrera .20 .50
NYM8 Michael Conforto .20 .50
NYM9 Curtis Granderson .20 .50
NYM10 Matt Harvey .20 .50
NYM11 Noah Syndergaard .20 .50
NYM12 Steven Matz .15 .40
NYM13 Zack Wheeler .20 .50
NYM14 Jeurys Familia .20 .50
NYM15 Juan Lagares .15 .40
NYM16 Bartolo Colon .15 .40
NYM17 Yoenis Cespedes .25 .60

2017 Mets Topps

COMPLETE SET (17) 3.00 8.00
NYM1 Yoenis Cespedes .25 .60
NYM2 Mr. Met .15 .40
NYM3 Neil Walker .15 .40
NYM4 Jacob deGrom .50 1.25
NYM5 Wilmer Flores .20 .50
NYM6 Lucas Duda .20 .50
NYM7 David Wright .20 .50
NYM8 Asdrubal Cabrera .20 .50
NYM9 Steven Matz .15 .40
NYM10 Curtis Granderson .20 .50
NYM11 Jose Reyes .20 .50
NYM12 Noah Syndergaard .20 .50
NYM13 Jeurys Familia .20 .50
NYM14 Seth Lugo .15 .40
NYM15 Matt Harvey .20 .50
NYM16 Travis d'Arnaud .20 .50
NYM17 Robert Gsellman .15 .40

2018 Mets Topps

COMPLETE SET (17) 2.50 6.00
NM1 Michael Conforto .20 .50
NM2 Noah Syndergaard .20 .50
NM3 Wilmer Flores .20 .50
NM4 Juan Lagares .15 .40
NM5 Travis d'Arnaud .20 .50
NM6 Dominic Smith .20 .50
NM7 Matt Harvey .20 .50
NM8 Amed Rosario .20 .50
NM9 Jerry Blevins .15 .40
NM10 Zack Wheeler .20 .50
NM11 Yoenis Cespedes .25 .60
NM12 Jacob deGrom .50 1.25
NM13 Jeurys Familia .20 .50
NM14 A.J. Ramos .15 .40
NM15 Seth Lugo .15 .40
NM16 Steven Matz .15 .40
NM17 Asdrubal Cabrera .20 .50

2019 Mets Topps

COMPLETE SET (17) 2.50 6.00
NM1 Jacob deGrom .50 1.25
NM2 Noah Syndergaard .20 .50
NM3 Michael Conforto .20 .50
NM4 Yoenis Cespedes .25 .60
NM5 Todd Frazier .15 .40
NM6 Robinson Cano .20 .50
NM7 Amed Rosario .20 .50
NM8 Jeff McNeil .40 1.00
NM9 Edwin Diaz .20 .50
NM10 Zack Wheeler .20 .50
NM11 Steven Matz .15 .40
NM12 Juan Lagares .15 .40
NM13 Jason Vargas .15 .40
NM14 Keon Broxton .15 .40
NM15 Seth Lugo .15 .40
NM16 Wilson Ramos .15 .40
NM17 Brandon Nimmo .20 .50

2020 Mets Topps

NYM1 Pete Alonso .60 1.50
NYM2 Jacob deGrom .50 1.25
NYM3 Amed Rosario .20 .50
NYM4 J.D. Davis .15 .40
NYM5 Brandon Nimmo .20 .50
NYM6 Michael Conforto .20 .50
NYM7 Noah Syndergaard .20 .50
NYM8 Marcus Stroman .20 .50
NYM9 Michael Wacha .20 .50
NYM10 Rick Porcello .20 .50
NYM11 Robinson Cano .20 .50
NYM12 Jeff McNeil .20 .50
NYM13 Edwin Diaz .20 .50
NYM14 Steven Matz .15 .40
NYM15 Dominic Smith .15 .40
NYM16 Jed Lowrie .15 .40
NYM17 Wilson Ramos .15 .40

2017 Mets Topps National Baseball Card Day

COMPLETE SET (9) 5.00 12.00
NYM1 Matt Harvey .75 2.00
NYM2 Noah Syndergaard .75 2.00
NYM3 Yoenis Cespedes 1.00 2.50
NYM4 Curtis Granderson .75 2.00
NYM5 David Wright .75 2.00
NYM6 Neil Walker .60 1.50
NYM7 Asdrubal Cabrera .75 2.00
NYM8 Steven Matz .60 1.50
NYM9 Mike Piazza 1.00 2.50

2008 Mets Topps Gift Set

1 Willie Randolph MG .15 .40
2 David Wright 30-30 .25 .60
3 David Wright .25 .60
4 Carlos Beltran/David Wright/Carlos Delgado .25 .60
5 Pedro Martinez .25 .60
6 Jose Reyes .25 .60
7 Johan Santana .25 .60
8 Carlos Delgado .15 .40
9 Pedro Martinez 3000th K .25 .60
10 Oliver Perez/Orlando Hernandez/John Maine .15 .40
11 John Maine .15 .40
12 Carlos Beltran .25 .60
13 Tom Glavine 300th Win .25 .60
14 Billy Wagner .15 .40
15 Jerry Manuel CO .15 .40
16 Jose Reyes POTM .25 .60
17 Luis Castillo .15 .40
18 Mike Pelfrey .15 .40
19 John Maine/Oliver Perez Orlando Hernandez .15 .40
20 Endy Chavez .15 .40
21 Endy Chavez/Carlos Beltran/Jose Reyes .25 .60
22 Aaron Heilman .15 .40
23 David Wright/Shawn Green/Jose Reyes.25 .60
24 John Maine POTM .15 .40
25 Moises Alou .15 .40
26 Tom Nieto CO .15 .40
27 Oliver Perez .15 .40
28 Billy Wagner 350th Save .15 .40
29 Ryan Church .15 .40
30 Orlando Hernandez .15 .40
31 John Maine/Oliver Perez/Tom Glavine.25 .60
32 Brian Schneider .15 .40
33 Scott Schoeneweis .15 .40
34 Sandy Alomar Sr. CO .15 .40
35 Jose Reyes Steals .25 .60
36 Ramon Castro .15 .40
37 Duaner Sanchez .15 .40
38 David Wright/Jose Reyes Carlos Beltran .25 .60
39 Damion Easley .15 .40
40 Willie Collazo .25 .60
41 Rick Peterson CO .15 .40
42 David Wright GG .25 .60
43 Angel Pagan .15 .40
44 Pedro Feliciano .15 .40
45 Tom Glavine/John Maine/Oliver Perez.25 .60
46 Oliver Perez K's .15 .40
47 Carlos Beltran/David Wright Carlos Delgado .25 .60
48 Brian Stokes .15 .40
49 David Wright/Carlos Beltran .25 .60
50 Marlon Anderson .15 .40
51 Howard Johnson CO .15 .40
52 Ramon Castro/Pedro Martinez .25 .60
53 Billy Wagner/Carlos Beltran David Wright/Jose Reyes .25 .60
54 Mr. Met .15 .40
55 Shea Stadium .15 .40

2008 Mets Topps Gift Set Autographs

ONE PER $49.99 TEAM SET BOX
DG Dwight Gooden 15.00 40.00
DJ Davey Johnson MG 15.00 40.00
DS Darryl Strawberry 40.00 80.00
GH Gary Carter 20.00 50.00
HJ Howard Johnson 20.00 50.00
JO Jesse Orosco 20.00 50.00
KH Keith Hernandez 20.00 50.00
KM Kevin Mitchell 20.00 50.00
RD Ron Darling 15.00 40.00
RK Ray Knight 15.00 40.00
SF Sid Fernandez 15.00 40.00

1993 Metz Baking

This 40-card standard-size set was produced by MSA (Michael Schechter Associates) for Metz Baking Co. The cards were issued in two series and feature on their fronts oval color drawings of the players with team names or logos airbrushed from their caps and uniforms. One card was inserted into packages of Metz products distributed in the Midwest. The cards are unnumbered and checklisted below in alphabetical order within each 20-card series.

COMPLETE SET (40) 6.00 15.00
1 Wade Boggs .20 .50
2 Barry Bonds .50 1.25
3 Bobby Bonilla .07 .20
4 Joe Carter .07 .20
5 Roger Clemens .50 1.25
6 Doug Drabek .07 .20
7 Cecil Fielder .07 .20
8 Dwight Gooden .12 .30
9 Ken Griffey Jr. .75 2.00
10 Tony Gwynn .50 1.25
11 Howard Johnson .07 .20
12 Wally Joyner .12 .30
13 Dave Justice .12 .30
14 Don Mattingly .75 2.00
15 Jack McDowell .07 .20
16 Kirby Puckett .20 .50
17 Cal Ripken 1.50 4.00
18 Ryne Sandberg .60 1.50
19 Darryl Strawberry .12 .30
20 Danny Tartabull .07 .20
21 Dante Bichette .12 .30
22 Jose Canseco .20 .50
23 Will Clark .20 .50
24 Shawon Dunston .07 .20
25 Dennis Eckersley .12 .30
26 Carlton Fisk .20 .50
27 Andres Galarraga .12 .30
28 Kirk Gibson .12 .30
29 Mark Grace .12 .30
30 Rickey Henderson .40 1.00
31 Kent Hrbek .12 .30
32 Barry Larkin .12 .30
33 Paul Molitor .20 .50
34 Terry Pendleton .07 .20
35 Nolan Ryan 1.50 4.00
36 Ozzie Smith .50 1.25
37 Mickey Tettleton .07 .20
38 Alan Trammell .12 .30
39 Andy Van Slyke .07 .20
40 Dave Winfield .12 .30

1927 Middy Bread

These 44 cards blank-backed, which measure approximately 2 1/4" by 4" were issued in the St Louis area and feature members of the Browns and Cardinals. It seems as if 22 cards for each of the teams were issued. Since the cards are unnumbered, we have sequenced them alphabetically by team with the Cardinals from card 1 through 22 and the Browns from 23 through 44. A Ross Youngs card was recently discovered and looks as if it fits in this set. More information about that card is certainly appreciated.

COMPLETE SET (44) 40000.00 80000.00
1 Grover Alexander 4000.00 8000.00
2 Herman Bell 1000.00 2000.00
3 Lester Bell 1000.00 2000.00
4 Ray Blades 1000.00 2000.00
5 Jim Bottomley 2000.00 4000.00
6 Danny Clark 1000.00 2000.00
7 Taylor Douthit 1000.00 2000.00
8 Frank Frisch 2500.00 5000.00
9 Chick Hafey 2000.00 4000.00
10 Jesse Haines 2000.00 4000.00
11 Vic Keen 1000.00 2000.00
12 Bob McGraw 1000.00 2000.00
13 Bob O'Farrell 1000.00 2000.00
14 Art Reinhardt 1000.00 2000.00
15 Jimmy Ring 1000.00 2000.00
16 Walter Roettger 1000.00 2000.00
17 Robert Schang 1000.00 2000.00
18 Willie Sherdel 1000.00 2000.00
19 Billy Southworth 1250.00 2500.00
20 Tommy Thevenow 1000.00 2000.00
21 George Toporcer 1000.00 2000.00
22 Spencer Adams 1000.00 2000.00
23 Win Ballou 1000.00 2000.00
24 Walter Beck 1000.00 2000.00
25 Herschel Bennett 1000.00 2000.00
26 Stewart Bolen 1000.00 2000.00
27 Leo Dixon 1000.00 2000.00
28 Chester Falk 1000.00 2000.00
29 Milt Gaston 1000.00 2000.00
30 Walter Gerber 1000.00 2000.00
31 Sam Jones 1250.00 2500.00
32 Carlisle Littlejohn 1000.00 2000.00
33 Oscar Melillo 1000.00 2000.00
34 Bing Miller 1250.00 2500.00
35 Otis Miller 1000.00 2000.00
36 Billie Mullen 1000.00 2000.00
37 Ernie Nevers 2000.00 4000.00
38 Steve O'Neil 1250.00 2500.00
39 Harry Rice 1000.00 2000.00
40 George Sisler 2500.00 5000.00
41 Walter Stewart 1000.00 2000.00
42 Elom Van Gilder 1000.00 2000.00
43 Ken Williams 1500.00 3000.00
44 Ernie Wingard 1000.00 2000.00
45 Ross Youngs 2000.00 4000.00

2005 Mid Mon Valley Hall of Fame

COMPLETE SET (36) 10.00 20.00
128 Bill Robinson BB .50 1.25
131 George Zuraw Scout BB .30 .75
142 Davey Russell BB .30 .75
143 Fred Uhlman Sr. BB .30 .75
153 Mitch Bailey CO BB .30 .75

2006 Mid Mon Valley Hall of Fame

COMPLETE SET (36) 10.00 20.00
97 Mouse Chacko BB BK .30 .75
106 Ducky LeJohn BB .30 .75
109 Danny Taylor BB .30 .75
158 Bobby Locke BB .30 .75
161 John Shelapinsky BB .30 .75
162 John Tener COMM BB .50 1.25

1993 Milk Bone Super Stars

This 20-card standard-size set was featured in specially marked packages of Milk Bone Flavor Snacks and Dog Treats. Two cards were inserted in each package. Also the complete set could be obtained by sending in a mail-in form along with three Super Star Seals plus 2.50.

COMPLETE SET (20) 8.00 20.00
1 Paul Molitor .60 1.50
2 Tom Glavine .60 1.50
3 Barry Larkin .40 1.00
4 Mark McGwire 1.50 4.00
5 Bill Swift .08 .25
6 Ken Caminiti .30 .75
7 Will Clark .60 1.50
8 Rafael Palmeiro .40 1.00
9 Matt Young .08 .25
10 Todd Zeile .20 .50
11 Wally Joyner .20 .50
12 Cal Ripken 3.00 8.00
13 Tom Foley .08 .25
14 Ben McDonald .08 .25
15 Larry Walker .40 1.00
16 Rob Dibble .08 .25
17 Brett Butler .20 .50
18 Joe Girardi .08 .25
19 Brady Anderson .20 .50
20 Craig Biggio .40 1.00

1971 Milk Duds

The cards in this 69-card set measure 1 13/16" by 2 5/8". The 1971 Milk Duds set contains 32 American League cards and 37 National League cards. The cards are actually numbered, but the very small number appears only on the flap of the box; nevertheless the numbers below are ordered alphabetically by player's name within league. American Leaguers are numbered 1-32 and National Leaguers 33-69. The cards are sepia toned on a tan background and were issued on the backs of five-cent boxes of Milk Duds candy. The prices listed in the checklist are for complete boxes. Cards cut from boxes are approximately one-half of the listed price. The names of three of the players in the set were misspelled and are noted in the checklist below as errors. Three of the boxes were double printed, i.e., twice as many were produced or printed compared to the other players. These double-printed players are indicated below by DP in the checklist after the player's name. According to published reports around the time of issue, Dick Bosman was supposedly going to be in this set but a bad photo negated his card being printed.

COMPLETE SET (69) 400.00 800.00
COMMON DP 4.00 10.00
1 Luis Aparicio 8.00 20.00
2 Stan Bahnsen 4.00 10.00
3 Danny Cater 4.00 10.00
4 Ray Culp 4.00 10.00
5 Ray Fosse 4.00 10.00
6 Bill Freehan 5.00 12.00
7 Jim Fregosi 5.00 12.00
8 Tommy Harper 4.00 10.00
9 Frank Howard 5.00 12.00
10 Jim Hunter 10.00 25.00
11 Tommy John 5.00 12.00
12 Alex Johnson 4.00 10.00
13 Dave Johnson 5.00 12.00
14 Harmon Killebrew DP 6.00 15.00
15 Sam McDowell 5.00 12.00
16 Dave McNally 4.00 10.00
17 Bill Melton 4.00 10.00
18 Andy Messersmith 4.00 10.00
19 Thurman Munson 20.00 50.00
20 Tony Oliva 6.00 15.00
21 Jim Palmer 8.00 20.00
22 Jim Perry 5.00 12.00
23 Fritz Peterson 4.00 10.00
24 Rico Petrocelli 4.00 10.00
25 Boog Powell 5.00 12.00
26 Brooks Robinson DP 6.00 15.00
27 Frank Robinson 12.50 30.00
28 George Scott 4.00 10.00
29 Reggie Smith 5.00 12.00
30 Mel Stottlemyer ERR/(sic, Stottlemyre) 5.00 12.00
31 Cesar Tovar 4.00 10.00
32 Roy White 4.00 10.00
33 Hank Aaron 30.00 60.00
34 Ernie Banks 12.50 40.00
35 Glen Beckert ERR/(sic, Glenn) 4.00 10.00
36 Johnny Bench 20.00 50.00
37 Lou Brock 12.50 30.00
38 Rico Carty 5.00 12.00
39 Orlando Cepeda 8.00 20.00
40 Roberto Clemente 50.00 100.00
41 Willie Davis 4.00 10.00
42 Dick Dietz 4.00 10.00
43 Bob Gibson 8.00 20.00
44 Bill Grabarkewitz 4.00 10.00
45 Bud Harrelson 4.00 10.00
46 Jim Hickman 4.00 10.00
47 Ken Holtzman 4.00 10.00
48 Randy Hundley 4.00 10.00
49 Fergie Jenkins 8.00 20.00
50 Don Kessinger 5.00 12.00
51 Willie Mays 50.00 100.00
52 Willie McCovey 8.00 20.00
53 Dennis Menke 4.00 10.00
54 Jim Merritt 4.00 10.00
55 Felix Millan 4.00 10.00
56 Claud Osteen ERR/(sic& Claude) 4.00 10.00
57 Milt Pappas/(pictured in Oriole uniform) 5.00 12.00
58 Tony Perez 8.00 20.00
59 Gaylord Perry 8.00 20.00
60 Pete Rose DP 40.00 80.00
61 Manny Sanguillen 5.00 12.00
62 Ron Santo 6.00 15.00
63 Tom Seaver 20.00 50.00
64 Wayne Simpson 4.00 10.00
65 Rusty Staub 5.00 12.00
66 Bobby Tolan 4.00 10.00
67 Joe Torre 6.00 15.00
68 Luke Walker 4.00 10.00
69 Billy Williams 8.00 20.00

1969 Milton Bradley

These cards were distributed as part of a baseball game produced by Milton Bradley in 1969. The cards each measure approximately 2" by 3" and have square corners. The card fronts show a black and white photo of the player with his name above the photo in a white border. The game outcomes are printed on the card backs. The game was played by rolling two dice. The outcomes (two through twelve) on the back of the player's card related to the sum of the two dice. The card backs are printed in red and black on white card stock; the player's name on back and successful outcomes for the batter such as hits are printed in red. Team logos have been airbrushed from the photos in this set. The cards are typically found with perforation notches visible. Since the cards are unnumbered, they are listed below in alphabetical order. One way to tell the 1969 and 1972 Milton Bradley sets apart is that the 1969 cards all the red digits 1 do not have a base while the 1972 red digit cards all have a base.

COMPLETE SET (296) 250.00 500.00
1 Hank Aaron 8.00 20.00
2 Ted Abernathy .40 1.00
3 Jerry Adair .40 1.00
4 Tommy Agee .40 1.00
5 Bernie Allen .40 1.00
6 Hank Allen .40 1.00
7 Richie Allen 1.25 3.00
8 Gene Alley .40 1.00
9 Bob Allison .60 1.50
10 Felipe Alou 1.25 3.00
11 Jesus Alou .40 1.00
12 Matty Alou .60 1.50
13 Max Alvis .40 1.00
14 Mike Andrews .40 1.00
15 Luis Aparicio 3.00 8.00
16 Jose Arcia .40 1.00
17 Bob Aspromonte .40 1.00
18 Joe Azcue .40 1.00
19 Ernie Banks 5.00 12.00
20 Steve Barber .40 1.00
21 John Bateman .40 1.00
22 Glenn Beckert .40 1.00
23 Gary Bell .40 1.00
24 Johnny Bench 8.00 20.00
25 Ken Berry .40 1.00
26 Frank Bertaina .40 1.00
27 Paul Blair .40 1.00
28 Wade Blasingame .40 1.00
29 Curt Blefary .40 1.00
30 John Boccabella .40 1.00
31 Bobby Bonds 3.00 8.00
32 Sam Bowens .40 1.00
33 Ken Boyer 1.25 3.00
34 Charles Bradford .40 1.00

Card		
35 Darrell Brandon	.40	1.00
36 Jim Brewer	.40	1.00
37 John Briggs	.40	1.00
38 Nelson Briles	.40	1.00
39 Ed Brinkman	.40	1.00
40 Lou Brock	5.00	12.00
41 Gates Brown	.40	1.00
42 Larry Brown	.40	1.00
43 George Brunet	.40	1.00
44 Jerry Buchek	.40	1.00
45 Don Buford	.40	1.00
46 Jim Bunning	3.00	8.00
47 Johnny Callison	1.00	2.50
48 Bert Campaneris	1.00	2.50
49 Jose Cardenal	.40	1.00
50 Leo Cardenas	.40	1.00
51 Don Cardwell	.40	1.00
52 Rod Carew	5.00	12.00
53 Paul Casanova	.40	1.00
54 Norm Cash	1.25	3.00
55 Danny Cater	.40	1.00
56 Orlando Cepeda	2.50	6.00
57 Dean Chance	.60	1.50
58 Ed Charles	.40	1.00
59 Horace Clarke	.40	1.00
60 Roberto Clemente	12.50	30.00
61 Donn Clendenon	.40	1.00
62 Ty Cline	.40	1.00
63 Nate Colbert	.40	1.00
64 Joe Coleman	.40	1.00
65 Bob Cox	2.50	6.00
66 Mike Cuellar	1.25	3.00
67 Ray Culp	.40	1.00
68 Clay Dalrymple	.40	1.00
69 Jim Davenport	.40	1.00
70 Vic Davalillo	.40	1.00
71 Ron Davis	.40	1.00
72 Tommy Davis	1.00	2.50
73 Willie Davis	.60	1.50
74 Chuck Dobson	.40	1.00
75 John Donaldson	.40	1.00
76 Al Downing	.40	1.00
77 Moe Drabowsky	.40	1.00
78 Dick Ellsworth	.40	1.00
79 Mike Epstein	.40	1.00
80 Andy Etchebarren	.40	1.00
81 Ron Fairly	.60	1.50
82 Dick Farrell	.40	1.00
83 Curt Flood	1.25	3.00
84 Joe Foy	.40	1.00
85 Tito Francona	.40	1.00
86 Bill Freehan	1.25	3.00
87 Jim Fregosi	1.00	2.50
88 Woodie Fryman	.40	1.00
89 Len Gabrielson	.40	1.00
90 Clarence Gaston	1.00	2.50
91 Jake Gibbs	.40	1.00
92 Russ Gibson	.40	1.00
93 Dave Giusti	.40	1.00
94 Tony Gonzalez	.40	1.00
95 Jim Gosger	.40	1.00
96 Julio Gotay	.40	1.00
97 Dick Green	.40	1.00
98 Jerry Grote	.60	1.50
99 Jimmie Hall	.40	1.00
100 Tom Haller	.40	1.00
101 Steve Hamilton	.40	1.00
102 Ron Hansen	.40	1.00
103 Jim Hardin	.40	1.00
104 Tommy Harper	.60	1.50
105 Bud Harrelson	.60	1.50
106 Ken Harrelson	1.25	3.00
107 Jim Ray Hart	.40	1.00
108 Woodie Held	.40	1.00
109 Tommy Helms	.40	1.00
110 Elrod Hendricks	.40	1.00
111 Mike Hershberger	.40	1.00
112 Jack Hiatt	.40	1.00
113 Jim Hickman	.40	1.00
114 John Hiller	.40	1.00
115 Chuck Hinton	.40	1.00
116 Ken Holtzman	.60	1.50
117 Joel Horlen	.40	1.00
118 Tony Horton	.60	1.50
119 Willie Horton	1.00	2.50
120 Frank Howard	1.25	3.00
121 Dick Howser	.40	1.00
122 Randy Hundley	.40	1.00
123 Ron Hunt	.40	1.00
124 Jim Hunter	3.00	8.00
125 Al Jackson	.40	1.00
126 Larry Jackson	.40	1.00
127 Reggie Jackson	10.00	25.00
128 Sonny Jackson	.40	1.00
129 Pat Jarvis	.40	1.00
130 Julian Javier	.40	1.00
131 Ferguson Jenkins	3.00	8.00
132 Manny Jimenez	.40	1.00
133 Tommy John	1.50	4.00
134 Bob Johnson	.40	1.00
135 Dave Johnson	1.25	3.00
136 Deron Johnson	.40	1.00
137 Lou Johnson	.40	1.00
138 Jay Johnstone	1.25	3.00
139 Cleon Jones	.60	1.50
140 Dalton Jones	.40	1.00
141 Duane Josephson	.40	1.00
142 Jim Kaat	1.50	4.00
143 Al Kaline	5.00	12.00
144 Don Kessinger	.60	1.50
145 Harmon Killebrew	4.00	10.00
146 Hal King	.40	1.00
147 Ed Kirkpatrick	.40	1.00
148 Fred Klages	.40	1.00
149 Ron Kline	.40	1.00
150 Bobby Knoop	.40	1.00
151 Gary Kolb	.40	1.00
152 Andy Kosco	.40	1.00
153 Ed Kranepool	.60	1.50
154 Lew Krausse	.40	1.00
155 Hal Lanier	.40	1.00
156 Jim LeFebvre	.40	1.00
157 Denny Lemaster	.40	1.00
158 Dave Leonhard	.40	1.00
159 Don Lock	.40	1.00
160 Mickey Lolich	1.25	3.00
161 Jim Lonborg	1.00	2.50
162 Mike Lum	.40	1.00
163 Sparky Lyle	2.00	5.00
164 Jim Maloney	.60	1.50
165 Juan Marichal	3.00	8.00
166 J.C. Martin	.40	1.00
167 Marty Martinez	.40	1.00
168 Tom Matchick	.40	1.00
169 Ed Mathews	4.00	10.00
170 Jerry May	.40	1.00
171 Lee May	.60	1.50
172 Lee Maye	.40	1.00
173 Willie Mays	8.00	20.00
174 Dal Maxvill	.40	1.00
175 Bill Mazeroski	1.50	4.00
176 Dick McAuliffe	.40	1.00
177 Al McBean	.40	1.00
178 Tim McCarver	1.25	3.00
179 Bill McCool	.40	1.00
180 Mike McCormick	.60	1.50
181 Willie McCovey	4.00	10.00
182 Tom McCraw	.40	1.00
183 Lindy McDaniel	.40	1.00
184 Sam McDowell	1.00	2.50
185 Orlando McFarlane	.40	1.00
186 Jim McGlothlin	.40	1.00
187 Denny McLain	1.25	3.00
188 Ken McMullen	.40	1.00
189 Dave McNally	1.00	2.50
190 Gerry McNertney	.40	1.00
191 Denis Menke	.40	1.00
192 Felix Millan	.40	1.00
193 Don Mincher	.40	1.00
194 Rick Monday	.60	1.50
195 Joe Morgan	4.00	10.00
196 Bubba Morton	.40	1.00
197 Manny Mota	.60	1.50
198 Jim Nash	.40	1.00
199 Dave Nelson	.40	1.00
200 Dick Nen	.40	1.00
201 Phil Niekro	3.00	8.00
202 Jim Northrup	.60	1.50
203 Rich Nye	.40	1.00
204 Johnny Odom	.40	1.00
205 Tony Oliva	1.50	4.00
206 Gene Oliver	.40	1.00
207 Phil Ortega	.40	1.00
208 Claude Osteen	.60	1.50
209 Ray Oyler	.40	1.00
210 Jose Pagan	.40	1.00
211 Jim Pagliaroni	.40	1.00
212 Milt Pappas	.60	1.50
213 Wes Parker	.40	1.00
214 Camilo Pascual	.40	1.00
215 Don Pavletich	.40	1.00
216 Joe Pepitone	1.00	2.50
217 Tony Perez	2.50	6.00
218 Gaylord Perry	3.00	8.00
219 Jim Perry	1.25	3.00
220 Gary Peters	.40	1.00
221 Rico Petrocelli	.60	1.50
222 Adolpho Phillips	.40	1.00
223 Tom Phoebus	.40	1.00
224 Vada Pinson	1.25	3.00
225 Boog Powell	1.50	4.00
226 Frank Quilici	.40	1.00
227 Doug Rader	.40	1.00
228 Rich Reese	.40	1.00
229 Phil Regan	.40	1.00
230 Rick Reichardt	.40	1.00
231 Rick Renick	.40	1.00
232 Roger Repoz	.40	1.00
233 Dave Ricketts	.40	1.00
234 Bill Robinson	.40	1.00
235 Brooks Robinson	5.00	12.00
236 Frank Robinson	5.00	12.00
237 Bob Rodgers	.40	1.00
238 Cookie Rojas	.40	1.00
239 Rich Rollins	.40	1.00
240 Phil Roof	.40	1.00
241 Pete Rose	6.00	15.00
242 John Roseboro	.60	1.50
243 Chico Ruiz	.40	1.00
244 Ray Sadecki	.40	1.00
245 Chico Salmon	.40	1.00
246 Jose Santiago	.40	1.00
247 Ron Santo	1.25	3.00
248 Tom Satriano	.40	1.00
249 Paul Schaal	.40	1.00
250 Tom Seaver	6.00	15.00
251 Art Shamsky	.40	1.00
252 Mike Shannon	1.00	2.50
253 Chris Short	.40	1.00
254 Dick Simpson	.40	1.00
255 Duke Sims	.40	1.00
256 Reggie Smith	1.25	3.00
257 Willie Smith	.40	1.00
258 Russ Snyder	.40	1.00
259 Al Spangler	.40	1.00
260 Larry Stahl	.40	1.00
261 Lee Stange	.40	1.00
262 Mickey Stanley	.40	1.00
263 Willie Stargell	4.00	10.00
264 Rusty Staub	1.25	3.00
265 Mel Stottlemyre	1.25	3.00
266 Ed Stroud	.40	1.00
267 Don Sutton	3.00	8.00
268 Ron Swoboda	.60	1.50
269 Jose Tartabull	.40	1.00
270 Tony Taylor	.60	1.50
271 Luis Tiant	1.25	3.00
272 Bill Tillman	.40	1.00
273 Bobby Tolan	.40	1.00
274 Jeff Torborg	.40	1.00
275 Joe Torre	2.00	5.00
276 Cesar Tovar	.40	1.00
277 Dick Tracewski	.40	1.00
278 Tom Tresh	1.25	3.00
279 Ted Uhlaender	.40	1.00
280 Del Unser	.40	1.00
281 Sandy Valdespino	.40	1.00
282 Fred Valentine	.40	1.00
283 Bob Veale	.40	1.00
284 Zoilo Versalles	.60	1.50
285 Pete Ward	.40	1.00
286 Al Weis	.40	1.00
287 Don Wert	.40	1.00
288 Bill White	1.25	3.00
289 Roy White	.60	1.50
290 Fred Whitfield	.40	1.00
291 Hoyt Wilhelm	3.00	8.00
292 Billy Williams	3.00	8.00
293 Maury Wills	1.50	4.00
294 Earl Wilson	.40	1.00
295 Wilbur Wood	.40	1.00
296 Jerry Zimmerman	.40	1.00

1970 Milton Bradley

These cards were distributed as part of a baseball game produced by Milton Bradley in 1970. The cards each measure approximately 2 3/16" by 3 1/2" and have rounded corners. The card fronts show a black and white photo of the player with his name and vital statistics below the photo in a white border. The game outcomes are printed on the card backs. The card backs are printed in red and black on white card stock; the player's name is printed in red at the top of the card. Team logos have been airbrushed from the photos in this set. Since the cards are unnumbered, they are listed below in alphabetical order. Thirty two game cards were also included in the original box, those cards are not priced here. This set is sometimes found in the original box and unwrapped. If the cards are in that condition, there is a 25 percent premium for the set.

Card		
COMPLETE SET (28)	50.00	100.00
1 Hank Aaron	4.00	10.00
2 Lou Brock	2.50	6.00
3 Ernie Banks	2.50	6.00
4 Rod Carew	3.00	8.00
5 Roberto Clemente	8.00	20.00
6 Tommy Davis	.50	1.25
7 Bill Freehan	.50	1.25
8 Jim Fregosi	.50	1.25
9 Tom Haller	.40	1.00
10 Frank Howard	.60	1.50
11 Reggie Jackson	5.00	12.00
12 Harmon Killebrew	1.50	4.00
13 Mickey Lolich	.60	1.50
14 Juan Marichal	1.50	4.00
15 Willie Mays	6.00	15.00
16 Willie McCovey	2.00	5.00
17 Sam McDowell	.50	1.25
18 Denis Menke	.40	1.00
19 Don Mincher	.40	1.00
20 Phil Niekro	1.50	4.00
21 Rico Petrocelli	.50	1.25
22 Boog Powell	.75	2.00
23 Frank Robinson	2.50	6.00
24 Pete Rose	4.00	10.00
25 Ron Santo	.75	2.00
26 Tom Seaver	4.00	10.00
27 Mel Stottlemyre	.50	1.25
28 Tony Taylor	.40	1.00

1972 Milton Bradley

These cards were distributed as part of a baseball game produced by Milton Bradley in 1972. The cards each measure approximately 2" by 3" and have square corners. The card fronts show a black and white photo of the player with his name above the photo in a white border. The game outcomes are printed on the card backs. The game was played by rolling two dice. The outcomes (two through twelve) on the back of the player's card related to the sum of the two dice. The card backs are printed in red and black on white card stock; successful outcomes for the batter such as hits are printed in red. Team logos have been airbrushed from the photos in this set. The cards are typically found with perforation notches visible. Since the cards are unnumbered, they are listed below in alphabetical order.

Card		
COMPLETE SET (372)	350.00	700.00
1 Hank Aaron	12.50	30.00
2 Tommie Aaron	.20	.50
3 Ted Abernathy	.20	.50
4 Jerry Adair	.20	.50
5 Tommy Agee	.40	1.00
6 Bernie Allen	.20	.50
7 Hank Allen	.20	.50
8 Richie Allen	1.25	3.00
9 Gene Alley	.20	.50
10 Bob Allison	.20	.50
11 Sandy Alomar	.20	.50
12 Felipe Alou	.75	2.00
13 Jesus Alou	.40	1.00
14 Matty Alou	.60	1.50
15 Max Alvis	.20	.50
16 Brant Alyea	.20	.50
17 Mike Andrews	.20	.50
18 Luis Aparicio	2.50	6.00
19 Jose Arcia	.20	.50
20 Jerry Arrigo	.20	.50
21 Bob Aspromonte	.20	.50
22 Joe Azcue	.20	.50
23 Bob Bailey	.20	.50
24 Sal Bando	.75	2.00
25 Ernie Banks	6.00	15.00
26 Steve Barber	.20	.50
27 Bob Barton	.20	.50
28 John Bateman	.20	.50
29 Glenn Beckert	.40	1.00
30 Johnny Bench	15.00	40.00
31 Ken Berry	.20	.50
32 Frank Bertaina	.20	.50
33 Paul Blair	.40	1.00
34 Steve Blass	.20	.50
35 Curt Blefary	.20	.50
36 Bobby Bolin	.20	.50
37 Bobby Bonds	1.25	3.00
38 Don Bosch	.20	.50
39 Dick Bosman	.20	.50
40 Dave Boswell	.20	.50
41 Ken Boswell	.20	.50
42 Cletis Boyer	.60	1.50
43 Charles Bradford	.20	.50
44 Ron Brand	.20	.50
45 Ken Brett	.20	.50
46 Jim Brewer	.20	.50
47 John Briggs	.20	.50
48 Nelson Briles	.20	.50
49 Ed Brinkman	.20	.50
50 Jim Britton	.20	.50
51 Lou Brock	5.00	12.00
52 Gates Brown	.20	.50
53 Larry Brown	.20	.50
54 Ollie Brown	.20	.50
55 George Brunet	.20	.50
56 Don Buford	.20	.50
57 Wally Bunker	.20	.50
58 Jim Bunning	2.50	6.00
59 Bill Butler	.20	.50
60 Johnny Callison	.60	1.50
61 Bert Campaneris	.60	1.50
62 Jose Cardenal	.20	.50
63 Leo Cardenas	.20	.50
64 Don Cardwell	.20	.50
65 Rod Carew	5.00	12.00
66 Cisco Carlos	.20	.50
67 Steve Carlton	6.00	15.00
68 Clay Carroll	.20	.50
69 Paul Casanova	.20	.50
70 Norm Cash	1.25	3.00
71 Danny Cater	.20	.50
72 Orlando Cepeda	2.00	5.00
73 Dean Chance	.40	1.00
74 Horace Clarke	.20	.50
75 Roberto Clemente	40.00	80.00
76 Donn Clendenon	.20	.50
77 Ty Cline	.20	.50
78 Nate Colbert	.20	.50
79 Joe Coleman	.20	.50
80 Billy Conigliaro	.20	.50
81 Casey Cox	.20	.50
82 Mike Cuellar	.60	1.50
83 Ray Culp	.20	.50
84 George Culver	.20	.50
85 Jim Davenport	.20	.50
86 Vic Davalillo	.20	.50
87 Tommy Davis	.60	1.50
88 Willie Davis	.40	1.00
89 Larry Dierker	.20	.50
90 Dick Dietz	.20	.50
91 Chuck Dobson	.20	.50
92 Pat Dobson	.20	.50
93 John Donaldson	.20	.50
94 Al Downing	.20	.50
95 Moe Drabowsky	.20	.50
96 John Edwards	.20	.50
97 Thomas Egan	.20	.50
98 Dick Ellsworth	.20	.50
99 Mike Epstein	.20	.50
100 Andy Etchebarren	.20	.50
101 Ron Fairly	.60	1.50
102 Frank Fernandez	.20	.50
103 Al Ferrara	.20	.50
104 Mike Fiore	.20	.50
105 Curt Flood	.75	2.00
106 Joe Foy	.20	.50
107 Tito Francona	.20	.50
108 Bill Freehan	.75	2.00
109 Jim Fregosi	.60	1.50
110 Woodie Fryman	.20	.50
111 Vern Fuller	.20	.50
112 Phil Gagliano	.20	.50
113 Clarence Gaston	.20	.50
114 Jake Gibbs	.20	.50
115 Russ Gibson	.20	.50
116 Dave Giusti	.20	.50
117 Fred Gladding	.20	.50
118 Tony Gonzalez	.20	.50
119 Jim Gosger	.20	.50
120 Jim Grant	.20	.50
121 Dick Green	.20	.50
122 Tom Griffin	.20	.50
123 Jerry Grote	.20	.50
124 Tom Hall	.20	.50
125 Tom Haller	.20	.50
126 Steve Hamilton	.20	.50
127 Bill Hands	.20	.50
128 Jim Hannan	.20	.50
129 Ron Hansen	.20	.50
130 Jim Hardin	.20	.50
131 Steve Hargan	.20	.50
132 Tommy Harper	.40	1.00
133 Bud Harrelson	.40	1.00
134 Ken Harrelson	.75	2.00
135 Jim Ray Hart	.20	.50
136 Richie Hebner	.40	1.00
137 Mike Hedlund	.20	.50
138 Tommy Helms	.20	.50
139 Elrod Hendricks	.20	.50
140 Ron Herbel	.20	.50
141 Jackie Hernandez	.20	.50
142 Mike Hershberger	.20	.50
143 Jack Hiatt	.20	.50
144 Dennis Higgins	.20	.50
146 John Hiller	.20	.50
147 Chuck Hinton	.20	.50
148 Larry Hisle	.20	.50
149 Ken Holtzman	.40	1.00
150 Joel Horlen	.20	.50
151 Tony Horton	.20	.50
152 Willie Horton	.60	1.50
153 Frank Howard	.75	2.00
154 Bob Humphreys	.20	.50
155 Randy Hundley	.20	.50
156 Ron Hunt	.20	.50
157 Jim Hunter	2.50	6.00
158 Grant Jackson	.20	.50
159 Reggie Jackson	15.00	40.00
160 Sonny Jackson	.20	.50
161 Pat Jarvis	.20	.50
162 Larry Jaster	.20	.50
163 Julian Javier	.20	.50
164 Ferguson Jenkins	2.50	6.00
165 Tommy John	1.25	3.00
166 Alex Johnson	.20	.50
167 Bob Johnson	.20	.50
168 Dave Johnson	.75	2.00
169 Deron Johnson	.20	.50
170 Jay Johnstone	.40	1.00
171 Cleon Jones	.40	1.00
172 Dalton Jones	.20	.50
173 Mack Jones	.20	.50
174 Rick Joseph	.20	.50
175 Duane Josephson	.20	.50
176 Jim Kaat	1.25	3.00
177 Al Kaline	5.00	12.00
178 Dick Kelley	.20	.50
179 Pat Kelly	.20	.50
180 Jerry Kenney	.20	.50
181 Don Kessinger	.40	1.00
182 Harmon Killebrew	4.00	10.00
183 Ed Kirkpatrick	.20	.50
184 Bobby Knoop	.20	.50
185 Cal Koonce	.20	.50
186 Jerry Koosman	.75	2.00
187 Andy Kosco	.20	.50
188 Ed Kranepool	.40	1.00
189 Ted Kubiak	.20	.50
190 Jose Laboy	.20	.50
191 Joe Lahoud	.20	.50
192 Bill Landis	.20	.50
193 Hal Lanier	.20	.50
194 Fred Lasher	.20	.50
195 John Lazar	.20	.50
196 Jim LeFebvre	.20	.50
197 Denny Lemaster	.20	.50
198 Dave Leonhard	.20	.50
199 Frank Linzy	.20	.50
200 Mickey Lolich	.75	2.00
201 Jim Lonborg	.40	1.00
202 Sparky Lyle	.75	2.00
203 Jim Maloney	.40	1.00
204 Juan Marichal	3.00	8.00
205 David Marshall	.20	.50
206 J.C. Martin	.20	.50
207 Marty Martinez	.20	.50
208 Tom Matchick	.20	.50
209 Carlos May	.20	.50
210 Jerry May	.20	.50
211 Lee May	.40	1.00
212 Lee Maye	.20	.50
213 Willie Mays	10.00	25.00
214 Dal Maxvill	.20	.50
215 Bill Mazeroski	.75	2.00
216 Dick McAuliffe	.40	1.00
217 Al McBean	.20	.50
218 Tim McCarver	.75	2.00
219 Bill McCool	.20	.50
220 Mike McCormick	.40	1.00
221 Willie McCovey	4.00	10.00
222 Tom McCraw	.20	.50
223 Lindy McDaniel	.20	.50
224 Sam McDowell	.60	1.50
225 Leon McFadden	.20	.50
226 Dan McGinn	.20	.50
227 Jim McGlothlin	.20	.50
228 Tug McGraw	.75	2.00
229 Denny McLain	.75	2.00
230 Ken McMullen	.20	.50
231 Dave McNally	.60	1.50
232 Gerry McNertney	.20	.50
233 Bill Melton	.20	.50
234 Denis Menke	.20	.50
235 Andy Messersmith	.40	1.00
236 Felix Millan	.20	.50
237 Norm Miller	.20	.50
238 Don Mincher	.20	.50
239 Rick Monday	.40	1.00
240 Don Money	.20	.50
241 Barry Moore	.20	.50
242 Bob Moose	.20	.50
243 Dave Morehead	.20	.50
244 Joe Morgan	4.00	10.00
245 Manny Mota	.40	1.00
246 Curt Motton	.20	.50
247 Bob Murcer	.75	2.00
248 Tom Murphy	.20	.50
249 Ivan Murrell	.20	.50
250 Jim Nash	.20	.50
251 Joe Niekro	.75	2.00
252 Phil Niekro	3.00	8.00
253 Gary Nolan	.20	.50
254 Jim Northrup	.40	1.00
255 Rich Nye	.20	.50
256 Johnny Odom	.20	.50
257 John O'Donoghue	.20	.50
258 Tony Oliva	.75	2.00
259 Bob Oliver	.20	.50
260 Claude Osteen	.40	1.00
261 Ray Oyler	.20	.50
262 Jose Pagan	.20	.50
263 Jim Palmer	3.00	8.00
264 Milt Pappas	.40	1.00
265 Wes Parker	.40	1.00
266 Freddie Patek	.20	.50
267 Mike Paul	.20	.50
268 Joe Pepitone	.60	1.50
269 Tony Perez	2.00	5.00
270 Gaylord Perry	3.00	8.00
271 Jim Perry	.60	1.50
272 Gary Peters	.20	.50
273 Rico Petrocelli	.60	1.50
274 Tom Phoebus	.20	.50
275 Lou Piniella	.75	2.00
276 Vada Pinson	.75	2.00
277 Boog Powell	.75	2.00
278 Jimmie Price	.20	.50
279 Frank Quilici	.20	.50
280 Doug Rader	.20	.50
281 Ron Reed	.20	.50
282 Rich Reese	.20	.50
283 Phil Regan	.20	.50
284 Rick Reichardt	.20	.50
285 Rick Renick	.20	.50
286 Roger Repoz	.20	.50
287 Merv Rettenmund	.20	.50
288 Dave Ricketts	.20	.50
289 Juan Rios	.20	.50
290 Bill Robinson	.20	.50
291 Brooks Robinson	5.00	12.00
292 Frank Robinson	5.00	12.00
293 Aurelio Rodriguez	.20	.50
294 Ellie Rodriguez	.20	.50
295 Cookie Rojas	.20	.50
296 Rich Rollins	.20	.50
297 Vincente Romo	.20	.50
298 Phil Roof	.20	.50
299 Pete Rose	40.00	80.00
300 John Roseboro	.40	1.00
301 Chico Ruiz	.20	.50
302 Mike Ryan	.20	.50
303 Ray Sadecki	.20	.50
304 Chico Salmon	.20	.50
305 Manny Sanguillen	.40	1.00
306 Ron Santo	.75	2.00
307 Tom Satriano	.20	.50
308 Ted Savage	.20	.50
309 Paul Schaal	.20	.50
310 Dick Schofield	.20	.50
311 George Scott	.40	1.00
312 Tom Seaver	8.00	20.00
313 Art Shamsky	.20	.50
314 Mike Shannon	.60	1.50
315 Chris Short	.20	.50
316 Duke Sims	.20	.50
317 Bill Singer	.20	.50
318 Reggie Smith	.75	2.00
319 Willie Smith	.20	.50
320 Russ Snyder	.20	.50
321 Al Spangler	.20	.50
322 Jim Spencer	.20	.50
323 Ed Spiezio	.20	.50
324 Larry Stahl	.20	.50
325 Lee Stange	.20	.50
326 Mickey Stanley	.40	1.00
327 Willie Stargell	5.00	12.00
328 Rusty Staub	.75	2.00
329 Jim Stewart	.20	.50
330 George Stone	.20	.50
331 Bill Stoneman	.40	1.00
332 Mel Stottlemyre	.75	2.00
333 Ed Stroud	.20	.50
334 Ken Suarez	.20	.50
335 Gary Sutherland	.20	.50
336 Don Sutton	2.50	6.00
337 Ron Swoboda	.40	1.00
338 Fred Talbot	.20	.50
339 Jose Tartabull	.20	.50
340 Ken Tatum	.20	.50
341 Tony Taylor	.40	1.00
342 Luis Tiant	.75	2.00
343 Bob Tillman	.20	.50
344 Bobby Tolan	.20	.50
345 Jeff Torborg	.20	.50
346 Joe Torre	.75	2.00
347 Cesar Tovar	.20	.50
348 Tom Tresh	.75	2.00
349 Ted Uhlaender	.20	.50
350 Del Unser	.20	.50
351 Bob Veale	.20	.50
352 Zoilo Versalles	.40	1.00
353 Luke Walker	.20	.50
354 Pete Ward	.20	.50
355 Eddie Watt	.20	.50
356 Ramon Webster	.20	.50
357 Al Weis	.20	.50
358 Don Wert	.20	.50
359 Bill White	.75	2.00
360 Roy White	.60	1.50
361 Hoyt Wilhelm	2.00	5.00
362 Billy Williams	4.00	10.00
363 Walt Williams	.20	.50
364 Maury Wills	.75	2.00
365 Don Wilson	.20	.50
366 Earl Wilson	.20	.50
367 Bobby Wine	.20	.50
368 Rick Wise	.40	1.00
369 Wilbur Wood	.20	.50
370 Woody Woodward	.20	.50
371 Clyde Wright	.20	.50
372 Jim Wynn	.75	2.00

1984 Milton Bradley

The cards in this 30-card set measure the standard size. This set of full color cards was produced by Topps for the Milton Bradley Co. The set was included in a board game entitled Championship Baseball. The fronts feature portraits of the players and the name, Championship Baseball, by Milton Bradley. The backs feature the Topps logo, statistics for the past year (pitchers' cards have career statistics), and dice rolls which are part of the board game. Pitcher cards have no dice roll charts. There are 15 players from each league. These unnumbered cards are listed below in alphabetical order. The cap logos and uniforms have been air-brushed to remove all team references. Many of these cards have been seen with bad centering.

Card		
COMPLETE SET (30)	6.00	15.00
1 Wade Boggs	1.25	3.00
2 George Brett	1.50	4.00
3 Rod Carew	.30	.75
4 Steve Carlton	.30	.75
5 Gary Carter	.30	.75
6 Dave Concepcion	.08	.25
7 Cecil Cooper	.08	.25
8 Andre Dawson	.25	.60
9 Carlton Fisk	.80	1.00
10 Steve Garvey	.08	.25
11 Pedro Guerrero	.02	.10
12 Ron Guidry	.08	.25
13 Rickey Henderson	.75	2.00
14 Reggie Jackson	.40	1.00
15 Ron Kittle	.02	.10
16 Bill Madlock	.02	.10
17 Dale Murphy	.40	1.00
18 Al Oliver	.02	.10
19 Darrell Porter	.02	.10
20 Cal Ripken	2.50	6.00
21 Pete Rose	.60	1.50
22 Steve Sax	.02	.10
23 Mike Schmidt	.60	1.50
24 Ted Simmons	.08	.25
25 Ozzie Smith	1.00	2.50
26 Dave Stieb	.02	.10
27 Fernando Valenzuela	.08	.25
28 Lou Whitaker	.25	.60
29 Dave Winfield	.40	1.00
30 Robin Yount	.40	1.00

1977 Johnny Mize

This 20-card set measures 3 1/8" by 3 3/4" and features both vertical and horizontal black-and-white photos of Johnny Mize at various stages of his life. The photos are bordered in gold and gray by a design similar to picture frame. The card title is printed below the photo in script. The backs are white and carry a variety of information. Some contain statistics, while others have quotes from other ball players or career information. The cards are unnumbered and checklisted below in alphabetical order according to either the card's title or the last name of an individual pictured with Johnny Mize. Two postage paid postcards were also included for buyers of the set to send to HOF Veteran Committee voters to support Mize's case for the HOF.

Card		
COMPLETE SET	6.00	15.00
COMMON CARD	.30	.75
1 Buddy Blattner	.60	1.50
Sid Gordon		
Ernie Lombardi		
Willar		
5 Johnny Mize	.60	1.50
Happy Chandler COMM		
Bucky Harris MG		
11 Johnny Mize	.40	1.00
Terry Moore		
13 Johnny Mize	.40	1.00
Allie Reynolds		
Billy Johnson		
14 Johnny Mize	.75	2.00
Roy Rogers		
16 Johnny Mize	.75	2.00
Enos Slaughter/1939		
20 Johnny Mize	.40	1.00
Gene Woodling		
Vic Raschi/1952		

1992 MJB Holographics Prototypes

Card		
COMPLETE SET (2)	1.25	3.00
R1 Jeff Bagwell	.75	2.00
R1 Chuck Knoblauch	.40	1.00

1992 MJB Holographics Bagwell

The premier edition of Holoprism 1991 Rookies of the Year presented Chuck Knoblauch, the American League Rookie of the Year, and Jeff Bagwell, the National League Rookie of the Year. Each four-card holographic set was issued in a plastic "jewel box," similar to that used for storing and protecting audio compact disks. The top has a window through which the consumer can view the top card, while the back of the case displays a certificate of authenticity with the serial number of the set and the production run (250,000 sets). Also Bagwell and Knoblauch each autographed 500 cards that were randomly inserted throughout the sets. These autograph cards are rarely seen in the secondary market.

Card		
COMPLETE SET (4)	.60	1.50
COMMON PLAYER (1-4)	.20	.50
AU Jeff Bagwell AU/500	25.00	60.00

1992 MJB Holographics Knoblauch

The premier edition of Holoprism 1991 Rookies of the Year presented Chuck Knoblauch, the American League Rookie of the Year, and Jeff Bagwell, the National League Rookie of the Year. Each four-card holographic set was issued in a plastic "jewel box," similar to that used for storing and protecting audio compact disks. The top has a window through which the consumer can view the top card, while the back of the case displays a certificate of authenticity with the serial number of the set and the production run (250,000 sets). Also Bagwell and Knoblauch each autographed 500 cards that were randomly inserted throughout the sets. These autograph cards are rarely seen in the secondary market.

Card		
COMPLETE SET (4)	.60	1.50
COMMON PLAYER (1-4)	.20	.50
AU Chuck Knoblauch AU/500	12.50	30.00

1969 MLB PhotoStamps

Each team is represented by nine players; hence the set consists of 216 player stamps each measuring approximately 1 3/4" by 2 7/8". There are two large albums available, one for each league. Also there are four smaller divisional albums each measuring approximately 4" by 7" and holding all the player stamps for a particular division. Stamps are unnumbered but are presented here in alphabetical order by team, Baltimore Orioles (1-9), Boston Red Sox (10-18), California Angels (19-27), Chicago White Sox (28-36), Cleveland Indians (37-45), Detroit Tigers (46-54), Kansas City Royals (55-63), Minnesota Twins (64-72), New York Yankees (73-81), Oakland A's (82-90), Seattle Pilots (91-99), Washington Senators (100-108), Atlanta Braves (109-117), Chicago Cubs (118-126), Cincinnati Reds (127-135), Houston Astros (136-144), Los Angeles Dodgers (145-153), Montreal Expos (154-162), New York Mets (163-171), Philadelphia Phillies (172-180), Pittsburgh Pirates (181-189), San Diego Padres (190-198), San Francisco Giants (199-207), and St. Louis Cardinals (208-216).

Card		
COMPLETE SET (216)	40.00	80.00
1 Paul Blair	.12	.30
2 Don Buford	.08	.20
3 Andy Etchebarren	.08	.20
4 Dave Johnson	.15	.40
5 Dave McNally	.12	.30
6 Tom Phoebus	.08	.20
7 Boog Powell	.20	.50
8 Brooks Robinson	.60	1.50
9 Frank Robinson	.60	1.50
10 Mike Andrews	.08	.20
11 Ray Culp	.08	.20
12 Dick Ellsworth	.08	.20
13 Ken Harrelson	.15	.40
14 Jim Lonborg	.12	.30
15 Rico Petrocelli	.12	.30
16 Jose Santiago	.08	.20
17 George Scott	.12	.30
18 Reggie Smith	.15	.40
19 George Brunet	.08	.20
20 Vic Davalillo	.08	.20
21 Jim Fregosi	.15	.40
22 Chuck Hinton	.08	.20
23 Bobby Knoop	.08	.20
24 Jim McGlothlin	.08	.20
25 Rick Reichardt	.08	.20
26 Roger Repoz	.08	.20
27 Bob Rodgers	.15	.40
28 Luis Aparicio	.40	1.00
29 Ken Berry	.08	.20
30 Joe Horlen	.08	.20
31 Tommy John	.20	.50
32 Duane Josephson	.08	.20
33 Tom McCraw	.08	.20
34 Gary Peters	.08	.20
35 Pete Ward	.08	.20
36 Wilbur Wood	.12	.30
37 Max Alvis	.08	.20
38 Joe Azcue	.08	.20
39 Larry Brown	.08	.20

40 Jose Cardenal .08 .20
41 Tony Horton .12 .30
42 Sam McDowell .12 .30
43 Sonny Siebert .08 .20
44 Luis Tiant .15 .40
45 Zoilo Versalles .08 .20
46 Norm Cash .15 .40
47 Bill Freehan .15 .40
48 Willie Horton .15 .40
49 Al Kaline .60 1.50
50 Mickey Lolich .15 .40
51 Dick McAuliffe .08 .20
52 Denny McLain .20 .50
53 Jim Northrup .08 .20
54 Mickey Stanley .08 .20
55 Jerry Adair .08 .20
56 Wally Bunker .08 .20
57 Moe Drabowsky .08 .20
58 Joe Foy .08 .20
59 Ed Kirkpatrick .08 .20
60 Dave Morehead .08 .20
61 Roger Nelson .08 .20
62 Paul Schaal .08 .20
63 Steve Whitaker .08 .20
64 Bob Allison .12 .30
65 Rod Carew .60 1.50
66 Dean Chance .12 .30
67 Jim Kaat .20 .50
68 Harmon Killebrew .40 1.00
69 Tony Oliva .20 .50
70 John Roseboro .08 .20
71 Cesar Tovar .08 .20
72 Ted Uhlaender .08 .20
73 Horace Clarke .08 .20
74 Jake Gibbs .08 .20
75 Steve Hamilton .08 .20
76 Joe Pepitone .12 .30
77 Fritz Peterson .08 .20
78 Bill Robinson .12 .30
79 Mel Stottlemyre .12 .30
80 Tom Tresh .15 .40
81 Roy White .12 .30
82 Sal Bando .12 .30
83 Bert Campaneris .15 .40
84 Danny Cater .08 .20
85 John Donaldson .08 .20
86 Mike Hershberger .08 .20
87 Jim Hunter .40 1.00
88 Rick Monday .12 .30
89 Jim Nash .08 .20
90 John Odom .08 .20
91 Jack Aker .08 .20
92 Steve Barber .08 .20
93 Gary Bell .08 .20
94 Tommy Davis .12 .30
95 Tommy Harper .08 .20
96 Don Mincher .08 .20
97 Ray Oyler .08 .20
98 Rich Rollins .08 .20
99 Chico Salmon .08 .20
100 Bernie Allen .08 .20
101 Ed Brinkman .08 .20
102 Paul Casanova .08 .20
103 Joe Coleman Jr. .08 .20
104 Mike Epstein .08 .20
105 Frank Howard .20 .50
106 Ken McMullen .08 .20
107 Camilo Pascual .08 .20
108 Ed Stroud .08 .20
109 Hank Aaron 1.00 2.50
110 Felipe Alou .15 .40
111 Bob Aspromonte .08 .20
112 Rico Carty .12 .30
113 Orlando Cepeda .30 .75
114 Pat Jarvis .08 .20
115 Felix Millan .08 .20
116 Phil Niekro .30 .75
117 Milt Pappas .08 .20
118 Ernie Banks .60 1.50
119 Glenn Beckert .08 .20
120 Bill Hands .08 .20
121 Randy Hundley .08 .20
122 Fergie Jenkins .30 .75
123 Don Kessinger .12 .30
124 Phil Regan .08 .20
125 Ron Santo .20 .50
126 Billy Williams .40 1.00
127 Johnny Bench .60 1.50
128 Tony Cloninger .08 .20
129 Tommy Helms .08 .20
130 Jim Maloney .12 .30
131 Lee May .12 .30
132 Jim Merritt .08 .20
133 Gary Nolan .08 .20
134 Tony Perez .30 .75
135 Pete Rose .75 2.00
136 Jesus Alou .08 .20
137 Curt Blefary .08 .20
138 Larry Dierker .08 .20
139 Johnny Edwards .08 .20
140 Denis Menke .08 .20
141 Joe Morgan .40 1.00
142 Doug Rader .12 .30
143 Don Wilson .08 .20
144 Jim Wynn .12 .30
145 Willie Davis .12 .30
146 Ron Fairly .12 .30
147 Len Gabrielson .08 .20
148 Tom Haller .08 .20
149 Jim LeFebvre .08 .20
150 Claude Osteen .08 .20
151 Wes Parker .12 .30
152 Bill Singer .08 .20
153 Don Sutton .30 .75
154 Bob Bailey .08 .20
155 John Bateman .08 .20
156 Ty Cline .08 .20
157 Jim Fairey .08 .20
158 Jim Grant .08 .20
159 Mack Jones .08 .20
160 Manny Mota .08 .20
161 Rusty Staub .20 .50
162 Maury Wills .20 .50
163 Tommy Agee .08 .20
164 Ed Charles .08 .20
165 Jerry Grote .12 .30
166 Bud Harrelson .15 .40
167 Cleon Jones .12 .30
168 Jerry Koosman .15 .40
169 Ed Kranepool .08 .20
170 Tom Seaver .75 2.00
171 Ron Swoboda .08 .20
172 Richie Allen .20 .50
173 Johnny Briggs .08 .20
174 Johnny Callison .12 .30
175 Woody Fryman .08 .20
176 Cookie Rojas .08 .20
177 Mike Ryan .08 .20
178 Chris Short .08 .20
179 Tony Taylor .08 .20
180 Rick Wise .12 .30
181 Gene Alley .08 .20
182 Matty Alou .12 .30
183 Jim Bunning .30 .75
184 Roberto Clemente 1.50 4.00
185 Ron Davis .08 .20
186 Jerry May .08 .20
187 Bill Mazeroski .20 .50
188 Willie Stargell .40 1.00
189 Bob Veale .08 .20
190 Ollie Brown .08 .20
191 Al Ferrara .08 .20
192 Tony Gonzales .08 .20
193 Dick Kelley .08 .20
194 Bill McCool .08 .20
195 Dick Selma .08 .20
196 Tommy Sisk .08 .20
197 Ed Spiezio .08 .20
198 Larry Stahl .08 .20
199 Jim Ray Hart .12 .30
200 Ron Hunt .08 .20
201 Hal Lanier .15 .40
202 Frank Linzy .08 .20
203 Juan Marichal .40 1.00
204 Willie Mays 1.00 2.50
205 Mike McCormick .12 .30
206 Willie McCovey .40 1.00
207 Gaylord Perry .30 .75
208 Nelson Briles .08 .20
209 Lou Brock .50 1.25
210 Curt Flood .20 .50
211 Bob Gibson .50 1.25
212 Julian Javier .08 .20
213 Dal Maxvill .08 .20
214 Tim McCarver .20 .50
215 Mike Shannon .12 .30
216 Joe Torre .20 .50

1970 MLB PhotoStamps

These unnumbered stamps are organized below alphabetically within teams; there are 24 teams each featuring 12 player stamps. This set is much tougher to find than the set produced the year before. They are essentially the same size at 1 7/8" by 2 15/16" and as with the prior set they are not gummed on the back. Stamps are unnumbered but are presented here in alphabetical order by team, Atlanta Braves (1-12), Chicago Cubs (13-24), Cincinnati Reds (25-36), Houston Astros (37-48), Los Angeles Dodgers (49-60), Montreal Expos (61-72), New York Mets (73-84), Philadelphia Phillies (85-96), Pittsburgh Pirates (97-108), San Diego Padres (109-120), San Francisco Giants (121-132), St. Louis Cardinals (133-144), Baltimore Orioles (145-156), Boston Red Sox (157-168), California Angels (169-180), Chicago White Sox (181-192), Cleveland Indians (193-204), Detroit Tigers (205-216), Kansas City Royals (217-228), Minnesota Twins (229-240), New York Yankees (241-252), Oakland A's (253-264), Seattle Pilots (265-276) and Washington Senators (277-288).

COMPLETE SET (288) 75.00 150.00
1 Hank Aaron 2.00 5.00
2 Bob Aspromonte .08 .20
3 Rico Carty .12 .30
4 Orlando Cepeda .20 .50
5 Bob Didier .08 .20
6 Tony Gonzales .08 .20
7 Pat Jarvis .08 .20
8 Felix Millan .08 .20
9 Jim Nash .08 .20
10 Phil Niekro .60 1.50
11 Milt Pappas .12 .30
12 Ron Reed .08 .20
13 Ernie Banks 1.00 2.50
14 Glenn Beckert .12 .30
15 Johnny Callison .12 .30
16 Bill Hands .08 .20
17 Randy Hundley .08 .20
18 Ken Holtzman .12 .30
19 Fergie Jenkins .60 1.50
20 Don Kessinger .12 .30
21 Phil Regan .08 .20
22 Ron Santo .20 .50
23 Dick Selma .08 .20
24 Billy Williams .60 1.50
25 Johnny Bench 1.00 2.50
26 Tony Cloninger .08 .20
27 Wayne Granger .08 .20
28 Tommy Helms .08 .20
29 Jim Maloney .12 .30
30 Lee May .12 .30
31 Jim McGlothlin .08 .20
32 Jim Merritt .08 .20
33 Gary Nolan .08 .20
34 Tony Perez .60 1.50
35 Pete Rose 1.50 4.00
36 Bobby Tolan .08 .20
37 Jesus Alou .08 .20
38 Tommy Davis .12 .30
39 Larry Dierker .08 .20
40 Johnny Edwards .08 .20
41 Fred Gladding .08 .20
42 Denver Lemaster .08 .20
43 Denis Menke .08 .20
44 Joe Morgan .60 1.50
45 Joe Pepitone .12 .30
46 Doug Rader .08 .20
47 Don Wilson .08 .20
48 Jim Wynn .12 .30
49 Willie Davis .12 .30
50 Len Gabrielson .08 .20
51 Tom Haller .08 .20
52 Jim LeFebvre .08 .20
53 Manny Mota .12 .30
54 Claude Osteen .12 .30
55 Wes Parker .12 .30
56 Bill Russell .20 .50
57 Bill Singer .08 .20
58 Ted Sizemore .08 .20
59 Don Sutton .60 1.50
60 Maury Wills .20 .50
61 Johnny Bateman .08 .20
62 Bob Bailey .08 .20
63 Ron Brand .08 .20
64 Ty Cline .08 .20
65 Ron Fairly .12 .30
66 Mack Jones .08 .20
67 Jose Laboy .08 .20
68 Claude Raymond .08 .20
69 Joe Sparma .08 .20
70 Rusty Staub .20 .50
71 Bill Stoneman .08 .20
72 Bobby Wine .08 .20
73 Tommy Agee .12 .30
74 Donn Clendenon .08 .20
75 Joe Foy .08 .20
76 Jerry Grote .12 .30
77 Bud Harrelson .12 .30
78 Cleon Jones .12 .30
79 Jerry Koosman .15 .40
80 Ed Kranepool .12 .30
81 Nolan Ryan 6.00 15.00
82 Tom Seaver 1.25 3.00
83 Ron Swoboda .12 .30
84 Al Weis .08 .20
85 Johnny Briggs .08 .20
86 Jim Bunning .60 1.50
87 Curt Flood .20 .50
88 Woody Fryman .08 .20
89 Larry Hisle .12 .30
90 Joe Hoerner .08 .20
91 Grant Jackson .08 .20
92 Tim McCarver .20 .50
93 Mike Ryan .08 .20
94 Chris Short .08 .20
95 Tony Taylor .08 .20
96 Rick Wise .12 .30
97 Gene Alley .08 .20
98 Matty Alou .12 .30
99 Roberto Clemente 4.00 10.00
100 Ron Davis .08 .20
101 Richie Hebner .08 .20
102 Jerry May .08 .20
103 Bill Mazeroski .30 .75
104 Bob Moose .08 .20
105 Al Oliver .20 .50
106 Manny Sanguillen .08 .20
107 Willie Stargell .75 2.00
108 Bob Veale .08 .20
109 Ollie Brown .08 .20
110 Dave Campbell .15 .40
111 Nate Colbert .08 .20
112 Pat Dobson .12 .30
113 Al Ferrara .08 .20
114 Dick Kelley .08 .20
115 Clay Kirby .08 .20
116 Bill McCool .08 .20
117 Frank Reberger .08 .20
118 Tommie Sisk .08 .20
119 Ed Spiezio .08 .20
120 Larry Stahl .08 .20
121 Bobby Bonds .20 .50
122 Jim Davenport .12 .30
123 Dick Dietz .08 .20
124 Jim Ray Hart .12 .30
125 Ron Hunt .08 .20
126 Hal Lanier .15 .40
127 Frank Linzy .08 .20
128 Juan Marichal .60 1.50
129 Willie Mays 3.00 8.00
130 Mike McCormick .12 .30
131 Willie McCovey .60 1.50
132 Gaylord Perry .60 1.50
133 Richie Allen .20 .50
134 Nelson Briles .08 .20
135 Lou Brock .75 2.00
136 Jose Cardenal .08 .20
137 Steve Carlton 1.00 2.50
138 Vic Davalillo .08 .20
139 Bob Gibson .75 2.00
140 Julian Javier .08 .20
141 Dal Maxvill .08 .20
142 Cookie Rojas .12 .30
143 Mike Shannon .15 .40
144 Joe Torre .20 .50
145 Mark Belanger .12 .30
146 Paul Blair .12 .30
147 Don Buford .08 .20
148 Mike Cuellar .12 .30
149 Andy Etchebarren .08 .20
150 Dave Johnson .15 .40
151 Dave McNally .12 .30
152 Tom Phoebus .08 .20
153 Boog Powell .20 .50
154 Brooks Robinson 1.00 2.50
155 Frank Robinson 1.00 2.50
156 Chico Salmon .08 .20
157 Mike Andrews .08 .20
158 Ray Culp .08 .20
159 Jim Lonborg .12 .30
160 Sparky Lyle .20 .50
161 Gary Peters .08 .20
162 Rico Petrocelli .15 .40
163 Vicente Romo .08 .20
164 Tom Satriano .08 .20
165 George Scott .12 .30
166 Sonny Siebert .08 .20
167 Reggie Smith .15 .40
168 Carl Yastrzemski 1.00 2.50
169 Sandy Alomar .12 .30
170 Jose Azcue .08 .20
171 Tom Egan .08 .20
172 Jim Fregosi .15 .40
173 Alex Johnson .12 .30
174 Jay Johnstone .12 .30
175 Rudy May .08 .20
176 Andy Messersmith .12 .30
177 Rick Reichardt .08 .20
178 Roger Repoz .08 .20
179 Aurelio Rodriguez .08 .20
180 Ken Tatum .08 .20
181 Luis Aparicio .60 1.50
182 Ken Berry .08 .20
183 Buddy Bradford .08 .20
184 Ron Hansen .08 .20
185 Joe Horlen .08 .20
186 Tommy John .40 1.00
187 Duane Josephson .08 .20
188 Bobby Knoop .08 .20
189 Tom McCraw .08 .20
190 Bill Melton .08 .20
191 Walt Williams .08 .20
192 Wilbur Wood .12 .30
193 Max Alvis .08 .20
194 Larry Brown .08 .20
195 Dean Chance .08 .20
196 Dick Ellsworth .12 .30
197 Vern Fuller .08 .20
198 Ken Harrelson .20 .50
199 Chuck Hinton .08 .20
200 Tony Horton .12 .30
201 Sam McDowell .15 .40
202 Vada Pinson .20 .50
203 Duke Sims .08 .20
204 Ted Uhlaender .08 .20
205 Norm Cash .15 .40
206 Bill Freehan .15 .40
207 Willie Horton .15 .40
208 Al Kaline .75 2.00
209 Mike Kilkenny .08 .20
210 Mickey Lolich .20 .50
211 Dick McAuliffe .12 .30
212 Denny McLain .20 .50
213 Jim Northrup .12 .30
214 Mickey Stanley .12 .30
215 Tom Tresh .12 .30
216 Earl Wilson .08 .20
217 Jerry Adair .08 .20
218 Wally Bunker .08 .20
219 Bill Butler .08 .20
220 Moe Drabowsky .08 .20
221 Jackie Hernandez .08 .20
222 Pat Kelly .08 .20
223 Ed Kirkpatrick .08 .20
224 Dave Morehead .08 .20
225 Roger Nelson .08 .20
226 Bob Oliver .08 .20
227 Lou Piniella .20 .50
228 Paul Schaal .08 .20
229 Bob Allison .12 .30
230 Dave Boswell .08 .20
231 Leo Cardenas .08 .20
232 Rod Carew 1.00 2.50
233 Jim Kaat .40 1.00
234 Harmon Killebrew .75 2.00
235 Tony Oliva .20 .50
236 Jim Perry .12 .30
237 Ron Perranoski .12 .30
238 Rich Reese .08 .20
239 Luis Tiant .20 .50
240 Cesar Tovar .12 .30
241 Jack Aker .08 .20
242 Curt Blefary .08 .20
243 Danny Cater .08 .20
244 Horace Clarke .08 .20
245 Jake Gibbs .08 .20
246 Steve Hamilton .08 .20
247 Bobby Murcer .20 .50
248 Fritz Peterson .08 .20
249 Bill Robinson .08 .20
250 Mel Stottlemyre .15 .40
251 Pete Ward .08 .20
252 Roy White .12 .30
253 Felipe Alou .15 .40
254 Sal Bando .15 .40
255 Bert Campaneris .12 .30
256 Chuck Dobson .08 .20
257 Tito Francona .08 .20
258 Dick Green .08 .20
259 Jim Hunter .60 1.50
260 Reggie Jackson 2.00 5.00
261 Don Mincher .08 .20
262 Rick Monday .12 .30
263 John Odom .08 .20
264 Ray Oyler .08 .20
265 Steve Barber .08 .20
266 Bobby Bolin .08 .20
267 George Brunet .08 .20
268 Wayne Comer .08 .20
269 John Donaldson .08 .20
270 Tommy Harper .12 .30
271 Mike Hegan .08 .20
272 Mike Hershberger .08 .20
273 Steve Hovley .08 .20
274 Bob Locker .08 .20
275 Gerry McNertney .08 .20
276 Rich Rollins .08 .20
277 Bernie Allen .08 .20
278 Dick Bosman .08 .20
279 Ed Brinkman .08 .20
280 Paul Casanova .08 .20
281 Joe Coleman .08 .20
282 Mike Epstein .08 .20
283 Frank Howard .20 .50
284 Ken McMullen .08 .20
285 John Roseboro .12 .30
286 Ed Stroud .08 .20
287 Del Unser .08 .20
288 Zoilo Versalles .12 .30

2000 MLB Showdown Promos

COMPLETE SET (35) 15.00 40.00
1 Bob Abreu .60 1.50
2 Sandy Alomar Jr. .60 1.50
3 Jeff Bagwell 1.00 2.50
4 Michael Barrett .60 1.50
5 Ron Belliard .60 1.50
6 Craig Biggio 1.00 2.50
7 Sean Casey .60 1.50
8 Luis Castillo .60 1.50
9 Carlos Delgado .60 1.50
10 J.D. Drew .60 1.50
11 Erubiel Durazo .60 1.50
12 Ray Durham .60 1.50
13 Damion Easley .60 1.50
14 Carlos Febles .60 1.50
15 Troy Glaus .60 1.50
16 Mark Grace 1.00 2.50
17 Rusty Greer .60 1.50
18 Ben Grieve .60 1.50
19 Tony Gwynn 1.50 4.00
20 Todd Helton 1.00 2.50
21 Andruw Jones .60 1.50
22 Andruw Jones OB8 .60 1.50
23 Andruw Jones OB10 .60 1.50
24 Chipper Jones 1.50 4.00
25 Jeff Kent .60 1.50
26 Corey Koskie .60 1.50
27 Edgar Martinez 1.00 2.50
28 Fred McGriff 1.00 2.50
29 Warren Morris .60 1.50
30 Rafael Palmeiro 1.00 2.50
31 Gary Sheffield .60 1.50
32 B.J. Surhoff .60 1.50
33 Jason Varitek 1.50 4.00
34 Robin Ventura .60 1.50
35 Bernie Williams 1.00 2.50

2000 MLB Showdown Diamond Star Promos

COMPLETE SET (19) 10.00 25.00
1 Sandy Alomar .60 1.50
2 Jeff Bagwell 1.00 2.50
3 Craig Biggio 1.00 2.50
4 Carlos Delgado .60 1.50
5 Ray Durham .60 1.50
6 Damion Easley .60 1.50
7 Mark Grace 1.00 2.50
8 Rusty Greer .60 1.50
9 Tony Gwynn 1.50 4.00
10 Chipper Jones 1.50 4.00
11 Jeff Kent .60 1.50
12 Edgar Martinez 1.00 2.50
13 Fred McGriff 1.00 2.50
14 Rafael Palmeiro 1.00 2.50
15 Gary Sheffield .60 1.50
16 B.J. Surhoff .60 1.50
17 Jason Varitek 1.50 4.00
18 Robin Ventura .60 1.50
19 Bernie Williams 1.00 2.50

2000 MLB Showdown Future Star Promos

COMPLETE SET (13) 5.00 12.00
1 Bob Abreu .60 1.50
2 Michael Barrett .60 1.50
3 Ron Belliard .60 1.50
4 Sean Casey .60 1.50
5 Luis Castillo .60 1.50
6 J.D. Drew .60 1.50
7 Erubiel Durazo .60 1.50
8 Carlos Febles .60 1.50
9 Troy Glaus .60 1.50
10 Ben Grieve .60 1.50
11 Todd Helton 1.00 2.50
12 Corey Koskie .60 1.50
13 Warren Morris .60 1.50

2000 MLB Showdown Home Run Hitter Promos

COMPLETE SET (14) 15.00 40.00
1 Barry Bonds 2.50 6.00
2 Jose Canseco 1.00 2.50
3 Nomar Garciaparra 1.00 2.50
4 Jason Giambi .60 1.50
5 Shawn Green .60 1.50
6 Ken Griffey Jr. 3.00 8.00
7 Andruw Jones .60 1.50
8 Chipper Jones 1.50 4.00
9 Mark McGwire 2.50 6.00
10 Rafael Palmeiro 1.00 2.50
11 Mike Piazza 1.50 4.00
12 Manny Ramirez 1.50 4.00
13 Alex Rodriguez 2.00 5.00
14 Sammy Sosa 1.50 4.00

2000 MLB Showdown 1st Edition

COMPLETE SET (462) 60.00 120.00
COMP.SET w/o FOIL (400) 30.00 60.00
COMMON CARD (1-462) .20 .50
COMMON FOIL 1.00 2.50
FOIL STATED ODDS 1:3
CONE/MADDUX IN EVERY STARTER DECK
1 Garret Anderson .20 .50
2 Tim Belcher .20 .50
3 Gary DiSarcina UER .20 .50
4 Darin Erstad .20 .50
5 Chuck Finley FOIL 1.00 2.50
6 Troy Glaus .20 .50
7 Todd Greene .20 .50
8 Jeff Huson .20 .50
9 Orlando Palmeiro .20 .50
10 Troy Percival .20 .50
11 Mark Petkovsek .20 .50
12 Tim Salmon .20 .50
13 Steve Sparks .20 .50
14 Mo Vaughn .20 .50
15 Matt Walbeck .20 .50
16 Jay Bell FOIL 1.00 2.50
17 Andy Benes .20 .50
18 Omar Daal .20 .50
19 Steve Finley .20 .50
20 Andy Fox .20 .50
21 Hanley Frias .20 .50
22 Bernard Gilkey .20 .50
23 Luis Gonzalez FOIL 1.00 2.50
24 Randy Johnson FOIL 2.50 6.00
25 Travis Lee .20 .50
26 Matt Mantei .20 .50
27 Dan Plesac .20 .50
28 Kelly Stinnett .20 .50
29 Greg Swindell .20 .50
30 Matt Williams FOIL 1.00 2.50
31 Tony Womack .20 .50
32 Bret Boone .20 .50
33 Tom Glavine .30 .75
34 Jose Hernandez .20 .50
35 Brian Hunter .20 .50
36 Andruw Jones .20 .50
37 Chipper Jones FOIL 2.50 6.00
38 Brian Jordan .20 .50
39 Ryan Klesko .20 .50
40 Keith Lockhart .20 .50
41 Greg Maddux FOIL * 3.00 8.00
42 Kevin Millwood FOIL 1.00 2.50
43 Eddie Perez .20 .50
44 Mike Remlinger .20 .50
45 John Rocker .20 .50
46 John Smoltz .50 1.25
47 Walt Weiss .20 .50
48 Gerald Williams .20 .50
49 Rich Amaral .20 .50
50 Brady Anderson .20 .50
51 Albert Belle .20 .50
52 Mike Bordick .20 .50
53 Jeff Conine .20 .50
54 Delino DeShields .20 .50
55 Scott Erickson .20 .50
56 Charles Johnson .20 .50
57 Mike Mussina .30 .75
58 Jesse Orosco .20 .50
59 Sidney Ponson .20 .50
60 Jeff Reboulet .20 .50
61 Cal Ripken FOIL 8.00 20.00
62 B.J. Surhoff .20 .50
63 Mike Timlin .20 .50
64 Rod Beck .20 .50
65 Damon Buford .20 .50
66 Rheal Cormier .20 .50
67 Nomar Garciaparra FOIL 1.50 4.00
68 Butch Huskey .20 .50
69 Darren Lewis .20 .50
70 Derek Lowe .20 .50
71 Pedro Martinez FOIL 1.50 4.00
72 Trot Nixon .20 .50
73 Jose Offerman .20 .50
74 Troy O'Leary .20 .50
75 Mark Portugal .20 .50
76 Pat Rapp .20 .50
77 Mike Stanley .20 .50
78 John Valentin .20 .50
79 Jason Varitek .50 1.25
80 Tim Wakefield .30 .75
81 Rick Aguilera .20 .50
82 Jeff Blauser .20 .50
83 Kyle Farnsworth .20 .50
84 Gary Gaetti .20 .50
85 Mark Grace .30 .75
86 Lance Johnson .20 .50
87 Jon Lieber .20 .50
88 Mickey Morandini .20 .50
89 Jose Nieves .20 .50
90 Jeff Reed .20 .50
91 Henry Rodriguez .20 .50
92 Scott Sanders .20 .50
93 Benito Santiago .20 .50
94 Sammy Sosa FOIL 2.50 6.00
95 Steve Trachsel .20 .50
96 James Baldwin .20 .50
97 Mike Caruso .20 .50
98 Ray Durham .20 .50
99 Brook Fordyce .20 .50
100 Bob Howry .20 .50
101 Paul Konerko .20 .50
102 Carlos Lee .20 .50
103 Greg Norton .20 .50
104 Magglio Ordonez .30 .75
105 Jim Parque .20 .50
106 Bill Simas .20 .50
107 Chris Singleton .20 .50
108 Mike Sirotka .20 .50
109 Frank Thomas FOIL 2.50 6.00
110 Craig Wilson .20 .50
111 Aaron Boone .20 .50
112 Mike Cameron .20 .50
113 Sean Casey FOIL 1.00 2.50
114 Danny Graves .20 .50
115 Pete Harnisch .20 .50
116 Barry Larkin FOIL 1.50 4.00
117 Pokey Reese .20 .50
118 Scott Sullivan .20 .50
119 Eddie Taubensee .20 .50
120 Brett Tomko .20 .50
121 Michael Tucker .20 .50
122 Greg Vaughn .20 .50
123 Ron Villone .20 .50
124 Scott Williamson FOIL 1.00 2.50
125 Dmitri Young .20 .50
126 Roberto Alomar FOIL 1.50 4.00
127 Harold Baines .30 .75
128 Dave Burba .20 .50
129 Bartolo Colon .20 .50
130 Einar Diaz .20 .50
131 Travis Fryman .20 .50
132 Mike Jackson .20 .50
133 David Justice .20 .50
134 Kenny Lofton FOIL 1.00 2.50
135 Charles Nagy .20 .50
136 Manny Ramirez FOIL 2.50 6.00
137 Richie Sexson .20 .50
138 Paul Shuey .20 .50
139 Jim Thome FOIL 1.50 4.00
140 Omar Vizquel .30 .75
141 Enrique Wilson .20 .50
142 Kurt Abbott .20 .50
143 Pedro Astacio .20 .50
144 Jeff Barry .20 .50
145 Dante Bichette .20 .50
146 Henry Blanco .20 .50
147 Brian Bohanon .20 .50
148 Vinny Castilla .20 .50
149 Jerry Dipoto .20 .50
150 Todd Helton .30 .75
151 Darryl Kile .20 .50
152 Curtis Leskanic .20 .50
153 Neifi Perez .20 .50
154 Terry Shumpert .20 .50
155 Dave Veres .20 .50
156 Larry Walker FOIL 1.50 4.00
157 Brad Ausmus .20 .50
158 Frank Catalanotto .20 .50
159 Tony Clark .20 .50
160 Deivi Cruz .20 .50
161 Damion Easley .20 .50
162 Juan Encarnacion .20 .50
163 Karim Garcia .20 .50
164 Bobby Higginson .20 .50
165 Todd Jones .20 .50
166 Gabe Kapler .20 .50
167 Dave Mlicki .20 .50
168 Brian Moehler .20 .50
169 C.J. Nitkowski .20 .50
170 Dean Palmer FOIL 1.00 2.50
171 Jeff Weaver .20 .50
172 Antonio Alfonseca .20 .50
173 Bruce Aven .20 .50
174 Dave Berg .20 .50
175 Luis Castillo FOIL 1.00 2.50
176 Ryan Dempster .20 .50
177 Brian Edmondson .20 .50
178 Alex Gonzalez .20 .50
179 Mark Kotsay .20 .50
180 Derrek Lee .20 .50
181 Braden Looper .20 .50
182 Mike Lowell .20 .50
183 Brian Meadows .20 .50
184 Mike Redmond .20 .50
185 Dennis Springer .20 .50
186 Preston Wilson .20 .50
187 Jeff Bagwell FOIL 1.50 4.00
188 Derek Bell .20 .50
189 Craig Biggio .30 .75
190 Tim Bogar .20 .50
191 Ken Caminiti .20 .50
192 Scott Elarton .20 .50
193 Tony Eusebio .20 .50
194 Carl Everett FOIL 1.00 2.50
195 Mike Hampton FOIL 1.00 2.50
196 Richard Hidalgo .20 .50
197 Stan Javier .20 .50
198 Jose Lima .20 .50
199 Jay Powell .20 .50
200 Shane Reynolds .20 .50
201 Bill Spiers .20 .50
202 Billy Wagner FOIL 1.00 2.50
203 Carlos Beltran FOIL 1.50 4.00
204 Johnny Damon .30 .75
205 Jermaine Dye .20 .50
206 Carlos Febles .20 .50
207 Jeremy Giambi .20 .50
208 Chad Kreuter .20 .50
209 Jeff Montgomery .20 .50
210 Joe Randa .20 .50
211 Jose Rosado .20 .50
212 Rey Sanchez .20 .50
213 Scott Service .20 .50
214 Tim Spehr .20 .50
215 Jeff Suppan .20 .50
216 Mike Sweeney .20 .50
217 Jay Witasick .20 .50
218 Adrian Beltre .50 1.25
219 Pedro Borbon .20 .50
220 Kevin Brown FOIL 1.00 2.50
221 Mark Grudzielanek .20 .50
222 Dave Hansen .20 .50
223 Todd Hundley .20 .50
224 Eric Karros .20 .50
225 Raul Mondesi .20 .50
226 Chan Ho Park .30 .75
227 Jeff Shaw .20 .50
228 Gary Sheffield FOIL 1.00 2.50
229 Ismael Valdes .20 .50
230 Jose Vizcaino .20 .50
231 Devon White .20 .50
232 Eric Young .20 .50
233 Ron Belliard .20 .50
234 Sean Berry .20 .50
235 Jeromy Burnitz FOIL 1.00 2.50
236 Jeff Cirillo .20 .50
237 Marquis Grissom .20 .50
238 Geoff Jenkins .20 .50
239 Scott Karl .20 .50
240 Mark Loretta .20 .50
241 Mike Myers .20 .50
242 David Nilsson FOIL 1.00 2.50
243 Hideo Nomo .50 1.25
244 Alex Ochoa .20 .50
245 Jose Valentin .20 .50
246 Bob Wickman .20 .50
247 Steve Woodard .20 .50
248 Chad Allen .20 .50
249 Ron Coomer .20 .50
250 Cristian Guzman .20 .50
251 Denny Hocking .20 .50
252 Torii Hunter .20 .50
253 Corey Koskie .20 .50
254 Matt Lawton .20 .50
255 Joe Mays .20 .50
256 Doug Mientkiewicz .20 .50
257 Eric Milton .20 .50
258 Brad Radke FOIL 1.00 2.50
259 Terry Steinbach .20 .50
260 Mike Trombley .20 .50
261 Todd Walker .20 .50
262 Bob Wells .20 .50
263 Shane Andrews .20 .50
264 Michael Barrett .20 .50
265 Orlando Cabrera .20 .50
266 Brad Fullmer .20 .50
267 Vladimir Guerrero FOIL 1.50 4.00
268 Wilton Guerrero .20 .50
269 Dustin Hermanson .20 .50
270 Steve Kline .20 .50
271 Manny Martinez .20 .50
272 Mike Thurman .20 .50
273 Ugueth Urbina .20 .50
274 Javier Vazquez .20 .50
275 Jose Vidro .20 .50
276 Rondell White .20 .50
277 Chris Widger .20 .50
278 Edgardo Alfonzo FOIL 1.00 2.50
279 Armando Benitez .30 .75
280 Roger Cedeno .20 .50
281 Dennis Cook .20 .50
282 Shawon Dunston .20 .50
283 Matt Franco .20 .50
284 Darryl Hamilton .20 .50
285 Rickey Henderson FOIL 2.50 6.00
286 Orel Hershiser .20 .50
287 Al Leiter .20 .50
288 John Olerud .20 .50
289 Rey Ordonez .20 .50
290 Mike Piazza FOIL 2.50 6.00
291 Kenny Rogers .20 .50
292 Robin Ventura .20 .50
293 Turk Wendell .20 .50
294 Masato Yoshii .20 .50
295 Scott Brosius .20 .50
296 Roger Clemens FOIL 3.00 8.00
297 David Cone FOIL * 1.00 2.50
298 Chad Curtis .20 .50
299 Chili Davis .20 .50
300 Orlando Hernandez .20 .50
301 Derek Jeter FOIL 6.00 15.00
302 Chuck Knoblauch .20 .50
303 Ricky Ledee .20 .50
304 Tino Martinez .20 .50
305 Ramiro Mendoza .20 .50
306 Paul O'Neill .30 .75
307 Andy Pettitte .30 .75
308 Jorge Posada .30 .75
309 Mariano Rivera FOIL 3.00 8.00
310 Mike Stanton .20 .50
311 Bernie Williams FOIL 1.50 4.00
312 Kevin Appier .20 .50

313 Eric Chavez .20 .50
314 Ryan Christenson .20 .50
315 Jason Giambi FOIL 1.00 2.50
316 Ben Grieve .20 .50
317 Buddy Groom .20 .50
318 Gil Heredia .20 .50
319 A.J. Hinch .20 .50
320 John Jaha .20 .50
321 Doug Jones .20 .50
322 Omar Olivares .20 .50
323 Tony Phillips .20 .50
324 Matt Stairs .20 .50
325 Miguel Tejada .30 .75
326 Randy Velarde FOIL 1.00 2.50
327 Bobby Abreu FOIL 1.00 2.50
328 Marlon Anderson .20 .50
329 Alex Arias .20 .50
330 Rico Brogna .20 .50
331 Paul Byrd .20 .50
332 Ron Gant .20 .50
333 Doug Glanville .20 .50
334 Wayne Gomes .20 .50
335 Kevin Jordan .20 .50
336 Mike Lieberthal .20 .50
337 Steve Montgomery .20 .50
338 Chad Ogea .20 .50
339 Scott Rolen .30 .75
340 Curt Schilling FOIL 1.50 4.00
341 Kevin Sefcik .20 .50
342 Mike Benjamin .20 .50
343 Kris Benson .20 .50
344 Adrian Brown .20 .50
345 Brant Brown .20 .50
346 Brad Clontz .20 .50
347 Brian Giles FOIL 1.00 2.50
348 Jason Kendall FOIL 1.00 2.50
349 Al Martin .20 .50
350 Warren Morris .20 .50
351 Todd Ritchie .20 .50
352 Scott Sauerbeck .20 .50
353 Jason Schmidt .20 .50
354 Ed Sprague .20 .50
355 Mike Williams .20 .50
356 Kevin Young .20 .50
357 Andy Ashby .20 .50
358 Ben Davis .20 .50
359 Tony Gwynn FOIL 2.50 6.00
360 Sterling Hitchcock .20 .50
361 Trevor Hoffman FOIL 1.50 4.00
362 Damian Jackson .20 .50
363 Wally Joyner .20 .50
364 Phil Nevin .20 .50
365 Eric Owens .20 .50
366 Ruben Rivera .20 .50
367 Reggie Sanders .20 .50
368 John Vander Wal .20 .50
369 Quilvio Veras .20 .50
370 Matt Whisenant .20 .50
371 Woody Williams .20 .50
372 Rich Aurilia .20 .50
373 Marvin Benard .20 .50
374 Barry Bonds FOIL 4.00 10.00
375 Ellis Burks .20 .50
376 Alan Embree .20 .50
377 Shawn Estes .20 .50
378 John Johnstone .20 .50
379 Jeff Kent .20 .50
380 Brent Mayne .20 .50
381 Bill Mueller .20 .50
382 Robb Nen .20 .50
383 Russ Ortiz .20 .50
384 Kirk Rueter .20 .50
385 F.P. Santangelo .20 .50
386 J.T. Snow .20 .50
387 David Bell .20 .50
388 Jay Buhner .20 .50
389 Russ Davis .20 .50
390 Freddy Garcia .20 .50
391 Ken Griffey Jr. FOIL 5.00 12.00
392 John Halama .20 .50
393 Brian Hunter .20 .50
394 Raul Ibanez .30 .75
395 Tom Lampkin .20 .50
396 Edgar Martinez FOIL 1.50 4.00
397 Jose Mesa .20 .50
398 Jamie Moyer .20 .50
399 Jose Paniagua .20 .50
400 Alex Rodriguez FOIL 3.00 8.00
401 Dan Wilson .20 .50
402 Manny Aybar .20 .50
403 Ricky Bottalico .20 .50
404 Kent Bottenfield .20 .50
405 Darren Bragg .20 .50
406 Alberto Castillo .20 .50
407 J.D. Drew .20 .50
408 Jose Jimenez .20 .50
409 Ray Lankford .20 .50
410 Joe McEwing .20 .50
411 Willie McGee .20 .50
412 Mark McGwire FOIL 4.00 10.00
413 Darren Oliver .20 .50
414 Lance Painter .20 .50
415 Edgar Renteria .20 .50
416 Fernando Tatis FOIL 1.00 2.50
417 Wilson Alvarez .20 .50
418 Rolando Arrojo .20 .50
419 Wade Boggs .30 .75
420 Miguel Cairo .20 .50
421 Jose Canseco FOIL 1.50 4.00
422 John Flaherty .20 .50
423 Roberto Hernandez .20 .50
424 Dave Martinez .20 .50
425 Fred McGriff .30 .75
426 Paul Sorrento .20 .50
427 Kevin Stocker .20 .50
428 Bubba Trammell .20 .50
429 Rick White .20 .50
430 Randy Winn .20 .50
431 Bobby Witt .20 .50
432 Royce Clayton .20 .50
433 Tim Crabtree .20 .50
434 Juan Gonzalez .20 .50
435 Tom Goodwin .20 .50
436 Rusty Greer .20 .50
437 Rick Helling .20 .50
438 Mark McLemore .20 .50
439 Mike Morgan .20 .50
440 Rafael Palmeiro FOIL 1.50 4.00
441 Ivan Rodriguez FOIL 1.50 4.00
442 Aaron Sele .20 .50
443 Lee Stevens .20 .50
444 Mike Venafro .20 .50
445 John Wetteland .20 .50
446 Todd Zeile .20 .50
447 Jeff Zimmerman FOIL 1.00 2.50
448 Tony Batista .20 .50
449 Homer Bush .20 .50
450 Jose Cruz Jr. .20 .50
451 Carlos Delgado .20 .50
452 Kelvim Escobar .20 .50
453 Tony Fernandez FOIL 1.00 2.50
454 Darrin Fletcher .20 .50
455 Shawn Green FOIL 1.00 2.50
456 Pat Hentgen .20 .50
457 Billy Koch .20 .50
458 Graeme Lloyd .20 .50
459 Brian McRae .20 .50
460 David Segui .20 .50
461 Shannon Stewart .20 .50
462 David Wells .20 .50

2000 MLB Showdown Unlimited

COMPLETE SET (462) 100.00 200.00
COMP.SET w/o FOIL (400) 25.00 50.00
*UNLIMITED: .25X TO .6X 1ST EDITION
*UNL.FOIL: .2X TO .5X BASIC FOIL
FOIL STATED ODDS 1:3
DISTRIBUTED ONLY IN STARTER SETS
UNLIMITED CARDS LACK EDITION LOGO

2000 MLB Showdown Strategy

COMPLETE SET (55) 12.50 30.00
FORTY STRATEGY PER STARTER SET
TWO STRATEGY PER PACK
S1 Umpire .20 .50
Bad Call
S2 M.Stanley .20 .50
Big Inning
S3 T.Phillips .20 .50
Bobbled in Outfield
S4 M.Ramirez .50 1.25
Clutch Hitting
S5 C.Knoblauch .20 .50
Do or Die
S6 Dodgers OF .20 .50
Down Middle
S7 C.Everett .20 .50
Ducks on Pond
S8 B.Bonds .75 2.00
Favorable Matchup
S9 D.Cruz .20 .50
Free Steal
S10 J.Offerman .20 .50
Get Under It
S11 R.Henderson .50 1.25
Great Lead
S12 D.Jackson .20 .50
Hard Slide
S13 D.Jeter 1.25 3.00
High Fives
S14 P.O'Neill .30 .75
Last Chance
S15 D.Jeter 1.25 3.00
Long Single
S16 Rangers Pitcher .20 .50
Out of Gas
S17 R.Henderson .50 1.25
Out of Position
S18 C.Jones .50 1.25
Percentages
S19 O.Vizquel .30 .75
Rally Cap
S20 M.Henneman .20 .50
Rattled
S21 M.Tejada .30 .75
Runner Not Held
S22 Rockies Pitcher .20 .50
Slow Roller
S23 Braves Pitcher .20 .50
Stick a Fork
S24 S.Sosa .50 1.25
Swing for Fences
S25 B.Williams .30 .75
Warning Track
S26 M.McGwire .75 2.00
Whiplash
S27 W.Clark .30 .75
Wide Throw
S28 E.Taubensee .20 .50
Wild Pitch
S29 W.Weiss .20 .50
By the Book
S30 B.Wagner .20 .50
Dominating
S31 O.Hernandez .20 .50
Full Windup
S32 Ordonez .20 .50
Klesko Fielding
S33 J.Kendall .20 .50
Gun 'Em Down!
S34 S.Sosa .50 1.25
He's Got a Gun
S35 D.Cone .20 .50
In the Groove
S36 P.Martinez .30 .75
In the Zone
S37 S.F. Giants .20 .50
Infield In
S38 R.Johnson .50 1.25
Intimidation
S39 K.Griffey Jr. 1.00 2.50
Just Over Wall
S40 Padres Pitcher .20 .50
Knock Down
S41 J.Orosco .20 .50
Lefty Specialist
S42 M.Rivera .60 1.50
Nerves of Steel
S43 R.Johnson .50 1.25
Nothing but Heat
S44 B.Hughes .20 .50
Pitchout
S45 J.Rocker .20 .50
Pumped Up
S46 G.Maddux .60 1.50
Quick Pitch
S47 Baerga-Klesko .20 .50
Rally Killer
S48 C.Knoblauch .20 .50
Short Fly
S49 P.Martinez .30 .75
Three Up-Down
S50 D.Jeter 1.25 3.00
Trick Pitch
S51 S.Sosa .50 1.25
Belt-High
S52 J.Torre .30 .75
Change in Strategy
S53 P.Reese .20 .50
Grounder to 2nd
S54 M.Grace .30 .75
Stealing Signals
S55 C.Ripken 1.50 4.00
Swing at Anything

2001 MLB Showdown Ace Pitcher Promo

COMPLETE SET (20) 8.00 20.00
1 Kris Benson .30 .75
2 Kevin Brown .30 .75
3 Roger Clemens 2.00 5.00
4 Bartolo Colon .60 1.50
5 Jeff D'Amico .20 .50
6 Ryan Dempster .30 .75
7 Adam Eaton .20 .50
8 Scott Elarton .20 .50
9 Livan Hernandez .40 1.00
10 Tim Hudson .60 1.50
11 Randy Johnson 1.00 2.50
12 Darryl Kile .20 .50
13 Al Leiter .40 1.00
14 Jon Lieber .30 .75
15 Greg Maddux 2.00 5.00
16 Pedro Martinez 1.20 3.00
17 Brad Radke .30 .75
18 Javier Vazquez .30 .75
19 Jeff Weaver .30 .75
20 David Wells .40 1.00

2001 MLB Showdown Diamond Star Promos

COMPLETE SET (20) 12.00 30.00
1 Roberto Alomar .60 1.50
2 Carlos Delgado .75 2.00
3 Jason Giambi .30 .75
4 Troy Glaus .80 2.50
5 Luis Gonzalez .60 1.50
6 Tony Gwynn 2.00 5.00
7 Todd Helton 1.00 2.50
8 Richard Hidalgo .20 .50
9 Bobby Higginson .20 .50
10 Andruw Jones .75 2.00
11 David Justice .40 1.00
12 Jeff Kent .60 1.50
13 Ivan Rodriguez 1.00 2.50
14 Gary Sheffield 1.00 2.50
15 Mike Sweeney .60 1.50
16 Miguel Tejada .60 2.50
17 Frank Thomas .75 2.00
18 Greg Vaughn .30 .75
19 Robin Ventura .30 .75
20 Rondell White .30 .75

2001 MLB Showdown Future Star Promos

COMPLETE SET (13) 4.00 10.00
1 Peter Bergeron .20 .50
2 Pat Burrell .60 1.50
3 Mike Cameron .40 1.00
4 Sean Casey .40 1.00
5 J.D. Drew .60 1.50
6 Corey Koskie .30 .75
7 Melvin Mora .40 1.00
8 Trot Nixon .60 1.50
9 Eric Owens .20 .50
10 Jay Payton .30 .75
11 Aramis Ramirez .60 1.50
12 Richie Sexson .40 1.00
13 Preston Wilson .30 .75

2001 MLB Showdown 1st Edition

COMPLETE SET (462) 250.00 400.00
COMP.SET w/o FOIL (400) 60.00 100.00
COMMON CARD (1-462) .08 .25
COMMON FOIL 1.25 3.00
STATED FOIL ODDS: 1:3
ERSTAD/VLADDIE IN EVERY STARTER DECK
1 Garret Anderson .30 .75
2 Darin Erstad FOIL * 1.25 3.00
3 Ron Gant .30 .75
4 Troy Glaus FOIL 1.25 3.00
5 Shigetoshi Hasegawa .30 .75
6 Adam Kennedy .08 .25
7 Al Levine RC .08 .25
8 Ben Molina .08 .25
9 Troy Percival .30 .75
10 Mark Petkovsek .08 .25
11 Tim Salmon .60 1.50
12 Scott Schoeneweis .08 .25
13 Scott Spiezio .08 .25
14 Mo Vaughn .30 .75
15 Jarrod Washburn .08 .25
16 Brian Anderson .08 .25
17 Danny Bautista .08 .25
18 Jay Bell .30 .75
19 Greg Colbrunn .08 .25
20 Steve Finley .30 .75
21 Luis Gonzalez 1.25 3.00
22 Randy Johnson FOIL 3.00 8.00
23 Byung-Hyun Kim .30 .75
24 Matt Mantei .08 .25
25 Mike Morgan .08 .25
26 Curt Schilling .30 .75
27 Kelly Stinnett .08 .25
28 Greg Swindell .08 .25
29 Matt Williams .30 .75
30 Tony Womack .08 .25
31 Andy Ashby .08 .25
32 Bobby Bonilla .30 .75
33 Rafael Furcal FOIL 1.25 3.00
34 Andres Galarraga .30 .75
35 Tom Glavine FOIL 2.00 5.00
36 Andruw Jones .60 1.50
37 Chipper Jones FOIL 3.00 8.00
38 Brian Jordan .30 .75
39 Wally Joyner .30 .75
40 Keith Lockhart .08 .25
41 Javy Lopez .30 .75
42 Greg Maddux FOIL 4.00 10.00
43 Kevin Millwood .30 .75
44 Mike Remlinger .08 .25
45 John Rocker .30 .75
46 B.J. Surhoff .30 .75
47 Quilvio Veras .08 .25
48 Brady Anderson .30 .75
49 Albert Belle .30 .75
50 Jeff Conine .30 .75
51 Delino DeShields .08 .25
52 Buddy Groom .08 .25
53 Trenidad Hubbard .08 .25
54 Luis Matos .08 .25
55 Jose Mercedes .08 .25
56 Melvin Mora .30 .75
57 Mike Mussina FOIL 2.00 5.00
58 Sidney Ponson .08 .25
59 Pat Rapp .08 .25
60 Chris Richard .08 .25
61 Cal Ripken FOIL 6.00 15.00
62 Mike Trombley .08 .25
63 Rolando Arrojo .08 .25
64 Dante Bichette .30 .75
65 Rheal Cormier .08 .25
66 Carl Everett .30 .75
67 Rich Garces .08 .25
68 Nomar Garciaparra FOIL 5.00 12.00
69 Mike Lansing .08 .25
70 Darren Lewis .08 .25
71 Derek Lowe .30 .75
72 Pedro Martinez FOIL 2.00 5.00
73 Ramon Martinez .08 .25
74 Trot Nixon .30 .75
75 Jose Offerman .08 .25
76 Troy O'Leary .08 .25
77 Jason Varitek 1.00 2.50
78 Rick Aguilera .08 .25
79 Damon Buford .08 .25
80 Joe Girardi .08 .25
81 Mark Grace .60 1.50
82 Willie Greene .08 .25
83 Ricky Gutierrez .08 .25
84 Felix Heredia .08 .25
85 Jon Lieber .08 .25
86 Jeff Reed .08 .25
87 Sammy Sosa FOIL 6.00 15.00
88 Kevin Tapani .08 .25
89 Todd Van Poppel .08 .25
90 Rondell White .30 .75
91 Kerry Wood .30 .75
92 Eric Young .08 .25
93 James Baldwin .08 .25
94 Ray Durham .30 .75
95 Keith Foulke FOIL 1.25 3.00
96 Bob Howry .08 .25
97 Charles Johnson FOIL 1.25 3.00
98 Mark Johnson .08 .25
99 Paul Konerko .30 .75
100 Carlos Lee .30 .75
101 Magglio Ordonez .30 .75
102 Jim Parque .08 .25
103 Herbert Perry .08 .25
104 Bill Simas .08 .25
105 Chris Singleton .08 .25
106 Mike Sirotka .08 .25
107 Frank Thomas FOIL 3.00 8.00
108 Jose Valentin .08 .25
109 Kelly Wunsch .08 .25
110 Aaron Boone .08 .25
111 Sean Casey .30 .75
112 Danny Graves .08 .25
113 Ken Griffey Jr. FOIL 6.00 15.00
114 Pete Harnisch .08 .25
115 Barry Larkin FOIL 2.00 5.00
116 Alex Ochoa .08 .25
117 Steve Parris .08 .25
118 Pokey Reese .08 .25
119 Chris Stynes .08 .25
120 Scott Sullivan .08 .25
121 Eddie Taubensee .08 .25
122 Michael Tucker .08 .25
123 Ron Villone .08 .25
124 Dmitri Young .30 .75
125 Roberto Alomar FOIL 2.00 5.00
126 Sandy Alomar Jr. .08 .25
127 Jason Bere .08 .25
128 Dave Burba .08 .25
129 Bartolo Colon .30 .75
130 Wil Cordero .08 .25
131 Chuck Finley .30 .75
132 Travis Fryman .30 .75
133 Steve Karsay .08 .25
134 Kenny Lofton .30 .75
135 Manny Ramirez FOIL 2.00 5.00
136 David Segui .08 .25
137 Jim Thome .60 1.50
138 Omar Vizquel .60 1.50
139 Bob Wickman .08 .25
140 Pedro Astacio .08 .25
141 Brian Bohanon .08 .25
142 Jeff Cirillo .08 .25
143 Jeff Frye .08 .25
144 Jeffrey Hammonds .08 .25
145 Todd Helton FOIL 2.00 5.00
146 Todd Hollandsworth .08 .25
147 Butch Huskey .08 .25
148 Jose Jimenez .08 .25
149 Brent Mayne .08 .25
150 Neifi Perez .08 .25
151 Terry Shumpert .08 .25
152 Larry Walker .30 .75
153 Gabe White FOIL 1.25 3.00
154 Masato Yoshii .08 .25
155 Matt Anderson .08 .25
156 Brad Ausmus .08 .25
157 Rich Becker .08 .25
158 Tony Clark .08 .25
159 Deivi Cruz .08 .25
160 Damion Easley .08 .25
161 Juan Encarnacion .08 .25
162 Juan Gonzalez .30 .75
163 Shane Halter .08 .25
164 Bobby Higginson .30 .75
165 Todd Jones FOIL 1.25 3.00
166 Brian Moehler .08 .25
167 Hideo Nomo 1.00 2.50
168 Dean Palmer .30 .75
169 Jeff Weaver .08 .25
170 Antonio Alfonseca .08 .25
171 Luis Castillo FOIL 1.25 3.00
172 Ryan Dempster FOIL 1.25 3.00
173 Cliff Floyd .30 .75
174 Alex Gonzalez .08 .25
175 Mark Kotsay .30 .75
176 Derrek Lee .60 1.50
177 Braden Looper .08 .25
178 Mike Lowell .30 .75
179 Brad Penny .08 .25
180 Mike Redmond .08 .25
181 Henry Rodriguez .08 .25
182 Jesus Sanchez .08 .25
183 Mark Smith .08 .25
184 Preston Wilson .30 .75
185 Moises Alou .30 .75
186 Jeff Bagwell FOIL 2.00 5.00
187 Lance Berkman .30 .75
188 Craig Biggio .60 1.50
189 Tim Bogar .08 .25
190 Jose Cabrera .08 .25
191 Octavio Dotel .08 .25
192 Scott Elarton FOIL 1.25 3.00
193 Richard Hidalgo .30 .75
194 Chris Holt .08 .25
195 Jose Lima .30 .75
196 Julio Lugo .08 .25
197 Mitch Meluskey .08 .25
198 Bill Spiers .08 .25
199 Daryle Ward .08 .25
200 Carlos Beltran .30 .75
201 Ricky Bottalico .08 .25
202 Johnny Damon FOIL 2.00 5.00
203 Jermaine Dye .30 .75
204 Carlos Febles .08 .25
205 Dave McCarty .08 .25
206 Mark Quinn .08 .25
207 Joe Randa .30 .75
208 Dan Reichert .08 .25
209 Rey Sanchez .08 .25
210 Jose Santiago .08 .25
211 Jeff Suppan .08 .25
212 Mac Suzuki .30 .75
213 Mike Sweeney .30 .75
214 Gregg Zaun .08 .25
215 Terry Adams .08 .25
216 Adrian Beltre .30 .75
217 Kevin Brown FOIL 1.25 3.00
218 Alex Cora .08 .25
219 Darren Dreifort .08 .25
220 Tom Goodwin .08 .25
221 Shawn Green .30 .75
222 Mark Grudzielanek .08 .25
223 Dave Hansen .08 .25
224 Todd Hundley .08 .25
225 Eric Karros .30 .75
226 Chad Kreuter .08 .25
227 Chan Ho Park .30 .75
228 Jeff Shaw .08 .25
229 Gary Sheffield FOIL 1.25 3.00
230 Juan Acevedo .08 .25
231 Ron Belliard .08 .25
232 Henry Blanco .08 .25
233 Jeromy Burnitz .30 .75
234 Jeff D'Amico FOIL 1.25 3.00
235 Valerio De Los Santos .08 .25
236 Marquis Grissom .30 .75
237 Charlie Hayes .08 .25
238 Jimmy Haynes .08 .25
239 Jose Hernandez .08 .25
240 Geoff Jenkins .30 .75
241 Curtis Leskanic .08 .25
242 Mark Loretta .08 .25
243 Richie Sexson .30 .75
244 Dave Weathers .08 .25
245 Jay Canizaro .08 .25
246 Ron Coomer .08 .25
247 Cristian Guzman .08 .25
248 LaTroy Hawkins .08 .25
249 Denny Hocking .08 .25
250 Torii Hunter .30 .75
251 Jacque Jones .30 .75
252 Corey Koskie .08 .25
253 Matt Lawton .08 .25
254 Matt LeCroy .08 .25
255 Eric Milton .08 .25
256 David Ortiz 1.00 2.50
257 Brad Radke FOIL 1.25 3.00
258 Mark Redman .08 .25
259 Bob Wells .08 .25
260 Michael Barrett .08 .25
261 Peter Bergeron .08 .25
262 Milton Bradley .30 .75
263 Orlando Cabrera .30 .75
264 Vladimir Guerrero FOIL * 3.00 8.00
265 Wilton Guerrero .08 .25
266 Dustin Hermanson .08 .25
267 Terry Jones .08 .25
268 Steve Kline .08 .25
269 Felipe Lira .08 .25
270 Mike Mordecai .08 .25
271 Lee Stevens .08 .25
272 Anthony Telford .08 .25
273 Javier Vazquez .30 .75
274 Jose Vidro FOIL 1.25 3.00
275 Edgardo Alfonzo FOIL 1.25 3.00
276 Derek Bell .08 .25
277 Armando Benitez .08 .25
278 Mike Bordick .08 .25
279 Mike Hampton FOIL 1.25 3.00
280 Lenny Harris .08 .25
281 Al Leiter .30 .75
282 Jay Payton .08 .25
283 Mike Piazza FOIL 4.00 10.00
284 Todd Pratt .08 .25
285 Glendon Rusch .08 .25
286 Bubba Trammell .08 .25
287 Robin Ventura .30 .75
288 Turk Wendell .08 .25
289 Rick White .08 .25
290 Todd Zeile .30 .75
291 Scott Brosius .30 .75
292 Roger Clemens FOIL 5.00 12.00
293 Jason Grimsley .08 .25
294 Orlando Hernandez .30 .75
295 Derek Jeter FOIL 5.00 12.00
296 Dave Justice .30 .75
297 Chuck Knoblauch .30 .75
298 Tino Martinez .60 1.50
299 Denny Neagle .08 .25
300 Jeff Nelson .08 .25
301 Paul O'Neill .60 1.50
302 Andy Pettitte .60 1.50
303 Jorge Posada .60 1.50
304 Mariano Rivera FOIL 3.00 8.00
305 Jose Vizcaino .08 .25
306 Bernie Williams FOIL 2.00 5.00
307 Kevin Appier .30 .75
308 Eric Chavez .30 .75
309 Ryan Christenson .08 .25
310 Jason Giambi FOIL 1.25 3.00
311 Jeremy Giambi .08 .25
312 Ben Grieve .08 .25
313 Gil Heredia .08 .25
314 Ramon Hernandez .08 .25
315 Tim Hudson FOIL 1.25 3.00
316 Jason Isringhausen .30 .75
317 Terrence Long FOIL 1.25 3.00
318 Jim Mecir .08 .25
319 Mark Mulder .30 .75
320 Matt Stairs .08 .25
321 Miguel Tejada .30 .75
322 Randy Velarde .08 .25
323 Bobby Abreu .30 .75
324 Jeff Brantley .08 .25
325 Pat Burrell .30 .75
326 Omar Daal .08 .25
327 Rob Ducey .08 .25
328 Doug Glanville .08 .25
329 Wayne Gomes .08 .25
330 Kevin Jordan .08 .25
331 Travis Lee .08 .25
332 Mike Lieberthal .30 .75
333 Vicente Padilla .08 .25
334 Robert Person .08 .25
335 Scott Rolen FOIL 2.00 5.00
336 Kevin Sefcik .08 .25
337 Randy Wolf .08 .25
338 Jimmy Anderson .08 .25
339 Mike Benjamin .08 .25
340 Kris Benson .08 .25
341 Adrian Brown .08 .25
342 Brian Giles FOIL 1.25 3.00
343 Jason Kendall FOIL 1.25 3.00
344 Pat Meares .08 .25
345 Warren Morris .08 .25
346 Aramis Ramirez .30 .75
347 Todd Ritchie .08 .25
348 Scott Sauerbeck .08 .25
349 Jose Silva .08 .25
350 John VanderWal .08 .25
351 Mike Williams .08 .25
352 Kevin Young .08 .25
353 Carlos Almanzar .08 .25
354 Bret Boone .30 .75
355 Matt Clement .30 .75
356 Adam Eaton .08 .25
357 Wiki Gonzalez .08 .25
358 Trevor Hoffman FOIL 1.25 3.00
359 Damian Jackson .08 .25
360 Ryan Klesko .30 .75
361 Phil Nevin FOIL 1.25 3.00
362 Eric Owens .08 .25
363 Desi Relaford .08 .25
364 Ruben Rivera .08 .25
365 Kevin Walker .08 .25
366 Woody Williams .08 .25
367 Jay Witasick .08 .25
368 Rich Aurilia .08 .25
369 Marvin Benard .08 .25
370 Barry Bonds FOIL 8.00 20.00
371 Ellis Burks .30 .75
372 Bobby Estalella .08 .25
373 Doug Henry .08 .25
374 Livan Hernandez .30 .75
375 Jeff Kent FOIL 1.25 3.00
376 Doug Mirabelli .08 .25
377 Bill Mueller .30 .75
378 Calvin Murray .08 .25
379 Robb Nen FOIL 1.25 3.00
380 Russ Ortiz .08 .25
381 Armando Rios .08 .25
382 Felix Rodriguez .08 .25
383 Kirk Rueter .08 .25
384 J.T. Snow .30 .75
385 Paul Abbott .08 .25
386 David Bell .08 .25
387 Jay Buhner .30 .75
388 Mike Cameron .30 .75
389 John Halama .08 .25
390 Rickey Henderson 1.00 2.50
391 Al Martin .08 .25
392 Edgar Martinez FOIL 2.00 5.00
393 Mark McLemore .08 .25
394 John Olerud .30 .75
395 Jose Paniagua .08 .25
396 Arthur Rhodes .08 .25
397 Alex Rodriguez FOIL 3.00 8.00
398 Kazuhiro Sasaki FOIL 1.25 3.00
399 Aaron Sele .08 .25
400 Dan Wilson .08 .25
401 Rick Ankiel FOIL 1.25 3.00
402 Will Clark .60 1.50
403 J.D. Drew .30 .75
404 Jim Edmonds FOIL 1.25 3.00
405 Pat Hentgen .08 .25
406 Darryl Kile .30 .75
407 Ray Lankford .30 .75
408 Mike Matheny .08 .25
409 Mark McGwire FOIL 8.00 20.00
410 Craig Paquette .08 .25
411 Placido Polanco .08 .25
412 Edgar Renteria .30 .75
413 Garrett Stephenson .08 .25
414 Fernando Tatis .08 .25
415 Mike Timlin .08 .25
416 Dave Veres .08 .25
417 Fernando Vina .08 .25
418 Miguel Cairo .08 .25
419 Vinny Castilla .30 .75
420 Steve Cox .08 .25
421 Doug Creek .08 .25
422 John Flaherty .08 .25
423 Jose Guillen .30 .75
424 Roberto Hernandez FOIL 1.25 3.00
425 Russ Johnson .08 .25
426 Albie Lopez .08 .25
427 Felix Martinez .08 .25
428 Fred McGriff .60 1.50
429 Bryan Rekar .08 .25
430 Greg Vaughn .08 .25
431 Gerald Williams .08 .25
432 Esteban Yan .08 .25
433 Luis Alicea .08 .25
434 Frank Catalanotto .08 .25
435 Royce Clayton .08 .25
436 Tim Crabtree .08 .25
437 Chad Curtis .08 .25
438 Rusty Greer .30 .75
439 Rick Helling .08 .25
440 Gabe Kapler .30 .75
441 Mike Lamb .08 .25
442 Ricky Ledee .08 .25
443 Rafael Palmeiro .60 1.50
444 Ivan Rodriguez FOIL 2.00 5.00
445 Kenny Rogers .30 .75
446 Mike Venafro .08 .25
447 John Wetteland .30 .75
448 Tony Batista FOIL 1.25 3.00
449 Jose Cruz Jr. .08 .25
450 Carlos Delgado FOIL 1.25 3.00
451 Kelvim Escobar .08 .25
452 Darrin Fletcher .08 .25
453 Brad Fullmer .08 .25
454 Alex Gonzalez .08 .25
455 Mark Guthrie .08 .25
456 Billy Koch .08 .25
457 Esteban Loaiza .08 .25
458 Raul Mondesi .30 .75
459 Mickey Morandini .08 .25
460 Paul Quantrill .08 .25
461 Shannon Stewart .30 .75
462 David Wells FOIL 1.25 3.00

2001 MLB Showdown Unlimited

COMPLETE SET (462) 125.00 200.00
COMP.SET w/o FOIL (400) 25.00 50.00
*UNLIMITED: .2X TO .5X 1ST EDITION
*UNL.FOIL: .2X TO .5X 1ST ED.FOIL

2001 MLB Showdown Strategy

COMPLETE SET (75) 6.00 15.00
S1 J.Posada .15 .40
Change Sides
S2 N.Garciaparra .30 .75
Clutch Hitter
S3 M.Ramirez Sox .15 .40
Clutch Hitting
S4 Williams .25 .60
Jeter
Contact
S5 S.Sosa .20 .50
Deep in the Gap
S6 B.Buchanan .08 .25
Dog Meat
S7 J.Canizaro .08 .25
Double Steal
S8 M.Tucker .08 .25
Down the Middle
S9 T. Wendell .08 .25
Drag Bunt
S10 L.Castillo .08 .25
Drained
S11 C.Everett .08 .25
Ducks on the Pond
S12 C.Delgado .08 .25
Matchup
S13 N.Garciaparra .08 .25
Fight it Off
S14 B.Molina .08 .25
Free Swinger
S15 E.Young .08 .25
Fuel on the Fire
S16 C.Carpenter .08 .25
Hiding an Injury
S17 N.Garciaparra .30 .75
In Motion
S18 A.Ochoa .08 .25
Last Chance
S19 Reds Player .08 .25
Lean Into It
S20 R.Henderson .20 .50
Nuisance
S21 A.Gonzalez .08 .25
Off Balance
S22 H.Nomo .20 .50
Out of Gas
S23 S.Casey .08 .25
Overthrow
S24 Angels Player .08 .25
Percentages
S25 Yankees Player .08 .25
Power Hitter
S26 C.Knoblauch .08 .25
Protect Runner
S27 T.Helton .15 .40
Pull The Ball
S28 T.Salmon .15 .40
Rally Cap
S29 R.Johnson .20 .50
Rough Outing
S30 J.Damon .15 .40
Runner not Held
S31 Cincinnati Reds .08 .25
Fumes
S32 A.Rodriguez .25 .60
Ruptured Duck
S33 P.Reese .08 .25
Sail Into Center
S34 M.McGwire .50 1.25
Magic Word
S35 Pirates .08 .25
Shell Shocked
S36 H.Bush .08 .25
Singles Hitter
S37 Cubs Player .08 .25
Up the Middle
S38 Twins Pitcher .08 .25

Stick a Fork
S39 J.Damon .08 .25
Take What's Given
S40 B.Giles .08 .25
Warning Track
S41 S.Dunston .08 .25
Turn On It
S42 C.Leskanic .08 .25
Anointed Closer
S43 Rangers Pitcher .08 .25
By the Book
S44 B.Higginson .08 .25
Cannon
S45 Orioles Player .08 .25
Choke
S46 G.Maddux .30 .75
Fast Worker
S47 Fans .08 .25
Flamethrower
S48 K.Brown .08 .25
Full Windup
S49 O.Vizquel .15 .40
Goose Egg
S50 T.Glavine .15 .40
Great Start
S51 N.Perez .08 .25
Great Throw
S52 M.Lamb .08 .25
Gutsy Play
S53 P.Reese .08 .25
Highlight Reel
S54 Yankees Player .08 .25
Insult to Injury
S55 R.Johnson .20 .50
In the Groove
S56 Red Sox Pitcher .08 .25
Well Done
S57 Fans .08 .25
Just Foul
S58 B.Williams .15 .40
Over the Wall
S59 B.Bonds .50 1.25
Leaping Catch
S60 J.Christiansen .08 .25
Lefty Special
S61 E.Taubensee .08 .25
Low and Away
S62 White Sox .08 .25
Conference
S63 T.Jones .08 .25
Nerves of Steel
S64 Pitchout .08 .25
S65 B.Moehler .08 .25
Scuff the Ball
S66 L.Hernandez .08 .25
Sloppy Bunt
S67 O.Vizquel .15 .40
Soft Hands
S68 B.Kim .08 .25
Submarine Pitch
S69 Mets Player(#Visibly Upset .08 .25
S70 B.Santiago .08 .25
Thinking
S71 K.Brown .08 .25
Air it Out
S72 P.Martinez .15 .40
Bear Down
S73 B.Cox .08 .25
Brainstorm
S74 D.Young .08 .25
Game of Inches
S75 M.Alou .08 .25
Second Look

2001 MLB Showdown Fanfest Promos

COMPLETE SET (6)

2002 MLB Showdown

COMP.SET w/o FOIL (300) 30.00 60.00
1 Garret Anderson .20 .50
2 David Eckstein .20 .50
3 Darin Erstad .20 .50
4 Troy Glaus FOIL 1.25 3.00
5 Adam Kennedy .20 .50
6 Ben Molina .20 .50
7 Ramon Ortiz .20 .50
8 Troy Percival .20 .50
9 Tim Salmon .20 .50
10 Scott Schoeneweis .20 .50
11 Scott Spiezio .20 .50
12 Jarrod Washburn .20 .50
13 Miguel Batista .20 .50
14 Jay Bell .20 .50
15 Craig Counsell .20 .50
16 David Dellucci .20 .50
17 Erubiel Durazo .20 .50
18 Steve Finley .20 .50
19 Luis Gonzalez FOIL 1.25 3.00
20 Mark Grace .30 .75
21 Randy Johnson FOIL 3.00 8.00
22 Byung-Hyun Kim .20 .50
23 Albie Lopez .20 .50
24 Curt Schilling FOIL 2.00 5.00
25 Matt Williams .20 .50
26 Tony Womack .20 .50
27 Marcus Giles FOIL 1.25 3.00
28 Tom Glavine .30 .75
29 Andruw Jones .20 .50
30 Chipper Jones FOIL 3.00 8.00
31 Brian Jordan .20 .50
32 Steve Karsay .20 .50
33 Javy Lopez .20 .50
34 Greg Maddux FOIL 5.00 12.00
35 Jason Marquis .20 .50
36 Mike Remlinger .20 .50
37 Rey Sanchez .20 .50
38 B. J. Surhoff .20 .50
39 Brady Anderson .20 .50
40 Tony Batista FOIL 1.25 3.00
41 Mike Bordick .20 .50
42 Jeff Conine .20 .50
43 Buddy Groom .20 .50
44 Jerry Hairston Jr. .20 .50
45 Jason Johnson .20 .50
46 Melvin Mora .20 .50
47 Chris Richard .20 .50
48 B. J. Ryan .20 .50
49 Josh Towers .20 .50
50 Rolando Arrojo .20 .50
51 Rod Beck .20 .50
52 Dante Bichette .20 .50
53 David Cone .20 .50
54 Carl Everett .20 .50
55 Rich Garces .20 .50
56 Derek Lowe .20 .50
57 Trot Nixon .20 .50
58 Hideo Nomo .50 1.25
59 Jose Offerman .20 .50
60 Troy O'Leary .20 .50
61 Manny Ramirez FOIL 2.00 5.00
62 Delino DeShields .20 .50
63 Kyle Farnsworth .20 .50
64 Jeff Fassero .20 .50
65 Ricky Gutierrez .20 .50
66 Todd Hundley .20 .50
67 Jon Lieber .20 .50
68 Fred McGriff .30 .75
69 Bill Mueller .20 .50
70 Corey Patterson .20 .50
71 Sammy Sosa FOIL 3.00 8.00
72 Julian Tavarez .20 .50
73 Kerry Wood .20 .50
74 Eric Young .20 .50
75 Mark Buehrle FOIL 2.00 5.00
76 Royce Clayton .20 .50
77 Joe Crede .20 .50
78 Ray Durham .20 .50
79 Keith Foulke .20 .50
80 Bob Howry .20 .50
81 Mark Johnson .20 .50
82 Paul Konerko .20 .50
83 Carlos Lee .20 .50
84 Sean Lowe .20 .50
85 Magglio Ordonez .30 .75
86 Jose Valentin .20 .50
87 Aaron Boone .20 .50
88 Jim Brower .20 .50
89 Sean Casey .20 .50
90 Brady Clark .20 .50
91 Adam Dunn FOIL 2.00 5.00
92 Danny Graves .20 .50
93 Ken Griffey Jr. FOIL 6.00 15.00
94 Pokey Reese .20 .50
95 Chris Reitsma .20 .50
96 Kelly Stinnett .20 .50
97 Dmitri Young .20 .50
98 Roberto Alomar FOIL 2.00 5.00
99 Danys Baez .20 .50
100 Russell Branyan .20 .50
101 Ellis Burks .20 .50
102 Bartolo Colon .20 .50
103 Marty Cordova .20 .50
104 Einar Diaz .20 .50
105 Juan Gonzalez .20 .50
106 Ricardo Rincon .20 .50
107 C. C. Sabathia FOIL 2.00 5.00
108 Paul Shuey .20 .50
109 Jim Thome FOIL 2.00 5.00
110 Omar Vizquel .30 .75
111 Bob Wickman .20 .50
112 Shawn Chacon .20 .50
113 Jeff Cirillo .20 .50
114 Mike Hampton .20 .50
115 Todd Helton FOIL 2.00 5.00
116 Greg Norton .20 .50
117 Ben Petrick .20 .50
118 Juan Pierre .20 .50
119 Terry Shumpert .20 .50
120 Larry Walker FOIL 2.00 5.00
121 Matt Anderson .20 .50
122 Roger Cedeno .20 .50
123 Tony Clark .20 .50
124 Deivi Cruz .20 .50
125 Damion Easley .20 .50
126 Shane Halter .20 .50
127 Bobby Higginson FOIL 1.25 3.00
128 Jose Macias .20 .50
129 Steve Sparks .20 .50
130 Jeff Weaver .20 .50
131 Antonio Alfonseca .20 .50
132 Josh Beckett FOIL 1.25 3.00
133 A. J. Burnett .20 .50
134 Luis Castillo .20 .50
135 Ryan Dempster .20 .50
136 Cliff Floyd .20 .50
137 Alex Gonzalez .20 .50
138 Braden Looper .20 .50
139 Mike Lowell .20 .50
140 Eric Owens .20 .50
141 Brad Penny .20 .50
142 Preston Wilson .20 .50
143 Moises Alou .20 .50
144 Brad Ausmus .20 .50
145 Jeff Bagwell FOIL 2.00 5.00
146 Lance Berkman FOIL 2.00 5.00
147 Craig Biggio .30 .75
148 Octavio Dotel .20 .50
149 Richard Hidalgo .20 .50
150 Julio Lugo .20 .50
151 Wade Miller .20 .50
152 Roy Oswalt FOIL 2.00 5.00
153 Shane Reynolds .20 .50
154 Jose Vizcaino .20 .50
155 Daryle Ward .20 .50
156 Carlos Beltran FOIL 1.25 3.00
157 Dee Brown .20 .50
158 Roberto Hernandez .20 .50
159 Mark Quinn .20 .50
160 Joe Randa .20 .50
161 Dan Reichert .20 .50
162 Jeff Suppan .20 .50
163 Mike Sweeney .20 .50
164 Kris Wilson .20 .50
165 Terry Adams .20 .50
166 Adrian Beltre .50 1.25
167 Alex Cora .30 .75
168 Tom Goodwin .20 .50
169 Shawn Green .30 .75
170 Marquis Grissom .20 .50
171 Mark Grudzielanek .20 .50
172 Eric Karros .20 .50
173 Paul LoDuca FOIL 1.25 3.00
174 Chan Ho Park .30 .75
175 Luke Prokopec .20 .50
176 Gary Sheffield .20 .50
177 Ronnie Belliard .20 .50
178 Henry Blanco .20 .50
179 Jeromy Burnitz .20 .50
180 Mike DeJean .20 .50
181 Chad Fox .20 .50
182 Jose Hernandez .20 .50
183 Geoff Jenkins .20 .50
184 Mark Loretta .20 .50
185 Nick Neugebauer .20 .50
186 Richie Sexson .20 .50
187 Ben Sheets FOIL 1.25 3.00
188 Devon White .20 .50
189 Cristian Guzman FOIL 1.25 3.00
190 Torii Hunter .20 .50
191 Jacque Jones .20 .50
192 Corey Koskie .20 .50
193 Joe Mays .20 .50
194 Doug Mientkiewicz .20 .50
195 Eric Milton .20 .50
196 David Ortiz .50 1.25
197 A. J. Pierzynski .20 .50
198 Brad Radke .20 .50
199 Luis Rivas .20 .50
200 Tony Armas Jr. .20 .50
201 Michael Barrett .20 .50
202 Peter Bergeron .20 .50
203 Orlando Cabrera .20 .50
204 Vladimir Guerrero FOIL 2.00 5.00
205 Graeme Lloyd .20 .50
206 Scott Strickland .20 .50
207 Fernando Tatis .20 .50
208 Mike Thurman .20 .50
209 Javier Vazquez .20 .50
210 Jose Vidro .20 .50
211 Brad Wilkerson .20 .50
212 Edgardo Alfonzo .20 .50
213 Kevin Appier .20 .50
214 Armando Benitez .20 .50
215 Alex Escobar .20 .50
216 John Franco .20 .50
217 Al Leiter .20 .50
218 Rey Ordonez .20 .50
219 Mike Piazza FOIL 3.00 8.00
220 Glendon Rusch .20 .50
221 Tsuyoshi Shinjo .20 .50
222 Steve Trachsel .20 .50
223 Todd Zeile .20 .50
224 Roger Clemens FOIL 4.00 10.00
225 Derek Jeter FOIL 8.00 20.00
226 Nick Johnson .20 .50
227 David Justice .20 .50
228 Tino Martinez .30 .75
229 Ramiro Mendoza .20 .50
230 Mike Mussina FOIL 2.00 5.00
231 Andy Pettitte .30 .75
232 Jorge Posada .30 .75
233 Mariano Rivera FOIL 3.00 8.00
234 Alfonso Soriano .30 .75
235 Mike Stanton .20 .50
236 Bernie Williams FOIL 2.00 5.00
237 Eric Chavez .20 .50
238 Johnny Damon Sox .30 .75
239 Jermaine Dye .20 .50
240 Jason Giambi FOIL 1.25 3.00
241 Jeremy Giambi .20 .50
242 Ramon Hernandez .20 .50
243 Tim Hudson FOIL 2.00 5.00
244 Jason Isringhausen .20 .50
245 Terrence Long .20 .50
246 Mark Mulder FOIL 1.25 3.00
247 Olmedo Saenz .20 .50
248 Miguel Tejada .30 .75
249 Barry Zito .20 .50
250 Bobby Abreu .20 .50
251 Marlon Anderson .20 .50
252 Ricky Bottalico .20 .50
253 Pat Burrell .20 .50
254 Omar Daal .20 .50
255 Johnny Estrada .20 .50
256 Nelson Figueroa .20 .50
257 Travis Lee .20 .50
258 Robert Person .20 .50
259 Scott Rolen FOIL 2.00 5.00
260 Jimmy Rollins FOIL 2.00 5.00
261 Randy Wolf .20 .50
262 Brian Giles FOIL 1.25 3.00
263 Jason Kendall .20 .50
264 Josias Manzanillo .20 .50
265 Warren Morris .20 .50
266 Aramis Ramirez .20 .50
267 Todd Ritchie .20 .50
268 Craig Wilson .20 .50
269 Jack Wilson .20 .50
270 Kevin Young .20 .50
271 Ben Davis .20 .50
272 Wiki Gonzalez .20 .50
273 Rickey Henderson .50 1.25
274 Junior Herndon .20 .50
275 Trevor Hoffman .30 .75
276 Damian Jackson .20 .50
277 D'Angelo Jimenez .20 .50
278 Mark Kotsay .20 .50
279 Phil Nevin FOIL 1.25 3.00
280 Bubba Trammell .20 .50
281 Rich Aurilia FOIL 1.25 3.00
282 Marvin Benard .20 .50
283 Barry Bonds FOIL 30.00 80.00
284 Shawn Estes .20 .50
285 Pedro Feliz .20 .50
286 Jeff Kent FOIL 1.25 3.00
287 Robb Nen .20 .50
288 Russ Ortiz .20 .50
289 Felix Rodriguez .20 .50
290 Kirk Rueter .20 .50
291 Benito Santiago .20 .50
292 J.T. Snow .20 .50
293 John Vander Wal .20 .50
294 Bret Boone FOIL 1.25 3.00
295 Mike Cameron .20 .50
296 Freddy Garcia FOIL 1.25 3.00
297 Carlos Guillen .20 .50
298 Edgar Martinez FOIL 2.00 5.00
299 Mark McLemore .20 .50
300 Jamie Moyer .20 .50
301 Jeff Nelson .20 .50
302 John Olerud .20 .50
303 Arthur Rhodes .20 .50
304 Kazuhiro Sasaki FOIL 1.25 3.00
305 Aaron Sele .20 .50
306 Ichiro Suzuki FOIL 4.00 10.00
307 Dan Wilson .20 .50
308 J.D. Drew FOIL 1.25 3.00
309 Jim Edmonds FOIL 2.00 5.00
310 Dustin Hermanson .20 .50
311 Darryl Kile .20 .50
312 Steve Kline .20 .50
313 Mike Matheny .20 .50
314 Matt Morris .20 .50
315 Craig Paquette .20 .50
316 Placido Polanco .20 .50
317 Albert Pujols FOIL 6.00 15.00
318 Edgar Renteria .20 .50
319 Bud Smith .20 .50
320 Dave Veres .20 .50
321 Fernando Vina .20 .50
322 Brent Abernathy .20 .50
323 Steve Cox .20 .50
324 Ben Grieve .20 .50
325 Aubrey Huff .20 .50
326 Joe Kennedy FOIL 1.25 3.00
327 Tanyon Sturtze .20 .50
328 Jason Tyner .20 .50
329 Greg Vaughn .20 .50
330 Paul Wilson .20 .50
331 Esteban Yan .20 .50
332 Frank Catalanotto .20 .50
333 Chad Curtis .20 .50
334 Doug Davis .20 .50
335 Gabe Kapler .20 .50
336 Mike Lamb .20 .50
337 Darren Oliver .20 .50
338 Rafael Palmeiro .30 .75
339 Alex Rodriguez FOIL 4.00 10.00
340 Ivan Rodriguez FOIL 2.00 5.00
341 Mike Venafro .20 .50
342 Michael Young .30 .75
343 Jeff Zimmerman .20 .50
344 Chris Carpenter .30 .75
345 Jose Cruz Jr. .20 .50
346 Carlos Delgado FOIL 1.25 3.00
347 Kelvim Escobar .20 .50
348 Darrin Fletcher .20 .50
349 Brad Fullmer .20 .50
350 Alex S.Gonzalez .20 .50
351 Billy Koch .20 .50
352 Esteban Loaiza .20 .50
353 Raul Mondesi .20 .50
354 Paul Quantrill .20 .50
355 Shannon Stewart .20 .50
356 Vernon Wells .20 .50

2002 MLB Showdown Strategy

COMPLETE SET (50) 4.00 10.00
S1 Bad Call .15 .40
B.Williams
S2 Clutch Hitting .30 .75
M.Piazza
S3 Crowd the Plate .08 .25
T.Glaus
S4 Down the Middle SP .20 .50
S5 Drag Bunt .20 .50
C.Patterson SP
S6 Ducks on the Pond .08 .25
S7 Fuel on the Fire .50 1.25
B.Bonds
S8 Last Chance .15 .40
C.Biggio
S9 Nuisance .20 .50
Mets SP
S10 Out of Gas .08 .25
Cubs
S11 Payoff Pitch .30 .75
M.Ramirez SP
S12 Pro Baserunner .20 .50
Phillies SP
S13 Protect the Runner SP .20 .50
S14 Pull the Ball .15 .40
R.Palmeiro
S15 Rally Cap .08 .25
T.Goodwin
S16 Rough Outing .08 .25
S17 Runner Not Held .08 .25
Cardinals
S18 Run on Fumes .20 .50
Giants SP
S19 Ruptured Duck SP .20 .50
S20 Sit on the Fastball .08 .25
J.Cruz
S21 Stick a Fork in Him .08 .25
K.Appier
S22 Sweet Swing .50 1.25
B.Bonds
S23 Take Given .30 .75
J.Damon SP
S24 Warning Track .08 .25
Pirates
S25 Turn On It .08 .25
L.Berkman
S26 By the Book .08 .25
B.Radke
S27 Cut Off in the Gap SP .20 .50
S28 Full Windup .15 .40
A.Pettitte
S29 Great Start .08 .25
B.Zito
S30 Great Throw .40 1.00
I.Suzuki
S31 HL Reel .20 .50
B.Abernathy SP
S32 Insult to Injury .08 .25
C.Schilling
S33 In the Groove .08 .25
M.Mulder
S34 Intimidation .20 .50
M.Rivera
S35 Job Well Done .20 .50
A.Rhodes SP
S36 Just Over the Wall SP .20 .50
S37 Knock Ball Down .08 .25
A.Nunez
S38 Lefty Specialist .08 .25
B.Wagner
S39 Low and Away .20 .50
R.Johnson
S40 Nerves of Steel .08 .25
T.Hoffman
S41 Pitchout SP .20 .50
S42 Pumped Up .08 .25
S43 Put Out the Fire .08 .25
K.Sasaki
S44 Rally Killer SP .20 .50
S45 Sloppy Bunt .20 .50
Indians SP
S46 Submarine Pitch .20 .50
B.Kim SP
S47 Change in Strategy .08 .25
S48 Grounder to 2nd .20 .50
Reds SP
S49 Crunch Time .20 .50
Dodgers SP
S50 Second Look .08 .25
S.Casey

2002 MLB Showdown All-Star Game

COMP.FACT.SET (100) 25.00 40.00
COMPLETE SET (50) 15.00 30.00
1 Garret Anderson .40 1.00
2 Tony Batista .40 1.00
3 Mark Buehrle .40 1.00
4 Johnny Damon Sox .60 1.50
5 Robert Fick .40 1.00
6 Freddy Garcia .40 1.00
7 Nomar Garciaparra 1.50 4.00
8 Jason Giambi .40 1.00
9 Roy Halladay .40 1.00
10 Shea Hillenbrand .40 1.00
11 Torii Hunter .40 1.00
12 Ichiro Suzuki 2.00 5.00
13 Derek Jeter 2.50 6.00
14 Paul Konerko .40 1.00
15 Derek Lowe .40 1.00
16 Jorge Posada .60 1.50
17 Manny Ramirez .60 1.50
18 Mariano Rivera 1.00 2.50
19 Alex Rodriguez 1.25 3.00
20 Kazuhiro Sasaki .40 1.00
21 Alfonso Soriano .40 1.00
22 Mike Sweeney .40 1.00
23 Robin Ventura .40 1.00
24 Omar Vizquel .60 1.50
25 Barry Zito .40 1.00
26 Lance Berkman .40 1.00
27 Barry Bonds 6.00 15.00
28 Luis Castillo .40 1.00
29 Adam Dunn .40 1.00
30 Eric Gagne .40 1.00
31 Luis Gonzalez .40 1.00
32 Shawn Green .40 1.00
33 Vladimir Guerrero 1.00 2.50
34 Todd Helton 1.00 2.50
35 Jose Hernandez .40 1.00
36 Andruw Jones .60 1.50
37 Mike Lowell .40 1.00
38 Robb Nen .40 1.00
39 Vicente Padilla .40 1.00
40 Odalis Perez .40 1.00
41 Mike Piazza 1.50 4.00
42 Scott Rolen .60 1.50
43 Jimmy Rollins .40 1.00
44 Benito Santiago .40 1.00
45 Curt Schilling .40 1.00
46 John Smoltz .60 1.50
47 Sammy Sosa 1.00 2.50
48 Junior Spivey .40 1.00
49 Jose Vidro .40 1.00
50 Mike Williams .40 1.00

2003 MLB Showdown

COMP.SET w/o FOIL (252) 30.00 60.00
COMMON CARD (1-304) .20 .50
COMMON FOIL 2.50 6.00
FOIL STATED ODDS 1:3
1 Garret Anderson FOIL 2.50 6.00
2 David Eckstein FOIL 2.50 6.00
3 Darin Erstad .20 .50
4 Brad Fullmer .20 .50
5 Troy Glaus .50 1.25
6 Adam Kennedy .20 .50
7 Bengie Molina .20 .50
8 Ramon Ortiz .20 .50
9 Orlando Palmeiro .20 .50
10 Troy Percival .20 .50
11 Tim Salmon .20 .50
12 Jarrod Washburn FOIL 2.50 6.00
13 Miguel Batista .20 .50
14 Danny Bautista .20 .50
15 Craig Counsell .20 .50
16 Steve Finley .20 .50
17 Luis Gonzalez FOIL 2.50 6.00
18 Mark Grace .30 .75
19 Randy Johnson FOIL 6.00 15.00
20 Byung-Hyun Kim .20 .50
21 Quinton McCracken .20 .50
22 Curt Schilling FOIL 4.00 10.00
23 Junior Spivey FOIL 2.50 6.00
24 Tony Womack .20 .50
25 Vinny Castilla .20 .50
26 Julio Franco .20 .50
27 Rafael Furcal FOIL 2.50 6.00
28 Marcus Giles .20 .50
29 Tom Glavine FOIL 4.00 10.00
30 Andruw Jones FOIL 2.50 6.00
31 Keith Lockhart .20 .50
32 Javy Lopez .20 .50
33 Greg Maddux FOIL 8.00 20.00
34 Kevin Millwood .20 .50
35 Gary Sheffield .20 .50
36 John Smoltz FOIL 6.00 15.00
37 Tony Batista .20 .50
38 Mike Bordick .20 .50
39 Jeff Conine .20 .50
40 Marty Cordova .20 .50
41 Jay Gibbons .20 .50
42 Geronimo Gil .20 .50
43 Jerry Hairston .20 .50
44 Jorge Julio .20 .50
45 Rodrigo Lopez .20 .50
46 Gary Matthews Jr. .20 .50
47 Melvin Mora .20 .50
48 Sidney Ponson .20 .50
49 Chris Singleton .20 .50
50 John Burkett .20 .50
51 Tony Clark .20 .50
52 Johnny Damon .30 .75
53 Alan Embree .20 .50
54 Nomar Garciaparra FOIL 4.00 10.00
55 Shea Hillenbrand .20 .50
56 Derek Lowe FOIL 2.50 6.00
57 Pedro Martinez FOIL 4.00 10.00
58 Trot Nixon .20 .50
59 Manny Ramirez .50 1.25
60 Rey Sanchez .20 .50
61 Ugueth Urbina .20 .50
62 Jason Varitek .50 1.25
63 Moises Alou .20 .50
64 Mark Bellhorn .20 .50
65 Roosevelt Brown .20 .50
66 Matt Clement .20 .50
67 Joe Girardi .30 .75
68 Alex Gonzalez .20 .50
69 Todd Hundley .20 .50
70 Jon Lieber .20 .50
71 Fred McGriff .30 .75
72 Bill Mueller .20 .50
73 Corey Patterson .20 .50
74 Mark Prior FOIL 4.00 10.00
75 Sammy Sosa FOIL 6.00 15.00
76 Mark Buehrle FOIL 4.00 10.00
77 Jon Garland .20 .50
78 Tony Graffanino .20 .50
79 Paul Konerko FOIL 4.00 10.00
80 Carlos Lee .20 .50
81 Magglio Ordonez FOIL 4.00 10.00
82 Frank Thomas .50 1.25
83 Dan Wright .20 .50
84 Aaron Boone .20 .50
85 Sean Casey .20 .50
86 Elmer Dessens .20 .50
87 Adam Dunn .30 .75
88 Danny Graves .20 .50
89 Joey Hamilton .20 .50
90 Jimmy Haynes .20 .50
91 Austin Kearns FOIL 2.50 6.00
92 Barry Larkin .30 .75
93 Jason LaRue .20 .50
94 Reggie Taylor .20 .50
95 Todd Walker .20 .50
96 Danys Baez .20 .50
97 Milton Bradley .20 .50
98 Ellis Burks .20 .50
99 Einar Diaz .20 .50
100 Ricky Gutierrez .20 .50
101 Matt Lawton .20 .50
102 Chris Magruder .20 .50
103 C. C. Sabathia .30 .75
104 Lee Stevens .20 .50
105 Jim Thome FOIL 4.00 10.00
106 Omar Vizquel .30 .75
107 Bob Wickman .20 .50
108 Gary Bennett .20 .50
109 Mike Hampton .20 .50
110 Todd Helton .30 .75
111 Jose Jimenez .20 .50
112 Denny Neagle .20 .50
113 Jose Ortiz .20 .50
114 Juan Pierre .20 .50
115 Juan Uribe .20 .50
116 Larry Walker FOIL 4.00 10.00
117 Todd Zeile .20 .50
118 Juan Acevedo .20 .50
119 Robert Fick .20 .50
120 Bobby Higginson .20 .50
121 Damian Jackson .20 .50
122 Craig Paquette .20 .50
123 Carlos Pena .30 .75
124 Mark Redman .20 .50
125 Randall Simon .20 .50
126 Steve Sparks .20 .50
127 Dmitri Young .20 .50
128 A. J. Burnett .20 .50
129 Luis Castillo .20 .50
130 Juan Encarnacion .20 .50
131 Alex Gonzalez .20 .50
132 Charles Johnson .20 .50
133 Derrek Lee .20 .50
134 Mike Lowell .20 .50
135 Vladimir Nunez .20 .50
136 Eric Owens .20 .50
137 Preston Wilson .20 .50
138 Brad Ausmus .20 .50
139 Lance Berkman FOIL 4.00 10.00
140 Craig Biggio .30 .75
141 Geoff Blum .20 .50
142 Richard Hidalgo .20 .50
143 Julio Lugo .20 .50
144 Orlando Merced .20 .50
145 Billy Wagner .20 .50
146 Carlos Beltran .30 .75
147 Paul Byrd .20 .50
148 Raul Ibanez .30 .75
149 Chuck Knoblauch .20 .50
150 Brent Mayne .20 .50
151 Neifi Perez .20 .50
152 Joe Randa .20 .50
153 Mike Sweeney .20 .50
154 Adrian Beltre .50 1.25
155 Eric Gagne FOIL 2.50 6.00
156 Shawn Green .20 .50
157 Marquis Grissom .20 .50
158 Mark Grudzielanek .20 .50
159 Kazuhisa Ishii FOIL 2.50 6.00
160 Cesar Izturis .20 .50
161 Brian Jordan .20 .50
162 Eric Karros .20 .50
163 Paul Lo Duca FOIL 2.50 6.00
164 Hideo Nomo .50 1.25
165 Jesse Orosco .20 .50
166 Odalis Perez .20 .50
167 Mike DeJean .20 .50
168 Jose Hernandez .20 .50
169 Geoff Jenkins .20 .50
170 Alex Sanchez .20 .50
171 Richie Sexson .20 .50
172 Ben Sheets .20 .50
173 Eric Young .20 .50
174 Eddie Guardado .20 .50
175 Cristian Guzman .20 .50
176 Torii Hunter FOIL 2.50 6.00
177 Jacque Jones .20 .50
178 Corey Koskie .20 .50
179 Doug Mientkiewicz .20 .50
180 Eric Milton .20 .50
181 A. J. Pierzynski .20 .50
182 Michael Barrett .20 .50
183 Orlando Cabrera .20 .50
184 Cliff Floyd .20 .50
185 Vladimir Guerrero FOIL 4.00 10.00
186 Tomo Ohka .20 .50
187 Fernando Tatis .20 .50
188 Javier Vazquez .20 .50
189 Jose Vidro FOIL 2.50 6.00
190 Brad Wilkerson .20 .50
191 Edgardo Alfonzo .20 .50
192 Roberto Alomar .30 .75
193 Pedro Astacio .20 .50
194 Armando Benitez .20 .50
195 Jeromy Burnitz .20 .50
196 Al Leiter .20 .50
197 Rey Ordonez .20 .50
198 Timo Perez .20 .50
199 Mike Piazza FOIL 6.00 15.00
200 Steve Trachsel .20 .50
201 Mo Vaughn .20 .50
202 Roger Clemens .60 1.50
203 Jason Giambi FOIL 2.50 6.00
204 Derek Jeter 1.25 3.00
205 Nick Johnson .20 .50
206 Steve Karsay .20 .50
207 Mike Mussina FOIL 4.00 10.00
208 Jorge Posada .30 .75
209 Mariano Rivera FOIL 8.00 20.00
210 Alfonso Soriano FOIL 4.00 10.00
211 Mike Stanton .20 .50
212 Robin Ventura .20 .50
213 Jeff Weaver .20 .50
214 Rondell White .20 .50
215 Bernie Williams FOIL 4.00 10.00
216 Eric Chavez .20 .50
217 Jermaine Dye .20 .50
218 Scott Hatteberg .20 .50
219 Tim Hudson .30 .75
220 Billy Koch .20 .50
221 Terrence Long .20 .50
222 Mark Mulder .20 .50
223 Miguel Tejada FOIL 4.00 10.00
224 Barry Zito FOIL 4.00 10.00
225 Bobby Abreu .20 .50
226 Marlon Anderson .20 .50
227 Pat Burrell .20 .50
228 Brandon Duckworth .20 .50
229 Jeremy Giambi .20 .50
230 Doug Glanville .20 .50
231 Mike Lieberthal .20 .50
232 Jose Mesa .20 .50
233 Vicente Padilla .20 .50
234 Jimmy Rollins .30 .75
236 Josh Fogg .20 .50
237 Brian Giles .20 .50
238 Jason Kendall .20 .50
239 Pokey Reese .20 .50
240 Kip Wells .20 .50
241 Mike Williams FOIL 2.50 6.00
242 Craig Wilson .20 .50
243 Jack Wilson .20 .50
244 Kevin Young .20 .50
245 Trevor Hoffman FOIL 4.00 10.00
246 Mark Kotsay .20 .50
247 Ray Lankford .20 .50
248 Brian Lawrence .20 .50
249 Phil Nevin .20 .50
250 Kurt Ainsworth .20 .50
251 David Bell .20 .50
252 Barry Bonds FOIL 50.00 120.00
253 Ryan Jensen .20 .50
254 Jeff Kent FOIL 2.50 6.00
255 Robb Nen .20 .50
256 Reggie Sanders .20 .50
257 Benito Santiago .20 .50
258 Tsuyoshi Shinjo .20 .50
259 J. T. Snow .20 .50
260 Bret Boone .20 .50
261 Mike Cameron .20 .50
262 Jeff Cirillo .20 .50
263 Freddy Garcia .20 .50
264 Carlos Guillen .20 .50
265 Mark McLemore .20 .50
266 Jamie Moyer .20 .50
267 John Olerud .20 .50
268 Joel Pineiro FOIL 2.50 6.00
269 Kazuhiro Sasaki FOIL 2.50 6.00
270 Ruben Sierra .20 .50
271 Dan Wilson .20 .50
272 Ichiro Suzuki FOIL 8.00 20.00
273 J.D. Drew .20 .50
274 Jim Edmonds FOIL 4.00 10.00
275 Jason Isringhausen .20 .50
276 Matt Morris FOIL 2.50 6.00
277 Albert Pujols FOIL 8.00 20.00
278 Edgar Renteria .20 .50
279 Scott Rolen FOIL 4.00 10.00
280 Jason Simontacchi .20 .50
281 Fernando Vina .20 .50
282 Brent Abernathy .20 .50
283 Steve Cox .20 .50
284 Chris Gomez .20 .50
285 Ben Grieve .20 .50
286 Joe Kennedy .20 .50
287 Tanyon Sturtze .20 .50
288 Paul Wilson .20 .50
289 Randy Winn FOIL 2.50 6.00
290 Juan Gonzalez .20 .50
291 Hideki Irabu .20 .50
292 Rafael Palmeiro FOIL 4.00 10.00
293 Herbert Perry .20 .50
294 Alex Rodriguez FOIL 8.00 20.00
295 Ivan Rodriguez .30 .75
296 Kenny Rogers .20 .50
297 Ismael Valdes .20 .50
298 Mike Young .20 .50
299 Dave Berg .20 .50
300 Carlos Delgado .20 .50
301 Kelvim Escobar .20 .50
302 Roy Halladay FOIL 4.00 10.00
303 Eric Hinske FOIL 2.50 6.00

304 Shannon Stewart .20 .50
P51 Pee Wee Reese Promo .30 .75

2003 MLB Showdown Strategy

COMPLETE SET (50) 3.00 8.00
S1 Bad Call .10 .25
S.Casey
S2 Clutch Hitting .10 .25
E.Burks
S3 Down Middle .10 .25
D.Graves
S4 Drag Bunt .10 .25
M.Mulder
S5 Ducks on the Pond .10 .25
S6 Fuel on Fire .10 .25
B.Santiago
S7 Goodbye BB .30 .75
Ichiro
S8 Great Addition .30 .75
Ichiro
S9 Last Chance .30 .75
Ichiro
S10 Nuisance .15 .40
B.Larkin
S11 Protect Runner .10 .25
J.Jones
S12 Pull the Ball .15 .40
J.Thome
S13 Rally Cap .10 .25
T.Martinez
S14 Rookie's Chance .10 .25
E.Hinske
S15 Runner Not Held .10 .25
S16 See Clearly .15 .40
V.Guerrero
S17 Serious Wheels .10 .25
D.Cruz
S18 Sit on Fastball .10 .25
C.Guillen
S19 Take Given .10 .25
D.Eckstein
S20 Turn On It .60 1.50
D.Jeter
S21 Valuable Asset .40 1.00
B.Bonds
S22 Aces Up .10 .25
M.Mulder
S23 By the Book .10 .25
D.Reichert
S24 Change It Up .10 .25
D.Neagle
S25 Cut Off Gap .10 .25
J.Encarnacion
S26 Full Windup .10 .25
C.Reitsma
S27 Good Leather .10 .25
J.Encarnacion
S28 Great Start .10 .25
M.Mulder
S29 Great Throw .10 .25
D.Bautista
S30 Highlight Reel .10 .25
J.Hernandez
S31 In the Groove .10 .25
S32 Insult to Injury .10 .25
D.Eckstein
S33 Job Well Done .10 .25
S34 Just Over Wall .10 .25
D.Justice
S35 Knock Ball Down .10 .25
L.Gonzalez
S36 Lefty Specialist .10 .25
R.Rincon
S37 Nerves of Steel .10 .25
E.Gagne
S38 Paint Corner .10 .25
C.Febles
S39 Pumped Up .15 .40
R.Ibanez
S40 Put Out Fire .10 .25
M.Wohlers
S41 Rally Killer .10 .25
A.Nunez
S42 Submarine Pitch .10 .25
B.Kim
S43 Throwing Heat .15 .40
D.Roberts
S44 What a Relief! .10 .25
S45 Change in Strategy .10 .25
S46 Feast or Famine .10 .25
G.Carrara
S47 Grounder to 2nd .15 .40
B.Larkin
S48 It's Crunch Time .10 .25
S49 Just Over Rail .10 .25
S.Halter
S50 Outmanaged .10 .25
Knight-Howe

2004 MLB Showdown

COMP.SET w/o FOIL (298) 30.00 60.00
COMMON CARD .20 .50
COMMON FOIL 2.50 6.00
FOIL STATED ODDS 1:3
1 Garret Anderson FOIL 2.50 6.00
2 David Eckstein .20 .50
3 Darin Erstad .20 .50
4 Troy Glaus .20 .50
5 Bengie Molina .20 .50
6 Ramon Ortiz .20 .50
7 Eric Owens .20 .50
8 Tim Salmon .20 .50
9 Scot Shields .20 .50
10 Scott Spiezio .20 .50
11 Jarrod Washburn .20 .50
12 Rod Barajas .20 .50
13 Alex Cintron .20 .50
14 Elmer Dessens .20 .50
15 Steve Finley .20 .50
16 Luis Gonzalez FOIL 2.50 6.00
17 Mark Grace .30 .75
18 Shea Hillenbrand .20 .50
19 Matt Kata .20 .50
20 Quinton McCracken .20 .50
21 Curt Schilling FOIL 4.00 10.00
22 Vinny Castilla .20 .50
23 Robert Fick .20 .50
24 Rafael Furcal .20 .50
25 Marcus Giles .20 .50
26 Andruw Jones .20 .50
27 Chipper Jones FOIL 6.00 15.00
28 Ray King .20 .50
29 Javy Lopez FOIL 2.50 6.00
30 Greg Maddux .60 1.50
31 Russ Ortiz .20 .50
32 Gary Sheffield FOIL 2.50 6.00
33 Tony Batista .20 .50
34 Deivi Cruz .20 .50
35 Travis Driskill .20 .50
36 Brook Fordyce .20 .50
37 Jay Gibbons .20 .50
38 Pat Hentgen .20 .50
39 Jorge Julio .20 .50
40 Rodrigo Lopez .20 .50
41 Luis Matos FOIL 2.50 6.00
42 Melvin Mora .20 .50
43 Brian Roberts .20 .50
44 B.J. Surhoff .20 .50
45 Johnny Damon .30 .75
46 Alan Embree .20 .50
47 Nomar Garciaparra FOIL 4.00 10.00
48 Byung-Hyun Kim .20 .50
49 Derek Lowe .20 .50
50 Pedro Martinez FOIL 4.00 10.00
51 Bill Mueller FOIL 2.50 6.00
52 Trot Nixon .20 .50
53 David Ortiz .50 1.25
54 Manny Ramirez .50 1.25
55 Jason Varitek .50 1.25
56 Tim Wakefield .30 .75
57 Todd Walker .20 .50
58 Antonio Alfonseca .20 .50
59 Moises Alou .20 .50
60 Paul Bako .20 .50
61 Alex Gonzalez .20 .50
62 Tom Goodwin .20 .50
63 Mark Grudzielanek .20 .50
64 Eric Karros .20 .50
65 Kenny Lofton .20 .50
66 Ramon E. Martinez .20 .50
67 Corey Patterson .20 .50
68 Mark Prior FOIL 4.00 10.00
69 Aramis Ramirez .20 .50
70 Mike Remlinger .20 .50
71 Sammy Sosa FOIL 6.00 15.00
72 Kerry Wood FOIL 2.50 6.00
73 Carlos Zambrano .30 .75
74 Mark Buehrle .30 .75
75 Bartolo Colon .20 .50
76 Joe Crede .20 .50
77 Tom Gordon .20 .50
78 Paul Konerko .30 .75
79 Carlos Lee .20 .50
80 Damaso Marte .20 .50
81 Miguel Olivo .20 .50
82 Magglio Ordonez FOIL 4.00 10.00
83 Frank Thomas .50 1.25
84 Jose Valentin .20 .50
85 Sean Casey .20 .50
86 Juan Castro .20 .50
87 Adam Dunn .30 .75
88 Danny Graves .20 .50
89 Ken Griffey Jr. 1.00 2.50
90 D'Angelo Jimenez .20 .50
91 Austin Kearns .20 .50
92 Barry Larkin .30 .75
93 Jason LaRue .20 .50
94 Chris Reitsma .20 .50
95 Reggie Taylor .20 .50
96 Paul Wilson .20 .50
97 Danys Baez .20 .50
98 Josh Bard .20 .50
99 Casey Blake .20 .50
100 Jason Boyd .20 .50
101 Milton Bradley FOIL 2.50 6.00
102 Ellis Burks .20 .50
103 Coco Crisp .20 .50
104 Jody Gerut .20 .50
105 Travis Hafner .20 .50
106 Matt Lawton .20 .50
107 John McDonald .20 .50
108 Terry Mulholland .20 .50
109 C.C. Sabathia .30 .75
110 Omar Vizquel .30 .75
111 Ronnie Belliard .20 .50
112 Shawn Chacon .20 .50
113 Todd Helton FOIL 4.00 10.00
114 Charles Johnson .20 .50
115 Darren Oliver .20 .50
116 Jay Payton .20 .50
117 Justin Speier .20 .50
118 Chris Stynes .20 .50
119 Larry Walker .30 .75
120 Preston Wilson .20 .50
121 Jeremy Bonderman .20 .50
122 Shane Halter .20 .50
123 Bobby Higginson .20 .50
124 Brandon Inge .20 .50
125 Wilfredo Ledezma .20 .50
126 Chris Mears .20 .50
127 Warren Morris .20 .50
128 Carlos Pena .30 .75
129 Ramon Santiago .20 .50
130 Andres Torres .20 .50
131 Dmitri Young .20 .50
132 Josh Beckett .20 .50
133 Miguel Cabrera .50 1.25
134 Luis Castillo .20 .50
135 Juan Encarnacion .20 .50
136 Alex Gonzalez .20 .50
137 Derrek Lee .20 .50
138 Braden Looper .20 .50
139 Mike Lowell .20 .50
140 Juan Pierre .20 .50
141 Mark Redman .20 .50
142 Ivan Rodriguez FOIL 4.00 10.00
143 Tim Spooneybarger .20 .50
144 Dontrelle Willis FOIL 2.50 6.00
145 Brad Ausmus .20 .50
146 Jeff Bagwell .30 .75
147 Lance Berkman .30 .75
148 Craig Biggio .30 .75
149 Geoff Blum .20 .50
150 Octavio Dotel FOIL 2.50 6.00
151 Morgan Ensberg .20 .50
152 Adam Everett .20 .50
153 Richard Hidalgo FOIL 2.50 6.00
154 Jeff Kent .20 .50
155 Brad Lidge .20 .50
156 Roy Oswalt .30 .75
157 Jeriome Robertson .20 .50
158 Billy Wagner FOIL 2.50 6.00
159 Carlos Beltran FOIL 4.00 10.00
160 Angel Berroa .20 .50
161 Jason Grimsley .20 .50
162 Aaron Guiel .20 .50
163 Runelvys Hernandez .20 .50
164 Raul Ibanez .30 .75
165 Curtis Leskanic .20 .50
166 Jose Lima .20 .50
167 Mike MacDougal .20 .50
168 Brent Mayne .20 .50
169 Joe Randa .20 .50
170 Desi Relaford .20 .50
171 Mike Sweeney .20 .50
172 Michael Tucker .20 .50
173 Adrian Beltre .50 1.25
174 Kevin Brown FOIL 2.50 6.00
175 Ron Coomer .20 .50
176 Alex Cora .30 .75
177 Eric Gagne FOIL 2.50 6.00
178 Shawn Green .20 .50
179 Cesar Izturis .20 .50
180 Brian Jordan .20 .50
181 Paul Lo Duca .20 .50
182 Fred McGriff .20 .50
183 Hideo Nomo .50 1.25
184 Paul Quantrill .20 .50
185 Dave Roberts .30 .75
186 Royce Clayton .20 .50
187 Keith Ginter .20 .50
188 Wes Helms .20 .50
189 Geoff Jenkins .20 .50
190 Brooks Kieschnick .20 .50
191 Eddie Perez .20 .50
192 Scott Podsednik FOIL 2.50 6.00
193 Richie Sexson FOIL 2.50 6.00
194 Ben Sheets .20 .50
195 John Vander Wal .20 .50
196 Chris Gomez .20 .50
197 Cristian Guzman .20 .50
198 LaTroy Hawkins .20 .50
199 Torii Hunter .20 .50
200 Jacque Jones .20 .50
201 Corey Koskie .20 .50
202 Doug Mientkiewicz .20 .50
203 A.J. Pierzynski
204 Brad Radke .20 .50
205 Shannon Stewart FOIL 2.50 6.00
206 Michael Barrett .20 .50
207 Orlando Cabrera FOIL 2.50 6.00
208 Endy Chavez .20 .50
209 Zach Day .20 .50
210 Vladimir Guerrero FOIL 4.00 10.00
211 Fernando Tatis .20 .50
212 Javier Vazquez .20 .50
213 Jose Vidro .20 .50
214 Brad Wilkerson .20 .50
215 Tony Clark .20 .50
216 Cliff Floyd .20 .50
217 John Franco .20 .50
218 Joe McEwing .20 .50
219 Timo Perez .20 .50
220 Jason Phillips .20 .50
221 Mike Piazza .50 1.25
222 Jose Reyes FOIL 4.00 10.00
223 Steve Trachsel .20 .50
224 Dave Weathers .20 .50
225 Ty Wigginton .20 .50
226 Roger Clemens FOIL 8.00 20.00
227 Chris Hammond .20 .50
228 Derek Jeter FOIL 15.00 40.00
229 Nick Johnson .20 .50
230 Hideki Matsui .75 2.00
231 Mike Mussina FOIL 4.00 10.00
232 Andy Pettitte .30 .75
233 Jorge Posada .30 .75
234 Mariano Rivera .60 1.50
235 Alfonso Soriano .30 .75
236 Jeff Weaver .20 .50
237 Bernie Williams .30 .75
238 Enrique Wilson .20 .50
239 Chad Bradford .20 .50
240 Eric Byrnes .20 .50
241 Mark Ellis .20 .50
242 Keith Foulke FOIL 2.50 6.00
243 Scott Hatteberg .20 .50
244 Ramon Hernandez .20 .50
245 Tim Hudson FOIL 4.00 10.00
246 Terrence Long .20 .50
247 Mark Mulder FOIL 2.50 6.00
248 Ricardo Rincon .20 .50
249 Chris Singleton .20 .50
250 Miguel Tejada .30 .75
251 Barry Zito .30 .75
252 Bobby Abreu .20 .50
253 David Bell .20 .50
254 Pat Burrell .20 .50
255 Marlon Byrd .20 .50
256 Rheal Cormier .20 .50
257 Vicente Padilla .20 .50
258 Tomas Perez .20 .50
259 Placido Polanco .20 .50
260 Jimmy Rollins .30 .75
261 Carlos Silva .20 .50
262 Jim Thome FOIL 4.00 10.00
263 Randy Wolf FOIL 2.50 6.00
264 Kris Benson .20 .50
265 Jeff D'Amico .20 .50
266 Adam Hyzdu .20 .50
267 Jason Kendall FOIL 2.50 6.00
268 Brian Meadows .20 .50
269 Abraham Nunez .20 .50
270 Reggie Sanders .20 .50
271 Matt Stairs .20 .50
272 Jack Wilson .20 .50
273 Gary Bennett .20 .50
274 Sean Burroughs .20 .50
275 Adam Eaton .20 .50
276 Luther Hackman .20 .50
277 Ryan Klesko .20 .50
278 Brian Lawrence .20 .50
279 Mark Loretta .20 .50
280 Phil Nevin .20 .50
281 Ramon Vazquez .20 .50
282 Edgardo Alfonzo .20 .50
283 Rich Aurilia .20 .50
284 Jim Brower .20 .50
285 Jose Cruz Jr. .20 .50
286 Ray Durham .20 .50
287 Andres Galarraga .30 .75
288 Marquis Grissom .20 .50
289 Neifi Perez .20 .50
290 Felix Rodriguez .20 .50
291 Benito Santiago .20 .50
292 Jason Schmidt FOIL 2.50 6.00
293 J.T. Snow .20 .50
294 Tim Worrell .20 .50
295 Bret Boone FOIL 2.50 6.00
296 Mike Cameron .20 .50
297 Ryan Franklin .20 .50
298 Carlos Guillen .20 .50
299 Shigetoshi Hasegawa .20 .50
300 Edgar Martinez .30 .75
301 Mark McLemore .20 .50
302 Jamie Moyer FOIL 2.50 6.00
303 John Olerud .20 .50
304 Ichiro Suzuki FOIL 8.00 20.00
305 Dan Wilson .20 .50
306 Randy Winn .20 .50
307 J.D. Drew .20 .50
308 Jeff Fassero .20 .50
309 Bo Hart .20 .50
310 Jason Isringhausen .20 .50
311 Tino Martinez .30 .75
312 Mike Matheny .20 .50
313 Orlando Palmeiro .20 .50
314 Albert Pujols FOIL 8.00 20.00
315 Edgar Renteria FOIL 2.50 6.00
316 Garrett Stephenson .20 .50
317 Woody Williams FOIL 2.50 6.00
318 Rocco Baldelli .20 .50
319 Lance Carter .20 .50
320 Carl Crawford .30 .75
321 Toby Hall .20 .50
322 Travis Harper .20 .50
323 Aubrey Huff FOIL 2.50 6.00
324 Travis Lee .20 .50
325 Julio Lugo .20 .50
326 Damian Rolls .20 .50
327 Jorge Sosa .20 .50
328 Hank Blalock .20 .50
329 Francisco Cordero .20 .50
330 Aaron Fultz .20 .50
331 Juan Gonzalez .20 .50
332 Rafael Palmeiro .30 .75
333 Alex Rodriguez FOIL 8.00 20.00
334 Mark Teixeira .30 .75
335 John Thomson .20 .50
336 Ismael Valdes .20 .50
337 Michael Young .20 .50
338 Frank Catalanotto .20 .50
339 Carlos Delgado .20 .50
340 Kelvim Escobar .20 .50
341 Roy Halladay FOIL 4.00 10.00
342 Eric Hinske .20 .50
343 Orlando Hudson .20 .50
344 Greg Myers .20 .50
345 Josh Phelps .20 .50
346 Cliff Politte .20 .50
347 Vernon Wells FOIL 2.50 6.00
348 Chris Woodward .20 .50
NNO Alex Rodriguez PROMO

2004 MLB Showdown Strategy

COMPLETE SET (50) 3.00 8.00
TWO PER BOOSTER PACK
S1 Bad Call .10 .25
L.Harris
S2 Burned .15 .40
A.Dunn
S3 Check Swing .30 .75
A.Rodriguez
S4 Deep in Gap .25 .60
M.Ramirez
S5 Drained .10 .25
P.Reese
S6 Ducks on Pond .08 .25
Wrigley Field
S7 Great Addition .30 .75
I.Suzuki
S8 Hard Slide .10 .25
A.Gonzalez
S9 Inside Park HR .10 .25
J.Pierre
S10 Options .10 .25
S.Casey
S11 Frying Pan .10 .25
S.Trachsel
S12 Play the Perc .10 .25
D.Willis
S13 Pointers .30 .75
A.Pujols
S14 Poor Positioning .10 .25
J.Cirillo
S15 Pull the Ball .10 .25
C.Delgado
S16 Rough Outing .15 .40
T.LaRussa
S17 Slow Roller .15 .40
N.Garciaparra
S18 Stick a Fork .10 .25
B.Cluck CO
S19 Sweet Swing .15 .40
B.Williams
S20 Take What's Given .15 .40
A.Dunn
S21 Think Again .10 .25
L.Bowa
S22 Turn on It .15 .40
J.Bagwell
S23 Aces Up .10 .25
R.Ortiz
S24 Caught Leaning .10 .25
B.Broussard
S25 Caught Corner .15 .40
M.Prior
S26 Choke .10 .25
M.Cuddyer
S27 Cover Second .10 .25
J.Wilson
S28 Dominating .15 .40
R.Halladay
S29 Foul Ball .25 .60
F.Thomas
S30 Good Leather .10 .25
R.Furcal
S31 Hooking Foul .10 .25
J.Giambi
S32 In the Zone .10 .25
A.Burnett
S33 Infield In .15 .40
O.Vizquel
S34 Lined Out Play .08 .25
Foul Pole
S35 Locate .15 .40
C.Schilling
S36 Locked In .08 .25
Padres Catcher
S37 Nerves Steel .08 .25
Marlins Pitcher
S38 Paint Corner .15 .40
C.Schilling
S39 Power Pitching .10 .25
K.Wood
S40 Short Fly .15 .40
A.Cora
S41 Sloppy Bunt .15 .40
N.Garciaparra
S42 Split-Finger .10 .25
K.Sasaki
S43 Top-Level .10 .25
M.Scioscia
S44 Tough Nails .10 .25
C.Hammond
S45 Change Strategy .10 .25
J.Moyer
S46 Close Call .10 .25
O.Cabrera
S47 New Strategies .10 .25
A.Howe
S48 Second Look .10 .25
R.Mackowiak
S49 Swing Anything .10 .25
M.Cuddyer
S50 Think Twice .10 .25
J.Schmidt

2005 MLB Showdown

COMP.SET w/o FOIL (298) 50.00 100.00
FOIL STATED ODDS 1:3
1 Garret Anderson .40 1.00
2 David Eckstein .40 1.00
3 Darin Erstad .40 1.00
4 Chone Figgins .40 1.00
5 Troy Glaus .40 1.00
6 Kevin Gregg .40 1.00
7 Vladimir Guerrero FOIL 3.00 8.00
8 Jose Guillen .40 1.00
9 Adam Kennedy .40 1.00
10 Troy Percival .40 1.00
11 Francisco Rodriguez FOIL 4.00 10.00
12 Tim Salmon .40 1.00
13 Danny Bautista .40 1.00
14 Alex Cintron .40 1.00
15 Luis Gonzalez .40 1.00
16 Scott Hairston .40 1.00
17 Shea Hillenbrand .40 1.00
18 Randy Johnson FOIL 6.00 15.00
19 Mike Koplove .40 1.00
20 Chad Tracy .40 1.00
21 Brandon Webb .60 1.50
22 Antonio Alfonseca .40 1.00
23 J.D. Drew FOIL 2.50 6.00
24 Johnny Estrada FOIL 2.50 6.00
25 Julio Franco .40 1.00
26 Rafael Furcal .40 1.00
27 Marcus Giles .40 1.00
28 Andruw Jones .40 1.00
29 Chipper Jones 1.00 2.50
30 Eli Marrero .40 1.00
31 John Smoltz 1.00 2.50
32 John Thomson .40 1.00
33 Jaret Wright .40 1.00
34 Buddy Groom .40 1.00
35 Jerry Hairston .40 1.00
36 Jorge Julio .40 1.00
37 Rodrigo Lopez .40 1.00
38 Melvin Mora FOIL 2.50 6.00
39 Rafael Palmeiro .60 1.50
40 Brian Roberts .40 1.00
41 B.J. Ryan .40 1.00
42 B.J. Surhoff .40 1.00
43 Miguel Tejada FOIL 4.00 10.00
44 Mark Bellhorn .40 1.00
45 Johnny Damon .60 1.50
46 Alan Embree .40 1.00
47 Keith Foulke .40 1.00
48 Gabe Kapler .40 1.00
49 Pedro Martinez .60 1.50
50 Bill Mueller .40 1.00
51 David Ortiz FOIL 6.00 15.00
52 Manny Ramirez FOIL 6.00 15.00
53 Pokey Reese .40 1.00
54 Curt Schilling FOIL 4.00 10.00
55 Mike Timlin .40 1.00
56 Jason Varitek 1.00 2.50
57 Moises Alou .40 1.00
58 Michael Barrett .40 1.00
59 Matt Clement .40 1.00
60 Kyle Farnsworth .40 1.00
61 Nomar Garciaparra .60 1.50
62 LaTroy Hawkins .40 1.00
63 Todd Hollandsworth .40 1.00
64 Derrek Lee .40 1.00
65 Greg Maddux 1.25 3.00
66 Kent Mercker .40 1.00
67 Corey Patterson .40 1.00
68 Aramis Ramirez .40 1.00
69 Kerry Wood .40 1.00
70 Mark Buehrle .60 1.50
71 Joe Crede .40 1.00
72 Freddy Garcia .40 1.00
73 Paul Konerko FOIL 4.00 10.00
74 Carlos Lee .40 1.00
75 Damaso Marte .40 1.00
76 Aaron Rowand .40 1.00
77 Shingo Takatsu .40 1.00
78 Juan Uribe .40 1.00
79 Jose Valentin .40 1.00
80 Sean Casey .40 1.00
81 Juan Castro .40 1.00
82 Adam Dunn FOIL 4.00 10.00
83 Ryan Freel .40 1.00
84 Aaron Harang .40 1.00
85 D'Angelo Jimenez .40 1.00
86 Barry Larkin .60 1.50
87 Jason LaRue .40 1.00
88 Wily Mo Pena .40 1.00
89 Phil Norton .40 1.00
90 John Riedling .40 1.00
91 Paul Wilson .40 1.00
92 Ronnie Belliard .40 1.00
93 Casey Blake .40 1.00
94 Ben Broussard .40 1.00
95 Coco Crisp .40 1.00
96 Travis Hafner FOIL 2.50 6.00
97 Matt Lawton .40 1.00
98 Cliff Lee .60 1.50
99 Victor Martinez .60 1.50
100 David Riske .40 1.00
101 C.C. Sabathia .60 1.50
102 Omar Vizquel .60 1.50
103 Jake Westbrook .40 1.00
104 Jeromy Burnitz .40 1.00
105 Vinny Castilla .40 1.00
106 Shawn Chacon .40 1.00
107 Royce Clayton .40 1.00
108 Todd Helton FOIL 4.00 10.00
109 Jason Jennings .40 1.00
110 Charles Johnson .40 1.00
111 Aaron Miles .40 1.00
112 Steve Reed .40 1.00
113 Mark Sweeney .40 1.00
114 Carlos Guillen .40 1.00
115 Omar Infante .40 1.00
116 Mike Maroth .40 1.00
117 Craig Monroe .40 1.00
118 Carlos Pena .60 1.50
119 Nate Robertson .40 1.00
120 Ivan Rodriguez FOIL 4.00 10.00
121 Alex Sanchez .40 1.00
122 Ugueth Urbina .40 1.00
123 Rondell White .40 1.00
124 Esteban Yan .40 1.00
125 Dmitri Young .40 1.00
126 Josh Beckett .40 1.00
127 Armando Benitez FOIL 2.50 6.00
128 Miguel Cabrera FOIL 6.00 15.00
129 Luis Castillo .40 1.00
130 Jeff Conine .40 1.00
131 Alex Gonzalez .40 1.00
132 Mike Lowell .40 1.00
133 Carl Pavano FOIL 2.50 6.00
134 Matt Perisho .40 1.00
135 Juan Pierre .40 1.00
136 Tim Spooneybarger .40 1.00
137 Dontrelle Willis .40 1.00
138 Brad Ausmus .40 1.00
139 Jeff Bagwell .60 1.50
140 Carlos Beltran FOIL 4.00 10.00
141 Lance Berkman FOIL 4.00 10.00
142 Craig Biggio .60 1.50
143 Roger Clemens FOIL 8.00 20.00
144 Morgan Ensberg .40 1.00
145 Adam Everett .40 1.00
146 Mike Gallo .40 1.00
147 Jeff Kent .40 1.00
148 Mike Lamb .40 1.00
149 Brad Lidge .40 1.00
150 Dan Miceli .40 1.00
151 Wade Miller .40 1.00
152 Roy Oswalt FOIL 4.00 10.00
153 Angel Berroa .40 1.00
154 Shawn Camp .40 1.00
155 Tony Graffanino .40 1.00
156 Ken Harvey .40 1.00
157 Darrell May .40 1.00
158 Joe Randa .40 1.00
159 Desi Relaford .40 1.00
160 Matt Stairs .40 1.00
161 Scott Sullivan .40 1.00
162 Mike Sweeney .40 1.00
163 Wilson Alvarez .40 1.00
164 Adrian Beltre FOIL 6.00 15.00
165 Milton Bradley .40 1.00
166 Hee Seop Choi .40 1.00
167 Eric Gagne FOIL 2.50 6.00
168 Shawn Green .40 1.00
169 Kazuhisa Ishii .40 1.00
170 Cesar Izturis .40 1.00
171 Jose Lima .40 1.00
172 Jeff Weaver .40 1.00
173 Jeff Bennett .40 1.00
174 Javy Lopez .40 1.00
175 Brady Clark .40 1.00
176 Craig Counsell .40 1.00
177 Doug Davis .40 1.00
178 Bill Hall .40 1.00
179 Geoff Jenkins .40 1.00
180 Brooks Kieschnick .40 1.00
181 Dan Kolb FOIL 2.50 6.00
182 Chad Moeller .40 1.00
183 Lyle Overbay .40 1.00
184 Scott Podsednik .40 1.00
185 Victor Santos .40 1.00
186 Henry Blanco .40 1.00
187 Michael Cuddyer .40 1.00
188 Lew Ford .40 1.00
189 Christian Guzman .40 1.00
190 Torii Hunter .40 1.00
191 Jacque Jones .40 1.00
192 Corey Koskie .40 1.00
193 Scott Linebrink .40 1.00
194 Brad Radke .40 1.00
195 Johan Santana FOIL 12.00 30.00
196 Ben Sheets .40 1.00
197 Wes Helms .40 1.00
198 Ken Griffey Jr. 2.00 5.00
199 Danny Graves .40 1.00
200 Runelvys Hernandez .40 1.00
201 Chris Woodward .40 1.00
202 Paul Lo Duca .40 1.00
203 Scot Shields .40 1.00
204 Todd Walker .40 1.00
205 Gregg Zaun .40 1.00
206 Ricky Bottalico .40 1.00
207 Mike Cameron .40 1.00
208 Cliff Floyd .40 1.00
209 Tom Glavine .60 1.50
210 Richard Hidalgo .40 1.00
211 Al Leiter .40 1.00
212 Braden Looper .40 1.00
213 Kazuo Matsui .40 1.00
214 Jason Phillips .40 1.00
215 Mike Piazza FOIL 6.00 15.00
216 Jose Reyes .60 1.50
217 David Wright .75 2.00
218 Kevin Brown .40 1.00
219 Miguel Cairo .40 1.00
220 Tom Gordon .40 1.00
221 Derek Jeter 2.50 6.00
222 Kenny Lofton .40 1.00
223 Jorge Posada FOIL 4.00 10.00
224 Paul Quantrill .40 1.00
225 Mariano Rivera 1.25 3.00
226 Alex Rodriguez FOIL 8.00 20.00
227 Gary Sheffield FOIL 2.50 6.00
228 Javier Vazquez FOIL 2.50 6.00
229 Enrique Wilson .40 1.00
230 Eric Byrnes .40 1.00
231 Eric Chavez FOIL 2.50 6.00
232 Bobby Crosby .40 1.00
233 Erubiel Durazo FOIL 2.50 6.00
234 Jermaine Dye .40 1.00
235 Scott Hatteberg .40 1.00
236 Bobby Kielty .40 1.00
237 Mark Kotsay .40 1.00
238 Mark Mulder FOIL 2.50 6.00
239 Ricardo Rincon .40 1.00
240 Marco Scutaro .60 1.50
241 Barry Zito .60 1.50
242 Bobby Abreu FOIL 2.50 6.00
243 David Bell .40 1.00
244 Pat Burrell .40 1.00
245 Rheal Cormier .40 1.00
246 Mike Lieberthal .40 1.00
247 Jason Michaels .40 1.00
248 Eric Milton FOIL 2.50 6.00
249 Vicente Padilla .40 1.00
250 Placido Polanco .40 1.00
251 Lance Carter .40 1.00
252 Jimmy Rollins .60 1.50
253 Jim Thome FOIL 4.00 10.00
254 Chase Utley .60 1.50
255 Billy Wagner .40 1.00
256 Randy Wolf .40 1.00
257 Jason Bay .40 1.00
258 Jose Castillo .40 1.00
259 Jason Kendall FOIL 2.50 6.00
260 Rob Mackowiak .40 1.00
261 Jose Mesa .40 1.00
262 Oliver Perez .40 1.00
263 Tike Redman .40 1.00
264 Salomon Torres .40 1.00
265 Daryle Ward .40 1.00
266 Kip Wells .40 1.00
267 Eric Munson .40 1.00
268 Craig Wilson .40 1.00
269 Jack Wilson .40 1.00
270 Sean Burroughs .40 1.00
271 Brian Giles .40 1.00
272 Khalil Greene .40 1.00
273 Ramon Hernandez .40 1.00
274 Trevor Hoffman .60 1.50
275 Ryan Klesko .40 1.00
276 Mark Loretta FOIL 2.50 6.00
277 Phil Nevin .40 1.00
278 Akinori Otsuka .40 1.00
279 Jay Payton .40 1.00
280 Jake Peavy FOIL 2.50 6.00
281 David Wells .40 1.00
282 Edgardo Alfonzo .40 1.00
283 Jim Brower .40 1.00
284 Deivi Cruz .40 1.00
285 Ray Durham .40 1.00
286 Scott Eyre .40 1.00
287 Marquis Grissom .40 1.00
288 Dustan Mohr .40 1.00
289 A.J. Pierzynski .40 1.00
290 Jason Schmidt FOIL 2.50 6.00
291 J.T. Snow FOIL 2.50 6.00
292 Brett Tomko .40 1.00
293 Michael Tucker .40 1.00
294 Bret Boone .40 1.00
295 Ryan Franklin .40 1.00
296 Eddie Guardado .40 1.00
297 Shigetoshi Hasegawa .40 1.00
298 Raul Ibanez .60 1.50
299 Edgar Martinez .60 1.50
300 Joel Pineiro .40 1.00
301 Scott Spiezio .40 1.00
302 Ichiro Suzuki FOIL 8.00 20.00
303 Dan Wilson .40 1.00
304 Randy Winn .40 1.00
305 Chris Carpenter FOIL 4.00 10.00
306 Jim Edmonds FOIL 4.00 10.00
307 Jason Isringhausen .40 1.00
308 Ray King .40 1.00
309 Mike Matheny .40 1.00
310 Matt Morris .40 1.00
311 Albert Pujols FOIL 8.00 20.00
312 Edger Renteria .40 1.00
313 Scott Rolen FOIL 4.00 10.00
314 Reggie Sanders .40 1.00
315 Julian Tavarez .40 1.00
316 Larry Walker .60 1.50
317 Woody Williams .40 1.00
318 Tony Womack .40 1.00
319 Danys Baez .40 1.00
320 Rocco Baldelli .40 1.00
321 Dewon Brazelton .40 1.00
322 Carl Crawford .60 1.50
323 Jose Cruz Jr. .40 1.00
324 Toby Hall .40 1.00
325 Travis Harper .40 1.00
326 Aubrey Huff .40 1.00
327 Julio Lugo .40 1.00
328 Tino Martinez .60 1.50
329 Rod Barajas .40 1.00
330 Hank Blalock FOIL 2.50 6.00
331 Francisco Cordero FOIL 2.50 6.00
332 Chan Ho Park .60 1.50
333 Kevin Mench .40 1.00
334 Laynce Nix .40 1.00
335 Kenny Rogers .40 1.00
336 Brian Shouse .40 1.00
337 Alfonso Soriano FOIL 4.00 10.00
338 Mark Teixeira .60 1.50
339 Michael Young .40 1.00
340 Miguel Batista .40 1.00
341 Frank Catalanotto .40 1.00
342 Carlos Delgado .40 1.00
343 Roy Halladay .60 1.50

344 Eric Hinske .40 1.00
345 Orlando Hudson .40 1.00
346 Reed Johnson .40 1.00
347 Justin Speier .40 1.00
348 Vernon Wells .40 1.00

2005 MLB Showdown Strategy

COMPLETE SET (50) 3.00 8.00
THREE PER BOOSTER PACK
S1 Goodbye Baseball .08 .25
S2 Great Addition .10 .25
J.Bay
S3 Hacker .08 .25
S4 Helping Himself .08 .25
S5 High Pitch Count .08 .25
S6 Hit the Foul Pole .08 .25
S7 Make Contact .15 .40
A.Soriano
S8 Pull the Ball .15 .40
A.Dunn
S9 Rattled .10 .25
J.Moyer
S10 Role Player .08 .25
S11 Scuffling .10 .25
K.Wood
S12 See it Clearly .15 .40
V.Guerrero
S13 Serious Wheels .10 .25
P.Polanco
S14 Sprint to Second .08 .25
S15 Steal the Sign .60 1.50
D.Jeter
S16 Turn On It .30 .75
A.Pujols
S17 Upper Deck Shot .15 .40
J.Edmonds
S18 Valuable Asset .08 .25
S19 Weakest Link .08 .25
S20 Work the Count .50 1.25
K.Griffey Jr.
S21 6/4/2003 .10 .25
D.Cruz
S22 Aces Up .30 .75
R.Clemens
S23 Can of Corn .30 .75
I.Suzuki
S24 De-Nied! .10 .25
N.Johnson
S25 Fireballer .10 .25
J.Schmidt
S26 Full Windup .10 .25
D.Willis
S27 Good Leather .30 .75
A.Rodriguez
S28 Hooking Foul .15 .40
S.Rolen
S29 Knuckleball .15 .40
T.Wakefield
S30 Lined Out of Play .10 .25
J.Castro
S31 Masterpiece .15 .40
J.Santana
S32 Out Pitch .10 .25
B.Colon
S33 Paint the Corner .08 .25
S34 Playing Shallow .08 .25
S35 Robbed! .10 .25
H.Blalock
S36 Shut the Door .10 .25
E.Gagne
S37 Up And In .15 .40
J.Edmonds
S38 Working the Edge .08 .25
S39 25th Man .10 .25
J.LaRue
S40 Change in Strategy .15 .40
T.LaRussa
S41 Close Call .30 .75
I.Suzuki
S42 Fake to Third .15 .40
J.Thome
S43 Fan Interference .10 .25
R.Freel
S44 Field General .60 1.50
Jeter-Brown
S45 Intensity .25 .60
S.Sosa
S46 Mind Games .10 .25
J.Washburn
S47 New Strategies .08 .25
S48 Scouting Report .15 .40
F.Robinson
S49 Second Look .08 .25
S50 Swing at Anything .10 .25
O.Cabrera

2000 MLB Showdown Pennant Run 1st Edition

COMPLETE SET (150) 50.00 100.00
COMP.SET w/o FOIL (130) 10.00 25.00
COMMON CARD (1-150) .20 .50
COMMON FOIL 1.00 2.50
FOIL STATED ODDS 1:3
1 Kent Bottenfield .20 .50
2 Ken Hill .20 .50
3 Adam Kennedy .20 .50
4 Ben Molina .20 .50
5 Scott Spiezio .20 .50
6 Brian Anderson .20 .50
7 Erubiel Durazo FOIL 1.00 2.50
8 Armando Reynoso .20 .50
9 Russ Springer .20 .50
10 Todd Stottlemyre .20 .50
11 Tony Womack .20 .50
12 Andres Galarraga FOIL 1.50 4.00
13 Javy Lopez FOIL 1.00 2.50
14 Kevin McGlinchy .20 .50
15 Terry Mulholland .20 .50
16 Reggie Sanders .20 .50
17 Harold Baines .30 .75
18 Will Clark .30 .75
19 Mike Trombley .20 .50
20 Manny Alexander .20 .50
21 Carl Everett FOIL 1.00 2.50
22 Ramon Martinez FOIL 1.00 2.50
23 Bret Saberhagen .20 .50
24 John Wasdin .20 .50
25 Joe Girardi .30 .75
26 Ricky Gutierrez .20 .50
27 Glenallen Hill .20 .50
28 Kevin Tapani .20 .50
29 Kerry Wood FOIL 1.00 2.50
30 Eric Young .20 .50
31 Keith Foulke FOIL 1.00 2.50
32 Mark Johnson .20 .50
33 Sean Lowe .20 .50
34 Jose Valentin .20 .50
35 Dante Bichette .20 .50
36 Ken Griffey Jr. FOIL 5.00 12.00
37 Denny Neagle .20 .50
38 Steve Parris .20 .50
39 Dennys Reyes .20 .50
40 Sandy Alomar Jr. .20 .50
41 Chuck Finley FOIL 1.00 2.50
42 Steve Karsay .20 .50
43 Steve Reed .20 .50
44 Jaret Wright .20 .50
45 Jeff Cirillo .20 .50
46 Tom Goodwin .20 .50
47 Jeffrey Hammonds .20 .50
48 Mike Lansing .20 .50
49 Aaron Ledesma .20 .50
50 Brent Mayne .20 .50
51 Doug Brocail .20 .50
52 Robert Fick .20 .50
53 Juan Gonzalez .20 .50
54 Hideo Nomo .50 1.25
55 Luis Polonia .20 .50
56 Brant Brown .20 .50
57 Alex Fernandez .20 .50
58 Cliff Floyd .20 .50
59 Dan Miceli .20 .50
60 Vladimir Nunez .20 .50
61 Moises Alou FOIL 1.00 2.50
62 Roger Cedeno FOIL 1.00 2.50
63 Octavio Dotel .20 .50
64 Mitch Meluskey .20 .50
65 Daryle Ward .20 .50
66 Mark Quinn FOIL 1.00 2.50
67 Brad Rigby .20 .50
68 Blake Stein .20 .50
69 Mac Suzuki .20 .50
70 Terry Adams .20 .50
71 Darren Dreifort .20 .50
72 Kevin Elster .20 .50
73 Shawn Green FOIL 1.00 2.50
74 Todd Hollandsworth .20 .50
75 Gregg Olson .20 .50
76 Kevin Barker .20 .50
77 Jose Hernandez .20 .50
78 Dave Weathers .20 .50
79 Hector Carrasco .20 .50
80 Eddie Guardado .20 .50
81 Jacque Jones .20 .50
82 David Ortiz .50 1.25
83 Peter Bergeron .20 .50
84 Hideki Irabu .20 .50
85 Lee Stevens .20 .50
86 Anthony Telford .20 .50
87 Derek Bell .20 .50
88 John Franco .20 .50
89 Mike Hampton FOIL 1.00 2.50
90 Bobby Jones .20 .50
91 Todd Pratt .20 .50
92 Todd Zeile .20 .50
93 Jason Grimsley .20 .50
94 Roberto Kelly .20 .50
95 Jim Leyritz .20 .50
96 Ramiro Mendoza .20 .50
97 Rich Becker .20 .50
98 Ramon Hernandez .20 .50
99 Tim Hudson FOIL 1.50 4.00
100 Jason Isringhausen .20 .50
101 Mike Magnante .20 .50
102 Olmedo Saenz .20 .50
103 Mickey Morandini .20 .50
104 Robert Person .20 .50
105 Desi Relaford .20 .50
106 Jason Christiansen .20 .50
107 Wil Cordero .20 .50
108 Francisco Cordova .20 .50
109 Chad Hermansen .20 .50
110 Pat Meares .20 .50
111 Aramis Ramirez .20 .50
112 Bret Boone .20 .50
113 Matt Clement .20 .50
114 Carlos Hernandez .20 .50
115 Ryan Klesko .20 .50
116 Dave Magadan .20 .50
117 Al Martin .20 .50
118 Bobby Estalella .20 .50
119 Livan Hernandez .20 .50
120 Doug Mirabelli .20 .50
121 Joe Nathan .20 .50
122 Mike Cameron .20 .50
123 Mark McLemore .20 .50
124 Gil Meche .20 .50
125 John Olerud .20 .50
126 Arthur Rhodes .20 .50
127 Aaron Sele FOIL 1.00 2.50
128 Jim Edmonds FOIL 1.00 2.50
129 Pat Hentgen .20 .50
130 Darryl Kile .20 .50
131 Eli Marrero .20 .50
132 Dave Veres .20 .50
133 Fernando Vina .20 .50
134 Vinny Castilla .20 .50
135 Juan Guzman .20 .50
136 Ryan Rupe .20 .50
137 Greg Vaughn FOIL 1.00 2.50
138 Gerald Williams .20 .50
139 Esteban Yan .20 .50
140 Tom Evans .20 .50
141 Gabe Kapler .20 .50
142 Ruben Mateo FOIL 1.00 2.50
143 Kenny Rogers .20 .50
144 David Segui .20 .50
145 Tony Batista .20 .50
146 Chris Carpenter .30 .75
147 Brad Fullmer .20 .50
148 Alex Gonzalez .20 .50
149 Roy Halladay .30 .75
150 Raul Mondesi FOIL 1.00 2.50

2000 MLB Showdown Pennant Run Strateg

COMPLETE SET (25) 5.00 12.00
S1 Aaron Boone .20 .50
S2 Chipper Jones .50 1.25
S3 Bob Abreu .20 .50
S4 Fernando Tatis .20 .50
S5 Rod Carew .30 .75
S6 J.D. Drew .20 .50
S7 John Vander Wal .20 .50
S8 Pokey Reese .20 .50
S9 Greg Maddux .60 1.50
S10 Cincinnati Reds .20 .50
S11 Larry Walker .30 .75
S12 Alex Rodriguez .60 1.50
S13 Alex Rodriguez .60 1.50
S14 New York Mets .20 .50
S15 Kevin Brown .20 .50
S16 Paul O'Neill .30 .75
S17 Scott Williamson .20 .50
S18 Jamie Moyer .20 .50
S19 Bernie Williams .30 .75
S20 John Franco .20 .50
S21 Pittsburgh Pirates .20 .50
S22 John Rocker .20 .50
S23 Mike Lansing .20 .50
S24 R.Clemens .60 1.50
J.Torre
S25 Derek Jeter 1.25 3.00

2000 MLB Showdown Pennant Run Unlimited

*UNLIMITED: 2X TO .5X 1ST EDITION
*UNL.FOIL: 2X TO .5X BASIC FOIL

2001 MLB Showdown Pennant Run

COMPLETE SET (175) 100.00 200.00
COMP.SET w/o FOIL (150) 15.00 40.00
COMMON CARD (1-175) .08 .25
COMMON FOIL 2.00 5.00
1 Randy Velarde .08 .25
2 Dustin Hermanson .08 .25
3 Jamie Moyer .30 .75
4 Aaron Fultz .08 .25
5 Barry Zito FOIL 3.00 8.00
6 Adam Piatt .08 .25
7 Ben Grieve .08 .25
8 C.C. Sabathia FOIL 2.00 5.00
9 Eddie Guardado .08 .25
10 Matt Kinney .08 .25
11 Blake Stein .08 .25
12 Billy Wagner FOIL 2.00 5.00
13 Chris Holt .08 .25
14 Homer Bush .08 .25
15 Vladimir Nunez .08 .25
16 C.J. Nitkowski .08 .25
17 Juan Pierre .30 .75
18 Jose Valentin .08 .25
19 Juan Gonzalez .30 .75
20 Derek Bell .08 .25
21 Wade Miller .08 .25
22 Shawn Estes .08 .25
23 Enrique Wilson .08 .25
24 Dave Magadan .08 .25
25 Jason Christiansen .08 .25
26 Paul Shuey .08 .25
27 Mark Wohlers .08 .25
28 John Riedling .08 .25
29 Francisco Cordova .08 .25
30 Craig House .08 .25
31 Scott Strickland .08 .25
32 Octavio Dotel .08 .25
33 Jimmy Rollins FOIL 2.00 5.00
34 Carl Pavano .30 .75
35 Sandy Alomar Jr. .08 .25
36 Hideki Irabu .08 .25
37 Tom Gordon .08 .25
38 Roosevelt Brown .08 .25
39 Alex Rodriguez FOIL 5.00 12.00
40 Andres Galarraga .08 .25
41 Rob Bell .08 .25
42 Jason Schmidt .30 .75
43 Rod Beck .08 .25
44 Paul Rigdon .08 .25
45 Dan Miceli .08 .25
46 Ricky Bones .08 .25
47 Mike Hampton FOIL 3.00 8.00
48 Cliff Politte .08 .25
49 Chris Stynes .08 .25
50 Ramiro Mendoza .08 .25
51 Todd Walker .08 .25
52 Fernando Seguignol .08 .25
53 Mark Guthrie .08 .25
54 Tony Armas Jr. .08 .25
55 Billy McMillon .08 .25
56 Gary Bennett .08 .25
57 Corey Patterson FOIL 2.00 5.00
58 Juan Guzman .08 .25
59 Joe Crede 1.00 2.50
60 A.J. Pierzynski .30 .75
61 Ben Davis .08 .25
62 Alan Embree .08 .25
63 Jon Garland FOIL 2.00 5.00
64 Ryan Kohlmeier .08 .25
65 Andy Benes .08 .25
66 Ron Gant .30 .75
67 Jerry Hairston Jr. .08 .25
68 Odalis Perez .08 .25
69 Lance Painter .08 .25
70 David Segui .08 .25
71 Russ Davis .08 .25
72 Jeff Zimmerman .08 .25
73 Dennys Reyes .08 .25
74 Jamey Wright .08 .25
75 Rico Brogna .08 .25
76 Geraldo Guzman .08 .25
77 Eric Gagne .30 .75
78 Bruce Chen .08 .25
79 Justin Speier .08 .25
80 Randy Keisler .08 .25
81 Ellis Burks FOIL 3.00 8.00
82 Alfonso Soriano .60 1.50
83 Jeff Nelson .08 .25
84 Wes Helms .08 .25
85 Freddy Garcia FOIL 2.00 5.00
86 Erubiel Durazo .08 .25
87 Ben Sheets FOIL 3.00 8.00
88 Jose Ortiz FOIL 2.00 5.00
89 Paul Wilson .08 .25
90 Onan Masaoka .08 .25
91 Jose Rosado .08 .25
92 A.J. Burnett .30 .75
93 Bubba Trammell .08 .25
94 Mike Fetters .08 .25
95 Jacob Cruz .08 .25
96 John Franco .30 .75
97 Armando Reynoso .30 .75
98 Lou Pote .08 .25
99 D'Angelo Jimenez FOIL 2.00 5.00
100 Julio Zuleta .08 .25
101 Charles Johnson FOIL 3.00 8.00
102 Tsuyoshi Shinjo RC .60 1.50
103 Brett Tomko .08 .25
104 Marcus Giles .30 .75
105 Craig Counsell .08 .25
106 Ruben Mateo .08 .25
107 Andy Ashby .08 .25
108 Marlon Anderson .08 .25
109 Mark Grace .60 1.50
110 Russ Branyan .08 .25
111 Julian Tavarez .08 .25
112 Joey Hamilton .08 .25
113 Jason LaRue .08 .25
114 Benji Gil .08 .25
115 Bill Mueller .30 .75
116 Mike Stanton .08 .25
117 Ray King .08 .25
118 Timo Perez .08 .25
119 Johnny Damon FOIL 3.00 8.00
120 Matt Morris .30 .75
121 Kevin Appier .30 .75
122 Frank Castillo .08 .25
123 Mike Darr .08 .25
124 Felipe Crespo .08 .25
125 John Smoltz FOIL 3.00 8.00
126 Ben Weber .08 .25
127 Luis Rivas .08 .25
128 Travis Harper .08 .25
129 Aubrey Huff .30 .75
130 Paul LoDuca .30 .75
131 Eric Davis .30 .75
132 Fernando Tatis .08 .25
133 Ugueth Urbina .08 .25
134 Steve Kline .08 .25
135 Tanyon Sturtze .08 .25
136 Scott Hatteberg .08 .25
137 Tomokazu Ohka FOIL 2.00 5.00
138 Melvin Mora .30 .75
139 Kip Wells .08 .25
140 Ken Caminiti .30 .75
141 Dave Martinez .08 .25
142 Robert Fick .08 .25
143 Mike Bordick .30 .75
144 Doug Mientkiewicz .30 .75
145 Darryl Hamilton .08 .25
146 Shane Reynolds .08 .25
147 Vernon Wells FOIL 2.00 5.00
148 Rey Ordonez .08 .25
149 Brad Ausmus .30 .75
150 Jay Powell .08 .25
151 Todd Hundley .08 .25
152 Travis Miller .08 .25
153 Tyler Houston .08 .25
154 Nelson Cruz .08 .25
155 Manny Ramirez FOIL 3.00 8.00
156 Luis Lopez .08 .25
157 Luis Sojo .08 .25
158 Tony Gwynn FOIL 3.00 8.00
159 Roger Cedeno .08 .25
160 Royce Clayton .08 .25
161 Olmedo Saenz .08 .25
162 Brook Fordyce .08 .25
163 Dee Brown .08 .25
164 David Wells FOIL 2.00 5.00
165 Jack Wilson RC .60 1.50
166 Pedro Feliz .08 .25
167 Hideo Nomo 1.00 2.50
168 Albert Pujols FOIL RC 15.00 40.00
169 Ichiro Suzuki FOIL RC 10.00 25.00
170 Ramon Ortiz .30 .75
171 Mike Holtz .08 .25
172 Chris Woodward .08 .25
173 Mike Mussina FOIL 3.00 8.00
174 Carlos Guillen .30 .75
175 Ben Petrick FOIL 2.00 5.00

2001 MLB Showdown Pennant Run Strategy

COMPLETE SET (25) 2.00 5.00
S1 J.Damon .15 .40
Advance on Throw
S2 R.Mateo .08 .25
Ball in the Dirt
S3 McGwire .50 1.25
Constant Pressure
S4 J.Lieber .08 .25
Emergency Bunt
S5 C.Ripken/1st-Pitch Swinging .60 1.50
S6 M.Piazza .30 .75
Go Up Hacking
S7 D.Jeter .50 1.25
Speedster
S8 J.Valentin .08 .25
Sprint to Second
S9 B.Santiago .08 .25
Wild Thing
S10 P.Reese .08 .25
Wipeout
S11 T.Gwynn .25 .60
Caught Napping
S12 G.Maddux .30 .75
Comebacker
S13 J.Zuleta .08 .25
Confusion
S14 R.Durham .08 .25
Double-Play
S15 A.Nunez .08 .25
Fired Up
S16 R.Ordonez .08 .25
Focused
S17 Clemens .40 1.00
Going the Distance
S18 R.Ankiel .08 .25
Great Pickoff Move
S19 Maddux .30 .75
Groundball Pitcher
S20 D.Graves .08 .25
Hung It
S21 M.McGwire .50 1.25
Pitch Around
S22 A.Leiter .08 .25
Pour It On
S23 B.Bonds .50 1.25
Clutch Performance
S24 Mascot .08 .25
Dot Racing
S25 D.Reyes .08 .25
It's Crunch Time

2002 MLB Showdown Pennant Run

COMP.SET w/o SP's (100) 15.00 40.00
COMMON CARD (1-125) .25 .60
COMMON FOIL 2.00 5.00
FOIL STATED ODDS 1:3
1 J.C. Romero .25 .60
2 Robb Nen .25 .60
3 Raul Mondesi .25 .60
4 Mike Piazza .60 1.50
5 Scott Rolen .40 1.00
6 Shigetoshi Hasegawa .25 .60
7 Shannon Stewart .25 .60
8 David Eckstein FOIL 2.00 5.00
9 Melvin Mora .25 .60
10 Jose Rijo .25 .60
11 Einar Diaz .25 .60
12 A.J. Burnett .25 .60
13 Mike Sweeney .25 .60
14 Jorge Posada FOIL 3.00 8.00
15 Mark Kotsay .25 .60
16 Doug Davis .25 .60
17 Steve Woodard .25 .60
18 Sun Woo Kim .25 .60
19 Sean Casey .25 .60
20 Juan Acevedo .25 .60
21 Dustan Mohr .25 .60
22 Mariano Rivera .60 1.50
23 Kip Wells .25 .60
24 Kenny Lofton FOIL 2.00 5.00
25 Steve Cox .25 .60
26 Josh Fogg FOIL 2.00 5.00
27 Ruben Sierra .25 .60
28 Sandy Alomar Jr. .25 .60
29 Vicente Padilla FOIL 2.00 5.00
30 Carlos Beltran .25 .60
31 Mike Lowell .25 .60
32 Omar Vizquel .40 1.00
33 Ricky Stone RC .25 .60
34 Geoff Jenkins .25 .60
35 Eric Karros .25 .60
36 Ryan Drese .25 .60
37 Adam Dunn .40 1.00
38 Hank Blalock .25 .60
39 Marcus Giles .25 .60
40 Joe Randa .25 .60
41 Bob Wickman .25 .60
42 Roy Halladay .25 .60
43 Craig Counsell .25 .60
44 Derek Lowe .25 .60
45 Ray Durham .25 .60
46 Paul Shuey .25 .60
47 Cliff Floyd .25 .60
48 Shawn Green .25 .60
49 Torii Hunter FOIL 2.00 5.00
50 Edgardo Alfonzo .25 .60
51 Carlos Pena .40 1.00
52 Sean Burroughs .25 .60
53 Placido Polanco .25 .60
54 Rafael Palmeiro .40 1.00
55 Nate Cornejo .25 .60
56 Tim Salmon .25 .60
57 Craig Biggio .40 1.00
58 Eric Hinske FOIL 2.00 5.00
59 Rickey Henderson .60 1.50
60 Nick Johnson .25 .60
61 Rey Ordonez .25 .60
62 Jose Hernandez .25 .60
63 Antonio Alfonseca .25 .60
64 Alfonso Soriano FOIL 3.00 8.00
65 Eric Chavez .25 .60
66 B.J. Surhoff FOIL 2.00 5.00
67 Austin Kearns FOIL 2.00 5.00
68 Jacob Cruz .25 .60
69 Armando Benitez .25 .60
70 Derek Jeter 1.50 4.00
71 Ryan Jensen .25 .60
72 Kevin Mench .25 .60
73 Mike Remlinger .25 .60
74 Luis Castillo .25 .60
75 Kazuhisa Ishii FOIL RC 3.00 8.00
76 Bobby Abreu .25 .60
77 Dave Veres .25 .60
78 Tony Batista .25 .60
79 Rey Sanchez .25 .60
80 Jason Grimsley .25 .60
81 Al Leiter FOIL 2.00 5.00
82 Kerry Wood FOIL 2.00 5.00
83 Ellis Burks .25 .60
84 Corey Patterson .25 .60
85 Adrian Beltre .60 1.50
86 Barry Zito .25 .60
87 Doug Mientkiewicz .25 .60
88 Jeffrey Hammonds .25 .60
89 Jeremy Giambi .25 .60
90 Tsuyoshi Shinjo .25 .60
91 Roger Clemens SS FOIL 6.00 15.00
92 John Franco SS .25 .60
93 Alex Rodriguez SS FOIL 6.00 15.00
94 Barry Bonds SS FOIL 25.00 60.00
95 Fred McGriff SS .40 1.00
96 Chuck Finley SS .25 .60
97 Jose Rijo SS .25 .60
98 Jeff Bagwell SS FOIL 12.00 30.00
99 Ron Gant SS .25 .60
100 Tom Glavine SS .40 1.00
101 Mike Mussina SS .40 1.00
102 Gary Sheffield SS .25 .60
103 Barry Larkin SS .40 1.00
104 Jim Thome SS .40 1.00
105 Chipper Jones SS FOIL 5.00 12.00
106 Rickey Henderson SS .60 1.50
107 Randy Johnson SS FOIL 5.00 12.00
108 Mike Piazza SS FOIL 5.00 12.00
109 John Smoltz SS .40 1.00
110 Edgar Martinez SS .40 1.00
111 Larry Walker SS .40 1.00
112 Pedro Martinez SS FOIL 12.00 30.00
113 Sammy Sosa SS FOIL 5.00 12.00
114 Roberto Alomar SS FOIL 12.00 30.00
115 Curt Schilling SS FOIL 3.00 8.00
116 Chuck Knoblauch SS .25 .60
117 Frank Thomas SS .60 1.50
118 Jeff Kent SS .25 .60
119 Kenny Lofton SS .25 .60
120 Ken Griffey Jr. SS 1.25 3.00
121 Trevor Hoffman SS FOIL 3.00 8.00
122 Mo Vaughn SS .25 .60
123 Robin Ventura SS .25 .60
124 Ellis Burks SS .25 .60
125 Tim Raines SS .40 1.00

2002 MLB Showdown Pennant Run Strategy

COMPLETE SET (23) 2.00 5.00
S1 Bad Call .15 .40
B.Williams
S2 Clutch Hitting .30 .75
M.Piazza
S3 Crowd Plate .08 .25
T.Glaus
S4 Down the Middle .08 .25
S5 Ducks on the Pond .08 .25
S6 Free Steal .25 .60
A.Rodriguez
S7 Overthrow .08 .25
S8 Payoff Pitch .08 .25
S9 Rally Cap .08 .25
T.Goodwin
S10 Rattled .08 .25
N.Cornejo
S11 Shell-Shocked .08 .25
R.Ankiel
S12 Shelled .08 .25
S.Sullivan
S13 Comebacker .08 .25
D.Williams
S14 Fast Worker .08 .25
S15 Full Windup .15 .40
A.Pettitte
S16 Great Throw .40 1.00
I.Suzuki
S17 Hung It .08 .25
S18 In Groove .08 .25
M.Mulder
S20 Insult Injury .08 .25
C.Schilling
S21 Nerves Steel .08 .25
T.Hoffman
S22 Pitchout .08 .25
S23 Scuff Ball .08 .25
B.Moehler
S25 Change in Strategy .08 .25

2003 MLB Showdown Pennant Run

COMP.SET w/o SP's (100) 15.00 40.00
FOIL STATED ODDS 1:3
1 Josh Beckett .20 .50
2 Jeremy Bonderman RC .75 2.00
3 Carlos Febles .20 .50
4 Tom Goodwin .20 .50
5 Luis Rivas .20 .50
6 Scott Sullivan .20 .50
7 John Thomson .20 .50
8 Lance Carter .20 .50
9 Terry Mulholland .20 .50
10 Jake Westbrook .20 .50
11 Chris George .20 .50
12 Jake Peavy .20 .50
13 Felix Rodriguez .20 .50
14 Marlon Byrd .20 .50
15 Toby Hall .20 .50
16 Rocky Biddle .20 .50
17 Brandon Lyon .20 .50
18 Roberto Hernandez .20 .50
19 Carlos Silva .20 .50
20 Chris Hammond .20 .50
21 Eric Munson .20 .50
22 David Dellucci .20 .50
23 R.A. Dickey .30 .75
24 Cliff Politte .20 .50
25 Russ Springer .20 .50
26 Kirk Rueter .20 .50
27 Vance Wilson .20 .50
28 Scott Williamson .20 .50
29 Ryan Franklin .20 .50
30 Juan Castro .20 .50
31 Craig Monroe .20 .50
32 Joe Beimel .20 .50
33 Scott Schoeneweis .20 .50
34 John Halama .20 .50
36 Felipe Lopez .20 .50
37 Casey Blake .20 .50
38 Mike MacDougal .20 .50
39 Kris Benson .20 .50
40 Francisco Cordero .20 .50
41 Tom Gordon .20 .50
42 Neifi Perez .20 .50
43 Chad Bradford .20 .50
44 Miguel Cairo .20 .50
45 Mike Matheny .20 .50
46 Mike Timlin .20 .50
47 D.J. Carrasco RC .20 .50
48 Eddie Perez .20 .50
49 Gregg Zaun .20 .50
50 Ronnie Belliard .20 .50
51 Ricardo Rodriguez .20 .50
52 B.J. Ryan .20 .50
53 Michael Tucker .20 .50
54 Rheal Cormier .20 .50
55 Felix Heredia .20 .50
56 Alex Cora .30 .75
57 Travis Lee .20 .50
58 Ted Lilly .20 .50
59 Tom Wilson .20 .50
60 Jeff D'Amico .20 .50
61 Adam Eaton .20 .50
62 Travis Harper .20 .50
63 Mark Loretta .20 .50
64 Ricky Stone .20 .50
65 Wil Cordero .20 .50
66 Cliff Floyd .20 .50
67 Livan Hernandez .20 .50
68 Paul Quantrill .20 .50
69 Ben Davis .20 .50
70 Shawn Estes .20 .50
71 Chris Stynes .20 .50
72 Jay Payton .20 .50
73 Ramon Hernandez .20 .50
74 Jason Johnson .20 .50
75 John Vander Wal .20 .50
76 Shawn Chacon FOIL 3.00 8.00
77 D'Angelo Jimenez .20 .50
78 Desi Relaford .20 .50
79 Rich Aurilia .20 .50
80 Rod Barajas .20 .50
81 Jose Cruz FOIL 3.00 8.00
82 Kyle Lohse .20 .50
83 Rondell White .20 .50
84 Gil Meche FOIL 3.00 8.00
85 Jose Guillen .20 .50
86 Kenny Lofton .20 .50
87 Zach Day FOIL 3.00 8.00
88 Mark Redman .20 .50
89 Melvin Mora FOIL 3.00 8.00
90 Todd Walker .20 .50
91 Torii Hunter .20 .50
92 Frank Catalanotto .20 .50
93 Andres Galarraga .30 .75
94 Jason Schmidt .20 .50
95 Eric Byrnes .20 .50
96 Hank Blalock FOIL 3.00 8.00
97 Jacque Jones FOIL 3.00 8.00
98 Michael Young .20 .50
99 Carl Everett .20 .50
100 Preston Wilson .20 .50
101 Esteban Loaiza .20 .50
102 Raul Mondesi FOIL 3.00 8.00
103 Carlos Delgado FOIL 3.00 8.00
104 Gary Sheffield FOIL 3.00 8.00
105 Kevin Appier .20 .50
106 Jesse Orosco SS .20 .50
107 Pat Hentgen SS .20 .50
108 Matt Williams SS .20 .50
109 David Cone SS FOIL 3.00 8.00
110 Mark Grace SS FOIL 5.00 12.00
111 Carlos Baerga SS FOIL 3.00 8.00
112 Greg Maddux SS FOIL 10.00 25.00
113 Kevin Brown SS FOIL 3.00 8.00
114 Ivan Rodriguez SS FOIL 5.00 12.00
115 John Olerud SS FOIL 3.00 8.00
116 Larry Doby CC .30 .75
117 Yogi Berra CC FOIL 8.00 20.00
118 Hoyt Wilhelm CC FOIL 5.00 12.00
119 Pee Wee Reese CC .30 .75
120 Brooks Robinson CC FOIL 5.00 12.00
121 Robin Yount CC FOIL 8.00 20.00
122 Reggie Jackson CC FOIL 5.00 12.00
123 Harmon Killebrew CC FOIL 8.00 20.00
124 Rod Carew CC FOIL 5.00 12.00
125 Nolan Ryan CC FOIL 25.00 60.00

2003 MLB Showdown Pennant Run Strategy

COMPLETE SET (25) 2.00 5.00
1 Change Sides .15 .40
O.Vizquel
2 Emergency Bunt .10 .25
J.Hairston
3 Get Under It .10 .25
B.Boone
4 In Motion .10 .25
D.Hansen
5 Out of Position .10 .25
6 Passed Ball .10 .25
E.Diaz
7 Magic Word .10 .25
J.McKeon
8 Suicide Squeeze .10 .25
9 Warning Track .10 .25
B.Giles
10 Block the Plate .10 .25
K.Osik
11 Comebacker .15 .40
Schilling-Butler
12 Good Matchup .10 .25
K.Ishii
13 Ground Rule Double .10 .25
A.Kearns
14 In the Zone .15 .40
P.Martinez
15 Infield In .10 .25
16 Pickoff Attempt .10 .25
W.Ruan
17 Play the Odds .30 .75
R.Clemens
18 Playing Shallow .10 .25
A.Kearns
19 Quick Pitch .10 .25
20 Sinker .10 .25
J.Jennings
21 Up and In .10 .25
J.Bell
22 Good Scouting .10 .25
D.Brown
23 Looking Ahead .10 .25
B.Showalter
24 Old Tricks .10 .25
25 Think Twice .30 .75
Showalter-A.Rod

2004 MLB Showdown Pennant Run

COMP.SET w/o FOIL (100) 15.00 40.00
COMMON CARD .20 .50
COMMON RC .20 .50
COMMON FOIL 1.25 3.00
COMMON HOF .20 .50
COMMON HOF FOIL 8.00 20.00
FOIL STATED ODDS 1:3
1 Shawn Chacon .20 .50
2 Bobby Crosby .20 .50
3 Russ Ortiz .20 .50
4 Jason Simontacchi .20 .50
5 Oscar Villarreal .20 .50
6 Rocky Biddle .20 .50
7 Joe Borowski .20 .50
8 Shawn Estes .20 .50
9 Adam LaRoche .20 .50
10 Carl Everett .20 .50
11 Willie Harris .20 .50
12 Carlos Silva .20 .50
13 Aaron Rowand .20 .50
14 Francisco Cordero .20 .50
15 Ryan Freel .20 .50
16 Trevor Hoffman .30 .75
17 Edgar Renteria AS .20 .50
18 Mike Maroth .20 .50
19 Carlos Pena .30 .75
20 John Smoltz .50 1.25
21 Carlos Guillen .20 .50
22 Buddy Groom .20 .50

23 Aaron Miles .20 .50
24 Jason Schmidt AS FOIL 1.25 3.00
25 Danny Kolb AS .20 .50
26 Marcos Scutaro .30 .75
27 Gary Sheffield AS .20 .50
28 Eric Gagne AS FOIL 1.25 3.00
29 Kazuhisa Ishii .20 .50
30 B.J. Ryan .20 .50
31 Mark Mulder AS FOIL 1.25 3.00
32 Gerald Laird .20 .50
33 Joe Mauer .40 1.00
34 Nate Robertson .20 .50
35 Hideki Matsui AS .75 2.00
36 Ray Lankford .20 .50
37 Jake Peavy .20 .50
38 Esteban Loaiza AS .20 .50
39 Mike Stanton .20 .50
40 Kevin Gregg .20 .50
41 Steve Trachsel .20 .50
42 Albert Pujols AS FOIL 4.00 10.00
43 Shingo Takatsu RC .20 .50
44 Ichiro Suzuki AS FOIL 4.00 10.00
45 Milton Bradley .20 .50
46 Eric Chavez .20 .50
47 Paul Lo Duca AS FOIL 1.25 3.00
48 Kip Wells .20 .50
49 Miguel Cabrera AS FOIL 3.00 8.00
50 Johnny Estrada AS .20 .50
51 Pedro Martinez FOIL 2.00 5.00
52 Jason Giambi AS .20 .50
53 Kenny Rogers AS .20 .50
54 Alex Rodriguez AS FOIL 4.00 10.00
55 Chone Figgins .20 .50
56 Ken Harvey AS .20 .50
57 Todd Helton AS .30 .75
58 Javy Lopez .20 .50
59 R.A. Dickey .30 .75
60 J.D. Drew .20 .50
61 Melvin Mora .20 .50
62 Danny Bautista .20 .50
63 Kerry Wood .20 .50
64 Randy Johnson AS .50 1.25
65 Scott Rolen AS FOIL 2.00 5.00
66 Roger Clemens AS FOIL 4.00 10.00
67 Brad Penny .20 .50
68 Matt Clement .20 .50
69 Ronnie Belliard AS FOIL 1.25 3.00
70 Alfonso Soriano AS FOIL 2.00 5.00
71 Lew Ford .20 .50
72 Sean Casey AS FOIL 1.25 3.00
73 Troy Glaus .20 .50
74 Mike Lowell AS .20 .50
75 Juan Uribe .20 .50
76 Adrian Beltre .50 1.25
77 Jack Wilson AS .20 .50
78 Craig Wilson .20 .50
79 Lyle Overbay FOIL 1.25 3.00
80 Jose Contreras .20 .50
81 Jason Jennings .20 .50
82 Matt Mantei .20 .50
83 Luis Vizcaino .20 .50
84 Luis Ayala .20 .50
85 Danny Patterson .20 .50
86 C.J. Nitkowski .20 .50
87 Larry Bigbie .20 .50
88 Mike Lieberthal .20 .50
89 Mike Timlin .20 .50
90 Rob Mackowiak .20 .50
91 Kevin Cash .20 .50
92 Danys Baez .20 .50
93 J.C. Romero .20 .50
94 Dan Miceli .20 .50
95 Armando Benitez AS .20 .50
96 Hank Blalock AS .20 .50
97 Vinny Castilla .20 .50
98 Danny Graves AS FOIL 1.25 3.00
99 Derek Jeter AS 1.25 3.00
100 Jim Thome AS FOIL 2.00 5.00
101 Mark Loretta AS .20 .50
102 Victor Martinez AS .30 .75
103 Ken Griffey Jr. AS 1.00 2.50
104 Miguel Tejada AS .30 .75
105 Mike Piazza AS .50 1.25
106 Ivan Rodriguez AS .30 .75
107 Tom Glavine AS .30 .75
108 Carl Crawford AS FOIL 2.00 5.00
109 Jeff Kent AS .20 .50
110 Ben Sheets AS .20 .50
111 Sammy Sosa AS .50 1.25
112 Vladimir Guerrero AS .30 .75
113 Curt Schilling AS .30 .75
114 Carl Pavano AS .20 .50
115 Manny Ramirez AS FOIL 3.00 8.00
116 Billy Williams HOF .30 .75
117 Ralph Kiner HOF .30 .75
118 Whitey Ford HOF FOIL 12.00 30.00
119 Jim Palmer HOF FOIL 10.00 25.00
120 Willie McCovey HOF FOIL 12.00 30.00
121 Phil Rizzuto HOF .30 .75
122 Orlando Cepeda HOF .30 .75
123 Eddie Mathews HOF FOIL 10.00 25.00
124 Tom Seaver HOF FOIL 12.00 30.00
125 Bob Feller HOF FOIL 12.00 30.00

2004 MLB Showdown Pennant Run Strategy

COMPLETE SET (25) 2.00 5.00
TWO PER BOOSTER PACK
S1 I.Rodriguez .15 .40
Down the Middle
S2 Carlos Pena .15 .40
Grooved
S3 A.Amezaga .10 .25
Lost in the Sun
S4 Protect the Runner .08 .25
S5 M.Herges .10 .25
Y.Torrealba
Fumes
S6 Neifi Perez .10 .25
Serious Wheels
S7 C.Counsell .10 .25
Smash up Middle
S8 Scott Rolen .15 .40
Superior Talent
S9 J.T. Snow .10 .25
Swat!
S10 Shigetoshi Hasegawa .10 .25
Timing
S11 Sean Casey .10 .25
Calculated Risk
S12 Reggie Sanders .10 .25
Chin Music
S13 Randy Johnson .25 .60
Great Start
S14 F.Thomas .25 .60
High and Tight
S15 Roger Clemens .30 .75
Intimidation
S16 Jose Valentin .10 .25
On Your Toes
S17 Ryan Klesko .10 .25
Rally Killer
S18 Chad Bradford .10 .25
Setup Man
S19 Darin Erstad .10 .25
Whiff!
S20 B.Snowalter .10 .25
Dugout General
S21 Jose Molina .10 .25
Old Tricks
S22 Out of Sync .08 .25
S23 Barry Larkin .15 .40
Revelation
S24 Mark Teixeira .15 .40
Stealing Signals
S25 Alex Rodriguez .30 .75
Superstar

2002 MLB Showdown Trading Deadline

COMP.SET w/o SP'S (125) 15.00 40.00
1 Jason Giambi FOIL 3.00 8.00
2 Chris Singleton .20 .50
3 Ben Davis .20 .50
4 Tsuyoshi Shinjo .40 1.00
5 Brian Jordan .40 1.00
6 Tony Clark .20 .50
7 Moises Alou FOIL 3.00 8.00
8 Todd Walker .20 .50
9 Ricky Gutierrez .20 .50
10 Brad Fullmer .20 .50
11 Jeromy Burnitz .40 1.00
12 Gary Sheffield FOIL 5.00 12.00
13 Marty Cordova FOIL 2.00 5.00
14 Todd Zeile .40 1.00
15 Alex Gonzalez .40 1.00
16 Kenny Lofton .40 1.00
17 Vinny Castilla .40 1.00
18 Craig Paquette .20 .50
19 Michael Tucker .20 .50
20 Cesar Izturis .20 .50
21 Eric Young .20 .50
22 Chuck Knoblauch .40 1.00
23 Roberto Alomar FOIL 5.00 12.00
24 David Bell .20 .50
25 Johnny Damon Sox .60 1.50
26 Roger Cedeno .20 .50
27 Robin Ventura .40 1.00
28 David Justice FOIL 3.00 8.00
29 Brady Anderson .40 1.00
30 Pokey Reese .20 .50
31 Reggie Sanders FOIL 3.00 8.00
32 Jeff Cirillo FOIL 2.00 5.00
33 Juan Encarnacion .20 .50
34 Tino Martinez FOIL 5.00 12.00
35 Carl Everett FOIL 3.00 8.00
36 Danny Bautista .20 .50
37 Rafael Furcal .40 1.00
38 Dmitri Young FOIL 3.00 8.00
39 Jay Gibbons .20 .50
40 Brian Buchanan .20 .50
41 David Segui .20 .50
42 Barry Larkin FOIL 5.00 12.00
43 John Vander Wal .20 .50
44 Brent Mayne .20 .50
45 Neifi Perez .20 .50
46 Lenny Harris .20 .50
47 Jason LaRue .20 .50
48 Travis Fryman .40 1.00
49 Juan Uribe .20 .50
50 Shea Hillenbrand .40 1.00
51 Aaron Rowand .40 1.00
52 Jose Ortiz .20 .50
53 Robert Fick .20 .50
54 Doug Glanville .20 .50
55 Charles Johnson FOIL 3.00 8.00
56 Derrek Lee .60 1.50
57 Carlos Febles .20 .50
58 Luis Rivas .20 .50
59 Lee Stevens .20 .50
60 Mike Lieberthal .40 1.00
61 Ryan Klesko FOIL 5.00 12.00
62 Chris Gomez .20 .50
63 Randy Winn .20 .50
64 Rusty Greer .40 1.00
65 Felipe Lopez .20 .50
66 Carlos Pena .20 .50
67 Toby Hall .20 .50
68 Milton Bradley .40 1.00
69 Matt Lawton .20 .50
70 Gregg Zaun .20 .50
71 Eric Hinske .20 .50
72 Alex Ochoa .20 .50
73 Rondell White .40 1.00
74 Armando Rios .20 .50
75 Desi Relaford .20 .50
76 Nomar Garciaparra FOIL 6.00 15.00
77 Frank Thomas FOIL 6.00 15.00
78 Mitch Meluskey .20 .50
79 Morgan Ensberg .40 1.00
80 Mo Vaughn FOIL 3.00 8.00
81 Adrian Brown .20 .50
82 Juan Gonzalez FOIL 3.00 8.00
83 Tom Wilson RC .40 1.00
84 Matt Stairs .20 .50
85 Andres Galarraga .40 1.00
86 Sidney Ponson .20 .50
87 Jesus Colome .20 .50
88 Juan Cruz .20 .50
89 Eddie Guardado .20 .50
90 Jon Garland .40 1.00
91 Denny Neagle .20 .50
92 Chad Durbin .20 .50
93 Kevin Brown FOIL 3.00 8.00
94 Elmer Dessens .20 .50
95 Eric Gagne .40 1.00
96 Jamey Wright .20 .50
97 Pedro Martinez FOIL 3.00 8.00
98 Jason Bere .20 .50
99 Ugueth Urbina .20 .50
100 Carl Pavano .40 1.00
101 Kip Wells .20 .50
102 Paul Abbott .20 .50
103 Billy Wagner FOIL 3.00 8.00
104 Erik Hiljus .20 .50
105 Brandon Duckworth .20 .50
106 Ruben Quevedo .20 .50
107 Jimmy Anderson .20 .50
108 Bobby Jones .20 .50
109 Livan Hernandez .40 1.00
110 Curtis Leskanic .20 .50
111 Tom Gordon .20 .50
112 Jeff Austin RC .40 1.00
113 Joel Pineiro .20 .50
114 Chad Bradford .20 .50
115 Woody Williams .20 .50
116 Victor Zambrano FOIL 2.00 5.00
117 Jose Mesa .20 .50
118 Roy Halladay .40 1.00
119 Steve Karsay .20 .50
120 Hideo Nomo 1.00 2.50
121 Jeff Farnsworth .20 .50
122 Dave Weathers .20 .50
123 Sean Lowe .20 .50
124 Mike Myers .20 .50
125 Jason Schmidt .40 1.00
126 Mike Williams .20 .50
127 Terry Adams .20 .50
128 Chan Ho Park FOIL 3.00 8.00
129 Jeff D'Amico .20 .50
130 Kevin Appier FOIL 3.00 8.00
131 Glendon Rusch .20 .50
132 Jason Isringhausen .40 1.00
133 Todd Ritchie .20 .50
134 Shawn Estes .20 .50
135 Kevin Millwood .40 1.00
136 Aaron Sele .20 .50
137 Rick Helling .20 .50
138 Billy Koch .20 .50
139 Paul Quantrill .20 .50
140 Tim Spooneybarger .20 .50
141 Jorge Julio .20 .50
142 Carlos Hernandez .20 .50
143 Rick Ankiel .20 .50
144 Scott Erickson .20 .50
145 Denny Hocking .20 .50
146 Kazuhisa Ishii RC .60 1.50
147 Pedro Astacio .20 .50
148 Satoru Komiyama RC .40 1.00
149 Kurt Ainsworth .20 .50
150 John Smoltz FOIL 5.00 12.00

2002 MLB Showdown Trading Deadline Strategy

COMPLETE SET (25) 2.00 5.00
S1 Big Inning .08 .25
L.Gonzalez
S2 Do or Die .08 .25
J.Cirillo
S3 Free Steal .25 .60
A.Rodriguez
S4 Lean Into It .08 .25
T.Shinjo
S5 Overthrow .08 .25
Cubs-Mets
S6 Pointers .08 .25
C.Patterson
S7 Pro Hitter .08 .25
D.Justice
S8 Rattled .08 .25
N.Cornejo
S9 Shelled .08 .25
S.Sullivan
S10 Shell-Shocked .08 .25
R.Ankiel
S11 Swing Fences .08 .25
Cubs
S12 Tricky Hop .08 .25
M.Anderson
S13 Whiplash .08 .25
S14 Choke .08 .25
A.Boone
S15 Comebacker .08 .25
D.Williams
S16 Fast Worker .08 .25
T.Nomura
S17 Focused .08 .25
P.Abbott
S18 Hung It .08 .25
S19 In the Zone .08 .25
R.Helling
S20 Scuff Ball .08 .25
B.Moehler
S21 Swiss Army .08 .25
J.Pineiro
S22 What Were You Thinking? .08 .25
S23 Whoops! .08 .25
A.Gonzalez
S24 Bear Down .08 .25
B.Giles
S25 Game Inches .08 .25
R.Aurilia

2003 MLB Showdown Trading Deadline

COMP.SET w/o SP's (120) 15.00 40.00
COMMON CARD (1-145) .20 .50
COMMON FOIL 1.50 4.00
COMMON FOIL RC 1.50 4.00
FOIL STATED ODDS 1:3
1 So Taguchi .20 .50
2 Ryan Drese .20 .50
3 Mike Hampton .20 .50
4 Sandy Alomar Jr. .20 .50
5 Steve Sparks .20 .50
6 Chan Ho Park .30 .75
7 Roger Cedeno .20 .50
8 Antonio Osuna .20 .50
9 Ryan Dempster .20 .50
10 Jesse Orosco .20 .50
11 Angel Berroa .20 .50
12 Sean Burroughs .20 .50
13 Matt Mantei .20 .50
14 Einar Diaz .20 .50
15 Ken Griffey Jr. 1.00 2.50
16 Rey Sanchez .20 .50
17 Antonio Alfonseca .20 .50
18 Carl Crawford .30 .75
19 Rey Ordonez .20 .50
20 Brandon Inge .20 .50
21 Hank Blalock .20 .50
22 Albie Lopez .20 .50
23 Aaron Sele .20 .50
24 Willie Bloomquist .20 .50
25 Shigetoshi Hasegawa .20 .50
26 Steve Kline .20 .50
27 Ramiro Mendoza .20 .50
28 Mike Stanton .20 .50
29 Carlos Zambrano .30 .75
30 Dean Palmer .20 .50
31 Mark Grudzielanek .20 .50
32 Matt Williams .20 .50
33 Michael Cuddyer .20 .50
34 Glendon Rusch .20 .50
35 Hee Seop Choi .20 .50
36 Mike Bordick .20 .50
37 Ray King .20 .50
38 Bill Mueller .20 .50
39 John McDonald .20 .50
40 Brent Butler .20 .50
41 Josh Bard .20 .50
42 Xavier Nady .20 .50
43 J.C. Romero .20 .50
44 Paul Shuey .20 .50
45 Eric Karros .20 .50
46 Runelvys Hernandez .20 .50
47 Braden Looper .20 .50
48 Dave Roberts .30 .75
49 Deivi Cruz .20 .50
50 Todd Hollandsworth .20 .50
51 Billy Koch .20 .50
52 Brandon Villafuerte .20 .50
53 Ricardo Rincon .20 .50
54 Joe Crede .20 .50
55 Juan Pierre .20 .50
56 Tsuyoshi Shinjo .20 .50
57 Ugueth Urbina .20 .50
58 Luis Vizcaino FOIL 1.50 4.00
59 Ben Weber .20 .50
60A Kerry Wood .20 .50
60B Kerry Wood FOIL 1.50 4.00
61 Tim Worrell .20 .50
62 Royce Clayton .20 .50
63 Chone Figgins .20 .50
64 Ken Huckaby .20 .50
65 Brian Anderson .20 .50
66 Aramis Ramirez .20 .50
67 Edgar Martinez .30 .75
68 Keith Foulke .20 .50
69 LaTroy Hawkins .20 .50
70 Mike Remlinger .20 .50
71 Lyle Overbay .20 .50
72 Buddy Groom .20 .50
73 Orlando Hudson .20 .50
74 Francisco Rodriguez FOIL 2.50 6.00
75 Craig Biggio .30 .75
76 Todd Zeile .20 .50
77 Vernon Wells .20 .50
78 Casey Fossum .20 .50
79 Wes Helms .20 .50
80 Robert Fick .20 .50
81 Scott Spiezio .20 .50
82 Ty Wigginton .20 .50
83 Elmer Dessens .20 .50
84 Arthur Rhodes .20 .50
85 Matt Stairs .20 .50
86 Miguel Olivo .20 .50
87 Tino Martinez .20 .50
88 Travis Hafner .20 .50
89 Octavio Dotel .20 .50
90 Jimmy Rollins .30 .75
91 Placido Polanco .20 .50
92 Kevin Brown .20 .50
93 John Patterson .20 .50
94 Andy Pettitte .30 .75
95 Bobby Kielty .20 .50
96 Jeremy Giambi .20 .50
97 Brandon Phillips .20 .50
98 Fred McGriff .30 .75
99 Damian Moss .20 .50
100 Russ Ortiz .20 .50
101 Mark Teixeira .30 .75
102 Tom Glavine FOIL 2.50 6.00
103 Chris Woodward .20 .50
104 Brad Radke .20 .50
105 Edgardo Alfonzo .20 .50
106 Jose Contreras FOIL RC 4.00 10.00
107 Josh Beckett .20 .50
108 Johan Santana .30 .75
109 Brandon Larson .20 .50
110 Randall Simon .20 .50
111 Randy Winn FOIL 1.50 4.00
112 Ray Durham .20 .50
113 Omar Daal FOIL 1.50 4.00
114 David Wells FOIL 1.50 4.00
115 Wade Miller .20 .50
116 Bartolo Colon FOIL 1.50 4.00
117 Ryan Klesko FOIL 1.50 4.00
118 Jeff Bagwell .30 .75
119 Roy Oswalt FOIL 2.50 6.00
120 Orlando Hernandez FOIL 1.50 4.00
121 Ivan Rodriguez FOIL 2.50 6.00
122 Tim Wakefield .30 .75
123 Josh Phelps .20 .50
124 Woody Williams .20 .50
125 Chipper Jones FOIL 4.00 10.00
126 Randy Wolf .20 .50
127 Kevin Millwood FOIL 1.50 4.00
128 Jeff Kent FOIL 1.50 4.00
129 Rocco Baldelli FOIL 1.50 4.00
130 Hideki Matsui FOIL RC 8.00 20.00
131 Jim Thome FOIL 2.50 6.00
132 Kazuhiro Sasaki RS .20 .50
133 Jason Jennings RS FOIL 1.50 4.00
134 Rafael Furcal RS .20 .50
135 Derek Jeter RS FOIL 10.00 25.00
136 Benito Santiago RS .20 .50
137 Jeff Bagwell RS .30 .75
138 Carlos Beltran RS .30 .75
139 Scott Rolen RS FOIL 2.50 6.00
141 Tim Salmon RS .20 .50
142 Ichiro Suzuki RS FOIL 5.00 12.00
143 Mike Piazza RS FOIL 4.00 10.00
144 Albert Pujols RS .60 1.50
145 Nomar Garciaparra RS FOIL 2.50 6.00

2003 MLB Showdown Trading Deadline Strategy

COMPLETE SET (25) 2.00 5.00
S1 Clutch Hitting .25 .60
S.Sosa
S2 Clutch Rookie .10 .25
B.Wilkerson
S3 Great Addition .50 1.25
H.Matsui
S4 Headed Home .10 .25
B.Mayne
S5 High Fives .15 .40
Vizcaino-Bagwell
S6 Long Gone! .40 1.00
B.Bonds
S7 On the Move .10 .25
S8 Take Given .15 .40
E.Martinez
S9 Who Is This Guy .10 .25
E.Hinske
S10 Add by Subtract .10 .25
J.Jennings
S11 De-nied! .10 .25
O.Hudson
S12 Digging Deep .30 .75
R.Clemens
S13 Lock It Down .25 .60
R.Johnson
S14 New Arrival .10 .25
M.Herges
S15 Not So Fast .10 .25
E.Diaz
S16 Pitch Around .30 .75
Ichiro
S17 Rookie Fireballer .15 .40
F.Rodriguez
S18 Split-Finger Fastball .25 .60
J.Smoltz
S19 Still Learning .10 .25
B.Buchanan
S20 3 up 3 Down .15 .40
B.Zito
S21 Triple Dip .10 .25
B.Butler
S22 Brainstorm .10 .25
S23 Outmanaged .10 .25
G.Varsho
S24 Stealing Signals .10 .25
M.McLemore
S25 Swing at Anything .10 .25
M.Cameron

2004 MLB Showdown Trading Deadline

COMP.SET w/o SP's (100) 15.00 40.00
FOIL STATED ODDS 1:3 BOOSTER
1 Jose Mesa .20 .50
2 Pokey Reese .20 .50
3 Rey Sanchez .20 .50
4 Jeff Weaver .20 .50
5 Todd Zeile .20 .50
6 Carlos Rivera .20 .50
7 Orlando Palmeiro .20 .50
8 Roberto Alomar .30 .75
9 Doug Glanville .20 .50
10 Khalil Greene .30 .75
11 Victor Martinez .30 .75
12 Jeffrey Hammonds .20 .50
13 Bobby Kielty .20 .50
14 Brian Schneider .20 .50
15 Arthur Rhodes .20 .50
16 David Dellucci .20 .50
17 Eric Young .20 .50
18 Grant Balfour .20 .50
19 Javier A. Lopez .20 .50
20 Jeff Nelson .20 .50
21 Kelvim Escobar .20 .50
22 Braden Looper .20 .50
23 Tino Martinez .30 .75
24 Laynce Nix .20 .50
25 Horacio Ramirez .20 .50
26 Hideki Matsui .75 2.00
27 Kevin Mench .20 .50
28 Scott Sullivan .20 .50
29 Michael Barrett .20 .50
30 Jose Cruz Jr. .20 .50
31 Robert Fick .20 .50
32 Brad Fullmer .20 .50
33 Eric Karros .20 .50
34 Mark Kotsay .20 .50
35 Fernando Vina .20 .50
36 Tim Worrell .20 .50
37 Mike Cameron .20 .50
38 Howie Clark .20 .50
39 Tom Gordon .20 .50
40 Adam Kennedy .20 .50
41 Rafael Palmeiro .30 .75
42 Reed Johnson .20 .50
43 Aquilino Lopez .20 .50
44 Julian Tavarez .20 .50
45 Ben Broussard .20 .50
46 Miguel Cabrera .50 1.25
47 Raul Ibanez .30 .75
48 Randall Simon .20 .50
49 Ronnie Belliard .20 .50
50 Scott Spiezio .20 .50
51 Ellis Burks .30 .75
52 LaTroy Hawkins .20 .50
53 Pat Hentgen .20 .50
54 Eddie Guardado .20 .50
55 Todd Walker .20 .50
56 Ivan Rodriguez .30 .75
57 Raul Mondesi .20 .50
58 Jeromy Burnitz .20 .50
59 Rich Aurilia .20 .50
60 Keith Foulke Sox .20 .50
61 Ramon Hernandez .20 .50
62 Kenny Lofton .20 .50
63 Rafael Soriano FOIL 1.00 2.50
64 Jody Gerut .20 .50
65 Randy Johnson .50 1.25
66 John Burkett .20 .50
67 Brian Giles FOIL 1.00 2.50
68 Matt Morris .20 .50
69 Derrek Lee .20 .50
70 Miguel Tejada .30 .75
71 Ted Lilly .20 .50
72 David Wells .20 .50
73 Carl Everett .20 .50
74 A.J. Pierzynski .20 .50
75 Gary Sheffield .20 .50
76 Juan Gonzalez .20 .50
77 Brandon Webb .20 .50
78 Joel Pineiro .20 .50
79 Scott Rolen FOIL 1.50 4.00
80 Jim Edmonds FOIL 1.50 4.00
81 Curt Schilling FOIL 1.50 4.00
82 Kevin Brown FOIL 1.00 2.50
83 Chad Cordero .20 .50
84 Rich Harden .20 .50
85 Lyle Overbay .20 .50
86 Paul Quantrill .20 .50
87 Rondell White .20 .50
88 Joe Nathan .20 .50
89 Jose Valverde .20 .50
90 Francisco Rodriguez .30 .75
91 Billy Wagner .20 .50
92 Jason Giambi .20 .50
93 Jason Lane .20 .50
94 Frank Thomas .50 1.25
95 Greg Maddux .60 1.50
96 Andy Pettitte .30 .75
97 Jay Payton .20 .50
98 Roger Clemens .60 1.50
99 Bartolo Colon FOIL 1.00 2.50
100 Vladimir Guerrero .30 .75
101 Kazuo Matsui FOIL RC 1.50 4.00
102 Javier Vazquez .20 .50
103 Esteban Loaiza FOIL 1.00 2.50
104 Alex Rodriguez FOIL 3.00 8.00
105 Javy Lopez FOIL 1.00 2.50
106 Tino Martinez SS .30 .75
107 Vladimir Guerrero SS FOIL 1.50 4.00
108 Derek Jeter SS FOIL 6.00 15.00
109 Craig Biggio SS .30 .75
110 Tom Glavine SS .30 .75
111 Nomar Garciaparra SS FOIL 1.50 4.00
112 Mike Mussina SS FOIL 1.50 4.00
113 Todd Helton SS FOIL 1.50 4.00
114 Greg Maddux SS FOIL 3.00 8.00
115 Roger Clemens SS FOIL 3.00 8.00
116 Rollie Fingers CC FOIL 12.00 30.00
117 Luis Aparicio CC .30 .75
118 Lou Brock CC .30 .75
119 Joe Morgan CC FOIL 12.00 30.00
120 Richie Ashburn CC FOIL 12.00 30.00
121 Al Kaline CC FOIL 20.00 50.00
122 Bob Gibson CC FOIL 12.00 30.00
123 Willie Stargell CC .30 .75
124 Warren Spahn CC FOIL 12.00 30.00
125 Mike Schmidt CC FOIL 30.00 80.00

2004 MLB Showdown Trading Deadline Strategy

COMPLETE SET (25) 2.00 5.00
COMMON CARD (S1-S25) .10 .25
COMMON RC YR .10 .25
STATED ODDS 2:1
S1 D.Wells .10 .25
Dialed-In
S2 A.Pujols .30 .75
En Fuego!
S3 S.Casey .10 .25
Last Chance
S4 On the Move .08 .25
S5 Opposite Field Power .08 .25
S6 L.Rothschild CO .10 .25
Out of Gas
S7 A.Soriano .15 .40
Quick Thinking
S8 R.Sexson .10 .25
Swing for Fences
S9 Wheelhouse .08 .25
S10 Beaned .08 .25
S11 M.Alou .10 .25
M.Giles
Broken Bat
S12 C.Everett .10 .25
Caught Napping
S13 R.Simon .10 .25
Chopper
S14 J.Pierre .10 .25
Dying Quail
S15 K.Matsui .15 .40
Great Reactions
S16 Piazza-Seo .25 .60
Insult to Injury
S17 T.Helton .15 .40
Lefty Shift
S18 A.Huff .10 .25
T.Hall
Pumped Up
S19 S.Sosa .25 .60
Punched Out
S20 Robbed! .08 .25
S21 F.Alou MG .10 .25
Feast or Famine
S22 Pac Bell Park .08 .25
Home Field
S23 Just Over the Rail .08 .25
S24 Umpires .08 .25
Late Call
S25 B.Melvin MG .10 .25
Outmanaged

2005 MLB Showdown Trading Deadline

COMP.SET w/o FOIL (150) 40.00 75.00
COMMON CARD (1-165) .40 1.00
COMMON FOIL 1-165 2.00 5.00
COMMON CARD (166-175) .40 1.00
COMMON FOIL (166-175) 4.00 10.00
FOIL STATED ODDS 1:3
1 Steve Finley .40 1.00
2 Josh Phelps .40 1.00
3 Magglio Ordonez .60 1.50
4 Nick Johnson .40 1.00
5 Carlos Lee FOIL 2.00 5.00
6 Quinton McCracken .40 1.00
7 Shawn Estes .40 1.00
8 J.J. Putz .40 1.00
9 Mike DeJean .40 1.00
10 Juan Gonzalez .40 1.00
11 Eric Young .40 1.00
12 Matt Mantei .40 1.00
13 Neal Cotts .40 1.00
14 Mark Sweeney .40 1.00
15 Glendon Rusch .40 1.00
16 Termel Sledge .40 1.00
17 Ron Villone .40 1.00
18 Troy Glaus .40 1.00
19 Wilson Valdez .40 1.00
20 B.J. Surhoff .40 1.00
21 Kazuhisa Ishii .40 1.00
22 Dustin Hermanson .40 1.00
23 Al Leiter .40 1.00
24 Octavio Dotel .40 1.00
25 Henry Blanco .40 1.00
26 J.D. Drew FOIL 2.00 5.00
27 Kevin Millwood .40 1.00
28 Sandy Alomar Jr. .40 1.00
29 John Riedling .40 1.00
30 Rich Harden FOIL 2.00 5.00
31 Aaron Sele .40 1.00
32 Carlos Beltran FOIL 3.00 8.00
33 Jose Lima .40 1.00
34 Richard Hidalgo .40 1.00
35 Placido Polanco .40 1.00
36 Neifi Perez .40 1.00
37 Wilson Alvarez .40 1.00
38 So Taguchi .40 1.00
39 Matt Perisho .40 1.00
40 Roberto Hernandez .40 1.00
41 Todd Walker .40 1.00
42 Jason Kendall .40 1.00
43 Brett Myers .40 1.00
44 Carlos Silva .40 1.00
45 Randy Johnson FOIL 5.00 12.00
46 Jeremy Bonderman .40 1.00
47 Orlando Cabrera .40 1.00
48 Carlos Delgado FOIL 2.00 5.00
49 A.J. Pierzynski .40 1.00
50 Omar Vizquel .60 1.50
51 Lenny Harris .40 1.00
52 Chris Carpenter .60 1.50
53 Miguel Cairo .40 1.00
54 Sammy Sosa FOIL 5.00 12.00
55 Royce Clayton .40 1.00
56 Cal Eldred .40 1.00
57 Rich Aurilia .40 1.00
58 Orlando Palmeiro .40 1.00
59 Bengie Molina .40 1.00
60 Ismael Valdez .40 1.00
61 Nate Bump .40 1.00
62 David Wells .40 1.00
63 Jermaine Dye .40 1.00
64 Carlos Zambrano .60 1.50
65 David Newhan .40 1.00
66 Russ Springer .40 1.00
67 Elmer Dessens .40 1.00
68 Kris Benson .40 1.00
69 Al Reyes .40 1.00
70 Tino Martinez .60 1.50
71 Ruben Sierra .40 1.00
72 Antonio Osuna .40 1.00
73 Moises Alou .40 1.00
74 Brad Wilkerson FOIL 2.00 5.00
75 Jason Christiansen .40 1.00
76 Geoff Blum .40 1.00
77 Dennys Reyes .40 1.00
78 Craig Counsell .40 1.00
79 Rey Sanchez .40 1.00
80 Mark Hendrickson .40 1.00
81 Doug Mirabelli .40 1.00
82 Jeromy Burnitz .40 1.00
83 Carl Pavano .40 1.00
84 Richie Sexson .40 1.00
85 Eric Milton .40 1.00
86 Mark DeRosa .40 1.00
87 Bob Wickman .40 1.00
88 Hideo Nomo 1.00 2.50
89 Tony Armas Jr. .40 1.00
90 Desi Relaford .40 1.00
91 Russ Ortiz .40 1.00
92 Jose Vidro .40 1.00
93 Jeff Kent FOIL 2.00 5.00
94 Esteban Yan .40 1.00
95 Tim Hudson FOIL 3.00 8.00
96 Jay Payton .40 1.00
97 Tony Womack .40 1.00
98 Gregg Zaun .40 1.00
99 David Weathers .40 1.00
100 Scott Podsednik FOIL 2.00 5.00
101 Mark Mulder FOIL 2.00 5.00
102 Jose Guillen .40 1.00
103 Grady Sizemore .60 1.50
104 Paul Bako .40 1.00
105 Jeff DaVanon .40 1.00
106 Jeff Nelson .40 1.00
107 Troy Percival .40 1.00
108 Brian Lawrence .40 1.00

109 Mike Redmond .40 1.00
110 Odalis Perez .40 1.00
111 John Franco .40 1.00
112 Doug Brocail .40 1.00
113 Einar Diaz .40 1.00
114 Mark Grudzielanek .40 1.00
115 Jason Marquis .40 1.00
116 Jayson Werth .60 1.50
117 John Mabry .40 1.00
118 Alexis Rios .40 1.00
119 Livan Hernandez .40 1.00
120 Zack Greinke 1.25 3.00
121 Chris Hammond .40 1.00
122 Kent Mercker .40 1.00
123 Ryan Drese .40 1.00
124 Pedro Martinez FOIL 3.00 8.00
125 Alex Cora .60 1.50
126 Kenny Lofton .40 1.00
127 Adrian Beltre FOIL 5.00 12.00
128 David Eckstein .40 1.00
129 Derek Lowe .40 1.00
130 Joe Randa .40 1.00
131 Jose Valentin .40 1.00
132 David Bush .40 1.00
133 Brian Schneider .40 1.00
134 Matt Clement .40 1.00
135 Paul Byrd .40 1.00
136 Jose Vizcaino .40 1.00
137 Todd Pratt .40 1.00
138 Jose Offerman .40 1.00
139 Dan Wilson .40 1.00
140 Frank Francisco .40 1.00
141 Woody Williams .40 1.00
142 Juan Castro .40 1.00
143 Jerry Hairston Jr. .40 1.00
144 Jeff Suppan .40 1.00
145 Steve Reed .40 1.00
146 Jon Lieber .40 1.00
147 Cristian Guzman .40 1.00
148 Shawn Green FOIL 2.00 5.00
149 Damion Easley .40 1.00
150 Bronson Arroyo .40 1.00
151 Raul Mondesi .40 1.00
152 Roger Cedeno .40 1.00
153 Carlos Baerga .40 1.00
154 Jose Hernandez .40 1.00
155 Antonio Alfonseca .40 1.00
156 Ricky Ledee .40 1.00
157 Armando Benitez .40 1.00
158 Esteban Loaiza .40 1.00
159 Steve Kline .40 1.00
160 Corey Koskie .40 1.00
161 Vinny Castilla FOIL 2.00 5.00
162 Tony Clark .40 1.00
163 Edgar Renteria FOIL 2.00 5.00
164 Brian Jordan .40 1.00
165 David Dellucci .40 1.00
166 Hoyt Wilhelm FOIL 6.00 15.00
167 Pee Wee Reese .60 1.50
168 Larry Doby .60 1.50
169 Yogi Berra FOIL 10.00 25.00
170 Robin Yount FOIL 10.00 25.00
171 Brooks Robinson FOIL 6.00 15.00
172 Reggie Jackson FOIL 6.00 15.00
173 Rod Carew FOIL 6.00 15.00
174 Harmon Killebrew FOIL 10.00 25.00
175 Nolan Ryan FOIL 20.00 50.00

2005 MLB Showdown Trading Deadline Strategy

COMPLETE SET (25) 3.00 8.00
TWO PER PACK
*FOIL: 2.5X TO 6X BASIC
FOIL STATED ODDS 1:3
1 Free Steal .08 .25
2 Get Under It .10 .25
G.Sheffield
3 Go Yard .15 .40
V.Guerrero
4 Just Called Up .08 .25
5 Leadoff Man .30 .75
Ichiro
6 Lofted .10 .25
B.Giles
7 Missed Cutoff .30 .75
Ichiro
8 Mom.Swing .25 .60
Piazza-Pedro
9 Shaken .08 .25
10 Shelled .15 .40
P.Konerko
11 Texas Leaguer .08 .25
12 Caught Looking .10 .25
M.Young
13 Great Range .10 .25
A.Jones
14 High Heat .30 .75
R.Clemens
15 Just Over the Wall .08 .25
16 Slider .25 .60
R.Johnson
17 Stranded .08 .25
18 Superior Athlete .10 .25
M.Loretta
19 Taking a Risk .15 .40
A.Pettitte
20 Team Defense .10 .25
T.Walker
21 Brainstorm .10 .25
E.Milton
22 Ch.Scorecard .08 .25
Busch Stad
23 Good Coaching .10 .25
M.Scioscia
24 Preparation .15 .40
M.Prior
25 Shell Game .08 .25

2003 MLB Stickers

COMPLETE SET (240) 6.00 15.00
1 David Eckstein .05 .10
2 Adam Kennedy .05 .10
3 Troy Glaus .05 .10
4 Garret Anderson .05 .10
5 Darin Erstad .05 .10
6 Tim Salmon .05 .10
7 Troy Percival .05 .10
8 Jarrod Washburn .05 .10
9 Tony Batista .05 .10
10 Deivi Cruz .05 .10
11 Jerry Hairston Jr .05 .10
12 Jeff Conine .05 .10
13 Jay Gibbons .05 .10
14 Rodrigo Lopez .05 .10
15 Omar Daal .05 .10
16 Jason Johnson .05 .10
17 Jason Varitek .10 .25
18 Nomar Garciaparra .05 .15
19 Shea Hillenbrand .05 .10
20 Johnny Damon .05 .15
21 Manny Ramirez .10 .25
22 Pedro Martinez .05 .15
23 Derek Lowe .05 .10
24 Tim Wakefield .05 .10
25 Magglio Ordonez .05 .15
26 Carlos Lee .05 .10
27 Joe Crede .05 .10
28 Paul Konerko .05 .15
29 Sandy Alomar Jr. .05 .10
30 Frank Thomas .10 .25
31 Bartolo Colon .05 .10
32 Mark Buehrle .05 .15
33 Ellis Burks .05 .10
34 Ricky Gutierrez .05 .10
35 Travis Hafner .05 .10
36 Omar Vizquel .05 .15
37 Milton Bradley .05 .15
38 Matt Lawton .05 .10
39 C.C. Sabathia .05 .15
40 Danys Baez .05 .10
41 Bobby Higginson .05 .10
42 Dean Palmer .05 .10
43 Craig Paquette .05 .10
44 Brandon Inge .05 .10
45 Dmitri Young .05 .10
46 Shane Halter .05 .10
47 Steve Sparks .05 .10
48 Mike Maroth .05 .10
49 Brent Mayne .05 .10
50 Carlos Febles .05 .10
51 Mike Sweeney .05 .10
52 Joe Randa .05 .10
53 Carlos Beltran .05 .15
54 Dee Brown .05 .10
55 Runelvys Hernandez .05 .10
56 Jeremy Affeldt .05 .10
57 Corey Koskie .05 .10
58 Doug Mientkiewicz .05 .10
59 Cristian Guzman .05 .10
60 Jacque Jones .05 .10
61 Torii Hunter .05 .10
62 A.J. Pierzynski .05 .10
63 Brad Radke .05 .10
64 Eddie Guardado .05 .10
65 Jason Giambi .05 .10
66 Derek Jeter .25 .60
67 Hideki Matsui .20 .50
68 Alfonso Soriano .05 .15
69 Bernie Williams .05 .15
70 Roger Clemens .12 .30
71 Mike Mussina .05 .15
72 Mariano Rivera .12 .30
73 Eric Chavez .05 .10
74 Miguel Tejada .05 .15
75 Scott Hatteberg .05 .10
76 Jermaine Dye .05 .10
77 Keith Foulke .05 .10
78 Mark Mulder .05 .10
79 Barry Zito .05 .15
80 Tim Hudson .05 .15
81 Ichiro Suzuki .12 .30
82 Edgar Martinez .05 .15
83 John Olerud .05 .10
84 Carlos Guillen .05 .10
85 Mike Cameron .05 .10
86 Freddy Garcia .05 .10
87 Bret Boone .05 .10
88 Kazuhiro Sasaki .05 .10
89 Toby Hall .05 .10
90 Rey Ordonez .05 .10
91 Carl Crawford .05 .10
92 Rocco Baldelli .05 .10
93 Seth McClung .05 .10
94 Ben Grieve .05 .10
95 Aubrey Huff .05 .10
96 Joe Kennedy .05 .10
97 Rafael Palmeiro .05 .15
98 Alex Rodriguez .12 .30
99 Hank Blalock .05 .10
100 Carl Everett .05 .10
101 Mike Young .05 .10
102 Juan Gonzalez .05 .10
103 Chan Ho Park .05 .10
104 Ugueth Urbina .05 .10
105 Carlos Delgado .05 .10
106 Vernon Wells .05 .10
107 Eric Hinske .05 .10
108 Shannon Stewart .05 .10
109 Orlando Hudson .05 .10
110 Kelvin Escobar .05 .10
111 Mark Hendrickson .05 .10
112 Roy Halladay .05 .10
113 Lyle Overbay .05 .10
114 Junior Spivey .05 .10
115 Tony Womack .05 .10
116 Matt Williams .05 .10
117 Steve Finley .05 .10
118 Luis Gonzalez .05 .10
119 Randy Johnson .10 .25
120 Curt Schilling .05 .15
121 Chipper Jones .10 .25
122 Andruw Jones .05 .10
123 Vinny Castilla .05 .10
124 Javy Lopez .05 .10
125 Rafael Furcal .05 .10
126 Greg Maddux .12 .30
127 Mike Hampton .05 .10
128 Russ Ortiz .05 .10
129 Sammy Sosa .10 .25
130 Corey Patterson .05 .10
131 Moises Alou .05 .10
132 Mark Bellhorn .05 .10
133 Alex Gonzalez .05 .10
134 Kerry Wood .05 .10
135 Matt Clement .05 .10
136 Mark Prior .05 .15
137 Ken Griffey Jr .20 .50
138 Adam Dunn .05 .15
139 Austin Kearns .05 .10
140 Sean Casey .05 .10
141 Barry Larkin .05 .15
142 Aaron Boone .05 .10
143 Ryan Dempster .05 .10
144 Danny Graves .05 .10
145 Larry Walker .05 .15
146 Todd Helton .05 .15
147 Charles Johnson .05 .10
148 Preston Wilson .05 .10
149 Gabe Kapler .05 .10
150 Ronnie Belliard .05 .10
151 Jason Jennings .05 .10
152 Shawn Chacon .05 .10
153 Ivan Rodriguez .05 .15
154 Juan Pierre .05 .10
155 Juan Encarnacion .05 .10
156 Todd Hollandsworth .05 .10
157 Luis Castillo .05 .10
158 Mike Lowell .05 .10
159 A.J. Burnett .05 .10
160 Josh Beckett .05 .15
161 Jeff Kent .05 .10
162 Craig Biggio .05 .15
163 Lance Berkman .05 .15
164 Morgan Ensberg .05 .10
165 Jeff Bagwell .05 .15
166 Brad Ausmus .05 .10
167 Roy Oswalt .05 .15
168 Wade Miller .05 .10
169 Fred McGriff .05 .15
170 Shawn Green .05 .10
171 Brian Jordan .05 .10
172 Paul LoDuca .05 .10
173 Adrian Beltre .10 .25
174 Kevin Brown .05 .10
175 Kazuhisa Ishii .05 .10
176 Eric Gagne .05 .10
177 Richie Sexson .05 .10
178 Geoff Jenkins .05 .10
179 Eddie Perez .05 .10
180 Jeffrey Hammonds .05 .10
181 Royce Clayton .05 .10
182 Mike DeJean .05 .10
183 Ben Sheets .05 .10
184 Glendon Rusch .05 .10
185 Vladimir Guerrero .05 .15
186 Jose Vidro .05 .10
187 Brad Wilkerson .05 .10
188 Michael Barrett .05 .10
189 Orlando Cabrera .05 .10
190 Jeff Liefer .05 .10
191 Joey Eischen .05 .10
192 Tomo Ohka .05 .10
193 Mo Vaughn UER .05 .10
Name spelled as Vaughan
194 Mike Piazza .10 .25
195 Roger Cedeno .05 .10
196 Jeromy Burnitz .05 .10
197 Cliff Floyd .05 .10
198 Al Leiter .05 .10
199 Tom Glavine .05 .15
200 Armando Benitez .05 .10
201 Jim Thome .05 .15
202 Mike Lieberthal .05 .10
203 Jimmy Rollins .05 .15
204 Pat Burrell .05 .10
205 Bobby Abreu .05 .10
206 David Bell .05 .10
207 Kevin Millwood .05 .10
208 Randy Wolf .05 .10
209 Jason Kendall .05 .10
210 Randall Simon .05 .10
211 Aramis Ramirez .05 .10
212 Pokey Reese .05 .10
213 Brian Giles .05 .10
214 Jack Wilson .05 .10
215 Kris Benson .05 .10
216 Josh Fogg .05 .10
217 Jim Edmonds .05 .15
218 J.D. Drew .05 .10
219 Albert Pujols .12 .30
220 Scott Rolen .05 .15
221 Tino Martinez .05 .10
222 Fernando Vina .05 .10
223 Edgar Renteria .05 .10
224 Matt Morris .05 .10
225 Sean Burroughs .05 .10
226 Ryan Klesko .05 .10
227 Phil Nevin .05 .10
228 Mark Kotsay .05 .10
229 Mark Loretta .05 .10
230 Xavier Nady .05 .10
231 Brian Lawrence .05 .10
232 Jake Peavy .05 .10
233 Barry Bonds .15 .40
234 Marquis Grissom .05 .10
235 Ray Durham .05 .10
236 J.T. Snow .05 .10
237 Edgardo Alfonzo .05 .10
238 Rich Aurilia .05 .10
239 Benito Santiago .05 .10
240 Robb Nen .05 .10

1977 Montefusco/D'Acquisto Restaurant

This postcard which features action shots of 1970's pitchers John "The Count" Montefusco as well as John D'Acquisto. In addition, there is a photo of the two Giant pitchers sitting at a table in their eatery. The back has information about this place.

1 John Montefusco 1.25 3.00
John D'Acquisto

1982 Montreal News

This 21-card set was cut out of the Montreal News and features various size color player photos of stars of different sports. The paper is printed in French. The cards are unnumbered and checklisted below in alphabetical order.

COMPLETE SET (21) 16.00 40.00
6 Steve Garvey BB 1.20 3.00
13 Pete Rose BB 3.20 8.00
14 Mike Schmidt BB 3.20 8.00
15 Willie Stargell BB 1.20 3.00
20 Fernando Valenzuela BB .80 2.00

1993-99 Moonlight Graham

These five standard-size cards honor Archibald Graham, who was immortalized in the movie "Field of Dreams". These cards were sold to benefit the Doc Graham scholarship funds. Each card has a different design. These cards are all currently available from the Moonlight Graham web site at three dollars per card.

COMPLETE SET (5) 4.00 10.00
COMMON CARD (1-5) 1.20 3.00
5 Archibald Graham 2.00 5.00
Joe Jackson
Play Ball/1999

1991 MooTown Snackers

This 24-card standard-size set was sponsored by MooTown Snackers. One player card and an attached mail-in certificate (with checklist on back) were included in five-ounce packages of MooTown Snackers cheese snacks. The complete set could be purchased through the mail by sending in the mail-in certificate, three MooTown Snackers UPC codes, and 5.95. The mail-in sets did not come with the attached mail-in tab; cards with tabs are valued approximately twice the prices listed in the checklist below.

COMPLETE SET (24) 12.50 30.00
1 Jose Canseco .60 1.50
2 Kirby Puckett 1.00 2.50
3 Barry Bonds 1.50 4.00
4 Ken Griffey Jr. 2.50 6.00
5 Ryne Sandberg 1.50 4.00
6 Tony Gwynn 1.50 4.00
7 Kal Daniels .08 .25
8 Ozzie Smith 1.50 4.00
9 Dave Justice .40 1.00
10 Sandy Alomar Jr. .20 .50
11 Wade Boggs .75 2.00
12 Ozzie Guillen .20 .50
13 Dave Magadan .08 .25
14 Cal Ripken 3.00 8.00
15 Don Mattingly 1.50 4.00
16 Ruben Sierra .20 .50
17 Robin Yount .60 1.50
18 Len Dykstra .20 .50
19 George Brett 1.50 4.00
20 Lance Parrish .08 .25
21 Chris Sabo .08 .25
22 Craig Biggio .40 1.00
23 Kevin Mitchell .08 .25
24 Cecil Fielder .20 .50

1992 MooTown Snackers

This 24-card standard-size set was produced by MSA (Michael Schechter Associates) for MooTown Snackers. The cards were inserted inside 5 ounce and 10 ounce cheese snack packages. It is reported that more than two million cards were produced. Collectors could also obtain the complete set through a mail-in offer. The cards obtained via mail did not come with the mail-in offer tabs. Cards with tabs have twice the value of the prices below. .

COMPLETE SET (24) 12.50 30.00
1 Albert Belle .20 .50
2 Jeff Bagwell .75 2.00
3 Jose Rijo .08 .25
4 Roger Clemens 1.50 4.00
5 Kevin Maas .08 .25
6 Kirby Puckett 1.00 2.50
7 Ken Griffey Jr. 2.50 6.00
8 Will Clark .60 1.50
9 Felix Jose .08 .25
10 Cecil Fielder .20 .50
11 Darryl Strawberry .20 .50
12 John Smiley .08 .25
13 Roberto Alomar .40 1.00
14 Paul Molitor .60 1.50
15 Andre Dawson .30 .75
16 Terry Mulholland .08 .25
17 Fred McGriff .30 .75
18 Dwight Gooden .20 .50
19 Rickey Henderson .75 2.00
20 Nolan Ryan 6.00 15.00
21 George Brett 1.50 4.00
22 Tom Glavine .40 1.00
23 Cal Ripken 3.00 8.00
24 Frank Thomas .75 2.00

1987 Mother's McGwire

This set consists of four, full-color, rounded-corner cards each showing a different pose of A's slugging rookie Mark McGwire. Cards were originally given out at the national Card Collectors Convention in San Francisco. Later they were available through a mail-in offer involving collectors sending in two proofs-of-purchase from any Mother's Cookies products to get one free card. Photos were taken by Doug McWilliams.

COMPLETE SET (4) 12.50 30.00
COMMON PLAYER (1-4) 3.00 8.00

1988 Mother's Will Clark

This regional set consists of four full-color, rounded-corner cards each showing a different pose of Giants' slugging first baseman Will Clark. Cards were originally found in 18 oz. packages of "Big Bags" of Mother's Cookies at stores in the Northern California area in February and March of 1988. Card backs are done in red and purple on white card stock.

COMPLETE SET (4) 6.00 15.00
COMMON PLAYER (1-4) 1.60 4.00

1988 Mother's McGwire

This regional set consists of four full-color, rounded-corner cards each showing a different pose of The Athletics' slugging first baseman Mark McGwire. Cards were originally found in 18 oz. packages of "Big Bags" of Mother's Cookies at stores in the Northern California area in February and March, 1988. Card backs are done in red and purple on white card stock.

COMPLETE SET (4) 12.50 30.00
COMMON PLAYER (1-4) 3.00 8.00

1989 Mother's Canseco

The 1989 Mother's Jose Canseco set contains four standard-size cards with rounded corners. The fronts have borderless color photos, and the horizontally oriented backs have biographical information. One card was included in each specially marked box of Mother's Cookies.

COMPLETE SET (4) 6.00 15.00
COMMON PLAYER (1-4) 1.50 4.00

1989 Mother's Will Clark

The 1989 Mother's Cookies Will Clark set contains four standard-size cards with rounded corners. The fronts have borderless color photos, and the horizontally oriented backs have biographical information. One card was included in each specially marked box of Mother's Cookies.

COMPLETE SET (4) 4.00 10.00
COMMON PLAYER (1-4) 1.20 3.00

1989 Mother's Griffey Jr.

The 1989 Mother's Cookies Ken Griffey Jr. set contains four standard-size cards with rounded corners. The fronts have borderless color photos, and the horizontal backs have biographical information. One card was included in each specially marked box of Mother's Cookies. The photos were shot by noted sports photographer Barry Colla. It has been reported that card No. 2 is a little more difficult to find than the other cards in the set.

COMPLETE SET (4) 10.00 25.00
COMMON PLAYER (1-4) 5.00 12.00
2 Ken Griffey Jr./(Baseball in hand) 8.00 20.00

1989 Mother's McGwire

The 1989 Mother's Cookies Mark McGwire set contains four standard-size cards with rounded corners. The fronts have borderless color photos, and the horizontal backs have biographical information. One card was included in each specially marked box of Mother's Cookies.

COMPLETE SET (4) 6.00 15.00
COMMON PLAYER (1-4) 1.50 4.00

1990 Mother's Canseco

This is a standard Mother's Cookies set with four cards each measuring the standard size with rounded corners issued to capitalize on Jose Canseco's popularity. This four-card set features Canseco in various batting poses.

COMPLETE SET (4) 6.00 15.00
COMMON PLAYER (1-4) 1.50 4.00

1990 Mother's Will Clark

This is a standard Mother's Cookies set with four cards each measuring the standard size with rounded corners issued to capitalize on Will Clark's popularity. This four-card set features Clark in various poses as indicated in the checklist below.

COMPLETE SET (4) 4.00 10.00
COMMON PLAYER (1-4) 1.20 3.00

1990 Mother's McGwire

This is a standard Mother's Cookies set with four cards each measuring the standard size with rounded corners issued to capitalize on Mark McGwire's popularity. This four-card set features McGwire in various poses as indicated in the checklist below.

COMPLETE SET (4) 6.00 15.00
COMMON PLAYER (1-4) 1.50 4.00

1990 Mother's Ryan

This is a typical Mother's Cookies set with four cards each measuring the standard size with rounded corners honoring Ryan's more than 5,000 strikeouts over his career. This four-card set features Ryan in various pitching poses. The second card in the set is considered tougher to find than the other three in the set. This four-card set was also issued as an unperforated strip.

COMPLETE SET (4) 6.00 15.00
COMMON PLAYER (1-4) 1.60 4.00
2 Nolan Ryan/(Dugout pose) 2.00 5.00

1990 Mother's Matt Williams

This is a standard Mother's Cookies set with four cards each measuring the standard size with rounded corners issued to capitalize on Matt Williams' popularity. This four-card set features Williams in various poses as indicated in the checklist below.

COMPLETE SET (4) 3.00 8.00
COMMON PLAYER (1-4) .80 2.00

1991 Mother's Griffeys

The 1991 Mother's Cookies Father and Son set featuring both major-league playing members of the Griffey family contains four standard-size cards with rounded corners measuring the standard size.

COMPLETE SET (4) 2.50 6.00
1 Ken Griffey Jr. 1.50 4.00
Holding bat
2 Ken Griffey Sr. .30 .75
Holding glove
3 Ken Griffey Sr. and 1.00 2.50
Ken Griffey Jr./(Pose with g
4 Ken Griffey Sr. and 1.00 2.50
Ken Griffey Jr./(Looking ove

1991 Mother's Ryan

This four-card standard-size rounded-corner set was sponsored by Mother's Cookies in honor of Nolan Ryan, baseball's latest 300-game winner. One card was packaged in each box of Mother's Cookies 18-ounce family size bags of five different flavored cookies (Chocolate Chip, Cookie Parade, Oatmeal Raisin, Fudge'N Chips, and Costadas). Also collectors could purchase an uncut strip of the four cards for 7.95 with four proof-of-purchase seals, and a protective sleeve for $1. This four-card set was also issued as an unperforated strip.

COMPLETE SET (4) 4.00 10.00
COMMON PLAYER (1-4) 1.00 2.50

1992 Mother's Bagwell

This four-card, standard-size set was sponsored by Mother's Cookies. The fronts have rounded corners and feature posed color full-bleed photos of Jeff Bagwell, the 1991 National League Rookie of the Year.

COMPLETE SET (4) 3.00 8.00
COMMON PLAYER (1-4) .80 2.00

1992 Mother's Knoblauch

This four-card set measures the standard size and was sponsored by Mother's Cookies in honor of the 1991 American League Rookie of the Year, Chuck Knoblauch.

COMPLETE SET (4) 3.00 8.00
COMMON PLAYER (1-4) .80 2.00

1992 Mother's Ryan Advertisement

These six ad sheets feature some of the actual card photos used in the 1992 Mothers Ryan set. The left side of the panel is used for the card while the right side tells you what type of cookies the cards are available in.

COMPLETE SET (6) 6.00 15.00
COMMON CARD (1-6) 1.20 3.00

1992 Mother's Ryan 7 No-Hitters

The 1992 Mother's Nolan Ryan Seven No-Hitters set contains eight standard-size cards with rounded corners and glossy full-bleed color photos. Card Nos. 1-4 were included in 18-ounce Mother's Cookies family size "Big Bag" cookies. Card Nos. 5-8 were in 16-ounce packages of "sandwich- cookies. The set was also available as an uncut sheet through a mail-in offer on specially marked packages for $7.95 plus four proofs of purchase. The horizontally oriented backs are printed in red and purple and feature biographical information, career notes, highlights, and statistics for each of his no-hitters (except card No. 8).

COMPLETE SET (8) 5.00 12.00
COMMON PLAYER (1-8) .60 1.50

1993 Mother's Ryan Farewell

This ten-card standard-size set has rounded corners and was issued by Mother's Cookies to bid farewell to Nolan Ryan. This set was also issued as a 7 5/8" by 14" sheet consisting of two rows with five cards in each row. This set was rereleased in 1994 with a 1994 date. The cards are valued the same for either year. The 1993 set is much more difficult to acquire as no extra quantities entered the secondary market.

COMPLETE SET (10) 4.00 10.00
COMMON PLAYER (1-10) .50 1.25

1994 Mother's Piazza

Issued to showcase the '93 NL ROY, these four standard-size cards have rounded corners and feature borderless posed color photos of Mike Piazza on their fronts. One card was included in each package of six varieties of Mother's Big Bag Cookies. The set was also issued as an uncut strip of four cards. The cards are numbered on the back as "X of 4."

COMPLETE SET (4) 3.00 8.00
COMMON PLAYER (1-4) .80 2.00

1994 Mother's Piazza/Salmon

This four-card standard-size rounded-corner set was issued to honor Mike Piazza and Tim Salmon as the 1993 Rookies of the Year. Featuring both players on each card, these cards were packaged one per bag of Mother's Major League Double Headers. The set was also issued as an uncut strip of four cards. The cards are numbered on the back as "X of 4." Mother's Cookies also produced two chase cards, which were issued in either red or blue foil versions, and were reportedly inserted at a rate of one card per 1,000 packages of Mother's Big Bag Cookies. Less than 10,000 of the foil cards were reportedly produced. The blue card is numbered on the back "1 in a 1000 Blue", the red card "1 in 1000 Red."

COMPLETE SET (4) 2.50 6.00
COMMON CARD (1-4) .60 1.50

1994 Mother's Salmon

This four-card standard size set sponsored by Mother's Cookies features Tim Salmon, the 1993 AL Rookie of the Year. One card was included in each package of six varieties of Mother's Big Bag Cookies. The cards are numbered on the back as "X of 4."

COMPLETE SET (4) 2.50 6.00
COMMON PLAYER (1-4) .60 1.50

1976 Motorola Old Timers

This 11-card standard-size set, issued by Motorola for their stockholders meeting in 1976, honored some of Baseball's all-time greats. The front of the cards were about the player while the backs of the cards talked in technical terms about Motorola products. The cards are also made on a thin (paper-like) card stock and are very flimsy. Certain dealers have reported that there was also an edible version made of organic substances of these cards issued. There are reports that this set was privately produced for Motorola by long time hobbyist Mike Cramer.

COMPLETE SET (11) 12.50 30.00
1 Honus Wagner 2.00 5.00
2 Nap Lajoie 1.00 2.50
3 Ty Cobb 3.00 8.00
4 William Wambsganss .40 1.00
5 Mordecai Brown .60 1.50
6 Ray Schalk .60 1.50
7 Frank Frisch .75 2.00
8 Pud Galvin .60 1.50
9 Babe Ruth 4.00 10.00
10 Grover C. Alexander 1.00 2.50
11 Frank L. Chance .75 2.00

1999 Mountain Dew Scratch-off

This scratch-off card was available at participating Subway Sandwich shops in 1999. Sponsored by Pepsi Cola, winning cards revealed one of three prizes: A Brady Anderson T-Shirt (1000 total), Brady Anderson autographed baseball glove (40 total), or a Brady Anderson autographed baseball bat (10 total).

1 Brady Anderson 1.25 3.00

1943 MP and Co. R302-1

The 1943 MP and Co. baseball card set consists of 24 player drawings each measuring 2 11/16" by 2 1/4". This company specialized in producing strips of cards to be sold in candy stores and provided a low quality but persistent challenge to other current sets. These unnumbered cards have been alphabetized and numbered in the checklist below. There is a variation on Foxx due to his acquisition by the Cubs from the Red Sox on June 1, 1942.

COMPLETE SET (24) 400.00 800.00
1 Ernie Bonham 7.50 15.00
2 Lou Boudreau 15.00 30.00
3 Dolph Camilli 10.00 20.00
4 Mort Cooper 7.50 15.00
5 Walker Cooper 7.00 12.00
6 Joe Cronin 15.00 30.00
7 Hank Danning 7.50 15.00
8 Bill Dickey 20.00 40.00
9 Joe DiMaggio 60.00 120.00
10 Bob Feller 20.00 40.00
11 Jimmy Foxx/(Chicago Cubs) 30.00 60.00
(Jimmie)
12 Hank Greenberg 30.00 60.00
13 Stan Hack 7.50 15.00
14 Tommy Henrich 12.50 25.00
15 Carl Hubbell 15.00 30.00
16 Joe Medwick 15.00 30.00
17 John Mize 15.00 30.00
18 Lou Novikoff 7.50 15.00
19 Mel Ott 20.00 40.00
20 Pee Wee Reese 20.00 40.00
21 Pete Reiser 12.50 25.00
22 Red Ruffing 15.00 30.00
23 Johnny Vander Meer 12.50 25.00
24 Ted Williams 60.00 120.00

1949 MP and Co. R302-2

The 1949 rendition of MP and Co. was basically a re-issue of the 1943 set with different players and numbers on the back. Cards again measure approximately 2 11/16" by 2 1/4". The card fronts are even more washed out than the previous set. Card numbers 104, 118, and 120 are unknown and may be related to the two unnumbered cards found in the set. The catalog also lists this set as W523.

COMPLETE SET 200.00 400.00
100 Lou Boudreau 10.00 20.00
101 Ted Williams 50.00 80.00
102 Buddy Kerr 5.00 10.00
103 Bob Feller 12.50 25.00
104 Unknown
105 Joe DiMaggio 50.00 80.00
106 Pee Wee Reese 12.50 25.00
107 Ferris Fain 5.00 10.00
108 Andy Pafko 5.00 10.00
109 Del Ennis 7.50 15.00
110 Ralph Kiner 12.50 25.00
111 Nippy Jones 5.00 10.00
112 Del Rice 5.00 10.00
113 Hank Sauer 6.00 12.00
114 Gil Coan 5.00 10.00
115 Eddie Joost 5.00 10.00
116 Alvin Dark 7.50 15.00
117 Larry Berra 15.00 30.00
118 Unknown
119 Bob Lemon 10.00 20.00
120 Unknown
121 Johnny Pesky 7.50 15.00
122 Johnny Sain 7.50 15.00
123 Hoot Evers 5.00 10.00
124 Larry Doby 12.50 25.00
xx Tom Henrich/(unnumbered) 7.50 15.00
xx Al Kozar/(unnumbered) 5.00 10.00

1992 Mr. Turkey Superstars

This 26-card set was sponsored by Mr. Turkey. One card was found on the back panel of Mr. Turkey products, such as Hardwood Smoked Turkey Pastrami. The standard-size player card is not perforated. The cards are numbered on the back; the card numbering is actually alphabetical by player's name.

COMPLETE SET (26) 10.00 25.00
1 Jim Abbott .20 .50
2 Roberto Alomar .40 1.00
3 Sandy Alomar Jr. .20 .50
4 Craig Biggio .30 .75
5 George Brett 1.00 2.50
6 Will Clark .50 1.25
7 Roger Clemens 1.00 2.50
8 Cecil Fielder .20 .50
9 Carlton Fisk .50 1.25
10 Andres Galarraga .40 1.00
11 Dwight Gooden .20 .50
12 Ken Griffey Jr. 1.50 4.00
13 Tony Gwynn 1.00 2.50
14 Rickey Henderson .50 1.25
15 Dave Justice .40 1.00
16 Don Mattingly 1.00 2.50
17 Dale Murphy .40 1.00
18 Kirby Puckett 1.00 2.50
19 Cal Ripken 2.00 5.00
20 Nolan Ryan 2.00 5.00
21 Chris Sabo .08 .25
22 Ryne Sandberg 1.00 2.50
23 Ozzie Smith .60 1.50
24 Darryl Strawberry .20 .50
25 Andy Van Slyke .20 .50
26 Robin Yount .50 1.25

1995 Mr. Turkey Baseball Greats

These five standard-size cards were sponsored by Mr. Turkey. The cards are unnumbered and checklisted below in alphabetical order.

COMPLETE SET (5) 3.00 8.00
1 Bob Feller 1.00 2.50
2 Al Kaline 1.00 2.50
3 Tug McGraw .40 1.00
4 Boog Powell .60 1.50
5 Warren Spahn 1.00 2.50

1977 MSA Discs

Produced under the auspices of Michael Scheter Associates (MSA) in 1977, the ballplayer on disc format was distributed by a number of different advertisers. There are many different back variations based on the particular area of distribution and sponsor. The discs are approximately 3 3/8" in diameter. Since these discs are unnumbered we have sequenced them in alphabetical order. Some of the other sponsors include Chilly Willie, Customized Sports, Dairy Isle, Detroit Ceasars, Dairy Isle, Holiday Inn, Saga, Wendy's and Zip'z. Unlike 1976, where these discs can be based off Crane Discs, these are priced only in each sponsor's area. Please check all the various sponsors for listings.

1981 MSA Mini Discs

This set of 32 discs, each measuring approximately 2 3/4" in diameter was apparently approved by the Major League Players Associations under the auspices of Mike Schecter Associates These blank backed discs and were distributed a couple of different ways. The discs are unnumbered and are listed alphabetically. One way to tell that these were issued in 1981 is that Reggie Jackson is listed as a New York Yankee. 1981 would prove to be Reggie's final year in New York.

COMPLETE SET (32) 10.00 25.00
1 Buddy Bell .08 .25
2 Johnny Bench .40 1.00
3 Bruce Bochte .02 .10

4 George Brett 3.00 8.00
5 Bill Buckner .02 .10
6 Rod Carew .40 1.00
7 Steve Carlton .40 1.00
8 Cesar Cedeno .08 .25
9 Jack Clark .02 .10
10 Cecil Cooper .02 .10
11 Bucky Dent .08 .25
12 Carlton Fisk 2.00 5.00
13 Steve Garvey .20 .50
14 Rich Gossage .08 .25
15 Mike Hargrove .08 .25
16 Keith Hernandez .08 .25
17 Bob Horner .02 .10
18 Reggie Jackson 2.00 5.00
19 Steve Kemp .02 .10
20 Ron LeFlore .02 .10
21 Fred Lynn .08 .25
22 Lee Mazzilli .02 .10
23 Eddie Murray 2.50 6.00
24 Mike Norris .02 .10
25 Dave Parker .08 .25
26 J.R. Richard .02 .10
27 Pete Rose 1.50 4.00
28 Mike Schmidt 1.50 4.00
29 Tom Seaver .40 1.00
30 Roy Smalley .02 .10
31 Willie Stargell .40 1.00
32 Garry Templeton .02 .10

1986 MSA Jay's Potato Chip Discs

Jay's Potato Chips produced a set of 20 discs in conjunction with Mike Schechter Associates and the Major League Baseball Players Association. The discs have a bright yellow border with red and blue trim. Each disc is approximately 2 3/4" in diameter. The discs are not numbered and hence are assigned numbers below alphabetically. The disc backs contain very sparse personal or statistical information about the player. The players featured are from the Chicago Cubs, Chicago White Sox and Milwaukee Brewers.

COMPLETE SET (20) 10.00 25.00
1 Harold Baines .40 1.00
2 Cecil Cooper .20 .50
3 Jody Davis .20 .50
4 Bob Dernier .20 .50
5 Richard Dotson .20 .50
6 Shawon Dunston .40 1.00
7 Carlton Fisk 2.50 6.00
8 Jim Gantner .20 .50
9 Ozzie Guillen .75 2.00
10 Teddy Higuera .20 .50
11 Ron Kittle .20 .50
12 Paul Molitor 2.50 6.00
13 Keith Moreland .20 .50
14 Earnest Riles .20 .50
15 Ryne Sandberg 4.00 10.00
16 Tom Seaver 2.50 6.00
17 Lee Smith .60 1.50
18 Rick Sutcliffe .20 .50
19 Greg Walker .20 .50
20 Robin Yount 2.50 6.00

1986 MSA Jiffy Pop Discs

Jiffy Pop Popcorn introduced a set of 20 discs produced in conjunction with the Major League Baseball Players Association and Mike Schechter Associates. A single disc was inserted inside each specially marked package. The discs are numbered on the back and have a yellow border on the front. Discs are approximately 2 3/4" in diameter. The disc backs contain very sparse personal or statistical information about the player.

COMPLETE SET (20) 15.00 40.00
1 Jim Rice .60 1.50
2 Wade Boggs 1.50 4.00
3 Lance Parrish .40 1.00
4 George Brett 2.50 6.00
5 Robin Yount 1.25 3.00
6 Don Mattingly 3.00 8.00
7 Dave Winfield 2.00 5.00
8 Reggie Jackson 2.50 6.00
9 Cal Ripken 4.00 10.00
10 Eddie Murray 3.00 8.00
11 Pete Rose 2.50 6.00
12 Ryne Sandberg 3.00 8.00
13 Nolan Ryan 4.00 10.00
14 Fernando Valenzuela .60 1.50
15 Willie McGee .60 1.50
16 Dale Murphy .75 2.00
17 Mike Schmidt 2.50 6.00
18 Steve Garvey .60 1.50
19 Gary Carter 1.50 4.00
20 Dwight Gooden .60 1.50

1987 MSA Iced Tea Discs

A set of 20 "Baseball Super Star" discs was produced in conjunction with the Major League Baseball Players Association and Mike Schechter Associates for various grocery chains. Sets were issued for Weis Markets, Key Foods, Our Own Tea and many others. The discs were issued as panels of three featuring two players and an offer disc. The discs have a bright yellow border on the front. Discs measure approximately 2 3/4" in diameter. Some dealers have speculated that noted hobby dealer John Broggi made the player selection for this set as well as the other iced tea disc sets. The disc backs contain very sparse personal or statistical information about the player. The base set is listed here but also complete player and price information can be found for each set listed in this description.

COMPLETE SET (20) 4.00 10.00
1 Darryl Strawberry .08 .25
2 Roger Clemens .60 1.50
3 Ron Darling .02 .10
4 Keith Hernandez .08 .25
5 Tony Pena .02 .10
6 Don Mattingly .60 1.50
7 Eric Davis .08 .25
8 Gary Carter .40 1.00
9 Dave Winfield .40 1.00
10 Wally Joyner .30 .75
11 Mike Schmidt .40 1.00
12 Robby Thompson .02 .10
13 Wade Boggs .40 1.00
14 Cal Ripken 1.25 3.00
15 Dale Murphy .20 .50
16 Tony Gwynn .75 2.00
17 Jose Canseco .40 1.00
18 Rickey Henderson .40 1.00
19 Lance Parrish .02 .10
20 Dave Righetti .02 .10

1987 MSA Jiffy Pop Discs

Jiffy Pop Popcorn introduced a set of 20 discs produced in conjunction with the Major League Baseball Players Association and Mike Schechter Associates. A single disc was inserted inside each specially marked package. The discs are numbered on the back and have a white border (with red stitching to resemble a baseball) on the front. Discs are approximately 2 3/4" in diameter. The disc backs contain very sparse personal or statistical information about the player.

COMPLETE SET (20) 12.50 30.00
1 Ryne Sandberg 3.00 8.00
2 Dale Murphy .75 2.00
3 Jack Morris .60 1.50
4 Keith Hernandez .60 1.50
5 George Brett 4.00 10.00
6 Don Mattingly 4.00 10.00
7 Ozzie Smith 3.00 8.00
8 Cal Ripken 6.00 15.00
9 Dwight Gooden .60 1.50
10 Pedro Guerrero .40 1.00
11 Lou Whitaker .60 1.50
12 Roger Clemens 5.00 12.00
13 Lance Parrish .40 1.00
14 Rickey Henderson 2.50 6.00
15 Fernando Valenzuela .60 1.50
16 Mike Schmidt 3.00 8.00
17 Darryl Strawberry .60 1.50
18 Mike Scott .40 1.00
19 Jim Rice .60 1.50
20 Wade Boggs 2.50 6.00

1988 MSA Fantastic Sam's Discs

Fantastic Sam's is a national chain of family haircutters with more than 1200 locations. There are 20 numbered discs in the set each with an orange border. The set was produced in conjunction with Mike Schechter Associates. One disc was given away free each time a customer visited a participating Fantastic Sam's. Each disc is connected by a perforation to a contest disc with a scratch-off for a potential (baseball related) prize. Each disc is approximately 2 3/4" in diameter. No team logos are shown in this set.

COMPLETE SET (20) 2.50 6.00
1 Kirby Puckett .60 1.50
2 George Brett .75 2.00
3 Mark McGwire .60 1.50
4 Wally Joyner .20 .50
5 Paul Molitor .60 1.50
6 Alan Trammell .30 .75
7 George Bell .08 .25
8 Wade Boggs .60 1.50
9 Don Mattingly .75 2.00
10 Julio Franco .30 .75
11 Ozzie Smith .60 1.50
12 Will Clark .40 1.00
13 Dale Murphy .30 .75
14 Eric Davis .08 .25
15 Andre Dawson .40 1.00
16 Tim Raines .20 .50
17 Darryl Strawberry .20 .50
18 Tony Gwynn .60 1.50
19 Mike Schmidt .50 1.25
20 Pedro Guerrero .08 .25

1988 MSA Hostess Discs

This set of 24 discs was produced by Hostess Potato Chips in conjunction with Mike Schechter Associates and the Major League Baseball Players Association. This set is one of the few disc sets to actually show the team logos. The set is subtitled Hostess Summer Doubleheaders and actually features a double disc (connected by a perforation) with a player from the Montreal Expos and a player from the Toronto Blue Jays. Each disc is approximately 2 5/8" in diameter. The discs are numbered; Montreal Expos are numbered 1-12 and Toronto Blue Jays are 13-24.

COMPLETE SET (24) 1.50 4.00
1 Mitch Webster .02 .10
2 Tim Burke .02 .10
3 Tom Foley .02 .10
4 Herm Winningham .02 .10
5 Hubie Brooks .02 .10
6 Mike Fitzgerald .04 .10
7 Tim Wallach .08 .25
8 Andres Galarraga .30 .75
9 Floyd Youmans .02 .10
10 Neal Heaton .02 .10
11 Tim Raines .20 .50
12 Casey Candaele .02 .10
13 Jim Clancy .02 .10
14 Rance Mulliniks .02 .10
15 Fred McGriff .30 .75
16 Ernie Whitt .02 .10
17 Dave Stieb .08 .25
18 Mark Eichhorn .02 .10
19 Jesse Barfield .08 .25
20 Lloyd Moseby .02 .10
21 Tony Fernandez .20 .50
22 George Bell .08 .25
23 Tom Henke .08 .25
24 Jimmy Key .30 .75

1988 MSA Iced Tea Discs

A set of 20 "Baseball Super Star" discs was produced in conjunction with the Major League Baseball Players Association and Mike Schechter Associates for various grocery chains. Sets were issued for Tetley Tea, Weis Markets, Key Foods, Our Own Tea and many others. The discs were issued as panels of three featuring two players and an offer disc. The discs have a blue border on the front. Discs are approximately 2 3/4" in diameter. The disc backs contain very sparse personal or statistical information about the player.

COMPLETE SET (20) 4.00 10.00
1 Wade Boggs .60 1.50
2 Ellis Burks .30 .75
3 Don Mattingly .75 2.00
4 Mark McGwire .75 2.00
5 Matt Nokes .02 .10
6 Kirby Puckett .75 2.00
7 Billy Ripken .02 .10
8 Kevin Seitzer .02 .10
9 Roger Clemens 1.00 2.50
10 Will Clark .30 .75
11 Vince Coleman .02 .10
12 Eric Davis .08 .25
13 Dave Magadan .02 .10
14 Dale Murphy .20 .50
15 Benito Santiago .08 .25
16 Mike Schmidt .40 1.00
17 Darryl Strawberry .08 .25
18 Dwight Gooden .08 .25
19 Steve Bedrosian .02 .10
20 Fernando Valenzuela .08 .25

1988 MSA Jiffy Pop Discs

Jiffy Pop Popcorn introduced a set of 20 discs produced in conjunction with the Major League Baseball Players Association and Mike Schechter Associates. A single disc was inserted inside each specially marked package. The discs are numbered (alphabetically) on the back and have a light blue border on the front. Discs are approximately 2 3/4" in diameter. The disc backs contain very sparse personal or statistical information about the player.

COMPLETE SET (20) 6.00 15.00
1 Buddy Bell .20 .50
2 Wade Boggs 1.50 4.00
3 Gary Carter 1.00 2.50
4 Jack Clark .20 .50
5 Will Clark 1.50 4.00
6 Roger Clemens 2.50 6.00
7 Vince Coleman .20 .50
8 Andre Dawson .75 2.00
9 Keith Hernandez .20 .50
10 Kent Hrbek .20 .50
11 Wally Joyner .40 1.00
12 Paul Molitor 1.00 2.50
13 Eddie Murray 1.00 2.50
14 Tim Raines .40 1.00
15 Bret Saberhagen .20 .50
16 Alan Trammell .60 1.50
17 Ozzie Virgil .20 .50
18 Tim Wallach .20 .50
19 Dave Winfield 1.50 4.00
20 Robin Yount 1.00 2.50

1989 MSA Holsum Discs

1989 Holsum Discs set is actually several sets of 20 discs issued for the following regional bakeries: Foxes Holsum (North Carolina and South Carolina), Butter Krust Bakeries (most of Pennsylvania), Phoenix Holsum (Arizona), Schafer's (Michigan) and Rainer Farms Homestyle. In Canada, Ben's Limited of Halifax distributed the discs under the Holsum/Schafer's imprint. The discs measure approximately 2 3/4" in diameter. This set was produced by MSA (Michael Schechter Associates) and like most of the MSA sets, there are no team logos on the discs. There is also an uncorrected error with Mark Grace's disc which pictures Vance Law on it.

COMPLETE SET (20) 5.00 12.00
1 Wally Joyner .20 .50
2 Wade Boggs .60 1.50
3 Ozzie Smith .75 2.00
4 Don Mattingly .75 2.00
5 Jose Canseco .60 1.50
6 Tony Gwynn 1.25 3.00
7 Eric Davis .20 .50
8 Kirby Puckett .60 1.50
9 Kevin Seitzer .08 .25
10 Darryl Strawberry .20 .50
11 Gregg Jefferies .08 .25
12 Mark Grace UER/(Photo actually Vance Law) 1.25 3.00
13 Matt Nokes .08 .25
14 Mark McGwire 1.00 2.50
15 Bobby Bonilla .20 .50
16 Roger Clemens 1.25 3.00
17 Frank Viola .08 .25
18 Orel Hershiser .20 .50
19 Dave Cone (David) .20 .50
20 Kirk Gibson .20 .50

1989 MSA Iced Tea Discs

These 20 discs of MSA's Third Annual Collectors' Edition measure approximately 2 5/8" in diameter and feature on their fronts posed color player head shots within red stars on yellow backgrounds. The player's name and team appear in black lettering near the bottom. There are no team logos featured on the discs. The backs carry player biography and 1988 statistics in blue lettering. The cards are numbered on the back as "X of 20." The sets were also produced under the Tetley Teas label and inserted into their tea bag boxes.

COMPLETE SET (20) 12.50 30.00
1 Don Mattingly 2.50 6.00
2 Dave Cone (David) 1.25 3.00
3 Mark McGwire 2.00 5.00
4 Will Clark 1.50 4.00
5 Darryl Strawberry .75 2.00
6 Dwight Gooden .75 2.00
7 Wade Boggs 2.00 5.00
8 Roger Clemens 2.50 6.00
9 Benito Santiago .75 2.00
10 Orel Hershiser .75 2.00
11 Eric Davis .75 2.00
12 Kirby Puckett 2.00 5.00
13 Dave Winfield 2.00 5.00
14 Andre Dawson 1.50 4.00
15 Steve Bedrosian .40 1.00
16 Cal Ripken 5.00 12.00
17 Andy Van Slyke .40 1.00
18 Jose Canseco 2.00 5.00
19 Jose Oquendo .40 1.00
20 Dale Murphy 1.50 4.00

1990 MSA Holsum Discs

The 1990 Holsum Discs set, subtitled "Superstars," is a 20-disc set with each disc measuring approximately 2 3/4" in diameter. The front of each disc features a full color player photo with a red border. The player's name, team and position appear below the photo. The white back carries the player's name and biography at the top, followed below by 1989 and career statistics. Typical of many of the sets produced by MSA (Michael Schechter Associates), the teams' logos are airbrushed out. The discs are numbered on the back. In Canada, Ben's Limited of Halifax distributed the discs under the Holsum imprint.

COMPLETE SET (20) 2.00 5.00
1 George Bell .02 .10
2 Tim Raines .08 .25
3 Tom Henke .02 .10
4 Andres Galarraga .30 .75
5 Bret Saberhagen .02 .10
6 Mark Davis .02 .10
7 Robin Yount .30 .75
8 Rickey Henderson .40 1.00
9 Kevin Mitchell .02 .10
10 Howard Johnson .02 .10
11 Will Clark .30 .75
12 Orel Hershiser .08 .25
13 Fred McGriff .20 .50
14 Dave Stewart .02 .10
15 Vince Coleman .02 .10
16 Steve Sax .02 .10
17 Kirby Puckett .40 1.00
18 Tony Gwynn .50 1.25
19 Jerome Walton .02 .10
20 Gregg Olson .02 .10

1990 MSA Iced Tea Discs

Issued in three-disc perforated strips, these 20 discs measure approximately 2 5/8" in diameter. Some of the discs have Tetley's Third Annual Collector's Edition on their fronts, while others read "Fourth Annual Collectors' Edition" and "Super Stars" on their fronts. Each strip contains two player discs and one disc for ordering a Tetley Press Sheet Calendar. Each red-bordered player disc features a color player head shot framed by a yellow line. The player's name and team name appear below the photo. The white back carries the player's name and team name at the bottom; above are the player's biography and 1989 stats. The discs are numbered on the back as "X of 20." Each disc is a tri-fold, consisting of two color player photos and a mail-in offer to receive a 15" by 25" press sheet calendar of the complete set of 20 players for only $3.50 plus four discs.

COMPLETE SET (20) 12.50 30.00
1 Will Clark .75 2.00
2 Howard Johnson .40 1.00
3 Chris Sabo .40 1.00
4 Jose Canseco 1.00 2.50
5 Bo Jackson .75 2.00
6 Kevin Mitchell .40 1.00
7 Wade Boggs 1.25 3.00
8 Ken Griffey Jr. 2.50 6.00
9 George Bell .40 1.00
10 Dwight Gooden .50 1.25
11 Bobby Bonilla .40 1.00
12 Ryne Sandberg 2.00 5.00
13 Kirby Puckett 1.25 3.00
14 Don Mattingly 2.00 5.00
15 Mark McGwire 2.00 5.00
16 Frank Viola .40 1.00
17 Bret Saberhagen .40 1.00
18 Mike Greenwell .40 1.00
19 Steve Sax .40 1.00
20 Nolan Ryan 4.00 10.00

1991 MSA Holsum Discs

The 1991 Holsum Discs set, subtitled "Superstars" is a 20-disc set with each disc measuring approximately 2 3/4" in diameter. The discs feature on their fronts white-bordered color player head shots. The player's name, team and position appear below the photo. The white back carries the player's name and biography at the top, followed below by 1990 statistics. Typical of many of the sets produced by MSA, (Michael Schechter Associates) the teams' logos are airbrushed out. In Canada, Ben's Limited of Halifax distributed the discs under the Holsum imprint.

COMPLETE SET (20) 125.00 250.00
1 Darryl Strawberry 1.25 3.00
2 Eric Davis 1.25 3.00
3 Tim Wallach .75 2.00
4 Kevin Mitchell .75 2.00
5 Tony Gwynn 10.00 25.00
6 Ryne Sandberg 8.00 20.00
7 Doug Drabek .75 2.00
8 Randy Myers .75 2.00
9 Ken Griffey Jr. 12.50 30.00
10 Alan Trammell 1.50 4.00
11 Ken Griffey Sr. .75 2.00
12 Rickey Henderson 8.00 20.00
13 Roger Clemens 10.00 25.00
14 Bob Welch .75 2.00
15 Kelly Gruber .75 2.00
16 Mark McGwire 10.00 25.00
17 Cecil Fielder 1.25 3.00
18 Dave Stieb .75 2.00
19 Nolan Ryan 20.00 50.00
20 Cal Ripken 20.00 50.00

1992 MSA Ben's Super Hitters Discs

The 1992 Ben's Disc set is a 20-disc set, with each disc measuring approximately 2 3/4" in diameter. The set is subtitled "Super Hitters". The discs feature on their fronts white-bordered color player head shots. The player's name, team and position appear below the photo. The white back carries the player's name and biography at the top, followed below by 1991 statistics. As is typical of many of the sets produced by MSA (Michael Schechter Associates), the teams' logos are airbrushed out.

COMPLETE SET (20) 12.50 30.00
1 Cecil Fielder .30 .75
2 Joe Carter .30 .75
3 Roberto Alomar .60 1.50
4 Devon White .20 .50
5 Kelly Gruber .20 .50
6 Cal Ripken Jr. 4.00 10.00
7 Kirby Puckett 2.00 5.00
8 Paul Molitor 1.25 3.00
9 Julio Franco .40 1.00
10 Ken Griffey Jr. 2.50 6.00
11 Frank Thomas 1.00 2.50
12 Jose Canseco 1.25 3.00
13 Danny Tartabull .20 .50
14 Terry Pendleton .20 .50
15 Tony Gwynn 2.00 5.00
16 Howard Johnson .20 .50
17 Will Clark .40 1.00
18 Barry Bonds 2.00 5.00
19 Ryne Sandberg 2.00 5.00
20 Bobby Bonilla .20 .50

1993 MSA Ben's Super Pitchers Discs

The 1993 Ben's Disc set is a 20-disc set, with each disc measuring approximately 2 3/4" in diameter. The set is subtitled "Super Pitchers". As is typical of many of the sets produced by MSA (Michael Schechter Associates), the teams' logos are airbrushed out. The discs feature white-bordered color player head shots on their fronts with the player's name, team and position appearing near the bottom. The white backs carry the player's name, biography and 1992 stats.

COMPLETE SET (20) 4.00 10.00
1 Dennis Eckersley .60 1.50
2 Chris Bosio .08 .25
3 Jack Morris .20 .50
4 Greg Maddux 1.25 3.00
5 Dennis Martinez .20 .50
6 Tom Glavine .50 1.25
7 Doug Drabek .08 .25
8 John Smoltz .30 .75
9 Randy Myers .20 .50
10 Jack McDowell .08 .25
11 John Wetteland .30 .75
12 Roger Clemens 1.00 2.50
13 Mike Mussina .40 1.00
14 Juan Guzman .08 .25
15 Jose Rijo .08 .25
16 Tom Henke .20 .50
17 Gregg Olson .08 .25
18 Jim Abbott .20 .50
19 Jimmy Key .08 .25
20 Rheal Cormier .08 .25

1992 MTV Rock n' Jock

This three-card standard-size set was sponsored by MTV to promote the Third Annual Rock n' Jock Softball Challenge held January 11, 1992, in Los Angeles. According to the card backs, 20,000 sets were produced. The fronts feature color player photos, and each card has a different color inner border (1-brick red; 2-kelly green; 3-blue). The outer border of all cards consists of yellow, orange, and purple stars on a white background. The backs have a black and white version of the outer border of the fronts and present an advertisement for the softball challenge. There has been some debate over the years about whether or not this is a legitimate set; however an MTV PR person at the time acknowledged that the set was produced for the event by MTV.

COMPLETE SET (3) 2.00 5.00
1 Hammer .08 .25
2 Frank Thomas .75 2.00
3 Ken Griffey Jr. 1.50 4.00

1988 Willard Mullin Postcards

These 24 postcards feature the drawings of Willard Mullin, among the most known sports cartoonists. These cards were issued by Holmes Publishing in 1988. The cards measure 3 1/2" by 5" and feature reprints of Mullin's best works.

COMPLETE SET (24) 5.00 12.00
1 Williard Mullin .02 .10
2 Casey Stengel .30 .75
3 Dizzy Dean Paul Dean .20 .50
4 Joe DiMaggio .75 2.00
5 Babe Ruth Hank Greenberg .75 2.00
6 Brooklyn Bum #1 .02 .10
7 Pete Reiser .08 .25
8 Dixie Walker .08 .25
9 Branch Rickey Bum #2 Flatbush Willie .08 .25
10 Jackie Robinson Abraham Lincoln 1.25 3.00
11 George Weiss Casey Stengel .20 .50
12 Flatbush Willie .02 .10
13 Flatbush Willie .02 .10
14 Jim Gilliam .08 .25
15 Duke Snider .30 .75
16 Flatbush Willie Walt Alston .08 .25
17 Flatbush Willie .02 .10
18 Stan Musial .60 1.50
19 Giants leave NY .02 .10
20 Flatbush Willie .02 .10
21 Unknown .02 .10
22 Willie Mays .75 2.00
23 Mickey Mantle 1.25 3.00
24 Amazing Mets .08 .25

1910 Murad College Silks S21

Each of these silks was issued by Murad Cigarettes around 1910 with a college emblem and an artist's rendering of a generic athlete on the front. The backs are blank. Each of the S21 silks measures roughly 5" by 7" and there was a smaller version created (roughly 3 1/2" by 5 1/2") of each and cataloged as S22.

*SMALLER S22: .3X TO .8X LARGER S21
1BB Army (West Point) baseball batter 30.00 60.00
2BB Brown baseball batter 30.00 60.00
3BB California baseball batter 30.00 60.00
4BB Chicago baseball batter 30.00 60.00
5BB Colorado baseball batter 30.00 60.00
6BB Columbia baseball batter 30.00 60.00
7BB Cornell baseball batter 30.00 60.00
8BB Dartmouth baseball batter 30.00 60.00
9BB Georgetown baseball batter 30.00 60.00
10BB Harvard baseball batter 30.00 60.00
11BB Illinois baseball batter 30.00 60.00
12BB Michigan baseball batter 30.00 60.00
13BB Minnesota baseball batter 30.00 60.00
14BB Missouri baseball batter 30.00 60.00
15BB Navy (Annapolis) baseball batter 30.00 60.00
16BB Ohio State baseball batter 30.00 60.00
17BB Pennsylvania baseball batter 30.00 60.00
18BB Purdue baseball batter 30.00 60.00
19BB Stanford baseball batter 30.00 60.00
1BBP Army (West Point) baseball pitcher 30.00 60.00
20BB Stanford baseball batter 30.00 60.00
21BB Syracuse baseball batter 30.00 60.00
22BB Texas baseball batter 30.00 60.00
23BB Wisconsin baseball batter 30.00 60.00
24BB Yale baseball batter 30.00 60.00
2BBP Brown baseball pitcher 30.00 60.00
3BBP California baseball pitcher 30.00 60.00
4BBP Chicago baseball pitcher 30.00 60.00
5BBP Colorado baseball pitcher 30.00 60.00
6BBP Columbia baseball pitcher 30.00 60.00
7BBP Cornell baseball pitcher 30.00 60.00
8BBP Dartmouth baseball pitcher 30.00 60.00
9BBP Georgetown baseball pitcher 30.00 60.00
10BBP Harvard baseball pitcher 30.00 60.00
11BBP Illinois baseball pitcher 30.00 60.00
12BBP Michigan baseball pitcher 30.00 60.00
13BBP Minnesota baseball pitcher 30.00 60.00
14BBP Missouri baseball pitcher 30.00 60.00
15BBP Navy (Annapolis) baseball pitcher 30.00 60.00
16BBP Ohio State baseball pitcher 30.00 60.00
17BBP Pennsylvania baseball pitcher 30.00 60.00
18BBP Purdue baseball pitcher 30.00 60.00
19BBP Stanford baseball pitcher 30.00 60.00
20BBP Stanford baseball pitcher 30.00 60.00
21BBP Syracuse baseball pitcher 30.00 60.00
22BBP Texas baseball pitcher 30.00 60.00
23BBP Wisconsin baseball pitcher 30.00 60.00
24BBP Yale baseball pitcher 30.00 60.00

1911 Murad College Series Premiums T6

9 Fordham Baseball fielder 250.00 400.00
19 State(Penn State) Baseball batter 250.00 400.00

1911 Murad College Series T51

These colorful cigarette cards featured several colleges and a variety of sports and recreations of the day and were issued in packs of Murad Cigarettes. The cards measure approximately 2" by 3". Two variations of each of the first 50 cards were produced; one variation says "College Series" on back, the other, "2nd Series". The drawings on cards of the 2nd Series are slightly different from those of the College Series. There are 6 different series of 25 in the College Series and they are listed here in the order that they appear on the checklist on the cardbacks. There is also a larger version (5" x 8") that was available for the first 25 cards as a premium (catalog designation T6) offer that could be obtained in exchange for 15 Murad cigarette coupons; the offers expired June 30, 1911.

*2ND SERIES: .4X TO 1X COLLEGE SERIES
9 Fordham Baseball fielder 25.00 50.00
19 State(Penn State) Baseball batter 25.00 50.00
38 S.U.K.(State Univ. of Kentucky) Baseball 25.00 50.00
92 O.S.U.(Ohio State) Baseball 25.00 50.00
109 H (Haverford) Baseball 25.00 50.00
128 Antioch#(Baseball 25.00 50.00
131 Bethany Baseball 25.00 50.00
146 K.W.C./(Kentucky Wesleyan College) Baseball 25.00 50.00

1981 Feg Murray's Cartoon Greats

This postcard set features the work of cartoonist Feg Murray. These cards feature reproductions of some of Murray's best works.

COMPLETE SET (21) 3.00 8.00
1 Feg Murray .08 .25
2 Ty Cobb .40 1.00
3 Dizzy Dean .30 .75
4 Bill Dickey .20 .50
5 Jimmy Foxx (Jimmie) .30 .75
6 Frank Frisch .20 .50
7 Lou Gehrig .40 1.00
8 Charles Gehringer .30 .75
9 Lefty Grove .30 .75
10 Gabby Hartnett .20 .50
11 Waite Hoyt .20 .50
12 Carl Hubbell .30 .75
13 John McGraw .30 .75
14 Mel Ott .30 .75
15 The Million-Dollar Baby George Herman (Babe) Rut .60 1.50
16 Babe Ruth Ain't It the Ruth .60 1.50
17 Al Simmons .30 .75
18 Casey Stengel .30 .75
19 Bill Terry .20 .50
20 Honus Wagner .50 1.25
21 Paul Waner .30 .75

1992 Musial AFUD

This five-card set, presented by the American Foundation for Urologic Disease, measures approximately 3 1/2" by 5 1/2". The fronts feature black-and-white photos of Stan Musial, spokesperson for the Prostate Cancer Education Campaign, during his career and now. Small pictures of Stan Musial are on all but one card. The set is packaged in a folder that includes information for obtaining materials to promote awareness of prostate cancer. The cards are unnumbered and checklisted.

COMPLETE SET (5) 6.00 15.00
COMMON PLAYER (1-5) 1.20 3.00

1963 Musial Colt 45 Tribute

This 5" by 7" one-card blank-backed set was issued to commemorate Stan Musial's last series in Houston during the 1963 season. The front has a posed photo of Stan along with the words "Farewell Houston Appearance August 23-24-25, 1963.

1 Stan Musial 6.00 15.00

1985 Musial TTC

This eight-card set of Stan Musial produced by TTC of Houston, Texas, in the 1952 Bowman style, measures approximately 2 1/8" by 3 3/8". The fronts feature black-and-white photos of Stan Musial in the various stages of swinging the bat. The backs carry his name, card number, and a different career fact on each card as checklisted below.

COMPLETE SET (8) 3.00 8.00
COMMON CARD (1-8) .40 1.00

1992 MVP 2 Highlights

Produced by MVP Sports, this 20-card set presents an outstanding baseball player from each league for the nine positions as well as one designated hitter from each league. The cards have rounded corners and measure 2 1/2" by 3 1/2."

COMPLETE SET (20) 4.00 10.00
1 Willie Mays .75 2.00
2 Hank Aaron .75 2.00
3 Ted Williams 1.00 2.50
4 Yogi Berra .40 1.00
5 Ernie Banks .40 1.00
6 Lou Brock .30 .75
7 Steve Carlton .40 1.00
8 Harmon Killebrew .30 .75
9 Gaylord Perry .30 .75
10 Rusty Staub .20 .50
11 Lou Boudreau .30 .75
12 Larry Doby .20 .50
13 Orlando Cepeda .20 .50
14 Bill Mazeroski .20 .50
15 Don Baylor .20 .50
16 Bill Madlock .08 .25
17 Joe Torre .30 .75
18 Boog Powell .20 .50
19 Graig Nettles .20 .50
20 Dave Johnson .20 .50

1992 MVP Game

Produced by MVP Sports, this 18-card set presents an outstanding baseball player at each position for both leagues. The cards have rounded corners and measure 2 1/4" by 3 1/2." The design but not the size is similar to that of playing cards. The backs of the American League (cards 1-9) cards are predominantly red and have the AL emblem, while the backs of the National League (cards 10-18) cards are predominantly purple and carry the NL emblem. Since the cards are unnumbered, we have checklisted them below alphabetically within leagues.

COMPLETE SET (18) 4.00 10.00
1 Don Baylor .20 .50
2 Yogi Berra .40 1.00
3 Lou Boudreau .30 .75
4 Larry Doby .30 .75
5 Dave Johnson .20 .50
6 Harmon Killebrew .30 .75
7 Graig Nettles .20 .50
8 Gaylord Perry .30 .75
9 Ted Williams 1.00 2.50
10 Hank Aaron .75 2.00
11 Ernie Banks .40 1.00
12 Lou Brock .30 .75
13 Steve Carlton .40 1.00
14 Orlando Cepeda .30 .75
15 Bill Madlock .08 .25
16 Willie Mays .75 2.00
17 Bill Mazeroski .20 .50
18 Joe Torre .30 .75

1889 N526 No. 7 Cigars

This set is comprised exclusively of members of the Boston Baseball Club, who are portrayed in black and white line drawings. The tobacco brand No. 7 Cigars has not yet been linked to a specific manufacturer. These cards were issued in 1889 and are similar to another series bearing Diamond S brand advertising.

COMPLETE SET (15) 3000.00 6000.00
1 Charles W. Bennett 400.00 800.00
2 Dennis (Dan) Brouthers 600.00 1200.00
3 Tom T. Brown 400.00 800.00
4 John G. Clarkson 600.00 1200.00
5 Charles W. Ganzell 400.00 800.00
6 James A. Hart 400.00 800.00
7 Richard F. Johnston 400.00 800.00
8 Mike King Kelly Captain 1000.00 2000.00
9 M.J. (Kid) Madden 400.00 800.00
10 William Nash 400.00 800.00
11 Jos. Quinn 400.00 800.00
12 Charles Radbourne 600.00 1200.00
13 J.B. Ray (sic) 400.00 800.00
14 Hardie Richardson 400.00 800.00
15 William Sowders 400.00 800.00

1976 Nabisco Sugar Daddy 1

This set of 25 tiny (approximately 1 1/16" by 2 3/4") cards features action scenes from a variety of popular sports from around the world. One card was included in specially marked Sugar Daddy and Sugar Mama candy bars. The set is referred to as "Sugar Daddy Sports World - Series 1" on the backs of the cards. The cards are in color with a relatively wide white border around the front of the cards.

COMPLETE SET (25) 40.00 80.00
12 Baseball Pete Rose 10.00 20.00

1976 Nabisco Sugar Daddy 2

This set of 25 tiny (approximately 1 1/16" by 2 3/4") cards features action scenes from a variety of popular sports from around the world. One card was included in specially marked Sugar Daddy and Sugar Mama candy bars. The set is referred to as "Sugar Daddy Sports World - Series 2" on the backs of the cards. The cards are in color with a relatively wide white border around the front of the cards.

COMPLETE SET (25) 40.00 80.00
25 Baseball 6.00 12.00

1969 Nabisco Team Flakes

The cards in this 24-card set measure either 1 15/16" by 3" or 1 3/4" by 2 15/16" depending on the amount of yellow border area provided between the "cut lines." The 1969 Nabisco Team Flakes set of full color, blank-backed and unnumbered cards was issued on the backs of Team Flakes cereal boxes. The cards are numbered in the checklist below in alphabetical order. There were three different panels or box backs containing eight cards each. The cards have yellow borders and are devoid of team insignias. The wider cards are tougher and should be valued at approximately 1.5X to 2X the narrower cards. The catalog designation is F275-34. Based on the alphabetical order of the player on the top left corner, we have identified the sheet that each player was on. The Aaron sheet is labelled S1, Pete Rose is labelled S2 and Ron Santo is labelled S3. These cards are actually called Mini Posters by Nabisco and all of these photos were also available in 2 feet by 3 feet posters that a kid could mail away for.

COMPLETE SET (24) 300.00 600.00
1 Hank Aaron S1 40.00 80.00
2 Richie Allen S1 6.00 15.00
3 Lou Brock S2 15.00 40.00
4 Paul Casanova S1 2.50 6.00
5 Roberto Clemente S3 50.00 100.00
6 Al Ferrara S3 2.50 6.00
7 Bill Freehan S2 4.00 10.00
8 Jim Fregosi S1 4.00 10.00
9 Bob Gibson S3 15.00 40.00
10 Tony Horton S2 4.00 10.00
11 Tommy John S3 6.00 15.00

12 Al Kaline S3 15.00 40.00
13 Jim Lonborg S2 2.50 6.00
14 Juan Marichal S1 15.00 40.00
15 Willie Mays S2 40.00 80.00
16 Rick Monday S2 2.50 6.00
17 Tony Oliva S1 6.00 15.00
18 Brooks Robinson S1 15.00 40.00
19 Frank Robinson S3 15.00 40.00
20 Pete Rose S2 30.00 60.00
21 Ron Santo S3 8.00 20.00
22 Tom Seaver S2 30.00 60.00
23 Rusty Staub S1 4.00 10.00
24 Mel Stottlemyre S3 2.50 6.00

1992 Nabisco

This 36-card standard-size set was sponsored by Nabisco and inserted in Shreddies cereal boxes and other Nabisco products in Canada. Three collector cards were protected by a cardboard sleeve that included two Bingo game symbols and a checklist on its back. The inside of each cereal box featured a Baseball Bingo Game Board. The collector became eligible to win prizes when he completed one vertical row, which consists of two required symbols and two correctly answered trivia questions. The odd number cards are Montreal Expos, while the even number cards are Toronto Blue Jays. Each card commemorates an outstanding achievement in the history of these two baseball franchises.

COMPLETE SET (36) 6.00 15.00
1 Bill Lee .30 .75
2 Cliff Johnson .20 .50
3 Ken Singleton .40 1.00
4 Al Woods .20 .50
5 Ron Hunt .30 .75
6 Barry Bonnell .20 .50
7 Tony Perez .60 1.50
8 Willie Upshaw .20 .50
9 Coco Laboy .20 .50
10 Famous Moments 1 .20 .50
October 5& 1985
Blue Jays win A
11 Bob Bailey .20 .50
12 Dave McKay .20 .50
13 Rodney Scott .20 .50
14 Jerry Garvin .20 .50
15 Famous Moments 2 .20 .50
October 11& 1981
Expos win NL E
16 Rick Bosetti .20 .50
17 Larry Parrish .30 .75
18 Bill Singer .20 .50
19 Ron Fairly .30 .75
20 Damaso Garcia .20 .50
21 Al Oliver .40 1.00
22 Famous Moments 3 .20 .50
September 30& 1989
Blue Jays ca
23 Claude Raymond .20 .50
24 Buck Martinez .30 .75
25 Rusty Staub .60 1.50
26 Otto Velez .20 .50
27 Mack Jones .20 .50
28 Garth Iorg .20 .50
29 Bill Stoneman .30 .75
30 Doug Ault .20 .50
31 Famous Moments 4 .20 .50
July 6& 1982
Expos hosts 1st AS
32 Jesse Jefferson .20 .50
33 Steve Rogers .30 .75
34 Ernie Whitt .20 .50
35 John Boccabella .20 .50
36 Bob Bailor .20 .50
xx Album .60 1.50

1993 Nabisco All-Star Autographs

Available by sending two proofs of purchase from specially marked Nabisco packages and 5.00, each card features an autographed color action photo of a former star on its front and comes in a special card holder along with a certificate of authenticity. Don Drysdale tragically passed away between his signing the cards and the beginning of the promotion. Nabisco honored all requests until they ran out of cards on Drysdale. The cards are unnumbered and are checklisted in alphabetical order.

COMPLETE SET (6) 50.00 120.00
1 Ernie Banks 10.00 25.00
2 Don Drysdale 15.00 40.00
3 Catfish Hunter 6.00 15.00
4 Phil Niekro 6.00 15.00
5 Brooks Robinson 6.00 15.00
6 Willie Stargell 6.00 15.00

1994 Nabisco All-Star Autographs

The Nabisco Biscuit Company and the Major League Baseball Players Alumni Association cosponsored the "Nabisco All-Star Legends" program, which featured these four autographed baseball cards as well as All-Star appearances nationwide and free tickets to minor league baseball games. Measuring the standard size, one card could be obtained by mailing 5.00 and two proofs of purchase from Oreo, Oreo Double Stuff, Chips Ahoy, Ritz, Wheat Thins, Better Cheddars, Nabisco Grahams, and Honey Maid Grahams crackers. Each autographed card was accompanied by an MLBPAA certificate of authenticity. The cards are unnumbered and checklisted below in alphabetical order.

COMPLETE SET (4) 25.00 60.00
1 Bob Gibson 6.00 15.00
2 Jim Palmer 6.00 15.00
3 Frank Robinson 6.00 15.00
4 Duke Snider 6.00 15.00

2000 Nabisco All Stars

COMPLETE SET (11) 8.00 20.00
1 Yogi Berra 1.00 2.50
2 Gary Carter .60 1.50
3 Orlando Cepeda .80 2.00
4 George Foster .20 .50
5 Steve Garvey .60 1.50
6 John Kruk .20 .50
7 Joe Morgan 1.00 2.50
8 Dot Richardson 2.00 5.00
9 Brooks Robinson 1.00 2.50
10 Mike Schmidt .80 2.00
11 Ozzie Smith 1.00 2.50

1909 E92-1 Dockman and Sons

The cards in this 40-card set measure 1 1/2" by 2 3/4". Additional advertising backs can also be found for Croft's Candy, Croft's Cocoa and Nadja - but pricing for these cards can be found in their own listings. The set contains poses identical to those in E101, E102, and E105. Book prices reference VgEx condition given the majority of cards found in this set are typically off-grade. Cards are unnumbered and checklisted alphabetically by each player's last name.

COMPLETE SET (62) 12500.00 25000.00
1 Harry Bemis 125.00 200.00
2 Chief Bender 350.00 600.00
3 Bill Bergen 125.00 200.00
4 Bob Bescher 125.00 200.00
5 Al Bridwell 125.00 200.00
6 Joe Casey 125.00 200.00
7 Frank Chance 350.00 600.00
8 Hal Chase 175.00 300.00
9 Sam Crawford 350.00 600.00
10 Harry Davis 125.00 200.00
11 Art Devlin 125.00 200.00
12 Bill Donovan 125.00 200.00
13 Mickey Doolan 125.00 200.00
14 Patsy Dougherty 125.00 200.00
15 Larry Doyle Batting 125.00 200.00
16 Larry Doyle Throwing 125.00 200.00
17 George Gibson 125.00 200.00
18 Topsy Hartsel 125.00 200.00
19 Hugh Jennings 350.00 600.00
20 Red Kleinow 125.00 200.00
21 Nap Lajoie 500.00 800.00
22 Hans Lobert 125.00 200.00
23 Sherry Magee 125.00 200.00
24 Christy Mathewson UER
(Matthewson) 1200.00 2000.00
25 John McGraw 350.00 600.00
26 Larry McLean 125.00 200.00
27 Dots Miller Batting 125.00 200.00
28 Danny Murphy 125.00 200.00
29 Bill O'Hara 125.00 200.00
30 Germany Schaefer 125.00 200.00
31 Admiral Schlei 125.00 200.00
32 Boss Smith (Schmidt) 125.00 200.00
33 Johnny Seigle (Siegle) 125.00 200.00
34 Dave Shean 125.00 200.00
35 Frank Smith 125.00 200.00
36 Joe Tinker 350.00 600.00
37 Honus Wagner Batting 2500.00 4000.00
38 Honus Wagner Throwing 1800.00 3000.00
39 Cy Young Cleveland 900.00 1500.00
40 Heinie Zimmerman 125.00 200.00

1910 Nadja E104

The cards in this 59-card set measure 1 1/2" by 2 3/4". The title of this set comes from the distinctive "Play Ball and eat Nadja Caramels" advertisement found on the reverse of some of the cards. The great majority of the known cards, however, are blank backed. They are grouped together because they have similar obverses and captions in blue print ("Nadja" cards with brown print captions belong to set E92). The cards are unnumbered and were issued in 1910. They have been alphabetized and numbered in our checklist Nadja reverses are valued at three times the prices below.

COMPLETE SET (59) 40000.00 80000.00
1 Bill Abstein 600.00 1200.00
2 Babe Adams 750.00 1500.00
3 Red Ames 600.00 1200.00
4 Home Run Baker 1000.00 2000.00
5 Jack Barry 500.00 1000.00
6 Johnny Bates 600.00 1200.00
7 Chief Bender 1000.00 2000.00
8 Kitty Bransfield 600.00 1200.00
9 Al Bridwell 600.00 1200.00
10 Hal Chase 750.00 1500.00
11 Fred Clarke 1000.00 2000.00
12 Eddie Collins 1000.00 2000.00
13 Doc Crandall 600.00 1200.00
14 Sam Crawford 2000.00 4000.00
15 Harry Davis 500.00 1000.00
16 Jim Delehanty (Delahanty) 600.00 1200.00
17 Art Devlin 500.00 1000.00
18 Red Dooin 500.00 1000.00
19 Mickey Doolan 500.00 1000.00
20 Larry Doyle 600.00 1200.00
21 Jimmy Dygert 500.00 1000.00
22 George Gibson 500.00 1000.00
23 Eddie Grant 600.00 1200.00
24 Topsy Hartsel 500.00 1000.00
25 Ham Hyatt 500.00 1000.00
26 Fred Jacklitsch 600.00 1200.00
27 Hugh Jennings 2000.00 4000.00
28 Davy Jones 600.00 1200.00
29 Tom Jones 600.00 1200.00
30 Otto Knabe 600.00 1200.00
31 Harry Krause 500.00 1000.00
32 John Lapp 500.00 1000.00
33 Tommy Leach 500.00 1000.00
34 Sam Leever 500.00 1000.00
35 Paddy Livingstone (Livingston) 500.00 1000.00
36 Bris Lord 500.00 1000.00
37 Connie Mack 2000.00 4000.00
38 Nick Maddox 500.00 1000.00
39 Sherry Magee 500.00 1000.00
40 John McGraw 2000.00 4000.00
41 Matthew McIntyre 600.00 1200.00
42 Dots Miller 500.00 1000.00
43 Earl Moore 600.00 1200.00
44 Pat Moren (Moran) 600.00 1200.00
45 Cy Morgan 500.00 1000.00
46 George Moriarty 600.00 1200.00
47 George Mullin 600.00 1200.00
48 Danny Murphy 500.00 1000.00
49 Red Murray 600.00 1200.00
50 Simon Nicholls 600.00 1200.00
51 Rube Oldring 500.00 1000.00
52 Charlie O'Leary 600.00 1200.00
53 Deacon Phillippe 600.00 1200.00
54 Eddie Plank 1500.00 3000.00
55 Admiral Schlei 600.00 1200.00
56 Boss Schmidt 500.00 1000.00
57 Cy Seymore (Seymour) 600.00 1200.00
58 Tully Sparks 600.00 1200.00
59 Amos Strunk 500.00 1000.00
60 Ed Summers 600.00 1200.00
62 Ira Thomas 500.00 1000.00
63 Honus Wagner 6000.00 10000.00
64 Ed Willett 600.00 1200.00
65 Vic Willis 1000.00 2000.00
66 Owen Wilson 500.00 1000.00
67 Hooks Wiltse 500.00 1000.00
61 Fred Tenney 3

1967 Nassau Health Ford

This one-card set was issued by Nassau Tuberculosis and Respiratory Disease Association and features a black-and-white photo of Whitey Ford. The back carries player information and a message about the dangers of cigarette smoking.

1 Whitey Ford 20.00 50.00

1921-23 National Caramel E220

The cards in this 120-card set measure 2" by 3 1/4". There are 114 different players and six variations known for the "Baseball Stars" set marketed by the National Caramel Company. The cards are unnumbered and contain black and white photos; they are similar to set E122 but the coarse screening effect of the latter is missing. Some players appear in two poses, Burns is found with two teams, and three names are misspelled on the cards. The set was probably issued in 1922, the same year as was E122. The cards have been alphabetized and numbered in the checklist below. The complete set price includes all variation cards listed in the checklist below.

COMPLETE SET (120) 8000.00 16000.00
1 Babe Adams 75.00 150.00
2 Grover C. Alexander 150.00 300.00
3 James Austin 60.00 120.00
4 Jim Bagbyk/(sic& Bagby) 60.00 120.00
5 Frank Baker 100.00 200.00
6 Dave Bancroft 100.00 200.00
7 Turner Barber 60.00 120.00
8 Geo.H. Burns/Cleveland 60.00 120.00
9 Geo.J. Burns/Cincinnati 60.00 120.00
10 Joe Bush 75.00 150.00
11 Leon Cadore 60.00 120.00
12 Max Carey 100.00 200.00
13 Ty Cobb 900.00 1800.00
14 Eddie Collins 150.00 300.00
15 John Collins 60.00 120.00
16 Wilbur Cooper 60.00 120.00
17 Stan Coveleskie 100.00 200.00
18 Walton Cruise 60.00 120.00
19 William Cunningham 60.00 120.00
20 George Cutshaw 60.00 120.00
21 Jake Daubert 75.00 150.00
22 Chas.A. Deal 60.00 120.00
23 Bill Doak 60.00 120.00
24 Joe Dugan 75.00 150.00
25A Jimmy Dykes/batting 75.00 150.00
25B Jimmy Dykes/fielding 75.00 150.00
26 Red Faber 100.00 200.00
27A Chick Fewster 75.00 150.00
27B Wilson Fewster 75.00 150.00
28 Ira Flagstead 60.00 120.00
29 Art Fletcher 60.00 120.00
30 Frankie Frisch 100.00 200.00
31 Larry Gardner 60.00 120.00
32 Walter Gerber 60.00 120.00
33 Charles Glazner 60.00 120.00
34 Hank Gowdy 75.00 150.00
35 J.C. Graney 60.00 120.00
36 Tommy Griffith 60.00 120.00
37 Charlie Grimm 75.00 150.00
38 Heine Groh 75.00 150.00
39 Byron Harris 60.00 120.00
40 Sam Harris 60.00 120.00
41 Harry Heilmann 100.00 200.00
42 Claude Hendrix 60.00 120.00
43 Walter Henline 60.00 120.00
44 Chas. Hollocher 60.00 120.00
45 Harry Hooper 100.00 200.00
46 Rogers Hornsby 300.00 600.00
47 Waite Hoyt 100.00 200.00
48 Wilbert Hubbell 75.00 150.00
49 Bill Jacobson 60.00 120.00
50 Walter Johnson 400.00 800.00
51 Jimmy Johnston 60.00 120.00
52 Joe Judge 60.00 120.00
53 George Kelly/N.Y. Giants 100.00 200.00
54 Dick Kerr 75.00 150.00
55A Pete Kilduff/bending 60.00 120.00
55B Pete Kilduff/leaping 60.00 120.00
56 Larry Kopf 60.00 120.00
57 Dutch Leonard 75.00 150.00
58 Nemo Leibold 60.00 120.00
59 Walter Mails 75.00 150.00
60 Walter Maranville 100.00 200.00
61 Carl Mays 75.00 150.00
62 Lee Meadows 60.00 120.00
63 Bob Meusel 75.00 150.00
64 Emil Meusel 60.00 120.00
65 Clyde Milan 75.00 150.00
66 Earl Neale 75.00 150.00
67 Robert Nehf/(picture actually/Arthur Nehf) 75.00
150.00
68 Bernie Neis 60.00 120.00
69 Joe Oeschger 60.00 120.00
70 Robert O'Farrell 75.00 150.00
71 Ivan Olson 60.00 120.00
72 Steve O'Neill 75.00 150.00
73 Geo. Paskert 60.00 120.00
74 Roger Peckinpaugh 75.00 150.00
75 Herb Pennock 100.00 200.00
76 Cy Perkins 60.00 120.00
77 Scott Perry 60.00 120.00
78 Jeff Pfeffer 60.00 120.00
79 Val Picinich 60.00 120.00
80 Wally Pipp 75.00 150.00
81 Derrill Pratt 60.00 120.00
82 Goldie Rapp 60.00 120.00
83 Edgar Rice 100.00 200.00
84 Jimmy Ring 60.00 120.00
85 Ed Roush 100.00 200.00
86 Babe Ruth 1100.00 2200.00
87 Wally Schang 60.00 120.00
88 Raymond Schmandt 60.00 120.00
89 Everett Scott 75.00 150.00
90 Joe Sewell 100.00 200.00
91 Maurice Shannon 60.00 120.00
92 Bob Shawkey 75.00 150.00
93 Urban Shocker 75.00 150.00
94 George Sisler 100.00 200.00
95 Earl Smith 60.00 120.00
96 John Smith 60.00 120.00
97 Sherrod Smith 60.00 120.00
98A Frank Snyder/crouching 60.00 120.00
98B Frank Snyder/standing 60.00 120.00
99 Tris Speaker 150.00 300.00
100 Vernon Spencer 60.00 120.00
101 Casey Stengel 250.00 500.00
102A Milton Stock/fielding 60.00 120.00
102B Milton Stock/batting 60.00 120.00
103 James Vaughn 60.00 120.00
104 Robert Veach 60.00 120.00
105 Bill Wambsganss 60.00 120.00
106 Aaron Ward 60.00 120.00
107 Zach Wheat 100.00 200.00
108A George Whitted/batting 60.00 120.00
108B George Whitted/fielding 60.00 120.00
109 Fred C. Williams 75.00 150.00
110 Art Wilson 60.00 120.00
111 Ivy Wingo 60.00 120.00
112 Lawton Witt 60.00 120.00
113 Pep Young 60.00 120.00
114 Ross Young 100.00 200.00

1936 National Chicle Fine Pen Premiums R313

The 1936 Fine Pen Premiums were issued anonymously by the National Chicle Company. The set is complete at 120 cards. Each card measures approximately 3 1/4" by 5 3/8". The cards are blank backed, unnumbered and could be obtained directly from a retail outlet rather than through the mail only. Three types of cards exist. The catalog designation for this set is R313.

COMPLETE SET (120) 1250.00 2500.00
1 Melo Almada 15.00 30.00
2 Paul Andrews 15.00 30.00
3 Elden Auker 15.00 30.00
4 Earl Averill 30.00 60.00
5 Jim Bucher 15.00 30.00
6 Moe Berg 75.00 150.00
7 Wally Berger 25.00 50.00
8 Charles Berry 15.00 30.00
9 Ralph Birkhofer 15.00 30.00
10 Cy Blanton 15.00 30.00
11 Ossie Bluege 20.00 40.00
12 Cliff Bolton 15.00 30.00
13 Zeke Bonura 15.00 30.00
14 Thos. Bridges 20.00 40.00
15 Sam Byrd 15.00 30.00
16 Dolph Camilli 25.00 50.00
17 Bruce Campbell 15.00 30.00
18 Walter Kit Carson 15.00 30.00
19 Ben Chapman 20.00 40.00
20 Rip Collins 20.00 40.00
21 Joe Cronin 30.00 60.00
22 Frank Crosetti 25.00 50.00
23 Paul Derringer 20.00 40.00
24 Bill Dietrich 15.00 30.00
25 Carl Doyle 15.00 30.00
26 Pete Fox 15.00 30.00
27 Frankie Frisch 30.00 60.00
28 Milton Galatzer 15.00 30.00
29 Charley Gehringer 30.00 60.00
30 Charley Gelbert 15.00 30.00
31 Jose Gomez 15.00 30.00
32 Lefty Gomez 30.00 60.00
33 Goose Goslin 30.00 60.00
34 Hank Gowdy 20.00 40.00
35 Hank Greenberg 30.00 60.00
36 Lefty Grove 30.00 60.00
37 Stan Hack 20.00 40.00
38 Odell Hale 15.00 30.00
39 Wild Bill Hallahan 15.00 30.00
40 Mel Harder 20.00 40.00
41 Bucky Harris 30.00 60.00
42 Frank Higgins 15.00 30.00
43 Oral C. Hildebrand 15.00 30.00
44 Myril Hoag 15.00 30.00
45 Rogers Hornsby 50.00 100.00
46 Waite Hoyt 30.00 60.00
47 Willis G. Hudlin(2) 15.00 30.00
48 Woody Jensen (2) 15.00 30.00
49 Wm. Knickerbocker 15.00 30.00
50 Joseph Kuhel 15.00 30.00
51 Cookie Lavagetto 20.00 40.00
52 Thornton Lee 15.00 30.00
53 Red Lucas 15.00 30.00
54 Pepper Martin 25.00 50.00
55 Joe Medwick 30.00 60.00
56 Oscar Melillo 15.00 30.00
57 Buddy Myer 15.00 30.00
58 Wally Moses 15.00 30.00
59 Van L. Mungo 15.00 30.00
60 Lamar Newsom 15.00 30.00
61 Buck Newsom 25.00 50.00
62 Steve O'Neill 20.00 40.00
63 Tommie Padden 15.00 30.00
64 Babe Phillips/(sic, Phelps) 15.00 30.00
65 Bill Rogel/(sic, Rogell) 15.00 30.00
66 Schoolboy Rowe 20.00 40.00
67 Al Simmons 30.00 60.00
68 Casey Stengel MG 60.00 120.00
69 Bill Swift 15.00 30.00
70 Cecil Travis 15.00 30.00
71 Pie Traynor 30.00 60.00
72 Wm. Urbansky/(sic, Urbanski) 15.00 30.00
73 Arky Vaughan 30.00 60.00
74 Joe Vosmik 15.00 30.00
75 Honus Wagner 60.00 120.00
76 Rube Walberg 20.00 40.00
77 Bill Walker 15.00 30.00
78 Gerald Walker 15.00 30.00
79 Bill Werber 15.00 30.00
80 Sam West 15.00 30.00
81 Pinkey Whitney 15.00 30.00
82 Vernon Wiltshere/(sic, Wilshere) 15.00 30.00
83 Pep Young 15.00 30.00
84 Babe and his babes 15.00 30.00
85 Bordagaray 15.00 30.00
Earnshaw
86 James Bucher and 15.00 30.00
John Babich
87 B. Chapman 15.00 30.00
B. Werber
88 Chicago White Sox/1936 15.00 30.00
89 Fence Busters 15.00 30.00
90 Fox 30.00 60.00
Simmons
Cochrane
91 G. Hartnett 30.00 60.00
K. Cuyler
92 L. Gomez 50.00 100.00
R. Ruffing
93 G. Hartnett 30.00 60.00
L. Warneke
94 C. Mack 60.00 120.00
J. McGraw
95 B. Myer 15.00 30.00
C. Dressen MG
96 P. Waner 30.00 60.00
L. Waner
Weaver
97 Wes Ferrell 30.00 60.00
Rick Ferrell
98 Nick Altrock 20.00 40.00
Al Schacht
99 Big Bosses Clash 15.00 30.00
Dykes safe
100 Bottomley tagging 20.00 40.00
Gelbert
101 Camilli catches 20.00 40.00
Jurges off first
102 CCS: Radcliffe safe 20.00 40.00
Harnett catching
103 CCS: L.Sewell blocks 15.00 30.00
runner at plate
104 CCS: Washington safe 15.00 30.00
105 Joe DiMaggio 250.00 500.00
106 Double Play-McQuinn 15.00 30.00
to Stine
107 J. Dykes 20.00 40.00
F. Crosetti
108 Glenn uses football 15.00 30.00
play at plate
109 H. Greenberg 30.00 60.00
B. Dickey
110 Hasset makes the out/(sic, Hassett) 15.00 30.00
111 Ernie Lombardi 30.00 60.00
112 McQuinn gets his man 15.00 30.00
113 Randy Moore hurt 15.00 30.00
stealing second
114 T. Moore out at 20.00 40.00
plate, Wilson catching
115 Sewell waits for 15.00 30.00
ball while
Clift scores
116 Talking it over 15.00 30.00
117 There she goes, CCS 15.00 30.00
118 Ump says No 15.00 30.00
Cleveland vs. Detroit
119 L. Waner 30.00 60.00
G. Hartnett
120 World Series 1935 30.00 60.00

1936 National Chicle Maranville Secrets R344

This paper set of 20 was issued in 1936 by the National Chicle Company. Each "card" measures 3 5/8" by 6". It carries the printing "Given only With Batter-Up Gum" on the back page. While the illustration shows the issue to be elongated. the papers were meant to be folded to create a four-page booklet. As the title implies. the set features instructional tips by Rabbit Maranville.

COMPLETE SET (20) 225.00 450.00
COMMON CARD (1-20) 12.50 25.00

1898 National Copper Plate

Measuring 9" by 12", these photos feature star players from the turn of the century. These photos were issued by National Copper Plate Co of Michigan. Since these are unnumbered, we have sequenced them in alphabetical order. There might be more photos known so any additions to this checklist is appreciated.

COMPLETE SET 3000.00 6000.00
1 Cap Anson 600.00 1200.00
2 Bob Becker 200.00 400.00
3 Tom Dowd 200.00 400.00
4 George Gillpatrick 200.00 400.00
5 Jot Goar 200.00 400.00
6 Mike Griffin 200.00 400.00
7 Clark Griffith 400.00 800.00
8 Bill Joyce 200.00 400.00
9 John McGraw 600.00 1200.00
10 Kid Nichols 400.00 800.00
11 Chief Zimmer 200.00 400.00

1913 National Game WG5

These cards were distributed as part of a baseball game produced in 1913 as indicated by the patent date on the backs of the cards. The cards each measure approximately 2 7/16" by 3 7/16" and have rounded corners. The card fronts show a sepia photo of the player, his name, his team, and the game outcome associated with that particular card. The card backs are all the same, each showing an ornate red and white design with "The National Game" and "Baseball" right in the middle all surrounded by a thick white outer border. Since the cards are unnumbered, they are listed below in alphabetical order. Some of the card photos are oriented horizontally (HOR).

COMPLETE SET (45) 2000.00 4000.00
COMMON ACTION CARD 10.00 25.00
1 Grover Alexander 300.00 600.00
2 Frank Baker 50.00 100.00
3 Chief Bender 40.00 80.00
4 Bob Bescher 15.00 40.00
5 Joe Birmingham 15.00 40.00
6 Roger Bresnahan 50.00 100.00
7 Nixey Callahan 15.00 40.00
8 Frank Chance 50.00 100.00
9 Hal Chase 20.00 50.00
10 Fred Clarke 40.00 80.00
11 Ty Cobb 300.00 600.00
12 Sam Crawford 50.00 100.00
13 Bill Dahlen 15.00 40.00
14 Jake Daubert 15.00 40.00
15 Red Dooin 15.00 40.00
16 Johnny Evers 50.00 100.00
17 Vean Gregg 15.00 40.00
18 Clark Griffith MG 40.00 80.00
19 Dick Hoblitzel 15.00 40.00
20 Miller Huggins 40.00 80.00
21 Joe Jackson 750.00 1500.00
22 Hugh Jennings MG 40.00 80.00
23 Walter Johnson 100.00 200.00
24 Ed Konetchy 15.00 40.00
25 Nap Lajoie 60.00 120.00
26 Connie Mack MG 50.00 100.00
27 Rube Marquard 40.00 80.00
28 Christy Mathewson 100.00 200.00
29 John McGraw MG 50.00 100.00
30 Larry McLean 15.00 40.00
31 Clyde Milan 15.00 40.00
32 Marty O'Toole 15.00 40.00
33 Nap Rucker 15.00 40.00
34 Tris Speaker 60.00 120.00
35 Jake Stahl 15.00 40.00
36 George Stallings MG 15.00 40.00
37 George Stovall 15.00 40.00
38 Bill Sweeney 15.00 40.00
39 Joe Tinker 50.00 100.00
40 Honus Wagner 300.00 600.00
41 Ed Walsh 50.00 100.00
42 Joe Wood 40.00 80.00
43 Cy Young 125.00 250.00
44 Batter Swinging
Looking forward
45 Batter Swinging
Looking back
46 Play at the plate
47 Runner looking back
48 Sliding
Fielder at base
49 Ty Cobb
Sliding
50 Slider
Hand on base
51 Sliding at the plate
Ump left
52 Sliding at the plate
Ump right
53 Rules Card
54 Score Card

2011 National League All-Stars Topps

NL1 Albert Pujols .50 1.25
NL2 Roy Halladay .25 .60
NL3 Chase Utley .25 .60
NL4 Cliff Lee .25 .60
NL5 Tim Lincecum .25 .60
NL6 Matt Holliday .40 1.00
NL7 David Wright .30 .75
NL8 Carlos Gonzalez .25 .60
NL9 Troy Tulowitzki .40 1.00
NL10 Zack Greinke .40 1.00
NL11 Ryan Braun .25 .60
NL12 Starlin Castro .25 .60
NL13 Buster Posey .50 1.25
NL14 Joey Votto .40 1.00
NL15 Stephen Strasburg .40 1.00
NL16 Jason Heyward .30 .75
NL17 Ryan Zimmerman .25 .60

2012 National League All-Stars Topps

NL1 Matt Kemp .30 .75
NL2 Ryan Braun .25 .60
NL3 Jose Reyes .25 .60
NL4 David Wright .30 .75
NL5 Ryan Howard .30 .75
NL6 Roy Halladay .30 .75
NL7 Tim Lincecum .30 .75
NL8 Clayton Kershaw .60 1.50
NL9 Troy Tulowitzki .40 1.00
NL10 Caros Gonzalez .30 .75
NL11 Dan Uggla .30 .75
NL12 Hanley Ramirez .30 .75
NL13 Buster Posey .50 1.25
NL14 Justin Upton .30 .75
NL15 Joey Votto .40 1.00
NL16 Mike Stanton .40 1.00
NL17 Stephen Strasburg .40 1.00

2013 National League All-Stars Topps

COMPLETE SET (17) 3.00 8.00
NL1 Bryce Harper .40 1.00
NL2 Matt Kemp .20 .50
NL3 Clayton Kershaw .40 1.00
NL4 Matt Cain .20 .50
NL5 Adrian Gonzalez .20 .50
NL6 Troy Tulowitzki .25 .60
NL7 Carlos Gonzalez .20 .50
NL8 Stephen Strasburg .25 .60
NL9 David Wright .20 .50
NL10 Pablo Sandoval .20 .50
NL11 Cole Hamels .20 .50
NL12 Buster Posey .30 .75
NL13 Giancarlo Stanton .25 .60
NL14 Joey Votto .40 1.00
NL15 Craig Kimbrel .30 .75
NL16 Andrew McCutchen .25 .60
NL17 Ryan Braun .20 .50

2014 National League All-Stars Topps

COMPLETE SET (17) 3.00 8.00
NL1 Bryce Harper .40 1.00
NL2 Buster Posey .30 .75
NL3 Clayton Kershaw .40 1.00
NL4 Adam Wainwright .20 .50
NL5 Freddie Freeman .30 .75
NL6 Troy Tulowitzki .25 .60
NL7 Carlos Gonzalez .20 .50
NL8 Stephen Strasburg .25 .60
NL9 David Wright .20 .50
NL10 Paul Goldschmidt .25 .60
NL11 Jose Fernandez .25 .60
NL12 Joey Votto .25 .60
NL13 Giancarlo Stanton .25 .60
NL14 Hanley Ramirez .20 .50
NL15 Craig Kimbrel .20 .50
NL16 Andrew McCutchen .25 .60
NL17 Ryan Braun .20 .50

2015 National League All-Stars Topps

COMPLETE SET (17) 3.00 8.00
NL1 Clayton Kershaw .40 1.00
NL2 Paul Goldschmidt .25 .60
NL3 Anthony Rizzo .30 .75
NL4 Freddie Freeman .30 .75
NL5 Javier Baez 1.25 3.00
NL6 Anthony Rendon .25 .60
NL7 Troy Tulowitzki .25 .60
NL8 Christian Yelich .30 .75
NL9 Bryce Harper .40 1.00
NL10 Andrew McCutchen .25 .60
NL11 Billy Hamilton .20 .50
NL12 Yasiel Puig .25 .60
NL13 Giancarlo Stanton .25 .60
NL14 Buster Posey .30 .75
NL15 Madison Bumgarner .20 .50
NL16 Johnny Cueto .20 .50
NL17 Craig Kimbrel .20 .50

2016 National League All-Stars Topps

COMPLETE SET (17) 3.00 8.00
NL1 Clayton Kershaw .40 1.00
NL2 Buster Posey .30 .75
NL3 Paul Goldschmidt .25 .60
NL4 Dee Gordon .15 .40
NL5 Kris Bryant .30 .75
NL6 Brandon Crawford .20 .50
NL7 Bryce Harper .40 1.00
NL8 Giancarlo Stanton .25 .60
NL9 Andrew McCutchen .25 .60
NL10 Jeurys Familia .20 .50
NL11 Zack Greinke .25 .60
NL12 Jake Arrieta .20 .50
NL13 Madison Bumgarner .20 .50
NL14 Jacob deGrom .50 1.25
NL15 Matt Harvey .20 .50
NL16 Yadier Molina .30 .75
NL17 Anthony Rizzo .30 .75

2017 National League All-Stars Topps

COMPLETE SET (17) 3.00 8.00
NL1 Kris Bryant .30 .75
NL2 Freddie Freeman .30 .75
NL3 Anthony Rizzo .30 .75
NL4 Yadier Molina .30 .75
NL5 Madison Bumgarner .20 .50
NL6 Nolan Arenado .40 1.00
NL7 Jake Arrieta .20 .50
NL8 Jon Lester .20 .50
NL9 Max Scherzer .25 .60
NL10 Bryce Harper .40 1.00
NL11 Daniel Murphy .20 .50
NL12 Yoenis Cespedes .25 .60
NL13 Noah Syndergaard .20 .50
NL14 Clayton Kershaw .40 1.00
NL15 Giancarlo Stanton .25 .60
NL16 Corey Seager .25 .60
NL17 Paul Goldschmidt .25 .60

2019 National League All-Stars Topps

COMPLETE SET (17) 4.00 10.00
NL1 Javier Baez .30 .75
NL2 Nolan Arenado .40 1.00
NL3 Paul Goldschmidt .25 .60
NL4 Freddie Freeman .30 .75
NL5 Ronald Acuna Jr. 1.25 3.00
NL6 Bryce Harper .40 1.00
NL7 Anthony Rizzo .30 .75
NL8 Kris Bryant .30 .75
NL9 Noah Syndergaard .20 .50
NL10 Max Scherzer .25 .60
NL11 Christian Yelich .30 .75
NL12 Joey Votto .25 .60
NL13 Yadier Molina .30 .75
NL14 J.T. Realmuto .25 .60
NL15 Jacob deGrom .50 1.25
NL16 Charlie Blackmon .25 .60
NL17 Clayton Kershaw .40 1.00

2020 National League All-Stars Topps

NL1 Bryce Harper .40 1.00
NL2 Christian Yelich .30 .75
NL3 Nolan Arenado .40 1.00
NL4 Cody Bellinger .50 1.25
NL5 Pete Alonso .60 1.50
NL6 Javier Baez .30 .75
NL7 Clayton Kershaw .40 1.00
NL8 Paul Goldschmidt .25 .60
NL9 Manny Machado .25 .60
NL10 Ronald Acuna Jr. 1.00 2.50
NL11 Max Scherzer .25 .60
NL12 Kris Bryant .30 .75
NL13 Jacob deGrom .50 1.25
NL14 Ozzie Albies .25 .60
NL15 Stephen Strasburg .25 .60
NL16 Juan Soto .75 2.00
NL17 Joey Votto .25 .60

1952 National Tea Labels

The bread labels in this set are often called "Red Borders" because of their distinctive trim. Each label measures 2 3/4" by 2 11/16". Issued with the bakery products of the National Tea Company, there are thought to be 48 different labels in the set. The six missing labels are thought to consist of two Yankees, two Indians and two Red Sox -- so that there would be exactly three representatives from each of the 16 teams. The labels are also known as the "Bread For Health" set and may have included an album. This set is the toughest of the bread label sets listed. These labels are unnumbered so we have sequenced them in alphabetical order. The catalog designation is D290-2.

COMPLETE SET (42) 5500.00 11000.00
1 Gene Bearden 175.00 350.00
2 Yogi Berra 300.00 600.00
3 Lou Brissie 175.00 350.00
4 Sam Chapman 175.00 350.00
5 Chuck Diering 175.00 350.00
6 Dom DiMaggio 300.00 600.00
7 Hank Edwards 175.00 350.00
8 Del Ennis 200.00 400.00
9 Ferris Fain 175.00 350.00
10 Howie Fox 175.00 350.00
11 Sid Gordon 200.00 400.00
12 Johhny Groth 175.00 350.00
13 Granny Hamner 175.00 350.00
14 Sam Jones 175.00 350.00
15 Howie Judson 175.00 350.00

16 Sherm Lollar 175.00 350.00
17 Clarence Marshall 175.00 350.00
18 Don Mueller 175.00 350.00
19 Danny Murtaugh 200.00 400.00
20 Dave Philley 175.00 350.00
21 Jerry Priddy 175.00 350.00
22 Bill Rigney 200.00 400.00
23 Robin Roberts 300.00 600.00
24 Eddie Robinson 175.00 350.00
25 Preacher Roe 250.00 500.00
26 Stan Rojek 175.00 350.00
27 Al Rosen 250.00 500.00
28 Bob Rush 175.00 350.00
29 Hank Sauer 200.00 400.00
30 Johnny Schmitz 175.00 350.00
31 Enos Slaughter 300.00 600.00
32 Duke Snider 600.00 1200.00
33 Warren Spahn 350.00 700.00
34 Gerry Staley 175.00 350.00
35 Virgil Stallcup 175.00 350.00
36 George Stirnweiss 175.00 350.00
37 Earl Torgeson 175.00 350.00
38 Dizzy Trout 200.00 400.00
39 Mickey Vernon 250.00 500.00
40 Wally Westlake 175.00 350.00
41 Johnny Wyrostek 175.00 350.00
42 Eddie Yost 200.00 400.00

1995 National Packtime

This 18-card standard-size set was sponsored by MLB, MLBPA, and the six licensed card companies from 1995 (Donruss, Fleer, Pacific, Pinnacle, Topps, and Upper Deck). Each of the six companies produced three cards for the set, which was available only through a mail-in offer for 28 wrappers from any of the six companies listed above plus $2.00 for shipping and handling. All orders had to be postmarked by June 30, 1995; any card sets not purchased by that date were destroyed. Except for the Topps card (which has a ragged white border), all the fronts display full-bleed color action photos. The backs carry a second color photo as well as biography and statistics. The cards are numbered on the back "X of 18." An unnumbered offer card, with a checklist on its back, was found in various 1995 baseball products.

COMPLETE SET (18) 3.00 8.00
1 Frank Thomas .25 .60
2 Matt Williams .10 .30
3 Juan Gonzalez .15 .40
4 Bob Hamelin .02 .10
5 Mike Piazza .60 1.50
6 Ken Griffey Jr. .60 1.50
7 Barry Bonds .50 1.25
8 Tim Salmon .10 .30
9 Jose Canseco .25 .60
10 Cal Ripken 1.00 2.50
11 Raul Mondesi .07 .20
12 Alex Rodriguez .60 1.50
13 Will Clark .15 .40
14 Fred McGriff .10 .30
15 Tony Gwynn .50 1.25
16 Kenny Lofton .07 .20
17 Deion Sanders .07 .20
18 Jeff Bagwell .30 .75

1995 National Packtime 2

This six-card set was sponsored by MLB, MLBPA and the six licensed card companies (Donruss, Fleer, Pacific, Pinnacle, Topps, and Upper Deck) who each produced one card for the set. The fronts feature borderless color action player photos, while the backs carry player information. The cards are checklisted below in alphabetical order.

COMPLETE SET (6) 1.50 4.00
1 Albert Belle .07 .20
2 Darren Daulton .02 .10
3 Randy Johnson .40 1.00
4 Greg Maddux .60 1.50
5 Don Mattingly .50 1.25
6 Hideo Nomo .40 1.00

2004 National Pastime

COMP.SET w/o SP's (60) 10.00 25.00
COMMON CARD (1-60) .30 .75
COMMON CARD (61-90) .75 2.00
61-90 ODDS 1:7 HOBBY, 1:48 RETAIL
61-90 PRINT RUN 699 SERIAL #'d SETS
1 Hideki Matsui 1.25 3.00
2 Khalil Greene .50 1.25
3 Pedro Martinez .50 1.25
4 Sammy Sosa .75 2.00
5 Mark Teixeira .50 1.25
6 Orlando Cabrera .30 .75
7 Scott Podsednik .30 .75
8 Miguel Tejada .50 1.25
9 Andruw Jones .30 .75
10 Manny Ramirez .75 2.00
11 Jose Reyes .50 1.25
12 Bobby Abreu .30 .75
13 Alex Rodriguez 1.00 2.50
14 Ivan Rodriguez .50 1.25
15 Jason Schmidt .30 .75
16 Mike Piazza .75 2.00
17 Eric Chavez .30 .75
18 Mark Prior .50 1.25
19 Adam Dunn .50 1.25
20 Richard Hidalgo .30 .75
21 Todd Helton .50 1.25
22 Rocco Baldelli .30 .75
23 Roy Oswalt .50 1.25
24 Angel Berroa .30 .75
25 Jason Giambi .30 .75
26 Jim Thome .50 1.25
27 Javy Lopez .30 .75
28 Derek Jeter 2.00 5.00
29 Tom Glavine .50 1.25
30 Magglio Ordonez .50 1.25
31 Austin Kearns .30 .75
32 Scott Rolen .50 1.25
33 Miguel Cabrera .75 2.00
34 Vernon Wells .30 .75
35 Frank Thomas .75 2.00
36 Jeff Bagwell .50 1.25
37 Shannon Stewart .30 .75
38 Richie Sexson .30 .75
39 Hideo Nomo .75 2.00
40 Nomar Garciaparra .50 1.25
41 C.C. Sabathia .50 1.25
42 Albert Pujols 1.00 2.50
43 Barry Zito .50 1.25
44 Hank Blalock .30 .75
45 Carlos Delgado .30 .75
46 Greg Maddux 1.00 2.50
47 Randy Johnson .75 2.00
48 Josh Beckett .30 .75
49 Kerry Wood .30 .75
50 Roger Clemens 1.00 2.50
51 Garret Anderson .30 .75
52 Ichiro Suzuki 1.00 2.50
53 Kip Wells .30 .75
54 Vladimir Guerrero .50 1.25
55 Shawn Green .30 .75
56 Chipper Jones .75 2.00
57 Aubrey Huff .30 .75
58 Ken Griffey Jr. 1.50 4.00
59 Torii Hunter .30 .75
60 Alfonso Soriano .50 1.25
61 Chris Shelton ROO RC .75 2.00
62 Graham Koonce ROO .75 2.00
63 Kaz Matsui ROO RC 1.25 3.00
64 Alfredo Simon ROO RC 1.25 3.00
65 Mike Gosling ROO RC .75 2.00
66 Mike Rouse ROO RC .75 2.00
67 Mariano Gomez ROO RC .75 2.00
68 Justin Leone ROO RC .75 2.00
69 Jose Capellan ROO RC .75 2.00
70 Donnie Kelly ROO RC 1.25 3.00
71 Merkin Valdez ROO RC .75 2.00
72 Greg Dobbs ROO RC .75 2.00
73 Shingo Takatsu ROO RC .75 2.00
74 Chris Aguila ROO RC .75 2.00
75 Jerome Gamble ROO RC .75 2.00
76 Onil Joseph ROO RC .75 2.00
77 Ramon Ramirez ROO RC .75 2.00
78 Angel Chavez ROO RC .75 2.00
79 Hector Gimenez ROO RC .75 2.00
80 Ivan Ochoa ROO RC .75 2.00
81 Aarom Baldiris ROO RC .75 2.00
82 Akinori Otsuka ROO RC .75 2.00
83 Ruddy Yan ROO .75 2.00
84 Jerry Gil ROO RC .75 2.00
85 Shawn Hill ROO RC .75 2.00
86 John Gall ROO RC .75 2.00
87 Jason Bartlett ROO RC 2.50 6.00
88 Jorge Sequea ROO RC .75 2.00
89 Luis A. Gonzalez ROO RC .75 2.00
90 Sean Henn ROO RC .75 2.00

2004 National Pastime Blue Foil

OVERALL PARALLEL ODDS 1:10 HOBBY
STATED PRINT RUN 1 SERIAL #'d SET
NO PRICING DUE TO SCARCITY

2004 National Pastime Red Foil

*RED 1-60: 1.25X TO 3X BASIC
*RED 61-90: .5X TO 1.2X BASIC
OVERALL PARALLEL ODDS 1:10 H, 1:48 R
STATED PRINT RUN 150 SERIAL #'d SETS

2004 National Pastime White Foil

*WHITE 1-60: 2.5X TO 6X BASIC
*WHITE 61-90: 1X TO 2.5X BASIC
OVERALL PARALLEL ODDS 1:10 H, 1:48 R
STATED PRINT RUN 50 SERIAL #'d SETS

2004 National Pastime 1959 Ted Williams Reprint

COMMON CARD (1-80) 2.00 5.00
STATED PRINT RUN 406 SERIAL #'d SETS
59 SET EXCH.PRINT RUN 1 #'d CARD
COMMON M'PIECE (1-80) 50.00 100.00
MASTERPIECE RANDOM IN HOBBY PACKS
MASTERPIECE PRINT RUN 1 #'d SET
OVERALL T.WILLIAMS ODDS 1:3 HOBBY

2004 National Pastime American Flag Patch

STATED ODDS 1:240 HOBBY BOXES
PRINT RUNS B/WN 1-3 COPIES PER
NO PRICING DUE TO SCARCITY

2004 National Pastime American Game

STATED ODDS 1:10 HOBBY; 1:12 RETAIL
1 Greg Maddux 1.25 3.00
2 Randy Johnson 1.00 2.50
3 Roger Clemens 1.25 3.00
4 Mark Prior .60 1.50
5 Mike Piazza 1.00 2.50
6 Alex Rodriguez 1.25 3.00
7 Adam Dunn .60 1.50
8 Jim Thome .60 1.50
9 Derek Jeter 2.50 6.00
10 Scott Rolen .60 1.50
11 Nomar Garciaparra .60 1.50
12 Kerry Wood .40 1.00
13 Chipper Jones 1.00 2.50
14 Frank Thomas 1.00 2.50
15 Jeff Bagwell .60 1.50

2004 National Pastime American Game Jersey

STATED ODDS 1:96 RETAIL
SP PRINT RUNS PROVIDED BY FLEER
SP'S ARE NOT SERIAL-NUMBERED
*PATCH p/r 37-50: 1.25X TO 3X JSY
*PATCH p/r 46: 1.25X TO 3X JSY SP
*PATCH p/r 30: 1.5X TO 4X JSY
*PATCH p/r 29-35: 1.5X TO 4X JSY SP
PATCH PRINTS B/WN 10-50 COPIES PER
NO PATCH PRICING ON QTY OF 13 OR LESS
PATCH M'PIECE PRINT RUN 1 #'d SET
NO PATCH MP PRICING DUE TO SCARCITY
OVERALL GU ODDS 1:60 H, AU-GU 1:24 R
PATCH MP ISSUED ONLY IN HOBBY PACKS
AD Adam Dunn 2.00 5.00
AR Alex Rodriguez 4.00 10.00
CJ Chipper Jones 3.00 8.00
DJ Derek Jeter 8.00 20.00
FT Frank Thomas SP/150 4.00 10.00
GM Greg Maddux SP/150 5.00 12.00
JB Jeff Bagwell 3.00 8.00
JT Jim Thome 3.00 8.00
KW Kerry Wood 2.00 5.00
MP Mike Piazza SP/200 5.00 12.00
MPR Mark Prior 3.00 8.00
RCL Roger Clemens 5.00 12.00
RJO Randy Johnson 3.00 8.00
SR Scott Rolen 3.00 8.00

2004 National Pastime American Game Retired GU

OVERALL GAME USED ODDS 1:60 HOBBY
PRINT RUNS B/WN 6-31 COPIES PER
NO PRICING ON QTY OF 10 OR LESS
BR Babe Ruth Bat/25 150.00 250.00
CF Carlton Fisk Patch/25 15.00 40.00
CR Cal Ripken Patch/25 60.00 120.00
DM Don Mattingly Pants/23 20.00 50.00
DW Dave Winfield Patch/31 20.00 50.00
MS Mike Schmidt Patch/25 50.00 100.00
RC Roberto Clemente Bat/25 60.00 120.00
TM Thurman Munson Bat/25 15.00 40.00

2004 National Pastime American Game Retired GU Autograph

OVERALL GAME USED ODDS 1:60 HOBBY
PRINT RUNS B/WN 5-25 COPIES PER
NO PRICING ON QTY OF 8 OR LESS
WM Willie McCovey Jsy/22 40.00 80.00

2004 National Pastime American Game Retired GU Dual

OVERALL GAME USED ODDS 1:60 HOBBY
PRINT RUNS B/WN 5-25 COPIES PER
NO PRICING ON QTY OF 10 OR LESS
JB Johnny Bench Bat-Patch/20 40.00 80.00
NR Nolan Ryan Bat-Jsy/25 40.00 80.00
RJ Reg Jackson Bat-Pants/25 15.00 40.00

2004 National Pastime Buyback Autographs

OVERALL AUTO ODDS 1:5 HOBBY
PRINT RUNS B/WN 1-174 #'d COPIES PER
L.DOBY PRINT RUN 447 COPIES
L.DOBY IS NOT SERIAL-NUMBERED
L.DOBY PRINT RUN PROVIDED BY FLEER
NO PRICING ON QTY OF 14 OR LESS
AD Andre Dawson 02 GG/130 6.00 15.00
BBL Bert Blyleven 00 GG/57 6.00 15.00
BBO1 Bobby Bonds 00 GG/24 40.00 80.00
BF Bob Feller 00 GG/36 10.00 25.00
BG2 B.Gibson 02 ULT FC/125 8.00 20.00
BM B.Maz 02 ULT FC/167 8.00 20.00
BR Brooks Robinson 02 GG/64 10.00 25.00
BS Bruce Sutter 00 GG/83 8.00 20.00
BW Billy Williams 02 GG/126 6.00 15.00
CB Clete Boyer 00 GG/65 6.00 15.00
CC Cecil Cooper 00 GG/28 5.00 12.00
CF1 C.Fisk 01 FOC ROY/15 15.00 40.00
DB Don Baylor 00 GG/24 8.00 20.00
DE Darrell Evans 00 GG/67 4.00 10.00
DG Dick Groat 00 GG/90 8.00 20.00
DL Don Larsen 00 GG/27 8.00 20.00
DP2 Dave Parker 02 GG/61 6.00 15.00
DS Duke Snider 02 GG/71 8.00 20.00
DW Dave Winfield 02 GG/64 6.00 15.00
EM1 Eddie Murray 02 GG/33 15.00 40.00
ES Enos Slaughter 00 GG/52 10.00 25.00
FH Frank Howard 00 GG/104 6.00 15.00
FJ Fergie Jenkins 00 GG/61 6.00 15.00
FL Fred Lynn 02 GG/126 4.00 10.00
FR F.Robinson 02 ULT FC/20 15.00 40.00
FW Frank White 00 GG/30 5.00 12.00
GK1 George Kell 00 GG/30 12.50 30.00
GK3 George Kell 02 GG Blue/40 10.00 25.00
GP1 Gaylord Perry 00 GG/70 6.00 15.00
GP2 Gaylord Perry 02 GG/52 6.00 15.00
GT Gorman Thomas 00 GG/85 4.00 10.00
HB2 Hank Bauer 02 GG/65 6.00 15.00
HM Hal McRae 00 GG/25 6.00 15.00
HS1 Herb Score 00 GG/56 6.00 15.00
HS2 Herb Score 00 GG ROY/46 6.00 15.00
HW2 H.Wilhelm 02 GG Black/36 10.00 25.00
HW3 H.Wilhelm 02 GG Blue/20 15.00 40.00
JB Jim Bouton 00 GG/71 4.00 10.00
JB1 Johnny Bench 02 GG/140 20.00 50.00
JK Jim Kaat 00 GG/58 6.00 15.00
JM Jack Morris 00 GG/80 6.00 15.00
JP Joe Pepitone 00 GG/82 6.00 15.00
JP1 Jim Palmer 02 GG/62 6.00 15.00
JP2 Jim Palmer 02 ULT FC/18 10.00 25.00
LA Luis Aparicio 00 GG/16 10.00 25.00
LBR Lou Brock 02 GG/18 15.00 40.00
LD Larry Doby 01 GG/447 * 15.00 40.00
LS Lee Smith 00 GG/24 10.00 25.00
ML Mickey Lolich 00 GG/40 10.00 25.00
MS Moose Skowron 00 GG/58 6.00 15.00
OC1 Orlando Cepeda 00 GG/31 8.00 20.00
OC2 O.Cepeda 02 GG/174 6.00 15.00
PB Paul Blair 02 GG/67 4.00 10.00
PG Phil Garner 00 GG/55 6.00 15.00
PR1 Phil Rizzuto 02 GG/49 12.50 30.00
PRO1 Preacher Roe 00 GG/52 10.00 25.00
PRO2 Preacher Roe 02 GG/68 8.00 20.00
RCE Ron Cey 00 GG/22 10.00 25.00
RCO Rocky Colavito 02 GG/72 15.00 40.00
RK Ralph Kiner 00 GG/17 15.00 40.00
RS Ryne Sandberg 02 GG/49 30.00 60.00
RY Robin Yount 02 ULT FC/24 40.00 80.00
SA S.Anderson 02 GG/112 6.00 15.00
SC Steve Carlton 02 GG/99 12.50 30.00
TO1 Tony Oliva 00 GG/110 6.00 15.00
TO3 Tony Oliva 02 GG/58 6.00 15.00
TP Tony Perez 02 ULT FC/160 8.00 20.00
VB1 Vida Blue 00 GG/124 4.00 10.00
VB2 Vida Blue 02 GG/60 4.00 10.00
WF Whitey Ford 02 GG/67 12.50 30.00
WM1 W.McCovey 01 GG/92 15.00 40.00
WM2 W.McCovey 02 GG/142 10.00 25.00
WM3 W.McCov 02 ULT FC/27 30.00 60.00
WS Warren Spahn 02 GG/63 12.50 30.00
YB Yogi Berra 02 GG/43 40.00 80.00

2004 National Pastime Buyback Game Used

OVERALL GAME USED ODDS 1:60 HOBBY
PRINT RUNS B/WN 1-32 COPIES PER
NO PRICING ON QTY OF 14 OR LESS
BG Bob Gibson 02 GG DD Jsy/17 10.00 25.00
(w/Duke Snider
BJ B.Jackson 02 GG TY Jsy/24 15.00 40.00
BR2 B.Rob 02 GG TY Bat/24 8.00 20.00
CF1 C.Fisk 02 GG TY Fld Jsy/25 8.00 20.00
CF2 C.Fisk 02 GG TY Hit Jsy/29 8.00 20.00
CR5 C.Rip 01 FUT BL Base/15 60.00 120.00
CR9 Ripken 02 GG DD Bat/17 60.00 120.00
CY C.Yaz 02 GG TY Jsy/22 15.00 40.00
DM3 Mattingly 02 GG DD Bat/23 15.00 40.00
DM5 Don Mattingly 02 GG TY Jsy/23 15.00 40.00
DS D.Sand 01 Auth DC Jsy/21 15.00 40.00
EMU E.Murray 02 GG TY Jsy/23 10.00 25.00
EMA2 Eddie Mathews 02 GG DD Bat /19 15.00 40.00
(w/Duke Snider
ES2 E.Slaughter 02 GG DD Bat/15 10.00 25.00
(w/Ted Kluszewski
GB2 Brett 02 GG DD Bat/18 20.00 50.00
GB3 G.Brett 02 GG TY Jsy/21 20.00 50.00
KP Puckett 02 GG DD Bat/15 20.00 50.00
LP L.Pin 01 LEG TM Jsy/29 6.00 15.00
MM1 M.McGw 01 Fut BL Base/18 30.00 60.00
MS M.Schm 01 FUT BF Bat/20 15.00 40.00
NF Nellie Fox GG DD Bat/15 15.00 40.00
(w/Rocky Colavito
NR1 N.Ryan 01 LEG TM Jsy/34 30.00 60.00
NR2 N.Ryan 02 GG TY Jsy/20 30.00 60.00
OC1 O.Cep 01 GG FGC Bat/16 10.00 25.00
OC2 O.Cep 01 LEG TM Jsy/32 6.00 15.00
PM3 Paul Molitor 02 GG DD Bat/16 8.00 20.00
(w/Dave Winfield
PM4 P.Mol 02 GG TY Brw Jsy/18 8.00 20.00
PM5 P.Mol 02 GG TY Jays Jsy/23 6.00 15.00
RJ1 R.Jackson 02 GG DD Bat/15 10.00 25.00
(w/Jim Rice
RJ2 R.Jack 02 GG TY A's Jsy/25 8.00 20.00
RY1 R.Yount 01 FUT BF Bat/19 15.00 40.00
RY2 R.Yount 02 GG TY Jsy/18 15.00 40.00
TG1 T.Gwy 01 AUTH DC Bat/32 15.00 40.00
TG2 T.Gwy 01 FUT BL Base/19 15.00 40.00
TK T.Klusz 02 GG TY Jsy/18 10.00 25.00
TP3 T.Perez 02 GG TY Jsy/22 8.00 20.00
WB W.Boggs 02 GG TY Jsy/26 8.00 20.00
WM3 W.McCov 02 GG TY Jsy/15 10.00 25.00
YB1 Y.Berra 02 GG DD Bat/15 10.00 25.00
YB2 Y.Berra 02 GG DD Bat/15 8.00 20.00
YB3 Y.Berra 02 GG DD F.Glv/15 15.00 40.00

2004 National Pastime History in the Making

STATED ODDS 1:5 HOBBY, 1:4 RETAIL
1 Pedro Martinez .60 1.50
2 Alex Rodriguez 1.25 3.00
3 Sammy Sosa 1.00 2.50
4 Mike Piazza 1.00 2.50
5 Jason Giambi .40 1.00
6 Jim Thome .60 1.50
7 Derek Jeter 2.50 6.00
8 Hideo Nomo 1.00 2.50
9 Nomar Garciaparra .60 1.50
10 Albert Pujols 1.25 3.00
11 Greg Maddux 1.25 3.00
12 Randy Johnson 1.00 2.50
13 Roger Clemens 1.25 3.00
14 Ichiro Suzuki 1.25 3.00
15 Vladimir Guerrero .60 1.50
16 Chipper Jones 1.00 2.50
17 Ken Griffey 2.00 5.00
18 Manny Ramirez 1.00 2.50
19 Ivan Rodriguez .60 1.50
20 Mark Prior .60 1.50
21 Austin Kearns .40 1.00
22 Alfonso Soriano .60 1.50
23 Barry Zito .60 1.50
24 Josh Beckett .40 1.00
25 Angel Berroa .40 1.00
26 Jose Reyes .60 1.50
27 Adam Dunn .60 1.50
28 Todd Helton .60 1.50
29 Hank Blalock .40 1.00
30 Kaz Matsui .60 1.50

2004 National Pastime History in the Making Dual Bat

OVERALL GAME USED ODDS 1:60 HOBBY
STATED PRINT RUN 5 SERIAL #'d CARDS
NO PRICING DUE TO SCARCITY

2004 National Pastime History in the Making Jersey

STATED ODDS 1:36 RETAIL
SP INFO PROVIDED BY FLEER
SP'S ARE NOT SERIAL-NUMBERED
*PATCH p/r 37-50: 1.25X TO 3X JSY
*PATCH p/r42-50: 1.2X TO 3X JSY SP 150-200
*PATCH p/r 41-49: 1X TO 2.5X JSY SP 75-100
*PATCH p/r 32: 1.5X TO 4X JSY SP 150-200
*PATCH p/r 26: 1.25X TO 3X JSY SP 75-100
*PATCH p/r 20-24: 2X TO 5X JSY
PATCH PRINTS B/WN 20-50 COPIES PER
K.MATSUI PATCH TOO VOLATILE TO PRICE
PATCH MASTERPIECE PRINT RUN 1 #'d SET
NO PATCH MP PRICING DUE TO SCARCITY
OVERALL GU ODDS 1:60 H, AU-GU 1:24 R
PATCH MP ISSUED ONLY IN HOBBY PACKS
AB Angel Berroa 2.00 5.00
AD Adam Dunn SP/100 3.00 8.00
AK Austin Kearns SP/100 3.00 8.00
AP Albert Pujols 6.00 15.00
AR Alex Rodriguez 4.00 10.00
AS Alfonso Soriano 2.00 5.00
BZ Barry Zito 2.00 5.00
CJ Chipper Jones 3.00 8.00
DJ Derek Jeter 8.00 20.00
GM Greg Maddux SP/150 5.00 12.00
HB Hank Blalock 2.00 5.00
HN Hideo Nomo 3.00 8.00
IR Ivan Rodriguez SP/150 4.00 10.00
JB Josh Beckett 2.00 5.00
JG Jason Giambi 2.00 5.00
JR Jose Reyes 2.00 5.00
JT Jim Thome 3.00 8.00
KM Kaz Matsui 4.00 10.00
MP Mike Piazza SP/200 5.00 12.00
MPR Mark Prior 3.00 8.00
MR Manny Ramirez 3.00 8.00
PM Pedro Martinez 3.00 8.00
RC Roger Clemens SP/75 6.00 15.00
RJ Randy Johnson 3.00 8.00
SS Sammy Sosa 3.00 8.00
TH Todd Helton SP/200 4.00 10.00
VG Vladimir Guerrero 3.00 8.00

2004 National Pastime National Treasures

STATED PRINT RUN 500 SERIAL #'d SETS
*GOLD p/r 75-94: .75X TO 2X BASIC
*GOLD p/r 49: 1X TO 2.5X BASIC
*GOLD p/r 19: 2X TO 5X BASIC
GOLD PRINT RUNS B/WN 2-94 COPIES PER
NO GOLD PRICING ON QTY OF 2 OR LESS
OVERALL NAT'L.TREA.ODDS 1:12 H, 1:240 R
GOLD ISSUED ONLY IN HOBBY PACKS
2 Kenesaw Landis .40 1.00
5 Leo Durocher .40 1.00
9 Peter Gammons .40 1.00
10 Ernie Harwell .60 1.50
11 Billy Martin .60 1.50
12 John McGraw .60 1.50
13 Red Barber .40 1.00
15 Casey Stengel .60 1.50
16 Sparky Anderson .60 1.50
17 Harry Caray .60 1.50
18 Ban Johnson .40 1.00
20 Ralph Kiner .60 1.50

2004 National Pastime National Treasures Autograph Red

STATED PRINT RUN 50 SERIAL #'d SETS
BLUE PRINT RUN 6 SERIAL #'d SETS
NO BLUE PRICING DUE TO SCARCITY
M'PIECE PRINT RUN 1 SERIAL #'d SET
NO M'PIECE PRICING DUE TO SCARCITY
*WHITE p/r 22-30: .6X TO 1.5X RED
WHITE PRINT RUNS B/WN 1-30 COPIES PER
NO WHITE PRICING ON QTY OF 2 OR LESS
OVERALL AUTO ODDS 1:5 HOBBY
EXCHANGE DEADLINE INDEFINITE

2004 National Pastime Signature Swings Gold

OVERALL AU ODDS 1:5 HOBBY, 1:24 RETAIL
PRINT RUNS B/WN 3-265 COPIES PER
NO PRICING ON QTY OF 10 OR LESS
EXCHANGE DEADLINE INDEFINITE
AJ Andruw Jones/23 15.00 40.00
AK1 Al Kaline/79 20.00 50.00
AK2 Austin Kearns/20 6.00 15.00
AT Alan Trammell/138 6.00 15.00
BD Bucky Dent/21 10.00 25.00
BM Bill Mazeroski/61 12.50 30.00
CF Carlton Fisk/36 12.50 30.00
CJ Chipper Jones/109 20.00 50.00
DE David Eckstein/161 10.00 25.00
DJ Derek Jeter/35 100.00 200.00
DM Don Mattingly/15 50.00 100.00
DP Dave Parker/57 8.00 20.00
EM Edgar Martinez/85 10.00 25.00
FH Frank Howard/60 8.00 20.00
GS Gary Sheffield/25 15.00 40.00
HB Hank Blalock/265 6.00 15.00
JC Joe Carter/95 6.00 15.00
LB Lance Berkman/172 6.00 15.00
LF Lew Ford/183 4.00 10.00
LG Luis Gonzalez/61 8.00 20.00
SC Sean Casey/169 6.00 15.00
SM Stan Musial/15 20.00 50.00
WS Warren Spahn/188 12.00 30.00

2004 National Pastime Signature Swings Red

*REDp/r106-109:.5X TO 1.2X GOLDp/r169-265
*RED p/r 106-109: .25X TO .6X GOLD p/r 61
*RED p/r 73-98: .6X TO 1.5X GOLDp/r161-173
*RED p/r 73-98: .5X TO 1.2X GOLDp/r109-138
*RED p/r 73-98: .3X TO .8X GOLD p/r 57
*RED p/r 73-98: .25X TO .6X GOLD p/r 15
*RED p/r 36-65: .75X TO 2X GOLD p/r 220
*RED p/r 36-65: .5X TO 1.2X GOLD p/r 79
*RED p/r 36-65: .4X TO 1X GOLD p/r 36-61
*RED p/r 36-65: .2X TO .5X GOLD p/r 15
*RED p/r 26-35: .5X TO 1.2X GOLD p/r 64
*RED p/r 26-35: .3X TO .8X GOLD p/r 21-25
*RED p/r 22-25: .75X TO 2X GOLD p/r 85-95
*RED p/r 22-25: .6X TO 1.5X GOLD p/r 60
*RED p/r 22-25: .5X TO 1.2X GOLD p/r 33-35
OVERALL AU ODDS 1:5 H, AU-GU 1:24 R
PRINT RUNS B/WN 22-109 COPIES PER
EXCHANGE DEADLINE INDEFINITE
GB George Brett/42 50.00 100.00
JE Jim Edmonds/22 20.00 50.00
JG2 Jay Gibbons/33 6.00 15.00
JP2 Juan Pierre/52 8.00 20.00
MS2 Moose Skowron/59 8.00 20.00

2004 National Pastime Signature Swings White

*WHITEp/r36-65: .75X TO 2X GOLDp/r173-220
*WHITEp/r36-65:.6X TO 1.5X GOLDp/r109-110
*WHITE p/r 36-65: .5X TO 1.2X GOLD p/r 85
*WHITE p/r 36-65: .4X TO 1X GOLD p/r 36-64
*WHITE p/r 36-65: .25X TO .6X GOLD p/r 25
*WHITE p/r 36-65: .2X TO .5X GOLD p/r 15
*WHITEp/r28-35:1X TO 2.5X GOLDp/r176-265
*WHITE p/r 28-35: .75X TO 2X GOLD p/r 138
*WHITE p/r 28-35: .6X TO 1.5X GOLDp/r79-95
*WHITE p/r 28-35: .5X TO 1.2X GOLD p/r 57
*WHITE p/r 28-35: .3X TO .8X GOLD p/r 15
*WHITE p/r 24-25: 1.25X TO 3X GOLD p/r 169
*WHITE p/r 24-25: .5X TO 1.2X GOLD p/r 35
*WHITE p/r 19: .75X TO 2X GOLD p/r 61
OVERALL AU ODDS 1:5 H, AU-GU 1:24 R
PRINT RUNS B/WN 1-57 COPIES PER
NO PRICING ON QTY OF 14 OR LESS
EXCHANGE DEADLINE INDEFINITE
AH Aubrey Huff/34 10.00 25.00
CR Cal Ripken/25 100.00 200.00
FT Frank Thomas/43 20.00 50.00
GB George Brett/30 60.00 120.00
IR Ivan Rodriguez/35 30.00 60.00
JE Jim Edmonds/42 12.50 30.00
JG2 Jay Gibbons/28 6.00 15.00
MS2 Moose Skowron/28 10.00 25.00
RP Rafael Palmeiro/47 20.00 50.00
SR Scott Rolen/28 15.00 40.00
VG Vladimir Guerrero/44 20.00 50.00

2004 National Pastime Signature Swings Bat Blue

PRINT RUNS B/WN 2-44 COPIES PER
NO PRICING ON QTY OF 14 OR LESS
M'PIECE PRINT RUN 1 SERIAL #'d SET
NO M'PIECE PRICING DUE TO SCARCITY
OVERALL AU ODDS 1:5 H, AU-GU 1:24 R
EXCHANGE DEADLINE INDEFINITE
AD Adam Dunn/31 15.00 40.00
AT Alan Trammell/19 15.00 40.00
BD Bucky Dent/15 15.00 40.00
BM Bill Mazeroski/39 15.00 40.00
CF Carlton Fisk/17 30.00 60.00
DE David Eckstein/44 15.00 40.00
DM Don Mattingly/23 60.00 120.00
DP Dave Parker/29 10.00 25.00
HB Hank Blalock/16 15.00 40.00
IR Ivan Rodriguez/19 40.00 80.00
JE Jim Edmonds/37 15.00 40.00
LF Lew Ford/44 6.00 15.00
RP Rafael Palmeiro/19 40.00 80.00
SC Sean Casey/37 10.00 25.00
SP Scott Podsednik/38 15.00 40.00

2004 National Pastime Signs of the Future Blue

*BLUE p/r 98: .2X TO .5X GOLD p/r 21
OVERALL AU ODDS 1:5 H, AU-GU 1:24 R
PRINT RUNS B/WN 1-98 COPIES PER
NO PRICING ON QTY OF 4 OR LESS
EXCHANGE DEADLINE INDEFINITE
KW Kerry Wood/98 10.00 25.00

2004 National Pastime Signs of the Future Gold

OVERALL AU ODDS 1:5 H, AU-GU 1:24 R
PRINT RUNS B/WN 21-340 COPIES PER
EXCHANGE DEADLINE INDEFINITE
AE Adam Everett/265 3.00 8.00
AL Adam LaRoche/78 4.00 10.00
AR Alexis Rios/45 6.00 15.00
AS Alfredo Simon/258 5.00 12.00
BC Bobby Crosby/299 4.00 10.00
DW Dontrelle Willis/47 10.00 25.00
JV Javier Vazquez/21 10.00 25.00
KG Khalil Greene/300 6.00 15.00
KH Koyie Hill/340 3.00 8.00
KY Kevin Youkilis/317 5.00 12.00
MC Miguel Cabrera/300 15.00 40.00
MG Mike Gosling/195 3.00 8.00
MN Michael Nakamura/231 3.00 8.00
RH1 Rich Harden/304 4.00 10.00
RH2 Ryan Howard/53 12.00 30.00
RW1 Ryan Wagner/251 3.00 8.00
SH Sean Henn/300 3.00 8.00
TH Tim Hudson/72 10.00 25.00

2004 National Pastime Signs of the Future Red

*REDp/r106-133:.5X TO 1.2X GOLDp/r195-317
*RED p/r 106-133: .3X TO .8X GOLD p/r 78
*RED p/r 98: .6X TO 1.5X GOLD p/r 251
*RED p/r 58: .75X TO 2X GOLD p/r 340
OVERALL AU ODDS 1:5 H, AU-GU 1:24 R
PRINT RUNS B/WN 52-133 COPIES PER
EXCHANGE DEADLINE INDEFINITE
AB1 Aarom Baldiris/64 6.00 15.00
AB2 A.J. Burnett/58 6.00 15.00
BN Bubba Nelson/99 4.00 10.00
CS Chris Shelton/55 15.00 40.00
EJ Edwin Jackson/52 4.00 10.00
GK Graham Koonce/55 4.00 10.00
JL1 Josh Labandeira/55 4.00 10.00
JL2 Justin Leone/68 6.00 15.00
JR Jose Reyes/93 6.00 15.00
KW Kerry Wood/55 10.00 25.00
MR Michael Rouse/124 3.00 8.00

2004 National Pastime Signs of the Future White

*WHITEp/r36-65: .75X TO 2X GOLDp/r195-317
*WHITE p/r 36-65: .5X TO 1.2X GOLD p/r 78
*WHITE p/r 36-65: .4X TO 1X GOLD p/r 45
*WHITEp/r26-35: 1X TO 2.5X GOLDp/r231-340
*WHITE p/r 26-35: .6X TO 1.5X GOLD p/r 72
*WHITE p/r 26-35: .3X TO .8X GOLD p/r 21
*WHITE p/r 20-21: 1.25X TO 3X GOLD p/r 300
*WHITE p/r 20-21: .6X TO 1.5X GOLD p/r 47
*WHITE p/r 15: .75X TO 2X GOLD p/r 53
OVERALL AU ODDS 1:5 H, AU-GU 1:24 R
PRINT RUNS B/WN 10-52 COPIES PER
NO PRICING ON QTY OF 10 OR LESS
NO RC YR PRICING ON QTY OF 25 OR LESS
EXCHANGE DEADLINE INDEFINITE
AB2 A.J. Burnett/22 10.00 25.00
EJ Edwin Jackson/24 6.00 15.00
GA Garrett Atkins/25 6.00 15.00
JR Jose Reyes/52 6.00 15.00
KW Kerry Wood/19 15.00 40.00
MR Michael Rouse/40 4.00 10.00
RW2 Rickie Weeks/17 10.00 25.00

2005 National Pastime

COMP.SET w/o SP's (50) 10.00 25.00
COMMON CARD (1-50) .30 .75
COMMON CARD (51-70) .75 2.00
COMMON CARD (71-80) .75 2.00
51-80 ODDS 1:11 HOBBY, 1:110 RETAIL
51-80 PRINT RUN 699 SERIAL #'d SETS
CARD 64 DOES NOT EXIST
1 Khalil Greene .30 .75
2 Pedro Martinez .50 1.25
3 Mark Teixeira .50 1.25
4 Jim Thome .50 1.25
5 Jack Wilson .30 .75
6 Johan Santana .50 1.25
7 Jason Bay .30 .75
8 Adam Dunn .50 1.25
9 Lyle Overbay .30 .75
10 Jason Schmidt .30 .75
11 Bobby Crosby .30 .75
12 J.D. Drew .30 .75
13 Ken Griffey Jr. 1.50 4.00
14 Sammy Sosa .75 2.00
15 Hank Blalock .30 .75
16 Victor Martinez .50 1.25
17 Randy Johnson .75 2.00
18 Vernon Wells .30 .75
19 Todd Helton .50 1.25
20 Javy Lopez .30 .75
21 Kaz Matsui .30 .75
22 Ben Sheets .30 .75
23 Brad Wilkerson .30 .75
24 Miguel Cabrera .75 2.00
25 Mike Sweeney .30 .75
26 Roger Clemens 1.00 2.50
27 Chipper Jones .75 2.00
28 Hideki Matsui 1.25 3.00
29 Manny Ramirez .75 2.00
30 Scott Rolen .50 1.25
31 Lance Berkman .50 1.25
32 Jim Edmonds .50 1.25
33 Derek Jeter 2.00 5.00
34 B.J. Upton .50 1.25
35 Carlos Delgado .30 .75
36 Ichiro Suzuki 1.00 2.50
37 Nomar Garciaparra .50 1.25
38 Albert Pujols 1.00 2.50
39 Ivan Rodriguez .50 1.25
40 Gary Sheffield .30 .75
41 Alfonso Soriano .50 1.25
42 Carlos Beltran .50 1.25
43 Magglio Ordonez .50 1.25
44 Alex Rodriguez 1.00 2.50
45 Curt Schilling .50 1.25
46 Greg Maddux 1.00 2.50
47 Vladimir Guerrero .50 1.25
48 Mike Piazza .75 2.00
49 Miguel Tejada .75 2.00
50 Adrian Beltre .75 2.00
51 Scott Kazmir IS 2.00 5.00
52 Gavin Floyd IS .75 2.00
53 Zack Greinke IS 2.50 6.00
54 David Wright IS 1.50 4.00
55 David Aardsma IS .75 2.00
56 Ryan Raburn IS .75 2.00
57 Joey Gathright IS .75 2.00
58 J.D. Durbin IS .75 2.00
59 Sean Burnett IS .75 2.00
60 Jose Lopez IS .75 2.00
61 Nick Swisher IS 1.25 3.00
62 Bobby Jenks IS .75 2.00
63 Kelly A. Johnson IS .75 2.00
65 Ronny Cedeno IS .75 2.00
66 Edwin Encarnacion IS 2.00 5.00
67 Jeff Baker IS .75 2.00
68 Taylor Buchholz IS .75 2.00
69 Justin Verlander IS RC 15.00 40.00
70 Luis Hernandez IS RC .75 2.00
71 Mike Schmidt AI 3.00 8.00
72 Al Kaline AI 2.00 5.00
73 Yogi Berra AI 2.00 5.00
74 Robin Yount AI 2.00 5.00
75 Nolan Ryan AI 6.00 15.00
76 Johnny Bench AI 2.00 5.00
77 Eddie Murray AI 1.25 3.00
78 Tom Seaver AI 1.25 3.00
79 Willie McCovey AI 1.25 3.00
80 Cal Ripken AI 6.00 15.00

2005 National Pastime Blue Foil

OVERALL PARALLEL ODDS 1:11 H
STATED PRINT RUN 1 SERIAL #'d SET
NO PRICING DUE TO SCARCITY

2005 National Pastime Red Foil

*RED 1-50: 1.25X TO 3X BASIC
*RED 51-70: .5X TO 1.2X BASIC
*RED 71-80: .5X TO 1.2X BASIC
OVERALL PARALLEL ODDS 1:11 H, 1:480 R
STATED PRINT RUN 150 SERIAL #'d SETS

2005 National Pastime White Foil

*WHITE 1-50 p/r 38-57: 2.5X TO 6X BASIC
*WHITE 1-50 p/r 21-31: 3X TO 8X BASIC
*WHITE 1-50 p/r 15-18: 4X TO 10X BASIC
*WHITE 71-80 p/r 41-44: 1X TO 2.5X BASIC
*WHITE 71-80 p/r 20-34: 1.25X TO 3X BASIC
*WHITE 71-80 p/r 19: 1.5X TO 4X BASIC
OVERALL PARALLEL ODDS 1:11 H, 1:480 R
PRINT RUNS B/WN 2-57 COPIES PER
NO PRICING ON QTY OF 13 OR LESS

2005 National Pastime Beltway Baseball

STATED ODDS 1:35 HOBBY, 1:920 RETAIL
STATED PRINT RUN 202 SERIAL #'d SETS
1 Ed Delahanty 2.50 6.00
2 Benjamin Harrison 2.50 6.00
3 William Howard Taft 2.50 6.00
4 Clark Griffith 2.50 6.00
5 Bobby Burke 2.50 6.00
6 Roy Seivers 2.50 6.00
7 Tom Cheney 2.50 6.00
8 Woodrow Wilson 2.50 6.00
9 Franklin D. Roosevelt 2.50 6.00
10 John F. Kennedy 3.00 8.00
11 Frank Howard 2.50 6.00
12 Griffith Stadium 2.50 6.00
13 RFK Stadium 2.50 6.00
14 All-Star Game 2.50 6.00
15 Ted Williams 12.00 30.00
16 Harmon Killebrew 6.00 15.00
17 Jeff Burroughs 2.50 6.00
18 All-Star Game 2.50 6.00
19 Unveiling the Nationals 2.50 6.00
20 New Logo 2.50 6.00

2005 National Pastime Buyback 1959 Ted Williams Autographs

OVERALL BUYBACK ODDS 1:10 HOBBY
STATED PRINT RUN ONE SET
25 UNSIGNED CARDS ALSO AVAIL.IN PACKS
NO PRICING DUE TO SCARCITY

2005 National Pastime Buyback Autographs

OVERALL BUYBACK ODDS 1:10 HOBBY
PRINT RUNS B/WN 1-84 COPIES PER
MOST CARDS HAND #'d IN BLUE INK
SERIAL #'d CARDS LACK HAND #ING
SERIAL #'d CARDS ARE NOT ACTUAL QTY
SEE BECKETT.COM FOR ACTUAL QTY
ALL CARDS INTENDED TO BE CRIMPED
CRIMPING ON MANY CARDS IS UNCLEAR
NO PRICING AVAILABLE

2005 National Pastime Buyback Game Used

OVERALL BUYBACK ODDS 1:10 HOBBY
PRINT RUNS B/WN 1-138 COPIES PER
MOST CARDS HAND #'d IN BLUE INK
SERIAL #'d CARDS LACK HAND #ING
SERIAL #'d CARDS ARE NOT ACTUAL QTY
SEE BECKETT.COM FOR ACTUAL QTY
ALL CARDS INTENDED TO BE CRIMPED

CRIMPING ON MANY CARDS IS UNCLEAR
NO PRICING AVAILABLE

2005 National Pastime Buyback Game Used Combos

OVERALL BUYBACK ODDS 1:10 HOBBY
PRINT RUNS B/WN 1-13 COPIES PER
MOST CARDS HAND #'d IN BLUE INK
SERIAL #'d CARDS LACK HAND #ING
SERIAL #'d CARDS ARE NOT ACTUAL QTY
SEE BECKETT.COM FOR ACTUAL QTY
ALL CARDS INTENDED TO BE CRIMPED
CRIMPING ON MANY CARDS IS UNCLEAR
NO PRICING DUE TO SCARCITY

2005 National Pastime First Name Bases Autograph Gold

*GOLDp/r126-149: .5XTO 1.2X SILVp/r225-401
*GOLDp/r73-99: .5X TO 1.2X SILVp/r158-316
OVERALL AU ODDS 1:5 H, AU-GU 1:24 R
PRINT RUNS B/WN 73-149 COPIES PER
AB Adrian Beltre/96 8.00 20.00
AP Albert Pujols/73 125.00 200.00
CR Cal Ripken/25 90.00 150.00

2005 National Pastime First Name Bases Autograph Red

*RED p/r 90-99: .5X TO 1.2X SILV p/r 225-401
OVERALL AU ODDS 1:5 H, AU-GU 1:24 R
PRINT RUNS B/WN 15-99 COPIES PER
NO PRICING ON QTY OF 25 OR LESS
BL Barry Larkin/27 30.00 60.00
JV Justin Verlander/99 20.00 50.00

2005 National Pastime First Name Bases Autograph Silver

OVERALL AU ODDS 1:5 H, AU-GU 1:24 R
PRINT RUNS B/WN 2-401 COPIES PER
NO PRICING ON QTY OF 19 OR LESS
JL Javy Lopez/158 6.00 15.00
JV Justin Verlander/401 15.00 40.00
MCAM Mike Cameron/375 4.00 10.00
MT Mark Teixeira/225 10.00 25.00
SH Shea Hillenbrand/316 6.00 15.00

2005 National Pastime First Name Bases Autograph White

*WHITE p/r 38-48: .6X TO 1.5X SILV p/r 225
*WHITE p/r 30-32: .75X TO 2X SILV p/r 375
OVERALL AU ODDS 1:5 H, AU-GU 1:24 R
PRINT RUNS B/WN 1-48 COPIES PER
NO PRICING ON QTY OF 18 OR LESS
AB Adrian Beltre/48 10.00 25.00
BL Barry Larkin/32 30.00 60.00

2005 National Pastime Grand Old Gamers

COMPLETE SET (35) 15.00 40.00
STATED ODDS 1:5 HOBBY, 1:12 RETAIL
1 Pedro Martinez .60 1.50
2 Jim Thome .60 1.50
3 Ken Griffey Jr. 2.00 5.00
4 Sammy Sosa 1.00 2.50
5 Hank Blalock .40 1.00
6 Randy Johnson 1.00 2.50
7 Roger Clemens 1.25 3.00
8 Chipper Jones 1.00 2.50
9 Hideki Matsui 1.50 4.00
10 Manny Ramirez 1.00 2.50
11 Derek Jeter 2.50 6.00
12 Ichiro Suzuki 1.25 3.00
13 Nomar Garciaparra .60 1.50
14 Albert Pujols 1.25 3.00
15 Gary Sheffield .40 1.00
16 Alfonso Soriano .60 1.50
17 Alex Rodriguez 1.25 3.00
18 Curt Schilling .60 1.50
19 Vladimir Guerrero .60 1.50
20 Mike Piazza 1.00 2.50
21 Greg Maddux 1.25 3.00
22 Frank Thomas 1.00 2.50
23 Adrian Beltre 1.00 2.50
24 Barry Larkin .60 1.50
25 Todd Helton .60 1.50
26 Kerry Wood .40 1.00
27 Kaz Matsui .40 1.00
28 Scott Rolen .60 1.50
29 Ivan Rodriguez .60 1.50
30 Miguel Tejada .60 1.50
31 Mark Teixeira .60 1.50
32 Rafael Palmeiro .60 1.50
33 Andruw Jones .40 1.00
34 Carlos Beltran .60 1.50
35 Jeff Bagwell .60 1.50

2005 National Pastime Grand Old Gamers Jersey

STATED ODDS 1:36 RETAIL
SP PRINT RUNS PROVIDED BY FLEER
SP'S ARE NOT SERIAL-NUMBERED
AB Adrian Beltre 2.00 5.00
AJ Andruw Jones 3.00 8.00
AP Albert Pujols 6.00 15.00
AS Alfonso Soriano 2.00 5.00
BL Barry Larkin 3.00 8.00
CB Carlos Beltran 2.00 5.00
CJ Chipper Jones 3.00 8.00
CS Curt Schilling 3.00 8.00
FT Frank Thomas 3.00 8.00
GM Greg Maddux SP/75 6.00 15.00
GS Gary Sheffield 2.00 5.00
HB Hank Blalock 2.00 5.00
HM Hideki Matsui SP/50 15.00 40.00
IR Ivan Rodriguez 3.00 8.00
JB Jeff Bagwell 3.00 8.00
JT Jim Thome 3.00 8.00
KM Kaz Matsui 2.00 5.00
KW Kerry Wood 2.00 5.00
MP Mike Piazza 3.00 8.00
MR Manny Ramirez 3.00 8.00
MT Mark Teixeira 3.00 8.00
PM Pedro Martinez 3.00 8.00
RC Roger Clemens SP/50 8.00 20.00
RJ Randy Johnson 3.00 8.00
RP Rafael Palmeiro 3.00 8.00
SR Scott Rolen 3.00 8.00
SS Sammy Sosa 3.00 8.00
TH Todd Helton 3.00 8.00
VG Vladimir Guerrero 3.00 8.00

2005 National Pastime Grand Old Gamers Patch Blue

PRINT RUNS B/WN 5-55 COPIES PER
NO PRICING ON QTY OF 25 OR LESS
MASTERPIECE PRINT RUN 1 #'d SET
NO MP PRICING DUE TO SCARCITY
OVERALL GU ODDS 1:120 HOBBY
CS Curt Schilling/38 15.00 40.00
FT Frank Thomas/35 15.00 40.00
GM Greg Maddux/31 20.00 50.00
HM Hideki Matsui/55 30.00 60.00
KW Kerry Wood/34 10.00 25.00
PM Pedro Martinez/45 15.00 40.00
VG Vladimir Guerrero/27 15.00 40.00

2005 National Pastime Grand Old Gamers Dual Patch

OVERALL GU ODDS 1:120 HOBBY
PRINT RUNS B/WN 5-33 COPIES PER
NO PRICING ON QTY OF 24 OR LESS
HBMT H.Blalock/M.Teixeira/33 20.00 50.00
IRMP I.Rodriguez/M.Piazza/31 20.00 50.00
RJPM R.Johnson/P.Martinez/32 20.00 50.00

2005 National Pastime Historical Record

COMPLETE SET (13) 15.00 40.00
STATED ODDS 1:6 H, OVERALL 1:10 R
PRINT RUNS B/WN 1987-2004 COPIES PER
1 Ichiro Suzuki/2004 2.00 5.00
2 Greg Maddux/2004 2.00 5.00
3 Alex Rodriguez/1998 2.00 5.00
4 Mike Piazza/2004 1.50 4.00
5 Nolan Ryan/1991 5.00 12.00
6 Albert Pujols/2001 2.00 5.00
7 Mike Schmidt/1987 2.50 6.00
8 Randy Johnson/2004 1.50 4.00
9 Sammy Sosa/2003 1.50 4.00
10 Cal Ripken/1996 5.00 12.00
11 Roger Clemens/2004 2.00 5.00
12 Hideki Matsui/2003 2.50 6.00
13 Hideo Nomo/1994 1.50 4.00

2005 National Pastime Historical Record Jersey

STATED ODDS 1:96 RETAIL
SP PRINT RUNS PROVIDED BY FLEER
SP'S ARE NOT SERIAL-NUMBERED
AP Albert Pujols 6.00 15.00
CR Cal Ripken SP/40 15.00 40.00
GM Greg Maddux 4.00 10.00
HM Hideki Matsui 6.00 15.00
HN Hideo Nomo 3.00 8.00
MP Mike Piazza 3.00 8.00
NRO Nolan Ryan 8.00 20.00
RC Roger Clemens 4.00 10.00
RJ Randy Johnson 3.00 8.00
SS Sammy Sosa 3.00 8.00

2005 National Pastime Historical Record Patch Blue

PRINT RUNS B/WN 5-55 COPIES PER
NO PRICING ON QTY OF 22 OR LESS
MASTERPIECE PRINT RUN 1 #'d SET
NO MP PRICING DUE TO SCARCITY
OVERALL GU ODDS 1:120 HOBBY
GM Greg Maddux/31 15.00 40.00
HM Hideki Matsui/55 30.00 60.00
MP Mike Piazza/31 15.00 40.00
NR Nolan Ryan/34 30.00 60.00
RJ Randy Johnson/51 15.00 40.00

2005 National Pastime Historical Record Dual Patch

OVERALL GU ODDS 1:120 HOBBY
PRINT RUNS B/WN 8-25 COPIES PER
NO PRICING DUE TO SCARCITY

2005 National Pastime Signature Swings Gold

*GOLD p/r 149-199: .4X TO 1X SILV
*GOLD p/r 71-100: .5X TO 1.2X SILV
*GOLD p/r 71-100: .4X TO 1X SILV SP/77
OVERALL AU ODDS 1:5 H, AU-GU 1:24 R
PRINT RUNS B/WN 50-199 COPIES PER
DN Dioner Navarro/175 4.00 10.00
DO David Ortiz/71 20.00 50.00
JB Johnny Bench/76 20.00 50.00
LB Lance Berkman/149 5.00 12.00
LO Lyle Overbay/50 6.00 15.00
MS Mike Schmidt/90 10.00 25.00
RJ Reggie Jackson/53 30.00 60.00

2005 National Pastime Signature Swings Silver

OVERALL AU ODDS 1:5 H, AU-GU 1:24 R
SP PRINT RUNS PROVIDED BY FLEER
SP'S ARE NOT SERIAL-NUMBERED
NO SP PRICING ON QTY OF 33 OR LESS
EXCHANGE DEADLINE TBD
AE Adam Everett 4.00 10.00
AH Aubrey Huff 6.00 15.00
BAY Jason Bay 6.00 15.00
BJU B.J. Upton 6.00 15.00
BR Brooks Robinson SP/77 12.50 30.00
CC Carl Crawford 6.00 15.00
CF Chone Figgins 4.00 10.00
CK Casey Kotchman 6.00 15.00
CU Chase Utley 10.00 25.00
DM Dallas McPherson 4.00 10.00
DW David Wright 20.00 50.00
JG Joey Gathright 4.00 10.00
JK Josh Kroeger 4.00 10.00
JM Joe Mauer 15.00 40.00
JMO Justin Morneau 12.50 30.00
JP Josh Phelps 4.00 10.00
KG Khalil Greene 10.00 25.00
KUB Jason Kubel 4.00 10.00
LF Lew Ford 4.00 10.00
MY Michael Young 6.00 15.00
NS Nick Swisher 6.00 15.00
SS Shannon Stewart 6.00 15.00
TH Travis Hafner 6.00 15.00
VAL Val Majewski 4.00 10.00
WMP Wily Mo Pena 6.00 15.00

2005 National Pastime Signature Swings Bat Red

*BAT RED p/r 76-99: .5X TO 1.2X SILV
*BAT RED p/r 42-64: .5X TO 1.2X SILV SP/77
OVERALL AU ODDS 1:5 H, AU-GU 1:24 R
PRINT RUNS B/WN 30-99 COPIES PER
JB Johnny Bench/42 30.00 60.00
LB Lance Berkman/99 6.00 15.00
MP Mike Piazza/30 60.00 120.00
MS Mike Schmidt/30 40.00 80.00
RJ Reggie Jackson/30 40.00 80.00
WB Wade Boggs/45 30.00 60.00

2005 National Pastime Signature Swings Jersey White

*JSY WHITE p/r 27-29: .75X TO 2X SILV
OVERALL AU ODDS 1:5 H, AU-GU 1:24 R
PRINT RUNS B/WN 3-29 COPIES PER
NO PRICING ON QTY OF 22 OR LESS
LB Lance Berkman/29 10.00 25.00

2005 National Pastime Signature Swings Patch Blue

*PATCH BLUE p/r 38-48: .75X TO 2X SILV
PRINT RUNS B/WN 3-48 COPIES PER
NO PRICING ON QTY OF 23 OR LESS
LOGO MP PRINT RUN 1 SERIAL #'d SET
NO LOGO MP PRICING DUE TO SCARCITY
OVERALL AU ODDS 1:5 H, AU-GU 1:24 R
DO David Ortiz/34 20.00 50.00

2005 Nationals Topps

COMP.FACT SET (55)
1 Washington Nationals Logo .10 .25
2 Jose Vidro .10 .25
3 Joe Horgan .10 .25
4 Danny Rueckel .10 .25
5 Wil Cordero .10 .25
6 Cristian Guzman .10 .25
7 Alex Escobar .10 .25
8 Tony Armas Jr. .10 .25
9 Zach Day .10 .25
10 Jamey Carroll .10 .25
11 Nick Johnson .10 .25
12 John Patterson .10 .25
13 Josh Karp .10 .25
14 Brendan Harris .10 .25
15 Gary Bennett .10 .25
16 Termel Sledge .10 .25
17 Tomo Ohka .10 .25
18 Chad Cordero .10 .25
19 Luis Ayala .10 .25
20 Tony Blanco .10 .25
21 Endy Chavez .10 .25
22 George Arias .10 .25
23 Chad Durbin .10 .25
24 Phil Hiatt .10 .25
25 Henry Mateo .10 .25
26 Livan Hernandez .10 .25
27 Larry Broadway .10 .25
28 T.J. Tucker .10 .25
29 J.J. Davis .10 .25
30 Brian Schneider .10 .25
31 Vinny Castilla .10 .25
32 Michael Hinckley .10 .25
33 Brandon Watson .10 .25
34 Claudio Vargas .10 .25
35 Ryan Church .10 .25
36 Jose Guillen .10 .25
37 Gary Majewski .10 .25
38 Jon Rauch .10 .25
39 Brad Wilkerson .10 .25
40 Francis Beltran .10 .25
41 Esteban Loaiza .10 .25
42 Carlos Baerga .10 .25
43 Sunny Kim .10 .25
44 Ian Desmond .25 .60
45 Jeffrey Hammonds .10 .25
46 Hector Carrasco .10 .25
47 Drew McMillan .10 .25
48 Jared Sandberg .10 .25
50 RFK Stadium .10 .25
51 Minnesota Twins .10 .25
52 Texas Rangers .10 .25
53 Baltimore Orioles .10 .25
54 Vinny Castilla .20 .50
Jose Guillen FM
55 Cristian Guzman .10 .25
Esteban Loaiza FM

2006 Nationals Topps

COMPLETE SET (14) 3.00 8.00
WAS1 Livan Hernandez .12 .30
WAS2 Jose Vidro .12 .30
WAS3 Nick Johnson .12 .30
WAS4 Cristian Guzman .12 .30
WAS5 Ryan Church .12 .30
WAS6 Alfonso Soriano .20 .50
WAS7 Jose Guillen .12 .30
WAS8 Brian Schneider .12 .30
WAS9 John Patterson .12 .30
WAS10 Chad Cordero .12 .30
WAS11 Marlon Byrd .12 .30
WAS12 Marlon Anderson .12 .30
WAS13 Brian Lawrence .12 .30
WAS14 Ryan Zimmerman .40 1.00

2007 Nationals Topps

COMPLETE SET (14) 3.00 8.00
WAS1 Ryan Zimmerman .20 .50
WAS2 Brian Schneider .12 .30
WAS3 John Patterson .12 .30
WAS4 Cristian Guzman .12 .30
WAS5 Nook Logan .12 .30
WAS6 Austin Kearns .12 .30
WAS7 Felipe Lopez .12 .30
WAS8 Alex Escobar .12 .30
WAS9 Chad Cordero .12 .30
WAS10 Ryan Church .12 .30
WAS11 Chris Snelling .12 .30
WAS12 Mike O'Connor .12 .30
WAS13 Nick Johnson .12 .30
WAS14 Jon Rauch .12 .30

2007 Nationals Upper Deck Mother's Day

COMPLETE SET 1.25 3.00
1 Brian Schneider .20 .50
2 John Patterson .20 .50
3 Chad Cordero .20 .50
4 Jon Rauch .20 .50
5 Nook Logan .20 .50
6 Austin Kearns .20 .50
7 Ryan Zimmerman .30 .75
8 Nick Johnson .20 .50
9 Ryan Church .20 .50

2008 Nationals Topps

COMPLETE SET (14) 3.00 8.00
WAS1 Ryan Zimmerman .20 .50
WAS2 Elijah Dukes .12 .30
WAS3 Matt Chico .12 .30
WAS4 Dmitri Young .12 .30
WAS5 Paul Lo Duca .12 .30
WAS6 Austin Kearns .12 .30
WAS7 Felipe Lopez .12 .30
WAS8 Shawn Hill .12 .30
WAS9 Chad Cordero .12 .30
WAS10 Lastings Milledge .12 .30
WAS11 Wily Mo Pena .12 .30
WAS12 Ronnie Belliard .12 .30
WAS13 Jason Bergmann .12 .30
WAS14 Jon Rauch .12 .30

2009 Nationals Topps

WAS1 Ryan Zimmerman .25 .60
WAS2 Collin Balester .15 .40
WAS3 Cristian Guzman .15 .40
WAS4 Daniel Cabrera .15 .40
WAS5 Lastings Milledge .15 .40
WAS6 Josh Willingham .25 .60
WAS7 Elijah Dukes .15 .40
WAS8 John Lannan .15 .40
WAS9 Ronnie Belliard .15 .40
WAS10 Scott Olsen .15 .40
WAS11 Austin Kearns .15 .40
WAS12 Joel Hanrahan .25 .60
WAS13 Jesus Flores .15 .40
WAS14 Nick Johnson .15 .40
WAS15 Teddy Roosevelt .15 .40

2010 Nationals Topps

WAS1 Ryan Zimmerman .25 .60
WAS2 Garrett Mock .15 .40
WAS3 Jason Marquis .15 .40
WAS4 Craig Stammen .15 .40
WAS5 John Lannan .15 .40
WAS6 Josh Willingham .25 .60
WAS7 Nyjer Morgan .15 .40
WAS8 Ivan Rodriguez .25 .60
WAS9 Shairon Martis .15 .40
WAS10 Adam Dunn .25 .60
WAS11 Ian Desmond .25 .60
WAS12 Cristian Guzman .15 .40
WAS13 Matt Capps .15 .40
WAS14 Jordan Zimmermann .25 .60
WAS15 Elijah Dukes .15 .40
WAS16 Jesus Flores .15 .40
WAS17 Scott Olsen .15 .40

2011 Nationals Topps

WAS1 Jayson Werth .25 .60
WAS2 Ryan Zimmerman .25 .60
WAS3 Jordan Zimmermann .25 .60
WAS4 Ivan Rodriguez .25 .60
WAS5 John Lannan .15 .40
WAS6 Tyler Clippard .15 .40
WAS7 Roger Bernadina .15 .40
WAS8 Ian Desmond .15 .40
WAS9 Livan Hernandez .15 .40
WAS10 Stephen Strasburg .40 1.00
WAS11 Danny Espinosa .15 .40
WAS12 Jason Marquis .15 .40
WAS13 Adam LaRoche .15 .40
WAS14 Nyjer Morgan .15 .40
WAS15 Mike Morse .15 .40
WAS16 Drew Storen .15 .40
WAS17 Nationals Park .15 .40

2012 Nationals Topps

WAS1 Stephen Strasburg .40 1.00
WAS2 Ian Desmond .25 .60
WAS3 Jayson Werth .30 .75
WAS4 John Lannan .25 .60
WAS5 Wilson Ramos .25 .60
WAS6 Glo Gonzalez .30 .75
WAS7 Ryan Zimmerman .30 .75
WAS8 Michael Morse .25 .60
WAS9 Steve Lombardozzi .25 .60
WAS10 Jordan Zimmermann .30 .75
WAS11 Chien-Ming Wang .30 .75
WAS12 Danny Espinosa .25 .60
WAS13 Adam LaRoche .25 .60
WAS14 Roger Bernadina .25 .60
WAS15 Drew Storen .25 .60
WAS16 Tyler Clippard .25 .60
WAS17 Nationals Park .15 .40

2013 Nationals Topps

COMPLETE SET (17) 3.00 8.00
WAS1 Bryce Harper .40 1.00
WAS2 Stephen Strasburg .25 .60
WAS3 Ryan Zimmerman .20 .50
WAS4 Gio Gonzalez .30 .75
WAS5 Jordan Zimmermann .20 .50
WAS6 Ian Desmond .15 .40
WAS7 Dan Haren .15 .40
WAS8 Jayson Werth .30 .75
WAS9 Drew Storen .25 .60
WAS10 Steve Lombardozzi .15 .40
WAS11 Denard Span .25 .60
WAS12 Adam LaRoche .25 .60
WAS13 Rafael Soriano .25 .60
WAS14 Danny Espinosa .25 .60
WAS15 Ross Detwiler .15 .40
WAS16 Kurt Suzuki .25 .60
WAS17 Nationals Park .15 .40

2014 Nationals Topps

COMPLETE SET (17) 3.00 8.00
WAS1 Bryce Harper .40 1.00
WAS2 Stephen Strasburg .25 .60
WAS3 Ryan Zimmerman .20 .50
WAS4 Gio Gonzalez .20 .50
WAS5 Jordan Zimmermann .20 .50
WAS6 Ian Desmond .15 .40
WAS7 Doug Fister .15 .40
WAS8 Jayson Werth .20 .50
WAS9 Drew Storen .15 .40
WAS10 Tyler Clippard .15 .40
WAS11 Denard Span .15 .40
WAS12 Adam LaRoche .15 .40
WAS13 Rafael Soriano .15 .40
WAS14 Wilson Ramos .15 .40
WAS15 Ross Detwiler .15 .40
WAS16 Anthony Rendon .25 .60
WAS17 Nationals Park .15 .40

2015 Nationals Topps

COMPLETE SET (17) 3.00 8.00
WN1 Bryce Harper .40 1.00
WN2 Doug Fister .15 .40
WN3 Gio Gonzalez .20 .50
WN4 Stephen Strasburg .25 .60
WN5 Wilson Ramos .15 .40
WN6 Anthony Rendon .25 .60
WN7 Jayson Werth .20 .50
WN8 Ryan Zimmerman .20 .50
WN9 Jordan Zimmermann .20 .50
WN10 Michael Taylor .15 .40
WN11 Danny Espinosa .15 .40
WN12 Ian Desmond .15 .40
WN13 Denard Span .15 .40
WN14 Max Scherzer .25 .60
WN15 Drew Storen .15 .40
WN16 Tanner Roark .15 .40
WN17 Jose Lobaton .15 .40

2016 Nationals Topps

COMPLETE SET (17) 3.00 8.00
WAS1 Bryce Harper .40 1.00
WAS2 Wilson Ramos .15 .40
WAS3 Ryan Zimmerman .20 .50
WAS4 Anthony Rendon .25 .60
WAS5 Daniel Murphy .20 .50
WAS6 Joe Ross .15 .40
WAS7 Jayson Werth .20 .50
WAS8 Stephen Strasburg .25 .60
WAS9 Max Scherzer .25 .60
WAS10 Gio Gonzalez .20 .50
WAS11 Tanner Roark .15 .40
WAS12 Jonathan Papelbon .20 .50
WAS13 Michael Taylor .15 .40
WAS14 Trea Turner .50 1.25
WAS15 Matt den Dekker .15 .40
WAS16 Danny Espinosa .15 .40
WAS17 Ben Revere .15 .40

2017 Nationals Topps

COMPLETE SET (17) 3.00 8.00
WAS1 Max Scherzer .25 .60
WAS2 Anthony Rendon .25 .60
WAS3 Shawn Kelley .15 .40
WAS4 Ryan Zimmerman .20 .50
WAS5 Daniel Murphy .20 .50
WAS6 Derek Norris .15 .40
WAS7 Gio Gonzalez .20 .50
WAS8 Jose Lobaton .15 .40
WAS9 Michael Taylor .15 .40
WAS10 Blake Treinen .25 .60
WAS11 Trea Turner .20 .50
WAS12 Joe Ross .15 .40
WAS13 Tanner Roark .15 .40
WAS14 Jayson Werth .20 .50
WAS15 Bryce Harper .40 1.00
WAS16 Stephen Strasburg .25 .60
WAS17 Adam Eaton .25 .60

2018 Nationals Topps

COMPLETE SET (17) 2.50 6.00
WN1 Bryce Harper .40 1.00
WN2 Anthony Rendon .25 .60
WN3 Ryan Madson .15 .40
WN4 Gio Gonzalez .20 .50
WN5 Adam Eaton .25 .60
WN6 Ryan Zimmerman .20 .50
WN7 Daniel Murphy .20 .50
WN8 Wilmer Difo .15 .40
WN9 Stephen Strasburg .25 .60
WN10 Sean Doolittle .15 .40
WN11 Max Scherzer .25 .60
WN12 Tanner Roark .15 .40
WN13 Michael Taylor .15 .40
WN14 Trea Turner .20 .50
WN15 Matt Wieters .25 .60
WN16 Erick Fedde .15 .40
WN17 Victor Robles .40 1.00

2019 Nationals Topps

COMPLETE SET (17) 2.50 6.00
WN1 Max Scherzer .25 .60
WN2 Juan Soto .75 2.00
WN3 Stephen Strasburg .25 .60
WN4 Ryan Zimmerman .20 .50
WN5 Adam Eaton .25 .60
WN6 Victor Robles .30 .75
WN7 Wilmer Difo .15 .40
WN8 Trea Turner .20 .50
WN9 Anthony Rendon .25 .60
WN10 Kyle Barraclough .15 .40
WN11 Kurt Suzuki .15 .40
WN12 Sean Doolittle .15 .40
WN13 Michael Taylor .15 .40
WN14 Joe Ross .15 .40
WN15 Yan Gomes .25 .60
WN16 Howie Kendrick .15 .40
WN17 Patrick Corbin .20 .50

2020 Nationals Topps

WAS1 Juan Soto .75 2.00
WAS2 Max Scherzer .25 .60
WAS3 Trea Turner .20 .50
WAS4 Victor Robles .30 .75
WAS5 Stephen Strasburg .25 .60
WAS6 Patrick Corbin .20 .50
WAS7 Wilmer Difo .15 .40
WAS8 Joe Ross .15 .40
WAS9 Sean Doolittle .15 .40
WAS10 Nationals Win World Series .15 .40
WAS11 Adam Eaton .25 .60
WAS12 Anibal Sanchez .20 .50
WAS13 Carter Kieboom .20 .50
WAS14 Yan Gomes .25 .60
WAS15 Kurt Suzuki .15 .40
WAS16 Daniel Hudson .15 .40
WAS17 Michael Taylor .15 .40

2017 Nationals Topps National Baseball Card Day

COMPLETE SET (10) 6.00 15.00
WAS1 Bryce Harper 1.50 4.00
WAS2 Daniel Murphy .75 2.00
WAS3 Stephen Strasburg 1.00 2.50
WAS4 Trea Turner .75 2.00
WAS5 Max Scherzer 1.00 2.50
WAS6 Adam Eaton 1.00 2.50
WAS7 Jayson Werth .75 2.00
WAS8 Ryan Zimmerman .75 2.00
WAS9 Tanner Roark .60 1.50
WAS10 Tim Raines .75 2.00

2004 National Trading Card Day

F1-F9 ISSUED IN FLEER PACK
T1-T12 ISSUED IN TOPPS PACK
DP1-DP6 ISSUED IN DONRUSS PACK
PP1-PP7 ISSUED IN PRESS PASS PACK
UD1-UD15 ISSUED IN UPPER DECK PACK
F1 Derek Jeter .60 1.50
F2 Alex Rodriguez Yanks .40 1.00
F3 Nomar Garciaparra .25 .60
F4 Jose Reyes .25 .60
T1 Rocco Baldelli .15 .40
T2 Mark Prior .15 .40
T3 Dontrelle Willis .15 .40
T4 Jason Giambi .15 .40
DP1 Albert Pujols .60 1.50
DP2 Roger Clemens .25 .60
DP3 Mike Piazza .25 .60
DP4 Alfonso Soriano .15 .40
UD2 Hideki Matsui .25 .60
UD3 Ichiro Suzuki .40 1.00
UD5 Ken Griffey Jr. .50 1.25
UD12 Sammy Sosa .25 .60

1986 Negro League Fritsch Samples

COMPLETE SET 8.00 20.00
1 Buck Leonard 1.00 2.50
7 Ray Dandridge 1.00 2.50
10 Satchel Paige 1.50 4.00
11 Jackie Robinson 1.50 4.00
20 Lou Dials .40 1.00
Sample in big bold letters
20A Lou Dials .40 1.00
Sample enclosed in a box
30 Josh Gibson 1.25 3.00
89 Monte Irvin 1.00 2.50
90 Cool Papa Bell 1.00 2.50

1986 Negro League Fritsch

This is a 119-card standard-size set of Negro League stars. The set features black and white photos framed by the title "Negro League Baseball Stars" in red above the player's name and the player's name in red below the photo. Each card back features a brief biography of the player pictured on the front of the card. The set was produced by long time Wisconsin card hobbyist Larry Fritsch and featured most of the great players of the old Negro Leagues. An earlier version of the set was produced in 1984 by Decathlon Corporation. Each Decathlon set has a serial number; Decathlon sets are valued at double the prices listed below.

COMPLETE SET (119) 12.50 30.00
1 Buck Leonard .20 .50
2 Ted Page .08 .25
3 Cool Papa Bell .20 .50
4 Charleston .15 .40
Gibson/
Page
Johnson
Oscar Charleston
5 Judy Johnson .15 .40
6 Monte Irvin .15 .40
7 Ray Dandridge .10 .30
8 Oscar Charleston .20 .50
9 Josh Gibson .40 1.00
10 Satchel Paige .40 1.00
11 Jackie Robinson .40 1.00
12 Lorenzo(Piper) Davis .05 .15
13 Josh Johnson .01 .05
14 Lou Dials .08 .25
15 Andy Porter .01 .05
16 John Henry Lloyd .10 .30
17 Andy Watts .01 .05
18 Rube Foster .10 .30
19 Martin DiHigo .20 .50
20 Lou Dials .08 .25
21 Satchel Paige .40 1.00
22 Crush Holloway .01 .05
23 Josh Gibson .40 1.00
24 Oscar Charleston .20 .50
25 Jackie Robinson .40 1.00
26 Larry Brown .01 .05
27 Hilton Smith .15 .40
28 Moses F. Walker .15 .40
29 Jimmie Crutchfield .10 .30
30 Josh Gibson .40 1.00
31 Josh Gibson .40 1.00
32 Bullet Rogan .10 .30
33 Clint Thomas .01 .05
34 Rats Henderson .01 .05
35 Pat Scantlebury .01 .05
36 Sydney Sy Morton .01 .05
37 Larry Kimbrough .01 .05
38 Sam Jethroe .08 .25
39 Normal(Tweed) Webb .01 .05
40 Mahlon Duckett .01 .05
41 Andy Anderson .01 .05
42 Buster Haywood .01 .05
43 Bob Trice .08 .25
44 Buster Clarkson .01 .05
45 Buck O'Neil .20 .50
46 Jim Zapp .01 .05
47 Lorenzo(Piper) Davis .08 .25
48 Ed Steel .01 .05
49 Bob Boyd .08 .25
50 Marlin Carter .01 .05
51 George Giles .01 .05
52 Bill Byrd .01 .05
53 Art Pennington .01 .05
54 Max Manning .01 .05
55 Ronald Teasley .01 .05
56 Ziggy Marcell .01 .05
57 Bill Cash .01 .05
58 Joe Scott .01 .05
59 Joe Fillmore .01 .05
60 Bob Thurman .08 .25
61 Larry Kimbrough .01 .05
62 Verdell Mathis .01 .05
63 Josh Johnson .08 .25
64 Ted Radcliffe .08 .25
65 William Bobby Robinson .05 .15
66 Bingo DeMoss .08 .25
67 John Beckwith .01 .05
68 Bill Jackman .01 .05
69 Bill Drake .01 .05
70 Charlie Grant .08 .25
71 Willie Wells .20 .50
72 Jose Fernandez .01 .05
73 Isidro Fabri .01 .05
74 Frank Austin .01 .05
75 Dick Lundy .01 .05
76 Junior Gilliam .08 .25
77 John Donaldson .01 .05
78 Rap Dixon .01 .05
79 Slim Jones .01 .05
80 Sam Jones .08 .25
81 Dave Hoskins .08 .25
82 Jerry Benjamin .01 .05
83 Luke Easter .08 .25
84 Ramon Herrera .01 .05
85 Matthew Carlisle .01 .05
86 Smokey Joe Williams .08 .25
87 Marvin Williams .01 .05
88 William Yancey .08 .25
89 Monte Irvin .20 .50
90 Cool Papa Bell .25 .60
91 Biz Mackey .15 .40
92 Harry Simpson .08 .25
93 Lazerio Salazar .01 .05
94 Bill Perkins .01 .05
95 Johnny Davis .01 .05
96 Jelly Jackson .08 .25
97 Sam Bankhead .08 .25
98 Hank Thompson .08 .25
99 William Bell .01 .05
100 Cliff Bell .01 .05
101 Dave Barnhill .01 .05
102 Dan Bankhead .08 .25
103 Pepper Bassett .01 .05
104 Newt Allen .08 .25
105 George Jefferson .01 .05
106 Pat Paterson .01 .05
107 Goose Tatum .40 1.00
108 Dave Malarcher .08 .25
109 Home Run Johnson .08 .25
110 Bill Monroe .01 .05
111 Sammy Hughes .01 .05
112 Dick Redding .08 .25
113 Fats Jenkins .01 .05
114 Jimmie Lyons .01 .05
115 Mule Suttles .08 .25
116 Ted Trent .01 .05
117 George Sweatt .01 .05
118 Frank Duncan .01 .05
119 Checklist Card .01 .05

1987 Negro League Phil Dixon

Produced by Phil Dixon, this 45-card set measures approximately 2 15/16" by 5". The fronts feature a mix of posed and action black-and-white player photos bordered in white. The horizontal backs carry the player's name, position, birth and death dates, and a brief career summary.

COMPLETE SET (45) 20.00 50.00
1 Samuel Hairston 1.25 3.00
2 Elander Victor Harris/(Vic) .72 2.00
3 Theodore(Ted) Trent .72 2.00
4 Edward Joseph Dwight/(Pee Wee) 1.25 3.00
5 Jessie Williams .72 2.00
6 Josh Gibson 5.00 12.00
7 Jose De La C. Mendez .72 2.00
8 Joe Green .72 2.00
9 Robert Boyd/(The Rope) 1.25 3.00
10 William(Plunk) Drake .72 2.00
11 Alfred(Army) Cooper .72 2.00
12 Charles Isam Taylor/(C.I.) .72 2.00
13 Dick Whitworth .72 2.00
14 Tobe Smith .72 2.00
15 William(Dizzy) .72 2.00
Dismukes
16 Richard Thomas Bayas/(Subby) .72 2.00
17 Hurley Allen McNair/(Mack) .72 2.00
18 Roy Partlow .72 2.00
19 Carroll Ray Mothell/(Dink) .72 2.00
20 John(Buck) O'Neil 2.50 6.00
21 Leroy(Satchel) Paige 5.00 12.00
22 Moses Fleetwood Walker 2.50 6.00
23 Quincy Jordan Gilmore .72 2.00
24 James(Cool Papa) Bell 2.50 6.00
25 Andrew(Rube) Foster 2.50 6.00
26 George Alexander .72 2.00
Sweatt
27 Hilton Lee Smith 2.50 6.00
28 Thomas Jefferson Young/(T.J.) .72 2.00
29 Chet Brewer 1.25 3.00
30 Buck Leonard 2.50 6.00
31 Walter Lee Joseph/(Newt) 1.25 3.00
32 Eugene Walter Baker/(Gene) 1.25 3.00
33 Jackie Robinson 5.00 12.00
34 Wilbur(Bullet) Rogan 1.25 3.00
35 Norman(Turkey) Stearns .72 2.00
36 Albert(Buster) Haywood .72 2.00
37 Lorenzo(Piper) Davis 1.25 3.00
38 Francisco Comimbre/(Pancho) .72 2.00
39 Bob Thurman 1.25 3.00
40 Booker T. McDaniel/(Cannonball) .72 2.00
41 Newton Henry Allen/(Colt) 1.25 3.00
42 Willie Wells 2.50 6.00
43 Connie Johnson 1.25 3.00
44 George Franklin Giles .72 2.00
45 Frank(Dunk) Duncan .72 2.00

1988 Negro League Duquesne

This 20-card set was sponsored by the Pittsburgh Pirates with the assistance of Rob Ruck of Chatham College and Duquesne Light Company. The set celebrates Negro League Baseball by depicting major black stars who played or were involved in the negro leagues in the Pittsburgh area. The set was given away at the Pittsburgh Pirates' home game on September 10, 1988. The set was issued in a sheet with five rows of four cards each; after perforation, the cards measure the standard size.

COMPLETE SET (20) 10.00 25.00
1 Andrew(Rube) Foster 1.00 2.50
2 1913 Homestead Grays .40 1.00
3 Cum Posey .40 1.00
4 1926 Pittsburgh .40 1.00
Crawfords
5 Gus Greenlee OWN .40 1.00
6 John Henry(Pop) Lloyd 1.00 2.50
7 Oscar Charleston 1.00 2.50
8 Smokey Joe Williams 1.00 2.50
9 William(Judy) Johnson 1.00 2.50
10 Martin Dihigo 1.00 2.50
11 LeRoy(Satchel) Paige 1.50 4.00
12 Josh Gibson 1.50 4.00
13 Sam Streeter .40 1.00
14 James(Cool Papa) Bell 1.00 2.50
15 Ted Page .75 2.00
16 Walter(Buck) Leonard 1.00 2.50
17 Ray(Hooks) Dandridge 1.00 2.50
18 Willis Moody and .40 1.00
Ralph(Lefty) Mellix
19 Harold Tinker .40 1.00
20 Monte Irvin 1.00 2.50

1989 Negro League Rini Postcards

This set of 12 postcards measures 3 1/2" by 5 1/2". The fronts feature color drawings by Susan Rini.

COMPLETE SET (12) 2.00 5.00
1 Monte Irvin .40 1.00
2 Martin Dihigo .30 .75
3 Clint Thomas .08 .25
4 Buster Haywood .08 .25
5 George Giles .08 .25
6 Isidro Fabri .08 .25
7 James(Cool Papa) Bell .40 1.00
8 Josh Gibson .40 1.00
9 Lou Dials .20 .50
10 Willie Wells .30 .75
11 Walter(Buck) Leonard .40 1.00
12 Jose Fernandez .08 .25

1990 Negro League Stars

The exclusion of black and Latino players from Major League Baseball from 1889 to 1947 resulted in these same players forming their own teams and leagues, and this 36-card set pays tribute to these men. These standard size cards feature beautiful water color portraits of the players, painted by Mark Chiarello.

COMPLETE SET (36) 30.00 60.00
1 Title Card .60 1.50
2 Josh Gibson 3.00 8.00
3 Cannonball Redding .60 1.50
4 Biz Mackey 1.00 2.50
5 Pop Lloyd 1.50 4.00
6 Bingo Demoss .60 1.50
7 Willard Brown .40 1.00
8 John Donaldson .40 1.00
9 Monte Irvin 1.50 4.00
10 Ben Taylor .40 1.00
11 Willie Wells 1.00 2.50
12 Dave Brown .40 1.00
13 Leon Day 1.50 4.00
14 Ray Dandridge 1.50 4.00
15 Turkey Stearnes .40 1.00
16 Rube Foster 1.50 4.00
17 Oliver Marcelle .40 1.00
18 Judy Johnson 1.50 4.00
19 Christobel Torrienti .60 1.50
20 Satchel Paige 3.00 8.00
21 Mule Suttles .60 1.50
22 John Beckwith .40 1.00
23 Martin Dihigo 1.50 4.00
24 Willie Foster .40 1.00
25 Dick Lundy .40 1.00
26 Buck Leonard 1.50 4.00
27 Smokey Joe Williams 1.50 4.00
28 Cool Papa Bell 1.50 4.00
29 Bullet Rogan .60 1.50
30 Newt Allen .60 1.50
31 Bruce Petway .60 1.50
32 Jose Mendez .40 1.00
33 Louis Santop .40 1.00
34 Jud Wilson .40 1.00
35 Sammy T. Hughes .40 1.00
36 Oscar Charleston 1.50 4.00

1991 Negro League Ron Lewis

This 30-card boxed set was produced by the Negro League Baseball Players Association and noted sports artist Ron Lewis and was subtitled Living Legends. Production quantities were limited to 10,000 sets, and each card of the set bears a unique serial number on the back. Also 200 uncut sheets were printed. The cards were issued in the postcard format and measure approximately 3 1/2" by 5 1/4". The front design features a full color painting of the player by Ron Lewis. These cards were also issued in 1995 as part of a two series Negro League set. The values are about the same for either set.

COMPLETE SET (30) 12.50 30.00
1 George Giles .40 1.00
2 Bill Cash .40 1.00
3 Bob Harvey .40 1.00
4 Lyman Bostock Sr. .60 1.50
5 Ray Dandridge 1.00 2.50
6 Leon Day 1.00 2.50
7 Lefty Mathis .40 1.00
8 Jimmie Crutchfield .60 1.50
9 Clyde McNeal .40 1.00
10 Bill Wright .40 1.00
11 Mahlon Duckett .40 1.00
12 Bobby Robinson .60 1.50
13 Max Manning .40 1.00
14 Armando Vazquez .40 1.00
15 Jehosie Heard .60 1.50
16 Quincy Trouppe .40 1.00
17 Wilmer Fields .40 1.00
18 Lonnie Blair .40 1.00
19 Garnett Blair .40 1.00
20 Monte Irvin 1.00 2.50
21 Willie Mays 2.50 6.00
22 Buck Leonard 1.00 2.50
23 Frank Evans .40 1.00
24 Josh Gibson Jr. .75 2.00
25 Ted Radcliffe .60 1.50
26 Josh Johnson .60 1.50
27 Gene Benson .40 1.00
28 Lester Lockett .60 1.50
29 Bubba Hyde .40 1.00
30 Rufus Lewis .40 1.00

1992 Negro League Kraft

On August 9, 1992, at Lackawanna County Stadium, in Scranton, Pennsylvania, Eclipse Enterprises Inc. sponsored the Negro League Baseball Players Association Night. This 18-card set was created especially for this event by Eclipse artist John Clapp and given out to fans in attendance. Reportedly only 11,000 of the 15,000 sets were distributed; the remainder were kept by Kraft General Foods of Glenville, Illinois.

COMPLETE SET (18) 6.00 15.00
1 Leon Day .60 1.50
2 Clinton(Casey) Jones .20 .50
3 Lester Lockett .30 .75
4 Monte Irvin 1.00 2.50
5 Armando Vazquez .20 .50
6 Jimmie Crutchfield .40 1.00
7 Ted Radcliffe .40 1.00
8 Albert Haywood .20 .50
9 Artie Wilson .30 .75
10 Sam Jethroe .30 .75
11 Edsall Walker .20 .50
12 Bill Wright .20 .50
13 Jim Cohen .20 .50
14 Andy Porter .20 .50
15 Tommy Sampson .20 .50
16 Buck Leonard 1.25 3.00
17 Josh Gibson 1.50 4.00
18 Martinez Jackson/(Reggie Jackson's .60 1.50
father)

1992 Negro League Paul Lee

On June 2, 1992 at Shea Stadium, Eclipse Enterprises Inc. sponsored the Negro League Baseball Players Association Night. This four-card set was created especially for this event by Eclipse artist Paul Lee, and they were given out to the first 50,000 fans in attendance. Each set included an insert outlining the goals of the association.

COMPLETE SET (4) 2.50 6.00
1 Monte Irvin .60 1.50
2 Walter(Buck) Leonard .60 1.50
3 Josh Gibson 1.25 3.00
4 Ray Dandridge .60 1.50

1992 Negro League Retort Legends I

This 100-card set was produced by R.D. Retort Enterprises of New Castle, Pennsylvania. The cards were issued in a brown box with the set name and logo stamped in gold. The production run was reported to be 10,000 individually numbered sets. Collectors who purchased the set received The Pictorial Negro League Legends Album, an 8 1/2" by 11" book containing more than 260 vintage Negro League photos, and an address list to facilitate the obtaining of autographs. The cards are "postcard" size, measuring approximately 3 1/2" by 5 1/2". The sepia-toned player photos have white borders, and player's name appears in the bottom white border. The backs carry a player profile and the serial number.

COMPLETE SET (100) 30.00 80.00
COMMON PLAYER (1-65) .40 1.00
COMMON CARD (66-100) .20 .50
1 Otha Bailey .60 1.50
2 Harry Barnes .40 1.00
3 Gene Benson .40 1.00
4 Bill Beverly .40 1.00
5 Charlie Biot .40 1.00
6 Bob Boyd .60 1.50
7 Allen Bryant .40 1.00
8 Marlin Carter .40 1.00
9 Bill Cash .40 1.00
10 Jim Cohen .40 1.00
11 Elliot Coleman .40 1.00
12 Johnnie Cowan .40 1.00
13 Jimmie Crutchfield .60 1.50
14 Saul Davis .40 1.00
15 Piper Davis .60 1.50
16 Leon Day 1.00 2.50
17 Lou Dials .75 2.00
18 Mahlon Duckett .60 1.50
19 Felix Evans .40 1.00
20 Rudy Fernandez .40 1.00
21 Joe Fillmore .40 1.00
22 George Giles .40 1.00
23 Louis Gillis .40 1.00
24 Stanley Glenn .40 1.00
25 Willie Grace .40 1.00
26 Wiley Griggs .40 1.00
27 Albert Haywood .40 1.00
28 Jimmy Hill .40 1.00
29 Cowan Hyde .40 1.00
30 Monte Irvin 1.25 3.00
31 Sam Jethroe .60 1.50
32 Connie Johnson .60 1.50
33 Josh Johnson .60 1.50
34 Clinton Jones .40 1.00
35 Larry Kimbrough .40 1.00
36 Clarence King .40 1.00
37 Jim LaMarque .40 1.00
38 Buck Leonard 1.25 3.00
39 Max Manning .40 1.00
40 Verdell Mathis .40 1.00
41 Nath McClinic .40 1.00
42 Clinton McCord .40 1.00
43 Clyde McNeal .40 1.00
44 John Miles .40 1.00
45 Buck O'Neil 1.25 3.00
46 Frank Pearson .40 1.00
47 Art Pennington .40 1.00
48 Nathaniel Peoples .40 1.00
49 Andy Porter .40 1.00
50 Ted(Double Duty) .60 1.50
Radcliffe
51 Chico Renfroe .40 1.00
52 Bobby Robinson .60 1.50
53 Tommy Sampson .40 1.00
54 Joe Scott .40 1.00
55 Joe Burt Scott .40 1.00
56 Herb Simpson .40 1.00
57 Lonnie Summers .40 1.00
58 Alfred Surratt .60 1.50
59 Bob Thurman .60 1.50
60 Harold Tinker .40 1.00
61 Quincy Trouppe .60 1.50
62 Edsall Walker .40 1.00
63 Al Wilmore .40 1.00
64 Artie Wilson .60 1.50
65 Jim Zapp .40 1.00
66 Grays vs. Stars 1937 .20 .50
67 Grays vs. Eagles 1943 .20 .50
68 Homestead Grays 1944 .20 .50
69 Grays vs. Cuban .20 .50
Stars 1944
70 Grays vs. Cubans 1944 .20 .50
71 Grays vs. Eagles 1945 .20 .50
72 Eagles pitching .20 .50
staff 1941
73 Buckeyes infield 1945 .20 .50
74 Homestead Grays 1948 .20 .50
75 Chicago .20 .50
Murderers Row 1943
76 Indianapolis Clowns/1945 .20 .50
77 East All-Stars 1937 .20 .50
78 East All-Stars 1938 .20 .50
79 East All-Stars 1939 .20 .50
80 East All-Stars 1948 .20 .50
81 West All-Stars 1948 .20 .50
82 Homestead Grays 1931 .20 .50
83 Homestead Grays 1938 .20 .50
84 Pittsburgh Crawfords/1936 .20 .50
85 K.C. Monarchs 1934 .20 .50
86 K.C. Monarchs 1949 .20 .50
87 Chicago American .20 .50
Giants 1941
88 Chicago American .20 .50
Giants 1947
89 Memphis Red Sox 1940 .20 .50
90 Memphis Red Sox 1946 .20 .50
91 Birmingham B.B. 1946 .20 .50
92 Birmingham B.B. 1948 .20 .50
93 Birmingham B.B. 1950 .20 .50
94 Harlem Globetrotters/1948 .20 .50
95 Cleveland Buckeyes/1947 .20 .50
96 Philadelphia Stars/1944 .20 .50
97 Newark Eagles 1939 .20 .50
98 Baltimore Elite .20 .50
Giants 1949
99 Indianapolis Clowns/1943 .20 .50
100 Cincinnati Tigers/1937 .20 .50

1993 Negro League Retort Legends II

This 100-card second series of R.D. Retort Enterprises' Negro League Legends was issued in a brown box that has the set logo on the top stamped in gold foil. The cards have a postcard design, measuring approximately 3 1/2" by 5 1/2", and feature white-bordered sepia-tone player photos on their fronts. The player's (or team's) name appears in the lower margin. The back carries the player's (or team's) name on the left side, which is highlighted by a baseball bat icon. The set's logo appears at the lower right, next to the set's production number (out of 10,000).

COMPLETE SET (100) 30.00 80.00
COMMON CARD (1-41) .40 1.00
COMMON CARD (42-100) .30 .75
1 Frank Barnes .40 1.00
2 John L. Bissant .40 1.00
3 Garnett E. Blair .40 1.00
4 Jim(Fire Ball) Bolden .40 1.00
5 Luther H. Branham .40 1.00
6 Sherwood(Woody) Brewer .40 1.00
7 Jimmy Dean .40 1.00
8 Frank Duncan Jr. .60 1.50
9 Wilmer(Red) Fields .40 1.00
10 Harold(Beebop) Gordon .40 1.00
11 Bill Greason .40 1.00
12 Acie(Skeet) Griggs .40 1.00
13 Napolean Gulley .40 1.00
14 Ray Haggins .40 1.00
15 Wilmer Harris .40 1.00
16 Bob Harvey .40 1.00
17 Jehosie Heard .60 1.50
18 Gordon(Hoppy) Hopkins .40 1.00
19 Herman(Doc) Horn .40 1.00
20 James(Sap) Ivory .40 1.00
21 Henry Kimbro .40 1.00
22 Milfred(Rick) Laurent .40 1.00
23 Ernest(The Kid) Long .40 1.00
24 Frank Marsh .40 1.00
25 Francis(Fran) Matthews .40 1.00
26 Jim McCurine .40 1.00
27 John Mitchell .40 1.00
28 Lee Moody .60 1.50
29 Rogers(Shape) Pierre .40 1.00
30 Nathaniel(Nat) Pollard .40 1.00
31 Merle Porter .40 1.00
32 William Powell .40 1.00
33 Ulysses A. Redd .40 1.00
34 Harry(Lefty) Rhodes .40 1.00
35 DeWitt Smallwood/(Woody) .40 1.00
36 Joseph B. Spencer .40 1.00
37 Riley A. Stewart .40 1.00
38 Earl Taborn .40 1.00
39 Ron Teasley .40 1.00
40 Joe Wiley .40 1.00
41 Walter(Buck) Leonard 1.25 3.00
42 Grays vs. B.E. Giants/1945 .30 .75
43 Grays vs. Monarchs/1945 .30 .75
44 Homestead Grays 1948 .30 .75
45 Pittsburgh Crawfords/1928 .30 .75
46 Pittsburgh Crawfords/1935 .30 .75
47 Kansas City Monarchs/1942 .30 .75
48 John(Buck) O'Neil MG .30 .75
William(Dizzy) Dismukes
49 Chicago American .30 .75
Giants 1942
50 Nashville Elite .30 .75
Giants 1935
51 Baltimore Elite .30 .75
Giants 1941
52 Birmingham Black .30 .75
Barons 1948
53 Birmingham Black .30 .75
Barons 1959
54 Memphis Red Sox 1954 .30 .75
55 Indianapolis ABC's/1923 .30 .75
56 Harlem Globetrotters/1948 .30 .75
57 Harlem Globetrotters/1948 .30 .75
58 Bismarck Barons 1955 .30 .75
59 Culiacan 1952 .30 .75
60 Santurce 1947 .30 .75
61 Pittsburgh Crawfords/1928 .30 .75
62 Pittsburgh Crawfords/1932 .30 .75
63 Pittsburgh Crawfords/1935 .30 .75
64 Homestead Grays 1937 .30 .75
65 Homestead Grays 1938 .30 .75
66 Homestead Grays 1940 .30 .75
67 Homestead Grays 1945 .30 .75
68 Homestead Grays 1948 .30 .75
69 Kansas City Monarchs/1932 .30 .75
70 Kansas City Monarchs/1934 .30 .75
71 Kansas City Monarchs/1941 .30 .75
72 Kansas City Monarchs/1946 .30 .75
73 Chicago American .30 .75
Giants 1950
74 Memphis Red Sox 1949 .30 .75
75 Birmingham Black .30 .75
Barons 1946
76 Birmingham Black .30 .75
Barons 1948
77 Birmingham Black .30 .75
Barons 1951
78 Birmingham Black .30 .75
Barons 1954
79 St. Louis Stars 1931 .30 .75
80 Newark Dodgers 1935 .30 .75
81 Brooklyn Eagles 1935 .30 .75
82 Newark Eagles 1946 .30 .75
83 Philadelphia Stars/1939 .30 .75
84 Philadelphia Stars/1946 .30 .75
85 Philadelphia Stars/1949 .30 .75
86 Nashville Elite .30 .75
Giants 1935
87 Baltimore Elite .30 .75
Giants 1939
88 Baltimore Elite .30 .75
Giants 1949
89 Cleveland Buckeyes/1947 .30 .75
90 Cincinnati Tigers 1936 .30 .75
91 Miami Ethiopian .30 .75
Clowns 1940
92 Indianapolis Clowns/1944 .30 .75
93 Indianapolis Clowns/1948 .30 .75
94 New York Cubans 1943 .30 .75
95 Harlem Globetrotters/1948 .30 .75
96 House of David 1938 .60 1.50
97 E.T. Community 1926 .30 .75
98 Bismarck Giants 1935 .30 .75
99 American All-Stars/1945 .30 .75
100 New York Stars 1949 .30 .75

1995 Negro League Legends I

This boxed set measures the standard size and was produced by the Negro League Baseball Players Association and noted sports artist Ron Lewis. Series I and II were both issued in one box. Just 25,000 sets were produced. The white-bordered fronts feature full color player paintings by Ron Lewis. The backs carry the player's name in white letters inside a pink bar and summarize the player's career.

COMPLETE SET (31) 12.50 30.00
1 George Giles .40 1.00
2 Bill Cash .40 1.00
3 Bob Harvey .40 1.00
4 Lyman Bostock Sr. .60 1.50
5 Ray Dandridge 1.00 2.50
6 Leon Day 1.00 2.50
7 Verdell Mathis .40 1.00
8 Jimmie Crutchfield .60 1.50
9 Clyde McNeal .40 1.00
10 Bill Wright .40 1.00
11 Mahlon Duckett .40 1.00
12 William (Bobby) Robinson .60 1.50
13 Max Manning .40 1.00
14 Armando Vasquez .40 1.00
15 Jehosie Heard .60 1.50
16 Quincy Trouppe .60 1.50
17 Wilmer Fields .40 1.00
18 Lonnie Blair .40 1.00
19 Garnett Blair .40 1.00
20 Monte Irvin 1.25 3.00
21 Willie Mays 2.50 6.00
22 Walter (Buck) Leonard 1.50 4.00
23 Frank Evans .40 1.00
24 Josh Gibson Jr. .75 2.00
25 Ted Radcliffe/(Double Duty) .60 1.50
26 Josh Johnson .60 1.50
27 Gene Benson .40 1.00
28 Lester Lockett .60 1.50
29 Cowan Hyde .40 1.00
30 Rufus Lewis .40 1.00
NNO Checklist .40 1.00

1995 Negro League Legends II

This boxed set measures the standard size and was produced by the Negro League Baseball Players Association and noted sports artist Ron Lewis. Series I and II were both issued in one box. Just 25,000 sets were produced. The white-bordered fronts feature full color player paintings by Ron Lewis. The backs carry the player's name in white letters inside a pink bar and summarize the player's career.

COMPLETE SET (33) 12.50 30.00
1 Willie Mays 2.00 5.00
Ernie Banks
Hank Aaron
2 Lester Lockett .40 1.00
Lyman Bostock Sr.
Bill Wright
3 Josh Gibson 1.00 2.50
Josh Gibson Jr.
Buck Leonard
4 Max Manning .75 2.00
Monte Irvin
Leon Day
5 Armando Vazquez .60 1.50
Minnie Minoso
Martin Dihigo
6 Ted Radcliffe .60 1.50
7 Bobby Robinson .40 1.00
Bill Owens
Turkey Stearnes
8 Wilmer Fields .40 1.00
Edsall Walker
Josh Johnson
9 Artie Wilson .60 1.50
Lionel Hampton
10 Earl Taborn .40 1.00
11 Barney Serrell .40 1.00
12 Rodolfo Fernandez .40 1.00
13 Willie Pope .40 1.00
14 Ray Noble .60 1.50
15 Jim Cohen .40 1.00
16 Henry Kimbro .40 1.00
17 Charlie Biot .40 1.00
18 Al Wilmore .40 1.00
19 Sam Jethroe .75 2.00
20 Tommy Sampson .40 1.00
21 Charlie Rivera .40 1.00
22 Claro Duany .40 1.00
23 Russell Awkard .40 1.00
24 Art Pennington .40 1.00
25 Wilmer Harris .40 1.00
26 Napoleon Gulley .40 1.00
27 Emilio Navarro .40 1.00
28 Andy Porter .40 1.00
29 Willie Grace .40 1.00
30 Red Moore .40 1.00
31 Buck O'Neill UER 1.00 2.50
Card back says Walter Buck O
32 Stanley Glenn .40 1.00
NNO Checklist UER .40 1.00
(Says last name of #31 is Leonard
should be O'Neill

1995 Negro League S.F. Examiner Tribute

This 12-card set was issued as a tribute by the San Francisco Examiner in honor of the Negro League's 75th Anniversary. The set was distributed in an uncut sepia and maroon sheet measuring approximately 14 1/4" by 11 1/4". The cards are unnumbered and checklisted below as they appear on the sheet from the top left to the bottom right.

COMPLETE SET (12) 4.00 10.00
1 Walter Buck Leonard .60 1.50
2 James Cool Papa Bell .75 2.00
3 Josh Gibson 1.25 3.00
4 William Judy Johnson .40 1.00
5 John Henry Pop Lloyd .40 1.00
6 Leon Day .60 1.50
7 Martin Dihigo .60 1.50
8 Monte Irvin .75 2.00
9 Oscar Charleston .40 1.00
10 Ray Dandridge .60 1.50
11 Andrew Rube Foster .40 1.00
12 Leroy Satchel Paige 1.25 3.00

1996 Negro League Baseball Museum

This nine-card set measures approximately 3 1/2" by 5 1/2" and features black-and-white player photos. The backs carry career information. The cards are unnumbered and checklisted below in alphabetical order.

COMPLETE SET (9) 4.00 10.00
1 Ulysses Hollimon .40 1.00
2 Herman Doc Horn Jr. .40 1.00
3 Clifford Connie Johnson .75 2.00
4 James Lefty LaMarque .40 1.00
5 Henry Pistol Mason .60 1.50
6 Bob Motley UMP .40 1.00
7 John Buck O'Neil 1.00 2.50
8 Jesse Rogers .40 1.00
9 Alfred Slick Surratt .60 1.50

1997 Negro League Playing Cards

This 56-card set honors the legendary players of the Negro Leagues and was distributed by the International Society of Athletes. The set could be obtained by sending in at least a $45 donation. The fronts of these rounded-corner cards feature black-and-white player photos in white borders. The player's name, position and team name are printed in black in the bottom border. The black backs carry the name of the set and the sponsor printed in gold. Since this set is similar to a playing card set, the set is checklisted below as if it were a playing card deck. In the checklist C means Clubs, D means Diamonds, H means Hearts and S means Spades. The cards are checklisted in playing order by suits and numbers are assigned to Aces (1), Jacks (11), Queens (12) and Kings (13).

COMPLETE SET (56) 75.00 150.00
1C Josh Gibson 4.00 10.00
1D Jackie Robinson 6.00 15.00
1H James(Cool Papa) Bell 1.50 4.00
1S Satchel Paige 4.00 10.00
2C Bill Cash .60 1.50
2D Sam Haynes .60 1.50
2H Samuel(Harriston) Hairston .75 2.00
2S Joe Greene .60 1.50
3C Fran Matthews .60 1.50
3D Bob(The Rope) Boyd .75 2.00
3H John(Buck) O'Neil 1.50 4.00
3S James(Red) Moore .60 1.50
4C Fred(Leap) Bankhead .60 1.50
4D William(Bonnie) Serrell .60 1.50
4H Lorenzo(Piper) Davis .75 2.00
4S Othello(Chico) Renfroe .60 1.50
5C Alex Radcliffe .60 1.50
5D Minnie Minoso 1.50 4.00
5H Parnell Woods .60 1.50
5S William(Judy) Johnson 1.50 4.00
6C Artie Wilson .75 2.00
6D John Henry(Pop) Lloyd 1.50 4.00
6H Thomas(Pee Wee) Butts .60 1.50
6S Willie(The Devil) Wells 1.50 4.00
7C Jim Zapp .60 1.50
7D Art(Superman) Pennington .60 1.50
7H Oscar Charleston 1.50 4.00
7S Gene Benson .75 2.00
8C Henry(Kimmie) Kimbro .60 1.50
8D Francisco(Pancho) Coimbre .60 1.50
8H Larry Doby 1.50 4.00
8S Willard(Sunnie) Brown 1.25 3.00
9C Chet Brewer .60 1.50
9D Sam(Jet) Jethroe 1.25 3.00
9H Hilton Smith 1.50 4.00
9S Martin Dihigo 1.50 4.00
10C Verdell(Lefty) Mathis .60 1.50
10D Joe Black 1.50 4.00
10H Leon Day .75 2.00
10S Don Newcombe 1.50 4.00
11C Junior Gilliam 1.50 4.00
11D Monte Irvin 1.50 4.00
11H Walter(Buck) Leonard 1.50 4.00
11S Ray(Hooks) Dandridge 1.25 3.00
12C Marcenia(Toni) Stone 1.50 4.00
12D Effie Manley OWN .75 2.00
Newark Eagles
12H Pamela Pryer-Fuller .60 1.50
Legends Reunion Organizer
12S Billie Harden OWN .60 1.50
Atlanta Black Crackers
13C Willie Mays 4.00 10.00
13D Hank Aaron 4.00 10.00
13H Ernie Banks 1.50 4.00
13S Roy(Campy) Campanella 1.50 4.00
JKO Ted(Double Duty) Radcliffe .75 2.00
SJKO Andrew(Rube) Foster .75 2.00
NNO Wilmer(Red) Fields .60 1.50
NNO Clifford(Connie) Johnson .75 2.00

2009 NEHF Sons of Italy Foundation

1 Ed Abbaticchio .30 .75
2 Johnny Antonelli• .30 .75
3 Bob Aspromonte UER .30 .75
(name is Ken on back)
4 Ken Aspromonte UER .30 .75
(name is Bob on back)
5 Rich Aurilia .30 .75
6 Steve Balboni• .30 .75
7 Sal Bando .30 .75
8 Mark Belanger .30 .75
9 Yogi Berra• .75 2.00
10 Craig Biggio .50 1.25
11 Ping Bodie .30 .75
12 Zeke Bonura .30 .75
13 Chris Bosio .30 .75
14 Ricky Bottalico .30 .75
15 Larry Bowa .30 .75
16 Ralph Branca .30 .75
17 Ernie Broglio .30 .75
18 Dolph Camilli .30 .75
19 Ken Caminiti .30 .75
20 Roy Campanella• .75 2.00
21 Tom Candiotti .30 .75
22 Bernie Carbo .30 .75
23 Jon Castino .30 .75
24 Phil Cavarretta .30 .75
25 Rick Cerone .30 .75
26 Jeff Cirillo .30 .75
27 Jack Clark .30 .75
28 Jerry Colangelo .30 .75
29 Rocky Colavito .30 .75
30 Tony Conigliaro .30 .75
31 Frankie Crosetti .30 .75
32 Tony Cuccinello .30 .75
33 Doug DeCinces .30 .75
34 Frank Demaree .30 .75
35 Mark DeRosa• .30 .75
36 Buttercup Dickerson .30 .75
37 Dom DiMaggio .30 .75
38 Joe DiMaggio• 1.50 4.00
39 Vince DiMaggio .30 .75
40 Dick Drago .30 .75
41 Jeff Fassero .30 .75
42 Joe Ferguson .30 .75
43 Ray Fosse .30 .75
44 John Franco .30 .75
45 Terry Francona .30 .75
46 Tito Francona .30 .75
47 Jim Fregosi .30 .75
48 Carl Furillo .30 .75
49 Gary Gaetti .30 .75
50 Joe Garagiola .30 .75
51 Bartlett Giamatti .30 .75
52 Jason Giambi .30 .75
53 Al Gionfrido .30 .75
54 Joe Girardi .50 1.25
55 Dave Giusti .30 .75
56 Tony Graffanino .30 .75
57 Pete Incaviglia .30 .75
58 Paul Konerko .50 1.25
59 Tony LaRussa• .50 1.25
60 Tom Lasorda• .30 .75
61 Cookie Lavagetto .30 .75
62 Tony Lazzeri• .30 .75
63 Ernie Lombardi• .30 .75
64 Sal Maglie .30 .75
65 Frank Malzone .30 .75
66 Gus Mancuso .30 .75
67 Billy Martin .50 1.25
68 Phil Masi .30 .75
69 Lee Mazzilli .30 .75
70 Leo Mazzone .30 .75
71 Sam Mele .30 .75
72 Doug Mirabelli• .30 .75
73 John Montefusco .30 .75
74 Don Mossi .30 .75
75 Tom Pagnozzi .30 .75
76 Eddie Pellagrini .30 .75
77 Joe Pepitone .30 .75
78 Rico Petrocelli .30 .75
79 Andy Pettitte .50 1.25
80 Mike Piazza .75 2.00
81 Babe Pinelli .30 .75
82 Vic Raschi .30 .75
83 Dave Righetti .30 .75
84 Phil Rizzuto• .50 1.25
85 Johnny Romano .30 .75
86 Ron Santo• .50 1.25
87 Steve Sax .30 .75
88 Mike Scioscia .30 .75
89 Sibby Sisti .30 .75
90 John Smoltz .75 2.00
91 Kevin Tapani .30 .75
92 Gene Tenace .30 .75
93 Joe Torre .50 1.25
94 Bobby Valentine .30 .75
95 Robin Ventura .30 .75
96 Frank Viola .30 .75
97 Barry Zito .50 1.25
98 Cover Card black .30 .75
Outstanding Achievement
99 Cover Card white .30 .75
Career Pitching Leaders
100 NEHF Cover Card .30 .75
Career Batting Leaders

1922 Neilson's Chocolates V61

The 1922 Neilson's Chocolate set, titled "Big League Baseball Stars", contains 120 cards and is essentially a reproduction of the E120 set. The cards measure approximately 2" by 3 1/4". The fronts feature oval-shaped black-and-white player photos with ornamented borders. The player's name, position and team also appear on the front. The backs give information about this set and carry an ad for Neilson's chocolate. There are two versions of this set: a numbered paper issue and an unnumbered cardboard issue. Cards of the unnumbered cardboard issue are worth approximately 50 percent more than the values listed in the checklist below.

COMPLETE SET (120) 4250.00 8500.00
1 George Burns 60.00 120.00
2 John Tobin 50.00 100.00
3 Tom Zachary 60.00 120.00
4 Joe Bush 60.00 120.00
5 Lu Blue 50.00 100.00
6 Tillie Walker 50.00 100.00
7 Carl Mays 60.00 120.00
8 Goose Goslin 100.00 200.00
9 Ed Rommel 60.00 120.00
10 Charles Robertson 50.00 100.00
11 Ralph Perkins 50.00 100.00
12 Joe Sewell 100.00 200.00
13 Harry Hooper 100.00 200.00
14 Red Faber 100.00 200.00
15 Bibb Falk 50.00 100.00
16 George Uhle 60.00 120.00
17 Emory Rigney 50.00 100.00
18 George Dauss 50.00 100.00
19 Herman Pillette 50.00 100.00
20 Wally Schang 60.00 120.00
21 Lawrence Woodall 50.00 100.00
22 Steve O'Neill 60.00 120.00
23 Bing Miller 50.00 100.00
24 Sylvester Johnson 50.00 100.00
25 Henry Severeid 50.00 100.00
26 Dave Danforth 50.00 100.00
27 Harry Heilmann 100.00 200.00
28 Bert Cole 50.00 100.00
29 Eddie Collins 100.00 200.00
30 Ty Cobb 1500.00 3000.00
31 Bill Wambsganss 60.00 120.00
32 George Sisler 100.00 200.00
33 Bob Veach 50.00 100.00
34 Earl Sheely 50.00 100.00
35 Pat Collins 50.00 100.00
36 Frank Davis 50.00 100.00
37 Babe Ruth 2500.00 5000.00
38 Bryan Harris 50.00 100.00
39 Bob Shawkey 75.00 150.00
40 Urban Shocker 60.00 120.00
41 Martin McManus 50.00 100.00
42 Clark Pittenger 50.00 100.00
43 Sam Jones 60.00 120.00
44 Waite Hoyt 100.00 200.00
45 Johnny Mostil 50.00 100.00
46 Mike Menosky 50.00 100.00
47 Walter Johnson 500.00 1000.00
48 Wally Pipp 60.00 120.00
49 Walter Gerber 50.00 100.00
50 Ed Gharrity 50.00 100.00
51 Frank Ellerbe 50.00 100.00
52 Kenneth Williams 75.00 150.00
53 Joe Hauser 60.00 120.00
54 Carson Bigbee 50.00 100.00
55 Irish Meusel 50.00 100.00
56 Milton Stock 50.00 100.00
57 Wilbur Cooper 60.00 120.00
58 Tom Griffith 50.00 100.00
59 Butch Henline 50.00 100.00
60 Bubbles Hargrave 50.00 100.00
61 Russel Wrightstone 50.00 100.00
62 Frankie Frisch 100.00 200.00
63 Frank Parkinson 50.00 100.00
64 Walter Ruether 60.00 120.00
65 Bill Doak 50.00 100.00
66 Marty Callaghan 50.00 100.00
67 Sammy Bohne 50.00 100.00
68 Earl Hamilton 50.00 100.00
69 Grover Alexander 200.00 400.00
70 George Burns 50.00 100.00
71 Max Carey 100.00 200.00
72 Adolph Luque 75.00 150.00
73 Dave Bancroft 100.00 200.00
74 Vic Aldridge 50.00 100.00
75 Jack Smith 50.00 100.00
76 Bob O'Farrell 60.00 120.00
77 Pete Donohue 50.00 100.00
78 Babe Pinelli 60.00 120.00
79 Ed Roush 100.00 200.00
80 Norman Boeckel 50.00 100.00
81 Rogers Hornsby 300.00 600.00
82 George Toporcer 50.00 100.00
83 Ivy Wingo 50.00 100.00
84 Virgil Cheeves 50.00 100.00
85 Vern Clemons 50.00 100.00
86 Lawrence Miller 50.00 100.00
87 Johnny Kelleher 50.00 100.00
88 Heinie Groh 60.00 120.00
89 Burleigh Grimes 100.00 200.00
90 Rabbit Maranville 100.00 200.00
91 Babe Adams 60.00 120.00
92 Lee King 50.00 100.00
93 Art Nehf 60.00 120.00
94 Frank Snyder 50.00 100.00
95 Raymond Powell 50.00 100.00
96 Wilbur Hubbell 50.00 100.00
97 Leon Cadore 50.00 100.00
98 Joe Oeschger 50.00 100.00
99 Jake Daubert 50.00 100.00
100 Will Sherdel 50.00 100.00
101 Hank DeBerry 50.00 100.00
102 Johnny Lavan 50.00 100.00
103 Jesse Haines 100.00 200.00
104 Joe Rapp 50.00 100.00
105 Oscar Ray Grimes 50.00 100.00
106 Ross Youngs 100.00 200.00
107 Art Fletcher 50.00 100.00
108 Clyde Barnhart 50.00 100.00
109 Pat Duncan 50.00 100.00
110 Charlie Hollocher 50.00 100.00
111 Horace Ford 50.00 100.00
112 Bill Cunningham 50.00 100.00
113 Walter Schmidt 50.00 100.00
114 Joe Schultz 50.00 100.00
115 John Morrison 50.00 100.00
116 Jimmy Caveney 50.00 100.00
117 Zach Wheat 100.00 200.00
118 Cy Williams 60.00 120.00
119 George Kelly 100.00 200.00
120 Jimmy Ring 50.00 100.00

1984 Nestle 792

The cards in this 792-card standard-size set are extremely similar to the 1984 Topps (egular issue (except for the Nestle logo instead of Topps logo on the front). In conjunction with Topps, the Nestle Company issued this set as six sheets available as a premium. The set was (as detailed on the back of the checklist card for the Nestle Dream Team cards) originally available from the Nestle Company in full sheets of 132 cards, 24" by 48", for 4.95 plus five Nestle candy wrappers per sheet. The backs are virtually identical to the Topps cards of this year, i.e., same player-number correspondence. These sheets have been cut up into individual cards and are available from a few dealers around the country. This is one of the few instances in this hobby where the complete uncut sheet is worth considerably less than the sum of the individual cards due to the expense required in having the sheet cut professionally (and precisely) into individual cards. Supposedly less than 5000 sets were printed. Since the checklist is exactly the same as that of the 1984 Topps, these Nestle cards are generally priced as a multiple of the corresponding Topps card. Beware also on this set to look for fakes and forgeries. Cards billed as Nestle proofs in black and white are fakes; there are even a few counterfeits in color.

COMPLETE CUT SET (792) 125.00 250.00
*STARS:4X to 8X BASIC CARDS
*ROOKIES: 3X to 6X BASIC CARDS
COMPLETE SET (22) 10.00 25.00
1 Eddie Murray .75 2.00
2 Lou Whitaker .40 1.00
3 George Brett 1.50 4.00
4 Cal Ripken 3.00 8.00
5 Jim Rice .30 .75
6 Dave Winfield .60 1.50
7 Lloyd Moseby .08 .25
8 Lance Parrish .30 .75
9 LaMarr Hoyt .08 .25
10 Ron Guidry .20 .50
11 Dan Quisenberry .08 .25
12 Steve Garvey .40 1.00
13 Johnny Ray .08 .25
14 Mike Schmidt 1.25 3.00
15 Ozzie Smith 1.25 3.00
16 Andre Dawson .40 1.00
17 Tim Raines .30 .75
18 Dale Murphy .40 1.00
19 Tony Pena .08 .25
20 John Denny .08 .25
21 Steve Carlton .40 1.00
22 Al Holland .08 .25
NNO Checklist .08 .25

1987 Nestle Dream Team

This 33-card standard-size set is, in a sense, three sets: Golden Era (1-11 gold), AL Modern Era (12-22 red), and NL Modern Era (23-33 blue). Cards have color coded borders by era. The first 11 card photos are in black and white. The Nestle set was apparently not licensed by Major League Baseball and hence the team logos are not shown in the photos. Six-packs of certain Nestle candy bars contained three cards; cards were also available through a send-in offer.

COMPLETE SET (33) 8.00 20.00
1 Lou Gehrig .60 1.50
2 Rogers Hornsby .08 .25
3 Pie Traynor .08 .25
4 Honus Wagner .30 .75
5 Babe Ruth 1.25 3.00
6 Tris Speaker .08 .25
7 Ty Cobb .75 2.00
8 Mickey Cochrane .08 .25
9 Walter Johnson .30 .75
10 Carl Hubbell .08 .25
11 Jimmy Foxx .30 .75
(Jimmie)
12 Rod Carew .30 .75
13 Nellie Fox .08 .25
14 Brooks Robinson .20 .50
15 Luis Aparicio .08 .25
16 Frank Robinson .08 .25
17 Mickey Mantle 1.25 3.00
18 Ted Williams .75 2.00
19 Yogi Berra .30 .75
20 Bob Feller .20 .50
21 Whitey Ford .20 .50
22 Harmon Killebrew .08 .25
23 Stan Musial .60 1.50
24 Jackie Robinson .75 2.00
25 Eddie Mathews .08 .25
26 Ernie Banks .20 .50
27 Roberto Clemente .75 2.00
28 Willie Mays .75 2.00
29 Hank Aaron .75 2.00
30 Johnny Bench .20 .50
31 Bob Gibson .20 .50
32 Warren Spahn .08 .25
33 Duke Snider .30 .75
NNO Checklist .05 .15

1988 Nestle

This 44-card standard-size set has yellow borders. This set was produced for Nestle by Mike Schechter Associates and was printed in Canada. The Nestle set was apparently not licensed by Major League Baseball and hence the team logos are not shown in the photos. The backs are printed in red and blue on white card stock.

COMPLETE SET (44) 15.00 40.00
1 Roger Clemens 1.50 4.00
2 Dale Murphy .40 1.00
3 Eric Davis .20 .50
4 Gary Gaetti .20 .50
5 Ozzie Smith 1.00 2.50
6 Mike Schmidt .75 2.00
7 Ozzie Guillen .20 .50
8 John Franco .20 .50
9 Andre Dawson .40 1.00
10 Mark McGwire 1.50 4.00
11 Bret Saberhagen .20 .50
12 Benito Santiago .08 .25
13 Jose Uribe .08 .25
14 Will Clark .60 1.50
15 Don Mattingly 1.50 4.00
16 Juan Samuel .08 .25
17 Jack Clark .08 .25
18 Darryl Strawberry .20 .50
19 Bill Doran .08 .25
20 Pete Incaviglia .08 .25
21 Dwight Gooden .20 .50
22 Willie Randolph .20 .50
23 Tim Wallach .08 .25
24 Pedro Guerrero .08 .25
25 Steve Bedrosian .08 .25
26 Gary Carter .60 1.50
27 Jeff Reardon .20 .50
28 Dave Righetti .08 .25
29 Frank White .20 .50
30 Buddy Bell .20 .50
31 Tim Raines .20 .50
32 Wade Boggs .60 1.50
33 Dave Winfield .60 1.50
34 George Bell .08 .25
35 Alan Trammell .30 .75
36 Joe Carter .30 .75
37 Jose Canseco .60 1.50
38 Carlton Fisk .60 1.50
39 Kirby Puckett .75 2.00
40 Tony Gwynn 1.50 4.00
41 Matt Nokes .08 .25
42 Keith Hernandez .20 .50
43 Nolan Ryan 3.00 8.00
44 Wally Joyner .20 .50

2002 Nestle

COMPLETE SET 4.00 10.00
1 Barry Bonds .60 1.50
2 Chipper Jones .60 1.50
3 Mike Piazza .75 2.00
4 Alex Rodriguez .50 1.50
5 Sammy Sosa .50 1.25
6 Ichiro Suzuki 1.25 3.00

1993 Nestle Quik Bunnies

This Nestle Quik set consists of one player card and 23 bunny cards in which the bunny is portrayed in cartoons participating in various sports activities. The card measures approximately 3 13/16" by 7 5/8" and have rounded corners. The Walker card has a color player action cutout superposed over a starry sky with Walker standing over the red maple leaf of the Canadian flag. The Nestle Quik logo appears at the upper left on a yellow diagonal section. A circular headshot of Walker and the bunny at the lower left overlays a brown diagonal section showing the card number. The horizontal back has bilingual major league highlights followed by stats. The left side carries bilingual instructions on how to order a Collector Cards Binder. The cards are numbered on the front and back.

COMPLETE SET (24) 2.50 6.00
COMMON BUNNY (2-24) .10 .25
1 Larry Walker .08 .25

1895 Newsboy N566

Newsboy Cut Plug was a tobacco brand by the National Tobacco Works of New York. The cabinet cards associated with this brand were offered as premiums in exchange for coupons or tags found in or on the packages. They were believed to have been issued around 1895. Although a number 841 has been seen, this series-which also contains actresses-has never been completely checklisted, and its exact length is not known. At this time, only 12 baseball players have been discovered. We have checklisted only the baseball players and priced them.

COMPLETE SET (13) 6000.00 15000.00
174 W.H. Murphy 1000.00 2000.00
175 Amos Rusie 4000.00 8000.00
176 Michael Tiernan 1000.00 2000.00
177 Eddie Burke 1000.00 2000.00
178 Jack Doyle 1000.00 2000.00
179 Shorty Fuller 1000.00 2000.00
180 George van Haltren 1000.00 2000.00
181 Dave Foutz 1000.00 2000.00
182 Jouett Meekin 1000.00 2000.00
201 W.H. (Dad) Clark/(street clothes) 1000.002000.00
202 Parke Wilson/(street clothes) 1000.00 2000.00
586 John M. Ward 2000.00 4000.00
portrait arms folded
587 John M. Ward 2000.00 4000.00
standing full length

1992 NewSport

This set of 30 glossy player photos was sponsored by NewSport and issued in France. The month when each card was issued is printed as a tagline on the card back. The set was also available in uncut strips. The cards measure approximately 4" by 6" and display glossy color player photos with white borders. The player's name and position appear in the top border, while the NewSport and MLB logos adorn the bottom of the card face. In French, the backs present biography, complete statistics, and career summary. The cards are unnumbered and checklisted below in alphabetical order.

COMPLETE SET (30) 150.00 300.00
1 Roberto Alomar 3.00 8.00
2 Wade Boggs 5.00 12.00
3 George Brett 10.00 25.00
4 Will Clark 4.00 10.00
5 Eric Davis 1.50 4.00
6 Rob Dibble .75 2.00
7 Doug Drabek .75 2.00
8 Julio Franco 1.50 4.00
9 Ken Griffey Jr. 12.50 30.00
10 Rickey Henderson 6.00 15.00
11 Kent Hrbek .75 2.00
12 Bo Jackson 3.00 8.00
13 Howard Johnson .75 2.00
14 Barry Larkin 3.00 8.00
15 Don Mattingly 10.00 25.00
16 Fred McGriff 2.50 6.00
17 Mark McGwire 10.00 25.00
18 Jack Morris .75 2.00
19 Lloyd Moseby .75 2.00
20 Terry Pendleton .75 2.00
21 Cal Ripken 20.00 50.00
22 Nolan Ryan 20.00 50.00
23 Bret Saberhagen .75 2.00
24 Ryne Sandberg 6.00 15.00
25 Benito Santiago 1.50 4.00
26 Mike Scioscia 1.50 4.00
27 Ozzie Smith 8.00 20.00
28 Darryl Strawberry 1.50 4.00
29 Andy Van Slyke .75 2.00
30 Frank Viola .75 2.00

1997 New Pinnacle

The 1997 New Pinnacle set was issued in one series totalling 200 cards and distributed in 10-card packs with a suggested retail price of $2.99. The fronts feature borderless color action player photos with gold printing. The backs carry another smaller player photo and biographical and statistical information. An Alex Rodriguez Sample card was distributed to dealers and hobby media several weeks prior to the product's release. Subsets include East meets West (178-187), Aura (188-197) and Checklists (198-200). Notable Rookie Cards include Brian Giles.

COMPLETE SET (200) 10.00 25.00
1 Ken Griffey Jr. .60 1.50
2 Sammy Sosa .30 .75
3 Greg Maddux .50 1.25
4 Matt Williams .10 .30
5 Jason Isringhausen .10 .30
6 Gregg Jefferies .10 .30
7 Chili Davis .10 .30
8 Paul O'Neill .20 .50
9 Larry Walker .10 .30
10 Ellis Burks .10 .30
11 Cliff Floyd .10 .30
12 Albert Belle .10 .30
13 Javier Lopez .10 .30
14 David Cone .10 .30
15 Jose Canseco .20 .50
16 Todd Zeile .10 .30
17 Bernard Gilkey .10 .30
18 Andres Galarraga .10 .30
19 Chris Snopek .10 .30
20 Tim Salmon .20 .50
21 Roger Clemens .60 1.50
22 Reggie Sanders .10 .30
23 John Jaha .10 .30
24 Andy Pettitte .20 .50
25 Kenny Lofton .10 .30
26 Robb Nen .10 .30
27 John Wetteland .10 .30
28 Bobby Bonilla .10 .30
29 Hideo Nomo .30 .75
30 Cecil Fielder .10 .30
31 Garret Anderson .10 .30
32 Pat Hentgen .10 .30
33 Dave Justice .10 .30
34 Billy Wagner .10 .30
35 Al Leiter .10 .30
36 Mark Wohlers .10 .30
37 Rondell White .10 .30
38 Charles Johnson .10 .30
39 Mark Grace .20 .50
40 Pedro Martinez .20 .50
41 Tom Goodwin .10 .30
42 Manny Ramirez .20 .50
43 Greg Vaughn .10 .30
44 Brian Jordan .10 .30
45 Mike Piazza .50 1.25
46 Roberto Hernandez .10 .30
47 Wade Boggs .20 .50
48 Scott Sanders .10 .30
49 Alex Gonzalez .10 .30
50 Kevin Brown .10 .30
51 Bob Higginson .10 .30
52 Ken Caminiti .10 .30
53 Derek Jeter .75 2.00
54 Carlos Baerga .10 .30
55 Jay Buhner .10 .30
56 Tim Naehring .10 .30
57 Jeff Bagwell .20 .50
58 Steve Finley .10 .30
59 Kevin Appier .10 .30
60 Jay Bell .10 .30
61 Ivan Rodriguez .20 .50
62 Terrell Wade .10 .30
63 Rusty Greer .10 .30
64 Juan Guzman .10 .30
65 Fred McGriff .20 .50
66 Tino Martinez .20 .50
67 Ray Lankford .10 .30
68 Juan Gonzalez .10 .30
69 Ron Gant .10 .30
70 Jack McDowell .10 .30
71 Tony Gwynn .40 1.00
72 Joe Carter .10 .30
73 Wilson Alvarez .10 .30
74 Jason Giambi .10 .30
75 Brian Hunter .10 .30
76 Michael Tucker .10 .30
77 Andy Benes .10 .30
78 Brady Anderson .10 .30
79 Ramon Martinez .10 .30
80 Troy Percival .10 .30
81 Alex Rodriguez .50 1.25
82 Jim Thome .20 .50
83 Denny Neagle .10 .30
84 Rafael Palmeiro .20 .50
85 Jose Valentin .10 .30
86 Marc Newfield .10 .30
87 Mariano Rivera .30 .75
88 Alan Benes .10 .30
89 Jimmy Key .10 .30
90 Joe Randa .10 .30
91 Cal Ripken 1.00 2.50
92 Craig Biggio .20 .50
93 Dean Palmer .10 .30
94 Gary Sheffield .10 .30
95 Ismael Valdes .10 .30
96 John Valentin .10 .30
97 Johnny Damon .20 .50
98 Mo Vaughn .10 .30
99 Paul Sorrento .10 .30
100 Randy Johnson .30 .75
101 Raul Mondesi .10 .30
102 Roberto Alomar .20 .50
103 Royce Clayton .10 .30
104 Mark Grudzielanek .10 .30
105 Wally Joyner .10 .30
106 Wil Cordero .10 .30
107 Will Clark .20 .50
108 Chuck Knoblauch .10 .30
109 Derek Bell .10 .30
110 Henry Rodriguez .10 .30
111 Edgar Renteria .10 .30
112 Travis Fryman .10 .30
113 Eric Young .10 .30
114 Sandy Alomar Jr. .10 .30
115 Darin Erstad .10 .30
116 Barry Larkin .20 .50
117 Barry Bonds .75 2.00
118 Frank Thomas .30 .75
119 Carlos Delgado .10 .30
120 Jason Kendall .10 .30
121 Todd Hollandsworth .10 .30
122 Jim Edmonds .10 .30
123 Chipper Jones .30 .75
124 Jeff Fassero .10 .30
125 Deion Sanders .20 .50
126 Matt Lawton .10 .30
127 Ryan Klesko .10 .30
128 Mike Mussina .20 .50
129 Paul Molitor .10 .30
130 Dante Bichette .10 .30
131 Bill Pulsipher .10 .30
132 Todd Hundley .10 .30
133 J.T. Snow .10 .30
134 Chuck Finley .10 .30
135 Shawn Green .10 .30
136 Charles Nagy .10 .30
137 Willie Greene .10 .30
138 Marty Cordova .10 .30
139 Eddie Murray .30 .75
140 Ryne Sandberg .50 1.25
141 Alex Fernandez .10 .30
142 Mark McGwire .75 2.00
143 Eric Davis .10 .30
144 Jermaine Dye .10 .30
145 Ruben Sierra .10 .30
146 Damon Buford .10 .30
147 John Smoltz .20 .50
148 Alex Ochoa .10 .30
149 Moises Alou .10 .30
150 Rico Brogna .10 .30
151 Terry Steinbach .10 .30
152 Jeff King .10 .30
153 Carlos Garcia .10 .30
154 Tom Glavine .20 .50
155 Edgar Martinez .20 .50
156 Kevin Elster .10 .30
157 Darryl Hamilton .10 .30
158 Jason Dickson .10 .30
159 Kevin Orie .10 .30
160 Bubba Trammell RC .10 .30
161 Jose Guillen .10 .30
162 Brant Brown .10 .30
163 Wendell Magee .10 .30
164 Scott Spiezio .10 .30
165 Todd Walker .10 .30
166 Rod Myers .10 .30
167 Damon Mashore .10 .30
168 Wilton Guerrero .10 .30
169 Vladimir Guerrero .30 .75
170 Nomar Garciaparra .50 1.25
171 Shannon Stewart .10 .30
172 Scott Rolen .20 .50
173 Bob Abreu .20 .50
174 Danny Patterson .10 .30
175 Andruw Jones .20 .50
176 Brian Giles RC .60 1.50
177 Dmitri Young .10 .30
178 Cal Ripken EMW .50 1.25
179 Chuck Knoblauch EMW .10 .30
180 Alex Rodriguez EMW .30 .75
181 Andres Galarraga EMW .10 .30
182 Pedro Martinez EMW .20 .50
183 Brady Anderson EMW .10 .30
184 Barry Bonds EMW .40 1.00
185 Ivan Rodriguez EMW .10 .30
186 Gary Sheffield EMW .10 .30
187 Denny Neagle EMW .10 .30
188 Mark McGwire AURA .40 1.00
189 Ellis Burks AURA .10 .30
190 Alex Rodriguez AURA .30 .75
191 Mike Piazza AURA .30 .75
192 Barry Bonds AURA .40 1.00
193 Albert Belle AURA .10 .30
194 Chipper Jones AURA .20 .50
195 Juan Gonzalez AURA .10 .30
196 Brady Anderson AURA .10 .30
197 Frank Thomas AURA .20 .50
198 Vladimir Guerrero CL .20 .50
199 Todd Walker CL .10 .30
200 Scott Rolen CL .10 .30
S81 Alex Rodriguez Sample .75 2.00

1997 New Pinnacle Artist's Proofs

COMMON RED 1.25 3.00
COMMON BLUE 2.50 6.00
COMMON GREEN 8.00 20.00
STATED ODDS 1:39
1 Ken Griffey Jr. G 10.00 25.00
2 Sammy Sosa B 4.00 10.00
3 Greg Maddux G 8.00 20.00
4 Matt Williams B 1.50 4.00
5 Jason Isringhausen R .60 1.50
6 Gregg Jefferies R .60 1.50
7 Chili Davis R .60 1.50
8 Paul O'Neill R 1.00 2.50
9 Larry Walker R .60 1.50
10 Ellis Burks B 1.50 4.00
11 Cliff Floyd R .60 1.50
12 Albert Belle G 2.00 5.00
13 Javier Lopez R .60 1.50
14 David Cone R .60 1.50
15 Jose Canseco B 2.50 6.00
16 Todd Zeile R 1.50 4.00
17 Bernard Gilkey B 1.50 4.00
18 Andres Galarraga B 1.50 4.00
19 Chris Snopek R .60 1.50
20 Tim Salmon B 2.50 6.00
21 Roger Clemens B 8.00 20.00
22 Reggie Sanders R .60 1.50
23 John Jaha R .60 1.50
24 Andy Pettitte B 2.50 6.00
25 Kenny Lofton G 2.00 5.00
26 Robb Nen R .60 1.50
27 John Wetteland B 1.50 4.00
28 Bobby Bonilla R .60 1.50
29 Hideo Nomo G 5.00 12.00
30 Cecil Fielder R .60 1.50
31 Garret Anderson R .60 1.50
32 Pat Hentgen R .60 1.50
33 Dave Justice R .60 1.50
34 Billy Wagner R .60 1.50
35 Al Leiter R .60 1.50
36 Mark Wohlers R .60 1.50
37 Rondell White R .60 1.50
38 Charles Johnson R .60 1.50
39 Mark Grace R 1.00 2.50
40 Pedro Martinez R 1.00 2.50
41 Tom Goodwin R .60 1.50
42 Manny Ramirez B 2.50 6.00
43 Greg Vaughn R .60 1.50
44 Brian Jordan B 1.50 4.00
45 Mike Piazza G 8.00 20.00
46 Roberto Hernandez R .60 1.50
47 Wade Boggs B 2.50 6.00
48 Scott Sanders R .60 1.50
49 Alex Gonzalez R .60 1.50
50 Kevin Brown R .60 1.50
51 Bob Higginson B 1.50 4.00
52 Ken Caminiti B 1.50 4.00
53 Derek Jeter G 12.50 30.00
54 Carlos Baerga R .60 1.50
55 Jay Buhner B 1.50 4.00
56 Tim Naehring R .60 1.50
57 Jeff Bagwell G 3.00 8.00
58 Steve Finley R .60 1.50
59 Kevin Appier R .60 1.50
60 Jay Bell R .60 1.50
61 Ivan Rodriguez B 2.50 6.00
62 Terrell Wade R .60 1.50
63 Rusty Greer R .60 1.50
64 Juan Guzman R .60 1.50
65 Fred McGriff R 1.00 2.50
66 Tino Martinez R 1.00 2.50
67 Ray Lankford R .60 1.50
68 Juan Gonzalez G 2.00 5.00
69 Ron Gant R .60 1.50
70 Jack McDowell R .60 1.50
71 Tony Gwynn B 5.00 12.00
72 Joe Carter B 1.50 4.00
73 Wilson Alvarez R .60 1.50
74 Jason Giambi R .60 1.50
75 Brian Hunter R .60 1.50
76 Michael Tucker R .60 1.50
77 Andy Benes R .60 1.50
78 Brady Anderson B 1.50 4.00
79 Ramon Martinez R .60 1.50
80 Troy Percival B 1.50 4.00
81 Alex Rodriguez G 8.00 20.00
82 Jim Thome B 2.50 6.00
83 Denny Neagle R .60 1.50
84 Rafael Palmeiro B 2.50 6.00
85 Jose Valentin R .60 1.50
86 Marc Newfield R .60 1.50
87 Mariano Rivera B 4.00 10.00
88 Alan Benes R .60 1.50
89 Jimmy Key R .60 1.50
90 Joe Randa R .60 1.50
91 Cal Ripken G 15.00 40.00
92 Craig Biggio R 1.00 2.50
93 Dean Palmer R .60 1.50
94 Gary Sheffield B 1.50 4.00
95 Ismael Valdes R .60 1.50
96 John Valentin R .60 1.50
97 Johnny Damon R 1.00 2.50
98 Mo Vaughn G 2.00 5.00
99 Paul Sorrento R .60 1.50
100 Randy Johnson B 4.00 10.00
101 Raul Mondesi B 1.50 4.00
102 Roberto Alomar B 2.50 6.00
103 Royce Clayton R .60 1.50
104 Mark Grudzielanek R .60 1.50
105 Wally Joyner R .60 1.50
106 Wil Cordero R .60 1.50
107 Will Clark B 3.00 8.00
108 Chuck Knoblauch B 2.00 5.00
109 Derek Bell R .60 1.50
110 Henry Rodriguez R .60 1.50
111 Edgar Renteria R .60 1.50
112 Travis Fryman R .60 1.50
113 Eric Young R .60 1.50
114 Sandy Alomar Jr. R .60 1.50
115 Darin Erstad B 1.50 4.00
116 Barry Larkin B 2.50 6.00
117 Barry Bonds B 10.00 25.00
118 Frank Thomas G 5.00 12.00
119 Carlos Delgado R .60 1.50
120 Jason Kendall R .60 1.50
121 Todd Hollandsworth R .60 1.50
122 Jim Edmonds R .60 1.50
123 Chipper Jones G 5.00 12.00
124 Jeff Fassero R .60 1.50
125 Deion Sanders B 2.50 6.00
126 Matt Lawton R .60 1.50
127 Ryan Klesko R .60 1.50
128 Mike Mussina R 1.00 2.50
129 Paul Molitor B 1.50 4.00
130 Dante Bichette R .60 1.50
131 Bill Pulsipher R .60 1.50
132 Todd Hundley B 1.50 4.00
133 J.T. Snow R .60 1.50
134 Chuck Finley R .60 1.50
135 Shawn Green R .60 1.50
136 Charles Nagy R .60 1.50
137 Willie Greene R .60 1.50
138 Marty Cordova R .60 1.50
139 Eddie Murray R 1.50 4.00
140 Ryne Sandberg R 2.50 6.00
141 Alex Fernandez R .60 1.50
142 Mark McGwire G 12.50 30.00
143 Eric Davis R .60 1.50
144 Jermaine Dye R .60 1.50
145 Ruben Sierra R .60 1.50
146 Damon Buford R .60 1.50
147 John Smoltz B 2.50 6.00
148 Alex Ochoa R .60 1.50
149 Moises Alou R .60 1.50
150 Rico Brogna R .60 1.50
151 Terry Steinbach R .60 1.50
152 Jeff King R .60 1.50
153 Carlos Garcia R .60 1.50
154 Tom Glavine R 1.00 2.50
155 Edgar Martinez B 2.50 6.00
156 Kevin Elster R .60 1.50
157 Darryl Hamilton R .60 1.50
158 Jason Dickson R .60 1.50
159 Kevin Orie R .60 1.50
160 Bubba Trammell R .25 .60
161 Jose Guillen B 1.50 4.00
162 Brant Brown R .60 1.50
163 Wendell Magee R .60 1.50
164 Scott Spiezio R .60 1.50
165 Todd Walker B 1.50 4.00
166 Rod Myers R .60 1.50
167 Damon Mashore R .60 1.50
168 Wilton Guerrero B 1.50 4.00
169 Vladimir Guerrero G 5.00 12.00
170 Nomar Garciaparra B 6.00 15.00
171 Shannon Stewart R .60 1.50
172 Scott Rolen R 1.00 2.50
173 Bob Abreu R 1.00 2.50
174 Danny Patterson R .60 1.50
175 Andruw Jones G 3.00 8.00
176 Brian Giles R 1.25 3.00
177 Dmitri Young R .60 1.50
178 Cal Ripken EMW G 8.00 20.00
179 Chuck Knoblauch EMW B 1.50 4.00
180 Alex Rodriguez EMW G 5.00 12.00
181 Andres Galarraga EMW R .60 1.50
182 Pedro Martinez EMW R 1.00 2.50
183 Brady Anderson EMW R .60 1.50
184 Barry Bonds EMW B 5.00 12.00
185 Ivan Rodriguez EMW B 1.50 4.00
186 Gary Sheffield EMW B 1.50 4.00
187 Denny Neagle EMW B 1.50 4.00
188 Mark McGwire AURA B 5.00 12.00
189 Ellis Burks AURA R .60 1.50
190 Alex Rodriguez AURA G 5.00 12.00
191 Mike Piazza AURA G 5.00 12.00
192 Barry Bonds AURA B 5.00 12.00
193 Albert Belle AURA G 2.00 5.00
194 Chipper Jones AURA G 3.00 8.00
195 Juan Gonzalez AURA G 2.00 5.00
196 Brady Anderson AURA B 1.50 4.00
197 Frank Thomas AURA G 3.00 8.00
198 Vladimir Guerrero CL R 1.00 2.50
199 Todd Walker CL R .60 1.50
200 Scott Rolen CL R .60 1.50

1997 New Pinnacle Museum Collection

*STARS: 2.5X TO 6X BASIC CARDS
*ROOKIES: 1X TO 2.5X BASIC CARDS
STATED DODS 1:9

1997 New Pinnacle Press Plates

COMMON FRONT 20.00 50.00
COMMON BACK 10.00 25.00
STATED ODDS 1:1250
BASE & INSERTS ALL HAVE PLATE PARALLEL
FOUR DIFT.COLORS FOR EVERY FRONT
FOUR DIFT.COLORS FOR EVERY BACK
NO STAR PRICING DUE TO SCARCITY

1997 New Pinnacle Interleague Encounter

COMPLETE SET (10) 125.00 250.00
STATED ODDS 1:240
1 A.Belle 2.50 6.00
B.Jordan
2 A.Jones 4.00 10.00
B.Anderson
3 K.Griffey Jr. 12.50 30.00
T.Gwynn
4 C.Ripken 20.00 50.00
C.Jones
5 M.Piazza 10.00 25.00
I.Rodriguez
6 D.Jeter 15.00 40.00
V.Guerrero
7 G.Maddux 10.00 25.00
M.Vaughn
8 A.Rodriguez 10.00 25.00
H.Nomo
9 J.Gonzalez 15.00 40.00
B.Bonds
10 F.Thomas 6.00 15.00
J.Bagwell

1997 New Pinnacle Keeping the Pace

STATED ODDS 1:89
1 Juan Gonzalez 1.00 2.50
2 Greg Maddux 4.00 10.00
3 Ivan Rodriguez 1.50 4.00
4 Ken Griffey Jr. 10.00 25.00
5 Alex Rodriguez 3.00 8.00
6 Barry Bonds 4.00 10.00
7 Frank Thomas 2.50 6.00
8 Chuck Knoblauch 1.00 2.50
9 Derek Jeter 6.00 15.00
10 Roger Clemens 3.00 8.00
11 Kenny Lofton 1.00 2.50
12 Tony Gwynn 2.50 6.00
13 Troy Percival 1.00 2.50
14 Cal Ripken 8.00 20.00
15 Andy Pettitte 1.50 4.00
16 Hideo Nomo 1.50 4.00
17 Randy Johnson 2.50 6.00
18 Mike Piazza 2.50 6.00

1997 New Pinnacle Spellbound

COMMON A.BELLE .75 2.00
COMMON A.JONES 2.00 5.00
COMMON A.RODRIGUEZ 4.00 10.00
COMMON C.JONES 2.00 5.00
COMMON C.RIPKEN 6.00 15.00
COMMON F.THOMAS 2.00 5.00
COMMON I.RODRIGUEZ 1.25 3.00
COMMON K.GRIFFEY JR. 4.00 10.00
COMMON M.PIAZZA 3.00 8.00
STATED ODDS 1:19
HOBBY: JUNIOR, ANDRUW, RIPKEN, CHIPPER
RETAIL: FRANK,PIAZZA, ALEX,PUDGE,BELLE

1969 New York Boy Scouts

This set of the New York Mets and Yankees, which measures 2 1/2" by 3 1/2" is believed to be a regional Long Island Boy Scout release and features black-and-white player photos with facsimile autographs. The backs carry the words, "Boy power-Manpower" and "Go Team for 1969." The following checklist may be incomplete and known additions are welcomed. Since these cards are unnumbered, we have sequenced them in alphabetical order.

COMPLETE SET 200.00 400.00
1 Tommie Agee 40.00 80.00
2 Bud Harrelson 40.00 80.00
3 Cleon Jones 40.00 80.00
4 Joe Pepitone 40.00 80.00
5 Tom Seaver 100.00 200.00
6 Art Shamsky 30.00 60.00
7 Mel Stottlemyre 40.00 80.00
8 Ron Swoboda 40.00 80.00

1954 New York Journal American

The cards in this 59-card set measure approximately 2" by 4". The 1954 New York Journal American set contains black and white, unnumbered cards issued in conjunction with the newspaper. News stands were given boxes of cards to be distributed with purchases and each card had a serial number for redemption in the contest. The set spotlights New York teams only and carries game schedules on the reverse. The cards have been assigned numbers in the listing below alphabetically within team so that Brooklyn Dodgers are 1-19, New York Giants are 20-39, and New York Yankees are 40-59. There is speculation that a 20th Dodger card may exist. The catalog designation for this set is M127.

COMPLETE SET (59) 1250.00 2500.00
1 Joe Black 7.50 15.00
2 Roy Campanella 60.00 120.00
3 Billy Cox 7.50 15.00
4 Carl Erskine 12.50 25.00
5 Carl Furillo 12.50 25.00
6 Jim Gilliam 12.50 25.00
7 Gil Hodges 40.00 80.00
8 Jim Hughes 7.50 15.00
9 Clem Labine 10.00 20.00
10 Billy Loes 7.50 15.00
11 Russ Meyer 7.50 15.00
12 Don Newcombe 12.50 25.00
13 Ervin Palica 7.50 15.00
14 Pee Wee Reese 60.00 120.00
15 Jackie Robinson 125.00 250.00
16 Preacher Roe 12.50 25.00
17 George Shuba 7.50 15.00
18 Duke Snider 75.00 150.00
19 Dick Williams 10.00 20.00
20 John Antonelli 7.50 15.00
21 Alvin Dark 10.00 20.00
22 Marv Grissom 7.50 15.00
23 Ruben Gomez 7.50 15.00
24 Jim Hearn 7.50 15.00
25 Bobby Hofman 7.50 15.00
26 Monte Irvin 25.00 50.00
27 Larry Jansen 7.50 15.00
28 Ray Katt 7.50 15.00
29 Don Liddle 7.50 15.00
30 Whitey Lockman 10.00 20.00
31 Sal Maglie 12.50 25.00
32 Willie Mays 150.00 300.00
33 Don Mueller 7.50 15.00
34 Dusty Rhodes 7.50 15.00
35 Hank Thompson 7.50 15.00
36 Wes Westrum 7.50 15.00
37 Hoyt Wilhelm 25.00 50.00
38 Davey Williams 7.50 15.00
39 Al Worthington 7.50 15.00
40 Hank Bauer 12.50 25.00
41 Yogi Berra 75.00 150.00
42 Harry Byrd 7.50 15.00
43 Andy Carey 7.50 15.00
44 Jerry Coleman 10.00 20.00
45 Joe Collins 7.50 15.00
46 Whitey Ford 50.00 100.00
47 Steve Kraly 7.50 15.00
48 Bob Kuzava 7.50 15.00
49 Frank Leja 7.50 15.00
50 Ed Lopat 12.50 25.00
51 Mickey Mantle 400.00 800.00
52 Gil McDougald 12.50 25.00
53 Bill Miller 7.50 15.00
54 Tom Morgan 7.50 15.00
55 Irv Noren 7.50 15.00
56 Allie Reynolds 12.50 25.00
57 Phil Rizzuto 40.00 80.00
58 Eddie Robinson 7.50 15.00
59 Gene Woodling 10.00 20.00

1973 New York Sunday News M138

These 22 newspaper cutouts feature color caricatures that measure 11 1/4" X 14 3/4". The complete page featuring both players measures 22.5" by 29.5". These are printed on newsprint and are unnumbered. Cards feature Mets and Yankees players. Two cards (One Yankee and one Met) were issued every Sunday from 6/17/73 through 8/26/73 in Cartoon section centerfold. Each pair of players played the same position.

COMPLETE SET (22) 75.00 150.00
1 Yogi Berra MG 5.00 12.00
2 Ralph Houk MG 2.50 6.00
3 Tom Seaver 6.00 15.00
4 Mel Stottlemyre 2.50 6.00
5 Ron Blomberg 2.00 5.00
6 John Milner 2.00 5.00
7 Horace Clarke 2.00 5.00
8 Felix Millan 2.00 5.00
9 Bud Harrelson 2.00 5.00
10 Gene Michael 2.00 5.00
11 Jim Fregosi 2.00 5.00
12 Graig Nettles 3.00 8.00
13 Jerry Grote 2.50 6.00
14 Thurman Munson 5.00 12.00
15 Cleon Jones 2.00 5.00
16 Roy White 2.50 6.00
17 Willie Mays 8.00 20.00
18 Bobby Murcer 3.00 8.00
19 Matty Alou 2.50 6.00
20 Rusty Staub 3.00 8.00
21 Sparky Lyle 2.50 6.00
22 Tug McGraw 4.00 10.00

1997 New York Lottery

This five-card set features color photos of legendary baseball players printed on a baseball diamond-shaped background. The set measures approximately 4" by 2" and was actually real New York scratch-off lottery ticket stubs that could be obtained for $1 a piece. The backs carry the lottery rules and prize information. The cards are unnumbered and checklisted below in alphabetical order.

COMPLETE SET (5)	3.00	8.00
1 Yogi Berra	1.00	2.50
2 Keith Hernandez	.60	1.50
3 Gil Hodges	1.00	2.50
4 Monte Irvin	.75	2.00
5 Don Larsen	.40	1.00

1974 New York News This Day in Sports

These cards are newspaper clippings of drawings by Hollreiser and are accompanied by textual description highlighting a player's unique sports feat. Cards are approximately 2" X 4 1/4". These are multisport cards and aranged in chronological order.

COMPLETE SET	50.00	120.00
1 Johnny Bench	2.00	4.00
Yogi Berra		
June 2, 1972; 1951		
3 Ted Williams	2.00	4.00
13-Jun-57		
5 Ezzard Charles	2.00	4.00
Sandy Koufax		
June 22, 1949; 1959		
6 Bobby Murcer	1.00	2.00
24-Jun-70		
7 Gil Hodges	2.00	4.00
Ralph Kiner		
June 25, 1949; 1950		
9 Dizzy Dean	1.25	2.50
1-Jul-34		
10 Billie Jean King	1.25	2.50
Carl Hubbell		
July 2, 1966; 1933		
11 Yogi Berra	1.25	2.50
3-Jul-57		
12 Arky Vaughan	2.00	4.00
Ted Williams		
July 8, 1941		
13 Tom Seaver	2.00	4.00
July 9, 1969; 1970		
14 Willie Stargell	1.25	2.50
11-Jul-73		
15 Nolan Ryan	5.00	10.00
15-Jul-73		
17 Casey Stengel	2.00	4.00
July 26, 1916; 1955		
18 Mickey Mantle	5.00	10.00
Whitey Ford		
July 29, 1966; 1955		
19 Robin Roberts	1.25	2.50
Aug. 19, 1955		
20 Lou Gehrig	2.00	4.00
Aug. 21, 1935; 1937		
21 Warren Spahn	1.25	2.50
Roy Face		
Aug. 30. 1960; 1959		
22 George Sisler	1.50	3.00
Pete Rose		
Sept. 4, 1920; 1973		
23 Sal Maglie	1.00	2.00
Tommy Henrich		
Sept. 9, 1950; 1941		
24 Hank Aaron	2.00	4.00
Sept. 21, 1958		
26 Dick Sisler	1.00	2.00
Oct. 1, 1950		
28 Pepper Martin	2.00	4.00
Yogi Berra		
Oct. 7, 1931; 1961		
29 Dizzy Dean	1.25	2.50
Daffy Dean		
Oct. 9, 1934		
30 Walter Johnson	1.25	2.50
Oct. 11, 1925		

1916 New York World Advertisements

These 9" by 4" card features four New York Area players. The cards have a player portrait and the rest of the card is devoted to advertising information about the New York World newspaper. Since the cards are unnumbered we have sequenced them in alphabetical order.

COMPLETE SET	250.00	800.00
1 Frank Baker	500.00	1000.00
2 Dave Bancroft	500.00	1000.00
3 Jake Daubert	500.00	1000.00
4 Buck Herzog	300.00	600.00
5 Dave Robertson	250.00	500.00

1983-85 Nike Poster Cards

The cards in this set measure approximately 5" by 7" and were produced for use by retailers of Nike full-size posters as a promotional counter display. The cards are plastic coated and feature color pictures of players posed in unique settings. The hole at the top was designed so that dealers could attach the cards to the display with a soft plastic fastener provided by Nike. The borders are black. Originally, 27-cards were issued together and others were added later as new posters were created. The backs are plain white and carry the poster name, item number, and the player names (except on group photos). The cards are numbered only by the item number on back and have been listed below according to the final two digits of that number.

COMPLETE SET (43)	125.00	225.00
18 MVP and CY	6.00	15.00
23 Fingers and Sutter	1.50	4.00
24 Penguin Power	1.25	3.00
31 K-Lord	1.50	4.00
37 Power Alley	1.50	4.00
38 Tigerrr Catcher	1.25	3.00
39 The Dodger Kid	1.25	3.00
52 Dr. K	1.25	3.00
54 Boss Boggs	3.00	6.00
55 Rick's World	1.25	3.00
56 Stickball	1.50	4.00
Gooden		
Murphy		

1985 Nike

This oversized (slightly larger than 3x5 cards) multisport set was issued by Nike to promote athletic shoe sales. Although the set contains an attractive rookie-season card of Michael Jordan, the fairly plentiful supply has kept the market value quite affordable. Sets were distributed in shrinkwrapped form. The cards are unnumbered and are listed here in alphabetical order.

COMP.FACTORY SET (5)	1250.00	2500.00
COMPLETE SET (5)	600.00	1200.00
1 Dwight Gooden	4.00	10.00
5 Lance Parrish	4.00	10.00

1990 Nike Mini-Posters

This two-card set features color action player photos and measures approximately 5" by 7". The cards are replicas of large 24" by 36" posters. The backs are blank. The cards are unnumbered and checklisted below in alphabetical order.

COMPLETE SET (2)	3.00	6.00
1 Mark Grace	1.25	3.00
2 Kirby Puckett	1.25	3.00

2003 Nike

COMPLETE SET	2.00	5.00
1 Torii Hunter	.40	1.00
2 Magglio Ordonez	.60	1.50
3 Alfonso Soriano	1.00	2.50

1989 Nissen

The 1989 J.J. Nissen set contains 20 standard-size cards. The fronts have airbrushed facial photos with white and yellow borders and orange trim. The backs are white and feature career stats. The complete set price below does not include the error version of Mark Grace.

COMPLETE SET (20)	3.00	8.00
1 Wally Joyner	.07	.20
2 Wade Boggs	.30	1.00
3 Ellis Burks	.10	.30
4 Don Mattingly	.75	2.00
5 Jose Canseco	.20	.50
6 Mike Greenwell	.02	.10
7 Eric Davis	.07	.20
8 Kirby Puckett	.40	1.00
9 Kevin Seitzer	.02	.10
10 Darryl Strawberry	.07	.20
11 Gregg Jefferies	.02	.10
12A Mark Grace ERR/(Photo actually Vance Law)	2.00	5.00
12B Mark Grace COR	.40	1.00
13 Matt Nokes	.02	.10
14 Mark McGwire	.75	2.00
15 Bobby Bonilla	.02	.10
16 Roger Clemens	.75	2.00
17 Frank Viola	.02	.10
18 Orel Hershiser	.07	.20
19 David Cone	.15	.40
20 Ted Williams	.75	2.00

1996 No Fear

This eight-card jumbo-sized set was issued through No Fear. It is a multi-sport set that features a posed color player shot on the front and a white back featuring a slogan by No Fear. The mode of distribution is unclear. The cards are not numbered and checklisted below in alphabetical order.

COMPLETE SET (8)	5.00	12.00
1 Wade Boggs BB	.80	2.00
5 Tony Gwynn BB	1.60	4.00
6 Eric Karros BB	.40	1.00
8 Mo Vaughn BB	.80	2.00

1953 Northland Bread Labels

This 32-label set features two players from each major league team and is one of the popular "Bread For Energy" sets. Each bread label measures 2 11/16" by 2 11/16". Although the labels are printed in black and white, the 1953 Northland Bread set includes a "Baseball Stars" album which provides additional information concerning "Baseball Immortals" and "Baseball Tips." These labels are unnumbered so we have checklisted them in alphabetical order. The amended catalog designation is D290-3A.

COMPLETE SET (32)	3500.00	7000.00
1 Cal Abrams	150.00	300.00
2 Richie Ashburn	250.00	500.00
3 Gus Bell	175.00	350.00
4 Jim Busby	150.00	300.00
5 Clint Courtney	150.00	300.00
6 Billy Cox	150.00	300.00
7 Jim Dyck	150.00	300.00
8 Nellie Fox	350.00	700.00
9 Sid Gordon	150.00	300.00
10 Warren Hacker	150.00	300.00
11 Jim Hearn	150.00	300.00
12 Fred Hutchinson	150.00	300.00
13 Monte Irvin	225.00	450.00
14 Jackie Jensen	175.00	350.00
15 Ted Kluszewski	225.00	450.00
16 Bob Lemon	225.00	450.00
17 Mickey McDermott	150.00	300.00
18 Minnie Minoso	175.00	350.00
19 Johnny Mize	225.00	450.00
20 Mel Parnell	150.00	300.00
21 Howie Pollet	150.00	300.00
22 Jerry Priddy	150.00	300.00
23 Allie Reynolds	175.00	350.00
24 Preacher Roe	175.00	350.00
25 Al Rosen	175.00	350.00
26 Connie Ryan	150.00	300.00
27 Hank Sauer	175.00	350.00
28 Red Schoendienst	225.00	450.00
29 Bobby Shantz	175.00	350.00
30 Enos Slaughter	225.00	450.00
31 Warren Spahn	350.00	700.00
32 Gus Zernial	175.00	350.00

1910 Notebook Covers

These eight cards are similar in size and appearance to the T-3 set. These cards measure 5" by 7 1/2". The cards are in full colors with red borders. We have checklisted the set in alphabetical order.

COMPLETE SET	2000.00	4000.00
1 Roger Breshnahan	200.00	400.00
2 Ty Cobb	750.00	1500.00
3 Eddie Collins	300.00	600.00
4 Johnny Evers	250.00	500.00
5 Clark Griffith	200.00	400.00
6 Nap Lajoie	300.00	600.00
7 Christy Mathewson	400.00	800.00
8 Honus Wagner	400.00	800.00

1960 Nu-Card Hi-Lites

The cards in this 72-card set measure approximately 3 1/4" by 5 3/8". In 1960, the Nu-Card Company introduced its Baseball Hi-Lites set of newspaper style cards. Each card singled out an individual baseball achievement with a picture and story. The reverses contain a baseball quiz. Cards 1-18 are more valuable if found printed totally in black on the front; these are copy-righted CVC as opposed to the NCI designation found on the red and black printed fronts.

COMPLETE SET (72)	400.00	800.00
1 Babe Ruth	20.00	50.00
Hits 3 Homers In		
A Series Game		
2 Johnny Podres	1.50	4.00
Pitching Wins Series		
3 Bill Bevans	1.50	4.00
Pitches No-Hitter, Almost		
4 Box Score Devised	1.50	4.00
By Reporter		
5 Johnny VanderMeer	1.50	4.00
Pitches Two No Hitters		
6 Indians Take Bums	1.50	4.00
7 Joe DiMaggio	15.00	40.00
Comes Thru		
8 Christy Mathewson	2.50	6.00
Pitches Three WS Shutouts		
9 Harvey Haddix	1.50	4.00
Pitches 12 Perfect Innings		
10 Bobby Thomson	5.00	12.00
Homer Sinks Dodgers		
11 Carl Hubbell	2.50	6.00
Strikes Out 5 A.L. Stars		
12 Pickoff Ends Series	1.50	4.00
13 Cards Take Series	1.50	4.00
From Yanks		
14 Dizzy And Daffy	2.50	6.00
Dean Win Series		
15 Mickey Owen	1.50	4.00
Drops Third Strike		
16 Babe Ruth	20.00	50.00
Calls Shot		
17 Fred Merkle	2.00	5.00
Pulls Boner		
18 Don Larsen	2.50	6.00
Hurls Perfect W.S. Game		
19 Mickey Cochrane	2.00	5.00
Bean Ball Ends Career		
20 Ernie Banks	8.00	20.00
Belts 47 Homers		
Earns MVP		
21 Stan Musial	8.00	20.00
Hits 5 Homers in One Day		
22 Mickey Mantle	30.00	60.00
Hits Longest Homer		
23 Roy Sievers	1.50	4.00
Captures Home Run Title		
24 Lou Gehrig/2130 Consecutive Game	15.00	40.00
Record Ends		
25 Red Schoendienst	2.00	5.00
Key Player		
Braves Pennant		
26 Midget Pinch-Hits	2.00	5.00
For St. Louis		
27 Willie Mays	12.50	30.00
Makes Greatest Catch		
28 Yogi Berra	6.00	15.00
Homer Puts Yanks In 1st		
29 Roy Campanella	6.00	15.00
NL MVP		
30 Bob Turley	1.50	4.00
Hurls Yankees To		
WS Champions		
31 Dodgers Take Series	1.50	4.00
From Sox in Six		
32 Carl Furillo Hero as	1.50	4.00
Dodgers Beat Chicago		
in 3rd		
33 Joe Adcock	1.50	4.00
Gets 4 Homers		
And A Double		
34 Bill Dickey	2.00	5.00
Chosen All-Star Catcher		
35 Lew Burdette Beats	1.50	4.00
Yanks In Three		
World Series G		
36 Umpires Clear	1.50	4.00
White Sox Bench		
37 Pee Wee Reese	5.00	12.00
38 Joe DiMaggio	15.00	40.00
Hits In 56 Straight		
39 Ted Williams	20.00	50.00
Hits .406 For Season		
40 Walter Johnson	3.00	8.00
Pitches 56 Straight		
41 Gil Hodges	2.00	5.00
Hits 4 Home Runs		
In Nite Game		
42 Hank Greenberg	2.50	6.00
Returns to Tigers From Army		
43 Ty Cobb	8.00	20.00
44 Robin Roberts	2.00	5.00
Wins 28 Games		
45 Phil Rizzuto	3.00	8.00
Two Runs Save 1st Place		
46 Tigers Beat Out	1.50	4.00
Senators For Pennant		
47 Babe Ruth	20.00	50.00
Hits 60th Home Run		
48 Cy Young	2.00	5.00
Honored		
49 Harmon Killebrew	5.00	12.00
Starts Spring Training		
50 Mickey Mantle	20.00	50.00
Hits Longest Homer		
at Stadium		
51 Braves Take Pennant	1.50	4.00
52 Ted Williams	15.00	40.00
Hero Of All-Star Game		
53 Jackie Robinson Saves	15.00	40.00
Dodgers For		
Play-off Serie		
54 Fred Snodgrass	1.50	4.00
Muffs Fly		
55 Duke Snider	8.00	20.00
Belts 2 Homers, Ties Record		
56 Giants Win 26 Straight	1.50	4.00
57 Ted Kluszewski	3.00	8.00
Stars In 1st Series Win		
58 Mel Ott	2.00	5.00
Walks 5 Times In Single Game		
59 Harvey Kuenn	1.50	4.00
Takes A.L. Batting Title		
60 Bob Feller	3.00	8.00
Hurls 3rd No-Hitter of Career		
61 Yankees Champs Again	1.50	4.00
62 Hank Aaron	8.00	20.00
Bat Beats Yankees		
In Series		
63 Warren Spahn	3.00	8.00
Beats Yanks in W.S.		
64 Ump's Wrong Call Helps	1.50	4.00
Dodgers Beat Yanks		
65 Al Kaline	5.00	12.00
Hits 3 Homers		
Two In Same Inning		
66 Bob Allison	1.50	4.00
Named AL ROY		
67 Willie McCovey	3.00	8.00
Blasts Way Into Giant Lineup		
68 Rocky Colavito	8.00	20.00
Hits 4 Homers in One Game		
69 Carl Erskine Sets	1.50	4.00
Strike Out Record		
in World Ser		
70 Sal Maglie	1.50	4.00
Pitches No-Hit Game		
71 Early Wynn	2.00	5.00
Victory Crushes Yanks		
72 Nellie Fox	8.00	20.00
AL MVP		

1961 Nu-Card Scoops

The cards in this 80-card set measure 2 1/2" by 3 1/2". This series depicts great moments in the history of individual ballplayers. Each card is designed as a miniature newspaper front-page, complete with data and picture. Both the number (401-480) and title are printed in red on the obverse, and the story is found on the back. An album was issued to hold the set. The set has been illegally reprinted, which has served to suppress the demand for the originals as well as the reprints.

COMPLETE SET (80)	200.00	400.00
401 Jim Gentile	.60	1.50
402 Warren Spahn/(No-hitter)	1.25	3.00
403 Bill Mazeroski	.75	2.00
404 Willie Mays:/(Three triples)	6.00	15.00
405 Woodie Held	.60	1.50
406 Vern Law	.60	1.50
407 Pete Runnels	.60	1.50
408 Lew Burdette/(No-hitter)	.60	1.50
409 Dick Stuart	.60	1.50
410 Don Cardwell	.60	1.50
411 Camilo Pascual	.60	1.50
412 Eddie Mathews	1.25	3.00
413 Dick Groat	.60	1.50
414 Gene Autry OWN	2.00	5.00
415 Bobby Richardson	.75	2.00
416 Roger Maris	4.00	10.00
417 Fred Merkle	.60	1.50
418 Don Larsen	.60	1.50
419 Mickey Cochrane	.75	2.00
420 Ernie Banks	1.50	4.00
421 Stan Musial	4.00	10.00
422 Mickey Mantle/(Longest homer)	12.50	30.00
423 Roy Sievers	.60	1.50
424 Lou Gehrig	8.00	20.00
425 Red Schoendienst	.75	2.00
426 Eddie Gaedel	1.25	3.00
427 Willie Mays/(Greatest catch)	8.00	20.00
428 Jackie Robinson	8.00	20.00
429 Roy Campanella	4.00	10.00
430 Bob Turley	.60	1.50
431 Larry Sherry	.60	1.50
432 Carl Furillo	.75	2.00
433 Joe Adcock	.60	1.50
434 Bill Dickey	.75	2.00
435 Lew Burdette 3 wins	.60	1.50
436 Umpire Clears Bench	.60	1.50
437 Pee Wee Reese	1.25	3.00
438 Joe DiMaggio/(56 Game Hit Streak)	8.00	20.00
439 Ted Williams/(Hits .406)	8.00	20.00
440 Walter Johnson	1.25	3.00
441 Gil Hodges	.75	2.00
442 Hank Greenberg	1.25	3.00
443 Ty Cobb	6.00	15.00
444 Robin Roberts	1.25	3.00
445 Phil Rizzuto	1.25	3.00
446 Hal Newhouser	1.25	3.00
447 Babe Ruth 60th Homer	15.00	40.00
448 Cy Young	1.25	3.00
449 Harmon Killebrew	1.25	3.00
450 Mickey Mantle/(Longest homer)	15.00	40.00
451 Braves Take Pennant	.60	1.50
452 Ted Williams/(All-Star Hero)	8.00	20.00
453 Yogi Berra	4.00	10.00
454 Fred Snodgrass	.60	1.50
455 Babe Ruth 3 Homers	12.50	30.00
456 Giants 26 Game Streak	.60	1.50
457 Ted Kluszewski	.60	1.50
458 Mel Ott	.75	2.00
459 Harvey Kuenn	.60	1.50
460 Bob Feller	1.50	4.00
461 Casey Stengel	1.25	3.00
462 Hank Aaron	8.00	20.00
463 Spahn Beats Yanks	.75	2.00
464 Ump's Wrong Call	.60	1.50
465 Al Kaline	1.50	4.00
466 Bob Allison	.60	1.50
467 Joe DiMaggio/(Four Homers)	8.00	20.00
468 Rocky Colavito	1.25	3.00
469 Carl Erskine	.60	1.50
470 Sal Maglie	.60	1.50
471 Early Wynn	.75	2.00
472 Nellie Fox	1.00	2.50
473 Marty Marion	.60	1.50
474 Johnny Podres	.60	1.50
475 Mickey Owen	.60	1.50
476 Dean Brothers/(Dizzy and Daffy)	1.00	2.50
477 Christy Mathewson	1.25	3.00
478 Harvey Haddix	.60	1.50
479 Carl Hubbell	.75	2.00
480 Bobby Thomson	.75	2.00

1983 O'Connell and Son Baseball Greats

This 20-card set features drawings of major league players in circles on color backgrounds and measures approximately 4 3/4" by 6 1/4". The player's name is printed on the front as is the player's team logo. The backs are blank. The cards are unnumbered and checklisted below in alphabetical order.

COMPLETE SET (20)	30.00	80.00
1 Hank Aaron	1.25	3.00
2 Johnny Bench	8.00	20.00
3 Yogi Berra	.40	1.00
4 George Brett	1.00	2.50
5 Roy Campanella	.40	1.00
6 Rod Carew	.40	1.00
7 Roberto Clemente	1.50	4.00
8 Bob Gibson	.40	1.00
9 Al Kaline	.40	1.00
10 Mickey Mantle	2.00	5.00
11 Joe Morgan	.20	.50
12 Stan Musial	.75	2.00
13 Jim Rice	.20	.50
14 Frank Robinson	.40	1.00
15 Pete Rose	20.00	50.00
16 Tom Seaver	.40	1.00
17 Duke Snider	.40	1.00
18 Honus Wagner	.40	1.00
19 Carl Yastrzemski	8.00	20.00
20 Robin Yount	.40	1.00

1984-89 O'Connell and Son Ink

This comprises the O'Connell and Son Ink Mini-Prints. The first series set (1-36) was released at the 1984 National Convention. With the inception of The Infield Dirt in 1991, an underground hobby publication, the cards have been included free with each issue. The December 1992 issue of The Infield Dirt, issued by the producers of this set, offered the entire set for $34.95. The cards feature pen and ink or pencil drawings of major league players on color backgrounds. The player's name is printed on the front as is the card number.

COMPLETE SET (250)	20.00	50.00
1 Ted Williams	.75	2.00
2 Minnie Minoso	.15	.40
3 Sandy Koufax	.40	1.00
4 Al Kaline	.15	.40
5 Whitey Ford	.15	.40
6 Wade Boggs	.15	.40
7 Nolan Ryan	.75	2.00
8 Greg Luzinski	.02	.10
9 Cal Ripken	.75	2.00
10 Carl Yastrzemski	.15	.40
11 Dale Murphy	.10	.30
12 Rocco Colavito	.15	.40
13 George Brett	.60	1.50
14 Willie McCovey	.15	.40
15 Rod Carew	.15	.40
16 Bob Gibson	.15	.40
17 Robin Yount	.15	.40
18 Steve Carlton	.15	.40
19 Harmon Killebrew	.15	.40
20 Willie Mays	.75	2.00
21 Reggie Jackson	.40	1.00
22 Eddie Mathews	.15	.40
23 Eddie Murray	.40	1.00
24 Johnny Bench	.30	.75
25 Mickey Mantle	1.00	2.50
26 Willie Stargell	.15	.40
27 Rickey Henderson	.15	.40
28 Roger Maris	.40	1.00
29 Darryl Strawberry	.07	.20
30 Pete Rose	.40	1.00
31 Jim Rice	.07	.20
32 Thurman Munson	.10	.30
33 Brooks Robinson	.15	.40
34 Fernando Valenzuela	.07	.20
35 Tony Oliva	.10	.30
36 Henry Aaron	.75	2.00
37 Joe Morgan	.15	.40
38 Kent Hrbek	.07	.20
39 Yogi Berra	.15	.40
40 Stan Musial	.60	1.50
41 Gary Matthews	.02	.10
42 Larry Doby	.15	.40
43 Steve Garvey	.10	.30
44 Bob Horner	.02	.10
45 Ron Guidry	.07	.20
46 Ernie Banks	.15	.40
47 Carlton Fisk	.15	.40
48 Pee Wee Reese	.15	.40
49 Bobby Shantz	.02	.10
50 Joe DiMaggio	.75	2.00
51 Enos Slaughter	.15	.40
52 Gary Carter	.15	.40
53 Bob Feller	.15	.40
54 Phil Rizzuto	.15	.40
55 Dave Concepcion	.07	.20
56 Ron Kittle	.02	.10
57 Dwight Evans	.07	.20
58 Johnny Mize	.15	.40
59 Richie Ashburn	.15	.40
60 Roberto Clemente	.75	2.00
61 Fred Lynn	.07	.20
62 Billy Williams	.15	.40
63 Dave Winfield	.15	.40
64 Robin Roberts	.15	.40
65 Billy Martin	.10	.30
66 Duke Snider	.15	.40
67 Luis Aparicio	.15	.40
68 Mickey Vernon	.07	.20
69 Mike Schmidt	.40	1.00
70 Frank Robinson	.15	.40
71 Bill Madlock	.02	.10
72 Rollie Fingers	.15	.40
73 Rod Carew	.15	.40
74 Carl Erskine	.02	.10
75 Lou Brock	.15	.40
76 Brooks Robinson	.15	.40
77 Roberto Clemente	.75	2.00
78 Nellie Fox	.15	.40
79 Bud Harrelson	.02	.10
80 Ted Williams	.75	2.00
81 Walter Johnson	.40	1.00
82 Cal Ripken	.75	2.00
83 Lefty Grove	.15	.40
84 Lou Whitaker	.07	.20
85 Johnny Bench	.30	.75
86 Ty Cobb	.75	2.00
87 Mike Schmidt	.40	1.00
88 George Brett	.60	1.50
89 Jim Bunning	.15	.40
90 Babe Ruth	1.00	2.50
91 Satchel Paige	.30	.75
92 Warren Spahn	.15	.40
93 Dale Murphy	.10	.30
94 Early Wynn	.15	.40
95 Reggie Jackson	.40	1.00
96 Charlie Gehringer	.15	.40
97 Jackie Robinson	.75	2.00
98 Lou Gehrig	.75	2.00
99 Hank Aaron	.75	2.00
100 Mickey Mantle	1.00	2.50
101 Sandy Koufax	.40	1.00
102 Ryne Sandberg	.30	.75
103 Don Mattingly	.30	1.00
104 Darryl Strawberry	.07	.20
105 Tom Seaver	.15	.40
106 Bil Klem	.07	.20
107 Dwight Gooden	.07	.20
108 Pete Rose	.40	1.00
109 Elston Howard	.07	.20
110 Honus Wagner	.15	.40
111 Waite Hoyt	.10	.30
112 Billy Bruton	.02	.10
113 Gil Hodges	.15	.40
114 Vic Power	.02	.10
115 Al Kaline	.15	.40
116 Al Lopez	.07	.20
117 Rocky Bridges	.02	.10
118 Junior Gilliam	.07	.20
119 Christy Mathewson	.15	.40
120 Hank Greenberg	.15	.40
121 Eddie Mathews	.15	.40
122 Van Lingle Mungo	.02	.10
123 Harry Suitcase Simpson	.02	.10
124 Carl Yastrzemski	.15	.40
125 Pete Rose	.40	1.00
126 Dizzy Dean	.15	.40
127 Chi Chi Olivo	.02	.10
128 Johnny Vander Meer	.02	.10
129 Roberto Clemente	.75	2.00
130 Carl Hubbell	.15	.40
131 Willie Mays	.75	2.00
132 Willie Stargell	.15	.40
133 Sam Jethroe	.02	.10
134 Pete Rose	.40	1.00
135 Jackie Robinson	.75	2.00
136 Yogi Berra	.15	.40
137 Grover Alexander	.15	.40
138 Joe Morgan	.15	.40
139 Rube Foster	.10	.30
140 Mickey Mantle	1.00	2.50
141 Ted Williams	.75	2.00
142 Jimmy Foxx	.15	.40
(Jimmie)		
143 Pepper Martin	.07	.20
144 Henry Aaron	.75	2.00
145 Vida Blue	.02	.10
146 Carl Furillo	.07	.20
147 Lloyd Waner	.10	.30
148 Eddie Dyer	.02	.10
149 Casey Stengel	.15	.40
150 Mickey Mantle	1.00	2.50
151 Gil Hodges	.15	.40
152 Don Mossi	.02	.10
153 Ron Swoboda	.02	.10
154 Hoyt Wilhelm	.10	.30
155 Ed Roush	.10	.30
156 Mickey Lolich	.07	.20
157 Jim Palmer	.15	.40
158 Thurman Munson	.10	.30
159 Don Zimmer	.02	.10
160 Henry Aaron	.75	2.00
161 Johnny Bench	.30	.75
162 Orlando Cepeda	.15	.40
163 Honus Wagner	.15	.40
164 Tom Seaver	.15	.40
165 Willie Mays	.75	2.00
166 Elmer Riddle	.02	.10
167 Tony Oliva	.10	.30
168 Elmer Flick	.07	.20
169 Curt Flood	.07	.20
170 Carl Yastrzemski	.15	.40
171 King Kong Keller	.07	.20
172 Christy Mathewson	.15	.40
173 Eddie Plank	.15	.40
174 Lou Gehrig	.75	2.00
175 John McGraw	.15	.40
176 Mule Haas	.02	.10
177 Paul Waner	.15	.40
178 Steve Blass	.02	.10
179 Honus Wagner	.15	.40
180 Jack Barry	.02	.10
181 Rocky Colavito	.15	.40
182 Danny Murtaugh	.02	.10
183 John Edwards	.02	.10
184 Pete Rose	.40	1.00
185 Roy Campanella	.15	.40
186 Jerry Grote	.02	.10
187 Leo Durocher	.15	.40
188 Rollie Fingers	.15	.40
189 Wes Parker	.02	.10
190 Joe Rudi	.02	.10
191 Bill Veeck	.07	.20
192 Mark Fidrych	.10	.30
193 George Foster	.07	.20
194 Early Wynn	.15	.40
195 Frank Howard	.07	.20
196 Graig Nettles	.07	.20
197 Juan Pizarro	.02	.10
198 Jose Cruz	.07	.20
199 Joe Jackson	.75	2.00
200 Stan Musial	.60	1.50
201 Chuck Klein	.15	.40
202 Ryne Sandberg	.30	.75
203 Richie Allen	.10	.30
204 Bo Jackson	.02	.10
205 Kevin Mitchell	.02	.10
206 Al Smith	.07	.20
Early Wynn		
Larry Doby		
207 Mickey Mantle	1.00	2.50
208 Will Clark	.10	.30
209 Cecil Fielder	.07	.20
210 Bobby Richardson	.07	.20
211 Nolan Ryan	.75	2.00
212 Casey Stengel	.15	.40
213 Ted Kluszewski	.15	.40
214 Gaylord Perry	.15	.40
215 Johnny Vander Meer	.07	.20
216 Willie Mays	.75	2.00
217 Goose Goslin	.10	.30
218 Bobby Shantz	.02	.10
219 Terry Pendleton	.02	.10
220 Richie Ashburn	.15	.40
221 Robin Yount	.15	.40
222 Cal Ripken	.75	2.00
223 Danny Ainge	.10	.30
224 Bob Friend	.02	.10
225 Orel Hershiser	.07	.20
226 Wade Boggs	.15	.40
227 Ballpark scene	.02	.10
228 Stan Musial	.60	1.50
229 Chris Short	.02	.10
230 Johnny Bench	.30	.75
231 Nellie Fox	.15	.40
232 Ron Santo	.15	.40
233 Tony Gwynn	.50	1.25
234 Phil Niekro	.15	.40
235 Frank Thomas	.75	2.00
236 Greg Gross	.02	.10
237 Ken Griffey Jr.	1.25	3.00
238 Benito Santiago	.02	.10
239 Dwight Gooden	.07	.20
240 Darryl Strawberry	.02	.10
241 Roy Campanella	.15	.40
242 Roger Clemens	.30	.75
243 Kirby Puckett	.50	1.25
244 Nolan Ryan	.75	2.00
NNO Checklist 6	.02	.10
NNO Checklist 2	.02	.10
NNO Checklist 1	.02	.10
NNO Checklist 4	.02	.10
NNO Checklist 3	.02	.10
NNO Checklist 5	.02	.10

1937 O-Pee-Chee Batter Ups V300

The cards in this 40-card set measure approximately 2 3/8" by 2 7/8". The fronts feature black-and-white die-cut player photos against a ballpark background with small players. The backs carry a short biography and career summary in English and French. The set is peculiar in that card numbering begins with 101. Cards without tops have greatly reduced value. The small ballplayer designs on the obverses are similar to those used on the 1934 American Goudey cards.

COMPLETE SET (40)	10000.00	20000.00
101 John Lewis	125.00	250.00
102 Jack Hayes	125.00	250.00
103 Earl Averill	250.00	500.00
104 Harland Clift	125.00	250.00
105 Beau Bell	125.00	250.00
106 Jimmie Foxx	750.00	1500.00
107 Hank Greenberg	750.00	1500.00
108 George Selkirk	150.00	300.00
109 Wally Moses	150.00	300.00
110 Gerry Walker	125.00	250.00
111 Goose Goslin	250.00	500.00
112 Charlie Gehringer	500.00	1000.00
113 Hal Trosky	125.00	250.00
114 Buddy Myer	125.00	250.00
115 Luke Appling	250.00	500.00
116 Zeke Bonura	125.00	250.00
117 Tony Lazzeri	250.00	500.00
118 Joe DiMaggio	5000.00	10000.00
119 Bill Dickey	600.00	1200.00
120 Bob Feller	1500.00	3000.00
121 Harry Kelley	125.00	250.00
122 Johnny Allen	150.00	300.00
123 Bob Johnson	150.00	300.00
124 Joe Cronin	250.00	500.00
125 Rip Radcliff	125.00	250.00
126 Cecil Travis	150.00	300.00
127 Joe Kuhel	125.00	250.00
128 Odell Hale	125.00	250.00
129 Sam West	125.00	250.00
130 Ben Chapman	150.00	300.00
131 Monte Pearson	125.00	250.00
132 Rick Ferrell	250.00	500.00
133 Tommy Bridges	150.00	300.00
134 Schoolboy Rowe	150.00	300.00
135 Vernon Kennedy	125.00	250.00
136 Red Ruffing	250.00	500.00
137 Lefty Grove	600.00	1200.00
138 Wes Ferrell	200.00	400.00
139 Buck Newsom	200.00	400.00
140 Rogers Hornsby	1000.00	2000.00

1965 O-Pee-Chee

The cards in this 283-card set measure the standard size. This set is essentially the same as the regular 1965 Topps set, except that the words "Printed in Canada" appear on the bottom of the back. On a white border, the fronts feature color player photos with rounded corners. The team name appears within a pennant design below the photo. The player's name and position are also printed on the front. On a blue background, the horizontal backs carry player biography and statistics on a gray card stock. Remember the prices below apply only to the O-Pee-Chee cards -- NOT to the 1965 Topps cards which are much more plentiful. Notable Rookie Cards include Bert Campaneris, Denny McLain, Joe Morgan and Luis Tiant.

COMPLETE SET (283)	1250.00	2500.00
COMMON PLAYER (1-198)	1.50	4.00
COMMON PLAYER (199-283)	2.50	6.00
1 Oliva	12.50	30.00
Howard		
Brooks LL !		
2 Clemente	15.00	40.00

Card	Low	High
Aaron		
Carty LL		
3 Kill	40.00	80.00
Mantle		
Powell LL		
4 Mays	10.00	25.00
Will		
Cepeda		
LL		
5 Brooks	30.00	60.00
Kill		
Mantle		
LL		
6 Boyer	8.00	20.00
Mays		
Santo LL		
7 Dean Chance	4.00	10.00
Joel Horlen LL		
8 Koufax	12.50	30.00
Drysdale LL		
9 AL Pitching Leaders	4.00	10.00
Dean Chance		
Gary Peters		
Dav		
10 NL Pitching Leaders	4.00	10.00
Larry Jackson		
Ray Sadecki		
J		
11 AL Strikeout Leaders	4.00	10.00
Al Downing		
Dean Chance		
Cam		
12 Veale	4.00	10.00
Drysdale		
Gibson LL		
13 Pedro Ramos	2.50	6.00
14 Len Gabrielson	1.50	4.00
15 Robin Roberts	6.00	15.00
16 Joe Morgan RC DP !	50.00	100.00
17 John Romano	1.50	4.00
18 Bill McCool	1.50	4.00
19 Gates Brown	2.50	6.00
20 Jim Bunning	6.00	15.00
21 Don Blasingame	1.50	4.00
22 Charlie Smith	1.50	4.00
23 Bob Tiefenauer	1.50	4.00
24 Twins Team	4.00	10.00
25 Al McBean	1.50	4.00
26 Bob Knoop	1.50	4.00
27 Dick Bertell	1.50	4.00
28 Barney Schultz	1.50	4.00
29 Felix Mantilla	1.50	4.00
30 Jim Bouton	4.00	10.00
31 Mike White	1.50	4.00
32 Herman Franks MG	1.50	4.00
33 Jackie Brandt	1.50	4.00
34 Cal Koonce	1.50	4.00
35 Ed Charles	1.50	4.00
36 Bob Wine	1.50	4.00
37 Fred Gladding	1.50	4.00
38 Jim King	1.50	4.00
39 Gerry Arrigo	1.50	4.00
40 Frank Howard	3.00	8.00
41 Bruce Howard	1.50	4.00
Marv Staehle		
42 Earl Wilson	2.50	6.00
43 Mike Shannon	2.50	6.00
44 Wade Blasingame	2.50	6.00
45 Roy McMillan	2.50	6.00
46 Bob Lee	1.50	4.00
47 Tommy Harper	2.50	6.00
48 Claude Raymond	2.50	6.00
49 Curt Blefary RC	2.50	6.00
50 Juan Marichal	6.00	15.00
51 Bill Bryan	1.50	4.00
52 Ed Roebuck	1.50	4.00
53 Dick McAuliffe	2.50	6.00
54 Joe Gibbon	1.50	4.00
55 Tony Conigliaro	8.00	20.00
56 Ron Kline	1.50	4.00
57 Cardinals Team	4.00	10.00
58 Fred Talbot	1.50	4.00
59 Nate Oliver	1.50	4.00
60 Jim O'Toole	2.50	6.00
61 Chris Cannizzaro	1.50	4.00
62 Jim Kaat UER(Misspelled Katt)	3.00	8.00
63 Ty Cline	1.50	4.00
64 Lou Burdette	2.50	6.00
65 Tony Kubek	6.00	15.00
66 Bill Rigney MG	1.50	4.00
67 Harvey Haddix	2.50	6.00
68 Del Crandall	2.50	6.00
69 Bill Virdon	2.50	6.00
70 Bill Skowron	3.00	8.00
71 John O'Donoghue	1.50	4.00
72 Tony Gonzalez	1.50	4.00
73 Dennis Ribant	1.50	4.00
74 Rico Petrocelli RC	6.00	15.00
75 Deron Johnson	2.50	6.00
76 Sam McDowell	3.00	8.00
77 Doug Camilli	1.50	4.00
78 Dal Maxvill	2.50	6.00
79 Checklist 1-88	4.00	10.00
80 Turk Farrell	1.50	4.00
81 Don Buford	2.50	6.00
82 Sandy Alomar RC	3.00	8.00
83 George Thomas	1.50	4.00
84 Ron Herbel	1.50	4.00
85 Willie Smith	1.50	4.00
86 Buster Narum	1.50	4.00
87 Nelson Mathews	1.50	4.00
88 Jack Lamabe	1.50	4.00
89 Mike Hershberger	1.50	4.00
90 Rich Rollins	2.50	6.00
91 Cubs Team	4.00	10.00
92 Dick Howser	2.50	6.00
93 Jack Fisher	1.50	4.00
94 Charlie Lau	2.50	6.00
95 Bill Mazeroski	6.00	15.00
96 Sonny Siebert	2.50	6.00
97 Pedro Gonzalez	1.50	4.00
98 Bob Miller	1.50	4.00
99 Gil Hodges MG	4.00	10.00
100 Ken Boyer	6.00	15.00
101 Fred Newman	1.50	4.00
102 Steve Boros	1.50	4.00
103 Harvey Kuenn	2.50	6.00
104 Checklist 89-176	4.00	10.00
105 Chico Salmon	1.50	4.00
106 Gene Oliver	1.50	4.00
107 Pat Corrales RC	2.50	6.00
108 Don Mincher	1.50	4.00
109 Walt Bond	1.50	4.00
110 Ron Santo	3.00	8.00
111 Lee Thomas	2.50	6.00
112 Derrell Griffith	1.50	4.00
113 Steve Barber	1.50	4.00
114 Jim Hickman	2.50	6.00
115 Bobby Richardson	6.00	15.00
116 Bob Tolan RC	2.50	6.00
117 Wes Stock	1.50	4.00
118 Hal Lanier	2.50	6.00
119 John Kennedy	1.50	4.00
120 Frank Robinson	30.00	60.00
121 Gene Alley	2.50	6.00
122 Bill Pleis	1.50	4.00
123 Frank Thomas	2.50	6.00
124 Tom Satriano	1.50	4.00
125 Juan Pizarro	1.50	4.00
126 Dodgers Team	4.00	10.00
127 Frank Lary	1.50	4.00
128 Vic Davalillo	1.50	4.00
129 Bennie Daniels	1.50	4.00
130 Al Kaline	30.00	60.00
131 Johnny Keane MG	1.50	4.00
132 World Series Game 1	4.00	10.00
Cards take opener/(Mike Shan		
133 Mel Stottlemyre WS	4.00	10.00
134 Mickey Mantle WS3	60.00	120.00
135 Ken Boyer WS	6.00	15.00
136 Tim McCarver WS	4.00	10.00
137 Jim Bouton WS	4.00	10.00
138 Bob Gibson WS7	8.00	20.00
139 World Series Summary	4.00	10.00
Cards celebrate		
140 Dean Chance	2.50	6.00
141 Charlie James	1.50	4.00
142 Bill Monbouquette	1.50	4.00
143 John Gelnar	1.50	4.00
Jerry May		
144 Ed Kranepool	2.50	6.00
145 Luis Tiant RC	8.00	20.00
146 Ron Hansen	1.50	4.00
147 Dennis Bennett	1.50	4.00
148 Willie Kirkland	1.50	4.00
149 Wayne Schurr	1.50	4.00
150 Brooks Robinson	30.00	60.00
151 Athletics Team	4.00	10.00
152 Phil Ortega	1.50	4.00
153 Norm Cash	4.00	10.00
154 Bob Humphreys	1.50	4.00
155 Roger Maris	50.00	100.00
156 Bob Sadowski	1.50	4.00
157 Zoilo Versalles	2.50	6.00
158 Dick Sisler MG	1.50	4.00
159 Jim Duffalo	1.50	4.00
160 Roberto Clemente !	125.00	250.00
161 Frank Baumann	1.50	4.00
162 Russ Nixon	1.50	4.00
163 John Briggs	1.50	4.00
164 Al Spangler	1.50	4.00
165 Dick Ellsworth	1.50	4.00
166 Tommie Agee RC	3.00	8.00
167 Bill Wakefield	1.50	4.00
168 Dick Green	2.50	6.00
169 Dave Vineyard	1.50	4.00
170 Hank Aaron	100.00	200.00
171 Jim Roland	1.50	4.00
172 Jim Piersall	3.00	8.00
173 Tigers Team	4.00	10.00
174 Joe Jay	1.50	4.00
175 Bob Aspromonte	1.50	4.00
176 Willie McCovey	12.50	30.00
177 Pete Mikkelsen	1.50	4.00
178 Dalton Jones	1.50	4.00
179 Hal Woodeshick	1.50	4.00
180 Bob Allison	2.50	6.00
181 Don Loun	1.50	4.00
Joe McCabe		
182 Mike de la Hoz	1.50	4.00
183 Dave Nicholson	1.50	4.00
184 John Boozer	1.50	4.00
185 Max Alvis	1.50	4.00
186 Bill Cowan	1.50	4.00
187 Casey Stengel MG	10.00	25.00
188 Sam Bowens	1.50	4.00
189 Checklist 177-264	4.00	10.00
190 Bill White	3.00	8.00
191 Phil Regan	2.50	6.00
192 Jim Coker	1.50	4.00
193 Gaylord Perry	10.00	25.00
194 Bill Kelso	2.50	6.00
Rick Reichardt		
195 Bob Veale	2.50	6.00
196 Ron Fairly	2.50	6.00
197 Diego Segui	1.50	4.00
198 Smoky Burgess	2.50	6.00
199 Bob Heffner	2.50	6.00
200 Joe Torre	4.00	10.00
201 Cesar Tovar RC	2.50	6.00
202 Leo Burke	2.50	6.00
203 Dallas Green	2.50	6.00
204 Russ Snyder	2.50	6.00
205 Warren Spahn	20.00	50.00
206 Willie Horton	4.00	10.00
207 Pete Rose	125.00	250.00
208 Tommy John	4.00	10.00
209 Pirates Team	4.00	10.00
210 Jim Fregosi	3.00	8.00
211 Steve Ridzik	2.50	6.00
212 Ron Brand	2.50	6.00
213 Jim Davenport	2.50	6.00
214 Bob Purkey	2.50	6.00
215 Pete Ward	2.50	6.00
216 Al Worthington	2.50	6.00
217 Walt Alston MG	4.00	10.00
218 Dick Schofield	2.50	6.00
219 Bob Meyer	2.50	6.00
220 Billy Williams	6.00	15.00
221 John Tsitouris	2.50	6.00
222 Bob Tillman	2.50	6.00
223 Dan Osinski	2.50	6.00
224 Bob Chance	2.50	6.00
225 Bo Belinsky	3.00	8.00
226 Elvio Jimenez	3.00	8.00
Jake Gibbs		
227 Bobby Klaus	2.50	6.00
228 Jack Sanford	2.50	6.00
229 Lou Clinton	2.50	6.00
230 Ray Sadecki	2.50	6.00
231 Jerry Adair	2.50	6.00
232 Steve Blass	2.50	6.00
233 Don Zimmer	3.00	8.00
234 White Sox Team	4.00	10.00
235 Chuck Hinton	2.50	6.00
236 Denny McLain RC	15.00	40.00
237 Bernie Allen	2.50	6.00
238 Joe Moeller	2.50	6.00
239 Doc Edwards	2.50	6.00
240 Bob Bruce	2.50	6.00
241 Mack Jones	2.50	6.00
242 George Brunet	2.50	6.00
243 Tommy Helms RC	3.00	8.00
244 Lindy McDaniel	3.00	8.00
245 Joe Pepitone	3.00	8.00
246 Tom Butters	3.00	8.00
247 Wally Moon	3.00	8.00
248 Gus Triandos	2.50	6.00
249 Dave McNally	3.00	8.00
250 Willie Mays	100.00	200.00
251 Billy Herman MG	3.00	8.00
252 Pete Richert	2.50	6.00
253 Danny Cater	2.50	6.00
254 Roland Sheldon	2.50	6.00
255 Camilo Pascual	3.00	8.00
256 Tito Francona	2.50	6.00
257 Jim Wynn	3.00	8.00
258 Larry Bearnarth	2.50	6.00
259 Jim Northrup RC	4.00	10.00
260 Don Drysdale	12.50	30.00
261 Duke Carmel	2.50	6.00
262 Bud Daley	2.50	6.00
263 Marty Keough	2.50	6.00
264 Bob Buhl	2.50	6.00
265 Jim Pagliaroni	2.50	6.00
266 Bert Campaneris RC	5.00	12.00
267 Senators Team	4.00	10.00
268 Ken McBride	2.50	6.00
269 Frank Bolling	2.50	6.00
270 Milt Pappas	2.50	6.00
271 Don Wert	2.50	6.00
272 Chuck Schilling	2.50	6.00
273 4th Series Checklist	5.00	12.00
274 Lum Harris MG	2.50	6.00
275 Dick Groat	4.00	10.00
276 Hoyt Wilhelm	6.00	15.00
277 Johnny Lewis	2.50	6.00
278 Ken Retzer	2.50	6.00
279 Dick Tracewski	2.50	6.00
280 Dick Stuart	3.00	8.00
281 Bill Stafford	2.50	6.00
282 Masanori Murakami RC	30.00	60.00
283 Fred Whitfield	3.00	8.00

1966 O-Pee-Chee

The cards in this 196-card set measure 2 1/2" by 3 1/2". This set is essentially the same as the regular 1966 Topps set, except that the words "Printed in Canada" appear on the bottom of the back, and the background colors are slightly different. On a white border, the fronts feature color player photos. The team name appears within a tilted bar in the top right corner, while the player's name and position are printed inside a bar under the photo. The horizontal backs carry player biography and statistics. The set was issued in five-card nickel packs which came 36 to a box. Remember the prices below apply only to the O-Pee-Chee cards -- NOT to the 1966 Topps cards which are much more plentiful. Notable Rookie Cards include Jim Palmer.

Card	Low	High
COMPLETE SET (196)	750.00	1500.00
1 Willie Mays	200.00	400.00
2 Ted Abernathy	1.25	3.00
3 Sam Mele MG	1.25	3.00
4 Ray Culp	1.25	3.00
5 Jim Fregosi	1.50	4.00
6 Chuck Schilling	1.25	3.00
7 Tracy Stallard	1.25	3.00
8 Floyd Robinson	1.25	3.00
9 Clete Boyer	1.50	4.00
10 Tony Cloninger	1.25	3.00
11 Brant Alyea	1.50	4.00
Pete Craig		
12 John Tsitouris	1.25	3.00
13 Lou Johnson	1.50	4.00
14 Norm Siebern	1.25	3.00
15 Vern Law	1.50	4.00
16 Larry Brown	1.25	3.00
17 John Stephenson	1.25	3.00
18 Roland Sheldon	1.25	3.00
19 Giants Team	2.50	6.00
20 Willie Horton	1.50	4.00
21 Don Nottebart	1.25	3.00
22 Joe Nossek	1.25	3.00
23 Jack Sanford	1.25	3.00
24 Don Kessinger RC	2.50	6.00
25 Pete Ward	1.50	4.00
26 Ray Sadecki	1.25	3.00
27 Darold Knowles	1.25	3.00
Andy Etchebarren		
28 Phil Niekro	12.50	30.00
29 Mike Brumley	1.25	3.00
30 Pete Rose	75.00	150.00
31 Jack Cullen	1.50	4.00
32 Adolfo Phillips	1.25	3.00
33 Jim Pagliaroni	1.25	3.00
34 Checklist 1-88	5.00	12.00
35 Ron Swoboda	2.50	6.00
36 Jim Hunter	12.50	30.00
37 Billy Herman MG	1.50	4.00
38 Ron Nischwitz	1.25	3.00
39 Ken Henderson	1.25	3.00
40 Jim Grant	1.25	3.00
41 Don LeJohn	1.25	3.00
42 Aubrey Gatewood	1.25	3.00
43 Don Landrum	1.25	3.00
44 Bill Davis	1.25	3.00
Tom Kelley		
45 Jim Gentile	1.50	4.00
46 Howie Koplitz	1.25	3.00
47 J.C. Martin	1.25	3.00
48 Paul Blair	1.50	4.00
49 Woody Woodward	1.25	3.00
50 Mickey Mantle	250.00	500.00
51 Gordon Richardson	1.25	3.00
52 Wes Covington	2.50	6.00
Johnny Callison		
53 Bob Duliba	1.25	3.00
54 Jose Pagan	1.25	3.00
55 Ken Harrelson	1.50	4.00
56 Sandy Valdespino	1.25	3.00
57 Jim Lefebvre	1.50	4.00
58 Dave Wickersham	1.25	3.00
59 Reds Team	2.50	6.00
60 Curt Flood	3.00	8.00
61 Bob Bolin	1.25	3.00
62 Merritt Ranew/(with sold line)	1.25	3.00
63 Jim Stewart	1.25	3.00
64 Bob Bruce	1.25	3.00
65 Leon Wagner	1.25	3.00
66 Al Weis	1.25	3.00
67 Cleon Jones	2.50	6.00
Dick Selma		
68 Hal Reniff	1.25	3.00
69 Ken Hamlin	1.25	3.00
70 Carl Yastrzemski	20.00	50.00
71 Frank Carpin	1.25	3.00
72 Tony Perez	15.00	40.00
73 Jerry Zimmerman	1.25	3.00
74 Don Mossi	1.50	4.00
75 Tommy Davis	1.50	4.00
76 Red Schoendienst MG	2.50	6.00
77 Johnny Orsino	1.25	3.00
78 Frank Linzy	1.25	3.00
79 Joe Pepitone	2.50	6.00
80 Richie Allen	3.00	8.00
81 Ray Oyler	1.25	3.00
82 Bob Hendley	1.25	3.00
83 Albie Pearson	1.50	4.00
84 Jim Beauchamp	1.25	3.00
Dick Kelley		
85 Eddie Fisher	1.25	3.00
86 John Bateman	1.25	3.00
87 Dan Napoleon	1.25	3.00
88 Fred Whitfield	1.25	3.00
89 Ted Davidson	1.25	3.00
90 Luis Aparicio	5.00	12.00
91 Bob Uecker/(with traded line)	6.00	15.00
92 Yankees Team	10.00	25.00
93 Jim Lonborg	1.50	4.00
94 Matty Alou	1.50	4.00
95 Pete Richert	1.25	3.00
96 Felipe Alou	2.50	6.00
97 Jim Merritt	1.25	3.00
98 Don Demeter	1.25	3.00
99 W.Stargell	3.00	8.00
Clendenon		
100 Sandy Koufax	75.00	150.00
101 Checklist 89-176	5.00	12.00
102 Ed Kirkpatrick	1.25	3.00
103 Dick Groat/(with traded line)	1.50	4.00
104 Alex Johnson/(with traded line)	1.50	4.00
105 Milt Pappas	1.50	4.00
106 Rusty Staub	2.50	6.00
107 Larry Stahl	1.25	3.00
Ron Tompkins		
108 Bobby Klaus	1.25	3.00
109 Ralph Terry	1.50	4.00
110 Ernie Banks	20.00	50.00
111 Gary Peters	1.25	3.00
112 Manny Mota	1.50	4.00
113 Hank Aguirre	1.25	3.00
114 Jim Gosger	1.25	3.00
115 Bill Henry	1.25	3.00
116 Walt Alston MG	2.50	6.00
117 Jake Gibbs	1.25	3.00
118 Mike McCormick	1.25	3.00
119 Art Shamsky	1.25	3.00
120 Harmon Killebrew	10.00	25.00
121 Ray Herbert	1.25	3.00
122 Joe Gaines	1.25	3.00
123 Frank Bork	1.25	3.00
Jerry May		
124 Tug McGraw	2.50	6.00
125 Lou Brock	12.50	30.00
126 Jim Palmer RC	75.00	150.00
127 Ken Berry	1.25	3.00
128 Jim Landis	1.25	3.00
129 Jack Kralick	1.25	3.00
130 Joe Torre	3.00	8.00
131 Angels Team	3.00	8.00
132 Orlando Cepeda	5.00	12.00
133 Don McMahon	1.25	3.00
134 Wes Parker	1.50	4.00
135 Dave Morehead	1.25	3.00
136 Woody Held	1.25	3.00
137 Pat Corrales	1.25	3.00
138 Roger Repoz	1.25	3.00
139 Byron Browne	1.25	3.00
Don Young		
140 Jim Maloney	1.50	4.00
141 Tom McCraw	1.25	3.00
142 Don Dennis	1.25	3.00
143 Jose Tartabull	1.50	4.00
144 Don Schwall	1.25	3.00
145 Bill Freehan	1.50	4.00
146 George Altman	1.25	3.00
147 Lum Harris MG	1.25	3.00
148 Bob Johnson	1.25	3.00
149 Dick Nen	1.25	3.00
150 Rocky Colavito	5.00	12.00
151 Gary Wagner	1.25	3.00
152 Frank Malzone	1.50	4.00
153 Rico Carty	1.50	4.00
154 Chuck Hiller	1.25	3.00
155 Marcelino Lopez	1.25	3.00
156 Dick Schofield	1.25	3.00
Hal Lanier		
157 Rene Lachemann	1.50	4.00
158 Jim Brewer	1.25	3.00
159 Chico Ruiz	1.25	3.00
160 Whitey Ford	20.00	50.00
161 Jerry Lumpe	1.25	3.00
162 Lee Maye	1.25	3.00
163 Tito Francona	1.25	3.00
164 Tommie Agee	1.50	4.00
Marv Staehle		
165 Don Lock	1.25	3.00
166 Chris Krug	1.25	3.00
167 Boog Powell	3.00	8.00
168 Dan Osinski	1.25	3.00
169 Duke Sims	1.25	3.00
170 Cookie Rojas	1.50	4.00
171 Nick Willhite	1.25	3.00
172 Mets Team	3.00	8.00
173 Al Spangler	1.25	3.00
174 Ron Taylor	1.50	4.00
175 Bert Campaneris	2.50	6.00
176 Jim Davenport	1.25	3.00
177 Hector Lopez	1.25	3.00
178 Bob Tillman	1.25	3.00
179 Dennis Aust	1.50	4.00
Bob Tolan		
180 Vada Pinson	2.50	6.00
181 Al Worthington	1.25	3.00
182 Jerry Lynch	1.25	3.00
183 Checklist 177-264	5.00	12.00
184 Denis Menke	1.25	3.00
185 Bob Buhl	1.50	4.00
186 Ruben Amaro	1.25	3.00
187 Chuck Dressen MG	1.50	4.00
188 Al Luplow	1.25	3.00
189 John Roseboro	1.50	4.00
190 Jimmie Hall	1.25	3.00
191 Darrell Sutherland	1.25	3.00
192 Vic Power	1.50	4.00
193 Dave McNally	1.50	4.00
194 Senators Team	3.00	8.00
195 Joe Morgan	10.00	25.00
196 Don Pavletich	1.50	4.00

1967 O-Pee-Chee

The cards in this 196-card set measure 2 1/2" by 3 1/2". This set is essentially the same as the regular 1967 Topps set, except that the words "Printed in Canada" appear on the bottom right corner of the back. On a white border, fronts feature color player photos with a thin black border. The player's name and position appear in the top part, while the team name is printed in big letters in the bottom part of the photo. On a green background, the backs carry player biography and statistics and two cartoon-like facts. Each checklist card features a small circular picture of a popular player included in that series. The set was issued in five card nickel packs which came 36 packs to a box. Remember the prices below apply only to the O-Pee-Chee cards -- NOT to the 1967 Topps cards which are much more plentiful.

Card	Low	High
COMPLETE SET (196)	600.00	1200.00
1 The Champs	12.50	30.00
Frank Robinson		
Hank Bauer		
Brooks Rob		
2 Jack Hamilton	1.25	3.00
3 Duke Sims	1.25	3.00
4 Hal Lanier	1.25	3.00
5 Whitey Ford	10.00	25.00
6 Dick Simpson	1.25	3.00
7 Don McMahon	1.25	3.00
8 Chuck Harrison	1.25	3.00
9 Ron Hansen	1.25	3.00
10 Matty Alou	1.50	4.00
11 Barry Moore	1.25	3.00
12 Jim Campanis	1.50	4.00
Bill Singer		
13 Joe Sparma	1.25	3.00
14 Phil Linz	1.50	4.00
15 Earl Battey	1.25	3.00
16 Bill Hands	1.25	3.00
17 Jim Gosger	1.25	3.00
18 Gene Oliver	1.25	3.00
19 Jim McGlothlin	1.25	3.00
20 Orlando Cepeda	4.00	10.00
21 Dave Bristol MG	1.25	3.00
22 Gene Brabender	1.25	3.00
23 Larry Elliot	1.25	3.00
24 Bob Allen	1.25	3.00
25 Elston Howard	2.50	6.00
26 Bob Priddy/(with traded line)	1.25	3.00
27 Bob Saverine	1.25	3.00
28 Barry Latman	1.25	3.00
29 Tommy McCraw	1.25	3.00
30 Al Kaline	10.00	25.00
31 Jim Brewer	1.25	3.00
32 Bob Bailey	1.50	4.00
33 Sal Bando RC	3.00	8.00
34 Pete Cimino	1.25	3.00
35 Rico Carty	1.50	4.00
36 Bob Tillman	1.25	3.00
37 Rick Wise	1.50	4.00
38 Bob Johnson	1.25	3.00
39 Curt Simmons	1.50	4.00
40 Rick Reichardt	1.25	3.00
41 Joe Hoerner	1.25	3.00
42 Mets Team	5.00	12.00
43 Chico Salmon	1.25	3.00
44 Joe Nuxhall	1.50	4.00
45 Roger Maris	30.00	60.00
46 Lindy McDaniel	1.50	4.00
47 Ken McMullen	1.25	3.00
48 Bill Freehan	1.50	4.00
49 Roy Face	1.50	4.00
50 Tony Oliva	3.00	8.00
51 Dave Adlesh	1.25	3.00
Wes Bales		
52 Dennis Higgins	1.25	3.00
53 Clay Dalrymple	1.25	3.00
54 Dick Green	1.25	3.00
55 Don Drysdale	8.00	20.00
56 Jose Tartabull	1.50	4.00
57 Pat Jarvis	1.50	4.00
58 Paul Schaal	1.25	3.00
59 Ralph Terry	1.50	4.00
60 Luis Aparicio	4.00	10.00
61 Gordy Coleman	1.25	3.00
62 Checklist 1-109	5.00	12.00
Frank Robinson		
63 Lou Brock	3.00	8.00
Curt Flood		
64 Fred Valentine	1.25	3.00
65 Tom Haller	1.50	4.00
66 Manny Mota	1.50	4.00
67 Ken Berry	1.25	3.00
68 Bob Buhl	1.50	4.00
69 Vic Davalillo	1.50	4.00
70 Ron Santo	3.00	8.00
71 Camilo Pascual	1.50	4.00
72 Tigers Rookies	1.50	4.00
George Korince/(photo actually		
J		
73 Rusty Staub	3.00	8.00
74 Wes Stock	1.25	3.00
75 George Scott	1.50	4.00
76 Jim Barbieri	1.25	3.00
77 Dooley Womack	1.25	3.00
78 Pat Corrales	1.25	3.00
79 Bubba Morton	1.25	3.00
80 Jim Maloney	1.25	3.00
81 Eddie Stanky MG	1.50	4.00
82 Steve Barber	1.25	3.00
83 Ollie Brown	1.25	3.00
84 Tommie Sisk	1.25	3.00
85 Johnny Callison	1.50	4.00
86 Mike McCormick/(with traded line)	1.50	4.00
87 George Altman	1.25	3.00
88 Mickey Lolich	2.50	6.00
89 Felix Millan	1.50	4.00
90 Jim Nash	1.50	4.00
91 Johnny Lewis	1.25	3.00
92 Ray Washburn	1.25	3.00
93 S.Bahnsen RC	2.50	6.00
B.Murcer		
94 Ron Fairly	1.50	4.00
95 Sonny Siebert	1.25	3.00
96 Art Shamsky	1.25	3.00
97 Mike Cuellar	2.50	6.00
98 Rich Rollins	1.25	3.00
99 Lee Stange	1.25	3.00
100 Frank Robinson	8.00	20.00
101 Ken Johnson	1.25	3.00
102 Phillies Team	2.50	6.00
103 Mickey Mantle CL2 DP	10.00	25.00
104 Minnie Rojas	1.25	3.00
105 Ken Boyer	3.00	8.00
106 Randy Hundley	1.50	4.00
107 Joel Horlen	1.25	3.00
108 Alex Johnson	1.50	4.00
109 R.Colavito	3.00	8.00
L.Wagner		
110 Jack Aker	1.25	3.00
111 John Kennedy	1.25	3.00
112 Dave Wickersham	1.25	3.00
113 Dave Nicholson	1.25	3.00
114 Jack Baldschun	1.25	3.00
115 Paul Casanova	1.25	3.00
116 Herman Franks MG	1.25	3.00
117 Darrell Brandon	1.25	3.00
118 Bernie Allen	1.25	3.00
119 Wade Blasingame	1.25	3.00
120 Floyd Robinson	1.25	3.00
121 Ed Bressoud	1.25	3.00
122 George Brunet	1.25	3.00
123 Jim Price	1.50	4.00
Luke Walker		
124 Jim Stewart	1.25	3.00
125 Moe Drabowsky	1.50	4.00
126 Tony Taylor	1.25	3.00
127 John O'Donoghue	1.25	3.00
128 Ed Spiezio	1.25	3.00
129 Phil Roof	1.25	3.00
130 Phil Regan	1.50	4.00
131 Yankees Team	5.00	12.00
132 Ozzie Virgil	1.25	3.00
133 Ron Kline	1.25	3.00
134 Gates Brown	1.25	3.00
135 Deron Johnson	1.50	4.00
136 Carroll Sembera	1.25	3.00
137 Ron Clark RC	1.25	3.00
Jim Ollom RC		
138 Dick Kelley	1.25	3.00
139 Dalton Jones	1.25	3.00
140 Willie Stargell	10.00	25.00
141 John Miller	1.25	3.00
142 Jackie Brandt	1.25	3.00
143 Pete Ward	2.50	6.00
Don Buford		
144 Bill Hepler	1.25	3.00
145 Larry Brown	1.25	3.00
146 Steve Carlton	30.00	60.00
147 Tom Egan	1.25	3.00
148 Adolfo Phillips	1.25	3.00
149 Joe Moeller	1.25	3.00
150 Mickey Mantle	200.00	400.00
151 World Series Game 1	2.50	6.00
Moe mows down 11/(Moe Drabow		
152 Jim Palmer WS2	4.00	10.00
153 World Series Game 3	2.50	6.00
Paul Blair's homer		
defeats L		
154 World Series Game 4	2.50	6.00
Orioles four straight/(Brook		
155 World Series Summary	2.50	6.00
Winners celebrate		
156 Ron Herbel	1.25	3.00
157 Danny Cater	1.25	3.00
158 Jimmie Coker	1.25	3.00
159 Bruce Howard	1.25	3.00
160 Willie Davis	1.50	4.00
161 Dick Williams MG	1.50	4.00
162 Billy O'Dell	1.25	3.00
163 Vic Roznovsky	1.25	3.00
164 Dwight Siebler	1.25	3.00
165 Cleon Jones	1.50	4.00
166 Eddie Mathews	8.00	20.00
167 Joe Coleman	1.25	3.00
Tim Cullen		
168 Ray Culp	1.25	3.00
169 Horace Clarke	1.25	3.00
170 Dick McAuliffe	1.50	4.00
171 Calvin Koonce	1.25	3.00
172 Bill Heath	1.25	3.00
173 Cardinals Team	2.50	6.00
174 Dick Radatz	1.50	4.00
175 Bobby Knoop	1.25	3.00
176 Sammy Ellis	1.25	3.00
177 Tito Fuentes	1.25	3.00
178 John Buzhardt	1.25	3.00
179 Charles Vaughan	1.50	4.00
Cecil Upshaw		
180 Curt Blefary	1.25	3.00
181 Terry Fox	1.25	3.00
182 Ed Charles	1.25	3.00
183 Jim Pagliaroni	1.25	3.00
184 George Thomas	1.25	3.00
185 Ken Holtzman RC	2.50	6.00
186 Ed Kranepool	2.50	6.00
Ron Swoboda		
187 Pedro Ramos	1.25	3.00
188 Ken Harrelson	1.50	4.00
189 Chuck Hinton	1.25	3.00
190 Turk Farrell	1.25	3.00
191 Checklist 197-283/(Willie Mays)	6.00	15.00
192 Fred Gladding	1.25	3.00
193 Jose Cardenal	1.50	4.00
194 Bob Allison	1.50	4.00
195 Al Jackson	1.25	3.00
196 Johnny Romano	1.50	4.00

1967 O-Pee-Chee Paper Inserts

Card	Low	High
COMPLETE SET (32)	175.00	350.00
1 Boog Powell	2.00	5.00
2 Bert Campaneris	1.25	3.00
3 Brooks Robinson	8.00	20.00
4 Tommie Agee	1.00	2.50
5 Carl Yastrzemski	10.00	25.00
6 Mickey Mantle	50.00	100.00
7 Frank Howard	1.50	4.00
8 Sam McDowell	1.25	3.00
9 Orlando Cepeda	3.00	8.00
10 Chico Cardenas	1.00	2.50
11 Bob Clemente	75.00	150.00
12 Willie Mays	15.00	40.00
13 Cleon Jones	1.00	2.50
14 John Callison	1.00	2.50
15 Hank Aaron	12.50	30.00
16 Don Drysdale	6.00	15.00
17 Bobby Knoop	1.00	2.50
18 Tony Oliva	2.00	5.00
19 Frank Robinson	6.00	15.00
20 Denny McLain	2.00	5.00
21 Al Kaline	10.00	25.00
22 Joe Pepitone	1.25	3.00
23 Harmon Killebrew	8.00	20.00
24 Leon Wagner	1.00	2.50
25 Joe Morgan	6.00	15.00
26 Ron Santo	2.00	5.00
27 Joe Torre	2.00	5.00
28 Juan Marichal	5.00	12.00
29 Matty Alou	1.25	3.00
30 Felipe Alou	1.50	4.00
31 Ron Hunt	1.00	2.50
32 Willie McCovey	6.00	15.00

1968 O-Pee-Chee

The cards in this 196-card set measure 2 1/2" by 3 1/2". This set is essentially the same as the regular 1968 Topps set, except that the words "Printed in Canada" appear on the bottom of the back and the backgrounds have a different color. The fronts feature color player photos with rounded corners. The player's name is printed under the photo, while his position and team name appear in a circle in the lower right. On a light brown background, the backs carry player biography and statistics and a cartoon-like trivia question. Each checklist card features a small circular picture of a popular player included in that series. Remember the prices below apply only to the O-Pee-Chee cards -- NOT to the 1968 Topps cards which are much more plentiful. The key card in the set is Nolan Ryan in his Rookie Card year. The first OPC cards of Hall of Famers Rod Carew and Tom Seaver also appear in this set.

Card	Low	High
COMPLETE SET (196)	1000.00	2000.00
1 Clemente	15.00	40.00
Gon		
M.Alou LL !		
2 Yaz	8.00	20.00
F.Rob		
Kaline LL		
3 Cepeda	10.00	25.00
Clemente		
Aar LL		
4 Yaz	8.00	20.00
Killebrew		
F.Rob LL		
5 Aaron	4.00	10.00
Santo		
McCovey LL		
6 Yaz	4.00	10.00
Killebrew		
Howard LL		
7 NL ERA Leaders	2.50	6.00
Phil Niekro		
Jim Bunning		
Chris Sh		
8 AL ERA Leaders	2.50	6.00
Joel Horlen		
Gary Peters		
Sonny Si		
9 McCorm	2.50	6.00
Jenk		
Bunn		
Ost LL		
10 AL Pitching Leaders	2.50	6.00
Jim Lonborg		
Earl Wilson		
Dea		
11 Bunning	3.00	8.00
Jenkins		
Perry LL		
12 AL Strikeout Leaders	2.50	6.00
Jim Lonborg		
Sam McDowell		
D		
13 Chuck Hartenstein	1.25	3.00
14 Jerry McNertney	1.25	3.00
15 Ron Hunt	1.25	3.00
16 Lou Piniella	3.00	8.00
17 Dick Hall	1.25	3.00
18 Mike Hershberger	1.25	3.00
19 Juan Pizarro	1.25	3.00
20 Brooks Robinson	12.50	30.00
21 Ron Davis	1.25	3.00
22 Pat Dobson	1.50	4.00
23 Chico Cardenas	1.50	4.00
24 Bobby Locke	1.25	3.00
25 Julian Javier	1.50	4.00
26 Darrell Brandon	1.25	3.00
27 Gil Hodges MG	4.00	10.00
28 Ted Uhlaender	1.25	3.00
29 Joe Verbanic	1.25	3.00
30 Joe Torre	3.00	8.00
31 Ed Stroud	1.25	3.00
32 Joe Gibbon	1.25	3.00
33 Pete Ward	1.50	4.00
34 Al Ferrara	1.25	3.00
35 Steve Hargan	1.25	3.00
36 Bob Moose	1.50	4.00
Bob Robertson		
37 Billy Williams	4.00	10.00
38 Tony Pierce	1.25	3.00
39 Cookie Rojas	1.25	3.00
40 Denny McLain	4.00	10.00
41 Julio Gotay	1.25	3.00

42 Larry Haney 1.25 3.00
43 Gary Bell 1.25 3.00
44 Frank Kostro 1.25 3.00
45 Tom Seaver 30.00 60.00
46 Dave Ricketts 1.25 3.00
47 Ralph Houk MG 1.50 4.00
48 Ted Davidson 1.25 3.00
49 Ed Brinkman 1.25 3.00
50 Willie Mays 40.00 80.00
51 Bob Locker 1.25 3.00
52 Hawk Taylor 1.25 3.00
53 Gene Alley 1.50 4.00
54 Stan Williams 1.25 3.00
55 Felipe Alou 2.50 6.00
56 Dave May RC 1.25 3.00
57 Dan Schneider 1.25 3.00
58 Eddie Mathews 8.00 20.00
59 Don Lock 1.25 3.00
60 Ken Holtzman 1.50 4.00
61 Reggie Smith 2.50 6.00
62 Chuck Dobson 1.25 3.00
63 Dick Kenworthy 1.25 3.00
64 Jim Merritt 1.25 3.00
65 John Roseboro 1.50 4.00
66 Casey Cox 1.25 3.00
67 Checklist 1-109 3.00 8.00
Jim Kaat
68 Ron Willis 1.25 3.00
69 Tom Tresh 1.50 4.00
70 Bob Veale 1.50 4.00
71 Vern Fuller 1.25 3.00
72 Tommy John 3.00 8.00
73 Jim Ray Hart 1.50 4.00
74 Milt Pappas 1.50 4.00
75 Don Mincher 1.25 3.00
76 Jim Britton 1.50 4.00
Ron Reed
77 Don Wilson 1.50 4.00
78 Jim Northrup 3.00 8.00
79 Ted Kubiak 1.25 3.00
80 Rod Carew 30.00 60.00
81 Larry Jackson 1.25 3.00
82 Sam Bowens 1.25 3.00
83 John Stephenson 1.25 3.00
84 Bob Tolan 1.25 3.00
85 Gaylord Perry 4.00 10.00
86 Willie Stargell 4.00 10.00
87 Dick Williams MG 1.50 4.00
88 Phil Regan 1.50 4.00
89 Jake Gibbs 1.50 4.00
90 Vada Pinson 2.50 6.00
91 Jim Ollom 1.25 3.00
92 Ed Kranepool 1.50 4.00
93 Tony Cloninger 1.25 3.00
94 Lee Maye 1.25 3.00
95 Bob Aspromonte 1.25 3.00
96 Frank Coggins 1.25 3.00
Dick Nold
97 Tom Phoebus 1.25 3.00
98 Gary Sutherland 1.25 3.00
99 Rocky Colavito 4.00 10.00
100 Bob Gibson 12.50 30.00
101 Glenn Beckert 1.50 4.00
102 Jose Cardenal 1.50 4.00
103 Don Sutton 4.00 10.00
104 Dick Dietz 1.25 3.00
105 Al Downing 1.50 4.00
106 Dalton Jones 1.25 3.00
107 Checklist 110-196 3.00 8.00
Juan Marichal
108 Don Pavletich 1.25 3.00
109 Bert Campaneris 1.50 4.00
110 Hank Aaron 40.00 80.00
111 Rich Reese 1.25 3.00
112 Woody Fryman 1.25 3.00
113 Tom Matchick 1.50 4.00
Daryl Patterson
114 Ron Swoboda 1.50 4.00
115 Sam McDowell 1.50 4.00
116 Ken McMullen 1.25 3.00
117 Larry Jaster 1.25 3.00
118 Mark Belanger 1.50 4.00
119 Ted Savage 1.25 3.00
120 Mel Stottlemyre 2.50 6.00
121 Jimmie Hall 1.25 3.00
122 Gene Mauch MG 1.50 4.00
123 Jose Santiago 1.25 3.00
124 Nate Oliver 1.25 3.00
125 Joel Horlen 1.25 3.00
126 Bobby Etheridge 1.25 3.00
127 Paul Lindblad 1.25 3.00
128 Tom Dukes 1.25 3.00
Alonzo Harris
129 Mickey Stanley 3.00 8.00
130 Tony Perez 4.00 10.00
131 Frank Bertaina 1.25 3.00
132 Bud Harrelson 1.50 4.00
133 Fred Whitfield 1.25 3.00
134 Pat Jarvis 1.25 3.00
135 Paul Blair 1.50 4.00
136 Randy Hundley 1.50 4.00
137 Twins Team 2.50 6.00
138 Ruben Amaro 1.25 3.00
139 Chris Short 1.25 3.00
140 Tony Conigliaro 4.00 10.00
141 Dal Maxvill 1.25 3.00
142 Buddy Bradford 1.25 3.00
Bill Voss
143 Pete Cimino 1.25 3.00
144 Joe Morgan 6.00 15.00
145 Don Drysdale 6.00 15.00
146 Sal Bando 1.50 4.00
147 Frank Linzy 1.25 3.00
148 Dave Bristol MG 1.25 3.00
149 Bob Saverine 1.25 3.00
150 Roberto Clemente 50.00 100.00
151 Lou Brock WS1 5.00 12.00
152 Carl Yastrzemski WS2 5.00 12.00
153 Nellie Briles WS 2.50 6.00
154 Bob Gibson WS4 5.00 12.00
155 Jim Lonborg WS 2.50 6.00
156 Rico Petrocelli WS 2.50 6.00
157 World Series Game 7 2.50 6.00
St. Louis wins it
158 World Series Summary 2.50 6.00
Cardinals celebrate
159 Don Kessinger 1.50 4.00
160 Earl Wilson 1.50 4.00
161 Norm Miller 1.25 3.00
162 Hal Gibson 1.50 4.00
Mike Torrez
163 Gene Brabender 1.25 3.00
164 Ramon Webster 1.25 3.00
165 Tony Oliva 3.00 8.00
166 Claude Raymond 1.50 4.00
167 Elston Howard 3.00 8.00
168 Dodgers Team 2.50 6.00
169 Bob Bolin 1.25 3.00
170 Jim Fregosi 1.50 4.00
171 Don Nottebart 1.25 3.00
172 Walt Williams 1.25 3.00
173 John Boozer 1.25 3.00
174 Bob Tillman 1.25 3.00
175 Maury Wills 3.00 8.00
176 Bob Allen 1.25 3.00
177 N.Ryan 300.00 600.00
J.Koosman RC !
178 Don Wert 1.50 4.00
179 Bill Stoneman 1.25 3.00
180 Curt Flood 2.50 6.00
181 Jerry Zimmerman 1.25 3.00
182 Dave Giusti 1.25 3.00
183 Bob Kennedy MG 1.50 4.00
184 Lou Johnson 1.25 3.00
185 Tom Haller 1.25 3.00
186 Eddie Watt 1.25 3.00
187 Sonny Jackson 1.25 3.00
188 Cap Peterson 1.25 3.00
189 Bill Landis 1.25 3.00
190 Bill White 1.50 4.00
191 Dan Frisella 1.25 3.00
192 Checklist 3 4.00 10.00
Carl Yastrzemski
193 Jack Hamilton 1.25 3.00
194 Don Buford 1.25 3.00
195 Joe Pepitone 1.50 4.00
196 Gary Nolan 1.50 4.00

1969 O-Pee-Chee

The cards in this 218-card set measure 2 1/2" by 3 1/2". This set is essentially the same as the regular 1969 Topps set, except that the words "Printed in Canada" appear on the bottom of the back and the backgrounds have a purple color. The fronts feature color player photos with rounded corners and thin black borders. The player's name and position are printed inside a circle in the top right corner, while the team name appears in the lower part of the photo. On a magenta background, the backs carry player biography and statistics. Each checklist card features a small circular picture of a popular player included in that series. Remember the prices below apply only to the O-Pee-Chee cards -- NOT to the 1969 Topps cards which are much more plentiful. Notable Rookie Cards include Graig Nettles.

COMPLETE SET (218) 500.00 1000.00
1 Yaz 8.00 20.00
Cater
Oliva LL DP!
2 Rose 4.00 10.00
M.Alou
F.Alou LL
3 AL RBI Leaders 2.50 6.00
Ken Harrelson
Frank Howard
Jim N
4 McCov 3.00 8.00
Santo
B.Will LL
5 AL Home Run Leaders 2.50 6.00
Frank Howard
Willie Horton/
6 McCov 3.00 8.00
R.Allen
Banks LL
7 AL ERA Leaders 2.50 6.00
Luis Tiant
Sam McDowell
Dave McN
8 Gibson 3.00 8.00
Bolin
Veale LL
9 AL Pitching Leaders 2.50 6.00
Denny McLain
Dave McNally
L
10 Marich 4.00 10.00
Gibson
Jenk LL
11 AL Strikeout Leaders 3.00 8.00
Sam McDowell
Denny McLain/
12 Gibson 2.50 6.00
Jenkins
LL DP
13 Mickey Stanley 1.50 4.00
14 Al McBean .75 2.00
15 Boog Powell 2.50 6.00
16 Cesar Gutierrez .75 2.00
Rich Robertson
17 Mike Marshall 1.50 4.00
18 Dick Schofield .75 2.00
19 Ken Suarez .75 2.00
20 Ernie Banks 10.00 25.00
21 Jose Santiago .75 2.00
22 Jesus Alou 1.50 4.00
23 Lew Krausse .75 2.00
24 Walt Alston MG 2.50 6.00
25 Roy White 1.50 4.00
26 Clay Carroll 1.50 4.00
27 Bernie Allen .75 2.00
28 Mike Ryan .75 2.00
29 Dave Morehead .75 2.00
30 Bob Allison 1.50 4.00
31 Amos Otis 2.50 6.00
G.Gentry RC
32 Sammy Ellis .75 2.00
33 Wayne Causey .75 2.00
34 Gary Peters .75 2.00
35 Joe Morgan 5.00 12.00
36 Luke Walker .75 2.00
37 Curt Motton .75 2.00
38 Zoilo Versalles 1.50 4.00
39 Dick Hughes .75 2.00
40 Mayo Smith MG .75 2.00
41 Bob Barton .75 2.00
42 Tommy Harper 1.50 4.00
43 Joe Niekro 1.50 4.00
44 Danny Cater .75 2.00
45 Maury Wills 2.50 6.00
46 Fritz Peterson 1.50 4.00
47 Paul Popovich .75 2.00
48 Brant Alyea .75 2.00
49 Steve Jones .75 2.00
Ellie Rodriguez
50 Roberto Clemente/(Bob on card) 40.00 80.00
51 Woody Fryman 1.50 4.00
52 Mike Andrews .75 2.00
53 Sonny Jackson .75 2.00
54 Cisco Carlos .75 2.00
55 Jerry Grote 1.50 4.00
56 Rich Reese .75 2.00
57 Denny McLain CL 3.00 8.00
58 Fred Gladding .75 2.00
59 Jay Johnstone 1.50 4.00
60 Nelson Briles 1.50 4.00
61 Jimmie Hall .75 2.00
62 Chico Salmon .75 2.00
63 Jim Hickman .75 2.00
64 Bill Monbouquette .75 2.00
65 Willie Davis 1.50 4.00
66 Mike Adamson .75 2.00
Merv Rettenmund
67 Bill Stoneman 1.50 4.00
68 Dave Duncan 1.50 4.00
69 Steve Hamilton 1.50 4.00
70 Tommy Helms 1.50 4.00
71 Steve Whitaker 1.50 4.00
72 Ron Taylor 1.50 4.00
73 Johnny Briggs .75 2.00
74 Preston Gomez MG .75 2.00
75 Luis Aparicio 3.00 8.00
76 Norm Miller .75 2.00
77 Ron Perranoski 1.50 4.00
78 Tom Satriano .75 2.00
79 Milt Pappas 1.50 4.00
80 Norm Cash 1.50 4.00
81 Mel Queen .75 2.00
82 Al Oliver RC 4.00 10.00
83 Mike Ferraro 1.50 4.00
84 Bob Humphreys .75 2.00
85 Lou Brock 10.00 25.00
86 Pete Richert .75 2.00
87 Horace Clarke 1.50 4.00
88 Rich Nye .75 2.00
89 Russ Gibson .75 2.00
90 Jerry Koosman 2.50 6.00
91 Al Dark MG 1.50 4.00
92 Jack Billingham 1.50 4.00
93 Joe Foy .75 2.00
94 Hank Aguirre .75 2.00
95 Johnny Bench 30.00 60.00
96 Denver LeMaster .75 2.00
97 Buddy Bradford .75 2.00
98 Dave Giusti .75 2.00
99 Twins Rookies 8.00 20.00
Danny Morris
Graig Nettles
100 Hank Aaron 30.00 60.00
101 Daryl Patterson .75 2.00
102 Jim Davenport .75 2.00
103 Roger Repoz .75 2.00
104 Steve Blass .75 2.00
105 Rick Monday 1.50 4.00
106 Jim Hannan .75 2.00
107 Checklist 110-218 3.00 8.00
Bob Gibson
108 Tony Taylor 1.50 4.00
109 Jim Lonborg 1.50 4.00
110 Mike Shannon 1.50 4.00
111 John Morris .75 2.00
112 J.C. Martin 1.50 4.00
113 Dave May .75 2.00
114 Alan Closter 1.50 4.00
John Cumberland
115 Bill Hands .75 2.00
116 Chuck Harrison .75 2.00
117 Jim Fairey 1.50 4.00
118 Stan Williams .75 2.00
119 Doug Rader 1.50 4.00
120 Pete Rose 30.00 60.00
121 Joe Grzenda .75 2.00
122 Ron Fairly 1.50 4.00
123 Wilbur Wood 1.50 4.00
124 Hank Bauer MG 1.50 4.00
125 Ray Sadecki .75 2.00
126 Dick Tracewski .75 2.00
127 Kevin Collins 1.50 4.00
128 Tommie Aaron 1.50 4.00
129 Bill McCool .75 2.00
130 Carl Yastrzemski 10.00 25.00
131 Chris Cannizzaro .75 2.00
132 Dave Baldwin .75 2.00
133 Johnny Callison 1.50 4.00
134 Jim Weaver .75 2.00
135 Tommy Davis 1.50 4.00
136 Steve Huntz .75 2.00
Mike Torrez
137 Wally Bunker .75 2.00
138 John Bateman .75 2.00
139 Andy Kosco .75 2.00
140 Jim Lefebvre 1.50 4.00
141 Bill Dillman .75 2.00
142 Woody Woodward .75 2.00
143 Joe Nossek .75 2.00
144 Bob Hendley .75 2.00
145 Max Alvis .75 2.00
146 Jim Perry 1.50 4.00
147 Leo Durocher MG 2.50 6.00
148 Lee Stange .75 2.00
149 Ollie Brown .75 2.00
150 Denny McLain 2.50 6.00
151 Clay Dalrymple/(Catching, Phillies) 1.50 4.00
152 Tommie Sisk .75 2.00
153 Ed Brinkman .75 2.00
154 Jim Britton .75 2.00
155 Pete Ward 1.50 4.00
156 Hal Gibson .75 2.00
Leon McFadden
157 Bob Rodgers 1.50 4.00
158 Joe Gibbon .75 2.00
159 Jerry Adair .75 2.00
160 Vada Pinson 2.50 6.00
161 John Purdin .75 2.00
162 Bob Gibson WS1 4.00 10.00
163 World Series Game 2 3.00 8.00
Tiger homers
deck the Cards#
164 T.McCarver 6.00 15.00
Maris WS3 DP
165 Lou Brock WS4 4.00 10.00
166 Al Kaline WS5 4.00 10.00
167 Jim Northrup WS 3.00 8.00
168 M.Lolich 4.00 10.00
B.Gibson WS7
169 World Series Summary 3.00 8.00
Tigers celebrate/(Dick McAu
170 Frank Howard 1.50 4.00
171 Glenn Beckert 1.50 4.00
172 Jerry Stephenson .75 2.00
173 Bob Christian .75 2.00
Gerry Nyman
174 Grant Jackson .75 2.00
175 Jim Bunning 3.00 8.00
176 Joe Azcue .75 2.00
177 Ron Reed .75 2.00
178 Ray Oyler 1.50 4.00
179 Don Pavletich .75 2.00
180 Willie Horton 1.50 4.00
181 Mel Nelson .75 2.00
182 Bill Rigney MG .75 2.00
183 Don Shaw 1.50 4.00
184 Roberto Pena .75 2.00
185 Tom Phoebus .75 2.00
186 John Edwards .75 2.00
187 Leon Wagner .75 2.00
188 Rick Wise 1.50 4.00
189 Joe Lahoud .75 2.00
John Thibodeau
190 Willie Mays 50.00 100.00
191 Lindy McDaniel 1.50 4.00
192 Jose Pagan .75 2.00
193 Don Cardwell 1.50 4.00
194 Ted Uhlaender .75 2.00
195 John Odom .75 2.00
196 Lum Harris MG .75 2.00
197 Dick Selma .75 2.00
198 Willie Smith .75 2.00
199 Jim French .75 2.00
200 Bob Gibson 6.00 15.00
201 Russ Snyder .75 2.00
202 Don Wilson 1.50 4.00
203 Dave Johnson 1.50 4.00
204 Jack Hiatt .75 2.00
205 Rick Reichardt .75 2.00
206 Larry Hisle 1.50 4.00
Barry Lersch
207 Roy Face 1.50 4.00
208 Donn Clendenon/(Montreal Expos) 1.50 4.00
209 Larry Haney UER/(Reversed negative) .75 2.00
210 Felix Millan .75 2.00
211 Galen Cisco .75 2.00
212 Tom Tresh 1.50 4.00
213 Gerry Arrigo .75 2.00
214 Checklist 3 3.00 8.00
With 69T deckle CL
on back (no playe
215 Rico Petrocelli 1.50 4.00
216 Don Sutton 3.00 8.00
217 John Donaldson .75 2.00
218 John Roseboro 1.50 4.00

1969 O-Pee-Chee Deckle

COMPLETE SET (24) 125.00 250.00
1 Richie Allen 2.00 5.00
2 Luis Aparicio 3.00 8.00
3 Rod Carew 4.00 10.00
4 Roberto Clemente 75.00 150.00
5 Curt Flood 1.50 4.00
6 Bill Freehan 1.50 4.00
7 Bob Gibson 4.00 10.00
8 Ken Harrelson 1.50 4.00
9 Tommy Helms 1.25 3.00
10 Tom Haller 1.25 3.00
11 Willie Horton 1.50 4.00
12 Frank Howard 2.00 5.00
13 Willie McCovey 4.00 10.00
14 Denny McLain 2.00 5.00
15 Juan Marichal 4.00 10.00
16 Willie Mays 40.00 80.00
17 Boog Powell 2.00 5.00
18 Brooks Robinson 6.00 15.00
19 Ron Santo 2.50 6.00
20 Rusty Staub 1.50 4.00
21 Mel Stottlemyre 1.25 3.00
22 Luis Tiant 1.25 3.00
23 Maury Wills 1.50 4.00
24 Carl Yastrzemski 8.00 20.00

1970 O-Pee-Chee

The cards in this 546-card set measure 2 1/2" by 3 1/2". This set is essentially the same as the regular 1970 Topps set, except that the words "Printed in Canada" appear on the backs and the backs are bilingual. On a gray border, the fronts feature color player photos with thin white borders. The player's name and position are printed under the photo, while the team name appears in the upper part of the picture. The horizontal backs carry player biography and statistics in French and English. The card stock is a deeper shade of yellow on the reverse for the O-Pee-Chee cards. The set was issued in eight-card dime packs which came 36 packs to a box. Remember the prices below apply only to the O-Pee-Chee cards -- NOT to the 1970 Topps cards which are much more plentiful. Notable Rookie Cards include Thurman Munson.

COMPLETE SET (546) 750.00 1500.00
COMMON PLAYER (1-459) .60 1.50
COMMON PLAYER (460-546) 1.00 2.50
1 Mets Team ! 12.50 40.00
2 Diego Segui .75 2.00
3 Darrel Chaney .60 1.50
4 Tom Egan .60 1.50
5 Wes Parker .75 2.00
6 Grant Jackson .60 1.50
7 Gary Boyd .60 1.50
Russ Nagelson
8 Jose Martinez .60 1.50
9 Checklist 1-132 6.00 15.00
10 Carl Yastrzemski 10.00 25.00
11 Nate Colbert .60 1.50
12 John Hiller .75 2.00
13 Jack Hiatt .60 1.50
14 Hank Allen .60 1.50
15 Larry Dierker .60 1.50
16 Charlie Metro MG .60 1.50
17 Hoyt Wilhelm 2.50 6.00
18 Carlos May .75 2.00
19 John Boccabella .60 1.50
20 Dave McNally .75 2.00
21 Vida Blue 2.50 6.00
G.Tenace RC
22 Ray Washburn .60 1.50
23 Bill Robinson .75 2.00
24 Dick Selma .60 1.50
25 Cesar Tovar .60 1.50
26 Tug McGraw 1.50 4.00
27 Chuck Hinton .60 1.50
28 Billy Wilson .60 1.50
29 Sandy Alomar .75 2.00
30 Matty Alou .75 2.00
31 Marty Pattin .75 2.00
32 Harry Walker MG .60 1.50
33 Don Wert .60 1.50
34 Willie Crawford .60 1.50
35 Joel Horlen .60 1.50
36 Danny Breeden .75 2.00
Bernie Carbo
37 Dick Drago .60 1.50
38 Mack Jones .60 1.50
39 Mike Nagy .60 1.50
40 Richie Allen 1.50 4.00
41 George Lauzerique .60 1.50
42 Tito Fuentes .60 1.50
43 Jack Aker .60 1.50
44 Roberto Pena .60 1.50
45 Dave Johnson .75 2.00
46 Ken Rudolph .60 1.50
47 Bob Miller .60 1.50
48 Gil Garrido .60 1.50
49 Tim Cullen .60 1.50
50 Tommie Agee .75 2.00
51 Bob Christian .60 1.50
52 Bruce Dal Canton .60 1.50
53 John Kennedy .60 1.50
54 Jeff Torborg .75 2.00
55 John Odom .60 1.50
56 Joe Lis .60 1.50
Scott Reid
57 Pat Kelly .60 1.50
58 Dave Marshall .60 1.50
59 Dick Ellsworth .60 1.50
60 Jim Wynn .75 2.00
61 Rose 6.00 15.00
Clemente
Jones LL
62 R.Carew 1.25 3.00
T.Oliva
LL
63 McCovey 1.25 3.00
Santo
Perez LL
64 Kill 2.50 6.00
Powell
Reggie LL
65 McCovey 2.50 6.00
Aaron
May LL
66 Kill 2.50 6.00
Howard
Reggie LL
67 Marich 3.00 8.00
Carlton
Gibs LL
68 Bosm .75 2.00
Palmer
Cuellar LL
69 Seav 3.00 8.00
Niek
Jenk
Mar LL
70 AL Pitching Leaders .75 2.00
Dennis McLain
Mike Cuellar/
71 F.Jenkins 1.25 3.00
B.Gibson
LL
72 AL Strikeout Leaders .75 2.00
Sam McDowell
Mickey Lolich#
73 Wayne Granger .60 1.50
74 Greg Washburn .60 1.50
Wally Wolf
75 Jim Kaat .75 2.00
76 Carl Taylor .60 1.50
77 Frank Linzy .60 1.50
78 Joe Lahoud .60 1.50
79 Clay Kirby .60 1.50
80 Don Kessinger .75 2.00
81 Dave May .60 1.50
82 Frank Fernandez .60 1.50
83 Don Cardwell .60 1.50
84 Paul Casanova .60 1.50
85 Max Alvis .60 1.50
86 Lum Harris MG .60 1.50
87 Steve Renko .75 2.00
88 Miguel Fuentes .75 2.00
Dick Baney
89 Juan Rios .60 1.50
90 Tim McCarver 1.25 3.00
91 Rich Morales .60 1.50
92 George Culver .60 1.50
93 Rick Renick .60 1.50
94 Fred Patek .75 2.00
95 Earl Wilson .75 2.00
96 Jerry Reuss RC 1.25 3.00
97 Joe Moeller .60 1.50
98 Gates Brown .75 2.00
99 Bobby Pfeil .60 1.50
100 Mel Stottlemyre .75 2.00
101 Bobby Floyd .60 1.50
102 Joe Rudi .75 2.00
103 Frank Reberger .60 1.50
104 Gerry Moses .60 1.50
105 Tony Gonzalez .60 1.50
106 Darold Knowles .60 1.50
107 Bobby Etheridge .60 1.50
108 Tom Burgmeier .60 1.50
109 Garry Jestadt .75 2.00
Carl Morton
110 Bob Moose .60 1.50
111 Mike Hegan .75 2.00
112 Dave Nelson .60 1.50
113 Jim Ray .60 1.50
114 Gene Michael .75 2.00
115 Alex Johnson .75 2.00
116 Sparky Lyle 1.25 3.00
117 Don Young .60 1.50
118 George Mitterwald .60 1.50
119 Chuck Taylor .60 1.50
120 Sal Bando .75 2.00
121 Fred Beene .60 1.50
Terry Crowley
122 George Stone .60 1.50
123 Don Gutteridge MG .60 1.50
124 Larry Jaster .60 1.50
125 Deron Johnson .60 1.50
126 Marty Martinez .60 1.50
127 Joe Coleman .60 1.50
128 Checklist 133-263 3.00 8.00
129 Jimmie Price .60 1.50
130 Ollie Brown .60 1.50
131 Ray Lamb .60 1.50
Bob Stinson
132 Jim McGlothlin .60 1.50
133 Clay Carroll .60 1.50
134 Danny Walton .60 1.50
135 Dick Dietz .60 1.50
136 Steve Hargan .60 1.50
137 Art Shamsky .60 1.50
138 Joe Foy .60 1.50
139 Rich Nye .60 1.50
140 Reggie Jackson 30.00 60.00
141 Dave Cash .75 2.00
Johnny Jeter
142 Fritz Peterson .60 1.50
143 Phil Gagliano .60 1.50
144 Ray Culp .60 1.50
145 Rico Carty .75 2.00
146 Danny Murphy .60 1.50
147 Angel Hermoso .60 1.50
148 Earl Weaver MG 2.00 5.00
149 Billy Champion .60 1.50
150 Harmon Killebrew 4.00 10.00
151 Dave Roberts .60 1.50
152 Ike Brown .60 1.50
153 Gary Gentry .60 1.50
154 Jim Miles .60 1.50
Jan Dukes
155 Denis Menke .60 1.50
156 Eddie Fisher .60 1.50
157 Manny Mota 1.25 3.00
158 Jerry McNertney .75 2.00
159 Tommy Helms .75 2.00
160 Phil Niekro 2.50 6.00
161 Richie Scheinblum .60 1.50
162 Jerry Johnson .60 1.50
163 Syd O'Brien .60 1.50
164 Ty Cline .60 1.50
165 Ed Kirkpatrick .60 1.50
166 Al Oliver 1.50 4.00
167 Bill Burbach .60 1.50
168 Dave Watkins .60 1.50
169 Tom Hall .60 1.50
170 Billy Williams 3.00 8.00
171 Jim Nash .60 1.50
172 Ralph Garr RC 1.25 3.00
173 Jim Hicks .60 1.50
174 Ted Sizemore .75 2.00
175 Dick Bosman .60 1.50
176 Jim Ray Hart .75 2.00
177 Jim Northrup .75 2.00
178 Denny LeMaster .60 1.50
179 Ivan Murrell .60 1.50
180 Tommy John 1.25 3.00
181 Sparky Anderson MG 3.00 8.00
182 Dick Hall .60 1.50
183 Jerry Grote .75 2.00
184 Ray Fosse .60 1.50
185 Don Mincher .75 2.00
186 Rick Joseph .60 1.50
187 Mike Hedlund .60 1.50
188 Manny Sanguillen .75 2.00
189 Thurman Munson RC 50.00 100.00
190 Joe Torre 1.50 4.00
191 Vicente Romo .60 1.50
192 Jim Qualls .60 1.50
193 Mike Wegener .60 1.50
194 Chuck Manuel RC 1.50 4.00
195 Tom Seaver NLCS1 8.00 20.00
196 Ken Boswell NLCS 1.50 4.00
197 Nolan Ryan NLCS3 12.50 40.00
198 Mets Celebrate 8.00 20.00
N.Ryan
199 AL Playoff Game 1 1.50 4.00
Orioles win squeaker/(Mike Cue
200 Boog Powell ALCS 1.50 4.00
201 AL Playoff Game 3 1.50 4.00
Birds wrap it up/(Boog Powell
202 AL Playoff Summary 1.50 4.00
Orioles celebrate
203 Rudy May .60 1.50
204 Len Gabrielson .60 1.50
205 Bert Campaneris .75 2.00
206 Clete Boyer .75 2.00
207 Norman McRae .60 1.50
Bob Reed
208 Fred Gladding .60 1.50
209 Ken Suarez .60 1.50
210 Juan Marichal 3.00 8.00
211 Ted Williams MG 8.00 20.00
212 Al Santorini .60 1.50
213 Andy Etchebarren .60 1.50
214 Ken Boswell .60 1.50
215 Reggie Smith 1.25 3.00
216 Chuck Hartenstein .60 1.50
217 Ron Hansen .60 1.50
218 Ron Stone .60 1.50
219 Jerry Kenney .60 1.50
220 Steve Carlton 8.00 20.00
221 Ron Brand .60 1.50
222 Jim Rooker .60 1.50
223 Nate Oliver .60 1.50
224 Steve Barber .75 2.00
225 Lee May .75 2.00
226 Ron Perranoski .60 1.50
227 John Mayberry RC .75 2.00
228 Aurelio Rodriguez .60 1.50
229 Rich Robertson .60 1.50
230 Brooks Robinson 8.00 20.00
231 Luis Tiant 1.25 3.00
232 Bob Didier .60 1.50
233 Lew Krausse .60 1.50
234 Tommy Dean .60 1.50
235 Mike Epstein .60 1.50
236 Bob Veale .60 1.50
237 Russ Gibson .60 1.50
238 Jose Laboy .75 2.00
239 Ken Berry .60 1.50
240 Fergie Jenkins 3.00 8.00
241 Al Fitzmorris .60 1.50
Scott Northey
242 Walt Alston MG 1.50 4.00
243 Joe Sparma .75 2.00
244 Checklist 264-372 3.00 8.00
245 Leo Cardenas .60 1.50
246 Jim McAndrew .60 1.50
247 Lou Klimchock .60 1.50
248 Jesus Alou .60 1.50
249 Bob Locker .60 1.50
250 Willie McCovey 5.00 12.00
251 Dick Schofield .60 1.50
252 Lowell Palmer .60 1.50
253 Ron Woods .60 1.50
254 Camilo Pascual .60 1.50
255 Jim Spencer .60 1.50
256 Vic Davalillo .60 1.50
257 Dennis Higgins .60 1.50
258 Paul Popovich .60 1.50
259 Tommie Reynolds .60 1.50
260 Claude Osteen .75 2.00
261 Curt Motton .60 1.50
262 Jerry Morales .60 1.50
Jim Williams
263 Duane Josephson .60 1.50
264 Rich Hebner .60 1.50
265 Randy Hundley .60 1.50
266 Wally Bunker .60 1.50
267 Herman Hill .60 1.50
Paul Ratliff
268 Claude Raymond .75 2.00
269 Cesar Gutierrez .60 1.50
270 Chris Short .60 1.50
271 Greg Goossen .75 2.00
272 Hector Torres .60 1.50
273 Ralph Houk MG .75 2.00
274 Gerry Arrigo .60 1.50
275 Duke Sims .60 1.50
276 Ron Hunt .60 1.50
277 Paul Doyle .60 1.50
278 Tommie Aaron .60 1.50
279 Bill Lee 1.25 3.00
280 Donn Clendenon .75 2.00
281 Casey Cox .60 1.50
282 Steve Huntz .60 1.50
283 Angel Bravo .60 1.50
284 Jack Baldschun .60 1.50
285 Paul Blair .75 2.00
286 Bill Buckner RC 3.00 8.00
287 Fred Talbot .60 1.50
288 Larry Hisle .75 2.00
289 Gene Brabender .60 1.50
290 Rod Carew 10.00 25.00
291 Leo Durocher MG 1.50 4.00
292 Eddie Leon .60 1.50
293 Bob Bailey .75 2.00
294 Jose Azcue .60 1.50
295 Cecil Upshaw .60 1.50
296 Woody Woodward .60 1.50
297 Curt Blefary .60 1.50
298 Ken Henderson .60 1.50
299 Buddy Bradford .60 1.50
300 Tom Seaver 12.50 40.00
301 Chico Salmon .60 1.50
302 Jeff James .60 1.50
303 Brant Alyea .60 1.50
304 Bill Russell RC 3.00 8.00
305 Don Buford WS 1.50 4.00
306 World Series Game 2 1.50 4.00
Donn Clendenon's homer
break
307 World Series Game 3 1.50 4.00
Tommie Agee's catch
saves th
308 World Series Game 4 1.50 4.00
J.C. Martin's bunt
ends dead
309 Jerry Koosman WS 1.50 4.00
310 WS Celebration Mets 3.00 8.00
311 Dick Green .60 1.50
312 Mike Torrez .60 1.50
313 Mayo Smith MG .60 1.50
314 Bill McCool .60 1.50
315 Luis Aparicio 3.00 8.00
316 Skip Guinn .60 1.50
317 Billy Conigliaro .75 2.00
Luis Alvarado
318 Willie Smith .60 1.50
319 Clay Dalrymple .60 1.50
320 Jim Maloney .75 2.00
321 Lou Piniella 1.25 3.00
322 Luke Walker .60 1.50
323 Wayne Comer .60 1.50
324 Tony Taylor .75 2.00
325 Dave Boswell .60 1.50
326 Bill Voss .60 1.50
327 Hal King RC .60 1.50
328 George Brunet .60 1.50
329 Chris Cannizzaro .60 1.50
330 Lou Brock 5.00 12.00
331 Chuck Dobson .60 1.50
332 Bobby Wine .75 2.00
333 Bobby Murcer 1.25 3.00
334 Phil Regan .60 1.50
335 Bill Freehan .75 2.00
336 Del Unser .60 1.50
337 Mike McCormick .75 2.00
338 Paul Schaal .60 1.50
339 Johnny Edwards .60 1.50
340 Tony Conigliaro 1.50 4.00

341 Bill Sudakis .60 1.50
342 Wilbur Wood .75 2.00
343 Checklist 373-459 3.00 8.00
344 Marcelino Lopez .60 1.50
345 Al Ferrara .60 1.50
346 Red Schoendienst MG .75 2.00
347 Russ Snyder .60 1.50
348 Mike Jorgensen .75 2.00
Jesse Hudson
349 Steve Hamilton .60 1.50
350 Roberto Clemente 40.00 80.00
351 Tom Murphy .60 1.50
352 Bob Barton .60 1.50
353 Stan Williams .60 1.50
354 Amos Otis .75 2.00
355 Doug Rader .60 1.50
356 Fred Lasher .60 1.50
357 Bob Burda .60 1.50
358 Pedro Borbon RC .75 2.00
359 Phil Roof .60 1.50
360 Curt Flood 1.25 3.00
361 Ray Jarvis .60 1.50
362 Joe Hague .60 1.50
363 Tom Shopay .60 1.50
364 Dan McGinn .75 2.00
365 Zoilo Versalles .60 1.50
366 Barry Moore .60 1.50
367 Mike Lum .60 1.50
368 Ed Herrmann .60 1.50
369 Alan Foster .60 1.50
370 Tommy Harper .75 2.00
371 Rod Gaspar .60 1.50
372 Dave Giusti .60 1.50
373 Roy White .75 2.00
374 Tommie Sisk .60 1.50
375 Johnny Callison 1.25 3.00
376 Lefty Phillips MG .60 1.50
377 Bill Butler .60 1.50
378 Jim Davenport .60 1.50
379 Tom Tischinski .60 1.50
380 Tony Perez 3.00 8.00
381 Bobby Brooks .60 1.50
Mike Olivo
382 Jack DiLauro .60 1.50
383 Mickey Stanley .75 2.00
384 Gary Neibauer .60 1.50
385 George Scott .75 2.00
386 Bill Dillman .60 1.50
387 Orioles Team 1.50 4.00
388 Byron Browne .60 1.50
389 Jim Shellenback .60 1.50
390 Willie Davis 1.25 3.00
391 Larry Brown .60 1.50
392 Walt Hriniak .75 2.00
393 John Gelnar .60 1.50
394 Gil Hodges MG 1.50 4.00
395 Walt Williams .60 1.50
396 Steve Blass .75 2.00
397 Roger Repoz .60 1.50
398 Bill Stoneman .60 1.50
399 Yankees Team 1.50 4.00
400 Denny McLain 1.50 4.00
401 John Harrell .60 1.50
Bernie Williams
402 Ellie Rodriguez .60 1.50
403 Jim Bunning 3.00 8.00
404 Rich Reese .60 1.50
405 Bill Hands .60 1.50
406 Mike Andrews .60 1.50
407 Bob Watson .75 2.00
408 Paul Lindblad .60 1.50
409 Bob Tolan .60 1.50
410 Boog Powell 1.50 4.00
411 Dodgers Team 1.50 4.00
412 Larry Burchart .60 1.50
413 Sonny Jackson .60 1.50
414 Paul Edmondson .60 1.50
415 Julian Javier .75 2.00
416 Joe Verbanic .60 1.50
417 John Bateman .60 1.50
418 John Donaldson .60 1.50
419 Ron Taylor .75 2.00
420 Ken McMullen .75 2.00
421 Pat Dobson .75 2.00
422 Royals Team 1.50 4.00
423 Jerry May .60 1.50
424 Mike Kilkenny .75 2.00
425 Bobby Bonds 3.00 8.00
426 Bill Rigney MG .60 1.50
427 Fred Norman .60 1.50
428 Don Buford .60 1.50
429 Randy Bobb .60 1.50
Jim Cosman
430 Andy Messersmith .75 2.00
431 Ron Swoboda .75 2.00
432 Checklist 460-546 3.00 8.00
433 Ron Bryant .60 1.50
434 Felipe Alou 1.25 3.00
435 Nelson Briles .75 2.00
436 Phillies Team 1.50 4.00
437 Danny Cater .60 1.50
438 Pat Jarvis .60 1.50
439 Lee Maye .60 1.50
440 Bill Mazeroski 3.00 8.00
441 John O'Donoghue .60 1.50
442 Gene Mauch MG .75 2.00
443 Al Jackson .60 1.50
444 Billy Farmer .60 1.50
John Matias
445 Vada Pinson 1.25 3.00
446 Billy Grabarkewitz .60 1.50
447 Lee Stange .60 1.50
448 Astros Team 1.50 4.00
449 Jim Palmer 6.00 15.00
450 Willie McCovey AS 3.00 8.00
451 Boog Powell AS 1.50 4.00
452 Felix Millan AS 1.25 3.00
453 Rod Carew AS 3.00 8.00
454 Ron Santo AS 1.50 4.00
455 Brooks Robinson AS 3.00 8.00
456 Don Kessinger AS 1.25 3.00
457 Rico Petrocelli AS 1.50 4.00
458 Pete Rose AS 8.00 20.00
459 Reggie Jackson AS 6.00 15.00
460 Matty Alou AS 1.50 4.00
461 Carl Yastrzemski AS 5.00 12.00
462 Hank Aaron AS 8.00 20.00
463 Frank Robinson AS 4.00 10.00
464 Johnny Bench AS 8.00 20.00
465 Bill Freehan AS 1.50 4.00
466 Juan Marichal AS 2.50 6.00
467 Denny McLain AS 2.50 6.00
468 Jerry Koosman AS 1.50 4.00
469 Sam McDowell AS 1.50 4.00
470 Willie Stargell 5.00 12.00
471 Chris Zachary 1.00 2.50
472 Braves Team 1.50 4.00
473 Don Bryant 1.00 2.50
474 Dick Kelley 1.00 2.50
475 Dick McAuliffe 1.50 4.00
476 Don Shaw 1.00 2.50
477 Al Severinsen 1.00 2.50
Roger Freed
478 Bob Heise 1.00 2.50
479 Dick Woodson 1.00 2.50
480 Glenn Beckert 1.50 4.00
481 Jose Tartabull 1.00 2.50
482 Tom Hilgendorf 1.00 2.50
483 Gail Hopkins 1.00 2.50
484 Gary Nolan 1.50 4.00
485 Jay Johnstone 1.50 4.00
486 Terry Harmon 1.00 2.50
487 Cisco Carlos 1.00 2.50
488 J.C. Martin 1.00 2.50
489 Eddie Kasko MG 1.00 2.50
490 Bill Singer 1.50 4.00
491 Graig Nettles 2.50 6.00
492 Keith Lampard 1.00 2.50
Scipio Spinks
493 Lindy McDaniel 1.50 4.00
494 Larry Stahl 1.00 2.50
495 Dave Morehead 1.00 2.50
496 Steve Whitaker 1.00 2.50
497 Eddie Watt 1.00 2.50
498 Al Weis 1.00 2.50
499 Skip Lockwood 1.00 2.50
500 Hank Aaron 30.00 60.00
501 White Sox Team 1.50 4.00
502 Rollie Fingers 5.00 12.00
503 Dal Maxvill 1.00 2.50
504 Don Pavletich 1.00 2.50
505 Ken Holtzman 1.50 4.00
506 Ed Stroud 1.00 2.50
507 Pat Corrales 1.00 2.50
508 Joe Niekro 1.50 4.00
509 Expos Team 2.50 6.00
510 Tony Oliva 2.50 6.00
511 Joe Hoerner 1.00 2.50
512 Billy Harris 1.00 2.50
513 Preston Gomez MG 1.00 2.50
514 Steve Hovley 1.00 2.50
515 Don Wilson 1.50 4.00
516 John Ellis 1.00 2.50
Jim Lyttle
517 Joe Gibbon 1.00 2.50
518 Bill Melton 1.00 2.50
519 Don McMahon 1.00 2.50
520 Willie Horton 1.50 4.00
521 Cal Koonce 1.00 2.50
522 Angels Team 1.50 4.00
523 Jose Pena 1.00 2.50
524 Alvin Dark MG 1.50 4.00
525 Jerry Adair 1.00 2.50
526 Ron Herbel 1.00 2.50
527 Don Bosch 1.50 4.00
528 Elrod Hendricks 1.00 2.50
529 Bob Aspromonte 1.00 2.50
530 Bob Gibson 8.00 20.00
531 Ron Clark 1.00 2.50
532 Danny Murtaugh MG 1.50 4.00
533 Buzz Stephen 1.00 2.50
534 Twins Team 1.50 4.00
535 Andy Kosco 1.00 2.50
536 Mike Kekich 1.00 2.50
537 Joe Morgan 5.00 12.00
538 Bob Humphreys 1.00 2.50
539 Larry Bowa RC 4.00 10.00
540 Gary Peters 1.00 2.50
541 Bill Heath 1.00 2.50
542 Checklist 547-633 3.00 8.00
543 Clyde Wright 1.00 2.50
544 Reds Team 2.50 6.00
545 Ken Harrelson 1.50 4.00
546 Ron Reed 1.50 4.00

1971 O-Pee-Chee

The cards in this 752-card set measure 2 1/2" by 3 1/2". The 1971 O-Pee-Chee set is a challenge to complete in "Mint" condition because the black borders are easily scratched and damaged. The O-Pee-Chee cards seem to have been cut (into individual cards) not as sharply as the Topps cards; the borders frequently appear slightly frayed. The players are also pictured in black and white on the back of the card. The next-to-last series (524-643) and the last series (644-752) are somewhat scarce. The O-Pee-Chee cards can be distinguished from Topps cards by the "Printed in Canada" on the bottom of the reverse. The reverse color is yellow instead of the green found on the backs of the 1971 Topps cards. The card backs are written in both French and English, except for cards 524-752 which were printed in English only. There are several cards which are different from the corresponding Topps card with a different pose or different team noted in bold type, i.e. "Recently Traded to ..." These changed cards are numbers 31, 32, 73, 144, 151, 161, 172, 182, 191, 202, 207, 248, 289 and 578. These cards were issued in eight-card dime packs which came 36 packs to a box. Remember, the prices below apply only to the 1971 O-Pee-Chee cards -- NOT Topps cards which are much more plentiful. Notable Rookie Cards include Dusty Baker and Don Baylor (Sharing the same card), Bert Blyleven, Dave Concepcion and Steve Garvey.

COMPLETE SET (752) 1250.00 2500.00
COMMON PLAYER (1-393) .60 1.50
COMMON PLAYER (394-523) 1.25 3.00
COMMON PLAYER (524-643) 1.50 4.00
COMMON PLAYER (644-752) 4.00 10.00
1 Orioles Team 10.00 25.00
2 Dock Ellis .60 1.50
3 Dick McAuliffe .75 2.00
4 Vic Davalillo .60 1.50
5 Thurman Munson 75.00 150.00
6 Ed Spiezio .60 1.50
7 Jim Holt .60 1.50
8 Mike McQueen .60 1.50
9 George Scott .75 2.00
10 Claude Osteen .75 2.00
11 Elliott Maddox .60 1.50
12 Johnny Callison .75 2.00
13 Charlie Brinkman .60 1.50
Dick Moloney
14 Dave Concepcion RC 10.00 25.00
15 Andy Messersmith .75 2.00
16 Ken Singleton RC 1.25 3.00
17 Billy Sorrell .60 1.50
18 Norm Miller .60 1.50
19 Skip Pitlock .60 1.50
20 Reggie Jackson 30.00 60.00
21 Dan McGinn .75 2.00
22 Phil Roof .60 1.50
23 Oscar Gamble .60 1.50
24 Rich Hand .60 1.50
25 Cito Gaston .75 2.00
26 Bert Blyleven RC 10.00 25.00
27 Fred Cambria .60 1.50
Gene Clines
28 Ron Klimkowski .60 1.50
29 Don Buford .60 1.50
30 Phil Niekro 3.00 8.00
31 John Bateman/(different pose) 1.25 3.00
32 Jerry DeVanon .75 2.00
Recently Traded To Orioles
33 Del Unser .60 1.50
34 Sandy Vance .60 1.50
35 Lou Piniella 1.25 3.00
36 Dean Chance .75 2.00
37 Rich McKinney .60 1.50
38 Jim Colborn .60 1.50
39 Gene Lamont RC .75 2.00
40 Lee May .75 2.00
41 Rick Austin .60 1.50
42 Boots Day .75 2.00
43 Steve Kealey .60 1.50
44 Johnny Edwards .60 1.50
45 Jim Hunter 3.00 8.00
46 Dave Campbell .75 2.00
47 Johnny Jeter .60 1.50
48 Dave Baldwin .60 1.50
49 Don Money .60 1.50
50 Willie McCovey 5.00 12.00
51 Steve Kline .60 1.50
52 Earl Williams RC .60 1.50
53 Paul Blair .75 2.00
54 Checklist 1-132 4.00 10.00
55 Steve Carlton 10.00 25.00
56 Duane Josephson .60 1.50
57 Von Joshua .60 1.50
58 Bill Lee .75 2.00
59 Gene Mauch MG .75 2.00
60 Dick Bosman .60 1.50
61 A.Johnson 1.25 3.00
Yaz
Oliva LL
62 NL Batting Leaders .75 2.00
Rico Carty
Joe Torre
Manny S
63 AL RBI Leaders 1.25 3.00
Frank Howard
Tony Conigliaro
B
64 Bench 3.00 8.00
Perez
B.Will LL
65 F.Howard 1.25 3.00
Kill
Yaz LL
66 Bench 3.00 8.00
B.Will
Perez LL
67 Segui 1.25 3.00
Palmer
Wright LL
68 Seaver 1.25 3.00
Simpson
Walker LL
69 AL Pitching Leaders .75 2.00
Mike Cuellar
Dave McNally
J
70 Gibson 3.00 8.00
Perry
Jenk LL
71 AL Strikeout Leaders .75 2.00
Sam McDowell
Mickey Lolich#
72 Seaver 3.00 8.00
Gibson
Jenk LL
73 George Brunet/(St. Louis Cardinals) .60 1.50
74 Pete Hamm .60 1.50
Jim Nettles
75 Gary Nolan .75 2.00
76 Ted Savage .60 1.50
77 Mike Compton .60 1.50
78 Jim Spencer .60 1.50
79 Wade Blasingame .60 1.50
80 Bill Melton .60 1.50
81 Felix Millan .60 1.50
82 Casey Cox .60 1.50
83 Tim Foli RC .75 2.00
84 Marcel Lachemann RC .60 1.50
85 Bill Grabarkewitz .60 1.50
86 Mike Kilkenny .75 2.00
87 Jack Heidemann .60 1.50
88 Hal King .60 1.50
89 Ken Brett .60 1.50
90 Joe Pepitone .75 2.00
91 Bob Lemon MG .75 2.00
92 Fred Wenz .60 1.50
93 Norm McRae .60 1.50
Denny Riddleberger
94 Don Hahn .75 2.00
95 Luis Tiant .75 2.00
96 Joe Hague .60 1.50
97 Floyd Wicker .60 1.50
98 Joe Decker .60 1.50
99 Mark Belanger .75 2.00
100 Pete Rose 50.00 100.00
101 Les Cain .60 1.50
102 Ken Forsch .75 2.00
Larry Howard
103 Rich Severson .60 1.50
104 Dan Frisella .60 1.50
105 Tony Conigliaro .75 2.00
106 Tom Dukes .60 1.50
107 Roy Foster .60 1.50
108 John Cumberland .60 1.50
109 Steve Hovley .60 1.50
110 Bill Mazeroski 3.00 8.00
111 Loyd Colson .60 1.50
Bobby Mitchell
112 Manny Mota .75 2.00
113 Jerry Crider .60 1.50
114 Billy Conigliaro .75 2.00
115 Donn Clendenon .75 2.00
116 Ken Sanders .60 1.50
117 Ted Simmons RC 4.00 10.00
118 Cookie Rojas .75 2.00
119 Frank Lucchesi MG .60 1.50
120 Willie Horton .75 2.00
121 Jim Dunegan .60 1.50
Roe Skidmore
122 Eddie Watt .60 1.50
123 Checklist 133-263 4.00 10.00
124 Don Gullett RC .75 2.00
125 Ray Fosse .60 1.50
126 Danny Coombs .60 1.50
127 Danny Thompson .75 2.00
128 Frank Johnson .60 1.50
129 Aurelio Monteagudo .60 1.50
130 Denis Menke .60 1.50
131 Curt Blefary .60 1.50
132 Jose Laboy .75 2.00
133 Mickey Lolich .75 2.00
134 Jose Arcia .60 1.50
135 Rick Monday .75 2.00
136 Duffy Dyer .60 1.50
137 Marcelino Lopez .60 1.50
138 Joe Lis .75 2.00
Willie Montanez
139 Paul Casanova .60 1.50
140 Gaylord Perry 3.00 8.00
141 Frank Quilici MG .60 1.50
142 Mack Jones .75 2.00
143 Steve Blass .75 2.00
144 Jackie Hernandez .75 2.00
145 Bill Singer .75 2.00
146 Ralph Houk MG .75 2.00
147 Bob Priddy .60 1.50
148 John Mayberry .75 2.00
149 Mike Hershberger .60 1.50
150 Sam McDowell .75 2.00
151 Tommy Davis/(Oakland A's) 1.25 3.00
152 Lloyd Allen .60 1.50
Winston Llenas
153 Gary Ross .60 1.50
154 Cesar Gutierrez .60 1.50
155 Ken Henderson .60 1.50
156 Bart Johnson .60 1.50
157 Bob Bailey 1.25 3.00
158 Jerry Reuss .75 2.00
159 Jarvis Tatum .60 1.50
160 Tom Seaver 12.50 40.00
161 Ron Hunt/(different pose) 2.50 6.00
162 Jack Billingham .60 1.50
163 Buck Martinez .75 2.00
164 Frank Duffy .75 2.00
Milt Wilcox
165 Cesar Tovar .60 1.50
166 Joe Hoerner .60 1.50
167 Tom Grieve RC .75 2.00
168 Bruce Dal Canton .60 1.50
169 Ed Herrmann .60 1.50
170 Mike Cuellar .75 2.00
171 Bobby Wine .75 2.00
172 Duke Sims/(Los Angeles Dodgers) .75 2.00
173 Gil Garrido .60 1.50
174 Dave LaRoche .60 1.50
175 Jim Hickman .60 1.50
176 Bob Montgomery RC .75 2.00
177 Hal McRae .75 2.00
178 Dave Duncan .75 2.00
179 Mike Corkins .60 1.50
180 Al Kaline 10.00 25.00
181 Hal Lanier .60 1.50
182 Al Downing/(Los Angeles Dodgers) .75 2.00
183 Gil Hodges MG 1.25 3.00
184 Stan Bahnsen .60 1.50
185 Julian Javier .60 1.50
186 Bob Spence .60 1.50
187 Ted Abernathy .60 1.50
188 Bobby Valentine RC 3.00 8.00
189 George Mitterwald .60 1.50
190 Bob Tolan .60 1.50
191 Mike Andrews/(Chicago White Sox) .75 2.00
192 Billy Wilson .60 1.50
193 Bob Grich RC 1.25 3.00
194 Mike Lum .60 1.50
195 Boog Powell ALCS .75 2.00
196 AL Playoff Game 2 .75 2.00
Dave McNally makes it
two stra
197 Jim Palmer ALCS2 1.25 3.00
198 AL Playoff Summary .75 2.00
Orioles Celebrate
199 NL Playoff Game 1 .75 2.00
Ty Cline pinch-triple
decides
200 NL Playoff Game 2 .75 2.00
Bobby Tolan scores for
third t
201 Ty Cline NLCS .75 2.00
202 Claude Raymond/(different pose) 2.50 6.00
203 Larry Gura .75 2.00
204 Bernie Smith .60 1.50
George Kopacz
205 Gerry Moses .60 1.50
206 Checklist 264-393 5.00 12.00
207 Alan Foster/(Cleveland Indians) .75 2.00
208 Billy Martin MG 1.25 3.00
209 Steve Renko .75 2.00
210 Rod Carew 8.00 20.00
211 Phil Hennigan .60 1.50
212 Rich Hebner .75 2.00
213 Frank Baker .60 1.50
214 Al Ferrara .60 1.50
215 Diego Segui .60 1.50
216 Reggie Cleveland .75 2.00
Luis Melendez
217 Ed Stroud .60 1.50
218 Tony Cloninger .60 1.50
219 Elrod Hendricks .60 1.50
220 Ron Santo 1.25 3.00
221 Dave Morehead .60 1.50
222 Bob Watson .75 2.00
223 Cecil Upshaw .60 1.50
224 Alan Gallagher .60 1.50
225 Gary Peters .60 1.50
226 Bill Russell .75 2.00
227 Floyd Weaver .60 1.50
228 Wayne Garrett .60 1.50
229 Jim Hannan .60 1.50
230 Willie Stargell 8.00 20.00
231 John Lowenstein RC .75 2.00
232 John Strohmayer .75 2.00
233 Larry Bowa .75 2.00
234 Jim Lyttle .60 1.50
235 Nate Colbert .60 1.50
236 Bob Humphreys .60 1.50
237 Cesar Cedeno RC .75 2.00
238 Chuck Dobson .60 1.50
239 Red Schoendienst MG .75 2.00
240 Clyde Wright .60 1.50
241 Dave Nelson .60 1.50
242 Jim Ray .60 1.50
243 Carlos May .60 1.50
244 Bob Tillman .60 1.50
245 Jim Kaat .75 2.00
246 Tony Taylor .60 1.50
247 Jerry Cram .75 2.00
Paul Splittorff
248 Hoyt Wilhelm/(Atlanta Braves) 4.00 10.00
249 Chico Salmon .60 1.50
250 Johnny Bench 30.00 60.00
251 Frank Reberger .60 1.50
252 Eddie Leon .60 1.50
253 Bill Sudakis .60 1.50
254 Cal Koonce .60 1.50
255 Bob Robertson .75 2.00
256 Tony Gonzalez .60 1.50
257 Nelson Briles .75 2.00
258 Dick Green .60 1.50
259 Dave Marshall .60 1.50
260 Tommy Harper .75 2.00
261 Darold Knowles .60 1.50
262 Jim Williams .60 1.50
Dave Robinson
263 John Ellis .60 1.50
264 Joe Morgan 4.00 10.00
265 Jim Northrup .75 2.00
266 Bill Stoneman .75 2.00
267 Rich Morales .60 1.50
268 Phillies Team 1.25 3.00
269 Gail Hopkins .60 1.50
270 Rico Carty .75 2.00
271 Bill Zepp .60 1.50
272 Tommy Helms .75 2.00
273 Pete Richert .60 1.50
274 Ron Slocum .60 1.50
275 Vada Pinson .75 2.00
276 George Foster RC 4.00 10.00
277 Gary Waslewski .60 1.50
278 Jerry Grote .75 2.00
279 Lefty Phillips MG .60 1.50
280 Fergie Jenkins 3.00 8.00
281 Danny Walton .60 1.50
282 Jose Pagan .60 1.50
283 Dick Such .60 1.50
284 Jim Gosger .75 2.00
285 Sal Bando .75 2.00
286 Jerry McNertney .60 1.50
287 Mike Fiore .60 1.50
288 Joe Moeller .60 1.50
289 Rusty Staub/(Different pose) 4.00 10.00
290 Tony Oliva 1.25 3.00
291 George Culver .60 1.50
292 Jay Johnstone .75 2.00
293 Pat Corrales .75 2.00
294 Steve Dunning .60 1.50
295 Bobby Bonds 2.50 6.00
296 Tom Timmermann .60 1.50
297 Johnny Briggs .60 1.50
298 Jim Nelson .60 1.50
299 Ed Kirkpatrick .60 1.50
300 Brooks Robinson 10.00 25.00
301 Earl Wilson .60 1.50
302 Phil Gagliano .60 1.50
303 Lindy McDaniel .75 2.00
304 Ron Brand .75 2.00
305 Reggie Smith .75 2.00
306 Jim Nash .60 1.50
307 Don Wert .60 1.50
308 Cardinals Team 1.25 3.00
309 Dick Ellsworth .60 1.50
310 Tommie Agee .75 2.00
311 Lee Stange .60 1.50
312 Harry Walker MG .60 1.50
313 Tom Hall .60 1.50
314 Jeff Torborg .75 2.00
315 Ron Fairly 1.25 3.00
316 Fred Scherman .60 1.50
317 Jim Driscoll .60 1.50
Angel Mangual
318 Rudy May .60 1.50
319 Ty Cline .60 1.50
320 Dave McNally .75 2.00
321 Tom Matchick .60 1.50
322 Jim Beauchamp .60 1.50
323 Billy Champion .60 1.50
324 Graig Nettles 1.25 3.00
325 Juan Marichal 4.00 10.00
326 Richie Scheinblum .60 1.50
327 World Series Game 1 .75 2.00
Boog Powell homers to
opposi
328 Don Buford WS .75 2.00
329 Frank Robinson WS3 1.25 3.00
330 World Series Game 4 .75 2.00
Reds stay alive
331 Brooks Robinson WS5 3.00 8.00
332 World Series Summary .75 2.00
Orioles Celebrate
333 Clay Kirby .60 1.50
334 Roberto Pena .60 1.50
335 Jerry Koosman .75 2.00
336 Tigers Team 1.25 3.00
337 Jesus Alou .60 1.50
338 Gene Tenace .75 2.00
339 Wayne Simpson .60 1.50
340 Rico Petrocelli .75 2.00
341 Steve Garvey RC 20.00 50.00
342 Frank Tepedino .75 2.00
343 Milt May RC .75 2.00
344 Ellie Rodriguez .60 1.50
345 Joel Horlen .60 1.50
346 Lum Harris MG .60 1.50
347 Ted Uhlaender .60 1.50
348 Fred Norman .60 1.50
349 Rich Reese .60 1.50
350 Billy Williams 3.00 8.00
351 Jim Shellenback .60 1.50
352 Denny Doyle .60 1.50
353 Carl Taylor .60 1.50
354 Don McMahon .60 1.50
355 Bud Harrelson 1.25 3.00
356 Bob Locker .60 1.50
357 Reds Team 1.25 3.00
358 Danny Cater .60 1.50
359 Ron Reed .60 1.50
360 Jim Fregosi .75 2.00
361 Don Sutton 3.00 8.00
362 Mike Adamson .60 1.50
Roger Freed
363 Mike Nagy .60 1.50
364 Tommy Dean .60 1.50
365 Bob Johnson .60 1.50
366 Ron Stone .60 1.50
367 Dalton Jones .60 1.50
368 Bob Veale .75 2.00
369 Checklist 394-523 4.00 10.00
370 Joe Torre 2.50 6.00
371 Jack Hiatt .60 1.50
372 Lew Krausse .60 1.50
373 Tom McCraw .60 1.50
374 Clete Boyer .75 2.00
375 Steve Hargan .60 1.50
376 Clyde Mashore .75 2.00
Ernie McAnally
377 Greg Garrett .60 1.50
378 Tito Fuentes .60 1.50
379 Wayne Granger .60 1.50
380 Ted Williams MG 6.00 15.00
381 Fred Gladding .60 1.50
382 Jake Gibbs .60 1.50
383 Rod Gaspar .60 1.50
384 Rollie Fingers 3.00 8.00
385 Maury Wills 2.50 6.00
386 Red Sox Team 1.25 3.00
387 Ron Herbel .60 1.50
388 Al Oliver 1.25 3.00
389 Ed Brinkman .60 1.50
390 Glenn Beckert .75 2.00
391 Steve Brye .75 2.00
Cotton Nash
392 Grant Jackson .60 1.50
393 Merv Rettenmund .75 2.00
394 Clay Carroll 1.25 3.00
395 Roy White 1.50 4.00
396 Dick Schofield 1.25 3.00
397 Alvin Dark MG 1.50 4.00
398 Howie Reed 1.50 4.00
399 Jim French 1.25 3.00
400 Hank Aaron 40.00 80.00
401 Tom Murphy 1.25 3.00
402 Dodgers Team 2.50 6.00
403 Joe Coleman 1.25 3.00
404 Buddy Harris 1.25 3.00
Roger Metzger
405 Leo Cardenas 1.25 3.00
406 Ray Sadecki 1.25 3.00
407 Joe Rudi 1.50 4.00
408 Rafael Robles 1.25 3.00
409 Don Pavletich 1.25 3.00
410 Ken Holtzman 1.50 4.00
411 George Spriggs 1.25 3.00
412 Jerry Johnson 1.25 3.00
413 Pat Kelly 1.25 3.00
414 Woodie Fryman 1.25 3.00
415 Mike Hegan 1.25 3.00
416 Gene Alley 1.25 3.00
417 Dick Hall 1.25 3.00
418 Adolfo Phillips 1.50 4.00
419 Ron Hansen 1.25 3.00
420 Jim Merritt 1.25 3.00
421 John Stephenson 1.25 3.00
422 Frank Bertaina 1.25 3.00
423 Dennis Saunders 1.25 3.00
Tim Marting
424 Roberto Rodriquez 1.25 3.00
425 Doug Rader 1.50 4.00
426 Chris Cannizzaro 1.25 3.00
427 Bernie Allen 1.25 3.00
428 Jim McAndrew 1.25 3.00
429 Chuck Hinton 1.25 3.00
430 Wes Parker 1.50 4.00
431 Tom Burgmeier 1.25 3.00
432 Bob Didier 1.25 3.00
433 Skip Lockwood 1.25 3.00
434 Gary Sutherland 1.50 4.00
435 Jose Cardenal 1.50 4.00
436 Wilbur Wood 1.50 4.00
437 Danny Murtaugh MG 1.50 4.00
438 Mike McCormick 1.50 4.00
439 Greg Luzinski RC 2.50 6.00
440 Bert Campaneris 1.50 4.00
441 Milt Pappas 1.50 4.00
442 Angels Team 2.50 6.00
443 Rich Robertson 1.25 3.00
444 Jimmie Price 1.25 3.00
445 Art Shamsky 1.25 3.00
446 Bobby Bolin 1.25 3.00
447 Cesar Geronimo 1.50 4.00
448 Dave Roberts 1.25 3.00
449 Brant Alyea 1.25 3.00
450 Bob Gibson 8.00 20.00
451 Joe Keough 1.25 3.00
452 John Boccabella 1.50 4.00
453 Terry Crowley 1.25 3.00
454 Mike Paul 1.25 3.00
455 Don Kessinger 1.50 4.00
456 Bob Meyer 1.25 3.00
457 Willie Smith 1.25 3.00
458 Ron Lolich 1.25 3.00
Dave Lemonds
459 Jim Lefebvre 1.25 3.00
460 Fritz Peterson 1.25 3.00
461 Jim Ray Hart 1.25 3.00
462 Senators Team 2.50 6.00
463 Tom Kelley 1.25 3.00
464 Aurelio Rodriguez 1.25 3.00
465 Tim McCarver 2.50 6.00
466 Ken Berry 1.25 3.00
467 Al Santorini 1.25 3.00
468 Frank Fernandez 1.25 3.00
469 Bob Aspromonte 1.25 3.00
470 Bob Oliver 1.25 3.00
471 Tom Griffin 1.25 3.00
472 Ken Rudolph 1.25 3.00
473 Gary Wagner 1.25 3.00
474 Jim Fairey 1.50 4.00
475 Ron Perranoski 1.25 3.00
476 Dal Maxvill 1.25 3.00
477 Earl Weaver MG 3.00 8.00
478 Bernie Carbo 1.25 3.00
479 Dennis Higgins 1.25 3.00
480 Manny Sanguillen 1.50 4.00
481 Daryl Patterson 1.25 3.00
482 Padres Team 2.50 6.00
483 Gene Michael 1.25 3.00
484 Don Wilson 1.25 3.00
485 Ken McMullen 1.25 3.00
486 Steve Huntz 1.25 3.00
487 Paul Schaal 1.25 3.00
488 Jerry Stephenson 1.25 3.00
489 Luis Alvarado 1.25 3.00
490 Deron Johnson 1.25 3.00
491 Jim Hardin 1.25 3.00
492 Ken Boswell 1.25 3.00
493 Dave May 1.25 3.00
494 Ralph Garr 1.50 4.00
Rick Kester
495 Felipe Alou 1.50 4.00
496 Woody Woodward 1.25 3.00
497 Horacio Pina 1.25 3.00
498 John Kennedy 1.25 3.00
499 Checklist 524-643 3.00 8.00
500 Jim Perry 1.50 4.00
501 Andy Etchebarren 1.25 3.00
502 Cubs Team 2.50 6.00
503 Gates Brown 1.50 4.00
504 Ken Wright 1.25 3.00
505 Ollie Brown 1.25 3.00
506 Bobby Knoop 1.25 3.00
507 George Stone 1.25 3.00
508 Roger Repoz 1.25 3.00
509 Jim Grant 1.25 3.00
510 Ken Harrelson 1.50 4.00
511 Chris Short 1.50 4.00
512 Dick Mills 1.25 3.00
Mike Garman
513 Nolan Ryan 100.00 200.00
514 Ron Woods 1.25 3.00
515 Carl Morton 1.50 4.00
516 Ted Kubiak 1.25 3.00
517 Charlie Fox MG 1.25 3.00
518 Joe Grzenda 1.25 3.00
519 Willie Crawford 1.25 3.00
520 Tommy John 2.50 6.00
521 Leron Lee 1.25 3.00
522 Twins Team 2.50 6.00
523 John Odom 1.25 3.00
524 Mickey Stanley 2.50 6.00
525 Ernie Banks 40.00 80.00
526 Ray Jarvis 1.50 4.00
527 Cleon Jones 2.50 6.00
528 Wally Bunker 1.50 4.00
529 Bill Buckner 2.50 6.00
530 Carl Yastrzemski 20.00 50.00
531 Mike Torrez 1.50 4.00
532 Bill Rigney MG 1.50 4.00
533 Mike Ryan 1.50 4.00
534 Luke Walker 1.50 4.00
535 Curt Flood 2.50 6.00
536 Claude Raymond 2.50 6.00
537 Tom Egan 1.50 4.00
538 Angel Bravo 1.50 4.00
539 Larry Brown 1.50 4.00
540 Larry Dierker 2.50 6.00
541 Bob Burda 1.50 4.00
542 Bob Miller 1.50 4.00
543 Yankees Team 6.00 15.00
544 Vida Blue 2.50 6.00
545 Dick Dietz 1.50 4.00
546 John Matias 1.50 4.00
547 Pat Dobson 1.50 4.00
548 Don Mason 1.50 4.00
549 Jim Brewer 1.50 4.00
550 Harmon Killebrew 12.50 40.00
551 Frank Linzy 1.50 4.00
552 Buddy Bradford 1.50 4.00
553 Kevin Collins 1.50 4.00
554 Lowell Palmer 1.50 4.00
555 Walt Williams 1.50 4.00
556 Jim McGlothlin 1.50 4.00
557 Tom Satriano 1.50 4.00
558 Hector Torres 1.50 4.00
559 AL Rookie Pitchers 1.50 4.00
Terry Cox
Bill Gogolewski
Ga
560 Rusty Staub 3.00 8.00
561 Syd O'Brien 1.50 4.00
562 Dave Giusti 1.50 4.00
563 Giants Team 3.00 8.00
564 Al Fitzmorris 1.50 4.00
565 Jim Wynn 2.50 6.00
566 Tim Cullen 1.50 4.00
567 Walt Alston MG 4.00 10.00
568 Sal Campisi 1.50 4.00
569 Ivan Murrell 1.50 4.00
570 Jim Palmer 20.00 50.00
571 Ted Sizemore 1.50 4.00
572 Jerry Kenney 1.50 4.00
573 Ed Kranepool 2.50 6.00
574 Jim Bunning 4.00 10.00
575 Bill Freehan 2.50 6.00
576 Cubs Rookies 1.50 4.00
Adrian Garrett
Brock Davis
Garry J
577 Jim Lonborg 2.50 6.00
578 Eddie Kasko/(Topps 578 is 2.50 6.00
Ron Hunt)
579 Marty Pattin 1.50 4.00
580 Tony Perez 12.50 30.00
581 Roger Nelson 1.50 4.00
582 Dave Cash 2.50 6.00
583 Ron Cook 1.50 4.00
584 Indians Team 3.00 8.00
585 Willie Davis 2.50 6.00

586 Dick Woodson 1.50 4.00
587 Sonny Jackson 1.50 4.00
588 Tom Bradley 1.50 4.00
589 Bob Barton 1.50 4.00
590 Alex Johnson 2.50 6.00
591 Jackie Brown 1.50 4.00
592 Randy Hundley 2.50 6.00
593 Jack Aker 1.50 4.00
594 Al Hrabosky RC 2.50 6.00
595 Dave Johnson 2.50 6.00
596 Mike Jorgensen 1.50 4.00
597 Ken Suarez 1.50 4.00
598 Rick Wise 2.50 6.00
599 Norm Cash 2.50 6.00
600 Willie Mays 75.00 150.00
601 Ken Tatum 1.50 4.00
602 Marty Martinez 1.50 4.00
603 Pirates Team 3.00 8.00
604 John Gelnar 1.50 4.00
605 Orlando Cepeda 4.00 10.00
606 Chuck Taylor 1.50 4.00
607 Paul Ratliff 1.50 4.00
608 Mike Wegener 2.50 6.00
609 Leo Durocher MG 3.00 8.00
610 Amos Otis 2.50 6.00
611 Tom Phoebus 1.50 4.00
612 Indians Rookies 1.50 4.00
Lou Camilli
Ted Ford
Steve Mingori
613 Pedro Borbon 1.50 4.00
614 Billy Cowan 1.50 4.00
615 Mel Stottlemyre 2.50 6.00
616 Larry Hisle 2.50 6.00
617 Clay Dalrymple 1.50 4.00
618 Tug McGraw 2.50 6.00
619 Checklist 644-752 4.00 10.00
620 Frank Howard 2.50 6.00
621 Ron Bryant 1.50 4.00
622 Joe Lahoud 1.50 4.00
623 Pat Jarvis 1.50 4.00
624 Athletics Team 3.00 8.00
625 Lou Brock 20.00 50.00
626 Freddie Patek 2.50 6.00
627 Steve Hamilton 1.50 4.00
628 John Bateman 2.50 6.00
629 John Hiller 3.00 8.00
630 Roberto Clemente 100.00 200.00
631 Eddie Fisher 1.50 4.00
632 Darrel Chaney 1.50 4.00
633 AL Rookie Outfielders 1.50 4.00
Bobby Brooks
Pete Koegel/
634 Phil Regan 1.50 4.00
635 Bobby Murcer 2.50 6.00
636 Denny LeMaster 1.50 4.00
637 Dave Bristol MG 1.50 4.00
638 Stan Williams 1.50 4.00
639 Tom Haller 1.50 4.00
640 Frank Robinson 30.00 60.00
641 Mets Team 10.00 25.00
642 Jim Roland 1.50 4.00
643 Rick Reichardt 1.50 4.00
644 Jim Stewart 4.00 10.00
645 Jim Maloney 5.00 12.00
646 Bobby Floyd 4.00 10.00
647 Juan Pizarro 4.00 10.00
648 Jon Matlack RC SP 8.00 20.00
649 Sparky Lyle 6.00 15.00
650 Richie Allen SP ! 20.00 50.00
651 Jerry Robertson 4.00 10.00
652 Braves Team 6.00 15.00
653 Russ Snyder 4.00 10.00
654 Don Shaw 4.00 10.00
655 Mike Epstein 4.00 10.00
656 Gerry Nyman 4.00 10.00
657 Jose Azcue 4.00 10.00
658 Paul Lindblad 4.00 10.00
659 Byron Browne 4.00 10.00
660 Ray Culp 4.00 10.00
661 Chuck Tanner MG 6.00 15.00
662 Mike Hedlund 4.00 10.00
663 Marv Staehle 4.00 10.00
664 Rookie Pitchers 6.00 15.00
Archie Reynolds
Bob Reynolds
Ke
665 Ron Swoboda 6.00 15.00
666 Gene Brabender 4.00 10.00
667 Pete Ward 5.00 12.00
668 Gary Neibauer 4.00 10.00
669 Ike Brown 4.00 10.00
670 Bill Hands 4.00 10.00
671 Bill Voss 4.00 10.00
672 Ed Crosby 4.00 10.00
673 Gerry Janeski 4.00 10.00
674 Expos Team 6.00 15.00
675 Dave Boswell 4.00 10.00
676 Tommie Reynolds 4.00 10.00
677 Jack DiLauro 4.00 10.00
678 George Thomas 4.00 10.00
679 Don O'Riley 4.00 10.00
680 Don Mincher 4.00 10.00
681 Bill Butler 4.00 10.00
682 Terry Harmon 4.00 10.00
683 Bill Burbach 4.00 10.00
684 Curt Motton 4.00 10.00
685 Moe Drabowsky 4.00 10.00
686 Chico Ruiz 4.00 10.00
687 Ron Taylor 5.00 12.00
688 Sparky Anderson MG 20.00 50.00
689 Frank Baker 4.00 10.00
690 Bob Moose 4.00 10.00
691 Bob Heise 4.00 10.00
692 AL Rookie Pitchers 4.00 10.00
Hal Haydel
Rogelio Moret
Way
693 Jose Pena 4.00 10.00
694 Rick Renick 4.00 10.00
695 Joe Niekro 5.00 12.00
696 Jerry Morales 4.00 10.00
697 Rickey Clark 4.00 10.00
698 Brewers Team 8.00 20.00
699 Jim Britton 5.00 12.00
700 Boog Powell 12.50 40.00
701 Bob Garibaldi 4.00 10.00
702 Milt Ramirez 4.00 10.00
703 Mike Kekich 4.00 10.00
704 J.C. Martin 4.00 10.00
705 Dick Selma 4.00 10.00
706 Joe Foy 4.00 10.00
707 Fred Lasher 4.00 10.00
708 Russ Nagelson 4.00 10.00
709 D.Baylor 60.00 120.00
D.Baker RC SP !
710 Sonny Siebert 4.00 10.00
711 Larry Stahl 4.00 10.00
712 Jose Martinez 4.00 10.00
713 Mike Marshall 8.00 20.00
714 Dick Williams MG 6.00 15.00
715 Horace Clarke 4.00 10.00
716 Dave Leonhard 4.00 10.00
717 Tommie Aaron 5.00 12.00
718 Billy Wynne 4.00 10.00
719 Jerry May 4.00 10.00
720 Matty Alou 5.00 12.00
721 John Morris 4.00 10.00
722 Astros Team 8.00 20.00
723 Vicente Romo 4.00 10.00
724 Tom Tischinski 4.00 10.00
725 Gary Gentry 4.00 10.00
726 Paul Popovich 4.00 10.00
727 Ray Lamb 4.00 10.00
728 NL Rookie Outfielders 4.00 10.00
Wayne Redmond
Keith Lampar
729 Dick Billings 4.00 10.00
730 Jim Rooker 4.00 10.00
731 Jim Qualls 4.00 10.00
732 Bob Reed 4.00 10.00
733 Lee Maye 4.00 10.00
734 Rob Gardner 4.00 10.00
735 Mike Shannon 6.00 15.00
736 Mel Queen 4.00 10.00
737 Preston Gomez MG 4.00 10.00
738 Russ Gibson 4.00 10.00
739 Barry Lersch 4.00 10.00
740 Luis Aparicio 20.00 50.00
741 Skip Guinn 4.00 10.00
742 Royals Team 6.00 15.00
743 John O'Donoghue 5.00 12.00
744 Chuck Manuel 4.00 10.00
745 Sandy Alomar 5.00 12.00
746 Andy Kosco 4.00 10.00
747 NL Rookie Pitchers 4.00 10.00
Al Severinsen
Scipio Spinks/
748 John Purdin 4.00 10.00
749 Ken Sczotkiewicz 4.00 10.00
750 Denny McLain 12.50 40.00
751 Al Weis 6.00 15.00
752 Dick Drago 5.00 12.00

1972 O-Pee-Chee

The cards in this 525-card set measure 2 1/2" by 3 1/2". The 1972 O-Pee-Chee set is very similar to the 1972 Topps set. On a white background, the fronts feature color player photos with multicolored frames, rounded bottom corners and the top part of the photo also rounded. The player's name and team name appear on the front. The horizontal backs carry player biography and statistics in French and English and have a different color than the 1972 Topps cards. Features appearing for the first time were "Boyhood Photos" (KP: 341-348 and 491-498) and "In Action" cards. The O-Pee-Chee cards can be distinguished from Topps cards by the "Printed in Canada" on the bottom of the back. This was the first year the cards denoted O.P.C. in the copyright line rather than T.C.G. There is one card in the set which is notably different from the corresponding Topps number on the back, No. 465 Gil Hodges, which notes his death in April of 1972. Remember, the prices below apply only to the O-Pee-Chee cards -- NOT Topps cards which are much more plentiful. The cards were packaged in 36 count boxes with eight cards per pack which cost ten cents each. Notable Rookie Cards include Carlton Fisk.

COMPLETE SET (525) 1000.00 2000.00
COMMON PLAYER (1-132) .40 1.00
COMMON PLAYER (133-263) .60 1.50
COMMON PLAYER (264-394) .75 2.00
COMMON PLAYER (395-525) 1.00 2.50
1 Pirates Team 5.00 12.00
2 Ray Culp .40 1.00
3 Bob Tolan .40 1.00
4 Checklist 1-132 2.50 6.00
5 John Bateman .75 2.00
6 Fred Scherman .40 1.00
7 Enzo Hernandez .40 1.00
8 Ron Swoboda .75 2.00
9 Stan Williams .40 1.00
10 Amos Otis .75 2.00
11 Bobby Valentine .75 2.00
12 Jose Cardenal .40 1.00
13 Joe Grzenda .40 1.00
14 Phillies Rookies .40 1.00
Pete Koegel
Mike Anderson
Wayn
15 Walt Williams .40 1.00
16 Mike Jorgensen .40 1.00
17 Dave Duncan .75 2.00
18 Juan Pizarro .40 1.00
19 Billy Cowan .40 1.00
20 Don Wilson .40 1.00
21 Braves Team .75 2.00
22 Rob Gardner .40 1.00
23 Ted Kubiak .40 1.00
24 Ted Ford .40 1.00
25 Bill Singer .40 1.00
26 Andy Etchebarren .40 1.00
27 Bob Johnson .40 1.00
28 Bob Gebhard .40 1.00
Steve Brye
Hal Haydel
29 Bill Bonham .40 1.00
30 Rico Petrocelli .75 2.00
31 Cleon Jones .75 2.00
32 Cleon Jones IA .40 1.00
33 Billy Martin MG 2.50 6.00
34 Billy Martin IA 1.50 4.00
35 Jerry Johnson .40 1.00
36 Jerry Johnson IA .40 1.00
37 Carl Yastrzemski 8.00 20.00
38 Carl Yastrzemski IA 3.00 8.00
39 Bob Barton .40 1.00
40 Bob Barton IA .40 1.00
41 Tommy Davis .75 2.00
42 Tommy Davis IA .40 1.00
43 Rick Wise .75 2.00
44 Rick Wise IA .40 1.00
45 Glenn Beckert .75 2.00
46 Glenn Beckert IA .40 1.00
47 John Ellis .40 1.00
48 John Ellis IA .40 1.00
49 Willie Mays 30.00 60.00
50 Willie Mays IA ! 12.50 30.00
51 Harmon Killebrew 5.00 12.00
52 Harmon Killebrew IA 2.50 6.00
53 Bud Harrelson .75 2.00
54 Bud Harrelson IA .40 1.00
55 Clyde Wright .40 1.00
56 Rich Chiles .40 1.00
57 Bob Oliver .40 1.00
58 Ernie McAnally .40 1.00
59 Fred Stanley .40 1.00
60 Manny Sanguillen .75 2.00
61 Burt Hooton RC .75 2.00
62 Angel Mangual .40 1.00
63 Duke Sims .40 1.00
64 Pete Broberg .40 1.00
65 Cesar Cedeno .75 2.00
66 Ray Corbin .40 1.00
67 Red Schoendienst MG 1.50 4.00
68 Jim York .40 1.00
69 Roger Freed .40 1.00
70 Mike Cuellar .75 2.00
71 Angels Team .75 2.00
72 Bruce Kison .40 1.00
73 Steve Huntz .40 1.00
74 Cecil Upshaw .40 1.00
75 Bert Campaneris .75 2.00
76 Don Carrithers .40 1.00
77 Ron Theobald .40 1.00
78 Steve Arlin .40 1.00
79 Carlton Fisk 40.00 80.00
Cooper RC !
80 Tony Perez 3.00 8.00
81 Mike Hedlund .40 1.00
82 Ron Woods .75 2.00
83 Dalton Jones .40 1.00
84 Vince Colbert .40 1.00
85 NL Batting Leaders 1.50 4.00
Joe Torre
Ralph Garr
Glenn B
86 AL Batting Leaders 1.50 4.00
Tony Oliva
Bobby Murcer
Merv
87 Torre 2.50 6.00
Starg
Aaron LL
88 Kill 2.50 6.00
F.Rob
R.Smith LL
89 Stargell 1.50 4.00
Aaron
May LL
90 Melton 1.50 4.00
Cash
Reggie LL
91 Seaver 1.50 4.00
Roberts
Wilson LL
92 Blue 1.50 4.00
Wood
Palmer LL
93 Jenk 2.50 6.00
Carlton
Seaver LL
94 AL Pitching Leaders 1.50 4.00
Mickey Lolich
Vida Blue
Wil
95 Seaver 2.50 6.00
Jenkins
Stone LL
96 AL Strikeout Leaders 1.50 4.00
Tom Sil
Mickey Lolich
Vida Blue
Jo
97 Tom Kelley .40 1.00
98 Chuck Tanner MG .75 2.00
99 Ross Grimsley .40 1.00
100 Frank Robinson 4.00 10.00
101 J.R.Richard RC 1.50 4.00
102 Lloyd Allen .40 1.00
103 Checklist 133-263 2.50 6.00
104 Toby Harrah RC .75 2.00
105 Gary Gentry .40 1.00
106 Brewers Team .75 2.00
107 Jose Cruz RC .75 2.00
108 Gary Waslewski .40 1.00
109 Jerry May .40 1.00
110 Ron Hunt .75 2.00
111 Jim Grant .40 1.00
112 Greg Luzinski .75 2.00
113 Rogelio Moret .40 1.00
114 Bill Buckner .75 2.00
115 Jim Fregosi .75 2.00
116 Ed Farmer .40 1.00
117 Cleo James .40 1.00
118 Skip Lockwood .40 1.00
119 Marty Perez .40 1.00
120 Bill Freehan .75 2.00
121 Ed Sprague .40 1.00
122 Larry Biittner .40 1.00
123 Ed Acosta .40 1.00
124 Yankees Rookies .40 1.00
Alan Closter
Rusty Torres
Roger
125 Dave Cash .75 2.00
126 Bart Johnson .40 1.00
127 Duffy Dyer .40 1.00
128 Eddie Watt .40 1.00
129 Charlie Fox MG .40 1.00
130 Bob Gibson 4.00 10.00
131 Jim Nettles .40 1.00
132 Joe Morgan 3.00 8.00
133 Joe Keough .60 1.50
134 Carl Morton 1.00 2.50
135 Vada Pinson 1.00 2.50
136 Darrel Chaney .60 1.50
137 Dick Williams MG 1.00 2.50
138 Mike Kekich .60 1.50
139 Tim McCarver 1.00 2.50
140 Pat Dobson 1.00 2.50
141 Mets Rookies 1.00 2.50
Buzz Capra
Leroy Stanton
Jon Matla
142 Chris Chambliss RC 2.00 5.00
143 Garry Jestadt .60 1.50
144 Marty Pattin .60 1.50
145 Don Kessinger 1.00 2.50
146 Steve Kealey .60 1.50
147 Dave Kingman RC 3.00 8.00
148 Dick Billings .60 1.50
149 Gary Neibauer .60 1.50
150 Norm Cash 1.00 2.50
151 Jim Brewer .60 1.50
152 Gene Clines .60 1.50
153 Rick Auerbach .60 1.50
154 Ted Simmons 2.00 5.00
155 Larry Dierker 1.00 2.50
156 Twins Team 1.00 2.50
157 Don Gullett .60 1.50
158 Jerry Kenney .60 1.50
159 John Boccabella 1.00 2.50
160 Andy Messersmith 1.00 2.50
161 Brock Davis .60 1.50
162 Darrell Porter RC UER 1.00 2.50
163 Tug McGraw 2.00 5.00
164 Tug McGraw IA 1.00 2.50
165 Chris Speier RC 1.00 2.50
166 Chris Speier IA .60 1.50
167 Deron Johnson .60 1.50
168 Deron Johnson IA .60 1.50
169 Vida Blue 2.00 5.00
170 Vida Blue IA 1.00 2.50
171 Darrell Evans 2.00 5.00
172 Darrell Evans IA 1.00 2.50
173 Clay Kirby .60 1.50
174 Clay Kirby IA .60 1.50
175 Tom Haller .60 1.50
176 Tom Haller IA .60 1.50
177 Paul Schaal .60 1.50
178 Paul Schaal IA .60 1.50
179 Dock Ellis .60 1.50
180 Dock Ellis IA .60 1.50
181 Ed Kranepool 1.00 2.50
182 Ed Kranepool IA .60 1.50
183 Bill Melton .60 1.50
184 Bill Melton IA .60 1.50
185 Ron Bryant .60 1.50
186 Ron Bryant IA .60 1.50
187 Gates Brown .60 1.50
188 Frank Lucchesi MG .60 1.50
189 Gene Tenace 1.00 2.50
190 Dave Giusti .60 1.50
191 Jeff Burroughs RC 2.00 5.00
192 Cubs Team 1.00 2.50
193 Kurt Bevacqua .60 1.50
194 Fred Norman .60 1.50
195 Orlando Cepeda 3.00 8.00
196 Mel Queen .60 1.50
197 Johnny Briggs .60 1.50
198 Charlie Hough RC 3.00 8.00
199 Mike Fiore .60 1.50
200 Lou Brock 4.00 10.00
201 Phil Roof .60 1.50
202 Scipio Spinks .60 1.50
203 Ron Blomberg .60 1.50
204 Tommy Helms .60 1.50
205 Dick Drago .60 1.50
206 Dal Maxvill .60 1.50
207 Tom Egan .60 1.50
208 Milt Pappas 1.00 2.50
209 Joe Rudi 1.00 2.50
210 Denny McLain 1.00 2.50
211 Gary Sutherland 1.00 2.50
212 Grant Jackson .60 1.50
213 Angels Rookies .60 1.50
Billy Parker
Art Kusnyer
Tom Sil
214 Mike McQueen .60 1.50
215 Alex Johnson 1.00 2.50
216 Joe Niekro 1.00 2.50
217 Roger Metzger .60 1.50
218 Eddie Kasko MG .60 1.50
219 Rennie Stennett 1.00 2.50
220 Jim Perry 1.00 2.50
221 NL Playoffs 1.00 2.50
Bucs champs
222 Brooks Robinson ALCS 2.00 5.00
223 Dave McNally WS 1.00 2.50
224 World Series Game 2/(Dave Johnson 1.00 2.50
and Mark Belan
225 Manny Sanguillen WS 1.00 2.50
226 Roberto Clemente WS4 4.00 10.00
227 Nellie Briles WS 1.00 2.50
228 World Series Game 6
(Frank Robinson and 2.00 5.00
Manny Sa
229 Steve Blass WS 1.00 2.50
230 World Series Summary 1.00 2.50
Pirates celebrate
231 Casey Cox .60 1.50
232 Chris Arnold .60 1.50
Jim Barr
Dave Rader
233 Jay Johnstone 1.00 2.50
234 Ron Taylor 2.00 5.00
235 Merv Rettenmund .60 1.50
236 Jim McGlothlin .60 1.50
237 Yankees Team 1.00 2.50
238 Leron Lee .60 1.50
239 Tom Timmermann .60 1.50
240 Richie Allen 1.00 2.50
241 Rollie Fingers 3.00 8.00
242 Don Mincher .60 1.50
243 Frank Linzy .60 1.50
244 Steve Braun .60 1.50
245 Tommie Agee 1.00 2.50
246 Tom Burgmeier .60 1.50
247 Milt May .60 1.50
248 Tom Bradley .60 1.50
249 Harry Walker MG .60 1.50
250 Boog Powell 1.00 2.50
251 Checklist 264-394 2.50 6.00
252 Ken Reynolds .60 1.50
253 Sandy Alomar 1.00 2.50
254 Boots Day 1.00 2.50
255 Jim Lonborg 1.00 2.50
256 George Foster 1.00 2.50
257 Jim Foor .60 1.50
Tim Hosley
Paul Jata
258 Randy Hundley .60 1.50
259 Sparky Lyle 1.00 2.50
260 Ralph Garr 1.00 2.50
261 Steve Mingori .60 1.50
262 Padres Team 1.00 2.50
263 Felipe Alou 1.00 2.50
264 Tommy John 1.25 3.00
265 Wes Parker 1.25 3.00
266 Bobby Bolin .75 2.00
267 Dave Concepcion 2.50 6.00
268 Dwain Anderson .75 2.00
Chris Floethe
269 Don Hahn .75 2.00
270 Jim Palmer 4.00 10.00
271 Ken Rudolph .75 2.00
272 Mickey Rivers RC 1.25 3.00
273 Bobby Floyd .75 2.00
274 Al Severinsen .75 2.00
275 Cesar Tovar .75 2.00
276 Gene Mauch MG 1.25 3.00
277 Elliott Maddox .75 2.00
278 Dennis Higgins .75 2.00
279 Larry Brown .75 2.00
280 Willie McCovey 3.00 8.00
281 Bill Parsons .75 2.00
282 Astros Team 1.25 3.00
283 Darrell Brandon .75 2.00
284 Ike Brown .75 2.00
285 Gaylord Perry 4.00 10.00
286 Gene Alley .75 2.00
287 Jim Hardin .75 2.00
288 Johnny Jeter .75 2.00
289 Syd O'Brien .75 2.00
290 Sonny Siebert .75 2.00
291 Hal McRae 1.25 3.00
292 Hal McRae IA .75 2.00
293 Danny Frisella .75 2.00
294 Danny Frisella IA .75 2.00
295 Dick Dietz .75 2.00
296 Dick Dietz IA .75 2.00
297 Claude Osteen 1.25 3.00
298 Claude Osteen IA .75 2.00
299 Hank Aaron 30.00 60.00
300 Hank Aaron IA 12.50 30.00
301 George Mitterwald .75 2.00
302 George Mitterwald IA .75 2.00
303 Joe Pepitone 1.25 3.00
304 Joe Pepitone IA .75 2.00
305 Ken Boswell .75 2.00
306 Ken Boswell IA .75 2.00
307 Steve Renko 1.25 3.00
308 Steve Renko IA .75 2.00
309 Roberto Clemente 40.00 80.00
310 Roberto Clemente IA 12.50 40.00
311 Clay Carroll .75 2.00
312 Clay Carroll IA .75 2.00
313 Luis Aparicio 4.00 10.00
314 Luis Aparicio IA 2.50 6.00
315 Paul Splittorff .75 2.00
316 Cardinals Rookies 1.25 3.00
Jim Bibby
Jorge Roque
Santiag
317 Rich Hand .75 2.00
318 Sonny Jackson .75 2.00
319 Aurelio Rodriguez .75 2.00
320 Steve Blass 1.25 3.00
321 Joe Lahoud .75 2.00
322 Jose Pena .75 2.00
323 Earl Weaver MG 3.00 8.00
324 Mike Ryan .75 2.00
325 Mel Stottlemyre 1.25 3.00
326 Pat Kelly .75 2.00
327 Steve Stone RC 1.25 3.00
328 Red Sox Team 1.25 3.00
329 Roy Foster .75 2.00
330 Jim Hunter 4.00 10.00
331 Stan Swanson 1.25 3.00
332 Buck Martinez .75 2.00
333 Steve Barber .75 2.00
334 Rangers Rookies .75 2.00
Bill Fahey
Jim Mason
Tom Raglan
335 Bill Hands .75 2.00
336 Marty Martinez .75 2.00
337 Mike Kilkenny 1.25 3.00
338 Bob Grich 1.25 3.00
339 Ron Cook .75 2.00
340 Roy White 1.25 3.00
341 Joe Torre KP 1.25 3.00
342 Wilbur Wood KP .75 2.00
343 Willie Stargell KP 1.25 3.00
344 Dave McNally KP .75 2.00
345 Rick Wise KP .75 2.00
346 Jim Fregosi KP .75 2.00
347 Tom Seaver KP 3.00 8.00
348 Sal Bando KP .75 2.00
349 Al Fitzmorris .75 2.00
350 Frank Howard 1.25 3.00
351 Braves Rookies 1.25 3.00
Tom House
Rick Kester
Jimmy Brit
352 Dave LaRoche .75 2.00
353 Art Shamsky .75 2.00
354 Tom Murphy .75 2.00
355 Bob Watson 1.25 3.00
356 Gerry Moses .75 2.00
357 Woodie Fryman .75 2.00
358 Sparky Anderson MG 3.00 8.00
359 Don Pavletich .75 2.00
360 Dave Roberts .75 2.00
361 Mike Andrews .75 2.00
362 Mets Team 2.50 6.00
363 Ron Klimkowski .75 2.00
364 Johnny Callison 1.25 3.00
365 Dick Bosman 1.25 3.00
366 Jimmy Rosario .75 2.00
367 Ron Perranoski .75 2.00
368 Danny Thompson .75 2.00
369 Jim Lefebvre 1.25 3.00
370 Don Buford .75 2.00
371 Denny LeMaster .75 2.00
372 Lance Clemons .75 2.00
Monty Montgomery
373 John Mayberry 1.25 3.00
374 Jack Heidemann .75 2.00
375 Reggie Cleveland 1.25 3.00
376 Andy Kosco .75 2.00
377 Terry Harmon .75 2.00
378 Checklist 395-525 3.00 8.00
379 Ken Berry .75 2.00
380 Earl Williams .75 2.00
381 White Sox Team 1.25 3.00
382 Joe Gibbon .75 2.00
383 Brant Alyea .75 2.00
384 Dave Campbell 1.25 3.00
385 Mickey Stanley 1.25 3.00
386 Jim Colborn .75 2.00
387 Horace Clarke 1.25 3.00
388 Charlie Williams .75 2.00
389 Bill Rigney MG .75 2.00
390 Willie Davis 1.25 3.00
391 Ken Sanders .75 2.00
392 Fred Cambria 1.25 3.00
Richie Zisk RC
393 Curt Motton .75 2.00
394 Ken Forsch 1.25 3.00
395 Matty Alou 1.25 3.00
396 Paul Lindblad 1.00 2.50
397 Phillies Team 2.50 6.00
398 Larry Hisle 1.25 3.00
399 Milt Wilcox 1.25 3.00
400 Tony Oliva 2.50 6.00
401 Jim Nash 1.00 2.50
402 Bobby Heise 1.00 2.50
403 John Cumberland 1.00 2.50
404 Jeff Torborg 1.25 3.00
405 Ron Fairly 1.25 3.00
406 George Hendrick RC 1.25 3.00
407 Chuck Taylor 1.00 2.50
408 Jim Northrup 1.25 3.00
409 Frank Baker 1.00 2.50
410 Fergie Jenkins 4.00 10.00
411 Bob Montgomery 1.00 2.50
412 Dick Kelley 1.00 2.50
413 Don Eddy 1.00 2.50
Dave Lemonds
414 Bob Miller 1.00 2.50
415 Cookie Rojas 1.00 2.50
416 Johnny Edwards 1.00 2.50
417 Tom Hall 1.00 2.50
418 Tom Shopay 1.00 2.50
419 Jim Spencer 1.00 2.50
420 Steve Carlton 12.50 30.00
421 Ellie Rodriguez 1.00 2.50
422 Ray Lamb 1.00 2.50
423 Oscar Gamble 1.25 3.00
424 Bill Gogolewski 1.00 2.50
425 Ken Singleton 1.25 3.00
426 Ken Singleton IA 1.00 2.50
427 Tito Fuentes 1.00 2.50
428 Tito Fuentes IA 1.00 2.50
429 Bob Robertson 1.00 2.50
430 Bob Robertson IA 1.00 2.50
431 Cito Gaston 1.25 3.00
432 Cito Gaston IA 1.00 2.50
433 Johnny Bench 12.50 40.00
434 Johnny Bench IA 8.00 20.00
435 Reggie Jackson 20.00 50.00
436 Reggie Jackson IA ! 10.00 25.00
437 Maury Wills 2.50 6.00
438 Maury Wills IA 1.25 3.00
439 Billy Williams 3.00 8.00
440 Billy Williams IA 2.50 6.00
441 Thurman Munson 10.00 25.00
442 Thurman Munson IA 5.00 12.00
443 Ken Henderson 1.00 2.50
444 Ken Henderson IA 1.00 2.50
445 Tom Seaver 20.00 50.00
446 Tom Seaver IA 10.00 25.00
447 Willie Stargell 4.00 10.00
448 Willie Stargell IA 2.50 6.00
449 Bob Lemon MG 1.25 3.00
450 Mickey Lolich 1.25 3.00
451 Tony LaRussa 3.00 8.00
452 Ed Herrmann 1.00 2.50
453 Barry Lersch 1.00 2.50
454 A's Team 2.50 6.00
455 Tommy Harper 1.25 3.00
456 Mark Belanger 1.25 3.00
457 Padres Rookies 1.00 2.50
Darcy Fast
Derrel Thomas
Mike Iv
458 Aurelio Monteagudo 1.00 2.50
459 Rick Renick 1.00 2.50
460 Al Downing 1.00 2.50
461 Tim Cullen 1.00 2.50
462 Rickey Clark 1.00 2.50
463 Bernie Carbo 1.00 2.50
464 Jim Roland 1.00 2.50
465 Gil Hodges MG/(Mentions his 12.50 40.00
death on 4/2/72)
466 Norm Miller 1.00 2.50
467 Steve Kline 1.00 2.50
468 Richie Scheinblum 1.00 2.50
469 Ron Herbel 1.00 2.50
470 Ray Fosse 1.00 2.50
471 Luke Walker 1.00 2.50
472 Phil Gagliano 1.00 2.50
473 Dan McGinn 1.00 2.50
474 J.Oates RC 10.00 25.00
Don Baylor
475 Gary Nolan 1.00 2.50
476 Lee Richard 1.00 2.50
477 Tom Phoebus 1.00 2.50
478 Checklist 5th Series 3.00 8.00
479 Don Shaw 1.00 2.50
480 Lee May 1.25 3.00
481 Billy Conigliaro 1.00 2.50
482 Joe Hoerner 1.00 2.50
483 Ken Suarez 1.00 2.50
484 Lum Harris MG 1.00 2.50
485 Phil Regan 1.00 2.50
486 John Lowenstein 1.00 2.50
487 Tigers Team 2.50 6.00
488 Mike Nagy 1.00 2.50
489 Terry Humphrey 1.00 2.50
Keith Lampard
490 Dave McNally 1.25 3.00
491 Lou Piniella KP 1.25 3.00
492 Mel Stottlemyre KP 1.25 3.00
493 Bob Bailey KP 1.25 3.00
494 Willie Horton KP 1.25 3.00
495 Bill Melton KP 1.00 2.50
496 Bud Harrelson KP 1.25 3.00
497 Jim Perry KP 1.25 3.00
498 Brooks Robinson KP 2.50 6.00
499 Vicente Romo 1.00 2.50
500 Joe Torre 3.00 8.00
501 Pete Hamm 1.00 2.50
502 Jackie Hernandez 1.00 2.50
503 Gary Peters 1.00 2.50
504 Ed Spiezio 1.00 2.50
505 Mike Marshall 1.25 3.00
506 Terry Ley 1.25 3.00
Jim Moyer
Dick Tidrow
507 Fred Gladding 1.00 2.50
508 Ellie Hendricks 1.00 2.50
509 Don McMahon 1.00 2.50
510 Ted Williams MG 8.00 20.00
511 Tony Taylor 1.00 2.50
512 Paul Popovich 1.00 2.50
513 Lindy McDaniel 1.25 3.00
514 Ted Sizemore 1.00 2.50
515 Bert Blyleven 2.50 6.00
516 Oscar Brown 1.00 2.50
517 Ken Brett 1.00 2.50
518 Wayne Garrett 1.00 2.50
519 Ted Abernathy 1.00 2.50
520 Larry Bowa 1.25 3.00
521 Alan Foster 1.00 2.50
522 Dodgers Team 2.50 6.00
523 Chuck Dobson 1.00 2.50
524 Ed Armbrister 1.00 2.50
Mel Behney
525 Carlos May 1.25 3.00

1973 O-Pee-Chee

The cards in this 660-card set measure 2 1/2" by 3 1/2". This set is essentially the same as the regular 1973 Topps set, except that the words "Printed in Canada" appear on the backs and the backs are bilingual. On a white border, the fronts feature color player photos with rounded corners and thin black borders. The player's name and position and the team name are also printed on the front. An "All-Time Leaders" series (471-478) appears in this set. Kid pictures appeared again for the second year in a row (341-346). The backs carry player biography and statistics in French and English. The cards are numbered on the back. The backs appear to be more "yellow" than the Topps backs. Remember, the prices below apply only to the O-Pee-Chee cards -- NOT Topps cards which are more plentiful. Unlike the 1973 Topps set, all cards in this set were issued equally and at the same time, i.e., there were no scarce series with the O-Pee-Chee cards. Although there are no scarce series, cards 529-660 attract a slight premium. Because of the premium that high series Topps cards attract, there is a perception that O-Pee-Chee cards of the same number sequence are less available. The key card in this set is the Mike Schmidt Rookie Card. The cards were packaged in 10 count packs with 36 cards in a box which cost 10 cents. Other Rookie Cards of note in this set include Bob Boone and Dwight Evans.

COMPLETE SET (660) 500.00 1000.00
COMMON PLAYER (1-528) .30 .75
COMMON PLAYER (529-660) 1.25 3.00
1 Aaron 20.00 50.00
Ruth
Mays !
2 Rich Hebner .60 1.50
3 Jim Lonborg .60 1.50
4 John Milner .30 .75
5 Ed Brinkman .30 .75
6 Mac Scarce .30 .75
7 Texas Rangers Team .60 1.50
8 Tom Hall .30 .75
9 Johnny Oates .30 .75
10 Don Sutton 2.50 6.00
11 Chris Chambliss .60 1.50
12 Padres Leaders .60 1.50
Don Zimmer MG
Dave Garcia CO
Joh
13 George Hendrick .60 1.50
14 Sonny Siebert .30 .75
15 Ralph Garr .60 1.50
16 Steve Braun .30 .75
17 Fred Gladding .30 .75
18 Leroy Stanton .30 .75
19 Tim Foli .30 .75
20 Stan Bahnsen .30 .75
21 Randy Hundley .60 1.50
22 Ted Abernathy .30 .75
23 Dave Kingman .60 1.50
24 Al Santorini .30 .75
25 Roy White .60 1.50
26 Pirates Team .60 1.50
27 Bill Gogolewski .30 .75
28 Hal McRae .60 1.50
29 Tony Taylor .60 1.50
30 Tug McGraw .60 1.50
31 Buddy Bell RC 1.00 2.50
32 Fred Norman .30 .75
33 Jim Breazeale .30 .75
34 Pat Dobson .30 .75
35 Willie Davis .60 1.50
36 Steve Barber .30 .75
37 Bill Robinson .60 1.50
38 Mike Epstein .30 .75
39 Dave Roberts .30 .75
40 Reggie Smith .60 1.50
41 Tom Walker .30 .75

42 Mike Andrews .30 .75
43 Randy Moffitt .30 .75
44 Rick Monday .60 1.50
45 Ellie Rodriguez(photo actually John Felske) .30 .75
46 Lindy McDaniel .60 1.50
47 Luis Melendez .30 .75
48 Paul Splittorff .30 .75
49 Twins Leaders .60 1.50
Frank Quilici MG
Vern Morgan CO
B
50 Roberto Clemente 20.00 50.00
51 Chuck Seelbach .30 .75
52 Denis Menke .30 .75
53 Steve Dunning .30 .75
54 Checklist 1-132 1.25 3.00
55 Jon Matlack .60 1.50
56 Merv Rettenmund .30 .75
57 Derrel Thomas .30 .75
58 Mike Paul .30 .75
59 Steve Yeager RC .60 1.50
60 Ken Holtzman .60 1.50
61 B.Williams 1.50 4.00
R.Carew LL
62 J.Bench 1.00 2.50
D.Allen LL
63 J.Bench 1.00 2.50
D.Allen LL
64 L.Brock .60 1.50
Campaneris LL
65 S.Carlton .60 1.50
L.Tiant LL
66 Carlton .60 1.50
Perry
Wood LL
67 S.Carlton 12.50 40.00
N.Ryan LL
68 C.Carroll .60 1.50
S.Lyle LL
69 Phil Gagliano .30 .75
70 Milt Pappas .60 1.50
71 Johnny Briggs .30 .75
72 Ron Reed .30 .75
73 Ed Herrmann .30 .75
74 Billy Champion .30 .75
75 Vada Pinson .60 1.50
76 Doug Rader .30 .75
77 Mike Torrez .60 1.50
78 Richie Scheinblum .30 .75
79 Jim Willoughby .30 .75
80 Tony Oliva 1.50 4.00
81 Chicago Cubs Leaders .60 1.50
Whitey Lockman MG
Hank Agui
82 Fritz Peterson .30 .75
83 Leron Lee .30 .75
84 Rollie Fingers 2.50 6.00
85 Ted Simmons .60 1.50
86 Tom McCraw .30 .75
87 Ken Boswell .30 .75
88 Mickey Stanley .60 1.50
89 Jack Billingham .30 .75
90 Brooks Robinson 4.00 10.00
91 Dodgers Team .60 1.50
92 Jerry Bell .30 .75
93 Jesus Alou .30 .75
94 Dick Billings .30 .75
95 Steve Blass .60 1.50
96 Doug Griffin .30 .75
97 Willie Montanez .60 1.50
98 Dick Woodson .30 .75
99 Carl Taylor .30 .75
100 Hank Aaron 20.00 50.00
101 Ken Henderson .30 .75
102 Rudy May .30 .75
103 Celerino Sanchez .30 .75
104 Reggie Cleveland .60 1.50
105 Carlos May .30 .75
106 Terry Humphrey .30 .75
107 Phil Hennigan .30 .75
108 Bill Russell .60 1.50
109 Doyle Alexander .60 1.50
110 Bob Watson .60 1.50
111 Dave Nelson .30 .75
112 Gary Ross .30 .75
113 Jerry Grote .60 1.50
114 Lynn McGlothen .30 .75
115 Ron Santo 1.50 4.00
116 Yankees Leaders .60 1.50
Ralph Houk MG
Jim Hegan CO
Elst
117 Ramon Hernandez .30 .75
118 John Mayberry .60 1.50
119 Larry Bowa .60 1.50
120 Joe Coleman .30 .75
121 Dave Rader .30 .75
122 Jim Strickland .30 .75
123 Sandy Alomar .60 1.50
124 Jim Hardin .30 .75
125 Ron Fairly .60 1.50
126 Jim Brewer .30 .75
127 Brewers Team .60 1.50
128 Ted Sizemore .30 .75
129 Terry Forster .60 1.50
130 Pete Rose 12.50 40.00
131 Red Sox Leaders .60 1.50
Eddie Kasko MG
Doug Camilli CO/
132 Matty Alou .60 1.50
133 Dave Roberts .30 .75
134 Milt Wilcox .30 .75
135 Lee May .60 1.50
136 Orioles Leaders 1.50 4.00
Earl Weaver MG
George Bamberger
137 Jim Beauchamp .30 .75
138 Horacio Pina .30 .75
139 Carmen Fanzone .30 .75
140 Lou Piniella 1.00 2.50
141 Bruce Kison .30 .75
142 Thurman Munson 4.00 10.00
143 John Curtis .30 .75
144 Marty Perez .30 .75
145 Bobby Bonds 1.50 4.00
146 Woodie Fryman .30 .75
147 Mike Anderson .30 .75
148 Dave Goltz .30 .75
149 Ron Hunt .30 .75
150 Wilbur Wood .60 1.50
151 Wes Parker .60 1.50
152 Dave May .30 .75
153 Al Hrabosky .60 1.50
154 Jeff Torborg .60 1.50
155 Sal Bando .60 1.50
156 Cesar Geronimo .30 .75
157 Denny Riddleberger .30 .75
158 Astros Team .60 1.50
159 Cito Gaston .60 1.50
160 Jim Palmer 3.00 8.00
161 Ted Martinez .30 .75
162 Pete Broberg .30 .75
163 Vic Davalillo .30 .75
164 Monty Montgomery .30 .75
165 Luis Aparicio 2.50 6.00
166 Terry Harmon .30 .75
167 Steve Stone .60 1.50
168 Jim Northrup .60 1.50
169 Ron Schueler RC .60 1.50
170 Harmon Killebrew 2.50 6.00
171 Bernie Carbo .30 .75
172 Steve Kline .30 .75
173 Hal Breeden .60 1.50
174 Goose Gossage RC 3.00 8.00
175 Frank Robinson 3.00 8.00
176 Chuck Taylor .30 .75
177 Bill Plummer .30 .75
178 Don Rose .30 .75
179 Oakland A's Leaders .60 1.50
Dick Williams MG
Jerry Adair
180 Fergie Jenkins 2.00 5.00
181 Jack Brohamer .30 .75
182 Mike Caldwell RC .60 1.50
183 Don Buford .30 .75
184 Jerry Koosman .60 1.50
185 Jim Wynn .60 1.50
186 Bill Fahey .30 .75
187 Luke Walker .30 .75
188 Cookie Rojas .60 1.50
189 Greg Luzinski 1.00 2.50
190 Bob Gibson 4.00 10.00
191 Tigers Team .60 1.50
192 Pat Jarvis .30 .75
193 Carlton Fisk 5.00 12.00
194 Jorge Orta .30 .75
195 Clay Carroll .30 .75
196 Ken McMullen .30 .75
197 Ed Goodson .30 .75
198 Horace Clarke .30 .75
199 Bert Blyleven 1.50 4.00
200 Billy Williams 2.50 6.00
201 A.L. Playoffs .60 1.50
A's over Tigers;
George Hendrick s
202 N.L. Playoffs .60 1.50
Reds over Pirates
George Foster's#
203 Gene Tenace WS .60 1.50
204 World Series Game 2 .60 1.50
A's two straight
205 World Series Game 3 1.00 2.50
Reds win squeeker/(Tony Pere
206 Gene Tenace WS .60 1.50
207 Blue Moon Odom WS .60 1.50
208 World Series Game 6 2.50 6.00
Reds' slugging
ties series/
209 World Series Game 7 .60 1.50
Bert Campaneris stars
winnin
210 World Series Summary .60 1.50
World champions:
A's Win
211 Balor Moore .30 .75
212 Joe Lahoud .30 .75
213 Steve Garvey 2.50 6.00
214 Dave Hamilton .30 .75
215 Dusty Baker 1.50 4.00
216 Toby Harrah .60 1.50
217 Don Wilson .30 .75
218 Aurelio Rodriguez .30 .75
219 Cardinals Team .60 1.50
220 Nolan Ryan 50.00 100.00
221 Fred Kendall .30 .75
222 Rob Gardner .30 .75
223 Bud Harrelson .60 1.50
224 Bill Lee .60 1.50
225 Al Oliver .60 1.50
226 Ray Fosse .30 .75
227 Wayne Twitchell .30 .75
228 Bobby Darwin .30 .75
229 Roric Harrison .30 .75
230 Joe Morgan 3.00 8.00
231 Bill Parsons .30 .75
232 Ken Singleton .60 1.50
233 Ed Kirkpatrick .30 .75
234 Bill North .30 .75
235 Jim Hunter 2.50 6.00
236 Tito Fuentes .30 .75
237 Braves Leaders 1.50 4.00
Eddie Mathews MG
Lew Burdette CO#
238 Tony Muser .30 .75
239 Pete Richert .30 .75
240 Bobby Murcer 1.00 2.50
241 Dwain Anderson .30 .75
242 George Culver .30 .75
243 Angels Team .60 1.50
244 Ed Acosta .30 .75
245 Carl Yastrzemski 5.00 12.00
246 Ken Sanders .30 .75
247 Del Unser .30 .75
248 Jerry Johnson .30 .75
249 Larry Biittner .30 .75
250 Manny Sanguillen .60 1.50
251 Roger Nelson .30 .75
252 Giants Leaders .60 1.50
Charlie Fox MG
Joe Amalfitano CO#
253 Mark Belanger .60 1.50
254 Bill Stoneman .60 1.50
255 Reggie Jackson 8.00 20.00
256 Chris Zachary .30 .75
257 N.Y. Mets Leaders 1.50 4.00
Yogi Berra MG
Roy McMillan CO#
258 Tommy John 1.00 2.50
259 Jim Holt .30 .75
260 Gary Nolan .60 1.50
261 Pat Kelly .30 .75
262 Jack Aker .30 .75
263 George Scott .60 1.50
264 Checklist 133-264 1.00 2.50
265 Gene Michael .60 1.50
266 Mike Lum .30 .75
267 Lloyd Allen .30 .75
268 Jerry Morales .30 .75
269 Tim McCarver 1.00 2.50
270 Luis Tiant 1.00 2.50
271 Tom Hutton .30 .75
272 Ed Farmer .30 .75
273 Chris Speier .30 .75
274 Darold Knowles .30 .75
275 Tony Perez 2.50 6.00
276 Joe Lovitto .30 .75
277 Bob Miller .30 .75
278 Orioles Team .60 1.50
279 Mike Strahler .30 .75
280 Al Kaline 4.00 10.00
281 Mike Jorgensen .30 .75
282 Steve Hovley .30 .75
283 Ray Sadecki .30 .75
284 Glenn Borgmann .30 .75
285 Don Kessinger .60 1.50
286 Frank Linzy .30 .75
287 Eddie Leon .30 .75
288 Gary Gentry .30 .75
289 Bob Oliver .30 .75
290 Cesar Cedeno .60 1.50
291 Rogelio Moret .30 .75
292 Jose Cruz .60 1.50
293 Bernie Allen .30 .75
294 Steve Arlin .30 .75
295 Bert Campaneris .60 1.50
296 Sparky Anderson MG 1.50 4.00
297 Walt Williams .30 .75
298 Ron Bryant .30 .75
299 Ted Ford .30 .75
300 Steve Carlton 5.00 12.00
301 Billy Grabarkewitz .30 .75
302 Terry Crowley .30 .75
303 Nelson Briles .30 .75
304 Duke Sims .30 .75
305 Willie Mays 20.00 50.00
306 Tom Burgmeier .30 .75
307 Boots Day .30 .75
308 Skip Lockwood .30 .75
309 Paul Popovich .30 .75
310 Dick Allen 1.00 2.50
311 Joe Decker .30 .75
312 Oscar Brown .30 .75
313 Jim Ray .30 .75
314 Ron Swoboda .60 1.50
315 John Odom .30 .75
316 Padres Team .60 1.50
317 Danny Cater .30 .75
318 Jim McGlothlin .30 .75
319 Jim Spencer .30 .75
320 Lou Brock 4.00 10.00
321 Rich Hinton .30 .75
322 Garry Maddox RC .60 1.50
323 Billy Martin MG 1.00 2.50
324 Al Downing .30 .75
325 Boog Powell .60 1.50
326 Darrell Brandon .30 .75
327 John Lowenstein .30 .75
328 Bill Bonham .30 .75
329 Ed Kranepool .60 1.50
330 Rod Carew 4.00 10.00
331 Carl Morton .30 .75
332 John Felske .30 .75
333 Gene Clines .30 .75
334 Freddie Patek .30 .75
335 Bob Tolan .30 .75
336 Tom Bradley .30 .75
337 Dave Duncan .60 1.50
338 Checklist 265-396 1.00 2.50
339 Dick Tidrow .30 .75
340 Nate Colbert .30 .75
341 Jim Palmer KP 1.00 2.50
342 Sam McDowell KP .60 1.50
343 Bobby Murcer KP .60 1.50
344 Jim Hunter KP 1.00 2.50
345 Chris Speier KP .30 .75
346 Gaylord Perry KP .60 1.50
347 Royals Team .60 1.50
348 Rennie Stennett .60 1.50
349 Dick McAuliffe .30 .75
350 Tom Seaver 6.00 15.00
351 Jimmy Stewart .30 .75
352 Don Stanhouse .30 .75
353 Steve Brye .30 .75
354 Billy Parker .30 .75
355 Mike Marshall .60 1.50
356 White Sox Leaders .60 1.50
Chuck Tanner MG
Joe Lonnett CO
357 Ross Grimsley .30 .75
358 Jim Nettles .30 .75
359 Cecil Upshaw .30 .75
360 Joe Rudi(photo actually Gene Tenace) .60 1.50
361 Fran Healy .30 .75
362 Eddie Watt .30 .75
363 Jackie Hernandez .30 .75
364 Rick Wise .30 .75
365 Rico Petrocelli .60 1.50
366 Brock Davis .30 .75
367 Burt Hooton .60 1.50
368 Bill Buckner .60 1.50
369 Lerrin LaGrow .30 .75
370 Willie Stargell 2.50 6.00
371 Mike Kekich .30 .75
372 Oscar Gamble .30 .75
373 Clyde Wright .30 .75
374 Darrell Evans 1.00 2.50
375 Larry Dierker .60 1.50
376 Frank Duffy .30 .75
377 Expos Leaders 1.00 2.50
Gene Mauch MG
Dave Bristol CO
Lar
378 Lenny Randle .30 .75
379 Cy Acosta .30 .75
380 Johnny Bench 6.00 15.00
381 Vicente Romo .30 .75
382 Mike Hegan .30 .75
383 Diego Segui .30 .75
384 Don Baylor 1.50 4.00
385 Jim Perry .60 1.50
386 Don Money .30 .75
387 Jim Barr .30 .75
388 Ben Oglivie .60 1.50
389 Mets Team 2.00 5.00
390 Mickey Lolich .60 1.50
391 Lee Lacy RC .60 1.50
392 Dick Drago .30 .75
393 Jose Cardenal .30 .75
394 Sparky Lyle .60 1.50
395 Roger Metzger .30 .75
396 Grant Jackson .30 .75
397 Dave Cash .60 1.50
398 Rich Hand .30 .75
399 George Foster .60 1.50
400 Gaylord Perry 2.50 6.00
401 Clyde Mashore .30 .75
402 Jack Hiatt .30 .75
403 Sonny Jackson .30 .75
404 Chuck Brinkman .30 .75
405 Cesar Tovar .30 .75
406 Paul Lindblad .30 .75
407 Felix Millan .30 .75
408 Jim Colborn .30 .75
409 Ivan Murrell .30 .75
410 Willie McCovey 3.00 8.00
411 Ray Corbin .30 .75
412 Manny Mota .60 1.50
413 Tom Timmerman .30 .75
414 Ken Rudolph .30 .75
415 Marty Pattin .30 .75
416 Paul Schaal .30 .75
417 Scipio Spinks .30 .75
418 Bobby Grich .60 1.50
419 Casey Cox .30 .75
420 Tommie Agee .30 .75
421 Angels Leaders .60 1.50
Bobby Winkles MG
Tom Morgan CO
S
422 Bob Robertson .30 .75
423 Johnny Jeter .30 .75
424 Denny Doyle .30 .75
425 Alex Johnson .30 .75
426 Dave LaRoche .30 .75
427 Rick Auerbach .30 .75
428 Wayne Simpson .30 .75
429 Jim Fairey .30 .75
430 Vida Blue .60 1.50
431 Gerry Moses .30 .75
432 Dan Frisella .30 .75
433 Willie Horton .60 1.50
434 Giants Team 1.00 2.50
435 Rico Carty .60 1.50
436 Jim McAndrew .30 .75
437 John Kennedy .30 .75
438 Enzo Hernandez .30 .75
439 Eddie Fisher .30 .75
440 Glenn Beckert .30 .75
441 Gail Hopkins .30 .75
442 Dick Dietz .30 .75
443 Danny Thompson .30 .75
444 Ken Brett .30 .75
445 Ken Berry .30 .75
446 Jerry Reuss .60 1.50
447 Joe Hague .30 .75
448 John Hiller .60 1.50
449 Indians Leaders 2.00 5.00
Ken Aspromonte MG
Rocky Colavito
450 Joe Torre 1.00 2.50
451 John Vuckovich .30 .75
452 Paul Casanova .30 .75
453 Checklist 397-528 1.00 2.50
454 Tom Haller .30 .75
455 Bill Melton .30 .75
456 Dick Green .30 .75
457 John Strohmayer .30 .75
458 Jim Mason .30 .75
459 Jimmy Howarth .30 .75
460 Bill Freehan .60 1.50
461 Mike Corkins .30 .75
462 Ron Blomberg .30 .75
463 Ken Tatum .30 .75
464 Chicago Cubs Team 1.00 2.50
465 Dave Giusti .30 .75
466 Jose Arcia .30 .75
467 Mike Ryan .30 .75
468 Tom Griffin .30 .75
469 Dan Monzon .30 .75
470 Mike Cuellar .60 1.50
471 Ty Cobb LDR 5.00 12.00
472 Lou Gehrig LDR 8.00 20.00
473 Hank Aaron LDR 5.00 12.00
474 Babe Ruth LDR 10.00 25.00
475 Ty Cobb LDR 4.00 10.00
476 Walter Johnson ATL/113 Shutouts 1.00 2.50
477 Cy Young ATL/511 Wins 1.00 2.50
478 Walter Johnson ATL/3508 Strikeouts 1.00 2.50
479 Hal Lanier .30 .75
480 Juan Marichal 2.50 6.00
481 White Sox Team Card 1.00 2.50
482 Rick Reuschel RC 1.00 2.50
483 Dal Maxvill .30 .75
484 Ernie McAnally .30 .75
485 Norm Cash .60 1.50
486 Phillies Leaders .60 1.50
Danny Ozark MG
Carroll Beringer
487 Bruce Dal Canton .30 .75
488 Dave Campbell .60 1.50
489 Jeff Burroughs .60 1.50
490 Claude Osteen .60 1.50
491 Bob Montgomery .30 .75
492 Pedro Borbon .30 .75
493 Duffy Dyer .30 .75
494 Rich Morales .30 .75
495 Tommy Helms .30 .75
496 Ray Lamb .30 .75
497 Cardinals Leaders 1.00 2.50
Red Schoendienst MG
Vern Benso
498 Graig Nettles 1.50 4.00
499 Bob Moose .30 .75
500 Oakland A's Team 1.00 2.50
501 Larry Gura .30 .75
502 Bobby Valentine 1.00 2.50
503 Phil Niekro 2.50 6.00
504 Earl Williams .30 .75
505 Bob Bailey .30 .75
506 Bart Johnson .30 .75
507 Darrel Chaney .30 .75
508 Gates Brown .30 .75
509 Jim Nash .30 .75
510 Amos Otis .60 1.50
511 Sam McDowell .60 1.50
512 Dalton Jones .30 .75
513 Dave Marshall .30 .75
514 Jerry Kenney .30 .75
515 Andy Messersmith .60 1.50
516 Danny Walton .30 .75
517 Pirates Leaders 1.00 2.50
Bill Virdon MG
Don Leppert CO
B
518 Bob Veale .30 .75
519 John Edwards .30 .75
520 Mel Stottlemyre .60 1.50
521 Atlanta Braves Team 1.00 2.50
522 Leo Cardenas .30 .75
523 Wayne Granger .30 .75
524 Gene Tenace .60 1.50
525 Jim Fregosi .60 1.50
526 Ollie Brown .30 .75
527 Dan McGinn .30 .75
528 Paul Blair .60 1.50
529 Milt May 1.25 3.00
530 Jim Kaat 1.50 4.00
531 Ron Woods 1.25 3.00
532 Steve Mingori 1.25 3.00
533 Larry Stahl 1.25 3.00
534 Dave Lemonds 1.25 3.00
535 John Callison 1.50 4.00
536 Phillies Team 2.50 6.00
537 Bill Slayback 1.25 3.00
538 Jim Ray Hart 1.50 4.00
539 Tom Murphy 1.25 3.00
540 Cleon Jones 1.50 4.00
541 Bob Bolin 1.25 3.00
542 Pat Corrales 1.50 4.00
543 Alan Foster 1.25 3.00
544 Von Joshua 1.25 3.00
545 Orlando Cepeda 4.00 10.00
546 Jim York 1.25 3.00
547 Bobby Heise 1.25 3.00
548 Don Durham 1.25 3.00
549 Whitey Herzog MG 1.50 4.00
550 Dave Johnson 1.50 4.00
551 Mike Kilkenny 1.50 4.00
552 J.C. Martin 1.25 3.00
553 Mickey Scott 1.25 3.00
554 Dave Concepcion 2.50 6.00
555 Bill Hands 1.25 3.00
556 Yankees Team 2.50 6.00
557 Bernie Williams 1.25 3.00
558 Jerry May 1.25 3.00
559 Barry Lersch 1.25 3.00
560 Frank Howard 1.50 4.00
561 Jim Geddes 1.25 3.00
562 Wayne Garrett 1.25 3.00
563 Larry Haney 1.25 3.00
564 Mike Thompson 1.25 3.00
565 Jim Hickman 1.25 3.00
566 Lew Krausse 1.25 3.00
567 Bob Fenwick 1.25 3.00
568 Ray Newman 1.25 3.00
569 Walt Alston MG 3.00 8.00
570 Bill Singer 1.50 4.00
571 Rusty Torres 1.25 3.00
572 Gary Sutherland 1.25 3.00
573 Fred Beene 1.25 3.00
574 Bob Didier 1.25 3.00
575 Dock Ellis 1.25 3.00
576 Expos Team 3.00 8.00
577 Eric Soderholm 1.25 3.00
578 Ken Wright 1.25 3.00
579 Tom Grieve 1.50 4.00
580 Joe Pepitone 1.50 4.00
581 Steve Kealey 1.25 3.00
582 Darrell Porter 1.50 4.00
583 Bill Greif 1.25 3.00
584 Chris Arnold 1.25 3.00
585 Joe Niekro 1.50 4.00
586 Bill Sudakis 1.25 3.00
587 Rich McKinney 1.25 3.00
588 Checklist 529-660 8.00 20.00
589 Ken Forsch 1.25 3.00
590 Deron Johnson 1.25 3.00
591 Mike Hedlund 1.25 3.00
592 John Boccabella 1.25 3.00
593 Royals Leaders 1.25 3.00
Jack McKeon MG
Galen Cisco CO
Ha
594 Vic Harris 1.25 3.00
595 Don Gullett 1.50 4.00
596 Red Sox Team 2.50 6.00
597 Mickey Rivers 1.50 4.00
598 Phil Roof 1.25 3.00
599 Ed Crosby 1.25 3.00
600 Dave McNally 1.50 4.00
601 Rookie Catchers 1.50 4.00
Sergio Robles
George Pena
Rick
602 Rookie Pitchers 1.50 4.00
Mel Behney
Ralph Garcia
Doug Ra
603 Rookie 3rd Basemen 1.50 4.00
Terry Hughes
Bill McNulty
Ke
604 Rookie Pitchers 1.50 4.00
Jesse Jefferson
Dennis O'Toole/
605 Enos Cabell RC 1.50 4.00
606 Gary Matthews RC 2.50 6.00
607 Rookie Shortstops 1.50 4.00
Pepe Frias
Ray Busse
Mario Gu
608 Steve Busby RC 2.50 6.00
609 Davey Lopes RC 2.50 6.00
610 Charlie Hough 1.50 4.00
611 Rookie Outfielders 1.50 4.00
Rich Coggins
Jim Wohlford
Ri
612 Rookie Pitchers 1.50 4.00
Steve Lawson
Bob Reynolds
Brent
613 Bob Boone RC 6.00 15.00
614 Dwight Evans RC 8.00 20.00
615 Mike Schmidt RC 100.00 250.00
Cey !
616 Rookie Pitchers 1.50 4.00
Norm Angelini
Steve Blateric
Mi
617 Rich Chiles 1.25 3.00
618 Andy Etchebarren 1.25 3.00
619 Billy Wilson 1.25 3.00
620 Tommy Harper 1.50 4.00
621 Joe Ferguson 1.50 4.00
622 Larry Hisle 1.50 4.00
623 Steve Renko 1.25 3.00
624 Leo Durocher MG 3.00 8.00
625 Angel Mangual 1.25 3.00
626 Bob Barton 1.25 3.00
627 Luis Alvarado 1.25 3.00
628 Jim Slaton 1.25 3.00
629 Indians Team 2.50 6.00
630 Denny McLain 2.50 6.00
631 Tom Matchick 1.25 3.00
632 Dick Selma 1.25 3.00
633 Ike Brown 1.25 3.00
634 Alan Closter 1.25 3.00
635 Gene Alley 1.50 4.00
636 Rickey Clark 1.25 3.00
637 Norm Miller 1.25 3.00
638 Ken Reynolds 1.25 3.00
639 Willie Crawford 1.25 3.00
640 Dick Bosman 1.25 3.00
641 Reds Team 2.50 6.00
642 Jose Laboy 1.25 3.00
643 Al Fitzmorris 1.25 3.00
644 Jack Heidemann 1.25 3.00
645 Bob Locker 1.25 3.00
646 Brewers Leaders 1.50 4.00
Del Crandall MG
Harvey Kuenn CO#
647 George Stone 1.25 3.00
648 Tom Egan 1.25 3.00
649 Rich Folkers 1.25 3.00
650 Felipe Alou 2.50 6.00
651 Don Carrithers 1.25 3.00
652 Ted Kubiak 1.25 3.00
653 Joe Hoerner 1.25 3.00
654 Twins Team 2.50 6.00
655 Clay Kirby 1.25 3.00
656 John Ellis 1.25 3.00
657 Bob Johnson 1.25 3.00
658 Elliott Maddox 1.25 3.00
659 Jose Pagan 1.25 3.00
660 Fred Scherman 2.50 6.00

1973 O-Pee-Chee Blue Team Checklists

COMPLETE SET (24) 60.00 120.00
COMMON TEAM (1-24) 2.50 6.00

1974 O-Pee-Chee

The cards in this 660-card set measure 2 1/2" by 3 1/2". The 1974 O-Pee-Chee cards are very similar to the 1974 Topps cards. Since the O-Pee-Chee cards were printed substantially later than the Topps cards, there was no "San Diego rumored moving to Washington" problem in the O-Pee-Chee set. On a white background, the fronts feature color player photos with rounded corners and blue borders. The player's name and position and the team name also appear on the front. The horizontal backs are golden yellow instead of green like the 1974 Topps and carry player biography and statistics in French and English. There are a number of obverse differences between the two sets as well; they are numbers 3, 4, 5, 6, 7, 8, 9, 99, 166 and 196. The Aaron Specials generally feature two past cards per card instead of four as in the Topps. Remember, the prices below apply only to O-Pee-Chee cards -- they are NOT prices for Topps cards as the Topps cards are generally much more available. The cards were issued in eight card packs with 36 packs to a box. Notable Rookie Cards include Dave Parker and Dave Winfield.

COMPLETE SET (660) 600.00 1000.00
1 Hank Aaron 30.00 60.00
Complete ML record
2 Aaron Special 54-57 5.00 12.00
Special 54-57
Records on back
3 Aaron Special 58-59 5.00 12.00
Special 58-59
4 Aaron Special 60-61 5.00 12.00
Special 60-61
5 Aaron Special 62-63 5.00 12.00
Special 62-63
6 Aaron Special 64-65 5.00 12.00
Special 64-65
7 Aaron Special 66-67 5.00 12.00
Special 66-67
8 Aaron Special 68-69 5.00 12.00
Special 68-69
9 Aaron Special 70-73 5.00 12.00
Special 70-73
Milestone homers
10 Johnny Bench 10.00 25.00
11 Jim Bibby .40 1.00
12 Dave May .40 1.00
13 Tom Hilgendorf .40 1.00
14 Paul Popovich .40 1.00
15 Joe Torre 1.50 4.00
16 Orioles Team .75 2.00
17 Doug Bird .40 1.00
18 Gary Thomasson .40 1.00
19 Gerry Moses .40 1.00
20 Nolan Ryan 40.00 80.00
21 Bob Gallagher .40 1.00
22 Cy Acosta .40 1.00
23 Craig Robinson .40 1.00
24 John Hiller .75 2.00
25 Ken Singleton .75 2.00
26 Bill Campbell .40 1.00
27 George Scott .75 2.00
28 Manny Sanguillen .75 2.00
29 Phil Niekro 2.50 6.00
30 Bobby Bonds 1.50 4.00
31 Astros Leaders .75 2.00
Preston Gomez MG
Roger Craig CO/
32 Johnny Grubb .40 1.00
33 Don Newhauser .40 1.00
34 Andy Kosco .40 1.00
35 Gaylord Perry 2.50 6.00
36 Cardinals Team .75 2.00
37 Dave Sells .40 1.00
38 Don Kessinger .75 2.00
39 Ken Suarez .40 1.00
40 Jim Palmer 5.00 12.00
41 Bobby Floyd .40 1.00
42 Claude Osteen .75 2.00
43 Jim Wynn .75 2.00
44 Mel Stottlemyre .75 2.00
45 Dave Johnson .75 2.00
46 Pat Kelly .40 1.00
47 Dick Ruthven .40 1.00
48 Dick Sharon .40 1.00
49 Steve Renko .40 1.00
50 Rod Carew 5.00 12.00
51 Bob Heise .40 1.00
52 Al Oliver .75 2.00
53 Fred Kendall .40 1.00
54 Elias Sosa .40 1.00
55 Frank Robinson 5.00 12.00
56 New York Mets Team .75 2.00
57 Darold Knowles .40 1.00
58 Charlie Spikes .40 1.00
59 Ross Grimsley .40 1.00
60 Lou Brock 4.00 10.00
61 Luis Aparicio 2.50 6.00
62 Bob Locker .40 1.00
63 Bill Sudakis .40 1.00
64 Doug Rau .40 1.00
65 Amos Otis .75 2.00
66 Sparky Lyle .75 2.00
67 Tommy Helms .40 1.00
68 Grant Jackson .40 1.00
69 Del Unser .40 1.00
70 Dick Allen 1.25 3.00
71 Dan Frisella .40 1.00
72 Aurelio Rodriguez .40 1.00
73 Mike Marshall 1.25 3.00
74 Twins Team .75 2.00
75 Jim Colborn .40 1.00
76 Mickey Rivers .75 2.00
77 Rich Troedson .40 1.00
78 Giants Leaders .75 2.00
Charlie Fox MG
John McNamara CO/
79 Gene Tenace .75 2.00
80 Tom Seaver 8.00 20.00
81 Frank Duffy .40 1.00
82 Dave Giusti .40 1.00
83 Orlando Cepeda 2.50 6.00
84 Rick Wise .40 1.00
85 Joe Morgan 5.00 12.00
86 Joe Ferguson .75 2.00
87 Fergie Jenkins 2.50 6.00
88 Fred Patek .75 2.00
89 Jackie Brown .40 1.00
90 Bobby Murcer .75 2.00
91 Ken Forsch .40 1.00
92 Paul Blair .75 2.00
93 Rod Gilbreath .40 1.00
94 Tigers Team .75 2.00
95 Steve Carlton 5.00 12.00
96 Jerry Hairston .40 1.00
97 Bob Bailey .75 2.00
98 Bert Blyleven 1.50 4.00
99 George Theodore/(Topps 99 is Brewers Leaders) 1.25 3.00
100 Willie Stargell 5.00 12.00
101 Bobby Valentine .75 2.00
102 Bill Greif .40 1.00
103 Sal Bando .75 2.00
104 Ron Bryant .40 1.00
105 Carlton Fisk 8.00 20.00
106 Harry Parker .40 1.00
107 Alex Johnson .40 1.00
108 Al Hrabosky .75 2.00
109 Bobby Grich .75 2.00
110 Billy Williams 2.50 6.00
111 Clay Carroll .40 1.00
112 Davey Lopes 1.25 3.00
113 Dick Drago .40 1.00
114 Angels Team .75 2.00
115 Willie Horton .75 2.00
116 Jerry Reuss .75 2.00
117 Ron Blomberg .40 1.00
118 Bill Lee .75 2.00
119 Phillies Leaders .75 2.00
Danny Ozark MG
Ray Rippelmeyer
120 Wilbur Wood .40 1.00
121 Larry Lintz .40 1.00
122 Jim Holt .40 1.00
123 Nellie Briles .75 2.00
124 Bobby Coluccio .40 1.00
125 Nate Colbert .40 1.00
126 Checklist 1-132 2.00 5.00
127 Tom Paciorek .75 2.00
128 John Ellis .40 1.00
129 Chris Speier .40 1.00
130 Reggie Jackson 10.00 25.00
131 Bob Boone 1.25 3.00
132 Felix Millan .40 1.00
133 David Clyde .40 1.00
134 Denis Menke .40 1.00
135 Roy White .75 2.00
136 Rick Reuschel .75 2.00
137 Al Bumbry .75 2.00
138 Eddie Brinkman .40 1.00
139 Aurelio Monteagudo .40 1.00
140 Darrell Evans 1.25 3.00
141 Pat Bourque .40 1.00
142 Pedro Garcia .40 1.00
143 Dick Woodson .40 1.00
144 Walt Alston MG 1.50 4.00
145 Dock Ellis .40 1.00
146 Ron Fairly .75 2.00
147 Bart Johnson .40 1.00
148 Dave Hilton .40 1.00

149 Mac Scarce .40 1.00
150 John Mayberry .75 2.00
151 Diego Segui .40 1.00
152 Oscar Gamble .75 2.00
153 Jon Matlack .75 2.00
154 Astros Team .75 2.00
155 Bert Campaneris .75 2.00
156 Randy Moffitt .40 1.00
157 Vic Harris .40 1.00
158 Jack Billingham .40 1.00
159 Jim Ray Hart .40 1.00
160 Brooks Robinson 5.00 12.00
161 Ray Burris .75 2.00
162 Bill Freehan .75 2.00
163 Ken Berry .40 1.00
164 Tom House .40 1.00
165 Willie Davis .75 2.00
166 Mickey Lolich/(Topps 166 is Royals Leaders) 1.50 4.00
167 Luis Tiant 1.25 3.00
168 Danny Thompson .40 1.00
169 Steve Rogers RC 1.25 3.00
170 Bill Melton .40 1.00
171 Eduardo Rodriguez .40 1.00
172 Gene Clines .40 1.00
173 Randy Jones RC 1.25 3.00
174 Bill Robinson .75 2.00
175 Reggie Cleveland .75 2.00
176 John Lowenstein .40 1.00
177 Dave Roberts .40 1.00
178 Garry Maddox .75 2.00
179 Yogi Berra MG 3.00 8.00
180 Ken Holtzman .75 2.00
181 Cesar Geronimo .40 1.00
182 Lindy McDaniel .75 2.00
183 Johnny Oates .40 1.00
184 Rangers Team .75 2.00
185 Jose Cardenal .40 1.00
186 Fred Scherman .40 1.00
187 Don Baylor 1.25 3.00
188 Rudy Meoli .40 1.00
189 Jim Brewer .40 1.00
190 Tony Oliva 1.25 3.00
191 Al Fitzmorris .40 1.00
192 Mario Guerrero .40 1.00
193 Tom Walker .40 1.00
194 Darrell Porter .75 2.00
195 Carlos May .40 1.00
196 Jim Hunter/(Topps 196 is Jim Fregosi) 2.50 6.00
197 Vicente Romo .40 1.00
198 Dave Cash .40 1.00
199 Mike Kekich .40 1.00
200 Cesar Cedeno .75 2.00
201 Rod Carew Pete Rose LL 3.00 8.00
202 Reggie W.Stargell LL 3.00 8.00
203 Reggie W.Stargell LL 3.00 8.00
204 T.Harper Lou Brock LL 1.25 3.00
205 Wilbur Wood Ron Bryant LL .75 2.00
206 Jim Palmer T.Seaver LL 2.50 6.00
207 Nolan Ryan T.Seaver LL 8.00 20.00
208 John Hiller Mike Marshall LL .75 2.00
209 Ted Sizemore .40 1.00
210 Bill Singer .40 1.00
211 Chicago Cubs Team .75 2.00
212 Rollie Fingers 2.50 6.00
213 Dave Rader .40 1.00
214 Bill Grabarkewitz .40 1.00
215 Al Kaline 6.00 15.00
216 Ray Sadecki .40 1.00
217 Tim Foli .40 1.00
218 John Briggs .40 1.00
219 Doug Griffin .40 1.00
220 Don Sutton 2.50 6.00
221 White Sox Leaders Chuck Tanner MG Jim Mahoney CO .75 2.00
222 Ramon Hernandez .40 1.00
223 Jeff Burroughs 1.25 3.00
224 Roger Metzger .40 1.00
225 Paul Splittorff .40 1.00
226 Padres Team Card 1.25 3.00
227 Mike Lum .40 1.00
228 Ted Kubiak .40 1.00
229 Fritz Peterson .40 1.00
230 Tony Perez 2.50 6.00
231 Dick Tidrow .40 1.00
232 Steve Brye .40 1.00
233 Jim Barr .40 1.00
234 John Milner .40 1.00
235 Dave McNally .75 2.00
236 Red Schoendienst MG 1.50 4.00
237 Ken Brett .40 1.00
238 Fran Healy .40 1.00
239 Bill Russell .75 2.00
240 Joe Coleman .40 1.00
241 Glenn Beckert .40 1.00
242 Bill Gogolewski .40 1.00
243 Bob Oliver .40 1.00
244 Carl Morton .40 1.00
245 Cleon Jones .40 1.00
246 A's Team 1.25 3.00
247 Rick Miller .40 1.00
248 Tom Hall .40 1.00
249 George Mitterwald .40 1.00
250 Willie McCovey 4.00 10.00
251 Graig Nettles 1.25 3.00
252 Dave Parker RC 6.00 15.00
253 John Boccabella .40 1.00
254 Stan Bahnsen .40 1.00
255 Larry Bowa .75 2.00
256 Tom Griffin .40 1.00
257 Buddy Bell 1.25 3.00
258 Jerry Morales .40 1.00
259 Bob Reynolds .40 1.00
260 Ted Simmons 1.50 4.00
261 Jerry Bell .40 1.00
262 Ed Kirkpatrick .40 1.00
263 Checklist 133-264 1.50 4.00
264 Joe Rudi .75 2.00
265 Tug McGraw 1.50 4.00
266 Jim Northrup .75 2.00
267 Andy Messersmith .75 2.00
268 Tom Grieve .75 2.00
269 Bob Johnson .40 1.00
270 Ron Santo 1.50 4.00
271 Bill Hands .40 1.00
272 Paul Casanova .40 1.00
273 Checklist 265-396 1.50 4.00
274 Fred Beene .40 1.00
275 Ron Hunt .40 1.00
276 Angels Leaders Bobby Winkles MG John Roseboro CO .75 2.00
277 Gary Nolan .75 2.00
278 Cookie Rojas .75 2.00
279 Jim Crawford .40 1.00
280 Carl Yastrzemski 8.00 20.00
281 Giants Team .75 2.00
282 Doyle Alexander .75 2.00
283 Mike Schmidt 12.50 40.00
284 Dave Duncan .75 2.00
285 Reggie Smith .75 2.00
286 Tony Muser .40 1.00
287 Clay Kirby .40 1.00
288 Gorman Thomas 1.25 3.00
289 Rick Auerbach .40 1.00
290 Vida Blue .75 2.00
291 Don Hahn .40 1.00
292 Chuck Seelbach .40 1.00
293 Milt May .40 1.00
294 Steve Foucault .40 1.00
295 Rick Monday .75 2.00
296 Ray Corbin .40 1.00
297 Hal Breeden .40 1.00
298 Roric Harrison .40 1.00
299 Gene Michael .40 1.00
300 Pete Rose 12.50 30.00
301 Bob Montgomery .40 1.00
302 Rudy May .40 1.00
303 George Hendrick .75 2.00
304 Don Wilson .40 1.00
305 Tito Fuentes .40 1.00
306 Earl Weaver MG 1.50 4.00
307 Luis Melendez .40 1.00
308 Bruce Dal Canton .40 1.00
309 Dave Roberts .40 1.00
310 Terry Forster .75 2.00
311 Jerry Grote .75 2.00
312 Deron Johnson .40 1.00
313 Barry Lersch .40 1.00
314 Brewers Team .75 2.00
315 Ron Cey 1.25 3.00
316 Jim Perry .75 2.00
317 Richie Zisk .75 2.00
318 Jim Merritt .40 1.00
319 Randy Hundley .40 1.00
320 Dusty Baker 1.25 3.00
321 Steve Braun .40 1.00
322 Ernie McAnally .40 1.00
323 Richie Scheinblum .40 1.00
324 Steve Kline .40 1.00
325 Tommy Harper .75 2.00
326 Sparky Anderson MG 1.50 4.00
327 Tom Timmermann .40 1.00
328 Skip Jutze .40 1.00
329 Mark Belanger .75 2.00
330 Juan Marichal 2.50 6.00
331 Carlton Fisk J.Bench AS 3.00 8.00
332 Dick Allen H.Aaron AS 4.00 10.00
333 Rod Carew J.Morgan AS 2.00 5.00
334 B.Robinson R.Santo AS 1.50 4.00
335 Bert Campaneris Chris Speier AS .75 2.00
336 Bobby Murcer P.Rose AS 2.50 6.00
337 Amos Otis Cesar Cedeno AS .75 2.00
338 R.Jackson B.Williams AS 3.00 8.00
339 Jim Hunter R.Wise AS 1.50 4.00
340 Thurman Munson 5.00 12.00
341 Dan Driessen RC .75 2.00
342 Jim Lonborg .75 2.00
343 Royals Team .75 2.00
344 Mike Caldwell .40 1.00
345 Bill North .40 1.00
346 Ron Reed .40 1.00
347 Sandy Alomar .75 2.00
348 Pete Richert .40 1.00
349 John Vukovich .40 1.00
350 Bob Gibson 4.00 10.00
351 Dwight Evans 1.50 4.00
352 Bill Stoneman .40 1.00
353 Rich Coggins .40 1.00
354 Chicago Cubs Leaders Whitey Lockman MG J.C. Mart .75 2.00
355 Dave Nelson .40 1.00
356 Jerry Koosman .75 2.00
357 Buddy Bradford .40 1.00
358 Dal Maxvill .40 1.00
359 Brent Strom .40 1.00
360 Greg Luzinski 1.25 3.00
361 Don Carrithers .40 1.00
362 Hal King .40 1.00
363 Yankees Team 1.25 3.00
364 Cito Gaston .75 2.00
365 Steve Busby .75 2.00
366 Larry Hisle .75 2.00
367 Norm Cash 1.25 3.00
368 Manny Mota .75 2.00
369 Paul Lindblad .40 1.00
370 Bob Watson .75 2.00
371 Jim Slaton .40 1.00
372 Ken Reitz .40 1.00
373 John Curtis .40 1.00
374 Marty Perez .40 1.00
375 Earl Williams .40 1.00
376 Jorge Orta .40 1.00
377 Ron Woods .40 1.00
378 Burt Hooton .75 2.00
379 Billy Martin MG 1.25 3.00
380 Bud Harrelson .75 2.00
381 Charlie Sands .40 1.00
382 Bob Moose .40 1.00
383 Phillies Team .75 2.00
384 Chris Chambliss .75 2.00
385 Don Gullett .75 2.00
386 Gary Matthews 1.25 3.00
387 Rich Morales .40 1.00
388 Phil Roof .40 1.00
389 Gates Brown .40 1.00
390 Lou Piniella 1.25 3.00
391 Billy Champion .40 1.00
392 Dick Green .40 1.00
393 Orlando Pena .40 1.00
394 Ken Henderson .40 1.00
395 Doug Rader .40 1.00
396 Tommy Davis .75 2.00
397 George Stone .40 1.00
398 Duke Sims .40 1.00
399 Mike Paul .40 1.00
400 Harmon Killebrew 4.00 10.00
401 Elliott Maddox .40 1.00
402 Jim Rooker .40 1.00
403 Red Sox Leaders Darrell Johnson MG Eddie Popowski .75 2.00
404 Jim Howarth .40 1.00
405 Ellie Rodriguez .40 1.00
406 Steve Arlin .40 1.00
407 Jim Wohlford .40 1.00
408 Charlie Hough .75 2.00
409 Ike Brown .40 1.00
410 Pedro Borbon .40 1.00
411 Frank Baker .40 1.00
412 Chuck Taylor .40 1.00
413 Don Money .75 2.00
414 Checklist 397-528 1.50 4.00
415 Gary Gentry .40 1.00
416 White Sox Team .75 2.00
417 Rich Folkers .40 1.00
418 Walt Williams .40 1.00
419 Wayne Twitchell .40 1.00
420 Ray Fosse .40 1.00
421 Dan Fife .40 1.00
422 Gonzalo Marquez .40 1.00
423 Fred Stanley .40 1.00
424 Jim Beauchamp .40 1.00
425 Pete Broberg .40 1.00
426 Rennie Stennett .40 1.00
427 Bobby Bolin .40 1.00
428 Gary Sutherland .40 1.00
429 Dick Lange .40 1.00
430 Matty Alou .75 2.00
431 Gene Garber RC .75 2.00
432 Chris Arnold .40 1.00
433 Lerrin LaGrow .40 1.00
434 Ken McMullen .40 1.00
435 Dave Concepcion 1.25 3.00
436 Don Hood .40 1.00
437 Jim Lyttle .40 1.00
438 Ed Herrmann .40 1.00
439 Norm Miller .40 1.00
440 Jim Kaat 1.50 4.00
441 Tom Ragland .40 1.00
442 Alan Foster .40 1.00
443 Tom Hutton .40 1.00
444 Vic Davalillo .40 1.00
445 George Medich .40 1.00
446 Len Randle .40 1.00
447 Twins Leaders Frank Quilici MG Ralph Rowe CO Bo .75 2.00
448 Ron Hodges .40 1.00
449 Tom McGraw .40 1.00
450 Rich Hebner .75 2.00
451 Tommy John 1.50 4.00
452 Gene Hiser .40 1.00
453 Balor Moore .40 1.00
454 Kurt Bevacqua .40 1.00
455 Tom Bradley .40 1.00
456 Dave Winfield RC 30.00 60.00
457 Chuck Goggin .40 1.00
458 Jim Ray .40 1.00
459 Reds Team 1.25 3.00
460 Boog Powell 1.25 3.00
461 John Odom .40 1.00
462 Luis Alvarado .40 1.00
463 Pat Dobson .40 1.00
464 Jose Cruz 1.25 3.00
465 Dick Bosman .40 1.00
466 Dick Billings .40 1.00
467 Winston Llenas .40 1.00
468 Pepe Frias .40 1.00
469 Joe Decker .40 1.00
470 Reggie Jackson ALCS 3.00 8.00
471 N.L. Playoffs Mets over Reds/(Jon Matlack pitchi .75 2.00
472 Darold Knowles WS .75 2.00
473 Willie Mays WS2 5.00 12.00
474 Bert Campaneris WS .75 2.00
475 Rusty Staub WS .75 2.00
476 Cleon Jones WS .75 2.00
477 Reggie Jackson WS6 3.00 8.00
478 Bert Campaneris WS .75 2.00
479 World Series Summary A's Celebrate; Win/2nd cons .75 2.00
480 Willie Crawford .40 1.00
481 Jerry Terrell .40 1.00
482 Bob Didier .40 1.00
483 Braves Team .75 2.00
484 Carmen Fanzone .40 1.00
485 Felipe Alou 1.25 3.00
486 Steve Stone .75 2.00
487 Ted Martinez .40 1.00
488 Andy Etchebarren .40 1.00
489 Pirates Leaders Danny Murtaugh MG Don Osborn CO# .75 2.00
490 Vada Pinson 1.25 3.00
491 Roger Nelson .40 1.00
492 Mike Rogodzinski .40 1.00
493 Joe Hoerner .40 1.00
494 Ed Goodson .40 1.00
495 Dick McAuliffe .75 2.00
496 Tom Murphy .40 1.00
497 Bobby Mitchell .40 1.00
498 Pat Corrales .40 1.00
499 Rusty Torres .40 1.00
500 Lee May .75 2.00
501 Eddie Leon .40 1.00
502 Dave LaRoche .40 1.00
503 Eric Soderholm .40 1.00
504 Joe Niekro .75 2.00
505 Bill Buckner .75 2.00
506 Ed Farmer .40 1.00
507 Larry Stahl .40 1.00
508 Expos Team 1.25 3.00
509 Jesse Jefferson .40 1.00
510 Wayne Garrett .40 1.00
511 Toby Harrah .75 2.00
512 Joe Lahoud .40 1.00
513 Jim Campanis .40 1.00
514 Paul Schaal .40 1.00
515 Willie Montanez .40 1.00
516 Horacio Pina .40 1.00
517 Mike Hegan .40 1.00
518 Derrel Thomas .40 1.00
519 Bill Sharp .40 1.00
520 Tim McCarver 1.25 3.00
521 Indians Leaders Ken Aspromonte MG Clay Bryant CO .75 2.00
522 J.R. Richard 1.25 3.00
523 Cecil Cooper 1.25 3.00
524 Bill Plummer .40 1.00
525 Clyde Wright .40 1.00
526 Frank Tepedino .75 2.00
527 Bobby Darwin .40 1.00
528 Bill Bonham .40 1.00
529 Horace Clarke .75 2.00
530 Mickey Stanley .75 2.00
531 Expos Leaders Gene Mauch MG Dave Bristol CO Cal 1.25 3.00
532 Skip Lockwood .40 1.00
533 Mike Phillips .40 1.00
534 Eddie Watt .40 1.00
535 Bob Tolan .40 1.00
536 Duffy Dyer .40 1.00
537 Steve Mingori .40 1.00
538 Cesar Tovar .40 1.00
539 Lloyd Allen .40 1.00
540 Bob Robertson .40 1.00
541 Indians Team .75 2.00
542 Goose Gossage 1.25 3.00
543 Danny Cater .40 1.00
544 Ron Schueler .40 1.00
545 Billy Conigliaro .75 2.00
546 Mike Corkins .40 1.00
547 Glenn Borgmann .40 1.00
548 Sonny Siebert .40 1.00
549 Mike Jorgensen .40 1.00
550 Sam McDowell .75 2.00
551 Von Joshua .40 1.00
552 Denny Doyle .40 1.00
553 Jim Willoughby .40 1.00
554 Tim Johnson .40 1.00
555 Woody Fryman .40 1.00
556 Dave Campbell .75 2.00
557 Jim McGlothlin .40 1.00
558 Bill Fahey .40 1.00
559 Darrell Chaney .40 1.00
560 Mike Cuellar .75 2.00
561 Ed Kranepool .75 2.00
562 Jack Aker .40 1.00
563 Hal McRae .75 2.00
564 Mike Ryan .40 1.00
565 Milt Wilcox .40 1.00
566 Jackie Hernandez .40 1.00
567 Red Sox Team .75 2.00
568 Mike Torrez .75 2.00
569 Rick Dempsey .75 2.00
570 Ralph Garr .75 2.00
571 Rich Hand .40 1.00
572 Enzo Hernandez .40 1.00
573 Mike Adams .40 1.00
574 Bill Parsons .40 1.00
575 Steve Garvey 1.50 4.00
576 Scipio Spinks .40 1.00
577 Mike Sadek .40 1.00
578 Ralph Houk MG .75 2.00
579 Cecil Upshaw .40 1.00
580 Jim Spencer .40 1.00
581 Fred Norman .40 1.00
582 Bucky Dent RC 2.50 6.00
583 Marty Pattin .40 1.00
584 Ken Rudolph .40 1.00
585 Merv Rettenmund .40 1.00
586 Jack Brohamer .40 1.00
587 Larry Christenson .40 1.00
588 Hal Lanier .40 1.00
589 Boots Day .75 2.00
590 Rogelio Moret .40 1.00
591 Sonny Jackson .40 1.00
592 Ed Bane .40 1.00
593 Steve Yeager .75 2.00
594 Leroy Stanton .40 1.00
595 Steve Blass .75 2.00
596 Rookie Pitchers Wayne Garland Fred Holdsworth M .40 1.00
597 Rookie Shortstops Dave Chalk John Gamble Pete M .75 2.00
598 Ken Griffey Sr. RC 6.00 15.00
599 Rookie Pitchers Ron Diorio Dave Freisleben Fran 1.25 3.00
600 Bill Madlock RC 3.00 8.00
601 Brian Downing RC 1.50 4.00
602 Rookie Pitchers Glenn Abbott Rick Henninger Cra .75 2.00
603 Rookie Catchers Barry Foote Tom Lundstedt Charl .75 2.00
604 A.Thornton F.White RC 3.00 8.00
605 Frank Tanana RC 2.00 5.00
606 Rookie Outfielders Jim Fuller Wilbur Howard Tom .75 2.00
607 Rookie Shortstops Leo Foster Tom Heintzelman Da .75 2.00
608 Rookie Pitchers Bob Apodaca Dick Baney John D'A 1.25 3.00
609 Rico Petrocelli .75 2.00
610 Dave Kingman 1.50 4.00
611 Rich Stelmaszek .40 1.00
612 Luke Walker .40 1.00
613 Dan Monzon .40 1.00
614 Adrian Devine .40 1.00
615 John Jeter .40 1.00
616 Larry Gura .40 1.00
617 Ted Ford .40 1.00
618 Jim Mason .40 1.00
619 Mike Anderson .40 1.00
620 Al Downing .40 1.00
621 Bernie Carbo .40 1.00
622 Phil Gagliano .40 1.00
623 Celerino Sanchez .40 1.00
624 Bob Miller .40 1.00
625 Ollie Brown .40 1.00
626 Pirates Team .75 2.00
627 Carl Taylor .40 1.00
628 Ivan Murrell .40 1.00
629 Rusty Staub 1.25 3.00
630 Tommy Agee .75 2.00
631 Steve Barber .40 1.00
632 George Culver .40 1.00
633 Dave Hamilton .40 1.00
634 Eddie Mathews MG 1.50 4.00
635 John Edwards .40 1.00
636 Dave Goltz .40 1.00
637 Checklist 529-660 1.50 4.00
638 Ken Sanders .40 1.00
639 Joe Lovitto .40 1.00
640 Milt Pappas .75 2.00
641 Chuck Brinkman .40 1.00
642 Terry Harmon .40 1.00
643 Dodgers Team .75 2.00
644 Wayne Granger .40 1.00
645 Ken Boswell .40 1.00
646 George Foster 1.25 3.00
647 Juan Beniquez .40 1.00
648 Terry Crowley .40 1.00
649 Fernando Gonzalez .40 1.00
650 Mike Epstein .40 1.00
651 Leron Lee .40 1.00
652 Gail Hopkins .40 1.00
653 Bob Stinson .75 2.00
654 Jesus Alou .75 2.00
655 Mike Tyson .40 1.00
656 Adrian Garrett .40 1.00
657 Jim Shellenback .40 1.00
658 Lee Lacy .40 1.00
659 Joe Lis .40 1.00
660 Larry Dierker 1.25 3.00

1974 O-Pee-Chee Team Checklists

COMPLETE SET (24) 20.00 50.00
COMMON TEAM (1-24) 1.00 2.50

1975 O-Pee-Chee

The cards in this 660-card set measure 2 1/2" by 3 1/2". The 1975 O-Pee-Chee cards are very similar to the 1975 Topps cards, yet rather different from previous years' issues. The most prominent change for the fronts is the use of a two-color frame colors surrounding the picture area rather than a single, subdued color. The fronts feature color player photos with rounded corners. The player's name and position, the team name and a facsimile autograph round out the front. The backs are printed in red and green on a yellow-vanilla card stock and carry player biography and statistics in French and English. Cards 189-212 depict the MVPs of both leagues from 1951 through 1974. The first six cards (1-6) feature players breaking records or achieving milestones during the previous season. Cards 306-313 picture league leaders in various statistical categories. Cards 459-466 depict the results of post-season action. Team cards feature a checklist back for players on that team. Remember, the prices below apply only to O-Pee-Chee cards -- they are NOT prices for Topps cards as the Topps cards are generally much more available. The cards were issued in eight card packs which cost 10 cents and came 48 packs to a box. Notable Rookie Cards include George Brett, Fred Lynn, Keith Hernandez, Jim Rice and Robin Yount.

COMPLETE SET (660) 500.00 1000.00
1 Hank Aaron HL 12.50 40.00
2 Lou Brock HL 1.50 4.00
3 Bob Gibson HL 1.50 4.00
4 Al Kaline HL 3.00 8.00
5 Nolan Ryan HL 12.50 30.00
6 Mike Marshall RB Hurls 106 Games .60 1.50
7 S.Busby Bosman N.Ryan HL 5.00 12.00
8 Rogelio Moret .30 .75
9 Frank Tepedino .60 1.50
10 Willie Davis .60 1.50
11 Bill Melton .30 .75
12 David Clyde .30 .75
13 Gene Locklear .60 1.50
14 Milt Wilcox .30 .75
15 Jose Cardenal .60 1.50
16 Frank Tanana 1.00 2.50
17 Dave Concepcion 1.00 2.50
18 Tigers Team CL Ralph Houk MG 1.00 2.50
19 Jerry Koosman .60 1.50
20 Thurman Munson 4.00 10.00
21 Rollie Fingers 2.00 5.00
22 Dave Cash .30 .75
23 Bill Russell .60 1.50
24 Al Fitzmorris .30 .75
25 Lee May .60 1.50
26 Dave McNally .60 1.50
27 Ken Reitz .30 .75
28 Tom Murphy .30 .75
29 Dave Parker 1.50 4.00
30 Bert Blyleven 1.00 2.50
31 Dave Rader .30 .75
32 Reggie Cleveland .60 1.50
33 Dusty Baker 1.00 2.50
34 Steve Renko .30 .75
35 Ron Santo .60 1.50
36 Joe Lovitto .30 .75
37 Dave Freisleben .30 .75
38 Buddy Bell 1.00 2.50
39 Andre Thornton .60 1.50
40 Bill Singer .30 .75
41 Cesar Geronimo .60 1.50
42 Joe Coleman .30 .75
43 Cleon Jones .60 1.50
44 Pat Dobson .30 .75
45 Joe Rudi .60 1.50
46 Phillies Team CL(Danny Ozark MG 1.00 2.50
47 Tommy John 1.00 2.50
48 Freddie Patek .60 1.50
49 Larry Dierker .60 1.50
50 Brooks Robinson 4.00 10.00
51 Bob Forsch .60 1.50
52 Darrell Porter .60 1.50
53 Dave Giusti .30 .75
54 Eric Soderholm .30 .75
55 Bobby Bonds 1.50 4.00
56 Rick Wise .60 1.50
57 Dave Johnson .60 1.50
58 Chuck Taylor .30 .75
59 Ken Henderson .30 .75
60 Fergie Jenkins 2.00 5.00
61 Dave Winfield 10.00 25.00
62 Fritz Peterson .30 .75
63 Steve Swisher .30 .75
64 Dave Chalk .30 .75
65 Don Gullett .60 1.50
66 Willie Horton .60 1.50
67 Tug McGraw 1.00 2.50
68 Ron Blomberg .30 .75
69 John Odom .30 .75
70 Mike Schmidt 12.50 30.00
71 Charlie Hough .60 1.50
72 Royals Team CL(Jack McKeon MG 1.00 2.50
73 J.R. Richard .60 1.50
74 Mark Belanger .60 1.50
75 Ted Simmons 1.00 2.50
76 Ed Sprague .60 1.50
77 Richie Zisk .60 1.50
78 Ray Corbin .30 .75
79 Gary Matthews .60 1.50
80 Carlton Fisk 4.00 10.00
81 Ron Reed .30 .75
82 Pat Kelly .30 .75
83 Jim Merritt .30 .75
84 Enzo Hernandez .30 .75
85 Bill Bonham .30 .75
86 Joe Lis .30 .75
87 George Foster 1.00 2.50
88 Tom Egan .30 .75
89 Jim Ray .30 .75
90 Rusty Staub 1.00 2.50
91 Dick Green .30 .75
92 Cecil Upshaw .30 .75
93 Davey Lopes 1.00 2.50
94 Jim Lonborg .60 1.50
95 John Mayberry .60 1.50
96 Mike Cosgrove .30 .75
97 Earl Williams .30 .75
98 Rich Folkers .30 .75
99 Mike Hegan .30 .75
100 Willie Stargell 2.50 6.00
101 Expos Team CL(Gene Mauch MG 1.00 2.50
102 Joe Decker .30 .75
103 Rick Miller .30 .75
104 Bill Madlock 1.00 2.50
105 Buzz Capra .30 .75
106 Mike Hargrove RC 1.50 4.00
107 Jim Barr .30 .75
108 Tom Hall .30 .75
109 George Hendrick .60 1.50
110 Wilbur Wood .30 .75
111 Wayne Garrett .30 .75
112 Larry Hardy .30 .75
113 Elliott Maddox .30 .75
114 Dick Lange .30 .75
115 Joe Ferguson .30 .75
116 Lerrin LaGrow .30 .75
117 Orioles Team CL Earl Weaver MG 1.50 4.00
118 Mike Anderson .30 .75
119 Tommy Helms .30 .75
120 Steve Busby/(photo actually Fran Healy) .60 1.50
121 Bill North .30 .75
122 Al Hrabosky .60 1.50
123 Johnny Briggs .30 .75
124 Jerry Reuss .60 1.50
125 Ken Singleton .60 1.50
126 Checklist 1-132 1.50 4.00
127 Glenn Borgmann .30 .75
128 Bill Lee .60 1.50
129 Rick Monday .60 1.50
130 Phil Niekro 1.50 4.00
131 Toby Harrah .60 1.50
132 Randy Moffitt .30 .75
133 Dan Driessen .60 1.50
134 Ron Hodges .30 .75
135 Charlie Spikes .30 .75
136 Jim Mason .30 .75
137 Terry Forster .60 1.50
138 Del Unser .30 .75
139 Horacio Pina .30 .75
140 Steve Garvey 1.50 4.00
141 Mickey Stanley .60 1.50
142 Bob Reynolds .30 .75
143 Cliff Johnson RC .60 1.50
144 Jim Wohlford .30 .75
145 Ken Holtzman .60 1.50
146 Padres Team CL John McNamara MG 1.00 2.50
147 Pedro Garcia .30 .75
148 Jim Rooker .30 .75
149 Tim Foli .30 .75
150 Bob Gibson 3.00 8.00
151 Steve Brye .30 .75
152 Mario Guerrero .30 .75
153 Rick Reuschel .60 1.50
154 Mike Lum .30 .75
155 Jim Bibby .30 .75
156 Dave Kingman 1.00 2.50
157 Pedro Borbon .60 1.50
158 Jerry Grote .30 .75
159 Steve Arlin .30 .75
160 Graig Nettles 1.00 2.50
161 Stan Bahnsen .30 .75
162 Willie Montanez .30 .75
163 Jim Brewer .30 .75
164 Mickey Rivers .60 1.50
165 Doug Rader .60 1.50
166 Woodie Fryman .30 .75
167 Rich Coggins .30 .75
168 Bill Greif .30 .75
169 Cookie Rojas .30 .75
170 Bert Campaneris .60 1.50
171 Ed Kirkpatrick .30 .75
172 Red Sox Team CL Darrell Johnson MG 1.50 4.00
173 Steve Rogers .60 1.50
174 Bake McBride .60 1.50
175 Don Money .60 1.50
176 Burt Hooton .60 1.50
177 Vic Correll .30 .75
178 Cesar Tovar .30 .75
179 Tom Bradley .30 .75
180 Joe Morgan 3.00 8.00
181 Fred Beene .30 .75
182 Don Hahn .30 .75
183 Mel Stottlemyre .60 1.50
184 Jorge Orta .30 .75
185 Steve Carlton 4.00 10.00
186 Willie Crawford .30 .75
187 Denny Doyle .30 .75
188 Tom Griffin .30 .75
189 Y.Berra R.Campanella MVP 2.50 6.00
190 Bobby Shantz Hank Sauer MVP 1.00 2.50
191 Al Rosen R.Campanella MV 1.00 2.50
192 Yogi Berra W.Mays MVP 2.50 6.00
193 Y.Berra R.Campanella MVP 1.50 4.00
194 M.Mantle D.Newcombe MVP 6.00 15.00
195 Mickey Mantle H.Aaron MV 8.00 20.00
196 Jackie Jensen Ernie Banks MVP 1.00 2.50
197 Nellie Fox E.Banks MVP 1.50 4.00
198 Roger Maris Dick Groat MVP 1.00 2.50
199 Rog.Maris F.Robinson MVP 1.50 4.00
200 Mickey Mantle M.Wills MV 6.00 15.00
201 Els.Howard S.Koufax MVP 1.00 2.50
202 B.Robinson K.Boyer MVP 1.00 2.50
203 Zoilo Versalles W.Mays M 1.00 2.50
204 R.Clemente F.Robinson MV 3.00 8.00
205 C.Yastrzemski Cepeda MVP 1.00 2.50
206 Denny McLain B.Gibson MV 1.00 2.50
207 H.Killebrew W.McCovey MV 1.00 2.50
208 Boog Powell J.Bench MVP 1.00 2.50
209 Vida Blue Joe Torre MVP 1.00 2.50
210 Dick Allen J.Bench MVP 1.00 2.50
211 Reggie Jackson P.Rose MV 3.00 8.00
212 Jeff Burroughs Steve Garvey MVP 1.00 2.50
213 Oscar Gamble .60 1.50
214 Harry Parker .30 .75
215 Bobby Valentine .60 1.50
216 Giants Team CL Wes Westrum MG 1.00 2.50
217 Lou Piniella 1.00 2.50
218 Jerry Johnson .30 .75
219 Ed Herrmann .30 .75
220 Don Sutton 1.50 4.00
221 Aurelio Rodriguez .30 .75
222 Dan Spillner .30 .75
223 Robin Yount RC 30.00 60.00
224 Ramon Hernandez .30 .75
225 Bob Grich .60 1.50
226 Bill Campbell .30 .75
227 Bob Watson .60 1.50
228 George Brett RC 50.00 100.00
229 Barry Foote .60 1.50
230 Jim Hunter 2.00 5.00
231 Mike Tyson .30 .75
232 Diego Segui .30 .75
233 Billy Grabarkewitz .30 .75
234 Tom Grieve .60 1.50
235 Jack Billingham .60 1.50
236 Angels Team CL Dick Williams MG 1.00 2.50
237 Carl Morton .30 .75
238 Dave Duncan .60 1.50
239 George Stone .30 .75
240 Garry Maddox .60 1.50
241 Dick Tidrow .30 .75
242 Jay Johnstone .60 1.50
243 Jim Kaat 1.00 2.50
244 Bill Buckner .60 1.50
245 Mickey Lolich 1.00 2.50
246 Cardinals Team CL Red Schoendienst MG 1.00 2.50

247 Enos Cabell .30 .75
248 Randy Jones 1.00 2.50
249 Danny Thompson .30 .75
250 Ken Brett .30 .75
251 Fran Healy .30 .75
252 Fred Scherman .30 .75
253 Jesus Alou .30 .75
254 Mike Torrez .60 1.50
255 Dwight Evans 1.00 2.50
256 Billy Champion .30 .75
257 Checklist 133-264 1.50 4.00
258 Dave LaRoche .30 .75
259 Len Randle .30 .75
260 Johnny Bench 8.00 20.00
261 Andy Hassler .30 .75
262 Rowland Office .30 .75
263 Jim Perry .60 1.50
264 John Milner .30 .75
265 Ron Bryant .30 .75
266 Sandy Alomar .60 1.50
267 Dick Ruthven .30 .75
268 Hal McRae .60 1.50
269 Doug Rau .30 .75
270 Ron Fairly .60 1.50
271 Jerry Moses .30 .75
272 Lynn McGlothen .30 .75
273 Steve Braun .30 .75
274 Vicente Romo .30 .75
275 Paul Blair .60 1.50
276 White Sox Team CL 1.00 2.50
Chuck Tanner MG
277 Frank Taveras .30 .75
278 Paul Lindblad .30 .75
279 Milt May .30 .75
280 Carl Yastrzemski 6.00 15.00
281 Jim Slaton .30 .75
282 Jerry Morales .30 .75
283 Steve Foucault .30 .75
284 Ken Griffey Sr. 2.00 5.00
285 Ellie Rodriguez .30 .75
286 Mike Jorgensen .30 .75
287 Roric Harrison .30 .75
288 Bruce Ellingsen .30 .75
289 Ken Rudolph .30 .75
290 Jon Matlack .30 .75
291 Bill Sudakis .30 .75
292 Ron Schueler .30 .75
293 Dick Sharon .30 .75
294 Geoff Zahn .30 .75
295 Vada Pinson 1.00 2.50
296 Alan Foster .30 .75
297 Craig Kusick .30 .75
298 Johnny Grubb .30 .75
299 Bucky Dent 1.00 2.50
300 Reggie Jackson 8.00 20.00
301 Dave Roberts .30 .75
302 Rick Burleson .60 1.50
303 Grant Jackson .30 .75
304 Pirates Team CL 1.00 2.50
Danny Murtaugh MG
305 Jim Colborn .30 .75
306 Rod Carew 1.00 2.50
R.Garr LL
307 Dick Allen 2.00 5.00
M.Schmidt LL
308 Jeff Burroughs 1.00 2.50
Bench LL
309 Billy North 1.00 2.50
Brock LL
310 Hunter 1.00 2.50
Jenk
Niekro LL
311 Jim Hunter 1.00 2.50
B.Capra LL
312 Nolan Ryan 8.00 20.00
S.Carlton LL
313 Terry Forster .60 1.50
Mike Marshall LL
314 Buck Martinez .30 .75
315 Don Kessinger .60 1.50
316 Jackie Brown .30 .75
317 Joe Lahoud .30 .75
318 Ernie McAnally .30 .75
319 Johnny Oates .30 .75
320 Pete Rose 12.50 40.00
321 Rudy May .30 .75
322 Ed Goodson .30 .75
323 Fred Holdsworth .30 .75
324 Ed Kranepool .60 1.50
325 Tony Oliva 1.00 2.50
326 Wayne Twitchell .30 .75
327 Jerry Hairston .30 .75
328 Sonny Siebert .30 .75
329 Ted Kubiak .30 .75
330 Mike Marshall .60 1.50
331 Indians Team CL(Frank Robinson MG 1.00 2.50
332 Fred Kendall .30 .75
333 Dick Drago .30 .75
334 Greg Gross .30 .75
335 Jim Palmer 3.00 8.00
336 Rennie Stennett .30 .75
337 Kevin Kobel .30 .75
338 Rick Stelmaszek .30 .75
339 Jim Fregosi .60 1.50
340 Paul Splittorff .30 .75
341 Hal Breeden .30 .75
342 Leroy Stanton .30 .75
343 Danny Frisella .30 .75
344 Ben Oglivie .60 1.50
345 Clay Carroll .60 1.50
346 Bobby Darwin .30 .75
347 Mike Caldwell .30 .75
348 Tony Muser .30 .75
349 Ray Sadecki .30 .75
350 Bobby Murcer .60 1.50
351 Bob Boone 1.00 2.50
352 Darold Knowles .30 .75
353 Luis Melendez .30 .75
354 Dick Bosman .30 .75
355 Chris Cannizzaro .30 .75
356 Rico Petrocelli .60 1.50
357 Ken Forsch .30 .75
358 Al Bumbry .60 1.50
359 Paul Popovich .30 .75
360 George Scott .60 1.50
361 Dodgers Team CL 1.00 2.50
Walter Alston MG
362 Steve Hargan .30 .75
363 Carmen Fanzone .30 .75
364 Doug Bird .30 .75
365 Bob Bailey .30 .75
366 Ken Sanders .30 .75
367 Craig Robinson .30 .75
368 Vic Albury .30 .75
369 Merv Rettenmund .30 .75
370 Tom Seaver 6.00 15.00
371 Gates Brown .30 .75
372 John D'Acquisto .30 .75
373 Bill Sharp .30 .75
374 Eddie Watt .30 .75
375 Roy White .60 1.50
376 Steve Yeager .60 1.50
377 Tom Hilgendorf .30 .75
378 Derrel Thomas .30 .75
379 Bernie Carbo .30 .75
380 Sal Bando .60 1.50
381 John Curtis .30 .75
382 Don Baylor 1.00 2.50
383 Jim York .30 .75
384 Brewers Team CL 1.00 2.50
Del Crandall MG
385 Dock Ellis .30 .75
386 Checklist 265-396 1.50 4.00
387 Jim Spencer .30 .75
388 Steve Stone .60 1.50
389 Tony Solaita .30 .75
390 Ron Cey 1.00 2.50
391 Don DeMola .30 .75
392 Bruce Bochte RC .60 1.50
393 Gary Gentry .30 .75
394 Larvell Blanks .30 .75
395 Bud Harrelson .60 1.50
396 Fred Norman .60 1.50
397 Bill Freehan .60 1.50
398 Elias Sosa .30 .75
399 Terry Harmon .30 .75
400 Dick Allen 1.00 2.50
401 Mike Wallace .30 .75
402 Bob Tolan .30 .75
403 Tom Buskey .30 .75
404 Ted Sizemore .30 .75
405 John Montague .30 .75
406 Bob Gallagher .30 .75
407 Herb Washington RC 1.00 2.50
408 Clyde Wright .30 .75
409 Bob Robertson .30 .75
410 Mike Cueller .60 1.50
sic, Cuellar
411 George Mitterwald .30 .75
412 Bill Hands .30 .75
413 Marty Pattin .30 .75
414 Manny Mota .60 1.50
415 John Hiller .60 1.50
416 Larry Lintz .30 .75
417 Skip Lockwood .30 .75
418 Leo Foster .30 .75
419 Dave Goltz .30 .75
420 Larry Bowa 1.00 2.50
421 Mets Team CL 1.50 4.00
Yogi Berra MG
422 Brian Downing .60 1.50
423 Clay Kirby .30 .75
424 John Lowenstein .30 .75
425 Tito Fuentes .30 .75
426 George Medich .30 .75
427 Clarence Gaston .60 1.50
428 Dave Hamilton .30 .75
429 Jim Dwyer .30 .75
430 Luis Tiant 1.00 2.50
431 Rod Gilbreath .30 .75
432 Ken Berry .30 .75
433 Larry Demery .30 .75
434 Bob Locker .30 .75
435 Dave Nelson .30 .75
436 Ken Frailing .30 .75
437 Al Cowens .60 1.50
438 Don Carrithers .30 .75
439 Ed Brinkman .30 .75
440 Andy Messersmith .60 1.50
441 Bobby Heise .30 .75
442 Maximino Leon .30 .75
443 Twins Team 1.00 2.50
Frank Quilici MG
444 Gene Garber .60 1.50
445 Felix Millan .30 .75
446 Bart Johnson .30 .75
447 Terry Crowley .30 .75
448 Frank Duffy .30 .75
449 Charlie Williams .30 .75
450 Willie McCovey 3.00 8.00
451 Rick Dempsey .60 1.50
452 Angel Mangual .30 .75
453 Claude Osteen .60 1.50
454 Doug Griffin .30 .75
455 Don Wilson .30 .75
456 Bob Coluccio .30 .75
457 Mario Mendoza .30 .75
458 Ross Grimsley .30 .75
459 1974 AL Champs .60 1.50
A's over Orioles/(Second base
ac
460 Steve Garvey NLCS 1.00 2.50
461 Reggie Jackson WS1 2.50 6.00
462 World Series Game 2
(Dodger dugout) .60 1.50
463 Rollie Fingers WS3 1.00 2.50
464 World Series Game 4/(A's batter) .60 1.50
465 Joe Rudi WS .60 1.50
466 WS Summary 1.00 2.50
A's
467 Ed Halicki .30 .75
468 Bobby Mitchell .30 .75
469 Tom Dettore .30 .75
470 Jeff Burroughs .60 1.50
471 Bob Stinson .30 .75
472 Bruce Dal Canton .30 .75
473 Ken McMullen .30 .75
474 Luke Walker .30 .75
475 Darrell Evans .60 1.50
476 Ed Figueroa .30 .75
477 Tom Hutton .30 .75
478 Tom Burgmeier .30 .75
479 Ken Boswell .30 .75
480 Carlos May .30 .75
481 Will McEnaney .60 1.50
482 Tom McCraw .30 .75
483 Steve Ontiveros .30 .75
484 Glenn Beckert .60 1.50
485 Sparky Lyle .60 1.50
486 Ray Fosse .30 .75
487 Astros Team CL 1.00 2.50
Preston Gomez MG
488 Bill Travers .30 .75
489 Cecil Cooper 1.00 2.50
490 Reggie Smith .60 1.50
491 Doyle Alexander .60 1.50
492 Rich Hebner .60 1.50
493 Don Stanhouse .30 .75
494 Pete LaCock .30 .75
495 Nelson Briles .60 1.50
496 Pepe Frias .30 .75
497 Jim Nettles .30 .75
498 Al Downing .30 .75
499 Marty Perez .30 .75
500 Nolan Ryan 40.00 80.00
501 Bill Robinson .60 1.50
502 Pat Bourque .30 .75
503 Fred Stanley .30 .75
504 Buddy Bradford .30 .75
505 Chris Speier .30 .75
506 Leron Lee .30 .75
507 Tom Carroll .30 .75
508 Bob Hansen .30 .75
509 Dave Hilton .30 .75
510 Vida Blue .60 1.50
511 Rangers Team CL 1.00 2.50
Billy Martin MG
512 Larry Milbourne .30 .75
513 Dick Pole .30 .75
514 Jose Cruz 1.00 2.50
515 Manny Sanguillen .60 1.50
516 Don Hood .30 .75
517 Checklist 397-528 1.50 4.00
518 Leo Cardenas .30 .75
519 Jim Todd .30 .75
520 Amos Otis .60 1.50
521 Dennis Blair .30 .75
522 Gary Sutherland .30 .75
523 Tom Paciorek .60 1.50
524 John Doherty .30 .75
525 Tom House .30 .75
526 Larry Hisle .60 1.50
527 Mac Scarce .30 .75
528 Eddie Leon .30 .75
529 Gary Thomasson .30 .75
530 Gaylord Perry 1.50 4.00
531 Reds Team 2.50 6.00
532 Gorman Thomas .60 1.50
533 Rudy Meoli .30 .75
534 Alex Johnson .30 .75
535 Gene Tenace .60 1.50
536 Bob Moose .30 .75
537 Tommy Harper .60 1.50
538 Duffy Dyer .30 .75
539 Jesse Jefferson .30 .75
540 Lou Brock 3.00 8.00
541 Roger Metzger .30 .75
542 Pete Broberg .30 .75
543 Larry Biittner .30 .75
544 Steve Mingori .30 .75
545 Billy Williams 1.50 4.00
546 John Knox .30 .75
547 Von Joshua .30 .75
548 Charlie Sands .30 .75
549 Bill Butler .30 .75
550 Ralph Garr .60 1.50
551 Larry Christenson .30 .75
552 Jack Brohamer .30 .75
553 John Boccabella .30 .75
554 Goose Gossage 1.00 2.50
555 Al Oliver 1.00 2.50
556 Tim Johnson .30 .75
557 Larry Gura .30 .75
558 Dave Roberts .30 .75
559 Bob Montgomery .30 .75
560 Tony Perez 2.00 5.00
561 A's Team CL 1.00 2.50
Alvin Dark MG
562 Gary Nolan .60 1.50
563 Wilbur Howard .30 .75
564 Tommy Davis .60 1.50
565 Joe Torre 1.00 2.50
566 Ray Burris .30 .75
567 Jim Sundberg RC 1.00 2.50
568 Dale Murray .30 .75
569 Frank White .60 1.50
570 Jim Wynn .60 1.50
571 Dave Lemanczyk .30 .75
572 Roger Nelson .30 .75
573 Orlando Pena .30 .75
574 Tony Taylor .30 .75
575 Gene Clines .30 .75
576 Phil Roof .30 .75
577 John Morris .30 .75
578 Dave Tomlin .30 .75
579 Skip Pitlock .30 .75
580 Frank Robinson 3.00 8.00
581 Darrel Chaney .30 .75
582 Eduardo Rodriguez .30 .75
583 Andy Etchebarren .30 .75
584 Mike Garman .30 .75
585 Chris Chambliss .60 1.50
586 Tim McCarver 1.00 2.50
587 Chris Ward .30 .75
588 Rick Auerbach .30 .75
589 Braves Team CL 1.00 2.50
Clyde King MG
590 Cesar Cedeno .60 1.50
591 Glenn Abbott .30 .75
592 Balor Moore .30 .75
593 Gene Lamont .30 .75
594 Jim Fuller .30 .75
595 Joe Niekro .60 1.50
596 Ollie Brown .30 .75
597 Winston Llenas .30 .75
598 Bruce Kison .30 .75
599 Nate Colbert .30 .75
600 Rod Carew 4.00 10.00
601 Juan Beniquez .30 .75
602 John Vukovich .30 .75
603 Lew Krausse .30 .75
604 Oscar Zamora .30 .75
605 John Ellis .30 .75
606 Bruce Miller .30 .75
607 Jim Holt .30 .75
608 Gene Michael .30 .75
609 Elrod Hendricks .30 .75
610 Ron Hunt .30 .75
611 Yankees: Team 1.00 2.50
MG
Bill Virdon
612 Terry Hughes .30 .75
613 Bill Parsons .30 .75
614 Rookie Pitchers .60 1.50
Jack Kucek
Dyar Miller
Vern Ruhle
615 Dennis Leonard RC 1.00 2.50
616 Jim Rice RC 8.00 20.00
617 Doug DeCinces RC 1.00 2.50
618 Rick Rhoden .60 1.50
McGregor RC
619 Rookie Outfielders .60 1.50
Benny Ayala
Nyls Nyman
Tommy
620 Gary Carter RC 10.00 25.00
621 John Denny RC 1.00 2.50
622 Fred Lynn RC 4.00 10.00
623 K.Hernandez 5.00 12.00
*P.Garner RC
624 Rookie Pitchers .60 1.50
Doug Konieczny
Gary Lavelle
Jim
625 Boog Powell 1.00 2.50
626 Larry Haney/(photo actually .30 .75
Dave Duncan)
627 Tom Walker .30 .75
628 Ron LeFlore RC .60 1.50
629 Joe Hoerner .30 .75
630 Greg Luzinski 1.00 2.50
631 Lee Lacy .30 .75
632 Morris Nettles .30 .75
633 Paul Casanova .30 .75
634 Cy Acosta .30 .75
635 Chuck Dobson .30 .75
636 Charlie Moore .30 .75
637 Ted Martinez .30 .75
638 Cubs Team CL 1.00 2.50
Jim Marshall MG
639 Steve Kline .30 .75
640 Harmon Killebrew 3.00 8.00
641 Jim Northrup .60 1.50
642 Mike Phillips .30 .75
643 Brent Strom .30 .75
644 Bill Fahey .30 .75
645 Danny Cater .30 .75
646 Checklist 529-660 1.50 4.00
647 Claudell Washington RC 1.00 2.50
648 Dave Pagan .60 1.50
649 Jack Heidemann .30 .75
650 Dave May .30 .75
651 John Morlan .30 .75
652 Lindy McDaniel .60 1.50
653 Lee Richard .30 .75
654 Jerry Terrell .30 .75
655 Rico Carty .60 1.50
656 Bill Plummer .30 .75
657 Bob Oliver .30 .75
658 Vic Harris .30 .75
659 Bob Apodaca .30 .75
660 Hank Aaron 12.50 40.00

1976 O-Pee-Chee

This is a 660-card standard-size set. The 1976 O-Pee-Chee cards are very similar to the 1976 Topps cards, yet rather different from previous years' issues. The most prominent change is that the backs are much brighter than their American counterparts. The cards parallel the American issue and it is a challenge to find well centered examples of these cards. Notable Rookie Cards include Dennis Eckersley and Ron Guidry.

COMPLETE SET (660) 400.00 800.00
1 Hank Aaron RB 10.00 25.00
Most RBI's, 2262
2 Bobby Bonds RB 1.25 3.00
Most leadoff
homers& 32;
Plus 3
3 Mickey Lolich RB .60 1.50
Lefthander& Most
Strikeouts 267
4 Dave Lopes RB .60 1.50
Most consecutive
SB attempts& 38
5 Tom Seaver RB 3.00 8.00
Most cons. seasons
with 200 SO's&
6 Rennie Stennett RB .60 1.50
Most hits in a 9
inning game&
7 Jim Umbarger .30 .75
8 Tito Fuentes .30 .75
9 Paul Lindblad .30 .75
10 Lou Brock 3.00 8.00
11 Jim Hughes .30 .75
12 Richie Zisk .60 1.50
13 John Wockenfuss .30 .75
14 Gene Garber .60 1.50
15 George Scott .60 1.50
16 Bob Apodaca .30 .75
17 New York Yankees 1.25 3.00
Team Card
18 Dale Murray .30 .75
19 George Brett 30.00 60.00
20 Bob Watson .60 1.50
21 Dave LaRoche .30 .75
22 Bill Russell .60 1.50
23 Brian Downing .60 1.50
24 Cesar Geronimo .60 1.50
25 Mike Torrez .60 1.50
26 Andre Thornton .60 1.50
27 Ed Figueroa .30 .75
28 Dusty Baker 1.25 3.00
29 Rick Burleson .60 1.50
30 John Montefusco RC .60 1.50
31 Len Randle .30 .75
32 Danny Frisella .30 .75
33 Bill North .30 .75
34 Mike Garman .30 .75
35 Tony Oliva 1.25 3.00
36 Frank Taveras .30 .75
37 John Hiller .60 1.50
38 Garry Maddox .60 1.50
39 Pete Broberg .30 .75
40 Dave Kingman 1.25 3.00
41 Tippy Martinez .60 1.50
42 Barry Foote .60 1.50
43 Paul Splittorff .30 .75
44 Doug Rader .60 1.50
45 Boog Powell 1.25 3.00
46 Los Angeles Dodgers 1.25 3.00
Team Card
Walt Alston MG/(C
47 Jesse Jefferson .30 .75
48 Dave Concepcion 1.25 3.00
49 Dave Duncan .60 1.50
50 Fred Lynn 1.25 3.00
51 Ray Burris .30 .75
52 Dave Chalk .30 .75
53 Mike Beard RC .30 .75
54 Dave Rader .30 .75
55 Gaylord Perry 2.00 5.00
56 Bob Tolan .30 .75
57 Phil Garner .60 1.50
58 Ron Reed .30 .75
59 Larry Hisle .60 1.50
60 Jerry Reuss .60 1.50
61 Ron LeFlore .60 1.50
62 Johnny Oates .60 1.50
63 Bobby Darwin .30 .75
64 Jerry Koosman .60 1.50
65 Chris Chambliss .60 1.50
66 Father and Son .60 1.50
Gus
Buddy Bell
67 Bob .60 1.50
Ray Boone FS
68 Father and Son .30 .75
Joe Coleman
Joe Coleman Jr.
69 Father and Son .30 .75
Jim
Mike Hegan
70 Father and Son .60 1.50
Roy Smalley
Roy Smalley Jr.
71 Steve Rogers 1.25 3.00
72 Hal McRae .60 1.50
73 Baltimore Orioles 1.25 3.00
Team Card
Earl Weaver MG/(Che
74 Oscar Gamble .60 1.50
75 Larry Dierker .60 1.50
76 Willie Crawford .30 .75
77 Pedro Borbon .60 1.50
78 Cecil Cooper .60 1.50
79 Jerry Morales .30 .75
80 Jim Kaat 1.50 4.00
81 Darrell Evans .60 1.50
82 Von Joshua .30 .75
83 Jim Spencer .30 .75
84 Brent Strom .30 .75
85 Mickey Rivers .60 1.50
86 Mike Tyson .30 .75
87 Tom Burgmeier .30 .75
88 Duffy Dyer .30 .75
89 Vern Ruhle .30 .75
90 Sal Bando .60 1.50
91 Tom Hutton .30 .75
92 Eduardo Rodriguez .30 .75
93 Mike Phillips .30 .75
94 Jim Dwyer .30 .75
95 Brooks Robinson 4.00 10.00
96 Doug Bird .30 .75
97 Wilbur Howard .30 .75
98 Dennis Eckersley RC 20.00 50.00
99 Lee Lacy .30 .75
100 Jim Hunter 2.00 5.00
101 Pete LaCock .30 .75
102 Jim Willoughby .30 .75
103 Biff Pocoroba RC .30 .75
104 Reds Team 1.50 4.00
105 Gary Lavelle .30 .75
106 Tom Grieve .60 1.50
107 Dave Roberts .30 .75
108 Don Kirkwood .30 .75
109 Larry Lintz .30 .75
110 Carlos May .30 .75
111 Danny Thompson .30 .75
112 Kent Tekulve RC 1.25 3.00
113 Gary Sutherland .30 .75
114 Jay Johnstone .60 1.50
115 Ken Holtzman .60 1.50
116 Charlie Moore .30 .75
117 Mike Jorgensen .30 .75
118 Boston Red Sox 1.25 3.00
Team Card
Darrell Johnson/(Check
119 Checklist 1-132 1.25 3.00
120 Rusty Staub .60 1.50
121 Tony Solaita .30 .75
122 Mike Cosgrove .30 .75
123 Walt Williams .30 .75
124 Doug Rau .30 .75
125 Don Baylor 1.50 4.00
126 Tom Dettore .30 .75
127 Larvell Blanks .30 .75
128 Ken Griffey Sr. 1.50 4.00
129 Andy Etchebarren .30 .75
130 Luis Tiant 1.25 3.00
131 Bill Stein .30 .75
132 Don Hood .30 .75
133 Gary Matthews .60 1.50
134 Mike Ivie .30 .75
135 Bake McBride .60 1.50
136 Dave Goltz .30 .75
137 Bill Robinson .60 1.50
138 Lerrin LaGrow .30 .75
139 Gorman Thomas .60 1.50
140 Vida Blue .60 1.50
141 Larry Parrish RC 1.25 3.00
142 Dick Drago .30 .75
143 Jerry Grote .30 .75
144 Al Fitzmorris .30 .75
145 Larry Bowa .60 1.50
146 George Medich .30 .75
147 Houston Astros 1.25 3.00
Team Card
Bill Virdon MG/(Checkl
148 Stan Thomas .30 .75
149 Tommy Davis .60 1.50
150 Steve Garvey 1.50 4.00
151 Bill Bonham .30 .75
152 Leroy Stanton .30 .75
153 Buzz Capra .30 .75
154 Bucky Dent .60 1.50
155 Jack Billingham .60 1.50
156 Rico Carty .60 1.50
157 Mike Caldwell .30 .75
158 Ken Reitz .30 .75
159 Jerry Terrell .30 .75
160 Dave Winfield 8.00 20.00
161 Bruce Kison .30 .75
162 Jack Pierce .30 .75
163 Jim Slaton .30 .75
164 Pepe Mangual .30 .75
165 Gene Tenace .60 1.50
166 Skip Lockwood .30 .75
167 Freddie Patek .60 1.50
168 Tom Hilgendorf .30 .75
169 Graig Nettles 1.25 3.00
170 Rick Wise .30 .75
171 Greg Gross .30 .75
172 Texas Rangers 1.25 3.00
Team Card
Frank Lucchesi MG/(Chec
173 Steve Swisher .30 .75
174 Charlie Hough .60 1.50
175 Ken Singleton .60 1.50
176 Dick Lange .30 .75
177 Marty Perez .30 .75
178 Tom Buskey .30 .75
179 George Foster 1.25 3.00
180 Goose Gossage 1.50 4.00
181 Willie Montanez .30 .75
182 Harry Rasmussen .30 .75
183 Steve Braun .30 .75
184 Bill Greif .30 .75
185 Dave Parker 1.50 4.00
186 Tom Walker .30 .75
187 Pedro Garcia .30 .75
188 Fred Scherman .30 .75
189 Claudell Washington .60 1.50
190 Jon Matlack .30 .75
191 NL Batting Leaders .60 1.50
Bill Madlock
Ted Simmons
Man
192 R.Carew 1.50 4.00
Lynn
T.Munson LL
193 Schmidt 2.00 5.00
Kingman
Luz LL
194 Reggie 2.00 5.00
Scott
Mayb LL
195 Luzin 1.25 3.00
Bench
Perez LL
196 AL RBI Leaders .60 1.50
George Scott
John Mayberry
Fred
197 Lopes 1.25 3.00
Morgan
Brock LL
198 AL Steals Leaders .60 1.50
Mickey Rivers
Claudell Washing
199 Seaver 1.50 4.00
Jones
Messers LL
200 Hunter 1.25 3.00
Palmer
Blue LL
201 R.Jones 1.25 3.00
Messer
Seaver LL
202 Palmer 2.00 5.00
Hunter
Eck LL
203 Seaver 1.50 4.00
Montef
Messer LL
204 Tanana .60 1.50
Blylev
Perry LL
205 Leading Firemen .60 1.50
Al Hrabosky
Rich Gossage
206 Manny Trillo .30 .75
207 Andy Hassler .30 .75
208 Mike Lum .30 .75
209 Alan Ashby .60 1.50
210 Lee May .60 1.50
211 Clay Carroll .60 1.50
212 Pat Kelly .30 .75
213 Dave Heaverlo .30 .75
214 Eric Soderholm .30 .75
215 Reggie Smith .60 1.50
216 Montreal Expos 1.25 3.00
Team Card
Karl Kuehl MG/(Checkli
217 Dave Freisleben .30 .75
218 John Knox .30 .75
219 Tom Murphy .30 .75
220 Manny Sanguillen .60 1.50
221 Jim Todd .30 .75
222 Wayne Garrett .30 .75
223 Ollie Brown .30 .75
224 Jim York .30 .75
225 Roy White .60 1.50
226 Jim Sundberg .60 1.50
227 Oscar Zamora .30 .75
228 John Hale .30 .75
229 Jerry Remy .30 .75
230 Carl Yastrzemski 6.00 15.00
231 Tom House .30 .75
232 Frank Duffy .30 .75
233 Grant Jackson .30 .75
234 Mike Sadek .30 .75
235 Bert Blyleven 1.50 4.00
236 Kansas City Royals 1.25 3.00
Team Card
Whitey Herzog MG/(
237 Dave Hamilton .30 .75
238 Larry Biittner .30 .75
239 John Curtis .30 .75
240 Pete Rose 12.50 40.00
241 Hector Torres .30 .75
242 Dan Meyer .30 .75
243 Jim Rooker .30 .75
244 Bill Sharp .30 .75
245 Felix Millan .30 .75
246 Cesar Tovar .30 .75
247 Terry Harmon .30 .75
248 Dick Tidrow .30 .75
249 Cliff Johnson .60 1.50
250 Fergie Jenkins 2.00 5.00
251 Rick Monday .60 1.50
252 Tim Nordbrook .30 .75
253 Bill Buckner .60 1.50
254 Rudy Meoli .30 .75
255 Fritz Peterson .30 .75
256 Rowland Office .30 .75
257 Ross Grimsley .30 .75
258 Nyls Nyman .30 .75
259 Darrel Chaney .30 .75
260 Steve Busby .30 .75
261 Gary Thomasson .30 .75
262 Checklist 133-264 1.25 3.00
263 Lyman Bostock RC 1.25 3.00
264 Steve Renko .30 .75
265 Willie Davis .60 1.50
266 Alan Foster .30 .75
267 Aurelio Rodriguez .30 .75
268 Del Unser .30 .75
269 Rick Austin .30 .75
270 Willie Stargell 2.00 5.00
271 Jim Lonborg .60 1.50
272 Rick Dempsey .60 1.50
273 Joe Niekro .60 1.50
274 Tommy Harper .60 1.50
275 Rick Manning .30 .75
276 Mickey Scott .30 .75
277 Chicago Cubs 1.25 3.00
Team Card
Jim Marshall MG/(Checkli
278 Bernie Carbo .30 .75
279 Roy Howell .30 .75
280 Burt Hooton .60 1.50
281 Dave May .30 .75
282 Dan Osborn .30 .75
283 Merv Rettenmund .30 .75
284 Steve Ontiveros .30 .75
285 Mike Cuellar .60 1.50
286 Jim Wohlford .30 .75
287 Pete Mackanin .30 .75
288 Bill Campbell .30 .75
289 Enzo Hernandez .30 .75
290 Ted Simmons .60 1.50
291 Ken Sanders .30 .75
292 Leon Roberts .30 .75
293 Bill Castro .30 .75
294 Ed Kirkpatrick .30 .75
295 Dave Cash .30 .75
296 Pat Dobson .30 .75
297 Roger Metzger .30 .75
298 Dick Bosman .30 .75
299 Champ Summers .30 .75
300 Johnny Bench 8.00 20.00
301 Jackie Brown .30 .75
302 Rick Miller .30 .75
303 Steve Foucault .30 .75
304 California Angels 1.25 3.00
Team Card
Dick Williams MG/(C
305 Andy Messersmith .60 1.50
306 Rod Gilbreath .30 .75
307 Al Bumbry .60 1.50
308 Jim Barr .30 .75
309 Bill Melton .30 .75
310 Randy Jones .60 1.50
311 Cookie Rojas .30 .75
312 Don Carrithers .30 .75
313 Dan Ford .30 .75
314 Ed Kranepool .30 .75
315 Al Hrabosky .60 1.50
316 Robin Yount 10.00 25.00
317 John Candelaria RC 1.25 3.00
318 Bob Boone 1.25 3.00
319 Larry Gura .30 .75
320 Willie Horton .60 1.50
321 Jose Cruz 1.25 3.00
322 Glenn Abbott .30 .75
323 Rob Sperring .30 .75
324 Jim Bibby .30 .75
325 Tony Perez 2.00 5.00
326 Dick Pole .30 .75
327 Dave Moates .30 .75
328 Carl Morton .30 .75
329 Joe Ferguson .30 .75
330 Nolan Ryan 20.00 50.00
331 San Diego Padres 1.25 3.00
Team Card
John McNamara MG/(Ch
332 Charlie Williams .30 .75
333 Bob Coluccio .30 .75
334 Dennis Leonard .60 1.50
335 Bob Grich .60 1.50
336 Vic Albury .30 .75
337 Bud Harrelson .60 1.50
338 Bob Bailey .30 .75
339 John Denny .60 1.50
340 Jim Rice 2.50 6.00
341 Lou Gehrig ATG 8.00 20.00
342 Rogers Hornsby ATG 1.50 4.00
343 Pie Traynor ATG 1.25 3.00
344 Honus Wagner ATG 3.00 8.00
345 Babe Ruth ATG 10.00 25.00
346 Ty Cobb ATG 8.00 20.00
347 Ted Williams ATG 8.00 20.00
348 Mickey Cochrane ATG 1.25 3.00
349 Walter Johnson ATG 3.00 8.00
350 Lefty Grove ATG 1.25 3.00
351 Randy Hundley .60 1.50
352 Dave Giusti .30 .75

353 Sixto Lezcano .60 1.50
354 Ron Blomberg .30 .75
355 Steve Carlton 4.00 10.00
356 Ted Martinez .30 .75
357 Ken Forsch .30 .75
358 Buddy Bell .60 1.50
359 Rick Reuschel .60 1.50
360 Jeff Burroughs .60 1.50
361 Detroit Tigers 1.25 3.00
Team Card
Ralph Houk MG/(Checkli
362 Will McEnaney .60 1.50
363 Dave Collins RC .60 1.50
364 Elias Sosa .30 .75
365 Carlton Fisk 3.00 8.00
366 Bobby Valentine .60 1.50
367 Bruce Miller .30 .75
368 Wilbur Wood .30 .75
369 Frank White .60 1.50
370 Ron Cey .60 1.50
371 Ellie Hendricks .30 .75
372 Rick Baldwin .30 .75
373 Johnny Briggs .30 .75
374 Dan Warthen .30 .75
375 Ron Fairly .60 1.50
376 Rich Hebner .60 1.50
377 Mike Hegan .30 .75
378 Steve Stone .60 1.50
379 Ken Boswell .30 .75
380 Bobby Bonds 1.50 4.00
381 Denny Doyle .30 .75
382 Matt Alexander .30 .75
383 John Ellis .30 .75
384 Philadelphia Phillies 1.25 3.00
Team Card
Danny Ozark MG/
385 Mickey Lolich .60 1.50
386 Ed Goodson .30 .75
387 Mike Miley .30 .75
388 Stan Perzanowski .30 .75
389 Glenn Adams .30 .75
390 Don Gullett .60 1.50
391 Jerry Hairston .30 .75
392 Checklist 265-396 1.25 3.00
393 Paul Mitchell .30 .75
394 Fran Healy .30 .75
395 Jim Wynn .60 1.50
396 Bill Lee .30 .75
397 Tim Foli .30 .75
398 Dave Tomlin .30 .75
399 Luis Melendez .30 .75
400 Rod Carew 3.00 8.00
401 Ken Brett .30 .75
402 Don Money .60 1.50
403 Geoff Zahn .30 .75
404 Enos Cabell .30 .75
405 Rollie Fingers 2.00 5.00
406 Ed Herrmann .30 .75
407 Tom Underwood .30 .75
408 Charlie Spikes .30 .75
409 Dave Lemanczyk .30 .75
410 Ralph Garr .60 1.50
411 Bill Singer .30 .75
412 Toby Harrah .60 1.50
413 Pete Varney .30 .75
414 Wayne Garland .30 .75
415 Vada Pinson 1.50 4.00
416 Tommy John 1.50 4.00
417 Gene Clines .30 .75
418 Jose Morales RC .60 1.50
419 Reggie Cleveland .30 .75
420 Joe Morgan 3.00 8.00
421 Oakland A's 1.25 3.00
Team Card/(No MG on front;
checklis
422 Johnny Grubb .30 .75
423 Ed Halicki .30 .75
424 Phil Roof .30 .75
425 Rennie Stennett .30 .75
426 Bob Forsch .30 .75
427 Kurt Bevacqua .30 .75
428 Jim Crawford .30 .75
429 Fred Stanley .30 .75
430 Jose Cardenal .60 1.50
431 Dick Ruthven .30 .75
432 Tom Veryzer .30 .75
433 Rick Waits .30 .75
434 Morris Nettles .30 .75
435 Phil Niekro 2.00 5.00
436 Bill Fahey .30 .75
437 Terry Forster .30 .75
438 Doug DeCinces .60 1.50
439 Rick Rhoden .60 1.50
440 John Mayberry .60 1.50
441 Gary Carter 3.00 8.00
442 Hank Webb .30 .75
443 San Francisco Giants 1.25 3.00
Team Card/(No MG on front;#
444 Gary Nolan .60 1.50
445 Rico Petrocelli .60 1.50
446 Larry Haney .30 .75
447 Gene Locklear .60 1.50
448 Tom Johnson .30 .75
449 Bob Robertson .30 .75
450 Jim Palmer 3.00 8.00
451 Buddy Bradford .30 .75
452 Tom Hausman .30 .75
453 Lou Piniella 1.25 3.00
454 Tom Griffin .30 .75
455 Dick Allen 1.25 3.00
456 Joe Coleman .30 .75
457 Ed Crosby .30 .75
458 Earl Williams .30 .75
459 Jim Brewer .30 .75
460 Cesar Cedeno .60 1.50
461 NL and AL Champs .60 1.50
Reds sweep Bucs;
Bosox surprise
462 World Series .60 1.50
Reds Champs
463 Steve Hargan .30 .75
464 Ken Henderson .30 .75
465 Mike Marshall .60 1.50
466 Bob Stinson .30 .75
467 Woodie Fryman .30 .75
468 Jesus Alou .30 .75
469 Rawly Eastwick .60 1.50
470 Bobby Murcer .60 1.50
471 Jim Burton .30 .75
472 Bob Davis .30 .75
473 Paul Blair .60 1.50
474 Ray Corbin .30 .75
475 Joe Rudi .60 1.50
476 Bob Moose .30 .75
477 Cleveland Indians 1.25 3.00
Team Card
Frank Robinson MG/(
478 Lynn McGlothen .30 .75
479 Bobby Mitchell .30 .75
480 Mike Schmidt 10.00 25.00
481 Rudy May .30 .75
482 Tim Hosley .30 .75
483 Mickey Stanley .30 .75
484 Eric Raich .30 .75
485 Mike Hargrove .60 1.50
486 Bruce Dal Canton .30 .75
487 Leron Lee .30 .75
488 Claude Osteen .60 1.50
489 Skip Jutze .30 .75
490 Frank Tanana .60 1.50
491 Terry Crowley .30 .75
492 Martin Pattin .30 .75
493 Derrel Thomas .30 .75
494 Craig Swan .60 1.50
495 Nate Colbert .30 .75
496 Juan Beniquez .30 .75
497 Joe McIntosh .30 .75
498 Glenn Borgmann .30 .75
499 Mario Guerrero .30 .75
500 Reggie Jackson 8.00 20.00
501 Billy Champion .30 .75
502 Tim McCarver 1.25 3.00
503 Elliott Maddox .30 .75
504 Pittsburgh Pirates 1.25 3.00
Team Card
Danny Murtaugh MG/
505 Mark Belanger .60 1.50
506 George Mitterwald .30 .75
507 Ray Bare .30 .75
508 Duane Kuiper .30 .75
509 Bill Hands .30 .75
510 Amos Otis .60 1.50
511 Jamie Easterley .30 .75
512 Ellie Rodriguez .30 .75
513 Bart Johnson .30 .75
514 Dan Driessen .60 1.50
515 Steve Yeager .60 1.50
516 Wayne Granger .30 .75
517 John Milner .30 .75
518 Doug Flynn .30 .75
519 Steve Brye .30 .75
520 Willie McCovey 3.00 8.00
521 Jim Colborn .30 .75
522 Ted Sizemore .30 .75
523 Bob Montgomery .30 .75
524 Pete Falcone .30 .75
525 Billy Williams 2.00 5.00
526 Checklist 397-528 1.25 3.00
527 Mike Anderson .30 .75
528 Dock Ellis .30 .75
529 Deron Johnson .30 .75
530 Don Sutton 2.00 5.00
531 New York Mets 1.25 3.00
Team Card
Joe Frazier MG/(Checkli
532 Milt May .30 .75
533 Lee Richard .30 .75
534 Stan Bahnsen .30 .75
535 Dave Nelson .30 .75
536 Mike Thompson .30 .75
537 Tony Muser .30 .75
538 Pat Darcy .30 .75
539 John Balaz .30 .75
540 Bill Freehan .60 1.50
541 Steve Mingori .30 .75
542 Keith Hernandez 1.25 3.00
543 Wayne Twitchell .30 .75
544 Pepe Frias .30 .75
545 Sparky Lyle .60 1.50
546 Dave Rosello .30 .75
547 Roric Harrison .30 .75
548 Manny Mota .60 1.50
549 Randy Tate .30 .75
550 Hank Aaron 12.50 40.00
551 Jerry DaVanon .30 .75
552 Terry Humphrey .30 .75
553 Randy Moffitt .30 .75
554 Ray Fosse .30 .75
555 Dyar Miller .30 .75
556 Minnesota Twins 1.25 3.00
Team Card
Gene Mauch MG/(Checkl
557 Dan Spillner .30 .75
558 Clarence Gaston .60 1.50
559 Clyde Wright .30 .75
560 Jorge Orta .30 .75
561 Tom Carroll .30 .75
562 Adrian Garrett .30 .75
563 Larry Demery .30 .75
564 Kurt Bevacqua Gum 1.25 3.00
565 Tug McGraw 1.25 3.00
566 Ken McMullen .30 .75
567 George Stone .30 .75
568 Rob Andrews .30 .75
569 Nelson Briles .60 1.50
570 George Hendrick .60 1.50
571 Don DeMola .30 .75
572 Rich Coggins .30 .75
573 Bill Travers .30 .75
574 Don Kessinger .60 1.50
575 Dwight Evans 1.25 3.00
576 Maximino Leon .30 .75
577 Marc Hill .30 .75
578 Ted Kubiak .30 .75
579 Clay Kirby .30 .75
580 Bert Campaneris .60 1.50
581 St. Louis Cardinals 1.25 3.00
Team Card
Red Schoendienst M
582 Mike Kekich .30 .75
583 Tommy Helms .30 .75
584 Stan Wall .30 .75
585 Joe Torre 1.50 4.00
586 Ron Schueler .30 .75
587 Leo Cardenas .30 .75
588 Kevin Kobel .30 .75
589 Mike Flanagan RC 1.25 3.00
590 Chet Lemon RC .60 1.50
591 Rookie Pitchers .60 1.50
Steve Grilli
Craig Mitchell
Jos
592 Willie Randolph RC 4.00 10.00
593 Rookie Pitchers .60 1.50
Larry Anderson
Ken Crosby
Mark
594 Rookie Catchers .60 1.50
OF
Andy Merchant
Ed Ott
Royle S
595 Rookie Pitchers .60 1.50
Art DeFillipis
Randy Lerch
Sid
596 Rookie Infielders .60 1.50
Craig Reynolds
Lamar Johnson/
597 Rookie Pitchers .60 1.50
Don Aase
Jack Kucek
Frank LaCor
598 Rookie Outfielders .60 1.50
Hector Cruz
Jamie Quirk
Jerr
599 Ron Guidry RC ! 5.00 12.00
600 Tom Seaver 6.00 15.00
601 Ken Rudolph .30 .75
602 Doug Konieczny .30 .75
603 Jim Holt .30 .75
604 Joe Lovitto .30 .75
605 Al Downing .30 .75
606 Milwaukee Brewers 1.25 3.00
Team Card
Alex Grammas MG/(Ch
607 Rich Hinton .30 .75
608 Vic Correll .30 .75
609 Fred Norman .30 .75
610 Greg Luzinski 1.25 3.00
611 Rich Folkers .30 .75
612 Joe Lahoud .30 .75
613 Tim Johnson .30 .75
614 Fernando Arroyo .30 .75
615 Mike Cubbage .30 .75
616 Buck Martinez .60 1.50
617 Darold Knowles .30 .75
618 Jack Brohamer .30 .75
619 Bill Butler .30 .75
620 Al Oliver .60 1.50
621 Tom Hall .30 .75
622 Rick Auerbach .30 .75
623 Bob Allietta .30 .75
624 Tony Taylor .30 .75
625 J.R. Richard .60 1.50
626 Bob Sheldon .30 .75
627 Bill Plummer .30 .75
628 John D'Acquisto .30 .75
629 Sandy Alomar .60 1.50
630 Chris Speier .30 .75
631 Atlanta Braves 1.25 3.00
Team Card
Dave Bristol MG/(Check
632 Rogelio Moret .30 .75
633 John Stearns RC .60 1.50
634 Larry Christenson .30 .75
635 Jim Fregosi .60 1.50
636 Joe Decker .30 .75
637 Bruce Bochte .30 .75
638 Doyle Alexander .60 1.50
639 Fred Kendall .30 .75
640 Bill Madlock 1.25 3.00
641 Tom Paciorek .60 1.50
642 Dennis Blair .30 .75
643 Checklist 529-660 1.25 3.00
644 Tom Bradley .30 .75
645 Darrell Porter .60 1.50
646 John Lowenstein .30 .75
647 Ramon Hernandez .30 .75
648 Al Cowens .30 .75
649 Dave Roberts .30 .75
650 Thurman Munson 4.00 10.00
651 John Odom .30 .75
652 Ed Armbrister .30 .75
653 Mike Norris RC .60 1.50
654 Doug Griffin .30 .75
655 Mike Vail .30 .75
656 Chicago White Sox 1.25 3.00
Team Card
Chuck Tanner MG/(Ch
657 Roy Smalley RC .60 1.50
658 Jerry Johnson .30 .75
659 Ben Oglivie .60 1.50
660 Davey Lopes ! 1.25 3.00

1977 O-Pee-Chee

The 1977 O-Pee-Chee set of 264 standard-size cards is not only much smaller numerically than its American counterpart, but also contains many different poses and is loaded with players from the two Canadian teams, including many players from the inaugural year of the Blue Jays and many single cards of players who were on multiplayer rookie cards. On a white background, the fronts feature color player photos with thin black borders. The player's name and position, a facsimile autograph, and the team name also appear on the front. The horizontal backs carry player biography and statistics in French and English. The numbering of this set is different than the U.S. issue, the backs have different colors and the words "O-Pee-Chee Printed in Canada" are printed on the back.

COMPLETE SET (264) 150.00 300.00
1 George Brett 4.00 10.00
Bill Madlock LL
2 Graig Nettles .75 2.00
Mike Schmidt LL
3 Lee May .60 1.50
George Foster LL
4 Bill North .30 .75
Dave Lopes LL
5 Jim Palmer .60 1.50
Randy Jones LL
6 Nolan Ryan 8.00 20.00
Tom Seaver LL
7 Mark Fidrych .30 .75
John Denny LL
8 Bill Campbell .30 .75
Rawly Eastwick LL
9 Mike Jorgensen .30 .75
10 Jim Hunter 1.00 2.50
11 Ken Griffey Sr. .60 1.50
12 Bill Campbell .12 .30
13 Otto Velez .30 .75
14 Milt May .12 .30
15 Dennis Eckersley 2.00 5.00
16 John Mayberry .30 .75
17 Larry Bowa .30 .75
18 Don Carrithers .30 .75
19 Ken Singleton .30 .75
20 Bill Stein .12 .30
21 Ken Brett .12 .30
22 Gary Woods .30 .75
23 Steve Swisher .12 .30
24 Don Sutton 1.00 2.50
25 Willie Stargell 1.00 2.50
26 Jerry Koosman .30 .75
27 Del Unser .30 .75
28 Bob Grich .30 .75
29 Jim Slaton .12 .30
30 Thurman Munson 2.00 5.00
31 Dan Driessen .12 .30
32 Tom Bruno .30 .75
33 Larry Hisle .30 .75
34 Phil Garner .12 .30
35 Mike Hargrove .30 .75
36 Jackie Brown .30 .75
37 Carl Yastrzemski 3.00 8.00
38 Dave Roberts .12 .30
39 Ray Fosse .12 .30
40 Dave McKay .30 .75
41 Paul Splittorff .12 .30
42 Garry Maddox .12 .30
43 Phil Niekro 1.00 2.50
44 Roger Metzger .12 .30
45 Gary Carter 1.00 2.50
46 Jim Spencer .12 .30
47 Ross Grimsley .12 .30
48 Bob Bailor .30 .75
49 Chris Chambliss .30 .75
50 Will McEnaney .30 .75
51 Lou Brock 1.50 4.00
52 Rollie Fingers 1.00 2.50
53 Chris Speier .12 .30
54 Bombo Rivera .30 .75
55 Pete Broberg .12 .30
56 Bill Madlock .75 2.00
57 Rick Rhoden .30 .75
58 Blue Jays Coaches .30 .75
Don Leppert
Bob Miller
Jackie
59 John Candelaria .12 .30
60 Ed Kranepool .12 .30
61 Dave LaRoche .12 .30
62 Jim Rice .75 2.00
63 Don Stanhouse .30 .75
64 Jason Thompson RC .30 .75
65 Nolan Ryan 12.50 40.00
66 Tom Poquette .12 .30
67 Leon Hooten .30 .75
68 Bob Boone .30 .75
69 Mickey Rivers .30 .75
70 Gary Nolan .12 .30
71 Sixto Lezcano .12 .30
72 Larry Parrish .30 .75
73 Dave Goltz .12 .30
74 Bert Campaneris .30 .75
75 Vida Blue .30 .75
76 Rick Cerone .30 .75
77 Ralph Garr .30 .75
78 Ken Forsch .12 .30
79 Willie Montanez .12 .30
80 Jim Palmer 1.50 4.00
81 Jerry White .30 .75
82 Gene Tenace .30 .75
83 Bobby Murcer .30 .75
84 Garry Templeton .60 1.50
85 Bill Singer .30 .75
86 Buddy Bell .30 .75
87 Luis Tiant .30 .75
88 Rusty Staub .60 1.50
89 Sparky Lyle .30 .75
90 Jose Morales .30 .75
91 Dennis Leonard .30 .75
92 Tommy Smith .12 .30
93 Steve Carlton 2.00 5.00
94 John Scott .30 .75
95 Bill Bonham .12 .30
96 Dave Lopes .30 .75
97 Jerry Reuss .30 .75
98 Dave Kingman .60 1.50
99 Dan Warthen .30 .75
100 Johnny Bench 4.00 10.00
101 Bert Blyleven .60 1.50
102 Cecil Cooper .30 .75
103 Mike Willis .30 .75
104 Dan Ford .12 .30
105 Frank Tanana .30 .75
106 Bill North .12 .30
107 Joe Ferguson .12 .30
108 Dick Williams MG .30 .75
109 John Denny .30 .75
110 Willie Randolph .60 1.50
111 Reggie Cleveland .30 .75
112 Doug Howard .30 .75
113 Randy Jones .12 .30
114 Rico Carty .30 .75
115 Mark Fidrych RC 2.00 5.00
116 Darrell Porter .30 .75
117 Wayne Garrett .30 .75
118 Greg Luzinski .60 1.50
119 Jim Barr .12 .30
120 George Foster .60 1.50
121 Phil Roof .30 .75
122 Bucky Dent .30 .75
123 Steve Braun .12 .30
124 Checklist 1-132 .60 1.50
125 Lee May .30 .75
126 Woodie Fryman .30 .75
127 Jose Cardenal .30 .75
128 Doug Rau .12 .30
129 Rennie Stennett .12 .30
130 Pete Vuckovich RC .30 .75
131 Cesar Cedeno .30 .75
132 Jon Matlack .12 .30
133 Don Baylor .60 1.50
134 Darrel Chaney .12 .30
135 Tony Perez 1.00 2.50
136 Aurelio Rodriguez .12 .30
137 Carlton Fisk 2.50 6.00
138 Wayne Garland .12 .30
139 Dave Hilton .30 .75
140 Rawly Eastwick .12 .30
141 Amos Otis .30 .75
142 Tug McGraw .30 .75
143 Rod Carew 2.50 6.00
144 Mike Torrez .30 .75
145 Sal Bando .30 .75
146 Dock Ellis .12 .30
147 Jose Cruz .30 .75
148 Alan Ashby .30 .75
149 Gaylord Perry 1.00 2.50
150 Keith Hernandez .30 .75
151 Dave Pagan .12 .30
152 Richie Zisk .12 .30
153 Steve Rogers .30 .75
154 Mark Belanger .30 .75
155 Andy Messersmith .30 .75
156 Dave Winfield 6.00 15.00
157 Chuck Hartenstein .30 .75
158 Manny Trillo .12 .30
159 Steve Yeager .30 .75
160 Cesar Geronimo .12 .30
161 Jim Rooker .12 .30
162 Tim Foli .30 .75
163 Fred Lynn .30 .75
164 Ed Figueroa .12 .30
165 Johnny Grubb .12 .30
166 Pedro Garcia .30 .75
167 Ron LeFlore .30 .75
168 Rich Hebner .30 .75
169 Larry Herndon RC .30 .75
170 George Brett 12.50 30.00
171 Joe Kerrigan .30 .75
172 Bud Harrelson .30 .75
173 Bobby Bonds .75 2.00
174 Bill Travers .12 .30
175 John Lowenstein .30 .75
176 Butch Wynegar RC .30 .75
177 Pete Falcone .12 .30
178 Claudell Washington .30 .75
179 Checklist 133-264 .60 1.50
180 Dave Cash .30 .75
181 Fred Norman .12 .30
182 Roy White .30 .75
183 Marty Perez .12 .30
184 Jesse Jefferson .30 .75
185 Jim Sundberg .30 .75
186 Dan Meyer .30 .75
187 Fergie Jenkins 1.00 2.50
188 Tom Veryzer .12 .30
189 Dennis Blair .30 .75
190 Rick Manning .12 .30
191 Doug Bird .12 .30
192 Al Bumbry .30 .75
193 Dave Roberts .12 .30
194 Larry Christenson .12 .30
195 Chet Lemon .30 .75
196 Ted Simmons .30 .75
197 Ray Burris .12 .30
198 Expos Coaches .30 .75
Jim Brewer
Billy Gardner
Mickey V
199 Ron Cey .30 .75
200 Reggie Jackson 4.00 10.00
201 Pat Zachry .12 .30
202 Doug Ault .30 .75
203 Al Oliver .30 .75
204 Robin Yount 4.00 10.00
205 Tom Seaver 3.00 8.00
206 Joe Rudi .30 .75
207 Barry Foote .30 .75
208 Toby Harrah .30 .75
209 Jeff Burroughs .30 .75
210 George Scott .30 .75
211 Jim Mason .30 .75
212 Vern Ruhle .12 .30
213 Fred Kendall .12 .30
214 Rick Reuschel .30 .75
215 Hal McRae .30 .75
216 Chip Lang .30 .75
217 Graig Nettles .60 1.50
218 George Hendrick .30 .75
219 Glenn Abbott .12 .30
220 Joe Morgan 2.00 5.00
221 Sam Ewing .30 .75
222 George Medich .12 .30
223 Reggie Smith .30 .75
224 Dave Hamilton .12 .30
225 Pepe Frias .30 .75
226 Jay Johnstone .30 .75
227 J.R. Richard .30 .75
228 Doug DeCinces .30 .75
229 Dave Lemanczyk .30 .75
230 Rick Monday .30 .75
231 Manny Sanguillen .30 .75
232 John Montefusco .12 .30
233 Duane Kuiper .12 .30
234 Ellis Valentine .30 .75
235 Dick Tidrow .12 .30
236 Ben Oglivie .30 .75
237 Rick Burleson .30 .75
238 Roy Hartsfield MG .30 .75
239 Lyman Bostock .30 .75
240 Pete Rose 8.00 20.00
241 Mike Ivie .12 .30
242 Dave Parker .60 1.50
243 Bill Greif .30 .75
244 Freddie Patek .30 .75
245 Mike Schmidt 6.00 15.00
246 Brian Downing .30 .75
247 Steve Hargan .12 .30
248 Dave Collins .30 .75
249 Felix Millan .12 .30
250 Don Gullett .30 .75
251 Jerry Royster .12 .30
252 Earl Williams .30 .75
253 Frank Duffy .12 .30
254 Tippy Martinez .12 .30
255 Steve Garvey .75 2.00
256 Alvis Woods .30 .75
257 John Hiller .30 .75
258 Dave Concepcion .60 1.50
259 Dwight Evans .60 1.50
260 Pete MacKanin .30 .75
261 George Brett RB 5.00 12.00
Most Consec. Games
Three Or More
262 Minnie Minoso RB .30 .75
Oldest Player To
Hit Safely
263 Jose Morales RB .30 .75
Most Pinch-hits, Season
264 Nolan Ryan RB 6.00 15.00
Most Seasons 300
Or More Strikeout

1978 O-Pee-Chee

The 242 standard-size cards comprising the 1978 O-Pee-Chee set differ from the cards of the 1978 Topps set by having a higher ratio of cards of players from the two Canadian teams, a practice begun by O-Pee-Chee in 1977 and continued to 1988. The fronts feature white-bordered color player photos, each framed by a colored line. The player's name appears in black lettering at the right of lower white margin. His team name appears in colored cursive lettering, interrupting the framing line at the bottom left of the photo; his position appears within a white baseball icon in an upper corner. The tan and brown horizontal backs carry the player's name, team and position in the brown border at the bottom. Biography, major league statistics, career highlights in both French and English and a bilingual result of an "at bat" in the "Play Ball" game also appear. The asterisked cards have an extra line on the front indicating team change. Double-printed (DP) cards are also noted below. The key card in this set is the Eddie Murray Rookie Card.

COMPLETE SET (242) 100.00 200.00
COMMON PLAYER (1-242) .10 .25
COMMON PLAYER DP (1-242) .08 .20
1 Dave Parker .60 1.50
Rod Carew LL
2 George Foster .25 .60
Jim Rice LL DP
3 George Foster .25 .60
Larry Hisle LL
4 Stolen Base Leaders DP .10 .25
Frank Taveras
Freddie Pat
5 Victory Leaders 1.00 2.50
Steve Carlton
Dave Goltz
Dennis
6 Phil Niekro 2.50 6.00
Nolan Ryan LL DP
7 John Candelaria .25 .60
Frank Tanana LL DP
8 Rollie Fingers .50 1.25
Bill Campbell LL
9 Steve Rogers DP .12 .30
10 Graig Nettles DP .30 .75
11 Doug Capilla .10 .25
12 George Scott .25 .60
13 Gary Woods .25 .60
14 Tom Veryzer .25 .60
Now with Cleveland as of 12-9-77
15 Wayne Garland .10 .25
16 Amos Otis .25 .60
17 Larry Christenson .10 .25
18 Dave Cash .25 .60
19 Jim Barr .10 .25
20 Ruppert Jones .10 .25
21 Eric Soderholm .10 .25
22 Jesse Jefferson .25 .60
23 Jerry Morales .10 .25
24 Doug Rau .10 .25
25 Rennie Stennett .10 .25
26 Lee Mazzilli .10 .25
27 Dick Williams MG .25 .60
28 Joe Rudi .25 .60
29 Robin Yount 4.00 10.00
30 Don Gullett DP .10 .25
31 Roy Howell DP .08 .20
32 Cesar Geronimo .10 .25
33 Rick Langford DP .08 .20
34 Dan Ford .10 .25
35 Gene Tenace .25 .60
36 Santo Alcala .25 .60
37 Rick Burleson .25 .60
38 Dave Rozema .10 .25
39 Duane Kuiper .10 .25
40 Ron Fairly .25 .60
Now with California as of 12-8-77
41 Dennis Leonard .25 .60
42 Greg Luzinski .50 1.25
43 Willie Montanez .25 .60
Now with N.Y. Mets as of 12-8-77
44 Enos Cabell .10 .25
45 Ellis Valentine .25 .60
46 Steve Stone .25 .60
47 Lee May DP .12 .30
48 Roy White .25 .60
49 Jerry Garvin .10 .25
50 Johnny Bench 3.00 8.00
51 Garry Templeton .25 .60
52 Doyle Alexander .25 .60
53 Steve Henderson .10 .25
54 Stan Bahnsen .10 .25
55 Dan Meyer .10 .25
56 Rick Reuschel .25 .60
57 Reggie Smith .25 .60
58 Blue Jays Team DP CL .30 .75
59 John Montefusco .10 .25
60 Dave Parker .50 1.25
61 Jim Bibby .10 .25
62 Fred Lynn .25 .60
63 Jose Morales .25 .60
64 Aurelio Rodriguez .10 .25
65 Frank Tanana .25 .60
66 Darrell Porter .25 .60
67 Otto Velez .10 .25
68 Larry Bowa .50 1.25
69 Jim Hunter 1.00 2.50
70 George Foster .50 1.25
71 Cecil Cooper DP .12 .30
72 Gary Alexander DP .08 .20
73 Paul Thormodsgard .10 .25
74 Toby Harrah .25 .60
75 Mitchell Page .10 .25
76 Alan Ashby .10 .25
77 Jorge Orta .10 .25
78 Dave Winfield 4.00 10.00
79 Andy Messersmith .25 .60
Now with N.Y. Yankees as of 12-8-
80 Ken Singleton .25 .60
81 Will McEnaney .25 .60
82 Lou Piniella .25 .60
83 Bob Forsch .10 .25
84 Dan Driessen .10 .25
85 Dave Lemanczyk .10 .25
86 Paul Dade .10 .25
87 Bill Campbell .10 .25
88 Ron LeFlore .25 .60
89 Bill Madlock .25 .60
90 Tony Perez DP .50 1.25
91 Freddie Patek .25 .60
92 Glenn Abbott .10 .25
93 Garry Maddox .25 .60
94 Steve Staggs .10 .25
95 Bobby Murcer .25 .60
96 Don Sutton 1.00 2.50
97 Al Oliver 1.00 2.50
Now with Texas Rangers as of 12-8-77
98 Jon Matlack .25 .60
Now with Texas Rangers as of 12-8-77
99 Sam Mejias .25 .60
100 Pete Rose DP 5.00 12.00
101 Randy Jones .10 .25
102 Sixto Lezcano .10 .25
103 Jim Clancy DP .12 .30
104 Butch Wynegar .10 .25
105 Nolan Ryan 12.50 40.00
106 Wayne Gross .10 .25
107 Bob Watson .25 .60
108 Joe Kerrigan .25 .60
Now with Baltimore as of 12-8-77
109 Keith Hernandez .25 .60
110 Reggie Jackson 3.00 8.00
111 Denny Doyle .10 .25
112 Sam Ewing .25 .60
113 Bert Blyleven 1.00 2.50
Now with Pittsburgh as of 12-8-77
114 Andre Thornton .25 .60
115 Milt May .10 .25
116 Jim Colborn .10 .25
117 Warren Cromartie RC .50 1.25
118 Ted Sizemore .10 .25
119 Checklist 1-121 .50 1.25
120 Tom Seaver 2.50 6.00
121 Luis Gomez .25 .60
122 Jim Spencer .25 .60
Now with N.Y. Yankees as of 12-12-77
123 Leroy Stanton .10 .25
124 Luis Tiant .25 .60
125 Mark Belanger .25 .60
126 Jackie Brown .10 .25
127 Bill Buckner .25 .60
128 Bill Robinson .25 .60
129 Rick Cerone .25 .60
130 Ron Cey .50 1.25
131 Jose Cruz .25 .60
132 Len Randle DP .08 .20
133 Bob Grich .25 .60
134 Jeff Burroughs .25 .60
135 Gary Carter 1.00 2.50
136 Milt Wilcox .10 .25
137 Carl Yastrzemski 2.50 6.00
138 Dennis Eckersley 1.25 3.00
139 Tim Nordbrook .10 .25
140 Ken Griffey Sr. .50 1.25
141 Bob Boone .50 1.25
142 Dave Goltz DP .08 .20
143 Al Cowens .10 .25
144 Bill Atkinson .10 .25
145 Chris Chambliss .25 .60
146 Jim Slaton .25 .60
Now with Detroit Tigers as of 12-9-77
147 Bill Stein .10 .25
148 Bob Bailor .25 .60
149 J.R. Richard .25 .60
150 Ted Simmons .25 .60
151 Rick Manning .10 .25
152 Lerrin LaGrow .10 .25
153 Larry Parrish .50 1.25
154 Eddie Murray RC! 30.00 60.00
155 Phil Niekro 1.00 2.50
156 Bake McBride .25 .60
157 Pete Vuckovich .25 .60
158 Ivan DeJesus .10 .25
159 Rick Rhoden .25 .60
160 Joe Morgan 1.25 3.00
161 Ed Ott .10 .25
162 Don Stanhouse .25 .60
163 Jim Rice .50 1.25
164 Bucky Dent .25 .60
165 Jim Kern .10 .25
166 Doug Rader .10 .25
167 Steve Kemp .10 .25
168 John Mayberry .25 .60
169 Tim Foli .25 .60
Now with N.Y. Mets as of 12-7-77
170 Steve Carlton 1.50 4.00
171 Pepe Frias .25 .60
172 Pat Zachry .10 .25
173 Don Baylor .50 1.25
174 Sal Bando DP .12 .30
175 Alvis Woods .25 .60
176 Mike Hargrove .25 .60
177 Vida Blue .25 .60
178 George Hendrick .25 .60
179 Jim Palmer 1.25 3.00
180 Andre Dawson 5.00 12.00
181 Paul Moskau .10 .25
182 Mickey Rivers .25 .60
183 Checklist 122-242 .50 1.25
184 Jerry Johnson .25 .60
185 Willie McCovey 1.25 3.00

186 Enrique Romo .10 .25
187 Butch Hobson .10 .25
188 Rusty Staub .50 1.25
189 Wayne Twitchell .25 .60
190 Steve Garvey 1.00 2.50
191 Rick Waits .10 .25
192 Doug DeCinces .25 .60
193 Tom Murphy .10 .25
194 Rich Hebner .25 .60
195 Ralph Garr .25 .60
196 Bruce Sutter .50 1.25
197 Tom Poquette .10 .25
198 Wayne Garrett .10 .25
199 Pedro Borbon .10 .25
200 Thurman Munson 1.50 4.00
201 Rollie Fingers 1.00 2.50
202 Doug Ault .25 .60
203 Phil Garner DP .08 .20
204 Lou Brock 1.25 3.00
205 Ed Kranepool .25 .60
206 Bobby Bonds .50 1.25
Now with White Sox as of 12-15-77
207 Expos Team DP .50 1.25
208 Bump Wills .10 .25
209 Gary Matthews .25 .60
210 Carlton Fisk 1.50 4.00
211 Jeff Byrd .25 .60
212 Jason Thompson .25 .60
213 Larvell Blanks .10 .25
214 Sparky Lyle .25 .60
215 George Brett 8.00 20.00
216 Del Unser .10 .25
217 Manny Trillo .10 .25
218 Roy Hartsfield MG .25 .60
219 Carlos Lopez .25 .60
Now with Baltimore as of 12-7-77
220 Dave Concepcion .50 1.25
221 John Candelaria .25 .60
222 Dave Lopes .25 .60
223 Tim Blackwell DP .12 .30
Now with Chicago Cubs as of 2-1-7
224 Chet Lemon .25 .60
225 Mike Schmidt 5.00 12.00
226 Cesar Cedeno .25 .60
227 Mike Willis .25 .60
228 Willie Randolph .50 1.25
229 Doug Bair .10 .25
230 Rod Carew 1.50 4.00
231 Mike Flanagan .25 .60
232 Chris Speier .10 .25
233 Don Aase .25 .60
Now with California as of 12-8-77
234 Buddy Bell .25 .60
235 Mark Fidrych 1.00 2.50
236 Lou Brock RB 1.25 3.00
Most Steals& Lifetime
237 Sparky Lyle RB .25 .60
Most Games Pure
Relief& Lifetime
238 Willie McCovey RB 1.00 2.50
Most Times 2 HR's
in Inning& L
239 Brooks Robinson RB 1.00 2.50
Most Consecutive
Seasons with
240 Pete Rose RB 3.00 8.00
Most Hits& Switch-
hitter& Lifetime
241 Nolan Ryan RB 6.00 15.00
Most games 10 or More
Strikeouts&
242 Reggie Jackson RB 1.50 4.00
Most Homers& One
World Series

1979 O-Pee-Chee

This set is an abridgement of the 1979 Topps set. The 374 standard-size cards comprising the 1979 O-Pee-Chee set differ from the cards of the 1979 Topps set by having a higher ratio of cards of players from the two Canadian teams, a practice begun by O-Pee-Chee in 1977 and continued to 1988. The 1979 O-Pee-Chee set was the largest (374) original baseball card set issued (up to that time) by O-Pee-Chee. The fronts feature white-bordered color player photos. The player's name, position, and team appear in colored lettering within the lower white margin. The green and white horizontal backs carry the player's name, team and position at the top. Biography, major league statistics, career highlights in both French and English and a bilingual trivia question and answer also appear. The asterisked cards have an extra line on the front indicating team change. Double-printed (DP) cards are also noted below. The fronts have an O-Pee-Chee logo in the lower left corner comparable to the Topps logo on the 1979 American Set. The cards are sequenced in the same order as the Topps cards; the O-Pee-Chee cards are in effect a compressed version of the Topps set. The key card in this set is the Ozzie Smith Rookie Card. This set was issued in 15 cent wax packs which came 24 boxes to a case.

COMPLETE SET (374) 100.00 200.00
COMMON PLAYER (1-374) .10 .25
COMMON PLAYER DP (1-374) .08 .20
1 Lee May .40 1.00
2 Dick Drago .10 .25
3 Paul Dade .10 .25
4 Ross Grimsley .10 .25
5 Joe Morgan DP 1.00 2.50
6 Kevin Kobel .10 .25
7 Terry Forster .10 .25
8 Paul Molitor 6.00 15.00
9 Steve Carlton 1.50 4.00
10 Dave Goltz .10 .25
11 Dave Winfield 2.50 6.00
12 Dave Rozema .10 .25
13 Ed Figueroa .10 .25
14 Alan Ashby .20 .50
Trade with Blue Jays 11-28-78
15 Dale Murphy 1.50 4.00
16 Dennis Eckersley .75 2.00
17 Ron Blomberg .10 .25
18 Wayne Twitchell .20 .50
Free Agent as of 3-1-79
19 Al Hrabosky .10 .25
20 Fred Norman .10 .25
21 Steve Garvey DP .40 1.00
22 Willie Stargell .75 2.00
23 John Hale .10 .25
24 Mickey Rivers .20 .50
25 Jack Brohamer .10 .25
26 Tom Underwood .10 .25
27 Mark Belanger .20 .50
28 Elliott Maddox .10 .25
29 John Candelaria .20 .50
30 Shane Rawley .10 .25
31 Steve Yeager .20 .50
32 Warren Cromartie .40 1.00
33 Jason Thompson .20 .50
34 Roger Erickson .10 .25
35 Gary Matthews .20 .50
36 Pete Falcone .20 .50
Traded 12-5-78
37 Dick Tidrow .10 .25
38 Bob Boone .40 1.00
39 Jim Bibby .10 .25
40 Len Barker .20 .50
Trade with Rangers 10-3-78
41 Robin Yount 2.50 6.00
42 Sam Mejias .20 .50
Traded 12-14-78
43 Ray Burris .10 .25
44 Tom Seaver DP 2.00 5.00
45 Roy Howell .10 .25
46 Jim Todd .20 .50
Free Agent 3-1-79
47 Frank Duffy .10 .25
48 Joel Youngblood .10 .25
49 Vida Blue .20 .50
50 Cliff Johnson .10 .25
51 Nolan Ryan 12.50 30.00
52 Ozzie Smith RC 40.00 80.00
53 Jim Sundberg .20 .50
54 Mike Paxton .10 .25
55 Lou Whitaker 2.50 6.00
56 Dan Schatzeder .10 .25
57 Rick Burleson .10 .25
58 Doug Bair .10 .25
59 Ted Martinez .10 .25
60 Bob Watson .20 .50
61 Jim Clancy .20 .50
62 Rowland Office .10 .25
63 Bobby Murcer .20 .50
64 Don Gullett .20 .50
65 Tom Paciorek .10 .25
66 Rick Rhoden .10 .25
67 Duane Kuiper .10 .25
68 Bruce Boisclair .10 .25
69 Manny Sarmiento .10 .25
70 Wayne Cage .10 .25
71 John Hiller .20 .50
72 Rick Cerone .10 .25
73 Dwight Evans .40 1.00
74 Buddy Solomon .10 .25
75 Roy White .20 .50
76 Mike Flanagan .40 1.00
77 Tom Johnson .10 .25
78 Glenn Burke .10 .25
79 Frank Taveras .10 .25
80 Don Sutton .75 2.00
81 Leon Roberts .10 .25
82 George Hendrick .40 1.00
83 Aurelio Rodriguez .10 .25
84 Ron Reed .10 .25
85 Alvis Woods .10 .25
86 Jim Beattie DP .08 .20
87 Larry Hisle .10 .25
88 Mike Garman .10 .25
89 Tim Johnson .10 .25
90 Paul Splittorff .10 .25
91 Darrel Chaney .10 .25
92 Mike Torrez .20 .50
93 Eric Soderholm .10 .25
94 Ron Cey .20 .50
95 Randy Jones .10 .25
96 Bill Madlock .20 .50
97 Steve Kemp DP .08 .20
98 Bob Apodaca .10 .25
99 Johnny Grubb .10 .25
100 Larry Milbourne .10 .25
101 Johnny Bench DP 2.50 6.00
102 Dave Lemanczyk .10 .25
103 Reggie Cleveland .10 .25
104 Larry Bowa .20 .50
105 Denny Martinez .60 1.50
106 Bill Travers .10 .25
107 Willie McCovey 1.00 2.50
108 Wilbur Wood .10 .25
109 Dennis Leonard .20 .50
110 Roy Smalley .20 .50
111 Cesar Geronimo .10 .25
112 Jesse Jefferson .20 .50
113 Dave Revering .10 .25
114 Goose Gossage .40 1.00
115 Steve Stone .20 .50
Free Agent 11-25-78
116 Doug Flynn .10 .25
117 Bob Forsch .10 .25
118 Paul Mitchell .10 .25
119 Toby Harrah .20 .50
Traded 12-8-78
120 Steve Rogers .20 .50
121 Checklist 1-125 DP .08 .20
122 Balor Moore .10 .25
123 Rick Reuschel .20 .50
124 Jeff Burroughs .20 .50
125 Willie Randolph .20 .50
126 Bob Stinson .10 .25
127 Rick Wise .10 .25
128 Luis Gomez .20 .50
129 Tommy John .60 1.50
Signed as Free Agent 11-22-78
130 Richie Zisk .10 .25
131 Mario Guerrero .10 .25
132 Oscar Gamble .20 .50
Trade with Padres 10-25-78
133 Don Money .10 .25
134 Joe Rudi .20 .50
135 Woodie Fryman .10 .25
136 Butch Hobson .10 .25
137 Jim Colborn .10 .25
138 Tom Grieve .10 .25
Traded 12-5-78
139 Andy Messersmith .20 .50
Free Agent 2-7-79
140 Andre Thornton .20 .50
141 Ken Kravec .10 .25
142 Bobby Bonds .60 1.50
Trade with Rangers 10-3-78
143 Jose Cruz .40 1.00
144 Dave Lopes .20 .50
145 Jerry Garvin .10 .25
146 Pepe Frias .10 .25
147 Mitchell Page .10 .25
148 Ted Sizemore .20 .50
Traded 2-23-79
149 Rich Gale .10 .25
150 Steve Ontiveros .10 .25
151 Rod Carew 1.50 4.00
Traded 2-5-79
152 Lary Sorensen DP .08 .20
153 Willie Montanez .10 .25
154 Floyd Bannister .20 .50
Traded 12-8-78
155 Bert Blyleven .40 1.00
156 Ralph Garr .20 .50
157 Thurman Munson 1.50 4.00
158 Bob Robertson .20 .50
Free Agent 3-1-79
159 Jon Matlack .10 .25
160 Carl Yastrzemski 2.50 6.00
161 Gaylord Perry .75 2.00
162 Mike Tyson .10 .25
163 Cecil Cooper .20 .50
164 Pedro Borbon .10 .25
165 Art Howe DP .08 .20
166 Joe Coleman .20 .50
Free Agent 3-1-79
167 George Brett 8.00 20.00
168 Gary Alexander .10 .25
169 Chet Lemon .20 .50
170 Craig Swan .10 .25
171 Chris Chambliss .20 .50
172 John Montague .10 .25
173 Ron Jackson .20 .50
Traded 12-4-78
174 Jim Palmer 1.25 3.00
175 Willie Upshaw .40 1.00
176 Tug McGraw .20 .50
177 Bill Buckner .20 .50
178 Doug Rau .10 .25
179 Andre Dawson 2.50 6.00
180 Jim Wright .10 .25
181 Garry Templeton .20 .50
182 Bill Bonham .10 .25
183 Lee Mazzilli .10 .25
184 Alan Trammell 3.00 8.00
185 Amos Otis .20 .50
186 Tom Dixon .10 .25
187 Mike Cubbage .10 .25
188 Sparky Lyle .40 1.00
Traded 11-10-78
189 Juan Bernhardt .10 .25
190 Bump Wills(Texas Rangers) .40 1.00
191 Dave Kingman .40 1.00
192 Lamar Johnson .10 .25
193 Lance Rautzhan .10 .25
194 Ed Herrmann .10 .25
195 Bill Campbell .10 .25
196 Gorman Thomas .20 .50
197 Paul Moskau .10 .25
198 Dale Murray .10 .25
199 John Mayberry .20 .50
200 Phil Garner .10 .25
201 Dan Ford .20 .50
Traded 12-4-78
202 Gary Thomasson .20 .50
Traded 2-15-79
203 Rollie Fingers .75 2.00
204 Al Oliver .20 .50
205 Doug Ault .20 .50
206 Scott McGregor .20 .50
207 Dave Cash .10 .25
208 Bill Plummer .10 .25
209 Ivan DeJesus .10 .25
210 Jim Rice .40 1.00
211 Ray Knight .20 .50
212 Paul Hartzell .20 .50
Traded 2-5-79
213 Tim Foli .10 .25
214 Butch Wynegar DP .08 .20
215 Darrell Evans .40 1.00
216 Ken Griffey Sr. .20 .50
217 Doug DeCinces .20 .50
218 Ruppert Jones .10 .25
219 Bob Montgomery .10 .25
220 Rick Manning .10 .25
221 Chris Speier .10 .25
222 Bobby Valentine .20 .50
223 Dave Parker .20 .50
224 Larry Biittner .10 .25
225 Ken Clay .10 .25
226 Gene Tenace .10 .25
227 Frank White .20 .50
228 Rusty Staub .40 1.00
229 Lee Lacy .10 .25
230 Doyle Alexander .10 .25
231 Bruce Bochte .10 .25
232 Steve Henderson .10 .25
233 Jim Lonborg .20 .50
234 Dave Concepcion .40 1.00
235 Jerry Morales .20 .50
Traded 12-4-78
236 Len Randle .10 .25
237 Bill Lee DP .12 .30
Traded 12-7-78
238 Bruce Sutter .75 2.00
239 Jim Essian .10 .25
240 Graig Nettles .40 1.00
241 Otto Velez .10 .25
242 Checklist 126-250 DP .08 .20
243 Reggie Smith .20 .50
244 Stan Bahnsen DP .08 .20
245 Garry Maddox DP .08 .20
246 Joaquin Andujar .20 .50
247 Dan Driessen .10 .25
248 Bob Grich .20 .50
249 Fred Lynn .20 .50
250 Skip Lockwood .10 .25
251 Craig Reynolds .20 .50
Traded 12-5-78
252 Willie Horton .20 .50
253 Rick Waits .10 .25
254 Bucky Dent .10 .25
255 Bob Knepper .10 .25
256 Miguel Dilone .10 .25
257 Bob Owchinko .10 .25
258 Al Cowens .10 .25
259 Bob Bailor .10 .25
260 Larry Christenson .10 .25
261 Tony Perez .75 2.00
262 Blue Jays Team .60 1.50
Roy Hartsfield MG/(Team checklist
263 Glenn Abbott .10 .25
264 Ron Guidry .20 .50
265 Ed Kranepool .10 .25
266 Charlie Hough .20 .50
267 Ted Simmons .40 1.00
268 Jack Clark .20 .50
269 Enos Cabell .10 .25
270 Gary Carter .75 2.00
271 Sam Ewing .10 .25
272 Tom Burgmeier .10 .25
273 Freddie Patek .10 .25
274 Frank Tanana .20 .50
275 Leroy Stanton .10 .25
276 Ken Forsch .10 .25
277 Ellis Valentine .10 .25
278 Greg Luzinski .20 .50
279 Rick Bosetti .10 .25
280 John Stearns .10 .25
281 Enrique Romo .20 .50
Traded 12-5-78
282 Bob Bailey .10 .25
283 Sal Bando .20 .50
284 Matt Keough .20 .50
285 Biff Pocoroba .10 .25
286 Mike Lum .20 .50
Free Agent 3-1-79
287 Jay Johnstone .20 .50
288 John Montefusco .10 .25
289 Ed Ott .10 .25
290 Dusty Baker .40 1.00
291 Rico Carty .40 1.00
Waivers from A's 10-2-78
292 Nino Espinosa .10 .25
293 Rich Hebner .20 .50
294 Cesar Cedeno .20 .50
295 Darrell Porter .20 .50
296 Rod Gilbreath .10 .25
297 Jim Kern .20 .50
Trade with Indians 10-3-78
298 Claudell Washington .20 .50
299 Luis Tiant .40 1.00
Signed as Free Agent 11-14-78
300 Mike Parrott .10 .25
301 Pete Broberg .20 .50
Free Agent 3-1-79
302 Greg Gross .20 .50
Traded 2-23-79
303 Darold Knowles .20 .50
Free Agent 2-12-79
304 Paul Blair .20 .50
305 Julio Cruz .10 .25
306 Hal McRae .40 1.00
307 Ken Reitz .10 .25
308 Tom Murphy .10 .25
309 Terry Whitfield .10 .25
310 J.R. Richard .20 .50
311 Mike Hargrove .40 1.00
Trade with Rangers 10-25-78
312 Rick Dempsey .20 .50
313 Phil Niekro .75 2.00
314 Bob Stanley .10 .25
315 Jim Spencer .10 .25
316 George Foster .20 .50
317 Dave LaRoche .10 .25
318 Rudy May .10 .25
319 Jeff Newman .10 .25
320 Rick Monday DP .08 .20
321 Omar Moreno .10 .25
322 Dave McKay .20 .50
323 Mike Schmidt 4.00 10.00
324 Ken Singleton .20 .50
325 Jerry Remy .10 .25
326 Bert Campaneris .20 .50
327 Pat Zachry .10 .25
328 Larry Herndon .10 .25
329 Mark Fidrych .60 1.50
330 Del Unser .10 .25
331 Gene Garber .20 .50
332 Bake McBride .20 .50
333 Jorge Orta .10 .25
334 Don Kirkwood .10 .25
335 Don Baylor .40 1.00
336 Bill Robinson .20 .50
337 Manny Trillo .20 .50
Traded 2-23-79
338 Eddie Murray 10.00 25.00
339 Tom Hausman .10 .25
340 George Scott DP .08 .20
341 Rick Sweet .10 .25
342 Lou Piniella .20 .50
343 Pete Rose 6.00 15.00
Free Agent 12-5-79
344 Stan Papi .20 .50
Traded 12-7-78
345 Jerry Koosman .40 1.00
Traded 12-8-78
346 Hosken Powell .10 .25
347 George Medich .10 .25
348 Ron LeFlore DP .08 .20
349 Montreal Expos Team .60 1.50
Dick Williams MG/(Team check
350 Lou Brock 1.25 3.00
351 Bill North .10 .25
352 Jim Hunter DP .60 1.50
353 Checklist 251-374 DP .12 .30
354 Ed Halicki .10 .25
355 Tom Hutton .10 .25
356 Mike Caldwell .20 .50
357 Larry Parrish .40 1.00
358 Geoff Zahn .10 .25
359 Derrel Thomas .20 .50
Signed as Free Agent 11-14-78
360 Carlton Fisk 1.25 3.00
361 John Henry Johnson .10 .25
362 Dave Chalk .10 .25
363 Dan Meyer DP .08 .20
364 Sixto Lezcano .10 .25
365 Rennie Stennett .10 .25
366 Mike Willis .20 .50
367 Buddy Bell DP .08 .20
Traded 12-8-78
368 Mickey Stanley .10 .25
369 Dave Rader .20 .50
Traded 2-23-79
370 Burt Hooton .20 .50
371 Keith Hernandez .40 1.00
372 Bill Stein .10 .25
373 Hal Dues .10 .25
374 Reggie Jackson DP 2.50 6.00

1980 O-Pee-Chee

This set is an abridgement of the 1980 Topps set. The cards are printed on white stock rather than the gray stock used by Topps. The 374 standard-size cards also differ from their Topps counterparts by having a higher ratio of cards of players from the two Canadian teams, a practice begun by O-Pee-Chee in 1977 and continued to 1988. The fronts feature white-bordered color player photos framed by a colored line. The player's name appears in the white border at the top and also as a facsimile autograph across the photo. The player's position appears within a colored banner at the upper left; his team name appears within a colored banner at the lower right. The blue and white horizontal backs carry the player's name, team and position at the top. Biography, major league statistics and career highlights in both French and English also appear. The cards are numbered on the back. The asterisked cards have an extra line, "Now with (new team name)" on the front indicating team change. Color changes, to correspond to the new team, are apparent on the pennant name and frame on the front. Double-printed (DP) cards are also noted below. The cards in this set were produced in lower quantities than other O-Pee-Chee sets of this era reportedly due to the company being on strike. The cards are sequenced in the same order as the Topps cards.

COMPLETE SET (374) 75.00 150.00
COMMON PLAYER (1-374) .08 .25
COMMON CARD DP (1-374) .02 .10
1 Craig Swan .08 .25
2 Dennis Martinez .40 1.00
3 Dave Cash (Now With Padres) .15 .40
4 Bruce Sutter .60 1.50
5 Ron Jackson .08 .25
6 Balor Moore .15 .40
7 Dan Ford .08 .25
8 Pat Putnam .08 .25
9 Derrel Thomas .08 .25
10 Jim Slaton .08 .25
11 Lee Mazzilli .15 .40
12 Del Unser .08 .25
13 Mark Wagner .08 .25
14 Vida Blue .30 .75
15 Jay Johnstone .15 .40
16 Julio Cruz DP .02 .10
17 Tony Scott .08 .25
18 Jeff Newman DP .02 .10
19 Luis Tiant .15 .40
20 Carlton Fisk 1.25 3.00
21 Dave Palmer .08 .25
22 Bombo Rivera .08 .25
23 Bill Fahey .08 .25
24 Frank White .30 .75
25 Rico Carty .15 .40
26 Bill Bonham DP .02 .10
27 Rick Miller .08 .25
28 J.R. Richard .15 .40
29 Joe Ferguson DP .02 .10
30 Bill Madlock .15 .40
31 Pete Vuckovich .08 .25
32 Doug Flynn .08 .25
33 Bucky Dent .15 .40
34 Mike Ivie .08 .25
35 Bob Stanley .08 .25
36 Al Bumbry .15 .40
37 Gary Carter .75 2.00
38 John Milner DP .02 .10
39 Sid Monge .08 .25
40 Bill Russell .15 .40
41 John Stearns .08 .25
42 Dave Stieb .40 1.00
43 .15 .40
44 Bob Owchinko .08 .25
45 Ron LeFlore .30 .75
Now with Expos
46 Ted Sizemore .08 .25
47 Ted Simmons .15 .40
48 Pepe Frias .15 .40
Now with Rangers
49 Ken Landreaux .08 .25
50 Manny Trillo .15 .40
51 Rick Dempsey .15 .40
52 Cecil Cooper .15 .40
53 Bill Lee .15 .40
54 Victor Cruz .08 .25
55 Johnny Bench 2.00 5.00
56 Rich Dauer .08 .25
57 Frank Tanana .15 .40
58 Francisco Barrios .08 .25
59 Bob Horner .15 .40
60 Fred Lynn DP .07 .20
61 Bob Knepper .15 .40
62 Sparky Lyle .15 .40
63 Larry Cox .08 .25
64 Dock Ellis .15 .40
Now with Pirates
65 Phil Garner .15 .40
66 Greg Luzinski .15 .40
67 Checklist 1-125 .30 .75
68 Dave Lemanczyk .08 .25
69 Tony Perez .60 1.50
Now with Red Sox
70 Gary Thomasson .08 .25
71 Craig Reynolds .08 .25
72 Amos Otis .15 .40
73 Biff Pocoroba .08 .25
74 Matt Keough .08 .25
75 Bill Buckner .15 .40
76 John Castino .08 .25
77 Rich Gossage .40 1.00
78 Gary Alexander .08 .25
79 Phil Huffman .08 .25
80 Bruce Bochte .08 .25
81 Darrell Evans .15 .40
82 Terry Puhl .15 .40
83 Jason Thompson .08 .25
84 Lary Sorensen .20 .50
85 Jerry Remy .08 .25
86 Tony Brizzolara .08 .25
87 Willie Wilson DP .07 .20
88 Eddie Murray 6.00 12.00
89 Larry Christenson .08 .25
90 Bob Randall .08 .25
91 Greg Pryor .08 .25
92 Glenn Abbott .08 .25
93 Jack Clark .15 .40
94 Rick Waits .08 .25
95 Luis Gomez .15 .40
Now with Braves
96 Burt Hooton .15 .40
97 John Henry Johnson .08 .25
98 Ray Knight .15 .40
99 Rick Reuschel .15 .40
100 Champ Summers .08 .25
101 Ron Davis .08 .25
102 Warren Cromartie .15 .40
103 Ken Reitz .08 .25
104 Hal McRae .15 .40
105 Alan Ashby .08 .25
106 Kevin Kobel .08 .25
107 Buddy Bell .15 .40
108 Dave Goltz .15 .40
Now with Dodgers
109 John Montefusco .08 .25
110 Lance Parrish .15 .40
111 Mike LaCoss .08 .25
112 Jim Rice .15 .40
113 Steve Carlton 1.25 3.00
114 Sixto Lezcano .08 .25
115 Ed Halicki .08 .25
116 Jose Morales .08 .25
117 Dave Concepcion .30 .75
118 Joe Cannon .08 .25
119 Willie Montanez .15 .40
Now with Padres
120 Lou Piniella .30 .75
121 Bill Stein .08 .25
122 Dave Winfield 2.00 5.00
123 Alan Trammell .75 2.00
124 Andre Dawson 1.25 3.00
125 Marc Hill .08 .25
126 Don Aase .08 .25
127 Dave Kingman .30 .75
128 Checklist 126-250 .30 .75
129 Dennis Lamp .08 .25
130 Phil Niekro .75 2.00
131 Tim Foli DP .02 .10
132 Jim Clancy .15 .40
133 Bill Atkinson .15 .40
Now with White Sox
134 Paul Dade DP .02 .10
135 Dusty Baker .15 .40
136 Al Oliver .30 .75
137 Dave Chalk .08 .25
138 Bill Robinson .08 .25
139 Robin Yount 2.50 6.00
140 Dan Schatzeder .15 .40
Now with Tigers
141 Mike Schmidt DP 2.00 5.00
142 Ralph Garr .15 .40
Now with Angels
143 Dale Murphy .75 2.00
144 Jerry Koosman .15 .40
145 Tom Veryzer .08 .25
146 Rick Bosetti .08 .25
147 Jim Spencer .08 .25
148 Gaylord Perry .75 2.00
Now with Rangers
149 Paul Blair .15 .40
150 Don Baylor .30 .75
151 Dave Rozema .08 .25
152 Steve Garvey .40 1.00
153 Elias Sosa .08 .25
154 Larry Gura .08 .25
155 Tim Johnson .08 .25
156 Steve Henderson .08 .25
157 Ron Guidry .15 .40
158 Mike Edwards .08 .25
159 Butch Wynegar .08 .25
160 Randy Jones .08 .25
161 Denny Walling .08 .25
162 Mike Hargrove .15 .40
163 Dave Parker .40 1.00
164 Roger Metzger .08 .25
165 Johnny Grubb .08 .25
166 Steve Kemp .08 .25
167 Bob Lacey .08 .25
168 Chris Speier .08 .25
169 Dennis Eckersley .60 1.50
170 Keith Hernandez .15 .40
171 Claudell Washington .15 .40
172 Tom Underwood .15 .40
Now with Yankees
173 Dan Driessen .08 .25
174 Al Cowens .15 .40
Now with Angels
175 Rich Hebner .15 .40
Now with Tigers
176 Willie McCovey .75 2.00
177 Carney Lansford .15 .40
178 Ken Singleton .15 .40
179 Jim Essian .08 .25
180 Mike Vail .08 .25
181 Randy Lerch .08 .25
182 Larry Parrish .30 .75
183 Checklist 251-374 .30 .75
184 George Hendrick .15 .40
185 Bob Davis .08 .25
186 Gary Matthews .08 .25
187 Lou Whitaker .75 2.00
188 Darrell Porter DP .07 .20
189 Wayne Gross .08 .25
190 Bobby Murcer .15 .40
191 Willie Aikens .15 .40
Now with Royals
192 Jim Kern .08 .25
193 Cesar Cedeno .08 .25
194 Joel Youngblood .08 .25
195 Ross Grimsley .15 .40
196 Jerry Mumphrey .15 .40
Now with Padres
197 Kevin Bell .08 .25
198 Garry Maddox .15 .40
199 Dave Freisleben .08 .25
200 Ed Ott .08 .25
201 Enos Cabell .08 .25
202 Pete LaCock .08 .25
203 Fergie Jenkins .75 2.00
204 Milt Wilcox .08 .25
205 Ozzie Smith 7.50 15.00
206 Ellis Valentine .15 .40
207 Dan Meyer .08 .25
208 Barry Foote .08 .25
209 George Foster .15 .40
210 Dwight Evans .15 .40
211 Paul Molitor 5.00 10.00
212 Tony Solaita .08 .25
213 Bill North .08 .25
214 Paul Splittorff .08 .25
215 Bobby Bonds .40 1.00
Now with Cardinals
216 Butch Hobson .08 .25
217 Mark Belanger .15 .40
218 Grant Jackson .08 .25
219 Tom Hutton DP .02 .10
220 Pat Zachry .08 .25
221 Duane Kuiper .08 .25
222 Larry Hisle DP .02 .10
223 Mike Krukow .08 .25
224 Johnnie LeMaster .08 .25
225 Billy Almon .15 .40
Now with Expos
226 Joe Niekro .15 .40
227 Dave Revering .08 .25
228 Don Sutton .60 1.50
229 John Hiller .15 .40
230 Alvis Woods .08 .25
231 Mark Fidrych .40 1.00
232 Duffy Dyer .08 .25
233 Nino Espinosa .08 .25
234 Doug Bair .08 .25
235 George Brett 7.50 16.00
236 Mike Torrez .08 .25
237 Frank Taveras .08 .25
238 Bert Blyleven .40 1.00
239 Willie Randolph .15 .40
240 Mike Sadek DP .02 .10
241 Jerry Royster .08 .25
242 John Denny .15 .40
Now with Indians
243 Rick Monday .08 .25
244 Jesse Jefferson .15 .40
245 Aurelio Rodriguez .15 .40
Now with Padres
246 Bob Boone .30 .75
247 Cesar Geronimo .08 .25
248 Bob Shirley .08 .25
249 Expos Checklist .40 1.00
250 Bob Watson .30 .75
Now with Yankees
251 Mickey Rivers .15 .40
252 Mike Tyson DP .07 .20
Now with Cubs
253 Wayne Nordhagen .08 .25
254 Roy Howell .08 .25
255 Lee May .15 .40
256 Jerry Martin .08 .25
257 Bake McBride .08 .25
258 Silvio Martinez .08 .25
259 Jim Mason .08 .25
260 Tom Seaver 2.00 5.00
261 Rick Wortham DP .02 .10
262 Mike Cubbage .08 .25
263 Gene Garber .15 .40
264 Bert Campaneris .15 .40
265 Tom Buskey .08 .25
266 Leon Roberts .08 .25
267 Ron Cey .30 .75
268 Steve Ontiveros .08 .25
269 Mike Caldwell .08 .25
270 Nelson Norman .08 .25
271 Steve Rogers .15 .40
272 Jim Morrison .08 .25
273 Clint Hurdle .15 .40
274 Dale Murray .08 .25
275 Jim Barr .08 .25
276 Jim Sundberg DP .07 .20
277 Willie Horton .15 .40
278 Andre Thornton .15 .40
279 Bob Forsch .08 .25
280 Joe Strain .08 .25
281 Rudy May .15 .40
Now with Yankees
282 Pete Rose 6.00 12.00
283 Jeff Burroughs .15 .40
284 Rick Langford .08 .25
285 Ken Griffey Sr. .30 .75
286 Bill Nahorodny .15 .40
Now with Braves
287 Art Howe .15 .40
288 Ed Figueroa .08 .25
289 Joe Rudi .15 .40
290 Alfredo Griffin .15 .40
291 Dave Lopes .15 .40
292 Rick Manning .08 .25
293 Dennis Leonard .15 .40
294 Bud Harrelson .15 .40
295 Skip Lockwood .15 .40
Now with Red Sox
296 Roy Smalley .08 .25
297 Kent Tekulve .15 .40
298 Scot Thompson .08 .25
299 Ken Kravec .08 .25
300 Blue Jays Checklist .40 1.00
301 Scott Sanderson .15 .40
302 Charlie Moore .15 .40
303 Nolan Ryan 12.50 25.00
Now with Astros
304 Bob Bailor .15 .40
305 Bob Stinson .08 .25
306 Al Hrabosky .15 .40
Now with Braves
307 Mitchell Page .08 .25
308 Garry Templeton .08 .25
309 Chet Lemon .15 .40
310 Jim Palmer .75 2.00
311 Rick Cerone .15 .40
Now with Yankees
312 Jon Matlack .08 .25
313 Don Money .08 .25
314 Reggie Jackson 2.50 6.00
315 Brian Downing .08 .25
316 Woodie Fryman .08 .25
317 Alan Bannister .08 .25
318 Ron Reed .08 .25
319 Willie Stargell .75 2.00
320 Jerry Garvin DP .02 .10
321 Cliff Johnson .08 .25
322 Doug DeCinces .15 .40

323 Gene Richards .08 .25
324 Joaquin Andujar .15 .40
325 Richie Zisk .08 .25
326 Bob Grich .15 .40
327 Gorman Thomas .15 .40
328 Chris Chambliss .30 .75
Now with Braves
329 Blue Jays Prospects .30 .75
Butch Edge
Pat Kelly
Ted Wi
330 Larry Bowa .15 .40
331 Barry Bonnell .15 .40
Now with Blue Jays
332 John Candelaria .15 .40
333 Toby Harrah .15 .40
334 Larry Biittner .08 .25
335 Mike Flanagan .15 .40
336 Ed Kranepool .08 .25
337 Ken Forsch DP .02 .10
338 John Mayberry .15 .40
339 Rick Burleson .08 .25
340 Milt May .15 .40
Now with Giants
341 Roy White .15 .40
342 Joe Morgan .75 2.00
343 Rollie Fingers .75 2.00
344 Mario Mendoza .08 .25
345 Stan Bahnsen .08 .25
346 Tug McGraw .15 .40
347 Rusty Staub .15 .40
348 Tommy John .30 .75
349 Ivan DeJesus .08 .25
350 Reggie Smith .15 .40
351 Expos Prospects .40 1.00
Tony Bernazard
Randy Miller
Joh
352 Floyd Bannister .08 .25
353 Rod Carew DP .60 1.50
354 Otto Velez .08 .25
355 Gene Tenace .15 .40
356 Freddie Patek .15 .40
Now with Angels
357 Elliott Maddox .08 .25
358 Pat Underwood .08 .25
359 Graig Nettles .30 .75
360 Rodney Scott .08 .25
361 Terry Whitfield .08 .25
362 Fred Norman .15 .40
Now with Expos
363 Sal Bando .15 .40
364 Greg Gross .08 .25
365 Carl Yastrzemski DP .75 2.00
366 Paul Hartzell .08 .25
367 Jose Cruz .15 .40
368 Shane Rawley .08 .25
369 Jerry White .08 .25
370 Rick Wise .15 .40
Now with Padres
371 Steve Yeager .30 .75
372 Omar Moreno .08 .25
373 Bump Wills .08 .25
374 Craig Kusick .15 .40
Now with Padres

1981 O-Pee-Chee

This set is an abridgement of the 1981 Topps set. The 374 standard-size cards comprising the 1981 O-Pee-Chee set differ from the cards of the 1981 Topps set by having a higher ratio of cards of players from the two Canadian teams, a practice begun by O-Pee-Chee in 1977 and continued to 1988. The fronts feature white-bordered color player photos framed by a colored line that is wider at the bottom. The player's name appears in that wider colored area. The player's position and team appear within a colored baseball cap icon at the lower left. The red and white horizontal backs carry the player's name and position at the top. Biography, major league statistics, and career highlights in both French and English also appear. In cases where a player changed teams or was traded before press time, a small line of print on the obverse makes note of the change. Double-printed (DP) cards are also noted below. The card backs are typically found printed on white card stock. There is, however, a "variation" set printed on gray card stock; gray backs are worth 50 percent more than corresponding white backs listed below. Notable Rookie Cards include Harold Baines, Kirk Gibson and Tim Raines.

COMPLETE SET (374) 25.00 60.00
COMMON PLAYER (1-374) .04 .10
COMMON PLAYER DP (1-374) .02 .05
1 Frank Pastore .02 .10
2 Phil Huffman .02 .10
3 Len Barker .02 .10
4 Robin Yount .75 2.00
5 Dave Stieb .08 .25
6 Gary Carter .40 1.00
7 Butch Hobson .02 .10
Now with Angels
8 Lance Parrish .08 .25
9 Bruce Sutter .40 1.00
Now with Cardinals
10 Mike Flanagan .08 .25
11 Paul Mirabella .02 .10
12 Craig Reynolds .02 .10
13 Joe Charboneau .20 .50
14 Dan Driessen .02 .10
15 Larry Parrish .02 .10
16 Ron Davis .02 .10
17 Cliff Johnson .02 .10
Now with Athletics
18 Bruce Bochte .02 .10
19 Jim Clancy .02 .10
20 Bill Russell .02 .10
21 Ron Oester .02 .10
22 Danny Darwin .02 .10
23 Willie Aikens .02 .10
24 Don Stanhouse .02 .10
25 Sixto Lezcano .02 .10
Now with Cardinals
26 U.L. Washington .02 .10
27 Champ Summers DP .01 .05
28 Enrique Romo .02 .10
29 Gene Tenace .08 .25
30 Jack Clark .08 .25
31 Checklist 1-125 DP .01 .05
32 Ken Oberkfell .02 .10
33 Rick Honeycutt .02 .10
Now with Rangers
34 Al Bumbry .02 .10
35 John Tamargo DP .01 .05
36 Ed Farmer .02 .10
37 Gary Roenicke .02 .10
38 Tim Foli DP .01 .05
39 Eddie Murray 2.50 6.00
40 Roy Howell .02 .10
Now with Brewers
41 Bill Gullickson .20 .50
42 Jerry White DP .01 .05
43 Tim Blackwell .02 .10
44 Steve Henderson .02 .10
45 Enos Cabell .02 .10
Now with Giants
46 Rick Bosetti .02 .10
47 Bill North .02 .10
48 Rich Gossage .20 .50
49 Bob Shirley .02 .10
Now with Cardinals
50 Dave Lopes .08 .25
51 Shane Rawley .02 .10
52 Lloyd Moseby .08 .25
53 Burt Hooton .02 .10
54 Ivan DeJesus .02 .10
55 Mike Norris .02 .10
56 Del Unser .02 .10
57 Dave Revering .02 .10
58 Joel Youngblood .02 .10
59 Steve McCatty .02 .10
60 Willie Randolph .08 .25
61 Butch Wynegar .02 .10
62 Gary Lavelle .02 .10
63 Willie Montanez .02 .10
64 Terry Puhl .02 .10
65 Scott McGregor .02 .10
66 Buddy Bell .08 .25
67 Toby Harrah .08 .25
68 Jim Rice .08 .25
69 Darrell Evans .08 .25
70 Al Oliver DP .07 .20
71 Hal Dues .02 .10
72 Barry Evans DP .01 .05
73 Doug Bair .02 .10
74 Mike Hargrove .08 .25
75 Reggie Smith .08 .25
76 Mario Mendoza .02 .10
Now with Rangers
77 Mike Barlow .02 .10
78 Garth Iorg .02 .10
79 Jeff Reardon RC .40 1.00
80 Roger Erickson .02 .10
81 Dave Stapleton .02 .10
82 Barry Bonnell .02 .10
83 Dave Concepcion .08 .25
84 Johnnie LeMaster .02 .10
85 Mike Caldwell .02 .10
86 Wayne Gross .02 .10
87 Rick Camp .02 .10
88 Joe Lefebvre .02 .10
89 Darrell Jackson .02 .10
90 Bake McBride .02 .10
91 Tim Stoddard DP .01 .05
92 Mike Easler .02 .10
93 Jim Bibby .02 .10
94 Kent Tekulve .08 .25
95 Jim Sundberg .08 .25
96 Tommy John .20 .50
97 Chris Speier .02 .10
98 Clint Hurdle .02 .10
99 Phil Garner .08 .25
100 Rod Carew .60 1.50
101 Steve Stone .02 .10
102 Joe Niekro .02 .10
103 Jerry Martin .02 .10
Now with Giants
104 Ron LeFlore DP .02 .10
Now with White Sox
105 Jose Cruz .08 .25
106 Don Money .02 .10
107 Bobby Brown .02 .10
108 Larry Herndon .02 .10
109 Dennis Eckersley .40 1.00
110 Carl Yastrzemski .60 1.50
111 Greg Minton .02 .10
112 Dan Schatzeder .02 .10
113 George Brett 3.00 8.00
114 Tom Underwood .02 .10
115 Roy Smalley .02 .10
116 Carlton Fisk .75 2.00
Now with White Sox
117 Pete Falcone .02 .10
118 Dale Murphy .60 1.50
119 Tippy Martinez .02 .10
120 Larry Bowa .08 .25
121 Julio Cruz .02 .10
122 Jim Gantner .08 .25
123 Al Cowens .02 .10
124 Jerry Garvin .02 .10
125 Andre Dawson .75 2.00
126 Charlie Leibrandt RC .20 .50
127 Willie Stargell .30 .75
128 Andre Thornton .08 .25
129 Art Howe .02 .10
130 Larry Gura .02 .10
131 Jerry Remy .02 .10
132 Rick Dempsey .08 .25
133 Alan Trammell DP .30 .75
134 Mike LaCoss .02 .10
135 Gorman Thomas .02 .10
136 Expos Future Stars 2.50 6.00
Tim Raines
Roberto Ramos
Bob
137 Bill Madlock .08 .25
138 Rich Dotson DP .02 .10
139 Oscar Gamble .02 .10
140 Bob Forsch .02 .10
141 Miguel Dilone .02 .10
142 Jackson Todd .02 .10
143 Dan Meyer .02 .10
144 Garry Templeton .02 .10
145 Mickey Rivers .08 .25
146 Alan Ashby .02 .10
147 Dale Berra .08 .25
148 Randy Jones .02 .10
Now with Mets
149 Joe Nolan .02 .10
150 Mark Fidrych .20 .50
151 Tony Armas .02 .10
152 Steve Kemp .02 .10
153 Jerry Reuss .08 .25
154 Rick Langford .02 .10
155 Chris Chambliss .08 .25
156 Bob McClure .02 .10
157 John Wathan .02 .10
158 John Curtis .02 .10
159 Steve Howe .08 .25
160 Garry Maddox .02 .10
161 Dan Graham .02 .10
162 Doug Corbett .02 .10
163 Rob Dressler .02 .10
164 Bucky Dent .08 .25
165 Alvis Woods .02 .10
166 Floyd Bannister .02 .10
167 Lee Mazzilli .02 .10
168 Don Robinson DP .01 .05
169 John Mayberry .02 .10
170 Woodie Fryman .02 .10
171 Gene Richards .02 .10
172 Rick Burleson .02 .10
Now with Angels
173 Bump Wills .02 .10
174 Glenn Abbott .02 .10
175 Dave Collins .02 .10
176 Mike Krukow .02 .10
177 Rick Monday .08 .25
178 Dave Parker .20 .50
179 Rudy May .02 .10
180 Pete Rose 1.25 3.00
181 Elias Sosa .02 .10
182 Bob Grich .08 .25
183 Fred Norman .02 .10
184 Jim Dwyer .02 .10
Now with Orioles
185 Dennis Leonard .02 .10
186 Gary Matthews .02 .10
187 Ron Hassey DP .01 .05
188 Doug DeCinces .08 .25
189 Craig Swan .02 .10
190 Cesar Cedeno .08 .25
191 Rick Sutcliffe .08 .25
192 Kiko Garcia .02 .10
193 Pete Vuckovich .02 .10
Now with Brewers
194 Tony Bernazard .02 .10
Now with White Sox
195 Keith Hernandez .08 .25
196 Jerry Mumphrey .02 .10
197 Jim Kern .02 .10
198 Jerry Dybzinski .02 .10
199 John Lowenstein .02 .10
200 George Foster .08 .25
201 Phil Niekro .30 .75
202 Bill Buckner .08 .25
203 Steve Carlton .60 1.50
204 John D'Acquisto .02 .10
Now with Angels
205 Rick Reuschel .08 .25
206 Dan Quisenberry .08 .25
207 Mike Schmidt DP .75 2.00
208 Bob Watson .08 .25
209 Jim Spencer .02 .10
210 Jim Palmer .30 .75
211 Derrel Thomas .02 .10
212 Steve Nicosia .02 .10
213 Omar Moreno .02 .10
214 Richie Zisk .02 .10
Now with Mariners
215 Larry Hisle .02 .10
216 Mike Torrez .02 .10
217 Rich Hebner .02 .10
218 Britt Burns RC .08 .25
219 Ken Landreaux .02 .10
220 Tom Seaver .75 2.00
221 Bob Davis .02 .10
Now with Angels
222 Jorge Orta .02 .10
223 Bobby Bonds .08 .25
224 Pat Zachry .02 .10
225 Ruppert Jones .02 .10
226 Duane Kuiper .02 .10
227 Rodney Scott .02 .10
228 Tom Paciorek .08 .25
229 Rollie Fingers .30 .75
Now with Brewers
230 George Hendrick .02 .10
231 Tony Perez .30 .75
232 Grant Jackson .02 .10
233 Damaso Garcia .02 .10
234 Lou Whitaker .50 1.25
235 Scott Sanderson .02 .10
236 Mike Ivie .02 .10
237 Charlie Moore .02 .10
238 Blue Jays Rookies .02 .10
Luis Leal
Brian Milner
Ken Sc
239 Rick Miller DP .01 .05
Now with Red Sox
240 Nolan Ryan 4.00 10.00
241 Checklist 126-250 DP .01 .05
242 Chet Lemon .02 .10
243 Dave Palmer .02 .10
244 Ellis Valentine .02 .10
245 Carney Lansford .08 .25
Now with Red Sox
246 Ed Ott DP .01 .05
247 Glenn Hubbard DP .01 .05
248 Joey McLaughlin .02 .10
249 Jerry Narron .02 .10
250 Ron Guidry .08 .25
251 Steve Garvey .20 .50
252 Victor Cruz .02 .10
253 Bobby Murcer .08 .25
254 Ozzie Smith 3.00 8.00
255 John Stearns .02 .10
256 Bill Campbell .02 .10
257 Rennie Stennett .02 .10
258 Rick Waits .02 .10
259 Gary Lucas .02 .10
260 Ron Cey .08 .25
261 Rickey Henderson 5.00 12.00
262 Sammy Stewart .02 .10
263 Brian Downing .02 .10
264 Mark Bomback .02 .10
265 John Candelaria .08 .25
266 Renie Martin .02 .10
267 Stan Bahnsen .02 .10
268 Montreal Expos CL .20 .50
269 Ken Forsch .02 .10
270 Greg Luzinski .08 .25
271 Ron Jackson .02 .10
272 Wayne Garland .02 .10
273 Milt May .02 .10
274 Rick Wise .02 .10
275 Dwight Evans .20 .50
276 Sal Bando .08 .25
277 Alfredo Griffin .02 .10
278 Rick Sofield .02 .10
279 Bob Knepper .02 .10
Now with Astros
280 Ken Griffey .08 .25
281 Ken Singleton .08 .25
282 Ernie Whitt .08 .25
283 Billy Sample .02 .10
284 Jack Morris .30 .75
285 Dick Ruthven .02 .10
286 Johnny Bench .75 2.00
287 Dave Smith .08 .25
288 Amos Otis .08 .25
289 Dave Goltz .02 .10
290 Bob Boone DP .07 .20
291 Aurelio Lopez .02 .10
292 Tom Hume .02 .10
293 Charlie Lea .02 .10
294 Bert Blyleven .20 .50
Now with Indians
295 Hal McRae .08 .25
296 Bob Stanley .02 .10
297 Bob Bailor .02 .10
Now with Mets
298 Jerry Koosman .08 .25
299 Elliott Maddox .02 .10
Now with Yankees
300 Paul Molitor 2.00 5.00
301 Matt Keough .02 .10
302 Pat Putnam .02 .10
303 Dan Ford .02 .10
304 John Castino .02 .10
305 Barry Foote .02 .10
306 Lou Piniella .08 .25
307 Gene Garber .02 .10
308 Rick Manning .02 .10
309 Don Baylor .20 .50
310 Vida Blue DP .07 .20
311 Doug Flynn .02 .10
312 Rick Rhoden .02 .10
313 Fred Lynn .08 .25
Now with Angels
314 Rich Dauer .02 .10
315 Kirk Gibson RC 2.00 5.00
316 Ken Reitz .02 .10
Now with Cubs
317 Lonnie Smith .08 .25
318 Steve Yeager .02 .10
319 Rowland Office .02 .10
320 Tom Burgmeier .02 .10
321 Leon Durham RC .08 .25
Now with Cubs
322 Neil Allen .02 .10
323 Ray Burris .02 .10
Now with Expos
324 Mike Willis .02 .10
325 Ray Knight .08 .25
326 Rafael Landestoy .02 .10
327 Moose Haas .02 .10
328 Ross Baumgarten .02 .10
329 Joaquin Andujar .08 .25
330 Frank White .08 .25
331 Toronto Blue Jays CL .08 .25
332 Dick Drago .02 .10
333 Sid Monge .02 .10
334 Joe Sambito .02 .10
335 Rick Cerone .02 .10
336 Eddie Whitson .02 .10
337 Sparky Lyle .08 .25
338 Checklist 251-374 .08 .25
339 Jon Matlack .02 .10
340 Ben Oglivie .02 .10
341 Dwayne Murphy .02 .10
342 Terry Crowley .02 .10
343 Frank Taveras .02 .10
344 Steve Rogers .02 .10
345 Warren Cromartie .02 .10
346 Bill Caudill .02 .10
347 Harold Baines RC 4.00 10.00
348 Frank LaCorte .02 .10
349 Glenn Hoffman .02 .10
350 J.R. Richard .02 .10
351 Otto Velez .02 .10
352 Ted Simmons .08 .25
Now with Brewers
353 Terry Kennedy .02 .10
Now with Padres
354 Al Hrabosky .02 .10
355 Bob Horner .08 .25
356 Cecil Cooper .08 .25
357 Bob Welch .08 .25
358 Paul Moskau .02 .10
359 Dave Rader .02 .10
Now with Angels
360 Willie Wilson .02 .10
361 Dave Kingman DP .08 .25
362 Joe Rudi .02 .10
Now with Red Sox
363 Rich Gale .02 .10
364 Steve Trout .02 .10
365 Graig Nettles DP .10 .30
366 Lamar Johnson .02 .10
367 Denny Martinez .30 .75
368 Manny Trillo .02 .10
369 Frank Tanana/Now with Red Sox .08 .25
370 Reggie Jackson .75 2.00
371 Bill Lee .08 .25
372 Jay Johnstone .08 .25
373 Jason Thompson .02 .10
374 Tom Hutton .02 .10

1981 O-Pee-Chee Posters

COMPLETE SET (24) 8.00 20.00
1 Willie Montanez .08 .25
2 Rodney Scott .08 .25
3 Chris Speier .08 .25
4 Larry Parrish .20 .50
5 Warren Cromartie .20 .50
6 Andre Dawson .75 2.00
7 Ellis Valentine .08 .25
8 Gary Carter .60 1.50
9 Steve Rogers .08 .25
10 Woodie Fryman .08 .25
11 Jerry White .08 .25
12 Scott Sanderson .08 .25
13 John Mayberry .20 .50
14 Damaso Garcia UER/(Misspelled Damasa) .08
.25
15 Alfredo Griffin .08 .25
16 Garth Iorg .08 .25
17 Alvis Woods .08 .25
18 Rick Bosetti .08 .25
19 Barry Bonnell .08 .25
20 Ernie Whitt .08 .25
21 Jim Clancy .08 .25
22 Dave Stieb .30 .75
23 Otto Velez .08 .25
24 Lloyd Moseby .20 .50

1982 O-Pee-Chee

This set is an abridgement of the 1982 Topps set. The 396 standard-size cards comprising the 1982 O-Pee-Chee set differ from the cards of the 1982 Topps set by having a higher ratio of cards of players from the two Canadian teams, a practice begun by O-Pee-Chee in 1977 and continued to 1988. The set contains virtually the same pictures for the players also featured in the 1982 Topps issue, but the O-Pee-Chee photos appear brighter. The fronts feature white-bordered color player photos with colored lines within the wide white margin on the left. The player's name, team and bilingual position appear in colored lettering within the wide bottom margin. The player's name also appears as a simulated autograph across the photo. The blue print on green horizontal backs carry the player's name, bilingual position and biography at the top. The player's major league statistics follow below. The cards are numbered on the back. The asterisked cards have an extra line on the front inside the picture area indicating team change. In Action (IA) and All-Star (AS) cards are indicated in the checklist below; these are included in the set in addition to the player's regular card. The 396 cards in the set were the largest "original" or distinct set total printed up to that time by O-Pee-Chee; the previous high had been 374 in 1979, 1980 and 1981.

COMPLETE SET (396) 20.00 50.00
1 Dan Spillner .02 .10
2 Ken Singleton AS .02 .10
3 John Candelaria .02 .10
4 Frank Tanana .08 .25
Traded to Rangers Jan. 15/82
5 Reggie Smith .08 .25
6 Rick Monday .02 .10
7 Scott Sanderson .02 .10
8 Rich Dauer .02 .10
9 Ron Guidry .08 .25
10 Ron Guidry IA .02 .10
11 Tom Brookens .02 .10
12 Moose Haas .02 .10
13 Chet Lemon .08 .25
Traded to Tigers Nov. 27/81
14 Steve Howe .02 .10
15 Ellis Valentine .02 .10
16 Toby Harrah .08 .25
17 Darrell Evans .08 .25
18 Johnny Bench .75 2.00
19 Ernie Whitt .02 .10
20 Garry Maddox .02 .10
21 Graig Nettles IA .08 .25
22 Al Oliver IA .08 .25
23 Bob Boone .08 .25
Traded to Angels Dec. 9/81
24 Pete Rose IA .60 1.50
25 Jerry Remy .02 .10
26 Jorge Orta .08 .25
Traded to Dodgers Dec 9/81
27 Bobby Bonds .08 .25
28 Jim Clancy .02 .10
29 Dwayne Murphy .02 .10
30 Tom Seaver .75 2.00
31 Tom Seaver IA .40 1.00
32 Claudell Washington .02 .10
33 Bob Shirley .02 .10
34 Bob Forsch .02 .10
35 Willie Aikens .08 .25
36 Rod Carew AS .30 .75
37 Willie Randolph .08 .25
38 Charlie Lea .02 .10
39 Lou Whitaker .30 .75
40 Dave Parker .08 .25
41 Dave Parker IA .02 .10
42 Mark Belanger .08 .25
Traded to Dodgers Dec. 24/81
43 Rick Langford .02 .10
44 Rollie Fingers IA .20 .50
45 Rick Cerone .02 .10
46 Johnny Wockenfuss .02 .10
47 Jack Morris AS .08 .25
48 Cesar Cedeno .02 .10
Traded to Reds Dec. 18/81
49 Alvis Woods .02 .10
50 Buddy Bell .08 .25
51 Mickey Rivers IA .02 .10
52 Steve Rogers .02 .10
53 Blue Jays Leaders .08 .25
John Mayberry
Dave Stieb/(Tea
54 Ron Hassey .02 .10
55 Rick Burleson .02 .10
56 Harold Baines .20 .50
57 Craig Reynolds .02 .10
58 Carlton Fisk AS .30 .75
59 Jim Kern .02 .10
Traded to Reds Feb. 10/82
60 Tony Armas .02 .10
61 Warren Cromartie .02 .10
62 Graig Nettles .08 .25
63 Jerry Koosman .08 .25
64 Pat Zachry .02 .10
65 Terry Kennedy .02 .10
66 Richie Zisk .02 .10
67 Rich Gale .08 .25
Traded to Giants Dec. 10/81
68 Steve Carlton .60 1.50
69 Greg Luzinski IA .08 .25
70 Tim Raines .75 2.00
71 Roy Lee Jackson .02 .10
72 Carl Yastrzemski .60 1.50
73 John Castino .02 .10
74 Joe Niekro .08 .25
75 Tommy John .08 .25
76 Dave Winfield AS .30 .75
77 Miguel Dilone .02 .10
78 Gary Gray .02 .10
79 Tom Hume .02 .10
80 Jim Palmer .50 1.25
81 Jim Palmer IA .30 .75
82 Vida Blue IA .08 .25
83 Garth Iorg .02 .10
84 Rennie Stennett .02 .10
85 Dave Lopes IA .08 .25
Traded to A's Feb. 8/82
86 Dave Concepcion .08 .25
87 Matt Keough .02 .10
88 Jim Spencer .02 .10
89 Steve Henderson .02 .10
90 Nolan Ryan 4.00 10.00
91 Carney Lansford .08 .25
92 Bake McBride .02 .10
93 Dave Stapleton .02 .10
94 Expos Team Leaders .08 .25
Warren Cromartie
Bill Gullick
95 Ozzie Smith 4.00 10.00
Traded to Cardinals Feb. 11/82
96 Rich Hebner .02 .10
97 Tim Foli .02 .10
Traded to Angels Dec. 11/82
98 Darrell Porter .02 .10
99 Barry Bonnell .02 .10
100 Mike Schmidt 1.25 3.00
101 Mike Schmidt IA .60 1.50
102 Dan Briggs .02 .10
103 Al Cowens .02 .10
104 Grant Jackson .08 .25
Traded to Royals Jan. 19/82
105 Kirk Gibson .30 .75
106 Dan Schatzeder .08 .25
Traded to Giants Dec. 9/81
107 Juan Berenguer .02 .10
108 Jack Morris .20 .50
109 Dave Revering .02 .10
110 Carlton Fisk .60 1.50
111 Carlton Fisk IA .30 .75
112 Billy Sample .02 .10
113 Steve McCatty .02 .10
114 Ken Landreaux .02 .10
115 Gaylord Perry .40 1.00
116 Elias Sosa .02 .10
117 Rich Gossage IA .08 .25
118 Expos Future Stars 2.00 5.00
Terry Francona
Brad Mills
Br
119 Billy Almon .02 .10
120 Gary Lucas .02 .10
121 Ken Oberkfell .02 .10
122 Steve Carlton IA .30 .75
123 Jeff Reardon .20 .50
124 Bill Buckner .08 .25
125 Danny Ainge .60 1.50
Voluntarily Retired Nov. 30/81
126 Paul Splittorff .02 .10
127 Lonnie Smith .02 .10
Traded to Cardinals Nov. 19/81
128 Rudy May .02 .10
129 Checklist 1-132 .02 .10
130 Julio Cruz .02 .10
131 Stan Bahnsen .02 .10
132 Pete Vuckovich .02 .10
133 Luis Salazar .02 .10
134 Dan Ford .08 .25
Traded to Orioles Jan. 28/82
135 Denny Martinez .30 .75
136 Lary Sorensen .02 .10
137 Fergie Jenkins .40 1.00
Traded to Cubs Dec. 15/81
138 Rick Camp .02 .10
139 Wayne Nordhagen .02 .10
140 Ron LeFlore .08 .25
141 Rick Sutcliffe .08 .25
142 Rick Waits .02 .10
143 Mookie Wilson .30 .75
144 Greg Minton .02 .10
145 Bob Horner .08 .25
146 Joe Morgan IA .30 .75
147 Larry Gura .02 .10
148 Alfredo Griffin .02 .10
149 Pat Putnam .02 .10
150 Ted Simmons .08 .25
151 Gary Matthews .08 .25
152 Greg Luzinski .08 .25
153 Mike Flanagan .08 .25
154 Jim Morrison .02 .10
155 Otto Velez .02 .10
156 Frank White .08 .25
157 Doug Corbett .02 .10
158 Brian Downing .02 .10
159 Willie Randolph IA .02 .10
160 Luis Tiant .08 .25
161 Andre Thornton .02 .10
162 Amos Otis .08 .25
163 Paul Mirabella .02 .10
164 Bert Blyleven .20 .50
165 Rowland Office .02 .10
166 Gene Tenace .08 .25
167 Cecil Cooper .08 .25
168 Bruce Benedict .02 .10
169 Mark Clear .02 .10
170 Jim Bibby .02 .10
171 Ken Griffey IA .08 .25
Traded to Yankees Nov 4/81
172 Bill Gullickson .02 .10
173 Mike Scioscia .02 .10
174 Doug DeCinces .08 .25
Traded to Angels Jan 28/82
175 Jerry Mumphrey .02 .10
176 Rollie Fingers .40 1.00
177 George Foster IA .08 .25
Traded to Mets Feb 10/82
178 Mitchell Page .02 .10
179 Steve Garvey .30 .75
180 Steve Garvey IA .08 .25
181 Woodie Fryman .02 .10
182 Larry Herndon .02 .10
Traded to Tigers Dec. 9/81
183 Frank White IA .08 .25
184 Alan Ashby .02 .10
185 Phil Niekro .40 1.00
186 Leon Roberts .02 .10
187 Rod Carew .60 1.50
188 Willie Stargell IA .30 .75
189 Joel Youngblood .02 .10
190 J.R. Richard .02 .10
191 Tim Wallach .30 .75
192 Broderick Perkins .02 .10
193 Johnny Grubb .02 .10
194 Larry Bowa .08 .25
Traded to Cubs Jan. 27/82
195 Paul Molitor 1.25 3.00
196 Willie Upshaw .02 .10
197 Roy Smalley .02 .10
198 Chris Speier .02 .10
199 Don Aase .02 .10
200 George Brett 2.50 6.00
201 George Brett IA 1.25 3.00
202 Rick Manning .02 .10
203 Blue Jays Prospects .30 .75
Jesse Barfield
Brian Milner#
204 Rick Reuschel .08 .25
205 Neil Allen .02 .10
206 Leon Durham .02 .10
207 Jim Gantner .08 .25
208 Joe Morgan .30 .75
209 Gary Lavelle .02 .10
210 Keith Hernandez .08 .25
211 Joe Charboneau .02 .10
212 Mario Mendoza .02 .10
213 Willie Randolph AS .08 .25
214 Lance Parrish .20 .50
215 Mike Krukow .02 .10
Traded to Phillies Dec. 8/81
216 Ron Cey .08 .25
217 Ruppert Jones .02 .10
218 Dave Lopes .08 .25
Traded to A's Feb. 8/82
219 Steve Yeager .02 .10
220 Manny Trillo .02 .10
221 Dave Concepcion IA .08 .25
222 Butch Wynegar .02 .10
223 Lloyd Moseby .02 .10
224 Bruce Bochte .02 .10
225 Ed Ott .02 .10
226 Checklist 133-264 .02 .10
227 Ray Burris .02 .10
228 Reggie Smith IA .08 .25
229 Oscar Gamble .02 .10
230 Willie Wilson .02 .10
231 Brian Kingman .02 .10
232 John Stearns .02 .10
233 Duane Kuiper .02 .10
Traded to Giants Nov. 16/81
234 Don Baylor .08 .25
235 Mike Easler .02 .10
236 Lou Piniella .08 .25
237 Robin Yount .60 1.50
238 Kevin Saucier .02 .10
239 Jon Matlack .02 .10
240 Bucky Dent .08 .25
241 Bucky Dent IA .02 .10
242 Milt May .02 .10
243 Lee Mazzilli .02 .10
244 Gary Carter .40 1.00
245 Ken Reitz .02 .10
246 Scott McGregor AS .02 .10
247 Pedro Guerrero .08 .25
248 Art Howe .02 .10
249 Dick Tidrow .02 .10
250 Tug McGraw .08 .25
251 Fred Lynn .08 .25
252 Fred Lynn IA .02 .10
253 Gene Richards .02 .10
254 Jorge Bell RC .40 1.00
George Bell
255 Tony Perez .40 1.00
256 Tony Perez IA .20 .50
257 Rich Dotson .02 .10
258 Bo Diaz .02 .10
Traded to Phillies Nov. 19/81
259 Rodney Scott .02 .10
260 Bruce Sutter .40 1.00
261 George Brett AS 1.25 3.00
262 Rick Dempsey .08 .25
263 Mike Phillips .02 .10
264 Jerry Garvin .02 .10
265 Al Bumbry .02 .10
266 Hubie Brooks .02 .10
267 Vida Blue .08 .25
268 Rickey Henderson 2.00 5.00
269 Rick Peters .02 .10
270 Rusty Staub .08 .25
271 Sixto Lezcano .02 .10
Traded to Padres Dec. 10/81
272 Bump Wills .02 .10
273 Gary Allenson .02 .10
274 Randy Jones .02 .10
275 Bob Watson .02 .10
276 Dave Kingman .08 .25

277 Terry Puhl .02 .10
278 Jerry Reuss .08 .25
279 Sammy Stewart .02 .10
280 Ben Oglivie .02 .10
281 Kent Tekulve .08 .25
282 Ken Macha .08 .25
283 Ron Davis .02 .10
284 Bob Grich .08 .25
285 Sparky Lyle .08 .25
286 Rich Gossage AS .08 .25
287 Dennis Eckersley .40 1.00
288 Garry Templeton .02 .10
Traded to Padres Dec. 10/81
289 Bob Stanley .02 .10
290 Ken Singleton .02 .10
291 Mickey Hatcher .02 .10
292 Dave Palmer .02 .10
293 Damaso Garcia .02 .10
294 Don Money .02 .10
295 George Hendrick .02 .10
296 Steve Kemp .02 .10
Traded to White Sox Nov. 27/81
297 Dave Smith .02 .10
298 Bucky Dent AS .02 .10
299 Steve Trout .02 .10
300 Reggie Jackson 1.25 3.00
Traded to Angels Jan. 26/82
301 Reggie Jackson IA .60 1.50
Traded to Angels Jan. 26/82
302 Doug Flynn .08 .25
Traded to Rangers Dec. 14/81
303 Wayne Gross .02 .10
304 Johnny Bench IA .30 .75
305 Don Sutton .40 1.00
306 Don Sutton IA .30 .75
307 Mark Bomback .02 .10
308 Charlie Moore .02 .10
309 Jeff Burroughs .02 .10
310 Mike Hargrove .08 .25
311 Enos Cabell .02 .10
312 Lenny Randle .02 .10
313 Ivan DeJesus .02 .10
Traded to Phillies Jan. 27/82
314 Buck Martinez .02 .10
315 Burt Hooton .02 .10
316 Scott McGregor .02 .10
317 Dick Ruthven .02 .10
318 Mike Heath .02 .10
319 Ray Knight .08 .25
Traded to Astros Dec. 18/81
320 Chris Chambliss .02 .10
321 Chris Chambliss IA .02 .10
322 Ross Baumgarten .02 .10
323 Bill Lee .08 .25
324 Gorman Thomas .02 .10
325 Jose Cruz .08 .25
326 Al Oliver .08 .25
327 Jackson Todd .02 .10
328 Ed Farmer .02 .10
Traded to Phillies Jan. 28/82
329 U.L. Washington .02 .10
330 Ken Griffey .08 .25
Traded to Yankees Nov. 4/81
331 John Milner .02 .10
332 Don Robinson .02 .10
333 Cliff Johnson .02 .10
334 Fernando Valenzuela .30 .75
335 Jim Sundberg .08 .25
336 George Foster .08 .25
Traded to Mets Feb. 10/82
337 Pete Rose AS .60 1.50
338 Dave Lopes AS .08 .25
Traded to A's Feb. 8/82
339 Mike Schmidt AS .60 1.50
340 Dave Concepcion AS .02 .10
341 Andre Dawson AS .30 .75
342 George Foster AS .08 .25
Traded to Mets Feb. 10/82
343 Dave Parker AS .08 .25
344 Gary Carter AS .08 .25
345 Fernando Valenzuela AS .20 .50
346 Tom Seaver AS .30 .75
347 Bruce Sutter AS .20 .50
348 Darrell Porter IA .02 .10
349 Dave Collins .02 .10
Traded to Yankees Dec. 23/81
350 Amos Otis IA .02 .10
351 Frank Taveras .02 .10
Traded to Expos Dec. 14/81
352 Dave Winfield .60 1.50
353 Larry Parrish .02 .10
354 Roberto Ramos .02 .10
355 Dwight Evans .08 .25
356 Mickey Rivers .02 .10
357 Butch Hobson .02 .10
358 Carl Yastrzemski IA .30 .75
359 Ron Jackson .02 .10
360 Len Barker .02 .10
361 Pete Rose 1.25 3.00
362 Kevin Hickey RC .02 .10
363 Rod Carew IA .30 .75
364 Hector Cruz .02 .10
365 Bill Madlock .08 .25
366 Jim Rice .08 .25
367 Ron Cey IA .08 .25
368 Luis Leal .04 .10
369 Dennis Leonard .02 .10
370 Mike Norris .02 .10
371 Tom Paciorek .08 .25
Traded to White Sox Dec. 11/81
372 Willie Stargell .40 1.00
373 Dan Driessen .02 .10
374 Larry Bowa IA .08 .25
Traded to Cubs Jan. 27/82
375 Dusty Baker .08 .25
376 Joey McLaughlin .02 .10
377 Reggie Jackson AS .60 1.50
Traded to Angels Jan. 26/82
378 Mike Caldwell .02 .10
379 Andre Dawson .60 1.50
380 Dave Stieb .02 .10
381 Alan Trammell .30 .75
382 John Mayberry .02 .10
383 John Wathan .02 .10
384 Hal McRae .08 .25
385 Ken Forsch .02 .10
386 Jerry White .02 .10
387 Tom Veryzer .02 .10
Traded to Mets Jan. 8/82
388 Joe Rudi .02 .10
Traded to A's Dec. 4/81
389 Bob Knepper .02 .10
390 Eddie Murray 1.50 4.00
391 Dale Murphy .30 .75
392 Bob Boone IA .08 .25
Traded to Angels Dec. 6/81
393 Al Hrabosky .02 .10
394 Checklist 265-396 .02 .10
395 Omar Moreno .02 .10
396 Rich Gossage .30 .75

1982 O-Pee-Chee Posters

COMPLETE SET (24) 3.00 8.00
1 John Mayberry .20 .50
2 Damaso Garcia .08 .25
3 Ernie Whitt .08 .25
4 Lloyd Moseby .08 .25
5 Alvis Woods .08 .25
6 Dave Stieb .30 .75
7 Roy Lee Jackson .08 .25
8 Joey McLaughlin .08 .25
9 Luis Leal .08 .25
10 Aurelio Rodriguez .08 .25
11 Otto Velez .08 .25
12 Juan Berenguer UER (Misspelled Berenger) .08 .25
13 Warren Cromartie .08 .25
14 Rodney Scott .08 .25
15 Larry Parrish .20 .50
16 Gary Carter 1.00 2.50
17 Tim Raines .40 1.00
18 Andre Dawson .75 2.00
19 Terry Francona .30 .75
20 Steve Rogers .08 .25
21 Bill Gullickson .08 .25
22 Scott Sanderson .08 .25
23 Jeff Reardon .40 1.00
24 Jerry White .08 .25

1983 O-Pee-Chee

This set is an abridgement of the 1983 Topps set. The 396 standard-size cards comprising the 1983 O-Pee-Chee set differ from the cards of the 1983 Topps set by having a higher ratio of cards of players from the two Canadian teams, a practice begun by O-Pee-Chee in 1977 and continued to 1988. The set contains virtually the same pictures for the players also featured in the 1983 Topps issue. The fronts feature white-bordered color player action photos framed by a colored line. A circular color player head shot also appears on the front at the lower right. The player's name, team and bilingual position appear at the lower left. The pink and white horizontal backs carry the player's name and biography at the top. The player's major league statistics and bilingual career highlights follow below. The asterisked cards have an extra line on the front inside the picture area indicating team change. The O-Pee-Chee logo appears on the front of every card. Super Veteran (SV) and All-Star (AS) cards are indicated in the checklist below; these are included in the set in addition to the player's regular card. The 1983 O-Pee-Chee set was issued in nine-card packs which cost 25 cents Canadian at time of issue. The set features Rookie Cards of Tony Gwynn and Ryne Sandberg.

COMPLETE SET (396) 25.00 60.00
1 Rusty Staub .07 .20
2 Larry Parrish .02 .10
3 George Brett 1.50 4.00
4 Carl Yastrzemski .50 1.25
5 Al Oliver SV .07 .20
6 Bill Virdon MG .02 .10
7 Gene Richards .02 .10
8 Steve Balboni .02 .10
9 Joey McLaughlin .02 .10
10 Gorman Thomas .02 .10
11 Chris Chambliss .07 .20
12 Ray Burris .02 .10
13 Larry Herndon .02 .10
14 Ozzie Smith 1.00 2.50
15 Ron Cey .07 .20
Now with Cubs
16 Willie Wilson .07 .20
17 Kent Tekulve .07 .20
18 Kent Tekulve SV .02 .10
19 Oscar Gamble .02 .10
20 Carlton Fisk .40 1.00
21 Dale Murphy AS .20 .50
22 Randy Lerch .02 .10
23 Dale Murphy .20 .50
24 Steve Mura .07 .20
Now with White Sox
25 Hal McRae .07 .20
26 Dennis Lamp .02 .10
27 Ron Washington .02 .10
28 Bruce Bochte .02 .10
29 Randy Jones .07 .20
Now with Pirates
30 Jim Rice .07 .20
31 Bill Gullickson .07 .20
32 Dave Concepcion AS .07 .20
33 Ted Simmons SV .07 .20
34 Bobby Cox MG .02 .10
35 Rollie Fingers .20 .50
36 Rollie Fingers SV .10 .30
37 Mike Hargrove .07 .20
38 Roy Smalley .02 .10
39 Terry Puhl .02 .10
40 Fernando Valenzuela .20 .50
41 Garry Maddox .02 .10
42 Dale Murray .07 .20
Now with Yankees
43 Bob Dernier .02 .10
44 Don Robinson .02 .10
45 John Mayberry .02 .10
46 Richard Dotson .02 .10
47 Wayne Nordhagen .02 .10
Now with Cubs
48 Lary Sorensen .02 .10
49 Willie McGee RC 1.25 3.00
50 Bob Horner .02 .10
51 Rusty Staub SV .07 .20
52 Tom Seaver 1.00 2.50
Now with Mets
53 Chet Lemon .02 .10
54 Scott Sanderson .02 .10
55 Mookie Wilson .07 .20
56 Reggie Jackson .60 1.50
57 Tim Blackwell .02 .10
58 Keith Moreland .02 .10
59 Alvis Woods .07 .20
Now with Athletics
60 Johnny Bench .60 1.50
61 Johnny Bench SV .30 .75
62 Jim Gott .02 .10
63 Rick Monday .02 .10
64 Gary Matthews .07 .20
65 Jack Morris .07 .20
66 Lou Whitaker .20 .50
67 U.L. Washington .02 .10
68 Eric Show .02 .10
69 Lee Lacy .02 .10
70 Steve Carlton .40 1.00
71 Steve Carlton SV .30 .75
72 Tom Paciorek .02 .10
73 Manny Trillo .07 .20
Now with Indians
74 Tony Perez SV .10 .30
75 Amos Otis .07 .20
76 Rick Mahler .02 .10
77 Hosken Powell .02 .10
78 Bill Caudill .02 .10
79 Dan Petry .02 .10
80 George Foster .07 .20
81 Joe Morgan .20 .50
Now with Phillies
82 Burt Hooton .02 .10
83 Ryne Sandberg RC 8.00 20.00
84 Alan Ashby .02 .10
85 Ken Singleton .07 .20
86 Tom Hume .02 .10
87 Dennis Leonard .02 .10
88 Jim Gantner .07 .20
89 Leon Roberts .07 .20
Now with Royals
90 Jerry Reuss .07 .20
91 Ben Oglivie .02 .10
92 Sparky Lyle SV .07 .20
93 John Castino .02 .10
94 Phil Niekro .20 .50
95 Alan Trammell .20 .50
96 Gaylord Perry .20 .50
97 Tom Herr .02 .10
98 Vance Law .02 .10
99 Dickie Noles .02 .10
100 Pete Rose 1.00 2.50
101 Pete Rose SV .50 1.25
102 Dave Concepcion .07 .20
103 Darrell Porter .02 .10
104 Ron Guidry .07 .20
105 Don Baylor .07 .20
Now with Yankees
106 Steve Rogers AS .02 .10
107 Greg Minton .02 .10
108 Glenn Hoffman .02 .10
109 Luis Leal .02 .10
110 Ken Griffey .07 .20
111 Expos Leaders .07 .20
Al Oliver
Steve Rogers/(Team chec
112 Luis Pujols .02 .10
113 Julio Cruz .02 .10
114 Jim Slaton .02 .10
115 Chili Davis .20 .50
116 Pedro Guerrero .07 .20
117 Mike Ivie .02 .10
118 Chris Welsh .02 .10
119 Frank Pastore .02 .10
120 Len Barker .02 .10
121 Chris Speier .02 .10
122 Bobby Murcer .07 .20
123 Bill Russell .02 .10
124 Lloyd Moseby .02 .10
125 Leon Durham .07 .20
126 Carl Yastrzemski SV .20 .50
127 John Candelaria .02 .10
128 Phil Garner .07 .20
129 Checklist 1-132 .02 .10
130 Dave Stieb .07 .20
131 Geoff Zahn .02 .10
132 Todd Cruz .02 .10
133 Tony Pena .07 .20
134 Hubie Brooks .07 .20
135 Dwight Evans .07 .20
136 Willie Aikens .02 .10
137 Woodie Fryman .02 .10
138 Rick Dempsey .07 .20
139 Bruce Berenyi .02 .10
140 Willie Randolph .07 .20
141 Eddie Murray 1.00 2.50
142 Mike Caldwell .02 .10
143 Tony Gwynn RC 12.00 30.00
144 Tommy John SV .07 .20
145 Don Sutton .40 1.00
146 Don Sutton SV .20 .50
147 Rick Manning .02 .10
148 George Hendrick .02 .10
149 Johnny Ray .02 .10
150 Bruce Sutter .07 .20
151 Bruce Sutter SV .02 .10
152 Jay Johnstone .07 .20
153 Jerry Koosman .07 .20
154 Johnnie LeMaster .02 .10
155 Dan Quisenberry .07 .20
156 Luis Salazar .02 .10
157 Steve Bedrosian .07 .20
158 Jim Sundberg .02 .10
159 Gaylord Perry SV .10 .30
160 Dave Kingman .10 .30
161 Dave Kingman SV .10 .30
162 Mark Clear .02 .10
163 Cal Ripken 4.00 10.00
164 Dave Palmer .02 .10
165 Dan Driessen .02 .10
166 Tug McGraw .10 .30
167 Dennis Martinez .07 .20
168 Juan Eichelberger .07 .20
Now with Indians
169 Doug Flynn .02 .10
170 Steve Howe .02 .10
171 Frank White .07 .20
172 Mike Flanagan .02 .10
173 Andre Dawson AS .10 .30
174 Manny Trillo AS .07 .20
Now with Indians
175 Bo Diaz .02 .10
176 Dave Righetti .07 .20
177 Harold Baines .20 .50
178 Vida Blue .07 .20
179 Luis Tiant SV .07 .20
180 Rickey Henderson 1.00 2.50
181 Rick Rhoden .02 .10
182 Fred Lynn .07 .20
183 Ed VandeBerg .02 .10
184 Dwayne Murphy .02 .10
185 Tim Lollar .02 .10
186 Dave Tobik .02 .10
187 Tug McGraw SV .07 .20
188 Rick Miller .02 .10
189 Dan Schatzeder .02 .10
190 Cecil Cooper .07 .20
191 Jim Beattie .02 .10
192 Rich Dauer .02 .10
193 Al Cowens .02 .10
194 Roy Lee Jackson .02 .10
195 Mike Gates .02 .10
196 Tommy John .20 .50
197 Bob Forsch .02 .10
198 Steve Garvey .20 .50
Now with Padres
199 Brad Mills .02 .10
200 Rod Carew .40 1.00
201 Rod Carew SV .20 .50
202 Blue Jays Leaders .07 .20
Dave Stieb
Damaso Garcia/(Tea
203 Floyd Bannister .07 .20
Now with White Sox
204 Bruce Benedict .02 .10
205 Dave Parker .07 .20
206 Ken Oberkfell .02 .10
207 Graig Nettles SV .07 .20
208 Sparky Lyle .07 .20
209 Jason Thompson .02 .10
210 Jack Clark .07 .20
211 Jim Kaat .07 .20
212 John Stearns .02 .10
213 Tom Burgmeier .02 .10
214 Jerry White .02 .10
215 Mario Soto .02 .10
216 Scott McGregor .02 .10
217 Tim Stoddard .07 .20
218 Bill Laskey .02 .10
219 Reggie Jackson SV .20 .50
220 Dusty Baker .07 .20
221 Joe Niekro .07 .20
222 Damaso Garcia .02 .10
223 John Montefusco .02 .10
224 Mickey Rivers .02 .10
225 Enos Cabell .02 .10
226 LaMarr Hoyt .02 .10
227 Tim Raines .20 .50
228 Joaquin Andujar .02 .10
229 Tim Wallach .07 .20
230 Fergie Jenkins .40 1.00
231 Fergie Jenkins SV .20 .50
232 Tom Brunansky .07 .20
233 Ivan DeJesus .02 .10
234 Bryn Smith .02 .10
235 Claudell Washington .02 .10
236 Steve Renko .02 .10
237 Dan Norman .02 .10
238 Cesar Cedeno .07 .20
239 Dave Stapleton .02 .10
240 Rich Gossage .20 .50
241 Rich Gossage SV .10 .30
242 Bob Stanley .02 .10
243 Rich Gale .07 .20
Now with Reds
244 Sixto Lezcano .02 .10
245 Steve Sax .07 .20
246 Jerry Mumphrey .02 .10
247 Dave Smith .02 .10
248 Bake McBride .02 .10
249 Checklist 133-264 .02 .10
250 Bill Buckner .07 .20
251 Kent Hrbek .20 .50
252 Gene Tenace .02 .10
Now with Pirates
253 Charlie Lea .02 .10
254 Rick Cerone .02 .10
255 Gene Garber .02 .10
256 Gene Garber SV .02 .10
257 Jesse Barfield .07 .20
258 Dave Winfield .40 1.00
259 Don Money .02 .10
260 Steve Kemp .02 .10
Now with Yankees
261 Steve Yeager .02 .10
262 Keith Hernandez .07 .20
263 Tippy Martinez .02 .10
264 Joe Morgan SV .20 .50
Now with Phillies
265 Joel Youngblood .02 .10
Now with Giants
266 Bruce Sutter AS .20 .50
267 Terry Francona .07 .20
268 Neil Allen .02 .10
269 Ron Oester .02 .10
270 Dennis Eckersley .40 1.00
271 Dale Berra .02 .10
272 Al Bumbry .02 .10
273 Lonnie Smith .02 .10
274 Terry Kennedy .02 .10
275 Ray Knight .02 .10
276 Mike Norris .02 .10
277 Rance Mulliniks .02 .10
278 Dan Spillner .02 .10
279 Bucky Dent .07 .20
280 Bert Blyleven .07 .20
281 Barry Bonnell .02 .10
282 Reggie Smith .02 .10
283 Reggie Smith SV .07 .20
284 Ted Simmons .07 .20
285 Lance Parrish .07 .20
286 Larry Christenson .02 .10
287 Ruppert Jones .02 .10
288 Bob Welch .02 .10
289 John Wathan .02 .10
290 Jeff Reardon .07 .20
291 Dave Revering .02 .10
292 Craig Swan .02 .10
293 Graig Nettles .07 .20
294 Alfredo Griffin .02 .10
295 Jerry Remy .02 .10
296 Joe Sambito .02 .10
297 Ron LeFlore .02 .10
298 Brian Downing .02 .10
299 Jim Palmer .20 .50
300 Mike Schmidt .75 2.00
301 Mike Schmidt SV .40 1.00
302 Ernie Whitt .02 .10
303 Andre Dawson .20 .50
304 Bobby Murcer SV .07 .20
305 Larry Bowa .07 .20
306 Lee Mazzilli .02 .10
Now with Pirates
307 Lou Piniella .07 .20
308 Buck Martinez .07 .20
309 Jerry Martin .02 .10
310 Greg Luzinski .07 .20
311 Al Oliver .07 .20
312 Mike Torrez .02 .10
Now with Mets
313 Dick Ruthven .02 .10
314 Gary Carter AS .20 .50
315 Rick Burleson .02 .10
316 Phil Niekro SV .10 .30
317 Moose Haas .02 .10
318 Carney Lansford .07 .20
Now with Athletics
319 Tim Foli .02 .10
320 Steve Rogers .02 .10
321 Kirk Gibson .20 .50
322 Glenn Hubbard .02 .10
323 Luis DeLeon .02 .10
324 Mike Marshall .02 .10
325 Von Hayes .02 .10
Now with Phillies
326 Garth Iorg .02 .10
327 Jose Cruz .07 .20
328 Jim Palmer SV .10 .30
329 Darrell Evans .07 .20
330 Buddy Bell .07 .20
331 Mike Krukow .02 .10
Now with Giants
332 Omar Moreno .02 .10
Now with Astros
333 Dave LaRoche .02 .10
334 Dave LaRoche SV .02 .10
335 Bill Madlock .07 .20
336 Garry Templeton .02 .10
337 John Lowenstein .02 .10
338 Willie Upshaw .02 .10
339 Dave Hostetler RC .02 .10
340 Larry Gura .02 .10
341 Doug DeCinces .07 .20
342 Mike Schmidt AS .40 1.00
343 Charlie Hough .07 .20
344 Andre Thornton .02 .10
345 Jim Clancy .02 .10
346 Ken Forsch .02 .10
347 Sammy Stewart .02 .10
348 Alan Bannister .02 .10
349 Checklist 265-396 .02 .10
350 Robin Yount .40 1.00
351 Warren Cromartie .02 .10
352 Tim Raines AS .20 .50
353 Tony Armas .02 .10
Now with Red Sox
354 Tom Seaver SV .50 1.25
Now with Mets
355 Tony Perez .30 .75
Now with Phillies
356 Toby Harrah .02 .10
357 Dan Ford .02 .10
358 Charlie Puleo .02 .10
Now with Reds
359 Dave Collins .02 .10
Now with Blue Jays
360 Nolan Ryan 3.00 8.00
361 Nolan Ryan SV 1.50 4.00
362 Bill Almon .02 .10
Now with Athletics
363 Eddie Milner .02 .10
364 Gary Lucas .02 .10
365 Dave Lopes .07 .20
366 Bob Boone .07 .20
367 Biff Pocoroba .02 .10
368 Richie Zisk .02 .10
369 Tony Bernazard .07 .20
370 Gary Carter .40 1.00
371 Paul Molitor .50 1.25
372 Art Howe .02 .10
373 Pete Rose AS .50 1.25
374 Glenn Adams .02 .10
375 Pete Vuckovich .02 .10
376 Gary Lavelle .02 .10
377 Lee May .07 .20
378 Lee May SV .07 .20
379 Butch Wynegar .02 .10
380 Ron Davis .02 .10
381 Bob Grich .07 .20
382 Gary Roenicke .02 .10
383 Jim Kaat SV .07 .20
384 Steve Carlton AS .20 .50
385 Mike Easler .02 .10
386 Rod Carew AS .20 .50
387 Bob Grich AS .07 .20
388 George Brett AS .75 2.00
389 Robin Yount AS .20 .50
390 Reggie Jackson AS .20 .50
391 Rickey Henderson AS .20 .50
392 Fred Lynn AS .07 .20
393 Carlton Fisk AS .20 .50
394 Pete Vuckovich AS .02 .10
395 Larry Gura AS .02 .10
396 Dan Quisenberry AS .02 .10

1984 O-Pee-Chee

This set is an abridgement of the 1984 Topps set. The 396 standard-size cards comprising the 1984 O-Pee-Chee set differ from the cards of the 1984 Topps set by having a higher ratio of cards of players from the two Canadian teams, a practice begun by O-Pee-Chee in 1977 and continued to 1988. The set contains virtually the same pictures for the players also featured in the 1984 Topps issue. The fronts feature white-bordered color player action photos. A color player head shot also appears on the front at the lower left. The player's name and position appear in colored lettering within the white margin at the lower right. His team name appears in vertical colored lettering within the white margin on the left. The red, white and blue horizontal backs carry the player's name and biography at the top. The player's major league statistics and bilingual career highlights follow below. The asterisked cards have an extra line on the front inside the picture area indicating team change. The O-Pee-Chee logo appears on the front of every card. All-Star (AS) cards are indicated in the checklist below; they are included in the set in addition to the player's regular card. The O-Pee-Chee set came in 12-card packs which cost 35 cents Canadian at time of issue. Notable Rookie Cards include Don Mattingly and Darryl Strawberry.

COMPLETE SET (396) 15.00 40.00
1 Pascual Perez .01 .05
2 Cal Ripken AS 1.25 3.00
3 Lloyd Moseby AS .01 .05
4 Mel Hall .01 .05
5 Willie Wilson .01 .05
6 Mike Morgan .01 .05
7 Gary Lucas .02 .10
Now with Expos
8 Don Mattingly RC 8.00 20.00
9 Jim Gott .01 .05
10 Robin Yount .20 .50
11 Joey McLaughlin .01 .05
12 Billy Sample .01 .05
13 Oscar Gamble .01 .05
14 Bill Russell .01 .05
15 Burt Hooton .01 .05
16 Omar Moreno .01 .05
17 Dave Lopes .02 .10
18 Dale Berra .01 .05
19 Rance Mulliniks .01 .05
20 Greg Luzinski .02 .10
21 Doug Sisk .01 .05
22 Don Robinson .01 .05
23 Keith Moreland .01 .05
24 Richard Dotson .01 .05
25 Glenn Hubbard .01 .05
26 Rod Carew .40 1.00
27 Alan Wiggins .01 .05
28 Frank Viola .20 .50
29 Phil Niekro .40 1.00
Now with Yankees
30 Wade Boggs 1.25 3.00
31 Dave Parker .08 .25
Now with Reds
32 Bobby Ramos .01 .05
33 Tom Burgmeier .01 .05
34 Eddie Milner .01 .05
35 Don Sutton .30 .75
36 Glenn Wilson .01 .05
37 Mike Krukow .01 .05
38 Dave Collins .01 .05
39 Garth Iorg .01 .05
40 Dusty Baker .08 .25
41 Tony Bernazard .02 .10
Now with Indians
42 Claudell Washington .01 .05
43 Cecil Cooper .02 .10
44 Dan Driessen .01 .05
45 Jerry Mumphrey .01 .05
46 Rick Rhoden .01 .05
47 Rudy Law .01 .05
48 Julio Franco .20 .50
49 Mike Norris .01 .05
50 Chris Chambliss .01 .05
51 Pete Falcone .01 .05
52 Mike Marshall .01 .05
53 Amos Otis .02 .10
Now with Pirates
54 Jesse Orosco .02 .10
55 Dave Concepcion .02 .10
56 Gary Allenson .01 .05
57 Dan Schatzeder .01 .05
58 Jerry Remy .01 .05
59 Carney Lansford .02 .10
60 Paul Molitor .40 1.00
61 Chris Codiroli .01 .05
62 Dave Hostetler .01 .05
63 Ed VandeBerg .01 .05
64 Ryne Sandberg 1.50 4.00
65 Kirk Gibson .20 .50
66 Nolan Ryan 2.50 6.00
67 Gary Ward .01 .05
Now with Rangers
68 Luis Salazar .01 .05
69 Dan Quisenberry AS .01 .05
70 Gary Matthews .01 .05
71 Pete O'Brien .02 .10
72 John Wathan .01 .05
73 Jody Davis .01 .05
74 Kent Tekulve .01 .05
75 Bob Forsch .01 .05
76 Alfredo Griffin .01 .05
77 Bryn Smith .01 .05
78 Mike Torrez .01 .05
79 Mike Hargrove .02 .10
80 Steve Rogers .01 .05
81 Bake McBride .01 .05
82 Doug DeCinces .01 .05
83 Richie Zisk .01 .05
84 Randy Bush .01 .05
85 Atlee Hammaker .01 .05
86 Chet Lemon .01 .05
87 Frank Pastore .01 .05
88 Alan Trammell .20 .50
89 Terry Francona .01 .05
90 Pedro Guerrero .01 .05
91 Dan Spillner .01 .05
92 Lloyd Moseby .01 .05
93 Bob Knepper .01 .05
94 Ted Simmons AS .02 .10
95 Aurelio Lopez .01 .05
96 Bill Buckner .02 .10
97 LaMarr Hoyt .01 .05
98 Tom Brunansky .01 .05
99 Ron Oester .01 .05
100 Reggie Jackson .50 1.25
101 Ron Davis .01 .05
102 Ken Oberkfell .01 .05
103 Dwayne Murphy .01 .05
104 Jim Slaton .01 .05
Now with Angels
105 Tony Armas .01 .05
106 Ernie Whitt .01 .05
107 Johnnie LeMaster .01 .05
108 Randy Moffitt .01 .05
109 Terry Forster .01 .05
110 Ron Guidry .02 .10
111 Bill Virdon MG .01 .05
112 Doyle Alexander .01 .05
113 Lonnie Smith .01 .05
114 Checklist 1-132 .01 .05
115 Andre Thornton .01 .05
116 Jeff Reardon .02 .10
117 Tom Herr .02 .10
118 Charlie Hough .02 .10
119 Phil Garner .02 .10
120 Keith Hernandez .08 .25
121 Rich Gossage .20 .50
Now with Padres
122 Ted Simmons .02 .10
123 Butch Wynegar .01 .05
124 Damaso Garcia .01 .05
125 Britt Burns .01 .05
126 Bert Blyleven .02 .10
127 Carlton Fisk .20 .50
128 Rick Manning .01 .05
129 Bill Laskey .01 .05
130 Ozzie Smith .75 2.00
131 Bo Diaz .01 .05
132 Tom Paciorek .01 .05
133 Dave Rozema .01 .05
134 Dave Stieb .01 .05
135 Brian Downing .01 .05
136 Rick Camp .01 .05
137 Willie Aikens .02 .10
Now with Blue Jays
138 Charlie Moore .01 .05
139 George Frazier .02 .10
Now with Indians
140 Storm Davis .01 .05
141 Glenn Hoffman .01 .05
142 Charlie Lea .01 .05
143 Mike Vail .01 .05
144 Steve Sax .02 .10
145 Gary Lavelle .01 .05
146 Gorman Thomas .02 .10
Now with Mariners
147 Dan Petry .01 .05
148 Mark Clear .01 .05
149 Dave Beard .02 .10
Now with Mariners
150 Dale Murphy .20 .50
151 Steve Trout .01 .05
152 Tony Pena .02 .10
153 Geoff Zahn .01 .05
154 Dave Henderson .01 .05
155 Frank White .02 .10
156 Dick Ruthven .01 .05
157 Gary Gaetti .08 .25
158 Lance Parrish .02 .10
159 Joe Price .01 .05
160 Mario Soto .01 .05
161 Tug McGraw .08 .25
162 Bob Ojeda .01 .05
163 George Hendrick .01 .05
164 Scott Sanderson .01 .05
Now with Cubs
165 Ken Singleton .01 .05
166 Terry Kennedy .01 .05
167 Gene Garber .01 .05
168 Juan Bonilla .01 .05
169 Larry Parrish .02 .10
170 Jerry Reuss .02 .10
171 John Tudor .02 .10
Now with Pirates
172 Dave Kingman .02 .10
173 Garry Templeton .01 .05
174 Bob Boone .02 .10
175 Graig Nettles .02 .10
176 Lee Smith .20 .50
177 LaMarr Hoyt AS .01 .05
178 Bill Krueger .01 .05
179 Buck Martinez .01 .05
180 Manny Trillo .02 .10
Now with Giants
181 Lou Whitaker AS .02 .10
182 Darryl Strawberry RC 1.50 4.00
183 Neil Allen .01 .05
184 Jim Rice AS .02 .10
185 Sixto Lezcano .01 .05
186 Tom Hume .01 .05
187 Garry Maddox .01 .05
188 Bryan Little .01 .05
189 Jose Cruz .02 .10
190 Ben Oglivie .01 .05
191 Cesar Cedeno .02 .10
192 Nick Esasky .01 .05
193 Ken Forsch .01 .05
194 Jim Palmer .20 .50
195 Jack Morris .02 .10
196 Steve Howe .02 .10
197 Harold Baines .02 .10
198 Bill Doran .02 .10
199 Willie Hernandez .02 .10
200 Andre Dawson .20 .50
201 Bruce Kison .01 .05
202 Bobby Cox MG .02 .10
203 Matt Keough .01 .05
204 Ron Guidry AS .02 .10
205 Greg Minton .01 .05
206 Al Holland .01 .05
207 Luis Leal .01 .05
208 Jose Oquendo RC .01 .05
209 Leon Durham .01 .05
210 Joe Morgan .30 .75
Now with Athletics
211 Lou Whitaker .02 .10
212 George Brett 1.25 3.00
213 Bruce Hurst .01 .05
214 Steve Carlton .40 1.00
215 Tippy Martinez .01 .05
216 Ken Landreaux .01 .05
217 Alan Ashby .01 .05
218 Dennis Eckersley .20 .50
219 Craig McMurtry .01 .05
220 Fernando Valenzuela .02 .10
221 Cliff Johnson .01 .05
222 Rick Honeycutt .01 .05
223 George Brett AS .60 1.50
224 Rusty Staub .02 .10
225 Lee Mazzilli .01 .05
226 Pat Putnam .01 .05
227 Bob Welch .02 .10
228 Rick Cerone .01 .05
229 Lee Lacy .01 .05
230 Rickey Henderson .75 2.00
231 Gary Redus .01 .05
232 Tim Wallach .02 .10

233 Checklist 133-264 .01 .05
234 Rafael Ramirez .01 .05
235 Matt Young RC .01 .05
236 Ellis Valentine .01 .05
237 John Castino .01 .05
238 Eric Show .01 .05
239 Bob Horner .01 .05
240 Eddie Murray .50 1.25
241 Billy Almon .01 .05
242 Greg Brock .01 .05
243 Bruce Sutter .02 .10
244 Dwight Evans .02 .10
245 Rick Sutcliffe .02 .10
246 Terry Crowley .01 .05
247 Fred Lynn .02 .10
248 Bill Dawley .01 .05
249 Dave Stapleton .01 .05
250 Bill Madlock .01 .05
251 Jim Sundberg .02 .10
Now with Brewers
252 Steve Yeager .01 .05
253 Jim Wohlford .01 .05
254 Shane Rawley .01 .05
255 Bruce Benedict .01 .05
256 Dave Geisel .01 .05
Now with Mariners
257 Julio Cruz .01 .05
258 Luis Sanchez .01 .05
259 Von Hayes .01 .05
260 Scott McGregor .01 .05
261 Tom Seaver .75 2.00
Now with White Sox
262 Doug Flynn .01 .05
263 Wayne Gross .01 .05
Now with Orioles
264 Larry Gura .01 .05
265 John Montefusco .01 .05
266 Dave Winfield AS .20 .50
267 Tim Lollar .01 .05
268 Ron Washington .01 .05
269 Mickey Rivers .01 .05
270 Mookie Wilson .02 .10
271 Moose Haas .01 .05
272 Rick Dempsey .02 .10
273 Dan Quisenberry .01 .05
274 Steve Henderson .01 .05
275 Len Matuszek .01 .05
276 Frank Tanana .02 .10
277 Dave Righetti .01 .05
278 Jorge Bell .08 .25
279 Ivan DeJesus .01 .05
280 Floyd Bannister .01 .05
281 Dale Murray .01 .05
282 Andre Robertson .01 .05
283 Rollie Fingers .20 .50
284 Tommy John .08 .25
285 Darrell Porter .01 .05
286 Lary Sorensen .02 .10
Now with Athletics
287 Warren Cromartie .02 .10
Now playing in Japan
288 Jim Beattie .01 .05
289 Blue Jays Leaders .02 .10
Lloyd Moseby
Dave Stieb/(Team
290 Dave Dravecky .02 .10
291 Eddie Murray AS .20 .50
292 Greg Bargar .01 .05
293 Tom Underwood .02 .10
Now with Orioles
294 U.L. Washington .01 .05
295 Mike Flanagan .01 .05
296 Rich Gedman .01 .05
297 Bruce Berenyi .01 .05
298 Jim Gantner .02 .10
299 Bill Caudill .02 .10
Now with Athletics
300 Pete Rose 1.00 2.50
Now with Expos
301 Steve Kemp .01 .05
302 Barry Bonnell .02 .10
Now with Mariners
303 Joel Youngblood .01 .05
304 Rick Langford .01 .05
305 Roy Smalley .01 .05
306 Ken Griffey .02 .10
307 Al Oliver .02 .10
308 Ron Hassey .01 .05
309 Len Barker .01 .05
310 Willie McGee .08 .25
311 Jerry Koosman .02 .10
Now with Phillies
312 Jorge Orta .02 .10
Now with Royals
313 Pete Vuckovich .01 .05
314 George Wright .01 .05
315 Bob Grich .02 .10
316 Jesse Barfield .02 .10
317 Willie Upshaw .01 .05
318 Bill Gullickson .01 .05
319 Ray Burris .02 .10
Now with Athletics
320 Bob Stanley .01 .05
321 Ray Knight .01 .05
322 Ken Schrom .01 .05
323 Johnny Ray .01 .05
324 Brian Giles .01 .05
325 Darrell Evans .02 .10
Now with Tigers
326 Mike Caldwell .01 .05
327 Ruppert Jones .01 .05
328 Chris Speier .01 .05
329 Bobby Castillo .01 .05
330 John Candelaria .01 .05
331 Bucky Dent .02 .10
332 Expos Leaders .02 .10
Al Oliver
Charlie Lea/(Team check
333 Larry Herndon .01 .05
334 Chuck Rainey .01 .05
335 Don Baylor .02 .10
336 Bob James .01 .05
337 Jim Clancy .01 .05
338 Duane Kuiper .01 .05
339 Roy Lee Jackson .01 .05
340 Hal McRae .02 .10
341 Larry McWilliams .01 .05
342 Tim Foli .02 .10
Now with Yankees
343 Fergie Jenkins .20 .50
344 Dickie Thon .01 .05
345 Kent Hrbek .08 .25
346 Larry Bowa .02 .10
347 Buddy Bell .02 .10
348 Toby Harrah .02 .10
Now with Yankees
349 Dan Ford .01 .05
350 George Foster .02 .10
351 Lou Piniella .02 .10
352 Dave Stewart .20 .50
353 Mike Easler .02 .10
Now with Red Sox
354 Jeff Burroughs .01 .05
355 Jason Thompson .01 .05
356 Glenn Abbott .01 .05
357 Ron Cey .02 .10
358 Bob Dernier .01 .05
359 Jim Acker .01 .05
360 Willie Randolph .02 .10
361 Mike Schmidt .60 1.50
362 David Green .01 .05
363 Cal Ripken 2.50 6.00
364 Jim Rice .02 .10
365 Steve Bedrosian .01 .05
366 Gary Carter .20 .50
367 Chili Davis .02 .10
368 Hubie Brooks .01 .05
369 Steve McCatty .01 .05
370 Tim Raines .20 .50
371 Joaquin Andujar .01 .05
372 Gary Roenicke .01 .05
373 Ron Kittle .01 .05
374 Rich Dauer .01 .05
375 Dennis Leonard .01 .05
376 Rick Burleson .01 .05
377 Eric Rasmussen .01 .05
378 Dave Winfield .20 .50
379 Checklist 265-396 .01 .05
380 Steve Garvey .08 .25
381 Jack Clark .02 .10
382 Odell Jones .01 .05
383 Terry Puhl .01 .05
384 Joe Niekro .02 .10
385 Tony Perez .30 .75
Now with Reds
386 George Hendrick AS .01 .05
387 Johnny Ray AS .01 .05
388 Mike Schmidt AS .20 .50
389 Ozzie Smith AS .40 1.00
390 Tim Raines AS .08 .25
391 Dale Murphy AS .08 .25
392 Andre Dawson AS .08 .25
393 Gary Carter AS .02 .10
394 Steve Rogers AS .01 .05
395 Steve Carlton AS .20 .50
396 Jesse Orosco AS .01 .05

1985 O-Pee-Chee

This set is an abridgement of the 1985 Topps set. The 396 standard-size cards comprising the 1985 O-Pee-Chee set differ from the cards of the 1985 Topps set by having a higher ratio of cards of players from the two Canadian teams, a practice begun by O-Pee-Chee in 1977 and continued to 1988. The set contains virtually the same pictures for the players also featured in the 1985 Topps issue. The fronts feature white-bordered color player photos. The player's name, position and team name and logo appear at the bottom of the photo. The green and white horizontal backs carry the player's name and biography at the top. The player's major league statistics and bilingual profile follow below. A bilingual trivia question and answer round out the back. The O-Pee-Chee logo appears on the front of every card. Notable Rookie Cards include Dwight Gooden and Kirby Puckett.

COMPLETE SET (396) 15.00 40.00
1 Tom Seaver .20 .50
2 Gary Lavelle .02 .10
Traded to Blue Jays 1-26-85
3 Tim Wallach .02 .10
4 Jim Wohlford .01 .05
5 Jeff Robinson .01 .05
6 Willie Wilson .01 .05
7 Cliff Johnson .02 .10
Free Agent with Rangers 12-20-84
8 Willie Randolph .02 .10
9 Larry Herndon .01 .05
10 Kirby Puckett RC 4.00 10.00
11 Mookie Wilson .02 .10
12 Dave Lopes .02 .10
Traded to Cubs 8-81-84
13 Tim Lollar .02 .10
Traded to White Sox 12-6-84
14 Chris Bando .01 .05
15 Jerry Koosman .02 .10
16 Bobby Meacham .01 .05
17 Mike Scott .01 .05
18 Rich Gedman .01 .05
19 George Frazier .01 .05
20 Chet Lemon .01 .05
21 Dave Concepcion .02 .10
22 Jason Thompson .01 .05
23 Bret Saberhagen RC* .40 1.00
24 Jesse Barfield .01 .05
25 Steve Bedrosian .01 .05
26 Roy Smalley .02 .10
Traded to Twins 2-19-85
27 Bruce Berenyi .01 .05
28 Butch Wynegar .01 .05
29 Alan Ashby .01 .05
30 Cal Ripken 1.50 4.00
31 Luis Leal .01 .05
32 Dave Dravecky .02 .10
33 Tito Landrum .01 .05
34 Pedro Guerrero .02 .10
35 Graig Nettles .02 .10
36 Fred Breining .01 .05
37 Roy Lee Jackson .01 .05
38 Steve Henderson .01 .05
39 Gary Pettis UER/(Photo actually .02 .10
Gary's little
b
40 Phil Niekro .20 .50
41 Dwight Gooden RC 1.25 3.00
42 Luis Sanchez .01 .05
43 Lee Smith .20 .50
44 Dickie Thon .01 .05
45 Greg Minton .01 .05
46 Mike Flanagan .01 .05
47 Bud Black .01 .05
48 Tony Fernandez .20 .50
49 Carlton Fisk .20 .50
50 John Candelaria .01 .05
51 Bob Watson .02 .10
Announced his Retirement
52 Rick Leach .01 .05
53 Rick Rhoden .01 .05
54 Cesar Cedeno .02 .10
55 Frank Tanana .01 .05
56 Larry Bowa .02 .10
57 Willie McGee .02 .10
58 Rich Dauer .01 .05
59 Jorge Bell .02 .10
60 George Hendrick .02 .10
Traded to Pirates 12-12-84
61 Donnie Moore .02 .10
Drafted by Angels 1-24-85
62 Mike Ramsey .01 .05
63 Nolan Ryan 1.25 3.00
64 Mark Bailey .01 .05
65 Bill Buckner .02 .10
66 Jerry Reuss .01 .05
67 Mike Schmidt .40 1.00
68 Von Hayes .01 .05
69 Phil Bradley .02 .10
70 Don Baylor .02 .10
71 Julio Cruz .01 .05
72 Rick Sutcliffe .01 .05
73 Storm Davis .01 .05
74 Mike Krukow .01 .05
75 Willie Upshaw .01 .05
76 Craig Lefferts .01 .05
77 Lloyd Moseby .01 .05
78 Ron Davis .01 .05
79 Rick Mahler .01 .05
80 Keith Hernandez .02 .10
81 Vance Law .02 .10
Traded to Expos 12-7-84
82 Joe Price .01 .05
83 Dennis Lamp .01 .05
84 Gary Ward .01 .05
85 Mike Marshall .01 .05
86 Marvell Wynne .01 .05
87 David Green .01 .05
88 Bryn Smith .01 .05
89 Sixto Lezcano .02 .10
Free Agent with Pirates 1-26-85
90 Rich Gossage .02 .10
91 Jeff Burroughs .02 .10
Purchased by Blue Jays 12-22-84
92 Bobby Brown .01 .05
93 Oscar Gamble .01 .05
94 Rick Dempsey .02 .10
95 Jose Cruz .02 .10
96 Johnny Ray .01 .05
97 Joel Youngblood .01 .05
98 Eddie Whitson .02 .10
Free Agent with 12-28-84
99 Milt Wilcox .01 .05
100 George Brett 1.25 3.00
101 Jim Acker .01 .05
102 Jim Sundberg .02 .10
Traded to Royals 1-18-85
103 Ozzie Virgil .01 .05
104 Mike Fitzgerald .02 .10
Traded to Expos 12-10-84
105 Ron Kittle .01 .05
106 Pascual Perez .01 .05
107 Barry Bonnell .01 .05
108 Lou Whitaker .08 .25
109 Gary Roenicke .01 .05
110 Alejandro Pena .01 .05
111 Doug DeCinces .01 .05
112 Doug Flynn .01 .05
113 Tom Herr .02 .10
114 Bob James .02 .10
Traded to White Sox 12-7-84
115 Rickey Henderson 1.25 3.00
Traded to Yankees 12-8-84
116 Pete Rose .20 .50
117 Greg Gross .01 .05
118 Eric Show .01 .05
119 Buck Martinez .02 .10
120 Steve Kemp .01 .05
Traded to Pirates 12-20-84
121 Checklist 1-132 .01 .05
122 Tom Brunansky .02 .10
123 Dave Kingman .02 .10
124 Garry Templeton .01 .05
125 Kent Tekulve .01 .05
126 Darryl Strawberry .20 .50
127 Mark Gubicza RC .02 .10
128 Ernie Whitt .01 .05
129 Don Robinson .01 .05
130 Al Oliver .02 .10
Traded to Dodgers 2-4-85
131 Mario Soto .01 .05
132 Jeff Leonard .01 .05
133 Andre Dawson .20 .50
134 Bruce Hurst .01 .05
135 Bobby Cox MG/(Team checklist back).02 .10
136 Matt Young .01 .05
137 Bob Forsch .01 .05
138 Ron Darling .02 .10
139 Steve Trout .01 .05
140 Geoff Zahn .01 .05
141 Ken Forsch .01 .05
142 Jerry Willard .01 .05
143 Bill Gullickson .01 .05
144 Mike Mason .01 .05
145 Alvin Davis .02 .10
146 Gary Redus .01 .05
147 Willie Aikens .01 .05
148 Steve Yeager .01 .05
149 Dickie Noles .01 .05
150 Jim Rice .02 .10
151 Moose Haas .01 .05
152 Steve Balboni .01 .05
153 Frank LaCorte .01 .05
154 Angel Salazar .02 .10
Drafted by Cardinals 1-24-85
155 Bob Grich .02 .10
156 Craig Reynolds .01 .05
157 Bill Madlock .01 .05
158 Pat Tabler .01 .05
159 Don Slaught .02 .10
Traded to Rangers 1-18-85
160 Lance Parrish .02 .10
161 Ken Schrom .01 .05
162 Wally Backman .01 .05
163 Dennis Eckersley .20 .50
164 Dave Collins .02 .10
Traded to A's 12-8-84
165 Dusty Baker .08 .25
166 Claudell Washington .01 .05
167 Rick Camp .01 .05
168 Garth Iorg .01 .05
169 Shane Rawley .01 .05
170 George Foster .02 .10
171 Tony Bernazard .01 .05
172 Don Sutton .30 .75
Traded to A's 12-8-84
173 Jerry Remy .01 .05
174 Rick Honeycutt .01 .05
175 Dave Parker .02 .10
176 Buddy Bell .02 .10
177 Steve Garvey .08 .25
178 Miguel Dilone .01 .05
179 Tommy John .08 .25
180 Dave Winfield .20 .50
181 Alan Trammell .08 .25
182 Rollie Fingers .20 .50
183 Larry McWilliams .01 .05
184 Carmen Castillo .01 .05
185 Al Holland .01 .05
186 Jerry Mumphrey .01 .05
187 Chris Chambliss .02 .10
188 Jim Clancy .01 .05
189 Glenn Wilson .01 .05
190 Rusty Staub .02 .10
191 Ozzie Smith .75 2.00
192 Howard Johnson .08 .25
Traded to Mets 12-7-84
193 Jimmy Key RC .20 .50
194 Terry Kennedy .01 .05
195 Glenn Hubbard .01 .05
196 Pete O'Brien .01 .05
197 Keith Moreland .01 .05
198 Eddie Milner .01 .05
199 Dave Engle .01 .05
200 Reggie Jackson .20 .50
201 Burt Hooton .02 .10
Free Agent with Rangers 1-3-85
202 Gorman Thomas .01 .05
203 Larry Parrish .01 .05
204 Bob Stanley .01 .05
205 Steve Rogers .01 .05
206 Phil Garner .01 .05
207 Ed VandeBerg .01 .05
208 Jack Clark .08 .25
Traded to Cardinals 2-1-85
209 Bill Campbell .01 .05
210 Gary Matthews .01 .05
211 Dave Palmer .01 .05
212 Tony Perez .20 .50
213 Sammy Stewart .01 .05
214 John Tudor .02 .10
Traded to Cardinals 12-12-84
215 Bob Brenly .02 .10
216 Jim Gantner .01 .05
217 Bryan Clark .01 .05
218 Doyle Alexander .01 .05
219 Bo Diaz .01 .05
220 Fred Lynn .02 .10
Free Agent with Orioles 12-11-84
221 Eddie Murray .20 .50
222 Hubie Brooks .01 .05
Traded to Expos 12-10-84
223 Tom Hume .01 .05
224 Al Cowens .01 .05
225 Mike Boddicker .01 .05
226 Len Matuszek .01 .05
227 Danny Darwin .02 .10
Traded to Brewers 1-18-85
228 Scott McGregor .01 .05
229 Dave LaPoint .02 .10
Traded to Giants 2-1-85
230 Gary Carter .30 .75
Traded to Mets 12-10-84
231 Joaquin Andujar .01 .05
232 Rafael Ramirez .01 .05
233 Wayne Gross .01 .05
234 Neil Allen .01 .05
235 Garry Maddox .01 .05
236 Mark Thurmond .01 .05
237 Julio Franco .08 .25
238 Ray Burris .02 .10
Traded to Brewers 12-8-84
239 Tim Teufel .01 .05
240 Dave Stieb .01 .05
241 Brett Butler .02 .10
242 Greg Brock .01 .05
243 Barbaro Garbey .01 .05
244 Greg Walker .01 .05
245 Chili Davis .02 .10
246 Darrell Porter .01 .05
247 Tippy Martinez .01 .05
248 Terry Forster .01 .05
249 Harold Baines .08 .25
250 Jesse Orosco .02 .10
251 Brad Gulden .01 .05
252 Mike Hargrove .02 .10
253 Nick Esasky .01 .05
254 Frank Williams .01 .05
255 Lonnie Smith .01 .05
256 Daryl Sconiers .01 .05
257 Bryan Little .02 .10
Traded to White Sox 12-7-84
258 Terry Francona .02 .10
259 Mark Langston RC .20 .50
260 Dave Righetti .02 .10
261 Checklist 133-264 .01 .05
262 Bob Horner .01 .05
263 Mel Hall .01 .05
264 John Shelby .01 .05
265 Juan Samuel .01 .05
266 Frank Viola .02 .10
267 Jim Fanning MG#Now Vice President
Player#Developme .01 .05
268 Dick Ruthven .01 .05
269 Bobby Ramos .01 .05
270 Dan Quisenberry .01 .05
271 Dwight Evans .02 .10
272 Andre Thornton .01 .05
273 Orel Hershiser .75 2.00
274 Ray Knight .01 .05
275 Bill Caudill .02 .10
Traded to Blue Jays 12-8-84
276 Charlie Hough .02 .10
277 Tim Raines .08 .25
278 Mike Squires .01 .05
279 Alex Trevino .01 .05
280 Ron Romanick .01 .05
281 Tom Niedenfuer .01 .05
282 Mike Stenhouse .02 .10
Traded to Twins 1-9-85
283 Terry Puhl .01 .05
284 Hal McRae .01 .05
285 Dan Driessen .01 .05
286 Rudy Law .01 .05
287 Walt Terrell .02 .10
Traded to Tigers 12-7-84
288 Jeff Kunkel .01 .05
289 Bob Knepper .01 .05
290 Cecil Cooper .02 .10
291 Bob Welch .01 .05
292 Frank Pastore .01 .05
293 Dan Schatzeder .01 .05
294 Tom Nieto .01 .05
295 Joe Niekro .02 .10
296 Ryne Sandberg .75 2.00
297 Gary Lucas .01 .05
298 John Castino .01 .05
299 Bill Doran .01 .05
300 Rod Carew .20 .50
301 John Montefusco .01 .05
302 Johnnie LeMaster .01 .05
303 Jim Beattie .01 .05
304 Gary Gaetti .02 .10
305 Dale Berra .02 .10
Traded to Yankees 12-20-84
306 Rick Reuschel .02 .10
307 Ken Oberkfell .01 .05
308 Kent Hrbek .02 .10
309 Mike Witt .01 .05
310 Manny Trillo .01 .05
311 Jim Gott .02 .10
Traded to Giants 1-26-85
312 LaMarr Hoyt .02 .10
Traded to Padres 12-6-84
313 Dave Schmidt .01 .05
314 Ron Oester .01 .05
315 Doug Sisk .01 .05
316 John Lowenstein .01 .05
317 Derrel Thomas .02 .10
Traded to Angels 9-6-84
318 Ted Simmons .02 .10
319 Darrell Evans .02 .10
320 Dale Murphy .08 .25
321 Ricky Horton .01 .05
322 Ken Phelps .01 .05
323 Lee Mazzilli .02 .10
324 Don Mattingly 1.50 4.00
325 John Denny .01 .05
326 Ken Singleton .01 .05
327 Brook Jacoby .01 .05
328 Greg Luzinski .02 .10
Announced his Retirement
329 Bob Ojeda .01 .05
330 Leon Durham .01 .05
331 Bill Laskey .01 .05
332 Ben Oglivie .01 .05
333 Willie Hernandez .01 .05
334 Bob Dernier .01 .05
335 Bruce Benedict .01 .05
336 Rance Mulliniks .01 .05
337 Rick Cerone .02 .10
Traded to Braves 12-6-84
338 Britt Burns .01 .05
339 Danny Heep .01 .05
340 Robin Yount .20 .50
341 Andy Van Slyke .08 .25
342 Curt Wilkerson .01 .05
343 Bill Russell .01 .05
344 Dave Henderson .01 .05
345 Charlie Lea .01 .05
346 Terry Pendleton RC .20 .50
347 Carney Lansford .01 .05
348 Bob Boone .02 .10
349 Mike Easler .01 .05
350 Wade Boggs .40 1.00
351 Atlee Hammaker .01 .05
352 Joe Morgan .20 .50
353 Damaso Garcia .01 .05
354 Floyd Bannister .01 .05
355 Bert Blyleven .02 .10
356 John Butcher .01 .05
357 Fernando Valenzuela .02 .10
358 Tony Pena .02 .10
359 Mike Smithson .01 .05
360 Steve Carlton .20 .50
361 Alfredo Griffin .02 .10
Traded to A's 12-8-84
362 Craig McMurtry .01 .05
363 Bill Dawley .01 .05
364 Richard Dotson .01 .05
365 Carmelo Martinez .01 .05
366 Ron Cey .02 .10
367 Tony Scott .01 .05
368 Dave Bergman .01 .05
369 Steve Sax .01 .05
370 Bruce Sutter .02 .10
371 Mickey Rivers .01 .05
372 Kirk Gibson .02 .10
373 Scott Sanderson .01 .05
374 Brian Downing .01 .05
375 Jeff Reardon .02 .10
376 Frank DiPino .01 .05
377 Checklist 265-396 .01 .05
378 Alan Wiggins .01 .05
379 Charles Hudson .01 .05
380 Ken Griffey .02 .10
381 Tom Paciorek .01 .05
382 Jack Morris .02 .10
383 Tony Gwynn 1.25 3.00
384 Jody Davis .01 .05
385 Jose DeLeon .01 .05
386 Bob Kearney .01 .05
387 George Wright .01 .05
388 Ron Guidry .02 .10
389 Rick Manning .01 .05
390 Sid Fernandez .02 .10
391 Bruce Bochte .01 .05
392 Dan Petry .01 .05
393 Tim Stoddard .02 .10
Free Agent with Padres 1-2-85
394 Tony Armas .01 .05
395 Paul Molitor .20 .50
396 Mike Heath .01 .05

1985 O-Pee-Chee Posters

COMPLETE SET (24) 2.50 6.00
1 Mike Fitzgerald .08 .25
2 Dan Driessen .08 .25
3 Dave Palmer .08 .25
4 U.L. Washington .08 .25
5 Hubie Brooks .08 .25
6 Tim Wallach .20 .50
7 Tim Raines .30 .75
8 Herm Winningham .08 .25
9 Andre Dawson .40 1.00
10 Charlie Lea .08 .25
11 Steve Rogers .08 .25
12 Jeff Reardon .20 .50
13 Buck Martinez .20 .50
14 Willie Upshaw .08 .25
15 Damaso Garcia UER .08 .25
(Misspelled Domaso)
16 Tony Fernandez .30 .75
17 Rance Mulliniks .08 .25
18 George Bell .20 .50
19 Lloyd Moseby .08 .25
20 Jesse Barfield .20 .50
21 Doyle Alexander .08 .25
22 Dave Stieb .20 .50
23 Bill Caudill .08 .25
24 Gary Lavelle .08 .25

1986 O-Pee-Chee

This set is an abridgement of the 1986 Topps set. The 396 standard-size cards comprising the 1986 O-Pee-Chee set differ from the cards of the 1986 Topps set by having a higher ratio of cards of players from the two Canadian teams, a practice begun by O-Pee-Chee in 1977 and continued to 1988. The fronts feature black-and white-bordered color player photos. The player's name appears within the white margin at the bottom. His team name appears within the black margin at the top and his position appears within a colored circle at the photo's lower left. The red horizontal backs carry the player's name and biography at the top. The player's major league statistics follow below. Some backs also have bilingual career highlights, some have bilingual baseball facts and still others have neither. The asterisked cards have an extra line on the front inside the picture area indicating team change. The O-Pee-Chee logo appears on the front of every card.

COMPLETE SET (396) 10.00 25.00
1 Pete Rose .75 2.00
2 Ken Landreaux .01 .05
3 Rob Picciolo .01 .05
4 Steve Garvey .05 .15
5 Andy Hawkins .01 .05
6 Rudy Law .01 .05
7 Lonnie Smith .01 .05
8 Dwayne Murphy .01 .05
9 Moose Haas .01 .05
10 Tony Gwynn .60 1.50
11 Bob Ojeda .02 .10
Now with Mets
12 Jose Uribe .01 .05
13 Bob Kearney .01 .05
14 Julio Cruz .01 .05
15 Eddie Whitson .01 .05
16 Rick Schu .01 .05
17 Mike Stenhouse .02 .10
Now with Red Sox
18 Lou Thornton .01 .05
19 Ryne Sandberg .30 .75
20 Lou Whitaker .02 .10
21 Mark Brouhard .01 .05
22 Gary Lavelle .01 .05
23 Manny Lee .01 .05
24 Don Slaught .01 .05
25 Willie Wilson .01 .05
26 Mike Marshall .01 .05
27 Ray Knight .01 .05
28 Mario Soto .01 .05
29 Dave Anderson .01 .05
30 Eddie Murray .30 .75
31 Dusty Baker .02 .10
32 Steve Yeager .02 .10
Now with Mariners
33 Andy Van Slyke .02 .10
34 Dave Righetti .01 .05
35 Jeff Reardon .02 .10
36 Burt Hooton .01 .05
37 Johnny Ray .01 .05
38 Glenn Hoffman .01 .05
39 Rick Mahler .01 .05
40 Ken Griffey .02 .10
41 Brad Wellman .01 .05
42 Joe Hesketh .01 .05
43 Mark Salas .01 .05
44 Jorge Orta .01 .05
45 Damaso Garcia .01 .05
46 Jim Acker .01 .05
47 Bill Madlock .02 .10
48 Bill Almon .01 .05
49 Rick Manning .01 .05
50 Dan Quisenberry .01 .05
51 Jim Gantner .01 .05
52 Kevin Bass .01 .05
53 Len Dykstra RC .40 1.00
54 John Franco .05 .15
55 Fred Lynn .02 .10
56 Jim Morrison .01 .05
57 Bill Doran .01 .05
58 Leon Durham .01 .05
59 Andre Thornton .01 .05
60 Dwight Evans .02 .10
61 Larry Herndon .01 .05
62 Bob Boone .02 .10
63 Kent Hrbek .05 .15
64 Floyd Bannister .01 .05
65 Harold Baines .05 .15
66 Pat Tabler .01 .05
67 Carmelo Martinez .01 .05
68 Ed Lynch .01 .05
69 George Foster .02 .10
70 Dave Winfield .15 .40
71 Ken Schrom .01 .05
Now with Indians
72 Toby Harrah .01 .05
73 Jackie Gutierrez .01 .05
Now with Orioles
74 Rance Mulliniks .01 .05
75 Jose DeLeon .01 .05
76 Ron Romanick .01 .05
77 Charlie Leibrandt .01 .05
78 Bruce Benedict .01 .05
79 Dave Schmidt .01 .05
Now with White Sox
80 Darryl Strawberry .05 .15
81 Wayne Krenchicki .01 .05
82 Tippy Martinez .01 .05
83 Phil Garner .02 .10
84 Darrell Porter .02 .10
Now with Rangers
85 Tony Perez .15 .40
Eric Davis also
shown in photo
86 Tom Waddell .01 .05
87 Tim Hulett .01 .05
88 Barbaro Garbey .01 .05
Now with A's
89 Randy St. Claire .01 .05
90 Garry Templeton .01 .05
91 Tim Teufel .02 .10
Now with Mets
92 Al Cowens .01 .05
93 Scot Thompson .01 .05
94 Tom Herr .01 .05
95 Ozzie Virgil .02 .10
Now with Braves
96 Jose Cruz .01 .05
97 Gary Gaetti .02 .10
98 Roger Clemens 2.00 5.00
99 Vance Law .01 .05
100 Nolan Ryan .60 1.50
101 Mike Smithson .01 .05
102 Rafael Santana .01 .05
103 Darrell Evans .02 .10
104 Rich Gossage .08 .25
105 Gary Ward .01 .05
106 Jim Gott .01 .05
107 Rafael Ramirez .01 .05
108 Ted Power .01 .05
109 Ron Guidry .02 .10
110 Scott McGregor .01 .05
111 Mike Scioscia .02 .10
112 Glenn Hubbard .01 .05
113 U.L. Washington .01 .05
114 Al Oliver .02 .10
115 Jay Howell .01 .05
116 Brook Jacoby .01 .05
117 Willie McGee .02 .10
118 Jerry Royster .01 .05
119 Barry Bonnell .01 .05
120 Steve Carlton .15 .40
121 Alfredo Griffin .01 .05
122 David Green .02 .10
Now with Brewers
123 Greg Walker .01 .05
124 Frank Tanana .01 .05
125 Dave Lopes .02 .10
126 Mike Krukow .01 .05
127 Jack Howell .01 .05
128 Greg Harris .01 .05
129 Herm Winningham .01 .05
130 Alan Trammell .05 .15
131 Checklist 1-132 .01 .05
132 Razor Shines .01 .05
133 Bruce Sutter .15 .40
134 Carney Lansford .01 .05
135 Joe Niekro .02 .10
136 Ernie Whitt .01 .05
137 Charlie Moore .01 .05
138 Mel Hall .01 .05
139 Roger McDowell .01 .05
140 John Candelaria .01 .05
141 Bob Rodgers MG CL .01 .05
142 Manny Trillo .02 .10
Now with Cubs
143 Dave Palmer .02 .10
Now with Braves
144 Robin Yount .08 .25
145 Pedro Guerrero .02 .10
146 Von Hayes .01 .05
147 Lance Parrish .02 .10
148 Mike Heath .02 .10
Now with Cardinals
149 Brett Butler .02 .10
150 Joaquin Andujar .02 .10
Now with A's
151 Graig Nettles .02 .10
152 Pete Vuckovich .01 .05
153 Jason Thompson .01 .05
154 Bert Roberge .01 .05
155 Bob Grich .02 .10
156 Roy Smalley .01 .05
157 Ron Hassey .01 .05
158 Bob Stanley .01 .05
159 Orel Hershiser .15 .40
160 Chet Lemon .01 .05
161 Terry Puhl .01 .05
162 Dave LaPoint .02 .10
Now with Tigers
163 Onix Concepcion .01 .05
164 Steve Balboni .01 .05
165 Mike Davis .01 .05
166 Dickie Thon .01 .05
167 Zane Smith .01 .05
168 Jeff Burroughs .01 .05
169 Alex Trevino .02 .10
Now with Dodgers
170 Gary Carter .15 .40
171 Tito Landrum .01 .05
172 Sammy Stewart .02 .10
Now with Red Sox
173 Wayne Gross .01 .05

174 Britt Burns .02 .10
Now with Yankees
175 Steve Sax .01 .05
176 Jody Davis .01 .05
177 Joel Youngblood .01 .05
178 Fernando Valenzuela .02 .10
179 Storm Davis .01 .05
180 Don Mattingly .50 1.25
181 Steve Bedrosian .02 .10
Now with Phillies
182 Jesse Orosco .02 .10
183 Gary Roenicke .02 .10
Now with Yankees
184 Don Baylor .02 .10
185 Rollie Fingers .15 .40
186 Ruppert Jones .01 .05
187 Scott Fletcher .02 .10
Now with Rangers
188 Bob Dernier .01 .05
189 Mike Mason .01 .05
190 George Hendrick .01 .05
191 Wally Backman .01 .05
192 Oddibe McDowell .01 .05
193 Bruce Hurst .01 .05
194 Ron Cey .02 .10
195 Dave Concepcion .02 .10
196 Doyle Alexander .01 .05
197 Dale Murphy .20 .50
198 Mark Langston .02 .10
199 Dennis Eckersley .15 .40
200 Mike Schmidt .15 .40
201 Nick Esasky .01 .05
202 Ken Dayley .01 .05
203 Rick Cerone .01 .05
204 Larry McWilliams .01 .05
205 Brian Downing .01 .05
206 Danny Darwin .01 .05
207 Bill Caudill .01 .05
208 Dave Rozema .01 .05
209 Eric Show .01 .05
210 Brad Komminsk .01 .05
211 Chris Bando .01 .05
212 Chris Speier .01 .05
213 Jim Clancy .01 .05
214 Randy Bush .01 .05
215 Frank White .02 .10
216 Dan Petry .01 .05
217 Tim Wallach .01 .05
218 Mitch Webster .01 .05
219 Dennis Lamp .01 .05
220 Bob Horner .01 .05
221 Dave Henderson .01 .05
222 Dave Smith .01 .05
223 Willie Upshaw .01 .05
224 Cesar Cedeno .02 .10
225 Ron Darling .01 .05
226 Lee Lacy .01 .05
227 John Tudor .01 .05
228 Jim Presley .01 .05
229 Bill Gullickson .02 .10
Now with Reds
230 Terry Kennedy .01 .05
231 Bob Knepper .01 .05
232 Rick Rhoden .01 .05
233 Richard Dotson .01 .05
234 Jesse Barfield .01 .05
235 Butch Wynegar .01 .05
236 Jerry Reuss .02 .10
237 Juan Samuel .01 .05
238 Larry Parrish .01 .05
239 Bill Buckner .02 .10
240 Pat Sheridan .01 .05
241 Tony Fernandez .05 .15
242 Rich Thompson .01 .05
Now with Brewers
243 Rickey Henderson .20 .50
244 Craig Lefferts .01 .05
245 Jim Sundberg .01 .05
246 Phil Niekro .15 .40
247 Terry Harper .01 .05
248 Spike Owen .01 .05
249 Bret Saberhagen .08 .25
250 Dwight Gooden .08 .25
251 Rich Dauer .01 .05
252 Keith Hernandez .02 .10
253 Bo Diaz .01 .05
254 Ozzie Guillen RC .60 1.50
255 Tony Armas .01 .05
256 Andre Dawson .08 .25
257 Doug DeCinces .01 .05
258 Tim Burke .01 .05
259 Dennis Boyd .01 .05
260 Tony Pena .01 .05
261 Sal Butera .02 .10
Now with Reds
262 Wade Boggs .30 .75
263 Checklist 133-264 .01 .05
264 Ron Oester .01 .05
265 Ron Davis .01 .05
266 Keith Moreland .01 .05
267 Paul Molitor .20 .50
268 John Denny .02 .10
Now with Reds
269 Frank Viola .02 .10
270 Jack Morris .02 .10
271 Dave Collins .02 .10
Now with Tigers
272 Bert Blyleven .02 .10
273 Jerry Willard .01 .05
274 Matt Young .01 .05
275 Charlie Hough .02 .10
276 Dave Dravecky .02 .10
277 Garth Iorg .01 .05
278 Hal McRae .01 .05
279 Curt Wilkerson .01 .05
280 Tim Raines .02 .10
281 Bill Laskey .02 .10
Now with Giants
282 Jerry Mumphrey .02 .10
Now with Cubs
283 Pat Clements .01 .05
284 Bob James .01 .05
285 Buddy Bell .02 .10
286 Tom Brookens .01 .05
287 Dave Parker .02 .10
288 Ron Kittle .01 .05
289 Johnnie LeMaster .01 .05
290 Carlton Fisk .15 .40
291 Jimmy Key .05 .15
292 Gary Matthews .01 .05
293 Marvell Wynne .01 .05
294 Danny Cox .01 .05
295 Kirk Gibson .02 .10
296 Mariano Duncan RC .05 .15
297 Ozzie Smith .40 1.00
298 Craig Reynolds .01 .05
299 Bryn Smith .01 .05
300 George Brett .40 1.00
301 Walt Terrell .01 .05
302 Greg Gross .01 .05
303 Claudell Washington .01 .05
304 Howard Johnson .02 .10
305 Phil Bradley .01 .05
306 R.J. Reynolds .01 .05
307 Bob Brenly .01 .05
308 Hubie Brooks .01 .05
309 Alvin Davis .01 .05
310 Donnie Hill .01 .05
311 Dick Schofield .01 .05
312 Tom Filer .01 .05
313 Mike Fitzgerald .01 .05
314 Marty Barrett .01 .05
315 Mookie Wilson .02 .10
316 Alan Knicely .01 .05
317 Ed Romero .01 .05
Now with Red Sox
318 Glenn Wilson .01 .05
319 Bud Black .01 .05
320 Jim Rice .02 .10
321 Terry Pendleton .05 .15
322 Dave Kingman .02 .10
323 Gary Pettis .01 .05
324 Dan Schatzeder .01 .05
325 Juan Beniquez .02 .10
Now with Orioles
326 Kent Tekulve .01 .05
327 Mike Pagliarulo .01 .05
328 Pete O'Brien .01 .05
329 Kirby Puckett .75 2.00
330 Rick Sutcliffe .01 .05
331 Alan Ashby .01 .05
332 Willie Randolph .02 .10
333 Tom Henke .02 .10
334 Ken Oberkfell .01 .05
335 Don Sutton .15 .40
336 Dan Gladden .01 .05
337 George Vukovich .01 .05
338 Jorge Bell .02 .10
339 Jim Dwyer .01 .05
340 Cal Ripken .60 1.50
341 Willie Hernandez .01 .05
342 Gary Redus .02 .10
Now with Phillies
343 Jerry Koosman .02 .10
344 Jim Wohlford .01 .05
345 Donnie Moore .01 .05
346 Floyd Youmans .01 .05
347 Gorman Thomas .01 .05
348 Cliff Johnson .01 .05
349 Ken Howell .01 .05
350 Jack Clark .02 .10
351 Gary Lucas .02 .10
Now with Angels
352 Bob Clark .01 .05
353 Dave Stieb .01 .05
354 Tony Bernazard .01 .05
355 Lee Smith .08 .25
356 Mickey Hatcher .01 .05
357 Ed VandeBerg .02 .10
Now with Dodgers
358 Rick Dempsey .01 .05
359 Bobby Cox MG .02 .10
360 Lloyd Moseby .01 .05
361 Shane Rawley .01 .05
362 Garry Maddox .01 .05
363 Buck Martinez .02 .10
364 Ed Nunez .01 .05
365 Luis Leal .01 .05
366 Dale Berra .01 .05
367 Mike Boddicker .01 .05
368 Greg Brock .01 .05
369 Al Holland .01 .05
370 Vince Coleman RC .08 .25
371 Rod Carew .15 .40
372 Ben Oglivie .01 .05
373 Lee Mazzilli .01 .05
374 Terry Francona .02 .10
375 Rich Gedman .01 .05
376 Charlie Lea .01 .05
377 Joe Carter .40 1.00
378 Bruce Bochte .01 .05
379 Bobby Meacham .01 .05
380 LaMarr Hoyt .01 .05
381 Jeff Leonard .01 .05
382 Ivan Calderon RC .02 .10
383 Chris Brown RC .01 .05
384 Steve Trout .01 .05
385 Cecil Cooper .02 .10
386 Cecil Fielder RC .60 1.50
387 Tim Flannery .01 .05
388 Chris Codiroli .01 .05
389 Glenn Davis .01 .05
390 Tom Seaver .15 .40
391 Julio Franco .05 .15
392 Tom Brunansky .01 .05
393 Rob Wilfong .01 .05
394 Reggie Jackson .15 .40
395 Scott Garrelts .01 .05
396 Checklist 265-396 .01 .05

1986 O-Pee-Chee Box Bottoms

COMPLETE SET (16) 6.00 15.00
A George Bell .08 .25
B Wade Boggs .60 1.50
C George Brett 1.50 4.00
D Vince Coleman .08 .25
E Carlton Fisk .60 1.50
F Dwight Gooden .30 .75
G Pedro Guerrero .08 .25
H Ron Guidry .20 .50
I Reggie Jackson .60 1.50
J Don Mattingly 1.50 4.00
K Oddibe McDowell .08 .25
L Willie McGee .20 .50
M Dale Murphy .40 1.00
N Pete Rose .60 1.50
O Bret Saberhagen .20 .50
P Fernando Valenzuela .20 .50

1987 O-Pee-Chee

This set is an abridgement of the 1987 Topps set. The 396 standard-size cards comprising the 1987 O-Pee-Chee set differ from the cards of the 1987 Topps set by having a higher ratio of cards of players from the two Canadian teams, a practice begun by O-Pee-Chee in 1977 and continued to 1988. The fronts feature wood grain bordered color player photos. The player's name appears in the colored rectangle at the lower right. His team logo appears at the upper left. The yellow, white and blue horizontal backs carry the player's name and bilingual position at the top. The player's major league statistics follow below. Some backs also have bilingual career highlights, some have bilingual baseball facts and still others have both or neither. The asterisked cards have an extra line on the front inside the picture area indicating team change. The O-Pee-Chee logo appears on the front of every card. Notable Rookie Cards include Barry Bonds.

COMPLETE SET (396) 6.00 15.00
1 Ken Oberkfell .01 .05
2 Jack Howell .01 .05
3 Hubie Brooks .01 .05
4 Bob Grich .02 .10
5 Rick Leach .01 .05
6 Phil Niekro .15 .40
7 Rickey Henderson .20 .50
8 Terry Pendleton .02 .10
9 Jay Tibbs .01 .05
10 Cecil Cooper .02 .10
11 Mario Soto .01 .05
12 George Bell .01 .05
13 Nick Esasky .01 .05
14 Larry McWilliams .01 .05
15 Dan Quisenberry .01 .05
16 Ed Lynch .01 .05
17 Pete O'Brien .01 .05
18 Luis Aguayo .01 .05
19 Matt Young .02 .10
Now with Dodgers
20 Gary Carter .15 .40
21 Tom Paciorek .01 .05
22 Doug DeCinces .01 .05
23 Lee Smith .05 .15
24 Jesse Barfield .01 .05
25 Bert Blyleven .02 .10
26 Greg Brock .02 .10
Now with Brewers
27 Dan Petry .01 .05
28 Rick Dempsey .02 .10
Now with Indians
29 Jimmy Key .05 .15
30 Tim Raines .02 .10
31 Bruce Hurst .01 .05
32 Manny Trillo .01 .05
33 Andy Van Slyke .02 .10
34 Ed VandeBerg .02 .10
Now with Indians
35 Sid Bream .01 .05
36 Dave Winfield .15 .40
37 Scott Garrelts .01 .05
38 Dennis Leonard .01 .05
39 Marty Barrett .01 .05
40 Dave Righetti .01 .05
41 Bo Diaz .01 .05
42 Gary Redus .01 .05
43 Tom Niedenfuer .01 .05
44 Greg Harris .01 .05
45 Jim Presley .01 .05
46 Danny Gladden .01 .05
47 Roy Smalley .01 .05
48 Wally Backman .01 .05
49 Tom Seaver .15 .40
50 Dave Smith .01 .05
51 Mel Hall .01 .05
52 Tim Flannery .01 .05
53 Julio Cruz .01 .05
54 Dick Schofield .01 .05
55 Tim Wallach .01 .05
56 Glenn Davis .01 .05
57 Darren Daulton .05 .15
58 Chico Walker .01 .05
59 Garth Iorg .01 .05
60 Tony Pena .01 .05
61 Ron Hassey .01 .05
62 Dave Dravecky .01 .05
63 Jorge Orta .01 .05
64 Al Nipper .01 .05
65 Tom Browning .01 .05
66 Marc Sullivan .01 .05
67 Todd Worrell .02 .10
68 Glenn Hubbard .01 .05
69 Carney Lansford .02 .10
70 Charlie Hough .01 .05
71 Lance McCullers .01 .05
72 Walt Terrell .01 .05
73 Bob Kearney .01 .05
74 Dan Pasqua .01 .05
75 Ron Darling .01 .05
76 Robin Yount .15 .40
77 Pat Tabler .01 .05
78 Tom Foley .01 .05
79 Juan Nieves .01 .05
80 Wally Joyner RC .20 .50
81 Wayne Krenchicki .01 .05
82 Kirby Puckett .30 .75
83 Bob Ojeda .01 .05
84 Mookie Wilson .02 .10
85 Kevin Bass .01 .05
86 Kent Tekulve .01 .05
87 Mark Salas .01 .05
88 Brian Downing .01 .05
89 Ozzie Guillen .02 .10
90 Dave Stieb .02 .10
91 Rance Mulliniks .01 .05
92 Mike Witt .01 .05
93 Charlie Moore .01 .05
94 Jose Uribe .01 .05
95 Oddibe McDowell .01 .05
96 Ray Soff .01 .05
97 Glenn Wilson .01 .05
98 Brook Jacoby .01 .05
99 Darryl Motley .02 .10
Now with Braves
100 Steve Garvey .05 .15
101 Frank White .02 .10
102 Mike Moore .01 .05
103 Rick Aguilera .02 .10
104 Buddy Bell .02 .10
105 Floyd Youmans .01 .05
106 Lou Whitaker .02 .10
107 Ozzie Smith .30 .75
108 Jim Gantner .01 .05
109 R.J. Reynolds .01 .05
110 John Tudor .01 .05
111 Alfredo Griffin .01 .05
112 Mike Flanagan .01 .05
113 Neil Allen .01 .05
114 Ken Griffey .02 .10
115 Donnie Moore .01 .05
116 Bob Horner .01 .05
117 Ron Shepherd .01 .05
118 Cliff Johnson .01 .05
119 Vince Coleman .01 .05
120 Eddie Murray .15 .40
121 Dwayne Murphy .01 .05
122 Jim Clancy .01 .05
123 Ken Landreaux .01 .05
124 Tom Nieto .02 .10
Now with Twins
125 Bob Brenly .01 .05
126 George Brett .30 .75
127 Vance Law .01 .05
128 Checklist 1-132 .01 .05
129 Bob Knepper .01 .05
130 Dwight Gooden .05 .15
131 Juan Bonilla .01 .05
132 Tim Burke .01 .05
133 Bob McClure .01 .05
134 Scott Bailes .01 .05
135 Mike Easler .02 .10
Now with Phillies
136 Ron Romanick .02 .10
Now with Yankees
137 Rich Gedman .01 .05
138 Bob Dernier .01 .05
139 John Denny .01 .05
140 Bret Saberhagen .02 .10
141 Herm Winningham .01 .05
142 Rick Sutcliffe .01 .05
143 Ryne Sandberg .15 .40
144 Mike Scioscia .02 .10
145 Charlie Kerfeld .01 .05
146 Jim Rice .02 .10
147 Steve Trout .01 .05
148 Jesse Orosco .02 .10
149 Mike Boddicker .01 .05
150 Wade Boggs .15 .40
151 Dane Iorg .01 .05
152 Rick Burleson .02 .10
Now with Orioles
153 Duane Ward RC .02 .10
154 Rick Reuschel .01 .05
155 Nolan Ryan .60 1.50
156 Bill Caudill .01 .05
157 Danny Darwin .01 .05
158 Ed Romero .01 .05
159 Bill Almon .01 .05
160 Julio Franco .02 .10
161 Kent Hrbek .02 .10
162 Chili Davis .05 .15
163 Kevin Gross .01 .05
164 Carlton Fisk .15 .40
165 Jeff Reardon .05 .15
Now with Twins
166 Bob Boone .02 .10
167 Rick Honeycutt .01 .05
168 Dan Schatzeder .01 .05
169 Jim Wohlford .01 .05
170 Phil Bradley .01 .05
171 Ken Schrom .01 .05
172 Ron Oester .01 .05
173 Juan Beniquez .02 .10
Now with Royals
174 Tony Armas .01 .05
175 Bob Stanley .01 .05
176 Steve Buechele .01 .05
177 Keith Moreland .01 .05
178 Cecil Fielder .05 .15
179 Gary Gaetti .02 .10
180 Chris Brown .01 .05
181 Tom Herr .01 .05
182 Lee Lacy .01 .05
183 Ozzie Virgil .01 .05
184 Paul Molitor .15 .40
185 Roger McDowell .01 .05
186 Mike Marshall .01 .05
187 Ken Howell .01 .05
188 Rob Deer .01 .05
189 Joe Hesketh .01 .05
190 Jim Sundberg .01 .05
191 Kelly Gruber .01 .05
192 Cory Snyder .01 .05
193 Dave Concepcion .02 .10
194 Kirk McCaskill .01 .05
195 Mike Pagliarulo .01 .05
196 Rick Manning .01 .05
197 Brett Butler .02 .10
198 Tony Gwynn .50 1.25
199 Mariano Duncan .01 .05
200 Pete Rose .15 .40
201 John Cangelosi .01 .05
202 Danny Cox .01 .05
203 Butch Wynegar .02 .10
Now with Angels
204 Chris Chambliss .02 .10
205 Graig Nettles .02 .10
206 Chet Lemon .01 .05
207 Don Aase .01 .05
208 Mike Mason .01 .05
209 Alan Trammell .05 .15
210 Lloyd Moseby .01 .05
211 Richard Dotson .01 .05
212 Mike Fitzgerald .01 .05
213 Darrell Porter .01 .05
214 Checklist 265-396 .01 .05
215 Mark Langston .01 .05
216 Steve Farr .01 .05
217 Dann Bilardello .01 .05
218 Gary Ward .02 .10
Now with Yankees
219 Cecilio Guante .02 .10
Now with Yankees
220 Joe Carter .08 .25
221 Ernie Whitt .01 .05
222 Denny Walling .01 .05
223 Charlie Leibrandt .01 .05
224 Wayne Tolleson .01 .05
225 Mike Smithson .01 .05
226 Zane Smith .01 .05
227 Terry Puhl .01 .05
228 Eric Davis .05 .15
229 Don Mattingly .30 .75
230 Don Baylor .02 .10
231 Frank Tanana .01 .05
232 Tom Brookens .01 .05
233 Steve Bedrosian .01 .05
234 Wallace Johnson .01 .05
235 Alvin Davis .01 .05
236 Tommy John .02 .10
237 Jim Morrison .01 .05
238 Ricky Horton .01 .05
239 Shane Rawley .01 .05
240 Steve Balboni .01 .05
241 Mike Krukow .01 .05
242 Rick Mahler .01 .05
243 Bill Doran .01 .05
244 Mark Clear .01 .05
245 Willie Upshaw .01 .05
246 Hal McRae .01 .05
247 Jose Canseco .60 1.50
248 George Hendrick .01 .05
249 Doyle Alexander .01 .05
250 Teddy Higuera .01 .05
251 Tom Hume .01 .05
252 Denny Martinez .02 .10
253 Eddie Milner .02 .10
Now with Giants
254 Steve Sax .01 .05
255 Juan Samuel .01 .05
256 Dave Bergman .01 .05
257 Bob Forsch .01 .05
258 Steve Yeager .01 .05
259 Don Sutton .15 .40
260 Vida Blue .05 .15
Now with A's
261 Tom Brunansky .01 .05
262 Joe Sambito .01 .05
263 Mitch Webster .01 .05
264 Checklist 133-264 .01 .05
265 Darrell Evans .02 .10
266 Dave Kingman .02 .10
267 Howard Johnson .01 .05
268 Greg Pryor .01 .05
269 Tippy Martinez .01 .05
270 Jody Davis .01 .05
271 Steve Carlton .15 .40
272 Andres Galarraga .20 .50
273 Fernando Valenzuela .02 .10
274 Jeff Hearron .01 .05
275 Ray Knight .02 .10
Now with Orioles
276 Bill Madlock .02 .10
277 Tom Henke .01 .05
278 Gary Pettis .01 .05
279 Jimy Williams MG CL .01 .05
280 Jeffrey Leonard .01 .05
281 Bryn Smith .01 .05
282 John Cerutti .01 .05
283 Gary Roenicke .02 .10
Now with Braves
284 Joaquin Andujar .01 .05
285 Dennis Boyd .01 .05
286 Tim Hulett .01 .05
287 Craig Lefferts .01 .05
288 Tito Landrum .01 .05
289 Manny Lee .01 .05
290 Leon Durham .01 .05
291 Johnny Ray .01 .05
292 Franklin Stubbs .01 .05
293 Bob Rodgers MG CL .01 .05
294 Terry Francona .02 .10
295 Len Dykstra .05 .15
296 Tom Candiotti .01 .05
297 Frank DiPino .01 .05
298 Craig Reynolds .01 .05
299 Jerry Hairston .01 .05
300 Reggie Jackson .20 .50
Now with A's
301 Luis Aquino .01 .05
302 Greg Walker .01 .05
303 Terry Kennedy .02 .10
Now with Orioles
304 Phil Garner .02 .10
305 John Franco .02 .10
306 Bill Buckner .02 .10
307 Kevin Mitchell RC .08 .25
Now with Padres
308 Don Slaught .01 .05
309 Harold Baines .02 .10
310 Frank Viola .01 .05
311 Dave Lopes .02 .10
312 Cal Ripken .60 1.50
313 John Candelaria .01 .05
314 Bob Sebra .01 .05
315 Bud Black .01 .05
316 Brian Fisher .02 .10
Now with Pirates
317 Clint Hurdle .02 .10
318 Earnest Riles .01 .05
319 Dave LaPoint .02 .10
Now with Cardinals
320 Barry Bonds RC 5.00 12.00
321 Tim Stoddard .01 .05
322 Ron Cey .05 .15
Now with A's
323 Al Newman .01 .05
324 Jerry Royster .02 .10
Now with White Sox
325 Garry Templeton .01 .05
326 Mark Gubicza .01 .05
327 Andre Thornton .01 .05
328 Bob Welch .02 .10
329 Tony Fernandez .02 .10
330 Mike Scott .01 .05
331 Jack Clark .02 .10
332 Danny Tartabull .02 .10
Now with Royals
333 Greg Minton .01 .05
334 Ed Correa .01 .05
335 Candy Maldonado .01 .05
336 Dennis Lamp .02 .10
Now with Indians
337 Sid Fernandez .01 .05
338 Greg Gross .01 .05
339 Willie Hernandez .01 .05
340 Roger Clemens .50 1.25
341 Mickey Hatcher .01 .05
342 Bob James .01 .05
343 Jose Cruz .02 .10
344 Bruce Sutter .15 .40
345 Andre Dawson .08 .25
346 Shawon Dunston .01 .05
347 Scott McGregor .01 .05
348 Carmelo Martinez .01 .05
349 Storm Davis .02 .10
Now with Padres
350 Keith Hernandez .02 .10
351 Andy McGaffigan .01 .05
352 Dave Parker .02 .10
353 Ernie Camacho .01 .05
354 Eric Show .01 .05
355 Don Carman .01 .05
356 Floyd Bannister .01 .05
357 Willie McGee .02 .10
358 Atlee Hammaker .01 .05
359 Dale Murphy .08 .25
360 Pedro Guerrero .01 .05
361 Will Clark RC .40 1.00
362 Bill Campbell .01 .05
363 Alejandro Pena .01 .05
364 Dennis Rasmussen .01 .05
365 Rick Rhoden .02 .10
Now with Yankees
366 Randy St. Claire .01 .05
367 Willie Wilson .02 .10
368 Dwight Evans .02 .10
369 Moose Haas .01 .05
370 Fred Lynn .02 .10
371 Mark Eichhorn .01 .05
372 Dave Schmidt .02 .10
Now with Orioles
373 Jerry Reuss .01 .05
374 Lance Parrish .02 .10
375 Ron Guidry .02 .10
376 Jack Morris .02 .10
377 Willie Randolph .02 .10
378 Joel Youngblood .01 .05
379 Darryl Strawberry .05 .15
380 Rich Gossage .08 .25
381 Dennis Eckersley .15 .40
382 Gary Lucas .01 .05
383 Ron Davis .01 .05
384 Pete Incaviglia .02 .10
385 Orel Hershiser .02 .10
386 Kirk Gibson .02 .10
387 Don Robinson .01 .05
388 Darnell Coles .01 .05
389 Von Hayes .01 .05
390 Gary Matthews .01 .05
391 Jay Howell .01 .05
392 Tim Laudner .01 .05
393 Rod Scurry .01 .05
394 Tony Bernazard .01 .05
395 Damaso Garcia .02 .10
Now with Braves
396 Mike Schmidt .15 .40

1987 O-Pee-Chee Box Bottoms

COMPLETE SET (8) 2.50 6.00
A Don Baylor .30 .75
B Steve Carlton .60 1.50
C Ron Cey .30 .75
D Cecil Cooper .30 .75
E Rickey Henderson .60 1.50
F Jim Rice .30 .75
G Don Sutton .60 1.50
H Dave Winfield .60 1.50

1988 O-Pee-Chee

This set is an abridgement of the 1988 Topps set. The 396 standard-size cards comprising the 1988 O-Pee-Chee set differ from the cards of the 1988 Topps set by having a higher ratio of cards of players from the two Canadian teams, a practice begun by O-Pee-Chee in 1977 and continued to 1988. The fronts feature white-bordered color player photos framed by a colored line. The player's name appears in the colored diagonal stripe at the lower right. His team name appears at the top. The orange horizontal backs carry the player's name, position and biography printed across the row of baseball icons at the top. The player's major league statistics follow below. Some backs also have bilingual career highlights, some have bilingual baseball facts and still others have both or neither. The asterisked cards have an extra line on the front inside the picture area indicating team change. They are styled like the 1988 Topps regular issue cards. The O-Pee-Chee logo appears on the front of every card. This set includes the first two 1987 draft picks of both the Montreal Expos and the Toronto Blue Jays.

COMPLETE SET (396) 4.00 10.00
1 Chris James .01 .05
2 Steve Buechele .01 .05
3 Mike Henneman .02 .10
4 Eddie Murray .15 .40
5 Bret Saberhagen .02 .10
6 Nathan Minchey .01 .05
Expos' second
draft choice
7 Harold Reynolds .02 .10
8 Bo Jackson .08 .25
9 Mike Easler .01 .05
10 Ryne Sandberg .15 .40
11 Mike Young .01 .05
12 Tony Phillips .01 .05
13 Andres Thomas .01 .05
14 Tim Burke .01 .05
15 Chili Davis .05 .15
Now with Angels
16 Jim Lindeman .01 .05
17 Ron Oester .01 .05
18 Craig Reynolds .01 .05
19 Juan Samuel .01 .05
20 Kevin Gross .01 .05
21 Cecil Fielder .02 .10
22 Greg Swindell .01 .05
23 Jose DeLeon .01 .05
24 Jim Deshaies .01 .05
25 Andres Galarraga .08 .25
26 Mitch Williams .01 .05
27 R.J. Reynolds .01 .05
28 Jose Nunez .01 .05
29 Angel Salazar .01 .05
30 Sid Fernandez .01 .05
31 Keith Moreland .01 .05
32 John Kruk .02 .10
33 Rob Deer .01 .05
34 Ricky Horton .01 .05
35 Harold Baines .05 .15
36 Jamie Moyer .02 .10
37 Kevin McReynolds .01 .05
38 Ron Darling .01 .05
39 Ozzie Smith .20 .50
40 Orel Hershiser .02 .10
41 Bob Melvin .02 .10
42 Alfredo Griffin .02 .10
Now with Dodgers
43 Dick Schofield .01 .05
44 Terry Steinbach .01 .05
45 Kent Hrbek .02 .10
46 Darnell Coles .01 .05
47 Jimmy Key .02 .10
48 Alan Ashby .01 .05
49 Julio Franco .02 .10
50 Hubie Brooks .01 .05
51 Chris Bando .01 .05
52 Fernando Valenzuela .02 .10
53 Kal Daniels .01 .05
54 Jim Clancy .01 .05
55 Phil Bradley .02 .10
Now with Phillies
56 Andy McGaffigan .01 .05
57 Mike LaValliere .01 .05
58 Dave Magadan .01 .05
59 Danny Cox .01 .05
60 Rickey Henderson .15 .40
61 Jim Rice .02 .10
62 Calvin Schiraldi .02 .10
Now with Cubs
63 Jerry Mumphrey .01 .05
64 Ken Caminiti RC .75 2.00
65 Leon Durham .01 .05
66 Shane Rawley .01 .05
67 Ken Oberkfell .01 .05
68 Keith Hernandez .02 .10
69 Bob Brenly .01 .05
70 Roger Clemens .40 1.00
71 Gary Pettis .02 .10
Now with Tigers
72 Dennis Eckersley .15 .40
73 Dave Smith .01 .05
74 Cal Ripken .60 1.50
75 Joe Carter .08 .25
76 Denny Martinez .02 .10
77 Juan Beniquez .01 .05
78 Tim Laudner .01 .05
79 Ernie Whitt .01 .05
80 Mark Langston .01 .05
81 Dale Sveum .01 .05
82 Dion James .01 .05
83 Dave Valle .01 .05
84 Bill Wegman .01 .05
85 Howard Johnson .01 .05
86 Benito Santiago .01 .05
87 Casey Candaele .01 .05
88 Delino DeShields XRC .20 .50
Expos' first
draft choice
89 Dave Winfield .15 .40
90 Dale Murphy .08 .25
91 Jay Howell .02 .10
Now with Dodgers
92 Ken Williams RC .05 .15
93 Bob Sebra .01 .05
94 Tim Wallach .01 .05
95 Lance Parrish .01 .05
96 Todd Benzinger .01 .05
97 Scott Garrelts .01 .05
98 Jose Guzman .01 .05
99 Jeff Reardon .02 .10
100 Jack Clark .02 .10
101 Tracy Jones .01 .05
102 Barry Larkin .30 .75
103 Curt Young .01 .05
104 Juan Nieves .01 .05
105 Terry Pendleton .02 .10
106 Rob Ducey RC .01 .05
107 Scott Bailes .01 .05
108 Eric King .01 .05
109 Mike Pagliarulo .01 .05
110 Teddy Higuera .01 .05
111 Pedro Guerrero .01 .05
112 Chris Brown .01 .05
113 Kelly Gruber .01 .05
114 Jack Howell .01 .05
115 Johnny Ray .01 .05
116 Mark Eichhorn .01 .05
117 Tony Pena .01 .05
118 Bob Welch .02 .10
Now with Athletics
119 Mike Kingery .01 .05
120 Kirby Puckett .30 .75
121 Charlie Hough .02 .10
122 Tony Bernazard .01 .05
123 Tom Candiotti .01 .05
124 Ray Knight .01 .05
125 Bruce Hurst .01 .05
126 Steve Jeltz .01 .05
127 Ron Guidry .02 .10
128 Duane Ward .01 .05
129 Greg Minton .01 .05
130 Buddy Bell .02 .10
131 Denny Walling .01 .05
132 Donnie Hill .01 .05
133 Wayne Tolleson .01 .05
134 Bob Rodgers MG CL .01 .05
135 Todd Worrell .02 .10
136 Brian Dayett .01 .05
137 Chris Bosio .01 .05
138 Mitch Webster .01 .05
139 Jerry Browne .01 .05

140 Jesse Barfield .01 .05
141 Doug DeCinces .02 .10
Now with Cardinals
142 Andy Van Slyke .02 .10
143 Doug Drabek .02 .10
144 Jeff Parrett .01 .05
145 Bill Madlock .02 .10
146 Larry Herndon .01 .05
147 Bill Buckner .02 .10
148 Carmelo Martinez .01 .05
149 Ken Howell .01 .05
150 Eric Davis .02 .10
151 Randy Ready .01 .05
152 Jeffrey Leonard .01 .05
153 Dave Stieb .02 .10
154 Jeff Stone .01 .05
155 Dave Righetti .01 .05
156 Gary Matthews .02 .10
157 Gary Carter .15 .40
158 Bob Boone .02 .10
159 Glenn Davis .01 .05
160 Willie McGee .02 .10
161 Bryn Smith .01 .05
162 Mark McLemore RC .02 .10
163 Dale Mohorcic .01 .05
164 Mike Flanagan .01 .05
165 Robin Yount .15 .40
166 Bill Doran .01 .05
167 Rance Mulliniks .01 .05
168 Wally Joyner .05 .15
169 Cory Snyder .01 .05
170 Rich Gossage .08 .25
171 Rick Mahler .01 .05
172 Henry Cotto .01 .05
173 George Bell .01 .05
174 B.J. Surhoff .02 .10
175 Kevin Bass .01 .05
176 Jeff Reed .01 .05
177 Frank Tanana .01 .05
178 Darryl Strawberry .02 .10
179 Lou Whitaker .02 .10
180 Terry Kennedy .01 .05
181 Mariano Duncan .01 .05
182 Ken Phelps .01 .05
183 Bob Dernier .02 .10
Now with Phillies
184 Ivan Calderon .01 .05
185 Rick Rhoden .01 .05
186 Rafael Palmeiro .20 .50
187 Kelly Downs .01 .05
188 Spike Owen .01 .05
189 Bobby Bonilla .02 .10
190 Candy Maldonado .01 .05
191 John Cerutti .01 .05
192 Devon White .02 .10
193 Brian Fisher .01 .05
194 Alex Sanchez 1st Draft .01 .05
195 Dan Quisenberry .01 .05
196 Dave Engle .01 .05
197 Lance McCullers .01 .05
198 Franklin Stubbs .01 .05
199 Scott Bradley .01 .05
200 Wade Boggs .15 .40
201 Kirk Gibson .02 .10
202 Brett Butler .02 .10
Now with Giants
203 Dave Anderson .01 .05
204 Donnie Moore .01 .05
205 Nelson Liriano RC .01 .05
206 Danny Gladden .01 .05
207 Dan Pasqua .02 .10
Now with White Sox
208 Robby Thompson .01 .05
209 Richard Dotson .02 .10
Now with Yankees
210 Willie Randolph .02 .10
211 Danny Tartabull .01 .05
212 Greg Brock .01 .05
213 Albert Hall .01 .05
214 Dave Schmidt .01 .05
215 Von Hayes .01 .05
216 Herm Winningham .01 .05
217 Mike Davis .02 .10
Now with Dodgers
218 Charlie Leibrandt .01 .05
219 Mike Stanley .02 .10
220 Tom Henke .01 .05
221 Dwight Evans .02 .10
222 Willie Wilson .01 .05
223 Stan Jefferson .01 .05
224 Mike Dunne .01 .05
225 Mike Scioscia .02 .10
226 Larry Parrish .01 .05
227 Mike Scott .01 .05
228 Wallace Johnson .01 .05
229 Jeff Musselman .01 .05
230 Pat Tabler .01 .05
231 Paul Molitor .15 .40
232 Bob James .01 .05
233 Joe Niekro .01 .05
234 Oddibe McDowell .01 .05
235 Gary Ward .01 .05
236 Ted Power .02 .10
Now with Royals
237 Pascual Perez .01 .05
238 Luis Polonia .01 .05
239 Mike Diaz .01 .05
240 Lee Smith .02 .10
Now with Red Sox
241 Willie Upshaw .01 .05
242 Tom Niedenfuer .01 .05
243 Tim Raines .02 .10
244 Jeff D. Robinson .01 .05
245 Rich Gedman .01 .05
246 Scott Bankhead .01 .05
247 Andre Dawson .08 .25
248 Brook Jacoby .01 .05
249 Mike Marshall .01 .05
250 Nolan Ryan .60 1.50
251 Tom Foley .01 .05
252 Bob Brower .01 .05
253 Checklist .01 .05
254 Scott McGregor .01 .05
255 Ken Griffey .02 .10
256 Ken Schrom .01 .05
257 Gary Gaetti .02 .10
258 Ed Nunez .01 .05
259 Frank Viola .01 .05
260 Vince Coleman .01 .05
261 Reid Nichols .01 .05
262 Tim Flannery .01 .05
263 Glenn Braggs .01 .05
264 Garry Templeton .01 .05
265 Bo Diaz .01 .05
266 Matt Nokes .01 .05
267 Barry Bonds .60 1.50
268 Bruce Ruffin .01 .05
269 Ellis Burks RC .20 .50
270 Mike Witt .01 .05
271 Ken Gerhart .01 .05
272 Lloyd Moseby .01 .05
273 Garth Iorg .01 .05
274 Mike Greenwell .01 .05
275 Kevin Seitzer .02 .10
276 Luis Salazar .01 .05
277 Shawon Dunston .01 .05
278 Rick Reuschel .01 .05
279 Randy St.Claire .01 .05
280 Pete Incaviglia .01 .05
281 Mike Boddicker .01 .05
282 Jay Tibbs .01 .05
283 Shane Mack .01 .05
284 Walt Terrell .01 .05
285 Jim Presley .01 .05
286 Greg Walker .01 .05
287 Dwight Gooden .02 .10
288 Jim Morrison .01 .05
289 Gene Garber .01 .05
290 Tony Fernandez .05 .15
291 Ozzie Virgil .01 .05
292 Carney Lansford .02 .10
293 Jim Acker .01 .05
294 Tommy Hinzo .01 .05
295 Bert Blyleven .08 .25
296 Ozzie Guillen .05 .15
297 Zane Smith .01 .05
298 Milt Thompson .01 .05
299 Len Dykstra .02 .10
300 Don Mattingly .30 .75
301 Bud Black .01 .05
302 Jose Uribe .01 .05
303 Manny Lee .01 .05
304 Sid Bream .01 .05
305 Steve Sax .01 .05
306 Billy Hatcher .01 .05
307 John Shelby .01 .05
308 Lee Mazzilli .01 .05
309 Bill Long .01 .05
310 Tom Herr .01 .05
311 Derek Bell XRC .15 .40
Blue Jays' second
draft choice
312 George Brett .30 .75
313 Bob McClure .01 .05
314 Jimy Williams MG CL .01 .05
315 Dave Parker .02 .10
Now with Athletics
316 Doyle Alexander .01 .05
317 Dan Plesac .01 .05
318 Mel Hall .01 .05
319 Ruben Sierra .01 .05
320 Alan Trammell .05 .15
321 Mike Schmidt .15 .40
322 Wally Ritchie .01 .05
323 Rick Leach .01 .05
324 Danny Jackson .01 .05
Now with Reds
325 Glenn Hubbard .01 .05
326 Frank White .02 .10
327 Larry Sheets .01 .05
328 John Cangelosi .01 .05
329 Bill Gullickson .01 .05
330 Eddie Whitson .01 .05
331 Brian Downing .01 .05
332 Gary Redus .01 .05
333 Wally Backman .01 .05
334 Dwayne Murphy .01 .05
335 Claudell Washington .01 .05
336 Dave Concepcion .02 .10
337 Jim Gantner .01 .05
338 Marty Barrett .01 .05
339 Mickey Hatcher .01 .05
340 Jack Morris .02 .10
341 John Franco .02 .10
342 Ron Robinson .01 .05
343 Greg Gagne .01 .05
344 Steve Bedrosian .01 .05
345 Scott Fletcher .01 .05
346 Vance Law .02 .10
Now with Cubs
347 Joe Johnson .02 .10
Now with Angels
348 Jim Eisenreich .08 .25
349 Alvin Davis .01 .05
350 Will Clark .20 .50
351 Mike Aldrete .01 .05
352 Billy Ripken .01 .05
353 Dave Stewart .02 .10
354 Neal Heaton .01 .05
355 Roger McDowell .01 .05
356 John Tudor .01 .05
357 Floyd Bannister .02 .10
Now with Royals
358 Rey Quinones .01 .05
359 Glenn Wilson .02 .10
Now with Mariners
360 Tony Gwynn .30 .75
361 Greg Maddux 1.00 2.50
362 Juan Castillo .01 .05
363 Willie Fraser .01 .05
364 Nick Esasky .01 .05
365 Floyd Youmans .01 .05
366 Chet Lemon .01 .05
367 Matt Young .02 .10
Now with A's
368 Gerald Young .01 .05
369 Bob Stanley .01 .05
370 Jose Canseco .15 .40
371 Joe Hesketh .01 .05
372 Rick Sutcliffe .02 .10
373 Checklist 133-264 .01 .05
374 Checklist 265-396 .01 .05
375 Tom Brunansky .01 .05
376 Jody Davis .01 .05
377 Sam Horn RC .01 .05
378 Mark Gubicza .01 .05
379 Rafael Ramirez .02 .10
Now with Astros
380 Joe Magrane .01 .05
381 Pete O'Brien .01 .05
382 Lee Guetterman .01 .05
383 Eric Bell .01 .05
384 Gene Larkin .02 .10
385 Carlton Fisk .15 .40
386 Mike Fitzgerald .01 .05
387 Kevin Mitchell .02 .10
388 Jim Winn .01 .05
389 Mike Smithson .01 .05
390 Darrell Evans .02 .10
391 Terry Leach .01 .05
392 Charlie Kerfeld .01 .05
393 Mike Krukow .01 .05
394 Mark McGwire 1.25 3.00
395 Fred McGriff .20 .50
396 DeWayne Buice .01 .05

1988 O-Pee-Chee Box Bottoms

COMPLETE SET (16) 6.00 15.00
A Don Baylor .08 .25
B Steve Bedrosian .02 .10
C Juan Beniquez .02 .10
D Bob Boone .08 .25
E Darrell Evans .08 .25
F Tony Gwynn 2.50 6.00
G John Kruk .08 .25
H Marvell Wynne .02 .10
I Joe Carter .30 .75
J Eric Davis .08 .25
K Howard Johnson .02 .10
L Darryl Strawberry .08 .25
M Rickey Henderson .75 2.00
N Nolan Ryan 4.00 10.00
O Mike Schmidt .60 1.50
P Kent Tekulve .02 .10

1989 O-Pee-Chee

The 1989 O-Pee-Chee baseball set contains 396 standard-size cards that feature white bordered color player photos framed by colored lines. The player's name and team appear at the lower right. The bilingual pinkish horizontal backs are bordered in black and carry the player's biography and statistics.

COMPLETE SET (396) 8.00 20.00
COMPLETE FACT. SET (396) 8.00 20.00
1 Brook Jacoby .01 .05
2 Atlee Hammaker .05 .15
3 Jack Clark .01 .05
4 Dave Stieb .02 .10
5 Bud Black .01 .05
6 Damon Berryhill .01 .05
7 Mike Scioscia .02 .10
8 Jose Uribe .01 .05
9 Mike Aldrete .01 .05
10 Andre Dawson .08 .25
11 Bruce Sutter .15 .40
12 Dale Sveum .01 .05
13 Dan Quisenberry .01 .05
14 Tom Niedenfuer .01 .05
15 Robby Thompson .01 .05
16 Ron Robinson .01 .05
17 Brian Downing .01 .05
18 Rick Rhoden .01 .05
19 Greg Gagne .01 .05
20 Allan Anderson .01 .05
21 Eddie Whitson .01 .05
22 Billy Ripken .01 .05
23 Mike Fitzgerald .01 .05
24 Shane Rawley .01 .05
25 Frank White .02 .10
26 Don Mattingly .40 1.00
27 Fred Lynn .01 .05
28 Mike Moore .01 .05
29 Kelly Gruber .01 .05
30 Dwight Gooden .02 .10
31 Dan Pasqua .01 .05
32 Dennis Rasmussen .01 .05
33 B.J. Surhoff .02 .10
34 Sid Fernandez .01 .05
35 John Tudor .01 .05
36 Mitch Webster .01 .05
37 Doug Drabek .01 .05
38 Bobby Witt .01 .05
39 Mike Maddux .01 .05
40 Steve Sax .01 .05
41 Orel Hershiser .02 .10
42 Pete Incaviglia .01 .05
43 Guillermo Hernandez .01 .05
44 Kevin Coffman .01 .05
45 Kal Daniels .01 .05
46 Carlton Fisk .15 .40
47 Carney Lansford .02 .10
48 Tim Burke .01 .05
49 Alan Trammell .60 1.50
50 George Bell .01 .05
51 Tony Gwynn .50 1.25
52 Bob Brenly .01 .05
53 Ruben Sierra .02 .10
54 Otis Nixon .01 .05
55 Julio Franco .02 .10
56 Pat Tabler .01 .05
57 Alvin Davis .01 .05
58 Kevin Seitzer .02 .10
59 Mark Davis .01 .05
60 Tom Brunansky .01 .05
61 Jeff Treadway .01 .05
62 Alfredo Griffin .01 .05
63 Keith Hernandez .02 .10
64 Alex Trevino .01 .05
65 Rick Reuschel .01 .05
66 Bob Walk .01 .05
67 Dave Palmer .01 .05
68 Pedro Guerrero .01 .05
69 Jose Oquendo .01 .05
70 Mark McGwire .60 1.50
71 Mike Boddicker .01 .05
72 Wally Backman .01 .05
73 Pascual Perez .01 .05
74 Joe Hesketh .01 .05
75 Tom Henke .01 .05
76 Nelson Liriano .01 .05
77 Doyle Alexander .01 .05
78 Tim Wallach .01 .05
79 Scott Bankhead .01 .05
80 Cory Snyder .01 .05
81 Dave Magadan .01 .05
82 Randy Ready .01 .05
83 Steve Buechele .01 .05
84 Bo Jackson .08 .25
85 Kevin McReynolds .01 .05
86 Jeff Reardon .02 .10
87 Tim Raines(Named Rock on card) .02 .10
88 Melido Perez .01 .05
89 Dave LaPoint .01 .05
90 Vince Coleman .01 .05
91 Floyd Youmans .01 .05
92 Buddy Bell .02 .10
93 Andres Galarraga .08 .25
94 Tony Pena .01 .05
95 Gerald Young .01 .05
96 Rick Cerone .01 .05
97 Ken Oberkfell .01 .05
98 Larry Sheets .01 .05
99 Chuck Crim .01 .05
100 Mike Schmidt .15 .40
101 Ivan Calderon .01 .05
102 Kevin Bass .01 .05
103 Chili Davis .02 .10
104 Randy Myers .02 .10
105 Ron Darling .01 .05
106 Willie Upshaw .01 .05
107 Jose DeLeon .01 .05
108 Fred Manrique .01 .05
109 Johnny Ray .01 .05
110 Paul Molitor .15 .40
111 Rance Mulliniks .01 .05
112 Jim Presley .01 .05
113 Lloyd Moseby .01 .05
114 Lance Parrish .01 .05
115 Jody Davis .01 .05
116 Matt Nokes .01 .05
117 Dave Anderson .01 .05
118 Checklist 1-132 .01 .05
119 Rafael Belliard .01 .05
120 Frank Viola .01 .05
121 Roger Clemens .40 1.00
122 Luis Salazar .01 .05
123 Mike Stanley .01 .05
124 Jim Traber .01 .05
125 Mike Krukow .01 .05
126 Sid Bream .01 .05
127 Joel Skinner .01 .05
128 Milt Thompson .01 .05
129 Terry Clark .01 .05
130 Gerald Perry .01 .05
131 Bryn Smith .01 .05
132 Kirby Puckett .40 1.00
133 Bill Long .01 .05
134 Jim Gantner .01 .05
135 Jose Rijo .01 .05
136 Joey Meyer .01 .05
137 Geno Petralli .01 .05
138 Wallace Johnson .01 .05
139 Mike Flanagan .01 .05
140 Shawon Dunston .01 .05
141 Eric Plunk .01 .05
142 Bobby Bonilla .02 .10
143 Jack McDowell .15 .40
144 Mookie Wilson .01 .05
145 Dave Stewart .02 .10
146 Gary Pettis .01 .05
147 Eric Show .01 .05
148 Eddie Murray .15 .40
149 Lee Smith .02 .10
150 Fernando Valenzuela .02 .10
151 Bob Welch .01 .05
152 Harold Baines .05 .15
153 Albert Hall .01 .05
154 Don Carman .01 .05
155 Marty Barrett .01 .05
156 Chris Sabo .01 .05
157 Bret Saberhagen .15 .40
158 Danny Cox .01 .05
159 Tom Foley .01 .05
160 Jeffrey Leonard .01 .05
161 Brady Anderson RC .30 .75
162 Rich Gossage .02 .10
163 Greg Brock .01 .05
164 Joe Carter .05 .15
165 Mike Dunne .01 .05
166 Jeff Russell .01 .05
167 Dan Plesac .01 .05
168 Willie Wilson .01 .05
169 Mike Jackson .02 .10
170 Tony Fernandez .05 .15
171 Jamie Moyer .05 .15
172 Jim Gott .01 .05
173 Mel Hall .01 .05
174 Mark McGwire .60 1.50
175 John Shelby .01 .05
176 Jeff Parrett .01 .05
177 Tim Belcher .01 .05
178 Rich Gedman .01 .05
179 Ozzie Virgil .01 .05
180 Mike Scott .01 .05
181 Dickie Thon .01 .05
182 Rob Murphy .01 .05
183 Oddibe McDowell .01 .05
184 Wade Boggs .15 .40
185 Claudell Washington .01 .05
186 Randy Johnson RC 1.50 4.00
187 Paul O'Neill .02 .10
188 Todd Benzinger .01 .05
189 Kevin Mitchell .02 .10
190 Mike Witt .01 .05
191 Sil Campusano .01 .05
192 Ken Gerhart .01 .05
193 Bob Rodgers MG .01 .05
194 Floyd Bannister .01 .05
195 Ozzie Guillen .05 .15
196 Ron Gant .02 .10
197 Neal Heaton .01 .05
198 Bill Swift .01 .05
199 Dave Parker .02 .10
200 George Brett .30 .75
201 Bo Diaz .01 .05
202 Brad Moore .01 .05
203 Rob Ducey .01 .05
204 Bert Blyleven .08 .25
205 Dwight Evans .02 .10
206 Roberto Alomar .30 .75
207 Henry Cotto .01 .05
208 Harold Reynolds .02 .10
209 Jose Guzman .01 .05
210 Dale Murphy .08 .25
211 Mike Pagliarulo .01 .05
212 Jay Howell .01 .05
213 Rene Gonzales .01 .05
214 Scott Garrelts .01 .05
215 Kevin Gross .01 .05
216 Jack Howell .01 .05
217 Kurt Stillwell .01 .05
218 Mike LaValliere .01 .05
219 Jim Clancy .01 .05
220 Gary Gaetti .02 .10
221 Hubie Brooks .01 .05
222 Bruce Ruffin .01 .05
223 Jay Buhner .08 .25
224 Cecil Fielder .02 .10
225 Willie McGee .02 .10
226 Bill Doran .01 .05
227 John Farrell .01 .05
228 Nelson Santovenia .01 .05
229 Jimmy Key .02 .10
230 Ozzie Smith .30 .75
231 Dave Schmidt .02 .10
232 Jody Reed .01 .05
233 Gregg Jefferies .01 .05
234 Tom Browning .01 .05
235 John Kruk .02 .10
236 Charles Hudson .01 .05
237 Todd Stottlemyre .02 .10
238 Don Slaught .01 .05
239 Tim Laudner .01 .05
240 Greg Maddux .50 1.25
241 Brett Butler .02 .10
242 Checklist 133-264 .01 .05
243 Bob Boone .02 .10
244 Willie Randolph .02 .10
245 Jim Rice .02 .10
246 Rey Quinones .01 .05
247 Checklist 265-396 .01 .05
248 Stan Javier .01 .05
249 Tim Leary .01 .05
250 Cal Ripken .60 1.50
251 John Dopson .01 .05
252 Billy Hatcher .01 .05
253 Robin Yount .15 .40
254 Mickey Hatcher .01 .05
255 Bob Horner .01 .05
256 Benny Santiago .02 .10
257 Luis Rivera .01 .05
258 Fred McGriff .08 .25
259 Dave Wells .01 .05
260 Dave Winfield .15 .40
261 Rafael Ramirez .01 .05
262 Nick Esasky .01 .05
263 Barry Bonds .40 1.00
264 Joe Magrane .05 .15
265 Kent Hrbek .02 .10
266 Jack Morris .02 .10
267 Jeff M. Robinson .01 .05
268 Ron Kittle .01 .05
269 Candy Maldonado .01 .05
270 Wally Joyner .02 .10
271 Glenn Braggs .01 .05
272 Ron Hassey .01 .05
273 Jose Lind .01 .05
274 Mark Eichhorn .01 .05
275 Danny Tartabull .01 .05
276 Paul Kilgus .01 .05
277 Mike Davis .01 .05
278 Andy McGaffigan .01 .05
279 Scott Bradley .01 .05
280 Bob Knepper .01 .05
281 Gary Redus .01 .05
282 Rickey Henderson .08 .25
283 Andy Allanson .01 .05
284 Rick Leach .01 .05
285 John Candelaria .01 .05
286 Dick Schofield .01 .05
287 Bryan Harvey .01 .05
288 Randy Bush .01 .05
289 Ernie Whitt .01 .05
290 John Franco .02 .10
291 Todd Worrell .01 .05
292 Teddy Higuera .01 .05
293 Keith Moreland .01 .05
294 Juan Berenguer .01 .05
295 Scott Fletcher .01 .05
296 Roger McDowell .02 .10
Now with Indians 12-6-88
297 Mark Grace .30 .75
298 Chris James .01 .05
299 Frank Tanana .01 .05
300 Darryl Strawberry .02 .10
301 Charlie Leibrandt .01 .05
302 Gary Ward .01 .05
303 Brian Fisher .01 .05
304 Terry Steinbach .01 .05
305 Dave Smith .01 .05
306 Greg Minton .01 .05
307 Lance McCullers .01 .05
308 Phil Bradley .01 .05
309 Terry Kennedy .01 .05
310 Rafael Palmeiro .08 .25
311 Ellis Burks .05 .15
312 Doug Jones .01 .05
313 Denny Martinez .02 .10
314 Pete O'Brien .01 .05
315 Greg Swindell .01 .05
316 Walt Weiss .01 .05
317 Pete Stanicek .01 .05
318 Gene Nelson .01 .05
319 Danny Jackson .01 .05
320 Lou Whitaker .02 .10
321 Will Clark .08 .25
322 John Smiley .01 .05
323 Mike Marshall .01 .05
324 Gary Carter .15 .40
325 Jesse Barfield .01 .05
326 Dennis Boyd .01 .05
327 Dave Henderson .01 .05
328 Chet Lemon .01 .05
329 Bob Melvin .02 .10
330 Eric Davis .02 .10
331 Ted Power .01 .05
332 Carmelo Martinez .01 .05
333 Bob Ojeda .01 .05
334 Steve Lyons .02 .10
335 Dave Righetti .02 .10
336 Steve Balboni .01 .05
337 Calvin Schiraldi .01 .05
338 Vance Law .01 .05
339 Zane Smith .01 .05
340 Kirk Gibson .02 .10
341 Jim Deshaies .01 .05
342 Tom Brookens .01 .05
343 Pat Borders .75 2.00
344 Devon White .02 .10
345 Charlie Hough .02 .10
346 Rex Hudler .01 .05
347 John Cerutti .01 .05
348 Kirk McCaskill .01 .05
349 Len Dykstra .02 .10
350 Andy Van Slyke .02 .10
351 Jeff D. Robinson .01 .05
352 Rick Schu .01 .05
353 Bruce Benedict .01 .05
354 Bill Wegman .01 .05
355 Mark Langston .01 .05
356 Steve Farr .01 .05
357 Richard Dotson .01 .05
358 Andres Thomas .01 .05
359 Alan Ashby .01 .05
360 Ryne Sandberg .30 .75
361 Kelly Downs .01 .05
362 Jeff Musselman .01 .05
363 Barry Larkin .08 .25
364 Rob Deer .01 .05
365 Mike Henneman .01 .05
366 Nolan Ryan .60 1.50
367 Johnny Paredes .01 .05
368 Bobby Thigpen .01 .05
369 Mickey Brantley .01 .05
370 Dennis Eckersley .15 .40
371 Manny Lee .01 .05
372 Juan Samuel .01 .05
373 Tracy Jones .01 .05
374 Mike Greenwell .01 .05
375 Terry Pendleton .02 .10
376 Steve Lombardozzi .01 .05
377 Mitch Williams .01 .05
378 Glenn Davis .01 .05
379 Mark Gubicza .01 .05
380 Orel Hershiser WS .20 .50
381 Jimy Williams MG .01 .05
382 Kirk Gibson WS .75 2.00
383 Howard Johnson .01 .05
384 David Cone .08 .25
385 Von Hayes .01 .05
386 Luis Polonia .01 .05
387 Danny Gladden .01 .05
388 Pete Smith .01 .05
389 Jose Canseco .20 .50
390 Mickey Hatcher .01 .05
391 Wil Tejada .01 .05
392 Duane Ward .01 .05
393 Rick Mahler .01 .05
394 Rick Sutcliffe .02 .10
395 Dave Martinez .01 .05
396 Ken Dayley .01 .05

1989 O-Pee-Chee Box Bottoms

COMPLETE SET (16) 5.00 12.00
A George Brett 1.00 2.50
B Bill Buckner .08 .25
C Darrell Evans .08 .25
D Rich Gossage .08 .25
E Greg Gross .02 .10
F Rickey Henderson .50 1.25
G Keith Hernandez .08 .25
H Tom Lasorda MG .08 .25
I Jim Rice .08 .25
J Cal Ripken 1.50 4.00
K Nolan Ryan 1.50 4.00
L Mike Schmidt .50 1.25
M Bruce Sutter .40 1.00
N Don Sutton .40 1.00
O Kent Tekulve .02 .10
P Dave Winfield .40 1.00

1990 O-Pee-Chee

The 1990 O-Pee-Chee baseball set was a 792-card standard-size set. For the first time since 1976, O-Pee-Chee issued the exact same set as Topps. The only distinctions are the bilingual text and the O-Pee-Chee copyright on the backs. The fronts feature color player photos bordered in various colors. The player's name appears at the bottom and his team name is printed at the top. The yellow horizontal backs carry the player's name, biography and position at the top, followed below by major league statistics. Cards 385-407 feature All-Stars, while cards 661-665 are Turn Back the Clock cards. Notable Rookie Cards include Juan Gonzalez, Sammy Sosa, Frank Thomas and Bernie Williams.

COMPLETE SET (792) 8.00 20.00
COMPLETE FACT.SET (792) 10.00 25.00
1 Nolan Ryan .75 2.00
2 Nolan Ryan Salute .40 1.00
3 Nolan Ryan Salute .40 1.00
4 Nolan Ryan Salute .40 1.00
5 Nolan Ryan Salute UER .40 1.00
Says Texas Stadium
rather than
Arlington Stadium
6 Vince Coleman RB .01 .05
7 Rickey Henderson RB .08 .25
8 Cal Ripken RB .30 .75
9 Eric Plunk .01 .05
10 Barry Larkin .08 .25
11 Paul Gibson .01 .05
12 Joe Girardi .02 .10
13 Mark Williamson .01 .05
14 Mike Fetters .01 .05
15 Teddy Higuera .01 .05
16 Kent Anderson .01 .05
17 Kelly Downs .01 .05
18 Carlos Quintana .01 .05
19 Al Newman .01 .05
20 Mark Gubicza .01 .05
21 Jeff Torborg MG .01 .05
22 Bruce Ruffin .01 .05
23 Randy Velarde .01 .05
24 Joe Hesketh .01 .05
25 Willie Randolph .02 .10
26 Don Slaught .02 .10
Now with Pirates
12
4
89
27 Rick Leach .01 .05
28 Duane Ward .01 .05
29 John Cangelosi .01 .05
30 David Cone .08 .25
31 Henry Cotto .01 .05
32 John Farrell .01 .05
33 Greg Walker .01 .05
34 Tony Fossas .01 .05
35 Benito Santiago .02 .10
36 John Costello .01 .05
37 Domingo Ramos .01 .05
38 Wes Gardner .01 .05
39 Curt Ford .01 .05
40 Jay Howell .01 .05
41 Matt Williams .05 .15
42 Jeff M. Robinson .01 .05
43 Dante Bichette .02 .10
44 Roger Salkeld FDP RC .01 .05
45 Dave Parker UER .05 .15
Born in Jackson
not Calhoun
46 Rob Dibble .01 .05
47 Brian Harper .01 .05
48 Zane Smith .01 .05
49 Tom Lawless .01 .05
50 Glenn Davis .01 .05
51 Doug Rader MG .01 .05
52 Jack Daugherty .01 .05
53 Mike LaCoss .01 .05
54 Joel Skinner .01 .05
55 Darrell Evans UER .02 .10
HR total should be
414, not 424
56 Franklin Stubbs .01 .05
57 Greg Vaughn .08 .25
58 Keith Miller .01 .05
59 Ted Power .02 .10
Now with Pirates
11/21/89
60 George Brett .30 .75
61 Deion Sanders .08 .25
62 Ramon Martinez .02 .10
63 Mike Pagliarulo .01 .05
64 Danny Darwin .01 .05
65 Devon White .01 .05
66 Greg Litton .01 .05
67 Scott Sanderson .02 .10
Now with Athletics
12/13/89
68 Dave Henderson .01 .05
69 Todd Frohwirth .01 .05
70 Mike Greenwell .01 .05
71 Allan Anderson .01 .05
72 Jeff Huson .01 .05
73 Bob Milacki .01 .05
74 Jeff Jackson FDP RC .01 .05
75 Doug Jones .01 .05
76 Dave Valle .01 .05
77 Dave Bergman .01 .05
78 Mike Flanagan .01 .05
79 Ron Kittle .01 .05
80 Jeff Russell .01 .05
81 Bob Rodgers MG .01 .05
82 Scott Terry .01 .05
83 Hensley Meulens .01 .05
84 Ray Searage .01 .05
85 Juan Samuel .02 .10
Now with Dodgers
12/20/89
86 Paul Kilgus .02 .10
Now with Blue Jays
12/7/89
87 Rick Luecken .02 .10
Now with Braves
12/17/89
88 Glenn Braggs .01 .05
89 Clint Zavaras .01 .05
90 Jack Clark .02 .10
91 Steve Frey .01 .05
92 Mike Stanley .01 .05
93 Shawn Hillegas .01 .05
94 Herm Winningham .01 .05
95 Todd Worrell .01 .05
96 Jody Reed .01 .05
97 Curt Schilling .60 1.50
98 Jose Gonzalez .01 .05
99 Rich Monteleone .01 .05
100 Will Clark -.08 .25
101 Shane Rawley .01 .05
Now with Red Sox
1/9/90
102 Stan Javier .01 .05
103 Marvin Freeman .01 .05
104 Bob Knepper .01 .05
105 Randy Myers .02 .10
Now with Reds
12/8/89
106 Charlie O'Brien .01 .05
107 Fred Lynn .02 .10
Now with Padres
12/7/89
108 Rod Nichols .01 .05
109 Roberto Kelly .01 .05
110 Tommy Helms MG .01 .05
111 Ed Whited .01 .05
112 Glenn Wilson .01 .05
113 Manny Lee .01 .05
114 Mike Bielecki .01 .05
115 Tony Pena .02 .10
Now with Red Sox
11/28/89
116 Floyd Bannister .01 .05
117 Mike Sharperson .01 .05
118 Erik Hanson .01 .05
119 Billy Hatcher .01 .05
120 John Franco .05 .15
Now with Mets
12/8/89
121 Robin Ventura .08 .25
122 Shawn Abner .01 .05
123 Rich Gedman .01 .05

Card	Low	High
124 Dave Dravecky	.01	.05
125 Kent Hrbek	.02	.10
126 Randy Kramer	.01	.05
127 Mike Devereaux	.01	.05
128 Checklist 1	.01	.05
129 Ron Jones	.01	.05
130 Bert Blyleven	.08	.25
131 Matt Nokes	.01	.05
132 Lance Blankenship	.01	.05
133 Ricky Horton	.01	.05
134 Earl Cunningham RC	.01	.05
135 Dave Magadan	.01	.05
136 Kevin Brown	.08	.25
137 Marty Pevey	.01	.05
138 Al Leiter	.08	.25
139 Greg Brock	.01	.05
140 Andre Dawson	.08	.25
141 John Hart MG	.01	.05
142 Jeff Wetherby	.01	.05
143 Rafael Belliard	.01	.05
144 Bud Black	.01	.05
145 Terry Steinbach	.01	.05
146 Rob Richie	.01	.05
147 Chuck Finley	.02	.10
148 Edgar Martinez	.05	.15
149 Steve Farr	.01	.05
150 Kirk Gibson	.02	.10
151 Rick Mahler	.01	.05
152 Lonnie Smith	.01	.05
153 Randy Milligan	.01	.05
154 Mike Maddux	.02	.10
Now with Dodgers		
12/21/89		
155 Ellis Burks	.05	.15
156 Ken Patterson	.01	.05
157 Craig Biggio	.08	.25
158 Craig Lefferts	.02	.10
Now with Padres		
12/7/89		
159 Mike Felder	.01	.05
160 Dave Righetti	.01	.05
161 Harold Reynolds	.02	.10
162 Todd Zeile	.05	.15
163 Phil Bradley	.01	.05
164 Jeff Juden FDP RC	.01	.05
165 Walt Weiss	.01	.05
166 Bobby Witt	.01	.05
167 Kevin Appier	.05	.15
168 Jose Lind	.01	.05
169 Richard Dotson	.02	.10
Now with Royals		
12/6/89		
170 George Bell	.01	.05
171 Russ Nixon MG	.01	.05
172 Tom Lampkin	.01	.05
173 Tim Belcher	.01	.05
174 Jeff Kunkel	.01	.05
175 Mike Moore	.01	.05
176 Luis Quinones	.01	.05
177 Mike Henneman	.01	.05
178 Chris James	.01	.05
Now with Indians		
12/6/89		
179 Brian Holton	.01	.05
180 Tim Raines	.02	.10
181 Juan Agosto	.01	.05
182 Mookie Wilson	.02	.10
183 Steve Lake	.01	.05
184 Danny Cox	.01	.05
185 Ruben Sierra	.02	.10
186 Dave LaPoint	.01	.05
187 Rick Wrona	.01	.05
188 Mike Smithson	.02	.10
Now with Angels		
12/19/89		
189 Dick Schofield	.01	.05
190 Rick Reuschel	.01	.05
191 Pat Borders	.01	.05
192 Don August	.01	.05
193 Andy Benes	.02	.10
194 Glenallen Hill	.01	.05
195 Tim Burke	.01	.05
196 Gerald Young	.01	.05
197 Doug Drabek	.01	.05
198 Mike Marshall	.02	.10
Now with Mets		
12/20/89		
199 Sergio Valdez	.01	.05
200 Don Mattingly	.40	1.00
201 Cito Gaston MG	.01	.05
202 Mike Macfarlane	.01	.05
203 Mike Roesler	.01	.05
204 Bob Dernier	.01	.05
205 Mark Davis	.02	.10
Now with Royals		
12/11/89		
206 Nick Esasky	.02	.10
Now with Braves		
11/17/89		
207 Bob Ojeda	.01	.05
208 Brook Jacoby	.01	.05
209 Greg Mathews	.01	.05
210 Ryne Sandberg	.20	.50
211 John Cerutti	.01	.05
212 Joe Orsulak	.01	.05
213 Scott Bankhead	.01	.05
214 Terry Francona	.02	.10
215 Kirk McCaskill	.01	.05
216 Ricky Jordan	.01	.05
217 Don Robinson	.01	.05
218 Wally Backman	.01	.05
219 Donn Pall	.01	.05
220 Barry Bonds	.40	1.00
221 Gary Mielke	.01	.05
222 Kurt Stillwell UER	.01	.05
Graduate misspelled		
as gradute		
223 Tommy Gregg	.01	.05
224 Delino DeShields RC	.08	.25
225 Jim Deshaies	.01	.05
226 Mickey Hatcher	.01	.05
227 Kevin Tapani RC	.08	.25
228 Dave Martinez	.01	.05
229 David Wells	.08	.25
230 Keith Hernandez	.05	.15
Now with Indians		
12/7/89		
231 Jack McKeon MG	.02	.10
232 Darnell Coles	.01	.05
233 Ken Hill	.02	.10
234 Mariano Duncan	.01	.05
235 Jeff Reardon	.02	.10
Now with Red Sox		
12/6/89		
236 Hal Morris	.01	.05
Now with Reds		
12/12/89		
237 Kevin Ritz	.01	.05
238 Felix Jose	.01	.05
239 Eric Show	.01	.05
240 Mark Grace	.08	.25
241 Mike Krukow	.01	.05
242 Fred Manrique	.01	.05
243 Barry Jones	.01	.05
244 Bill Schroeder	.01	.05
245 Roger Clemens	.40	1.00
246 Jim Eisenreich	.01	.05
247 Jerry Reed	.01	.05
248 Dave Anderson	.02	.10
Now with Giants		
11/29/89		
249 MikeTexas Smith	.01	.05
250 Jose Canseco	.15	.40
251 Jeff Blauser	.01	.05
252 Otis Nixon	.01	.05
253 Mark Portugal	.01	.05
254 Francisco Cabrera	.01	.05
255 Bobby Thigpen	.01	.05
256 Marvell Wynne	.01	.05
257 Jose DeLeon	.01	.05
258 Barry Lyons	.01	.05
259 Lance McCullers	.01	.05
260 Eric Davis	.02	.10
261 Whitey Herzog MG	.02	.10
262 Checklist 2	.01	.05
263 Mel Stottlemyre Jr.	.01	.05
264 Bryan Clutterbuck	.01	.05
265 Pete O'Brien	.02	.10
Now with Mariners		
12/7/89		
266 German Gonzalez	.01	.05
267 Mark Davidson	.01	.05
268 Rob Murphy	.01	.05
269 Dickie Thon	.01	.05
270 Dave Stewart	.02	.10
271 Chet Lemon	.01	.05
272 Bryan Harvey	.01	.05
273 Bobby Bonilla	.01	.05
274 Mauro Gozzo	.01	.05
275 Mickey Tettleton	.02	.10
276 Gary Thurman	.01	.05
277 Lenny Harris	.01	.05
278 Pascual Perez	.02	.10
Now with Yankees		
11/27/89		
279 Steve Buechele	.01	.05
280 Lou Whitaker	.02	.10
281 Kevin Bass	.02	.10
Now with Giants		
11/20/89		
282 Derek Lilliquist	.01	.05
283 Joey Belle	.08	.25
284 Mark Gardner	.01	.05
285 Willie McGee	.02	.10
286 Lee Guetterman	.01	.05
287 Vance Law	.01	.05
288 Greg Briley	.01	.05
289 Norm Charlton	.01	.05
290 Robin Yount	.20	.50
291 Dave Johnson MG	.02	.10
292 Jim Gott	.02	.10
Now with Dodgers		
12/7/89		
293 Mike Gallego	.01	.05
294 Craig McMurtry	.01	.05
295 Fred McGriff	.08	.25
296 Jeff Ballard	.01	.05
297 Tom Herr	.01	.05
298 Dan Gladden	.01	.05
299 Adam Peterson	.01	.05
300 Bo Jackson	.08	.25
301 Don Aase	.01	.05
302 Marcus Lawton	.01	.05
303 Rick Cerone	.02	.10
Now with Yankees		
12/19/89		
304 Marty Clary	.01	.05
305 Eddie Murray	.15	.40
306 Tom Niedenfuer	.01	.05
307 Bip Roberts	.01	.05
308 Jose Guzman	.01	.05
309 Eric Yelding	.01	.05
310 Steve Bedrosian	.01	.05
311 Dwight Smith	.01	.05
312 Dan Quisenberry	.01	.05
313 Gus Polidor	.01	.05
314 Donald Harris FDP	.01	.05
315 Bruce Hurst	.01	.05
316 Carney Lansford	.02	.10
317 Mark Guthrie	.01	.05
318 Wallace Johnson	.01	.05
319 Dion James	.01	.05
320 Dave Stieb	.02	.10
321 Joe Morgan MG	.01	.05
322 Junior Ortiz	.01	.05
323 Willie Wilson	.01	.05
324 Pete Harnisch	.01	.05
325 Robby Thompson	.01	.05
326 Tom McCarthy	.01	.05
327 Ken Williams	.02	.10
328 Curt Young	.01	.05
329 Oddibe McDowell	.01	.05
330 Ron Darling	.01	.05
331 Juan Gonzalez RC	.60	1.50
332 Paul O'Neill	.08	.25
333 Bill Wegman	.01	.05
334 Johnny Ray	.01	.05
335 Andy Hawkins	.01	.05
336 Ken Griffey Jr.	.75	2.00
337 Lloyd McClendon	.01	.05
338 Dennis Lamp	.01	.05
339 Dave Clark	.02	.10
Now with Cubs		
11/20/89		
340 Fernando Valenzuela	.02	.10
341 Tom Foley	.01	.05
342 Alex Trevino	.01	.05
343 Frank Tanana	.01	.05
344 George Canale	.01	.05
345 Harold Baines	.05	.15
346 Jim Presley	.01	.05
347 Junior Felix	.01	.05
348 Gary Wayne	.01	.05
349 Steve Finley	.08	.25
350 Bret Saberhagen	.02	.10
351 Roger Craig MG	.01	.05
352 Bryn Smith	.02	.10
Now with Cardinals		
11/29/89		
353 Sandy Alomar Jr.	.05	.15
Now with Indians		
12/6/89		
354 Stan Belinda	.01	.05
355 Marty Barrett	.01	.05
356 Randy Ready	.01	.05
357 Dave West	.01	.05
358 Andres Thomas	.01	.05
359 Jimmy Jones	.01	.05
360 Paul Molitor	.15	.40
361 Randy McCament	.01	.05
362 Damon Berryhill	.01	.05
363 Dan Petry	.01	.05
364 Rolando Roomes	.01	.05
365 Ozzie Guillen	.02	.10
366 Mike Heath	.01	.05
367 Mike Morgan	.01	.05
368 Bill Doran	.01	.05
369 Todd Burns	.01	.05
370 Tim Wallach	.01	.05
371 Jimmy Key	.02	.10
372 Terry Kennedy	.01	.05
373 Alvin Davis	.01	.05
374 Steve Cummings RC	.01	.05
375 Dwight Evans	.02	.10
376 Checklist 3 UER	.01	.05
Higuera misalphabet-		
ized in Brewer list		
377 Mickey Weston	.01	.05
378 Luis Salazar	.01	.05
379 Steve Rosenberg	.01	.05
380 Dave Winfield	.15	.40
381 Frank Robinson MG	.05	.15
382 Jeff Musselman	.01	.05
383 John Morris	.01	.05
384 Pat Combs	.01	.05
385 Fred McGriff AS	.02	.10
386 Julio Franco AS	.01	.05
387 Wade Boggs AS	.08	.25
388 Cal Ripken AS	.30	.75
389 Robin Yount AS	.08	.25
390 Ruben Sierra AS	.01	.05
391 Kirby Puckett AS	.08	.25
392 Carlton Fisk AS	.08	.25
393 Bret Saberhagen AS	.01	.05
394 Jeff Ballard AS	.01	.05
395 Jeff Russell AS	.01	.05
396 Bart Giamatti RC MEM	.08	.25
397 Will Clark AS	.02	.10
398 Ryne Sandberg AS	.08	.25
399 Howard Johnson AS	.01	.05
400 Ozzie Smith AS	.08	.25
401 Kevin Mitchell AS	.01	.05
402 Eric Davis AS	.01	.05
403 Tony Gwynn AS	.08	.25
404 Craig Biggio AS	.05	.15
405 Mike Scott AS	.01	.05
406 Joe Magrane AS	.01	.05
407 Mark Davis AS	.01	.05
Now with Royals		
12/11/89		
408 Trevor Wilson	.01	.05
409 Tom Brunansky	.01	.05
410 Joe Boever	.01	.05
411 Ken Phelps	.01	.05
412 Jamie Moyer	.01	.05
413 Brian DuBois	.01	.05
414 Frank Thomas RC	1.50	4.00
415 Shawon Dunston	.01	.05
416 Dave Johnson P	.01	.05
417 Jim Gantner	.01	.05
418 Tom Browning	.01	.05
419 Beau Allred RC	.01	.05
420 Carlton Fisk	.15	.40
421 Greg Minton	.01	.05
422 Pat Sheridan	.01	.05
423 Fred Toliver	.02	.10
Now with Yankees		
9		
27/89		
424 Jerry Reuss	.01	.05
425 Bill Landrum	.01	.05
426 Jeff Hamilton UER	.01	.05
Stats say he fanned		
197 times in 1987		
but he only had 147 at bats		
427 Carmen Castillo	.01	.05
428 Steve Davis	.02	.10
Now with Dodgers		
12/12/89		
429 Tom Kelly MG	.01	.05
430 Pete Incaviglia	.01	.05
431 Randy Johnson	.30	.75
432 Damaso Garcia	.02	.10
Now with Yankees		
12/22/89		
433 Steve Olin	.02	.10
434 Mark Carreon	.01	.05
435 Kevin Seitzer	.01	.05
436 Mel Hall	.01	.05
437 Les Lancaster	.01	.05
438 Greg Myers	.01	.05
439 Jeff Parrett	.01	.05
440 Alan Trammell	.05	.15
441 Bob Kipper	.01	.05
442 Jerry Browne	.01	.05
443 Cris Carpenter	.01	.05
444 Kyle Abbott FDP	.01	.05
445 Danny Jackson	.01	.05
446 Dan Pasqua	.01	.05
447 Atlee Hammaker	.01	.05
448 Greg Gagne	.01	.05
449 Dennis Rasmussen	.01	.05
450 Rickey Henderson	.30	.75
451 Mark Lemke	.01	.05
452 Luis DeLosSantos	.01	.05
453 Jody Davis	.01	.05
454 Jeff King	.01	.05
455 Jeffrey Leonard	.01	.05
456 Chris Gwynn	.01	.05
457 Gregg Jefferies	.01	.05
458 Bob McClure	.01	.05
459 Jim Lefebvre MG	.01	.05
460 Mike Scott	.01	.05
461 Carlos Martinez	.01	.05
462 Denny Walling	.01	.05
463 Drew Hall	.01	.05
464 Jerome Walton	.01	.05
465 Kevin Gross	.01	.05
466 Rance Mulliniks	.01	.05
467 Juan Nieves	.01	.05
468 Bill Ripken	.01	.05
469 John Kruk	.02	.10
470 Frank Viola	.01	.05
471 Mike Brumley	.02	.10
Now with Orioles		
1		
10/90		
472 Jose Uribe	.01	.05
473 Joe Price	.01	.05
474 Rich Thompson	.01	.05
475 Bob Welch	.01	.05
476 Brad Komminsk	.01	.05
477 Willie Fraser	.01	.05
478 Mike LaValliere	.01	.05
479 Frank White	.02	.10
480 Sid Fernandez	.01	.05
481 Garry Templeton	.01	.05
482 Steve Carter	.01	.05
483 Alejandro Pena	.02	.10
Now with Mets		
12/20/89		
484 Mike Fitzgerald	.01	.05
485 John Candelaria	.01	.05
486 Jeff Treadway	.01	.05
487 Steve Searcy	.01	.05
488 Ken Oberkfell	.02	.10
Now with Astros		
12/6/89		
489 Nick Leyva MG	.01	.05
490 Dan Plesac	.01	.05
491 Dave Cochrane RC	.01	.05
492 Ron Oester	.01	.05
493 Jason Grimsley	.01	.05
494 Terry Puhl	.01	.05
495 Lee Smith	.02	.10
496 Cecil Espy UER	.01	.05
'88 stats have 3 SB's		
should be 33		
497 Dave Schmidt	.02	.10
Now with Expos		
12/13/89		
498 Rick Schu	.01	.05
499 Bill Long	.01	.05
500 Kevin Mitchell	.01	.05
501 Matt Young	.02	.10
Now with Mariners		
12/8/89		
502 Mitch Webster	.02	.10
Now with Indians		
11/20/89		
503 Randy St.Claire	.01	.05
504 Tom O'Malley	.01	.05
505 Kelly Gruber	.01	.05
506 Tom Glavine	.08	.25
507 Gary Redus	.01	.05
508 Terry Leach	.01	.05
509 Tom Pagnozzi	.01	.05
510 Dwight Gooden	.02	.10
511 Clay Parker	.01	.05
512 Gary Pettis	.02	.10
Now with Rangers		
11/24/89		
513 Mark Eichhorn	.02	.10
Now with Angels		
12/13/89		
514 Andy Allanson	.01	.05
515 Len Dykstra	.02	.10
516 Tim Leary	.01	.05
517 Roberto Alomar	.08	.25
518 Bill Krueger	.01	.05
519 Bucky Dent MG	.01	.05
520 Mitch Williams	.01	.05
521 Craig Worthington	.01	.05
522 Mike Dunne	.02	.10
Now with Padres		
12/4/89		
523 Jay Bell	.01	.05
524 Daryl Boston	.01	.05
525 Wally Joyner	.02	.10
526 Checklist 4	.01	.05
527 Ron Hassey	.01	.05
528 Kevin Wickander UER	.02	.10
Monthly scoreboard		
strikeout total was 2.2		
that was his innings		
pitched total		
529 Greg A. Harris	.01	.05
530 Mark Langston	.02	.10
Now with Angels		
12/4/89		
531 Ken Caminiti	.08	.25
532 Cecilio Guante	.02	.10
Now with Indians		
11/21/89		
533 Tim Jones	.01	.05
534 Louie Meadows	.01	.05
535 John Smoltz	.08	.25
536 Bob Geren	.01	.05
537 Mark Grant	.01	.05
538 Bill Spiers UER	.01	.05
Photo actually George Canale		
539 Neal Heaton	.01	.05
540 Danny Tartabull	.01	.05
541 Pat Perry	.01	.05
542 Darren Daulton	.02	.10
543 Nelson Liriano	.01	.05
544 Dennis Boyd	.02	.10
Now with Expos		
12/7/89		
545 Kevin McReynolds	.01	.05
546 Kevin Hickey	.01	.05
547 Jack Howell	.01	.05
548 Pat Clements	.01	.05
549 Don Zimmer MG	.01	.05
550 Julio Franco	.02	.10
551 Tim Crews	.01	.05
552 MikeMiss. Smith	.01	.05
553 Scott Scudder UER	.01	.05
Cedar Rapids		
554 Jay Buhner	.08	.25
555 Jack Morris	.02	.10
556 Gene Larkin	.01	.05
557 Jeff Innis	.01	.05
558 Rafael Ramirez	.01	.05
559 Andy McGaffigan	.01	.05
560 Steve Sax	.01	.05
561 Ken Dayley	.01	.05
562 Chad Kreuter	.01	.05
563 Alex Sanchez	.01	.05
564 Tyler Houston FDP RC	.01	.05
565 Scott Fletcher	.01	.05
566 Mark Knudson	.01	.05
567 Ron Gant	.02	.10
568 John Smiley	.01	.05
569 Ivan Calderon	.01	.05
570 Cal Ripken	.60	1.50
571 Brett Butler	.02	.10
572 Greg W. Harris	.01	.05
573 Danny Heep	.01	.05
574 Bill Swift	.01	.05
575 Lance Parrish	.01	.05
576 Mike Dyer RC	.01	.05
577 Charlie Hayes	.01	.05
578 Joe Magrane	.01	.05
579 Art Howe MG	.01	.05
580 Joe Carter	.02	.10
581 Ken Griffey Sr.	.02	.10
582 Rick Honeycutt	.01	.05
583 Bruce Benedict	.01	.05
584 Phil Stephenson	.01	.05
585 Kal Daniels	.01	.05
586 Edwin Nunez	.01	.05
587 Lance Johnson	.01	.05
588 Rick Rhoden	.01	.05
589 Mike Aldrete	.01	.05
590 Ozzie Smith	.20	.50
591 Todd Stottlemyre	.02	.10
592 R.J. Reynolds	.01	.05
593 Scott Bradley	.01	.05
594 Luis Sojo	.01	.05
595 Greg Swindell	.01	.05
596 Jose DeJesus	.01	.05
597 Chris Bosio	.01	.05
598 Brady Anderson	.08	.25
599 Frank Williams	.01	.05
600 Darryl Strawberry	.02	.10
601 Luis Rivera	.01	.05
602 Scott Garrelts	.01	.05
603 Tony Armas	.01	.05
604 Ron Robinson	.01	.05
605 Mike Scioscia	.02	.10
606 Storm Davis	.02	.10
Now with Royals		
12/7/89		
607 Steve Jeltz	.01	.05
608 Eric Anthony	.01	.05
609 Sparky Anderson MG	.02	.10
610 Pedro Guerrero	.01	.05
611 Walt Terrell	.02	.10
Now with Pirates		
11/29/89		
612 Dave Gallagher	.01	.05
613 Jeff Pico	.01	.05
614 Nelson Santovenia	.01	.05
615 Rob Deer	.01	.05
616 Brian Holman	.01	.05
617 Geronimo Berroa	.01	.05
618 Ed Whitson	.01	.05
619 Rob Ducey	.01	.05
620 Tony Castillo	.01	.05
621 Melido Perez	.01	.05
622 Sid Bream	.01	.05
623 Jim Corsi	.01	.05
624 Darrin Jackson	.01	.05
625 Roger McDowell	.01	.05
626 Bob Melvin	.02	.10
627 Jose Rijo	.01	.05
628 Candy Maldonado	.02	.10
Now with Indians		
11/28/89		
629 Eric Hetzel	.01	.05
630 Gary Gaetti	.02	.10
631 John Wetteland	.08	.25
632 Scott Lusader	.01	.05
633 Dennis Cook	.01	.05
634 Luis Polonia	.01	.05
635 Brian Downing	.01	.05
636 Jesse Orosco	.02	.10
637 Craig Reynolds	.01	.05
638 Jeff Montgomery	.02	.10
639 Tony LaRussa MG	.02	.10
640 Rick Sutcliffe	.02	.10
641 Doug Strange	.01	.05
642 Jack Armstrong	.01	.05
643 Alfredo Griffin	.01	.05
644 Paul Assenmacher	.01	.05
645 Jose Oquendo	.01	.05
646 Checklist 5	.01	.05
647 Rex Hudler	.02	.10
648 Jim Clancy	.01	.05
649 Dan Murphy	.01	.05
650 Mike Witt	.01	.05
651 Rafael Santana	.02	.10
Now with Indians		
1/10/90		
652 Mike Boddicker	.01	.05
653 John Moses	.01	.05
654 Paul Coleman FDP RC	.01	.05
655 Gregg Olson	.01	.05
656 Mackey Sasser	.01	.05
657 Terry Mulholland	.01	.05
658 Donell Nixon	.01	.05
659 Greg Cadaret	.01	.05
660 Vince Coleman	.01	.05
661 Dick Howser TBC'85	.01	.05
UER		
Seaver's 300th on 7/11/85		
should be 8/4/85		
662 Mike Schmidt TBC'80	.08	.25
663 Fred Lynn TBC'75	.01	.05
664 Johnny Bench TBC'70	.08	.25
665 Sandy Koufax TBC'65	.20	.50
666 Brian Fisher	.01	.05
667 Curt Wilkerson	.01	.05
668 Joe Oliver	.01	.05
669 Tom Lasorda MG	.08	.25
670 Dennis Eckersley	.15	.40
671 Bob Boone	.02	.10
672 Roy Smith	.01	.05
673 Joey Meyer	.01	.05
674 Spike Owen	.01	.05
675 Jim Abbott	.05	.15
676 Randy Kutcher	.01	.05
677 Jay Tibbs	.01	.05
678 Kirt Manwaring UER	.01	.05
88 Phoenix stats repeated		
679 Gary Ward	.01	.05
680 Howard Johnson	.01	.05
681 Mike Schooler	.01	.05
682 Dann Bilardello	.01	.05
683 Kenny Rogers	.02	.10
684 Julio Machado	.01	.05
685 Tony Fernandez	.01	.05
686 Carmelo Martinez	.02	.10
Now with Phillies		
12/4/89		
687 Tim Birtsas	.01	.05
688 Milt Thompson	.01	.05
689 Rich Yett	.02	.10
Now with Twins		
12/26/89		
690 Mark McGwire	.30	.75
691 Chuck Cary	.01	.05
692 Sammy Sosa RC	1.50	4.00
693 Calvin Schiraldi	.01	.05
694 Mike Stanton	.01	.05
695 Tom Henke	.01	.05
696 B.J. Surhoff	.02	.10
697 Mike Davis	.01	.05
698 Omar Vizquel	.08	.25
699 Jim Leyland MG	.01	.05
700 Kirby Puckett	.30	.75
701 Bernie Williams RC	.60	1.50
702 Tony Phillips	.01	.05
Now with Tigers		
12/5/89		
703 Jeff Brantley	.01	.05
704 Chip Hale	.01	.05
705 Claudell Washington	.01	.05
706 Geno Petralli	.01	.05
707 Luis Aquino	.01	.05
708 Larry Sheets	.02	.10
Now with Tigers		
1/10/90		
709 Juan Berenguer	.01	.05
710 Von Hayes	.01	.05
711 Rick Aguilera	.04	.10
712 Todd Benzinger	.01	.05
713 Tim Drummond	.01	.05
714 Marquis Grissom RC	.20	.50
715 Greg Maddux	.40	1.00
716 Steve Balboni	.01	.05
717 Ron Karkovice	.01	.05
718 Gary Sheffield	.20	.50
719 Wally Whitehurst	.01	.05
720 Andres Galarraga	.08	.25
721 Lee Mazzilli	.01	.05
722 Felix Fermin	.01	.05
723 Jeff D. Robinson	.01	.05
Now with Yankees		
12/4/89		
724 Juan Bell	.01	.05
725 Terry Pendleton	.02	.10
726 Gene Nelson	.01	.05
727 Pat Tabler	.01	.05
728 Jim Acker	.01	.05
729 Bobby Valentine MG	.01	.05
730 Tony Gwynn	.30	.75
731 Don Carman	.01	.05
732 Ernest Riles	.01	.05
733 John Dopson	.01	.05
734 Kevin Elster	.01	.05
735 Charlie Hough	.02	.10
736 Rick Dempsey	.01	.05
737 Chris Sabo	.01	.05
738 Gene Harris	.01	.05
739 Dale Sveum	.01	.05
740 Jesse Barfield	.01	.05
741 Steve Wilson	.01	.05
742 Ernie Whitt	.01	.05
743 Tom Candiotti	.01	.05
744 Kelly Mann	.01	.05
745 Hubie Brooks	.01	.05
746 Dave Smith	.01	.05
747 Randy Bush	.01	.05
748 Doyle Alexander	.01	.05
749 Mark Parent UER	.01	.05
'87 BA .80, should be .080		
750 Dale Murphy	.08	.25
751 Steve Lyons	.02	.10
752 Tom Gordon	.05	.15
753 Chris Speier	.01	.05
754 Bob Walk	.01	.05
755 Rafael Palmeiro	.08	.25
756 Ken Howell	.01	.05
757 Larry Walker RC	.60	1.50
758 Mark Thurmond	.01	.05
759 Tom Trebelhorn MG	.01	.05
760 Wade Boggs	.15	.40
761 Mike Jackson	.02	.10
762 Doug Dascenzo	.01	.05
763 Dennis Martinez	.02	.10
764 Tim Teufel	.01	.05
765 Chili Davis	.02	.10
766 Brian Meyer	.01	.05
767 Tracy Jones	.01	.05
768 Chuck Crim	.01	.05
769 Greg Hibbard	.01	.05
770 Cory Snyder	.01	.05
771 Pete Smith	.01	.05
772 Jeff Reed	.01	.05
773 Dave Leiper	.01	.05
774 Ben McDonald	.01	.05
775 Andy Van Slyke	.02	.10
776 Charlie Leibrandt	.02	.10
Now with Braves		
12/17/89		
777 Tim Laudner	.01	.05
778 Mike Jeffcoat	.01	.05
779 Lloyd Moseby	.02	.10
Now with Tigers		
12/7/89		
780 Orel Hershiser	.02	.10
781 Mario Diaz	.01	.05
782 Jose Alvarez	.02	.10
Now with Giants		
12/4/89		
783 Checklist 6	.01	.05
784 Scott Bailes	.02	.10
Now with Angels		
1/9/90		
785 Jim Rice	.02	.10
786 Eric King	.01	.05
787 Rene Gonzales	.01	.05
788 Frank DiPino	.01	.05
789 John Wathan MG	.01	.05
790 Gary Carter	.15	.40
791 Alvaro Espinoza	.01	.05
792 Gerald Perry	.01	.05

1990 O-Pee-Chee Box Bottoms

Card	Low	High
COMPLETE SET (16)	4.00	10.00
A Wade Boggs	.40	1.00
B George Brett	.75	2.00
C Andre Dawson	.20	.50
D Darrell Evans	.07	.20
E Dwight Gooden	.07	.20
F Rickey Henderson	.50	1.25
G Tom Lasorda MG	.20	.50
H Fred Lynn	.02	.10
I Mark McGwire	1.00	2.50
J Dave Parker	.07	.20
K Jeff Reardon	.07	.20
L Rick Reuschel	.02	.10
M Jim Rice	.07	.20
N Cal Ripken	1.50	4.00
O Nolan Ryan	1.50	4.00
P Ryne Sandberg	.75	2.00

1991 O-Pee-Chee

The 1991 O-Pee-Chee baseball set contains 792 standard-size cards. For the second time since 1976, O-Pee-Chee issued the exact same set as Topps. The only distinctions are the bilingual text and the O-Pee-Chee copyright on the backs. The fronts feature white-bordered color action player photos framed by two different colored lines. The player's name and position appear at the bottom of the photo, with his team name appearing just above. The Topps 40th anniversary logo appears in the upper left corner. The traded players have their new teams and dates of trade printed on the photo. The pinkish horizontal backs present player biography, statistics and bilingual career highlights. Cards 386-407 are an All-Star subset. Notable Rookie Cards include Carl Everett and Chipper Jones.

Card	Low	High
COMPLETE SET (792)	6.00	15.00
COMPLETE FACT.SET (792)	8.00	20.00
1 Nolan Ryan	.75	2.00
2 George Brett RB	.15	.40
3 Carlton Fisk RB	.08	.25
4 Kevin Maas RB	.01	.05
5 Cal Ripken RB	.30	.75
6 Nolan Ryan RB	.40	1.00
7 Ryne Sandberg RB	.08	.25
8 Bobby Thigpen RB	.01	.05
9 Darrin Fletcher	.01	.05
10 Gregg Olson	.01	.05
11 Roberto Kelly	.01	.05
12 Paul Assenmacher	.01	.05
13 Mariano Duncan	.01	.05
14 Dennis Lamp	.01	.05
15 Von Hayes	.01	.05
16 Mike Heath	.01	.05
17 Jeff Brantley	.01	.05
18 Nelson Liriano	.01	.05
19 Jeff D. Robinson	.01	.05
20 Pedro Guerrero	.01	.05
21 Joe Morgan MG	.01	.05
22 Storm Davis	.01	.05
23 Jim Gantner	.01	.05
24 Dave Martinez	.01	.05
25 Tim Belcher	.01	.05
26 Luis Sojo UER/(Born in Barquisimeto&	.01	.05
not Caracas		
27 Bobby Witt	.01	.05
28 Alvaro Espinoza	.01	.05
29 Bob Walk	.01	.05
30 Gregg Jefferies	.01	.05
31 Colby Ward	.01	.05
32 Mike Simms	.01	.05
33 Barry Jones	.01	.05
34 Atlee Hammaker	.01	.05
35 Greg Maddux	.40	1.00
36 Donnie Hill	.01	.05
37 Tom Bolton	.01	.05
38 Scott Bradley	.01	.05
39 Jim Neidlinger	.01	.05
40 Kevin Mitchell	.01	.05
41 Ken Dayley	.02	.10
Now with Blue Jays/11/26/90		
42 Chris Hoiles	.01	.05
43 Roger McDowell	.01	.05
44 Mike Felder	.01	.05
45 Chris Sabo	.01	.05
46 Tim Drummond	.01	.05
47 Brook Jacoby	.01	.05
48 Dennis Boyd	.01	.05
49 Pat Borders	.01	.05
50 Bob Welch	.01	.05
51 Art Howe MG	.01	.05
52 Francisco Oliveras	.01	.05
53 Mike Sharperson UER	.01	.05
Born in 1961, not 1960		
54 Gary Mielke	.01	.05
55 Jeffrey Leonard	.01	.05
56 Jeff Parrett	.01	.05
57 Jack Howell	.01	.05
58 Mel Stottlemyre Jr.	.01	.05
59 Eric Yelding	.01	.05
60 Frank Viola	.01	.05

61 Stan Javier .01 .05
62 Lee Guetterman .01 .05
63 Milt Thompson .01 .05
64 Tom Herr .01 .05
65 Bruce Hurst .01 .05
66 Terry Kennedy .01 .05
67 Rick Honeycutt .01 .05
68 Gary Sheffield .20 .50
69 Steve Wilson .01 .05
70 Ellis Burks .02 .10
71 Jim Acker .01 .05
72 Junior Ortiz .01 .05
73 Craig Worthington .01 .05
74 Shane Andrews RC .01 .05
75 Jack Morris .02 .10
76 Jerry Browne .01 .05
77 Drew Hall .01 .05
78 Geno Petralli .01 .05
79 Frank Thomas .25 .60
80 Fernando Valenzuela .02 .10
81 Cito Gaston MG .01 .05
82 Tom Glavine .15 .40
83 Daryl Boston .01 .05
84 Bob McClure .01 .05
85 Jesse Barfield .01 .05
86 Les Lancaster .01 .05
87 Tracy Jones .01 .05
88 Bob Tewksbury .01 .05
89 Darren Daulton .02 .10
90 Danny Tartabull .01 .05
91 Greg Colbrunn .01 .05
92 Danny Jackson .02 .10
Now with Cubs/11/21/90
93 Ivan Calderon .01 .05
94 John Dopson .01 .05
95 Paul Molitor .15 .40
96 Trevor Wilson .01 .05
97 Brady Anderson .08 .25
98 Sergio Valdez .01 .05
99 Chris Gwynn .01 .05
100 Don Mattingly .40 1.00
101 Rob Ducey .01 .05
102 Gene Larkin .01 .05
103 Tim Costo .01 .05
104 Don Robinson .01 .05
105 Kevin McReynolds .01 .05
106 Ed Nunez .02 .10
Now with Brewers/12/4/90
107 Luis Polonia .01 .05
108 Matt Young .02 .10
Now with Red Sox/12/4/90
109 Greg Riddoch MG .01 .05
110 Tom Henke .01 .05
111 Andres Thomas .01 .05
112 Frank DiPino .01 .05
113 Carl Everett RC .40 1.00
114 Lance Dickson .01 .05
115 Hubie Brooks .02 .10
Now with Mets/12/15/90
116 Mark Davis .01 .05
117 Dion James .01 .05
118 Tom Edens .01 .05
119 Carl Nichols .01 .05
120 Joe Carter .05 .15
Now with Blue Jays/12/5/90
121 Eric King .02 .10
Now with Indians/12/4/90
122 Paul O'Neill .15 .40
123 Greg A. Harris .01 .05
124 Randy Bush .01 .05
125 Steve Bedrosian .02 .10
Now with Twins/12/5/90
126 Bernard Gilkey .02 .10
127 Joe Price .01 .05
128 Travis Fryman .08 .25
Front has SS, back has SS-3B
129 Mark Eichhorn .01 .05
130 Ozzie Smith .20 .50
131 Checklist 1 .01 .05
132 Jamie Quirk .01 .05
133 Greg Briley .01 .05
134 Kevin Elster .01 .05
135 Jerome Walton .01 .05
136 Dave Schmidt .01 .05
137 Randy Ready .01 .05
138 Jamie Moyer .05 .15
Now with Cardinals/1/10/91
139 Jeff Treadway .01 .05
140 Fred McGriff .08 .25
Now with Padres/12/5/90
141 Nick Leyva MG .01 .05
142 Curt Wilkerson .02 .10
Now with Pirates/1/9/91
143 John Smiley .01 .05
144 Dave Henderson .01 .05
145 Lou Whitaker .02 .10
146 Dan Plesac .01 .05
147 Carlos Baerga .01 .05
148 Rey Palacios .01 .05
149 Al Osuna UER/(Shown with glove on .01 .05
right hand& bi
150 Cal Ripken .60 1.50
151 Tom Browning .01 .05
152 Mickey Hatcher .01 .05
153 Bryan Harvey .01 .05
154 Jay Buhner .02 .10
155 Dwight Evans .05 .15
Now with Orioles/12/6/90
156 Carlos Martinez .01 .05
157 John Smoltz .08 .25
158 Jose Uribe .01 .05
159 Joe Boever .01 .05
160 Vince Coleman .01 .05
161 Tim Leary .01 .05
162 Ozzie Canseco .01 .05
163 Dave Johnson .01 .05
164 Edgar Diaz .01 .05
165 Sandy Alomar Jr. .02 .10
166 Harold Baines .05 .15
167 Randy Tomlin .01 .05
168 John Olerud .08 .25
169 Luis Aquino .01 .05
170 Carlton Fisk .15 .40
171 Tony LaRussa MG .02 .10
172 Pete Incaviglia .01 .05
173 Jason Grimsley .01 .05
174 Ken Caminiti .08 .25
175 Jack Armstrong .01 .05
176 John Orton .01 .05
177 Reggie Harris .01 .05
178 Dave Valle .01 .05
179 Pete Harnisch .01 .05
Now with Astros/1/10/91
180 Tony Gwynn .30 .75
181 Duane Ward .01 .05
182 Junior Noboa .01 .05
183 Clay Parker .01 .05
184 Gary Green .01 .05
185 Joe Magrane .01 .05
186 Rod Booker .01 .05
187 Greg Cadaret .01 .05
188 Damon Berryhill .01 .05
189 Daryl Irvine .01 .05
190 Matt Williams .05 .15
191 Willie Blair .02 .10
Now with Indians/11/6/90
192 Rob Deer .02 .10
Now with Tigers/11/21/90
193 Felix Fermin .01 .05
194 Xavier Hernandez .01 .05
195 Wally Joyner .02 .10
196 Jim Vatcher .01 .05
197 Chris Nabholz .01 .05
198 R.J. Reynolds .01 .05
199 Mike Hartley .01 .05
200 Darryl Strawberry .05 .15
Now with Dodgers/11/8/90
201 Tom Kelly MG .01 .05
202 Jim Leyritz .01 .05
203 Gene Harris .01 .05
204 Herm Winningham .01 .05
205 Mike Perez .01 .05
206 Carlos Quintana .01 .05
207 Gary Wayne .01 .05
208 Willie Wilson .01 .05
209 Ken Howell .01 .05
210 Lance Parrish .01 .05
211 Brian Barnes .01 .05
212 Steve Finley .08 .25
Now with Astros/1/10/91
213 Frank Wills .01 .05
214 Joe Girardi .02 .10
215 Dave Smith .02 .10
Now with Cubs/12/17/90
216 Greg Gagne .01 .05
217 Chris Bosio .01 .05
218 Rick Parker .01 .05
219 Jack McDowell .01 .05
220 Tim Wallach .01 .05
221 Don Slaught .01 .05
222 Brian McRae RC .08 .25
223 Allan Anderson .01 .05
224 Juan Gonzalez .08 .25
225 Randy Johnson .25 .60
226 Alfredo Griffin .01 .05
227 Steve Avery UER
(Pitched 13 games for .01 .05
Durham in
228 Rex Hudler .01 .05
229 Rance Mulliniks .01 .05
230 Sid Fernandez .01 .05
231 Doug Rader MG .01 .05
232 Jose DeJesus .01 .05
233 Al Leiter .01 .05
234 Scott Erickson .01 .05
235 Dave Parker .02 .10
236 Frank Tanana .01 .05
237 Rick Cerone .01 .05
238 Mike Dunne .01 .05
239 Darren Lewis .02 .10
Now with Giants/12/4/90
240 Mike Scott .01 .05
241 Dave Clark UER/(Career totals 19 HR .01 .05
and 5 3B& sh
242 Mike LaCoss .01 .05
243 Lance Johnson .01 .05
244 Mike Jeffcoat .01 .05
245 Kal Daniels .01 .05
246 Kevin Wickander .01 .05
247 Jody Reed .01 .05
248 Tom Gordon .02 .10
249 Bob Melvin .01 .05
250 Dennis Eckersley .15 .40
251 Mark Lemke .01 .05
252 Mel Rojas .02 .10
253 Garry Templeton .01 .05
254 Shawn Boskie .01 .05
255 Brian Downing .01 .05
256 Greg Hibbard .01 .05
257 Tom O'Malley .01 .05
258 Chris Hammond .01 .05
259 Hensley Meulens .01 .05
260 Harold Reynolds .02 .10
261 Bud Harrelson MG .01 .05
262 Tim Jones .01 .05
263 Checklist 2 .01 .05
264 Dave Hollins .01 .05
265 Mark Gubicza .01 .05
266 Carmelo Castillo .01 .05
267 Mark Knudson .01 .05
268 Tom Brookens .01 .05
269 Joe Hesketh .01 .05
270 Mark McGwire .30 .75
271 Omar Olivares .01 .05
272 Jeff King .01 .05
273 Johnny Ray .01 .05
274 Ken Williams .02 .10
275 Alan Trammell .05 .15
276 Bill Swift .01 .05
277 Scott Coolbaugh .02 .10
Now with Padres/12/12/90
278 Alex Fernandez UER .01 .05
No '90 White Sox stats
279 Jose Gonzalez .01 .05
280 Bret Saberhagen .02 .10
281 Larry Sheets .01 .05
282 Don Carman .01 .05
283 Marquis Grissom .02 .10
284 Billy Spiers .01 .05
285 Jim Abbott .02 .10
286 Ken Oberkfell .01 .05
287 Mark Grant .01 .05
288 Derrick May .01 .05
289 Tim Birtsas .01 .05
290 Steve Sax .01 .05
291 John Wathan MG .01 .05
292 Bud Black .01 .05
293 Jay Bell .01 .05
294 Mike Moore .01 .05
295 Rafael Palmeiro .08 .25
296 Mark Williamson .01 .05
297 Manny Lee .01 .05
298 Omar Vizquel .08 .25
299 Scott Radinsky .01 .05
300 Kirby Puckett .25 .60
301 Steve Farr .02 .10
Now with Yankees/11/26/90
302 Tim Teufel .01 .05
303 Mike Boddicker .02 .10
Now with Royals/11/21/90
304 Kevin Reimer .01 .05
305 Mike Scioscia .02 .10
306 Lonnie Smith .01 .05
307 Andy Benes .01 .05
308 Tom Pagnozzi .01 .05
309 Norm Charlton .01 .05
310 Gary Carter .15 .40
311 Jeff Pico .01 .05
312 Charlie Hayes .01 .05
313 Ron Robinson .01 .05
314 Gary Pettis .01 .05
315 Roberto Alomar .15 .40
316 Gene Nelson .01 .05
317 Mike Fitzgerald .01 .05
318 Rick Aguilera .02 .10
319 Jeff McKnight .01 .05
320 Tony Fernandez .02 .10
Now with Padres/12/5/90
321 Bob Rodgers MG .01 .05
322 Terry Shumpert .01 .05
323 Cory Snyder .01 .05
324 Ron Kittle .01 .05
325 Brett Butler .02 .10
Now with Dodgers/12/15/90
326 Ken Patterson .01 .05
327 Ron Hassey .01 .05
328 Walt Terrell .01 .05
329 David Justice UER .15 .40
330 Dwight Gooden .02 .10
331 Eric Anthony .01 .05
332 Kenny Rogers .05 .15
Now with White Sox/12/4/90
333 Chipper Jones RC 15.00 40.00
334 Todd Benzinger .01 .05
335 Mitch Williams .01 .05
336 Matt Nokes .01 .05
337 Keith Comstock .01 .05
338 Luis Rivera .01 .05
339 Larry Walker .08 .25
340 Ramon Martinez .01 .05
341 John Moses .01 .05
342 Mickey Morandini .01 .05
343 Jose Oquendo .01 .05
344 Jeff Russell .01 .05
345 Len Dykstra .02 .10
346 Jesse Orosco .02 .10
347 Greg Vaughn .08 .25
348 Todd Stottlemyre .02 .10
349 Dave Gallagher .02 .10
Now with Angels/12/4/90
350 Glenn Davis .01 .05
351 Joe Torre MG .02 .10
352 Frank White .02 .10
353 Tony Castillo .01 .05
354 Sid Bream .02 .10
Now with Braves/12/5/90
355 Chili Davis .02 .10
356 Mike Marshall .01 .05
357 Jack Savage .01 .05
358 Mark Parent .02 .10
Now with Rangers/12/12/90
359 Chuck Cary .01 .05
360 Tim Raines .05 .15
Now with White Sox/12/23/90
361 Scott Garrelts .01 .05
362 Hector Villanueva .01 .05
363 Rick Mahler .01 .05
364 Dan Pasqua .01 .05
365 Mike Schooler .01 .05
366 Checklist 3 .01 .05
367 Dave Walsh RC .01 .05
368 Felix Jose .01 .05
369 Steve Searcy .01 .05
370 Kelly Gruber .01 .05
371 Jeff Montgomery .01 .05
372 Spike Owen .01 .05
373 Darrin Jackson .01 .05
374 Larry Casian .01 .05
375 Tony Pena .01 .05
376 Mike Harkey .01 .05
377 Rene Gonzales .01 .05
378 Wilson Alvarez .02 .10
379 Randy Velarde .01 .05
380 Willie McGee .05 .15
Now with Giants/12/3/90
381 Jim Leyland MG .01 .05
382 Mackey Sasser .01 .05
383 Pete Smith .01 .05
384 Gerald Perry .02 .10
Now with Cardinals/12/13/90
385 Mickey Tettleton .02 .10
Now with Tigers/1/12/90
386 Cecil Fielder AS .02 .10
387 Julio Franco AS .01 .05
388 Kelly Gruber AS .01 .05
389 Alan Trammell AS .02 .10
390 Jose Canseco AS .08 .25
391 Rickey Henderson AS .15 .40
392 Ken Griffey Jr. AS .40 1.00
393 Carlton Fisk AS .02 .10
394 Bob Welch AS .01 .05
395 Chuck Finley AS .01 .05
396 Bobby Thigpen AS .01 .05
397 Eddie Murray AS .02 .10
398 Ryne Sandberg AS .05 .15
399 Matt Williams AS .05 .15
400 Barry Larkin AS .02 .10
401 Barry Bonds AS .20 .50
402 Darryl Strawberry AS .02 .10
403 Bobby Bonilla AS .01 .05
404 Mike Scioscia AS .01 .05
405 Doug Drabek AS .01 .05
406 Frank Viola AS .01 .05
407 John Franco AS .01 .05
408 Ernie Riles .02 .10
Now with Athletics/12/4/90
409 Mike Stanley .01 .05
410 Dave Righetti .02 .10
Now with Giants/12/4/90
411 Lance Blankenship .01 .05
412 Dave Bergman .01 .05
413 Terry Mulholland .01 .05
414 Sammy Sosa .15 .40
415 Rick Sutcliffe .02 .10
416 Randy Milligan .01 .05
417 Bill Krueger .01 .05
418 Nick Esasky .01 .05
419 Jeff Reed .01 .05
420 Bobby Thigpen .01 .05
421 Alex Cole .01 .05
422 Rick Reuschel .01 .05
423 Rafael Ramirez UER .01 .05
Born 1959, not 1958
424 Calvin Schiraldi .01 .05
425 Andy Van Slyke .01 .05
426 Joe Grahe .01 .05
427 Rick Dempsey .01 .05
428 John Barfield .01 .05
429 Stump Merrill MG .01 .05
430 Gary Gaetti .02 .10
431 Paul Gibson .01 .05
432 Delino DeShields .02 .10
433 Pat Tabler .01 .05
Now with Blue Jays/12/5/90
434 Julio Machado .01 .05
435 Kevin Maas .01 .05
436 Scott Bankhead .01 .05
437 Doug Dascenzo .01 .05
438 Vicente Palacios .01 .05
439 Dickie Thon .01 .05
440 George Bell .01 .05
Now with Cubs/12/6/90
441 Zane Smith .01 .05
442 Charlie O'Brien .01 .05
443 Jeff Innis .01 .05
444 Glenn Braggs .01 .05
445 Greg Swindell .01 .05
446 Craig Grebeck .01 .05
447 John Burkett .01 .05
448 Craig Lefferts .01 .05
449 Juan Berenguer .01 .05
450 Wade Boggs .15 .40
451 Neal Heaton .01 .05
452 Bill Schroeder .01 .05
453 Lenny Harris .01 .05
454 Kevin Appier .02 .10
455 Walt Weiss .01 .05
456 Charlie Leibrandt .01 .05
457 Todd Hundley .08 .25
458 Brian Holman .01 .05
459 Tom Trebelhorn MG .01 .05
460 Dave Stieb .02 .10
461 Robin Ventura .08 .25
462 Steve Frey .01 .05
463 Dwight Smith .01 .05
464 Steve Buechele .01 .05
465 Ken Griffey Sr. .02 .10
466 Charles Nagy .02 .10
467 Dennis Cook .01 .05
468 Tim Hulett .01 .05
469 Chet Lemon .01 .05
470 Howard Johnson .01 .05
471 Mike Lieberthal RC .20 .50
472 Kirt Manwaring .01 .05
473 Curt Young .01 .05
474 Phil Plantier .01 .05
475 Teddy Higuera .01 .05
476 Glenn Wilson .01 .05
477 Mike Fetters .01 .05
478 Kurt Stillwell .01 .05
479 Bob Patterson .01 .05
480 Dave Magadan .01 .05
481 Eddie Whitson .01 .05
482 Tino Martinez .08 .25
483 Mike Aldrete .01 .05
484 Dave LaPoint .01 .05
485 Terry Pendleton .05 .15
Now with Braves/12/3/90
486 Tommy Greene .01 .05
487 Rafael Belliard .02 .10
Now with Braves/12/18/90
488 Jeff Manto .01 .05
489 Bobby Valentine MG .01 .05
490 Kirk Gibson .05 .15
Now with Royals/12/1/90
491 Kurt Miller .01 .05
492 Ernie Whitt .01 .05
493 Jose Rijo .01 .05
494 Chris James .01 .05
495 Charlie Hough .05 .15
Now with White Sox/12/20/90
496 Marty Barrett .01 .05
497 Ben McDonald .01 .05
498 Mark Salas .01 .05
499 Melido Perez .01 .05
500 Will Clark .15 .40
501 Mike Bielecki .01 .05
502 Carney Lansford .02 .10
503 Roy Smith .01 .05
504 Julio Valera .01 .05
505 Chuck Finley .02 .10
506 Darnell Coles .01 .05
507 Steve Jeltz .01 .05
508 Mike York .01 .05
509 Glenallen Hill .01 .05
510 John Franco .02 .10
511 Steve Balboni .01 .05
512 Jose Mesa .01 .05
513 Jerald Clark .01 .05
514 Mike Stanton .01 .05
515 Alvin Davis .01 .05
516 Karl Rhodes .01 .05
517 Joe Oliver .01 .05
518 Cris Carpenter .01 .05
519 Sparky Anderson MG .02 .10
520 Mark Grace .15 .40
521 Joe Orsulak .01 .05
522 Stan Belinda .01 .05
523 Rodney McCray .01 .05
524 Darrel Akerfelds .01 .05
525 Willie Randolph .02 .10
526 Moises Alou .02 .10
527 Checklist 4 .01 .05
528 Denny Martinez .02 .10
529 Marc Newfield .01 .05
530 Roger Clemens .40 1.00
531 Dave Rohde .01 .05
532 Kirk McCaskill .01 .05
533 Oddibe McDowell .01 .05
534 Mike Jackson .02 .10
535 Ruben Sierra .02 .10
536 Mike Witt .01 .05
537 Jose Lind .01 .05
538 Bip Roberts .01 .05
539 Scott Terry .01 .05
540 George Brett .30 .75
541 Domingo Ramos .01 .05
542 Rob Murphy .01 .05
543 Junior Felix .01 .05
544 Alejandro Pena .01 .05
545 Dale Murphy .15 .40
546 Jeff Ballard .01 .05
547 Mike Pagliarulo .01 .05
548 Jaime Navarro .01 .05
549 John McNamara MG .01 .05
550 Eric Davis .02 .10
551 Bob Kipper .01 .05
552 Jeff Hamilton .01 .05
553 Joe Klink .01 .05
554 Brian Harper .01 .05
555 Turner Ward .01 .05
556 Gary Ward .01 .05
557 Wally Whitehurst .01 .05
558 Otis Nixon .02 .10
559 Adam Peterson .01 .05
560 Greg Smith .02 .10
Now with Dodgers/12/14/90
561 Tim McIntosh .01 .05
562 Jeff Kunkel .01 .05
563 Brent Knackert .01 .05
564 Dante Bichette .02 .10
565 Craig Biggio .05 .15
566 Craig Wilson .01 .05
567 Dwayne Henry .01 .05
568 Ron Karkovice .01 .05
569 Curt Schilling .25 .60
Now with Astros/1/10/91
570 Barry Bonds .30 .75
571 Pat Combs .01 .05
572 Dave Anderson .01 .05
573 Rich Rodriguez UER
(Stats say drafted 4th& .01 .05
but b.
574 John Marzano .01 .05
575 Robin Yount .15 .40
576 Jeff Kaiser .01 .05
577 Bill Doran .01 .05
578 Dave West .01 .05
579 Roger Craig MG .01 .05
580 Dave Stewart .02 .10
581 Luis Quinones .01 .05
582 Marty Clary .01 .05
583 Tony Phillips .01 .05
584 Kevin Brown .05 .15
585 Pete O'Brien .01 .05
586 Fred Lynn .01 .05
587 Jose Offerman UER .01 .05
588 Mark Whiten .01 .05
589 Scott Ruskin .01 .05
590 Eddie Murray .15 .40
591 Ken Hill .01 .05
592 B.J. Surhoff .02 .10
593 Mike Walker .01 .05
594 Rich Garces .01 .05
595 Bill Landrum .01 .05
596 Ronnie Walden .01 .05
597 Jerry Don Gleaton .01 .05
598 Sam Horn .01 .05
599 Greg Myers .01 .05
600 Bo Jackson .08 .25
601 Bob Ojeda .02 .10
Now with Dodgers/12/15/90
602 Casey Candaele .01 .05
603 Wes Chamberlain .01 .05
604 Billy Hatcher .01 .05
605 Jeff Reardon .02 .10
606 Jim Gott .01 .05
607 Edgar Martinez .05 .15
608 Todd Burns .01 .05
609 Jeff Torborg MG .01 .05
610 Andres Galarraga .08 .25
611 Dave Eiland .01 .05
612 Steve Lyons .02 .10
613 Eric Show .02 .10
Now with Athletics/12/10/90
614 Luis Salazar .01 .05
615 Bert Blyleven .02 .10
616 Todd Zeile .02 .10
617 Bill Wegman .01 .05
618 Sil Campusano .01 .05
619 David Wells .05 .15
620 Ozzie Guillen .02 .10
621 Ted Power .02 .10
Now with Reds/12/14/90
622 Jack Daugherty .01 .05
623 Jeff Blauser .01 .05
624 Tom Candiotti .01 .05
625 Terry Steinbach .01 .05
626 Gerald Young .01 .05
627 Tim Layana .01 .05
628 Greg Litton .01 .05
629 Wes Gardner .02 .10
Now with Padres/12/15/90
630 Dave Winfield .15 .40
631 Mike Morgan .01 .05
632 Lloyd Moseby .01 .05
633 Kevin Tapani .01 .05
634 Henry Cotto .01 .05
635 Andy Hawkins .01 .05
636 Geronimo Pena .01 .05
637 Bruce Ruffin .01 .05
638 Mike Macfarlane .01 .05
639 Frank Robinson MG .08 .25
640 Andre Dawson .08 .25
641 Mike Henneman .01 .05
642 Hal Morris .01 .05
643 Jim Presley .01 .05
644 Chuck Crim .01 .05
645 Juan Samuel .01 .05
646 Andujar Cedeno .01 .05
647 Mark Portugal .01 .05
648 Lee Stevens .01 .05
649 Bill Sampen .01 .05
650 Jack Clark .05 .15
Now with Red Sox/12/15/90
651 Alan Mills .01 .05
652 Kevin Romine .01 .05
653 Anthony Telford .01 .05
654 Paul Sorrento .02 .10
655 Erik Hanson .01 .05
656 Checklist 5 .01 .05
657 Mike Kingery .01 .05
658 Scott Aldred .01 .05
659 Oscar Azocar .01 .05
660 Lee Smith .02 .10
661 Steve Lake .01 .05
662 Rob Dibble .01 .05
663 Greg Brock .01 .05
664 John Farrell .01 .05
665 Mike LaValliere .01 .05
666 Danny Darwin .01 .05
Now with Red Sox/12/19/90
667 Kent Anderson .01 .05
668 Bill Long .01 .05
669 Lou Piniella MG .02 .10
670 Rickey Henderson .30 .75
671 Andy McGaffigan .01 .05
672 Shane Mack .01 .05
673 Greg Olson UER/(6 RBI in '88 at Tide- .01 .05
water and
674 Kevin Gross .02 .10
Now with Dodgers/12/3/90
675 Tom Brunansky .01 .05
676 Scott Chiamparino .01 .05
677 Billy Ripken .01 .05
678 Mark Davidson .01 .05
679 Bill Bathe .01 .05
680 David Cone .08 .25
681 Jeff Schaefer .01 .05
682 Ray Lankford .08 .25
683 Derek Lilliquist .01 .05
684 Milt Cuyler .01 .05
685 Doug Drabek .01 .05
686 Mike Gallego .01 .05
687 John Cerutti .01 .05
688 Rosario Rodriguez .02 .10
Now with Pirates/12/20/90
689 John Kruk .02 .10
690 Orel Hershiser .02 .10
691 Mike Blowers .01 .05
692 Efrain Valdez .01 .05
693 Francisco Cabrera .01 .05
694 Randy Veres .01 .05
695 Kevin Seitzer .01 .05
696 Steve Olin .01 .05
697 Shawn Abner .01 .05
698 Mark Guthrie .01 .05
699 Jim Lefebvre MG .01 .05
700 Jose Canseco .15 .40
701 Pascual Perez .01 .05
702 Tim Naehring .01 .05
703 Juan Agosto .02 .10
Now with Cardinals/12/14/90
704 Devon White .05 .15
Now with Blue Jays/12/2/90
705 Robby Thompson .01 .05
706 Brad Arnsberg .01 .05
707 Jim Eisenreich .01 .05
708 John Mitchell .01 .05
709 Matt Sinatro .01 .05
710 Kent Hrbek .02 .10
711 Jose DeLeon .01 .05
712 Ricky Jordan .01 .05
713 Scott Scudder .01 .05
714 Marvell Wynne .01 .05
715 Tim Burke .01 .05
716 Bob Geren .01 .05
717 Phil Bradley .01 .05
718 Steve Crawford .01 .05
719 Keith Miller .01 .05
720 Cecil Fielder .02 .10
721 Mark Lee .01 .05
722 Wally Backman .01 .05
723 Candy Maldonado .01 .05
724 David Segui .01 .05
725 Ron Gant .02 .10
726 Phil Stephenson .01 .05
727 Mookie Wilson .02 .10
728 Scott Sanderson .02 .10
Now with Yankees/12/31/90
729 Don Zimmer MG .01 .05
730 Barry Larkin .15 .40
731 Jeff Gray .01 .05
732 Franklin Stubbs .02 .10
Now with Brewers/12/5/90
733 Kelly Downs .01 .05
734 John Russell .01 .05
735 Ron Darling .01 .05
736 Dick Schofield .01 .05
737 Tim Crews .01 .05
738 Mel Hall .01 .05
739 Russ Swan .01 .05
740 Ryne Sandberg .20 .50
741 Jimmy Key .02 .10
742 Tommy Gregg .01 .05
743 Bryn Smith .01 .05
744 Nelson Santovenia .01 .05
745 Doug Jones .01 .05
746 John Shelby .01 .05
747 Tony Fossas .01 .05
748 Al Newman .01 .05
749 Greg W. Harris .01 .05
750 Bobby Bonilla .01 .05
751 Wayne Edwards .01 .05
752 Kevin Bass .01 .05
753 Paul Marak UER/(Stats say drafted in .01 .05
May& but bi
754 Bill Pecota .01 .05
755 Mark Langston .01 .05
756 Jeff Huson .01 .05
757 Mark Gardner .01 .05
758 Mike Devereaux .01 .05
759 Bobby Cox MG .02 .10
760 Benny Santiago .02 .10
761 Larry Andersen .02 .10
Now with Padres/12/21/90
762 Mitch Webster .01 .05
763 Dana Kiecker .01 .05
764 Mark Carreon .01 .05
765 Shawon Dunston .01 .05
766 Jeff M. Robinson .02 .10
Now with Orioles/1/12/91
767 Dan Wilson RC .08 .25
768 Donn Pall .01 .05
769 Tim Sherrill .01 .05
770 Jay Howell .01 .05
771 Gary Redus UER/(Born in Tanner& .01 .05
should say Athen
772 Kent Mercker UER
(Born in Indianapolis& .01 .05
should s
773 Tom Foley .01 .05
774 Dennis Rasmussen .01 .05
775 Julio Franco .02 .10
776 Brent Mayne .01 .05
777 John Candelaria .01 .05
778 Dan Gladden .01 .05
779 Carmelo Martinez .01 .05
780 Randy Myers .02 .10
781 Darryl Hamilton .01 .05
782 Jim Deshaies .01 .05
783 Joel Skinner .01 .05
784 Willie Fraser .02 .10
Now with Blue Jays/12/2/90
785 Scott Fletcher .01 .05
786 Eric Plunk .01 .05
787 Checklist 6 .01 .05
788 Bob Milacki .01 .05
789 Tom Lasorda MG .15 .40
790 Ken Griffey Jr. .75 2.00
791 Mike Benjamin .01 .05
792 Mike Greenwell .01 .05

1991 O-Pee-Chee Box Bottoms

COMPLETE SET (16) 4.00 10.00
A Bert Blyleven .30 .75
B George Brett .75 2.00
C Brett Butler .08 .25
D Andre Dawson .30 .75
E Dwight Evans .08 .25
F Carlton Fisk .50 1.25
G Alfredo Griffin .02 .10
H Rickey Henderson .50 1.25
I Willie McGee .08 .25
J Dale Murphy .30 .75
K Eddie Murray .50 1.25
L Dave Parker .08 .25
M Jeff Reardon .08 .25
N Nolan Ryan 1.50 4.00
O Juan Samuel .02 .10
P Robin Yount .50 1.25

1992 O-Pee-Chee

The 1992 O-Pee-Chee set contains 792 standard-size cards. These cards were sold in ten-card wax packs with a stick of bubble gum. The fronts have either posed or action color player photos on a white card face. Different color stripes frame the pictures, and the player's name and team name appear in two short color stripes respectively at the bottom. In English and French, the horizontally oriented backs have biography and complete career batting or pitching record. In addition, some of the cards have a picture of a baseball field and stadium on the back. Special subsets included are Record Breakers (2-5), Prospects (58, 126, 179, 473, 551, 591, 618, 656, 676) and a five-card tribute to Gary Carter (45, 387, 389, 399, 402). Each wax pack wrapper served as an entry blank offering each collector the chance to win one of 1,000 complete factory sets of 1992 O-Pee-Chee Premier baseball cards.

COMPLETE SET (792) 10.00 25.00
COMPLETE FACT.SET (792) 12.50 30.00
1 Nolan Ryan .75 2.00
2 Rickey Henderson RB .15 .40
Some cards have print
marks that show 1.991
on the front
3 Jeff Reardon RB .01 .05
4 Nolan Ryan RB .40 1.00
5 Dave Winfield RB .05 .15
6 Brien Taylor RC .01 .05
7 Jim Olander .01 .05
8 Bryan Hickerson .01 .05
9 Jon Farrell .01 .05
10 Wade Boggs .15 .40
11 Jack McDowell .01 .05
12 Luis Gonzalez .15 .40
13 Mike Scioscia .02 .10
14 Wes Chamberlain .01 .05
15 Dennis Martinez .02 .10
16 Jeff Montgomery .02 .10
17 Randy Milligan .01 .05
18 Greg Cadaret .01 .05
19 Jamie Quirk .01 .05
20 Bip Roberts .01 .05
21 Buck Rodgers MG .01 .05
22 Bill Wegman .01 .05
23 Chuck Knoblauch .08 .25
24 Randy Myers .02 .10
25 Ron Gant .01 .05
26 Mike Bielecki .01 .05
27 Juan Gonzalez .08 .25
28 Mike Schooler .01 .05
29 Mickey Tettleton .01 .05
30 John Kruk .02 .10
31 Bryn Smith .01 .05
32 Chris Nabholz .01 .05
33 Carlos Baerga .01 .05
34 Jeff Juden .01 .05
35 Dave Righetti .01 .05
36 Scott Ruffcorn .01 .05
37 Luis Polonia .01 .05
38 Tom Candiotti .02 .10
Now with Dodgers
12-3-91
39 Greg Olson .01 .05
40 Cal Ripken 1.50 4.00
Lou Gehrig
41 Craig Lefferts .01 .05
42 Mike Macfarlane .01 .05

43 Jose Lind .01 .05
44 Rick Aguilera .02 .10
45 Gary Carter .20 .50
46 Steve Farr .01 .05
47 Rex Hudler .02 .10
48 Scott Scudder .01 .05
49 Damon Berryhill .01 .05
50 Ken Griffey Jr. .50 1.25
51 Tom Runnells MG .01 .05
52 Juan Bell .01 .05
53 Tommy Gregg .01 .05
54 David Wells .05 .15
55 Rafael Palmeiro .15 .40
56 Charlie O'Brien .01 .05
57 Donn Pall .01 .05
58 Brad Ausmus RC .60 1.50
Jim Campanis Jr.
Dave Nilsson
Doug Robbins
59 Mo Vaughn .08 .25
60 Tony Fernandez .01 .05
61 Paul O'Neill .15 .40
62 Gene Nelson .01 .05
63 Randy Ready .01 .05
64 Bob Kipper .02 .10
Now with Twins
12-17-91
65 Willie McGee .02 .10
66 Scott Stahoviak .01 .05
67 Luis Salazar .01 .05
68 Marvin Freeman .01 .05
69 Kenny Lofton .15 .40
Now with Indians
12-10-91
70 Gary Gaetti .02 .10
71 Erik Hanson .01 .05
72 Eddie Zosky .01 .05
73 Brian Barnes .01 .05
74 Scott Leius .01 .05
75 Bret Saberhagen .02 .10
76 Mike Gallego .01 .05
77 Jack Armstrong .02 .10
Now with Indians
11-15-91
78 Ivan Rodriguez .20 .50
79 Jesse Orosco .02 .10
80 David Justice .05 .15
81 Ced Landrum .01 .05
82 Doug Simons .01 .05
83 Tommy Greene .01 .05
84 Leo Gomez .01 .05
85 Jose DeLeon .01 .05
86 Steve Finley .02 .10
87 Bob MacDonald .01 .05
88 Darrin Jackson .01 .05
89 Neal Heaton .01 .05
90 Robin Yount .15 .40
91 Jeff Reed .01 .05
92 Lenny Harris .01 .05
93 Reggie Jefferson .01 .05
94 Sammy Sosa .15 .40
95 Scott Bailes .01 .05
96 Tom McKinnon .01 .05
97 Luis Rivera .01 .05
98 Mike Harkey .01 .05
99 Jeff Treadway .01 .05
100 Jose Canseco .15 .40
101 Omar Vizquel .02 .10
102 Scott Kamieniecki .01 .05
103 Ricky Jordan .01 .05
104 Jeff Ballard .01 .05
105 Felix Jose .01 .05
106 Mike Boddicker .01 .05
107 Dan Pasqua .01 .05
108 Mike Timlin .01 .05
109 Roger Craig MG .01 .05
110 Ryne Sandberg .20 .50
111 Mark Carreon .01 .05
112 Oscar Azocar .01 .05
113 Mike Greenwell .01 .05
114 Mark Portugal .01 .05
115 Terry Pendleton .01 .05
116 Willie Randolph .02 .10
Now with Mets
12-20-91
117 Scott Terry .01 .05
118 Chili Davis .02 .10
119 Mark Gardner .01 .05
120 Alan Trammell .05 .15
121 Derek Bell .02 .10
122 Gary Varsho .01 .05
123 Bob Ojeda .01 .05
124 Shawn Livsey .01 .05
125 Chris Hoiles .01 .05
126 Ryan Klesko .08 .25
John Jaha
Rico Brogna
Dave Staton
127 Carlos Quintana .01 .05
128 Kurt Stillwell .01 .05
129 Melido Perez .01 .05
130 Alvin Davis .01 .05
131 Checklist 1-132 .01 .05
132 Eric Show .01 .05
133 Rance Mulliniks .01 .05
134 Darryl Kile .01 .05
135 Von Hayes .02 .10
Now with Angels
12-8-91
136 Bill Doran .01 .05
137 Jeff D. Robinson .01 .05
138 Monty Fariss .01 .05
139 Jeff Innis .01 .05
140 Mark Grace UER .15 .40
Home Calie., should be Calif.
141 Jim Leyland MG UER .01 .05
No closed parenthesis
after East in 1991
142 Todd Van Poppel .01 .05
143 Paul Gibson .01 .05
144 Bill Swift .01 .05
145 Danny Tartabull .02 .10
Now with Yankees
1-6-92
146 Al Newman .01 .05
147 Cris Carpenter .01 .05
148 Anthony Young .01 .05
149 Brian Bohanon .01 .05
150 Roger Clemens UER .40 1.00
League leading ERA in
1990 not italicized
151 Jeff Hamilton .01 .05
152 Charlie Leibrandt .01 .05
153 Ron Karkovice .01 .05
154 Hensley Meulens .01 .05
155 Scott Bankhead .01 .05
156 Manny Ramirez RC 2.00 5.00
157 Keith Miller .02 .10
Now with Royals
12-11-91
158 Todd Frohwirth .01 .05
159 Darrin Fletcher .02 .10
Now with Expos
12-9-91
160 Bobby Bonilla .01 .05
161 Casey Candaele .01 .05
162 Paul Faries .01 .05
163 Dana Kiecker .01 .05
164 Shane Mack .01 .05
165 Mark Langston .01 .05
166 Geronimo Pena .01 .05
167 Andy Allanson .01 .05
168 Dwight Smith .01 .05
169 Chuck Crim .02 .10
Now with Angels
12-10-91
170 Alex Cole .01 .05
171 Bill Plummer MG .01 .05
172 Juan Berenguer .01 .05
173 Brian Downing .01 .05
174 Steve Frey .01 .05
175 Orel Hershiser .02 .10
176 Ramon Garcia .01 .05
177 Dan Gladden .02 .10
Now with Tigers
12-19-91
178 Jim Acker .01 .05
179 Bobby DeJardin .01 .05
Cesar Bernhardt
Armando Moreno
Andy Stankiewicz
180 Kevin Mitchell .02 .10
181 Hector Villanueva .01 .05
182 Jeff Reardon .02 .10
183 Brent Mayne .01 .05
184 Jimmy Jones .01 .05
185 Benito Santiago .02 .10
186 Cliff Floyd .40 1.00
187 Ernie Riles .01 .05
188 Jose Guzman .01 .05
189 Junior Felix .01 .05
190 Glenn Davis .01 .05
191 Charlie Hough .02 .10
192 Dave Fleming .01 .05
193 Omar Olivares .01 .05
194 Eric Karros .08 .25
195 David Cone .08 .25
196 Frank Castillo .01 .05
197 Glenn Braggs .01 .05
198 Scott Aldred .01 .05
199 Jeff Blauser .01 .05
200 Len Dykstra .02 .10
201 Buck Showalter MG RC .08 .25
202 Rick Honeycutt .01 .05
203 Greg Myers .01 .05
204 Trevor Wilson .01 .05
205 Jay Howell .01 .05
206 Luis Sojo .01 .05
207 Jack Clark .02 .10
208 Julio Machado .01 .05
209 Lloyd McClendon .01 .05
210 Ozzie Guillen .02 .10
211 Jeremy Hernandez .01 .05
212 Randy Velarde .01 .05
213 Les Lancaster .01 .05
214 Andy Mota .01 .05
215 Rich Gossage .02 .10
216 Brent Gates .01 .05
217 Brian Harper .01 .05
218 Mike Flanagan .01 .05
219 Jerry Browne .01 .05
220 Jose Rijo .01 .05
221 Skeeter Barnes .01 .05
222 Jaime Navarro .01 .05
223 Mel Hall .01 .05
224 Bret Barberie .01 .05
225 Roberto Alomar .15 .40
226 Pete Smith .01 .05
227 Daryl Boston .01 .05
228 Eddie Whitson .01 .05
229 Shawn Boskie .01 .05
230 Dick Schofield .01 .05
231 Brian Drahman .01 .05
232 John Smiley .01 .05
233 Mitch Webster .01 .05
234 Terry Steinbach .01 .05
235 Jack Morris .05 .15
Now with Blue Jays
12-18-91
236 Bill Pecota .02 .10
Now with Mets
12-11-91
237 Jose Hernandez .01 .05
238 Greg Litton .01 .05
239 Brian Holman .01 .05
240 Andres Galarraga .08 .25
241 Gerald Young .01 .05
242 Mike Mussina .25 .60
243 Alvaro Espinoza .01 .05
244 Darren Daulton .02 .10
245 John Smoltz .08 .25
246 Jason Pruitt .01 .05
247 Chuck Finley .02 .10
248 Jim Gantner .01 .05
249 Tony Fossas .01 .05
250 Ken Griffey Sr. .02 .10
251 Kevin Elster .01 .05
252 Dennis Rasmussen .01 .05
253 Terry Kennedy .01 .05
254 Ryan Bowen .01 .05
255 Robin Ventura .02 .10
256 Mike Aldrete .01 .05
257 Jeff Russell .01 .05
258 Jim Lindeman .01 .05
259 Ron Darling .01 .05
260 Devon White .02 .10
261 Tom Lasorda MG .08 .25
262 Terry Lee .01 .05
263 Bob Patterson .01 .05
264 Checklist 133-264 .01 .05
265 Teddy Higuera .01 .05
266 Roberto Kelly .01 .05
267 Steve Bedrosian .01 .05
268 Brady Anderson .05 .15
269 Ruben Amaro Jr. .01 .05
270 Tony Gwynn .30 .75
271 Tracy Jones .01 .05
272 Jerry Don Gleaton .01 .05
273 Craig Grebeck .01 .05
274 Bob Scanlan .01 .05
275 Todd Zeile .02 .10
276 Shawn Green RC 1.50 4.00
277 Scott Chiamparino .01 .05
278 Darryl Hamilton .01 .05
279 Jim Clancy .01 .05
280 Carlos Martinez .01 .05
281 Kevin Appier .02 .10
282 John Wehner .01 .05
283 Reggie Sanders .02 .10
284 Gene Larkin .01 .05
285 Bob Welch .01 .05
286 Gilberto Reyes .01 .05
287 Pete Schourek .01 .05
288 Andujar Cedeno .01 .05
289 Mike Morgan .02 .10
Now with Cubs
12-3-91
290 Bo Jackson .02 .10
291 Phil Garner MG .01 .05
292 Ray Lankford .08 .25
293 Mike Henneman .01 .05
294 Dave Valle .01 .05
295 Alonzo Powell .01 .05
296 Tom Brunansky .01 .05
297 Kevin Brown .05 .15
298 Kelly Gruber .01 .05
299 Charles Nagy .01 .05
300 Don Mattingly .40 1.00
301 Kirk McCaskill .02 .10
Now with White Sox
12-28-91
302 Joey Cora .01 .05
303 Dan Plesac .01 .05
304 Joe Oliver .01 .05
305 Tom Glavine .15 .40
306 Al Shirley .01 .05
307 Bruce Ruffin .01 .05
308 Craig Shipley .01 .05
309 Dave Martinez .02 .10
Now with Reds
12-11-91
310 Jose Mesa .01 .05
311 Henry Cotto .01 .05
312 Mike LaValliere .01 .05
313 Kevin Tapani .01 .05
314 Jeff Huson .01 .05
315 Juan Samuel .01 .05
316 Curt Schilling .15 .40
317 Mike Bordick .01 .05
318 Steve Howe .01 .05
319 Tony Phillips .01 .05
320 George Bell .01 .05
321 Lou Piniella MG .02 .10
322 Tim Burke .01 .05
323 Milt Thompson .01 .05
324 Danny Darwin .01 .05
325 Joe Orsulak .01 .05
326 Eric King .01 .05
327 Jay Buhner .05 .15
328 Joel Johnston .01 .05
329 Franklin Stubbs .01 .05
330 Will Clark .15 .40
331 Steve Lake .01 .05
332 Chris Jones .02 .10
Now with Astros
12-19-91
333 Pat Tabler .01 .05
334 Kevin Gross .01 .05
335 Dave Henderson .01 .05
336 Greg Anthony .01 .05
337 Alejandro Pena .01 .05
338 Shawn Abner .01 .05
339 Tom Browning .01 .05
340 Otis Nixon .01 .05
341 Bob Geren .02 .10
Now with Reds
12-2-91
342 Tim Spehr .01 .05
343 John Vander Wal .01 .05
344 Jack Daugherty .01 .05
345 Zane Smith .01 .05
346 Rheal Cormier .01 .05
347 Kent Hrbek .02 .10
348 Rick Wilkins .01 .05
349 Steve Lyons .02 .10
350 Gregg Olson .01 .05
351 Greg Riddoch MG .01 .05
352 Ed Nunez .01 .05
353 Braulio Castillo .01 .05
354 Dave Bergman .01 .05
355 Warren Newson .01 .05
356 Luis Quinones .01 .05
Now with Twins
1-9-92
357 Mike Witt .01 .05
358 Ted Wood .01 .05
359 Mike Moore .01 .05
360 Lance Parrish .01 .05
361 Barry Jones .01 .05
362 Javier Ortiz .01 .05
363 John Candelaria .01 .05
364 Glenallen Hill .01 .05
365 Duane Ward .01 .05
366 Checklist 265-396 .01 .05
367 Rafael Belliard .01 .05
368 Bill Krueger .01 .05
369 Steve Whitaker .01 .05
370 Shawon Dunston .01 .05
371 Dante Bichette .02 .10
372 Kip Gross .02 .10
Now with Dodgers
11-27-91
373 Don Robinson .01 .05
374 Bernie Williams .15 .40
375 Bert Blyleven .02 .10
376 Chris Donnels .01 .05
377 Bob Zupcic .01 .05
378 Joel Skinner .01 .05
379 Steve Chitren .01 .05
380 Barry Bonds .40 1.00
381 Sparky Anderson MG .02 .10
382 Sid Fernandez .01 .05
383 Dave Hollins .01 .05
384 Mark Lee .01 .05
385 Tim Wallach .01 .05
386 Lance Blankenship .01 .05
387 Gary Carter TRIB .08 .25
388 Ron Tingley .01 .05
389 Gary Carter TRIB .08 .25
390 Gene Harris .01 .05
391 Jeff Schaefer .01 .05
392 Mark Grant .01 .05
393 Carl Willis .01 .05
394 Al Leiter .02 .10
395 Ron Robinson .01 .05
396 Tim Hulett .01 .05
397 Craig Worthington .01 .05
398 John Orton .01 .05
399 Gary Carter TRIB .08 .25
400 John Dopson .01 .05
401 Moises Alou .08 .25
402 Gary Carter TRIB .08 .25
403 Matt Young .01 .05
404 Wayne Edwards .01 .05
405 Nick Esasky .01 .05
406 Dave Eiland .01 .05
407 Mike Brumley .01 .05
408 Bob Milacki .01 .05
409 Geno Petralli .01 .05
410 Dave Stewart .02 .10
411 Mike Jackson .02 .10
412 Luis Aquino .01 .05
413 Tim Teufel .01 .05
414 Jeff Ware .01 .05
415 Jim Deshaies .01 .05
416 Ellis Burks .02 .10
417 Allan Anderson .01 .05
418 Alfredo Griffin .01 .05
419 Wally Whitehurst .01 .05
420 Sandy Alomar Jr. .02 .10
421 Juan Agosto .01 .05
422 Sam Horn .01 .05
423 Jeff Fassero .01 .05
424 Paul McClellan .01 .05
425 Cecil Fielder .02 .10
426 Tim Raines .02 .10
427 Eddie Taubensee .02 .10
428 Dennis Boyd .01 .05
429 Tony LaRussa MG .02 .10
430 Steve Sax .01 .05
431 Tom Gordon .02 .10
432 Billy Hatcher .01 .05
433 Cal Eldred .01 .05
434 Wally Backman .01 .05
435 Mark Eichhorn .01 .05
436 Mookie Wilson .02 .10
437 Scott Servais .01 .05
438 Mike Maddux .01 .05
439 Chico Walker .01 .05
440 Doug Drabek .01 .05
441 Rob Deer .01 .05
442 Dave West .01 .05
443 Spike Owen .01 .05
444 Tyrone Hill .01 .05
445 Matt Williams .05 .15
446 Mark Lewis .01 .05
447 David Segui .01 .05
448 Tom Pagnozzi .01 .05
449 Jeff Johnson .01 .05
450 Mark McGwire .40 1.00
451 Tom Henke .01 .05
452 Wilson Alvarez .02 .10
453 Gary Redus .01 .05
454 Darren Holmes .01 .05
455 Pete O'Brien .01 .05
456 Pat Combs .01 .05
457 Hubie Brooks .01 .05
Now with Angels
12-10-91
458 Frank Tanana .01 .05
459 Tom Kelly MG .01 .05
460 Andre Dawson .05 .15
461 Doug Jones .01 .05
462 Rich Rodriguez .01 .05
463 Mike Simms .01 .05
464 Mike Jeffcoat .01 .05
465 Barry Larkin .15 .40
466 Stan Belinda .01 .05
467 Lonnie Smith .01 .05
468 Greg A. Harris .01 .05
469 Jim Eisenreich .01 .05
470 Pedro Guerrero .01 .05
471 Jose DeJesus .01 .05
472 Rich Rowland .01 .05
473 Frank Bolick .15 .40
Craig Paquette
Tom Redington
Paul Russo UER
Line around top border
474 Mike Rossiter .01 .05
475 Robby Thompson .01 .05
476 Randy Bush .01 .05
477 Greg Hibbard .01 .05
478 Dale Sveum .02 .10
Now with Phillies
12-11-91
479 Chito Martinez .01 .05
480 Scott Sanderson .01 .05
481 Tino Martinez .08 .25
482 Jimmy Key .01 .05
483 Terry Shumpert .01 .05
484 Mike Hartley .01 .05
485 Chris Sabo .01 .05
486 Bob Walk .01 .05
487 John Cerutti .01 .05
488 Scott Cooper .01 .05
489 Bobby Cox MG .02 .10
490 Julio Franco .02 .10
491 Jeff Brantley .02 .10
492 Mike Devereaux .01 .05
493 Jose Offerman .01 .05
494 Gary Thurman .01 .05
495 Carney Lansford .02 .10
496 Joe Grahe .01 .05
497 Andy Ashby .02 .10
498 Gerald Perry .01 .05
499 Dave Otto .01 .05
500 Vince Coleman .01 .05
501 Rob Mallicoat .01 .05
502 Greg Briley .01 .05
503 Pascual Perez .01 .05
504 Aaron Sele RC .40 1.00
505 Bobby Thigpen .01 .05
506 Todd Benzinger .01 .05
507 Candy Maldonado .01 .05
508 Bill Gullickson .01 .05
509 Doug Dascenzo .01 .05
510 Frank Viola .01 .05
511 Kenny Rogers .01 .05
512 Mike Heath .01 .05
513 Kevin Bass .01 .05
514 Kim Batiste .01 .05
515 Delino DeShields .02 .10
516 Ed Sprague .01 .05
517 Jim Gott .01 .05
518 Jose Melendez .01 .05
519 Hal McRae MG .01 .05
520 Jeff Bagwell .30 .75
521 Joe Hesketh .01 .05
522 Milt Cuyler .01 .05
523 Shawn Hillegas .01 .05
524 Don Slaught .01 .05
525 Randy Johnson .20 .50
526 Doug Platt .01 .05
527 Checklist 397-528 .01 .05
528 Steve Foster .01 .05
529 Joe Girardi .02 .10
530 Jim Abbott .02 .10
531 Larry Walker .05 .15
532 Mike Huff .01 .05
533 Mackey Sasser .01 .05
534 Benji Gil .01 .05
535 Dave Stieb .01 .05
536 Willie Wilson .01 .05
537 Mark Leiter .01 .05
538 Jose Uribe .01 .05
539 Thomas Howard .01 .05
540 Ben McDonald .01 .05
541 Jose Tolentino .01 .05
542 Keith Mitchell .01 .05
543 Jerome Walton .01 .05
544 Cliff Brantley .01 .05
545 Andy Van Slyke .02 .10
546 Paul Sorrento .01 .05
547 Herm Winningham .01 .05
548 Mark Guthrie .01 .05
549 Joe Torre MG .02 .10
550 Darryl Strawberry .02 .10
551 Wilfredo Cordero .75 2.00
Chipper Jones
Manny Alexander
Alex Arias UER
No line around top border
552 Dave Gallagher .01 .05
553 Edgar Martinez .05 .15
554 Donald Harris .01 .05
555 Frank Thomas .20 .50
556 Storm Davis .01 .05
557 Dickie Thon .01 .05
558 Scott Garrelts .01 .05
559 Steve Olin .01 .05
560 Rickey Henderson .30 .75
561 Jose Vizcaino .01 .05
562 Wade Taylor .01 .05
563 Pat Borders .01 .05
564 Jimmy Gonzalez .01 .05
565 Lee Smith .02 .10
566 Bill Sampen .01 .05
567 Dean Palmer .02 .10
568 Bryan Harvey .01 .05
569 Tony Pena .01 .05
570 Lou Whitaker .02 .10
571 Randy Tomlin .01 .05
572 Greg Vaughn .02 .10
573 Kelly Downs .01 .05
574 Steve Avery UER .01 .05
Should be 13 games
for Durham in 1989
575 Kirby Puckett .40 1.00
576 Heathcliff Slocumb .01 .05
577 Kevin Seitzer .01 .05
578 Lee Guetterman .01 .05
579 Johnny Oates MG .01 .05
580 Greg Maddux .40 1.00
581 Stan Javier .01 .05
582 Vicente Palacios .01 .05
583 Mel Rojas .01 .05
584 Wayne Rosenthal .01 .05
585 Lenny Webster .01 .05
586 Rod Nichols .01 .05
587 Mickey Morandini .01 .05
588 Russ Swan .01 .05
589 Mariano Duncan .01 .05
Now with Phillies
12-10-91
590 Howard Johnson .01 .05
591 Jeromy Burnitz .08 .25
Jacob Brumfield
Alan Cockrell
D.J. Dozier
592 Denny Neagle .02 .10
593 Steve Decker .01 .05
594 Brian Barber .01 .05
595 Bruce Hurst .01 .05
596 Kent Mercker .01 .05
597 Mike Magnante .01 .05
598 Jody Reed .01 .05
599 Steve Searcy .01 .05
600 Paul Molitor .15 .40
601 Dave Smith .01 .05
602 Mike Fetters .01 .05
603 Luis Mercedes .01 .05
604 Chris Gwynn .02 .10
Now with Royals
12-11-91
605 Scott Erickson .01 .05
606 Brook Jacoby .01 .05
607 Todd Stottlemyre .01 .05
608 Scott Bradley .01 .05
609 Mike Hargrove MG .01 .05
610 Eric Davis .02 .10
611 Brian Hunter .01 .05
612 Pat Kelly .01 .05
613 Pedro Munoz .01 .05
614 Al Osuna .01 .05
615 Matt Merullo .01 .05
616 Larry Andersen .01 .05
617 Junior Ortiz .01 .05
618 Cesar Hernandez .01 .05
Steve Hosey
Jeff McNeely
Dan Peltier
619 Danny Jackson .01 .05
620 George Brett .30 .75
621 Dan Gakeler .01 .05
622 Steve Buechele .01 .05
623 Bob Tewksbury .01 .05
624 Shawn Estes RC .40 1.00
625 Kevin McReynolds .01 .05
626 Chris Haney .01 .05
627 Mike Sharperson .01 .05
628 Mark Williamson .01 .05
629 Wally Joyner .02 .10
630 Carlton Fisk .15 .40
631 Armando Reynoso .01 .05
632 Felix Fermin .01 .05
633 Mitch Williams .01 .05
634 Manuel Lee .01 .05
635 Harold Baines .05 .15
636 Greg W. Harris .01 .05
637 Orlando Merced .01 .05
638 Chris Bosio .01 .05
639 Wayne Housie .01 .05
640 Xavier Hernandez .01 .05
641 David Howard .01 .05
642 Tim Crews .01 .05
643 Rick Cerone .01 .05
644 Terry Leach .01 .05
645 Deion Sanders .08 .25
646 Craig Wilson .01 .05
647 Marquis Grissom .02 .10
648 Scott Fletcher .01 .05
649 Norm Charlton .01 .05
650 Jesse Barfield .01 .05
651 Joe Slusarski .01 .05
652 Bobby Rose .01 .05
653 Dennis Lamp .01 .05
654 Allen Watson .01 .05
655 Brett Butler .02 .10
656 1992 Prospects OF .05 .15
Rudy Pemberton
Henry Rodriguez
657 Dave Johnson .01 .05
658 Checklist 529-660 .01 .05
659 Brian McRae .01 .05
660 Fred McGriff .05 .15
661 Bill Landrum .01 .05
662 Juan Guzman .01 .05
663 Greg Gagne .01 .05
664 Ken Hill .02 .10
Now with Expos
11-25-91
665 Dave Haas .01 .05
666 Tom Foley .01 .05
667 Roberto Hernandez .02 .10
668 Dwayne Henry .01 .05
669 Jim Fregosi MG .01 .05
670 Harold Reynolds .02 .10
671 Mark Whiten .01 .05
672 Eric Plunk .01 .05
673 Todd Hundley .02 .10
674 Mo Sanford .01 .05
675 Bobby Witt .01 .05
676 Sam Militello .01 .05
Pat Mahomes
Turk Wendell
Roger Salkeld
677 John Marzano .01 .05
678 Joe Klink .01 .05
679 Pete Incaviglia .01 .05
680 Dale Murphy .15 .40
681 Rene Gonzales .01 .05
682 Andy Benes .01 .05
683 Jim Poole .01 .05
684 Trever Miller .01 .05
685 Scott Livingstone .01 .05
686 Rich DeLucia .01 .05
687 Harvey Pulliam .01 .05
688 Tim Belcher .01 .05
689 Mark Lemke .01 .05
690 John Franco .02 .10
691 Walt Weiss .01 .05
692 Scott Ruskin .02 .10
Now with Reds
12-11-91
693 Jeff King .01 .05
694 Mike Gardiner .01 .05
695 Gary Sheffield .20 .50
696 Joe Boever .01 .05
697 Mike Felder .01 .05
698 John Habyan .01 .05
699 Cito Gaston MG .01 .05
700 Ruben Sierra .02 .10
701 Scott Radinsky .01 .05
702 Lee Stevens .01 .05
703 Mark Wohlers .01 .05
704 Curt Young .01 .05
705 Dwight Evans .02 .10
706 Rob Murphy .01 .05
707 Gregg Jefferies .02 .10
Now with Royals
12-11-91
708 Tom Bolton .01 .05
709 Chris James .01 .05
710 Kevin Maas .01 .05
711 Ricky Bones .01 .05
712 Curt Wilkerson .01 .05
713 Roger McDowell .01 .05
714 Pokey Reese RC .15 .40
715 Craig Biggio .05 .15
716 Kirk Dressendorfer .01 .05
717 Ken Dayley .01 .05
718 B.J. Surhoff .02 .10
719 Terry Mulholland .01 .05
720 Kirk Gibson .02 .10
721 Mike Pagliarulo .01 .05
722 Walt Terrell .01 .05
723 Jose Oquendo .01 .05
724 Kevin Morton .01 .05
725 Dwight Gooden .02 .10
726 Kirt Manwaring .01 .05
727 Chuck McElroy .01 .05
728 Dave Burba .01 .05
729 Art Howe MG .01 .05
730 Ramon Martinez .01 .05
731 Donnie Hill .01 .05
732 Nelson Santovenia .01 .05
733 Bob Melvin .02 .10
734 Scott Hatteberg .01 .05
735 Greg Swindell .02 .10
Now with Reds
11-15-91
736 Lance Johnson .01 .05
737 Kevin Reimer .01 .05
738 Dennis Eckersley .15 .40
739 Rob Ducey .01 .05
740 Ken Caminiti .05 .15
741 Mark Gubicza .01 .05
742 Billy Spiers .01 .05
743 Darren Lewis .01 .05
744 Chris Hammond .01 .05
745 Dave Magadan .02 .10
746 Bernard Gilkey .02 .10
747 Willie Banks .01 .05
748 Matt Nokes .01 .05
749 Jerald Clark .01 .05
750 Travis Fryman .02 .10
751 Steve Wilson .01 .05
752 Billy Ripken .01 .05
753 Paul Assenmacher .01 .05
754 Charlie Hayes .01 .05
755 Alex Fernandez .01 .05
756 Gary Pettis .01 .05
757 Rob Dibble .01 .05
758 Tim Naehring .01 .05
759 Jeff Torborg MG .01 .05
760 Ozzie Smith .20 .50
761 Mike Fitzgerald .01 .05
762 John Burkett .01 .05
763 Kyle Abbott .01 .05
764 Tyler Green .01 .05
765 Pete Harnisch .01 .05
766 Mark Davis .01 .05
767 Kal Daniels .01 .05
768 Jim Thome .15 .40
769 Jack Howell .01 .05
770 Sid Bream .01 .05
771 Arthur Rhodes .01 .05
772 Garry Templeton .01 .05
773 Hal Morris .01 .05
774 Bud Black .01 .05
775 Ivan Calderon .01 .05
776 Doug Henry .01 .05
777 John Olerud .05 .15
778 Tim Leary .01 .05
779 Jay Bell .01 .05
780 Eddie Murray .20 .50
Now with Mets
11-27-91
781 Paul Abbott .01 .05
782 Phil Plantier .01 .05
783 Joe Magrane .01 .05
784 Ken Patterson .01 .05
785 Albert Belle .05 .15
786 Royce Clayton .01 .05
787 Checklist 661-792 .01 .05
788 Mike Stanton .01 .05
789 Bobby Valentine MG .01 .05
790 Joe Carter .02 .10
791 Danny Cox .01 .05
792 Dave Winfield .20 .50
Now with Blue Jays
12-19-91

1992 O-Pee-Chee Box Bottoms

COMPLETE SET (4) 1.25 3.00
1 Pirates Prevail .20 .50
2 Braves Beat Bucs .30 .75
3 Blue Jays Claim Crown .40 1.00
4 Kirby Puckett .75 2.00
Twins Tally in Tenth

1993 O-Pee-Chee

The 1993 O-Pee-Chee baseball set consists of 396 standard-size cards. This is the first year that the regular series does not parallel in design the series that Topps issued. The set was sold in wax packs with eight cards plus a random insert card from either a four-card World Series Heroes subset or an 18-card World Series Champions subset. The fronts features color action player photos with white borders. The player's name appears in a silver stripe across the bottom that overlaps the O-Pee-Chee logo. The backs display color close-ups next to a panel containing biographical data. The panel and a stripe at the bottom reflect the team colors. A white box in the center of the card contains statistics and bilingual (English and French) career highlights.

COMPLETE SET (396) 20.00 50.00
1 Jim Abbott .15 .40
Now with Yankees/12/6/92
2 Eric Anthony .02 .10
3 Harold Baines .07 .20
4 Roberto Alomar .25 .60
5 Steve Avery .02 .10
6 Jim Austin .02 .10
7 Mark Wohlers .02 .10
8 Steve Buechele .02 .10
9 Pedro Astacio .02 .10
10 Moises Alou .07 .20
11 Rod Beck .02 .10
12 Sandy Alomar .07 .20
13 Bret Boone .15 .40
14 Bryan Harvey .02 .10
15 Bobby Bonilla .02 .10
16 Brady Anderson .07 .20
17 Andy Benes .02 .10
18 Ruben Amaro Jr. .02 .10
19 Jay Bell .02 .10
20 Kevin Brown .15 .40
21 Scott Bankhead .07 .20

Now with Red Sox/12/8/92
22 Denis Boucher .02 .10
23 Kevin Appier .07 .20
24 Pat Kelly .02 .10
25 Rick Aguilera .02 .10
26 George Bell .02 .10
27 Steve Farr .02 .10
28 Chad Curtis .02 .10
29 Jeff Bagwell .60 1.50
30 Lance Blankenship .02 .10
31 Derek Bell .02 .10
32 Damon Berryhill .02 .10
33 Ricky Bones .02 .10
34 Rheal Cormier .02 .10
35 Andre Dawson .25 .60
Now with Red Sox/12/2/92
36 Brett Butler .07 .20
37 Sean Berry .02 .10
38 Bud Black .02 .10
39 Carlos Baerga .07 .20
40 Jay Buhner .15 .40
41 Charlie Hough .07 .20
42 Sid Fernandez .02 .10
43 Luis Mercedes .02 .10
44 Jerald Clark .07 .20
Now with Rockies/11/17/92
45 Wes Chamberlain .02 .10
46 Barry Bonds .75 2.00
Now with Giants/12/8/92
47 Jose Canseco .30 .75
48 Tim Belcher .02 .10
49 David Nied .02 .10
50 George Brett .60 1.50
51 Cecil Fielder .07 .20
52 Chili Davis .07 .20
Now with Angels/12/11/92
53 Alex Fernandez .02 .10
54 Charlie Hayes .07 .20
Now with Rockies/11/17/92
55 Rob Ducey .02 .10
56 Craig Biggio .25 .60
57 Mike Bordick .02 .10
58 Pat Borders .02 .10
59 Jeff Blauser .02 .10
60 Chris Bosio .07 .20
Now with Mariners/12/3/92
61 Bernard Gilkey .02 .10
62 Shawon Dunston .02 .10
63 Tom Candiotti .02 .10
64 Darrin Fletcher .02 .10
65 Jeff Brantley .07 .20
66 Albert Belle .07 .20
67 Dave Fleming .02 .10
68 John Franco .07 .20
69 Glenn Davis .02 .10
70 Tony Fernandez .07 .20
Now with Mets/10/26/92
71 Darren Daulton .07 .20
72 Doug Drabek .07 .20
Now with Astros/12/1/92
73 Julio Franco .07 .20
74 Tom Browning .02 .10
75 Tom Gordon .07 .20
76 Travis Fryman .07 .20
77 Scott Erickson .02 .10
78 Carlton Fisk .25 .60
79 Roberto Kelly .07 .20
Now with Reds/11/3/92
80 Gary DiSarcina .02 .10
81 Ken Caminiti .15 .40
82 Ron Darling .02 .10
83 Joe Carter .07 .20
84 Sid Bream .02 .10
85 Cal Eldred .02 .10
86 Mark Grace .15 .40
87 Eric Davis .07 .20
88 Ivan Calderon .07 .20
Now with Red Sox/12/8/92
89 John Burkett .02 .10
90 Felix Fermin .02 .10
91 Ken Griffey Jr. 1.00 2.50
92 Dwight Gooden .07 .20
93 Mike Devereaux .02 .10
94 Tony Gwynn .75 2.00
95 Mariano Duncan .02 .10
96 Jeff King .02 .10
97 Juan Gonzalez .25 .60
98 Norm Charlton .07 .20
Now with Mariners/11/17/92
99 Mark Gubicza .02 .10
100 Danny Gladden .02 .10
101 Greg Gagne .07 .20
Now with Royals/12/8/92
102 Ozzie Guillen .07 .20
103 Don Mattingly .75 2.00
104 Damion Easley .02 .10
105 Casey Candaele .02 .10
106 Dennis Eckersley .30 .75
107 David Cone .15 .40
Now with Royals/12/8/92
108 Ron Gant .02 .10
109 Mike Fetters .02 .10
110 Mike Harkey .02 .10
111 Kevin Gross .02 .10
112 Archi Cianfrocco .02 .10
113 Will Clark .25 .60
114 Glenallen Hill .02 .10
115 Erik Hanson .02 .10
116 Todd Hundley .07 .20
117 Leo Gomez .02 .10
118 Bruce Hurst .02 .10
119 Len Dykstra .07 .20
120 Jose Lind .07 .20
Now with Royals/11/19/92
121 Jose Guzman .07 .20
Now with Cubs/12/1/92
122 Rob Dibble .02 .10
123 Gregg Jefferies .02 .10
124 Bill Gullickson .02 .10
125 Brian Harper .02 .10
126 Roberto Hernandez .07 .20
127 Sam Militello .02 .10
128 Junior Felix .07 .20
Now with Marlins/11/17/92
129 Andujar Cedeno .02 .10
130 Rickey Henderson .40 1.00
131 Bob MacDonald .02 .10
132 Tom Glavine .30 .75
133 Scott Fletcher .07 .20
Now with Red Sox/11/30/92
134 Brian Jordan .07 .20
135 Greg Maddux 1.00 2.50
Now with Braves/12/9/92
136 Orel Hershiser .07 .20
137 Greg Colbrunn .02 .10
138 Royce Clayton .02 .10
139 Thomas Howard .02 .10
140 Randy Johnson .40 1.00
141 Jeff Innis .02 .10
142 Chris Hoiles .02 .10
143 Darrin Jackson .02 .10
144 Tommy Greene .02 .10
145 Mike LaValliere .02 .10
146 David Hulse .02 .10
147 Barry Larkin .15 .40
148 Wally Joyner .07 .20
149 Mike Henneman .02 .10
150 Kent Hrbek .07 .20
151 Bo Jackson .25 .60
152 Rich Monteleone .02 .10
153 Chuck Finley .07 .20
154 Steve Finley .07 .20
155 Dave Henderson .02 .10
156 Kelly Gruber .07 .20
Now with Angels/12/8/92
157 Brian Hunter .02 .10
158 Darryl Hamilton .02 .10
159 Derrick May .02 .10
160 Jay Howell .02 .10
161 Wil Cordero .02 .10
162 Bryan Hickerson .02 .10
163 Reggie Jefferson .02 .10
164 Edgar Martinez .15 .40
165 Nigel Wilson .02 .10
166 Howard Johnson .02 .10
167 Tim Hulett .02 .10
168 Mike Maddux .07 .20
Now with Mets/12/17/92
169 Dave Hollins .02 .10
170 Zane Smith .02 .10
171 Rafael Palmeiro .25 .60
172 Dave Martinez .07 .20
Now with Giants/12/9/92
173 Rusty Meacham .02 .10
174 Mark Leiter .02 .10
175 Chuck Knoblauch .25 .60
176 Lance Johnson .02 .10
177 Matt Nokes .02 .10
178 Luis Gonzalez .25 .60
179 Jack Morris .07 .20
180 David Justice .25 .60
181 Doug Henry .02 .10
182 Felix Jose .02 .10
183 Delino DeShields .02 .10
184 Rene Gonzales .02 .10
185 Pete Harnisch .02 .10
186 Mike Moore .07 .20
Now with Tigers/12/9/92
187 Juan Guzman .02 .10
188 John Olerud .15 .40
189 Ryan Klesko .07 .20
190 John Jaha .02 .10
191 Ray Lankford .07 .20
192 Jeff Fassero .02 .10
193 Darren Lewis .02 .10
194 Mark Lewis .02 .10
195 Alan Mills .02 .10
196 Wade Boggs .40 1:00
Now with Yankees/12/15/92
197 Hal Morris .02 .10
198 Ron Karkovice .02 .10
199 Joe Grahe .02 .10
200 Butch Henry .07 .20
Now with Rockies/11/17/92
201 Mark McGwire 1.00 2.50
202 Tom Henke .07 .20
Now with Rangers/12/15/92
203 Ed Sprague .02 .10
204 Charlie Leibrandt .07 .20
Now with Rangers/12/9/92
205 Pat Listach .02 .10
206 Omar Olivares .02 .10
207 Mike Morgan .02 .10
208 Eric Karros .15 .40
209 Marquis Grissom .07 .20
210 Willie McGee .07 .20
211 Derek Lilliquist .02 .10
212 Tino Martinez .25 .60
213 Jeff Kent .15 .40
214 Mike Mussina .25 .60
215 Randy Myers .07 .20
Now with Cubs/12/9/92
216 John Kruk .07 .20
217 Tom Brunansky .02 .10
218 Paul O'Neill .15 .40
Now with Yankees/11/3/92
219 Scott Livingstone .02 .10
220 John Valentin .02 .10
221 Eddie Zosky .02 .10
222 Pete Smith .02 .10
223 Bill Wegman .02 .10
224 Todd Zeile .07 .20
225 Tim Wallach .07 .20
Now with Dodgers/12/24/92
226 Mitch Williams .02 .10
227 Tim Wakefield .15 .40
228 Frank Viola .02 .10
229 Nolan Ryan 1.25 3.00
230 Kirk McCaskill .02 .10
231 Melido Perez .02 .10
232 Mark Langston .02 .10
233 Xavier Hernandez .02 .10
234 Jerry Browne .02 .10
235 Dave Stieb .07 .20
Now with White Sox/12/8/92
236 Mark Lemke .02 .10
237 Paul Molitor .25 .60
Now with Blue Jays/12/7/92
238 Geronimo Pena .02 .10
239 Ken Hill .02 .10
240 Jack Clark .02 .10
241 Greg Myers .02 .10
242 Pete Incaviglia .07 .20
Now with Phillies/12/8/92
243 Ruben Sierra .07 .20
244 Todd Stottlemyre .02 .10
245 Pat Hentgen .07 .20
246 Melvin Nieves .02 .10
247 Jaime Navarro .02 .10
248 Donovan Osborne .02 .10
249 Brian Barnes .02 .10
250 Cory Snyder .07 .20
Now with Dodgers/12/5/92
251 Kenny Lofton .15 .40
252 Kevin Mitchell .07 .20
Now with Reds/11/17/92
253 Dave Magadan .07 .20
Now with Marlins/12/8/92
254 Ben McDonald .02 .10
255 Fred McGriff .15 .40
256 Mickey Morandini .02 .10
257 Randy Tomlin .02 .10
258 Dean Palmer .07 .20
259 Roger Clemens .75 2.00
260 Joe Oliver .02 .10
261 Jeff Montgomery .07 .20
262 Tony Phillips .02 .10
263 Shane Mack .02 .10
264 Jack McDowell .02 .10
265 Mike Macfarlane .02 .10
266 Luis Polonia .02 .10
267 Doug Jones .02 .10
268 Terry Steinbach .02 .10
269 Jimmy Key .07 .20
Now with Yankees/12/10/92
270 Pat Tabler .02 .10
271 Otis Nixon .02 .10
272 Dave Nilsson .02 .10
273 Tom Pagnozzi .02 .10
274 Ryne Sandberg .60 1.50
275 Ramon Martinez .02 .10
276 Tim Laker .02 .10
277 Bill Swift .02 .10
278 Charles Nagy .02 .10
279 Harold Reynolds .15 .40
Now with Orioles/12/11/92
280 Eddie Murray .30 .75
281 Gregg Olson .02 .10
282 Frank Seminara .02 .10
283 Terry Mulholland .02 .10
284 Kevin Reimer .07 .20
Now with Brewers/11/17/92
285 Mike Greenwell .02 .10
286 Jose Rijo .02 .10
287 Brian McRae .02 .10
288 Frank Tanana .07 .20
Now with Mets/12/10/92
289 Pedro Munoz .02 .10
290 Tim Raines .07 .20
291 Andy Stankiewicz .02 .10
292 Tim Salmon .25 .60
293 Jimmy Jones .02 .10
294 Dave Stewart .07 .20
Now with Blue Jays/12/8/92
295 Mike Timlin .02 .10
296 Greg Olson .02 .10
297 Dan Plesac .07 .20
Now with Cubs/12/8/92
298 Mike Perez .02 .10
299 Jose Offerman .02 .10
300 Denny Martinez .07 .20
301 Robby Thompson .02 .10
302 Bret Saberhagen .07 .20
303 Joe Orsulak .07 .20
Now with Mets/12/18/92
304 Tim Naehring .02 .10
305 Bip Roberts .02 .10
306 Kirby Puckett .60 1.50
307 Steve Sax .02 .10
308 Danny Tartabull .02 .10
309 Jeff Juden .02 .10
310 Duane Ward .02 .10
311 Alejandro Pena .07 .20
Now with Pirates/12/10/92
312 Kevin Seitzer .02 .10
313 Ozzie Smith .40 1.00
314 Mike Piazza 1.25 3.00
315 Chris Nabholz .02 .10
316 Tony Pena .07 .20
317 Gary Sheffield .40 1.00
318 Mark Portugal .02 .10
319 Walt Weiss .07 .20
Now with Marlins/11/17/92
320 Manuel Lee .07 .20
Now with Rangers/12/19/92
321 David Wells .15 .40
322 Terry Pendleton .02 .10
323 Billy Spiers .02 .10
324 Lee Smith .07 .20
325 Bob Scanlan .02 .10
326 Mike Scioscia .07 .20
327 Spike Owen .07 .20
Now with Yankees/12/4/92
328 Mackey Sasser .07 .20
Now with Mariners/12/23/92
329 Arthur Rhodes .02 .10
330 Ben Rivera .02 .10
331 Ivan Rodriguez .40 1.00
332 Phil Plantier .07 .20
Now with Padres/12/10/92
333 Chris Sabo .02 .10
334 Mickey Tettleton .02 .10
335 John Smiley .07 .20
Now with Reds/11/30/92
336 Bobby Thigpen .02 .10
337 Randy Velarde .02 .10
338 Luis Sojo .07 .20
Now with Blue Jays/12/8/92
339 Scott Servais .02 .10
340 Bob Welch .02 .10
341 Devon White .02 .10
342 Jeff Reardon .07 .20
343 B.J. Surhoff .07 .20
344 Bob Tewksbury .02 .10
345 Jose Vizcaino .02 .10
346 Mike Sharperson .02 .10
347 Mel Rojas .02 .10
348 Matt Williams .15 .40
349 Steve Olin .02 .10
350 Mike Schooler .02 .10
351 Ryan Thompson .02 .10
352 Cal Ripken 1.25 3.00
353 Benito Santiago .15 .40
Now with Marlins/12/16/92
354 Curt Schilling .30 .75
355 Andy Van Slyke .02 .10
356 Kenny Rogers .02 .10
357 Jody Reed .07 .20
Now with Dodgers/11/17/92
358 Reggie Sanders .15 .40
359 Kevin McReynolds .02 .10
360 Alan Trammell .15 .40
361 Kevin Tapani .02 .10
362 Frank Thomas .30 .75
363 Bernie Williams .25 .60
364 John Smoltz .07 .20
365 Robin Yount .40 1.00
366 John Wetteland .07 .20
367 Bob Zupcic .02 .10
368 Julio Valera .02 .10
369 Brian Williams .02 .10
370 Willie Wilson .02 .10
Now with Cubs/12/18/92
371 Dave Winfield .40 1.00
Now with Twins/12/17/92
372 Deion Sanders .15 .40
373 Greg Vaughn .07 .20
374 Todd Worrell .07 .20
Now with Dodgers/12/9/92
375 Darryl Strawberry .07 .20
376 John Vander Wal .02 .10
377 Mike Benjamin .02 .10
378 Mark Whiten .02 .10
379 Omar Vizquel .07 .20
380 Anthony Young .02 .10
381 Rick Sutcliffe .02 .10
382 Candy Maldonado .07 .20
Now with Cubs/12/11/92
383 Francisco Cabrera .02 .10
384 Larry Walker .15 .40
385 Scott Cooper .02 .10
386 Gerald Williams .02 .10
387 Robin Ventura .15 .40
388 Carl Willis .02 .10
389 Lou Whitaker .07 .20
390 Hipolito Pichardo .02 .10
391 Rudy Seanez .02 .10
392 Greg Swindell .07 .20
Now with Astros/12/4/92
393 Mo Vaughn .25 .60
394 Checklist 1-132 .02 .10
395 Checklist 133-264 .02 .10
396 Checklist 265-396 .02 .10

1993 O-Pee-Chee World Champions

COMPLETE SET (18) 2.00 5.00
1 Roberto Alomar .60 1.50
2 Pat Borders .02 .10
3 Joe Carter .08 .25
4 David Cone .40 1.00
5 Kelly Gruber .02 .10
6 Juan Guzman .02 .10
7 Tom Henke .02 .10
8 Jimmy Key .08 .25
9 Manuel Lee .02 .10
10 Candy Maldonado .02 .10
11 Jack Morris .08 .25
12 John Olerud .20 .50
13 Ed Sprague .08 .25
14 Todd Stottlemyre .08 .25
15 Duane Ward .02 .10
16 Devon White .02 .10
17 Dave Winfield .75 2.00
18 Cito Gaston MG .02 .10

1993 O-Pee-Chee World Series Heroes

COMPLETE SET (4) .75 2.00
1 Pat Borders .08 .25
2 Jimmy Key .20 .50
3 Ed Sprague .08 .25
4 Dave Winfield .60 1.50

1994 O-Pee-Chee

The 1994 O-Pee-Chee baseball set consists of 270 standard-size cards. Production was limited to 2,500 individually numbered cases. Each display box contained 36 packs and one 5" by 7" All-Star Jumbo card. Each foil pack contained 14 regular cards plus either one chase card or one redemption card.

COMPLETE SET (270) 6.00 15.00
1 Paul Molitor .15 .40
2 Kirt Manwaring .01 .05
3 Brady Anderson .02 .10
4 Scott Cooper .01 .05
5 Kevin Stocker .01 .05
6 Alex Fernandez .01 .05
7 Jeff Montgomery .02 .10
8 Danny Tartabull .01 .05
9 Damion Easley .01 .05
10 Andujar Cedeno .01 .05
11 Steve Karsay .01 .05
12 Dave Stewart .02 .10
13 Fred McGriff .05 .15
14 Jaime Navarro .01 .05
15 Allen Watson .01 .05
16 Ryne Sandberg .30 .75
17 Arthur Rhodes .01 .05
18 Marquis Grissom .02 .10
19 John Burkett .01 .05
20 Robby Thompson .01 .05
21 Denny Martinez .02 .10
22 Ken Griffey Jr. .75 2.00
23 Orestes Destrade .01 .05
24 Dwight Gooden .02 .10
25 Rafael Palmeiro .08 .25
26 Pedro A.Martinez .01 .05
27 Wes Chamberlain .01 .05
28 Juan Gonzalez .08 .25
29 Kevin Mitchell .01 .05
30 Dante Bichette .02 .10
31 Howard Johnson .01 .05
32 Mickey Tettleton .01 .05
33 Robin Ventura .05 .15
34 Terry Mulholland .01 .05
35 Bernie Williams .08 .25
36 Eduardo Perez .01 .05
37 Rickey Henderson .20 .50
38 Terry Pendleton .01 .05
39 John Smoltz .08 .25
40 Derrick May .01 .05
41 Pedro Martinez .20 .50
42 Mark Portugal .01 .05
43 Albert Belle .04 .10
44 Edgar Martinez .05 .15
45 Gary Sheffield .20 .50
46 Bret Saberhagen .02 .10
47 Ricky Gutierrez .01 .05
48 Orlando Merced .01 .05
49 Mike Greenwell .01 .05
50 Jose Rijo .01 .05
51 Jeff Granger .01 .05
52 Mike Henneman .01 .05
53 Dave Winfield .15 .40
54 Don Mattingly .40 1.00
55 J.T. Snow .02 .10
56 Todd Van Poppel .01 .05
57 Chipper Jones .30 .75
58 Darryl Hamilton .01 .05
59 Delino DeShields .01 .05
60 Rondell White .02 .10
61 Eric Anthony .01 .05
62 Charlie Hough .01 .05
63 Sid Fernandez .01 .05
64 Derek Bell .01 .05
65 Phil Plantier .01 .05
66 Curt Schilling .15 .40
67 Roger Clemens .40 1.00
68 Jose Lind .01 .05
69 Andres Galarraga .08 .25
70 Tim Belcher .01 .05
71 Ron Karkovice .01 .05
72 Alan Trammell .05 .15
73 Pete Harnisch .01 .05
74 Mark McGwire .50 1.25
75 Ryan Klesko .02 .10
76 Ramon Martinez .01 .05
77 Gregg Jefferies .01 .05
78 Steve Buechele .01 .05
79 Bill Swift .01 .05
80 Matt Williams .05 .15
81 Randy Johnson .20 .50
82 Mike Mussina .08 .25
83 Andy Benes .01 .05
84 Dave Staton .01 .05
85 Steve Cooke .01 .05
86 Andy Van Slyke .01 .05
87 Ivan Rodriguez .20 .50
88 Frank Viola .01 .05
89 Aaron Sele .02 .10
90 Ellis Burks .02 .10
91 Wally Joyner .02 .10
92 Rick Aguilera .01 .05
93 Kirby Puckett .40 1.00
94 Roberto Hernandez .01 .05
95 Mike Stanley .01 .05
96 Roberto Alomar .08 .25
97 James Mouton .01 .05
98 Chad Curtis .01 .05
99 Mitch Williams .01 .05
100 Carlos Delgado .20 .50
101 Greg Maddux .40 1.00
102 Brian Harper .01 .05
103 Tom Pagnozzi .01 .05
104 Jose Offerman .01 .05
105 John Wetteland .02 .10
106 Carlos Baerga .02 .10
107 Dave Magadan .01 .05
108 Bobby Jones .01 .05
109 Tony Gwynn .40 1.00
110 Jeromy Burnitz .05 .15
111 Bip Roberts .01 .05
112 Carlos Garcia .01 .05
113 Jeff Russell .01 .05
114 Armando Reynoso .01 .05
115 Ozzie Guillen .02 .10
116 Bo Jackson .05 .15
117 Terry Steinbach .01 .05
118 Deion Sanders .08 .25
119 Randy Myers .01 .05
120 Mark Whiten .01 .05
121 Manny Ramirez .20 .50
122 Ben McDonald .01 .05
123 Darren Daulton .02 .10
124 Kevin Young ..01 .05
125 Barry Larkin .08 .25
126 Cecil Fielder .02 .10
127 Frank Thomas .20 .50
128 Luis Polonia .01 .05
129 Steve Finley .02 .10
130 John Olerud .02 .10
131 John Jaha .01 .05
132 Darren Lewis .01 .05
133 Orel Hershiser .02 .10
134 Chris Bosio .01 .05
135 Ryan Thompson .01 .05
136 Chris Sabo .01 .05
137 Tommy Greene .01 .05
138 Andre Dawson .08 .25
139 Roberto Kelly .01 .05
140 Ken Hill .01 .05
141 Greg Gagne .01 .05
142 Julio Franco .02 .10
143 Chili Davis .02 .10
144 Dennis Eckersley .15 .40
145 Joe Carter .02 .10
146 Mark Grace .05 .15
147 Mike Piazza .40 1.00
148 J.R. Phillips .01 .05
149 Rich Amaral .01 .05
150 Benny Santiago .02 .10
151 Jeff King .01 .05
152 Dean Palmer .02 .10
153 Hal Morris .01 .05
154 Mike Macfarlane .01 .05
155 Chuck Knoblauch .02 .10
156 Pat Kelly .01 .05
157 Greg Swindell .01 .05
158 Chuck Finley .02 .10
159 Devon White .02 .10
160 Duane Ward .01 .05
161 Sammy Sosa .25 .60
162 Javy Lopez .05 .15
163 Eric Karros .02 .10
164 Royce Clayton .01 .05
165 Salomon Torres .01 .05
166 Jeff Kent .02 .10
167 Chris Hoiles .01 .05
168 Len Dykstra .02 .10
169 Jose Canseco .15 .40
170 Bret Boone .02 .10
171 Charlie Hayes .01 .05
172 Lou Whitaker .02 .10
173 Jack McDowell .01 .05
174 Jimmy Key .02 .10
175 Mark Langston .01 .05
176 Darryl Kile .01 .05
177 Juan Guzman .01 .05
178 Pat Borders .01 .05
179 Cal Eldred .01 .05
180 Jose Guzman .01 .05
181 Ozzie Smith .25 .60
182 Rod Beck .01 .05
183 Dave Fleming .01 .05
184 Eddie Murray .15 .40
185 Cal Ripken .75 2.00
186 Dave Hollins .01 .05
187 Will Clark .08 .25
188 Otis Nixon .01 .05
189 Joe Oliver .01 .05
190 Roberto Mejia .01 .05
191 Felix Jose .01 .05
192 Tony Phillips .01 .05
193 Wade Boggs .20 .50
194 Tim Salmon .05 .15
195 Ruben Sierra .02 .10
196 Steve Avery .01 .05
197 B.J. Surhoff .02 .10
198 Todd Zeile .02 .10
199 Raul Mondesi .08 .25
200 Barry Bonds .40 1.00
201 Sandy Alomar .02 .10
202 Bobby Bonilla .01 .05
203 Mike Devereaux .01 .05
204 Ricky Bottalico RC .01 .05
205 Kevin Brown .05 .15
206 Jason Bere .01 .05
207 Reggie Sanders .02 .10
208 David Nied .01 .05
209 Travis Fryman .02 .10
210 James Baldwin .01 .05
211 Jim Abbott .02 .10
212 Jeff Bagwell .30 .75
213 Bob Welch .02 .10
214 Jeff Blauser .01 .05
215 Brett Butler .02 .10
216 Pat Listach .01 .05
217 Bob Tewksbury .01 .05
218 Mike Lansing .01 .05
219 Wayne Kirby .01 .05
220 Chuck Carr .01 .05
221 Harold Baines .02 .10
222 Jay Bell .01 .05
223 Cliff Floyd .05 .15
224 Rob Dibble .01 .05
225 Kevin Appier .02 .10
226 Eric Davis .02 .10
227 Matt Walbeck .01 .05
228 Tim Raines .02 .10
229 Paul O'Neill .02 .10
230 Craig Biggio .08 .25
231 Brent Gates .01 .05
232 Rob Butler .01 .05
233 David Justice .05 .15
234 Rene Arocha .01 .05
235 Mike Morgan .01 .05
236 Denis Boucher .01 .05
237 Kenny Lofton .02 .10
238 Jeff Conine .02 .10
239 Bryan Harvey .01 .05
240 Danny Jackson .01 .05
241 Al Martin .01 .05
242 Tom Henke .01 .05
243 Erik Hanson .01 .05
244 Walt Weiss .01 .05
245 Brian McRae .01 .05
246 Kevin Tapani .01 .05
247 David McCarty .01 .05
248 Doug Drabek .01 .05
249 Troy Neel .01 .05
250 Tom Glavine .08 .25
251 Ray Lankford .02 .10
252 Wil Cordero .01 .05
253 Larry Walker .05 .15
254 Charles Nagy .01 .05
255 Kirk Rueter .01 .05
256 John Franco .02 .10
257 John Kruk .02 .10
258 Alex Gonzalez .01 .05
259 Mo Vaughn .08 .25
260 David Cone .05 .15
261 Kent Hrbek .02 .10
262 Lance Johnson .01 .05
263 Luis Gonzalez .08 .25
264 Mike Bordick .01 .05
265 Ed Sprague .01 .05
266 Moises Alou .05 .15
267 Omar Vizquel .02 .10
268 Jay Buhner .02 .10
269 Checklist .01 .05
270 Checklist .01 .05

1994 O-Pee-Chee All-Star Redemptions

COMPLETE SET (25) 5.00 12.00
1 Frank Thomas .30 .75
2 Paul Molitor .40 1.00
3 Barry Bonds .60 1.50
4 Juan Gonzalez .25 .60
5 Jeff Bagwell .50 1.25
6 Carlos Baerga .07 .20
7 Ryne Sandberg .40 1.00
8 Ken Griffey Jr. 1.00 2.50
9 Mike Piazza .75 2.00
10 Tim Salmon .10 .30
11 Marquis Grissom .10 .30
12 Albert Belle .10 .30
13 Fred McGriff .15 .40
14 Jack McDowell .07 .20
15 Cal Ripken 1.25 3.00
16 John Olerud .10 .30
17 Kirby Puckett .50 1.25
18 Roger Clemens .75 2.00
19 Larry Walker .10 .30
20 Cecil Fielder .10 .30
21 Roberto Alomar .25 .60
22 Greg Maddux 1.00 2.50
23 Joe Carter .10 .30
24 David Justice .10 .30
25 Kenny Lofton .15 .40

1994 O-Pee-Chee Jumbo All-Stars

COMPLETE SET (25) 15.00 40.00
FOIL: SAME VALUE AS BASIC JUMBOS
1 Frank Thomas .75 2.00
2 Paul Molitor .60 1.50
3 Barry Bonds 1.50 4.00
4 Juan Gonzalez .40 1.00
5 Jeff Bagwell .75 2.00
6 Carlos Baerga .08 .25
7 Ryne Sandberg 1.25 3.00
8 Ken Griffey Jr. 2.50 6.00
9 Mike Piazza 2.00 5.00
10 Tim Salmon .40 1.00
11 Marquis Grissom .20 .50
12 Albert Belle .20 .50
13 Fred McGriff .30 .75
14 Jack McDowell .08 .25
15 Cal Ripken 3.00 8.00
16 John Olerud .20 .50
17 Kirby Puckett 1.00 2.50
18 Roger Clemens 1.50 4.00
19 Larry Walker .30 .75
20 Cecil Fielder .20 .50
21 Roberto Alomar .40 1.00
22 Greg Maddux 2.00 5.00
23 Joe Carter .20 .50
24 David Justice .20 .50
25 Kenny Lofton .30 .75

1994 O-Pee-Chee Jumbo All-Stars Foil

These cards, parallel to the Jumbo All-Stars a collector received when buying a 1994 O-Pee-Chee Box were given a foil treatment. These cards were available by a collector accumulating five cards from the All-Star redemption set and sending in $20 Canadian. These cards were to be available to collectors by early October, 1994.

COMPLETE SET (25) 8.00 20.00
*SAME PRICE AS REGULAR JUMBO ALL-STAR

1994 O-Pee-Chee Diamond Dynamos

COMPLETE SET (18) 10.00 25.00
1 Mike Piazza 8.00 20.00
2 Robert Mejia .40 1.00
3 Wayne Kirby .40 1.00
4 Kevin Stocker .40 1.00
5 Chris Gomez .40 1.00
6 Bobby Jones .40 1.00
7 David McCarty .40 1.00
8 Kirk Rueter .40 1.00
9 J.T. Snow .60 1.50
10 Wil Cordero .40 1.00
11 Tim Salmon 2.50 6.00
12 Jeff Conine .75 2.00
13 Jason Bere .40 1.00
14 Greg McMichael .40 1.00
15 Brent Gates .40 1.00
16 Allen Watson .40 1.00
17 Aaron Sele .60 1.50
18 Carlos Garcia .40 1.00

1994 O-Pee-Chee Hot Prospects

COMPLETE SET (9) 8.00 20.00
1 Cliff Floyd .75 2.00
2 James Mouton .20 .50
3 Salomon Torres .20 .50
4 Raul Mondesi .40 1.00
5 Carlos Delgado 2.00 5.00
6 Manny Ramirez 2.50 6.00
7 Javy Lopez 1.00 2.50
8 Alex Gonzalez .20 .50
9 Ryan Klesko 1.50 4.00

1994 O-Pee-Chee World Champions

COMPLETE SET (9) 6.00 15.00
1 Rickey Henderson 3.00 8.00
2 Devon White .60 1.50
3 Paul Molitor 1.25 3.00
4 Joe Carter .60 1.50
5 John Olerud .75 2.00
6 Roberto Alomar 1.00 2.50
7 Ed Sprague .40 1.00
8 Pat Borders .40 1.00
9 Tony Fernandez .75 2.00

2009 O-Pee-Chee

COMPLETE SET (600) 60.00 120.00
COMMON CARD (1-560) .15 .40
COMMON RC (561-600) .40 1.00
RC ODDS 1:3 HOBBY/RETAIL
CL ODDS 1:3 HOBBY/RETAIL
MOMENT ODDS 1:6 HOBBY/RETAIL
LL ODDS 1:8 HOBBY/RETAIL
1 Melvin Mora .15 .40
2 Jim Thome .25 .60
3 Jonathan Sanchez .15 .40
4 Cesar Izturis .15 .40
5 A.J. Pierzynski .15 .40
6 Adam LaRoche .15 .40
7 J.D. Drew .15 .40
8 Brian Schneider .15 .40
9 John Grabow .15 .40
10 Jimmy Rollins .25 .60
11 Jeff Baker .15 .40
12 Daniel Cabrera .15 .40
13 Kyle Lohse .15 .40
14 Jason Giambi .15 .40
15 Nate McLouth .15 .40
16 Gary Matthews .15 .40
17 Cody Ross .15 .40
18 Justin Masterson .15 .40
19 Jose Lopez .15 .40
20 Brian Roberts .15 .40
21 Cla Meredith .15 .40
22 Ben Francisco .15 .40
23 Brian McCann .25 .60
24 Carlos Guillen .15 .40
25 Chien-Ming Wang .25 .60

26 Brandon Phillips .15 .40
27 Saul Rivera .15 .40
28 Torii Hunter .15 .40
29 Jamie Moyer .15 .40
30 Kevin Youkilis .15 .40
31 Martin Prado .15 .40
32 Magglio Ordonez .25 .60
33 Nomar Garciaparra .25 .60
34 Takashi Saito .15 .40
35 Chase Headley .15 .40
36 Mike Pelfrey .15 .40
37 Ronny Cedeno .15 .40
38 Dallas McPherson .15 .40
39 Zack Greinke .40 1.00
40 Matt Cain .25 .60
41 Xavier Nady .15 .40
42 Willie Aybar .15 .40
43 Edgar Gonzalez .15 .40
44 Gabe Gross .15 .40
45 Joey Votto .40 1.00
46 Jason Michaels .15 .40
47 Eric Chavez .15 .40
48 Jason Bartlett .15 .40
49 Jeremy Guthrie .15 .40
50 Matt Holliday .40 1.00
51 Ross Ohlendorf .15 .40
52 Gil Meche .15 .40
53 B.J. Upton .25 .60
54 Ryan Doumit .15 .40
55 Jay Bruce .25 .60
56 Huston Street .15 .40
57 Bobby Crosby .15 .40
58 Jose Valverde .15 .40
59 Brian Tallet .15 .40
60 Adam Dunn .25 .60
61 Victor Martinez .25 .60
62 Jeff Francoeur .25 .60
63 Emilio Bonifacio .15 .40
64 Chone Figgins .15 .40
65 Alexei Ramirez .25 .60
66 Brian Giles .15 .40
67 Khalil Greene .15 .40
68 Phil Hughes .15 .40
69 Mike Aviles .15 .40
70 Ryan Braun .25 .60
71 Braden Looper .15 .40
72 Jhonny Peralta .15 .40
73 Ian Stewart .15 .40
74 James Loney .15 .40
75 Chase Utley .25 .60
76 Reed Johnson .15 .40
77 Jorge Cantu .15 .40
78 Julio Lugo .15 .40
79 Raul Ibanez .25 .60
80 Lance Berkman .25 .60
81 Joel Peralta .15 .40
82 Mark Hendrickson .15 .40
83 Jeff Suppan .15 .40
84 Scott Olsen .15 .40
85 Joba Chamberlain .15 .40
86 Fausto Carmona .15 .40
87 Andy Pettitte .25 .60
88 Jim Johnson .15 .40
89 Chris Snyder .15 .40
90 Nick Swisher .25 .60
91 Edgar Renteria .15 .40
92 Brandon Inge .15 .40
93 Aubrey Huff .15 .40
94 Stephen Drew .15 .40
95 Denard Span .15 .40
96 Carl Crawford .25 .60
97 Felix Pie .15 .40
98 Jeremy Sowers .15 .40
99 Trevor Hoffman .25 .60
100 Albert Pujols .50 1.25
101 Radhames Liz .15 .40
102 Doug Davis .15 .40
103 Joel Hanrahan .25 .60
104 Seth Smith .15 .40
105 Francisco Liriano .15 .40
106 Bobby Abreu .15 .40
107 Willie Harris .15 .40
108 Travis Ishikawa .20 .50
109 Travis Hafner .15 .40
110 Adrian Gonzalez .30 .75
111 Shin-Soo Choo .25 .60
112 Robinson Cano .25 .60
113 Matt Capps .15 .40
114 Gerald Laird .15 .40
115 Max Scherzer .40 1.00
116 Mike Jacobs .15 .40
117 Asdrubal Cabrera .25 .60
118 J.J. Hardy .15 .40
119 Justin Upton .25 .60
120 Mariano Rivera .50 1.25
121 Jack Cust .15 .40
122 Orlando Hudson .15 .40
123 Brian Wilson .40 1.00
124 Heath Bell .15 .40
125 Chipper Jones .40 1.00
126 Jason Marquis .15 .40
127 Rocco Baldelli .15 .40
128 Rafael Perez .15 .40
129 Carlos Gomez .15 .40
130 Kerry Wood .15 .40
131 Adam Wainwright .25 .60
132 Michael Bourn .15 .40
133 Cristian Guzman .15 .40
134 Dustin McGowan .15 .40
135 James Shields .15 .40
136 Matt Lindstrom .15 .40
137 Rick Ankiel .15 .40
138 J.P. Howell .15 .40
139 Ben Zobrist .25 .60
140 Tim Hudson .25 .60
141 Clayton Kershaw .60 1.50
142 Edwin Encarnacion .40 1.00
143 Kevin Millwood .15 .40
144 Jack Hannahan .15 .40
145 Alex Gordon .25 .60
146 Chad Durbin .15 .40
147 Derrek Lee .15 .40
148 Kevin Gregg .15 .40
149 Clint Barmes .15 .40
150 Dustin Pedroia .40 1.00
151 Brad Hawpe .15 .40
152 Steven Shell .15 .40
153 Jesse Crain .15 .40
154 Edwar Ramirez .15 .40
155 Jair Jurrjens .15 .40
156 Matt Albers .15 .40
157 Endy Chavez .15 .40
158 Steve Pearce .40 1.00
159 John Maine .15 .40
160 Ryan Theriot .15 .40
161 Eric Stults .15 .40
162 Cha-Seung Baek .15 .40
163 Alex Gonzalez .15 .40
164 Dan Haren .15 .40
165 Edwin Jackson .15 .40
166 Felipe Lopez .15 .40
167 David DeJesus .15 .40
168 Todd Wellemeyer .15 .40
169 Joey Gathright .15 .40
170 Roy Oswalt .25 .60
171 Carlos Pena .25 .60
172 Nick Hundley .15 .40
173 Adrian Beltre .40 1.00
174 Omar Vizquel .25 .60
175 Cole Hamels .30 .75
176 Jarrod Saltalamacchia .15 .40
177 Yuniesky Betancourt .15 .40
178 Placido Polanco .15 .40
179 Ryan Spilborghs .15 .40
180 Josh Beckett .15 .40
181 Cory Wade .15 .40
182 Aaron Laffey .15 .40
183 Kosuke Fukudome .25 .60
184 Miguel Montero .15 .40
185 Edinson Volquez .15 .40
186 Jon Garland .15 .40
187 Andruw Jones .15 .40
188 Vernon Wells .15 .40
189 Zach Duke .15 .40
190 David Wright .30 .75
191 Ryan Madson .15 .40
192 Hideki Okajima .15 .40
193 Ryan Church .15 .40
194 Adam Jones .25 .60
195 Geovany Soto .25 .60
196 Jeremy Hermida .15 .40
197 Juan Rivera .15 .40
198 David Weathers .15 .40
199 Jorge Campillo .15 .40
200 Derek Jeter 1.00 2.50
201 Brett Myers .15 .40
202 Brett Gardner .25 .60
203 Rafael Furcal .15 .40
204 Wandy Rodriguez .15 .40
205 Ricky Nolasco .15 .40
206 Ryan Freel .15 .40
207 Jeremy Bonderman .15 .40
208 Michael Wuertz .15 .40
209 Hank Blalock .15 .40
210 Alfonso Soriano .25 .60
211 Jeff Clement .15 .40
212 Garrett Atkins .15 .40
213 Luis Vizcaino .15 .40
214 Tim Redding .15 .40
215 Ryan Ludwick .25 .60
216 Mark Teahen .15 .40
217 Chris Young .15 .40
218 David Aardsma .15 .40
219 Ubaldo Jimenez .15 .40
220 Ryan Howard .30 .75
221 Skip Schumaker .15 .40
222 Craig Counsell .15 .40
223 Chris Iannetta .15 .40
224 Jason Kubel .15 .40
225 Johan Santana .25 .60
226 Luke Hochevar .15 .40
227 Jason Bay .25 .60
228 Alex Hinshaw .15 .40
229 Jon Rauch .15 .40
230 Carlos Quentin .15 .40
231 Coco Crisp .15 .40
232 Casey Blake .15 .40
233 Carlos Marmol .25 .60
234 Fernando Rodney .15 .40
235 Jed Lowrie .15 .40
236 Brad Penny .15 .40
237 Reggie Willits .15 .40
238 Mike Hampton .15 .40
239 Mike Lowell .15 .40
240 Randy Johnson .40 1.00
241 Jarrod Washburn .15 .40
242 B.J. Ryan .15 .40
243 Javier Vazquez .15 .40
244 Todd Helton .25 .60
245 Matt Garza .15 .40
246 Ramon Hernandez .15 .40
247 Johnny Cueto .25 .60
248 Willy Taveras .15 .40
249 Carlos Silva .15 .40
250 Manny Ramirez .40 1.00
251 A.J. Burnett .15 .40
252 Aaron Cook .15 .40
253 Josh Bard .15 .40
254 Aaron Harang .15 .40
255 Jeff Samardzija .25 .60
256 Brad Lidge .15 .40
257 Pedro Feliz .15 .40
258 Kazuo Matsui .15 .40
259 Joe Blanton .15 .40
260 Ian Kinsler .25 .60
261 Rich Harden .15 .40
262 Kelly Johnson .15 .40
263 Anibal Sanchez .15 .40
264 Mike Adams .15 .40
265 Chad Billingsley .25 .60
266 Chris Davis .25 .60
267 Brandon Moss .15 .40
268 Matt Kemp .30 .75
269 Jose Arredondo .15 .40
270 Mark Teixeira .25 .60
271 Glen Perkins .15 .40
272 Pat Burrell .15 .40
273 Luke Scott .15 .40
274 Scott Feldman .25 .60
275 Ichiro Suzuki .50 1.25
276 Cliff Floyd .15 .40
277 Bill Hall .15 .40
278 Bronson Arroyo .15 .40
279 Lyle Overbay .15 .40
280 Aramis Ramirez .15 .40
281 Jeff Keppinger .15 .40
282 Brandon Morrow .15 .40
283 Ryan Shealy .15 .40
284 Andy Sonnanstine .15 .40
285 Josh Johnson .25 .60
286 Carlos Ruiz .15 .40
287 Gregg Zaun .15 .40
288 Kenji Johjima .25 .60
289 Mike Gonzalez .15 .40
290 Carlos Delgado .15 .40
291 Gary Sheffield .15 .40
292 Brian Anderson .15 .40
293 Josh Hamilton .25 .60
294 Tom Gorzelanny .15 .40
295 Yunel Escobar .15 .40
296 Scott Hairston .15 .40
297 Luis Castillo .15 .40
298 Gabe Kapler .15 .40
299 Nelson Cruz .40 1.00
300 Tim Lincecum .25 .60
301 Brian Bannister .15 .40
302 Frank Francisco .15 .40
303 Jose Guillen .15 .40
304 Erick Aybar .15 .40
305 Brad Ziegler .15 .40
306 John Baker .15 .40
307 Hong-Chih Kuo .15 .40
308 Jo Jo Reyes .15 .40
309 Josh Willingham .25 .60
310 Billy Wagner .15 .40
311 Nick Blackburn .15 .40
312 David Purcey .15 .40
313 Rafael Soriano .15 .40
314 Zach Miner .15 .40
315 Andre Ethier .25 .60
316 Rickie Weeks .15 .40
317 Akinori Iwamura .15 .40
318 Hideki Matsui .40 1.00
319 Ryan Rowland-Smith .15 .40
320 Miguel Cabrera .40 1.00
321 Manny Parra .15 .40
322 Jack Wilson .15 .40
323 Jeremy Reed .15 .40
324 Chris Coste .15 .40
325 Grady Sizemore .25 .60
326 Andy LaRoche .15 .40
327 Joel Pineiro .15 .40
328 Brian Buscher .15 .40
329 Randy Wolf .15 .40
330 Jake Peavy .15 .40
331 Curtis Granderson .30 .75
332 Kyle Kendrick .15 .40
333 Joe Saunders .15 .40
334 Russell Martin .15 .40
335 Conor Jackson .15 .40
336 Paul Konerko .25 .60
337 Kevin Slowey .25 .60
338 Mark DeRosa .25 .60
339 Garret Anderson .15 .40
340 Michael Young .15 .40
341 Greg Dobbs .15 .40
342 Brian Moehler .15 .40
343 Alex Rios .15 .40
344 Mike Napoli .15 .40
345 Bobby Jenks .15 .40
346 Daric Barton .15 .40
347 Jason Kendall .15 .40
348 Chad Qualls .15 .40
349 Milton Bradley .15 .40
350 Joe Mauer .30 .75
351 Livan Hernandez .15 .40
352 Chris Ray .15 .40
353 Bob Howry .15 .40
354 Manny Corpas .15 .40
355 Ervin Santana .15 .40
356 Billy Butler .15 .40
357 Russ Springer .15 .40
358 Micah Owings .15 .40
359 Corey Hart .15 .40
360 Francisco Rodriguez .25 .60
361 Ted Lilly .15 .40
362 Adam Everett .15 .40
363 Scott Rolen .25 .60
364 Troy Tulowitzki .40 1.00
365 Jacoby Ellsbury .30 .75
366 Jayson Werth .25 .60
367 Gio Gonzalez .25 .60
368 Mark Ellis .15 .40
369 Brendan Harris .15 .40
370 David Ortiz .40 1.00
371 Carlos Lee .15 .40
372 Jonathan Broxton .15 .40
373 Jesse Litsch .15 .40
374 Barry Zito .25 .60
375 Daisuke Matsuzaka .25 .60
376 Kevin Kouzmanoff .15 .40
377 Jesse Carlson .15 .40
378 Brian Fuentes .15 .40
379 Mark Reynolds .15 .40
380 Brandon Webb .25 .60
381 Scott Kazmir .15 .40
382 Blake DeWitt .15 .40
383 Kurt Suzuki .15 .40
384 Chris Volstad .15 .40
385 Gavin Floyd .15 .40
386 Paul Maholm .15 .40
387 Freddy Sanchez .15 .40
388 Scott Baker .15 .40
389 John Danks .15 .40
390 CC Sabathia .25 .60
391 Ryan Dempster .15 .40
392 Tim Wakefield .25 .60
393 Mike Cameron .15 .40
394 Aaron Rowand .15 .40
395 Howie Kendrick .15 .40
396 Marlon Byrd .15 .40
397 Dave Bush .15 .40
398 George Sherrill .15 .40
399 Francisco Cordero .15 .40
400 Evan Longoria .25 .60
401 Hiroki Kuroda .15 .40
402 Sean Gallagher .15 .40
403 Yovani Gallardo .15 .40
404 Ryan Sweeney .15 .40
405 Chris Dickerson .15 .40
406 Jason Varitek .40 1.00
407 Erik Bedard .15 .40
408 J.J. Putz .15 .40
409 Wily Mo Pena .15 .40
410 Rich Hill .15 .40
411 Delmon Young .25 .60
412 David Eckstein .15 .40
413 Marcus Thames .15 .40
414 Dontrelle Willis .15 .40
415 Joakim Soria .15 .40
416 Chan Ho Park .25 .60
417 Jered Weaver .25 .60
418 Justin Duchscherer .15 .40
419 Casey Kotchman .15 .40
420 John Lackey .25 .60
421 Peter Moylan .15 .40
422 Bengie Molina .15 .40
423 Mark Loretta .15 .40
424 Dan Wheeler .15 .40
425 Ken Griffey Jr. .75 2.00
426 Justin Verlander .40 1.00
427 Troy Glaus .15 .40
428 Daniel Murphy RC 1.50 4.00
429 Brandon Backe .15 .40
430 Nick Markakis .30 .75
431 Travis Metcalf .15 .40
432 Austin Kearns .15 .40
433 Adam Lind .15 .40
434 Jody Gerut .15 .40
435 Jonathan Papelbon .25 .60
436 Duaner Sanchez .15 .40
437 David Murphy .15 .40
438 Eddie Guardado .15 .40
439 Johnny Damon .25 .60
440 Derek Lowe .15 .40
441 Miguel Olivo .15 .40
442 Shaun Marcum .15 .40
443 Ty Wigginton .25 .60
444 Elijah Dukes .15 .40
445 Felix Hernandez .25 .60
446 Joe Inglett .15 .40
447 Kelly Shoppach .15 .40
448 Eric Hinske .15 .40
449 Fred Lewis .15 .40
450 Cliff Lee .25 .60
451 Miguel Tejada .25 .60
452 Jensen Lewis .15 .40
453 Ryan Zimmerman .25 .60
454 Jon Lester .25 .60
455 Justin Morneau .25 .60
456 John Smoltz .40 1.00
457 Emmanuel Burriss .15 .40
458 Joe Nathan .15 .40
459 Jeff Niemann .15 .40
460 Roy Halladay .25 .60
461 Matt Diaz .15 .40
462 Oscar Salazar .15 .40
463 Chris Perez .15 .40
464 Matt Joyce .15 .40
465 Dan Uggla .15 .40
466 Jermaine Dye .15 .40
467 Shane Victorino .15 .40
468 Chris Getz .15 .40
469 Chris B. Young .15 .40
470 Prince Fielder .25 .60
471 Juan Pierre .15 .40
472 Travis Buck .15 .40
473 Dioner Navarro .15 .40
474 Mark Buehrle .25 .60
475 Hanley Ramirez .25 .60
476 John Lannan .15 .40
477 Lastings Milledge .15 .40
478 Dallas Braden .15 .40
479 Orlando Cabrera .15 .40
480 Jose Reyes .25 .60
481 Jorge Posada .25 .60
482 Jason Isringhausen .15 .40
483 Rich Aurilia .15 .40
484 Hunter Pence .25 .60
485 Carlos Zambrano .25 .60
486 Randy Winn .15 .40
487 Carlos Beltran .25 .60
488 Armando Galarraga .15 .40
489 Wilson Betemit .15 .40
490 Vladimir Guerrero .25 .60
491 Ryan Garko .15 .40
492 Ian Snell .15 .40
493 Yadier Molina .50 1.25
494 Tom Glavine .25 .60
495 Cameron Maybin .15 .40
496 Vicente Padilla .15 .40
497 Keiichi Yabu .15 .40
498 Oliver Perez .15 .40
499 Carlos Villanueva .15 .40
500 Alex Rodriguez .50 1.25
501 Baltimore Orioles CL .15 .40
502 Boston Red Sox CL .25 .60
503 Chicago White Sox CL .15 .40
504 Houston Astros CL .15 .40
505 Oakland Athletics CL .15 .40
506 Toronto Blue Jays CL .15 .40
507 Atlanta Braves CL .15 .40
508 Milwaukee Brewers CL .15 .40
509 St. Louis Cardinals CL .25 .60
510 Chicago Cubs CL .25 .60
511 Arizona Diamondbacks CL .15 .40
512 Los Angeles Dodgers CL .25 .60
513 San Francisco Giants CL .15 .40
514 Cleveland Indians CL .15 .40
515 Seattle Mariners CL .15 .40
516 Florida Marlins CL .15 .40
517 New York Mets CL .25 .60
518 Washington Nationals CL .15 .40
519 San Diego Padres CL .15 .40
520 Pittsburgh Pirates CL .15 .40
521 Tampa Bay Rays CL .15 .40
522 Cincinnati Reds CL .15 .40
523 Colorado Rockies CL .15 .40
524 Kansas City Royals CL .15 .40
525 Detroit Tigers CL .15 .40
526 Minnesota Twins CL .15 .40
527 New York Yankees CL .25 .60
528 Philadelphia Phillies CL .15 .40
529 Los Angeles Angels CL .15 .40
530 Texas Rangers CL .15 .40
531 Bradley/Mauer/Pedroia .40 1.00
532 Chipper/Holliday/Pujols .50 1.25
533 M.Cabrera/ARod/Quentin .50 1.25
534 Delgado/Dunn/Howard .30 .75
535 Morneau/Hamilton/Cabrera .40 1.00
536 Howard/Wright/A.Gon .30 .75
537 C.Lee/D.Matsu/Halladay .25 .60
538 Santana/Peavy/Lince .25 .60
539 C.Lee/D.Matsu/Halladay .25 .60
540 Lince/Dempster/Webb .25 .60
541 Ervin Santana
Roy Halladay/A.J. Burnett .25 .60
542 Santana/Lince/Haren .25 .60
543 Grady Sizemore .25 .60
544 Ichiro Suzuki .50 1.25
545 Hanley Ramirez .25 .60
546 Jose Reyes .25 .60
547 Johan Santana .25 .60
548 Adrian Gonzalez .30 .75
549 Carlos Zambrano .25 .60
550 Jonathan Papelbon .25 .60
551 Josh Hamilton .25 .60
552 Derek Jeter 1.00 2.50
553 Kevin Youkilis .15 .40
554 Joe Mauer .30 .75
555 Kosuke Fukudome .25 .60
Ryan Theriot
556 Chipper Jones .40 1.00
557 Lance Berkman .25 .60
558 Michael Young .15 .40
559 Evan Longoria .25 .60
560 Alex Rodriguez .50 1.25
561 Travis Snider RC .60 1.50
562 James McDonald RC 1.00 2.50
563 Brian Duensing RC .60 1.50
564 Josh Outman RC .60 1.50
565 Josh Geer (RC) .40 1.00
566 Kevin Jepsen (RC) .40 1.00
567 Scott Lewis (RC) .40 1.00
568 Jason Motte (RC) .60 1.50
569 Ricky Romero (RC) .60 1.50
570 Landon Powell (RC) .40 1.00
571 Scott Elbert (RC) .40 1.00
572 Bobby Parnell RC .60 1.50
573 Ryan Perry RC 1.00 2.50
574 Phil Coke RC .60 1.50
575 Trevor Cahill RC 1.00 2.50
576 Jesse Chavez RC .40 1.00
577 George Kottaras (RC) .40 1.00
578 Trevor Crowe RC .40 1.00
579 David Freese RC 1.25 3.00
580 Matt Tuiasosopo (RC) .40 1.00
581 Brett Anderson RC .60 1.50
582 Casey McGehee (RC) .40 1.00
583 Elvis Andrus RC 1.00 2.50
584 Shawn Kelley RC .60 1.50
585 Mike Hinckley (RC) .40 1.00
586 Donald Veal RC .60 1.50
587 Colby Rasmus (RC) .60 1.50
588 Shairon Martis RC .60 1.50
589 Walter Silva RC .60 1.50
590 Chris Jakubauskas RC .60 1.50
591 Brad Nelson (RC) .40 1.00
592 Alfredo Simon (RC) .40 1.00
593 Koji Uehara RC 1.00 2.50
594 Rick Porcello RC 1.25 3.00
595 Kenshin Kawakami RC .60 1.50
596 Dexter Fowler (RC) .60 1.50
597 Jordan Schafer (RC) .60 1.50
598 David Patton RC .60 1.50
599 Luis Cruz RC .40 1.00
600 Joe Martinez RC .60 1.50

2009 O-Pee-Chee Black

*BLACK VET: 1X TO 2.5X BASIC
*BLACK RC: .75X TO 2X BASIC
STATED ODDS 1:6 HOBBY/RETAIL

2009 O-Pee-Chee Black Blank Back

RANDOM INSERTS IN PACKS
NO PRICING DUE TO SCARCITY

2009 O-Pee-Chee Black Mini

*BLK MINI VET: 4X TO 10X BASIC
*BLK MINI RC: 1.5X TO 4X BASIC
STATED ODDS 1:216 HOBBY/RETAIL

2009 O-Pee-Chee All-Rookie Team

STATED ODDS 1:40 HOBBY/RETAIL
AR1 Geovany Soto .60 1.50
AR2 Joey Votto 1.00 2.50
AR3 Alexei Ramirez .60 1.50
AR4 Evan Longoria .60 1.50
AR5 Mike Aviles .40 1.00
AR6 Jacoby Ellsbury .75 2.00
AR7 Jay Bruce .60 1.50
AR8 Kosuke Fukudome .60 1.50
AR9 Jair Jurrjens .40 1.00
AR10 Denard Span .40 1.00

2009 O-Pee-Chee Box Bottoms

CARDS LISTED ALPHABETICALLY
1 Ryan Braun .60 1.50
2 Miguel Cabrera 1.00 2.50
3 Adrian Gonzalez .75 2.00
4 Vladimir Guerrero .60 1.50
5 Josh Hamilton .60 1.50
6 Derek Jeter 2.50 6.00
7 Chipper Jones 1.00 2.50
8 Clayton Kershaw 1.50 4.00
9 Evan Longoria .60 1.50
10 Dustin Pedroia 1.00 2.50
11 Albert Pujols 1.25 3.00
12 Hanley Ramirez .60 1.50
13 Grady Sizemore .60 1.50
14 Alfonso Soriano .60 1.50
15 Ichiro Suzuki 1.25 3.00
16 Chase Utley .60 1.50

2009 O-Pee-Chee Face of the Franchise

STATED ODDS 1:13 HOBBY/RETAIL
FF1 Vladimir Guerrero .60 1.50
FF2 Roy Oswalt .60 1.50
FF3 Eric Chavez .40 1.00
FF4 Roy Halladay .60 1.50
FF5 Chipper Jones 1.00 2.50
FF6 Ryan Braun .60 1.50
FF7 Albert Pujols 1.25 3.00
FF8 Carlos Zambrano .60 1.50
FF9 Brandon Webb .60 1.50
FF10 Russell Martin .40 1.00
FF11 Tim Lincecum .60 1.50
FF12 Grady Sizemore .60 1.50
FF13 Ichiro Suzuki 1.25 3.00
FF14 Hanley Ramirez .60 1.50
FF15 David Wright .75 2.00
FF16 Ryan Zimmerman .60 1.50
FF17 Brian Roberts .40 1.00
FF18 Adrian Gonzalez .75 2.00
FF19 Jimmy Rollins .60 1.50
FF20 Nate McLouth .40 1.00
FF21 Michael Young .40 1.00
FF22 Evan Longoria .60 1.50
FF23 David Ortiz 1.00 2.50
FF24 Jay Bruce .60 1.50
FF25 Troy Tulowitzki 1.00 2.50
FF26 Alex Gordon .60 1.50
FF27 Miguel Cabrera 1.00 2.50
FF28 Joe Mauer .75 2.00
FF29 Carlos Quentin .40 1.00
FF30 Derek Jeter 2.50 6.00

2009 O-Pee-Chee Highlights and Milestones

STATED ODDS 1:27 HOBBY/RETAIL
HM1 Brad Lidge .40 1.00
HM2 Ken Griffey Jr. 2.00 5.00
HM3 Melvin Mora .40 1.00
HM4 Derek Jeter 2.50 6.00
HM5 Josh Hamilton .60 1.50
HM6 Alfonso Soriano .60 1.50
HM7 Francisco Rodriguez .60 1.50
HM8 Jon Lester .60 1.50
HM9 Carlos Zambrano .60 1.50
HM10 Adrian Beltre 1.00 2.50
HM11 Carlos Gomez .40 1.00
HM12 Kelly Shoppach .40 1.00
HM13 Manny Ramirez 1.00 2.50
HM14 Carlos Delgado .40 1.00
HM15 CC Sabathia .60 1.50

2009 O-Pee-Chee Materials

STATED ODDS 1:108 HOBBY
STATED ODDS 1:216 RETAIL
BBP Brad Penny/Josh Beckett/A.J. Burnett 4.00 10.00
BHH Rocco Baldelli/Corey Hart
Jeremy Hermida 4.00 10.00
BMY Youkilis/Beltre/Mora 8.00 20.00
BYP Jonathan Papelbon
Kevin Youkilis/Josh Beckett 6.00 15.00
CBG Chad Billingsley
Fausto Carmona/Zack Greinke 4.00 10.00
CFM Nick Markakis/Jeff Francoeur
Michael Cuddyer 6.00 15.00
CKR Ian Kinsler/Brian Roberts
Robinson Cano 5.00 12.00
CSW Nick Swisher/Michael Cuddyer
Josh Willingham 6.00 15.00
DLO Magglio Ordonez/Carlos Lee
Jermaine Dye 6.00 15.00
EFG Jacoby Ellsbury/Curtis
Granderson/Chone Figgins 6.00 15.00
ELK Kemp/Ethier/Loney 8.00 20.00
FOD David Ortiz/Carlos
Delgado/Prince Fielder 5.00 12.00
GDH J.J. Hardy/Stephen
Drew/Khalil Greene 4.00 10.00
HAG Garrett Atkins/Carlos
Gonzalez/Todd Helton 4.00 10.00
HMC Justin Morneau/Miguel
Cabrera/Travis Hafner 6.00 15.00
HML Long/Morn/Hamil 8.00 20.00
HMW Jake Westbrook/Travis
Hafner/Victor Martinez 4.00 10.00
HRR Halladay/Rios/Rolen 8.00 20.00
JCP Posada/Cano/Jeter 10.00 25.00
KJN Jayson Nix/Kelly Johnson
Howie Kendrick 4.00 10.00
LRF Kosuke Fukudome/Derrek
Lee/Aramis Ramirez 4.00 10.00
LWS Brad Lidge/Takashi Saito
Billy Wagner 4.00 10.00
MFJ Kelly Johnson/Jeff Francoeur
Brian McCann 4.00 10.00
MMM Russell Martin/Victor
Martinez/Joe Mauer 6.00 15.00
NMC Mauer/Nathan/Cuddyer 8.00 20.00
OHG Hafner/Ortiz/Giambi 4.00 10.00
OHP Roy Halladay/Brad
Penny/Roy Oswalt 5.00 12.00
PBO Ortiz/Pap/Buchholz 5.00 12.00
PCF Pujols/Fielder/M.Cabrera 10.00 25.00
PHB Cole Hamels/Erik Bedard
Andy Pettitte 5.00 12.00
RPV Ivan Rodriguez/Jorge
Posada/Jason Varitek 5.00 12.00
VWB Clay Buchholz/Justin
Verlander/Jered Weaver 4.00 10.00
YDR Chris B. Young/Mark
Reynolds/Stephen Drew 5.00 12.00
YKM Michael Young/Ian
Kinsler/Kevin Millwood 4.00 10.00

2009 O-Pee-Chee Midsummer Memories

STATED ODDS 1:27 HOBBY/RETAIL
MM1 Ken Griffey Jr. 2.00 5.00
MM2 Hank Blalock .40 1.00
MM3 Michael Young .40 1.00
MM4 Ichiro Suzuki 1.25 3.00
MM5 Miguel Tejada .60 1.50
MM6 Alfonso Soriano .60 1.50
MM7 Jimmy Rollins .60 1.50
MM8 Derek Jeter 2.50 6.00
MM9 Justin Morneau .60 1.50
MM10 J.D. Drew .40 1.00
MM11 Carl Crawford .60 1.50
MM12 Vladimir Guerrero .60 1.50
MM13 Mark Teixeira .60 1.50
MM14 David Ortiz 1.00 2.50
MM15 Manny Ramirez 1.00 2.50

2009 O-Pee-Chee New York New York

STATED ODDS 1:40 HOBBY/RETAIL
NY1 CC Sabathia 1.00 2.50
NY2 Jorge Posada 1.00 2.50
NY3 Derek Jeter 4.00 10.00
NY4 Alex Rodriguez 2.00 5.00
NY5 Chien-Ming Wang 1.00 2.50
NY6 Joba Chamberlain .60 1.50
NY7 A.J. Burnett .60 1.50
NY8 Mariano Rivera 2.00 5.00
NY9 Nick Swisher 1.00 2.50
NY10 Robinson Cano 1.00 2.50
NY11 Mark Teixeira 1.00 2.50
NY12 Johnny Damon 1.00 2.50
NY13 Hideki Matsui 1.50 4.00
NY14 Andy Pettitte 1.00 2.50
NY15 Xavier Nady .60 1.50
NY16 Jose Reyes 1.00 2.50
NY17 David Wright 1.25 3.00
NY18 John Maine .60 1.50
NY19 Daniel Murphy 2.50 6.00
NY20 Francisco Rodriguez 1.00 2.50
NY21 Carlos Delgado .60 1.50
NY22 Luis Castillo .60 1.50
NY23 Ryan Church .60 1.50
NY24 Brian Schneider .60 1.50
NY25 J.J. Putz .60 1.50
NY26 Mike Pelfrey .60 1.50
NY27 Oliver Perez .60 1.50
NY28 Jeremy Reed .60 1.50
NY29 Johan Santana 1.00 2.50
NY30 Carlos Beltran 1.00 2.50

2009 O-Pee-Chee New York New York Multi Sport

RANDOM INSERTS IN PACKS
MS1 CC Sabathia 1.50 4.00
MS2 Henrik Lundqvist 4.00 10.00
MS3 Jose Reyes 1.50 4.00
MS4 Derek Jeter 6.00 15.00
MS5 David Wright 2.00 5.00
MS6 Rick DiPietro 2.50 6.00
MS7 Joba Chamberlain 1.00 2.50
MS8 Alex Rodriguez 3.00 8.00
MS9 Johan Santana 1.50 4.00
MS10 Carlos Beltran 1.50 4.00

2009 O-Pee-Chee Retro

RM1 Sidney Crosby 6.00 15.00
RM2 Alexander Ovechkin 6.00 15.00
RM3 Carey Price 3.00 8.00
RM4 Henrik Lundqvist 2.50 6.00
RM5 Jonathan Toews 3.00 8.00
RM6 Martin Brodeur 3.00 8.00
RM7 Evgeni Malkin 5.00 12.00
RM8 Jarome Iginla 2.50 6.00
RM9 Henrik Zetterberg 2.50 6.00
RM10 Roberto Luongo 2.50 6.00
RM11 Travis Snider 1.25 3.00
RM12 Russell Martin .75 2.00
RM13 Justin Morneau 1.25 3.00
RM14 Joey Votto 2.00 5.00
RM15 Alex Rios .75 2.00
RM16 Jon Lester 1.25 3.00
RM17 Ryan Howard 1.50 4.00
RM18 Johan Santana 1.25 3.00
RM19 CC Sabathia 1.25 3.00
RM20 Roy Halladay 1.25 3.00
RM21 Chase Utley 1.25 3.00
RM22 Chipper Jones 2.00 5.00
RM23 Ryan Braun 1.25 3.00
RM24 Ken Griffey Jr. 4.00 10.00
RM25 B.J. Upton 1.25 3.00
RM26 Hanley Ramirez 1.25 3.00
RM27 Alex Rodriguez 2.50 6.00
RM28 Cole Hamels 1.50 4.00
RM29 Albert Pujols 2.50 6.00
RM30 Derek Jeter 5.00 12.00
RM31 Manny Ramirez 2.00 5.00
RM32 David Wright 1.50 4.00
RM33 Evan Longoria 1.25 3.00

2009 O-Pee-Chee Signatures

STATED ODDS 1:216 HOBBY
STATED ODDS 1:1080 RETAIL
SAJ Joaquin Arias 4.00 10.00
SAL Aaron Laffey 6.00 15.00
SAR Alexei Ramirez 10.00 25.00
SBJ Brandon Jones 3.00 8.00
SBR Brian Barton 3.00 8.00
SCD Chris Duncan 10.00 25.00
SCH Corey Hart 5.00 12.00
SCS Clint Sammons 3.00 8.00
SCW Cory Wade 5.00 12.00
SDM David Murphy 3.00 8.00
SED Elijah Dukes 4.00 10.00
SEV Edinson Volquez 6.00 15.00
SFC Fausto Carmona 3.00 8.00
SHE Chase Headley 6.00 15.00
SHJ J.A. Happ 8.00 20.00
SIK Ian Kennedy 4.00 10.00
SJA Jonathan Albaladejo 4.00 10.00
SJB Jeremy Bonderman 15.00 40.00
SJC Jeff Clement 6.00 15.00
SJH Justin Hampson 3.00 8.00
SJL Jed Lowrie 4.00 10.00
SKJ Kelly Johnson 3.00 8.00
SKK Kevin Kouzmanoff 3.00 8.00
SKM Kyle McClellan 6.00 15.00
SKS Kurt Suzuki 6.00 15.00
SMB Michael Bourn 8.00 20.00
SMH Micah Hoffpauir 8.00 20.00
SMR Mike Rabelo 10.00 25.00
SNB Nick Blackburn 3.00 8.00
SRO Ross Ohlendorf 6.00 15.00
SSA Jarrod Saltalamacchia 6.00 15.00
SSM Sean Marshall 5.00 12.00
SSP Steve Pearce 5.00 12.00

2009 O-Pee-Chee The Award Show

STATED ODDS 1:20 HOBBY/RETAIL
AW1 Yadier Molina 1.25 3.00
AW2 Adrian Gonzalez .75 2.00
AW3 Brandon Phillips .40 1.00
AW4 David Wright .75 2.00
AW5 Jimmy Rollins .60 1.50
AW6 Carlos Beltran .60 1.50
AW7 Shane Victorino .40 1.00
AW8 Geovany Soto .60 1.50
AW9 Tim Lincecum .60 1.50
AW10 Albert Pujols 1.25 3.00
AW11 Joe Mauer .75 2.00
AW12 Carlos Pena .60 1.50
AW13 Dustin Pedroia 1.00 2.50
AW14 Adrian Beltre 1.00 2.50
AW15 Torii Hunter .40 1.00
AW16 Grady Sizemore .60 1.50
AW17 Ichiro Suzuki 1.25 3.00
AW18 Evan Longoria .60 1.50
AW19 Cliff Lee .60 1.50
AW20 Dustin Pedroia 1.00 2.50

2009 O-Pee-Chee Walk-Off Winners

STATED ODDS 1:40 HOBBY/RETAIL
WK1 Ryan Braun .60 1.50
WK2 Ryan Zimmerman .60 1.50
WK3 Michael Young .40 1.00

Card	Low	High
WK4 J.D. Drew	.40	1.00
WK5 Carlos Ruiz	.40	1.00
WK6 Dan Uggla	.40	1.00
WK7 Johnny Damon	.60	1.50
WK8 Jed Lowrie	.40	1.00
WK9 Ryan Ludwick	.60	1.50
WK10 Dioner Navarro	.40	1.00

1991 O-Pee-Chee Premier

The 1991 OPC Premier set contains 132 standard-size cards. The fronts feature color action player photos on a white card face. All the pictures are bordered in gold above, while the color of the border stripes on the other three sides varies from card to card. The player's name, team name, and position (the last item in English and French) appear below the picture. In a horizontal format, the backs have a color head shot and the team logo in a circular format. Biography and statistics (1990 and career) are presented on an orange and yellow striped background. The cards are arranged in alphabetical order and numbered on the back. Small packs of these cards were given out at the Fan Fest to commemorate the 1991 All-Star Game in Canada.

Card	Low	High
COMPLETE SET (132)	4.00	10.00
COMPLETE FACT.SET (132)	6.00	15.00
1 Roberto Alomar	.08	.25
2 Sandy Alomar Jr.	.02	.10
3 Moises Alou	.02	.10
4 Brian Barnes	.01	.05
5 Steve Bedrosian	.01	.05
6 George Bell	.01	.05
7 Juan Bell	.01	.05
8 Albert Belle	.02	.10
9 Bud Black	.01	.05
10 Mike Boddicker	.01	.05
11 Wade Boggs	.15	.40
12 Barry Bonds	.30	.75
13 Denis Boucher RC	.01	.05
14 George Brett	.30	.75
15 Hubie Brooks	.01	.05
16 Brett Butler	.02	.10
17 Ivan Calderon	.01	.05
18 Jose Canseco	.15	.40
19 Gary Carter	.15	.40
20 Joe Carter	.02	.10
21 Jack Clark	.02	.10
22 Will Clark	.08	.25
23 Roger Clemens	.30	.75
24 Alex Cole	.01	.05
25 Vince Coleman	.01	.05
26 Jeff Conine RC	.05	.15
27 Milt Cuyler	.01	.05
28 Danny Darwin	.01	.05
29 Eric Davis	.02	.10
30 Glenn Davis	.01	.05
31 Andre Dawson	.08	.25
32 Ken Dayley	.01	.05
33 Steve Decker	.01	.05
34 Delino DeShields	.02	.10
35 Lance Dickson RC	.01	.05
36 Kirk Dressendorfer RC	.01	.05
37 Shawon Dunston	.01	.05
38 Dennis Eckersley	.15	.40
39 Dwight Evans	.02	.10
40 Howard Farmer	.01	.05
41 Junior Felix	.01	.05
42 Alex Fernandez	.01	.05
43 Tony Fernandez	.02	.10
44 Cecil Fielder	.02	.10
45 Carlton Fisk	.15	.40
46 Willie Fraser	.01	.05
47 Gary Gaetti	.02	.10
48 Andres Galarraga	.08	.25
49 Ron Gant	.02	.10
50 Kirk Gibson	.02	.10
51 Bernard Gilkey	.01	.05
52 Leo Gomez	.01	.05
53 Rene Gonzales	.01	.05
54 Juan Gonzalez	.15	.40
55 Dwight Gooden	.02	.10
56 Ken Griffey Jr.	.25	.60
57 Kelly Gruber	.01	.05
58 Pedro Guerrero	.01	.05
59 Tony Gwynn	.30	.75
60 Chris Hammond	.01	.05
61 Ron Hassey	.01	.05
62 Rickey Henderson	.20	.50
63 Tom Henke	.01	.05
64 Orel Hershiser	.02	.10
65 Chris Hoiles	.01	.05
66 Todd Hundley	.02	.10
67 Pete Incaviglia	.01	.05
68 Danny Jackson	.01	.05
69 Barry Jones	.01	.05
70 David Justice	.08	.25
71 Jimmy Key	.02	.10
72 Ray Lankford	.08	.25
73 Darren Lewis	.01	.05
74 Kevin Maas	.01	.05
75 Denny Martinez	.02	.10
76 Tino Martinez	.08	.25
77 Don Mattingly	.30	.75
78 Willie McGee	.02	.10
79 Fred McGriff	.05	.15
80 Hensley Meulens	.01	.05
81 Kevin Mitchell	.01	.05
82 Paul Molitor	.15	.40
83 Mickey Morandini	.01	.05
84 Jack Morris	.02	.10
85 Dale Murphy	.08	.25
86 Eddie Murray	.15	.40
87 Chris Nabholz	.01	.05
88 Tim Naehring	.01	.05
89 Otis Nixon	.01	.05
90 Jose Offerman	.01	.05
91 Bob Ojeda	.01	.05
92 John Olerud	.05	.15
93 Gregg Olson	.01	.05
94 Dave Parker	.02	.10
95 Terry Pendleton	.02	.10
96 Kirby Puckett	.25	.60
97 Tim Raines	.02	.10
98 Jeff Reardon	.02	.10
99 Dave Righetti	.02	.10
100 Cal Ripken	.60	1.50
101 Mel Rojas	.01	.05
102 Nolan Ryan	.60	1.50
103 Ryne Sandberg	.20	.50
104 Scott Sanderson	.01	.05
105 Benny Santiago	.02	.10
106 Pete Schourek RC	.01	.05
107 Gary Scott	.01	.05
108 Terry Shumpert	.01	.05
109 Ruben Sierra	.02	.10
110 Doug Simons	.01	.05
111 Dave Smith	.01	.05
112 Ozzie Smith	.30	.75
113 Cory Snyder	.01	.05
114 Luis Sojo	.01	.05
115 Dave Stewart	.02	.10
116 Dave Stieb	.02	.10
117 Darryl Strawberry	.02	.10
118 Pat Tabler	.01	.05
119 Wade Taylor	.01	.05
120 Bobby Thigpen	.01	.05
121 Frank Thomas	.20	.50
122 Mike Timlin RC	.01	.05
123 Alan Trammell	.05	.15
124 Mo Vaughn	.02	.10
125 Tim Wallach	.01	.05
126 Devon White	.02	.10
127 Mark Whiten	.01	.05
128 Bernie Williams	.20	.50
129 Willie Wilson	.01	.05
130 Dave Winfield	.15	.40
131 Robin Yount	.15	.40
132 Checklist 1-132	.01	.05

1992 O-Pee-Chee Premier

The 1992 OPC Premier baseball set consists of 198 standard-size cards. The fronts feature a mix of color action and posed player photos bordered in white. Gold stripes edge the picture on top and below, while colored stripes edge the pictures on the left and right sides. The player's name, position, and team appear in the bottom white border. In addition to a color head shot, the backs carry biography and the team logo on a panel that shades from green to blue as well as statistics on a black panel.

Card	Low	High
COMPLETE SET (198)	3.00	8.00
COMPLETE FACT.SET (198)	5.00	12.00
1 Wade Boggs	.15	.40
2 John Smiley	.01	.05
3 Checklist 1-99	.01	.05
4 Ron Gant	.02	.10
5 Mike Bordick	.01	.05
6 Charlie Hayes	.01	.05
7 Kevin Morton	.01	.05
8 Checklist 100-198	.01	.05
9 Chris Gwynn	.01	.05
10 Melido Perez	.01	.05
11 Dan Gladden	.01	.05
12 Brian McRae	.01	.05
13 Dennis Martinez	.02	.10
14 Bob Scanlan	.01	.05
15 Julio Franco	.02	.10
16 Ruben Amaro Jr.	.01	.05
17 Mo Sanford	.01	.05
18 Scott Bankhead	.01	.05
19 Dickie Thon	.01	.05
20 Chris James	.01	.05
21 Mike Huff	.01	.05
22 Orlando Merced	.01	.05
23 Chris Sabo	.01	.05
24 Jose Canseco	.15	.40
25 Reggie Sanders	.02	.10
26 Chris Nabholz	.01	.05
27 Kevin Seitzer	.01	.05
28 Ryan Bowen	.01	.05
29 Gary Carter	.15	.40
30 Wayne Rosenthal	.01	.05
31 Alan Trammell	.05	.15
32 Doug Drabek	.01	.05
33 Craig Shipley	.01	.05
34 Ryne Sandberg	.15	.40
35 Chuck Knoblauch	.02	.10
36 Bret Barberie	.01	.05
37 Tim Naehring	.01	.05
38 Omar Olivares	.01	.05
39 Royce Clayton	.01	.05
40 Brent Mayne	.01	.05
41 Darrin Fletcher	.01	.05
42 Howard Johnson	.01	.05
43 Steve Sax	.01	.05
44 Greg Swindell	.01	.05
45 Andre Dawson	.08	.25
46 Kent Hrbek	.02	.10
47 Dwight Gooden	.02	.10
48 Mark Leiter	.01	.05
49 Tom Glavine	.08	.25
50 Mo Vaughn	.08	.25
51 Doug Jones	.01	.05
52 Brian Barnes	.01	.05
53 Rob Dibble	.02	.10
54 Kevin McReynolds	.01	.05
55 Ivan Rodriguez	.20	.50
56 Scott Livingstone UER/(Photo actually.01 Travis Fry		.05
57 Mike Magnante	.01	.05
58 Pete Schourek	.01	.05
59 Frank Thomas	.20	.50
60 Kirk McCaskill	.01	.05
61 Wally Joyner	.02	.10
62 Rick Aguilera	.02	.10
63 Eric Karros	.08	.25
64 Tino Martinez	.08	.25
65 Bryan Hickerson	.01	.05
66 Ruben Sierra	.02	.10
67 Willie Randolph	.04	.10
68 Bill Landrum	.01	.05
69 Bip Roberts	.01	.05
70 Cecil Fielder	.02	.10
71 Pat Kelly	.01	.05
72 Kenny Lofton	.15	.40
73 John Franco	.02	.10
74 Phil Plantier	.01	.05
75 Dave Martinez	.01	.05
76 Warren Newson	.01	.05
77 Chito Martinez	.01	.05
78 Brian Hunter	.01	.05
79 Jack Morris	.02	.10
80 Eric King	.01	.05
81 Nolan Ryan	.60	1.50
82 Bret Saberhagen	.02	.10
83 Roberto Kelly	.01	.05
84 Ozzie Smith	.30	.75
85 Chuck McElroy	.01	.05
86 Carlton Fisk	.08	.25
87 Mike Mussina	.20	.50
88 Mark Carreon	.01	.05
89 Ken Hill	.01	.05
90 Rick Cerone	.01	.05
91 Deion Sanders	.08	.25
92 Don Mattingly	.30	.75
93 Danny Tartabull	.01	.05
94 Keith Miller	.01	.05
95 Gregg Jefferies	.01	.05
96 Barry Larkin	.08	.25
97 Kevin Mitchell	.02	.10
98 Rick Sutcliffe	.01	.05
99 Mark McGwire	.30	.75
100 Albert Belle	.02	.10
101 Gregg Olson	.01	.05
102 Kirby Puckett	.25	.60
103 Luis Gonzalez	.08	.25
104 Randy Myers	.02	.10
105 Roger Clemens	.30	.75
106 Tony Gwynn	.30	.75
107 Jeff Bagwell	.20	.50
108 John Wetteland	.02	.10
109 Bernie Williams	.08	.25
110 Scott Kamieniecki	.01	.05
111 Robin Yount	.15	.40
112 Dean Palmer	.02	.10
113 Tim Belcher	.01	.05
114 George Brett	.30	.75
115 Frank Viola	.01	.05
116 Kelly Gruber	.01	.05
117 David Justice	.08	.25
118 Scott Leius	.01	.05
119 Jeff Fassero	.02	.10
120 Sammy Sosa	.20	.50
121 Al Osuna	.01	.05
122 Wilson Alvarez	.02	.10
123 Jose Offerman	.01	.05
124 Mel Rojas	.01	.05
125 Shawon Dunston	.01	.05
126 Pete Incaviglia	.01	.05
127 Von Hayes	.01	.05
128 Dave Gallagher	.01	.05
129 Eric Davis	.02	.10
130 Roberto Alomar	.08	.25
131 Mike Gallego	.01	.05
132 Robin Ventura	.02	.10
133 Bill Swift	.01	.05
134 John Kruk	.02	.10
135 Craig Biggio	.08	.25
136 Eddie Taubensee	.02	.10
137 Cal Ripken	.60	1.50
138 Charles Nagy	.01	.05
139 Jose Melendez	.01	.05
140 Jim Abbott	.02	.10
141 Paul Molitor	.15	.40
142 Tom Candiotti	.01	.05
143 Bobby Bonilla	.01	.05
144 Matt Williams	.05	.15
145 Brett Butler	.02	.10
146 Will Clark	.08	.25
147 Rickey Henderson	.20	.50
148 Ray Lankford	.02	.10
149 Bill Pecota	.01	.05
150 Dave Winfield	.15	.40
151 Darren Lewis	.01	.05
152 Bob MacDonald	.01	.05
153 David Segui	.02	.10
154 Benny Santiago	.02	.10
155 Chuck Finley	.02	.10
156 Andujar Cedeno	.01	.05
157 Barry Bonds	.30	.75
158 Joe Grahe	.01	.05
159 Frank Castillo	.01	.05
160 Dave Burba	.01	.05
161 Leo Gomez	.01	.05
162 Orel Hershiser	.02	.10
163 Delino DeShields	.02	.10
164 Sandy Alomar Jr.	.02	.10
165 Denny Neagle	.01	.05
166 Fred McGriff	.05	.15
167 Ken Griffey Jr.	.50	1.25
168 Juan Guzman	.01	.05
169 Bobby Rose	.01	.05
170 Steve Avery	.01	.05
171 Rich DeLucia	.01	.05
172 Mike Timlin	.01	.05
173 Randy Johnson	.20	.50
174 Paul Gibson	.01	.05
175 David Cone	.08	.25
176 Marquis Grissom	.02	.10
177 Kurt Stillwell	.01	.05
178 Mark Whiten	.01	.05
179 Darryl Strawberry	.02	.10
180 Mike Morgan	.01	.05
181 Scott Scudder	.01	.05
182 George Bell	.01	.05
183 Alvin Davis	.01	.05
184 Len Dykstra	.02	.10
185 Kyle Abbott	.01	.05
186 Chris Haney	.01	.05
187 Junior Noboa	.01	.05
188 Dennis Eckersley	.15	.40
189 Derek Bell	.01	.05
190 Lee Smith	.02	.10
191 Andres Galarraga	.08	.25
192 Jack Armstrong	.01	.05
193 Eddie Murray	.15	.40
194 Joe Carter	.02	.10
195 Terry Pendleton	.01	.05
196 Darryl Kile	.02	.10
197 Rod Beck RC	.08	.25
198 Hubie Brooks	.01	.05

1993 O-Pee-Chee Premier

The 1993 OPC Premier set consists of 132 standard-size cards. The foil packs contain eight regular cards and one Star Performer insert card. The white-bordered fronts feature a mix of color action and posed player photos. The player's name and position are printed in the lower left border. The backs carry a color head shot, biography, 1992 statistics, and the team logo. According to O-Pee-Chee, only 4,000 cases were produced.

Card	Low	High
COMPLETE SET (132)	2.00	5.00
1 Barry Bonds	.20	.50
2 Chad Curtis	.01	.05
3 Chris Bosio	.01	.05
4 Cal Eldred	.01	.05
5 Dan Walters	.01	.05
6 Rene Arocha RC	.01	.05
7 Delino DeShields	.01	.05
8 Spike Owen	.01	.05
9 Jeff Russell	.01	.05
10 Phil Plantier	.01	.05
11 Mike Christopher	.01	.05
12 Darren Daulton	.02	.10
13 Scott Cooper	.01	.05
14 Paul O'Neill	.02	.10
15 Jimmy Key	.02	.10
16 Dickie Thon	.01	.05
17 Greg Gohr	.01	.05
18 Andre Dawson	.07	.20
19 Steve Cooke	.01	.05
20 Tony Fernandez	.05	.15
21 Mark Gardner	.01	.05
22 Dave Martinez	.01	.05
23 Jose Guzman	.01	.05
24 Chili Davis	.02	.10
25 Randy Knorr	.01	.05
26 Mike Piazza	.40	1.00
27 Benji Gil	.01	.05
28 Dave Winfield	.08	.25
29 Wil Cordero	.01	.05
30 Butch Henry	.01	.05
31 Eric Young	.01	.05
32 Orestes Destrade	.01	.05
33 Randy Myers	.02	.10
34 Tom Brunansky	.01	.05
35 Dan Wilson	.02	.10
36 Juan Guzman	.01	.05
37 Tim Salmon	.05	.15
38 Bill Krueger	.01	.05
39 Larry Walker	.07	.20
40 David Hulse RC	.01	.05
41 Ken Ryan RC	.01	.05
42 Jose Lind	.01	.05
43 Benny Santiago	.02	.10
44 Ray Lankford	.02	.10
45 Dave Stewart	.02	.10
46 Don Mattingly	.20	.50
47 Fernando Valenzuela	.02	.10
48 Scott Fletcher	.01	.05
49 Wade Boggs	.08	.25
50 Norm Charlton	.01	.05
51 Carlos Baerga	.02	.10
52 John Olerud	.05	.15
53 Willie Wilson	.01	.05
54 Dennis Moeller	.01	.05
55 Joe Orsulak	.01	.05
56 John Smiley	.01	.05
57 Al Martin	.01	.05
58 Andres Galarraga	.07	.20
59 Billy Ripken	.01	.05
60 Dave Stieb	.02	.10
61 Dave Magadan	.01	.05
62 Todd Worrell	.02	.10
63 Sherman Obando RC	.01	.05
64 Kent Bottenfield	.01	.05
65 Vinny Castilla	.15	.40
66 Charlie Hayes	.01	.05
67 Mike Hartley	.01	.05
68 Harold Baines	.05	.15
69 John Cummings RC	.01	.05
70 J.T.Snow RC	.08	.25
71 Graeme Lloyd RC	.01	.05
72 Frank Bolick	.01	.05
73 Doug Drabek	.01	.05
74 Milt Thompson	.01	.05
75 Tim Pugh RC	.01	.05
76 John Kruk	.02	.10
77 Tom Henke	.01	.05
78 Kevin Young	.01	.05
79 Ryan Thompson	.01	.05
80 Mike Hampton	.07	.20
81 Jose Canseco	.08	.25
82 Mike Lansing RC	.02	.10
83 Candy Maldonado	.01	.05
84 Alex Arias	.01	.05
85 Troy Neel	.01	.05
86 Greg Swindell	.01	.05
87 Tim Wallach	.01	.05
88 Andy Van Slyke	.01	.05
89 Harold Reynolds	.02	.10
90 Bryan Harvey	.01	.05
91 Jerald Clark	.01	.05
92 David Cone	.05	.15
93 Ellis Burks	.02	.10
94 Scott Bankhead	.01	.05
95 Pete Incaviglia	.01	.05
96 Cecil Fielder	.02	.10
97 Sean Berry	.01	.05
98 Gregg Jefferies	.01	.05
99 Billy Brewer	.01	.05
100 Scott Sanderson	.01	.05
101 Walt Weiss	.01	.05
102 Travis Fryman	.02	.10
103 Barry Larkin	.07	.20
104 Darren Holmes	.01	.05
105 Ivan Calderon	.01	.05
106 Terry Jorgensen	.01	.05
107 David Nied	.01	.05
108 Tim Bogar RC	.01	.05
109 Roberto Kelly	.01	.05
110 Mike Moore	.01	.05
111 Carlos Garcia	.01	.05
112 Mike Bielecki	.01	.05
113 Trevor Hoffman	.07	.20
114 Rich Amaral	.01	.05
115 Jody Reed	.01	.05
116 Charlie Liebrandt	.01	.05
117 Greg Gagne	.01	.05
118 Darrell Sherman RC	.01	.05
119 Jeff Conine	.01	.05
120 Tim Laker RC	.01	.05
121 Kevin Seitzer	.01	.05
122 Jeff Mutis	.01	.05
123 Rico Rossy	.01	.05
124 Paul Molitor	.08	.25
125 Cal Ripken	.40	1.00
126 Greg Maddux	.30	.75
127 Greg McMichael RC	.01	.05
128 Felix Jose	.01	.05
129 Dick Schofield	.01	.05
130 Jim Abbott	.02	.10
131 Kevin Reimer	.01	.05
132 Checklist 1-132	.01	.05

1993 O-Pee-Chee Premier Star Performers

*FOIL STARS: 12.5X TO 25X HI COLUMN
FOIL STARS RANDOM INSERTS IN PACKS

Card	Low	High
1 Frank Thomas	.20	.50
2 Fred McGriff	.07	.20
3 Roberto Alomar	.08	.25
4 Ryne Sandberg	.25	.60
5 Edgar Martinez	.07	.20
6 Gary Sheffield	.15	.40
7 Juan Gonzalez	.15	.40
8 Eric Karros	.07	.20
9 Ken Griffey Jr.	.60	1.50
10 Deion Sanders	.07	.20
11 Kirby Puckett	.25	.60
12 Will Clark	.08	.25
13 Joe Carter	.05	.15
14 Barry Bonds	.30	.75
15 Pat Listach	.02	.10
16 Mark McGwire	.30	.75
17 Kenny Lofton	.08	.25
18 Roger Clemens	.40	1.00
19 Greg Maddux	.50	1.25
20 Nolan Ryan	.75	2.00
21 Tom Glavine	.15	.40
22 Dennis Eckersley	.15	.40

1993 O-Pee-Chee Premier Top Draft Picks

Card	Low	High
COMPLETE SET (4)	2.50	6.00
RANDOM INSERTS IN PACKS		
1 B.J.Wallace	.40	1.00
2 Shannon Stewart	1.25	3.00
3 Rod Henderson	.40	1.00
4 Todd Steverson	.40	1.00

1982-90 Ohio Hall of Fame

This set of tri-colored cards measures 3" x 6" and contains biographies and statistics on the backs. Cards are numbered and checklisted below. This set was continued for many years thereafter and our list is incomplete and all help is appreciated.

Card	Low	High
COMPLETE SET	30.00	80.00
1 Ohio Hall of Fame	.30	.75
2 Checklist	.30	.75
3 Nick Cullop	.30	.75
4 Dean Chance	.30	.75
5 Bob Feller	1.50	4.00
6 Jesse Haines	.60	1.50
7 Waite Hoyt	.60	1.50
8 Ernie Lombardi	.60	1.50
9 Mike Powers	.30	.75
10 Edd Roush	.60	1.50
11 Red Ruffing	.60	1.50
12 Luke Sewell	.30	.75
13 Tris Speaker	1.25	3.00
14 Cy Young	1.25	3.00
15 Walter Alston	.40	1.00
16 Lou Boudreau	.60	1.50
17 Warren Giles	.40	1.00
18 Ted Kluszewski	.60	1.50
19 William McKinley	.60	1.50
20 Roger Peckinpaugh	.30	.75
21 Johnny VanderMeer	.40	1.00
22 Early Wynn	.60	1.50
23 Earl Averill	.60	1.50
24 Stan Coveleskie	.60	1.50
25 Lefty Grove	.75	2.00
26 Nap Lajoie	.75	2.00
27 Al Lopez	.40	1.00
28 Eddie Onslow	.30	.75
29 Branch Rickey	.40	1.00
30 Frank Robinson	.75	2.00
31 George Sisler	.60	1.50
32 Bob Lemon	.60	1.50
33 Satchel Paige	2.00	5.00
34 Bucky Walters	.40	1.00
35 Gus Bell	.30	.75
36 Rocky Colavito	.60	1.50
37 Mel Harder	.40	1.00
38 Tom Henrich	.40	1.00
39 Miller Huggins	.40	1.00
40 Fred Hutchinson	.30	.75
41 Eppa Rixey	.60	1.50
42 Joe Sewell	.60	1.50
43 George Uhle	.30	.75
44 Bill Veeck	.40	1.00
45 Estel Crabtree	.30	.75
46 Harvey Haddix	.30	.75
47 Noodles Hahn	.30	.75
48 Joe Jackson	2.50	6.00
49 Kenesaw Landis	.40	1.00
50 Thurman Munson	.60	1.50
51 Gabe Paul	.30	.75
52 Vada Pinson	.40	1.00
53 Wally Post	.30	.75
54 Vic Wertz	.30	.75
55 Paul Derringer	.30	.75
56 John Galbreath	.30	.75
57 Rube Marquard	.60	1.50
58 Bill McKechnie	.40	1.00
59 Rocky Nelson	.30	.75
60 Al Rosen	.40	1.00
61 Lew Fonseca	.30	.75
62 Larry MacPhail	.40	1.00
63 Joe Nuxhall	.30	.75
64 Birdie Tebbetts	.30	.75
65 Gene Woodling	.30	.75
66 Ethan Allen	.30	.75
70 Tot Pressnell	.30	.75
76 George Sisler Jr	.30	.75
79 Woody English	.30	.75
81 Frank Baumholz	.30	.75
83 Sam McDowell	.40	1.00
91 Denny Galehouse	.30	.75
92 Brooks Lawrence	.30	.75
99 Bob Wren CO	.30	.75
102 Willis Hudlin	.30	.75
103 Gene Michael	.30	.75

1997 Ohio Lottery

This five-card set features color head photos of legendary baseball players printed on a diamond and baseball background. The set measures approximately 4" by 2 1/4" and was actually real Ohio scratch-off lottery ticket stubs that could be obtained for $1 a piece. The backs carry the lottery rules and prize information. The cards are unnumbered and checklisted below in alphabetical order.

Card	Low	High
COMPLETE SET (5)	3.00	8.00
1 Rocky Colavito	.75	2.00
2 Larry Doby	1.00	2.50
3 George Foster	.40	1.00
4 Tony Perez	1.00	2.50
5 Gaylord Perry	1.00	2.50

1959 Oklahoma Today Major Leaguers

These 20 cards which measure 1 11/16" by 2 3/4" were featured on the back cover of the Summer 1959 Issue of Oklahoma Today. The card fronts feature Black and White photos on color backgrounds (8 green, 8 gold and 4 light blue). The bottom 1/4" of the front has a white panel with the players name in red. The backs are grey with the player's name, position team and league. The checklist below is as the players appear on the uncut covers in 4 rows of 5 cards starting on the top left. In the complete book form -- this set is valued at two to three times the values listed below.

Card	Low	High
COMPLETE SET (20)	125.00	250.00
1 Paul Waner	7.50	15.00
2 Lloyd Waner	7.50	15.00
3 Jerry Walker	3.00	6.00
4 Tom Sturdivant	3.00	6.00
5 Warren Spahn	12.50	25.00
6 Allie Reynolds	5.00	10.00
7 Dale Mitchell	3.00	6.00
8 Cal McLish	3.00	6.00
9 Von McDaniel	3.00	6.00
10 Lindy McDaniel	3.00	6.00
11 Pepper Martin	6.00	12.00
12 Mickey Mantle	150.00	300.00
13 Carl Hubbell	7.50	15.00
14 Paul Dean	3.00	6.00
15 Dizzy Dean	7.50	15.00
16 Don Demeter	3.00	6.00
17 Alvin Dark	5.00	10.00
18 Johnny Callison	5.00	10.00
19 Harry Brecheen	3.00	6.00
20 Jerry Adair	3.00	6.00

1887-90 Old Judge N172

The Goodwin Company's baseball series depicts hundreds of ballplayers from more than 40 major and minor league teams as well as boxers and wrestlers. The cards (approximately 1 1/2" by 2 1/2") are actually photographs from the Hall studio in New York which were pasted onto thick cardboard. The pictures are sepia in color with either a white or pink cast, and the cards are blank backed. They are found either numbered or unnumbered, with or without a copyright date, and with hand printed or machine printed names. All known cards have the name "Goodwin Co., New York" at the base. The cards were marketed during the period 1887-1890 in packs of "Old Judge" and "Gypsy Queen" cigarettes (cards marked with the latter brand are worth double the values listed below). They have been listed alphabetically and assigned numbers in the checklist below for simplicity's sake; the various poses known for some players also have not been listed for the same reason. Some of the players are pictured in horizontal (HOR) poses. In all, more than 2300 different Goodwin cards are known to collectors, with more being discovered every year. Cards from the "Spotted Tie" sub-series are denoted in the checklist below by SPOT. The Lee Gibson and Egyptian Healey cards are currently considered unique and are not priced due to market scarcity. The Stephen Behel card is drawing extra interest as there is debate as to whether or not he is the first Jewish player depicted on a card.

Card	Low	High
COMPLETE SET	500000.00	1000000.00
COMMON PLAYER	150.00	300.00
COMMON PLAYER (DOUBLE)	200.00	400.00
COMMON BROWNS CHAMP	250.00	500.00
COMMON PLAYER (PCL)	20000.00	50000.00
COMMON SPOTTED TIE	500.00	1000.00
1 Gus Albert	300.00	500.00
2 Charles Alcott	300.00	500.00
3 Alexander	300.00	500.00
4 Myron Allen	300.00	500.00
5 Bob Allen	300.00	500.00
6 Uncle Bill Alvord	300.00	500.00
7 Varney Anderson	300.00	500.00
8 Ed Andrews	300.00	500.00
9 Ed Andrews w B.Hoover	350.00	600.00
10 Wally Andrews	300.00	500.00
11 Bill Annis	300.00	500.00
12A Cap Anson in Uniform		
12B Cap Anson Street Clothes	5000.00	8000.00
13 Old Hoss Ardner	300.00	500.00
14 Tug Arundel	300.00	500.00
15 Jersey Bakley	300.00	500.00
16 Clarence Baldwin	300.00	500.00
17 Mark (Fido) Baldwin	300.00	500.00
18 Lady Baldwin	350.00	600.00
19 James Banning	300.00	500.00
20 Samuel Barkley	300.00	500.00
21 Bald Billy Barnie MG	350.00	600.00
22 Charles Bassett	300.00	500.00
23 Charles Bastian	300.00	500.00
24 Charles Bastian w P.Schriver	350.00	600.00
25 Ebenezer Beatin	300.00	500.00
26 Jake Beckley	2500.00	4000.00
27 Stephen Behel SPOT	6000.00	10000.00
28 Charles Bennett	300.00	500.00
29 Louis Bierbauer	300.00	500.00
30 Louis Bierbauer w R.Gamble	350.00	600.00
31 Bill Bishop	300.00	500.00
32 William Blair	300.00	500.00
33 Ned Bligh	300.00	500.00
34 Bogart	300.00	500.00
35 Boyce	300.00	500.00
36 Jake Boyd	350.00	600.00
37 Honest John Boyle	300.00	500.00
38 Handsome Henry Boyle	300.00	500.00
39 Nick Bradley	300.00	500.00
40 George (Grin) Bradley	300.00	500.00
41 Stephen Brady SPOT	900.00	1500.00
42 E.L. Breckinridge PCL		
43 Timothy Brosnan Minn	300.00	500.00
44 Timothy Brosnan Sioux	300.00	500.00
45 Cal Broughton	300.00	500.00
46 Big Dan Brouthers	1500.00	2500.00
47 Thomas Brown	300.00	500.00
48 California Brown	300.00	500.00
49 Pete Browning	3000.00	5000.00
50 Charles Brynan	300.00	500.00
51 Al Buckenberger MG	300.00	500.00
52 Dick Buckley	300.00	500.00
53 Charles Buffington	300.00	500.00
54 Ernest Burch	300.00	500.00
55 Bill Burdick	300.00	500.00
56 Black Jack Burdock	300.00	500.00
57 Robert Burks	300.00	500.00
58 George (Watch) Burnham MG	350.00	600.00
59 James Burns Omaha	300.00	500.00
60 Jimmy Burns KC	300.00	500.00
61 Tommy (Oyster) Burns	350.00	600.00
62 Thomas E. Burns	300.00	500.00
63 Doc Bushong Brooklyn	300.00	500.00
64 Doc Bushong Browns Champs	500.00	800.00
65 Patsy Cahill	300.00	500.00
66 Count Campau	300.00	500.00
67 Jimmy Canavan	300.00	500.00
68 Bart Cantz	300.00	500.00
69 Handsome Jack Carney	300.00	500.00
70 Hick Carpenter	300.00	500.00
71 Cliff Carroll	300.00	500.00
72 Scrappy Carroll	300.00	500.00
73 Frederick Carroll	300.00	500.00
74 Jumbo Cartwright	300.00	500.00
75 Bob Caruthers Brooklyn	500.00	800.00
76 Bob Caruthers Browns Champs	500.00	800.00
77 Daniel Casey	300.00	500.00
78 Icebox Chamberlain	300.00	500.00
79 Cupid Childs	300.00	500.00
80 Bob Clark	300.00	500.00
81 Owen Clark	300.00	500.00
82 William H. Clarke w/M.Hughes	350.00	600.00
83 William (Dad) Clarke	300.00	500.00
84 Pete Connell	300.00	500.00
85 John Clarkson	1200.00	2000.00
86 Jack Clements	300.00	500.00
87 Elmer Cleveland	300.00	500.00
88 Monk Cline	300.00	500.00
89 Mike Cody	300.00	500.00
90 John Coleman	300.00	500.00
91 Bill Collins	300.00	500.00
92 Hub Collins	300.00	500.00
93 Charles Comiskey	2500.00	4000.00
94 Commy Comiskey	1800.00	3000.00
95 Roger Connor Script	2500.00	4000.00
96 Roger Connor New York	2500.00	4000.00
97 Richard Conway	300.00	500.00
98 Peter Conway	300.00	500.00
99 James Conway	300.00	500.00
100 Paul Cook	300.00	500.00
101 Jimmy Cooney	300.00	500.00
102 Larry Corcoran	500.00	800.00
103 Pop Corkhill	300.00	500.00
104 Cannon Ball Crane	300.00	500.00
105 Samuel Crane	300.00	500.00
106 Jack Crogan	350.00	600.00
107 John Crooks	300.00	500.00
108 Lave Cross	300.00	500.00
109 Bill Crossley	300.00	500.00
110 Joe Crotty SPOT	900.00	1500.00
111 Joe Crotty	300.00	500.00
112 Billy Crowell	300.00	500.00
113 Jim Cudworth	300.00	500.00
114 Bert Cunningham	300.00	500.00
115 Tacks Curtis	300.00	500.00
116 Ed Cushman SPOT	900.00	1500.00
117 Ed Cushman	300.00	500.00
118 Tony Cusick	300.00	500.00
119 Vincent Dailey PCL		
120 Edward Dailey Phi-Wash	300.00	500.00
121 Edward Dailey Columbus	500.00	800.00
122 Bill Daley	300.00	500.00
123 Con Daley	300.00	500.00
124 Abner Dalrymple	300.00	500.00
125 Tom Daly	350.00	600.00
126 James Daly	300.00	500.00
127 Law Daniels	300.00	500.00
128 Dell Darling	300.00	500.00
129 William Darnbrough	300.00	500.00
130 D. Davin	300.00	1500.00
131 Jumbo Davis	300.00	500.00
132 Pat Dealey	300.00	500.00
133 Thomas Deasley Throwing	300.00	500.00
134 Thomas Deasley Fielding	300.00	500.00
135 Edward Decker	300.00	500.00
136 Big Ed Delahanty	5000.00	8000.00
137 Jeremiah Denny	300.00	500.00
138 James Devlin	300.00	500.00
139 Thomas Dolan	300.00	500.00
140 Jack Donahue PCL		
141 James Donahue SPOT	900.00	1500.00
142 James Donahue	300.00	500.00
143 James Donnelly	300.00	500.00
144 Charles Dooley PCL		
145 J. Doran		
146 Michael Dorgan	300.00	500.00
147 Cornelius Doyle PCL		
148 Home Run Duffe	300.00	500.00
149 Hugh Duffy	1500.00	2500.00
150 Dan Dugdale	350.00	600.00
151 Duck Duke	300.00	500.00
152 Sure Shot Dunlap	300.00	500.00
153 J. Dunn	350.00	600.00
154 Jesse (Cyclone) Duryea	300.00	500.00
155 John Dwyer	350.00	600.00
156 Billy Earle	300.00	500.00
157 Buck Ebright	300.00	500.00
158 Red Ehret	300.00	500.00
159 R. Emmerke	300.00	500.00
160 Dude Esterbrook	300.00	500.00
161 Henry Esterday	300.00	500.00
162 Long John Ewing	300.00	500.00
163 Buck Ewing	1500.00	2500.00
164 Buck Ewing w Mascot	1500.00	2500.00

165 Jay Faatz 300.00 500.00
166 Clinkgers Fagan 300.00 500.00
167 William Farmer 300.00 500.00
168 Sidney Farrar 350.00 600.00
169 John (Moose) Farrell 300.00 500.00
170 Charles(Duke) Farrell 300.00 500.00
171 Frank Fennelly 300.00 500.00
172 Charlie Ferguson 300.00 500.00
173 Colonel Ferson 300.00 500.00
174 Wallace Fessenden UMP 350.00 600.00
175 Jocko Fields 300.00 500.00
176 Fischer 350.00 600.00
177 Thomas Flanigan 300.00 500.00
178 Silver Flint 300.00 500.00
179 Thomas Flood 300.00 500.00
180 Flynn 1500.00
181 James Fogarty 300.00 500.00
182 Frank (Monkey) Foreman 300.00 500.00
183 Thomas Forster 300.00 500.00
184 Elmer E. Foster SPOT 900.00 1500.00
185 Elmer Foster NY-Chi 300.00 500.00
186 F.W. Foster SPOT 900.00 1500.00
187 Scissors Foutz Browns Champ 500.00 800.00
188 Scissors Foutz Brooklyn 300.00 500.00
189 Julie Freeman 300.00 500.00
190 Will Fry 300.00 500.00
191 Fred Fudger PCL
192 William Fuller 300.00 500.00
193 Shorty Fuller 300.00 500.00
194 Christopher Fullmer 300.00 500.00
195 Christopher Fullmer w T.Tucker 350.00 600.00
196 Honest John Gaffney MGR 500.00 800.00
197 Pud Galvin 1800.00 3000.00
198 Robert Gamble 300.00 500.00
199 Charles Ganzel 300.00 500.00
200 Gid Gardner 300.00 500.00
201 Gid Gardner w M.Murray 350.00 600.00
202 Hank Gastreich 300.00 500.00
203 Emil Geiss 300.00 500.00
204 Frenchy Genins 300.00 500.00
205 William George 300.00 500.00
206 Joe Gerhardt 300.00 500.00
207 Pretzels Getzein 300.00 500.00
208 Lee Gibson 300.00 500.00
209 Robert Gilks 300.00 500.00
210 Pete Gillespie 300.00 500.00
211 Barney Gilligan 300.00 500.00
212 Frank Gilmore 300.00 500.00
213 Pebbly Jack Glasscock 500.00 800.00
214 Kid Gleason 500.00 800.00
215 Brother Bill Gleason 300.00 500.00
216 William Bill Gleason 500.00 800.00
217 Mouse Glenn 300.00 500.00
218 Michael Goodfellow 300.00 500.00
219 George (Piano Legs) Gore 300.00 500.00
220 Frank Graves: Minn. 300.00 500.00
221 William Greenwood 300.00 500.00
222 Michael Greer 300.00 500.00
223 Mike Griffin 300.00 500.00
224 Clark Griffith 1800.00 3000.00
225 Henry Gruber 300.00 500.00
226 Addison Gumbert 300.00 500.00
227 Thomas Gunning 300.00 500.00
228 Joseph Gunson 300.00 500.00
229 George Haddock 300.00 500.00
230 William Hafner 300.00 500.00
231 Willie Hahm Mascot 300.00 500.00
232 William Hallman 300.00 500.00
233 Billy Hamilton 1200.00 2000.00
234 Willie Hamm w N.Williamson 500.00 800.00
235 Frank Hankinson SPOT 900.00 1500.00
236 Frank Hankinson 300.00 500.00
237 Ned Hanlon 1200.00 2000.00
238 William Hanrahan 350.00 600.00
239 A.G. Hapeman PCL
240 Pa Harkins 300.00 500.00
241 William Hart 300.00 500.00
242 William (Bill) Hasamdear 300.00 500.00
243 Colonel Hatfield 300.00 500.00
244 Egyptian Healey Wash-Ind 300.00 500.00
245 Egyptian Healey Washington 300.00 500.00
246 J.C. Healy 300.00 500.00
247 Guy Hecker 300.00 500.00
248 Tony Hellman 300.00 500.00
249 Hardie Henderson 300.00 500.00
250 Hardie Henderson w M.Greer 350.00 600.00
251 Moxie Hengle 350.00 600.00
252 John Henry 300.00 500.00
253 Edward Herr 300.00 500.00
254 Hunkey Hines 300.00 500.00
255 Paul Hines 300.00 500.00
256 Texas Wonder Hoffman 300.00 500.00
257 Eddie Hogan 300.00 500.00
258 William Holbert SPOT 900.00 1500.00
259 William Holbert 300.00 500.00
260 James (Bugs) Holliday 300.00 500.00
261 Charles Hoover 350.00 600.00
262 Buster Hoover 300.00 500.00
263 Jack Horner 300.00 500.00
264 Jack Horner w E.Warner 350.00 600.00
265 Michael Horning 300.00 500.00
266 Pete Hotaling 300.00 500.00
267 William Howes 300.00 500.00
268 Dummy Hoy 1800.00 3000.00
269 Nat Hudson Browns Champs 500.00 800.00
270 Nat Hudson St. Louis 300.00 500.00
271 Mickey Hughes 300.00 500.00
272 Hungler 300.00 500.00
273 Wild Bill Hutchinson 300.00 500.00
274 John Irwin 300.00 500.00
275 Arthur (Cut Rate) Irwin 300.00 500.00
276 A.C. Jantzen 300.00 500.00
277 Frederick Jevne 300.00 500.00
278 John Johnson 300.00 500.00
279 Richard Johnston 300.00 500.00
280 Jordan 300.00 500.00
281 Heinie Kappell 300.00 500.00
282 Timothy Keefe 1200.00 2000.00
283 Tim Keefe w D.Richardson 700.00 1200.00
284 George Keefe 300.00 500.00
285 James Keenan 300.00 500.00
286 King Kelly 10,000-Bos-Chic 3000.00 5000.00
287 Honest John Kelly MGR 500.00 800.00
288 Kelly UMP 350.00 600.00
289 Charles Kelly 600.00 1000.00
290 Kelly and Powell UMP-MGR 350.00 600.00
291 Rudolph Kemmler Browns Champs 500.00800.00
292 Rudolph Kemmler St. Paul 300.00 500.00
293 Theodore Kennedy 350.00 600.00
294 J.J. Kenyon 300.00 500.00
295 John Kerins 300.00 500.00
296 Matthew Kilroy 300.00 500.00
297 Charles King 300.00 500.00
298 August Kloff 300.00 500.00
299 William Klusman 300.00 500.00
300 Phillip Knell 300.00 500.00
301 Fred Knouf 300.00 500.00
302 Charles Kremmeyer PCL
303 William Krieg 300.00 500.00
304 William Krieg w/A.Kloff 350.00 600.00
305 Gus Krock 300.00 500.00
306 Willie Kuehne 300.00 500.00
307 Frederick Lange 350.00 600.00
308 Ted Larkin 300.00 500.00
309 Arlie Latham Browns Champs 600.00 1000.00
310 Arlie Latham Stl-Chi 500.00 800.00
311 John Lauer 300.00 500.00
312 John Leighton 300.00 500.00
313 Rube Levy PCL
314 Tom Loftus MGR 300.00 500.00
315 Herman (Germany) Long 500.00 800.00
316 Danny Long PCL
317 Tom Lovett 300.00 500.00
318 Bobby (Link) Lowe 500.00 800.00
319 Jack Lynch SPOT 900.00 1500.00
320 John Lynch 300.00 500.00
321 Dennis Lyons 300.00 500.00
322 Harry Lyons 300.00 500.00
323 Connie Mack 3500.00 6000.00
324 Joe (Reddie) Mack 300.00 500.00
325 James (Little Mack) Macullar 300.00 500.00
326 Kid Madden 300.00 500.00
327 Daniel Mahoney 300.00 500.00
328 Willard (Grasshopper) Maines 300.00 500.00
329 Fred Mann 300.00 500.00
330 Jimmy Manning 300.00 500.00
331 Charles (Lefty) Marr 300.00 500.00
332 Mascot (Willie) Breslin 350.00 600.00
333 Samuel Maskery 300.00 500.00
334 Bobby Mathews 300.00 500.00
335 Michael Mattimore 300.00 500.00
336 Albert Maul 300.00 500.00
337 Albert Mays SPOT 900.00 1500.00
338 Albert Mays 300.00 500.00
339 James McAleer 300.00 500.00
340 Thomas McCarthy 1500.00 2500.00
341 John McCarthy 300.00 500.00
342 James McCauley 350.00 600.00
343 William McClellan 300.00 500.00
344 John McCormack 300.00 500.00
345 Big Jim McCormick 300.00 500.00
346 McCreachery MGR
347 James (Chippy) McGarr 300.00 500.00
348 Jack McGeachy 300.00 500.00
349 John McGlone 300.00 500.00
350 James (Deacon) McGuire 300.00 500.00
351 Bill McGunnigle MGR 500.00 800.00
352 Ed McKean 300.00 500.00
353 Alex McKinnon 300.00 500.00
354 Thomas McLaughlin SPOT 900.00 1500.00
355 John (Bid) McPhee 3000.00 5000.00
356 James McQuaid 300.00 500.00
357 John McQuaid UMP 350.00 600.00
358 Jame McTamany 300.00 500.00
359 George McVey 300.00 500.00
360 Peter Meegan PCL
361 John Messitt 300.00 500.00
362 George (Doggie) Miller 300.00 500.00
363 Joseph Miller 300.00 500.00
364 Jocko Milligan 300.00 500.00
365 E.L. Mills 300.00 500.00
366 Daniel Minnehan 300.00 500.00
367 Samuel Moffet 300.00 500.00
368 Honest Morrell 300.00 500.00
369 Ed Morris 300.00 500.00
370 Morrisey 300.00 500.00
371 Tony (Count) Mullane 500.00 800.00
372 Joseph Mulvey 300.00 500.00
373 P.L. Murphy 300.00 500.00
374 Pat J. Murphy 300.00 500.00
375 Miah Murray 300.00 500.00
376 Truthful Mutrie MGR 350.00 600.00
377 George Myers 300.00 500.00
378 Al (Cod) Myers 300.00 500.00
379 Thomas Nagle 300.00 500.00
380 Billy Nash 300.00 500.00
381 Candy Nelson SPOT 900.00 1500.00
382 Kid Nichols 2500.00 4000.00
383 Samuel Nichols 300.00 500.00
384 J.W. Nicholson 350.00 600.00
385 Tom Nicholson (Parson) 300.00 500.00
386 Nicholls Nicol 500.00 800.00
387 Hugh Nicol 300.00 500.00
388 Hugh Nicol w J.Reilly 350.00 600.00
389 Frederick Nyce 300.00 500.00
390 Doc Oberlander 300.00 500.00
391 Jack O'Brien 300.00 500.00
392 William O'Brien 300.00 500.00
393 William O'Brien w/J.Irwin 350.00 600.00
394 Darby O'Brien 300.00 500.00
395 John O'Brien 300.00 500.00
396 P.J. O'Connell 300.00 500.00
397 John O'Connor 300.00 500.00
398 Hank O'Day 500.00 800.00
399 O'Day 300.00 500.00
400 James O'Neil Stl-Chi 300.00 500.00
401 James O'Neil Browns Champs 500.00 800.00
402 Norris (Tip) O'Neill PCL
403 Jim O'Rourke 1800.00 3000.00
404 Thomas O'Rourke 300.00 500.00
405 David Orr SPOT 900.00 1500.00
406 David Orr 300.00 500.00
407 Parsons 300.00 500.00
408 Owen Patton 300.00 500.00
409 James Peeples 300.00 500.00
410 James Peeples w H.Henderson 350.00 600.00
411 Hip Perrier PCL
412 Patrick Pettee 300.00 500.00
413 Patrick Pettee w B.Lowe 350.00 600.00
414 Dandelion Pfeffer 300.00 500.00
415 Dick Phelan 300.00 500.00
416 William Phillips 300.00 500.00
417 John Pickett 300.00 500.00
418 George Pinkney 300.00 500.00
419 Thomas Poorman 300.00 500.00
420 Henry Porter 300.00 500.00
421 James Powell 300.00 500.00
422 Tom Powers PCL
423 Bill (Blondie) Purcell 300.00 500.00
424 Thomas Quinn 300.00 500.00
425 Joseph Quinn 300.00 500.00
426 Old Hoss Radbourne Portrait 2500.00 4000.00
427 Old Hoss Radbourne Non-Portrait 2500.00 4000.00
428 Shorty Radford 300.00 500.00
429 Tom Ramsey 300.00 500.00
430 Rehse 300.00 500.00
431 Long John Reilly 300.00 500.00
432 Charles (Princeton) Reilly 300.00 500.00
433 Charles Reynolds 300.00 500.00
434 Hardie Richardson 300.00 500.00
435 Danny Richardson 300.00 500.00
436 Charles Ripslager SPOT 900.00 1500.00
437 John Roach 300.00 500.00
438 Wilbert (Uncle Robbie) Robinson 1500.002500.00
439 M.C. Robinson 300.00 500.00
440 Yank Robinson Stl 300.00 500.00
441 Yank Robinson Browns Champs 500.00 800.00
442 George Rooks 350.00 600.00
443 James (Chief) Roseman SPOT 900.00 1500.00
444 Davis Rowe MGR 300.00 500.00
445 Jack Rowe 300.00 500.00
446 Amos Rusie Indianapolis 3500.00 6000.00
447 Amos Rusie New York 3500.00 6000.00
448 James Ryan 500.00 800.00
449 Henry Sage 300.00 500.00
450 Henry Sage w W.Van Dyke 350.00 600.00
451 Sanders 300.00 500.00
452 Al (Ben) Sanders 300.00 500.00
453 Frank Scheibeck 300.00 500.00
454 Albert Schellhase 300.00 500.00
455 William Schenkle 300.00 500.00
456 Bill Schildknecht 300.00 500.00
457 Gus (Pink Whiskers) Schmelz MGR 300.00500.00
458 Lewis (Jumbo) Schoeneck 350.00 600.00
459 Pop Schriver 300.00 500.00
460 John Seery 300.00 500.00
461 William Serad 300.00 500.00
462 Edward Seward 300.00 500.00
463 George (Orator) Shafer 300.00 500.00
464 Frank Shafer 300.00 500.00
465 Daniel Shannon 300.00 500.00
466 William Sharsig 350.00 600.00
467 Samuel Shaw 300.00 500.00
468 John Shaw 300.00 500.00
469 William Shindle 300.00 500.00
470 George Shock 300.00 500.00
471 Otto Shomberg 300.00 500.00
472 Lev Shrev 300.00 500.00
473 Ed (Baldy) Silch 300.00 500.00
474 Michael Slattery 300.00 500.00
475 Sam (Sky Rocket) Smith 300.00 500.00
476 John (Phenomenal) Smith Portrait 1500.00 2500.00
477 John (Phenomenal) Smith Non-Portrait 300.00 500.00
478 Elmer Smith 300.00 500.00
479 Fred (Sam) Smith 300.00 500.00
480 George (Germany) Smith 300.00 500.00
481 Pop Smith 300.00 500.00
482 Nick Smith 300.00 500.00
483 P.T. Somers 300.00 500.00
484 Joe Sommer 300.00 500.00
485 Pete Sommers 300.00 500.00
486 William Sowders 300.00 500.00
487 John Sowders 300.00 500.00
488 Charles Sprague 350.00 600.00
489 Edward Sproat 300.00 500.00
490 Harry Staley 300.00 500.00
491 Daniel Stearns 300.00 500.00
492 Billy (Cannonball) Stemmyer 300.00 500.00
493 B.F. Stephens 300.00 500.00
494 John C. Sterling 300.00 500.00
495 Leonard Stockwell PCL
496 Harry Stovey 600.00 1000.00
497 C. Scott Stratton 300.00 500.00
498 Joseph Straus 300.00 500.00
499 John (Cub) Stricker 300.00 500.00
500 Marty Sullivan 300.00 500.00
501 Michael Sullivan 300.00 500.00
502 Billy Sunday 900.00 1500.00
503 Sy Sutcliffe 300.00 500.00
504 Ezra Sutton 300.00 500.00
505 Ed Cyrus Swartwood 300.00 500.00
506 Parke Swartzel 300.00 500.00
507 Peter Sweeney 300.00 500.00
508 Louis Sylvester PCL
509 Ed (Dimples) Tate 300.00 500.00
510 Patsy Tebeau 500.00 800.00
511 John Tener 350.00 600.00
512 Bill (Adonis) Terry 300.00 500.00
513 Big Sam Thompson 1500.00 2500.00
514 Silent Mike Tiernan 350.00 600.00
515 Ledell Titcomb 300.00 500.00
516 Phillip Tomney 300.00 500.00
517 Stephen Toole 300.00 500.00
518 George Townsend 300.00 500.00
519 William Traffley 300.00 500.00
520 George Treadway 300.00 500.00
521 Samuel Trott 300.00 500.00
522 Samuel Trott w T.Burns 350.00 600.00
523 Tom (Foghorn) Tucker 300.00 500.00
524 William Tuckerman 300.00 500.00
525 George Turner 300.00 500.00
526 Lawrence Twitchell 300.00 500.00
527 James Tyng 300.00 500.00
528 William Van Dyke 300.00 500.00
529 George (Rip) Van Haltren 300.00 500.00
530 Farmer Harry Vaughn 300.00 500.00
531 Peek-a-Boo Veach 500.00 800.00
532 Veach PCL
533 Leon Viau 300.00 500.00
534 William Vinton 300.00 500.00
535 Joseph Visner 300.00 500.00
536 Christian Von Der Ahe OWNER 500.00 800.00
537 Joseph Walsh 300.00 500.00
538 John M. Ward 1800.00 3000.00
539 E.H. Warner 500.00 800.00
540 William Watkins MGR 350.00 600.00
541 Farmer Bill Weaver 300.00 500.00
542 Charles Weber 300.00 500.00
543 George (Stump) Weidman 300.00 500.00
544 William Weidner 300.00 500.00
545 Curtis Welch Browns Champ 500.00 800.00
546 Curtis Welch A's 350.00 600.00
547 Curtis Welch w B.Gleason 500.00 800.00
548 Smilin' Mickey Welch 1800.00 3000.00
549 Jake Wells 300.00 500.00
550 Frank Wells 350.00 600.00
551 Joseph Werrick 300.00 500.00
552 Milton (Buck) West 300.00 500.00
553 Gus (Cannonball) Weyhing 300.00 500.00
554 John Weyhing 300.00 500.00
555 Bobby Wheelock 300.00 500.00
556 Whitacre 300.00 500.00
557 Pat Whitaker 300.00 500.00
558 Deacon White 500.00 800.00
559 William White 300.00 500.00
560 Jim (Grasshopper) Whitney 300.00 500.00
561 Arthur Whitney 300.00 500.00
562 G. Whitney 300.00 500.00
563 James Williams MGR 350.00 600.00
564 Ned Williamson 500.00 800.00
565 Williamson and Mascot 350.00 600.00
566 C.H. Willis 300.00 500.00
567 Walt Wilmot 300.00 500.00
568 George Winkleman Hartford 600.00 1000.00
569 Samuel Wise 300.00 500.00
570 William (Chicken) Wolf 300.00 500.00
571 George (Dandy) Wood 300.00 500.00
572 Peter Wood 300.00 500.00
573 Harry Wright MGR 5000.00 8000.00
574 Charles (Chief) Zimmer 300.00 500.00
575 Frank Zinn 300.00 500.00
576 John Barnes (Barns) MG 500.00 800.00

1887-89 Old Judge Cabinets N173

These cabinets measuure approximately 4 1/2" by 6". These feature the same poses as on the N172 Old Judge Set. As a note we are listing these cabinets by player's name and not by poses. This list is in alphabetical order and all additions to the checklist are appreciated.

COMPLETE SET

1949 Olmes Studios

This set measures 3 1/2" by 5 1/2" and features Philadelphia players only. Seven poses of Ferris Fain exist. The Olmes Studio identification is printed on the back of the postcard. There have been several additions to this set in recent years so any further additions are appreciated.

COMPLETE SET 400.00 800.00
1 Lou Brissie 25.00 50.00
2 Sam Chapman 25.00 50.00
3 Joe Coleman 25.00 50.00
4 Ferris Fain 40.00 80.00
5 Frank Fanovich 25.00 50.00
6 Dick Fowler 25.00 50.00
7 Bob Hooper 25.00 50.00
8 Skeeter Kell 25.00 50.00
9 Paul Lehner 25.00 50.00
10 Lou Limmer 25.00 50.00
11 Barney McCoskey 25.00 50.00
12 Robin Roberts 50.00 100.00
13 Carl Scheib 25.00 50.00
14 Joe Tipton 25.00 50.00
15 Gus Zernial 25.00 50.00

1982 On Deck Discs

These discs, which were distributed in On Deck Cookie packaging features the same players as the 1981 MSA Discs. This set, however -- unlike the 1981 MSA Discs clearly state on the back that they are from a 1982 Collector series set.

COMPLETE SET (32) 10.00 25.00
1 Buddy Bell .08 .25
2 Johnny Bench .30 1.00
3 Bruce Bochte .08 .25
4 George Brett 3.00 8.00
5 Bill Buckner .08 .25
6 Rod Carew .30 1.00
7 Steve Carlton .30 1.00
8 Cesar Cedeno .08 .25
9 Jack Clark .08 .25
10 Cecil Cooper .08 .25
11 Bucky Dent .08 .25
12 Carlton Fisk 2.00 5.00
13 Steve Garvey .20 .50
14 Rich Gossage .20 .50
15 Mike Hargrove .08 .25
16 Keith Hernandez .08 .25
17 Bob Horner .08 .25
18 Reggie Jackson 2.00 5.00
19 Steve Kemp .08 .25
20 Ron LeFlore .08 .25
21 Fred Lynn .08 .25
22 Lee Mazzilli .08 .25
23 Eddie Murray 1.50 4.00
24 Mike Norris .08 .25
25 Dave Parker .08 .25
26 J.R. Richard .08 .25
27 Pete Rose 1.50 4.00
28 Mike Schmidt 1.50 4.00
29 Tom Seaver .30 1.00
30 Roy Smalley .08 .25
31 Willie Stargell .20 1.00
32 Garry Templeton .08 .25

2000 Opening Day 2K

COMPLETE SET (32) 10.00 25.00
STATED ODDS 1:5
1-8 DIST.IN TOPPS OPENING DAY
9-16 DIST.IN FLEER RETAIL
17-24 DIST.IN UD VICTORY & UD HIT.CLUB
25-32 DIST. IN PACIFIC RETAIL
1 Mark McGwire TOPPS .75 2.00
2 Barry Bonds TOPPS .75 2.00
3 Ivan Rodriguez TOPPS .30 .75
4 Sean Casey TOPPS .20 .50
5 Derek Jeter TOPPS 1.25 3.00
6 Vladimir Guerrero TOPPS .30 .75
7 Preston Wilson TOPPS .20 .50
8 Ben Grieve TOPPS .20 .50
9 Cal Ripken FLEER 1.50 4.00
10 Alex Rodriguez FLEER .60 1.50
11 Mike Piazza FLEER .50 1.25
12 Jeff Bagwell FLEER .30 .75
13 Randy Johnson FLEER .50 1.25
14 Jason Kendall FLEER .20 .50
15 Maggilo Ordonez FLEER .30 .75
16 Carlos Delgado FLEER .20 .50
17 Ken Griffey Jr. UD 1.00 2.50
18 Sammy Sosa UD .50 1.25
19 Pedro Martinez UD .30 .75
20 Manny Ramirez UD .50 1.25
21 Shawn Green UD .20 .50
22 Carlos Beltran UD .30 .75
23 Juan Gonzalez UD .20 .50
24 Jeromy Burnitz UD .20 .50
25 Mo Vaughn PAC .20 .50
26 Chipper Jones PAC .50 1.25
27 Nomar Garciaparra PAC .30 .75
28 Larry Walker PAC .30 .75
29 Corey Koskie PAC .20 .50
30 Scott Rolen PAC .30 .75
31 Tony Gwynn PAC .50 1.25
32 Jose Canseco PAC .30 .75

1979 Open Pantry

This set is an unnumbered, 12-card issue featuring players from Milwaukee area professional sports teams with five Brewers baseball (1-5), five Bucks basketball (6-10), and two Packers football (11-12). Cards are black and white with red trim and measure approximately 5" by 6". Cards were sponsored by Open Pantry, Lake to Lake, and MACC (Milwaukee Athletes against Childhood Cancer). The cards are unnumbered and hence are listed and numbered below alphabetically within sport.

COMPLETE SET (12) 12.50 25.00
1 Jerry Augustine 1.00 2.00
2 Sal Bando 1.50 3.00
3 Cecil Cooper 1.50 3.00
4 Larry Hisle 1.25 2.50
5 Lary Sorensen 1.00 2.00

1939 Orcajo Photo Art PC786

The postcards in this set measures 3 1/2" by 5 1/2" and comes in three styles. The first contains an Orcajo Photo Art back. Type 2 is marked "Courtesy of Val Decker Packing Co., Piquality Brand Meats" on the front. Type 3 is marked "Metropolitan Clothing Co" on the front. The cards are listed in the checklist below by type. The set is broken down this way: Type 1 are cards 1-26; Type 2 are 27-31 and Type 3 are cards 32-33. The set was issued in 1939 and features a card of Joe DiMaggio, the only apparent non-Cincinnati player. The cards are sepia in color and feature white borders.

COMPLETE SET (33) 1750.00 3500.00
1 Wally Berger 50.00 100.00
2 Nino Bongiovanni 40.00 80.00
3 Frenchy Bordagray 40.00 80.00
4 Harry Craft 50.00 100.00
5 Ray Davis 40.00 80.00
6 Paul Derringer 50.00 100.00
7 Joe DiMaggio 400.00 800.00
8 Linus Frey 40.00 80.00
9 Lee Gamble 40.00 80.00
10 Ival Goodman 40.00 80.00
11 Hank Gowdy CO 40.00 80.00
12 Lee Grissom 40.00 80.00
13 Williard Herschberger Name in White 50.00 100.00
14 Eddie Joost 50.00 100.00
15 Frank McCormick 50.00 100.00
16 Bill McKecknie MG 75.00 150.00
17 Billy Meyers 40.00 80.00
18 Whitey Moore 40.00 80.00
19 Lew Riggs 40.00 80.00
20 Les Scarsella 40.00 80.00
21 Milburn Shoffner 40.00 80.00
22 Junior Thompson 40.00 80.00
23 Bucky Walters 60.00 120.00
24 Bill Werber 50.00 100.00
25 Dick West 40.00 80.00
26 Jimmie Wilson 40.00 80.00
27 Alan Cooke 40.00 80.00
28 Linus Frey small projection 40.00 80.00
29 Williard Herschberger Name in black 40.00 80.00
30 Ernie Lombardi Name plain 75.00 150.00
31 Johnny Vander Meer 60.00 120.00
32 Ernie Lombardi name fancy 75.00 150.00
33 Johnny Vander Meer 60.00 120.00

2001 Oreo/Ritz

COMPLETE SET (4) 2.50 5.00
COMMON JETER .75 2.00
COMMON GRIFFEY .40 1.00

2005 Origins

COMMON CARD (1-100) .30 .75
COMMON CARD (101-150) .30 .75
COMMON CARD (151-200) .30 .75
1-200 ODDS APPX EIGHT PER TIN
COMMON CARD (201-286) .30 .75
201-286 ODDS 1:2 '05 UD UPDATE
1 Jim Edmonds .50 1.25
2 Jason Schmidt .30 .75
3 J.D. Drew .30 .75
4 Luis Gonzalez .30 .75
5 Nomar Garciaparra .50 1.25
6 Jake Peavy .30 .75
7 Rafael Furcal .30 .75
8 Craig Biggio .50 1.25
9 Ken Griffey Jr. 1.50 4.00
10 Mike Piazza .75 2.00
11 Jose Vidro .30 .75
12 Ivan Rodriguez .50 1.25
13 Carl Crawford .50 1.25
14 Roger Clemens 1.00 2.50
15 Kerry Wood .30 .75
16 Vernon Wells .30 .75
17 Carlos Guillen .30 .75
18 Tim Hudson .50 1.25
19 Carl Pavano .30 .75
20 Carlos Beltran .50 1.25
21 Pedro Martinez .50 1.25
22 Hideki Matsui 1.25 3.00
23 Frank Thomas .75 2.00
24 Curt Schilling .50 1.25
25 Manny Ramirez .75 2.00
26 Alex Rodriguez 1.00 2.50
27 Aubrey Huff .30 .75
28 David Ortiz .75 2.00
29 Mark Prior .50 1.25
30 Albert Pujols 1.00 2.50
31 Miguel Cabrera .75 2.00
32 Brad Penny .30 .75
33 Carlos Delgado .30 .75
34 Aramis Ramirez .30 .75
35 Josh Beckett .30 .75
36 Rafael Palmeiro .50 1.25
37 Bret Boone .30 .75
38 Lance Berkman .50 1.25
39 Carlos Zambrano .50 1.25
40 Adam Dunn .50 1.25
41 Livan Hernandez .30 .75
42 Mike Mussina .50 1.25
43 Ben Sheets .30 .75
44 Derek Jeter 2.00 5.00
45 Kazuo Matsui .30 .75
46 Bobby Abreu .30 .75
47 Jeff Bagwell .50 1.25
48 Travis Hafner .30 .75
49 Torii Hunter .30 .75
50 Kevin Brown .30 .75
51 Alfonso Soriano .50 1.25
52 Jim Thome .50 1.25
53 John Smoltz .75 2.00
54 Mike Sweeney .30 .75
55 Andy Pettitte .50 1.25
56 Chipper Jones .75 2.00
57 Randy Johnson .75 2.00
58 Steve Finley .30 .75
59 Larry Walker .50 1.25
60 Troy Glaus .30 .75
61 Greg Maddux 1.00 2.50
62 Shawn Green .30 .75
63 Roy Halladay .50 1.25
64 Jeff Kent .30 .75
65 Scott Podsednik .30 .75
66 Miguel Tejada .50 1.25
67 Lyle Overbay .30 .75
68 Bernie Williams .50 1.25
69 Todd Helton .50 1.25
70 Melvin Mora .30 .75
71 Magglio Ordonez .50 1.25
72 Carlos Lee .30 .75
73 Roy Oswalt .50 1.25
74 Victor Martinez .50 1.25
75 Scott Rolen .50 1.25
76 Eric Chavez .30 .75
77 Paul Konerko .50 1.25
78 Jose Reyes .50 1.25
79 Barry Larkin .50 1.25
80 Johnny Damon .50 1.25
81 Eric Gagne .30 .75
82 Andruw Jones .30 .75
83 Gary Sheffield .30 .75
84 Richie Sexson .30 .75
85 Sammy Sosa .75 2.00
86 Mark Teixeira .50 1.25
87 Vladimir Guerrero .50 1.25
88 Michael Young .30 .75
89 Johan Santana .50 1.25
90 Adrian Beltre .75 2.00
91 Tom Glavine .50 1.25
92 Hank Blalock .30 .75
93 Preston Wilson .30 .75
94 Jason Kendall .30 .75
95 Mike Lowell .30 .75
96 Craig Wilson .30 .75
97 Ichiro Suzuki 1.00 2.50
98 Mark Mulder .30 .75
99 Garret Anderson .30 .75
100 Brian Giles .30 .75
101 Robin Yount RET .75 2.00
102 Ernie Banks RET .75 2.00
103 Mike Schmidt RET 1.25 3.00
104 Enos Slaughter RET .50 1.25
105 Red Schoendienst RET .50 1.25
106 Hoyt Wilhelm RET .50 1.25
107 Lou Brock RET .50 1.25
108 Rollie Fingers RET .50 1.25
109 Gaylord Perry RET .50 1.25
110 Bobby Doerr RET .50 1.25
111 Larry Doby RET .50 1.25
112 Al Lopez RET .30 .75
113 Joe Morgan RET .50 1.25
114 Luis Aparicio RET .50 1.25
115 Willie McCovey RET .50 1.25
116 Bob Lemon RET .50 1.25
117 Early Wynn RET .50 1.25
118 Bob Feller RET .50 1.25
119 Cal Ripken RET 2.50 6.00
120 George Kell RET .50 1.25
121 Juan Marichal RET .50 1.25
122 Monte Irvin RET .50 1.25
123 Harmon Killebrew RET .75 2.00
124 Lou Boudreau RET .50 1.25
125 Mickey Mantle RET 2.50 6.00
126 Richie Ashburn RET .50 1.25
127 Pee Wee Reese RET .50 1.25
128 Whitey Ford RET .50 1.25
129 Tom Seaver RET .50 1.25
130 Phil Rizzuto RET .50 1.25
131 Yogi Berra RET .75 2.00
132 Warren Spahn RET .50 1.25
133 Billy Williams RET .50 1.25
134 Jim Bunning RET .50 1.25
135 Ralph Kiner RET .50 1.25
136 Ted Williams RET 1.50 4.00
137 Rick Ferrell RET .30 .75
138 Robin Roberts RET .50 1.25
139 Brooks Robinson RET .50 1.25
140 Hal Newhouser RET .50 1.25
141 Catfish Hunter RET .50 1.25
142 Phil Niekro RET .50 1.25
143 Fergie Jenkins RET .50 1.25
144 Al Kaline RET .75 2.00
145 Stan Musial RET 1.25 3.00
146 Joe DiMaggio RET 1.50 4.00
147 Willie Stargell RET .50 1.25
148 Nolan Ryan RET 2.50 6.00
149 Babe Ruth RET 2.00 5.00
150 Bob Gibson RET .50 1.25
151 David DeJesus YS .30 .75
152 Chris Burke YS .30 .75
153 Chad Cordero YS .30 .75
154 Kevin Youkilis YS .30 .75
155 Bucky Jacobsen YS .30 .75
156 B.J. Upton YS .50 1.25
157 Aaron Rowand YS .30 .75
158 Jose Capellan YS .30 .75
159 David Wright YS .60 1.50
160 Jason Bay YS .30 .75
161 Edwin Jackson YS .30 .75
162 Scott Kazmir YS .75 2.00
163 J.D. Closser YS .30 .75
164 Chase Utley YS .50 1.25
165 Nick Swisher YS .50 1.25
166 Casey Kotchman YS .30 .75
167 Bobby Crosby YS .30 .75
168 Zack Greinke YS 1.00 2.50
169 Gavin Floyd YS .30 .75
170 Jeff Francis YS .30 .75
171 Dallas McPherson YS .30 .75
172 Gabe Gross YS .30 .75
173 Brandon Claussen YS .30 .75
174 Wily Mo Pena YS .30 .75
175 Robb Quinlan YS .30 .75
176 Oliver Perez YS .30 .75
177 Guillermo Quiroz YS .30 .75
178 Ryan Howard YS .60 1.50
179 Gerald Laird YS .30 .75
180 Jayson Werth YS .50 1.25
181 Bobby Madritsch YS .30 .75
182 Laynce Nix YS .30 .75
183 Eddy Rodriguez YS .30 .75
184 Rickie Weeks YS .30 .75
185 Scott Proctor YS .30 .75
186 Adam LaRoche YS .30 .75
187 Yhency Brazoban YS .30 .75
188 Adrian Gonzalez YS .60 1.50
189 Jason Lane YS .30 .75
190 Ryan Wagner YS .30 .75
191 Roman Colon YS .30 .75
192 Alexis Rios YS .30 .75
193 Joe Mauer YS .60 1.50
194 Garrett Atkins YS .30 .75
195 Daniel Cabrera YS .30 .75
196 Khalil Greene YS .30 .75
197 Joe Blanton YS .30 .75
198 Jason DuBois YS .30 .75
199 Angel Guzman YS .30 .75
200 Jesse Crain YS .30 .75
201 Adam Shabala YS RC .30 .75
202 Ambiorix Burgos YS RC .30 .75
203 Ambiorix Concepcion YS RC .30 .75
204 Anibal Sanchez YS RC 1.25 3.00
205 Bill McCarthy YS RC .30 .75
206 Brandon McCarthy YS RC .50 1.25
207 Brian Burres YS RC .30 .75
208 Carlos Ruiz YS RC .50 1.25
209 Casey Rogowski YS RC .50 1.25
210 Chad Orvella YS RC .30 .75
211 Chris Resop YS RC .30 .75
212 Chris Roberson YS RC .30 .75
213 Chris Seddon YS RC .30 .75
214 Colter Bean YS RC .30 .75
215 Dae-Sung Koo YS RC .30 .75
216 Yuniesky Betancourt YS RC 1.25 3.00
217 Dave Gassner YS RC .30 .75
218 Brian Anderson YS RC .50 1.25
219 D.J. Houlton YS RC .30 .75
220 Derek Wathan YS RC .30 .75
221 Devon Lowery YS RC .30 .75
222 Enrique Gonzalez YS RC .30 .75
223 Ryan Zimmerman YS RC 1.50 4.00
224 Eude Brito YS RC .30 .75
225 Francisco Butto YS RC .30 .75
226 Franquelis Osoria YS RC .30 .75
227 Garrett Jones YS RC .50 1.25
228 Geovany Soto YS RC 1.50 4.00
229 Hayden Penn YS RC .30 .75
230 Ismael Ramirez YS RC .30 .75
231 Jared Gothreaux YS RC .30 .75
232 Jason Hammel YS RC .75 2.00
233 Chris Denorfia YS RC .30 .75
234 Jeff Miller YS RC .30 .75
235 Jeff Niemann YS RC .75 2.00
236 Dana Eveland YS RC .30 .75
237 Joel Peralta YS RC .30 .75
238 John Hattig YS RC .30 .75
239 Jorge Campillo YS RC .30 .75
240 Juan Morillo YS RC .30 .75
241 Justin Verlander YS RC 5.00 12.00
242 Ryan Garko YS RC .30 .75
243 Keiichi Yabu YS RC .30 .75
244 Kendry Morales YS RC .75 2.00
245 Luis Hernandez YS RC .30 .75
246 Jermaine Van Buren YS .30 .75
247 Luis Pena YS RC .30 .75
248 Luis O.Rodriguez YS RC .30 .75
249 Luke Scott YS RC .75 2.00
250 Marcos Carvajal YS RC .30 .75
251 Mark Woodyard YS RC .30 .75
252 Matt A.Smith YS RC .30 .75
253 Matthew Lindstrom YS RC .30 .75
254 Miguel Negron YS RC .50 1.25
255 Mike Morse YS RC 1.00 2.50
256 Nate McLouth YS RC .50 1.25
257 Nelson Cruz YS RC 4.00 10.00
258 Nick Masset YS RC .30 .75
259 Mark McLemore YS RC .30 .75
260 Oscar Robles YS RC .30 .75
261 Paulino Reynoso YS RC .30 .75
262 Pedro Lopez YS RC .30 .75
263 Pete Orr YS RC .50 1.25
264 Philip Humber YS RC .75 2.00
265 Prince Fielder YS RC 1.50 4.00
266 Randy Messenger YS RC .30 .75
267 Randy Williams YS RC .30 .75
268 Raul Tablado YS RC .30 .75
269 Ronny Paulino YS RC .50 1.25
270 Russ Rohlicek YS RC .30 .75

271 Russell Martin YS RC 1.00 2.50
272 Scott Baker YS RC .50 1.25
273 Ryan Spilborghs YS RC .75 2.00
274 Scott Munter YS RC .30 .75
275 Sean Thompson YS RC .30 .75
276 Sean Tracey YS RC .30 .75
277 Shane Costa YS RC .30 .75
278 Stephen Drew YS RC 1.00 2.50
279 Steve Schmoll YS RC .30 .75
280 Tadahito Iguchi YS RC .50 1.25
281 Tony Giarratano YS RC .30 .75
282 Tony Pena YS RC .30 .75
283 Travis Bowyer YS RC .30 .75
284 Ubaldo Jimenez YS RC .75 2.00
285 Wladimir Balentien YS RC .50 1.25
286 Yorman Bazardo YS RC .30 .75

2005 Origins Blue

*BLUE 1-100: 1.25X TO 3X BASIC
*BLUE 101-150: 1.5X TO 4X BASIC
*BLUE 101-150 PRE-WAR: 1.25X TO 3X BASIC
*BLUE 151-200: 1.25X TO 3X BASIC
1-200 OVERALL PARALLEL ODDS 1 PER TIN
*BLUE 201-286: 2X TO 5X BASIC
201-286 ISSUED IN '05 UD UPDATE PACKS
201-286 ONE #'d CARD OR AU PER PACK
STATED PRINT RUN 50 SERIAL #'d SETS

2005 Origins Red

*RED 1-100: .75X TO 2X BASIC
*RED 101-150: 1X TO 2.5X BASIC
*RED 151-200: .75X TO 2X BASIC
1-200 OVERALL PARALLEL ODDS 1 PER TIN
*RED 201-286: 1.25X TO 3X BASIC
201-286 ISSUED IN '05 UD UPDATE PACKS
201-286 ONE #'d CARD OR AU PER PACK
STATED PRINT RUN 99 SERIAL #'d SETS
1 Jim Edmonds 3.00 8.00

2005 Origins UD Promos

*PROMOS: .6X TO 1.5X BASIC

2005 Origins Materials Jersey

OVERALL GU ODDS TWO PER TIN
SP INFO PROVIDED BY UPPER DECK
AB Adrian Beltre 3.00 8.00
AJ Andruw Jones 4.00 10.00
AP Albert Pujols 6.00 15.00
AS Alfonso Soriano 3.00 8.00
BS Ben Sheets 3.00 8.00
CB Carlos Beltran 3.00 8.00
CJ Chipper Jones 4.00 10.00
CR Cal Ripken SP 12.50 30.00
CS Curt Schilling 4.00 10.00
DJ Derek Jeter 8.00 20.00
DO David Ortiz 4.00 10.00
EC Eric Chavez 3.00 8.00
FT Frank Thomas 4.00 10.00
GL Troy Glaus 3.00 8.00
GM Greg Maddux 4.00 10.00
GS Gary Sheffield 3.00 8.00
HB Hank Blalock 3.00 8.00
HE Todd Helton 4.00 10.00
HM Hideki Matsui 6.00 15.00
HU Torii Hunter 3.00 8.00
IR Ivan Rodriguez 4.00 10.00
IS Ichiro Suzuki 5.00 12.00
JB Jeff Bagwell 4.00 10.00
JD J.D. Drew 3.00 8.00
JT Jim Thome 4.00 10.00
KG Ken Griffey Jr. 6.00 15.00
KM Kazuo Matsui 3.00 8.00
KW Kerry Wood 3.00 8.00
LB Lance Berkman 3.00 8.00
MC Miguel Cabrera 4.00 10.00
MP Mark Prior 4.00 10.00
MR Manny Ramirez 4.00 10.00
MT Mark Teixeira 4.00 10.00
NR Nolan Ryan SP 12.50 30.00
PI Mike Piazza 4.00 10.00
RJ Randy Johnson 4.00 10.00
SR Scott Rolen 4.00 10.00
SS Sammy Sosa 4.00 10.00
TE Miguel Tejada 3.00 8.00
TG Tony Gwynn SP 6.00 15.00
TH Tim Hudson 3.00 8.00
VG Vladimir Guerrero 4.00 10.00

2005 Origins Signatures

OVERALL AU ODDS ONE PER TIN
TIER 3 QTY 350 OR MORE COPIES PER
TIER 2 QTY B/WN 200-250 COPIES PER
TIER 1 QTY B/WN 5-100 COPIES PER
C.RIPKEN PRINT RUN 25 CARDS
C.BELTRAN PRINT RUN 5 CARDS
PRINT RUN INFO PROVIDED BY UD
CARDS ARE NOT SERIAL-NUMBERED
C.BELTRAN T1 TOO SCARCE TO PRICE
EXCHANGE DEADLINE 06/08/08
AB1 Adrian Beltre T2 8.00 20.00
AH1 Aubrey Huff T3 6.00 15.00
AO1 Akinori Otsuka T3 10.00 25.00
BD1 Bobby Doerr T3 6.00 15.00
BF1 Bob Feller T2 10.00 25.00
BR1 Brooks Robinson T2 10.00 25.00
BS1 Ben Sheets T2 6.00 15.00
BU1 B.J. Upton T3 6.00 15.00
CC1 Carl Crawford T3 6.00 15.00
CK1 Casey Kotchman T3 6.00 15.00
CR1 Cal Ripken T1/25 * 125.00 200.00
CU1 Chase Utley T3 20.00 50.00
CZ1 Carlos Zambrano T3 10.00 25.00
DG1 Dwight Gooden T3 6.00 15.00
DJ1 Derek Jeter T1 100.00 175.00
DK1 Dave Kingman T3 6.00 15.00
DM1 Dallas McPherson T3 4.00 10.00
DW1 David Wright T3 10.00 25.00
FH1 Frank Howard T3 6.00 15.00
GR1 Khalil Greene T3 10.00 25.00
HO1 Ryan Howard T3 12.50 30.00
JB1 Jason Bay T3 6.00 15.00
JP1 Jim Palmer T2 6.00 15.00
JS1 Johan Santana T2 4.00 10.00
KG1 Ken Griffey Jr. T2 75.00 200.00
KH1 Keith Hernandez T3 6.00 15.00
MA1 Don Mattingly T1 40.00 100.00
MC1 Miguel Cabrera T2 15.00 40.00
MG1 Marcus Giles T3 6.00 15.00
MS1 Mike Schmidt T1 75.00 150.00
MT1 Mark Teixeira T2 10.00 25.00
OP1 Oliver Perez T3 4.00 10.00
OS1 Roy Oswalt T2 6.00 15.00
PE1 Jake Peavy T3 10.00 25.00
PM1 Paul Molitor T1 10.00 25.00
RG1 Ron Guidry T3 10.00 25.00
RH1 Rich Harden T3 6.00 15.00
RO1 Al Rosen T3 6.00 15.00
RS1 Ron Santo T3 6.00 15.00
RW1 Rickie Weeks T2 6.00 15.00
RY1 Robin Yount T1 20.00 50.00
SK1 Scott Kazmir T3 8.00 20.00
SL1 Sparky Lyle T3 6.00 15.00
ST1 Shingo Takatsu T3 6.00 15.00
TG1 Tony Gwynn T1 20.00 50.00
TH1 Travis Hafner T3 6.00 15.00
VM1 Victor Martinez T3 6.00 15.00

2005 Origins Nostalgic Signs

COMPLETE SET (41) 75.00 150.00
ONE SIGN PER SEALED TIN
AB Adrian Beltre 2.00 5.00
AP Albert Pujols 2.50 6.00
AR Alex Rodriguez 2.50 6.00
AS Alfonso Soriano 1.25 3.00
BR Babe Ruth 5.00 12.00
CB Carlos Beltran 1.25 3.00
CJ Chipper Jones 2.00 5.00
CR Cal Ripken 6.00 15.00
CS Curt Schilling 1.25 3.00
DJ Derek Jeter 5.00 12.00
DO David Ortiz 2.00 5.00
EC Eric Chavez .75 2.00
FT Frank Thomas 2.00 5.00
HB Hank Blalock .75 2.00
HM Hideki Matsui 3.00 8.00
HW Honus Wagner 1.25 3.00
IR Ivan Rodriguez 1.25 3.00
IS Ichiro Suzuki 2.50 6.00
JD Joe DiMaggio 4.00 10.00
JR Jackie Robinson 1.25 3.00
JS Johan Santana 1.25 3.00
JT Jim Thome 1.25 3.00
KG Ken Griffey Jr. 4.00 10.00
LG Lou Gehrig 4.00 10.00
MC Miguel Cabrera 2.00 5.00
MP Mike Piazza 2.00 5.00
MPR Mark Prior 1.25 3.00
MR Manny Ramirez 2.00 5.00
MT Miguel Tejada 1.25 3.00
NR Nolan Ryan 6.00 15.00
PM Pedro Martinez 1.25 3.00
RC Roger Clemens 2.50 6.00
RJ Randy Johnson 2.00 5.00
SP Satchel Paige 2.00 5.00
SR Scott Rolen 1.25 3.00
SS Sammy Sosa 2.00 5.00
TC Ty Cobb 3.00 8.00
TH Todd Helton 1.25 3.00
TW Ted Williams 4.00 10.00
VG Vladimir Guerrero 1.25 3.00
WJ Walter Johnson 1.25 3.00

2005 Origins Tins

ISSUED AS COLLECTIBLE PACKAGING
DJ Derek Jeter 5.00 12.00
HW Honus Wagner 1.25 3.00
TC Ty Cobb 3.00 8.00
WJ Walter Johnson 1.25 3.00

2005 Origins Old Judge

*OLD JUDGE 1-200: .4X TO 1X ORIGINS
1-200 ODDS APPX EIGHT CARDS PER TIN
*OLD JUDGE 201-286: .4X TO 1X ORIGINS
201-286 ODDS 1:2 '05 UD UPDATE

2005 Origins Old Judge Blue

*OJ BLUE: .4X TO 1X ORIGINS BLUE
1-200 OVERALL PARALLEL ODDS 1 PER TIN
201-286 ISSUED IN '05 UD UPDATE PACKS
201-286 ONE #'d CARD OR AU PER PACK
STATED PRINT RUN 50 SERIAL #'d SETS

2005 Origins Old Judge Red

*OJ RED: .4X TO 1X ORIGINS RED
1-200 OVERALL PARALLEL ODDS 1 PER TIN
201-286 ISSUED IN '05 UD UPDATE PACKS
201-286 ONE #'d CARD OR AU PER PACK
STATED PRINT RUN 99 SERIAL #'d SETS

2005 Origins Old Judge Autographs

*OLD JUDGE AU: .4X TO 1X ORIGINS AU
OVERALL AU ODDS ONE PER TIN
TIER 3 QTY 350 OR MORE COPIES PER
TIER 2 QTY B/WN 200-250 COPIES PER
TIER 1 QTY B/WN 5-100 COPIES PER
C.RIPKEN PRINT RUN 25 CARDS
C.BELTRAN PRINT RUN 5 CARDS
TIERED PRINT RUN INFO PROVIDED BY UD
CARDS ARE NOT SERIAL-NUMBERED
C.BELTRAN T1 TOO SCARCE TO PRICE
EXCHANGE DEADLINE 06/08/08
AB Adrian Beltre T2 8.00 20.00
AH Aubrey Huff T3 6.00 15.00
AO Akinori Otsuka T3 10.00 25.00
BD Bobby Doerr T3 6.00 15.00
BF Bob Feller T2 10.00 25.00
BR Brooks Robinson T2 10.00 25.00
BS Ben Sheets T2 6.00 15.00
BU B.J. Upton T3 10.00 25.00
CC Carl Crawford T3 6.00 15.00
CK Casey Kotchman T3 6.00 15.00
CR Cal Ripken T1/25 * 75.00 200.00
CU Chase Utley T3 10.00 25.00
CZ Carlos Zambrano T3 10.00 25.00
DG Dwight Gooden T3 6.00 15.00
DJ Derek Jeter T1 125.00 300.00
DK Dave Kingman T3 6.00 15.00
DM Dallas McPherson T3 4.00 10.00
DW David Wright T3 5.00 12.00
FH Frank Howard T3 6.00 15.00
GR Khalil Greene T3 10.00 25.00
HO Ryan Howard T3 6.00 15.00
JB Jason Bay T3 6.00 15.00
JP Jim Palmer T2 6.00 15.00
KG Ken Griffey Jr. T2 40.00 100.00
KH Keith Hernandez T3 6.00 15.00
MA Don Mattingly T1 30.00 80.00
MC Miguel Cabrera T2 15.00 40.00
MS Mike Schmidt T1 20.00 50.00
MT Mark Teixeira T2 10.00 25.00
OP Oliver Perez T3 4.00 10.00
OS Roy Oswalt T2 6.00 15.00
PE Jake Peavy T3 10.00 25.00
PM Paul Molitor T1 10.00 25.00
RG Ron Guidry T3 10.00 25.00
RH Rich Harden T3 6.00 15.00
RO Al Rosen T3 6.00 15.00
RS Ron Santo T3 8.00 20.00
RW Rickie Weeks T2 6.00 15.00
RY Robin Yount T1 20.00 50.00
SK Scott Kazmir T3 8.00 20.00
SL Sparky Lyle T3 6.00 15.00
ST Shingo Takatsu T3 6.00 15.00
TG Tony Gwynn T1 20.00 50.00
TH Travis Hafner T3 5.00 12.00
VM Victor Martinez T3 6.00 15.00

2005 Origins Old Judge Materials Jersey

*OLD JUDGE GU: .4X TO 1X ORIGINS GU
OVERALL GU ODDS TWO PER TIN
SP INFO PROVIDED BY UPPER DECK

1994 Origins of Baseball

Published by the American Archives Publishing Co. (Beverly Hills, CA), this boxed set of 100 standard-size cards recounts the historic origins of baseball from 1744 to 1899. According to the title card, limited edition uncut sheets of the set as well as 8" by 10" reproductions of certain cards were also produced.

COMP. FACT SET (104) 4.00 10.00
1 Abner Doubleday .08 .25
2 Doubleday Field .01 .05
3 Rounders 1744 .01 .05
4 Early Baseball 700 AD .01 .05
5 The Knickerbockers .01 .05
6 Alexander Cartwright .08 .25
7 Baseball in the 1850's .01 .05
8 Social Clubs .01 .05
9 Brooklyn Eckfords .01 .05
10 New England Baseball .01 .05
11 Henry Chadwick .08 .25
12 Brooklyn Excelsiors .01 .05
13 Abraham Lincoln .30 .75
14 Andrew Johnson .05 .15
15 First Enclosed Park .01 .05
16 Brooklyn Atlantics .01 .05
17 James Creighton .05 .15
18 Baseball in the 1860's .01 .05
19 1869 Red Stockings .01 .05
20 Cincinnati Celebration .01 .05
21 Harry Wright .08 .25
22 Boston Ball Club 1872 .01 .05
23 Arthur Cummings .08 .25
24 William Hulbert .05 .15
25 George Wright .08 .25
26 Albert Spalding .08 .25
27 Albert Bushong .05 .15
28 Bid McPhee .05 .15
29 James O'Rourke .05 .15
30 Pud Galvin .08 .25
31 Edwin Bligh .05 .15
32 William Purcell .05 .15
33 Roger Connor .08 .25
34 Cincinnati Ball Club .01 .05
35 Peter Browning .05 .15
36 William Gleason .05 .15
37 Paul Hines .05 .15
38 Baseball in the 1880's .01 .05
39 Robert Carruthers .05 .15
40 New York Metropolitans .01 .05
41 Saint George's Field .01 .05
42 Charles Radbourne .08 .25
43 George Andrews .05 .15
44 William Hoy .08 .25
45 Chicago Ball Club .01 .05
46 Cap Anson .30 .75
47 John Clarkson .08 .25
48 Mike Kelly .30 .75
49 Buffalo Bisons 1887 .01 .05
50 Moses Walker .30 .75
51 Detroit Ball Club .01 .05
52 Little League .01 .05
53 Louisville Ball Club .01 .05
54 John Farrell .05 .15
55 Walter Latham .05 .15
56 Fred Dunlap .05 .15
57 Tim Keefe .08 .25
58 Cincinnati Ball Club .01 .05
59 1889 World Tour .01 .05
60 Dan Brouthers .08 .25
61 John M. Ward .08 .25
62 Albert Spalding .08 .25
63 The Baseball Cap .01 .05
64 Tom Esterbrook .05 .15
65 Mark Baldwin .05 .15
66 Tony Mullane .08 .25
67 John Glasscock .05 .15
68 Amos Rusie .08 .25
69 Jake Beckley .08 .25
70 Jimmy Collins .08 .25
71 Charles Comiskey .08 .25
72 Tom Connolly .08 .25
73 Mickey Welch .08 .25
74 Ed Delahanty .08 .25
75 Hugh Duffy .08 .25
76 Buck Ewing .08 .25
77 Clark Griffith .08 .25
78 Kid Nichols .08 .25
79 Billy Hamilton .08 .25
80 Ban Johnson .05 .15
81 Willie Keeler .08 .25
82 Bobby Wallace .08 .25
83 Nap Lajoie .30 .75
84 Connie Mack .30 .75
85 Fred Clarke .08 .25
86 Tommy McCarthy .08 .25
87 John McGraw .30 .75
88 Jesse Burkett .08 .25
89 Frank Chance .08 .25
90 Mordecai Brown .08 .25
91 New York Nationals .01 .05
92 Jack Chesbro .05 .15
93 Sam Thompson .08 .25
94 Boston vs. New York .01 .05
95 Rube Waddell .08 .25
96 Joe Kelley .08 .25
97 Addie Joss .08 .25
98 Boston Beaneaters .01 .05
99 Baltimore Baseball Club .01 .05
100 The Game in 1899 .01 .05
z3 Acknowledgments .01 .05
zNNO0 Title card/(Proof of ownership) .01 .05
zNNO0 Bibliography card .01 .05
NNO0 Certificate of Authenticity .01 .05

1894 Orioles Alpha

These cards which measure 3 7/8" by 2 3/8" featured players from the great Baltimore Oriole teams of the 1890's. This set has the players photographed in black tie regalia. The back of each card credits the Alpha Photo Engraving Company of Baltimore, Maryland.

COMPLETE SET (14) 6000.00 12000.00
1 Frank Bonner 10000.00 20000.00
2 Walter Brodie 10000.00 20000.00
3 Dan Brouthers 20000.00 40000.00
4 Charles Esper 10000.00 20000.00
5 Kid Gleason 12500.00 25000.00
6 Ned Hanlon MG 15000.00 30000.00
7 William Hawke 10000.00 20000.00
8 George Hemmings 10000.00 20000.00
9 Hugh Jennings 20000.00 40000.00
10 Joe Kelley 20000.00 40000.00
11 John McGraw 25000.00 50000.00
12 John McMahon 10000.00 20000.00
13 Henry Reitz 10000.00 20000.00
14 Wilbert Robinson 20000.00 40000.00

1954 Orioles Esskay

The cards in this 36-card set measure 2 1/4" by 3 1/2". The 1954 Esskay Meats set contains color, unnumbered cards featuring Baltimore Orioles only. The cards were issued in panels of two on boxes of Esskay hot dogs; consequently, many have grease stains on the cards and are quite difficult to obtain in mint condition. The 1954 Esskay set can be distinguished from the 1955 Esskay set supposedly by the white or off-white (the 1955 set) backs of the cards. The backs of the 1954 cards are also supposedly "waxed" to a greater degree than the 1955 cards. The catalog designation is F181-1. Since the cards are unnumbered, they are ordered below in alphabetical order for convenience. These cards were issued in conjunction with the "Bobo Newsome" TV Show. In addition, 8 by 10 photos of Bobo Newsome pitching Esskay photos are known to exist. It is considered a photo premium for this product

COMPLETE SET (36) 10000.00 20000.00
1 Cal Abrams 300.00 600.00
2 Neil Berry 300.00 600.00
3 Michael Blyzka 300.00 600.00
4 Harry Brecheen 400.00 800.00
5 Gil Coan 300.00 600.00
6 Joe Coleman 300.00 600.00
7 Clint Courtney 400.00 800.00
8 Charles E. Diering 300.00 600.00
9 Jimmie Dykes 400.00 800.00
10 Frank Fanovich 300.00 600.00
11 Howard Fox 300.00 600.00
12 Jim Fridley 300.00 600.00
13 Chico Garcia 300.00 600.00
14 Jehosie Heard 300.00 600.00
15 Darrell Johnson 400.00 800.00
16 Robert D. Kennedy 400.00 800.00
17 Dick Kokos 300.00 600.00
18 Dave Koslo 300.00 600.00
19 Lou Kretlow 300.00 600.00
20 Dick Kryhoski 300.00 600.00
21 Bob Kuzava 300.00 600.00
22 Don Larsen 600.00 1200.00
23 Don Lenhardt 300.00 600.00
24 Dick Littlefield 300.00 600.00
25 Sam Mele 300.00 600.00
26 Les Moss 300.00 600.00
27 Ray L. Murray 300.00 600.00
28 Bobo Newsom 400.00 800.00
29 Tom Oliver 300.00 600.00
30 Duane Pillette 300.00 600.00
31 Francis M. Skaff 300.00 600.00
32 Marlin Stuart 300.00 600.00
33 Bob Turley 600.00 1200.00
34 Eddie Waitkus 300.00 600.00
35 Vic Wertz 400.00 800.00
36 Robert G. Young 300.00 600.00
NNO Bobo Newsom Photo 500.00 1000.00

1954 Orioles Photos

These blank-backed black and white photos featured members of the 1954 Baltimore Orioles, in their first year in Baltimore. This listing we are running was found as a set, however it is possible that these photos were issued throughout the 1954 season. Since these are unnumbered, we have sequenced them in alphabetical order.

COMPLETE SET 250.00 500.00
1 Cal Abrams 10.00 20.00
2 Neil Berry 10.00 20.00
3 Vern Bickford 10.00 20.00
4 Gil Coan 10.00 20.00
5 Joe Coleman 10.00 20.00
6 Chuck Diering 10.00 20.00
7 Jim Dyck 10.00 20.00
8 Howie Fox 10.00 20.00
9 Jim Fridley 10.00 20.00
10 Jehosie Heard 10.00 20.00
11 Billy Hunter 10.00 20.00
12 Darrell Johnson 10.00 20.00
13 Dick Kokos 10.00 20.00
14 Lou Kretlow 10.00 20.00
15 Dick Kryhoski 10.00 20.00
16 Don Larsen 20.00 40.00
17 Don Lenhardt 10.00 20.00
18 Dick Littlefield 10.00 20.00
19 Sam Mele 10.00 20.00
20 Les Moss 10.00 20.00
21 Duane Pillette 10.00 20.00
22 Vern Stephens 12.50 25.00
23 Marlin Stuart 10.00 20.00
24 Bob Turley 20.00 40.00
25 Vic Wertz 12.50 25.00
26 Bob Young 10.00 20.00

1954-55 Orioles Postcards

This set features glossy black-and-white portraits of the Baltimore Orioles with white borders. The backs carry a postcard format. The cards are unnumbered and checklisted below in alphabetical order.

COMPLETE SET 1500.00 3000.00
1 Cal Abrams 40.00 80.00
2 Bob Alexander 40.00 80.00
3 Mike Blyzka 40.00 80.00
4 Jim Brideweser 40.00 80.00
5 Hal Brown 40.00 80.00
6 Harry Byrd 40.00 80.00
7 Bob Chakales 40.00 80.00
8 Wayne Causey 40.00 80.00
9 Gil Coan 40.00 80.00
10 Joe Coleman 40.00 80.00
11 Clint Courtney 40.00 80.00
12 Billy Cox 50.00 100.00
13 Chuck Diering 40.00 80.00
14 Harry Dorish 40.00 80.00
15 Jim Dyck 40.00 80.00
16 Jimmy Dykes 50.00 100.00
17 Howie Fox 40.00 80.00
18 Jim Fridley 40.00 80.00
19 Chico Garcia 40.00 80.00
20 Ted Gray 40.00 80.00
21 Bob Hale 40.00 80.00
22 Bill Hunter 50.00 100.00
23 Don Johnson 40.00 80.00
24 Bob Kennedy 40.00 80.00
25 Lou Kretlow 40.00 80.00
26 Dick Kryhoski 40.00 80.00
27 Bob Kuzava 40.00 80.00
28 Don Larsen 60.00 120.00
29 Don Leppert 40.00 80.00
30 Ed Lopat 50.00 100.00
31 Fred Marsh 40.00 80.00
32 Jim McDonald 40.00 80.00
33 Sam Mele 40.00 80.00
34 Willie Miranda 40.00 80.00
35 Les Moss 40.00 80.00
36 Ray Murray 40.00 80.00
37 Bob Nelson 40.00 80.00
38 Billy O'Dell 40.00 80.00
39 Dave Philley 40.00 80.00
40 Erv Palica 40.00 80.00
41 Duane Pillette 40.00 80.00
42 Dave Pope 40.00 80.00
43 Paul Richards 50.00 100.00
44 Saul Rogovin 40.00 80.00
45 Art Schallock 40.00 80.00
46 Frank Skaff 40.00 80.00
47 Hal Smith 40.00 80.00
48 Vern Stephens 50.00 100.00
49 Marlin Stuart 40.00 80.00
50 Gus Triandos 50.00 100.00
51 Bob Turley/(Portrait) 50.00 100.00
52 Bob Turley/(Throwing) 50.00 100.00
53 Eddie Waitkus 50.00 100.00
54 Wally Westlake 40.00 80.00
55 Bill Wright 40.00 80.00
56 Gene Woodling 50.00 100.00
57 Bobby Young 40.00 80.00
58 George Zuverink 40.00 80.00

1954 Orioles Zip Large

Little is known about these cards, which were issued over a two-year period. Believed to be called Zip Cards. These cards measure 2 3/4" by 3 5/8" and a total of twenty-five total cards are known to be issued between 1954 and 1955. The biggest difference between the large and small zip cards is in the larger photos, the photos are basically full bordered and take up a great deal of the card while in the small cards, the player's photo are in a circle. All the cards have a year and card number along with the zip cards name on the bottom.

COMPLETE SET (4) 400.00 800.00
1 Billy O'Dell 100.00 200.00
2 Joe Durham 100.00 200.00
3 Eddie Waitkus 100.00 200.00
4 Chuck Diering 100.00 200.00

1954 Orioles Zip Small

These cards, measure 2" and 2 5/8" and are significantly smaller than their larger counterparts

1 Marlin Stuart 100.00 200.00
2 Chico Garcia 100.00 200.00
3 Jim Fridley 100.00 200.00
4 Jimmy Dykes MG 100.00 200.00
5 Bob Chakales 100.00 200.00
6 Jim Brideweser 100.00 200.00
7 Tom Oliver CO 100.00 200.00
8 Frank Skaff CO 100.00 200.00

1955 Orioles Esskay

The cards in this 27-card set measure 2 1/4" by 3 1/2". The 1955 Esskay Meats set was issued in panels of two on boxes of Esskay hot dogs. This set of full color, blank back, unnumbered cards features Baltimore Orioles only. Many of the players in the 1954 Esskay set were also issued in this set. The catalog designation is F181-2. Since the cards are unnumbered, they are ordered below in alphabetical order for convenience. The 1955 set is supposedly somewhat more difficult to find than the 1954 set.

COMPLETE SET (27) 7500.00 15000.00
1 Cal Abrams 300.00 600.00
2 Robert Alexander 300.00 600.00
3 Harry Brecheen 400.00 800.00
4 Harry Byrd 300.00 600.00
5 Gil Coan 300.00 600.00
6 Joe Coleman 300.00 600.00
7 William Cox 400.00 800.00
8 Charles E. Diering 300.00 600.00
9 Walter Evers 400.00 800.00
10 Don Johnson 300.00 600.00
11 Robert D. Kennedy 400.00 800.00
12 Lou Kretlow 300.00 600.00
13 Bob Kuzava 300.00 600.00
14 Fred Marsh 300.00 600.00
15 Charles Maxwell 400.00 800.00
16 Jim McDonald 300.00 600.00
17 Bill Miller 300.00 600.00
18 Willie Miranda 400.00 800.00
19 Raymond L. Moore 300.00 600.00
20 Les Moss 300.00 600.00
21 Bobo Newsom 400.00 800.00
22 Duane Pillette 300.00 600.00
23 Harold W. Smith 300.00 600.00
24 Gus Triandos 400.00 800.00
25 Eddie Waitkus 300.00 600.00
26 Gene Woodling 500.00 1000.00
27 Robert G. Young 300.00 600.00

1955 Orioles Zip Large

For the second year, the company "zip cards" issued a few cards of the fledgling Baltimore Orioles. These cards, just as the 1954 cards measure 2 3/4" by 3 5/8". Any further information about these cards as well as additions to our checklists is very appreciated.

COMPLETE SET (5) 500.00 1000.00
1 Les Moss 100.00 200.00
2 Don Leppert 100.00 200.00
3 Bobby Young 100.00 200.00
4 Hoot Evers 100.00 200.00
5 Bob Kennedy 100.00 200.00

1955 Orioles Zip Small

COMPLETE SET (8) 750.00 1500.00
1 Wayne Causey 100.00 200.00
2 Bob Hale 100.00 200.00
3 Dave Philley 100.00 200.00
4 Tom Gastall 100.00 200.00
5 Jim Dyck 100.00 200.00
6 Lum Harris 100.00 200.00
7 Art Schallock 100.00 200.00
8 Bob Nelson 100.00 200.00

1956 Orioles Postcards

This 38-card set features glossy black-and-white portraits of the Baltimore Orioles in white borders and printed on a postcard format. Cards 1-28 were blank in the bottom margins for autographs. Card 29-37 had the player's name and nickname printed on the front. There were two cards of different players numbered 20. Please note that there is some duplications in the Orioles Postcards lists and years. We will continue to work on further clarifying each set and year.

COMPLETE SET (38) 750.00 1500.00
1 George Zuverink 30.00 60.00
2 Wayne Causey 30.00 60.00
3 Bob Nelson 30.00 60.00
4 Jim Pyburn 30.00 60.00
5 Willie Miranda 30.00 60.00
6 Jim Dyck 30.00 60.00
7 Dave Philley 30.00 60.00
8 Erv Palica 30.00 60.00
9 Gus Triandos 40.00 80.00
10 Hal Smith 30.00 60.00
11 Dave Pope 30.00 60.00
12 Tom Gastall 30.00 60.00
13 Jim Wilson 30.00 60.00
14 Hal Brown 30.00 60.00
15 Harry Dorish 30.00 60.00
16 Ray Moore 30.00 60.00
17 Bob Hale 30.00 60.00
18 Tito Francona 30.00 60.00
19 Don Ferrarese 30.00 60.00
20 Bob Boyd 30.00 60.00
20 George Kell 60.00 120.00
21 Babe Birrer 30.00 60.00
22 Bill Wright 30.00 60.00
23 Billy Gardner 40.00 80.00
24 Paul Richards MG 40.00 80.00
25 Mel Held 30.00 60.00
26 Chuck Diering 30.00 60.00
27 Fred Marsh 30.00 60.00
28 Bobby Adams 30.00 60.00
29 Walter Evers 30.00 60.00
30 Robert Nieman 30.00 60.00
31 George Kell 60.00 120.00
32 Jose Fornieles 30.00 60.00
33 William Loes 40.00 80.00
34 John Schmitz 30.00 60.00
35 Clifford Johnson 30.00 60.00
36 Joseph Frazier 30.00 60.00
37 Richard Williams 40.00 80.00

1958 Orioles Jay Publishing

This 12-card set of the Baltimore Orioles measures approximately 5" by 7" and features black-and-white player photos in a white border. These cards were packaged 12 to a packet. The backs are blank. The cards are unnumbered and checklisted below in alphabetical order.

COMPLETE SET (12) 20.00 40.00
1 Bob Boyd 1.50 3.00
2 Jim Busby 1.50 3.00
3 Billy Gardner 1.50 3.00
4 Connie Johnson 1.50 3.00
5 Billy Loes 2.00 4.00
6 Willy Miranda 1.50 3.00
7 Bob Nieman 1.50 3.00
8 Bill O'Dell 1.50 3.00
9 Al Pilarcik 1.50 3.00
10 Paul Richards MG 2.50 5.00
11 Gus Triandos 2.50 5.00
12 George Zuverink 1.50 3.00

1959 Orioles Jay Publishing

This 12-card set of the Baltimore Orioles measures approximately 5" by 7" and features black-and-white player photos in a white border. These cards were packaged 12 to a packet. The backs are blank. The cards are unnumbered and checklisted below in alphabetical order.

COMPLETE SET (12) 25.00 50.00
1 Bob Boyd 1.50 3.00
2 Chico Carrasquel 1.50 3.00
3 Billy Gardner 1.50 3.00
4 Bob Nieman 1.50 3.00
5 Billy O'Dell 1.50 3.00
6 Milt Pappas 2.50 5.00
7 Brooks Robinson 7.50 15.00
8 Willie Tasby 1.50 3.00
9 Gus Triandos 1.50 3.00
10 Jerry Walker 1.50 3.00
11 James(Hoyt) Wilhelm 5.00 10.00
12 Gene Woodling 1.50 3.00

1960 Orioles Jay Publishing

This 12-card set of the Baltimore Orioles measures approximately 5" by 7" and features black-and-white player photos in a white border. These cards were packaged 12 to a packet and originally sold for 25 cents. The backs are blank. The cards are unnumbered and checklisted below in alphabetical order.

COMPLETE SET (12) 15.00 40.00
1 Jackie Brandt 1.00 2.50
2 Marv Breeding 1.00 2.50
3 Jack Fisher 1.00 2.50
4 Ron Hansen 1.00 2.50
5 Milt Pappas 1.25 3.00
6 Paul Richards MG 1.25 3.00
7 Brooks Robinson 5.00 12.00
8 Willie Tasby 1.00 2.50
9 Gus Triandos 1.00 2.50
10 Jerry Walker 1.00 2.50
11 Hoyt Wilhelm 3.00 8.00
12 Gene Woodling 1.25 3.00

1960 Orioles Postcards

This 12-card set of the Baltimore Orioles features black-and-white player portraits in white borders. The backs are blank. The cards are unnumbered and checklisted below in alphabetical order.

COMPLETE SET (12) 75.00 150.00
1 Jackie Brandt 8.00 20.00
2 Harry Brecheen 8.00 20.00
3 Marv Breeding 8.00 20.00
4 Chuck Estrada 8.00 20.00
5 Jack Fisher 8.00 20.00
6 Jim Gentil/(After Swing) 10.00 25.00
7 Gordon Jones/(Pitching) 8.00 20.00
8 Dave Philley 8.00 20.00
9 Willie Tasby 8.00 20.00
10 Gus Triandos 8.00 20.00
11 Jerry Walker 8.00 20.00
12 Gene Woodling 10.00 25.00

1961 Orioles Jay Publishing

This 12-card set of the Baltimore Orioles measures approximately 5" by 7". The fronts feature black-and-white posed player photos with the player's and team name printed below in the white border. These cards were packaged 12 in a packet. The backs are blank. The cards are unnumbered and checklisted below in alphabetical order.

COMPLETE SET (12) 8.00 20.00
1 Jackie Brandt 1.25 3.00
2 Chuck Estrada 1.25 3.00
3 Jack Fisher 1.25 3.00
4 Jim Gentile 1.50 4.00
5 Ron Hansen 1.25 3.00
6 Whitey Herzog
7 Milt Pappas 1.50 4.00
8 Paul Richards MG 1.25 3.00
9 Brooks Robinson 4.00 10.00
10 Russ Snyder 1.25 3.00
11 Gus Triandos 1.25 3.00
12 Jerry Walker 1.25 3.00

1961 Orioles Postcards

This 22-card set features black-and-white portraits of the Baltimore Orioles with white borders and printed on a cream colored paper. The backs are blank. The cards are unnumbered and checklisted below in alphabetical order.

COMPLETE SET (22) 150.00 300.00
1 Jerry Adair 8.00 20.00
2 Jackie Brandt 8.00 20.00
3 Marv Breeding 8.00 20.00
4 Hal Brown 8.00 20.00
5 Jim Busby 8.00 20.00
6 Walt Dropo 8.00 20.00
7 Chuck Estrada 8.00 20.00
8 Jack Fisher 8.00 20.00
9 Hank Foiles 8.00 20.00
10 Jim Gentile 8.00 20.00
11 Ron Hansen 8.00 20.00
12 Whitey Herzog 8.00 20.00
13 Billy Hoeft 8.00 20.00
14 Milt Pappas 8.00 20.00
15 Dave Philley 8.00 20.00
16 Brooks Robinson 10.00 25.00
17 Russ Snyder 8.00 20.00
18 Gene Stephens 8.00 20.00
19 Wes Stock 8.00 20.00
20 Gus Triandos 8.00 20.00
21 Jerry Walker 8.00 20.00
22 Hoyt Wilhelm 8.00 20.00

1962 Orioles Jay Publishing

This 12-card set of the Baltimore Orioles measures approximately 5" by 7". The fronts feature black-and-white posed player photos with the player's and team name printed below in the white border. These cards were packaged 12 to a packet. The backs are blank. The cards are unnumbered and checklisted below in alphabetical order.

COMPLETE SET (12) 12.50 30.00
1 Jerry Adair .75 2.00
2 Steve Barber .75 2.00
3 Jackie Brandt .75 2.00
4 Marv Breeding .75 2.00
5 Hector Brown .75 2.00
6 Chuck Estrada .75 2.00
7 Jim Gentile 1.25 3.00
8 Ron Hansen .75 2.00
9 Milt Pappas 1.00 2.50
10 Brooks Robinson 4.00 10.00
11 Earl Robinson .75 2.00
12 Gus Triandos .75 2.00

1962 Orioles Postcards

This 33-card set features black-and-white player portraits with white borders. The backs are blank. The cards are unnumbered and checklisted below in alphabetical order. Boog Powell appears in his Rookie Card season.

COMPLETE SET (33) 200.00 400.00
1 Jerry Adair 4.00 10.00
2 Steve Barber/(Portrait) 4.00 10.00
3 Steve Barber/(Ready to throw) 4.00 10.00
4 Jackie Brandt 4.00 10.00
5 Marv Breeding 4.00 10.00
6 Hal Brown 4.00 10.00
7 Chuck Estrada 4.00 10.00
8 Jack Fisher 4.00 10.00
9 Jim Gentile 6.00 15.00
10 Dick Hall 4.00 10.00
11 Ron Hansen 4.00 10.00
12 Whitey Herzog 6.00 15.00
13 Billy Hitchcock 6.00 15.00
14 Billy Hoeft 4.00 10.00
15 Hobie Landrith 4.00 10.00
16 Charlie Lau 4.00 10.00
17 Jim Lehew 4.00 10.00
18 Dave Nicholson 4.00 10.00

19 Milt Pappas 6.00 15.00
20 Boog Powell 10.00 25.00
21 Art Quirk 4.00 10.00
22 Robin Roberts 8.00 20.00
23 Brooks Robinson 10.00 25.00
24 Earl Robinson 4.00 10.00
25 Billy Short 4.00 10.00
26 Russ Snyder 4.00 10.00
27 Wes Stock 4.00 10.00
28 Johnny Temple 4.00 10.00
29 Marv Throneberry 5.00 12.00
30 Gus Triandos 4.00 10.00
31 Ozzie Virgil 4.00 10.00
32 Hoyt Wilhelm 8.00 20.00
33 Dick Williams 5.00 12.00

1963 Orioles Jay Publishing

This 12-card set of the Baltimore Orioles measures approximately 5" by 7". The fronts feature black-and-white posed player photos with the player's and team name printed below in the white border. These cards were packaged 12 to a packet. The backs are blank. The cards are unnumbered and checklisted below in alphabetical order.

COMPLETE SET (12) 15.00 40.00
1 Jerry Adair .75 2.00
2 Luis Aparicio 2.50 6.00
3 Steve Barber .75 2.00
4 Jackie Brandt .75 2.00
5 Chuck Estrada .75 2.00
6 Jim Gentile 1.25 3.00
7 Billy Hitchcock MG .75 2.00
8 John Orsino .75 2.00
9 Milt Pappas 1.25 3.00
10 Robin Roberts 2.50 6.00
11 Brooks Robinson 3.00 8.00
12 Wes Stock .75 2.00

1963 Orioles Postcards

This 34-card set features black-and-white portraits of the Baltimore Orioles with white borders. The backs are blank. The cards are unnumbered and checklisted below in alphabetical order.

COMPLETE SET (34) 200.00 400.00
1 Jerry Adair 4.00 10.00
2 Luis Aparicio 8.00 20.00
3 Luke Appling 8.00 20.00
4 Steve Barber 6.00 15.00
5 Hank Bauer CO 6.00 15.00
6 Jack Brandt 4.00 10.00
7 Harry Brecheen CO 6.00 15.00
8 Dick Brown 4.00 10.00
9 Pete Burnside 4.00 10.00
10 Chuck Estrada 4.00 10.00
11 Joe Gaines 4.00 10.00
12 Jim Gentile 6.00 15.00
13 Dick Hall 4.00 10.00
14 Billy Hitchcock MG 6.00 15.00
15 Bob Johnson 4.00 10.00
16 Hobie Landrith 4.00 10.00
17 Charlie Lau 5.00 12.00
18 Mike McCormick 4.00 10.00
19 Dave McNally 8.00 20.00
20 John Miller 4.00 10.00
21 Stu Miller 4.00 10.00
22 Buster Narum 4.00 10.00
23 John Orsino/(Catching) 4.00 10.00
24 John Orsino 4.00 10.00
25 Milt Pappas 6.00 15.00
26 Boog Powell 8.00 20.00
27 Robin Roberts 8.00 20.00
28 Brooks Robinson 10.00 25.00
29 Bob Saverine 4.00 10.00
30 Al Smith 4.00 10.00
31 Russ Snyder 4.00 10.00
32 Wes Stock 4.00 10.00
33 Dean Stone 4.00 10.00
34 Fred Valentine 4.00 10.00

1964 Orioles Jay Publishing

This 12-card set of the Baltimore Orioles measures approximately 5" by 7". The fronts feature black-and-white posed player photos with the player's and team name printed below in the white border. These cards were packaged 12 to a packet. The backs are blank. The cards are unnumbered and checklisted below in alphabetical order.

COMPLETE SET (12) 15.00 40.00
1 Luis Aparicio 2.00 5.00
2 Steve Barber 1.25 3.00
3 Hank Bauer MG 1.50 4.00
4 Jackie Brandt 1.00 2.50
5 Chuck Estrada 1.00 2.50
6 Willie Kirkland 1.00 2.50
7 John Orsino 1.00 2.50
8 Milt Pappas 1.25 3.00
9 Boog Powell 2.00 5.00
10 Robin Roberts 2.00 5.00
11 Brooks Robinson 4.00 10.00
12 Norm Siebern 1.00 2.50

1964 Orioles Postcards

This 36-card set features black-and-white portraits of the Baltimore Orioles with white borders. The backs are blank. The cards are unnumbered and checklisted below in alphabetical order.

COMPLETE SET (36) 150.00 300.00
1 Jerry Adair 3.00 8.00
2 Luis Aparicio 6.00 15.00
3 Steve Barber/(Light ink autograph) 5.00 12.00
4 Steve Barber/(Dark ink autograph) 5.00 12.00
5 Hank Bauer MG 5.00 12.00
6 Frank Bertaina 3.00 8.00
7 Sam Bowens/(Closer head shot) 3.00 8.00
8 Sam Bowens 3.00 8.00
9 Jack Brandt 3.00 8.00
10 Harry Brecheen CO 5.00 12.00
11 Dick Brown 3.00 8.00
12 Wally Bunker 3.00 8.00
13 Chuck Estrada 3.00 8.00
14 Joe Gaines 3.00 8.00
15 Harvey Haddix 3.00 8.00
16 Dick Hall 3.00 8.00
17 Larry Haney 3.00 8.00
18 Billy Hunter CO 3.00 8.00
19 Lou Jackson 3.00 8.00
20 Bob Johnson 3.00 8.00
21 Willie Kirkland 3.00 8.00
22 Charley Lau 3.00 8.00
23 Mike McCormick 3.00 8.00
24 Dave McNally 5.00 12.00
25 Stu Miller 3.00 8.00
26 John Orsino 3.00 8.00
27 Milt Pappas 5.00 12.00
28 Boog Powell 6.00 15.00
29 Robin Roberts 6.00 15.00
30 Brooks Robinson 8.00 20.00
31 Earl Robinson 3.00 8.00
32 Bob Saverine 3.00 8.00
33 Norm Siebern 3.00 8.00
34 Russ Snyder 3.00 8.00
35 Wes Stock 3.00 8.00
36 Dave Vineyard 3.00 8.00

1965 Orioles Jay Publishing

This 12-card set of the Pittsburgh Pirates measures approximately 5" by 7". The fronts feature black-and-white posed player photos with the player's and team name printed below in the white border. These cards were packaged 12 to a packet. The backs are blank. The cards are unnumbered and checklisted below in alphabetical order.

COMPLETE SET (12) 12.50 30.00
1 Jerry Adair .75 2.00
2 Luis Aparicio 1.50 4.00
3 Steve Barber 1.00 2.50
4 Hank Bauer MG 1.25 3.00
5 Sam Bowens .75 2.00
6 Wally Bunker .75 2.00
7 John Orsino .75 2.00
8 Milt Pappas 1.00 2.50
9 Boog Powell 1.50 4.00
10 Brooks Robinson 2.50 6.00
11 Norm Siebern .75 2.00
12 Dave Vineyard .75 2.00

1965 Orioles Postcards

This 34-card set features black-and-white portraits of the Baltimore Orioles with white borders. The backs are blank. The cards are unnumbered and checklisted below in alphabetical order. Jim Palmer's postcard predates his Rookie Card.

COMPLETE SET (34) 150.00 300.00
1 Jerry Adair 3.00 8.00
2 Luis Aparicio 6.00 15.00
3 Steve Barber 5.00 12.00
4 Hank Bauer MG 5.00 12.00
5 Paul Blair 5.00 12.00
6 Curt Blefary 3.00 8.00
7 Sam Bowens 3.00 8.00
8 Jack Brandt 3.00 8.00
9 Harry Brecheen CO 4.00 10.00
10 Dick Brown 3.00 8.00
11 Wally Bunker 3.00 8.00
12 Sam Bowens 3.00 8.00
13 Dick Hall 3.00 8.00
14 Billy Hunter CO 4.00 10.00
15 Bob Johnson 3.00 8.00
16 Davey Johnson 6.00 15.00
17 Darold Knowles 3.00 8.00
18 Don Larsen 6.00 15.00
19 Charley Lau 3.00 8.00
20 Sherm Lollar CO 3.00 8.00
21 Dave McNally 6.00 15.00
22 John Miller 3.00 8.00
23 Stu Miller 3.00 8.00
24 John Orsino 3.00 8.00
25 Jim Palmer 12.50 30.00
26 Milt Pappas 5.00 12.00
27 Boog Powell 6.00 15.00
28 Robin Roberts 6.00 15.00
29 Brooks Robinson 10.00 25.00
30 Norm Siebern 3.00 8.00
31 Russ Snyder 3.00 8.00
32 Dave Vineyard 3.00 8.00
33 Carl Warwick 3.00 8.00
34 Gene Woodling CO 4.00 10.00

1966 Orioles Postcards

This 34-card set features black-and-white portraits of the Baltimore Orioles with white borders. The backs are blank. The cards are unnumbered and checklisted below in alphabetical order. Jim Palmer has a postcard in his Rookie Card year.

COMPLETE SET (34) 150.00 300.00
1 Luis Aparicio 6.00 15.00
2 Steve Barber 4.00 10.00
3 Frank Bertaina 3.00 8.00
4 Paul Blair 4.00 10.00
5 Curt Blefary 3.00 8.00
6 Sam Bowens 3.00 8.00
7 Gene Brabender 3.00 8.00
8 Harry Brecheen 3.00 8.00
9 Wally Bunker/(Looking forward) 3.00 8.00
10 Wally Bunker/(Looking to the side) 3.00 8.00
11 Camilo Carreon 3.00 8.00
12 Moe Drabowsky 3.00 8.00
13 Andy Etchebarren 3.00 8.00
14 Eddie Fisher 3.00 8.00
15 Dick Hall 3.00 8.00
16 Woodie Held 3.00 8.00
17 Billy Hunter 3.00 8.00
18 Bob Johnson 3.00 8.00
19 Davey Johnson 5.00 12.00
20 Charley Lau 3.00 8.00
21 Sherm Lollar/(Closer head photo) 3.00 8.00
22 Sherm Lollar 3.00 8.00
23 Dave McNally 4.00 10.00
24 John Miller 3.00 8.00
25 Stu Miller 3.00 8.00
26 Jim Palmer 6.00 15.00
27 Boog Powell 6.00 15.00
28 Brooks Robinson 8.00 20.00
29 Frank Robinson 8.00 20.00
30 Vic Roznovsky 3.00 8.00
31 Billy Short 3.00 8.00
32 Russ Snyder 3.00 8.00
33 Eddie Watt 3.00 8.00
34 Gene Woodling 3.00 8.00

1967-69 Orioles Postcards

This 107-card set features black-and-white portraits of the Baltimore Orioles with white borders. The backs are blank. Some of the cards carry facsimile autographs. The cards are unnumbered and checklisted below in alphabetical order.

COMPLETE SET (107) 300.00 600.00
1 Mike Adamson 2.00 5.00
2 Luis Aparicio 4.00 10.00
3 George Bamberger CO 2.00 5.00
Larger head shot
4 George Bamberger CO 2.00 5.00
5 Steve Barber 2.00 5.00
6 Hank Bauer MG 3.00 8.00
7 Fred Beene 2.00 5.00
8 Mark Belanger 2.50 6.00
9 Mark Belanger 2.50 6.00
Closer head shot
10 Mark Belanger 2.50 6.00
Artist's rendition
11 Frank Bertaina 2.00 5.00
12 Frank Bertaina 2.00 5.00
Lighter portrait
13 Paul Blair 2.50 6.00
Lighter looking to left
14 Paul Blair 2.50 6.00
Darker looking to left
15 Paul Blair 2.50 6.00
Looking straight ahead
16 Curt Blefary 2.00 5.00
17 Sam Bowens 2.00 5.00
18 Gene Brabender 2.00 5.00
19 Harry Brecheen CO 2.00 5.00
20 Don Buford 2.00 5.00
Looking straight ahead
21 Don Buford 2.00 5.00
Dark closer head shot
22 Don Buford 2.00 5.00
Lighter closer head shot
23 Don Buford 2.00 5.00
Name in bold print
24 Wally Bunker 2.00 5.00
Dark portrait
25 Wally Bunker 2.00 5.00
Lighter protrait
26 Terry Crowley 2.00 5.00
27 Mike Cuellar 3.00 8.00
Light portrait
28 Mike Cuellar 3.00 8.00
Dark portrait
29 Clay Dalrymple 2.00 5.00
30 Bill Dillman 2.00 5.00
31 Moe Drabowsky 2.00 5.00
Looking to the left
32 Moe Drabowsky 2.00 5.00
Looking straight ahead
33 Mike Epstein 2.00 5.00
34 Andy Etchebarren 2.00 5.00
Looking to the left
35 Andy Etchebarren 2.00 5.00
Cream colored paper
36 Andy Etchebarren 2.00 5.00
Clearer looking to left
37 Andy Etchebarren 2.00 5.00
Looking straight ahead
38 Chico Fernandez 2.00 5.00
39 Eddie Fisher 2.00 5.00
40 Bobby Floyd 2.00 5.00
41 Jim Frey CO 2.00 5.00
42 Dick Hall 2.00 5.00
43 Larry Haney 2.00 5.00
44 Larry Haney 2.00 5.00
Larger portrait
45 Jim Hardin 2.00 5.00
46 Elrod Hendricks 2.00 5.00
Looking straight ahead
47 Elrod Hendricks 2.00 5.00
Looking slightly to the left
48 Elrod Hendricks 2.00 5.00
Closer looking to the left photo
49 Vern Hoscheit CO 2.00 5.00
50 Bruce Howard 2.00 5.00
51 Billy Hunter CO 2.00 5.00
Looking to the left
52 Bill Hunter CO 2.00 5.00
Darker looking to left
53 Billy Hunter/(Autographed and looking straight ah
2.00 5.00
54 Bob Johnson 2.00 5.00
55 Dave Johnson 3.00 8.00
Autographed artist's version
56 Davey Johnson 3.00 8.00
57 Dave Johnson 3.00 8.00
Darker portrait
58 Charlie Lau 2.00 5.00
59 Dave Leonhard 2.00 5.00
Autographed
60 Dave Leonhard 2.00 5.00
Name is spelled as Leonard
61 Dave Leonhard 2.00 5.00
Closer head view
62 Dave Leonhard 2.00 5.00
Different cap
63 Sherm Lollar CO 2.00 5.00
64 Marcelino Lopez 2.00 5.00
65 Dave May 2.00 5.00
66 Dave May 2.00 5.00
Closer head shot
67 Dave McNally 3.00 8.00
Looking to left
68 Dave McNally 3.00 8.00
Looking straight ahead
69 Stu Miller 2.00 5.00
70 John Morris 2.00 5.00
71 Curt Motton 2.00 5.00
Light portrait
72 Curt Motton 2.00 5.00
Darker portrait
73 Roger Nelson 2.00 5.00
74 John O'Donoghue 2.00 5.00
75 Jim Palmer 6.00 15.00
Looking to the right
76 Jim Palmer 6.00 15.00
Head turned straight
77 Jim Palmer 6.00 15.00
Looking to the left
78 Tom Phoebus 2.00 5.00
79 Tom Phoebus 2.00 5.00
Darker portrait
80 Tom Phoebus 2.00 5.00
Lighter portrait
81 Boog Powell 4.00 10.00
Light portrait
82 Boog Powell 4.00 10.00
Larger head shot
83 Boog Powell 4.00 10.00
Lighter portrait
84 Merv Rettenmund 2.00 5.00
85 Merv Rettenmund 2.00 5.00
Darker portrait
86 Merv Rettenmund 2.00 5.00
Lighter portrait
87 Pete Richert 2.00 5.00
Not smiling
88 Pete Richert 2.00 5.00
Smiling
89 Brooks Robinson 6.00 15.00
90 Brooks Robinson 6.00 15.00
Darker autographed version
91 Brooks Robinson 6.00 15.00
Lighter portrait
92 Brooks Robinson 6.00 15.00
Shows mail cancellation
93 Brooks Robinson 6.00 15.00
Farther away head shot
94 Frank Robinson 6.00 15.00
95 Vic Roznovsky 2.00 5.00
96 Chico Salmon 2.00 5.00
97 Ray Scarborough CO 2.00 5.00
98 Al Severinsen 2.00 5.00
99 Russ Snyder 2.00 5.00
100 George Staller CO 2.00 5.00
101 Fred Valentine 2.00 5.00
102 Eddie Watt 2.00 5.00
103 Ed Watt 2.00 5.00
Autographed
104 Earl Weaver MG 4.00 10.00
105 Gene Woodling CO 2.00 5.00
Looking straight ahead
106 Gene Woodling CO 2.00 5.00
Autographed and darker
107 Gene Woodling CO 2.00 5.00
Autographed and lighter

1968 Orioles Dexter Press/Coca Cola Postcards

This 12-card set features posed borderless color photos of the Baltimore Orioles printed on postcard-size cards. The backs carry the player's biography and a facsimile autograph with a Dexter press serial number.

COMPLETE SET (12) 40.00 80.00
1 Mark Belanger 2.50 6.00
2 Paul Blair 2.50 6.00
3 Curt Blefary 2.00 5.00
4 Don Buford 2.00 5.00
5 Moe Drabowsky 2.00 5.00
6 Andy Etchebarren 2.00 5.00
7 Dave Johnson 4.00 10.00
8 Dave McNally 3.00 8.00
9 Tom Phoebus 2.00 5.00
10 Boog Powell 4.00 10.00
11 Brooks Robinson 6.00 15.00
12 Frank Robinson 6.00 15.00

1969 Orioles Postcards Color

This three-card set features borderless color portraits of the Baltimore Orioles printed on postcard size cards. The backs are blank. The cards are unnumbered and checklisted below in alphabetical order.

COMPLETE SET (3) 10.00 25.00
1 Bob Grich 3.00 8.00
2 Dave Johnson 3.00 8.00
3 Brooks Robinson 6.00 15.00

1970 Orioles Black and White

This 15-piece set features blank-backed, white-bordered, 8" X 10" black-and-white photos. The player's name appears in black within the bottom border. A facsimile autograph is printed across the photo. The word "Tadder" is pasted into photos at lower right. Photos are unnumbered and checklisted below in alphabetical order.

COMPLETE SET (15) 20.00 50.00
1 Mark Belanger 2.00 5.00
2 Don Buford 1.25 3.00
3 Mike Cuellar 2.00 5.00
4 Clay Dalrymple 1.25 3.00
5 Andy Etchebarren 1.25 3.00
6 Dave Johnson 2.50 6.00
7 Dave McNally 2.00 5.00
8 Curt Motton 1.25 3.00
9 Jim Palmer 4.00 10.00
10 Boog Powell 2.50 6.00
11 Merv Rettenmund 1.25 3.00
12 Frank Robinson 4.00 10.00
13 Chico Salmon 1.25 3.00
14 Eddie Watt 1.25 3.00
15 Earl Weaver MG 2.50 6.00

1970 Orioles Matchbooks

These matchbooks are known to be issued by Universal Match and are known to be an 24 matchbook set. The front shows a portrait of the featured player in an team logo while the reverse has the Baltimore Oriole mascot. Since these are unnumbered, we have sequenced them in alphabetical order and any help in finishing this checklist is appreciated.

COMPLETE SET (24) 100.00 175.00
NNO Paul Blair 3.00 8.00
NNO Don Buford 3.00 8.00
NNO Mike Cuellar 3.00 8.00
NNO Clay Dalrymple 3.00 8.00
NNO Andy Etchebarren 3.00 8.00
NNO Bobby Floyd 3.00 8.00
NNO Dick Hall 3.00 8.00
NNO Jim Hardin 3.00 8.00
NNO Elrod Hendricks 3.00 8.00
NNO Dave Johnson 3.00 8.00
NNO Dave Leonhard 3.00 8.00
NNO Dave McNally 3.00 8.00
NNO Curt Motton 3.00 8.00
NNO Jim Palmer 6.00 15.00
NNO Tom Phoebus 3.00 8.00
NNO Boog Powell 10.00 25.00
NNO Merv Rettenmund 3.00 8.00
NNO Pete Richert 3.00 8.00
NNO Brooks Robinson 20.00 50.00
NNO Frank Robinson 15.00 40.00
NNO Chico Salmon 3.00 8.00
NNO Eddie Watt 3.00 8.00
NNO Earl Weaver MG 3.00 8.00

1970 Orioles Postcards

This 32-card set features color portraits of the Baltimore Orioles with white borders and printed on postcard size cards. The backs are blank. The cards are unnumbered and checklisted below in alphabetical order. According to information published at the time, these cards could be ordered from the Orioles at 10 cents each, 12 cards for a dollar or $2.50 for the whole set.

COMPLETE SET (32) 75.00 150.00
1 George Bamberger CO 1.50 4.00
2 Mark Belanger 2.00 5.00
3 Paul Blair 2.50 6.00
4 Don Buford 1.50 4.00
5 Terry Crowley 1.50 4.00
6 Mike Cuellar 2.50 6.00
7 Clay Dalrymple 1.50 4.00
8 Moe Drabowsky 1.50 4.00
9 Andy Etchebarren 1.50 4.00
10 Jim Frey CO 1.50 4.00
11 Dick Hall 1.50 4.00
12 Jim Hardin 1.50 4.00
13 Elrod Hendricks/(No buttons showing) 1.50 4.00
14 Elrod Hendricks/(One button showing) 1.50 4.00
15 Billy Hunter CO 1.50 4.00
16 Dave Johnson 2.50 6.00
17 Dave Leonhard 1.50 4.00
18 Marcelino Lopez 1.50 4.00
19 Dave McNally 2.50 6.00
20 Dave McNally/(Darker portrait) 2.50 6.00
21 Curt Motton 1.50 4.00
22 Jim Palmer 5.00 12.00
23 Tom Phoebus 1.50 4.00
24 Boog Powell 3.00 8.00
25 Merv Rettenmund 1.50 4.00
26 Pete Richert 1.50 4.00
27 Brooks Robinson 5.00 12.00
28 Frank Robinson 5.00 12.00
29 Chico Salmon 1.50 4.00
30 George Staller CO 1.50 4.00
31 Eddie Watt 1.50 4.00
32 Earl Weaver MG 3.00 8.00

1971 Orioles Aldana

This crude 12 card blank backed cards are credited to artist Carl Aldana. A drawing of the player along with his last name is on the front. There are two different Brooks Robinson cards in this set.

COMPLETE SET (12) 75.00 150.00
1 Mark Belanger 1.00 2.50
2 Paul Blair .75 2.00
3 Mike Cuellar 1.25 3.00
4 Ellie Hendricks .75 2.00
5 Dave Johnson 2.00 5.00
6 Dave McNally 1.25 3.00
7 Jim Palmer 6.00 15.00
8 Boog Powell 2.00 5.00
9 Brooks Robinson 15.00 40.00
Uniform number visible on back
10 Brooks Robinson 15.00 40.00
Facing front
11 Frank Robinson 12.50 30.00
12 Earl Weaver MG 3.00 8.00

1971 Orioles Champions

Subtitled "Pictures of Champions," this 16-card set measures 2 1/8" by 2 3/4". Since the card stock is orange, the close-up photos on the fronts are orange-tinted and have orange borders. The orange backs have the jersey number, player's name and the set subtitle. The cards are unnumbered and checklisted below in alphabetical order.

COMPLETE SET (16) 75.00 150.00
1 Mark Belanger 4.00 10.00
2 Don Buford 2.50 6.00
3 Mike Cuellar 4.00 10.00
4 Andy Etchebarren 2.50 6.00
5 Dick Hall 2.50 6.00
6 Ellie Hendricks 2.50 6.00
7 Dave Johnson 5.00 12.00
8 Dave Leonhard 2.50 6.00
9 Dave May 2.50 6.00
10 Dave McNally 4.00 10.00
11 Jim Palmer 8.00 20.00
12 Pete Richert 2.50 6.00
13 Brooks Robinson 15.00 40.00
14 Frank Robinson 12.50 30.00
15 Eddie Watt 2.50 6.00
16 Earl Weaver MG 5.00 12.00

1971 Orioles Postcards

This 30-card set features color portraits of the Baltimore Orioles with white borders and printed on postcard size cards. The backs are blank. The cards are unnumbered and checklisted below in alphabetical order.

COMPLETE SET (30) 75.00 150.00
1 George Bamberger CO 1.50 4.00
2 Mark Belanger 2.00 5.00
3 Paul Blair 2.50 6.00
4 Don Buford 1.50 4.00
5 Mike Cuellar 2.50 6.00
6 Clay Dalrymple 1.50 4.00
7 Jerry DaVanon 1.50 4.00
8 Pat Dobson 2.00 5.00
9 Tom Dukes 1.50 4.00
10 Andy Etchebarren 1.50 4.00
11 Jim Frey CO 1.50 4.00
12 Dick Hall 1.50 4.00
13 Jim Hardin 1.50 4.00
14 Elrod Hendricks 1.50 4.00
15 Billy Hunter CO 1.50 4.00
16 Grant Jackson 1.50 4.00
17 Dave Johnson 2.50 6.00
18 Dave McNally 2.50 6.00
19 Curt Motton 1.50 4.00
20 Jim Palmer 4.00 10.00
21 Boog Powell 3.00 8.00
22 Merv Rettenmund 1.50 4.00
23 Pete Richert 1.50 4.00
24 Brooks Robinson 4.00 10.00
25 Frank Robinson 4.00 10.00
26 Chico Salmon 1.50 4.00
27 Tom Shopay 1.50 4.00
28 George Staller CO 1.50 4.00
29 Ed Watt 1.50 4.00
30 Earl Weaver MG 3.00 8.00

1972 Orioles DMV

The 1972 Baltimore Orioles Police/Safety set was issued on a thin unperforated cardboard sheet measuring 12 1/2" by 8". When the players are cut into individual cards, they measure approximately 2 1/2" by 4". The color of the sheet is pale yellow, and consequently the black and white borderless player photos have a similar cast. The player's name, position, and team name appear below the pictures. The backs have different safety messages sponsored by the Office of Traffic Safety, D.C. Department of Motor Vehicles. The cards are unnumbered and checklisted below in alphabetical order.

COMPLETE SET (10) 15.00 40.00
1 Mark Belanger 1.50 4.00
2 Paul Blair 1.25 3.00
3 Don Buford 1.25 3.00
4 Mike Cuellar 1.25 3.00
5 Dave Johnson 1.50 4.00
6 Dave McNally 1.50 4.00
7 Boog Powell 2.00 5.00
8 Brooks Robinson 4.00 10.00
9 Merv Rettenmund .75 2.00
10 Earl Weaver MG 2.00 5.00

1972 Orioles Postcards

This 33-card set features color portraits of the Baltimore Orioles with white borders and printed on postcard size cards. The backs are blank. The cards are unnumbered and checklisted below in alphabetical order.

COMPLETE SET (33) 75.00 150.00
1 Doyle Alexander 1.50 4.00
2 George Bamberger CO 1.50 4.00
3 Don Baylor 2.50 6.00
4 Mark Belanger 2.00 5.00
5 Paul Blair 2.50 6.00
6 Dave Boswell 1.50 4.00
7 Don Buford 1.50 4.00
8 Richie Coggins 1.50 4.00
9 Terry Crowley 1.50 4.00
10 Mike Cuellar 2.50 6.00
11 Pat Dobson 1.50 4.00
12 Andy Etchebarren 1.50 4.00
13 Jim Frey CO 1.50 4.00
14 Bobby Grich 2.50 6.00
15 Roric Harrison 1.50 4.00
16 Elrod Hendricks 1.50 4.00
17 Billy Hunter CO 1.50 4.00
18 Grant Jackson 1.50 4.00
19 Dave Johnson 2.50 6.00
20 Dave Leonhard 1.50 4.00
21 Dave McNally 2.50 6.00
22 Johnny Oates 2.00 5.00
23 Jim Palmer 5.00 12.00
24 Boog Powell 3.00 8.00
25 John Boog Powell 3.00 8.00
26 Merv Rettenmund 1.50 4.00
27 Brooks Robinson 5.00 12.00
28 Chico Salmon 1.50 4.00
29 Mickey Scott 1.50 4.00
30 Tom Shopay 1.50 4.00
31 George Staller CO 1.50 4.00
32 Eddie Watt 1.50 4.00
33 Earl Weaver MG 3.00 8.00

1973 Orioles Johnny Pro

This 25-card set measures approximately 4 1/4" by 7 1/4" and features members of the 1973 Baltimore Orioles. The cards were designed to be pushed-out in a style similar to the 1964 Topps Stand Ups. The sides of the cards have a small advertisement for Johnny Pro Enterprises and even gives a phone number where they could have been reached. Oddly, the Orlando Pena card was not available in a die-cut version. The cards have the player's photo against a distinctive solid green background. The cards are blank backed. There are several variations within the set; the complete set price below includes all of the variation cards. The set is checklisted in order by uniform number. According to informed sources, there were 15,000 sets produced.

COMPLETE SET (25) 100.00 200.00
1 Al Bumbry 1.50 4.00
2 Rich Coggins 1.50 4.00
3A Bobby Grich/(Fielding) 3.00 8.00
3B Bobby Grich/(Batting) 12.50 30.00
4 Earl Weaver 4.00 10.00
5A Brooks Robinson/(Fielding) 8.00 20.00
5B Brooks Robinson/(Batting) 12.50 40.00
6 Paul Blair 2.50 6.00
7 Mark Belanger 2.50 6.00
8 Andy Etchebarren 1.50 4.00
10 Elrod Hendricks 1.50 4.00
11 Terry Crowley 1.50 4.00
12 Tommy Davis 2.50 6.00
13 Doyle Alexander 2.50 6.00
14 Merv Rettenmund 1.50 4.00
15 Frank Baker 1.50 4.00
16 Dave McNally 2.50 6.00
21 Larry Brown 1.50 4.00
22A Jim Palmer 8.00 20.00
22B Jim Palmer/(Pitching) 12.50 30.00
23 Grant Jackson 1.50 4.00
25 Don Baylor 3.00 8.00
26 John(Boog) Powell 5.00 12.00
27 Orlando Pena/(NOT die-cut) 1.50 4.00
32 Earl Williams 1.50 4.00
34 Bob Reynolds 1.50 4.00
35 Mike Cuellar 2.50 6.00
39 Eddie Watt 1.50 4.00

1973-74 Orioles Postcards

These 43 cards feature color portraits of the Baltimore Orioles with white borders and printed on postcard size cards. The backs are blank. The cards are unnumbered and checklisted below in alphabetical order.

COMPLETE SET (43) 30.00 60.00
1 Doyle Alexander/(Dark) .40 1.00
2 Doyle Alexander/(Light) .40 1.00
3 Frank Baker .40 1.00
4 George Bamberger CO .40 1.00
5 Don Baylor 1.00 2.50
6 Mark Belanger .75 2.00
7 Paul Blair .60 1.50
8 Larry Brown .40 1.00
9 Al Bumbry .40 1.00
10 Al Bumbry .40 1.00
11 Enos Cabell .40 1.00
12 Rich Coggins .40 1.00
13 Terry Crowley .40 1.00
14 Jim Fuller .40 1.00
15 Wayne Garland .40 1.00
16 Mike Cuellar .60 1.50
17 Tommy Davis .60 1.50
18 Andy Etchebarren .40 1.00
19 Jim Frey CO .40 1.00
20 Bob Grich 1.00 2.50
21 Ross Grimsley .40 1.00
22 Roric Harrison .40 1.00
23 Ellie Hendricks .40 1.00
24 Don Hood .40 1.00
25 Billy Hunter CO .40 1.00
26 Grant Jackson .40 1.00
27 Jesse Jefferson .40 1.00
28 Dave McNally/(Looking right) .75 2.00
29 Dave McNally/(Looking left) .75 2.00
30 Johnny Oates .40 1.00
31 Jim Palmer/(Autographed) 2.00 5.00
32 Jim Palmer/(Eyes looking left) 2.00 5.00
33 Orlando Pena .40 1.00
34 Boog Powell 1.25 3.00
35 Merv Rettenmund .40 1.00
36 Bob Reynolds .40 1.00
37 Brooks Robinson 2.00 5.00
38 Mickey Scott .40 1.00
39 George Staller .40 1.00
40 Eddie Watt .40 1.00
41 Earl Weaver MG 1.00 2.50
42 Earl Williams/(Smiling) .40 1.00
43 Earl Williams/(Non-smiling) .40 1.00

1975 Orioles Postcards

This 30-card set of the Baltimore Orioles features player photos on postcard-size cards. The cards are unnumbered and checklisted below in alphabetical order.

COMPLETE SET (30) 12.50 30.00
1 Doyle Alexander .30 .75
2 George Bamberger CO .30 .75
3 Don Baylor .75 2.00
4 Mark Belanger .30 .75
5 Paul Blair .40 1.00
6 Al Bumbry .30 .75
7 Mike Cuellar .40 1.00
8 Tommy Davis .40 1.00
9 Doug DeCinces .60 1.50
10 Dave Duncan .30 .75
11 Jim Frey CO .30 .75
12 Wayne Garland .30 .75
13 Bob Grich .30 .75
14 Ross Grimsley .30 .75
15 Elrod Hendricks .30 .75
16 Billy Hunter CO .30 .75
17 Grant Jackson .30 .75
18 Jesse Jefferson .30 .75
19 Dave Johnson .30 .75
20 Lee May .40 1.00
21 Tim Nordbrook .30 .75
22 Jim Northrup .30 .75
23 Jim Palmer 1.50 4.00
24 Bob Reynolds .30 .75
25 Brooks Robinson 2.00 5.00
26 Tom Shopay .30 .75
27 Ken Singleton .60 1.50
28 George Staller CO .30 .75
29 Mike Torrez .30 .75
30 Earl Weaver MG .75 2.00

1976 Orioles English's Chicken Lids

This set features round black-and-white player photos and measures approximately 8 1/4" in diameter. The backs are blank. The cards are unnumbered and checklisted below in alphabetical order; however, the checklist is incomplete. Cuellar, Holtzman and Palmer are all the large size cards. Ten other cards were issued and those lids measure 7" in diameter.

COMPLETE SET 40.00 80.00
1 Mark Belanger 2.50 6.00
2 Paul Blair 2.00 5.00
3 Al Bumbry 2.00 5.00
4 Mike Cuellar 2.00 5.00
5 Dave Duncan 2.50 6.00
6 Bobby Grich 2.00 5.00
7 Ross Grimsley 2.00 5.00
8 Ellie Hendricks 2.00 5.00
9 Ken Holtzman 2.00 5.00
10 Lee May 2.50 6.00
11 Jim Palmer 5.00 12.00
12 Brooks Robinson 5.00 12.00
13 Ken Singleton 2.50 6.00

1976 Orioles Postcards

This 38-card set of the Baltimore Orioles features glossy player photos with white borders on postcard-size cards. The cards are unnumbered and checklisted below in alphabetical order. An important card in this set is of Reggie Jackson, during his only season as an Oriole and one of the few Jackson Oriole cards available.

COMPLETE SET (38) 15.00 40.00
1 Doyle Alexander .30 .75
2 Bob Bailor .30 .75
3 George Bamberger CO .30 .75
4 Mark Belanger .60 1.50
5 Paul Blair .30 .75
6 Al Bumbry .30 .75
7 Terry Crowley .30 .75
8 Mike Cuellar .40 1.00
9 Doug DeCinces .40 1.00
10 Rick Dempsey .40 1.00
11 Dave Duncan .30 .75
12 Mike Flanagan .30 .75
13 Jim Frey CO .30 .75
14 Wayne Garland .30 .75
15 Bobby Grich .40 1.00
16 Ross Grimsley .30 .75
17 Tommy Harper .30 .75
18 Elrod Hendricks .30 .75
19 Fred Holdsworth .30 .75
20 Bill Hunter CO .30 .75
21 Grant Jackson .30 .75
22 Reggie Jackson 4.00 10.00
23 Tippy Martinez .30 .75
24 Lee May .40 1.00
25 Rudy May .30 .75
26 Dyar Miller .30 .75
27 Andres Mora .30 .75
28 Tony Muser .30 .75
29 Tim Nordbrook .30 .75

30 Dave Pagan .30 .75
31 Jim Palmer 1.50 4.00
32 Cal Ripken Sr. CO .30 .75
33 Brooks Robinson 1.50 4.00
34 Brooks Robinson 1.50 4.00
Triangle in lower right corner
35 Tom Shopay .30 .75
36 Ken Singleton .40 1.00
37 Royle Stillman .30 .75
38 Earl Weaver MG .75 2.00

1977 Orioles Photo Album

Issued as a photo album, but with easily perforated photos, which measure approximately 5 1/4" by 8 1/2" when seperated, these pictures feature members of the Baltimore Orioles. Since the photos were issued in alphabetical order, we have notated these photos in that order as well. This set is noticable for one of the very first appearences of Eddie Murray.

COMPLETE SET 10.00 25.00
1 Earl Weaver MG .60 1.50
2 George Bamberger CO .30 .75
3 Jim Frey CO .30 .75
4 Cal Ripken Sr CO .30 .75
5 Mark Belanger .40 1.00
6 Al Bumbry .30 .75
7 Rich Dauer .30 .75
8 Doug DeCinces .40 1.00
9 Rick Dempsey .40 1.00
10 Dick Drago .30 .75
11 Mike Flanagan .30 .75
12 Kiko Garcia .30 .75
13 Ross Grimsley .30 .75
14 Pat Kelly .30 .75
15 Elliott Maddox .30 .75
16 Dennis Martinez .40 1.00
17 Tippy Martinez .30 .75
18 Lee May .40 1.00
19 Rudy May .30 .75
20 Scott McGregor .30 .75
21 Andres Mora .30 .75
22 Eddie Murray 3.00 8.00
23 Tony Muser .30 .75
24 Jim Palmer 1.25 3.00
25 Brooks Robinson 1.25 3.00
26 Tom Shopay .30 .75
27 Ken Singleton .40 1.00
28 Dave Skaggs .30 .75
29 Billy Smith .30 .75
30 Dave Criscione .30 .75
31 Ken Rudolph .30 .75

1977 Orioles Postcards

This 22-card set features glossy color portraits of the Baltimore Orioles with white borders and measures approximately 3 3/8" by 5 1/4". The backs are blank. The cards are unnumbered and checklisted below in alphabetical order. The Eddie Murray postcard predates his Rookie Card.

COMPLETE SET (22) 10.00 25.00
1 Mark Belanger .40 1.00
2 Al Bumbry .30 .75
3 Rich Dauer .30 .75
4 Doug DeCinces .40 1.00
5 Rick Dempsey .40 1.00
6 Kiko Garcia .30 .75
7 Ross Grimsley .30 .75
8 Larry Harlow .30 .75
9 Fred Holdsworth .30 .75
10 Bill Hunter CO .30 .75
11 Pat Kelly .30 .75
12 Dennis Martinez .75 2.00
13 Tippy Martinez .30 .75
14 Scott McGregor .30 .75
15 Eddie Murray 3.00 8.00
16 Brooks Robinson/(Light background) 1.50 4.00
17 Brooks Robinson/(Dark background) 1.50 4.00
18 Tom Shopay .30 .75
19 Ken Singleton .40 1.00
20 Dave Skaggs .30 .75
21 Billy Smith .30 .75
22 Earl Weaver MG .75 2.00

1978 Orioles Postcards

This 34-card set features glossy color portraits of the Baltimore Orioles with white borders and measures approximately 3 3/8" by 5 1/4". The backs are blank. The cards are unnumbered and checklisted below in alphabetical order.

COMPLETE SET (34) 12.50 30.00
1 Mark Belanger .40 1.00
2 Nelson Briles .30 .75
3 Al Bumbry .40 1.00
4 Terry Crowley .30 .75
5 Rich Dauer .30 .75
6 Doug DeCinces .40 1.00
7 Rick Dempsey .40 1.00
8 Mike Flanagan .60 1.50
9 Jim Frey CO .30 .75
10 Kiko Garcia .30 .75
11 Larry Harlow .30 .75
12 Ellie Hendricks .30 .75
13 Pat Kelly .30 .75
14 Joe Kerrigan .30 .75
15 Carlos Lopez .30 .75
16 Dennis Martinez .75 2.00
17 Tippy Martinez .30 .75
18 Lee May .40 1.00
19 Scott McGregor .30 .75
20 Ray Miller CO .30 .75
21 Andres Mora .30 .75
22 Eddie Murray 1.25 3.00
23 Tony Muser .30 .75
24 Jim Palmer 1.25 3.00
25 Cal Ripken Sr. CO .30 .75
26 Frank Robinson CO .75 2.00
27 Gary Roenicke .30 .75
28 Ken Singleton .40 1.00
29 Dave Skaggs .30 .75
30 Billy Smith .30 .75
31 Don Stanhouse .30 .75
32 Earl Stephenson .30 .75
33 Tim Stoddard .40 1.00
34 Earl Weaver MG .75 2.00

1979 Orioles Postcards

This 18-card set features glossy color portraits of the Baltimore Orioles with white borders and measures approximately 3 3/8" by 5 1/4". The backs are blank. The cards are unnumbered and checklisted below in alphabetical order.

COMPLETE SET (18) 6.00 15.00
1 Benny Ayala .30 .75
2 Al Bumbry .30 .75
3 Rich Dauer .30 .75
4 Doug DeCinces .40 1.00
5 Rick Dempsey .40 1.00
6 Mike Flanagan .40 1.00
7 Jim Frey CO .30 .75
8 Joe Kerrigan .30 .75
9 John Lowenstein .30 .75
10 Scott McGregor .30 .75
11 Ray Miller CO .30 .75
12 Eddie Murray 1.25 3.00
13 Jim Palmer 1.25 3.00
14 Sammy Stewart/(Red trim) .30 .75
15 Sammy Stewart/(Orange trim) .30 .75
16 Steve Stone .60 1.50
17 Earl Weaver MG .75 2.00
18 The Bird(Mascot) .30 .75

1980 Orioles Postcards

This 24-card blank-backed set features glossy color portraits of the Baltimore Orioles with white borders and measures approximately 3 3/8" by 5 1/4". The cards are unnumbered and checklisted below in alphabetical order. Any of these cards were available from the team for 10 cents each.

COMPLETE SET (24) 8.00 20.00
1 Benny Ayala .20 .50
2 Mark Belanger .20 .50
3 Al Bumbry
4 Terry Crowley .20 .50
5 Rich Dauer
6 Doug DeCinces .30 .75
7 Rick Dempsey
8 Mike Flanagan .30 .75
9 Dave Ford .20 .50
10 Kiko Garcia .20 .50
11 Dan Graham .20 .50
12 Ellie Hendricks .20 .50
13 Pat Kelly .20 .50
14 Joe Kerrigan .20 .50
15 John Lowenstein .20 .50
16 Dennis Martinez
17 Tippy Martinez
18 Lee May
19 Scott McGregor .20 .50
20 Ray Miller .20 .50
21 Eddie Murray 1.50 4.00
22 Jim Palmer 1.25 3.00
23 Cal Ripken Sr. CO
24 Frank Robinson CO
25 Gary Roenicke .20 .50
26 Lenn Sakata .20 .50
27 Ken Singleton .30 .75
27 Tim Stoddard .30 .75
28 Steve Stone .30 .75
29 Earl Weaver .60 1.50
30 The Bird(Mascot) .20 .50
31 Memorial Stadium .20 .50

1981 Orioles 1966 Franchise

This 32 card standard-size set was issued by the Franchise of Bel Air, Maryland. This set commemorated the 15th anniversary of the first Orioles World Championship.

COMPLETE SET 25.00 60.00
1 Title Card .75 2.00
2 Team Card .75 2.00
3 Luis Aparicio 1.50 4.00
4 Steve Barber 1.00 2.50
5 Hank Bauer MG 1.00 2.50
6 Paul Blair 1.25 3.00
7 Curt Blefary .75 2.00
8 Sam Bowens .75 2.00
9 Gene Brabender .75 2.00
10 Harry Brecheen CO .75 2.00
11 Wally Bunker .75 2.00
12 Moe Drabowsky .75 2.00
13 Andy Etchebarren .75 2.00
14 Eddie Fisher .75 2.00
15 Dick Hall .75 2.00
16 Larry Haney .75 2.00
17 Woodie Held .75 2.00
18 Billy Hunter CO .75 2.00
19 Bob Johnson .75 2.00
20 Dave Johnson 1.25 3.00
21 Sherm Lollar CO .75 2.00
22 Dave McNally 1.00 2.50
23 John Miller .75 2.00
24 Stu Miller .75 2.00
25 Jim Palmer 2.50 6.00
26 John (Boog) Powell 1.50 4.00
27 Brooks Robinson 2.50 6.00
28 Frank Robinson 2.50 6.00
29 Vic Roznovsky .75 2.00
30 Russ Snyder .80 2.00
31 Eddie Watt .75 2.00
32 Gene Woodling CO .75 2.00

1981 Orioles Postcards

This 25-card set features glossy color portraits of the Baltimore Orioles with white borders and measures approximately 3 1/2" by 5 1/4". The backs carry a postcard format with Memorial Stadium address. The cards are unnumbered and checklisted below in alphabetical order. An early major league Cal Ripken Jr. card is in this set.

COMPLETE SET (25) 12.50 30.00
1 Benny Ayala .20 .50
2 Al Bumbry .20 .50
3 Terry Crowley .20 .50
4 Rich Dauer .20 .50
5 Rick Dempsey .30 .75
6 Jim Dwyer .20 .50
7 Elrod Hendricks .20 .50
8 Wayne Krenchicki .20 .50
9 Dennis Martinez .40 1.00
10 Tippy Martinez .20 .50
11 Ray Miller .20 .50
12 Jose Morales .20 .50
13 Eddie Murray 1.25 3.00
14 Jim Palmer 1.00 2.50
15 Cal Ripken Jr. 8.00 20.00
16 Ralph Rowe .20 .50
17 Lenn Sakata .20 .50
18 Jeff Schneider .20 .50
19 John Shelby .20 .50
20 Ken Singleton .30 .75
21 Sammy Stewart .20 .50
22 Steve Stone .20 .50
23 Jimmy Williams .20 .50
24 The Bird(Mascot) .20 .50
25 Memorial Stadium .20 .50

1982 Orioles Postcards

This six-card set features glossy color portraits of the Baltimore Orioles with white borders and measures approximately 3 1/2" by 5 1/4". The backs carry a postcard format and Memorial Stadium address. The cards are unnumbered and checklisted below in alphabetical order. Cal Ripken Jr. has a card in his Rookie Card season.

COMPLETE SET (6) 3.00 8.00
1 Rich Dauer .20 .50
2 Mike Flanagan .40 1.00
3 Ross Grimsley .20 .50
4 Cal Ripken Jr. 5.00 12.00
5 Ken Singleton .40 1.00
6 Sammy Stewart .20 .50

1983 Orioles Postcards

This 33-card set of the Baltimore Orioles measures 3 1/2" by 5 1/8" and features white-bordered, color player portraits with the player's name in the bottom margin. The backs carry a postcard format. The cards are unnumbered and checklisted below in alphabetical order.

COMPLETE SET (33) 6.00 15.00
1 Joe Altobelli MG .20 .50
2 Benny Ayala .20 .50
3 Mike Boddicker .40 1.00
4 Bob Bonner .20 .50
5 Al Bumbry .20 .50
6 Todd Cruz .20 .50
7 Rich Dauer .20 .50
8 Storm Davis .30 .75
9 Rick Dempsey .30 .75
10 Jim Dwyer .20 .50
11 Mike Flanagan .20 .50
12 Dan Ford .20 .50
13 Ellie Hendricks CO .20 .50
14 John Lowenstein .20 .50
15 Dennis Martinez .40 1.00
16 Tippy Martinez .20 .50
17 Scott McGregor .20 .50
18 Ray Miller CO .20 .50
19 Eddie Murray 1.25 3.00
20 Joe Nolan .20 .50
21 Jim Palmer .60 1.50
22 Allan Ramirez .20 .50
23 Cal Ripken Jr. 2.50 6.00
24 Cal Ripken Sr. CO .20 .50
25 Gary Roenicke .20 .50
26 Ralph Rowe CO .20 .50
27 Lenn Sakata .20 .50
28 Ken Singleton .30 .75
29 Sammy Stewart .20 .50
30 Tim Stoddard .30 .75
31 Earl Weaver MG .60 1.50
32 Jimmy Williams CO .20 .50
33 Memorial Stadium .20 .50

1984 Orioles English's Discs

This disc set salutes the 1983 Baltimore Orioles Champion team; the discs come into two sizes, measuring either 7 1/4" or 8 3/8" in diameter. The fronts feature a black-and-white head shot on a white background encircled by orange. His name, position, team name biographical information and brief statistics are printed on the white circle. The phrase "English's Salutes" and "1983 Champions" are printed in black print in the orange border. The discs are unnumbered and checklisted below in alphabetical order. The backs are blank so we have sequenced this set in alphabetical order.

COMPLETE SET (13) 20.00 50.00
1 Mike Boddicker .20 .50
2 Rich Dauer .20 .50
3 Storm Davis .20 .50
4 Rick Dempsey .40 1.00
5 Mike Flanagan .40 1.00
6 John Lowenstein .20 .50
7 Tippy Martinez .20 .50
8 Scott McGregor .20 .50
9 Eddie Murray 4.00 10.00
10 Jim Palmer 2.50 6.00
11 Cal Ripken 15.00 40.00
12 Gary Roenicke .20 .50
13 Ken Singleton .40 1.00

1984 Orioles Postcards

This 43-card set features glossy color portraits of the Baltimore Orioles with white borders and measures approximately 3 1/2" by 5 1/4". The backs carry a postcard format and Memorial Stadium address. The cards are unnumbered and checklisted below in alphabetical order.

COMPLETE SET (43) 10.00 25.00
1 Joe Altobelli MG .20 .50
2 Bennie Ayala .20 .50
3 Mike Boddicker/(Autographed) .30 .75
4 Mike Boddicker .30 .75
5 Mark Brown .20 .50
6 Al Bumbry .20 .50
7 Todd Cruz .20 .50
8 Rich Dauer .20 .50
9 Storm Davis .20 .50
10 Rick Dempsey .30 .75
11 Ken Dixon .20 .50
12 Jim Dwyer .20 .50
13 Mike Flanagan .30 .75
14 Dan Ford .20 .50
15 Wayne Gross .20 .50
16 Ellie Hendricks CO .20 .50
17 John Lowenstein .20 .50
18 Dennis Martinez .40 1.00
19 Tippy Martinez .20 .50
20 Scott McGregor .20 .50
21 Ray Miller CO/(Higher name) .20 .50
22 Ray Miller CO/(Lower name) .20 .50
23 Eddie Murray 1.00 2.50
24 Joe Nolan .20 .50
25 Jim Palmer .60 1.50
26 Floyd Rayford .20 .50
27 Cal Ripken Jr. 2.00 5.00
28 Cal Ripken Sr. CO .20 .50
29 Vic Rodriguez .20 .50
30 Gary Roenicke .20 .50
31 Ralph Rowe CO .20 .50
32 Lenn Sakata .20 .50
33 Larry Sheets .20 .50
34 John Shelby .20 .50
35 Ken Singleton .30 .75
36 Nate Snell .20 .50
37 Sammy Stewart .20 .50
38 Bill Swaggerty .20 .50
39 Jim Traber .20 .50
40 Tom Underwood .20 .50
41 Jimmy Williams CO .20 .50
42 Mike Young .20 .50
43 The Bird(Mascot) .20 .50
44 Memorial Stadium .20 .50

1985 Orioles Health

This 20-card set features color player portraits that measure approximately 3 1/2" by 5 1/4" in a white border. The backs carry a "Health Message" and the player's signature above his name. Some of the players have two cards with the same picture but a different health message on the back. Cal Ripken Jr. has three cards with three different health messages. The cards are unnumbered and checklisted below in alphabetical order. A set in considered complete with any one card of the players for whom more than one card was issued.

COMPLETE SET (20) 4.00 10.00
1 Don Aase .08 .25
2 Mike Boddicker (2) .20 .50
3 Storm Davis .08 .25
4 Rick Dempsey (2) .20 .50
5 Ken Dixon .08 .25
6 Jim Dwyer .08 .25
7 Mike Flanagan (2) .20 .50
8 Lee Lacy .08 .25
9 Fred Lynn (2) .20 .50
10 Dennis Martinez .30 .75
11 Tippy Martinez .08 .25
12 Scott McGregor .08 .25
13 Eddie Murray (2) 1.00 2.50
14 Floyd Rayford (2) .08 .25
15 Cal Ripken Jr. (3) 2.00 5.00
16 Larry Sheets (2) .08 .25
17 John Shelby .08 .25
18 Earl Weaver .40 1.00
19 Alan Wiggins .08 .25
20 Mike Young .08 .25

1985 Orioles Postcards

This 38-card set features glossy color portraits of the Baltimore Orioles with white borders and measures approximately 3 1/2" by 5 1/4". The backs carry a postcard format and Memorial Stadium address. The cards are unnumbered and checklisted below in alphabetical order.

COMPLETE SET (38) 10.00 25.00
1 Don Aase .20 .50
2 Mike Boddicker .30 .75
3 Al Bumbry .20 .50
4 Fritz Connally .20 .50
5 Terry Crowley .20 .50
6 Rich Dauer .20 .50
7 Rick Dempsey .30 .75
8 Ken Dixon .20 .50
9 Mike Flanagan .30 .75
10 Ellie Hendricks CO/(Darker portrait) .20 .50
11 Ellie Hendricks CO .20 .50
12 Lee Lacy .20 .50
13 Fred Lynn .30 .75
14 Fred Lynn .30 .75
15 Dennis Martinez .40 1.00
16 Tippy Martinez .20 .50
17 Scott McGregor .20 .50
18 Ray Miller CO .20 .50
19 Eddie Murray 1.00 2.50
20 Joe Nolan .20 .50
21 Al Pardo .20 .50
22 Floyd Rayford .20 .50
23 Floyd Rayford/(Darker portrait) .20 .50
24 Cal Ripken Jr. 2.00 5.00
25 Cal Ripken Sr. CO .20 .50
26 Frank Robinson CO .60 1.50
27 Gary Roenicke .20 .50
28 Ken Rowe .20 .50
29 Lenn Sakata .20 .50
30 Larry Sheets .20 .50
31 John Shelby .20 .50
32 Nate Snell .20 .50
33 Sammy Stewart .20 .50
34 Bill Swaggerty .20 .50
35 Alan Wiggins .20 .50
36 Jimmy Williams CO .20 .50
37 Mike Young .20 .50
38 Memorial Stadium .20 .50

1986 Orioles Greats TCMA

This 12-card standard-size set features some of the best Baltimore Orioles since 1954. The fronts display player photos, his name as well as a position identification. The back has vital statistics, career totals and a biography.

COMPLETE SET (12) 2.50 6.00
1 Hoyt Wilhelm .40 1.00
2 Hank Bauer MG .20 .50
3 Jim Palmer .60 1.50
4 Dave McNally .20 .50
5 Paul Blair .08 .25
6 Gus Triandos .08 .25
7 Frank Robinson .60 1.50
8 Ken Singleton .08 .25
9 Luis Aparicio .40 1.00
10 Brooks Robinson .60 1.50
11 John Boog Powell .40 1.00
12 Dave Johnson .20 .50

1986 Orioles Health

This 21-card set features color player portraits that measure approximately 3 1/2" by 5 1/4" in a white border. The backs carry a "Health Message" and the player's signature above his name. Some of the players have two or three cards with the same picture but a different health message on the back. One of Mike Flanagan's cards displays a "Safety Message." The cards are unnumbered and checklisted below in alphabetical order. The complete set price includes only one card for each player who have mulitple cards issued.

COMPLETE SET (21) 8.00 20.00
1 Don Aase (2) .20 .50
2 Mike Boddicker (2) .20 .50
3 Storm Davis (2) .20 .50
4 Rick Dempsey (2) .30 .75
5 Ken Dixon .20 .50
6 Jim Dwyer .20 .50
7 Mike Flanagan (3) .30 .75
8 Lee Lacy .20 .50
9 Fred Lynn (2) .30 .75
10 Dennis Martinez .40 1.00
11 Tippy Martinez .20 .50
12 Scott McGregor .20 .50
13 Eddie Murray (3) 1.00 2.50
14 Floyd Rayford (2) .20 .50
15 Cal Ripken Jr. (3) 2.00 5.00
16 Larry Sheets (2) .20 .50
17 John Shelby .20 .50
18 Nate Snell .20 .50
19 Earl Weaver .60 1.50
20 Alan Wiggins .20 .50
21 Mike Young (2) .20 .50

1986 Orioles Postcards

This 27-card set features glossy color portraits of the Baltimore Orioles with white borders and measures approximately 3 1/2" by 5 1/4". The backs carry a postcard format and Memorial Stadium address. The cards are unnumbered and checklisted below in alphabetical order.

COMPLETE SET (27) 8.00 20.00
1 Juan Beniquez .20 .50
2 Mike Boddicker .20 .50
3 Juan Bonilla .20 .50
4 Rich Bordi .20 .50
5 Storm Davis .20 .50
6 Rick Dempsey .30 .75
7 Ken Dixon .20 .50
8 Jim Dwyer .20 .50
9 Brad Havens .20 .50
10 Elrod Hendricks .20 .50
11 Scott McGregor .20 .50
12 Eddie Murray 1.00 2.50
13 Tom O'Malley .20 .50
14 Floyd Rayford .20 .50
15 Cal Ripken Jr. 2.00 5.00
16 Cal Ripken Sr. .20 .50
17 Frank Robinson .60 1.50
18 Ken Rowe .20 .50
19 Larry Sheets .20 .50
20 John Shelby .20 .50
21 Nate Snell .20 .50
22 Jim Traber .20 .50
23 Earl Weaver .60 1.50
24 Alan Wiggins .20 .50
25 Jimmy Williams .20 .50
26 Mike Young .20 .50
27 The Bird(Mascot) .20 .50

1987 Orioles French Bray

The 1987 French Bray set contains 30 cards (featuring members of the Baltimore Orioles) measuring approximately 2 1/4" by 3". The fronts have facial photos with white and orange borders; the horizontally oriented backs are white and feature career stats. The cards were given away in perforated sheet form on Photo Card Day at the Orioles home game on July 26, 1987. A large team photo was also included as one of the three panels in this perforated card set. The cards are unnumbered except for uniform number.

COMPLETE SET (30) 8.00 20.00
2 Alan Wiggins .08 .25
3 Bill Ripken .20 .50
6 Floyd Rayford .08 .25
7 Cal Ripken Sr. MG .08 .25
8 Cal Ripken Jr. 4.00 10.00
9 Jim Dwyer .08 .25
10 Terry Crowley CO .08 .25
15 Terry Kennedy .08 .25
16 Scott McGregor .08 .25
18 Larry Sheets .08 .25
19 Fred Lynn .20 .50
20 Frank Robinson CO .75 2.00
24 Dave Schmidt .08 .25
25 Ray Knight .08 .25
27 Lee Lacy .08 .25
31 Mark Wiley CO .08 .25
32 Mark Williamson .08 .25
33 Eddie Murray 1.25 3.00
38 Ken Gerhart .08 .25
39 Ken Dixon .08 .25
40 Jimmy Williams CO .08 .25
42 Mike Griffin .08 .25
43 Mike Young .08 .25
44 Elrod Hendricks CO .08 .25
45 Eric Bell .08 .25
46 Mike Flanagan .20 .50
49 Tom Niedenfuer .08 .25
52 Mike Boddicker .20 .50
54 John Habyan .08 .25
57 Tony Arnold .08 .25

1987 Orioles Postcards

This 45-card set features glossy color portraits of the Baltimore Orioles with white borders and measures approximately 3 1/2" by 5 1/4". The backs carry a postcard format and Memorial Stadium address. The Mike Griffin, Mike Hart, Bill Ripken and Ron Washington cards display black-and-white player photos and have blank backs. There is another Bill Ripken card with a glossy front but it also has a blank back. All the aforementioned blank backed cards were issued late in 1987 and are in shorter supply. Hence, they are labeled with a SP designation below. The cards are unnumbered and checklisted below in alphabetical order.

COMPLETE SET (45) 15.00 40.00
COMMON CARD (1-45) .20 .50
COMMON SP 4.00
1 Don Aase .20 .50
2 Tony Arnold .20 .50
3 Jeff Ballard .20 .50
4 Eric Bell .20 .50
5 Mike Boddicker .30 .75
6 Rick Burleson .20 .50
7 Terry Crowley CO .20 .50
8 Luis De Leon .20 .50
9 Ken Dixon .20 .50
10 Jim Dwyer .20 .50
11 Mike Flanagan .30 .75
12 Ken Gerhart .20 .50
13 Rene Gonzales .20 .50
14 Mike Griffin 1.50 4.00
15 John Habyan .20 .50
16 Mike Hart SP 1.50 4.00
17 Elrod Hendricks CO .20 .50
18 Elrod Hendricks
(Larger bottom margin) .20 .50
19 Terry Kennedy .20 .50
20 Ray Knight .20 .50
21 Lee Lacy .20 .50
22 Fred Lynn .30 .75
23 Scott McGregor .20 .50
24 Eddie Murray 1.25 3.00
25 Tom Niedenfuer .20 .50
26 Jack O'Connor .20 .50
27 Floyd Rayford .20 .50
28 Bill Ripken (2) SP 2.00 5.00
29 Cal Ripken Jr. 2.00 5.00
30 Cal Ripken Sr. MG .20 .50
31 Brooks Robinson .60 1.50
32 Frank Robinson CO .60 1.50
33 Dave Schmidt .20 .50
34 Larry Sheets .20 .50
35 John Shelby .20 .50
36 Dave Van Gorder .20 .50
37 Ron Washington SP 1.50 4.00
38 Alan Wiggins .20 .50
39 Mark Wiley CO .20 .50
40 Jimmy Williams CO .20 .50
41 Mark Williamson .20 .50
42 Mike Young .20 .50
43 The Bird(Mascot) .20 .50
44 Memorial Stadium .20 .50

1988 Orioles French Bray

This set was distributed as a perforated set of 30 full-color cards attached to a large team photo on July 31, 1988, the Baltimore Orioles' Photo Card Day. The cards measure approximately 2 1/4" by 3 1/16". Card backs are simply done in black and white with statistics but no narrative or any personal information. Cards are unnumbered except for uniform number. Card front have a thin orange inner border and have the French Bray (Printing and Graphic Communication) logo in the lower right corner.

COMPLETE SET (30) 6.00 15.00
2 Don Buford CO .08 .25
6 Joe Orsulak .08 .25
7 Bill Ripken .20 .50
8 Cal Ripken 3.00 8.00
9 Jim Dwyer .08 .25
10 Terry Crowley CO .08 .25
12 Mike Morgan .08 .25
14 Mickey Tettleton .40 1.00
15 Terry Kennedy .08 .25
17 Pete Stanicek .08 .25
18 Larry Sheets .08 .25
19 Fred Lynn .30 .75
20 Frank Robinson MG .40 1.00
23 Oswald Peraza .08 .25
24 Dave Schmidt .08 .25
25 Rick Schu .08 .25
28 Jim Traber .08 .25
31 Herm Starrette CO .08 .25
33 Eddie Murray 1.00 2.50
34 Jeff Ballard .08 .25
38 Ken Gerhart .08 .25
40 Minnie Mendoza CO .08 .25
41 Don Aase .08 .25
44 Elrod Hendricks CO .08 .25
47 John Hart CO .08 .25
48 Jose Bautista .08 .25
49 Tom Niedenfuer .08 .25
52 Mike Boddicker .20 .50
53 Jay Tibbs .08 .25
88 Rene Gonzales .08 .25

1988 Orioles Postcards

This 42-card set features glossy color portraits of the Baltimore Orioles with white borders and measures approximately 3 1/2" by 5 1/4". The backs carry a postcard format and Memorial Stadium address. The cards are unnumbered and checklisted below in alphabetical order. Similar to 1987; a couple of players were issued later in the year in Black and White with Blank Backs. In 1988, it was Brady Anderson and Joe Durham.

COMPLETE SET (42) 15.00 40.00
COMMON CARD (1-42) .20 .50
COMMON SP 4.00
1 Don Aase .20 .50
2 Brady Anderson SP 3.00 8.00
3 Jeff Ballard .20 .50
4 Jose Bautista .20 .50
5 Eric Bell .20 .50
6 Mike Boddicker .20 .50
7 Don Buford CO .20 .50
8 Terry Crowley CO .20 .50
9 Joe Durham CO SP 1.50 4.00
10 Jim Dwyer .20 .50
11 Ken Gerhart .20 .50
12 Rene Gonzales .20 .50
13 John Habyan .20 .50
14 John Hart CO .20 .50
15 Ellie Hendricks CO .20 .50
16 Keith Hughes .20 .50
17 Terry Kennedy .20 .50
18 Fred Lynn .30 .75
19 Scott McGregor .20 .50
20 Minnie Mendoza CO .20 .50
21 Mike Morgan .20 .50
21 Tom Niedenfuer .20 .50
22 Eddie Murray 1.00 2.50
23 John Oates CO .20 .50
24 Joe Orsulak .20 .50
25 Oswald Peraza .20 .50
26 Bill Ripken .20 .50
27 Cal Ripken Jr. 2.00 5.00
28 Cal Ripken Sr. MG .20 .50
29 Frank Robinson .60 1.50
30 Wade Rowdon .20 .50
31 Dave Schmidt .20 .50
32 Rick Schu .20 .50
33 Larry Sheets .20 .50
34 Doug Sisk .20 .50
35 Pete Stanicek .20 .50
36 Herm Starrette CO .20 .50
37 Mickey Tettleton .60 1.50
38 Mark Thurmond .20 .50
39 Jay Tibbs .20 .50
40 Jim Traber .20 .50
41 Mark Williamson .20 .50
42 The Bird(Mascot) .20 .50
43 Memorial Stadium .20 .50

1989 Orioles French Bray

The 1989 French Bray/WWF Orioles set contains 31 cards measuring approximately 2 1/4" by 3". The fronts have facial photos with orange and white borders; the backs are white and feature career stats. The set was given away at a Baltimore home game on May 12, 1989. The cards are numbered by the players' uniform numbers.

COMPLETE SET (32) 5.00 12.00
3 Bill Ripken .08 .25
6 Joe Orsulak .08 .25
7 Cal Ripken Sr. CO .08 .25
8 Cal Ripken Jr. 2.00 5.00
9 Brady Anderson 1.00 2.50
10 Steve Finley 1.00 2.50
11 Craig Worthington .08 .25
12 Mike Devereaux .08 .25
14 Mickey Tettleton .30 .75
15 Randy Milligan .08 .25
16 Phil Bradley .08 .25
18 Bob Milacki .08 .25
19 Larry Sheets .08 .25
20 Frank Robinson MG .40 1.00
21 Mark Thurmond .08 .25
23 Kevin Hickey .08 .25
24 Dave Schmidt .08 .25
28 Jim Traber .08 .25
29 Jeff Ballard .08 .25
30 Gregg Olson .40 1.00
31 Al Jackson CO .08 .25
32 Mark Williamson .08 .25
36 Bob Melvin .20 .50
37 Brian Holton .08 .25
40 Tom McCraw CO .08 .25
42 Pete Harnisch .20 .50
43 Francisco Melendez .08 .25
44 Elrod Hendricks CO .08 .25
46 Johnny Oates CO .08 .25
48 Jose Bautista .08 .25
88 Rene Gonzales .08 .25
NNO Sponsor ad .08 .25

1989 Orioles Postcards

This 41-card set features glossy color portraits of the Baltimore Orioles with white borders and measures approximately 3 1/2" by 5 1/4". The backs carry a postcard format and Memorial Stadium address. The Dave Johnson, Ben McDonald, and Curt Schilling cards display black-and-white player photos with blank backs. Similar to the previous two years, these cards were printed later in the year and are shorter supply. Therefore, they are marked as SP's below. The cards are unnumbered and checklisted below in alphabetical order. The Curt Schiling postcard is one from his Rookie Card year.

COMPLETE SET (41) 15.00 40.00
COMMON CARD (1-41) .20 .50
COMMON SP 1.50 4.00
1 Brady Anderson .60 1.50
2 Jeff Ballard .20 .50
3 Jose Bautista .20 .50
4 Phil Bradley .20 .50
5 Mike Devereaux .20 .50
6 Joe Durham CO .20 .50
7 Steve Finley .60 1.50
8 Rene Gonzales .20 .50
9 John Habyan .20 .50
10 Pete Harnisch .20 .50
11 Elrod Hendricks .20 .50
12 Kevin Hickey .20 .50
13 Brian Holton .20 .50
14 Al Jackson CO .20 .50
15 Dave Johnson SP 1.50 4.00
16 Tom McCraw CO .20 .50
17 Ben McDonald SP 2.00 5.00
18 Bob Melvin .30 .75
19 Bob Milacki .20 .50
20 Randy Milligan .20 .50
21 Curt Motton CO .20 .50
22 John Oates CO .20 .50
23 Gregg Olson .60 1.50
24 Joe Orsulak .20 .50
25 Bill Ripken .20 .50
26 Cal Ripken Jr. 2.50 6.00
27 Cal Ripken Sr. CO .20 .50
28 Frank Robinson MG .60 1.50
29 Curt Schilling SP 8.00 20.00
30 Dave Schmidt .20 .50
31 Rick Schu .20 .50
32 Larry Sheets .20 .50
33 Pete Stanicek .20 .50
34 Mickey Tettleton .40 1.00
35 Mark Thurmond .20 .50
36 Jay Tibbs .20 .50
37 Jim Traber .20 .50
38 Mark Williamson .20 .50
39 Craig Worthington .20 .50
40 The Bird(Mascot) .20 .50
41 Memorial Stadium .20 .50

1990 Orioles Postcards

This 19-card set features glossy color portraits of the Baltimore Orioles with white borders and measures approximately 3 1/2" by 5 1/4". The backs display a postcard format and Memorial Stadium address. Many of the cards in this set were issued in Black and White with blank backs. They are notated below with BW. The cards are unnumbered and checklisted below in alphabetical order.

COMPLETE SET (19) 20.00 50.00
COMMON CARD (1-19) .20 .50
COMMON BW 1.20 3.00
1 Jeff Ballard BW 1.25 3.00
2 Rex Barney ANN BW 1.50 4.00
3 Marty Brown .20 .50
4 Joe Durham BW 1.25 3.00
5 Steve Finley .60 1.50

6 Dave Gallagher BW 1.25 3.00
7 Rene Gonzales .20 .50
8 Dick Hall BW 1.25 3.00
9 Kevin Hickey BW 1.25 3.00
10 Sam Horn .20 .50
11 Tim Hulett .20 .50
12 Dave Johnson .20 .50
13 Dave Johnson BW 1.25 3.00
14 Ron Kittle BW 1.25 3.00
15 Brad Komminsk .20 .50
16 Ben McDonald BW 1.50 4.00
17 Jose Mesa BW 1.50 4.00
18 Jon Miller ANN BW 1.50 4.00
19 Randy Milligan .20 .50
20 Randy Milligan BW 1.25 3.00
21 John Mitchell .20 .50
22 Joe Price .20 .50
23 Bill Ripken BW 1.25 3.00
24 Frank Robinson .60 1.50
25 Dave Segui UER .60 1.50
Spelled Sequi on front
26 Anthony Telford BW 1.25 3.00
27 Jay Tibbs .20 .50
28 Mickey Weston .20 .50
29 Orioles Ball Girls BW 1.50 4.00
30 The Bird(Mascot) .20 .50
31 Memorial Stadium .20 .50

1991 Orioles Crown

This 501-card set was produced by the Baltimore Orioles in conjunction with Crown Gasoline Stations and Coca-Cola. The cards measure approximately 2 1/2" by 3 1/8" and feature every Oriole player in the team's modern history (1954-1991). The cards were issued in four series, with ten twelve-card sheets per set. The first set was given away at the Orioles May 17th game against the California Angels, and the following day the set went on sale at Baltimore area Crown gasoline stations for 1.99 with an eight gallon fill-up. The second set was given away at the Orioles June 28th game against the Boston Red Sox, and again it went on sale the following day at Crown gasoline stations. The third set was given away at the Orioles August 11th game against the Chicago White Sox and went on sale on the same day. The fourth set went on sale at Crown gasoline stations on September 16. The cards are arranged alphabetically by player and checklisted below accordingly.

COMPLETE SET (501) 25.00 60.00
1 Don Aase .20 .50
2 Cal Abrams .20 .50
3 Jerry Adair .20 .50
4 Bobby Adams .20 .50
5 Mike Adamson .20 .50
6 Jay Aldrich .20 .50
7 Bob Alexander .20 .50
8 Doyle Alexander .20 .50
9 Brady Anderson .25 .60
10 John Anderson .20 .50
11 Mike Anderson .20 .50
12 Luis Aparicio .60 1.50
13 Tony Arnold .20 .50
14 Bobby Avila .20 .50
15 Benny Ayala .20 .50
16 Bob Bailor .20 .50
17 Frank Baker .20 .50
18 Jeff Ballard .20 .50
19 George Bamberger .20 .50
20 Steve Barber .20 .50
21 Ray(Buddy) Barker .20 .50
22 Ed Barnowski .20 .50
23 Jose Bautista .20 .50
24 Don Baylor .30 .75
25 Charlie Beamon .20 .50
26 Fred Beene .20 .50
27 Mark Belanger .25 .60
28 Eric Bell .20 .50
29 Juan Bell .20 .50
30 Juan Beniquez .20 .50
31 Neil Berry .20 .50
32 Frank Bertaina .20 .50
33 Fred Besana .20 .50
34 Vern Bickford .20 .50
35 Babe Birrer .20 .50
36 Paul Blair .25 .60
37 Curt Blefary .20 .50
38 Mike Blyzka .20 .50
39 Mike Boddicker .20 .50
40 Juan Bonilla .20 .50
41 Bob Bonner .20 .50
42 Dan Boone .20 .50
43 Rich Bordi .20 .50
44 Dave Boswell .20 .50
45 Sam Bowens .20 .50
46 Bob Boyd .20 .50
47 Gene Brabender .20 .50
48 Phil Bradley .20 .50
49 Jackie Brandt .20 .50
50 Marv Breeding .20 .50
51 Jim Brideweser .20 .50
52 Nelson Briles .20 .50
53 Dick Brown .20 .50
54 Hal Brown .20 .50
55 Larry Brown .20 .50
56 Mark Brown .20 .50
57 Marty Brown .20 .50
58 George Brunet .20 .50
59 Don Buford .20 .50
60 Al Bumbry .20 .50
61 Wally Bunker .20 .50
62 Leo Burke .20 .50
63 Rick Burleson .20 .50
64 Pete Burnside .20 .50
65 Jim Busby .20 .50
66 John Buzhardt .20 .50
67 Harry Byrd .20 .50
68 Enos Cabell .20 .50
69 Chico Carrasquel .20 .50
70 Camilo Carreon .20 .50
71 Foster Castleman .20 .50
72 Wayne Causey .20 .50
73 Art Ceccarelli .20 .50
74 Bob Chakales .20 .50
75 Tony Chevez .20 .50
76 Tom Chism .20 .50
77 Gino Cimoli .20 .50
78 Gil Coan .20 .50
79 Rich Coggins .20 .50
80 Joe Coleman .20 .50
81 Rip Coleman .20 .50
82 Fritz Connally .20 .50
83 Sandy Consuegra .20 .50
84 Doug Corbett .20 .50
85 Mark Corey .20 .50
86 Clint Courtney .20 .50
87 Billy Cox .20 .50
88 Dave Criscione .20 .50
89 Terry Crowley .20 .50
90 Todd Cruz .20 .50
91 Mike Cuellar .25 .60
92 Angie Dagres .20 .50
93 Clay Dalrymple .20 .50
94 Rich Dauer .20 .50
95 Jerry DaVanon .20 .50
96 Butch Davis .20 .50
97 Storm Davis .20 .50
98 Tommy Davis .25 .60
99 Doug DeCinces .20 .50
100 Luis DeLeon .20 .50
101 Ike Delock .20 .50
102 Rick Dempsey .20 .50
103 Mike Devereaux .25 .60
104 Chuck Diering .20 .50
105 Gordon Dillard .20 .50
106 Bill Dillman .20 .50
107 Mike Dimmel .20 .50
108 Ken Dixon .20 .50
109 Pat Dobson .20 .50
110 Tom Dodd .20 .50
111 Harry Dorish .20 .50
112 Moe Drabowsky .20 .50
113 Dick Drago .20 .50
114 Walt Dropo .20 .50
115 Tom Dukes .20 .50
116 Dave Duncan .20 .50
117 Ryne Duren .25 .60
118 Joe Durham .20 .50
119 Jim Dwyer .20 .50
120 Jim Dyck .20 .50
121 Mike Epstein .20 .50
122 Chuck Essegian .20 .50
123 Chuck Estrada .20 .50
124 Andy Etchebarren .20 .50
125 Hoot Evers .20 .50
126 Ed Farmer .20 .50
127 Chico Fernandez .20 .50
128 Don Ferrarese .20 .50
129 Jim Finigan .20 .50
130 Steve Finley .30 .75
131 Mike Fiore .20 .50
132 Eddie Fisher .20 .50
133 Jack Fisher .20 .50
134 Tom Fisher .20 .50
135 Mike Flanagan .25 .60
136 John Flinn .20 .50
137 Bobby Floyd .20 .50
138 Hank Foiles .20 .50
139 Dan Ford .20 .50
140 Dave Ford .20 .50
141 Mike Fornieles .20 .50
142 Howie Fox .20 .50
143 Tito Francona .20 .50
144 Joe Frazier .20 .50
145 Roger Freed .20 .50
146 Jim Fridley .20 .50
147 Jim Fuller .20 .50
148 Joe Gaines .20 .50
149 Vinicio(Chico) Garcia .20 .50
150 Kiko Garcia .20 .50
151 Billy Gardner .20 .50
152 Wayne Garland .20 .50
153 Tommy Gastall .20 .50
154 Jim Gentile .25 .60
155 Ken Gerhart .20 .50
156 Paul Gilliford .20 .50
157 Joe Ginsberg .20 .50
158 Leo Gomez .20 .50
159 Rene Gonzales .20 .50
160 Billy Goodman .20 .50
161 Dan Graham .20 .50
162 Ted Gray .20 .50
163 Gene Green .20 .50
164 Lenny Green .20 .50
165 Bobby Grich .25 .60
166 Nuje Griffin .20 .50
167 Ross Grimsley .20 .50
168 Wayne Gross .20 .50
169 Glenn Gulliver .20 .50
170 Jackie Gutierrez .20 .50
171 John Habyan .20 .50
172 Harvey Haddix .20 .50
173 Bob Hale .20 .50
174 Dick Hall .20 .50
175 Bert Hamric .20 .50
176 Larry Haney .20 .50
177 Ron Hansen .20 .50
178 Jim Hardin .20 .50
179 Larry Harlow .20 .50
180 Pete Harnisch .20 .50
181 Tommy Harper .20 .50
182 Bob Harrison .20 .50
183 Roric Harrison .20 .50
184 Jack Harshman .20 .50
185 Mike Hart .20 .50
186 Pete Hartzell .20 .50
187 Grady Hatton .20 .50
188 Brad Havens .20 .50
189 Drungo Hazewood .20 .50
190 Jehosie Heard .20 .50
191 Mel Held .20 .50
192 Woodie Held .20 .50
193 Ellie Hendricks .20 .50
194 Leo Hernandez .20 .50
195 Whitey Herzog .30 .75
196 Kevin Hickey .20 .50
197 Billy Hoeft .20 .50
198 Chris Hoiles .25 .60
199 Fred Holdsworth .20 .50
200 Brian Holton .20 .50
201 Ken Holtzman .20 .50
202 Don Hood .20 .50
203 Sam Horn .20 .50
204 Art Houtteman .20 .50
205 Bruce Howard .20 .50
206 Rex Hudler .20 .50
207 Phil Huffman .20 .50
208 Keith Hughes .20 .50
209 Mark Huismann .20 .50
210 Tim Hulett .20 .50
211 Billy Hunter .20 .50
212 Dave Huppert .20 .50
213 Jim Hutto .20 .50
214 Dick Hyde .20 .50
215 Grant Jackson .20 .50
216 Lou Jackson .20 .50
217 Reggie Jackson 2.00 5.00
218 Ron Jackson .20 .50
219 Jesse Jefferson .20 .50
220 Stan Jefferson .20 .50
221 Bob Johnson .20 .50
222 Connie Johnson .20 .50
223 Darrell Johnson .20 .50
224 Dave Johnson .20 .50
225 Davey Johnson .30 .75
226 David Johnson .20 .50
227 Don Johnson .20 .50
228 Ernie Johnson .20 .50
229 Gordon Jones .20 .50
230 Ricky Jones .20 .50
231 O'Dell Jones .20 .50
232 Sam Jones .20 .50
233 George Kell .60 1.50
234 Frank Kellert .20 .50
235 Pat Kelly .20 .50
236 Bub Kennedy .20 .50
237 Terry Kennedy .20 .50
238 Joe Kerrigan .20 .50
239 Mike Kinnunen .20 .50
240 Willie Kirkland .20 .50
241 Ron Kittle .20 .50
242 Billy Klaus .20 .50
243 Ray Knight .25 .60
244 Darold Knowles .20 .50
245 Dick Kokos .20 .50
246 Brad Komminsk .20 .50
247 Dave Koslo .20 .50
248 Wayne Krenchicki .20 .50
249 Lou Kretlow .20 .50
250 Dick Kryhoski .20 .50
251 Bob Kuzava .20 .50
252 Lee Lacy .20 .50
253 Hobie Landrith .20 .50
254 Tito Landrum .20 .50
255 Don Larsen .25 .60
256 Charlie Lau .20 .50
257 Jim Lehew .20 .50
258 Ken Lehman .20 .50
259 Don Lenhardt .20 .50
260 Dave Leonhard .20 .50
261 Don Leppert .20 .50
262 Dick Littlefield .20 .50
263 Charlie Locke .20 .50
264 Whitey Lockman .20 .50
265 Billy Loes .20 .50
266 Ed Lopat .25 .60
267 Carlos Lopez .20 .50
268 Marcelino Lopez .20 .50
269 John Lowenstein .20 .50
270 Steve Luebber .20 .50
271 Dick Luebke .20 .50
272 Fred Lynn .25 .60
273 Bobby Mabe .20 .50
274 Elliott Maddox .20 .50
275 Hank Majeski .20 .50
276 Roger Marquis .20 .50
277 Freddie Marsh .20 .50
278 Jim Marshall .20 .50
279 Morrie Martin .20 .50
280 Dennis Martinez .30 .75
281 Tippy Martinez .20 .50
282 Tom Matchick .20 .50
283 Charlie Maxwell .20 .50
284 Dave May .20 .50
285 Lee May .25 .60
286 Rudy May .20 .50
287 Mike McCormick .20 .50
288 Ben McDonald .20 .50
289 Jim McDonald .20 .50
290 Scott McGregor .20 .50
291 Mickey McGuire .20 .50
292 Jeff McKnight .20 .50
293 Dave McNally .30 .75
294 Sam Mele .20 .50
295 Francisco Melendez .20 .50
296 Bob Melvin .20 .50
297 Jose Mesa .30 .75
298 Eddie Miksis .20 .50
299 Bob Milacki .20 .50
300 Bill Miller .20 .50
301 Dyar Miller .20 .50
302 John Miller .20 .50
303 Randy Miller .20 .50
304 Stu Miller .20 .50
305 Randy Milligan .20 .50
306 Paul Mirabella .20 .50
307 Willie Miranda .20 .50
308 John Mitchell .20 .50
309 Paul Mitchell .20 .50
310 Ron Moeller .20 .50
311 Bob Molinaro .20 .50
312 Ray Moore .20 .50
313 Andres Mora .20 .50
314 Jose Morales .20 .50
315 Keith Moreland .20 .50
316 Mike Morgan .20 .50
317 Dan Morogiello .20 .50
318 John Morris .20 .50
319 Les Moss .20 .50
320 Curt Motton .20 .50
321 Eddie Murray 2.00 5.00
322 Ray Murray .20 .50
323 Tony Muser .20 .50
324 Buster Narum .20 .50
325 Bob Nelson .20 .50
326 Roger Nelson .20 .50
327 Carl Nichols .20 .50
328 Dave Nicholson .20 .50
329 Tim Niedenfuer .20 .50
330 Bob Nieman .20 .50
331 Donell Nixon .20 .50
332 Joe Nolan .20 .50
333 Dickie Noles .20 .50
334 Tim Nordbrook .20 .50
335 Jim Northrup .20 .50
336 Jack O'Connor .20 .50
337 Billy O'Dell .20 .50
338 John O'Donoghue .20 .50
339 Tom O'Malley .20 .50
340 Johnny Oates .20 .50
341 Chuck Oertel .20 .50
342 Bob Oliver .20 .50
343 Gregg Olson .25 .60
344 John Orsino .20 .50
345 Joe Orsulak .20 .50
346 John Pacella .20 .50
347 Dave Pagan .20 .50
348 Erv Palica .20 .50
349 Jim Palmer 2.00 5.00
350 John Papa .20 .50
351 Milt Pappas .25 .60
352 Al Pardo .20 .50
353 Kelly Paris .20 .50
354 Mike Parrott .20 .50
355 Tom Patton .20 .50
356 Albie Pearson .20 .50
357 Orlando Pena .20 .50
358 Oswald Peraza .20 .50
359 Buddy Peterson .20 .50
360 Dave Philley .20 .50
361 Tom Phoebus .20 .50
362 Al Pilarcik .20 .50
363 Duane Pillette .20 .50
364 Lou Piniella/(Pictured wearing a KC Royals cap) .30 .75
365 Dave Pope .20 .50
366 Arnie Portocarrero .20 .50
367 Boog Powell .30 .75
368 Johnny Powers .20 .50
369 Carl Powis .20 .50
370 Joe Price .20 .50
371 Jim Pyburn .20 .50
372 Art Quirk .20 .50
373 Jamie Quirk .20 .50
374 Allan Ramirez .20 .50
375 Floyd Rayford .20 .50
376 Mike Reinbach .20 .50
377 Merv Rettenmund .20 .50
378 Bob Reynolds .20 .50
379 Del Rice/(Wearing St. Louis Cardinals cap) .20 .50
380 Pete Richert .20 .50
381 Jeff Rineer .20 .50
382 Bill Ripken .20 .50
383 Cal Ripken 4.00 10.00
384 Robin Roberts .60 1.50
385 Brooks Robinson 2.00 5.00
386 Earl Robinson .20 .50
387 Eddie Robinson .20 .50
388 Frank Robinson 2.00 5.00
389 Sergio Robles .20 .50
390 Aurelio Rodriguez .20 .50
391 Vic Rodriguez .20 .50
392 Gary Roenicke .20 .50
393 Saul Rogovin/(Wearing Philadelphia Phillies cap) .20 .50
394 Wade Rowdon .20 .50
395 Ken Rowe .20 .50
396 Willie Royster .20 .50
397 Vic Roznovsky .20 .50
398 Ken Rudolph .20 .50
399 Lenn Sakata .20 .50
400 Chico Salmon .20 .50
401 Orlando Sanchez (Pictured wearing St. Louis Card .20 .50
402 Bob Saverine .20 .50
403 Art Schallock .20 .50
404 Bill Scherrer/(Wearing Detroit Tigers cap) .20 .50
405 Curt Schilling .75 2.00
406 Dave Schmidt .20 .50
407 Johnny Schmitz .20 .50
408 Jeff Schneider .20 .50
409 Rick Schu .20 .50
410 Mickey Scott .20 .50
411 Kal Segrist .20 .50
412 David Segui .25 .60
413 Al Severinsen .20 .50
414 Larry Sheets .20 .50
415 John Shelby .20 .50
416 Barry Shetrone .20 .50
417 Tom Shopay .20 .50
418 Bill Short .20 .50
419 Norm Siebern .20 .50
420 Nelson Simmons .20 .50
421 Ken Singleton .25 .60
422 Doug Sisk .20 .50
423 Dave Skaggs .20 .50
424 Lou Sleater .20 .50
425 Al Smith .20 .50
426 Billy Smith .20 .50
427 Hal Smith .20 .50
428 Mike(Texas) Smith .20 .50
429 Nate Smith .20 .50
430 Nate Snell .20 .50
431 Russ Snyder .20 .50
432 Don Stanhouse .20 .50
433 Pete Stanicek .20 .50
434 Herm Starrette .20 .50
435 John Stefaro .20 .50
436 Gene Stephens .20 .50
437 Vern Stephens .20 .50
438 Earl Stephenson .20 .50
439 Sammy Stewart .20 .50
440 Royle Stillman .20 .50
441 Wes Stock .20 .50
442 Tim Stoddard .20 .50
443 Dean Stone .20 .50
444 Jeff Stone .20 .50
445 Steve Stone .20 .50
446 Marlin Stuart .20 .50
447 Gordie Sundin .20 .50
448 Bill Swaggerty .20 .50
449 Willie Tasby .20 .50
450 Joe Taylor .20 .50
451 Dorn Taylor .20 .50
452 Anthony Telford .20 .50
453 Johnny Temple .20 .50
454 Mickey Tettleton .25 .60
455 Valmy Thomas/(Wearing Philadelphia Phillies cap) .20 .50
456 Bobby Thomson/(Wearing Boston Red Sox cap) .30 .75
457 Marv Throneberry .25 .60
458 Mark Thurmond .20 .50
459 Jay Tibbs .20 .50
460 Mike Torrez .20 .50
461 Jim Traber .20 .50
462 Gus Triandos .25 .60
463 Paul(Dizzy) Trout/(Wearing Detroit Tigers cap) .20 .50
464 Bob Turley .25 .60
465 Tom Underwood .20 .50
466 Fred Valentine .20 .50
467 Dave Van Gorder .20 .50
468 Dave Vineyard .20 .50
469 Ozzie Virgil .20 .50
470 Eddie Waitkus .20 .50
471 Greg Walker .20 .50
472 Jerry Walker .20 .50
473 Pete Ward .20 .50
474 Carl Warwick .20 .50
475 Ron Washington .20 .50
476 Eddie Watt .20 .50
477 Don Welchel .20 .50
478 George Werley .20 .50
479 Vic Wertz .20 .50
480 Wally Westlake/(Wearing a Pittsburgh Pirates cap .20 .50
481 Mickey Weston .20 .50
482 Alan Wiggins .20 .50
483 Bill Wight .20 .50
484 Hoyt Wilhelm .60 1.50
485 Dallas Williams .20 .50
486 Dick Williams .25 .60
487 Earl Williams .20 .50
488 Mark Williamson .20 .50
489 Jim Wilson .20 .50
490 Gene Woodling .20 .50
491 Craig Worthington .20 .50
492 Bobby Young .20 .50
493 Mike Young .20 .50
494 Frank Zupo .20 .50
495 George Zuverink .20 .50
496 Glenn Davis .20 .50
497 Dwight Evans .30 .75
498 Dave Gallagher .20 .50
499 Paul Kilgus .20 .50
500 Jeff Robinson .20 .50
501 Ernie Whitt .20 .50

1991 Orioles Postcards

This 36-card set features glossy color portraits of the Baltimore Orioles with white borders and measures approximately 3 1/2" by 5 1/4". The backs display a postcard format and Memorial Stadium address. The cards of Kevin Hickey, Chito Martinez, Jim Poole, and Anthony Telford carry black-and-white player photos and blank backs. The cards of Glenn Davis, Dwight Evans, and Bob Milacki are also available with blank backs. The cards are unnumbered and checklisted below in alphabetical order.

COMPLETE SET (36) 12.50 30.00
COMMON CARD (1-36) .20 .50
COMMON BW 1.20 3.00
1 Brady Anderson .60 1.50
2 Jeff Ballard .20 .50
3 Juan Bell .20 .50
4 Glenn Davis .30 .75
5 Mike Devereaux .20 .50
6 Dwight Evans .40 1.00
7 Mike Flanagan .30 .75
8 Todd Frohwirth .20 .50
9 Leo Gomez .20 .50
10 Elrod Hendricks CO .20 .50
11 Kevin Hickey BW 1.25 3.00
12 Chris Hoiles .20 .50
13 Sam Horn .20 .50
14 Dave Johnson .20 .50
15 Paul Kilgus .20 .50
16 Chito Martinez BW 1.25 3.00
17 Ben McDonald .20 .50
18 Jeff McKnight .20 .50
19 Jose Mesa .30 .75
20 Bob Milacki .20 .50
21 Randy Milligan .20 .50
22 Gregg Olson .30 .75
23 Joe Orsulak .20 .50
24 Mark Williamson .20 .50
24 Jim Poole BW 1.25 3.00
25 Bill Ripken .20 .50
26 Cal Ripken Jr. 2.00 5.00
27 Brooks Robinson .60 1.50
28 Frank Robinson .60 1.50
29 Jeff Robinson .20 .50
30 Dave Segui .30 .75
31 Roy Smith .20 .50
32 Anthony Telford BW 1.25 3.00
33 Ernie Whitt .20 .50
35 The Bird(Mascot) .20 .50
36 Memorial Stadium .20 .50

1992 Orioles Postcards

This 40-card set features borderless color photos of the Baltimore Orioles. The backs carry a message to the Orioles fans with a facsimile player signature. The backs of the cards of John Oates and Arthur Rhodes display a postcard format. The photo of Arthur Rhodes is black-and-white. The cards are unnumbered and checklisted below in alphabetical order.

COMPLETE SET (40) 12.50 30.00
1 Brady Anderson/(Running) .60 1.50
2 Brady Anderson/(With bat) .60 1.50
3 Greg Biagini CO .20 .50
4 Dick Bosman CO .20 .50
5 Glenn Davis .30 .75
6 Storm Davis .20 .50
7 Rick Dempsey .30 .75
8 Mike Devereaux .20 .50
9 Mike Flanagan .30 .75
10 Todd Frohwirth .20 .50
11 Leo Gomez .20 .50
12 Elrod Hendricks CO .20 .50
13 Chris Hoiles .20 .50
14 Sam Horn .20 .50
15 Tim Hulett .20 .50
16 Davey Lopes CO .30 .75
17 Chito Martinez .20 .50
18 Ben McDonald .20 .50
19 Mark McLemore .30 .75
20 Jose Mesa .30 .75
21 Bob Milacki .20 .50
22 Randy Milligan .20 .50
23 Alan Mills .20 .50
24 Mike Mussina/(Arms extended) 1.25 3.00
25 Mike Mussina/(Beginning of pitch) 1.25 3.00
26 John Oates MG .20 .50
27 Gregg Olson .30 .75
28 Joe Orsulak .20 .50
29 Jim Poole .20 .50
30 Arthur Rhodes .20 .50
31 Bill Ripken .20 .50
32 Cal Ripken Jr. 2.00 5.00
33 David Segui .30 .75
34 Rick Sutcliffe .30 .75
35 Jeff Tackett/(End of batting swing) .20 .50
36 Jeff Tackett/(Batting) .20 .50
37 Mark Williamson .20 .50
38 Oriole Bird(Mascot) .20 .50
39 Postcard Back .20 .50
40 Camden Yards .20 .50

1993 Orioles Crown Action Stand Ups

This set was issued in three distict series through Crown Petroleum service stations. These cards featured mainly retired Orioles players. Even though this set was issued in three distinct series, we have numbered them and priced them as one complete set. However, within each series, we have grouped the cards in alphabetical order.

COMPLETE SET (12) 8.00 20.00
1 Rick Dempsey .60 1.50
2 Jim Palmer 1.50 4.00
3 Brooks Robinson 1.50 4.00
4 Frank Robinson 1.50 4.00
5 Bobby Grich .60 1.50
6 Tippy Martinez .40 1.00
7 Cal Ripken Jr. 3.00 8.00
8 Earl Weaver MG 1.00 2.50
9 Paul Blair .40 1.00
10 Terry Crowley .40 1.00
11 Boog Powell 1.00 2.50
12 Ken Singleton .60 1.50

1993 Orioles Postcards

This 38-card set features borderless glossy color portraits and action photos of the Baltimore Orioles and measures approximately 3 1/2" by 5 1/4". The backs display a message to the Orioles fan with a facsimile signature. The photos of Paul Carey and Dick Hall are black-and-white. The cards of Dick Hall, Dave Johnson, Jim Palmer, and Harold Reynolds carry postcard format backs. The cards are unnumbered and checklisted below in alphabetical order.

COMPLETE SET (38) 12.50 30.00
COMMON CARD (1-38) .20 .50
COMMON BW .80 2.00
1 Brady Anderson .60 1.50
2 Harold Baines .40 1.00
3 Greg Biagini CO .20 .50
4 Dick Bosman CO .20 .50
5 Damon Buford .20 .50
6 Paul Carey BW .75 2.00
7 Mike Devereaux/(Hatless) .20 .50
8 Mike Devereaux (Wearing batting helmet) .20 .50
9 Mike Ferraro CO .20 .50
10 Leo Gomez .20 .50
11 Dick Hall .75 2.00
12 Jeffrey Hammonds .20 .50
13 Elrod Hendricks CO .20 .50
14 Chris Hoiles .20 .50
15 Dave Johnson .60 1.50
16 Ben McDonald .20 .50
17 Mark McLemore .30 .75
18 Alan Mills .20 .50
19 Jamie Moyer .60 1.50
20 Mike Mussina 1.25 3.00
21 Jerry Narron CO .20 .50
22 Johnny Oates MG .20 .50
23 Sherman Obando .20 .50
24 Gregg Olson .30 .75
25 Jim Palmer 1.00 2.50
26 Brad Pennington .20 .50
27 Jim Poole .20 .50
28 Harold Reynolds/(Portrait) 1.25 3.00
29 Harold Reynolds/(Batting) .30 .75
30 Arthur Rhodes .20 .50
31 Cal Ripken Jr. 2.00 5.00
32 David Segui .30 .75
33 Rick Sutcliffe .30 .75
34 Jeff Tackett .20 .50
35 Fernando Valenzuela Wind-Up .40 1.00
36 Fernando Valenzuela Follow-Thru .40 1.00
37 Jack Voigt .20 .50
38 Mark Williamson .20 .50
39 Camden Yards .20 .50

1994 Orioles Postcards

This 37-card set features borderless color photos of the Baltimore Orioles with a matte finish and measures approximately 3 1/2" by 5". The backs display one of 13 different messages with a facsimile signature printed below. The Paul Blair and Boog Powell cards carry black-and-white player photos with blank backs. The cards are unnumbered and checklisted below in alphabetical order.

COMPLETE SET (37) 12.50 30.00
COMMON CARD (1-37) .20 .50
COMMON BW 1.50
1 Brady Anderson .60 1.50
2 Harold Baines .40 1.00
3 Greg Biagini CO .20 .50
4 Paul Blair BW .60 1.50
5 Tom Bolton .20 .50
6 Dick Bosman CO .20 .50
7 Don Buford CO .20 .50
8 Mike Devereaux .20 .50
9 Mark Eichhorn .20 .50
10 Sid Fernandez .20 .50
11 Leo Gomez .20 .50
12 Jeffrey Hammonds .20 .50
13 Elrod Hendricks CO .20 .50
14 Chris Hoiles .20 .50
15 Tim Hulett .20 .50
16 Davey Lopes CO .30 .75
17 Ben McDonald .20 .50
18 Mark McLemore .30 .75
19 Alan Mills .20 .50
20 Jamie Moyer .60 1.50
21 Mike Mussina 1.00 2.50
22 Jerry Narron CO .20 .50
23 Johnny Oates MG .20 .50
24 Mike Oquist .20 .50
25 Rafael Palmeiro .60 1.50
26 Jim Poole .20 .50
27 Boog Powell BW 1.25 3.00
28 Arthur Rhodes .20 .50
29 Cal Ripken Jr. 2.00 5.00
30 Chris Sabo .20 .50
31 Lee Smith .30 .75
32 Lonnie Smith .20 .50
33 Jeff Tackett .20 .50
34 Jack Voigt .20 .50
35 Mark Williamson .20 .50
36 The Oriole Bird Mascot .20 .50
37 Camden Yards .20 .50

1994 Orioles Program

This 108-card set includes all current and minor league players in the Baltimore Orioles' organization. The set was issued in twelve nine-card perforated sheets, with each sheet issued in game day programs which sold for 3.00. Reportedly only 21,000 of each unperforated sheet were produced. Each 7 1/2" by 10 1/2" sheet consists of nine standard-size cards. The cards are unnumbered and checklisted below in alphabetical order.

COMPLETE SET (108) 12.50 30.00
1 Manny Alexander .08 .25
2 Brady Anderson .40 1.00
3 Matt Anderson .08 .25
4 Harold Baines .40 1.00
5 Miles Barnden .08 .25
6 Kimera Bartee .08 .25
7 Juan Bautista .08 .25
8 Armando Benitez .40 1.00
9 Joe Borowski .08 .25
10 Brian Brewer .08 .25
11 Brandon Bridgers .08 .25
12 Cory Brown .08 .25
13 Damon Buford .08 .25
14 Clayton Byrne .08 .25
15 Rocco Cafaro .08 .25
16 Paul Carey .08 .25
17 Carlos Chavez .08 .25
18 Eric Chavez .08 .25
19 Steve Chitren .08 .25
20 Mike Cook .08 .25
21 Shawn Curran .08 .25
22 Kevin Curtis .08 .25
23 Joey Dawley .08 .25
24 Jim Dedrick .08 .25
25 Cesar Devarez .08 .25
26 Mike Devereaux .08 .25
27 Brian DuBois .08 .25
28 Keith Eaddy .08 .25
29 Mark Eichhorn .08 .25
30 Scott Emerson .08 .25
31 Vaughn Eshelman .08 .25
32 Craig Faulkner .08 .25
33 Sid Fernandez .20 .50
34 Rick Forney .08 .25
35 Jim Foster .08 .25
36 Jesse Garcia .08 .25
37 Mike Garguilo .08 .25
38 Rich Gedman .08 .25
39 Leo Gomez .08 .25
40 Rene Gonzales .08 .25
41 Curtis Goodwin .08 .25
42 Kris Gresham .08 .25
43 Shane Hale .08 .25
44 Jeffrey Hammonds .20 .50
45 Jimmy Haynes .08 .25
46 Chris Hoiles .08 .25
47 Tim Hulett .08 .25
48 Matt Jarvis .08 .25
49 Scott Klingenbeck .08 .25
50 Rick Krivda .08 .25
51 David Lamb .08 .25
52 Chris Lemp .08 .25
53 T.R. Lewis .08 .25
54 Bryan Link .08 .25
55 John Lombardi .08 .25
56 Rob Lukachyk .08 .25
57 Calvin Maduro .08 .25
58 Barry Manuel .08 .25
59 Lincoln Martin .08 .25
60 Scott McClain .08 .25
61 Ben McDonald .08 .25
62 Kevin McGehee .08 .25
63 Mark McLemore .20 .50
64 Miguel Mejia .08 .25
65 Feliciano Mercedes .08 .25
66 Jose Millares .08 .25
67 Brent Miller .08 .25
68 Alan Mills .08 .25
69 Jamie Moyer .40 1.00
70 Mike Mussina 1.00 2.50
71 Sherman Obando .08 .25
72 Alex Ochoa .08 .25
73 John O'Donoghue .08 .25
74 Mike Oquist .08 .25
75 Bo Ortiz .08 .25
76 Billy Owens .08 .25
77 Rafael Palmeiro .75 2.00
78 Dave Paveloff .08 .25
79 Brad Pennington .08 .25
80 Bill Percibal .08 .25
81 Jim Poole .08 .25
82 Jay Powell .20 .50
83 Arthur Rhodes .08 .25
84 Matt Riemer .08 .25
85 Cal Ripken 2.00 5.00
86 Kevin Ryan .08 .25
87 Chris Sabo .08 .25
88 Brian Sackinsky .08 .25
89 Francisco Saneaux .08 .25
90 Jason Satre .08 .25

91 David Segui .20 .50
92 Jose Serra .08 .25
93 Larry Shenk .08 .25
94 Lee Smith .30 .75
95 Lonnie Smith .20 .50
96 Mark Smith .08 .25
97 Garrett Stephenson .08 .25
98 Jeff Tackett .08 .25
99 Brad Tyler .08 .25
100 Pedro Ulises .08 .25
101 Jack Voigt .08 .25
102 Jim Walker .08 .25
103 B.J. Waszgis .08 .25
104 Jim Wawruck .08 .25
105 Mel Wearing .08 .25
106 Mark Williamson .08 .25
107 Brian Wood .08 .25
108 Greg Zaun .08 .25

1994 Orioles U.S. Playing Cards

These 56 playing standard-size cards have rounded corners, and feature color posed and action player photos on their white-bordered fronts. The player's name and position appear near the bottom. The white and black backs carry the logos for the Orioles, baseball's 125th Anniversary, MLBPA, and Bicycle Sports Collection. The set is checklisted below in playing card order by suits and assigned numbers to aces (1), jacks (11), queens (12), and kings (13).

COMPLETE SET (56) 2.00 5.00
1C Chris Hoiles .01 .05
1D Mike Mussina .30 .75
1H Cal Ripken Jr. .60 1.50
1S Mark McLemore .02 .10
2C Mike Cook .01 .05
2D Mike Oquist .01 .05
2H Harold Baines .05 .15
2S Manny Alexander .01 .05
3C Paul Carey .01 .05
3D Brad Pennington .01 .05
3H John O'Donoghue .01 .05
3S Kevin McGehee .01 .05
4C Jeff Tackett .01 .05
4D Jeffrey Hammonds .01 .05
4H Sid Fernandez .01 .05
4S Jim Poole .01 .05
5C Arthur Rhodes .01 .05
5D Jack Voigt .01 .05
5H Alan Mills .01 .05
5S Leo Gomez .01 .05
6C Damon Buford .01 .05
6D Chris Sabo .01 .05
6H Jamie Moyer .05 .15
6S Tim Hulett .01 .05
7C David Segui .02 .10
7D Rafael Palmeiro .30 .75
7H Harold Baines .05 .15
7S Mike Devereaux .01 .05
8C Ben McDonald .01 .05
8D Chris Hoiles .01 .05
8H Mark McLemore .02 .10
8S Brady Anderson .20 .50
9C Cal Ripken Jr. .60 1.50
9D Jim Poole .01 .05
9H Jeff Tackett .01 .05
9S Mike Mussina .30 .75
10C Brad Pennington .01 .05
10D Leo Gomez .01 .05
10H Arthur Rhodes .01 .05
10S Sherman Obando .01 .05
11C Jack Voigt .01 .05
11D Tim Hulett .01 .05
11H Damon Buford .01 .05
11S Alan Mills .01 .05
12C Jeffrey Hammonds .01 .05
12D Mike Devereaux .01 .05
12H David Segui .02 .10
12S Jamie Moyer .05 .15
13C Rafael Palmeiro .30 .75
13D Brady Anderson .20 .50
13H Ben McDonald .01 .05
13S Harold Baines .05 .15
NNO Featured Players .01 .05

1995 Orioles Postcards

This set features borderless color photos of the Baltimore Orioles with a matte finish and measures approximately 3 1/2" by 5". The backs carry one of 10 different messages with a facsimile signature printed below. The cards of Bobby Bonilla, Al Bumbry, Jim Dedrick, Jeff Huson, Rick Krivda, and Mike Smith display a postcard format on the backs with a Camden Yards return address. The cards are unnumbered and checklisted below in alphabetical order. Some cards were issued for the Orioles Winter Caravan. The are also interspersed with the regular cards. The players featured on the Winter Carnival Cards were usually retired players. They are notated with a WC after their names.

COMPLETE SET (52) 12.50 30.00
1 Manny Alexander .20 .50
2 Brady Anderson .60 1.50
3 Harold Baines .40 1.00
4 Bret Barberie .20 .50
5 Rex Barney ANN WC .40 1.00
6 Kevin Bass .20 .50
7 Armando Benitez .60 1.50
8 Paul Blair .30 .75
9 Bobby Bonilla .30 .75
10 Steve Boros CO .20 .50
11 Kevin Brown .60 1.50
12 Al Bumbry CO .20 .50
Also in the WC set
13 Terry Clark .20 .50
14 Chuck Cottier CO .20 .50
15 Jim Dedrick .20 .50
16 Mark Eichhorn .20 .50
17 Scott Erickson .20 .50
18 Sid Fernandez .30 .75
19 Mike Flanagan CO .30 .75
20 Leo Gomez .20 .50
21 Curtis Goodwin .20 .50
22 Dick Hall WC .20 .50
23 Jeffrey Hammonds .20 .50
24 Gene Harris .20 .50
25 Chris Hoiles .20 .50
26 Jeff Huson .20 .50
27 Doug Jones .30 .75
28 Rick Krivda .20 .50
29 Mark Lee .20 .50
30 Jeff Manto .20 .50
31 Tippy Martinez WC .20 .50
32 Lee May CO .30 .75
33 Jon Miller ANN WC .30 .75
34 Alan Mills .20 .50
35 Jamie Moyer .60 1.50
36 Mike Mussina 1.00 2.50
37 Mike Oquist .20 .50
38 Jesse Orosco .30 .75
39 Jim Palmer WC 1.00 2.50
40 Rafael Palmiero .60 1.50
41 Boog Powell WC .60 1.50
42 Phil Regan MG .20 .50
43 Arthur Rhodes .20 .50
44 Cal Ripken Jr. 2.00 5.00
45 Brooks Robinson WC 1.00 2.50
46 Larry Sheets WC .20 .50
47 Mark Smith .20 .50
48 Bill Swaggerty WC .20 .50
49 Chuck Thompson ANN WC .30 .75
50 Gregg Zaun .20 .50
51 The Oriole Bird(Mascot) .20 .50
52 Camden Yards .20 .50

1996 Orioles Fleer

These 20 standard-size cards feature the same design as the regular Fleer issue, except they are UV coated, use silver foil and are numbered "x of 20". The team set packs were available at retail locations and hobby shops in 10-card packs for a suggested retail price of $1.99.

COMPLETE SET (20) 2.50 6.00
1 Roberto Alomar .30 .75
2 Brady Anderson .15 .40
3 Armando Benitez .15 .40
4 Bobby Bonilla .07 .20
5 Scott Erickson .07 .20
6 Jeffrey Hammonds .02 .10
7 Jimmy Haynes .02 .10
8 Chris Hoiles .02 .10
9 Rick Krivda .02 .10
10 Kent Mercker .02 .10
11 Mike Mussina .40 1.00
12 Randy Myers .07 .20
13 Jesse Orosco .07 .20
14 Rafael Palmeiro .30 .75
15 Cal Ripken 1.25 3.00
16 B.J. Surhoff .07 .20
17 Tony Tarasco .02 .10
18 David Wells .20 .50
19 Logo card .02 .10
20 Checklist .02 .10

1996 Orioles Postcards

This 39-card set features borderless color photos of the Baltimore Orioles with a matte finish and measures approximately 3 1/2" by 5". The backs display one of seven different messages or a postcard format. The cards are unnumbered and checklisted below in alphabetical order.

COMPLETE SET (39) 8.00 20.00
1 Manny Alexander .20 .50
2 Roberto Alomar .60 1.50
3 Brady Anderson .60 1.50
4 Armando Benitez .60 1.50
5 Bobby Bonilla .30 .75
6 Jim Dedrick .20 .50
7 Mike Devereaux .20 .50
8 Pat Dobson CO .20 .50
9 Rick Down CO .20 .50
10 Scott Erickson .30 .75
11 Andy Etchebarren CO .20 .50
12 Jeffrey Hammonds .20 .50
13 Jimmy Haynes .20 .50
14 Ellie Hendricks CO .20 .50
15 Chris Hoiles .20 .50
16 Jeff Huson .20 .50
17 Davey Johnson MG .30 .75
18 Rick Krivda .20 .50
19 Roger McDowell .20 .50
20 Roger McDowell/(Black-and-white) .20 .50
21 Kent Mercker .20 .50
22 Alan Mills .20 .50
23 Mike Mussina 1.00 2.50
24 Randy Myers .30 .75
25 Jesse Orosco .30 .75
26 Rafael Palmiero .60 1.50
27 Sam Perlozzo CO .20 .50
28 Luis Polonia .20 .50
29 Arthur Rhodes .20 .50
30 Bill Ripken .20 .50
31 Cal Ripken Jr. 2.00 5.00
32 Mark Smith .20 .50
33 John Steams CO .20 .50
34 B.J. Surhoff .40 1.00
35 Earl Weaver MG .60 1.50
36 David Wells .60 1.50
37 Gregg Zaun .20 .50
38 The Bird .20 .50
39 Camden Yards .20 .50

1997 Orioles Postcards

This 35-card set features borderless color postcards of the Baltimore Orioles. Each photo has a matte finish and measures approximately 3 1/2" by 5". The backs display either a blank autograph back, a "Profile" back, or one of two different postcard format backs. The cards are unnumbered and checklisted below in alphabetical order.

COMPLETE SET (35) 6.00 15.00
1 Roberto Alomar .60 1.50
2 Brady Anderson .60 1.50
3 Armando Benitez .60 1.50
4 Mike Bordick/(Portrait) .20 .50
5 Mike Bordick/(Leaning back) .20 .50
6 Shawn Boskie .20 .50
7 Rocky Coppinger .20 .50
8 Rocky Coppinger/(Closer view) .20 .50
9 Eric Davis/(Portrait) .30 .75
10 Eric Davis/(Batting) .30 .75
11 David Dellucci .20 .50
12 Scott Erickson .30 .75
13 Jeffrey Hammonds .20 .50
14 Chris Hoiles .20 .50
15 Pete Incaviglia/(Lighter photo) .20 .50
16 Pete Incaviglia/(Darker photo) .20 .50
17 Mike Johnson .20 .50
18 Scott Kamieniecki .20 .50
19 Jimmy Key .20 .50
20 Terry Mathews .20 .50
21 Ray Miller .20 .50
22 Alan Mills .20 .50
23 Mike Mussina 1.00 2.50
24 Randy Myers .30 .75
25 Jesse Orosco .30 .75
26 Rafael Palmeiro .60 1.50
27 Jeff Reboulet .20 .50
28 Arthur Rhodes .20 .50
29 Cal Ripken Jr. 2.00 5.00
30 Nerio Rodriguez .20 .50
31 B.J. Surhoff .30 .75
32 Tony Tarasco .20 .50
33 Lenny Webster .20 .50
34 Brian Williams .20 .50
35 The Bird(Mascot) .20 .50

1997 Orioles Score

This 15-card set of the Baltimore Orioles was issued in five-card packs with a suggested retail price of $1.30 each. The fronts feature color player photos with special team specific color foil stamping. The backs carry player information. Only 100 cases were made for each team. Platinum parallel cards were inserted at a rate of 1:6, Premier parallel cards at a rate of 1:31.

COMPLETE SET (15) 3.00 8.00
*PLATINUM: 5X BASIC CARDS
*PREMIER: 20X BASIC CARDS
1 Rafael Palmeiro .30 .75
2 Eddie Murray .40 1.00
3 Roberto Alomar .30 .75
4 Rocky Coppinger .08 .25
5 Brady Anderson .25 .60
6 Bobby Bonilla .15 .40
7 Cal Ripken 1.50 4.00
8 Mike Mussina .30 .75
9 Nerio Rodriguez .08 .25
10 Randy Myers .15 .40
11 B.J. Surhoff .15 .40
12 Jeffrey Hammonds .08 .25
13 Chris Hoiles .08 .25
14 Jimmy Haynes .08 .25
15 David Wells .30 .75

1997 Orioles Sun

This seven-card set distributed by the Baltimore Sun measures approximately 9 3/4" by 13" and features color player photos of the Baltimore Orioles. Most of the cards are two-sided with pictures on both sides. The cards are unnumbered and checklisted below in alphabetical order.

COMPLETE SET (7) 4.00 10.00
1 All-Stars .75 2.00
Jimmy Key
2 Roberto Alomar .60 1.50
Todd Zeile
Chris Hoiles
Cal Ripk
3 Roberto Alomar .40 1.00
Rafael Palmeiro
4 Brady Anderson .40 1.00
Randy Myers
5 Mike Bordick 1.00 2.50
Cal Ripken Jr.
6 Mike Mussina .40 1.00
Scott Erickson
7 1997 All-Stars .60 1.50
Brady Anderson
Roberto Alomar
Ca

1998 Orioles Score

This 15-card set was issued in special retail packs and features color photos of the Baltimore Orioles team. The backs carry player information. A special platinum parallel set was also issued and randomly inserted in packs.

COMPLETE SET (15) 3.00 8.00
*PLATINUM: 5X BASIC CARDS
1 Roberto Alomar .40 1.00
2 Jimmy Key .20 .50
3 Cal Ripken 1.50 4.00
4 Brady Anderson .20 .50
5 Geronimo Berroa .08 .25
6 Chris Holles .08 .25
7 Rafael Palmeiro .40 1.00
8 Mike Mussina .40 1.00
9 Randy Myers .20 .50
10 Mike Bordick .08 .25
11 Scott Erickson .20 .50
12 Armando Benitez .40 1.00
13 B.J. Surhoff .20 .50
14 Jeffrey Hammonds .08 .25
15 Arthur Rhodes .08 .25

1999 Orioles Postcards

These postcards were issued by the Baltimore Orioles and feature members of the 1999 Orioles. Some of the poses were repeats of the postcards released in previous years and a few of the early releases have postcards backs. The players with postcards backs who were acquired by the Orioles before the season began are: Chip Alley, Albert Belle, Will Clark, Terry Crowley CO, Delino DeShields, Charles Johnson, Ryan Minor, Calvin Pickering and Alvie Shepard. We have sequenced these postcards in alphabetical order.

COMPLETE SET (45) 12.50 30.00
1 Brady Anderson .30 .75
2 Chip Alley .20 .50
3 Rich Amaral .20 .50
4 Harold Baines .30 .75
5 Albert Belle .30 .75
Player Profile Back
6 Albert Belle .30 .75
PC Back
7 Ricky Bones .20 .50
8 Mike Bordick .20 .50
9 Will Clark .60 1.50
Player Profile Back
10 Will Clark .60 1.50
PC Back
11 Jeff Conine .20 .50
12 Rocky Coppinger .20 .50
13 Terry Crowley CO .20 .50
PC Back
14 Terry Crowley CO .20 .50
Player Profile Back
15 Delino DeShields .20 .50
Early Release
16 Delino DeShields .20 .50
PC Back
17 Scott Erickson .30 .75
18 Mike Fetters .20 .50
19 Mike Figga .20 .50
20 Marv Foley CO .20 .50
21 Juan Guzman .20 .50
22 Ellie Hendricks CO .20 .50
Message Back
23 Doug Johns .20 .50
24 Charles Johnson .20 .50
PC Back
25 Charles Johnson .20 .50
Player Profile Back
26 Jason Johnson .20 .50
27 Scott Kamienicki .20 .50
28 Bruce Kison CO .20 .50
29 Ray Miller MG .20 .50
30 Ryan Minor .20 .50
31 Eddie Murray CO .60 1.50
32 Mike Mussina .60 1.50
33 Jesse Orosco .30 .75
34 Sam Perlozzo CO .20 .50
35 Calvin Pickering .20 .50
36 Sidney Ponson .20 .50
37 Jeff Reboulet .20 .50
38 Arthur Rhodes .20 .50
39 Cal Ripken Jr. 1.50 4.00
40 Alvie Shepard .20 .50
41 B.J. Surhoff .30 .75
42 Mike Timlin .20 .50
43 Lenny Webster .20 .50
44 Bird .20 .50
Mascot
45 Camden Yards .20 .50

1999 Orioles Sheet Coke

This commemorative sheet was issued at the end of the 1999 Orioles season to honor individual highlights attained by various Orioles during the 1999 season. Six players are featured and the sheets are individually numbered.

1 Cal Ripken 2.00 5.00
Will Clark
Jesse Orosco
Harold Baine

2001 Orioles Postcards

COMPLETE SET (36) 8.00 20.00
1 Brady Anderson .40 1.00
2 Mike Bordick .20 .50
3 Jeff Conine .30 .75
4 Terry Crowley CO .20 .50
5 Delino DeShields .20 .50
6 Scott Erickson .30 .75
7 Brook Fordyce .20 .50
8 Jay Gibbons .60 1.50
9 Buddy Groom .20 .50
10 Jerry Hairston Jr. .40 1.00
11 Mike Hargrove MG .20 .50
12 Elrod Hendricks CO .20 .50
13 Pat Hentgen .30 .75
14 Jason Johnson .20 .50
15 Mike Kinkade .20 .50
16 Ryan Kohlmeier .20 .50
17 Fernando Lunar .20 .50
18 Luis Matos .40 1.00
19 Chuck McElroy .20 .50
20 Jose Mercedes .20 .50
21 Alan Mills .20 .50
22 Melvin Mora .20 .50
23 Eddie Murray CO .60 1.50
24 Greg Myers .20 .50
25 Chad Paronto .20 .50
26 Sam Perlozzo CO .20 .50
27 Sidney Ponson .20 .50
28 Chris Richard .20 .50
29 Cal Ripken Jr 1.20 3.00
30 B.J. Ryan .30 .75
31 David Segui .30 .75
32 Willis Roberts .20 .50
33 Josh Towers .20 .50
34 Mike Trombley .20 .50
35 Tom Trebelhorn CO .20 .50
36 Mark Wiley CO .20 .50

2002 Orioles Postcards

COMPLETE SET (41) 8.00 20.00
1 Tony Batista .30 .75
2 Rick Bauer .20 .50
3 Erik Bedard .20 .50
4 Larry Bigbie .20 .50
5 Mike Bordick .20 .50
6 Jeff Conine .30 .75
7 Marty Cordova .20 .50
8 Terry Crowley CO .20 .50
9 Rick Dempsey CO .30 .75
10 Sean Douglass .20 .50
11 Travis Driskill .20 .50
12 Scott Erickson .30 .75
13 Brook Fordyce .20 .50
14 Luis Garcia .20 .50
15 Jay Gibbons .40 1.00
16 Geronimo Gil .20 .50
17 Buddy Groom .20 .50
18 Jerry Hairston .30 .75
19 Mike Hargrove MG .20 .50
20 Elrod Hendricks CO .20 .50
21 Pat Hentgen .20 .50
22 Jason Johnson .20 .50
23 Jorge Julio .40 1.00
24 Rodrigo Lopez .40 1.00
25 Calvin Maduro .20 .50
26 Luis Matos .40 1.00
27 Gary Matthews Jr. .30 .75
28 Melvin Mora .60 1.50
29 Mike Moriarty .20 .50
30 John Parrish .20 .50
31 Sam Perlozzo CO .20 .50
32 Sidney Ponson .20 .50
33 Chris Richard .20 .50
34 Brian Roberts .75 2.00
35 Willis Roberts .20 .50
36 B.J. Ryan .60 1.50
37 David Segui .30 .75
38 Chris Singleton .20 .50
39 Josh Towers .20 .50
40 Tom Trebelhorn CO .20 .50
41 Mark Wiley CO .20 .50

2002 Orioles Program

COMPLETE SET (48) 4.00 10.00
1 Checklist .08 .25
2 John Bale .08 .25
3 Tony Batista .20 .50
4 Rick Bauer .08 .25
5 Erik Bedard .08 .25
6 Larry Bigbie .08 .25
7 Mike Bordick .08 .25
8 Jeff Conine .20 .50
9 Marty Cordova .08 .25
10 Sean Douglass .08 .25
11 Scott Erickson .20 .50
12 Brook Fordyce .08 .25
13 Kris Foster .08 .25
14 Jay Gibbons .30 .75
15 Geronimo Gil .08 .25
16 Buddy Groom .08 .25
17 Jerry Hairston .30 .75
18 Pat Hentgen .08 .25
19 Jason Johnson .08 .25
20 Jorge Julio .30 .75
21 Fernando Lunar .08 .25
22 Calvin Maduro .08 .25
23 Luis Matos .30 .75
24 Melvin Mora .60 1.50
25 John Parrish .08 .25
26 Sydney Ponson .08 .25
27 Chris Richard .08 .25
28 Luis Rivera .08 .25
29 Brian Roberts .60 1.50
30 Willis Roberts .08 .25
31 Eddie Rogers .08 .25
32 B.J. Ryan .40 1.00
33 David Segui .20 .50
34 Chris Singleton .08 .25
35 John Stephens .08 .25
36 Josh Towers .08 .25
37 Mike Hargrove .20 .50
38 Terry Crowley .08 .25
39 Rick Dempsey .08 .25
40 Elrod Hendricks .20 .50
41 Sam Perlozzo .08 .25
42 Tom Treblehorn .08 .25
43 Mark Wiley .08 .25
44 The Bird .08 .25
45 OPCY Birds Eye .08 .25
46 OPCY Interior .08 .25
47 OPCY Façade .08 .25
48 Eutaw Street .08 .25

2006 Orioles Topps

COMPLETE SET (14) 3.00 8.00
BAL1 Miguel Tejada .20 .50
BAL2 Corey Patterson .12 .30
BAL3 Melvin Mora .12 .30
BAL4 Brian Roberts .12 .30
BAL5 Jay Gibbons .12 .30
BAL6 Luis Matos .12 .30
BAL7 Javy Lopez .12 .30
BAL8 Rodrigo Lopez .12 .30
BAL9 Erik Bedard .12 .30
BAL10 Daniel Cabrera .12 .30
BAL11 Bruce Chen .12 .30
BAL12 Jorge Julio .12 .30
BAL13 David Newhan .12 .30
BAL14 Ramon Hernandez .12 .30

2007 Orioles Topps

COMPLETE SET (14) 3.00 8.00
BAL1 Miguel Tejada .20 .50
BAL2 Ramon Hernandez .12 .30
BAL3 Jay Gibbons .12 .30
BAL4 Aubrey Huff .12 .30
BAL5 Kris Benson .12 .30
BAL6 Jay Payton .12 .30
BAL7 Chris Ray .12 .30
BAL8 Melvin Mora .12 .30
BAL9 Corey Patterson .12 .30
BAL10 Daniel Cabrera .12 .30
BAL11 Adam Loewen .12 .30
BAL12 Brian Roberts .12 .30
BAL13 Erik Bedard .12 .30
BAL14 Nick Markakis .25 .60

2008 Orioles Topps

COMPLETE SET (14) 3.00 8.00
BAL1 Nick Markakis .25 .60
BAL2 Brian Roberts .12 .30
BAL3 Ramon Hernandez .12 .30
BAL4 Kevin Millar .12 .30
BAL5 Aubrey Huff .12 .30
BAL6 Jeremy Guthrie .12 .30
BAL7 Jay Payton .12 .30
BAL8 Chris Ray .12 .30
BAL9 Melvin Mora .12 .30
BAL10 Adam Loewen .12 .30
BAL11 Daniel Cabrera .12 .30
BAL12 Brian Burres .12 .30
BAL13 Luke Scott .12 .30
BAL14 Erik Bedard .12 .30

2009 Orioles Topps

BAL1 Nick Markakis .30 .75
BAL2 Adam Jones .25 .60
BAL3 Radhames Liz .15 .40
BAL4 Aubrey Huff .15 .40
BAL5 Cesar Izturis .15 .40
BAL6 Brian Roberts .15 .40
BAL7 Lou Montañez .15 .40
BAL8 Ryan Freel .15 .40
BAL9 Melvin Mora .15 .40
BAL10 Luke Scott .15 .40
BAL11 George Sherrill .15 .40
BAL12 Jeremy Guthrie .15 .40
BAL13 Chris Ray .15 .40
BAL14 Felix Pie .15 .40
BAL15 Oriole Park At Camden Yards .15 .40

2010 Orioles Topps

BAL1 Adam Jones .25 .60
BAL2 Luke Scott .15 .40
BAL3 Nick Markakis .30 .75
BAL4 Ty Wigginton .15 .40
BAL5 David Hernandez .15 .40
BAL6 Jeremy Guthrie .15 .40
BAL7 Brian Roberts .15 .40
BAL8 Cesar Izturis .15 .40
BAL9 Felix Pie .15 .40
BAL10 Nolan Reimold .15 .40
BAL11 Koji Uehara .15 .40
BAL12 Chris Tillman .15 .40
BAL13 Mike Gonzalez .15 .40
BAL14 Kevin Millwood .15 .40
BAL15 Garrett Atkins .15 .40
BAL16 Brad Bergesen .15 .40
BAL17 Cla Meredith .15 .40

2011 Orioles Topps

BAL1 Nick Markakis .30 .75
BAL2 Adam Jones .25 .60
BAL3 Brian Matusz .15 .40
BAL4 Chris Tillman .15 .40
BAL5 Felix Pie .15 .40
BAL6 Nolan Reimold .15 .40
BAL7 Brian Roberts .15 .40
BAL8 Luke Scott .15 .40
BAL9 Koji Uehara .15 .40
BAL10 Derrek Lee .15 .40
BAL11 Jake Arrieta .30 .75
BAL12 Josh Bell .15 .40
BAL13 Kevin Gregg .15 .40
BAL14 Jeremy Guthrie .15 .40
BAL15 J.J. Hardy .15 .40
BAL16 Mark Reynolds .15 .40
BAL17 Oriole Park at Camden Yards .15 .40

2012 Orioles Topps

BALT1 Adam Jones .30 .75
BALT2 Nick Markakis .30 .75
BALT3 Nolan Reimold .25 .60
BALT4 Brian Roberts .25 .60
BALT5 Chris Davis .25 .60
BALT6 Alfredo Simon .25 .60
BALT7 Kevin Gregg .25 .60
BALT8 J.J. Hardy .25 .60
BALT9 Endy Chavez .25 .60
BALT10 Tommy Hunter .25 .60
BALT11 Jake Arrieta .30 .75
BALT12 Robert Andino .25 .60
BALT13 Jim Johnson .15 .40
BALT14 Brian Matusz .25 .60
BALT15 Mark Reynolds .25 .60
BALT16 Zach Britton .30 .75
BALT17 Oriole Park at Camden Yards .15 .40

2013 Orioles Topps

COMPLETE SET (17) 3.00 8.00
BAL1 Adam Jones .30 .75
BAL2 Manny Machado 1.00 2.50
BAL3 Nick Markakis .30 .75
BAL4 Jim Johnson .25 .60
BAL5 J.J. Hardy .25 .60
BAL6 Jason Hammel .30 .75
BAL7 Dylan Bundy .40 1.00
BAL8 Wei-Yin Chen .15 .40
BAL9 Chris Davis .20 .50
BAL10 Brian Roberts .25 .60
BAL11 Jake Arrieta .20 .50
BAL12 Brian Matusz .15 .40
BAL13 Nolan Reimold .25 .60
BAL14 Nate McLouth .15 .40
BAL15 Miguel Gonzalez .25 .60
BAL16 Chris Tillman .25 .60
BAL17 Oriole Park at Camden Yards .15 .40

2014 Orioles Topps

COMPLETE SET (17) 3.00 8.00
BAL1 Adam Jones .20 .50
BAL2 Manny Machado .25 .60
BAL3 Nick Markakis .20 .50
BAL4 Bud Norris .15 .40
BAL5 J.J. Hardy .15 .40
BAL6 Brian Matusz .15 .40
BAL7 Dylan Bundy .20 .50
BAL8 Wei-Yin Chen .15 .40
BAL9 Chris Davis .15 .40
BAL10 Mike Belfiore .15 .40
BAL11 Kevin Gausman .25 .60
BAL12 Miguel Gonzalez .15 .40
BAL13 Steve Pearce .15 .40
BAL14 Nolan Reimold .15 .40
BAL15 Jonathan Schoop .15 .40
BAL16 Chris Tillman .15 .40
BAL17 Oriole Park at Camden Yards .15 .40

2015 Orioles Topps

COMPLETE SET (17) 3.00 8.00
BO1 Adam Jones .20 .50
BO2 Alejandro De Aza .15 .40
BO3 Miguel Gonzalez .15 .40
BO4 Ubaldo Jimenez .15 .40
BO5 Zach Britton .20 .50
BO6 Darren O'Day .15 .40
BO7 Manny Machado .25 .60
BO8 Bud Norris .15 .40
BO9 Jonathan Schoop .15 .40
BO10 Steve Pearce .25 .60
BO11 J.J. Hardy .15 .40
BO12 Chris Davis .15 .40
BO13 Delmon Young .20 .50
BO14 Chris Tillman .15 .40
BO15 Wei-Yin Chen .15 .40
BO16 Tommy Hunter .15 .40
BO17 Caleb Joseph .15 .40

2016 Orioles Topps

COMPLETE SET (17) 3.00 8.00
BAL1 Manny Machado .25 .60
BAL2 Caleb Joseph .15 .40
BAL3 Darren O'Day .15 .40
BAL4 Jonathan Schoop .15 .40
BAL5 J.J. Hardy .15 .40
BAL6 Chris Davis .15 .40
BAL7 Adam Jones .20 .50
BAL8 Mark Trumbo .15 .40
BAL9 Jimmy Paredes .15 .40
BAL10 T.J. McFarland .15 .40
BAL11 Chris Tillman .15 .40
BAL12 Ubaldo Jimenez .15 .40
BAL13 Zach Britton .20 .50
BAL14 Ryan Flaherty .15 .40
BAL15 Brian Matusz .15 .40
BAL16 Miguel Gonzalez .15 .40
BAL17 Kevin Gausman .25 .60

2017 Orioles Topps

COMPLETE SET (17) 3.00 8.00
BAL1 Manny Machado .25 .60
BAL2 J.J. Hardy .15 .40
BAL3 Caleb Joseph .15 .40
BAL4 Chris Davis .15 .40
BAL5 Brad Brach .15 .40
BAL6 Jonathan Schoop .15 .40
BAL7 Hyun-Soo Kim .20 .50
BAL8 Zach Britton .20 .50
BAL9 Adam Jones .20 .50
BAL10 Chris Tillman .15 .40
BAL11 Kevin Gausman .25 .60
BAL12 Darren O'Day .15 .40
BAL13 Oriole Park at Camden Yards .15 .40
BAL14 Mychal Givens .15 .40
BAL15 Wellington Castillo .15 .40
BAL16 Dylan Bundy .20 .50
BAL17 Joey Rickard .15 .40

2018 Orioles Topps

COMPLETE SET (17) 2.00 5.00
BO1 Jonathan Schoop .15 .40
BO2 Manny Machado .25 .60
BO3 Joey Rickard .15 .40
BO4 Caleb Joseph .15 .40
BO5 Tim Beckham .20 .50
BO6 Trey Mancini .20 .50
BO7 Adam Jones .20 .50
BO8 Kevin Gausman .25 .60
BO9 Mark Trumbo .15 .40
BO10 Anthony Santander .15 .40
BO11 Zach Britton .15 .40
BO12 Austin Hays .25 .60
BO13 Chris Davis .15 .40
BO14 Darren O'Day .15 .40
BO15 Dylan Bundy .20 .50
BO16 Brad Brach .15 .40
BO17 Chance Sisco .20 .50

2019 Orioles Topps

COMPLETE SET (17) 2.00 5.00
BO1 Trey Mancini .20 .50
BO2 Rio Ruiz .15 .40
BO3 Jonathan Villar .15 .40
BO4 Mark Trumbo .15 .40
BO5 Dylan Bundy .20 .50
BO6 Andrew Cashner .15 .40
BO7 Alex Cobb .15 .40
BO8 Cedric Mullins .30 .75
BO9 Joey Rickard .15 .40
BO10 Jace Peterson .15 .40
BO11 Chris Davis .15 .40
BO12 Renato Nunez .20 .50
BO13 Mychal Givens .15 .40
BO14 DJ Stewart .20 .50
BO15 Richard Bleier .15 .40
BO16 David Hess .15 .40
BO17 Chance Sisco .15 .40

2020 Orioles Topps

BAL1 Trey Mancini .25 .60
BAL2 DJ Stewart .15 .40
BAL3 Chance Sisco .15 .40
BAL4 John Means .25 .60
BAL5 Hunter Harvey .25 .60
BAL6 Pedro Severino .15 .40
BAL7 Austin Hays .25 .60
BAL8 Anthony Santander .15 .40
BAL9 Mychal Givens .15 .40
BAL10 Stevie Wilkerson .25 .60
BAL11 Alex Cobb .15 .40
BAL12 Rio Ruiz .15 .40
BAL13 Hanser Alberto .15 .40
BAL14 Renato Nunez .20 .50
BAL15 Dwight Smith Jr. .15 .40
BAL16 Richard Bleier .15 .40
BAL17 Chris Davis .15 .40

2017 Orioles Topps National Baseball Card Day

COMPLETE SET (10) 6.00 15.00
BAL1 Manny Machado 1.00 2.50
BAL2 Adam Jones .75 2.00
BAL3 Chris Tillman .60 1.50
BAL4 J.J. Hardy .60 1.50
BAL5 Mark Trumbo .60 1.50
BAL6 Zach Britton .75 2.00
BAL7 Chris Davis .60 1.50
BAL8 Kevin Gausman 1.00 2.50
BAL9 Jonathan Schoop .60 1.50
BAL10 Cal Ripken Jr. 3.00 8.00

1994 Oscar Mayer Round-Ups

The 1994 Oscar Mayer Superstar Round-Up set consists of 30 circular pop-up cards measuring about 2 1/2" in diameter and features 15 players from the American (1-15) and National (16-30) Leagues. One card was inserted in each specially marked 16-oz. package of Oscar Mayer bologna available in April and May. On-pack and in-store point-of-purchase mail-in offers enabled consumers to order a boxed American and/or National League 15-card set for 1.95 plus proof-of-purchase for each set. The black-bordered fronts feature color action player shots that are perforated and cut out in such a way so that when the tab at the top is pulled, the photo becomes three-dimensional. Also revealed is a trivia question and answer, and the player's statistics. The set's title appears at the top within the black border in blue lettering on American League cards and green lettering on National League cards. The player's name, position, and team appear below the photo. The back displays the player's name, position, team, and career highlights. A color player action cutout appears alongside. The cards are numbered on the front toward the lower right, following alphabetical order by league.

COMPLETE SET (30) 5.00 12.00
1 Jim Abbott .15 .40
2 Kevin Appier .07 .20
3 Roger Clemens .60 1.50
4 Cecil Fielder .15 .40
5 Juan Gonzalez .30 .75
6 Ken Griffey Jr. 1.00 2.50
7 Kenny Lofton .25 .60
8 Jack McDowell .07 .20
9 Paul Molitor .40 1.00
10 Kirby Puckett .50 1.25
11 Cal Ripken Jr. 1.25 3.00
12 Tim Salmon .25 .60
13 Ruben Sierra .15 .40

14 Frank Thomas .40 1.00
15 Greg Vaughn .15 .40
16 Jeff Bagwell .40 1.00
17 Barry Bonds .60 1.50
18 Bobby Bonilla .15 .40
19 Jeff Conine .07 .20
20 Lenny Dykstra .15 .40
21 Andres Galarraga .30 .75
22 Marquis Grissom .07 .20
23 Tony Gwynn .60 1.50
24 Gregg Jefferies .07 .20
25 John Kruk .15 .40
26 Greg Maddux .75 2.00
27 Mike Piazza .75 2.00
28 Jose Rijo .07 .20
29 Ryne Sandberg .40 1.00
30 Andy Van Slyke .15 .40

1987 Our Own Tea Discs

These Discs, which feature the Our Own Tea name on the front, are a parallel issue to the 1987 MSA Iced Tea Discs. They are valued the same as the regular Discs.

COMPLETE SET (20) 3.00 8.00
1 Darryl Strawberry .07 .20
2 Roger Clemens .60 1.50
3 Ron Darling .02 .10
4 Keith Hernandez .07 .20
5 Tony Pena .02 .10
6 Don Mattingly .60 1.50
7 Eric Davis .07 .20
8 Gary Carter .30 .75
9 Dave Winfield .30 .75
10 Wally Joyner .25 .60
11 Mike Schmidt .30 .75
12 Robby Thompson .02 .10
13 Wade Boggs .30 .75
14 Cal Ripken 1.25 3.00
15 Dale Murphy .15 .40
16 Tony Gwynn .75 2.00
17 Jose Canseco .30 .75
18 Rickey Henderson .40 1.25
19 Lance Parrish .02 .10
20 Dave Righetti .02 .10

1988 Our Own Tea Discs

For the second year, MSA issued iced tea discs with the Our Own Tea label on the front. These discs are parallel to the regular Iced Tea Discs and are valued the same

COMPLETE SET (20) 4.00 10.00
1 Wade Boggs .30 .75
2 Ellis Burks .25 .60
3 Don Mattingly .60 1.50
4 Mark McGwire .50 1.25
5 Matt Nokes .02 .10
6 Kirby Puckett .40 1.00
7 Billy Ripken .02 .10
8 Kevin Seitzer .02 .10
9 Roger Clemens .60 1.50
10 Will Clark .25 .60
11 Vince Coleman .02 .10
12 Eric Davis .07 .20
13 Dave Magadan .02 .10
14 Dale Murphy .15 .40
15 Benito Santiago .07 .20
16 Mike Schmidt .30 .75
17 Darryl Strawberry .07 .20
18 Steve Bedrosian .02 .10
19 Dwight Gooden .07 .20
20 Fernando Valenzuela .07 .20

1989 Our Own Tea Discs

For the third season, Our Own Tea was one of the companies which distributed the MSA Iced Tea Discs. These discs say Our Own on the front and are valued the same as the MSA Iced Tea discs.

COMPLETE SET (20) 12.50 30.00
1 Don Mattingly 2.50 6.00
2 Dave Cone (David) .75 2.00
3 Mark McGwire 2.00 5.00
4 Will Clark 1.00 2.50
5 Darryl Strawberry .60 1.50
6 Dwight Gooden .60 1.50
7 Wade Boggs 1.25 3.00
8 Roger Clemens 2.50 6.00
9 Benito Santiago .60 1.50
10 Orel Hershiser .60 1.50
11 Eric Davis .60 1.50
12 Kirby Puckett 2.00 5.00
13 Dave Winfield 1.25 3.00
14 Andre Dawson 1.00 2.50
15 Steve Bedrosian .40 1.00
16 Cal Ripken 6.00 15.00
17 Andy Van Slyke .40 1.00
18 Jose Canseco 1.25 3.00
19 Jose Oquendo .40 1.00
20 Dale Murphy 1.00 2.50

1936-41 Overland Candy R301

These unnumbered cards (which are actually wrappers) measure 5" by 5 1/4" and were issued over a period of time in the 1930's. A drawing of the player is on the top of the wrapper with his name and biography underneath him. The Overland Candy Co logo is noted on the bottom. Wrappers are known with or without the ingredient list. No extra value is given for either variation.

COMPLETE SET 7500.00 15000.00
1 Mel Almada 200.00 400.00
2 Luke Appling 400.00 800.00
3 Earl Averill 400.00 800.00
4 Wally Berger 250.00 500.00
5 Zeke Bonura 250.00 500.00
6 Dolph Camilli 250.00 500.00
7 Phil Cavaretta 250.00 500.00
8 Ben Chapman 200.00 400.00
9 Harland Clift 200.00 400.00
10A Johnny Cooney Boston 200.00 400.00
10B Johnny Cooney Brooklyn 200.00 400.00
11A Bill Dietrich Chicago 200.00 400.00
11B Bill Dietrich Philadelphia 200.00 400.00
12 Joe DiMaggio 2000.00 4000.00
13 Jimmie Foxx 400.00 800.00
14 Lou Gehrig 1500.00 3000.00
15 Charley Gehringer 400.00 800.00
16 Jose Luis Gomez 200.00 400.00
17 Lefty Gomez 400.00 800.00
18 Joe Gordon 300.00 600.00
19 Hank Greenberg 400.00 800.00
20 Lefty Grove 400.00 800.00
21 Mule Haas 200.00 400.00
22 Rollie Hemsley 200.00 400.00
23 Pinky Higgins 200.00 400.00
24 Oral Hildebrand 200.00 400.00
25 Bob Johnson 250.00 500.00
26 Buck Jordan 200.00 400.00
27 Fabian Kowalik 200.00 400.00
28 Ken Keltner 250.00 500.00
29 Cookie Lavagetto 200.00 400.00
30 Tony Lazzeri 400.00 800.00
31 Samuel A. Leslie 200.00 400.00
32 Danny Litwhiler 200.00 400.00
33 Ted Lyons 400.00 800.00
34 George McQuinn 200.00 400.00
35 Johnny Mize 400.00 800.00
36 Terry Moore 200.00 400.00
37 Bill Nicholson 200.00 400.00
38 Frankie Pytlak 200.00 400.00
39 Rip Radcliff 200.00 400.00
40 Pete Reiser 300.00 600.00
41 Red Rolfe 250.00 500.00
42 Schoolboy Rowe 250.00 500.00
43 Al Simmons 400.00 800.00
44 Cecil Travis 250.00 500.00
45 Hal Trosky 250.00 500.00
46 Joe Vosmik 200.00 400.00
47 Bill Werber 200.00 400.00
48 Max West 200.00 400.00
49 Sam West 200.00 400.00
50 Whit Wyatt 200.00 400.00

1921 Oxford Confectionery E253

This 20 card set measures 1 5/8" by 2 3/4" and almost the whole front is a player photo. The player's name and team is on the bottom. The backs note that these cards are produced solely for the Oxford Confectionery Company and lists a player checklist.

COMPLETE SET (20) 3000.00 6000.00
1 Grover C. Alexander 750.00 1500.00
2 Dave Bancroft 400.00 800.00
3 Max Carey 400.00 800.00
4 Ty Cobb 3000.00 6000.00
5 Eddie Collins 750.00 1500.00
6 Frankie Frisch 600.00 1200.00
7 Burleigh Grimes 400.00 800.00
8 Bill Holke 200.00 400.00
9 Rogers Hornsby 1000.00 2000.00
10 Walter Johnson 1500.00 3000.00
11 Lee Meadows 200.00 400.00
12 Cy Perkins 200.00 400.00
13 Del Pratt 200.00 400.00
14 Ed Roush 400.00 800.00
15 Babe Ruth 5000.00 10000.00
16 Ray Schalk 400.00 800.00
17 George Sisler 600.00 1200.00
18 Tris Speaker 750.00 1500.00
19 Cy Williams 200.00 400.00
20 Whitey Witt 200.00 400.00

1990 Pacific Candy Wade Boggs

COMPLETE SET (1) .75 2.00
NNO Wade Boggs .75 2.00

1980-83 Pacific Legends

This 120-card standard-size set is actually four 30-card subsets plus a four-card wax box bottom panel (cards 121-124). The golden-toned set was distributed by series over several years beginning in 1980 with the first 30 cards. The set was produced by Pacific Trading Cards and is frequently referred to as Cramer Legends, for the founder of Pacific Trading cards, Mike Cramer. Even though the wax box cards are numbered from 121-124 and called "Series 5," the set is considered complete without them. Each series was originally available from Pacific Trading card for $2.95 each.

COMPLETE SET (120) 12.50 30.00
COMMON PLAYER (1-120) .10
COMMON PLAYER (121-124) .50
1 Babe Ruth 1.25 3.00
2 Heinie Manush .07 .20
3 Rabbit Maranville .07 .20
4 Earl Averill .07 .20
5 Joe DiMaggio 1.00 2.50
6 Mickey Mantle 1.25 3.00
7 Hank Aaron .60 1.50
8 Stan Musial .30 .75
9 Bill Terry .07 .20
10 Sandy Koufax .20 .50
11 Ernie Lombardi .07 .20
12 Dizzy Dean .20 .50
13 Lou Gehrig 1.00 2.50
14 Walter Alston .07 .20
15 Jackie Robinson .60 1.50
16 Jimmie Foxx .10 .30
17 Billy Southworth .02 .10
18 Honus Wagner .30 .75
19 Duke Snider .20 .50
20 Rogers Hornsby UER (At bat total of/1873 is inco .20 .50
21 Paul Waner .07 .20
22 Luke Appling .07 .20
23 Billy Herman .07 .20
24 Lloyd Waner .07 .20
25 Fred Hutchinson .02 .10
26 Eddie Collins .07 .20
27 Lefty Grove .10 .30
28 Chuck Connors .10 .30
29 Lefty O'Doul .02 .10
30 Hank Greenberg .20 .50
31 Ty Cobb .75 2.00
32 Enos Slaughter .07 .20
33 Ernie Banks .20 .50
34 Christy Mathewson .20 .50
35 Mel Ott .10 .30
36 Pie Traynor .07 .20
37 Clark Griffith .07 .20
38 Mickey Cochrane .07 .20
39 Joe Cronin .07 .20
40 Leo Durocher .07 .20
41 Home Run Baker .07 .20
42 Joe Tinker .07 .20
43 John McGraw .07 .20
44 Bill Dickey .07 .20
45 Walter Johnson .20 .50
46 Frankie Frisch .07 .20
47 Casey Stengel .10 .30
48 Willie Mays .60 1.50
49 Johnny Mize .07 .20
50 Roberto Clemente .75 2.00
51 Burleigh Grimes .07 .20
52 Pee Wee Reese .20 .50
53 Bob Feller .20 .50
54 Brooks Robinson .20 .50
55 Sam Crawford .07 .20
56 Robin Roberts .10 .30
57 Warren Spahn .10 .30
58 Joe McCarthy .07 .20
59 Jocko Conlan .07 .20
60 Satchel Paige 1.00
61 Ted Williams .75 2.00
62 George Kelly .07 .20
63 Gil Hodges .10 .30
64 Jim Bottomley .07 .20
65 Al Kaline .20 .50
66 Harvey Kuenn .02 .10
67 Yogi Berra .20 .50
68 Nellie Fox .02 .10
69 Harmon Killebrew .10 .30
70 Edd Roush .07 .20
71 Mordecai Brown .07 .20
72 Gabby Hartnett .07 .20
73 Early Wynn .07 .20
74 Nap Lajoie .07 .20
75 Charlie Grimm .02 .10
76 Joe Garagiola .07 .20
77 Ted Lyons .02 .10
78 Mickey Vernon .02 .10
79 Lou Boudreau .07 .20
80 Al Dark .02 .10
81 Ralph Kiner .10 .30
82 Phil Rizzuto .10 .30
83 Stan Hack .02 .10
84 Frank Chance .07 .20
85 Ray Schalk .07 .20
86 Bill McKechnie .07 .20
87 Travis Jackson .07 .20
88 Pete Reiser .02 .10
89 Carl Hubbell .10 .30
90 Roy Campanella .20 .50
91 Cy Young .10 .30
92 Kiki Cuyler .07 .20
93 Chief Bender .07 .20
94 Richie Ashburn .10 .30
95 Riggs Stephenson .02 .10
96 Minnie Minoso .02 .10
97 Hack Wilson .07 .20
98 Al Lopez .07 .20
99 Willie Keeler .07 .20
100 Fred Lindstrom .07 .20
101 Roger Maris .10 .30
102 Roger Bresnahan .07 .20
103 Monty Stratton .07 .20
104 Goose Goslin .07 .20
105 Earle Combs .07 .20
106 Pepper Martin .02 .10
107 Joe Jackson .60 1.50
108 George Sisler .07 .20
109 Red Ruffing .07 .20
110 Johnny Vander Meer .02 .10
111 Herb Pennock .07 .20
112 Chuck Klein .07 .20
113 Paul Derringer .02 .10
114 Addie Joss .07 .20
115 Bobby Thomson .02 .10
116 Chick Hafey .07 .20
117 Lefty Gomez .07 .20
118 George Kell .07 .20
119 Al Simmons .07 .20
120 Bob Lemon .07 .20
121 Hoyt Wilhelm/(Wax box card) .20 .50
122 Arky Vaughan/(Wax box card) .20 .50
123 Frank Robinson/(Wax box card) .60 1.50
124 Grover Alexander/(Wax box card) 1.00

1984 Pacific Trading Cards Postcards

These postcards were sent from Pacific Trading Cards to members of their mailing list to announce events in what was then their flagship store. The fronts feature famous major leaguers while the backs feature information about upcoming events at Pacific's store

COMPLETE SET 4.00 10.00
1 Bob Feller 1.25 3.00
2 Babe Ruth 4.00 10.00

1988 Pacific Eight Men Out

This 110-card standard-size set, produced by Mike Cramer's Pacific Trading Cards of Edmonds, Washington, was released in conjunction with the popular movie of the same name, which told the story of the "fix" of the 1919 World Series between the Cincinnati Reds and the Chicago "Black" Sox. The cards have a raspberry-colored border on the card fronts as well as raspberry-colored print on the white card stock backs. The cards were available either as wax packs or as collated sets. Generally the cards relating to the movie (showing actors) are in full-color whereas the vintage photography showing the actual players involved is in a sepia tone.

COMPLETE SET (110) 3.00 8.00
COMP.FACT SET (110) 3.00 8.00
1 We're Going To See The Sox .05 .15
2 White Sox Win The Pennant .01 .05
3 The Series .01 .05
4 1919 Chicago White Sox .01 .05
5 The Black Sox Scandal .01 .05
6 Eddie Cicotte 29-7 in 1919 .05 .15
7 Buck's Their Favorite .05 .15
8 Eddie Collins .08 .25
9 Michael Rooker as Chick Gandil .01 .05
10 Charlie Sheen as Hap Felsch .20 .50
11 James Read as Lefty Williams .01 .05
12 John Cusack as Buck Weaver .08 .25
13 D.B. Sweeney as Joe Jackson .08 .25
14 David Strathairn as Eddie Cicotte .01 .05
15 Perry Lang as Fred McMullin .05 .15
16 Don Harvey as Swede Risberg .01 .05
17 The Gambler Burns And Maharg .01 .05
18 Sleepy Bill Burns .01 .05
19 The Key is Cicotte .01 .05
20 C'mon Betsy .01 .05
21 The Fix .01 .05
22 Chick Approaches Cicotte .01 .05
23 Kid Gleason MG .01 .05
24 Charles Comiskey OWN .01 .05
25 Chick Gandil/1st Baseman .05 .15
26 Swede Risberg .01 .05
27 Sport Sullivan .01 .05
28 Abe Attell And Arnold Rothstein .01 .05
29 Hugh Fullerton Sportswriter .01 .05
30 Ring Lardner Sportswriter .01 .05
31 Shoeless Joe His Batting Eye .08 .25
32 Shoeless Joe .20 .50
33 Buck Can't Sleep .01 .05
34 George Buck Weaver .05 .15
35 Hugh and Ring Confront Kid .01 .05
36 Joe Doesn't Want To Play .05 .15
37 Shoeless Joe Jackson .20 .50
38 Sore Arm, Cicotte Old Man Cicotte .01 .05
39 The Fix Is On .01 .05
40 Buck Plays To Win .01 .05
41 Hap Makes A Great Catch .01 .05
42 Hugh and Ring Suspect .01 .05
43 Ray Gets Things Going .01 .05
44 Lefty Loses Game Two .01 .05
45 Lefty Crosses Up Catcher Ray Schalk .01 .05
46 Chick's RBI Wins Game Three .01 .05
47 Dickie Kerr Wins Game Three .01 .05
48 Chick Leaves Buck At Third .01 .05
49 Williams Loses Game Five .01 .05
50 Ray Schalk .01 .05
51 Schalk Blocks The Plate .01 .05
52 Schalk Is Thrown Out .01 .05
53 Chicago Stickball Game .01 .05
54 I'm Forever Blowing Ball Games .01 .05
55 Felsch Scores Jackson .08 .25
56 Kerr Wins Game Six .01 .05
57 Where's The Money .01 .05
58 Cicotte Wins Game Seven .01 .05
59 Kid Watches Eddie .01 .05
60 Lefty Is Threatened .01 .05
61 James Get Your Arm Ready Fast .01 .05
62 Shoeless Joe's Home Run .20 .50
63 Buck Played His Best .05 .15
64 Hugh Exposes The Fix .01 .05
65 Sign The Petition .01 .05
66 Baseball Owners Hire A Commissioner .01 .05
67 Judge Kenesaw Mountain Landis .05 .15
68 Grand Jury Summoned .01 .05
69 Say It Ain't So, Joe .08 .25
70 The Swede's A Hard Guy .01 .05
71 Buck Loves The Game .01 .05
72 The Trial .01 .05
73 Kid Gleason Takes The Stand .01 .05
74 The Verdict .01 .05
75 Eight Men Out .01 .05
76 Oscar(Happy) Felsch .05 .15
77 Who's Joe Jackson .08 .25
78 Ban Johnson PRES .05 .15
79 Judge Landis COMM .05 .15
80 Charles Comiskey OWN .05 .15
81 Heinie Groh .01 .05
82 Slim Sallee .01 .05
83 Dutch Ruether .01 .05
84 Edd Roush .08 .25
85 Morrie Rath .01 .05
86 Bill Rariden .01 .05
87 Jimmy Ring .01 .05
88 Greasy Neale .05 .15
89 Pat Moran MG .01 .05
90 Adolfo Luque .01 .05
91 Larry Kopf .01 .05
92 Ray Fisher .01 .05
93 Hod Eller .01 .05
94 Pat Duncan .01 .05
95 Jake Daubert .01 .05
96 Red Faber .08 .25
97 Dickie Kerr .01 .05
98 Shano Collins .01 .05
99 Eddie Collins .08 .25
100 Ray Schalk .08 .25
101 Nemo Leibold .01 .05
102 Kid Gleason MG .05 .15
103 Swede Risberg .05 .15
104 Eddie Cicotte .05 .15
105 Fred McMullin .01 .05
106 Chick Gandil .08 .25
107 Buck Weaver .08 .25
108 Lefty Williams .05 .15
109 Happy Felsch .05 .15
110 Joe Jackson .40 1.00

1988 Pacific Legends I

This attractive set of 110 full-color standard-size silver-bordered cards was produced by Mike Cramer's Pacific Trading Cards of Edmonds, Washington. Card backs are printed in yellow, black, and gray on white card stock. The cards were available either as wax packs or as collated sets. The players pictured in the set had retired many years before, but most are still well remembered. The statistics on the card backs give the player's career and "best season" statistics. The set was licensed by Major League Baseball Players Alumni.

COMPLETE SET (110) 5.00 12.00
COMP. FACT SET (110) 4.00 10.00
1 Hank Aaron .60 1.50
2 Red Schoendienst .05 .15
3 Brooks Robinson .08 .25
4 Luke Appling .05 .15
5 Gene Woodling .01 .05
6 Stan Musial .30 .75
7 Mickey Mantle 1.25 3.00
8 Richie Ashburn .08 .25
9 Ralph Kiner .08 .25
10 Phil Rizzuto .08 .25
11 Harvey Haddix .01 .05
12 Ken Boyer .02 .10
13 Clete Boyer .01 .05
14 Ken Harrelson .02 .10
15 Robin Roberts .08 .25
16 Catfish Hunter .08 .25
17 Frank Howard .02 .10
18 Jim Perry .01 .05
19A Elston Howard ERR (Reversed negative) .08 .25
19B Elston Howard COR .08 .25
20 Jim Bouton .02 .10
21 Pee Wee Reese .08 .25
22A Mel Stottlemyre ERR (Spelled Stottlemyer on card) .05 .15
22B Mel Stottlemyre COR .05 .15
23 Hank Sauer .01 .05
24 Willie Mays .60 1.50
25 Tom Tresh .01 .05
26 Roy Sievers .01 .05
27 Leo Durocher .08 .25
28 Al Dark .01 .05
29 Tony Kubek .02 .10
30 Johnny VanderMeer .02 .10
31 Joe Adcock .01 .05
32 Bob Lemon .08 .25
33 Don Newcombe .02 .10
34 Thurman Munson .08 .25
35 Earl Battey .01 .05
36 Ernie Banks .20 .50
37 Matty Alou .01 .05
38 Dave McNally .01 .05
39 Mickey Lolich .02 .10
40 Jackie Robinson .75 2.00
41 Allie Reynolds .02 .10
42A Don Larsen ERR/(Misspelled Larson on card front) .05 .15
42B Don Larsen COR .05 .15
43 Fergie Jenkins .08 .25
44 Jim Gilliam .02 .10
45 Bobby Thomson .02 .10
46 Sparky Anderson .02 .10
47 Roy Campanella .20 .50
48 Marv Throneberry .01 .05
49 Bill Virdon .01 .05
50 Ted Williams .60 1.50
51 Minnie Minoso .02 .10
52 Bob Turley .01 .05
53 Yogi Berra .20 .50
54 Juan Marichal .08 .25
55 Duke Snider .20 .50
56 Harvey Kuenn .01 .05
57 Nellie Fox .08 .25
58 Felipe Alou .02 .10
59 Tony Oliva .02 .10
60 Bill Mazeroski .08 .25
61 Bobby Shantz .01 .05
62 Mark Fidrych .05 .15
63 Johnny Mize .08 .25
64 Ralph Terry .01 .05
65 Gus Bell .01 .05
66 Jerry Koosman .02 .10
67 Mike McCormick .01 .05
68 Lou Burdette .01 .05
69 George Kell .08 .25
70 Vic Raschi .01 .05
71 Chuck Connors .08 .25
72 Ted Kluszewski .08 .25
73 Bobby Doerr .08 .25
74 Bobby Richardson .02 .10
75 Carl Erskine .02 .10
76 Hoyt Wilhelm .08 .25
77 Bob Purkey .01 .05
78 Bob Friend .01 .05
79 Monte Irvin .08 .25
80A Jim Lonborg ERR (Misspelled Longborg on card fro .05 .15
80B Jim Lonborg COR .05 .15
81 Wally Moon .01 .05
82 Moose Skowron .01 .05
83 Tommy Davis .01 .05
84 Enos Slaughter .08 .25
85 Sal Maglie UER/(1945-1917 on back) .01 .05
86 Harmon Killebrew .08 .25
87 Gil Hodges .05 .15
88 Jim Kaat .02 .10
89 Roger Maris .20 .50
90 Billy Williams .08 .25
91 Luis Aparicio .08 .25
92 Jim Bunning .08 .25
93 Bill Freehan .02 .10
94 Orlando Cepeda .05 .15
95 Early Wynn .08 .25
96 Tug McGraw .02 .10
97 Ron Santo .08 .25
98 Del Crandall .01 .05
99 Sal Bando .01 .05
100 Joe DiMaggio 1.00 2.50
101 Bob Feller .20 .50
102 Larry Doby .05 .15
103 Rollie Fingers .08 .25
104 Al Kaline .08 .25
105 Johnny Podres .01 .05
106 Lou Boudreau .08 .25
107 Zoilo Versalles .01 .05
108 Dick Groat .01 .05
109 Warren Spahn .08 .25
110 Johnny Bench .20 .50

1989 Pacific Griffey Candy Bar

Produced by the Pacific Candy Co., this set features a color batting image of Ken Griffey, Jr. of the Seattle Mariners on a blue, white, or yellow background with silver borders and advertises the milk chocolate Ken Griffey, Jr. Candy Bar available at stores throughout the Northwest. The back displays player information. Griffey is allergic to chocolate so he could not eat the candy bar named for him.

COMPLETE SET (3) 6.00 15.00
COMMON CARD (1A-1C) 2.00 5.00

1989 Pacific Legends II

The 1989 Pacific Legends Series II set contains 110 standard-size cards. The fronts have vintage color photos with silver borders. The backs are gray and feature career highlights and lifetime statistics. The cards were distributed as factory sets as well as in ten-card wax packs.

COMPLETE SET (110) 4.00 10.00
COMP.FACT SET (110) 4.00 10.00
111 Reggie Jackson .20 .50
112 Rich Reese .01 .05
113 Frankie Frisch .05 .15
114 Ed Kranepool .01 .05
115 Al Hrabosky .01 .05
116 Eddie Mathews .08 .25
117 Ty Cobb .60 1.50
118 Jim Davenport .01 .05
119 Buddy Lewis .01 .05
120 Virgil Trucks .01 .05
121 Del Ennis .01 .05
122 Dick Radatz .01 .05
123 Andy Pafko .01 .05
124 Wilbur Wood .01 .05
125 Joe Sewell .05 .15
126 Herb Score .01 .05
127 Paul Waner .05 .15
128 Lloyd Waner .05 .15
129 Brooks Robinson .20 .50
130 Bo Belinsky .02 .10
131 Phil Cavarretta .01 .05
132 Claude Osteen .01 .05
133 Tito Francona .01 .05
134 Billy Pierce .02 .10
135 Roberto Clemente .60 1.50
136 Spud Chandler .01 .05
137 Enos Slaughter .05 .15
138 Ken Holtzman .01 .05
139 John Hopp .01 .05
140 Tony LaRussa .02 .10
141 Ryne Duren .01 .05
142 Glenn Beckert UER (Misspelled Glen on card front .01 .05
143 Ken Keltner .01 .05
144 Hank Bauer .02 .10
145 Roger Craig .02 .10
146 Frank Baker .05 .15
147 Jim O'Toole .01 .05
148 Rogers Hornsby .15 .40
149 Jose Cardenal .01 .05
150 Bobby Doerr .05 .15
151 Mickey Cochrane .05 .15
152 Gaylord Perry .05 .15
153 Frank Thomas .01 .05
154 Ted Williams .60 1.50
155 Sam McDowell .01 .05
156 Bob Feller .20 .50
157 Bert Campaneris .01 .05
158 Thornton Lee UER (Misspelled Thorton on card fro .01 .05
159 Gary Peters .01 .05
160 Joe Medwick .05 .15
161 Joe Nuxhall .01 .05
162 Joe Schultz .01 .05
163 Harmon Killebrew .08 .25
164 Bucky Walters .01 .05
165 Bob Allison .01 .05
166 Lou Boudreau .05 .15
167 Joe Cronin .05 .15
168 Mike Torrez .01 .05
169 Rich Rollins .01 .05
170 Tony Cuccinello .01 .05
171 Hoyt Wilhelm .05 .15
172 Ernie Harwell ANN .02 .10
173 George Foster .01 .05
174 Lou Gehrig .60 1.50
175 Dave Kingman .02 .10
176 Babe Ruth .75 2.00
177 Joe Black .01 .05
178 Roy Face .01 .05
179 Earl Weaver MG .05 .15
180 Johnny Mize .05 .15
181 Roger Cramer .01 .05
182 Jim Piersall .02 .10
183 Ned Garver .01 .05
184 Billy Williams .05 .15
185 Lefty Grove .05 .15
186 Jim Grant .01 .05
187 Elmer Valo .01 .05
188 Ewell Blackwell .01 .05
189 Mel Ott .05 .15
190 Harry Walker .01 .05
191 Bill Campbell .01 .05
192 Walter Johnson .08 .25
193 Catfish Hunter .05 .15
194 Charlie Keller .01 .05
195 Hank Greenberg .05 .15
196 Bobby Murcer .02 .10
197 Al Lopez .02 .10
198 Vida Blue .02 .10
199 Shag Crawford UMP .01 .05
200 Arky Vaughan .05 .15
201 Smoky Burgess .01 .05
202 Rip Sewell .01 .05
203 Earl Averill .05 .15
204 Milt Pappas .01 .05
205 Mel Harder .01 .05
206 Sam Jethroe .01 .05
207 Randy Hundley .01 .05
208 Jesse Haines .01 .05
209 Jack Brickhouse ANN .01 .05
210 Whitey Ford .08 .25
211 Honus Wagner .20 .50
212 Phil Niekro .05 .15
213 Gary Bell .01 .05
214 Jon Matlack .01 .05
215 Moe Drabowsky .01 .05
216 Edd Roush .05 .15
217 Joel Horlen .01 .05
218 Casey Stengel .08 .25
219 Burt Hooton .01 .05
220 Joe Jackson .60 1.50

1989-90 Pacific Senior League

The 1989-90 Pacific Trading Cards Senior League set contains 220 standard-size cards. The fronts feature color photos with silver borders and player names and positions at the bottom. The horizontally oriented backs are red, white, and blue, and show vital statistics and career highlights. The cards were distributed as a boxed set with 15 card-sized logo stickers/puzzle pieces as well as in wax packs. There are several In Action cards in the set, designated by IA in the checklist below. The Nettles card was corrected very late according to the set's producer.

COMPLETE SET (220) 4.00 10.00
COMP. FACT SET (220) 4.00 10.00
1 Bobby Tolan MG .02 .10
2 Sergio Ferrer .01 .05
3 David Rajsich .01 .05
4 Ron LeFlore .02 .10
5 Steve Henderson .01 .05
6 Jerry Martin .01 .05
7 Gary Rajsich .01 .05
8 Elias Sosa .01 .05
9 Jon Matlack .02 .10
10 Steve Kemp .02 .10
11 Lenny Randle .01 .05
12 Roy Howell .01 .05
13 Milt Wilcox .01 .05
14 Alan Bannister .01 .05
15 Dock Ellis .02 .10
16 Mike Williams .01 .05
17 Luis Gomez .01 .05
18 Joe Sambito .01 .05
19 Bake McBride .01 .05
20 Pat Zachry UER/(Photo actually Dick Bosman) .01 .05
21 Dwight Lowry .01 .05
22 Ozzie Virgil Sr. CO .01 .05
23 Randy Lerch .01 .05
24 Butch Benton .01 .05
25 Tom Zimmer CO UER (No bio information) .01 .05
26 Al Holland UER/(Photo actually Nardi Contreras) .01 .05
27 Sammy Stewart .01 .05
28 Bill Lee .02 .10
29 Ferguson Jenkins .20 .50
30 Leon Roberts .01 .05
31 Rick Wise .02 .10
32 Butch Hobson .01 .05
33 Pete LaCock .01 .05
34 Bill Campbell .01 .05
35 Doug Simunic .01 .05
36 Mario Guerrero .01 .05
37 Jim Willoughby .01 .05
38 Joe Pittman .01 .05
39 Mark Bomback .01 .05
40 Tommy McMillan .01 .05
41 Gary Allenson .01 .05
42 Cecil Cooper .05 .15
43 John LaRosa .01 .05
44 Darrell Brandon .01 .05
45 Bernie Carbo .01 .05
46 Mike Cuellar .05 .15
47 Al Bumbry .01 .05
48 Gene Richards .01 .05
49 Pedro Borbon .01 .05
50 Julio Solo .01 .05
51 Ed Nottle MG .01 .05
52 Jim Bibby .01 .05
53 Doug Griffin CO .01 .05
54 Ed Clements .01 .05
55 Dalton Jones .01 .05
56 Earl Weaver MG .20 .50
57 Jesus De La Rosa .01 .05
58 Paul Casanova .01 .05
59 Frank Riccelli .01 .05
60 Rafael Landestoy UER (Misspelled Raphael on card .01 .05
61 George Hendrick .02 .10
62 Cesar Cedeno .05 .15
63 Bert Campaneris .05 .15
64 Derrel Thomas .01 .05
65 Bobby Ramos .01 .05
66 Grant Jackson .01 .05
67 Steve Whitaker .01 .05
68 Pedro Ramos .01 .05
69 Joe Hicks UER (No height or weight information) .01 .05
70 Taylor Duncan .01 .05
71 Tom Shopay .01 .05
72 Ken Clay .01 .05
73 Mike Kekich .01 .05
74 Ed Halicki .01 .05
75 Ed Figueroa .01 .05
76 Paul Blair .01 .05
77 Luis Tiant .05 .15
78 Stan Bahnsen .01 .05
79 Rennie Stennett .01 .05
80 Bobby Molinaro .01 .05
81 Jim Gideon .01 .05
82 Orlando Gonzalez .01 .05
83 Amos Otis .02 .10

84 Dennis Leonard .01 .05
85 Pat Putnam .01 .05
86 Rick Manning .01 .05
87 Pat Dobson MG .01 .05
88 Marty Castillo .01 .05
89 Steve McCatty .01 .05
90 Doug Bird .01 .05
91 Rick Waits .01 .05
92 Ron Jackson .01 .05
93 Tim Hosley .01 .05
94 Steve Luebber .01 .05
95 Rich Gale .01 .05
96 Champ Summers .01 .05
97 Dave LaRoche .01 .05
98 Bobby Jones .01 .05
99 Kim Allen .01 .05
100 Wayne Garland .01 .05
101 Tom Spencer .01 .05
102 Dan Driessen .02 .10
103 Ron Pruitt .01 .05
104 Tim Ireland .01 .05
105 Dan Driessen IA .01 .05
106 Pepe Frias UER/(Misspelled Pepi on card front) .01 .05
107 Eric Rasmussen .01 .05
108 Don Hood .01 .05
109 Joe Coleman CO UER/(Photo actually Tony Torchia) .01 .05
110 Jim Slaton .01 .05
111 Clint Hurdle .02 .10
112 Larry Milbourne .01 .05
113 Al Holland .01 .05
114 George Foster .02 .10
115 Graig Nettles MG .05 .15
116 Oscar Gamble .02 .10
117 Ross Grimsley .01 .05
118 Bill Travers .01 .05
119 Jose Beniquez .01 .05
120 Jerry Grote IA .01 .05
121 John D'Acquisto .01 .05
122 Tom Murphy .01 .05
123 Walt Williams UER/(Listed as pitcher) .01 .05
124 Roy Thomas .01 .05
125 Jerry Grote .02 .10
126A Jim Nettles ERR/(Writing on bat knob) .08 .25
126B Jim Nettles COR 1.00 2.50
127 Randy Niemann .01 .05
128 Bobby Bonds .20 .50
129 Ed Glynn .01 .05
130 Ed Hicks .01 .05
131 Ivan Murrell .01 .05
132 Graig Nettles MG .08 .25
133 Hal McRae .08 .25
134 Pat Kelly .01 .05
135 Sammy Stewart .01 .05
136 Bruce Kison .01 .05
137 Jim Morrison .01 .05
138 Omar Moreno .01 .05
139 Tom Brown .01 .05
140 Steve Dillard .01 .05
141 Gary Alexander .01 .05
142 Al Oliver .08 .25
143 Rick Lysander .01 .05
144 Tippy Martinez .01 .05
145 Al Cowens .01 .05
146 Gene Clines .01 .05
147 Willie Aikens .01 .05
148 Tommy Moore .01 .05
149 Clete Boyer MG .02 .10
150 Stan Cliburn .01 .05
151 Ken Kravec .01 .05
152 Garth Iorg .01 .05
153 Rick Peterson .01 .05
154 Wayne Nordhagen UER (Misspelled Nordgahen on car .01 .05
155 Danny Meyer .01 .05
156 Wayne Garrett .01 .05
157 Wayne Krenchicki .01 .05
158 Graig Nettles .08 .25
159 Earl Stephenson .01 .05
160 Carl Taylor .01 .05
161 Rollie Fingers .20 .50
162 Toby Harrah .02 .10
163 Mickey Rivers .02 .10
164 Dave Kingman .05 .15
165 Paul Mirabella .01 .05
166 Dick Williams MG .02 .10
167 Luis Pujols .01 .05
168 Tito Landrum .01 .05
169 Tom Underwood .01 .05
170 Mark Wagner .01 .05
171 Odell Jones .01 .05
172 Doug Capilla .01 .05
173 Alfie Rondon .01 .05
174 Lowell Palmer .01 .05
175 Juan Eichelberger .01 .05
176 Wes Clements .01 .05
177 Rodney Scott .01 .05
178 Ron Washington .01 .05
179 Al Hrabosky .02 .10
180 Sid Monge .01 .05
181 Randy Johnson .01 .05
182 Tim Stoddard .02 .10
183 Dick Williams MG .02 .10
184 Lee Lacy .01 .05
185 Jerry White .01 .05
186 Dave Kingman .05 .15
187 Checklist 1-110 .01 .05
188 Jose Cruz .02 .10
189 Jamie Easterly .01 .05
190 Ike Blessit .01 .05
191 Johnny Grubb .01 .05
192 Dave Cash .01 .05
193 Doug Corbett .01 .05
194 Bruce Bochy .01 .05
195 Mark Corey .01 .05
196 Gil Rondon .01 .05
197 Jerry Martin .01 .05
198 Gerry Pirtle .01 .05
199 Gates Brown MG .01 .05
200 Bob Galasso .01 .05
201 Bake McBride .01 .05
202 Wayne Granger .01 .05
203 Larry Milbourne .01 .05
204 Tom Paciorek .01 .05
205 U.L. Washington .01 .05
206 Larvell Blanks .01 .05
207 Bob Shirley .01 .05
208 Pete Falcone .01 .05
209 Sal Butera .01 .05
210 Roy Branch .01 .05
211 Dyar Miller .01 .05
212 Paul Siebert .01 .05
213 Ken Reitz .01 .05
214 Bill Madlock .05 .15
215 Vida Blue .05 .15
216 Dave Hilton .01 .05
217 Pedro Ramos CO and Charlie Bree CO .01 .05
218 Checklist 111-220 .01 .05
219 Pat Dobson MG and Earl Weaver MG .05 .15
220 Curt Flood COMM .05 .15

1990 Pacific Gwynn Candy Bar

Produced by the Pacific Candy Co., this card features a color action player photo of Tony Gwynn of the San Diego Padres on a tan background in a silver frame and advertises the milk chocolate Tony Gwynn Base Hit Candy Bar. The back displays player information.

1 Tony Gwynn 1.25 3.00

1990 Pacific Legends

The 1990 Pacific Legends issue was a 110-card standard-size set issued by Pacific Trading Cards. The set numbering is basically arranged in two alphabetical sequences. This set was available in both factory set and wax packs form. The set does include some active players, Willie Wilson and Jesse Barfield, the last two players in the set.

COMPLETE SET (110) 4.00 10.00
COMP. FACT SET (110) 4.00 10.00
1 Hank Aaron .30 .75
2 Tommie Agee .01 .05
3 Luke Appling .05 .15
4 Sal Bando .01 .05
5 Ernie Banks .20 .50
6 Don Baylor .02 .10
7 Yogi Berra .20 .50
8 Vida Blue .01 .05
9 Lou Boudreau .05 .15
10 Clete Boyer .01 .05
11 George Bamberger .01 .05
12 Lou Brock .08 .25
13 Ralph Branca .01 .05
14 Carl Erskine .01 .05
15 Bert Campaneris .01 .05
16 Steve Carlton .08 .25
17 Rod Carew .08 .25
18 Rocky Colavito .08 .25
19 Frankie Crosetti .02 .10
20 Larry Doby .05 .15
21 Bobby Doerr .05 .15
22 Walt Dropo .01 .05
23 Rick Ferrell .05 .15
24 Joe Garagiola .02 .10
25 Ralph Garr .01 .05
26 Dick Groat .01 .05
27 Steve Garvey .02 .10
28 Bob Gibson .08 .25
29 Don Drysdale .08 .25
30 Billy Herman .05 .15
31 Bobby Grich .01 .05
32 Monte Irvin .05 .15
33 Dave Johnson .01 .05
34 Don Kessinger .01 .05
35 Harmon Killebrew .05 .15
36 Ralph Kiner .05 .15
37 Vern Law .01 .05
38 Ed Lopat .01 .05
39 Bill Mazeroski .05 .15
40 Rick Monday .01 .05
41 Manny Mota .01 .05
42 Don Newcombe .02 .10
43 Gaylord Perry .05 .15
44 Jim Piersall .02 .10
45 Johnny Podres .02 .10
46 Boog Powell .05 .15
47 Robin Roberts .05 .15
48 Ron Santo .05 .15
49 Herb Score .02 .10
50 Enos Slaughter .05 .15
51 Warren Spahn .08 .25
52 Rusty Staub .02 .10
53 Frank Torre .01 .05
54 Bob Horner .01 .05
55 Lee May .01 .05
56 Bill White .02 .10
57 Hoyt Wilhelm .05 .15
58 Billy Williams .05 .15
59 Ted Williams .30 .75
60 Tom Seaver .20 .50
61 Carl Yastrzemski .08 .25
62 Marv Throneberry .01 .05
63 Steve Stone .01 .05
64 Rico Petrocelli .01 .05
65 Orlando Cepeda .05 .15
66 Eddie Mathews .05 .15
67 Joe Sewell .05 .15
68 Catfish Hunter .05 .15
69 Alvin Dark .02 .10
70 Richie Ashburn .05 .15
71 Dusty Baker .02 .10
72 George Foster .01 .05
73 Eddie Yost .01 .05
74 Buddy Bell .01 .05
75 Manny Sanguillen .01 .05
76 Jim Bunning .05 .15
77 Smoky Burgess .01 .05
78 Al Rosen .01 .05
79 Gene Conley .01 .05
80 Dave Dravecky .01 .05
81 Charlie Gehringer .05 .15
82 Billy Pierce .01 .05
83 Willie Horton .01 .05
84 Ron Hunt .01 .05
85 Bob Feller .08 .25
86 George Kell .05 .15
87 Dave Kingman .05 .15
88 Jerry Koosman .02 .10
89 Clem Labine .01 .05
90 Tony LaRussa .02 .10
91 Dennis Leonard .01 .05
92 Dale Long .01 .05
93 Sparky Lyle .01 .05
94 Gil McDougald .01 .05
95 Don Mossi .01 .05
96 Phil Niekro .05 .15
97 Tom Paciorek .01 .05
98 Mel Parnell .01 .05
99 Lou Piniella .02 .10
100 Bobby Richardson .02 .10
101 Phil Rizzuto .08 .25
102 Brooks Robinson .08 .25
103 Pete Runnels .01 .05
104 Diego Segui .01 .05
105 Bobby Shantz .01 .05
106 Bobby Thomson .02 .10
107 Joe Torre .02 .10
108 Earl Weaver MG .05 .15
109 Willie Wilson .01 .05
110 Jesse Barfield .01 .05

1991 Pacific Prototype

This standard-size card was produced by Pacific Trading Cards in order to help them secure a liscense with Major League Baseball. The front has a photo of Ryne Sandberg along with the necessary identification. The back is basically blank. The card has room for vital statistics, a brief biography and some statistics and each section is framed in red. A very limited number of these cards were produced. Almost all of these cards were destroyed. A prototype card of Leon Durham was produced in 1988. As far as is known, no copies of the Durham card have ever surfaced in the secondary market.

1 Ryne Sandberg 500.00 1200.00

1991 Pacific Ryan Texas Express I

This 110-card standard-size set, Texas Express, traces the career of Nolan Ryan from the start of his career into the 1991 season as well as his personal life with his family on his ranch in Alvin, Texas. This set was issued by Pacific Trading cards and was the first set featuring an individual baseball player to be sold in wax packs since the 1959 Fleer Ted Williams issue. The cards were available in 12-card foil packs and factory sets. Moreover, eight unnumbered bonus cards (1-6 No Hitters, 1991 25th Season, and Rookie year with the Mets) were produced in quantities of 1,000 of each card in gold foil and 10,000 of each card in silver foil; these bonus cards were randomly inserted in foil packs only. After the first and second series of Pacific Nolan Ryan Texas Express had sold out, Pacific reissued card numbers 1-220 in 1993, and the cards produced in this reissue may be distinguished by the 27th season logo, which was introduced to collectors in the 30-card 27th Season series. Currently there is no value differential between the two types.

COMPLETE SET (110) 5.00 12.00
COMP. FACT (110) 5.00 12.00
COMMON PLAYER (1-110) .04 .10
1 Nolan Ryan Future Hall of Famer .15 .40
11 Nolan Ryan Gil Hodges Keep the Ball Down .08 .25
29 Nolan Ryan Fastest Pitch Ever Thrown Clocked at .05 .15
30 Nolan Ryan No-Hitter Number 3 .05 .15
31 Nolan Ryan No-Hitter Number 4 .05 .15
32 Nolan Ryan Frank Tanana .05 .15
36 Nolan Ryan Starting Pitcher .05 .15
40 Nolan Ryan Home Run .05 .15
42 Nolan Ryan Record 5th No-Hitter .05 .15
43 Nolan Ryan No-Hitter Number 5 .05 .15
45 Nolan Ryan Passes Walter Johnson .08 .25
46 Nolan Ryan Strikeout 4000 .05 .15
61 Nolan Ryan Dan Smith .05 .15
63 Nolan Ryan Last Pitch No-Hitter Number 6 .05 .15
64 Nolan Ryan Sweet Number 6 .05 .15
68 Nolan Ryan Brad Arnsberg Geno Petralli/300 Game .08 .25
75 Nolan Ryan Pitcher Texas Rangers .05 .15
77 Nolan Ryan Throwing Spirals .08 .25
92 Nolan's a Real Gamer/(Bloody lip and blood all o .40 1.00
93 Nolan Ryan Jim Sundberg Ranger Battery Mates .08 .25
107 Nolan Ryan The Ryan Family .05 .15
110 Nolan Ryan Lynn Nolan Ryan .15 .40

1991 Pacific Ryan Inserts 8

These eight standard-size cards were inserts in 1991 Pacific Nolan Ryan Texas Express foil packs. As with the regular issue, the fronts display glossy color photos that are bordered in silver foil and either purple/red or red/orange border stripes. The cards are unnumbered and checklisted in chronological order. Besides the silver cards, they were also issued on a much more limited basis in gold. The gold versions are valued at quadruple the prices listed below.

COMPLETE SET (8) 40.00 100.00
COMMON PLAYER (1-8) 6.00 15.00

1991 Pacific Ryan 7th No-Hitter

This seven-card standard-size set was produced by Pacific Trading Cards Inc. to capture various moments of Nolan Ryan's 7th no-hitter. These cards were produced in the following numbers: 1,000 of each card in gold foil and 10,000 of each card in silver foil. These cards were randomly inserted in foil packs only. Supposedly as many as half of the cards were destroyed and never released. The prices below refer to the silver versions; the gold versions would be valued at quadruple the prices below. In addition to silver and gold, two other border versions have surfaced. One type has silver prism borders, the other has gold hologram-like borders. It is not known how these cards were distributed, but they are scarcer than the gold border cards and are valued at six times the prices below.

COMPLETE SET (7) 40.00 100.00
COMMON PLAYER (1-7) 6.00 15.00

1991 Pacific Senior League

Pacific Trading Cards released this 160-card set just after the Senior League suspended operations. The standard size cards were sold in wax packs and as complete sets.There are two different versions of cards for the following players: Dan Driessen, Rafael Landestoy, Amos Otis, Cesar Cedeno, Ron LeFlore, Dan Norman, Dave Cash, Vida Blue, Rollie Fingers and Jim Rice.

COMPLETE SET (170) 3.00 8.00
COMP.FACT SET (170) 3.00 8.00
1A Dan Driessen Leading off .02 .10
1B Dan Driessen Fielding .02 .10
2 Marty Castillo .01 .05
3 Jerry White .01 .05
4 Bud Anderson .01 .05
5 Ron Jackson .01 .05
6 Fred Stanley CO .01 .05
7 Steve Luebber .01 .05
8 Jerry Terrell CO .01 .05
9 Pat Dobson .02 .10
10 Ken Kravec .01 .05
11 Gil Rondon .01 .05
12 Dyar Miller CO .01 .05
13 Bobby Molinaro .01 .05
14 Jerry Martin .01 .05
15 Rick Waits .01 .05
16 Steve McCatty .01 .05
17 Roger Slagle .01 .05
18 Mike Ramsey .01 .05
19 Rich Gale .01 .05
20 Larry Harlow .01 .05
21 Dan Rohn .01 .05
22 Don Cooper .01 .05
23 Marv Foley .01 .05
24A Rafael Landestoy Batting .01 .05
24B Rafael Landestoy Leading off .01 .05
25 Eddie Milner .01 .05
26A Amos Otis White jersey .02 .10
26B Amos Otis Green jersey .02 .10
27 Odell Jones .01 .05
28 Tippy Martinez .01 .05
29 Stu Cliburn .01 .05
30 Stan Cliburn .01 .05
31 Tony Cloninger CO .01 .05
32 Jeff Jones .01 .05
33 Ken Reitz .01 .05
34 Dave Sax .01 .05
35 Orlando Gonzalez .01 .05
36 Jose Cruz .02 .10
37 Mickey Mahler .01 .05
38 Derek Botelho .01 .05
39 Rick Lysander .01 .05
40A Cesar Cedeno On base .02 .10
40B Cesar Cedeno Kneeling .02 .10
41 Garth Iorg .01 .05
42 Wayne Krenchicki .01 .05
43 Clete Boyer CO .02 .10
44 Dan Boone .01 .05
45 George Vukovich .01 .05
46 Omar Moreno .01 .05
47 Ron Washington .01 .05
48 Ron Washington MVP .01 .05
49 Rick Peterson .01 .05
50 Tack Wilson .01 .05
51 Stan Cliburn Stu Cliburn .01 .05
52 Rick Lysander POY .01 .05
53 Cesar Cedeno Pete LaCock .02 .10
54 Jim Marshall MG Clete Boyer MG .01 .05
55 Doug Simunic .01 .05
56 Pat Kelly .01 .05
57 Roy Branch .01 .05
58 Dave Cash .02 .10
59 Bobby Jones .01 .05
60 Hector Cruz .01 .05
61 Reggie Cleveland .01 .05
62 Gary Lance .01 .05
63A Ron LeFlore Orange cap .02 .10
63B Ron LeFlore Blue helmet .02 .10
64A Dan Norman Batting .01 .05
64B Dan Norman Leading off .01 .05
65 Renie Martin .01 .05
66 Pete Mackanin MG .01 .05
67 Frank Riccelli .01 .05
68 Alfie Rondon .01 .05
69 Rodney Scott .01 .05
70 Jim Tracy .01 .05
71 Ed Dennis .01 .05
72 Rick Lindell .01 .05
73 Stu Pepper .01 .05
74 Jeff Youngbauer .01 .05
75 Russ Foster .01 .05
76 Jeff Capriati .01 .05
77 Art DeFreites .01 .05
78 Alfie Rondon .01 .05
79 Reggie Cleveland IA .01 .05
80A Dave Cash Orange cap .01 .05
80B Dave Cash Blue helmet .01 .05
81A Vida Blue Ball showing .05 .15
81B Vida Blue Ball hidden .05 .15
82 Ed Glynn .01 .05
83 Bob Owchinko .01 .05
84 Bill Fleming .01 .05
85 Ron Roenicke Gary Roenicke .01 .05
86 Tom Thompson CO .01 .05
87 Derrel Thomas UER Name misspelled Derrell .01 .05
88 Jim Willoughby .01 .05
89 Jim Pankovits .01 .05
90 Jack Cooley CO .01 .05
91 Lenn Sakata .01 .05
92 Mike Brocki .01 .05
93 Chuck Fick .01 .05
94 Tom Benedict .01 .05
95 Anthony Davis .08 .25
96 Cardell Camper .01 .05
97 Leon Roberts .01 .05
98 Roger Erickson .01 .05
99 Kim Allen .01 .05
100 Dave Skaggs .01 .05
101 Joe Decker .01 .05
102 U.L. Washington .01 .05
103 Don Fletcher .01 .05
104 Gary Roenicke .01 .05
105 Rich Dauer MG .01 .05
106 Ron Roenicke .01 .05
107 Mike Norris .01 .05
108 Ferguson Jenkins .20 .50
109 Ronn Reynolds .01 .05
110 Pete Falcone .01 .05
111 Gary Allenson .01 .05
112 Mark Wagner .01 .05
113 Jack Lazorko .01 .05
114 Bob Galasso .01 .05
115 Ron Davis .01 .05
116 Lenny Randle .01 .05
117 Ricky Peters .01 .05
118 Jim Dwyer .01 .05
119 Juan Eichelberger .01 .05
120 Pete LaCock .02 .10
121 Tony Scott .01 .05
122 Rick Lancellotti .01 .05
123 Barry Bonnell .01 .05
124 Dave Hilton .01 .05
125 Bill Campbell .01 .05
126A Rollie Fingers Ball in air .20 .50
126B Rollie Fingers Ball in hand .20 .50
127 Jim Marshall MG .01 .05
128 Razor Shines .02 .10
129 Guy Sularz .01 .05
130 Roy Thomas .01 .05
131 Joel Youngblood .01 .05
132 Ernie Camacho .01 .05
133 Dave Hilton CO Jim Marshall MG Fred Stanle .01 .05
134 Ken Landreaux .01 .05
135 Dave Rozema .01 .05
136 Tom Zimmer CO .01 .05
137 Elias Sosa .01 .05
138 Ossie Virgil Sr. CO .01 .05
139 Al Holland .01 .05
140 Milt Wilcox .01 .05
141 Jerry Reed .01 .05
142 Chris Welsh .01 .05
143 Luis Gomez .01 .05
144 Steve Henderson .01 .05
145 Butch Benton .01 .05
146 Bill Lee .02 .10
147 Todd Cruz .01 .05
148A Jim Rice Bat up .08 .25
148B Jim Rice Bat at waist .08 .25
149 Tito Landrum .01 .05
150 Ozzie Virgil Jr. .01 .05
151 Joe Pittman .01 .05
152 Bobby Tolan MG .01 .05
153 Len Barker .01 .05
154 Dave Rajsich .01 .05
155 Glenn Gulliver .01 .05
156 Gary Rajsich .01 .05
157 Joe Sambito .01 .05
158 Frank Vito .01 .05
159 Ozzie Virgil Jr. Ozzie Virgil Sr. .01 .05
160 Dave Rajsich Gary Rajsich .01 .05

1992 Pacific Ryan Magazine 6

These six standard size cards were inserted (bound) into the July 1992 Volume 2, Issue 2 of Trading Cards magazine as a pair of two-card strips. These are very similar to the hard-to-find inserts that Pacific inserted into the Ryan Texas Express second series foil packs. These "magazine cards" are only differentiable by the fact that they lack the words "Limited Edition" on the copyright line on their backs.

COMPLETE SET (6) 3.00 8.00
COMMON PLAYER (1-6) .60 1.50

1992 Pacific Ryan Texas Express II

For the second year, Pacific issued a 110-card standard-size set titled Texas Express. A six-card insert set was randomly inserted in foil packs, with 1,000 autographed and numbered of card number 1. This set was also issued in a factory set form with no inserts. This set is essentially an extension or second series of the 1991 Pacific Nolan Ryan set and is numbered that way. After the first and second series of Pacific Nolan Ryan Texas Express had sold out, Pacific reissued card numbers 1-220 in 1993, and the cards produced in this reissue may be distinguished by the 27th season logo, which was introduced to collectors in the 30-card 27th Season series. Currently there is no value differential between the two types.

COMPLETE SET (110) 4.00 10.00
COMP.FACT (110) 4.00 10.00
COMMON PLAYER (111-220) .04 .10
111 Nolan Ryan The Golden Arm .08 .25
118 Nolan Ryan The Cowboy .05 .15
122 Nolan Ryan New York Strikeout Record .05 .15
124 Nolan Ryan Hall of Fame Victims .08 .25
129 Nolan Ryan Strikeout Record .05 .15
130 Nolan Ryan Number One .05 .15
132 Nolan Ryan Number Two .05 .15
134 Nolan Ryan Number Three .05 .15
135 Nolan Ryan Bob Feller Pure Speed .08 .25
138 Nolan Ryan Number Four .05 .15
142 Nolan Ryan Strong Houston Staff .05 .15
143 Nolan Ryan Number Five .05 .15
148 Nolan Ryan Breaks Walter Johnson's Record .08 .25
149 Nolan Ryan Reese Ryan .08 .25
156 Nolan Ryan Like Father Like Son .05 .15
170 Nolan Ryan Number Six .05 .15
171 Nolan Ryan/300th Win .05 .15
173 Nolan Ryan Man of the Year .08 .25
177 Nolan Ryan Mike Stanley Stanley's Delight .05 .15
178 Nolan Ryan After Nolan's 7th No-Hitter .05 .15
187 Nolan Ryan Number Seven .05 .15
188 Nolan Ryan Passes Phil Niekro .05 .15
189 Nolan Ryan Trails Don Sutton .05 .15
198 Nolan Ryan Goose Gossage .08 .25
200 Nolan Ryan Roger Clemens Don't Mess With Texas .15 .40
204 Nolan Ryan Bobby Valentine Manager's Delight .05 .15
206 Nolan Ryan The Quarterback .08 .25
208 Nolan Ryan Tom House Passing Along Wisdom .05 .15
211 Nolan Ryan Seven No-Hitters .05 .15
219 Nolan Ryan Receives The Victor Award .05 .15
220 Nolan Ryan/1992: Nolan's 26th Season .08 .25

1992 Pacific Ryan Gold

These eight standard size cards were one of two insert subsets randomly packed in 1992 Pacific Nolan Ryan Texas Express II 12-card and 24-card foil packs. Supposedly 10,000 of each card were produced. The cards feature high gloss color action photos of Ryan pitching his seven no-hitters. The pictures are bordered in gold foil and either red/orange (1-4) or purple/red border (5-8) stripes. Inside a flaming baseball design, the backs of cards 1-7 display statistics for that no-hitter while card No. 8 summarizes all seven no-hitters. The cards are unnumbered and checklisted in chronological order of the events.

COMPLETE SET (8) 100.00 200.00
COMMON PLAYER (1-8) 10.00 25.00

1992 Pacific Ryan Limited

These six standard size cards were one of two insert subsets randomly packed in 1992 Pacific Nolan Ryan Texas Express II 12-card and 24-card foil packs. Only 3,000 of each card were produced and, as an added bonus, 1,000 of card number 1 were autographed by Ryan. A similar-looking pair of two-card strips was inserted (bound) into all issues of the July 1992 Volume 2, Issue 2 of Trading Cards magazine. However these "magazine cards" lack the words "Limited Edition" on the copyright line on their backs. Nolan's name appears in a red, white, and blue bar above a red box containing either career highlights (2, 3, 6), statistics (4) or a poem (5).

COMPLETE SET (6) 60.00 120.00
COMMON PLAYER (1-6) 10.00 25.00
AU Nolan Ryan Card #1, 1000 signed 75.00 200.00

1992 Pacific Seaver

This 110-card standard-size set traces the career of Tom Seaver. The set was sold in 12-card foil packs or as a factory set for $12.95 through a mail-in offer. Autograph cards of Tom Seaver were randomly inserted into packs.

COMPLETE SET (110) 3.00 8.00
COMP.FACT SET (110) 3.00 8.00
COMMON PLAYER (1-110) .04 .10
1 Tom Seaver Stand-out High School Basketball Play .15 .40
8 Tom Seaver/1967 Rookie of the Year .05 .15
15 Tom Seaver/1969 Cy Young Winner .05 .15
16 Tom Seaver Pitcher of the Year .05 .15
22 Tom Seaver Second Cy Young Award .05 .15
57 Tom Seaver Luke Appling Ozzie Guillen Blast Fro .08 .25
59 Tom Seaver LaMarr Hoyt Cy Young Winners .05 .15
60 Tom Seaver Carlton Fisk Two Legends of the Game .08 .25
61 Tom Seaver Placido Domingo Singing Praise .05 .15
63 Tom Seaver Sarah Seaver Anne Seaver Nancy Seave .05 .15
65 Tom Seaver Traded to the Red Sox .05 .15
67 Tom Seaver Red Sox Man .05 .15
68 Tom Seaver Boston Red Sox Pitcher .05 .15
82 Tom Seaver Nolan Ryan .15 .40
85 Tom Seaver Nolan Ryan/300 Win Club .15 .40
91 Tom Seaver Tom Terrific .05 .15
104 Tom Seaver George Thomas Seaver .05 .15
106 Tom Seaver Receives the Judge Emil Fuchs Award .05 .15
110 Tom Seaver Breaking Walter Johnson's Strikeout R .05 .15

1992 Pacific Seaver Inserts 6

These six standard-size cards were one of two insert subsets (depicting career highlights of Tom Seaver) randomly packed in 1992 Pacific Tom Seaver 12-card foil packs. The two insert sets are numbered the same, the primary physical difference being a white border or a gold foil border on the card front. Only 3,000 of each non-gold card were produced and, as an added bonus, 1,000 of card number 1 were autographed by Seaver. According to Pacific, 10,000 of each gold card were produced. However, it seems like the numbers reported by Pacific were actually transposed when the cards were issued. There seem to be more non-gold (White) card issued than Gold cards. The six career highlight cards feature high gloss color action player photos on their fronts edged by a color stripe on the left and framed by a white (or gold) outer border. The "Tom Terrific" logo overlays the stripe at the lower left corner. The backs of the gold foil insert cards are identical to those of the regular inserts and are distinguished only by their non-glossy finish. The values for the gold and white versions are the same at this time.

COMPLETE SET (6) 60.00 120.00
COMMON PLAYER (1-6) 10.00 25.00
AU1 Tom Seaver AU 30.00 80.00

1993 Pacific Ryan 27th Season

Pacific issued this 30-card standard-size set to honor Nolan Ryan being the first player in Major League Baseball history to appear in 27 seasons. The series was available in collector sets inside an attractive complete set box as well as in 25-cent five-card foil packs; the foil packs contained series I, series II, 27th Season series, and randomly inserted bonus cards. The cards are numbered on the back in continuation of the Texas Express first and second series. Beginning in mid-June, displays of Advil featuring Ryan and two-card packs appeared in stores nationwide. The two-card foil packs were available with the purchase of a bottle of 24 or more Advil Tablets or Caplets. On June 20, 1993, an offer to purchase the entire set was featured in Sunday newspapers. By mailing the Advil proof of purchase and $3.49 plus $1.50 for shipping to Pacific, the complete 30-card set could be obtained; the offer expired Dec. 31, 1993.

COMPLETE SET (251) 12.00 30.00
COMP.FACT.SET (1-30) 5.00 12.00
COMMON RYAN .10 .25
241 Nolan Ryan Tom Seaver .10 .25
242 Nolan Ryan Rod Carew Angels' Number 30 Retired .10 .25
245 Nolan Ryan Jimmie Reese Great Friends .10 .25
246 Nolan Ryan Gene Autry Cowboys .10 .25
250 Nolan Ryan Tom Seaver Pacific Pride .10 .25
NNO Pacific Trading Cards Cover card .10 .25

1993 Pacific Ryan Farewell McCormick

Given away to fans attending a Texas Rangers game at Arlington Stadium during Nolan Ryan Appreciation Week, this 21-card, standard-size set was produced by Pacific Trading Cards, Inc. for McCormick and Company.

COMPLETE SET (21) 4.00 10.00
COMMON PLAYER (1-20) .20 .50

1993 Pacific Ryan Limited

Six more standard-size cards (7-12), numbered in continuation of the 1992 set, were issued in 1993 and have a 1993 copyright notice on the card back. The card design was not significantly altered, and the backs contain the words "Limited Edition", as do the first six cards. Card numbers 7-12 were issued with gold foil borders, and the production run was 3,000 of each card. Gold foil versions of card Nos. 7-9 were given away only at the Bellevue (WA) Sports Collectors Classic IV each day of the show; card numbers 10-12 were randomly inserted in the 25-cent Changemaker packs. Although the cards are most commonly found with gold borders, white border cards have also been reported.

COMPLETE SET (6) 20.00 50.00
COMMON CARD (7-12) 10.00 25.00

1993 Pacific Ryan Prism Inserts

This 20-card prism standard-size set was issued by Pacific to honor the career of Nolan Ryan. The cards were randomly inserted into 1993 Nolan Ryan 25-cent Changemaker five-card packs. The production figures were reportedly 10,000 of each card. Gold versions of these sets are known as well. The Gold versions are

currently valued at 2X the prices listed below.
COMPLETE SET (20) 60.00 120.00
COMMON PLAYER (1-20) 3.00 8.00
*GOLD: 2X PRISM

1993 Pacific Spanish

Issued in two 330-card series, these 660 standard-size cards represent Pacific's first effort at a nationally distributed, MLB-licensed card set. All text on both sides is in Spanish. The cards are numbered on the back, grouped alphabetically within teams, and checklisted below alphabetically according to teams in both series. Each series card numbering is alphabetical by players within teams with the teams themselves in order by team nickname. Very early in the printing, Rob Maurer (number 313) was printed with, very obviously, someone else's photo on the card. This very tough card is rarely seen in the hobby and since it is so thinly traded there is no established market value. On the Third Annual Latin Night at Yankee Stadium (July 22, 1993; New York Yankees versus California Angels), four-card foil packs, featuring a title card and three player cards, were given away.

COMPLETE SET (660) 15.00 40.00
COMPLETE SERIES 1 (330) 10.00 25.00
COMPLETE SERIES 2 (330) 6.00 15.00
COMMON PLAYER (1-330) .02 .05
COMMON CARD (331-660) .04 .10
1 Rafael Belliard .01 .05
2 Sid Bream .01 .05
3 Francisco Cabrera .01 .05
4 Marvin Freeman .01 .05
5 Ron Gant .02 .10
6 Tom Glavine .20 .50
7 Brian Hunter .01 .05
8 David Justice .10 .30
9 Ryan Klesko .02 .10
10 Melvin Nieves .01 .05
11 Deion Sanders .10 .30
12 John Smoltz .10 .30
13 Mark Wohlers .01 .05
14 Brady Anderson .02 .10
15 Glenn Davis .01 .05
16 Mike Devereaux .01 .05
17 Leo Gomez .01 .05
18 Chris Hoiles .01 .05
19 Chito Martinez .01 .05
20 Ben McDonald .01 .05
21 Mike Mussina .10 .30
22 Gregg Olson .01 .05
23 Joe Orsulak .01 .05
24 Cal Ripken 1.25 3.00
25 David Segui .01 .05
26 Rick Sutcliffe .02 .10
27 Wade Boggs .30 .75
28 Tom Brunansky .01 .05
29 Ellis Burks .02 .10
30 Roger Clemens .60 1.50
31 John Dopson .01 .05
32 John Flaherty .01 .05
33 Mike Greenwell .01 .05
34 Tony Pena .01 .05
35 Carlos Quintana .01 .05
36 Luis Rivera .01 .05
37 Mo Vaughn :10 .30
38 Frank Viola .01 .05
39 Matt Young .01 .05
40 Scott Bailes .01 .05
41 Bert Blyleven .10 .30
42 Chad Curtis .01 .05
43 Gary DiSarcina .01 .05
44 Chuck Finley .02 .10
45 Mike Fitzgerald .01 .05
46 Gary Gaetti .02 .10
47 Rene Gonzales .01 .05
48 Mark Langston .01 .05
49 Scott Lewis .01 .05
50 Luis Polonia .01 .05
51 Tim Salmon .10 .30
52 Lee Stevens .01 .05
53 Steve Buechele .01 .05
54 Frank Castillo .01 .05
55 Doug Dascenzo .01 .05
56 Andre Dawson .10 .30
57 Shawon Dunston .01 .05
58 Mark Grace .07 .20
59 Mike Morgan .01 .05
60 Luis Salazar .01 .05
61 Rey Sanchez .01 .05
62 Ryne Sandberg .40 1.00
63 Dwight Smith .01 .05
64 Jerome Walton .01 .05
65 Rick Wilkins .01 .05
66 Wilson Alvarez .02 .10
67 George Bell .01 .05
68 Joey Cora .01 .05
69 Alex Fernandez .01 .05
70 Carlton Fisk .20 .50
71 Craig Grebeck .01 .05
72 Ozzie Guillen .07 .20
73 Jack McDowell .01 .05
74 Scott Radinsky .01 .05
75 Tim Raines .02 .10
76 Bobby Thigpen .01 .05
77 Frank Thomas .30 .75
78 Robin Ventura .10 .30
79 Tom Browning .01 .05
80 Jacob Brumfield .01 .05
81 Rob Dibble .01 .05
82 Bill Doran .01 .05
83 Billy Hatcher .01 .05
84 Barry Larkin .10 .30
85 Hal Morris .01 .05
86 Joe Oliver .01 .05
87 Jeff Reed .01 .05
88 Jose Rijo .01 .05
89 Bip Roberts .01 .05
90 Chris Sabo .01 .05
91 Sandy Alomar Jr. .02 .10
92 Brad Arnsberg .01 .05
93 Carlos Baerga .02 .10
94 Albert Belle .02 .10
95 Felix Fermin .01 .05
96 Mark Lewis .01 .05
97 Kenny Lofton .07 .20
98 Carlos Martinez .01 .05
99 Rod Nichols .01 .05
100 Dave Rohde .01 .05
101 Scott Scudder .01 .05
102 Paul Sorrento .01 .05
103 Mark Whiten .01 .05
104 Mark Carreon .01 .05
105 Milt Cuyler .01 .05
106 Rob Deer .01 .05
107 Cecil Fielder .02 .10
108 Travis Fryman .02 .10
109 Dan Gladden .01 .05
110 Bill Gullickson .01 .05
111 Les Lancaster .01 .05
112 Mark Leiter .01 .05
113 Tony Phillips .01 .05
114 Mickey Tettleton .01 .05
115 Alan Trammell .07 .20
116 Lou Whitaker .02 .10
117 Jeff Bagwell .40 1.00
118 Craig Biggio .10 .30
119 Joe Boever .01 .05
120 Casey Candaele .01 .05
121 Andujar Cedeno .01 .05
122 Steve Finley .07 .20
123 Luis Gonzalez .10 .30
124 Pete Harnisch .01 .05
125 Jimmy Jones .01 .05
126 Mark Portugal .01 .05
127 Rafael Ramirez .01 .05
128 Mike Simms .01 .05
129 Eric Yelding .01 .05
130 Luis Aquino .01 .05
131 Kevin Appier .02 .10
132 Mike Boddicker .01 .05
133 George Brett .60 1.50
134 Tom Gordon .01 .05
135 Mark Gubicza .01 .05
136 David Howard .01 .05
137 Gregg Jefferies .01 .05
138 Wally Joyner .02 .10
139 Brian McRae .01 .05
140 Jeff Montgomery .01 .05
141 Terry Shumpert .01 .05
142 Curtis Wilkerson .01 .05
143 Brett Butler .02 .10
144 Eric Davis .02 .10
145 Kevin Gross .01 .05
146 Dave Hansen .01 .05
147 Lenny Harris .01 .05
148 Carlos Hernandez .01 .05
149 Orel Hershiser .02 .10
150 Jay Howell .01 .05
151 Eric Karros .07 .20
152 Ramon Martinez .01 .05
153 Jose Offerman .01 .05
154 Mike Sharperson .01 .05
155 Darryl Strawberry .02 .10
156 Jim Gantner .01 .05
157 Darryl Hamilton .01 .05
158 Doug Henry .01 .05
159 John Jaha .01 .05
160 Pat Listach .01 .05
161 Jaime Navarro .01 .05
162 Dave Nilsson .01 .05
163 Jesse Orosco .02 .10
164 Kevin Seitzer .01 .05
165 B.J. Surhoff .02 .10
166 Greg Vaughn .02 .10
167 Robin Yount .20 .50
168 Rick Aguilera .02 .10
169 Scott Erickson .02 .10
170 Mark Guthrie .01 .05
171 Kent Hrbek .02 .10
172 Chuck Knoblauch .10 .30
173 Gene Larkin .01 .05
174 Shane Mack .01 .05
175 Pedro Munoz .01 .05
176 Mike Pagliarulo .01 .05
177 Kirby Puckett .30 .75
178 Kevin Tapani .01 .05
179 Gary Wayne .01 .05
180 Moises Alou .02 .10
181 Brian Barnes .01 .05
182 Archi Cianfrocco .01 .05
183 Delino DeShields .02 .10
184 Darrin Fletcher .01 .05
185 Marquis Grissom .02 .10
186 Ken Hill .01 .05
187 Dennis Martinez .02 .10
188 Bill Sampen .01 .05
189 John Vander Wal .01 .05
190 Larry Walker .10 .30
191 Tim Wallach .01 .05
192 Bobby Bonilla .01 .05
193 Daryl Boston .01 .05
194 Vince Coleman .01 .05
195 Kevin Elster .01 .05
196 Sid Fernandez .01 .05
197 John Franco .02 .10
198 Dwight Gooden .02 .10
199 Howard Johnson .01 .05
200 Willie Randolph .02 .10
201 Bret Saberhagen .02 .10
202 Dick Schofield .01 .05
203 Pete Schourek .01 .05
204 Greg Cadaret .01 .05
205 John Habyan .01 .05
206 Pat Kelly .01 .05
207 Kevin Maas .01 .05
208 Don Mattingly .60 1.50
209 Matt Nokes .01 .05
210 Melido Perez .01 .05
211 Scott Sanderson .01 .05
212 Andy Stankiewicz .01 .05
213 Danny Tartabull .01 .05
214 Randy Velarde .02 .10
215 Bernie Williams .10 .30
216 Harold Baines .02 .10
217 Mike Bordick .01 .05
218 Scott Brosius .02 .10
219 Jerry Browne .01 .05
220 Ron Darling .01 .05
221 Dennis Eckersley .15 .40
222 Rickey Henderson .30 .75
223 Rick Honeycutt .01 .05
224 Mark McGwire .60 1.50
225 Ruben Sierra .02 .10
226 Terry Steinbach .01 .05
227 Bob Welch .01 .05
228 Willie Wilson .01 .05
229 Ruben Amaro .01 .05
230 Kim Batiste .01 .05
231 Juan Bell .01 .05
232 Wes Chamberlain .01 .05
233 Darren Daulton .02 .10
234 Mariano Duncan .01 .05
235 Lenny Dykstra .02 .10
236 Dave Hollins .01 .05
237 Stan Javier .01 .05
238 John Kruk .02 .10
239 Mickey Morandini .01 .05
240 Terry Mulholland .01 .05
241 Mitch Williams .01 .05
242 Stan Belinda .01 .05
243 Jay Bell .01 .05
244 Carlos Garcia .01 .05
245 Jeff King .01 .05
246 Mike LaValliere .01 .05
247 Lloyd McClendon .01 .05
248 Orlando Merced .01 .05
249 Paul Miller .01 .05
250 Gary Redus .01 .05
251 Don Slaught .01 .05
252 Zane Smith .01 .05
253 Andy Van Slyke .01 .05
254 Tim Wakefield .15 .40
255 Andy Benes .01 .05
256 Dann Bilardello .01 .05
257 Tony Gwynn .60 1.50
258 Greg W. Harris .01 .05
259 Darrin Jackson .01 .05
260 Mike Maddux .01 .05
261 Fred McGriff .07 .20
262 Rich Rodriguez .01 .05
263 Benito Santiago .02 .10
264 Gary Sheffield .20 .50
265 Kurt Stillwell .01 .05
266 Tim Teufel .01 .05
267 Bud Black .01 .05
268 John Burkett .01 .05
269 Will Clark .10 .30
270 Royce Clayton .01 .05
271 Bryan Hickerson .01 .05
272 Chris James .01 .05
273 Darren Lewis .01 .05
274 Willie McGee .02 .10
275 Jim McNamara .01 .05
276 Francisco Oliveras .01 .05
277 Robby Thompson .01 .05
278 Matt Williams .08 .20
279 Trevor Wilson .01 .05
280 Bret Boone .07 .20
281 Greg Briley .01 .05
282 Jay Buhner .02 .10
283 Henry Cotto .01 .05
284 Rich DeLucia .01 .05
285 Dave Fleming .01 .05
286 Ken Griffey Jr. 1.00 2.50
287 Erik Hanson .01 .05
288 Randy Johnson .30 .75
289 Tino Martinez .07 .20
290 Edgar Martinez .07 .20
291 Dave Valle .01 .05
292 Omar Vizquel .07 .20
293 Luis Alicea .01 .05
294 Bernard Gilkey .01 .05
295 Felix Jose .01 .05
296 Ray Lankford .02 .10
297 Omar Olivares .01 .05
298 Jose Oquendo .01 .05
299 Tom Pagnozzi .01 .05
300 Geronimo Pena .01 .05
301 Gerald Perry .01 .05
302 Ozzie Smith .40 1.00
303 Lee Smith .02 .10
304 Bob Tewksbury .01 .05
305 Todd Zeile .07 .20
306 Kevin Brown .07 .20
307 Todd Burns .01 .05
308 Jose Canseco .20 .50
309 Hector Fajardo .01 .05
310 Julio Franco .01 .05
311A Juan Gonzalez .50 1.25
White uniform on back
311B Juan Gonzalez .50 1.25
Blue uniform on back
312 Jeff Huson .01 .05
313A Rob Maurer ERR
Believed to be Donald Harris pictu
313B Rob Maurer .01 .05
314 Rafael Palmeiro .10 .30
315 Dean Palmer .02 .10
316 Ivan Rodriguez .30 .75
317 Nolan Ryan 1.25 3.00
318 Dickie Thon .01 .05
319 Roberto Alomar .10 .30
320 Derek Bell .01 .05
321 Pat Borders .01 .05
322 Joe Carter .02 .10
323 Kelly Gruber .01 .05
324 Juan Guzman .01 .05
325 Manny Lee .01 .05
326 Jack Morris .02 .10
327 John Olerud .07 .20
328 Ed Sprague .01 .05
329 Todd Stottlemyre .01 .05
330 Duane Ward .01 .05
331 Steve Avery .02 .10
332 Damon Berryhill .02 .10
333 Jeff Blauser .02 .10
334 Mark Lemke .02 .10
335 Greg Maddux 1.25 3.00
336 Kent Mercker .02 .10
337 Otis Nixon .02 .10
338 Greg Olson .02 .10
339 Bill Pecota .02 .10
340 Terry Pendleton .07 .20
341 Mike Stanton .02 .10
342 Todd Frohwirth .02 .10
343 Tim Hulett .02 .10
344 Mark McLemore .07 .20
345 Luis Mercedes .02 .10
346 Alan Mills .02 .10
347 Sherman Obando .02 .10
348 Jim Poole .02 .10
349 Harold Reynolds .07 .20
350 Arthur Rhodes .02 .10
351 Jeff Tackett .02 .10
352 Fernando Valenzuela .07 .20
353 Scott Bankhead .02 .10
354 Ivan Calderon .02 .10
355 Scott Cooper .02 .10
356 Danny Darwin .02 .10
357 Scott Fletcher .02 .10
358 Tony Fossas .02 .10
359 Greg A. Harris .02 .10
360 Joe Hesketh .02 .10
361 Jose Melendez .02 .10
362 Paul Quantrill .02 .10
363 John Valentin .02 .10
364 Mike Butcher .02 .10
365 Chuck Crim .02 .10
366 Chili Davis .07 .20
367 Damion Easley .02 .10
368 Steve Frey .02 .10
369 Joe Grahe .02 .10
370 Greg Myers .02 .10
371 John Orton .02 .10
372 J.T. Snow .30 .75
373 Ron Tingley .02 .10
374 Julio Valera .02 .10
375 Paul Assenmacher .02 .10
376 Jose Bautista .02 .10
377 Jose Guzman .02 .10
378 Greg Hibbard .02 .10
379 Candy Maldonado .02 .10
380 Derrick May .02 .10
381 Dan Plesac .02 .10
382 Tommy Shields .02 .10
383 Sammy Sosa .75 2.00
384 Jose Vizcaino .02 .10
385 Matt Walbeck .02 .10
386 Ellis Burks .07 .20
387 Roberto Hernandez .07 .20
388 Mike Huff .02 .10
389 Bo Jackson .20 .50
390 Lance Johnson .02 .10
391 Ron Karkovice .02 .10
392 Kirk McCaskill .02 .10
393 Donn Pall .02 .10
394 Dan Pasqua .02 .10
395 Steve Sax .02 .10
396 Dave Stieb .02 .10
397 Bobby Ayala .02 .10
398 Tim Belcher .02 .10
399 Jeff Branson .02 .10
400 Cesar Hernandez .02 .10
401 Roberto Kelly .02 .10
402 Randy Milligan .02 .10
403 Kevin Mitchell .02 .10
404 Juan Samuel .02 .10
405 Reggie Sanders .07 .20
406 John Smiley .02 .10
407 Dan Wilson .02 .10
408 Mike Christopher .02 .10
409 Dennis Cook .02 .10
410 Alvaro Espinoza .02 .10
411 Glenallen Hill .02 .10
412 Reggie Jefferson .02 .10
413 Derek Lilliquist .02 .10
414 Jose Mesa .07 .20
415 Charles Nagy .02 .10
416 Junior Ortiz .02 .10
417 Eric Plunk .02 .10
418 Ted Power .02 .10
419 Scott Aldred .02 .10
420 Andy Ashby .02 .10
421 Freddie Benavides .02 .10
422 Dante Bichette .07 .20
423 Willie Blair .02 .10
424 Vinny Castilla .10 .30
425 Jerald Clark .02 .10
426 Alex Cole .02 .10
427 Andres Galarraga .20 .50
428 Joe Girardi .07 .20
429 Charlie Hayes .02 .10
430 Butch Henry .02 .10
431 Darren Holmes .02 .10
432 Dale Murphy .20 .50
433 David Nied .02 .10
434 Jeff Parrett .02 .10
435 Steve Reed .02 .10
436 Armando Reynoso .02 .10
437 Bruce Ruffin .02 .10
438 Bryn Smith .02 .10
439 Jim Tatum .02 .10
440 Eric Young .07 .20
441 Skeeter Barnes .02 .10
442 Tom Bolton .02 .10
443 Kirk Gibson .07 .20
444 Chad Kreuter .02 .10
445 Bill Krueger .02 .10
446 Scott Livingstone .02 .10
447 Bob MacDonald .02 .10
448 Mike Moore .02 .10
449 Mike Munoz .02 .10
450 Gary Thurman .02 .10
451 David Wells .20 .50
452 Alex Arias .02 .10
453 Jack Armstrong .02 .10
454 Bret Barberie .02 .10
455 Ryan Bowen .02 .10
456 Cris Carpenter .02 .10
457 Chuck Carr .02 .10
458 Jeff Conine .07 .20
459 Steve Decker .02 .10
460 Orestes Destrade .02 .10
461 Monty Fariss .02 .10
462 Junior Felix .02 .10
463 Bryan Harvey .02 .10
464 Trevor Hoffman .20 .50
465 Charlie Hough .07 .20
466 Dave Magadan .02 .10
467 Bob McClure .02 .10
468 Rob Natal .02 .10
469 Scott Pose .02 .10
470 Rich Renteria .02 .10
471 Benito Santiago .07 .20
472 Matt Turner .02 .10
473 Walt Weiss .02 .10
474 Eric Anthony .02 .10
475 Chris Donnels .02 .10
476 Doug Drabek .02 .10
477 Xavier Hernandez .02 .10
478 Doug Jones .02 .10
479 Darryl Kile .02 .10
480 Scott Servais .02 .10
481 Greg Swindell .02 .10
482 Eddie Taubensee .02 .10
483 Jose Uribe .02 .10
484 Brian Williams .02 .10
485 Billy Brewer .02 .10
486 David Cone .10 .30
487 Greg Gagne .02 .10
488 Phil Hiatt .02 .10
489 Jose Lind .02 .10
490 Brent Mayne .02 .10
491 Kevin McReynolds .02 .10
492 Keith Miller .02 .10
493 Hipolito Pichardo .02 .10
494 Harvey Pulliam .02 .10
495 Rico Rossy .02 .10
496 Pedro Astacio .02 .10
497 Tom Candiotti .02 .10
498 Tom Goodwin .02 .10
499 Jim Gott .02 .10
500 Pedro Martinez .60 1.50
501 Roger McDowell .02 .10
502 Mike Piazza 1.50 4.00
503 Jody Reed .02 .10
504 Rick Trlicek .02 .10
505 Mitch Webster .02 .10
506 Steve Wilson .02 .10
507 Jim Austin .02 .10
508 Ricky Bones .02 .10
509 Alex Diaz .02 .10
510 Mike Fetters .02 .10
511 Teddy Higuera .02 .10
512 Graeme Lloyd .02 .10
513 Carlos Maldonado .02 .10
514 Josias Manzanillo .02 .10
515 Kevin Reimer .02 .10
516 Bill Spiers .02 .10
517 Bill Wegman .02 .10
518 Willie Banks .02 .10
519 J.T. Bruett .02 .10
520 Brian Harper .02 .10
521 Terry Jorgensen .02 .10
522 Scott Leius .02 .10
523 Pat Mahomes .02 .10
524 Dave McCarty .02 .10
525 Jeff Reboulet .02 .10
526 Mike Trombley .02 .10
527 Carl Willis .02 .10
528 Dave Winfield .50 1.25
529 Sean Berry .02 .10
530 Frank Bolick .02 .10
531 Kent Bottenfield .02 .10
532 Wilfredo Cordero .02 .10
533 Jeff Fassero .02 .10
534 Tim Laker .02 .10
535 Mike Lansing .07 .20
536 Chris Nabholz .02 .10
537 Mel Rojas .02 .10
538 John Wetteland .07 .20
539 Ted Wood .02 .10
540 Mike Draper .02 .10
541 Tony Fernandez .07 .20
542 Todd Hundley .07 .20
543 Jeff Innis .02 .10
544 Jeff McKnight .02 .10
545 Eddie Murray .50 1.25
546 Charlie O'Brien .02 .10
547 Frank Tanana .07 .20
548 Ryan Thompson .02 .10
549 Chico Walker .02 .10
550 Anthony Young .02 .10
551 Jim Abbott .07 .20
552 Wade Boggs .50 1.25
553 Steve Farr .02 .10
554 Neal Heaton .02 .10
555 Steve Howe .02 .10
556 Dion James .02 .10
557 Scott Kamieniecki .02 .10
558 Jimmy Key .07 .20
559 Jim Leyritz .02 .10
560 Paul O'Neill .10 .30
561 Spike Owen .02 .10
562 Lance Blankenship .02 .10
563 Joe Boever .02 .10
564 Storm Davis .02 .10
565 Kelly Downs .02 .10
566 Eric Fox .02 .10
567 Rich Gossage .20 .50
568 Dave Henderson .02 .10
569 Shawn Hillegas .02 .10
570 Mike Mohler .02 .10
571 Troy Neel .02 .10
572 Dale Sveum .02 .10
573 Larry Andersen .02 .10
574 Bob Ayrault .02 .10
575 Jose DeLeon .02 .10
576 Jim Eisenreich .07 .20
577 Pete Incaviglia .02 .10
578 Danny Jackson .02 .10
579 Ricky Jordan .02 .10
580 Ben Rivera .02 .10
581 Curt Schilling .40 1.00
582 Milt Thompson .02 .10
583 David West .02 .10
584 John Candelaria .02 .10
585 Steve Cooke .02 .10
586 Tom Foley .02 .10
587 Al Martin .02 .10
588 Blas Minor .02 .10
589 Dennis Moeller .02 .10
590 Denny Neagle .07 .20
591 Tom Prince .02 .10
592 Randy Tomlin .02 .10
593 Bob Walk .02 .10
594 Kevin Young .07 .20
595 Pat Gomez .02 .10
596 Ricky Gutierrez .02 .10
597 Gene Harris .02 .10
598 Jeremy Hernandez .02 .10
599 Phil Plantier .02 .10
600 Tim Scott .02 .10
601 Frank Seminara .02 .10
602 Darrell Sherman .02 .10
603 Craig Shipley .02 .10
604 Guillermo Velasquez .02 .10
605 Dan Walters .02 .10
606 Mike Benjamin .02 .10
607 Barry Bonds .75 2.00
608 Jeff Brantley .07 .20
609 Dave Burba .02 .10
610 Craig Colbert .02 .10
611 Mike Jackson .02 .10
612 Kirt Manwaring .02 .10
613 Dave Martinez .02 .10
614 Dave Righetti .07 .20
615 Kevin Rogers .02 .10
616 Bill Swift .02 .10
617 Rich Amaral .02 .10
618 Mike Blowers .02 .10
619 Chris Bosio .02 .10
620 Norm Charlton .02 .10
621 John Cummings .02 .10
622 Mike Felder .02 .10
623 Bill Haselman .02 .10
624 Tim Leary .02 .10
625 Pete O'Brien .02 .10
626 Russ Swan .02 .10
627 Fernando Vina .20 .50
628 Rene Arocha .02 .10
629 Rod Brewer .02 .10
630 Ozzie Canseco .02 .10
631 Rheal Cormier .02 .10
632 Brian Jordan .07 .20
633 Joe Magrane .02 .10
634 Donovan Osborne .02 .10
635 Mike Perez .02 .10
636 Stan Royer .02 .10
637 Hector Villanueva .02 .10
638 Tracy Woodson .02 .10
639 Benji Gil .02 .10
640 Tom Henke .07 .20
641 David Hulse .02 .10
642 Charlie Leibrandt .02 .10
643 Robb Nen .07 .20
644 Dan Peltier .02 .10
645 Billy Ripken .02 .10
646 Kenny Rogers .07 .20
647 John Russell .02 .10
648 Dan Smith .02 .10
649 Matt Whiteside .02 .10
650 William Canate .02 .10
651 Darnell Coles .02 .10
652 Al Leiter .07 .20
653 Domingo Martinez .02 .10
654 Paul Molitor .40 1.00
655 Luis Sojo .02 .10
656 Dave Stewart .07 .20
657 Mike Timlin .02 .10
658 Turner Ward .02 .10
659 Devon White .07 .20
660 Eddie Zosky .02 .10

1993 Pacific Beisbol Amigos

COMPLETE SET (30) 30.00 80.00
1 Edgar Martinez .75 2.00
2 Luis Polonia .40 1.00
Stan Javier
3 George Bell .40 1.00
Julio Franco
4 Ozzie Guillen 1.50 4.00
Ivan Rodriguez
5 Carlos Baerga .60 1.50
Sandy Alomar Jr.
6 Intercambio Extranjero .60 1.50
Sandy Alomar Jr.
Alvaro E
7 Sandy Alomar Jr. 1.50 4.00
Roberto Alomar
8 Jose Lind .40 1.00
Felix Jose
9 Ricky Bones .40 1.00
Jaime Navarro
10 Jamie Navarro .40 1.00
Jesse Orosco
11 Tino Martinez .75 2.00
Edgar Martinez
12 Juan Gonzalez 5.00 12.00
Ivan Rodriguez
13 Juan Gonzalez 2.50 6.00
Julio Franco
14 Julio Franco 4.00 10.00
Jose Canseco
Rafael Palmeiro
15 Juan Gonzalez 6.00 15.00
Jose Canseco
16 Ivan Rodriguez 1.00 2.50
Benji Gil
17 Jose Guzman .40 1.00
Frank Castillo
18 Rey Sanchez .40 1.00
Jose Vizcaino
19 Derrick May 4.00 10.00
Sammy Sosa
20 Sammy Sosa UER 4.00 10.00
Candy Maldonado/(Sammy is from
D
21 Jose Rijo .40 1.00
Juan Samuel
22 Freddie Benavides .75 2.00
Andres Galarraga
23 Guillermo Velasquez .40 1.00
Benito Santiago
24 Luis Gonzalez .75 2.00
Andujar Cedeno
25 Wilfredo Cordero .60 1.50
Dennis Martinez
26 Moises Alou .60 1.50
Wilfredo Cordero
27 Ozzie Canseco 1.00 2.50
Jose Canseco
28 Jose Oquendo .40 1.00
Luis Alicea
29 Luis Alicea .40 1.00
Rene Arocha
30 Geronimo Pena .40 1.00
Luis Alicea

1993 Pacific Spanish Gold Estrellas

COMPLETE SET (20) 6.00 15.00
1 Moises Alou .40 1.00
2 Bobby Bonilla .20 .50
3 Tony Fernandez .20 .50
4 Felix Jose .20 .50
5 Dennis Martinez .40 1.00
6 Orlando Merced .20 .50
7 Jose Oquendo .20 .50
8 Geronimo Pena .20 .50
9 Jose Rijo .20 .50
10 Benito Santiago .40 1.00
11 Sandy Alomar Jr. .40 1.00
12 Carlos Baerga .40 1.00
13 Jose Canseco 1.50 4.00
14 Juan Gonzalez 1.00 2.50
15 Juan Guzman .20 .50
16 Edgar Martinez .60 1.50
17 Rafael Palmeiro .75 2.00
18 Ruben Sierra .40 1.00
19 Danny Tartabull .20 .50
20 Omar Vizquel .40 1.00

1993 Pacific Jugadores Calientes

COMPLETE SET (36) 100.00 200.00
1 Rich Amaral .40 1.00
2 George Brett 6.00 15.00
3 Jay Buhner 1.25 3.00
4 Roger Clemens 6.00 15.00
5 Kirk Gibson .75 2.00
6 Juan Gonzalez 2.50 6.00
7 Ken Griffey Jr. 10.00 25.00
8 Bo Jackson 1.50 4.00
9 Kenny Lofton 1.25 3.00
10 Mark McGwire 6.00 15.00
11 Sherman Obando .40 1.00
12 John Olerud 1.25 3.00
13 Carlos Quintana .40 1.00
14 Ivan Rodriguez 3.00 8.00
15 Nolan Ryan 12.50 30.00
16 J.T. Snow 2.50 6.00
17 Fernando Valenzuela .75 2.00
18 Dave Winfield 3.00 8.00
19 Moises Alou .75 2.00
20 Jeff Bagwell 5.00 12.00
21 Barry Bonds 5.00 12.00
22 Bobby Bonilla .40 1.00
23 Vinny Castilla 1.50 4.00
24 Andujar Cedeno .40 1.00
25 Orestes Destrade .40 1.00
26 Andres Galarraga 1.50 4.00
27 Mark Grace 1.50 4.00
28 Tony Gwynn 6.00 15.00
29 Roberto Kelly .40 1.00
30 John Kruk .75 2.00
31 Dave Magadan .40 1.00
32 Derrick May .40 1.00
33 Orlando Merced .40 1.00
34 Mike Piazza 10.00 25.00
35 Armando Reynoso .40 1.00
36 Jose Vizcaino .40 1.00

1993 Pacific Spanish Prism Inserts

COMPLETE SET (20) 30.00 60.00
1 Francisco Cabrera 1.25 3.00
2 Jose Lind 1.25 3.00
3 Dennis Martinez 1.50 4.00
4 Ramon Martinez 1.25 3.00
5 Jose Rijo 1.25 3.00
6 Benito Santiago 1.50 4.00
7 Roberto Alomar 2.50 6.00
8 Sandy Alomar Jr. 1.25 3.00
9 Carlos Baerga 1.50 4.00
10 George Bell 1.25 3.00
11 Jose Canseco 3.00 8.00
12 Alex Fernandez 1.25 3.00
13 Julio Franco 1.50 4.00
14 Juan Gonzalez 2.50 6.00
15 Ozzie Guillen 2.00 5.00
16 Teddy Higuera 1.25 3.00
17 Edgar Martinez 2.00 5.00
18 Hipolito Pichardo 1.25 3.00
19 Luis Polonia 1.25 3.00
20 Ivan Rodriguez 4.00 10.00

1994 Pacific Promos

COMPLETE SET (8) 4.00 10.00
P1 Carlos Baerga .20 .50
P2 Joe Carter .20 .50
P3 Juan Gonzalez .40 1.00
P4 Ken Griffey Jr. 1.25 3.00
P5 Greg Maddux .75 2.00
P6 Mike Piazza 1.00 2.50
P7 Tim Salmon .30 .75
P8 Frank Thomas .40 1.00

1994 Pacific

The 660 standard-size cards comprising this set feature color player action shots on their fronts that are borderless, except at the bottom, where a team color-coded marbleized border set off by a gold-foil line carries the team color-coded player's name. The cards are grouped alphabetically within teams. The set closes with an Award Winners subset (655-660). There are no key Rookie Cards in this set.

COMPLETE SET (660) 20.00 50.00
CL: RANDOM INSERTS IN PACKS
1 Steve Avery .02 .10
2 Steve Bedrosian .02 .10
3 Damon Berryhill .02 .10
4 Jeff Blauser .02 .10
5 Sid Bream .02 .10
6 Francisco Cabrera .02 .10
7 Ramon Caraballo .02 .10
8 Ron Gant .07 .20
9 Tom Glavine .10 .30
10 Chipper Jones .20 .50
11 David Justice .07 .20
12 Ryan Klesko .07 .20
13 Mark Lemke .02 .10
14 Javier Lopez .07 .20
15 Greg Maddux .30 .75
16 Fred McGriff .10 .30
17 Greg McMichael .02 .10
18 Kent Mercker .02 .10
19 Otis Nixon .02 .10
20 Terry Pendleton .07 .20
21 Deion Sanders .10 .30
22 John Smoltz .10 .30
23 Tony Tarasco .02 .10
24 Manny Alexander .02 .10
25 Brady Anderson .07 .20
26 Harold Baines .07 .20
27 Damon Buford .02 .10
28 Paul Carey .02 .10
29 Mike Devereaux .02 .10
30 Todd Frohwirth .02 .10
31 Leo Gomez .02 .10
32 Jeffrey Hammonds .02 .10
33 Chris Hoiles .02 .10
34 Tim Hulett .02 .10
35 Ben McDonald .02 .10
36 Mark McLemore .02 .10
37 Alan Mills .02 .10

38 Mike Mussina .10 .30
39 Sherman Obando .02 .10
40 Gregg Olson .02 .10
41 Mike Pagliarulo .02 .10
42 Jim Poole .02 .10
43 Harold Reynolds .07 .20
44 Cal Ripken .60 1.50
45 David Segui .02 .10
46 Fernando Valenzuela .07 .20
47 Jack Voigt .02 .10
48 Scott Bankhead .02 .10
49 Roger Clemens .40 1.00
50 Scott Cooper .02 .10
51 Danny Darwin .02 .10
52 Andre Dawson .07 .20
53 John Dopson .02 .10
54 Scott Fletcher .02 .10
55 Tony Fossas .02 .10
56 Mike Greenwell .02 .10
57 Billy Hatcher .02 .10
58 Jeff McNeely .02 .10
59 Jose Melendez .02 .10
60 Tim Naehring .02 .10
61 Tony Pena .02 .10
62 Paul Quantrill .02 .10
63 Carlos Quintana .02 .10
64 Luis Rivera .02 .10
65 Jeff Russell .02 .10
66 Aaron Sele .02 .10
67 John Valentin .02 .10
68 Mo Vaughn .07 .20
69 Frank Viola .07 .20
70 Bob Zupcic .02 .10
71 Mike Butcher .02 .10
72 Rod Correia .02 .10
73 Chad Curtis .02 .10
74 Chili Davis .07 .20
75 Gary DiSarcina .02 .10
76 Damion Easley .02 .10
77 John Farrell .02 .10
78 Chuck Finley .07 .20
79 Joe Grahe .02 .10
80 Stan Javier .02 .10
81 Mark Langston .02 .10
82 Phil Leftwich RC .02 .10
83 Torey Lovullo .02 .10
84 Joe Magrane .02 .10
85 Greg Myers .02 .10
86 Eduardo Perez .02 .10
87 Luis Polonia .02 .10
88 Tim Salmon .10 .30
89 J.T. Snow .07 .20
90 Kurt Stillwell .02 .10
91 Ron Tingley .02 .10
92 Chris Turner .02 .10
93 Julio Valera .02 .10
94 Jose Bautista .02 .10
95 Shawn Boskie .02 .10
96 Steve Buechele .02 .10
97 Frank Castillo .02 .10
98 Mark Grace UER/(stats have
98 home runs in 1993;# .10 .30
99 Jose Guzman .02 .10
100 Mike Harkey .02 .10
101 Greg Hibbard .02 .10
102 Doug Jennings .02 .10
103 Derrick May .02 .10
104 Mike Morgan .02 .10
105 Randy Myers .02 .10
106 Karl Rhodes .02 .10
107 Kevin Roberson .02 .10
108 Rey Sanchez .02 .10
109 Ryne Sandberg .30 .75
110 Tommy Shields .02 .10
111 Dwight Smith .02 .10
112 Sammy Sosa .20 .50
113 Jose Vizcaino .02 .10
114 Turk Wendell .02 .10
115 Rick Wilkins .02 .10
116 Willie Wilson .02 .10
117 Eddie Zambrano RC .02 .10
118 Wilson Alvarez .02 .10
119 Tim Belcher .02 .10
120 Jason Bere .02 .10
121 Rodney Bolton .02 .10
122 Ellis Burks .07 .20
123 Joey Cora .02 .10
124 Alex Fernandez .02 .10
125 Ozzie Guillen .07 .20
126 Craig Grebeck .02 .10
127 Roberto Hernandez .02 .10
128 Bo Jackson .20 .50
129 Lance Johnson .02 .10
130 Ron Karkovice .02 .10
131 Mike LaValliere .02 .10
132 Norberto Martin .02 .10
133 Kirk McCaskill .02 .10
134 Jack McDowell .02 .10
135 Scott Radinsky .02 .10
136 Tim Raines .07 .20
137 Steve Sax .02 .10
138 Frank Thomas .20 .50
139 Dan Pasqua .02 .10
140 Robin Ventura .07 .20
141 Jeff Branson .02 .10
142 Tom Browning .02 .10
143 Jacob Brumfield .02 .10
144 Tim Costo .02 .10
145 Rob Dibble .07 .20
145 Brian Dorsett ERR
146 Brian Dorsett .02 .10
147 Steve Foster .02 .10
148 Cesar Hernandez .02 .10
149 Roberto Kelly .02 .10
150 Barry Larkin .10 .30
151 Larry Luebbers .02 .10
152 Kevin Mitchell .02 .10
153 Tim Pugh .02 .10
154 Joe Oliver .02 .10
155 Jeff Reardon .07 .20
156 Jose Rijo .02 .10
157 Bip Roberts .02 .10
158 Chris Sabo .02 .10
159 Juan Samuel .02 .10
160 Reggie Sanders .07 .20
161 John Smiley .02 .10
162 Jerry Spradlin .02 .10
163 Gary Varsho .02 .10
164 Sandy Alomar Jr. .02 .10
165 Albert Belle .07 .20
166 Carlos Baerga .02 .10
167 Mark Clark .02 .10
168 Alvaro Espinoza .02 .10
169 Felix Fermin .02 .10
170 Reggie Jefferson .02 .10
171 Wayne Kirby .02 .10
172 Tom Kramer .02 .10
173 Kenny Lofton .07 .20
174 Jesse Levis .02 .10
175 Candy Maldonado .02 .10
175 Carlos Martinez ERR
176 Carlos Martinez .02 .10
177 Jose Mesa .02 .10
178 Jeff Mutis .02 .10
179 Charles Nagy .02 .10
180 Bob Ojeda .02 .10
181 Junior Ortiz .02 .10
182 Eric Plunk .02 .10
183 Manny Ramirez .20 .50
184 Jeff Treadway .02 .10
185 Bill Wertz .02 .10
186 Paul Sorrento .02 .10
187 Freddie Benavides .02 .10
188 Dante Bichette .07 .20
189 Willie Blair .02 .10
190 Daryl Boston .02 .10
191 Pedro Castellano .02 .10
192 Vinny Castilla .07 .20
193 Jerald Clark .02 .10
194 Alex Cole .02 .10
195 Andres Galarraga .07 .20
196 Joe Girardi .02 .10
197 Charlie Hayes .02 .10
198 Darren Holmes .02 .10
199 Chris Jones .02 .10
200 Curt Leskanic .02 .10
201 Roberto Mejia .02 .10
202 David Nied .02 .10
203 Jayhawk Owens .02 .10
204 Steve Reed .02 .10
205 Armando Reynoso .02 .10
206 Bruce Ruffin .02 .10
207 Keith Shepherd .02 .10
208 Jim Tatum .02 .10
209 Eric Young .02 .10
210 Skeeter Barnes .02 .10
211 Danny Bautista .02 .10
212 Tom Bolton .02 .10
213 Eric Davis .07 .20
214 Storm Davis .02 .10
215 Cecil Fielder .07 .20
216 Travis Fryman .07 .20
217 Kirk Gibson .07 .20
218 Dan Gladden .02 .10
219 John Doherty .02 .10
220 Chris Gomez .02 .10
221 David Haas .02 .10
222 Bill Krueger .02 .10
223 Chad Kreuter .02 .10
224 Mark Leiter .02 .10
225 Bob MacDonald .02 .10
226 Mike Moore .02 .10
227 Tony Phillips .02 .10
228 Rich Rowland .02 .10
229 Mickey Tettleton .02 .10
230 Alan Trammell .07 .20
231 Lou Whitaker .07 .20
232 David Wells .07 .20
233 Luis Aquino .02 .10
234 Alex Arias .02 .10
235 Jack Armstrong .02 .10
236 Ryan Bowen .02 .10
237 Chuck Carr .02 .10
238 Matias Carrillo .02 .10
239 Jeff Conine .07 .20
240 Henry Cotto .02 .10
241 Orestes Destrade .02 .10
242 Chris Hammond .02 .10
243 Bryan Harvey .02 .10
244 Charlie Hough .07 .20
245 Richie Lewis .02 .10
246 Mitch Lyden .02 .10
247 Dave Magadan .02 .10
248 Bob Natal .02 .10
249 Benito Santiago .07 .20
250 Gary Sheffield .07 .20
251 Matt Turner .02 .10
252 David Weathers .02 .10
253 Walt Weiss .02 .10
254 Darrell Whitmore .02 .10
255 Nigel Wilson .02 .10
256 Eric Anthony .02 .10
257 Jeff Bagwell .10 .30
258 Kevin Bass .02 .10
259 Craig Biggio .10 .30
260 Ken Caminiti .07 .20
261 Andujar Cedeno .02 .10
262 Chris Donnels .02 .10
263 Doug Drabek .02 .10
264 Tom Edens .02 .10
265 Steve Finley .07 .20
266 Luis Gonzalez .07 .20
267 Pete Harnisch .02 .10
268 Xavier Hernandez .02 .10
269 Todd Jones .02 .10
270 Darryl Kile .07 .20
271 Al Osuna .02 .10
272 Rick Parker .02 .10
273 Mark Portugal .02 .10
274 Scott Servais .02 .10
275 Greg Swindell .02 .10
276 Eddie Taubensee .02 .10
277 Jose Uribe .02 .10
278 Brian Williams .02 .10
279 Kevin Appier .07 .20
280 Billy Brewer .02 .10
281 David Cone .07 .20
282 Greg Gagne .02 .10
283 Tom Gordon .02 .10
284 Chris Gwynn .02 .10
285 John Habyan .02 .10
286 Chris Haney .02 .10
287 Phil Hiatt .02 .10
288 David Howard .02 .10
289 Felix Jose .02 .10
290 Wally Joyner .07 .20
291 Kevin Koslofski .02 .10
292 Jose Lind .02 .10
293 Brent Mayne .02 .10
294 Mike Macfarlane .02 .10
295 Brian McRae .02 .10
296 Kevin McReynolds .02 .10
297 Keith Miller .02 .10
298 Jeff Montgomery .02 .10
299 Hipolito Pichardo .02 .10
300 Rico Rossy .02 .10
301 Curtis Wilkerson .02 .10
302 Pedro Astacio .02 .10
303 Rafael Bournigal .02 .10
304 Brett Butler .07 .20
305 Tom Candiotti .02 .10
306 Omar Daal .02 .10
307 Jim Gott .02 .10
308 Kevin Gross .02 .10
309 Dave Hansen .02 .10
310 Carlos Hernandez .02 .10
311 Orel Hershiser .07 .20
312 Eric Karros .07 .20
313 Pedro Martinez .20 .50
314 Ramon Martinez .02 .10
315 Roger McDowell .02 .10
316 Raul Mondesi .07 .20
317 Jose Offerman .02 .10
318 Mike Piazza .40 1.00
319 Jody Reed .02 .10
320 Henry Rodriguez .02 .10
321 Cory Snyder .02 .10
322 Darryl Strawberry .07 .20
323 Tim Wallach .02 .10
324 Steve Wilson .02 .10
325 Juan Bell .02 .10
326 Ricky Bones .02 .10
327 Alex Diaz RC .02 .10
328 Cal Eldred .02 .10
329 Darryl Hamilton .02 .10
330 Doug Henry .02 .10
331 John Jaha .02 .10
332 Pat Listach .02 .10
333 Graeme Lloyd .02 .10
334 Carlos Maldonado .02 .10
335 Angel Miranda .02 .10
336 Jaime Navarro .02 .10
337 Dave Nilsson .02 .10
338 Rafael Novoa .02 .10
339 Troy O'Leary .02 .10
340 Jesse Orosco .02 .10
341 Kevin Seitzer .02 .10
342 Bill Spiers .02 .10
343 William Suero .02 .10
344 B.J. Surhoff .07 .20
345 Dickie Thon .02 .10
346 Jose Valentin .02 .10
347 Greg Vaughn .02 .10
348 Robin Yount .30 .75
349 Willie Banks .02 .10
350 Bernardo Brito .02 .10
351 Scott Erickson .02 .10
352 Mark Guthrie .02 .10
353 Chip Hale .02 .10
354 Brian Harper .02 .10
355 Kent Hrbek .07 .20
356 Terry Jorgensen .02 .10
357 Chuck Knoblauch .07 .20
358 Gene Larkin .02 .10
359 Scott Leius .02 .10
360 Shane Mack .02 .10
361 David McCarty .02 .10
362 Pat Meares .02 .10
363 Pedro Munoz .02 .10
364 Derek Parks .02 .10
365 Kirby Puckett .20 .50
366 Jeff Reboulet .02 .10
367 Kevin Tapani .02 .10
368 Mike Trombley .02 .10
369 George Tsamis .02 .10
370 Carl Willis .02 .10
371 Dave Winfield .07 .20
372 Moises Alou .07 .20
373 Brian Barnes .02 .10
374 Sean Berry .02 .10
375 Frank Bolick .02 .10
376 Wil Cordero .02 .10
377 Delino DeShields .02 .10
378 Jeff Fassero .02 .10
379 Darrin Fletcher .02 .10
380 Cliff Floyd .07 .20
381 Lou Frazier .02 .10
382 Marquis Grissom .07 .20
383 Gil Heredia .02 .10
384 Mike Lansing .07 .20
385 Oreste Marrero RC .02 .10
386 Dennis Martinez .07 .20
387 Curtis Pride RC .07 .20
388 Mel Rojas .02 .10
389 Kirk Rueter .07 .20
390 Joe Siddall .02 .10
391 John Vander Wal .02 .10
392 Larry Walker .07 .20
393 John Wetteland .07 .20
394 Rondell White .07 .20
395 Tim Bogar .02 .10
396 Bobby Bonilla .07 .20
397 Jeromy Burnitz .07 .20
398 Mike Draper .02 .10
399 Sid Fernandez .02 .10
400 John Franco .07 .20
401 Dave Gallagher .02 .10
402 Dwight Gooden .07 .20
403 Eric Hillman .02 .10
404 Todd Hundley .02 .10
405 Butch Huskey .02 .10
406 Jeff Innis .02 .10
407 Howard Johnson .02 .10
408 Jeff Kent .07 .20
409 Ced Landrum .02 .10
410 Mike Maddux .02 .10
411 Josias Manzanillo .02 .10
412 Jeff McKnight .02 .10
413 Eddie Murray .20 .50
414 Tito Navarro .02 .10
415 Joe Orsulak .02 .10
416 Bret Saberhagen .07 .20
417 Dave Telgheder .02 .10
418 Ryan Thompson .02 .10
419 Chico Walker .02 .10
420 Jim Abbott .10 .30
421 Wade Boggs .10 .30
422 Mike Gallego .02 .10
423 Mark Hutton .02 .10
424 Dion James .02 .10
425 Domingo Jean .02 .10
426 Pat Kelly .02 .10
427 Jimmy Key .07 .20
428 Jim Leyritz .02 .10
429 Kevin Maas .02 .10
430 Don Mattingly .50 1.25
431 Bobby Munoz .02 .10
432 Matt Nokes .02 .10
433 Paul O'Neill .10 .30
434 Spike Owen .02 .10
435 Melido Perez .02 .10
436 Lee Smith .07 .20
437 Andy Stankiewicz .02 .10
438 Mike Stanley .02 .10
439 Danny Tartabull .02 .10
440 Randy Velarde .02 .10
441 Bernie Williams .10 .30
442 Gerald Williams .02 .10
443 Mike Witt .02 .10
444 Marcos Armas .02 .10
445 Lance Blankenship .02 .10
446 Mike Bordick .02 .10
447 Ron Darling .02 .10
448 Dennis Eckersley .07 .20
449 Brent Gates .02 .10
450 Rich Gossage .07 .20
451 Scott Hemond .02 .10
452 Dave Henderson .02 .10
453 Shawn Hillegas .02 .10
454 Rick Honeycutt .02 .10
455 Scott Lydy .02 .10
456 Mark McGwire .50 1.25
457 Henry Mercedes .02 .10
458 Mike Mohler .02 .10
459 Troy Neel .02 .10
460 Edwin Nunez .02 .10
461 Craig Paquette .02 .10
462 Ruben Sierra .07 .20
463 Terry Steinbach .02 .10
464 Todd Van Poppel .02 .10
465 Bob Welch .02 .10
466 Bobby Witt .02 .10
467 Ruben Amaro .02 .10
468 Larry Andersen .02 .10
469 Kim Batiste .02 .10
470 Wes Chamberlain .02 .10
471 Darren Daulton .07 .20
472 Mariano Duncan .02 .10
473 Len Dykstra .07 .20
474 Jim Eisenreich .02 .10
475 Tommy Greene .02 .10
476 Dave Hollins .02 .10
477 Pete Incaviglia .02 .10
478 Danny Jackson .02 .10
479 John Kruk .07 .20
480 Tony Longmire .02 .10
481 Jeff Manto .02 .10
482 Mickey Morandini .02 .10
483 Terry Mulholland .02 .10
484 Todd Pratt .07 .20
485 Ben Rivera .02 .10
486 Curt Schilling .07 .20
487 Kevin Stocker .02 .10
488 Milt Thompson .02 .10
489 David West .02 .10
490 Mitch Williams .02 .10
491 Jeff Ballard .02 .10
492 Jay Bell .07 .20
493 Scott Bullett .02 .10
494 Dave Clark .02 .10
495 Steve Cooke .02 .10
496 Midre Cummings .02 .10
497 Mark Dewey .02 .10
498 Carlos Garcia .02 .10
499 Jeff King .02 .10
500 Al Martin .02 .10
501 Lloyd McClendon .02 .10
502 Orlando Merced .02 .10
503 Blas Minor .02 .10
504 Denny Neagle .07 .20
505 Tom Prince .02 .10
506 Don Slaught .02 .10
507 Zane Smith .02 .10
508 Randy Tomlin .02 .10
509 Andy Van Slyke .10 .30
510 Paul Wagner .02 .10
511 Tim Wakefield .10 .30
512 Bob Walk .02 .10
513 John Wehner .02 .10
514 Kevin Young .02 .10
515 Billy Bean .02 .10
516 Andy Benes .02 .10
517 Derek Bell .02 .10
518 Doug Brocail .02 .10
519 Jarvis Brown .02 .10
520 Phil Clark .02 .10
521 Mark Davis .02 .10
522 Jeff Gardner .02 .10
523 Pat Gomez .02 .10
524 Ricky Gutierrez .02 .10
525 Tony Gwynn .25 .60
526 Gene Harris .02 .10
527 Kevin Higgins .02 .10
528 Trevor Hoffman .10 .30
529 Luis Lopez .02 .10
530 Pedro A.Martinez RC .02 .10
531 Melvin Nieves .02 .10
532 Phil Plantier .02 .10
533 Frank Seminara .02 .10
534 Craig Shipley .02 .10
535 Tim Teufel .02 .10
536 Guillermo Velasquez .02 .10
537 Wally Whitehurst .02 .10
538 Rod Beck .02 .10
539 Todd Benzinger .02 .10
540 Barry Bonds .60 1.50
541 Jeff Brantley .02 .10
542 Dave Burba .02 .10
543 John Burkett .02 .10
544 Will Clark .10 .30
545 Royce Clayton .02 .10
546 Bryan Hickerson .02 .10
547 Mike Jackson .02 .10
548 Darren Lewis .02 .10
549 Kirt Manwaring .02 .10
550 Dave Martinez .02 .10
551 Willie McGee .07 .20
552 Jeff Reed .02 .10
553 Dave Righetti .07 .20
554 Kevin Rogers .02 .10
555 Steve Scarsone .02 .10
556 Bill Swift .02 .10
557 Robby Thompson .02 .10
558 Salomon Torres .02 .10
559 Matt Williams .07 .20
560 Trevor Wilson .02 .10
561 Rich Amaral .02 .10
562 Mike Blowers .02 .10
563 Chris Bosio .02 .10
564 Jay Buhner .07 .20
565 Norm Charlton .07 .20
566 Jim Converse .02 .10
567 Rich DeLucia .02 .10
568 Mike Felder .02 .10
569 Dave Fleming .02 .10
570 Ken Griffey Jr. .40 1.00
571 Bill Haselman .02 .10
572 Dwayne Henry .02 .10
573 Brad Holman .02 .10
574 Randy Johnson .20 .50
575 Greg Litton .02 .10
576 Edgar Martinez .10 .30
577 Tino Martinez .10 .30
578 Jeff Nelson .02 .10
579 Marc Newfield .02 .10
580 Roger Salkeld .02 .10
581 Mackey Sasser .02 .10
582 Brian Turang RC .02 .10
583 Omar Vizquel .10 .30
584 Dave Valle .02 .10
585 Luis Alicea .02 .10
586 Rene Arocha .02 .10
587 Rheal Cormier .02 .10
588 Tripp Cromer .02 .10
589 Bernard Gilkey .02 .10
590 Lee Guetterman .02 .10
591 Gregg Jefferies .02 .10
592 Tim Jones .02 .10
593 Paul Kilgus .02 .10
594 Les Lancaster .02 .10
595 Omar Olivares .02 .10
596 Jose Oquendo .02 .10
597 Donovan Osborne .02 .10
598 Tom Pagnozzi .02 .10
599 Erik Pappas .02 .10
600 Geronimo Pena .02 .10
601 Mike Perez .02 .10
602 Gerald Perry .02 .10
603 Stan Royer .02 .10
604 Ozzie Smith .30 .75
605 Bob Tewksbury .02 .10
606 Allen Watson .02 .10
607 Mark Whiten .02 .10
608 Todd Zeile .02 .10
609 Jeff Bronkey .02 .10
610 Kevin Brown .07 .20
611 Jose Canseco .10 .30
612 Doug Dascenzo .02 .10
613 Butch Davis .02 .10
614 Mario Diaz .02 .10
615 Julio Franco .07 .20
616 Benji Gil .02 .10
617 Juan Gonzalez .07 .20
618 Tom Henke .02 .10
619 Jeff Huson .02 .10
620 David Hulse .02 .10
621 Craig Lefferts .02 .10
622 Rafael Palmeiro .10 .30
623 Dean Palmer .07 .20
624 Bob Patterson .02 .10
625 Roger Pavlik .02 .10
626 Gary Redus .02 .10
627 Ivan Rodriguez .10 .30
628 Kenny Rogers .07 .20
629 Jon Shave .02 .10
630 Doug Strange .02 .10
631 Matt Whiteside .02 .10
632 Roberto Alomar .10 .30
633 Pat Borders .02 .10
634 Scott Brow .02 .10
635 Rob Butler .02 .10
636 Joe Carter .07 .20
637 Tony Castillo .02 .10
638 Mark Eichhorn .02 .10
639 Tony Fernandez .02 .10
640 Huck Flener RC .02 .10
641 Alfredo Griffin .02 .10
642 Juan Guzman .02 .10
643 Rickey Henderson .20 .50
644 Pat Hentgen .02 .10
645 Randy Knorr .02 .10
646 Al Leiter .07 .20
647 Domingo Martinez .02 .10
648 Paul Molitor .07 .20
649 Jack Morris .07 .20
650 John Olerud .07 .20
651 Ed Sprague .02 .10
652 Dave Stewart .07 .20
653 Devon White .07 .20
654 Woody Williams .07 .20
655 Barry Bonds MVP .30 .75
656 Greg Maddux CY .20 .50
657 Jack McDowell CY .02 .10
658 Mike Piazza ROY .20 .50
659 Tim Salmon ROY .07 .20
660 Frank Thomas MVP .10 .30

1994 Pacific All-Latino

COMPLETE SET (20) 10.00 25.00
STATED ODDS 1:25 PURPLE
1 Benito Santiago 1.00 2.50
2 Dave Magadan .50 1.25
3 Andres Galarraga 1.00 2.50
4 Luis Gonzalez 1.00 2.50
5 Jose Offerman .50 1.25
6 Bobby Bonilla 1.00 2.50
7 Dennis Martinez 1.00 2.50
8 Mariano Duncan .50 1.25
9 Orlando Merced .50 1.25
10 Jose Rijo .50 1.25
11 Danny Tartabull .50 1.25
12 Ruben Sierra 1.00 2.50
13 Ivan Rodriguez 1.50 4.00
14 Juan Gonzalez 1.00 2.50
15 Jose Canseco 1.50 4.00
16 Rafael Palmeiro 1.50 4.00
17 Roberto Alomar 1.50 4.00
18 Eduardo Perez .50 1.25
19 Alex Fernandez .50 1.25
20 Omar Vizquel 1.50 4.00

1994 Pacific Checklists

COMPLETE SET (6) .75 2.00
COMMON CARD (1-6) .16 .40

1994 Pacific Gold Prisms

COMPLETE SET (20) 12.00 30.00
STATED ODDS 1:25 PURPLE
1 Juan Gonzalez 1.00 2.50
2 Ken Griffey Jr. 5.00 12.00
3 Frank Thomas 2.50 6.00
4 Albert Belle 1.00 2.50
5 Rafael Palmeiro 1.50 4.00
6 Joe Carter 1.00 2.50
7 Dean Palmer 1.00 2.50
8 Mickey Tettleton .50 1.25
9 Tim Salmon 1.50 4.00
10 Danny Tartabull .50 1.25
11 Barry Bonds 8.00 20.00
12 David Justice 1.00 2.50
13 Matt Williams 1.00 2.50
14 Fred McGriff 1.50 4.00
15 Ron Gant 1.00 2.50
16 Mike Piazza 5.00 12.00
17 Bobby Bonilla 1.00 2.50
18 Phil Plantier .50 1.25
19 Sammy Sosa 2.50 6.00
20 Rick Wilkins .50 1.25

1994 Pacific Silver Prisms

COMPLETE SET (36) 60.00 120.00
TRIANGULAR INSERTS IN PURPLE PACKS
*CIRCULAR: 2X TO .5X SILVER PRISM
ONE CIRCULAR PER BLACK RETAIL PACK
1 Robin Yount 3.00 8.00
2 Juan Gonzalez .75 2.00
3 Rafael Palmeiro 1.25 3.00
4 Paul Molitor .75 2.00
5 Roberto Alomar 1.25 3.00
6 John Olerud .75 2.00
7 Randy Johnson 2.00 5.00
8 Ken Griffey Jr. 4.00 10.00
9 Wade Boggs 1.25 3.00
10 Don Mattingly 5.00 12.00
11 Kirby Puckett 2.00 5.00
12 Tim Salmon 1.25 3.00
13 Frank Thomas 2.00 5.00
14 Fernando Valenzuela .75 2.00
15 Cal Ripken 6.00 15.00
16 Carlos Baerga .40 1.00
17 Kenny Lofton .75 2.00
18 Cecil Fielder .75 2.00
19 John Burkett .40 1.00
20 Andres Galarraga .75 2.00
21 Charlie Hayes .40 1.00
22 Orestes Destrade .40 1.00
23 Jeff Conine .75 2.00
24 Jeff Bagwell 1.25 3.00
25 Mark Grace 1.25 3.00
26 Ryne Sandberg 3.00 8.00
27 Gregg Jefferies .40 1.00
28 Barry Bonds 6.00 15.00
29 Mike Piazza 4.00 10.00
30 Greg Maddux 3.00 8.00
31 Darren Daulton .75 2.00
32 John Kruk .75 2.00
33 Lenny Dykstra .75 2.00
34 Orlando Merced .40 1.00
35 Tony Gwynn 2.50 6.00
36 Robby Thompson .40 1.00

1995 Pacific

This 450-card standard-size set was issued in one series. The full-bleed fronts have action photos; the "Pacific Collection" logo is on the upper left and the player's name is at the bottom. The horizontal backs have a player photo on the left with 1994 stats and some career highlights on the right. The career highlights are in both English and Spanish. The cards are numbered in the lower right corner. The cards are grouped alphabetically within teams and checklisted below alphabetically according to teams for each league. There are no key Rookie Cards in this set.

COMPLETE SET (450) 20.00 50.00
1 Steve Avery .02 .10
2 Rafael Belliard .02 .10
3 Jeff Blauser .02 .10
4 Tom Glavine .10 .30
5 David Justice .07 .20
6 Mike Kelly .02 .10
7 Roberto Kelly .02 .10
8 Ryan Klesko .07 .20
9 Mark Lemke .02 .10
10 Javier Lopez .07 .20
11 Greg Maddux .30 .75
12 Fred McGriff .10 .30
13 Greg McMichael .02 .10
14 Jose Oliva .02 .10
15 John Smoltz .10 .30
16 Tony Tarasco .02 .10
17 Brady Anderson .07 .20
18 Harold Baines .07 .20
19 Armando Benitez .02 .10
20 Mike Devereaux .02 .10
21 Leo Gomez .02 .10
22 Jeffrey Hammonds .02 .10
23 Chris Hoiles .02 .10
24 Ben McDonald .02 .10
25 Mark McLemore .02 .10
26 Jamie Moyer .07 .20
27 Mike Mussina .10 .30
28 Rafael Palmeiro .10 .30
29 Jim Poole .02 .10
30 Cal Ripken .60 1.50
31 Lee Smith .07 .20
32 Mark Smith .02 .10
33 Jose Canseco .10 .30
34 Roger Clemens .40 1.00
35 Scott Cooper .02 .10
36 Andre Dawson .07 .20
37 Tony Fossas .02 .10
38 Mike Greenwell .02 .10
39 Chris Howard .02 .10
40 Jose Melendez .02 .10
41 Nate Minchey .02 .10
42 Tim Naehring .02 .10
43 Otis Nixon .02 .10
44 Carlos Rodriguez .02 .10
45 Aaron Sele .02 .10
46 Lee Tinsley .02 .10
47 Sergio Valdez .02 .10
48 John Valentin .02 .10
49 Mo Vaughn .07 .20
50 Brian Anderson .02 .10
51 Garret Anderson .07 .20
52 Rod Correia .02 .10
53 Chad Curtis .02 .10
54 Mark Dalesandro .02 .10
55 Chili Davis .07 .20
56 Gary DiSarcina .02 .10
57 Damion Easley .02 .10
58 Jim Edmonds .10 .30
59 Jorge Fabregas .02 .10
60 Chuck Finley .07 .20
61 Bo Jackson .20 .50
62 Mark Langston .02 .10
63 Eduardo Perez .02 .10
64 Tim Salmon .10 .30
65 J.T. Snow .07 .20
66 Willie Banks .02 .10
67 Jose Bautista .02 .10
68 Shawon Dunston .02 .10
69 Kevin Foster .02 .10
70 Mark Grace .10 .30
71 Jose Guzman .02 .10
72 Jose Hernandez .02 .10
73 Blaise Ilsley .02 .10
74 Derrick May .02 .10
75 Randy Myers .02 .10
76 Karl Rhodes .02 .10
77 Kevin Roberson .02 .10
78 Rey Sanchez .02 .10
79 Sammy Sosa .20 .50
80 Steve Trachsel .02 .10
81 Eddie Zambrano .02 .10
82 Wilson Alvarez .02 .10
83 Jason Bere .02 .10
84 Joey Cora .02 .10
85 Jose DeLeon .02 .10
86 Alex Fernandez .02 .10
87 Julio Franco .07 .20
88 Ozzie Guillen .07 .20
89 Joe Hall .02 .10
90 Roberto Hernandez .02 .10
91 Darrin Jackson .02 .10
92 Lance Johnson .02 .10
93 Norberto Martin .02 .10
94 Jack McDowell .02 .10
95 Tim Raines .07 .20
96 Olmedo Saenz .02 .10
97 Frank Thomas .20 .50
98 Robin Ventura .07 .20
99 Bret Boone .07 .20
100 Jeff Brantley .02 .10
101 Jacob Brumfield .02 .10
102 Hector Carrasco .02 .10
103 Brian Dorsett .02 .10
104 Tony Fernandez .02 .10
105 Willie Greene .02 .10
106 Erik Hanson .02 .10
107 Kevin Jarvis .02 .10
108 Barry Larkin .10 .30
109 Kevin Mitchell .02 .10
110 Hal Morris .02 .10
111 Jose Rijo .02 .10
112 Johnny Ruffin .02 .10
113 Deion Sanders .10 .30
114 Reggie Sanders .07 .20
115 Sandy Alomar Jr. .02 .10
116 Ruben Amaro .02 .10
117 Carlos Baerga .02 .10
118 Albert Belle .07 .20
119 Alvaro Espinoza .02 .10
120 Rene Gonzales .02 .10
121 Wayne Kirby .02 .10
122 Kenny Lofton .07 .20
123 Candy Maldonado .02 .10
124 Dennis Martinez .07 .20
125 Eddie Murray .20 .50
126 Charles Nagy .02 .10
127 Tony Pena .02 .10
128 Manny Ramirez .10 .30
129 Paul Sorrento .02 .10
130 Jim Thome .10 .30
131 Omar Vizquel .10 .30
132 Dante Bichette .07 .20
133 Ellis Burks .07 .20
134 Vinny Castilla .07 .20
135 Marvin Freeman .02 .10
136 Andres Galarraga .07 .20
137 Joe Girardi .02 .10
138 Charlie Hayes .02 .10
139 Mike Kingery .02 .10
140 Nelson Liriano .02 .10
141 Roberto Mejia .02 .10
142 David Nied .02 .10
143 Steve Reed .02 .10
144 Armando Reynoso .02 .10
145 Bruce Ruffin .02 .10
146 John Vander Wal .02 .10
147 Walt Weiss .02 .10
148 Skeeter Barnes .02 .10
149 Tim Belcher .02 .10
150 Junior Felix .02 .10
151 Cecil Fielder .07 .20
152 Travis Fryman .07 .20
153 Kirk Gibson .07 .20
154 Chris Gomez .02 .10
155 Buddy Groom .02 .10
156 Chad Kreuter .02 .10
157 Mike Moore .02 .10
158 Tony Phillips .02 .10

159 Juan Samuel .02 .10
160 Mickey Tettleton .02 .10
161 Alan Trammell .07 .20
162 David Wells .07 .20
163 Lou Whitaker .07 .20
164 Kurt Abbott .02 .10
165 Luis Aquino .02 .10
166 Alex Arias .02 .10
167 Bret Barberie .02 .10
168 Jerry Browne .02 .10
169 Chuck Carr .02 .10
170 Matias Carrillo .02 .10
171 Greg Colbrunn .02 .10
172 Jeff Conine .07 .20
173 Carl Everett .07 .20
174 Robb Nen .07 .20
175 Yorkis Perez .02 .10
176 Pat Rapp .02 .10
177 Benito Santiago .07 .20
178 Gary Sheffield .07 .20
179 Darrell Whitmore .02 .10
180 Jeff Bagwell .10 .30
181 Kevin Bass .02 .10
182 Craig Biggio .10 .30
183 Andujar Cedeno .02 .10
184 Doug Drabek .02 .10
185 Tony Eusebio .02 .10
186 Steve Finley .07 .20
187 Luis Gonzalez .07 .20
188 Pete Harnisch .02 .10
189 John Hudek .02 .10
190 Orlando Miller .02 .10
191 James Mouton .02 .10
192 Roberto Petagine .02 .10
193 Shane Reynolds .02 .10
194 Greg Swindell .02 .10
195 Dave Veres .02 .10
196 Kevin Appier .07 .20
197 Stan Belinda .02 .10
198 Vince Coleman .02 .10
199 David Cone .07 .20
200 Gary Gaetti .07 .20
201 Greg Gagne .02 .10
202 Mark Gubicza .02 .10
203 Bob Hamelin .02 .10
204 Dave Henderson .02 .10
205 Felix Jose .02 .10
206 Wally Joyner .07 .20
207 Jose Lind .02 .10
208 Mike MacFarlane .02 .10
209 Brian McRae .02 .10
210 Jeff Montgomery .02 .10
211 Hipolito Pichardo .02 .10
212 Pedro Astacio .02 .10
213 Brett Butler .07 .20
214 Omar Daal .02 .10
215 Delino DeShields .02 .10
216 Darren Dreifort .02 .10
217 Carlos Hernandez .02 .10
218 Orel Hershiser .07 .20
219 Garey Ingram .02 .10
220 Eric Karros .07 .20
221 Ramon Martinez .02 .10
222 Raul Mondesi .07 .20
223 Jose Offerman .02 .10
224 Mike Piazza .30 .75
225 Henry Rodriguez .02 .10
226 Ismael Valdes .02 .10
227 Tim Wallach .02 .10
228 Jeff Cirillo .02 .10
229 Alex Diaz .02 .10
230 Cal Eldred .02 .10
231 Mike Fetters .02 .10
232 Brian Harper .02 .10
233 Ted Higuera .02 .10
234 John Jaha .02 .10
235 Graeme Lloyd .02 .10
236 Jose Mercedes .02 .10
237 Jaime Navarro .02 .10
238 Dave Nilsson .02 .10
239 Jesse Orosco .02 .10
240 Jody Reed .02 .10
241 Jose Valentin .02 .10
242 Greg Vaughn .02 .10
243 Turner Ward .02 .10
244 Rick Aguilera .02 .10
245 Rich Becker .02 .10
246 Jim Deshaies .02 .10
247 Steve Dunn .02 .10
248 Scott Erickson .02 .10
249 Kent Hrbek .07 .20
250 Chuck Knoblauch .07 .20
251 Scott Leius .02 .10
252 David McCarty .02 .10
253 Pat Meares .02 .10
254 Pedro Munoz .02 .10
255 Kirby Puckett .20 .50
256 Carlos Pulido .02 .10
257 Kevin Tapani .02 .10
258 Matt Walbeck .02 .10
259 Dave Winfield .07 .20
260 Moises Alou .07 .20
261 Juan Bell .02 .10
262 Freddie Benavides .02 .10
263 Sean Berry .02 .10
264 Wil Cordero .02 .10
265 Jeff Fassero .02 .10
266 Darrin Fletcher .02 .10
267 Cliff Floyd .07 .20
268 Marquis Grissom .07 .20
269 Gil Heredia .02 .10
270 Ken Hill .02 .10
271 Pedro Martinez .10 .30
272 Mel Rojas .02 .10
273 Larry Walker .07 .20
274 John Wetteland .07 .20
275 Rondell White .07 .20
276 Tim Bogar .02 .10
277 Bobby Bonilla .07 .20
278 Rico Brogna .02 .10
279 Jeromy Burnitz .07 .20
280 John Franco .07 .20
281 Eric Hillman .02 .10
282 Todd Hundley .02 .10
283 Jeff Kent .07 .20
284 Mike Maddux .02 .10
285 Joe Orsulak .02 .10
286 Luis Rivera .02 .10
287 Bret Saberhagen .07 .20
288 David Segui .02 .10
289 Ryan Thompson .02 .10
290 Fernando Vina .02 .10
291 Jose Vizcaino .02 .10
292 Jim Abbott .10 .30
293 Wade Boggs .10 .30
294 Russ Davis .02 .10
295 Mike Gallego .02 .10
296 Xavier Hernandez .02 .10
297 Steve Howe .02 .10
298 Jimmy Key .07 .20
299 Don Mattingly .50 1.25
300 Terry Mulholland .02 .10
301 Paul O'Neill .10 .30
302 Luis Polonia .02 .10
303 Mike Stanley .02 .10
304 Danny Tartabull .02 .10
305 Randy Velarde .02 .10
306 Bob Wickman .02 .10
307 Bernie Williams .10 .30
308 Mark Acre .02 .10
309 Geronimo Berroa .02 .10
310 Mike Bordick .02 .10
311 Dennis Eckersley .07 .20
312 Rickey Henderson .20 .50
313 Stan Javier .02 .10
314 Miguel Jimenez .02 .10
315 Francisco Matos RC .02 .10
316 Mark McGwire .50 1.25
317 Troy Neel .02 .10
318 Steve Ontiveros .02 .10
319 Carlos Reyes .02 .10
320 Ruben Sierra .07 .20
321 Terry Steinbach .02 .10
322 Bob Welch .02 .10
323 Bobby Witt .02 .10
324 Larry Andersen .02 .10
325 Kim Batiste .02 .10
326 Darren Daulton .07 .20
327 Mariano Duncan .02 .10
328 Lenny Dykstra .07 .20
329 Jim Eisenreich .02 .10
330 Danny Jackson .02 .10
331 John Kruk .07 .20
332 Tony Longmire .02 .10
333 Tom Marsh .02 .10
334 Mickey Morandini .02 .10
335 Bobby Munoz .02 .10
336 Todd Pratt .02 .10
337 Tom Quinlan .02 .10
338 Kevin Stocker .02 .10
339 Fernando Valenzuela .07 .20
340 Jay Bell .07 .20
341 Dave Clark .02 .10
342 Steve Cooke .02 .10
343 Carlos Garcia .02 .10
344 Jeff King .02 .10
345 Jon Lieber .02 .10
346 Ravelo Manzanillo .02 .10
347 Al Martin .02 .10
348 Orlando Merced .02 .10
349 Denny Neagle .07 .20
350 Alejandro Pena .02 .10
351 Don Slaught .02 .10
352 Zane Smith .02 .10
353 Andy Van Slyke .10 .30
354 Rick White .02 .10
355 Kevin Young .02 .10
356 Andy Ashby .02 .10
357 Derek Bell .02 .10
358 Andy Benes .02 .10
359 Phil Clark .02 .10
360 Donnie Elliott .02 .10
361 Ricky Gutierrez .02 .10
362 Tony Gwynn .25 .60
363 Trevor Hoffman .07 .20
364 Tim Hyers .02 .10
365 Luis Lopez .02 .10
366 Jose Martinez .02 .10
367 Pedro A.Martinez .02 .10
368 Phil Plantier .02 .10
369 Bip Roberts .02 .10
370 A.J.Sager .02 .10
371 Jeff Tabaka .02 .10
372 Todd Benzinger .02 .10
373 Barry Bonds .40 1.00
374 John Burkett .02 .10
375 Mark Carreon .02 .10
376 Royce Clayton .02 .10
377 Pat Gomez .02 .10
378 Erik Johnson .02 .10
379 Darren Lewis .02 .10
380 Kirt Manwaring .02 .10
381 Dave Martinez .02 .10
382 John Patterson .02 .10
383 Mark Portugal .02 .10
384 Darryl Strawberry .07 .20
385 Salomon Torres .02 .10
386 Wm. VanLandingham .02 .10
387 Matt Williams .07 .20
388 Rich Amaral .02 .10
389 Bobby Ayala .02 .10
390 Mike Blowers .02 .10
391 Chris Bosio .02 .10
392 Jay Buhner .07 .20
393 Jim Converse .02 .10
394 Tim Davis .02 .10
395 Felix Fermin .02 .10
396 Dave Fleming .02 .10
397 Goose Gossage .07 .20
398 Ken Griffey Jr. .40 1.00
399 Randy Johnson .20 .50
400 Edgar Martinez .10 .30
401 Tino Martinez .10 .30
402 Alex Rodriguez .50 1.25
403 Dan Wilson .02 .10
404 Luis Alicea .02 .10
405 Rene Arocha .02 .10
406 Bernard Gilkey .02 .10
407 Gregg Jefferies .02 .10
408 Ray Lankford .07 .20
409 Terry McGriff .02 .10
410 Omar Olivares .02 .10
411 Jose Oquendo .02 .10
412 Vicente Palacios .02 .10
413 Geronimo Pena .02 .10
414 Mike Perez .02 .10
415 Gerald Perry .02 .10
416 Ozzie Smith .30 .75
417 Bob Tewksbury .02 .10
418 Mark Whiten .02 .10
419 Todd Zeile .02 .10
420 Esteban Beltre .02 .10
421 Kevin Brown .07 .20
422 Cris Carpenter .02 .10
423 Will Clark .10 .30
424 Hector Fajardo .02 .10
425 Jeff Frye .02 .10
426 Juan Gonzalez .07 .20
427 Rusty Greer .07 .20
428 Rick Honeycutt .02 .10
429 David Hulse .02 .10
430 Manny Lee .02 .10
431 Junior Ortiz .02 .10
432 Dean Palmer .07 .20
433 Ivan Rodriguez .10 .30
434 Dan Smith .02 .10
435 Roberto Alomar .10 .30
436 Pat Borders .02 .10
437 Scott Brow .02 .10
438 Rob Butler .02 .10
439 Joe Carter .07 .20
440 Tony Castillo .02 .10
441 Domingo Cedeno .02 .10
442 Brad Cornett .02 .10
443 Carlos Delgado .07 .20
444 Alex Gonzalez .02 .10
445 Juan Guzman .02 .10
446 Darren Hall .02 .10
447 Paul Molitor .07 .20
448 John Olerud .07 .20
449 Robert Perez .02 .10
450 Devon White .07 .20

1995 Pacific Gold Crown Die Cuts

COMPLETE SET (20) 75.00 150.00
STATED ODDS 1:18
1 Greg Maddux 5.00 12.00
2 Fred McGriff 2.00 5.00
3 Rafael Palmeiro 2.00 5.00
4 Cal Ripken 10.00 25.00
5 Jose Canseco 2.00 5.00
6 Frank Thomas 3.00 8.00
7 Albert Belle 1.25 3.00
8 Manny Ramirez 2.00 5.00
9 Andres Galarraga 1.25 3.00
10 Jeff Bagwell 2.00 5.00
11 Chan Ho Park .60 1.50
12 Raul Mondesi 1.25 3.00
13 Mike Piazza 5.00 12.00
14 Kirby Puckett 3.00 8.00
15 Barry Bonds 6.00 15.00
16 Ken Griffey Jr. 6.00 15.00
17 Alex Rodriguez 8.00 20.00
18 Juan Gonzalez 1.25 3.00
19 Roberto Alomar 2.00 5.00
20 Carlos Delgado 1.25 3.00

1995 Pacific Gold Prisms

COMPLETE SET (36) 60.00 120.00
STATED ODDS 1:12
1 Jose Canseco 1.50 4.00
2 Gregg Jefferies .50 1.25
3 Fred McGriff 1.50 4.00
4 Joe Carter 1.00 2.50
5 Tim Salmon 1.50 4.00
6 Wade Boggs 1.50 4.00
7 Dave Winfield 1.00 2.50
8 Bob Hamelin .50 1.25
9 Cal Ripken 8.00 20.00
10 Don Mattingly 6.00 15.00
11 Juan Gonzalez 1.00 2.50
12 Carlos Delgado 1.00 2.50
13 Barry Bonds 5.00 12.00
14 Albert Belle 1.00 2.50
15 Raul Mondesi 1.00 2.50
16 Jeff Bagwell 1.50 4.00
17 Mike Piazza 4.00 10.00
18 Rafael Palmeiro 1.50 4.00
19 Frank Thomas 2.50 6.00
20 Matt Williams 1.00 2.50
21 Ken Griffey Jr. 5.00 12.00
22 Will Clark 1.50 4.00
23 Bobby Bonilla 1.00 2.50
24 Kenny Lofton 1.00 2.50
25 Paul Molitor 1.00 2.50
26 Kirby Puckett 2.50 6.00
27 David Justice 1.00 2.50
28 Jeff Conine 1.00 2.50
29 Bret Boone 1.00 2.50
30 Larry Walker 1.00 2.50
31 Cecil Fielder 1.00 2.50
32 Manny Ramirez 1.50 4.00
33 Javier Lopez 1.00 2.50
34 Jimmy Key 1.00 2.50
35 Andres Galarraga 1.00 2.50
36 Tony Gwynn 3.00 8.00

1995 Pacific Latinos Destacados

COMPLETE SET (36) 20.00 50.00
STATED ODDS 1:9
1 Roberto Alomar 1.25 3.00
2 Moises Alou .75 2.00
3 Wilson Alvarez .40 1.00
4 Carlos Baerga .40 1.00
5 Geronimo Berroa .40 1.00
6 Jose Canseco 1.25 3.00
7 Hector Carrasco .40 1.00
8 Wil Cordero .40 1.00
9 Carlos Delgado .75 2.00
10 Damion Easley .40 1.00
11 Tony Eusebio .40 1.00
12 Hector Fajardo .40 1.00
13 Andres Galarraga .75 2.00
14 Carlos Garcia .40 1.00
15 Chris Gomez .40 1.00
16 Alex Gonzalez .40 1.00
17 Juan Gonzalez .75 2.00
18 Luis Gonzalez .75 2.00
19 Felix Jose .40 1.00
20 Javier Lopez .75 2.00
21 Luis Lopez .40 1.00
22 Dennis Martinez .75 2.00
23 Orlando Miller .40 1.00
24 Raul Mondesi .75 2.00
25 Jose Oliva .40 1.00
26 Rafael Palmeiro 1.25 3.00
27 Yorkis Perez .40 1.00
28 Manny Ramirez 1.25 3.00
29 Jose Rijo .40 1.00
30 Alex Rodriguez 5.00 12.00
31 Ivan Rodriguez 1.25 3.00
32 Carlos Rodriguez .40 1.00
33 Sammy Sosa 2.00 5.00
34 Tony Tarasco .40 1.00
35 Ismael Valdes .40 1.00
36 Bernie Williams 1.25 3.00

1995 Pacific Harvey Riebe

Produced by Pacific, this standard-size card celebrates the baseball career of Harvey Riebe. The card is unnumbered. Riebe had never before been featured on any card.

1 Harvey Riebe .40 1.00

1996 Pacific

This 450-card set was issued in 12-card packs. The fronts feature borderless color action player photos with double-etched gold foil printing. The horizontal backs carry a color player portrait with player information in both English and Spanish and 1995 season player statistics.

COMPLETE SET (450) 15.00 40.00
SUBSET CARDS HALF VALUE OF BASE CARDS
1 Steve Avery .07 .20
2 Ryan Klesko .07 .20
3 Pedro Borbon .07 .20
4 Chipper Jones .20 .50
5 Kent Mercker .07 .20
6 Greg Maddux .30 .75
7 Greg McMichael .07 .20
8 Mark Wohlers .07 .20
9 Fred McGriff .10 .30
10 John Smoltz .10 .30
11 Rafael Belliard .07 .20
12 Mark Lemke .07 .20
13 Tom Glavine .10 .30
14 Javier Lopez .07 .20
15 Jeff Blauser .07 .20
16 David Justice .07 .20
17 Marquis Grissom .07 .20
18 Greg Maddux CY .20 .50
19 Randy Myers .07 .20
20 Scott Servais .07 .20
21 Sammy Sosa .20 .50
22 Kevin Foster .07 .20
23 Jose Hernandez .07 .20
24 Jim Bullinger .07 .20
25 Mike Perez .07 .20
26 Shawon Dunston .07 .20
27 Rey Sanchez .07 .20
28 Frank Castillo .07 .20
29 Jaime Navarro .07 .20
30 Brian McRae .07 .20
31 Mark Grace .10 .30
32 Roberto Rivera .07 .20
33 Luis Gonzalez .07 .20
34 Hector Carrasco .07 .20
35 Bret Boone .07 .20
36 Thomas Howard .07 .20
37 Hal Morris .07 .20
38 John Smiley .07 .20
39 Jeff Brantley .07 .20
40 Barry Larkin .10 .30
41 Mariano Duncan .07 .20
42 Xavier Hernandez .07 .20
43 Pete Schourek .07 .20
44 Reggie Sanders .07 .20
45 Dave Burba .07 .20
46 Jeff Branson .07 .20
47 Mark Portugal .07 .20
48 Ron Gant .07 .20
49 Benito Santiago .07 .20
50 Barry Larkin MVP .07 .20
51 Steve Reed .07 .20
52 Kevin Ritz .07 .20
53 Dante Bichette .07 .20
54 Darren Holmes .07 .20
55 Ellis Burks .07 .20
56 Walt Weiss .07 .20
57 Armando Reynoso .07 .20
58 Vinny Castilla .07 .20
59 Jason Bates .07 .20
60 Mike Kingery .07 .20
61 Bryan Rekar .07 .20
62 Curtis Leskanic .07 .20
63 Bret Saberhagen .07 .20
64 Andres Galarraga .07 .20
65 Larry Walker .07 .20
66 Joe Girardi .07 .20
67 Quilvio Veras .07 .20
68 Robb Nen .07 .20
69 Mario Diaz .07 .20
70 Chuck Carr .07 .20
71 Alex Arias .07 .20
72 Pat Rapp .07 .20
73 Rich Garces .07 .20
74 Kurt Abbott .07 .20
75 Andre Dawson .07 .20
76 Greg Colbrunn .07 .20
77 John Burkett .07 .20
78 Terry Pendleton .07 .20
79 Jesus Tavarez .07 .20
80 Charles Johnson .07 .20
81 Yorkis Perez .07 .20
82 Jeff Conine .07 .20
83 Gary Sheffield .07 .20
84 Brian L. Hunter .07 .20
85 Derrick May .07 .20
86 Greg Swindell .07 .20
87 Derek Bell .07 .20
88 Dave Veres .07 .20
89 Jeff Bagwell .10 .30
90 Todd Jones .07 .20
91 Orlando Miller .07 .20
92 Pedro A. Martinez .07 .20
93 Tony Eusebio .07 .20
94 Craig Biggio .10 .30
95 Shane Reynolds .07 .20
96 James Mouton .07 .20
97 Doug Drabek .07 .20
98 Dave Magadan .07 .20
99 Ricky Gutierrez .07 .20
100 Hideo Nomo .20 .50
101 Delino DeShields .07 .20
102 Tom Candiotti .07 .20
103 Mike Piazza .30 .75
104 Ramon Martinez .07 .20
105 Pedro Astacio .07 .20
106 Chad Fonville .07 .20
107 Raul Mondesi .07 .20
108 Ismael Valdes .07 .20
109 Jose Offerman .07 .20
110 Todd Worrell .07 .20
111 Eric Karros .07 .20
112 Brett Butler .07 .20
113 Juan Castro .07 .20
114 Roberto Kelly .07 .20
115 Omar Daal .07 .20
116 Antonio Osuna .07 .20
117 Hideo Nomo ROY .10 .30
118 Mike Lansing .07 .20
119 Mel Rojas .07 .20
120 Sean Berry .07 .20
121 David Segui .07 .20
122 Tavo Alvarez .07 .20
123 Pedro Martinez .10 .30
124 F.P. Santangelo .07 .20
125 Rondell White .07 .20
126 Cliff Floyd .07 .20
127 Henry Rodriguez .07 .20
128 Tony Tarasco .07 .20
129 Yamil Benitez .07 .20
130 Carlos Perez .07 .20
131 Wil Cordero .07 .20
132 Jeff Fassero .07 .20
133 Moises Alou .07 .20
134 John Franco .07 .20
135 Rico Brogna .07 .20
136 Dave Mlicki .07 .20
137 Bill Pulsipher .07 .20
138 Jose Vizcaino .07 .20
139 Carl Everett .07 .20
140 Edgardo Alfonzo .07 .20
141 Bobby Jones .07 .20
142 Alberto Castillo .07 .20
143 Joe Orsulak .07 .20
144 Jeff Kent .07 .20
145 Ryan Thompson .07 .20
146 Jason Isringhausen .07 .20
147 Todd Hundley .07 .20
148 Alex Ochoa .07 .20
149 Charlie Hayes .07 .20
150 Michael Mimbs .07 .20
151 Darren Daulton .07 .20
152 Toby Borland .07 .20
153 Andy Van Slyke .10 .30
154 Mickey Morandini .07 .20
155 Sid Fernandez .07 .20
156 Tom Marsh .07 .20
157 Kevin Stocker .07 .20
158 Paul Quantrill .07 .20
159 Gregg Jefferies .07 .20
160 Ricky Bottalico .07 .20
161 Lenny Dykstra .07 .20
162 Mark Whiten .07 .20
163 Tyler Green .07 .20
164 Jim Eisenreich .07 .20
165 Heathcliff Slocumb .07 .20
166 Esteban Loaiza .07 .20
167 Rich Aude .07 .20
168 Jason Christiansen .07 .20
169 Ramon Morel .07 .20
170 Orlando Merced .07 .20
171 Paul Wagner .07 .20
172 Jeff King .07 .20
173 Jay Bell .07 .20
174 Jacob Brumfield .07 .20
175 Nelson Liriano .07 .20
176 Dan Miceli .07 .20
177 Carlos Garcia .07 .20
178 Denny Neagle .07 .20
179 Angelo Encarnacion .07 .20
180 Al Martin .07 .20
181 Midre Cummings .07 .20
182 Eddie Williams .07 .20
183 Roberto Petagine .07 .20
184 Tony Gwynn .25 .60
185 Andy Ashby .07 .20
186 Melvin Nieves .07 .20
187 Phil Clark .07 .20
188 Brad Ausmus .07 .20
189 Bip Roberts .07 .20
190 Fernando Valenzuela .07 .20
191 Marc Newfield .07 .20
192 Steve Finley .07 .20
193 Trevor Hoffman .07 .20
194 Andujar Cedeno .07 .20
195 Jody Reed .07 .20
196 Ken Caminiti .07 .20
197 Joey Hamilton .07 .20
198 Tony Gwynn BAC .10 .30
199 Shawn Barton .07 .20
200 Deion Sanders .10 .30
201 Rikkert Faneyte .07 .20
202 Barry Bonds .60 1.50
203 Matt Williams .07 .20
204 Jose Bautista .07 .20
205 Mark Leiter .07 .20
206 Mark Carreon .07 .20
207 Robby Thompson .07 .20
208 Terry Mulholland .07 .20
209 Rod Beck .07 .20
210 Royce Clayton .07 .20
211 J.R. Phillips .07 .20
212 Kirt Manwaring .07 .20
213 Glenallen Hill .07 .20
214 William VanLandingham .07 .20
215 Scott Cooper .07 .20
216 Bernard Gilkey .07 .20
217 Allen Watson .07 .20
218 Donovan Osborne .07 .20
219 Ray Lankford .07 .20
220 Tony Fossas .07 .20
221 Tom Pagnozzi .07 .20
222 John Mabry .07 .20
223 Tripp Cromer .07 .20
224 Mark Petkovsek .07 .20
225 Mike Morgan .07 .20
226 Ozzie Smith .30 .75
227 Tom Henke .07 .20
228 Jose Oquendo .07 .20
229 Brian Jordan .07 .20
230 Cal Ripken .60 1.50
231 Scott Erickson .07 .20
232 Harold Baines .07 .20
233 Jeff Manto .07 .20
234 Jesse Orosco .07 .20
235 Jeffrey Hammonds .07 .20
236 Brady Anderson .07 .20
237 Manny Alexander .07 .20
238 Chris Hoiles .07 .20
239 Rafael Palmeiro .10 .30
240 Ben McDonald .07 .20
241 Curtis Goodwin .07 .20
242 Bobby Bonilla .07 .20
243 Mike Mussina .10 .30
244 Kevin Brown .07 .20
245 Armando Benitez .07 .20
246 Jose Canseco .10 .30
247 Erik Hanson .07 .20
248 Mo Vaughn .07 .20
249 Tim Naehring .07 .20
250 Vaughn Eshelman .07 .20
251 Mike Greenwell .07 .20
252 Troy O'Leary .07 .20
253 Tim Wakefield .07 .20
254 Dwayne Hosey .07 .20
255 John Valentin .07 .20
256 Rick Aguilera .07 .20
257 Mike MacFarlane .07 .20
258 Roger Clemens .40 1.00
259 Luis Alicea .07 .20
260 Mo Vaughn MVP .07 .20
261 Mark Langston .07 .20
262 Jim Edmonds .07 .20
263 Rod Correia .07 .20
264 Tim Salmon .10 .30
265 J.T. Snow .07 .20
266 Orlando Palmeiro .07 .20
267 Jorge Fabregas .07 .20
268 Jim Abbott .10 .30
269 Eduardo Perez .07 .20
270 Lee Smith .07 .20
271 Gary DiSarcina .07 .20
272 Damion Easley .07 .20
273 Tony Phillips .07 .20
274 Garret Anderson .07 .20
275 Chuck Finley .07 .20
276 Chili Davis .07 .20
277 Lance Johnson .07 .20
278 Alex Fernandez .07 .20
279 Robin Ventura .07 .20
280 Chris Snopek .07 .20
281 Brian Keyser .07 .20
282 Lyle Mouton .07 .20
283 Luis Andujar .07 .20
284 Tim Raines .07 .20
285 Larry Thomas .07 .20
286 Ozzie Guillen .07 .20
287 Frank Thomas .20 .50
288 Roberto Hernandez .07 .20
289 Dave Martinez .07 .20
290 Ray Durham .07 .20
291 Ron Karkovice .07 .20
292 Wilson Alvarez .07 .20
293 Omar Vizquel .10 .30
294 Eddie Murray .20 .50
295 Sandy Alomar Jr. .07 .20
296 Orel Hershiser .07 .20
297 Jose Mesa .07 .20
298 Julian Tavarez .07 .20
299 Dennis Martinez .07 .20
300 Carlos Baerga .07 .20
301 Manny Ramirez .10 .30
302 Jim Thome .10 .30
303 Kenny Lofton .07 .20
304 Tony Pena .07 .20
305 Alvaro Espinoza .07 .20
306 Paul Sorrento .07 .20
307 Albert Belle .07 .20
308 Danny Bautista .07 .20
309 Chris Gomez .07 .20
310 Jose Lima .07 .20
311 Phil Nevin .07 .20
312 Alan Trammell .07 .20
313 Chad Curtis .07 .20
314 John Flaherty .07 .20
315 Travis Fryman .07 .20
316 Todd Steverson .07 .20
317 Brian Bohanon .07 .20
318 Lou Whitaker .07 .20
319 Bobby Higginson .07 .20
320 Steve Rodriguez .07 .20
321 Cecil Fielder .07 .20
322 Felipe Lira .07 .20
323 Juan Samuel .07 .20
324 Bob Hamelin .07 .20
325 Tom Goodwin .07 .20
326 Johnny Damon .10 .30
327 Hipolito Pichardo .07 .20
328 Dilson Torres .07 .20
329 Kevin Appier .07 .20
330 Mark Gubicza .07 .20
331 Jon Nunnally .07 .20
332 Gary Gaetti .07 .20
333 Brent Mayne .07 .20
334 Brent Cookson .07 .20
335 Tom Gordon .07 .20
336 Wally Joyner .07 .20
337 Greg Gagne .07 .20
338 Fernando Vina .07 .20
339 Joe Oliver .07 .20
340 John Jaha .07 .20
341 Jeff Cirillo .07 .20
342 Pat Listach .07 .20
343 Dave Nilsson .07 .20
344 Steve Sparks .07 .20
345 Ricky Bones .07 .20
346 David Hulse .07 .20
347 Scott Karl .07 .20
348 Darryl Hamilton .07 .20
349 B.J. Surhoff .07 .20
350 Angel Miranda .07 .20
351 Sid Roberson .07 .20
352 Matt Mieske .07 .20
353 Jose Valentin .07 .20
354 Matt Lawton RC .15 .40
355 Eddie Guardado .07 .20
356 Brad Radke .07 .20
357 Pedro Munoz .07 .20
358 Scott Stahoviak .07 .20
359 Erik Schullstrom .07 .20
360 Pat Meares .07 .20
361 Marty Cordova .07 .20
362 Scott Leius .07 .20
363 Matt Walbeck .07 .20
364 Rich Becker .07 .20
365 Kirby Puckett .20 .50
366 Oscar Munoz .07 .20
367 Chuck Knoblauch .07 .20
368 Marty Cordova ROY .07 .20
369 Bernie Williams .10 .30
370 Mike Stanley .07 .20
371 Andy Pettitte .10 .30
372 Jack McDowell .07 .20
373 Sterling Hitchcock .07 .20
374 David Cone .07 .20
375 Randy Velarde .07 .20
376 Don Mattingly .50 1.25
377 Melido Perez .07 .20
378 Wade Boggs .10 .30
379 Ruben Sierra .07 .20
380 Tony Fernandez .07 .20
381 John Wetteland .07 .20
382 Mariano Rivera .40 1.00
383 Derek Jeter .50 1.25
384 Paul O'Neill .10 .30
385 Mark McGwire .50 1.25
386 Scott Brosius .07 .20
387 Don Wengert .07 .20
388 Terry Steinbach .07 .20
389 Brent Gates .07 .20
390 Craig Paquette .07 .20
391 Mike Bordick .07 .20
392 Ariel Prieto .07 .20
393 Dennis Eckersley .07 .20
394 Carlos Reyes .07 .20
395 Todd Stottlemyre .07 .20
396 Rickey Henderson .20 .50
397 Geronimo Berroa .07 .20
398 Steve Ontiveros .07 .20
399 Mike Gallego .07 .20
400 Stan Javier .07 .20
401 Randy Johnson .20 .50
402 Norm Charlton .07 .20
403 Mike Blowers .07 .20
404 Tino Martinez .10 .30
405 Dan Wilson .07 .20
406 Andy Benes .07 .20
407 Alex Diaz .07 .20
408 Edgar Martinez .10 .30
409 Chris Bosio .07 .20
410 Ken Griffey Jr. .40 1.00
411 Luis Sojo .07 .20
412 Bob Wolcott .07 .20
413 Vince Coleman .07 .20
414 Rich Amaral .07 .20
415 Jay Buhner .07 .20
416 Alex Rodriguez .40 1.00
417 Joey Cora .07 .20
418 Randy Johnson CY .10 .30
419 Edgar Martinez BAC .07 .20
420 Ivan Rodriguez .10 .30
421 Mark McLemore .07 .20
422 Mickey Tettleton .07 .20
423 Juan Gonzalez .07 .20
424 Will Clark .10 .30
425 Kevin Gross .07 .20
426 Dean Palmer .07 .20
427 Kenny Rogers .07 .20
428 Bob Tewksbury .07 .20
429 Benji Gil .07 .20
430 Jeff Russell .07 .20
431 Rusty Greer .07 .20
432 Roger Pavlik .07 .20
433 Esteban Beltre .07 .20
434 Otis Nixon .07 .20
435 Paul Molitor .07 .20
436 Carlos Delgado .07 .20
437 Ed Sprague .07 .20
438 Juan Guzman .07 .20
439 Domingo Cedeno .07 .20
440 Pat Hentgen .07 .20
441 Tomas Perez .07 .20
442 John Olerud .07 .20
443 Shawn Green .07 .20
444 Al Leiter .07 .20
445 Joe Carter .07 .20
446 Robert Perez .07 .20
447 Devon White .07 .20
448 Tony Castillo .07 .20
449 Alex Gonzalez .07 .20
450 Roberto Alomar .10 .30

1996 Pacific Cramer's Choice

COMPLETE SET (10) 50.00 100.00
STATED ODDS 1:721
CC1 Roberto Alomar 3.00 8.00
CC2 Wade Boggs 3.00 8.00
CC3 Cal Ripken 15.00 40.00
CC4 Greg Maddux 8.00 20.00
CC5 Frank Thomas 20.00 50.00
CC6 Tony Gwynn 5.00 12.00
CC7 Mike Piazza 5.00 12.00
CC8 Ken Griffey Jr. 20.00 50.00
CC9 Manny Ramirez 3.00 8.00
CC10 Edgar Martinez 3.00 8.00

1996 Pacific Estrellas Latinas

COMPLETE SET (36) 15.00 40.00
STATED ODDS 1:9
EL1 Roberto Alomar .75 2.00
EL2 Moises Alou .50 1.25
EL3 Carlos Baerga .50 1.25
EL4 Geronimo Berroa .50 1.25
EL5 Ricky Bones .50 1.25
EL6 Bobby Bonilla .50 1.25
EL7 Jose Canseco .75 2.00
EL8 Vinny Castilla .50 1.25
EL9 Pedro Martinez .75 2.00
EL10 John Valentin .50 1.25

EL11 Andres Galarraga .50 1.25
EL12 Juan Gonzalez .50 1.25
EL13 Ozzie Guillen .50 1.25
EL14 Esteban Loaiza .50 1.25
EL15 Javier Lopez .50 1.25
EL16 Dennis Martinez .50 1.25
EL17 Edgar Martinez .75 2.00
EL18 Tino Martinez .75 2.00
EL19 Orlando Merced .50 1.25
EL20 Jose Mesa .50 1.25
EL21 Raul Mondesi .50 1.25
EL22 Jaime Navarro .50 1.25
EL23 Rafael Palmeiro .75 2.00
EL24 Carlos Perez .50 1.25
EL25 Manny Ramirez .75 2.00
EL26 Alex Rodriguez 2.50 6.00
EL27 Ivan Rodriguez .75 2.00
EL28 David Segui .50 1.25
EL29 Ruben Sierra .50 1.25
EL30 Sammy Sosa 1.25 3.00
EL31 Julian Tavarez .50 1.25
EL32 Ismael Valdes .50 1.25
EL33 Fernando Valenzuela .50 1.25
EL34 Quilvio Veras .50 1.25
EL35 Omar Vizquel .75 2.00
EL36 Bernie Williams .75 2.00

1996 Pacific Gold Crown Die Cuts

COMPLETE SET (36) 40.00 100.00
STATED ODDS 1:37
DC1 Roberto Alomar 1.00 2.50
DC2 Will Clark 1.00 2.50
DC3 Johnny Damon 1.00 2.50
DC4 Don Mattingly 3.00 8.00
DC5 Edgar Martinez 1.00 2.50
DC6 Manny Ramirez 1.00 2.50
DC7 Mike Piazza 1.50 4.00
DC8 Quilvio Veras .60 1.50
DC9 Rickey Henderson 1.50 4.00
DC10 Jeff Bagwell 1.00 2.50
DC11 Andres Galarraga 1.00 2.50
DC12 Tim Salmon .60 1.50
DC13 Ken Griffey Jr. 3.00 8.00
DC14 Sammy Sosa 1.50 4.00
DC15 Cal Ripken 5.00 12.00
DC16 Raul Mondesi .60 1.50
DC17 Jose Canseco 1.00 2.50
DC18 Frank Thomas 1.50 4.00
DC19 Hideo Nomo 1.50 4.00
DC20 Wade Boggs 1.00 2.50
DC21 Reggie Sanders .60 1.50
DC22 Carlos Baerga .60 1.50
DC23 Mo Vaughn .60 1.50
DC24 Ivan Rodriguez 1.00 2.50
DC25 Kirby Puckett 1.50 4.00
DC26 Albert Belle .60 1.50
DC27 Vinny Castilla .60 1.50
DC28 Greg Maddux 2.50 6.00
DC29 Dante Bichette .60 1.50
DC30 Deion Sanders 1.00 2.50
DC31 Chipper Jones 1.50 4.00
DC32 Cecil Fielder .60 1.50
DC33 Randy Johnson 1.50 4.00
DC34 Mark McGwire 2.50 6.00
DC35 Tony Gwynn 1.50 4.00
DC36 Barry Bonds 2.50 6.00

1996 Pacific Hometowns

COMPLETE SET (20) 25.00 60.00
STATED ODDS 1:18
HP1 Mike Piazza 2.50 6.00
HP2 Greg Maddux 2.50 6.00
HP3 Tony Gwynn 2.00 5.00
HP4 Carlos Baerga .60 1.50
HP5 Don Mattingly 4.00 10.00
HP6 Cal Ripken 5.00 12.00
HP7 Chipper Jones 1.50 4.00
HP8 Andres Galarraga .60 1.50
HP9 Manny Ramirez 1.00 2.50
HP10 Roberto Alomar 1.00 2.50
HP11 Ken Griffey Jr. 3.00 8.00
HP12 Jose Canseco 1.00 2.50
HP13 Frank Thomas 1.50 4.00
HP14 Vinny Castilla .60 1.50
HP15 Roberto Kelly .60 1.50
HP16 Dennis Martinez .60 1.50
HP17 Kirby Puckett 1.50 4.00
HP18 Raul Mondesi .60 1.50
HP19 Hideo Nomo 1.50 4.00
HP20 Edgar Martinez 1.00 2.50

1996 Pacific Milestones

COMPLETE SET (10) 20.00 50.00
STATED ODDS 1:37
M1 Albert Belle .60 1.50
M2 Don Mattingly 4.00 10.00
M3 Tony Gwynn 2.00 5.00
M4 Jose Canseco 1.00 2.50
M5 Marty Cordova .60 1.50
M6 Wade Boggs 1.00 2.50
M7 Greg Maddux 2.50 6.00
M8 Eddie Murray 1.50 4.00
M9 Ken Griffey Jr. 3.00 8.00
M10 Cal Ripken 5.00 12.00

1996 Pacific October Moments

COMPLETE SET (20) 20.00 50.00
STATED ODDS 1:37
OM1 Carlos Baerga .75 2.00
OM2 Albert Belle .75 2.00
OM3 Dante Bichette .75 2.00
OM4 Jose Canseco 1.25 3.00
OM5 Tom Glavine 1.25 3.00
OM6 Ken Griffey Jr. 4.00 10.00
OM7 Randy Johnson 2.00 5.00
OM8 Chipper Jones 2.00 5.00
OM9 David Justice .75 2.00
OM10 Ryan Klesko .75 2.00
OM11 Kenny Lofton .75 2.00
OM12 Javier Lopez .75 2.00
OM13 Greg Maddux 3.00 8.00
OM14 Edgar Martinez 1.25 3.00
OM15 Don Mattingly 4.00 10.00
OM16 Hideo Nomo 2.00 5.00
OM17 Mike Piazza 2.00 5.00
OM18 Manny Ramirez 1.25 3.00
OM19 Reggie Sanders .75 2.00
OM20 Jim Thome 1.25 3.00

1996 Pacific/Advil Nolan Ryan

This 27-card standard-size set features all-time strikeout king, Nolan Ryan. The set was available directly with a proof of purchase of Advil products. Each full-bleed card features a different highlight of Ryan's career. There was also an A and B card which were included at retail stores as part of the store display. A collector got a pack with these cards if they a big enough package. They were not available as part of the regular set.

COMPLETE SET (27) 6.00 15.00
COMMON CARD (1-27) .24 .60
A Nolan Ryan 1.00 2.50
B Nolan Ryan 1.00 2.50

1996 Pacific Baerga Softball

This eight card set features major league baseball players who donated their time to participate in the Second Annual Carlos Baerga Celebrities Softball Game, played Dec. 8 in Bayamon, Puerto Rico. Two cards from the set were distributed to each attendee of the game. The fronts carry colored action player photos from the softball game. The backs display color player portraits with player information in both Spanish and English.

COMPLETE SET (8) 2.50 6.00
1 Carlos Baerga .08 .25
2 Mike Piazza 1.00 2.50
3 Bernie Williams .40 1.00
4 Frank Thomas .50 1.25
5 Roberto Alomar .40 1.00
6 Edgar Martinez .30 .75
7 Kenny Lofton .30 .75
8 Sammy Sosa .60 1.50

1997 Pacific

This 450-card set was issued in one series and distributed in 12-card packs. The fronts feature color action player photos foiled in gold. The backs carry player information in both English and Spanish with player statistics. No subsets are featured as the manufacturer focused on providing collectors with the most comprehensive selection of major league players as possible. Rookie Cards include Brian Giles.

COMPLETE SET (450) 20.00 50.00
1 Garret Anderson .10 .30
2 George Arias .10 .30
3 Chili Davis .10 .30
4 Gary DiSarcina .10 .30
5 Jim Edmonds .10 .30
6 Darin Erstad .10 .30
7 Jorge Fabregas .10 .30
8 Chuck Finley .10 .30
9 Rex Hudler .10 .30
10 Mark Langston .10 .30
11 Orlando Palmeiro .10 .30
12 Troy Percival .10 .30
13 Tim Salmon .20 .50
14 J.T. Snow .10 .30
15 Randy Velarde .10 .30
16 Manny Alexander .10 .30
17 Roberto Alomar .20 .50
18 Brady Anderson .10 .30
19 Armando Benitez .10 .30
20 Bobby Bonilla .10 .30
21 Rocky Coppinger .10 .30
22 Scott Erickson .10 .30
23 Jeffrey Hammonds .10 .30
24 Chris Hoiles .10 .30
25 Eddie Murray .30 .75
26 Mike Mussina .20 .50
27 Randy Myers .10 .30
28 Rafael Palmeiro .20 .50
29 Cal Ripken 1.00 2.50
30 B.J. Surhoff .10 .30
31 Tony Tarasco .10 .30
32 Esteban Beltre .10 .30
33 Darren Bragg .10 .30
34 Jose Canseco .20 .50
35 Roger Clemens .60 1.50
36 Wil Cordero .10 .30
37 Alex Delgado .10 .30
38 Jeff Frye .10 .30
39 Nomar Garciaparra .50 1.25
40 Tom Gordon .10 .30
41 Mike Greenwell .10 .30
42 Reggie Jefferson .10 .30
43 Tim Naehring .10 .30
44 Troy O'Leary .10 .30
45 Heathcliff Slocumb .10 .30
46 Lee Tinsley .10 .30
47 John Valentin .10 .30
48 Mo Vaughn .10 .30
49 Wilson Alvarez .10 .30
50 Harold Baines .10 .30
51 Ray Durham .10 .30
52 Alex Fernandez .10 .30
53 Ozzie Guillen .10 .30
54 Roberto Hernandez .10 .30
55 Ron Karkovice .10 .30
56 Darren Lewis .10 .30
57 Norberto Martin .10 .30
58 Dave Martinez .10 .30
59 Lyle Mouton .10 .30
60 Jose Munoz .10 .30
61 Tony Phillips .10 .30
62 Kevin Tapani .10 .30
63 Danny Tartabull .10 .30
64 Frank Thomas .30 .75
65 Robin Ventura .10 .30
66 Sandy Alomar Jr. .10 .30
67 Albert Belle .10 .30
68 Julio Franco .10 .30
69 Brian Giles RC .60 1.50
70 Danny Graves .10 .30
71 Orel Hershiser .10 .30
72 Jeff Kent .10 .30
73 Kenny Lofton .10 .30
74 Dennis Martinez .10 .30
75 Jack McDowell .10 .30
76 Jose Mesa .10 .30
77 Charles Nagy .10 .30
78 Manny Ramirez .20 .50
79 Julian Tavarez .10 .30
80 Jim Thome .20 .50
81 Jose Vizcaino .10 .30
82 Omar Vizquel .20 .50
83 Brad Ausmus .10 .30
84 Kimera Bartee .10 .30
85 Raul Casanova .10 .30
86 Tony Clark .10 .30
87 Travis Fryman .10 .30
88 Bobby Higginson .10 .30
89 Mark Lewis .10 .30
90 Jose Lima .10 .30
91 Felipe Lira .10 .30
92 Phil Nevin .10 .30
93 Melvin Nieves .10 .30
94 Curtis Pride .10 .30
95 Ruben Sierra .10 .30
96 Alan Trammell .10 .30
97 Kevin Appier .10 .30
98 Tim Belcher .10 .30
99 Johnny Damon .20 .50
100 Tom Goodwin .10 .30
101 Bob Hamelin .10 .30
102 David Howard .10 .30
103 Jason Jacome .10 .30
104 Keith Lockhart .10 .30
105 Mike Macfarlane .10 .30
106 Jeff Montgomery .10 .30
107 Jose Offerman .10 .30
108 Hipolito Pichardo .10 .30
109 Joe Randa .10 .30
110 Bip Roberts .10 .30
111 Chris Stynes .10 .30
112 Mike Sweeney .10 .30
113 Joe Vitiello .10 .30
114 Jeromy Burnitz .10 .30
115 Chuck Carr .10 .30
116 Jeff Cirillo .10 .30
117 Mike Fetters .10 .30
118 David Hulse .10 .30
119 John Jaha .10 .30
120 Scott Karl .10 .30
121 Jesse Levis .10 .30
122 Mark Loretta .10 .30
123 Mike Matheny .10 .30
124 Ben McDonald .10 .30
125 Matt Mieske .10 .30
126 Angel Miranda .10 .30
127 Dave Nilsson .10 .30
128 Jose Valentin .10 .30
129 Fernando Vina .10 .30
130 Ron Villone .10 .30
131 Gerald Williams .10 .30
132 Rick Aguilera .10 .30
133 Rich Becker .10 .30
134 Ron Coomer .10 .30
135 Marty Cordova .10 .30
136 Eddie Guardado .10 .30
137 Denny Hocking .10 .30
138 Roberto Kelly .10 .30
139 Chuck Knoblauch .10 .30
140 Matt Lawton .10 .30
141 Pat Meares .10 .30
142 Paul Molitor .10 .30
143 Greg Myers .10 .30
144 Jeff Reboulet .10 .30
145 Scott Stahoviak .10 .30
146 Todd Walker .10 .30
147 Wade Boggs .20 .50
148 David Cone .10 .30
149 Mariano Duncan .10 .30
150 Cecil Fielder .10 .30
151 Dwight Gooden .10 .30
152 Derek Jeter .75 2.00
153 Jim Leyritz .10 .30
154 Tino Martinez .20 .50
155 Paul O'Neill .20 .50
156 Andy Pettitte .20 .50
157 Tim Raines .10 .30
158 Mariano Rivera .30 .75
159 Ruben Rivera .10 .30
160 Kenny Rogers .10 .30
161 Darryl Strawberry .10 .30
162 John Wetteland .10 .30
163 Bernie Williams .20 .50
164 Tony Batista .10 .30
165 Geronimo Berroa .10 .30
166 Mike Bordick .10 .30
167 Scott Brosius .10 .30
168 Brent Gates .10 .30
169 Jason Giambi .10 .30
170 Jose Herrera .10 .30
171 Brian Lesher RC .10 .30
172 Damon Mashore .10 .30
173 Mark McGwire .75 2.00
174 Ariel Prieto .10 .30
175 Carlos Reyes .10 .30
176 Matt Stairs .10 .30
177 Terry Steinbach .10 .30
178 John Wasdin .10 .30
179 Ernie Young .10 .30
180 Rich Amaral .10 .30
181 Bobby Ayala .10 .30
182 Jay Buhner .10 .30
183 Rafael Carmona .10 .30
184 Norm Charlton .10 .30
185 Joey Cora .10 .30
186 Ken Griffey Jr. .60 1.50
187 Sterling Hitchcock .10 .30
188 Dave Hollins .10 .30
189 Randy Johnson .30 .75
190 Edgar Martinez .20 .50
191 Jamie Moyer .10 .30
192 Alex Rodriguez .50 1.25
193 Paul Sorrento .10 .30
194 Salomon Torres .10 .30
195 Bob Wells .10 .30
196 Dan Wilson .10 .30
197 Will Clark .20 .50
198 Kevin Elster .10 .30
199 Rene Gonzales .10 .30
200 Juan Gonzalez .10 .30
201 Rusty Greer .10 .30
202 Darryl Hamilton .10 .30
203 Mike Henneman .10 .30
204 Ken Hill .10 .30
205 Mark McLemore .10 .30
206 Darren Oliver .10 .30
207 Dean Palmer .10 .30
208 Roger Pavlik .10 .30
209 Ivan Rodriguez .20 .50
210 Kurt Stillwell .10 .30
211 Mickey Tettleton .10 .30
212 Bobby Witt .10 .30
213 Tilson Brito .10 .30
214 Jacob Brumfield .10 .30
215 Miguel Cairo .10 .30
216 Joe Carter .10 .30
217 Felipe Crespo .10 .30
218 Carlos Delgado .10 .30
219 Alex Gonzalez .10 .30
220 Shawn Green .10 .30
221 Juan Guzman .10 .30
222 Pat Hentgen .10 .30
223 Charlie O'Brien .10 .30
224 John Olerud .10 .30
225 Robert Perez .10 .30
226 Tomas Perez .10 .30
227 Juan Samuel .10 .30
228 Ed Sprague .10 .30
229 Mike Timlin .10 .30
230 Rafael Belliard .10 .30
231 Jermaine Dye .10 .30
232 Tom Glavine .20 .50
233 Marquis Grissom .10 .30
234 Andruw Jones .20 .50
235 Chipper Jones .30 .75
236 David Justice .10 .30
237 Ryan Klesko .10 .30
238 Mark Lemke .10 .30
239 Javier Lopez .10 .30
240 Greg Maddux .50 1.25
241 Fred McGriff .20 .50
242 Denny Neagle .10 .30
243 Eddie Perez .10 .30
244 John Smoltz .20 .50
245 Mark Wohlers .10 .30
246 Brant Brown .10 .30
247 Scott Bullett .10 .30
248 Leo Gomez .10 .30
249 Luis Gonzalez .10 .30
250 Mark Grace .20 .50
251 Jose Hernandez .10 .30
252 Brooks Kieschnick .10 .30
253 Brian McRae .10 .30
254 Jaime Navarro .10 .30
255 Mike Perez .10 .30
256 Rey Sanchez .10 .30
257 Ryne Sandberg .50 1.25
258 Scott Servais .10 .30
259 Sammy Sosa .30 .75
260 Pedro Valdes .10 .30
261 Turk Wendell .10 .30
262 Bret Boone .10 .30
263 Jeff Branson .10 .30
264 Jeff Brantley .10 .30
265 Dave Burba .10 .30
266 Hector Carrasco .10 .30
267 Eric Davis .10 .30
268 Willie Greene .10 .30
269 Lenny Harris .10 .30
270 Thomas Howard .10 .30
271 Barry Larkin .20 .50
272 Hal Morris .10 .30
273 Joe Oliver .10 .30
274 Eric Owens .10 .30
275 Jose Rijo .10 .30
276 Reggie Sanders .10 .30
277 Eddie Taubensee .10 .30
278 Jason Bates .10 .30
279 Dante Bichette .10 .30
280 Ellis Burks .10 .30
281 Vinny Castilla .10 .30
282 Andres Galarraga .10 .30
283 Quinton McCracken .10 .30
284 Jayhawk Owens .10 .30
285 Jeff Reed .10 .30
286 Bryan Rekar .10 .30
287 Armando Reynoso .10 .30
288 Kevin Ritz .10 .30
289 Bruce Ruffin .10 .30
290 John Vander Wal .10 .30
291 Larry Walker .10 .30
292 Walt Weiss .10 .30
293 Eric Young .10 .30
294 Kurt Abbott .10 .30
295 Alex Arias .10 .30
296 Miguel Batista .10 .30
297 Kevin Brown .10 .30
298 Luis Castillo .10 .30
299 Greg Colbrunn .10 .30
300 Jeff Conine .10 .30
301 Charles Johnson .10 .30
302 Al Leiter .10 .30
303 Robb Nen .10 .30
304 Joe Orsulak .10 .30
305 Yorkis Perez .10 .30
306 Edgar Renteria .10 .30
307 Gary Sheffield .10 .30
308 Jesus Tavarez .10 .30
309 Quilvio Veras .10 .30
310 Devon White .10 .30
311 Jeff Bagwell .20 .50
312 Derek Bell .10 .30
313 Sean Berry .10 .30
314 Craig Biggio .20 .50
315 Doug Drabek .10 .30
316 Tony Eusebio .10 .30
317 Ricky Gutierrez .10 .30
318 Xavier Hernandez .10 .30
319 Brian L. Hunter .10 .30
320 Darryl Kile .10 .30
321 Derrick May .10 .30
322 Orlando Miller .10 .30
323 James Mouton .10 .30
324 Bill Spiers .10 .30
325 Pedro Astacio .10 .30
326 Brett Butler .10 .30
327 Juan Castro .10 .30
328 Roger Cedeno .10 .30
329 Delino DeShields .10 .30
330 Karim Garcia .10 .30
331 Todd Hollandsworth .10 .30
332 Eric Karros .10 .30
333 Oreste Marrero .10 .30
334 Ramon Martinez .10 .30
335 Raul Mondesi .10 .30
336 Hideo Nomo .30 .75
337 Antonio Osuna .10 .30
338 Chan Ho Park .10 .30
339 Mike Piazza .50 1.25
340 Ismael Valdes .10 .30
341 Moises Alou .10 .30
342 Omar Daal .10 .30
343 Jeff Fassero .10 .30
344 Cliff Floyd .10 .30
345 Mark Grudzielanek .10 .30
346 Mike Lansing .10 .30
347 Pedro Martinez .20 .50
348 Sherman Obando .10 .30
349 Jose Paniagua .10 .30
350 Henry Rodriguez .10 .30
351 Mel Rojas .10 .30
352 F.P. Santangelo .10 .30
353 David Segui .10 .30
354 Dave Silvestri .10 .30
355 Ugueth Urbina .10 .30
356 Rondell White .10 .30
357 Edgardo Alfonzo .10 .30
358 Carlos Baerga .10 .30
359 Tim Bogar .10 .30
360 Rico Brogna .10 .30
361 Alvaro Espinoza .10 .30
362 Carl Everett .10 .30
363 John Franco .10 .30
364 Bernard Gilkey .10 .30
365 Todd Hundley .10 .30
366 Butch Huskey .10 .30
367 Jason Isringhausen .10 .30
368 Bobby Jones .10 .30
369 Lance Johnson .10 .30
370 Brent Mayne .10 .30
371 Alex Ochoa .10 .30
372 Rey Ordonez .10 .30
373 Ron Blazier .10 .30
374 Ricky Bottalico .10 .30
375 David Doster .10 .30
376 Lenny Dykstra .10 .30
377 Jim Eisenreich .10 .30
378 Bobby Estalella .10 .30
379 Gregg Jefferies .10 .30
380 Kevin Jordan .10 .30
381 Ricardo Jordan .10 .30
382 Mickey Morandini .10 .30
383 Ricky Otero .10 .30
384 Benito Santiago .10 .30
385 Gene Schall .10 .30
386 Curt Schilling .10 .30
387 Kevin Sefcik .10 .30
388 Kevin Stocker .10 .30
389 Jermaine Allensworth .10 .30
390 Jay Bell .10 .30
391 Jason Christiansen .10 .30
392 Francisco Cordova .10 .30
393 Mark Johnson .10 .30
394 Jason Kendall .10 .30
395 Jeff King .10 .30
396 Jon Lieber .10 .30
397 Nelson Liriano .10 .30
398 Esteban Loaiza .10 .30
399 Al Martin .10 .30
400 Orlando Merced .10 .30
401 Ramon Morel .10 .30
402 Luis Alicea .10 .30
403 Alan Benes .10 .30
404 Andy Benes .10 .30
405 Terry Bradshaw .10 .30
406 Royce Clayton .10 .30
407 Dennis Eckersley .10 .30
408 Gary Gaetti .10 .30
409 Mike Gallego .10 .30
410 Ron Gant .10 .30
411 Brian Jordan .10 .30
412 Ray Lankford .10 .30
413 John Mabry .10 .30
414 Willie McGee .10 .30
415 Tom Pagnozzi .10 .30
416 Ozzie Smith .50 1.25
417 Todd Stottlemyre .10 .30
418 Mark Sweeney .10 .30
419 Andy Ashby .10 .30
420 Ken Caminiti .10 .30
421 Archi Cianfrocco .10 .30
422 Steve Finley .10 .30
423 Chris Gomez .10 .30
424 Tony Gwynn .40 1.00
425 Joey Hamilton .10 .30
426 Rickey Henderson .30 .75
427 Trevor Hoffman .10 .30
428 Brian Johnson .10 .30
429 Wally Joyner .10 .30
430 Scott Livingstone .10 .30
431 Jody Reed .10 .30
432 Craig Shipley .10 .30
433 Fernando Valenzuela .10 .30
434 Greg Vaughn .10 .30
435 Rich Aurilia .10 .30
436 Kim Batiste .10 .30
437 Jose Bautista .10 .30
438 Rod Beck .10 .30
439 Marvin Benard .10 .30
440 Barry Bonds .75 2.00
441 Shawon Dunston .10 .30
442 Shawn Estes .10 .30
443 Osvaldo Fernandez .10 .30
444 Stan Javier .10 .30
445 David McCarty .10 .30
446 Bill Mueller RC .50 1.25
447 Steve Scarsone .10 .30
448 Robby Thompson .10 .30
449 Rick Wilkins .10 .30
450 Matt Williams .10 .30

1997 Pacific Light Blue

*STARS: 2.5X TO 6X BASIC CARDS
*ROOKIES: 1.25X TO 3X BASIC CARDS
ONE PER SPECIAL RETAIL PACK

1997 Pacific Silver

*STARS: 20X TO 50X HI COLUMN
*ROOKIES: 6X TO 15X HI COLUMN
STATED ODDS 1:73
STATED PRINT RUN 67 SETS

1997 Pacific Card-Supials

COMPLETE SET (72) 75.00 150.00
COMP.LARGE SET (36) 40.00 100.00
*MINIS: .25X TO .6X LARGE SUPIALS
STATED ODDS 1:37
LARGE CARDS LISTED BELOW
1 Roberto Alomar 1.50 4.00
2 Brady Anderson 1.00 2.50
3 Eddie Murray 2.50 6.00
4 Cal Ripken 8.00 20.00
5 Jose Canseco 1.50 4.00
6 Mo Vaughn 1.00 2.50
7 Frank Thomas 2.50 6.00
8 Albert Belle 1.00 2.50
9 Omar Vizquel 1.50 4.00
10 Chuck Knoblauch 1.00 2.50
11 Paul Molitor 1.00 2.50
12 Wade Boggs 1.50 4.00
13 Derek Jeter 6.00 15.00
14 Andy Pettitte 1.50 4.00
15 Mark McGwire 6.00 15.00
16 Jay Buhner 1.00 2.50
17 Ken Griffey Jr. 5.00 12.00
18 Alex Rodriguez 4.00 10.00
19 Juan Gonzalez 1.00 2.50
20 Ivan Rodriguez 1.50 4.00
21 Andruw Jones 1.50 4.00
22 Chipper Jones 2.50 6.00
23 Ryan Klesko 1.00 2.50
24 Greg Maddux 4.00 10.00
25 Ryne Sandberg 4.00 10.00
26 Andres Galarraga 1.00 2.50
27 Gary Sheffield 1.00 2.50
28 Jeff Bagwell 1.50 4.00
29 Todd Hollandsworth 1.00 2.50
30 Hideo Nomo 2.50 6.00
31 Mike Piazza 4.00 10.00
32 Todd Hundley 1.00 2.50
33 Dennis Eckersley 1.00 2.50
34 Ken Caminiti 1.00 2.50
35 Tony Gwynn 3.00 8.00
36 Barry Bonds 6.00 15.00

1997 Pacific Cramer's Choice

STATED ODDS 1:721
1 Roberto Alomar 4.00 10.00
2 Frank Thomas 6.00 15.00
3 Albert Belle 2.50 6.00
4 Andy Pettitte 4.00 10.00
5 Ken Griffey Jr. 12.00 30.00
6 Alex Rodriguez 8.00 20.00
7 Chipper Jones 6.00 15.00
8 John Smoltz 4.00 10.00
9 Mike Piazza 6.00 15.00
10 Tony Gwynn 6.00 15.00

1997 Pacific Fireworks Die Cuts

COMPLETE SET (20) 50.00 120.00
STATED ODDS 1:73
1 Roberto Alomar 2.00 5.00
2 Brady Anderson 1.25 3.00
3 Eddie Murray 2.00 5.00
4 Cal Ripken 10.00 25.00
5 Frank Thomas 3.00 8.00
6 Albert Belle 1.25 3.00
7 Derek Jeter 8.00 20.00
8 Andy Pettitte 2.00 5.00
9 Bernie Williams 2.00 5.00
10 Mark McGwire 5.00 12.00
11 Ken Griffey Jr. 10.00 25.00
12 Alex Rodriguez 4.00 10.00
13 Juan Gonzalez 1.25 3.00
14 Andruw Jones 1.25 3.00
15 Chipper Jones 3.00 8.00
16 Hideo Nomo 2.00 5.00
17 Mike Piazza 3.00 8.00
18 Henry Rodriguez 1.25 3.00
19 Tony Gwynn 3.00 8.00
20 Barry Bonds 5.00 12.00

1997 Pacific Gold Crown Die Cuts

COMPLETE SET (36) 30.00 80.00
STATED ODDS 1:37
1 Roberto Alomar 1.00 2.50
2 Brady Anderson .60 1.50
3 Mike Mussina 1.00 2.50
4 Eddie Murray 1.00 2.50
5 Cal Ripken 5.00 12.00
6 Jose Canseco 1.00 2.50
7 Frank Thomas 1.50 4.00
8 Albert Belle .60 1.50
9 Omar Vizquel 1.00 2.50
10 Wade Boggs 1.00 2.50
11 Derek Jeter 4.00 10.00
12 Andy Pettitte 1.00 2.50
13 Mariano Rivera 2.00 5.00
14 Bernie Williams 1.00 2.50
15 Mark McGwire 2.50 6.00
16 Ken Griffey Jr. 3.00 8.00
17 Edgar Martinez 1.00 2.50
18 Alex Rodriguez 2.00 5.00
19 Juan Gonzalez .60 1.50
20 Ivan Rodriguez 1.00 2.50
21 Andruw Jones .60 1.50
22 Chipper Jones 1.50 4.00
23 Ryan Klesko .60 1.50
24 John Smoltz 1.00 2.50
25 Ryne Sandberg 2.50 6.00
26 Andres Galarraga 1.00 2.50
27 Edgar Renteria .60 1.50
28 Jeff Bagwell 1.00 2.50
29 Todd Hollandsworth .60 1.50
30 Hideo Nomo 1.00 2.50
31 Mike Piazza 1.50 4.00
32 Todd Hundley .60 1.50
33 Brian Jordan .60 1.50
34 Ken Caminiti .60 1.50
35 Tony Gwynn 1.50 4.00
36 Barry Bonds 2.50 6.00

1997 Pacific Latinos of the Major Leagues

COMPLETE SET (36) 20.00 50.00
STATED ODDS 1:18
1 George Arias .60 1.50
2 Roberto Alomar 1.00 2.50
3 Rafael Palmeiro 1.00 2.50
4 Bobby Bonilla .60 1.50
5 Jose Canseco 1.00 2.50
6 Wilson Alvarez .60 1.50
7 Dave Martinez .60 1.50
8 Julio Franco .60 1.50
9 Manny Ramirez 1.00 2.50
10 Omar Vizquel 1.00 2.50
11 Marty Cordova .60 1.50
12 Roberto Kelly .60 1.50
13 Tino Martinez 1.00 2.50
14 Mariano Rivera 1.50 4.00
15 Ruben Rivera .60 1.50
16 Bernie Williams 1.00 2.50
17 Geronimo Berroa .60 1.50
18 Joey Cora .60 1.50
19 Edgar Martinez 1.00 2.50
20 Alex Rodriguez 2.50 6.00
21 Juan Gonzalez .60 1.50
22 Ivan Rodriguez 1.00 2.50
23 Andruw Jones 1.00 2.50
24 Javier Lopez .60 1.50
25 Sammy Sosa 1.50 4.00
26 Vinny Castilla .60 1.50
27 Andres Galarraga .60 1.50
28 Ramon Martinez .60 1.50
29 Raul Mondesi .60 1.50
30 Ismael Valdes .60 1.50
31 Pedro Martinez 1.00 2.50
32 Henry Rodriguez .60 1.50
33 Carlos Baerga .60 1.50
34 Rey Ordonez .60 1.50
35 Fernando Valenzuela .60 1.50
36 Osvaldo Fernandez .60 1.50

1997 Pacific Triple Crown Die Cuts

COMPLETE SET (20) 100.00 200.00
STATED ODDS 1:145
1 Brady Anderson 2.50 6.00
2 Rafael Palmeiro 4.00 10.00
3 Mo Vaughn 2.50 6.00
4 Frank Thomas 6.00 15.00
5 Albert Belle 2.50 6.00
6 Jim Thome 4.00 10.00
7 Cecil Fielder 2.50 6.00
8 Mark McGwire 15.00 40.00
9 Ken Griffey Jr. 12.50 30.00
10 Alex Rodriguez 10.00 25.00
11 Juan Gonzalez 2.50 6.00
12 Andruw Jones 4.00 10.00
13 Chipper Jones 6.00 15.00
14 Dante Bichette 2.50 6.00
15 Ellis Burks 2.50 6.00
16 Andres Galarraga 2.50 6.00
17 Jeff Bagwell 4.00 10.00
18 Mike Piazza 10.00 25.00
19 Ken Caminiti 2.50 6.00
20 Barry Bonds 15.00 40.00

1997 Pacific Baerga Softball

This 10-card set features major league baseball players who donated their time to participate in the Fourth Annual Carlos Baerga Celebrities Softball Game, played December 14 in Hayto Rey, Puerto Rico, with proceeds from the game going to various Children's foundations throughout Puerto Rico. Two cards from the set were distributed in promo packs to the first 12,000 people at the game. The fronts carry color action player photos from the previous year's softball game, gold-foil stamping, and the game's official logo. The backs display color player portraits with player information in both Spanish and English.

COMPLETE SET (10) 3.00 8.00
1 Carlos Baerga .08 .25
2 Bernie Williams .40 1.00
3 Ivan Rodriguez .50 1.25
4 Sandy Alomar Jr. .20 .50
5 Joey Cora .08 .25
6 Roberto Alomar .40 1.00
7 Moises Alou .20 .50
8 Rey Ordonez .08 .25
9 Derek Jeter 2.00 5.00
10 David Justice .20 .50

1998 Pacific

The 1998 Pacific set was issued in one series totalling 450 cards and distributed in 12-card packs with a suggested retail price of $2.49. The fronts features borderless color player photos with gold foil highlights. The backs carry player information in both Spanish and English. As is standard with base-brand Pacific, the entire set is devoid of subset cards, instead focusing on a comprehensive selection of major league players.

COMPLETE SET (450) 25.00 60.00
1 Luis Alicea .10 .30
2 Garret Anderson .10 .30
3 Jason Dickson .10 .30
4 Gary DiSarcina .10 .30
5 Jim Edmonds .10 .30
6 Darin Erstad .10 .30
7 Chuck Finley .10 .30
8 Shigetoshi Hasegawa .10 .30
9 Rickey Henderson .30 .75
10 Dave Hollins .10 .30
11 Mark Langston .10 .30
12 Orlando Palmeiro .10 .30
13 Troy Percival .10 .30
14 Tony Phillips .10 .30
15 Tim Salmon .20 .50
16 Allen Watson .10 .30
17 Roberto Alomar .20 .50
18 Brady Anderson .10 .30
19 Harold Baines .10 .30
20 Armando Benitez .10 .30
21 Geronimo Berroa .10 .30
22 Mike Bordick .10 .30
23 Eric Davis .10 .30
24 Scott Erickson .10 .30
25 Chris Hoiles .10 .30
26 Jimmy Key .10 .30
27 Aaron Ledesma .10 .30
28 Mike Mussina .20 .50
29 Randy Myers .10 .30
30 Jesse Orosco .10 .30
31 Rafael Palmeiro .20 .50
32 Jeff Reboulet .10 .30
33 Cal Ripken 1.00 2.50
34 B.J. Surhoff .10 .30
35 Steve Avery .10 .30
36 Darren Bragg .10 .30
37 Wil Cordero .10 .30

38 Jeff Frye .10 .30
39 Nomar Garciaparra .50 1.25
40 Tom Gordon .10 .30
41 Bill Haselman .10 .30
42 Scott Hatteberg .10 .30
43 Butch Henry .10 .30
44 Reggie Jefferson .10 .30
45 Tim Naehring .10 .30
46 Troy O'Leary .10 .30
47 Jeff Suppan .10 .30
48 John Valentin .10 .30
49 Mo Vaughn .10 .30
50 Tim Wakefield .10 .30
51 James Baldwin .10 .30
52 Albert Belle .10 .30
53 Tony Castillo .10 .30
54 Doug Drabek .10 .30
55 Ray Durham .10 .30
56 Jorge Fabregas .10 .30
57 Ozzie Guillen .10 .30
58 Matt Karchner .10 .30
59 Norberto Martin .10 .30
60 Dave Martinez .10 .30
61 Lyle Mouton .10 .30
62 Jaime Navarro .10 .30
63 Frank Thomas .30 .75
64 Mario Valdez .10 .30
65 Robin Ventura .10 .30
66 Sandy Alomar Jr. .10 .30
67 Paul Assenmacher .10 .30
68 Tony Fernandez .10 .30
69 Brian Giles .10 .30
70 Marquis Grissom .10 .30
71 Orel Hershiser .10 .30
72 Mike Jackson .10 .30
73 David Justice .10 .30
74 Albie Lopez .10 .30
75 Jose Mesa .10 .30
76 Charles Nagy .10 .30
77 Chad Ogea .10 .30
78 Manny Ramirez .20 .50
79 Jim Thome .20 .50
80 Omar Vizquel .20 .50
81 Matt Williams .10 .30
82 Jaret Wright .10 .30
83 Willie Blair .10 .30
84 Raul Casanova .10 .30
85 Tony Clark .10 .30
86 Deivi Cruz .10 .30
87 Damion Easley .10 .30
88 Travis Fryman .10 .30
89 Bobby Higginson .10 .30
90 Brian L. Hunter .10 .30
91 Todd Jones .10 .30
92 Dan Miceli .10 .30
93 Brian Moehler .10 .30
94 Mel Nieves .10 .30
95 Jody Reed .10 .30
96 Justin Thompson .10 .30
97 Bubba Trammell .10 .30
98 Kevin Appier .10 .30
99 Jay Bell .10 .30
100 Yamil Benitez .10 .30
101 Johnny Damon .20 .50
102 Chili Davis .10 .30
103 Jermaine Dye .10 .30
104 Jed Hansen .10 .30
105 Jeff King .10 .30
106 Mike Macfarlane .10 .30
107 Felix Martinez .10 .30
108 Jeff Montgomery .10 .30
109 Jose Offerman .10 .30
110 Dean Palmer .10 .30
111 Hipolito Pichardo .10 .30
112 Jose Rosado .10 .30
113 Jeromy Burnitz .10 .30
114 Jeff Cirillo .10 .30
115 Cal Eldred .10 .30
116 John Jaha .10 .30
117 Doug Jones .10 .30
118 Scott Karl .10 .30
119 Jesse Levis .10 .30
120 Mark Loretta .10 .30
121 Ben McDonald .10 .30
122 Jose Mercedes .10 .30
123 Matt Mieske .10 .30
124 Dave Nilsson .10 .30
125 Jose Valentin .10 .30
126 Fernando Vina .10 .30
127 Gerald Williams .10 .30
128 Rick Aguilera .10 .30
129 Rich Becker .10 .30
130 Ron Coomer .10 .30
131 Marty Cordova .10 .30
132 Eddie Guardado .10 .30
133 LaTroy Hawkins .10 .30
134 Denny Hocking .10 .30
135 Chuck Knoblauch .10 .30
136 Matt Lawton .10 .30
137 Pat Meares .10 .30
138 Paul Molitor .10 .30
139 David Ortiz .40 1.00
140 Brad Radke .10 .30
141 Terry Steinbach .10 .30
142 Bob Tewksbury .10 .30
143 Javier Valentin .10 .30
144 Wade Boggs .20 .50
145 David Cone .10 .30
146 Chad Curtis .10 .30
147 Cecil Fielder .10 .30
148 Joe Girardi .10 .30
149 Dwight Gooden .10 .30
150 Hideki Irabu .10 .30
151 Derek Jeter .75 2.00
152 Tino Martinez .20 .50
153 Ramiro Mendoza .10 .30
154 Paul O'Neill .20 .50
155 Andy Pettitte .20 .50
156 Jorge Posada .20 .50
157 Mariano Rivera .30 .75
158 Rey Sanchez .10 .30
159 Luis Sojo .10 .30
160 David Wells .10 .30
161 Bernie Williams .20 .50
162 Rafael Bournigal .10 .30
163 Scott Brosius .10 .30
164 Jose Canseco .20 .50
165 Jason Giambi .10 .30
166 Ben Grieve .10 .30
167 Dave Magadan .10 .30
168 Brent Mayne .10 .30
169 Jason McDonald .10 .30
170 Izzy Molina .10 .30
171 Ariel Prieto .10 .30
172 Carlos Reyes .10 .30
173 Scott Spiezio .10 .30
174 Matt Stairs .10 .30
175 Bill Taylor .10 .30
176 Dave Telgheder .10 .30
177 Steve Wojciechowski .10 .30
178 Rich Amaral .10 .30
179 Bobby Ayala .10 .30
180 Jay Buhner .10 .30
181 Rafael Carmona .10 .30
182 Ken Cloude .10 .30
183 Joey Cora .10 .30
184 Russ Davis .10 .30
185 Jeff Fassero .10 .30
186 Ken Griffey Jr. .60 1.50
187 Raul Ibanez .10 .30
188 Randy Johnson .30 .75
189 Roberto Kelly .10 .30
190 Edgar Martinez .20 .50
191 Jamie Moyer .10 .30
192 Omar Olivares .10 .30
193 Alex Rodriguez .50 1.25
194 Heathcliff Slocumb .10 .30
195 Paul Sorrento .10 .30
196 Dan Wilson .10 .30
197 Scott Bailes .10 .30
198 John Burkett .10 .30
199 Domingo Cedeno .10 .30
200 Will Clark .20 .50
201 Hanley Frias RC .10 .30
202 Juan Gonzalez .10 .30
203 Tom Goodwin .10 .30
204 Rusty Greer .10 .30
205 Wilson Heredia .10 .30
206 Darren Oliver .10 .30
207 Bill Ripken .10 .30
208 Ivan Rodriguez .20 .50
209 Lee Stevens .10 .30
210 Fernando Tatis .10 .30
211 John Wetteland .10 .30
212 Bobby Witt .10 .30
213 Jacob Brumfield .10 .30
214 Joe Carter .10 .30
215 Roger Clemens .60 1.50
216 Felipe Crespo .10 .30
217 Jose Cruz Jr. .10 .30
218 Carlos Delgado .10 .30
219 Mariano Duncan .10 .30
220 Carlos Garcia .10 .30
221 Alex Gonzalez .10 .30
222 Juan Guzman .10 .30
223 Pat Hentgen .10 .30
224 Orlando Merced .10 .30
225 Tomas Perez .10 .30
226 Paul Quantrill .10 .30
227 Benito Santiago .10 .30
228 Woody Williams .10 .30
229 Rafael Belliard .10 .30
230 Jeff Blauser .10 .30
231 Pedro Borbon .10 .30
232 Tom Glavine .20 .50
233 Tony Graffanino .10 .30
234 Andruw Jones .20 .50
235 Chipper Jones .30 .75
236 Ryan Klesko .10 .30
237 Mark Lemke .10 .30
238 Kenny Lofton .10 .30
239 Javier Lopez .10 .30
240 Fred McGriff .20 .50
241 Greg Maddux .50 1.25
242 Denny Neagle .10 .30
243 John Smoltz .20 .50
244 Michael Tucker .10 .30
245 Mark Wohlers .10 .30
246 Manny Alexander .10 .30
247 Miguel Batista .10 .30
248 Mark Clark .10 .30
249 Doug Glanville .10 .30
250 Jeremi Gonzalez .10 .30
251 Mark Grace .20 .50
252 Jose Hernandez .10 .30
253 Lance Johnson .10 .30
254 Brooks Kieschnick .10 .30
255 Kevin Orie .10 .30
256 Ryne Sandberg .50 1.25
257 Scott Servais .10 .30
258 Sammy Sosa .30 .75
259 Kevin Tapani .10 .30
260 Ramon Tatis .10 .30
261 Bret Boone .10 .30
262 Dave Burba .10 .30
263 Brook Fordyce .10 .30
264 Willie Greene .10 .30
265 Barry Larkin .20 .50
266 Pedro A. Martinez .10 .30
267 Hal Morris .10 .30
268 Joe Oliver .10 .30
269 Eduardo Perez .10 .30
270 Pokey Reese .10 .30
271 Felix Rodriguez .10 .30
272 Deion Sanders .20 .50
273 Reggie Sanders .10 .30
274 Jeff Shaw .10 .30
275 Scott Sullivan .10 .30
276 Brett Tomko .10 .30
277 Roger Bailey .10 .30
278 Dante Bichette .10 .30
279 Ellis Burks .10 .30
280 Vinny Castilla .10 .30
281 Frank Castillo .10 .30
282 Mike DeJean RC .10 .30
283 Andres Galarraga .10 .30
284 Darren Holmes .10 .30
285 Kirt Manwaring .10 .30
286 Quinton McCracken .10 .30
287 Neifi Perez .10 .30
288 Steve Reed .10 .30
289 John Thomson .10 .30
290 Larry Walker .10 .30
291 Walt Weiss .10 .30
292 Kurt Abbott .10 .30
293 Antonio Alfonseca .10 .30
294 Moises Alou .10 .30
295 Alex Arias .10 .30
296 Bobby Bonilla .10 .30
297 Kevin Brown .20 .50
298 Craig Counsell .10 .30
299 Darren Daulton .10 .30
300 Jim Eisenreich .10 .30
301 Alex Fernandez .10 .30
302 Felix Heredia .10 .30
303 Livan Hernandez .10 .30
304 Charles Johnson .10 .30
305 Al Leiter .10 .30
306 Robb Nen .10 .30
307 Edgar Renteria .10 .30
308 Gary Sheffield .10 .30
309 Devon White .10 .30
310 Bob Abreu .10 .30
311 Brad Ausmus .10 .30
312 Jeff Bagwell .20 .50
313 Derek Bell .10 .30
314 Sean Berry .10 .30
315 Craig Biggio .20 .50
316 Ramon Garcia .10 .30
317 Luis Gonzalez .10 .30
318 Ricky Gutierrez .10 .30
319 Mike Hampton .10 .30
320 Richard Hidalgo .10 .30
321 Thomas Howard .10 .30
322 Darryl Kile .10 .30
323 Jose Lima .10 .30
324 Shane Reynolds .10 .30
325 Bill Spiers .10 .30
326 Tom Candiotti .10 .30
327 Roger Cedeno .10 .30
328 Greg Gagne .10 .30
329 Karim Garcia .10 .30
330 Wilton Guerrero .10 .30
331 Todd Hollandsworth .10 .30
332 Eric Karros .10 .30
333 Ramon Martinez .10 .30
334 Raul Mondesi .10 .30
335 Otis Nixon .10 .30
336 Hideo Nomo .30 .75
337 Antonio Osuna .10 .30
338 Chan Ho Park .10 .30
339 Mike Piazza .50 1.25
340 Dennis Reyes .10 .30
341 Ismael Valdes .10 .30
342 Todd Worrell .10 .30
343 Todd Zeile .10 .30
344 Darrin Fletcher .10 .30
345 Mark Grudzielanek .10 .30
346 Vladimir Guerrero .30 .75
347 Dustin Hermanson .10 .30
348 Mike Lansing .10 .30
349 Pedro Martinez .20 .50
350 Ryan McGuire .10 .30
351 Jose Paniagua .10 .30
352 Carlos Perez .10 .30
353 Henry Rodriguez .10 .30
354 F.P. Santangelo .10 .30
355 David Segui .10 .30
356 Ugueth Urbina .10 .30
357 Marc Valdes .10 .30
358 Jose Vidro .10 .30
359 Rondell White .10 .30
360 Juan Acevedo .10 .30
361 Edgardo Alfonzo .10 .30
362 Carlos Baerga .10 .30
363 Carl Everett .10 .30
364 John Franco .10 .30
365 Bernard Gilkey .10 .30
366 Todd Hundley .10 .30
367 Butch Huskey .10 .30
368 Bobby Jones .10 .30
369 Takashi Kashiwada RC .10 .30
370 Greg McMichael .10 .30
371 Brian McRae .10 .30
372 Alex Ochoa .10 .30
373 John Olerud .10 .30
374 Rey Ordonez .10 .30
375 Turk Wendell .10 .30
376 Ricky Bottalico .10 .30
377 Rico Brogna .10 .30
378 Len Dykstra .10 .30
379 Bobby Estalella .10 .30
380 Wayne Gomes .10 .30
381 Tyler Green .10 .30
382 Gregg Jefferies .10 .30
383 Mark Leiter .10 .30
384 Mike Lieberthal .10 .30
385 Mickey Morandini .10 .30
386 Scott Rolen .20 .50
387 Curt Schilling .10 .30
388 Kevin Stocker .10 .30
389 Danny Tartabull .10 .30
390 Jermaine Allensworth .10 .30
391 Adrian Brown .10 .30
392 Jason Christiansen .10 .30
393 Steve Cooke .10 .30
394 Francisco Cordova .10 .30
395 Jose Guillen .10 .30
396 Jason Kendall .10 .30
397 Jon Lieber .10 .30
398 Esteban Loaiza .10 .30
399 Al Martin .10 .30
400 Kevin Polcovich .10 .30
401 Joe Randa .10 .30
402 Ricardo Rincon .10 .30
403 Tony Womack .10 .30
404 Kevin Young .10 .30
405 Andy Benes .10 .30
406 Royce Clayton .10 .30
407 Delino DeShields .10 .30
408 Mike Difelice RC .10 .30
409 Dennis Eckersley .10 .30
410 John Frascatore .10 .30
411 Gary Gaetti .10 .30
412 Ron Gant .10 .30
413 Brian Jordan .10 .30
414 Ray Lankford .10 .30
415 Willie McGee .10 .30
416 Mark McGwire .75 2.00
417 Matt Morris .10 .30
418 Luis Ordaz .10 .30
419 Todd Stottlemyre .10 .30
420 Andy Ashby .10 .30
421 Jim Bruske .10 .30
422 Ken Caminiti .10 .30
423 Will Cunnane .10 .30
424 Steve Finley .10 .30
425 John Flaherty .10 .30
426 Chris Gomez .10 .30
427 Tony Gwynn .40 1.00
428 Joey Hamilton .10 .30
429 Carlos Hernandez .10 .30
430 Sterling Hitchcock .10 .30
431 Trevor Hoffman .10 .30
432 Wally Joyner .10 .30
433 Greg Vaughn .10 .30
434 Quilvio Veras .10 .30
435 Wilson Alvarez .10 .30
436 Rod Beck .10 .30
437 Barry Bonds .75 2.00
438 Jacob Cruz .10 .30
439 Shawn Estes .10 .30
440 Darryl Hamilton .10 .30
441 Roberto Hernandez .10 .30
442 Glenallen Hill .10 .30
443 Stan Javier .10 .30
444 Brian Johnson .10 .30
445 Jeff Kent .10 .30
446 Bill Mueller .10 .30
447 Kirk Rueter .10 .30
448 J.T. Snow .10 .30
449 Julian Tavarez .10 .30
450 Jose Vizcaino .10 .30

1998 Pacific Platinum Blue

*STARS: 8X TO 20X BASIC CARDS
STATED ODDS 1:73
STATED PRINT RUN 67 SETS

1998 Pacific Red Threatt

*STARS: 2.5X TO 6X BASIC CARDS
ONE PER WAL-MART PACK

1998 Pacific Silver

*STARS: 2X TO 5X BASIC CARDS

1998 Pacific Cramer's Choice

STATED ODDS 1:721
1 Greg Maddux 8.00 20.00
2 Roberto Alomar 4.00 10.00
3 Cal Ripken 20.00 50.00
4 Nomar Garciaparra 4.00 10.00
5 Larry Walker 4.00 10.00
6 Mike Piazza 6.00 15.00
7 Mark McGwire 10.00 25.00
8 Tony Gwynn 6.00 15.00
9 Ken Griffey Jr. 15.00 40.00
10 Roger Clemens 8.00 20.00

1998 Pacific Gold Crown Die Cuts

COMPLETE SET (36) 125.00 250.00
STATED ODDS 1:37
1 Chipper Jones 4.00 10.00
2 Greg Maddux 6.00 15.00
3 Denny Neagle 1.50 4.00
4 Roberto Alomar 2.50 6.00
5 Rafael Palmeiro 2.50 6.00
6 Cal Ripken 12.50 30.00
7 Nomar Garciaparra 6.00 15.00
8 Mo Vaughn 1.50 4.00
9 Frank Thomas 4.00 10.00
10 Sandy Alomar Jr. 1.50 4.00
11 David Justice 1.50 4.00
12 Manny Ramirez 2.50 6.00
13 Andres Galarraga 1.50 4.00
14 Larry Walker 1.50 4.00
15 Moises Alou 1.50 4.00
16 Livan Hernandez 1.50 4.00
17 Gary Sheffield 1.50 4.00
18 Jeff Bagwell 2.50 6.00
19 Raul Mondesi 1.50 4.00
20 Hideo Nomo 4.00 10.00
21 Mike Piazza 6.00 15.00
22 Derek Jeter 10.00 25.00
23 Tino Martinez 2.50 6.00
24 Bernie Williams 2.50 6.00
25 Ben Grieve 1.50 4.00
26 Mark McGwire 10.00 25.00
27 Tony Gwynn 5.00 12.00
28 Barry Bonds 10.00 25.00
29 Ken Griffey Jr. 8.00 20.00
30 Randy Johnson 4.00 10.00
31 Edgar Martinez 2.50 6.00
32 Alex Rodriguez 6.00 15.00
33 Juan Gonzalez 1.50 4.00
34 Ivan Rodriguez 2.50 6.00
35 Roger Clemens 8.00 20.00
36 Jose Cruz Jr. 1.50 4.00

1998 Pacific Home Run Hitters

COMPLETE SET (20) 75.00 150.00
STATED ODDS 1:73
1 Rafael Palmeiro 3.00 8.00
2 Mo Vaughn 2.00 5.00
3 Sammy Sosa 5.00 12.00
4 Albert Belle 2.00 5.00
5 Frank Thomas 5.00 12.00
6 David Justice 2.00 5.00
7 Jim Thome 3.00 8.00
8 Matt Williams 2.00 5.00
9 Vinny Castilla 2.00 5.00
10 Andres Galarraga 2.00 5.00
11 Larry Walker 2.00 5.00
12 Jeff Bagwell 3.00 8.00
13 Mike Piazza 8.00 20.00
14 Tino Martinez 3.00 8.00
15 Mark McGwire 12.50 30.00
16 Barry Bonds 12.50 30.00
17 Jay Buhner 2.00 5.00
18 Ken Griffey Jr. 10.00 25.00
19 Alex Rodriguez 8.00 20.00
20 Juan Gonzalez 2.00 5.00

1998 Pacific In The Cage

COMPLETE SET (20) 75.00 150.00
STATED ODDS 1:145
1 Chipper Jones 5.00 12.00
2 Roberto Alomar 3.00 8.00
3 Cal Ripken 15.00 40.00
4 Nomar Garciaparra 8.00 20.00
5 Frank Thomas 5.00 12.00
6 Sandy Alomar Jr. 2.00 5.00
7 David Justice 2.00 5.00
8 Larry Walker 2.00 5.00
9 Bobby Bonilla 2.00 5.00
10 Mike Piazza 8.00 20.00
11 Tino Martinez 3.00 8.00
12 Bernie Williams 3.00 8.00
13 Mark McGwire 12.50 30.00
14 Tony Gwynn 6.00 15.00
15 Barry Bonds 12.50 30.00
16 Ken Griffey Jr. 12.50 30.00
17 Edgar Martinez 3.00 8.00
18 Alex Rodriguez 8.00 20.00
19 Juan Gonzalez 2.00 5.00
20 Ivan Rodriguez 3.00 8.00

1998 Pacific Latinos of the Major Leagues

COMPLETE SET (36) 30.00 80.00
STATED ODDS 2:37
1 Andruw Jones 1.25 3.00
2 Javier Lopez .75 2.00
3 Roberto Alomar 1.25 3.00
4 Geronimo Berroa .75 2.00
5 Rafael Palmeiro 1.25 3.00
6 Nomar Garciaparra 3.00 8.00
7 Sammy Sosa 2.00 5.00
8 Ozzie Guillen .75 2.00
9 Sandy Alomar Jr. .75 2.00
10 Manny Ramirez 1.25 3.00
11 Omar Vizquel 1.25 3.00
12 Vinny Castilla .75 2.00
13 Andres Galarraga .75 2.00
14 Moises Alou .75 2.00
15 Bobby Bonilla .75 2.00
16 Livan Hernandez .75 2.00
17 Edgar Renteria .75 2.00
18 Wilton Guerrero .75 2.00
19 Raul Mondesi .75 2.00
20 Ismael Valdes .75 2.00
21 Fernando Vina .75 2.00
22 Pedro Martinez 1.25 3.00
23 Edgardo Alfonzo .75 2.00
24 Carlos Baerga .75 2.00
25 Rey Ordonez .75 2.00
26 Tino Martinez 1.25 3.00
27 Mariano Rivera 2.00 5.00
28 Bernie Williams 1.25 3.00
29 Jose Canseco 1.25 3.00
30 Joey Cora .75 2.00
31 Roberto Kelly .75 2.00
32 Edgar Martinez 1.25 3.00
33 Alex Rodriguez 3.00 8.00
34 Juan Gonzalez .75 2.00
35 Ivan Rodriguez 1.25 3.00
36 Jose Cruz Jr. .75 2.00

1998 Pacific Team Checklists

COMPLETE SET (30) 75.00 150.00
STATED ODDS 1:37
1 T.Salmon 1.25 3.00
J.Edmonds
2 C.Ripken 10.00 25.00
R.Alomar
3 N.Garciaparra 5.00 12.00
M.Vaughn
4 F.Thomas 3.00 8.00
A.Belle
5 S.Alomar Jr. 2.00 5.00
M.Ramirez
6 J.Thompson 1.25 3.00
T.Clark
7 J.Damon 2.00 5.00
J.Dye
8 D.Nilsson 1.25 3.00
J.Cirillo
9 P.Molitor 1.25 3.00
C.Knoblauch
10 T.Martinez 8.00 20.00
D.Jeter
11 B.Grieve 2.00 5.00
J.Canseco
12 K.Griffey Jr. 10.00 25.00
A.Rodriguez
13 J.Gonzalez 2.00 5.00
I.Rodriguez
14 J.Cruz Jr. 6.00 15.00
R.Clemens
15 G.Maddux 5.00 12.00
C.Jones
16 S.Sosa 3.00 8.00
M.Grace
17 B.Larkin 2.00 5.00
D.Sanders
18 L.Walker 1.25 3.00
A.Galarraga
19 M.Alou 1.25 3.00
B.Bonilla
20 J.Bagwell 2.00 5.00
C.Biggio
21 M.Piazza 5.00 12.00
H.Nomo
22 P.Martinez 2.00 5.00
H.Rodriguez
23 R.Ordonez 1.25 3.00
C.Baerga
24 C.Schilling 2.00 5.00
S.Rolen
25 A.Martin 1.25 3.00
T.Womack
26 M.McGwire 8.00 20.00
D.Eckersley
27 T.Gwynn 4.00 10.00
W.Joyner
28 B.Bonds 8.00 20.00
J.T.Snow
29 M.Williams 1.25 3.00
J.Bell
30 F.McGriff 2.00 5.00
R.Hernandez

1998 Pacific Home Run Heroes

This six-card standard-size set was issued exclusively through Wal-Mart. The set was issued in a special can and retailed for $4.95 when issued.

COMPLETE SET (6) 2.00 5.00
1 Mark McGwire .75 2.00
2 Sammy Sosa .50 1.25
3 Ken Griffey Jr. 1.00 2.50
4 Greg Vaughn '07 .20
5 Albert Belle .10 .30
6 Jose Canseco .30 .75

1998 Pacific Home Run History

This 72-card set honors Mark McGwire's and Sammy Sosa's record-breaking home run race during the 1998 season. The set was created exclusively for QVC and was available during a 24-hour period on the cable television shopping channel on September 28, 1998. The cards feature color action player photos and the home run number or some other important fact about the player. Two bonus cards were included in the set: Mark McGwire as the Home Run Champion and Cal Ripken Jr. as the Consecutive Games Champion. Only 142,500 sets were produced.

COMPLETE SET (72) 12.50 30.00
COMMON SOSA (1-70) .20 .50
COMMON MCGWIRE 1.00
43 Mark McGwire/70!!! .75 2.00
67 Mark McGwire .40 1.00
Sammy Sosa
68 Mark McGwire .40 1.00
Sammy Sosa
69 Mark McGwire .40 1.00
Sammy Sosa
70 Mark McGwire .40 1.00
Sammy Sosa
HRC1 Mark McGwire 1.25 3.00
Home Run Champion
HRC2 Cal Ripken CHAMP 1.25 3.00

1998 Pacific Nestle

This 20-card set features color action player photos in a red border. The backs carry a player portrait with career statistics and information about the player in Spanish in a blue border. The first five numbers have two cards with different players and card design. The harder to obtain cards have the letter "B" after their number in the checklist below.

COMPLETE SET (20) 6.00 15.00
1A Bernie Williams .40 1.00
1B Ismael Valdes .08 .25
2A Tino Martinez .15 .40
2B Juan Gonzalez .50 1.25
3A Alex Rodriguez 1.25 3.00
3B Ivan Rodriguez .50 1.25
4A Edgar Martinez .25 .60
4B Joey Cora .08 .25
5A Andres Galarraga .25 .60
5B Livan Hernandez .08 .25
6 Manny Ramirez .50 1.25
7 Carlos Baerga .08 .25
8 Pedro Martinez .50 1.25
9 Vinny Castilla .15 .40
10 Sammy Sosa .75 2.00
11 Nomar Garciaparra 1.25 3.00
12 Javy Lopez .15 .40
13 Sandy Alomar Jr. .08 .25
14 Roberto Alomar .40 1.00
15 Jose Canseco .50 1.25

1999 Pacific

This 500 card standard-size set was issued in 10 card packs that had a SRP of $2.19 per pack. Each Box containted 36 packs and each case had 20 boxes. Continuing the trend begun in 1998 with Pacific On-Line, Pacific issued two versions of 50 of the star or leading prospect players in the set with both an action version as well as a head shot. Thus the cards are actually numbered from 1 through 450, but the 50 additional headshot cards (carrying identical numbering to the action cards) bring the total number of cards in the set to 500. The complete set includes both versions of each player. The head shots were inserted one per pack. An unnumbered Tony Gwynn sample card was distributed to dealers and hobby media prior to the product's release. The card is easy to recognize by the bold, diagonal "SAMPLE" text running across the back.

COMPLETE SET (500) 30.00 80.00
EACH ASTERISK CARD HAS TWO VERSIONS
BOTH VERSIONS EQUALLY VALUED
ASTERISK CARDS AS FOLLOWS: 12/22/27/28
32/36/37/40/45/49/54/57/60/65/66/70/87/106
134/136/141/142/143/144/146/154/184/186
196/204/250/270/286/293/294/296/305/308
311/322/352/368/378/387/396/423/429/436
438/440
1 Garret Anderson .10 .30
2 Jason Dickson .10 .30
3 Gary DiSarcina .10 .30
4 Jim Edmonds .10 .30
5 Darin Erstad .10 .30
6 Chuck Finley .10 .30
7 Shigetoshi Hasegawa .10 .30
8 Ken Hill .10 .30
9 Dave Hollins .10 .30
10 Phil Nevin .10 .30
11 Troy Percival .10 .30
12 Tim Salmon * .20 .50
12A Tim Salmon Headshot .20 .50
13 Brian Anderson .10 .30
14 Tony Batista .10 .30
15 Jay Bell .10 .30
16 Andy Benes .10 .30
17 Yamil Benitez .10 .30
18 Omar Daal .10 .30
19 David Dellucci .10 .30
20 Karim Garcia .10 .30
21 Bernard Gilkey .10 .30
22 Travis Lee * .10 .30
22A Travis Lee Headshot .10 .30
23 Aaron Small .10 .30
24 Kelly Stinnett .10 .30
25 Devon White .10 .30
26 Matt Williams .10 .30
27 Bruce Chen * .10 .30
27A Bruce Chen Headshot .10 .30
28 Andres Galarraga * .10 .30
28A A. Galarraga Headshot .10 .30
29 Tom Glavine .20 .50
30 Ozzie Guillen .10 .30
31 Andruw Jones .20 .50
32 Chipper Jones * .30 .75
32A Chipper Jones Headshot .30 .75
33 Ryan Klesko .10 .30
34 George Lombard .10 .30
35 Javy Lopez .10 .30
36 Greg Maddux * .50 1.25
36A Greg Maddux Headshot .50 1.25
37 Marty Malloy * .10 .30
37A Marty Malloy Headshot .10 .30
38 Dennis Martinez .10 .30
39 Kevin Millwood .10 .30
40 Alex Rodriguez * .50 1.25
40A Alex Rodriguez Headshot .50 1.25
41 Denny Neagle .10 .30
42 John Smoltz .20 .50
43 Michael Tucker .10 .30
44 Walt Weiss .10 .30
45 Roberto Alomar * .20 .50
45A R.Alomar Headshot .20 .50
46 Brady Anderson .10 .30
47 Harold Baines .10 .30
48 Mike Bordick .10 .30
49 Danny Clyburn * .10 .30
49A Danny Clyburn Headshot .10 .30
50 Eric Davis .10 .30
51 Scott Erickson .10 .30
52 Chris Hoiles .10 .30
53 Jimmy Key .10 .30
54 Ryan Minor * .10 .30
54A Ryan Minor Headshot .10 .30
55 Mike Mussina .20 .50
56 Jesse Orosco .10 .30
57 Rafael Palmeiro * .20 .50
57A R.Palmeiro Headshot .20 .50
58 Sidney Ponson .10 .30
59 Arthur Rhodes .10 .30
60 Cal Ripken * 1.00 2.50
60A Cal Ripken Headshot 1.00 2.50
61 B.J. Surhoff .10 .30
62 Steve Avery .10 .30
63 Darren Bragg .10 .30
64 Dennis Eckersley .10 .30
65 Nomar Garciaparra * .50 1.25
65A N.Garciaparra Headshot .50 1.25
66 Sammy Sosa * .30 .75
66A Sammy Sosa Headshot .30 .75
67 Tom Gordon .10 .30
68 Reggie Jefferson .10 .30
69 Darren Lewis .10 .30
70 Mark McGwire * .75 2.00
70A Mark McGwire Headshot .75 2.00
71 Pedro Martinez .20 .50
72 Troy O'Leary .10 .30
73 Bret Saberhagen .10 .30
74 Mike Stanley .10 .30
75 John Valentin .10 .30
76 Jason Varitek .30 .75
77 Mo Vaughn .10 .30
78 Tim Wakefield .10 .30
79 Manny Alexander .10 .30
80 Rod Beck .10 .30
81 Brant Brown .10 .30
82 Mark Clark .10 .30
83 Gary Gaetti .10 .30
84 Mark Grace .20 .50
85 Jose Hernandez .10 .30
86 Lance Johnson .10 .30
87 Jason Maxwell * .10 .30
87A Jason Maxwell Headshot .10 .30
88 Mickey Morandini .10 .30
89 Terry Mulholland .10 .30
90 Henry Rodriguez .10 .30
91 Scott Servais .10 .30
92 Kevin Tapani .10 .30
93 Pedro Valdes .10 .30
94 Kerry Wood .10 .30
95 Jeff Abbott .10 .30
96 James Baldwin .10 .30
97 Albert Belle .10 .30
98 Mike Cameron .10 .30
99 Mike Caruso .10 .30
100 Wil Cordero .10 .30
101 Ray Durham .10 .30
102 Jaime Navarro .10 .30
103 Greg Norton .10 .30
104 Magglio Ordonez .10 .30
105 Mike Sirotka .10 .30
106 Frank Thomas * .30 .75
106A F.Thomas Headshot .30 .75
107 Robin Ventura .10 .30
108 Craig Wilson .10 .30
109 Aaron Boone .10 .30
110 Bret Boone .10 .30
111 Sean Casey .10 .30
112 Pete Harnisch .10 .30
113 John Hudek .10 .30
114 Barry Larkin .20 .50
115 Eduardo Perez .10 .30
116 Mike Remlinger .10 .30
117 Reggie Sanders .10 .30
118 Chris Stynes .10 .30
119 Eddie Taubensee .10 .30
120 Brett Tomko .10 .30
121 Pat Watkins .10 .30
122 Dmitri Young .10 .30
123 Sandy Alomar Jr. .10 .30
124 Dave Burba .10 .30
125 Bartolo Colon .10 .30
126 Joey Cora .10 .30
127 Brian Giles .10 .30
128 Dwight Gooden .10 .30
129 Mike Jackson .10 .30
130 David Justice .10 .30
131 Kenny Lofton .10 .30
132 Charles Nagy .10 .30
133 Chad Ogea .10 .30
134 Manny Ramirez * .20 .50
134A M.Ramirez Headshot .20 .50
135 Richie Sexson .10 .30
136 Jim Thome * .20 .50
136A Jim Thome Headshot .20 .50
137 Omar Vizquel .20 .50
138 Jaret Wright .10 .30
139 Pedro Astacio .10 .30
140 Jason Bates .10 .30
141 Dante Bichette * .10 .30
141A D. Bichette Headshot .10 .30
142 Vinny Castilla * .10 .30
142A Vinny Castilla Headshot .10 .30
143 Edgard Clemente * .10 .30
143A E. Clemente Headshot .10 .30

144 Derrick Gibson * .10 .30
144A D. Gibson Headshot .10 .30
145 Curtis Goodwin .10 .30
146 Todd Helton * .20 .50
146A Todd Helton Headshot .20 .50
147 Bobby Jones .10 .30
148 Darryl Kile .10 .30
149 Mike Lansing .10 .30
150 Chuck McElroy .10 .30
151 Neifi Perez .10 .30
152 Jeff Reed .10 .30
153 John Thomson .10 .30
154 Larry Walker * .10 .30
154A Larry Walker Headshot .10 .30
155 Jamey Wright .10 .30
156 Kimera Bartee .10 .30
157 Geronimo Berroa .10 .30
158 Raul Casanova .10 .30
159 Frank Catalanotto .10 .30
160 Tony Clark .10 .30
161 Deivi Cruz .10 .30
162 Damion Easley .10 .30
163 Juan Encarnacion .10 .30
164 Luis Gonzalez .10 .30
165 Seth Greisinger .10 .30
166 Bob Higginson .10 .30
167 Brian L.Hunter .10 .30
168 Todd Jones .10 .30
169 Justin Thompson .10 .30
170 Antonio Alfonseca .10 .30
171 Dave Berg .10 .30
172 John Cangelosi .10 .30
173 Craig Counsell .10 .30
174 Todd Dunwoody .10 .30
175 Cliff Floyd .10 .30
176 Alex Gonzalez .10 .30
177 Livan Hernandez .10 .30
178 Ryan Jackson .10 .30
179 Mark Kotsay .10 .30
180 Derrek Lee .20 .50
181 Matt Mantei .10 .30
182 Brian Meadows .10 .30
183 Edgar Renteria .10 .30
184 Moises Alou * .10 .30
184A Moises Alou Headshot .10 .30
185 Brad Ausmus .10 .30
186 Jeff Bagwell * .20 .50
186A Jeff Bagwell Headshot .20 .50
187 Derek Bell .10 .30
188 Sean Berry .10 .30
189 Craig Biggio .20 .50
190 Carl Everett .10 .30
191 Ricky Gutierrez .10 .30
192 Mike Hampton .10 .30
193 Doug Henry .10 .30
194 Richard Hidalgo .10 .30
195 Randy Johnson .30 .75
196 Russ Johnson * .10 .30
196A Russ Johnson Headshot .10 .30
197 Shane Reynolds .10 .30
198 Bill Spiers .10 .30
199 Kevin Appier .10 .30
200 Tim Belcher .10 .30
201 Jeff Conine .10 .30
202 Johnny Damon .20 .50
203 Jermaine Dye .10 .30
204 Jeremy Giambi * .10 .30
204A Je. Giambi Headshot .10 .30
205 Jeff King .10 .30
206 Shane Mack .10 .30
207 Jeff Montgomery .10 .30
208 Hal Morris .10 .30
209 Jose Offerman .10 .30
210 Dean Palmer .10 .30
211 Jose Rosado .10 .30
212 Glendon Rusch .10 .30
213 Larry Sutton .10 .30
214 Mike Sweeney .10 .30
215 Bobby Bonilla .10 .30
216 Alex Cora .10 .30
217 Darren Dreifort .10 .30
218 Mark Grudzielanek .10 .30
219 Todd Hollandsworth .10 .30
220 Trenidad Hubbard .10 .30
221 Charles Johnson .10 .30
222 Eric Karros .10 .30
223 Matt Luke .10 .30
224 Ramon Martinez .10 .30
225 Raul Mondesi .10 .30
226 Chan Ho Park .10 .30
227 Jeff Shaw .10 .30
228 Gary Sheffield .10 .30
229 Eric Young .10 .30
230 Jeromy Burnitz .10 .30
231 Jeff Cirillo .10 .30
232 Marquis Grissom .10 .30
233 Bobby Hughes .10 .30
234 John Jaha .10 .30
235 Geoff Jenkins .10 .30
236 Scott Karl .10 .30
237 Mark Loretta .10 .30
238 Mike Matheny .10 .30
239 Mike Myers .10 .30
240 Dave Nilsson .10 .30
241 Bob Wickman .10 .30
242 Jose Valentin .10 .30
243 Fernando Vina .10 .30
244 Rick Aguilera .10 .30
245 Ron Coomer .10 .30
246 Marty Cordova .10 .30
247 Denny Hocking .10 .30
248 Matt Lawton .10 .30
249 Pat Meares .10 .30
250 Paul Molitor * .10 .30
250A Paul Molitor Headshot .10 .30
251 Otis Nixon .10 .30
252 Alex Ochoa .10 .30
253 David Ortiz .30 .75
254 A.J. Pierzynski .10 .30
255 Brad Radke .10 .30
256 Terry Steinbach .10 .30
257 Bob Tewksbury .10 .30
258 Todd Walker .10 .30
259 Shane Andrews .10 .30
260 Shayne Bennett .10 .30
261 Orlando Cabrera .10 .30
262 Brad Fullmer .10 .30
263 Vladimir Guerrero .30 .75
264 Wilton Guerrero .10 .30
265 Dustin Hermanson .10 .30
266 Terry Jones RC .10 .30
267 Steve Kline .10 .30
268 Carl Pavano .10 .30
269 F.P. Santangelo .10 .30
270 Fernando Seguignol * .10 .30
270A F.Seguignol Headshot .10 .30
271 Ugueth Urbina .10 .30
272 Jose Vidro .10 .30
273 Chris Widger .10 .30
274 Edgardo Alfonzo .10 .30
275 Carlos Baerga .10 .30
276 John Franco .10 .30
277 Todd Hundley .10 .30
278 Butch Huskey .10 .30
279 Bobby Jones .10 .30
280 Al Leiter .10 .30
281 Greg McMichael .10 .30
282 Brian McRae .10 .30
283 Hideo Nomo .30 .75
284 John Olerud .10 .30
285 Rey Ordonez .10 .30
286 Mike Piazza * .50 1.25
286A Mike Piazza Headshot .50 1.25
287 Turk Wendell .10 .30
288 Masato Yoshii .10 .30
289 David Cone .10 .30
290 Chad Curtis .10 .30
291 Joe Girardi .10 .30
292 Orlando Hernandez .10 .30
293 Hideki Irabu * .10 .30
293A Hideki Irabu Headshot .10 .30
294 Derek Jeter * .75 2.00
294A Derek Jeter Headshot .75 2.00
295 Chuck Knoblauch .10 .30
296 Mike Lowell * .10 .30
296A Mike Lowell Headshot .10 .30
297 Tino Martinez .20 .50
298 Ramiro Mendoza .10 .30
299 Paul O'Neill .20 .50
300 Andy Pettitte .20 .50
301 Jorge Posada .20 .50
302 Tim Raines .10 .30
303 Mariano Rivera .30 .75
304 David Wells .10 .30
305 Bernie Williams * .20 .50
305A B. Williams Headshot .20 .50
306 Mike Blowers .10 .30
307 Tom Candiotti .10 .30
308 Eric Chavez * .10 .30
308A Eric Chavez Headshot .10 .30
309 Ryan Christenson .10 .30
310 Jason Giambi .10 .30
311 Ben Grieve * .10 .30
311A Ben Grieve Headshot .10 .30
312 Rickey Henderson .30 .75
313 A.J. Hinch .10 .30
314 Jason McDonald .10 .30
315 Bip Roberts .10 .30
316 Kenny Rogers .10 .30
317 Scott Spiezio .10 .30
318 Matt Stairs .10 .30
319 Miguel Tejada .10 .30
320 Bob Abreu .10 .30
321 Alex Arias .10 .30
322 Gary Bennett RC * .10 .30
322A Gary Bennett Headshot .10 .30
323 Ricky Bottalico .10 .30
324 Rico Brogna .10 .30
325 Bobby Estalella .10 .30
326 Doug Glanville .10 .30
327 Kevin Jordan .10 .30
328 Mark Leiter .10 .30
329 Wendell Magee .10 .30
330 Mark Portugal .10 .30
331 Desi Relaford .10 .30
332 Scott Rolen .20 .50
333 Curt Schilling .10 .30
334 Kevin Sefcik .10 .30
335 Adrian Brown .10 .30
336 Emil Brown .10 .30
337 Lou Collier .10 .30
338 Francisco Cordova .10 .30
339 Freddy Garcia .10 .30
340 Jose Guillen .10 .30
341 Jason Kendall .10 .30
342 Al Martin .10 .30
343 Abraham Nunez .10 .30
344 Aramis Ramirez .10 .30
345 Ricardo Rincon .10 .30
346 Jason Schmidt .10 .30
347 Turner Ward .10 .30
348 Tony Womack .10 .30
349 Kevin Young .10 .30
350 Juan Acevedo .10 .30
351 Delino DeShields .10 .30
352 J.D. Drew * .10 .30
352A J.D. Drew Headshot .10 .30
353 Ron Gant .10 .30
354 Brian Jordan .10 .30
355 Ray Lankford .10 .30
356 Eli Marrero .10 .30
357 Kent Mercker .10 .30
358 Matt Morris .10 .30
359 Luis Ordaz .10 .30
360 Donovan Osborne .10 .30
361 Placido Polanco .10 .30
362 Fernando Tatis .10 .30
363 Andy Ashby .10 .30
364 Kevin Brown .20 .50
365 Ken Caminiti .10 .30
366 Steve Finley .10 .30
367 Chris Gomez .10 .30
368 Tony Gwynn * .40 1.00
368A Tony Gwynn Headshot .40 1.00
369 Joey Hamilton .10 .30
370 Carlos Hernandez .10 .30
371 Trevor Hoffman .10 .30
372 Wally Joyner .10 .30
373 Jim Leyritz .10 .30
374 Ruben Rivera .10 .30
375 Greg Vaughn .10 .30
376 Quilvio Veras .10 .30
377 Rich Aurilia .10 .30
378 Barry Bonds * .75 2.00
378A Barry Bonds Headshot .60 1.50
379 Ellis Burks .10 .30
380 Joe Carter .10 .30
381 Stan Javier .10 .30
382 Brian Johnson .10 .30
383 Jeff Kent .10 .30
384 Jose Mesa .10 .30
385 Bill Mueller .10 .30
386 Robb Nen .10 .30
387 Armando Rios * .10 .30
387A Armando Rios Headshot .10 .30
388 Kirk Rueter .10 .30
389 Rey Sanchez .10 .30
390 J.T. Snow .10 .30
391 David Bell .10 .30
392 Jay Buhner .10 .30
393 Ken Cloude .10 .30
394 Russ Davis .10 .30
395 Jeff Fassero .10 .30
396 Ken Griffey Jr. * .60 1.50
396A K.Griffey Jr. Headshot .60 1.50
397 Giomar Guevara RC .10 .30
398 Carlos Guillen .10 .30
399 Edgar Martinez .20 .50
400 Shane Monahan .10 .30
401 Jamie Moyer .10 .30
402 David Segui .10 .30
403 Makoto Suzuki .10 .30
404 Mike Timlin .10 .30
405 Dan Wilson .10 .30
406 Wilson Alvarez .10 .30
407 Rolando Arrojo .10 .30
408 Wade Boggs .20 .50
409 Miguel Cairo .10 .30
410 Roberto Hernandez .10 .30
411 Mike Kelly .10 .30
412 Aaron Ledesma .10 .30
413 Albie Lopez .10 .30
414 Dave Martinez .10 .30
415 Quinton McCracken .10 .30
416 Fred McGriff .20 .50
417 Bryan Rekar .10 .30
418 Paul Sorrento .10 .30
419 Randy Winn .10 .30
420 John Burkett .10 .30
421 Will Clark .20 .50
422 Royce Clayton .10 .30
423 Juan Gonzalez * .10 .30
423A J. Gonzalez Headshot .10 .30
424 Tom Goodwin .10 .30
425 Rusty Greer .10 .30
426 Rick Helling .10 .30
427 Roberto Kelly .10 .30
428 Mark McLemore .10 .30
429 Ivan Rodriguez * .20 .50
429A Ivan Rodriguez Headshot .20 .50
430 Aaron Sele .10 .30
431 Lee Stevens .10 .30
432 Todd Stottlemyre .10 .30
433 John Wetteland .10 .30
434 Todd Zeile .10 .30
435 Jose Canseco * .20 .50
435A Jose Canseco Headshot .20 .50
436 Roger Clemens * .60 1.50
436A R.Clemens Headshot .60 1.50
437 Felipe Crespo .10 .30
438 Jose Cruz Jr. .10 .30
439 Carlos Delgado .10 .30
440 Tom Evans * .10 .30
440A Tom Evans Headshot .10 .30
441 Tony Fernandez .10 .30
442 Darrin Fletcher .10 .30
443 Alex Gonzalez .10 .30
444 Shawn Green .10 .30
445 Roy Halladay .30 .75
446 Pat Hentgen .10 .30
447 Juan Samuel .10 .30
448 Benito Santiago .10 .30
449 Shannon Stewart .10 .30
450 Woody Williams .10 .30
NNO Tony Gwynn Sample .40 1.00

1999 Pacific Platinum Blue

*STARS: 10X TO 25X BASIC CARDS
STATED ODDS 1:73

1999 Pacific Red

*STARS: 2X TO 5X BASIC CARDS
ONE PER RETAIL PACK

1999 Pacific Cramer's Choice

COMPLETE SET (10) 60.00 120.00
STATED PRINT RUN 299 SERIAL #'d SETS
1 Cal Ripken 15.00 40.00
2 Nomar Garciaparra 3.00 8.00
3 Frank Thomas 5.00 12.00
4 Ken Griffey Jr. 40.00 100.00
5 Alex Rodriguez 6.00 15.00
6 Greg Maddux 6.00 15.00
7 Sammy Sosa 5.00 12.00
8 Kerry Wood 2.00 5.00
9 Mark McGwire 8.00 20.00
10 Tony Gwynn 5.00 12.00

1999 Pacific Dynagon Diamond

COMPLETE SET (20) 15.00 40.00
STATED ODDS 4:37
*TITANIUM: 2.5X TO 6X BASIC DYN.DIAM.
TITANIUM: RANDOM INS.IN HOBBY PACKS
TITANIUM PRINT RUN 99 SERIAL #'d SETS
1 Cal Ripken 3.00 8.00
2 Nomar Garciaparra .60 1.50
3 Frank Thomas 1.00 2.50
4 Derek Jeter 2.50 6.00
5 Ben Grieve .40 1.00
6 Ken Griffey Jr. 2.00 5.00
7 Alex Rodriguez 1.25 3.00
8 Juan Gonzalez .40 1.00
9 Travis Lee .40 1.00
10 Chipper Jones 1.00 2.50
11 Greg Maddux 1.25 3.00
12 Sammy Sosa 1.00 2.50
13 Kerry Wood .40 1.00
14 Jeff Bagwell .60 1.50
15 Hideo Nomo 1.00 2.50
16 Mike Piazza 1.00 2.50
17 J.D. Drew .40 1.00
18 Mark McGwire 1.50 4.00
19 Tony Gwynn 1.00 2.50
20 Barry Bonds 1.50 4.00

1999 Pacific Gold Crown Die Cuts

COMPLETE SET (36) 125.00 250.00
STATED ODDS 1:37
1 Darin Erstad 1.50 4.00
2 Cal Ripken 12.50 30.00
3 Nomar Garciaparra 6.00 15.00
4 Pedro Martinez 2.50 6.00
5 Mo Vaughn 1.50 4.00
6 Frank Thomas 4.00 10.00
7 Kenny Lofton 1.50 4.00
8 Manny Ramirez 2.50 6.00
9 Paul Molitor 1.50 4.00
10 Derek Jeter 10.00 25.00
11 Bernie Williams 2.50 6.00
12 Ben Grieve 1.50 4.00
13 Ken Griffey Jr. 8.00 20.00
14 Alex Rodriguez 6.00 15.00
15 Wade Boggs 2.50 6.00
16 Juan Gonzalez 1.50 4.00
17 Ivan Rodriguez 2.50 6.00
18 Jose Canseco 2.50 6.00
19 Roger Clemens 8.00 20.00
20 Travis Lee 1.50 4.00
21 Chipper Jones 4.00 10.00
22 Greg Maddux 6.00 15.00
23 Sammy Sosa 4.00 10.00
24 Kerry Wood 1.50 4.00
25 Todd Helton 2.50 6.00
26 Larry Walker 1.50 4.00
27 Jeff Bagwell 2.50 6.00
28 Craig Biggio 2.50 6.00
29 Raul Mondesi 1.50 4.00
30 Vladimir Guerrero 4.00 10.00
31 Mike Piazza 6.00 15.00
32 Scott Rolen 2.50 6.00
33 J.D. Drew 1.50 4.00
34 Mark McGwire 10.00 25.00
35 Tony Gwynn 5.00 12.00
36 Barry Bonds 10.00 25.00

1999 Pacific Hot Cards

COMPLETE SET (10) 20.00 50.00
ONE PER HOT CARD REGISTRY EXCHANGE
STATED PRINT RUN 500 SERIAL #'d SETS
1 Alex Rodriguez 3.00 8.00
2 Tony Gwynn 2.50 6.00
3 Ken Griffey Jr. 5.00 12.00
4 Sammy Sosa 2.50 6.00
5 Ivan Rodriguez 1.50 4.00
6 Derek Jeter 6.00 15.00
7 Cal Ripken 8.00 20.00
8 Mark McGwire 4.00 10.00
9 J.D. Drew 1.00 2.50
10 Bernie Williams 1.50 4.00

1999 Pacific Team Checklists

COMPLETE SET (30) 75.00 150.00
STATED ODDS 2:37
1 Darin Erstad .75 2.00
2 Cal Ripken 6.00 15.00
3 Nomar Garciaparra 3.00 8.00
4 Frank Thomas 2.00 5.00
5 Manny Ramirez 1.25 3.00
6 Damion Easley .75 2.00
7 Jeff King .75 2.00
8 Paul Molitor .75 2.00
9 Derek Jeter 5.00 12.00
10 Ben Grieve .75 2.00
11 Ken Griffey Jr. 4.00 10.00
12 Wade Boggs 1.25 3.00
13 Juan Gonzalez .75 2.00
14 Roger Clemens 4.00 10.00
15 Travis Lee .75 2.00
16 Chipper Jones 2.00 5.00
17 Sammy Sosa 2.00 5.00
18 Barry Larkin 1.25 3.00
19 Todd Helton 1.25 3.00
20 Mark Kotsay .75 2.00
21 Jeff Bagwell 1.25 3.00
22 Raul Mondesi .75 2.00
23 Jeff Cirillo .75 2.00
24 Vladimir Guerrero 2.00 5.00
25 Mike Piazza 3.00 8.00
26 Scott Rolen 1.25 3.00
27 Jason Kendall .75 2.00
28 Mark McGwire 5.00 12.00
29 Tony Gwynn 2.50 6.00
30 Barry Bonds 5.00 12.00

1999 Pacific Timelines

STATED ODDS 1:181 HOBBY
STATED PRINT RUN 199 SERIAL #'d SETS
1 Cal Ripken 15.00 40.00
2 Frank Thomas 5.00 12.00
3 Jim Thome 3.00 8.00
4 Paul Molitor 5.00 12.00
5 Bernie Williams 3.00 8.00
6 Derek Jeter 12.00 30.00
7 Ken Griffey Jr. 10.00 25.00
8 Alex Rodriguez 6.00 15.00
9 Wade Boggs 3.00 8.00
10 Jose Canseco 3.00 8.00
11 Roger Clemens 6.00 15.00
12 Andres Galarraga 3.00 8.00
13 Chipper Jones 5.00 12.00
14 Greg Maddux 6.00 15.00
15 Sammy Sosa 5.00 12.00
16 Larry Walker 3.00 8.00
17 Randy Johnson 5.00 12.00
18 Mike Piazza 5.00 12.00
19 Mark McGwire 8.00 20.00
20 Tony Gwynn 5.00 12.00

1999 Pacific Players Choice

These cards, which are 1999 Pacific cards but were specially stamped for the Players Choice ceremony are parallels of the regular 1999 Pacific Cards. They are printed in different amounts so we have put the number of each card printed next to the players name.

COMPLETE SET 100.00 200.00
32 Chipper Jones/70 12.50 30.00
36 Greg Maddux/71 12.50 30.00
60 Cal Ripken/71 20.00 50.00
66 Sammy Sosa/70 10.00 25.00
71 Pedro Martinez/36 6.00 15.00
134 Manny Ramirez/71 6.00 15.00
186 Jeff Bagwell/71 6.00 15.00
234 John Jaha/33 2.50 6.00
378 Barry Bonds/70 10.00 25.00
396 Ken Griffey Jr./100 12.50 30.00

2000 Pacific

COMPLETE SET (500) 20.00 50.00
COMMON CARD (1-450) .10 .30
DUAL VERSIONS EXIST FOR FOLLOWING:
BOTH VERSIONS VALUED EQUALLY
6/16/31/37/38/42/49/60/64/68/91/107/111
114/123/132/134/143/154/187190/201/214
224/230/263/282/284/289/294/304/331/332
341/352/356/363/373/377/381/392/393/402
406/408/415/420/429/440/444
1 Garret Anderson .12 .30
2 Tim Belcher .12 .30
3 Gary DiSarcina .12 .30
4 Trent Durrington .12 .30
5 Jim Edmonds .12 .30
6 Darin Erstad* .12 .30
6A Darin Erstad POR .12 .30
7 Chuck Finley .12 .30
8 Troy Glaus .12 .30
9 Todd Greene .12 .30
10 Bret Hemphill .12 .30
11 Ken Hill .12 .30
12 Ramon Ortiz .12 .30
13 Troy Percival .12 .30
14 Mark Petkovsek .12 .30
15 Tim Salmon .12 .30
16 Mo Vaughn* .12 .30
16A Mo Vaughn POR .12 .30
17 Jay Bell .12 .30
18 Omar Daal .12 .30
19 Erubiel Durazo .12 .30
20 Steve Finley .12 .30
21 Bernard Gilkey .12 .30
22 Luis Gonzalez .12 .30
23 Randy Johnson .30 .75
24 Byung-Hyun Kim .12 .30
25 Travis Lee .12 .30
26 Matt Mantei .12 .30
27 Armando Reynoso .12 .30
28 Rob Ryan .12 .30
29 Kelly Stinnett .12 .30
30 Todd Stottlemyre .12 .30
31 Matt Williams* .12 .30
31A Matt Williams POR .12 .30
32 Tony Womack .12 .30
33 Bret Boone .12 .30
34 Andres Galarraga .20 .50
35 Tom Glavine .20 .50
36 Ozzie Guillen .12 .30
37 Andruw Jones* .12 .30
37A Andruw Jones POR .12 .30
38 Chipper Jones* .30 .75
38A Chipper Jones POR .30 .75
39 Brian Jordan .12 .30
40 Ryan Klesko .12 .30
41 Javy Lopez .12 .30
42 Greg Maddux* .40 1.00
42A Greg Maddux POR .40 1.00
43 Kevin Millwood .12 .30
44 John Rocker .12 .30
45 Randall Simon .12 .30
46 John Smoltz .30 .75
47 Gerald Williams .12 .30
48 Brady Anderson .12 .30
49 Albert Belle* .12 .30
49A Albert Belle POR .12 .30
50 Mike Bordick .12 .30
51 Will Clark .20 .50
52 Jeff Conine .12 .30
53 Delino DeShields .12 .30
54 Jerry Hairston Jr. .12 .30
55 Charles Johnson .12 .30
56 Eugene Kingsale .12 .30
57 Ryan Minor .12 .30
58 Mike Mussina .20 .50
59 Sidney Ponson .12 .30
60 Cal Ripken* 1.00 2.50
60A Cal Ripken POR 1.00 2.50
61 B.J. Surhoff .12 .30
62 Mike Timlin .12 .30
63 Rod Beck .12 .30
64 Nomar Garciaparra* .20 .50
64A Nomar Garciaparra POR .20 .50
65 Tom Gordon .12 .30
66 Butch Huskey .12 .30
67 Derek Lowe .12 .30
68 Pedro Martinez* .20 .50
68A Pedro Martinez POR .20 .50
69 Trot Nixon .12 .30
70 Jose Offerman .12 .30
71 Troy O'Leary .12 .30
72 Pat Rapp .12 .30
73 Donnie Sadler .12 .30
74 Mike Stanley .12 .30
75 John Valentin .12 .30
76 Jason Varitek .30 .75
77 Wilton Veras .12 .30
78 Tim Wakefield .20 .50
79 Rick Aguilera .12 .30
80 Manny Alexander .12 .30
81 Roosevelt Brown .12 .30
82 Mark Grace .20 .50
83 Glenallen Hill .12 .30
84 Lance Johnson .12 .30
85 Jon Lieber .12 .30
86 Cole Liniak .12 .30
87 Chad Meyers .12 .30
88 Mickey Morandini .12 .30
89 Jose Nieves .12 .30
90 Henry Rodriguez .12 .30
91 Sammy Sosa* .30 .75
91A Sammy Sosa POR .30 .75
92 Kevin Tapani .12 .30
93 Kerry Wood .12 .30
94 Mike Caruso .12 .30
95 Ray Durham .12 .30
96 Brook Fordyce .12 .30
97 Bobby Howry .12 .30
98 Paul Konerko .12 .30
99 Carlos Lee .12 .30
100 Aaron Myette .12 .30
101 Greg Norton .12 .30
102 Maggio Ordonez .20 .50
103 Jim Parque .12 .30
104 Liu Rodriguez .12 .30
105 Chris Singleton .12 .30
106 Mike Sirotka .12 .30
107 Frank Thomas* .30 .75
107A Frank Thomas POR .30 .75
108 Kip Wells .12 .30
109 Aaron Boone .12 .30
110 Mike Cameron .12 .30
111 Sean Casey* .12 .30
111A Sean Casey POR .12 .30
112 Jeffrey Hammonds .12 .30
113 Pete Harnisch .12 .30
114 Barry Larkin* .20 .50
114A Barry Larkin POR .20 .50
115 Jason LaRue .12 .30
116 Denny Neagle .12 .30
117 Pokey Reese .12 .30
118 Scott Sullivan .12 .30
119 Eddie Taubensee .12 .30
120 Greg Vaughn .12 .30
121 Scott Williamson .12 .30
122 Dmitri Young .12 .30
123 Roberto Alomar* .20 .50
123A Roberto Alomar POR .20 .50
124 Sandy Alomar Jr. .12 .30
125 Harold Baines .20 .50
126 Russell Branyan .12 .30
127 Dave Burba .12 .30
128 Bartolo Colon .12 .30
129 Travis Fryman .12 .30
130 Mike Jackson .12 .30
131 David Justice .12 .30
132 Kenny Lofton* .12 .30
132A Kenny Lofton POR .12 .30
133 Charles Nagy .12 .30
134 Manny Ramirez* .30 .75
134A Manny Ramirez POR .30 .75
135 Dave Roberts .20 .50
136 Richie Sexson .12 .30
137 Jim Thome .20 .50
138 Omar Vizquel .20 .50
139 Jaret Wright .12 .30
140 Pedro Astacio .12 .30
141 Dante Bichette .12 .30
142 Brian Bohanon .12 .30
143 Vinny Castilla* .12 .30
143A Vinny Castilla POR .12 .30
144 Edgard Clemente .12 .30
145 Derrick Gibson .12 .30
146 Todd Helton .20 .50
147 Darryl Kile .12 .30
148 Mike Lansing .12 .30
149 Kirt Manwaring .12 .30
150 Neifi Perez .12 .30
151 Ben Petrick .12 .30
152 Juan Sosa RC .12 .30
153 Dave Veres .12 .30
154 Larry Walker* .20 .50
154A Larry Walker POR .20 .50
155 Brad Ausmus .12 .30
156 Dave Borkowski .12 .30
157 Tony Clark .12 .30
158 Francisco Cordero .12 .30
159 Deivi Cruz .12 .30
160 Damion Easley .12 .30
161 Juan Encarnacion .12 .30
162 Robert Fick .12 .30
163 Bobby Higginson .12 .30
164 Gabe Kapler .12 .30
165 Brian Moehler .12 .30
166 Dean Palmer .12 .30
167 Luis Polonia .12 .30
168 Justin Thompson .12 .30
169 Jeff Weaver .12 .30
170 Antonio Alfonseca .12 .30
171 Bruce Aven .12 .30
172 A.J. Burnett .12 .30
173 Luis Castillo .12 .30
174 Ramon Castro .12 .30
175 Ryan Dempster .12 .30
176 Alex Fernandez .12 .30
177 Cliff Floyd .12 .30
178 Amaury Garcia .12 .30
179 Alex Gonzalez .12 .30
180 Mark Kotsay .12 .30
181 Mike Lowell .12 .30
182 Brian Meadows .12 .30
183 Kevin Orie .12 .30
184 Julio Ramirez .12 .30
185 Preston Wilson .12 .30
186 Moises Alou .12 .30
187 Jeff Bagwell* .20 .50
187A Jeff Bagwell POR .20 .50
188 Glen Barker .12 .30
189 Derek Bell .12 .30
190 Craig Biggio* .20 .50
190A Craig Biggio POR .20 .50
191 Ken Caminiti .12 .30
192 Scott Elarton .12 .30
193 Carl Everett .12 .30
194 Mike Hampton .12 .30
195 Carlos E. Hernandez .12 .30
196 Richard Hidalgo .12 .30
197 Jose Lima .12 .30
198 Shane Reynolds .12 .30
199 Bill Spiers .12 .30
200 Billy Wagner .12 .30
201 Carlos Beltran* .20 .50
201A Carlos Beltran POR .20 .50
202 Dermal Brown .12 .30
203 Johnny Damon .20 .50
204 Jermaine Dye .12 .30
205 Carlos Febles .12 .30
206 Jeremy Giambi .12 .30
207 Mark Quinn .12 .30
208 Joe Randa .12 .30
209 Dan Reichert .12 .30
210 Jose Rosado .12 .30
211 Rey Sanchez .12 .30
212 Jeff Suppan .12 .30
213 Mike Sweeney .12 .30
214 Kevin Brown* .12 .30
214A Kevin Brown POR .12 .30
215 Darren Dreifort .12 .30
216 Eric Gagne .12 .30
217 Mark Grudzielanek .12 .30
218 Todd Hollandsworth .12 .30
219 Todd Hundley .12 .30
220 Eric Karros .12 .30
221 Raul Mondesi .12 .30
222 Chan Ho Park .20 .50
223 Jeff Shaw .12 .30
224 Gary Sheffield* .12 .30
224A Gary Sheffield POR .12 .30
225 Ismael Valdes .12 .30
226 Devon White .12 .30
227 Eric Young .12 .30
228 Kevin Barker .12 .30
229 Ron Belliard .12 .30
230 Jeromy Burnitz* .12 .30
230A Jeromy Burnitz POR .12 .30
231 Jeff Cirillo .12 .30
232 Marquis Grissom .12 .30
233 Geoff Jenkins .12 .30
234 Mark Loretta .12 .30
235 David Nilsson .12 .30
236 Hideo Nomo .30 .75
237 Alex Ochoa .12 .30
238 Kyle Peterson .12 .30
239 Fernando Vina .12 .30
240 Bob Wickman .12 .30
241 Steve Woodard .12 .30
242 Chad Allen .12 .30
243 Ron Coomer .12 .30
244 Marty Cordova .12 .30
245 Cristian Guzman .12 .30
246 Denny Hocking .12 .30
247 Jacque Jones .12 .30
248 Corey Koskie .12 .30
249 Matt Lawton .12 .30
250 Joe Mays .12 .30
251 Eric Milton .12 .30
252 Brad Radke .12 .30
253 Mark Redman .12 .30
254 Terry Steinbach .12 .30
255 Todd Walker .12 .30
256 Tony Armas Jr. .12 .30
257 Michael Barrett .12 .30
258 Peter Bergeron .12 .30
259 Geoff Blum .12 .30
260 Orlando Cabrera .12 .30
261 Trace Coquillette RC .12 .30
262 Brad Fullmer .12 .30
263 Vladimir Guerrero* .20 .50
263A Vladimir Guerrero POR .20 .50
264 Wilton Guerrero .12 .30
265 Dustin Hermanson .12 .30
266 Manny Martinez RC .12 .30
267 Ryan McGuire .12 .30
268 Ugueth Urbina .12 .30
269 Jose Vidro .12 .30
270 Rondell White .12 .30
271 Chris Widger .12 .30
272 Edgardo Alfonzo .12 .30
273 Armando Benitez .12 .30
274 Roger Cedeno .12 .30
275 Dennis Cook .12 .30
276 Octavio Dotel .12 .30
277 John Franco .12 .30
278 Darryl Hamilton .12 .30
279 Rickey Henderson .30 .75
280 Orel Hershiser .12 .30
281 Al Leiter .12 .30
282 John Olerud* .12 .30
282A John Olerud POR .12 .30
283 Rey Ordonez .12 .30
284 Mike Piazza* .30 .75
284A Mike Piazza POR .30 .75
285 Kenny Rogers .12 .30
286 Jorge Toca .12 .30
287 Robin Ventura .12 .30
288 Scott Brosius .12 .30
289 Roger Clemens* .40 1.00
289A Roger Clemens POR .40 1.00
290 David Cone .12 .30
291 Chili Davis .12 .30
292 Orlando Hernandez .12 .30
293 Hideki Irabu .12 .30
294 Derek Jeter* .75 2.00
294A Derek Jeter POR .75 2.00
295 Chuck Knoblauch .12 .30
296 Ricky Ledee .12 .30
297 Jim Leyritz .12 .30
298 Tino Martinez .12 .30
299 Paul O'Neill .20 .50
300 Andy Pettitte .20 .50
301 Jorge Posada .20 .50
302 Mariano Rivera .40 1.00
303 Alfonso Soriano .30 .75
304 Bernie Williams* .20 .50
304A Bernie Williams POR .20 .50
305 Ed Yarnall .12 .30
306 Kevin Appier .12 .30
307 Rich Becker .12 .30
308 Eric Chavez .12 .30
309 Jason Giambi .12 .30
310 Ben Grieve .12 .30
311 Ramon Hernandez .12 .30
312 Tim Hudson .20 .50
313 John Jaha .12 .30
314 Doug Jones .12 .30
315 Omar Olivares .12 .30
316 Mike Oquist .12 .30
317 Matt Stairs .12 .30
318 Miguel Tejada .20 .50
319 Randy Velarde .12 .30
320 Bob Abreu .12 .30
321 Marlon Anderson .12 .30
322 Alex Arias .12 .30
323 Rico Brogna .12 .30
324 Paul Byrd .12 .30
325 Ron Gant .12 .30
326 Doug Glanville .12 .30
327 Wayne Gomes .12 .30
328 Mike Lieberthal .12 .30
329 Robert Person .12 .30
330 Desi Relaford .12 .30
331 Scott Rolen* .20 .50
331A Scott Rolen POR .20 .50
332 Curt Schilling* .20 .50
332A Curt Schilling POR .20 .50
333 Kris Benson .12 .30
334 Adrian Brown .12 .30

335 Brant Brown .12 .30
336 Brian Giles .12 .30
337 Chad Hermansen .12 .30
338 Jason Kendall .12 .30
339 Al Martin .12 .30
340 Pat Meares .12 .30
341 Warren Morris* .12 .30
341A Warren Morris POR .12 .30
342 Todd Ritchie .12 .30
343 Jason Schmidt .12 .30
344 Ed Sprague .12 .30
345 Mike Williams .12 .30
346 Kevin Young .12 .30
347 Rick Ankiel .20 .50
348 Ricky Bottalico .12 .30
349 Kent Bottenfield .12 .30
350 Darren Bragg .12 .30
351 Eric Davis .12 .30
352 J.D. Drew* .12 .30
352A J.D. Drew POR .12 .30
353 Adam Kennedy .12 .30
354 Ray Lankford .12 .30
355 Joe McEwing .12 .30
356 Mark McGwire* .50 1.25
356A Mark McGwire POR .50 1.25
357 Matt Morris .12 .30
358 Darren Oliver .12 .30
359 Edgar Renteria .12 .30
360 Fernando Tatis .12 .30
361 Andy Ashby .12 .30
362 Ben Davis .12 .30
363 Tony Gwynn* .30 .75
363A Tony Gwynn POR .30 .75
364 Sterling Hitchcock .12 .30
365 Trevor Hoffman .20 .50
366 Damian Jackson .12 .30
367 Wally Joyner .12 .30
368 Dave Magadan .12 .30
369 Gary Matthews Jr. .12 .30
370 Phil Nevin .12 .30
371 Eric Owens .12 .30
372 Ruben Rivera .12 .30
373 Reggie Sanders* .12 .30
373A Reggie Sanders POR .12 .30
374 Quilvio Veras .12 .30
375 Rich Aurilia .12 .30
376 Marvin Benard .12 .30
377 Barry Bonds* .50 1.25
377A Barry Bonds POR .50 1.25
378 Ellis Burks .12 .30
379 Shawn Estes .12 .30
380 Livan Hernandez .12 .30
381 Jeff Kent* .12 .30
381A Jeff Kent POR .12 .30
382 Brent Mayne .12 .30
383 Bill Mueller .12 .30
384 Calvin Murray .12 .30
385 Robb Nen .12 .30
386 Russ Ortiz .12 .30
387 Kirk Rueter .12 .30
388 J.T. Snow .12 .30
389 David Bell .12 .30
390 Jay Buhner .12 .30
391 Russ Davis .12 .30
392 Freddy Garcia* .12 .30
392A Freddy Garcia POR .12 .30
393 Ken Griffey Jr.* .60 1.50
393A Ken Griffey Jr. POR .60 1.50
394 Carlos Guillen .12 .30
395 John Halama .12 .30
396 Brian L.Hunter .12 .30
397 Ryan Jackson .12 .30
398 Edgar Martinez .20 .50
399 Gil Meche .12 .30
400 Jose Mesa .12 .30
401 Jamie Moyer .12 .30
402 Alex Rodriguez* .40 1.00
402A Alex Rodriguez POR .40 1.00
403 Dan Wilson .12 .30
404 Wilson Alvarez .12 .30
405 Rolando Arrojo .12 .30
406 Wade Boggs* .20 .50
406A Wade Boggs POR .20 .50
407 Miguel Cairo .12 .30
408 Jose Canseco* .20 .50
408A Jose Canseco POR .20 .50
409 John Flaherty .12 .30
410 Jose Guillen .12 .30
411 Roberto Hernandez .12 .30
412 Terrell Lowery .12 .30
413 Dave Martinez .12 .30
414 Quinton McCracken .12 .30
415 Fred McGriff* .20 .50
415A Fred McGriff POR .20 .50
416 Ryan Rupe .12 .30
417 Kevin Stocker .12 .30
418 Bubba Trammell .12 .30
419 Royce Clayton .12 .30
420 Juan Gonzalez* .12 .30
420A Juan Gonzalez POR .12 .30
421 Tom Goodwin .12 .30
422 Rusty Greer .12 .30
423 Rick Helling .12 .30
424 Roberto Kelly .12 .30
425 Ruben Mateo .12 .30
426 Mark McLemore .12 .30
427 Mike Morgan .12 .30
428 Rafael Palmeiro .20 .50
429 Ivan Rodriguez* .20 .50
429A Ivan Rodriguez POR .20 .50
430 Aaron Sele .12 .30
431 Lee Stevens .12 .30
432 John Wetteland .12 .30
433 Todd Zeile .12 .30
434 Jeff Zimmerman .12 .30
435 Tony Batista .12 .30
436 Casey Blake .12 .30
437 Homer Bush .12 .30
438 Chris Carpenter .20 .50
439 Jose Cruz Jr. .12 .30
440 Carlos Delgado* .12 .30
440A Carlos Delgado POR .12 .30
441 Tony Fernandez .12 .30
442 Darrin Fletcher .12 .30
443 Alex Gonzalez .12 .30
444 Shawn Green* .12 .30
444A Shawn Green POR .12 .30
445 Roy Halladay .20 .50
446 Billy Koch .12 .30
447 David Segui .12 .30
448 Shannon Stewart .12 .30
449 David Wells .12 .30
450 Vernon Wells .12 .30
SAMP Tony Gwynn Sample .40 1.00

2000 Pacific Copper

*COPPER: 8X TO 20X BASIC CARDS
STATED PRINT RUN 99 SERIAL #'d SETS
DUAL VERSIONS EXIST IN PARALLEL SET

2000 Pacific Emerald Green

*EM.GREEN: 8X TO 20X BASIC CARDS
STATED PRINT RUN 99 SERIAL #'d SETS
DUAL VERSIONS EXIST IN PARALLEL SET

2000 Pacific Gold

*GOLD: 5X TO 12X BASIC CARDS
STATED PRINT RUN 199 SERIAL #'d SETS
DUAL VERSIONS EXIST IN PARALLEL SET

2000 Pacific Platinum Blue

*PLAT.BLUE: 10X TO 25X BASIC CARDS
STATED PRINT RUN 75 SERIAL #'d SETS
DUAL VERSIONS EXIST IN PARALLEL SET

2000 Pacific Premiere Date

*PREMIERE DATE: 20X TO 50X BASIC
STATED ODDS 1:24 HOBBY
STATED PRINT RUN 37 SERIAL #'d SETS
DUAL VERSIONS EXIST IN PARALLEL SET

2000 Pacific Ruby

COMPLETE SET (500) 125.00 250.00
*RUBY: 1.25X TO 3X BASIC CARDS
12 CARDS PER JEWEL RETAIL PACK
DUAL VERSIONS EXIST IN PARALLEL SET

2000 Pacific Command Performers

COMPLETE SET (20) 30.00 60.00
STATED ODDS 1:24 JEWEL RETAIL
PROOFS PRINT RUN 10 SERIAL #'d SETS
PROOFS TOO SCARCE TO PRICE
1 Chipper Jones 1.50 4.00
2 Greg Maddux 2.00 5.00
3 Cal Ripken 5.00 12.00
4 Nomar Garciaparra 1.00 2.50
5 Sammy Sosa 1.50 4.00
6 Sean Casey .60 1.50
7 Manny Ramirez 1.50 4.00
8 Larry Walker 1.00 2.50
9 Jeff Bagwell 1.00 2.50
10 Vladimir Guerrero 1.00 2.50
11 Mike Piazza 1.50 4.00
12 Roger Clemens 2.00 5.00
13 Derek Jeter 4.00 10.00
14 Mark McGwire 2.50 6.00
15 Tony Gwynn 1.50 4.00
16 Barry Bonds 2.50 6.00
17 Ken Griffey Jr. 3.00 8.00
18 Alex Rodriguez 2.00 5.00
19 Ivan Rodriguez 1.00 2.50
20 Shawn Green .60 1.50

2000 Pacific Cramer's Choice

STATED ODDS 1:721
1 Chipper Jones 5.00 12.00
2 Cal Ripken 15.00 40.00
3 Nomar Garciaparra 3.00 8.00
4 Sammy Sosa 5.00 12.00
5 Mike Piazza 5.00 12.00
6 Derek Jeter 12.00 30.00
7 Mark McGwire 8.00 20.00
8 Tony Gwynn 5.00 12.00
9 Ken Griffey Jr. 10.00 25.00
10 Alex Rodriguez 6.00 15.00

2000 Pacific Diamond Leaders

COMPLETE SET (30) 20.00 50.00
STATED ODDS 2:25
1 G.And .40 1.00
Finley
Perc
Vaughn
2 Belle .60 1.50
Mussina
Surhoff
3 G'parra .60 1.50
P.Martinez
O'Leary
4 Durham 1.00 2.50
Ordonez
Thomas
5 Colon 1.00 2.50
Ramirez
Vizquel
6 Cruz .40 1.00
Mlicki
Palmer
7 Damon .60 1.50
Dye
Rosado
Sweeney
8 Koskie .40 1.00
Milton
Radke
9 Hern/Jeter/Riv/Will 2.50 6.00
10 Giambi .60 1.50
Hudson
Stairs
11 Garcia 2.00 5.00
Griffey
Martinez
12 Canseco .60 1.50
R.Hern
McGriff
13 Palmeiro .60 1.50
I.Rod
Wetteland
14 Delgado .40 1.00
Stewart
Wells
15 R.Johnson 1.00 2.50
M.Will
L.Gonz
16 C.Jones 1.25 3.00
Jordan
Maddux
17 Grace 1.00 2.50
Lieber
Sosa
18 Casey .40 1.00
Harnisch
Vaughn
19 Astacio .60 1.50
Bichette
Walker
20 L.Castillo .40 1.00
A.Fern
P.Wilson
21 Bagwell .60 1.50
Hampton
Wagner
22 K.Brown .40 1.00
Grudz
Karros
23 Burnitz 1.00 2.50
Cirillo
Grissom
Nomo
24 V.Guerrero .60 1.50
D.Herm
Urbina
25 Cedeno 1.00 2.50
Henderson
Piazza
26 Abreu .60 1.50
Lieberthal
Schilling
27 Giles .40 1.00
Kendall
K.Young
28 Botten 1.50 4.00
Lankford
McGwire
29 Gwynn 1.00 2.50
Hoffman
Sanders
30 Bonds 1.50 4.00
Kent
R.Ortiz

2000 Pacific Gold Crown Die Cuts

STATED ODDS 1:25
1 Mo Vaughn .75 2.00
2 Matt Williams .75 2.00
3 Andruw Jones .75 2.00
4 Chipper Jones 2.00 5.00
5 Greg Maddux 2.50 6.00
6 Cal Ripken 6.00 15.00
7 Nomar Garciaparra 1.25 3.00
8 Pedro Martinez 1.25 3.00
9 Sammy Sosa 2.00 5.00
10 Magglio Ordonez 1.25 3.00
11 Frank Thomas 2.00 5.00
12 Sean Casey .75 2.00
13 Roberto Alomar 1.25 3.00
14 Manny Ramirez 2.00 5.00
15 Larry Walker 1.25 3.00
16 Jeff Bagwell 1.25 3.00
17 Craig Biggio 1.25 3.00
18 Carlos Beltran 1.25 3.00
19 Vladimir Guerrero 1.25 3.00
20 Mike Piazza 2.00 5.00
21 Roger Clemens 2.50 6.00
22 Derek Jeter 5.00 12.00
23 Bernie Williams 1.25 3.00
24 Scott Rolen 1.25 3.00
25 Warren Morris .75 2.00
26 J.D. Drew .75 2.00
27 Mark McGwire 3.00 8.00
28 Tony Gwynn 2.00 5.00
29 Barry Bonds 3.00 8.00
30 Ken Griffey Jr. 4.00 10.00
31 Alex Rodriguez 2.50 6.00
32 Jose Canseco 1.25 3.00
33 Juan Gonzalez .75 2.00
34 Rafael Palmeiro 1.25 3.00
35 Ivan Rodriguez 1.25 3.00
36 Shawn Green .75 2.00

2000 Pacific Ornaments

COMPLETE SET (20) 40.00 80.00
STATED ODDS 2:25
1 Mo Vaughn .75 2.00
2 Chipper Jones 2.00 5.00
3 Greg Maddux 2.50 6.00
4 Cal Ripken 6.00 15.00
5 Nomar Garciaparra 1.25 3.00
6 Sammy Sosa 2.00 5.00
7 Frank Thomas 2.00 5.00
8 Manny Ramirez 2.00 5.00
9 Larry Walker 1.25 3.00
10 Jeff Bagwell 1.25 3.00
11 Mike Piazza 2.00 5.00
12 Roger Clemens 2.50 6.00
13 Derek Jeter 5.00 12.00
14 Scott Rolen 1.25 3.00
15 J.D. Drew .75 2.00
16 Mark McGwire 3.00 8.00
17 Tony Gwynn 2.00 5.00
18 Ken Griffey Jr. 4.00 10.00
19 Alex Rodriguez 2.50 6.00
20 Ivan Rodriguez 1.25 3.00

2000 Pacific Past and Present

COMPLETE SET (20) 60.00 120.00
STATED ODDS 1:49
PROOFS PRINT RUN 1 SERIAL #'d SET
PROOFS NOT PRICED DUE TO SCARCITY
1 Chipper Jones 2.50 6.00
2 Greg Maddux 3.00 8.00
3 Cal Ripken 8.00 20.00
4 Nomar Garciaparra 1.50 4.00
5 Pedro Martinez 1.50 4.00
6 Sammy Sosa 2.50 6.00
7 Frank Thomas 2.50 6.00
8 Manny Ramirez 2.50 6.00
9 Larry Walker 1.50 4.00
10 Jeff Bagwell 1.50 4.00
11 Mike Piazza 2.50 6.00
12 Roger Clemens 3.00 8.00
13 Derek Jeter 6.00 15.00
14 Mark McGwire 4.00 10.00
15 Tony Gwynn 2.50 6.00
16 Barry Bonds 4.00 10.00
17 Ken Griffey Jr. 5.00 12.00
18 Alex Rodriguez 3.00 8.00
19 Wade Boggs 1.50 4.00
20 Ivan Rodriguez 1.50 4.00

2000 Pacific Reflections

COMPLETE SET (20) 100.00 200.00
STATED ODDS 1:97
1 Andruw Jones 2.50 6.00
2 Chipper Jones 6.00 15.00
3 Cal Ripken 20.00 50.00
4 Nomar Garciaparra 4.00 10.00
5 Sammy Sosa 6.00 15.00
6 Frank Thomas 6.00 15.00
7 Manny Ramirez 6.00 15.00
8 Jeff Bagwell 4.00 10.00
9 Vladimir Guerrero 4.00 10.00
10 Mike Piazza 6.00 15.00
11 Derek Jeter 15.00 40.00
12 Bernie Williams 4.00 10.00
13 Scott Rolen 4.00 10.00
14 J.D. Drew 2.50 6.00
15 Mark McGwire 10.00 25.00
16 Tony Gwynn 6.00 15.00
17 Ken Griffey Jr. 12.00 30.00
18 Alex Rodriguez 8.00 20.00
19 Juan Gonzalez 2.50 6.00
20 Ivan Rodriguez 4.00 10.00

2000 Pacific Backyard Baseball

COMPLETE SET (11) 5.00 12.00
1 Nomar Garciaparra .30 .75
2 Juan Gonzalez .20 .50
3 Ken Griffey Jr 1.00 2.50
4 Tony Gwynn .50 1.25
5 Chipper Jones .50 1.25
6 Derek Jeter 1.25 3.00
7 Mark McGwire .75 2.00
8 Cal Ripken Jr 1.50 4.00
9 Ivan Rodriguez .30 .75
10 Annie Frazier .20 .50
Cartoon
11 Pablo Sanchez .20 .50
Cartoon

2001 Pacific

COMPLETE SET (500) 50.00 100.00
1 Garret Anderson .10 .30
2 Gary DiSarcina .10 .30
3 Darin Erstad .10 .30
4 Seth Etherton .10 .30
5 Ron Gant .10 .30
6 Troy Glaus .10 .30
7 Shigetoshi Hasegawa .10 .30
8 Adam Kennedy .10 .30
9 Ben Molina .10 .30
10 Ramon Ortiz .10 .30
11 Troy Percival .10 .30
12 Tim Salmon .20 .50
13 Scott Schoeneweis .10 .30
14 Mo Vaughn .10 .30
15 Jarrod Washburn .10 .30
16 Brian Anderson .10 .30
17 Danny Bautista .10 .30
18 Jay Bell .10 .30
19 Greg Colbrunn .10 .30
20 Erubiel Durazo .10 .30
21 Steve Finley .10 .30
22 Luis Gonzalez .10 .30
23 Randy Johnson .30 .75
24 Byung-Hyun Kim .10 .30
25 Matt Mantei .10 .30
26 Armando Reynoso .10 .30
27 Todd Stottlemyre .10 .30
28 Matt Williams .10 .30
29 Tony Womack .10 .30
30 Andy Ashby .10 .30
31 Bobby Bonilla .10 .30
32 Rafael Furcal .10 .30
33 Andres Galarraga .10 .30
34 Tom Glavine .20 .50
35 Andruw Jones .20 .50
36 Chipper Jones .30 .75
37 Brian Jordan .10 .30
38 Wally Joyner .10 .30
39 Keith Lockhart .10 .30
40 Javy Lopez .10 .30
41 Greg Maddux .50 1.25
42 Kevin Millwood .10 .30
43 John Rocker .10 .30
44 Reggie Sanders .10 .30
45 John Smoltz .20 .50
46 B.J. Surhoff .10 .30
47 Quilvio Veras .10 .30
48 Walt Weiss .10 .30
49 Brady Anderson .10 .30
50 Albert Belle .10 .30
51 Jeff Conine .10 .30
52 Delino DeShields .10 .30
53 Brook Fordyce .10 .30
54 Jerry Hairston Jr. .10 .30
55 Mark Lewis .10 .30
56 Luis Matos .10 .30
57 Melvin Mora .10 .30
58 Mike Mussina .20 .50
59 Chris Richard .10 .30
60 Cal Ripken 1.00 2.50
61 Manny Alexander .10 .30
62 Rolando Arrojo .10 .30
63 Midre Cummings .10 .30
64 Carl Everett .10 .30
65 Nomar Garciaparra .50 1.25
66 Mike Lansing .10 .30
67 Darren Lewis .10 .30
68 Derek Lowe .10 .30
69 Pedro Martinez .20 .50
70 Ramon Martinez .10 .30
71 Trot Nixon .10 .30
72 Troy O'Leary .10 .30
73 Jose Offerman .10 .30
74 Tomo Ohka .10 .30
75 Jason Varitek .30 .75
76 Rick Aguilera .10 .30
77 Shane Andrews .10 .30
78 Brant Brown .10 .30
79 Damon Buford .10 .30
80 Joe Girardi .10 .30
81 Mark Grace .20 .50
82 Willie Greene .10 .30
83 Ricky Gutierrez .10 .30
84 Jon Lieber .10 .30
85 Sammy Sosa .30 .75
86 Kevin Tapani .10 .30
87 Rondell White .10 .30
88 Kerry Wood .10 .30
89 Eric Young .10 .30
90 Harold Baines .10 .30
91 James Baldwin .10 .30
92 Ray Durham .10 .30
93 Cal Eldred .10 .30
94 Keith Foulke .10 .30
95 Charles Johnson .10 .30
96 Paul Konerko .10 .30
97 Carlos Lee .10 .30
98 Magglio Ordonez .10 .30
99 Jim Parque .10 .30
100 Herbert Perry .10 .30
101 Chris Singleton .10 .30
102 Mike Sirotka .10 .30
103 Frank Thomas .30 .75
104 Jose Valentin .10 .30
105 Rob Bell .10 .30
106 Aaron Boone .10 .30
107 Sean Casey .10 .30
108 Danny Graves .10 .30
109 Ken Griffey Jr. .60 1.50
110 Pete Harnisch .10 .30
111 Brian Hunter .10 .30
112 Barry Larkin .20 .50
113 Pokey Reese .10 .30
114 Benito Santiago .10 .30
115 Chris Stynes .10 .30
116 Michael Tucker .10 .30
117 Ron Villone .10 .30
118 Scott Williamson .10 .30
119 Dmitri Young .10 .30
120 Roberto Alomar .20 .50
121 Sandy Alomar Jr. .10 .30
122 Russell Branyan .10 .30
123 Dave Burba .10 .30
124 Bartolo Colon .10 .30
125 Wil Cordero .10 .30
126 Einar Diaz .10 .30
127 Chuck Finley .10 .30
128 Travis Fryman .10 .30
129 Kenny Lofton .10 .30
130 Charles Nagy .10 .30
131 Manny Ramirez .20 .50
132 David Segui .10 .30
133 Jim Thome .20 .50
134 Omar Vizquel .20 .50
135 Brian Bohanon .10 .30
136 Jeff Cirillo .10 .30
137 Jeff Frye .10 .30
138 Jeffrey Hammonds .10 .30
139 Todd Helton .20 .50
140 Todd Hollandsworth .10 .30
141 Jose Jimenez .10 .30
142 Brent Mayne .10 .30
143 Neifi Perez .10 .30
144 Ben Petrick .10 .30
145 Juan Pierre .10 .30
146 Larry Walker .10 .30
147 Todd Walker .10 .30
148 Masato Yoshii .10 .30
149 Brad Ausmus .10 .30
150 Rich Becker .10 .30
151 Tony Clark .10 .30
152 Deivi Cruz .10 .30
153 Damion Easley .10 .30
154 Juan Encarnacion .10 .30
155 Robert Fick .10 .30
156 Juan Gonzalez .10 .30
157 Bobby Higginson .10 .30
158 Todd Jones .10 .30
159 Wendell Magee Jr. .10 .30
160 Brian Moehler .10 .30
161 Hideo Nomo .30 .75
162 Dean Palmer .10 .30
163 Jeff Weaver .10 .30
164 Antonio Alfonseca .10 .30
165 Dave Berg .10 .30
166 A.J. Burnett .10 .30
167 Luis Castillo .10 .30
168 Ryan Dempster .10 .30
169 Cliff Floyd .10 .30
170 Alex Gonzalez .10 .30
171 Mark Kotsay .10 .30
172 Derrek Lee .20 .50
173 Mike Lowell .10 .30
174 Mike Redmond .10 .30
175 Henry Rodriguez .10 .30
176 Jesus Sanchez .10 .30
177 Preston Wilson .10 .30
178 Moises Alou .10 .30
179 Jeff Bagwell .20 .50
180 Glen Barker .10 .30
181 Lance Berkman .10 .30
182 Craig Biggio .20 .50
183 Tim Bogar .10 .30
184 Ken Caminiti .10 .30
185 Roger Cedeno .10 .30
186 Scott Elarton .10 .30
187 Tony Eusebio .10 .30
188 Richard Hidalgo .10 .30
189 Jose Lima .10 .30
190 Mitch Meluskey .10 .30
191 Shane Reynolds .10 .30
192 Bill Spiers .10 .30
193 Billy Wagner .10 .30
194 Daryle Ward .10 .30
195 Carlos Beltran .10 .30
196 Ricky Bottalico .10 .30
197 Johnny Damon .20 .50
198 Jermaine Dye .10 .30
199 Jorge Fabregas .10 .30
200 David McCarty .10 .30
201 Mark Quinn .10 .30
202 Joe Randa .10 .30
203 Jeff Reboulet .10 .30
204 Rey Sanchez .10 .30
205 Blake Stein .10 .30
206 Jeff Suppan .10 .30
207 Mac Suzuki .10 .30
208 Mike Sweeney .10 .30
209 Greg Zaun .10 .30
210 Adrian Beltre .10 .30
211 Kevin Brown .10 .30
212 Alex Cora .10 .30
213 Darren Dreifort .10 .30
214 Tom Goodwin .10 .30
215 Shawn Green .10 .30
216 Mark Grudzielanek .10 .30
217 Todd Hundley .10 .30
218 Eric Karros .10 .30
219 Chad Kreuter .10 .30
220 Jim Leyritz .10 .30
221 Chan Ho Park .10 .30
222 Jeff Shaw .10 .30
223 Gary Sheffield .10 .30
224 Devon White .10 .30
225 Ron Belliard .10 .30
226 Henry Blanco .10 .30
227 Jeromy Burnitz .10 .30
228 Jeff D'Amico .10 .30
229 Marquis Grissom .10 .30
230 Charlie Hayes .10 .30
231 Jimmy Haynes .10 .30
232 Tyler Houston .10 .30
233 Geoff Jenkins .10 .30
234 Mark Loretta .10 .30
235 James Mouton .10 .30
236 Richie Sexson .10 .30
237 Jamey Wright .10 .30
238 Jay Canizaro .10 .30
239 Ron Coomer .10 .30
240 Cristian Guzman .10 .30
241 Denny Hocking .10 .30
242 Torii Hunter .10 .30
243 Jacque Jones .10 .30
244 Corey Koskie .10 .30
245 Matt Lawton .10 .30
246 Matt LeCroy .10 .30
247 Eric Milton .10 .30
248 David Ortiz .30 .75
249 Brad Radke .10 .30
250 Mark Redman .10 .30
251 Michael Barrett .10 .30
252 Peter Bergeron .10 .30
253 Milton Bradley .10 .30
254 Orlando Cabrera .10 .30
255 Vladimir Guerrero .30 .75
256 Wilton Guerrero .10 .30
257 Dustin Hermanson .10 .30
258 Hideki Irabu .10 .30
259 Fernando Seguignol .10 .30
260 Lee Stevens .10 .30
261 Andy Tracy .10 .30
262 Javier Vazquez .10 .30
263 Jose Vidro .10 .30
264 Edgardo Alfonzo .10 .30
265 Derek Bell .10 .30
266 Armando Benitez .10 .30
267 Mike Bordick .10 .30
268 John Franco .10 .30
269 Darryl Hamilton .10 .30
270 Mike Hampton .10 .30
271 Lenny Harris .10 .30
272 Al Leiter .10 .30
273 Joe McEwing .10 .30
274 Rey Ordonez .10 .30
275 Jay Payton .10 .30
276 Mike Piazza .50 1.25
277 Glendon Rusch .10 .30
278 Bubba Trammell .10 .30
279 Robin Ventura .10 .30
280 Todd Zeile .10 .30
281 Scott Brosius .10 .30
282 Jose Canseco .20 .50
283 Roger Clemens .60 1.50
284 David Cone .10 .30
285 Dwight Gooden .10 .30
286 Orlando Hernandez .10 .30
287 Glenallen Hill .10 .30
288 Derek Jeter .75 2.00
289 David Justice .10 .30
290 Chuck Knoblauch .10 .30
291 Tino Martinez .20 .50
292 Denny Neagle .10 .30
293 Paul O'Neill .20 .50
294 Andy Pettitte .20 .50
295 Jorge Posada .20 .50
296 Mariano Rivera .30 .75
297 Luis Sojo .10 .30
298 Jose Vizcaino .10 .30
299 Bernie Williams .20 .50
300 Kevin Appier .10 .30
301 Eric Chavez .10 .30
302 Ryan Christenson .10 .30
303 Jason Giambi .10 .30
304 Jeremy Giambi .10 .30
305 Ben Grieve .10 .30
306 Gil Heredia .10 .30
307 Ramon Hernandez .10 .30
308 Tim Hudson .10 .30
309 Jason Isringhausen .10 .30
310 Terrence Long .10 .30
311 Mark Mulder .10 .30
312 Adam Piatt .10 .30
313 Matt Stairs .10 .30
314 Miguel Tejada .10 .30
315 Randy Velarde .10 .30
316 Alex Arias .10 .30
317 Pat Burrell .10 .30
318 Omar Daal .10 .30
319 Travis Lee .10 .30
320 Mike Lieberthal .10 .30
321 Randy Wolf .10 .30
322 Bobby Abreu .10 .30
323 Jeff Brantley .10 .30
324 Bruce Chen .10 .30
325 Doug Glanville .10 .30
326 Kevin Jordan .10 .30
327 Robert Person .10 .30
328 Scott Rolen .20 .50
329 Jimmy Anderson .10 .30
330 Mike Benjamin .10 .30
331 Kris Benson .10 .30
332 Adrian Brown .10 .30
333 Brian Giles .10 .30
334 Jason Kendall .10 .30
335 Pat Meares .10 .30
336 Warren Morris .10 .30
337 Aramis Ramirez .10 .30
338 Todd Ritchie .10 .30
339 Jason Schmidt .10 .30
340 John VanderWal .10 .30
341 Mike Williams .10 .30
342 Enrique Wilson .10 .30
343 Kevin Young .10 .30
344 Rick Ankiel .10 .30
345 Andy Benes .10 .30
346 Will Clark .20 .50
347 Eric Davis .10 .30
348 J.D. Drew .10 .30
349 Shawon Dunston .10 .30
350 Jim Edmonds .10 .30
351 Pat Hentgen .10 .30
352 Darryl Kile .10 .30
353 Ray Lankford .10 .30
354 Mike Matheny .10 .30
355 Mark McGwire .75 2.00
356 Craig Paquette .10 .30
357 Edgar Renteria .10 .30
358 Garrett Stephenson .10 .30
359 Fernando Tatis .10 .30
360 Dave Veres .10 .30
361 Fernando Vina .10 .30
362 Bret Boone .10 .30
363 Matt Clement .10 .30
364 Ben Davis .10 .30
365 Adam Eaton .10 .30
366 Wiki Gonzalez .10 .30
367 Tony Gwynn .40 1.00
368 Damian Jackson .10 .30
369 Ryan Klesko .10 .30
370 John Mabry .10 .30
371 Dave Magadan .10 .30
372 Phil Nevin .10 .30
373 Eric Owens .10 .30
374 Desi Relaford .10 .30
375 Ruben Rivera .10 .30
376 Woody Williams .10 .30
377 Rich Aurilia .10 .30
378 Marvin Benard .10 .30
379 Barry Bonds .75 2.00
380 Ellis Burks .10 .30
381 Bobby Estalella .10 .30
382 Shawn Estes .10 .30
383 Mark Gardner .10 .30
384 Livan Hernandez .10 .30
385 Jeff Kent .10 .30
386 Bill Mueller .10 .30
387 Robb Nen .10 .30
388 Russ Ortiz .10 .30
389 Armando Rios .10 .30
390 Kirk Rueter .10 .30
391 J.T. Snow .10 .30
392 David Bell .10 .30
393 Jay Buhner .10 .30
394 Mike Cameron .10 .30
395 Freddy Garcia .10 .30
396 Carlos Guillen .10 .30
397 John Halama .10 .30
398 Rickey Henderson .30 .75
399 Al Martin .10 .30
400 Edgar Martinez .20 .50
401 Mark McLemore .10 .30
402 Jamie Moyer .10 .30
403 John Olerud .10 .30
404 Joe Oliver .10 .30
405 Alex Rodriguez .40 1.00
406 Kazuhiro Sasaki .10 .30
407 Aaron Sele .10 .30
408 Dan Wilson .10 .30
409 Miguel Cairo .10 .30
410 Vinny Castilla .10 .30
411 Steve Cox .10 .30
412 John Flaherty .10 .30
413 Jose Guillen .10 .30
414 Roberto Hernandez .10 .30
415 Russ Johnson .10 .30
416 Felix Martinez .10 .30
417 Fred McGriff .20 .50
418 Greg Vaughn .10 .30
419 Gerald Williams .10 .30
420 Luis Alicea .10 .30
421 Frank Catalanotto .10 .30
422 Royce Clayton .10 .30
423 Chad Curtis .10 .30
424 Rusty Greer .10 .30
425 Bill Haselman .10 .30
426 Rick Helling .10 .30
427 Gabe Kapler .10 .30
428 Mike Lamb .10 .30
429 Ricky Ledee .10 .30
430 Ruben Mateo .10 .30
431 Rafael Palmeiro .20 .50
432 Ivan Rodriguez .20 .50
433 Kenny Rogers .10 .30
434 John Wetteland .10 .30
435 Jeff Zimmerman .10 .30
436 Tony Batista .10 .30
437 Homer Bush .10 .30
438 Chris Carpenter .10 .30
439 Marty Cordova .10 .30
440 Jose Cruz Jr. .10 .30
441 Carlos Delgado .10 .30
442 Darrin Fletcher .10 .30
443 Brad Fullmer .10 .30
444 Alex Gonzalez .10 .30
445 Billy Koch .10 .30
446 Raul Mondesi .10 .30
447 Mickey Morandini .10 .30
448 Shannon Stewart .10 .30
449 Steve Trachsel .10 .30
450 David Wells .10 .30
451 Juan Alvarez .10 .30
452 Shawn Wooten .10 .30
453 Ismael Villegas .10 .30
454 Carlos Casimiro .10 .30
455 Morgan Burkhart .10 .30
456 Paxton Crawford .10 .30
457 Dernell Stenson .10 .30
458 Ross Gload .10 .30
459 Raul Gonzalez .10 .30
460 Corey Patterson .10 .30
461 Julio Zuleta .10 .30
462 Rocky Biddle .10 .30
463 Joe Crede .30 .75
464 Matt Ginter .10 .30

465 Aaron Myette .10 .30
466 Mike Bell .10 .30
467 Travis Dawkins .10 .30
468 Mark Watson .10 .30
469 Elvis Pena .10 .30
470 Eric Munson .10 .30
471 Pablo Ozuna .10 .30
472 Frank Charles .10 .30
473 Mike Judd .10 .30
474 Hector Ramirez .10 .30
475 Jack Cressend .10 .30
476 Talmadge Nunnari .10 .30
477 Jorge Toca .10 .30
478 Alfonso Soriano .20 .50
479 Jay Tessmer .10 .30
480 Jake Westbrook .10 .30
481 Eric Byrnes .10 .30
482 Jose Ortiz .10 .30
483 Tike Redman .10 .30
484 Domingo Guzman .10 .30
485 Rodrigo Lopez .10 .30
486 Xavier Nady .10 .30
487 Pedro Feliz .10 .30
488 Damon Minor .10 .30
489 Ryan Vogelsong .10 .30
490 Joel Pineiro .10 .30
491 Justin Brunette .10 .30
492 Keith McDonald .10 .30
493 Aubrey Huff .10 .30
494 Kenny Kelly .10 .30
495 Damian Rolls .10 .30
496 John Bale .10 .30
497 Pasqual Coco .10 .30
498 Matt DeWitt .10 .30
499 Leo Estrella .10 .30
500 Josh Phelps .10 .30

2001 Pacific Extreme LTD

*STARS: 20X TO 50X BASIC CARDS
STATED PRINT RUN 45 SERIAL #'d SETS

2001 Pacific Hobby LTD

*STARS: 12.5X TO 30X BASIC CARDS
STATED PRINT RUN 70 SERIAL #'d SETS

2001 Pacific Premiere Date

*STARS: 25X TO 60X BASIC CARDS
STATED ODDS 1:24 HOBBY
STATED PRINT RUN 36 SERIAL #'d SETS

2001 Pacific Retail LTD

*STARS: 10X TO 25X BASIC CARDS
STATED PRINT RUN 85 SERIAL #'d SETS

2001 Pacific Cramer's Choice

STATED ODDS 1:721
*CANVAS: .75X TO 2X BASIC CRAMER
*STYRENE: .6X TO 1.5X BASIC CRAMER
STYRENE RANDOM INSERTS IN PACKS
1 Cal Ripken 15.00 40.00
2 Nomar Garciaparra 3.00 8.00
3 Sammy Sosa 3.00 8.00
4 Frank Thomas 5.00 12.00
5 Ken Griffey Jr. 10.00 25.00
6 Mike Piazza 5.00 12.00
7 Derek Jeter 12.00 30.00
8 Mark McGwire 8.00 20.00
9 Barry Bonds 8.00 20.00
10 Alex Rodriguez 6.00 15.00

2001 Pacific Decade's Best

COMPLETE SET (36) 50.00 120.00
STATED ODDS 2:37
A1 Rickey Henderson 1.25 3.00
A2 Rafael Palmeiro .75 2.00
A3 Cal Ripken 4.00 10.00
A4 Jose Canseco .75 2.00
A5 Juan Gonzalez .50 1.25
A6 Frank Thomas 1.25 3.00
A7 Albert Belle .50 1.25
A8 Edgar Martinez .75 2.00
A9 Mo Vaughn .50 1.25
A10 Derek Jeter 3.00 8.00
A11 Mark McGwire 3.00 8.00
A12 Alex Rodriguez 1.50 4.00
A13 Ken Griffey Jr. 2.50 6.00
A14 Nomar Garciaparra 2.00 5.00
A15 Roger Clemens 2.50 6.00
A16 Bernie Williams .75 2.00
A17 Ivan Rodriguez .75 2.00
A18 Pedro Martinez .75 2.00
N1 Barry Bonds 3.00 8.00
N2 Jeff Bagwell .75 2.00
N3 Tom Glavine .75 2.00
N4 Gary Sheffield .50 1.25
N5 Fred McGriff .75 2.00
N6 Greg Maddux 2.00 5.00
N7 Mike Piazza 2.00 5.00
N8 Tony Gwynn 1.50 4.00
N9 Hideo Nomo 1.25 3.00
N10 Andres Galarraga .50 1.25
N11 Larry Walker .50 1.25
N12 Scott Rolen .75 2.00
N13 Pedro Martinez .75 2.00
N14 Sammy Sosa 1.25 3.00
N15 Mark McGwire 3.00 8.00
N16 Kerry Wood .50 1.25
N17 Chipper Jones 1.25 3.00
N18 Mark Grace .75 2.00

2001 Pacific Game Jersey

SKIP-NUMBERED SET
3 Gary Sheffield 4.00 10.00
5 Scott Rolen 6.00 15.00
7 Tony Gwynn 8.00 20.00
8 Alex Rodriguez 10.00 25.00
9 Rafael Palmeiro 6.00 15.00

2001 Pacific Game Jersey Patch

PRINT RUNS LISTED BELOW
5-CARD SKIP-NUMBERED SET
3 Gary Sheffield/226 10.00 25.00
5 Scott Rolen/157 15.00 40.00
7 Tony Gwynn/183 30.00 60.00
8 Alex Rodriguez/221 20.00 50.00
9 Rafael Palmeiro/154 15.00 40.00

2001 Pacific Gold Crown Die Cuts

STATED ODDS 1:73
*BLUE: .6X TO 1.5X BASIC CROWN
BLUE RANDOM INSERTS IN PACKS
BLUE PRINT RUN 100 SERIAL #'d SETS
*PURPLE: 1X TO 2.5X BASIC CROWN
PURPLE RANDOM INSERTS IN PACKS
PURPLE PRINT RUN 50 SERIAL #'d SETS
CARD NUMBER 27 DOES NOT EXIST
ANKIEL/BURRELL BOTH NUMBERED 26
1 Darin Erstad 1.50 4.00
2 Troy Glaus 1.50 4.00
3 Randy Johnson 1.50 4.00
4 Rafael Furcal 1.50 4.00
5 Andruw Jones 1.50 4.00
6 Chipper Jones 1.50 4.00
7 Greg Maddux 2.50 6.00
8 Cal Ripken 5.00 12.00
9 Nomar Garciaparra 2.50 6.00
10 Pedro Martinez 1.50 4.00
11 Corey Patterson 1.50 4.00
12 Sammy Sosa 1.50 4.00
13 Frank Thomas 1.50 4.00
14 Ken Griffey Jr. 3.00 8.00
15 Manny Ramirez 1.50 4.00
16 Todd Helton 1.50 4.00
17 Jeff Bagwell 1.50 4.00
18 Shawn Green 1.50 4.00
19 Gary Sheffield 1.50 4.00
20 Vladimir Guerrero 1.50 4.00
21 Mike Piazza 2.50 6.00
22 Jose Canseco 1.50 4.00
23 Roger Clemens 3.00 8.00
24 Derek Jeter 4.00 10.00
25 Jason Giambi 1.50 4.00
26 Rick Ankiel 1.50 4.00
26 Pat Burrell 1.50 4.00
28 Jim Edmonds 1.50 4.00
29 Mark McGwire 4.00 10.00
30 Tony Gwynn 2.00 5.00
31 Barry Bonds 4.00 10.00
32 Rickey Henderson 1.50 4.00
33 Edgar Martinez 1.50 4.00
34 Alex Rodriguez 2.00 5.00
35 Ivan Rodriguez 1.50 4.00
36 Carlos Delgado 1.50 4.00

2001 Pacific Gold Crown Die Cuts Autograph

6-CARD SKIP-NUMBERED SET
6 Chipper Jones 50.00 100.00
11 Corey Patterson 10.00 25.00
13 Frank Thomas 30.00 60.00
19 Gary Sheffield 15.00 40.00
28 Jim Edmonds 15.00 40.00
31 Barry Bonds 40.00 80.00

2001 Pacific On the Horizon

COMPLETE SET (10) 40.00 100.00
STATED ODDS 1:145
1 Rafael Furcal 4.00 10.00
2 Corey Patterson 4.00 10.00
3 Russell Branyan 4.00 10.00
4 Juan Pierre 4.00 10.00
5 Mark Quinn 4.00 10.00
6 Alfonso Soriano 6.00 15.00
7 Adam Piatt 4.00 10.00
8 Pat Burrell 4.00 10.00
9 Kazuhiro Sasaki 4.00 10.00
10 Aubrey Huff 4.00 10.00

2001 Pacific Ornaments

COMPLETE SET (24) 75.00 150.00
STATED ODDS 2:37
1 Rafael Furcal 1.50 4.00
2 Chipper Jones 2.00 5.00
3 Greg Maddux 3.00 8.00
4 Cal Ripken 6.00 15.00
5 Nomar Garciaparra 3.00 8.00
6 Pedro Martinez 1.50 4.00
7 Sammy Sosa 2.00 5.00
8 Frank Thomas 2.00 5.00
9 Ken Griffey Jr. 4.00 10.00
10 Manny Ramirez 1.50 4.00
11 Todd Helton 1.50 4.00
12 Vladimir Guerrero 2.00 5.00
13 Mike Piazza 3.00 8.00
14 Roger Clemens 4.00 10.00
15 Derek Jeter 5.00 12.00
16 Pat Burrell 1.50 4.00
17 Rick Ankiel 1.50 4.00
18 Mark McGwire 5.00 12.00
19 Barry Bonds 5.00 12.00
20 Alex Rodriguez 2.50 6.00
21 Troy Glaus 1.50 4.00
22 Tom Glavine 1.50 4.00
23 Jim Edmonds 1.50 4.00
24 Ivan Rodriguez 1.50 4.00

1999 Pacific Crown Collection

The 1999 Pacific Crown Collection was issued in one series totalling 300 cards and was distributed in 12-card packs. The cards were intended for distribution primarily to Latin America and Mexico, thus the text on them is bilingual but predominantly Spanish. The same pattern holds true for Crown Collection insert cards. The fronts feature color action player photos. The backs carry player information and career statistics. An unnumbered Tony Gwynn sample card was distributed to dealers and hobby media prior to the product's release. The card is easy to recognize by the bold, diagonal "SAMPLE" text running across the back.

COMPLETE SET (300) 20.00 50.00
1 Garret Anderson .10 .30
2 Gary DiSarcina .10 .30
3 Jim Edmonds .10 .30
4 Darin Erstad .10 .30
5 Shigetoshi Hasegawa .10 .30
6 Norberto Martin .10 .30
7 Omar Olivares .10 .30
8 Orlando Palmeiro .10 .30
9 Tim Salmon .20 .50
10 Randy Velarde .10 .30
11 Tony Batista .10 .30
12 Jay Bell .10 .30
13 Yamil Benitez .10 .30
14 Omar Daal .10 .30
15 David Dellucci .10 .30
16 Karim Garcia .10 .30
17 Travis Lee .10 .30
18 Felix Rodriguez .10 .30
19 Devon White .10 .30
20 Matt Williams .10 .30
21 Andres Galarraga .10 .30
22 Tom Glavine .20 .50
23 Ozzie Guillen .10 .30
24 Andruw Jones .20 .50
25 Chipper Jones .30 .75
26 Ryan Klesko .10 .30
27 Javy Lopez .10 .30
28 Greg Maddux .50 1.25
29 Dennis Martinez .10 .30
30 Odalis Perez .10 .30
31 Rudy Seanez .10 .30
32 John Smoltz .20 .50
33 Roberto Alomar .20 .50
34 Armando Benitez .10 .30
35 Scott Erickson .10 .30
36 Juan Guzman .10 .30
37 Mike Mussina .20 .50
38 Jesse Orosco .10 .30
39 Rafael Palmeiro .20 .50
40 Sidney Ponson .10 .30
41 Cal Ripken 1.00 2.50
42 B.J. Surhoff .10 .30
43 Lenny Webster .10 .30
44 Dennis Eckersley .10 .30
45 Nomar Garciaparra .50 1.25
46 Darren Lewis .10 .30
47 Pedro Martinez .20 .50
48 Troy O'Leary .10 .30
49 Bret Saberhagen .10 .30
50 John Valentin .10 .30
51 Mo Vaughn .10 .30
52 Tim Wakefield .10 .30
53 Manny Alexander .10 .30
54 Rod Beck .10 .30
55 Gary Gaetti .10 .30
56 Mark Grace .20 .50
57 Felix Heredia .10 .30
58 Jose Hernandez .10 .30
59 Henry Rodriguez .10 .30
60 Sammy Sosa .30 .75
61 Kevin Tapani .10 .30
62 Kerry Wood .10 .30
63 James Baldwin .10 .30
64 Albert Belle .10 .30
65 Mike Caruso .10 .30
66 Carlos Castillo .10 .30
67 Wil Cordero .10 .30
68 Jaime Navarro .10 .30
69 Magglio Ordonez .10 .30
70 Frank Thomas .30 .75
71 Robin Ventura .10 .30
72 Bret Boone .10 .30
73 Sean Casey .10 .30
74 Guillermo Garcia RC .10 .30
75 Barry Larkin .20 .50
76 Melvin Nieves .10 .30
77 Eduardo Perez .10 .30
78 Roberto Petagine .10 .30
79 Reggie Sanders .10 .30
80 Eddie Taubensee .10 .30
81 Brett Tomko .10 .30
82 Sandy Alomar Jr. .10 .30
83 Bartolo Colon .10 .30
84 Joey Cora .10 .30
85 Einar Diaz .10 .30
86 David Justice .10 .30
87 Kenny Lofton .10 .30
88 Manny Ramirez .20 .50
89 Jim Thome .20 .50
90 Omar Vizquel .20 .50
91 Enrique Wilson .10 .30
92 Pedro Astacio .10 .30
93 Dante Bichette .10 .30
94 Vinny Castilla .10 .30
95 Edgard Clemente .10 .30
96 Todd Helton .20 .50
97 Darryl Kile .10 .30
98 Mike Munoz .10 .30
99 Neifi Perez .10 .30
100 Jeff Reed .10 .30
101 Larry Walker .10 .30
102 Gabe Alvarez .10 .30
103 Kimera Bartee .10 .30
104 Frank Castillo .10 .30
105 Tony Clark .10 .30
106 Deivi Cruz .10 .30
107 Damion Easley .10 .30
108 Luis Gonzalez .10 .30
109 Marino Santana .10 .30
110 Justin Thompson .10 .30
111 Antonio Alfonseca .10 .30
112 Alex Fernandez .10 .30
113 Cliff Floyd .10 .30
114 Alex Gonzalez .10 .30
115 Livan Hernandez .10 .30
116 Mark Kotsay .10 .30
117 Derrek Lee .20 .50
118 Edgar Renteria .10 .30
119 Jesus Sanchez .10 .30
120 Moises Alou .10 .30
121 Jeff Bagwell .20 .50
122 Derek Bell .10 .30
123 Craig Biggio .20 .50
124 Tony Eusebio .10 .30
125 Ricky Gutierrez .10 .30
126 Richard Hidalgo .10 .30
127 Randy Johnson .30 .75
128 Jose Lima .10 .30
129 Shane Reynolds .10 .30
130 Johnny Damon .20 .50
131 Carlos Febles .10 .30
132 Jeff King .10 .30
133 Mendy Lopez .10 .30
134 Hal Morris .10 .30
135 Jose Offerman .10 .30
136 Jose Rosado .10 .30
137 Jose Santiago RC .10 .30
138 Bobby Bonilla .10 .30
139 Roger Cedeno .10 .30
140 Alex Cora .10 .30
141 Eric Karros .10 .30
142 Raul Mondesi .10 .30
143 Antonio Osuna .10 .30
144 Chan Ho Park .10 .30
145 Gary Sheffield .10 .30
146 Ismael Valdes .10 .30
147 Jeromy Burnitz .10 .30
148 Jeff Cirillo .10 .30
149 Valerio De Los Santos .10 .30
150 Marquis Grissom .10 .30
151 Scott Karl .10 .30
152 Dave Nilsson .10 .30
153 Al Reyes .10 .30
154 Rafael Roque RC .10 .30
155 Jose Valentin .10 .30
156 Fernando Vina .10 .30
157 Rick Aguilera .10 .30
158 Hector Carrasco .10 .30
159 Marty Cordova .10 .30
160 Eddie Guardado .10 .30
161 Paul Molitor .10 .30
162 Otis Nixon .10 .30
163 Alex Ochoa .10 .30
164 David Ortiz .30 .75
165 Frank Rodriguez .10 .30
166 Todd Walker .10 .30
167 Miguel Batista .10 .30
168 Orlando Cabrera .10 .30
169 Vladimir Guerrero .30 .75
170 Wilton Guerrero .10 .30
171 Carl Pavano .10 .30
172 Robert Perez .10 .30
173 F.P. Santangelo .10 .30
174 Fernando Seguignol .10 .30
175 Ugueth Urbina .10 .30
176 Javier Vazquez .10 .30
177 Edgardo Alfonzo .10 .30
178 Carlos Baerga .10 .30
179 John Franco .10 .30
180 Luis Lopez .10 .30
181 Hideo Nomo .30 .75
182 John Olerud .10 .30
183 Rey Ordonez .10 .30
184 Mike Piazza .50 1.25
185 Armando Reynoso .10 .30
186 Masato Yoshii .10 .30
187 David Cone .10 .30
188 Orlando Hernandez .10 .30
189 Hideki Irabu .10 .30
190 Derek Jeter .75 2.00
191 Ricky Ledee .10 .30
192 Tino Martinez .20 .50
193 Ramiro Mendoza .10 .30
194 Paul O'Neill .20 .50
195 Jorge Posada .20 .50
196 Mariano Rivera .30 .75
197 Luis Sojo .10 .30
198 Bernie Williams .20 .50
199 Rafael Bournigal .10 .30
200 Eric Chavez .10 .30
201 Ryan Christenson .10 .30
202 Jason Giambi .10 .30
203 Ben Grieve .10 .30
204 Rickey Henderson .30 .75
205 A.J. Hinch .10 .30
206 Kenny Rogers .10 .30
207 Miguel Tejada .10 .30
208 Jorge Velandia .10 .30
209 Bobby Abreu .10 .30
210 Marlon Anderson .10 .30
211 Alex Arias .10 .30
212 Bobby Estalella .10 .30
213 Doug Glanville .10 .30
214 Scott Rolen .20 .50
215 Curt Schilling .10 .30
216 Kevin Sefcik .10 .30
217 Adrian Brown .10 .30
218 Francisco Cordova .10 .30
219 Freddy Garcia .10 .30
220 Jose Guillen .10 .30
221 Jason Kendall .10 .30
222 Al Martin .10 .30
223 Abraham Nunez .10 .30
224 Aramis Ramirez .10 .30
225 Ricardo Rincon .10 .30
226 Kevin Young .10 .30
227 J.D. Drew .10 .30
228 Ron Gant .10 .30
229 Jose Jimenez .10 .30
230 Brian Jordan .10 .30
231 Ray Lankford .10 .30
232 Eli Marrero .10 .30
233 Mark McGwire .75 2.00
234 Luis Ordaz .10 .30
235 Placido Polanco .10 .30
236 Fernando Tatis .10 .30
237 Andy Ashby .10 .30
238 Kevin Brown .20 .50
239 Ken Caminiti .10 .30
240 Steve Finley .10 .30
241 Chris Gomez .10 .30
242 Tony Gwynn .40 1.00
243 Carlos Hernandez .10 .30
244 Trevor Hoffman .10 .30
245 Wally Joyner .10 .30
246 Ruben Rivera .10 .30
247 Greg Vaughn .10 .30
248 Quilvio Veras .10 .30
249 Rich Aurilia .10 .30
250 Barry Bonds .75 2.00
251 Stan Javier .10 .30
252 Jeff Kent .10 .30
253 Ramon E.Martinez RC .10 .30
254 Jose Mesa .10 .30
255 Armando Rios .10 .30
256 Rich Rodriguez .10 .30
257 Rey Sanchez .10 .30
258 J.T. Snow .10 .30
259 Julian Tavarez .10 .30
260 Jeff Fassero .10 .30
261 Ken Griffey Jr. .60 1.50
262 Giomar Guevara RC .10 .30
263 Carlos Guillen .10 .30
264 Raul Ibanez .10 .30
265 Edgar Martinez .20 .50
266 Jamie Moyer .10 .30
267 Alex Rodriguez .50 1.25
268 David Segui .10 .30
269 Makato Suzuki .10 .30
270 Wilson Alvarez .10 .30
271 Rolando Arrojo .10 .30
272 Wade Boggs .20 .50
273 Miguel Cairo .10 .30
274 Roberto Hernandez .10 .30
275 Aaron Ledesma .10 .30
276 Albie Lopez .10 .30
277 Quinton McCracken .10 .30
278 Fred McGriff .20 .50
279 Esteban Yan .10 .30
280 Luis Alicea .10 .30
281 Will Clark .20 .50
282 Juan Gonzalez .10 .30
283 Rusty Greer .10 .30
284 Rick Helling .10 .30
285 Xavier Hernandez .10 .30
286 Roberto Kelly .10 .30
287 Esteban Loaiza .10 .30
288 Ivan Rodriguez .20 .50
289 Aaron Sele .10 .30
290 John Wetteland .10 .30
291 Jose Canseco .20 .50
292 Roger Clemens .60 1.50
293 Felipe Crespo .10 .30
294 Jose Cruz Jr. .10 .30
295 Carlos Delgado .10 .30
296 Kelvim Escobar .10 .30
297 Tony Fernandez .10 .30
298 Alex Gonzalez .10 .30
299 Tomas Perez .10 .30
300 Juan Samuel .10 .30
NNO Tony Gwynn Sample .40 1.00

1999 Pacific Crown Collection Platinum Blue

*STARS: 10X TO 25X BASIC CARDS
STATED ODDS 1:73

1999 Pacific Crown Collection Red

*STARS: 2X TO 5X BASIC CARDS
STATED ODDS 4:37 RETAIL

1999 Pacific Crown Collection In The Cage

COMPLETE SET (20) 60.00 120.00
STATED ODDS 1:145
1 Chipper Jones 3.00 8.00
2 Cal Ripken 10.00 25.00
3 Nomar Garciaparra 2.00 5.00
4 Sammy Sosa 3.00 8.00
5 Frank Thomas 3.00 8.00
6 Manny Ramirez 3.00 8.00
7 Todd Helton 2.00 5.00
8 Moises Alou 1.25 3.00
9 Vladimir Guerrero 2.00 5.00
10 Mike Piazza 3.00 8.00
11 Derek Jeter 8.00 20.00
12 Ben Grieve 1.25 3.00
13 J.D. Drew 1.25 3.00
14 Mark McGwire 5.00 12.00
15 Tony Gwynn 3.00 8.00
16 Ken Griffey Jr. 20.00 50.00
17 Edgar Martinez 2.00 5.00
18 Alex Rodriguez 4.00 10.00
19 Juan Gonzalez 1.25 3.00
20 Ivan Rodriguez 2.00 5.00

1999 Pacific Crown Collection Latinos of the Major Leagues

COMPLETE SET (36) 30.00 80.00
STATED ODDS 2:37
1 Roberto Alomar 1.25 3.00
2 Rafael Palmeiro 1.25 3.00
3 Nomar Garciaparra 3.00 8.00
4 Pedro Martinez 1.25 3.00
5 Magglio Ordonez .75 2.00
6 Sandy Alomar Jr. .75 2.00
7 Bartolo Colon .75 2.00
8 Manny Ramirez 1.25 3.00
9 Omar Vizquel 1.25 3.00
10 Enrique Wilson .75 2.00
11 David Ortiz 2.00 5.00
12 Orlando Hernandez .75 2.00
13 Tino Martinez 1.25 3.00
14 Mariano Rivera 2.00 5.00
15 Bernie Williams 1.25 3.00
16 Edgar Martinez 1.25 3.00
17 Alex Rodriguez 3.00 8.00
18 David Segui .75 2.00
19 Rolando Arrojo .75 2.00
20 Juan Gonzalez .75 2.00
21 Ivan Rodriguez 1.25 3.00
22 Jose Canseco 1.25 3.00
23 Jose Cruz Jr. .75 2.00
24 Andres Galarraga .75 2.00
25 Andruw Jones 1.25 3.00
26 Javy Lopez .75 2.00
27 Sammy Sosa 2.00 5.00
28 Vinny Castilla .75 2.00
29 Alex Gonzalez .75 2.00
30 Moises Alou .75 2.00
31 Bobby Bonilla .75 2.00
32 Raul Mondesi .75 2.00
33 Fernando Vina .75 2.00
34 Vladimir Guerrero 2.00 5.00
35 Carlos Baerga .75 2.00
36 Rey Ordonez .75 2.00

1999 Pacific Crown Collection Pacific Cup

COMPLETE SET (10) 40.00 80.00
STATED ODDS 1:721
1 Cal Ripken 10.00 25.00
2 Nomar Garciaparra 2.00 5.00
3 Frank Thomas 3.00 8.00
4 Ken Griffey Jr. 6.00 15.00
5 Alex Rodriguez 4.00 10.00
6 Greg Maddux 4.00 10.00
7 Sammy Sosa 3.00 8.00
8 Kerry Wood 1.25 3.00
9 Mark McGwire 5.00 12.00
10 Tony Gwynn 3.00 8.00

1999 Pacific Crown Collection Tape Measure

COMPLETE SET (20) 60.00 120.00
STATED ODDS 1:73
1 Andres Galarraga 1.50 4.00
2 Chipper Jones 4.00 10.00
3 Nomar Garciaparra 6.00 15.00
4 Sammy Sosa 4.00 10.00
5 Frank Thomas 4.00 10.00
6 Manny Ramirez 2.50 6.00
7 Vinny Castilla 1.50 4.00
8 Moises Alou 1.50 4.00
9 Jeff Bagwell 2.50 6.00
10 Raul Mondesi 1.50 4.00
11 Vladimir Guerrero 4.00 10.00
12 Mike Piazza 6.00 15.00
13 J.D. Drew 1.50 4.00
14 Mark McGwire 10.00 25.00
15 Greg Vaughn 1.50 4.00
16 Ken Griffey Jr. 8.00 20.00
17 Alex Rodriguez 6.00 15.00
18 Juan Gonzalez 1.50 4.00
19 Ivan Rodriguez 2.50 6.00
20 Jose Canseco 2.50 6.00

1999 Pacific Crown Collection Team Checklists

COMPLETE SET (30) 75.00 150.00
STATED ODDS 1:37
1 Darin Erstad 1.25 3.00
2 Travis Lee 1.25 3.00
3 Chipper Jones 3.00 8.00
4 Cal Ripken 10.00 25.00
5 Nomar Garciaparra 5.00 12.00
6 Sammy Sosa 3.00 8.00
7 Frank Thomas 3.00 8.00
8 Barry Larkin 2.00 5.00
9 Manny Ramirez 2.00 5.00
10 Larry Walker 1.25 3.00
11 Bob Higginson 1.25 3.00
12 Livan Hernandez 1.25 3.00
13 Moises Alou 1.25 3.00
14 Jeff King 1.25 3.00
15 Raul Mondesi 1.25 3.00
16 Marquis Grissom 1.25 3.00
17 David Ortiz 3.00 8.00
18 Vladimir Guerrero 3.00 8.00
19 Mike Piazza 5.00 12.00
20 Derek Jeter 8.00 20.00
21 Ben Grieve 1.25 3.00
22 Scott Rolen 2.00 5.00
23 Jason Kendall 1.25 3.00
24 Mark McGwire 8.00 20.00
25 Tony Gwynn 4.00 10.00
26 Barry Bonds 8.00 20.00
27 Ken Griffey Jr. 6.00 15.00
28 Wade Boggs 2.00 5.00
29 Juan Gonzalez 1.25 3.00
30 Jose Canseco 2.00 5.00

1999 Pacific Crown Collection Players Choice

These cards, which parallel the regular Crown Collection Cards were issued by Pacific to be given away at the Players Choice award ceremony. The cards have a "Players Choice" stamp on them and are skip numbered to match their number. These cards were produced in varying quantites so we have put the print run next to the players name

COMPLETE SET 100.00 200.00
10 Randy Velarde/35 4.00 10.00
41 Cal Ripken Jr./25
47 Pedro Martinez/38 12.50 30.00
88 Manny Ramirez/39 12.50 30.00
112 Alex Fernandez/39 4.00 10.00
128 Jose Lima/38 4.00 10.00

2000 Pacific Crown Collection

COMPLETE SET (300) 15.00 40.00
COMMON CARD (1-300) .10 .30
1 Garret Anderson .12 .30
2 Darin Erstad .12 .30
3 Ben Molina .12 .30
4 Ramon Ortiz .12 .30
5 Orlando Palmeiro .12 .30
6 Troy Percival .12 .30
7 Tim Salmon .12 .30
8 Mo Vaughn .12 .30
9 Mo Vaughn TC .12 .30
10 Jay Bell .12 .30
11 Omar Daal .12 .30
12 Erubiel Durazo .12 .30
13 Steve Finley .12 .30
14 Hanley Frias .12 .30
15 Luis Gonzalez .12 .30
16 Randy Johnson .30 .75
17 Matt Williams .12 .30
18 Matt Williams TC .12 .30
19 Andres Galarraga .20 .50
20 Tom Glavine .20 .50
21 Andruw Jones .12 .30
22 Chipper Jones .30 .75
23 Brian Jordan .12 .30
24 Javy Lopez .12 .30
25 Greg Maddux .40 1.00
26 Kevin Millwood .12 .30
27 Eddie Perez .12 .30
28 John Smoltz .30 .75
29 Chipper Jones TC .30 .75
30 Albert Belle .12 .30
31 Jesse Garcia .12 .30
32 Jerry Hairston Jr. .12 .30
33 Charles Johnson .12 .30
34 Mike Mussina .20 .50
35 Sidney Ponson .12 .30
36 Cal Ripken 1.00 2.50
37 B.J. Surhoff .12 .30
38 Cal Ripken TC 1.00 2.50
39 Nomar Garciaparra .20 .50
40 Pedro Martinez .20 .50
41 Ramon Martinez .12 .30
42 Trot Nixon .12 .30
43 Jose Offerman .12 .30
44 Troy O'Leary .12 .30
45 John Valentin .12 .30
46 Wilton Veras .12 .30
47 Nomar Garciaparra TC .20 .50
48 Mark Grace .20 .50
49 Felix Heredia .12 .30
50 Jose Molina .12 .30
51 Jose Nieves .12 .30
52 Henry Rodriguez .12 .30
53 Sammy Sosa .30 .75
54 Kerry Wood .12 .30
55 Sammy Sosa TC .30 .75
56 Mike Caruso .12 .30
57 Carlos Castillo .12 .30
58 Jason Dellaero .12 .30
59 Carlos Lee .12 .30
60 Magglio Ordonez .20 .50
61 Jesus Pena .12 .30
62 Liu Rodriguez .12 .30
63 Frank Thomas .30 .75
64 Magglio Ordonez TC .20 .50
65 Aaron Boone .12 .30
66 Mike Cameron .12 .30
67 Sean Casey .12 .30
68 Juan Guzman .12 .30
69 Barry Larkin .20 .50
70 Pokey Reese .12 .30
71 Eddie Taubensee .12 .30
72 Greg Vaughn .12 .30
73 Sean Casey TC .12 .30
74 Roberto Alomar .20 .50
75 Sandy Alomar Jr. .12 .30
76 Bartolo Colon .12 .30
77 Jacob Cruz .12 .30
78 Einar Diaz .12 .30
79 David Justice .12 .30
80 Kenny Lofton .12 .30
81 Manny Ramirez .30 .75
82 Richie Sexson .12 .30
83 Jim Thome .20 .50
84 Omar Vizquel .20 .50
85 Enrique Wilson .12 .30
86 Manny Ramirez TC .30 .75
87 Pedro Astacio .12 .30
88 Henry Blanco .12 .30
89 Vinny Castilla .12 .30
90 Edgard Clemente .12 .30
91 Todd Helton .20 .50
92 Neifi Perez .12 .30
93 Terry Shumpert .12 .30
94 Juan Sosa RC .12 .30
95 Larry Walker .20 .50
96 Larry Walker TC .20 .50
97 Tony Clark .12 .30
98 Deivi Cruz .12 .30
99 Damion Easley .12 .30
100 Juan Encarnacion .12 .30
101 Karim Garcia .12 .30
102 Luis Garcia RC .12 .30
103 Juan Gonzalez .12 .30
104 Jose Macias .12 .30
105 Dean Palmer .12 .30
106 Juan Encarnacion TC .12 .30
107 Antonio Alfonseca .12 .30
108 Armando Almanza .12 .30
109 Bruce Aven .12 .30
110 Luis Castillo .12 .30
111 Ramon Castro .12 .30
112 Alex Fernandez .12 .30
113 Cliff Floyd .12 .30
114 Alex Gonzalez .12 .30
115 Michael Tejera RC .12 .30
116 Preston Wilson .12 .30
117 Luis Castillo TC .12 .30
118 Jeff Bagwell .20 .50
119 Craig Biggio .20 .50
120 Jose Cabrera .12 .30
121 Tony Eusebio .12 .30
122 Carl Everett .12 .30
123 Ricky Gutierrez .12 .30
124 Mike Hampton .12 .30
125 Richard Hidalgo .12 .30
126 Jose Lima .12 .30
127 Billy Wagner .12 .30
128 Jeff Bagwell TC .20 .50
129 Carlos Beltran .20 .50
130 Johnny Damon .20 .50
131 Jermaine Dye .12 .30
132 Carlos Febles .12 .30
133 Jeremy Giambi .12 .30
134 Jose Rosado .12 .30
135 Rey Sanchez .12 .30
136 Jose Santiago .12 .30
137 Carlos Beltran TC .20 .50
138 Chad Allen .12 .30
139 Craig Counsell .12 .30
140 Shawn Green .12 .30
141 Eric Karros .12 .30
142 Chan Ho Park .20 .50
143 Angel Pena .12 .30
144 Gary Sheffield .12 .30
145 Jose Vizcaino .12 .30
146 Devon White .12 .30
147 Eric Karros TC .12 .30
148 Ron Belliard .12 .30
149 Jason Bere .12 .30
150 Jeromy Burnitz .12 .30
151 Marquis Grissom .12 .30
152 Geoff Jenkins .12 .30
153 Dave Nilsson .12 .30
154 Rafael Roque .12 .30
155 Jose Valentin .12 .30
156 Fernando Vina .12 .30
157 Jeromy Burnitz TC .12 .30
158 Chad Allen .12 .30
159 Ron Coomer .12 .30
160 Eddie Guardado .12 .30
161 Cristian Guzman .12 .30
162 Jacque Jones .12 .30
163 Javier Valentin .12 .30
164 Todd Walker .12 .30
165 Ron Coomer TC .12 .30
166 Michael Barrett .12 .30
167 Miguel Batista .12 .30
168 Vladimir Guerrero .20 .50
169 Wilton Guerrero .12 .30
170 Fernando Seguignol .12 .30
171 Ugueth Urbina .12 .30
172 Javier Vazquez .12 .30
173 Jose Vidro .12 .30
174 Rondell White .12 .30
175 Vladimir Guerrero TC .20 .50
176 Edgardo Alfonzo .12 .30
177 Armando Benitez .12 .30
178 Roger Cedeno .12 .30
179 Octavio Dotel .12 .30
180 Melvin Mora .12 .30
181 Rey Ordonez .12 .30
182 Mike Piazza .30 .75
183 Jorge Toca .12 .30
184 Robin Ventura .12 .30
185 Edgardo Alfonzo TC .12 .30
186 Roger Clemens .40 1.00
187 David Cone .12 .30

188 Orlando Hernandez .12 .30
189 Derek Jeter .75 2.00
190 Ricky Ledee .12 .30
191 Tino Martinez .12 .30
192 Ramiro Mendoza .12 .30
193 Jorge Posada .20 .50
194 Mariano Rivera .40 1.00
195 Alfonso Soriano .30 .75
196 Bernie Williams .20 .50
197 Derek Jeter TC .75 2.00
198 Eric Chavez .12 .30
199 Jason Giambi .12 .30
200 Ben Grieve .12 .30
201 Ramon Hernandez .12 .30
202 Tim Hudson .20 .50
203 John Jaha .12 .30
204 Omar Olivares .12 .30
205 Olmedo Saenz .12 .30
206 Matt Stairs .12 .30
207 Miguel Tejada .20 .50
208 Tim Hudson TC .20 .50
209 Rico Brogna .12 .30
210 Bob Abreu .12 .30
211 Marlon Anderson .12 .30
212 Alex Arias .12 .30
213 Doug Glanville .12 .30
214 Robert Person .12 .30
215 Scott Rolen .20 .50
216 Curt Schilling .20 .50
217 Scott Rolen TC .20 .50
218 Francisco Cordova .12 .30
219 Brian Giles .12 .30
220 Jason Kendall .12 .30
221 Warren Morris .12 .30
222 Abraham Nunez .12 .30
223 Aramis Ramirez .12 .30
224 Jose Silva .12 .30
225 Kevin Young .12 .30
226 Brian Giles TC .12 .30
227 Rick Ankiel .20 .50
228 Ricky Bottalico .12 .30
229 J.D. Drew .12 .30
230 Ray Lankford .12 .30
231 Mark McGwire .50 1.25
232 Eduardo Perez .12 .30
233 Placido Polanco .12 .30
234 Edgar Renteria .12 .30
235 Fernando Tatis .12 .30
236 Mark McGwire TC .50 1.25
237 Carlos Almanzar .12 .30
238 Wiki Gonzalez .12 .30
239 Tony Gwynn .30 .75
240 Trevor Hoffman .20 .50
241 Damian Jackson .12 .30
242 Wally Joyner .12 .30
243 Ruben Rivera .12 .30
244 Reggie Sanders .12 .30
245 Quilvio Veras .12 .30
246 Tony Gwynn TC .30 .75
247 Rich Aurilia .12 .30
248 Marvin Benard .12 .30
249 Barry Bonds .50 1.25
250 Ellis Burks .12 .30
251 Miguel Del Toro .12 .30
252 Edwards Guzman .12 .30
253 Livan Hernandez .12 .30
254 Jeff Kent .12 .30
255 Russ Ortiz .12 .30
256 Armando Rios .12 .30
257 Barry Bonds TC .50 1.25
258 Rafael Bournigal .12 .30
259 Freddy Garcia .12 .30
260 Ken Griffey Jr. .60 1.50
261 Carlos Guillen .12 .30
262 Raul Ibanez .20 .50
263 Edgar Martinez .20 .50
264 Jose Mesa .12 .30
265 Jamie Moyer .12 .30
266 John Olerud .12 .30
267 Jose Paniagua .12 .30
268 Alex Rodriguez .40 1.00
269 Alex Rodriguez TC .40 1.00
270 Wilson Alvarez .12 .30
271 Wade Boggs .20 .50
272 Miguel Cairo .12 .30
273 Jose Canseco .20 .50
274 Jose Guillen .12 .30
275 Roberto Hernandez .12 .30
276 Albie Lopez .12 .30
277 Quinton McCracken .12 .30
278 Fred McGriff .20 .50
279 Esteban Yan .12 .30
280 Jose Canseco TC .20 .50
281 Rusty Greer .12 .30
282 Roberto Kelly .12 .30
283 Esteban Loaiza .12 .30
284 Ruben Mateo .12 .30
285 Rafael Palmeiro .20 .50
286 Ivan Rodriguez .20 .50
287 Aaron Sele .12 .30
288 John Wetteland .12 .30
289 Ivan Rodriguez TC .20 .50
290 Tony Batista .12 .30
291 Jose Cruz Jr. .12 .30
292 Carlos Delgado .12 .30
293 Kelvim Escobar .12 .30
294 Tony Fernandez .12 .30
295 Billy Koch .12 .30
296 Raul Mondesi .12 .30
297 Willis Otanez .12 .30
298 David Segui .12 .30
299 David Wells .12 .30
300 Carlos Delgado TC .12 .30
SAMP Tony Gwynn Sample .30 .75

2000 Pacific Crown Collection Holographic Purple

*HOLO.PURPLE: 5X TO 10X BASIC
STATED PRINT RUN 199 SERIAL #'d SETS

2000 Pacific Crown Collection Platinum Blue

*PLAT.BLUE: 12.5X TO 25X BASIC CARDS
STATED PRINT RUN 67 SERIAL #'d SETS

2000 Pacific Crown Collection Premiere Date

*PREM.DATE: 30X TO 60X BASIC
STATED ODDS 1:36
STATED PRINT RUN 27 SERIAL #'d SETS

2000 Pacific Crown Collection In the Cage

COMPLETE SET (20) 50.00 100.00
1 Mo Vaughn 1.00 2.50
2 Chipper Jones 2.50 6.00
3 Cal Ripken 6.00 15.00
4 Nomar Garciaparra 1.50 4.00
5 Sammy Sosa 2.50 6.00
6 Frank Thomas 6.00 15.00
7 Roberto Alomar 1.50 4.00
8 Manny Ramirez 2.50 6.00
9 Larry Walker 1.50 4.00
10 Jeff Bagwell 1.50 4.00
11 Vladimir Guerrero 1.50 4.00
12 Mike Piazza 2.50 6.00
13 Derek Jeter 12.00 30.00
14 Bernie Williams 1.50 4.00
15 Mark McGwire 4.00 10.00
16 Tony Gwynn 2.50 6.00
17 Ken Griffey Jr. 12.00 30.00
18 Alex Rodriguez 3.00 8.00
19 Rafael Palmeiro 1.50 4.00
20 Ivan Rodriguez 1.50 4.00

2000 Pacific Crown Collection Latinos of the Major Leagues

COMPLETE SET (36) 12.50 30.00
STATED ODDS 2:37
*PARALLELS: 1.25X TO 3X BASIC LATINOS
PARALLELS PRINT RUN 99 SERIAL #'d SETS
1 Erubiel Durazo .40 1.00
2 Luis Gonzalez .40 1.00
3 Andruw Jones .40 1.00
4 Nomar Garciaparra .60 1.50
5 Pedro Martinez .60 1.50
6 Sammy Sosa 1.00 2.50
7 Carlos Lee .40 1.00
8 Magglio Ordonez .60 1.50
9 Roberto Alomar .60 1.50
10 Manny Ramirez 1.00 2.50
11 Omar Vizquel .60 1.50
12 Vinny Castilla .40 1.00
13 Juan Gonzalez .40 1.00
14 Luis Castillo .40 1.00
15 Jose Lima .40 1.00
16 Carlos Beltran .60 1.50
17 Vladimir Guerrero .60 1.50
18 Edgardo Alfonzo .40 1.00
19 Roger Cedeno .40 1.00
20 Rey Ordonez .40 1.00
21 Orlando Hernandez .40 1.00
22 Tino Martinez .40 1.00
23 Mariano Rivera 1.25 3.00
24 Bernie Williams .60 1.50
25 Miguel Tejada .60 1.50
26 Bob Abreu .40 1.00
27 Fernando Tatis .40 1.00
28 Freddy Garcia .40 1.00
29 Edgar Martinez .60 1.50
30 Alex Rodriguez 1.25 3.00
31 Jose Canseco .60 1.50
32 Ruben Mateo .40 1.00
33 Rafael Palmeiro .60 1.50
34 Ivan Rodriguez .60 1.50
35 Carlos Delgado .40 1.00
36 Raul Mondesi .40 1.00

2000 Pacific Crown Collection Moment of Truth

COMPLETE SET (30) 20.00 50.00
STATED ODDS 1:37
1 Mo Vaughn .40 1.00
2 Chipper Jones 1.00 2.50
3 Greg Maddux 1.25 3.00
4 Albert Belle .40 1.00
5 Cal Ripken 3.00 8.00
6 Nomar Garciaparra .60 1.50
7 Pedro Martinez .60 1.50
8 Sammy Sosa 1.00 2.50
9 Frank Thomas 1.00 2.50
10 Barry Larkin .60 1.50
11 Kenny Lofton .40 1.00
12 Manny Ramirez 1.00 2.50
13 Larry Walker .60 1.50
14 Juan Gonzalez .40 1.00
15 Jeff Bagwell .60 1.50
16 Craig Biggio .60 1.50
17 Carlos Beltran .60 1.50
18 Vladimir Guerrero .60 1.50
19 Mike Piazza 1.00 2.50
20 Roger Clemens 1.25 3.00
21 Derek Jeter 2.50 6.00
22 Bernie Williams .60 1.50
23 Mark McGwire 1.50 4.00
24 Tony Gwynn 1.00 2.50
25 Barry Bonds 1.50 4.00
26 Ken Griffey Jr. 2.00 5.00
27 Alex Rodriguez 1.25 3.00
28 Rafael Palmeiro .60 1.50
29 Ivan Rodriguez .60 1.50
30 Carlos Delgado .40 1.00

2000 Pacific Crown Collection Pacific Cup

COMPLETE SET (10) 60.00 120.00
STATED ODDS 1:721
1 Cal Ripken 15.00 40.00
2 Nomar Garciaparra 3.00 8.00
3 Pedro Martinez 3.00 8.00
4 Sammy Sosa 5.00 12.00
5 Vladimir Guerrero 3.00 8.00
6 Derek Jeter 12.00 30.00
7 Mark McGwire 8.00 20.00
8 Tony Gwynn 5.00 12.00
9 Ken Griffey Jr. 10.00 25.00
10 Alex Rodriguez 6.00 15.00

2000 Pacific Crown Collection Timber 2000

COMPLETE SET (20) 40.00 80.00
STATED ODDS 1:73
1 Chipper Jones 2.50 6.00
2 Nomar Garciaparra 1.50 4.00
3 Sammy Sosa 2.50 6.00
4 Magglio Ordonez 1.50 4.00
5 Manny Ramirez 2.50 6.00
6 Vinny Castilla 1.00 2.50
7 Juan Gonzalez 1.00 2.50
8 Jeff Bagwell 1.50 4.00
9 Shawn Green 1.00 2.50
10 Vladimir Guerrero 1.50 4.00
11 Mike Piazza 2.50 6.00
12 Derek Jeter 6.00 15.00
13 Bernie Williams 1.50 4.00
14 Mark McGwire 4.00 10.00
15 Ken Griffey Jr. 5.00 12.00
16 Alex Rodriguez 3.00 8.00
17 Jose Canseco 1.50 4.00
18 Rafael Palmeiro 1.50 4.00
19 Ivan Rodriguez 1.50 4.00
20 Carlos Delgado 1.00 2.50

1998 Pacific Invincible

The 1998 Pacific Invincible set was issued in one series totalling 150 cards and was distributed in five-card packs with an SRP of $2.99. The fronts feature a color action player photo as well as a head shot printed on an inlaid cel window with gold foil printing. The backs carry another player photo with a paragraph highlighting the player's career accomplishments.

COMPLETE SET (150) 40.00 100.00
1 Garret Anderson .60 1.50
2 Jim Edmonds .60 1.50
3 Darin Erstad .60 1.50
4 Chuck Finley .60 1.50
5 Tim Salmon 1.00 2.50
6 Roberto Alomar 1.00 2.50
7 Brady Anderson .60 1.50
8 Geronimo Berroa .40 1.00
9 Eric Davis .60 1.50
10 Mike Mussina 1.00 2.50
11 Rafael Palmeiro 1.00 2.50
12 Cal Ripken 5.00 12.00
13 Steve Avery .40 1.00
14 Nomar Garciaparra 2.50 6.00
15 John Valentin .40 1.00
16 Mo Vaughn .60 1.50
17 Albert Belle .60 1.50
18 Ozzie Guillen .60 1.50
19 Norberto Martin .40 1.00
20 Frank Thomas 1.50 4.00
21 Robin Ventura .60 1.50
22 Sandy Alomar Jr. .40 1.00
23 David Justice .60 1.50
24 Kenny Lofton .60 1.50
25 Manny Ramirez 1.00 2.50
26 Jim Thome 1.00 2.50
27 Omar Vizquel 1.00 2.50
28 Matt Williams .60 1.50
29 Jaret Wright .40 1.00
30 Raul Casanova .40 1.00
31 Tony Clark .40 1.00
32 Deivi Cruz .40 1.00
33 Bobby Higginson .60 1.50
34 Justin Thompson .40 1.00
35 Yamil Benitez .40 1.00
36 Johnny Damon 1.00 2.50
37 Jermaine Dye .60 1.50
38 Jed Hansen .40 1.00
39 Larry Sutton .40 1.00
40 Jeromy Burnitz .60 1.50
41 Jeff Cirillo .40 1.00
42 Dave Nilsson .40 1.00
43 Jose Valentin .40 1.00
44 Fernando Vina .40 1.00
45 Marty Cordova .40 1.00
46 Chuck Knoblauch .60 1.50
47 Paul Molitor .60 1.50
48 Brad Radke .60 1.50
49 Terry Steinbach .40 1.00
50 Wade Boggs 1.00 2.50
51 Hideki Irabu .40 1.00
52 Derek Jeter 4.00 10.00
53 Tino Martinez 1.00 2.50
54 Andy Pettitte 1.00 2.50
55 Mariano Rivera 1.50 4.00
56 Bernie Williams 1.00 2.50
57 Jose Canseco 1.00 2.50
58 Jason Giambi .60 1.50
59 Ben Grieve .40 1.00
60 Aaron Small .40 1.00
61 Jay Buhner .60 1.50
62 Ken Cloude .40 1.00
63 Joey Cora .40 1.00
64 Ken Griffey Jr. 3.00 8.00
65 Randy Johnson 1.50 4.00
66 Edgar Martinez 1.00 2.50
67 Alex Rodriguez 2.50 6.00
68 Will Clark 1.00 2.50
69 Juan Gonzalez .60 1.50
70 Rusty Greer .60 1.50
71 Ivan Rodriguez 1.00 2.50
72 Joe Carter .60 1.50
73 Roger Clemens 3.00 8.00
74 Jose Cruz Jr. .40 1.00
75 Carlos Delgado .60 1.50
76 Andruw Jones 1.00 2.50
77 Chipper Jones 1.50 4.00
78 Ryan Klesko .60 1.50
79 Javier Lopez .60 1.50
80 Greg Maddux 2.50 6.00
81 Miguel Batista .40 1.00
82 Jeremi Gonzalez .40 1.00
83 Mark Grace 1.00 2.50
84 Kevin Orie .40 1.00
85 Sammy Sosa 1.50 4.00
86 Barry Larkin 1.00 2.50
87 Deion Sanders 1.00 2.50
88 Reggie Sanders .60 1.50
89 Chris Stynes .40 1.00
90 Dante Bichette .60 1.50
91 Vinny Castilla .60 1.50
92 Andres Galarraga .60 1.50
93 Neifi Perez .40 1.00
94 Larry Walker .60 1.50
95 Moises Alou .60 1.50
96 Bobby Bonilla .60 1.50
97 Kevin Brown 1.00 2.50
98 Craig Counsell .40 1.00
99 Livan Hernandez .60 1.50
100 Edgar Renteria .60 1.50
101 Gary Sheffield .60 1.50
102 Jeff Bagwell 1.00 2.50
103 Craig Biggio 1.00 2.50
104 Luis Gonzalez .60 1.50
105 Darryl Kile .60 1.50
106 Wilton Guerrero .40 1.00
107 Eric Karros .60 1.50
108 Ramon Martinez .40 1.00
109 Raul Mondesi .60 1.50
110 Hideo Nomo 1.50 4.00
111 Chan Ho Park .60 1.50
112 Mike Piazza 2.50 6.00
113 Mark Grudzielanek .40 1.00
114 Vladimir Guerrero 1.50 4.00
115 Pedro Martinez 1.00 2.50
116 Henry Rodriguez .40 1.00
117 David Segui .40 1.00
118 Edgardo Alfonzo .40 1.00
119 Carlos Baerga .40 1.00
120 John Franco .60 1.50
121 John Olerud .60 1.50
122 Rey Ordonez .40 1.00
123 Ricky Bottalico .40 1.00
124 Gregg Jefferies .40 1.00
125 Mickey Morandini .40 1.00
126 Scott Rolen 1.00 2.50
127 Curt Schilling .60 1.50
128 Jose Guillen .60 1.50
129 Esteban Loaiza .40 1.00
130 Al Martin .40 1.00
131 Tony Womack .40 1.00
132 Dennis Eckersley .60 1.50
133 Gary Gaetti .60 1.50
134 Curtis King .40 1.00
135 Ray Lankford .60 1.50
136 Mark McGwire 4.00 10.00
137 Ken Caminiti .60 1.50
138 Steve Finley .60 1.50
139 Tony Gwynn 2.00 5.00
140 Carlos Hernandez .40 1.00
141 Wally Joyner .60 1.50
142 Barry Bonds 4.00 10.00
143 Jacob Cruz .40 1.00
144 Shawn Estes .40 1.00
145 Stan Javier .40 1.00
146 J.T. Snow .60 1.50
147 Nomar Garciaparra ROY 1.50 4.00
148 Scott Rolen ROY 1.00 2.50
149 Ken Griffey Jr. MVP 2.00 5.00
150 Larry Walker MVP .40 1.00

1998 Pacific Invincible Platinum Blue

*STARS: 2X TO 5X BASIC CARDS
STATED ODDS 1:73

1998 Pacific Invincible Silver

*STARS: 1X TO 2.5X BASIC CARDS
STATED ODDS 2:37

1998 Pacific Invincible Cramer's Choice Green

COMP.GREEN SET (10) 200.00 400.00
GREEN PRINT RUN 99 SERIAL #'d SETS
*DARK BLUE: .5X TO 1.2X GREEN
DARK BLUE PRINT RUN 80 SERIAL #'d SETS
GOLD PRINT RUN 15 SERIAL #'d SETS
NO GOLD PRICES DUE TO SCARCITY
*LIGHT BLUE: .6X TO 1.5X GREEN
LIGHT BLUE PRINT RUN 50 SERIAL #'d SETS
PURPLE PRINT RUN 10 SERIAL #'d SETS
NO PURPLE PRICES DUE TO SCARCITY
*RED: 1X TO 2.5X GREEN
RED PRINT RUN 25 SERIAL#'d SETS
RANDOM INSERTS IN PACKS
GREEN CARDS LISTED BELOW!
1 Greg Maddux 20.00 50.00
2 Roberto Alomar 8.00 20.00
3 Cal Ripken 40.00 100.00
4 Nomar Garciaparra 20.00 50.00
5 Larry Walker 8.00 20.00
6 Mike Piazza 20.00 50.00
7 Mark McGwire 30.00 80.00
8 Tony Gwynn 15.00 40.00
9 Ken Griffey Jr. 25.00 60.00
10 Roger Clemens 25.00 60.00

1998 Pacific Invincible Gems of the Diamond

COMPLETE SET (220) 20.00 50.00
1 Jim Edmonds .10 .30
2 Todd Greene .10 .30
3 Ken Hill .10 .30
4 Mike Holtz .10 .30
5 Mike James .10 .30
6 Chad Kreuter .10 .30
7 Tim Salmon .20 .50
8 Roberto Alomar .20 .50
9 Brady Anderson .10 .30
10 Dave Dellucci .20 .50
11 Jeffrey Hammonds .10 .30
12 Mike Mussina .20 .50
13 Rafael Palmeiro .20 .50
14 Arthur Rhodes .10 .30
15 Cal Ripken 1.00 2.50
16 Nerio Rodriguez .10 .30
17 Tony Tarasco .10 .30
18 Lenny Webster .10 .30
19 Mike Benjamin .10 .30
20 Rich Garces .10 .30
21 Nomar Garciaparra .50 1.25
22 Shane Mack .10 .30
23 Jose Malave .10 .30
24 Jesus Tavarez .10 .30
25 Mo Vaughn .10 .30
26 John Wasdin .10 .30
27 Jeff Abbott .10 .30
28 Albert Belle .10 .30
29 Mike Cameron .10 .30
30 Al Levine .10 .30
31 Robert Machado .10 .30
32 Greg Norton .10 .30
33 Magglio Ordonez .60 1.50
34 Mike Sirotka .10 .30
35 Frank Thomas .30 .75
36 Mario Valdez .10 .30
37 Sandy Alomar Jr. .10 .30
38 David Justice .10 .30
39 Jack McDowell .10 .30
40 Eric Plunk .10 .30
41 Manny Ramirez .20 .50
42 Kevin Seitzer .10 .30
43 Paul Shuey .10 .30
44 Omar Vizquel .20 .50
45 Kimera Bartee .10 .30
46 Glenn Dishman .10 .30
47 Orlando Miller .10 .30
48 Mike Myers .10 .30
49 Phil Nevin .10 .30
50 A.J. Sager .10 .30
51 Ricky Bones .10 .30
52 Scott Cooper .10 .30
53 Shane Halter .10 .30
54 David Howard .10 .30
55 Glendon Rusch .10 .30
56 Joe Vitiello .10 .30
57 Jeff D'Amico .10 .30
58 Mike Fetters .10 .30
59 Mike Matheny .10 .30
60 Jose Mercedes .10 .30
61 Ron Villone .10 .30
62 Jack Voigt .10 .30
63 Brent Brede .10 .30
64 Chuck Knoblauch .10 .30
65 Paul Molitor .10 .30
66 Todd Ritchie .10 .30
67 Frankie Rodriguez .10 .30
68 Scott Stahoviak .10 .30
69 Greg Swindell .10 .30
70 Todd Walker .10 .30
71 Wade Boggs .20 .50
72 Hideki Irabu .10 .30
73 Derek Jeter .75 2.00
74 Pat Kelly .10 .30
75 Graeme Lloyd .10 .30
76 Tino Martinez .20 .50
77 Jeff Nelson .10 .30
78 Scott Pose .10 .30
79 Mike Stanton .10 .30
80 Darryl Strawberry .10 .30
81 Bernie Williams .20 .50
82 Tony Batista .10 .30
83 Mark Bellhorn .10 .30
84 Ben Grieve .10 .30
85 Pat Lennon .10 .30
86 Brian Lesher .10 .30
87 Miguel Tejada .30 .75
88 George Williams .10 .30
89 Joey Cora .10 .30
90 Rob Ducey .10 .30
91 Ken Griffey Jr. .60 1.50
92 Randy Johnson .30 .75
93 Edgar Martinez .20 .50
94 John Marzano .10 .30
95 Greg McCarthy .10 .30
96 Alex Rodriguez .50 1.25
97 Andy Sheets .10 .30
98 Mike Timlin .10 .30
99 Lee Tinsley .10 .30
100 Damon Buford .10 .30
101 Alex Diaz .10 .30
102 Benji Gil .10 .30
103 Juan Gonzalez .10 .30
104 Eric Gunderson .10 .30
105 Danny Patterson .10 .30
106 Ivan Rodriguez .20 .50
107 Mike Simms .10 .30
108 Luis Andujar .10 .30
109 Joe Carter .10 .30
110 Roger Clemens .60 1.50
111 Jose Cruz Jr. .10 .30
112 Shawn Green .10 .30
113 Robert Perez .10 .30
114 Juan Samuel .10 .30
115 Ed Sprague .10 .30
116 Shannon Stewart .10 .30
117 Danny Bautista .10 .30
118 Chipper Jones .30 .75
119 Ryan Klesko .10 .30
120 Keith Lockhart .10 .30
121 Javier Lopez .10 .30
122 Greg Maddux .50 1.25
123 Kevin Millwood .30 .75
124 Mike Mordecai .10 .30
125 Eddie Perez .10 .30
126 Randall Simon .10 .30
127 Miguel Cairo .10 .30
128 Dave Clark .10 .30
129 Kevin Foster .10 .30
130 Mark Grace .20 .50
131 Tyler Houston .10 .30
132 Mike Hubbard .10 .30
133 Kevin Orie .10 .30
134 Ryne Sandberg .50 1.25
135 Sammy Sosa .30 .75
136 Lenny Harris .10 .30
137 Kent Mercker .10 .30
138 Mike Morgan .10 .30
139 Deion Sanders .20 .50
140 Chris Stynes .10 .30
141 Gabe White .10 .30
142 Jason Bates .10 .30
143 Vinny Castilla .10 .30
144 Andres Galarraga .10 .30
145 Curtis Leskanic .10 .30
146 Jeff McCurry .10 .30
147 Mike Munoz .10 .30
148 Larry Walker .10 .30
149 Jamey Wright .10 .30
150 Moises Alou .10 .30
151 Bobby Bonilla .10 .30
152 Kevin Brown .20 .50
153 John Cangelosi .10 .30
154 Jeff Conine .10 .30
155 Cliff Floyd .10 .30
156 Jay Powell .10 .30
157 Edgar Renteria .10 .30
158 Tony Saunders .10 .30
159 Gary Sheffield .10 .30
160 Jeff Bagwell .20 .50
161 Tim Bogar .10 .30
162 Tony Eusebio .10 .30
163 Chris Holt .10 .30
164 Ray Montgomery .10 .30
165 Luis Rivera .10 .30
166 Eric Anthony .10 .30
167 Brett Butler .10 .30
168 Juan Castro .10 .30
169 Tripp Cromer .10 .30
170 Raul Mondesi .10 .30
171 Hideo Nomo .30 .75
172 Mike Piazza .50 1.25
173 Tom Prince .10 .30
174 Adam Riggs .10 .30
175 Shane Andrews .10 .30
176 Shayne Bennett .10 .30
177 Raul Chavez .10 .30
178 Pedro Martinez .20 .50
179 Sherman Obando .10 .30
180 Andy Stankiewicz .10 .30
181 Alberto Castillo .10 .30
182 Shawn Gilbert .10 .30
183 Luis Lopez .10 .30
184 Roberto Petagine .10 .30
185 Armando Reynoso .10 .30
186 Midre Cummings .10 .30
187 Kevin Jordan .10 .30
188 Desi Relaford .10 .30
189 Scott Rolen .20 .50
190 Ken Ryan .10 .30
191 Kevin Sefcik .10 .30
192 Emil Brown .10 .30
193 Lou Collier .10 .30
194 Francisco Cordova .10 .30
195 Kevin Elster .10 .30
196 Mark Smith .10 .30
197 Marc Wilkins .10 .30
198 Manny Aybar .10 .30
199 Jose Bautista .10 .30
200 David Bell .10 .30
201 Rigo Beltran .10 .30
202 Delino DeShields .10 .30
203 Dennis Eckersley .10 .30
204 John Mabry .10 .30
205 Eli Marrero .10 .30
206 Willie McGee .10 .30
207 Mark McGwire .75 2.00
208 Ken Caminiti .10 .30
209 Tony Gwynn .40 1.00
210 Chris Jones .10 .30
211 Craig Shipley .10 .30
212 Pete Smith .10 .30
213 Jorge Velandia .10 .30
214 Dario Veras .10 .30
215 Rich Aurilia .10 .30
216 Damon Berryhill .10 .30
217 Barry Bonds .75 2.00
218 Osvaldo Fernandez .10 .30
219 Dante Powell .10 .30
220 Rich Rodriguez .10 .30

1998 Pacific Invincible Interleague Players

COMPLETE SET (30) 200.00 400.00
STATED ODDS 1:73
1A Roberto Alomar 4.00 10.00
1N Craig Biggio 4.00 10.00
2A Cal Ripken 20.00 50.00
2N Chipper Jones 6.00 15.00
3A Nomar Garciaparra 10.00 25.00
3N Scott Rolen 4.00 10.00
4A Mo Vaughn 2.50 6.00
4N Andres Galarraga 2.50 6.00
5A Frank Thomas 6.00 15.00
5N Tony Gwynn 8.00 20.00
6A Albert Belle 2.50 6.00
6N Barry Bonds 15.00 40.00
7A Hideki Irabu 1.50 4.00
7N Hideo Nomo 6.00 15.00
8A Derek Jeter 15.00 40.00
8N Rey Ordonez 1.50 4.00
9A Tino Martinez 4.00 10.00
9N Mark McGwire 15.00 40.00
10A Alex Rodriguez 10.00 25.00
10N Edgar Renteria 2.50 6.00
11A Ken Griffey Jr. 12.50 30.00
11N Larry Walker 2.50 6.00
12A Randy Johnson 6.00 15.00
12N Greg Maddux 10.00 25.00
13A Ivan Rodriguez 4.00 10.00
13N Mike Piazza 10.00 25.00
14A Roger Clemens 12.50 30.00
14N Pedro Martinez 4.00 10.00
15A Jose Cruz Jr. 1.50 4.00
15N Wilton Guerrero 1.50 4.00

1998 Pacific Invincible Moments in Time

COMPLETE SET (20) 50.00 100.00
STATED ODDS 1:145
1 Chipper Jones 3.00 8.00
2 Cal Ripken 10.00 25.00
3 Frank Thomas 3.00 8.00
4 David Justice 1.25 3.00
5 Andres Galarraga 2.00 5.00
6 Larry Walker 2.00 5.00
7 Livan Hernandez 1.25 3.00
8 Wilton Guerrero 1.25 3.00
9 Hideo Nomo 3.00 8.00
10 Mike Piazza 3.00 8.00
11 Pedro Martinez 2.00 5.00
12 Bernie Williams 2.00 5.00
13 Ben Grieve 1.25 3.00
14 Scott Rolen 2.00 5.00
15 Mark McGwire 5.00 12.00
16 Tony Gwynn 3.00 8.00
17 Ken Griffey Jr. 12.50 30.00
18 Alex Rodriguez 4.00 10.00
19 Juan Gonzalez 1.25 3.00
20 Jose Cruz Jr. 1.25 3.00

1998 Pacific Invincible Photoengravings

COMPLETE SET (18) 40.00 100.00
STATED ODDS 1:37
1 Greg Maddux 4.00 10.00
2 Cal Ripken 8.00 20.00
3 Nomar Garciaparra 4.00 10.00
4 Frank Thomas 2.50 6.00
5 Larry Walker 1.00 2.50
6 Mike Piazza 4.00 10.00
7 Hideo Nomo 2.50 6.00
8 Pedro Martinez 1.50 4.00
9 Derek Jeter 6.00 15.00
10 Tino Martinez 1.50 4.00
11 Mark McGwire 6.00 15.00
12 Tony Gwynn 3.00 8.00
13 Barry Bonds 6.00 15.00
14 Ken Griffey Jr. 5.00 12.00
15 Alex Rodriguez 4.00 10.00
16 Ivan Rodriguez 1.50 4.00
17 Roger Clemens 5.00 12.00
18 Jose Cruz Jr. .60 1.50

1998 Pacific Invincible Team Checklists

COMPLETE SET (30) 60.00 120.00
STATED ODDS 2:37
1 R.Henderson 2.50 6.00
Erstad
Salmon
2 G.Maddux 3.00 8.00
Chipper
Andruw
3 C.Ripken 8.00 20.00
Muss
Alom
Palm
4 N.Garciaparra 4.00 10.00
M.Vaughn
5 S.Sosa 4.00 10.00
Sandberg
Grace
6 Thom 2.50 6.00
Belle
Vent
Guillen
7 B.Larkin 1.50 4.00
D.Sanders
8 M.Ramirez 1.50 4.00
Thome
Justice
9 L.Walker 1.00 2.50
A.Galarraga
10 T.Clark 1.00 2.50
B.Higginson
11 G.Sheffield 1.00 2.50
L.Hern
C.John
12 J.Bagwell 1.50 4.00
Biggio
Hidalgo
13 J.Damon 1.50 4.00
C.Davis
14 M.Piazza 4.00 10.00
Nomo
Mondesi
15 Nil 1.00 2.50
Vina
Burn
Franco
Cir
16 P.Molitor 1.00 2.50
C.Knoblauch
17 V.Guerrero 2.50 6.00
P.Martinez
18 Alfonzo 1.00 2.50
Hundley
Olerud
19 D.Jeter 6.00 15.00
A.Pettitte
T.Mart
20 J.Giambi 1.50 4.00
J.Canseco
21 S.Rolen 1.50 4.00
C.Schilling
22 J.Guillen 1.00 2.50
T.Womack
23 M.McGwire 6.00 15.00
Lankford
Eck
24 Gwynn 3.00 8.00
Cam
Fin
Joyner
25 B.Bonds 6.00 15.00
J.T.Snow
26 K.Griffey 5.00 12.00
A.Rod
R.John
27 J.Gonz 1.50 4.00
I.Rod
W.Clark
28 J.Cruz Jr. 5.00 12.00
R.Clemens
29 M.Williams 1.00 2.50
J.Bell
30 W.Boggs 1.50 4.00
F.McGriff

1999 Pacific Invincible

The 1999 Pacific Invincible set was issued in one series totalling 150 cards and was distributed in three-card packs with an SRP of $2.99. The fronts feature a color action player photo as well as a head shot printed on an inlaid cel window with gold foil printing. The backs carry information about the player.

COMPLETE SET (150) 100.00 200.00
1 Jim Edmonds .50 1.25
2 Darin Erstad .50 1.25
3 Troy Glaus .75 2.00
4 Tim Salmon .75 2.00
5 Mo Vaughn .50 1.25
6 Steve Finley .50 1.25
7 Randy Johnson 1.25 3.00
8 Travis Lee .30 .75
9 Dante Powell .30 .75
10 Matt Williams .50 1.25
11 Bret Boone .50 1.25
12 Andruw Jones .75 2.00
13 Chipper Jones 1.25 3.00
14 Brian Jordan .50 1.25
15 Ryan Klesko .50 1.25
16 Javy Lopez .50 1.25
17 Greg Maddux 2.00 5.00
18 Brady Anderson .50 1.25
19 Albert Belle .50 1.25
20 Will Clark .75 2.00
21 Mike Mussina .75 2.00
22 Cal Ripken 4.00 10.00
23 Nomar Garciaparra 2.00 5.00
24 Pedro Martinez .75 2.00
25 Trot Nixon .50 1.25
26 Jose Offerman .30 .75
27 Donnie Sadler .30 .75
28 John Valentin .30 .75
29 Mark Grace .75 2.00
30 Lance Johnson .30 .75
31 Henry Rodriguez .30 .75
32 Sammy Sosa 1.25 3.00
33 Kerry Wood .50 1.25
34 McKay Christensen .30 .75
35 Ray Durham .50 1.25
36 Jeff Liefer .30 .75
37 Frank Thomas 1.25 3.00
38 Mike Cameron .30 .75
39 Barry Larkin .75 2.00
40 Greg Vaughn .30 .75

41 Dmitri Young .50 1.25
42 Roberto Alomar .75 2.00
43 Sandy Alomar Jr. .30 .75
44 David Justice .50 1.25
45 Kenny Lofton .50 1.25
46 Manny Ramirez .75 2.00
47 Jim Thome .75 2.00
48 Dante Bichette .50 1.25
49 Vinny Castilla .50 1.25
50 Darryl Hamilton .30 .75
51 Todd Helton .75 2.00
52 Neifi Perez .30 .75
53 Larry Walker .50 1.25
54 Tony Clark .30 .75
55 Damion Easley .30 .75
56 Bob Higginson .50 1.25
57 Brian L.Hunter .30 .75
58 Gabe Kapler .50 1.25
59 Cliff Floyd .50 1.25
60 Alex Gonzalez .30 .75
61 Mark Kotsay .50 1.25
62 Derrek Lee .75 2.00
63 Braden Looper .30 .75
64 Moises Alou .50 1.25
65 Jeff Bagwell .75 2.00
66 Craig Biggio .75 2.00
67 Ken Caminiti .50 1.25
68 Scott Elarton .30 .75
69 Mitch Meluskey .30 .75
70 Carlos Beltran .75 2.00
71 Johnny Damon .75 2.00
72 Carlos Febles .30 .75
73 Jeremy Giambi .30 .75
74 Kevin Brown .75 2.00
75 Todd Hundley .30 .75
76 Paul LoDuca .50 1.25
77 Raul Mondesi .50 1.25
78 Gary Sheffield .50 1.25
79 Geoff Jenkins .30 .75
80 Jeromy Burnitz .50 1.25
81 Marquis Grissom .50 1.25
82 Jose Valentin .30 .75
83 Fernando Vina .30 .75
84 Corey Koskie .30 .75
85 Matt Lawton .30 .75
86 Christian Guzman .30 .75
87 Torii Hunter .50 1.25
88 Doug Mientkiewicz RC .75 2.00
89 Michael Barrett .30 .75
90 Brad Fullmer .30 .75
91 Vladimir Guerrero 1.25 3.00
92 Fernando Seguignol .30 .75
93 Ugueth Urbina .30 .75
94 Bobby Bonilla .50 1.25
95 Rickey Henderson 1.25 3.00
96 Rey Ordonez .30 .75
97 Mike Piazza 2.00 5.00
98 Robin Ventura .50 1.25
99 Roger Clemens 2.50 6.00
100 Derek Jeter 3.00 8.00
101 Chuck Knoblauch .50 1.25
102 Tino Martinez .75 2.00
103 Paul O'Neill .75 2.00
104 Bernie Williams .75 2.00
105 Eric Chavez .50 1.25
106 Ryan Christenson .30 .75
107 Jason Giambi .50 1.25
108 Ben Grieve .30 .75
109 Miguel Tejada .50 1.25
110 Marlon Anderson .30 .75
111 Doug Glanville .30 .75
112 Scott Rolen .75 2.00
113 Curt Schilling .50 1.25
114 Brian Giles .50 1.25
115 Warren Morris .30 .75
116 Jason Kendall .50 1.25
117 Kris Benson .30 .75
118 J.D. Drew .50 1.25
119 Ray Lankford .50 1.25
120 Mark McGwire 3.00 8.00
121 Matt Clement .50 1.25
122 Tony Gwynn 1.50 4.00
123 Trevor Hoffman .50 1.25
124 Wally Joyner .50 1.25
125 Reggie Sanders .50 1.25
126 Barry Bonds 3.00 8.00
127 Ellis Burks .50 1.25
128 Jeff Kent .50 1.25
129 Stan Javier .30 .75
130 J.T. Snow .50 1.25
131 Jay Buhner .50 1.25
132 Freddy Garcia RC 1.25 3.00
133 Ken Griffey Jr. 2.50 6.00
134 Russ Davis .30 .75
135 Edgar Martinez .75 2.00
136 Alex Rodriguez 2.00 5.00
137 David Segui .30 .75
138 Rolando Arrojo .30 .75
139 Wade Boggs .75 2.00
140 Jose Canseco .75 2.00
141 Quinton McCracken .30 .75
142 Fred McGriff .75 2.00
143 Juan Gonzalez .50 1.25
144 Tom Goodwin .30 .75
145 Rusty Greer .50 1.25
146 Ivan Rodriguez .75 2.00
147 Jose Cruz Jr. .30 .75
148 Carlos Delgado .50 1.25
149 Shawn Green .50 1.25
150 Roy Halladay 10.00 25.00

1999 Pacific Invincible Opening Day

*STARS: 4X TO 10X BASIC CARDS
*ROOKIES: 2.5X TO 6X BASIC CARDS
STATED ODDS 1:25 HOBBY
STATED PRINT RUN 69 SERIAL #'d SETS

1999 Pacific Invincible Platinum Blue

*STARS: 4X TO 10X BASIC CARDS
*ROOKIES: 2.5X TO 6X BASIC CARDS
RANDOM INSERTS IN PACKS
STATED PRINT RUN 67 SERIAL #'d SETS

1999 Pacific Invincible Diamond Magic

COMPLETE SET (10) 15.00 40.00
STATED ODDS 1:49
1 Cal Ripken 5.00 12.00
2 Nomar Garciaparra 1.00 2.50
3 Sammy Sosa 1.50 4.00
4 Frank Thomas 1.50 4.00
5 Mike Piazza 1.50 4.00
6 J.D. Drew .60 1.50
7 Mark McGwire 2.50 6.00
8 Tony Gwynn 1.50 4.00
9 Ken Griffey Jr. 3.00 8.00
10 Alex Rodriguez 2.00 5.00

1999 Pacific Invincible Flash Point

COMPLETE SET (20) 12.50 30.00
STATED ODDS 1:25
1 Mo Vaughn 1.00 2.50
2 Chipper Jones 2.50 6.00
3 Greg Maddux 4.00 10.00
4 Cal Ripken 8.00 20.00
5 Nomar Garciaparra 4.00 10.00
6 Sammy Sosa 2.50 6.00
7 Frank Thomas 2.50 6.00
8 Manny Ramirez 1.50 4.00
9 Vladimir Guerrero 2.50 6.00
10 Mike Piazza 4.00 10.00
11 Roger Clemens 5.00 12.00
12 Derek Jeter 6.00 15.00
13 Ben Grieve .60 1.50
14 Scott Rolen 1.50 4.00
15 J.D. Drew 1.00 2.50
16 Mark McGwire 6.00 15.00
17 Tony Gwynn 3.00 8.00
18 Ken Griffey Jr. 5.00 12.00
19 Alex Rodriguez 4.00 10.00
20 Juan Gonzalez 1.00 2.50

1999 Pacific Invincible Giants of the Game

RANDOM INSERTS IN PACKS
STATED PRINT RUN 10 SERIAL #'d SETS
NO PRICING AVAILABLE DUE TO SCARCITY
1 Cal Ripken
2 Nomar Garciaparra
3 Sammy Sosa
4 Frank Thomas
5 Mike Piazza
6 J.D. Drew
7 Mark McGwire
8 Tony Gwynn
9 Ken Griffey Jr.
10 Alex Rodriguez

1999 Pacific Invincible Sandlot Heroes

COMPLETE SET (40) 10.00 25.00
ONE PER PACK
TWO VERSIONS OF EACH CARD EXIST
A/B VERSIONS VALUED EQUALLY
1 Mo Vaughn .08 .25
1B Mo Vaughn .08 .25
2 Chipper Jones Wearing Cap .25 .60
2B Chipper Jones Wearing Helmet .25 .60
3 G.Maddux Ball Up .40 1.00
4 C.Ripken Fielding .75 2.00
5 Garciaparra No Bat .40 1.00
6 Sammy Sosa Fielding .25 .60
6B Sammy Sosa Hitting .25 .60
7 Frank Thomas Standing .25 .60
7B Frank Thomas Running .25 .60
8 Manny Ramirez Running .15 .40
8B Manny Ramirez Batting .15 .40
9 Vladimir Guerrero Fielding .25 .60
9B Vladimir Guerrero Batting .25 .60
10 M.Piazza No Bat .40 1.00
11 Roger Clemens .50 1.25
12 D.Jeter Fielding .60 1.50
13 Eric Chavez Throwing .08 .25
13B Eric Chavez Batting .08 .25
14 Ben Grieve .05 .15
14B Ben Grieve .05 .15
15 J.D. Drew No Bat .08 .25
15B J.D. Drew w Bat .08 .25
16 M.McGwire Fielding .60 1.50
17 T.Gwynn No Bat .30 .75
18 Ken Griffey Jr. .50 1.25
19 ARod Wearing Helmet .40 1.00
20 Juan Gonzalez .08 .25
20B Juan Gonzalez .08 .25

1999 Pacific Invincible Seismic Force

COMPLETE SET (40) 10.00 25.00
ONE PER PACK
TWO VERSIONS OF EACH CARD EXIST
A/B VERSIONS VALUED EQUALLY
1 Mo Vaughn Wearing hat .08 .25
2 Chipper Jones Portrait .25 .60
3 Greg Maddux .40 1.00
4 Cal Ripken Portrait .75 2.00
5 Nomar Garciaparra Portrait with bat .40 1.00
6 Sammy Sosa No hat .25 .60
7 Frank Thomas Portrait with bat .25 .60
8 Manny Ramirez Portrait with bat .15 .40
9 Vladimir Guerrero Portrait with bat .25 .60
10 Mike Piazza Portrait with bat .40 1.00
11 Bernie Williams Portrait with bat .15 .40
12 Derek Jeter Portrait with bat .60 1.50
13 Ben Grieve Portrait with bat .05 .15
14 J.D. Drew Portrait with bat .08 .25
15 Mark McGwire Red jersey .60 1.50
16 Tony Gwynn Portrait .30 .75
17 Ken Griffey Jr. Sitting in dugout .50 1.25
18 Alex Rodriguez Portrait with bat .40 1.00
19 Juan Gonzalez Portrait with bat .08 .25
20 Ivan Rodriguez Portrait with bat .15 .40

1999 Pacific Invincible Thunder Alley

STATED ODDS 1:121
1 Mo Vaughn .75 2.00
2 Chipper Jones 2.00 5.00
3 Cal Ripken 6.00 15.00
4 Nomar Garciaparra 1.25 3.00
5 Sammy Sosa 2.00 5.00
6 Frank Thomas 2.00 5.00
7 Manny Ramirez 2.00 5.00
8 Todd Helton 1.25 3.00
9 Vladimir Guerrero 1.25 3.00
10 Mike Piazza 2.00 5.00
11 Derek Jeter 5.00 12.00
12 Ben Grieve .75 2.00
13 Scott Rolen 1.25 3.00
14 J.D. Drew .75 2.00
15 Mark McGwire 3.00 8.00
16 Tony Gwynn 2.00 5.00
17 Ken Griffey Jr. 4.00 10.00
18 Alex Rodriguez 2.50 6.00
19 Juan Gonzalez .75 2.00
20 Ivan Rodriguez 1.25 3.00

1999 Pacific Invincible Players Choice

These cards, which parallel the regular Pacific Invincible cards were issued by Pacific to be given away at the Players Choice award ceremony. The cards have a "Players Choice" stamp on them and are skip numbered to match their number. These cards were produced in varying quantites so we have put the print run next to the players name

7 Randy Johnson/131 6.00 15.00
10 Matt Williams/130 2.50 6.00
13 Chipper Jones/118 8.00 20.00
17 Greg Maddux/133 10.00 25.00
22 Cal Ripken Jr./137 16.00 40.00
24 Pedro Martinez/130 5.00 12.00
32 Sammy Sosa/124 8.00 20.00
42 Roberto Alomar/118 4.00 10.00
65 Jeff Bagwell/118 5.00 12.00
70 Carlos Beltran/142 2.50 6.00
115 Warren Morris/133 2.00 5.00
126 Barry Bonds/137 8.00 20.00
132 Freddy Garcia/100 2.00 5.00
133 Ken Griffey Jr./113 10.00 25.00

2000 Pacific Invincible

COMPLETE SET (150) 40.00 100.00
COMMON CARD (1-150) .30 .75
1 Darin Erstad .30 .75
2 Troy Glaus .30 .75
3 Ramon Ortiz .30 .75
4 Tim Salmon .30 .75
5 Mo Vaughn .30 .75
6 Erubiel Durazo .30 .75
7 Luis Gonzalez .30 .75
8 Randy Johnson .75 2.00
9 Matt Williams .30 .75
10 Rafael Furcal .50 1.25
11 Andres Galarraga .50 1.25
12 Tom Glavine .50 1.25
13 Andruw Jones .30 .75
14 Chipper Jones .75 2.00
15 Greg Maddux 1.00 2.50
16 Kevin Millwood .30 .75
17 Albert Belle .30 .75
18 Will Clark .50 1.25
19 Mike Mussina .50 1.25
20 Matt Riley .30 .75
21 Cal Ripken 2.50 6.00
22 Carl Everett .30 .75
23 Nomar Garciaparra .50 1.25
24 Steve Lomasney .30 .75
25 Pedro Martinez .50 1.25
26 Tomo Ohka RC .30 .75
27 Wilton Veras .30 .75
28 Mark Grace .50 1.25
29 Sammy Sosa .75 2.00
30 Kerry Wood .30 .75
31 Eric Young .30 .75
32 Julio Zuleta RC .30 .75
33 Paul Konerko .30 .75
34 Carlos Lee .30 .75
35 Maggio Ordonez .50 1.25
36 Josh Paul .30 .75
37 Frank Thomas .75 2.00
38 Rob Bell .30 .75
39 Dante Bichette .30 .75
40 Sean Casey .30 .75
41 Ken Griffey Jr. 1.50 4.00
42 Barry Larkin .50 1.25
43 Pokey Reese .30 .75
44 Roberto Alomar .50 1.25
45 Manny Ramirez .75 2.00
46 Richie Sexson .30 .75
47 Jim Thome .50 1.25
48 Omar Vizquel .50 1.25
49 Jeff Cirillo .30 .75
50 Todd Helton .50 1.25
51 Neifi Perez .30 .75
52 Larry Walker .50 1.25
53 Tony Clark .30 .75
54 Juan Encarnacion .30 .75
55 Juan Gonzalez .30 .75
56 Hideo Nomo .75 2.00
57 Luis Castillo .30 .75
58 Alex Gonzalez .30 .75
59 Brad Penny .30 .75
60 Preston Wilson .30 .75
61 Moises Alou .30 .75
62 Jeff Bagwell .50 1.25
63 Lance Berkman .50 1.25
64 Craig Biggio .50 1.25
65 Roger Cedeno .30 .75
66 Jose Lima .30 .75
67 Carlos Beltran .50 1.25
68 Johnny Damon .50 1.25
69 Chad Durbin RC .30 .75
70 Jermaine Dye .30 .75
71 Carlos Febles .30 .75
72 Mark Quinn .30 .75
73 Kevin Brown .30 .75
74 Eric Gagne .30 .75
75 Shawn Green .30 .75
76 Eric Karros .30 .75
77 Gary Sheffield .30 .75
78 Kevin Barker .30 .75
79 Ron Belliard .30 .75
80 Jeromy Burnitz .30 .75
81 Geoff Jenkins .30 .75
82 Jacque Jones .30 .75
83 Corey Koskie .30 .75
84 Matt LeCroy .30 .75
85 David Ortiz .75 2.00
86 Johan Santana RC 5.00 12.00
87 Todd Walker .30 .75
88 Peter Bergeron .30 .75
89 Vladimir Guerrero .50 1.25
90 Jose Vidro .30 .75
91 Rondell White .30 .75
92 Edgardo Alfonzo .30 .75
93 Derek Bell .30 .75
94 Mike Hampton .30 .75
95 Rey Ordonez .30 .75
96 Mike Piazza .75 2.00
97 Robin Ventura .30 .75
98 Roger Clemens 1.00 2.50
99 Orlando Hernandez .30 .75
100 Derek Jeter 2.00 5.00
101 Alfonso Soriano .75 2.00
102 Bernie Williams .50 1.25
103 Eric Chavez .30 .75
104 Jason Giambi .30 .75
105 Ben Grieve .30 .75
106 Tim Hudson .50 1.25
107 Miguel Tejada .50 1.25
108 Bob Abreu .30 .75
109 Doug Glanville .30 .75
110 Mike Lieberthal .30 .75
111 Scott Rolen .50 1.25
112 Brian Giles .30 .75
113 Chad Hermansen .30 .75
114 Jason Kendall .30 .75
115 Warren Morris .30 .75
116 Aramis Ramirez .30 .75
117 Rick Ankiel .50 1.25
118 J.D. Drew .30 .75
119 Mark McGwire 1.25 3.00
120 Fernando Tatis .30 .75
121 Fernando Vina .30 .75
122 Bret Boone .30 .75
123 Ben Davis .30 .75
124 Tony Gwynn .75 2.00
125 Trevor Hoffman .50 1.25
126 Ryan Klesko .30 .75
127 Rich Aurilia .30 .75
128 Barry Bonds 1.25 3.00
129 Ellis Burks .30 .75
130 Jeff Kent .30 .75
131 Freddy Garcia .30 .75
132 Carlos Guillen .30 .75
133 Edgar Martinez .50 1.25
134 John Olerud .30 .75
135 Rob Ramsay .30 .75
136 Alex Rodriguez 1.00 2.50
137 Kazuhiro Sasaki RC .75 2.00
138 Jose Canseco .50 1.25
139 Vinny Castilla .30 .75
140 Fred McGriff .50 1.25
141 Greg Vaughn .30 .75
142 Dan Wheeler .30 .75
143 Gabe Kapler .30 .75
144 Ruben Mateo .30 .75
145 Rafael Palmeiro .50 1.25
146 Ivan Rodriguez .50 1.25
147 Tony Batista .30 .75
148 Carlos Delgado .30 .75
149 Raul Mondesi .30 .75
150 Vernon Wells .30 .75

2000 Pacific Invincible Holographic Purple

*HOLO.PUPRLE: 1.2X TO 3X BASIC
STATED PRINT RUN 299 SERIAL #'d SETS

2000 Pacific Invincible Platinum Blue

*PLAT.BLUE: 4X TO 10X BASIC
STATED PRINT RUN 67 SERIAL #'d SETS

2000 Pacific Invincible Diamond Aces

COMPLETE SET (20) 2.50 6.00
ONE PER PACK
*ACES 399: 3X TO 8X BASIC ACES
ACES 399 PRINT RUN 399 SERIAL #'d SETS
1 Randy Johnson .30 .75
2 Greg Maddux .40 1.00
3 Tom Glavine .20 .50
4 John Smoltz .30 .75
5 Mike Mussina .20 .50
6 Pedro Martinez .20 .50
7 Kerry Wood .12 .30
8 Bartolo Colon .12 .30
9 Brad Penny .12 .30
10 Billy Wagner .12 .30
11 Kevin Brown .12 .30
12 Mike Hampton .12 .30
13 Roger Clemens .40 1.00
14 David Cone .12 .30
15 Orlando Hernandez .12 .30
16 Mariano Rivera .40 1.00
17 Tim Hudson .20 .50
18 Trevor Hoffman .20 .50
19 Rick Ankiel .20 .50
20 Freddy Garcia .12 .30

2000 Pacific Invincible Eyes of the World

COMPLETE SET (20) 12.50 30.00
STATED ODDS 1:37
1 Erubiel Durazo .40 1.00
2 Andruw Jones .40 1.00
3 Cal Ripken 3.00 8.00
4 Nomar Garciaparra .60 1.50
5 Pedro Martinez .60 1.50
6 Sammy Sosa 1.00 2.50
7 Ken Griffey Jr. 2.00 5.00
8 Manny Ramirez 1.00 2.50
9 Larry Walker .60 1.50
10 Juan Gonzalez .40 1.00
11 Carlos Beltran .60 1.50
12 Vladimir Guerrero .60 1.50
13 Orlando Hernandez .40 1.00
14 Derek Jeter 2.50 6.00
15 Mark McGwire 1.50 4.00
16 Tony Gwynn 1.00 2.50
17 Freddy Garcia .40 1.00
18 Alex Rodriguez 1.25 3.00
19 Jose Canseco .60 1.50
20 Ivan Rodriguez .60 1.50

2000 Pacific Invincible Game Gear

PRINT RUNS B/WN 65-1000 COPIES PER
1 J.Bagwell Jsy/1000 2.50 6.00
2 T.Glavine Jsy/1000 2.50 6.00
3 M.Grace Jsy/1000 2.50 6.00
4 E.Karros Jsy/1000 1.50 4.00
5 E.Martinez Jsy/800 2.50 6.00
6 M.Ramirez Jsy/975 4.00 10.00
7 C.Ripken Jsy/1000 6.00 15.00
8 A.Rodriguez Jsy/900 5.00 12.00
9 I.Rodriguez Jsy/675 2.50 6.00
10 M.Vaughn Jsy/1000 1.50 4.00
11 E.Martinez Bat-Jsy/200 4.00 10.00
12 M.Ramirez Bat-Jsy/145 6.00 15.00
13 A.Rodriguez Bat-Jsy/200 8.00 20.00
14 I.Rodriguez Bat-Jsy/200 4.00 10.00
15 E.Martinez Bat/200 4.00 10.00
16 M.Ramirez Bat/200 6.00 15.00
17 I.Rodriguez Bat/200 4.00 10.00
18 A.Rodriguez Bat/200 8.00 20.00
19 J.Bagwell Patch/125 10.00 25.00
20 T.Glavine Patch/110 10.00 25.00
21 M.Grace Patch/125 10.00 25.00
22 T.Gwynn Patch/65 15.00 40.00
23 C.Jones Patch/80 15.00 40.00
24 E.Karros Patch/125 6.00 15.00
25 G.Maddux Patch/80 20.00 50.00
26 E.Martinez Patch/125 10.00 25.00
27 M.Ramirez Patch/125 15.00 40.00
28 C.Ripken Patch/125 30.00 80.00
29 A.Rodriguez Patch/125 20.00 50.00
30 I.Rodriguez Patch/125 10.00 25.00
31 F.Thomas Patch/125 15.00 40.00
32 M.Vaughn Patch/125 6.00 15.00

2000 Pacific Invincible Kings of the Diamond

COMPLETE SET (30) 8.00 20.00
ONE PER PACK
*KINGS 299: 4X TO 10X BASIC KINGS
KINGS 299 PRINT RUN 299 SERIAL #'d SETS
1 Mo Vaughn .12 .30
2 Erubiel Durazo .12 .30
3 Andruw Jones .12 .30
4 Chipper Jones .30 .75
5 Cal Ripken 1.00 2.50
6 Nomar Garciaparra .20 .50
7 Sammy Sosa .30 .75
8 Frank Thomas .30 .75
9 Sean Casey .12 .30
10 Ken Griffey Jr. .60 1.50
11 Manny Ramirez .30 .75
12 Larry Walker .20 .50
13 Juan Gonzalez .12 .30
14 Jeff Bagwell .20 .50
15 Craig Biggio .20 .50
16 Carlos Beltran .20 .50
17 Shawn Green .12 .30
18 Vladimir Guerrero .20 .50
19 Mike Piazza .30 .75
20 Derek Jeter .75 2.00
21 Bernie Williams .20 .50
22 Ben Grieve .12 .30
23 Scott Rolen .20 .50
24 Mark McGwire .50 1.25
25 Tony Gwynn .30 .75
26 Barry Bonds .50 1.25
27 Alex Rodriguez .40 1.00
28 Jose Canseco .20 .50
29 Rafael Palmeiro .20 .50
30 Ivan Rodriguez .20 .50

2000 Pacific Invincible Lighting the Fire

COMPLETE SET (20) 60.00 120.00
STATED ODDS 1:73
1 Chipper Jones 2.50 6.00
2 Greg Maddux 3.00 8.00
3 Cal Ripken 8.00 20.00
4 Nomar Garciaparra 1.50 4.00
5 Pedro Martinez 1.50 4.00
6 Ken Griffey Jr. 5.00 12.00
7 Sammy Sosa 2.50 6.00
8 Manny Ramirez 2.50 6.00
9 Juan Gonzalez 1.00 2.50
10 Jeff Bagwell 1.50 4.00
11 Shawn Green 1.00 2.50
12 Vladimir Guerrero 1.50 4.00
13 Mike Piazza 2.50 6.00
14 Roger Clemens 3.00 8.00
15 Derek Jeter 6.00 15.00
16 Mark McGwire 4.00 10.00
17 Tony Gwynn 2.50 6.00
18 Alex Rodriguez 3.00 8.00
19 Jose Canseco 1.50 4.00
20 Ivan Rodriguez 1.50 4.00

2000 Pacific Invincible Ticket to Stardom

STATED ODDS 1:181
1 Andruw Jones 2.50 6.00
2 Chipper Jones 6.00 15.00
3 Cal Ripken 20.00 50.00
4 Nomar Garciaparra 4.00 10.00
5 Pedro Martinez 4.00 10.00
6 Ken Griffey Jr. 12.00 30.00
7 Sammy Sosa 6.00 15.00
8 Manny Ramirez 6.00 15.00
9 Jeff Bagwell 4.00 10.00
10 Shawn Green 2.50 6.00
11 Vladimir Guerrero 4.00 10.00
12 Mike Piazza 6.00 15.00
13 Derek Jeter 15.00 40.00
14 Alfonso Soriano 6.00 15.00
15 Scott Rolen 4.00 10.00
16 Rick Ankiel 4.00 10.00
17 Mark McGwire 10.00 25.00
18 Tony Gwynn 6.00 15.00
19 Alex Rodriguez 8.00 20.00
20 Ivan Rodriguez 4.00 10.00

2000 Pacific Invincible Wild Vinyl

STATED PRINT RUN 10 SERIAL #'d SETS
NO PRICING DUE TO SCARCITY

1998 Pacific Omega

The 1998 Pacific Omega set was issued in one series totalling 250 cards. The cards were issued in eight-card packs with an SRP of $1.99. In addition, a Tony Gwynn sample card was issued prior to the product's release. The card was distributed to dealers and hobby media to preview the product. It's identical in design to a standard Aurora card except for the word "SAMPLE" printed diagonally against the back of the card coupled with a large MLB "Genuine Merchandise" sticker. Notable Rookie Cards include Kevin Millwood and Maggio Ordonez,

COMPLETE SET (250) 15.00 40.00
1 Garret Anderson .10 .30
2 Gary DiSarcina .10 .30
3 Jim Edmonds .10 .30
4 Darin Erstad .10 .30
5 Cecil Fielder .10 .30
6 Chuck Finley .10 .30
7 Shigetoshi Hasegawa .10 .30
8 Tim Salmon .20 .50
9 Brian Anderson .10 .30
10 Jay Bell .10 .30
11 Andy Benes .10 .30
12 Yamil Benitez .10 .30
13 Jorge Fabregas .10 .30
14 Travis Lee .10 .30
15 Devon White .10 .30
16 Matt Williams .10 .30
17 Andres Galarraga .10 .30
18 Tom Glavine .20 .50
19 Andruw Jones .20 .50
20 Chipper Jones .30 .75
21 Ryan Klesko .10 .30
22 Javy Lopez .10 .30
23 Greg Maddux .50 1.25
24 Kevin Millwood RC .40 1.00
25 Denny Neagle .10 .30
26 John Smoltz .20 .50
27 Roberto Alomar .20 .50
28 Brady Anderson .10 .30
29 Joe Carter .10 .30
30 Eric Davis .10 .30
31 Jimmy Key .10 .30
32 Mike Mussina .20 .50
33 Rafael Palmeiro .20 .50
34 Cal Ripken 1.00 2.50
35 B.J. Surhoff .10 .30
36 Dennis Eckersley .10 .30
37 Nomar Garciaparra .50 1.25
38 Reggie Jefferson .10 .30
39 Derek Lowe .10 .30
40 Pedro Martinez .20 .50
41 Brian Rose .10 .30
42 John Valentin .10 .30
43 Jason Varitek .30 .75
44 Mo Vaughn .10 .30
45 Jeff Blauser .10 .30
46 Jeremi Gonzalez .10 .30
47 Mark Grace .20 .50
48 Lance Johnson .10 .30
49 Kevin Orie .10 .30
50 Henry Rodriguez .10 .30
51 Sammy Sosa .30 .75
52 Kerry Wood .15 .40
53 Albert Belle .10 .30
54 Mike Cameron .10 .30
55 Mike Caruso .10 .30
56 Ray Durham .10 .30
57 Jaime Navarro .10 .30
58 Greg Norton .10 .30
59 Magglio Ordonez RC 1.00 2.50
60 Frank Thomas .30 .75
61 Robin Ventura .10 .30
62 Bret Boone .10 .30
63 Willie Greene .10 .30
64 Barry Larkin .20 .50
65 Jon Nunnally .10 .30
66 Eduardo Perez .10 .30
67 Reggie Sanders .10 .30
68 Brett Tomko .10 .30
69 Sandy Alomar Jr. .10 .30
70 Travis Fryman .10 .30
71 David Justice .10 .30
72 Kenny Lofton .10 .30
73 Charles Nagy .10 .30
74 Manny Ramirez .20 .50
75 Jim Thome .20 .50
76 Omar Vizquel .20 .50
77 Enrique Wilson .10 .30
78 Jaret Wright .10 .30
79 Dante Bichette .10 .30
80 Ellis Burks .10 .30
81 Vinny Castilla .10 .30
82 Todd Helton .20 .50
83 Darryl Kile .10 .30
84 Mike Lansing .10 .30
85 Neifi Perez .10 .30
86 Larry Walker .10 .30
87 Raul Casanova .10 .30
88 Tony Clark .10 .30
89 Luis Gonzalez .10 .30
90 Bobby Higginson .10 .30
91 Brian Hunter .10 .30
92 Bip Roberts .10 .30
93 Justin Thompson .10 .30
94 Josh Booty .10 .30
95 Craig Counsell .10 .30
96 Livan Hernandez .10 .30
97 Ryan Jackson RC .10 .30
98 Mark Kotsay .10 .30
99 Derrek Lee .20 .50
100 Mike Piazza .50 1.25
101 Edgar Renteria .10 .30
102 Cliff Floyd .10 .30
103 Moises Alou .10 .30
104 Jeff Bagwell .20 .50
105 Derek Bell .10 .30
106 Sean Berry .10 .30
107 Craig Biggio .20 .50
108 John Halama RC .10 .30
109 Richard Hidalgo .10 .30
110 Shane Reynolds .10 .30
111 Tim Belcher .10 .30
112 Brian Bevil .10 .30
113 Jeff Conine .10 .30
114 Johnny Damon .20 .50
115 Jeff King .10 .30
116 Jeff Montgomery .10 .30
117 Dean Palmer .10 .30
118 Terry Pendleton .10 .30
119 Bobby Bonilla .10 .30
120 Wilton Guerrero .10 .30
121 Todd Hollandsworth .10 .30
122 Charles Johnson .10 .30
123 Eric Karros .10 .30
124 Paul Konerko .10 .30
125 Ramon Martinez .10 .30
126 Raul Mondesi .10 .30
127 Hideo Nomo .30 .75
128 Gary Sheffield .10 .30
129 Ismael Valdes .10 .30
130 Jeromy Burnitz .10 .30
131 Jeff Cirillo .10 .30
132 Todd Dunn .10 .30
133 Marquis Grissom .10 .30
134 John Jaha .10 .30
135 Scott Karl .10 .30
136 Dave Nilsson .10 .30
137 Jose Valentin .10 .30
138 Fernando Vina .10 .30
139 Rick Aguilera .10 .30
140 Marty Cordova .10 .30
141 Pat Meares .10 .30
142 Paul Molitor .10 .30
143 David Ortiz .40 1.00
144 Brad Radke .10 .30
145 Terry Steinbach .10 .30
146 Todd Walker .10 .30
147 Shane Andrews .10 .30
148 Brad Fullmer .10 .30
149 Mark Grudzielanek .10 .30
150 Vladimir Guerrero .30 .75
151 F.P. Santangelo .10 .30
152 Jose Vidro .10 .30
153 Rondell White .10 .30
154 Carlos Baerga .10 .30
155 Bernard Gilkey .10 .30
156 Todd Hundley .10 .30
157 Butch Huskey .10 .30
158 Bobby Jones .10 .30
159 Brian McRae .10 .30
160 John Olerud .10 .30
161 Rey Ordonez .10 .30
162 Masato Yoshii RC .15 .40
163 David Cone .10 .30
164 Hideki Irabu .10 .30
165 Derek Jeter .75 2.00
166 Chuck Knoblauch .10 .30
167 Tino Martinez .20 .50
168 Paul O'Neill .20 .50
169 Andy Pettitte .20 .50
170 Mariano Rivera .30 .75
171 Darryl Strawberry .10 .30
172 David Wells .10 .30
173 Bernie Williams .20 .50
174 Ryan Christenson RC .10 .30
175 Jason Giambi .10 .30
176 Ben Grieve .10 .30
177 Rickey Henderson .30 .75
178 A.J. Hinch .10 .30
179 Kenny Rogers .10 .30
180 Ricky Bottalico .10 .30
181 Rico Brogna .10 .30
182 Doug Glanville .10 .30
183 Gregg Jefferies .10 .30
184 Mike Lieberthal .10 .30
185 Scott Rolen .20 .50
186 Curt Schilling .10 .30
187 Jermaine Allensworth .10 .30
188 Lou Collier .10 .30
189 Jose Guillen .10 .30
190 Jason Kendall .10 .30
191 Al Martin .10 .30
192 Tony Womack .10 .30
193 Kevin Young .10 .30
194 Royce Clayton .10 .30
195 Delino DeShields .10 .30
196 Gary Gaetti .10 .30
197 Ron Gant .10 .30
198 Brian Jordan .10 .30
199 Ray Lankford .10 .30
200 Mark McGwire .75 2.00
201 Todd Stottlemyre .10 .30
202 Kevin Brown .20 .50
203 Ken Caminiti .10 .30
204 Steve Finley .10 .30
205 Tony Gwynn .40 1.00
206 Carlos Hernandez .10 .30
207 Wally Joyner .10 .30
208 Greg Vaughn .10 .30
209 Barry Bonds .75 2.00
210 Shawn Estes .10 .30
211 Orel Hershiser .10 .30
212 Stan Javier .10 .30
213 Jeff Kent .10 .30
214 Bill Mueller .10 .30
215 Robb Nen .10 .30
216 J.T. Snow .10 .30
217 Jay Buhner .10 .30
218 Ken Cloude .10 .30
219 Joey Cora .10 .30
220 Ken Griffey Jr. .60 1.50
221 Glenallen Hill .10 .30
222 Randy Johnson .30 .75
223 Edgar Martinez .20 .50
224 Jamie Moyer .10 .30
225 Alex Rodriguez .50 1.25
226 David Segui .10 .30
227 Dan Wilson .10 .30
228 Rolando Arrojo RC .15 .40
229 Wade Boggs .20 .50
230 Miguel Cairo .10 .30

231 Roberto Hernandez .10 .30
232 Quinton McCracken .10 .30
233 Fred McGriff .20 .50
234 Paul Sorrento .10 .30
235 Kevin Stocker .10 .30
236 Will Clark .20 .50
237 Juan Gonzalez .10 .30
238 Rusty Greer .10 .30
239 Rick Helling .10 .30
240 Roberto Kelly .10 .30
241 Ivan Rodriguez .20 .50
242 Aaron Sele .10 .30
243 John Wetteland .10 .30
244 Jose Canseco .20 .50
245 Roger Clemens .60 1.50
246 Jose Cruz Jr. .10 .30
247 Carlos Delgado .10 .30
248 Alex Gonzalez .10 .30
249 Ed Sprague .10 .30
250 Shannon Stewart .10 .30
NNO Tony Gwynn Sample .40 1.00

1998 Pacific Omega Red

*STARS: 5X TO 12X BASIC CARDS
*ROOKIES: 2.5X TO 6X BASIC CARDS
STATED ODDS 1:4 RETAIL

1998 Pacific Omega EO Portraits

COMPLETE SET (20) 75.00 150.00
STATED ODDS 1:73
PORTRAIT 1 OF 1 PRINT RUN 1 #'d SET
PORT.1/1 NOT PRICED DUE TO SCARCITY
1 Cal Ripken 15.00 40.00
2 Nomar Garciaparra 8.00 20.00
3 Mo Vaughn 2.00 5.00
4 Frank Thomas 5.00 12.00
5 Manny Ramirez 3.00 8.00
6 Ben Grieve 2.00 5.00
7 Ken Griffey Jr. 10.00 25.00
8 Alex Rodriguez 8.00 20.00
9 Juan Gonzalez 2.00 5.00
10 Ivan Rodriguez 3.00 8.00
11 Travis Lee 2.00 5.00
12 Greg Maddux 8.00 20.00
13 Chipper Jones 5.00 12.00
14 Kerry Wood 2.50 6.00
15 Larry Walker 2.00 5.00
16 Jeff Bagwell 3.00 8.00
17 Mike Piazza 8.00 20.00
18 Mark McGwire 12.50 30.00
19 Tony Gwynn 6.00 15.00
20 Barry Bonds 12.50 30.00

1998 Pacific Omega Face To Face

COMPLETE SET (10) 75.00 150.00
STATED ODDS 1:145
1 A.Rodriguez 8.00 20.00
N.Garciaparra
2 M.McGwire 15.00 40.00
K.Griffey Jr.
3 M.Piazza 8.00 20.00
S.Alomar Jr.
4 K.Wood 10.00 25.00
R.Clemens
5 C.Ripken 15.00 40.00
P.Molitor
6 T.Gwynn 6.00 15.00
W.Boggs
7 C.Jones 5.00 12.00
F.Thomas
8 T.Lee 2.00 5.00
B.Grieve
9 H.Nomo 5.00 12.00
H.Irabu
10 J.Gonzalez 3.00 8.00
M.Ramirez

1998 Pacific Omega Online Inserts

COMPLETE SET (36) 60.00 120.00
STATED ODDS 4:37
1 Cal Ripken 6.00 15.00
2 Nomar Garciaparra 3.00 8.00
3 Pedro Martinez 1.25 3.00
4 Mo Vaughn .75 2.00
5 Frank Thomas 2.00 5.00
6 Sandy Alomar Jr. .75 2.00
7 Manny Ramirez 1.25 3.00
8 Jaret Wright .75 2.00
9 Paul Molitor .75 2.00
10 Derek Jeter 5.00 12.00
11 Bernie Williams 1.25 3.00
12 Ben Grieve .75 2.00
13 Ken Griffey Jr. 4.00 10.00
14 Edgar Martinez 1.25 3.00
15 Alex Rodriguez 3.00 8.00
16 Wade Boggs 1.25 3.00
17 Juan Gonzalez .75 2.00
18 Ivan Rodriguez 1.25 3.00
19 Roger Clemens 4.00 10.00
20 Travis Lee .75 2.00
21 Matt Williams .75 2.00
22 Andres Galarraga .75 2.00
23 Chipper Jones 2.00 5.00
24 Greg Maddux 3.00 8.00
25 Sammy Sosa 2.00 5.00
26 Kerry Wood 1.00 2.50
27 Barry Larkin 1.25 3.00
28 Larry Walker .75 2.00
29 Derrek Lee 1.25 3.00
30 Jeff Bagwell 1.25 3.00
31 Hideo Nomo 2.00 5.00
32 Mike Piazza 3.00 8.00
33 Scott Rolen 1.25 3.00
34 Mark McGwire 5.00 12.00
35 Tony Gwynn 2.50 6.00
36 Barry Bonds 5.00 12.00

1998 Pacific Omega Prisms

COMPLETE SET (20) 75.00 150.00
STATED ODDS 1:37
1 Cal Ripken 8.00 20.00
2 Nomar Garciaparra 4.00 10.00
3 Pedro Martinez 1.50 4.00
4 Frank Thomas 2.50 6.00
5 Manny Ramirez 1.50 4.00
6 Brian Giles 2.50 6.00
7 Derek Jeter 6.00 15.00
8 Ben Grieve 1.00 2.50
9 Ken Griffey Jr. 5.00 12.00
10 Alex Rodriguez 4.00 10.00
11 Juan Gonzalez 1.00 2.50
12 Travis Lee 1.00 2.50
13 Chipper Jones 2.50 6.00
14 Greg Maddux 4.00 10.00
15 Kerry Wood 1.25 3.00
16 Larry Walker 1.00 2.50
17 Hideo Nomo 2.50 6.00
18 Mike Piazza 4.00 10.00
19 Mark McGwire 6.00 15.00
20 Tony Gwynn 3.00 8.00

1998 Pacific Omega Rising Stars

COMPLETE SET (30) 20.00 50.00
STATED ODDS 4:37 HOBBY
*TIER 1: 2.5X TO 6X BASIC RS
TIER 1 PRINT RUN 100 SERIAL #'d SETS
TIER 1 CARDS ARE 2/10/16/19/20/25
*TIER 2: 3X TO 8X BASIC RS
TIER 2 PRINT RUN 75 SERIAL #'d SETS
TIER 2 CARDS ARE 3/12/18/23/26/27
*TIER 3: 4X TO 10X BASIC RS
TIER 3 PRINT RUN 50 SERIAL #'d SETS
TIER 3 CARDS ARE 1/7/15/17/22/28
*TIER 4: 6X TO 15X BASIC RS
TIER 4 PRINT RUN 25 SERIAL #'d SETS
TIER 4 CARDS ARE 6/9/11/14/21/29
TIER 5 STATED PRINT RUN 1 SET
TIER 5 CARDS ARE 4/5/8/13/24/30
TIER 5 NOT PRICED DUE TO SCARCITY
TIER 1-5: RANDOM INSERTS IN PACKS
1 N.Rodriguez .75 2.00
S.Ponson
2 F.Catalanotto 1.25 3.00
Duran
Runyan
3 K.Brown .75 2.00
C.Almanzar
4 A.Boone .75 2.00
Watkins
Winch
5 B.Meadows .75 2.00
Larkin
Alfonseca
6 T.Moore .75 2.00
S.Bennett
Stovall
7 F.Martinez .75 2.00
L.Sutton
B.Bevil
8 H.Bush .75 2.00
M.Buddie
9 R.Butler .75 2.00
E.Yan
10 D.Hollins .75 2.00
B.Edmondson
11 L.Collier .75 2.00
J.Silva
J.Martinez
12 S.Sinclair .75 2.00
M.Dalesandro
13 J.Varitek 2.00 5.00
B.Rose
B.Shouse
14 M.Caruso .75 2.00
J.Abbott
T.Fordh
15 B.Smith .75 2.00
J.Johnson
16 M.Kotsay .75 2.00
Berg
J.Sanchez
17 R.Hidalgo .75 2.00
Halama
T.Miller
18 G.Jenkins .75 2.00
Hughes
Woodard
19 E.Marrero .75 2.00
Politte
Busby
20 D.Relaford .75 2.00
D.Winston
21 T.Helton 1.25 3.00
B.Jones
22 R.Arrojo 2.00 5.00
M.Cairo
D.Carlson
23 D.Ortiz 2.50 6.00
J.Valentin
E.Milton
24 M.Ordonez/G.Norton 2.00 5.00
25 B.Fullmer .75 2.00
Vazquez
DeHart
26 P.Konerko .75 2.00
M.Luke
27 D.Lee 1.25 3.00
R.Jackson
Roskos
28 B.Grieve .75 2.00
Hinch
Christenson
29 T.Lee 1.25 3.00
K.Garcia
Dellucci
30 K.Wood 1.00 2.50
M.Pisciotta

1999 Pacific Omega

The 1999 Pacific Omega set was issued in one series for a total of 250 cards and distributed in six-card packs. The set features color player photos printed on silver foiled cards in a three-panel horizontal design. A Tony Gwynn Sample card was distributed to dealers and hobby media several weeks prior to the release of the product. The card can be readily identified by the bold "SAMPLE" text running across the back. An embossed stamped version of this same sample card was distributed exclusively at the 1999 Chicago Sportsfest card at the Pacific booth.

COMPLETE SET (250) 15.00 40.00
COMMON CARD (1-250) .10 .30
COMMON DUAL-PLAYER .15 .40
1 Garret Anderson .10 .30
2 Jim Edmonds .10 .30
3 Darin Erstad .10 .30
4 Chuck Finley .10 .30
5 Troy Glaus .20 .50
6 Troy Percival .10 .30
7 Chris Pritchett .10 .30
8 Tim Salmon .20 .50
9 Mo Vaughn .10 .30
10 Jay Bell .10 .30
11 Steve Finley .10 .30
12 Luis Gonzalez .10 .30
13 Randy Johnson .30 .75
14 Byung-Hyun Kim RC .40 1.00
15 Travis Lee .10 .30
16 Matt Williams .10 .30
17 Tony Womack .10 .30
18 Bret Boone .10 .30
19 Mark DeRosa .10 .30
20 Tom Glavine .20 .50
21 Andruw Jones .20 .50
22 Chipper Jones .30 .75
23 Brian Jordan .10 .30
24 Ryan Klesko .10 .30
25 Javy Lopez .10 .30
26 Greg Maddux .50 1.25
27 John Smoltz .20 .50
28 B.Chen .15 .40
O.Perez
29 Brady Anderson .10 .30
30 Harold Baines .10 .30
31 Albert Belle .10 .30
32 Will Clark .20 .50
33 Delino DeShields .10 .30
34 Jerry Hairston Jr. .10 .30
35 Charles Johnson .10 .30
36 Mike Mussina .20 .50
37 Cal Ripken 1.00 2.50
38 B.J. Surhoff .10 .30
39 Jin Ho Cho .10 .30
40 Nomar Garciaparra .50 1.25
41 Pedro Martinez .20 .50
42 Jose Offerman .10 .30
43 Troy O'Leary .10 .30
44 John Valentin .10 .30
45 Jason Varitek .30 .75
46 J.Pena RC .15 .40
B.Rose
47 Mark Grace .20 .50
48 Glenallen Hill .10 .30
49 Tyler Houston .10 .30
50 Mickey Morandini .10 .30
51 Henry Rodriguez .10 .30
52 Sammy Sosa .30 .75
53 Kevin Tapani .10 .30
54 Mike Caruso .10 .30
55 Ray Durham .10 .30
56 Paul Konerko .10 .30
57 Carlos Lee .10 .30
58 Magglio Ordonez .10 .30
59 Mike Sirotka .10 .30
60 Frank Thomas .30 .75
61 M.Johnson .15 .40
C.Singleton
62 Mike Cameron .10 .30
63 Sean Casey .10 .30
64 Pete Harnisch .10 .30
65 Barry Larkin .20 .50
66 Pokey Reese .10 .30
67 Greg Vaughn .10 .30
68 Scott Williamson .10 .30
69 Dmitri Young .10 .30
70 Roberto Alomar .20 .50
71 Sandy Alomar Jr. .10 .30
72 Travis Fryman .10 .30
73 David Justice .10 .30
74 Kenny Lofton .10 .30
75 Manny Ramirez .20 .50
76 Richie Sexson .10 .30
77 Jim Thome .20 .50
78 Omar Vizquel .20 .50
79 Jaret Wright .10 .30
80 Dante Bichette .10 .30
81 Vinny Castilla .10 .30
82 Todd Helton .20 .50
83 Darryl Hamilton .10 .30
84 Darryl Kile .10 .30
85 Neifi Perez .10 .30
86 Larry Walker .10 .30
87 Tony Clark .10 .30
88 Damion Easley .10 .30
89 Juan Encarnacion .10 .30
90 Bobby Higginson .10 .30
91 Gabe Kapler .10 .30
92 Dean Palmer .10 .30
93 Justin Thompson .10 .30
94 Jeff Weaver RC .25 .60
95 Bruce Aven .10 .30
96 Luis Castillo .10 .30
97 Alex Fernandez .10 .30
98 Cliff Floyd .10 .30
99 Alex Gonzalez .10 .30
100 Mark Kotsay .10 .30
101 Preston Wilson .10 .30
102 Moises Alou .10 .30
103 Jeff Bagwell .20 .50
104 Craig Biggio .20 .50
105 Derek Bell .10 .30
106 Mike Hampton .10 .30
107 Richard Hidalgo .10 .30
108 Jose Lima .10 .30
109 Billy Wagner .10 .30
110 R.Johnson .15 .40
D.Ward
111 Carlos Beltran .20 .50
112 Johnny Damon .20 .50
113 Jermaine Dye .10 .30
114 Carlos Febles .10 .30
115 Jeremy Giambi .10 .30
116 Joe Randa .10 .30
117 Mike Sweeney .10 .30
118 O.Moreno .15 .40
J.Santiago RC
119 Kevin Brown .20 .50
120 Todd Hundley .10 .30
121 Eric Karros .10 .30
122 Raul Mondesi .10 .30
123 Chan Ho Park .10 .30
124 Angel Pena .10 .30
125 Gary Sheffield .10 .30
126 Devon White .10 .30
127 Eric Young .10 .30
128 Ron Belliard .10 .30
129 Jeromy Burnitz .10 .30
130 Jeff Cirillo .10 .30
131 Marquis Grissom .10 .30
132 Geoff Jenkins .10 .30
133 David Nilsson .10 .30
134 Hideo Nomo .30 .75
135 Fernando Vina .10 .30
136 Ron Coomer .10 .30
137 Marty Cordova .10 .30
138 Corey Koskie .10 .30
139 Brad Radke .10 .30
140 Todd Walker .10 .30
141 C.Allen RC .15 .40
T.Hunter
142 C.Guzman .15 .40
J.Jones
143 Michael Barrett .10 .30
144 Orlando Cabrera .10 .30
145 Vladimir Guerrero .30 .75
146 Wilton Guerrero .10 .30
147 Ugueth Urbina .10 .30
148 Rondell White .10 .30
149 Chris Widger .10 .30
150 Edgardo Alfonzo .10 .30
151 Roger Cedeno .10 .30
152 Octavio Dotel .10 .30
153 Rickey Henderson .30 .75
154 John Olerud .10 .30
155 Rey Ordonez .10 .30
156 Mike Piazza .50 1.25
157 Robin Ventura .10 .30
158 Scott Brosius .10 .30
159 Roger Clemens .60 1.50
160 David Cone .10 .30
161 Chili Davis .10 .30
162 Orlando Hernandez .10 .30
163 Derek Jeter .75 2.00
164 Chuck Knoblauch .10 .30
165 Tino Martinez .20 .50
166 Paul O'Neill .20 .50
167 Bernie Williams .20 .50
168 Jason Giambi .10 .30
169 Ben Grieve .10 .30
170 Chad Harville RC .10 .30
171 Tim Hudson RC 1.00 2.50
172 Tony Phillips .10 .30
173 Kenny Rogers .10 .30
174 Matt Stairs .10 .30
175 Miguel Tejada .10 .30
176 E.Chavez .15 .40
O.Saenz
177 Bobby Abreu .10 .30
178 Ron Gant .10 .30
179 Doug Glanville .10 .30
180 Mike Lieberthal .10 .30
181 Desi Relaford .10 .30
182 Scott Rolen .20 .50
183 Curt Schilling .10 .30
184 M.Anderson .15 .40
R.Wolf
185 Brant Brown .10 .30
186 Brian Giles .10 .30
187 Jason Kendall .10 .30
188 Al Martin .10 .30
189 Ed Sprague .10 .30
190 Kevin Young .10 .30
191 K.Benson .15 .40
W.Morris
192 Kent Bottenfield .10 .30
193 Eric Davis .10 .30
194 J.D. Drew .10 .30
195 Ray Lankford .10 .30
196 Joe McEwing RC .10 .30
197 Mark McGwire .75 2.00
198 Edgar Renteria .10 .30
199 Fernando Tatis .10 .30
200 Andy Ashby .10 .30
201 Ben Davis .10 .30
202 Tony Gwynn .40 1.00
203 Trevor Hoffman .10 .30
204 Wally Joyner .10 .30
205 Gary Matthews Jr. .10 .30
206 Ruben Rivera .10 .30
207 Reggie Sanders .10 .30
208 Rich Aurilia .10 .30
209 Marvin Benard .10 .30
210 Barry Bonds .75 2.00
211 Ellis Burks .10 .30
212 Stan Javier .10 .30
213 Jeff Kent .10 .30
214 Robb Nen .10 .30
215 J.T. Snow .10 .30
216 Gil Meche .10 .30
217 David Bell .10 .30
218 Freddy Garcia RC .30 .75
219 Ken Griffey Jr. .60 1.50
220 Brian L.Hunter .10 .30
221 John Halama .10 .30
222 Edgar Martinez .20 .50
223 Jamie Moyer .10 .30
224 Alex Rodriguez .50 1.25
225 Jay Buhner .10 .30
226 Rolando Arrojo .10 .30
227 Wade Boggs .20 .50
228 Miguel Cairo .10 .30
229 Jose Canseco .20 .50
230 Dave Martinez .10 .30
231 Fred McGriff .20 .50
232 Kevin Stocker .10 .30
233 M.Duvall RC .15 .40
D.Lamb
234 Royce Clayton .10 .30
235 Juan Gonzalez .10 .30
236 Rusty Greer .10 .30
237 Ruben Mateo .10 .30
238 Rafael Palmeiro .20 .50
239 Ivan Rodriguez .20 .50
240 John Wetteland .10 .30
241 Todd Zeile .10 .30
242 Jeff Zimmerman RC .10 .30
243 Homer Bush .10 .30
244 Jose Cruz Jr. .10 .30
245 Carlos Delgado .10 .30
246 Tony Fernandez .10 .30
247 Shawn Green .10 .30
248 Shannon Stewart .10 .30
249 David Wells .10 .30
250 R.Halladay .40 1.00
B.Koch
S1 Tony Gwynn Sample .75 2.00
S1A T.Gwynn Samp. Stamp 2.00 5.00

1999 Pacific Omega Copper

*STARS: 8X TO 20X BASIC CARDS
*RC'S/DUAL: 5X TO 12X BASIC CARDS
RANDOM INSERTS IN HOBBY PACKS
STATED PRINT RUN 99 SERIAL #'d SETS

1999 Pacific Omega Gold

*STARS: 4X TO 10X BASIC CARDS
*RC'S/DUAL: 2X TO 5X BASIC CARDS
RANDOM INSERTS IN RETAIL PACKS
STATED PRINT RUN 299 SERIAL #'d SETS

1999 Pacific Omega Platinum Blue

*STARS: 10X TO 25X BASIC CARDS
*RC'S/DUAL: 6X TO 15X BASIC CARDS
RANDOM INSERTS IN ALL PACKS
STATED PRINT RUN 75 SERIAL #'d SETS

1999 Pacific Omega Premiere Date

*STARS: 12.5X TO 30X BASIC CARDS
*RC'S/DUAL: 8X TO 20X BASIC CARDS
ONE PER HOBBY BOX
STATED PRINT RUN 50 SERIAL #'d SETS

1999 Pacific Omega 5-Tool Talents

COMPLETE SET (30) 30.00 80.00
STATED ODDS 4:37
1 Randy Johnson 1.25 3.00
2 Greg Maddux 2.00 5.00
3 Pedro Martinez .75 2.00
4 Kevin Brown .75 2.00
5 Roger Clemens 2.50 6.00
6 Carlos Lee .50 1.25
7 Gabe Kapler .50 1.25
8 Carlos Beltran .75 2.00
9 J.D. Drew .50 1.25
10 Ruben Mateo .50 1.25
11 Chipper Jones 1.25 3.00
12 Sammy Sosa 1.25 3.00
13 Manny Ramirez .75 2.00
14 Vladimir Guerrero 1.25 3.00
15 Mark McGwire 3.00 8.00
16 Ken Griffey Jr. 2.50 6.00
17 Jose Canseco .75 2.00
18 Nomar Garciaparra 2.00 5.00
19 Frank Thomas 1.25 3.00
20 Larry Walker .50 1.25
21 Jeff Bagwell .75 2.00
22 Mike Piazza 2.00 5.00
23 Tony Gwynn 1.50 4.00
24 Juan Gonzalez .50 1.25
25 Cal Ripken 4.00 10.00
26 Derek Jeter 3.00 8.00
27 Scott Rolen .75 2.00
28 Barry Bonds 3.00 8.00
29 Alex Rodriguez 2.00 5.00
30 Ivan Rodriguez .75 2.00

1999 Pacific Omega 5-Tool Talents Tiers

*TIER 1: 2.5X TO 6X BASIC 5-TOOL
TIER 1 PRINT RUN 100 SERIAL #'d SETS
TIER 1 CARDS ARE 1/6/11/18/21/28
TIER 1 CARDS HAVE BLUE FOIL
*TIER 2: 3X TO 8X BASIC 5-TOOL
TIER 2 PRINT RUN 75 SERIAL #'d SETS
TIER 2 CARDS ARE 2/7/13/16/19/30
TIER 2 CARDS HAVE RED FOIL
*TIER 3: 5X TO 12X BASIC 5-TOOL
TIER 3 PRINT RUN 50 SERIAL #'d SETS
TIER 3 CARDS ARE 3/8/15/20/25/26
TIER 3 CARDS HAVE GREEN FOIL
*TIER 4: 8X TO 20X BASIC 5-TOOL
TIER 4 PRINT RUN 25 SERIAL #'d SETS
TIER 4 CARDS ARE 4/9/12/17/23/29
TIER 4 CARDS HAVE PURPLE FOIL
TIER 5 PRINT RUN 1 SERIAL #'d SET
TIER 5 CARDS ARE 5/10/14/22/24/27
TIER 5 CARDS HAVE GOLD FOIL
TIER 5 NO PRICING DUE TO SCARCITY

1999 Pacific Omega Debut Duos

COMPLETE SET (10) 60.00 120.00
STATED ODDS 1:145
1 N.Garciaparra 8.00 20.00
V.Guerrero
2 D.Jeter/A.Pettitte 12.50 30.00
3 G.Anderson/A.Rodriguez 8.00 20.00
4 C.Jones/R.Mondesi 5.00 12.00
5 P.Martinez/M.Piazza 8.00 20.00
6 M.Vaughn/B.Williams 3.00 8.00
7 J.Gonzalez/K.Griffey Jr. 10.00 25.00
8 S.Sosa/L.Walker 5.00 12.00
9 B.Bonds/M.McGwire 12.50 30.00
10 W.Boggs/T.Gwynn 6.00 15.00

1999 Pacific Omega Diamond Masters

COMPLETE SET (36) 40.00 100.00
STATED ODDS 4:37
1 Darin Erstad .60 1.50
2 Mo Vaughn .60 1.50
3 Matt Williams .60 1.50
4 Andruw Jones 1.00 2.50
5 Chipper Jones 1.50 4.00
6 Greg Maddux 2.50 6.00
7 Cal Ripken 5.00 12.00
8 Nomar Garciaparra 2.50 6.00
9 Pedro Martinez 1.00 2.50
10 Sammy Sosa 1.50 4.00
11 Frank Thomas 1.50 4.00
12 Kenny Lofton .60 1.50
13 Manny Ramirez 1.00 2.50
14 Larry Walker .60 1.50
15 Gabe Kapler .60 1.50
16 Jeff Bagwell 1.00 2.50
17 Craig Biggio 1.00 2.50
18 Raul Mondesi .60 1.50
19 Vladimir Guerrero 1.50 4.00
20 Mike Piazza 2.50 6.00
21 Roger Clemens 3.00 8.00
22 Derek Jeter 4.00 10.00
23 Bernie Williams 1.00 2.50
24 Scott Rolen 1.00 2.50
25 J.D. Drew .60 1.50
26 Mark McGwire 4.00 10.00
27 Fernando Tatis .60 1.50
28 Tony Gwynn 2.00 5.00
29 Barry Bonds 4.00 10.00
30 Ken Griffey Jr. 3.00 8.00
31 Alex Rodriguez 2.50 6.00
32 Jose Canseco 1.00 2.50
33 Juan Gonzalez .60 1.50
34 Ruben Mateo .60 1.50
35 Ivan Rodriguez 1.00 2.50
36 Shawn Green .60 1.50

1999 Pacific Omega EO Portraits

COMPLETE SET (20) 125.00 250.00
STATED ODDS 1:73
EO PORTRAIT 1 OF 1 PARALLELS EXIST
EO PORT.1 OF 1'S TOO SCARCE TO PRICE
1 Mo Vaughn 2.00 5.00
2 Chipper Jones 5.00 12.00
3 Greg Maddux 8.00 20.00
4 Cal Ripken 15.00 40.00
5 Nomar Garciaparra 8.00 20.00
6 Sammy Sosa 5.00 12.00
7 Frank Thomas 5.00 12.00
8 Manny Ramirez 3.00 8.00
9 Jeff Bagwell 3.00 8.00
10 Mike Piazza 8.00 20.00
11 Roger Clemens 10.00 25.00
12 Derek Jeter 12.50 30.00
13 Scott Rolen 3.00 8.00
14 Mark McGwire 12.50 30.00
15 Tony Gwynn 6.00 15.00
16 Barry Bonds 12.50 30.00
17 Ken Griffey Jr. 10.00 25.00
18 Alex Rodriguez 8.00 20.00
19 Jose Canseco 3.00 8.00
20 Juan Gonzalez 2.00 5.00

1999 Pacific Omega Hit Machine 3000

COMPLETE SET (20) 60.00 120.00
COMMON CARD (1-20) 4.00 10.00
RANDOM INSERTS IN PACKS
STATED PRINT RUN 3000 SERIAL #'d SETS
CARD 21 DIST.AT '99 SPORTSFEST SHOW
21 T.Gwynn Philly Sportsfest 6.00 15.00

1999 Pacific Omega HR 99

COMPLETE SET (20) 40.00 100.00
STATED ODDS 1:37
1 Mo Vaughn 1.00 2.50
2 Matt Williams 1.00 2.50
3 Chipper Jones 2.50 6.00
4 Albert Belle 1.00 2.50
5 Nomar Garciaparra 4.00 10.00
6 Sammy Sosa 2.50 6.00
7 Frank Thomas 2.50 6.00
8 Manny Ramirez 1.50 4.00
9 Jeff Bagwell 1.50 4.00
10 Raul Mondesi 1.00 2.50
11 Vladimir Guerrero 2.50 6.00
12 Mike Piazza 4.00 10.00
13 Derek Jeter 6.00 15.00
14 Mark McGwire 6.00 15.00
15 Fernando Tatis 1.00 2.50
16 Barry Bonds 6.00 15.00
17 Ken Griffey Jr. 5.00 12.00
18 Alex Rodriguez 4.00 10.00
19 Jose Canseco 1.50 4.00
20 Juan Gonzalez 1.00 2.50

1999 Pacific Omega Players Choice

These cards, which parallel the regular Pacific Omega set, were distributed with a special "Players Choice" logo at the Players Choice award ceremony. We have listed these cards in skip number order to match their regular number in the set. And since they were all printed in different numbers we have printed the print run next to the players name.

68 Scott Williamson/45 3.00 8.00
97 Alex Fernandez/45 3.00 8.00
101 Preston Wilson/45 3.00 8.00
111 Carlos Beltran/40 3.00 8.00
192 Kent Bottenfeld/45 3.00 8.00
218 Freddy Garcia/28 5.00 12.00
238 Rafael Palmeiro/40 5.00 12.00
242 Jeff Zimmerman/45 3.00 8.00

2000 Pacific Omega

COMP.SET w/o SP's (150) 8.00 20.00
COMMON CARD (1-150) .12 .30
COMMON CARD (151-255) .50 1.25
151-255 RANDOM INSERTS IN PACKS
151-255 PRINT RUN 999 SERIAL #'d SETS
1 Garret Anderson .12 .30
2 Darin Erstad .12 .30
3 Troy Glaus .12 .30
4 Tim Salmon .12 .30
5 Mo Vaughn .12 .30
6 Jay Bell .12 .30
7 Steve Finley .12 .30
8 Luis Gonzalez .12 .30
9 Randy Johnson .30 .75
10 Matt Williams .12 .30
11 Andres Galarraga .20 .50
12 Andruw Jones .12 .30
13 Chipper Jones .30 .75
14 Brian Jordan .12 .30
15 Greg Maddux .40 1.00
16 B.J. Surhoff .12 .30
17 Brady Anderson .12 .30
18 Albert Belle .12 .30
19 Mike Mussina .20 .50
20 Cal Ripken 1.00 2.50
21 Carl Everett .12 .30
22 Nomar Garciaparra .20 .50
23 Pedro Martinez .20 .50
24 Jason Varitek .30 .75
25 Mark Grace .20 .50
26 Sammy Sosa .30 .75
27 Rondell White .12 .30
28 Kerry Wood .12 .30
29 Eric Young .12 .30
30 Ray Durham .12 .30
31 Carlos Lee .12 .30
32 Magglio Ordonez .20 .50
33 Frank Thomas .30 .75
34 Sean Casey .12 .30
35 Ken Griffey Jr. .60 1.50
36 Barry Larkin .20 .50
37 Pokey Reese .12 .30
38 Roberto Alomar .20 .50
39 Kenny Lofton .12 .30
40 Manny Ramirez .30 .75
41 David Segui .12 .30
42 Jim Thome .20 .50
43 Omar Vizquel .20 .50
44 Jeff Cirillo .12 .30
45 Jeffrey Hammonds .12 .30
46 Todd Helton .20 .50
47 Todd Hollandsworth .12 .30
48 Larry Walker .20 .50
49 Tony Clark .12 .30
50 Juan Encarnacion .12 .30
51 Juan Gonzalez .12 .30
52 Bobby Higginson .12 .30
53 Hideo Nomo .30 .75
54 Dean Palmer .12 .30
55 Luis Castillo .12 .30
56 Cliff Floyd .12 .30
57 Derrek Lee .12 .30
58 Mike Lowell .12 .30
59 Henry Rodriguez .12 .30
60 Preston Wilson .12 .30
61 Moises Alou .12 .30
62 Jeff Bagwell .20 .50
63 Craig Biggio .20 .50
64 Ken Caminiti .12 .30
65 Richard Hidalgo .12 .30
66 Carlos Beltran .20 .50
67 Johnny Damon .20 .50
68 Jermaine Dye .12 .30
69 Joe Randa .12 .30
70 Mike Sweeney .12 .30
71 Adrian Beltre .30 .75
72 Kevin Brown .12 .30
73 Shawn Green .12 .30
74 Eric Karros .12 .30
75 Chan Ho Park .20 .50
76 Gary Sheffield .12 .30
77 Ron Belliard .12 .30
78 Jeromy Burnitz .12 .30
79 Geoff Jenkins .12 .30
80 Richie Sexson .12 .30
81 Ron Coomer .12 .30
82 Jacque Jones .12 .30
83 Corey Koskie .12 .30
84 Matt Lawton .12 .30
85 Vladimir Guerrero .20 .50
86 Lee Stevens .12 .30
87 Jose Vidro .12 .30
88 Edgardo Alfonzo .12 .30
89 Derek Bell .12 .30
90 Mike Bordick .12 .30
91 Mike Piazza .30 .75
92 Robin Ventura .12 .30
93 Jose Canseco .20 .50
94 Roger Clemens .40 1.00
95 Orlando Hernandez .12 .30
96 Derek Jeter .75 2.00
97 David Justice .12 .30
98 Tino Martinez .12 .30
99 Jorge Posada .20 .50
100 Bernie Williams .20 .50
101 Eric Chavez .12 .30
102 Jason Giambi .12 .30
103 Ben Grieve .12 .30
104 Miguel Tejada .20 .50
105 Bobby Abreu .12 .30
106 Doug Glanville .12 .30
107 Travis Lee .12 .30
108 Mike Lieberthal .12 .30
109 Scott Rolen .20 .50
110 Brian Giles .12 .30
111 Jason Kendall .12 .30
112 Warren Morris .12 .30
113 Kevin Young .12 .30
114 Will Clark .20 .50
115 J.D. Drew .12 .30
116 Jim Edmonds .12 .30
117 Mark McGwire .50 1.25
118 Edgar Renteria .12 .30
119 Fernando Tatis .12 .30
120 Fernando Vina .12 .30
121 Bret Boone .12 .30
122 Tony Gwynn .30 .75
123 Trevor Hoffman .20 .50
124 Phil Nevin .12 .30
125 Eric Owens .12 .30
126 Barry Bonds .50 1.25
127 Ellis Burks .12 .30
128 Jeff Kent .12 .30
129 J.T. Snow .12 .30
130 Jay Buhner .12 .30

131 Mike Cameron .12 .30
132 Rickey Henderson .30 .75
133 Edgar Martinez .20 .50
134 John Olerud .12 .30
135 Alex Rodriguez .40 1.00
136 Kazuhiro Sasaki RC .30 .75
137 Fred McGriff .20 .50
138 Greg Vaughn .12 .30
139 Gerald Williams .12 .30
140 Rusty Greer .12 .30
141 Gabe Kapler .12 .30
142 Ricky Ledee .12 .30
143 Rafael Palmeiro .20 .50
144 Ivan Rodriguez .20 .50
145 Tony Batista .12 .30
146 Jose Cruz Jr. .12 .30
147 Carlos Delgado .12 .30
148 Brad Fullmer .12 .30
149 Shannon Stewart .12 .30
150 David Wells .12 .30
151 J.Alvarez .50 1.25
J.DaVanon RC
152 S.Etherton .50 1.25
A.Kennedy
153 R.Ortiz .50 1.25
L.Pote
154 D.Turnbow RC .50 1.25
E.Weaver
155 R.Barajas .50 1.25
J.Conti
156 B.Kim .50 1.25
R.Ryan
157 D.Cortes RC .50 1.25
G.Lombard
158 I.Coffie .50 1.25
M.Mora
159 R.Kohlmeier .50 1.25
L.Matos RC
160 W.Morales .50 1.25
J.Parrish RC
161 C.Richard .50 1.25
J.Spurgeon RC
162 I.Alcantara .50 1.25
T.Ohka RC
163 P.Crawford .50 1.25
S.Lee RC
164 M.Mahoney RC .50 1.25
W.Veras
165 D.Garibay .50 1.25
R.Gload RC
166 G.Matthews Jr. .50 1.25
P.Norton
167 R.Brown .50 1.25
R.Quevedo
168 L.Barcelo .50 1.25
R.Biddle RC
169 M.Buehrle RC 4.00 10.00
J.Garland
170 A.Myette .50 1.25
J.Paul
171 K.Wells .50 1.25
K.Wunsch
172 R.Bell .50 1.25
T.Dawkins
173 H.Mercado .50 1.25
J.Riedling RC
174 R.Branyan .50 1.25
S.DePaula RC
175 M.Watson RC .50 1.25
T.Drew
176 C.House RC .50 1.25
B.Petrick
177 R.Fick .50 1.25
J.Macias
178 J.Cardona .50 1.25
B.Villafuerte RC
179 A.Almanza .50 1.25
A.Burnett
180 R.Castro .50 1.25
P.Ozuna
181 L.Berkman .75 2.00
J.Green
182 J.Lugo .50 1.25
T.McKnight
183 M.Meluskey .50 1.25
W.Miller
184 C.Durbin .50 1.25
H.Ortiz RC
185 D.Brown .50 1.25
M.Quinn
186 E.Gagne .50 1.25
M.Judd
187 K.Davis RC .50 1.25
V.DeLosSantos
188 S.Perez .50 1.25
P.Rigdon RC
189 M.Kinney .50 1.25
M.LeCroy
190 J.Maxwell .50 1.25
A.Pierzynski
191 J.Romero 8.00 20.00
J.Santana RC
192 T.Armas Jr. .50 1.25
P.Bergeron
193 M.Blank .50 1.25
M.Bradley
194 T.De La Rosa .50 1.25
S.Forster RC
195 Y.Lara .50 1.25
T.Nunnari RC
196 B.Schneider .50 1.25
A.Tracy RC
197 S.Strickland .50 1.25
T.Tucker
198 E.Cammack .50 1.25
J.Mann RC
199 G.Roberts .50 1.25
J.Toca
200 A.Soriano 1.25 3.00
J.Tessmer
201 T.Long .50 1.25
M.Mulder
202 P.Burrell .50 1.25
C.Pollitte
203 J.Anderson .50 1.25
B.Arroyo
204 M.Darr .50 1.25
K.DeHaan
205 A.Eaton .50 1.25
W.Gonzalez
206 B.Kolb .50 1.25
K.Walker RC
207 D.Minor .50 1.25
C.Murray
208 K.Hodges 6.00 15.00
J.Pineiro RC
209 R.Ramsay 1.25 3.00
K.Sasaki
210 R.Ankiel .75 2.00
M.Matthews
211 S.Cox .50 1.25
T.Harper
212 K.Kelly .50 1.25
D.Rolls RC
213 D.Davis .50 1.25
S.Sheldon
214 B.Sikorski .50 1.25
P.Valdes
215 F.Cordero .50 1.25
B.Waszgis RC
216 J.Phelps .50 1.25
M.DeWitt RC
217 V.Wells .50 1.25
D.Wise
218 G.Guzman RC .50 1.25
J.Marquis
219 R.Furcal .75 2.00
S.Sisco RC
220 B.Ryan .50 1.25
K.Beirne
221 M.Ginter RC .50 1.25
B.Penny
222 J.Zuleta RC .50 1.25
E.Munson
223 D.Reichert .50 1.25
J.Williams RC
224 J.LaRue .50 1.25
D.Ardoin RC
225 R.King .50 1.25
M.Redman
226 J.Crede .50 1.25
M.Bell
227 J.Pierre RC 2.50 6.00
J.Payton
228 W.Franklin .50 1.25
R.Choate RC
229 C.Truby .50 1.25
A.Piatt
230 K.Nicholson .50 1.25
C.Woodward
231 B.Zito 4.00 10.00
J.Boyd RC
232 B.O'Connor RC .50 1.25
M.Del Toro
233 C.Guillen .50 1.25
A.Huff
234 C.Hermansen .50 1.25
J.Tyner
235 A.Fultz 5.00 12.00
R.Vogelsong RC
236 S.Wooten .50 1.25
V.Wilson
237 D.Klassen .50 1.25
M.Lamb RC
238 C.Bradford .50 1.25
G.Stechshulte RC
239 Villegas .50 1.25
Ramirez
Will
Vizc
240 Garcia .50 1.25
Guzman
Brun
Coco
241 F.Charles .50 1.25
K.McDonald RC
242 C.Casimiro .50 1.25
M.Burkhart RC
243 R.Gonzalez RC .50 1.25
S.Gilbert
244 D.Einertson .50 1.25
J.Sparks RC
245 E.Byrnes RC .50 1.25
B.Clark
246 L.Estrella RC .50 1.25
C.Greene
247 T.Coquillette 1.25 3.00
P.Feliz RC
248 T.Redman RC .50 1.25
D.Newhan
249 R.Lopez .50 1.25
J.Bale RC
250 C.Patterson .50 1.25
J.Ortiz RC
251 B.Reames .50 1.25
O.Mairena RC
252 X.Nady 1.25 3.00
T.Perez RC
253 T.Jacquez 1.25 3.00
V.Padilla RC
254 E.Pena .50 1.25
A.Melhuse RC
255 B.Weber .50 1.25
A.Cabrera RC

2000 Pacific Omega Copper

*COPPER: 15X TO 30X BASIC
STATED ODDS 1:73 HOBBY
STATED PRINT RUN 45 SERIAL #'d SETS

2000 Pacific Omega Gold

*GOLD 1-150: 4X TO 10X BASIC
STATED ODDS 1:37 RETAIL
STATED PRINT RUN 120 SERIAL #'d SETS

2000 Pacific Omega Platinum Blue

*PLAT.BLUE 1-150: 6X TO 15X BASIC
STATED ODDS 1:145
STATED PRINT RUN 55 SERIAL #'d SETS

2000 Pacific Omega Premiere Date

*PREM.DATE 1-150: 4X TO 10X BASIC
STATED ODDS: 1:37 HOBBY
STATED PRINT RUN 77 SERIAL #'d SETS

2000 Pacific Omega AL/NL Contenders

COMPLETE AL SET (18) 10.00 25.00
COMPLETE NL SET (18) 10.00 25.00
STATED ODDS 2:37
AL1 Darin Erstad .40 1.00
AL2 Troy Glaus .40 1.00
AL3 Mo Vaughn .40 1.00
AL4 Albert Belle .40 1.00
AL5 Cal Ripken 3.00 8.00
AL6 Nomar Garciaparra .60 1.50
AL7 Pedro Martinez .60 1.50
AL8 Frank Thomas 1.00 2.50
AL9 Manny Ramirez 1.00 2.50
AL10 Jim Thome .60 1.50
AL11 Juan Gonzalez .40 1.00
AL12 Roger Clemens 1.25 3.00
AL13 Derek Jeter 2.50 6.00
AL14 Bernie Williams .60 1.50
AL15 Jason Giambi .40 1.00
AL16 Alex Rodriguez 1.25 3.00
AL17 Edgar Martinez .60 1.50
AL18 Carlos Delgado .40 1.00
NL1 Randy Johnson 1.00 2.50
NL2 Chipper Jones 1.00 2.50
NL3 Greg Maddux 1.25 3.00
NL4 Sammy Sosa 1.00 2.50
NL5 Sean Casey .40 1.00
NL6 Ken Griffey Jr. 2.00 5.00
NL7 Todd Helton .60 1.50
NL8 Jeff Bagwell .60 1.50
NL9 Shawn Green .40 1.00
NL10 Gary Sheffield .40 1.00
NL11 Vladimir Guerrero .60 1.50
NL12 Mike Piazza 1.00 2.50
NL13 Scott Rolen .60 1.50
NL14 Rick Ankiel .60 1.50
NL15 J.D. Drew .40 1.00
NL16 Jim Edmonds .40 1.00
NL17 Mark McGwire 1.50 4.00
NL18 Barry Bonds 1.50 4.00

2000 Pacific Omega EO Portraits

COMPLETE SET (20) 30.00 60.00
STATED ODDS 1:73
ONE OF ONE PARALLEL RANDOM IN PACKS
ONE OF ONE PRINT RUN 1 SERIAL #'d SET
NO ONE OF ONE PRICING AVAILABLE
1 Chipper Jones 1.50 4.00
2 Greg Maddux 2.00 5.00
3 Cal Ripken 5.00 12.00
4 Pedro Martinez 1.00 2.50
5 Nomar Garciaparra 1.00 2.50
6 Sammy Sosa 1.50 4.00
7 Frank Thomas 1.50 4.00
8 Ken Griffey Jr. 3.00 8.00
9 Gary Sheffield .60 1.50
10 Vladimir Guerrero 1.00 2.50
11 Mike Piazza 1.50 4.00
12 Roger Clemens 2.00 5.00
13 Derek Jeter 4.00 10.00
14 Pat Burrell .60 1.50
15 Rick Ankiel .60 1.50
16 Mark McGwire 2.50 6.00
17 Tony Gwynn 1.50 4.00
18 Barry Bonds 2.50 6.00
19 Alex Rodriguez 2.00 5.00
20 Ivan Rodriguez 1.00 2.50

2000 Pacific Omega Full Count

COMPLETE SET (36) 20.00 50.00
STATED ODDS 4:37 HOBBY
1 Magglio Ordonez .60 1.50
2 Manny Ramirez 1.00 2.50
3 Todd Helton .60 1.50
4 David Justice .40 1.00
5 Bernie Williams .60 1.50
6 Jason Giambi .40 1.00
7 Scott Rolen .60 1.50
8 Jeff Kent .40 1.00
9 Edgar Martinez .60 1.50
10 Randy Johnson 1.00 2.50
11 Greg Maddux 1.25 3.00
12 Mike Mussina .60 1.50
13 Pedro Martinez .60 1.50
14 Chuck Finley .40 1.00
15 Kevin Brown .40 1.00
16 Roger Clemens 1.25 3.00
17 Tim Hudson .60 1.50
18 Rick Ankiel .60 1.50
19 Troy Glaus .40 1.00
20 Chipper Jones 1.00 2.50
21 Nomar Garciaparra .60 1.50
22 Jeff Bagwell .60 1.50
23 Shawn Green .40 1.00
24 Vladimir Guerrero .60 1.50
25 Mike Piazza 1.00 2.50
26 Jim Edmonds .40 1.00
27 Rafael Palmeiro .60 1.50
28 Cal Ripken 3.00 8.00
29 Sammy Sosa 1.00 2.50
30 Frank Thomas 1.00 2.50
31 Ken Griffey Jr. 2.00 5.00
32 Gary Sheffield .40 1.00
33 Barry Bonds 1.50 4.00
34 Alex Rodriguez 1.25 3.00
35 Mark McGwire 1.50 4.00
36 Carlos Delgado .40 1.00

2000 Pacific Omega MLB Generations

COMPLETE SET (20) 75.00 150.00
STATED ODDS 1:145
1 M.McGwire 6.00 15.00
P.Burrell
2 C.Ripken 12.00 30.00
A.Rodriguez
3 R.Johnson 4.00 10.00
R.Ankiel
4 T.Gwynn 4.00 10.00
D.Erstad
5 B.Bonds 6.00 15.00
M.Ordonez
6 F.Thomas 4.00 10.00
J.Giambi
7 R.Clemens 5.00 12.00
K.Wood
8 M.Piazza 4.00 10.00
M.Meluskey
9 K.Griffey Jr. 8.00 20.00
A.Jones
10 B.Williams 2.50 6.00
J.Drew
11 C.Jones 4.00 10.00
T.Glaus
12 A.Galarraga 2.50 6.00
T.Helton
13 J.Gonzalez 2.50 6.00
V.Guerrero
14 C.Biggio 2.50 6.00
R.Furcal
15 S.Sosa 4.00 10.00
J.Dye
16 L.Walker 2.50 6.00
R.Hidalgo
17 G.Maddux 5.00 12.00
A.Eaton
18 B.Larkin 10.00 25.00
D.Jeter
19 R.Alomar 2.50 6.00
J.Vidro
20 J.Kent 1.50 4.00
E.Alfonzo

2000 Pacific Omega Signatures

1 Darin Erstad 10.00 25.00
2 Nomar Garciaparra 10.00 25.00
4 Magglio Ordonez 6.00 15.00
5 Frank Thomas 20.00 50.00
6 Brady Clark 10.00 25.00
7 Richard Hidalgo 6.00 15.00
8 Gary Sheffield 6.00 15.00
9 Pat Burrell 10.00 25.00
10 Jim Edmonds 15.00 40.00

2000 Pacific Omega Stellar Performers

COMPLETE SET (20) 30.00 60.00
STATED ODDS 1:37
1 Darin Erstad .60 1.50
2 Chipper Jones 1.50 4.00
3 Greg Maddux 2.00 5.00
4 Cal Ripken 5.00 12.00
5 Pedro Martinez 1.00 2.50
6 Nomar Garciaparra 1.00 2.50
7 Sammy Sosa 1.50 4.00
8 Frank Thomas 1.50 4.00
9 Ken Griffey Jr. 3.00 8.00
10 Todd Helton 1.00 2.50
11 Jeff Bagwell 1.00 2.50
12 Vladimir Guerrero 1.00 2.50
13 Mike Piazza 1.50 4.00
14 Derek Jeter 4.00 10.00
15 Roger Clemens 2.00 5.00
16 Tony Gwynn 1.50 4.00
17 Barry Bonds 2.50 6.00
18 Alex Rodriguez 2.00 5.00
19 Mark McGwire 2.50 6.00
20 Ivan Rodriguez 1.00 2.50

1998 Pacific Online

The 1998 Pacific Online set was issued in one series totalling 800 cards, but numbered to only 780. To add some spice to the set, the manufacturer decided to create two versions of twenty top stars. These cards are designed and (unfortunately) numbered identically, but feature totally different photos on both the front and back. For simplification to checklisting, we've added A and B suffixes to these cards, and added descriptions of the photos in an attempt to differentiate them. Cards were initially distributed in nine-card packs with an SRP of $1.49. An unnumbered Tony Gwynn Sample card (featuring entirely different photos and cardback text from the regular issue Gwynn cards) was distributed in dealer order forms several weeks prior to the products shipping date. Notable Rookie Cards include Kevin Millwood and Magglio Ordonez.

COMPLETE SET (800) 100.00 200.00
DUAL VERSIONS EXIST FOR FOLLOWING:
41/63/67/101/113/157/182/260/311/485/505
530/621/637/655/686/693/704/732/743
1 Garret Anderson .15 .40
2 Rich DeLucia .15 .40
3 Jason Dickson .15 .40
4 Gary DiSarcina .15 .40
5 Jim Edmonds .15 .40
6 Darin Erstad .15 .40
7 Cecil Fielder .15 .40
8 Chuck Finley .15 .40
9 Carlos Garcia .15 .40
10 Shigetoshi Hasegawa .15 .40
11 Ken Hill .15 .40
13 Mike Holtz .15 .40
14 Mike James .15 .40
15 Norberto Martin .15 .40
16 Damon Mashore .15 .40
17 Jack McDowell .15 .40
18 Phil Nevin .15 .40
19 Omar Olivares .15 .40
20 Troy Percival .15 .40
21 Rich Robertson .15 .40
22 Tim Salmon .25 .60
23 Craig Shipley .15 .40
24 Matt Walbeck .15 .40
25 Allen Watson .15 .40
26 Jim Edmonds TC .15 .40
27 Brian Anderson .15 .40
28 Tony Batista .15 .40
29 Jay Bell .15 .40
30 Andy Benes .15 .40
31 Yamil Benitez .15 .40
32 Willie Blair .15 .40
33 Brent Brede .15 .40
34 Scott Brow .15 .40
35 Omar Daal .15 .40
36 Dave Dellucci RC .40 1.00
37 Edwin Diaz .15 .40
38 Jorge Fabregas .15 .40
39 Andy Fox .15 .40
40 Karim Garcia .15 .40
41 Travis Lee* .15 .40
41A T.Lee Hitting .15 .40
42 Barry Manuel .15 .40
43 Gregg Olson .15 .40
44 Felix Rodriguez .15 .40
45 Clint Sodowsky .15 .40
46 Russ Springer .15 .40
47 Andy Stankiewicz .15 .40
48 Kelly Stinnett .15 .40
49 Jeff Suppan .15 .40
50 Devon White .15 .40
51 Matt Williams .15 .40
52 Travis Lee TC .15 .40
53 Danny Bautista .15 .40
54 Rafael Belliard .15 .40
55 Adam Butler RC .15 .40
56 Mike Cather RC .15 .40
57 Brian Edmondson .15 .40
58 Alan Embree .15 .40
59 Andres Galarraga .15 .40
60 Tom Glavine .25 .60
61 Tony Graffanino .15 .40
62 Andruw Jones .25 .60
63 Chipper Jones* .40 1.00
63A C.Jones Hitting .40 1.00
64 Ryan Klesko .15 .40
65 Keith Lockhart .15 .40
66 Javy Lopez .15 .40
67 Greg Maddux* .60 1.50
67A G.Maddux Pitching .60 1.50
68 Dennis Martinez .15 .40
69 Kevin Millwood RC .60 1.50
70 Denny Neagle .15 .40
71 Eddie Perez .15 .40
72 Curtis Pride .15 .40
73 John Smoltz .25 .60
74 Michael Tucker .15 .40
75 Walt Weiss .15 .40
76 Gerald Williams .15 .40
77 Mark Wohlers .15 .40
78 Chipper Jones TC .25 .60
79 Roberto Alomar .25 .60
80 Brady Anderson .15 .40
81 Harold Baines .15 .40
82 Armando Benitez .15 .40
83 Mike Bordick .15 .40
84 Joe Carter .15 .40
85 Norm Charlton .15 .40
86 Eric Davis .15 .40
87 Doug Drabek .15 .40
88 Scott Erickson .15 .40
89 Jeffrey Hammonds .15 .40
90 Chris Hoiles .15 .40
91 Scott Kamieniecki .15 .40
92 Jimmy Key .15 .40
93 Terry Mathews .15 .40
94 Alan Mills .15 .40
95 Mike Mussina .25 .60
96 Jesse Orosco .15 .40
97 Rafael Palmeiro .25 .60
98 Sidney Ponson .15 .40
99 Jeff Reboulet .15 .40
100 Arthur Rhodes .15 .40
101 Cal Ripken* 1.25 3.00
101A C.Ripken Hitting Close-Up 1.25 3.00
102 Nerio Rodriguez .15 .40
103 B.J. Surhoff .15 .40
104 Lenny Webster .15 .40
105 Cal Ripken TC .60 1.50
106 Steve Avery .15 .40
107 Mike Benjamin .15 .40
108 Darren Bragg .15 .40
109 Damon Buford .15 .40
110 Jim Corsi .15 .40
111 Dennis Eckersley .15 .40
112 Rich Garces .15 .40
113 Nomar Garciaparra* .60 1.50
113A N.Garciaparra Hitting .60 1.50
114 Tom Gordon .15 .40
115 Scott Hatteberg .15 .40
116 Butch Henry .15 .40
117 Reggie Jefferson .15 .40
118 Mark Lemke .15 .40
119 Darren Lewis .15 .40
120 Jim Leyritz .15 .40
121 Derek Lowe .15 .40
122 Pedro Martinez .25 .60
123 Troy O'Leary .15 .40
124 Brian Rose .15 .40
125 Bret Saberhagen .15 .40
126 Donnie Sadler .15 .40
127 Brian Shouse RC .25 .60
128 John Valentin .15 .40
129 Jason Varitek .40 1.00
130 Mo Vaughn .15 .40
131 Tim Wakefield .15 .40
132 John Wasdin .15 .40
133 Nomar Garciaparra TC .40 1.00
134 Terry Adams .15 .40
135 Manny Alexander .15 .40
136 Rod Beck .15 .40
137 Jeff Blauser .15 .40
138 Brant Brown .15 .40
139 Mark Clark .15 .40
140 Jeremi Gonzalez .15 .40
141 Mark Grace .25 .60
142 Jose Hernandez .15 .40
143 Tyler Houston .15 .40
144 Lance Johnson .15 .40
145 Sandy Martinez .15 .40
146 Matt Mieske .15 .40
147 Mickey Morandini .15 .40
148 Terry Mulholland .15 .40
149 Kevin Orie .15 .40
150 Bob Patterson .15 .40
151 Marc Pisciotta RC .15 .40
152 Henry Rodriguez .15 .40
153 Scott Servais .15 .40
154 Sammy Sosa .40 1.00
155 Kevin Tapani .15 .40
156 Steve Trachsel .15 .40
157 Kerry Wood* .20 .50
157A K.Wood Pitching Close-Up .20 .50
158 Kerry Wood TC .10 .30
159 Jeff Abbott .15 .40
160 James Baldwin .15 .40
161 Albert Belle .15 .40
162 Jason Bere .15 .40
163 Mike Cameron .15 .40
164 Mike Caruso .15 .40
165 Carlos Castillo .15 .40
166 Tony Castillo .15 .40
167 Ray Durham .15 .40
168 Scott Eyre .15 .40
169 Tom Fordham .15 .40
170 Keith Foulke .15 .40
171 Lou Frazier .15 .40
172 Matt Karchner .15 .40
173 Chad Kreuter .15 .40
174 Jaime Navarro .15 .40
175 Greg Norton .15 .40
176 Charlie O'Brien .15 .40
177 Magglio Ordonez RC 1.25 3.00
178 Ruben Sierra .15 .40
179 Bill Simas .15 .40
180 Mike Sirotka .15 .40
181 Chris Snopek .15 .40
182 Frank Thomas* .40 1.00
182A F.Thomas Swing .40 1.00
183 Robin Ventura .15 .40
184 Frank Thomas TC .25 .60
185 Stan Belinda .15 .40
186 Aaron Boone .15 .40
187 Bret Boone .15 .40
188 Brook Fordyce .15 .40
189 Willie Greene .15 .40
190 Pete Harnisch .15 .40
191 Lenny Harris .15 .40
192 Mark Hutton .15 .40
193 Damian Jackson .15 .40
194 Ricardo Jordan .15 .40
195 Barry Larkin .25 .60
196 Eduardo Perez .15 .40
197 Pokey Reese .15 .40
198 Mike Remlinger .15 .40
199 Reggie Sanders .15 .40
200 Jeff Shaw .15 .40
201 Chris Stynes .15 .40
202 Scott Sullivan .15 .40
203 Eddie Taubensee .15 .40
204 Brett Tomko .15 .40
205 Pat Watkins .15 .40
206 David Weathers .15 .40
207 Gabe White .15 .40
208 Scott Winchester .15 .40
209 Barry Larkin TC .15 .40
210 Sandy Alomar Jr. .15 .40
211 Paul Assenmacher .15 .40
212 Geronimo Berroa .15 .40
213 Pat Borders .15 .40
214 Jeff Branson .15 .40
215 Dave Burba .15 .40
216 Bartolo Colon .15 .40
217 Shawon Dunston .15 .40
218 Travis Fryman .15 .40
219 Brian Giles .15 .40
220 Dwight Gooden .15 .40
221 Mike Jackson .15 .40
222 David Justice .15 .40
223 Kenny Lofton .15 .40
224 Jose Mesa .15 .40
225 Alvin Morman .15 .40
226 Charles Nagy .15 .40
227 Chad Ogea .15 .40
228 Eric Plunk .15 .40
229 Manny Ramirez .25 .60
230 Paul Shuey .15 .40
231 Jim Thome .25 .60
232 Ron Villone .15 .40
233 Omar Vizquel .25 .60
234 Enrique Wilson .15 .40
235 Jaret Wright .15 .40
236 Manny Ramirez TC .15 .40
237 Pedro Astacio .15 .40
238 Jason Bates .15 .40
239 Dante Bichette .15 .40
240 Ellis Burks .15 .40
241 Vinny Castilla .15 .40
242 Greg Colbrunn .15 .40
243 Mike DeJean RC .15 .40
244 Jerry Dipoto .15 .40
245 Curtis Goodwin .15 .40
246 Todd Helton .25 .60
247 Bobby Jones RC .15 .40
248 Darryl Kile .15 .40
249 Mike Lansing .15 .40
250 Curtis Leskanic .15 .40
251 Nelson Liriano .15 .40
252 Kirt Manwaring .15 .40
253 Chuck McElroy .15 .40
254 Mike Munoz .15 .40
255 Neifi Perez .15 .40
256 Jeff Reed .15 .40
257 Mark Thompson .15 .40
258 John Vander Wal .15 .40
259 Dave Veres .15 .40
260 Larry Walker* .15 .40
260A L.Walker Hitting Close-Up .15 .40
261 Jamey Wright .15 .40
262 Larry Walker TC .15 .40
263 Kimera Bartee .15 .40
264 Doug Brocail .15 .40
265 Raul Casanova .15 .40
266 Frank Castillo .15 .40
267 Frank Catalanotto RC .40 1.00
268 Tony Clark .15 .40
269 Deivi Cruz .15 .40
270 Roberto Duran RC .15 .40
271 Damion Easley .15 .40
272 Bryce Florie .15 .40
273 Luis Gonzalez .15 .40
274 Bobby Higginson .15 .40
275 Brian Hunter .15 .40
276 Todd Jones .15 .40
277 Greg Keagle .15 .40
278 Jeff Manto .15 .40
279 Brian Moehler .15 .40
280 Joe Oliver .15 .40
281 Joe Randa .15 .40
282 Bill Ripken .15 .40
283 Bip Roberts .15 .40
284 Sean Runyan .15 .40
285 A.J. Sager .15 .40
286 Justin Thompson .15 .40
287 Tony Clark TC .15 .40
288 Antonio Alfonseca .15 .40
289 Dave Berg RC .25 .60
290 Josh Booty .15 .40
291 John Cangelosi .15 .40
292 Craig Counsell .15 .40
293 Vic Darensbourg .15 .40
294 Cliff Floyd .15 .40
295 Oscar Henriquez .15 .40
296 Felix Heredia .15 .40
297 Ryan Jackson RC .15 .40
298 Mark Kotsay .15 .40
299 Andy Larkin .15 .40
300 Derrek Lee .25 .60
301 Brian Meadows .15 .40
302 Rafael Medina .15 .40
303 Jay Powell .15 .40
304 Edgar Renteria .15 .40
305 Jesus Sanchez RC .15 .40
306 Rob Stanifer RC .15 .40
307 Gregg Zaun .15 .40
308 Derrek Lee TC .15 .40
309 Moises Alou .15 .40
310 Brad Ausmus .15 .40
311 Jeff Bagwell* .25 .60
311A J.Bagwell Hitting .25 .60
312 Derek Bell .15 .40
313 Sean Bergman .15 .40
314 Sean Berry .15 .40
315 Craig Biggio .25 .60
316 Tim Bogar .15 .40
317 Jose Cabrera RC .15 .40
318 Dave Clark .15 .40
319 Tony Eusebio .15 .40
320 Carl Everett .15 .40
321 Ricky Gutierrez .15 .40
322 John Halama RC .25 .60
323 Mike Hampton .15 .40
324 Doug Henry .15 .40
325 Richard Hidalgo .15 .40
326 Jack Howell .15 .40
327 Jose Lima .15 .40
328 Mike Magnante .15 .40
329 Trever Miller .15 .40
330 C.J. Nitkowski .15 .40
331 Shane Reynolds .15 .40
332 Bill Spiers .15 .40
333 Billy Wagner .15 .40
334 Jeff Bagwell TC .15 .40
335 Tim Belcher .15 .40
336 Brian Bevil .15 .40
337 Johnny Damon .25 .60
338 Jermaine Dye .15 .40
339 Sal Fasano .15 .40
340 Shane Halter .15 .40
341 Chris Haney .15 .40
342 Jed Hansen .15 .40
343 Jeff King .15 .40
344 Jeff Montgomery .15 .40
345 Hal Morris .15 .40
346 Jose Offerman .15 .40
347 Dean Palmer .15 .40
348 Terry Pendleton .15 .40
349 Hipolito Pichardo .15 .40
350 Jim Pittsley .15 .40
351 Pat Rapp .15 .40
352 Jose Rosado .15 .40
353 Glendon Rusch .15 .40
354 Scott Service .15 .40
355 Larry Sutton .15 .40
356 Mike Sweeney .15 .40
357 Joe Vitiello .15 .40
358 Matt Whisenant .15 .40
359 Ernie Young .15 .40
360 Jeff King TC .15 .40
361 Bobby Bonilla .15 .40
362 Jim Bruske .15 .40
363 Juan Castro .15 .40
364 Roger Cedeno .15 .40
365 Mike Devereaux .15 .40
366 Darren Dreifort .15 .40
367 Jim Eisenreich .15 .40
368 Wilton Guerrero .15 .40
369 Mark Guthrie .15 .40
370 Darren Hall .15 .40
371 Todd Hollandsworth .15 .40
372 Thomas Howard .15 .40
373 Trenidad Hubbard .15 .40
374 Charles Johnson .15 .40
375 Eric Karros .15 .40
376 Paul Konerko .15 .40
377 Matt Luke .15 .40
378 Ramon Martinez .15 .40
379 Raul Mondesi .15 .40
380 Hideo Nomo .40 1.00
381 Antonio Osuna .15 .40
382 Chan Ho Park .15 .40
383 Tom Prince .15 .40

384 Scott Radinsky .15 .40
385 Gary Sheffield .15 .40
386 Ismael Valdes .15 .40
387 Jose Vizcaino .15 .40
388 Eric Young .15 .40
389 Gary Sheffield TC .15 .40
390 Jeromy Burnitz .15 .40
391 Jeff Cirillo .15 .40
392 Cal Eldred .15 .40
393 Chad Fox RC .15 .40
394 Marquis Grissom .15 .40
395 Bob Hamelin .15 .40
396 Bobby Hughes .15 .40
397 Darrin Jackson .15 .40
398 John Jaha .15 .40
399 Geoff Jenkins .15 .40
400 Doug Jones .15 .40
401 Jeff Juden .15 .40
402 Scott Karl .15 .40
403 Jesse Levis .15 .40
404 Mark Loretta .15 .40
405 Mike Matheny .15 .40
406 Jose Mercedes .15 .40
407 Mike Myers .15 .40
408 Marc Newfield .15 .40
409 Dave Nilsson .15 .40
410 Al Reyes .15 .40
411 Jose Valentin .15 .40
412 Fernando Vina .15 .40
413 Paul Wagner .15 .40
414 Bob Wickman .15 .40
415 Steve Woodard .15 .40
416 Marquis Grissom TC .15 .40
417 Rick Aguilera .15 .40
418 Ron Coomer .15 .40
419 Marty Cordova .15 .40
420 Brent Gates .15 .40
421 Eddie Guardado .15 .40
422 Denny Hocking .15 .40
423 Matt Lawton .15 .40
424 Pat Meares .15 .40
425 Orlando Merced .15 .40
426 Eric Milton .15 .40
427 Paul Molitor .15 .40
428 Mike Morgan .15 .40
429 Dan Naulty .15 .40
430 Otis Nixon .15 .40
431 Alex Ochoa .15 .40
432 David Ortiz .50 1.25
433 Brad Radke .15 .40
434 Todd Ritchie .15 .40
435 Frank Rodriguez .15 .40
436 Terry Steinbach .15 .40
437 Greg Swindell .15 .40
438 Bob Tewksbury .15 .40
439 Mike Trombley .15 .40
440 Javier Valentin .15 .40
441 Todd Walker .15 .40
442 Paul Molitor TC .15 .40
443 Shane Andrews .15 .40
444 Miguel Batista .15 .40
445 Shayne Bennett .15 .40
446 Rick DeHart RC .15 .40
447 Brad Fullmer .15 .40
448 Mark Grudzielanek .15 .40
449 Vladimir Guerrero .40 1.00
450 Dustin Hermanson .15 .40
451 Steve Kline .15 .40
452 Scott Livingstone .15 .40
453 Mike Maddux .15 .40
454 Derrick May .15 .40
455 Ryan McGuire .15 .40
456 Trey Moore .15 .40
457 Mike Mordecai .15 .40
458 Carl Pavano .15 .40
459 Carlos Perez .15 .40
460 F.P. Santangelo .15 .40
461 DaRond Stovall .15 .40
462 Anthony Telford .15 .40
463 Ugueth Urbina .15 .40
464 Marc Valdes .15 .40
465 Jose Vidro .15 .40
466 Rondell White .15 .40
467 Chris Widger .15 .40
468 Vladimir Guerrero TC .25 .60
469 Edgardo Alfonzo .15 .40
470 Carlos Baerga .15 .40
471 Rich Becker .15 .40
472 Brian Bohanon .15 .40
473 Alberto Castillo .15 .40
474 Dennis Cook .15 .40
475 John Franco .15 .40
476 Matt Franco .15 .40
477 Bernard Gilkey .15 .40
478 John Hudek .15 .40
479 Butch Huskey .15 .40
480 Bobby Jones .15 .40
481 Al Leiter .15 .40
482 Luis Lopez .15 .40
483 Brian McRae .15 .40
484 Dave Mlicki .15 .40
485 John Olerud .15 .40
486 Rey Ordonez .15 .40
487 Craig Paquette .15 .40
488 Mike Piazza* .60 1.50
488A M.Piazza Close-Up .60 1.50
489 Todd Pratt .15 .40
490 Mel Rojas .15 .40
491 Tim Spehr .15 .40
492 Turk Wendell .15 .40
493 Masato Yoshii RC .25 .60
494 Mike Piazza TC .40 1.00
495 Willie Banks .15 .40
496 Scott Brosius .15 .40
497 Mike Buddie RC .15 .40
498 Homer Bush .15 .40
499 David Cone .15 .40
500 Chad Curtis .15 .40
501 Chili Davis .15 .40
502 Joe Girardi .15 .40
503 Darren Holmes .15 .40
504 Hideki Irabu .15 .40
505 Derek Jeter* 1.00 2.50
505A D.Jeter Hitting 1.00 2.50
506 Chuck Knoblauch .15 .40
507 Graeme Lloyd .15 .40
508 Tino Martinez .25 .60
509 Ramiro Mendoza .15 .40
510 Jeff Nelson .15 .40
511 Paul O'Neill .25 .60
512 Andy Pettitte .25 .60
513 Jorge Posada .25 .60
514 Tim Raines .15 .40
515 Mariano Rivera .40 1.00
516 Luis Sojo .15 .40
517 Mike Stanton .15 .40
518 Darryl Strawberry .15 .40
519 Dale Sveum .15 .40
520 David Wells .15 .40
521 Bernie Williams .25 .60
522 Bernie Williams TC .15 .40
523 Kurt Abbott .15 .40
524 Mike Blowers .15 .40
525 Rafael Bournigal .15 .40
526 Tom Candiotti .15 .40
527 Ryan Christenson RC .15 .40
528 Mike Fetters .15 .40
529 Jason Giambi .15 .40
530 Ben Grieve* .15 .40
530A B.Grieve Swinging .15 .40
531 Buddy Groom .15 .40
532 Jimmy Haynes .15 .40
533 Rickey Henderson .40 1.00
534 A.J. Hinch .15 .40
535 Mike Macfarlane .15 .40
536 Dave Magadan .15 .40
537 T.J. Mathews .15 .40
538 Jason McDonald .15 .40
539 Kevin Mitchell .15 .40
540 Mike Mohler .15 .40
541 Mike Oquist .15 .40
542 Ariel Prieto .15 .40
543 Kenny Rogers .15 .40
544 Aaron Small .15 .40
545 Scott Spiezio .15 .40
546 Matt Stairs .15 .40
547 Bill Taylor .15 .40
548 Dave Telgheder .15 .40
549 Jack Voigt .15 .40
550 Ben Grieve TC .15 .40
551 Bob Abreu .15 .40
552 Ruben Amaro .15 .40
553 Alex Arias .15 .40
554 Matt Beech .15 .40
555 Ricky Bottalico .15 .40
556 Billy Brewer .15 .40
557 Rico Brogna .15 .40
558 Doug Glanville .15 .40
559 Wayne Gomes .15 .40
560 Mike Grace .15 .40
561 Tyler Green .15 .40
562 Rex Hudler .15 .40
563 Gregg Jefferies .15 .40
564 Kevin Jordan .15 .40
565 Mark Leiter .15 .40
566 Mark Lewis .15 .40
567 Mike Lieberthal .15 .40
568 Mark Parent .15 .40
569 Yorkis Perez .15 .40
570 Desi Relaford .15 .40
571 Scott Rolen .25 .60
572 Curt Schilling .15 .40
573 Kevin Sefcik .15 .40
574 Jerry Spradlin .15 .40
575 Garrett Stephenson .15 .40
576 Darrin Winston RC .15 .40
577 Scott Rolen TC .15 .40
578 Jermaine Allensworth .15 .40
579 Jason Christiansen .15 .40
580 Lou Collier .15 .40
581 Francisco Cordova .15 .40
582 Elmer Dessens .15 .40
583 Freddy Garcia .15 .40
584 Jose Guillen .15 .40
585 Jason Kendall .15 .40
586 Jon Lieber .15 .40
587 Esteban Loaiza .15 .40
588 Al Martin .15 .40
589 Javier Martinez RC .15 .40
590 Chris Peters .15 .40
591 Kevin Polcovich .15 .40
592 Ricardo Rincon .15 .40
593 Jason Schmidt .15 .40
594 Jose Silva .15 .40
595 Mark Smith .15 .40
596 Doug Strange .15 .40
597 Turner Ward .15 .40
598 Marc Wilkins .15 .40
599 Mike Williams .15 .40
600 Tony Womack .15 .40
601 Kevin Young .15 .40
602 Tony Womack TC .15 .40
603 Manny Aybar RC .25 .60
604 Kent Bottenfield .15 .40
605 Jeff Brantley .15 .40
606 Mike Busby .15 .40
607 Royce Clayton .15 .40
608 Delino DeShields .15 .40
609 John Frascatore .15 .40
610 Gary Gaetti .15 .40
611 Ron Gant .15 .40
612 David Howard .15 .40
613 Brian Hunter .15 .40
614 Brian Jordan .15 .40
615 Tom Lampkin .15 .40
616 Ray Lankford .15 .40
617 Braden Looper .15 .40
618 John Mabry .15 .40
619 Eli Marrero .15 .40
620 Willie McGee .15 .40
621 Mark McGwire* 1.00 2.50
621A M.McGwire Hitting 1.00 2.50
622 Kent Mercker .15 .40
623 Matt Morris .15 .40
624 Donovan Osborne .15 .40
625 Tom Pagnozzi .15 .40
626 Lance Painter .15 .40
627 Mark Petkovsek .15 .40
628 Todd Stottlemyre .15 .40
629 Mark McGwire TC .50 1.25
630 Andy Ashby .15 .40
631 Brian Boehringer .15 .40
632 Kevin Brown .25 .60
633 Ken Caminiti .15 .40
634 Steve Finley .15 .40
635 Ed Giovanola .15 .40
636 Chris Gomez .15 .40
637 Tony Gwynn* .50 1.25
637A T.Gwynn White Jersey .50 1.25
638 Joey Hamilton .15 .40
639 Carlos Hernandez .15 .40
640 Sterling Hitchcock .15 .40
641 Trevor Hoffman .15 .40
642 Wally Joyner .15 .40
643 Dan Miceli .15 .40
644 James Mouton .15 .40
645 Greg Myers .15 .40
646 Carlos Reyes .15 .40
647 Andy Sheets .15 .40
648 Pete Smith .15 .40
649 Mark Sweeney .15 .40
650 Greg Vaughn .15 .40
651 Quilvio Veras .15 .40
652 Tony Gwynn TC .25 .60
653 Rich Aurilia .15 .40
654 Marvin Benard .15 .40
655 Barry Bonds* 1.00 2.50
655A B.Bonds Close-Up 1.00 2.50
656 Danny Darwin .15 .40
657 Shawn Estes .15 .40
658 Mark Gardner .15 .40
659 Darryl Hamilton .15 .40
660 Charlie Hayes .15 .40
661 Orel Hershiser .15 .40
662 Stan Javier .15 .40
663 Brian Johnson .15 .40
664 John Johnstone .15 .40
665 Jeff Kent .15 .40
666 Brent Mayne .15 .40
667 Bill Mueller .15 .40
668 Robb Nen .15 .40
669 Jim Poole .15 .40
670 Steve Reed .15 .40
671 Rich Rodriguez .15 .40
672 Kirk Rueter .15 .40
673 Rey Sanchez .15 .40
674 J.T. Snow .15 .40
675 Julian Tavarez .15 .40
676 Barry Bonds TC .50 1.25
677 Rich Amaral .15 .40
678 Bobby Ayala .15 .40
679 Jay Buhner .15 .40
680 Ken Cloude .15 .40
681 Joey Cora .15 .40
682 Russ Davis .15 .40
683 Rob Ducey .15 .40
684 Jeff Fassero .15 .40
685 Tony Fossas .15 .40
686 Ken Griffey Jr.* .75 2.00
686A K.Griffey Jr. Hitting .75 2.00
687 Glenallen Hill .15 .40
688 Jeff Huson .15 .40
689 Randy Johnson .40 1.00
690 Edgar Martinez .25 .60
691 John Marzano .15 .40
692 Jamie Moyer .15 .40
693 Alex Rodriguez* .60 1.50
693A A.Rodriguez Hitting .60 1.50
694 David Segui .15 .40
695 Heathcliff Slocumb .15 .40
696 Paul Spoljaric .15 .40
697 Bill Swift .15 .40
698 Mike Timlin .15 .40
699 Bob Wells .15 .40
700 Dan Wilson .15 .40
701 Ken Griffey Jr. TC .50 1.25
702 Wilson Alvarez .15 .40
703 Rolando Arrojo RC .25 .60
704 Wade Boggs* .25 .60
704A W.Boggs Hitting .25 .60
705 Rich Butler RC .15 .40
706 Miguel Cairo .15 .40
707 Mike Difelice RC .25 .60
708 John Flaherty .15 .40
709 Roberto Hernandez .15 .40
710 Mike Kelly .15 .40
711 Aaron Ledesma .15 .40
712 Albie Lopez .15 .40
713 Dave Martinez .15 .40
714 Quinton McCracken .15 .40
715 Fred McGriff .25 .60
716 Jim Mecir .15 .40
717 Tony Saunders .15 .40
718 Bobby Smith .15 .40
719 Paul Sorrento .15 .40
720 Dennis Springer .15 .40
721 Kevin Stocker .15 .40
722 Ramon Tatis .15 .40
723 Bubba Trammell .15 .40
724 Esteban Yan RC .25 .60
725 Wade Boggs TC .15 .40
726 Luis Alicea .15 .40
727 Scott Bailes .15 .40
728 John Burkett .15 .40
729 Domingo Cedeno .15 .40
730 Will Clark .25 .60
731 Kevin Elster .15 .40
732 Juan Gonzalez .15 .40
732A J.Gonzalez Without Bat .15 .40
733 Tom Goodwin .15 .40
734 Rusty Greer .15 .40
735 Eric Gunderson .15 .40
736 Bill Haselman .15 .40
737 Rick Helling .15 .40
738 Roberto Kelly .15 .40
739 Mark McLemore .15 .40
740 Darren Oliver .15 .40
741 Danny Patterson .15 .40
742 Roger Pavlik .15 .40
743 Ivan Rodriguez* .25 .60
743A I.Rodriguez Hitting .25 .60
744 Aaron Sele .15 .40
745 Mike Simms .15 .40
746 Lee Stevens .15 .40
747 Fernando Tatis .15 .40
748 John Wetteland .15 .40
749 Bobby Witt .15 .40
750 Juan Gonzalez TC .15 .40
751 Carlos Almanzar RC .25 .60
752 Kevin Brown .25 .60
753 Jose Canseco .25 .60
754 Chris Carpenter .15 .40
755 Roger Clemens .75 2.00
756 Felipe Crespo .15 .40
757 Jose Cruz Jr. .15 .40
758 Mark Dalesandro .15 .40
759 Carlos Delgado .15 .40
760 Kelvim Escobar .15 .40
761 Tony Fernandez .15 .40
762 Darrin Fletcher .15 .40
763 Alex Gonzalez .15 .40
764 Craig Grebeck .15 .40
765 Shawn Green .15 .40
766 Juan Guzman .15 .40
767 Erik Hanson .15 .40
768 Pat Hentgen .15 .40
769 Randy Myers .15 .40
770 Robert Person .15 .40
771 Dan Plesac .15 .40
772 Paul Quantrill .15 .40
773 Bill Risley .15 .40
774 Juan Samuel .15 .40
775 Steve Sinclair RC .15 .40
776 Ed Sprague .15 .40
777 Mike Stanley .15 .40
778 Shannon Stewart .15 .40
779 Woody Williams .15 .40
780 Roger Clemens TC .40 1.00
SAMP Tony Gwynn Sample .75 2.00

1998 Pacific Online Red

COMPLETE SET (800) 100.00 200.00
*STARS: 1.25X TO 3X BASIC CARDS
*ROOKIES: .75X TO 2X BASIC CARDS
EIGHT CARDS PER RETAIL PACK

1998 Pacific Online Web Cards

COMPLETE SET (800) 300.00 600.00
*STARS: 1.5X TO 4X BASIC CARDS
*ROOKIES: .75X TO 2X BASIC CARDS
ONE PER PACK

1998 Pacific Online Winners

*WINNER CARDS: 4X TO 10X BASIC CARDS

1995 Pacific Prisms

This 144-card standard-size set was issued for the first time as a stand alone set instead as an insert set. Total production of this product was 2,999 individually numbered cases that contained 20 boxes of 36 packs. The full-bleed fronts feature a player photo against a silver prismatic background with the player's name on the bottom. The backs have a full-color photo with some biographical information. The cards are grouped alphabetically according to teams for each league with AL and NL intermingled. There are no key Rookie Cards in this set. A checklist or team logo card was seeded into every pack.

COMPLETE SET (144) 40.00 100.00
ONE CL OR TEAM LOGO PER PACK
1 David Justice .50 1.25
2 Ryan Klesko .50 1.25
3 Javier Lopez .50 1.25
4 Greg Maddux 2.00 5.00
5 Fred McGriff .75 2.00
6 Tony Tarasco .30 .75
7 Jeffrey Hammonds .30 .75
8 Mike Mussina .75 2.00
9 Rafael Palmeiro .75 2.00
10 Cal Ripken 4.00 10.00
11 Lee Smith .50 1.25
12 Roger Clemens 2.50 6.00
13 Scott Cooper .30 .75
14 Mike Greenwell .30 .75
15 Carlos Rodriguez .30 .75
16 Mo Vaughn .50 1.25
17 Chili Davis .50 1.25
18 Jim Edmonds .75 2.00
19 Jorge Fabregas .30 .75
20 Bo Jackson 1.25 3.00
21 Tim Salmon .75 2.00
22 Mark Grace .75 2.00
23 Jose Guzman .30 .75
24 Randy Myers .30 .75
25 Rey Sanchez .30 .75
26 Sammy Sosa 1.25 3.00
27 Wilson Alvarez .30 .75
28 Julio Franco .50 1.25
29 Ozzie Guillen .50 1.25
30 Jack McDowell .30 .75
31 Frank Thomas 1.25 3.00
32 Bret Boone .50 1.25
33 Barry Larkin .75 2.00
34 Hal Morris .30 .75
35 Jose Rijo .30 .75
36 Deion Sanders .75 2.00
37 Carlos Baerga .30 .75
38 Albert Belle .50 1.25
39 Kenny Lofton .50 1.25
40 Dennis Martinez .50 1.25
41 Manny Ramirez .75 2.00
42 Omar Vizquel .75 2.00
43 Dante Bichette .50 1.25
44 Marvin Freeman .30 .75
45 Andres Galarraga .50 1.25
46 Mike Kingery .30 .75
47 Danny Bautista .30 .75
48 Cecil Fielder .50 1.25
49 Travis Fryman .50 1.25
50 Tony Phillips .30 .75
51 Alan Trammell .50 1.25
52 Lou Whitaker .50 1.25
53 Alex Arias .30 .75
54 Bret Barberie .30 .75
55 Jeff Conine .50 1.25
56 Charles Johnson .50 1.25
57 Gary Sheffield .50 1.25
58 Jeff Bagwell .75 2.00
59 Craig Biggio .75 2.00
60 Doug Drabek .30 .75
61 Tony Eusebio .30 .75
62 Luis Gonzalez .50 1.25
63 David Cone .50 1.25
64 Bob Hamelin .30 .75
65 Felix Jose .30 .75
66 Wally Joyner .50 1.25
67 Brian McRae .30 .75
68 Brett Butler .50 1.25
69 Garey Ingram .30 .75
70 Ramon Martinez .30 .75
71 Raul Mondesi .50 1.25
72 Mike Piazza 2.00 5.00
73 Henry Rodriguez .30 .75
74 Ricky Bones .30 .75
75 Pat Listach .30 .75
76 Dave Nilsson .30 .75
77 Jose Valentin .30 .75
78 Rick Aguilera .30 .75
79 Denny Hocking .30 .75
80 Shane Mack .30 .75
81 Pedro Munoz .30 .75
82 Kirby Puckett 1.25 3.00
83 Dave Winfield .50 1.25
84 Moises Alou .50 1.25
85 Wil Cordero .30 .75
86 Cliff Floyd .50 1.25
87 Marquis Grissom .50 1.25
88 Pedro Martinez .75 2.00
89 Larry Walker .50 1.25
90 Bobby Bonilla .50 1.25
91 Jeromy Burnitz .50 1.25
92 John Franco .50 1.25
93 Jeff Kent .50 1.25
94 Jose Vizcaino .30 .75
95 Wade Boggs .75 2.00
96 Jimmy Key .50 1.25
97 Don Mattingly 4.00 10.00
98 Paul O'Neill .75 2.00
99 Luis Polonia .30 .75
100 Danny Tartabull .30 .75
101 Geronimo Berroa .30 .75
102 Rickey Henderson 1.25 3.00
103 Ruben Sierra .50 1.25
104 Terry Steinbach .30 .75
105 Darren Daulton .50 1.25
106 Mariano Duncan .30 .75
107 Lenny Dykstra .50 1.25
108 Mike Lieberthal .50 1.25
109 Tony Longmire .30 .75
110 Tom Marsh .30 .75
111 Jay Bell .50 1.25
112 Carlos Garcia .30 .75
113 Orlando Merced .30 .75
114 Andy Van Slyke .75 2.00
115 Derek Bell .30 .75
116 Tony Gwynn 1.50 4.00
117 Luis Lopez .30 .75
118 Bip Roberts .30 .75
119 Rod Beck .30 .75
120 Barry Bonds 3.00 8.00
121 Darryl Strawberry .50 1.25
122 Wm. Van Landingham .30 .75
123 Matt Williams .50 1.25
124 Jay Buhner .50 1.25
125 Felix Fermin .30 .75
126 Ken Griffey Jr. 2.50 6.00
127 Randy Johnson 1.25 3.00
128 Edgar Martinez .75 2.00
129 Alex Rodriguez 3.00 8.00
130 Rene Arocha .30 .75
131 Gregg Jefferies .30 .75
132 Mike Perez .30 .75
133 Ozzie Smith 2.00 5.00
134 Jose Canseco .75 2.00
135 Will Clark .75 2.00
136 Juan Gonzalez .50 1.25
137 Ivan Rodriguez .75 2.00
138 Roberto Alomar .75 2.00
139 Joe Carter .50 1.25
140 Carlos Delgado .50 1.25
141 Alex Gonzalez .30 .75
142 Juan Guzman .30 .75
143 Paul Molitor .50 1.25
144 John Olerud .50 1.25

1995 Pacific Prisms Checklist

COMMON CARD (1-2) .10 .25

1995 Pacific Prisms Team Logo

COMPLETE SET (28) 2.00 5.00
COMMON CARD (1-28) .10 .25

1996 Pacific Prisms

This 144-card set features a color action player cut-out over a double-etched silver foil prismatic background. The backs carry a color player portrait with information about the player in both English and Spanish.

COMPLETE SET (144) 60.00 120.00
P1 Tom Glavine 1.00 2.50
P2 Chipper Jones 1.50 4.00
P3 David Justice .60 1.50
P4 Ryan Klesko .60 1.50
P5 Javy Lopez .60 1.50
P6 Greg Maddux 2.50 6.00
P7 Fred McGriff 1.00 2.50
P8 Frank Castillo .60 1.50
P9 Luis Gonzalez .60 1.50
P10 Mark Grace 1.00 2.50
P11 Brian McRae .60 1.50
P12 Jaime Navarro .60 1.50
P13 Sammy Sosa 1.50 4.00
P14 Bret Boone .60 1.50
P15 Ron Gant .60 1.50
P16 Barry Larkin 1.00 2.50
P17 Reggie Sanders .60 1.50
P18 Benito Santiago .60 1.50
P19 Dante Bichette .60 1.50
P20 Vinny Castilla .60 1.50
P21 Andres Galarraga .60 1.50
P22 Bryan Rekar .60 1.50
P23 Roberto Alomar 1.00 2.50
P24 Jeff Conine .60 1.50
P25 Andre Dawson .60 1.50
P26 Charles Johnson .60 1.50
P27 Gary Sheffield .60 1.50
P28 Quilvio Veras .60 1.50
P29 Jeff Bagwell 1.00 2.50
P30 Derek Bell .60 1.50
P31 Craig Biggio 1.00 2.50
P32 Tony Eusebio .60 1.50
P33 Karim Garcia .60 1.50
P34 Eric Karros .60 1.50
P35 Ramon Martinez .60 1.50
P36 Raul Mondesi .60 1.50
P37 Hideo Nomo 1.50 4.00
P38 Mike Piazza 2.50 6.00
P39 Ismael Valdes .60 1.50
P40 Moises Alou .60 1.50
P41 Wil Cordero .60 1.50
P42 Pedro Martinez 1.00 2.50
P43 Mel Rojas .60 1.50
P44 David Segui .60 1.50
P45 Edgardo Alfonzo .60 1.50
P46 Rico Brogna .60 1.50
P47 John Franco .60 1.50
P48 Jason Isringhausen .60 1.50
P49 Jose Vizcaino .60 1.50
P50 Ricky Bottalico .60 1.50
P51 Darren Daulton .60 1.50
P52 Lenny Dykstra .60 1.50
P53 Tyler Green .60 1.50
P54 Gregg Jefferies .60 1.50
P55 Jay Bell .60 1.50
P56 Jason Christiansen .60 1.50
P57 Carlos Garcia .60 1.50
P58 Esteban Loaiza .60 1.50
P59 Orlando Merced .60 1.50
P60 Andujar Cedeno .60 1.50
P61 Tony Gwynn 2.00 5.00
P62 Melvin Nieves .60 1.50
P63 Phil Plantier .60 1.50
P64 Fernando Valenzuela .60 1.50
P65 Barry Bonds 4.00 10.00
P66 J.R. Phillips .60 1.50
P67 Deion Sanders 1.00 2.50
P68 Matt Williams .60 1.50
P69 Bernard Gilkey .60 1.50
P70 Tom Henke .60 1.50
P71 Brian Jordan .60 1.50
P72 Ozzie Smith 2.50 6.00
P73 Manny Alexander .60 1.50
P74 Bobby Bonilla .60 1.50
P75 Mike Mussina 1.00 2.50
P76 Rafael Palmeiro 1.00 2.50
P77 Cal Ripken 5.00 12.00
P78 Jose Canseco 1.00 2.50
P79 Roger Clemens 3.00 8.00
P80 John Valentin .60 1.50
P81 Mo Vaughn .60 1.50
P82 Tim Wakefield .60 1.50
P83 Garret Anderson .60 1.50
P84 Damion Easley .60 1.50
P85 Jim Edmonds .60 1.50
P86 Tim Salmon 1.00 2.50
P87 Wilson Alvarez .60 1.50
P88 Alex Fernandez .60 1.50
P89 Ozzie Guillen .60 1.50
P90 Roberto Hernandez .60 1.50
P91 Frank Thomas 1.50 4.00
P92 Robin Ventura .60 1.50
P93 Carlos Baerga .60 1.50
P94 Albert Belle .60 1.50
P95 Kenny Lofton .60 1.50
P96 Dennis Martinez .60 1.50
P97 Eddie Murray 1.50 4.00
P98 Manny Ramirez 1.00 2.50
P99 Omar Vizquel 1.00 2.50
P100 Chad Curtis .60 1.50
P101 Cecil Fielder .60 1.50
P102 Felipe Lira .60 1.50
P103 Alan Trammell .60 1.50
P104 Kevin Appier .60 1.50
P105 Johnny Damon 1.00 2.50
P106 Gary Gaetti .60 1.50
P107 Wally Joyner .60 1.50
P108 Ricky Bones .60 1.50
P109 John Jaha .60 1.50
P110 B.J. Surhoff .60 1.50
P111 Jose Valentin .60 1.50
P112 Fernando Vina .60 1.50
P113 Marty Cordova .60 1.50
P114 Chuck Knoblauch .60 1.50
P115 Scott Leius .60 1.50
P116 Pedro Munoz .60 1.50
P117 Kirby Puckett 1.50 4.00
P118 Wade Boggs 1.00 2.50
P119 Don Mattingly 4.00 10.00
P120 Jack McDowell .60 1.50
P121 Paul O'Neill 1.00 2.50
P122 Ruben Rivera .60 1.50
P123 Bernie Williams 1.00 2.50
P124 Geronimo Berroa .60 1.50
P125 Rickey Henderson 1.50 4.00
P126 Mark McGwire 4.00 10.00
P127 Terry Steinbach .60 1.50
P128 Danny Tartabull .60 1.50
P129 Jay Buhner .60 1.50
P130 Joey Cora .60 1.50
P131 Ken Griffey Jr. 3.00 8.00
P132 Randy Johnson 1.50 4.00
P133 Edgar Martinez 1.00 2.50
P134 Tino Martinez 1.00 2.50
P135 Will Clark 1.00 2.50
P136 Juan Gonzalez .60 1.50
P137 Dean Palmer .60 1.50
P138 Ivan Rodriguez 1.00 2.50
P139 Mickey Tettleton .60 1.50
P140 Larry Walker .60 1.50
P141 Joe Carter .60 1.50
P142 Carlos Delgado .60 1.50
P143 Alex Gonzalez .60 1.50
P144 Paul Molitor .60 1.50

1996 Pacific Prisms Gold

COMPLETE SET (144) 400.00 800.00
*GOLD: 1.25X TO 3X BASIC CARDS
STATED ODDS 1:18

1996 Pacific Prisms Fence Busters

COMPLETE SET (20) 75.00 150.00
STATED ODDS 1:37
FB1 Albert Belle 1.25 3.00
FB2 Dante Bichette 1.25 3.00
FB3 Barry Bonds 8.00 20.00
FB4 Jay Buhner 1.25 3.00
FB5 Jose Canseco 2.00 5.00
FB6 Ken Griffey Jr. 6.00 15.00
FB7 Chipper Jones 3.00 8.00
FB8 Dave Justice 1.25 3.00
FB9 Eric Karros 1.25 3.00
FB10 Edgar Martinez 2.00 5.00
FB11 Mark McGwire 8.00 20.00
FB12 Eddie Murray 3.00 8.00
FB13 Mike Piazza 5.00 12.00
FB14 Kirby Puckett 3.00 8.00
FB15 Cal Ripken 10.00 25.00
FB16 Tim Salmon 2.00 5.00
FB17 Sammy Sosa 3.00 8.00
FB18 Frank Thomas 3.00 8.00
FB19 Mo Vaughn 1.25 3.00
FB20 Larry Walker 1.25 3.00

1996 Pacific Prisms Flame Throwers

COMPLETE SET (10) 30.00 60.00
STATED ODDS 1:73
FT1 Randy Johnson 5.00 12.00
FT2 Mike Mussina 3.00 8.00
FT3 Roger Clemens 6.00 15.00
FT4 Tom Glavine 3.00 8.00
FT5 Hideo Nomo 5.00 12.00
FT6 Jose Rijo 2.00 5.00
FT7 Greg Maddux 8.00 20.00
FT8 David Cone 2.00 5.00
FT9 Ramon Martinez 2.00 5.00
FT10 Jose Mesa 2.00 5.00

1996 Pacific Prisms Red Hot Stars

COMPLETE SET (20) 100.00 200.00
STATED ODDS 1:37
RH1 Roberto Alomar 2.00 5.00
RH2 Jose Canseco 2.00 5.00
RH3 Chipper Jones 3.00 8.00
RH4 Mike Piazza 5.00 12.00
RH5 Tim Salmon 2.00 5.00
RH6 Jeff Bagwell 2.00 5.00
RH7 Ken Griffey Jr. 6.00 15.00
RH8 Greg Maddux 5.00 12.00
RH9 Kirby Puckett 3.00 8.00
RH10 Frank Thomas 3.00 8.00
RH11 Albert Belle 1.25 3.00
RH12 Tony Gwynn 4.00 10.00
RH13 Edgar Martinez 2.00 5.00
RH14 Manny Ramirez 2.00 5.00
RH15 Barry Bonds 8.00 20.00
RH16 Wade Boggs 2.00 5.00
RH17 Randy Johnson 3.00 8.00
RH18 Don Mattingly 8.00 20.00
RH19 Cal Ripken 10.00 25.00
RH20 Mo Vaughn 1.25 3.00

1996 Pacific Prisms Team Logos

COMPLETE SET (30) 5.00 12.00
PB1 Oakland Athletics .25 .60
PB2 California Angels .25 .60
PB3 Houston Astros .25 .60
PB4 Toronto Blue Jays .25 .60
PB5 Atlanta Braves .25 .60
PB6 Milwaukee Brewers .25 .60
PB7 St. Louis Cardinals .40 1.00
PB8 Chicago Cubs .40 1.00
PB9 Tampa Bay Devil Rays .25 .60
PB10 Arizona Diamondbacks .25 .60
PB11 Los Angeles Dodgers .40 1.00
PB12 Montreal Expos .25 .60
PB13 San Francisco Giants .25 .60
PB14 Cleveland Indians .25 .60
PB15 Seattle Mariners .25 .60
PB16 Florida Marlins .25 .60
PB17 New York Mets .25 .60
PB18 Baltimore Orioles .25 .60
PB19 San Diego Padres .25 .60
PB20 Philadelphia Phillies .25 .60
PB21 Pittsburgh Pirates .25 .60
PB22 Texas Rangers .25 .60
PB23 Boston Red Sox .40 1.00
PB24 Cincinnati Reds .25 .60
PB25 Colorado Rockies .25 .60
PB26 Kansas City Royals .25 .60
PB27 Detroit Tigers .25 .60
PB28 Minnesota Twins .25 .60
PB29 Chicago White Sox .25 .60
PB30 New York Yankees .40 1.00

1997 Pacific Prisms

The 1997 Pacific Prism set was issued in one series totalling 150 cards and displays color action photos of many of the top players from last season. Foiled in gold, the set features a visually stunning inlaid transparent cel on each card. The backs carry player information in both Spanish and English.

COMPLETE SET (150) 40.00 100.00
1 Chili Davis .50 1.25
2 Jim Edmonds .50 1.25
3 Darin Erstad .50 1.25
4 Orlando Palmeiro .50 1.25
5 Tim Salmon .75 2.00
6 J.T. Snow .50 1.25
7 Roberto Alomar .75 2.00
8 Brady Anderson .50 1.25
9 Eddie Murray 1.25 3.00
10 Mike Mussina .75 2.00
11 Rafael Palmeiro .75 2.00
12 Cal Ripken 4.00 10.00
13 Jose Canseco .75 2.00
14 Roger Clemens 2.50 6.00
15 Nomar Garciaparra 2.00 5.00
16 Reggie Jefferson .50 1.25
17 Mo Vaughn .50 1.25
18 Wilson Alvarez .50 1.25
19 Harold Baines .50 1.25
20 Alex Fernandez .50 1.25
21 Danny Tartabull .50 1.25
22 Frank Thomas 1.25 3.00
23 Robin Ventura .50 1.25
24 Sandy Alomar Jr. .50 1.25
25 Albert Belle .50 1.25
26 Kenny Lofton .50 1.25
27 Jim Thome .75 2.00
28 Omar Vizquel .75 2.00
29 Raul Casanova .50 1.25
30 Tony Clark .50 1.25
31 Travis Fryman .50 1.25
32 Bobby Higginson .50 1.25
33 Melvin Nieves .50 1.25
34 Justin Thompson .50 1.25
35 Johnny Damon .75 2.00
36 Tom Goodwin .50 1.25
37 Jeff Montgomery .50 1.25
38 Jose Offerman .50 1.25
39 John Jaha .50 1.25
40 Jeff Cirillo .50 1.25
41 Dave Nilsson .50 1.25
42 Jose Valentin .50 1.25
43 Fernando Vina .50 1.25
44 Marty Cordova .50 1.25
45 Roberto Kelly .50 1.25
46 Chuck Knoblauch .50 1.25
47 Paul Molitor .50 1.25
48 Todd Walker .50 1.25
49 Wade Boggs .75 2.00
50 Cecil Fielder .50 1.25
51 Derek Jeter 2.50 6.00
52 Tino Martinez .75 2.00
53 Andy Pettitte .75 2.00

54 Mariano Rivera 1.25 3.00
55 Bernie Williams .75 2.00
56 Tony Batista .50 1.25
57 Geronimo Berroa .50 1.25
58 Jason Giambi .50 1.25
59 Mark McGwire 3.00 8.00
60 Terry Steinbach .50 1.25
61 Jay Buhner .50 1.25
62 Joey Cora .50 1.25
63 Ken Griffey Jr. 2.50 6.00
64 Edgar Martinez .75 2.00
65 Alex Rodriguez 2.00 5.00
66 Paul Sorrento .50 1.25
67 Will Clark .75 2.00
68 Juan Gonzalez .50 1.25
69 Rusty Greer .50 1.25
70 Dean Palmer .50 1.25
71 Ivan Rodriguez .75 2.00
72 Joe Carter .50 1.25
73 Carlos Delgado .50 1.25
74 Juan Guzman .50 1.25
75 Pat Hentgen .50 1.25
76 Ed Sprague .50 1.25
77 Jermaine Dye .50 1.25
78 Andruw Jones .75 2.00
79 Chipper Jones 1.25 3.00
80 Ryan Klesko .50 1.25
81 Javier Lopez .50 1.25
82 Greg Maddux 2.50 6.00
83 John Smoltz .75 2.00
84 Mark Grace .75 2.00
85 Luis Gonzalez .50 1.25
86 Brooks Kieschnick .50 1.25
87 Jaime Navarro .50 1.25
88 Ryne Sandberg 2.00 5.00
89 Sammy Sosa 1.25 3.00
90 Bret Boone .50 1.25
91 Jeff Brantley .50 1.25
92 Eric Davis .50 1.25
93 Barry Larkin .75 2.00
94 Reggie Sanders .50 1.25
95 Ellis Burks .50 1.25
96 Dante Bichette .50 1.25
97 Vinny Castilla .50 1.25
98 Andres Galarraga .50 1.25
99 Eric Young .50 1.25
100 Kevin Brown .50 1.25
101 Jeff Conine .50 1.25
102 Charles Johnson .50 1.25
103 Edgar Renteria .50 1.25
104 Gary Sheffield .50 1.25
105 Jeff Bagwell .75 2.00
106 Derek Bell .50 1.25
107 Sean Berry .50 1.25
108 Craig Biggio .75 2.00
109 Shane Reynolds .50 1.25
110 Karim Garcia .50 1.25
111 Todd Hollandsworth .50 1.25
112 Ramon Martinez .50 1.25
113 Raul Mondesi .50 1.25
114 Hideo Nomo 1.25 3.00
115 Mike Piazza 2.00 5.00
116 Ismael Valdes .50 1.25
117 Moises Alou .50 1.25
118 Mark Grudzielanek .50 1.25
119 Pedro Martinez .75 2.00
120 Henry Rodriguez .50 1.25
121 F.P. Santangelo .50 1.25
122 Carlos Baerga .50 1.25
123 Bernard Gilkey .50 1.25
124 Todd Hundley .50 1.25
125 Lance Johnson .50 1.25
126 Alex Ochoa .50 1.25
127 Rey Ordonez .50 1.25
128 Lenny Dykstra .50 1.25
129 Gregg Jefferies .50 1.25
130 Ricky Otero .50 1.25
131 Benito Santiago .50 1.25
132 Jermaine Allensworth .50 1.25
133 Francisco Cordova .50 1.25
134 Carlos Garcia .50 1.25
135 Jason Kendall .50 1.25
136 Al Martin .50 1.25
137 Dennis Eckersley .50 1.25
138 Ron Gant .50 1.25
139 Brian Jordan .50 1.25
140 John Mabry .50 1.25
141 Ozzie Smith 2.00 5.00
142 Ken Caminiti .50 1.25
143 Steve Finley .50 1.25
144 Tony Gwynn 1.50 4.00
145 Wally Joyner .50 1.25
146 Fernando Valenzuela .50 1.25
147 Barry Bonds 3.00 8.00
148 Jacob Cruz .50 1.25
149 Osvaldo Fernandez .50 1.25
150 Matt Williams .50 1.25

1997 Pacific Prisms Light Blue

*STARS: 1.25X TO 3X BASIC CARDS
STATED ODDS 1:18 WAL-MART/SAM'S

1997 Pacific Prisms Platinum

*STARS: 1.25X TO 3X BASIC CARDS
STATED ODDS 1:18 HOBBY

1997 Pacific Prisms Gate Attractions

COMPLETE SET (32) 75.00 150.00
STATED ODDS 1:73
GA1 Roberto Alomar 2.00 5.00
GA2 Brady Anderson 1.25 3.00
GA3 Cal Ripken 10.00 25.00
GA4 Frank Thomas 3.00 8.00
GA5 Kenny Lofton 1.25 3.00
GA6 Omar Vizquel 2.00 5.00
GA7 Paul Molitor 3.00 8.00
GA8 Wade Boggs 2.00 5.00
GA9 Derek Jeter 8.00 20.00
GA10 Andy Pettitte 2.00 5.00
GA11 Bernie Williams 2.00 5.00
GA12 Geronimo Berroa 1.25 3.00
GA13 Mark McGwire 5.00 12.00
GA14 Ken Griffey Jr. 6.00 15.00
GA15 Alex Rodriguez 4.00 10.00
GA16 Juan Gonzalez 1.25 3.00
GA17 Andruw Jones 1.25 3.00
GA18 Chipper Jones 3.00 8.00
GA19 Greg Maddux 5.00 12.00
GA20 Ryne Sandberg 5.00 12.00
GA21 Sammy Sosa 2.00 5.00
GA22 Andres Galarraga 2.00 5.00
GA23 Jeff Bagwell 2.00 5.00
GA24 Todd Hollandsworth 1.25 3.00
GA25 Hideo Nomo 2.00 5.00
GA26 Mike Piazza 3.00 8.00
GA27 Todd Hundley 1.25 3.00
GA28 Lance Johnson 1.25 3.00
GA29 Ozzie Smith 4.00 10.00
GA30 Ken Caminiti 1.25 3.00
GA31 Tony Gwynn 3.00 8.00
GA32 Barry Bonds 5.00 12.00

1997 Pacific Prisms Gems of the Diamond

COMPLETE SET (220) 25.00 60.00
STATED ODDS 2:1
GD1 Jim Abbott .25 .60
GD2 Shawn Boskie .08 .25
GD3 Gary Disarcina .08 .25
GD4 Jim Edmonds .15 .40
GD5 Todd Greene .08 .25
GD6 Jack Howell .08 .25
GD7 Jeff Schmidt .08 .25
GD8 Shad Williams .08 .25
GD9 Roberto Alomar .25 .60
GD10 Cesar Devarez .08 .25
GD11 Alan Mills .08 .25
GD12 Eddie Murray .40 1.00
GD13 Jesse Orosco .08 .25
GD14 Arthur Rhodes .08 .25
GD15 Bill Ripken .08 .25
GD16 Cal Ripken 1.50 4.00
GD17 Mark Smith .08 .25
GD18 Roger Clemens 1.00 2.50
GD19 Vaughn Eshelman .08 .25
GD20 Rich Garces .08 .25
GD21 Bill Haselman .08 .25
GD22 Dwayne Hosey .08 .25
GD23 Mike Maddux .08 .25
GD24 Jose Malave .08 .25
GD25 Aaron Sele .08 .25
GD26 James Baldwin .08 .25
GD27 Pat Borders .08 .25
GD28 Mike Cameron .08 .25
GD29 Tony Castillo .08 .25
GD30 Domingo Cedeno .08 .25
GD31 Greg Norton .08 .25
GD32 Frank Thomas .40 1.00
GD33 Albert Belle .15 .40
GD34 Einar Diaz .08 .25
GD35 Alan Embree .08 .25
GD36 Albie Lopez .08 .25
GD37 Chad Ogea .08 .25
GD38 Tony Pena .08 .25
GD39 Joe Roa .08 .25
GD40 Fausto Cruz .08 .25
GD41 Joey Eischen .08 .25
GD42 Travis Fryman .15 .40
GD43 Mike Myers .08 .25
GD44 A.J. Sager .08 .25
GD45 Duane Singleton .08 .25
GD46 Justin Thompson .08 .25
GD47 Jeff Granger .08 .25
GD48 Les Norman .08 .25
GD49 Jon Nunnally .08 .25
GD50 Craig Paquette .08 .25
GD51 Michael Tucker .08 .25
GD52 Julio Valera .08 .25
GD53 Kevin Young .08 .25
GD54 Cal Eldred .08 .25
GD55 Ramon Garcia .08 .25
GD56 Marc Newfield .08 .25
GD57 Al Reyes .08 .25
GD58 Tim Unroe .08 .25
GD59 Tim Vanegmond .08 .25
GD60 Turner Ward .08 .25
GD61 Bob Wickman .08 .25
GD62 Chuck Knoblauch .15 .40
GD63 Paul Molitor .15 .40
GD64 Kirby Puckett .40 1.00
GD65 Tom Quinlan .08 .25
GD66 Rich Robertson .08 .25
GD67 Dave Stevens .08 .25
GD68 Matt Walbeck .08 .25
GD69 Wade Boggs .25 .60
GD70 Tony Fernandez .08 .25
GD71 Andy Fox .08 .25
GD72 Joe Girardi .08 .25
GD73 Charlie Hayes .08 .25
GD74 Pat Kelly .08 .25
GD75 Jeff Nelson .08 .25
GD76 Melido Perez .08 .25
GD77 Mark Acre .08 .25
GD78 Allen Battle .08 .25
GD79 Rafael Bournigal .08 .25
GD80 Mark McGwire 1.25 3.00
GD81 Pedro Munoz .08 .25
GD82 Scott Spiezio .08 .25
GD83 Don Wengert .08 .25
GD84 Steve Wojciechowski .08 .25
GD85 Alex Diaz .08 .25
GD86 Ken Griffey Jr. 1.00 2.50
GD87 Raul Ibanez .08 .25
GD88 Mike Jackson .08 .25
GD89 John Marzano .08 .25
GD90 Greg McCarthy .08 .25
GD91 Alex Rodriguez .75 2.00
GD92 Andy Sheets .08 .25
GD93 Mac Suzuki .08 .25
GD94 Benji Gil .08 .25
GD95 Juan Gonzalez .15 .40
GD96 Kevin Gross .08 .25
GD97 Gil Heredia .08 .25
GD98 Luis Ortiz .08 .25
GD99 Jeff Russell .08 .25
GD100 Dave Valle .08 .25
GD101 Marty Janzen .08 .25
GD102 Sandy Martinez .08 .25
GD103 Julio Mosquera .08 .25
GD104 Otis Nixon .08 .25
GD105 Paul Spoljaric .08 .25
GD106 Shannon Stewart .15 .40
GD107 Woody Williams .08 .25
GD108 Steve Avery .08 .25
GD109 Mike Bielecki .08 .25
GD110 Pedro Borbon .08 .25
GD111 Ed Giovanola .08 .25
GD112 Chipper Jones .40 1.00
GD113 Greg Maddux .75 2.00
GD114 Mike Mordecai .08 .25
GD115 Terrell Wade .08 .25
GD116 Terry Adams .08 .25
GD117 Brian Dorsett .08 .25
GD118 Doug Glanville .08 .25
GD119 Tyler Houston .08 .25
GD120 Robin Jennings .08 .25
GD121 Ryne Sandberg .75 2.00
GD122 Terry Shumpert .08 .25
GD123 Amaury Telemaco .08 .25
GD124 Steve Trachsel .08 .25
GD125 Curtis Goodwin .08 .25
GD126 Mike Kelly .08 .25
GD127 Chad Mottola .08 .25
GD128 Mark Portugal .08 .25
GD129 Roger Salkeld .08 .25
GD130 John Smiley .08 .25
GD131 Lee Smith .15 .40
GD132 Roger Bailey .08 .25
GD133 Andres Galarraga .15 .40
GD134 Darren Holmes .08 .25
GD135 Curtis Leskanic .08 .25
GD136 Mike Munoz .08 .25
GD137 Jeff Reed .08 .25
GD138 Mark Thompson .08 .25
GD139 Jamey Wright .08 .25
GD140 Andre Dawson .15 .40
GD141 Craig Grebeck .08 .25
GD142 Matt Mantei .08 .25
GD143 Billy McMillon .08 .25
GD144 Kurt Miller .08 .25
GD145 Ralph Milliard .08 .25
GD146 Bob Natal .08 .25
GD147 Joe Siddall .08 .25
GD148 Bob Abreu .25 .60
GD149 Doug Brocail .08 .25
GD150 Danny Darwin .08 .25
GD151 Mike Hampton .15 .40
GD152 Todd Jones .08 .25
GD153 Kirt Manwaring .08 .25
GD154 Alvin Morman .08 .25
GD155 Billy Ashley .08 .25
GD156 Tom Candiotti .08 .25
GD157 Darren Dreifort .08 .25
GD158 Greg Gagne .08 .25
GD159 Wilton Guerrero .08 .25
GD160 Hideo Nomo .40 1.00
GD161 Mike Piazza .75 2.00
GD162 Tom Prince .08 .25
GD163 Todd Worrell .08 .25
GD164 Moises Alou .15 .40
GD165 Shane Andrews .08 .25
GD166 Derek Aucoin .08 .25
GD167 Raul Chavez .08 .25
GD168 Darrin Fletcher .08 .25
GD169 Mark Leiter .08 .25
GD170 Henry Rodriguez .08 .25
GD171 Dave Veres .08 .25
GD172 Paul Byrd .08 .25
GD173 Alberto Castillo .08 .25
GD174 Mark Clark .08 .25
GD175 Rey Ordonez .08 .25
GD176 Roberto Petagine .08 .25
GD177 Andy Tomberlin .08 .25
GD178 Derek Wallace .08 .25
GD179 Paul Wilson .08 .25
GD180 Ruben Amaro Jr. .08 .25
GD181 Toby Borland .08 .25
GD182 Rich Hunter .08 .25
GD183 Tony Longmire .08 .25
GD184 Wendell Magee .08 .25
GD185 Bobby Munoz .08 .25
GD186 Scott Rolen .25 .60
GD187 Mike Williams .08 .25
GD188 Trey Beamon .08 .25
GD189 Jason Christiansen .08 .25
GD190 Elmer Dessens .08 .25
GD191 Angelo Encarnacion .08 .25
GD192 Carlos Garcia .08 .25
GD193 Mike Kingery .08 .25
GD194 Chris Peters .08 .25
GD195 Tony Womack .15 .40
GD196 Brian Barber .08 .25
GD197 David Bell .08 .25
GD198 Tony Fossas .08 .25
GD199 Rick Honeycutt .08 .25
GD200 T.J. Mathews .08 .25
GD201 Miguel Mejia .08 .25
GD202 Donovan Osborne .08 .25
GD203 Ozzie Smith .60 1.50
GD204 Andres Berumen .08 .25
GD205 Ken Caminiti .15 .40
GD206 Chris Gwynn .08 .25
GD207 Tony Gwynn .60 1.50
GD208 Rickey Henderson .40 1.00
GD209 Scott Sanders .08 .25
GD210 Jason Thompson .08 .25
GD211 Fernando Valenzuela .15 .40
GD212 Tim Worrell .08 .25
GD213 Barry Bonds 1.25 3.00
GD214 Jay Canizaro .08 .25
GD215 Doug Creek .08 .25
GD216 Jacob Cruz .08 .25
GD217 Glenallen Hill .08 .25
GD218 Tom Lampkin .08 .25
GD219 Jim Poole .08 .25
GD220 Desi Wilson .08 .25

1997 Pacific Prisms Sizzling Lumber

COMPLETE SET (36) 40.00 100.00
STATED ODDS 1:37
SL1A Cal Ripken 6.00 15.00
SL1B Rafael Palmeiro .75 2.00
SL1C Roberto Alomar 1.25 3.00
SL2A Frank Thomas 2.00 5.00
SL2B Robin Ventura .75 2.00
SL2C Harold Baines 1.25 3.00
SL3A Albert Belle .75 2.00
SL3B Manny Ramirez 1.25 3.00
SL3C Kenny Lofton .75 2.00
SL4A Derek Jeter 5.00 12.00
SL4B Bernie Williams 1.25 3.00
SL4C Wade Boggs 1.25 3.00
SL5A Mark McGwire 3.00 8.00
SL5B Jason Giambi .75 2.00
SL5C Geronimo Berroa .75 2.00
SL6A Ken Griffey Jr. 4.00 10.00
SL6B Alex Rodriguez 2.50 6.00
SL6C Jay Buhner .75 2.00
SL7A Juan Gonzalez .75 2.00
SL7B Dean Palmer .75 2.00
SL7C Ivan Rodriguez 1.25 3.00
SL8A Ryan Klesko .75 2.00
SL8B Chipper Jones 2.00 5.00
SL8C Andruw Jones .75 2.00
SL9A Dante Bichette .75 2.00
SL9B Andres Galarraga 1.25 3.00
SL9C Vinny Castilla .75 2.00
SL10A Jeff Bagwell 1.25 3.00
SL10B Craig Biggio 1.25 3.00
SL10C Derek Bell .75 2.00
SL11A Mike Piazza 2.00 5.00
SL11B Raul Mondesi .75 2.00
SL11C Karim Garcia .75 2.00
SL12A Tony Gwynn 2.00 5.00
SL12B Ken Caminiti .75 2.00
SL12C Greg Vaughn .75 2.00

1997 Pacific Prisms Sluggers and Hurlers

STATED ODDS 1:145
SH1A Cal Ripken 8.00 20.00
SH1B Mike Mussina 1.50 4.00
SH2A Jose Canseco 1.50 4.00
SH2B Roger Clemens 3.00 8.00
SH3A Frank Thomas 2.50 6.00
SH3B Wilson Alvarez 1.00 2.50
SH4A Kenny Lofton 1.00 2.50
SH4B Orel Hershiser 1.00 2.50
SH5A Derek Jeter 6.00 15.00
SH5B Andy Pettitte 1.50 4.00
SH6A Ken Griffey Jr. 10.00 25.00
SH6B Randy Johnson 2.50 6.00
SH7A Alex Rodriguez 3.00 8.00
SH7B Jamie Moyer 1.00 2.50
SH8A Andruw Jones 1.00 2.50
SH8B Greg Maddux 4.00 10.00
SH9A Chipper Jones 2.50 6.00
SH9B John Smoltz 1.50 4.00
SH10A Jeff Bagwell 1.50 4.00
SH10B Shane Reynolds 1.00 2.50
SH11A Mike Piazza 2.50 6.00
SH11B Hideo Nomo 1.50 4.00
SH12A Tony Gwynn 2.50 6.00
SH12B Fernando Valenzuela 1.00 2.50

1999 Pacific Prism

The 1999 Pacific Prism set was issued in one series totalling 150 cards. The fronts feature a color action player cropped photo printed on holographic silver foil cards. The backs carry two more player photos and career statistics. An unnumbered Tony Gwynn sample card was distributed to dealers and hobby media prior to the product's release. The card is easy to recognize by the bold, diagonal "SAMPLE" text running across the back. An additional version of this sample card was distributed to attendees of a private party hosted by Pacific at Hawaii XIV Trade Seminar in February, 1999. This special sample card features a bold gold foil "Pacific Hawaii XIV" logo at the lower right corner of the card front and is also serial numbered to 200 in red ink by hand on the card front.

COMPLETE SET (150) 25.00 60.00
1 Garret Anderson .25 .60
2 Jim Edmonds .25 .60
3 Darin Erstad .25 .60
4 Chuck Finley .25 .60
5 Tim Salmon .40 1.00
6 Jay Bell .25 .60
7 David Dellucci .15 .40
8 Travis Lee .15 .40
9 Matt Williams .25 .60
10 Andres Galarraga .25 .60
11 Tom Glavine .40 1.00
12 Andruw Jones .40 1.00
13 Chipper Jones .60 1.50
14 Ryan Klesko .25 .60
15 Javy Lopez .25 .60
16 Greg Maddux 1.00 2.50
17 Roberto Alomar .40 1.00
18 Ryan Minor .15 .40
19 Mike Mussina .40 1.00
20 Rafael Palmeiro .40 1.00
21 Cal Ripken 2.00 5.00
22 Nomar Garciaparra 1.00 2.50
23 Pedro Martinez .40 1.00
24 John Valentin .15 .40
25 Mo Vaughn .25 .60
26 Tim Wakefield .25 .60
27 Rod Beck .15 .40
28 Mark Grace .40 1.00
29 Lance Johnson .15 .40
30 Sammy Sosa .60 1.50
31 Kerry Wood .25 .60
32 Albert Belle .25 .60
33 Mike Caruso .15 .40
34 Magglio Ordonez .25 .60
35 Frank Thomas .60 1.50
36 Robin Ventura .25 .60
37 Aaron Boone .25 .60
38 Barry Larkin .40 1.00
39 Reggie Sanders .25 .60
40 Brett Tomko .15 .40
41 Sandy Alomar Jr. .15 .40
42 Bartolo Colon .25 .60
43 David Justice .25 .60
44 Kenny Lofton .25 .60
45 Manny Ramirez .40 1.00
46 Richie Sexson .25 .60
47 Jim Thome .40 1.00
48 Omar Vizquel .40 1.00
49 Dante Bichette .25 .60
50 Vinny Castilla .25 .60
51 Edgard Clemente .15 .40
52 Todd Helton .40 1.00
53 Quinton McCracken .15 .40
54 Larry Walker .25 .60
55 Tony Clark .15 .40
56 Damion Easley .15 .40
57 Luis Gonzalez .25 .60
58 Bob Higginson .25 .60
59 Brian Hunter .15 .40
60 Cliff Floyd .25 .60
61 Alex Gonzalez .15 .40
62 Livan Hernandez .25 .60
63 Derrek Lee .40 1.00
64 Edgar Renteria .25 .60
65 Moises Alou .25 .60
66 Jeff Bagwell .40 1.00
67 Derek Bell .15 .40
68 Craig Biggio .40 1.00
69 Randy Johnson .60 1.50
70 Johnny Damon .40 1.00
71 Jeff King .15 .40
72 Hal Morris .15 .40
73 Dean Palmer .25 .60
74 Eric Karros .25 .60
75 Raul Mondesi .25 .60
76 Chan Ho Park .25 .60
77 Gary Sheffield .25 .60
78 Jeromy Burnitz .25 .60
79 Jeff Cirillo .15 .40
80 Marquis Grissom .25 .60
81 Jose Valentin .15 .40
82 Fernando Vina .15 .40
83 Paul Molitor .25 .60
84 Otis Nixon .15 .40
85 David Ortiz .60 1.50
86 Todd Walker .15 .40
87 Vladimir Guerrero .60 1.50
88 Carl Pavano .25 .60
89 Fernando Seguignol .15 .40
90 Ugueth Urbina .15 .40
91 Carlos Baerga .15 .40
92 Bobby Bonilla .25 .60
93 Hideo Nomo .60 1.50
94 John Olerud .25 .60
95 Rey Ordonez .15 .40
96 Mike Piazza 1.00 2.50
97 David Cone .25 .60
98 Orlando Hernandez .25 .60
99 Hideki Irabu .15 .40
100 Derek Jeter 1.50 4.00
101 Tino Martinez .40 1.00
102 Bernie Williams .40 1.00
103 Eric Chavez .25 .60
104 Jason Giambi .25 .60
105 Ben Grieve .15 .40
106 Rickey Henderson .60 1.50
107 Bob Abreu .25 .60
108 Doug Glanville .15 .40
109 Scott Rolen .40 1.00
110 Curt Schilling .25 .60
111 Emil Brown .15 .40
112 Jose Guillen .25 .60
113 Jason Kendall .25 .60
114 Al Martin .15 .40
115 Aramis Ramirez .25 .60
116 Kevin Young .25 .60
117 J.D. Drew .25 .60
118 Ron Gant .25 .60
119 Brian Jordan .25 .60
120 Eli Marrero .15 .40
121 Mark McGwire 1.50 4.00
122 Kevin Brown .40 1.00
123 Tony Gwynn .75 2.00
124 Trevor Hoffman .25 .60
125 Wally Joyner .25 .60
126 Greg Vaughn .15 .40
127 Barry Bonds 1.50 4.00
128 Ellis Burks .25 .60
129 Jeff Kent .25 .60
130 Robb Nen .25 .60
131 J.T. Snow .25 .60
132 Jay Buhner .25 .60
133 Ken Griffey Jr. 1.25 3.00
134 Edgar Martinez .40 1.00
135 Alex Rodriguez 1.00 2.50
136 David Segui .15 .40
137 Rolando Arrojo .15 .40
138 Wade Boggs .40 1.00
139 Aaron Ledesma .15 .40
140 Fred McGriff .40 1.00
141 Will Clark .40 1.00
142 Juan Gonzalez .25 .60
143 Rusty Greer .25 .60
144 Ivan Rodriguez .40 1.00
145 Aaron Sele .15 .40
146 Jose Canseco .40 1.00
147 Roger Clemens 1.25 3.00
148 Jose Cruz Jr. .15 .40
149 Carlos Delgado .25 .60
150 Alex Gonzalez .15 .40
SA Tony Gwynn Sample .40 1.00
SAH Tony Gwynn Hawaii/200 6.00 15.00

1999 Pacific Prism Holographic Blue

*STARS: 6X TO 15X BASIC CARDS
RANDOM INSERTS IN PACKS
STATED PRINT RUN 80 SERIAL #'d SETS

1999 Pacific Prism Holographic Gold

*STARS: 2X TO 5X BASIC CARDS
RANDOM INSERTS IN PACKS
STATED PRINT RUN 480 SERIAL #'d SETS

1999 Pacific Prism Holographic Mirror

*STARS: 4X TO 10X BASIC CARDS
RANDOM INSERTS IN PACKS
STATED PRINT RUN 160 SERIAL #'d SETS

1999 Pacific Prism Holographic Purple

*STARS: 2.5X TO 6X BASIC CARDS
RANDOM INSERTS IN HOBBY PACKS
STATED PRINT RUN 320 SERIAL #'d SETS

1999 Pacific Prism Red

*STARS: 1.5X TO 4X BASIC CARDS
STATED ODDS 2:25 RETAIL

1999 Pacific Prism Ahead of the Game

COMPLETE SET (20) 60.00 120.00
STATED ODDS 1:49
1 Darin Erstad 1.25 3.00
2 Travis Lee .75 2.00
3 Chipper Jones 3.00 8.00
4 Cal Ripken 10.00 25.00
5 Nomar Garciaparra 5.00 12.00
6 Sammy Sosa 3.00 8.00
7 Kerry Wood 1.25 3.00
8 Frank Thomas 3.00 8.00
9 Manny Ramirez 2.00 5.00
10 Todd Helton 2.00 5.00
11 Jeff Bagwell 2.00 5.00
12 Mike Piazza 5.00 12.00
13 Derek Jeter 8.00 20.00
14 Bernie Williams 2.00 5.00
15 J.D. Drew 1.25 3.00
16 Mark McGwire 8.00 20.00
17 Tony Gwynn 4.00 10.00
18 Ken Griffey Jr. 6.00 15.00
19 Alex Rodriguez 5.00 12.00
20 Ivan Rodriguez 2.00 5.00

1999 Pacific Prism Ballpark Legends

COMPLETE SET (10) 75.00 150.00
STATED ODDS 1:193
1 Cal Ripken 20.00 50.00
2 Nomar Garciaparra 10.00 25.00
3 Frank Thomas 6.00 15.00
4 Ken Griffey Jr. 12.50 30.00
5 Alex Rodriguez 10.00 25.00
6 Greg Maddux 10.00 25.00
7 Sammy Sosa 6.00 15.00
8 Kerry Wood 2.50 6.00
9 Mark McGwire 15.00 40.00
10 Tony Gwynn 8.00 20.00

1999 Pacific Prism Diamond Glory

COMPLETE SET (20) 20.00 50.00
STATED ODDS 2:25
1 Darin Erstad .50 1.25
2 Travis Lee .30 .75
3 Chipper Jones 1.25 3.00
4 Greg Maddux 2.00 5.00
5 Cal Ripken 4.00 10.00
6 Nomar Garciaparra 2.00 5.00
7 Sammy Sosa 1.25 3.00
8 Kerry Wood .50 1.25
9 Frank Thomas 1.25 3.00
10 Todd Helton .75 2.00
11 Jeff Bagwell .75 2.00
12 Mike Piazza 2.00 5.00
13 Derek Jeter 3.00 8.00
14 Bernie Williams .75 2.00
15 J.D. Drew .50 1.25
16 Mark McGwire 3.00 8.00
17 Tony Gwynn 1.50 4.00
18 Ken Griffey Jr. 2.50 6.00
19 Alex Rodriguez 2.00 5.00
20 Juan Gonzalez .50 1.25

1999 Pacific Prism Epic Performers

COMPLETE SET (10) 40.00 100.00
STATED ODDS 1:97 HOBBY
1 Cal Ripken 12.50 30.00
2 Nomar Garciaparra 6.00 15.00
3 Frank Thomas 4.00 10.00
4 Ken Griffey Jr. 8.00 20.00
5 Alex Rodriguez 6.00 15.00
6 Greg Maddux 6.00 15.00
7 Sammy Sosa 4.00 10.00
8 Kerry Wood 1.50 4.00
9 Mark McGwire 10.00 25.00
10 Tony Gwynn 5.00 12.00

2000 Pacific Prism

COMPLETE SET (150) 10.00 25.00
COMMON CARD (1-150) .15 .40
COMMON RC .15 .40
1 Jeff DaVanon RC .15 .40
2 Troy Glaus .15 .40
3 Tim Salmon .15 .40
4 Mo Vaughn .15 .40
5 Jay Bell .15 .40
6 Erubiel Durazo .15 .40
7 Luis Gonzalez .15 .40
8 Randy Johnson .40 1.00
9 Matt Williams .15 .40
10 Andres Galarraga .25 .60
11 Andruw Jones .15 .40
12 Chipper Jones .40 1.00
13 Brian Jordan .15 .40
14 Greg Maddux .50 1.25
15 Kevin Millwood .15 .40
16 John Smoltz .40 1.00
17 Albert Belle .15 .40
18 Mike Mussina .25 .60
19 Calvin Pickering .15 .40
20 Cal Ripken 1.25 3.00
21 B.J. Surhoff .15 .40
22 Nomar Garciaparra .25 .60
23 Pedro Martinez .25 .60
24 Troy O'Leary .15 .40
25 John Valentin .15 .40
26 Jason Varitek .40 1.00
27 Mark Grace .25 .60
28 Henry Rodriguez .15 .40
29 Sammy Sosa .40 1.00
30 Kerry Wood .15 .40
31 Ray Durham .15 .40
32 Carlos Lee .15 .40
33 Magglio Ordonez .25 .60
34 Chris Singleton .15 .40
35 Frank Thomas .40 1.00
36 Sean Casey .15 .40
37 Travis Dawkins .15 .40
38 Barry Larkin .25 .60
39 Pokey Reese .15 .40
40 Scott Williamson .15 .40
41 Roberto Alomar .25 .60
42 Bartolo Colon .15 .40
43 David Justice .15 .40
44 Manny Ramirez .40 1.00
45 Richie Sexson .15 .40
46 Jim Thome .25 .60
47 Omar Vizquel .25 .60
48 Pedro Astacio .15 .40
49 Todd Helton .25 .60
50 Neifi Perez .15 .40
51 Ben Petrick .15 .40
52 Larry Walker .25 .60
53 Tony Clark .15 .40
54 Damion Easley .15 .40
55 Juan Gonzalez .15 .40
56 Dean Palmer .15 .40
57 A.J. Burnett .15 .40
58 Luis Castillo .15 .40
59 Cliff Floyd .15 .40
60 Alex Gonzalez .15 .40
61 Preston Wilson .15 .40
62 Jeff Bagwell .25 .60
63 Craig Biggio .25 .60
64 Ken Caminiti .15 .40
65 Jose Lima .15 .40
66 Billy Wagner .15 .40
67 Carlos Beltran .25 .60
68 Johnny Damon .25 .60
69 Jermaine Dye .15 .40
70 Carlos Febles .15 .40
71 Mike Sweeney .15 .40
72 Kevin Brown .15 .40
73 Shawn Green .15 .40
74 Eric Karros .15 .40
75 Chan Ho Park .25 .60
76 Gary Sheffield .15 .40
77 Ron Belliard .15 .40
78 Jeromy Burnitz .15 .40
79 Marquis Grissom .15 .40
80 Geoff Jenkins .15 .40
81 Mark Loretta .15 .40
82 Ron Coomer .15 .40
83 Jacque Jones .15 .40
84 Corey Koskie .15 .40
85 Brad Radke .15 .40
86 Todd Walker .15 .40
87 Michael Barrett .15 .40
88 Peter Bergeron .15 .40
89 Vladimir Guerrero .25 .60
90 Jose Vidro .15 .40
91 Rondell White .15 .40
92 Edgardo Alfonzo .15 .40
93 Rickey Henderson .40 1.00
94 Rey Ordonez .15 .40
95 Mike Piazza .40 1.00
96 Robin Ventura .15 .40
97 Roger Clemens .50 1.25
98 Orlando Hernandez .15 .40
99 Derek Jeter 1.00 2.50
100 Tino Martinez .15 .40
101 Mariano Rivera .50 1.25
102 Alfonso Soriano .40 1.00
103 Bernie Williams .25 .60
104 Eric Chavez .15 .40
105 Jason Giambi .15 .40
106 Ben Grieve .15 .40
107 Tim Hudson .25 .60
108 John Jaha .15 .40
109 Bobby Abreu .15 .40
110 Doug Glanville .15 .40
111 Mike Lieberthal .15 .40
112 Scott Rolen .25 .60
113 Curt Schilling .25 .60
114 Brian Giles .15 .40
115 Jason Kendall .15 .40
116 Warren Morris .15 .40
117 Kevin Young .15 .40
118 Rick Ankiel .25 .60
119 J.D. Drew .15 .40
120 Chad Hutchinson .15 .40
121 Ray Lankford .15 .40
122 Mark McGwire .60 1.50
123 Fernando Tatis .15 .40
124 Bret Boone .15 .40
125 Ben Davis .15 .40
126 Tony Gwynn .40 1.00
127 Trevor Hoffman .25 .60
128 Barry Bonds .60 1.50
129 Ellis Burks .15 .40
130 Jeff Kent .15 .40
131 J.T. Snow .15 .40
132 Freddy Garcia .15 .40
133 Ken Griffey Jr. .75 2.00
134 Edgar Martinez .25 .60
135 John Olerud .15 .40
136 Alex Rodriguez .50 1.25
137 Jose Canseco .25 .60
138 Vinny Castilla .15 .40
139 Roberto Hernandez .15 .40
140 Fred McGriff .25 .60
141 Rusty Greer .15 .40
142 Ruben Mateo .15 .40
143 Rafael Palmeiro .25 .60
144 Ivan Rodriguez .25 .60
145 Lee Stevens .15 .40
146 Tony Batista .15 .40
147 Carlos Delgado .15 .40
148 Shannon Stewart .15 .40
149 David Wells .15 .40
150 Vernon Wells .15 .40

2000 Pacific Prism Drops Silver

*PRIS.DROPS: .75X TO 2X BASIC
STATED PRINT RUN 799 SETS
ASTERISK PRINT RUN 916 SETS
50 PLAYERS HAVE 916 OF EACH CARD

2000 Pacific Prism Holographic Blue

*HOLO.BLUE: 6X TO 15X BASIC
STATED PRINT RUN 80 SERIAL #'d SETS

2000 Pacific Prism Holographic Gold

*HOLO.GOLD: 2X TO 5X BASIC
STATED PRINT RUN 480 SERIAL #'d SETS

2000 Pacific Prism Holographic Mirror

*HOLO.MIRROR: 3X TO 8X BASIC
STATED PRINT RUN 160 SERIAL #'d SETS

2000 Pacific Prism Holographic Purple

*HOLO.PURP: 5X TO 12X BASIC
STATED PRINT RUN 99 SERIAL #'d SETS

2000 Pacific Prism Pebbly Dots

*PEBBLY: 1.25X TO 3X BASIC
STATED PRINT RUN 691 SETS
ASTERISK PRINT RUN 448 SETS
50 PLAYERS HAVE 448 OF EACH CARD

2000 Pacific Prism Premiere Date

*PREM.DATE: 8X TO 20X BASIC
STATED ODDS 1:24 HOBBY
STATED PRINT RUN 61 SERIAL #'d SETS

2000 Pacific Prism Proofs

NO PRICING DUE TO SCARCITY

2000 Pacific Prism Rapture Gold

*RAP.GOLD: 1.5X TO 4X BASIC
STATED PRINT RUN 565 SETS

2000 Pacific Prism Rapture Silver

*RAP.SILVER: .75X TO 2X BASIC
STATED PRINT RUN 916 SETS

2000 Pacific Prism Sheen Silver

*SHEEN.SILV: 1.25X TO 3X BASIC
STATED PRINT RUN 448 SETS
50 PLAYERS HAVE 565 OF EACH CARD
ASTERISK PRINT RUN 565 SETS
SKIP-NUMBERED 100-CARD SET
1 Jeff DaVanon * .50 1.25
2 Troy Glaus * .50 1.25
3 Tim Salmon * .50 1.25
5 Jay Bell * .50 1.25
6 Erubiel Durazo * .50 1.25
7 Luis Gonzalez * .50 1.25
10 Andres Galarraga * .75 2.00
13 Brian Jordan * .50 1.25
15 Kevin Millwood * .50 1.25
16 John Smoltz * 1.25 3.00
17 Albert Belle * .50 1.25
19 Calvin Pickering * .50 1.25
21 B.J. Surhoff * .50 1.25
24 Troy O'Leary * .50 1.25
25 John Valentin * .50 1.25
26 Jason Varitek * 1.25 3.00
27 Mark Grace * .75 2.00
28 Henry Rodriguez * .50 1.25
31 Ray Durham * .50 1.25
32 Carlos Lee * .50 1.25
34 Chris Singleton * .50 1.25
37 Travis Dawkins * .50 1.25
38 Barry Larkin * .75 2.00
39 Pokey Reese * .50 1.25
40 Scott Williamson * .50 1.25
42 Bartolo Colon .50 1.25
43 David Justice .50 1.25
45 Richie Sexson .50 1.25
47 Omar Vizquel .75 2.00
48 Pedro Astacio .50 1.25
50 Neifi Perez .50 1.25
51 Ben Petrick .50 1.25
53 Tony Clark .50 1.25
54 Damion Easley .50 1.25
56 Dean Palmer .50 1.25
57 A.J. Burnett .50 1.25
58 Luis Castillo .50 1.25
59 Cliff Floyd .50 1.25
60 Alex Gonzalez .50 1.25
64 Ken Caminiti .50 1.25
65 Jose Lima .50 1.25
66 Billy Wagner .50 1.25
68 Johnny Damon .75 2.00
69 Jermaine Dye .50 1.25
70 Carlos Febles .50 1.25
71 Mike Sweeney .50 1.25
74 Eric Karros .50 1.25
75 Chan Ho Park .75 2.00
77 Ron Belliard .50 1.25
79 Marquis Grissom .50 1.25
80 Geoff Jenkins * .50 1.25
81 Mark Loretta * .50 1.25
82 Ron Coomer * .50 1.25
83 Jacque Jones * .50 1.25
84 Corey Koskie * .50 1.25
85 Brad Radke * .50 1.25
86 Todd Walker * .50 1.25
87 Michael Barrett * .50 1.25
88 Peter Bergeron * .50 1.25
90 Jose Vidro * .50 1.25
91 Rondell White * .50 1.25
93 Rickey Henderson * 1.25 3.00
94 Rey Ordonez * .50 1.25
96 Robin Ventura * .50 1.25
98 Orlando Hernandez * .50 1.25
100 Tino Martinez * .50 1.25
101 Mariano Rivera * 1.50 4.00
102 Alfonso Soriano * 1.25 3.00
104 Eric Chavez * .50 1.25
105 Jason Giambi * .50 1.25
106 Ben Grieve * .50 1.25
107 Tim Hudson * .75 2.00
108 John Jaha * .50 1.25
109 Bobby Abreu * .50 1.25
110 Doug Glanville * .50 1.25
111 Mike Lieberthal .50 1.25
113 Curt Schilling .75 2.00
115 Jason Kendall .50 1.25
116 Warren Morris .50 1.25
117 Kevin Young .50 1.25
120 Chad Hutchinson .50 1.25
121 Ray Lankford .50 1.25
123 Fernando Tatis .50 1.25
124 Bret Boone .50 1.25
125 Ben Davis .50 1.25
127 Trevor Hoffman .75 2.00
129 Ellis Burks .50 1.25
130 Jeff Kent .50 1.25
131 J.T. Snow .50 1.25
134 Edgar Martinez .75 2.00
135 John Olerud .50 1.25
138 Vinny Castilla .50 1.25
139 Roberto Hernandez .50 1.25
140 Fred McGriff .75 2.00
141 Rusty Greer .50 1.25
145 Lee Stevens .50 1.25
146 Tony Batista .50 1.25
148 Shannon Stewart .50 1.25
149 David Wells .50 1.25
150 Vernon Wells .50 1.25

2000 Pacific Prism Slider Silver

*SLID.SILVER: 1.25X TO 3X BASIC
TIER 1 PRINT RUN 334 SETS
TIER 2 PRINT RUN 448 SETS
TIER 3 PRINT RUN 565 SETS
RANDOM INSERTS IN HOB/RET PACKS
1 Jeff DaVanon T1 .60 1.50
2 Troy Glaus T1 .60 1.50
3 Tim Salmon T1 .60 1.50
4 Mo Vaughn T3 .60 1.50
5 Jay Bell T1 .60 1.50
6 Erubiel Durazo T1 .60 1.50
7 Luis Gonzalez T1 .60 1.50
8 Randy Johnson T3 1.50 4.00
9 Matt Williams T3 .60 1.50
10 Andres Galarraga T1 1.00 2.50
11 Andruw Jones T3 .60 1.50
12 Chipper Jones T3 1.50 4.00
13 Brian Jordan T1 .60 1.50
14 Greg Maddux T3 2.00 5.00
15 Kevin Millwood T1 .60 1.50
16 John Smoltz T1 1.50 4.00
17 Albert Belle T1 .60 1.50
18 Mike Mussina T3 1.00 2.50
19 Calvin Pickering T1 .60 1.50
20 Cal Ripken T3 5.00 12.00
21 B.J. Surhoff T1 .60 1.50
22 Nomar Garciaparra T3 1.00 2.50
23 Pedro Martinez T3 1.00 2.50
24 Troy O'Leary T1 .60 1.50
25 John Valentin T1 .60 1.50
26 Jason Varitek T1 1.50 4.00
27 Mark Grace T1 1.00 2.50
28 Henry Rodriguez T1 .60 1.50
29 Sammy Sosa T3 1.50 4.00
30 Kerry Wood T3 .60 1.50
31 Ray Durham T1 .60 1.50
32 Carlos Lee T1 .60 1.50
33 Magglio Ordonez T3 1.00 2.50
34 Chris Singleton T1 .60 1.50
35 Frank Thomas T3 1.50 4.00
36 Sean Casey T3 .60 1.50
37 Travis Dawkins T1 .60 1.50
38 Barry Larkin T1 1.00 2.50
39 Pokey Reese T1 .60 1.50
40 Scott Williamson T1 .60 1.50
41 Roberto Alomar T3 1.00 2.50
42 Bartolo Colon T2 .60 1.50
43 David Justice T2 .60 1.50
44 Manny Ramirez T3 1.50 4.00
45 Richie Sexson T2 .60 1.50
46 Jim Thome T3 1.00 2.50
47 Omar Vizquel T2 1.00 2.50
48 Pedro Astacio T2 .60 1.50
49 Todd Helton T3 1.00 2.50
50 Neifi Perez T2 .60 1.50
51 Ben Petrick T2 .60 1.50
52 Larry Walker T3 1.00 2.50
53 Tony Clark T2 .60 1.50
54 Damion Easley T2 .60 1.50
55 Juan Gonzalez T3 .60 1.50
56 Dean Palmer T2 .60 1.50
57 A.J. Burnett T2 .60 1.50
58 Luis Castillo T2 .60 1.50
59 Cliff Floyd T2 .60 1.50
60 Alex Gonzalez T2 .60 1.50
61 Preston Wilson T3 .60 1.50
62 Jeff Bagwell T3 1.00 2.50
63 Craig Biggio T3 1.00 2.50
64 Ken Caminiti T2 .60 1.50
65 Jose Lima T2 .60 1.50
66 Billy Wagner T2 .60 1.50
67 Carlos Beltran T3 1.00 2.50
68 Johnny Damon T2 1.00 2.50
69 Jermaine Dye T2 .60 1.50
70 Carlos Febles T2 .60 1.50
71 Mike Sweeney T2 .60 1.50
72 Kevin Brown T3 .60 1.50
73 Shawn Green T3 .60 1.50
74 Eric Karros T2 .60 1.50
75 Chan Ho Park T2 1.00 2.50
76 Gary Sheffield T3 .60 1.50
77 Ron Belliard T2 .60 1.50
78 Jeromy Burnitz T3 .60 1.50
79 Marquis Grissom T2 .60 1.50
80 Geoff Jenkins T1 .60 1.50
81 Mark Loretta T1 .60 1.50
82 Ron Coomer T1 .60 1.50
83 Jacque Jones T1 .60 1.50
84 Corey Koskie T1 .60 1.50
85 Brad Radke T1 .60 1.50
86 Todd Walker T1 .60 1.50
87 Michael Barrett T1 .60 1.50
88 Peter Bergeron T1 .60 1.50
89 Vladimir Guerrero T3 1.00 2.50
90 Jose Vidro T1 .60 1.50
91 Rondell White T1 .60 1.50
92 Edgardo Alfonzo T3 .60 1.50
93 Rickey Henderson T1 1.50 4.00
94 Rey Ordonez T1 .60 1.50
95 Mike Piazza T3 1.50 4.00
96 Robin Ventura T1 .60 1.50
97 Roger Clemens T3 2.00 5.00
98 Orlando Hernandez T1 .60 1.50
99 Derek Jeter T3 4.00 10.00
100 Tino Martinez T1 .60 1.50
101 Mariano Rivera T1 2.00 5.00
102 Alfonso Soriano T1 1.50 4.00
103 Bernie Williams T3 1.00 2.50
104 Eric Chavez T1 .60 1.50
105 Jason Giambi T1 .60 1.50
106 Ben Grieve T1 .60 1.50
107 Tim Hudson T1 1.00 2.50
108 John Jaha T1 .60 1.50
109 Bobby Abreu T1 .60 1.50
110 Doug Glanville T1 .60 1.50
111 Mike Lieberthal T2 .60 1.50
112 Scott Rolen T3 1.00 2.50
113 Curt Schilling T2 1.00 2.50
114 Brian Giles T3 .60 1.50
115 Jason Kendall T2 .60 1.50
116 Warren Morris T2 .60 1.50
117 Kevin Young T2 .60 1.50
118 Rick Ankiel T3 1.00 2.50
119 J.D. Drew T3 .60 1.50
120 Chad Hutchinson T2 .60 1.50
121 Ray Lankford T2 .60 1.50
122 Mark McGwire T3 2.50 6.00
123 Fernando Tatis T2 .60 1.50
124 Bret Boone T2 .60 1.50
125 Ben Davis T2 .60 1.50
126 Tony Gwynn T3 1.50 4.00
127 Trevor Hoffman T2 1.00 2.50
128 Barry Bonds T3 2.50 6.00
129 Ellis Burks T2 .60 1.50
130 Jeff Kent T2 .60 1.50
131 J.T. Snow T2 .60 1.50
132 Freddy Garcia T3 .60 1.50
133 Ken Griffey Jr. T3 3.00 8.00
134 Edgar Martinez T2 1.00 2.50
135 John Olerud T2 .60 1.50
136 Alex Rodriguez T3 2.00 5.00
137 Jose Canseco T3 1.00 2.50
138 Vinny Castilla T2 .60 1.50
139 Roberto Hernandez T2 .60 1.50
140 Fred McGriff T2 1.00 2.50
141 Rusty Greer T2 .60 1.50
142 Ruben Mateo T3 .60 1.50
143 Rafael Palmeiro T3 1.00 2.50
144 Ivan Rodriguez T3 1.00 2.50
145 Lee Stevens T2 .60 1.50
146 Tony Batista T2 .60 1.50
147 Carlos Delgado T3 .60 1.50
148 Shannon Stewart T2 .60 1.50
149 David Wells T2 .60 1.50
150 Vernon Wells T2 .60 1.50

2000 Pacific Prism Texture Silver

*TEX.SILVER: 1.25X TO 3X BASIC
STATED PRINT RUN 448 SETS

2000 Pacific Prism Tinsel Silver

*TINS.SILVER: 2X TO 5X BASIC
STATED PRINT RUN 331 SETS

2000 Pacific Prism Woodgrain Silver

*WOOD.SILVER: 2X TO 5X BASIC
STATED PRINT RUN 331 SETS

2000 Pacific Prism AL/NL Legends

COMPLETE AL SET (10) 8.00 20.00
COMPLETE NL SET (10) 8.00 20.00
STATED ODDS 1:25
A1 Mo Vaughn .40 1.00
A2 Cal Ripken 3.00 8.00
A3 Nomar Garciaparra .60 1.50
A4 Manny Ramirez 1.00 2.50
A5 Roger Clemens 1.25 3.00
A6 Derek Jeter 2.50 6.00
A7 Ken Griffey Jr. 2.00 5.00
A8 Alex Rodriguez 1.25 3.00
A9 Jose Canseco .60 1.50
A10 Rafael Palmeiro .60 1.50
N1 Chipper Jones 1.00 2.50
N2 Greg Maddux 1.25 3.00
N3 Sammy Sosa 1.00 2.50
N4 Larry Walker .60 1.50
N5 Jeff Bagwell .60 1.50
N6 Vladimir Guerrero .60 1.50
N7 Mike Piazza 1.00 2.50
N8 Mark McGwire 1.50 4.00
N9 Tony Gwynn 1.00 2.50
N10 Barry Bonds 1.50 4.00

2000 Pacific Prism Center Stage

COMPLETE SET (20) 15.00 40.00
STATED ODDS 1:25
1 Chipper Jones 1.00 2.50
2 Cal Ripken 3.00 8.00
3 Nomar Garciaparra .60 1.50
4 Pedro Martinez .60 1.50
5 Sammy Sosa 1.00 2.50
6 Sean Casey .40 1.00
7 Manny Ramirez 1.00 2.50
8 Jim Thome .60 1.50
9 Jeff Bagwell .60 1.50
10 Carlos Beltran .60 1.50
11 Vladimir Guerrero .60 1.50
12 Mike Piazza 1.00 2.50
13 Derek Jeter 2.50 6.00
14 Bernie Williams .60 1.50
15 Scott Rolen .60 1.50
16 Mark McGwire 1.50 4.00
17 Tony Gwynn 1.00 2.50
18 Ken Griffey Jr. 2.00 5.00
19 Alex Rodriguez 1.25 3.00
20 Ivan Rodriguez .60 1.50

2000 Pacific Prism Dial-A-Stats

STATED ODDS 1:193
1 Chipper Jones 3.00 8.00
2 Greg Maddux 4.00 10.00
3 Cal Ripken 10.00 25.00
4 Sammy Sosa 3.00 8.00
5 Mike Piazza 3.00 8.00
6 Roger Clemens 4.00 10.00
7 Mark McGwire 5.00 12.00
8 Tony Gwynn 3.00 8.00
9 Ken Griffey Jr. 6.00 15.00
10 Alex Rodriguez 4.00 10.00

2000 Pacific Prism Prospects Hobby

COMPLETE SET (10) 6.00 15.00
STATED ODDS 1:97 HOBBY
RETAIL PROSPECTS ODDS 1:97 RETAIL
RETAIL PROSPECTS HAVE DIF'T PHOTOS
1 Erubiel Durazo .75 2.00
2 Wilton Veras .75 2.00
3 Ben Petrick .75 2.00
4 Mark Quinn .75 2.00
5 Peter Bergeron .75 2.00
6 Alfonso Soriano 2.00 5.00
7 Tim Hudson 1.25 3.00
8 Chad Hermansen .75 2.00
9 Rick Ankiel 1.25 3.00
10 Ruben Mateo .75 2.00

2000 Pacific Prism Prospects Retail

*RETAIL: .4X TO 1X HOBBY PROSPECTS
STATED ODDS 1:97 RETAIL

1958 Packard Bell

This seven-card set includes members of the Los Angeles Dodgers and San Francisco Giants and was issued in both teams' first year on the West Coast. This black and white, unnumbered set features cards measuring approximately 3 3/8" by 5 3/8". The backs are advertisements for Packard Bell (a television and radio manufacturer) along with a schedule for either the Giants or Dodgers. There were four Giants printed and three Dodgers. The catalog designation for this set is H805-5. Since the cards are unnumbered, they are listed below alphabetically.

COMPLETE SET (7) 600.00 1200.00
1 Walt Alston MG 125.00 250.00
2 Johnny Antonelli 60.00 120.00
3 Jim Gilliam 75.00 150.00
4 Gil Hodges 150.00 300.00
5 Willie Mays 400.00 800.00
6 Bill Rigney MG 60.00 120.00
7 Hank Sauer 60.00 120.00

1969 Padres Team Issue

Measuring approximately 5" by 7", these cards feature members of the 1969 San Diego Padres during their debut season. Since these cards are unnumbered, we have sequenced them in alphabetical order. This list may be incomplete so any additions are appreciated.

COMPLETE SET 30.00 60.00
1 Nate Colbert 3.00 8.00
2 Bill Davis 2.00 5.00
3 Tom Dukes 2.00 5.00
4 Tony Gonzalez 2.00 5.00
5 Walt Hriniak 3.00 8.00
6 Chris Krug 2.00 5.00
7 Billy McCool 2.00 5.00
8 Ivan Murrell 2.00 5.00
9 John Podres 2.50 6.00
10 Frank Reberger 2.00 5.00
11 Rafael Robles 2.00 5.00
12 John Ruberto
13 John Sipin 2.00 5.00
14 Tommie Sisk 2.00 5.00
15 Larry Stahl 2.00 5.00

1969 Padres Volpe

These eight 8 1/2" by 11 cards feature members of the San Diego Padres in their inagural season. These cards feature two drawings (a large portrait shot as well as an smaller action pose) by noted sport artist Nicholas Volpe on the front. The backs have the Padres logo as well as a biography of Volpe. These cards are unnumbered and we have sequenced them in alphabetical order.

COMPLETE SET (8) 10.00 25.00
1 Ollie Brown 1.25 3.00
2 Tommy Dean 1.00 2.50
3 Al Ferrera 1.00 2.50
4 Clarence Gaston 2.00 5.00
5 Preston Gomez MG 1.25 3.00
6 Johnny Podres 1.50 4.00
7 Al Santorini 1.00 2.50
8 Ed Spiezio 1.00 2.50

1971 Padres Team Issue

Measuring approximately 5" by 7", these cards feature members of the 1971 San Diego Padres. Since these cards are unnumbered, we have sequenced them in alphabetical order.

COMPLETE SET 5.00 12.00
1 Dave Campbell .75 2.00
2 Chris Cannizzaro .40 1.00
3 Tommy Dean .40 1.00
4 Al Ferrara .40 1.00
5 Enzo Hernandez .40 1.00
6 Steve Huntz .40 1.00
7 Van Kelly .40 1.00
8 Bill Laxton .40 1.00
9 Gerry Nyman .40 1.00
10 Tom Phoebus .40 1.00
11 Al Santorini .40 1.00
12 Ron Slocum .40 1.00
13 Ramon Webster .40 1.00

1972 Padres Colbert Commemorative

This 8 1/2" by 11" photo features Nate Colbert and honors his spectacular doubleheader feat of August 1, 1972 in which he hit five homers and drove in 13 runs. Colbert is posed with a bat and balls which show what occured that day.

1 Nate Colbert 4.00 10.00

1972 Padres Postcards

This 28-card set of the San Diego Padres features borderless black-and-white player photos measuring approximately 3 3/8" by 5 3/8". The backs are blank. The cards are unnumbered and checklisted below in alphabetical order.

COMPLETE SET (28) 50.00 100.00
1 Ed Acosta 1.50 4.00
2 Steve Arlin 1.50 4.00
3 Bob Barton 1.50 4.00
4 Ollie Brown 2.00 5.00
5 Mike Caldwell 1.50 4.00
6 Dave Campbell 2.50 6.00
7 Nate Colbert 2.50 6.00
8 Mike Corkins 1.50 4.00
9 Roger Craig 2.50 6.00
10 Clarence Gaston 3.00 8.00
11 Bill Greif 1.50 4.00
12 Enzo Hernandez 1.50 4.00
13 Gary Jestadt 1.50 4.00
14 John Jeter 1.50 4.00
15 Fred Kendall 1.50 4.00
16 Clay Kirby 1.50 4.00
17 Leron Lee 1.50 4.00
18 Jerry Morales 1.50 4.00
19 Ivan Murrell 1.50 4.00
20 Fred Norman 1.50 4.00
21 Raefle Robles 1.50 4.00
22 Gary Ross 1.50 4.00
23 Mark Schaeffer 1.50 4.00
24 Ed Spiezio 1.50 4.00
25 Ron Taylor 1.50 4.00
26 Darrel Thomas 1.50 4.00
27 W. Whiettlemann CO 1.50 4.00
28 Don Zimmer MG 2.50 6.00

1973 Padres Dean's

This 30-card set of the San Diego Padres was issued in five series. The cards measure 5 1/2" by 8 1/2" and are printed on very thin paper. The fronts feature white-bordered black-and-white player portraits with the player's name and position, sponsor and team logos below the photo. The backs are blank. The cards are unnumbered and checklisted below in alphabetical order. Dave Winfield is featured in his rookie season in an item which predates his Rookie Card.

COMPLETE SET (30) 40.00 80.00
1 Steve Arlin .75 2.00
2 Mike Caldwell .75 2.00
3 Dave Campbell 1.50 4.00
4 Nate Colbert 1.25 3.00
5 Mike Corkins .75 2.00
6 Pat Corrales .75 2.00
7 Dave Garcia .75 2.00
8 Clarence Gaston 1.25 3.00
9 Bill Greif .75 2.00
10 John Grubb .75 2.00
11 Enzo Hernandez .75 2.00
12 Randy Jones 2.00 5.00
13 Fred Kendall .75 2.00
14 Clay Kirby .75 2.00
15 Leron Lee .75 2.00
16 Dave Marshall .75 2.00
17 Don Mason .75 2.00
18 Jerry Morales .75 2.00
19 Ivan Murrell .75 2.00
20 Fred Norman .75 2.00
21 Johnny Podres 1.25 3.00
22 Dave Roberts .75 2.00
23 Vicente Romo .75 2.00
24 Gary Ross .75 2.00
25 Bob Skinner .75 2.00
26 Derrel Thomas .75 2.00
27 Rich Troedson .75 2.00
28 Whitey Wietelmann CO .75 2.00
29 Dave Winfield 20.00 50.00
30 Don Zimmer 1.25 3.00

1974 Padres Dean's

These cards measure 5 1/2" by 8 1/2" and are printed on very thin paper. The fronts feature white-bordered black-and-white player photos with the player's name and position, and sponsor and team logos below the photo. The backs carry the player's career summary, biography and statistics. The cards are unnumbered and checklisted below in alphabetical order. Some of these cards are also known to come with blank backs. Dave Winfield appears in his Rookie Card season.

COMPLETE SET (30) 40.00 80.00
1 Matty Alou 1.25 3.00
2 Bob Barton .75 2.00
3 Glenn Beckert .75 2.00
4 Jack Bloomfield CO .75 2.00
5 Nate Colbert .75 2.00
6 Mike Corkins .75 2.00
7 Jim Davenport CO .75 2.00
8 Dave Freisleben .75 2.00
9 Cito Gaston 1.50 4.00
10 Bill Greif .75 2.00
11 John Grubb .75 2.00
12 Larry Hardy .75 2.00
13 Enzo Hernandez .75 2.00
14 Dave Hilton .75 2.00
15 Randy Jones 1.50 4.00
16 Fred Kendall .75 2.00
17 Gene Locklear .75 2.00
18 Willie McCovey 4.00 10.00
19 John McNamara MG .75 2.00
20 Rich Morales .75 2.00
21 Bill Poesdel CO .75 2.00
22 Dave Roberts .75 2.00
23 Vicente Romo .75 2.00
24 Dan Spillner .75 2.00
25 Derrel Thomas .75 2.00
26 Bob Tolan .75 2.00
27 Rich Troedson .75 2.00
28 Whitey Wietelmann CO 1.25 3.00
29 Bernie Williams .75 2.00
30 Dave Winfield 8.00 20.00

1974 Padres McDonald Discs

Measuring approximately 2 3/8" in diameter, members of the 1974 Padres are featured in this set. Among the players featured in this set is Dave Winfield during his Rookie Card season. These items were given out at the July 30th Padres game. According to informed sources, 60,000 photo balls were produced for the event. A baseball holder was also produced. These have a value of approximately $25. The set was originally available for $3 from the manufacturer.

COMPLETE SET (15) 20.00 50.00
1 Matty Alou 2.00 5.00
2 Glen Beckert 1.25 3.00
3 Nate Colbert 1.50 4.00
4 Bill Greif 1.25 3.00
5 John Grubb 1.25 3.00
6 Enzo Hernandez 1.25 3.00
7 Randy Jones 1.50 4.00
8 Fred Kendall 1.25 3.00
9 Willie McCovey 4.00 10.00
10 John McNamara MG 1.25 3.00
11 Dave Roberts 1.25 3.00
12 Bobby Tolan 1.50 4.00
13 Dave Winfield 8.00 20.00
14 Ronald McDonald 1.25 3.00
Has giveaway dates
15 Padres Sked 1.25 3.00

1974 Padres Team Issue

This 18-card set features black-and-white photos of the San Diego Padres measuring approximately 3 5/16" by 5 5/16". The cards are unnumbered and checklisted below in alphabetical order.

COMPLETE SET (18) 8.00 20.00
1 Bob Barton .20 .50
2 Glenn Beckert .20 .50
3 Mike Corkins .20 .50
4 Dave Freisleben .20 .50
5 Bill Greif .20 .50
6 Larry Hardy .20 .50
7 Randy Jones .30 .75
8 Willie McCovey/(Batting) 2.00 5.00
9 Willie McCovey/(Leaning on bat) 2.00 5.00
10 Dave Roberts/(Catching) .20 .50
11 Dave Roberts/(Leaning on bat) .20 .50
12 Vicente Romo .20 .50
13 Dan Spillner .20 .50
14 Derrel Thomas .20 .50
15 Bobby Tolan .20 .50
16 Dave Tomlin .20 .50
17 Rich Troedson .20 .50
18 Dave Winfield 4.00 10.00

1975 Padres Dean's

These cards measure 5 1/2" by 8 1/2" and are printed on very thin paper. The fronts feature black-and-white player photos with the player's name and position, and sponsor and team logos below the photo. The backs carry the player's career summary, biography and statistics. The cards are unnumbered and checklisted below in alphabetical order. Randy Hundley and Hector Torres were late season trade and their cards have blank backs.

COMPLETE SET (30) 40.00 80.00
1 Jim Davenport CO .75 2.00
2 Bob Davis .75 2.00
3 Rich Folkers .75 2.00
4 Alan Foster .75 2.00
5 Dave Freisleben .75 2.00
6 Tito Fuentes .75 2.00
7 Danny Frisella .75 2.00
8 Bill Greif .75 2.00
9 Johnny Grubb .75 2.00
10 Enzo Hernandez .75 2.00
11 Randy Hundley 1.25 3.00
12 Mike Ivie .75 2.00
13 Jerry Johnson .75 2.00
14 Randy Jones 1.50 4.00
15 Fred Kendall .75 2.00
16 Ted Kubiak .75 2.00
17 Gene Locklear .75 2.00
18 Willie McCovey 4.00 10.00
19 Joe McIntosh .75 2.00
20 John McNamara MG .75 2.00
21 Tom Morgan CO .75 2.00
22 Dick Sharon .75 2.00
23 Dick Sisler CO .75 2.00
24 Dan Spillner .75 2.00
25 Brent Strom .75 2.00
26 Bobby Tolan .75 2.00
27 Dave Tomlin .75 2.00
28 Hector Torres .75 2.00
29 Whitey Wietelmann CO .75 2.00
30 Dave Winfield 6.00 15.00

1977 Padres Family Fun

This set of the San Diego Padres was produced by Huish Family Fun Centers and measures approximately 5 1/2" by 8 1/2". The fronts feature black-and-white player photos with white borders. The backs carry biographical information and career statistics. The set was distributed in eight-card packs with sponsor coupons printed on the pack wrappers. The cards are unnumbered and checklisted below in alphabetical order.

COMPLETE SET (8) 6.00 15.00
1 Joey Amalfitano CO .75 2.00
2 Alvin Dark MG 1.25 3.00
3 Randy Jones 1.00 2.50
4 Bob Owchinko .75 2.00
5 Dave Roberts .75 2.00
6 Rick Sawyer .75 2.00
7 Pat Scanlon .75 2.00
8 Jerry Turner .75 2.00

1977 Padres Schedule Cards

This 89-card set was issued in 1977 and features members of the 1977 San Diego Padres as well as former Padres and others connected with the Padres in some capacity. The cards measure approximately 2 1/4" by 3 3/8" and have brown and white photos on the front of the cards with a schedule of the 1977 Padres special events on the back. A thin line borders the front photo with the team name and player name appearing below in the same sepia tone. The set is checklisted alphabetically in the list below. The complete set price below refers to the set with all variations listed. The blank-backed cards may have been issued in a different year than the other schedule-back cards.

COMPLETE SET (89) 20.00 50.00
1A Bill Almon .20 .50
Kneeling
1B Bill Almon .30 .75
Shown chest up
bat on shoulder
2 Matty Alou .30 .75
3 Joe Amalfitano CO .10 .25
4A Steve Arlin .20 .50
Follow through
4B Steve Arlin .20 .50
Glove to chest
5 Bob Barton .30 .75
6 Buzzie Bavasi GM .20 .50
7 Glenn Beckert .30 .75
8 Vic Bernal .10 .25
9 Ollie Brown .30 .75
10A Dave Campbell .30 .75
Bat on shoulder
10B Dave Campbell .30 .75
Kneeling, capless
11 Mike Champion .10 .25
12 Mike Champion and .10 .25
Bill Almon
13A Nate Colbert .30 .75
Shown waist up
13B Nate Colbert .40 1.00
Shown full figure;
blank back
14 Nate Colbert and .30 .75
friend Kneeling next
to child with bat
15 Jerry Coleman ANN .30 .75
16 Roger Craig CO .20 .50
17 John D'Acquisto .10 .25
18 Bob Davis .10 .25
19 Willie Davis .40 1.00
20 Jim Eakle .10 .25
Tuba Man
21A Rollie Fingers .75 2.00
Shown waist up
both hands in glove
in front of body
21B Rollie Fingers .75 2.00
Head shot
22A Dave Freisleben 1.00 2.50
Washington jersey and
cap blank back
22B Dave Freisleben .20 .50
Kneeling
23A Clarence Gaston .40 1.00
Bat on shoulder Padres on jersey
23B Clarence Gaston .40 1.00
Bat on shoulder Padre on jersey
24 Tom Griffin .10 .25
25 Johnny Grubb .20 .50
26A George Hendrick .30 .75
Shown chest up
wearing warm-up jacket
26B George Hendrick .30 .75
Shown waist up
wearing white jersey
27 Enzo Hernandez .10 .25
28 Enzo Hernandez and .30 .75
Nate Colbert
29A Mike Ivie .30 .75
Batting pose, shown
from thighs up
29B Mike Ivie .30 .75
Batting pose
shown from shoulders up
blank back
29C Mike Ivie/(Bat on shoulder) .30 .75
30A Randy Jones .30 .75
Following Through
30B Randy Jones .40 1.00
Holding Cy Young Award
31 Randy Jones and .40 1.00
Bowie Kuhn COMM
Randy holding trophy
32A Fred Kendall .30 .75
Batting pose
32B Fred Kendall .30 .75
Ball in right hand
33 Mike Kilkenny .30 .75
Blank back
34A Clay Kirby .30 .75
Follow through
34B Clay Kirby .30 .75
Glove near to chest
35 Ray Kroc OWN .40 1.00
Blank back
36 Dave Marshall .30 .75
37A Willie McCovey 1.25 3.00
With mustache
bat on shoulder
37B Willie McCovey 1.25 3.00
Without mustache
blank back
38A John McNamara MG .30 .75
Looking to his left
blank back
38B John McNamara MG .30 .75
Looking to his right
38C John McNamara MG .30 .75
Looking straight
ahead, smiling
39 Luis Melendez .10 .25
40 Butch Metzger .10 .25
41 Bob Miller CO .10 .25
42A Fred Norman .30 .75
Short hair, kneeling
42B Fred Norman .30 .75
Long hair, arms
over head
43 Bob Owchinko .10 .25
44 Doug Rader .30 .75
45 Merv Rettenmund .10 .25
46A Gene Richards .30 .75
Shown chest up
stands in background
46B Gene Richards .20 .50
Shown from thighs up
47 Dave Roberts .10 .25
48 Rick Sawyer .10 .25
49 Bob Shirley .10 .25
50 Bob Skinner CO .20 .50
51 Ballard Smith GM .30 .75
52 Ed Spiezio .30 .75
53 Dan Spillner .10 .25
54 Brent Strom .10 .25
55 Gary Sutherland .10 .25
56 Gene Tenace .30 .75
57A Derrell Thomas .30 .75
Head shot
wearing glasses
57B Derrell Thomas .30 .75
Kneeling, not
wearing glasses
58A Bobby Tolan .30 .75
Batting pose
58B Bobby Tolan .30 .75
Kneeling, holding
cleats in hand
59 Dave Tomlin .10 .25
60A Jerry Turner .30 .75
Batting pose, gloveless
wall in background
60B Jerry Turner .30 .75
Batting pose
both hands gloved
61 Bobby Valentine .40 1.00
62 Dave Wehrmeister .10 .25
63 Whitey Wietelmann CO .10 .25
64 Don Williams CO .10 .25
65A Dave Winfield 4.00 10.00
Batting pose, waist up#field in background
65B Dave Winfield 4.00 10.00
Batting, stands in
background, black bat
telescoped
65C Dave Winfield 4.00 10.00
Two bats on shoulder
65D Dave Winfield 4.00 10.00
Full figure, leaning
on bat, blank back

1978 Padres Family Fun

This 39-card set features members of the 1978 San Diego Padres. These large cards measure approximately 3 1/2" by 5 1/2" and are framed in a style similar to the 1962 Topps set with wood-grain borders. The cards have full color photos on the front of the card along with the Padres logo and Family Fun Centers underneath the photo in circles and the name of the player on the bottom of the card. The backs of the card asked each person what their greatest thrill in baseball was. This set is especially noteworthy for having one of the earliest Ozzie Smith cards printed. The set is checklisted alphabetically in the list below. This set was also available in uncut sheet form.

COMPLETE SET (39) 20.00 50.00
1 Bill Almon .20 .50
2 Tucker Ashford .20 .50
3 Chuck Baker .20 .50
4 Dave Campbell ANN .30 .75
5 Mike Champion .20 .50
6 Jerry Coleman ANN .30 .75
7 Roger Craig MG .40 1.00
8 John D'Acquisto .20 .50
9 Bob Davis .20 .50

10 Chuck Estrada CO .20 .50
11 Rollie Fingers 1.50 4.00
12 Dave Freisleben .20 .50
13 Oscar Gamble .30 .75
14 Fernando Gonzalez .20 .50
15 Billy Herman CO .60 1.50
16 Randy Jones .30 .75
17 Ray Kroc OWN .60 1.50
18 Mark Lee .20 .50
19 Mickey Lolich .40 1.00
20 Bob Owchinko .20 .50
21 Broderick Perkins .20 .50
22 Gaylord Perry 1.50 4.00
23 Eric Rasmussen .20 .50
24 Don Reynolds .20 .50
25 Gene Richards .20 .50
26 Dave Roberts .20 .50
27 Phil Roof CO .20 .50
28 Bob Shirley .20 .50
29 Ozzie Smith 10.00 25.00
30 Dan Spillner .20 .50
31 Rick Sweet .20 .50
32 Gene Tenace .30 .75
33 Derrel Thomas .20 .50
34 Jerry Turner .20 .50
35 Dave Wehrmeister .20 .50
36 Whitey Wietelmann CO .20 .50
37 Don Williams CO .20 .50
38 Dave Winfield 4.00 10.00
39 1978 All-Star Game .30 .75

1979 Padres Family Fun

This set features photos of the San Diego Padres and has Family Fun Center printed in a bar on the front. These cards were also produced by Dean's photo processors.

COMPLETE SET 12.50 30.00
1 Roger Craig MG .20 .50
2 John D'Acquisto .20 .50
3 Ozzie Smith 4.00 10.00
4 KGB Chicken .60 1.50
5 Gene Richards .20 .50
6 Jerry Turner .20 .50
7 Bob Owchinko .20 .50
8 Gene Tenace .40 1.00
9 Whitey Wietelmann CO .20 .50
10 Bill Almon .20 .50
11 Dave Winfield 2.00 5.00
12 Mike Hargrove .30 .75
13 Fernando Gonzalez .20 .50
14 Barry Evans .20 .50
15 Steve Mura .20 .50
16 Chuck Estrada CO .20 .50
17 Bill Fahey .20 .50
18 Gaylord Perry 1.25 3.00
19 Dan Briggs .20 .50
20 Billy Herman CO .60 1.50
21 Mickey Lolich .40 1.00
22 Broderick Perkins .20 .50
23 Fred Kendall .20 .50
24 Rollie Fingers 1.25 3.00
25 Kurt Bevacqua .20 .50
26 Jerry Coleman ANN .40 1.00
27 Don Williams .20 .50
28 Paul Dade .20 .50
29 Randy Jones .30 .75
30 Eric Rasmussen .20 .50
31 Bobby Tolan .20 .50
32 Doug Rader .20 .50
33 Dave Campbell .30 .75
34 Jay Johnstone .40 1.00
35 Mark Lee .20 .50
36 Bob Shirley .20 .50

1980 Padres Family Fun

This 36 card set was issued in six card increments six times during the 1980 season. We have sequenced these cards in the order they were given out during the season.

COMPLETE SET 10.00 25.00
1 Randy Jones .30 .75
2 John D'Acquisto .20 .50
3 Jerry Coleman CO .60 1.50
4 Ozzie Smith 2.00 5.00
5 Gene Richards .20 .50
6 Bill Fahey .20 .50
7 John Curtis .20 .50
8 Al Heist CO .20 .50
9 Gary Lucas .20 .50
10 Gene Tenace .20 .50
11 Willie Montanez .20 .50
12 Aurelio Rodriguez .20 .50
13 Eric Rasmussen .20 .50
14 Tim Flannery .20 .50
15 Chuck Estrada CO .20 .50
16 Eddie Doucette ANN .20 .50
17 Bob Shirley .20 .50
18 The Chicken .60 1.50
19 Dave Winfield 1.25 3.00
20 Kurt Bevacqua .20 .50
21 Paul Dade .20 .50
22 Dave Cash .20 .50
23 Don Williams CO .20 .50
24 Rollie Fingers .75 2.00
25 Jerry Mumphrey .20 .50
26 Fred Kendall .20 .50
27 Steve Mura .20 .50
28 Dennis Kinney .20 .50
29 Von Joshua .20 .50
30 Dick Phillips CO .20 .50
31 Dave Campbell .30 .75
32 Juan Eichelberger .20 .50
33 Rick Wise .20 .50
34 Bobby Tolan .20 .50
35 Jerry Turner .20 .50
36 Barry Evans .20 .50

1981 Padres Family Fun

These cards were issued as part of six-card sheets given out at various games during the strike-laden 1981 season. Six players as well as a coupon were issued on each sheet. We are pricing all cards indivually as cut off from these sheets. There is a premium of 25 percent for a complete sheet. We have catalogued these cards individually and sequenced them in alphabetical order.

COMPLETE SET (24) 6.00 15.00
1 Randy Bass .20 .50
2 Kurt Bevacqua .20 .50
3 Daniel Boone .20 .50
4 Ed Brinkman CO .20 .50
5 Dave Cash .20 .50
6 Paul Dade .20 .50
7 Dave Edwards .20 .50
8 Chuck Estrada CO .20 .50
9 Rollie Fingers .60 1.50
10 Frank Howard MG .40 1.00
11 Jack Krol CO .20 .50
12 Joe Lefebvre .20 .50
13 Tim Lollar .20 .50
14 Gary Lucas .20 .50
15 Gene Richards .20 .50
16 Luis Salazar .20 .50
17 Ozzie Smith 1.25 3.00
18 Ed Stevens .20 .50
19 Craig Stimac .20 .50
20 Steve Swisher .20 .50
21 Jerry Turner .20 .50
22 John Urrea .20 .50
23 Don Williams .20 .50
24 Dave Winfield .75 2.00

1983 Padres Team Issue

This 32-card set of the San Diego Padres features color player photos and measures approximately 3 1/2" by 5 1/2". The cards are unnumbered and checklisted below in alphabetical order.

COMPLETE SET (32) 10.00 25.00
1 Kurt Bevacqua .20 .50
2 Juan Bonilla .20 .50
3 Greg Booker .20 .50
4 Nate Colbert CO .20 .50
5 Luis DeLeon .20 .50
6 Dave Dravecky .20 .50
7 Tim Flannery .20 .50
8 Steve Garvey .60 1.50
9 Tony Gwynn 6.00 15.00
10 Ruppert Jones .20 .50
11 Terry Kennedy .20 .50
12 Jack Krol CO .20 .50
13 Sixto Lezcano .20 .50
14 Tim Lollar .20 .50
15 Gary Lucas .20 .50
16 Jack McKeon GM .30 .75
17 Kevin McReynolds .60 1.50
18 Sid Monge .20 .50
19 John Montefusco .20 .50
20 Mario Ramirez .20 .50
21 Gene Richards .20 .50
22 Luis Salazar .20 .50
23 Norm Sherry CO .20 .50
24 Eric Show .20 .50
25 Elias Sosa .20 .50
26 Mark Thurmond .20 .50
27 Bobby Tolan CO .20 .50
28 Jerry Turner .20 .50
29 Ossie Virgil CO .20 .50
30 Ed Whitson .20 .50
31 Alan Wiggins .20 .50
32 Dick Williams MG .30 .75

1984 Padres Gwynn Lite

This one-card postcard set features Tony Gwynn just after he won the first of what turned out to be myriad batting titles. This card, which measure 5" by 7" hard yellow borders and a photo of Gywnn on the front posing with a big bat. The back has biographical information, career highlights and complete statistics.

COMPLETE SET
1 Tony Gwynn 5.00 10.00

1984 Padres Mother's

The cards in this 28-card set measure 2 1/2" by 3 1/2". In 1984, the Los Angeles based Mother's Cookies Co. issued five sets of cards featuring players from major league teams. The San Diego Padres set features current players depicted by photos. Similar to their 1952 and 1953 issues, the cards have rounded corners. The backs of the cards contain the Mother's Cookies logo. The cards were distributed in partial sets to fans at the respective stadiums of the teams involved. Whereas 20 cards were given to each patron, a redemption card, redeemable for eight more cards was included. Unfortunately, the eight cards received by redeeming the coupon were not necessarily the eight needed to complete a set. Hobbyist Barry Colla was involved in the production of these sets.

COMPLETE SET (28) 8.00 20.00
1 Dick Williams MG .20 .50
2 Rich Gossage .40 1.00
3 Tim Lollar .08 .25
4 Eric Show .08 .25
5 Terry Kennedy .08 .25
6 Kurt Bevacqua .20 .50
7 Steve Garvey .75 2.00
8 Garry Templeton .20 .50
9 Tony Gwynn 5.00 12.00
10 Alan Wiggins .08 .25
11 Dave Dravecky .40 1.00
12 Tim Flannery .08 .25
13 Kevin McReynolds .40 1.00
14 Bobby Brown .08 .25
15 Ed Whitson .08 .25
16 Doug Gwosdz .08 .25
17 Luis DeLeon .08 .25
18 Andy Hawkins .20 .50
19 Craig Lefferts .20 .50
20 Carmelo Martinez .08 .25
21 Sid Monge .08 .25
22 Graig Nettles .40 1.00
23 Mario Ramirez .08 .25
24 Luis Salazar .08 .25
25 Champ Summers .08 .25
26 Mark Thurmond .08 .25
27 Padres' Coaches .08 .25
Harry Dunlop
Jack Krol
Ozzie Vi
28 Padres' Checklist .08 .25

1984 Padres Smokey

The cards in this 29-card set measure 2 1/2" by 3 3/4". This unnumbered, full color set features the Fire Prevention Bear and a Padres player, coach, manager, or associate on each card. The set was given out at the ballpark at the May 14th game against the Expos. Logos of the California Department of Forestry and the U.S. Forest Service appear in conjunction with a Smokey the Bear logo on the obverse. The set commemorates the 40th birthday of Smokey the Bear. The backs contain short biographical data, statistics and a fire prevention hint from the player pictured on the front.

COMPLETE SET (29) 5.00 12.00
1 Kurt Bevacqua .20 .50
2 Bobby Brown .08 .25
3 Dave Campbell ANN .20 .50
4 The Chicken .40 1.00
Mascot
5 Jerry Coleman ANN .20 .50
6 Luis DeLeon .08 .25
7 Dave Dravecky .40 1.00
8 Harry Dunlop CO .08 .25
9 Tim Flannery .08 .25
10 Steve Garvey .40 1.00
11 Doug Gwosdz .08 .25
12 Tony Gwynn 2.50 6.00
13 Doug Harvey UMP .30 .75
14 Terry Kennedy .20 .50
15 Jack Krol CO .08 .25
16 Tim Lollar .08 .25
17 Jack McKeon VP .20 .50
18 Kevin McReynolds .30 .75
19 Sid Monge .08 .25
20 Luis Salazar .08 .25
21 Norm Sherry CO .08 .25
22 Eric Show .08 .25
23 Smokey the Bear .08 .25
24 Garry Templeton .08 .25
25 Mark Thurmond .08 .25
26 Ozzie Virgil CO .08 .25
27 Ed Whitson .08 .25
28 Alan Wiggins .08 .25
29 Dick Williams MG .20 .50

1985 Padres Mother's

The cards in this 28-card set measure 2 1/2" by 3 1/2". In 1985, the Los Angeles based Mother's Cookies Co. again issued five sets of cards featuring players from major league teams. The San Diego Padres set features current players depicted by photos on cards with rounded corners. The backs of the cards contain the Mother's Cookies logo. Cards were passed out at the stadium on August 11.

COMPLETE SET (28) 4.00 10.00
1 Dick Williams MG .20 .50
2 Tony Gwynn 2.00 5.00
3 Kevin McReynolds .20 .50
4 Graig Nettles .40 1.00
5 Rich Gossage .40 1.00
6 Steve Garvey .40 1.00
7 Garry Templeton .08 .25
8 Dave Dravecky .30 .75
9 Eric Show .08 .25
10 Terry Kennedy .20 .50
11 Luis DeLeon .08 .25
12 Bruce Bochy .20 .50
13 Andy Hawkins .08 .25
14 Kurt Bevacqua .20 .50
15 Craig Lefferts .08 .25
16 Mario Ramirez .08 .25
17 LaMarr Hoyt .08 .25
18 Jerry Royster .08 .25
19 Tim Stoddard .20 .50
20 Tim Flannery .08 .25
21 Mark Thurmond .08 .25
22 Greg Booker .08 .25
23 Bobby Brown .08 .25
24 Carmelo Martinez .08 .25
25 Al Bumbry .08 .25
26 Jerry Davis .08 .25
27 Padres' Coaches .08 .25
Jack Krol
Harry Dunlop
Deacon J
28 Padres' Checklist .08 .25
Jack Murphy Stadium

1986 Padres Greats TCMA

This 12-card standard-size set features some of the leading Padres players from their first two decades. The player's photo and name are on the front. The backs are used to give more player information.

COMPLETE SET (12) 1.50 4.00
1 Nate Colbert .20 .50
2 Tito Fuentes .08 .25
3 Enzo Hernandez .08 .25
4 Dave Roberts .08 .25
5 Gene Richards .08 .25
6 Ollie Brown .08 .25
7 Clarence Gaston .30 .75
8 Fred Kendall .08 .25
9 Gaylord Perry .40 1.00
10 Randy Jones .20 .50
11 Rollie Fingers .40 1.00
12 Preston Gomez MG .08 .25

1987 Padres Bohemian Hearth Bread

The Bohemian Hearth Bread Company issued this 22-card set of San Diego Padres. The cards measure 2 1/2" by 3 1/2" and feature a distinctive yellow border on the front of the cards. Card backs provide career year-by-year statistics and are numbered.

COMPLETE SET (22) 20.00 50.00
1 Garry Templeton .40 1.00
4 Joey Cora 1.00 2.50
5 Randy Ready .40 1.00
6 Steve Garvey 2.00 5.00
7 Kevin Mitchell 1.00 2.50
8 John Kruk 1.50 4.00
9 Benito Santiago 4.00 10.00
10 Larry Bowa MG .60 1.50
11 Tim Flannery .40 1.00
14 Carmelo Martinez .40 1.00
16 Marvell Wynne .40 1.00
19 Tony Gwynn 10.00 25.00
21 James Steels .40 1.00
22 Stan Jefferson .40 1.00
30 Eric Show .40 1.00
31 Ed Whitson .40 1.00
34 Storm Davis .40 1.00
37 Craig Lefferts .40 1.00
40 Andy Hawkins .40 1.00
41 Lance McCullers .40 1.00
43 Dave Dravecky 1.50 4.00
54 Rich Gossage 2.00 5.00

1986-87 Padres Fire Prevention Tips Booklets

These four Fire Prevention Booklets feature members of the San Diego Padres. The first three booklets issued are somewhat smaller and were issued in 1986. than than the fourth and fifth books issued and were issued in 1987. These booklets are unnumbered and we have sequenced them in alphabetical order

COMPLETE SET (5) 6.00 15.00
1 Dave Dravecky 1.25 3.00
Pitching Tips
2 Tim Flannery .75 2.00
Fielding Tips
3 Tony Gwynn 4.00 10.00
Batting Tips
4 Lance McCullers .75 2.00
Tips on Receiving the Pitch
5 Benito Santiago 2.00 5.00
The Pick-Off Move to First

1988 Padres Coke

These cards were actually issued as two separate promotions. The first eight cards were issued as a perforated sheet (approximately 7 1/2" by 10 1/2") as a Coca Cola Junior Padres Club promotion. The other 12 cards were issued later on specific game days to members of the Junior Padres Club. All the cards are standard size, 2 1/2" by 3 1/2" and are unnumbered. Cards that were on the perforated panel are indicated by PAN in the checklist below. Since the cards are unnumbered, they are listed below by uniform number, which is featured prominently on the card fronts.

COMPLETE SET (21) 15.00 40.00
COMMON PANEL PLAYER .20 .50
COMMON NON-PAN PLAYER .60 1.50
1 Garry Templeton PAN .30 .75
5 Randy Ready PAN .20 .50
7 Keith Moreland .60 1.50
8 John Kruk 2.00 5.00
9 Benito Santiago .75 2.00
10 Larry Bowa MG PAN .40 1.00
11 Tim Flannery PAN .20 .50
14 Carmelo Martinez .60 1.50
15 Jack McKeon MG .75 2.00
19 Tony Gwynn 8.00 20.00
22 Stan Jefferson .60 1.50
27 Mark Parent .60 1.50
30 Eric Show .60 1.50
31 Eddie Whitson .60 1.50
35 Chris Brown PAN .20 .50
41 Lance McCullers .60 1.50
45 Jimmy Jones PAN .20 .50
48 Mark Davis PAN .30 .75
51 Greg Booker .60 1.50
55 Mark Grant PAN .20 .50
NNO Padres Logo PAN
(Program explanation on reverse) .20 .50

1988 Padres Smokey

The cards in this 31-card set measure approximately 3 3/4" by 5 3/4". This unnumbered, full color set features the Fire Prevention Bear, Smokey, and a Padres player, coach, manager, or associate on each card. The set was given out at Jack Murphy Stadium to fans under the age of 14 during the Smokey Bear Day game promotion. The logo of the California Department of Forestry appears on the reverse in conjunction with a Smokey the Bear logo on the obverse. The backs contain short biographical data and a fire prevention hint from Smokey. The set is numbered below in alphabetical order. The card backs are actually postcards that can be addressed and mailed. Cards of Larry Bowa and Candy Sierra were printed but were not officially released since they were no longer members of the Padres by the time the cards were to be distributed. Roberto Alomar appears in his Rookie Card year in this set.

COMPLETE SET (31) 12.50 30.00
1 Shawn Abner .20 .50
2 Roberto Alomar 3.00 8.00
3 Sandy Alomar CO .40 1.00
4 Greg Booker .20 .50
5 Chris Brown .20 .50
6 Mark Davis .40 1.00
7 Pat Dobson CO .20 .50
8 Tim Flannery .20 .50
9 Mark Grant .20 .50
10 Tony Gwynn 5.00 12.00
11 Andy Hawkins .20 .50
12 Stan Jefferson .20 .50
13 Jimmy Jones .20 .50
14 John Kruk .75 2.00
15 Dave Leiper .20 .50
16 Shane Mack .20 .50
17 Carmelo Martinez .20 .50
18 Lance McCullers .20 .50
19 Keith Moreland .20 .50
20 Eric Nolte .20 .50
21 Amos Otis CO .20 .50
22 Mark Parent .20 .50
23 Randy Ready .20 .50
24 Greg Riddoch CO .20 .50
25 Benito Santiago .60 1.50
26 Eric Show .20 .50
27 Denny Sommers CO .20 .50
28 Garry Templeton .40 1.00
29 Dickie Thon .20 .50
30 Ed Whitson .20 .50
31 Marvell Wynne .20 .50

1989 Padres Coke

These cards were actually issued as two separate promotions. The first nine cards were issued as a perforated sheet (approximately 7 1/2" by 10 1/2") as a Coca Cola Junior Padres Club promotion. The other 12 cards were issued later on specific game days to members of the Junior Padres Club. All the cards are standard size and are unnumbered. Cards that were on the perforated panel are indicated by PAN in the checklist below. Since the cards are unnumbered, they are listed below in alphabetical order by subject. Marvell Wynne was planned for the set but was not issued since he was traded before the set was released; Walt Terrell also is tougher to find due to his mid-season trade.

COMPLETE SET (21) 15.00 40.00
COMMON PANEL CARD .20 .50
COMMON NON-PAN CARD .60 1.50
1 Roberto Alomar PAN 2.50 6.00
2 Jack Clark .60 1.50
3 Mark Davis .60 1.50
4 Tim Flannery .60 1.50
5 Mark Grant .60 1.50
6 Tony Gwynn 6.00 15.00
7 Bruce Hurst .60 1.50
8 Chris James .60 1.50
9 Carmelo Martinez PAN .20 .50
10 Jack McKeon MG PAN .20 .50
11 Mark Parent .60 1.50
12 Dennis Rasmussen PAN .20 .50
13 Randy Ready PAN .20 .50
14 Bip Roberts .60 1.50
15 Luis Salazar .60 1.50
16 Benito Santiago .60 1.50
17 Eric Show PAN .20 .50
18 Garry Templeton PAN .20 .50
19 Walt Terrell SP .60 1.50
20 Ed Whitson PAN .20 .50
NNO Padres Logo PAN .20 .50

1989 Padres Magazine

These 2 1/2" by 3 1/2" cards came as an insert in issues of "Padres" magazine sold in San Diego. These cards were sponsored by San Diego Sports Collectibles, a major hobby dealer. The cards feature beautiful full-color photos on the front and interesting did-you-know facts on the back along with one line of career statistics. The cards of retired Padres feature a highlight of their career in San Diego. The suggested retail price of each of the six different Padres magazines was 1.50.

COMPLETE SET (24) 6.00 15.00
1 Jack McKeon MG .08 .25
2 Sandy Alomar Jr. .40 1.00
3 Tony Gwynn 4.00 10.00
4 Willie McCovey/(McCovey hits 16th .40 1.00
career grand s
5 John Kruk .20 .50
6 Jack Clark .20 .50
7 Eric Show .08 .25
8 Rollie Fingers/(Fingers wins NL Saves.40 1.00
title for
9 The Alomars .75 2.00
Sandy Alomar Sr.
Sandy Alomar Jr.
R
10 Carmelo Martinez .08 .25
11 Benito Santiago .20 .50
12 Nate Colbert/(Colbert 5 HR's&/13 RBI's in .08
.25
Doubl
13 Mark Davis .08 .25
14 Roberto Alomar 2.50 6.00
15 Tim Flannery .08 .25
16 Randy Jones .20 .50
Wins Cy Young Award
17 Dennis Rasmussen .08 .25
18 Greg W. Harris .08 .25
19 Garry Templeton .08 .25
20 Steve Garvey .30 .75
Home Run ties NLCS
21 Bruce Hurst .08 .25
22 Ed Whitson .08 .25
23 Chris James .08 .25
24 Gaylord Perry/(Perry Wins Cy Young.40 1.00
Award in Both

1989 Padres Postcards

This 36-card set of the San Diego Padres features color player photos on a postcard format and measures approximately 3 3/4" by 5 3/4". The cards are unnumbered and checklisted below in alphabetical order.

COMPLETE SET (36) 8.00 20.00
1 Shawn Abner .20 .50
2 Roberto Alomar 1.25 3.00
3 Sandy Alomar Jr. .60 1.50
4 Sandy Alomar Sr. CO .20 .50
5 Jack Clark .30 .75
6 Jerald Clark .20 .50
7 Pat Clements .20 .50
8 Mark Davis .20 .50
9 Pat Dobson CO .20 .50
10 Tim Flannery .20 .50
11 Mark Grant .20 .50
12 Gary Green .20 .50
13 Tony Gwynn 2.00 5.00
14 Greg Harris .20 .50
15 Bruce Hurst .20 .50
16 Chris James .20 .50
17 Dave Leiper .20 .50
18 Carmelo Martinez .20 .50
19 Jack McKeon MG .30 .75
20 Rob Nelson .20 .50
21 Amos Otis CO .20 .50
22 Mike Pagliarulo .20 .50
23 Mark Parent .20 .50
24 Dennis Rasmussen .20 .50
25 Greg Riddoch CO .20 .50
26 Bip roberts .20 .50
27 Luis Salazar .20 .50
28 Benito Santiago .40 1.00
29 Eric Show .20 .50
30 Don Schulze .20 .50
31 Tony Siegle VP .20 .50
32 Denny Sommers CO .20 .50
33 Garry Templeton .20 .50
34 Fred Toliver .20 .50
35 Ed Whitson .20 .50
36 Marvell Wynne .20 .50

1989 Padres Show Kay

This one-card set measures approximately 2 1/2" by 4 7/8" and featues a color photo of San Diego Padres pitcher, Eric Show, on the top portion of the card with player information and career statistics on the back. The part below the picture held a lapel pin commemorating Eric Show becoming the Padres all-time victory leader with 93 wins. This portion could be torn off and brought to any Kay Jewelers for a chance to win a Longines watch.

1 Eric Show 2.00 5.00

1990 Padres Coke

These standard-size cards were issued in two forms: a 7 1/2" by 10 5/8" perforated sheet featuring eight player cards and the Padre logo card (marked by PAN below) as well as 12 individual player cards. The sheet was issued to Coca-Cola Junior Padres Club Members as a starter set, and club members who attended the first six Junior Padres Club games received two additional cards per game. The cards are unnumbered and checklisted below in alphabetical order, with the team logo card listed at the end.

COMPLETE SET (21) 12.50 30.00
COMMON PANEL CARD .20 .50
COMMON NON-PAN CARD .40 1.00
1 Roberto Alomar 3.00 8.00
2 Andy Benes PAN .40 1.00
3 Joe Carter 2.50 6.00
4 Jack Clark .60 1.50
5 Mark Grant PAN .20 .50
6 Tony Gwynn 5.00 12.00
7 Greg W. Harris .40 1.00
8 Bruce Hurst .40 1.00
9 Craig Lefferts .40 1.00
10 Fred Lynn .60 1.50
11 Jack McKeon MG PAN .20 .50
12 Mike Pagliarulo .40 1.00
13 Mark Parent PAN .20 .50
14 Dennis Rasmussen PAN .20 .50
15 Bip Roberts PAN .30 .75
16 Benito Santiago .75 2.00
17 Calvin Schiraldi .40 1.00
18 Eric Show PAN .20 .50
19 Garry Templeton .40 1.00
20 Ed Whitson PAN .20 .50
NNO Padres Logo PAN .20 .50

1990 Padres Magazine/Unocal

This 24-card set was sponsored by Unocal 76 and was available in the San Diego Padres' game programs for 17.50. The cards were divided into six series, and each series was issued on a 5" by 9" sheet of four cards with a sponsor's coupon. After perforation, the cards measure the standard size. Some players appear in more than one series. Coupons from the magazine were to be turned into Unocal for 25 Jack McKeon, 26 Bip Roberts, and 27 Joe Carter.

COMPLETE SET (27) 8.00 20.00
COMMON CARD (1-24) .10 .25
COMMON CARD (25-27) .30 .75
1 Tony Gwynn 2.50 6.00
2 Benito Santiago .30 .75
3 Mike Pagliarulo .08 .25
4 Dennis Rasmussen .08 .25
5 Eric Show .08 .25
6 Darrin Jackson .08 .25
7 Mark Parent .08 .25
8 Padres Announcers .20 .50
Jerry Coleman
Rick Monday
9 Andy Benes .40 1.00
10 Roberto Alomar 1.50 4.00
11 Craig Lefferts .08 .25
12 Ed Whitson .08 .25
13 Calvin Schiraldi .08 .25
14 Garry Templeton .08 .25
15 Tony Gwynn 3.00 8.00
16 Padres Announcers .08 .25
Bob Chandler and
Ted Leitner
17 Fred Lynn .20 .50
18 Jack Clark .20 .50
19 Mike Dunne .08 .25
20 Mark Grant .08 .25
21 Benito Santiago .30 .75
22 The Coaches .20 .50
Sandy Alomar Sr.
Pat Dobson
Amos Ot
23 Bruce Hurst .08 .25
24 Greg W. Harris .08 .25
25 Jack McKeon MG .40 1.00
26 Bip Roberts .40 1.00
27 Joe Carter 1.25 3.00

1990 Padres Postcards

These postcards feature the members of the 1990 San Diego Padres. The year can be identified as 1990 was Joe Carter's only year with the Padres. Since these cards are unnumbered, we have sequenced them in alphabetical order.

COMPLETE SET 8.00 20.00
1 Shawn Abner .20 .50
2 Roberto Alomar .75 2.00
3 Sandy Alomar Sr. CO .20 .50
4 Andy Benes .20 .50
5 Joe Carter .30 .75
6 Jerald Clark .20 .50
7 Jack Clark .30 .75
8 Pat Clements .20 .50
9 Joey Cora .20 .50
10 Pat Dobson CO .20 .50
11 Mike Dunne .20 .50
12 Mark Grant .20 .50
13 Tony Gwynn 1.50 4.00
14 Bruce Hurst .20 .50
15 Greg Harris .20 .50
16 Darrin Jackson .20 .50
17 Craig Lefferts .20 .50
18 Fred Lynn .30 .75
19 Jack McKeon MG .30 .75
20 Amos Otis CO .20 .50
21 Mike Pagliarulo .20 .50
22 Mark Parent .20 .50
23 Dennis Rasmussen .20 .50
24 Greg Riddoch CO .20 .50
25 Bip Roberts .20 .50
26 Benito Santiago .40 1.00
27 Calvin Schiraldi .20 .50
28 Eric Show .20 .50
29 Denny Sommers CO .20 .50
30 Phil Stephenson .20 .50
31 Garry Templeton .20 .50
32 Ed Whitson .20 .50

1991 Padres Coke

These nine standard-size cards were sponsored by Coca-Cola and issued in perforated sheets that measure approximately 7 3/4" by 10 3/4". They feature on their fronts posed studio shots of players and announcers for the Padres. The cards are unnumbered and checklisted below in alphabetical order.

COMPLETE SET (9) 3.00 8.00
1 Bob Chandler ANN .40 1.00
2 Jerry Coleman ANN .60 1.50
3 Paul Faries .40 1.00
4 Craig Lefferts .40 1.00
5 Ted Leitner ANN .40 1.00
6 Rick Monday ANN .40 1.00
7 Greg Riddoch MG .40 1.00
8 Bip Roberts .40 1.00
9 Title card .40 1.00

1991 Padres Magazine/Rally's

This 30-card set was sponsored by Rally's Hamburgers. The first 27 cards were divided into six series, and each series was issued on a 5" by 9" sheet of four cards with a sponsor's coupon. After perforation, the cards measure the standard size. Some players appear on more than one sheet, and there are variations involving Schiraldi, Gardner, and Presley, who were released during the season. For example, on the fourth sheet (13-16), Clark replaced Schiraldi; likewise Hurst replaced Gardner on the fifth sheet (17-20) and Roberts (who also appears on the third sheet) replaced Presley on the sixth sheet (21-24). The last three cards were available as part of a promotion whereby fans could tear out a coupon from the Padres Magazine and bring the coupon to one of eight Rally's Hamburgers locations in San Diego County in order to redeem one card.

COMPLETE SET (30) 10.00 25.00
COMMON CARD (1-24) .10 .25
COMMON CARD (25-27) .40 1.00
COMMON SP 3.00
1 Greg Riddoch MG .08 .25
2 Dennis Rasmussen .08 .25
3 Thomas Howard .08 .25
4 Tom Lampkin .08 .25
5 Bruce Hurst .08 .25
6 Darrin Jackson .08 .25
7 Jerald Clark .08 .25
8 Shawn Abner .08 .25
9 Bip Roberts .40 1.00
10 Marty Barrett .08 .25
11 Jim Vatcher .08 .25
12 Greg Gross .08 .25
13 Greg W. Harris .08 .25
14 Ed Whitson .08 .25
15A Calvin Schiraldi SP 1.25 3.00
15B Jerald Clark .40 1.00
16 Rich Rodriguez .08 .25
17 Larry Andersen .08 .25
18 Andy Benes .50 1.25
19A Wes Gardner SP 1.25 3.00
19B Bruce Hurst .40 1.00
20 Paul Faries .08 .25
21 Craig Lefferts .08 .25
22 Tony Gwynn 3.00 8.00
23A Jim Presley SP 1.25 3.00
23B Bip Roberts .40 1.00
24 Fred McGriff 1.50 4.00
25 Gaylord Perry .75 2.00
26 Benito Santiago .50 1.25
27 Tony Fernandez .40 1.00

1991 Padres Smokey

This 39-card set of the San Diego Padres measures approximately 3 1/2" by 5" and features color player photos on the fronts.

COMPLETE SET (39) 6.00 15.00
1 Shawn Abner .08 .25
2 Larry Andersen .08 .25
3 Andy Benes .08 .25
4 Jerald Clark .08 .25
5 Pat Clements .08 .25
6 Scott Coolbaugh .08 .25
7 John Costello .08 .25
8 Bruce Dorsett .08 .25
9 Paul Faries .08 .25
10 Tony Fernandez .30 .75
11 Tony Gwynn 4.00 10.00
12 Atlee Hammaker .08 .25
13 Greg Harris .08 .25
14 Thomas Howard .08 .25
15 Bruce Hurst .08 .25
16 Darrin Jackson .08 .25
17 Bruce Kimm CO .08 .25
18 Tom Lampkin .08 .25
19 Craig Lefferts .08 .25
20 Mike Maddux .08 .25
21 Fred McGriff .75 2.00
22 Joe McIlvaine GM .08 .25
23 Jose Melendez .08 .25
24 Jose Mota .08 .25
25 Adam Peterson .08 .25
26 Rob Picciolo CO .08 .25
27 Dennis Rasmussen .08 .25
28 Merv Rettenmund CO .08 .25
29 Greg Riddoch MG .08 .25
30 Mike Roarke CO .08 .25
31 Bip Roberts .08 .25
32 Steve Rosenberg .08 .25
33 Benito Santiago .20 .50
34 Jim Snyder CO .08 .25
35 Phil Stephenson .08 .25
36 Tim Teufel .08 .25
37 Jim Vatcher .08 .25
38 Kevin Ward .08 .25
39 Ed Whitson .08 .25

1992 Padres Carl's Jr.

This 25-card set was sponsored by Carl's Jr. restaurants and issued in perforated nine-card sheets or in a precut set. The cards are printed on thick card stock and measure slightly larger than standard size (2 9/16" by 3 9/16"). The cards are unnumbered and checklisted below in alphabetical order.

COMPLETE SET (25) 6.00 15.00
1 Larry Andersen .08 .25
2 Oscar Azocar .08 .25
3 Andy Benes .08 .25
4 Dann Bilardello .08 .25
5 Jerald Clark .08 .25
6 Tony Fernandez .20 .50
7 Tony Gwynn 2.50 6.00
8 Greg W. Harris .08 .25
9 Bruce Hurst .08 .25
10 Darrin Jackson .08 .25
11 Craig Lefferts .08 .25
12 Mike Maddux .08 .25
13 Fred McGriff 1.25 3.00
14 Jose Melendez .08 .25
15 Randy Myers .30 .75
16 Greg Riddoch MG .08 .25
17 Rich Rodriguez .08 .25
18 Benito Santiago .30 .75
19 Gary Sheffield .75 2.00
20 Craig Shipley .08 .25
21 Kurt Stillwell .08 .25
22 Tim Teufel .08 .25
23 Kevin Ward .08 .25
24 Ed Whitson .08 .25
25 All-Star Game Logo .08 .25

1992 Padres Mother's

The 1992 Mother's Cookies Padres set contains 28 cards with rounded corners measuring the standard size.

COMPLETE SET (28) 5.00 12.00
1 Greg Riddoch MG .08 .25
2 Greg W. Harris .08 .25
3 Gary Sheffield .75 2.00
4 Fred McGriff .75 2.00
5 Kurt Stillwell .08 .25
6 Benito Santiago .30 .75
7 Tony Gwynn 2.00 5.00
8 Tony Fernandez .20 .50
9 Jerald Clark .08 .25
10 Dave Eiland .08 .25
11 Randy Myers .30 .75
12 Oscar Azocar .08 .25
13 Dann Bilardello .08 .25
14 Jose Melendez .08 .25
15 Darrin Jackson .08 .25
16 Andy Benes .08 .25
17 Tim Teufel .08 .25
18 Jeremy Hernandez .08 .25
19 Kevin Ward .08 .25
20 Bruce Hurst .08 .25
21 Larry Andersen .08 .25
22 Rich Rodriguez .08 .25
23 Pat Clements .08 .25
24 Craig Lefferts .08 .25
25 Craig Shipley .08 .25
26 Mike Maddux .08 .25
27 Coaches .08 .25
Jim Snyder
Mike Roarke
Rob Picciolo
Me
28 Checklist .08 .25

1992 Padres Police DARE

Sponsored by DARE (Drug Abuse Resistance Education) America, this 30-card standard-size set is printed on thin card stock. The cards are unnumbered and checklisted below in alphabetical order, with multi-player cards listed at the end.

COMPLETE SET (27) 12.50 30.00
1 Oscar Azocar .20 .50
2 Bluepper (Mascot) .20 .50
3 Andy Benes .20 .50
4 Jerald Clark .20 .50
5 Jim Deshaies .20 .50
6 Dave Eiland .20 .50
7 Tony Fernandez .40 1.00
8 Tony Gwynn 4.00 10.00
9 Greg W. Harris .20 .50
10 Bruce Hurst .20 .50
11 Darrin Jackson .20 .50
12 Tom Lampkin .20 .50
13 Craig Lefferts .20 .50
14 Fred McGriff 2.00 5.00
15 Rob Picciolo .20 .50
16 Merv Rettenmund CO .20 .50
17 Greg Riddoch MG .20 .50
18 Benito Santiago .75 2.00
19 Frank Seminara .20 .50
20 Gary Sheffield 1.50 4.00
21 Craig Shipley .20 .50
22 Phil Stephenson .20 .50
23 Kurt Stillwell .20 .50
24 Tim Teufel .20 .50
25 Dan Walters .20 .50
26 Kevin Ward .20 .50
27 Jack Murphy Stadium .20 .50
28 Coaches Card .20 .50
Bruce Kimm
Rob Picciolo
Merv Rette
29 Padres Relievers .20 .50
Larry Andersen
Mike Maddux
Jos
30 Fred McGriff .75 2.00
Tony Fernandez
Gary Sheffield
Tony Gwynn

1992 Padres Smokey

This 36-card set was issued in the postcard format and measures approximately 3 13/16" by 5 11/16". The cards are unnumbered and checklisted below in alphabetical order.

COMPLETE SET (36) 8.00 20.00
1 Larry Andersen .20 .50
2 Oscar Azocar .20 .50
3 Andy Benes .30 .75
4 Dann Bilardello .20 .50
5 Jerald Clark .20 .50
6 Pat Clements .20 .50
7 Dave Eiland .20 .50
8 Tony Fernandez .30 .75
9 Tony Gwynn 4.00 10.00
10 Gene Harris .20 .50
11 Greg W. Harris .20 .50
12 Jeremy Hernandez .20 .50
13 Bruce Hurst .20 .50
14 Darrin Jackson .20 .50
15 Tom Lampkin .20 .50
16 Bruce Kimm CO .20 .50
17 Craig Lefferts .20 .50
18 Mike Maddux .20 .50
19 Fred McGriff .75 2.00
20 Jose Melendez .20 .50
21 Randy Myers .30 .75
22 Gary Pettis .20 .50
23 Rob Picciolo CO .20 .50
24 Merv Rettenmund CO .20 .50
25 Greg Riddoch MG .20 .50
26 Mike Roarke CO .20 .50
27 Rich Rodriguez .20 .50
28 Benito Santiago .40 1.00
29 Frank Seminara .20 .50
30 Gary Sheffield 1.00 2.50
31 Craig Shipley .20 .50
32 Jim Snyder CO .20 .50
33 Dave Staton .20 .50
34 Kurt Stillwell .20 .50
35 Tim Teufel .20 .50
36 Kevin Ward .20 .50

1993 Padres Mother's

The 1993 Mother's Cookies Padres set consists of 28 standard-size cards with rounded corners.

COMPLETE SET (28) 5.00 12.00
1 Jim Riggleman MG .08 .25
2 Gary Sheffield .60 1.50
3 Tony Gwynn 1.50 4.00
4 Fred McGriff .40 1.00
5 Greg W. Harris .08 .25
6 Tim Teufel .08 .25
7 Dave Eiland .08 .25
8 Phil Plantier .08 .25
9 Bruce Hurst .08 .25
10 Ricky Gutierrez .08 .25
11 Rich Rodriguez .08 .25
12 Derek Bell .08 .25
13 Bob Geren .08 .25
14 Andy Benes .08 .25
15 Darrell Sherman .08 .25
16 Frank Seminara .08 .25
17 Guillermo Velasquez .08 .25
18 Gene Harris .08 .25
19 Dan Walters .08 .25
20 Craig Shipley .08 .25
21 Phil Clark .08 .25
22 Jeff Gardner .08 .25
23 Mike Scioscia .20 .50
24 Wally Whitehurst .08 .25
25 Roger Mason .08 .25
26 Kerry Taylor .08 .25
27 Tim Scott .08 .25
28 Checklist .08 .25
Coaches
Bruce Bochy
Dan Radison
Mike

1994 Padres Mother's

The 1994 Mother's Cookies Padres set consists of 28 standard-size cards with rounded corners.

COMPLETE SET (28) 3.00 8.00
1 Jim Riggleman MG .08 .25
2 Tony Gwynn 1.25 3.00
3 Andy Benes .08 .25
4 Bip Roberts .08 .25
5 Phil Clark .08 .25
6 Wally Whitehurst .08 .25
7 Archi Cianfrocco .08 .25
8 Derek Bell .08 .25
9 Ricky Gutierrez .08 .25
10 Mark Davis .08 .25
11 Phil Plantier .08 .25
12 Brian Johnson .08 .25
13 Billy Bean .20 .50
14 Craig Shipley .08 .25
15 Tim Hyers .08 .25
16 Gene Harris .08 .25
17 Scott Sanders .08 .25
18 A.J. Sager .08 .25
19 Keith Lockhart .08 .25
20 Tim Mauser .08 .25
21 Andy Ashby .20 .50
22 Brad Ausmus .08 .25
23 Trevor Hoffman .40 1.00
24 Luis Lopez .08 .25
25 Doug Brocail .08 .25
26 Dave Staton .08 .25
27 Pedro Martinez .08 .25
28 Checklist .08 .25
Coaches
Sonny Siebert
Rob Picciolo
Da

1995 Padres CHP

Sponsored by the California Highway Patrol, this 16-card set features color player photos in a blue frame. The backs carry player information and a safety tip.

COMPLETE SET (16) 6.00 15.00
1 Tony Gwynn 4.00 10.00
2 Brad Ausmus .20 .50
3 Andy Ashby .20 .50
4 Brian Johnson .20 .50
5 Trevor Hoffman .60 1.50
6 Scott Sanders .20 .50
7 Bip Roberts .20 .50
8 Roberto Petagine .20 .50
9 Fernando Valenzuela .40 1.00
10 Ken Caminiti .75 2.00
11 Steve Finley .60 1.50
12 Andujar Cedeno .20 .50
13 Jody Reed .20 .50
14 Eddie Williams .20 .50
15 Joey Hamilton .20 .50
16 Bruce Bochy MG .20 .50
Chief Don Watkins

1995 Padres Mother's

The 1995 Mother's Cookies San Diego Padres set consists of 28 standard-size cards with rounded corners.

COMPLETE SET (28) 4.00 10.00
1 Bruce Bochy MG .08 .25
2 Tony Gwynn 1.25 3.00
3 Ken Caminiti .50 1.25
4 Bip Roberts .08 .25
5 Andujar Cedeno .08 .25
6 Andy Benes .20 .50
7 Phil Clark .08 .25
8 Fernando Valenzuela .30 .75
9 Roberto Petagine .08 .25
10 Brian Johnson .08 .25
11 Scott Livingstone .08 .25
12 Brian Williams .08 .25
13 Jody Reed .08 .25
14 Steve Finley .40 1.00
15 Jeff Tabaka .08 .25
16 Ray Holbert .08 .25
17 Tim Worrell .08 .25
18 Eddie Williams .08 .25
19 Brad Ausmus .08 .25
20 Willie Blair .08 .25
21 Trevor Hoffman .40 1.00
22 Scott Sanders .08 .25
23 Andy Ashby .08 .25
24 Joey Hamilton .08 .25
25 Andres Berumen .08 .25
26 Melvin Nieves .08 .25
27 Bryce Florie .08 .25
28 Coaches .20 .50
Checklist
Merv Rettenmund
Graig Nettles#

1996 Padres Mother's

This 28-card set consists of borderless posed color player portraits in stadium settings.

COMPLETE SET (28) 4.00 10.00
1 Bruce Bochy MG .08 .25
2 Tony Gwynn 1.25 3.00
3 Wally Joyner .40 1.00
4 Rickey Henderson .60 1.50
5 Ken Caminiti .50 1.25
6 Scott Sanders .08 .25
7 Steve Finley .40 1.00
8 Fernando Valenzuela .30 .75
9 Brian Johnson .08 .25
10 Jody Reed .08 .25
11 Bob Tewksbury .08 .25
12 Andujar Cedeno .08 .25
13 Sean Bergman .08 .25
14 Marc Newfield .08 .25
15 Craig Shipley .08 .25
16 Scott Livingstone .08 .25
17 Trevor Hoffman .40 1.00
18 Doug Bochtler .08 .25
19 Archi Cianfrocco .08 .25
20 Joey Hamilton .08 .25
21 Andy Ashby .08 .25
22 Chris Gwynn .08 .25
23 Luis Lopez .08 .25
24 Tim Worrell .08 .25
25 Brad Ausmus .08 .25
26 Willie Blair .08 .25
27 Bryce Florie .08 .25
28 Coaches Card CL .08 .25
Dan Warthen
Rob Picciolo
Davey

1997 Padres Mother's

This 28-card set of the San Diego Padres sponsored by Mother's Cookies consists of posed color player photos with rounded corners.

COMPLETE SET (28) 5.00 12.00
1 Bruce Bochy MG .08 .25
2 Tony Gwynn 1.25 3.00
3 Ken Caminiti .50 1.25
4 Wally Joyner .20 .50
5 Rickey Henderson .50 1.25
6 Greg Vaughn .20 .50
7 Steve Finley .40 1.00
8 Fernando Valenzuela .30 .75
9 John Flaherty .08 .25
10 Sterling Hitchcock .08 .25
11 Quilvio Veras .08 .25
12 Don Slaught .08 .25
13 Sean Bergman .08 .25
14 Chris Gomez .08 .25
15 Craig Shipley .08 .25
16 Joey Hamilton .08 .25
17 Scott Livingstone .08 .25
18 Trevor Hoffman .40 1.00
19 Doug Bochtler .08 .25
20 Chris Jones .08 .25
21 Andy Ashby .08 .25
22 Archi Cianfrocco .08 .25
23 Tim Worrell .08 .25
24 Will Cunnane .08 .25
25 Carlos Hernandez .08 .25
26 Tim Scott .08 .25
27 Dario Veras .08 .25
28 Coaches Card CL .08 .25
Greg Booker
Tim Flannery
Davey

1998 Padres Junior Hoffman

This 5" by 7" full-bleed blank-backed photo features star reliver Trevor Hoffman. In the upper left is a trademark for the "Junior Padres", with the sponsors, Sparkletts and The Sports Authority noted on the bottom. This was used as a premium for kids joining the "Junior Padres"

1 Trevor Hoffman 1.25 3.00

1998 Padres Mother's

This 28-card set of the San Diego Padres sponsored by Mother's Cookies consists of posed color player photos with rounded corners.

COMPLETE SET (28) 4.00 10.00
1 Bruce Bochy MG .08 .25
2 Tony Gwynn 1.25 3.00
3 Ken Caminiti .50 1.25
4 Kevin Brown .40 1.00
5 Wally Joyner .20 .50
6 Sterling Hitchcock .08 .25
7 Greg Vaughn .20 .50
8 Steve Finley .30 .75
9 Joey Hamilton .08 .25
10 Carlos Hernandez .08 .25
11 Quilvio Veras .08 .25
12 Trevor Hoffman .40 1.00
13 Chris Gomez .08 .25
14 Andy Ashby .08 .25
15 Greg Myers .08 .25
16 Mark Langston .08 .25
17 Andy Sheets .08 .25
18 Dan Miceli .08 .25
19 James Mouton .08 .25
20 Brian Boehringer .08 .25
21 Archi Cianfrocco .08 .25
22 Mark Sweeney .08 .25
23 Pete Smith .08 .25
24 Eddie Williams .08 .25
25 Ed Giovanola .08 .25
26 Carlos Reyes .08 .25
27 Donne Wall .08 .25
28 Coaches Card CL .08 .25
Greg Booker
Tim Flannery
Davey

1999 Padres Keebler

This 28 card standard-size set was designed by long time Mother Cookies card creator Wayne Bebb. However, for 1999, Mother's Cookies did not participate in a card promotion so this set was issued by Keebler. Similar to the Mothers promotions, a collector received 20 different cards and 8 same cards that he/she would have to trade to complete their set.

COMPLETE SET (28) 4.00 10.00
1 Bruce Bochy MG .08 .25
2 Tony Gwynn 1.00 2.50
3 Wally Joyner .20 .50
4 Sterling Hitchcock .08 .25
5 Jim Leyritz .08 .25
6 Trevor Hoffman .30 .75
7 Quilvio Veras .08 .25
8 Dave Magadan .08 .25
9 Andy Ashby .08 .25
10 Damian Jackson .08 .25
11 Dan Miceli .08 .25
12 Reggie Sanders .20 .50
13 Chris Gomez .08 .25
14 Ruben Rivera .08 .25
15 Greg Myers .08 .25
16 Ed Vosberg .08 .25
17 John Vander Wal .10 .25
18 Donne Wall .08 .25
19 Eric Owens .08 .25
20 Brian Boehringer .08 .25
21 Woody Williams .08 .25
22 Matt Clement .40 1.00
23 Carlos Reyes .08 .25
24 Stan Spencer .08 .25
25 George Arias .08 .25
26 Carlos Almanzar .08 .25
27 Phil Nevin .40 1.00
28 Greg Booker CO .08 .25
Tim Flannery CO
Davey Lopes CO
R

1999 Padres MADD

These slightly oversize cards feature both current members of the 1999 San Diego Padres as well as some of the leading players from the first 30 years of the Padres history. Since the cards are unnumbered, we have sequenced them in alphabetical order. Please note that a couple of players have cards in both Spanish and English.

COMPLETE SET (23) 8.00 20.00
1 George Arias .40 1.00
2 Andy Ashby .40 1.00
3 Ben Davis .40 1.00
4 Tim Flannery .40 1.00
5 Steve Garvey 3.00 8.00
6 Chris Gomez .40 1.00
7 Rich Gossage 1.25 3.00
8 Tony Gwynn 3.00 8.00
9 Sterling Hitchcock .40 1.00
10 Trevor Hoffman .75 2.00
11 Damian Jackson .40 1.00
12 Randy Jones .60 1.50
13 Wally Joyner .60 1.50
14 Jim Leyritz .40 1.00
15 Phil Nevin 1.25 3.00
16 Eric Owens .40 1.00
17 Ruben Rivera .40 1.00
Outfielder
18 Ruben Rivera .40 1.00
Jardinero
19 Reggie Sanders .60 1.50
20 John Vander Wal .40 1.00
21 Quilvio Veras .40 1.00
Second Base
22 Quilvio Veras .40 1.00
Base Segundo
23 Dave Winfield 2.50 6.00

1999 Padres Postcards

These 4" by 6" postcards feature members of the San Diego Padres. The fronts have a full color player photo while the backs have the players name and position in bold across the top and then some information about him. Since the cards are unnumbered, we have sequenced them in alphabetical order

COMPLETE SET 4.00 10.00
1 George Arias .20 .50
2 Greg Booker CO .20 .50
3 Matt Clement .60 1.50
4 Mike Darr .20 .50
5 Ben Davis .20 .50
6 Chris Gomez .20 .50
7 Damian Jackson .20 .50
8 Jim Leyritz .20 .50
9 Dave Magadan .20 .50
10 Gary Matthews Jr. .20 .50
11 Heath Murray .20 .50
12 David Newhan .20 .50
13 Phil Nevin .30 .75
14 Eric Owens .20 .50
15 Ruben Rivera .20 .50
16 Dave Smith CO .20 .50
17 John Vander Wal .20 .50
18 Woody Williams .30 .75
19 San Diego Padres/1998 NL Champs .20 .50
20 Logo Card .20 .50

2000 Padres Keebler

COMPLETE SET (28) 4.00 10.00
1 Bruce Bochy MG .10 .25
2 Tony Gwynn .80 2.00
3 Ryan Klesko .30 .75
4 Sterling Hitchcock .10 .25
5 Al Martin .10 .25
6 Trevor Hoffman .40 1.00
7 Bret Boone .20 .50
8 Dave Magadan .10 .25
9 Steve Montgomery .10 .25
10 Damian Jackson .10 .25
11 Woody Williams .20 .50
12 Wiki Gonzalez .10 .25
13 Chris Gomez .10 .25
14 Ruben Rivera .10 .25
15 Ed Sprague .10 .25
16 Carlton Loewer .10 .25
17 Kory DeHaan .10 .25
18 Donne Wall .10 .25
19 Eric Owens .10 .25
20 Brian Boehringer .10 .25
21 Phil Nevin .20 .50
22 Matt Clement .40 1.00
23 Brian Meadows .10 .25
24 Vicente Palacios .10 .25
25 Carlos Hernandez .10 .25
26 Carlos Almanzar .10 .25
27 Kevin Walker .10 .25
28 Greg Booker CO .20 .50
Tim Flannery CO
Ben Oglivie CO
R

2000 Padres MADD

COMPLETE SET (15) 12.00 30.00
1 Bret Boone .80 2.00
2 Sean Burroughs 2.50 6.00
3 Buddy Carlyle .40 1.00
4 Matt Clement 1.20 3.00
5 Mike Darr .40 1.00
6 Ben Davis .40 1.00
7 Tony Gwynn 4.00 10.00
8 Carlos Hernandez .40 1.00
9 Trevor Hoffman 1.20 3.00
10 Ryan Klesko 1.20 3.00
11 Al Martin .40 1.00
12 Phil Nevin .60 1.50
13 Eric Owens .40 1.00
14 Ruben Rivera .40 1.00
15 Woody Williams .60 1.50

2000 Padres Postcards

COMPLETE SET 4.80 12.00
1 Carlos Almanzar .20 .50
2 Bret Boone .30 .75
3 Ben Davis .20 .50
4 Adam Eaton .40 1.00
5 Todd Erdos .20 .50
6 Duane Espy .20 .50
7 Wiki Gonzalez .20 .50
8 Trevor Hoffman .60 1.50
9 Damian Jackson .20 .50
10 Ryan Klesko .60 1.50
11 Carlton Loewer .20 .50
12 John Mabry .20 .50
13 Steve Montgomery .20 .50
14 Phil Nevin .30 .75
15 Kevin Nicholson .20 .50
16 Eric Owens .20 .50
17 Desi Relaford .20 .50
18 Brian Tollberg .20 .50
19 Joe Vitiello .20 .50
20 Kevin Walker .20 .50
21 Jay Witasick .20 .50

2001 Padres Keebler

COMPLETE SET 4.00 10.00
1 Bruce Bochy MG .10 .25
2 Tony Gwynn .80 2.00
3 Trevor Hoffman .40 1.00
4 Ryan Klesko .40 1.00
5 Woody Williams .20 .50
6 Chris Gomez .10 .25
7 Ben Davis .10 .25
8 Dave Magadan .10 .25
9 Rickey Henderson .50 1.25
10 Wiki Gonzalez .10 .25
11 Bobby J. Jones .10 .25
12 Damian Jackson .10 .25
13 Kevin Jarvis .10 .25
14 Bubba Trammell .10 .25
15 Kevin Walker .10 .25
16 Mark Kotsay .40 1.00
17 Alex Arias .10 .25
18 Phil Nevin .20 .50
19 Jay Witasick .10 .25
20 Mike Darr .10 .25
21 Adam Eaton .20 .50
22 Wascar Serrano .10 .25
23 Jose Nunez .10 .25
24 Brian Tolberg .10 .25
25 Donaldo Mendez .10 .25
26 Tom Davey .10 .25
27 Rodney Myers .10 .25
28 Greg Booker CO .10 .25
Duane Espy CO
Tim Flannery CO
Ro

2001 Padres MADD

COMPLETE SET 10.00 25.00
1 Bruce Bochy MG .40 1.00
2 Mike Darr .40 1.00
3 Ben Davis .40 1.00
4 Adam Eaton .60 1.50
5 Chris Gomez .40 1.00
6 Tony Gwynn 2.40 6.00
7 Sterling Hitchcock .40 1.00
8 Trevor Hoffman 1.00 2.50
9 Damian Jackson .40 1.00
10 Bobby Jones .40 1.00
11 Ryan Klesko 1.00 2.50
12 Dave Magadan .40 1.00
13 Phil Nevin .60 1.50
14 Bubba Trammell .40 1.00
15 Kevin Walker .40 1.00
16 Woody Williams .60 1.50
NNO Swinging Friar .40 1.00
Mascot

2001 Padres Postcards

COMPLET SET (32) 4.80 20.00
1 Alex Arias .10 .50
2 Bruce Bochy MG .10 .50
3 Greg Booker CO .10 .50
4 Mike Colangelo .10 .50
5 Ben Davis .10 .50
6 Mike Darr .10 .50
7 Tom Davey .10 .50
8 Adam Eaton .20 .75
9 Duane Espy CO .10 .50
10 Tim Flannery CO .10 .50
11 Wiki Gonzalez .10 .50
12 Tony Gwynn 1.20 4.00
13 Rickey Henderson .80 3.00
14 Trevor Hoffman .40 1.50
15 Damian Jackson .10 .50
16 Kevin Jarvis .10 .50
17 Bobby Jones .10 .50
18 Ryan Klesko .40 1.50
19 Mark Kotsay .40 1.50
20 Carlton Loewer .10 .50
21 Dave Magadan .10 .50
22 Donaldo Mendez .10 .50
23 Mark Merila CO .10 .50
24 Rodney Myers .10 .50
25 Phil Nevin .20 .75
26 Santiago Perez .10 .50
27 Rob Picciolo CO .10 .50
28 Brian Tollberg .10 .50
29 Alan Trammell CO .20 .75
30 Kevin Walker .10 .50
31 Woody Williams .20 .75
32 Jay Witasick .10 .50

2002 Padres Hall of Fame Upper Deck

1 Ozzie Smith 2.00 5.00
Gaylord Perry
Dave Winfield
Willie

2002 Padres Keebler

1 Bruce Bochy MG .08 .25
2 Trevor Hoffman .40 1.00
3 Sean Burroughs .20 .50
4 Ryan Klesko .40 1.00
5 Phil Nevin .20 .50
6 Kevin Jarvis .08 .25
7 Ron Gant .20 .50
8 Ramon Vazquez .08 .25
9 Alan Embree .08 .25
10 Wiki Gonzalez .08 .25
11 Bobby J. Jones .08 .25
12 Mark Kotsay .40 1.00
13 Brett Tomko .08 .25
14 Bubba Trammell .08 .25
15 Tom Lampkin .08 .25
16 Steve Reed .08 .25
17 Deivi Cruz .08 .25
18 Brian Tollberg .08 .25
19 Trenidad Hubbard .08 .25
20 Jose Nunez .08 .25
21 Ray Lankford .20 .50
22 Kevin Walker .08 .25
23 Dennis Tankersley .08 .25
24 Jeremy Fikac .08 .25
25 D'Angelo Jimenez .08 .25
26 Brian Lawrence .08 .25
27 Adam Eaton .20 .50
28 Darrel Akerfelds CO .08 .25
Greg Booker CO
Duane Espy CO

2003 Padres Carl's Jr.

COMPLETE SET 4.00 10.00
1 Roberto Alomar .40 1.00
2 Bruce Bochy MG .10 .25
3 Kevin Brown .30 .75
4 Ken Caminiti .50 1.25
5 Steve Finley .40 1.00
6 Steve Garvey .40 1.00
7 Tony Gwynn .75 2.00
8 Trevor Hoffman .40 1.00
9 Randy Jones .10 .25
10 Gaylord Perry .40 1.00
11 Benito Santiago .20 .50
12 Ozzie Smith .60 1.50
13 Dave Winfield .60 1.50

2003 Padres Keebler

1 Bruce Bochy MG .10 .25
2 Trevor Hoffman .40 1.00
3 Phil Nevin .20 .50
4 Ryan Klesko .40 1.00
5 Sean Burroughs .20 .50
6 Brian Lawrence .10 .25
7 Rondell White .20 .50
8 Ramon Vazquez .10 .25
9 Mark Kotsay .40 1.00
10 Dave Hansen .10 .25
11 Jaret Wright .10 .25
12 Gary Bennett .10 .25
13 Brandon Villafuerte .10 .25
14 Lou Merloni .10 .25
15 Jesse Orosco .20 .50
16 Keith Lockhart .10 .25
17 Kevin Walker .10 .25
18 Mark Loretta .20 .50
19 Kevin Jarvis .10 .25
20 Xavier Nady .30 .75
21 Jake Peavy .60 1.50
22 Mike Mathews .10 .25
23 Brian Buchanan .10 .25
24 Luther Hackman .10 .25
25 Adam Eaton .20 .50
26 Matt Herges .10 .25
27 Jay Witasick .10 .25
28 Darren Balsley CO .10 .25
Dave Lopes CO
Dave Magadan CO#

2006 Padres Topps

COMPLETE SET (14) 3.00 8.00
SDP1 Jake Peavy .12 .30
SDP2 Woody Williams .12 .30
SDP3 Ryan Klesko .12 .30
SDP4 Khalil Greene .12 .30
SDP5 Brian Giles .12 .30
SDP6 Geoff Blum .12 .30
SDP7 Dave Roberts .20 .50
SDP8 Trevor Hoffman .20 .50
SDP9 Mike Cameron .12 .30
SDP10 Vinny Castilla .12 .30
SDP11 Chris Young .12 .30
SDP12 Chan Ho Park .20 .50
SDP13 Mark Bellhorn .12 .30
SDP14 Ben Johnson .12 .30

2007 Padres Topps

COMPLETE SET (14) 3.00 8.00
SAD1 Greg Maddux .40 1.00
SAD2 Jake Peavy .12 .30
SAD3 Adrian Gonzalez .25 .60
SAD4 Clay Hensley .12 .30
SAD5 Kevin Kouzmanoff .12 .30
SAD6 Brian Giles .12 .30
SAD7 Termel Sledge .12 .30
SAD8 Marcus Giles .12 .30
SAD9 Cla Meredith .12 .30
SAD10 Josh Bard .12 .30
SAD11 Chris Young .12 .30
SAD12 Trevor Hoffman .20 .50
SAD13 Khalil Greene .12 .30
SAD14 Mike Cameron .12 .30

2008 Padres Topps

COMPLETE SET (14) 3.00 8.00
SAD1 Greg Maddux .40 1.00
SAD2 Jake Peavy .12 .30
SAD3 Adrian Gonzalez .20 .50
SAD4 Jim Edmonds .20 .50
SAD5 Kevin Kouzmanoff .12 .30
SAD6 Brian Giles .12 .30
SAD7 Scott Hairston .12 .30
SAD8 Tadahito Iguchi .12 .30
SAD9 Michael Barrett .12 .30
SAD10 Josh Bard .12 .30
SAD11 Chris Young .12 .30
SAD12 Trevor Hoffman .20 .50
SAD13 Khalil Greene .12 .30
SAD14 Cla Meredith .12 .30

2009 Padres Topps

SDP1 Adrian Gonzalez .30 .75
SDP2 Jake Peavy .15 .40
SDP3 Kevin Kouzmanoff .15 .40
SDP4 Chris Young .15 .40
SDP5 Chase Headley .15 .40
SDP6 Matt Antonelli .25 .60
SDP7 Jody Gerut .15 .40
SDP8 Josh Banks .15 .40
SDP9 Brian Giles .15 .40
SDP10 Cha-Seung Baek .15 .40
SDP11 Will Venable .15 .40
SDP12 Edgar Gonzalez .15 .40
SDP13 Wade LeBlanc .25 .60
SDP14 Scott Hairston .15 .40
SDP15 Swinging Friar .15 .40

2010 Padres Topps

SDP1 Adrian Gonzalez .30 .75
SDP2 Aaron Poreda .15 .40
SDP3 Kyle Blanks .15 .40
SDP4 Tony Gwynn Jr. .15 .40
SDP5 Kevin Correia .15 .40
SDP6 Mat Latos .25 .60
SDP7 Will Venable .15 .40
SDP8 David Eckstein .15 .40
SDP9 Chase Headley .15 .40
SDP10 Chris Young .15 .40
SDP11 Everth Cabrera .15 .40
SDP12 Luis Durango .15 .40
SDP13 Scott Hairston .15 .40
SDP14 Nick Hundley .15 .40
SDP15 Heath Bell .15 .40
SDP16 Clayton Richard .15 .40
SDP17 Tim Stauffer .15 .40

2011 Padres Topps

SDP1 Mat Latos .25 .60
SDP2 Chase Headley .15 .40
SDP3 Wade LeBlanc .15 .40
SDP4 Ryan Ludwick .15 .40
SDP5 Everth Cabrera .15 .40
SDP6 Heath Bell .15 .40
SDP7 Orlando Hudson .15 .40
SDP8 Cameron Maybin .15 .40
SDP9 Brad Hawpe .15 .40
SDP10 Jason Bartlett .15 .40
SDP11 Clayton Richard .15 .40
SDP12 Nick Hundley .15 .40
SDP13 Aaron Harang .15 .40
SDP14 Will Venable .15 .40
SDP15 Cory Luebke .15 .40
SDP16 Kyle Blanks .15 .40
SDP17 PETCO Park .15 .40

2012 Padres Topps

SD1 Cameron Maybin .25 .60
SD2 Will Venable .25 .60
SD3 Kyle Blanks .25 .60
SD4 Huston Street .25 .60
SD5 Orlando Hudson .25 .60
SD6 Nick Hundley .25 .60
SD7 Yonder Alonso .25 .60

SD8 Jason Bartlett .25 .60
SD9 Carlos Quentin .25 .60
SD10 Edinson Volquez .25 .60
SD11 Clayton Richard .25 .60
SD12 Chase Headley .25 .60
SD13 Jesus Guzman .25 .60
SD14 Tim Stauffer .25 .60
SD15 Cory Luebke .25 .60
SD16 Dustin Moseley .25 .60
SD17 PETCO Park .15 .40

2013 Padres Topps

COMPLETE SET (17) 3.00 8.00
SDP1 Chase Headley .25 .60
SDP2 Yonder Alonso .15 .40
SDP3 Logan Forsythe .25 .60
SDP4 Yasmani Grandal .25 .60
SDP5 Carlos Quentin .25 .60
SDP6 Cameron Maybin .25 .60
SDP7 Everth Cabrera .15 .40
SDP8 Clayton Richard .15 .40
SDP9 Edinson Volquez .15 .40
SDP10 Andrew Cashner .15 .40
SDP11 Casey Kelly .30 .75
SDP12 Jason Marquis .15 .40
SDP13 Huston Street .25 .60
SDP14 Jesus Guzman .25 .60
SDP15 Nick Hundley .25 .60
SDP16 Will Venable .15 .40
SDP17 Petco Park .15 .40

2014 Padres Topps

COMPLETE SET (17) 3.00 8.00
SDP1 Chase Headley .15 .40
SDP2 Yonder Alonso .15 .40
SDP3 Seth Smith .15 .40
SDP4 Yasmani Grandal .15 .40
SDP5 Carlos Quentin .15 .40
SDP6 Huston Street .15 .40
SDP7 Everth Cabrera .15 .40
SDP8 Ian Kennedy .15 .40
SDP9 Jedd Gyorko .15 .40
SDP10 Andrew Cashner .15 .40
SDP11 Josh Johnson .20 .50
SDP12 Tyson Ross .15 .40
SDP13 Cameron Maybin .15 .40
SDP14 Joaquin Benoit .15 .40
SDP15 Nick Hundley .15 .40
SDP16 Will Venable .15 .40
SDP17 Petco Park .15 .40

2015 Padres Topps

COMPLETE SET (17) 3.00 8.00
SDP1 Matt Kemp .20 .50
SDP2 Alexi Amarista .15 .40
SDP3 Andrew Cashner .15 .40
SDP4 Will Middlebrooks .15 .40
SDP5 Jedd Gyorko .15 .40
SDP6 Justin Upton .20 .50
SDP7 Ian Kennedy .15 .40
SDP8 Tommy Medica .15 .40
SDP9 Carlos Quentin .15 .40
SDP10 Wil Myers .20 .50
SDP11 Rymer Liriano .15 .40
SDP12 Cory Spangenberg .15 .40
SDP13 Yonder Alonso .15 .40
SDP14 Yangervis Solarte .15 .40
SDP15 Tyson Ross .15 .40
SDP16 Derek Norris .15 .40
SDP17 Joaquin Benoit .15 .40

2016 Padres Topps

COMPLETE SET (17) 3.00 8.00
SDP1 Matt Kemp .20 .50
SDP2 James Shields .15 .40
SDP3 Derek Norris .15 .40
SDP4 Wil Myers .20 .50
SDP5 Alexi Amarista .15 .40
SDP6 Yangervis Solarte .15 .40
SDP7 Jon Jay .15 .40
SDP8 Travis Jankowski .15 .40
SDP9 Andrew Cashner .15 .40
SDP10 Colin Rea .15 .40
SDP11 Tyson Ross .15 .40
SDP12 Melvin Upton Jr. .20 .50
SDP13 Brett Wallace .15 .40
SDP14 Alex Dickerson .15 .40
SDP15 Cory Spangenberg .15 .40
SDP16 Odrisamer Despaigne .15 .40
SDP17 Robbie Erlin .15 .40

2017 Padres Topps

COMPLETE SET (17) 3.00 8.00
SD1 Wil Myers .20 .50
SD2 Yangervis Solarte .15 .40
SD3 Jabari Blash .15 .40
SD4 Christian Friedrich .15 .40
SD5 Cory Spangenberg .15 .40
SD6 Hunter Renfroe .20 .50
SD7 Christian Bethancourt .15 .40
SD8 Luis Sardinas .15 .40
SD9 Adam Rosales .15 .40
SD10 Colin Rea .15 .40
SD11 Alex Dickerson .15 .40
SD12 Jarred Cosart .15 .40
SD13 Ryan Schimpf .15 .40
SD14 Carlos Asuaje .15 .40
SD15 Austin Hedges .15 .40
SD16 Manny Margot .15 .40
SD17 Travis Jankowski .15 .40

2018 Padres Topps

COMPLETE SET (17) 2.00 5.00
SP1 Wil Myers .20 .50
SP2 Hunter Renfroe .15 .40
SP3 Cory Spangenberg .15 .40
SP4 Clayton Richard .15 .40
SP5 Erick Aybar .15 .40
SP6 Manny Margot .15 .40
SP7 Luis Perdomo .15 .40
SP8 Jose Pirela .15 .40
SP9 Dinelson Lamet .15 .40
SP10 Travis Jankowski .15 .40
SP11 Brad Hand .15 .40
SP12 Travis Wood .15 .40
SP13 Robbie Erlin .15 .40
SP14 Freddy Galvis .15 .40
SP15 Colin Rea .15 .40
SP16 Carlos Asuaje .15 .40
SP17 Austin Hedges .15 .40

2019 Padres Topps

COMPLETE SET (17) 2.00 5.00
SP1 Eric Hosmer .20 .50
SP2 Wil Myers .20 .50
SP3 Hunter Renfroe .15 .40
SP4 Austin Hedges .15 .40
SP5 Francisco Mejia .20 .50
SP6 Joey Lucchesi .15 .40
SP7 Luis Urias .25 .60
SP8 Craig Stammen .15 .40
SP9 Franmil Reyes .15 .40
SP10 Manny Margot .15 .40
SP11 Greg Garcia .15 .40
SP12 Eric Lauer .15 .40
SP13 Robbie Erlin .15 .40
SP14 Ian Kinsler .20 .50
SP15 Kirby Yates .20 .50
SP16 Travis Jankowski .15 .40
SP17 Jacob Nix .20 .50

2020 Padres Topps

SD1 Manny Machado .25 .60
SD2 Wil Myers .20 .50
SD3 Fernando Tatis Jr. 1.25 3.00
SD4 Joey Lucchesi .15 .40
SD5 Eric Hosmer .20 .50
SD6 Trent Grisham .60 1.50
SD7 Pedro Avila
SD8 Francisco Mejia .20 .50
SD9 Kirby Yates .15 .40
SD10 Chris Paddack .25 .60
SD11 Dinelson Lamet .15 .40
SD12 Adrian Morejon .15 .40
SD13 Josh Naylor .15 .40
SD14 David Bednar .15 .40
SD15 Ian Kinsler .20 .50
SD16 Cal Quantrill .15 .40
SD17 Michel Baez .15 .40

2017 Padres Topps National Baseball Card Day

COMPLETE SET (10) 5.00 12.00
SDP1 Travis Jankowski .60 1.50
SDP2 Yangervis Solarte .60 1.50
SDP3 Hunter Renfroe .75 2.00
SDP4 Wil Myers .75 2.00
SDP5 Luis Sardinas .60 1.50
SDP6 Ryan Schimpf .60 1.50
SDP7 Erick Aybar .60 1.50
SDP8 Austin Hedges .60 1.50
SDP9 Manny Margot .60 1.50
SDP10 Tony Gwynn 1.00 2.50

1996 Paige NoirTech

This 12-card set measures approximately 3 1/2" by 5 1/2" and features black-and-white photos of Satchel Paige. The backs carry discriptions of the front pictures in a postcard format.

COMPLETE SET (12) 3.00 8.00
COMMON CARD (1-12) .20 .50
1 Satchel Paige .75 2.00
Josh Gibson
Cy Perkins
2 Satchel Paige All-Stars .30 .75
3 Satchel Paige .40 1.00
Dizzy Dean
Cecil Travis
10 Satchel Paige .60 1.50
Billie Holiday
12 Satchel Paige .40 1.00
Vernon Gomez

2003 Palmeiro Donruss 500 Homer

1 Rafael Palmeiro 2.00 5.00

2002 Palmeiro Viagra

COMPLETE SET 2.00 5.00
1 Rafael Palmeiro .75 2.00
Portrait
2 Rafael Palmeiro .75 2.00
Batting Pose
3 Rafael Palmeiro .40 1.00
Shows Palmeiro's Back

1988 Palmer Healthfest

This one card standard-size set feature retired Oriole great Jim Palmer. The front has a full color photo of Palmer surrounded by blue borders. The bottom part of the card mentions the sponsor "Sentars Leigh Hospital" and this card was given out at Healthfest 88. The back has vital stats, World Series stats and some facts about Palmer.

1 Jim Palmer 2.00 5.00

2013 Panini America's Pastime

1-275 PRINT RUN 125 SER.#'d SETS
276-311 PRINT RUN 99 SER.#'d SETS
EXCHANGE DEADLINE 07/09/2015
1 Adam Dunn 2.00 5.00
2 Jonathan Papelbon 2.00 5.00
3 David Wright 2.00 5.00
4 Ian Kinsler 2.00 5.00
5 Mark Trumbo 1.50 4.00
6 Derek Jeter 6.00 15.00
7 Brian Wilson 2.50 6.00
8 Joe Mauer 2.00 5.00
9 Justin Masterson 1.50 4.00
10 Jim Johnson 1.50 4.00
11 Nick Swisher 2.00 5.00
12 Elvis Andrus 2.00 5.00
13 Chris Davis 2.00 5.00
14 Mitch Moreland 1.50 4.00
15 Hunter Pence 2.00 5.00
16 Yadier Molina 3.00 8.00
17 Robinson Cano 2.00 5.00
18 Joey Votto 2.50 6.00
19 B.J. Upton 2.00 5.00
20 Adam Jones 2.00 5.00
21 David Price 2.00 5.00
22 Matt Kemp 2.00 5.00
23 Todd Helton 2.00 5.00
24 Sergio Romo 1.50 4.00
25 Freddie Freeman 3.00 8.00
26 Albert Pujols 3.00 8.00
27 Jacoby Ellsbury 2.00 5.00
28 Dustin Pedroia 2.50 6.00
29 Jordan Zimmermann 2.00 5.00
30 Wei-Yin Chen 1.50 4.00
31 Miguel Cabrera 2.50 6.00
32 Raul Ibanez 2.00 5.00
33 Zack Greinke 2.50 6.00
34 Mike Trout 20.00 50.00
35 Adam LaRoche 1.50 4.00
36 Chris Sale 2.50 6.00
37 Giancarlo Stanton 2.50 6.00
38 Jose Reyes 2.00 5.00
39 Evan Longoria 2.00 5.00
40 Buster Posey 3.00 8.00
41 Anthony Rizzo 3.00 8.00
42 Adam Wainwright 2.00 5.00
43 Eric Hosmer 2.00 5.00
44 Bartolo Colon 1.50 4.00
45 Clayton Kershaw 4.00 10.00
46 Ichiro 3.00 8.00
47 Justin Morneau 2.00 5.00
48 Shin-Soo Choo 2.00 5.00
49 Yu Darvish 2.50 6.00
50 Chris Carter 1.50 4.00
51 Adrian Beltre 2.50 6.00
52 Edwin Encarnacion 2.50 6.00
53 Starlin Castro 1.50 4.00
54 Paul Konerko 2.00 5.00
55 Jose Bautista 2.00 5.00
56 Curtis Granderson 2.00 5.00
57 Adrian Gonzalez 2.00 5.00
58 Alfonso Soriano 2.00 5.00
59 Billy Butler 1.50 4.00
60 CC Sabathia 2.00 5.00
61 Yoenis Cespedes 2.50 6.00
62 Troy Tulowitzki 2.50 6.00
63 Stephen Strasburg 2.50 6.00
64 Ryan Zimmerman 2.00 5.00
65 Max Scherzer 2.50 6.00
66 Justin Upton 2.00 5.00
67 Ryan Howard 2.00 5.00
68 Paul Goldschmidt 2.50 6.00
69 Matt Harvey 2.00 5.00
70 Josh Hamilton 2.00 5.00
71 Allen Craig 2.00 5.00
72 Carlos Beltran 2.00 5.00
73 Chase Headley 1.50 4.00
74 Justin Verlander 2.50 6.00
75 Michael Young 1.50 4.00
76 Roy Halladay 2.00 5.00
77 Andrew McCutchen 2.50 6.00
78 Andy Pettitte 2.00 5.00
79 Anibal Sanchez 1.50 4.00
80 Brandon Phillips 1.50 4.00
81 Bryce Harper 4.00 10.00
82 Chase Utley 2.00 5.00
83 Chris Johnson 1.50 4.00
84 R.A. Dickey 2.00 5.00
85 Prince Fielder 2.00 5.00
86 Pedro Alvarez 1.50 4.00
87 Michael Cuddyer 1.50 4.00
88 Jose Altuve 2.00 5.00
89 Felix Hernandez 2.00 5.00
90 Mike Napoli 1.50 4.00
91 Mariano Rivera 3.00 8.00
92 Carlos Gonzalez 2.00 5.00
93 Joe Nathan 1.50 4.00
94 Pablo Sandoval 2.00 5.00
95 James Shields 1.50 4.00
96 Domonic Brown 2.00 5.00
97 David Ortiz 2.50 6.00
98 Craig Kimbrel 2.00 5.00
99 Matt Carpenter 2.50 6.00
100 Jorge De La Rosa 1.50 4.00
101 Don Mattingly 5.00 12.00
102 Pete Rose 5.00 12.00
103 Ken Griffey Jr. 5.00 12.00
104 Reggie Jackson 2.50 6.00
105 Cal Ripken Jr. 8.00 20.00
106 George Brett 5.00 12.00
107 Mike Piazza 2.50 6.00
108 Alan Trammell 2.00 5.00
109 Bo Jackson 2.50 6.00
110 Rickey Henderson 2.50 6.00
111 Mike Schmidt 4.00 10.00
112 Joe Morgan 2.00 5.00
113 Darryl Strawberry 1.50 4.00
114 Bob Gibson 2.00 5.00
115 Roberto Alomar 2.00 5.00
116 Ozzie Smith 3.00 8.00
117 Eddie Murray 2.00 5.00
118 Chipper Jones 2.50 6.00
119 Frank Robinson 2.00 5.00
120 Randy Johnson 2.50 6.00
121 Curt Schilling 2.00 5.00
122 Craig Biggio 2.00 5.00
123 Steve Carlton 2.00 5.00
124 Goose Gossage 2.00 5.00
125 Jim Palmer 2.00 5.00
126 Don Sutton 1.50 4.00
127 Robin Yount 2.50 6.00
128 Fergie Jenkins 2.00 5.00
129 Bernie Williams 2.00 5.00
130 Johnny Bench 2.50 6.00
131 Mark Grace 2.50 6.00
132 Roger Clemens 3.00 8.00
133 Barry Larkin 2.00 5.00
134 Carlton Fisk 2.00 5.00
135 Ryne Sandberg 5.00 12.00
136 Carl Yastrzemski 4.00 10.00
137 Tony Gwynn 2.50 6.00
138 Ernie Banks 2.50 6.00
139 Paul O'Neill 2.00 5.00
140 Bobby Doerr 1.50 4.00
141 Al Kaline 2.50 6.00
142 Bill Mazeroski 2.00 5.00
143 Nomar Garciaparra 2.00 5.00
144 Dennis Eckersley 2.00 5.00
145 Tom Seaver 2.00 5.00
146 Pedro Martinez 2.00 5.00
147 Mike Mussina 2.00 5.00
148 Brooks Robinson 2.00 5.00
149 Jim Rice 2.00 5.00
150 Frank Thomas 2.50 6.00
151 John Kruk 1.50 4.00
152 Will Clark 2.00 5.00
153 Dwight Gooden 1.50 4.00
154 Rod Carew 2.00 5.00
155 Jim Thome 2.00 5.00
156 Tom Glavine 1.50 4.00
157 Jose Canseco 2.00 5.00
158 Nolan Ryan 8.00 20.00
159 Ivan Rodriguez 2.00 5.00
160 Yogi Berra 2.50 6.00
161 Cy Young 2.50 6.00
162 Satchel Paige 2.50 6.00
163 Kirby Puckett 2.50 6.00
164 Ty Cobb 4.00 10.00
165 Lou Gehrig 5.00 12.00
166 Honus Wagner 2.50 6.00
167 Joe DiMaggio 5.00 12.00
168 Ted Williams 5.00 12.00
169 Stan Musial 4.00 10.00
170 Bill Dickey 1.50 4.00
171 Sam Crawford 1.50 4.00
172 Warren Spahn 2.00 5.00
173 Josh Gibson 2.50 6.00
174 Jackie Robinson 2.50 6.00
175 Roy Campanella 2.50 6.00
176 Alberto Cabrera RC 1.50 4.00
177 Carter Capps RC 1.50 4.00
178 Yoervis Medina RC 1.50 4.00
179 Donovan Hand RC 1.50 4.00
180 John Gast RC 1.00 2.50
181 Nick Noonan RC 2.00 5.00
182 A.J. Ramos RC 2.00 5.00
183 Nate Freiman RC 1.00 2.50
184 Donnie Joseph RC 1.00 2.50
185 Alex Wood RC 2.00 5.00
186 Steve Ames RC 1.00 2.50
187 Andrew Werner RC 1.50 4.00
188 Brock Holt RC 2.00 5.00
189 Cody Asche RC 2.50 6.00
190 Hiram Burgos RC 1.50 4.00
191 Jermaine Curtis RC 2.50 6.00
192 Marcell Ozuna RC 4.00 10.00
193 Seth Maness RC 1.50 4.00
194 Kevin Siegrist RC 2.50 6.00
195 Matt Magill RC 1.50 4.00
196 Corey Kluber RC 5.00 12.00
197 Bryan Morris RC 1.50 4.00
198 Derek Dietrich RC 2.00 5.00
199 Jose Dominguez RC 1.50 4.00
200 Alex Colome RC 1.50 4.00
201 Nathan Karns RC 1.50 4.00
202 Jeurys Familia RC 2.50 6.00
203 Brandon Workman RC 1.00 2.50
204 David Adams RC 2.00 5.00
205 Todd Cunningham RC 1.50 4.00
206 Brooks Raley RC 1.50 4.00
207 Robbie Grossman RC 1.50 4.00
208 Ryan Pressly RC 2.00 5.00
209 Oswaldo Arcia RC 1.50 4.00
210 Ian Krol RC 1.00 2.50
211 Michael Tonkin RC 1.00 2.50
212 Leury Garcia RC 1.50 4.00
213 Josh Phegley RC 1.50 4.00
214 Munenori Kawasaki RC 2.50 6.00
215 Keith Butler RC 1.50 4.00
216 Paul Clemens RC 1.50 4.00
217 Jose Ortega RC 1.50 4.00
218 Taylor Jordan RC 1.00 2.50
219 Jean Machi RC 1.50 4.00
220 Pedro Villarreal RC 1.50 4.00
221 Justin Grimm RC 1.50 4.00
222 Rafael Ortega RC 1.50 4.00
223 Robert Carson RC 1.50 4.00
224 Brett Oberholtzer RC 1.00 2.50
225 Will Smith RC 1.50 4.00
226 Chris Herrmann RC 1.50 4.00
227 Brad Miller RC 1.50 4.00
228 Thomas Neal RC 1.50 4.00
229 Michael Wacha RC 2.50 6.00
230 Tyler Lyons RC 1.50 4.00
231 Jose Cisnero RC 1.50 4.00
232 Nick Tepesch RC 1.50 4.00
233 Cesar Hernandez RC 1.50 4.00
234 Joey Terdoslavich RC 1.50 4.00
235 Jarred Cosart RC 2.00 5.00
236 Adam Warren JSY RC 3.00 8.00
237 Alex Wilson JSY RC 3.00 8.00
238 Carlos Triunfel JSY RC 3.00 8.00
239 Cory Rasmus RC 1.00 2.50
240 Derrick Robinson JSY RC 3.00 8.00
241 Hector Rondon JSY RC 3.00 8.00
242 Jordy Mercer JSY RC 3.00 8.00
243 Juan Lagares JSY RC
244 Kyle Gibson RC 2.50 6.00
245 Neftali Soto JSY RC 3.00 8.00
246 Scott Rice JSY RC 3.00 8.00
247 T.J. McFarland JSY RC 3.00 8.00
248 Tom Koehler JSY RC 3.00 8.00
249 Vidal Nuno JSY RC 3.00 8.00
250 Yan Gomes RC 3.00 8.00
251 Aaron Loup AU RC 4.00 10.00
252 Alfredo Marte AU RC
253 Sonny Gray AU RC 6.00 15.00
254 Brandon Maurer AU RC 4.00 10.00
255 Bruce Rondon AU RC 4.00 10.00
256 Jonathan Pettibone AU RC 4.00 10.00
257 Casey Kelly AU RC 4.00 10.00
258 Mike Olt AU RC 4.00 10.00
259 Allen Webster AU RC 4.00 10.00
260 Collin McHugh AU RC 6.00 15.00
261 David Lough AU RC 4.00 10.00
262 Denis Phipps AU RC
263 Eury Perez AU RC 4.00 10.00
264 Henry M. Rodriguez AU RC 4.00 10.00
265 Jaye Chapman AU RC 4.00 10.00
266 Kyle Skipworth AU RC 4.00 10.00
267 Kyuji Fujikawa AU RC
268 L.J. Hoes AU RC 4.00 10.00
269 Melky Mesa AU RC
270 Nick Maronde AU RC 4.00 10.00
271 Paco Rodriguez AU RC 4.00 10.00
272 Rob Brantly AU RC 4.00 10.00
273 Rob Scahill AU RC 4.00 10.00
274 Shawn Tolleson AU RC 4.00 10.00
275 Tyler Cloyd AU RC 4.00 10.00
276 Aaron Hicks JSY AU/99 RC
277 Adam Eaton JSY AU/99 RC 12.00 30.00
278 Yasiel Puig JSY Bat/99 RC 15.00 40.00
281 Brandon Barnes JSY AU/99 RC
283 Christian Yelich JSY AU/99 RC 25.00 60.00
285 Didi Gregorius JSY AU/99 RC 5.00 12.00
287 Evan Gattis JSY AU/99 RC 10.00 25.00
289 Hyun-Jin Ryu JSY AU/99 RC
290 Jackie Bradley Jr. JSY AU/99 RC 12.50 30.00
291 Jake Odorizzi JSY AU/99 RC 6.00 15.00
293 Jose Fernandez JSY AU/99 RC 40.00 80.00
294 Junior Lake JSY AU/99 RC 5.00 12.00
295 Justin Wilson JSY AU/99 RC
297 Kevin Gausman JSY AU/99 RC
298 Manny Machado JSY AU/99 RC 20.00 50.00
299 Chris Rusin JSY AU/99 RC 6.00 15.00
300 Mike Zunino JSY AU/69 RC 15.00 40.00
301 Nick Franklin JSY AU/99 RC
302 Nolan Arenado JSY AU/99 RC
303 Preston Claiborne JSY AU/99 RC 5.00 12.00
304 Scott Van Slyke JSY AU/99 RC 8.00 20.00
307 Tyler Skaggs JSY AU/99 RC 5.00 12.00
308 Wil Myers JSY AU/99 RC 15.00 40.00
309 Zoilo Almonte JSY AU/99 RC EXCH
310 Zack Wheeler JSY AU/99 RC 15.00 40.00
311 Bruce Rondon JSY AU/85 RC 5.00 12.00

2013 Panini America's Pastime Gold

*GLD 1-235/239/244/250: .75X TO 2X BASIC
STATED PRINT RUN 25 SER.#'d SETS
NO MEM OR AU RC PRICING AVAILABLE
EXCHANGE DEADLINE 07/09/2015

2013 Panini America's Pastime Red

*RED: .5X TO 1.2X BASIC
STATED PRINT RUN 49 SER.#'d SETS
NO PRICING ON MOST DUE TO LACK OF INFO

2013 Panini America's Pastime All-Panini Autographs

PRINT RUNS B/WN 10-125 COPIES PER
NO PRICING ON QTY 10
EXCHANGE DEADLINE 07/09/2015
1 Curt Schilling/25 10.00 25.00
2 Alan Trammell/49 12.50 30.00
3 Dusty Baker/25 5.00 12.00
4 Billy Williams/25 6.00 15.00
5 Joe Morgan/57 10.00 25.00
6 Bernie Williams/25 10.00 25.00
8 Ken Griffey Jr./25 75.00 150.00
9 Don Mattingly/25 40.00 80.00
10 Mike Piazza/39 15.00 40.00
11 Roger Clemens/25 20.00 50.00
12 Yogi Berra/40 25.00 60.00
13 Mariano Rivera/42 90.00 150.00
14 Ivan Nova/27 6.00 15.00
15 Clayton Kershaw/25 20.00 50.00
16 David Freese/25 8.00 20.00
17 Fred McGriff/25 8.00 20.00
18 Josh Reddick/25
19 Maury Wills/125 5.00 12.00
20 Monte Irvin/25
21 Edgar Martinez/49 20.00 50.00
23 Buster Posey/25 20.00 50.00
24 Denny McLain/79 8.00 20.00
25 Devon White/25 5.00 12.00

2013 Panini America's Pastime All-Panini Autographs Gold

*GOLD: .4X TO 1X BASIC
PRINT RUNS B/WN 5-25 COPIES PER
NO PRICING ON QTY 10 OR LESS
EXCHANGE DEADLINE 07/09/2015
2 Alan Trammell/25 15.00 40.00
19 Maury Wills/25 6.00 15.00

2013 Panini America's Pastime America's Best Autographs

PRINT RUNS B/WN 10-99 COPIES PER
NO PRICING ON QTY 10
EXCHANGE DEADLINE 07/09/2015
1 Ben Sheets/49 4.00 10.00
2 Matt Harvey/15 40.00 80.00
3 Rick Monday/50 4.00 10.00
4 Stephen Strasburg/50 20.00 50.00
6 Troy Glaus/25 6.00 15.00
7 Troy Tulowitzki/49 8.00 20.00
8 Chris Sale/19 6.00 15.00
9 Adam Jones/25 15.00 40.00
10 Mike Trout/27 75.00 200.00
11 Ben McDonald/25 10.00 25.00
12 Wally Joyner/64 8.00 20.00
13 Will Clark/25 12.50 30.00
15 Fred McGriff/49 10.00 25.00
17 Josh Reddick/25 4.00 10.00
18 Ron Blomberg/25 4.00 10.00
19 David Freese/49 6.00 15.00
20 Colby Rasmus/25 12.50 30.00
22 Matt Moore/28 6.00 15.00
23 Ron Cey/25 5.00 12.00
24 Chris Davis/25 10.00 25.00
25 Evan Longoria/49 8.00 20.00

2013 Panini America's Pastime Barnstorming Brilliance

STATED PRINT RUN 125 SER.#'d SETS
1 Satchel Paige 4.00 10.00
2 Jackie Robinson 2.00 5.00
3 Monte Irvin 2.00 5.00
4 Roy Campanella 2.00 5.00
5 Ted Radcliffe 2.00 5.00
6 Buck O'Neil 4.00 10.00
7 Ernie Banks 2.00 5.00
8 Minnie Minoso 2.00 5.00
9 Larry Doby 2.00 5.00

2013 Panini America's Pastime Barnstorming Brilliance Gold

*GOLD: .6X TO 1.5X BASIC
STATED PRINT RUN 25 SER.#'d SETS

2013 Panini America's Pastime Between the Seams

PRINT RUNS B/WN 1-25 COPIES PER
NO PRICING ON QTY 10 OR LESS
EXCHANGE DEADLINE 07/09/2015

2013 Panini America's Pastime Boys of Summer Autographs

PRINT RUNS B/WN 10-125 COPIES PER
NO PRICING ON QTY 13 OR LESS
EXCHANGE DEADLINE 07/09/2015
1 Bill Buckner/15 6.00 15.00
2 Bucky Dent/25 4.00 10.00
3 Cody Ross/125 4.00 10.00
4 Dusty Baker/125 5.00 12.00
5 Lenny Dykstra/125 4.00 10.00
9 Mookie Wilson/86 5.00 12.00
10 Oscar Gamble/25 4.00 10.00
11 Paul Lo Duca/15 4.00 10.00
12 Ron Gant/15 8.00 20.00
13 Steve Garvey/25 90.00 150.00
14 Steve Sax/15 8.00 20.00
15 Willie Horton/49 8.00 20.00
16 Darryl Strawberry/25 10.00 25.00
17 Tommy Lasorda /25 15.00 40.00
18 Steve Carlton/57 8.00 20.00
19 Boog Powell/15 10.00 25.00
21 Jim Rice/25 10.00 25.00
22 Dennis Eckersley/25 10.00 25.00
23 Todd Helton/36 8.00 20.00
24 Tony Perez/20 6.00 15.00
25 Minnie Minoso/25 10.00 25.00
26 Ron Guidry/25 10.00 25.00
27 Tommy John/25 4.00 10.00
28 Pete Rose/25 20.00 50.00
30 Jay Buhner/25 20.00 50.00

2013 Panini America's Pastime Boys of Summer Autographs Gold

*GOLD: .4X TO 1X BASIC
PRINT RUNS B/WN 5-25 COPIES PER
NO PRICING ON QTY 10 OR LESS
EXCHANGE DEADLINE 07/09/2015
9 Mookie Wilson/25 10.00 25.00
10 Oscar Gamble/25 6.00 15.00
29 Frank White/25 5.00 12.00

2013 Panini America's Pastime Career Numbers

STATED PRINT RUN 125 SER.#'d SETS
CNAD Andre Dawson 3.00 8.00
CNAK Al Kaline 4.00 10.00
CNBJ Bo Jackson 4.00 10.00
CNBW Bernie Williams 3.00 8.00
CNCB Craig Biggio 3.00 8.00
CNCJ Chipper Jones 4.00 10.00
CNFM Fred McGriff 3.00 8.00
CNFR Frank Robinson 3.00 8.00
CNGP Gaylord Perry 3.00 8.00
CNHK Harmon Killebrew 4.00 10.00
CNPM Paul Molitor 4.00 10.00

2013 Panini America's Pastime Career Numbers Gold

*GOLD: .5X TO 1.2X BASIC
STATED PRINT RUN 25 SER.#'d SETS

2013 Panini America's Pastime Characters of the Game

STATED PRINT RUN 125 SER.#'d SETS
1 Bernie Williams 3.00 8.00
2 David Ortiz 4.00 10.00
3 Gaylord Perry 3.00 8.00
4 Jered Weaver 3.00 8.00
5 John Kruk 2.50 6.00
6 Johnny Damon 3.00 8.00
7 Lenny Dykstra 2.50 6.00
8 Phil Niekro 3.00 8.00
9 Rickey Henderson 4.00 10.00
10 Tim Wakefield 2.50 6.00

2013 Panini America's Pastime Characters of the Game Gold

*GOLD: .75X TO 2X BASIC
STATED PRINT RUN 25 SER.#'d SETS

2013 Panini America's Pastime Characters of the Game Signatures

PRINT RUNS B/WN 10-50 COPIES PER
NO PRICING ON QTY 10
EXCHANGE DEADLINE 07/09/2015
1 Bernie Williams/15 20.00 50.00
2 Carlton Fisk/25 15.00 40.00
3 David Ortiz/25 20.00 50.00
4 Freddie Freeman/25 12.00 30.00
6 Jered Weaver/25 EXCH 5.00 12.00
8 John Kruk/25 8.00 20.00
9 Johnny Damon/25 5.00 12.00
10 Lenny Dykstra/23 6.00 15.00
11 Phil Niekro/15 20.00 50.00
12 Rafael Palmeiro/50 5.00 12.00
13 Rickey Henderson/15 75.00 150.00
14 Tim Wakefield/15 60.00 120.00
15 Willie McGee/25 15.00 40.00

2013 Panini America's Pastime Characters of the Game Signatures Gold

*GOLD: .4X TO 1X BASIC
PRINT RUNS B/WN 5-25 COPIES PER
NO PRICING ON QTY 14 OR LESS
EXCHANGE DEADLINE 07/09/2015

2013 Panini America's Pastime Combo Swatches

STATED PRINT RUN 125 SER.#'d SETS
1 Prince Fielder/125 3.00 8.00
2 Tony Gwynn/125 4.00 10.00
3 Rickey Henderson/125 10.00 25.00
4 Jose Bautista/25
5 Yasiel Puig/125 12.50 30.00
6 Ian Kinsler/99 3.00 8.00
7 Nomar Garciaparra/125 3.00 8.00
8 Andre Dawson/49 6.00 15.00
9 Bo Jackson/99 6.00 15.00
10 Dwight Gooden/125 3.00 8.00
11 Wade Boggs/49 6.00 15.00
12 Jacoby Ellsbury/125 3.00 8.00
13 Adam Jones/99 3.00 8.00
14 Craig Biggio/99 4.00 10.00
15 Goose Gossage/125 3.00 8.00
16 Felix Hernandez/125 4.00 10.00
17 Mike Piazza/125 5.00 12.00
18 Roger Clemens/125 3.00 8.00
19 David Ortiz /125 5.00 12.00
20 Jose Canseco/125 8.00 20.00

2013 Panini America's Pastime Combo Swatches Gold

*GOLD: .75X TO 2X BASIC
STATED PRINT RUN 25 SER.#'d SETS

2013 Panini America's Pastime Decades

STATED PRINT RUN 125 SER.#'d SETS
1 Pete Rose 6.00 15.00
2 Reggie Jackson 2.50 6.00
3 Rod Carew 2.50 6.00
4 Nolan Ryan 10.00 25.00
5 Cal Ripken Jr. 10.00 25.00
6 George Brett 6.00 15.00
7 Rickey Henderson 3.00 8.00
8 Ryne Sandberg 6.00 15.00
9 Ken Griffey Jr. 6.00 15.00
10 Ivan Rodriguez 2.00 5.00
11 Frank Thomas 3.00 8.00
12 Mike Piazza 3.00 8.00
13 Derek Jeter 8.00 20.00
14 Albert Pujols 4.00 10.00
15 Ichiro 4.00 10.00
16 Todd Helton 2.50 6.00
17 Miguel Cabrera 3.00 8.00
18 Mike Trout 25.00 60.00
19 Buster Posey 4.00 10.00
20 Bryce Harper 5.00 12.00

2013 Panini America's Pastime Decades Gold

*GOLD: .6X TO 1.5X BASIC
STATED PRINT RUN 25 SER.#'d SETS

2013 Panini America's Pastime Dual Exhibits Booklets

PRINT RUNS B/WN 10-99 COPIES PER
3 B.Harper/Y.Puig/50 40.00 80.00
4 A.Rodriguez/R.Palmeiro/99 6.00 15.00
5 T.Milone/J.Parker/99 5.00 12.00
6 W.Rosario/J.Rutledge/99 4.00 10.00
7 R.Clemens/R.Johnson/99 8.00 20.00
8 J.Rice/D.Evans/49 8.00 20.00
9 M.Piazza/R.Clemens/99 12.50 30.00
10 A.Pujols/O.Smith/99 10.00 25.00
11 T.Gwynn/R.Hndrsn/99 10.00 25.00
12 M.Grace/A.Rizzo/50 15.00 40.00
13 A.Soriano/Sabathia/99 5.00 12.00
14 P.Fielder/M.Cabrera/99 6.00 15.00
15 G.Maddux/T.Glavine/99 15.00 40.00
16 T.Lasorda/F.Valenzuela/49 10.00 25.00

2013 Panini America's Pastime Dual Exhibits Booklets Gold

*GOLD: .5X TO 1.2X BASIC
PRINT RUNS B/WN 5-49 COPIES PER
NO PRICING ON QTY 10 OR LESS

2013 Panini America's Pastime Dual Exhibits Booklets Red

*RED: .5X TO 1.2X BASIC
PRINT RUNS B/WN 2-25 COPIES PER
NO PRICING ON QTY 10 OR LESS

2013 Panini America's Pastime First Class

STATED PRINT RUN 125 SER.#'d SETS
1 Nolan Ryan 6.00 15.00
2 Chipper Jones 2.00 5.00
3 Cal Ripken Jr. 6.00 15.00
4 Tony Gwynn 2.00 5.00
5 Ken Griffey Jr. 8.00 20.00
6 Bernie Williams 1.50 4.00
7 Kirby Puckett 10.00 25.00
8 Paul O'Neill 1.50 4.00
9 Yogi Berra 2.00 5.00
10 Ozzie Smith 2.50 6.00
11 Ernie Banks 2.00 5.00
12 Willie McCovey 1.50 4.00
13 Carl Yastrzemski 3.00 8.00
14 Don Mattingly 4.00 10.00
15 Craig Biggio 1.50 4.00

2013 Panini America's Pastime First Class Gold

*GOLD: .6X TO 1.5X BASIC
STATED PRINT RUN 25 SER.#'d SETS

2013 Panini America's Pastime Front Row Fabrics Booklets

PRINT RUNS B/WN 25-125 COPIES PER
1 R.Clemens/N.Garciaparra/125 8.00 20.00
2 K.Puckett/H.Killebrew/40 25.00 60.00
3 R.Hndrsn/D.Eckrsly/115 15.00 40.00
4 A.Rdrguez/I.Rdrguez/99 8.00 20.00
5 D.Gooden/D.Strawberry/60 8.00 20.00
6 T.Gwynn/D.Mattingly/99 10.00 25.00
7 A.Pujols/K.Griffey Jr./75 12.50 30.00
8 A.Jackson/C.Grndrsn/99 5.00 12.00
9 D.Murphy/B.Horner/75 10.00 25.00
10 G.Hodges/R.Campanella/25 30.00 60.00
11 R.Jackson/L.Piniella/75 12.50 30.00
12 J.Marichal/W.McCovey/59 20.00 50.00

2013 Panini America's Pastime Front Row Fabrics Booklets Gold

*GOLD: .5X TO 1.2X BASIC
PRINT RUNS B/WN 15-49 COPIES PER

2013 Panini America's Pastime Front Row Fabrics Booklets Red

*RED: .5X TO 1.2X BASIC
PRINT RUNS B/WN 10-25 COPIES PER
NO PRICING QTY 14 OR LESS

2013 Panini America's Pastime Future Fabrics

PRINT RUNS B/WN 50-125 COPIES PER
1 Aaron Hicks/125 3.00 8.00
2 Tom Koehler/125 3.00 8.00
3 Yasiel Puig/125 6.00 15.00
4 Neftali Soto/125 3.00 8.00
5 Wil Myers/50 4.00 10.00
6 Evan Gattis/50 8.00 20.00
7 Tyler Skaggs/99 3.00 8.00
8 Didi Gregorius/125 3.00 8.00
10 Vidal Nuno/125 3.00 8.00
11 Carlos Triunfel/125 3.00 8.00
12 Juan Lagares/125 4.00 10.00
13 Zack Wheeler/50 3.00 8.00
14 Derrick Robinson/125 3.00 8.00
15 Hector Rondon/125 3.00 8.00
16 Scott Rice/125 3.00 8.00
17 Jackie Bradley Jr./125 3.00 8.00
18 Adam Warren/125 3.00 8.00
19 Cory Rasmus/125 3.00 8.00
20 Alex Wilson/125 3.00 8.00
21 Junior Lake/75 5.00 12.00
22 T.J. McFarland/125 3.00 8.00
24 Jordy Mercer/125 3.00 8.00
25 Manny Machado/50 12.50 30.00

2013 Panini America's Pastime Future Fabrics Gold

*GOLD: .4X TO 1X BASIC
PRINT RUNS B/WN 10-25 COPIES PER
NO PRICING ON QTY 10

2013 Panini America's Pastime Hitters Ink Booklets

PRINT RUNS B/WN 10-99 COPIES PER

NO PRICING ON QTY 10
2013 Panini America's Pastime
All-Panini Autographs Red
1 A.Galarraga/V.Castilla/99 10.00 25.00
2 E.Martinez/J.Buhner/49 30.00 60.00
3 Y.Cespedes/J.Donaldson/49 15.00 40.00
4 P.Konerko/H.Baines/49 40.00 80.00
5 P.O'Neill/D.Mattingly/25
6 T.Gwynn/S.Garvey/25 75.00 150.00
7 W.Clark/K.Mitchell/25
8 E.Burks/D.Bichette/99 12.00 30.00
9 R.Sandberg/B.Dernier/25
10 M.Hargrove/A.Thornton/99 6.00 15.00
11 T.Glaus/T.Salmon/99 5.00 12.00
12 W.Boggs/D.Mattingly/25 90.00 150.00
13 J.Kruk/C.Ruiz/25 12.50 30.00
14 B.Madlock/D.Parker/49
16 D.Ortiz/K.Millar/25
17 M.Williams/K.Mitchell/99
18 J.Clark/T.Pendleton/99 10.00 25.00

2013 Panini America's Pastime Hitters Ink Booklets Gold

*GOLD: .4X TO 1X BASIC
PRINT RUNS B/WN 7-49 COPIES PER
NO PRICING ON QTY 7
EXCHANGE DEADLINE 07/09/2015
3 Y.Cespedes/J.Donaldson/25 20.00 50.00

2013 Panini America's Pastime Hitters Ink Booklets Red

*RED: .5X TO 1.2X BASIC
PRINT RUNS B/WN 5-25 COPIES PER
NO PRICING ON QTY 10 OR LESS
EXCHANGE DEADLINE 07/09/2015

2013 Panini America's Pastime Impact Ink

PRINT RUNS B/WN 15-125 COPIES PER
NO PRICING ON QTY 10
EXCHANGE DEADLINE 07/09/2015
1 Anthony Rizzo/49 8.00 20.00
2 Brandon Phillips/25
3 Dexter Fowler/100 4.00 10.00
4 Lance Lynn/25 8.00 20.00
5 Troy Tulowitzki/25 12.00 30.00
6 Brandon McCarthy/25
7 Wilin Rosario/125 4.00 10.00
8 Pablo Sandoval/15 30.00 60.00
9 Alex Avila/25 20.00 50.00
10 Colby Rasmus/25 6.00 15.00
11 Josh Reddick/25 4.00 10.00
12 Brett Gardner/15 15.00 40.00
13 Clayton Kershaw/25 40.00 80.00
14 Carl Crawford/20 6.00 15.00
15 Starlin Castro/15
16 Dustin Ackley/25 6.00 15.00
17 Elvis Andrus/15
18 David Freese/25 4.00 10.00
19 Alex Wood/125 4.00 10.00
20 Billy Hamilton /25 15.00 40.00
21 Brandon Beachy/25 5.00 12.00
22 Carlos Gomez/25
23 Chad Billingsley/15 4.00 10.00
25 Jackie Bradley Jr./25 15.00 40.00

2013 Panini America's Pastime Impact Ink Gold

*GOLD: .4X TO 1X BASIC
PRINT RUNS B/WN 10-25 COPIES PER
NO PRICING ON QTY 10 OR LESS
EXCHANGE DEADLINE 07/09/2015

2013 Panini America's Pastime Inked

PRINT RUNS B/WN 10-125 COPIES PER
NO PRICING ON QTY 10
EXCHANGE DEADLINE 07/09/2015
1 Anthony Rizzo/49 10.00 25.00
2 Asdrubal Cabrera/125 4.00 10.00
3 Billy Hamilton/25 15.00 40.00
4 Bruce Rondon/125 4.00 10.00
5 Chris Davis/25 10.00 25.00
6 Chris Sale/125 4.00 10.00
7 Dexter Fowler/50 4.00 10.00
8 Edwin Encarnacion/15
9 Evan Longoria/15 15.00 40.00
10 Hyun-Jin Ryu/25 12.50 30.00
11 Ike Davis/25
12 Ivan Nova/15 4.00 10.00
13 James Shields/49 4.00 10.00
14 Jason Grilli/25
15 Jose Fernandez/25 20.00 50.00
16 Junior Lake/125 4.00 10.00
17 Mark Trumbo/25 10.00 25.00
18 Matt Harvey/15 20.00 50.00
19 Michael Morse/25 6.00 15.00
20 Oscar Taveras/125 15.00 40.00
21 Wilin Rosario/125 4.00 10.00
22 Zach McAllister/125 4.00 10.00
23 Tyler Flowers/125 4.00 10.00
25 Elvis Andrus/15
26 Aaron Loup/125 4.00 10.00
27 Adeiny Hechavarria/125 4.00 10.00
28 Brandon Maurer/125 4.00 10.00
29 Brooks Raley/89 4.00 10.00
30 Carlos Gomez/25
32 Jean Segura/15
33 Matt Adams/25 10.00 25.00
34 Yovani Gallardo/49 4.00 10.00
35 Alex Avila/25 10.00 25.00
36 Colby Rasmus/25 10.00 25.00
37 Josh Rutledge/125 4.00 10.00
38 Josh Vitters/15 5.00 12.00
39 Dustin Ackley/25
40 Chris Rusin/25 4.00 10.00
41 Yasmani Grandal/25
42 Xavier Avery/125 4.00 10.00
43 Jonathan Lucroy/33 12.00 30.00
44 Tyler Chatwood/125 4.00 10.00
45 Leonys Martin/68
46 Wellington Castillo/28 4.00 10.00
47 Aaron Hicks/125 6.00 15.00
48 Adam Warren/89 4.00 10.00
49 Andrew Taylor/89
50 Starling Marte/25

2013 Panini America's Pastime Inked Gold

*GOLD: .4X TO 1X BASIC
PRINT RUNS B/WN 5-25 COPIES PER
NO PRICING ON QTY 10 OR LESS
EXCHANGE DEADLINE 07/09/2015

2013 Panini America's Pastime Invincible

STATED PRINT RUN 125 SER.#'d SETS
1 Lou Gehrig 5.00 12.00
2 Ty Cobb 4.00 10.00
3 Jackie Robinson 2.50 6.00
4 Cy Young 2.50 6.00
5 Honus Wagner 2.50 6.00
6 Bob Gibson 2.00 5.00
7 Ozzie Smith 3.00 8.00
8 Cal Ripken Jr. 8.00 20.00
9 Rickey Henderson 2.50 6.00
10 Pete Rose 5.00 12.00
11 Roger Clemens 3.00 8.00
12 Nolan Ryan 8.00 20.00
13 Yogi Berra 2.50 6.00
14 Mike Schmidt 4.00 10.00
15 Ken Griffey Jr. 8.00 20.00

2013 Panini America's Pastime Invincible Gold

*GOLD: .75X TO 2X BASIC
STATED PRINT RUN 25 SER.#'d SETS

2013 Panini America's Pastime Jumbo Swatches

PRINT RUNS B/WN 4-125 SER.#'d SETS
NO PRICING ON QTY 10 OR LESS
2 Bo Jackson/75 12.50 30.00
3 Derek Jeter/125 20.00 50.00
5 George Brett/15 50.00 100.00
6 Miguel Cabrera/125 5.00 12.00
7 Andy Pettitte/25 5.00 12.00
8 Billy Martin/35 20.00 50.00
10 Ted Williams/50 30.00 60.00
11 Prince Fielder/125 3.00 8.00
12 Dustin Pedroia/75 5.00 12.00
14 Eric Hosmer/75 6.00 15.00
15 Leo Durocher/25 20.00 50.00
16 Ed Kranepool/40 6.00 15.00
17 Fernando Valenzuela/25 6.00 15.00
18 Goose Gossage/25 5.00 12.00
19 Jimmy Rollins/75 5.00 12.00
20 Roger Clemens/25
21 Buster Posey/25 10.00 25.00
22 Cliff Lee/15 4.00 10.00
23 Frank Thomas/25 12.50 30.00
24 Lou Piniella/25 3.00 8.00
25 Evan Longoria/125 5.00 12.00
26 Ian Kinsler/75 3.00 8.00
27 Pete Rose/25 15.00 40.00
28 Will Clark/25 10.00 25.00
29 Mike Piazza/25 12.50 30.00
30 Max Scherzer/125 4.00 10.00

2013 Panini America's Pastime Jumbo Swatches Gold

*GOLD: .4X TO 1X BASIC
PRINT RUNS B/WN 1-25 COPIES PER
NO PRICING ON QTY 10 OR LESS
3 Derek Jeter/25 25.00 60.00
12 Dustin Pedroia/15 15.00 40.00

2013 Panini America's Pastime Majestic Marks

PRINT RUNS B/WN 12-125 COPIES PER
NO PRICING ON QTY 12
EXCHANGE DEADLINE 07/09/2015
1 Aramis Ramirez/15
2 Darryl Strawberry/49 8.00 20.00
3 Dave Stieb/25 5.00 12.00
4 Dwayne Murphy/125 4.00 10.00
5 Harold Baines/15 6.00 15.00
6 Harold Reynolds/125 4.00 10.00
7 Kerry Wood/25 8.00 20.00
8 Steve Avery/15 15.00 40.00
9 Fernando Valenzuela/49 10.00 25.00
10 Fergie Jenkins/24 12.50 30.00
11 Greg Maddux/29 25.00 60.00
13 Buddy Bell/125 6.00 15.00
14 Jay Bruce/25 5.00 12.00
15 Jean Segura/15
16 Jerome Walton/15
17 Jesse Barfield/15 4.00 10.00
18 Joe Mauer/25 10.00 25.00
19 John Kruk/49 8.00 20.00
20 Josh Donaldson/25 12.00 30.00
21 Kevin Millar/125 6.00 15.00
22 Kris Medlen/25 6.00 15.00
23 Larry Bowa/125 6.00 15.00
24 Pat Tabler/15 4.00 10.00
25 Pat Corbin/125 4.00 10.00
26 Terry Pendleton/15 6.00 15.00
27 Tony Pena/25 4.00 10.00
28 Don Larsen/25
29 Tony Kubek/25 20.00 50.00
30 Fred Lynn/25 5.00 12.00

2013 Panini America's Pastime Majestic Marks Gold

*GOLD: .4X TO 1X BASIC
PRINT RUNS B/WN 8-25 COPIES PER
NO PRICING ON QTY 10
EXCHANGE DEADLINE 07/09/2015

2013 Panini America's Pastime National Treasures Rookies

STATED PRINT RUN 99 SER.#'d SETS
EXCHANGE DEADLINE 07/09/2015
312 Aaron Hicks JSY AU 5.00 12.00
313 Adam Eaton JSY AU
314 Yasiel Puig JSY 40.00 100.00
315 Anthony Rendon AU EXCH 15.00 40.00
316 Brandon Barnes JSY AU 5.00 12.00
317 Carlos Martinez AU 6.00 15.00
318 Christian Yelich JSY AU 20.00 50.00
319 Darin Ruf AU 10.00 25.00
320 Didi Gregorius JSY AU 5.00 12.00
321 Dylan Bundy AU 12.50 30.00
322 Evan Gattis JSY AU 5.00 12.00
323 Gerrit Cole JSY AU EXCH 15.00 40.00
324 Hyun-Jin Ryu JSY AU EXCH 20.00 50.00
325 Jedd Gyorko AU
326 Jose Fernandez JSY AU 25.00 60.00
327 Junior Lake JSY AU
328 Jurickson Profar Bat AU EXCH 12.50 30.00
329 Kevin Gausman JSY AU 10.00 25.00
330 Manny Machado JSY AU 30.00 60.00
331 Mike Zunino JSY AU
332 Shelby Miller AU 12.50 30.00
333 Wil Myers JSY AU 10.00 25.00
334 Zoilo Almonte JSY AU EXCH 5.00 12.00
335 Zack Wheeler JSY AU 10.00 25.00
336 Chris Rusin JSY AU 5.00 12.00

2013 Panini America's Pastime Past Present and Future

PRINT RUNS B/WN 10-125 COPIES PER
NO PRICING ON QTY 10
1 Dvis/Ghrig/Pjols/99 30.00 60.00
2 Brtt/Lngria/Mchdo/50 15.00 40.00
3 Sphn/Krshw/Bmgrnr/20 30.00 60.00
4 Ryan/Vrlndr/Hrvey/99 10.00 25.00
5 Rdrguez/Psey/Wters/75 12.00 30.00
7 Rbnsn/Cano/Pdroia/99 15.00 40.00
8 Snder/Kemp/Puig/125 8.00 20.00
9 Brra/Mer/Znino/25 10.00 25.00
10 Spker/McCtchn/Trout/20 25.00 60.00
11 Wnfld/Ichiro/Hrper/20 20.00 50.00
12 Rbnsn/Bltre/Mchdo/50 12.00 30.00
13 Hrnndz/Paige/Drvish/50 20.00 50.00
14 Brck/Ellsbry/Trout/50 12.00 30.00
15 Frnndz/Schrzr/Ryan/15

2013 Panini America's Pastime Past Present and Future Gold

*GOLD: .4X TO 1X BASIC
PRINT RUNS B/WN 5-25 COPIES PER
NO PRICING ON QTY 10 OR LESS
1 Dvis/Ghrig/Pjols/99 40.00 80.00
4 Ryan/Vrlndr/Hrvey/99 12.50 30.00
7 Rbnsn/Cano/Pdroia/99 20.00 50.00

2013 Panini America's Pastime Pastime Signatures

PRINT RUNS B/WN 25-125 COPIES PER
EXCHANGE DEADLINE 07/09/2015
1 Al Kaline/49
2 Asdrubal Cabrera/125
3 Barry Larkin/99 20.00 50.00
4 Bill Buckner/125 5.00 12.00
5 Bo Jackson/99 20.00 50.00
6 Bret Saberhagen/49 8.00 20.00
7 Bucky Dent/25 4.00 10.00
8 Cal Ripken Jr./75 25.00 60.00
9 Carlos Ruiz/25 6.00 15.00
10 Pete Rose/125 10.00 25.00
11 Cody Ross/125 4.00 10.00
12 Craig Biggio/49 10.00 25.00
13 Curt Schilling/125 6.00 15.00
14 Allen Craig/25 20.00 50.00
15 Dave Kingman/125 4.00 10.00
16 Dave Parker/49
17 David Ortiz/49 15.00 40.00
18 Don Mattingly/49 15.00 40.00
19 Dwayne Murphy/125 4.00 10.00
20 Edgar Martinez/125 5.00 12.00
21 Goose Gossage/49 5.00 12.00
22 Harold Reynolds/125 4.00 10.00
23 Jose Canseco/125 10.00 25.00
24 Kevin Mitchell/125 4.00 10.00
25 Kevin Seitzer/125 4.00 10.00
26 Lucas Duda/125 4.00 10.00
27 Martin Prado/125 4.00 10.00
28 Mike Greenwell/125 4.00 10.00
29 Nolan Ryan/125 25.00 60.00
30 Paul Lo Duca/125 4.00 10.00
31 Rick Monday/125 5.00 12.00
32 Rob Dibble/125 4.00 10.00
33 Robinson Cano/125 10.00 25.00
34 Ryne Sandberg/75 15.00 40.00
35 Stephen Strasburg/125 10.00 25.00
36 Steve Garvey/99 10.00 25.00
37 Steve Sax/125 5.00 12.00
38 Steve Yeager/125 4.00 10.00
39 Tom Seaver/75 20.00 50.00
40 Mike Schmidt/125 12.50 30.00
41 Reggie Jackson/125 12.50 30.00
42 Ernie Banks/125 20.00 50.00
43 David Price/75 12.50 30.00
44 David Wright/125 10.00 25.00
45 Kris Medlen/125 5.00 12.00
46 Chris Davis/75 10.00 25.00
47 Matt Harvey/125 20.00 50.00
48 Oscar Taveras/125 4.00 10.00
49 Yoenis Cespedes/49 12.00 30.00
50 Brandon Phillips/25 10.00 25.00
51 Willie McGee/49 12.50 30.00
52 George Brett/75 25.00 60.00
53 Alex Wood/125 4.00 10.00
54 Bernie Williams/99 12.00 30.00
55 Bob Gibson/75 12.50 30.00
56 Bobby Doerr/49 4.00 10.00
57 Brandon Beachy/125 4.00 10.00
58 Chad Billingsley/25 4.00 10.00
59 Chipper Jones/64 20.00 50.00
60 Chris Perez/125 4.00 10.00
61 Daniel Murphy/125 10.00 25.00
62 Don Sutton/49 4.00 10.00
63 Fergie Jenkins/75 4.00 10.00
64 Frank White/125 10.00 25.00
65 J.J. Hardy/25
66 Jack Clark/125 4.00 10.00
67 Jason Kipnis/49 4.00 10.00
68 Jay Bruce/125 5.00 12.00
69 Jay Buhner/49 6.00 15.00
70 Jean Segura/125 4.00 10.00
71 Jeff Bagwell/75 15.00 40.00
72 Jered Weaver/75 5.00 12.00
73 Jesse Barfield/125 4.00 10.00
74 Jim Palmer/49 5.00 12.00
75 Jon Jay/125 4.00 10.00
76 Jorge Posada/49 20.00 50.00
77 Josh Donaldson/125 5.00 12.00
78 Kevin Millar/125 6.00 15.00
79 Kyuji Fujikawa/125
80 Lance Lynn/125 6.00 15.00
81 Lance Parrish/25 15.00 40.00
82 Larry Bowa/125 4.00 10.00
83 Mark Grace/25 10.00 25.00
84 Mike Mussina/49 10.00 25.00
85 Mike Napoli/25 5.00 12.00
86 Mike Trout/75 100.00 200.00
87 Mitch Moreland/125 4.00 10.00
88 Nomar Garciaparra/49 12.50 30.00
89 Pat Tabler/125 4.00 10.00
90 Pat Corbin/125 4.00 10.00
91 Pedro Martinez/49 20.00 50.00
92 Rickey Henderson/125 25.00 60.00
93 Steve Finley/25 4.00 10.00
94 Terry Pendleton/125 4.00 10.00
95 Tim Wakefield/75 6.00 15.00
96 Tom Glavine/49 12.50 30.00
97 Robin Ventura/25 15.00 40.00
98 Mike Hargrove/125 4.00 10.00
99 Kirk Gibson/25
100 Joe Girardi/25

2013 Panini America's Pastime Pastime Signatures Gold

*GOLD: .5X TO 1.2X BASIC
PRINT RUNS B/WN 10-25 COPIES PER
NO PRICING ON QTY 10
EXCHANGE DEADLINE 07/09/2015

2013 Panini America's Pastime Prime 9

STATED PRINT RUN 125 SER.#'d SETS
1 Roger Clemens 3.00 8.00
2 Yogi Berra 2.50 6.00
3 Albert Pujols 3.00 8.00
4 Jackie Robinson 2.50 6.00
5 George Brett 5.00 12.00
6 Derek Jeter 6.00 15.00
7 Ted Williams 5.00 12.00
8 Ken Griffey Jr. 5.00 12.00
9 Ichiro 3.00 8.00

2013 Panini America's Pastime Prime 9 Gold

*GOLD: .6X TO 1.5X BASIC
STATED PRINT RUN 25 SER.#'d SETS

2013 Panini America's Pastime Silhouettes Memorabilia

PRINT RUNS B/WN 25-125 SER.#'d SETS
1 Adam Jones/125 4.00 10.00
2 Dustin Pedroia/75 6.00 15.00
3 Evan Longoria/25 4.00 10.00
4 Andy Pettitte/25 6.00 15.00
5 Prince Fielder/125 4.00 10.00
6 Clay Buchholz/50 3.00 8.00
7 Josh Reddick/99 3.00 8.00
8 Starlin Castro/25 5.00 12.00
9 Felix Hernandez/25 5.00 12.00
10 Matt Wieters/125 3.00 8.00
11 CC Sabathia/125 3.00 8.00
12 Ian Kinsler/50 3.00 8.00
13 Troy Tulowitzki/25 4.00 10.00
14 Curtis Granderson/99 5.00 12.00
15 Michael Morse/50 3.00 8.00
16 Alex Avila/50 5.00 12.00
17 Mark Teixeira/50 4.00 10.00
18 Cliff Lee/25 4.00 10.00
19 Stephen Strasburg/25 8.00 20.00
20 Matt Harvey/25 15.00 40.00
21 Jason Heyward/50 5.00 12.00
22 Matt Holliday/50 5.00 12.00
23 Matt Cain/50 5.00 12.00
24 Anthony Rizzo/99 4.00 10.00
25 Johnny Cueto/50 4.00 10.00
26 Yovani Gallardo/50 4.00 10.00
27 Alfonso Soriano/125 4.00 10.00
28 Matt Kemp/25 4.00 10.00
29 Pablo Sandoval/50 3.00 8.00
30 Adrian Beltre/25 3.00 8.00
31 Aroldis Chapman/25 4.00 10.00
32 Ryan Howard/25 5.00 12.00
33 Miguel Cabrera/50 5.00 12.00
34 Kendrys Morales/125 3.00 8.00
35 Nick Markakis/25 6.00 15.00
36 Carlos Gonzalez/25 3.00 8.00
37 Todd Helton/25 5.00 12.00
38 Alex Rodriguez/25 8.00 20.00
39 Devin Mesoraco/125 3.00 8.00
40 Nelson Cruz/25 3.00 8.00
41 Rickey Henderson/25 12.50 30.00
42 Dale Murphy/25 6.00 15.00
43 Nomar Garciaparra/125 3.00 8.00
44 Tony Gwynn/125 6.00 15.00
45 Ken Griffey Jr./50 10.00 25.00
46 Darryl Strawberry/125 4.00 10.00
47 Reggie Jackson/25 8.00 20.00
49 Frank Thomas/50 4.00 10.00
50 Don Mattingly/25 20.00 50.00

2013 Panini America's Pastime Silhouettes Memorabilia Gold

*GOLD: .4X TO 1X BASIC
PRINT RUNS B/WN 10-25 COPIES PER
NO PRICING ON QTY 10

2013 Panini America's Pastime Standing O

STATED PRINT RUN 125 SER.#'d SETS
1 Derek Jeter 6.00 15.00
2 Mariano Rivera 3.00 8.00
3 Miguel Cabrera 2.50 6.00
4 David Wright 2.00 5.00
5 David Ortiz 2.50 6.00
6 Yu Darvish 2.50 6.00
7 Joe Mauer 2.00 5.00
8 Dustin Pedroia 2.50 6.00
9 Evan Longoria 2.00 5.00
10 Ichiro 3.00 8.00
11 Clayton Kershaw 4.00 10.00
12 Will Clark 2.00 5.00
13 Jorge Posada 2.00 5.00
14 Al Kaline 2.50 6.00
15 Craig Biggio 2.00 5.00
16 George Brett 5.00 12.00
17 Rickey Henderson
18 Nolan Ryan 8.00 20.00
19 Chipper Jones 2.50 6.00
20 Reggie Jackson 2.00 5.00
21 Cal Ripken Jr. 8.00 20.00

2013 Panini America's Pastime Standing O Gold

*GOLD: .6X TO 1.5X BASIC
STATED PRINT RUN 25 SER.#'d SETS

2013 Panini America's Pastime Superstar Scripts Booklets

PRINT RUNS B/WN 25-125 COPIES PER
EXCHANGE DEADLINE 07/09/2015
1 A.Trammell/L.Parrish/20
2 D.Strwbrry/D.Gooden/20 40.00 80.00
3 M.Harvey/Z.Wheeler/25
4 C.Biggio/J.Bagwell/15
5 J.Canseco/D.Eckersley/15 75.00 150.00
6 K.Wood/M.Grace/20
7 W.McGee/V.Coleman/20 30.00 60.00
8 F.White/B.Sbrhgen/99 10.00 25.00
10 T.Glavine/S.Avery/20 30.00 60.00
11 V.Coleman/O.Guillen/99
12 B.Williams/J.Posada/15
13 C.Schilling/T.Wakefield/15 100.00 200.00
14 S.Castro/A.Rizzo/20
15 G.Cole/Z.Wheeler/20
16 D.Price/R.A.Dickey/15
17 S.Strasburg/M.Trout/15
18 T.Lasorda /T.LaRussa/15

2013 Panini America's Pastime Superstar Scripts Booklets Gold

*GOLD: .4X TO 1X BASIC
PRINT RUNS B/WN 8-49 COPIES PER
NO PRICING ON QTY 10 OR LESS
EXCHANGE DEADLINE 07/09/2015

2013 Panini America's Pastime Superstar Scripts Booklets Red

*RED: .5X TO 1.2X BASIC
PRINT RUNS B/WN 5-25 COPIES PER
NO PRICING ON QTY 10 OR LESS
EXCHANGE DEADLINE 07/09/2015

2013 Panini America's Pastime Trading Swatches

PRINT RUNS B/WN 25-125 SER.#'d SETS
1 Rickey Henderson/125 12.50 30.00
2 Alex Rodriguez/125 8.00 20.00
3 Carlton Fisk/125 4.00 10.00
4 Pete Rose/25
5 Darryl Strawberry/125 3.00 8.00
6 Dennis Eckersley/125 4.00 10.00
7 Greg Maddux/125 8.00 20.00
8 Hunter Pence/125 3.00 8.00
9 David Ortiz /125 4.00 10.00
10 Rafael Palmeiro/125 3.00 8.00
11 Randy Johnson/125 5.00 12.00
12 Reggie Jackson/36 10.00 25.00
13 Roberto Alomar/125 6.00 15.00
14 Roger Clemens/125 3.00 8.00
15 Tom Glavine/125 4.00 10.00
16 Wade Boggs/125 6.00 15.00
17 Adrian Beltre/125 3.00 8.00
18 Justin Upton/99 3.00 8.00
19 Mark Grace/50 10.00 25.00
20 Mike Piazza/99 12.50 30.00
21 Nick Swisher/125 4.00 10.00
22 Nolan Ryan/25 40.00 80.00
23 Prince Fielder/125 3.00 8.00
24 Mike Napoli/125 3.00 8.00
25 Johan Santana/125 4.00 10.00

2013 Panini America's Pastime Trading Swatches Gold

*GOLD: .5X TO 1.2X BASIC
PRINT RUNS B/WN 10-25 COPIES PER
NO PRICING ON QTY 10

2013 Panini America's Pastime USA Baseball Jerseys

STATED PRINT RUN 125 SER.#'d SETS
1 Tyler Beede 4.00 10.00
2 David Berg 3.00 8.00
3 Skye Bolt 4.00 10.00
4 Alex Bregman 4.00 10.00
5 Ryan Burr 3.00 8.00
6 Matt Chapman 4.00 10.00
7 Michael Conforto 5.00 12.00
8 Austin Cousino 3.00 8.00
9 Chris Diaz 3.00 8.00
10 Riley Ferrell 3.00 8.00
11 Brandon Finnegan 5.00 12.00
12 Grayson Greiner 3.00 8.00
13 Erick Fedde 3.00 8.00
14 Matt Imhof 3.00 8.00
15 Daniel Mengden 3.00 8.00
16 Preston Morrison 3.00 8.00
17 Carlos Rodon 6.00 15.00
18 Kyle Schwarber 5.00 12.00
19 Taylor Sparks 3.00 8.00
20 Sam Travis 4.00 10.00
21 Trea Turner 3.00 8.00
22 Bradley Zimmer 3.00 8.00

2013 Panini America's Pastime USA Baseball Jerseys Gold

*GOLD: .5X TO 1.2X BASIC
STATED PRINT RUN 25 SER.#'d SETS
18 Kyle Schwarber 6.00 15.00

2019 Panini America's Pastime Autographs

RANDOM INSERTS IN PACKS
STATED PRINT RUN 99 SER.#'d SETS
EXCHANGE DEADLINE 2/21/2021
*GOLD: .6X TO 1.5X
1 Taylor Ward 3.00 8.00
2 Kevin Newman 5.00 12.00
3 Jeff McNeil 8.00 20.00
4 Michael Kopech 10.00 25.00
5 Jake Bauers 5.00 12.00
6 Stephen Gonsalves 3.00 8.00
7 Dennis Santana 3.00 8.00
8 Ryan O'Hearn 3.00 8.00
9 Sean Reid-Foley 3.00 8.00
10 Kevin Kramer 4.00 10.00
11 Nick Senzel 10.00 25.00
12 Jonathan Davis 4.00 10.00
13 Daniel Ponce de Leon 5.00 12.00
14 Vladimir Guerrero Jr. 40.00 100.00
15 Josh James 5.00 12.00
16 Garrett Hampson 5.00 12.00
17 Danny Jansen 3.00 8.00
18 Luis Urias 5.00 12.00
19 Jacob Nix 4.00 10.00
20 Patrick Wisdom 3.00 8.00
21 Justus Sheffield 5.00 12.00
22 Corbin Burnes 10.00 25.00
23 Brad Keller 3.00 8.00
25 Ryan Borucki 3.00 8.00
26 Luis Ortiz 3.00 8.00
27 Jake Cave 4.00 10.00
28 Eloy Jimenez 12.00 30.00
29 Touki Toussaint 4.00 10.00
30 Kyle Wright 5.00 12.00
31 Kolby Allard 5.00 12.00
32 Dakota Hudson 4.00 10.00
33 Framber Valdez 3.00 8.00
34 David Fletcher 10.00 25.00
35 Brandon Lowe 8.00 20.00
36 Ramon Laureano 8.00 20.00
37 Jonathan Loaisiga 4.00 10.00
38 Cionel Perez 3.00 8.00
39 Myles Straw 5.00 12.00
40 Reese McGuire 5.00 12.00
41 Enyel De Los Santos 3.00 8.00
42 Chris Shaw 3.00 8.00
43 Cedric Mullins 10.00 25.00
44 Bryse Wilson 4.00 10.00
45 Rowdy Tellez 5.00 12.00
46 Fernando Tatis Jr. 40.00 100.00
47 Kyle Tucker 8.00 20.00
48 Chance Adams 3.00 8.00
49 Christin Stewart 4.00 10.00
50 Caleb Ferguson 4.00 10.00

2019 Panini America's Pastime Boys of Summer Autographs

RANDOM INSERTS IN PACKS
PRINT RUNS B/WN 10-99 COPIES PER
NO PRICING QTY 15 OR LESS
EXCHANGE DEADLINE 2/21/2021
*GOLD/25: .6X TO 1.5X p/r 99
*GOLD/25: .5X TO 1.2X p/r 35
2 Harrison Bader/20 6.00 15.00
4 Cameron Gallagher/35 4.00 10.00
8 Juan Soto/35 20.00 50.00
12 Darrell Evans/20 5.00 12.00
15 Victor Victor Mesa/99 6.00 15.00
16 Pete Alonso/99 25.00 60.00
17 Dillon Peters/99 3.00 8.00
18 Zack Granite/99 3.00 8.00
20 Andrew Stevenson/99 3.00 8.00

2019 Panini America's Pastime Material Signatures

RANDOM INSERTS IN PACKS
STATED PRINT RUN 99 SER.#'d SETS
EXCHANGE DEADLINE 2/21/2021
*GOLD: .6X TO 1.5X
1 Kevin Newman 5.00 12.00
2 Jeff McNeil 8.00 20.00
3 Michael Kopech 10.00 25.00
4 Jake Bauers 5.00 12.00
5 Stephen Gonsalves 3.00 8.00
6 Dennis Santana 3.00 8.00
7 Ryan O'Hearn 3.00 8.00
8 Kevin Kramer 4.00 10.00
9 Nick Senzel 10.00 25.00
10 Vladimir Guerrero Jr. 20.00 50.00
11 Josh James 5.00 12.00
12 Danny Jansen 3.00 8.00
13 Luis Urias 5.00 12.00
14 Justus Sheffield 5.00 12.00
15 Corbin Burnes 10.00 25.00
16 Brad Keller 3.00 8.00
18 Jake Cave 4.00 10.00
19 Eloy Jimenez 12.00 30.00
20 Touki Toussaint 4.00 10.00
21 Kyle Tucker 8.00 20.00
22 Dakota Hudson 4.00 10.00
23 Christin Stewart 4.00 10.00
24 David Fletcher 10.00 25.00
25 Ramon Laureano 8.00 20.00
26 Framber Valdez 3.00 8.00
27 Cedric Mullins 10.00 25.00
28 Rowdy Tellez 5.00 12.00
29 Fernando Tatis Jr. 40.00 100.00
30 Kyle Wright 5.00 12.00

2020 Panini America's Pastime

RANDOM INSERTS IN PACKS
PRINT RUNS B/WN 25-99 COPIES PER
EXCHANGE DEADLINE 3/18/2022
1 Josh Rojas/99 3.00 8.00
2 Yordan Alvarez/25 50.00 125.00
3 Sean Murphy/25 8.00 20.00
4 Ronald Bolanos/99 3.00 8.00
5 Yu Chang/99 5.00 12.00
6 Anthony Kay/99 3.00 8.00
7 Andres Munoz/99 5.00 12.00
8 Domingo Leyba/99 4.00 10.00
9 Michael King/99 5.00 12.00
10 Gavin Lux/99 15.00 40.00
11 Jesus Luzardo/99 6.00 15.00
12 Bo Bichette/99 60.00 150.00
13 Brendan McKay/99 5.00 12.00
14 Logan Allen/99 3.00 8.00
15 Nico Hoerner/99 12.00 30.00
16 Mauricio Dubon/99 4.00 10.00
17 Deivy Grullon/99 3.00 8.00
18 Aaron Civale/99 6.00 15.00
19 Logan Webb/99 5.00 12.00
20 Danny Mendick/99 10.00 25.00
21 Brock Burke/99 3.00 8.00
22 Sheldon Neuse/99 4.00 10.00
23 Tres Barrera/99 6.00 15.00
24 Randy Arozarena/99 75.00 200.00
25 Adbert Alzolay/99 4.00 10.00
26 Zac Gallen/99 8.00 20.00
27 Matt Thaiss/49 5.00 12.00
28 Tyrone Taylor/99 3.00 8.00
29 Willi Castro/99 5.00 12.00
30 Dylan Cease/99 5.00 12.00
31 Jaylin Davis/99 5.00 12.00
32 Bryan Abreu/99 3.00 8.00
33 Aristides Aquino/99 8.00 20.00
34 Abraham Toro/99 4.00 10.00
35 Edwin Rios/99 8.00 20.00
36 Jonathan Hernandez/99 3.00 8.00
37 Nick Solak/99 6.00 15.00
39 Donnie Walton/99 8.00 20.00
40 Kyle Lewis/99 30.00 80.00
41 Bobby Bradley/99 3.00 8.00
42 Justin Dunn/99 4.00 10.00
43 Adrian Morejon/99 3.00 8.00
44 Travis Demeritte/99 5.00 12.00
45 A.J. Puk/99 5.00 12.00
46 Trent Grisham/99 12.00 30.00
47 Brusdar Graterol/99 5.00 12.00
48 Zack Collins/99 4.00 10.00
49 Jordan Yamamoto/99 3.00 8.00
50 Isan Diaz/99 5.00 12.00
51 Yoshitomo Tsutsugo/99 8.00 20.00

2020 Panini America's Pastime Boys of Summer

RANDOM INSERTS IN PACKS
PRINT RUNS B/WN 15-99 COPIES PER
NO PRICING QTY 15 OR LESS
EXCHANGE DEADLINE 3/18/2022
1 Ronald Acuna Jr./25
2 Steve Garvey/99 15.00 40.00
3 Jose Canseco/25 15.00 40.00
4 Blake Snell/49 5.00 12.00
5 Cavan Biggio EXCH/99 6.00 15.00
6 Corbin Burnes/99 10.00 25.00
7 Dennis Eckersley/25 6.00 15.00
8 Fernando Tatis Jr./49 75.00 200.00
9 Goose Gossage/25 6.00 15.00
10 J.D. Martinez/25
12 Jose Ramirez/25 6.00 15.00
13 Keith Hernandez/25 12.00 30.00
15 Pete Rose/25 25.00 60.00
16 Trevor Hoffman/25 15.00 40.00
17 Vladimir Guerrero Jr./25 30.00 80.00
18 Walker Buehler/49 20.00 50.00

2020 Panini America's Pastime Boys of Summer Gold

*GOLD/25: .6X TO 1.5X p/r 99
*GOLD/25: .5X TO 1.2X p/r 49
RANDOM INSERTS IN PACKS
PRINT RUNS B/WN 10-25 COPIES PER
NO PRICING QTY 15 OR LESS
EXCHANGE DEADLINE 3/18/2022
2 Steve Garvey/25 30.00 80.00

2020 Panini America's Pastime Material Signatures

RANDOM INSERTS IN PACKS
STATED PRINT RUN 99 SER.#'d SETS
EXCHANGE DEADLINE 3/18/2022
*GOLD/25: .6X TO 1.5X
1 Yordan Alvarez 30.00 80.00
2 Jake Rogers 3.00 8.00
3 Sean Murphy 5.00 12.00
4 Yu Chang 5.00 12.00
5 Gavin Lux 15.00 40.00
6 Bo Bichette 40.00 100.00
7 Jesus Luzardo 6.00 15.00
8 Brendan McKay 5.00 12.00
9 Logan Allen 3.00 8.00
10 Nico Hoerner 12.00 30.00
11 Mauricio Dubon 4.00 10.00
12 Logan Webb 5.00 12.00
13 Sheldon Neuse 4.00 10.00
14 Sam Hilliard 5.00 12.00
15 Zac Gallen 8.00 20.00
16 Matt Thaiss 4.00 10.00
17 Willi Castro 5.00 12.00
18 Dylan Cease 5.00 12.00
19 Aristides Aquino 8.00 20.00
21 Kyle Lewis 30.00 80.00
22 Bobby Bradley 3.00 8.00
23 Justin Dunn 4.00 10.00
24 Adrian Morejon 3.00 8.00
25 A.J. Puk 5.00 12.00
26 Trent Grisham 12.00 30.00
27 Brusdar Graterol 5.00 12.00
28 Zack Collins 4.00 10.00
29 Jordan Yamamoto 3.00 8.00
30 Isan Diaz 5.00 12.00

2019 Panini Ascension

RANDOM INSERTS IN PACKS
*GOLD/199: 1.2X TO 3X
*BLUE/99: 1.5X TO 4X
*RED/50: 2X TO 5X
*HOLO SLVR/25: 3X TO 8X
1 Pete Alonso RC 2.00 5.00
2 Eloy Jimenez RC .60 1.50
3 Fernando Tatis Jr. RC 4.00 10.00
4 Nathaniel Lowe RC .75 2.00
5 Kyle Tucker RC .40 1.00
6 Yusei Kikuchi RC .25 .60
7 Chris Paddack RC .30 .75
8 Mike Trout 2.50 6.00
9 Bryce Harper .40 1.00
10 Aaron Judge .60 1.50
11 Michael Chavis RC .25 .60
12 Shohei Ohtani .40 1.00
13 Charlie Blackmon .25 .60
14 Taylor Hearn .15 .40
15 Vladimir Guerrero Jr. RC 2.50 6.00
16 Kyle Freeland .20 .50
17 Mark Zagunis .15 .40
18 Thairo Estrada RC .25 .60
19 Lorenzo Cain .15 .40
20 Elvis Andrus .20 .50

2020 Panini Ascension Autographs

RANDOM INSERTS IN PACKS
EXCHANGE DEADLINE 3/18/2022
*GOLD/75-99: .5X TO 1.2X BASIC
*GOLD/50: .6X TO 1.5X BASIC
*RED/50: .6X TO 1.5X BASIC
*RED/25: .8X TO 2X BASIC
*BLUE/25: .8X TO 2X BASIC
1 David Bote 3.00 8.00
2 Roman Quinn 2.50 6.00
3 Dylan Carlson 10.00 25.00
4 Aaron Judge
5 Zach Davies 2.50 6.00
6 Tyler Mahle 2.50 6.00
7 Billy McKinney 2.50 6.00
8 Kaleb Cowart 2.50 6.00
9 DJ Stewart 2.50 6.00
10 Michael Lorenzen 2.50 6.00
11 Luke Farrell 2.50 6.00
12 Tanner Rainey 2.50 6.00
13 Jason Martin 3.00 8.00
15 Mitch Moreland 2.50 6.00
16 Cameron Gallagher 2.50 6.00
17 Chance Adams 2.50 6.00
18 Garrett Hampson 2.50 6.00
19 Nathaniel Lowe 6.00 15.00
20 Huascar Ynoa 4.00 10.00
21 J.T. Realmuto 6.00 15.00
22 Anthony Banda 2.50 6.00
23 Jonathan Loaisiga 3.00 8.00
24 Pablo Reyes 2.50 6.00
25 Ronald Acuna Jr. EXCH 50.00 120.00

2011 Panini Black Friday

14 Josh Hamilton .60 1.50
15 Albert Pujols 1.50 4.00
16 Mariano Rivera .60 1.50

17 Adrian Gonzalez .40 1.00
18 Matt Kemp .40 1.00
19 Starlin Castro .60 1.50
JH Josh Hamilton .60 1.50

2011 Panini Black Friday Rookies
RC11 Anthony Rendon 3.00 8.00
RC12 Dylan Bundy 2.00 5.00
RC13 Bubba Starling 2.50 6.00

2012 Panini Black Friday
1-23 CRACKED ICE/25: 6X TO 15X BASE HI
24-50 CRACKED ICE/25: 2.5X TO 6X BASE HI
18 Josh Hamilton .75 2.00
19 Miguel Cabrera .75 2.00
20 Derek Jeter 2.00 5.00
21 Albert Pujols 1.50 4.00
22 David Price .50 1.25
23 Stephen Strasburg 1.00 2.50
39 Trevor Bauer/599 1.00 2.50
40 Yu Darvish/599 3.00 8.00
41 Bryce Harper/599 6.00 15.00
42 Brett Lawrie/599 1.50 4.00
43 Mike Trout/599 6.00 15.00
44 Matt Moore/599 1.00 2.50
45 Yoenis Cespedes/599 2.50 6.00
46 Jarrod Parker/599 .60 1.50

2012 Panini Black Friday Black Holofoil
CRACKED ICE/25: 3X TO 8X BASE HI
15 Andrew McCutchen 1.00 2.50
16 Prince Fielder .60 1.50
17 Bryce Harper 6.00 15.00

2012 Panini Black Friday Kings
CRACKED ICE/25: 2X TO 5X BASE HI
4 Barry Larkin .40 1.00
5 George Brett .75 2.00

2012 Panini Black Friday Rookie Kings
CRACKED ICE/25: 2X TO 5X BASE HI
7 Mike Trout 6.00 15.00
8 Yu Darvish 3.00 8.00
RT Ryan Tatusko .40 1.00

2013 Panini Black Friday
CRACKED ICE/35: 5X TO 12X BASIC CARDS
LAVA FLOW/150: 2X TO 5X BASIC CARDS
4 Mike Trout BB 1.00 2.50
8 Miguel Cabrera BB .50 1.25
12 Chris Davis BB .25 .60
16 Paul Goldschmidt BB .30 .75
20 Matt Harvey BB .20 .50
23 Max Scherzer BB .25 .60
26 Yadier Molina BB .30 .75
31 Hyun-Jin Ryu BB .25 .60
42 Yasiel Puig/299 BB 2.50 6.00
43 Evan Gattis/299 BB 1.25 3.00
44 Shelby Miller/299 BB 1.00 2.50
45 Wil Myers/299 BB 1.25 3.00
46 Jose Fernandez/299 BB 4.00 10.00
47 Jurickson Profar/299 BB 1.00 2.50
62 Manny Machado JSY/99 BB 6.00 15.00

2013 Panini Black Friday Collection
CRACKED ICE/35: 4X TO 10X BASIC CARDS
LAVA FLOW/150: 1.5X TO 4X BASIC CARDS
1 Yasiel Puig .75 2.00
2 Andrew McCutchen .40 1.00
3 Bryce Harper .50 1.25
4 Robinson Cano .40 1.00
5 Troy Tulowitzki .40 1.00

2013 Panini Black Friday Happy Holidays
JP Jurickson Profar 1.50 4.00

2013 Panini Black Friday VIP
CRACKED ICE/35: 2.5X TO 6X BASIC CARDS
LAVA FLOW/150: 1.2X TO 3X BASIC CARDS
1 Yasiel Puig 1.50 4.00
2 Manny Machado .75 2.00

2014 Panini Black Friday
*1-21 ICE VETS/25: 6X TO 15X BASIC CARDS
*22-50 ICE ROOKIE/25: 2X TO 5X BASIC CARDS/499
*JSY ICE/25: 1.2X TO 3X BASIC JSY/99
1-21 THICK STOCK/50: 1.5X TO 4X BASIC CARDS
22-50 THICK STOCK/50: .8X TO 2X BASIC CARDS
15 Mike Trout BB 1.00 2.50
16 Clayton Kershaw BB .50 1.25
17 Felix Hernandez BB .25 .60
18 Jose Altuve BB .25 .60
19 Giancarlo Stanton BB .30 .75
20 Miguel Cabrera BB .50 1.25
21 Carlos Gomez BB .20 .50
40 Jacob deGrom BB 3.00 8.00
41 Jose Abreu BB 3.00 8.00
42 Arismendy Alcantara BB .50 1.25
43 George Springer BB 1.00 2.50
44 Yordano Ventura BB .50 1.25
45 Matt Shoemaker BB .50 1.25
46 Masahiro Tanaka BB 2.00 5.00
47 Gregory Polanco BB .75 2.00
48 Xander Bogaerts BB 1.25 3.00
49 Rougned Odor BB .50 1.25
50 Marcus Stroman BB .50 1.25
63 Oscar Taveras BB JSY 3.00 8.00
64 Taijuan Walker BB JSY 3.00 8.00
JB Javier Baez BB JSY 3.00 8.00

2014 Panini Black Friday Collection
*CRACKED ICE/25: 4X TO 10X BASIC CARDS
THICK STOCK/50: 1.2X TO 3X BASIC CARDS
1 Bo Jackson BB .50 1.25
2 Bryce Harper BB .60 1.50
3 David Ortiz BB .40 1.00
4 Jose Abreu BB 2.50 6.00
21 Yasiel Puig BB 1.00 2.50

2014 Panini Black Friday Manufactured Patch Autographs
BH Billy Hamilton 6.00 15.00
DS Danny Salazar 6.00 15.00
JA Jose Abreu 50.00 100.00
KZ Kyle Zimmer 5.00 12.00
MC Michael Choice 8.00 20.00
TW Taijuan Walker 12.00 30.00
YV Yordano Ventura 12.00 30.00

2014 Panini Black Friday Manufactured Patch Autographs MLBPA
GS George Springer 12.00 30.00
MC Michael Choice 8.00 20.00
YV Yordano Ventura 12.00 30.00

2014 Panini Black Friday Manufactured Patches MLBPA
CK Clayton Kershaw 3.00 8.00
GS George Springer 5.00 12.00
JA Jose Abreu 6.00 15.00
MT Masahiro Tanaka 4.00 10.00
MT Mike Trout 8.00 20.00
NR Nolan Ryan 12.00 30.00
TG Tony Gwynn 2.00 5.00

2014 Panini Black Friday Rookie Manufactured Patch Autographs
JN Jimmy Nelson 8.00 20.00
JR Jose Ramirez 10.00 25.00
MS Matt Shoemaker 12.00 30.00
RF Reymond Fuentes
TM Tommy Medica 10.00 25.00

2014 Panini Black Friday Rookie Portraits
*CRACKED ICE/25: 3X TO 8X BASIC CARDS
THICK STOCK/50: 1X TO 2.5X BASIC CARDS
18 Masahiro Tanaka BB 1.50 4.00
19 Jose Abreu BB 2.50 6.00
20 George Springer BB .75 2.00

2014 Panini Black Friday Rookie Portraits Autographs
19 Jose Abreu BB 40.00 100.00
20 George Springer BB 10.00 25.00

2015 Panini Black Friday
*CRACKED/25: 1X TO 2.5X BASIC CARDS
*THICK/50: .8X TO 2X BASIC CARDS
17 Andrew McCutchen .75 2.00
18 Bryce Harper 1.00 2.50
19 Paul Goldschmidt .75 2.00
20 Mike Trout 1.25 3.00
21 Nolan Arenado .75 2.00
22 Aroldis Chapman .75 2.00
23 Albert Pujols .75 2.00
24 Dallas Keuchel .75 2.00
45 Kris Bryant 8.00 20.00
46 Carlos Correa 1.25 3.00
47 Carlos Rodon 1.25 3.00
48 Joc Pederson 2.00 5.00
49 Miguel Sano 1.25 3.00
50 Matt Duffy 1.25 3.00
52 Jung-Ho Kang 1.25 3.00

2015 Panini Black Friday Collection
*CRACKED/25: 1X TO 2.5X BASIC CARDS
*THICK/50: .8X TO 2X BASIC CARDS
1 Bryce Harper 1.25 3.00
2 Alex Rodriguez 1.25 3.00
3 George Brett 1.25 3.00
4 Kris Bryant 1.25 3.00
5 Pete Rose 1.25 3.00
6 Clayton Kershaw 1.25 3.00
7 Josh Donaldson 1.25 3.00

2015 Panini Black Friday Happy Holidays Materials
*CRACKED/25: .8X TO 2X BASIC HAT
KB Kris Bryant 6.00 15.00
YT Yasmany Tomas 2.50 6.00

2015 Panini Black Friday Manufactured Patches
*CRACKED/25: .8X TO 2X BASIC PATCH
5 Bo Jackson 2.50 6.00
BH Bryce Harper 2.50 6.00

2015 Panini Black Friday Rookie Materials Jerseys
*CRACKED/25: .8X TO 2X BASIC JSY
1 Jorge Soler 2.50 6.00
3 Addison Russell 2.50 6.00
4 Kris Bryant 6.00 15.00
5 Yasmany Tomas 2.50 6.00
6 Javier Baez 2.50 6.00
7 Maikel Franco 2.50 6.00

2016 Panini Black Friday Collegiate Jerseys
*CRACKED/25: .8X TO 2X BASIC JSY
C1 Dansby Swanson 2.50 6.00
C2 Kyle Schwarber 2.50 6.00
C3 Alex Bregman 2.50 6.00
C4 Andrew Benintendi 2.50 6.00
C5 Trea Turner 2.50 6.00

2016 Panini Black Friday Jerseys
*CRACKED/25: .8X TO 2X BASE JSY
1 Corey Seager 2.50 6.00
2 Trevor Story 2.50 6.00
3 Miguel Sano 2.50 6.00
4 Nomar Mazara 2.50 6.00
5 Andrew Benintendi 2.50 6.00
6 Stephen Piscotty 2.50 6.00
7 Mookie Betts 2.50 6.00
8 Addison Russell 2.50 6.00
9 Anthony Rizzo 2.50 6.00
10 Kris Bryant 2.50 6.00
11 Byron Buxton 2.50 6.00
12 Jacob deGrom 2.50 6.00
13 Gary Sanchez 2.50 6.00
14 Alex Bregman 2.50 6.00
15 Yoan Moncada 2.50 6.00

2017 Panini Black Friday Happy Holiday Memorabilia
*CRACKED/25: .8X TO 2X BASIC MEM
HHAR Alex Reyes 2.50 6.00
HHCF Carson Fulmer 2.50 6.00
HHGT Gleyber Torres 2.50 6.00
HHMM Manuel Margot 2.50 6.00

2017 Panini Black Friday Memorabilia
*CRACKED/25: .8X TO 2X BASIC MEM
MAJ Aaron Judge 10.00 25.00
MCB Cody Bellinger 2.50 6.00

2017 Panini Black Friday Memorabilia Small
*CRACKED/25: .8X TO 2X BASIC MEM
MSAJ Aaron Judge 10.00 25.00
MSCB Cody Bellinger 2.50 6.00

2017 Panini Black Friday Panini Collection
*DECOY/50: .6X TO 1.5X BASIC INSERTS
*WEDGE/50: .6X TO 1.5X BASIC INSERTS
14 Giancarlo Stanton 1.50 4.00
15 Cody Bellinger 1.50 4.00
16 Aaron Judge 3.00 8.00
17 Bryce Harper 1.50 4.00
18 Ian Happ 1.50 4.00
AJ Aaron Judge 3.00 8.00
CB Cody Bellinger 1.50 4.00

2017 Panini Black Friday Panini Collection Cracked Ice
16 Aaron Judge 12.00 30.00
AJ Aaron Judge 12.00 30.00

2017 Panini Black Friday Patches
*CRACKED/25: .8X TO 2X BASIC PATCH
BFAJ Aaron Judge 4.00 10.00
BFBH Bryce Harper 2.50 6.00
BFCB Cody Bellinger 2.50 6.00
BFCK Clayton Kershaw SP 2.50 6.00
BFIC Ichiro 2.50 6.00
BFMT Mike Trout 2.50 6.00

2019 Panini Black Friday Autographs
29 Cody Bellinger/10
30 Christian Yelich
31 Mike Trout
32 Ronald Acuna Jr.
33 Nolan Arenado
34 Javier Baez
35 Kris Bryant
36 Alex Bregman/25 12.00 30.00
37 Justin Verlander
38 Mookie Betts
39 Cal Ripken
40 Ken Griffey Jr./10

2019 Panini Black Friday Happy Holidays Memorabilia
CW Coby White 12.00 30.00
EJ Eloy Jimenez 4.00 10.00
VG Vladimir Guerrero Jr./42 5.00 12.00

2019 Panini Black Friday Massive Materials
AR Austin Riley/50 6.00 15.00
BB Bo Bichette/50 6.00 15.00
CK Carter Kieboom/50 6.00 15.00
EJ Eloy Jimenez/10
FT Fernando Tatis Jr./10
JA Jo Adell/50 6.00 15.00
LR Luis Robert/10
PA Pete Alonso/50 6.00 15.00
VG Vladimir Guerrero Jr./10
YA Yordan Alvarez/10

2019 Panini Black Friday Panini Collection
CB Cody Bellinger 2.00 5.00
PA Pete Alonso 2.00 5.00
VG Vladimir Guerrero Jr. 2.00 5.00
WF Wander Franco 2.00 5.00

2019 Panini Black Friday Panini Collection Future Frames
*FRAMES/99: .8X TO 2X BASIC CARDS

2019 Panini Black Friday Panini Collection Galactic Windows
*GALACTIC/25: 1.2X TO 3X BASIC CARDS

2019 Panini Black Friday Panini Collection Holo
*HOLO/199: .6X TO 1.5X BASIC CARDS

2019 Panini Black Friday Panini Collection Swirlorama
*SWIRL/50: 1X TO 2.5X BASIC CARDS

2019 Panini Black Friday Private Signings
CF Clint Frazier 4.00 10.00
KT Kyle Tucker 4.00 10.00
RH Rhys Hoskins
TT Trea Turner 6.00 15.00

2019 Panini Black Friday Rookies
RC15 Eloy Jimenez 2.00 5.00
RC16 Fernando Tatis Jr. 2.00 5.00
RC17 Pete Alonso 2.00 5.00
RC18 Chris Paddack 2.00 5.00
RC19 Vladimir Guerrero Jr. 2.00 5.00

2019 Panini Black Friday Rookies Future Frames
*FUTURE/99: 1X TO 2.5X BASIC CARDS

2019 Panini Black Friday Rookies Galactic Windows
*WINDOWS/25: 1.5X TO 4X BASIC CARDS

2019 Panini Black Friday Rookies Holo
*HOLO/199: .8X TO 2X BASIC CARDS

2019 Panini Black Friday Rookies Swirlorama
*SWIRL/50: 1.2X TO 3X BASIC CARDS

2010 Panini Century
COMPLETE SET (100)

2010 Panini Century Air Mail Bats
STATED PRINT RUN 3-250
NO PRICING QTY 5 OR LESS
1 Joe Jackson/50 60.00 120.00
2 Pete Rose/250 12.50 30.00
4 Eddie Mathews/250 4.00 10.00
6 Joe Morgan/250 3.00 8.00
8 Mike Schmidt/250 4.00 10.00
9 Minnie Minoso/250 5.00 12.00
11 Orlando Cepeda/250 4.00 10.00
12 Reggie Jackson/250 3.00 8.00

2010 Panini Century Air Mail Jerseys
STATED PRINT RUN 3-250
NO PRICING ON QTY 25 OR LESS
4 Eddie Mathews/250 4.00 10.00
5 Robin Yount/40 20.00 50.00
12 Reggie Jackson/150 4.00 10.00
14 Duke Snider/50 6.00 15.00

2010 Panini Century Air Mail Bats Autographs
STATED PRINT RUN 1-50
NO PRICING ON QTY 25 OR LESS
2 Pete Rose/50 20.00 50.00
11 Orlando Cepeda/50 8.00 20.00
13 Brooks Robinson/27 10.00 25.00

2010 Panini Century Air Mail Jerseys Autographs
STATED PRINT RUN 1-25
NO PRICING DUE TO SCARCITY

2010 Panini Century Ballpark Autographs
STATED PRINT RUN 5-50
NO PRICING ON QTY 25 OR LESS
4 Fergie Jenkins/35 10.00 25.00
11 Andre Dawson/50 10.00 25.00

2010 Panini Century Ballpark Materials
STATED PRINT RUN 1-250
NO PRICING ON QTY 25 OR LESS
3 Duke Snider/50 6.00 15.00
4 Fergie Jenkins/50 4.00 10.00
5 Steve Carlton/250 3.00 8.00
6 Rod Carew/200 3.00 8.00
7 Frank Robinson/99 4.00 10.00
8 Dale Murphy/99 6.00 15.00
10 Lou Brock/250 3.00 8.00
11 Andre Dawson/99 3.00 8.00
14 Wade Boggs/250 3.00 8.00

2010 Panini Century Ballpark Materials Prime
STATED PRINT RUN 2-30
NO PRICING ON QTY 25 OR LESS
8 Dale Murphy/30 12.50 30.00

2010 Panini Century Ballpark Materials Autographs
STATED PRINT RUN 2-49
NO PRICING ON QTY 25 OR LESS
11 Andre Dawson/49 6.00 15.00

2010 Panini Century Ballpark Materials Prime Autographs
STATED PRINT RUN 1-50
NO PRICING ON QTY 25 OR LESS
8 Dale Murphy/50 40.00 80.00
15 Joe Morgan/50 15.00 40.00

2010 Panini Century Baseball Six Cent Stamp Autographs
STATED PRINT RUN 2-50
NO PRICING ON QTY 25 OR LESS
3 Billy Williams/32 10.00 25.00
7 Dennis Eckersley/50 12.50 30.00
15 Johnny Pesky/50 12.50 30.00
31 Steve Carlton/32 15.00 40.00
47 Carlton Fisk/38 12.50 30.00
48 Gary Carter/50 12.50 30.00
54 Brooks Robinson/50 15.00 40.00
68 Frank Howard/31 10.00 25.00
69 Dale Murphy/26 20.00 50.00
75 Joe Morgan/50 12.50 30.00

2010 Panini Century Baseball Six Cent Stamp Materials
STATED PRINT RUN 1-250
NO PRICING ON QTY 25 OR LESS
2 Orel Hershiser/100 3.00 8.00
14 Joe Jackson/50 50.00 100.00
17 Lou Brock/100 6.00 15.00
24 Pete Rose/100 12.50 30.00
25 Phil Niekro/50 4.00 10.00
27 Robin Yount/50 10.00 25.00
28 Rod Carew/50 5.00 12.00
45 Tony Gwynn/250 6.00 15.00
63 Dave Winfield/99 3.00 8.00
69 Dale Murphy/30 10.00 25.00
71 Fergie Jenkins/33 5.00 12.00

2010 Panini Century Baseball Six Cent Stamp Materials Autographs
STATED PRINT RUN 1-34
NO PRICING ON QTY 25 OR LESS
74 Harmon Killebrew/34 60.00 120.00

2010 Panini Century Baseball Three Cent Stamp Autographs
STATED PRINT RUN 1-42
NO PRICING ON QTY 25 OR LESS
7 Dennis Eckersley/40 12.50 30.00
40 Don Mattingly/34 40.00 80.00
48 Gary Carter/37 12.50 30.00
54 Brooks Robinson/34 12.50 30.00
75 Joe Morgan/28 15.00 40.00

2010 Panini Century Baseball Three Cent Stamp Materials
STATED PRINT RUN 1-250
NO PRICING ON QTY 25 OR LESS
2 Orel Hershiser/50 4.00 10.00
14 Joe Jackson/50 50.00 100.00
24 Pete Rose/100 12.50 30.00
25 Phil Niekro/50 4.00 10.00
27 Robin Yount/50 20.00 50.00
28 Rod Carew/50 5.00 12.00
45 Tony Gwynn/250 6.00 15.00
63 Dave Winfield/31 4.00 10.00

2010 Panini Century Bats
NO PRICING ON QTY 25 OR LESS
1 Bo Jackson/50 6.00 15.00
6 Arky Vaughan/250 8.00 20.00
8 Reggie Jackson/250 3.00 8.00
10 Wade Boggs/250 3.00 8.00
17 Orlando Cepeda/100 6.00 15.00
19 Will Clark/250 4.00 10.00
21 Andre Dawson/100 3.00 8.00
35 Pete Rose/100 12.50 30.00
40 Joe Jackson/50 50.00 100.00
41 Reggie Jackson/50 3.00 8.00
47 Pete Rose/100 12.50 30.00
53 Eddie Mathews/250 4.00 10.00
59 Minnie Minoso/250 5.00 12.00
63 Dale Murphy/50 6.00 15.00
64 Eddie Murray/250 3.00 8.00
69 Dave Parker/100 4.00 10.00
79 Pete Rose/100 10.00 25.00
82 Ryne Sandberg/250 5.00 12.00
85 Mike Schmidt/100 5.00 12.00
90 Willie Stargell/250 5.00 12.00
94 Larry Walker/100 3.00 8.00

2010 Panini Century Bats Autographs
STATED PRINT RUN 1-99
NO PRICING ON QTY 25 OR LESS
17 Orlando Cepeda/50 6.00 15.00
18 Gary Carter/50 15.00 40.00
21 Andre Dawson/50 6.00 15.00
22 Bobby Doerr/50 6.00 15.00
27 Carlton Fisk/50 12.50 30.00
33 Dwight Gooden/99 6.00 15.00
35 Pete Rose/50 60.00 120.00
47 Pete Rose/50 20.00 50.00
69 Dave Parker/50 8.00 20.00
79 Pete Rose/50 30.00 60.00

2010 Panini Century Blast from the Past Bats
STATED PRINT RUN 1-250
NO PRICING ON QTY 25 OR LESS
1 Reggie Jackson/250 3.00 8.00
2 Ryne Sandberg/150 6.00 15.00
3 Mike Schmidt/250 4.00 10.00
5 Paul Molitor/150 4.00 10.00
6 Don Mattingly/30 5.00 12.00
7 Barry Larkin/99 4.00 10.00
9 Wade Boggs/250 3.00 8.00
14 Carlton Fisk/27 5.00 12.00
15 Kirk Gibson/40 4.00 10.00
16 Will Clark/250 4.00 10.00
18 Dale Murphy/50 6.00 15.00
20 Joe Morgan/250 3.00 8.00

2010 Panini Century Blast from the Past Jerseys
STATED PRINT RUN 1-250
NO PRICING ON QTY 25 OR LESS
1 Reggie Jackson/250 3.00 8.00
2 Ryne Sandberg/100 6.00 15.00
3 Mike Schmidt/50 6.00 15.00
7 Barry Larkin/99 4.00 10.00
8 Tony Gwynn/250 6.00 15.00
9 Wade Boggs/175 4.00 10.00
11 Jim Palmer/50 4.00 10.00
12 Jim Rice/250 4.00 10.00
16 Will Clark/250 4.00 10.00
18 Dale Murphy/99 5.00 12.00

2010 Panini Century Cut Autographs
STATED PRINT RUN 1-100
NO PRICING ON QTY 25 OR LESS
1 Al Barlick/100 10.00 25.00
6 Bill Terry/65 20.00 50.00
7 Bob Lemon/55 20.00 50.00
11 Catfish Hunter/40 30.00 60.00
12 Charlie Gehringer/40 20.00 50.00
18 Enos Slaughter/52 15.00 40.00
21 George Kell/100 8.00 20.00
24 Happy Chandler/34 15.00 40.00
29 Joe Sewell/100 10.00 25.00
30 Johnny Mize/100 15.00 40.00
34 Lou Boudreau/58 12.50 30.00
36 Billy Herman/50 8.00 20.00
37 Edd Roush/27 20.00 50.00
39 Pee Wee Reese/31 40.00 80.00
40 Phil Rizzuto/52 15.00 40.00
42 Rick Ferrell/88 10.00 25.00

2010 Panini Century Jerseys
STATED PRINT RUN 15-250
NO PRICING ON QTY 25 OR LESS
1 Bo Jackson/50 6.00 15.00
3 Luis Aparicio/250 3.00 8.00
4 Richie Ashburn/250 5.00 12.00
9 Bert Blyleven/100 5.00 12.00
10 Wade Boggs/100 5.00 12.00
11 Lou Boudreau/175 5.00 12.00
15 Rod Carew/100 4.00 10.00
19 Will Clark/100 8.00 20.00
20 Joe Cronin/250 4.00 10.00
21 Andre Dawson/50 4.00 10.00
22 Bobby Doerr/250 4.00 10.00
27 Carlton Fisk/100 5.00 12.00
34 Tony Gwynn/250 6.00 15.00
36 Orel Hershiser/50 4.00 10.00
37 Gil Hodges/250 8.00 20.00
38 Frank Howard/250 4.00 10.00
47 Pete Rose/50 15.00 40.00
51 Juan Marichal/50 3.00 8.00
53 Eddie Mathews/250 4.00 10.00
62 Jack Morris/50 5.00 12.00
64 Eddie Murray/250 3.00 8.00
67 Tony Oliva/100 6.00 15.00
69 Dave Parker/250 3.00 8.00
74 Jim Rice/250 4.00 10.00
89 Warren Spahn/250 4.00 10.00
90 Willie Stargell/100 6.00 15.00

2010 Panini Century Jerseys Autographs
STATED PRINT RUN 1-100
NO PRICING ON QTY 25 OR LESS
1 Bo Jackson/30 40.00 80.00
21 Andre Dawson/50 10.00 25.00
22 Bobby Doerr/50 12.50 30.00
23 Dennis Eckersley/50 10.00 25.00
25 Bob Feller/50 10.00 25.00
33 Dwight Gooden/99 6.00 15.00
36 Orel Hershiser/50 5.00 12.00
38 Frank Howard/65 10.00 25.00
42 Fergie Jenkins/50 8.00 20.00
44 Al Kaline/45 15.00 40.00
47 Pete Rose/50 40.00 80.00
62 Jack Morris/100 6.00 15.00
68 Jim Palmer/50 8.00 20.00
69 Dave Parker/100 6.00 15.00
71 Gaylord Perry/99 6.00 15.00
74 Jim Rice/100 6.00 15.00
86 Red Schoendienst/50 10.00 25.00
92 Don Sutton/100 6.00 15.00
95 Billy Williams/30 10.00 25.00
100 Robin Yount/50 15.00 40.00

2010 Panini Century Jerseys Prime Autographs
STATED PRINT RUN 1-50
NO PRICING ON QTY 25 OR LESS
1 Bo Jackson/50 20.00 50.00
13 Lou Brock/50 10.00 25.00
18 Gary Carter/50 15.00 40.00
21 Andre Dawson/50 10.00 25.00
23 Dennis Eckersley/50 10.00 25.00
42 Kirk Gibson/50 10.00 25.00
33 Dwight Gooden/50 8.00 20.00
35 Pete Rose/40 40.00 80.00
36 Orel Hershiser/50 5.00 12.00
38 Frank Howard/50 12.50 30.00
42 Fergie Jenkins/45 8.00 20.00
51 Juan Marichal/50 10.00 25.00
62 Jack Morris/50 10.00 25.00
63 Dale Murphy/50 6.00 15.00
68 Jim Palmer/45 8.00 20.00
69 Dave Parker/50 8.00 20.00
74 Jim Rice/50 10.00 25.00
85 Mike Schmidt/35 20.00 50.00
87 Tom Seaver/35 30.00 80.00
92 Don Sutton/50 8.00 20.00
93 Alan Trammell/50 30.00 60.00
95 Billy Williams/50 8.00 20.00
100 Robin Yount/50 30.00 60.00

2010 Panini Century Postcards Materials
STATED PRINT RUN 5-250
NO PRICING ON QTY 25 OR LESS
1 Andre Dawson/100 3.00 8.00
5 Harmon Killebrew/100 10.00 25.00
6 Stan Musial/99 8.00 20.00
10 Nolan Ryan/100 10.00 25.00
16 Tony Gwynn/250 6.00 15.00
20 Paul Molitor/250 3.00 8.00

2010 Panini Century Postcards Materials Prime
STATED PRINT RUN 1-25
NO PRICING DUE TO SCARCITY

2010 Panini Century Postcards Materials Autographs
STATED PRINT RUN 1-50
NO PRICING ON QTY 25 OR LESS
1 Andre Dawson/50 6.00 15.00
10 Nolan Ryan/50 50.00 100.00

2010 Panini Century Postcards Materials Prime Autographs
STATED PRINT RUN 1-50
NO PRICING ON QTY 25 OR LESS
1 Andre Dawson/50 6.00 15.00
10 Nolan Ryan/50 50.00 100.00
20 Paul Molitor/50 15.00 40.00

2010 Panini Century Postmark Autographs Silver
STATED PRINT RUN 1-250
NO PRICING ON QTY 25 OR LESS
5 Harold Baines/163 6.00 15.00
14 Jim Bunning/79 6.00 15.00
16 Steve Carlton/50 10.00 25.00
18 Gary Carter/250 12.50 30.00
21 Andre Dawson/250 6.00 15.00
22 Bobby Doerr/250 6.00 15.00
23 Dennis Eckersley/250 6.00 15.00
24 Carl Erskine/250 6.00 15.00
25 Bob Feller/50 15.00 40.00
26 Mark Fidrych/50 15.00 40.00
33 Dwight Gooden/250 6.00 15.00
39 Monte Irvin/250 6.00 15.00
42 Fergie Jenkins/250 6.00 15.00
44 Al Kaline/250 15.00 40.00
45 George Kell/150 6.00 15.00
49 Don Larsen/38 5.00 12.00
52 Marty Marion/98 6.00 15.00
57 Denny McLain/43 10.00 25.00
62 Jack Morris/74 5.00 12.00
63 Dale Murphy/250 6.00 15.00
68 Jim Palmer/213 8.00 20.00
69 Dave Parker/75 6.00 15.00
70 Tony Perez/50 6.00 15.00
71 Gaylord Perry/250 6.00 15.00
73 Tim Raines/75 5.00 12.00
74 Jim Rice/250 4.00 10.00
77 Brooks Robinson/50 15.00 40.00
86 Red Schoendienst/250 8.00 20.00
88 Duke Snider/40 10.00 25.00
91 Bruce Sutter/223 8.00 20.00
92 Don Sutton/149 5.00 12.00
93 Alan Trammell/226 6.00 15.00
97 Maury Wills/250 6.00 15.00

2017 Panini Chronicles
COMP.SET w/o RCs (100) 8.00 20.00
101-150 PRINT RUN 499 SER.#'d SETS
1 Bryce Harper .40 1.00
2 Robbie Ray .15 .40
3 Yonder Alonso .15 .40
4 Jay Bruce .20 .50
5 Andrew McCutchen .25 .60
6 Jacob deGrom .50 1.25
7 Mickey Mantle .75 2.00
8 Joey Gallo .20 .50
9 George Springer .20 .50
10 Chris Sale .25 .60
11 Justin Verlander .25 .60
12 Hunter Pence .20 .50
13 Giancarlo Stanton .25 .60
14 Jason Kipnis .20 .50
15 Jose Altuve .20 .50
16 Josh Donaldson .20 .50
17 Ben Gamel .20 .50
18 Matt Carpenter .25 .60
19 Odubel Herrera .20 .50
20 Salvador Perez .20 .50
21 Ryan Zimmerman .20 .50
22 Corey Seager .25 .60
23 Gerrit Cole .25 .60
24 Freddie Freeman .30 .75
25 Adrian Beltre .25 .60
26 Matt Holliday .25 .60
27 Scott Schebler .20 .50
28 Max Scherzer .25 .60
29 Yoenis Cespedes .25 .60
30 Trevor Story .25 .60
31 Elvis Andrus .20 .50
32 Joe Mauer .20 .50
33 Francisco Lindor .25 .60
34 Khris Davis .25 .60
35 Justin Bour .20 .50
36 Rougned Odor .20 .50
37 Miguel Sano .20 .50
38 Ryne Sandberg .50 1.25
39 Kole Calhoun .15 .40
40 Ryan Braun .20 .50
41 Zack Greinke .25 .60
42 Mike Schmidt .40 1.00
43 Yangervis Solarte .15 .40
44 Adam Jones .20 .50
45 Logan Morrison .15 .40
46 Bo Jackson .25 .60
47 Mike Trout 1.25 3.00
48 Mike Moustakas .20 .50
49 Buster Posey .30 .75
50 Felix Hernandez .20 .50
51 Joey Votto .25 .60
52 Nolan Arenado .40 1.00
53 Justin Smoak .15 .40
54 Lorenzo Cain .15 .40
55 Josh Harrison .15 .40
56 Nolan Ryan .75 2.00
57 Gary Sanchez .25 .60
58 Todd Frazier .15 .40
59 Edwin Encarnacion .25 .60
60 Corey Dickerson .15 .40
61 Pete Rose .50 1.25
62 Eric Thames .20 .50
63 Cal Ripken .75 2.00
64 Adam Duvall .20 .50
65 Paul Goldschmidt .25 .60
66 Corey Kluber .20 .50
67 Madison Bumgarner .20 .50
68 Billy Hamilton .20 .50
69 Clayton Kershaw .40 1.00
70 Chris Archer .15 .40
71 Kris Bryant .30 .75
72 Yadier Molina .30 .75
73 Charlie Blackmon .25 .60
74 Anthony Rizzo .30 .75
75 Albert Pujols .30 .75
76 Roger Clemens .30 .75
77 Jake Lamb .20 .50
78 Miguel Cabrera .25 .60
79 Wil Myers .20 .50
80 Yu Darvish .25 .60
81 Mark Reynolds .15 .40
82 George Brett .50 1.25
83 Bartolo Colon .15 .40
84 Dexter Fowler .20 .50
85 Trea Turner .20 .50
86 Mookie Betts .50 1.25
87 Carlos Correa .25 .60
88 Matt Davidson .20 .50
89 Javier Baez .30 .75
90 Marcell Ozuna .25 .60
91 Brian Dozier .25 .60
92 Ken Griffey Jr. .50 1.25
93 Alex Rodriguez .30 .75
94 Manny Machado .25 .60
95 Evan Longoria .20 .50
96 Rickey Henderson .25 .60
97 Dee Gordon .15 .40
98 Jose Bautista .20 .50
99 Robinson Cano .20 .50
100 Matt Kemp .20 .50
101 Hunter Renfroe RC .50 1.25
102 Andrew Benintendi RC 1.00 2.50
103 Alex Reyes RC .40 1.00
104 Sam Travis RC .40 1.00
105 Alex Bregman RC 1.50 4.00
106 Josh Hader RC .40 1.00
107 Carson Fulmer RC .30 .75
108 Dansby Swanson RC .75 2.00
109 David Dahl RC .40 1.00
110 Aaron Judge RC 6.00 15.00
111 Jordan Montgomery RC .50 1.25
112 Josh Bell RC .75 2.00
113 Manuel Margot RC .30 .75
114 Mitch Haniger RC .50 1.25
115 Orlando Arcia RC .50 1.25
116 Franklin Barreto RC .30 .75
117 Trey Mancini RC .60 1.50
118 Tyler Glasnow RC 1.25 3.00
119 Yoan Moncada RC 1.00 2.50
120 Cody Bellinger RC 5.00 12.00
121 Ian Happ RC .60 1.50
122 Antonio Senzatela RC .30 .75
123 Jesse Winker RC 1.25 3.00
124 Andrew Toles RC .30 .75
125 Francis Martes RC .30 .75
126 Christian Arroyo RC .50 1.25
127 Bradley Zimmer RC .40 1.00
128 Anthony Alford RC .30 .75
129 German Marquez RC .50 1.25
130 Dinelson Lamet RC .30 .75
131 Magneuris Sierra RC .30 .75
132 Derek Fisher RC .40 1.00
133 Jorge Bonifacio RC .30 .75
134 Bruce Maxwell RC .30 .75
135 Adam Frazier RC .30 .75
136 Guillermo Heredia RC .50 1.25
137 Jose De Leon RC .30 .75
138 J.T. Riddle RC .30 .75
139 Jeff Hoffman RC .30 .75
140 Luis Castillo RC 1.00 2.50
141 Chad Pinder RC .30 .75
142 Ryon Healy RC .40 1.00
143 Adam Engel RC .30 .75
144 Erik Gonzalez RC .30 .75
145 Jake Thompson RC .30 .75
146 Lewis Brinson RC .50 1.25
147 Jacoby Jones RC .40 1.00
148 Tzu-Wei Lin RC .30 .75
149 Raimel Tapia RC .40 1.00
150 Paul DeJong RC 1.00 2.50

2017 Panini Chronicles Blue
*BLUE/399: .75X TO 2X BASIC
*BLUE RC/299: .4X TO 1X BASIC RC

RANDOM INSERTS IN PACKS
PRINT RUNS B/WN 299-399 COPIES PER

2017 Panini Chronicles Gold

*GOLD/999: .6X TO 1.5X BASIC
*GOLD RC/399: .4X TO 1X BASIC RC
RANDOM INSERTS IN PACKS
PRINT RUNS B/WN 399-999 COPIES PER

2017 Panini Chronicles Green

*GREEN: .75X TO 2X BASIC
*GREEN RC: .5X TO 1.2X BASIC RC
RANDOM INSERTS IN PACKS
STATED PRINT RUN 199 SER.#'d SETS

2017 Panini Chronicles Purple

*PURPLE: 1.2X TO 3X BASIC
*PURPLE RC: .6X TO 1.5X BASIC RC
RANDOM INSERTS IN PACKS
STATED PRINT RUN 99 SER.#'d SETS

2017 Panini Chronicles Red

*RED: 5X TO 12X BASIC
*RED RC: 1.5X TO 4X BASIC RC
RANDOM INSERTS IN PACKS
STATED PRINT RUN 25 SER.#'d SETS

2017 Panini Chronicles Autographs

RANDOM INSERTS IN PACKS
EXCHANGE DEADLINE 5/22/2019
*GOLD/49-99: .5X TO 1.2X BASIC
*GOLD/25: .6X TO 1.5X BASIC
*BLUE/25: .6X TO 1.5X BASIC
1 Aaron Judge 60.00 150.00
2 Cody Bellinger 75.00 200.00
3 Yoan Moncada
4 Andrew Benintendi 10.00 25.00
5 Magneuris Sierra 2.50 6.00
6 Dansby Swanson 10.00 25.00
7 Ryon Healy 3.00 8.00
8 Mitch Haniger 4.00 10.00
9 Antonio Senzatela 2.50 6.00
10 Ian Happ 5.00 12.00
11 Trey Mancini 6.00 15.00
12 Jordan Montgomery 4.00 10.00
13 Bradley Zimmer 3.00 8.00
14 Hunter Renfroe 3.00 8.00
15 Lewis Brinson 4.00 10.00
16 Alex Bregman 12.00 30.00
17 Josh Bell 8.00 20.00
18 Derek Fisher 3.00 8.00
19 Sam Travis 3.00 8.00
20 Franklin Barreto 2.50 6.00
21 Dinelson Lamet 2.50 6.00
22 David Dahl 3.00 8.00
23 Orlando Arcia 4.00 10.00
24 John Farrell 4.00 10.00
25 Francis Martes 2.50 6.00
26 Jose Abreu 8.00 20.00
27 Yoenis Cespedes
28 Ryne Sandberg 15.00 40.00
29 Tom Glavine
30 Anthony Alford 2.50 6.00
31 Wade Boggs
32 German Marquez 4.00 10.00
33 Chad Pinder 2.50 6.00
34 Jorge Alfaro 3.00 8.00
35 Adalberto Mejia 2.50 6.00
36 Renato Nunez 5.00 12.00
37 Gabriel Ynoa 2.50 6.00
38 Jose Rondon 2.50 6.00
39 Theo Epstein
40 Robin Yount 15.00 40.00
41 Keith Hernandez
42 Roger Clemens 20.00 50.00
43 Andres Galarraga 3.00 8.00
44 Robert Gsellman 2.50 6.00
45 Corey Seager
46 Gerrit Cole 4.00 10.00
47 Jason Kipnis 3.00 8.00
48 Yandy Diaz 5.00 12.00
49 Joc Pederson 3.00 8.00
50 Roy Halladay

2017 Panini Chronicles Signature Swatches

RANDOM INSERTS IN PACKS
PRINT RUNS B/WN 5-299 COPIES PER
NO PRICING ON QTY 10 OR LESS
EXCHANGE DEADLINE 5/22/2019
1 Aaron Judge/99 EXCH 60.00 150.00
6 Ian Happ/299 6.00 15.00
7 Andrew Benintendi/199 15.00 40.00
10 Bradley Zimmer/99 4.00 10.00
15 Paul Molitor/25 15.00 40.00
16 Paul Molitor/25 15.00 40.00
17 Paul Molitor/25 15.00 40.00
21 Edgar Martinez/299 4.00 10.00
22 Corey Seager/25 12.00 30.00
24 Josh Donaldson/25
25 Dave Concepcion/25 15.00 40.00
26 Todd Helton/25 12.00 30.00
28 Starling Marte/299 4.00 10.00
29 Andres Galarraga/49 5.00 12.00
31 Pete Rose/49 15.00 40.00
33 Fred McGriff/49 10.00 25.00
34 Luis Gonzalez/25
37 Ozzie Smith/25 15.00 40.00

2017 Panini Chronicles Signature Swatches Purple

*PURPLE: .5X TO 1.2X p/r 199-299
RANDOM INSERTS IN PACKS
PRINT RUNS B/WN 49-99 COPIES PER
EXCHANGE DEADLINE 5/22/2019
4 Alex Bregman/49 20.00 50.00
8 Trey Mancini/99 8.00 20.00

2017 Panini Chronicles Signature Swatches Red

*RED: .6X TO 1.5X p/r 199-299
*RED: .5X TO 1.2X p/r 49-99
RANDOM INSERTS IN PACKS
PRINT RUNS B/WN 3-25 COPIES PER
NO PRICING ON QTY 15 OR LESS
EXCHANGE DEADLINE 5/22/2019
4 Alex Bregman/25 25.00 60.00
8 Trey Mancini/25 10.00 25.00

2017 Panini Chronicles Swatches

RANDOM INSERTS IN PACKS
PRINT RUNS B/WN 10-499 COPIES PER
NO PRICING ON QTY 10
*PURPLE/49-99: .5X TO 1.2X p/r 149-499
*PURPLE/49-99: .4X TO 1X p/r 49-99
*PURPLE/25: .6X TO 1.5X p/r 149-499
*PURPLE/25: .5X TO 1.2X p/r 49-99
*RED/25: .6X TO 1.5X p/r 149-499
*RED/25: .5X TO 1.2X p/r 49-99
1 Mike Trout/99 15.00 40.00
2 Kris Bryant/49 5.00 12.00
3 Adrian Beltre/99 3.00 8.00
4 Alex Rodriguez/499 3.00 8.00
5 Justin Verlander/499 2.50 6.00
6 Eddie Mathews/49 5.00 12.00
8 Andrew Benintendi/499 3.00 8.00
9 Don Sutton/149 2.00 5.00
10 Yoan Moncada/499 3.00 8.00
11 Cody Bellinger/49 8.00 20.00
12 Rollie Fingers/299 4.00 10.00
13 Rick Ferrell/25
14 Harmon Killebrew/25 10.00 25.00
15 Tony Gwynn/499 2.50 6.00
16 Craig Biggio/499 2.00 5.00
17 George Brett/199 10.00 25.00
18 Mike Piazza/499 2.50 6.00
20 Duke Snider/25 5.00 12.00
21 Jake Arrieta/499 2.00 5.00
22 Max Scherzer/49 3.00 8.00
23 Clayton Kershaw/49 5.00 12.00
24 Anthony Rizzo/299 3.00 8.00
25 Madison Bumgarner/299 2.00 5.00
26 Xander Bogaerts/499 2.50 6.00
27 Paul Goldschmidt/99 3.00 8.00
28 Dansby Swanson/499 3.00 8.00
29 Nolan Arenado/499 4.00 10.00
30 Marcell Ozuna/499 2.50 6.00
31 Miguel Cabrera/499 2.50 6.00
32 Jose Canseco/199 4.00 10.00
33 Carlos Delgado/499 1.50 4.00
34 Bill Buckner/49 2.00 5.00
35 Aaron Judge/499 12.00 30.00
36 Paul Konerko/499 2.00 5.00
37 Andruw Jones/499 1.50 4.00
38 Miguel Sano/499 2.00 5.00
39 George Springer/499 2.00 5.00
40 Andy Pettitte/299 2.00 5.00
41 Curt Schilling/99 2.50 6.00
42 Josh Bell/499 3.00 8.00
43 Dale Murphy/99 5.00 12.00
44 Bert Blyleven/49 6.00 15.00
45 Juan Gonzalez/499 2.50 6.00
46 Lewis Brinson/499 2.50 6.00
47 Chipper Jones/499 2.50 6.00
48 Ken Griffey Jr./499 4.00 10.00
49 Jose Altuve/49 2.50 6.00
50 Harold Baines/499 2.00 5.00
51 Gary Sheffield/49 2.00 5.00
52 Andre Dawson/99 2.50 6.00
53 Edgar Martinez/499 2.00 5.00
54 Sparky Anderson/25 10.00 25.00
55 Bryce Harper/25 5.00 12.00
56 Dustin Pedroia/199 3.00 8.00
57 Joe Torre/499 2.00 5.00
58 Hideki Matsui/499 2.50 6.00
59 John Farrell/499 1.50 4.00
60 Gary Sanchez/499 2.50 6.00

2018 Panini Chronicles

INSERTED IN '18 CHRONICLES PACKS
*SLVR VET/199: 1X TO 2.5X BASE
*SLVR RC/199: .6X TO 1.5X BASE RC
*GOLD VET/99: 1.2X TO 3X BASE
*GOLD RC/99: .75X TO 2X BASE RC
1 Shohei Ohtani RC 6.00 15.00
2 Austin Hays RC .40 1.00
3 Noah Syndergaard .20 .50
4 Freddie Freeman .30 .75
5 Justin Bour .15 .40
6 Khris Davis .25 .60
7 Miguel Cabrera .25 .60
8 Giancarlo Stanton .25 .60
9 Yadier Molina .30 .75
10 Mookie Betts .50 1.25
11 Starling Marte .20 .50
12 Walker Buehler RC 1.25 3.00
13 Rafael Devers RC .75 2.00
14 Robinson Cano .20 .50
15 Victor Robles RC .60 1.50
16 Eric Hosmer .20 .50
17 Joey Votto .25 .60
18 Max Scherzer .25 .60
19 Paul Goldschmidt .25 .60
20 Clint Frazier RC .50 1.25
21 Clayton Kershaw .40 1.00
22 Kris Bryant .30 .75
23 Dustin Fowler RC .25 .60
24 Willie Calhoun RC .40 1.00
25 Chris Sale .25 .60
26 Dominic Smith RC .30 .75
27 Miguel Andujar RC 1.00 2.50
28 Nicky Delmonico RC .25 .60
29 Jake Arrieta .20 .50
30 Shohei Ohtani RC 6.00 15.00
31 Eric Thames .20 .50
32 Luiz Gohara RC .25 .60
33 Jose Altuve .20 .50
34 Adrian Beltre .25 .60
35 Nolan Arenado .40 1.00
36 Corey Seager .25 .60
37 Ronald Acuna Jr. RC 8.00 20.00
38 Gary Sanchez .25 .60
39 Jose Abreu .25 .60
40 Manny Machado .25 .60
41 Ozzie Albies RC .75 2.00
42 Rhys Hoskins RC 1.00 2.50
43 Harrison Bader RC .40 1.00
44 J.P. Crawford RC .25 .60
45 Carlos Correa .25 .60
46 Corey Kluber .20 .50
47 Mike Trout 1.25 3.00
48 Anthony Rizzo .30 .75
49 Alex Gordon .20 .50
50 Josh Donaldson .20 .50
51 Albert Pujols .30 .75
52 Amed Rosario RC .30 .75
53 Andrew McCutchen .25 .60
54 Aaron Judge .60 1.50
55 Francisco Lindor .25 .60
56 Cody Bellinger .50 1.25
57 Chance Sisco RC .30 .75
58 Miguel Sano .20 .50
59 Bryce Harper .40 1.00
60 Gleyber Torres RC 2.50 6.00

2018 Panini Chronicles Blue

*BLUE: 1.5X TO 4X BASIC
*BLUE RC: 1X TO 2.5X BASIC RC
INSERTED IN '18 CHRONICLES PACKS
STATED PRINT RUN 49 SER.#'d SETS

2018 Panini Chronicles Holo Gold

*GOLD: 1.2X TO 3X BASIC
*GOLD RC: .75X TO 2X BASIC RC
INSERTED IN '18 CHRONICLES PACKS
STATED PRINT RUN 99 SER.#'d SETS

2018 Panini Chronicles Pink

*PINK: 2.5X TO 6X BASIC
*PINK RC: 1.5X TO 4X BASIC RC
INSERTED IN '18 CHRONICLES PACKS
STATED PRINT RUN 25 SER.#'d SETS

2018 Panini Chronicles Press Proof

*PP: .75X TO 2X BASIC
*PP RC: .5X TO 1.2X BASIC RC
INSERTED IN '18 CHRONICLES PACKS
STATED PRINT RUN 299 SER.#'d SETS

2018 Panini Chronicles Teal

*TEAL: 1X TO 2.5X BASIC
*TEAL RC: .6X TO 1.5X BASIC RC
INSERTED IN '18 CHRONICLES PACKS
STATED PRINT RUN 199 SER.#'d SETS

2018 Panini Chronicles Autographs

RANDOM INSERTS IN PACKS
CAAH Austin Hays 3.00 8.00
CACG Cameron Gallagher 2.50 6.00
CACP Chad Pinder 2.50 6.00
CADP Dillon Peters 2.50 6.00
CAFP Freddy Peralta 2.50 6.00
CAFR Franmil Reyes 4.00 10.00
CAGM German Marquez 2.50 6.00
CAGY Gabriel Ynoa 2.50 6.00
CAJE Jeurys Familia 3.00 8.00
CAJG Javier Guerra 2.50 6.00
CAJP James Paxton 3.00 8.00
CAJR Jose Rondon 2.50 6.00
CAKF Kyle Farmer 2.50 6.00
CALG Luiz Gohara 2.50 6.00
CALS Lucas Sims 2.50 6.00
CAMA Miguel Andujar 12.00 30.00
CAMG Mitch Garver 2.50 6.00
CARR Robbie Ray 2.50 6.00
CATW Tyler Wade 3.00 8.00
CAVC Victor Caratini 3.00 8.00

2018 Panini Chronicles Autographs Holo Silver

*PURPLE/25: .75X TO 2X BASE
RANDOM INSERTS IN PACKS
PRINT RUNS B/WN 5-25 COPIES PER
NO PRICING ON QTY 5
CADF Dustin Fowler/25 5.00 12.00

2018 Panini Chronicles Autographs Purple

*PURPLE/99: .5X TO 1.2X BASE
*PURPLE/35-49: .6X TO 1.5X BASE
RANDOM INSERTS IN PACKS
PRINT RUNS B/WN 10-99 COPIES PER
NO PRICING ON QTY 10
CADF Dustin Fowler/99 3.00 8.00

2018 Panini Chronicles Autographs Red

*RED/75-199: .5X TO 1.2X BASE
*RED/49: .6X TO 1.5X BASE
RANDOM INSERTS IN PACKS
PRINT RUNS B/WN 15-199 COPIES PER
NO PRICING ON QTY 15
CADF Dustin Fowler/199 3.00 8.00

2018 Panini Chronicles Signature Swatches

RANDOM INSERTS IN PACKS
*GOLD/99-149: .5X TO 1.2X BASIC
*RED/25: .75X TO 2X BASIC
CCSDP DJ Peters 6.00 15.00
CCSJB Jaime Barria 3.00 8.00
CCSWA Willy Adames 3.00 8.00

2018 Panini Chronicles Signature Swatches Blue

*BLUE/99: .5X TO 1.2X BASIC
RANDOM INSERTS IN PACKS
PRINT RUNS B/WN 49-99 COPIES PER
CCSAM Austin Meadows/49 10.00 25.00

2018 Panini Chronicles Signature Swatches Holo Gold

*RED/49: .5X TO 1.2X BASIC
*RED/25: .75X TO 2X BASIC
RANDOM INSERTS IN PACKS
PRINT RUNS B/WN 25-49 COPIES PER
CCSAM Austin Meadows/25 12.00 30.00

2018 Panini Chronicles Swatches

INSERTED IN '18 CHRONICLES PACKS
CSSO Shohei Ohtani 10.00 25.00
CSAR Amed Rosario 2.00 5.00
CSAH Austin Hays 2.50 6.00
CSVR Victor Robles 4.00 10.00
CSOA Ozzie Albies 5.00 12.00
CSRM Ryan McMahon 4.00 10.00
CSRH Rhys Hoskins 4.00 10.00
CSRD Rafael Devers 5.00 12.00
CSMA Miguel Andujar 4.00 10.00
CSMT Mike Trout 8.00 20.00
CSAJ Aaron Judge
CSRA Ronald Acuna Jr. 8.00 20.00
CSFT Fernando Tatis Jr. 15.00 40.00
CSMB Mookie Betts 5.00 12.00
CSCK Clayton Kershaw 4.00 10.00
CSJA Jose Altuve 2.00 5.00
CSKG Ken Griffey Jr. 8.00 20.00
CSGT Gleyber Torres 5.00 12.00
CSKP Kirby Puckett
CSNA Nolan Arenado 4.00 10.00
CSBH Bryce Harper 4.00 10.00
CSFL Francisco Lindor 2.50 6.00
CSMM Manny Machado 2.50 6.00

2018 Panini Chronicles Swatches Holo Gold

*HOLO GOLD/49: .5X TO 1.2X BASIC
*HOLO GOLD/25: .6X TO 1.5X BASIC
INSERTED IN '18 CHRONICLES PACKS
PRINT RUNS B/WN 25-49 COPIES PER
CSCF Clint Frazier/49 4.00 10.00

2018 Panini Chronicles Swatches Red

*RED/25: .6X TO 1.5X BASIC
INSERTED IN '18 CHRONICLES PACKS
PRINT RUNS B/WN 10-25 COPIES PER
NO PRICING ON QTY 10
CSCF Clint Frazier/25 5.00 12.00

2019 Panini Chronicles

RANDOM INSERTS IN PACKS
*RED/99: 1.5X TO 4X
*BLUE/50: 2X TO 5X
*PINK/25: 3X TO 8X
1 Joey Votto .25 .60
2 Joey Gallo .20 .50
3 Cody Bellinger .50 1.25
4 Pete Alonso RC 2.00 5.00
5 Bryce Harper .40 1.00
6 Fernando Tatis Jr. RC 4.00 10.00
7 Clayton Kershaw .40 1.00
8 Max Scherzer .25 .60
9 Javier Baez .30 .75
10 Nolan Arenado .40 1.00
11 Aaron Judge .60 1.50
12 Ryan O'Hearn RC .15 .40
13 Jose Altuve .20 .50
14 Madison Bumgarner .20 .50
15 Christian Yelich .30 .75
16 Adam Jones .20 .50
17 Chris Paddack RC .30 .75
18 Ichiro .30 .75
19 Kyle Tucker RC .40 1.00
20 Noah Syndergaard .20 .50
21 Blake Snell .20 .50
22 Christin Stewart RC .20 .50
23 Yusei Kikuchi RC .25 .60
24 Ronald Acuna Jr. 1.25 3.00
25 Anthony Rizzo .30 .75
26 Carlos Correa .25 .60
27 Giancarlo Stanton .25 .60
28 Michael Kopech RC .50 1.25
29 Paul Goldschmidt .25 .60
30 Shohei Ohtani .40 1.00
31 Mookie Betts .50 1.25
32 Austin Riley RC .75 2.00
33 Francisco Lindor .25 .60
34 Eloy Jimenez RC .60 1.50
35 Jose Ramirez .20 .50
36 Kris Bryant .30 .75
37 Mike Trout 1.25 3.00
38 David Fletcher RC .50 1.25
39 Brandon Lowe RC .25 .60
40 Jake Bauers RC .25 .60
41 Touki Toussaint RC .20 .50
42 Rowdy Tellez RC .25 .60
43 Justus Sheffield RC .25 .60
44 Jason Martin RC .20 .50
45 Bryan Reynolds RC .50 1.25
46 Michael Chavis RC .25 .60
47 Cole Tucker RC .25 .60
48 Carter Kieboom RC .25 .60
49 Vladimir Guerrero Jr. RC 2.50 6.00
50 Nathaniel Lowe RC .75 2.00

2020 Panini Chronicles

RANDOM INSERTS IN PACKS
1 Mike Trout 2.00 5.00
2 Vladimir Guerrero Jr. .40 1.00
3 Ronald Acuna Jr. 1.50 4.00
4 Juan Soto .75 2.00
5 Pete Alonso .60 1.50
6 Gleyber Torres .50 1.25
7 Aaron Judge .60 1.50
8 Shohei Ohtani .40 1.00
9 Anthony Rizzo .30 .75
10 Fernando Tatis Jr. 4.00 10.00
11 Cody Bellinger .50 1.25
12 Christian Yelich .30 .75
13 Max Scherzer .25 .60
14 Jacob deGrom .50 1.25
15 Gerrit Cole .40 1.00
16 Nolan Arenado .40 1.00
17 Mookie Betts .50 1.25
18 Francisco Lindor .25 .60
19 Alex Bregman .25 .60
20 Rafael Devers .30 .75
21 Xander Bogaerts .25 .60
22 Jonathan Villar .15 .40
23 Blake Snell .20 .50
24 Keston Hiura .30 .75
25 Trea Turner .20 .50
26 Starling Marte .20 .50
27 Kris Bryant .30 .75
28 Paul Goldschmidt .25 .60
29 Trevor Bauer .30 .75
30 Bryce Harper .40 1.00
31 Bo Bichette RC 5.00 12.00
32 Yordan Alvarez RC 2.50 6.00
33 Nico Hoerner RC 1.00 2.50
34 Aristides Aquino RC .60 1.50
35 Gavin Lux RC 1.25 3.00
36 Dustin May RC .75 2.00
37 Dylan Cease RC .40 1.00
38 Luis Robert RC 4.00 10.00
39 Zac Gallen RC .60 1.50
40 Brendan McKay RC .40 1.00
41 Yoshitomo Tsutsugo RC .60 1.50
42 Shogo Akiyama RC .40 1.00
43 A.J. Puk RC .40 1.00
44 Jesus Luzardo RC .50 1.25
45 Shun Yamaguchi RC .30 .75

2020 Panini Chronicles Blue

RANDOM INSERTS IN PACKS
STATED PRINT RUN 50 SER.#'d SETS
*BLUE VET: 1.5X TO 4X BASIC
*BLUE RC: 1X TO 2.5X BASIC RC

2020 Panini Chronicles Signatures

RANDOM INSERTS IN PACKS
PRINT RUNS B/WN 5-99 COPIES PER
NO PRICING QTY 15 OR LESS
EXCHANGE DEADLINE 3/18/2022
6 Gleyber Torres EXCH/25 20.00 50.00
18 Francisco Lindor/49 6.00 15.00
25 Trea Turner/25 6.00 15.00
31 Bo Bichette/30 30.00 80.00
32 Yordan Alvarez/50 40.00 100.00
33 Nico Hoerner/99 12.00 30.00
34 Aristides Aquino/60 8.00 20.00
37 Dylan Cease/90 5.00 12.00
38 Luis Robert EXCH/99 75.00 200.00
39 Zac Gallen/49 6.00 15.00
41 Yoshitomo Tsutsugo/99 8.00 20.00
42 Shogo Akiyama/49 6.00 15.00
43 A.J. Puk/99 5.00 12.00
45 Shun Yamaguchi/99 4.00 10.00

2015 Panini Contenders

COMPLETE SET (99) 15.00 40.00
PLATE PRINT RUN 1 SET PER COLOR
NO PLATE PRICING DUE TO SCARCITY
1 A.J. Minter .25 .60
2 Corey Seager 1.00 2.50
3 Aaron Judge 3.00 8.00
4 Aaron Nola .30 .75
5 Alex Bregman 1.00 2.50
6 Alex Young .20 .50
7 Trea Turner .60 1.50
8 Andrew Benintendi 1.00 2.50
9 Richie Martin .20 .50
10 Andrew Stevenson .20 .50
11 Anthony Hermelyn .20 .50
12 Mikey White .25 .60
13 Austin Rei .25 .60
14 Barry Larkin .25 .60
15 Blake Trahan .20 .50
16 Bo Jackson .30 .75
17 Bob Gibson .25 .60
18 Braden Bishop .20 .50
19 Braden Shipley .20 .50
20 Brandon Koch .20 .50
21 Brandon Lowe .30 .75
22 Breckin Williams .20 .50
23 Brett Lilek .20 .50
24 Carson Fulmer .20 .50
25 Casey Hughston .20 .50
26 Chris Shaw .20 .50
27 J.P. Crawford .20 .50
28 Cody Poteet .20 .50
29 Craig Biggio .25 .60
30 D.J. Peterson .20 .50
31 Dansby Swanson 1.25 3.00
32 Dave Winfield .25 .60
33 David Thompson .25 .60
34 Matt Olson 1.00 2.50
35 Zack Erwin .20 .50
36 Dillon Tate .25 .60
37 Andrew Suarez .25 .60
38 Donnie Dewees .30 .75
39 Drew Smith .20 .50
40 Erick Fedde .20 .50
41 Frank Howard .20 .50
42 Frank Thomas .30 .75
43 Fred Lynn .20 .50
44 Garrett Cleavinger .25 .60
45 Grayson Long .20 .50
46 Harrison Bader .30 .75
47 Hunter Dozier .20 .50
48 Hunter Renfroe .30 .75
49 Ian Happ .75 2.00
50 Jake Lemoine .20 .50
51 Matt Chapman .60 1.50
52 Jeff Degano .25 .60
53 Jeff Hendrix .25 .60
54 Jeff Hoffman .25 .60
55 John Elway .50 1.25
56 Jon Harris .25 .60
57 Josh Graham .25 .60
58 Tyler Beede .25 .60
59 Kevin Kramer .25 .60
60 Kevin Newman .50 1.25
61 Mike Schmidt .50 1.25
62 Ryan Burr .20 .50
63 Dansby Swanson 1.25 3.00
64 Alex Bregman 1.00 2.50
65 Luke Weaver .30 .75
66 Dillon Tate .25 .60
67 Mark Mathias .25 .60
68 Mark McGwire .50 1.25
69 Matt Chapman .60 1.50
70 Michael Conforto .25 .60
71 Michael Matuella .25 .60
72 Mikey White .25 .60
73 Nathan Kirby .25 .60
74 Ozzie Smith .40 1.00
75 Paul Molitor .30 .75
76 Peter O'Brien .30 .75
77 Phil Bickford .20 .50
78 Philip Pfeifer .20 .50
79 Randy Johnson .30 .75
80 Reggie Jackson .25 .60
81 Rhett Wiseman .20 .50
82 Riley Ferrell .20 .50
83 Robert Refsnyder .25 .60
84 Roger Clemens .40 1.00
85 Scott Kingery .30 .75
86 Skye Bolt .25 .60
87 Stephen Piscotty .25 .60
88 Tate Matheny .20 .50
89 Taylor Ward .30 .75
90 Thomas Eshelman .20 .50
91 Tony Gwynn .30 .75
92 Trea Turner .60 1.50
93 Tyler Alexander .20 .50
94 Tyler Beede .25 .60
95 Tyler Jay .20 .50
96 Tyler Krieger .20 .50
97 Tyler Naquin .30 .75
98 Walker Buehler 1.25 3.00
99 Will Clark .25 .60

2015 Panini Contenders Cracked Ice

*CRACKED ICE: 6X TO 15X BASIC
RANDOM INSERTS IN PACKS
STATED PRINT RUN 23 SER.#'d SETS

2015 Panini Contenders Draft

*DRAFT: 3X TO 8X BASIC
RANDOM INSERTS IN PACKS
STATED PRINT RUN 99 SER.#'d SETS

2015 Panini Contenders Alumni Ink

OVERALL AUTO ODDS 1:4 HOBBY
2 Aaron Judge 25.00 60.00
4 Braden Shipley 3.00 8.00
5 D.J. Peterson 3.00 8.00
7 Erick Fedde 3.00 8.00
9 Hunter Renfroe 5.00 12.00
10 Kyle Schwarber 30.00 80.00
13 Peter O'Brien 5.00 12.00
16 Trea Turner 10.00 25.00
17 Tyler Naquin 5.00 12.00
24 Barry Larkin 12.00 30.00
25 Mike Schmidt 20.00 100.00

2015 Panini Contenders Class Reunion

COMPLETE SET (25) 6.00 15.00
APPX.ODDS 1:4 HOBBY
1 Dansby Swanson 2.00 5.00
2 Alex Bregman 1.50 4.00
3 Dillon Tate .40 1.00
4 Tyler Jay .30 .75
5 Andrew Benintendi 1.50 4.00
6 Carson Fulmer .30 .75
7 Ian Happ 1.25 3.00
8 Breckin Williams .30 .75
9 Phil Bickford .30 .75
10 Kevin Newman .75 2.00
11 Richie Martin .30 .75
12 Walker Buehler 2.00 5.00
13 Cody Poteet .30 .75
14 Taylor Ward .50 1.25
15 Jon Harris .40 1.00
16 Chris Shaw .30 .75
17 Garrett Cleavinger .40 1.00
18 Ryan Burr .30 .75
19 Nathan Kirby .40 1.00
20 Alex Young .30 .75
21 Thomas Eshelman .30 .75
22 Donnie Dewees .50 1.25
23 Scott Kingery .50 1.25
24 Brett Lilek .30 .75
25 Jeff Degano .40 1.00

2015 Panini Contenders College Ticket Autographs

OVERALL AUTO ODDS 1:4 HOBBY
*BLUE FOIL: .4X TO 1X BASIC
*RED FOIL: .4X TO 1X BASIC
*DRAFT/99: .5X TO 1.2X BASIC
*CRACKED/23: 1.2X TO 3X BASIC
PLATE PRINT RUN 1 SET PER COLOR
BLACK-CYAN-MAGENTA-YELLOW ISSUED
NO PLATE PRICING DUE TO SCARCITY
1 Swanson Thrwng 12.00 30.00
2 Tate Arm back 4.00 10.00
3 Bregman Prple jsy 15.00 40.00
4 Fulmer Frnt leg up 10.00 25.00
5 Benintendi Wht jsy 15.00 40.00
6 W.Buehler Wht jrsy 6.00 15.00
7 Tyler Jay 3.00 8.00
Throwing
8 Drew Smith 3.00 8.00
9 Kaprielian Fcng rght 6.00 15.00
10 Michael Matuella 4.00 10.00
Black jersey
11 Happ Fldng 6.00 15.00
12 Jon Harris 4.00 10.00
Arm back
13 Nathan Kirby 4.00 10.00
Looking straight
14 Phil Bickford 3.00 8.00
Arm down
15 Kevin Newman 8.00 20.00
Batting
16 DJ Stewart 4.00 10.00
Fielding
17 Richie Martin 3.00 8.00
Batting
18 Alex Young 3.00 8.00
Pitching
19 Cody Ponce 3.00 8.00
Front leg down
20 Kingery Fldng 5.00 12.00
22 Thomas Eshelman 3.00 8.00
Facing forward
23 Riley Ferrell 3.00 8.00
Arm back
24 Blake Trahan 3.00 8.00
Ball visible
25 Donnie Dewees 3.00 8.00
Swinging
26 Mikey White 4.00 10.00
Fielding
27 Rei Gld jsy 4.00 10.00
28 Brett Lilek 3.00 8.00
Black jersey
29 Taylor Ward 5.00 12.00
Catching
30 Andrew Stevenson 3.00 8.00
Purple jersey
31 Andrew Suarez 4.00 10.00
White jersey
32 Kevin Kramer 4.00 10.00
Sunglasses
33 Braden Bishop 3.00 8.00
34 Jeff Degano 3.00 8.00
Facing left
35 Christin Stewart 4.00 10.00
Pinstripe jersey
36 Bader Fcng lft 5.00 12.00
37 Wiseman Fldng 6.00 15.00
38 Brandon Koch 3.00 8.00
Arm down
39 Brandon Lowe 8.00 20.00
Arm up
40 David Thompson 3.00 8.00
Fielding
41 Mark Mathias 4.00 10.00
Fielding
42 Casey Hughston 3.00 8.00
Batting
43 Skye Bolt 4.00 10.00
Batting
44 Tate Matheny 3.00 8.00
Maroon jersey
45 Tyler Alexander 3.00 8.00
Facing forward
46 Tyler Krieger 3.00 8.00
Orange jersey
47 Philip Pfeifer 3.00 8.00
Arm back
50 A.J. Minter 4.00 10.00
White jersey

2015 Panini Contenders College Ticket Autographs Photo Variation

OVERALL AUTO ODDS 1:4 HOBBY
*BLUE FOIL: .4X TO 1X BASIC
*RED FOIL: .4X TO 1X BASIC
*DRAFT/99: .5X TO 1.2X BASIC
*CRACKED/23: 1.2X TO 3X BASIC
PLATE PRINT RUN 1 SET PER COLOR
BLACK-CYAN-MAGENTA-YELLOW ISSUED
NO PLATE PRICING DUE TO SCARCITY
1 Swanson Undr-hnd 30.00 80.00
2 Tate Arm DOWN 4.00 10.00
3 Bregman Yllw jsy 12.00 30.00
4 Fulmer Frnt leg down 10.00 25.00
5 Benintendi Red jsy 25.00 60.00
6 Walker Buehler 20.00 50.00
7 Tyler Jay 3.00 8.00
Arm back
8 Drew Smith 3.00 8.00
9 Kaprielian Fcng left 6.00 15.00
10 Michael Matuella 4.00 10.00
Blue jersey
11 Happ Bttng 12.00 30.00
12 Jon Harris 4.00 10.00
Arm up
13 Nathan Kirby 4.00 10.00
Looking down
14 Phil Bickford 3.00 8.00
Hands together
15 Kevin Newman 8.00 20.00
Throwing
16 DJ Stewart 4.00 10.00
Running
17 Richie Martin 3.00 8.00
Fielding
18 Alex Young 3.00 8.00
Hand on cap
19 Cody Ponce 3.00 8.00
Front leg up
20 Kingery Running 5.00 12.00
22 Thomas Eshelman 3.00 8.00
Facing right
23 Riley Ferrell 3.00 8.00
Arm down
24 Blake Trahan 3.00 8.00
No ball
25 Donnie Dewees 5.00 12.00
w/Bat
26 Mikey White 4.00 10.00
Throwing
27 Rei Blue jsy 4.00 10.00
28 Brett Lilek 3.00 8.00
Red jersey
29 Taylor Ward 5.00 12.00
Swinging
30 Andrew Stevenson 3.00 8.00
White jersey
31 Andrew Suarez 4.00 10.00
Black jersey
32 Kevin Kramer 4.00 10.00
Throwing
33 Braden Bishop 3.00 8.00
34 Jeff Degano 4.00 10.00
Facing forward
35 Christin Stewart 4.00 10.00
Orange jersey
36 Bader Fcng right 5.00 12.00
37 Wiseman Bttng 6.00 15.00
38 Brandon Koch 3.00 8.00
Arm up
39 Brandon Lowe 8.00 20.00
Arm back
40 David Thompson 4.00 10.00
Batting
41 Mark Mathias 4.00 10.00
Batting
42 Casey Hughston 3.00 8.00
Fielding
43 Skye Bolt 4.00 10.00
Fielding
44 Tate Matheny 3.00 8.00
White jersey
45 Tyler Alexander 3.00 8.00
Facing right
46 Tyler Krieger 3.00 8.00
Blue jersey
47 Philip Pfeifer 3.00 8.00
Leg up
50 A.J. Minter 4.00 10.00
Maroon jersey

2015 Panini Contenders Collegiate Connections

COMPLETE SET (25) 6.00 15.00
APPX.ODDS 1:4 HOBBY
1 Rafael Palmeiro .40 1.00
Will Clark
2 Bo Jackson .50 1.25
Frank Thomas
3 C.Fulmer/D.Swanson 2.00 5.00
4 Dave Winfield .50 1.25
Paul Molitor
5 Fulmer/Buehler 2.00 5.00
6 D.Swanson/R.Wiseman 2.00 5.00
7 A.Bregman/A.Stevenson 1.50 4.00
8 Cody Poteet .40 1.00
Kevin Kramer
9 Jon Harris .40 1.00
Tate Matheny
10 Carson Fulmer .40 1.00
Tyler Beede
11 Phil Bickford .30 .75
Thomas Eshelman
12 Newman/Kingery .75 2.00
13 Winston/Weaver .50 1.25
14 H.Bader/R.Martin .50 1.25

15 Alex Young .30 .75
Riley Ferrell
16 Riley Ferrell .30 .75
Tyler Alexander
17 Alex Young .30 .75
Tyler Alexander
18 Casey Hughston .40 1.00
Mikey White
19 A.Judge/T.Ward 5.00 12.00
20 Andrew Suarez .40 1.00
David Thompson
21 R.Wilson/T.Turner 1.00 2.50
22 Tyler Krieger .30 .75
Zack Erwin
23 Brandon Koch .30 .75
Drew Smith
24 Austin Rei .40 1.00
Braden Bishop
25 Philip Pfeifer .30 .75
Rhett Wiseman

2015 Panini Contenders Collegiate Connections Signatures

OVERALL AUTO ODDS 1:4 HOBBY
1 Palmeiro/Clark 30.00 80.00
7 Bregman/Stevenson 25.00 60.00
9 Harris/Matheny 5.00 12.00
15 Young/Ferrell 4.00 10.00
19 Judge/Ward 15.00 40.00
20 Suarez/Thompson 8.00 20.00
21 Wilson/Turner 30.00 80.00
24 Rei/Bishop 15.00 40.00

2015 Panini Contenders Draft Ticket Autographs

OVERALL AUTO ODDS 1:4 HOBBY
*BLUE FOIL: .4X TO 1X BASIC
*RED FOIL: .4X TO 1X BASIC
*DRAFT/99: .5X TO 1.2X BASIC
*CRACKED/23: 1.2X TO 3X BASIC
PLATE PRINT RUN 1 SET PER COLOR
BLACK-CYAN-MAGENTA-YELLOW ISSUED
NO PLATE PRICING DUE TO SCARCITY
1 Brendan Rodgers 6.00 15.00
2 Daz Cameron 4.00 10.00
3 Garrett Whitley 4.00 10.00
4 Kyle Tucker 10.00 25.00
5 Trenton Clark 2.50 6.00
6 Nick Plummer 3.00 8.00
7 Tyler Stephenson 6.00 15.00
8 Mike Nikorak 2.50 6.00
10 Kolby Allard 2.50 6.00
11 Cornelius Randolph 2.50 6.00
12 Ryan Mountcastle 12.00 30.00
14 Chris Betts 3.00 8.00
15 Beau Burrows 2.50 6.00
16 Dakota Chalmers 2.50 6.00
17 Jalen Miller 2.50 6.00
18 Jacob Nix 2.50 6.00
19 Austin Riley 25.00 60.00
20 Demi Orimoloye 3.00 8.00
21 Eric Jenkins 2.50 6.00
22 Mitchell Hansen 2.50 6.00
23 Austin Smith 2.50 6.00
24 Peter Lambert 2.50 6.00
25 Jake Woodford 2.50 6.00
26 Juan Hillman 2.50 6.00
27 Triston McKenzie 10.00 25.00
28 Lucas Herbert 2.50 6.00
30 Mac Marshall 2.50 6.00
31 Nick Neidert 2.50 6.00
32 Nolan Watson 2.50 6.00
33 Ke'Bryan Hayes 12.00 30.00
34 Desmond Lindsay 4.00 10.00
35 Bryce Denton 4.00 10.00
36 Josh Naylor 3.00 8.00
37 Thomas Szapucki 2.50 6.00
38 Blake Perkins 2.50 6.00
39 Javier Medina 2.50 6.00
40 Jahmai Jones 3.00 8.00
41 Travis Blankenhorn 3.00 8.00
45 Max Wotell 2.50 6.00
46 Jordan Hicks 6.00 15.00
47 Nash Walters 2.50 6.00
48 Tyler Nevin 4.00 10.00
49 Drew Finley 2.50 6.00
50 Mike Soroka 8.00 20.00

2015 Panini Contenders Game Day Tickets

COMPLETE SET (24) 6.00 15.00
OVERALL AUTO ODDS 1:4 HOBBY
1 Dansby Swanson 2.00 5.00
2 Alex Bregman 1.50 4.00
3 Dillon Tate .40 1.00
4 Tyler Jay .30 .75
5 Andrew Benintendi 1.50 4.00
6 Carson Fulmer .30 .75
7 Ian Happ 1.25 3.00
8 Breckin Williams .30 .75
9 Phil Bickford .30 .75
10 Kevin Newman .75 2.00
11 Richie Martin .30 .75
12 Walker Buehler 2.00 5.00
13 Cody Poteet .30 .75
14 Taylor Ward .50 1.25
15 Jon Harris .40 1.00
16 Chris Shaw .30 .75
17 Jake Lemoine .30 .75
18 Drew Smith .30 .75
19 Nathan Kirby .40 1.00
20 Alex Young .30 .75
21 Thomas Eshelman .30 .75
22 Donnie Dewees .50 1.25
23 Scott Kingery .50 1.25
24 Brett Lilek .30 .75
25 Jeff Degano .40 1.00

2015 Panini Contenders International Ticket Autographs

OVERALL AUTO ODDS 1:4 HOBBY
*BLUE FOIL: .4X TO 1X BASIC
*RED FOIL: .4X TO 1X BASIC
*CRACKED/23: 1.2X TO 3X BASIC
PLATE PRINT RUN 1 SET PER COLOR
BLACK-CYAN-MAGENTA-YELLOW ISSUED
NO PLATE PRICING DUE TO SCARCITY
2 Christian Pache 15.00 40.00
4 Yadier Alvarez 5.00 12.00
8 Lucius Fox 5.00 12.00
9 Jeison Guzman 4.00 10.00
10 Jonathan Arauz 3.00 8.00
12 Vladimir Guerrero Jr. 75.00 200.00
13 Orlando Arcia 4.00 10.00
15 Yoan Moncada 20.00 50.00
16 Aristides Aquino 40.00 100.00
20 Franklin Barreto 4.00 10.00
21 Gilbert Lara 4.00 10.00
23 Jairo Labourt 3.00 8.00
24 Jarlin Garcia 4.00 10.00
25 Wei-Chieh Huang 4.00 10.00
26 Jorge Mateo 12.00 30.00
27 Julian Leon 3.00 8.00
29 Yoan Lopez 3.00 8.00
30 Victor Robles 12.00 30.00

2015 Panini Contenders Old School Colors

COMPLETE SET (47) 8.00 20.00
RANDOM INSERTS IN PACKS
1 Roger Clemens .50 1.25
2 Reggie Jackson .30 .75
3 Randy Johnson .40 1.00
4 Craig Biggio .30 .75
5 Frank Thomas .40 1.00
6 Will Clark .30 .75
7 Barry Larkin .30 .75
8 Mike Schmidt .60 1.50
9 Dave Winfield .30 .75
10 Bo Jackson .40 1.00
11 Rafael Palmeiro .30 .75
12 Paul Molitor .40 1.00
13 Richie Martin .25 .60
14 Tony Gwynn .40 1.00
15 Frank Howard .25 .60
16 John Elway .75 2.00
17 Fred Lynn .25 .60
18 A.J. Reed .30 .75
19 Aaron Nola .40 1.00
20 Kevin Newman .60 1.50
21 Peter O'Brien .40 1.00
22 Stephen Piscotty .30 .75
23 Aaron Judge 4.00 10.00
24 Braden Shipley .25 .60
25 D.J. Peterson .25 .60
26 Erick Fedde .25 .60
27 Hunter Dozier .25 .60
28 Hunter Renfroe .40 1.00
29 Kyle Schwarber 1.00 2.50
30 Luke Weaver .40 1.00
31 Michael Conforto .30 .75
32 Robert Refsnyder .30 .75
33 Trea Turner .75 2.00
34 Tyler Naquin .40 1.00
35 Alex Bregman 1.25 3.00
36 Andrew Benintendi 1.25 3.00
37 Carson Fulmer .25 .60
38 Dansby Swanson 1.50 4.00
39 Breckin Williams .25 .60
40 Dillon Tate .30 .75
41 Ian Happ 1.00 2.50
42 Andrew Suarez .30 .75
43 Mark McGwire .60 1.50
44 Ozzie Smith .50 1.25
45 Bob Gibson .30 .75
46 Tyler Jay .25 .60
47 Phil Bickford .25 .60

2015 Panini Contenders Old School Colors Signatures

OVERALL AUTO ODDS 1:4 HOBBY
2 Reggie Jackson 10.00 25.00
3 Randy Johnson 25.00 60.00
7 Barry Larkin 10.00 25.00
11 Rafael Palmeiro 10.00 25.00
14 Tony Gwynn 50.00 120.00
18 John Elway 40.00 100.00

2015 Panini Contenders Passports

COMPLETE SET (25) 6.00 15.00
APPX.ODDS 1:4 HOBBY
1 Yoan Moncada 1.50 4.00
2 Aristides Aquino 6.00 15.00
3 Domingo Leyba .30 .75
4 Edmundo Sosa .40 1.00
5 Francisco Mejia .75 2.00
6 Franklin Barreto .40 1.00
7 Gilbert Lara .40 1.00
8 Gleyber Torres 5.00 12.00
9 Yoan Lopez .30 .75
10 Jorge Mateo 1.00 2.50
11 Julian Leon .30 .75
12 Luis Encarnacion .30 .75
13 Magneuris Sierra .50 1.25
14 Manuel Margot .30 .75
15 Marcos Molina .30 .75
16 Ozhaino Albies 3.00 8.00
17 Rafael Devers 2.00 5.00
18 Reynaldo Lopez .40 1.00
19 Richard Urena .50 1.25
20 Sergio Alcantara .30 .75
21 Teoscar Hernandez 1.25 3.00
22 Willy Adames .50 1.25
23 Yairo Munoz .40 1.00
24 Julio Urias 1.00 2.50
25 Luis Severino .40 1.00

2015 Panini Contenders Prospect Ticket Autographs

OVERALL AUTO ODDS 1:4 HOBBY
*BLUE FOIL: .4X TO 1X BASIC
*RED FOIL: .4X TO 1X BASIC
*CRACKED/23: 1.2X TO 3X BASIC
PLATE PRINT RUN 1 SET PER COLOR
BLACK-CYAN-MAGENTA-YELLOW ISSUED
NO PLATE PRICING DUE TO SCARCITY
2 Adam Walker 2.50 6.00
3 Brett Phillips 2.50 6.00
4 Correlle Prime 2.50 6.00
5 D.J. Peterson 2.50 6.00
6 Kyle Schwarber 6.00 15.00
8 Nick Kingham 2.50 6.00
9 Trea Turner 10.00 25.00
10 Tyrone Taylor 2.50 6.00
12 Andrew Faulkner 2.50 6.00
13 Jace Fry 2.50 6.00
14 Yoan Moncada 10.00 25.00
15 Aristides Aquino 40.00 100.00
17 Edmundo Sosa 3.00 8.00
18 Francisco Mejia 5.00 12.00
19 Franklin Barreto 6.00 15.00
20 Gilbert Lara 3.00 8.00
21 Gleyber Torres 25.00 60.00
22 Jairo Labourt 2.50 6.00
24 Javier Guerra 10.00 25.00
25 Jorge Mateo 4.00 10.00
28 Magneuris Sierra 6.00 15.00
29 Manuel Margot 2.50 6.00
31 Ozhaino Albies 20.00 50.00
32 Rafael Devers 15.00 40.00
34 Richard Urena 4.00 10.00
37 Willy Adames 4.00 10.00
39 Julio Urias 8.00 20.00
40 Luis Severino 3.00 8.00
41 Brent Honeywell 4.00 10.00
42 Mauricio Dubon 3.00 8.00
43 Micker Adolfo 3.00 8.00
45 Antonio Senzatela 3.00 8.00
46 Jake Lemoine 2.50 6.00
47 Corey Seager 15.00 40.00
48 Garrett Cleavinger 3.00 8.00
49 Grayson Long 2.50 6.00

2015 Panini Contenders School Colors

COMPLETE SET (52) 8.00 20.00
RANDOM INSERTS IN PACKS
1 Dansby Swanson 1.50 4.00
2 Alex Bregman 1.25 3.00
3 Dillon Tate .30 .75
4 Tyler Jay .25 .60
5 Andrew Benintendi 1.25 3.00
6 Carson Fulmer .25 .60
7 Ian Happ 1.00 2.50
8 Breckin Williams .25 .60
9 Phil Bickford .25 .60
10 Kevin Newman .60 1.50
11 Richie Martin .25 .60
12 Walker Buehler 1.50 4.00
13 Cody Poteet .25 .60
14 Taylor Ward .40 1.00
15 Jon Harris .30 .75
16 Chris Shaw .25 .60
17 Jake Lemoine .25 .60
18 Ryan Burr .25 .60
19 Nathan Kirby .30 .75
20 Alex Young .25 .60
21 Thomas Eshelman .25 .60
22 Donnie Dewees .40 1.00
23 Scott Kingery .40 1.00
24 Brett Lilek .25 .60
25 Jeff Degano .30 .75
26 Andrew Stevenson .25 .60
27 Andrew Suarez .30 .75
28 Kevin Kramer .30 .75
29 Mikey White .30 .75
30 Tyler Alexander .25 .60
31 Anthony Hermelyn .25 .60
32 Grayson Long .25 .60
33 Garrett Cleavinger .30 .75
34 A.J. Minter .30 .75
35 Michael Matuella .30 .75
36 Riley Ferrell .25 .60
37 Austin Rei .30 .75
38 Blake Trahan .25 .60
39 Brandon Lowe .40 1.00
40 Braden Bishop .25 .60
41 Casey Hughston .25 .60
42 Drew Smith .25 .60
43 Harrison Bader .40 1.00
44 Philip Pfeifer .25 .60
45 Rhett Wiseman .25 .60
46 Tate Matheny .25 .60
47 Zack Erwin .25 .60
48 Brandon Koch .25 .60
49 David Thompson .30 .75
50 Tyler Krieger .25 .60
51 Skye Bolt .30 .75
52 A.J. Reed .30 .75

2015 Panini Contenders School Colors Signatures

OVERALL AUTO ODDS 1:4 HOBBY
1 Aaron Judge 75.00 200.00
4 Erick Fedde 8.00 20.00
5 Hunter Dozier 3.00 8.00
7 Kyle Schwarber 10.00 25.00
8 Luke Weaver 5.00 12.00
9 Michael Conforto 20.00 50.00
10 Robert Refsnyder 4.00 10.00
12 Tyler Naquin 5.00 12.00
13 Dansby Swanson 10.00 25.00
14 Alex Bregman 10.00 25.00
15 Dillon Tate 4.00 10.00
17 Andrew Benintendi 10.00 25.00
18 Carson Fulmer 3.00 8.00
19 Ian Happ 15.00 40.00
20 James Kaprielian 3.00 8.00
21 Phil Bickford 3.00 8.00
22 Kevin Newman 8.00 20.00
23 Richie Martin 3.00 8.00
24 Walker Buehler 6.00 15.00
25 DJ Stewart 4.00 10.00

2015 Panini Contenders USA Baseball Ticket Autographs

*BLUE FOIL: .4X TO 1X BASIC
*RED FOIL: .4X TO 1X BASIC
*DRAFT/99: .5X TO 1.2X BASIC
*CRACKED/23: 1.2X TO 3X BASIC
PLATE PRINT RUN 1 SET PER COLOR
BLACK-CYAN-MAGENTA-YELLOW ISSUED
NO PLATE PRICING DUE TO SCARCITY
1 Corey Seager 20.00 50.00
2 D.J. Peterson 2.50 6.00
3 Kyle Schwarber 10.00 25.00
4 Matt Olson 6.00 15.00
5 Michael Conforto 25.00 60.00
7 Alex Bregman 12.00 30.00
9 Kevin Kramer 3.00 8.00
13 Carson Fulmer 2.50 6.00
14 Riley Ferrell 2.50 6.00
16 Christin Stewart 3.00 8.00
17 Matt Chapman 8.00 20.00
18 Dansby Swanson 12.00 30.00
19 Daz Cameron 4.00 10.00
21 DJ Stewart 4.00 10.00
24 James Kaprielian 2.50 6.00
25 Thomas Eshelman 3.00 8.00
26 Taylor Ward 4.00 10.00
27 Ke'Bryan Hayes 20.00 50.00
29 Kolby Allard 2.50 6.00
31 Trenton Clark 3.00 8.00
32 Kyle Tucker 20.00 50.00
33 Lucas Herbert 3.00 8.00
34 Tyler Jay 3.00 8.00
35 Tyler Beede 3.00 8.00
36 Mark Mathias 3.00 8.00
37 Mikey White 4.00 10.00
42 A.J. Minter 3.00 8.00
45 Buddy Reed 10.00 25.00
46 Nick Banks 8.00 20.00
47 Garrett Hampson 5.00 12.00
48 Corey Ray 10.00 25.00
50 Ryan Howard 4.00 10.00
51 Anfernee Grier 3.00 8.00
52 Daulton Jefferies 4.00 10.00
54 Stephen Nogosek 3.00 8.00
55 Mike Shawaryn 3.00 8.00
56 Matt Thaiss 5.00 12.00
57 JJ Schwarz 15.00 40.00
58 Robert Tyler 3.00 8.00
59 Anthony Kay 3.00 8.00
60 Bobby Dalbec 15.00 40.00
61 Chris Okey 3.00 8.00
63 A.J. Puk 4.00 10.00
64 Tanner Houck 12.00 30.00
65 Zach Jackson 4.00 10.00
66 KJ Harrison 5.00 12.00
67 Logan Shore 10.00 25.00
68 Brendan McKay 10.00 25.00

2017 Panini Contenders College Tickets

INSERTED IN '17 EEE PACKS
EXCHANGE DEADLINE 6/6/2019
*CRACKED ICE/24: .75X TO 2X BASIC
1 Jake Burger 8.00 20.00
2 Evan White 6.00 15.00
3 Alex Faedo 8.00 20.00
4 David Peterson 5.00 12.00
5 Logan Warmoth 4.00 10.00
6 Tanner Houck 5.00 12.00
7 Brian Miller 3.00 8.00
8 Stuart Fairchild 3.00 8.00
9 Gavin Sheets 4.00 10.00
10 Joseph Dunand 5.00 12.00
12 Wil Crowe 4.00 10.00
13 KJ Harrison 5.00 12.00
14 Trevor Stephan 4.00 10.00
15 A.J. Minter 3.00 8.00
16 Casey Gillaspie 2.50 6.00
17 Harrison Bader 4.00 10.00
18 Zack Collins 3.00 8.00
19 Greg Deichmann 5.00 12.00
20 Drew Ellis 4.00 10.00
22 Morgan Cooper 3.00 8.00
23 Jake Thompson 2.50 6.00
24 Tommy Doyle
25 Ernie Clement 3.00 8.00
26 J.J. Matijevic 3.00 8.00
27 Connor Seabold 2.50 6.00
28 Will Gaddis 2.50 6.00
29 Dylan Busby 2.50 6.00
30 Brendan McKay 10.00 25.00
31 Joey Morgan 3.00 8.00
32 Quinn Brodey 2.50 6.00
33 Cody Sedlock 2.50 6.00
34 Kyle Wright 8.00 20.00

2017 Panini Contenders Rookie Ticket

INSERTED IN '17 CHRONICLES PACKS
EXCHANGE DEADLINE 5/22/2019
*CHAMP/35-49: .6X TO 1.5X BASIC
*CHAMP/25: .75X TO 2X BASIC
*CRACKED ICE/24: .75X TO 2X BASIC
*PLAYOFF/99: .5X TO 1.2X BASIC
*PLAYOFF/49: .6X TO 1.5X BASIC
*PLAYOFF/25: .75X TO 2X BASIC
1 Aaron Judge 50.00 120.00
2 Cody Bellinger
3 Yoan Moncada
4 Andrew Benintendi 15.00 40.00
5 Reynaldo Lopez 2.50 6.00
6 Dansby Swanson
7 Carson Fulmer 2.50 6.00
8 Ryon Healy 3.00 8.00
9 Mitch Haniger 4.00 10.00
10 Antonio Senzatela 2.50 6.00
11 Ian Happ 6.00 15.00
12 Trey Mancini
13 Jordan Montgomery 4.00 10.00
14 Bradley Zimmer 3.00 8.00
15 Hunter Renfroe 3.00 8.00
16 Jorge Bonifacio 2.50 6.00
17 Renato Nunez 5.00 12.00
18 Jacoby Jones 3.00 8.00
19 Alex Bregman 12.00 30.00
20 Josh Bell 6.00 15.00
21 Derek Fisher 3.00 8.00
22 Erik Gonzalez 2.50 6.00
23 Sam Travis 3.00 8.00
24 Franklin Barreto 2.50 6.00
25 Dinelson Lamet 2.50 6.00
26 Andrew Toles
27 Lewis Brinson
28 Orlando Arcia 4.00 10.00
29 Kyle Freeland 3.00 8.00
30 Jose De Leon 2.50 6.00
31 David Dahl 3.00 8.00
32 Yandy Diaz 5.00 12.00
33 Jorge Alfaro 3.00 8.00
34 Magneuris Sierra 2.50 6.00
35 Luke Weaver 5.00 12.00
36 Alex Reyes 5.00 12.00
37 Anthony Alford 2.50 6.00
38 Brock Stewart 2.50 6.00
39 Tyler Glasnow 8.00 20.00
40 Carson Kelly 3.00 8.00
41 Adam Frazier 2.50 6.00
42 Gavin Cecchini 2.50 6.00
43 Guillermo Heredia 8.00 20.00
44 German Marquez 4.00 10.00
45 Francis Martes 2.50 6.00
46 Matt Chapman 8.00 20.00
47 Hunter Dozier 2.50 6.00
48 Josh Hader 3.00 8.00
49 Aaron Judge 50.00 120.00
50 Cody Bellinger

2017 Panini Contenders USA Baseball 15U and Collegiate National Team Tickets

INSERTED IN '17 EEE PACKS
EXCHANGE DEADLINE 6/6/2019
*CRACKED ICE/24: .75X TO 2X BASIC
1 Seth Beer 8.00 20.00
2 Steven Gingery 6.00 15.00
3 Nick Madrigal 5.00 12.00
4 Jake McCarthy 3.00 8.00
5 Nick Meyer 3.00 8.00
6 Casey Mize 15.00 40.00
7 Konnor Pilkington 5.00 12.00
8 Dallas Woolfolk 2.50 6.00
9 Tyler Frank 3.00 8.00
10 Cadyn Grenier 3.00 8.00
11 Gianluca Dalatri 2.50 6.00
12 Braden Shewmake 8.00 20.00
13 Bryce Tucker
14 Andrew Vaughn 12.00 30.00
15 Steele Walker 3.00 8.00
16 Jeremy Eierman 5.00 12.00
17 Patrick Raby 4.00 10.00
18 Grant Koch 2.50 6.00
19 Travis Swaggerty 6.00 15.00
20 Tim Cate 3.00 8.00
21 Nick Sprengel 2.50 6.00
22 Johnny Aiello 3.00 8.00
23 Ryley Gilliam 2.50 6.00
24 Jon Olsen 2.50 6.00
25 Tyler Holton 2.50 6.00
26 Sean Wymer 2.50 6.00
27 Nelson Berkwich 2.50 6.00
28 Alek Boychuk 2.50 6.00
29 Michael Brooks 2.50 6.00
30 Dylan Crews 4.00 10.00
31 Pete Crow-Armstrong 10.00 25.00
32 Davis Diaz 2.50 6.00
33 Michael Flores 4.00 10.00
34 Lucas Gordon 3.00 8.00
35 Mac Guscette 3.00 8.00
36 Petey Halpin 6.00 15.00
37 Joshua Hartle 3.00 8.00
38 Rawley Hector 4.00 10.00
39 Jackson Miller 2.50 6.00
40 Robert Moore 2.50 6.00
41 Roc Riggio 2.50 6.00
42 Alejandro Rosario 5.00 12.00
43 Grant Taylor 4.00 10.00
44 Masyn Winn 2.50 6.00
45 Tanner Witt 3.00 8.00
46 Giuseppe Ferraro 3.00 8.00

2017 Panini Contenders USA Baseball 18U Tickets

INSERTED IN '17 EEE PACKS
EXCHANGE DEADLINE 6/6/2019
*CRACKED ICE/24: .75X TO 2X BASIC
1 Will Banfield 4.00 10.00
2 Raynel Delgado 5.00 12.00
3 Triston Casas 3.00 8.00
4 Carter Young 4.00 10.00
5 Cole Wilcox 3.00 8.00
6 Ryan Weathers 2.50 6.00
7 Brice Turang 8.00 20.00
8 Mason Denaburg 4.00 10.00
9 Brandon Dieter 2.50 6.00
10 Alek Thomas 4.00 10.00
11 JT Ginn 3.00 8.00
12 Nolan Gorman 12.00 30.00
13 Michael Siani 3.00 8.00
14 Kumar Rocker 6.00 15.00
15 Joseph Menefee 3.00 8.00
16 Ethan Hankins 12.00 30.00
17 Anthony Seigler 6.00 15.00
18 Landon Marceaux 2.50 6.00
19 Jarred Kelenic 30.00 80.00
20 Matthew Liberatore 3.00 8.00

2018 Panini Contenders Playoff Ticket Autographs

RANDOM INSERTS IN PACKS
PRINT RUNS B/WN 10-99 COPIES PER
NO PRICING ON QTY 10
3 Lucas Sims/49 4.00 10.00
4 Austin Hays/25 8.00 20.00
6 Gleyber Torres/10
8 Nicky Delmonico/99 3.00 8.00
10 Greg Allen/99 3.00 8.00
15 Kyle Farmer/49 4.00 10.00
16 Brian Anderson/99 4.00 10.00
17 Brandon Woodruff/99 10.00 25.00
21 Tyler Wade/99 4.00 10.00
22 Dustin Fowler/99 3.00 8.00
30 David Bote/99 12.00 30.00
32 Juan Soto/49 75.00 200.00

2018 Panini Contenders Season Ticket Autographs

INSERTED IN '18 CHRONICLES PACKS
1 Max Fried
2 Ozzie Albies 15.00 40.00
3 Lucas Sims 2.50 6.00
4 Austin Hays 4.00 10.00
5 Chance Sisco
6 Gleyber Torres 40.00 100.00
7 Rafael Devers
8 Nicky Delmonico 2.50 6.00
9 Francisco Mejia 3.00 8.00
10 Greg Allen 2.50 6.00
11 Ryan McMahon 10.00 25.00
12 J.D. Davis 3.00 8.00
13 Walker Buehler
14 Alex Verdugo 4.00 10.00
15 Kyle Farmer 2.50 6.00
16 Brian Anderson 3.00 8.00
17 Brandon Woodruff 8.00 20.00
18 Amed Rosario
19 Clint Frazier
20 Miguel Andujar 20.00 50.00
23 J.P. Crawford
24 Nick Williams
25 Rhys Hoskins
26 Jack Flaherty 10.00 25.00
27 Ronald Acuna Jr. 60.00 150.00
28 Willie Calhoun
29 Victor Robles
30 David Bote 10.00 25.00
32 Juan Soto 50.00 120.00

2018 Panini Contenders Season Tickets Autographs Cracked Ice

RANDOM INSERTS IN PACKS
STATED PRINT RUN 24 SER.#'d SETS
1 Max Fried 20.00 50.00
2 Ozzie Albies 40.00 100.00
3 Lucas Sims 5.00 12.00
4 Austin Hays 8.00 20.00
5 Chance Sisco 6.00 15.00
6 Gleyber Torres 75.00 200.00
7 Rafael Devers 12.00 30.00
8 Nicky Delmonico 5.00 12.00
9 Francisco Mejia 6.00 15.00
10 Greg Allen 5.00 12.00
11 Ryan McMahon 15.00 40.00
12 J.D. Davis 6.00 15.00
13 Walker Buehler 25.00 60.00
14 Alex Verdugo 8.00 20.00
15 Kyle Farmer 5.00 12.00
16 Brian Anderson 6.00 15.00
17 Brandon Woodruff 15.00 40.00
18 Amed Rosario 6.00 15.00
19 Clint Frazier 15.00 40.00
20 Miguel Andujar 50.00 210.00
21 Tyler Wade 6.00 15.00
22 Dustin Fowler 5.00 12.00
23 J.P. Crawford 5.00 12.00
24 Nick Williams 6.00 15.00
25 Rhys Hoskins 40.00 100.00
26 Jack Flaherty 20.00 50.00
27 Ronald Acuna Jr. 250.00 600.00
28 Willie Calhoun 8.00 20.00
29 Victor Robles 12.00 30.00
30 David Bote 40.00 100.00
31 Austin Meadows 12.00 30.00
32 Juan Soto 125.00 300.00

2018 Panini Contenders Season Tickets Autographs Red

RANDOM INSERTS IN PACKS
PRINT RUNS B/WN 25-199 COPIES PER
3 Lucas Sims/99 3.00 8.00
4 Austin Hays/49 6.00 15.00
6 Gleyber Torres/25 75.00 200.00
8 Nicky Delmonico/199 3.00 8.00
10 Greg Allen/199 3.00 8.00
15 Kyle Farmer/99 3.00 8.00
16 Brian Anderson/199 4.00 10.00
17 Brandon Woodruff/199 10.00 25.00
21 Tyler Wade/199 4.00 10.00
22 Dustin Fowler/199 3.00 8.00
30 David Bote/199 12.00 30.00
32 Juan Soto/99 60.00 150.00

2019 Panini Contenders Season Ticket Autographs

RANDOM INSERTS IN PACKS
EXCHANGE DEADLINE 2/21/2021
*GOLD/99: .5X TO 1.2X
*GOLD/50: .6X TO 1.5X
*RED/50: .6X TO 1.5X
*RED/25: .75X TO 2X
*CRACKED ICE/23: .75X TO 2X
1 Pete Alonso 40.00 100.00
2 Michael Kopech 8.00 20.00
3 Eloy Jimenez 10.00 25.00
4 Fernando Tatis Jr. EXCH 50.00 120.00
5 Yusei Kikuchi 4.00 10.00
6 Cole Tucker 4.00 10.00
8 Jeff McNeil 6.00 15.00
9 Chris Paddack 5.00 12.00
10 Kyle Tucker 6.00 15.00
13 Corbin Burnes 8.00 20.00
14 Jake Bauers 4.00 10.00
15 Jon Duplantier 2.50 6.00
16 Cal Quantrill 2.50 6.00
17 Vladimir Guerrero Jr. 40.00 100.00
18 Ramon Laureano 6.00 15.00
19 Brandon Lowe 6.00 15.00
20 Carter Kieboom 4.00 10.00
21 Nick Senzel 8.00 20.00
22 Michael Chavis 10.00 25.00
23 Danny Jansen 2.50 6.00
24 Luis Urias 4.00 10.00
25 Nathaniel Lowe 12.00 30.00
26 Keston Hiura 10.00 25.00
27 Austin Riley 8.00 20.00
28 Brendan Rodgers 4.00 10.00
29 Corbin Martin 4.00 10.00
30 Cavan Biggio 12.00 30.00
31 Mitch Keller 3.00 8.00

2020 Panini Contenders

AUTOGRAPHS RANDOM INSERTS IN PACKS
EXCHANGE DEADLINE 4/30/22
1 Anthony Rendon .30 .75
2 Max Muncy .25 .60
3 Francisco Lindor .30 .75
4 Elvis Andrus .25 .60
5 Mike Soroka .30 .75
6 Josh Bell .25 .60
7 Justin Verlander .30 .75
8 Chris Paddack .30 .75
9 Cavan Biggio .40 1.00
10 Eugenio Suarez .25 .60
11 Hyun-Jin Ryu .25 .60
12 Kyle Seager .20 .50
13 Matt Olson .30 .75
14 Yadier Molina .40 1.00
15 Xander Bogaerts .30 .75
16 Matt Boyd .20 .50
17 Gleyber Torres .60 1.50
18 Christian Yelich .40 1.00
19 Aaron Nola .25 .60
20 Trey Mancini .30 .75
21 Jonathan Villar .20 .50
22 George Springer .25 .60
23 Mike Clevinger .25 .60
24 Austin Meadows .30 .75
25 Bryce Harper .50 1.25
26 Lucas Giolito .25 .60
27 Joey Votto .30 .75
28 Charlie Morton .30 .75
29 Kyle Hendricks .30 .75
30 J.T. Realmuto .30 .75
31 Ozzie Albies .30 .75
32 Anthony Rizzo .40 1.00
33 John Means .30 .75
34 Shane Bieber .30 .75
35 Shohei Ohtani .50 1.25
36 Rafael Devers .40 1.00
37 Trevor Story .30 .75
38 Josh Hader .25 .60
39 Jose Berrios .25 .60
40 Jacob deGrom .60 1.50
41 Jorge Soler .30 .75
42 Josh Donaldson .25 .60
43 Manny Machado .30 .75
44 Mike Moustakas .25 .60
45 Juan Soto 1.00 2.50
46 Freddie Freeman .40 1.00
47 Joey Gallo .30 .75
48 Kevin Newman .30 .75
49 Fernando Tatis Jr. 1.50 4.00
50 Matt Chapman .30 .75
51 Buster Posey .40 1.00
52 Miguel Cabrera .30 .75
53 Nelson Cruz .30 .75
54 Aaron Judge .75 2.00
55 DJ LeMahieu .30 .75
56 Yoan Moncada .30 .75
57 Whit Merrifield .30 .75
58 Alex Bregman .30 .75
59 Kris Bryant .40 1.00
60 Nolan Arenado .50 1.25
61 Jack Flaherty .30 .75
62 Jose Altuve .25 .60
63 Lance Lynn .20 .50
64 Ronald Acuna Jr. 1.25 3.00
65 Eduardo Escobar .20 .50
66 Cody Bellinger .60 1.50
67 Rhys Hoskins .40 1.00
68 Mike Minor .20 .50
69 Bryan Reynolds .25 .60
70 Paul Goldschmidt .30 .75
71 Ketel Marte .25 .60
72 Gerrit Cole .50 1.25
73 Vladimir Guerrero Jr. .50 1.25
74 Marco Gonzales .20 .50
75 Zack Greinke .30 .75
76 Tyler Glasnow .30 .75
77 Brandon Crawford .25 .60
78 J.D. Martinez .30 .75
79 Trea Turner .25 .60
80 Javier Baez .40 1.00
81 Eduardo Rodriguez .20 .50
82 Marcus Semien .30 .75
83 Jorge Polanco .25 .60
84 Tim Anderson .30 .75
85 Luis Castillo .25 .60
86 Mookie Betts .60 1.50
87 David Fletcher .30 .75
88 Clayton Kershaw .50 1.25
89 Pete Alonso .75 2.00
90 Sandy Alcantara .20 .50
91 Charlie Blackmon .30 .75
92 Brian Anderson .20 .50
93 Blake Snell .25 .60
94 Mike Trout 1.50 4.00
95 Albert Pujols .40 1.00
96 Jose Ramirez .25 .60
97 Hunter Dozier .20 .50
98 Eloy Jimenez .60 1.50
99 Max Scherzer .30 .75
100 Jeff McNeil .25 .60
101 A.J. Puk AU RC EXCH 8.00 20.00
102 Zac Gallen AU RC 6.00 15.00
103 Yoshitomo Tsutsugo AU RC 6.00 15.00
104 Aaron Civale AU RC 5.00 12.00
105 Yordan Alvarez AU RC 20.00 50.00
106 Shun Yamaguchi AU RC 3.00 8.00
107 Adbert Alzolay AU RC 3.00 8.00
108 Adrian Morejon AU RC 2.50 6.00
109 Aristides Aquino AU RC 10.00 25.00
110 Bo Bichette AU RC 25.00 60.00
111 Shogo Akiyama AU RC 6.00 15.00
112 Sheldon Neuse AU RC 3.00 8.00
113 Brendan McKay AU RC EXCG 4.00 10.00
114 Brusdar Graterol AU RC 4.00 10.00
115 Dustin May AU RC 8.00 20.00
116 Sean Murphy AU RC 4.00 10.00
117 Nico Hoerner AU RC 10.00 25.00
118 Nick Solak AU RC 5.00 12.00
119 Luis Robert AU RC 40.00 100.00
120 Kyle Lewis AU RC 25.00 60.00
121 Kwang-Hyun Kim AU RC 5.00 12.00
123 Isan Diaz AU RC 4.00 10.00
124 Dylan Cease AU RC EXCH
125 Gavin Lux AU RC 12.00 30.00
126 Brock Burke AU RC 2.50 6.00
127 Randy Arozarena AU RC 25.00 60.00
129 Edwin Rios AU RC 6.00 15.00
130 Jake Rogers AU RC 2.50 6.00
131 Tony Gonsolin AU RC 10.00 25.00
132 Trent Grisham AU RC 10.00 25.00
134 Deivy Grullon AU RC 2.50 6.00
135 Jose Urquidy AU RC 3.00 8.00
136 Andres Munoz AU RC 4.00 10.00
137 Yonathan Daza AU RC 3.00 8.00
138 Bobby Bradley AU RC 2.50 6.00
139 Jonathan Hernandez AU RC 2.50 6.00
140 Matt Thaiss AU RC 3.00 8.00
141 Tres Barrera AU RC 5.00 12.00
142 Abraham Toro AU RC 3.00 8.00
143 Ronald Bolanos AU RC 2.50 6.00
145 T.J. Zeuch AU RC 2.50 6.00
146 Logan Webb AU RC 4.00 10.00
147 Domingo Leyba AU RC 3.00 8.00
148 Rico Garcia AU RC 4.00 10.00
149 Mauricio Dubon AU RC 3.00 8.00
150 Willi Castro AU RC 4.00 10.00
151 Anthony Kay AU RC 2.50 6.00
152 Michel Baez AU RC 2.50 6.00
153 Danny Mendick AU RC 3.00 8.00
154 Sam Hilliard AU RC 4.00 10.00
155 Lewis Thorpe AU RC 2.50 6.00
156 Justin Dunn AU RC 3.00 8.00
157 Logan Allen AU RC 2.50 6.00
158 Michael King AU RC 4.00 10.00
159 Bryan Abreu AU RC 2.50 6.00
160 Travis Demeritte AU RC 4.00 10.00
161 Jake Fraley AU RC 3.00 8.00
162 Jaylin Davis AU RC 4.00 10.00
163 Yu Chang AU RC 4.00 10.00

165 Patrick Sandoval AU RC 4.00 10.00
166 Zack Collins AU RC 3.00 8.00
167 Jordan Yamamoto AU RC 2.50 6.00

2020 Panini Contenders Cracked Ice Ticket

*CRCKD ICE: 3X TO 8X BASIC
*CRCKD ICE AU: .8X TO 2X BASIC
RANDOM INSERTS IN PACKS
STATED PRINT RUN 23 SER.#'d SETS
EXCHANGE DEADLINE 4/30/22
17 Gleyber Torres 8.00 20.00
45 Juan Soto 12.00 30.00
49 Fernando Tatis Jr. 25.00 60.00
86 Mookie Betts 12.00 30.00
88 Clayton Kershaw 10.00 25.00
98 Eloy Jimenez 8.00 20.00
103 Yoshitomo Tsutsugo AU 15.00 40.00
105 Yordan Alvarez AU 50.00 120.00
109 Aristides Aquino AU 20.00 50.00
110 Bo Bichette AU 60.00 150.00
111 Shogo Akiyama AU 15.00 40.00
113 Brendan McKay AU EXCH 12.00 30.00
119 Luis Robert AU 125.00 300.00
120 Kyle Lewis AU 100.00 250.00
121 Kwang-Hyun Kim AU 25.00 60.00
124 Dylan Cease AU EXCH 12.00 30.00
149 Mauricio Dubon AU 10.00 25.00

2020 Panini Contenders Draft Ticket Blue

*DRAFT BLUE: 1.2X TO 3X BASIC
*DRAFT BLUE AU: .5X TO 1.2X BASIC
RANDOM INSERTS IN PACKS
1-100 PRINT RUN 149 SER.#'d SETS
101-167 PRINT RUN B/TW 15-99 COPIES PER
NO PRICING ON QTY 15
EXCHANGE DEADLINE 4/30/22
17 Gleyber Torres 3.00 8.00
86 Mookie Betts 5.00 12.00
88 Clayton Kershaw 4.00 10.00
98 Eloy Jimenez 3.00 8.00
110 Bo Bichette AU 40.00 100.00
119 Luis Robert AU 75.00 200.00
122 Jesus Luzardo AU EXCH

2020 Panini Contenders Draft Ticket Purple

*DRAFT PRPL: 1.5X TO 4X BASIC
RANDOM INSERTS IN PACKS
17 Gleyber Torres 4.00 10.00
86 Mookie Betts 6.00 15.00
88 Clayton Kershaw 5.00 12.00
98 Eloy Jimenez 4.00 10.00

2020 Panini Contenders Draft Ticket Red

*DRAFT RED: 1.5X TO 4X BASIC
*DRAFT RED AU: .5X TO 1.2X BASIC
RANDOM INSERTS IN PACKS
1-100 PRINT RUN 99 SER.#'d SETS
101-167 PRINT RUN B/TW 15-75 COPIES PER
NO PRICING ON QTY 15
EXCHANGE DEADLINE 4/30/22
17 Gleyber Torres 4.00 10.00
86 Mookie Betts 6.00 15.00
88 Clayton Kershaw 5.00 12.00
98 Eloy Jimenez 4.00 10.00
110 Bo Bichette AU 40.00 100.00
119 Luis Robert AU 75.00 200.00

2020 Panini Contenders Variations

*VAR.: .4X TO 1X BASIC
RANDOM INSERTS IN PACKS
EXCHANGE DEADLINE 4/30/22
101 A.J. Puk AU EXCH 8.00 20.00
102 Zac Gallen AU 6.00 15.00
105 Yordan Alvarez AU 12.00 30.00
109 Aristides Aquino AU 10.00 25.00
110 Bo Bichette AU 25.00 60.00
111 Shogo Akiyama AU 6.00 15.00
117 Nico Hoerner AU 10.00 25.00
119 Luis Robert AU 40.00 100.00
120 Kyle Lewis AU 25.00 60.00
121 Kwang-Hyun Kim AU 5.00 12.00
125 Gavin Lux AU 12.00 30.00
126 Trent Grisham AU 10.00 25.00
127 Randy Arozarena AU 20.00 50.00
129 Edwin Rios AU 6.00 15.00
132 Trent Grisham AU 10.00 25.00

2020 Panini Contenders Variations Cracked Ice Ticket

*VAR.CRCKD ICE: .8X TO 2X BASIC
RANDOM INSERTS IN PACKS
STATED PRINT RUN 23 SER.#'d SETS
EXCHANGE DEADLINE 4/30/22
103 Yoshitomo Tsutsugo AU 15.00 40.00
105 Yordan Alvarez AU 50.00 120.00
109 Aristides Aquino AU 20.00 50.00
110 Bo Bichette AU 60.00 150.00
111 Shogo Akiyama AU 15.00 40.00
113 Brendan McKay AU EXCH 12.00 30.00
119 Luis Robert AU 125.00 300.00
120 Kyle Lewis AU 100.00 250.00
121 Kwang-Hyun Kim AU 25.00 60.00
124 Dylan Cease AU EXCH 12.00 30.00
149 Mauricio Dubon AU 10.00 25.00

2020 Panini Contenders Variations Draft Ticket Blue

*VAR.DRAFT BLUE: .5X TO 1.2X BASIC
RANDOM INSERTS IN PACKS
PRINT RUN B/TW 35-99 COPIES PER
EXCHANGE DEADLINE 4/30/22
110 Bo Bichette AU 40.00 100.00
119 Luis Robert AU 75.00 200.00

2020 Panini Contenders Variations Draft Ticket Red

*VAR.DRAFT RED: .5X TO 1.2X BASIC
RANDOM INSERTS IN PACKS
STATED PRINT RUN 75 SER.#'d SETS
EXCHANGE DEADLINE 4/30/22
110 Bo Bichette AU 40.00 100.00
119 Luis Robert AU 75.00 200.00

2020 Panini Contenders Contenders Autographs

RANDOM INSERTS IN PACKS
EXCHANGE DEADLINE 4/30/22
*CRCKD ICE/23: .8X TO 2X BASIC
1 Miguel Amaya 2.50 6.00
2 Brandon Lowe 3.00 8.00
3 Jordan Romano 4.00 10.00
4 Colton Welker 2.50 6.00
5 Brennen Davis 5.00 12.00
6 Cionel Perez 2.50 6.00
7 Matthew Thompson 3.00 8.00
8 Evan White 6.00 15.00
9 Pablo Reyes 2.50 6.00
10 Malfrin Sosa 3.00 8.00
11 Kameron Misner 4.00 10.00
12 Joey Cantillo 2.50 6.00
13 Ryne Nelson 3.00 8.00
14 Seth Johnson 2.50 6.00
15 Drey Jameson 2.50 6.00
16 Nick Neidert 2.50 6.00
17 Sammy Siani 2.50 6.00
18 Adonis Rosa 4.00 10.00
19 Nick Maton 2.50 6.00
20 Je'Von Ward 2.50 6.00
21 Matt Mervis 2.50 6.00
22 Mason McCoy 2.50 6.00
23 Josh Fleming 3.00 8.00
24 Junior Martina 2.50 6.00
25 Victor Bericoto 5.00 12.00
26 Ronny Mauricio 6.00 15.00
27 Shay Whitcomb 3.00 8.00
28 Shed Long Jr. 3.00 8.00
29 Wander Franco 25.00 60.00
30 Bryce Elder 3.00 8.00
31 Brandon Williamson 4.00 10.00
32 Antoine Kelly 5.00 12.00
33 Austin Shenton 2.50 6.00
34 D'Shawn Knowles 3.00 8.00
35 Eddy Diaz 2.50 6.00
36 Evan Fitterer 5.00 12.00
37 Gilberto Jimenez 10.00 25.00
38 Ismael Mena 4.00 10.00
39 Austin Allen 3.00 8.00
40 Isaac Galloway 2.50 6.00
41 Yoan Lopez 2.50 6.00
42 A.J. Vukovich 5.00 12.00
43 Travis Blankenhorn 5.00 12.00
44 Sam Hentges 2.50 6.00
45 Chad Sobotka 2.50 6.00

2020 Panini Contenders Draft Pick Ticket Autographs

RANDOM INSERTS IN PACKS
EXCHANGE DEADLINE 4/30/22
1 Austin Martin 12.00 30.00
2 Spencer Torkelson 60.00 150.00
3 Emerson Hancock 10.00 25.00
4 Zac Veen 10.00 25.00
5 Asa Lacy 15.00 40.00
6 Nick Gonzales 15.00 40.00
7 Garrett Mitchell 15.00 40.00
8 Mick Abel 6.00 15.00
9 Austin Hendrick 10.00 25.00
10 Jared Kelley 6.00 15.00
11 Garrett Crochet 15.00 40.00
12 Casey Martin 10.00 25.00
13 Jordan Walker 12.00 30.00
14 Nick Bitsko 4.00 10.00
15 Ed Howard 15.00 40.00
16 Reid Detmers 6.00 15.00
18 Cade Cavalli 4.00 10.00
19 Daniel Cabrera 8.00 20.00
20 Max Meyer 10.00 25.00

2020 Panini Contenders Draft Pick Ticket Autographs Cracked Ice

*CRCKD ICE: .8X TO 2X BASIC
RANDOM INSERTS IN PACKS
STATED PRINT RUN 23 SER.#'d SETS
EXCHANGE DEADLINE 4/30/22
1 Austin Martin 50.00 120.00
6 Nick Gonzales 40.00 100.00
8 Mick Abel 25.00 60.00
9 Austin Hendrick 25.00 60.00

2020 Panini Contenders Draft Pick Ticket Autographs Draft Blue

*DRAFT BLUE: .5X TO 1.2X BASIC
RANDOM INSERTS IN PACKS
PRINT RUN B/TW 49-99 COPIES PER
EXCHANGE DEADLINE 4/30/22
1 Austin Martin/49 30.00 80.00

2020 Panini Contenders Draft Pick Ticket Autographs Draft Red

*DRAFT RED: .5X TO 1.2X BASIC
RANDOM INSERTS IN PACKS
STATED PRINT RUN 75 SER.#'d SETS
EXCHANGE DEADLINE 4/30/22
1 Austin Martin 30.00 80.00
6 Nick Gonzales 25.00 60.00
8 Mick Abel 15.00 40.00

2020 Panini Contenders Draft Pick Ticket Autographs 2

RANDOM INSERTS IN PACKS
EXCHANGE DEADLINE 4/30/22
*DRAFT BLUE/99: .5X TO 1.2X BASIC
*DRAFT RED/75: .5X TO 1.2X BASIC
1 Patrick Bailey 6.00 15.00
2 Heston Kjerstad 15.00 40.00
4 Pete Crow-Armstrong 8.00 20.00
5 Tyler Soderstrom 10.00 25.00
6 Austin Wells 10.00 25.00
7 Jared Shuster 8.00 20.00
8 Carmen Mlodzinski 3.00 8.00
9 Tanner Burns 4.00 10.00
10 Bobby Miller 6.00 15.00
11 Nick Loftin 5.00 12.00
13 Alika Williams 3.00 8.00
14 Slade Cecconi 3.00 8.00
15 Jordan Westburg 6.00 15.00
16 Aaron Sabato 12.00 30.00
17 Bryce Jarvis 3.00 8.00
18 Dillon Dingler 6.00 15.00
19 Drew Romo 6.00 15.00
20 Justin Lange 2.50 6.00
21 Justin Foscue 6.00 15.00
22 Carson Tucker 6.00 15.00

2020 Panini Contenders Draft Pick Ticket Autographs 2 Cracked Ice

*CRCKD ICE: .8X TO 2X BASIC
RANDOM INSERTS IN PACKS
STATED PRINT RUN 23 SER.#'d SETS
EXCHANGE DEADLINE 4/30/22
4 Pete Crow-Armstrong 40.00 100.00
11 Nick Loftin 20.00 50.00

2020 Panini Contenders First Rounders

RANDOM INSERTS IN PACKS
*GOLD: .8X TO 2X BASIC
1 Garrett Mitchell 2.50 6.00
2 Robert Hassell 2.50 6.00
3 Pete Crow-Armstrong 1.00 2.50
4 Spencer Torkelson 3.00 8.00
5 Austin Martin 1.00 2.50
6 Asa Lacy 2.00 5.00
7 Nick Gonzales 1.50 4.00
8 Zac Veen 1.50 4.00
9 Emerson Hancock 1.25 3.00
10 Reid Detmers .75 2.00
11 Max Meyer 1.25 3.00
12 Heston Kjerstad 2.50 6.00
13 Patrick Bailey 1.00 2.50
14 Tyler Soderstrom 1.25 3.00
15 Austin Hendrick 3.00 8.00

2020 Panini Contenders First Rounders Cracked Ice

*CRCKD ICE: 1.5X TO 4X BASIC
RANDOM INSERTS IN PACKS
STATED PRINT RUN 23 SER.#'d SETS
8 Zac Veen 10.00 25.00

2020 Panini Contenders Future Stars

RANDOM INSERTS IN PACKS
1 Wander Franco 2.50 6.00
2 Jo Adell 1.25 3.00
3 Casey Mize 1.00 2.50
4 Nate Pearson 1.00 2.50
5 Drew Waters .75 2.00
6 Hunter Greene .50 1.25
7 Nick Madrigal 1.25 3.00
8 Andrew Vaughn 1.25 3.00
9 Bobby Dalbec 2.00 5.00
10 Sixto Sanchez 1.00 2.50
11 Tyler Freeman .40 1.00
12 Evan White .75 2.00
13 Nolan Jones .50 1.25
14 Alex Kirilloff .60 1.50
15 Jasson Dominguez 8.00 20.00
16 MacKenzie Gore .60 1.50
17 Dylan Carlson 1.25 3.00
18 Brady Singer 1.50 4.00
19 Ryan Mountcastle 1.50 4.00
20 Joey Bart 1.00 2.50

2020 Panini Contenders Future Stars Cracked Ice

*CRCKD ICE: 1.5X TO 4X BASIC
RANDOM INSERTS IN PACKS
STATED PRINT RUN 23 SER.#'d SETS
5 Drew Waters 10.00 25.00
16 MacKenzie Gore 6.00 15.00

2020 Panini Contenders Future Stars Gold

*GOLD: .8X TO 2X BASIC
RANDOM INSERTS IN PACKS
STATED PRINT RUN 99 SER.#'d SETS
16 MacKenzie Gore 3.00 8.00

2020 Panini Contenders Game Day

RANDOM INSERTS IN PACKS
*GOLD: .8X TO 2X BASIC
1 Gleyber Torres 1.00 2.50
2 Alex Bregman .50 1.25
3 Javier Baez .60 1.50
4 Shohei Ohtani .75 2.00
5 Francisco Lindor .50 1.25
6 Justin Verlander .50 1.25
7 Bryce Harper .75 2.00
8 Manny Machado .50 1.25
9 Nolan Arenado .75 2.00
10 Jacob deGrom 1.00 2.50

2020 Panini Contenders Game Day Cracked Ice

*CRCKD ICE: 1.5X TO 4X BASIC
RANDOM INSERTS IN PACKS
STATED PRINT RUN 23 SER.#'d SETS
1 Gleyber Torres 12.00 30.00

2020 Panini Contenders Gold Rush

RANDOM INSERTS IN PACKS
1 Mike Trout 60.00 150.00
2 Pete Alonso 25.00 60.00
3 Yordan Alvarez 30.00 80.00
4 Juan Soto 40.00 100.00

2020 Panini Contenders Legacy

RANDOM INSERTS IN PACKS
1 Ken Griffey Jr. 1.00 2.50
2 Greg Maddux .60 1.50
3 Frank Thomas 1.00 2.50
4 Jim Thome .40 1.00
5 Cal Ripken 1.50 4.00
6 Reggie Jackson .40 1.00
7 Nolan Ryan 1.50 4.00
8 Randy Johnson 1.00 2.50
9 Mark McGwire .75 2.00
10 Pedro Martinez .40 1.00

2020 Panini Contenders Legacy Cracked Ice

*CRCKD ICE: 1.5X TO 4X BASIC
RANDOM INSERTS IN PACKS
STATED PRINT RUN 23 SER.#'d SETS
1 Ken Griffey Jr. 25.00 60.00
3 Frank Thomas 10.00 25.00
7 Nolan Ryan 12.00 30.00
8 Randy Johnson 12.00 30.00
9 Mark McGwire 10.00 25.00

2020 Panini Contenders Legacy Gold

*GOLD: .8X TO 2X BASIC
RANDOM INSERTS IN PACKS
STATED PRINT RUN 99 SER.#'d SETS
3 Frank Thomas 5.00 12.00
7 Nolan Ryan 6.00 15.00
8 Randy Johnson 6.00 15.00

2020 Panini Contenders Legendary

RANDOM INSERTS IN PACKS
1 Sandy Koufax 1.00 2.50
2 Ichiro .60 1.50
3 Tony Gwynn .50 1.25
4 Alex Rodriguez .60 1.50
5 George Brett 1.00 2.50
6 Vladimir Guerrero .40 1.00
7 Ryne Sandberg 1.00 2.50
8 Rickey Henderson .50 1.25

2020 Panini Contenders Legendary Cracked Ice

*CRCKD ICE: 1.5X TO 4X BASIC
RANDOM INSERTS IN PACKS
STATED PRINT RUN 23 SER.#'d SETS
3 Tony Gwynn 15.00 40.00
4 Alex Rodriguez 15.00 40.00
8 Rickey Henderson 12.00 30.00

2020 Panini Contenders Legendary Gold

*GOLD: .8X TO 2X BASIC
RANDOM INSERTS IN PACKS
STATED PRINT RUN 99 SER.#'d SETS
4 Alex Rodriguez 3.00 8.00
8 Rickey Henderson 4.00 10.00

2020 Panini Contenders Potential

RANDOM INSERTS IN PACKS
1 Luis Robert 2.50 6.00
2 Gilberto Jimenez 1.50 4.00
3 Roberto Campos 1.50 4.00
4 Erick Pena 1.00 2.50
5 Taylor Trammell .50 1.25
6 Logan Gilbert .40 1.00
7 CJ Abrams 1.00 2.50
8 Nate Pearson 1.00 2.50
9 Cristian Pache 1.00 2.50
10 Matthew Liberatore .40 1.00
11 Jarred Kelenic 1.50 4.00
12 Oscar Colas 1.00 2.50

2020 Panini Contenders Potential Cracked Ice

*CRCKD ICE: 1.5X TO 4X BASIC
RANDOM INSERTS IN PACKS
STATED PRINT RUN 23 SER.#'d SETS
1 Luis Robert 25.00 60.00
9 Cristian Pache 6.00 23.00
12 Oscar Colas 12.00 30.00

2020 Panini Contenders Potential Gold

*GOLD: .8X TO 2X BASIC
RANDOM INSERTS IN PACKS
STATED PRINT RUN 99 SER.#'d SETS
1 Luis Robert 12.00 30.00
12 Oscar Colas 6.00 15.00

2020 Panini Contenders Prospect Ticket Autographs

RANDOM INSERTS IN PACKS
EXCHANGE DEADLINE 4/30/22
1 Adley Rutschman 15.00 40.00
2 Evan White 5.00 12.00
3 Cristian Pache 10.00 25.00
4 Nick Madrigal 10.00 25.00
5 Hunter Greene 8.00 20.00

2020 Panini Contenders Prospect Ticket Autographs Cracked Ice

*CRCKD ICE: .8X TO 2X BASIC
RANDOM INSERTS IN PACKS
STATED PRINT RUN 23 SER.#'d SETS
EXCHANGE DEADLINE 4/30/22
1 Adley Rutschman 40.00 100.00

2020 Panini Contenders Prospect Ticket Autographs Draft Blue

*DRAFT BLUE: .5X TO 1.2X BASIC
RANDOM INSERTS IN PACKS
PRINT RUN B/TW 35-99 COPIES PER
EXCHANGE DEADLINE 4/30/22
1 Adley Rutschman/35 25.00 60.00

2020 Panini Contenders Prospect Ticket Autographs Draft Red

*DRAFT RED/75: .5X TO 1.2X BASIC
*DRAFT RED/25: .8X TO 2X BASIC
RANDOM INSERTS IN PACKS
PRINT RUN B/TW 25-75 COPIES PER
EXCHANGE DEADLINE 4/30/22
1 Adley Rutschman/25 40.00 100.00

2020 Panini Contenders Prospect Ticket Autographs 2

RANDOM INSERTS IN PACKS
EXCHANGE DEADLINE 4/30/22
*DRAFT BLUE/99: .5X TO 1.2X BASIC
*DRAFT RED/75: .5X TO 1.2X BASIC
*CRCKD ICE/23: .8X TO 2X BASIC
1 Jeremy Arocho 2.50 6.00
2 Malcom Nunez 5.00 12.00
3 Grant McCray 4.00 10.00
4 Norge Vera 3.00 8.00
5 Vaughn Grissom 4.00 10.00
6 Yiddi Cappe 5.00 12.00
7 Roberto Campos 15.00 40.00
8 Victor Vodnik 5.00 12.00
9 Yoelqui Cespedes 25.00 60.00
10 Oscar Colas 15.00 40.00

2020 Panini Contenders Retro '98 Rookie Ticket Autographs

RANDOM INSERTS IN PACKS
EXCHANGE DEADLINE 4/30/22
*DRAFT BLUE/30-99: .5X TO 1.2X BASIC
*DRAFT RED/75: .5X TO 1.2X BASIC
*CRCKD ICE/23: .8X TO 2X BASIC
1 Yordan Alvarez 15.00 40.00
2 Gavin Lux 20.00 50.00
3 A.J. Puk EXCH 8.00 20.00
4 Kyle Lewis 30.00 80.00
5 Nico Hoerner 8.00 20.00
6 Luis Robert EXCH 50.00 120.00
7 Sheldon Neuse 3.00 8.00
8 Zac Gallen 5.00 12.00
9 Adbert Alzolay 3.00 8.00
10 Isan Diaz 4.00 10.00
11 Matt Thaiss 3.00 8.00
12 Jordan Yamamoto 2.50 6.00
13 Lewis Thorpe 2.50 6.00
14 Sam Hilliard 4.00 10.00
15 Tony Gonsolin 5.00 12.00

2020 Panini Contenders Retro '99 Rookie Ticket Autographs

RANDOM INSERTS IN PACKS
EXCHANGE DEADLINE 4/30/22
1 Sean Murphy 4.00 10.00
2 Aristides Aquino 8.00 20.00
3 Shogo Akiyama 4.00 10.00
4 Yu Chang 4.00 10.00
5 Shun Yamaguchi 3.00 8.00
6 Jesus Luzardo EXCH 5.00 12.00
7 Dylan Cease 4.00 10.00
8 Brendan McKay EXCH 4.00 10.00
9 Yoshitomo Tsutsugo 8.00 20.00
10 Abraham Toro 3.00 8.00

2020 Panini Contenders Retro '99 Rookie Ticket Autographs Cracked Ice

*CRCKD ICE: .8X TO 2X BASIC
RANDOM INSERTS IN PACKS
STATED PRINT RUN 23 SER.#'d SETS
EXCHANGE DEADLINE 4/30/22
3 Shogo Akiyama 12.00 30.00
9 Yoshitomo Tsutsugo 30.00 80.00

2020 Panini Contenders Retro '99 Rookie Ticket Autographs Draft Blue

3 Shogo Akiyama/49 8.00 20.00
9 Yoshitomo Tsutsugo/33 10.00 25.00

2020 Panini Contenders Retro '99 Rookie Ticket Autographs Draft Red

*DRAFT RED: .5X TO 1.2X BASIC
RANDOM INSERTS IN PACKS
STATED PRINT RUN 75 SER.#'d SETS
EXCHANGE DEADLINE 4/30/22
3 Shogo Akiyama 8.00 20.00
9 Yoshitomo Tsutsugo 10.00 25.00

2020 Panini Contenders Rookie of the Year Contenders Autographs

RANDOM INSERTS IN PACKS
EXCHANGE DEADLINE 4/30/22
1 A.J. Puk 4.00 10.00
3 Aristides Aquino 6.00 15.00
4 Bo Bichette
5 Brendan McKay 4.00 10.00
6 Brusdar Graterol 4.00 10.00
7 Dylan Cease 4.00 10.00
8 Gavin Lux 12.00 30.00
9 Isan Diaz 4.00 10.00
10 Jesus Luzardo 5.00 12.00
11 Kwang-Hyun Kim
12 Kyle Lewis
13 Luis Robert
14 Nico Hoerner 10.00 25.00
15 Sean Murphy 6.00 15.00
16 Shogo Akiyama 4.00 10.00
17 Shun Yamaguchi 3.00 8.00
18 Yordan Alvarez 25.00 60.00
19 Yoshitomo Tsutsugo 6.00 15.00
20 Zac Gallen 5.00 12.00

2020 Panini Contenders Rookie of the Year Contenders Autographs Cracked Ice

*CRCKD ICE: .8X TO 2X BASIC
RANDOM INSERTS IN PACKS
STATED PRINT RUN 23 SER.#'d SETS
EXCHANGE DEADLINE 4/30/22
11 Kwang-Hyun Kim 30.00 80.00
13 Luis Robert 150.00 400.00

2020 Panini Contenders Rookie Roundup Autographs

RANDOM INSERTS IN PACKS
EXCHANGE DEADLINE 4/30/22
3 Tim Lopes 3.00 8.00
4 Dom Nunez 3.00 8.00
5 Kean Wong 4.00 10.00
6 Zach Green 2.50 6.00
7 Jacob Waguespack 3.00 8.00
8 Mike Brosseau 5.00 12.00
9 Seth Brown 2.50 6.00
10 Jorge Alcala 2.50 6.00
11 Ryan McBroom 6.00 15.00
13 Kevin Ginkel 2.50 6.00
14 Kyle Garlick 4.00 10.00
15 LaMonte Wade Jr. 4.00 10.00
16 Dillon Tate 2.50 6.00
17 Robel Garcia 2.50 6.00
18 Scott Heineman 2.50 6.00

2020 Panini Contenders Rookie Roundup Autographs Cracked Ice

*CRCKD ICE: .8X TO 2X BASIC
RANDOM INSERTS IN PACKS
STATED PRINT RUN 23 SER.#'d SETS
EXCHANGE DEADLINE 4/30/22

2020 Panini Contenders Round Numbers Dual Autographs

RANDOM INSERTS IN PACKS
EXCHANGE DEADLINE 4/30/22
*CRCKD ICE/23: .6X TO 1.5X BASIC
1 A.Martin/S.Torkelson 60.00 150.00
4 P.Bailey/T.Soderstrom
11 S.Beer/T.Casas 10.00 25.00
14 B.Baty/J.Jung 15.00 40.00

2020 Panini Contenders Up and Coming

RANDOM INSERTS IN PACKS
*GOLD: .8X TO 2X BASIC
*CRCKD ICE: 1.5X TO 4X BASIC
1 Dylan Carlson 1.25 3.00
2 Luis Matos .50 1.25
3 Brailyn Marquez .75 2.00
4 Kristian Robinson 1.00 2.50
5 Tarik Skubal 1.50 4.00
6 Julio Rodriguez 2.00 5.00
7 Andrew Vaughn 1.25 3.00
8 Malcom Nunez .60 1.50
9 Luis V. Garcia 1.25 3.00
10 Ji-Hwan Bae .50 1.25

2020 Panini Contenders Winning Tickets

RANDOM INSERTS IN PACKS
1 Jasson Dominguez 5.00 12.00
2 Bo Bichette 2.50 6.00
3 Yordan Alvarez 3.00 8.00
4 Pete Alonso 1.25 3.00
5 Wander Franco 3.00 8.00
6 Vladimir Guerrero Jr. .75 2.00
7 Mike Trout 2.50 6.00
8 Javier Baez .60 1.50
9 Cody Bellinger 1.00 2.50
10 Christian Yelich .60 1.50
11 Ronald Acuna Jr. 2.00 5.00
12 Juan Soto 1.50 4.00
13 Rafael Devers .60 1.50
14 Aaron Judge 1.25 3.00
15 Fernando Tatis Jr. 2.50 6.00

2020 Panini Contenders Winning Tickets Cracked Ice

*CRCKD ICE: 1.5X TO 4X BASIC
RANDOM INSERTS IN PACKS
STATED PRINT RUN 23 SER.#'d SETS
1 Jasson Dominguez 40.00 100.00
2 Bo Bichette 20.00 50.00
11 Ronald Acuna Jr. 12.00 30.00
12 Juan Soto 10.00 25.00
15 Fernando Tatis Jr. 25.00 60.00

2020 Panini Contenders Winning Tickets Gold

*GOLD: .8X TO 2X BASIC
RANDOM INSERTS IN PACKS
STATED PRINT RUN 99 SER.#'d SETS
1 Jasson Dominguez 20.00 50.00
11 Ronald Acuna Jr. 6.00 15.00
12 Juan Soto 5.00 12.00

2017 Panini Contenders Draft Picks

ALL VERSIONS EQUALLY PRICED
EXCHANGE DEADLINE 03/06/2019
1A A.J. Puk .30 .75
Blue jersey
1B A.J. Puk .30 .75
White jersey
2A Barry Larkin .25 .60
Batting
2B Barry Larkin .25 .60
Running
3A Bo Jackson .30 .75
Black and white photo
3B Bo Jackson .30 .75
Color photo
4A Cal Quantrill .20 .50
Glove down
4B Cal Quantrill .20 .50
Glove up
5A Corey Ray .25 .60
Holding bat
5B Corey Ray .25 .60
Running
6A Craig Biggio .25 .60
Pirates jersey
6B Craig Biggio .25 .60
Seton Hall jersey
7A Dave Winfield .25 .60
Bierman Field on card back
7B Dave Winfield .25 .60
Siebert Field on card back
8A Frank Thomas .30 .75
Black and white photo
8B Frank Thomas .30 .75
Color photo
9A Fred Lynn .20 .50
Hat
9B Fred Lynn .20 .50
Helmet
10A John Elway .50 1.25
10B John Elway .50 1.25
11A Justin Dunn .20 .50
Number showing
11B Justin Dunn .20 .50
No number
12A Kyle Lewis .40 1.00
12B Kyle Lewis .40 1.00
13A Mark McGwire .50 1.25
13B Mark McGwire .50 1.25
14A Matt Thaiss .20 .50
Gray jersey
14B Matt Thaiss .20 .50
White jersey
15A Nick Senzel .60 1.50
15B Nick Senzel .60 1.50
16A Ozzie Smith .40 1.00
16B Ozzie Smith .40 1.00
17A Brent Rooker .50 1.25
17B Brent Rooker .50 1.25
18A Paul Molitor .30 .75
Bierman Field on card back
18B Paul Molitor .30 .75
Siebert Field on card back
19A Rafael Palmeiro .25 .60
Maroon jersey
19B Rafael Palmeiro .25 .60
White jersey
20A Reggie Jackson .25 .60
Full bat
20B Reggie Jackson .25 .60
Partial bat
21A Roger Clemens .40 1.00
21B Roger Clemens .40 1.00
22A T.J. Zeuch .20 .50
Ball showing
22B T.J. Zeuch .20 .50
Ball in hand
23A Tony Gwynn .30 .75
Zoomed in
23B Tony Gwynn .30 .75
Zoomed out
24A Will Clark .25 .60
Batting gloves on both hands
24B Will Clark .25 .60
Batting gloves on one hand
25A Zack Collins .25 .60
Orange jersey
25B Zack Collins .25 .60
White jersey
27A Brendan McKay AU 12.00 30.00
27B Brendan McKay AU 12.00 30.00
28A Royce Lewis AU 25.00 60.00
28B Royce Lewis AU 25.00 60.00
29A Austin Beck AU 12.00 30.00
29B Austin Beck AU 12.00 30.00
30A Kendall AU Glass 6.00 15.00
30B Kendall AU No Glass 6.00 15.00
31A Faedo AU 5.00 12.00
31B Faedo AU 5.00 12.00
32A Kyle Wright AU 10.00 25.00
32B Kyle Wright AU 10.00 25.00
33A DL Hall AU 4.00 10.00
Glove up
33B DL Hall AU 4.00 10.00
Glove down
34A Keston Hiura AU 6.00 15.00
Blue jersey
34B Keston Hiura AU 6.00 15.00
Gray jersey
35A Jo Adell AU EXCH 12.00 30.00
35B Jo Adell AU EXCH 12.00 30.00
36A Shane Baz AU 5.00 12.00
Arm back
36B Shane Baz AU 5.00 12.00
Arm down
37A Seth Romero AU 3.00 8.00
Ball showing
37B Seth Romero AU 3.00 8.00
No ball
38A Alex Lange AU 5.00 12.00
Glove next to face
38B Alex Lange AU 5.00 12.00
Ball behind head
39A MacKenzie Gore AU 25.00 60.00
39B MacKenzie Gore AU 25.00 60.00
40A Clarke Schmidt AU 5.00 12.00
Gray jersey
40B Clarke Schmidt AU 5.00 12.00
White jersey
41A Griffin Canning AU 5.00 12.00
Pinstripe jersey
41B Griffin Canning AU 5.00 12.00
White jersey
42A Nick Pratto AU 5.00 12.00
42B Nick Pratto AU 5.00 12.00
43A Pavin Smith AU 5.00 12.00
43B Pavin Smith AU 5.00 12.00
44A J.B. Bukauskas AU 5.00 12.00
Side view
44B J.B. Bukauskas AU 5.00 12.00
Front view
45A Adam Haseley AU 6.00 15.00
Batting
45B Adam Haseley AU 6.00 15.00
Sunglasses on
46 Logan Warmoth AU 5.00 12.00
47 Jake Burger AU 6.00 15.00
48 Heliot Ramos AU 8.00 20.00
49 David Peterson AU 6.00 15.00
50 Tanner Houck AU 15.00 40.00
51 Mark Vientos AU 5.00 12.00
52 Trevor Rogers AU 8.00 20.00
53 Bubba Thompson AU 5.00 12.00
54 Christopher Seise AU 5.00 12.00
55 Matt Sauer AU 4.00 10.00
56 Evan White AU 8.00 20.00
57 Sam Carlson AU 4.00 10.00
58 Quentin Holmes AU 4.00 10.00
59 Brian Miller AU 3.00 8.00
60 Tristen Lutz AU 5.00 12.00

2017 Panini Contenders Draft Picks Cracked Ice Ticket

*ICE 1-25: 4X TO 10X BASIC
*ICE AU 27-60: 1X TO 2.5X BASIC
RANDOM INSERTS IN PACKS
STATED PRINT RUN 23 SER.#'d SETS
EXCHANGE DEADLINE 03/06/2019

2017 Panini Contenders Draft Picks Draft Ticket

*DRAFT 1-25: 2.5X TO 6X BASIC
*DRAFT AU 27-60: .5X TO 1.2X BASIC
RANDOM INSERTS IN PACKS
STATED PRINT RUN 99 SER.#'d SETS
EXCHANGE DEADLINE 03/06/2019

2017 Panini Contenders Draft Picks Game Day Tickets

RANDOM INSERTS IN PACKS
1 Brendan McKay 1.00 2.50
2 Brian Miller .25 .60
3 Alex Faedo .40 1.00
4 Kyle Wright .75 2.00
5 Keston Hiura 1.25 3.00
6 Evan White .60 1.50
7 Nick Senzel .75 2.00
8 Clarke Schmidt .40 1.00
9 Griffin Canning .40 1.00
10 Pavin Smith .40 1.00
11 David Peterson .50 1.25
12 Adam Haseley .50 1.25
13 Jake Burger .50 1.25
14 Tanner Houck 1.25 3.00
15 Logan Warmoth .40 1.00

2017 Panini Contenders Draft Picks Alumni Ink

RANDOM INSERTS IN PACKS
EXCHANGE DEADLINE 03/06/2019
1 Reggie Jackson 15.00 40.00
2 Barry Bonds 60.00 150.00
3 Frank Thomas
4 John Elway
5 Bo Jackson 50.00 120.00
6 Mark McGwire
7 Barry Larkin
8 Roger Clemens
9 Ozzie Smith
10 Paul Molitor

2017 Panini Contenders Draft Picks Collegiate Connections Dual Signatures

RANDOM INSERTS IN PACKS
EXCHANGE DEADLINE 03/06/2019
1 Kendall/Wright 15.00 40.00
2 Schmidt/Crowe 15.00 40.00
3 Smith/Haseley
4 Bukauskas/Warmoth 6.00 15.00
5 Bo Jackson
Frank Thomas
7 Bonds/Jackson 100.00 250.00
8 Palmeiro/Clark 75.00 200.00
9 Winfield/Molitor 20.00 50.00
10 Miller/Warmoth 12.00 30.00

2017 Panini Contenders Draft Picks International Ticket Autographs

RANDOM INSERTS IN PACKS
EXCHANGE DEADLINE 03/06/2019
*DRAFT/99: .5X TO 1.2X BASIC
*ICE/23: .75X TO 2X BASIC
1 Luis Robert 40.00 100.00
2 Ronny Mauricio 5.00 12.00
3 Julio Rodriguez 20.00 50.00
4 George Valera EXCH 6.00 15.00
6 Jeffry Marte 5.00 12.00
7 Adrian Hernandez 3.00 8.00
8 Larry Ernesto 3.00 8.00
9 Ynmanol Marinez 4.00 10.00
10 Ronny Rojas 3.00 8.00
11 Carlos Aguiar 4.00 10.00
12 Luis Garcia 5.00 12.00

2017 Panini Contenders Draft Picks Old School Colors

COMPLETE SET (10) 4.00 10.00
RANDOM INSERTS IN PACKS
1 Reggie Jackson .30 .75
2 Craig Biggio .30 .75
3 Frank Thomas .40 1.00
4 John Elway .60 1.50
5 Bo Jackson .40 1.00
6 Mark McGwire .60 1.50
7 Barry Larkin .30 .75
8 Roger Clemens .50 1.25
9 Ozzie Smith .50 1.25
10 Paul Molitor .40 1.00

2017 Panini Contenders Draft Picks Old School Colors Signatures

RANDOM INSERTS IN PACKS
EXCHANGE DEADLINE 03/06/2019
1 Reggie Jackson 15.00 40.00
2 Craig Biggio
3 Frank Thomas
4 John Elway 40.00 100.00
5 Bo Jackson 50.00 120.00
7 Barry Larkin
8 Roger Clemens 15.00 40.00
9 Ozzie Smith
10 Paul Molitor 10.00 25.00

2017 Panini Contenders Draft Picks Prospect Ticket Autographs

RANDOM INSERTS IN PACKS
EXCHANGE DEADLINE 03/06/2019
*DRAFT/99: .5X TO 1.2X BASIC
*ICE/23: .75X TO 2X BASIC
1 Nick Senzel 12.00 30.00
2 Eloy Jimenez 40.00 100.00
3 Carlos Rincon 3.00 8.00
4 Vladimir Guerrero Jr. 100.00 250.00
5 Kevin Maitan 5.00 12.00
6 Andres Gimenez 8.00 20.00
7 Ronald Acuna 75.00 200.00
8 Jomar Reyes 5.00 12.00
9 Willi Castro 5.00 12.00
10 Albert Abreu 4.00 10.00
11 Gleyber Torres 50.00 125.00
12 Amed Rosario 5.00 12.00
13 David Garcia 4.00 10.00
14 Luis Almanzar 3.00 8.00
15 Luis V. Garcia 4.00 10.00
16 Yoan Moncada
17 Cristian Pache
18 Willy Adames 4.00 10.00
19 Abraham Gutierrez 5.00 12.00
20 Victor Robles 6.00 15.00
21 Rafael Devers 12.00 30.00
22 Francisco Mejia 5.00 12.00
23 Blake Rutherford 5.00 12.00

2017 Panini Contenders Draft Picks School Colors

COMPLETE SET (15) 4.00 10.00
RANDOM INSERTS IN PACKS
1 Brendan McKay 1.00 2.50
2 Brian Miller .25 .60
3 Alex Faedo .40 1.00
4 Kyle Wright .75 2.00
5 Keston Hiura 1.25 3.00
6 Evan White .60 1.50
7 Nick Senzel .75 2.00
8 Clarke Schmidt .40 1.00
9 Griffin Canning .40 1.00
10 Pavin Smith .40 1.00
11 David Peterson .50 1.25
12 Adam Haseley .50 1.25
13 Jake Burger .50 1.25
14 Tanner Houck 1.25 3.00
15 Logan Warmoth .40 1.00

2017 Panini Contenders Draft Picks School Colors Signatures

RANDOM INSERTS IN PACKS
EXCHANGE DEADLINE 03/06/2019
1 Brendan McKay 15.00 40.00
2 Jeren Kendall
3 Alex Faedo
4 Kyle Wright
5 Keston Hiura
6 Seth Romero
7 Alex Lange
8 Clarke Schmidt
9 Griffin Canning
10 Pavin Smith
11 J.B. Bukauskas
12 Adam Haseley 12.00 30.00
13 Jake Burger 12.00 30.00
14 Tanner Houck
15 Logan Warmoth
16 David Peterson 12.00 30.00
18 Evan White
19 Brian Miller
20 Wil Crowe

2018 Panini Contenders Draft Picks

1 A.J. Puk .30 .75
Puk...
2 Adam Haseley .30 .75
3 Alex Faedo .30 .75
Against...
4 Barry Larkin .25 .60
Larkin...
5 Bo Jackson .30 .75
Before...
6 Reggie Jackson .25 .60
While...
7 Brendan McKay .30 .75
McKay...
8 Brent Rooker .25 .60
By...
9 Chance Adams .30 .75
Transferring...
10 Clarke Schmidt .30 .75
Equally...
11 Craig Biggio .25 .60
As a...
12 Dave Winfield .25 .60
During...
13 David Peterson .40 1.00
Peterson...
14 Evan White .50 1.25
Kentucky...
15 Frank Thomas .30 .75
After...
16 Fred Lynn .20 .50
USC...
17 J.B. Bukauskas .20 .50
If...
18 Jake Burger .20 .50
Missouri...
19 Jon Duplantier .20 .50
After...
20 Keston Hiura .50 1.25
A...
21 Kyle Wright .50 1.25
22 Mark McGwire .50 1.25
23 Nick Senzel .60 1.50
24 Ozzie Smith .40 1.00
25 Paul Molitor .30 .75
Molitor...

2018 Panini Contenders Draft Picks Cracked Ice Ticket

*ICE: 4X TO 10X BASIC
RANDOM INSERTS IN PACKS
STATED PRINT RUN 23 SER.#'d SETS

2018 Panini Contenders Draft Picks Variations

*VAR: .4X TO 1X BASIC
RANDOM INSERTS IN PACKS

2018 Panini Contenders Draft Picks Variations Cracked Ice Ticket

*ICE: 4X TO 10X BASIC
RANDOM INSERTS IN PACKS
STATED PRINT RUN 23 SER.#'d SETS

2018 Panini Contenders Draft Picks Variations Draft Ticket

*DRAFT: 2.5X TO 6X BASIC
RANDOM INSERTS IN PACKS
STATED PRINT RUN 99 SER.#'d SETS

2018 Panini Contenders Draft Picks Collegiate Connections Signatures

RANDOM INSERTS IN PACKS
*ICE/23: .5X TO 1.2X BASIC
1 Singer/Kower 20.00 50.00
3 Bohm/Jenista
4 Knight/Cole 15.00 40.00
5 Grenier/Madrigal 15.00 40.00
6 Cortes/Hill 15.00 40.00
7 Tristan Beck 10.00 25.00
Kris Bubic
9 Singer/Faedo 20.00 50.00
10 Rooker/Pilkington 8.00 20.00

2018 Panini Contenders Draft Picks Draft Ticket

*DRAFT: 2.5X TO 6X BASIC
RANDOM INSERTS IN PACKS
STATED PRINT RUN 99 SER.#'d SETS

2018 Panini Contenders Draft Picks Draft Ticket Autographs

RANDOM INSERTS IN PACKS
*VAR DRFT/99: .5X TO 1.2X BASIC
*DRAFT/99: .5X TO 1.2X BASIC
1 Brady Singer 8.00 20.00
2 Shane McClanahan 5.00 12.00
3 Casey Mize 12.00 30.00
4 Matthew Liberatore 4.00 10.00
5 Brice Turang 10.00 25.00
6 Nolan Gorman 20.00 50.00
7 Joey Bart 25.00 60.00
8 Ryan Rolison 6.00 15.00
9 Travis Swaggerty 10.00 25.00
10 Jackson Kowar 6.00 15.00
11 Nick Madrigal 12.00 30.00
12 Steele Walker 4.00 10.00
13 Trevor Larnach 8.00 20.00
15 Jarred Kelenic 50.00 120.00
16 Seth Beer 15.00 40.00
18 Logan Gilbert 5.00 12.00
19 Jonathan India 20.00 50.00
20 Alec Bohm 10.00 25.00
21 Ryan Weathers 4.00 10.00
23 Tristan Beck 4.00 10.00
24 Griffin Conine 6.00 15.00
25 Will Banfield 4.00 10.00
26 Daniel Lynch 4.00 10.00
27 Triston Casas 8.00 20.00
30 Grant Lavigne 8.00 20.00
31 Kody Clemens 5.00 12.00
32 Cole Winn 4.00 10.00
33 Eric Cole 4.00 10.00
34 Jake McCarthy 5.00 12.00
36 Xavier Edwards 5.00 12.00
37 Tim Cate 5.00 12.00
38 Connor Scott 4.00 10.00
39 Luken Baker 5.00 12.00
40 Blaine Knight 4.00 10.00
41 Bo Naylor 4.00 10.00
42 Joe Gray 5.00 12.00
43 Parker Meadows 4.00 10.00
44 Lyon Richardson 5.00 12.00
45 Konnor Pilkington 4.00 10.00
46 Simeon Woods-Richardson 4.00 10.00
47 Tanner Dodson 4.00 10.00
48 Osiris Johnson 4.00 10.00
49 Braxton Ashcraft 4.00 10.00
50 Cadyn Grenier 4.00 10.00
51 Anthony Seigler 8.00 20.00
52 Josh Stowers 8.00 20.00
53 Colton Eastman 4.00 10.00
54 Jeremiah Jackson 4.00 10.00
55 Tristan Pompey 3.00 8.00
56 Tyler Frank 3.00 8.00
57 Jonathan Bowlan 3.00 8.00
58 Ryan Jeffers 6.00 15.00
59 Josh Breaux 4.00 10.00
60 Kris Bubic 5.00 12.00
61 Owen White 5.00 12.00
63 Jordan Groshans 6.00 15.00
64 Griffin Roberts 3.00 8.00
65 Greyson Jenista 6.00 15.00
66 Nico Hoerner 12.00 30.00
67 Brennen Davis 10.00 25.00
68 Adam Hill 3.00 8.00
69 Carlos Cortes 4.00 10.00
70 Alek Thomas 8.00 20.00
71 Jayson Schroeder 3.00 8.00
72 Grayson Rodriguez 6.00 15.00
73 Jameson Hannah 5.00 12.00
75 Nick Decker 6.00 15.00
76 Lenny Torres Jr. 4.00 10.00
77 Nick Schnell 3.00 8.00
78 Ethan Hankins 4.00 10.00
79 Nick Sandlin 3.00 8.00
80 Mason Denaburg 4.00 10.00

2018 Panini Contenders Draft Picks Draft Ticket Autographs Cracked Ice

ICE: .75X TO 2X BASIC
RANDOM INSERTS IN PACKS
STATED PRINT RUN 23 SER.#'d SETS
20 Alec Bohm 40.00 100.00

2018 Panini Contenders Draft Picks Draft Ticket Variation Autographs

*VAR: .4X TO 1X BASIC
RANDOM INSERTS IN PACKS
17 Jeremy Eierman 3.00 8.00

2018 Panini Contenders Draft Picks Draft Ticket Variation Autographs Cracked Ice

*VAR ICE: .75X TO 2X BASIC
RANDOM INSERTS IN PACKS
STATED PRINT RUN 23 SER.#'d SETS
17 Jeremy Eierman 6.00 15.00
20 Alec Bohm 40.00 100.00

2018 Panini Contenders Draft Picks Game Day Tickets

RANDOM INSERTS IN PACKS
*ICE/23: 2.5X TO 6X BASIC
1 Brady Singer 1.25 3.00
2 Shane McClanahan .40 1.00
3 Casey Mize 2.00 5.00
4 Ryan Rolison .50 1.25
5 Travis Swaggerty .75 2.00
6 Jackson Kowar .75 2.00
7 Nick Madrigal 1.00 2.50
8 Cadyn Grenier .30 .75
9 Logan Gilbert .40 1.00
10 Greyson Jenista .40 1.00
11 Alec Bohm 1.50 4.00
12 Joey Bart 2.50 6.00
13 Trevor Larnach 1.50 4.00
14 Nico Hoerner 1.25 3.00
15 Kris Bubic .40 1.00
16 Griffin Roberts .25 .60
17 Steele Walker .30 .75
18 Seth Beer 1.00 2.50
19 Jake McCarthy .40 1.00
20 Jonathan India 1.50 4.00

2018 Panini Contenders Draft Picks International Ticket Autographs

RANDOM INSERTS IN PACKS
*DRAFT/99: .5X TO 1.2X BASIC
*ICE/23: .75X TO 2X BASIC
1 Robert Puason 10.00 25.00
2 Jhon Diaz 5.00 12.00
3 Noelvi Marte 6.00 15.00
4 Frankely Hurtado 3.00 8.00
5 Jeffrey Diaz 3.00 8.00
6 Estanli Castillo 3.00 8.00
7 Julio Pablo Martinez 15.00 40.00

2018 Panini Contenders Draft Picks Old School Colors

RANDOM INSERTS IN PACKS
*ICE/23: 4X TO 10X BASIC
1 Reggie Jackson .30 .75
2 Frank Thomas .40 1.00
3 Bo Jackson .40 1.00
4 Mark McGwire .60 1.50
5 Barry Larkin .30 .75
6 Craig Biggio .30 .75
7 Paul Molitor .40 1.00
8 Roger Clemens .50 1.25
9 Ozzie Smith .50 1.25

2018 Panini Contenders Draft Picks Old School Colors Signatures

RANDOM INSERTS IN PACKS
*ICE/23: .6X TO 1.5X BASIC
1 Reggie Jackson 10.00 25.00
2 Dave Winfield
3 Frank Thomas 20.00 50.00
4 Bo Jackson 25.00 60.00
5 Mark McGwire 15.00 40.00
6 Barry Larkin 8.00 20.00
7 Will Clark 15.00 40.00
8 Paul Molitor 10.00 25.00
9 Roger Clemens 12.00 30.00
10 Ozzie Smith 15.00 40.00

2018 Panini Contenders Draft Picks Prospect Ticket Autographs

RANDOM INSERTS IN PACKS
*VAR: .4X TO 1X BASIC
*VAR DRFT/99: .5X TO 1.2X BASIC
*DRAFT/99: .5X TO 1.2X BASIC
1 Aramis Ademan 4.00 10.00
2 Yordan Alvarez 40.00 100.00
3 Keibert Ruiz 5.00 12.00
4 DJ Peters 6.00 15.00
5 Estevan Florial 5.00 12.00
6 Luis Robert 50.00 125.00
7 Fernando Tatis Jr. 40.00 100.00
8 Miguel Aparicio 3.00 8.00
9 Vladimir Guerrero Jr. 75.00 200.00
10 Eloy Jimenez 15.00 40.00
11 D.J. Wilson 3.00 8.00
12 Michael Kopech 12.00 30.00
13 Jose Siri 3.00 8.00
14 Brendan Rodgers 5.00 12.00
15 Jeisson Rosario 5.00 12.00
16 Sandro Fabian 3.00 8.00
17 Leody Taveras 5.00 12.00
18 Akil Baddoo 20.00 50.00
19 Brendan McKay 5.00 12.00
20 Jesus Sanchez 5.00 12.00
21 Kyle Tucker 8.00 20.00
22 James Nelson 3.00 8.00
23 Forrest Whitley 5.00 12.00
24 Carter Kieboom 8.00 20.00
25 Austin Riley 40.00 100.00
26 Mitch Keller 4.00 10.00
27 Franklin Perez 4.00 10.00
28 Chance Adams 5.00 12.00
29 Sixto Sanchez 12.00 30.00
30 Justus Sheffield 5.00 12.00
31 Bo Bichette 15.00 40.00
32 Brent Honeywell 5.00 12.00

2018 Panini Contenders Draft Picks Prospect Ticket Autographs Cracked Ice

*ICE: .75X TO 2X BASIC
RANDOM INSERTS IN PACKS
STATED PRINT RUN 23 SER.#'d SETS
3 Keibert Ruiz 25.00 60.00

2018 Panini Contenders Draft Picks School Colors

RANDOM INSERTS IN PACKS
*ICE/23: 2.5X TO 6X BASIC
1 Brady Singer 1.25 3.00
2 Shane McClanahan .40 1.00
3 Casey Mize 2.00 5.00
4 Ryan Rolison .50 1.25
5 Travis Swaggerty .75 2.00
6 Jackson Kowar .75 2.00
7 Nick Madrigal 1.00 2.50
8 Cadyn Grenier .30 .75
9 Logan Gilbert .40 1.00
10 Greyson Jenista .40 1.00
11 Alec Bohm 1.50 4.00
12 Joey Bart 2.50 6.00
13 Trevor Larnach 1.50 4.00
14 Griffin Conine .50 1.25
15 Kris Bubic .40 1.00
16 Griffin Roberts .25 .60
17 Steele Walker .30 .75
18 Seth Beer 1.00 2.50
19 Jake McCarthy .40 1.00
20 Jonathan India 1.50 4.00
21 Nico Hoerner 1.25 3.00

2018 Panini Contenders Draft Picks School Colors Signatures

RANDOM INSERTS IN PACKS
*ICE/23: .6X TO 1.5X BASIC
1 Brady Singer 10.00 25.00
2 Shane McClanahan 5.00 12.00
3 Casey Mize 15.00 40.00
4 Ryan Rolison 6.00 15.00
5 Travis Swaggerty 10.00 25.00
6 Jackson Kowar 10.00 25.00
7 Nick Madrigal 12.00 30.00
8 Cadyn Grenier 4.00 10.00
9 Logan Gilbert 5.00 12.00
10 Trevor Larnach 20.00 50.00
13 Kris Bubic
14 Griffin Roberts 3.00 8.00
15 Jonathan India 20.00 50.00
17 Steele Walker 4.00 10.00
18 Seth Beer 12.00 30.00
19 Jake McCarthy 5.00 12.00
20 Nico Hoerner 15.00 40.00

2019 Panini Contenders Draft Picks

1 Adley Rutschman 1.25 3.00
2 Alek Manoah .40 1.00
3 Andrew Vaughn .60 1.50
4 Frank Thomas .30 .75
5 Reggie Jackson .25 .60
6 Braden Shewmake .60 1.50
7 Bryson Stott .60 1.50
8 Casey Mize .50 1.25
9 Hunter Bishop .60 1.50
10 JJ Bleday 1.00 2.50
11 Joey Bart .60 1.50
12 Jonathan India 1.25 3.00
13 Josh Jung .60 1.50
14 Kameron Misner .60 1.50
15 Kody Hoese .60 1.50
16 Davis Wendzel .30 .75
17 Logan Davidson .20 .50
18 Logan Wyatt .30 .75
19 Michael Busch .60 1.50
20 Nick Lodolo .40 1.00
21 Nick Madrigal .75 2.00
22 Nico Hoerner .60 1.50
23 Shea Langeliers .40 1.00
24 Will Wilson .30 .75
25 Zack Thompson .30 .75

2019 Panini Contenders Draft Picks Cracked Ice Ticket

*CRCKD ICE: 2X TO 5X BASIC
RANDOM INSERTS IN PACKS
STATED PRINT RUN 23 SER.#'d SETS

2019 Panini Contenders Draft Picks Variations

*VAR: .4X TO 1X BASIC
RANDOM INSERTS IN PACKS

2019 Panini Contenders Draft Picks Variations Cracked Ice Ticket

*VAR CRCKD ICE: 2X TO 5X BASIC
RANDOM INSERTS IN PACKS
STATED PRINT RUN 23 SER.#'d SETS

2019 Panini Contenders Draft Picks Variations Draft Ticket

*VAR DRAFT: 1X TO 2.5X BASIC
RANDOM INSERTS IN PACKS
STATED PRINT RUN 99 SER.#'d SETS

2019 Panini Contenders Draft Picks Collegiate Connections Signatures

RANDOM INSERTS IN PACKS
EXCHANGE DEADLINE 10/24/2020
*CRCKD ICE/23: .5X TO 1.2X BASIC
1 Rutschman/Madrigal 50.00 120.00
2 Wendzel/Langeliers
4 Strumpf/Toglia 10.00 25.00
9 Fletcher/Campbell 12.00 30.00
10 Busch/Baum 20.00 50.00

2019 Panini Contenders Draft Picks Draft Ticket Autographs

RANDOM INSERTS IN PACKS
EXCHANGE DEADLINE 10/24/2020
*PRSPCT/99: .5X TO 1.2X BASIC
*CRCKD ICE/23: .75X TO 2X BASIC
1 Logan Davidson 2.50 6.00
2 Daniel Espino 3.00 8.00
3 Zack Thompson 4.00 10.00
4 Brennan Malone 2.50 6.00
5 Jackson Rutledge 5.00 12.00
6 George Kirby 4.00 10.00
7 Michael Busch 3.00 8.00
8 Rece Hinds 3.00 8.00
9 Logan Wyatt 4.00 10.00
11 Seth Johnson 2.50 6.00
14 J.J. Goss 3.00 8.00
15 Matt Canterino 3.00 8.00
16 Drey Jameson 2.50 6.00
17 Treiyn Fletcher 4.00 10.00
18 Chase Strumpf 5.00 12.00
21 Gunnar Henderson 5.00 12.00
22 Kyle Stowers 4.00 10.00
23 Kendall Williams 4.00 10.00
24 Nasim Nunez 2.50 6.00
25 Tyler Baum 3.00 8.00
26 Sammy Siani 3.00 8.00
27 Ethan Small 3.00 8.00
28 Josh Wolf 3.00 8.00
30 Logan Driscoll 4.00 10.00
31 T.J. Sikkema 4.00 10.00
32 Ryan Jensen 4.00 10.00
33 Anthony Volpe 10.00 25.00
34 Michael Toglia 4.00 10.00
35 Korey Lee 5.00 12.00
36 Kody Hoese 8.00 20.00
37 Davis Wendzel 4.00 10.00
38 John Doxakis 3.00 8.00
40 Matt Wallner 5.00 12.00
42 Ryan Garcia 2.50 6.00
43 Brady McConnell 4.00 10.00
44 Tommy Henry 3.00 8.00
45 Matt Gorski 4.00 10.00
47 Greg Jones 3.00 8.00
48 Aaron Schunk 5.00 12.00
51 Isaiah Campbell 5.00 12.00
52 Josh Smith 5.00 12.00
53 Karl Kauffmann 2.50 6.00
54 Kyren Paris 2.50 6.00
56 Yordys Valdes 5.00 12.00
58 Alec Marsh 3.00 8.00
59 Dominic Fletcher 2.50 6.00
60 Jared Triolo 4.00 10.00

2019 Panini Contenders Draft Picks Game Day Tickets

RANDOM INSERTS IN PACKS
*CRCKD ICE/23: 1.5X TO 4X BASIC
1 Adley Rutschman 1.50 4.00
2 Alek Manoah .50 1.25
3 Andrew Vaughn .75 2.00
4 Bobby Witt Jr. 1.50 4.00
5 Braden Shewmake .75 2.00
6 Bryson Stott .75 2.00
7 CJ Abrams 1.25 3.00
8 Riley Greene 1.50 4.00
9 Hunter Bishop .75 2.00
10 JJ Bleday 1.25 3.00
11 Josh Jung .75 2.00
12 Kameron Misner .60 1.50
13 Kody Hoese .75 2.00
14 Logan Davidson .25 .60
15 Logan Wyatt .40 1.00
16 Michael Busch .75 2.00
17 Nick Lodolo .50 1.25
18 Shea Langeliers .50 1.25
19 Will Wilson .40 1.00
20 Zack Thompson .40 1.00

2019 Panini Contenders Draft Picks International Ticket Autographs

RANDOM INSERTS IN PACKS
EXCHANGE DEADLINE 10/24/2020
*DRAFT/99: .5X TO 1.2X BASIC
*CRCKD ICE/23: .75X TO 2X BASIC
1 Noelvi Marte 6.00 15.00
2 Kevin Alcantara 5.00 12.00
3 Richard Gallardo 3.00 8.00
4 Diego Cartaya 5.00 12.00
5 Marco Luciano 10.00 25.00
6 Osiel Rodriguez 4.00 10.00
7 Orelvis Martinez 4.00 10.00

2019 Panini Contenders Draft Picks Legacy

RANDOM INSERTS IN PACKS
*CRCKD ICE/23: 1.5X TO 4X BASIC
1 Bobby Witt Jr. 1.50 4.00
2 Josh Jung .75 2.00
3 Shea Langeliers .50 1.25
4 Adley Rutschman 1.50 4.00
5 Andrew Vaughn .75 2.00
6 Will Wilson .40 1.00
7 Nolan Gorman .75 2.00
8 Adley Rutschman 1.50 4.00
9 Riley Greene 1.50 4.00
10 CJ Abrams 1.25 3.00

2019 Panini Contenders Draft Picks Legacy Signatures

RANDOM INSERTS IN PACKS
EXCHANGE DEADLINE 10/24/2020
*CRCKD ICE/23: .75X TO 2X
1 Bobby Witt Jr. 15.00 40.00
4 Adley Rutschman 25.00 60.00
5 Andrew Vaughn 10.00 25.00
7 Nolan Gorman 8.00 20.00
8 Adley Rutschman 25.00 60.00
9 Riley Greene 10.00 25.00
10 CJ Abrams 15.00 40.00

2019 Panini Contenders Draft Picks Prospect Ticket Autographs

RANDOM INSERTS IN PACKS
EXCHANGE DEADLINE 10/24/2020
*DRAFT/99: .5X TO 1.2X BASIC
*CRCKD ICE/23: .75X TO 2X BASIC
1 Wander Franco 25.00 60.00
2 Shervyen Newton 4.00 10.00
3 Royce Lewis 5.00 12.00
4 Casey Mize 6.00 15.00
5 Jhoan Duran 4.00 10.00
6 Moises Gomez 4.00 10.00
8 Carlos Rodriguez 2.50 6.00
9 Gavin Lux 10.00 25.00
10 Yordan Alvarez 40.00 100.00
11 Nick Madrigal 8.00 20.00
12 Jonathan India 10.00 25.00
13 Nolan Gorman 8.00 20.00
14 Luis Robert 25.00 60.00
15 Randy Florentino 2.50 6.00
16 Livan Soto 3.00 8.00
17 Victor Victor Mesa 5.00 12.00
18 Vidal Brujan 8.00 20.00
19 Nico Hoerner 8.00 20.00
20 Michael King 4.00 10.00
21 Miguel Vargas 12.00 30.00
22 Gabriel Maciel 2.50 6.00
23 Jarred Kelenic 25.00 60.00
24 Antonio Cabello 5.00 12.00
25 Luis Toribio 2.50 6.00

2019 Panini Contenders Draft Picks RPS Draft Ticket Autographs

RANDOM INSERTS IN PACKS
EXCHANGE DEADLINE 10/24/2020
*VAR: .4X TO 1X BASIC
*DRAFT/99: .5X TO 1.2X BASIC
*VAR DRAFT/99: .5X TO 1.2X BASIC
*CRCKD ICE/23: .75X TO 2X BASIC
*VAR CRCKD ICE/23: .75X TO 2X BASIC
1 Adley Rutschman 20.00 50.00
2 Bobby Witt Jr. EXCH 15.00 40.00
3 CJ Abrams 12.00 30.00
4 Andrew Vaughn 8.00 20.00
5 Riley Greene EXCH 15.00 40.00
6 Shea Langeliers 8.00 20.00
7 Corbin Carroll 4.00 10.00
8 Josh Jung 8.00 20.00
9 Hunter Bishop 8.00 20.00
10 Kameron Misner EXCH 6.00 15.00
11 Bryson Stott 4.00 10.00
12 Brett Baty 5.00 12.00
13 Nick Lodolo 4.00 10.00
14 JJ Bleday 12.00 30.00
15 Alek Manoah EXCH 5.00 12.00
16 Will Wilson 4.00 10.00

2019 Panini Contenders Draft Picks School Colors

RANDOM INSERTS IN PACKS
*CRCKD ICE/23: 1.5X TO 4X BASIC
1 Adley Rutschman 1.50 4.00
2 Alek Manoah .50 1.25
3 Andrew Vaughn .75 2.00
4 Bobby Witt Jr. 1.50 4.00
5 Braden Shewmake .75 2.00
6 Bryson Stott .75 2.00
7 CJ Abrams 1.25 3.00
8 Riley Greene 1.50 4.00
9 Hunter Bishop .75 2.00
10 JJ Bleday 1.25 3.00
11 Josh Jung .75 2.00
12 Kameron Misner .60 1.50
13 Kody Hoese .75 2.00
14 Logan Davidson .25 .60
15 Logan Wyatt .40 1.00
16 Michael Busch .75 2.00
17 Nick Lodolo .50 1.25
18 Shea Langeliers .50 1.25
19 Will Wilson .40 1.00
20 Zack Thompson .40 1.00

2019 Panini Contenders Draft Picks School Colors Signatures

RANDOM INSERTS IN PACKS
EXCHANGE DEADLINE 10/24/2020
*CRCKD ICE/23: .75X TO 2X
1 Adley Rutschman 25.00 60.00
2 Andrew Vaughn 10.00 25.00
3 Bobby Witt Jr. 20.00 50.00
4 Bryson Stott 10.00 25.00
5 CJ Abrams 15.00 40.00
6 Corbin Carroll 5.00 12.00
7 Kody Hoese 10.00 25.00
8 Hunter Bishop 10.00 25.00
9 JJ Bleday 15.00 40.00
10 Josh Jung 12.00 30.00
13 Logan Davidson 3.00 8.00
14 Logan Wyatt 5.00 12.00
15 Michael Busch 10.00 25.00
16 Nick Lodolo 6.00 15.00
17 Riley Greene 6.00 15.00
18 Shea Langeliers 6.00 15.00
19 Will Wilson 5.00 12.00
20 Zack Thompson 5.00 12.00

2018 Panini Contenders Optic

1 Amed Rosario .30 .75
2 Austin Hays .40 1.00
3 Clint Frazier .50 1.25
4 Ronald Acuna Jr. 8.00 20.00
5 Miguel Andujar 1.00 2.50
6 Ozzie Albies .75 2.00
7 Rafael Devers .75 2.00
8 Rhys Hoskins 1.00 2.50
9 Shohei Ohtani 6.00 15.00
10 Gleyber Torres RC 2.50 6.00

2019 Panini Contenders Optic

RANDOM INSERTS IN PACKS
*HOLO: .75X TO 2X
*HYPER/299: .75X TO 2X
*RUBY/199: 1X TO 2.5X
*BLUE/99: 1.2X TO 3X
*PURPLE/75: 1.2X TO 3X
*GREEN/50: 1.5X TO 4X
*PINK/25: 2.5X TO 6X
1 Pete Alonso RC 4.00 10.00
2 Eloy Jimenez RC .60 1.50
3 Fernando Tatis Jr. RC 3.00 8.00
4 Michael Kopech RC .50 1.25
5 Kyle Tucker RC .40 1.00
6 Yusei Kikuchi RC .25 .60
7 Chris Paddack RC .30 .75
8 Mike Trout 2.50 6.00
9 Nick Senzel RC .50 1.25
10 Aaron Judge .60 1.50
11 Kris Bryant .30 .75
12 Shohei Ohtani .40 1.00
13 Ozzie Albies .25 .60
14 Andrew Benintendi .25 .60
15 Juan Soto .75 2.00
16 Felix Hernandez .20 .50
17 Jose Ramirez .20 .50
18 Ronald Acuna Jr. 2.50 6.00
19 Trea Turner .20 .50
20 Vladimir Guerrero Jr. RC 2.50 6.00
21 Corey Kluber .20 .50
22 Carter Kieboom RC .25 .60
23 Trevor Story .25 .60
24 Brandon Lowe RC .25 .60
25 Michael Chavis RC .25 .60

2019 Panini Contenders Optic Draft Picks Autographs

RANDOM INSERTS IN PACKS
EXCHANGE DEADLINE 10/24/2020
*HYPER/20: .75X TO 2X BASIC
1 Adley Rutschman 25.00 60.00
2 Bobby Witt Jr. EXCH 20.00 50.00
3 CJ Abrams 15.00 40.00
4 Andrew Vaughn 20.00 50.00
5 Riley Greene EXCH 12.00 30.00
6 Shea Langeliers 8.00 20.00
7 Corbin Carroll 5.00 12.00
8 Josh Jung 8.00 20.00
9 Hunter Bishop 10.00 25.00
10 Kameron Misner EXCH 6.00 15.00
11 Bryson Stott 10.00 25.00
12 Logan Davidson 3.00 8.00
13 Nick Lodolo 6.00 15.00
14 Michael Busch 10.00 25.00
15 Zack Thompson 5.00 12.00
16 Brett Baty 6.00 15.00
17 Will Wilson 5.00 12.00
18 Alek Manoah EXCH 10.00 25.00
19 JJ Bleday 15.00 40.00
20 Jackson Rutledge 6.00 15.00

2020 Panini Contenders Optic

RANDOM INSERTS IN '20 CHRONICLES
1 Bo Bichette RC 3.00 8.00
2 Yordan Alvarez RC 2.50 6.00
3 Gavin Lux RC 1.25 3.00
4 Brendan McKay RC .40 1.00
5 Aristides Aquino RC .60 1.50
6 Yoshitomo Tsutsugo RC .60 1.50
7 Luis Robert RC 4.00 10.00
8 Aaron Judge .60 1.50
9 Mike Trout 2.00 5.00
10 Cody Bellinger .50 1.25
11 Fernando Tatis Jr. 2.00 5.00
12 Vladimir Guerrero Jr. .40 1.00
13 Shohei Ohtani .40 1.00
14 Mookie Betts .50 1.25
15 Manny Machado .25 .60
16 Bryce Harper .40 1.00
17 Francisco Lindor .25 .60
18 Rafael Devers .30 .75
19 Alex Bregman .25 .60
20 Matt Chapman .25 .60
21 Ronald Acuna Jr. 1.50 4.00
22 Juan Soto .75 2.00
23 Pete Alonso .60 1.50
24 Christian Yelich .30 .75
25 Clayton Kershaw .40 1.00
26 Shogo Akiyama RC .40 1.00
27 Isan Diaz RC .40 1.00
28 Nico Hoerner RC 1.00 2.50
29 Xander Bogaerts .25 .60
30 Josh Bell .20 .50

2020 Panini Contenders Optic Blue Ice

*BLUE VET: 1.5X TO 4X BASIC
*BLUE RC: 1X TO 2.5X BASIC RC
RANDOM INSERTS IN '20 CHRONICLES
STATED PRINT RUN 99 SER.#'d SETS
1 Bo Bichette 20.00 50.00
2 Yordan Alvarez 10.00 25.00
7 Luis Robert 30.00 80.00
9 Mike Trout 12.00 30.00

2020 Panini Contenders Optic Green

*GREEN VET: 2.5X TO X BASIC
*GREEN RC: 1.5X TO 4X BASIC RC
RANDOM INSERTS IN '20 CHRONICLES
STATED PRINT RUN 50 SER.#'d SETS
1 Bo Bichette 30.00 80.00
2 Yordan Alvarez 25.00 60.00

7 Luis Robert 40.00 100.00
9 Mike Trout 25.00 60.00

2020 Panini Contenders Optic Holo

*HOLO VET: 1X TO 2.5X BASIC
*HOLO RC: .6X TO 1.5X BASIC RC
RANDOM INSERTS IN '20 CHRONICLES
7 Luis Robert 8.00 20.00

2020 Panini Contenders Optic Hyper

*HYPER VET: 1.2X TO 3X BASIC
*HYPER RC: .8X TO 2X BASIC RC
RANDOM INSERTS IN '20 CHRONICLES
STATED PRINT RUN 299 SER.#'d SETS
7 Luis Robert 15.00 40.00

2020 Panini Contenders Optic Pink

*PINK VET: 4X TO 10X BASIC
*PINK RC: 2.5X TO 6X BASIC RC
RANDOM INSERTS IN '20 CHRONICLES
STATED PRINT RUN 25 SER.#'d SETS
1 Bo Bichette 50.00 120.00
2 Yordan Alvarez 40.00 100.00
7 Luis Robert 60.00 150.00
9 Mike Trout 30.00 80.00

2020 Panini Contenders Optic Purple Mojo

*PURPLE VET: 1.5X TO 4X BASIC
*PURPLE RC: 1X TO 2.5X BASIC RC
RANDOM INSERTS IN '20 CHRONICLES
STATED PRINT RUN 75 SER.#'d SETS
1 Bo Bichette 20.00 50.00
2 Yordan Alvarez 15.00 40.00
7 Luis Robert 30.00 80.00
9 Mike Trout 20.00 50.00

2020 Panini Contenders Optic Ruby Wave

*RUBY VET: 1.2X TO 3X BASIC
*RUBY RC: .8X TO 2X BASIC RC
RANDOM INSERTS IN '20 CHRONICLES
STATED PRINT RUN 199 SER.#'d SETS
7 Luis Robert 15.00 40.00

2020 Panini Contenders Optic Draft Pick Ticket Autographs

RANDOM INSERTS IN '20 CONTENDERS
EXCHANGE DEADLINE 4/30/22
1 Austin Martin
2 Spencer Torkelson
3 Emerson Hancock 12.00 30.00
4 Zac Veen
5 Asa Lacy 10.00 25.00

2020 Panini Contenders Optic Draft Pick Ticket Autographs Cracked Ice

*CRCKD ICE: .8X TO 2X BASIC
RANDOM INSERTS IN '20 CONTENDERS
STATED PRINT RUN 23 SER.#'d SETS
EXCHANGE DEADLINE 4/30/22
2 Spencer Torkelson 400.00 800.00

2020 Panini Contenders Optic Rookie Ticket Autograph Variations

RANDOM INSERTS IN '20 CONTENDERS
EXCHANGE DEADLINE 4/30/22
1 Bo Bichette EXCH 30.00 80.00
2 Yordan Alvarez 20.00 50.00
3 Gavin Lux 15.00 40.00
4 Brendan McKay 5.00 12.00
5 Aristides Aquino 12.00 30.00
6 Yoshitomo Tsutsugo 8.00 20.00
7 Luis Robert EXCH 50.00 120.00
8 Dustin May 10.00 25.00
9 Dylan Cease EXCH 5.00 12.00
10 Zac Gallen 6.00 15.00
11 A.J. Puk EXCH 5.00 12.00
12 Brusdar Graterol 5.00 12.00
13 Adbert Alzolay 4.00 10.00
14 Aaron Civale 6.00 15.00
15 Tony Gonsolin 6.00 15.00
16 Sean Murphy 5.00 12.00
17 Kwang-Hyun Kim 15.00 40.00
18 Shun Yamaguchi 4.00 10.00
19 Jesus Luzardo
20 Bryan Abreu 3.00 8.00
21 Shogo Akiyama 8.00 20.00
22 Isan Diaz EXCH 5.00 12.00
23 Nico Hoerner 10.00 25.00
24 Brendan McKay 5.00 12.00
25 Mauricio Dubon 4.00 10.00

2020 Panini Contenders Optic Rookie Ticket Autograph Variations Cracked Ice

*CRCKD ICE: .8X TO 2X BASIC
RANDOM INSERTS IN '20 CONTENDERS
STATED PRINT RUN 23 SER.#'d SETS
EXCHANGE DEADLINE 4/30/22
2 Yordan Alvarez 60.00 150.00
8 Dustin May 30.00 80.00

2020 Panini Contenders Optic Rookie Ticket Autographs

RANDOM INSERTS IN '20 CONTENDERS
EXCHANGE DEADLINE 4/30/22
1 Bo Bichette EXCH 30.00 80.00
2 Yordan Alvarez 20.00 50.00
3 Gavin Lux 15.00 40.00
4 Brendan McKay 5.00 12.00
5 Aristides Aquino 12.00 30.00
6 Yoshitomo Tsutsugo 8.00 20.00
7 Luis Robert EXCH 50.00 120.00
8 Dustin May 10.00 25.00
9 Dylan Cease EXCH 5.00 12.00
10 Zac Gallen 6.00 15.00
11 A.J. Puk EXCH 5.00 12.00
12 Brusdar Graterol 5.00 12.00
13 Adbert Alzolay 4.00 10.00
14 Aaron Civale 6.00 15.00
15 Tony Gonsolin 6.00 15.00
16 Sean Murphy 5.00 12.00
17 Kwang-Hyun Kim 15.00 40.00
18 Shun Yamaguchi 4.00 10.00
19 Jesus Luzardo
20 Bryan Abreu 3.00 8.00
21 Shogo Akiyama 8.00 20.00
22 Isan Diaz EXCH 5.00 12.00
23 Nico Hoerner 10.00 25.00
24 Brendan McKay 5.00 12.00
25 Mauricio Dubon 4.00 10.00

2020 Panini Contenders Optic Rookie Ticket Autographs Cracked Ice

*CRCKD ICE: .8X TO 2X BASIC
RANDOM INSERTS IN '20 CONTENDERS
STATED PRINT RUN 23 SER.#'d SETS
EXCHANGE DEADLINE 4/30/22
2 Yordan Alvarez 60.00 150.00
8 Dustin May 30.00 80.00

2020 Panini Contenders Optic Season Ticket

RANDOM INSERTS IN PACKS
31 Trea Turner .60 1.50
32 Gerrit Cole 1.25 3.00
33 Jacob deGrom 1.50 4.00
34 Miguel Cabrera .75 2.00
35 Albert Pujols 1.00 2.50
36 Robinson Cano .60 1.50
37 Nolan Arenado 1.25 3.00
38 Walker Buehler 1.00 2.50
39 Jack Flaherty .75 2.00
40 Gleyber Torres 1.50 4.00
41 Kris Bryant 1.00 2.50
42 Whit Merrifield .75 2.00
43 Starling Marte .60 1.50
44 Ozzie Albies .75 2.00
45 Freddie Freeman 1.00 2.50
46 Trevor Story .75 2.00
47 Paul Goldschmidt .75 2.00
48 J.D. Martinez .75 2.00
49 Austin Meadows .75 2.00
50 Shane Bieber .75 2.00
51 Anthony Rendon .75 2.00
52 Alex Verdugo .60 1.50
53 Charlie Blackmon .75 2.00
54 Chris Paddack .75 2.00
55 Keston Hiura 1.00 2.50
56 Max Scherzer .75 2.00
57 Yoan Moncada .75 2.00
58 Max Muncy .60 1.50
59 Cavan Biggio 1.00 2.50
60 Victor Robles 1.00 2.50
61 Tommy Edman .75 2.00
62 Jose Ramirez .60 1.50
63 Amed Rosario .60 1.50
64 Adalberto Mondesi .60 1.50
65 Willy Adames .50 1.25
66 Mike Soroka .75 2.00
67 Eloy Jimenez 1.50 4.00
68 Justin Verlander .75 2.00
69 Nelson Cruz .75 2.00
70 Javier Baez 1.00 2.50
71 Stephen Strasburg .75 2.00

2020 Panini Contenders Optic Season Ticket Cracked Ice

*CRCKD ICE: 1.2X TO 3X BASIC
RANDOM INSERTS IN '20 CONTENDERS
STATED PRINT RUN 23 SER.#'d SETS
34 Miguel Cabrera 8.00 20.00
38 Walker Buehler 6.00 15.00
45 Freddie Freeman 8.00 20.00

2012 Panini Cooperstown

1 Ty Cobb .60 1.50
2 Walter Johnson .40 1.00
3 Honus Wagner .40 1.00
4 Christy Mathewson .40 1.00
5 Nap Lajoie .40 1.00
6 Lou Gehrig .75 2.00
7 Ban Johnson .15 .40
8 Connie Mack .15 .40
9 Alexander Cartwright .25 .60
10 Ozzie Smith .50 1.25
11 Buck Ewing .15 .40
12 Don Sutton .25 .60
13 Willie Keeler .15 .40
14 Nolan Ryan 1.25 3.00
15 Al Spalding .15 .40
16 Rod Carew .25 .60
17 Eddie Collins .25 .60
18 Roberto Clemente 1.00 2.50
19 Paul Molitor .40 1.00
20 George Sisler .25 .60
21 Charles Comiskey .15 .40
22 Rogers Hornsby .25 .60
23 Barry Larkin .25 .60
24 George Brett .75 2.00
25 Fred Clarke .15 .40
26 Ed Delahanty .15 .40
27 Hugh Duffy .25 .60
28 King Kelly .15 .40
29 Rube Marquard .25 .60
30 Ron Santo .25 .60
31 Harry Heilmann .25 .60
32 Gary Carter .25 .60
33 Joe Tinker .25 .60
34 Johnny Evers .15 .40
35 Frank Chance .25 .60
36 Lefty Grove .25 .60
37 Frankie Frisch .25 .60
38 Tommy McCarthy .15 .40
39 Mike Schmidt .60 1.50
40 Bill Mazeroski .25 .60
41 Mickey Cochrane .25 .60
42 Dennis Eckersley .25 .60
43 Eddie Murray .25 .60
44 Ryne Sandberg .75 2.00
45 Carlton Fisk .25 .60
46 Carl Hubbell .25 .60
47 Herb Pennock .25 .60
48 Pie Traynor .25 .60
49 Charlie Gehringer .15 .40
50 Mel Ott .40 1.00
51 Jimmie Foxx .40 1.00
52 Paul Waner .25 .60
53 Lloyd Waner .25 .60
54 Bruce Sutter .25 .60
55 Bill Dickey .15 .40
56 Roberto Alomar .25 .60
57 Phil Niekro .25 .60
58 Ted Williams .75 2.00
59 Richie Ashburn .25 .60
60 Ray Schalk .15 .40
61 Gaylord Perry .25 .60
62 Rabbit Maranville .25 .60
63 Sam Crawford .25 .60
64 Jim Rice .25 .60
65 Zack Wheat .25 .60
66 Wade Boggs .25 .60
67 Dave Winfield .25 .60
68 Joe Cronin .15 .40
69 Bob Feller .25 .60
70 Billy Hamilton .30 .75
71 Hank Greenberg .40 1.00
72 Jackie Robinson .40 1.00
73 Miller Huggins .15 .40
74 Luke Appling .25 .60
75 Satchel Paige .40 1.00
76 Bob Lemon .25 .60
77 Bobby Doerr .25 .60
78 Yogi Berra .40 1.00
79 Early Wynn .25 .60
80 Carl Yastrzemski .60 1.50
81 Frank Robinson .25 .60
82 Tommy Lasorda .25 .60
83 Burleigh Grimes .25 .60
84 Andre Dawson .25 .60
85 Duke Snider .25 .60
86 Whitey Ford .25 .60
87 Whitey Herzog .15 .40
88 Joe Medwick .15 .40
89 Tony Perez .25 .60
90 Lou Boudreau .25 .60
91 Tom Seaver .25 .60
92 Stan Musial .60 1.50
93 Sparky Anderson .25 .60
94 Jim Bunning .25 .60
95 Hal Newhouser .25 .60
96 Phil Rizzuto .25 .60
97 Al Barlick .25 .60
98 Ralph Kiner .25 .60
99 Eddie Mathews .40 1.00
100 George Kell .25 .60
101 Enos Slaughter .25 .60
102 Al Kaline .40 1.00
103 Johnny Mize .25 .60
104 Bob Gibson .25 .60
105 Addie Joss .25 .60
106 Robin Yount .40 1.00
107 Rollie Fingers .25 .60
108 Roy Campanella .40 1.00
109 Bert Blyleven .25 .60
110 Tony Gwynn .40 1.00
111 Frank Robinson .25 .60
112 Walter Alston .25 .60
113 Joe DiMaggio .75 2.00
114 Warren Spahn .25 .60
115 Ernie Banks .40 1.00
116 Earl Weaver .25 .60
117 Steve Carlton .25 .60
118 Orlando Cepeda .25 .60
119 Al Lopez .15 .40
120 Rickey Henderson .40 1.00
121 Harry Hooper .15 .40
122 Goose Goslin .25 .60
123 Nellie Fox .25 .60
124 Jim Palmer .25 .60
125 Monte Irvin .25 .60
126 Buck Leonard .15 .40
127 Goose Gossage .25 .60
128 Hack Wilson .25 .60
129 Sam Thompson .15 .40
130 Willie McCovey .25 .60
131 Cal Ripken Jr. 1.25 3.00
132 Ralph Kiner .25 .60
133 Arky Vaughan .15 .40
134 Juan Marichal .25 .60
135 Brooks Robinson .25 .60
136 Luis Aparicio .25 .60
137 Rick Ferrell .15 .40
138 Johnny Bench .40 1.00
139 Harmon Killebrew .40 1.00
140 Pee Wee Reese .25 .60
141 Hoyt Wilhelm .25 .60
142 Lou Brock .25 .60
143 Catfish Hunter .25 .60
144 Red Schoendienst .25 .60
145 Joe Morgan .25 .60
146 Willie Stargell .25 .60
147 Reggie Jackson .25 .60
148 Fergie Jenkins .25 .60
149 Tony Lazzeri .25 .60
150 Billy Williams .25 .60
151 Lou Gehrig SP 5.00 12.00
152 Tris Speaker SP 3.00 8.00
153 Christy Mathewson SP 3.00 8.00
154 Home Run Baker SP 3.00 8.00
155 Dizzy Dean SP 3.00 8.00
156 Al Simmons SP 3.00 8.00
157 Cy Young SP 3.00 8.00
158 Jim Bottomley SP 3.00 8.00
159 Honus Wagner SP 3.00 8.00
160 Walter Johnson SP 3.00 8.00
161 Mel Ott SP 3.00 8.00
162 Jesse Burkett SP 3.00 8.00
163 Cap Anson SP 3.00 8.00
164 Nap Lajoie SP 3.00 8.00
165 Edd Roush SP 3.00 8.00
166 Rogers Hornsby SP 3.00 8.00
167 Hank Greenberg SP 3.00 8.00
168 Eddie Plank SP 3.00 8.00
169 Jimmie Foxx SP 3.00 8.00
170 Oscar Charleston SP 3.00 8.00

2012 Panini Cooperstown Crystal Collection

CRYSTAL 1-150: 2X TO 5X BASIC
STATED PRINT RUN 299 SER.#'d SETS
14 Nolan Ryan 10.00 25.00
131 Cal Ripken Jr. 40.00 80.00
151 Lou Gehrig 4.00 10.00
152 Tris Speaker 1.25 3.00
153 Christy Mathewson 2.00 5.00
154 Home Run Baker 2.00 5.00
155 Dizzy Dean 1.25 3.00
156 Al Simmons .75 2.00
157 Cy Young 2.00 5.00
158 Jim Bottomley .75 2.00
159 Honus Wagner 2.00 5.00
160 Walter Johnson 2.00 5.00
161 Mel Ott 2.00 5.00
162 Jesse Burkett .75 2.00
163 Cap Anson 1.25 3.00
164 Nap Lajoie 2.00 5.00
165 Edd Roush 1.25 3.00
166 Rogers Hornsby 1.25 3.00
167 Hank Greenberg 2.00 5.00
168 Eddie Plank 1.25 3.00
169 Jimmie Foxx 2.00 5.00
170 Oscar Charleston .75 2.00

2012 Panini Cooperstown Crystal Collection Blue

CRYSTAL BLUE: 2X TO 5X BASIC
STATED PRINT RUN 499 SER.#'d SETS
14 Nolan Ryan 10.00 25.00

2012 Panini Cooperstown Crystal Collection Red

CRYSTAL RED: 2X TO 5X BASIC
STATED PRINT RUN 399 SER.#'d SETS
14 Nolan Ryan 10.00 25.00

2012 Panini Cooperstown Ballparks

COMPLETE SET (10) 8.00 20.00
1 Huntington Avenue Grounds 1.00 2.50
2 Polo Grounds 1905 1.00 2.50
3 Shibe Park 1.00 2.50
4 Polo Grounds 1913 1.00 2.50
5 Exposition Park 1.00 2.50
6 Bennett Park 1.00 2.50
7 South Side Park 1.00 2.50
8 West Side Park 1.00 2.50
9 Polo Grounds 1903 1.00 2.50
10 Polo Grounds 1910 1.00 2.50

2012 Panini Cooperstown Bronze History

STATED PRINT RUN 599 SER.#'d SETS
1 Grover Alexander 1.25 3.00
2 Cap Anson 2.00 5.00
3 Frank Baker 3.00 8.00
4 Al Barlick 1.25 3.00
5 Jake Beckley 1.25 3.00
6 Cool Papa Bell 1.25 3.00
7 Chief Bender 1.25 3.00
8 Yogi Berra 3.00 8.00
9 Jim Bottomley 1.25 3.00
10 Roger Bresnahan 1.25 3.00
11 Dan Brouthers 1.25 3.00
12 Mordecai Brown 1.25 3.00
13 Jesse Burkett 1.25 3.00
14 Alexander Cartwright 1.25 3.00
15 Henry Chadwick 1.25 3.00
16 Happy Chandler 1.25 3.00
17 Oscar Charleston 1.25 3.00
18 Jack Chesbro 1.25 3.00
19 Fred Clarke 1.25 3.00
20 John Clarkson 3.00 8.00
21 Eddie Collins 1.25 3.00
22 Jimmy Collins 2.00 5.00
23 Charles Comiskey 1.25 3.00
24 Jocko Conlan 2.00 5.00
25 Roger Connor 1.25 3.00
26 Andy Cooper 2.00 5.00
27 Ed Delahanty 1.25 3.00
28 Martin Dihigo 1.25 3.00
29 Hugh Duffy 1.25 3.00
30 Johnny Evers 1.25 3.00
31 Buck Ewing 1.25 3.00
32 Elmer Flick 1.25 3.00
33 Rube Foster 1.25 3.00
34 Frankie Frisch 2.00 5.00
35 Charlie Gehringer 1.25 3.00
36 Pat Gillick 3.00 8.00
37 Chick Hafey 2.00 5.00
38 Jesse Haines 2.00 5.00
39 Doug Harvey 2.00 5.00
40 Harry Heilmann 1.25 3.00
41 Harry Hooper 1.25 3.00
42 Rogers Hornsby 2.00 5.00
43 Cal Hubbard 2.00 5.00
44 Catfish Hunter 1.25 3.00
45 Ban Johnson 1.25 3.00
46 Judy Johnson 2.00 5.00
47 Tim Keefe 3.00 8.00
48 Joe Kelley 1.25 3.00
49 King Kelly 1.25 3.00
50 Bowie Kuhn 2.00 5.00
51 Nap Lajoie 2.00 5.00
52 Kenesaw Landis 1.25 3.00
53 Buck Leonard 1.25 3.00
54 Pop Lloyd 1.25 3.00
55 Connie Mack 1.25 3.00
56 Larry MacPhail 1.25 3.00
57 Effa Manley 1.25 3.00
58 Rube Marquard 1.25 3.00
59 Joe McGinnity 2.00 5.00
60 Bid McPhee 2.00 5.00
61 Joe Medwick 1.25 3.00
62 Johnny Mize 1.25 3.00
63 Kid Nichols 2.00 5.00
64 Walter O'Malley 1.25 3.00
65 Jim O'Rourke 3.00 8.00
66 Mel Ott 3.00 8.00
67 Satchel Paige 3.00 8.00
68 Herb Pennock 1.25 3.00
69 Eddie Plank 1.25 3.00
70 Cum Posey 2.00 5.00
71 Charles Radbourn 1.25 3.00
72 Branch Rickey 1.25 3.00
73 Wilbert Robinson 3.00 8.00
74 Amos Rusie 1.25 3.00
75 Ray Schalk 1.25 3.00
76 George Sisler 2.00 5.00
77 Al Spalding 1.25 3.00
78 Tris Speaker 2.00 5.00
79 Turkey Stearnes 3.00 8.00
80 Sam Thompson 1.25 3.00
81 Joe Tinker 1.25 3.00
82 Bill Veeck 3.00 8.00
83 Rube Waddell 3.00 8.00
84 Ed Walsh 1.25 3.00
85 George Weiss 1.25 3.00
86 Mickey Welch 3.00 8.00
87 Sol White 3.00 8.00
88 Vic Willis 3.00 8.00
89 George Wright 3.00 8.00
90 Harry Wright 3.00 8.00
91 Tom Yawkey 3.00 8.00
92 Monte Ward 3.00 8.00
93 Mule Suttles 2.00 5.00
94 Ned Hanlon 3.00 8.00
95 Candy Cummings 1.25 3.00
96 Ed Barrow 2.00 5.00
97 Will Harridge 2.00 5.00
98 Nestor Chylak 1.25 3.00
99 Clark Griffith 2.00 5.00
100 Bill McGowan 2.00 5.00

2012 Panini Cooperstown Credentials

1 Tom Seaver .60 1.50
2 Willie McCovey .60 1.50
3 Eddie Murray .60 1.50
4 Don Drysdale .60 1.50
5 Steve Carlton .60 1.50
6 Ernie Banks 1.00 2.50
7 Robin Yount 1.00 2.50
8 Dave Winfield .60 1.50
9 Don Sutton .60 1.50
10 Ozzie Smith 1.25 3.00
11 Frank Robinson .60 1.50
12 Juan Marichal .60 1.50
13 Phil Niekro .60 1.50
14 Roberto Clemente 2.50 6.00
15 Bert Blyleven .60 1.50
16 Bob Gibson .60 1.50
17 Mike Schmidt 1.50 4.00
18 Barry Larkin .60 1.50
19 Gaylord Perry .60 1.50

2012 Panini Cooperstown Famed Cuts

PRINT RUNS B/WN 1-33 COPIES PER
NO PRICING ON QTY 25 OR LESS
9 Joe Sewell/33 15.00 40.00

2012 Panini Cooperstown Famous Moments

1 Cy Young 1.00 2.50
2 Bill Mazeroski .60 1.50
3 Tom Seaver .60 1.50
4 Roy Campanella 1.00 2.50
5 Nolan Ryan 3.00 8.00
6 Babe Ruth 2.50 6.00
7 Mickey Mantle 3.00 8.00
8 Mel Ott 1.00 2.50
9 Jackie Robinson 1.00 2.50
10 Harmon Killebrew 1.00 2.50
11 Tony Gwynn 1.00 2.50
12 Charlie Gehringer .40 1.00
13 Don Larsen .40 1.00
14 Ted Williams 2.00 5.00
15 Willie Mays 2.00 5.00
16 Bob Feller .60 1.50
17 Carl Yastrzemski 1.50 4.00
18 Maury Wills .40 1.00
19 Frank Robinson .60 1.50
20 Cy Young 1.00 2.50

2012 Panini Cooperstown Famous Moments Signatures

1 Don Larsen 20.00 50.00
2 Carl Yastrzemski 20.00 50.00
3 Maury Wills 10.00 25.00
4 Denny McLain 8.00 20.00
6 Shawn Green 6.00 15.00
7 Don Mattingly 40.00 80.00
8 Tom Seaver 30.00 80.00
9 Nate Colbert 4.00 10.00

2012 Panini Cooperstown Field Generals

1 Johnny Bench 1.00 2.50
2 Yogi Berra 1.00 2.50
3 Mickey Cochrane .60 1.50
4 Gary Carter .60 1.50
5 Ray Schalk .40 1.00
6 Roy Campanella 1.00 2.50
7 Carlton Fisk .60 1.50
8 Rick Ferrell .40 1.00
9 Roger Bresnahan .60 1.50
10 Bill Dickey .40 1.00

2012 Panini Cooperstown Hall History

1 Inaugural Class .40 1.00
2 Ty Cobb 1.50 4.00
3 Baseball Hall of Fame .40 1.00
4 Abner Doubleday .40 1.00
5 Lou Gehrig 2.00 5.00
6 Roberto Clemente 2.50 6.00
7 Effa Manley .40 1.00
8 Ted Williams 2.00 5.00
9 Tom Seaver .60 1.50
10 Honus Wagner 1.00 2.50

2012 Panini Cooperstown High Praise

1 Luis Aparicio .75 2.00
2 Nolan Ryan 4.00 10.00
3 Johnny Bench 1.25 3.00
4 Yogi Berra 1.25 3.00
5 George Brett 2.50 6.00
6 Lou Brock .75 2.00
7 Rod Carew .75 2.00
8 Whitey Ford .75 2.00
9 Eddie Murray .75 2.00
10 Tony Gwynn 1.25 3.00
11 Reggie Jackson .75 2.00
12 Al Kaline 1.25 3.00
13 Joe Morgan .75 2.00
14 Cal Ripken Jr. 4.00 10.00
15 Robin Yount 1.25 3.00
16 Tom Seaver .75 2.00
17 Johnny Mize .75 2.00
18 Harmon Killebrew 1.25 3.00
19 Brooks Robinson .75 2.00
20 Jim Bunning .75 2.00

2012 Panini Cooperstown HOF Classes Induction Year

1 Ty Cobb 3.00 8.00
2 Walter Johnson 2.00 5.00
3 Lou Gehrig 4.00 10.00
4 Rogers Hornsby 1.25 3.00
5 Jimmie Foxx 2.00 5.00
6 Mel Ott 2.00 5.00
7 Frank Baker 2.00 5.00
8 Joe DiMaggio 4.00 10.00
9 Jackie Robinson 2.00 5.00
10 Ted Williams 4.00 10.00
11 Stan Musial 3.00 8.00
12 Yogi Berra 2.00 5.00
13 Al Kaline 2.00 5.00
14 Brooks Robinson 1.25 3.00
15 Reggie Jackson 1.25 3.00
16 George Brett 4.00 10.00
17 Nolan Ryan 6.00 15.00
18 Cal Ripken Jr. 6.00 15.00
19 Rickey Henderson 2.00 5.00
20 Barry Larkin 1.25 3.00

2012 Panini Cooperstown Induction

1 George Brett 3.00 8.00
2 Al Kaline 1.50 4.00
3 Rickey Henderson 1.50 4.00
4 Harmon Killebrew 1.50 4.00
5 Mike Schmidt 2.50 6.00
6 Ted Williams 3.00 8.00
7 Johnny Bench 1.50 4.00
8 Whitey Ford 1.00 2.50
9 Cal Ripken Jr. 5.00 12.00
10 Jim Palmer 1.00 2.50
11 Joe DiMaggio 3.00 8.00
12 Nolan Ryan 5.00 12.00
13 Tom Seaver 1.00 2.50
14 Billy Williams 1.00 2.50
15 Tony Gwynn 1.50 4.00
16 Robin Yount 1.50 4.00
17 Roberto Alomar 1.00 2.50
18 Richie Ashburn 1.00 2.50
19 Bob Feller 1.00 2.50
20 Lou Brock 1.00 2.50
21 Brooks Robinson 1.00 2.50
22 Ryne Sandberg 3.00 8.00
23 Reggie Jackson 1.00 2.50
24 Bob Gibson 1.00 2.50
25 Yogi Berra 1.50 4.00

2012 Panini Cooperstown Museum Pieces

1 Ty Cobb 1.50 4.00
2 Ernie Banks 1.00 2.50
3 Christy Mathewson 1.00 2.50
4 Babe Ruth 2.50 6.00
5 Hank Aaron 2.00 5.00
6 Buck Leonard .40 1.00
7 Johnny Bench 1.00 2.50
8 George Brett 2.00 5.00
9 Willie Mays 2.00 5.00
10 Carlton Fisk .60 1.50
11 Rickey Henderson 1.00 2.50
12 Al Kaline 1.00 2.50
13 Walter Johnson 1.00 2.50
14 Lou Gehrig 2.00 5.00
15 Johnny Evers .40 1.00
16 Mel Ott 1.00 2.50
17 Mickey Mantle 3.00 8.00
18 Joe DiMaggio 2.00 5.00
19 Paul Waner .60 1.50
20 Lefty Grove .60 1.50

2012 Panini Cooperstown Signatures

OVERALL AUTO ODDS ONE PER BOX
PRINT RUNS B/WN 5-799 COPIES PER
NO PRICING ON QTY 25 OR LESS
1 Luis Aparicio/149 10.00 25.00
2 Yogi Berra/99 40.00 100.00
3 Johnny Bench/100 40.00 100.00
4 Wade Boggs/100 25.00 60.00
5 George Brett/30 150.00 400.00
6 Lou Brock/199 10.00 25.00
7 Jim Bunning/350 4.00 10.00
8 Rod Carew/149 15.00 40.00
9 Gary Carter/75 30.00 80.00
10 Orlando Cepeda/330 6.00 15.00
11 Bobby Doerr/250 6.00 15.00
12 Bob Feller/40 40.00 100.00
13 Whitey Ford/75 15.00 40.00
14 Goose Gossage/499 6.00 15.00
15 Tony Gwynn/99 30.00 80.00
16 Doug Harvey/500 5.00 12.00
18 Reggie Jackson/75 30.00 60.00
19 Fergie Jenkins/599 5.00 12.00
20 Al Kaline/349 15.00 40.00
21 George Kell/250 6.00 15.00
22 Ernie Banks/25 100.00 250.00
23 Bert Blyleven/399 5.00 12.00
24 Andre Dawson/324 6.00 15.00
25 Stan Musial/50 125.00 300.00
27 Tommy Lasorda/149 30.00 80.00
28 Juan Marichal/179 12.00 30.00
29 Bill Mazeroski/149 12.00 30.00
30 Willie McCovey/99 30.00 80.00
31 Steve Carlton/199 10.00 25.00
32 Paul Molitor/399 6.00 15.00
33 Joe Morgan/100 30.00 80.00
34 Eddie Murray/100 25.00 60.00
35 Phil Niekro/299 5.00 12.00
36 Jim Palmer/350 5.00 12.00
37 Carlton Fisk/239 15.00 40.00
38 Frank Robinson/90 30.00 80.00
39 Tony Perez/648 6.00 15.00
40 Carl Yastrzemski/75 40.00 100.00
41 Mike Schmidt/100 25.00 60.00
42 Cal Ripken Jr./50 75.00 200.00
43 Brooks Robinson/349 10.00 25.00
44 Nolan Ryan/75 75.00 150.00
45 Ryne Sandberg/99 30.00 80.00
46 Red Schoendienst/549 6.00 15.00
48 Rickey Henderson/50 75.00 150.00
49 Bruce Sutter/799 5.00 12.00
50 Earl Weaver /299 8.00 20.00
51 Don Sutton/788 4.00 10.00
53 Jim Rice/599 5.00 12.00
54 Barry Larkin/199 20.00 50.00
55 Billy Williams/299 6.00 15.00
56 Dave Winfield/50 25.00 60.00
57 Robin Yount/100 20.00 50.00
58 Gaylord Perry/549 4.00 10.00
59 Rollie Fingers/799 6.00 15.00
60 Duke Snider/25 75.00 200.00
61 Whitey Herzog/550 6.00 15.00
62 Paul Molitor/100 10.00 25.00
63 Reggie Jackson/25 40.00 100.00
64 Nolan Ryan/50 60.00 150.00
66 Pat Gillick/500 4.00 10.00
67 Gaylord Perry/50 8.00 20.00
68 Bob Gibson/99 12.00 30.00
69 Dennis Eckersley/650 6.00 15.00
70 Rickey Henderson/50 75.00 150.00
71 Ozzie Smith/149 20.00 50.00
72 Dick Williams/49 20.00 50.00
73 Robin Roberts/25 40.00 100.00
75 Wade Boggs/25 25.00 60.00
76 Andre Dawson/75 15.00 40.00
78 Bert Blyleven/25 15.00 40.00
79 Dave Winfield/25 25.00 60.00
80 Orlando Cepeda/19 75.00 200.00
83 Vin Scully/100 250.00 500.00
84 Joe Garagiola/125 20.00 50.00
85 Milo Hamilton/500 6.00 15.00
86 Bob Wolff/500 8.00 20.00
87 Marty Brennaman/500 12.00 30.00
88 Jerry Coleman/300 6.00 15.00
90 Gene Elston/500 4.00 10.00
91 Denny Matthews/500 5.00 12.00
92 Jon Miller/500 8.00 20.00
93 Tony Kubek/200 15.00 40.00
94 Dave Van Horne/500 4.00 10.00
95 Tim McCarver/50 50.00 100.00
96 Peter Gammons/300 10.00 25.00
97 Murray Chass/500 4.00 10.00
100 Tony Perez/50 15.00 40.00

2012 Panini Cooperstown The Village

COMPLETE SET (10) 8.00 20.00
1 Main Street 1.00 2.50
2 Otsego Lake 1.00 2.50
3 Outside the Museum 1.00 2.50
4 Otesaga Hotel 1.00 2.50
5 James Fenimore Cooper Statue 1.00 2.50
6 The Landmark Inn 1.00 2.50
7 Cooperstown Sidewalk 1.00 2.50
8 Cooperstown Mountains 1.00 2.50
9 The Farmers' Museum 1.00 2.50
10 Fresh Snowfall in Cooperstown 1.00 2.50

2012 Panini Cooperstown Voices of Summer

COMPLETE SET (10) 8.00 20.00
COMMON CARD 1.00 2.50
1 Mel Allen 1.00 2.50
2 Harry Caray 1.00 2.50
3 Ernie Harwell 1.00 2.50
4 Jack Buck 1.00 2.50
5 Red Barber 1.00 2.50
6 Joe Garagiola 1.00 2.50
7 Denny Matthews 1.00 2.50
8 Russ Hodges 1.00 2.50
9 Vin Scully 1.00 2.50
10 Harry Kalas 1.00 2.50

2012 Panini Cooperstown With Honors

COMPLETE SET (10) 8.00 20.00
1 Jackie Robinson 1.00 2.50
2 Bobby Doerr .60 1.50
3 Bob Feller .60 1.50
4 Charlie Gehringer .40 1.00
5 Joe DiMaggio 2.00 5.00
6 Hank Greenberg 1.00 2.50
7 Stan Musial 1.50 4.00
8 Whitey Ford .60 1.50
9 Ted Williams 2.00 5.00
10 Johnny Mize .60 1.50

2013 Panini Cooperstown

COMPLETE SET (110) 40.00 80.00
COMP.SET w/o SP's (100) 15.00 40.00
1 Lou Gehrig .50 1.25
2 Cy Young .25 .60
3 Tris Speaker .20 .50
4 Christy Mathewson .25 .60
5 Ty Cobb .40 1.00
6 Rogers Hornsby .20 .50
7 Walter Johnson .25 .60
8 Joe Tinker .20 .50
9 Johnny Evers .15 .40
10 Frank Chance .20 .50
11 Cap Anson .20 .50
12 Frank Baker .25 .60
13 Dan Brouthers .15 .40
14 Honus Wagner .25 .60
15 Frankie Frisch .20 .50
16 Edd Roush .20 .50
17 Satchel Paige .25 .60
18 Miller Huggins .15 .40
19 Nap Lajoie .25 .60
20 Rube Marquard .20 .50
21 Tony Lazzeri .20 .50
22 Zack Wheat .20 .50
23 Hack Wilson .20 .50
24 Goose Goslin .20 .50
25 Lefty Grove .20 .50
26 Lloyd Waner .20 .50
27 Paul Waner .20 .50
28 Buck Leonard .15 .40
29 Jim Bottomley .15 .40
30 George Sisler .20 .50
31 Mel Ott .25 .60
32 Jimmie Foxx .25 .60
33 Burleigh Grimes .20 .50
34 Harry Heilmann .20 .50
35 Joe Medwick .15 .40
36 Bill Dickey .15 .40
37 Arky Vaughan .15 .40
38 Mickey Cochrane .20 .50
39 Dizzy Dean .20 .50
40 Bill Terry .20 .50
41 Carl Hubbell .20 .50
42 Jackie Robinson .25 .60
43 Bobby Doerr .20 .50
44 Dave Bancroft .15 .40
45 Billy Southworth .15 .40
46 Charlie Gehringer .15 .40
47 Al Lopez .15 .40
48 Rick Ferrell .15 .40
49 Bob Lemon .20 .50
50 Luke Appling .20 .50
51 Bob Feller .20 .50
52 Hal Newhouser .20 .50
53 Lou Boudreau .20 .50
54 George Kell .20 .50
55 Roy Campanella .25 .60
56 Stan Musial .40 1.00
57 Al Barlick .20 .50
58 Duke Snider .20 .50

59 Phil Rizzuto .20 .50
60 Whitey Ford .20 .50
61 Nellie Fox .20 .50
62 Casey Stengel .20 .50
63 Warren Spahn .20 .50
64 Pee Wee Reese .20 .50
65 Vin Scully .25 .60
66 Billy Williams .20 .50
67 Hoyt Wilhelm .20 .50
68 Yogi Berra .25 .60
69 Red Schoendienst .20 .50
70 Jim Bunning .20 .50
71 Frank Robinson .20 .50
72 Robin Roberts .20 .50
73 Richie Ashburn .20 .50
74 Luis Aparicio .20 .50
75 Al Kaline .25 .60
76 Willie McCovey .20 .50
77 Steve Carlton .20 .50
78 Brooks Robinson .20 .50
79 Bill Mazeroski .20 .50
80 Johnny Bench .25 .60
81 Orlando Cepeda .20 .50
82 Rod Carew .20 .50
83 Willie Stargell .20 .50
84 Bob Gibson .20 .50
85 Joe Morgan .20 .50
86 Phil Niekro .20 .50
87 Tom Seaver .20 .50
88 Bruce Sutter .20 .50
89 Juan Marichal .20 .50
90 Carl Yastrzemski .40 1.00
91 Tony Perez .20 .50
92 Reggie Jackson .20 .50
93 Carlton Fisk .20 .50
94 Jim Palmer .20 .50
95 Catfish Hunter .20 .50
96 Mike Schmidt .40 1.00
97 Robin Yount .25 .60
98 Dave Winfield .20 .50
99 George Brett .50 1.25
100 Nolan Ryan .75 2.00
101 Cal Ripken Jr. SP 3.00 8.00
102 Tommy Lasorda SP .75 2.00
103 Carlton Fisk SP .75 2.00
104 Wade Boggs SP .75 2.00
105 Eddie Murray SP .75 2.00
106 Ryne Sandberg SP 2.00 5.00
107 Rickey Henderson SP 1.00 2.50
108 Jim Rice SP .75 2.00
109 Tony Gwynn SP 1.00 2.50
110 Gaylord Perry SP .75 2.00

2013 Panini Cooperstown Blue Crystal

*BLUE: 2X TO 5X BASIC
STATED PRINT RUN 499 SER.#'d SETS

2013 Panini Cooperstown Gold Crystal

*GOLD: 2.5X TO 6X BASIC
STATED PRINT RUN 299 SER.#'d SETS

2013 Panini Cooperstown Green Crystal

*GREEN: 1.5X TO 4X BASIC
100 Nolan Ryan 10.00 25.00

2013 Panini Cooperstown Red Crystal

*RED: 2X TO 5X BASIC
STATED PRINT RUN 399 SER.#'d SETS

2013 Panini Cooperstown Orange

*ORANGE: 2.5X TO 6X BASIC
STATED PRINT RUN 325 SER.#'d SETS

2013 Panini Cooperstown Colgan's Chips

1 Roberto Alomar 1.00 2.50
2 Sparky Anderson 1.00 2.50
3 Cap Anson 1.00 2.50
4 Luis Aparicio 1.00 2.50
5 Luke Appling 1.00 2.50
6 Richie Ashburn 1.00 2.50
7 Home Run Baker 1.25 3.00
8 Ernie Banks 1.25 3.00
9 Johnny Bench 1.25 3.00
10 Yogi Berra 1.25 3.00
11 Yogi Berra 1.25 3.00
12 Bert Blyleven 1.00 2.50
13 Wade Boggs 1.00 2.50
14 Jim Bottomley .75 2.00
15 Lou Boudreau 1.00 2.50
16 Roger Bresnahan 1.00 2.50
17 George Brett 2.50 6.00
18 Lou Brock 1.00 2.50
19 Dan Brouthers .75 2.00
20 Jim Bunning 1.00 2.50
21 Jesse Burkett .75 2.00
22 Roy Campanella 1.25 3.00
23 Rod Carew 1.00 2.50
24 Steve Carlton 1.00 2.50
25 Gary Carter 1.00 2.50
26 Gary Carter 1.00 2.50
27 Orlando Cepeda 1.00 2.50
28 Frank Chance 1.00 2.50
29 Ty Cobb 2.00 5.00
30 Mickey Cochrane 1.00 2.50
31 Joe Cronin .75 2.00
32 Charles Comiskey .75 2.00
33 Stan Coveleski 1.00 2.50
34 Sam Crawford .75 2.00
35 Andre Dawson 1.00 2.50
36 Dizzy Dean 1.00 2.50
37 Bill Dickey .75 2.00
38 Bobby Doerr 1.00 2.50
39 Dennis Eckersley 1.00 2.50
40 Johnny Evers .75 2.00
41 Buck Ewing .50 1.25
42 Bob Feller 1.00 2.50
43 Rick Ferrell .75 2.00
44 Rollie Fingers .50 1.25
45 Carlton Fisk 1.00 2.50
46 Whitey Ford 1.00 2.50
47 Nellie Fox 1.00 2.50
48 Frankie Frisch 1.00 2.50
49 Lou Gehrig 2.50 6.00
50 Charlie Gehringer .75 2.00
51 Bob Gibson 1.00 2.50
52 Josh Gibson 1.25 3.00
53 Lefty Gomez .50 1.25
54 Goose Goslin 1.00 2.50
55 Goose Gossage 1.00 2.50
56 Burleigh Grimes 1.00 2.50
57 Lefty Grove 1.00 2.50
58 Tony Gwynn 1.25 3.00
59 Doug Harvey .50 1.25
60 Rickey Henderson 1.25 3.00
61 Whitey Herzog .50 1.25
62 Harry Hooper .50 1.25
63 Rogers Hornsby 1.00 2.50
64 Waite Hoyt .50 1.25
65 Carl Hubbell 1.00 2.50
66 Miller Huggins .75 2.00
67 Catfish Hunter 1.00 2.50
68 Catfish Hunter 1.00 2.50
69 Monte Irvin .75 2.00
70 Reggie Jackson 1.00 2.50
71 Reggie Jackson 1.00 2.50
72 Fergie Jenkins 1.00 2.50
73 Walter Johnson 1.25 3.00
74 Addie Joss .75 2.00
75 Al Kaline 1.25 3.00
76 George Kell 1.00 2.50
77 King Kelly .50 1.25
78 Harmon Killebrew 1.25 3.00
79 Ralph Kiner .75 2.00
80 Bowie Kuhn .75 2.00
81 Nap Lajoie 1.25 3.00
82 Kenesaw Landis .50 1.25
83 Barry Larkin 1.00 2.50
84 Tommy Lasorda 1.00 2.50
85 Bob Lemon 1.00 2.50
86 Buck Leonard .75 2.00
87 Fred Lindstrom .50 1.25
88 Al Lopez .75 2.00
89 Connie Mack .50 1.25
90 Heinie Manush .50 1.25
91 Rabbit Maranville .50 1.25
92 Juan Marichal 1.00 2.50
93 Rube Marquard 1.00 2.50
94 Eddie Mathews 1.25 3.00
95 Christy Mathewson 1.25 3.00
96 Bill Mazeroski 1.00 2.50
97 Willie McCovey 1.00 2.50
98 John McGraw .75 2.00
99 Joe Medwick .75 2.00
100 Paul Molitor 1.25 3.00
101 Joe Morgan 1.00 2.50
102 Joe Morgan 1.00 2.50
103 Eddie Murray 1.00 2.50
104 Stan Musial 2.00 5.00
105 Hal Newhouser 1.00 2.50
106 Phil Niekro 1.00 2.50
107 Walter O'Malley .50 1.25
108 Mel Ott 1.25 3.00
109 Satchel Paige 1.25 3.00
110 Jim Palmer 1.00 2.50
111 Tony Perez 1.00 2.50
112 Gaylord Perry 1.00 2.50
113 Eddie Plank .50 1.25
114 Effa Manley .50 1.25
115 Kirby Puckett 1.25 3.00
116 Charles Radbourn .50 1.25
117 Pee Wee Reese 1.00 2.50
118 Jim Rice 1.00 2.50
119 Sam Rice .75 2.00
120 Cal Ripken Jr. 4.00 10.00
121 Phil Rizzuto 1.00 2.50
122 Robin Roberts 1.00 2.50
123 Brooks Robinson 1.00 2.50
124 Frank Robinson 1.00 2.50
125 Jackie Robinson 1.25 3.00
126 Edd Roush 1.00 2.50
127 Nolan Ryan 4.00 10.00
128 Nolan Ryan 4.00 10.00
129 Ryne Sandberg 2.50 6.00
130 Ron Santo .75 2.00
131 Mike Schmidt 2.00 5.00
132 Red Schoendienst 1.00 2.50
133 Tom Seaver 1.00 2.50
134 Tom Seaver 1.00 2.50
135 Al Simmons 1.00 2.50
136 George Sisler 1.00 2.50
137 Ozzie Smith 1.50 4.00
138 Duke Snider 1.00 2.50
139 Warren Spahn 1.00 2.50
140 Tris Speaker 1.00 2.50
141 Willie Stargell 1.00 2.50
142 Casey Stengel 1.00 2.50
143 Bruce Sutter 1.00 2.50
144 Don Sutton .75 2.00
145 Bill Terry 1.00 2.50
146 Joe Tinker 1.00 2.50
147 Pie Traynor .50 1.25
148 Dazzy Vance .75 2.00
149 Arky Vaughan .75 2.00
150 Honus Wagner 1.25 3.00
151 Ed Walsh .50 1.25
152 Lloyd Waner 1.00 2.50
153 Paul Waner 1.00 2.50
154 Earl Weaver .75 2.00
155 Zack Wheat 1.00 2.50
156 Hoyt Wilhelm 1.00 2.50
157 Billy Williams 1.00 2.50
158 Dick Williams .50 1.25
159 Hack Wilson 1.00 2.50
160 Dave Winfield 1.00 2.50
161 George Wright .50 1.25
162 Early Wynn 1.00 2.50
163 Carl Yastrzemski 2.00 5.00
164 Cy Young 1.25 3.00
165 Robin Yount 1.25 3.00

2013 Panini Cooperstown Historic Tickets

1 1916 World Series .30 .75
2 1919 World Series .30 .75
3 1920 World Series .30 .75
4 1922 World Series .30 .75
5 1922 World Series .30 .75
6 1924 World Series .30 .75
7 1925 World Series .30 .75
8 1931 US Tour of Japan .30 .75
9 1931 World Series .30 .75
10 1934 World Series .30 .75
11 1936 World Series .30 .75
12 1936 World Series .30 .75
13 1940 World Series .30 .75
14 1942 World Series .30 .75
15 1944 World Series .30 .75
16 1944 World Series .30 .75
17 1946 World Series .30 .75
18 Baseball Hall of Fame Opening .30 .75
19 Roy Campanella .75 2.00
20 Roberto Clemente 2.00 5.00
21 Lou Gehrig 1.50 4.00
22 Lou Gehrig 1.50 4.00
23 Roger Maris .75 2.00
24 Jackie Robinson .75 2.00
25 Bobby Thomson .50 1.25

2013 Panini Cooperstown Induction

COMPLETE SET (20) 12.50 30.00
1 Frank Robinson 1.00 2.50
2 Joe Morgan 1.00 2.50
3 Phil Niekro 1.00 2.50
4 Phil Rizzuto 1.00 2.50
5 Willie Stargell 1.00 2.50
6 Ernie Banks 1.25 3.00
7 Carl Yastrzemski 2.00 5.00
8 Steve Carlton 1.00 2.50
9 Andre Dawson 1.00 2.50
10 Wade Boggs 1.00 2.50
11 Eddie Murray 1.00 2.50
12 Barry Larkin 1.00 2.50
13 Warren Spahn 1.00 2.50
14 Duke Snider 1.00 2.50
15 Paul Molitor 1.25 3.00
16 Carlton Fisk 1.00 2.50
17 Early Wynn 1.00 2.50
18 Rod Carew 1.00 2.50
19 Ozzie Smith 1.50 4.00
20 Catfish Hunter 1.00 2.50

2013 Panini Cooperstown International Play

COMPLETE SET (10) 8.00 20.00
1 Luis Aparicio 2.00 5.00
2 Bert Blyleven 2.00 5.00
3 Orlando Cepeda 2.00 5.00
4 Roberto Alomar 2.00 5.00
5 Rod Carew 2.00 5.00
6 Fergie Jenkins 2.00 5.00
7 Juan Marichal 2.00 5.00
8 Tony Perez 2.00 5.00
9 Harry Wright 1.00 2.50
10 Cristobal Torriente 1.00 2.50

2013 Panini Cooperstown Lumberjacks

ALL VERSIONS EQUALLY PRICED
1 Cap Anson 2.50 6.00
2 Cap Anson 2.50 6.00
3 Cap Anson 2.50 6.00
4 Ty Cobb 5.00 12.00
5 Ty Cobb 5.00 12.00
6 Ty Cobb 5.00 12.00
7 Johnny Evers 2.00 5.00
8 Johnny Evers 2.00 5.00
9 Johnny Evers 2.00 5.00
10 Joe Tinker 2.50 6.00
11 Joe Tinker 2.50 6.00
12 Joe Tinker 2.50 6.00
13 Frank Chance 2.50 6.00
14 Frank Chance 2.50 6.00
15 Frank Chance 2.50 6.00
16 Dan Brouthers 2.00 5.00
17 Dan Brouthers 2.00 5.00
18 Dan Brouthers 2.00 5.00
19 Nap Lajoie 3.00 8.00
20 Nap Lajoie 3.00 8.00
21 Nap Lajoie 3.00 8.00
22 Connie Mack 1.25 3.00
23 Connie Mack 1.25 3.00
24 Connie Mack 1.25 3.00
25 Harry Hooper 1.25 3.00
26 Harry Hooper 1.25 3.00
27 Harry Hooper 1.25 3.00
28 Ed Walsh 1.25 3.00
29 Ed Walsh 1.25 3.00
30 Ed Walsh 1.25 3.00
31 Buck Ewing 1.25 3.00
32 Buck Ewing 1.25 3.00
33 Buck Ewing 1.25 3.00
34 Roger Bresnahan 2.50 6.00
35 Roger Bresnahan 2.50 6.00
36 Roger Bresnahan 2.50 6.00
37 Fred Clarke 2.00 5.00
38 Fred Clarke 2.00 5.00
39 Fred Clarke 2.00 5.00
40 Joe McGinnity 1.25 3.00
41 Joe McGinnity 1.25 3.00
42 Joe McGinnity 1.25 3.00
43 Hugh Duffy 1.25 3.00
44 Hugh Duffy 1.25 3.00
45 Hugh Duffy 1.25 3.00
46 Charles Radbourn 1.25 3.00
47 Charles Radbourn 1.25 3.00
48 Charles Radbourn 1.25 3.00
49 Cy Young 3.00 8.00
50 Cy Young 3.00 8.00
51 Cy Young 3.00 8.00
52 John McGraw 2.00 5.00
53 John McGraw 2.00 5.00
54 John McGraw 2.00 5.00
55 King Kelly 1.25 3.00
56 King Kelly 1.25 3.00
57 King Kelly 1.25 3.00
58 Home Run Baker 3.00 8.00
59 Home Run Baker 3.00 8.00
60 Home Run Baker 3.00 8.00
61 Jimmy Collins 2.00 5.00
62 Jimmy Collins 2.00 5.00
63 Jimmy Collins 2.00 5.00
64 Max Carey 2.00 5.00
65 Max Carey 2.00 5.00
66 Max Carey 2.00 5.00
67 Addie Joss 2.00 5.00
68 Addie Joss 2.00 5.00
69 Addie Joss 2.00 5.00
70 Rube Marquard 2.50 6.00
71 Rube Marquard 2.50 6.00
72 Rube Marquard 2.50 6.00
73 Sam Thompson 1.25 3.00
74 Sam Thompson 1.25 3.00
75 Sam Thompson 1.25 3.00
76 Elmer Flick 2.00 5.00
77 Elmer Flick 2.00 5.00
78 Elmer Flick 2.00 5.00
79 Sam Crawford 2.00 5.00
80 Sam Crawford 2.00 5.00
81 Sam Crawford 2.00 5.00
82 Honus Wagner 3.00 8.00
83 Honus Wagner 3.00 8.00
84 Honus Wagner 3.00 8.00
85 Bobby Wallace 1.25 3.00
86 Bobby Wallace 1.25 3.00
87 Bobby Wallace 1.25 3.00
88 John Montgomery Ward 2.00 5.00
89 John Montgomery Ward 2.00 5.00
90 John Montgomery Ward 2.00 5.00
91 Zack Wheat 2.50 6.00
92 Zack Wheat 2.50 6.00
93 Zack Wheat 2.50 6.00
94 John Clarkson 2.00 5.00
95 John Clarkson 2.00 5.00
96 John Clarkson 2.00 5.00
97 Chief Bender 2.50 6.00
98 Chief Bender 2.50 6.00
99 Chief Bender 2.50 6.00
100 Eddie Plank 1.25 3.00

2013 Panini Cooperstown Lumberjacks Die Cut

STATED PRINT RUN 175 SER.#'d SETS
1 Ty Cobb 10.00 25.00
2 Tris Speaker 8.00 20.00
3 Nap Lajoie 8.00 20.00
4 Walter Johnson 15.00 40.00
5 Zack Wheat 6.00 15.00
6 King Kelly 8.00 20.00
7 Home Run Baker 6.00 15.00
8 Roger Bresnahan 6.00 15.00
9 Honus Wagner 10.00 25.00
10 Sam Crawford 6.00 15.00
11 Harry Hooper 6.00 15.00
12 John McGraw 8.00 20.00
13 Max Carey 6.00 15.00
14 Jimmy Collins 6.00 15.00
15 Eddie Plank
16 Dan Brouthers
17 Fred Clarke 6.00 15.00
18 Connie Mack 6.00 15.00
19 Buck Ewing 6.00 15.00
20 Joe Tinker 6.00 15.00
21 Frankie Frisch 6.00 15.00
22 Johnny Evers 6.00 15.00
23 Addie Joss 8.00 20.00
24 Frank Chance

2013 Panini Cooperstown Museum Pieces

1 Johnny Evers .40 1.00
2 Bob Feller .50 1.25
3 Hank Greenberg .60 1.50
4 George Brett 1.25 3.00
5 Roy Campanella .60 1.50
6 Paul Waner .50 1.25
7 Tony Gwynn .60 1.50
8 Bobby Doerr .50 1.25
9 Reggie Jackson .50 1.25
10 Buck Leonard .40 1.00
11 Mickey Mantle 2.00 5.00
12 Hank Aaron 1.25 3.00
13 Nolan Ryan 2.00 5.00
14 Walter Johnson .60 1.50
15 Bob Gibson .50 1.25

2013 Panini Cooperstown Numbers Game

1 Cy Young 1.00 2.50
2 Cy Young/Walter Johnson 1.00 2.50
3 Ed Walsh .40 1.00
4 Addie Joss/Ed Walsh .60 1.50
5 Hack Wilson .75 2.00
6 H.Wilson/L.Gehrig 2.00 5.00
7 Hugh Duffy .40 1.00
8 Billy Hamilton .75 2.00
9 Tris Speaker .75 2.00
10 Lou Brock/Rickey Henderson 1.00 2.50
11 Hugh Jennings .75 2.00
12 Nolan Ryan 3.00 8.00
13 Walter Johnson 1.00 2.50
14 Cy Young 1.00 2.50
15 Ty Cobb 1.50 4.00
16 R.Hornsby/T.Cobb 1.50 4.00
17 Ted Williams 2.00 5.00
18 Jake Beckley .60 1.50
19 Rickey Henderson 1.00 2.50
20 R.Henderson/T.Cobb 1.50 4.00

2013 Panini Cooperstown Pennants Blue

1 Satchel Paige 6.00 15.00
2 Lou Gehrig 5.00 12.00
3 Joe Medwick 1.50 4.00
4 Roy Campanella 2.50 6.00
5 Warren Spahn 2.00 5.00
6 Casey Stengel 2.00 5.00
7 Carlton Fisk 2.00 5.00
8 Edd Roush 2.00 5.00
9 Tony Lazzeri 2.00 5.00
10 Mickey Cochrane 2.00 5.00
11 Ron Santo 1.50 4.00
12 Rickey Henderson 2.50 6.00
13 Ozzie Smith 3.00 8.00
14 Willie McCovey 2.00 5.00
15 Goose Goslin 2.00 5.00
16 Robin Yount 2.50 6.00
17 Tom Seaver 2.00 5.00
18 Barry Larkin 2.00 5.00
19 Mel Ott 2.50 6.00
20 Tris Speaker 2.00 5.00
21 Christy Mathewson 2.50 6.00
22 Ryne Sandberg 5.00 12.00
23 Johnny Bench 2.50 6.00
24 Steve Carlton 2.00 5.00
25 George Brett 5.00 12.00
26 Eddie Mathews 2.50 6.00
27 Walter Johnson 2.50 6.00
28 Nolan Ryan 8.00 20.00
29 Yogi Berra 2.50 6.00
30 Stan Musial 4.00 10.00
31 Reggie Jackson 2.00 5.00
32 Jackie Robinson 2.50 6.00
33 Brooks Robinson 2.00 5.00
34 Bob Gibson 2.00 5.00
35 Rogers Hornsby 2.00 5.00
36 Nap Lajoie 2.50 6.00
37 Eddie Murray 2.00 5.00
38 Duke Snider 2.00 5.00
39 Dizzy Dean 2.00 5.00
40 Ernie Banks 2.50 6.00
41 Carl Hubbell 2.00 5.00
42 Cal Ripken Jr. 8.00 20.00
43 Mike Schmidt 4.00 10.00
44 Lou Brock 2.00 5.00
45 Sam Crawford 1.50 4.00
46 Josh Gibson 2.50 6.00
47 Connie Mack 1.00 2.50
48 Eddie Plank 1.00 2.50

2013 Panini Cooperstown Pennants Red

*RED: .4X TO 1X BLUE

2013 Panini Cooperstown Signatures

EXCHANGE DEADLINE 02/28/2015
2 Roberto Alomar/25
5 Johnny Bench/90 30.00 60.00
RAL Roberto Alomar/125 15.00 40.00
HOFALK Al Kaline/325 15.00 40.00
HOFBCS Bruce Sutter/100 4.00 10.00
HOFBGS Wade Boggs/90
HOFBIL Billy Williams/330 8.00 20.00
HOFBLY Bert Blyleven/99 4.00 10.00
HOFBOB Bobby Doerr/350 5.00 12.00
HOFBRC Bruce Sutter/390 8.00 20.00
HOFBRK Brooks Robinson/350 10.00 25.00
HOFBRT Bert Blyleven/591 4.00 10.00
HOFCAL Cal Ripken Jr./100 40.00 80.00
HOFCAR Rod Carew/100 15.00 40.00
HOFCAR Steve Carlton/180 6.00 15.00
HOFCEP Orlando Cepeda/375 10.00 25.00
HOFDAW Andre Dawson/599 6.00 15.00
HOFDEN Dennis Eckersley/500 4.00 10.00
HOFDNS Dennis Eckersley/200 4.00 10.00
HOFDON Don Sutton/75 4.00 10.00
HOFDST Don Sutton/200 10.00 25.00
HOFDVE Dave Winfield/50 15.00 40.00
HOFECK Dennis Eckersley/400 4.00 10.00
HOFEDI Phil Niekro/350 4.00 10.00
HOFERN Ernie Banks/90 40.00 100.00
HOFFER Fergie Jenkins/450 10.00 25.00
HOFFIN Rollie Fingers/199 4.00 10.00
HOFFIS Carlton Fisk/90 15.00 40.00
HOFFNK Frank Robinson/50 12.00 30.00
HOFFRK Frank Robinson/20
HOFGAD Gaylord Perry/330 6.00 15.00
HOFGEO George Brett/50 50.00 100.00
HOFGIB Bob Gibson/90 20.00 50.00
HOFGIL Pat Gillick/550 5.00 12.00
HOFGOS Goose Gossage/150 8.00 20.00
HOFGSG Goose Gossage/20
HOFGWY Tony Gwynn/125 25.00 60.00
HOFGYL Gaylord Perry/20
HOFHAR Doug Harvey/510 4.00 10.00
HOFHED Rickey Henderson/10
HOFHND Rickey Henderson/30 60.00 120.00
HOFJAK Reggie Jackson/30 30.00 60.00
HOFJAX Reggie Jackson/50
HOFJBU Jim Bunning/6
HOFJEN Fergie Jenkins/49
HOFJIM Jim Bunning/340 4.00 10.00
HOFJIM Jim Rice/799 6.00 15.00
HOFJOE Joe Morgan/120 10.00 25.00
HOFLAR Barry Larkin/190 20.00 50.00
HOFLOU Lou Brock/125 15.00 40.00
HOFMAR Juan Marichal/200 10.00 25.00
HOFMAZ Bill Mazeroski/300 10.00 25.00
HOFMCC Willie McCovey/40
HOFMIK Mike Schmidt/100 25.00 60.00
HOFMOL Paul Molitor/490 6.00 15.00
HOFMOR Joe Morgan/10
HOFMUR Eddie Murray/75 20.00 50.00
HOFNOL Nolan Ryan/10
HOFNOR Nolan Ryan/10
HOFNRY Nolan Ryan/90
HOFORL Orlando Cepeda/25 15.00 40.00
HOFOZZ Ozzie Smith/90 15.00 40.00
HOFPAL Jim Palmer/400 10.00 25.00
HOFPAU Paul Molitor/60 12.00 30.00
HOFPER Gaylord Perry/39 8.00 20.00
HOFPRY Gaylord Perry/210 6.00 15.00
HOFPRZ Tony Perez/99 12.00 30.00
HOFRED Red Schoendienst/500 10.00 25.00
HOFREG Reggie Jackson/10 60.00 150.00
HOFRIC Goose Gossage/430 6.00 15.00
HOFRKY Rickey Henderson/40 75.00 150.00
HOFROB Frank Robinson/10
HOFROB Robin Yount/90 20.00 50.00
HOFROD Rod Carew/20
HOFROL Rollie Fingers/700 4.00 10.00
HOFRYA Nolan Ryan/10
HOFRYN Ryne Sandberg/90 20.00 50.00
HOFSEA Tom Seaver/40 12.00 30.00
HOFSEV Tom Seaver/40 EXCH 25.00 60.00
HOFSMT Ozzie Smith/20
HOFSTN Don Sutton/100 8.00 20.00
HOFSTV Steve Carlton/20
HOFSUT Bruce Sutter/100
HOFSVR Tom Seaver/20
HOFTNY Tony Perez/300 10.00 25.00
HOFTOM Tommy Lasorda/150 30.00 80.00
HOFTPZ Tony Perez/201 6.00 15.00
HOFWDE Wade Boggs/20
HOFWHI Whitey Ford/50 15.00 40.00
HOFWIL Willie McCovey/10
HOFWIL Billy Williams/20
HOFWIN Dave Winfield/25
HOFWTY Whitey Herzog/699 8.00 20.00
HOFYAZ Carl Yastrzemski/75 40.00 80.00
HOFYBR Yogi Berra/100 40.00 100.00
HOFYOG Yogi Berra/25

2015 Panini Cooperstown

PRINTING PLATES RANDOMLY INSERTED
PLATE PRINT RUN 1 SET PER COLOR
NO PLATE PRICING DUE TO SCARCITY
1 Al Kaline 1.00 2.50
2 Al Simmons .75 2.00
3 Andre Dawson .75 2.00
4 Arky Vaughan .60 1.50
5 Babe Ruth 2.50 6.00
6 Barry Larkin .75 2.00
7 Bert Blyleven .75 2.00
8 Bill Dickey .60 1.50
9 Bill Mazeroski .75 2.00
10 Bill Terry .60 1.50
11 Billy Williams .75 2.00
12 Bob Feller .75 2.00
13 Bob Gibson .75 2.00
14 Bobby Doerr .75 2.00
15 Brooks Robinson .75 2.00
16 Bruce Sutter .75 2.00
17 Cal Ripken 3.00 8.00
18 Carl Yastrzemski 1.50 4.00
19 Carlton Fisk .75 2.00
20 Charlie Gehringer .60 1.50
21 Craig Biggio .75 2.00
22 Dave Bancroft .60 1.50
23 Dennis Eckersley .75 2.00
24 Dizzy Dean .75 2.00
25 Don Drysdale .75 2.00
26 Don Sutton .75 2.00
27 Doug Harvey .60 1.50
28 Duke Snider .75 2.00
29 Eddie Collins .75 2.00
30 Eddie Mathews 1.00 2.50
31 Eddie Murray .75 2.00
32 Fergie Jenkins .75 2.00
33 Frank Chance .75 2.00
34 Frank Robinson .75 2.00
35 Frank Thomas 1.00 2.50
36 Frankie Frisch .75 2.00
37 Gabby Hartnett .60 1.50
38 Gary Carter .75 2.00
39 Gaylord Perry .75 2.00
40 George Brett 2.00 5.00
41 George Kelly .60 1.50
42 Goose Gossage .75 2.00
43 Greg Maddux 1.25 3.00
44 Hack Wilson .75 2.00
45 Harmon Killebrew 1.00 2.50
46 Herb Pennock .75 2.00
47 Honus Wagner 1.00 2.50
48 Jackie Robinson 1.00 2.50
49 Jim Bottomley .60 1.50
50 Jim Bunning .75 2.00
51 Jim Palmer .75 2.00
52 Jim Rice .75 2.00
53 Jimmie Foxx 1.00 2.50
54 Joe Cronin .60 1.50
55 Joe DiMaggio 2.00 5.00
56 Joe Morgan .75 2.00
57 John Smoltz 1.00 2.50
58 Johnny Bench 1.00 2.50
59 Juan Marichal .75 2.00
60 Lefty Gomez .60 1.50
61 Leo Durocher .60 1.50
62 Lou Brock .75 2.00
63 Lou Gehrig 2.00 5.00
64 Luke Appling .75 2.00
65 Mel Ott 1.00 2.50
66 Miller Huggins .60 1.50
67 Monte Irvin .75 2.00
68 Nap Lajoie 1.00 2.50
69 Nolan Ryan 3.00 8.00
70 Orlando Cepeda .75 2.00
71 Pat Gillick .60 1.50
72 Paul Molitor 1.00 2.50
73 Pedro Martinez .75 2.00
74 Pee Wee Reese .75 2.00
75 Phil Niekro .75 2.00
76 Randy Johnson 1.00 2.50
77 Red Schoendienst .75 2.00
78 Reggie Jackson .75 2.00
79 Rickey Henderson 1.00 2.50
80 Roberto Alomar .75 2.00
81 Roberto Clemente 2.50 6.00
82 Robin Yount 1.00 2.50
83 Rod Carew .75 2.00
84 Rogers Hornsby .75 2.00
85 Rollie Fingers .75 2.00
86 Ryne Sandberg 2.00 5.00
87 Sam Crawford .75 2.00
88 Stan Musial 1.50 4.00
89 Steve Carlton .75 2.00
90 Ted Williams 2.00 5.00
91 Tom Glavine .75 2.00
92 Tommy Lasorda .75 2.00
93 Tony Gwynn 1.00 2.50
94 Tony La Russa .75 2.00
95 Tony Perez .75 2.00
96 Ty Cobb 1.50 4.00
97 Wade Boggs .75 2.00
98 Whitey Ford .75 2.00
99 Whitey Herzog .60 1.50
100 Yogi Berra 1.00 2.50

2015 Panini Cooperstown Blue

*BLUE: 1.5X TO 4X BASIC
RANDOM INSERTS IN PACKS
STATED PRINT RUN 25 SER.#'d SETS

2015 Panini Cooperstown Red

*RED: 1.5X TO 4X BASIC
RANDOM INSERTS IN PACKS
STATED PRINT RUN 35 SER.#'d SETS

2015 Panini Cooperstown '14 Elite ReCollection Collection Autographs

RANDOM INSERTS IN PACKS
PRINT RUNS B/WN 5-25 COPIES PER
NO PRICING ON QTY 5
32 Andre Dawson/25 20.00 50.00

2015 Panini Cooperstown '14 Crusades ReCollection Collection Autographs

RANDOM INSERTS IN PACKS
PRINT RUNS B/WN 5-50 COPIES PER
NO PRICING ON QTY 5
51 Al Kaline/25 15.00 40.00
68 Jim Palmer/50 15.00 40.00
93 Jim Rice/50 10.00 25.00

2015 Panini Cooperstown Dead Ball ERA All Stars

RANDOM INSERTS IN PACKS
*GOLD/25: 1.5X TO 4X BASIC
1 Frank Chance .75 2.00
2 Honus Wagner 1.00 2.50
3 Dave Bancroft .60 1.50
4 Roger Bresnahan .75 2.00
5 Miller Huggins .60 1.50
6 Rogers Hornsby .75 2.00
7 Tris Speaker .75 2.00
8 Sam Crawford .75 2.00
9 Ty Cobb 1.50 4.00
10 Eddie Collins .75 2.00
11 Nap Lajoie 1.00 2.50
12 Willie Keeler .60 1.50
13 George Sisler .75 2.00

2015 Panini Cooperstown Etched in Cooperstown Silver

RANDOM INSERTS IN PACKS
*HOLO SILVER/25: .5X TO 1.2X BASIC
1 Al Kaline 3.00 8.00
2 Al Simmons 2.50 6.00
3 Arky Vaughan 2.00 5.00
4 Babe Ruth 8.00 20.00
5 Bill Dickey 2.00 5.00
6 Bill Terry 2.00 5.00
7 Bob Gibson 2.50 6.00
8 Brooks Robinson 2.50 6.00
9 Cal Ripken 10.00 25.00
10 Carl Yastrzemski 5.00 12.00
11 Carlton Fisk 2.50 6.00
12 Charlie Gehringer 2.00 5.00
13 Craig Biggio 2.50 6.00
14 Dave Bancroft 2.00 5.00
15 Dizzy Dean 2.50 6.00
16 Don Drysdale 2.50 6.00
17 Duke Snider 2.50 6.00
18 Eddie Collins 2.50 6.00
19 Eddie Mathews 3.00 8.00
20 Eddie Murray 2.50 6.00
21 Frank Chance 2.50 6.00
22 Frank Robinson 2.50 6.00
23 Frank Thomas 3.00 8.00
24 Frankie Frisch 2.50 6.00
25 Gabby Hartnett 2.00 5.00
26 George Brett 6.00 15.00
27 George Kelly 2.00 5.00
28 Greg Maddux 4.00 10.00
29 Hack Wilson 2.50 6.00
30 Harmon Killebrew 3.00 8.00
31 Herb Pennock 2.50 6.00
32 Honus Wagner 3.00 8.00
33 Jackie Robinson 3.00 8.00
34 Jim Bottomley 2.00 5.00
35 Jim Palmer 2.50 6.00
36 Jim Rice 2.50 6.00
37 Jimmie Foxx 3.00 8.00
38 Joe Cronin 2.00 5.00
39 Joe DiMaggio 6.00 15.00
40 Joe Morgan 2.50 6.00
41 John Smoltz 3.00 8.00
42 Johnny Bench 3.00 8.00
43 Juan Marichal 2.50 6.00
44 Lefty Gomez 2.00 5.00
45 Leo Durocher 2.00 5.00
46 Lou Brock 2.50 6.00
47 Lou Gehrig 6.00 15.00
48 Luke Appling 2.50 6.00
49 Mel Ott 3.00 8.00
50 Miller Huggins 2.00 5.00
51 Nap Lajoie 3.00 8.00
52 Nolan Ryan 10.00 25.00
53 Orlando Cepeda 2.50 6.00
54 Paul Molitor 3.00 8.00
55 Pedro Martinez 2.50 6.00
56 Randy Johnson 3.00 8.00
57 Reggie Jackson 2.50 6.00
58 Rickey Henderson 3.00 8.00
59 Roberto Clemente 8.00 20.00
60 Robin Yount 3.00 8.00
61 Rod Carew 2.50 6.00
62 Rogers Hornsby 2.50 6.00
63 Ryne Sandberg 6.00 15.00
64 Sam Crawford 2.50 6.00
65 Stan Musial 5.00 12.00
66 Steve Carlton 2.50 6.00
67 Ted Williams 6.00 15.00
68 Tom Glavine 2.50 6.00
69 Tony Gwynn 3.00 8.00
70 Ty Cobb 5.00 12.00

2015 Panini Cooperstown Etched in Cooperstown Dual Silver

RANDOM INSERTS IN PACKS
*HOLO SILVER/25: .5X TO 1.2X BASIC
1 P.Martinez/R.Johnson 3.00 8.00
2 C.Biggio/J.Smoltz 3.00 8.00
3 T.Glavine/G.Maddux 4.00 10.00
4 F.Robinson/B.Robinson 2.50 6.00
5 C.Ripken/E.Murray 10.00 25.00
6 C.Yastrzemski/J.Rice 5.00 12.00
7 J.Robinson/D.Snider 3.00 8.00
8 F.Chance/G.Hartnett 2.50 6.00
9 J.Morgan/J.Bench 3.00 8.00
10 T.Cobb/S.Crawford 5.00 12.00
11 P.Molitor/R.Yount 3.00 8.00
12 B.Ruth/L.Gehrig 8.00 20.00
13 B.Dickey/L.Gomez 2.00 5.00
14 H.Pennock/M.Huggins 2.50 6.00
15 H.Wagner/R.Clemente 8.00 20.00
16 D.Dean/R.Hornsby 2.50 6.00
17 H.Wilson/R.Sandberg 6.00 15.00
18 C.Fisk/F.Thomas 3.00 8.00
19 B.Feller/N.Lajoie 3.00 8.00
20 R.Jackson/R.Henderson 3.00 8.00
21 A.Kaline/C.Gehringer 3.00 8.00
22 B.Blyleven/H.Killebrew 3.00 8.00
23 B.Terry/M.Ott 3.00 8.00
24 J.Foxx/E.Collins 3.00 8.00
25 J.Marichal/O.Cepeda 2.50 6.00
26 L.Brock/B.Gibson 2.50 6.00
27 F.Frisch/S.Musial 5.00 12.00
28 G.Brett/N.Ryan 10.00 25.00
29 M.Schmidt/S.Carlton 5.00 12.00
30 N.Ryan/R.Carew 10.00 25.00

2015 Panini Cooperstown HOF Chronicles

PRINTING PLATES RANDOMLY INSERTED
PLATE PRINT RUN 1 SET PER COLOR
BLACK-CYAN-MAGENTA-YELLOW ISSUED
NO PLATE PRICING DUE TO SCARCITY

2015 Panini Cooperstown Crown Royale

RANDOM INSERTS IN PACKS
*SILVER/75: .5X TO 1.2X BASIC
*PURPLE/50: .6X TO 1.5X BASIC
*BLUE/25: 1X TO 2.5X BASIC
1 Al Kaline 2.50 6.00
2 Al Simmons 2.00 5.00
3 Andre Dawson 2.00 5.00
4 Arky Vaughan 1.50 4.00
5 Babe Ruth 6.00 15.00
6 Barry Larkin 2.00 5.00
7 Bert Blyleven 2.00 5.00
8 Bill Dickey 1.50 4.00
9 Bill Mazeroski 2.00 5.00
10 Bill Terry 1.50 4.00
11 Billy Williams 2.00 5.00
12 Bob Feller 2.00 5.00
13 Bob Gibson 2.00 5.00
14 Bobby Doerr 2.00 5.00
15 Brooks Robinson 2.00 5.00
16 Bruce Sutter 2.00 5.00
17 Cal Ripken 8.00 20.00
18 Carl Yastrzemski 4.00 10.00
19 Carlton Fisk 2.00 5.00
20 Charlie Gehringer 1.50 4.00
21 Craig Biggio 2.00 5.00
22 Dave Bancroft 1.50 4.00
23 Dennis Eckersley 2.00 5.00
24 Dizzy Dean 2.00 5.00
25 Don Drysdale 2.00 5.00
26 Don Sutton 2.00 5.00
27 Doug Harvey 1.50 4.00
28 Duke Snider 2.00 5.00
29 Eddie Collins 2.00 5.00
30 Eddie Mathews 2.50 6.00
31 Eddie Murray 2.00 5.00
32 Fergie Jenkins 2.00 5.00
33 Frank Chance 2.00 5.00
34 Frank Robinson 2.00 5.00
35 Frank Thomas 2.50 6.00
36 Frankie Frisch 2.00 5.00
37 Gabby Hartnett 1.50 4.00
38 Gary Carter 2.00 5.00
39 Gaylord Perry 2.00 5.00
40 George Brett 5.00 12.00
41 George Kelly 1.50 4.00
42 Goose Gossage 2.00 5.00
43 Greg Maddux 3.00 8.00
44 Hack Wilson 2.00 5.00
45 Harmon Killebrew 2.50 6.00
46 Herb Pennock 2.00 5.00
47 Honus Wagner 2.50 6.00
48 Jackie Robinson 2.50 6.00
49 Jim Bottomley 1.50 4.00
50 Jim Bunning 2.00 5.00
51 Jim Palmer 2.00 5.00
52 Jim Rice 2.00 5.00
53 Jimmie Foxx 2.50 6.00
54 Joe Cronin 1.50 4.00
55 Joe DiMaggio 5.00 12.00
56 Joe Morgan 2.00 5.00
57 John Smoltz 2.50 6.00
58 Johnny Bench 2.50 6.00
59 Juan Marichal 2.00 5.00
60 Lefty Gomez 1.50 4.00
61 Leo Durocher 1.50 4.00
62 Lou Brock 2.00 5.00
63 Lou Gehrig 5.00 12.00
64 Luke Appling 2.00 5.00
65 Mel Ott 2.50 6.00
66 Miller Huggins 1.50 4.00
67 Monte Irvin 2.00 5.00
68 Nap Lajoie 2.50 6.00
69 Nolan Ryan 8.00 20.00
70 Orlando Cepeda 2.00 5.00
71 Pat Gillick 1.50 4.00
72 Paul Molitor 2.50 6.00
73 Pedro Martinez 2.00 5.00
74 Pee Wee Reese 2.00 5.00
75 Phil Niekro 2.00 5.00
76 Randy Johnson 2.50 6.00
77 Red Schoendienst 2.00 5.00
78 Reggie Jackson 2.00 5.00
79 Rickey Henderson 2.50 6.00
80 Roberto Alomar 2.00 5.00
81 Roberto Clemente 6.00 15.00
82 Robin Yount 2.50 6.00
83 Rod Carew 2.00 5.00
84 Rogers Hornsby 2.00 5.00
85 Rollie Fingers 2.00 5.00
86 Ryne Sandberg 5.00 12.00
87 Sam Crawford 2.00 5.00
88 Stan Musial 4.00 10.00
89 Steve Carlton 2.00 5.00
90 Ted Williams 5.00 12.00
91 Tom Glavine 2.00 5.00
92 Tommy Lasorda 2.00 5.00
93 Tony Gwynn 2.50 6.00
94 Tony La Russa 2.00 5.00
95 Tony Perez 2.00 5.00
96 Ty Cobb 4.00 10.00
97 Wade Boggs 2.00 5.00
98 Whitey Ford 2.00 5.00
99 Whitey Herzog 1.50 4.00
100 Yogi Berra 2.50 6.00

2015 Panini Cooperstown Diamond Kings ReCollection Collection Autographs

RANDOM INSERTS IN PACKS
PRINT RUNS B/WN 3-50 COPIES PER
NO PRICING ON QTY 5
51 Al Kaline/25 25.00 50.00
56 Brooks Robinson/25 15.00 40.00
93 Jim Rice/50 10.00 25.00
96 Bert Blyleven/25 10.00 25.00

2015 Panini Cooperstown Golf Classic

RANDOM INSERTS IN PACKS
*GOLD/25: .5X TO 1.2X BASIC
1 Yogi Berra 3.00 8.00
2 Bert Blyleven 2.50 6.00
3 Wade Boggs 2.50 6.00
4 George Brett 6.00 15.00
5 Andre Dawson 2.50 6.00
6 Dennis Eckersley 2.50 6.00
7 Rollie Fingers 2.50 6.00
8 Tom Glavine 2.50 6.00
9 Goose Gossage 2.50 6.00
10 Tony Gwynn 3.00 8.00
11 Whitey Herzog 2.00 5.00
12 Reggie Jackson 2.50 6.00
13 Barry Larkin 2.50 6.00
14 Tony La Russa 2.50 6.00
15 Greg Maddux 4.00 10.00
16 Eddie Murray 2.50 6.00
17 Phil Niekro 2.50 6.00
18 Kirby Puckett 3.00 8.00
19 Jim Rice 2.50 6.00
20 Cal Ripken 10.00 25.00
21 Frank Robinson 2.50 6.00
22 Jackie Robinson 3.00 8.00
23 Ryne Sandberg 6.00 15.00
24 Mike Schmidt 5.00 12.00
25 Carl Yastrzemski 5.00 12.00
26 Johnny Bench 3.00 8.00
27 Randy Johnson 3.00 8.00
28 Paul Molitor 3.00 8.00
29 Joe Morgan 2.50 6.00
30 Ted Williams 6.00 15.00
31 Ozzie Smith 4.00 10.00
32 Dick Williams 2.00 5.00
33 Ernie Banks 3.00 8.00
34 G.Brett/Y.Berra 6.00 15.00
35 G.Carter/D.Winfield 2.50 6.00
36 Bob Gibson 2.50 6.00
37 B.Larkin/O.Smith 4.00 10.00
38 Nolan Ryan 10.00 25.00
39 J.Bench/R.Fingers 3.00 8.00
40 C.Yastrzemski/J.Bench 5.00 12.00

2015 Panini Cooperstown Armed Forces

RANDOM INSERTS IN PACKS
*GOLD/25: 1.2X TO 3X BASIC
1 Joe DiMaggio 2.00 5.00
2 Bobby Doerr .75 2.00
3 Bob Feller .75 2.00
4 Whitey Ford .75 2.00
5 Charlie Gehringer .60 1.50
6 Hank Greenberg 1.00 2.50
7 Stan Musial 1.50 4.00
8 Jackie Robinson 1.00 2.50
9 Larry Doby .75 2.00
10 Bill Dickey .60 1.50
11 Phil Rizzuto .75 2.00

2015 Panini Cooperstown HOF Induction

*INDUCTION: .4X TO 1X BASE CARDS
*RED/35: 1.5X TO 4X BASIC
*BLUE/25: 1.5X TO 4X BASIC
PRINTING PLATES RANDOMLY INSERTED
PLATE PRINT RUN 1 SET PER COLOR
BLACK-CYAN-MAGENTA-YELLOW ISSUED
NO PLATE PRICING DUE TO SCARCITY

2015 Panini Cooperstown Induction

RANDOM INSERTS IN PACKS
*GOLD/25: 1.5X TO 4X BASIC
1 Roberto Alomar .75 2.00
2 Craig Biggio .75 2.00
3 Bert Blyleven .75 2.00
4 Wade Boggs .75 2.00
5 Dennis Eckersley .75 2.00
6 Tom Glavine .75 2.00
7 Goose Gossage .75 2.00
8 Greg Maddux 1.25 3.00
9 Pedro Martinez .75 2.00
10 Bill Mazeroski .75 2.00
11 Paul Molitor 1.00 2.50
12 Eddie Murray .75 2.00
13 Doug Harvey .60 1.50
14 Rickey Henderson 1.00 2.50
15 Randy Johnson 1.00 2.50
16 Barry Larkin .75 2.00
17 Tony La Russa .75 2.00
18 Tony Perez .75 2.00
19 Jim Rice .75 2.00
20 Cal Ripken 3.00 8.00
21 Ryne Sandberg 2.00 5.00
22 John Smoltz 1.00 2.50
23 Bruce Sutter .75 2.00
24 Don Sutton .75 2.00
25 Frank Thomas 1.00 2.50
26 Robin Yount 1.00 2.50

2015 Panini Cooperstown Induction Signatures

RANDOM INSERTS IN PACKS
*RED/49: .4X TO 1X BASIC
*BLUE/25: .5X TO 1.2X BASIC
2 Andre Dawson 10.00 25.00
3 Barry Larkin 12.00 30.00
4 Bert Blyleven 5.00 12.00
6 Billy Williams 5.00 12.00
7 Brooks Robinson 12.00 30.00
8 Bruce Sutter 5.00 12.00
10 Carlton Fisk 20.00 50.00
11 Craig Biggio 15.00 40.00
12 Dennis Eckersley 5.00 12.00
13 Don Sutton 5.00 12.00
14 Doug Harvey 8.00 20.00
15 Eddie Murray 50.00 120.00
16 Fergie Jenkins 5.00 12.00
17 Frank Thomas 30.00 80.00
18 Gaylord Perry 5.00 12.00
20 Goose Gossage 5.00 12.00
22 Jim Bunning 5.00 12.00
23 Jim Palmer 5.00 12.00
24 Jim Rice 5.00 12.00
26 John Smoltz 12.00 30.00
29 Lou Brock 5.00 12.00
30 Nolan Ryan 60.00 150.00
31 Orlando Cepeda 5.00 12.00
32 Pat Gillick 4.00 10.00
33 Paul Molitor 6.00 15.00
34 Pedro Martinez 40.00 100.00
35 Phil Niekro 5.00 12.00
36 Randy Johnson 75.00 200.00
37 Red Schoendienst 6.00 15.00
43 Rollie Fingers 5.00 12.00
46 Tom Glavine 15.00 40.00
47 Tony La Russa 8.00 20.00
48 Tony Perez 5.00 12.00
50 Whitey Herzog 4.00 10.00

2015 Panini Cooperstown Signatures

RANDOM INSERTS IN PACKS
*RED/49: .4X TO 1X BASIC
*BLUE/25: .5X TO 1.2X BASIC
1 Al Kaline 8.00 20.00
2 Andre Dawson 5.00 12.00
3 Bert Blyleven 5.00 12.00
4 Bill Mazeroski 30.00 80.00
5 Billy Williams 5.00 12.00
7 Bobby Doerr 4.00 10.00
8 Brooks Robinson 8.00 20.00
9 Bruce Sutter 5.00 12.00
10 Carl Yastrzemski 50.00 120.00
11 Carlton Fisk 15.00 40.00
12 Craig Biggio 15.00 40.00
13 Dennis Eckersley 5.00 12.00
14 Don Sutton 5.00 12.00
15 Doug Harvey 6.00 15.00
17 Fergie Jenkins 5.00 12.00
18 Frank Robinson 10.00 25.00
19 Gaylord Perry 5.00 12.00
20 Goose Gossage 8.00 20.00
21 Jim Bunning 5.00 12.00
22 Jim Palmer 5.00 12.00
23 Jim Rice 5.00 12.00
24 John Smoltz 10.00 25.00
25 Johnny Bench 25.00 60.00
26 Juan Marichal 12.00 30.00
27 Lou Brock 12.00 30.00
28 Monte Irvin 5.00 12.00
29 Orlando Cepeda 5.00 12.00
30 Pat Gillick 4.00 10.00
31 Paul Molitor 6.00 15.00
32 Pedro Martinez 40.00 100.00
33 Phil Niekro 5.00 12.00
34 Randy Johnson 75.00 200.00
35 Red Schoendienst 6.00 15.00
36 Reggie Jackson 15.00 40.00
38 Roberto Alomar EXCH 10.00 25.00
40 Rod Carew 12.00 30.00
41 Rollie Fingers 5.00 12.00
44 Tom Glavine 8.00 20.00
46 Tony La Russa 5.00 12.00
47 Tony Perez 8.00 20.00
49 Whitey Herzog 4.00 10.00

2015 Panini Cooperstown Names of the Game

RANDOM INSERTS IN PACKS
*GOLD/25: .5X TO 1.2X BASIC
1 Al Kaline 3.00 8.00
2 Al Simmons 2.50 6.00
3 Andre Dawson 2.50 6.00
4 Babe Ruth 8.00 20.00
5 Bill Terry 2.00 5.00
6 Brooks Robinson 2.50 6.00
7 Cal Ripken 10.00 25.00
8 Dave Bancroft 2.00 5.00
9 Eddie Murray 2.50 6.00
10 Frank Chance 2.50 6.00
11 Frank Robinson 2.50 6.00
12 Frank Thomas 3.00 8.00
13 Frankie Frisch 2.50 6.00
14 George Kelly 2.00 5.00
15 Greg Maddux 4.00 10.00
16 Herb Pennock 2.50 6.00
17 Honus Wagner 3.00 8.00
18 Jim Bottomley 2.00 5.00
19 Jim Palmer 2.50 6.00
20 Jimmie Foxx 3.00 8.00
21 Joe Cronin 2.50 6.00
22 Johnny Bench 3.00 8.00
23 Lefty Gomez 2.00 5.00
24 Leo Durocher 2.50 6.00
25 Lou Gehrig 6.00 15.00
26 Luke Appling 2.50 6.00
27 Mel Ott 3.00 8.00
28 Miller Huggins 2.00 5.00
29 Nap Lajoie 3.00 8.00
30 Nolan Ryan 10.00 25.00
31 Orlando Cepeda 2.50 6.00
32 Paul Molitor 3.00 8.00
33 Pedro Martinez 3.00 8.00
34 Randy Johnson 3.00 8.00
35 Reggie Jackson 2.50 6.00
36 Roberto Clemente 8.00 20.00
37 Rogers Hornsby 2.50 6.00
38 Sam Crawford 2.50 6.00
39 Tony Gwynn 3.00 8.00
40 Ty Cobb 5.00 12.00
41 Bill Mazeroski 2.50 6.00
42 Hack Wilson 2.50 6.00
43 Enos Slaughter 2.50 6.00
44 Rick Ferrell 2.00 5.00
45 Duke Snider 2.50 6.00
46 Juan Marichal 2.50 6.00
47 Lou Brock 2.50 6.00

2018 Panini Cornerstones

1 Jack Flaherty JSY AU RC 12.00 30.00
2 Rhys Hoskins JSY AU RC 20.00 50.00
3 Ozzie Albies JSY AU RC 15.00 40.00
4 Miguel Andujar JSY AU RC 25.00 60.00
5 Rafael Devers JSY AU RC 20.00 50.00
6 Chance Sisco JSY AU RC 4.00 10.00
7 Victor Caratini JSY AU RC 8.00 20.00
8 Francisco Mejia JSY AU RC 10.00 25.00
9 Kyle Farmer JSY AU RC 3.00 8.00
10 Austin Hays JSY AU RC 5.00 12.00
11 Alex Verdugo JSY AU RC 8.00 20.00
12 Zack Granite JSY AU RC 3.00 8.00
13 Clint Frazier JSY AU RC 8.00 20.00
14 Nick Williams JSY AU RC 4.00 10.00
15 Harrison Bader JSY AU RC 12.00 30.00
16 Willie Calhoun JSY AU RC 5.00 12.00
17 Victor Robles JSY AU RC 12.00 30.00
18 Max Fried JSY AU RC 12.00 30.00
19 Lucas Sims JSY AU RC 3.00 8.00
20 Walker Buehler JSY AU RC 12.00 30.00
21 Erick Fedde JSY AU RC 3.00 8.00
22 Amed Rosario JSY AU RC 5.00 12.00
23 Tyler Wade JSY AU RC 4.00 10.00
24 J.P. Crawford JSY AU RC 3.00 8.00
25 Shohei Ohtani JSY AU RC 150.00 300.00
26 Mike Trout 5.00 12.00
27 Bryce Harper 1.25 3.00
28 Aaron Judge 5.00 12.00
29 Cody Bellinger 1.50 4.00
30 Jose Altuve .60 1.50
31 Ichiro 1.00 2.50
32 Clayton Kershaw 1.25 3.00
33 Buster Posey 1.00 2.50
34 Giancarlo Stanton .75 2.00
35 Shohei Ohtani 12.00 30.00
36 J.D. Martinez .75 2.00
37 Paul Goldschmidt .75 2.00
38 Joey Votto .75 2.00
39 George Springer .60 1.50
40 Jose Ramirez .60 1.50
41 Max Scherzer .75 2.00
42 Albert Pujols 1.00 2.50
43 Francisco Lindor .75 2.00
44 Kris Bryant 1.00 2.50
45 Manny Machado .75 2.00
46 Gary Sanchez .75 2.00
47 Miguel Cabrera .75 2.00
48 Andrew McCutchen .75 2.00
49 Carlos Correa .75 2.00
50 Nolan Arenado 1.25 3.00

2018 Panini Cornerstones Reserve Materials

INSERTED IN '18 CHRONICLES PACKS
PRINT RUNS B/WN 49-99 COPIES PER
*QARTZ/49: .5X TO 1.2X p/r 99
*QARTZ/25: .6X TO 1.5X p/r 49
*GRANITE/25: .6X TO 1.5X p/r 99
*GRANITE/25: .5X TO 1.2X p/r 49
1 Ozzie Albies/99 4.00 10.00
2 Rafael Devers/99 6.00 15.00
3 Clint Frazier/99 4.00 10.00
4 Rhys Hoskins/99 4.00 10.00
5 Amed Rosario/99 2.50 6.00
6 Nick Williams/99 2.50 6.00
7 Francisco Mejia/99 2.50 6.00
8 Willie Calhoun/99 3.00 8.00
9 Victor Robles/99 4.00 10.00
10 J.P. Crawford/99 2.00 5.00
11 Kyle Farmer/99 2.00 5.00
12 Paul Blackburn/99 2.00 5.00
13 Miguel Andujar/99 5.00 12.00
14 Walker Buehler/99 4.00 10.00
15 Chance Sisco/99 2.50 6.00
16 Gary Sanchez/99 3.00 8.00
17 George Springer/99 2.50 6.00
18 Adrian Beltre/49 4.00 10.00
19 Andrew Benintendi/99 3.00 8.00
20 Buster Posey/49 4.00 10.00
21 Clayton Kershaw/49 4.00 10.00
22 Corey Seager/99 3.00 8.00
23 Giancarlo Stanton/99 4.00 10.00
24 Shohei Ohtani/99 10.00 25.00
25 Marcell Ozuna/99 3.00 8.00

2018 Panini Cornerstones Rookie Reserve Signatures

RANDOM INSERTS IN PACKS
STATED PRINT RUN 99 SER.#'d SETS
*QUARTZ/49: .5X TO 1.2X BASIC
*GRANITE/25: .75X TO 2X BASIC
1 Brandon Woodruff 10.00 25.00
2 Rhys Hoskins 12.00 30.00
3 Ozzie Albies 12.00 30.00
4 Miguel Andujar 6.00 15.00
5 Rafael Devers 8.00 20.00
6 Chance Sisco 4.00 10.00
7 Victor Caratini 4.00 10.00
8 Francisco Mejia 4.00 10.00
9 Kyle Farmer 3.00 8.00
10 Austin Hays 5.00 12.00
11 Alex Verdugo 5.00 12.00
12 Zack Granite 3.00 8.00
13 Clint Frazier 6.00 15.00
14 Nick Williams 4.00 10.00
15 Harrison Bader 5.00 12.00
16 Willie Calhoun 5.00 12.00
17 Victor Robles 8.00 20.00
18 Max Fried 12.00 30.00
20 Walker Buehler 15.00 40.00
21 Erick Fedde 3.00 8.00
22 Amed Rosario 4.00 10.00
23 Tyler Wade 3.00 8.00
24 J.P. Crawford 3.00 8.00
25 Richard Urena 3.00 8.00

2019 Panini Cornerstones

INSERTED IN '19 CHRONICLES PACKS
STATED PRINT RUN 99 SER.#'d SETS
26 Mike Trout 6.00 15.00
27 Shohei Ohtani 1.25 3.00
28 Aaron Judge 2.00 5.00
29 Mookie Betts 1.50 4.00
30 Alex Bregman .75 2.00
31 Christian Yelich 1.00 2.50
32 Francisco Lindor .75 2.00
33 Javier Baez 1.00 2.50
34 Nolan Arenado 1.25 3.00
35 Ronald Acuna Jr. 4.00 10.00

2019 Panini Cornerstones Prospect Quad Relic Autographs

INSERTED IN '19 CHRONICLES PACKS
PRINT RUNS B/WN 25-99 COPIES PER
EXCHANGE DEADLINE 2/21/2021
*CRYSTAL/49: .5X TO 1.2X p/r 99
*CRYSTAL/25: .5X TO 1.2X p/r 49
1 Forrest Whitley/49 6.00 15.00
2 Brendan Rodgers/49 6.00 15.00
3 Bo Bichette/99 30.00 80.00
4 Wander Franco/25 50.00 120.00
6 Ian Anderson/49 12.00 30.00
8 Mitch Keller/49 5.00 12.00
9 Leody Taveras/49 6.00 15.00
12 Sean Murphy/25 6.00 15.00
14 Adbert Alzolay/49 4.00 10.00
15 Kyle Lewis/49 8.00 20.00
16 Julio Pablo Martinez/49 4.00 10.00
17 Khalil Lee/49 4.00 10.00
18 Brent Honeywell/49 5.00 12.00
19 Yordan Alvarez/49 40.00 100.00
20 Corey Ray/49 4.00 10.00

2019 Panini Cornerstones Prospect Quad Relic Autographs Crystal

*CRYSTAL/49: .5X TO 1.2X p/r 99
*CRYSTAL/25: .5X TO 1.2X p/r 49
INSERTED IN '19 CHRONICLES PACKS
PRINT RUNS B/WN 25-49 COPIES PER
EXCHANGE DEADLINE 2/21/2021
1 Forrest Whitley/25 12.00 30.00

2019 Panini Cornerstones Quad Relic Autographs

INSERTED IN '19 CHRONICLES PACKS
PRINT RUNS B/WN 7-49 COPIES PER
NO PRICING ON QTY 15 OR LESS
EXCHANGE DEADLINE 2/21/2021
*CRYSTAL/25: .5X TO 1.2X p/r 49
2 Juan Soto/49 30.00 80.00
3 Jose Ramirez/25 6.00 15.00
4 Justin Turner/25 8.00 20.00
5 Jose Canseco/49 20.00 50.00
6 Rod Carew/15
7 Tom Glavine/15
8 Al Oliver/25 5.00 12.00
9 Mitch Haniger/25 6.00 15.00
10 Juan Gonzalez/49 4.00 10.00
11 Omar Vizquel/25 6.00 15.00
12 Whit Merrifield/25 8.00 20.00
13 Aaron Judge/10
14 Shohei Ohtani/7
15 Ichiro/7

2018 Panini Crusade

INSERTED IN '18 CHRONICLES PACKS
1 Gleyber Torres RC 2.50 6.00
2 Giancarlo Stanton .25 .60
3 Rhys Hoskins RC 1.00 2.50
4 Jose Altuve .20 .50
5 Manny Machado .25 .60
6 Clint Frazier RC .50 1.25
7 Aaron Judge .60 1.50
8 Kris Bryant .30 .75
9 Miguel Andujar RC 1.00 2.50
10 Rafael Devers RC .75 2.00
11 Alex Verdugo RC .40 1.00
12 Bryce Harper .40 1.00
13 Nick Williams RC .30 .75
14 Shohei Ohtani RC 6.00 15.00
15 Ryan McMahon RC .60 1.50
16 Victor Robles RC .60 1.50
17 Austin Hays RC .40 1.00
18 Ronald Acuna Jr. RC 8.00 20.00
19 Mike Trout 1.25 3.00
20 Dominic Smith RC .30 .75
21 Cody Bellinger .50 1.25
22 Nolan Arenado .40 1.00
23 Amed Rosario RC .30 .75
24 J.P. Crawford RC .25 .60
25 Ozzie Albies RC .75 2.00

2018 Panini Crusade Blue Ice

*BLUE: 1X TO 2.5X BASIC
*BLUE RC: .6X TO 1.5X BASIC
INSERTED IN '18 CHRONICLES PACKS
STATED PRINT RUN 149 SER.#'d SETS
3 Rhys Hoskins 4.00 10.00
14 Shohei Ohtani 6.00 15.00
18 Ronald Acuna Jr. 6.00 15.00
19 Mike Trout 6.00 15.00

2018 Panini Crusade Green

*GREEN: 1.5X TO 4X BASIC
*GREEN RC: 1X TO 2.5X BASIC
INSERTED IN '18 CHRONICLES PACKS
STATED PRINT RUN 50 SER.#'d SETS
1 Gleyber Torres 8.00 20.00
3 Rhys Hoskins 6.00 15.00
7 Aaron Judge 12.00 30.00
9 Miguel Andujar 10.00 25.00
14 Shohei Ohtani 10.00 25.00
18 Ronald Acuna Jr. 10.00 25.00
19 Mike Trout 10.00 25.00

2018 Panini Crusade Holo

*HOLO: .75X TO 2X BASIC
*HOLO RC: .5X TO 1.2X BASIC
INSERTED IN '18 CHRONICLES PACKS
3 Rhys Hoskins 3.00 8.00
14 Shohei Ohtani 5.00 12.00
18 Ronald Acuna Jr. 5.00 12.00
19 Mike Trout 5.00 12.00

2018 Panini Crusade Hyper

*HYPER: .75X TO 2X BASIC
*HYPER RC: .5X TO 1.2X BASIC
INSERTED IN '18 CHRONICLES PACKS
STATED PRINT RUN 299 SER.#'d SETS
3 Rhys Hoskins 3.00 8.00
14 Shohei Ohtani 5.00 12.00
18 Ronald Acuna Jr. 5.00 12.00
19 Mike Trout 5.00 12.00

2018 Panini Crusade Pink

*PINK: 2.5X TO 6X BASIC
*PINK RC: 1.5X TO 4X BASIC
INSERTED IN '18 CHRONICLES PACKS
STATED PRINT RUN 25 SER.#'d SETS
1 Gleyber Torres 12.00 30.00
3 Rhys Hoskins 10.00 25.00
7 Aaron Judge 20.00 50.00
9 Miguel Andujar 15.00 40.00
14 Shohei Ohtani 15.00 40.00
18 Ronald Acuna Jr. 15.00 40.00
19 Mike Trout 15.00 40.00

2018 Panini Crusade Purple Mojo

*PURPLE: 1.2X TO 3X BASIC
*PURPLE RC: .75X TO 2X BASIC
INSERTED IN '18 CHRONICLES PACKS
STATED PRINT RUN 99 SER.#'d SETS
1 Gleyber Torres 6.00 15.00
3 Rhys Hoskins 5.00 12.00
14 Shohei Ohtani 8.00 20.00
18 Ronald Acuna Jr. 8.00 20.00
19 Mike Trout 8.00 20.00

2018 Panini Crusade Ruby Wave

*RUBY: 1X TO 2.5X BASIC
*RUBY RC: .6X TO 1.5X BASIC
INSERTED IN '18 CHRONICLES PACKS
STATED PRINT RUN 199 SER.#'d SETS
3 Rhys Hoskins 4.00 10.00
14 Shohei Ohtani 6.00 15.00
18 Ronald Acuna Jr. 6.00 15.00
19 Mike Trout 6.00 15.00

2018 Panini Crusade Signatures

RANDOM INSERTS IN PACKS
8 Felix Jorge 2.50 6.00
9 Andrew Stevenson 2.50 6.00
10 Jimmie Sherfy 2.50 6.00
15 Trevor Story 6.00 15.00
18 Franmil Reyes 4.00 10.00
20 Yairo Munoz 6.00 15.00

2019 Panini Crusade

RANDOM INSERTS IN PACKS
*HOLO: .75X TO 2X
*HYPER/299: .75X TO 2X
*RUBY/199: 1X TO 2.5X
*BLUE/99: 1.2X TO 3X
*PURPLE/75: 1.2X TO 3X
*GREEN/50: 1.5X TO 4X
*PINK/25: 2.5X TO 6X
1 Pete Alonso RC 5.00 12.00
2 Eloy Jimenez RC .60 1.50
3 Fernando Tatis Jr. RC 4.00 10.00
4 Michael Kopech RC .50 1.25
5 Kyle Tucker RC .40 1.00
6 Yusei Kikuchi RC .25 .60
7 Chris Paddack RC .30 .75
8 Mike Trout 1.25 3.00
9 Bryce Harper .40 1.00
10 Aaron Judge .60 1.50
11 Kris Bryant .30 .75
12 Shohei Ohtani .40 1.00
13 Jacob deGrom .50 1.25
14 Nick Senzel RC .50 1.25
15 Shaun Anderson RC .15 .40
16 Gleyber Torres .50 1.25
17 Juan Soto .75 2.00
18 Carter Kieboom RC .25 .60
19 Jose Altuve .20 .50
20 Brandon Lowe RC .25 .60
21 Vladimir Guerrero Jr. RC 4.00 10.00
22 Cody Bellinger .50 1.25
23 Rhys Hoskins .30 .75
24 Blake Snell .20 .50
25 Max Scherzer .25 .60

2020 Panini Crusade

RANDOM INSERTS IN PACKS
1 Bo Bichette RC 3.00 8.00
2 Yordan Alvarez RC 2.50 6.00
3 Gavin Lux RC 1.25 3.00
4 Brendan McKay RC .40 1.00
5 Aristides Aquino RC .60 1.50
6 Yoshitomo Tsutsugo RC .60 1.50
7 Luis Robert RC 4.00 10.00
8 Aaron Judge .60 1.50
9 Mike Trout 2.00 5.00
10 Cody Bellinger .50 1.25
11 Fernando Tatis Jr. 2.00 5.00
12 Vladimir Guerrero Jr. .40 1.00
13 Kwang-Hyun Kim RC .50 1.25
14 Ketel Marte .20 .50
15 Blake Snell .20 .50
16 Pete Alonso .60 1.50
17 Kris Bryant .30 .75
18 Kyle Lewis RC 4.00 10.00
19 Nick Solak RC 1.00 2.50
20 A.J. Puk RC .40 1.00

2019 Panini Cyber Monday

*FRAMES/99: .6X TO 1.5X BASIC CARDS
*SWIRL/50: .8X TO 2X BASIC CARDS
*GALACTIC/25: 1X TO 2.5X BASIC CARDS
13 Cody Bellinger .75 2.00
14 Christian Yelich .75 2.00
15 Mike Trout .75 2.00
16 Ronald Acuna Jr. .75 2.00
17 Nolan Arenado .75 2.00
18 Alex Bregman .75 2.00

2012 Panini Father's Day

RANDOM INSERTS IN FATHER'S DAY PACKS
CRACKED ICE/25: 5X TO 12X BASE HI
7 Josh Hamilton .40 1.00
8 Albert Pujols .75 2.00
9 Ryan Howard .50 1.25
10 Stephen Strasburg .75 2.00
11 Prince Fielder .30 .75
12 Ichiro Suzuki .60 1.50
13 David Ortiz .30 .75
14 Eric Hosmer .40 1.00

2012 Panini Father's Day Legends

RANDOM INSERTS IN FATHERS DAY PACKS
CRACKED ICE/25: 5X TO 12X BASE HI
8 Stan Musial .60 1.50
9 Ken Griffey Jr. .75 2.00
10 Nolan Ryan 1.25 3.00
11 Don Mattingly .75 2.00

2012 Panini Father's Day Rookies

STATED PRINT RUN 499 SER.#'d SETS
7 Yu Darvish 4.00 10.00
8 Bubba Starling 2.00 5.00
9 Mike Trout 6.00 15.00
10 Jesus Montero 1.50 4.00
11 Dylan Bundy 2.50 6.00

2012 Panini Father's Day Rookies Cracked Ice

CRACKED ICE/25: 2.5X TO 6X BASE HI
ANNOUNCED PRINT RUN 25

2012 Panini Father's Day Thick Portraits

RANDOM INSERTS IN FATHERS DAY PACKS
ANNOUNCED PRINT RUN 50
3 Yu Darvish 15.00 40.00

2013 Panini Father's Day Elite

CRACKED ICE/25: 3X TO 8X BASIC CARDS
LAVA FLOW/25: 3X TO 8X BASIC CARDS
2 Stephen Strasburg

2013 Panini Father's Day Museum Collection

*CRACKED ICE/25: 2.5X TO 6X BASIC
*LAVA FLOW/25: 2.5X TO 6X BASIC
MC1 George Brett 2.00 5.00
MC2 Carlton Fisk .75 2.00
MC3 Tony Gwynn 1.00 2.50
MC4 Whitey Ford .75 2.00
MC5 Wade Boggs .75 2.00
MC6 Johnny Bench 1.00 2.50
MC7 Brooks Robinson .75 2.00
MC8 Rickey Henderson 1.00 2.50
MC9 Andre Dawson .75 2.00

2013 Panini Father's Day Museum Collection Cracked Ice Autographs

MC1 George Brett
MC2 Carlton Fisk
MC3 Tony Gwynn
MC4 Whitey Ford 20.00 50.00
MC5 Wade Boggs
MC6 Johnny Bench 25.00 60.00
MC7 Brooks Robinson
MC8 Rickey Henderson
MC9 Andre Dawson 12.00 30.00

2013 Panini Father's Day Rookie of the Year Materials

LAVA FLOW/25: 1.5X TO 4X BASIC JSY
ROYBH Bryce Harper

2013 Panini Father's Day Team Pinnacle

CRACKED ICE/25: 3X TO 8X BASIC CARDS
LAVA FLOW/25: 3X TO 8X BASIC CARDS
8 Bryce Harper/Stephen Strasburg
9 Josh Hamilton/Albert Pujols
10 Matt Kemp/Clayton Kershaw
15 Mike Olt/Jurickson Profar

2014 Panini Father's Day

COMPLETE SET (55) 20.00 50.00
*1-24 THICK STOCK: 1X TO 2.5X BASIC CARDS
*25-55 THICK STOCK: .5X TO 1.2X BASIC CARDS
*1-24 ICE VETS/25: 5X TO 12X BASIC CARDS
*25-55 ICE ROOKIE/25: 2X TO 5X BASIC CARDS/499
18 Mike Trout BB 1.00 2.50
19 Miguel Cabrera BB .50 1.25
20 Bryce Harper BB .60 1.50
21 Andrew McCutchen BB .50 1.25
22 Paul Goldschmidt BB .40 1.00
23 Jose Fernandez BB .40 1.00
24 Yu Darvish BB .30 .75
25 Xander Bogaerts BB 1.25 3.00
26 Nick Castellanos BB .60 1.50
27 Taijuan Walker BB .60 1.50
28 Michael Choice BB .50 1.25
29 Jose Abreu BB 3.00 8.00
30 Kolten Wong BB .60 1.50
31 Masahiro Tanaka BB 2.00 5.00
32 George Springer BB 1.00 2.50
33 Yordano Ventura BB .50 1.25

2014 Panini Father's Day Elite

3 Masahiro Tanaka BB

2014 Panini Father's Day Legends

COMPLETE SET (10)
3 Greg Maddux BB
4 Frank Thomas BB
5 Tom Glavine BB

2014 Panini Father's Day Rookies

COMPLETE SET (20) 10.00 25.00
*CRACKED ICE/25: 3X TO 8X BASIC CARDS
*THICK STOCK: 1X TO 2.5X BASIC CARDS
R19 Masahiro Tanaka BB 1.50 4.00
R20 Jose Abreu BB 2.50 6.00

2015 Panini Father's Day

17 Mike Trout 1.50 3.00
18 Clayton Kershaw .60 1.50
19A Dustin Pedroia .50 1.25
19B Dustin Pedroia .50 1.25
20 Giancarlo Stanton .60 1.50
21 Miguel Cabrera .60 1.50
22 Yasiel Puig .60 1.50
23A Buster Posey .60 1.50
23B Buster Posey .60 1.50
24 Jose Abreu .60 1.50
41 Joc Pederson 2.00 5.00
42 Daniel Norris 1.25 3.00
43 Jorge Soler 1.25 3.00
44 Maikel Franco 1.00 2.50
45A Brandon Finnegan 1.00 2.50
45B Brandon Finnegan 1.00 2.50
46 Dalton Pompey 1.00 2.50
47 Devon Travis 1.25 3.00
48 Yasmany Tomas 1.00 2.50
49 Addison Russell 1.25 3.00
50 Kris Bryant 8.00 20.00
58 Javier Baez JSY 3.00 8.00
59 Rusney Castillo JSY 2.00 5.00
60 Michael Taylor JSY 2.00 5.00

2015 Panini Father's Day Elements

15 Bryce Harper 1.50 4.00

2015 Panini Father's Day Sketch

*THICK: 2X TO 5X BASIC CARDS
*CRACKED/25: 2X TO 5X BASIC CARDS
11 Giancarlo Stanton 1.00 2.50
12 Mike Trout 1.50 4.00
13 Kris Bryant 1.50 4.00

2019 Panini Father's Day

1 Shohei Ohtani .75 2.00
2 Mike Trout .75 2.00
3 Mookie Betts .75 2.00
4 Francisco Lindor .75 2.00
5 Bryce Harper .75 2.00
6 Aaron Judge .75 2.00
7 Manny Machado .75 2.00
8 Ronald Acuna Jr. .75 2.00
9 Kris Bryant .75 2.00
10 Alex Bregman .75 2.00
11 Bo Jackson .75 2.00
12 Ken Griffey Jr. .75 2.00
13 Rickey Henderson .75 2.00
14 Cal Ripken .75 2.00
49 Mariano Rivera .75 2.00
50 Lincoln Riley .75 2.00
51 Brandon Lowe 1.25 3.00
52 Cedric Mullins 1.25 3.00
53 Chance Adams 1.25 3.00
54 Danny Jansen 1.25 3.00
55 Jake Bauers 1.25 3.00
56 Jeff McNeil 1.25 3.00
57 Jonathan Loaisiga 1.25 3.00
58 Justus Sheffield 1.25 3.00
59 Kolby Allard 1.25 3.00
60 Kyle Tucker 1.25 3.00

61 Luis Urias 1.25 3.00
62 Michael Kopech 1.25 3.00
63 Ryan O'Hearn 1.25 3.00
64 Steven Duggar 1.25 3.00
65 Touki Toussaint 1.25 3.00
75 Eloy Jimenez 1.25 3.00
76 Fernando Tatis Jr. 1.25 3.00
77 Pete Alonso 1.25 3.00
78 Chris Paddack 1.25 3.00
79 Yusei Kikuchi 1.25 3.00
81 Victor Victor Mesa 1.25 3.00
83 Vladimir Guerrero Jr. 1.25 3.00
85 Alex Kirilloff 1.25 3.00

2016 Panini Flawless

STATED PRINT RUN 20 SER.#'d SETS
1 Albert Pujols 25.00 60.00
2 Babe Ruth 60.00 150.00
3 Bill Dickey 12.00 30.00
4 Bryce Harper 75.00 200.00
5 Buster Posey 15.00 40.00
6 Cal Ripken 40.00 100.00
7 Carl Yastrzemski 25.00 60.00
8 Carlos Correa 50.00 120.00
9 Clayton Kershaw 20.00 50.00
10 Dizzy Dean 15.00 40.00
11 Eddie Collins 12.00 30.00
12 Frank Chance 12.00 30.00
13 Frank Thomas 30.00 80.00
14 George Brett 50.00 120.00
15 George Sisler 12.00 30.00
16 Greg Maddux 30.00 80.00
17 Herb Pennock 10.00 25.00
18 Honus Wagner 20.00 50.00
19 Ichiro Suzuki 60.00 150.00
20 Jackie Robinson 25.00 60.00
21 Jimmie Foxx 15.00 40.00
22 Joe DiMaggio 25.00 60.00
23 Joe Jackson 30.00 80.00
24 Jose Abreu 12.00 30.00
25 Josh Donaldson 12.00 30.00
26 Ken Griffey Jr. 75.00 200.00
27 Kirby Puckett 60.00 150.00
28 Kris Bryant 60.00 150.00
29 Lefty Gomez 10.00 25.00
30 Lou Gehrig 60.00 150.00
31 Mark McGwire 20.00 50.00
32 Masahiro Tanaka 20.00 50.00
33 Mel Ott 20.00 50.00
34 Miguel Cabrera 25.00 60.00
35 Mike Schmidt 20.00 50.00
36 Mike Trout 75.00 200.00
37 Nolan Ryan 50.00 120.00
38 Pete Rose 25.00 60.00
39 Roberto Clemente 40.00 100.00
40 Roger Maris 20.00 50.00
41 Rogers Hornsby 20.00 50.00
42 Ryne Sandberg 25.00 60.00
43 Stan Musial 20.00 50.00
44 Ted Williams 30.00 80.00
45 Tony Gwynn 40.00 100.00
46 Tony Lazzeri 15.00 40.00
47 Tris Speaker 10.00 25.00
48 Ty Cobb 30.00 80.00
49 Willie Keeler 20.00 50.00
50 Yadier Molina 30.00 80.00
51 Barry Bonds AM 30.00 80.00
52 Bo Jackson AM 25.00 60.00
53 Randy Johnson AM 20.00 50.00
54 Frank Thomas AM 30.00 80.00
55 Mark McGwire AM 20.00 50.00
56 Buster Posey AM 15.00 40.00
57 Dustin Pedroia AM 15.00 40.00
58 Kyle Schwarber AM 25.00 60.00
59 Jake Arrieta AM 20.00 50.00
60 Michael Conforto AM 20.00 50.00
61 Stephen Piscotty AM 15.00 40.00
62 Trea Turner AM 15.00 40.00
63 David Price AM 20.00 50.00
64 Max Scherzer AM 12.00 30.00
65 Will Clark AM 25.00 60.00
66 Jackie Robinson AM 25.00 60.00
67 Craig Biggio AM 15.00 40.00
68 Tony Gwynn AM 40.00 100.00
69 Josh Donaldson AM 12.00 30.00
70 Matt Harvey AM 15.00 40.00
71 Clayton Kershaw USA 60.00 150.00
72 Kris Bryant USA 125.00 300.00
73 Buster Posey USA 50.00 120.00
74 Manny Machado USA 40.00 100.00
75 Kyle Schwarber USA 40.00 100.00
76 Corey Seager USA 75.00 150.00
77 Michael Conforto USA 40.00 100.00
78 Trea Turner USA 40.00 100.00
79 Mark McGwire USA 60.00 150.00
80 Frank Thomas USA 50.00 120.00
81 Ken Griffey Jr. USA 100.00 250.00
82 Bryce Harper USA 75.00 200.00
83 Mike Trout USA 125.00 300.00
84 Andrew McCutchen USA 50.00 120.00
85 Alex Rodriguez USA 60.00 150.00
86 Kyle Schwarber RC 25.00 60.00
87 Corey Seager RC 40.00 100.00
88 Miguel Sano RC 12.00 30.00
89 Michael Conforto RC 20.00 50.00
90 Stephen Piscotty RC 15.00 40.00
91 Trea Turner RC 15.00 40.00
92 Luis Severino RC 10.00 25.00
93 Rob Refsnyder RC 10.00 25.00
94 Aaron Nola RC 15.00 40.00
95 Ketel Marte RC 12.00 30.00
96 Raul Mondesi RC 12.00 30.00
97 Henry Owens RC 10.00 25.00
98 Greg Bird RC 10.00 25.00
99 Jose Peraza RC 10.00 25.00
100 Hector Olivera RC 10.00 25.00
101 Trevor Story RC 40.00 100.00
102 Byung-ho Park RC 20.00 50.00
103 Kenta Maeda RC 20.00 50.00

2016 Panini Flawless Ruby

*RUBY: .4X TO 1X BASIC
RANDOM INSERTS IN PACKS
STATED PRINT RUN 15 SER.#'d SETS

2016 Panini Flawless Dual Diamond Memorabilia Ruby

RANDOM INSERTS IN PACKS
PRINT RUNS B/WN 15-20 COPIES PER
1 Adam Wainwright 25.00 60.00
Yadier Molina/20
4 Belt/Bumgarner/20 60.00 150.00
8 Chris Archer 15.00 40.00
Kevin Kiermaier/20
9 Ichiro/Gordon/15 25.00 60.00
20 Kyle Seager 20.00 50.00
Robinson Cano/20
22 Harvey/Syndrgrd/20 30.00 80.00

2016 Panini Flawless Dual Diamond Memorabilia Sapphire

RANDOM INSERTS IN PACKS
PRINT RUNS B/WN 10-20 COPIES PER
NO PRICING ON QTY 10
1 Wnwrght/Mlna/15 60.00 150.00
3 McCtchn/Marte/15 50.00 120.00
4 Belt/Bumgarner/15 75.00 200.00
7 Dallas Keuchel 15.00 40.00
Collin McHugh/15
8 Chris Archer 15.00 40.00
Kevin Kiermaier/15
12 Stanton/Fernandez/15 20.00 50.00
14 Velander/Martinez/15 20.00 50.00
15 McCann/Ellsbury/15 30.00 80.00
20 Seager/Cano/15 25.00 60.00
22 Harvey/Syndrgrd/15 40.00 100.00

2016 Panini Flawless Dual Patches

RANDOM INSERTS IN PACKS
STATED PRINT RUN 25 SER.#'d SETS
10 Dallas Keuchel 8.00 20.00

2016 Panini Flawless Dual Patches Ruby

*RUBY/15-20: .4X TO 1X BASIC
RANDOM INSERTS IN PACKS
PRINT RUNS B/WN 15-20 COPIES PER
3 Andrew McCutchen/15 50.00 120.00
38 Manny Machado/15 20.00 50.00

2016 Panini Flawless Dual Patches Sapphire

*SAPPHIRE/15: .4X TO 1X BASIC
RANDOM INSERTS IN PACKS
PRINT RUNS B/WN 10-15 COPIES PER
NO PRICING ON QTY 10
1 Adam Wainwright/15 10.00 25.00
3 Andrew McCutchen/15 50.00 120.00
11 Dee Gordon/15 6.00 15.00
17 J.D. Martinez/15 12.00 30.00
22 Jose Altuve/15 50.00 120.00
34 Jung-Ho Kang/15 20.00 50.00
37 Madison Bumgarner/15 15.00 40.00
38 Manny Machado/15 20.00 50.00

2016 Panini Flawless Dual Signatures

STATED PRINT RUN 25 SER.#'d SETS
*RUBY/20: .4X TO 1X BASIC
*SAPPHIRE/15: .4X TO 1X BASIC
FDAL A.Nola/L.Severino 15.00 40.00
FDCJ C.Seager/J.Peraza 25.00 60.00
FDCK C.Edwards Jr./K.Schwarber 8.00 20.00
FDJT J.Gray/T.Murphy 6.00 15.00
FDKS K.Schwarber/T.Murphy 20.00 50.00
FDMM M.Kepler/M.Sano 15.00 40.00
FDRG R.Refsnyder/G.Bird 8.00 20.00
FDTC T.Turner/C.Seager 60.00 150.00

2016 Panini Flawless Flawless Cuts

RANDOM INSERTS IN PACKS
PRINT RUNS B/WN 1-25 COPIES PER
NO PRICING ON QTY 10 OR LESS
2 Bob Meusel/25 60.00 150.00
21 Sam Rice/15 75.00 200.00
22 Stan Musial/25 40.00 100.00
23 Ted Williams/25 250.00 400.00

2016 Panini Flawless Flawless Cuts Memorabilia

RANDOM INSERTS IN PACKS
PRINT RUNS B/WN 1-25 COPIES PER
NO PRICING ON QTY 10 OR LESS
*PRIME/25: .5X TO 1.2X BASIC
2 Bob Meusel/25 60.00 150.00
7 George Sisler/15 250.00 400.00
13 Lefty Gomez/15 60.00 150.00
21 Sam Rice/25 100.00 250.00
22 Stan Musial/25 60.00 150.00
23 Ted Williams/25 400.00 600.00

2016 Panini Flawless Greats Autographs

RANDOM INSERTS IN PACKS
PRINT RUNS B/WN 5-25 COPIES PER
NO PRICING ON QTY 5
*RUBY/20: .4X TO 1X BASIC
*SAPPHIRE/15: .4X TO 1X BASIC
GAAG Andres Galarraga/25 10.00 25.00
GAAP Albert Pujols/15 60.00 150.00
GABB Barry Bonds/15 100.00 250.00
GABJ Bo Jackson/25 40.00 100.00
GACJ Chipper Jones/15 40.00 100.00
GACR Cal Ripken/15 50.00 120.00
GADM Dale Murphy/25 10.00 25.00
GADO David Ortiz/25 50.00 120.00
GAFT Frank Thomas/25 40.00 100.00
GAGB George Brett/15 100.00 250.00
GAIR Ivan Rodriguez/15 60.00 150.00
GAJC Jose Canseco/25 25.00 60.00
GAMM Mark McGwire/15 60.00 150.00
GAMP Mike Piazza/15 50.00 120.00
GAMR Mariano Rivera/15 75.00 200.00
GAMS Mike Schmidt/15 30.00 80.00
GANR Nolan Ryan/25 50.00 120.00
GAOV Omar Vizquel/25 10.00 25.00
GARS Ryne Sandberg/15 30.00 80.00
GATH Todd Helton/15 15.00 40.00
GAWC Will Clark/15 30.00 80.00
GAWM Willie McGee/25 15.00 40.00

2016 Panini Flawless Greats Dual Memorabilia Autographs

RANDOM INSERTS IN PACKS
PRINT RUNS B/WN 15-25 COPIES PER
GDBBP Barry Bonds/15 250.00 400.00
GDBBS Barry Bonds/15 250.00 400.00
GDBJ Bo Jackson/15 60.00 150.00
GDCB Craig Biggio/15 50.00 120.00
GDCF Carlton Fisk/15 50.00 120.00
GDCJ Chipper Jones/15 60.00 150.00
GDEM Eddie Murray/15 50.00 120.00
GDGB George Brett/15 250.00 500.00
GDGMA Greg Maddux/15 75.00 200.00
GDGMC Greg Maddux/15 75.00 200.00
GDJB Johnny Bench/15 75.00 200.00
GDJM Joe Morgan/15 40.00 100.00
GDJS John Smoltz/15 60.00 150.00
GDMMO Mark McGwire/15 150.00 300.00
GDMMS Mark McGwire/15 150.00 300.00
GDMR Mariano Rivera/15 150.00 300.00
GDPM Pedro Martinez/15 60.00 150.00
GDRC Rod Carew/15 60.00 150.00
GDRH Rickey Henderson/15
GDRJO Reggie Jackson/15 50.00 120.00
GDRJC Reggie Jackson/15 50.00 120.00
GDRP Rafael Palmeiro/25 25.00 60.00
GDRS Red Schoendienst/25 60.00 150.00
GDRS Ryne Sandberg/15 30.00 80.00
GDSC Steve Carlton/15 50.00 120.00

2016 Panini Flawless Greats Dual Memorabilia Autographs Ruby

*RUBY/20: .4X TO 1X BASIC
RANDOM INSERTS IN PACKS
PRINT RUNS B/WN 10-20 COPIES PER
NO PRICING ON QTY 10
GDGP Gaylord Perry/20 25.00 60.00
GDNR Nolan Ryan/20 125.00 300.00
GDPM Paul Molitor/20 30.00 80.00

2016 Panini Flawless Greats Dual Memorabilia Autographs Sapphire

*SAPPHIRE/15: .4X TO 1X BASIC
RANDOM INSERTS IN PACKS
PRINT RUNS B/WN 5-15 COPIES PER
NO PRICING ON QTY 5
GDDO David Ortiz/15 200.00 400.00
GDFTC Frank Thomas/15 75.00 200.00
GDFTT Frank Thomas/15 75.00 200.00
GDGP Gaylord Perry/15 25.00 60.00
GDNR Nolan Ryan/15 125.00 300.00
GDPM Paul Molitor/15 30.00 80.00

2016 Panini Flawless Hall of Fame Autographs

RANDOM INSERTS IN PACKS
PRINT RUNS B/WN 5-25 COPIES PER
NO PRICING ON QTY 10 OR LESS
*RUBY/15-20: .4X TO 1X BASIC
*SAPPHIRE/15: .4X TO 1X BASIC
HOFAD Andre Dawson/25 15.00 40.00
HOFBL Barry Larkin/15 30.00 80.00
HOFCB Craig Biggio/15 20.00 50.00
HOFCR Cal Ripken/15 50.00 120.00
HOFCY Carl Yastrzemski/15 60.00 150.00
HOFFT Frank Thomas/25 40.00 100.00
HOFGB George Brett/15 100.00 250.00
HOFJR Jim Rice/25 10.00 25.00
HOFJS John Smoltz/15 25.00 60.00
HOFLB Lou Brock/15 20.00 50.00
HOFMS Mike Schmidt/15 30.00 80.00
HOFNR Nolan Ryan/25 50.00 120.00
HOFRC Rod Carew/15 20.00 50.00
HOFRJ Reggie Jackson/15 20.00 50.00
HOFRS Ryne Sandberg/15 30.00 80.00
HOFSC Steve Carlton/15 15.00 40.00

2016 Panini Flawless Material Greats

RANDOM INSERTS IN PACKS
PRINT RUNS B/WN 5-25 COPIES PER
NO PRICING ON QTY 10 OR LESS
*RUBY/20: .4X TO 1X BASIC
*SAPPHIRE/15: .4X TO 1X BASIC
1 Babe Ruth/25 200.00 400.00
2 Bill Dickey/25 10.00 25.00
3 Bob Feller/25 10.00 25.00
4 Charlie Gehringer/25 12.00 30.00
5 Duke Snider/25 12.00 30.00
7 Herb Pennock/25 10.00 25.00
9 Jackie Robinson/25 40.00 100.00
10 John McGraw/25 25.00 60.00
11 Joe DiMaggio/25 50.00 120.00
12 Lefty O'Doul/25 12.00 30.00
13 Lefty Gomez/25 25.00 60.00
14 Lou Gehrig/25 100.00 250.00
15 Mel Ott/25 12.00 30.00
16 Roberto Clemente/25 30.00 80.00
18 Rogers Hornsby/25 12.00 30.00
19 Stan Musial/25 20.00 50.00
20 Ted Williams/25 25.00 60.00
21 Tony Gwynn/25 15.00 40.00
22 Tony Lazzeri/25 20.00 50.00
23 Sam Rice/25 25.00 60.00
25 Warren Spahn/25 12.00 30.00

2016 Panini Flawless Patch Autographs

RANDOM INSERTS IN PACKS
PRINT RUNS B/WN 10-25 COPIES PER
NO PRICING ON QTY 10
PAAR Addison Russell/25 25.00 60.00
PACS Chris Sale/25 25.00 60.00
PADA Dale Murphy/25 40.00 100.00
PADK Dallas Keuchel/25 15.00 40.00
PADW David Wright/25 30.00 80.00
PAEM Edgar Martinez/25 15.00 40.00
PAFH Felix Hernandez/25 30.00 80.00
PAFL Fred Lynn/25 12.00 30.00
PAFV Fernando Valenzuela/15
PAJD Jacob deGrom/25 50.00 120.00
PAKB Kris Bryant/25 150.00 300.00
PASG Sonny Gray/25 20.00 50.00
PAYM Yoan Moncada/15 150.00 300.00
PAYAM Yadier Molina/25 100.00 250.00

2016 Panini Flawless Patch Autographs Ruby

*RUBY/20: .4X TO 1X BASIC
RANDOM INSERTS IN PACKS
PRINT RUNS B/WN 5-20 COPIES PER
NO PRICING ON QTY 10 OR LESS
PATF Todd Frazier/20 12.00 30.00

2016 Panini Flawless Patch Autographs Sapphire

*SAPPHIRE/15: .4X TO 1X BASIC
RANDOM INSERTS IN PACKS
PRINT RUNS B/WN 5-15 COPIES PER
NO PRICING ON QTY 5
PADO David Ortiz/15 75.00 200.00
PAJP Joc Pederson/15 20.00 50.00
PATF Todd Frazier/15 12.00 30.00

2016 Panini Flawless Patches

RANDOM INSERTS IN PACKS
PRINT RUNS B/WN 15-25 COPIES PER
3 Andrew McCutchen/25 25.00 60.00
12 Devin Mesoraco/15 6.00 15.00
22 Jose Altuve/15 20.00 50.00

2016 Panini Flawless Patches Ruby

*RUBY/20: .4X TO 1X BASIC
RANDOM INSERTS IN PACKS
PRINT RUNS B/WN 10-20 COPIES PER
NO PRICING ON QTY 10 OR LESS
1 Adam Wainwright/20 10.00 25.00
14 Freddie Freeman/20 12.00 30.00
37 Madison Bumgarner/20 15.00 40.00

2016 Panini Flawless Patches Sapphire

*SAPPHIRE/15: .4X TO 1X BASIC
RANDOM INSERTS IN PACKS
PRINT RUNS B/WN 10-15 COPIES PER
NO PRICING ON QTY 10
1 Adam Wainwright/15 10.00 25.00
7 Carlos Gonzalez/15 8.00 20.00
10 Dallas Keuchel/15 8.00 20.00
11 Dee Gordon/15 6.00 15.00
14 Freddie Freeman/15 12.00 30.00
15 Giancarlo Stanton/15 12.00 30.00
17 J.D. Martinez/15 12.00 30.00
25 Prince Fielder/15
34 Jung-Ho Kang/15 20.00 50.00
36 Kevin Kiermaier/15 12.00 30.00
37 Madison Bumgarner/15 15.00 40.00
50 Yu Darvish/15 10.00 25.00

2016 Panini Flawless Players Collection

1 Al Simmons/25 15.00 40.00
4 Barry Bonds/25 20.00 50.00
5 Bill Dickey/25 20.00 50.00
7 Bob Meusel/25 15.00 40.00
8 Cal Ripken/25 30.00 80.00
9 Chuck Klein/25 20.00 50.00
10 Dave Bancroft/25 12.00 30.00
12 Earl Averill/25 40.00 100.00
14 Frank Chance/25 30.00 80.00
16 Gabby Hartnett/25 20.00 50.00
17 George Brett/25 20.00 50.00
18 George Sisler/25 20.00 50.00
19 Goose Goslin/25 15.00 40.00
21 Herb Pennock/25 15.00 40.00
22 Honus Wagner/25 75.00 200.00
24 Jim Bottomley/25 15.00 40.00
26 Joe DiMaggio/25 60.00 150.00
27 Joe Jackson/25 100.00 250.00
28 John McGraw/25 30.00 80.00
29 Ken Griffey Jr./25 30.00 80.00
30 Kirby Puckett/25 50.00 120.00
31 Lefty Gomez/25 40.00 100.00
32 Lefty O'Doul/25 20.00 50.00
33 Lou Gehrig/25 100.00 250.00
34 Mel Ott/25 30.00 80.00
35 Miller Huggins/25 20.00 50.00
36 Nap Lajoie/25 40.00 100.00
37 Roberto Clemente/25 75.00 200.00
38 Roger Bresnahan/25 20.00 50.00
39 Roger Maris/25 30.00 80.00
40 Rogers Hornsby/25 30.00 80.00
41 Sam Crawford/25 20.00 50.00
42 Sam Rice/25 30.00 80.00
43 Stan Musial/25 25.00 60.00
44 Ted Williams/25 60.00 150.00
45 Tom Yawkey/25 30.00 80.00
46 Tony Gwynn/25 25.00 60.00
47 Tony Lazzeri/25 30.00 80.00
48 Tris Speaker/25 30.00 80.00
49 Ty Cobb/25 100.00 250.00
50 Willie Keeler/25 40.00 100.00

2016 Panini Flawless Autographs Red

RANDOM INSERTS IN PACKS
STATED PRINT RUN 25 SER.#'d SETS
*BLUE/25: .4X TO 1X BASIC
*RED/25: .4X TO 1X BASIC
1 Addison Russell/25 15.00 40.00
2 Brian Johnson/25 6.00 15.00
6 Corey Seager/25 30.00 80.00
8 Frank Thomas/25 40.00 100.00
11 Kris Bryant/25 75.00 200.00
12 Kyle Schwarber/25 15.00 40.00
13 Mac Williamson/25 8.00 20.00
14 Manny Machado/25 60.00 150.00
16 Michael Conforto/25 12.00 30.00
17 Peter O'Brien/25 6.00 15.00
18 Richie Shaffer/25 6.00 15.00
19 Rob Refsnyder/25 10.00 25.00
20 Todd Frazier/25 10.00 25.00
22 Tom Murphy/25 6.00 15.00
23 Travis Jankowski/25 6.00 15.00
24 Trea Turner/25 20.00 50.00

2016 Panini Flawless Rookie Autographs

RANDOM INSERTS IN PACKS
STATED PRINT RUN 25 SER.#'d SETS
*RUBY/20: .4X TO 1X BASIC
*SAPPHIRE/15: .4X TO 1X BASIC
RAAN Aaron Nola 15.00 40.00
RABD Brandon Drury 10.00 25.00
RABJ Brian Johnson 6.00 15.00
RABP Byung-ho Park 30.00 80.00
RACE Carl Edwards Jr. 8.00 20.00
RACS Corey Seager 60.00 150.00
RAGB Greg Bird 8.00 20.00
RAJG Jonathan Gray 6.00 15.00
RAJP Jose Peraza 8.00 20.00
RAKM Ketel Marte 12.00 30.00
RAKS Kyle Schwarber 20.00 50.00
RAKW Kyle Waldrop 8.00 20.00
RALS Luis Severino 8.00 20.00
RAMC Michael Conforto 8.00 20.00
RAMK Max Kepler 25.00 60.00
RAMS Miguel Sano 20.00 50.00
RAMW Mac Williamson 8.00 20.00
RAPO Peter O'Brien 6.00 15.00
RARM Raul Mondesi 12.00 30.00
RARR Rob Refsnyder 8.00 20.00
RARS Richie Shaffer 6.00 15.00
RASP Stephen Piscotty 20.00 50.00
RATJ Travis Jankowski 6.00 15.00
RATM Tom Murphy 6.00 15.00
RATS Trevor Story 40.00 100.00
RATT Trea Turner 20.00 50.00

2016 Panini Flawless Rookie Patch Autographs

RANDOM INSERTS IN PACKS
STATED PRINT RUN 25 SER.#'d SETS
RPAAN Aaron Nola 25.00 60.00
RPABD Brandon Drury 12.00 30.00
RPACS Corey Seager 100.00 250.00
RPADA Dariel Alvarez 6.00 15.00
RPAKC Kaleb Cowart 10.00 25.00
RPAKM Ketel Marte 15.00 40.00
RPAKS Kyle Schwarber 60.00 150.00
RPAKS Kyle Schwarber 60.00 150.00
RPALS Luis Severino 8.00 20.00
RPAMC Michael Conforto 60.00 150.00
RPAMS Miguel Sano 30.00 80.00
RPAMW Mac Williamson 40.00 100.00
RPAPO Peter O'Brien 20.00 50.00
RPARM Raul Mondesi 20.00 50.00
RPARR Rob Refsnyder 15.00 40.00
RPARS Richie Shaffer 10.00 25.00
RPASP Stephen Piscotty 6.00 15.00
RPATS Trevor Story 25.00 60.00
RPATT Trea Turner 30.00 80.00
RPAZD Zach Davies 30.00 80.00

2016 Panini Flawless Rookie Patch Autographs Ruby

*RUBY: .4X TO 1X BASIC
RANDOM INSERTS IN PACKS
STATED PRINT RUN 20 SER.#'d SETS
RPAJG Jonathan Gray 10.00 25.00
RPAKW Kyle Waldrop 10.00 25.00

2016 Panini Flawless Rookie Patch Autographs Sapphire

*SAPPHIRE: .4X TO 1X BASIC
RANDOM INSERTS IN PACKS
STATED PRINT RUN 15 SER.#'d SETS
RPABJ Brian Johnson 10.00 25.00
RPAGB Greg Bird 8.00 20.00
RPAJG Jonathan Gray 10.00 25.00
RPAKW Kyle Waldrop 10.00 25.00

2016 Panini Flawless Rookie Patches

RANDOM INSERTS IN PACKS
STATED PRINT RUN 25 SER.#'d SETS
1 Kyle Schwarber 15.00 40.00
2 Corey Seager 20.00 50.00
3 Miguel Sano 10.00 25.00
4 Michael Conforto 8.00 20.00
5 Stephen Piscotty 15.00 40.00
6 Trea Turner 20.00 50.00
7 Luis Severino 8.00 20.00
8 Rob Refsnyder 8.00 20.00
9 Aaron Nola 12.00 30.00
10 Ketel Marte 12.00 30.00
11 Raul Mondesi 12.00 30.00
12 Jonathan Gray 6.00 15.00
13 Greg Bird 8.00 20.00
14 Richie Shaffer 6.00 15.00
15 Travis Jankowski 6.00 15.00
16 Mac Williamson 10.00 25.00
17 Brian Johnson 6.00 15.00
18 Peter O'Brien 6.00 15.00
19 Kyle Waldrop 8.00 20.00
20 Brandon Drury 10.00 25.00
21 Dariel Alvarez 6.00 15.00
24 Colin Rea 6.00 15.00

2016 Panini Flawless Rookie Patches Ruby

*RUBY: .4X TO 1X BASIC
RANDOM INSERTS IN PACKS
STATED PRINT RUN 20 SER.#'d SETS
23 Gary Sanchez 30.00 80.00

2016 Panini Flawless Rookie Patches Sapphire

*SAPPHIRE: .4X TO 1X BASIC
RANDOM INSERTS IN PACKS
STATED PRINT RUN 15 SER.#'d SETS
23 Gary Sanchez 30.00 80.00

2016 Panini Flawless Rookie Signatures

RANDOM INSERTS IN PACKS
STATED PRINT RUN 25 SER.#'d SETS
*RUBY/20: .4X TO 1X BASIC
*SAPPHIRE/15: .4X TO 1X BASIC
RFAN Aaron Nola 15.00 40.00
RFBD Brandon Drury 10.00 25.00
RFBJ Brian Johnson 6.00 15.00
RFBP Byung-ho Park 30.00 80.00
RFCE Carl Edwards Jr. 8.00 20.00
RFCS Corey Seager 60.00 150.00
RFGB Greg Bird 8.00 20.00
RFJG Jonathan Gray 6.00 15.00
RFJP Jose Peraza 8.00 20.00
RFKM Ketel Marte 12.00 30.00
RFKS Kyle Schwarber 20.00 50.00
RFKW Kyle Waldrop 8.00 20.00
RFLS Luis Severino 8.00 20.00
RFMC Michael Conforto 8.00 20.00
RFMK Max Kepler 25.00 60.00
RFMS Miguel Sano 20.00 50.00
RFPO Peter O'Brien 6.00 15.00
RFRM Raul Mondesi 12.00 30.00
RFRR Rob Refsnyder 8.00 20.00
RFRS Richie Shaffer 6.00 15.00
RFSP Stephen Piscotty 10.00 25.00
RFTJ Travis Jankowski 6.00 15.00
RFTM Tom Murphy 6.00 15.00
RFTT Trea Turner 20.00 50.00
RFTT Trevor Story 40.00 100.00
RFWM Mac Williamson 8.00 20.00

2016 Panini Flawless Signatures

RANDOM INSERTS IN PACKS
PRINT RUNS B/WN 5-25 COPIES PER
NO PRICING ON QTY 10 OR LESS
*RUBY/20: .4X TO 1X BASIC
*SAPPHIRE/15: .4X TO 1X BASIC
FSAG Andres Galarraga/25 10.00 25.00
FSAR Anthony Rizzo/25 30.00 80.00
FSBJ Bo Jackson/25 40.00 100.00
FSCJ Chipper Jones/15 40.00 100.00
FSCR Cal Ripken/15 50.00 120.00
FSDM Daniel Murphy/25
FSDM Don Mattingly/15 50.00 120.00
FSDO David Ortiz/25 50.00 120.00
FSFT Frank Thomas/25 40.00 100.00
FSGB George Brett/15 100.00 250.00
FSJA Jose Abreu/15 15.00 40.00
FSJC Jose Canseco/25 25.00 60.00
FSJD Josh Donaldson/15 15.00 40.00
FSJG Jacob deGrom/25 25.00 60.00
FSJS John Smoltz/15 15.00 40.00
FSKB Kris Bryant/25 75.00 200.00
FSNR Nolan Ryan/25 50.00 120.00
FSOV Omar Vizquel/25 15.00 40.00
FSRJ Reggie Jackson/15 20.00 50.00
FSRS Ryne Sandberg/15 30.00 80.00
FSSC Steve Carlton/15 15.00 40.00
FSWC Wei-Yin Chen/25 50.00 120.00
FSWM Willie McGee/25 15.00 40.00
FSYM Yoan Moncada/15 60.00 150.00
FSYAM Yadier Molina/25 50.00 120.00

2016 Panini Flawless Teammates Triple Relics

RANDOM INSERTS IN PACKS
PRINT RUNS B/WN 5-25 COPIES PER
NO PRICING ON QTY 5
*RUBY/20: .4X TO 1X BASIC
*SAPPHIRE/15: .4X TO 1X BASIC
1 Msl/Ghrg/Ruth/25 250.00 500.00
5 Dcky/DMggo/Gmz/25 40.00 100.00
6 Goslin/Rice/Sisler/25 20.00 50.00
8 Hggns/Ruth/Ghrg/25 250.00 500.00
9 Msl/Ghrg/Lzzri/25 75.00 200.00
10 Ruth/Pnnck/Ghrg/25 250.00 500.00
11 Ghrngr/Cobb/Hlmn/25 40.00 100.00
12 Sthwrth/Bttmly/Hrnsby/15 30.00 80.00
13 Herman/Klein/Hartnett/25 20.00 50.00
14 Gehringer/Goslin/Greenberg/25 25.00 60.00
15 Greenberg/Herman/Kiner/25 25.00 60.00
18 Kelly/Bancroft/Frisch/25 20.00 50.00
20 Foxx/Wlams/DMggo/25 50.00 125.00
23 McGraw/Ott/Hornsby/25 25.00 60.00
25 Spahn/Sain/Waner/25 20.00 50.00

2016 Panini Flawless Transitions Signatures

RANDOM INSERTS IN PACKS
PRINT RUNS B/WN 15-25 COPIES PER
*RUBY/20: .4X TO 1X BASIC
*SAPPHIRE/15: .4X TO 1X BASIC
TAG Alex Gordon/25
TBJ Brian Johnson/25 6.00 15.00
TBL Barry Larkin/15 30.00 80.00
TDP David Price/25 20.00 50.00
TDPE Dustin Pedroia/15
TFT Frank Thomas/25 25.00 60.00
TGC Gerrit Cole/25 20.00 50.00
TKS Kyle Schwarber/25 20.00 50.00
TMC Michael Conforto/25 8.00 20.00
TMM Mark McGwire/15 60.00 150.00
TMW Mac Williamson/25 8.00 20.00
TPO Peter O'Brien/25 6.00 15.00
TRR Rob Refsnyder/25 8.00 20.00
TRS Richie Shaffer/25 6.00 15.00
TSG Sonny Gray/25
TTF Todd Frazier/25 10.00 25.00
TTH Todd Helton/15 15.00 40.00
TTJ Travis Jankowski/25 6.00 15.00
TTM Tom Murphy/25 6.00 15.00
TTT Trea Turner/25 20.00 50.00
TWC Will Clark/15 30.00 80.00

2017 Panini Flawless

RANDOM INSERTS IN PACKS
STATED PRINT RUN 20 SER.#'d SETS
1 Babe Ruth 60.00 150.00
2 Lou Gehrig 25.00 60.00
3 Ty Cobb 25.00 60.00
4 Roberto Clemente 60.00 150.00
5 Honus Wagner 25.00 60.00
6 Joe DiMaggio 30.00 80.00
7 Mickey Mantle 50.00 120.00
8 Ted Williams 40.00 100.00
9 Jackie Robinson 20.00 50.00
10 Stan Musial 20.00 50.00
11 Kirby Puckett 40.00 100.00
12 Joe Jackson 50.00 120.00
13 Roger Maris 30.00 80.00
14 Ken Griffey Jr. 40.00 100.00
15 Cal Ripken 25.00 60.00
16 George Brett 20.00 50.00
17 Nolan Ryan 25.00 60.00
18 Mike Trout 30.00 80.00
19 Kris Bryant 25.00 60.00
20 Clayton Kershaw 20.00 50.00
21 Buster Posey 15.00 40.00
22 Ichiro 30.00 80.00
23 Frank Thomas 20.00 50.00
24 Andrew Benintendi RC 25.00 60.00
25 Corey Seager 20.00 50.00
26 Gary Sanchez 25.00 60.00
27 David Ortiz 20.00 50.00
28 Dansby Swanson RC 15.00 40.00
29 Albert Pujols 20.00 50.00
30 Bryce Harper 60.00 150.00
31 Ken Griffey Jr. 40.00 100.00
32 Alex Bregman RC 15.00 40.00
33 Ichiro 30.00 80.00
34 Yoan Moncada RC 25.00 60.00
35 Bo Jackson 25.00 60.00
36 Jimmie Foxx 25.00 60.00
37 Rogers Hornsby 20.00 50.00
38 Tony Gwynn 30.00 80.00
39 Mike Piazza 25.00 60.00
40 Nolan Ryan 25.00 60.00
41 Nolan Ryan 25.00 60.00
42 Mel Ott 20.00 50.00
43 Thurman Munson 50.00 120.00
44 Carlos Correa 20.00 50.00
45 Pete Rose 25.00 60.00
46 Jackie Robinson AM 20.00 50.00
47 Bo Jackson AM 25.00 60.00
48 Tony Gwynn AM -30.00 80.00
50 George Sisler AM 10.00 25.00
51 Will Clark AM 15.00 40.00
52 Frank Thomas AM 20.00 50.00
53 Andrew Benintendi AM 25.00 60.00
54 Dansby Swanson AM 15.00 40.00
55 Alex Bregman AM 15.00 40.00
56 Kris Bryant USA 25.00 60.00
57 Corey Seager USA 20.00 50.00
58 Mike Trout USA 30.00 80.00
59 Ken Griffey Jr. USA 40.00 100.00
60 Manny Machado USA 15.00 40.00
61 Clayton Kershaw USA 20.00 50.00
62 Buster Posey USA 15.00 40.00
63 Dansby Swanson USA 15.00 40.00
64 Alex Bregman USA 15.00 40.00
65 Roger Clemens USA 15.00 40.00
66 Babe Ruth 30.00 80.00
67 Lou Gehrig 25.00 60.00
68 Joe DiMaggio 30.00 80.00
69 Ted Williams 40.00 100.00
70 Mickey Mantle 50.00 120.00
71 Jackie Robinson 20.00 50.00
72 Ken Griffey Jr. 40.00 100.00
73 Ty Cobb 25.00 60.00
74 Roberto Clemente 60.00 150.00
75 Honus Wagner 25.00 60.00
76 Babe Ruth 60.00 150.00
77 Ty Cobb 25.00 60.00
78 Ted Williams 40.00 100.00
79 Lou Gehrig 25.00 60.00
80 Roberto Clemente 60.00 150.00
81 Mike Trout 30.00 80.00
82 Mickey Mantle 50.00 120.00
83 Cal Ripken 25.00 60.00
84 Honus Wagner 25.00 60.00
85 Albert Pujols 20.00 50.00
86 Babe Ruth AS 60.00 150.00
87 Lou Gehrig AS 25.00 60.00
88 Joe DiMaggio AS 30.00 80.00
89 Ted Williams AS 40.00 100.00
90 Stan Musial AS 20.00 50.00
91 Roberto Clemente AS 60.00 150.00
92 Kirby Puckett AS 40.00 100.00
93 Ken Griffey Jr. AS 40.00 100.00
94 Bo Jackson AS 25.00 60.00
95 Kris Bryant AS 25.00 60.00
96 Cal Ripken AS 25.00 60.00
97 Reggie Jackson AS 20.00 50.00
98 Ichiro AS 30.00 80.00
99 Mike Trout AS 30.00 80.00
100 Mickey Mantle AS 25.00 60.00
101 Aaron Judge RC 75.00 200.00
102 Aaron Judge AM 75.00 200.00
103 Aaron Judge 75.00 200.00
104 Aaron Judge AS 75.00 200.00
105 Cody Bellinger RC 125.00 300.00
106 Cody Bellinger 125.00 300.00
107 Cody Bellinger AS 125.00 300.00

2017 Panini Flawless Ruby

*RUBY: .4X TO 1X BASIC
RANDOM INSERTS IN PACKS
STATED PRINT RUN 15 SER.#'d SETS

2017 Panini Flawless Cuts

RANDOM INSERTS IN PACKS
PRINT RUNS B/WN 1-25 COPIES PER
NO PRICING ON QTY 10 OR LESS
2 Stan Musial/25 40.00 100.00
3 Harmon Killebrew/25 25.00 60.00
8 Bobby Thomson/25 20.00 50.00
9 Carl Hubbell/15 30.00 80.00
12 Ed Barrow/15 150.00 400.00
13 Gary Carter/25 20.00 50.00
14 Ralph Kiner/25 20.00 50.00
15 Joe Medwick/15 40.00 100.00
16 Joe Sewell/25 20.00 50.00
17 Johnny Mize/25 40.00 100.00

2017 Panini Flawless Cuts Memorabilia

RANDOM INSERTS IN PACKS
PRINT RUNS B/WN 2-25 COPIES PER
NO PRICING ON QTY 10 OR LESS
7 Ted Williams/25 300.00 800.00

2017 Panini Flawless Dual Player Signatures

RANDOM INSERTS IN PACKS
PRINT RUNS B/WN 15-25 COPIES PER
*SAPPHIRE/15: .4X TO 1X BASIC
1 Naquin/Turner/25 12.00 30.00
2 Seager/Schwarber/25 30.00 80.00
5 Benintendi/Moncada/25 25.00 60.00
6 Sanchez/Story/25
7 Sale/Kluber/25 30.00 80.00
8 Lindor/Kluber/15 40.00 100.00
9 David Dahl 10.00 25.00
Raimel Tapia/25
10 Bell/Glasnow/25 15.00 40.00
11 Fulmer/Moncada/25 15.00 40.00
12 Alex Reyes 10.00 25.00
Jose De Leon/25
13 Henderson/Brock/25 40.00 100.00
14 ThomasySandberg/25 50.00 120.00
15 Dawson/Grace/15 40.00 100.00
16 Griffey Jr./Griffey Sr./25 100.00 250.00
17 Ryan/Clemens/20 100.00 250.00
18 Mattingly/McGee/15 40.00 100.00
19 Jimenez/Happ/25 30.00 80.00
20 Frazier/Torres/25 60.00 150.00

2017 Panini Flawless Dual Player Signatures Ruby

*RUBY/15-20: .4X TO 1X BASIC
RANDOM INSERTS IN PACKS
PRINT RUNS B/WN 10-20 COPIES PER
NO PRICING ON QTY 10
3 Machado/Beltre/15

2017 Panini Flawless USA Signatures

RANDOM INSERTS IN PACKS
PRINT RUNS B/WN 15-25 COPIES PER
*SAPPHIRE/15: .4X TO 1X BASIC
1 Francisco Lindor/15 30.00 80.00
3 Addison Russell/20 15.00 40.00
6 Dansby Swanson/25 20.00 50.00
7 Frank Thomas/15 40.00 100.00
8 Nomar Garciaparra/25 20.00 50.00
9 Jason Giambi/25 8.00 20.00

2017 Panini Flawless USA Signatures Ruby
*RUBY/15-20: .4X TO 1X BASIC
RANDOM INSERTS IN PACKS
PRINT RUNS B/WN 10-20 COPIES PER
NO PRICING ON QTY 10
10 Shawn Green/15 8.00 20.00

2019 Panini Flawless
STATED PRINT RUN 20 SER.#'d SETS
1 Mike Trout 75.00 200.00
2 Mookie Betts 40.00 100.00
3 Nolan Arenado 15.00 40.00
4 Christian Yelich 15.00 40.00
5 Aaron Judge 30.00 80.00
6 Bryce Harper 50.00 120.00
7 Ichiro 20.00 50.00
8 Albert Pujols 30.00 80.00
9 Ronald Acuna Jr. 60.00 150.00
10 Juan Soto 40.00 100.00
11 Gleyber Torres 25.00 60.00
12 Shohei Ohtani 30.00 80.00
13 Javier Baez 15.00 40.00
14 Cody Bellinger 30.00 80.00
15 Kris Bryant 15.00 40.00
16 Aaron Judge 30.00 80.00
17 Anthony Rizzo 15.00 40.00
18 Yadier Molina 15.00 40.00
19 Mike Trout 75.00 200.00
20 Aaron Judge 30.00 80.00
21 Johnny Bench LEG 12.00 30.00
22 Joe Jackson LEG 60.00 150.00
23 Al Kaline LEG 12.00 30.00
24 Christy Mathewson LEG 30.00 80.00
25 Lloyd Waner LEG 10.00 25.00
26 Harmon Killebrew LEG 12.00 30.00
27 Bob Feller LEG 15.00 40.00
28 Babe Ruth LEG 30.00 80.00
29 Joe Medwick LEG 8.00 20.00
30 Lefty Gomez LEG 15.00 40.00
31 Mickey Mantle LEG 40.00 100.00
32 Mule Suttles LEG 12.00 30.00
33 Cy Young LEG 20.00 50.00
34 Grover Alexander LEG 10.00 25.00
35 Hank Greenberg LEG 20.00 50.00
36 Yogi Berra LEG 20.00 50.00
37 Jackie Robinson LEG 25.00 60.00
38 Roberto Clemente LEG 60.00 150.00
39 Ty Cobb LEG
40 Honus Wagner LEG 50.00 120.00
41 Mike Trout AS 75.00 200.00
42 Aaron Judge AS 30.00 80.00
43 Cody Bellinger AS 30.00 80.00
44 Kirby Puckett AS 25.00 60.00
45 Mickey Mantle AS 40.00 100.00
46 Roger Maris AS 20.00 50.00
47 Roy Campanella AS 20.00 50.00
48 Pedro Martinez AS 20.00 50.00
49 Ken Griffey Jr. AS 40.00 100.00
50 Joe Cronin AS 8.00 20.00
51 Mariano Rivera AS 25.00 60.00
52 Randy Johnson AS 12.00 30.00
53 Ted Williams AS 25.00 60.00
54 Babe Ruth AS 30.00 80.00
55 Bob Gibson AS 15.00 40.00
56 Fernando Tatis Jr. RC 125.00 300.00
57 Pete Alonso RC 60.00 150.00
58 Vladimir Guerrero Jr. RC 50.00 125.00
59 Eloy Jimenez RC 40.00 100.00
60 Jeff McNeil RC 30.00 80.00
61 Yusei Kikuchi RC 12.00 30.00
62 Austin Riley RC 20.00 50.00
63 Vladimir Guerrero Jr. 50.00 125.00
64 Fernando Tatis Jr. 125.00 300.00
65 Pete Alonso 60.00 150.00

2019 Panini Flawless Autographs
RANDOM INSERTS IN PACKS
STATED PRINT RUN 25 SER.#'d SETS
*RUBY/20: .4X TO 1X BASIC
2 David Ross 15.00 40.00
3 Luis Severino 12.00 30.00
6 Blake Snell 12.00 30.00
7 J.T. Realmuto 30.00 80.00
8 Jason Giambi 10.00 25.00
10 Frank Thomas 40.00 100.00
11 Kyle Hendricks 50.00 120.00
12 David Wright 15.00 40.00
13 Lou Brock 20.00 50.00
14 Walker Buehler 20.00 50.00
15 Ronald Acuna Jr. 80.00 200.00
16 Corey Seager 15.00 40.00
17 Matt Carpenter 15.00 40.00
18 Andre Dawson 12.00 30.00
19 J.D. Martinez 15.00 40.00
20 Juan Soto 100.00 250.00
21 Tom Glavine 12.00 30.00
23 Keith Hernandez 10.00 25.00
24 Omar Vizquel 12.00 30.00
26 Juan Marichal 12.00 30.00
27 Josh Hader 12.00 30.00
28 Kyle Schwarber 15.00 40.00
30 Tony Perez 15.00 40.00
32 Pete Rose 25.00 60.00
33 Goose Gossage 12.00 30.00
36 Paul Molitor 15.00 40.00
37 Paul Molitor 15.00 40.00
38 Mark Grace 12.00 30.00

2019 Panini Flawless Dual Patch Autographs
RANDOM INSERTS IN PACKS
STATED PRINT RUN 25 SER.#'d SETS
*RUBY: .4X TO 1X BASIC
1 Pete Alonso 100.00 250.00
2 Jon Duplantier 10.00 25.00
4 Dawinzon Hernandez 10.00 25.00
5 Dylan Cease 15.00 40.00
7 Brendan Rodgers 15.00 40.00
9 Keston Hiura 30.00 80.00
12 Carter Kieboom 15.00 40.00
13 Yordan Alvarez 75.00 200.00
14 Jonathan Loaisiga 12.00 30.00
16 Touki Toussaint 12.00 30.00
17 Bo Bichette 40.00 100.00
19 Willy Adames 10.00 25.00

2019 Panini Flawless Dual Patches
RANDOM INSERTS IN PACKS
PRINT RUNS B/WN 7-25 COPIES PER
NO PRICING ON QTY 15 OR LESS
*RUBY/20: .4X TO 1X BASIC
2 Gary Carter/25 15.00 40.00
17 Justin Verlander/25 8.00 20.00
19 Matt Chapman/25 8.00 20.00
20 Austin Riley/25 12.00 30.00

2019 Panini Flawless Dual Signature Patches
RANDOM INSERTS IN PACKS
PRINT RUNS B/WN 15-25 COPIES PER
NO PRICING ON QTY 15 OR LESS
*RUBY/20: .4X TO 1X BASIC
5 Hoskins/Alonso/25 80.00 200.00

2019 Panini Flawless Dual Signatures
RANDOM INSERTS IN PACKS
PRINT RUNS B/WN 15-25 COPIES PER
NO PRICING ON QTY 15 OR LESS
*RUBY/20: .4X TO 1X BASIC
4 Acuna Jr./Ohtani/25 125.00 300.00
5 Soto/Acuna Jr./25 200.00 500.00
7 Mesa/Franco/25 75.00 200.00
8 Tatis Jr./Vlad Jr./25 150.00 400.00
9 Whitley/Tucker/25 25.00 60.00
10 Jimenez/Kopech/25 40.00 100.00

2019 Panini Flawless Legendary Dual Materials
RANDOM INSERTS IN PACKS
PRINT RUNS B/WN 15-25 COPIES PER
NO PRICING ON QTY 15 OR LESS
*RUBY/20: .4X TO 1X BASIC
2 Mule Suttles/25 15.00 40.00
3 Stan Musial/25 15.00 40.00
4 Hank Greenberg/25 15.00 40.00
5 Roberto Clemente/25 40.00 100.00
6 Joe Cronin/25 10.00 25.00
7 Roger Maris/25 15.00 40.00
8 Tommy Henrich/25 10.00 25.00
9 Bill Dickey/25 12.00 30.00
11 Jimmie Foxx/25 25.00 60.00
12 Jackie Robinson/25 30.00 80.00
13 Joe Jackson/25 60.00 150.00
15 Joe McCarthy/25 10.00 25.00
18 Tony Lazzeri/25 12.00 30.00
19 Bob Meusel/25 15.00 40.00
20 Miller Huggins/25 10.00 25.00
23 Jackie Robinson/20 30.00 80.00

2019 Panini Flawless Legends Jumbo Material
RANDOM INSERTS IN PACKS
PRINT RUNS B/WN 7-25 COPIES PER
NO PRICING ON QTY 15 OR LESS
*RUBY/20: .4X TO 1X BASIC
8 Bill Dickey/25 15.00 40.00
10 Tommy Henrich/25 10.00 25.00
11 Elston Howard/25 10.00 25.00
15 Dom DiMaggio/25 10.00 25.00
18 Mule Suttles/25 15.00 40.00
19 Roberto Clemente/25 50.00 120.00

2019 Panini Flawless Legends Jumbo Material Ruby
*RUBY/20: .4X TO 1X BASIC
RANDOM INSERTS IN PACKS
PRINT RUNS B/WN 10-20 COPIES PER
NO PRICING ON QTY 15 OR LESS
5 Roger Bresnahan/20 25.00 60.00
13 Tom Yawkey/20 10.00 25.00
14 Ernie Lombardi/20 15.00 40.00
17 Carl Furillo/20 10.00 25.00

2019 Panini Flawless Memorable Marks Autographs
RANDOM INSERTS IN PACKS
PRINT RUNS B/WN 15-25 COPIES PER
NO PRICING ON QTY 15 OR LESS
*RUBY/20: .4X TO 1X BASIC
2 Adrian Beltre/25 15.00 40.00
3 Carlton Fisk/25 12.00 30.00
4 David Ross/25 15.00 40.00
5 Lou Whitaker/25 20.00 50.00
7 Charlie Blackmon/25 15.00 40.00
9 Joe Carter/25 10.00 25.00
12 Tim Wakefield/25 10.00 25.00
13 Ken Griffey Sr./25 10.00 25.00
14 Dennis Eckersley/25 12.00 30.00
15 Francisco Lindor/25 15.00 40.00
16 Matt Chapman/25 15.00 40.00
17 Austin Riley/25 20.00 50.00
18 Royce Lewis/25 20.00 50.00
20 Rod Carew/20 12.00 30.00

2019 Panini Flawless Milestones Jersey Autographs
RANDOM INSERTS IN PACKS
PRINT RUNS B/WN 15-25 COPIES PER
NO PRICING ON QTY 15 OR LESS
*RUBY/20: .4X TO 1X BASIC
2 Austin Riley/25 20.00 50.00
19 Blake Snell/25 12.00 30.00

2019 Panini Flawless Moments Jersey Autographs
RANDOM INSERTS IN PACKS
STATED PRINT RUN 25 SER.#'d SETS
*RUBY/20: .4X TO 1X BASIC
18 Jordan Hicks 15.00 40.00
20 Austin Riley 20.00 50.00

2019 Panini Flawless Patch Autographs
RANDOM INSERTS IN PACKS
PRINT RUNS B/WN 15-25 COPIES PER
NO PRICING ON QTY 15 OR LESS
*RUBY/20: .4X TO 1X BASIC
5 Jordan Hicks/25 15.00 40.00
12 Austin Riley/25 20.00 50.00
14 Blake Snell/25 12.00 30.00
17 Chris Paddack/25 20.00 50.00
19 Josh Naylor/25 12.00 30.00
21 Ronald Acuna Jr./25 100.00 250.00
24 Pete Alonso/25 60.00 150.00
26 Carter Kieboom/25 15.00 40.00
29 Rhys Hoskins/20 30.00 80.00

2019 Panini Flawless Patches
RANDOM INSERTS IN PACKS
PRINT RUNS B/WN 3-25 COPIES PER
NO PRICING ON QTY 15 OR LESS
*RUBY/20: .4X TO 1X BASIC
1 Yusei Kikuchi/25 12.00 30.00
6 Fernando Tatis Jr./25 80.00 200.00
23 Eloy Jimenez/20 50.00 120.00
31 Michael Kopech/20 15.00 40.00

2019 Panini Flawless Penmanship Materials Dual Patch Autographs
RANDOM INSERTS IN PACKS
STATED PRINT RUN 25 SER.#'d SETS
4 Oscar Mercado 25.00 60.00
9 Keston Hiura 40.00 100.00

2019 Panini Flawless Performances Patch Autographs
RANDOM INSERTS IN PACKS
PRINT RUNS B/WN 20-25 COPIES PER
*RUBY/20: .4X TO 1X BASIC
1 Rhys Hoskins/20 30.00 80.00
4 Juan Soto/25 75.00 200.00

2019 Panini Flawless Quad Patch Signatures
RANDOM INSERTS IN PACKS
STATED PRINT RUN 25 SER.#'d SETS
*RUBY/20: .4X TO 1X BASIC
4 Paul DeJong 25.00 60.00
9 Cal Quantrill 10.00 25.00

2019 Panini Flawless Rookie Dual Patch Autographs
RANDOM INSERTS IN PACKS
STATED PRINT RUN 25 SER.#'d SETS
*RUBY/20: .4X TO 1X BASIC
1 Vladimir Guerrero Jr. 75.00 200.00
2 Eloy Jimenez 40.00 100.00
3 Ryan O'Hearn 10.00 25.00
4 Fernando Tatis Jr. 125.00 300.00
5 Reese McGuire 15.00 40.00
6 Jake Bauers 15.00 40.00
8 Justus Sheffield 15.00 40.00
9 Michael Kopech 30.00 80.00
10 Kyle Tucker 25.00 60.00
11 Luis Urias 15.00 40.00
12 Jeff McNeil 25.00 60.00
13 Kyle Wright 15.00 40.00
14 Ramon Laureano 25.00 60.00
15 Steven Duggar 12.00 30.00
16 Josh James 15.00 40.00
17 Dennis Santana 10.00 25.00
18 Christin Stewart 12.00 30.00
19 Cedric Mullins 30.00 80.00
20 Corbin Burnes 30.00 80.00

2019 Panini Flawless Rookie Patch Autographs
RANDOM INSERTS IN PACKS
STATED PRINT RUN 25 SER.#'d SETS
*RUBY: .4X TO 1X BASIC
1 Vladimir Guerrero Jr. 75.00 200.00
2 Eloy Jimenez 40.00 100.00
3 Ryan O'Hearn 10.00 25.00
4 Fernando Tatis Jr. 125.00 300.00
5 Reese McGuire 15.00 40.00
6 Jake Bauers 15.00 40.00
8 Justus Sheffield 15.00 40.00
9 Michael Kopech 30.00 80.00
10 Kyle Tucker 25.00 60.00
11 Luis Urias 10.00 25.00
12 Jeff McNeil 30.00 80.00
13 Kyle Wright 15.00 40.00
14 Ramon Laureano 25.00 60.00
15 Steven Duggar 12.00 30.00
16 Josh James 15.00 40.00
17 Dennis Santana 10.00 25.00
18 Christin Stewart 12.00 30.00
19 Cedric Mullins 30.00 80.00
20 Corbin Burnes 30.00 80.00

2019 Panini Flawless Rookie Triple Patch Autographs
RANDOM INSERTS IN PACKS
STATED PRINT RUN 25 SER.#'d SETS
*RUBY: .4X TO 1X BASIC
1 Vladimir Guerrero Jr. 75.00 200.00
2 Eloy Jimenez 40.00 100.00
3 Ryan O'Hearn 10.00 25.00
4 Fernando Tatis Jr. 125.00 300.00
5 Reese McGuire 15.00 40.00
6 Jake Bauers 15.00 40.00
8 Justus Sheffield 15.00 40.00
9 Michael Kopech 30.00 80.00
10 Kyle Tucker 25.00 60.00
11 Luis Urias 15.00 40.00
12 Jeff McNeil 25.00 60.00
13 Kyle Wright 15.00 40.00
14 Ramon Laureano 25.00 60.00
15 Steven Duggar 12.00 30.00
16 Josh James 15.00 40.00
17 Dennis Santana 10.00 25.00
18 Christin Stewart 12.00 30.00
19 Cedric Mullins 30.00 80.00
20 Corbin Burnes 30.00 80.00

2019 Panini Flawless Signature Patches
RANDOM INSERTS IN PACKS
STATED PRINT RUN 25 SER.#'d SETS
*RUBY/20: .4X TO 1X BASIC
11 Nathaniel Lowe 50.00 125.00
19 Matt Chapman 20.00 50.00

2019 Panini Flawless Signatures
RANDOM INSERTS IN PACKS
PRINT RUNS B/WN 15-25 COPIES PER
NO PRICING ON QTY 15 OR LESS
*RUBY/20: .4X TO 1X BASIC
1 Vladimir Guerrero Jr./25 60.00 150.00
2 Aaron Judge/20 60.00 150.00
3 Shohei Ohtani/25 60.00 150.00
4 Ken Griffey Jr./20 100.00 250.00
5 Ken Griffey Jr./20 100.00 250.00
8 Frank Thomas/20 40.00 100.00
11 Shohei Ohtani/25 60.00 150.00
18 Jason Giambi/20 10.00 25.00

2019 Panini Flawless Signatures Ruby
*RUBY/20: .4X TO 1X BASIC
RANDOM INSERTS IN PACKS
PRINT RUNS B/WN 10-20 COPIES PER
NO PRICING ON QTY 15 OR LESS
14 Steve Garvey/20 40.00 100.00

2019 Panini Flawless Spikes
RANDOM INSERTS IN PACKS
PRINT RUNS B/WN 5-20 COPIES PER
NO PRICING ON QTY 15 OR LESS
2 Jeff McNeil/20 60.00 150.00
11 Jake Bauers/20 20.00 50.00
13 Albert Pujols/17 150.00 400.00
17 Carlos Correa/16 50.00 120.00

2019 Panini Flawless Triple Legends Relics
RANDOM INSERTS IN PACKS
STATED PRINT RUN 25 SER.#'d SETS
*RUBY/20: .4X TO 1X BASIC
2 Greenberg/Kaline/Cobb 40.00 100.00
3 Foxx/Williams/Cronin 25.00 60.00
4 Jackson/Wagner/Hornsby 75.00 200.00
5 DiMaggio/Clemente/Robinson 100.00 250.00
6 Ott/Maris/Musial 30.00 80.00
8 Sewell/Speaker/Lemon 15.00 40.00
9 Maris/Howard/Mantle 40.00 100.00

2019 Panini Flawless Triple Legends Relics Ruby
*RUBY/20: .4X TO 1X BASIC
RANDOM INSERTS IN PACKS
PRINT RUNS B/WN 10-20 COPIES PER
NO PRICING ON QTY 15 OR LESS
1 Gehrig/Mantle/Ruth/20 300.00 600.00
10 Wagner/Ruth/Cobb/20 150.00 400.00

2019 Panini Flawless Triple Patch Autographs
RANDOM INSERTS IN PACKS
PRINT RUNS B/WN 20-25 COPIES PER
*RUBY/20: .4X TO 1X BASIC
3 Juan Soto/20 75.00 200.00
5 Nathaniel Lowe/25 50.00 125.00
8 Luis Arraez/25 40.00 100.00

2019 Panini Flawless Triple Patch Signatures
RANDOM INSERTS IN PACKS
PRINT RUNS B/WN 15-25 COPIES PER
NO PRICING ON QTY 15 OR LESS
*RUBY/20: .4X TO 1X BASIC
6 Ronald Acuna Jr./25 100.00 250.00
9 David Fletcher/25 30.00 80.00
10 Corbin Martin/25 15.00 40.00

2019 Panini Flawless Two Player Dual Rookie Patch Autographs
RANDOM INSERTS IN PACKS
STATED PRINT RUN 25 SER.#'d SETS
*RUBY: .4X TO 1X BASIC
2 Tucker/Jimenez 40.00 100.00
3 Tatis Jr/Urias 75.00 200.00
4 Tucker/Mullins 10.00 25.00
5 Eloy/Vlad Jr 60.00 150.00
6 Kopech/Sheffield 15.00 40.00
7 Bauers/O'Hearn 10.00 25.00
9 Urias/McNeil 15.00 40.00

2020 Panini Flawless
STATED PRINT RUN 20 SER.#'d SETS
1 Mike Trout 100.00 250.00
2 Aaron Judge 50.00 120.00
3 Pete Alonso 30.00 80.00
4 Fernando Tatis Jr. 60.00 150.00
5 Vladimir Guerrero Jr. 40.00 100.00
6 Bryce Harper 40.00 100.00
7 Yadier Molina 40.00 100.00
8 Cody Bellinger 40.00 100.00
9 Shohei Ohtani 40.00 100.00
10 Albert Pujols 30.00 80.00
11 Anthony Rizzo 40.00 100.00
12 Juan Soto 40.00 100.00
13 Ronald Acuna Jr. 100.00 250.00
14 Gleyber Torres 25.00 60.00
15 Mookie Betts 125.00 300.00
16 Javier Baez 30.00 80.00
17 Clayton Kershaw 40.00 100.00
18 Mike Trout 100.00 250.00
19 Pete Alonso 30.00 80.00
20 Vladimir Guerrero Jr. 40.00 100.00
21 Mariano Rivera 40.00 100.00
22 Babe Ruth 100.00 250.00
23 Ichiro 50.00 120.00
24 Sandy Koufax 50.00 120.00
25 Sammy Sosa 40.00 100.00
26 Mickey Mantle 60.00 150.00
27 Honus Wagner 40.00 100.00
28 Al Kaline 50.00 120.00
29 Roberto Clemente 50.00 120.00
30 Lou Gehrig 50.00 120.00
31 Ty Cobb 50.00 120.00
32 Ken Griffey Jr. 50.00 120.00
33 Joe Jackson 40.00 100.00
34 Cal Ripken 50.00 120.00
35 Mike Schmidt 40.00 100.00
36 Mark McGwire 40.00 100.00
37 Jackie Robinson 40.00 100.00
38 Nolan Ryan 60.00 150.00
39 George Brett 30.00 80.00
40 Kirby Puckett 50.00 120.00
41 Luis Robert RC 125.00 300.00
42 Bo Bichette RC 60.00 150.00
43 Yordan Alvarez RC 80.00 200.00
44 Gavin Lux RC 40.00 100.00
45 Brendan McKay RC 20.00 50.00
46 Jesus Luzardo RC 20.00 50.00
47 Aristides Aquino RC 25.00 60.00
48 Nico Hoerner RC 30.00 80.00
49 Dustin May RC 25.00 60.00
50 Yoshitomo Tsutsugo RC 15.00 40.00
51 Shogo Akiyama RC 12.00 30.00

2020 Panini Flawless Variations
STATED PRINT RUN 20 SER.#'d SETS
1 Mike Trout 100.00 250.00
2 Aaron Judge 50.00 120.00
8 Cody Bellinger 40.00 100.00
9 Shohei Ohtani 40.00 100.00
12 Juan Soto 40.00 100.00
13 Ronald Acuna Jr. 100.00 250.00
21 Mariano Rivera 40.00 100.00
22 Babe Ruth 100.00 250.00
24 Sandy Koufax 50.00 120.00
25 Sammy Sosa 40.00 100.00
30 Lou Gehrig 50.00 120.00
32 Ken Griffey Jr. 50.00 120.00
38 Nolan Ryan 40.00 100.00
41 Luis Robert 125.00 300.00
42 Bo Bichette 60.00 150.00
43 Yordan Alvarez 80.00 200.00
44 Gavin Lux 40.00 100.00
46 Kwang-Hyun Kim 40.00 100.00
47 Aristides Aquino 25.00 60.00
49 Shun Yamaguchi 10.00 25.00

2020 Panini Flawless Dual Patch Autographs
RANDOM INSERTS IN PACKS
PRINT RUNS B/WN 15-25 COPIES PER
NO PRICING ON QTY 15 OR LESS
1 Adley Rutschman/25 75.00 200.00
2 Chris Paddack/24 15.00 40.00
4 Josh Hader/25 12.00 30.00
7 Kwang-Hyun Kim/25 20.00 50.00
9 Shogo Akiyama/25 25.00 60.00
12 Steve Garvey/25 40.00 100.00
14 Luis Robert/25 150.00 400.00
15 Ketel Marte/21 12.00 30.00
18 Evan White/25 15.00 40.00
19 Corey Seager/25 30.00 80.00
26 Keston Hiura/25 20.00 50.00
27 Kyle Hendricks/25 30.00 80.00
29 Shun Yamaguchi/25 15.00 40.00

2020 Panini Flawless Dual Patch Autographs Ruby
*RUBY/20: .4X TO 1X BASIC
RANDOM INSERTS IN PACKS
PRINT RUNS B/WN 10-20 COPIES PER
NO PRICING ON QTY 15 OR LESS
16 Josh Bell/20 12.00 30.00
19 Corey Seager/20 40.00 100.00
21 Alex Bregman/20 30.00 80.00

2020 Panini Flawless Dual Patches
RANDOM INSERTS IN PACKS
PRINT RUNS B/WN 20-25 COPIES PER
1 Satchel Paige/25 40.00 100.00
2 George Brett/20 25.00 60.00
4 Gavin Lux/20 15.00 40.00
5 Yordan Alvarez/25 50.00 120.00
8 Luis Aparicio/25 15.00 40.00
10 Albert Pujols/25 20.00 50.00
12 Tom Glavine/25 15.00 40.00
14 Roger Clemens/20 10.00 25.00

2020 Panini Flawless Dual Patches Ruby
*RUBY/20: .4X TO 1X BASIC
RANDOM INSERTS IN PACKS
PRINT RUNS B/WN 10-20 COPIES PER
NO PRICING ON QTY 15 OR LESS
1 Satchel Paige/20 50.00 120.00
7 Vladimir Guerrero/20 15.00 40.00
10 Albert Pujols/20 25.00 60.00
19 Nolan Ryan/20 25.00 60.00
20 Alex Rodriguez/20 15.00 40.00

2020 Panini Flawless Dual Signature Patches
RANDOM INSERTS IN PACKS
PRINT RUNS B/WN 15-25 COPIES PER
NO PRICING ON QTY 15 OR LESS
1 P.Alonso/Y.Alvarez/25 60.00 150.00
2 Brendan McKay 15.00 40.00
Brusdar Graterol/25
3 B.Bichette/V.Guerrero Jr/25 200.00 500.00
4 A.Aquino/Y.Alvarez/25 100.00 250.00
8 J.Adell/L.Robert/25 150.00 400.00

2020 Panini Flawless Dual Signature Patches Ruby
*RUBY/20: .4X TO 1X BASIC
RANDOM INSERTS IN PACKS
PRINT RUNS B/WN 10-20 COPIES PER
NO PRICING ON QTY 15 OR LESS
1 P.Alonso/Y.Alvarez/20 75.00 200.00
3 B.Bichette/V.Guerrero Jr/20 250.00 600.00
8 J.Adell/L.Robert/20 200.00 500.00

2020 Panini Flawless Dual Signatures
RANDOM INSERTS IN PACKS
PRINT RUNS B/WN 15-25 COPIES PER
NO PRICING ON QTY 15 OR LESS
*RUBY/20: .4X TO 1X BASIC
8 Pete Alonso 60.00 150.00
Yordan Alvarez/25

2020 Panini Flawless Greats Autographs
RANDOM INSERTS IN PACKS
PRINT RUNS B/WN 15-25 COPIES PER
NO PRICING ON QTY 15 OR LESS
*RUBY/20: .4X TO 1X BASIC
2 Frank Thomas/25 50.00 120.00
3 Juan Marichal/25 20.00 50.00
5 Nolan Ryan/20 60.00 150.00
6 Ozzie Smith/20 25.00 60.00
7 Paul Molitor/20 20.00 50.00
9 Tom Glavine/20 20.00 50.00
10 Ken Griffey Jr./20 125.00 300.00
12 Alan Trammell/25 20.00 50.00

2020 Panini Flawless Greats Dual Memorabilia Autographs
RANDOM INSERTS IN PACKS
PRINT RUNS B/WN 10-25 COPIES PER
NO PRICING ON QTY 15 OR LESS
4 Elroy Face/25 25.00 60.00

2020 Panini Flawless Greats Dual Memorabilia Autographs Ruby
*RUBY/20: .4X TO 1X BASIC
RANDOM INSERTS IN PACKS
PRINT RUNS B/WN 7-20 COPIES PER
NO PRICING ON QTY 15 OR LESS
14 Alan Trammell/20 50.00 120.00

2020 Panini Flawless Horizontal Rookie Patch Autographs
RANDOM INSERTS IN PACKS
PRINT RUNS B/WN 15-25 COPIES PER
NO PRICING ON QTY 15 OR LESS
2 Dylan Cease/25 12.00 30.00
3 Aristides Aquino/25 25.00 60.00
6 Bo Bichette/25 100.00 250.00
7 Gavin Lux/25 40.00 100.00
8 Brendan McKay/25 15.00 40.00

2020 Panini Flawless Horizontal Rookie Patch Autographs Ruby
*RUBY/20: .4X TO 1X BASIC
RANDOM INSERTS IN PACKS
PRINT RUNS B/WN 10-20 COPIES PER
NO PRICING ON QTY 15 OR LESS
5 Yordan Alvarez/20 75.00 200.00
6 Bo Bichette/20 125.00 300.00

2020 Panini Flawless Legendary Materials
RANDOM INSERTS IN PACKS
PRINT RUNS B/WN 7-25 COPIES PER
NO PRICING ON QTY 15 OR LESS
1 Lou Gehrig/25 75.00 200.00
3 Ted Williams/25 25.00 60.00
4 Ty Cobb/25 50.00 120.00
5 Jackie Robinson/25 50.00 120.00
7 Mickey Mantle/25 40.00 100.00
8 Joe Jackson/25 50.00 120.00
9 Jimmie Foxx/25 25.00 60.00
11 Stan Musial/25 15.00 40.00
12 Mel Ott/25 25.00 60.00
14 Cool Papa Bell/25 25.00 60.00
15 Hank Greenberg/25 20.00 50.00
16 Roger Maris/25 25.00 60.00
17 Rogers Hornsby/25 30.00 80.00
18 Joe Cronin/25 10.00 25.00
19 Bill Dickey/25 20.00 50.00
20 Mule Suttles/20 20.00 50.00

2020 Panini Flawless Legendary Materials Ruby
*RUBY/20: .4X TO 1X BASIC
RANDOM INSERTS IN PACKS
PRINT RUNS B/WN 10-20 COPIES PER
NO PRICING ON QTY 15 OR LESS
1 Lou Gehrig/20 100.00 250.00
11 Stan Musial/20 20.00 50.00

2020 Panini Flawless Legendary Signatures
RANDOM INSERTS IN PACKS
PRINT RUNS B/WN 15-25 COPIES PER
NO PRICING ON QTY 15 OR LESS
*RUBY/20: .4X TO 1X BASIC
3 Ryne Sandberg/25 30.00 80.00
4 Rickey Henderson/25 40.00 100.00
10 Barry Larkin/25 25.00 60.00

2020 Panini Flawless Legends Jumbo Materials
RANDOM INSERTS IN PACKS
PRINT RUNS B/WN 7-25 COPIES PER
NO PRICING ON QTY 15 OR LESS
*RUBY/20: .4X TO 1X BASIC
1 Bob Lemon/25 15.00 40.00
6 Early Wynn/25 30.00 80.00
12 Addie Joss/25 100.00 250.00
13 Roger Maris/20 40.00 100.00
16 Joe McCarthy/20 20.00 50.00
17 Ted Lyons/25 15.00 40.00
20 Luis Aparicio/25 12.00 30.00

2020 Panini Flawless Memorable Marks
RANDOM INSERTS IN PACKS
PRINT RUNS B/WN 10-25 COPIES PER
NO PRICING ON QTY 15 OR LESS
*RUBY/20: .4X TO 1X BASIC
2 Dave Stewart/25 10.00 25.00
3 Anthony Rizzo/25 30.00 80.00
4 Andre Dawson/25 15.00 40.00
5 Austin Meadows/25 15.00 40.00
6 Don Mattingly/25 40.00 100.00
8 Justin Turner/25 20.00 50.00
9 Keith Hernandez/25 20.00 50.00
10 Mark Grace/25 20.00 50.00
11 Ronald Acuna Jr./25 75.00 200.00
13 Tony Perez/25 25.00 60.00
16 Ryan Zimmerman/25 12.00 30.00
18 Gleyber Torres/25 40.00 100.00
19 Bryan Reynolds/25 12.00 30.00

2020 Panini Flawless Milestones
RANDOM INSERTS IN PACKS
PRINT RUNS B/WN 10-25 COPIES PER
NO PRICING ON QTY 15 OR LESS
3 CC Sabathia/25 25.00 60.00
8 Sammy Sosa/21 100.00 250.00
19 Pete Rose/20 100.00 250.00
23 Yordan Alvarez/25 100.00 250.00

2020 Panini Flawless Milestones Ruby
*RUBY/20: .4X TO 1X BASIC
RANDOM INSERTS IN PACKS
PRINT RUNS B/WN 7-20 COPIES PER
NO PRICING ON QTY 15 OR LESS
5 David Wright/20 40.00 100.00

2020 Panini Flawless Moments
RANDOM INSERTS IN PACKS
PRINT RUNS B/WN 10-25 COPIES PER
NO PRICING ON QTY 15 OR LESS
2 CC Sabathia/25 25.00 60.00
5 Aristides Aquino/25 30.00 80.00
22 Josh Bell/25 12.00 30.00
23 Aroldis Chapman/25 20.00 50.00

2020 Panini Flawless Moments Ruby
*RUBY/20: .4X TO 1X BASIC
RANDOM INSERTS IN PACKS
PRINT RUNS B/WN 7-20 COPIES PER
NO PRICING ON QTY 15 OR LESS
1 Adrian Beltre/20 30.00 80.00

2020 Panini Flawless Patch Autographs
RANDOM INSERTS IN PACKS
PRINT RUNS B/WN 15-25 COPIES PER
NO PRICING ON QTY 15 OR LESS
1 Gavin Lux/25 50.00 125.00
15 Austin Riley/25 15.00 40.00
16 Cavan Biggio/25 20.00 50.00
18 Fernando Tatis Jr./25 125.00 300.00
24 Keston Hiura/25 25.00 60.00

2020 Panini Flawless Patch Autographs Ruby
*RUBY/20: .4X TO 1X BASIC
RANDOM INSERTS IN PACKS
PRINT RUNS B/WN 10-20 COPIES PER
NO PRICING ON QTY 15 OR LESS
17 Chris Paddack/20 15.00 40.00
18 Fernando Tatis Jr./20 150.00 400.00
19 Andrew Vaughn/20 40.00 100.00

2020 Panini Flawless Patches
RANDOM INSERTS IN PACKS
PRINT RUNS B/WN 10-25 COPIES PER
NO PRICING ON QTY 15 OR LESS
3 Bo Bichette/23 30.00 80.00
4 Yordan Alvarez/25 50.00 120.00
5 Aristides Aquino/25 15.00 40.00
6 Brendan McKay/25 8.00 20.00
7 Gavin Lux/25 15.00 40.00
8 Luis Robert/25 60.00 150.00
9 A.J. Puk/25 12.00 30.00
15 Jasson Dominguez/25 50.00 120.00
16 Wander Franco/20 50.00 125.00
17 Dylan Cease/25 15.00 40.00
19 Nico Hoerner/20 8.00 20.00
28 Chris Paddack/25 8.00 20.00
31 Keston Hiura/25 10.00 25.00
38 Austin Meadows/25 10.00 25.00

2020 Panini Flawless Patches Ruby
*RUBY/20: .4X TO 1X BASIC
RANDOM INSERTS IN PACKS
PRINT RUNS B/WN 15-20 COPIES PER
NO PRICING ON QTY 15
3 Bo Bichette/20 40.00 100.00
20 Jesus Luzardo/20 10.00 25.00
40 Mike Soroka/20 10.00 25.00

2020 Panini Flawless Penmanship Materials
RANDOM INSERTS IN PACKS
PRINT RUNS B/WN 10-25 COPIES PER
NO PRICING ON QTY 15 OR LESS
*RUBY/20: .4X TO 1X BASIC
5 Michael Chavis/25 12.00 30.00
9 Bert Blyleven/25 12.00 30.00

2020 Panini Flawless Premium Ink
RANDOM INSERTS IN PACKS
PRINT RUNS B/WN 10-25 COPIES PER
NO PRICING ON QTY 15 OR LESS
*RUBY/20: .4X TO 1X BASIC
3 Vladimir Guerrero Jr./25 60.00 150.00
6 Don Mattingly/25 40.00 100.00
7 Dennis Eckersley/25 12.00 30.00
8 Dale Murphy/25 20.00 50.00
10 Luis Severino/25 12.00 30.00
11 Craig Biggio/25 20.00 50.00
14 David Ross/25 25.00 60.00

2020 Panini Flawless Quad Patch Signatures
RANDOM INSERTS IN PACKS
PRINT RUNS B/WN 15-25 COPIES PER
NO PRICING ON QTY 15
4 Royce Lewis/25 30.00 80.00
6 Cavan Biggio/25 20.00 50.00
14 Austin Meadows/25 20.00 50.00
15 Jeff McNeil/25 30.00 80.00
18 Alec Bohm/25 75.00 200.00
20 Estevan Florial/25 30.00 80.00

2020 Panini Flawless Quad Patch Signatures Ruby
*RUBY/20: .4X TO 1X BASIC
RANDOM INSERTS IN PACKS
PRINT RUNS B/WN 10-20 COPIES PER
NO PRICING ON QTY 15 OR LESS
4 Royce Lewis/20 40.00 100.00
6 Cavan Biggio/20 30.00 80.00
7 Luis Robert/20 150.00 400.00
14 Austin Meadows/20 25.00 60.00
19 Elroy Face/20 20.00 50.00
23 Sixto Sanchez/20 30.00 80.00
25 Yordan Alvarez/20 75.00 200.00

2020 Panini Flawless Rookie Dual Patch Autographs
RANDOM INSERTS IN PACKS
PRINT RUNS B/WN 15-25 COPIES PER
NO PRICING ON QTY 15 OR LESS
6 Aristides Aquino/25 25.00 60.00
9 A.J. Puk/25 15.00 40.00
13 Dylan Cease/25 12.00 30.00
18 Brendan McKay/25 15.00 40.00
19 Gavin Lux/25 40.00 100.00
20 Bo Bichette/25 100.00 250.00

2020 Panini Flawless Rookie Dual Patch Autographs Ruby
*RUBY/20: .4X TO 1X BASIC
RANDOM INSERTS IN PACKS
PRINT RUNS B/WN 10-20 COPIES PER
NO PRICING ON QTY 15 OR LESS
10 Yordan Alvarez/20 75.00 200.00
20 Bo Bichette/20 125.00 300.00

2020 Panini Flawless Rookie Patch Autographs
RANDOM INSERTS IN PACKS
PRINT RUNS B/WN 15-25 COPIES PER
NO PRICING ON QTY 15 OR LESS
3 Dylan Cease/25 12.00 30.00
7 Gavin Lux/25 40.00 100.00
8 Bo Bichette/25 100.00 250.00
9 A.J. Puk/25 15.00 40.00
11 Aristides Aquino/25 25.00 60.00
19 Brendan McKay/25 15.00 40.00
20 Yordan Alvarez/25 60.00 150.00

2020 Panini Flawless Rookie Patch Autographs Ruby
*RUBY/20: .4X TO 1X BASIC
RANDOM INSERTS IN PACKS

PRINT RUNS B/WN 10-20 COPIES PER
NO PRICING ON QTY 15 OR LESS
8 Bo Bichette/20 125.00 300.00
20 Yordan Alvarez/20 75.00 200.00

2020 Panini Flawless Rookie Signatures

RANDOM INSERTS IN PACKS
STATED PRINT RUN 25 SER.#'d SETS
*RUBY/20: .4X TO 1X BASIC
7 Gavin Lux 30.00 80.00
8 Bo Bichette 80.00 200.00
9 A.J. Puk 10.00 25.00
11 Aristides Aquino 15.00 40.00
19 Brendan McKay 10.00 25.00
20 Yordan Alvarez 100.00 250.00
21 Yoshitomo Tsutsugo 25.00 60.00

2020 Panini Flawless Signature Prime Materials

RANDOM INSERTS IN PACKS
PRINT RUNS B/WN 15-25 COPIES PER
NO PRICING ON QTY 15 OR LESS
11 Royce Lewis/25 40.00 100.00
14 Austin Riley/25 20.00 50.00
16 Cavan Biggio/25 20.00 50.00
19 Max Muncy/20 15.00 40.00
35 Kyle Hendricks/25 25.00 60.00
38 Josh Bell/25 12.00 30.00

2020 Panini Flawless Signature Prime Materials Ruby

*RUBY/20: .4X TO 1X BASIC
RANDOM INSERTS IN PACKS
PRINT RUNS B/WN 10-20 COPIES PER
NO PRICING ON QTY 15 OR LESS
15 Brendan Rodgers/20 10.00 25.00
17 Chris Paddack/20 15.00 40.00
21 Luis Robert/20 150.00 400.00
26 Sixto Sanchez/20 40.00 100.00
34 J.D. Martinez/20 20.00 50.00

2020 Panini Flawless Signatures

RANDOM INSERTS IN PACKS
PRINT RUNS B/WN 15-25 COPIES PER
NO PRICING ON QTY 15 OR LESS
7 Aaron Judge/25 75.00 200.00
8 Gleyber Torres/25 40.00 100.00
10 Ken Griffey Jr./20 200.00 500.00
11 Kenny Lofton/20 20.00 50.00
12 Ivan Rodriguez/20
14 Nolan Ryan/20 60.00 150.00
15 Paul Molitor/20 15.00 40.00
16 Pete Rose/20 30.00 80.00
17 Pete Alonso/25 50.00 120.00
18 Reggie Jackson/20 30.00 80.00
20 Walker Buehler/25 30.00 80.00
23 Steve Garvey/20 30.00 80.00
24 Ronald Acuna Jr./25 150.00 400.00
26 Luis Severino/25 12.00 30.00
28 Xander Bogaerts/20 15.00 40.00
29 John Smoltz/25 20.00 50.00
31 Eloy Jimenez/25 30.00 80.00
33 Jose Ramirez/25 15.00 40.00
38 Fernando Tatis Jr./25 125.00 300.00
39 Andre Dawson/25 15.00 40.00
40 Adrian Beltre/25 25.00 60.00

2020 Panini Flawless Signatures Ruby

*RUBY/20: .4X TO 1X BASIC
RANDOM INSERTS IN PACKS
PRINT RUNS B/WN 10-20 COPIES PER
NO PRICING ON QTY 15 OR LESS
3 Clayton Kershaw/20 60.00 150.00
4 David Wright/20 30.00 80.00
5 George Brett/20 50.00 120.00
7 Aaron Judge/20 100.00 250.00
9 J.D. Martinez/20 15.00 40.00
24 Ronald Acuna Jr./20 200.00 500.00
33 Jose Ramirez/20 20.00 50.00

2020 Panini Flawless Spikes

RANDOM INSERTS IN PACKS
PRINT RUNS B/WN 8-22 COPIES PER
NO PRICING ON QTY 14 OR LESS
5 Alex Rodriguez/16 75.00 200.00
6 Andrew Vaughn/16 60.00 150.00
11 Vladimir Guerrero Jr./22 60.00 150.00
18 Spencer Torkelson/18 75.00 200.00

2020 Panini Flawless Star Swatch Signatures

RANDOM INSERTS IN PACKS
PRINT RUNS B/WN 20-25 COPIES PER
1 Bo Bichette/25 125.00 300.00
3 Gavin Lux/25 30.00 80.00
4 A.J. Puk/25 15.00 40.00
5 Brendan McKay/25 15.00 40.00
10 Aristides Aquino/25 25.00 60.00
15 Dylan Cease/25 10.00 25.00
22 Keston Hiura/20 15.00 40.00

2020 Panini Flawless Star Swatch Signatures Ruby

*RUBY/20: .4X TO 1X BASIC
RANDOM INSERTS IN PACKS
PRINT RUNS B/WN 10-20 COPIES PER
NO PRICING ON QTY 15 OR LESS
2 Yordan Alvarez/20 60.00 150.00
3 Gavin Lux/20 40.00 100.00
23 Chris Paddack/20 15.00 40.00

2020 Panini Flawless Triple Legends Relics

RANDOM INSERTS IN PACKS
PRINT RUNS B/WN 15-25 COPIES PER
NO PRICING ON QTY 15 OR LESS
2 Chance/Hartnett/Santo/25 60.00 150.00
3 Goslin/Cronin/Rice/25 25.00 60.00
4 Terry/McGraw/Ott/25 30.00 80.00
6 Greenberg/Williams/Berra/25 60.00 150.00
7 Combs/Waner/Waner/25 25.00 60.00
8 Robinson/DiMaggio/Williams/25 75.00 200.00

2020 Panini Flawless Triple Legends Relics Ruby

*RUBY/20: .4X TO 1X BASIC
RANDOM INSERTS IN PACKS
PRINT RUNS B/WN 10-20 COPIES PER
NO PRICING ON QTY 15 OR LESS
8 Robinson/DiMaggio/Williams/20 100.00 250.00

2020 Panini Flawless Triple Patch Autographs

RANDOM INSERTS IN PACKS
PRINT RUNS B/WN 15-25 COPIES PER
NO PRICING ON QTY 15
*RUBY/20: .4X TO 1X BASIC
4 Bo Bichette/25 100.00 250.00
5 Aristides Aquino/25 30.00 80.00
6 Brendan McKay/25 15.00 40.00
18 Fernando Tatis Jr./25 150.00 400.00
22 Juan Soto/20 100.00 250.00
23 Adley Rutschman/25 75.00 200.00

2017 Panini Gold Standard

1-25 PRINT RUN 269 SER.#'d SETS
INSERTED IN '17 CHRONICLES PACKS
JSY AU PRINT RUNS B/WN 99-199 COPIES PER
EXCHANGE DEADLINE 5/22/2019
1 Mike Trout/269 5.00 12.00
2 Ichiro/269 1.25 3.00
3 Kris Bryant/269 1.25 3.00
4 Bryce Harper/269 1.50 4.00
5 Carlos Correa/269 1.00 2.50
6 Buster Posey/269 1.25 3.00
7 Mickey Mantle/269 3.00 8.00
8 Clayton Kershaw/269 1.50 4.00
9 Anthony Rizzo/269 1.25 3.00
10 Francisco Lindor/269 1.00 2.50
11 Paul Goldschmidt/269 1.00 2.50
12 Nolan Arenado/269 1.50 4.00
13 Mookie Betts/269 2.00 5.00
14 Corey Seager/269 1.00 2.50
15 Albert Pujols/269 1.25 3.00
16 Noah Syndergaard/269 .75 2.00
17 Chris Sale/269 1.00 2.50
18 Justin Turner/269 1.00 2.50
19 Xander Bogaerts/269 1.00 2.50
20 Gary Sanchez/269 1.00 2.50
21 Yadier Molina/269 1.25 3.00
22 Yoenis Cespedes/269 1.00 2.50
23 Josh Donaldson/269 .75 2.00
24 Jose Altuve/269 .75 2.00
25 Andrew McCutchen/269 1.00 2.50
26 Andrew Benintendi AU JSY/199 RC 15.00 40.00
27 Yoan Moncada AU JSY/99 RC 10.00 25.00
28 Alex Bregman AU JSY/199 RC 40.00 100.00
29 Dansby Swanson AU JSY/199 RC 6.00 15.00
30 Ian Happ AU JSY/199 RC 8.00 20.00
31 Cody Bellinger AU JSY/99 RC 30.00 80.00
32 Aaron Judge AU JSY/199 RC 60.00 150.00
33 Trey Mancini AU JSY/199 RC 8.00 20.00
34 Jordan Montgomery AU JSY/199 RC 10.00 25.00
35 Bradley Zimmer AU JSY/199 RC 4.00 10.00
36 Mitch Haniger AU JSY/199 RC 6.00 15.00
37 Andrew Toles AU JSY/199 RC 3.00 8.00
38 Alex Reyes AU JSY/99 RC 6.00 15.00
39 Tyler Glasnow AU JSY/199 RC 10.00 25.00
40 Manuel Margot AU JSY/99 RC 4.00 10.00
41 Hunter Renfroe AU JSY/99 RC 5.00 12.00
42 Jorge Bonifacio AU JSY/99 RC 4.00 10.00
43 Antonio Senzatela AU JSY/199 RC 3.00 8.00
44 Amir Garrett AU JSY/199 RC 5.00 12.00
45 David Dahl AU JSY/199 RC 4.00 10.00
46 Sam Travis AU JSY/199 RC 5.00 12.00
47 Ryon Healy AU JSY/199 RC 5.00 12.00
48 Carson Fulmer AU JSY/199 RC 3.00 8.00
49 Lewis Brinson AU JSY/99 RC 6.00 15.00
50 Jacoby Jones AU JSY/199 RC 4.00 10.00

2017 Panini Gold Standard Blue

*BLUE: .75X TO 2X BASIC
INSERTED IN '17 CHRONICLES PACKS
STATED PRINT RUN 79 SER.#'d SETS
1 Mike Trout 8.00 20.00

2017 Panini Gold Standard Newly Minted Memorabilia

INSERTED IN '17 CHRONICLES PACKS
STATED PRINT RUN 99 SER.#'d SETS
*BLUE/25: .5X TO 1.2X BASIC
1 Andrew Benintendi 6.00 15.00
2 Yoan Moncada 5.00 12.00
3 Alex Bregman 6.00 15.00
4 Dansby Swanson 5.00 12.00
5 Ian Happ 4.00 10.00
6 Cody Bellinger 5.00 12.00
7 Aaron Judge 15.00 40.00
8 Trey Mancini 4.00 10.00
9 Jordan Montgomery 3.00 8.00
10 Bradley Zimmer 2.50 6.00
11 Mitch Haniger 3.00 8.00
13 Alex Reyes 2.50 6.00
14 Tyler Glasnow 8.00 20.00
15 Manuel Margot 2.00 5.00
16 Hunter Renfroe 2.50 6.00
17 Jorge Bonifacio 2.00 5.00
18 Antonio Senzatela 2.00 5.00
19 Gleyber Torres 4.00 10.00
20 David Dahl 2.50 6.00
21 Sam Travis 2.50 6.00
22 Ryon Healy 2.50 6.00
24 Lewis Brinson 3.00 8.00
25 Jacoby Jones 2.50 6.00

2017 Panini Gold Standard Rookie Jersey Autographs Double

INSERTED IN '17 CHRONICLES PACKS
PRINT RUNS B/WN 99-199 COPIES PER
EXCHANGE DEADLINE 5/22/2019
*PRIME/25: .6X TO 1.5X p/r 199
*PRIME/25: .5X TO 1.2X p/r 99
1 Andrew Benintendi/199 15.00 40.00
2 Yoan Moncada/99 10.00 25.00
3 Alex Bregman/199 20.00 50.00
4 Dansby Swanson/199 12.00 30.00
5 Ian Happ/199 8.00 20.00
6 Cody Bellinger/99 25.00 60.00
7 Aaron Judge/199 75.00 200.00
8 Trey Mancini/199 8.00 20.00
9 Jordan Montgomery/199 10.00 25.00
10 Bradley Zimmer/199 4.00 10.00
11 Mitch Haniger/199 6.00 15.00
12 Raimel Tapia/199 4.00 10.00
13 Alex Reyes/99 6.00 15.00
14 Tyler Glasnow/99 12.00 30.00
15 Manuel Margot/99 4.00 10.00
16 Hunter Renfroe/99 5.00 12.00
17 Jorge Bonifacio/199 3.00 8.00
18 Antonio Senzatela/199 3.00 8.00
19 Amir Garrett/199 5.00 12.00
20 David Dahl/199 4.00 10.00
21 Sam Travis/199 5.00 12.00
22 Ryon Healy/199 5.00 12.00
23 Chad Pinder/199
24 Lewis Brinson/99 6.00 15.00
25 Jacoby Jones/199 4.00 10.00

2017 Panini Gold Standard Rookie Jersey Autographs Prime

*PRIME/25: .6X TO 1.5X p/r 199
*PRIME/25: .5X TO 1.2X p/r 99
INSERTED IN '17 CHRONICLES PACKS
PRINT RUNS B/WN 13-25 COPIES PER
NO PRICING ON QTY 13
EXCHANGE DEADLINE 5/22/2019

2012 Panini Golden Age

COMP.SET w/o SP's (146) 15.00 40.00
SP ANNCD PRINT RUN OF 92 PER
1 Edgar Allan Poe .20 .50
2 Ty Cobb .75 2.00
3 Jack Johnson .30 .75
4 Theodore Roosevelt .20 .50
5 Sam Crawford .30 .75
6 Battling Nelson .20 .50
7 Titanic .20 .50
8 W.K. Kellogg .20 .50
9 Joe Jackson .60 1.50
10 Lefty Williams .20 .50
11 Buck Weaver .30 .75
12 Happy Felsch .20 .50
13 Eddie Cicotte .20 .50
14 Swede Risberg .30 .75
15 Chick Gandil .20 .50
16 Fred McMullin .20 .50
17 Eddie Collins .30 .75
18 Buster Keaton .20 .50
19 Burleigh Grimes .30 .75
20 Man o' War .20 .50
20SP Man o' War SP 6.00 15.00
21 Bobby Jones .30 .75
21SP Bobby Jones SP 30.00 60.00
22 John Heisman .20 .50
23 Rudolph Valentino .20 .50
24 Dizzy Dean .30 .75
25 Walter Hagen .20 .50
26 Jack Dempsey .30 .75
27 Johnny Weissmuller .20 .50
28 Spirit of St. Louis .20 .50
29 Rogers Hornsby .30 .75
30 Charlie Chaplin .20 .50
31 Loch Ness Monster .20 .50
31SP Loch Ness Monster SP 8.00 20.00
32 Franklin D. Roosevelt .20 .50
33 Red Grange .60 1.50
33SP Red Grange SP 10.00 25.00
34 Jimmie Foxx .50 1.25
35 Arky Vaughan .20 .50
36 Hindenburg .20 .50
37 Citation .20 .50
38 Eddie Arcaro .20 .50
39 Charlie Gehringer .20 .50
40 Ted Williams 1.00 2.50
41 Jackie Robinson .50 1.25
42 Joe DiMaggio 1.00 2.50
43 Early Wynn .30 .75
44 Buck Leonard .20 .50
45 Byron Nelson .30 .75
46 Ralph Kiner .30 .75
47 Bill Dickey .20 .50
48 Eddie Mathews .50 1.25
49 Joe Garagiola .20 .50
50 Babe Didrikson Zaharias .20 .50
51 Hal Newhouser .30 .75
52 Stan Musial .75 2.00
52SP Stan Musial SP 50.00 100.00
53 Harry Truman .20 .50
54 Moe Howard .30 .75
55 Larry Fine .30 .75
56 Curly Howard .30 .75
57 The Three Stooges .30 .75
58 Duke Ellington .20 .50
59 Bobby Thomson .30 .75
60 Phil Rizzuto .30 .75
61 Dwight D. Eisenhower .20 .50
62 Ben Hogan .20 .50
62SP Ben Hogan SP 20.00 50.00
63 Ava Gardner .20 .50
64 Bob Feller .30 .75
65 Whitey Ford .30 .75
66 Red Schoendienst .30 .75
67 Al Kaline .50 1.25
68 Duke Snider .30 .75
69 Pee Wee Reese .30 .75
70 Don Larsen .20 .50
71 Minnie Minoso .20 .50
72 Jayne Mansfield .20 .50
72SP Jayne Mansfield SP 10.00 25.00
73 Tony Kubek .20 .50
74 Bob Beamon .20 .50
75 Jim Ryun .20 .50
76 Bill Mazeroski .30 .75
77 John F. Kennedy .50 1.25
78 Willie McCovey .30 .75
79 Warren Spahn .30 .75
80 Dick Fosbury .20 .50
81 Elizabeth Montgomery .20 .50
82 Jim Bunning .30 .75
83 Nancy Lopez .20 .50
84 Frank Robinson .30 .75
85 Carl Yastrzemski .75 2.00
86 Denny McLain .20 .50
87 Bill Russell .75 2.00
87SP Bill Russell SP 10.00 25.00
88 Luis Aparicio .30 .75
89 Frank Howard .20 .50
90 Rusty Staub .20 .50
91 Earl Weaver .30 .75
92 Joe Namath .75 2.00
93 Richard Petty 1.00 2.50
94 Meadowlark Lemon .50 1.25
95 Maureen McCormick .20 .50
96 Sam Snead .20 .50
97 Harmon Killebrew .50 1.25
98 Vida Blue .20 .50
99 Billy Martin .30 .75
100 Gene Tenace .20 .50
101 Ron Blomberg .20 .50
102 Bob Gibson .30 .75
103 Tom Seaver .30 .75
104 Barbara Eden .20 .50
104SP Barbara Eden SP 6.00 15.00
105 John Dean .20 .50
105SP John Dean SP 6.00 15.00
106 Frankie Frisch .30 .75
107 Penny Chenery .20 .50
108 Secretariat .30 .75
108SP Secretariat SP 8.00 20.00
109 Ron Turcotte .20 .50
109SP Ron Turcotte SP 6.00 15.00
110 Catfish Hunter .30 .75
111 Rollie Fingers .30 .75
112 Bobby Allison .50 1.25
112SP Bobby Allison SP 6.00 15.00
113 Grace Kelly .20 .50
114 Seattle Slew .30 .75
114SP Seattle Slew SP 8.00 20.00
115 Jean Cruguet .20 .50
116 Mark Spitz .30 .75
117 Johnny Bench .50 1.25
118 Pete Rose 1.00 2.50
119 Tony Perez .30 .75
120 Frank Tanana .20 .50
121 Bill Walton .50 1.25
122 Al Unser .50 1.25
123 Joe Torre .30 .75
124 Affirmed .20 .50
125 Steve Cauthen .20 .50
126 Nolan Ryan 1.50 4.00
127 Fred Lynn .20 .50
128 John Blue Moon Odom .20 .50
129 Reggie Jackson .30 .75
130 Lou Piniella .20 .50
131 Kareem Abdul-Jabbar .75 2.00
131SP Kareem Abdul-Jabbar SP 6.00 15.00
132 Mickey Lolich .20 .50
133 Bobby Fischer .20 .50
134 Thurman Munson .50 1.25
135 Boog Powell .20 .50
136 Bob Woodward .20 .50
137 Carl Bernstein .20 .50
138 Richard Nixon .20 .50
139 Steve Garvey .20 .50
140 Maury Wills .20 .50
141 Nate Colbert .20 .50
142 Jerry West .60 1.50
143 Gordie Howe 1.00 2.50
144 Cleon Jones .20 .50
145 Russell Johnson .20 .50
146 Dawn Wells .20 .50

2012 Panini Golden Age Mini Broadleaf Blue Ink

*MINI BLUE: 2.5X TO 6X BASIC

2012 Panini Golden Age Mini Broadleaf Brown Ink

*MINI BROWN: .6X TO 1.5X BASIC
APPX.ODDS ONE PER PACK

2012 Panini Golden Age Mini Crofts Candy Blue Ink

*MINI BLUE: 1.5X TO 4X BASIC

2012 Panini Golden Age Mini Crofts Candy Red Ink

*MINI RED: 1.5X TO 4X BASIC
APPX.ODDS 1:8 HOBBY

2012 Panini Golden Age Mini Ty Cobb Tobacco

*MINI COBB: 2.5X TO 6X BASIC

2012 Panini Golden Age Batter-Up

APPX.ODDS 1:12 HOBBY
1 Duke Snider 1.50 4.00
2 Whitey Ford 1.50 4.00
3 Man o' War 1.50 4.00
4 Buck Weaver 1.50 4.00
5 Harmon Killebrew 2.50 6.00
6 Jack Johnson 1.50 4.00
7 Bobby Jones 1.50 4.00
8 Red Grange 1.50 4.00
9 Early Wynn 1.50 4.00
10 Al Kaline 2.50 6.00
11 Babe Didrikson Zaharias 1.00 2.50
12 Ben Hogan 2.50 6.00
13 Jayne Mansfield 1.50 4.00
14 Curly Howard 2.50 6.00
15 Walter Hagen 1.00 2.50
16 Luis Aparicio 1.50 4.00
17 Billy Williams 1.50 4.00
18 Ava Gardner 1.50 4.00
19 Brooks Robinson 1.50 4.00
20 Eddie Mathews 2.50 6.00
21 Seattle Slew 1.50 4.00
22 Jack Dempsey 1.50 4.00
23 Yogi Berra 2.50 6.00
24 Nolan Ryan 8.00 20.00
25 Swede Risberg 1.50 4.00

2012 Panini Golden Age Black Sox Bats

PRINT RUNS B/WN 99-199 COPIES PER
1 Joe Jackson/99 75.00 150.00
2 Lefty Williams/199 40.00 80.00

2012 Panini Golden Age Ferguson Bakery Pennants Blue

ISSUED AS BOX TOPPERS
1 Jack Johnson 3.00 8.00
2 Bobby Allison 2.00 5.00
3 Joe Jackson 6.00 15.00
4 Buck Weaver 3.00 8.00
5 Battling Nelson 2.00 5.00
6 Man o' War 3.00 8.00
7 Bobby Jones 3.00 8.00
8 Spirit of St. Louis 3.00 8.00
9 Frankie Frisch 3.00 8.00
10 Dawn Wells 3.00 8.00
11 Russell Johnson 2.00 5.00
12 Walter Hagen 3.00 8.00
13 Harry Truman 2.00 5.00
14 Red Grange 6.00 15.00
15 Harry Heilmann 3.00 8.00
16 Citation 3.00 8.00
17 Eddie Arcaro 2.00 5.00
18 Jimmie Foxx 5.00 12.00
19 Joe Namath 8.00 20.00
20 Bill Dickey 2.00 5.00
21 Ted Williams 10.00 25.00
22 Vida Blue 2.00 5.00
23 Jackie Robinson 5.00 12.00
24 Stan Musial 8.00 20.00
25 Jack Dempsey 3.00 8.00
26 Byron Nelson 2.00 5.00
27 Ben Hogan 3.00 8.00
28 Ty Cobb 8.00 20.00
29 The Three Stooges 10.00 25.00
30 Ava Gardner 3.00 8.00
31 Sam Snead 3.00 8.00
32 Babe Didrikson Zaharias 2.00 5.00
33 Jayne Mansfield 3.00 8.00
34 Nap Lajoie 5.00 12.00
35 Frank Robinson 3.00 8.00
36 Pete Rose 10.00 25.00
37 Al Kaline 5.00 12.00
38 Richard Nixon 2.00 5.00
39 Secretariat 8.00 20.00
40 Ron Turcotte 5.00 12.00
41 Richard Petty 8.00 20.00
42 Seattle Slew 3.00 8.00
43 Jean Cruguet 2.00 5.00
44 Affirmed 2.00 5.00
45 Steve Cauthen 2.00 5.00
46 Al Unser 2.00 5.00
47 Johnny Bench 5.00 12.00
48 Sam Crawford 3.00 8.00

2012 Panini Golden Age Ferguson Bakery Pennants Yellow

ISSUED AS BOX TOPPERS
1 Jack Johnson 3.00 8.00
2 Bobby Allison 2.00 5.00
3 Joe Jackson 6.00 15.00
4 Buck Weaver 3.00 8.00
5 Battling Nelson 2.00 5.00
6 Man o' War 3.00 8.00
7 Bobby Jones 3.00 8.00
8 Spirit of St. Louis 3.00 8.00
9 Frankie Frisch 3.00 8.00
10 Dawn Wells 3.00 8.00
11 Russell Johnson 2.00 5.00
12 Walter Hagen 3.00 8.00
13 Harry Truman 2.00 5.00
14 Red Grange 6.00 15.00
15 Harry Heilmann 3.00 8.00
16 Citation 3.00 8.00
17 Eddie Arcaro 2.00 5.00
18 Jimmie Foxx 5.00 12.00
19 Joe Namath 8.00 20.00
20 Bill Dickey 2.00 5.00
21 Ted Williams 10.00 25.00
22 Vida Blue 2.00 5.00
23 Jackie Robinson 5.00 12.00
24 Stan Musial 8.00 20.00
25 Jack Dempsey 3.00 8.00
26 Byron Nelson 2.00 5.00
27 Ben Hogan 3.00 8.00
28 Ty Cobb 8.00 20.00
29 The Three Stooges 10.00 25.00
30 Ava Gardner 3.00 8.00
31 Sam Snead 3.00 8.00
32 Babe Didrikson Zaharias 2.00 5.00
33 Jayne Mansfield 3.00 8.00
34 Nap Lajoie 5.00 12.00
35 Frank Robinson 3.00 8.00
36 Pete Rose 10.00 25.00
37 Al Kaline 5.00 12.00
38 Richard Nixon 2.00 5.00
39 Secretariat 8.00 20.00
40 Ron Turcotte 5.00 12.00
41 Richard Petty 8.00 20.00
42 Seattle Slew 3.00 8.00
43 Jean Cruguet 2.00 5.00
44 Affirmed 2.00 5.00
45 Steve Cauthen 2.00 5.00
46 Al Unser 2.00 5.00
47 Johnny Bench 5.00 12.00
48 Sam Crawford 3.00 8.00

2012 Panini Golden Age Headlines

COMPLETE SET (15) 12.50 30.00
APPX.ODDS 1:12 HOBBY
1 The Wright Brothers 1.00 2.50
2 Titanic 1.00 2.50
3 Franklin D. Roosevelt 1.00 2.50
4 V-J Day 1.00 2.50
5 Harry Truman 1.00 2.50
6 Martin Luther King 1.00 2.50
7 Tom Seaver 1.50 4.00
8 Apollo 11 1.00 2.50
9 Bobby Fischer 1.00 2.50
10 Secretariat 4.00 10.00
11 Eddie Arcaro 1.00 2.50
12 Richard Nixon 1.00 2.50
13 Wall Street 1.00 2.50
14 Joe Namath 4.00 10.00
15 Jackie Robinson 2.50 6.00

2012 Panini Golden Age Historic Signatures

STATED ODDS 1:24 HOBBY
1 Joe Garagiola 10.00 25.00
2 Ron LeFlore 4.00 10.00
3 Don Larsen 4.00 10.00
4 Denny McLain 5.00 12.00
5 Rusty Staub 6.00 15.00
6 Fred Lynn 4.00 15.00
7 Ron Turcotte 12.00 30.00
8 Jean Cruguet 4.00 10.00
9 Steve Cauthen 4.00 10.00
10 Lou Piniella 8.00 20.00
11 Jim Palmer 8.00 20.00
12 Mickey Lolich 4.00 10.00
13 Bill Madlock 10.00 25.00
14 Penny Chenery 20.00 50.00
15 Vida Blue 5.00 12.00
16 Jim Ryun 10.00 25.00
17 Ron Blomberg 4.00 10.00
18 Nancy Lopez 6.00 15.00
19 Al Kaline 15.00 40.00
21 Barbara Eden 15.00 40.00
22 Bill Walton 8.00 20.00
23 Ralph Branca 6.00 15.00
24 Nolan Ryan 100.00 175.00
25 Frank Tanana 4.00 10.00
26 Tony Oliva 4.00 10.00
27 Boog Powell 6.00 15.00
28 Bob Woodward 15.00 40.00
29 Carl Bernstein 12.00 30.00
30 John Dean 6.00 15.00
31 Meadowlark Lemon 12.00 30.00
33 Joe Torre 10.00 25.00
36 Mark Spitz 12.00 30.00
37 Al Unser 8.00 20.00
39 Maureen McCormick 25.00 60.00
40 Bobby Allison 5.00 12.00
41 Rollie Fingers 6.00 15.00
42 John Blue Moon Odom 5.00 12.00
43 Russell Johnson 6.00 15.00
44 Dawn Wells 20.00 50.00
46 Maury Wills 8.00 20.00
47 Steve Garvey 8.00 20.00
48 Cleon Jones 5.00 12.00
49 Richard Petty 20.00 50.00
50 Gene Tenace 4.00 10.00

2012 Panini Golden Age Movie Posters

ISSUED AS HOBBY BOX TOPPERS
STATED PRINT RUN 60 SER.#'d SETS
1 Orson Welles 4.00 10.00
2 G.Cooper Yankees 20.00 50.00
3 H.Bogart Falcon 6.00 15.00
6 Cary Grant 8.00 20.00
8 G.Cooper Noon 8.00 20.00
11 John Wayne 10.00 25.00

2012 Panini Golden Age Movie Posters Memorabilia

ISSUED AS HOBBY BOX TOPPERS
STATED PRINT RUN 99 SER.#'d SETS
1 A.Moorehead/O.Welles 8.00 20.00
2 G.Cooper/T.Wright 12.50 30.00
3 M.Astor/H.Bogart 20.00 50.00
4 M.Monroe/J.Russell 20.00 50.00
5 V.Leigh/M.Brando 8.00 20.00
6 C.Grant/J.Mason 20.00 50.00
7 H.Bogart/K.Hepburn 20.00 50.00
8 G.Cooper/G.Kelly 20.00 50.00
9 D.Reed/B.Lancaster 10.00 25.00
10 L.Bacall/H.Bogart 15.00 40.00
11 John Wayne 20.00 50.00

2012 Panini Golden Age Museum Age Memorabilia

STATED ODDS 1:24 HOBBY
2 Burleigh Grimes Pants 12.00 30.00
3 Dizzy Dean FldGlv 50.00 100.00
4 Eddie Collins Bat 12.00 30.00
5 Charlie Chaplin Jkt 15.00 40.00
6 Arky Vaughan Bat 10.00 25.00
7 Johnny Weissmuller Jkt 6.00 15.00
8 Vida Blue Jsy 4.00 10.00
9 Lou Piniella Pants 4.00 10.00
10 Ava Gardner 5.00 12.00
11 Rusty Staub Bat 4.00 10.00
12 Sam Snead 8.00 20.00
13 Grace Kelly 6.00 15.00
14 Minnie Minoso Bat 4.00 10.00
15 Mary Pickford 6.00 15.00
16 Ken Boyer Bat 4.00 10.00
17 Rod Carew Bat 4.00 10.00
19 Bobby Allison Shirt 4.00 10.00
20 Secretariat 60.00 120.00
21 Billy Martin Jkt 4.00 10.00
22 Dave Parker Jsy 4.00 10.00
23 Reggie Jackson Bat 4.00 10.00
24 Maureen McCormick Shirt 4.00 10.00
25 Ted Williams Jsy 20.00 50.00
26 Jayne Mansfield 5.00 12.00
27 Ron Turcotte Jkt 12.00 30.00
28 Nap Lajoie Bat 12.00 30.00
29 Carole Lombard 5.00 12.00
30 Bill Madlock Jsy 4.00 10.00
31 Dawn Wells Shirt 10.00 25.00
32 Russell Johnson Shirt 4.00 10.00
33 Duke Ellington 20.00 50.00
34 Luis Aparicio Pants 5.00 12.00
35 Gary Carter Bat 4.00 10.00
36 Joe Torre Jsy 6.00 15.00
37 Rudolph Valentino Hat 12.00 30.00
38 Thurman Munson Jsy 6.00 15.00
39 Nellie Fox Bat 4.00 10.00
40 Pee Wee Reese Jsy 8.00 20.00

2012 Panini Golden Age Newark Evening World Supplement

APPX.ODDS 1:24 HOBBY
1 Jack Dempsey 3.00 8.00
2 Nancy Lopez 1.00 2.50
3 Johnny Bench 2.50 6.00
4 Citation 1.50 4.00
5 Man o' War 1.50 4.00
6 Red Grange 3.00 8.00
7 Joe Jackson 3.00 8.00
8 Bob Feller 1.50 4.00
9 Buck Leonard 1.00 2.50
10 Buck Weaver 1.50 4.00
11 Juan Marichal 1.50 4.00
12 Gary Carter 1.50 4.00
13 Jayne Mansfield 1.00 2.50
14 Pete Rose 5.00 12.00
15 Ron Turcotte 1.50 4.00
16 Ron LeFlore 1.00 2.50
17 Bobby Doerr 1.50 4.00
18 Joe Garagiola 1.00 2.50
19 Affirmed 1.50 4.00
20 Bill Russell 3.00 8.00
21 Jim Ryun 1.00 2.50
22 Jerry West 3.00 8.00
23 Jean Cruguet 1.00 2.50
24 Steve Cauthen 1.00 2.50
25 Thurman Munson 2.50 6.00

2013 Panini Golden Age

1 Abraham Lincoln .50 1.25
2A Billy Sunday .30 .75
2B Billy Sunday SP 10.00 25.00
3 John L. Sullivan .30 .75
4 Wyatt Earp .20 .50
5 Joe Wood .30 .75
6A Henry Ford .20 .50
6B Henry Ford SP 10.00 25.00
7 Joe Tinker .40 1.00
8 Johnny Evers .30 .75
9 Frank Chance .40 1.00
10 William Howard Taft .30 .75
11 Gene Tunney .30 .75
12 Fred Merkle .30 .75
13 Tris Speaker .40 1.00
14 Fielding Yost .20 .50
15A Unsinkable Molly Brown .20 .50
15B Al Kaline SP 10.00 25.00
16 Woodrow Wilson .30 .75
17A Grantland Rice .30 .75
17B Grantland Rice SP 10.00 25.00
18 Knute Rockne .75 2.00
19 Jake Daubert .30 .75
20 Edd Roush .40 1.00
21 Arnold Rothstein .20 .50
22 Abe Attell .20 .50
23 Alexander Graham Bell .20 .50
24 Rudolph Valentino .20 .50
25A Harry Houdini .30 .75
25B Harry Houdini SP 10.00 25.00
26 Bobby Jones .30 .75
27 Helen Wills .20 .50
28A Jim Bottomley .30 .75
28B Jim Bottomley SP 10.00 25.00
29 Jacob Ruppert .30 .75
30 Miller Huggins .30 .75
31A War Admiral .30 .75
31B War Admiral SP 10.00 25.00
32A Hack Wilson .40 1.00
32B Hack Wilson SP 10.00 25.00
33 Dave Bancroft .30 .75
34A Jim Thorpe .60 1.50
34B Jim Thorpe SP 15.00 40.00
35 Herbert Hoover .30 .75
36A Spanky McFarland .30 .75
36B Spanky McFarland SP 10.00 25.00
37 Buckwheat Thomas .30 .75
38 Stymie Beard .30 .75
39 Al Simmons .40 1.00
40A Walter Hagen .30 .75
40B Walter Hagen SP 10.00 25.00
41 The Three Stooges .50 1.25
42 Wally Pipp .30 .75
43 Rocky Marciano .30 .75
44 Doak Walker .50 1.25
45A Bill Terry .40 1.00
45B Bill Terry SP 10.00 25.00
46 Red Grange .60 1.50
47 Mel Ott .50 1.25
48 Seabiscuit .30 .75
49 Branch Rickey .30 .75
50 Flight 19 .20 .50
51 Stan Musial .75 2.00
52 Warren Spahn .40 1.00
53 Bob Hope .30 .75
54 Jane Russell .20 .50
55 Jean Harlow .20 .50
56A Henry Fonda .20 .50
56B Henry Fonda SP 10.00 25.00
57 Richie Ashburn .40 1.00
58 Lou Boudreau .40 1.00
59 Al Lopez .30 .75
60 Lana Turner .20 .50
61 Gil Hodges .30 .75
62 Red Schoendienst .40 1.00
63A Grace Kelly .30 .75
63B Grace Kelly SP 10.00 25.00
64A Yogi Berra .50 1.25
64B Yogi Berra SP 10.00 25.00
65A Bobby Richardson .30 .75
65B Bobby Richardson SP 10.00 25.00
66A Walter Cronkite .20 .50
66B Walter Cronkite SP 10.00 25.00
67 Lyndon Johnson .30 .75
68 Al Kaline .50 1.25
69 Ralph Terry .30 .75
70 Elizabeth Montgomery .20 .50
71 Sam McDowell .30 .75
72 Apollo 11 .20 .50
73 Bob Denver .20 .50
74 Alan Hale .20 .50
75 Mario Andretti .30 .75
76A Laffit Pincay .20 .50
76B Laffit Pincay SP 10.00 25.00
77 Norm Cash .30 .75
78 Ed Kranepool .30 .75
79 Ron Swoboda .30 .75
80 Sham .20 .50
81 Penny Marshall .20 .50
82 Rod Serling .20 .50
83 Joe Morgan .40 1.00
84 Brooks Robinson .40 1.00
85 Henry Winkler .20 .50
86 Eve Plumb .20 .50
87 Stanley Livingston .20 .50
88 Barry Livingston .20 .50
89 Ted Simmons .40 1.00
90 Bowie Kuhn .30 .75
91 Eva Gabor .20 .50
92A Riva Ridge .20 .50
92B Riva Ridge SP 10.00 25.00
93 Gerald Ford .30 .75
94 Angel Cordero .20 .50
95 Tommy Davis .30 .75
96 Bill Freehan .30 .75
97 Donna Douglas .20 .50
98 Max Baer Jr. .20 .50
99 Bob Gibson .40 1.00
100 Fred Biletnikoff .30 .75
101 Jim Rice .40 1.00
102 Lou Brock .40 1.00
103 Carl Eller .20 .50
104 Jerry Lewis .20 .50
105 Bob Griese .50 1.25
106A Jim Kiick .20 .50
106B Jim Kiick SP 10.00 25.00
107 Don Maynard .30 .75
108 Johnny Bench .50 1.25
109 Steve Cauthen .20 .50
110 Affirmed .30 .75
111 Evel Knievel .20 .50
112 Sugar Ray Leonard .30 .75
113 George Brett 1.00 2.50
114A Bigfoot .20 .50
114B Bigfoot SP 10.00 25.00
115A Earl Campbell .50 1.25
115B Earl Campbell SP 10.00 25.00
116 Lem Barney .20 .50

117 Bo Schembechler .30 .75
118 Jimmy Carter .30 .75
119A Bo Derek .30 .75
119B Bo Derek SP 10.00 25.00
120 Barry Williams .20 .50
121 Joe Frazier .30 .75
122 Darrell Waltrip .30 .75
123 Johnny Carson .20 .50
124 Tommy Smothers .20 .50
125 Dick Smothers .20 .50
126 Stan Lee .30 .75
127 The Edmund Fitzgerald .20 .50
128A Jan Stephenson .20 .50
128B Jan Stephenson SP 10.00 25.00
129 Bobby Hull .50 1.25
130 Karen and Mickey Taylor .20 .50
131 Barry Switzer .30 .75
132 Keith Hernandez .30 .75
133 John Belushi .20 .50
134 Tommy John .30 .75
135 Mike Schmidt .75 2.00
136A Thomas Hearns .20 .50
136B Thomas Hearns SP 10.00 25.00
137 Steve Stone .30 .75
138 Pete Rose 1.00 2.50
139 Curly Neal .50 1.25
140 Carlton Fisk .40 1.00
141 Sparky Anderson .40 1.00
142 Ron Guidry .30 .75
143 Dale Murphy .50 1.25
144 Lyman Bostock .30 .75
145 Tatum O'Neal .30 .75
146 Erin Blunt .20 .50
147 Jackie Earle Haley .20 .50
148 David Stambaugh .20 .50
149 David Pollock .20 .50
150 Gary Lee Cavagnaro .20 .50

2013 Panini Golden Age White
*WHITE: 3X TO 8X BASIC
NO WHITE SP PRICING AVAILABLE

2013 Panini Golden Age Bread For Energy
1 Hack Wilson .75 2.00
2 Warren Spahn .75 2.00
3 Norm Cash .60 1.50
4 Nolan Ryan 3.00 8.00
5 Sham .40 1.00
6 Jim Kiick .40 1.00
7 Thomas Hearns 1.00 2.50
8 Eddie Cicotte .40 1.00
9 Buck Leonard .60 1.50
10 Nancy Lopez .40 1.00

2013 Panini Golden Age Delong Gum
COMPLETE SET (30) 40.00 80.00
1 Al Simmons 1.50 4.00
2 Harmon Killebrew 2.00 5.00
3 Secretariat 2.00 5.00
4 Stan Musial 3.00 8.00
5 Al Kaline 2.00 5.00
6 Johnny Bench 2.00 5.00
7 Pete Rose 4.00 10.00
8 Curly Neal 1.25 3.00
9 Darrell Waltrip .75 2.00
10 Bo Schembechler .75 2.00
11 Jim Kiick 1.25 3.00
12 Carl Yastrzemski 3.00 8.00
13 Mel Ott 2.00 5.00
14 Seabiscuit 1.25 3.00
15 Rocky Marciano 1.25 3.00
16 Billy Sunday 1.25 3.00
17 Buck Weaver 1.25 3.00
18 Hack Wilson 1.50 4.00
19 Earl Campbell 1.25 3.00
20 Mark Fidrych .75 2.00
21 Bo Derek 2.00 5.00
22 Grantland Rice 1.25 3.00
23 Bobby Jones 1.25 3.00
24 Nap Lajoie 2.00 5.00
25 Steve Cauthen .75 2.00
26 Elizabeth Montgomery .75 2.00
27 Frankie Frisch 1.50 4.00
28 Joe Wood 1.25 3.00
29 War Admiral .75 2.00
30 Walter Hagen 1.25 3.00

2013 Panini Golden Age Exhibits
1 Jim Thorpe 6.00 15.00
2 Tris Speaker 5.00 12.00
3 Jane Russell 2.50 6.00
4 Carlton Fisk 5.00 12.00
5 Evel Knievel 2.50 6.00
6 John Belushi 4.00 10.00
7 Secretariat 6.00 15.00
8 Bo Derek 4.00 10.00
9 Harry Houdini 4.00 10.00
10 Johnny Bench 6.00 15.00
11 Joe Tinker 5.00 12.00
12 Johnny Evers 4.00 10.00
13 Frank Chance 5.00 12.00
14 Lana Turner 2.50 6.00
15 Seabiscuit 4.00 10.00
16 Al Kaline 6.00 15.00
17 Tatum O'Neal 4.00 10.00
18 Grace Kelly 6.00 15.00
19 Hack Wilson 5.00 12.00
20 Harmon Killebrew 6.00 15.00
21 Buck Weaver 4.00 10.00
22 Walter Hagen 4.00 10.00
23 Billy Sunday 4.00 10.00
24 Gene Tunney 4.00 10.00
25 Jack Johnson 6.00 15.00
26 Apollo 11 2.50 6.00
27 Harry Truman 6.00 15.00
28 The Edmund Fitzgerald 2.50 6.00
29 Jim Bottomley 4.00 10.00
30 Abraham Lincoln 6.00 15.00
31 Citation 4.00 10.00
32 Steve Cauthen 2.50 6.00
33 Bobby Jones 4.00 10.00
34 Alan Hale 2.50 6.00
35 Bob Feller 5.00 12.00
36 Reggie Jackson 5.00 12.00
37 Sugar Ray Leonard 6.00 15.00
38 Jan Stephenson 4.00 10.00
39 Lem Barney 4.00 10.00
40 Affirmed 2.50 6.00

2013 Panini Golden Age Headlines
COMPLETE SET (15) 8.00 20.00
1 Henry Ford .60 1.50
2 Red Grange 2.00 5.00
3 Sir Barton .60 1.50
4 Hindenburg .60 1.50
5 Brooks Robinson 1.25 3.00
6 Stan Musial 2.50 6.00
7 Bob Griese 1.50 4.00
8 Lyndon Johnson .60 1.50
9 Pearl Harbor .60 1.50
10 The Edmund Fitzgerald .60 1.50
11 1906 San Francisco Earthquake .60 1.50
12 Gil Hodges 1.00 2.50
13 Denny McLain 1.00 2.50
14 Bobby Hull 1.50 4.00
15 Earl Campbell 1.50 4.00

2013 Panini Golden Age Historic Signatures
EXCHANGE DEADLINE 12/26/2014
AC Angel Cordero 6.00 15.00
AK Al Kaline 25.00 50.00
BD Bo Derek 20.00 50.00
BH Bobby Hull 15.00 40.00
BL Barry Livingston 8.00 20.00
BOB Bob Watson 6.00 15.00
BR Brooks Robinson 5.00 12.00
BRD Bobby Richardson 5.00 12.00
BS Barry Switzer 20.00 50.00
BW Barry Williams 5.00 10.00
CE Carl Eller 6.00 15.00
CF Carlton Fisk 15.00 40.00
CN Curly Neal 20.00 50.00
DD Donna Douglas 15.00 40.00
DP David Pollock 5.00 10.00
DSM Dick Smothers 12.00 30.00
DST David Stambaugh 8.00 20.00
DW Darrell Waltrip 6.00 15.00
EB Erin Blunt 5.00 12.00
EC Earl Campbell
EK Ed Kranepool 5.00 12.00
EP Eve Plumb 8.00 20.00
FB Fred Biletnikoff 6.00 15.00
GLC Gary Lee Cavagnaro 5.00 12.00
HW Henry Winkler 20.00 50.00
JEH Jackie Earle Haley 50.00 100.00
JK Jim Kiick 5.00 12.00
JL Jerry Lewis 50.00 100.00
JS Jan Stephenson 5.00 12.00
LB Lem Barney 8.00 20.00
LP Laffit Pincay 5.00 12.00
MA Mario Andretti 10.00 25.00
MBJ Max Baer Jr. 8.00 20.00
PM Penny Marshall 12.00 30.00
RC Ron Cey 5.00 12.00
RON Ron Swoboda 5.00 12.00
RS Red Schoendienst 6.00 15.00
RT Ralph Terry 5.00 12.00
SC Steve Cauthen 8.00 20.00
SL Stanley Livingston 8.00 20.00
SM Sam McDowell 5.00 12.00
SRL Sugar Ray Leonard 25.00 60.00
SS Steve Stone 5.00 12.00
STL Stan Lee 75.00 200.00
TD Tommy Davis 5.00 12.00
TH Thomas Hearns 12.00 30.00
TNL Tatum O'Neal 20.00 50.00
TS Ted Simmons 6.00 15.00
TSM Tommy Smothers 6.00 15.00
YB Yogi Berra 50.00 120.00

2013 Panini Golden Age Mini American Caramel Blue Back
*MINI BLUE: 1.2X TO 3X BASIC

2013 Panini Golden Age Mini American Caramel Red Back
*MINI RED: 2X TO 5X BASIC

2013 Panini Golden Age Mini Carolina Brights Green Back
*MINI GREEN: .75X TO 2X BASIC

2013 Panini Golden Age Mini Carolina Brights Purple Back
*MINI PURPLE: 2X TO 5X BASIC

2013 Panini Golden Age Mini Nadja Caramels Back
*MINI NADJA: 2X TO 5X BASIC

2013 Panini Golden Age Museum Age Memorabilia
1 Carlton Fisk 4.00 10.00
2 Hindenburg
3 Henry Fonda 5.00 12.00
4 Maureen McCormick 8.00 20.00
5 Barry Williams 4.00 10.00
6 Tim McCarver 4.00 10.00
7 George Brett 6.00 15.00
8 Bill Terry 6.00 15.00
9 Al Kaline 6.00 15.00
10 Dale Murphy 4.00 10.00
11 Knute Rockne 10.00 25.00
12 Jim Bottomley 6.00 15.00
13 Gene Tunney 40.00 80.00
14 John Belushi 30.00 60.00
15 Carole Lombard 5.00 12.00
16 Jane Russell 5.00 12.00
17 Jean Harlow 12.50 30.00
18 Grace Kelly 5.00 12.00
19 Joe Frazier 6.00 15.00
20 Lou Brock 4.00 10.00
21 Max Baer Jr. 5.00 12.00
22 Ron Guidry 4.00 10.00
23 Gil Hodges 4.00 10.00
24 Johnny Carson 6.00 15.00
25 Bob Hope 6.00 15.00
26 Lana Turner 5.00 12.00
27 Elizabeth Montgomery 12.50 30.00
28 Jake Daubert 6.00 15.00
29 Dave Bancroft 6.00 15.00
30 Eva Gabor 4.00 10.00
31 Ava Gardner 4.00 10.00
32 Yogi Berra 6.00 15.00
33 Willie McCovey 10.00 25.00
34 Norm Cash 20.00 50.00
35 Nolan Ryan 30.00 60.00
36 Nap Lajoie 30.00 60.00
38 Bill Freehan 4.00 10.00
39 Bobby Hull 15.00 40.00
40 Bob Denver 5.00 12.00

2013 Panini Golden Age Playing Cards
COMPLETE SET (53) 50.00 100.00
1 Mario Andretti .75 2.00
2 Alexander Graham Bell .75 2.00
3 Jim Bottomley .75 2.00
4 Steve Cauthen .50 1.25
5 Frank Chance 1.00 2.50
6 Jean Cruguet .50 1.25
7 Bob Denver .50 1.25
8 Bo Derek .75 2.00
9 Johnny Evers .75 2.00
10 Bobby Fischer 3.00 8.00
11 Henry Ford 1.25 3.00
12 Frankie Frisch 1.00 2.50
13 Bob Gibson 1.00 2.50
14 Goose Goslin 1.25 3.00
15 Red Grange 1.50 4.00
16 Alan Hale .50 1.25
17 Thomas Hearns .50 1.25
18 Harry Houdini .75 2.00
19 Jack Johnson 1.25 3.00
20 Joker .50 1.25
21 Al Kaline 1.25 3.00
22 Grace Kelly .75 2.00
23 John F. Kennedy 1.25 3.00
24 Evel Knievel .75 2.00
25 Nap Lajoie 1.25 3.00
26 Jerry Lewis .75 2.00
27 Carole Lombard .75 2.00
28 Nancy Lopez 1.25 3.00
29 Rocky Marciano 1.25 3.00
30 Elizabeth Montgomery 1.25 3.00
31 Curly Neal 1.25 3.00
32 Richard Petty 1.25 3.00
33 Theodore Roosevelt 1.25 3.00
34 Nolan Ryan 4.00 10.00
35 Bo Schembechler 1.25 3.00
36 Seabiscuit .75 2.00
37 Secretariat 1.25 3.00
38 Sham .75 2.00
39 Jan Stephenson .75 2.00
40 Barry Switzer .50 1.25
41 Bill Terry 1.00 2.50
42 Joe Tinker 1.00 2.50
43 Titanic .75 2.00
44 Harry Truman 1.25 3.00
45 Arky Vaughan .75 2.00
46 War Admiral .75 2.00
47 Buck Weaver .75 2.00
48 Dawn Wells 1.25 3.00
49 Lefty Williams .50 1.25
50 Hack Wilson 1.00 2.50
51 Woodrow Wilson 1.25 3.00
52 Joe Wood .75 2.00
53 Carl Yastrzemski 2.00 5.00

2013 Panini Golden Age Three Stooges
COMMON CARD 2.00 5.00

2013 Panini Golden Age Tip Top Bread Labels
COMPLETE SET (10) 10.00 25.00
1 Stan Musial 2.50 6.00
2 Yogi Berra 1.50 4.00
3 Brooks Robinson 1.25 3.00
4 Man o' War 1.00 2.50
5 Buck Weaver 1.00 2.50
6 Curly Neal 1.00 2.50
7 Pete Rose 3.00 8.00
8 Red Grange 2.00 5.00
9 Kelly Leak 1.50 4.00
10 Mel Ott 1.50 4.00

2014 Panini Golden Age
COMP.SET w/o SP's (150) 12.00 30.00
1 Cy Young .30 .75
2 King Kelly .20 .50
3 Dan Brouthers .20 .50
4 Harry Wright .20 .50
5 Butch Cassidy .20 .50
6 Sundance Kid .20 .50
7 Doc Holliday .20 .50
8 Rube Waddell .20 .50
9 Jim Thorpe .50 1.25
10 Ulysses S. Grant .20 .50
11 Ed Delahanty .20 .50
12 Christy Mathewson .30 .75
13 John Pemberton .20 .50
14 Eddie Plank .25 .60
15 John McGraw .25 .60
16 P.T. Barnum .20 .50
17 Willis Carrier .20 .50
18 William McKinley .20 .50
19 Addie Joss .25 .60
SP19 Addie Joss SP 8.00 20.00
20 Captain Edward Smith .20 .50
21 Model T Ford .20 .50
22 Ty Cobb .50 1.25
23 Lusitania .20 .50
24 C.W. Post .20 .50
25 Joe Jackson .40 1.00
26 Sleepy Bill Burns .20 .50
27 Kid Gleason .20 .50
28 Frank Baker .30 .75
29 King Tut's Tomb .20 .50
30 Harold Lloyd .20 .50
31 Connie Mack .20 .50
32 Zack Wheat .25 .60
33 Fatty Arbuckle .20 .50
34 Nap Lajoie .30 .75
35 Casey Stengel .25 .60
36 Lefty Grove .25 .60
37 Dizzy Dean .25 .60
38 Mark Koenig .20 .50
39 Rube Marquard .25 .60
40 Carl Alfalfa Switzer .20 .50
SP40 Carl Alfalfa Switzer SP 3.00 8.00
41 Claudette Colbert .20 .50
42 Assault .20 .50
SP42 Assault SP 8.00 20.00
43 Moe Berg .20 .50
44 Lon Chaney Jr. .20 .50
45 Fay Wray .20 .50
46 Amelia Earhart's Lockheed Electra .20 .50
47 William Randolph Hearst .20 .50
48 Baseball Hall of Fame .20 .50
49 Orson Welles .20 .50
50 Kenesaw Mountain Landis .20 .50
51 Tom Harmon .25 .60
52 Eddie Gaedel .20 .50
53 Patsy Cline .20 .50
54 Red Pollard .20 .50
55 Enos Slaughter .25 .60
56 Joe Louis .30 .75
57 Rita Hayworth .20 .50
58 Ernie Nevers .25 .60
59 Dom DiMaggio .20 .50
60 Bob Lemon .25 .60
61 Elroy Hirsch .25 .60
62 Josh Gibson .30 .75
63 Dead Sea Scrolls .20 .50
64 Rabbit Maranville .25 .60
65 Chuck Connors .20 .50
66 Tommy Lasorda .25 .60
67 Eddie Waitkus .20 .50
68 Jack Johnson .30 .75
69 Buddy Holly .20 .50
70 Clyde Bulldog Turner .25 .60
71 Tony Dow .20 .50
72 Ken Osmond .20 .50
73 Ernie Banks .30 .75
74 Harvey Haddix .20 .50
75 Liberace .20 .50
SP75 Liberace SP 3.00 8.00
76 Vada Pinson .20 .50
77 Northern Dancer .20 .50
78 Don Knotts .20 .50
79 Geese Ausbie .25 .60
80 Robin Roberts .25 .60
81 Rocky Colavito .25 .60
82 Martin Luther King Jr. .30 .75
83 Jerry West .40 1.00
84 Jacqueline Kennedy .30 .75
SP84 Jacqueline Kennedy SP 8.00 20.00
85 Jack Ruby .20 .50
86 Pete Rose .60 1.50
87 Junior Johnson .20 .50
88 Mackinac Bridge .20 .50
89 Phil Cavarretta .20 .50
90 Marques Haynes .25 .60
91 Vivien Leigh .20 .50
92 Bob Hayes .20 .50
93 Jim Bouton .20 .50
94 Charlton Heston .20 .50
95 Pat Priest .20 .50
96 Curt Flood .20 .50
97 Willie Horton .20 .50
98 Angela Cartwright .20 .50
SP98 Frank Robinson SP 3.00 8.00
99 Bill Mumy .20 .50
100 Marta Kristen .20 .50
101 Bill Russell .50 1.25
102 Frank Robinson .25 .60
103 Gene Tierney .20 .50
104 Butch Patrick .20 .50
105 Jimi Hendrix .20 .50
106 Jackie Gleason .20 .50
107 Haystacks Calhoun .20 .50
108 Gaylord Perry .25 .60
109 Bill Shoemaker .20 .50
110 Cadillac Ranch .20 .50
111 Mike Lookinland .20 .50
112 Susan Olsen .20 .50
113 Christopher Knight .20 .50
114 Steve Carlton .25 .60
115 Angie Dickinson .20 .50
116 Great Sphinx of Giza .20 .50
117 Phil Niekro .25 .60
118 Charlene Tilton .20 .50
119 Ronald Reagan .30 .75
120 Dusty Baker .20 .50
121 Catherine Bach .20 .50
SP121 Catherine Bach SP 3.00 8.00
122 Alydar .20 .50
123 Jorge Velasquez .20 .50
124 Jake LaMotta .25 .60
125 Richard Dreyfuss .20 .50
126 Oscar Gamble .20 .50
127 Lee Majors .20 .50
128 Lindsay Wagner .20 .50
129 Bucky Dent .20 .50
130 Willie Nelson .20 .50
131 Farrah Fawcett .20 .50
132 D. Wayne Lukas .20 .50
133 Dave Kingman .20 .50
134 Mickey Rivers .20 .50
135 Artis Gilmore .25 .60
136 Frederick Valentich .20 .50
137 Tatum O'Neal .20 .50
138 Steve Yeager .20 .50
139 Davey Lopes .20 .50
140 Spectacular Bid .20 .50
SP140 Spectacular Bid SP 6.00 15.00
141 Chris McCarron .20 .50
142 Gary Carter .25 .60
143 George Gervin .30 .75
144 Michael Spinks .20 .50
145 Joey Ramone .20 .50
146 Loretta Swit .20 .50
147 Nolan Ryan 1.00 2.50
148 Steve Yzerman .60 1.50
149 Hank Williams .20 .50
SP149 Hank Williams SP 3.00 8.00
150 Terry Bradshaw .40 1.00

2014 Panini Golden Age White
*WHITE: 2.5X TO 6X BASIC

2014 Panini Golden Age Mini Croft's Swiss Milk Cocoa
*MINI CROFTS: 2.5X TO 6X BASIC
86 Pete Rose 8.00 20.00
147 Nolan Ryan 12.00 30.00

2014 Panini Golden Age Mini Hindu Brown Back
*MINI HINDU BROWN: 2X TO 5X BASIC

2014 Panini Golden Age Mini Hindu Red Back
*MINI HINDU RED: 2.5X TO 6X BASIC

2014 Panini Golden Age Mini Mono Brand Blue Back
*MINI MONO BLUE: 1.5X TO 4X BASIC

2014 Panini Golden Age Mini Mono Brand Green Back
*MINI MONO GREEN: 1.5X TO 4X BASIC

2014 Panini Golden Age Mini Smith's Mello Mint
*MINI MELLO: 5X TO 12X BASIC

2014 Panini Golden Age '13 National Game
COMPLETE SET (12) 8.00 20.00
1 Ted Williams 1.50 4.00
2 George Brett 1.50 4.00
3 Goose Goslin .60 1.50
4 Joe Medwick .50 1.25
5 Josh Gibson .75 2.00
6 Eddie Plank .60 1.50
7 Willie Stargell .60 1.50
8 Zack Wheat .60 1.50
9 Gabby Hartnett .50 1.25
10 Pete Rose 1.50 4.00
11 Frank Baker .75 2.00
12 Nolan Ryan 2.50 6.00

2014 Panini Golden Age 5x7 Box Toppers
1 Jimi Hendrix 6.00 15.00
2 Ted Williams 8.00 20.00
3 Warren Spahn 3.00 8.00
4 Willie McCovey 3.00 8.00
5 George H. W. Bush 6.00 15.00
6 Johnny Carson 3.00 8.00
7 Gene Tunney 6.00 15.00
8 Joe Medwick 2.50 6.00
9 Duke Snider 3.00 8.00
10 Rodney Dangerfield 6.00 15.00
11 Jacqueline Kennedy 6.00 15.00
12 Joe Frazier 3.00 8.00

2014 Panini Golden Age 5x7 Box Toppers Memorabilia
PRINT RUNS B/WN 10-50 COPIES PER
NO PRICING ON QTY 10
5 George H. W. Bush/50 50.00 100.00
8 Joe Medwick/40 30.00 60.00
9 Duke Snider/25 40.00 80.00
12 Joe Frazier/50 50.00 100.00

2014 Panini Golden Age Box Bottoms Black Back
*RED BACK: .4X TO 1X BLK BACK
*BLANK BACK: .6X TO 1.5X BLK BACK
1 Hack Wilson 1.50 4.00
2 Gallant Fox 1.25 3.00
3 Red Grange 2.50 6.00
4 Nap Lajoie 2.00 5.00
5 Jack Johnson 2.00 5.00
6 Clyde Bulldog Turner 1.50 4.00
7 Dan Brouthers 1.25 3.00
8 Jacqueline Kennedy 2.00 5.00
9 Ernie Nevers 1.50 4.00

2014 Panini Golden Age Box Bottoms Black Back Panels
COMPLETE SET (3) 5.00 12.00
*RED BACK: .4X TO 1X BLK BACK
*BLANK BACK: .6X TO 1.5X BLK BACK
1 Hack Wilson 2.00 5.00
Gallant Fox
Red Grange
2 Nap Lajoie 2.00 5.00
Jack Johnson
Clyde Bulldog Turner
3 Dan Brouthers 2.00 5.00
Jacqueline Kennedy
Ernie Nevers

2014 Panini Golden Age Darby Chocolate
1 Bobby Jones 2.00 5.00
2 Walter Hagen 2.00 5.00
3 Byron Nelson 2.00 5.00
4 Ty Cobb 3.00 8.00
5 Jim Thorpe 3.00 8.00
6 Nap Lajoie 2.00 5.00
7 Whirlaway 1.25 3.00
8 Eddie Arcaro 1.25 3.00
9 Citation 1.25 3.00
10 Eddie Cicotte 1.25 3.00
11 Joe Jackson 2.50 6.00
12 Swede Risberg 1.25 3.00
13 Ulysses S. Grant 1.25 3.00
14 Douglas MacArthur 1.25 3.00
15 Dwight D. Eisenhower 1.25 3.00
16 Christy Mathewson 2.00 5.00
17 Cy Young 2.00 5.00
18 Lefty Grove 1.50 4.00
19 Jack Johnson 2.00 5.00
20 Joe Louis 2.00 5.00
21 Jake LaMotta 2.00 5.00
22 Dizzy Dean 1.50 4.00
23 Zack Wheat 1.50 4.00
24 Rube Marquard 1.50 4.00
25 Rabbit Maranville 1.50 4.00
26 Cal Ripken Jr. 5.00 12.00
27 Ozzie Smith 2.50 6.00
28 Johnny Bench 2.00 5.00
29 Ted Simmons 1.50 4.00
30 Gary Carter 1.50 4.00

2014 Panini Golden Age Darby Chocolate Panels
1 Bobby Jones 5.00 12.00
Walter Hagen
Byron Nelson
2 Ty Cobb 5.00 12.00
Jim Thorpe
Nap Lajoie
3 Whirlaway 5.00 12.00
Eddie Arcaro
Citation
4 Eddie Cicotte 5.00 12.00
Joe Jackson
Swede Risberg
5 Ulysses S. Grant 5.00 12.00
Douglas MacArthur
Dwight D. Eisenhower
6 Christy Mathewson 5.00 12.00
Cy Young
Lefty Grove
7 Jack Johnson 5.00 12.00
Joe Louis
Jake LaMotta
8 Dizzy Dean 5.00 12.00
Zack Wheat
Rube Marquard
9 Mrnvlle/Ripken/Ozzie 6.00 15.00
10 Johnny Bench 5.00 12.00
Ted Simmons
Gary Carter

2014 Panini Golden Age Fan Craze
COMPLETE SET (8) 6.00 15.00
1 Joe Louis .75 2.00
2 Ty Cobb 1.25 3.00
3 Tom Harmon .75 2.00
4 Christy Mathewson .75 2.00
5 Whitey Ford .60 1.50
6 Tatum O'Neal .50 1.25
7 Alydar .75 2.00
8 Gene Tierney .50 1.25

2014 Panini Golden Age First Fifty
*1ST FIFTY: 3X TO 8X BASIC
STATED PRINT RUN 50 SER.#'d SETS

2014 Panini Golden Age Headlines
COMPLETE SET (9) 10.00 25.00
1 John Pemberton 1.25 3.00
2 Kenesaw Mountain Landis 1.25 3.00
3 Franklin D. Roosevelt 1.25 3.00
4 1958 NFL Championship Game 1.25 3.00
5 Hawaii Becomes 50th State 1.25 3.00
6 John F. Kennedy 1.25 3.00
7 The Beatles 1.25 3.00
8 Monday Night Football 1.25 3.00
9 Nolan Ryan 2.00 5.00

2014 Panini Golden Age Historic Signatures
EXCHANGE DEADLINE 01/02/2016
ANC Angela Cartwright 15.00 40.00
ANG Angie Dickinson 10.00 25.00
ART Artis Gilmore 5.00 12.00
AUS Geese Ausbie 5.00 12.00
BAK Dusty Baker 5.00 12.00
BCH Catherine Bach 15.00 40.00
BDE Bo Derek 25.00 60.00
BOU Jim Bouton 5.00 12.00
BPT Butch Patrick 10.00 25.00
CHA Charlene Tilton 5.00 12.00
CMC Chris McCarron 8.00 20.00
COL Rocky Colavito 15.00 40.00
DNT Bucky Dent 8.00 20.00
DVD Dick Van Dyke 100.00 175.00
DWL D. Wayne Lukas 40.00 80.00
EBK Ernie Banks 40.00 80.00
FNK Frank Robinson 25.00 60.00
GAM Oscar Gamble 5.00 12.00
GRV George Gervin 8.00 20.00
HYN Marques Haynes 5.00 12.00
JLA Jake LaMotta 15.00 40.00
JSC John Schneider 8.00 20.00
JUN Junior Johnson 10.00 25.00
KNG Dave Kingman 8.00 20.00
KNT Christopher Knight 6.00 15.00
KOS Ken Osmond 6.00 15.00
LAF Laffit Pincay 6.00 15.00
LOP Davey Lopes 5.00 12.00
MAJ Lee Majors 15.00 40.00
MAK Marta Kristen 6.00 15.00
MIC Mickey Rivers 5.00 12.00
MKL Mike Lookinland 5.00 12.00
MUM Bill Mumy 6.00 15.00
PPT Pat Priest 10.00 25.00
PRK Dave Parker 5.00 12.00
PTE Pete Rose 12.00 30.00
RHB Richie Hebner 6.00 15.00
RMO Rick Monday 5.00 12.00
SCT Steve Carlton 10.00 25.00
SNO Susan Olsen 5.00 12.00
SPK Michael Spinks 10.00 25.00
STV Steve Yeager 5.00 12.00
SWT Loretta Swit 10.00 25.00
TAO Tatum O'Neal 12.00 30.00
TDW Tony Dow 8.00 20.00
TWO Tom Wopat 10.00 25.00
VEL Jorge Velasquez 6.00 15.00
WAG Lindsay Wagner 15.00 40.00
WHT Willie Horton 5.00 12.00

2014 Panini Golden Age Legends of Music Memorabilia
1 Hank Williams 12.00 30.00
2 Liberace 12.00 30.00
3 Willie Nelson 12.00 30.00
4 Joey Ramone 12.00 30.00
5 Hank Williams 12.00 30.00
6 Liberace 12.00 30.00
7 Willie Nelson 12.00 30.00
8 Willie Nelson 12.00 30.00

2014 Panini Golden Age Museum Age Memorabilia
1 Vivien Leigh 12.00 30.00
2 Angie Dickinson 5.00 12.00
3 Buddy Holly 20.00 50.00
6 Jack Ruby 10.00 25.00
7 Michael Spinks 5.00 12.00
8 Farrah Fawcett 15.00 40.00
11 Charlton Heston 6.00 15.00
13 Gary Carter 4.00 10.00
16 Claudette Colbert 5.00 12.00
17 Lon Chaney Jr. 8.00 20.00
19 Ed Kranepool 6.00 15.00
21 Marta Kristen 8.00 20.00
22 Bill Mumy 5.00 12.00
23 Junior Johnson 5.00 12.00
24 Pat Priest 5.00 12.00
25 Lee Majors 5.00 12.00
27 Enos Slaughter 4.00 10.00
28 Patsy Cline 15.00 40.00
29 Frankie Frisch 10.00 25.00
30 Susan Olsen 5.00 12.00
31 Christopher Knight 5.00 12.00
32 Mike Lookinland 5.00 12.00
33 Charlene Tilton 6.00 15.00
34 Sparky Anderson 6.00 15.00
35 Tommy Lasorda 4.00 10.00
36 Jacqueline Kennedy 12.00 30.00
38 Gene Tierney 6.00 15.00

2014 Panini Golden Age Newsmakers
COMPLETE SET (8) 10.00 25.00
1 The Wright Brothers 1.25 3.00
2 Henry Ford 1.25 3.00
3 Man o' War 1.25 3.00
4 Franklin D. Roosevelt 1.25 3.00
5 Joe Louis 1.25 3.00
6 Yogi Berra 2.00 5.00
7 Martin Luther King Jr. 1.25 3.00
8 Farrah Fawcett 1.25 3.00

2014 Panini Golden Age Star Stamps
1 Titanic 2.00 5.00
Captain Edward Smith
The Unsinkable Molly Brown
Lusitania
2 Addie Joss 2.50 6.00
Lefty Williams
Rube Waddell
Eddie Plank
3 Al Kaline 5.00 12.00
Catfish Hunter
Carl Yastrzemski
Willie Horton
4 Rose/Morg/Bench/Perez 6.00 15.00
5 Fay Wray 2.00 5.00
Vivien Leigh
Fatty Arbuckle
Carl Alfalfa Switzer
6 Steve Carlton 2.50 6.00
Phil Niekro
Juan Marichal
Tom Seaver
7 Jacqueline Kennedy 2.00 5.00
Elizabeth Montgomery
Vivien Leigh
Loretta Swit
8 Man o' War 2.00 5.00
Bobby Jones
Red Grange
Hack Wilson
9 Lou/DiMag/Harm/ Musial 5.00 12.00
10 Henry Ford 2.00 5.00
William Randolph Hearst
C.W. Post
Joseph Pulitzer
11 Ryan/Reggie/Maz/Ashburn 10.00 25.00
12 John McGraw 2.50 6.00
Kid Gleason
Connie Mack
Casey Stengel
13 Happy Felsch 2.00 5.00
Kenesaw Mountain Landis
Eddie Cicotte
Swede Risberg
14 John Havlicek 3.00 8.00
Jerry West
George Gervin
Bill Russell
15 Early Wynn 2.50 6.00
Bob Lemon
Bob Feller
Robin Roberts
16 Gabby Hartnett 3.00 8.00
Yogi Berra
Johnny Bench
Gary Carter
17 Citation 2.00 5.00
Eddie Arcaro
Northern Dancer
Bill Shoemaker
18 Jacqueline Kennedy 2.00 5.00
Grace Kelly
Rita Hayworth
Claudette Colbert
19 John L. Sullivan 3.00 8.00
Jack Johnson
Joe Louis
Joe Frazier
20 Fay Wray 2.00 5.00
Lon Chaney Jr.
Vivien Leigh
Pat Priest
22 George Kell 3.00 8.00
Tom Tresh
Yogi Berra
Willie Horton
23 Bobby Jones 2.00 5.00
Walter Hagen
Gene Tunney
Jim Thorpe
24 Brooks/Math/Brett/Schmidt 6.00 15.00
25 Ulysses S. Grant 2.00 5.00
Theodore Roosevelt
Harry S. Truman
Dwight D. Eisenhower
26 Ceped/Yount/Ryan/Brett 10.00 25.00
27 Monte Irvin 2.50 6.00
Enos Slaughter
Lou Boudreau
Willie Stargell
28 Christy Mathewson 4.00 10.00
Cy Young
Joe Jackson
Zack Wheat
29 Butch Patrick 2.00 5.00
Pat Priest
Bill Mumy
Marta Kristen
30 Dick Van Dyke 2.00 5.00
Don Knotts
Jackie Gleason
Henry Winkler

2014 Panini Hall of Fame Blue Frame
RANDOM INSERTS IN PACKS
STATED PRINT RUN 75 SER.#'d SETS
1 Ty Cobb 4.00 10.00
2 Walter Johnson 2.50 6.00
3 Christy Mathewson 2.50 6.00
4 Honus Wagner 2.50 6.00
5 Nap Lajoie 2.50 6.00
6 Tris Speaker 2.00 5.00
7 Cy Young 2.50 6.00

8 Grover Alexander 2.00 5.00
9 Alexander Cartwright 2.00 5.00
10 Eddie Collins 2.00 5.00
11 Lou Gehrig 5.00 12.00
12 Willie Keeler 1.50 4.00
13 George Sisler 2.00 5.00
14 Rogers Hornsby 2.00 5.00
15 Frank Chance 2.00 5.00
16 Johnny Evers 1.50 4.00
17 Frankie Frisch 2.00 5.00
18 Lefty Grove 2.00 5.00
19 Carl Hubbell 2.00 5.00
20 Herb Pennock 2.00 5.00
21 Pie Traynor 2.00 5.00
22 Mordecai Brown 1.50 4.00
23 Jimmie Foxx 2.50 6.00
24 Mel Ott 2.50 6.00
25 Dizzy Dean 2.00 5.00
26 Rabbit Maranville 2.00 5.00
27 Bill Terry 1.50 4.00
28 Joe DiMaggio 5.00 12.00
29 Zack Wheat 2.00 5.00
30 Bob Feller 2.00 5.00
31 Jackie Robinson 2.50 6.00
32 Edd Roush 2.00 5.00
33 Burleigh Grimes 2.00 5.00
34 Miller Huggins 1.50 4.00
35 Casey Stengel 2.00 5.00
36 Roy Campanella 2.50 6.00
37 Stan Musial 4.00 10.00
38 Dave Bancroft 1.50 4.00
39 Rube Marquard 2.00 5.00
40 Satchel Paige 2.50 6.00
41 Yogi Berra 2.50 6.00
42 Josh Gibson 2.50 6.00
43 Early Wynn 2.00 5.00
44 Roberto Clemente 10.00 25.00
45 Warren Spahn 2.00 5.00
46 Jim Bottomley 1.50 4.00
47 Whitey Ford 2.00 5.00
48 Ernie Banks 2.50 6.00
49 Eddie Mathews 2.50 6.00
50 Hack Wilson 2.00 5.00
51 Al Kaline 2.50 6.00
52 Duke Snider 2.00 5.00
53 Bob Gibson 2.00 5.00
54 Frank Robinson 2.00 5.00
55 Juan Marichal 2.00 5.00
56 Brooks Robinson 2.00 5.00
57 Don Drysdale 2.00 5.00
58 Rick Ferrell 1.50 4.00
59 Harmon Killebrew 2.50 6.00
60 Pee Wee Reese 2.00 5.00
61 Enos Slaughter 2.00 5.00
62 Arky Vaughan 1.50 4.00
63 Willie McCovey 2.00 5.00
64 Catfish Hunter 2.00 5.00
65 Johnny Bench 2.50 6.00
66 Carl Yastrzemski 4.00 10.00
67 Joe Morgan 2.00 5.00
68 Jim Palmer 2.00 5.00
69 Rod Carew 2.00 5.00
70 Tony Lazzeri 2.00 5.00
71 Hal Newhouser 2.00 5.00
72 Tom Seaver 2.00 5.00
73 Reggie Jackson 2.00 5.00
74 Steve Carlton 2.00 5.00
75 Leo Durocher 1.50 4.00
76 Phil Rizzuto 2.00 5.00
77 Richie Ashburn 2.00 5.00
78 Mike Schmidt 4.00 10.00
79 Larry Doby 2.00 5.00
80 George Brett 15.00 40.00
81 Orlando Cepeda 2.00 5.00
82 Nolan Ryan 12.00 30.00
83 Robin Yount 2.50 6.00
84 Carlton Fisk 2.00 5.00
85 Ozzie Smith 3.00 8.00
86 Eddie Murray 2.00 5.00
87 Paul Molitor 2.50 6.00
88 Wade Boggs 2.00 5.00
89 Ryne Sandberg 5.00 12.00
90 Tony Gwynn 2.50 6.00
91 Cal Ripken Jr. 10.00 25.00
92 Rickey Henderson 2.50 6.00
93 Jim Rice 2.00 5.00
94 Andre Dawson 2.00 5.00
95 Roberto Alomar 2.00 5.00
96 Bert Blyleven 2.00 5.00
97 Barry Larkin 2.00 5.00
98 Tom Glavine 2.00 5.00
99 Greg Maddux 3.00 8.00
100 Frank Thomas 2.50 6.00

2014 Panini Hall of Fame Blue Frame Blue

*BLUE-BLUE: .6X TO 1.5X BLUE FRAME
RANDOM INSERTS IN PACKS
STATED PRINT RUN 25 SER.#'d SETS

2014 Panini Hall of Fame Blue Frame Red

*BLUE-RED: .5X TO 1.2X BLUE FRAME
RANDOM INSERTS IN PACKS
STATED PRINT RUN 50 SER.#'d SETS

2014 Panini Hall of Fame Green Frame

*GRN FRAME: .4X TO 1X BLUE FRAME 1.50 4.00
RANDOM INSERTS IN PACKS
STATED PRINT RUN 75 SER.#'d SETS
*GRN-RED/50: .5X TO 1.2X BLUE FRAME
*GRN-BLUE/25: .6X TO 1.5X BLUE FRAME

2014 Panini Hall of Fame Red Frame

*RED FRAME: .4X TO 1X BLUE FRAME
RANDOM INSERTS IN PACKS
STATED PRINT RUN 75 SER.#'d SETS
*RED-RED/50: .5X TO 1.2X BLUE FRAME
*RED-BLUE/25: .6X TO 1.5X BLUE FRAME

2014 Panini Hall of Fame Crusades

OVERALL ONE CRUSADE PER BOX
*RED/75: .75X TO 2X BASIC
*PURPLE/50: 1X TO 2.5X BASIC
PLATES ISSUED IN '15 COOPERSTOWN
PLATE PRINT RUN 1 SET PER COLOR
BLACK-CYAN-MAGENTA-YELLOW ISSUED
NO PLATE PRICING DUE TO SCARCITY
1 Ty Cobb 2.50 6.00
2 Walter Johnson 1.50 4.00
3 Christy Mathewson 1.50 4.00
4 Honus Wagner 1.50 4.00
5 Nap Lajoie 1.50 4.00
6 Tris Speaker 1.25 3.00
7 Cy Young 1.50 4.00
8 Grover Alexander 1.25 3.00
9 Alexander Cartwright 1.25 3.00
10 Eddie Collins 1.25 3.00
11 Lou Gehrig 3.00 8.00
12 Willie Keeler 1.00 2.50
13 George Sisler 1.25 3.00
14 Rogers Hornsby 1.25 3.00
15 Frank Chance 1.25 3.00
16 Johnny Evers 1.00 2.50
17 Frankie Frisch 1.25 3.00
18 Lefty Grove 1.25 3.00
19 Carl Hubbell 1.25 3.00
20 Herb Pennock 1.25 3.00
21 Pie Traynor 1.25 3.00
22 Mordecai Brown 1.00 2.50
23 Jimmie Foxx 1.50 4.00
24 Mel Ott 1.50 4.00
25 Dizzy Dean 1.25 3.00
26 Rabbit Maranville 1.25 3.00
27 Bill Terry 1.00 2.50
28 Joe DiMaggio 3.00 8.00
29 Zack Wheat 1.25 3.00
30 Bob Feller 1.25 3.00
31 Jackie Robinson 1.50 4.00
32 Edd Roush 1.25 3.00
33 Burleigh Grimes 1.25 3.00
34 Miller Huggins 1.00 2.50
35 Casey Stengel 1.25 3.00
36 Roy Campanella 1.50 4.00
37 Stan Musial 2.50 6.00
38 Dave Bancroft 1.00 2.50
39 Rube Marquard 1.25 3.00
40 Satchel Paige 1.50 4.00
41 Yogi Berra 1.50 4.00
42 Josh Gibson 1.50 4.00
43 Early Wynn 1.25 3.00
44 Roberto Clemente 4.00 10.00
45 Warren Spahn 1.25 3.00
46 Jim Bottomley 1.00 2.50
47 Whitey Ford 1.25 3.00
48 Ernie Banks 1.50 4.00
49 Eddie Mathews 1.50 4.00
50 Hack Wilson 1.25 3.00
51 Al Kaline 1.50 4.00
52 Duke Snider 1.25 3.00
53 Bob Gibson 1.25 3.00
54 Frank Robinson 1.25 3.00
55 Juan Marichal 1.25 3.00
56 Brooks Robinson 1.25 3.00
57 Don Drysdale 1.25 3.00
58 Rick Ferrell 1.00 2.50
59 Harmon Killebrew 1.50 4.00
60 Pee Wee Reese 1.25 3.00
61 Enos Slaughter 1.25 3.00
62 Arky Vaughan 1.00 2.50
63 Willie McCovey 1.25 3.00
64 Catfish Hunter 1.25 3.00
65 Johnny Bench 1.50 4.00
66 Carl Yastrzemski 2.50 6.00
67 Joe Morgan 1.25 3.00
68 Jim Palmer 1.25 3.00
69 Rod Carew 1.25 3.00
70 Tony Lazzeri 1.25 3.00
71 Hal Newhouser 1.25 3.00
72 Tom Seaver 1.25 3.00
73 Reggie Jackson 1.25 3.00
74 Steve Carlton 1.25 3.00
75 Leo Durocher 1.00 2.50
76 Phil Rizzuto 1.25 3.00
77 Richie Ashburn 1.25 3.00
78 Mike Schmidt 2.50 6.00
79 Larry Doby 1.25 3.00
80 George Brett 3.00 8.00
81 Orlando Cepeda 1.25 3.00
82 Nolan Ryan 5.00 12.00
83 Robin Yount 1.50 4.00
84 Carlton Fisk 1.25 3.00
85 Ozzie Smith 2.00 5.00
86 Eddie Murray 1.25 3.00
87 Paul Molitor 1.50 4.00
88 Wade Boggs 1.25 3.00
89 Ryne Sandberg 3.00 8.00
90 Tony Gwynn 1.50 4.00
91 Cal Ripken Jr. 5.00 12.00
92 Rickey Henderson 1.50 4.00
93 Jim Rice 1.25 3.00
94 Andre Dawson 1.25 3.00
95 Roberto Alomar 1.25 3.00
96 Bert Blyleven 1.25 3.00
97 Barry Larkin 1.25 3.00
98 Tom Glavine 1.25 3.00
99 Greg Maddux 2.00 5.00
100 Frank Thomas 1.50 4.00

2014 Panini Hall of Fame Crusades Orange Die-Cut

*ORANGE DC: 1.5X TO 4X BASIC
OVERALL ONE CRUSADE PER BOX
STATED PRINT RUN 25 SER.#'d SETS
82 Nolan Ryan 30.00 80.00

2014 Panini Hall of Fame Cut Signatures

OVERALL AUTO ODDS 2 PER BOX
PRINT RUNS B/WN 1-99 COPIES PER
NO PRICING ON QTY 19 OR LESS
EXCHANGE DEADLINE 4/8/2016
6 Billy Herman/25 20.00 50.00
8 Bob Lemon/25 10.00 25.00
20 Enos Slaughter/24 20.00 50.00
30 Joe Sewell/99 12.00 30.00
32 Lee MacPhail/25 20.00 50.00
37 Ralph Kiner/99 12.00 30.00
42 Stan Musial/99 30.00 80.00
46 Warren Spahn/99 20.00 50.00
47 Joe Sewell/99 12.00 30.00
48 Ralph Kiner/99 12.00 30.00
49 Stan Musial/99 20.00 80.00
50 Warren Spahn/99 20.00 50.00
61 George Kell/25 12.00 30.00
64 Lou Boudreau/49 12.00 30.00

2014 Panini Hall of Fame Diamond Kings

OVERALL ONE DK PER BOX
*RED/75: .75X TO 2X BASIC
*BLUE/50: 1X TO 2.5X BASIC
1 Ty Cobb 2.50 6.00
2 Walter Johnson 1.50 4.00
3 Christy Mathewson 1.50 4.00
4 Honus Wagner 1.50 4.00
5 Nap Lajoie 1.50 4.00
6 Tris Speaker 1.25 3.00
7 Cy Young 1.50 4.00
8 Grover Alexander 1.25 3.00
9 Alexander Cartwright 1.25 3.00
10 Eddie Collins 1.25 3.00
11 Lou Gehrig 3.00 8.00
12 Willie Keeler 1.00 2.50
13 George Sisler 1.25 3.00
14 Rogers Hornsby 1.25 3.00
15 Frank Chance 1.25 3.00
16 Johnny Evers 1.00 2.50
17 Frankie Frisch 1.25 3.00
18 Lefty Grove 1.25 3.00
19 Carl Hubbell 1.25 3.00
20 Herb Pennock 1.25 3.00
21 Pie Traynor 1.25 3.00
22 Mordecai Brown 1.00 2.50
23 Jimmie Foxx 1.50 4.00
24 Mel Ott 1.50 4.00
25 Dizzy Dean 1.25 3.00
26 Rabbit Maranville 1.25 3.00
27 Bill Terry 1.00 2.50
28 Joe DiMaggio 3.00 8.00
29 Zack Wheat 1.25 3.00
30 Bob Feller 1.25 3.00
31 Jackie Robinson 1.50 4.00
32 Edd Roush 1.25 3.00
33 Burleigh Grimes 1.25 3.00
34 Miller Huggins 1.00 2.50
35 Casey Stengel 1.25 3.00
36 Roy Campanella 1.50 4.00
37 Stan Musial 2.50 6.00
38 Dave Bancroft 1.00 2.50
39 Rube Marquard 1.25 3.00
40 Satchel Paige 1.50 4.00
41 Yogi Berra 1.50 4.00
42 Josh Gibson 1.50 4.00
43 Early Wynn 1.25 3.00
44 Roberto Clemente 4.00 10.00
45 Warren Spahn 1.25 3.00
46 Jim Bottomley 1.00 2.50
47 Whitey Ford 1.25 3.00
48 Ernie Banks 1.50 4.00
49 Eddie Mathews 1.50 4.00
50 Hack Wilson 1.25 3.00
51 Al Kaline 1.50 4.00
52 Duke Snider 1.25 3.00
53 Bob Gibson 1.25 3.00
54 Frank Robinson 1.25 3.00
55 Juan Marichal 1.25 3.00
56 Brooks Robinson 1.25 3.00
57 Don Drysdale 1.25 3.00
58 Rick Ferrell 1.00 2.50
59 Harmon Killebrew 1.50 4.00
60 Pee Wee Reese 1.25 3.00
61 Enos Slaughter 1.25 3.00
62 Arky Vaughan 1.00 2.50
63 Willie McCovey 1.25 3.00
64 Catfish Hunter 1.25 3.00
65 Johnny Bench 1.50 4.00
66 Carl Yastrzemski 2.50 6.00
67 Joe Morgan 1.25 3.00
68 Jim Palmer 1.25 3.00
69 Rod Carew 1.25 3.00
70 Tony Lazzeri 1.25 3.00
71 Hal Newhouser 1.25 3.00
72 Tom Seaver 1.25 3.00
73 Reggie Jackson 1.25 3.00
74 Steve Carlton 1.25 3.00
75 Leo Durocher 1.00 2.50
76 Phil Rizzuto 1.25 3.00
77 Richie Ashburn 1.25 3.00
78 Mike Schmidt 2.50 6.00
79 Larry Doby 1.25 3.00
80 George Brett 3.00 8.00
81 Orlando Cepeda 1.25 3.00
82 Nolan Ryan 5.00 12.00
83 Robin Yount 1.50 4.00
84 Carlton Fisk 1.25 3.00
85 Ozzie Smith 2.00 5.00
86 Eddie Murray 1.25 3.00
87 Paul Molitor 1.50 4.00
88 Wade Boggs 1.25 3.00
89 Ryne Sandberg 3.00 8.00
90 Tony Gwynn 1.50 4.00
91 Cal Ripken Jr. 5.00 12.00
92 Rickey Henderson 1.50 4.00
93 Jim Rice 1.25 3.00
94 Andre Dawson 1.25 3.00
95 Roberto Alomar 1.25 3.00
96 Bert Blyleven 1.25 3.00
97 Barry Larkin 1.25 3.00
98 Tom Glavine 1.25 3.00
99 Greg Maddux 2.00 5.00
100 Frank Thomas 1.50 4.00

2014 Panini Hall of Fame Elite Dominator

OVERALL ONE DOMINATOR PER BOX
*GOLD/25: .6X TO 1.5X BASIC
1 Bob Gibson 1.50 4.00
2 Burleigh Grimes 1.50 4.00
3 Cal Ripken Jr. 6.00 15.00
4 Christy Mathewson 2.00 5.00
5 Cy Young 2.00 5.00
6 Dizzy Dean 1.50 4.00
7 Duke Snider 1.50 4.00
8 Eddie Collins 1.50 4.00
9 Ernie Banks 2.00 5.00
10 Frank Chance 1.50 4.00
11 Frank Robinson 1.50 4.00
12 George Brett 4.00 10.00
13 Hack Wilson 1.50 4.00
14 Honus Wagner 2.00 5.00
15 Jackie Robinson 2.00 5.00
16 Jimmie Foxx 2.00 5.00
17 Joe DiMaggio 4.00 10.00
18 Johnny Bench 2.00 5.00
19 Johnny Evers 1.25 3.00
20 Josh Gibson 2.00 5.00
21 Lou Gehrig 4.00 10.00
22 Mel Ott 2.00 5.00
23 Mike Schmidt 10.00 25.00
24 Miller Huggins 1.25 3.00
25 Nap Lajoie 2.00 5.00
26 Nolan Ryan 6.00 15.00
27 Reggie Jackson 1.50 4.00
28 Rickey Henderson 2.00 5.00
29 Roberto Clemente 6.00 15.00
30 Rod Carew 1.50 4.00
31 Rogers Hornsby 1.50 4.00
32 Roy Campanella 2.00 5.00
33 Ryne Sandberg 4.00 10.00
34 Satchel Paige 2.00 5.00
35 Tom Seaver 1.50 4.00
36 Tony Gwynn 2.00 5.00
37 Tony Lazzeri 1.50 4.00
38 Warren Spahn 1.50 4.00
39 Ty Cobb 3.00 8.00
40 Walter Johnson 2.00 5.00

2014 Panini Hall of Fame Elite Series

OVERALL ONE ELITE SERIES PER BOX
*GOLD/25: 2X TO 5X BASIC
1 Bob Gibson 1.50 4.00
2 Burleigh Grimes 1.50 4.00
3 Cal Ripken Jr. 6.00 15.00
4 Carl Yastrzemski 3.00 8.00
5 Yogi Berra 2.00 5.00
6 Ozzie Smith 2.50 6.00
7 Duke Snider 1.50 4.00
8 Whitey Ford 1.50 4.00
9 Eddie Murray 1.50 4.00
10 Ernie Banks 2.00 5.00
11 Joe Morgan 1.50 4.00
12 Frank Robinson 1.50 4.00
13 Frank Thomas 2.00 5.00
14 Frankie Frisch 1.50 4.00
15 George Brett 6.00 15.00
16 George Sisler 1.50 4.00
17 Greg Maddux 2.50 6.00
18 Hack Wilson 1.50 4.00
19 Willie McCovey 1.50 4.00
20 Johnny Bench 2.00 5.00
21 Roberto Alomar 1.50 4.00
22 Lefty Grove 1.50 4.00
23 Eddie Mathews 2.00 5.00
24 Mike Schmidt 5.00 12.00
25 Miller Huggins 1.25 3.00
26 Nap Lajoie 2.00 5.00
27 Nolan Ryan 8.00 20.00
28 Reggie Jackson 1.50 4.00
29 Rickey Henderson 2.00 5.00
30 Rod Carew 1.50 4.00
31 Catfish Hunter 1.50 4.00
32 Andre Dawson 1.50 4.00
33 Ryne Sandberg 6.00 15.00
34 Carlton Fisk 1.50 4.00
35 Tom Glavine 1.50 4.00
36 Tony Gwynn 2.00 5.00
37 Tony Lazzeri 1.50 4.00
38 Tris Speaker 1.50 4.00
39 Warren Spahn 1.50 4.00
40 Willie Keeler 1.25 3.00

2014 Panini Hall of Fame Heroes Buyback Autographs

OVERALL AUTO ODDS 2 PER BOX
PRINT RUNS B/WN 1-64 COPIES PER
NO PRICING ON QTY 19 OR LESS
EXCHANGE DEADLINE 4/8/2016
7 Charlie Gehringer/22 10.00 25.00
16 Lou Boudreau/26 12.00 30.00
22 Robin Roberts/52 12.00 30.00

2014 Panini Hall of Fame Signatures

OVERALL AUTO ODDS 2 PER BOX
EXCHANGE DEADLINE 4/8/2016
1 Al Kaline 10.00 25.00
2 Andre Dawson 6.00 15.00
4 Bert Blyleven 6.00 15.00
6 Billy Williams 6.00 15.00
8 Bobby Cox 12.00 30.00
9 Bobby Doerr 6.00 15.00
10 Brooks Robinson 15.00 40.00
11 Bruce Sutter 5.00 12.00
14 Carlton Fisk 10.00 25.00
16 Dennis Eckersley 6.00 15.00
18 Don Sutton 6.00 15.00
19 Doug Harvey 5.00 12.00
23 Fergie Jenkins 6.00 15.00
27 Gaylord Perry 6.00 15.00
30 Goose Gossage 6.00 15.00
33 Jim Bunning 6.00 15.00
34 Jim Palmer 6.00 15.00
35 Jim Rice 6.00 15.00
40 Lou Brock 15.00 40.00
41 Luis Aparicio 6.00 15.00
45 Orlando Cepeda 6.00 15.00
47 Pat Gillick 5.00 12.00
48 Paul Molitor 8.00 20.00
49 Phil Niekro 6.00 15.00
51 Red Schoendienst 6.00 15.00
54 Roberto Alomar 5.00 12.00
57 Rollie Fingers 6.00 15.00
61 Tom Glavine 15.00 40.00
65 Tony La Russa 10.00 25.00
66 Tony Perez 10.00 25.00
69 Whitey Herzog 5.00 12.00
72 Andre Dawson 6.00 15.00
73 Bert Blyleven 6.00 15.00
74 Billy Williams 6.00 15.00
75 Bobby Doerr 6.00 15.00
76 Brooks Robinson 15.00 40.00
77 Bruce Sutter 5.00 12.00
78 Dennis Eckersley 6.00 15.00
79 Don Sutton 6.00 15.00
80 Doug Harvey 5.00 12.00
81 Fergie Jenkins 6.00 15.00
82 Gaylord Perry 6.00 15.00
83 Goose Gossage 6.00 15.00
84 Jim Bunning 6.00 15.00
85 Jim Palmer 6.00 15.00
86 Jim Rice 6.00 15.00
87 Orlando Cepeda 6.00 15.00
88 Pat Gillick 5.00 12.00
89 Paul Molitor 8.00 20.00
90 Red Schoendienst 8.00 20.00
91 Rollie Fingers 6.00 15.00
92 Tom Glavine 15.00 40.00
93 Tony La Russa 10.00 25.00
94 Tony Perez 8.00 20.00
95 Whitey Herzog 5.00 12.00
96 Al Kaline 12.00 30.00

2014 Panini Hall of Fame Signatures Blue

*BLUE: .5X TO 1.2X BASIC
OVERALL AUTO ODDS 2 PER BOX
PRINT RUNS B/WN 18-25 COPIES PER
NO PRICING ON QTY 18
EXCHANGE DEADLINE 4/8/2016
5 Bill Mazeroski/20 20.00 50.00
12 Cal Ripken Jr./25 40.00 100.00
15 Dave Winfield/25 60.00 120.00
22 Ernie Banks/25 50.00 100.00
25 Frank Thomas/25 60.00 150.00
29 George Kell/25 8.00 20.00
36 Joe Morgan/22 8.00 20.00
43 Monte Irvin/25 15.00 40.00
46 Ozzie Smith/25 15.00 40.00
52 Reggie Jackson/25 30.00 80.00
55 Robin Yount/25 10.00 25.00
58 Ryne Sandberg/25 20.00 50.00
64 Tony Gwynn/25 50.00 100.00
97 Bob Feller/25 40.00 80.00
99 Monte Irvin/25 15.00 40.00
100 Whitey Ford/25 20.00 50.00

2014 Panini Hall of Fame Signatures Red

*RED: .5X TO 1.2X BASIC
OVERALL AUTO ODDS 2 PER BOX
PRINT RUNS B/WN 36-50 COPIES PER
EXCHANGE DEADLINE 4/8/2016
43 Monte Irvin/50 8.00 20.00
98 Bobby Doerr/50 8.00 20.00
99 Monte Irvin/50 8.00 20.00
100 Whitey Ford/50 15.00 40.00

2018 Panini Illusions

INSERTED IN '18 CHRONICLES PACKS
1 Gleyber Torres RC 2.50 6.00
2 Mike Trout 1.25 3.00
3 Bryce Harper .40 1.00
4 Kris Bryant .30 .75
5 Aaron Judge .60 1.50
6 Ichiro .30 .75
7 Mickey Mantle .75 2.00
8 Joey Lucchesi RC .25 .60
9 Scott Kingery RC .40 1.00
10 Clint Frazier RC .50 1.25
11 Rafael Devers RC .75 2.00
12 Shohei Ohtani RC 6.00 15.00
13 Rhys Hoskins RC 1.00 2.50
14 Ronald Acuna Jr. RC 8.00 20.00
15 Amed Rosario RC .30 .75
16 Austin Hays RC .40 1.00
17 Ozzie Albies RC .75 2.00
18 Miguel Andujar RC 1.00 2.50
19 Jordan Hicks RC .50 1.25
20 Juan Soto RC 6.00 15.00
21 Victor Robles RC .60 1.50
22 Willie Calhoun RC .40 1.00
23 Max Fried RC 1.00 2.50
24 Richard Urena RC .25 .60
25 Alex Verdugo RC .40 1.00
26 Chris Flexen RC .25 .60
27 Harrison Bader RC .40 1.00
28 Brandon Woodruff RC .75 2.00
29 Zack Granite RC .25 .60
30 Giancarlo Stanton .25 .60

2018 Panini Illusions Trophy Collection Blue

*BLUE: 1.2X TO 3X BASIC
*BLUE RC: .75X TO 2X BASIC
INSERTED IN '18 CHRONICLES PACKS
STATED PRINT RUN 99 SER.#'d SETS
12 Shohei Ohtani 8.00 20.00

2018 Panini Illusions Trophy Collection Red

*RED: 2X TO 5X BASIC
*RED RC: 1.2X TO 3X BASIC
INSERTED IN '18 CHRONICLES PACKS
STATED PRINT RUN 25 SER.#'d SETS
2 Mike Trout 15.00 40.00
12 Shohei Ohtani 12.00 30.00

2018 Panini Illusions Autographs

RANDOM INSERTS IN PACKS
*GOLD/25: .75X TO 2X BASIC
8 Joey Lucchesi 2.50 6.00
9 Scott Kingery 4.00 10.00
18 Miguel Andujar 10.00 25.00
19 Jordan Hicks 5.00 12.00
20 Juan Soto 50.00 120.00
26 Chris Flexen 2.50 6.00
28 Brandon Woodruff 8.00 20.00
29 Zack Granite 2.50 6.00

2019 Panini Leather and Lumber

101-151 RANDOMLY INSERTED
101-151 PRINT RUN B/WN 99-175 PER
EXCHANGE DEADLINE 11/29/2020
1 Miles Mikolas .40 1.00
2 Brandon Crawford .30 .75
3 Noah Syndergaard .30 .75
4 Kevin Pillar .25 .60
5 Max Scherzer .40 1.00
6 Nolan Arenado .60 1.50
7 Felix Hernandez .30 .75
8 Jameson Taillon .30 .75
9 Francisco Lindor .40 1.00
10 Jacob deGrom .75 2.00
11 Andrelton Simmons .25 .60
12 Chris Sale .40 1.00
13 Lorenzo Cain .25 .60
14 Manny Machado .40 1.00
15 Blake Snell .30 .75
16 Javier Baez .50 1.25
17 Carlos Rodon .40 1.00
18 Luis Severino .30 .75
19 Stephen Strasburg .40 1.00
20 Carlos Carrasco .25 .60
21 David Peralta .25 .60
22 Jose Urena .25 .60
23 Chris Archer .25 .60
24 Jackie Bradley Jr. .40 1.00
25 Madison Bumgarner .30 .75
26 Carlos Correa .40 1.00
27 James Paxton .30 .75
28 Paul Goldschmidt .40 1.00
29 Aaron Nola .30 .75
30 Gerrit Cole .40 1.00
31 Justin Smoak .25 .60
32 Justin Verlander .40 1.00
33 Anthony Rendon .40 1.00
34 Jose Berrios .30 .75
35 Matt Chapman .40 1.00
36 Kyle Freeland .30 .75
37 Clayton Kershaw .60 1.50
38 Corey Kluber .30 .75
39 Francisco Mejia .30 .75
40 Adam Jones .30 .75
41 Matt Carpenter .40 1.00
42 Gleyber Torres .75 2.00
43 Jose Ramirez .30 .75
44 Walker Buehler .50 1.25
45 Brandon Belt .30 .75
46 Miguel Andujar .40 1.00
47 Charlie Blackmon .40 1.00
48 Yadier Molina .50 1.25
49 Jon Lester .30 .75
50 Alex Bregman .40 1.00
51 Trey Mancini .30 .75
52 Eric Hosmer .30 .75
53 Starling Marte .30 .75
54 Joey Votto .40 1.00
55 J.T. Realmuto .40 1.00
56 Miguel Cabrera .40 1.00
57 Trea Turner .30 .75
58 Nicholas Castellanos .40 1.00
59 Wilson Ramos .25 .60
60 Harrison Bader .30 .75
61 Salvador Perez .30 .75
62 Kris Bryant .50 1.25
63 Aaron Judge 1.00 2.50
64 Anthony Rizzo .50 1.25
65 Matt Olson .40 1.00
66 Freddie Freeman .50 1.25
67 Christian Yelich .50 1.25
68 Jesus Aguilar .30 .75
69 Trevor Story .40 1.00
70 Mike Trout 2.00 5.00
71 Albert Pujols .50 1.25
72 Khris Davis .40 1.00
73 Ronald Acuna Jr. 2.00 5.00
74 Rafael Devers .50 1.25
75 Mike Moustakas .30 .75
76 Joey Wendle .30 .75
77 Rhys Hoskins .50 1.25
78 Eugenio Suarez .30 .75
79 Willy Adames .25 .60
80 Eddie Rosario .30 .75
81 Shohei Ohtani .60 1.50
82 Joey Gallo .30 .75
83 Ozzie Albies .40 1.00
84 Mitch Haniger .30 .75
85 Austin Meadows .40 1.00
86 Cody Bellinger .75 2.00
87 Mookie Betts .75 2.00
88 A.J. Pollock .25 .60
89 J.D. Martinez .40 1.00
90 Nomar Mazara .25 .60
91 Jose Abreu .40 1.00
92 Whit Merrifield .40 1.00
93 Jose Altuve .30 .75
94 Odubel Herrera .30 .75
95 Andrew Benintendi .40 1.00
96 Michael Conforto .30 .75
97 Juan Soto 1.25 3.00
98 Bryce Harper .60 1.50
99 Giancarlo Stanton .40 1.00
100 Nelson Cruz .40 1.00
101 Dakota Hudson AU/149 RC 4.00 10.00
102 Cedric Mullins AU/149 RC 10.00 25.00
103 Kyle Tucker AU/149 RC 8.00 20.00
104 Ramon Laureano AU/149 RC 5.00 12.00
105 Jake Cave AU/149 RC 4.00 10.00
106 Jake Bauers AU/149 RC 5.00 12.00
107 Rowdy Tellez AU/149 RC 5.00 12.00
108 Enyel De Los Santos AU/149 RC 3.00 8.00
109 Ryan Borucki AU/149 RC 3.00 8.00
110 Stephen Gonsalves AU/149 RC 3.00 8.00
111 Brandon Lowe AU/149 RC 8.00 20.00
112 Kevin Newman AU/149 RC 5.00 12.00
113 Luis Urias AU/149 RC 4.00 10.00
114 Framber Valdez AU/149 RC 3.00 8.00
115 Dennis Santana AU/149 RC
116 Jonathan Loaisiga AU/149 RC
117 Sean Reid-Foley AU/149 RC 3.00 8.00
118 Chris Shaw AU/99 RC 3.00 8.00
119 Justus Sheffield AU/149 RC 5.00 12.00
120 Danny Jansen AU/149 RC 3.00 8.00
121 Jeff McNeil AU/99 RC 8.00 20.00
122 Steven Duggar AU/149 RC 4.00 10.00
123 Corbin Burnes AU/149 RC 10.00 25.00
124 Kyle Wright AU/149 RC 5.00 12.00
125 Kolby Allard AU/149 RC 5.00 12.00
126 Kevin Kramer AU/149 RC 4.00 10.00
127 Brad Keller AU/149 RC 3.00 8.00
128 Ryan O'Hearn AU/149 RC 3.00 8.00
129 Touki Toussaint AU/149 RC 4.00 10.00
130 Chance Adams AU/149 RC 3.00 8.00
131 David Fletcher AU/149 RC 10.00 25.00
132 Michael Kopech AU/149 RC 10.00 25.00
133 Josh James AU/149 RC 5.00 12.00
134 Christin Stewart AU/149 RC 4.00 10.00
135 Caleb Ferguson AU/149 RC 3.00 8.00
136 Taylor Ward AU/149 RC 3.00 8.00
137 Vladimir Guerrero Jr. AU/149 RC 25.00 60.00
138 Garrett Hampson AU/149 RC 5.00 12.00
139 Eloy Jimenez AU/99 RC 20.00 50.00
140 Fernando Tatis Jr. AU/149 RC 50.00 120.00
141 Yusei Kikuchi AU/149 RC 12.00 30.00
142 Cionel Perez AU/175 RC 3.00 8.00
143 Daniel Ponce de Leon AU/175 RC 5.00 12.00
144 Bryse Wilson AU/175 RC 4.00 10.00
145 Jacob Nix AU/175 RC 3.00 8.00
146 Jonathan Davis AU/175 RC 4.00 10.00
147 Luis Ortiz AU/175 RC 3.00 8.00
148 Myles Straw AU/175 RC 6.00 15.00
149 Patrick Wisdom AU/175 RC 3.00 8.00
150 Reese McGuire AU/175 RC 5.00 12.00
151 Pete Alonso AU/149 RC 50.00 120.00

2019 Panini Leather and Lumber Die Cut

*DIE CUT: .5X TO 1.2X BASIC
RANDOM INSERTS IN PACKS

2019 Panini Leather and Lumber Die Cut Blue

*DIE CUT BLUE: 1.5X TO 4X BASIC
RANDOM INSERTS IN PACKS
STATED PRINT RUN 25 SER.#'d SETS

2019 Panini Leather and Lumber Die Cut Gold

*DIE CUT GOLD: 1X TO 2.5X BASIC
RANDOM INSERTS IN PACKS
STATED PRINT RUN 99 SER.#'d SETS

2019 Panini Leather and Lumber Embossed

*EMBOSSED: .5X TO 1.2X BASIC
RANDOM INSERTS IN PACKS

2019 Panini Leather and Lumber Embossed Gold Proof

*EMBOSSED GOLD: .6X TO 1.5X BASIC
RANDOM INSERTS IN PACKS

2019 Panini Leather and Lumber 500 HR Club Bats

RANDOM INSERTS IN PACKS
1 Eddie Murray 6.00 15.00
2 Ken Griffey Jr. 15.00 40.00
3 Frank Robinson 6.00 15.00
4 Willie McCovey 6.00 15.00
5 Harmon Killebrew 8.00 20.00
6 Reggie Jackson 6.00 15.00
7 Albert Pujols 12.00 30.00
8 Frank Thomas 8.00 20.00
9 Gary Sheffield 5.00 12.00
10 David Ortiz 8.00 20.00

2019 Panini Leather and Lumber Autographs

RANDOM INSERTS IN PACKS
EXCHANGE DEADLINE 11/29/2020
1 Yohander Mendez 2.50 6.00
4 Stephen Piscotty 2.50 6.00
5 Matt Barnes 2.50 6.00
7 Marcell Ozuna 4.00 10.00
9 Mitch Haniger 3.00 8.00
10 Marwin Gonzalez 2.50 6.00
11 Shohei Ohtani 100.00 250.00
12 Tom Glavine
14 Jackie Bradley Jr.
15 Mitch Garver 2.50 6.00
16 J.T. Realmuto 12.00 30.00
17 Jason Kipnis 3.00 8.00
18 Francisco Lindor 12.00 30.00
19 Sean Newcomb 2.50 6.00
20 Ryne Sandberg
21 Jedd Gyorko 2.50 6.00
22 Yadier Molina 25.00 60.00
24 Julio Urias 4.00 10.00
25 Nolan Arenado 25.00 60.00
26 Stephen Strasburg
27 Aaron Nola
29 Wilson Ramos 4.00 10.00
30 Edgar Martinez 8.00 20.00
32 Luis Severino 3.00 8.00
33 Mike Leake 2.50 6.00
34 Tony Kemp 2.50 6.00
36 Mike Mussina 8.00 20.00
39 John Smoltz
40 Max Muncy 6.00 15.00

2019 Panini Leather and Lumber Autographs Blue

*BLUE p/r 60-150: .5X TO 1.2X BASIC
*BLUE p/r 50: .6X TO 1.5X BASIC
*BLUE p/r 25: .75X TO 2X BASIC
RANDOM INSERTS IN PACKS
PRINT RUNS B/WN 5-150 COPIES PER
NO PRICING ON QTY 15 OR LESS
EXCHANGE DEADLINE 11/29/2020
2 J.D. Davis/50 4.00 10.00
23 Juan Soto/25 EXCH 20.00 50.00

2019 Panini Leather and Lumber Autographs Gold

*GOLD p/r 75-200: .5X TO 1.2X BASIC
*GOLD p/r 20-25: .75X TO 2X BASIC
RANDOM INSERTS IN PACKS
PRINT RUNS B/WN 7-200 COPIES PER
NO PRICING ON QTY 15 OR LESS
EXCHANGE DEADLINE 11/29/2020
23 Juan Soto/25 EXCH 20.00 50.00

2019 Panini Leather and Lumber Autographs Holo Gold

*HOLO GLD p/r 25: .75X TO 2X BASIC
RANDOM INSERTS IN PACKS
PRINT RUNS B/WN 2-25 COPIES PER
NO PRICING ON QTY 10 OR LESS
EXCHANGE DEADLINE 11/29/2020
3 Anthony Banda/25 10.00 25.00
8 Alex Reyes/25 6.00 15.00

2019 Panini Leather and Lumber Autographs Holo Silver

*HOLO SLV p/r 99: .5X TO 1.2X BASIC
*HOLO SLV p/r 49-50: .6X TO 1.5X BASIC
*HOLO SLV p/r 25: .75X TO 2X BASIC
RANDOM INSERTS IN PACKS
PRINT RUNS B/WN 3-99 COPIES PER
NO PRICING ON QTY 15 OR LESS
EXCHANGE DEADLINE 11/29/2020
2 J.D. Davis/25 5.00 12.00
3 Anthony Banda/50 8.00 20.00
8 Alex Reyes/50 5.00 12.00

2019 Panini Leather and Lumber Baseball Signatures

RANDOM INSERTS IN PACKS
EXCHANGE DEADLINE 11/29/2020
*BLK GLD p/r 22: .75X TO 2X BASIC
1 Aaron Judge 60.00 150.00
2 Adrian Beltre
3 Andres Galarraga 6.00 15.00
4 Don Mattingly 40.00 100.00
5 Dwight Gooden 4.00 10.00
6 Kerry Wood 5.00 12.00

8 Miguel Cabrera EXCH
9 Orlando Hernandez 2.50 6.00
11 Wade Boggs 20.00 50.00
13 Cesar Hernandez
16 Jim Rice
19 Gleyber Torres 8.00 20.00
20 Cody Bellinger EXCH
26 Tim Wakefield
27 Ronald Guzman 2.50 6.00
30 Cameron Gallagher
33 Amed Rosario 5.00 12.00
34 Jordan Hicks
35 Trey Mancini
38 Chance Sisco
39 Harrison Bader
41 Ronald Acuna Jr. EXCH 40.00 100.00
42 Andrew Stevenson 2.50 6.00
43 Omar Vizquel
44 Mike Mussina 8.00 20.00
45 Gary Sheffield
46 Chris Sale EXCH 6.00 15.00
47 Shohei Ohtani 100.00 250.00
48 George Brett 60.00 150.00
49 Kevin Mitchell

2019 Panini Leather and Lumber Baseball Signatures Black

*BLACK p/r 25: .75X TO 2X BASIC
RANDOM INSERTS IN PACKS
PRINT RUNS B/WN 5-25 COPIES PER
NO PRICING ON QTY 15 OR LESS
EXCHANGE DEADLINE 11/29/2020
36 Juan Soto/25 EXCH 20.00 50.00

2019 Panini Leather and Lumber Baseball Signatures Blue

*BLUE p/r 49: .6X TO 1.5X BASIC
*BLUE p/r 20-25: .75X TO 2X BASIC
RANDOM INSERTS IN PACKS
PRINT RUNS B/WN 5-49 COPIES PER
NO PRICING ON QTY 20 OR LESS
EXCHANGE DEADLINE 11/29/2020
36 Juan Soto/25 EXCH 20.00 50.00

2019 Panini Leather and Lumber Baseball Signatures Light Blue

*LGHT BLUE p/r 20-25: .75X TO 2X BASIC
RANDOM INSERTS IN PACKS
PRINT RUNS B/WN 5-25 COPIES PER
NO PRICING ON QTY 18 OR LESS
EXCHANGE DEADLINE 11/29/2020
25 David Bote/20
28 Freddy Peralta/20
36 Juan Soto/25 EXCH 20.00 50.00
37 Willy Adames/20 8.00 20.00

2019 Panini Leather and Lumber Baseball Signatures Pink

*PINK p/r 25: .75X TO 2X BASIC
RANDOM INSERTS IN PACKS
PRINT RUNS B/WN 5-25 COPIES PER
NO PRICING ON QTY 15 OR LESS
EXCHANGE DEADLINE 11/29/2020
36 Juan Soto/25 EXCH 20.00 50.00

2019 Panini Leather and Lumber Bat Patrol

RANDOM INSERTS IN PACKS
*GOLD/99: .75X TO 2X BASIC
*HOLO SILVER/25: 1.2X TO 3X BASIC
1 Joe Jackson .75 2.00
2 Tony Gwynn .60 1.50
3 Ichiro .75 2.00
4 Joe DiMaggio 1.25 3.00
5 Rod Carew .50 1.25
6 Edd Roush .50 1.25
7 Ken Griffey Jr. 1.25 3.00
8 Juan Soto 2.00 5.00
9 Robinson Cano .50 1.25
10 Tony Lazzeri .50 1.25
11 Wade Boggs .50 1.25
12 Paul Molitor .60 1.50
13 Jose Altuve .50 1.25
14 Christian Yelich .75 2.00
15 Dustin Pedroia .60 1.50

2019 Panini Leather and Lumber Benchmarks

RANDOM INSERTS IN PACKS
*GOLD/99: .75X TO 2X BASIC
*HOLO SILVER/25: 1.2X TO 3X BASIC
1 Frank Thomas .60 1.50
2 Shohei Ohtani 1.00 2.50
3 Mike Trout 3.00 8.00
4 Jacob deGrom 1.25 3.00
5 Greg Maddux .75 2.00
6 Jose Altuve .50 1.25
7 Ronald Acuna Jr. 3.00 8.00
8 Alex Rodriguez .75 2.00
9 Joey Votto .60 1.50
10 Yogi Berra .60 1.50
11 Tony Gwynn .60 1.50
12 Randy Johnson .60 1.50
13 Mookie Betts 1.25 3.00
14 Cal Ripken 2.00 5.00
15 Justin Verlander .60 1.50
16 Aaron Nola .50 1.25
17 Ichiro .75 2.00
18 Max Scherzer .60 1.50
19 Chris Sale .60 1.50
20 Vladimir Guerrero .50 1.25

2019 Panini Leather and Lumber Big Bats

RANDOM INSERTS IN PACKS
PRINT RUNS B/WN 35-199 COPIES PER
2 Bo Jackson/50 8.00 20.00
4 George Springer/84 4.00 10.00
5 Jorge Soler/71 5.00 12.00
7 Vladimir Guerrero Jr./199 15.00 40.00
8 Rickey Henderson/49 8.00 20.00
9 Fernando Tatis Jr./99 8.00 20.00
10 Kirby Puckett/35 25.00 60.00
11 Adam Jones/79 4.00 10.00
12 Mike Piazza/119 5.00 12.00
15 Yasmani Grandal/50 4.00 10.00

2019 Panini Leather and Lumber Big Bats Gold

*GOLD/99: .4X TO 1X p/r 199
*GOLD/35-49: .5X TO 1.2X p/r 71-199
*GOLD/35-49: .4X TO 1X p/r 35-49
*GOLD/25: .6X TO 1.5X p/r 71-199
*GOLD/25: .5X TO 1.2X p/r 35-49
RANDOM INSERTS IN PACKS
PRINT RUNS B/WN 25-99 COPIES PER
3 Kris Bryant/49 8.00 20.00
6 Eloy Jimenez/49 6.00 15.00
13 Jose Canseco/49 5.00 12.00
14 Miguel Andujar/49 6.00 15.00

2019 Panini Leather and Lumber Big Bats Holo Silver

*SILVR 20-25: .6X TO 1.5X p/r 71-199
*SILVR 20-25: .5X TO 1.2X p/r 35-50
RANDOM INSERTS IN PACKS
PRINT RUNS B/WN 10-25 COPIES PER
NO PRICING ON QTY 15 OR LESS
3 Kris Bryant/25 10.00 25.00
6 Eloy Jimenez/25 8.00 20.00
13 Jose Canseco/25 6.00 15.00
14 Miguel Andujar/25 8.00 20.00

2019 Panini Leather and Lumber Equalizers

RANDOM INSERTS IN PACKS
*GOLD/99: .75X TO 2X BASIC
*HOLO SILVER/25: 1.2X TO 3X BASIC
1 Nolan Arenado 1.00 2.50
2 Babe Ruth
3 Giancarlo Stanton .60 1.50
4 Mike Trout 3.00 8.00
5 Ken Griffey Jr. 1.25 3.00
6 Alex Rodriguez .75 2.00
7 Miguel Cabrera .60 1.50
8 Javier Baez .75 2.00
9 Joe DiMaggio 1.25 3.00
10 Joey Votto .60 1.50
11 Mookie Betts 1.25 3.00
12 Christian Yelich .75 2.00
13 Francisco Lindor .60 1.50
14 Alex Bregman .60 1.50
15 Anthony Rizzo .75 2.00
16 Bryce Harper 1.00 2.50
17 Aaron Judge 1.50 4.00
18 Manny Machado .60 1.50
19 Vladimir Guerrero .50 1.25
20 Trevor Story .60 1.50

2019 Panini Leather and Lumber Flashing the Leather

RANDOM INSERTS IN PACKS
PRINT RUNS B/WN 55-299 COPIES PER
*BLUE/49: .5X TO 1.2X BASIC
*GOLD/99: .4X TO 1X BASIC
*GOLD/25: .6X TO 1.5X BASIC
*SLVR/25: .6X TO 1.5X BASIC
1 Jose Peraza/299 3.00 8.00
2 Andrew Benintendi/299 5.00 12.00
3 Ozzie Albies/174 4.00 10.00
4 Shohei Ohtani/99 6.00 15.00
5 Francisco Lindor/55 4.00 10.00
6 Byron Buxton/125 4.00 10.00
7 J.P. Crawford/299 2.50 6.00
8 Cody Bellinger/199 5.00 12.00
9 Dansby Swanson/249 4.00 10.00
10 Billy Martin/99 8.00 20.00
11 Gil Hodges/99 10.00 25.00
12 Ken Griffey Jr./99 10.00 25.00
13 Clint Frazier/299 3.00 8.00
14 Jim Rice/199 3.00 8.00
15 Alex Bregman/125 4.00 10.00

2019 Panini Leather and Lumber Grip It 'n Rip It

RANDOM INSERTS IN PACKS
PRINT RUNS B/WN 25-99 COPIES PER
*GOLD/35-49: .5X TO 1.2X p/r 56-99
*GOLD/20: .4X TO 1X p/r 25
1 Kyle Tucker/99 6.00 15.00
2 Cedric Mullins/75 5.00 12.00
3 Jake Bauers /99 4.00 10.00
4 Garrett Hampson/72 4.00 10.00
5 Christin Stewart/50 4.00 10.00
6 Myles Straw/72 4.00 10.00
7 Ryan O'Hearn/99 2.50 6.00
8 David Fletcher/99 8.00 20.00
9 Taylor Ward/80 2.50 6.00
10 Jake Cave/56 3.00 8.00
11 Ramon Laureano/88 5.00 12.00
12 Shohei Ohtani/25 12.00 30.00
13 Brandon Lowe/77 4.00 10.00
14 Jonathan Davis/99 3.00 8.00

2019 Panini Leather and Lumber Grip It 'n Rip It Holo Silver

*SLVR/25: .6X TO 1.5X p/r 56-99
*SLVR/25: .5X TO 1.2X p/r 50
RANDOM INSERTS IN PACKS
PRINT RUNS B/WN 15-25 COPIES PER
NO PRICING ON QTY 15
15 Danny Jansen/25 4.00 10.00

2019 Panini Leather and Lumber Hit-N-Run

RANDOM INSERTS IN PACKS
*GOLD/99: .75X TO 2X BASIC
*HOLO SILVER/25: 1.2X TO 3X BASIC
1 Ichiro .75 2.00
2 Mookie Betts 1.25 3.00
3 Rickey Henderson .60 1.50
4 Charlie Blackmon .60 1.50
5 Mike Trout 3.00 8.00
6 Jose Altuve .50 1.25
7 Kevin Kiermaier .50 1.25
8 Alex Rodriguez .75 2.00
9 Lorenzo Cain .40 1.00
10 Jose Ramirez .50 1.25
11 Whit Merrifield .60 1.50
12 Trea Turner .50 1.25
13 Dee Gordon .40 1.00
14 Starling Marte .50 1.25
15 Vladimir Guerrero .50 1.25

2019 Panini Leather and Lumber Hitter Inc. Signatures Bat

RANDOM INSERTS IN PACKS
PRINT RUNS B/WN 5-25 COPIES PER
EXCHANGE DEADLINE 11/29/2020
1 Victor Robles/20 10.00 25.00
17 Alex Verdugo/25 6.00 15.00

2019 Panini Leather and Lumber Hitter Inc. Signatures Bat Gold

*GOLD/50: .25X TO .6X BASIC
RANDOM INSERTS IN PACKS
PRINT RUNS B/WN 7-50 COPIES PER
NO PRICING ON QTY 15 OR LESS
EXCHANGE DEADLINE 11/29/2020
5 Rafael Devers/25 10.00 25.00

2019 Panini Leather and Lumber Hitter Inc. Signatures Jersey

RANDOM INSERTS IN PACKS
PRINT RUN B/WN 5-25 COPIES PER
NO PRICING ON QTY 15 OR LESS
EXCHANGE DEADLINE 11/29/2020
16 Dontrelle Willis/25 5.00 12.00
17 Alex Verdugo/25 6.00 15.00
21 Dustin Fowler/25 5.00 12.00
22 Michael Taylor/25 5.00 12.00

2019 Panini Leather and Lumber Home Run Kings

RANDOM INSERTS IN PACKS
*GOLD/99: .75X TO 2X BASIC
*HOLO SILVER/25: 1.2X TO 3X BASIC
1 Babe Ruth 1.50 4.00
2 Jimmie Foxx .60 1.50
3 Willie McCovey .50 1.25
4 Harmon Killebrew .60 1.50
5 David Ortiz .60 1.50
6 Ken Griffey Jr. 1.25 3.00
7 Albert Pujols .75 2.00
8 Alex Rodriguez .75 2.00
9 Frank Thomas .60 1.50
10 Frank Robinson .50 1.25

2019 Panini Leather and Lumber Knothole Gang

RANDOM INSERTS IN PACKS
*GOLD/99: .75X TO 2X BASIC
*HOLO SILVER/25: 1.2X TO 3X BASIC
1 Roy Campanella .60 1.50
2 Shohei Ohtani 1.00 2.50
3 Ozzie Albies .60 1.50
4 Trevor Story .60 1.50
5 Christian Yelich .75 2.00
6 Mitch Haniger .50 1.25
7 Kris Bryant .75 2.00
8 Bryce Harper 1.00 2.50
9 Aaron Judge 1.50 4.00
10 Gleyber Torres 1.25 3.00
11 Starling Marte .50 1.25
12 Eugenio Suarez .50 1.25
13 Cody Bellinger 1.25 3.00
14 Anthony Rendon .60 1.50
15 Rhys Hoskins .75 2.00

2019 Panini Leather and Lumber Leather and Lace Signatures

RANDOM INSERTS IN PACKS
STATED PRINT RUN 25 SER.#'d SETS
EXCHANGE DEADLINE 11/29/2020
1 Jacob Nix 6.00 15.00
2 Francisco Mejia 6.00 15.00
3 Fernando Tatis Jr. 50.00 120.00
4 Enyel De Los Santos 5.00 12.00
5 Justus Sheffield 8.00 20.00
6 Dakota Hudson 6.00 15.00
7 Daniel Ponce de Leon 8.00 20.00
8 Reese McGuire 8.00 20.00
9 Vladimir Guerrero Jr. 30.00 80.00
11 Kyle Tucker 12.00 30.00
12 Jonathan Loaisiga 6.00 15.00
13 Chance Adams 5.00 12.00
14 Michael Kopech 15.00 40.00
15 Brad Keller 5.00 12.00

2019 Panini Leather and Lumber Leather and Lace Signatures Gold

*GOLD: .4X TO 1X BASIC
RANDOM INSERTS IN PACKS
STATED PRINT RUN 20 SER.#'d SETS
EXCHANGE DEADLINE 11/29/2020
10 Eloy Jimenez 20.00 50.00

2019 Panini Leather and Lumber Leather and Lumber

RANDOM INSERTS IN PACKS
*GOLD/99: .75X TO 2X BASIC
*HOLO SILVER/25: 1.2X TO 3X BASIC
1 Anthony Rizzo .75 2.00
2 Alex Bregman .60 1.50
3 Manny Machado .60 1.50
4 Mike Trout 3.00 8.00
5 Javier Baez .75 2.00
6 Nolan Arenado 1.00 2.50
7 Matt Chapman .60 1.50
8 Adrian Beltre .60 1.50
9 Francisco Lindor .60 1.50
10 Yadier Molina .75 2.00

2019 Panini Leather and Lumber Leather and Lumber Dual Bat Relics

RANDOM INSERTS IN PACKS
PRINT RUNS B/WN 49-299 COPIES PER
1 Adrian Beltre/49 5.00 12.00
3 Alex Verdugo/199 3.00 8.00
4 Carlos Correa/299 4.00 10.00
5 Corey Seager/199 4.00 10.00
6 David Dahl/199 2.50 6.00
7 Eddie Murray/299 3.00 8.00
8 Eric Thames/249 2.50 6.00
9 Gary Carter/199 3.00 8.00
10 J.P. Crawford/199 2.50 6.00
11 Miguel Andujar/125 4.00 10.00
12 Max Kepler/199 3.00 8.00
14 Nicky Delmonico/249 2.50 6.00
15 Rickey Henderson/199 8.00 20.00
16 Ryan McMahon/249 4.00 10.00
17 Shohei Ohtani/99 8.00 20.00
18 Stephen Piscotty/299 2.50 6.00
19 Yoan Moncada/30 5.00 12.00
20 Kirby Puckett/130 6.00 15.00
21 Harrison Bader/299 3.00 8.00
22 Francisco Mejia/99 3.00 8.00
23 Dustin Pedroia/99 4.00 10.00
24 Lewis Brinson/199 2.50 6.00
25 Rhys Hoskins/99 5.00 12.00
26 Tony Gwynn/199 4.00 10.00
27 Willson Contreras/299 3.00 8.00
28 Willie Stargell/149 3.00 8.00
29 Willie Calhoun/199 2.50 6.00
30 Hanley Ramirez/299 3.00 8.00

2019 Panini Leather and Lumber Leather and Lumber Dual Bat-Jersey Relics

RANDOM INSERTS IN PACKS
PRINT RUNS B/WN 35-99 COPIES PER
1 Adrian Beltre/35 5.00 12.00
2 Alex Bregman/99 4.00 10.00
3 Alex Verdugo/99 3.00 8.00
4 Carlos Correa/99 4.00 10.00
5 Corey Seager/99 4.00 10.00
6 David Dahl/99 2.50 6.00
7 Eddie Murray/99 3.00 8.00
8 Eric Thames/99 2.50 6.00
9 Gary Carter/99 3.00 8.00
10 J.P. Crawford/99 2.50 6.00
11 Miguel Andujar/99 4.00 10.00
12 Max Kepler/99 3.00 8.00
13 Miguel Sano/49 4.00 10.00
14 Nicky Delmonico/99 2.50 6.00
15 Rickey Henderson/49 10.00 25.00
16 Ryan McMahon/99 4.00 10.00
17 Shohei Ohtani/99 8.00 20.00
18 Stephen Piscotty/99 2.50 6.00
19 Yoan Moncada/50 5.00 12.00
20 Kirby Puckett/49 8.00 20.00
21 Harrison Bader/99 3.00 8.00
22 Francisco Mejia/49 4.00 10.00
23 Dustin Pedroia/49 5.00 12.00
24 Lewis Brinson/99 2.50 6.00
25 Rhys Hoskins/49 6.00 15.00
26 Tony Gwynn/49 5.00 12.00
27 Willson Contreras/99 3.00 8.00
28 Willie Stargell/99 3.00 8.00
29 Willie Calhoun/99 2.50 6.00
30 Hanley Ramirez/99 3.00 8.00

2019 Panini Leather and Lumber Leather and Lumber Dual Jersey Relics

RANDOM INSERTS IN PACKS
PRINT RUNS B/WN 49-349 COPIES PER
1 Adrian Beltre/349 4.00 10.00
2 Alex Bregman/349 4.00 10.00
3 Alex Verdugo/349 3.00 8.00
4 Carlos Correa/249 4.00 10.00
5 Corey Seager/349 4.00 10.00
6 David Dahl/349 2.50 6.00
7 Eddie Murray/249 3.00 8.00
8 Eric Thames/349 2.50 6.00
9 Gary Carter/49 4.00 10.00
10 J.P. Crawford/349 2.50 6.00
11 Miguel Andujar/349 4.00 10.00
12 Max Kepler/349 3.00 8.00
13 Miguel Sano/349 3.00 8.00
14 Nicky Delmonico/349 2.50 6.00
15 Rickey Henderson/99 8.00 20.00
16 Ryan McMahon/349 4.00 10.00
17 Shohei Ohtani/349 8.00 20.00
18 Stephen Piscotty/349 2.50 6.00
19 Yoan Moncada/349 4.00 10.00
21 Harrison Bader/349 3.00 8.00
22 Francisco Mejia/349 3.00 8.00
23 Dustin Pedroia/249 4.00 10.00
24 Lewis Brinson/349 2.50 6.00
25 Rhys Hoskins/349 5.00 12.00
26 Tony Gwynn/249 4.00 10.00
27 Willson Contreras/349 3.00 8.00
28 Willie Stargell/349 3.00 8.00
29 Willie Calhoun/349 2.50 6.00
30 Hanley Ramirez/349 3.00 8.00

2019 Panini Leather and Lumber Leather and Lumber Dual Jersey-Glove Relics

RANDOM INSERTS IN PACKS
STATED PRINT RUN 25 SER.#'d SETS
2 Alex Bregman 8.00 20.00
4 Carlos Correa 8.00 20.00
5 Corey Seager 8.00 20.00
6 David Dahl 5.00 12.00
8 Eric Thames 5.00 12.00
9 Gary Carter 6.00 15.00
10 J.P. Crawford 5.00 12.00
11 Miguel Andujar 8.00 20.00
12 Max Kepler 6.00 15.00
13 Miguel Sano 6.00 15.00
14 Nicky Delmonico 5.00 12.00
15 Rickey Henderson 5.00 40.00
16 Ryan McMahon 8.00 20.00
17 Shohei Ohtani 15.00 40.00
18 Stephen Piscotty 5.00 12.00
19 Yoan Moncada 8.00 20.00
20 Kirby Puckett 12.00 30.00
21 Harrison Bader 6.00 15.00
22 Francisco Mejia 6.00 15.00
23 Dustin Pedroia 8.00 20.00
24 Lewis Brinson 5.00 12.00
25 Rhys Hoskins 10.00 25.00
27 Willson Contreras 6.00 15.00
28 Willie Stargell 6.00 15.00
29 Willie Calhoun 5.00 12.00
30 Hanley Ramirez 6.00 15.00

2019 Panini Leather and Lumber Leather and Lumber Signatures

RANDOM INSERTS IN PACKS
PRINT RUNS B/WN 10-150 COPIES PER
NO PRICING ON QTY 10
EXCHANGE DEADLINE 11/29/2020
3 Jake Bauers/25 8.00 20.00
4 Kyle Tucker/25 12.00 30.00
6 Garrett Hampson/40 6.00 15.00
8 Myles Straw/99 5.00 12.00
10 David Fletcher/150 10.00 25.00
11 Jake Cave/99 4.00 10.00
14 Brandon Lowe/25 12.00 30.00
16 Kevin Kramer/99 4.00 10.00
18 Francisco Mejia/25 6.00 15.00
20 Patrick Wisdom/99 3.00 8.00

2019 Panini Leather and Lumber Leather and Lumber Signatures Blue

RANDOM INSERTS IN PACKS
PRINT RUNS B/WN 7-75 COPIES PER
NO PRICING ON QTY 15 OR LESS
EXCHANGE DEADLINE 11/29/2020
3 Jake Bauers/50 6.00 15.00
5 Cedric Mullins/50 12.00 30.00
6 Garrett Hampson/50 6.00 15.00
7 Christin Stewart/50 5.00 12.00
8 Myles Straw/50 6.00 15.00
9 Ryan O'Hearn/50 4.00 10.00
10 David Fletcher/75 10.00 25.00
11 Jake Cave/50 5.00 12.00
12 Jeff McNeil/50 10.00 25.00
13 Danny Jansen/25 5.00 12.00
15 Ramon Laureano/50 10.00 25.00
16 Kevin Kramer/50 5.00 12.00
17 Kevin Newman/50 6.00 15.00
18 Francisco Mejia/50 5.00 12.00
19 Chris Shaw/50 4.00 10.00
20 Patrick Wisdom/50 4.00 10.00

2019 Panini Leather and Lumber Leather and Lumber Signatures Gold

RANDOM INSERTS IN PACKS
PRINT RUNS B/WN 9-99 COPIES PER
NO PRICING ON QTY 9
EXCHANGE DEADLINE 11/29/2020
3 Jake Bauers/75 5.00 12.00
4 Kyle Tucker/20 12.00 30.00
5 Cedric Mullins/75 10.00 25.00
6 Garrett Hampson/75 5.00 12.00
8 Myles Straw/75 5.00 12.00
9 Ryan O'Hearn/75 3.00 8.00
10 David Fletcher/99 10.00 25.00
11 Jake Cave/75 4.00 10.00
12 Jeff McNeil/75 8.00 20.00
14 Brandon Lowe/20 12.00 30.00
15 Ramon Laureano/75 8.00 20.00
16 Kevin Kramer/75 4.00 10.00
17 Kevin Newman/75 5.00 12.00
18 Francisco Mejia/75 4.00 10.00
20 Patrick Wisdom/75 3.00 8.00

2019 Panini Leather and Lumber Leather and Lumber Signatures Holo Silver

RANDOM INSERTS IN PACKS
PRINT RUNS B/WN 5-25 COPIES PER
NO PRICING ON QTY 15 OR LESS
EXCHANGE DEADLINE 11/29/2020
3 Jake Bauers/25 8.00 20.00
5 Cedric Mullins/25 15.00 40.00
6 Garrett Hampson/25 8.00 20.00
7 Christin Stewart/25 6.00 15.00
8 Myles Straw/25 8.00 20.00
9 Ryan O'Hearn/25 5.00 12.00
10 David Fletcher/25 15.00 40.00
11 Jake Cave/25 6.00 15.00
12 Jeff McNeil/25 12.00 30.00
15 Ramon Laureano/25 12.00 30.00
16 Kevin Kramer/25 6.00 15.00
17 Kevin Newman/25 8.00 20.00
18 Francisco Mejia/25 6.00 15.00
19 Chris Shaw/25 5.00 12.00
20 Patrick Wisdom/25 5.00 12.00

2019 Panini Leather and Lumber Leather and Lumber Triple Bat-Jersey Relics

RANDOM INSERTS IN PACKS
*GOLD/75-299: .5X TO 1.2X BASIC
*GOLD/49: .6X TO 1.5X BASIC
*GOLD/25: .75X TO 2X BASIC
*HOLO GLD/25: .75X TO 2X BASIC
1 Eloy Jimenez 4.00 10.00
2 Kyle Tucker 4.00 10.00
3 Cedric Mullins 3.00 8.00
4 Jake Bauers 2.50 6.00
5 Christin Stewart 2.00 5.00
6 Ryan O'Hearn 1.50 4.00
7 Jeff McNeil 3.00 8.00
8 Ramon Laureano 3.00 8.00
9 Corey Seager 2.50 6.00
10 Brandon Lowe 2.50 6.00
11 Amed Rosario 2.00 5.00
12 Chance Sisco 1.50 4.00
13 J.P. Crawford 1.50 4.00
14 Jose Peraza 2.00 5.00
15 Shohei Ohtani 6.00 15.00
16 Max Kepler 2.00 5.00
17 Willson Contreras 2.00 5.00
18 Austin Hays 2.50 6.00
20 Bernie Williams 2.00 5.00
21 Carlton Fisk 2.00 5.00
22 Francisco Mejia 2.00 5.00
23 Delino DeShields Jr. 1.50 4.00
24 Gregory Polanco 2.00 5.00
25 Jake Cave 2.00 5.00
26 Craig Biggio 2.00 5.00
27 Jose Canseco 2.00 5.00
28 Jose Reyes 2.00 5.00
29 Kevin Kramer 2.00 5.00
30 Alex Verdugo 2.00 5.00
31 Taylor Ward 1.50 4.00
32 Omar Vizquel 2.00 5.00
33 Jose Canseco 2.00 5.00
34 Willie McCovey 3.00 8.00
35 Kevin Newman 2.50 6.00
36 David Fletcher 5.00 12.00
37 Chris Shaw 1.50 4.00
38 Patrick Wisdom 1.50 4.00
39 Danny Jansen 1.50 4.00
40 Rowdy Tellez 2.50 6.00

2019 Panini Leather and Lumber Leather and Lumber Triple Jersey Relics

RANDOM INSERTS IN PACKS
1 Eloy Jimenez 4.00 10.00
2 Kyle Tucker 4.00 10.00
3 Cedric Mullins 3.00 8.00
4 Jake Bauers 2.50 6.00
5 Christin Stewart 2.00 5.00
6 Ryan O'Hearn 1.50 4.00
7 Jeff McNeil 3.00 8.00
8 Ramon Laureano 3.00 8.00
9 Corey Seager 2.50 6.00
10 Brandon Lowe 2.50 6.00
11 Amed Rosario 2.00 5.00
12 Chance Sisco 1.50 4.00
13 J.P. Crawford 1.50 4.00
14 Jose Peraza 2.00 5.00
15 Shohei Ohtani 5.00 12.00
16 Max Kepler 2.00 5.00
17 Willson Contreras 2.00 5.00
18 Austin Hays 2.50 6.00
20 Bernie Williams 2.00 5.00
21 Carlton Fisk 2.00 5.00
22 Francisco Mejia 2.00 5.00
23 Delino DeShields Jr. 1.50 4.00
24 Gregory Polanco 2.00 5.00
25 Jake Cave 2.00 5.00
26 Craig Biggio 2.00 5.00
27 Jose Canseco 2.00 5.00
28 Jose Reyes 4.00 10.00
29 Kevin Kramer 2.00 5.00
30 Alex Verdugo 2.00 5.00
31 Taylor Ward 1.50 4.00
32 Omar Vizquel 2.00 5.00
33 Jose Canseco 2.00 5.00
35 Kevin Newman 2.50 6.00
36 David Fletcher 5.00 12.00
37 Chris Shaw 1.50 4.00
38 Patrick Wisdom 1.50 4.00
39 Danny Jansen 1.50 4.00
40 Rowdy Tellez 2.50 6.00

2019 Panini Leather and Lumber Leather and Lumber Triple Jersey Relics Holo Silver

*SLVR/75-99: .5X TO 1.5X BASIC
*SLVR/49: .6X TO 1.5X BASIC
RANDOM INSERTS IN PACKS
PRINT RUN B/WN 49-99 COPIES PER
19 Mike Piazza/49 4.00 10.00

2019 Panini Leather and Lumber Leather Signatures

RANDOM INSERTS IN PACKS
EXCHANGE DEADLINE 11/29/2020
*DRK BRWN/20: .75X TO 2X BASIC
1 Josh Donaldson 8.00 20.00
2 Omar Vizquel
3 Pete Rose EXCH 10.00 25.00
4 Jose Canseco EXCH 8.00 20.00
5 Steve Garvey
6 Don Mattingly 40.00 100.00
7 Ozzie Smith
8 Brooks Robinson
9 Ivan Rodriguez EXCH 12.00 30.00

2019 Panini Leather and Lumber Legendary Lumber

RANDOM INSERTS IN PACKS
PRINT RUNS B/WN 10-99 COPIES PER
NO PRICING ON QTY 15 OR LESS
*GOLD/49: .5X TO 1.2X p/r 99
*GOLD/25: .5X TO 1.2X p/r 49
*SLVR/25: .6X TO 1.5X p/r 99
2 Frank Chance/49 8.00 20.00
4 Edd Roush/49 8.00 20.00
8 Roy Campanella/25 8.00 20.00
9 Tony Lazzeri/99 5.00 12.00
10 Kirby Puckett/99 6.00 15.00

2019 Panini Leather and Lumber Life on the Edge

RANDOM INSERTS IN PACKS
*GOLD/99: .75X TO 2X BASIC
*HOLO SILVER/25: 1.2X TO 3X BASIC
1 Kyle Freeland .50 1.25
2 Chris Sale .60 1.50
3 Clayton Kershaw 1.00 2.50
4 Max Scherzer .60 1.50
5 Greg Maddux .75 2.00
6 Justin Verlander .60 1.50
7 Corey Kluber .50 1.25
8 Blake Snell .50 1.25
9 Aaron Nola .50 1.25
10 Jacob deGrom 1.25 3.00

2019 Panini Leather and Lumber Lumber Signatures

RANDOM INSERTS IN PACKS
EXCHANGE DEADLINE 11/29/2020
1 Don Mattingly 40.00 100.00
2 Wade Boggs 20.00 50.00
3 Ted Simmons 15.00 40.00
7 Andrew Benintendi EXCH 12.00 30.00
8 Jose Canseco EXCH 8.00 20.00
9 Andres Galarraga 6.00 15.00

2019 Panini Leather and Lumber Lumber Signatures Blue

*BLUE/20: .75X TO 2X BASIC
RANDOM INSERTS IN PACKS
PRINT RUNS B/WN 10-20 COPIES PER
NO PRICING ON QTY 15 OR LESS
EXCHANGE DEADLINE 11/29/2020
6 Kyle Schwarber/20

2019 Panini Leather and Lumber Lumberjacks

RANDOM INSERTS IN PACKS
*GOLD/99: .75X TO 2X BASIC
*HOLO SILVER/25: 1.2X TO 3X BASIC
1 Jose Abreu .60 1.50
2 David Ortiz .60 1.50
3 Khris Davis .60 1.50
4 Paul Goldschmidt .60 1.50
5 Nelson Cruz .60 1.50
6 Roy Campanella .60 1.50
7 Jose Ramirez .50 1.25
8 Edwin Encarnacion .60 1.50
9 Bryce Harper 1.00 2.50
10 J.D. Martinez .60 1.50
11 Joey Gallo .50 1.25
12 Miguel Cabrera .60 1.50
13 Kyle Schwarber .60 1.50
14 Rhys Hoskins .75 2.00
15 Aaron Judge 1.50 4.00

2019 Panini Leather and Lumber Maple and Ash

RANDOM INSERTS IN PACKS
*GOLD/99: .75X TO 2X BASIC
*HOLO SILVER/25: 1.2X TO 3X BASIC
1 Charlie Blackmon .60 1.50
2 Gleyber Torres 1.25 3.00
3 Ryne Sandberg 1.25 3.00
4 Joe Jackson .75 2.00
5 Joe DiMaggio 1.25 3.00
6 Cal Ripken 2.00 5.00
7 Shohei Ohtani 1.00 2.50
8 Matt Chapman .60 1.50
9 Yogi Berra .60 1.50
10 Cody Bellinger 1.25 3.00

2019 Panini Leather and Lumber Naturals

RANDOM INSERTS IN PACKS
*GOLD/99: .75X TO 2X BASIC
*HOLO SILVER/25: 1.2X TO 3X BASIC
1 Rickey Henderson .60 1.50
2 Chipper Jones .60 1.50
3 Ken Griffey Jr. 1.25 3.00
4 Barry Larkin .50 1.25
5 Robinson Cano .50 1.25
6 Miguel Cabrera .60 1.50
7 Mike Trout 3.00 8.00
8 Mookie Betts 1.25 3.00
9 Joe Jackson .75 2.00
10 Babe Ruth 1.50 4.00
11 Ichiro .75 2.00
12 Vladimir Guerrero .50 1.25
13 Ronald Acuna Jr. 3.00 8.00
14 Joe DiMaggio 1.25 3.00
15 Juan Soto 2.00 5.00

2019 Panini Leather and Lumber Power Alley

RANDOM INSERTS IN PACKS
*GOLD/99: .75X TO 2X BASIC
*HOLO SILVER/25: 1.2X TO 3X BASIC
1 Andrew McCutchen .60 1.50
2 Alex Bregman .60 1.50
3 Christian Yelich .75 2.00
4 Whit Merrifield .60 1.50
5 Barry Larkin .50 1.25
6 Lorenzo Cain .40 1.00
7 Juan Soto 2.00 5.00
8 Kris Bryant .75 2.00
9 Javier Baez .75 2.00
10 Ken Boyer .40 1.00
11 Joe DiMaggio 1.25 3.00
12 Gleyber Torres 1.25 3.00
13 Mike Trout 3.00 8.00
14 Miguel Cabrera .60 1.50
15 Gil Hodges .50 1.25

2019 Panini Leather and Lumber Rivals Materials

RANDOM INSERTS IN PACKS
PRINT RUNS B/WN 15-199 COPIES PER
NO PRICING ON QTY 15
*GOLD/99: .4X TO 1X p/r 99-199
*GOLD/35-49: .5X TO 1.2X p/r 99-199
*GOLD/25: .5X TO 1.2X p/r 49-50
1 Rodriguez/Ortiz/199 5.00 12.00
2 Piazza/Clemens/149 5.00 12.00
3 Jose Bautista 3.00 8.00
Rougned Odor/199
4 Madison Bumgarner 4.00 10.00
Yasiel Puig/199
5 Judge/Betts/199 10.00 25.00
6 Smith/Yount/199 5.00 12.00
8 Aaron Nola 5.00 12.00
Max Scherzer/50
10 Campy/Berra/49 12.00 30.00
11 Pujols/Ichiro/49 6.00 15.00
12 Soto/Acuna/199 6.00 15.00
13 Cabrera/Clemens/199 5.00 12.00
14 Adrian Beltre 4.00 10.00
Felix Hernandez/99
15 Bryant/Molina/199 5.00 12.00

2019 Panini Leather and Lumber Rivals Materials Holo Silver

*SLVR/25: .6X TO 1.5X p/r 99-199
*SLVR/25: .5X TO 1.2X p/r 49-50
RANDOM INSERTS IN PACKS
PRINT RUNS B/WN 5-25 COPIES PER
NO PRICING ON QTY 10 OR LESS
7 Snell/Sale/25 6.00 15.00

2019 Panini Leather and Lumber Rookie Baseball Signatures Black

*BLACK p/r 75-149: .4X TO 1X BASIC
*BLACK p/r 25: .6X TO 1.5X BASIC
RANDOM INSERTS IN PACKS
PRINT RUNS BW/N 1-149 COPIES PER
NO PRICING ON QTY 4 OR LESS
EXCHANGE DEADLINE 11/29/2020

2019 Panini Leather and Lumber Rookie Baseball Signatures Black Gold

*BLCK GLD: .6X TO 1.5X BASIC
RANDOM INSERTS IN PACKS
STATED PRINT RUN 25 SER.#'d SETS
EXCHANGE DEADLINE 11/29/2020

2019 Panini Leather and Lumber Rookie Baseball Signatures Blue

*BLUE p/r 60-99: .4X TO 1X BASIC
*BLUE p/r 25: .6X TO 1.5X BASIC
RANDOM INSERTS IN PACKS
PRINT RUNS BW/N 4-99 COPIES PER
NO PRICING ON QTY 4
EXCHANGE DEADLINE 11/29/2020

2019 Panini Leather and Lumber Rookie Baseball Signatures Light Blue

*LT BLUE p/r 49-50: .5X TO 1.2X BASIC
*LT BLUE p/r 35: .6X TO 1.5X BASIC
RANDOM INSERTS IN PACKS
PRINT RUNS BW/N 35-50 COPIES PER
EXCHANGE DEADLINE 11/29/2020

2019 Panini Leather and Lumber Rookie Baseball Signatures Pink

*PINK p/r 75-99: .4X TO 1X BASIC
*PINK p/r 50: .5X TO 1.2X BASIC
*PINK p/r 25: .6X TO 1.5X BASIC
RANDOM INSERTS IN PACKS
PRINT RUNS BW/N 1-75 COPIES PER
NO PRICING ON QTY 1
EXCHANGE DEADLINE 11/29/2020

2019 Panini Leather and Lumber Rookie Leather Signatures

*LEATHER p/r 99-149: .4X TO 1X BASIC

RANDOM INSERTS IN PACKS
PRINT RUNS BW/N 99-149 COPIES PER
EXCHANGE DEADLINE 11/29/2020

2019 Panini Leather and Lumber Rookie Leather Signatures Black and Silver

*BLK SLVR: .6X TO 1.5X BASIC
RANDOM INSERTS IN PACKS
STATED PRINT RUN 25 SER.#'d SETS
EXCHANGE DEADLINE 11/29/2020

2019 Panini Leather and Lumber Rookie Leather Signatures Dark Brown

*DRK BRWN p/r 75-99: .4X TO 1X BASIC
*DRK BRWN p/r 49: .5X TO 1.2X BASIC
RANDOM INSERTS IN PACKS
PRINT RUNS BW/N 49-99 COPIES PER
EXCHANGE DEADLINE 11/29/2020

2019 Panini Leather and Lumber Rookie Lumber Signatures

*LUMBER p/r 99-149: .4X TO 1X BASIC
RANDOM INSERTS IN PACKS
PRINT RUNS BW/N 99-149 COPIES PER
EXCHANGE DEADLINE 11/29/2020

2019 Panini Leather and Lumber Rookie Lumber Signatures Blue

*BLUE p/r 75-99: .4X TO 1X BASIC
*BLUE p/r 49: .5X TO 1.2X BASIC
RANDOM INSERTS IN PACKS
PRINT RUNS BW/N 49-99 COPIES PER
EXCHANGE DEADLINE 11/29/2020

2019 Panini Leather and Lumber Rookie Lumber Signatures Holo Silver

*HOLO SLVR: .6X TO 1.5X BASIC
RANDOM INSERTS IN PACKS
STATED PRINT RUN 25 SER.#'d SETS
EXCHANGE DEADLINE 11/29/2020

2019 Panini Leather and Lumber Slugfest

RANDOM INSERTS IN PACKS
*GOLD/99: .75X TO 2X BASIC
*HOLO SILVER/25: 1.2X TO 3X BASIC
1 Jose Abreu .60 1.50
2 Adrian Beltre .60 1.50
3 Albert Pujols .75 2.00
4 Rhys Hoskins .75 2.00
5 Ronald Acuna Jr. 3.00 8.00
6 Jimmie Foxx .60 1.50
7 Bryce Harper 1.00 2.50
8 J.D. Martinez .60 1.50
9 Ken Boyer .40 1.00
10 Paul Goldschmidt .60 1.50
11 Giancarlo Stanton .60 1.50
12 Babe Ruth 1.50 4.00
13 Alex Rodriguez .75 2.00
14 Shohei Ohtani 1.00 2.50
15 Aaron Judge 1.50 4.00
16 Josh Donaldson .50 1.25
17 Kris Bryant .75 2.00
18 Frank Thomas .60 1.50
19 Roy Campanella .60 1.50
20 Khris Davis .60 1.50

2019 Panini Leather and Lumber Sweet Feet

RANDOM INSERTS IN PACKS
PRINT RUNS B/WN 50-194 COPIES PER
5 Corey Seager/50 5.00 12.00
6 Darryl Strawberry/99 4.00 10.00
10 Joc Pederson/194 3.00 8.00
15 Vladimir Guerrero/99 6.00 15.00

2019 Panini Leather and Lumber Sweet Feet Blue

*BLUE/49: .5X TO 1.2X p/r 99-194
RANDOM INSERTS IN PACKS
PRINT RUNS B/WN 15-99 COPIES PER
NO PRICING ON QTY 15
1 Myles Straw/23 6.00 15.00
2 Amed Rosario/30 4.00 10.00
3 Austin Hays/48 5.00 12.00
4 Victor Robles/25 8.00 20.00
7 Gleyber Torres/49 6.00 15.00
8 Ichiro/49 12.00 30.00
11 Manuel Margot/49 3.00 8.00
12 Mike Trout/25 40.00 100.00
13 Nick Williams/25 4.00 10.00
14 Shohei Ohtani/99 8.00 20.00
16 Paul Molitor/95 8.00 20.00
17 Juan Soto/25 10.00 25.00
19 Orlando Arcia/25 4.00 10.00
20 Javier Baez/25 8.00 20.00

2019 Panini Leather and Lumber Sweet Feet Gold

*GOLD/75-99: .4X TO 1X p/r 99-194
*GOLD/20: .6X TO 1.5X p/r 99
*GOLD/20: .5X TO 1.2X p/r 50
RANDOM INSERTS IN PACKS
PRINT RUNS B/WN 20-199 COPIES PER
2 Amed Rosario/50 4.00 10.00
7 Gleyber Torres/50 6.00 15.00
8 Ichiro/70 10.00 25.00
12 Mike Trout/49 30.00 80.00
13 Nick Williams/49 3.00 8.00
14 Shohei Ohtani/199 8.00 20.00
17 Juan Soto/42 8.00 20.00

2019 Panini Leather and Lumber Sweet Feet Holo Silver

*SLVR/25: .6X TO 1.5X p/r 99-194
RANDOM INSERTS IN PACKS
PRINT RUNS B/WN 10-25 COPIES PER
NO PRICING ON QTY 10
2 Amed Rosario/25 5.00 12.00
3 Austin Hays/25 6.00 15.00
7 Gleyber Torres/25 8.00 20.00
8 Ichiro/25 15.00 40.00
11 Manuel Margot/25 4.00 10.00
14 Shohei Ohtani/25 12.00 30.00
16 Paul Molitor/25 12.00 30.00
18 Ronald Acuna Jr./25 10.00 25.00

2019 Panini Leather and Lumber W.A.R. Daddys

RANDOM INSERTS IN PACKS
*GOLD/99: .75X TO 2X BASIC
*HOLO SILVER/25: 1.2X TO 3X BASIC
1 Jimmie Foxx .60 1.50
2 J.D. Martinez .60 1.50
3 Alex Rodriguez .75 2.00
4 Frank Robinson .50 1.25
5 Randy Johnson .60 1.50
6 Ken Griffey Jr. 1.25 3.00
7 Giancarlo Stanton .60 1.50
8 Babe Ruth 1.50 4.00
9 Clayton Kershaw 1.00 2.50
10 Nolan Ryan 2.00 5.00

2020 Panini Legacy

RANDOM INSERTS IN PACKS
1 Shogo Akiyama RC .40 1.00
2 Yordan Alvarez RC 2.50 6.00
3 Bo Bichette RC 3.00 8.00
4 Aristides Aquino RC .60 1.50
5 Gavin Lux RC 1.25 3.00
6 Yoshitomo Tsutsugo RC .60 1.50
7 Brendan McKay RC .40 1.00
8 Luis Robert RC 4.00 10.00
9 Adrian Morejon RC .25 .60
10 Michael King RC .40 1.00
11 Rafael Devers .30 .75
12 Justin Verlander .25 .60
13 Anthony Rendon .25 .60
14 Jose Ramirez .20 .50
15 Clayton Kershaw .40 1.00

2020 Panini Legacy Signatures

RANDOM INSERTS IN PACKS
PRINT RUNS B/WN 10-99 COPIES PER
NO PRICING QTY 15 OR LESS
EXCHANGE DEADLINE 3/18/2022
1 Shogo Akiyama/49 6.00 15.00
2 Yordan Alvarez/50 40.00 100.00
3 Bo Bichette/30 30.00 80.00
4 Aristides Aquino/60 8.00 20.00
6 Yoshitomo Tsutsugo/99 8.00 20.00
8 Luis Robert EXCH/99 75.00 200.00
9 Adrian Morejon/96 3.00 8.00
10 Michael King/99 5.00 12.00
14 Jose Ramirez/25 6.00 15.00

2020 Panini Luminance Autographs

RANDOM INSERTS IN PACKS
EXCHANGE DEADLINE 3/18/2022
*GOLD/75-99: .5X TO 1.2X BASIC
*GOLD/50: .6X TO 1.5X BASIC
*GOLD/25: .8X TO 2X BASIC
*RED/50: .6X TO 1.5X BASIC
*RED/25: .8X TO 2X BASIC
*BLUE/25: .8X TO 2X BASIC
1 Kyle Wright 4.00 10.00
2 Evan White 6.00 15.00
3 J.D. Davis 2.50 6.00
4 Myles Straw 3.00 8.00
5 Jeff McNeil 3.00 8.00
6 Stephen Piscotty 2.50 6.00
7 Daniel Robertson 2.50 6.00
8 Andrew Stevenson 2.50 6.00
9 Odubel Herrera 3.00 8.00
10 Jose Ramirez 6.00 15.00
11 Jonathan Davis 3.00 8.00
12 Luis Ortiz 2.50 6.00
13 Austin Voth 2.50 6.00
14 Josh Hader 3.00 8.00
15 Tyler Glasnow 4.00 10.00
16 Derek Fisher 2.50 6.00
17 Jake Cave 3.00 8.00
18 Yohander Mendez 2.50 6.00
19 Cesar Hernandez 2.50 6.00
20 Brian Anderson 2.50 6.00
21 Rio Ruiz 2.50 6.00
22 Josh James 2.50 6.00
23 Carlos Martinez 3.00 8.00
24 Michael Chavis 6.00 15.00
25 Connor Sadzeck 2.50 6.00

2020 Panini Magnitude

RANDOM INSERTS IN PACKS
1 Mike Trout 2.00 5.00
2 Aaron Judge .60 1.50
3 Shohei Ohtani .40 1.00
4 Cody Bellinger .50 1.25
5 Christian Yelich .30 .75
6 Juan Soto .75 2.00
7 Ronald Acuna Jr. 1.50 4.00
8 Vladimir Guerrero Jr. .40 1.00
9 Pete Alonso .60 1.50
10 Fernando Tatis Jr. 2.00 5.00
11 Yordan Alvarez RC 2.50 6.00
12 Gavin Lux RC 1.25 3.00
13 Luis Robert RC 4.00 10.00
14 Aristides Aquino RC .60 1.50
15 Bo Bichette RC 3.00 8.00
16 Brendan McKay RC .40 1.00
17 Dustin May RC .75 2.00
18 Kris Bryant .30 .75
19 Francisco Lindor .25 .60
20 Bryce Harper .40 1.00
21 Javier Baez .30 .75
22 Shogo Akiyama RC .40 1.00
23 Gerrit Cole .40 1.00
24 Mookie Betts .50 1.25
25 Yoshitomo Tsutsugo RC .60 1.50

2020 Panini Mosaic

RANDOM INSERTS IN PACKS
1 Josh Rojas RC .25 .60
2 Rico Garcia RC .40 1.00
3 Yordan Alvarez RC 2.50 6.00
4 Jesus Luzardo RC .50 1.25
5 Jake Rogers RC .25 .60
6 Sean Murphy RC .40 1.00
7 Ronald Bolanos RC .25 .60
8 Yu Chang RC .40 1.00
9 Anthony Kay RC .25 .60
10 Andres Munoz RC .40 1.00
11 Domingo Leyba RC .30 .75
12 Michael King RC .40 1.00
13 Gavin Lux RC 1.25 3.00
14 Bo Bichette RC 3.00 8.00
15 Brendan McKay RC .40 1.00
16 Logan Allen RC .25 .60
17 Nico Hoerner RC 1.00 2.50
18 Mauricio Dubon RC .30 .75
19 Joe Palumbo RC .25 .60
20 Deivy Grullon RC .25 .60
21 Aaron Civale RC .50 1.25
22 Tony Gonsolin RC 1.00 2.50
23 Logan Webb RC .40 1.00
24 Danny Mendick RC .30 .75
25 Brock Burke RC .25 .60
26 Sheldon Neuse RC .30 .75
27 Tres Barrera RC .50 1.25
28 Randy Arozarena RC 2.00 5.00
29 Adbert Alzolay RC .30 .75
30 Sam Hilliard RC .40 1.00
31 Zac Gallen RC .60 1.50
32 Matt Thaiss RC .30 .75
33 Tyrone Taylor RC .25 .60
34 Patrick Sandoval RC .40 1.00
35 Willi Castro RC .40 1.00
36 Lewis Thorpe RC .25 .60
37 Dylan Cease RC .40 1.00
38 Jaylin Davis RC .40 1.00
39 Bryan Abreu RC .25 .60
40 Aristides Aquino RC .60 1.50
41 Abraham Toro RC .30 .75
42 Edwin Rios RC .60 1.50
43 Jonathan Hernandez RC .25 .60
44 Michel Baez RC .25 .60
45 Nick Solak RC 1.00 2.50
46 Dustin May RC .75 2.00
47 Donnie Walton RC .60 1.50
48 Jake Fraley RC .30 .75
49 Kyle Lewis RC 8.00 20.00
50 Bobby Bradley RC .25 .60
51 Justin Dunn RC .30 .75
52 Adrian Morejon RC .25 .60
53 Travis Demeritte RC .40 1.00
54 A.J. Puk RC .40 1.00
55 Trent Grisham RC 1.00 2.50
56 Brusdar Graterol RC .40 1.00
57 Zack Collins RC .30 .75
58 Jordan Yamamoto RC .25 .60
59 Isan Diaz RC .40 1.00
60 T.J. Zeuch RC .25 .60
61 Yonathan Daza RC .30 .75
62 Shun Yamaguchi RC .30 .75
63 Kwang-Hyun Kim RC .50 1.25
64 Shogo Akiyama RC .40 1.00
65 Yoshitomo Tsutsugo RC .60 1.50
66 Luis Robert RC 8.00 20.00
67 Trey Mancini .25 .60
68 Rafael Devers .30 .75
69 J.D. Martinez .25 .60
70 Aaron Judge .60 1.50
71 Gleyber Torres .50 1.25
72 Vladimir Guerrero Jr. .40 1.00
73 Josh Bell .20 .50
74 Blake Snell .20 .50
75 Eloy Jimenez .50 1.25
76 Jose Ramirez .20 .50
77 Francisco Lindor .25 .60
78 Miguel Cabrera .25 .60
79 Whit Merrifield .25 .60
80 Nelson Cruz .25 .60
81 Nolan Arenado .40 1.00
82 Mike Trout 2.00 5.00
83 Shohei Ohtani .40 1.00
84 Cody Bellinger .50 1.25
85 Manny Machado .25 .60
86 Alex Bregman .25 .60
87 Jose Altuve .20 .50
88 Gerrit Cole .40 1.00
89 Ronald Acuna Jr. 1.50 4.00
90 Ozzie Albies .25 .60
91 Juan Soto .75 2.00
92 Max Scherzer .25 .60
93 Fernando Tatis Jr. 2.00 5.00
94 Pete Alonso .60 1.50
95 Bryce Harper .40 1.00
96 Javier Baez .30 .75
97 Christian Yelich .30 .75
98 Keston Hiura .30 .75
99 Paul Goldschmidt .25 .60
100 Joey Votto .25 .60

2020 Panini Mosaic Blue

*BLUE VET: 2X TO 5X BASIC
*BLUE RC: 1.2X TO 3X BASIC RC
RANDOM INSERTS IN PACKS
STATED PRINT RUN 99 SER.#'d SETS
3 Yordan Alvarez 15.00 40.00
14 Bo Bichette 40.00 100.00
28 Randy Arozarena 30.00 80.00
49 Kyle Lewis 25.00 60.00
63 Kwang-Hyun Kim 12.00 30.00
66 Luis Robert 40.00 100.00
70 Aaron Judge 10.00 25.00
71 Gleyber Torres 6.00 15.00
82 Mike Trout 25.00 60.00
84 Cody Bellinger 10.00 25.00
89 Ronald Acuna Jr. 15.00 40.00
93 Fernando Tatis Jr. 20.00 50.00

2020 Panini Mosaic Mosaic

*MOSAIC VET: 1X TO 2.5X BASIC
*MOSAIC RC: .6X TO 1.5X BASIC RC
RANDOM INSERTS IN PACKS
3 Yordan Alvarez 10.00 25.00
14 Bo Bichette 10.00 25.00
28 Randy Arozarena 15.00 40.00
66 Luis Robert 15.00 40.00
82 Mike Trout 12.00 30.00
89 Ronald Acuna Jr. 8.00 20.00
93 Fernando Tatis Jr. 10.00 25.00

2020 Panini Mosaic Purple

*PURPLE VET: 2.5X TO 6X BASIC
*PURPLE RC: 1.5X TO 4X BASIC RC
RANDOM INSERTS IN PACKS
STATED PRINT RUN 49 SER.#'d SETS
3 Yordan Alvarez 20.00 50.00
14 Bo Bichette 50.00 120.00
17 Nico Hoerner 15.00 40.00
28 Randy Arozarena 40.00 100.00
49 Kyle Lewis 30.00 80.00
63 Kwang-Hyun Kim 15.00 40.00
66 Luis Robert 50.00 120.00
70 Aaron Judge 12.00 30.00
71 Gleyber Torres 8.00 20.00
82 Mike Trout 40.00 100.00
84 Cody Bellinger 12.00 30.00
89 Ronald Acuna Jr. 20.00 50.00
93 Fernando Tatis Jr. 25.00 60.00

2020 Panini Mosaic Silver

3 Yordan Alvarez 10.00 25.00
14 Bo Bichette 10.00 25.00
28 Randy Arozarena 15.00 40.00
66 Luis Robert 15.00 40.00
82 Mike Trout 12.00 30.00
89 Ronald Acuna Jr. 8.00 20.00
93 Fernando Tatis Jr. 10.00 25.00

2020 Panini Mosaic White

*WHITE VET: 10X TO 25X BASIC
*WHITE RC: 6X TO 15X BASIC RC
RANDOM INSERTS IN PACKS
STATED PRINT RUN 25 SER.#'d SETS
3 Yordan Alvarez 30.00 80.00
13 Gavin Lux 25.00 60.00
14 Bo Bichette 150.00 400.00
17 Nico Hoerner 30.00 80.00
28 Randy Arozarena 125.00 300.00
49 Kyle Lewis 40.00 100.00
55 Trent Grisham 20.00 50.00
63 Kwang-Hyun Kim 30.00 80.00
66 Luis Robert 125.00 300.00
70 Aaron Judge 25.00 60.00
71 Gleyber Torres 15.00 40.00
82 Mike Trout 200.00 500.00
84 Cody Bellinger 25.00 60.00
89 Ronald Acuna Jr. 50.00 120.00
91 Juan Soto 125.00 300.00
93 Fernando Tatis Jr. 50.00 120.00

2012 Panini National Convention

1-20 CRACKED ICE/25: 5X TO 12X BASE HI
21-40 CRACKED ICE/25: 1.5X TO 4X BASE HI
*HOLO 1-20: 1X TO 2.5X BASIC CARDS
*HOLO 21-40: .6X TO 1.5X BASIC CARDS
*1-20 HOLO LAVA: 2X TO 5X BASE HI
*21-40 HOLO LAVA: 1X TO 2.5X BASE HI
UNPRICED PLATE ANNCD PRINT RUN 5 SETS
13 Josh Hamilton .40 1.00
14 Derek Jeter .75 2.00
15 Albert Pujols .60 1.50
18 Ken Griffey Jr. .60 1.50
31 Yu Darvish/499 3.00 8.00
32 Bryce Harper/499 4.00 10.00
33 Yoenis Cespedes/499 2.00 5.00
34 Dylan Bundy/499 2.50 6.00

2012 Panini National Convention Diamond Kings

BK1 Yu Darvish 1.50 4.00
BK2 Bryce Harper 10.00 25.00

2012 Panini National Convention Diamond Kings Holofoil

BK1 Yu Darvish 2.50 6.00
BK2 Bryce Harper 3.00 8.00

2012 Panini National Convention Team Colors Baltimore

CRACKED ICE/25: 4X TO 10X BASE HI
1 Cal Ripken Jr. 2.50 6.00
2 Dylan Bundy 1.25 3.00
3 Adam Jones .40 1.00

2012 Panini National Convention Team Colors Washington

CRACKED ICE/25: 4X TO 10X BASE HI
1 Stephen Strasburg 1.00 2.50

2013 Panini National Convention

1-24 CRACKED ICE/25: 4X TO 10X BASIC CARDS
25-47 CRACKED ICE/25: 2X TO 5X BASIC CARDS
*1-24 LAVA FLOW/99: 2.5X TO 6X BASIC CARDS
*25-47 LAVA FLOW/99: 1.2X TO 3X BASIC CARDS
1 Mike Trout
2 Bryce Harper
3 Felix Hernandez
4 Clayton Kershaw
5 Matt Harvey
6 Stephen Strasburg
38 Byron Buxton
40 Manny Machado
41 Evan Gattis
42 Yasiel Puig 12.50 30.00
43 Oscar Taveras
44 Shelby Miller

2013 Panini National Convention Kings

CRACKED ICE/25: 2.5X TO 6X BASIC CARDS
*LAVA FLOW: 1.5X TO 4X BASIC CARDS
1 Ken Griffey Jr.
2 Carlton Fisk
3 Courtney Hawkins
4 Chris Sale
5 Ernie Banks
6 Javier Baez
7 Starlin Castro
R1 Jurickson Profar
R2 Mike Zunino

2013 Panini National Convention VIP

COMPLETE SET (6) 3.00 8.00
3 Oscar Taveras

2014 Panini National Convention

*1-21 CRACKED ICE VETS/25: 4X TO 10X
*22-50 CRACKED ICE ROOKIE/25: 2X TO 5X
*THICK STOCK: .6X TO 1.5X BASIC CARDS
1 Mike Trout BB 1.00 2.50
2 Derek Jeter BB .75 2.00
3 Yasiel Puig BB .75 2.00
4 Paul Goldschmidt BB .40 1.00
5 Clayton Kershaw BB .40 1.00
6 Troy Tulowitzki BB .40 1.00
7 David Wright BB .40 1.00
22 Masahiro Tanaka BB 1.00 2.50
23 Jose Abreu BB 1.00 2.50
24 Yangervis Solarte BB .75 2.00
25 Xander Bogaerts BB .75 2.00
26 George Springer BB 1.00 2.50
27 Michael Choice BB .60 1.50
28 Taijuan Walker BB .60 1.50
29 Yordano Ventura BB .75 2.00
30 Gregory Polanco BB .60 1.50
32 Jon Singleton BB .60 1.50
KB Kris Bryant BB 1.00 2.50

2014 Panini National Convention City of Cleveland

*THICK STOCK: .6X TO 1.5X BASIC CARDS
*CRACKED ICE/25: 3X TO 8X BASIC CARDS
5 Michael Brantley BB
6 Lonnie Chisenhall BB
7 Justin Masterson BB

2014 Panini National Convention Legends

*CRACKED ICE/25: 5X TO 12X BASIC CARDS
*THICK STOCK: .6X TO 1.5X BASIC CARDS
1 Nolan Ryan BB
2 Cal Ripken Jr. BB
3 Don Mattingly BB

2014 Panini National Convention VIP

PRIZM BLUE VETS/25: 2.5X TO 6X BASIC CARDS
PRIZM BLUE ROOKIES/25: 1.2X TO 3X
1 Derek Jeter BB
2 Bryce Harper BB
3 Mike Trout BB
4 Yasiel Puig BB
5 Nolan Ryan BB
6 Don Mattingly BB
7 Cal Ripken BB
8 Ken Griffey Jr. BB
9 Ichiro Suzuki BB
10 Miguel Cabrera BB
11 Jose Abreu BB
12 Masahiro Tanaka BB
13 Xander Bogaerts BB
16 Taijuan Walker BB
17 Yordano Ventura BB
18 Billy Hamilton BB
19 Nick Castellanos BB
20 Oscar Taveres BB

2014 Panini National Convention VIP Cracked Ice Patch

4 Yasiel Puig BB/10
7 Cal Ripken BB/10
8 Ken Griffey Jr. BB/10
9 Ichiro Suzuki BB/10
13 Xander Bogaerts BB/10
16 Taijuan Walker BB/25
17 Yordano Ventura BB/25
18 Billy Hamilton BB/25
19 Nick Castellanos BB/10

2014 Panini National Convention VIP Party

BP1 Javier Baez 3.00 8.00
BP2 Jonathan Gray 1.00 2.50

2014 Panini National Convention VIP Rookies

COMPLETE SET (6) 6.00 15.00
3 Jose Abreu BB 1.50 4.00
4 Masahiro Tanaka BB 2.50 6.00

2014 Panini National Convention

1 Evan Longoria .30 .75
2 Yadier Molina .50 1.25
3 Ryan Braun .30 .75
4 Adrian Beltre .40 1.00
5 Josh Donaldson .30 .75
6 Gregory Polanco .40 1.00
7 Oscar Taveras .30 .75
8 Masahiro Tanaka .75 2.00
9 Jose Abreu 2.00 5.00

2015 Panini National Convention

1 Mike Trout
2 Clayton Kershaw
3A Matt Harvey
3B Matt Harvey
College photo
4 Jose Abreu
5 Bryce Harper
6A Paul Goldschmidt
6B Paul Goldschmidt
College photo
29 Carlos Correa
30 Eduardo Rodriguez
31 Francisco Lindor
41 Joey Gallo
42 Daniel Norris
43 Joc Pederson
44 Dalton Pompey
45 Devon Travis
46 Noah Syndergaard
47 Carlos Rodon
48 Mike Foltynewicz
49 Blake Swihart
50 Chi Chi Gonzalez
66 Jorge Soler JSY/99 BB
67 Rusney Castillo JSY/99 BB
68 Addison Russell JSY/99 BB
69A Kris Bryant JSY/99 BB
69B Kris Bryant
College photo
70 Yasmany Tomas JSY/99 BB
71 Javier Baez JSY/99 BB
72 Maikel Franco JSY/99 BB
73 Brandon Finnegan JSY/99 BB
74 Michael Taylor JSY/99 BB
75 Archie Bradley JSY/99 BB

2015 Panini National Convention College Legends

*CRACKED ICE/25: 5X TO 12X BASIC CARDS
*THICK STOCK: .6X TO 1.5X BASIC CARDS
1 Buster Posey
2 Trevor Bauer
3 David Price
4 Alex Gordon
5 Tim Lincecum
6 Kris Bryant

2015 Panini National Convention Rookie Jerseys

*CRACKED ICE/25: .6X TO 1.5X BASIC JSY
1BB Kris Bryant
2BB Addison Russell
3BB Yasmany Tomas

2015 Panini National Convention Tools of the Trade Jerseys

*CRACKED ICE/25: 1X TO 2.5X BASIC JSY
1 Bryce Harper
2 Giancarlo Stanton
3 Alex Rodriguez 4.00 10.00
4 Paul Goldschmidt
5 Felix Hernandez
6 Buster Posey

2015 Panini National Convention VIP

COMPLETE SET (6) 3.00 8.00
*CRACKED ICE/25: 5X TO 12X BASIC CARDS
1 Kris Bryant BB 1.25 3.00
2 Joc Pederson BB

2019 Panini National Convention

*FUR/99: .6X TO 1.5X BASIC CARDS
*SPOKES/50: .8X TO 2X BASIC CARDS
*EXPLOSION/40: .8X TO 2X BASIC CARDS
*SQUARES/25: 1X TO 2.5X BASIC CARDS

2019 Panini National Convention College

*FUR/99: .6X TO 1.5X BASIC CARDS
*SPOKES/50: .8X TO 2X BASIC CARDS
*EXPLOSION/40: .8X TO 2X BASIC CARDS
*SQUARES/25: 1X TO 2.5X BASIC CARDS

2019 Panini National Convention Legends

*FUR/99: .6X TO 1.5X BASIC CARDS
*SPOKES/50: .8X TO 2X BASIC CARDS
*EXPLOSION/40: .8X TO 2X BASIC CARDS
*SQUARES/25: 1X TO 2.5X BASIC CARDS
CR Cal Ripken .75 2.00
DM Don Mattingly .75 2.00
GB George Brett .75 2.00
MR Mariano Rivera .75 2.00
NR Nolan Ryan .75 2.00
NR Nolan Ryan .75 2.00

2019 Panini National Convention Massive Materials

AJ Aaron Judge 6.00 15.00
EJ Eloy Jimenez 6.00 15.00
FT Fernando Tatis Jr. 6.00 15.00
GT Gleyber Torres 6.00 15.00
MA Miguel Andujar 6.00 15.00
NS Nick Senzel 6.00 15.00
RA Ronald Acuna Jr. 6.00 15.00
RH Rhys Hoskins 6.00 15.00
SO Shohei Ohtani 6.00 15.00
VG Vladimir Guerrero Jr. 6.00 15.00

2019 Panini National Convention Memorabilia

*CRACKED: .6X TO 1.5X BASIC JSY
*RAPTURE/50: .8X TO 2X BASIC JSY
*SPOKES/25: 1X TO 2.5X BASIC JSY

2019 Panini National Convention Prospects

*FUR/99: .6X TO 1.5X BASIC CARDS
*SPOKES/50: .8X TO 2X BASIC CARDS
*EXPLOSION/40: .8X TO 2X BASIC CARDS
*SQUARES/25: 1X TO 2.5X BASIC CARDS

2012 Panini National Treasures

1-150 PRINT RUNS B/WN 1-99 COPIES PER
NO PRICING ON QTY 25 OR LESS
151-225 PRINT RUN 99 SER.#'d SETS
PRICING LISTED IS FOR ONE-COLOR JSYS
EXCHANGE DEADLINE 8/27/2014
1 Ty Cobb/99 30.00 60.00
4 Nap Lajoie/99 15.00 40.00
5 Eddie Collins/99 15.00 40.00
10 Charlie Gehringer/99 10.00 25.00
12 Mei Ott/99 10.00 25.00
13 Paul Waner/49 8.00 20.00
14 Harry Heilmann/99 12.50 30.00
16 Bill Dickey/49 10.00 25.00
17 Joe DiMaggio/49 30.00 60.00
18 Bill Terry/99 8.00 20.00
19 Joe Cronin/99 8.00 20.00
20 Hank Greenberg/99 12.50 30.00
21 Bob Feller/99 8.00 20.00
22 Jackie Robinson/99 20.00 50.00
23 Luke Appling/99 12.50 30.00
25 Miller Huggins/99 10.00 25.00
26 Ted Williams/99 12.50 30.00
27 Billy Martin/99 10.00 25.00
28 Lloyd Waner/49 12.50 30.00
29 Joe Medwick/99 10.00 25.00
30 Roy Campanella/99 12.50 30.00
32 Dave Bancroft/99 15.00 40.00
35 Yogi Berra/25 10.00 25.00
36 Roberto Clemente/49 20.00 50.00
37 Heinie Groh/99 5.00 12.00
39 George Kelly/99 8.00 20.00
40 Jim Bottomley/99 8.00 20.00
43 Billy Herman/99 4.00 10.00
44 Ralph Kiner/99 5.00 12.00
45 Tris Speaker/99 12.50 30.00
48 Hack Wilson/49 20.00 50.00
49 Chuck Klein/99 6.00 15.00
50 Al Kaline/99 5.00 12.00
52 Carl Furillo/99 5.00 12.00
54 Frank Robinson/99 8.00 20.00
55 Walter Alston/99 5.00 12.00
56 Juan Marichal/99 4.00 10.00
57 Brooks Robinson/99 5.00 12.00
58 Luis Aparicio/49 6.00 15.00
59 Don Drysdale/99 6.00 15.00
61 Pee Wee Reese/99 12.50 30.00
64 Willie Keeler/99 12.00 30.00
65 Hoyt Wilhelm/49 6.00 15.00
67 Willie McCovey/99 5.00 12.00
68 Catfish Hunter/99 5.00 12.00
75 Jim Palmer/49 4.00 10.00
76 Rod Carew/99 4.00 10.00
80 Hal Newhouser/49 10.00 25.00
81 Tom Seaver/99 4.00 10.00
82 Reggie Jackson/99 5.00 12.00
83 Steve Carlton/99 3.00 8.00
84 Leo Durocher/99 8.00 20.00
87 Mike Schmidt/99 6.00 15.00
90 Tommy Lasorda/99 4.00 10.00
92 Don Sutton/99 4.00 10.00
94 Orlando Cepeda/25 8.00 20.00
96 Robin Yount/25 10.00 25.00
98 Carlton Fisk/99 3.00 8.00
100 Adrian Beltre/99 3.00 8.00
101 Andrew McCutchen/99 5.00 12.00
102 Ozzie Smith/99 5.00 12.00
103 Gary Carter/99 4.00 10.00
104 Eddie Murray/49 6.00 15.00
105 Dennis Eckersley/99 3.00 8.00
107 Al Simmons/99 10.00 25.00
109 Tony Gwynn/99 4.00 10.00
110 Cal Ripken Jr./99 10.00 25.00
111 Goose Gossage/99 3.00 8.00
113 Rickey Henderson/99 8.00 20.00
114 Jim Rice/49 6.00 15.00
115 Andre Dawson/99 4.00 10.00
116 Roberto Alomar/99 3.00 8.00
117 Bert Blyleven/49 5.00 12.00
118 Barry Larkin/49 10.00 25.00
120 Albert Pujols/99 4.00 10.00
122 Buster Posey/99 8.00 20.00
123 Robinson Cano/99 8.00 20.00
124 Dale Murphy/99 3.00 8.00
125 Derek Jeter/99 8.00 20.00
126 Eddie Stanky/99 6.00 15.00
128 Frank Howard/99 5.00 12.00
129 Harvey Kuenn/99 5.00 12.00
130 Ryan Braun/99 5.00 12.00
132 Ivan Rodriguez/99 5.00 12.00
133 Jake Daubert/99 10.00 25.00
135 Joe Jackson/49 40.00 80.00
137 Josh Hamilton/99 3.00 8.00
138 Justin Verlander/99 5.00 12.00
139 Ken Griffey Jr./99 10.00 25.00
140 Lefty Williams/99 10.00 25.00
141 Mariano Rivera/99 10.00 25.00
142 Matt Kemp/99 3.00 8.00
143 Miguel Cabrera/99 5.00 12.00
144 Pete Reiser/99 10.00 25.00
146 Randy Johnson/99 4.00 10.00
147 Goose Goslin/99 15.00 40.00
148 Ted Kluszewski/99 10.00 25.00
149 Tommy Henrich/99 5.00 12.00
150 Willie Kamm/99 8.00 20.00
151 A.J. Pollock AU RC 6.00 15.00
152 Addison Reed AU RC 8.00 20.00
153 Adeiny Hechavarria AU RC 5.00 12.00
154 Andrelton Simmons AU RC 12.00 30.00
155 Anthony Gose Jsy AU RC 6.00 15.00
156 Austin Romine Jsy AU RC 6.00 15.00
157 Brad Peacock Jsy AU RC 5.00 12.00
158 Brett Jackson Jsy AU RC 6.00 15.00
159 Brett Lawrie Jsy AU RC 6.00 15.00
160 Bryce Harper Jsy RC 25.00 60.00
161 Casey Crosby Jsy AU RC 5.00 12.00
162 Chris Archer AU RC 5.00 12.00
163 Chris Marrero Jsy AU RC 5.00 12.00
164 Chris Parmelee AU RC 4.00 10.00
165 Dan Straily AU RC 6.00 15.00
166 David Phelps Jsy AU RC 10.00 25.00
167 Dellin Betances Jsy AU RC 5.00 12.00
168 Derek Norris AU RC 4.00 10.00
169 Devin Mesoraco Jsy AU RC 6.00 15.00
170 Drew Hutchison AU RC 4.00 10.00
171 Drew Pomeranz AU RC 5.00 12.00
172 Drew Smyly Jsy AU RC 8.00 20.00
173 Eric Surkamp Jsy AU RC 6.00 15.00
174 Freddy Galvis AU RC 6.00 15.00
175 Garrett Richards Jsy AU RC 10.00 25.00
176 Hector Sanchez Jsy AU RC 8.00 20.00
177 Jarrod Parker Jsy AU RC 6.00 15.00
178 Jean Segura Jsy AU RC 6.00 15.00
179 Jeff Locke AU RC 10.00 25.00
180 Jemile Weeks Jsy AU RC 4.00 10.00
181 Jesus Montero Jsy AU RC 8.00 20.00
182 Joe Benson AU RC 4.00 10.00
183 Joe Wieland AU RC 4.00 10.00
184 Jordan Lyles Jsy AU 6.00 15.00
185 Valdespin Jsy AU EXCH RC 6.00 15.00
186 Josh Rutledge AU RC 4.00 10.00
187 Josh Vitters Jsy AU RC 10.00 25.00
188 Justin De Fratus AU RC 5.00 12.00
189 Kelvin Herrera Jsy AU RC 6.00 15.00
190 Kirk Nieuwenhuis Jsy AU RC 6.00 15.00
191 Leonys Martin Jsy AU RC 6.00 15.00
192 Liam Hendriks Jsy AU RC 10.00 25.00
193 Lucas Luetge AU RC 4.00 10.00
194 Martin Perez Jsy AU RC 5.00 12.00
195 Matt Adams AU RC 5.00 12.00
196 Matt Dominguez AU RC 5.00 12.00
197 Matt Harvey Jsy AU RC 10.00 25.00
198 Matt Moore Jsy AU RC 10.00 25.00
199 Mike Trout Jsy AU 1500.00 3000.00
200 Nick Hagadone AU RC 4.00 10.00
201 Pat Corbin AU RC 15.00 40.00
202 Rafael Dolis AU RC 4.00 10.00
203 Robbie Ross Jsy AU RC 8.00 20.00
204 Ryan Cook Jsy AU RC 5.00 12.00
205 Scott Barnes AU RC 4.00 10.00
206 Starling Marte Jsy AU RC 12.50 30.00
207 Steve Lombardozzi AU RC 5.00 12.00
208 Taylor Green Jsy AU RC 5.00 12.00
209 Feder Jsy AU RC 6.00 15.00
210 Milone Jsy AU RC 6.00 15.00
211 Trevor Bauer AU RC 25.00 60.00
212 T.Rosenthal Jsy AU EXCH RC 40.00 80.00
213 Tyler Moore Jsy AU RC 10.00 25.00
214 Tyler Pastornicky Jsy AU RC 5.00 12.00
215 Tyler Thornburg Jsy AU RC 8.00 20.00
216 Wade Miley Jsy RC 4.00 10.00
217 Wei-Yin Chen Jsy AU RC 100.00 200.00
218 Wellington Castillo Jsy AU 5.00 12.00
219 Wilin Rosario Jsy AU RC 10.00 25.00
220 Will Middlebrooks Jsy AU RC 15.00 40.00
221 Xavier Avery Jsy AU RC 5.00 12.00
222 Yasmani Grandal Jsy AU RC 10.00 25.00
223 Yoenis Cespedes AU RC 25.00 60.00
224 Yu Darvish Jsy RC 12.00 30.00
225 Zach McAllister AU RC 4.00 10.00

2012 Panini National Treasures All Decade Combo Materials

PRINT RUNS B/WN 1-99 COPIES PER
NO PRICING ON QTY 25 OR LESS
EXCHANGE DEADLINE 8/27/2014
10 Jackie Robinson 30.00 60.00
Duke Snider/99

2012 Panini National Treasures All Decade Materials
PRINT RUNS B/WN 5-99 COPIES PER
NO PRICING ON QTY 25 OR LESS
EXCHANGE DEADLINE 8/27/2014
1 Nap Lajoie/99 15.00 40.00
2 Honus Wagner/25 60.00 120.00
3 Ty Cobb/99 30.00 60.00
4 Jake Daubert/99 10.00 25.00
6 Joe Jackson/49 60.00 120.00
8 Dave Bancroft/99 15.00 40.00
9 Jim Bottomley/49 10.00 25.00
12 Harry Heilmann/99 10.00 25.00
13 Miller Huggins/99 15.00 40.00
14 George Kelly/99 8.00 20.00
15 Willie Kamm/99 8.00 20.00
16 Hack Wilson/99 15.00 40.00
17 Bill Terry/99 8.00 20.00
18 Lou Gehrig/30 75.00 150.00
23 Joe Cronin/99 6.00 15.00
25 Joe DiMaggio/49 50.00 100.00
27 Paul Waner/99 6.00 15.00
32 Chuck Klein/99 6.00 15.00
33 Hank Greenberg/99 12.50 30.00
34 Al Simmons/99 10.00 25.00
35 Goose Goslin/99 8.00 20.00
36 Lloyd Waner/99 8.00 20.00
37 Willie Keeler/99 12.50 30.00
38 Tris Speaker/99 12.50 30.00
39 Pee Wee Reese/99 12.50 30.00
40 Jackie Robinson/99 20.00 50.00

2012 Panini National Treasures All Decade Signatures
PRINT RUNS B/WN 10-60 COPIES PER
NO PRICING ON QTY 25 OR LESS
EXCHANGE DEADLINE 8/27/2014
1 George Kell/40 10.00 25.00
2 Maury Wills/60 10.00 25.00

2012 Panini National Treasures Greatness Materials
PRINT RUNS B/WN 5-99 COPIES PER
NO PRICING ON QTY 25 OR LESS
EXCHANGE DEADLINE 8/27/2014
1 Ty Cobb/99 20.00 50.00
3 Lou Gehrig/99 50.00 100.00
4 Ted Williams/99 12.50 30.00
6 Stan Musial/99 10.00 25.00
7 Joe DiMaggio/99 40.00 80.00
11 Roberto Clemente/99 20.00 50.00
17 Mike Schmidt/49 8.00 20.00
18 Nap Lajoie/99 12.50 30.00
19 Al Simmons/99 10.00 25.00
21 Joe Jackson/49 60.00 120.00
22 Bob Feller/99 8.00 20.00
23 Hank Greenberg/99 12.50 30.00
26 Nolan Ryan/99 10.00 25.00
28 Jackie Robinson/99 12.50 30.00
30 Reggie Jackson/99 10.00 25.00
32 Harry Heilmann/99 8.00 20.00
34 Bill Terry/99 8.00 20.00
35 Paul Waner/99 6.00 15.00
39 Willie Keeler/99 15.00 40.00
40 Tris Speaker/99 15.00 40.00

2012 Panini National Treasures Immortal Cut Signatures
PRINT RUNS B/WN 5-99 COPIES PER
NO PRICING ON QTY 25 OR LESS
EXCHANGE DEADLINE 8/27/2014
4 Bobby Thomson/99 12.00 30.00
5 Harmon Killebrew/99 15.00 40.00
6 Ralph Kiner/99 8.00 20.00
7 Joe Sewell/99 8.00 20.00

2012 Panini National Treasures Jumbo Materials
PRINT RUNS B/WN 49-99 COPIES PER
NO PRICING ON QTY 25 OR LESS
EXCHANGE DEADLINE 8/27/2014
1 Albert Pujols/99 10.00 25.00
2 Alex Rodriguez/99 12.50 30.00
3 Curtis Granderson/99 6.00 15.00
4 Derek Jeter/99 25.00 60.00
5 Evan Longoria/99 6.00 15.00
6 Hunter Pence/99 10.00 25.00
7 Matt Kemp/99 10.00 25.00
8 Jacoby Ellsbury/99 8.00 20.00
9 Jimmy Rollins/99 5.00 12.00
10 Joe Mauer/99 8.00 20.00
11 Joey Votto/99 12.50 30.00
12 Justin Verlander/99 12.50 30.00
13 Lance Berkman/99 10.00 25.00
14 Mark Teixeira/99 6.00 15.00
15 Matt Wieters/99 5.00 12.00
16 Michael Bourn/99 5.00 12.00
17 Michael Young/99 8.00 20.00
18 Paul Konerko/99 8.00 20.00
19 Prince Fielder/99 12.50 30.00
20 Robinson Cano/99 8.00 20.00
21 Roy Halladay/99 10.00 25.00
22 Ryan Howard/99 5.00 12.00
23 Tim Lincecum/99 10.00 25.00
24 Troy Tulowitzki/99 10.00 25.00
25 Yu Darvish/49 15.00 40.00

2012 Panini National Treasures Jumbo Materials Nickname
PRINT RUNS B/WN 5-99 COPIES PER
NO PRICING ON QTY 25 OR LESS
EXCHANGE DEADLINE 8/27/2014
1 Albert Pujols/99 10.00 25.00
2 Alex Rodriguez/99 10.00 25.00
4 Derek Jeter/99 25.00 60.00
5 Evan Longoria/99 6.00 15.00
8 Jacoby Ellsbury/99 8.00 20.00
9 Jimmy Rollins/99 5.00 12.00
11 Joey Votto/99 12.50 30.00
13 Lance Berkman/99 5.00 12.00
14 Mark Teixeira/99 6.00 15.00
18 Paul Konerko/99 8.00 20.00
19 Prince Fielder/99 10.00 25.00
22 Ryan Howard/99 6.00 15.00
23 Tim Lincecum/99 10.00 25.00

2012 Panini National Treasures Jumbo Signature Materials Die-Cut Player
PRINT RUNS B/WN 5-49 COPIES PER
NO PRICING ON QTY 25 OR LESS
EXCHANGE DEADLINE 8/27/2014
1 Adam Jones/49 12.50 30.00
2 Adrian Beltre/49 12.50 30.00
3 Adrian Gonzalez/49 10.00 25.00
5 Austin Jackson/49 10.00 25.00
9 Dale Murphy/49 10.00 25.00
10 David Wright/49 20.00 50.00
11 Felix Hernandez/49 30.00 60.00
12 Jose Bautista/49 6.00 15.00
13 Josh Hamilton/49 20.00 50.00
14 Justin Upton/49 8.00 20.00

2012 Panini National Treasures League Leaders Materials
PRINT RUNS B/WN 10-99 COPIES PER
NO PRICING ON QTY 25 OR LESS
EXCHANGE DEADLINE 8/27/2014
1 Nap Lajoie/99 20.00 50.00
2 Ty Cobb/99 30.00 60.00
4 Joe Jackson/49 60.00 120.00
7 George Kelly/99 8.00 20.00
8 Jim Bottomley/49 10.00 25.00
9 Harry Heilmann/99 8.00 20.00
10 Paul Waner/99 6.00 15.00
11 Lou Gehrig/99 50.00 100.00
12 Lloyd Waner/99 10.00 25.00
13 Hack Wilson/99 15.00 40.00
14 Chuck Klein/99 6.00 15.00
16 Joe Cronin/99 8.00 20.00
17 Goose Goslin/99 10.00 25.00
18 Billy Herman/99 4.00 10.00
19 Hank Greenberg/99 12.50 30.00
20 Luke Appling/99 10.00 25.00
21 Joe Medwick/49 12.50 30.00
22 Joe DiMaggio/49 30.00 60.00
23 Al Simmons/99 10.00 25.00
24 Ted Williams/99 12.50 30.00
25 Stan Musial/99 10.00 25.00
26 Jackie Robinson/99 20.00 50.00
27 Willie Keeler/99 10.00 25.00
28 Carl Furillo/99 5.00 12.00
29 Tris Speaker/99 12.50 30.00
30 Jake Daubert/99 10.00 25.00

2012 Panini National Treasures Nicknames
PRINT RUNS B/WN 5-99 COPIES PER
NO PRICING ON QTY 25 OR LESS
EXCHANGE DEADLINE 8/27/2014
1 Ty Cobb/99 30.00 60.00
12 Mel Ott/49 12.50 30.00
18 Bill Terry/49 10.00 25.00
19 Joe Cronin/49 12.00 30.00
20 Hank Greenberg/49 15.00 40.00
21 Bob Feller/49 10.00 25.00
23 Luke Appling/49 12.50 30.00
25 Miller Huggins/49 12.50 30.00
26 Ted Williams/49 12.50 30.00
45 Tris Speaker/49 15.00 40.00
49 Chuck Klein/49 8.00 20.00
50 Al Kaline/99 6.00 15.00
56 Juan Marichal/49 5.00 12.00
82 Reggie Jackson/99 5.00 12.00
84 Leo Durocher/49 10.00 25.00
95 Nolan Ryan/49 12.50 30.00
102 Ozzie Smith/99 5.00 12.00
107 Al Simmons/49 12.50 30.00
109 Tony Gwynn/99 4.00 10.00
110 Cal Ripken Jr./99 10.00 25.00
120 Albert Pujols/99 4.00 10.00
123 Carl Furillo/49 6.00 15.00
125 Derek Jeter/49 12.00 30.00

2012 Panini National Treasures Treasure Materials
PRINT RUNS B/WN 10-99 COPIES PER
NO PRICING ON QTY 25 OR LESS
EXCHANGE DEADLINE 8/27/2014
1 Albert Pujols/99 8.00 20.00
2 Alex Rodriguez/99 4.00 10.00
3 Carlos Beltran/99 3.00 8.00
4 Curtis Granderson/99 3.00 8.00
5 Derek Jeter/99 12.00 30.00
6 Evan Longoria/99 3.00 8.00
7 Ian Kinsler/99 3.00 8.00
9 Jacoby Ellsbury/99 3.00 8.00
10 Jason Heyward/99 4.00 10.00
11 Joe Mauer/99 8.00 20.00
12 Joey Votto/99 10.00 25.00
13 Jose Reyes/99 3.00 8.00
14 Justin Verlander/99 5.00 12.00
15 Mark Teixeira/99 3.00 8.00
16 Matt Holliday/99 3.00 8.00
17 Matt Kemp/99 3.00 8.00
18 Michael Bourn/99 4.00 10.00
19 Michael Young/99 3.00 8.00
20 Paul Konerko/99 6.00 15.00
21 Prince Fielder/99 10.00 25.00
22 Robinson Cano/99 4.00 10.00
24 Ryan Howard/99 8.00 20.00
25 Starlin Castro/99 3.00 8.00
26 Tim Lincecum/99 6.00 15.00
27 Troy Tulowitzki/99 8.00 20.00
28 Yu Darvish/99 10.00 25.00
29 Adam Dunn/99 3.00 8.00
30 Alfonso Soriano/99 3.00 8.00
31 Anthony Rizzo/99 4.00 10.00
32 Aroldis Chapman/99 8.00 20.00
34 Buster Posey/99 8.00 20.00
35 Carlos Gonzalez/99 3.00 8.00
36 Chipper Jones/99 4.00 10.00
37 Johnny Cueto/99 3.00 8.00
38 Josh Hamilton/99 3.00 8.00
39 Justin Morneau/99 3.00 8.00
40 Lance Berkman/99 8.00 20.00
41 Matt Wieters/99 4.00 10.00
42 Max Scherzer/99 3.00 8.00
43 Miguel Cabrera/99 6.00 15.00
44 Michael Fiers/99 3.00 8.00
45 Mike Moustakas/99 4.00 10.00
46 Mike Napoli/99 3.00 8.00
47 Wei-Yin Chen/99 8.00 20.00
48 Ryan Braun/99 5.00 12.00
49 Ryan Zimmerman/99 3.00 8.00
50 Yonder Alonso/99 3.00 8.00

2012 Panini National Treasures Treasure Signature Materials
PRINT RUNS B/WN 1-99 COPIES PER
NO PRICING ON QTY 25 OR LESS
EXCHANGE DEADLINE 8/27/2014
1 Adam Jones/49 12.00 30.00
4 Alex Avila/49 12.50 30.00
5 Andrew McCutchen/49 25.00 60.00
6 Austin Jackson/49 10.00 25.00
11 Brett Gardner/49 10.00 25.00
18 Dave Parker/49 10.00 25.00
25 Drew Stubbs/49 5.00 12.00
27 Dwight Gooden/49 10.00 25.00
30 Tim Federowicz/99 4.00 10.00
31 Frank Howard/49 12.50 30.00
37 Jemile Weeks/99 4.00 10.00
44 Justin Upton/49 12.50 30.00
45 Keith Hernandez/49 12.50 30.00
53 Minnie Minoso/49 12.50 30.00
61 Ron Cey/49 6.00 15.00
66 Tommy John/49 10.00 25.00
67 Tony Oliva/49 12.50 30.00
68 Scott Barnes/99 4.00 10.00
72 Yovani Gallardo/49 8.00 20.00
74 Anthony Gose/49 6.00 15.00
75 Austin Romine/99 5.00 12.00
76 Brad Peacock/49 4.00 10.00
77 Brett Jackson/49 10.00 25.00
79 David Phelps/49 6.00 15.00
80 Dellin Betances/99 12.00 30.00
82 Devin Mesoraco/99 8.00 20.00
83 Drew Smyly/99 8.00 20.00
84 Dustin Ackley/49 10.00 25.00
85 Garrett Richards/99 10.00 25.00
86 Jarrod Parker/99 8.00 20.00
87 Jean Segura/49 6.00 15.00
88 Jesus Montero/99 8.00 20.00
89 Casey Crosby/49 4.00 10.00
90 Kelvin Herrera/99 4.00 10.00
91 Leonys Martin/49 10.00 25.00
92 Martin Perez/99 12.00 30.00
93 Starling Marte/49 15.00 40.00
94 Matt Harvey/99 60.00 120.00
95 Matt Moore/99 10.00 25.00
96 Tyler Thornburg/49 6.00 15.00
97 Wellington Castillo/99 4.00 10.00
98 Wilin Rosario/99 8.00 20.00
100 Yasmani Grandal/99 5.00 12.00

2012 Panini National Treasures Triple Crown Winners Materials
PRINT RUNS B/WN 1-99 COPIES PER
NO PRICING ON QTY 25 OR LESS
EXCHANGE DEADLINE 8/27/2014
1 Nap Lajoie/99 15.00 40.00
2 Ty Cobb/99 30.00 60.00
6 Chuck Klein/99 10.00 25.00
7 Lou Gehrig/99 50.00 100.00
8 Joe Medwick/99 10.00 25.00
9 Ted Williams/99 12.50 30.00
10 Ted Williams/99 20.00 50.00
11 Frank Robinson/99 5.00 12.00
12 Carl Yastrzemski/99 8.00 20.00
18 Bob Feller/99 8.00 20.00
21 Randy Johnson/99 4.00 10.00
22 Clayton Kershaw/99 6.00 15.00
23 Justin Verlander/99 10.00 25.00
24 Miguel Cabrera/99 12.50 30.00

2014 Panini National Treasures
1-150 PRINT RUNS B/WN 10-99 COPIES PER
NO PRICING ON QTY 25 OR LESS
151-225 PRINT RUN 99 SER.#'d SETS
PRICING LISTED IS FOR ONE-COLOR JSYS
EXCHANGE DEADLINE 6/30/2016
1 Ty Cobb JSY/25 40.00 100.00
3 Nap Lajoie JSY/25 25.00 60.00
4 Tris Speaker BAT/25 20.00 50.00
5 Eddie Collins JSY/25 20.00 50.00
6 Lou Gehrig JSY/25 90.00 150.00
7 Willie Keeler BAT/25 20.00 50.00
8 George Sisler JSY/25 20.00 50.00
9 Rogers Hornsby JSY/25 20.00 50.00
10 Roger Bresnahan JSY/25 20.00 50.00
11 Frank Chance BAT/25 20.00 50.00
12 Frankie Frisch JSY/25 20.00 50.00
14 Jimmie Foxx BAT/25 25.00 60.00
15 Mel Ott JSY/25 25.00 60.00
16 Harry Heilmann JSY/25 20.00 50.00
17 Paul Waner JSY/25 15.00 40.00
18 Al Simmons JSY/25 20.00 50.00
19 Bill Dickey JSY/25 20.00 50.00
20 Joe DiMaggio JSY/25 20.00 50.00
22 Hank Greenberg JSY/99 10.00 25.00
23 Sam Crawford JSY/99 12.00 30.00
24 Bob Feller JSY/99 5.00 12.00
26 Luke Appling JSY/99 5.00 12.00
27 Miller Huggins JSY/27 12.00 30.00
28 Ted Williams JSY/99 10.00 25.00
29 Lloyd Waner JSY/25 10.00 25.00
30 Goose Goslin JSY/99 5.00 12.00
31 Roy Campanella JSY/99 8.00 20.00
32 Stan Musial JSY/99 8.00 20.00
33 Dave Bancroft JSY/99 10.00 25.00
34 Satchel Paige JSY/25 40.00 100.00
36 Roberto Clemente JSY/25 40.00 100.00
37 George Kelly JSY/25 20.00 50.00
38 Warren Spahn JSY/25 20.00 50.00
39 Jim Bottomley JSY/25 20.00 50.00
40 Whitey Ford JSY/99 4.00 10.00
41 Billy Herman JSY/99 3.00 8.00
42 Ralph Kiner JSY/99 4.00 10.00
43 Hack Wilson BAT/25 20.00 50.00
44 Al Kaline JSY/99 5.00 12.00
45 Chuck Klein JSY/99 8.00 20.00
46 Duke Snider JSY/25 8.00 20.00
47 Tom Yawkey JSY/99 12.00 30.00
48 Johnny Mize JSY/25 15.00 40.00
49 Frank Robinson JSY/99 4.00 10.00
50 Walter Alston JSY/99 4.00 10.00
51 Brooks Robinson JSY/99 6.00 15.00
52 Luis Aparicio JSY/99 4.00 10.00
53 Don Drysdale JSY/99 4.00 10.00
54 Rick Ferrell JSY/25 20.00 50.00
55 Harmon Killebrew JSY/99 5.00 12.00
56 Pee Wee Reese JSY/99 10.00 25.00
57 Lou Brock JSY/99 6.00 15.00
58 Enos Slaughter JSY/25 20.00 50.00
59 Willie McCovey JSY/75 10.00 25.00
60 Billy Williams JSY/25 4.00 10.00
61 Willie Stargell JSY/99 8.00 20.00
62 Johnny Bench JSY/99 10.00 25.00
64 Carl Yastrzemski JSY/25 10.00 25.00
65 Tony Lazzeri JSY/27 15.00 40.00
66 Rollie Fingers JSY/99 4.00 10.00
67 Tom Seaver JSY/25 10.00 25.00
68 Reggie Jackson JSY/99 4.00 10.00
69 Leo Durocher JSY/25 10.00 25.00
70 Mike Schmidt JSY/25 8.00 20.00
71 Nellie Fox JSY/99 10.00 25.00
72 George Brett JSY/25 50.00 120.00
73 Orlando Cepeda JSY/99 8.00 20.00
74 Nolan Ryan JSY/25 15.00 40.00
75 Robin Yount JSY/25 15.00 40.00
76 Carlton Fisk JSY/49 4.00 10.00
78 Ozzie Smith JSY/99 6.00 15.00
79 Eddie Murray JSY/25 4.00 10.00
80 Dennis Eckersley JSY/99 4.00 10.00
81 Paul Molitor JSY/99 5.00 12.00
82 Wade Boggs JSY/99 4.00 10.00
83 Ryne Sandberg JSY/25 10.00 25.00
84 Tony Gwynn JSY/99 6.00 15.00
85 Cal Ripken JSY/99 6.00 15.00
86 Rickey Henderson JSY/99 5.00 12.00
87 Andre Dawson JSY/99 4.00 10.00
88 Roberto Alomar JSY/25 4.00 10.00
89 Tom Glavine JSY/99 4.00 10.00
90 Greg Maddux JSY/25 10.00 25.00
91 Frank Thomas JSY/99 8.00 20.00
92 Joe Torre JSY/99 6.00 15.00
93 Bob Gibson JSY/25 10.00 25.00
94 Bob Meusel JSY/27 15.00 40.00
95 Carl Furillo JSY/99 3.00 8.00
96 Dom DiMaggio JSY/25 10.00 25.00
97 Eddie Stanky JSY/99 6.00 15.00
98 Elston Howard JSY/25 15.00 40.00
99 Gil Hodges JSY/99 10.00 25.00
100 Heinie Groh JSY/99 8.00 20.00
101 Jim Gilliam JSY/99 6.00 15.00
102 Joe Jackson JSY/25 60.00 150.00
103 Ken Boyer JSY/99 10.00 25.00
104 Lefty Williams JSY/99 10.00 25.00
105 Pete Reiser JSY/99 3.00 8.00
106 Roger Maris JSY/99 15.00 40.00
107 Ted Kluszewski JSY/99 6.00 15.00
108 Thurman Munson JSY/99 8.00 20.00
109 Tommy Henrich JSY/99 3.00 8.00
110 Willie Kamm JSY/99 6.00 15.00
111 Earl Averill BAT/25 6.00 15.00
112 Adam Jones JSY/99 4.00 10.00
113 Adrian Beltre JSY/99 6.00 15.00
114 Adrian Gonzalez JSY/99 4.00 10.00
115 Albert Pujols JSY/99 6.00 15.00
116 Andrew McCutchen JSY/99 10.00 25.00
117 Anthony Rizzo JSY/99 10.00 25.00
118 Bryce Harper BAT/25 10.00 25.00
119 Buster Posey JSY/25 15.00 40.00
120 Carlos Gomez JSY/99 3.00 8.00
121 Chris Davis JSY/25 3.00 8.00
122 Clayton Kershaw JSY/99 4.00 10.00
123 David Ortiz JSY/99 5.00 12.00
124 David Wright JSY/99 4.00 10.00
125 Derek Jeter JSY/99 12.00 30.00
126 Dustin Pedroia JSY/99 5.00 12.00
127 Edwin Encarnacion JSY/99 5.00 12.00
128 Evan Longoria JSY/99 4.00 10.00
129 Felix Hernandez JSY/99 4.00 10.00
130 Freddie Freeman JSY/25 6.00 15.00
131 Giancarlo Stanton JSY/25 5.00 12.00
132 Hanley Ramirez JSY/99 4.00 10.00
133 Ichiro Suzuki JSY/25 12.00 30.00
134 Joey Votto JSY/99 5.00 12.00
135 Jose Bautista JSY/99 4.00 10.00
136 Jose Fernandez JSY/25 12.00 30.00
137 Josh Donaldson JSY/99 4.00 10.00
138 Justin Upton JSY/99 4.00 10.00
139 Manny Machado JSY/25 5.00 12.00
140 Max Scherzer JSY/99 5.00 12.00
141 Miguel Cabrera JSY/99 6.00 15.00
142 Mike Trout JSY/99 10.00 25.00
143 Paul Goldschmidt JSY/99 5.00 12.00
144 Robinson Cano JSY/25 4.00 10.00
145 Sonny Gray JSY/99 4.00 10.00
146 Starlin Castro JSY/99 3.00 8.00
147 Stephen Strasburg JSY/25 20.00 50.00
148 Yasiel Puig JSY/99 5.00 12.00
149 Yoenis Cespedes JSY/99 5.00 12.00
150 Yu Darvish JSY/99 5.00 12.00
151 Xander Bogaerts JSY AU RC 12.00 30.00
152 Masahiro Tanaka JSY RC 10.00 25.00
153 Taijuan Walker JSY AU RC 5.00 12.00
154 George Springer JSY AU RC 20.00 50.00
155 Nick Castellanos JSY AU RC 15.00 40.00
156 Yordano Ventura JSY AU RC 8.00 20.00
157 Jose Abreu JSY AU RC 12.00 30.00
158 Travis d'Arnaud JSY AU RC 12.00 30.00
159 Odor JSY AU RC EXCH 12.00 30.00
160 Billy Hamilton JSY AU RC 6.00 15.00
161 Marcus Stroman JSY AU RC 15.00 40.00
162 Kolten Wong JSY AU RC 12.00 30.00
163 Jesse Hahn JSY AU RC 6.00 15.00
164 Chris Owings JSY AU RC 5.00 12.00
165 Rafael Montero JSY AU RC 5.00 12.00
167 Matt Davidson JSY AU RC 6.00 15.00
168 Jake Marisnick JSY AU RC 5.00 12.00
169 Marcus Semien JSY AU RC 8.00 20.00
170 Jimmy Nelson JSY AU RC 5.00 12.00
171 Michael Choice JSY AU RC 5.00 12.00
172 Andrew Susac JSY AU RC 10.00 25.00
173 C.J. Cron JSY AU RC 5.00 12.00
174 J.R. Murphy JSY AU RC 5.00 12.00
175 Jonathan Schoop JSY AU RC 8.00 20.00
176 Wilmer Flores JSY AU RC 4.00 10.00
177 Luis Sardinas JSY AU RC 5.00 12.00
178 David Hale JSY AU RC 5.00 12.00
180 Alex Guerrero JSY AU RC 6.00 15.00
181 Jace Peterson JSY AU RC 5.00 12.00
182 Ramirez JSY AU RC EXCH 20.00 50.00
183 Danny Santana JSY AU RC 10.00 25.00
184 Chris Taylor AU RC 15.00 40.00
185 Tucker Barnhart JSY AU RC 5.00 12.00
186 Randal Grichuk JSY AU RC 10.00 25.00
187 Josmil Pinto JSY AU RC 5.00 12.00
188 Yangervis Solarte JSY AU RC 5.00 12.00
190 Roenis Elias JSY AU RC 5.00 12.00
191 Nick Martinez JSY AU RC 5.00 12.00
192 David Holmberg JSY AU RC 5.00 12.00
193 Erisbel Arruebarrena JSY AU RC 5.00 12.00
194 Anthony DeSclafani JSY AU RC 5.00 12.00
195 Jacob deGrom JSY AU RC 600.00 1500.00
196 Wei-Chung Wang JSY AU RC 15.00 40.00
197 Polanco JSY AU RC EXCH 10.00 25.00
199 Adrian Nieto JSY AU RC 5.00 12.00
200 Chase Whitley JSY AU RC 5.00 12.00
201 Andrew Heaney JSY AU RC 5.00 12.00
202 Eugenio Suarez JSY AU RC 20.00 50.00
203 Garin Cecchini JSY AU RC 5.00 12.00
204 Joe Panik JSY AU RC 20.00 50.00
205 Kevin Kiermaier JSY AU RC 10.00 25.00
206 Matt Shoemaker JSY AU RC 8.00 20.00
207 Despaigne JSY AU RC 5.00 12.00
208 Tommy La Stella JSY AU RC 5.00 12.00
209 Carlos Contreras JSY AU RC 5.00 12.00
210 Mookie Betts JSY AU RC 60.00 150.00
212 Domingo Santana JSY AU RC 8.00 20.00
213 Carlos Sanchez JSY AU RC 5.00 12.00
214 Alcantara JSY AU RC 8.00 20.00
215 Shane Greene JSY AU RC 20.00 50.00
216 Tyler Collins JSY AU RC 5.00 12.00
217 Enny Romero JSY AU RC 5.00 12.00
218 Aaron Altherr JSY AU RC 5.00 12.00
219 Christian Vazquez JSY AU RC 15.00 40.00
220 James Paxton JSY AU RC 10.00 25.00
221 Kyle Parker JSY AU RC 6.00 15.00
222 Chase Anderson JSY AU RC 5.00 12.00
223 Robbie Ray JSY AU RC 5.00 12.00
224 Aaron Sanchez AU RC 5.00 12.00

2014 Panini National Treasures Jerseys Prime
*PRIME: .6X TO 1.5X BASIC
RANDOM INSERTS IN PACKS
PRINT RUNS B/WN 1-25 COPIES PER
NO PRICING ON QTY 10 OR LESS

2014 Panini National Treasures Rookie Material Signatures Gold
*GOLD: .6X TO 1.5X BASIC
RANDOM INSERTS IN PACKS
PRINT RUNS B/WN 10-25 COPIES PER
NO PRICING ON QTY 10
EXCHANGE DEADLINE 6/30/2016
152 Masahiro Tanaka/25 40.00 100.00
157 Jose Abreu/25 150.00 250.00

2014 Panini National Treasures Rookie Material Signatures Purple
*PURPLE: .5X TO 1.2X BASIC
RANDOM INSERTS IN PACKS
STATED PRINT RUN 49 SER.#'d SETS
EXCHANGE DEADLINE 6/30/2016
152 Masahiro Tanaka 20.00 50.00

2014 Panini National Treasures All Decade Materials
RANDOM INSERTS IN PACKS
PRINT RUNS B/WN 25-99 COPIES PER
1 Frank Chance/25 60.00 150.00
3 Herb Pennock/25 15.00 40.00
5 Heinie Groh/99 6.00 15.00
6 Lefty Gomez/25 20.00 50.00
7 Nap Lajoie/25 25.00 60.00
8 Carl Furillo/99 4.00 10.00
9 Joe Cronin/99 6.00 15.00
10 Bob Meusel/27 15.00 40.00
11 Eddie Collins/25 25.00 60.00
12 Goose Goslin/25 10.00 25.00
13 Whitey Ford/99 5.00 12.00
14 Early Wynn/25 10.00 25.00
15 Yogi Berra/99 10.00 25.00
16 Rick Ferrell/25 20.00 50.00
17 Billy Herman/99 4.00 10.00
18 Luke Appling/99 5.00 12.00
19 Larry Doby/25 20.00 50.00
20 Earl Averill/25 12.00 30.00
21 Ernie Banks/25 12.00 30.00
22 Tommy Henrich/99 6.00 15.00
23 Bob Feller/99 10.00 25.00
24 Ralph Kiner/99 5.00 12.00
25 Eddie Stanky/99 4.00 10.00

2014 Panini National Treasures All Decade Materials Combos
RANDOM INSERTS IN PACKS
PRINT RUNS B/WN 10-25 COPIES PER
NO PRICING ON QTY 10
1 Chance/Bresnahan/25 100.00 200.00
2 Collins/Lajoie/25 40.00 100.00
3 Bancroft/Wagner/25 50.00 120.00
4 Ford/Berra/99 15.00 40.00
5 Gomez/Grove/25 50.00 120.00
6 Simmons/Goslin/25 20.00 50.00
8 Gehringer/Lazzeri/25 25.00 60.00
10 DiMaggio/Henrich/25 20.00 50.00

2014 Panini National Treasures All Decade Materials Triples
RANDOM INSERTS IN PACKS
PRINT RUNS B/WN 10-99 COPIES PER
NO PRICING ON QTY 10
1 Crwfrd/Cbb/Klr/25 60.00 150.00
2 Chnce/Wgnr/Brsnhn/25 100.00 200.00
4 Smmns/Wlsn/Hlmnn/25 30.00 80.00
5 Smmns/Avrll/Gsln/25 30.00 80.00
6 Slghtr/Knr/Msl/25 30.00 80.00
8 Sndr/Msl/Sphn/25 40.00 100.00
9 Pjls/Szki/Rvra/99 12.00 30.00
10 Rpkn/Grffy Jr./Gwnn/99 20.00 50.00

2014 Panini National Treasures Armory Booklet Materials
RANDOM INSERTS IN PACKS
STATED PRINT RUN 25 SER.#'d SETS
1 Jose Abreu 50.00 120.00
2 Masahiro Tanaka 50.00 120.00
3 Mike Trout 75.00 200.00
4 Yasiel Puig 40.00 100.00
5 Yu Darvish 25.00 60.00

2014 Panini National Treasures Baseball Signature Die Cuts
RANDOM INSERTS IN PACKS
PRINT RUNS B/WN 10-99 COPIES PER
NO PRICING ON QTY 10 OR LESS
EXCHANGE DEADLINE 6/30/2016
1 Aaron Sanchez/99 4.00 10.00
2 Adam Eaton/99 4.00 10.00
3 Adam Jones/25 12.00 30.00
5 Adrian Gonzalez/25 12.00 30.00
7 Alex Wood/99 4.00 10.00
8 Anthony Rendon/99 10.00 25.00
9 Anthony Rizzo/99 12.00 30.00
10 Archie Bradley/99 4.00 10.00
12 Brian McCann/25 5.00 12.00
14 Byron Buxton/25 12.00 30.00
16 Carlos Correa/99 20.00 50.00
18 Carlos Gonzalez/25 6.00 15.00
21 Chris Sale/99 10.00 25.00
22 Clayton Kershaw/25 60.00 150.00
23 Clint Frazier/99 15.00 40.00
25 David Price/25 15.00 40.00
26 David Wright/25 20.00 50.00
27 Arismendy Alcantara/99 4.00 10.00
28 Dillon Gee/99 4.00 10.00
29 Dustin Pedroia/25 25.00 60.00
30 Eric Hosmer/25 12.00 30.00
35 Gerrit Cole/25 12.00 30.00
38 George Springer/99 15.00 40.00
40 Gregory Polanco/99 EXCH 6.00 15.00
43 Jason Kipnis/99 10.00 25.00
44 Javier Baez/99 12.00 30.00
47 Jedd Gyorko/99 4.00 10.00
48 Jered Weaver/25 10.00 25.00
49 Jimmy Nelson/99 4.00 10.00
50 Joe Mauer/25 15.00 40.00
52 Jonathan Gray/99 5.00 12.00
53 Jose Abreu/99 25.00 60.00
55 Josh Donaldson/99 6.00 15.00
56 Junior Lake/99 4.00 10.00
57 Justin Upton/25 6.00 15.00
59 Kyle Zimmer/99 4.00 10.00
63 Matt Carpenter/99 15.00 40.00
65 Max Scherzer/25 20.00 50.00
67 Miguel Sano/99 5.00 12.00
71 Mike Zunino/99 4.00 10.00
72 Nick Castellanos/99 12.00 30.00
73 Noah Syndergaard/99 20.00 50.00
77 Pete Rose/25 40.00 100.00
80 Robert Stephenson/99 4.00 10.00
82 Ryan Braun/25 20.00 50.00
84 Salvador Perez/99 15.00 40.00
85 Shelby Miller/99 5.00 12.00
86 Starling Marte/99 12.00 30.00
88 Taijuan Walker/99 4.00 10.00
89 Todd Helton/25 12.00 30.00
90 Tom Glavine/25 30.00 80.00
91 Tom Koehler/99 4.00 10.00
92 Kris Bryant/99 100.00 250.00
93 Tony La Russa/25 15.00 40.00
96 Wil Myers/25 6.00 15.00
97 Xander Bogaerts/99 15.00 40.00
98 Mookie Betts/99 EXCH 50.00 120.00
99 Yoenis Cespedes/25 12.00 30.00
100 Yordano Ventura/99 EXCH 12.00 30.00

2014 Panini National Treasures Boston St. Patrick's Day Jerseys
RANDOM INSERTS IN PACKS
STATED PRINT RUN 49 SER.#'d SETS
*PRIME/25: .6X TO 1.5X BASIC
1 David Ortiz 15.00 40.00
2 Dustin Pedroia 15.00 40.00
3 Jackie Bradley Jr. 15.00 40.00
4 Xander Bogaerts 12.00 30.00

2014 Panini National Treasures Boston St. Patrick's Day Jerseys Signatures
RANDOM INSERTS IN PACKS
STATED PRINT RUN 25 SER.#'d SETS
EXCHANGE DEADLINE 6/30/2016
1 David Ortiz 50.00 120.00
2 Dustin Pedroia 40.00 100.00
4 Xander Bogaerts 40.00 100.00

2014 Panini National Treasures Colossal Materials
RANDOM INSERTS IN PACKS
PRINT RUNS B/WN 25-99 COPIES PER
*JSY NUM/25: .75X TO 2X BASIC
*NAMEPLATE/25: .75X TO 2X BASIC
1 Adam Jones/99 4.00 10.00
2 Anthony Rizzo/99 6.00 15.00
3 Aroldis Chapman/99 5.00 12.00
4 Yoenis Cespedes/25 5.00 12.00
5 Bryce Harper/25 10.00 25.00
6 Chris Davis/99 3.00 8.00
7 Cliff Lee/99 4.00 10.00
8 David Ortiz/25 6.00 15.00
9 Dustin Pedroia/25 5.00 12.00
10 Edwin Encarnacion/99 4.00 10.00
11 Eric Hosmer/99 4.00 10.00
12 Evan Longoria/99 4.00 10.00
13 Felix Hernandez/99 4.00 10.00
14 Gerrit Cole/99 5.00 12.00
15 Gregory Polanco/99 5.00 12.00
16 Joey Votto/25 5.00 12.00
17 Jose Bautista/99 4.00 10.00
18 Jose Fernandez/25 6.00 15.00
19 Justin Upton/99 4.00 10.00
20 Madison Bumgarner/99 4.00 10.00
21 Manny Machado/25 6.00 15.00
22 Max Scherzer/25 5.00 12.00
23 Miguel Cabrera/99 6.00 15.00
24 Brock Holt/25 3.00 8.00
25 Paul Goldschmidt/25 5.00 12.00
26 Starlin Castro/99 3.00 8.00
27 Taijuan Walker/99 3.00 8.00
28 Wil Myers/25 3.00 8.00
29 Yasiel Puig/25 5.00 12.00
30 Matt Shoemaker/99 5.00 12.00
31 Chase Utley/99 4.00 10.00
32 Jason Heyward/99 4.00 10.00
33 Johnny Cueto/99 4.00 10.00
34 Julio Teheran/25 4.00 10.00
35 Devin Mesoraco/99 3.00 8.00
36 Dee Gordon/99 3.00 8.00
37 Hunter Pence/25 12.00 30.00
38 A.J. Pollock/99 4.00 10.00
39 Salvador Perez/99 4.00 10.00
40 Michael Brantley/99 4.00 10.00
41 Alex Gordon/99 4.00 10.00
42 Victor Martinez/99 4.00 10.00
43 Jon Lester/99 4.00 10.00
44 Dallas Keuchel/99 4.00 10.00
45 Koji Uehara/25 8.00 20.00
46 Kyle Seager/99 3.00 8.00
47 Hyun-Jin Ryu/99 4.00 10.00
48 Tom Koehler/99 3.00 8.00
49 Ryan Howard/99 4.00 10.00
50 Rick Porcello/99 4.00 10.00

2014 Panini National Treasures Colossal Materials Prime Jersey Number
*JSY NUM: .75X TO 2X BASIC
RANDOM INSERTS IN PACKS
PRINT RUNS B/WN 4-25 COPIES PER
NO PRICING ON QTY 15 OR LESS

2014 Panini National Treasures Colossal Materials Prime Nameplate
*NAMEPLATE: .75X TO 2X BASIC
RANDOM INSERTS IN PACKS
PRINT RUNS B/WN 1-25 COPIES PER
NO PRICING ON QTY 15 OR LESS

2014 Panini National Treasures Combo Materials Booklet
RANDOM INSERTS IN PACKS
STATED PRINT RUN 25 SER.#'d SETS
1 M.Tanaka/Y.Darvish 20.00 50.00
2 Y.Puig/Y.Cespedes 10.00 25.00
3 G.Springer/J.Singleton 6.00 15.00
4 Polanco/Taveras 10.00 25.00
5 A.Pujols/M.Trout 50.00 125.00
6 A.Pujols/M.McGwire 20.00 50.00
8 D.Jeter/I.Suzuki 60.00 150.00
9 D.Ortiz/D.Pedroia 20.00 50.00
10 M.Scherzer/M.Cabrera 10.00 25.00
11 F.Hernandez/R.Cano 15.00 40.00
12 E.Encarnacion/J.Bautista 10.00 25.00
13 C.Davis/N.Cruz 10.00 25.00

2014 Panini National Treasures Flawless
RANDOM INSERTS IN PACKS
STATED PRINT RUN 20 SER.#'d SETS
1 Al Simmons 20.00 50.00
2 Albert Pujols 150.00 250.00
3 Alexander Cartwright 20.00 50.00
4 Bill Dickey 15.00 40.00
5 Bill Terry 15.00 40.00
6 Bob Gibson 20.00 50.00
7 Brooks Robinson 20.00 50.00
8 Bryce Harper 150.00 250.00
9 Burleigh Grimes 20.00 50.00
10 Cal Ripken 60.00 150.00
11 Carl Hubbell 20.00 50.00
12 Carl Yastrzemski 40.00 100.00
13 Carlton Fisk 20.00 50.00
14 Charlie Gehringer 15.00 40.00
15 Christy Mathewson 25.00 60.00
16 Chuck Klein 15.00 40.00
17 Clayton Kershaw 40.00 100.00
18 Cy Young 60.00 150.00
19 David Ortiz 40.00 100.00
20 Derek Jeter 300.00 400.00
21 Dizzy Dean 20.00 50.00
22 Don Drysdale 20.00 50.00
23 Duke Snider 20.00 50.00
24 Edd Roush 20.00 50.00
25 Eddie Collins 20.00 50.00
26 Eddie Murray 20.00 50.00
27 Ernie Banks 25.00 60.00
28 Frank Chance 20.00 50.00
29 Frank Robinson 20.00 50.00
30 Frank Thomas 30.00 80.00
31 Frankie Frisch 20.00 50.00
32 Freddie Freeman 30.00 80.00
33 Gabby Hartnett 15.00 40.00
34 George Brett 50.00 125.00
35 George Sisler 20.00 50.00
36 George Springer 50.00 120.00
37 Giancarlo Stanton 25.00 60.00
38 Goose Goslin 20.00 50.00
39 Greg Maddux 30.00 80.00
40 Gregory Polanco 150.00 300.00
41 Grover Alexander 40.00 100.00
42 Hack Wilson 20.00 50.00
43 Hank Greenberg 25.00 60.00
44 Harry Heilmann 20.00 50.00
45 Herb Pennock 20.00 50.00
46 Honus Wagner 25.00 60.00
47 Ichiro Suzuki 150.00 250.00
48 Jackie Robinson 25.00 60.00
49 Jim Thorpe 150.00 250.00
50 Jimmie Foxx 25.00 60.00
51 Joe DiMaggio 50.00 125.00
52 Joe Jackson 30.00 80.00
53 Joe Medwick 15.00 40.00
54 Johnny Evers 15.00 40.00
55 Jose Abreu 150.00 250.00
56 Josh Gibson 25.00 60.00
57 Ken Griffey Jr. 50.00 125.00
58 Lefty Grove 20.00 50.00
59 Lou Gehrig 50.00 125.00
60 Mariano Rivera 30.00 80.00
61 Mark McGwire 50.00 125.00
62 Masahiro Tanaka 50.00 125.00
63 Mel Ott 25.00 60.00
64 Miguel Cabrera 25.00 60.00
65 Mike Schmidt 40.00 100.00
66 Mike Trout 125.00 300.00
67 Miller Huggins 15.00 40.00
68 Mordecai Brown 15.00 40.00
69 Nap Lajoie 25.00 60.00
70 Nolan Ryan 60.00 150.00
71 Oscar Taveras 20.00 50.00
72 Paul Waner 20.00 50.00
73 Pete Rose 50.00 125.00
74 Pie Traynor 20.00 50.00
75 Rabbit Maranville 20.00 50.00
76 Reggie Jackson 20.00 50.00
77 Rickey Henderson 25.00 60.00
78 Roberto Clemente 60.00 150.00
79 Rod Carew 20.00 50.00
80 Roger Bresnahan 20.00 50.00
81 Roger Maris 25.00 60.00
82 Rogers Hornsby 20.00 50.00
83 Roy Campanella 25.00 60.00
84 Rube Marquard 20.00 50.00
85 Ryne Sandberg 50.00 125.00
86 Sam Crawford 20.00 50.00
87 Satchel Paige 25.00 60.00
88 Stan Musial 40.00 100.00
89 Ted Williams 50.00 125.00
90 Thurman Munson 25.00 60.00

91 Tony Gwynn 40.00 100.00
92 Tony Lazzeri 20.00 50.00
93 Tris Speaker 20.00 50.00
94 Ty Cobb 40.00 100.00
95 Walter Johnson 25.00 60.00
96 Willie Keeler 15.00 40.00
97 Xander Bogaerts 50.00 125.00
98 Yasiel Puig 25.00 60.00
99 Yu Darvish 25.00 60.00
100 Zack Wheat 20.00 50.00

2014 Panini National Treasures Franchise Materials

RANDOM INSERTS IN PACKS
PRINT RUNS B/WN 25-99 COPIES PER
1 Andrew McCutchen/99 12.00 30.00
2 Anthony Rizzo/99 5.00 12.00
3 Bryce Harper/25 10.00 25.00
4 Buster Posey/25 12.00 30.00
5 Clayton Kershaw/99 6.00 15.00
6 David Ortiz/99 4.00 10.00
7 David Wright/99 3.00 8.00
8 Derek Jeter/99 12.00 30.00
9 Felix Hernandez/99 3.00 8.00
10 Freddie Freeman/99 5.00 12.00
11 George Springer/25 10.00 25.00
12 Giancarlo Stanton/25 4.00 10.00
13 Jose Bautista/99 3.00 8.00
14 Miguel Cabrera/99 4.00 10.00
15 Mike Trout/99 20.00 50.00
16 Paul Goldschmidt/99 4.00 10.00
17 Robinson Cano/99 3.00 8.00
18 Troy Tulowitzki/99 4.00 10.00
19 Yasiel Puig/99 4.00 10.00
20 Yu Darvish/99 4.00 10.00

2014 Panini National Treasures Game Ball Signatures

RANDOM INSERTS IN PACKS
PRINT RUNS B/WN 1-99 COPIES PER
NO PRICING ON QTY 10 OR LESS
EXCHANGE DEADLINE 6/30/2016
17 Chris Owings/99 5.00 12.00
19 Christian Bethancourt/99 5.00 12.00
21 David Hale/99 5.00 12.00
27 Erik Johnson/99 5.00 12.00
37 George Springer/99 12.00 30.00
41 J.R. Murphy/99 5.00 12.00
44 James Paxton/99 5.00 12.00
51 Jimmy Nelson/99 5.00 12.00
55 Jonathan Schoop/99 5.00 12.00
56 Jose Abreu/25 12.00 30.00
66 Marcus Semien/99 25.00 60.00
69 Matt Davidson/99 6.00 15.00
71 Michael Choice/99 5.00 12.00
75 Nick Castellanos/99 15.00 40.00
87 Taijuan Walker/99 8.00 20.00
88 Tanner Roark/99 5.00 12.00
98 Xander Bogaerts/99 15.00 40.00
99 Yangervis Solarte/99 5.00 12.00
100 Yordano Ventura/99 EXCH 6.00 15.00

2014 Panini National Treasures HOF 75th Anniversary Souvenir Cuts

RANDOM INSERTS IN PACKS
PRINT RUNS B/WN 1-25 COPIES PER
NO PRICING ON QTY 1
EXCHANGE DEADLINE 6/30/2016
29 Ralph Kiner/25 20.00 50.00

2014 Panini National Treasures HOF Logo Signatures

RANDOM INSERTS IN PACKS
PRINT RUNS B/WN 10-25 COPIES PER
NO PRICING ON QTY 10 OR LESS
EXCHANGE DEADLINE 6/30/2016
1 Al Kaline/25 25.00 50.00
2 Andre Dawson/25 15.00 40.00
5 Billy Williams/25 15.00 40.00
8 Brooks Robinson/25 15.00 40.00
11 Carlton Fisk/25 15.00 40.00
12 Don Sutton/25 15.00 40.00
15 Fergie Jenkins/25 15.00 40.00
21 Jim Bunning/25 15.00 40.00
22 Jim Palmer/25 15.00 40.00
23 Jim Rice/25 20.00 50.00
33 Paul Molitor/25 20.00 50.00
34 Phil Niekro/25 15.00 40.00
35 Red Schoendienst/25 15.00 40.00
41 Rollie Fingers/25 15.00 40.00
44 Tom Glavine/25 20.00 50.00
48 Tony Perez/25 20.00 50.00

2014 Panini National Treasures Immortalized Materials

RANDOM INSERTS IN PACKS
PRINT RUNS B/WN 10-99 COPIES PER
NO PRICING ON QTY 10
1 Bill Dickey/25 20.00 50.00
2 Charlie Gehringer/25 12.00 30.00
3 Earl Averill/25 12.00 30.00
4 Eddie Collins/25 25.00 60.00
5 Herb Pennock/25 25.00 60.00
6 Gabby Hartnett/25 30.00 80.00
7 Lefty Gomez/25 20.00 50.00
8 Lefty O'Doul/99 8.00 20.00
10 Carl Furillo/99 4.00 10.00
11 Nap Lajoie/25 25.00 60.00
12 Rick Ferrell/25 20.00 50.00
14 Yogi Berra/99 6.00 15.00
15 Whitey Ford/99 8.00 20.00
16 Stan Musial/99 10.00 25.00
17 Duke Snider/99 5.00 12.00
18 Ernie Banks/25 20.00 50.00
19 Ron Santo/99 8.00 20.00
20 Willie Keeler/99 15.00 40.00

2014 Panini National Treasures League Leaders Materials

RANDOM INSERTS IN PACKS
PRINT RUNS B/WN 10-99 COPIES PER
NO PRICING ON QTY 10
1 Frank Chance/25 60.00 150.00
2 Roger Bresnahan/25 50.00 120.00
3 Tony Lazzeri/25 15.00 40.00
4 Bob Meusel/27 15.00 40.00
5 Earl Averill/25 12.00 30.00
6 Duke Snider/99 5.00 12.00
7 George Case/99 8.00 20.00
8 Carl Furillo/99 4.00 10.00
9 Barry Bonds/99 12.00 30.00
10 Nap Lajoie/25 25.00 60.00
11 Willie Keeler/25 50.00 120.00
12 Herb Pennock/25 25.00 60.00
13 Lefty Gomez/25 20.00 50.00
14 Harry Heilmann/25 15.00 40.00
15 Bill Terry/25 12.00 30.00
16 Jimmie Foxx/25 20.00 50.00
17 Lefty O'Doul/99 8.00 20.00
19 Lefty Grove/25 40.00 100.00
20 Bob Feller/99 6.00 15.00
21 Mark McGwire/25 15.00 40.00
22 George Kelly/99 8.00 20.00
23 Johnny Pesky/99 6.00 15.00
24 Paul Waner/25 12.00 30.00
25 Hack Wilson/25 25.00 60.00

2014 Panini National Treasures League Leaders Materials Prime

*PRIME: .75X TO 2X BASIC
RANDOM INSERTS IN PACKS
PRINT RUNS B/WN 1-25 COPIES PER
NO PRICING ON QTY 5 OR LESS
9 Barry Bonds/25 100.00 250.00

2014 Panini National Treasures League Leaders Materials Combos

RANDOM INSERTS IN PACKS
PRINT RUNS B/WN 10-99 COPIES PER
NO PRICING ON QTY 10
1 F.Chance/H.Wagner/25 60.00 150.00
2 N.Lajoie/W.Keeler/25 40.00 100.00
5 C.Klein/L.O'Doul/25 20.00 50.00
6 H.Groh/R.Hornsby/25 25.00 60.00
7 G.Hartnett/R.Hornsby/25 50.00 120.00
8 H.Wilson/J.Bottomley/25 25.00 60.00
9 C.Klein/H.Wilson/25 25.00 60.00
10 A.Simmons/H.Heilmann/25 20.00 50.00

2014 Panini National Treasures League Leaders Materials Quads

RANDOM INSERTS IN PACKS
PRINT RUNS B/WN 1-25 COPIES PER
NO PRICING ON QTY 5 OR LESS
4 Kln/Wlsn/Ott/Hrnsby/25 60.00 150.00
5 Smmns/Msl/Gsln/Hlmnn/25 40.00 100.00

2014 Panini National Treasures League Leaders Materials Triples

RANDOM INSERTS IN PACKS
PRINT RUNS B/WN 1-25 COPIES PER
NO PRICING ON QTY 10 OR LESS
1 Cllns/Crwfrd/Cbb/25 200.00 300.00
3 Sslr/Spkr/Cbb/25 200.00 300.00
5 Wnr/Wnr/Hrnsby/25 40.00 100.00
7 Wlsn/O'Dl/Wnr/25 40.00 100.00
8 Vghn/Kln/Crnn/25 25.00 60.00
9 Hrmn/Slghtr/Cse/25 25.00 60.00
10 Wlkr/Mze/Knr/25 30.00 80.00

2014 Panini National Treasures Legends Cuts Jumbo Materials

RANDOM INSERTS IN PACKS
PRINT RUNS B/WN 1-25 COPIES PER
NO PRICING ON QTY 10 OR LESS
EXCHANGE DEADLINE 6/30/2016
71 Bobby Thomson/25 20.00 50.00
76 Gil McDougald/25 25.00 60.00
77 Harry Walker/25 40.00 100.00
79 Johnny Pesky/25 40.00 100.00
80 Ken Griffey Jr./25 150.00 250.00
81 Mariano Rivera/25 150.00 300.00
82 Mark McGwire/25 EXCH 60.00 120.00
83 Pete Rose/25 50.00 120.00

2014 Panini National Treasures Legends Cuts Jumbo Materials Bat

RANDOM INSERTS IN PACKS
PRINT RUNS B/WN 1-25 COPIES PER
NO PRICING ON QTY 10 OR LESS
EXCHANGE DEADLINE 6/30/2016
82 Mark McGwire/25 EXCH 50.00 120.00

2014 Panini National Treasures Legends Cuts Jumbo Materials Cuts

RANDOM INSERTS IN PACKS
PRINT RUNS B/WN 1-25 COPIES PER
NO PRICING ON QTY 10 OR LESS
EXCHANGE DEADLINE 6/30/2016
71 Bobby Thomson/25 20.00 50.00
76 Gil McDougald/25 40.00 100.00
77 Harry Walker/25 40.00 100.00
79 Johnny Pesky/25 40.00 100.00

2014 Panini National Treasures Legends Cuts Jumbo Materials Nickname

RANDOM INSERTS IN PACKS
PRINT RUNS B/WN 1-25 COPIES PER
NO PRICING ON QTY 10 OR LESS
EXCHANGE DEADLINE 6/30/2016
71 Bobby Thomson/25 20.00 50.00
76 Gil McDougald/25 40.00 100.00
77 Harry Walker/25 40.00 100.00
79 Johnny Pesky/25 40.00 100.00
80 Ken Griffey Jr./25 150.00 250.00
81 Mariano Rivera/25 150.00 300.00
82 Mark McGwire/25 EXCH 50.00 120.00
83 Pete Rose/25 50.00 120.00

2014 Panini National Treasures Legends Cuts Jumbo Materials Nickname Bat

RANDOM INSERTS IN PACKS
PRINT RUNS B/WN 1-25 COPIES PER
NO PRICING ON QTY 10 OR LESS
EXCHANGE DEADLINE 6/30/2016
82 Mark McGwire/25 EXCH 60.00 150.00

2014 Panini National Treasures Legends Cuts Jumbo Materials Team Nickname Stat

RANDOM INSERTS IN PACKS
PRINT RUNS B/WN 1-25 COPIES PER
NO PRICING ON QTY 10 OR LESS
EXCHANGE DEADLINE 6/30/2016
71 Bobby Thomson/25 20.00 50.00

2014 Panini National Treasures Legends Jumbo Materials

RANDOM INSERTS IN PACKS
PRINT RUNS B/WN 1-25 COPIES PER
NO PRICING ON QTY 10 OR LESS
EXCHANGE DEADLINE 6/30/2016
21 Tom Yawkey/25 30.00 80.00

2014 Panini National Treasures Made In Autographs

RANDOM INSERTS IN PACKS
PRINT RUNS B/WN 10-99 COPIES PER
NO PRICING ON QTY 10 OR LESS
EXCHANGE DEADLINE 6/30/2016
1 Aaron Sanchez/99 12.00 30.00
2 Adam Jones/25 20.00 50.00
3 Addison Russell/99 25.00 60.00
4 Anthony Rizzo/99 20.00 50.00
5 Archie Bradley/99 5.00 12.00
6 Billy Hamilton/99 6.00 15.00
9 Byron Buxton/25 20.00 50.00
13 Chris Owings/99 5.00 12.00
14 Chris Sale/99 12.00 30.00
15 Clayton Kershaw/25 100.00 200.00
16 Clint Frazier/99 12.00 30.00
19 Dustin Pedroia/25 40.00 100.00
20 Eric Hosmer/25 20.00 50.00
22 Freddie Freeman/99 12.00 30.00
23 George Springer/99 15.00 40.00
24 Gerrit Cole/25 20.00 50.00
26 Joe Mauer/25 20.00 50.00
27 Jonathan Gray/99 10.00 25.00
28 Josh Donaldson/99 10.00 25.00
29 Justin Upton/25 12.00 30.00
31 Kyle Zimmer/99 8.00 20.00
33 Marcus Stroman/99 8.00 20.00
35 Matt Carpenter/99 20.00 50.00
37 Max Scherzer/25 20.00 50.00
40 Nick Castellanos/99 10.00 25.00
41 Noah Syndergaard/99 15.00 40.00
43 Barry Bonds/15 150.00 300.00
44 Pete Rose/25 50.00 120.00
49 Robert Stephenson/99 5.00 12.00
51 Ryan Braun/25 12.00 30.00
53 Shelby Miller/99 6.00 15.00
55 Taijuan Walker/99 5.00 12.00
56 Todd Helton/25 20.00 50.00
57 Tom Koehler/99 5.00 12.00
58 Kris Bryant/99 100.00 200.00
59 Travis d'Arnaud/99 EXCH 6.00 15.00
60 Wil Myers/25 12.00 30.00
61 Zack Wheeler/99 12.00 30.00
62 Carlos Correa/99 60.00 150.00
64 Orlando Cepeda/25 10.00 25.00
65 Bernie Williams/25 20.00 50.00
67 Salvador Perez/99 10.00 25.00
68 Odor/99 EXCH 12.00 30.00
69 Andres Galarraga/99 6.00 15.00
70 Carlos Gonzalez/25 10.00 25.00
71 Raicel Iglesias/99 12.00 30.00
75 Victor Martinez/25 15.00 40.00
78 Gregory Polanco/99 EXCH 8.00 20.00
79 Miguel Sano/99 6.00 15.00
86 Starling Marte/99 10.00 25.00
90 Yordano Ventura/99 EXCH 12.00 30.00
92 Aroldis Chapman/25 15.00 40.00
93 Jose Abreu/99 12.00 30.00
94 Jose Canseco/25 20.00 50.00
96 Luis Tiant/25 20.00 50.00
97 Rafael Palmeiro/25 12.00 30.00
98 Tony Perez/25 20.00 50.00
99 Yasmany Tomas/99 EXCH 10.00 25.00
100 Yoenis Cespedes/25 12.00 30.00

2014 Panini National Treasures Nicknames Materials

*NICKNAME: .4X TO 1X BASIC
RANDOM INSERTS IN PACKS
PRINT RUNS B/WN 4-99 COPIES PER
NO PRICING ON QTY 10 OR LESS
*PRIME: .6X TO 1.5X BASIC
32 Stan Musial/25 10.00 25.00
45 Chuck Klein/25 10.00 25.00

2014 Panini National Treasures Notable Nicknames Autographs

RANDOM INSERTS IN PACKS
PRINT RUNS B/WN 10-99 COPIES PER
NO PRICING ON QTY 10
EXCHANGE DEADLINE 6/30/2016
1 Jose Abreu/99 50.00 125.00
2 Jose Abreu/99 50.00 125.00
3 Matt Adams/25 12.00 30.00
10 Billy Butler/25 12.00 30.00
11 Jose Canseco/25 25.00 60.00
13 Joe Charboneau/99 6.00 15.00
14 Orlando Cepeda/25 20.00 50.00
15 Yoenis Cespedes/25 12.00 30.00
16 Yoenis Cespedes/25 12.00 30.00
17 Aroldis Chapman/25 12.00 30.00
20 Gerrit Cole/25 30.00 80.00
22 Andre Dawson/25 25.00 60.00
26 Carlton Fisk/25 25.00 60.00
27 Andres Galarraga/99 10.00 25.00
29 Adrian Gonzalez/25 12.00 30.00
30 Carlos Gonzalez/25 12.00 30.00
31 Luis Gonzalez/25 12.00 30.00
33 Sonny Gray/25 20.00 50.00
37 Gregory Polanco/99 EXCH 15.00 40.00
38 Noah Syndergaard/99 15.00 40.00
39 Roy Halladay/25 25.00 60.00
42 Willie Horton/99 10.00 25.00
43 Frank Howard/25 25.00 60.00
44 Frank Howard/25 25.00 60.00
46 Odor/99 EXCH 15.00 40.00
47 Travis d'Arnaud/99 EXCH 8.00 20.00
49 Al Kaline/25 30.00 80.00
50 Clayton Kershaw/25 60.00 150.00
58 Fred McGriff/25 20.00 50.00
61 Minnie Minoso/99 25.00 60.00
62 Paul Molitor/25 20.00 50.00
66 Don Newcombe/25 12.00 30.00
70 Jim Palmer/25 12.00 30.00
71 Dave Parker/99 12.00 30.00
72 Dustin Pedroia/25 40.00 100.00
73 Dustin Pedroia/25 40.00 100.00
74 Yordano Ventura/99 EXCH 12.00 30.00
80 Brooks Robinson/25 30.00 80.00
81 Brooks Robinson/25 30.00 80.00
94 Andre Thornton/99 6.00 15.00
95 Luis Tiant/25 12.00 30.00
97 Fernando Valenzuela/25 30.00 80.00
98 Billy Williams/25 20.00 50.00
99 David Wright/25 125.00 250.00

2014 Panini National Treasures NT Star Jumbo Materials

RANDOM INSERTS IN PACKS
PRINT RUNS B/WN 25-99 COPIES PER
1 Paul Goldschmidt/99 10.00 25.00
2 Justin Upton/99 6.00 15.00
3 Chris Davis/99 5.00 12.00
4 Manny Machado/25 8.00 20.00
5 Adam Jones/99 6.00 15.00
6 David Ortiz/99 10.00 25.00
7 Dustin Pedroia/25 8.00 20.00
8 Anthony Rizzo/99 10.00 25.00
9 Joey Votto/25 15.00 40.00
10 Miguel Cabrera/99 8.00 20.00
11 Albert Pujols/25 20.00 50.00
12 Yasiel Puig/99 8.00 20.00
13 David Wright/99 10.00 25.00
14 Derek Jeter/99 40.00 100.00
15 Masahiro Tanaka/25 15.00 40.00
16 Sonny Gray/99 6.00 15.00
17 Andrew McCutchen/25 40.00 100.00
18 Buster Posey/25 20.00 50.00
19 Felix Hernandez/99 8.00 20.00
20 Evan Longoria/25 12.00 30.00
21 Adrian Beltre/99 6.00 15.00
22 Yu Darvish/99 10.00 25.00
23 Edwin Encarnacion/99 8.00 20.00
24 Jose Bautista/99 6.00 15.00
25 Bryce Harper/25 15.00 40.00

2014 Panini National Treasures NT Star Jumbo Materials Bat

RANDOM INSERTS IN PACKS
PRINT RUNS B/WN 2-25 COPIES PER
NO PRICING ON QTY 10 OR LESS
2 Justin Upton/25 10.00 25.00
6 David Ortiz/25 20.00 50.00
12 Yasiel Puig/25 12.00 30.00
20 Evan Longoria/25 10.00 25.00
21 Adrian Beltre/25 12.00 30.00
23 Edwin Encarnacion/25 12.00 30.00

2014 Panini National Treasures NT Star Jumbo Materials Signatures

17 Ozzie Smith/25 25.00 60.00

2014 Panini National Treasures Rookie Colossal Materials Signatures

RANDOM INSERTS IN PACKS
STATED PRINT RUN 99 SER.#'d SETS
EXCHANGE DEADLINE 6/30/2016
1 Xander Bogaerts 15.00 40.00
2 Arismendy Alcantara 4.00 10.00
3 Taijuan Walker 12.00 30.00
4 George Springer 10.00 25.00
5 Nick Castellanos 12.00 30.00
6 Yordano Ventura EXCH 8.00 20.00
7 Jose Abreu 20.00 50.00
8 Travis d'Arnaud 5.00 12.00
9 Billy Hamilton 10.00 25.00
10 Kolten Wong 12.00 30.00
11 Chris Owings 4.00 10.00
12 Matt Davidson 5.00 12.00
13 Marcus Semien 20.00 50.00
14 Jimmy Nelson 4.00 10.00
15 Michael Choice 4.00 10.00
16 J.R. Murphy 4.00 10.00
19 David Hale 4.00 10.00
23 Roenis Elias 4.00 10.00
24 David Holmberg 4.00 10.00
25 Gregory Polanco 10.00 25.00

2014 Panini National Treasures Rookie Silhouette Autographs

RANDOM INSERTS IN PACKS
STATED PRINT RUN 99 SER.#'d SETS
EXCHANGE DEADLINE 6/30/2016
*GOLD: .6X TO 1.5X BASIC
1 Xander Bogaerts EXCH 15.00 40.00
2 Arismendy Alcantara 5.00 12.00
3 Taijuan Walker 15.00 40.00
4 George Springer 15.00 40.00
5 Nick Castellanos 15.00 40.00
6 Yordano Ventura EXCH 10.00 25.00
7 Jose Abreu 40.00 100.00
8 Travis d'Arnaud EXCH 6.00 15.00
9 Odor EXCH 12.00 30.00
10 Billy Hamilton 15.00 40.00
11 Marcus Stroman 8.00 20.00
12 Kolten Wong 6.00 15.00
14 Chris Owings 5.00 12.00
15 Rafael Montero 5.00 12.00
17 Matt Davidson 6.00 15.00
18 Chase Whitley 5.00 12.00
19 Marcus Semien 25.00 60.00
20 Jimmy Nelson 5.00 12.00
21 Michael Choice 5.00 12.00
23 C.J. Cron 5.00 12.00
24 J.R. Murphy 5.00 12.00
28 David Hale 5.00 12.00
29 Matt Shoemaker 10.00 25.00
30 Alex Guerrero 6.00 15.00
31 Tommy La Stella 5.00 12.00
33 Shane Greene 15.00 40.00
34 Andrew Heaney 5.00 12.00
35 Tucker Barnhart 5.00 12.00
36 Kevin Kiermaier 12.00 30.00
40 Roenis Elias 5.00 12.00
41 Nick Martinez 5.00 12.00
42 David Holmberg 5.00 12.00
43 Enny Romero 5.00 12.00
44 Anthony DeSclafani 5.00 12.00
45 Wei-Chung Wang 30.00 80.00
47 Gregory Polanco EXCH 10.00 25.00

2014 Panini National Treasures Silhouette Autographs

RANDOM INSERTS IN PACKS
PRINT RUNS B/WN 10-99 COPIES PER
EXCHANGE DEADLINE 6/30/2016
*GOLD: .5X TO 1.2X BASIC
1 Adam Jones/49 12.00 30.00
2 Adrian Beltre/49 30.00 80.00
4 Anthony Rizzo/99 12.00 30.00
6 Byron Buxton/99 10.00 25.00
10 Carlton Fisk/49 20.00 50.00
14 David Wright/49 15.00 40.00
16 Dustin Pedroia/49 12.00 30.00
18 Eric Hosmer/49 12.00 30.00
23 Gerrit Cole/49 15.00 40.00
25 Jose Abreu/99 20.00 50.00
27 Javier Baez/99 15.00 40.00
31 Justin Upton/49 6.00 15.00
32 Kyle Zimmer/99 10.00 25.00
37 Max Scherzer/49 20.00 50.00
41 Kris Bryant/99 150.00 300.00
43 Barry Bonds/25 200.00 300.00
44 Pete Rose/49 30.00 80.00
49 Ken Griffey Jr./25 100.00 200.00
50 Ryne Sandberg/25 25.00 60.00
51 Archie Bradley/99 5.00 12.00
53 Barry Bonds/25 200.00 300.00
NNO Jonathan Gray/99 6.00 15.00

2014 Panini National Treasures Teammates Materials

RANDOM INSERTS IN PACKS
PRINT RUNS B/WN 5-99 COPIES PER
NO PRICING ON QTY 10 OR LESS
1 C.Klein/L.O'Doul/25 20.00 50.00
2 B.Meusel/T.Lazzeri/27 25.00 60.00
6 L.Gomez/Y.Berra/25 25.00 60.00
7 H.Pennock/L.Gomez/25 30.00 80.00
9 C.Gehringer/H.Greenberg/25 25.00 60.00
14 E.Howard/R.Maris/49 20.00 50.00
16 A.Pujols/M.Trout/99 30.00 80.00
17 Stanton/Fernandez/99 6.00 15.00
18 D.Jeter/I.Suzuki/99 15.00 40.00
19 D.Jeter/M.Tanaka/99 15.00 40.00
20 I.Suzuki/M.Tanaka/99 12.00 30.00

2014 Panini National Treasures Timeline Box Scores

RANDOM INSERTS IN PACKS
PRINT RUNS B/WN 13-32 SER.#'d SETS
NO PRICING ON QTY 13

2014 Panini National Treasures Treasure Materials

RANDOM INSERTS IN PACKS
PRINT RUNS B/WN 25-99 COPIES PER
*PRIME/25: .6X TO 1.5X BASIC
1 Adam Jones/99 3.00 8.00
2 Adrian Beltre/99 4.00 10.00
3 Adrian Gonzalez/99 3.00 8.00
4 Albert Pujols/99 6.00 15.00
5 Andrew McCutchen/99 6.00 15.00
6 Aroldis Chapman/99 4.00 10.00
7 Anthony Rizzo/99 5.00 12.00
8 Billy Hamilton/99 3.00 8.00
9 Bryce Harper/25 10.00 25.00
10 Byron Buxton/99 5.00 12.00
11 Chris Davis/25 2.50 6.00
12 Cliff Lee/99 3.00 8.00
13 David Ortiz/99 4.00 10.00
14 Derek Jeter/99 10.00 25.00
15 Dustin Pedroia/99 4.00 10.00
16 Edwin Encarnacion/99 4.00 10.00
17 Evan Gattis/99 2.50 6.00
18 Evan Longoria/99 3.00 8.00
19 Felix Hernandez/99 3.00 8.00
20 Freddie Freeman/25 5.00 12.00
21 George Springer/25 5.00 12.00
22 Gerrit Cole/99 4.00 10.00
23 Giancarlo Stanton/25 4.00 10.00
24 Gregory Polanco/99 4.00 10.00
25 Hyun-Jin Ryu/99 3.00 8.00
26 Ichiro Suzuki/25 12.00 30.00
27 Jameson Taillon/99 3.00 8.00
28 Javier Baez/99 5.00 12.00
29 Jimmy Nelson/99 2.50 6.00
30 Joey Votto/99 4.00 10.00
31 Jonathan Gray/99 3.00 8.00
32 Justin Upton/99 3.00 8.00
33 Manny Machado/25 4.00 10.00
34 Mark McGwire/25 12.00 30.00
35 Masahiro Tanaka/25 20.00 50.00
36 Max Scherzer/99 4.00 10.00
37 Michael Choice/99 2.50 6.00
38 Miguel Cabrera/99 6.00 15.00
39 Oscar Taveras/99 3.00 8.00
40 Pablo Sandoval/99 3.00 8.00
41 Robinson Cano/99 3.00 8.00
42 Ryan Braun/99 3.00 8.00
43 Sonny Gray/99 3.00 8.00
44 Stephen Strasburg/25 4.00 10.00
45 Taijuan Walker/99 2.50 6.00
46 Travis d'Arnaud/99 3.00 8.00
47 Xander Bogaerts/25 8.00 20.00
48 Yasiel Puig/99 6.00 15.00
49 Yordano Ventura/99 3.00 8.00
50 Yu Darvish/99 4.00 10.00

2014 Panini National Treasures Treasure Signature Materials

RANDOM INSERTS IN PACKS
PRINT RUNS B/WN 5-99 COPIES PER
NO PRICING ON QTY 5
EXCHANGE DEADLINE 6/30/2016
7 Alex Guerrero/99 5.00 12.00
8 Andrew Heaney/99 4.00 10.00
9 Anthony DeSclafani/99 4.00 10.00
11 Billy Hamilton/99 10.00 25.00
12 C.J. Cron/99 4.00 10.00
17 Chase Whitley/99 4.00 10.00
19 Chris Owings/99 4.00 10.00
22 David Holmberg/99 4.00 10.00
23 David Hale/99 4.00 10.00
25 Danny Santana/99 10.00 25.00
33 Eugenio Suarez/99 20.00 50.00
39 George Springer/99 12.00 30.00
40 Gregory Polanco/99 10.00 25.00
44 Jimmy Nelson/99 4.00 10.00
45 J.R. Murphy/99 4.00 10.00
46 Jace Peterson/99 4.00 10.00
47 Jacob deGrom/99 125.00 300.00
48 Jake Marisnick/99 4.00 10.00
51 Jon Singleton/99 5.00 12.00
55 Jose Abreu/99 30.00 80.00
59 Kolten Wong/99 5.00 12.00
62 Luis Sardinas/99 4.00 10.00
64 Marcus Semien/99 20.00 50.00
65 Marcus Stroman/99 6.00 15.00
67 Matt Davidson/99 5.00 12.00
69 Matt Shoemaker/99 12.00 30.00
71 Michael Choice/99 4.00 10.00
76 Nick Castellanos/99 10.00 25.00
77 Nick Martinez/99 4.00 10.00
78 Odrisamer Despaigne/99 4.00 10.00
82 Rafael Montero/99 4.00 10.00
83 Randal Grichuk/99 8.00 20.00
86 Roenis Elias/99 4.00 10.00
87 Odor/99 EXCH 10.00 25.00
92 Taijuan Walker/99 4.00 10.00
93 Tanner Roark/99 4.00 10.00
96 Travis d'Arnaud/99 8.00 20.00
97 Xander Bogaerts/99 12.00 30.00
98 Yangervis Solarte/99 4.00 10.00
100 Yordano Ventura/99 12.00 30.00

2014 Panini National Treasures Treasure Signatures

RANDOM INSERTS IN PACKS
PRINT RUNS B/WN 25-99 COPIES PER
EXCHANGE DEADLINE 6/30/2016
*GOLD: .5X TO 1.2X BASIC p/r 99
*GOLD: .4X TO 1X BASIC p/r 25
21 Corey Knebel/99 4.00 10.00
29 Eddie Butler/99 4.00 10.00
30 Erik Johnson/99 4.00 10.00
36 Garin Cecchini/99 4.00 10.00
49 James Paxton/99 6.00 15.00
73 Miguel Sano/99 5.00 12.00
88 Shelby Miller/25 5.00 12.00
91 Steven Souza/25 5.00 12.00

2015 Panini National Treasures

1-150 PRINT RUN B/WN 10-99 COPIES PER
NO PRICING ON QTY 10
151-237 PRINT RUN B/WN 20-99 COPIES PER
EXCHANGE DEADLINE 7/8/2017
1 Babe Ruth JSY/25 200.00 400.00
2 Bill Dickey JSY/25 12.00 30.00
3 Billy Herman JSY/49 3.00 8.00
4 Billy Martin JSY/25 8.00 20.00
5 Bobby Thomson JSY/99 4.00 10.00
8 Charlie Gehringer JSY/99 8.00 20.00
10 Don Drysdale JSY/99 4.00 10.00
12 Eddie Stanky JSY/99 5.00 12.00
13 Frank Chance JSY/25 25.00 60.00
14 George Case JSY/99 3.00 8.00
15 George Kelly JSY/99 5.00 12.00
16 George Sisler JSY/99 8.00 20.00
17 Gil Hodges JSY/99 6.00 15.00
18 Hank Greenberg JSY/99 10.00 25.00
19 Harry Heilmann JSY/25 6.00 15.00
20 Harvey Kuenn JSY/99 3.00 8.00
21 Herb Pennock JSY/99 6.00 15.00
22 Honus Wagner JSY/25 30.00 120.00
23 Jackie Robinson JSY/99 15.00 40.00
24 Jimmie Foxx JSY/99 12.00 30.00
25 Joe Cronin JSY/99 3.00 8.00
26 Joe DiMaggio JSY/99 20.00 50.00
27 Joe Jackson Bat/25 50.00 120.00
28 Joe Medwick JSY/25 15.00 40.00
29 Johnny Mize JSY/99 4.00 10.00
30 Ken Boyer JSY/49 5.00 12.00
31 Lefty Gomez JSY/25 15.00 40.00
32 Lefty Grove JSY/25 30.00 80.00
33 Leo Durocher JSY/99 3.00 8.00
34 Lloyd Waner JSY/99 6.00 15.00
35 Lou Gehrig JSY/99 40.00 100.00
36 Luke Appling JSY/99 5.00 12.00
37 Mel Ott JSY/99 8.00 20.00
38 Nellie Fox JSY/99 4.00 10.00
39 Paul Waner JSY/99 6.00 15.00
40 Pee Wee Reese JSY/99 5.00 12.00
41 Pete Reiser JSY/99 5.00 12.00
42 Roberto Clemente JSY/99 20.00 50.00
43 Roger Maris JSY/99 12.00 30.00
44 Rogers Hornsby JSY/99 12.00 30.00
45 Ron Santo JSY/99 4.00 10.00
46 Roy Campanella JSY/25 12.00 30.00
48 Stan Musial JSY/25 12.00 30.00
49 Ted Kluszewski JSY/99 5.00 12.00
50 Ted Williams JSY/25 30.00 80.00
51 Thurman Munson JSY/25 15.00 40.00
52 Tommy Henrich JSY/99 3.00 8.00
53 Tony Lazzeri JSY/25 30.00 80.00
54 Tris Speaker JSY/99 12.00 30.00
55 Ty Cobb JSY/99 15.00 40.00
56 Walter Alston JSY/99 4.00 10.00
57 Willie Keeler JSY/99 10.00 25.00
58 Bill Mazeroski JSY/25 12.00 30.00
59 Al Kaline BAT/49 6.00 15.00
60 Billy Williams JSY/25 5.00 12.00
61 Bob Lemon JSY/25 8.00 20.00
62 Bobby Doerr JSY/49 8.00 20.00
63 Brooks Robinson JSY/49 8.00 20.00
64 Dave Winfield JSY/99 4.00 10.00
65 Bob Feller JSY/99 6.00 15.00
66 Mark McGwire JSY/99 8.00 20.00
67 Duke Snider JSY/99 6.00 15.00
68 Earl Weaver JSY/99 5.00 12.00
69 Early Wynn JSY/99 6.00 15.00
70 E.Mathews JSY/99 6.00 15.00
71 Eddie Murray JSY/99 4.00 10.00
72 Enos Slaughter JSY/99 8.00 20.00
73 Felix Hernandez JSY/99 4.00 10.00
74 Gary Carter JSY/99 4.00 10.00
75 Hal Newhouser JSY/25 8.00 20.00
76 Harmon Killebrew JSY/25 6.00 15.00
77 Hoyt Wilhelm JSY/99 4.00 10.00
78 Bo Jackson JSY/49 10.00 25.00
79 Jim Palmer JSY/99 4.00 10.00
80 Joe Morgan JSY/99 4.00 10.00
81 J.Bench JSY/99 6.00 15.00
82 Juan Marichal JSY/25 10.00 25.00
83 Larry Doby JSY/99 6.00 15.00
84 Lou Brock JSY/99 4.00 10.00
85 Orlando Cepeda JSY/99 4.00 10.00
86 George Brett JSY/99 6.00 15.00
87 Nolan Ryan JSY/99 8.00 20.00
88 Frank Thomas JSY/99 5.00 12.00
89 Randy Johnson JSY/49 5.00 12.00
90 Ozzie Smith JSY/99 6.00 15.00
91 Paul Molitor JSY/99 5.00 12.00
92 Don Mattingly JSY/99 8.00 20.00
93 Barry Bonds JSY/49 8.00 20.00
94 Reggie Jackson JSY/99 4.00 10.00
95 M.Rivera JSY/99 6.00 15.00
96 Rod Carew JSY/99 4.00 10.00
97 Adam Jones JSY/49 4.00 10.00
98 R.Sandberg JSY/99 6.00 15.00
99 John McGraw JSY/99 20.00 50.00
100 Tommy Lasorda JSY/99 4.00 10.00
101 Tony Gwynn JSY/99 5.00 12.00
102 Warren Spahn JSY/25 10.00 25.00
103 Ken Griffey Jr. JSY/99 10.00 25.00
104 Cal Ripken JSY/99 6.00 15.00
105 Willie McCovey JSY/99 4.00 10.00
106 Craig Biggio JSY/99 4.00 10.00
107 Pedro Martinez JSY/99 4.00 10.00
108 John Smoltz JSY/99 5.00 12.00
109 Kirby Puckett JSY/99 8.00 20.00
110 Frank Robinson JSY/99 4.00 10.00
111 Bob Gibson JSY/49 5.00 12.00
112 Yastrzemski JSY/99 6.00 15.00
113 Rickey Henderson JSY/99 5.00 12.00
114 Pete Rose JSY/99 8.00 20.00
115 Josh Donaldson JSY/99 4.00 10.00
116 C.Kershaw JSY/99 8.00 20.00
117 Mike Trout JSY/99 12.00 30.00
118 Ichiro Bat/99 6.00 15.00
119 Bryce Harper JSY/99 8.00 20.00
120 Buster Posey JSY/99 6.00 15.00
121 Giancarlo Stanton JSY/99 5.00 12.00
122 Albert Pujols JSY/99 5.00 12.00
123 Todd Frazier JSY/99 3.00 8.00
124 Manny Machado JSY/99 5.00 12.00
125 Anthony Rizzo JSY/99 6.00 15.00
126 Madison Bumgarner JSY/99 4.00 10.00
127 Johnny Sain JSY/99 5.00 12.00
128 Jacob deGrom JSY/99 5.00 12.00
129 Jose Altuve JSY/99 4.00 10.00
130 Yadier Molina JSY/99 6.00 15.00
131 Paul Goldschmidt JSY/99 5.00 12.00
132 Jose Bautista JSY/99 4.00 10.00
133 Miguel Cabrera JSY/99 5.00 12.00
134 Andrew McCutchen JSY/99 5.00 12.00
135 Nelson Cruz JSY/99 5.00 12.00
136 Jose Abreu JSY/99 5.00 12.00
137 David Ortiz JSY/99 5.00 12.00
138 Alex Rodriguez JSY/99 5.00 12.00
139 Moose Skowron JSY/99 3.00 8.00
140 Prince Fielder JSY/99 4.00 10.00
141 Eric Hosmer JSY/99 4.00 10.00
142 Matt Kemp JSY/99 4.00 10.00
143 Evan Longoria JSY/99 4.00 10.00
144 Bob Turley JSY/99 3.00 8.00
145 Michael Brantley JSY/99 4.00 10.00
146 Carlos Gonzalez JSY/99 4.00 10.00
147 Frankie Crosetti JSY/99 6.00 15.00
148 Joe Mauer JSY/99 4.00 10.00
149 Ryan Howard JSY/99 4.00 10.00
150 Sonny Gray JSY/99 4.00 10.00
151 Kris Bryant JSY AU/99 RC 75.00 200.00
152 Archie Bradley JSY AU/99 RC EXCH 4.00 10.00
153 Yasmany Tomas JSY AU/99 RC 5.00 12.00
154 Matt Barnes JSY AU/99 RC 4.00 10.00
155 Brandon Finnegan JSY AU/99 RC 6.00 15.00
156 Kendall Graveman JSY AU/99 RC 6.00 15.00
157 Maikel Franco JSY AU/99 RC 10.00 25.00
158 Addison Russell JSY AU/99 RC 20.00 50.00
160 Javier Baez JSY AU/99 RC 100.00 250.00
161 Michael Taylor JSY AU/99 RC 6.00 15.00
162 Christian Walker JSY AU/99 RC 6.00 15.00
164 Lane Adams JSY AU/99 RC 4.00 10.00
165 Matt Szczur JSY AU/99 RC 5.00 12.00
166 Andy Wilkins JSY AU/99 RC 4.00 10.00
167 Ryan Rua JSY AU/99 RC 6.00 15.00
169 Edwin Escobar JSY AU/99 RC 6.00 15.00
170 Rymer Liriano JSY AU/99 RC 4.00 10.00
171 R.J. Alvarez JSY AU/99 RC 4.00 10.00
172 Cory Spangenberg JSY AU/99 RC 4.00 10.00
173 Trevor May JSY AU/99 RC 4.00 10.00
174 Steven Moya JSY AU/99 RC 5.00 12.00
175 Wilmer Difo JSY AU/99 RC 4.00 10.00
178 Terrance Gore JSY AU/99 RC 4.00 10.00
179 Lindor JSY AU/99 RC EXCH 40.00 100.00
180 James McCann JSY AU/99 RC 10.00 25.00
181 Daniel Norris JSY AU/99 RC 4.00 10.00
182 Bryan Mitchell JSY AU/99 RC 4.00 10.00
183 Gary Brown JSY AU/99 RC 4.00 10.00
184 Mike Foltynewicz JSY AU/99 RC 4.00 10.00
185 Jorge Soler JSY AU/99 RC 6.00 15.00
186 Kevin Plawecki JSY AU/99 RC 3.00 80.00
187 Joc Pederson JSY AU/99 RC 12.00 30.00
188 Chris Heston JSY AU/99 RC 4.00 10.00
190 Jake Lamb JSY AU/99 RC 6.00 15.00
191 Rusney Castillo JSY AU/99 RC 5.00 12.00
192 Devon Travis JSY AU/99 RC 4.00 10.00
194 Dalton Pompey JSY AU/99 RC 5.00 12.00
195 Byron Buxton JSY AU/99 RC EXCH 20.00 50.00
196 Jung-Ho Kang JSY AU/99 RC EXCH 15.00 40.00
197 Blake Swihart JSY AU/99 RC 12.00 30.00
199 Daniel Corcino JSY AU/99 RC 4.00 10.00
200 Joey Gallo JSY AU/99 RC 12.00 30.00
201 Deven Marrero JSY AU/99 RC 6.00 15.00
202 Carlos Correa JSY/99 RC 30.00 80.00
203 Austin Hedges JSY AU/99 RC 4.00 10.00
204 David Peralta JSY AU/99 RC 4.00 10.00
206 Preston Tucker JSY AU/99 RC 10.00 25.00
208 Carlos Rodon JSY AU/99 RC EXCH 10.00 25.00
209 Noah Syndergaard JSY AU/99 RC EXCH 50.00 120.00
211 Matt Duffy JSY AU/99 RC 5.00 12.00
212 Lance McCullers JSY AU/99 RC 6.00 15.00
213 Steven Matz JSY AU/99 RC 4.00 10.00
214 Eddie Rosario JSY AU/99 RC 8.00 20.00
215 Williams Perez JSY AU/99 RC 5.00 12.00
216 Eduardo Rodriguez JSY AU/99 RC EXCH 4.00 10.00
217 A.J. Cole JSY AU/20 RC 4.00 10.00
218 Mark Canha JSY AU/99 RC 6.00 15.00
220 Corey Knebel JSY AU/99 RC 4.00 10.00
221 J.T. Realmuto JSY AU/99 RC 40.00 100.00
222 Steven Souza JSY AU/99 RC 5.00 12.00
223 Nick Ahmed JSY AU/99 RC 10.00 25.00
225 Sean Gilmartin JSY AU/99 RC 6.00 15.00
226 David Rollins JSY AU/99 RC 6.00 15.00
229 Andrew Chafin JSY AU/49 RC 4.00 10.00
230 Hunter Strickland JSY AU/99 RC 12.00 30.00
234 Taylor Jungmann JSY AU/99 RC 4.00 10.00
237 Billy Burns JSY AU/99 RC 4.00 10.00

2015 Panini National Treasures 42 Tribute Materials

RANDOM INSERTS IN PACKS
PRINT RUNS B/WN 25-99 COPIES PER
*PRIME/25: 1X TO 2.5X BASIC

1 Jorge Soler/99 4.00 10.00
2 Andrew McCutchen/99 4.00 10.00
3 Gerrit Cole/99 4.00 10.00
4 Starling Marte/99 3.00 8.00
5 Josh Harrison/99 2.50 6.00
6 Jacob deGrom/99 8.00 20.00
7 Lucas Duda/99 3.00 8.00
8 David Peralta/25 5.00 12.00
9 Jake Lamb/99 4.00 10.00
10 Andrew Chafin/99 2.50 6.00
11 Stephen Strasburg/99 4.00 10.00
12 Keone Kela/99 3.00 8.00
13 Collin McHugh/99 2.50 6.00
14 Paul Molitor/99 4.00 10.00
15 Eric Hosmer/99 3.00 8.00
16 Jose Bautista/99 3.00 8.00
17 Josh Donaldson/99 3.00 8.00
18 Wil Myers/99 3.00 8.00
19 Joey Votto/99 4.00 10.00
20 Troy Tulowitzki/25 6.00 15.00
21 Freddie Freeman/99 5.00 12.00
22 Paul Goldschmidt/99 4.00 10.00
23 Carlos Gonzalez/99 3.00 8.00
24 Matt Kemp/99 3.00 8.00
25 James Shields/99 2.50 6.00
26 Torii Hunter/25 2.50 6.00
27 Jason Kipnis/99 3.00 8.00

2015 Panini National Treasures All Century Materials
RANDOM INSERTS IN PACKS
PRINT RUNS B/WN 5-99 COPIES PER
NO PRICING ON QTY 10 OR LESS
2 Bill Dickey/25 12.00 30.00
3 Charlie Gehringer/25 10.00 25.00
5 George Sisler/49 8.00 20.00
6 Harry Heilmann/99 6.00 15.00
7 Honus Wagner/25 60.00 150.00
8 Jackie Robinson/25 30.00 80.00
9 Jimmie Foxx/25 12.00 30.00
10 Joe Cronin/99 5.00 12.00
11 Joe DiMaggio/25 25.00 60.00
12 Joe Jackson/25 30.00 80.00
15 Lou Gehrig/25 40.00 100.00
16 Mel Ott/99 6.00 15.00
17 Nellie Fox/99 8.00 20.00
18 Roberto Clemente/25 40.00 100.00
19 Rogers Hornsby/99 10.00 25.00
20 Roy Campanella/25 15.00 40.00
21 Satchel Paige/25 40.00 100.00
22 Harmon Killebrew/25 6.00 15.00
23 Ted Williams/99 12.00 30.00
24 Tris Speaker/49 10.00 25.00
25 Ty Cobb/25 40.00 100.00

2015 Panini National Treasures All Century Materials Combos
PRINT RUNS B/WN 10-99 COPIES PER
NO PRICING ON QTY 10
2 Jackson/Fox/25 50.00 120.00
3 Williams/Musial/99 25.00 60.00
4 Foxx/Cobb/49 30.00 80.00
5 Gehringer/Heilmann/25 20.00 50.00
6 Sisler/Hornsby/49 20.00 50.00
7 Dickey/Cronin/25 20.00 50.00
8 Paige/Feller/25 40.00 100.00
9 Gehrig/DiMaggio/25 60.00 150.00
10 Clemente/Robinson/49 75.00 150.00

2015 Panini National Treasures All Century Materials Quads
RANDOM INSERTS IN PACKS
PRINT RUNS B/WN 10-25 COPIES PER
NO PRICING ON QTY 10
2 Sphn/Mthws/Hrnsby/Msl/25 40.00 100.00
3 Ghrngr/Frsch/Hrtntt/Spkr/25 40.00 100.00
4 Clmnte/Wllms/Kllbrw/Rbnsn/25 100.00 200.00

2015 Panini National Treasures All Century Materials Triples
PRINT RUNS B/WN 5-25 COPIES PER
NO PRICING ON QTY 10 OR LESS
2 Sndr/Rbnsn/Cmpnlla/25 40.00 100.00
3 Wgnr/Jcksn/Cobb/25 150.00 300.00
4 Clins/Smmns/Foxx/25 40.00 100.00
6 Ghrngr/Grnbrg/Hlmnn/25 30.00 80.00
7 Sslr/Msl/Hrnsby/25 30.00 80.00
9 Fox/Clmnte/Wllms/25 100.00 200.00
10 DMggo/Mdwck/Spkr/25 40.00 100.00

2015 Panini National Treasures All Star Materials
RANDOM INSERTS IN PACKS
PRINT RUNS B/WN 22-99 COPIES PER
*PRIME/25: .75X TO 2X BASIC
1 Kris Bryant/99 12.00 30.00
2 Joc Pederson/99 10.00 25.00
3 Josh Donaldson/99 3.00 8.00
4 Felix Hernandez/99 3.00 8.00
5 Nelson Cruz/99 4.00 10.00
6 Mike Trout/99 20.00 50.00
7 Jose Altuve/99 3.00 8.00
8 Salvador Perez/99 3.00 8.00
9 Miguel Cabrera/99 4.00 10.00
10 Albert Pujols/99 5.00 12.00
11 Paul Goldschmidt/99 4.00 10.00
12 Clayton Kershaw/22 8.00 20.00
13 Manny Machado/99 4.00 10.00
14 Mike Moustakas/99 3.00 8.00
15 Madison Bumgarner/99 3.00 8.00
16 Gerrit Cole/99 4.00 10.00
17 Jacob deGrom/99 8.00 20.00
18 Yadier Molina/99 5.00 12.00
19 Andrew McCutchen/22 4.00 10.00
20 Justin Upton/99 3.00 8.00
21 Buster Posey/25 12.00 30.00
22 Dee Gordon/99 2.50 6.00
23 Bryce Harper/34 10.00 25.00
24 Todd Frazier/99 2.50 6.00
25 Giancarlo Stanton/99 4.00 10.00

2015 Panini National Treasures All Star Materials Combos
STATED PRINT RUN 25 SER.#'d SETS
1 B.Harper/K/Bryant 30.00 80.00
2 A.Pujols/M/Trout 20.00 50.00
3 P.Goldschmidt/A/Pollock 5.00 12.00
4 G.Cole/A/McCutchen 5.00 12.00
5 D.Gordon/G/Stanton 5.00 12.00
6 J.Bautista/J/Donaldson 10.00 25.00
7 J.Iglesias/M/Cabrera 10.00 25.00
8 F.Hernandez/N/Cruz 5.00 12.00
9 B.Holt/X/Bogaerts 5.00 12.00
10 J.Pederson/K/Bryant 15.00 40.00

2015 Panini National Treasures All Star Materials Quads
RANDOM INSERTS IN PACKS
STATED PRINT RUN 25 SER.#'d SETS
1 Brynt/Hrpr/Stntn/Trt 75.00 150.00
2 Krshw/Hrnndz/dGrm/Bmgrnr 20.00 50.00
3 Pdrsn/Brynt/Pnk/Arndo 20.00 50.00
4 Trt/Pjls/Psy/Pnk 25.00 60.00
5 Jns/Gnzlz/McCtchn/Tulo 10.00 25.00

2015 Panini National Treasures All Star Materials Triples
STATED PRINT RUN 25 SER.#'d SETS
1 Hrpr/Pdrsn/Brynt 25.00 60.00
2 Psy/Pnk/Bmgrnr 25.00 60.00
3 Gnzlz/Pdrsn/Krshw 20.00 50.00
4 Machado/Donaldson/Frazier 6.00 15.00
5 Grdn/Prz/Mstks 25.00 60.00
6 Psy/Mlna/Prz 20.00 50.00
7 Gnzlz/Rizzo/Gldschmdt 10.00 25.00
8 Dozier/Kipnis/Altuve 6.00 15.00
9 Brynt/Trt/Hrpr 60.00 150.00
10 Cole/deGrom/Gray 6.00 15.00

2015 Panini National Treasures Armory Booklet Materials
RANDOM INSERTS IN PACKS
STATED PRINT RUN 25 SER.#'d SETS
1 Kris Bryant 40.00 100.00
2 Francisco Lindor 30.00 80.00
3 Kyle Schwarber 30.00 80.00
4 Corey Seager 25.00 60.00
5 Byron Buxton 25.00 60.00
6 Maikel Franco 20.00 50.00
7 Yoan Moncada 25.00 60.00
8 Yasmany Tomas 12.00 30.00
9 Addison Russell 20.00 50.00
10 Javier Baez 80.00 200.00

2015 Panini National Treasures Baseball Signature Die Cuts
RANDOM INSERTS IN PACKS
PRINT RUNS B/WN 5-99 COPIES PER
NO PRICING ON QTY 15 OR LESS
4 Adrian Gonzalez/25 6.00 15.00
5 Alex Gordon/99 10.00 25.00
7 Andres Galarraga/25 15.00 40.00
8 Andy Pettitte/25 15.00 40.00
10 Anthony Rizzo/25 15.00 40.00
11 Archie Bradley/25 EXCH 8.00 20.00
13 Billy Butler/25 3.00 8.00
14 Blake Swihart/99 10.00 25.00
17 Carlos Rodon/99 6.00 15.00
18 Charlie Blackmon/25 5.00 12.00
19 Chris Davis/25 10.00 25.00
21 Corey Kluber/25 10.00 25.00
22 Corey Seager/25 40.00 100.00
25 Dave Winfield/25 20.00 50.00
26 David Ortiz/25 30.00 80.00
27 David Wright/25 20.00 50.00
28 Don Mattingly/25 30.00 80.00
31 Eric Hosmer/99 12.00 30.00
Inserted in '16 NT
33 Evan Longoria/25 10.00 25.00
37 Frank Howard/25 8.00 20.00
38 Freddie Freeman/99 8.00 20.00
39 George Springer/25 10.00 25.00
40 Gregory Polanco/99 6.00 15.00
41 Jacob deGrom/25 50.00 120.00
42 Jason Heyward/99 8.00 20.00
43 Matt Duffy/99 4.00 10.00
44 Joc Pederson/99 12.00 30.00
46 Joe Panik/99 12.00 30.00
47 Jonathan Lucroy/99 4.00 10.00
50 Jose Fernandez/99 10.00 25.00
51 Josh Donaldson/99 12.00 30.00
52 Josh Harrison/25 8.00 20.00
53 Jung-Ho Kang/75 EXCH 15.00 40.00
54 Justin Upton/25 6.00 15.00
56 Steven Matz/99 20.00 50.00
57 Kris Bryant/99 75.00 150.00
58 Kyle Seager/25 6.00 15.00
59 Luis Severino/25 15.00 40.00
62 Lorenzo Cain/99 15.00 40.00
67 Noah Syndergaard/25 40.00 100.00
69 Will Clark/25 20.00 50.00
70 Paul Goldschmidt/25 20.00 50.00
74 Rusney Castillo/99 4.00 10.00
78 Kyle Schwarber/25 50.00 120.00
80 Jake Arrieta/99 25.00 60.00
81 Todd Frazier/25 8.00 20.00
82 Troy Tulowitzki/25 12.00 30.00
83 Tyler Glasnow/99 4.00 10.00
86 Willie Horton/99 6.00 15.00
88 Yasmany Tomas/99 10.00 25.00
89 Yoan Moncada/99 30.00 80.00
90 Yoenis Cespedes/25 20.00 50.00
96 James McCann/99 4.00 10.00
97 Maikel Franco/99 4.00 10.00
98 Nathan Karns/99 3.00 8.00
99 Michael Taylor/99 3.00 8.00
101 Adam Jones/25 20.00 50.00
102 Addison Russell/99 20.00 50.00

2015 Panini National Treasures Baseball Signature Die Cuts Jose Abreu
RANDOM INSERTS IN PACKS
STATED PRINT RUN 99 SER.#'d SETS
EXCHANGE DEADLINE 7/8/2017
1 Jose Abreu 12.00 30.00
2 Jose Abreu 12.00 30.00

2015 Panini National Treasures Booklet Materials Combos
PRINT RUNS B/WN 5-25 COPIES PER
NO PRICING ON QTY 10 OR LESS
1 Bryant/Russell/25 20.00 50.00
3 Bryant/Schwrbr/25 30.00 80.00
7 Encrncn/Dnldsn/25 8.00 20.00
8 Russell/Baez/25 25.00 60.00
9 B.Buxton/M.Sano/25 12.00 30.00
10 Soler/Moncada/25 12.00 30.00
11 Bryant/Seager/25 20.00 50.00
12 Jones/Machado/25 25.00 60.00
13 Gldschmdt/Tomas/25 8.00 20.00
15 Pettitte/Boggs/25 12.00 30.00
18 Jackson/Sanders/25 20.00 50.00
19 Wright/deGrom/25 25.00 60.00

2015 Panini National Treasures Booklet Signatures Combos
RANDOM INSERTS IN PACKS
PRINT RUNS B/WN 5-25 COPIES PER
NO PRICING ON QTY 10 OR LESS
EXCHANGE DEADLINE 7/8/2017
1 K.Bryant/A.Russell 125.00 250.00
3 K.Bryant/K.Schwarber 150.00 300.00
9 B.Buxton/M.Sano 75.00 150.00
11 C.Seager/K.Bryant 150.00 300.00

2015 Panini National Treasures Career Year Materials
RANDOM INSERTS IN PACKS
PRINT RUNS B/WN 5-99 COPIES PER
NO PRICING ON QTY 10 OR LESS
2 Bill Dickey/25 12.00 30.00
5 Bobby Thomson/49 8.00 20.00
8 Charlie Gehringer/25 10.00 25.00
12 Eddie Stanky/25 6.00 15.00
14 George Case/25 8.00 20.00
16 George Sisler/25 8.00 20.00
17 Gil Hodges/99 6.00 15.00
18 Hank Greenberg/25 20.00 50.00
20 Harvey Kuenn/99 3.00 8.00
21 Herb Pennock/25 15.00 40.00
23 Jackie Robinson/25 30.00 80.00
34 Lloyd Waner/25 10.00 25.00
36 Luke Appling/99 5.00 12.00
37 Mel Ott/99 6.00 15.00
38 Nellie Fox/25 25.00 60.00
39 Paul Waner/25 10.00 25.00
40 Pee Wee Reese/25 8.00 20.00
41 Pete Reiser/99 5.00 12.00
43 Roger Maris/99 12.00 30.00
44 Rogers Hornsby/25 20.00 50.00
49 Ted Kluszewski/99 6.00 15.00
54 Tris Speaker/25 15.00 40.00
57 Willie Keeler/49 10.00 25.00
86 George Brett/25 12.00 30.00
87 Nolan Ryan/25 12.00 30.00
89 Randy Johnson/49 5.00 12.00
93 Barry Bonds/49 8.00 20.00
103 Ken Griffey Jr./99 8.00 20.00
104 Cal Ripken/49 8.00 20.00
106 Craig Biggio/25 4.00 10.00
107 Pedro Martinez/25 4.00 10.00
108 John Smoltz/25 5.00 12.00
109 Kirby Puckett/99 6.00 15.00

2015 Panini National Treasures Colossal Materials
RANDOM INSERTS IN PACKS
PRINT RUNS B/WN 25-99 COPIES PER
*PRIME NAME/20-25: .75X TO 2X BASIC
*PRIME NUM/20-25: .75X TO 2X BASIC
1 Adam Jones/25 3.00 8.00
2 Aroldis Chapman/99 4.00 10.00
3 Barry Bonds/49 12.00 30.00
4 Billy Hamilton/99 3.00 8.00
5 Brandon Belt/25 3.00 8.00
6 Brian Dozier/99 3.00 8.00
7 Brock Holt/49 2.50 6.00
8 Buster Posey/25 10.00 25.00
9 Byron Buxton/99 12.00 30.00
10 CC Sabathia/99 3.00 8.00
11 Chris Archer/99 2.50 6.00
12 Dallas Keuchel/99 3.00 8.00
13 Lorenzo Cain/99 2.50 6.00
14 Dustin Pedroia/25 4.00 10.00
15 Addison Russell/99 6.00 15.00
16 Edwin Encarnacion/99 4.00 10.00
17 Evan Longoria/25 3.00 8.00
18 Felix Hernandez/25 3.00 8.00
19 Francisco Lindor/99 20.00 50.00
20 Freddie Freeman/99 5.00 12.00
21 Gerrit Cole/99 4.00 10.00
22 Hanley Ramirez/99 3.00 8.00
23 Jacoby Ellsbury/99 3.00 8.00
24 Jason Heyward/99 3.00 8.00
25 Jason Kipnis/99 3.00 8.00
26 Johnny Cueto/99 3.00 8.00
27 Jose Abreu/25 4.00 10.00
28 Jose Bautista/99 3.00 8.00
29 Jose Fernandez/25 4.00 10.00
30 Jose Iglesias/99 3.00 8.00
31 Josh Donaldson/99 3.00 8.00
32 Josh Harrison/99 2.50 6.00
33 Justin Upton/99 3.00 8.00
34 Ken Griffey Jr./99 12.00 30.00
35 Kolten Wong/99 3.00 8.00
36 Kris Bryant/99 12.00 30.00
37 Madison Bumgarner/49 3.00 8.00
38 Maikel Franco/99 3.00 8.00
39 Manny Machado/25 6.00 15.00
40 Michael Brantley/49 3.00 8.00
41 Nelson Cruz/49 4.00 10.00
42 Prince Fielder/99 3.00 8.00
43 Ryan Braun/99 3.00 8.00
44 Sonny Gray/99 3.00 8.00
45 Starling Marte/99 3.00 8.00
46 Torii Hunter/99 2.50 6.00
47 Wil Myers/99 3.00 8.00
48 Yasiel Puig/25 4.00 10.00
49 Yasmany Tomas/99 3.00 8.00
50 Yu Darvish/25 4.00 10.00

2015 Panini National Treasures Game Ball Signatures
RANDOM INSERTS IN PACKS
PRINT RUNS B/WN 5-99 COPIES PER
NO PRICING ON QTY 15 OR LESS
1 Adam Jones 20.00 50.00
4 Andre Dawson/49 12.00 30.00
5 Andre Thornton/20 10.00 25.00
6 Andres Galarraga/20 15.00 40.00
9 Boog Powell/49 10.00 25.00
10 Brandon Phillips/25 10.00 25.00
15 Carlos Gonzalez/25 5.00 12.00
21 Dave Parker/25 10.00 25.00
23 David Justice/49 12.00 30.00
26 Dennis Eckersley/49 12.00 30.00
28 Dick Williams/40 3.00 8.00
29 Doug Harvey/49 3.00 8.00
31 Dusty Baker/49 6.00 15.00
32 Dwight Gooden/99 10.00 25.00
33 Edgar Martinez/49 12.00 30.00
34 Eric Davis/49 15.00 40.00
35 Fergie Jenkins/20 6.00 15.00
39 Fred Lynn/25 10.00 25.00
40 Fred McGriff/50 10.00 25.00
41 Freddie Freeman/30 12.00 30.00
42 Gary Sheffield/20 12.00 30.00
43 Gaylord Perry/49 10.00 25.00
45 George Kell/30 10.00 25.00
46 Gerrit Cole/25 4.00 10.00
48 Jason Kipnis/40 6.00 15.00
49 Jeff Bagwell/25 20.00 50.00
50 Jered Weaver/25 10.00 25.00
51 Jim Bunning/65 10.00 25.00
52 Jim Palmer/20 12.00 30.00
53 Jim Rice/25 25.00 50.00
54 Joe Girardi/49 6.00 15.00
58 Jose Canseco 10.00 25.00
60 Josh Donaldson/30 20.00 50.00
63 Kerry Wood/50 12.00 30.00
67 Matt Williams/50 10.00 25.00
68 Max Scherzer/20 25.00 60.00
75 Paul Konerko/40 15.00 40.00
80 Rafael Palmeiro/25 12.00 30.00
81 Red Schoendienst/25 20.00 50.00
85 Robin Ventura/25 20.00 50.00
89 Shelby Miller/30 6.00 15.00
95 Tony La Russa/99 10.00 25.00
96 Tony Perez/25 15.00 40.00
100 Willie McGee/49 10.00 25.00

2015 Panini National Treasures Leather and Lumber Signatures Leather
RANDOM INSERTS IN PACKS
PRINT RUNS B/WN 5-99 COPIES PER
NO PRICING ON QTY 15 OR LESS
1 Fergie Jenkins/20 12.00 30.00
2 Pete Rose/20 30.00 80.00
3 Craig Biggio/20 15.00 40.00
4 Bruce Sutter/25 10.00 25.00
5 Bob Feller/20 20.00 50.00
6 Dick Williams/25 10.00 25.00
9 Juan Gonzalez/99 10.00 25.00
11 Jose Abreu/25 15.00 40.00
12 Fred Lynn/25 10.00 25.00
13 Will Clark/25 25.00 60.00
15 Paul Molitor/25 12.00 30.00
20 Joey Gallo/30 20.00 50.00
24 Michael Brantley/96 4.00 10.00
27 Jim Rice/25 10.00 25.00
29 Tony Perez/20 15.00 40.00

2015 Panini National Treasures Leather and Lumber Signatures Lumber
RANDOM INSERTS IN PACKS
PRINT RUNS B/WN 5-49 COPIES PER
NO PRICING ON QTY 15 OR LESS
1 Fergie Jenkins/49 10.00 25.00
4 Bruce Sutter/49 10.00 25.00
6 Dick Williams/25 10.00 25.00
20 Joey Gallo/25 20.00 50.00
24 Michael Brantley/32 10.00 25.00
32 Dwight Gooden/49 12.00 30.00

2015 Panini National Treasures Legends Booklet Materials
RANDOM INSERTS IN PACKS
PRINT RUNS B/WN 1-25 COPIES PER
NO PRICING ON QTY 10 OR LESS
5 Bob Feller/25 20.00 50.00
6 Tommy Henrich/25 12.00 30.00
8 Billy Martin/25 15.00 40.00
11 Duke Snider/25 20.00 50.00
12 Eddie Stanky/25 12.00 30.00
15 Gil Hodges/25 15.00 40.00
20 Leo Durocher/25 12.00 30.00

2015 Panini National Treasures Made in Autographs
RANDOM INSERTS IN PACKS
PRINT RUNS B/WN 5-99 COPIES PER
NO PRICING ON QTY 15 OR LESS
EXCHANGE DEADLINE 7/8/2017
1 Adam Jones/25 20.00 50.00
2 Addison Russell/99 5.00 12.00
5 Andres Galarraga/25 15.00 40.00
6 Andy Pettitte/25 25.00 60.00
8 Anthony Rizzo/25 20.00 50.00
9 Archie Bradley/25 8.00 20.00
11 Bert Blyleven/25 10.00 25.00
12 Bert Campaneris/25 12.00 30.00
13 Juan Gonzalez/99 10.00 25.00
14 Blake Swihart/99 4.00 10.00
17 Byron Buxton/25 EXCH 20.00 50.00
20 Carlos Rodon/25 15.00 40.00
21 Chris Davis/25 10.00 25.00
23 Corey Kluber/25 8.00 20.00
24 Corey Seager/25 40.00 100.00
27 David Ortiz/25 50.00 120.00
28 David Wright/25 12.00 30.00
33 Evan Longoria/25 10.00 25.00
38 Freddie Freeman/99 10.00 25.00
40 Joc Pederson/99 5.00 12.00
42 Jonathan Lucroy/25 4.00 10.00
43 Jorge Soler/99 6.00 15.00
45 Jose Canseco/25 20.00 50.00
46 Jose Fernandez/25 20.00 50.00
47 Josh Donaldson/99 12.00 30.00
48 Josh Harrison/25 8.00 20.00
51 Jung-Ho Kang/75 EXCH 15.00 40.00
55 Kris Bryant/99 60.00 150.00
56 Kyle Schwarber/99 8.00 20.00
57 Luis Severino/99 12.00 30.00
59 Maikel Franco/99 6.00 30.00
63 Max Scherzer/25 25.00 60.00
67 Robert Refsnyder/99 4.00 10.00
68 Noah Syndergaard/49 15.00 40.00
69 Nolan Ryan/25 50.00 120.00
73 Paul Goldschmidt/25 20.00 50.00
84 Rusney Castillo/99 4.00 10.00
89 Jake Arrieta/99 30.00 80.00
92 Troy Tulowitzki/25 12.00 30.00
94 Wade Boggs/25 25.00 60.00
96 Will Clark/25 20.00 50.00
98 Yasmany Tomas/99 8.00 20.00
99 Yoan Moncada/25 75.00 200.00
100 Yoenis Cespedes/25 20.00 50.00

2015 Panini National Treasures Materials Prime
*PRIME: 1.2X TO 3X BASIC
RANDOM INSERTS IN PACKS
PRINT RUNS B/WN 1-25 COPIES PER
NO PRICING ON QUANTY 15 OR LESS

2015 Panini National Treasures Notable Nicknames Autographs
RANDOM INSERTS IN PACKS
PRINT RUNS B/WN 10-99 COPIES PER
NO PRICING ON QTY 10
EXCHANGE DEADLINE 7/8/2017
5 Bert Blyleven/25 20.00 50.00
9 Jimmy Wynn/99 3.00 8.00
11 Jose Canseco/25 15.00 40.00
15 Kris Bryant/99 60.00 150.00
16 Yoenis Cespedes/25 25.00 60.00
17 Bert Campaneris/25 12.00 30.00
22 Andre Dawson/25 20.00 50.00
23 Chris Davis/25 30.00 80.00
25 Jose Fernandez/25 10.00 25.00
27 Andres Galarraga/99 8.00 20.00
28 Will Clark/25 40.00 100.00
29 Adrian Gonzalez/25 12.00 30.00
32 Troy Tulowitzki/25 25.00 60.00
36 Byron Buxton/25 EXCH 12.00 30.00
38 Noah Syndergaard/99 25.00 60.00
40 Dennis Eckersley/25 10.00 25.00
44 Frank Howard/25 12.00 30.00
45 Reggie Jackson/25 20.00 50.00
47 Rollie Fingers/25 15.00 40.00
50 Bob Gibson/25 15.00 40.00
56 Bob Gibson/25 15.00 40.00
57 Paul Goldschmidt/25 20.00 50.00
58 Dwight Gooden/99 12.00 30.00
60 Dwight Gooden/99 12.00 30.00
61 Billy Hamilton/25 8.00 20.00
62 Paul Molitor/25 15.00 40.00
63 Todd Frazier/25 20.00 50.00
64 Dale Murphy/25 12.00 30.00
69 John Smoltz/25 15.00 40.00
70 Jim Palmer/25 10.00 25.00
71 Jim Rice/25 25.00 60.00
72 Dustin Pedroia/25 25.00 60.00
73 Dustin Pedroia/25 25.00 60.00
74 Dave Winfield/25 12.00 30.00
75 Gaylord Perry/99 8.00 20.00
88 Alex Gordon/25 25.00 60.00
89 Josh Donaldson/25 20.00 50.00
92 Corey Kluber/99 4.00 10.00
94 Evan Longoria/25 15.00 40.00
98 Phil Niekro/25 12.00 30.00
99 David Wright/25 12.00 30.00
101 Kyle Schwarber/99 15.00 40.00
102 Jacob deGrom/25 100.00 250.00

2015 Panini National Treasures Notable Nicknames Autographs Jose Abreu
RANDOM INSERTS IN PACKS
STATED PRINT RUN 99 SER.#'d SETS
EXCHANGE DEADLINE 7/8/2017
1 Jose Abreu 6.00 15.00
2 Jose Abreu 6.00 15.00

2015 Panini National Treasures NT Stars Booklet Materials Prime
RANDOM INSERTS IN PACKS
PRINT RUNS B/WN 1-25 COPIES PER
NO PRICING ON QTY 15 OR LESS
6 Felix Hernandez/25 6.00 15.00
7 Freddie Freeman/25 6.00 15.00
8 Gerrit Cole/25 12.00 30.00
16 Matt Kemp/25 5.00 12.00
23 Ryan Braun/25 6.00 15.00

2015 Panini National Treasures NT Stars Booklet Materials Bat
RANDOM INSERTS IN PACKS
PRINT RUNS B/WN 10-25 COPIES PER
NO PRICING ON QTY 15 OR LESS
1 Adrian Gonzalez/25 5.00 12.00
5 David Ortiz/25 10.00 25.00
7 Freddie Freeman/25 6.00 15.00
9 Giancarlo Stanton/25 10.00 25.00
12 Jose Bautista/25 8.00 20.00
14 Hanley Ramirez/25 5.00 12.00
16 Matt Kemp/25 5.00 12.00
17 Miguel Cabrera/25 12.00 30.00
19 Nelson Cruz/25 6.00 15.00
24 Buster Posey/25 15.00 40.00

2015 Panini National Treasures NT Stars Booklet Materials Bat Stat
RANDOM INSERTS IN PACKS
PRINT RUNS B/WN 1-25 COPIES PER
NO PRICING ON QTY 15 OR LESS
5 David Ortiz/25 10.00 25.00
7 Freddie Freeman/25 6.00 15.00
9 Giancarlo Stanton/25 10.00 25.00
12 Jose Bautista/25 8.00 20.00
14 Hanley Ramirez/25 5.00 12.00
16 Matt Kemp/25 5.00 12.00
17 Miguel Cabrera/25 12.00 30.00
19 Nelson Cruz/25 6.00 15.00
24 Buster Posey/25 15.00 40.00

2015 Panini National Treasures NT Stars Booklet Materials Multi Swatch Quads
RANDOM INSERTS IN PACKS
PRINT RUNS B/WN 10-25 COPIES PER
NO PRICING ON QTY 10 OR LESS
2 Albert Pujols/25 8.00 20.00
3 Alex Rodriguez/25 12.00 30.00
5 David Ortiz/25 10.00 25.00
6 Felix Hernandez/25 6.00 15.00
7 Freddie Freeman/25 6.00 15.00
8 Gerrit Cole/25 12.00 30.00
9 Giancarlo Stanton/25 10.00 25.00
10 Jose Abreu/25 10.00 25.00
11 Jose Altuve/25 12.00 30.00
12 Jose Bautista/25 8.00 20.00
13 Josh Donaldson/25 5.00 12.00
16 Matt Kemp/25 5.00 12.00
17 Miguel Cabrera/25 12.00 30.00
18 Mike Trout/25 40.00 100.00
19 Nelson Cruz/25 6.00 15.00
20 Paul Goldschmidt/25 10.00 25.00
21 Prince Fielder/25 5.00 12.00
22 Robinson Cano/25 6.00 15.00
23 Ryan Braun/25 6.00 15.00
24 Buster Posey/25 15.00 40.00
25 Yasiel Puig/25 6.00 15.00

2015 Panini National Treasures NT Stars Booklet Materials Multi Swatch Trios
RANDOM INSERTS IN PACKS
PRINT RUNS B/WN 5-25 COPIES PER
NO PRICING ON QTY 10 OR LESS
2 Albert Pujols/25 8.00 20.00
3 Alex Rodriguez/25 12.00 30.00
5 David Ortiz/25 10.00 25.00
6 Felix Hernandez/25 6.00 15.00
9 Giancarlo Stanton/25 10.00 25.00
10 Jose Abreu/25 10.00 25.00
11 Jose Altuve/25 12.00 30.00
12 Jose Bautista/25 8.00 20.00
13 Josh Donaldson/25 5.00 12.00
17 Miguel Cabrera/25 12.00 30.00
18 Mike Trout/25 40.00 100.00
19 Nelson Cruz/25 6.00 15.00
20 Paul Goldschmidt/25 10.00 25.00
21 Prince Fielder/25 5.00 12.00
22 Robinson Cano/25 6.00 15.00
24 Buster Posey/25 15.00 40.00
25 Yasiel Puig/25 6.00 15.00

2015 Panini National Treasures NT Stars Booklet Materials Nickname
RANDOM INSERTS IN PACKS
PRINT RUNS B/WN 10-25 COPIES PER
NO PRICING ON QTY 10
1 Adrian Gonzalez/25 5.00 12.00
2 Albert Pujols/25 8.00 20.00
3 Alex Rodriguez/25 12.00 30.00
5 David Ortiz/25 10.00 25.00
6 Felix Hernandez/25 6.00 15.00
7 Freddie Freeman/25 6.00 15.00
8 Gerrit Cole/25 12.00 30.00
9 Giancarlo Stanton/25 10.00 25.00
10 Jose Abreu/25 10.00 25.00
11 Jose Altuve/25 12.00 30.00
13 Josh Donaldson/25 5.00 12.00
15 Kris Bryant/25 30.00 80.00
17 Miguel Cabrera/25 12.00 30.00
18 Mike Trout/25 40.00 100.00
19 Nelson Cruz/25 6.00 15.00
20 Paul Goldschmidt/25 10.00 25.00
21 Prince Fielder/25 5.00 12.00
22 Robinson Cano/25 6.00 15.00
23 Ryan Braun/25 6.00 15.00
24 Buster Posey/25 15.00 40.00

2015 Panini National Treasures NT Stars Booklet Materials Nickname Bat
RANDOM INSERTS IN PACKS
PRINT RUNS B/WN 1-25 COPIES PER
NO PRICING ON QTY 15 OR LESS
5 David Ortiz/25 10.00 25.00
7 Freddie Freeman/25 6.00 15.00
9 Giancarlo Stanton/25 10.00 25.00
12 Jose Bautista/25 8.00 20.00
14 Hanley Ramirez/25 5.00 12.00
16 Matt Kemp/25 5.00 12.00
17 Miguel Cabrera/25 12.00 30.00
19 Nelson Cruz/25 6.00 15.00
24 Buster Posey/25 15.00 40.00

2015 Panini National Treasures Panini Signatures Jose Abreu
RANDOM INSERTS IN PACKS
STATED PRINT RUN 99 SER.#'d SETS
EXCHANGE DEADLINE 7/8/2017
1 Jose Abreu 12.00 30.00
2 Jose Abreu 12.00 30.00

2015 Panini National Treasures Silhouette Autographs
38 Mookie Betts/25 50.00 120.00

2015 Panini National Treasures Souvenir Cuts
RANDOM INSERTS IN PACKS
PRINT RUNS B/WN 1-99 COPIES PER
NO PRICING ON QTY 10 OR LESS
EXCHANGE DEADLINE 7/8/2017
2 Bobby Thomson/99 12.00 30.00
3 Harmon Killebrew/99 20.00 50.00
4 Gary Carter/25 25.00 60.00
5 Johnny Pesky/99 15.00 40.00
6 Ralph Kiner/99 15.00 40.00
8 Stan Musial/99 25.00 60.00
9 Warren Spahn/25 30.00 80.00
10 Lou Boudreau/25 15.00 40.00

2015 Panini National Treasures St. Patrick's Day Jerseys
RANDOM INSERTS IN PACKS
PRINT RUNS B/WN 10-49 COPIES PER
NO PRICING ON QTY 15 OR LESS
*PRIME/20-25: .75X TO 2X BASIC
1 Blake Swihart/49 4.00 10.00
2 David Ortiz/49 10.00 25.00
4 Jackie Bradley Jr./49 5.00 12.00
5 Pablo Sandoval/49 4.00 10.00
6 Rusney Castillo/49 4.00 10.00
7 Xander Bogaerts/25 10.00 25.00
8 Matt Barnes/49 3.00 8.00
9 Eduardo Rodriguez/49 3.00 8.00
10 Brian Johnson/49 3.00 8.00
11 Edwin Escobar/49 3.00 8.00
12 Deven Marrero/49 3.00 8.00
13 Brandon Finnegan/49 3.00 8.00
14 Lane Adams/49 3.00 8.00
15 Hunter Dozier/49 3.00 8.00
16 Terrance Gore/49 3.00 8.00
17 Raul Mondesi/49 5.00 12.00
18 Maikel Franco/49 12.00 30.00
19 Odubel Herrera/49 5.00 12.00
20 Matt Holliday/49 5.00 12.00
21 Yadier Molina/49 15.00 40.00
22 Stephen Piscotty/25 4.00 10.00
23 Marco Gonzales/49 5.00 12.00
27 Wilmer Difo/21 3.00 8.00

2015 Panini National Treasures Timeline Materials
RANDOM INSERTS IN PACKS
PRINT RUNS B/WN 10-25 COPIES PER
NO PRICING ON QTY 10
*CITIES/20-25: .4X TO 1X BASIC
*CITIES PRIME/25: .75X TO 2X BASIC
*PRIME/25: .75X TO 2X BASIC
2 Joc Pederson/25 6.00 15.00
3 Joc Pederson/25 6.00 15.00
4 Jorge Soler/25 5.00 12.00
5 Aroldis Chapman/25 5.00 12.00
6 Preston Tucker/25 5.00 12.00
7 Carlos Correa/20 25.00 60.00
8 Carlos Correa/25 25.00 60.00
9 Jake Lamb/25 5.00 12.00
10 Noah Syndergaard/25 8.00 20.00
11 Noah Syndergaard/25 8.00 20.00
12 Giancarlo Stanton/25 5.00 12.00
13 Kris Bryant/25 25.00 60.00
14 Jose Bautista/25 4.00 10.00
15 Hanley Ramirez/25 4.00 10.00
16 Nelson Cruz/25 5.00 12.00
19 Johnny Cueto/25 4.00 10.00
21 Justin Upton/25 4.00 10.00
22 Adrian Gonzalez/25 4.00 10.00
25 Johnny Cueto/25 4.00 10.00

2015 Panini National Treasures Timeline Materials Team Cities
*TEAM CITIES: .4X TO 1X BASIC
RANDOM INSERTS IN PACKS
PRINT RUNS B/WN 5-25 COPIES PER
NO PRICING ON QTY 15 OR LESS

2015 Panini National Treasures Treasured Materials
RANDOM INSERTS IN PACKS
PRINT RUNS B/WN 25-99 COPIES PER
*PRIME/25: .75X TO 2X BASIC
1 Adam Jones/99 3.00 8.00
2 Adrian Beltre/99 4.00 10.00
3 Adrian Gonzalez/99 3.00 8.00
4 Albert Pujols/49 5.00 12.00
5 Andrew McCutchen/99 4.00 10.00
6 Dallas Keuchel/99 3.00 8.00
7 Anthony Rizzo/99 5.00 12.00
8 Jose Altuve/25 3.00 8.00
9 Bryce Harper/25 10.00 25.00
10 Byron Buxton/99 12.00 30.00
11 Jose Abreu/25 4.00 10.00
12 Clayton Kershaw/99 6.00 15.00
13 David Ortiz/25 4.00 10.00
14 Kris Bryant/99 12.00 30.00
15 Dustin Pedroia/25 4.00 10.00
16 Edwin Encarnacion/25 4.00 10.00
17 Kyle Schwarber/99 12.00 30.00
18 Evan Longoria/25 3.00 8.00
19 Felix Hernandez/25 3.00 8.00
20 Freddie Freeman/25 5.00 12.00
21 Corey Seager/99 6.00 15.00
22 Lorenzo Cain/99 2.50 6.00
23 Giancarlo Stanton/99 4.00 10.00
24 Prince Fielder/99 3.00 8.00
25 Paul Goldschmidt/25 4.00 10.00
26 Ichiro/25 5.00 12.00
27 Francisco Lindor/99 20.00 50.00
28 Todd Frazier/99 2.50 6.00
29 Jose Bautista/49 3.00 8.00
30 Joey Votto/99 4.00 10.00
31 Josh Donaldson/99 3.00 8.00
32 Justin Upton/49 3.00 8.00
33 Manny Machado/99 4.00 10.00
34 Mark McGwire/99 6.00 15.00
35 Masahiro Tanaka/99 3.00 8.00
36 Chris Sale/99 4.00 10.00
37 Yasiel Puig/99 4.00 10.00
38 Miguel Cabrera/99 4.00 10.00
39 Matt Harvey/99 3.00 8.00
40 Pablo Sandoval/99 3.00 8.00
41 Robinson Cano/99 3.00 8.00
42 Mike Trout/99 20.00 50.00
43 Sonny Gray/99 3.00 8.00
44 Yu Darvish/99 4.00 10.00
45 Madison Bumgarner/25 3.00 8.00
46 Buster Posey/49 5.00 12.00

2015 Panini National Treasures Treasured Signature Materials
RANDOM INSERTS IN PACKS
PRINT RUNS B/WN 5-99 COPIES PER
NO PRICING ON QTY 15 OR LESS
69 Mookie Betts/99 50.00 60.00

2016 Panini National Treasures
1-150 RANDOMLY INSERTED IN PACKS
1-150 PRINT RUNS B/WN 10-99 COPIES PER
NO PRICING ON QTY 10
151-218 RANDOMLY INSERTED IN PACKS
151-218 PRINT RUNS B/WN 49-99 COPIES PER
EXCHANGE DEADLINE 6/14/2018
1 Babe Ruth Bat/25 100.00 250.00
2 Joe DiMaggio Bat/25 20.00 50.00
3 Ty Cobb Bat/25 40.00 100.00
4 Roberto Clemente Bat/25 25.00 60.00
5 Jackie Robinson Jsy/25 30.00 80.00
6 Billy Herman Bat/25 4.00 10.00
7 Billy Martin Jsy/99 4.00 10.00
8 Lou Gehrig Jsy/20 60.00 150.00
9 Honus Wagner Jsy/25 50.00 120.00
10 Ted Williams Jsy/25 25.00 60.00
11 Stan Musial Bat/25 10.00 25.00
12 Don Drysdale Jsy/99 4.00 10.00
13 Walter Alston Jsy/99 4.00 10.00
14 Tris Speaker Jsy/25 20.00 50.00
15 Eddie Stanky Bat/99 3.00 8.00
16 Luke Appling Jsy/99 4.00 10.00
17 Hank Greenberg Bat/25 15.00 40.00
18 Joe Cronin Bat/49 10.00 25.00
19 Nellie Fox Jsy/25 12.00 30.00
20 Roy Campanella Bat/25 12.00 30.00
21 Joe Medwick Jsy/25
22 Lloyd Waner Bat/49 6.00 15.00
24 Ron Santo Jsy/25 10.00 25.00
25 Roger Maris Bat/25 20.00 50.00
26 Pee Wee Reese Jsy/25 6.00 15.00
27 Tommy Henrich Jsy/25 8.00 20.00
28 Bobby Thomson Jsy/49 8.00 20.00
29 Satchel Paige Jsy/25 20.00 50.00
30 Paul Waner Bat/25 10.00 25.00

31 Dave Bancroft Bat/25 12.00 30.00
32 Harmon Killebrew Jsy/25 10.00 25.00
33 Jake Daubert Bat/25 8.00 20.00
34 Al Simmons Bat/49 6.00 15.00
35 Elston Howard Jsy/99 4.00 10.00
36 Charlie Keller Jsy/49 8.00 20.00
38 Arky Vaughan Bat/49 10.00 25.00
39 Ernie Lombardi Bat/49 10.00 25.00
40 Lou Brock Jsy/49 4.00 10.00
41 Cal Ripken Jsy/49 12.00 30.00
42 Ken Griffey Jr. Jsy/99 6.00 15.00
43 Pedro Martinez Jsy/99 4.00 10.00
44 Greg Maddux Bat/99 6.00 15.00
45 Craig Biggio Jsy/99 4.00 10.00
46 Mike Piazza Bat/99 5.00 12.00
47 Don Mattingly Jsy/99 6.00 15.00
48 Paul Molitor Jsy/49 5.00 12.00
49 Max Carey Bat/25 40.00 100.00
50 Ted Lyons Jsy/25 20.00 50.00
51 Sam Rice Bat/25 20.00 50.00
52 Mariano Rivera Jsy/49 6.00 15.00
53 Nap Lajoie Bat/25 40.00 100.00
54 Bob Feller Jsy/99 4.00 10.00
56 Ralph Kiner Bat/25 10.00 25.00
57 Kirby Puckett Bat/99 8.00 20.00
58 Duke Snider Jsy/99 4.00 10.00
59 Gary Carter Bat/99 4.00 10.00
60 Lefty O'Doul Jsy/49 12.00 30.00
61 Tony Gwynn Jsy/99 5.00 12.00
62 Rickey Henderson Jsy/49 10.00 25.00
63 Nolan Ryan Jsy/99 8.00 20.00
64 Mark McGwire Jsy/99 6.00 15.00
65 Barry Bonds Jsy/25 10.00 25.00
66 Barry Bonds Jsy/99 5.00 12.00
67 Ryne Sandberg Bat/25 10.00 25.00
68 Earl Weaver Jsy/49 4.00 10.00
69 Chuck Klein Jsy/25 12.00 30.00
70 Frankie Frisch Bat/49 8.00 20.00
71 Roger Bresnahan Bat/99 10.00 25.00
72 Enos Slaughter Jsy/25 15.00 40.00
73 Johnny Sain Jsy/49 6.00 15.00
74 Don Hoak Jsy/49 6.00 15.00
75 Goose Goslin Bat/49 8.00 20.00
76 Mike Trout Jsy/49 12.00 30.00
77 Frank Thomas Jsy/99 5.00 12.00
78 George Brett Jsy/25 10.00 25.00
79 Bryce Harper Jsy/25 8.00 20.00
80 Josh Donaldson Jsy/99 4.00 10.00
81 Jake Arrieta Jsy/49 4.00 10.00
82 Manny Machado Jsy/99 5.00 12.00
83 Kris Bryant Jsy/99 8.00 20.00
84 Madison Bumgarner Jsy/99 5.00 12.00
85 Adam Wainwright Jsy/99 4.00 10.00
86 Clayton Kershaw Jsy/99 5.00 12.00
87 Jose Altuve Jsy/49 4.00 10.00
88 Xander Bogaerts Jsy/99 4.00 10.00
89 David Ortiz Jsy/99 5.00 12.00
90 Alex Rodriguez Jsy/99 5.00 12.00
91 Pete Rose Jsy/49 5.00 12.00
92 Albert Pujols Jsy/99 6.00 15.00
93 Johnny Bench Jsy/99 6.00 15.00
94 Frank Robinson Bat/49 4.00 10.00
95 Frank Robinson Jsy/99 4.00 10.00
96 Roger Clemens Jsy/25 8.00 20.00
97 Nolan Arenado Jsy/49 8.00 20.00
98 Anthony Rizzo Jsy/49 6.00 15.00
99 Eric Hosmer Jsy/99 4.00 10.00
100 Salvador Perez Jsy/25 20.00 50.00
101 Giancarlo Stanton Jsy/99 5.00 12.00
102 Carlos Correa Jsy/49 10.00 25.00
103 Daniel Murphy Jsy/99 4.00 10.00
104 Max Scherzer Jsy/25 6.00 15.00
105 Jacob deGrom Jsy/99 10.00 25.00
106 Stephen Strasburg Jsy/99 5.00 12.00
107 Jose Fernandez Jsy/99 5.00 12.00
108 Todd Frazier Jsy/99 3.00 8.00
109 Chris Sale Jsy/99 5.00 12.00
110 Johnny Cueto Jsy/99 4.00 10.00
111 Yadier Molina Jsy/99 6.00 15.00
112 Buster Posey Jsy/49 5.00 12.00
113 Robinson Cano Jsy/25 5.00 12.00
114 Francisco Lindor Jsy/99 4.00 10.00
115 Addison Russell Jsy/99 5.00 12.00
116 Evan Longoria Jsy/99 4.00 10.00
117 Miguel Cabrera Jsy/99 5.00 12.00
118 Ian Desmond Jsy/99 3.00 8.00
120 Justin Verlander Jsy/99 5.00 12.00
121 Wil Myers Jsy/99 4.00 10.00
122 Mookie Betts Jsy/99 5.00 12.00
123 Carlos Gonzalez Jsy/99 4.00 10.00
124 David Price Jsy/99 4.00 10.00
125 Jake Lamb Jsy/99 4.00 10.00
126 Jose Bautista Jsy/99 4.00 10.00
127 Victor Martinez Jsy/99 4.00 10.00
128 Edwin Encarnacion Jsy/99 5.00 12.00
129 Kyle Seager Jsy/99 3.00 8.00
130 Andrew McCutchen Jsy/99 6.00 15.00
131 Jonathan Schoop Jsy/99 3.00 8.00
132 Jose Abreu Bat/25 6.00 15.00
133 Dustin Pedroia Jsy/99 5.00 12.00
134 David Wright Jsy/99 4.00 10.00
135 Gary Sheffield Jsy/49 3.00 8.00
136 Darryl Strawberry Jsy/99 3.00 8.00
138 Andres Galarraga Jsy/99 4.00 10.00
139 Omar Vizquel Jsy/49 4.00 10.00
140 Carl Yastrzemski Jsy/49 6.00 15.00
141 Mike Schmidt Bat/49 5.00 12.00
142 Bob Gibson Jsy/49 4.00 10.00
143 Steve Carlton Jsy/25 5.00 12.00
144 Reggie Jackson Jsy/25 5.00 12.00
145 Rod Carew Jsy/25 5.00 12.00
146 Ozzie Smith Jsy/99 5.00 12.00
147 Ken Griffey Jr. Jsy/25 30.00 80.00
148 Chris Davis Jsy/99 3.00 8.00
149 Barry Larkin Jsy/99 4.00 10.00
150 Yu Darvish JSY/99 6.00 15.00
151 Schwarber JSY AU/99 RC 15.00 40.00
152 C.Seager JSY AU/99 RC 20.00 50.00
153 M.Sano JSY AU/99 RC 12.00 30.00
154 T.Story JSY AU/49 RC 20.00 50.00
155 A.Nola JSY AU/99 RC 8.00 20.00
156 A.Diaz JSY AU/99 RC 20.00 50.00
157 Alex Dickerson JSY AU/99 RC 4.00 10.00
158 Brandon Drury JSY AU/99 RC 6.00 15.00
159 Brian Ellington JSY AU/99 RC 4.00 10.00
160 Brian Johnson JSY AU/99 RC 4.00 10.00
161 Byung-ho Park JSY AU/99 RC 5.00 12.00
162 Edwards Jr. JSY AU/99 RC 5.00 12.00
163 Colin Rea JSY AU/99 RC 4.00 10.00
164 Dae-ho Lee JSY AU/99 RC 6.00 15.00
165 Dariel Alvarez JSY AU/99 RC 4.00 10.00
166 Elias Diaz JSY AU/99 RC 6.00 15.00
167 Frankie Montas JSY AU/99 RC 5.00 12.00
168 G.Bird JSY AU/99 RC 5.00 12.00
169 Henry Owens JSY AU/99 RC 5.00 12.00
171 J.Eickhoff JSY AU/99 RC 6.00 15.00
173 Joey Rickard JSY AU/99 RC 4.00 10.00
174 John Lamb JSY AU/99 RC 4.00 10.00
175 Jonathan Gray JSY AU/99 RC 5.00 12.00
176 Jorge Lopez JSY AU/99 RC 4.00 10.00
177 Jose Peraza JSY AU/99 RC 5.00 12.00
178 Kaleb Cowart JSY AU/99 RC 4.00 10.00
179 Kelby Tomlinson JSY AU/99 RC 5.00 12.00
180 Ketel Marte JSY AU/99 RC 6.00 15.00
181 Kyle Waldrop JSY AU/99 RC 5.00 12.00
182 L.Severino JSY AU/99 RC 15.00 40.00
183 Luke Jackson JSY AU/99 RC 4.00 10.00
184 Mac Williamson JSY AU/99 RC 6.00 15.00
185 Mallex Smith JSY AU/99 RC 5.00 12.00
186 M.Kepler JSY AU/99 RC 10.00 25.00
188 Michael Reed JSY AU/99 RC 4.00 10.00
189 N.Mazara JSY AU/99 RC 12.00 30.00
190 Pedro Severino JSY AU/99 RC 4.00 10.00
191 Peter O'Brien JSY AU/99 RC 4.00 10.00
192 R.Mondesi JSY AU/99 RC 6.00 15.00
193 Richie Shaffer JSY AU/79 RC 4.00 10.00
194 Rob Refsnyder JSY AU/99 RC 6.00 15.00
195 Robert Stephenson JSY AU/99 RC 4.00 10.00
196 Ross Stripling JSY AU/99 RC 4.00 10.00
197 S.Oh JSY AU/99 RC 10.00 25.00
198 Socrates Brito JSY AU/99 RC 4.00 10.00
199 S.Piscotty JSY AU/99 RC 8.00 20.00
200 Tom Murphy JSY AU/99 RC 4.00 10.00
201 Travis Jankowski JSY AU/99 RC 4.00 10.00
202 Trayce Thompson JSY AU/99 RC 6.00 15.00
203 T.Turner JSY AU/99 RC 12.00 50.00
204 Tyler Duffey JSY AU/99 RC 4.00 10.00
205 Tyler Naquin JSY AU/99 RC 6.00 15.00
206 Tyler White JSY AU/99 RC 4.00 10.00
207 Brett Eibner JSY AU/99 RC 4.00 10.00
208 Zack Godley JSY AU/99 RC 4.00 10.00
209 J.Urias JSY AU/99 RC 10.00 25.00
211 Greg Mahle JSY AU/99 RC 4.00 10.00
212 J.Taillon JSY AU/99 RC 20.00 50.00
213 Contreras JSY AU/99 RC 10.00 25.00
214 Tim Anderson JSY AU/99 RC 50.00 120.00
215 A.J. Reed JSY AU/99 RC 4.00 10.00
216 Brandon Nimmo JSY AU/99 RC 6.00 15.00
217 Merrifield JSY AU/99 RC 100.00 250.00
218 L.Giolito JSY AU/99 RC 6.00 15.00

2016 Panini National Treasures 12 Player Materials

RANDOM INSERTS IN PACKS
PRINT RUNS B/WN 10-99 COPIES PER
NO PRICING ON QTY 10
2 Lrkn/Rbnsn/Cal/Jones/etc 30.00 80.00
3 ARod/Thms/Brtt/Bgwll/etc 40.00 100.00

2016 Panini National Treasures 16 Player Materials

RANDOM INSERTS IN PACKS
PRINT RUNS B/WN 16-99 COPIES PER
NO PRICING ON QTY 16
1 Gib/Mat/Rob/Thom/etc 75.00 200.00
3 Reed/Drry/Park/Sgr/etc 20.00 50.00

2016 Panini National Treasures 42 Tribute Material Signatures

RANDOM INSERTS IN PACKS
PRINT RUNS B/WN 15-99 COPIES PER
NO PRICING ON QTY 15
EXCHANGE DEADLINE 6/14/2018
42CA Chris Archer/25 5.00 12.00
42CG Carlos Gonzalez/25 6.00 15.00
42JD Josh Donaldson/49 10.00 25.00
42JH Jason Heyward/25 12.00 30.00
42JL Jake Lamb/99 4.00 10.00
42PM Paul Molitor/49 6.00 15.00
42RS Ross Stripling/99 3.00 8.00
42TH Todd Helton/25 12.00 30.00
42TN Tyler Naquin/99 5.00 12.00
42TS Trevor Story/99 10.00 25.00
42TW Tyler White/99 3.00 8.00
42WM Wil Myers/49 5.00 12.00

2016 Panini National Treasures 42 Tribute Materials

RANDOM INSERTS IN PACKS
PRINT RUNS BW/N 20-99 COPIES PER
42AB Adrian Beltre/99 5.00 12.00
42AM Andrew McCutchen/49 8.00 20.00
42CK Clayton Kershaw/49 5.00 12.00
42CM Collin McHugh/99 3.00 8.00
42DP David Peralta/99 3.00 8.00
42JB Jose Bautista/49 4.00 10.00
42JH Josh Harrison/99 3.00 8.00
42JH Jason Heyward/99 4.00 10.00
42JL Jake Lamb/20 5.00 12.00
42JU Justin Upton/25 5.00 12.00
42JV Joey Votto/25 6.00 15.00
42LD Lucas Duda/99 4.00 10.00
42MK Matt Kemp/49 4.00 10.00
42NA Nolan Arenado/49 8.00 20.00
42PK Paul Konerko/99 4.00 10.00
42PM Paul Molitor/99 5.00 12.00
42SC Starlin Castro/99 4.00 10.00
42SM Starling Marte/99 4.00 10.00
42SS Stephen Strasburg/99 5.00 12.00
42TH Todd Helton/99 4.00 10.00
42TN Tyler Naquin/99 5.00 12.00
42TS Trevor Story/99 6.00 15.00
42TW Tyler White/99 3.00 8.00
42WM Wil Myers/99 4.00 10.00
42ZC Zack Cozart/99 3.00 8.00

2016 Panini National Treasures All Out Jerseys

RANDOM INSERTS IN PACKS
PRINT RUNS BW/N 5-99 COPIES PER
1 Cal Ripken/25 20.00 50.00
3 Dustin Pedroia/25 15.00 40.00
4 Jason Heyward/25 8.00 20.00
5 Willson Contreras/25 20.00 50.00
6 Craig Biggio/25 10.00 25.00
8 Josh Harrison/25 4.00 10.00
9 Byron Buxton/99 8.00 20.00
10 Salvador Perez/25 12.00 30.00

2016 Panini National Treasures Armory Booklet Materials

RANDOM INSERTS IN PACKS
PRINT RUNS BW/N 25-99 COPIES PER
*PRIME/25: .6X TO 1.5X p/r 49-99
AMBAR Alex Reyes/99 6.00 15.00
AMBAR A.J. Reed/99 8.00 20.00
AMBCS Corey Seager/99 20.00 50.00
AMBDW David Wright/99 12.00 30.00
AMBJG Jonathan Gray/25 8.00 20.00
AMBJP Jose Peraza/99 6.00 15.00
AMBKS Kyle Schwarber/99 25.00 60.00
AMBLG Lou Gehrig/25 400.00 800.00
AMBLG Lucas Giolito/49 8.00 20.00
AMBLS Luis Severino/49 12.00 30.00
AMBMK Max Kepler/25 10.00 25.00
AMBMS Mike Schmidt/25 40.00 100.00
AMBMS Miguel Sano/99 10.00 25.00
AMBSP Stephen Piscotty/25 12.00 30.00
AMBTG Tony Gwynn/25 50.00 120.00
AMBWC Willson Contreras/99 15.00 40.00

2016 Panini National Treasures Baseball Signatures

RANDOM INSERTS IN PACKS
PRINT RUNS B/WN 10-99 COPIES PER
NO PRICING ON QTY 10
EXCHANGE DEADLINE 6/14/2018
1 Aledmys Diaz/99 10.00 25.00
2 Dae-ho Lee/99 6.00 15.00
4 Ji-Man Choi/99 10.00 25.00
5 Joey Rickard/99 4.00 10.00
6 Mallex Smith/99 4.00 10.00
7 Nomar Mazara/99
8 Ross Stripling/99 4.00 10.00
9 Seung-Hwan Oh/99
10 Tyler Naquin/99 6.00 15.00
11 Tyler White/99 6.00 15.00
12 Henry Owens/99 5.00 12.00
13 Byung-ho Park/99 5.00 12.00
14 Miguel Sano/99 10.00 25.00
15 Stephen Piscotty/99 6.00 15.00
16 Aaron Nola/99 8.00 20.00
17 Julio Urias/99 12.00 30.00
18 Albert Almora Jr./99
19 Jameson Taillon/99 5.00 12.00
21 Jacob deGrom/25
22 Todd Frazier/25 5.00 12.00
23 Jose Abreu/99 6.00 15.00
24 Dustin Pedroia/25
25 Randal Grichuk/99 4.00 10.00
26 Joe Panik/99 5.00 12.00
27 David Peralta/99 4.00 10.00
28 Lorenzo Cain/99 8.00 20.00
29 Anthony Rizzo/25
30 Omar Vizquel/99 5.00 12.00
31 Don Mattingly/25 40.00 100.00
33 Steven Souza/99 5.00 12.00
36 Joc Pederson/99 5.00 12.00
38 Trevor Story/99 20.00 50.00
40 Tim Anderson/49 50.00 120.00
41 Paul Molitor/99 6.00 15.00
45 Juan Gonzalez/25 12.00 30.00
46 Rafael Devers/99 8.00 20.00
49 Steve Carlton/25 6.00 15.00

2016 Panini National Treasures Clear Signatures

RANDOM INSERTS IN PACKS
PRINT RUNS B/WN 10-99 COPIES PER
NO PRICING ON QTY 15 OR LESS
EXCHANGE DEADLINE 6/14/2018
CSAD Andre Dawson/25 8.00 20.00
CSAJ Adam Jones/99 5.00 12.00
CSAK Al Kaline/25 25.00 50.00
CSAR Addison Russell/99 15.00 40.00
CSBB Bert Blyleven/25 8.00 20.00
CSBG Bob Gibson/25 15.00 40.00
CSBM Bill Mazeroski/25 12.00 30.00
CSCG Carlos Gomez/99 4.00 10.00
CSCK Clayton Kershaw/25 40.00 100.00
CSCM Carlos Martinez/99 5.00 12.00
CSCO Corey Seager/40 20.00 50.00
CSCS Chris Sale/99 10.00 25.00
CSCY Corey Kluber/49 5.00 12.00
CSDK Dallas Keuchel/75 15.00 20.00
CSDO Don Sutton/99 5.00 12.00
CSDS Darryl Strawberry/99 6.00 15.00
CSEB Ernie Banks/25 30.00 80.00
CSEG Evan Gattis/99 4.00 10.00
CSEH Eric Hosmer/49 12.00 30.00
CSGC Gerrit Cole/49 6.00 15.00
CSGG Goose Gossage/99 5.00 12.00
CSGP Gregory Polanco/99 5.00 12.00
CSGS George Springer/99 6.00 15.00
CSJA Jose Altuve/75 15.00 40.00
CSJA Jose Abreu/99 6.00 15.00
CSJB Jeff Bagwell/25 20.00 50.00
CSJC Jose Canseco/99 6.00 15.00
CSJF Jose Fernandez/56 8.00 20.00
CSJG Jonathan Gray/99 4.00 10.00
CSJK Jason Kipnis/99 5.00 12.00
CSJS Jonathan Schoop/99 4.00 10.00
CSJW Jered Weaver/25 6.00 15.00
CSKS Kyle Schwarber/99 25.00 60.00
CSMB Mookie Betts/49 50.00 120.00
CSMC Michael Conforto/99 10.00 25.00
CSMS Max Scherzer/99 25.00 60.00
CSNC Nick Castellanos/99 6.00 15.00
CSOS Ozzie Smith/25 10.00 25.00
CSRA Roberto Alomar/25 12.00 30.00
CSSG Sonny Gray/75 5.00 12.00
CSTN Tyler Naquin/99 6.00 15.00
CSVM Victor Martinez/49 5.00 12.00

2016 Panini National Treasures Colossal Material Signatures

RANDOM INSERTS IN PACKS
PRINT RUNS B/WN 10-99 COPIES PER
NO PRICING ON QTY 15 OR LESS
EXCHANGE DEADLINE 6/14/2018
*PURPLE/30-49: .5X TO 1.2X p/r 99
*PURPLE/30-49: .4X TO 1X p/r 49
*PURPLE/25: .6X TO 1.5X p/r 99
*PURPLE/25: .5X TO 1.2X p/r 49
*PURPLE/25: .4X TO 1X p/r 25
*GOLD/25: .6X TO 1.5X p/r 99
*GOLD/25: .5X TO 1.2X p/r 49
*GOLD/25: .4X TO 1X p/r 25
CSAG Andres Galarraga/99 4.00 10.00
CSAR A.J. Reed/99 3.00 8.00
CSAR Anthony Rizzo/25 20.00 50.00
CSAR Alex Reyes/99 6.00 15.00
CSBN Brandon Nimmo/99 5.00 12.00
CSBP Byung-ho Park/99 4.00 10.00
CSCS Corey Seager/99 40.00 100.00
CSDA Dariel Alvarez/99 3.00 8.00
CSDM Don Mattingly/25 25.00 60.00
CSDP David Price/49 8.00 20.00
CSDP Dustin Pedroia/25 20.00 50.00
CSDR Daniel Robertson/99 3.00 8.00
CSGC Gerrit Cole/25 10.00 25.00
CSJD Jacob deGrom/20
CSJG Juan Gonzalez/25 15.00 40.00
CSMG Mike Gerber/99 3.00 8.00
CSMK Max Kepler/99
CSMM Manuel Margot/99 8.00 20.00
CSMO Matt Olson/99 10.00 25.00
CSMS Miguel Sano/99 5.00 12.00
CSOV Omar Vizquel/25 8.00 20.00
CSPK Paul Konerko/25 8.00 20.00
CSRT Raimel Tapia/99 4.00 10.00
CSSP Stephen Piscotty/99 5.00 12.00
CSSS Steven Souza/99 4.00 10.00
CSTA Tim Anderson/99 40.00 100.00
CSTF Todd Frazier/25 5.00 12.00
CSTS Trevor Story/99 10.00 25.00
CSWC Willson Contreras/99 10.00 25.00

2016 Panini National Treasures Colossal Materials

RANDOM INSERTS IN PACKS
PRINT RUNS BW/N 4-99 COPIES PER
NO PRICING ON QTY 10 OR LESS
*PRIME/20-25: .6X TO 1.5X p/r 49-99
*PRIME/20-25: .5X TO 1.2X p/r 25
CAD Aledmys Diaz/99 4.00 10.00
CAG Andres Galarraga/25 5.00 12.00
CAM Andrew McCutchen/25 10.00 25.00
CAW Adam Wainwright/99 4.00 10.00
CBB Bert Blyleven/25 5.00 12.00
CBJ Bo Jackson/49 12.00 30.00
CBP Byung-ho Park/99 4.00 10.00
CCA Chris Archer/99 3.00 8.00
CCH Chase Headley/99 3.00 8.00
CCJ Chipper Jones/49 5.00 12.00
CCK Clayton Kershaw/25 6.00 15.00
CCR Cal Ripken/49 15.00 40.00
CCS Corey Seager/99 6.00 15.00
CDH Dilson Herrera/99 4.00 10.00
CDM Daniel Murphy/99 4.00 10.00
CDW David Wright/99 4.00 10.00
CEA Elvis Andrus/99 4.00 10.00
CEL Evan Longoria/49 4.00 10.00
CFF Freddie Freeman/99 6.00 15.00
CGC Gerrit Cole/99 5.00 12.00
CGM Greg Maddux/25 8.00 20.00
CGS Giancarlo Stanton/25 6.00 15.00
CJB Jackie Bradley Jr./25 6.00 15.00
CJD Josh Donaldson/25 5.00 12.00
CJH Jason Heyward/99 4.00 10.00
CJK Jung-Ho Kang/25 4.00 10.00
CJM J.D. Martinez/99 5.00 12.00
CJO Jake Odorizzi/99 3.00 8.00
CJP Joe Panik/99 4.00 10.00
CJV Justin Verlander/49 5.00 12.00
CKM Kenta Maeda/25 4.00 10.00
CKS Kyle Schwarber/99 6.00 15.00
CMC Michael Conforto/99 4.00 10.00
CMF Maikel Franco/49 4.00 10.00
CMS Miguel Sano/99 5.00 12.00
CMT Michael Taylor/99 3.00 8.00
CNM Nomar Mazara/99 4.00 10.00
CNW Neil Walker/99 3.00 8.00
COV Omar Vizquel/49 4.00 10.00
CRY Robin Yount/49 8.00 20.00
CSM Steven Matz/99 3.00 8.00
CSP Stephen Piscotty/99 5.00 12.00
CTN Tyler Naquin/49 5.00 12.00
CTS Trevor Story/99 6.00 15.00
CTT Trea Turner/99 6.00 15.00
CVM Victor Martinez/99 4.00 10.00
CWM Wil Myers/99 4.00 10.00
CYM Yadier Molina/99 6.00 15.00

2016 Panini National Treasures Combo Materials

RANDOM INSERTS IN PACKS
PRINT RUNS BW/N 10-99 COPIES PER
NO PRICING ON QTY 15 OR LESS
1 Giancarlo Stanton/25 6.00 15.00
2 Todd Frazier/25 4.00 10.00
3 Adrian Beltre/25 6.00 15.00
4 Victor Martinez/25 5.00 12.00
6 Anthony Rendon/25 6.00 15.00
7 Adam Wainwright/25 5.00 12.00
10 Chris Sale/25 6.00 15.00

2016 Panini National Treasures Game Ball Signatures

RANDOM INSERTS IN PACKS
PRINT RUNS B/WN 5-75 COPIES PER
NO PRICING ON QTY 10 OR LESS
EXCHANGE DEADLINE 6/14/2018
GBSAK Al Kaline/25 25.00 50.00
GBSBW Bernie Williams/25 12.00 30.00
GBSDE Dennis Eckersley/60 6.00 15.00
GBSDG Dwight Gooden/75 5.00 12.00
GBSDJ David Justice/55 10.00 25.00
GBSDO David Ortiz/25 40.00 100.00
GBSFM Fred McGriff/75 6.00 15.00
GBSJB Jose Bautista/25 12.00 30.00
GBSJC Jose Canseco/49 12.00 30.00
GBSJP Jim Palmer/40 5.00 12.00
GBSJR Jim Rice/60 10.00 25.00
GBSMM Manny Machado/25 20.00 50.00
GBSTL Tommy Lasorda/25

2016 Panini National Treasures Game Dated Material Signatures

RANDOM INSERTS IN PACKS
PRINT RUNS B/WN 10-99 COPIES PER
NO PRICING ON QTY 15 OR LESS
EXCHANGE DEADLINE 6/14/2018
GDSAJ Austin Jackson/99 3.00 8.00
GDSDP David Price/25 10.00 25.00
GDSFF Freddie Freeman/25 12.00 30.00
GDSJL Junior Lake/99 3.00 8.00
GDSJM Joe Mauer/25 12.00 30.00
GDSKM Ketel Marte/99 5.00 12.00
GDSMS Matt Szczur/99 4.00 10.00
GDSSP Salvador Perez/49 12.00 30.00
GDSSP Stephen Piscotty/99 5.00 12.00
GDSSS Stephen Strasburg/20 20.00 50.00
GDSWM Wil Myers/25 6.00 15.00
GDSXB Xander Bogaerts/49 15.00 40.00

2016 Panini National Treasures Game Dated Material Signatures Prime

*GOLD/25: .6X TO 1.5X p/r 99
*GOLD/25: .5X TO 1.2X p/r 49
*GOLD/25: .4X TO 1X p/r 20-25
RANDOM INSERTS IN PACKS
PRINT RUNS B/WN 5-25 COPIES PER
NO PRICING ON QTY 10 OR LESS
EXCHANGE DEADLINE 6/14/2018
GDSAC Aroldis Chapman/25 8.00 20.00

2016 Panini National Treasures Game Dated Materials

RANDOM INSERTS IN PACKS
PRINT RUNS BW/N 20-99 COPIES PER
*PRIME/25: .6X TO 1.5X p/r 49-99
*PRIME/25: .5X TO 1.2X p/r 25
GDAM Andrew McCutchen/25 10.00 25.00
GDAR Addison Russell/99 5.00 12.00
GDAW Adam Wainwright/99 4.00 10.00
GDBB Billy Butler/99 3.00 8.00
GDBD Brian Dozier/99 4.00 10.00
GDCB Carlos Beltran/49 4.00 10.00
GDCD Chris Davis/49 3.00 8.00
GDCG Curtis Granderson/49 4.00 10.00
GDCM Collin McHugh/99 3.00 8.00
GDCU Chase Utley/49 4.00 10.00
GDEA Elvis Andrus/99 4.00 10.00
GDEG Evan Gattis/99 3.00 8.00
GDFF Freddie Freeman/99 6.00 15.00
GDHR Hanley Ramirez/99 4.00 10.00
GDIK Ian Kinsler/25 5.00 12.00
GDIN Ivan Nova/99 4.00 10.00
GDJA Jose Altuve/25 5.00 12.00
GDJC Johnny Cueto/99 4.00 10.00
GDJD Jacob deGrom/25 12.00 30.00
GDJE Jacoby Ellsbury/49 4.00 10.00
GDJM Joe Mauer/25 5.00 12.00
GDJM J.D. Martinez/49 5.00 12.00
GDJP Joe Panik/49 4.00 10.00

2016 Panini National Treasures July 4th Jersey Signatures

RANDOM INSERTS IN PACKS
PRINT RUNS B/WN 25-99 COPIES PER
EXCHANGE DEADLINE 6/14/2018
1 Joey Rickard/99 3.00 8.00
3 Julio Urias/25 20.00 50.00

2016 Panini National Treasures July 4th Jerseys

*PRIME/25: .6X TO 1.5X BASIC
RANDOM INSERTS IN PACKS
PRINT RUNS B/WN 10-49 COPIES PER
NO PRICING ON QTY 10
1 Joey Rickard/49 3.00 8.00
2 Hyun Soo Kim/49 5.00 12.00

2016 Panini National Treasures Leagues Best Jerseys

RANDOM INSERTS IN PACKS
PRINT RUNS BW/N 1-99 COPIES PER
NO PRICING ON QTY 10 OR LESS
*GOLD/24-25: .6X TO 1.5X p/r 49-99
*GOLD/24-25: .5X TO 1.2X p/r 25
LLAS Al Simmons/25 12.00 30.00
LLBF Bob Feller/49 8.00 20.00
LLDD Don Drysdale/49 6.00 15.00
LLDS Duke Snider/99 4.00 10.00
LLGB George Brett/49 10.00 25.00
LLGG Goose Goslin/25 10.00 25.00
LLHG Heinie Groh/99 3.00 8.00
LLJP Jim Palmer/25 5.00 12.00
LLKG Ken Griffey Jr./49 8.00 20.00
LLKP Kirby Puckett/49 15.00 40.00
LLLD Larry Doby/25 10.00 25.00
LLLO Lefty O'Doul/49 3.00 8.00
LLMR Mariano Rivera/99 6.00 15.00
LLPR Pete Rose/25 12.00 30.00
LLRJ Reggie Jackson/99 4.00 10.00
LLTG Tony Gwynn/99 5.00 12.00
LLTW Ted Williams/25 25.00 60.00
LLWS Willie Stargell/99 4.00 10.00

2016 Panini National Treasures Leagues Best Jerseys Combo

RANDOM INSERTS IN PACKS
PRINT RUNS B/WN 25-49 COPIES PER
*GOLD/25: 1X TO 2.5X BASIC
1 Thomas/Gwynn/99 6.00 15.00
4 Averill/Medwick/25 10.00 25.00
5 McCovey/Killebrew/25 10.00 25.00
7 Williams/Robinson/25 40.00 100.00
8 Rose/Carew/25 15.00 40.00
9 Harper/Trout/25 25.00 60.00
10 Arenado/Donaldson/99 10.00 25.00

2016 Panini National Treasures Leagues Best Jerseys Quads

RANDOM INSERTS IN PACKS
PRINT RUNS B/WN 25-49 COPIES PER
*GOLD/25: 2X TO 5X BASIC
1 Mrry/Hndrsn/Clmns/Sndbrg/99 6.00 15.00
2 Schit/Hndrsn/Crltn/Brtt/99 12.00 30.00
3 DMggo/Vghn/Grnbrg/Ghrg/25
5 Mris/Rbnsn/Cpda/Ford/99 20.00 50.00

2016 Panini National Treasures Leagues Best Jerseys Trios

RANDOM INSERTS IN PACKS
PRINT RUNS B/WN 5-49 COPIES PER
NO PRICING ON QTY 10 OR LESS
2 Crnn/Vghn/Kln/25 12.00 30.00
3 Hrmn/Applng/Msl/25 12.00 30.00
4 Snider/Furillo/Mathews/49 8.00 20.00
6 Rose/Clmnte/Yaz/25
7 Lje/Crwfrd/Cobb/25 50.00 120.00
8 Brtt/Hndrsn/Bggs/49 15.00 40.00
9 Drysdale/Robinson/Banks/49 8.00 20.00
10 DMggo/Feller/Wllms/25 40.00 100.00

2016 Panini National Treasures Legends Booklet Materials

RANDOM INSERTS IN PACKS
PRINT RUNS BW/N 1-99 COPIES PER
NO PRICING ON QTY 10 OR LESS
LBMBB Barry Bonds/49 6.00 15.00
LBMEM Eddie Murray/25 6.00 15.00
LBMES Enos Slaughter/25 20.00 50.00
LBMFT Frank Thomas/49 10.00 25.00
LBMJB Johnny Bench/99 10.00 25.00
LBMKG Ken Griffey Jr./25 10.00 25.00
LBMKP Kirby Puckett/49 15.00 40.00
LBMNR Nolan Ryan/25 30.00 80.00
LBMRC Rod Carew/49 6.00 15.00
LBMPWR Pee Wee Reese/49 12.00 30.00

2016 Panini National Treasures Legends Booklet Materials Bat

RANDOM INSERTS IN PACKS
PRINT RUNS BW/N 5-49 COPIES PER
NO PRICING ON QTY 15 OR LESS
LBMEM Eddie Murray/25 6.00 15.00
LBMFH Frank Howard/49 8.00 20.00
LBMFT Frank Thomas/49 10.00 25.00
LBMJB Johnny Bench/25 12.00 30.00
LBMKP Kirby Puckett/25 20.00 50.00

2016 Panini National Treasures Legends Booklet Materials Nickname

RANDOM INSERTS IN PACKS
PRINT RUNS BW/N 1-25 COPIES PER
NO PRICING ON QTY 15 OR LESS
LBMKP Kirby Puckett/25 20.00 50.00
LBMPM Paul Molitor/25 6.00 15.00
LBMRC Rod Carew/25 8.00 20.00

2016 Panini National Treasures Legends Booklet Materials Nickname Bat

RANDOM INSERTS IN PACKS
PRINT RUNS BW/N 3-49 COPIES PER
NO PRICING ON QTY 15 OR LESS
LBMFH Frank Howard/49 8.00 20.00
LBMMS Mike Schmidt/25 12.00 30.00
LBMRC Rod Carew/25 8.00 20.00

2016 Panini National Treasures Legends Booklet Materials Stats

RANDOM INSERTS IN PACKS
PRINT RUNS BW/N 1-49 COPIES PER
NO PRICING ON QTY 15 OR LESS
LBMBB Barry Bonds/49 6.00 15.00
LBMKP Kirby Puckett/49 15.00 40.00
LBMRS Ryne Sandberg/25 8.00 20.00
LBMPWR Pee Wee Reese/49 12.00 30.00

2016 Panini National Treasures Legends Booklet Materials Stats Bat

RANDOM INSERTS IN PACKS
PRINT RUNS BW/N 1-25 COPIES PER
NO PRICING ON QTY 10 OR LESS
LBMFH Frank Howard/20 8.00 20.00
LBMMS Mike Schmidt/25 12.00 30.00

2016 Panini National Treasures Legends Cuts Booklet Materials Bat

RANDOM INSERTS IN PACKS
PRINT RUNS B/WN 1-20 COPIES PER
NO PRICING ON QTY 15 OR LESS
EXCHANGE DEADLINE 6/14/2018
LCBMRC Rocky Colavito/20 50.00 120.00

2016 Panini National Treasures Legends Cuts Booklet Materials Nickname Bat

RANDOM INSERTS IN PACKS
PRINT RUNS B/WN 1-25 COPIES PER
NO PRICING ON QTY 10 OR LESS
EXCHANGE DEADLINE 6/14/2018
LCBMCK Charlie Keller/20
LCBMGC Gary Carter/25 20.00 50.00
LCBMGC Gary Carter/25 20.00 50.00

2016 Panini National Treasures Legends Cuts Booklet Materials Stats Bat

RANDOM INSERTS IN PACKS
PRINT RUNS B/WN 1-20 COPIES PER
NO PRICING ON QTY 15 OR LESS
EXCHANGE DEADLINE 6/14/2018
LCBMCK Charlie Keller/20 50.00 120.00

2016 Panini National Treasures Legends Materials

RANDOM INSERTS IN PACKS
PRINT RUNS BW/N 10-99 COPIES PER
NO PRICING ON QTY 15 OR LESS
LTBH Billy Herman/25 4.00 10.00
LTES Eddie Stanky/99 3.00 8.00
LTJC Joe Cronin/25 10.00 25.00
LTJR Jackie Robinson/25 30.00 80.00
LTLW Lloyd Waner/25 12.00 30.00
LTNF Nellie Fox/25 20.00 50.00
LTPR Pee Wee Reese/25 15.00 40.00
LTRC Roy Campanella/25 12.00 30.00
LTRC Roberto Clemente/25 25.00 60.00
LTRM Roger Maris/25 20.00 50.00
LTRS Ron Santo/25 15.00 40.00
LTSM Stan Musial/25 10.00 25.00
LTSP Satchel Paige/25 20.00 50.00
LTTC Ty Cobb/25 40.00 100.00
LTTH Tommy Henrich/25 10.00 25.00
LTTS Tris Speaker/25 20.00 50.00
LTTW Ted Williams/25 25.00 60.00

2016 Panini National Treasures Legends Materials Combo

RANDOM INSERTS IN PACKS
PRINT RUNS BW/N 5-25 COPIES PER
NO PRICING ON QTY 10 OR LESS
LTPW Paul Waner/25 20.00 50.00
LTRC Roberto Clemente/25 25.00 60.00
LTSM Stan Musial/25 10.00 25.00
LTTC Ty Cobb/25 40.00 100.00
LTTW Ted Williams/25 25.00 60.00

2016 Panini National Treasures Legends Materials Quads

RANDOM INSERTS IN PACKS
PRINT RUNS BW/N 10-25 COPIES PER
NO PRICING ON QTY 15 OR LESS
LTBF Bob Feller/25 10.00 25.00
LTFC Frankie Crosetti/25 15.00 40.00
LTSC Sam Crawford/25 20.00 50.00

2016 Panini National Treasures Legends Materials Trios

RANDOM INSERTS IN PACKS
PRINT RUNS BW/N 10-99 COPIES PER
NO PRICING ON QTY 10
LTAV Arky Vaughan/99 10.00 25.00
LTCK Charlie Keller/25 10.00 25.00
LTEL Ernie Lombardi/25 20.00 50.00
LTNL Nap Lajoie/25 25.00 60.00
LTRK Ralph Kiner/25 12.00 30.00
LTSR Sam Rice/99 12.00 30.00
LTTL Ted Lyons/25 20.00 50.00

2016 Panini National Treasures Made In Autographs

RANDOM INSERTS IN PACKS
PRINT RUNS B/WN 10-99 COPIES PER
NO PRICING ON QTY 10 OR LESS
EXCHANGE DEADLINE 6/14/2018
MIAD Aledmys Diaz/99 10.00 25.00
MIAH Alen Hanson/99 5.00 12.00
MIAR Anthony Rizzo/25
MIBB Billy Burns/99 4.00 10.00
MIBP Byung-ho Park/99 5.00 12.00
MICD Carlos Delgado/49
MICP Chan Ho Park/25
MIDP David Peralta/99 4.00 10.00
MIEM Edgar Martinez/99 5.00 12.00
MIJD Jacob deGrom/25
MIJP Joe Panik/99 5.00 12.00
MIKS Kyle Schwarber/25 60.00 150.00
MILC Lorenzo Cain/25 10.00 25.00
MILF Lucius Fox/99 6.00 15.00
MIMK Max Kepler/99
MIMP Mark Prior/99 5.00 12.00
MING Nomar Garciaparra/25 20.00 50.00
MINR Nolan Ryan/25 40.00 100.00
MIOA Orlando Arcia/99
MIOV Omar Vizquel/25 6.00 15.00
MIPM Paul Molitor/25 8.00 20.00
MIRG Randal Grichuk/99 4.00 10.00
MIRS Ryne Sandberg/25 25.00 60.00
MISC Steve Carlton/25 6.00 15.00
MISO Seung-Hwan Oh/99
MISS Steven Souza/99 5.00 12.00
MITF Todd Frazier/25 5.00 12.00
MITH Todd Helton/25 10.00 25.00
MIWB Wade Boggs/25 8.00 20.00

2016 Panini National Treasures Material Variations

*VAR/49-99: .4X TO 1X BASE p/r 49-99
*VAR/25: .5X TO 1.2X BASE p/r 49-99
*VAR/25: .4X TO 1X BASE p/r 20-25
RANDOM INSERTS IN PACKS
PRINT RUNS B/WN 5-99 COPIES PER
NO PRICING ON QTY 15 OR LESS

2016 Panini National Treasures Material Variations Prime

*PRIME/25: .5X TO 1.2X BASE p/r 49-99
*PRIME/25: .4X TO 1X BASE p/r 20-25
RANDOM INSERTS IN PACKS
PRINT RUNS B/WN 1-25 COPIES PER
NO PRICING ON QTY 10 OR LESS
63 Nolan Ryan/25 20.00 50.00

2016 Panini National Treasures Materials Prime

*PRIME/25: .5X TO 1.2X BASE p/r 49-99
*PRIME/25: .4X TO 1X BASE p/r 20-25
RANDOM INSERTS IN PACKS
PRINT RUNS B/WN 1-25 COPIES PER
NO PRICING ON QTY 16 OR LESS
54 Bob Feller/25 12.00 30.00
63 Nolan Ryan/25 20.00 50.00
95 Frank Robinson/25 10.00 25.00
137 Juan Gonzalez/25 25.00 60.00

2016 Panini National Treasures Memorial Day Jersey Signatures

RANDOM INSERTS IN PACKS
PRINT RUNS B/WN 15-99 COPIES PER
NO PRICING ON QTY 15
EXCHANGE DEADLINE 6/14/2018
1 Anthony Rendon/49 20.00 50.00
2 Seung-Hwan Oh/99
3 Aledmys Diaz/99 8.00 20.00
7 Byung-ho Park/99 4.00 10.00

2016 Panini National Treasures Memorial Day Jerseys

RANDOM INSERTS IN PACKS
PRINT RUNS BW/N 35-99 COPIES PER
*PRIME/25: .6X TO 1.5X p/r 99
*PRIME/25: .5X TO 1.2X p/r 35
1 Anthony Rendon/35 6.00 15.00
2 Seung-Hwan Oh/99 4.00 10.00
3 Aledmys Diaz/99 4.00 10.00
4 Jeremy Hazelbaker/99 4.00 10.00
6 Rob Refsnyder/99 4.00 10.00
7 Byung-ho Park/99 4.00 10.00

2016 Panini National Treasures Mother's Day Jersey Signatures

RANDOM INSERTS IN PACKS
STATED PRINT RUN 49 SER.#'d SETS
EXCHANGE DEADLINE 6/14/2018
1 Salvador Perez 12.00 30.00
2 Omar Vizquel 6.00 15.00

2016 Panini National Treasures Mother's Day Jerseys

RANDOM INSERTS IN PACKS
STATED PRINT RUN 99 SER.#'d SETS
1 Salvador Perez 4.00 10.00

2016 Panini National Treasures Notable Nicknames Autographs

RANDOM INSERTS IN PACKS
PRINT RUNS B/WN 10-99 COPIES PER
NO PRICING ON QTY 10 OR LESS
EXCHANGE DEADLINE 6/14/2018
NNAG Andres Galarraga/99 10.00 25.00
NNAO Al Oliver/25 10.00 25.00
NNAT Alan Trammell/25 25.00 60.00
NNBB Bill Buckner/25

NNDC David Cone/49 10.00 25.00
NNDG Dwight Gooden/25 6.00 15.00
NNDL Dae-ho Lee/99 6.00 15.00
NNDM Don Mattingly/25 40.00 100.00
NNDW David Wells/25
NNFM Fred McGriff/25 8.00 20.00
NNGS Gary Sheffield/25 10.00 25.00
NNJA Jose Abreu/99 6.00 15.00
NNJA Jose Abreu/99 6.00 15.00
NNJC Jose Canseco/99 10.00 25.00
NNJD Josh Donaldson/25
NNJD Jacob deGrom/25
NNJG Jason Giambi/25 5.00 12.00
NNJG Juan Gonzalez/25 40.00 100.00
NNMG Mark Grace/25 25.00 60.00
NNNG Nomar Garciaparra/25 20.00 50.00
NNOV Omar Vizquel/99 5.00 12.00
NNPM Paul Molitor/99 15.00 40.00
NNPR Pete Rose/49 40.00 100.00
NNSG Steve Garvey/25 20.00 50.00
NNTF Todd Frazier/49 12.00 30.00
NNVG Vladimir Guerrero/99

2016 Panini National Treasures Parchment Signatures

RANDOM INSERTS IN PACKS
PRINT RUNS B/WN 3-65 COPIES PER
NO PRICING ON QTY 15 OR LESS
EXCHANGE DEADLINE 6/14/2018
2 Pete Rose/49 20.00 50.00
3 Andre Dawson/49 6.00 15.00
4 Dennis Eckersley/65 6.00 15.00
5 Don Sutton/60 5.00 12.00
6 Ron Guidry/50 5.00 12.00
7 Brooks Robinson/25 15.00 40.00
10 Phil Niekro/40 5.00 12.00
11 Billy Williams/25 25.00 60.00
13 Al Kaline/25 25.00 50.00
14 Paul Goldschmidt/25 10.00 25.00
15 Edgar Martinez/25 8.00 20.00
19 Jonathan Lucroy/20 10.00 25.00
20 David Ortiz/20 40.00 100.00
21 Jose Bautista/20 6.00 15.00
23 Fergie Jenkins/20 10.00 25.00
25 Johnny Pesky/25 20.00 50.00

2016 Panini National Treasures Player's Collection Signature Materials

RANDOM INSERTS IN PACKS
PRINT RUNS B/WN 5-99 COPIES PER
NO PRICING ON QTY 15 OR LESS
EXCHANGE DEADLINE 6/14/2018
PCSAB Adrian Beltre/25 25.00 60.00
PCSAB Aaron Blair/99 3.00 8.00
PCSAD Alex Dickerson/99 3.00 8.00
PCSAR Alex Reyes/99 6.00 15.00
PCSAR A.J. Reed/99 3.00 8.00
PCSBB Brandon Belt/25
PCSBD Brandon Drury/99 5.00 12.00
PCSBJ Bo Jackson/25 30.00 80.00
PCSBN Brandon Nimmo/99 5.00 12.00
PCSBP Brett Phillips/99 3.00 8.00
PCSBP Byung-ho Park/99 4.00 10.00
PCSBR Brooks Robinson/25 20.00 50.00
PCSCE Carl Edwards Jr./99 10.00 25.00
PCSCF Clint Frazier/99 25.00 60.00
PCSCR Colin Rea/99 3.00 8.00
PCSCS Corey Seager/99 40.00 100.00
PCSDP Dustin Pedroia/25 20.00 50.00
PCSDP David Peralta/99 3.00 8.00
PCSED Elias Diaz/99
PCSEM Edgar Martinez/25 8.00 20.00
PCSFJ Fergie Jenkins/25 12.00 30.00
PCSFT Frank Thomas/25 30.00 80.00
PCSGM Greg Maddux/20 50.00 120.00
PCSJA Jose Abreu/25 8.00 20.00
PCSJA Jose Abreu/49 6.00 15.00
PCSJB Jose Berrios/99 5.00 12.00
PCSJD Josh Donaldson/25 12.00 30.00
PCSJE Jerad Eickhoff/99 5.00 12.00
PCSJG Jonathan Gray/49 4.00 10.00
PCSJG Jacob deGrom/25
PCSJP Joe Panik/99 6.00 15.00
PCSJT Jameson Taillon/99 8.00 20.00
PCSKS Kyle Schwarber/99
PCSLG Lucas Giolito/99 5.00 12.00
PCSLS Luis Severino/99 8.00 20.00
PCSMC Matt Carpenter/25 10.00 25.00
PCSMR Michael Reed/99 3.00 8.00
PCSMS Miguel Sano/99 8.00 20.00
PCSMS Mallex Smith/99 3.00 8.00
PCSNM Nomar Mazara/99
PCSOA Orlando Arcia/99
PCSOV Omar Vizquel/99 5.00 12.00
PCSOV Omar Vizquel/25 8.00 20.00
PCSPM Paul Molitor/25 8.00 20.00
PCSPM Pedro Martinez/25
PCSPN Phil Niekro/25 6.00 15.00
PCSPR Pete Rose/25 30.00 80.00
PCSRD Rafael Devers/99
PCSRF Rollie Fingers/20 15.00 40.00
PCSRG Randal Grichuk/99 3.00 8.00
PCSRM Raul A. Mondesi/99
PCSRR Rob Refsnyder/99 4.00 10.00
PCSRS Robert Stephenson/99 3.00 8.00
PCSRS Ross Stripling/99 3.00 8.00
PCSRS Ryne Sandberg/20 20.00 50.00
PCSSB Socrates Brito/99 3.00 8.00
PCSSM Sean Manaea/99 3.00 8.00
PCSSN Sean Newcomb/99 8.00 20.00
PCSSP Stephen Piscotty/99 5.00 12.00
PCSTF Todd Frazier/25 5.00 12.00
PCSTG Tyler Glasnow/99 8.00 20.00
PCSTJ Travis Jankowski/99 3.00 8.00
PCSTM Tom Murphy/99 3.00 8.00
PCSTN Tyler Naquin/99 5.00 12.00
PCSTW Tyler White/99 3.00 8.00
PCSWC Willson Contreras/99 10.00 25.00
PCSYL Yoan Lopez/99 3.00 8.00
PCSYM Yadier Molina/25 30.00 80.00
PCSYM Yoan Moncada/99 25.00 60.00

2016 Panini National Treasures Quad Player Materials Booklet

RANDOM INSERTS IN PACKS
PRINT RUNS B/WN 3-99 COPIES PER
NO PRICING ON QTY 15 OR LESS
2 Sgr/Schwrbr/Sano/Stry/99 10.00 25.00
3 Krshw/dGrm/Bmgrnr/Arrta/20 15.00 40.00
4 Park/Mzra/Nqn/Psctty/49 8.00 20.00

2016 Panini National Treasures Rookie Jersey Signatures Vertical

RANDOM INSERTS IN PACKS
STATED PRINT RUN 99 SER.#'d SETS
EXCHANGE DEADLINE 6/14/2018
*PURPLE/49: .5X TO 1.2X BASE
*GOLD/25: .6X TO 1.5X BASE
RJSVAD Alex Dickerson/99 3.00 8.00
RJSVBE Brian Ellington/99 3.00 8.00
RJSVBP Byung-ho Park/99 4.00 10.00
RJSVCE Carl Edwards Jr./99 10.00 25.00
RJSVCR Colin Rea/99 3.00 8.00
RJSVCS Corey Seager/99 40.00 100.00
RJSVDA Daniel Alvarez/99 3.00 8.00
RJSVED Elias Diaz/99
RJSVFM Frankie Montas/99 4.00 10.00
RJSVGB Greg Bird/25 6.00 15.00
RJSVJE Jerad Eickhoff/99 5.00 12.00
RJSVJG Jonathan Gray/99 3.00 8.00
RJSVJL Jorge Lopez/99 3.00 8.00
RJSVJL John Lamb/99 3.00 8.00
RJSVJP Jose Peraza/99 4.00 10.00
RJSVKM Ketel Marte/99 5.00 12.00
RJSVKS Kyle Schwarber/99
RJSVKT Kelby Tomlinson/99 3.00 8.00
RJSVKW Kyle Waldrop/99 4.00 10.00
RJSVLS Luis Severino/99 8.00 20.00
RJSVMK Max Kepler/99
RJSVMS Miguel Sano/99 8.00 20.00
RJSVMW Mac Williamson/99 5.00 12.00
RJSVRM Raul A. Mondesi/99
RJSVSP Stephen Piscotty/99 5.00 12.00
RJSVTD Tyler Duffey/99 5.00 12.00
RJSVTJ Travis Jankowski/99 3.00 8.00
RJSVTM Tom Murphy/99 3.00 8.00
RJSVTS Trevor Story/99 10.00 25.00
RJSVTT Trayce Thompson/99 5.00 12.00

2016 Panini National Treasures Rookie Material Signatures Gold

*PURPLE/25: .6X TO 1.5X BASE JSY AU
RANDOM INSERTS IN PACKS
PRINT RUNS B/WN 10-25 COPIES PER
NO PRICING ON QTY 15 OR LESS
EXCHANGE DEADLINE 6/14/2018

2016 Panini National Treasures Rookie Material Signatures Purple

*PURPLE/49: .5X TO 1.2X BASE JSY AU
*PURPLE/25: .6X TO 1.5X BASE JSY AU
RANDOM INSERTS IN PACKS
PRINT RUNS B/WN 15-49 COPIES PER
NO PRICING ON QTY 15
EXCHANGE DEADLINE 6/14/2018

2016 Panini National Treasures Signatures

RANDOM INSERTS IN PACKS
PRINT RUNS B/WN 10-99 COPIES PER
NO PRICING ON QTY 10
EXCHANGE DEADLINE 6/14/2018
SAG Andres Galarraga/25 6.00 15.00
SAN Aaron Nola/99 10.00 25.00
SAR Anthony Rizzo/25
SBB Billy Burns/99 4.00 10.00
SBP Byung-ho Park/99 5.00 12.00
SBW Billy Williams/49
SCF Carlton Fisk/25 12.00 30.00
SDL Dae-ho Lee/99 6.00 15.00
SEE Edwin Encarnacion/49 6.00 15.00
SEM Edgar Martinez/99 5.00 12.00
SJA Jose Abreu/99 6.00 15.00
SJC Joe Carter/25 10.00 25.00
SJD Josh Donaldson/25
SJG Jason Giambi/25 5.00 12.00
SJP Jorge Posada/25 20.00 50.00
SLS Luis Severino/25 15.00 40.00
SMS Miguel Sano/25 12.00 30.00
SMS Max Scherzer/49 25.00 60.00
SNM Nomar Mazara/99
SNS Noah Syndergaard/25
SOH Orel Hershiser/49 25.00 60.00
SRG Ron Guidry/99 5.00 12.00
SRP Rafael Palmeiro/25 6.00 15.00
STH Todd Helton/25 10.00 25.00
STS Trevor Story/25 12.00 30.00
SVG Vladimir Guerrero/99
SVM Victor Martinez/25 6.00 15.00
SWB Wade Boggs/25 8.00 20.00
SYM Yadier Molina/25 25.00 60.00

2016 Panini National Treasures Six Swatch Signatures

RANDOM INSERTS IN PACKS
PRINT RUNS B/WN 10-99 COPIES PER
NO PRICING ON QTY 15 OR LESS
EXCHANGE DEADLINE 6/14/2018
*PRPLE/49: .5X TO 1.2X p/r 99
*PRPLE/49: .4X TO 1X p/r 49
*PRPLE/25: .6X TO 1.5X p/r 99
*PRPLE/25: .5X TO 1.2X p/r 49
*PRPLE/25: .4X TO 1X p/r 20-25
*GOLD/25: .6X TO 1.5X p/r 99
*GOLD/25: .5X TO 1.2X p/r 49
*GOLD/25: .4X TO 1X p/r 20-25
SSSAB Adrian Beltre/25 25.00 60.00
SSSAD Aledmys Diaz/99 8.00 20.00
SSSBD Brandon Drury/49 6.00 15.00
SSSBJ Brian Johnson/99 3.00 8.00
SSSBP Byung-ho Park/99 4.00 10.00
SSSCE Carl Edwards Jr./99 10.00 25.00
SSSDG Dwight Gooden/25 10.00 25.00
SSSDL Dae-ho Lee/99 6.00 15.00
SSSDR Daniel Robertson/99 5.00 12.00
SSSFT Frank Thomas/20 30.00 80.00
SSSGC Gerrit Cole/25 10.00 25.00
SSSHB Harold Baines/25 12.00 30.00
SSSJD Jacob deGrom/25
SSSJH Jason Heyward/25 12.00 30.00
SSSJP Joe Panik/99 6.00 15.00
SSSJP Jose Peraza/99 4.00 10.00
SSSKM Ketel Marte/99 5.00 12.00
SSSLS Lucas Sims/99 3.00 8.00
SSSMS Miguel Sano/99 8.00 20.00
SSSMW Mac Williamson/99 5.00 12.00
SSSNM Nomar Mazara/99
SSSPS Pedro Severino/99 3.00 8.00
SSSRR Rob Refsnyder/99 4.00 10.00
SSSSO Seung-Hwan Oh/99
SSSTF Todd Frazier/25 5.00 12.00
SSSTJ Travis Jankowski/99 3.00 8.00
SSSTS Trevor Story/99 10.00 25.00
SSSTT Trea Turner/99 15.00 40.00
SSSZG Zack Godley/99 3.00 8.00

2016 Panini National Treasures Souvenir Cuts

RANDOM INSERTS IN PACKS
PRINT RUNS B/WN 1-99 COPIES PER
NO PRICING ON QTY 15 OR LESS
EXCHANGE DEADLINE 6/14/2018
2 Burleigh Grimes/25 60.00 150.00
4 Ralph Kiner/49 12.00 30.00
5 Stan Musial/99 20.00 50.00
6 Harmon Killebrew/25 20.00 50.00
7 Bobby Thomson/98 10.00 25.00
9 Gary Carter/25 15.00 40.00
14 Al Lopez/20 12.00 30.00

2016 Panini National Treasures St. Patrick's Day Jersey Signatures

RANDOM INSERTS IN PACKS
PRINT RUNS B/WN 15-99 COPIES PER
NO PRICING ON QTY 15
EXCHANGE DEADLINE 6/14/2018
1 Henry Owens/49 5.00 12.00
2 Jose Peraza/99 4.00 10.00
3 Kyle Waldrop/99 4.00 10.00
4 Robert Stephenson/99 3.00 8.00
5 John Lamb/99 3.00 8.00
7 Mallex Smith/99 3.00 8.00
8 Ozhaino Albies/21 20.00 50.00
9 Omar Vizquel/25 8.00 20.00
10 Mookie Betts/25
14 Dansby Swanson/20 20.00 50.00
15 Aaron Blair/99 3.00 8.00
16 George Springer/49 12.00 30.00

2016 Panini National Treasures St. Patrick's Day Jerseys

RANDOM INSERTS IN PACKS
PRINT RUNS B/WN 25-99 COPIES PER
*PRIME/25: .6X TO 1.5X p/r 49-99
*PRIME/25: .5X TO 1.2X p/r 25
SPDAD Aledmys Diaz/99 4.00 10.00
SPDBF Brandon Finnegan/99 3.00 8.00
SPDBS Blake Swihart/99 4.00 10.00
SPDCC Carl Crawford/99 4.00 10.00
SPDDF David Freese/99 3.00 8.00
SPDDO David Ortiz/25 12.00 30.00
SPDDP Dustin Pedroia/25 15.00 40.00
SPDDS Dansby Swanson/49 10.00 25.00
SPDGS George Springer/25 5.00 12.00
SPDHD Hunter Dozier/99 3.00 8.00
SPDHO Henry Owens/99 4.00 10.00
SPDHO Hector Olivera/99 4.00 10.00
SPDJB Jackie Bradley Jr./99 5.00 12.00
SPDJH Josh Hamilton/49 4.00 10.00
SPDJK Jung-Ho Kang/49 3.00 8.00
SPDMB Mookie Betts/99 10.00 25.00
SPDMF Maikel Franco/99 4.00 10.00
SPDMH Matt Holliday/99 5.00 12.00
SPDMS Mallex Smith/99 3.00 8.00
SPDMT Mike Trout/99 12.00 30.00
SPDOH Odubel Herrera/99 4.00 10.00
SPDPS Pablo Sandoval/99 4.00 10.00
SPDRC Rusney Castillo/99 3.00 8.00
SPDRM Raul A. Mondesi/99 6.00 15.00
SPDSP Stephen Piscotty/99 5.00 12.00
SPDXB Xander Bogaerts/96 5.00 12.00
SPDYM Yadier Molina/99 6.00 15.00

2016 Panini National Treasures Stars Booklet Material Signatures

RANDOM INSERTS IN PACKS
PRINT RUNS B/WN 5-49 COPIES PER
NO PRICING ON QTY 15 OR LESS
EXCHANGE DEADLINE 6/14/2018
SBMSCS Corey Seager/25 50.00 120.00
SBMSJH Jason Heyward/25 12.00 30.00
SBMSJL Jake Lamb/49 5.00 12.00
SBMSJS Jonathan Schoop/49 12.00 30.00
SBMSSG Sonny Gray/25 6.00 15.00
SBMSTS Trevor Story/25 15.00 40.00

2016 Panini National Treasures Stars Booklet Material Signatures Bat

RANDOM INSERTS IN PACKS
PRINT RUNS B/WN 2-49 COPIES PER
NO PRICING ON QTY 15 OR LESS
EXCHANGE DEADLINE 6/14/2018
SBMSBB Brandon Belt/49 5.00 12.00
SBMSWM Wil Myers/25 6.00 15.00

2016 Panini National Treasures Stars Booklet Material Signatures Nickname

RANDOM INSERTS IN PACKS
PRINT RUNS B/WN 2-49 COPIES PER
NO PRICING ON QTY 17 OR LESS
EXCHANGE DEADLINE 6/14/2018
SBMSAR Anthony Rendon/25 10.00 25.00
SBMSCS Corey Seager/25 50.00 120.00
SBMSEH Eric Hosmer/25 15.00 40.00
SBMSFF Freddie Freeman/25 12.00 30.00
SBMSGC Gerrit Cole/25 10.00 25.00
SBMSJH Jason Heyward/25 12.00 30.00
SBMSJL Jake Lamb/25 6.00 15.00
SBMSJP Joe Panik/25 10.00 25.00
SBMSJS Jonathan Schoop/49 12.00 30.00
SBMSSG Sonny Gray/25 6.00 15.00
SBMSTS Trevor Story/25 15.00 40.00

2016 Panini National Treasures Stars Booklet Material Signatures Nickname Bat

RANDOM INSERTS IN PACKS
PRINT RUNS B/WN 1-25 COPIES PER
NO PRICING ON QTY 15 OR LESS
EXCHANGE DEADLINE 6/14/2018
SBMSBB Brandon Belt/25
SBMSTS Trevor Story/25 15.00 40.00
SBMSWM Wil Myers/25 6.00 15.00

2016 Panini National Treasures Stars Booklet Material Signatures Stats

RANDOM INSERTS IN PACKS
PRINT RUNS B/WN 2-25 COPIES PER
NO PRICING ON QTY 15 OR LESS
EXCHANGE DEADLINE 6/14/2018
SBMSAR Anthony Rendon/25 10.00 25.00
SBMSCS Corey Seager/25 50.00 120.00
SBMSEH Eric Hosmer/25 15.00 40.00
SBMSFF Freddie Freeman/25 12.00 30.00
SBMSGC Gerrit Cole/25 10.00 25.00
SBMSJP Joe Panik/25 10.00 25.00
SBMSSG Sonny Gray/25 6.00 15.00

2016 Panini National Treasures Stars Booklet Material Signatures Stats Bat

RANDOM INSERTS IN PACKS
PRINT RUNS B/WN 1-25 COPIES PER
NO PRICING ON QTY 15 OR LESS
EXCHANGE DEADLINE 6/14/2018
SBMSBB Brandon Belt/25
SBMSTS Trevor Story/25 15.00 40.00

2016 Panini National Treasures Stars Booklet Materials

RANDOM INSERTS IN PACKS
PRINT RUNS B/WN 10-99 COPIES PER
NO PRICING ON QTY 15 OR LESS
SBMAB Adrian Beltre/99 5.00 12.00
SBMAG Adrian Gonzalez/49 4.00 10.00
SBMAM Andrew McCutchen/49 8.00 20.00
SBMAR Anthony Rizzo/25 10.00 25.00
SBMBP Buster Posey/25 8.00 20.00
SBMDO David Ortiz/99 10.00 25.00
SBMJA Jose Altuve/25 5.00 12.00
SBMJB Jose Bautista/99 4.00 10.00
SBMJD Josh Donaldson/25 5.00 12.00
SBMKB Kris Bryant/25 8.00 20.00
SBMMB Madison Bumgarner/99 5.00 12.00
SBMMC Miguel Cabrera/49 5.00 12.00
SBMNA Nolan Arenado/49 8.00 20.00
SBMXB Xander Bogaerts/25 6.00 15.00

2016 Panini National Treasures Stars Booklet Materials Bat

RANDOM INSERTS IN PACKS
PRINT RUNS B/WN 10-49 COPIES PER
NO PRICING ON QTY 16 OR LESS
SBMAM Andrew McCutchen/25 10.00 25.00
SBMCC Carlos Correa/49 6.00 15.00
SBMDO David Ortiz/25 12.00 30.00
SBMJB Jose Bautista/25 5.00 12.00
SBMMC Miguel Cabrera/25 6.00 15.00
SBMMM Manny Machado/25 6.00 15.00

2016 Panini National Treasures Stars Booklet Materials Nickname

RANDOM INSERTS IN PACKS
PRINT RUNS B/WN 5-99 COPIES PER
NO PRICING ON QTY 10 OR LESS
SBMAB Adrian Beltre/49 5.00 12.00
SBMAG Adrian Gonzalez/25 5.00 12.00
SBMAM Andrew McCutchen/25 10.00 25.00
SBMAR Anthony Rizzo/25 10.00 25.00
SBMBH Bryce Harper/25 20.00 50.00
SBMCC Carlos Correa/25 8.00 20.00
SBMDO David Ortiz/49 10.00 25.00
SBMJA Jose Altuve/25 5.00 12.00
SBMJB Jose Bautista/49 4.00 10.00
SBMKB Kris Bryant/99 6.00 15.00
SBMMB Madison Bumgarner/25 6.00 15.00
SBMMM Manny Machado/25 6.00 15.00
SBMMT Mike Trout/25 30.00 80.00
SBMNA Nolan Arenado/25 8.00 20.00
SBMXB Xander Bogaerts/25 6.00 15.00

2016 Panini National Treasures Stars Booklet Materials Nickname Bat

RANDOM INSERTS IN PACKS
PRINT RUNS B/WN 10-99 COPIES PER
NO PRICING ON QTY 15 OR LESS
SBMAB Adrian Beltre/49 5.00 12.00
SBMAG Adrian Gonzalez/25 5.00 12.00
SBMAM Andrew McCutchen/25 10.00 25.00
SBMBH Bryce Harper/49 15.00 40.00
SBMCC Carlos Correa/99 6.00 15.00
SBMDO David Ortiz/99 8.00 20.00
SBMJB Jose Bautista/99 4.00 10.00
SBMMC Miguel Cabrera/25 6.00 15.00
SBMMT Mike Trout/25 30.00 80.00
SBMNC Nelson Cruz/25 6.00 15.00

2016 Panini National Treasures Stars Booklet Materials Stats

RANDOM INSERTS IN PACKS
PRINT RUNS B/WN 5-99 COPIES PER
NO PRICING ON QTY 10 OR LESS
SBMAB Adrian Beltre/49 5.00 12.00
SBMAG Adrian Gonzalez/25 5.00 12.00
SBMAM Andrew McCutchen/25 10.00 25.00
SBMAR Anthony Rizzo/25 10.00 25.00
SBMBH Bryce Harper/25 20.00 50.00
SBMCC Carlos Correa/25 8.00 20.00
SBMDO David Ortiz/49 10.00 25.00
SBMGS Giancarlo Stanton/49 5.00 12.00
SBMJA Jose Altuve/25 5.00 12.00
SBMJB Jose Bautista/99 4.00 10.00
SBMJD Josh Donaldson/49 4.00 10.00
SBMKB Kris Bryant/49 6.00 15.00
SBMMB Madison Bumgarner/25 6.00 15.00
SBMMC Miguel Cabrera/25 6.00 15.00
SBMMM Manny Machado/25 6.00 15.00
SBMMT Mike Trout/25 30.00 80.00
SBMNA Nolan Arenado/25 10.00 25.00
SBMXB Xander Bogaerts/25 6.00 15.00

2016 Panini National Treasures Stars Booklet Materials Stats Bat

RANDOM INSERTS IN PACKS
PRINT RUNS B/WN 10-99 COPIES PER
NO PRICING ON QTY 15 OR LESS
SBMAB Adrian Beltre/25 6.00 15.00
SBMAM Andrew McCutchen/49 8.00 20.00
SBMBP Buster Posey/25 8.00 20.00
SBMCC Carlos Correa/99 6.00 15.00
SBMDO David Ortiz/99 10.00 25.00
SBMGS Giancarlo Stanton/99 5.00 12.00
SBMJB Jose Bautista/49 4.00 10.00
SBMMC Matt Carpenter/25 6.00 15.00
SBMMC Miguel Cabrera/25 6.00 15.00
SBMMT Mike Trout/25 30.00 80.00
SBMNC Nelson Cruz/25 6.00 15.00

2016 Panini National Treasures Treasure Chest 24 Materials

RANDOM INSERTS IN PACKS
STATED PRINT RUN 99 SER.#'d SETS
1 24 Players 60.00 150.00

2016 Panini National Treasures Treasure Chest 32 Materials

RANDOM INSERTS IN PACKS
STATED PRINT RUN 99 SER.#'d SETS
1 32 Players 40.00 100.00

2016 Panini National Treasures Treasure Materials

RANDOM INSERTS IN PACKS
PRINT RUNS B/WN 10-99 COPIES PER
NO PRICING ON QTY 10
*PRIME/25: .6X TO 1.5X p/r 49-99
*PRIME/25: .5X TO 1.2X p/r 20-25
TMAB Adrian Beltre/99 5.00 12.00
TMAG Alex Gordon/99 4.00 10.00
TMAM Andrew McCutchen/99 8.00 20.00
TMBH Bryce Harper/25 20.00 50.00
TMBP Buster Posey/25 8.00 20.00
TMCC Carlos Correa/49 5.00 12.00
TMCK Clayton Kershaw/49 5.00 12.00
TMCS Chris Sale/99 5.00 12.00
TMDO David Ortiz/99 10.00 25.00
TMEH Eric Hosmer/99 4.00 10.00
TMGS Giancarlo Stanton/49 5.00 12.00
TMID Ian Desmond/99 3.00 8.00
TMJA Jose Abreu/49 5.00 12.00
TMJA Jake Arrieta/25 5.00 12.00
TMJA Jose Altuve/25 5.00 12.00
TMJB Jose Bautista/49 4.00 10.00
TMJC Johnny Cueto/99 4.00 10.00
TMJD Jacob deGrom/99 10.00 25.00
TMJD Josh Donaldson/49 4.00 10.00
TMJF Jose Fernandez/99 5.00 12.00
TMKB Kris Bryant/49 6.00 15.00
TMMB Madison Bumgarner/49 4.00 10.00
TMMC Matt Carpenter/20 6.00 15.00
TMMC Miguel Cabrera/49 5.00 12.00
TMMM Manny Machado/25 6.00 15.00
TMMT Masahiro Tanaka/99 4.00 10.00
TMMT Mike Trout/99 25.00 60.00
TMNA Nolan Arenado/49 8.00 20.00
TMRC Robinson Cano/25 5.00 12.00
TMSP Salvador Perez/25 5.00 12.00
TMYD Yu Darvish/49 5.00 12.00
TMYM Yadier Molina/99 6.00 15.00

2016 Panini National Treasures Treasure Signature Materials

RANDOM INSERTS IN PACKS
PRINT RUNS B/WN 10-99 COPIES PER
NO PRICING ON QTY 17 OR LESS
EXCHANGE DEADLINE 6/14/2018
*GLD/24-25: .6X TO 1.5X p/r 85-99
*GLD/24-25: .5X TO 1.2X p/r 45-49
*GLD/24-25: .4X TO 1X p/r 20-25
TSMAB Adrian Beltre/45 4.00 10.00
TSMAG Alex Gordon/49 8.00 20.00
TSMAR A.J. Reed/99 3.00 8.00
TSMAR Anthony Rendon/99 6.00 15.00
TSMAR Anthony Rizzo/25 20.00 50.00
TSMBB Brandon Belt/25
TSMBE Brian Ellington/99 3.00 8.00
TSMBL Brett Lawrie/99 4.00 10.00
TSMBM Brian McCann/99 4.00 10.00
TSMBN Brandon Nimmo/99 5.00 12.00
TSMBP Brandon Phillips/49 4.00 10.00
TSMBR Brooks Robinson/25 20.00 50.00
TSMCD Chris Davis/25 5.00 12.00
TSMCF Clint Frazier/99 25.00 60.00
TSMCG Carlos Gonzalez/25 6.00 15.00
TSMCH Cole Hamels/25 6.00 15.00
TSMCK Clayton Kershaw/25 40.00 100.00
TSMCR Cameron Rupp/99 3.00 8.00
TSMCS CC Sabathia/25 6.00 15.00
TSMDA Daniel Alvarez/99 3.00 8.00
TSMDP David Price/25 10.00 25.00
TSMDS Darryl Strawberry/99 8.00 20.00
TSMDW David Wright/25 8.00 20.00
TSMEH Eric Hosmer/49 12.00 30.00
TSMEL Evan Longoria/25 8.00 20.00
TSMEM Edgar Martinez/49 6.00 15.00
TSMFF Freddie Freeman/49 10.00 25.00
TSMGB Greg Bird/99 4.00 10.00
TSMJA Jose Abreu/25 10.00 25.00
TSMJB Jeff Bagwell/49 15.00 40.00
TSMJB Jose Berrios/99 5.00 12.00
TSMJD Jacob deGrom/25
TSMJG Jason Giambi/49
TSMJL Jake Lamb/99 4.00 10.00
TSMJM James McCann/99 4.00 10.00
TSMJP Jose Peraza/99 4.00 10.00
TSMJP Jorge Posada/49 25.00 60.00
TSMJP Joc Pederson/49 5.00 12.00
TSMKM Ketel Marte/99 5.00 12.00
TSMKT Kelby Tomlinson/99 3.00 8.00
TSMKW Kyle Waldrop/99 4.00 10.00
TSMLB Lou Brock/25 20.00 50.00
TSMLM Logan Morrison/99 3.00 8.00
TSMLS Luis Severino/99 8.00 20.00
TSMMB Michael Brantley/99 4.00 10.00
TSMMC Matt Carpenter/25 10.00 25.00
TSMMM Manny Machado/99 15.00 40.00
TSMMS Max Scherzer/99 20.00 50.00
TSMMS Mallex Smith/99 3.00 8.00
TSMMT Mark Trumbo/99 3.00 8.00
TSMMT Michael Taylor/99 3.00 8.00
TSMOC Orlando Cepeda/99 10.00 25.00
TSMOV Omar Vizquel/99 5.00 12.00
TSMPF Prince Fielder/25 6.00 15.00
TSMPG Paul Goldschmidt/25 10.00 25.00
TSMPO Paulo Orlando/99 3.00 8.00
TSMPS Pedro Severino/99 3.00 8.00
TSMRA Roberto Alomar/25 10.00 25.00
TSMRA Roberto Alomar/99 10.00 25.00
TSMRB Ryan Braun/25 8.00 20.00
TSMRS Ross Stripling/99 3.00 8.00
TSMSC Starlin Castro/85 3.00 8.00
TSMSG Sonny Gray/99 4.00 10.00
TSMSM Steven Matz/99 3.00 8.00
TSMSM Sean Manaea/99 3.00 8.00
TSMSP Salvador Perez/49 12.00 30.00
TSMTA Tim Anderson/99 12.00 30.00
TSMTH Todd Helton/20 12.00 30.00
TSMTJ Tommy John/99 6.00 15.00
TSMTT Trayce Thompson/99 5.00 12.00
TSMVG Vladimir Guerrero/25 10.00 25.00
TSMWB Wade Boggs/25 15.00 40.00
TSMWC Willson Contreras/99 10.00 25.00
TSMWM Wil Myers/99 4.00 10.00
TSMYM Yadier Molina/25 30.00 80.00
TSMYM Yoan Moncada/25 40.00 100.00
TSMYT Yasmany Tomas/49 4.00 10.00
TSMZD Zach Davies/25 6.00 15.00

2016 Panini National Treasures Triple Player Materials Booklet

RANDOM INSERTS IN PACKS
PRINT RUNS B/WN 3-25 COPIES PER
NO PRICING ON QTY 5 OR LESS
3 Ripken/Brett/Piazza/25 60.00 150.00

2017 Panini National Treasures

1-150 RANDOMLY INSERTED IN PACKS
1-150 PRINT RUNS B/WN 10-99 COPIES PER
NO PRICING ON QTY 10
151-220 RANDOMLY INSERTED IN PACKS
151-220 PRINT RUNS B/WN 49-99 COPIES PER
EXCHANGE DEADLINE 4/25/2019
2 Casey Stengel/99 5.00 12.00
3 Don Drysdale/99 5.00 12.00
5A Ernie Banks/49 6.00 15.00
5B Ernie Banks/99 8.00 20.00
6 Frank Chance/25 15.00 40.00
9 Gil Hodges/25 12.00 30.00
10 Herb Pennock/99 5.00 12.00
11A Jackie Robinson/25 25.00 60.00
11B Jackie Robinson/25 25.00 60.00
16 Leo Durocher/99 5.00 12.00
17 Lou Gehrig/25 75.00 200.00
18A Mel Ott/25 12.00 30.00
18B Mel Ott/25 12.00 30.00
19 Pee Wee Reese/49 8.00 20.00
20A Rogers Hornsby/49 10.00 25.00
20B Rogers Hornsby/25 12.00 30.00
22 Thurman Munson/99 12.00 30.00
23 Tony Lazzeri/49 10.00 25.00
26 Willie Keeler/49 10.00 25.00
28 Billy Martin/99 6.00 15.00
30 Carl Furillo/99 3.00 8.00
31 Charlie Gehringer/25
32 Charlie Keller/99 3.00 8.00
33 Eddie Stanky/49 3.00 8.00
34 George Kelly/99 5.00 12.00
36 Harry Hooper/25 20.00 50.00
38 Joe Cronin/25
41 Ken Boyer/25 8.00 20.00
42 Kiki Cuyler/49 10.00 25.00
44 Lloyd Waner/25 6.00 15.00
45 Luke Appling/49 3.00 8.00
46 Max Carey/49 2.50 6.00
47 Nellie Fox/99 5.00 12.00
48 Paul Waner/49 5.00 12.00
49A Roberto Clemente/25 30.00 80.00
50A Roger Maris/25 15.00 40.00
50B Roger Maris/25 15.00 40.00
51 Ron Santo/49 10.00 25.00
52A Stan Musial/25 8.00 20.00
52B Stan Musial/99 6.00 15.00
53 Ted Lyons/49 4.00 10.00
54A Ted Williams/25 20.00 50.00
54B Ted Williams/25 20.00 50.00
55 Tommy Henrich/49 6.00 15.00
56 Walter Alston/99 5.00 12.00
57 Al Simmons/25 20.00 50.00
58 Arky Vaughan/49 6.00 15.00
60 Bob Turley/99 3.00 8.00
61 Dom DiMaggio/25
62A Elston Howard/99 3.00 8.00
62B Elston Howard/99 3.00 8.00
63 Frankie Frisch/25 8.00 20.00
65 Ernie Lombardi/25 10.00 25.00
66 Jim Bottomley/49 6.00 15.00
68 Roger Bresnahan/25 10.00 25.00
69 Sam Crawford/25
71A Kirby Puckett/49 15.00 40.00
71B Kirby Puckett/25 20.00 50.00
73 Frankie Crosetti/25 8.00 20.00
74 Gil McDougald/99 3.00 8.00
75 Don Hoak/99 5.00 12.00
76 Gabby Hartnett/25 50.00 120.00
77 Goose Goslin/25 15.00 40.00
78 Harry Brecheen/99 6.00 15.00
79 Harry Walker/99 3.00 8.00
80 Heinie Groh/49 6.00 15.00
81 Jim Gilliam/99 3.00 8.00
82 John McGraw/49 20.00 50.00
83 Johnny Pesky/25 3.00 8.00
84 Johnny Sain/25 5.00 12.00
85 Lefty O'Doul/49 8.00 20.00
86 Lefty Williams/99 8.00 20.00
88 Tom Yawkey/99 5.00 12.00
89 Willie Kamm/99 3.00 8.00
90A Mike Trout/99 10.00 25.00
90B Mike Trout/49 10.00 25.00
91A Kris Bryant/99 5.00 12.00
91B Kris Bryant/99 5.00 12.00
92A Manny Machado/99 4.00 10.00
92B Manny Machado/99 4.00 10.00
93A Francisco Lindor/49 4.00 10.00
93B Francisco Lindor/99 4.00 10.00
94 Miguel Cabrera/99 4.00 10.00
95 Daniel Murphy/49 3.00 8.00
96 Carlos Correa/99 3.00 8.00
97A Noah Syndergaard/99 3.00 8.00
97B Noah Syndergaard/99 3.00 8.00
98A Bryce Harper/49 10.00 25.00
98B Bryce Harper/25 8.00 20.00
99A Anthony Rizzo/99 6.00 15.00
99B Anthony Rizzo/99 6.00 15.00
100A Clayton Kershaw/99 5.00 12.00
100B Clayton Kershaw/99 5.00 12.00
101A Buster Posey/99 5.00 12.00
101B Buster Posey/99 5.00 12.00
102A Gary Sanchez/99 10.00 25.00
102B Gary Sanchez/99 10.00 25.00
103A Corey Seager/99 4.00 10.00
103B Corey Seager/99 4.00 10.00
104 Javier Baez/99 5.00 12.00
105A Yadier Molina/99 5.00 12.00
105B Yadier Molina/99 12.00 30.00
106 Josh Donaldson/99 3.00 8.00
107 Yoenis Cespedes/99 4.00 10.00
108 Kyle Schwarber/99 4.00 10.00
109A Mookie Betts/49 8.00 20.00
109B Mookie Betts/99 8.00 20.00
110 Freddie Freeman/99 5.00 12.00
111 Jose Altuve/99 3.00 8.00
112A Madison Bumgarner/49 3.00 8.00
112B Madison Bumgarner/99 3.00 8.00
113 Dustin Pedroia/99 4.00 10.00
114A Nolan Arenado/99 6.00 15.00
114B Nolan Arenado/99 6.00 15.00
115 Joey Gallo/99 3.00 8.00
116 Giancarlo Stanton/99 4.00 10.00
117 George Springer/99 4.00 10.00
118 Marcell Ozuna/49 4.00 10.00
119 Nomar Mazara/99 2.50 6.00
120 Wil Myers/99 3.00 8.00
121A Albert Pujols/49 5.00 12.00
121B Albert Pujols/99 5.00 12.00
122A Ichiro/49 5.00 12.00
122B Ichiro/99 5.00 12.00
123 Robinson Cano/99 3.00 8.00
124 Chris Sale/99 4.00 10.00
125 Max Scherzer/99 4.00 10.00
126A Adrian Beltre/99 4.00 10.00
126B Adrian Beltre/99 4.00 10.00
127 Justin Verlander/99 4.00 10.00
128 Kevin Kiermaier/99 3.00 8.00
129 Paul Goldschmidt/99 4.00 10.00
130A Xander Bogaerts/99 4.00 10.00
130B Xander Bogaerts/99 4.00 10.00
131 Trea Turner/99 3.00 8.00
132 Christian Yelich/99 5.00 12.00
133 Aaron Sanchez/99 3.00 8.00
134 Addison Russell/99 4.00 10.00
135 Michael Fulmer/65 2.50 6.00
136A Ken Griffey Jr./99 8.00 20.00
136B Ken Griffey Jr./99 8.00 20.00
137A George Brett/99 8.00 20.00
137B George Brett/99 8.00 20.00
138A Cal Ripken/99 8.00 20.00
138B Cal Ripken/99 8.00 20.00
139A Nolan Ryan/99 8.00 20.00
139B Nolan Ryan/25 10.00 25.00
140A Tony Gwynn/99 4.00 10.00
140B Tony Gwynn/99 4.00 10.00
141A Greg Maddux/99 5.00 12.00
141B Greg Maddux/99 5.00 12.00
142A Frank Thomas/99 4.00 10.00
142B Frank Thomas/99 4.00 10.00
143 Harmon Killebrew/99 4.00 10.00
144 Mike Piazza/99 4.00 10.00
145 Bob Feller/99 5.00 12.00
146 Willie McCovey/99 3.00 8.00
147A Pete Rose/99 6.00 15.00
147B Pete Rose/99 6.00 15.00
148 David Ortiz/99 4.00 10.00
149A Rickey Henderson/49 6.00 15.00
149B Rickey Henderson/49 6.00 15.00
150 Bob Gibson/25
151 Benintendi JSY AU/99 RC EX 15.00 40.00
152 Moncada JSY AU/99 RC 30.00 80.00
153 Swanson JSY AU/99 RC EX 10.00 25.00
154 Bregman JSY AU/99 RC EX 40.00 100.00
155 Dahl JSY AU/99 RC 8.00 20.00
156 Koda Glover JSY AU/99 RC 4.00 10.00
157 Alex Reyes JSY AU/99 RC EXCH 6.00 15.00
158 Tyler Glasnow JSY AU/99 RC 6.00 15.00
159 Jose De Leon JSY AU/99 RC 4.00 10.00
160 Joe Musgrove JSY AU/99 RC 50.00 120.00
161 Manuel Margot JSY AU/99 RC 4.00 10.00
162 Judge JSY AU/49 RC 75.00 200.00
163 David Paulino JSY AU/99 RC 5.00 12.00
164 Reynaldo Lopez JSY AU/99 RC 4.00 10.00
165 Bradley Zimmer JSY AU/99 RC 5.00 12.00
166 Braden Shipley JSY AU/99 RC 4.00 10.00
167 Renfroe JSY AU/99 RC 5.00 12.00
168 Alfaro JSY AU/99 RC 8.00 20.00
169 Carson Fulmer JSY AU/99 RC 6.00 15.00
170 Weaver JSY AU/99 RC 5.00 12.00
171 Raimel Tapia JSY AU/99 RC 5.00 12.00
172 Adalberto Mejia JSY AU/99 RC 4.00 10.00
173 Amir Garrett JSY AU/99 RC 8.00 20.00
174 Renato Nunez JSY AU/99 RC 8.00 20.00
175 Jacoby Jones JSY AU/99 RC EXCH 5.00 12.00
176 Gabriel Ynoa JSY AU/99 RC 4.00 10.00
177 Chad Pinder JSY AU/99 RC 4.00 10.00
178 Kelly JSY AU/49 RC 5.00 12.00
179 Mancini JSY AU/99 RC 8.00 20.00
180 Jose Rondon JSY AU/99 RC 4.00 10.00
181 Teoscar Hernandez JSY AU/99 RC EXCH 15.00 40.00
182 Healy JSY AU/49 RC 6.00 15.00
183 Erik Gonzalez JSY AU/99 RC 4.00 10.00
184 Quinn JSY AU/99 RC 4.00 10.00
185 Olson JSY AU/99 RC 10.00 25.00
186 German Marquez JSY AU/99 RC 6.00 15.00
187 Jharel Cotton JSY AU/99 RC 4.00 10.00
188 Jake Thompson JSY AU/99 RC 4.00 10.00
190 Hunter Dozier JSY AU/49 RC 5.00 12.00
191 Adam Plutko JSY AU/49 RC 4.00 10.00
192 Bellinger JSY AU/49 RC EX 40.00 100.00
193 Happ JSY AU/99 RC 5.00 12.00
196 Haniger JSY AU/99 RC 15.00 40.00
198 Dan Vogelbach JSY AU/99 RC 6.00 15.00
201 Bell JSY AU/25 RC 15.00 40.00
203 Gavin Cecchini JSY AU/99 RC 6.00 15.00
204 Jeff Hoffman JSY AU/99 RC 4.00 10.00
205 Yohander Mendez JSY AU/99 RC 4.00 10.00
206 Montgomery JSY AU/99 RC 8.00 20.00
207 Sierra JSY AU/99 RC 12.00 30.00
208 Antonio Senzatela JSY AU/99 RC 4.00 10.00
210 Heredia JSY AU/99 RC 12.00 30.00
211 Arcia JSY AU/99 RC 10.00 25.00
212 Sam Travis JSY AU/49 RC 6.00 15.00
213 Anthony Alford JSY AU/99 RC 4.00 10.00
214 Jorge Bonifacio JSY AU/99 RC 6.00 15.00
215 Brinson JSY AU/49 RC 10.00 25.00
217 Frazier JSY AU/99 RC 12.00 30.00
218 Dinelson Lamet JSY AU/99 RC 4.00 10.00
219 Fisher JSY AU/99 RC 4.00 10.00
220 Barreto JSY AU/99 RC 6.00 15.00

2017 Panini National Treasures Gold

*GOLD/20-25: .5X TO 1.2 BASIC p/r 49-99
*GOLD JSY AU/25-49: .5X TO 1.2X BASIC
RANDOM INSERTS IN PACKS
PRINT RUNS B/WN 3-49 COPIES PER
NO PRICING ON QTY 15 OR LESS
EXCHANGE DEADLINE 4/25/2019
194 Andrew Toles JSY AU/49

2017 Panini National Treasures Holo Gold

*HOLO JSY AU/25: .6X TO 1.5X BASIC
RANDOM INSERTS IN PACKS
PRINT RUNS B/WN 3-25 COPIES PER
NO PRICING ON QTY 15 OR LESS
EXCHANGE DEADLINE 4/25/2019
194 Andrew Toles JSY AU/25

2017 Panini National Treasures 16 Player Materials Booklet

RANDOM INSERTS IN PACKS
PRINT RUNS B/WN 15-99 COPIES PER
NO PRICING ON QTY 15
1 Retired Stars/99 100.00 250.00
3 Rookies/99 50.00 120.00

2017 Panini National Treasures All Century Relics

2 Robin Yount/99
3 Yogi Berra/25
4 Dennis Eckersley/49
5 Harmon Killebrew/25
6 Rod Carew/25
7 Cal Ripken/49
8 Paul Molitor/99
9 Lou Brock/49
10 Ken Griffey Jr./99
11 Tony Gwynn/99
12 Al Kaline/25
13 Willie Stargell/99

2017 Panini National Treasures All Decade Dual Relics

RANDOM INSERTS IN PACKS
PRINT RUNS B/WN 10-25 COPIES PER
NO PRICING ON QTY 10
*HOLO GOLD/25: .6X TO 1.5X BASIC
3 Frisch/Rice/99 8.00 20.00
4 Gehringer/Ott/49 12.00 30.00
5 Mize/Williams/99 12.00 30.00
6 Mantle/Berra/25 40.00 100.00
7 Killebrew/Clemente/49 40.00 100.00
8 Palmer/Seaver/99 4.00 10.00
9 Brett/Henderson/99 15.00 40.00
10 Maddux/Piazza/99 6.00 15.00

2017 Panini National Treasures All Decade Quad Relics

RANDOM INSERTS IN PACKS
PRINT RUNS B/WN 10-25 COPIES PER
NO PRICING ON QTY 10
1 Bncrft/Bttmly/Hrnsby/Kmm/25 20.00 50.00
3 Thms/IRod/Grfty/Gwnn/25 30.00 80.00
4 Pjls/Arod/Grffy/Hltn/25 15.00 40.00
5 Bnks/Mntle/Wllms/Brra/25 75.00 200.00

2017 Panini National Treasures All Decade Relics

1 Albert Pujols/99
2 David Ortiz/99
3 Roy Halladay/49
4 Joe Mauer/99
5 Mike Piazza/99
6 Ken Griffey Jr./99
8 Frank Thomas/99
9 Ryne Sandberg/99
10 Cal Ripken/99
11 Mike Schmidt/99
12 Pete Rose/49
13 Johnny Bench/99
14 Reggie Jackson/49
15 Harmon Killebrew/49
16 Stan Musial/99
17 Arky Vaughan/25

2017 Panini National Treasures All Decade Triple Relics

RANDOM INSERTS IN PACKS
PRINT RUNS B/WN 10-25 COPIES PER
NO PRICING ON QTY 10
1 Ghrngr/Foxx/Ghrg/25 75.00 200.00
3 Sndr/Mthws/Mntle/25 40.00 100.00
4 Ruth/Hnsby/Spkr/25 75.00 200.00
5 Mrphy/Mrry/Brtt/25 30.00 80.00

2017 Panini National Treasures Armory Materials Booklet

1 Cody Bellinger/99
2 Andrew Benintendi/99
3 Yoan Moncada/99
4 Alex Bregman/99
5 Aaron Judge/99
6 Dansby Swanson/99
8 J.P. Crawford/99
9 Vladimir Guerrero Jr./99
10 Eloy Jimenez/99

2017 Panini National Treasures Chicago World Champions Tribute Relics

1 Anthony Rizzo
2 Addison Russell
3 Javier Baez
4 Jake Arrieta
5 Matt Szczur
6 Willson Contreras
7 Jason Heyward
8 Carl Edwards Jr.
9 Kyle Schwarber
10 Jorge Soler
11 Jon Lester

2017 Panini National Treasures Chicago World Champions Tribute Signatures

RANDOM INSERTS IN PACKS
PRINT RUNS B/WN 5-99 COPIES PER
NO PRICING ON QTY 15 OR LESS
EXCHANGE DEADLINE 4/25/2019
1 Theo Epstein/25 100.00 250.00
2 Anthony Rizzo/25 60.00 150.00
3 Addison Russell/49 15.00 40.00
4 Javier Baez/25
5 Jake Arrieta/25
6 Matt Szczur/99 12.00 30.00
7 Willson Contreras/99 20.00 50.00
9 Carl Edwards Jr./49 15.00 40.00
10 Kyle Schwarber/99 20.00 50.00

2017 Panini National Treasures College Rookie Materials Signatures

1 Dansby Swanson/99
2 Andrew Benintendi/99
3 Alex Bregman/99
4 Carson Fulmer/99
5 Hunter Renfroe/99
6 Ian Happ/99
7 Aaron Judge/99
8 Luke Weaver/49

2017 Panini National Treasures Colossal Material Signatures

1 Alex Gordon/25
3 Jonathan Lucroy/25
4 Ian Kinsler/49
5 Marcell Ozuna/25
6 George Springer/25
7 Hunter Pence/49
8 Wil Myers/20
10 Byron Buxton/25
11 Brendan Rodgers/20
12 Adam Duvall/99
18 Brandon Belt/99
21 Odubel Herrera/25
23 Edwin Encarnacion/20
25 Tyler Naquin/99
26 Adrian Gonzalez/49
28 Freddie Freeman/20
29 Edgar Martinez/49
32 Michael Kopech/99
33 Orel Hershiser/25
34 Paul Molitor/25
35 Pete Rose/25
39 Eric Hosmer/49
40 Nomar Mazara/25
45 Gary Sanchez/25
48 Lou Brock/20
49 Lucius Fox/99

2017 Panini National Treasures Colossal Materials

1 Kyle Schwarber/99
2 Kyle Seager/99
3 Jose Abreu/99
4 Jon Lester/99
5 Nelson Cruz/99
6 Brandon Belt/99
7 Dustin Pedroia/99
8 Buster Posey/49
9 J.A. Happ/99
10 Alex Gordon/99
11 Adam Duvall/99
12 Alex Rodriguez/49
13 Alfonso Soriano/99
14 Andruw Jones/99
15 Barry Larkin/49
16 Brandon Crawford/99
17 Brett Phillips/99
18 Carlton Fisk/99
19 CC Sabathia/99
20 Christian Yelich/99
21 Earl Weaver/99
22 Evan Gattis/99
23 Felix Hernandez/99
24 George Springer/99
25 Goose Gossage/99
26 Hanley Ramirez/99
27 Ian Happ/99
28 J.P. Crawford/99
29 Jackie Bradley Jr./99
30 Joe Torre/99
31 Jose Reyes/99
32 Josh Donaldson/25
33 Justin Upton/99
34 Kevin Maitan/99
35 Eloy Jimenez/99
36 Madison Bumgarner/99
37 Michael Conforto/99
38 Miguel Cabrera/99
39 Miguel Sano/99
40 Nelson Cruz/99
41 Ozzie Albies/99
42 Rick Porcello/99
43 Mike Trout/25
44 Robinson Cano/99
45 Ryne Sandberg/49
46 Sean Newcomb/99
47 Stephen Piscotty/99
48 Steven Matz/99
49 Todd Frazier/99
50 Tommy Lasorda/99
51 Wil Myers/99
52 Yoenis Cespedes/99
53 Zack Cozart/99
54 Bert Blyleven/49
55 Brian Dozier/99

2017 Panini National Treasures Colossal Stat Relics

1 Harmon Killebrew/25
3 Xander Bogaerts/25
4 Cody Bellinger/25
5 Aaron Judge/25
6 Buster Posey/25
7 Clayton Kershaw/25
8 Corey Seager/25
9 Alfonso Soriano/25
10 Dwight Gooden/25
11 Evan Longoria/25
12 Felix Hernandez/25
13 Gary Carter/25
14 Mike Piazza/25
15 Max Scherzer/25

2017 Panini National Treasures Dual Signature Material Booklet

2 George Springer
Jose Altuve/25
3 Francisco Lindor
Xander Bogaerts/25
5 Addison Russell
Javier Baez/25
7 Corey Seager
Trea Turner/25

2017 Panini National Treasures Greatness Relics

1 Roger Maris/49
2 Jackie Robinson/25
3 Roberto Clemente/25
4 Ted Williams/49
5 Al Simmons/49
6 Frankie Frisch/25
7 Mickey Mantle/25
8 Heinie Groh/99
9 Elston Howard/99
10 Kirby Puckett/49
11 Phil Rizzuto/25
12 Eddie Murray/99
13 Bobby Doerr/49
14 Sparky Anderson/25
15 Larry Doby/49

2017 Panini National Treasures Hometown Heroes Autographs

RANDOM INSERTS IN PACKS
PRINT RUNS B/WN 5-99 COPIES PER
NO PRICING ON QTY 15 OR LESS
EXCHANGE DEADLINE 4/25/2019
1 Yoan Moncada/20 20.00 50.00
2 George Springer/25 20.00 50.00
3 Nolan Arenado/20
5 Marcell Ozuna/25
7 Hunter Pence/49 8.00 20.00
11 Billy Wagner/89 6.00 15.00
12 Mike Napoli/99 3.00 8.00
15 Andres Galarraga/99 4.00 10.00
16 Paul Molitor/25 15.00 40.00
18 Francisco Lindor/25 25.00 60.00
19 Xander Bogaerts/25 20.00 50.00
20 Corey Seager/25 25.00 60.00
22 Al Oliver/99 3.00 8.00
23 Chris Sale/25 12.00 30.00
24 Brian Dozier/99 12.00 30.00
26 Andre Dawson/20 10.00 25.00
28 Jackie Bradley Jr./99 5.00 12.00
29 Max Scherzer/20
33 Freddie Freeman/20 10.00 25.00
35 Stephen Piscotty/99 4.00 10.00
36 Gary Sanchez/25 15.00 40.00
37 Edgar Renteria/49 4.00 10.00
40 Trea Turner/25 12.00 30.00
41 Addison Russell/25 20.00 50.00
45 Alex Bregman/49 15.00 40.00
46 Andrew Benintendi/99 20.00 80.00
47 Dansby Swanson/49 15.00 40.00
48 Trey Mancini/99 8.00 20.00
49 Mitch Haniger/99 8.00 20.00
50 Aaron Judge/99 75.00 200.00

2017 Panini National Treasures League Leaders Dual Relics

RANDOM INSERTS IN PACKS
PRINT RUNS B/WN 5-25 COPIES PER
NO PRICING ON QTY 10 OR LESS
1 Mattingly/Gwynn/25 20.00 50.00
2 Adrian Beltre 6.00 15.00
Manny Ramirez/25
5 Cepeda/Maris/25

2017 Panini National Treasures League Leaders Quad Relics

RANDOM INSERTS IN PACKS
PRINT RUNS B/WN 15-25 COPIES PER
NO PRICING ON QTY 15
1 Mttngly/Brtt/Hndrsn/Bggs/25 40.00 100.00
3 Lynn/Brtt/Mrgn/Crw/25 20.00 50.00
4 Ortz/Trt/Btts/Arndo/25
5 Bggo/Mrtnz/Thms/Gwnn/25 25.00 60.00

2017 Panini National Treasures League Leaders Relics

1 Tony Gwynn/99
2 Rickey Henderson/99
3 Pete Rose/25
4 Ichiro/49
5 Rickey Henderson/99
6 Edd Roush/49
7 Wade Boggs/99
8 Albert Pujols/99
9 Jose Canseco/99
10 Jeff Bagwell/99
11 Manny Ramirez/99
12 Billy Williams/49
13 Duke Snider/25
14 Hack Wilson/25
15 Sam Crawford/25

2017 Panini National Treasures League Leaders Triple Relics

RANDOM INSERTS IN PACKS
PRINT RUNS B/WN 15-25 COPIES PER
NO PRICING ON QTY 15
1 Rbnsn/Clmnte/Wllms/25 60.00 150.00
2 Rose/Carew/Gwynn/25 20.00 50.00
3 Foxx/Gehrig/Mantle/25 75.00 200.00
4 Harper/Bryant/Trout/25 25.00 60.00

2017 Panini National Treasures Legends Booklet Dual Materials

1 Frank Thomas/99
2 George Brett/99
3 Harmon Killebrew/49
4 Mike Piazza/99
5 Barry Larkin/99
6 Eddie Mathews/99
7 Mickey Mantle/25
8 Cal Ripken/99
9 Gary Carter/99
10 Ken Griffey Jr./99
12 Johnny Bench/99
13 Bert Blyleven/99
14 Duke Snider/99
15 Al Kaline/99
16 Paul Molitor/99
17 Robin Yount/99
18 Reggie Jackson/99
19 Ryne Sandberg/99
20 Tom Seaver/99
22 Kirby Puckett/25
23 Ken Griffey Jr./99
24 Albert Pujols/99
25 Ichiro/25
26 Yogi Berra/99

2017 Panini National Treasures Legends Booklet Quad Materials

3 George Kelly/25
5 Mickey Mantle/25
6 Joe Cronin/25

2017 Panini National Treasures Legends Booklet Triple Materials

1 Mariano Rivera/25
2 Rickey Henderson/25
4 Roger Maris/25
5 Tony Gwynn/49
6 Pete Rose/25
7 Ron Santo/25
8 Elston Howard/25
9 Willie Kamm/20

2017 Panini National Treasures Legends Cuts Booklet

RANDOM INSERTS IN PACKS
PRINT RUNS B/WN 5-99 COPIES PER
NO PRICING ON QTY 10 OR LESS
EXCHANGE DEADLINE 4/25/2019
1 Harmon Killebrew/99 20.00 50.00
2 Ralph Kiner/25 20.00 50.00
3 Gary Carter/99 15.00 40.00
4 Stan Musial/49 25.00 60.00
5 Bobby Thomson/49 12.00 30.00
6 Johnny Mize/25
9 Pete Rose/25 40.00 100.00

2017 Panini National Treasures Legends Cuts Booklet Dual Materials

3 Bill Dickey/20
28 Stan Musial/20
45 Gary Carter/25
59 Gary Carter/25
60 Harmon Killebrew/25
62 Warren Spahn/20
70 Bob Gibson/25
90 Mariano Rivera/25

2017 Panini National Treasures Legends Cuts Booklet Materials

59 Gary Carter/25
82 Steve Carlton/20

2017 Panini National Treasures Legends Cuts Booklet Moments

RANDOM INSERTS IN PACKS
PRINT RUNS B/WN 1-99 COPIES PER
NO PRICING ON QTY 15 OR LESS
EXCHANGE DEADLINE 4/25/2019
1 Harmon Killebrew/99 15.00 40.00
3 Gary Carter/99 12.00 30.00
4 Stan Musial/49 25.00 60.00
5 Bobby Thomson/99 12.00 30.00

2017 Panini National Treasures Legends Cuts Booklet Nickname

RANDOM INSERTS IN PACKS
PRINT RUNS B/WN 1-99 COPIES PER
NO PRICING ON QTY 15 OR LESS
EXCHANGE DEADLINE 4/25/2019
1 Harmon Killebrew/99 15.00 40.00
2 Ralph Kiner/25 20.00 50.00
3 Gary Carter/99 12.00 30.00
4 Stan Musial/49 25.00 60.00
5 Bobby Thomson/99 12.00 30.00
9 Pete Rose/20 25.00 60.00

2017 Panini National Treasures Legends Cuts Booklet Quad Materials

45 Gary Carter/25
59 Gary Carter/25

2017 Panini National Treasures Legends Cuts Booklet Stats

RANDOM INSERTS IN PACKS
PRINT RUNS B/WN 1-99 COPIES PER
NO PRICING ON QTY 10 OR LESS
EXCHANGE DEADLINE 4/25/2019
1 Harmon Killebrew/99 15.00 40.00
2 Ralph Kiner/25 20.00 50.00
3 Gary Carter/99 12.00 30.00
4 Stan Musial/49 25.00 60.00

2017 Panini National Treasures Legends Cuts Booklet Triple Materials

45 Gary Carter/25
59 Gary Carter/25

2017 Panini National Treasures Legends Dual Cuts Booklet

RANDOM INSERTS IN PACKS
PRINT RUNS B/WN 1-49 COPIES PER
NO PRICING ON QTY 5 OR LESS
EXCHANGE DEADLINE 4/25/2019
4 Killebrew/Musial/49 40.00 100.00

2017 Panini National Treasures Legends Dual Relics

2 Roger Clemens/25
6 Tom Seaver/25
10 Mariano Rivera/25
11 Jackie Robinson/25
16 Alex Rodriguez/25
17 Johnny Mize/25
18 Sam Crawford/25

2017 Panini National Treasures Legends Quad Relics

1 Harmon Killebrew
2 Paul Molitor
3 Nolan Ryan
4 Cal Ripken

2017 Panini National Treasures Legends Triple Relics

1 Eddie Mathews/25
3 Tony Gwynn/25
4 Ken Griffey Jr./25
5 Mike Piazza/25

2017 Panini National Treasures Material Ink

1 Eloy Jimenez/99
2 Nomar Mazara/25
3 Andre Dawson/30
4 Dwight Gooden/49
7 Starling Marte/99
10 Trea Turner/25
11 Joe Panik/99
14 Freddie Freeman/25
15 Stephen Piscotty/99
16 Gary Sanchez/49
17 Charlie Blackmon/49
18 Corey Kluber/25
19 Kyle Seager/99
20 Jason Kipnis/99
23 Cole Hamels/20
24 Manny Machado/25
30 Marcell Ozuna/25
31 Salvador Perez/25
32 Orel Hershiser/49
33 Adam Duvall/99
34 Hunter Pence/49
36 Alex Gordon/25
40 George Springer/25
42 Wil Myers/25
44 Odubel Herrera/99
45 Gleyber Torres/99
48 Craig Biggio/25
49 Jim Rice/25
50 Edgar Martinez/49

2017 Panini National Treasures Monumental Materials Booklets

RANDOM INSERTS IN PACKS
PRINT RUNS B/WN 3-99 COPIES PER
NO PRICING ON QTY 10 OR LESS
2 Bllvn/Ryan/Clmns/Crltn/25 20.00 50.00
3 Cncptn/Mrgn/Bnch/Rse/99 25.00 60.00
4 Mthws/Bnks/Kllbrw/Ott/49 25.00 60.00
8 Rickey Henderson/99 15.00 40.00

2017 Panini National Treasures Notable Nicknames Autographs

RANDOM INSERTS IN PACKS
PRINT RUNS B/WN 5-99 COPIES PER
NO PRICING ON QTY 15 OR LESS
EXCHANGE DEADLINE 4/25/2019
1 Darrell Evans/99 6.00 15.00
3 Paul Molitor/49 10.00 25.00
5 Darryl Strawberry/99 12.00 30.00
7 Edgar Martinez/49 12.00 30.00
9 Edgar Renteria/49 10.00 25.00
10 Lee Smith/99 8.00 20.00
13 Billy Wagner/99 12.00 30.00
17 Orel Hershiser/25 50.00 120.00
20 Lou Brock/25
25 Frank Thomas/20 40.00 100.00
26 Nomar Mazara/25
27 Keith Hernandez/25 30.00 80.00
28 Alex Gordon/25 15.00 40.00
29 Trey Mancini/99 25.00 60.00
30 Gary Sanchez/25
31 Craig Kimbrel/49 15.00 40.00
32 Hunter Pence/49 12.00 30.00
39 Terry Francona/49 20.00 50.00
40 Josh Tomlin/99 4.00 10.00
49 Mike Napoli/99 4.00 10.00

2017 Panini National Treasures Pastime Signatures

RANDOM INSERTS IN PACKS
PRINT RUNS B/WN 5-99 COPIES PER
NO PRICING ON QTY 15 OR LESS
EXCHANGE DEADLINE 4/25/2019
*GOLD/25: .6X TO 1.5X p/r 99
*GOLD/25: .5X TO 1.2X p/r 49
1 Willie McGee/99 6.00 15.00
3 Jose Canseco/99 6.00 15.00
5 Chris Sale/25 12.00 30.00
6 Adrian Beltre/20 15.00 40.00
8 Keith Hernandez/25 10.00 25.00
9 Mark Grace/99 8.00 20.00
10 Fred Lynn/25
13 Craig Kimbrel/49 10.00 25.00
14 Francisco Lindor/25 25.00 60.00
16 Phil Niekro/20 6.00 15.00
19 Andre Dawson/20 10.00 25.00
21 Jackie Bradley Jr./99 5.00 12.00
22 Max Scherzer/20
25 Gary Sanchez/25 25.00 60.00
26 Charlie Blackmon/49 6.00 15.00
27 Josh Tomlin/25 5.00 12.00
28 Terry Francona/49 12.00 30.00
29 Edgar Renteria/49 4.00 10.00
31 Gleyber Torres/99 25.00 60.00
34 Andres Galarraga/99 4.00 10.00
35 Ken Griffey Sr./49 4.00 10.00
41 Marcell Ozuna/25
44 Frank Thomas/20 25.00 60.00
45 Lou Brock/25 12.00 30.00
46 Lee Smith/99 3.00 8.00

2017 Panini National Treasures Player's Collection Signatures

1 Yoan Moncada/20
2 Andrew Benintendi/99
3 Alex Bregman/49
4 Dansby Swanson/99
5 Trey Mancini/99
6 Aaron Judge/99
7 Corey Seager/25
10 Nolan Arenado/20
14 Eloy Jimenez/99
17 Frank Thomas/25
24 David Dahl/99
25 Mitch Haniger/99
26 Edgar Martinez/25
27 Adam Duvall/99
29 Dwight Gooden/49
30 Chris Sale/25
31 Gary Sanchez/25
32 Hunter Pence/49
33 Adrian Beltre/20
34 Jonathan Lucroy/25
39 Francisco Lindor/25
40 Salvador Perez/25
43 Cole Hamels/20
44 Freddie Freeman/25
45 Xander Bogaerts/25
47 Kyle Seager/99
48 Gleyber Torres/99
51 Josh Bell/99
52 Alex Reyes/99
53 Tyler Glasnow/99
54 Jose De Leon/99
55 Joe Musgrove/99
56 Manuel Margot/99
57 Hunter Renfroe/99
58 Jorge Alfaro/99
59 Carson Fulmer/99
60 Koda Glover/99
62 Ryon Healy/99
63 Luke Weaver/99
64 Gavin Cecchini/99
65 Cody Bellinger/99
66 Amed Rosario/99
67 Hunter Dozier/99
68 Erik Gonzalez/99
69 Jose Rondon/99
70 Matt Olson/99
71 Yohander Mendez/99
72 Chad Pinder/99
73 Carson Kelly/99
75 Roman Quinn/99
76 German Marquez/99
77 Jharel Cotton/99
78 Jake Thompson/99
80 Adam Plutko/99
81 Gabriel Ynoa/99
84 David Paulino/99
85 Reynaldo Lopez/99
86 Jeff Hoffman/99
87 Braden Shipley/99
88 Raimel Tapia/99
89 Adalberto Mejia/99
90 Renato Nunez/99
93 Byron Buxton/25
94 Eric Hosmer/25
98 Marcell Ozuna/25
99 Odubel Herrera/49
100 Lou Brock/25

2017 Panini National Treasures Quad Player Materials Booklet

RANDOM INSERTS IN PACKS
PRINT RUNS B/WN 3-9 COPIES PER
NO PRICING ON QTY 3
1 Jdge/Bllngr/Swnsn/Mncda/99 30.00 80.00
2 Rzzo/Bnks/Brnt/Sndbrg/25 75.00 200.00
3 Brtt/Pcktt/Pzza/Gwnn/25 50.00 120.00
4 Sgr/Lndr/Mchdo/Btts/49 20.00 50.00

2017 Panini National Treasures Retro Signatures

RANDOM INSERTS IN PACKS
PRINT RUNS B/WN 5-99 COPIES PER
NO PRICING ON QTY 15 OR LESS
EXCHANGE DEADLINE 4/25/2019
1 Yoan Moncada/25 15.00 40.00
2 Bert Campaneris/99 6.00 15.00
8 Pete Rose/25 20.00 50.00
9 Jose Canseco/25 12.00 30.00
11 Edwin Encarnacion/20 8.00 20.00
12 Jonathan Lucroy/25
13 Tony Oliva/25 12.00 30.00
18 Tommy John/25 5.00 12.00
25 Edgar Martinez/49 8.00 20.00
26 Andres Galarraga/99 4.00 10.00
27 Nomar Mazara/25 8.00 20.00
31 Paul Molitor/25 15.00 40.00
35 Ken Griffey Sr./49 4.00 10.00
36 Josh Donaldson/25 10.00 25.00
39 Johnny Damon/20
41 Adrian Gonzalez/25 6.00 15.00
42 John Farrell/49 8.00 20.00
43 Joe Carter/25 12.00 30.00
44 Jim Rice/25
45 Alan Trammell/99 10.00 25.00
46 Hunter Pence/49 8.00 20.00
47 Andy Pettitte/25 8.00 20.00
48 Andruw Jones/99 3.00 8.00

2017 Panini National Treasures Rookie Jersey Signatures Vertical

1 Yoan Moncada/25
2 Dansby Swanson/25
3 Alex Bregman/25
4 Cody Bellinger/25
5 Alex Reyes/25
7 Jose De Leon/25
8 Joe Musgrove/25
9 Manuel Margot/25
10 David Paulino/25
11 Reynaldo Lopez/25
12 Braden Shipley/25
13 Hunter Renfroe/25
14 Carson Fulmer/25
15 Luke Weaver/25
16 Amir Garrett/25
17 Renato Nunez/25
18 Ian Happ/25
19 Chad Pinder/25
20 Trey Mancini/25
21 Jose Rondon/25
22 Teoscar Hernandez/25
23 Erik Gonzalez/25
24 Roman Quinn/25
25 German Marquez/25
26 Jharel Cotton/25
27 Jake Thompson/25

2017 Panini National Treasures Rookie Signature Jumbo Material Booklet

1 Yoan Moncada
4 Dansby Swanson
5 Aaron Judge
7 Ian Happ
8 Orlando Arcia
9 Hunter Renfroe
10 Trey Mancini

2017 Panini National Treasures Rookie Timeline Materials

2 Andrew Benintendi
3 Yoan Moncada
4 Trey Mancini
5 Aaron Judge
6 Dansby Swanson
7 Jordan Montgomery
8 Alex Bregman
9 Mitch Haniger
10 Amir Garrett
11 Orlando Arcia
12 Josh Bell
13 David Dahl
14 Manuel Margot
15 Carson Fulmer
16 Ian Happ
17 Hunter Renfroe

2017 Panini National Treasures Rookie Timeline Materials Signatures

1 Cody Bellinger/99
2 Andrew Benintendi/99
3 Yoan Moncada/99
4 Trey Mancini/99
5 Aaron Judge/99
6 Dansby Swanson/99
7 Jordan Montgomery/99
8 Alex Bregman/49
9 Mitch Haniger/99
10 Amir Garrett/99
11 Ian Happ/99

2017 Panini National Treasures Signature Material Booklet

1 Eric Hosmer/25
3 Jose Altuve/25
7 Freddie Freeman/25

2017 Panini National Treasures Six Swatch Signatures

1 Mark Prior/99
3 Pete Rose/25
4 Rafael Palmeiro/49
6 Jim Rice/49
7 Jake Arrieta/25
8 David Ortiz/25
9 Manny Machado/25
12 Francisco Lindor/25
14 Frank Thomas/25
18 Aledmys Diaz/99
19 Adrian Beltre/35
20 Edwin Encarnacion/49
23 Lee Smith/49
24 Lou Brock/25
27 Nomar Garciaparra/20
29 Ozzie Smith/25
31 Tony Oliva/20
32 Ryne Sandberg/25
33 Dwight Gooden/49
36 Mike Napoli/99
37 John Farrell/49
39 Fred Lynn/25
40 Addison Russell/49
43 Nomar Mazara/49
45 Jose Altuve/25
47 Corey Kluber/25
48 Josh Tomlin/25
49 Corey Seager/25
50 Yoan Moncada/25

2017 Panini National Treasures Stars Booklet Material Signatures

2 Nelson Cruz/25
3 Aaron Judge/99
4 Andrew Benintendi/99
5 Yoan Moncada/25
6 Cody Bellinger/25
7 Alex Bregman/25
8 Dansby Swanson/25
9 Ian Happ/99
12 Jackie Bradley Jr./25
13 George Springer/25
15 Jose Abreu/25
16 Joey Votto/20

2017 Panini National Treasures Timeline Materials Names

1 Alex Rodriguez/25
2 Mike Trout/25
3 Manny Machado/25
4 David Ortiz/25
5 Chipper Jones/25
6 Corey Kluber/25
7 Dee Gordon/25
8 Ken Griffey Jr./25
9 Harmon Killebrew/25
10 Dustin Pedroia/25
11 Fred Lynn/25
12 Giancarlo Stanton/25
13 Greg Maddux/25
14 Ivan Rodriguez/25
15 Nolan Ryan/25

2017 Panini National Treasures Timeline Materials Nicknames

1 Alex Rodriguez/25
2 Mike Trout/25
3 Manny Machado/25
4 David Ortiz/25
5 Chipper Jones/25
6 Corey Kluber/25
7 Dee Gordon/25
8 Ken Griffey Jr./25
10 Dustin Pedroia/25
13 Greg Maddux/25
14 Ivan Rodriguez/25
15 Nolan Ryan/25

2017 Panini National Treasures Timeline Materials Signatures Names

1 Byron Buxton/99
2 Corey Seager/99
3 Edwin Encarnacion/49
4 Yogi Berra/25
6 Barry Larkin/49
8 Omar Vizquel/49
9 Sean Newcomb/99
10 Sam Travis/99
11 Bradley Zimmer/99
12 Francis Martes/25
13 Adrian Gonzalez/25
14 Alfonso Soriano/99
15 Gary Sanchez/25

2017 Panini National Treasures Timeline Materials Signatures Team Cities

1 Byron Buxton/99
2 Corey Seager/99
3 Edwin Encarnacion/25

4 Yogi Berra/25
6 Barry Larkin/49
8 Omar Vizquel/99
9 Sean Newcomb/99
10 Sam Travis/99
11 Bradley Zimmer/99
12 Francis Martes/25
13 Adrian Gonzalez/25
14 Alfonso Soriano/49
15 Gary Sanchez/25

2017 Panini National Treasures Timeline Materials Team Cities

1 Alex Rodriguez/25
2 Mike Trout/25
3 Manny Machado/25
4 David Ortiz/25
5 Chipper Jones/25
6 Corey Kluber/25
7 Dee Gordon/25
8 Ken Griffey Jr./25
10 Dustin Pedroia/25
11 Fred Lynn/25
12 Giancarlo Stanton/25
13 Greg Maddux/25
14 Ivan Rodriguez/25
15 Nolan Ryan/25

2017 Panini National Treasures Timeline Rookie Materials

1 Cody Bellinger

2017 Panini National Treasures Treasure Chest 24 Materials Booklet

RANDOM INSERTS IN PACKS
STATED PRINT RUN 99 SER.#'d SETS
1 24 Material Booklet 75.00 200.00

2017 Panini National Treasures Treasure Chest 32 Materials Booklet

RANDOM INSERTS IN PACKS
STATED PRINT RUN 99 SER.#'d SETS
1 32 Material Booklet 125.00 300.00

2017 Panini National Treasures Treasure Materials

1 Mike Trout/49
2 Kris Bryant/49
3 Bryce Harper/49
4 Aaron Judge/99
5 Giancarlo Stanton/99
6 Joey Gallo/99
7 Buster Posey/99
8 Marcell Ozuna/99
9 Jose Altuve/99
10 Jose Abreu/99
11 Eric Hosmer/99
12 Joey Votto/99
13 Michael Conforto/99
14 Nolan Arenado/99
15 Joe Mauer/99
16 Miguel Sano/99
17 Dallas Keuchel/99
18 Clayton Kershaw/99
19 Corey Seager/99
20 Kevin Kiermaier/99
21 Xander Bogaerts/99
22 Daniel Murphy/99
23 Miguel Cabrera/99
24 Carlos Correa/99
25 Manny Machado/99

2017 Panini National Treasures Treasure Signature Materials

1 Manny Machado/49
2 Rickey Henderson/49
3 Jose Abreu/99
4 Yasmany Tomas/99
5 Wade Boggs/99
6 Ivan Rodriguez/49
7 Tom Glavine/49
8 Tom Glavine/99
9 Yoan Moncada/99
10 Dave Winfield/49
11 Brooks Robinson/49
12 Stephen Strasburg/49
13 Ryne Sandberg/49
14 David Dahl/99
15 Luis Aparicio/49
16 Ozzie Smith/49
17 Willie McCovey/49
18 Tommy Lasorda/49
19 Alex Bregman/99
20 Gavin Cecchini/99
21 Don Mattingly/49
22 Don Mattingly/49
23 Francisco Lindor/89
24 Corey Seager/99
25 David Ortiz/49
26 David Ortiz/49
27 Joey Votto/49
28 Robin Yount/49
29 Xander Bogaerts/99
30 Aaron Judge/99
31 Carson Fulmer/99
32 Ian Happ/99
33 Andrew McCutchen/25
34 Alfonso Soriano/99
35 Andre Dawson/49
36 Andrew Benintendi/99
37 Josh Donaldson/99
38 Andres Galarraga/99
39 Yadier Molina/99
40 David Wright/49
41 Antonio Senzatela/99
42 Yandy Diaz/99
43 Trey Mancini/99
44 Victor Robles/99
45 Nolan Arenado/49
46 Bob Gibson/25
47 Jose Canseco/99
48 Lazaro Armenteros/99
49 Jonathan Lucroy/99
50 Starling Marte/99
51 Jose Ramirez/99
52 Ken Griffey Jr./25
54 Cal Ripken/25
55 Nolan Ryan/25
56 Kevin Maitan/99
57 Gleyber Torres/99
58 Amed Rosario/99
59 Dave Concepcion/99
60 Jeff Bagwell/49
61 Noah Syndergaard/49
62 Carlos Gonzalez/25
63 Albert Pujols/25
64 Dustin Pedroia/49
65 Anthony Rizzo/49
66 Hunter Pence/49
67 Edwin Encarnacion/49
68 Frank Thomas/49
69 Joe Torre/49
71 Paul Goldschmidt/49
72 Chris Sale/49
73 Max Scherzer/49
74 Jose Altuve/49

2017 Panini National Treasures Treasured Signatures

RANDOM INSERTS IN PACKS
PRINT RUNS B/WN 5-99 COPIES PER
NO PRICING ON QTY 15 OR LESS
EXCHANGE DEADLINE 4/25/2019
1 Yoan Moncada/20 30.00 80.00
3 Corey Seager/25 25.00 60.00
4 Trea Turner/25 12.00 30.00
5 Xander Bogaerts/25 20.00 50.00
6 Jose Altuve/25 20.00 50.00
9 Nolan Arenado/20
10 Bert Campaneris/99 6.00 15.00
11 Tony Oliva/25 12.00 30.00
14 Nomar Mazara/25 5.00 12.00
15 Orel Hershiser/25 30.00 80.00
17 Ian Kinsler/25 15.00 40.00
18 Andy Pettitte/25 12.00 30.00
21 Marcell Ozuna/25
22 Chris Sale/25 12.00 30.00
23 Chuck Finley/99 3.00 8.00
25 Corey Kluber/25 12.00 30.00
26 Craig Biggio/20 8.00 20.00
27 Craig Kimbrel/49 12.00 30.00
30 Dennis Eckersley/49 8.00 20.00
31 Edgar Martinez/49 8.00 20.00
32 Fergie Jenkins/25 12.00 30.00
33 Francisco Lindor/25 25.00 60.00
34 Fred Lynn/25
35 Gaylord Perry/99 5.00 12.00
36 Mike Napoli/49 4.00 10.00
37 Don Mattingly/20
40 John Franco/99 5.00 12.00
44 Eloy Jimenez/99 20.00 50.00
46 Frank Howard/99 10.00 25.00
47 Mark Grace/99 8.00 20.00

2017 Panini National Treasures Triple Crown Winners Relics

1 Miguel Cabrera/99
2 Ted Williams/99
9 Rogers Hornsby/25
13 Steve Carlton/99
14 Clayton Kershaw/99
15 Justin Verlander/99
16 Dwight Gooden/99

2017 Panini National Treasures Triple Player Materials Booklet

RANDOM INSERTS IN PACKS
PRINT RUNS B/WN 3-99 COPIES PER
NO PRICING ON QTY 3
2 Rpkn/Thms/Grffy/99 30.00 80.00
3 Bnntndi/Bllngr/Happ/99 12.00 30.00

2019 Panini National Treasures

RANDOMLY INSERTED IN PACKS
PRINT RUNS B/WN 1-99 COPIES PER
NO PRICING ON QTY 15 OR LESS
EXCHANGE DEADLINE 3/25/21
1 Bryse Wilson JSY AU/99 RC 5.00 12.00
2 Touki Toussaint JSY AU/99 RC 5.00 12.00
3 M.Kopech JSY AU/99 RC 10.00 25.00
4 R.Laureano JSY AU/99 RC 15.00 40.00
5 Garrett Hampson JSY AU/99 RC 6.00 15.00
6 Dennis Santana JSY AU/99 RC 4.00 10.00
7 Ryan O'Hearn JSY AU/99 RC 6.00 15.00
8 Jonathan Loaisiga JSY AU/99 RC 6.00 15.00
9 E.Jimenez JSY AU/99 RC 25.00 60.00
10 Reese McGuire JSY AU/99 RC 6.00 15.00
11 Corbin Burnes JSY AU/99 RC 12.00 30.00
12 Jake Cave JSY AU/99 RC 5.00 12.00
13 Luis Ortiz JSY AU/99 RC 4.00 10.00
14 Kyle Wright JSY AU/99 RC 6.00 15.00
15 Chris Shaw JSY AU/99 RC 4.00 10.00
16 Kevin Kramer JSY AU/99 RC 6.00 15.00
17 Framber Valdez JSY AU/99 RC 4.00 10.00
18 D.Hudson JSY AU/99 RC 12.00 30.00
19 K.Newman JSY AU/99 RC 15.00 40.00
20 Danny Jansen JSY AU/99 RC 4.00 10.00
21 Brad Keller JSY AU/99 RC 4.00 10.00
22 Chance Adams JSY AU/99 RC 4.00 10.00
23 Enyel De Los Santos JSY AU/99 RC 4.00 10.00
24 Taylor Ward JSY AU/99 RC 4.00 10.00
26 K.Tucker JSY AU/99 RC 15.00 40.00
27 Patrick Wisdom JSY AU/99 RC 4.00 10.00
28 J.McNeil JSY AU/99 RC 20.00 50.00
29 Guerrero Jr. JSY AU/99 RC 100.00 250.00
30 Cionel Perez JSY AU/99 RC 4.00 10.00
31 Kolby Allard JSY AU/99 RC 6.00 15.00
32 Stephen Gonsalves JSY AU/99 RC 6.00 15.00
33 B.Lowe JSY AU/99 RC 8.00 20.00
34 Myles Straw JSY AU/99 RC 6.00 15.00
35 Tatis Jr. JSY AU/99 RC 125.00 300.00
36 Sean Reid-Foley JSY AU/99 RC 4.00 10.00
37 Jonathan Davis JSY AU/99 RC 5.00 12.00
38 Ryan Borucki JSY AU/99 RC 4.00 10.00
39 Christin Stewart JSY AU/99 RC 5.00 12.00
40 Cedric Mullins JSY AU/99 RC 12.00 30.00
41 Justus Sheffield JSY AU/99 RC 6.00 15.00
42 Caleb Ferguson JSY AU/99 RC 5.00 12.00
43 Jacob Nix JSY AU/99 RC 5.00 12.00
44 Daniel Ponce de Leon JSY AU/99 RC 6.00 15.00
45 Josh James JSY AU/99 RC 6.00 15.00
46 David Fletcher JSY AU/99 RC 8.00 20.00
47 Steven Duggar JSY AU/99 RC 5.00 12.00
48 Rowdy Tellez JSY AU/99 RC 6.00 15.00
49 Luis Urias JSY AU/99 RC 6.00 15.00
50 Jake Bauers JSY AU/99 RC 6.00 15.00
51 P.Alonso JSY AU/49 RC 125.00 300.00
53 C.Paddack JSY AU/75 RC 15.00 40.00
54 B.Reynolds JSY AU/99 RC 40.00 100.00
55 C.Tucker JSY AU/99 RC 20.00 50.00
56 M.Chavis JSY AU/99 RC 12.00 30.00
57 Y.Kikuchi JSY AU/99 RC 10.00 25.00
58 D.Hernandez JSY AU/86 RC 4.00 10.00
59 Ty France JSY AU/99 RC 15.00 40.00
60 Taylor Hearn JSY AU/99 RC 4.00 10.00
61 C.Kieboom JSY AU/99 RC 15.00 40.00
63 Cal Quantrill JSY AU/25 RC 6.00 15.00
64 Nathaniel Lowe JSY AU/99 RC 20.00 50.00
66 A.Riley JSY AU/99 RC 20.00 50.00
67 Shaun Anderson JSY AU/99 RC 4.00 10.00
68 K.Hiura JSY AU/99 RC 15.00 40.00
69 Nicky Lopez JSY AU/49 RC 8.00 20.00
71 Brendan Rodgers JSY AU/99 RC 6.00 15.00
72 L.Arraez JSY AU/99 RC 25.00 60.00
73 O.Mercado JSY AU/79 RC 20.00 50.00
74 Addie Joss JSY/25 25.00 60.00
75 Mitch Haniger JSY/99 2.50 6.00
76 Rafael Devers JSY/99 4.00 10.00
77 Franmil Reyes JSY/99 2.00 5.00
78 Roger Maris JSY/25
79 Tommy Pham JSY/99 2.00 5.00
80 Juan Soto JSY/99 10.00 25.00
81 Adrian Beltre JSY/99 3.00 8.00
82 Nicholas Castellanos JSY/99 3.00 8.00
83 Jose Urena JSY/99 2.00 5.00
84 Rhys Hoskins JSY/99 4.00 10.00
85 David Peralta JSY/99 2.00 5.00
86 Joey Gallo JSY/99 2.50 6.00
87 Ichiro Suzuki JSY/99 4.00 10.00
88 Felix Hernandez JSY/99 2.50 6.00
89 Marcell Ozuna JSY/99 3.00 8.00
90 Ron Santo JSY/49 10.00 25.00
91 Mookie Betts JSY/49 8.00 20.00
92 Evan Longoria JSY/99 2.50 6.00
93 Eugenio Suarez JSY/99 2.50 6.00
94 Justin Verlander JSY/99 3.00 8.00
95 Luke Weaver JSY/99 2.00 5.00
96 Roberto Clemente JSY/99 25.00 60.00
97 Tommy Henrich JSY/49 2.50 6.00
98 Bobby Thomson JSY/25
99 Gleyber Torres JSY/99 12.00 30.00
100 Josh Bell JSY/49 3.00 8.00
101 Trevor Story JSY/99 3.00 8.00
102 Jose Altuve JSY/49 3.00 8.00
103 Shohei Ohtani JSY/99 15.00 40.00
104 Gerrit Cole JSY/99 3.00 8.00
105 David Price JSY/99 2.50 6.00
106 Bryce Harper JSY/99 10.00 25.00
107 Hunter Dozier JSY/99 2.00 5.00
108 German Marquez JSY/99 2.00 5.00
109 Xander Bogaerts JSY/99 6.00 15.00
110 Michael Conforto JSY/99 2.50 6.00
111 Paul Goldschmidt JSY/91 3.00 8.00
112 Freddie Freeman JSY/49 5.00 12.00
113 Mike Trout JSY/99 12.00 30.00
114 Lucas Giolito JSY/99 2.50 6.00
115 Chris Sale JSY/99 3.00 8.00
116 Trey Mancini JSY/99 2.50 6.00
117 Corey Kluber JSY/99 2.50 6.00
118 Jake Arrieta JSY/99 2.50 6.00
119 Mickey Mantle JSY/99 25.00 60.00
120 Eddie Stanky JSY/99 4.00 10.00
121 Aaron Nola JSY/99 2.50 6.00
122 Manny Machado JSY/99 3.00 8.00
123 Billy Martin JSY/49 12.00 30.00
124 Giancarlo Stanton JSY/99 3.00 8.00
125 Francisco Lindor JSY/99 3.00 8.00
126 Christian Yelich JSY/99 4.00 10.00
127 Stephen Strasburg JSY/99 3.00 8.00
128 Edwin Diaz JSY/49 3.00 8.00
129 Masahiro Tanaka JSY/49 3.00 8.00
131 Marcus Stroman JSY/99 2.50 6.00
132 Patrick Corbin JSY/99 2.50 6.00
133 Adalberto Mondesi JSY/99 2.50 6.00
134 Noah Syndergaard JSY/99 2.50 6.00
135 Anthony Rizzo JSY/99 4.00 10.00
136 Miguel Cabrera JSY/99 3.00 8.00
137 Jacob deGrom JSY/49 8.00 20.00
138 Javier Baez JSY/99 4.00 10.00
139 Max Scherzer JSY/99 3.00 8.00
140 Albert Pujols JSY/49 5.00 12.00
141 Starling Marte JSY/99 2.50 6.00
142 Harvey Kuenn JSY/99 2.00 5.00
143 Jose Abreu JSY/99 3.00 8.00
144 Mike Soroka JSY/99 3.00 8.00
145 George Springer JSY/99 2.50 6.00
146 Aaron Judge JSY/99 8.00 20.00
147 Lorenzo Cain JSY/99 2.00 5.00
149 Austin Meadows JSY/49 4.00 10.00
150 J.D. Martinez JSY/99 3.00 8.00
151 Ronald Acuna Jr. JSY/99 12.00 30.00
152 Clayton Kershaw JSY/99 5.00 12.00
153 Buster Posey JSY/49 5.00 12.00
154 Matt Chapman JSY/99 3.00 8.00
155 Ken Boyer JSY/49 6.00 15.00
156 Alex Bregman JSY/99 3.00 8.00
157 Jose Berrios JSY/99 2.50 6.00
159 Michael Brantley JSY/99 2.50 6.00
160 Jack Flaherty JSY/99 3.00 8.00
161 Nolan Arenado JSY/99 5.00 12.00
162 Madison Bumgarner JSY/99 2.50 6.00
163 Carl Furillo JSY/49 2.50 6.00
164 Cody Bellinger JSY/49 8.00 20.00
165 Ozzie Albies JSY/99 3.00 8.00
166 Eddie Rosario JSY/99 2.50 6.00
167 Andrew Benintendi JSY/99 3.00 8.00
168 Whit Merrifield JSY/99 3.00 8.00
169 J.T. Realmuto JSY/99 3.00 8.00
170 Max Fried JSY/99 3.00 8.00
171 Jose Ramirez JSY/99 2.50 6.00
172 Kris Bryant JSY/99 12.00 30.00
173 Paul DeJong JSY/99 3.00 8.00
174 Herb Pennock JSY/49 3.00 8.00
175 Rogers Hornsby JSY/25 10.00 25.00
176 Luke Appling JSY/99 3.00 8.00
177 Leo Durocher JSY/99 3.00 8.00
178 Mule Suttles JSY/99 20.00 50.00
181 Tom Seaver JSY/49 3.00 8.00
182 Charlie Keller JSY/99 2.00 5.00
183 Yogi Berra JSY/99 15.00 40.00
184 Ted Williams JSY/25 20.00 50.00
185 Bill Dickey JSY/25 12.00 30.00
186 Joe Cronin JSY/25 3.00 8.00
188 Paul Waner JSY/99 6.00 15.00
189 Walter Alston JSY/99 2.50 6.00
191 Don Drysdale JSY/99 2.50 6.00
192 Satchel Paige JSY/25 30.00 80.00
193 Billy Herman JSY/25 3.00 8.00
194 Lloyd Waner JSY/25
195 Willie Keeler JSY/99 10.00 25.00
196 Tony Lazzeri JSY/49 6.00 15.00
197 Casey Stengel JSY/49 3.00 8.00
198 Johnny Mize JSY/49 5.00 12.00
200 Ted Lyons JSY/49 6.00 15.00
201 Jimmie Foxx JSY/25 15.00 40.00
202 Honus Wagner JSY/25 50.00 120.00
203 Joe Jackson JSY/49 40.00 100.00
204 Harry Hooper JSY/25 3.00 8.00
205 Hank Greenberg JSY/99 10.00 25.00
206 Jackie Robinson JSY/99 25.00 60.00
209 Roy Campanella JSY/25
210 Gil Hodges JSY/99 4.00 10.00
212 Ty Cobb JSY/25
214 Joe Sewell JSY/49 8.00 20.00
215 Stan Musial JSY/49 10.00 25.00
216 Joe McCarthy JSY/25 15.00 40.00
218 Frank Chance JSY/99 8.00 20.00
220 Max Carey JSY/49 2.50 6.00
222 Tris Speaker JSY/25 15.00 40.00
223 Edd Roush JSY/99 6.00 15.00

2019 Panini National Treasures Gold

*GOLD/49: .5X TO 1.2X p/r 79-99
*GOLD/25: .8X TO 2X p/r 79-99
*GOLD/25: .6X TO 1.5X pr/49
RANDOM INSERTS IN PACKS
PRINT RUNS B/WN 25-49 COPIES PER
EXCHANGE DEADLINE 3/25/21
51 Pete Alonso JSY AU/25 200.00 500.00
68 Keston Hiura JSY AU/49 30.00 80.00

2019 Panini National Treasures Holo Gold

*HOLO GOLD/20-25: .8X TO 2X p/r 49
*HOLO GOLD/20-25: .6X TO 1.5X p/r 49
RANDOM INSERTS IN PACKS
PRINT RUNS B/WN 15-25 COPIES PER
NO PRICING ON QTY 15 OR LESS
EXCHANGE DEADLINE 3/25/21
51 Pete Alonso JSY AU/20 200.00 500.00
68 Keston Hiura JSY AU/25 40.00 100.00

2019 Panini National Treasures Cleats

RANDOM INSERTS IN PACKS
PRINT RUNS B/WN 7-25 COPIES PER
NO PRICING ON QTY 15 OR LESS
1 Mike Piazza/25 5.00 12.00
2 Starlin Castro/22 6.00 15.00
3 Brendan Rodgers/25 5.00 12.00
4 Nick Senzel/22 10.00 25.00
5 Fernando Tatis Jr./25 10.00 25.00
6 Brandon Lowe/25 5.00 12.00
7 Michael Kopech/25 10.00 25.00
8 Kyle Schwarber/25 5.00 12.00
9 Eloy Jimenez/25 12.00 30.00
12 Kyle Tucker/25 8.00 20.00
13 Ken Griffey Jr./20 25.00 60.00
14 Vladimir Guerrero Jr./25 15.00 40.00
15 Pete Alonso/25 30.00 80.00

2019 Panini National Treasures Colossal Material Signatures

RANDOM INSERTS IN PACKS
PRINT RUNS B/WN 5-99 COPIES PER
NO PRICING ON QTY 15 OR LESS
EXCHANGE DEADLINE 3/25/21
4 George Springer/25 6.00 15.00
5 Xander Bogaerts/25 15.00 40.00
6 Stephen Strasburg/25 12.00 30.00
7 Michael Brantley/99 8.00 20.00
8 Jonathan Villar/75 3.00 8.00
9 Adalberto Mondesi/99 6.00 15.00
10 Miguel Cabrera/25 25.00 60.00
11 Hunter Dozier/99 3.00 8.00
12 Cal Ripken/25 50.00 120.00
13 Ronald Acuna Jr./25 50.00 120.00
14 Dick Williams/25 5.00 12.00
15 Ralph Kiner/25 15.00 40.00
16 Luis Aparicio/25 20.00 50.00
17 Ozzie Smith/25 15.00 40.00
18 Fernando Tatis Jr./99 50.00 120.00
19 Eloy Jimenez/25 EXCH 25.00 60.00
20 Jose Canseco/99 10.00 25.00

2019 Panini National Treasures Colossal Materials

RANDOM INSERTS IN PACKS
PRINT RUNS B/WN 5-49 COPIES PER
NO PRICING ON QTY 15 OR LESS
*HOLO GOLD/25: .6X TO 1.5X p/r 66-99
*HOLO GOLD/25: .5X TO 1.2X p/r 49
1 Mike Trout/49 20.00 50.00
2 Kris Bryant/25 6.00 15.00
3 Anthony Rizzo/49 5.00 12.00
4 Jose Altuve/25 4.00 10.00
5 Rafael Devers/99 4.00 10.00
6 Franmil Reyes/99 2.00 5.00
7 Matt Chapman/99 3.00 8.00
8 Josh Bell/99 2.50 6.00
9 Justin Verlander/99 3.00 8.00
10 Aaron Judge/99 8.00 20.00
11 Shohei Ohtani/99 5.00 12.00
12 Miguel Cabrera/49 4.00 10.00
13 Noah Syndergaard/49 3.00 8.00
14 Gerrit Cole/99 3.00 8.00
15 German Marquez/99 2.00 5.00
16 Patrick Corbin/66 2.50 6.00
17 Marcell Ozuna/99 3.00 8.00
18 Tommy Pham/99 2.00 5.00
19 Adrian Beltre/49 4.00 10.00
20 Albert Pujols/49 5.00 12.00
21 Brandon Woodruff/99 3.00 8.00
23 Clayton Kershaw/49 6.00 15.00
24 Clint Frazier/99 2.50 6.00
25 David Bote/99 2.50 6.00
26 David Ortiz/49 4.00 10.00
27 David Wright/99 2.50 6.00
28 Evan Longoria/99 2.50 6.00
29 Felix Hernandez/99 2.50 6.00
30 Frank Thomas/49 4.00 10.00
31 Freddie Freeman/49 5.00 12.00
32 Giancarlo Stanton/49 4.00 10.00
33 Ivan Rodriguez/49 3.00 8.00
34 Joey Votto/99 3.00 8.00
35 Jose Abreu/99 3.00 8.00
36 Larry Walker/99 2.50 6.00
37 Ozzie Albies/99 5.00 12.00
38 Victor Robles/99 4.00 10.00
39 Walker Buehler/99 4.00 10.00
40 Miguel Andujar/99 3.00 8.00

2019 Panini National Treasures Cut Signature Booklets

RANDOM INSERTS IN PACKS
PRINT RUNS B/WN 5-49 COPIES PER
NO PRICING ON QTY 15 OR LESS
EXCHANGE DEADLINE 3/25/21
*NAMES/20-25: .5X TO 1.2X p/r 49
*NAMES/20-25: .5X TO 1.2X p/r 25
*STAT./20-25: .5X TO 1.2X p/r 49
*STAT./20-25: .4X TO 1X p/r 25
*STAT.VAR./20-25: .5X TO 1.2X p/r 49
*STAT.VAR./20-25: .4X TO 1X p/r 25
4 Bobby Thomson/49 12.00 30.00
5 Gary Carter/49 12.00 30.00
6 Harmon Killebrew/49 25.00 60.00
11 Stan Musial/25 30.00 80.00
15 Ryne Sandberg/25 40.00 100.00
16 Vladimir Guerrero/25 15.00 40.00
18 Harmon Killebrew/25 30.00 80.00
19 Gary Carter/25 15.00 40.00
20 John Smoltz/25 30.00 80.00
22 Cal Ripken/25 EXCH 25.00 60.00
31 Aaron Judge/49 60.00 150.00
33 Roger Clemens/25 30.00 80.00

2019 Panini National Treasures Cut Signature Material Booklets

RANDOM INSERTS IN PACKS
PRINT RUNS B/WN 3-30 COPIES PER
NO PRICING ON QTY 15 OR LESS
EXCHANGE DEADLINE 3/25/21
*NAMES/20: .4X TO 1X BASIC
*STAT./20: .4X TO 1X BASIC
3 Adrian Beltre/30 20.00 50.00
9 Craig Biggio/20
15 Paul Molitor/20
25 Pete Rose/20 30.00 80.00
30 Gary Carter/25 20.00 50.00

2019 Panini National Treasures Debut Material Signature Booklets

RANDOM INSERTS IN PACKS
PRINT RUNS B/WN 25-99 COPIES PER
EXCHANGE DEADLINE 3/25/21
*HOLO GOLD: .6X TO 1.5X p/r 99
1 Pete Alonso/99 60.00 150.00
2 Jon Duplantier/99 3.00 8.00
3 Chris Paddack/25
4 Cole Tucker/99 10.00 25.00
6 Carter Kieboom/25 15.00 40.00
7 Cal Quantrill/25 5.00 12.00
8 Nathaniel Lowe/99 15.00 40.00
10 Vladimir Guerrero Jr./99 50.00 120.00
DMSFT Fernando Tatis Jr./49 60.00 150.00
12 Eloy Jimenez/49 15.00 40.00
13 Michael Kopech/25 15.00 40.00
14 Jonathan Loaisiga/99 4.00 10.00
15 Jake Bauers/25 8.00 20.00
16 Brendan Rodgers/25 EXCH 10.00 25.00

2019 Panini National Treasures Decades Signatures Booklets

RANDOM INSERTS IN PACKS
PRINT RUNS B/WN 5-25 COPIES PER
NO PRICING ON QTY 15 OR LESS
EXCHANGE DEADLINE 3/25/21
6 Andres Galarraga 100.00 250.00
Joey Votto
Jose Ramirez
Mark Grace
Roberto Alomar
Trevor Story/25

2019 Panini National Treasures Game Gear

RANDOM INSERTS IN PACKS
PRINT RUNS B/WN 25-99 COPIES PER
*HOLO GOLD/25: .6X TO 1.5X p/r 99
*HOLO GOLD/25: .5X TO 1.2X p/r 49
1 Alex Rodriguez/99 4.00 10.00
2 Eric Thames/99 2.00 5.00
3 Albert Pujols/49 5.00 12.00
4 Rafael Devers/99 4.00 10.00
5 Tony Gwynn/99 3.00 8.00
6 Mike Trout/49 15.00 40.00
7 CC Sabathia/99 2.50 6.00
8 Don Mattingly/49 8.00 20.00
9 Frank Robinson/99 8.00 20.00
10 George Brett/49 8.00 20.00
11 Leo Durocher/49 5.00 12.00
12 Nolan Ryan/99 12.00 30.00
13 Rod Carew/49 3.00 8.00
14 Ryne Sandberg/49 8.00 20.00
15 Steve Garvey/99 15.00 40.00
16 Lou Gehrig/25 50.00 120.00
17 Edwin Encarnacion/49 4.00 10.00
18 Carl Furillo/99 2.00 5.00
19 Mark Grace/99 2.50 6.00
20 Joe Jackson/49 40.00 100.00
21 Harmon Killebrew/49 6.00 15.00
22 Mike Piazza/49 4.00 10.00
23 Mickey Mantle/49 25.00 60.00
24 Roberto Alomar/49 3.00 8.00
25 Buster Posey/49 5.00 12.00

2019 Panini National Treasures Game Gear Holo Gold

*HOLO GOLD/25: .6X TO 1.5X p/r 99
*HOLO GOLD/25: .5X TO 1.2X p/r 49
RANDOM INSERTS IN PACKS
PRINT RUNS B/WN 10-25 COPIES PER
NO PRICING ON QTY 15 OR LESS
20 Joe Jackson/25 100.00 250.00

2019 Panini National Treasures Game Gear Duals

RANDOM INSERTS IN PACKS
PRINT RUNS B/WN 25-99 COPIES PER
*HOLO GOLD/25: .6X TO 1.5X p/r 99
*HOLO GOLD/25: .5X TO 1.2X p/r 49
1 Alex Rodriguez/99 4.00 10.00
2 Eric Thames/99 2.00 5.00
3 Albert Pujols/99 4.00 10.00
4 Rafael Devers/99 4.00 10.00
5 Tony Gwynn/49 4.00 10.00
6 Mike Trout/27 20.00 50.00
7 CC Sabathia/99 2.50 6.00
8 Don Mattingly/49 8.00 20.00
9 Frank Robinson/49 3.00 8.00
10 George Brett/25 10.00 25.00
11 Leo Durocher/49 5.00 12.00
12 Nolan Ryan/99 10.00 25.00
13 Rod Carew/49 3.00 8.00
14 Ryne Sandberg/99 6.00 15.00
15 Steve Garvey/99 15.00 40.00
17 Edwin Encarnacion/99 3.00 8.00
18 Carl Furillo/99 2.00 5.00
19 Mark Grace/99 2.50 6.00
20 Joe Jackson/25 100.00 250.00
21 Harmon Killebrew/25 8.00 20.00
22 Mike Piazza/99 3.00 8.00
23 Mickey Mantle/49 25.00 60.00
24 Roberto Alomar/99 2.50 6.00
25 Buster Posey/99 4.00 10.00

2019 Panini National Treasures Game Gear Eights

RANDOM INSERTS IN PACKS
PRINT RUNS B/WN 25-99 COPIES PER
*HOLO GOLD/25: .6X TO 1.5X p/r 99
*HOLO GOLD/25: .5X TO 1.2X p/r 49
1 Vladimir Guerrero Jr./99 10.00 25.00
2 Eloy Jimenez/99 8.00 20.00
3 Fernando Tatis Jr./99 8.00 80.00
4 Shohei Ohtani/99 5.00 12.00
5 Aaron Judge/99 8.00 20.00
6 Justus Sheffield/99 3.00 8.00
7 Pete Alonso/99 15.00 40.00
8 Michael Kopech/99 6.00 15.00
9 Wander Franco/99 8.00 20.00
10 Victor Victor Mesa/99 4.00 10.00
11 Brendan Rodgers/99 3.00 8.00
12 Jeff McNeil/99 5.00 12.00
13 Bo Bichette/99 6.00 15.00
15 Keston Hiura/99 6.00 15.00
16 Nick Senzel/99 6.00 15.00
17 Kyle Wright/99 3.00 8.00
18 Christin Stewart/99 2.50 6.00
19 Ryan O'Hearn/99 2.00 5.00
20 Dennis Santana/99 2.00 5.00
21 Jonathan Loaisiga/99 2.50 6.00
22 Touki Toussaint/99 2.50 6.00
23 Chance Adams/99 2.00 5.00
24 Bryse Wilson/99 2.50 6.00
25 Garrett Hampson/99 3.00 8.00
26 Enyel De Los Santos/99 2.00 5.00
27 Danny Jansen/99 2.00 5.00
29 Mike Trout/27 20.00 50.00
30 Dakota Hudson/99 2.50 6.00
31 Jonathan Davis/99 2.50 6.00
32 Adrian Beltre/49 4.00 10.00
35 Ronald Acuna Jr./99 15.00 40.00
36 Juan Soto/99 10.00 25.00
37 Jo Adell/99 8.00 20.00
38 Rafael Devers/99 4.00 10.00
44 Ivan Rodriguez/25 8.00 20.00
47 Estevan Florial/99 3.00 8.00
48 Forrest Whitley/99 3.00 8.00
49 Nathaniel Lowe/99 10.00 25.00
50 Corbin Burnes/99 5.00 12.00

2019 Panini National Treasures Game Gear Sevens

RANDOM INSERTS IN PACKS
PRINT RUNS B/WN 25-99 COPIES PER
*HOLO GOLD/25: .6X TO 1.5X p/r 99
*HOLO GOLD/25: .5X TO 1.2X p/r 49
1 Vladimir Guerrero Jr./99 10.00 25.00
2 Eloy Jimenez/99 8.00 20.00
3 Fernando Tatis Jr./99 8.00 20.00
4 Shohei Ohtani/99 5.00 12.00
5 Aaron Judge/99 8.00 20.00
6 Justus Sheffield/99 3.00 8.00
7 Pete Alonso/99 15.00 40.00
8 Michael Kopech/99 6.00 15.00
9 Wander Franco/99 8.00 20.00
10 Victor Victor Mesa/99 4.00 10.00
11 Brendan Rodgers/99 3.00 8.00
12 Jeff McNeil/99 5.00 12.00
13 Bo Bichette/99 6.00 15.00
15 Keston Hiura/99 6.00 15.00
16 Nick Senzel/99 6.00 15.00
17 Kyle Wright/99 3.00 8.00
18 Christin Stewart/99 2.50 6.00
19 Ryan O'Hearn/99 2.00 5.00
20 Dennis Santana/99 2.00 5.00
21 Jonathan Loaisiga/99 2.50 6.00
22 Touki Toussaint/99 2.50 6.00
23 Chance Adams/99 2.00 5.00
24 Bryse Wilson/99 2.50 6.00
25 Garrett Hampson/99 3.00 8.00
26 Enyel De Los Santos/99 2.00 5.00
27 Danny Jansen/99 2.00 5.00
29 Mike Trout/27 20.00 50.00
30 Dakota Hudson/99 2.50 6.00
31 Jonathan Davis/99 2.50 6.00
32 Adrian Beltre/49 4.00 10.00
35 Ronald Acuna Jr./99 15.00 40.00
36 Juan Soto/99 10.00 25.00
37 Jo Adell/99 8.00 20.00
38 Rafael Devers/99 4.00 10.00
42 Christian Yelich/49 5.00 12.00
44 Ivan Rodriguez/25 8.00 20.00
46 Ken Griffey Jr./25 15.00 40.00
47 Estevan Florial/99 3.00 8.00
48 Forrest Whitley/99 3.00 8.00
49 Nathaniel Lowe/99 10.00 25.00
50 Corbin Burnes/99 5.00 12.00

2019 Panini National Treasures Game Gear Signatures

RANDOM INSERTS IN PACKS
PRINT RUNS B/WN 49-99 COPIES PER
EXCHANGE DEADLINE 3/25/21
*HOLO GOLD: .6X TO 1.5X p/r 99
*HOLO GOLD: .5X TO 1.2X p/r 49
1 Vladimir Guerrero Jr./49 25.00 60.00
2 Eloy Jimenez/49 15.00 40.00
3 Fernando Tatis Jr./49 50.00 120.00
4 Pete Alonso/99 60.00 150.00
6 Kyle Tucker/49 10.00 25.00
8 Justus Sheffield/99 5.00 12.00
9 Christin Stewart/49 5.00 12.00
10 Ramon Laureano/99 8.00 20.00
11 Michael Kopech/99 10.00 25.00
13 Jonathan Loaisiga/99 4.00 10.00
14 Luis Ortiz/99 3.00 8.00
15 Kevin Newman/99 5.00 12.00
16 Jon Duplantier/99 3.00 8.00
18 Bryan Reynolds/99 8.00 20.00
19 Michael Chavis/99 12.00 30.00
21 Austin Riley/49 20.00 50.00
22 Keston Hiura/99 15.00 40.00
24 Nathaniel Lowe/99 15.00 40.00

2019 Panini National Treasures Game Gear Signatures Dual

RANDOM INSERTS IN PACKS
PRINT RUNS B/WN 25-99 COPIES PER
EXCHANGE DEADLINE 3/25/21
1 Vladimir Guerrero Jr./25 30.00 80.00
2 Eloy Jimenez/25 20.00 50.00
3 Fernando Tatis Jr./49 50.00 120.00
4 Pete Alonso/99 60.00 150.00
6 Kyle Tucker/25 12.00 30.00
8 Justus Sheffield/99 5.00 12.00
9 Christin Stewart/25 6.00 15.00
10 Ramon Laureano/99 8.00 20.00
11 Michael Kopech/99 10.00 25.00
13 Jonathan Loaisiga/99 4.00 10.00
14 Luis Ortiz/99 3.00 8.00
15 Kevin Newman/99 5.00 12.00
16 Jon Duplantier/99 3.00 8.00
17 Chris Paddack/99 6.00 15.00
18 Bryan Reynolds/99 8.00 20.00
19 Michael Chavis/99 12.00 30.00
21 Austin Riley/25 25.00 60.00
22 Keston Hiura/99 15.00 40.00
24 Nathaniel Lowe/99 15.00 40.00

2019 Panini National Treasures Game Gear Signatures Trio

RANDOM INSERTS IN PACKS
PRINT RUNS B/WN 25-99 COPIES PER
EXCHANGE DEADLINE 3/25/21
1 Vladimir Guerrero Jr./25 30.00 80.00
2 Eloy Jimenez/25 20.00 50.00
3 Fernando Tatis Jr./49 50.00 120.00
4 Pete Alonso/99 60.00 150.00
6 Kyle Tucker/25 12.00 30.00
8 Justus Sheffield/99 5.00 12.00
9 Christin Stewart/25 6.00 15.00
10 Ramon Laureano/99 8.00 20.00
11 Michael Kopech/99 10.00 25.00
13 Jonathan Loaisiga/99 4.00 10.00
14 Luis Ortiz/99 3.00 8.00
15 Kevin Newman/99 5.00 12.00
16 Jon Duplantier/99 3.00 8.00
17 Chris Paddack/99 6.00 15.00
18 Bryan Reynolds/99 8.00 20.00
19 Michael Chavis/99 12.00 30.00
21 Austin Riley/25 25.00 60.00
22 Keston Hiura/99 15.00 40.00
24 Nathaniel Lowe/99 15.00 40.00

2019 Panini National Treasures Game Gear Sixes

RANDOM INSERTS IN PACKS
PRINT RUNS B/WN 10-99 COPIES PER
NO PRICING ON QTY 15 OR LESS
*HOLO GOLD/25: .6X TO 1.5X p/r 99
*HOLO GOLD/25: .5X TO 1.2X p/r 49
1 Vladimir Guerrero Jr./99 8.00 20.00
2 Eloy Jimenez/99 8.00 20.00
3 Fernando Tatis Jr./99 8.00 20.00
4 Shohei Ohtani/99 5.00 12.00
5 Aaron Judge/99 8.00 20.00
6 Justus Sheffield/99 5.00 12.00
7 Pete Alonso/99 15.00 40.00
8 Michael Kopech/99 6.00 15.00
9 Wander Franco/99 8.00 20.00
10 Victor Victor Mesa/99 4.00 10.00
11 Brendan Rodgers/99 3.00 8.00
12 Jeff McNeil/99 5.00 12.00
13 Bo Bichette/99 12.00 30.00
15 Keston Hiura/99 6.00 15.00
16 Nick Senzel/99 6.00 15.00
17 Kyle Wright/99 3.00 8.00
18 Christin Stewart/99 2.50 6.00
19 Ryan O'Hearn/99 2.00 5.00
20 Dennis Santana/99 2.00 5.00
21 Jonathan Loaisiga/99 2.50 6.00
22 Touki Toussaint/99 6.00 15.00
23 Chance Adams/99 2.00 5.00
24 Bryse Wilson/99 2.50 6.00
25 Garrett Hampson/99 3.00 8.00
26 Enyel De Los Santos/99 2.00 5.00
27 Danny Jansen/99 2.00 5.00
29 Mike Trout/27 20.00 50.00
30 Dakota Hudson/99 2.50 6.00
31 Jonathan Davis/99 2.50 6.00
32 Adrian Beltre/49 4.00 10.00
33 Carlos Correa/49 4.00 10.00
35 Ronald Acuna Jr./99 15.00 40.00
36 Juan Soto/99 10.00 25.00
37 Jo Adell/99 8.00 20.00
38 Rafael Devers/99 4.00 10.00
42 Christian Yelich/99 4.00 10.00
44 Ivan Rodriguez/25 8.00 20.00
46 Ken Griffey Jr./25 15.00 40.00
47 Estevan Florial/99 3.00 8.00
48 Forrest Whitley/99 3.00 8.00
49 Nathaniel Lowe/99 10.00 25.00
50 Corbin Burnes/99 5.00 12.00

2019 Panini National Treasures Game Gear Trios

RANDOM INSERTS IN PACKS
PRINT RUNS B/WN 10-99 COPIES PER
NO PRICING ON QTY 15 OR LESS
*HOLO GOLD/25: .6X TO 1.5X p/r 99
*HOLO GOLD/25: .5X TO 1.2X p/r 49
1 Alex Rodriguez/99 4.00 10.00
2 Eric Thames/99 2.00 5.00
3 Albert Pujols/49 5.00 12.00
4 Rafael Devers/99 4.00 10.00
5 Tony Gwynn/49 4.00 10.00
6 Mike Trout/27 20.00 50.00
7 CC Sabathia/99 2.50 6.00
8 Don Mattingly/49 8.00 20.00
9 Frank Robinson/49 3.00 8.00
10 George Brett/25 10.00 25.00
11 Leo Durocher/49 5.00 12.00
12 Nolan Ryan/99 10.00 25.00
13 Rod Carew/25 4.00 10.00
14 Ryne Sandberg/99 6.00 15.00

15 Steve Garvey/99 15.00 40.00
17 Edwin Encarnacion/99 3.00 8.00
18 Carl Furillo/49 2.50 6.00
19 Mark Grace/99 2.50 6.00
22 Mike Piazza/49 4.00 10.00
23 Mickey Mantle/49 25.00 60.00
24 Roberto Alomar/99 2.50 6.00
25 Buster Posey/99 4.00 10.00

2019 Panini National Treasures Hall of Fame Materials

RANDOM INSERTS IN PACKS
PRINT RUNS B/WN 25-99 COPIES PER
*PRIME/25: .6X TO 1.5X p/r 99
*PRIME/25: .5X TO 1.2X p/r 49
1 Eddie Murray/99 2.50 6.00
2 Catfish Hunter/49 3.00 8.00
3 Ivan Rodriguez/99 2.50 6.00
4 Mike Piazza/99 3.00 8.00
5 Greg Maddux/99 4.00 10.00
6 Cal Ripken/99 10.00 25.00
7 Pedro Martinez/99 2.50 6.00
8 Fergie Jenkins/99 2.50 6.00
9 Joe Morgan/99 2.50 6.00
10 Wade Boggs/99 2.50 6.00
11 Goose Gossage/99 2.50 6.00
12 Rollie Fingers/99 2.50 6.00
13 Dave Winfield/99 2.50 6.00
14 Tony Gwynn/99 5.00 12.00
15 Barry Larkin/99 2.50 6.00
16 Tom Seaver/49 3.00 8.00
17 Andre Dawson/99 2.50 6.00
18 Johnny Bench/99 6.00 15.00
19 Craig Biggio/99 2.50 6.00
20 Bert Blyleven/99 2.50 6.00
21 Frank Robinson/99 2.50 6.00
22 Duke Snider/25 4.00 10.00
23 Rickey Henderson/49 6.00 15.00
24 George Brett/49 8.00 20.00
25 Robin Yount/99 3.00 8.00
26 Harmon Killebrew/25 5.00 12.00
27 Randy Johnson/99 3.00 8.00
28 Brooks Robinson/99 2.50 6.00
29 Orlando Cepeda/99 2.50 6.00
30 Mule Suttles/99 20.00 50.00
31 Ryne Sandberg/99 6.00 15.00
32 Ozzie Smith/99 4.00 10.00
33 Ken Griffey Jr./99 6.00 15.00
34 Roberto Alomar/99 2.50 6.00
35 John Smoltz/99 3.00 8.00
36 Frank Thomas/49 6.00 15.00
37 Rod Carew/99 6.00 15.00
38 Jim Palmer/25 4.00 10.00
39 Paul Molitor/99 5.00 12.00
40 Kirby Puckett/49 20.00 50.00
41 Lou Brock/49 8.00 20.00
42 Gary Carter/99 2.50 6.00
43 Willie McCovey/99 2.50 6.00
44 Nolan Ryan/99 10.00 25.00
45 Al Kaline/49 4.00 10.00
46 Reggie Jackson/99 2.50 6.00
47 Alan Trammell/99 2.50 6.00
48 Juan Marichal/20 4.00 10.00
49 Vladimir Guerrero/99 2.50 6.00
50 Tom Glavine/99 2.50 6.00

2019 Panini National Treasures Hall of Fame Signatures

RANDOM INSERTS IN PACKS
PRINT RUNS B/WN 10-49 COPIES PER
NO PRICING ON QTY 18 OR LESS
EXCHANGE DEADLINE 3/25/21
12 Monte Irvin/49 5.00 12.00

2019 Panini National Treasures Legendary Jumbo Materials Booklets

RANDOM INSERTS IN PACKS
PRINT RUNS B/WN 10-49 COPIES PER
NO PRICING ON QTY 15 OR LESS
*HOLO GOLD/25: .5X TO 1.2X p/r 49
1 Bill Mazeroski/49 6.00 15.00
2 Mike Trout/49 25.00 60.00
3 Ichiro Suzuki/49 10.00 25.00
6 Leo Durocher/25 3.00 8.00
7 Joe Cronin/25 3.00 8.00
8 Tom Yawkey/49 12.00 30.00
9 Paul Molitor/49 4.00 10.00
10 Eddie Stanky/49 2.50 6.00
11 Tommy Lasorda/49 3.00 8.00
12 Tommy Henrich/49 8.00 20.00
15 Ron Santo/21 15.00 40.00

2019 Panini National Treasures Legendary Jumbo Materials Booklets Holo Gold

*HOLO GOLD/25: .5X TO 1.2X p/r 49
RANDOM INSERTS IN PACKS
PRINT RUNS B/WN 7-25 COPIES PER
NO PRICING ON QTY 15 OR LESS
1 Bill Mazeroski/25 15.00 40.00
3 Ichiro Suzuki/25 15.00 40.00

2019 Panini National Treasures Legendary Silhouette Duals Booklets

RANDOM INSERTS IN PACKS
PRINT RUNS B/WN 5-49 COPIES PER
NO PRICING ON QTY 15 OR LESS
*HOLO GOLD/25: .5X TO 1.2X p/r 49
1 A.Pujols/I.Suzuki 20.00 50.00
3 H.Pennock/J.Cronin 12.00 30.00
4 B.Lemon/T.Speaker
5 M.Mantle/R.Maris 125.00 400.00
6 H.Killebrew/K.Puckett 30.00 80.00
7 E.Sawyer/J.McCarthy 25.00 60.00
8 A.Kaline/H.Kuenn 20.00 50.00

2019 Panini National Treasures Legends Materials Booklets

RANDOM INSERTS IN PACKS
PRINT RUNS B/WN 10-49 COPIES PER
NO PRICING ON QTY 15 OR LESS
*HOLO GOLD/25: .5X TO 1.2X p/r 49
2 Babe Ruth/25 75.00 200.00
4 Red Schoendienst/49 3.00 8.00
5 Miller Huggins/49 8.00 20.00
6 Ty Cobb/25 50.00 120.00
7 Tom Yawkey/49 12.00 30.00
8 Heinie Groh/49 2.50 6.00
9 Tris Speaker/49 15.00 40.00
10 Max Carey/49 5.00 12.00
11 Joe Dugan/49 6.00 15.00
12 Mule Suttles/49 25.00 60.00
13 Doc Cramer/49 8.00 20.00
14 Dom DiMaggio/49 20.00 50.00
15 Carl Furillo/49 2.50 6.00
16 Richie Ashburn/49 20.00 50.00

2019 Panini National Treasures Legends Materials Booklets Duals Holo Gold

*HOLO GOLD/25: .5X TO 1.2X p/r 49
RANDOM INSERTS IN PACKS
PRINT RUNS B/WN 10-25 COPIES PER
NO PRICING ON QTY 15 OR LESS
16 Richie Ashburn/25 75.00 200.00

2019 Panini National Treasures Player's Weekend Signatures

RANDOM INSERTS IN PACKS
STATED PRINT RUN 99 SER.#'d SETS
EXCHANGE DEADLINE 3/25/21
1 Dennis Santana 3.00 8.00
2 Ryan O'Hearn 3.00 8.00
3 Corbin Burnes 10.00 25.00
4 Jake Cave 4.00 10.00
5 Dakota Hudson 4.00 10.00
6 Brad Keller 3.00 8.00
7 Jeff McNeil 8.00 20.00
8 David Fletcher 10.00 25.00
9 Steven Duggar 4.00 10.00

2019 Panini National Treasures Retro Materials

RANDOM INSERTS IN PACKS
PRINT RUNS B/WN 5-99 COPIES PER
NO PRICING ON QTY 15 OR LESS
*HOLO GOLD/25: .6X TO 1.5X p/r 99
*HOLO GOLD/25: .5X TO 1.2X p/r 49
1 Ron Santo/49 10.00 25.00
2 Ken Griffey Jr./99 20.00 50.00
3 Cal Ripken/49 12.00 30.00
4 Kirby Puckett/49 20.00 50.00
5 Frank Robinson/49 3.00 8.00
6 Jose Canseco/49 3.00 8.00
7 Ichiro Suzuki/99 4.00 10.00
8 Orlando Cepeda/25 4.00 10.00
11 Gary Carter/49 3.00 8.00
12 Mariano Rivera/49 8.00 20.00
13 Frank Thomas/99 3.00 8.00
14 Goose Gossage/99 2.50 6.00
15 Ivan Rodriguez/99 2.50 6.00
16 Mark McGwire/49 6.00 15.00
17 Rollie Fingers/49 3.00 8.00
19 Eddie Murray/49 3.00 8.00
21 Red Schoendienst/25 10.00 25.00
22 Steve Garvey/99 8.00 20.00
23 Larry Walker/99 2.50 6.00
24 John Smoltz/49 4.00 10.00
25 Tommy Henrich/25 10.00 25.00
26 Eddie Sawyer/49 2.50 6.00
27 Casey Stengel/25 6.00 15.00
28 Roberto Alomar/49 3.00 8.00
29 Ted Williams/25 50.00

2019 Panini National Treasures Retro Signatures

RANDOM INSERTS IN PACKS
PRINT RUNS B/WN 10-99 COPIES PER
NO PRICING ON QTY 15 OR LESS
EXCHANGE DEADLINE 3/25/21
1 Ken Griffey Jr./49 75.00 200.00
2 Frank Thomas/49 25.00 60.00
3 Juan Soto/99 30.00 80.00
4 Max Muncy/49 EXCH 5.00 12.00
5 Walker Buehler/49 25.00 60.00
6 Jose Canseco/49 8.00 20.00
7 Vladimir Guerrero/25 15.00 40.00
RSRA Ronald Acuna Jr./99 50.00 120.00
9 Gleyber Torres/99 30.00 80.00
11 Willie McGee/25 10.00 25.00
12 Roger Clemens/25 30.00 80.00
13 Whit Merrifield/49 6.00 15.00
14 Joey Votto/25 EXCH 20.00 50.00
15 Roger Clemens/25 30.00 80.00
16 Craig Biggio/25 EXCH 10.00 25.00
17 Alex Rodriguez/25 30.00 80.00
18 Chris Sale/49 10.00 25.00
19 Ichiro Suzuki/25
20 Ivan Rodriguez/25 15.00 40.00
21 Nolan Arenado/49 30.00 80.00
22 Lou Whitaker/49 12.00 30.00
23 Bob Gibson/25 20.00 50.00
26 Ken Griffey Jr./25 100.00 250.00
28 Cal Ripken/25 30.00 80.00
30 Nolan Ryan/25 50.00 120.00
31 Nolan Ryan/25 50.00 120.00
32 Nolan Ryan/25 50.00 120.00
33 Nolan Ryan/25 50.00 120.00
34 Rickey Henderson/25 30.00 80.00
35 Alan Trammell/49 25.00 60.00
36 Shohei Ohtani/99 50.00 120.00
37 Aaron Judge/99 50.00 120.00
38 David Ross/25 25.00 60.00
39 Frank Robinson/25 15.00 40.00
40 Frank Robinson/25 15.00 40.00

2019 Panini National Treasures Rookie Signature Jumbo Material Booklets

RANDOM INSERTS IN PACKS
STATED PRINT RUN 99 SER.#'d SETS
EXCHANGE DEADLINE 3/25/21
1 Michael Kopech 10.00 25.00
2 Ramon Laureano 15.00 40.00
3 Ryan O'Hearn 3.00 8.00
4 Eloy Jimenez 20.00 50.00
5 Corbin Burnes 10.00 25.00
6 Kyle Wright 5.00 12.00
7 Nick Senzel EXCH 20.00 50.00
8 Kyle Tucker 8.00 20.00
9 Jeff McNeil 15.00 20.00
10 Vladimir Guerrero Jr. 50.00 120.00
11 Fernando Tatis Jr. 50.00 120.00
12 Christin Stewart 4.00 10.00
13 Cedric Mullins 10.00 25.00
14 Justus Sheffield 5.00 12.00
16 Jake Bauers 5.00 12.00

2019 Panini National Treasures Rookie Signature Material Names

RANDOM INSERTS IN PACKS
STATED PRINT RUN 99 SER.#'d SETS
EXCHANGE DEADLINE 3/25/21
*GOLD: .5X TO 1.2X BASIC
*HOLO GOLD: .6X TO 1.5X BASIC
1 Kyle Tucker 10.00 25.00
2 Patrick Wisdom 3.00 8.00
3 Jeff McNeil 10.00 25.00
4 Vladimir Guerrero Jr. 50.00 120.00
5 Cionel Perez 3.00 8.00
6 Kolby Allard 5.00 12.00
7 Stephen Gonsalves 3.00 8.00
8 Brandon Lowe 8.00 20.00
9 Eloy Jimenez 15.00 40.00
10 Fernando Tatis Jr. 60.00 150.00
11 Sean Reid-Foley 3.00 8.00
12 Jonathan Davis 4.00 10.00
13 Ryan Borucki 3.00 8.00
14 Christin Stewart 4.00 10.00
15 Cedric Mullins 10.00 25.00
16 Justus Sheffield 5.00 12.00
17 Caleb Ferguson 4.00 10.00
18 Jacob Nix 4.00 10.00
19 Daniel Ponce de Leon 5.00 12.00
20 Josh James 5.00 12.00
21 David Fletcher 10.00 25.00
22 Steven Duggar 4.00 10.00
23 Rowdy Tellez 5.00 12.00
24 Luis Urias 5.00 12.00
25 Jake Bauers 5.00 12.00

2019 Panini National Treasures Rookie Signature Material Names Holo Gold

*HOLO GOLD: .6X TO 1.5X BASIC
RANDOM INSERTS IN PACKS
STATED PRINT RUN 25 SER.#'d SETS
EXCHANGE DEADLINE 3/25/21
1 Kyle Tucker 25.00 60.00
3 Jeff McNeil 30.00 80.00

2019 Panini National Treasures Rookie Signatures

RANDOM INSERTS IN PACKS
STATED PRINT RUN 99 SER.#'d SETS
EXCHANGE DEADLINE 3/25/21
1 Touki Toussaint 4.00 10.00
2 Michael Kopech 10.00 25.00
3 Ramon Laureano 8.00 20.00
4 Ryan O'Hearn 3.00 8.00
5 Eloy Jimenez 15.00 40.00
6 Corbin Burnes 10.00 25.00
7 Kyle Wright 5.00 12.00
8 Dakota Hudson 4.00 10.00
9 Danny Jansen 3.00 8.00
11 Kyle Tucker 8.00 20.00
12 Jeff McNeil 8.00 20.00
13 Vladimir Guerrero Jr. 50.00 120.00
14 Fernando Tatis Jr. 40.00 100.00
15 Christin Stewart 4.00 10.00
16 Cedric Mullins 10.00 25.00
17 Justus Sheffield 5.00 12.00
18 David Fletcher 6.00 15.00
19 Luis Urias EXCH 8.00 20.00
20 Jake Bauers EXCH 5.00 12.00

2019 Panini National Treasures Rookie Silhouette Signatures

RANDOM INSERTS IN PACKS
PRINT RUNS B/WN 10-25 COPIES PER
NO PRICING ON QTY 15 OR LESS
EXCHANGE DEADLINE 3/25/21
1 Yusei Kikuchi/25 EXCH 8.00 20.00
2 Ramon Laureano/25 20.00 50.00
3 Ryan O'Hearn/25 5.00 12.00
4 Eloy Jimenez/25 20.00 50.00
5 Corbin Burnes/25 15.00 40.00
6 Kyle Wright/25 8.00 20.00
7 Dakota Hudson/25 6.00 15.00
9 Brad Keller/25 5.00 12.00
10 Kyle Tucker/25 15.00 40.00
12 Vladimir Guerrero Jr./25 60.00 150.00
13 Brandon Lowe/25 12.00 30.00
14 Fernando Tatis Jr./25 100.00 250.00
16 Cedric Mullins/25 15.00 40.00
17 Justus Sheffield/25 8.00 20.00
18 Luis Urias/25 8.00 20.00
19 Jake Bauers/25 8.00 20.00
20 Jon Duplantier/25 5.00 12.00
21 Chris Paddack/25 12.00 30.00
22 Pete Alonso/25 60.00 150.00
23 Michael Chavis/25 20.00 50.00
24 Cole Tucker/25 8.00 20.00
25 Bryan Reynolds/25 15.00 40.00

2019 Panini National Treasures Rookie Triple Material Ink

RANDOM INSERTS IN PACKS
STATED PRINT RUN 99 SER.#'d SETS
EXCHANGE DEADLINE 3/25/21
*GOLD: .5X TO 1.2X BASIC
*HOLO GOLD: .6X TO 1.5X BASIC
1 Bryse Wilson 4.00 10.00
2 Touki Toussaint 4.00 10.00
3 Michael Kopech 10.00 25.00
4 Ramon Laureano 10.00 25.00
5 Garrett Hampson 5.00 12.00
6 Dennis Santana 3.00 8.00
7 Ryan O'Hearn 3.00 8.00
8 Jonathan Loaisiga 4.00 10.00
9 Eloy Jimenez 15.00 40.00
10 Reese McGuire 5.00 12.00
11 Corbin Burnes 10.00 25.00
12 Jake Cave 10.00 25.00
13 Luis Ortiz 3.00 8.00
14 Kyle Wright 5.00 12.00
15 Chris Shaw 3.00 8.00
16 Kevin Kramer 4.00 10.00
17 Framber Valdez 3.00 8.00
18 Dakota Hudson 4.00 10.00
19 Kevin Newman 5.00 12.00
20 Danny Jansen 3.00 8.00
21 Vladimir Guerrero Jr. 50.00 120.00
22 Chance Adams 3.00 8.00
23 Enyel De Los Santos 3.00 8.00
24 Taylor Ward 3.00 8.00

2019 Panini National Treasures Shadowbox Material Signatures

RANDOM INSERTS IN PACKS
PRINT RUNS B/WN 5-49 COPIES PER
NO PRICING ON QTY 15 OR LESS
EXCHANGE DEADLINE 3/25/21
2 Pete Alonso/25 75.00 200.00
3 Chris Paddack/25 25.00 60.00
4 Yusei Kikuchi/25 EXCH 8.00 20.00
5 Jon Duplantier/25 5.00 12.00
6 Mitch Moreland/25 5.00 12.00
7 Andres Galarraga/25 15.00 40.00
8 Kerry Wood/25 5.00 12.00
9 Scooter Gennett/35 5.00 12.00
10 Miguel Cabrera/25 30.00 80.00
11 Vladimir Guerrero/25 15.00 40.00
12 Rhys Hoskins/25
14 Ozzie Albies/25 EXCH
15 Rafael Devers/25 EXCH 20.00 50.00
16 Ozzie Smith/25 15.00 40.00
17 Keith Hernandez/25 10.00 25.00
18 Larry Walker/25 15.00 40.00
19 Jason Giambi/25 5.00 12.00
20 Max Muncy/25
22 Whit Merrifield/35 8.00 20.00
23 Nolan Arenado/25
24 Omar Vizquel/25 EXCH 6.00 15.00
25 Patrick Corbin/25 8.00 20.00
26 Yandy Diaz/35 5.00 12.00
27 David Bote/25 6.00 15.00
28 Jose Berrios/25 6.00 15.00
29 Alex Verdugo/25 6.00 15.00
30 Juan Soto/25 60.00 150.00
33 Walker Buehler/25 20.00 50.00
34 Corey Seager/25 EXCH 12.00 30.00
36 Luis Severino/25 15.00 40.00
38 Shohei Ohtani/20 60.00 150.00
41 Ronald Acuna Jr./25 75.00 200.00
43 Charlie Blackmon/25 8.00 20.00
44 Mitch Haniger/49 6.00 15.00
45 Trey Mancini/25 6.00 15.00
46 Adrian Beltre/25
47 Joey Votto/25 EXCH
49 Blake Snell/25 10.00 25.00

2019 Panini National Treasures Signature Jumbo Material Booklets

RANDOM INSERTS IN PACKS
PRINT RUNS B/WN 15-99 COPIES PER
NO PRICING ON QTY 15 OR LESS
EXCHANGE DEADLINE 3/25/21
1 Shohei Ohtani/25 75.00 200.00
2 Aaron Judge/49 100.00 250.00
4 Forrest Whitley/99 8.00 20.00
5 Kyle Lewis/99 50.00 120.00
8 Wander Franco/99 75.00 200.00
10 Nolan Ryan/25 60.00 150.00

2019 Panini National Treasures Signatures

RANDOM INSERTS IN PACKS
PRINT RUNS B/WN 10-99 COPIES PER
NO PRICING ON QTY 15 OR LESS
EXCHANGE DEADLINE 3/25/21
2 Charlie Blackmon/49 6.00 15.00
5 Max Muncy/99 12.00 30.00
6 Odubel Herrera/99 4.00 10.00
9 Shane Bieber/34 40.00 100.00
10 Trevor Story/99 5.00 12.00
11 Walker Buehler/99 40.00 100.00
13 Alex Verdugo/99 4.00 10.00
14 Chris Sale/25 8.00 20.00
18 Dansby Swanson/49 6.00 15.00
20 J.T. Realmuto/99 10.00 25.00
22 Orlando Hernandez/25 5.00 12.00
24 Ozzie Guillen/99 3.00 8.00
25 Goose Gossage/99 6.00 15.00
26 Jim Rice/99 4.00 10.00
27 Kerry Wood/99 3.00 8.00
28 Omar Vizquel/99 4.00 10.00
29 Ted Simmons/25 10.00 25.00
32 Andres Galarraga/99 4.00 10.00
36 Mitch Haniger/99 4.00 10.00

2019 Panini National Treasures Six Pack Material Signatures Booklets

RANDOM INSERTS IN PACKS
STATED PRINT RUN 99 SER.#'d SETS
EXCHANGE DEADLINE 3/25/21
1 Michael Kopech 10.00 25.00
2 Ryan O'Hearn 3.00 8.00
3 Eloy Jimenez 20.00 50.00
5 Kyle Tucker 12.00 30.00
6 Jeff McNeil 12.00 30.00
7 Vladimir Guerrero Jr. 50.00 120.00
8 Fernando Tatis Jr. 75.00 200.00
9 Justus Sheffield 5.00 12.00

2019 Panini National Treasures Social Signatures

RANDOM INSERTS IN PACKS
STATED PRINT RUN 99 SER.#'d SETS
EXCHANGE DEADLINE 3/25/21
1 Vladimir Guerrero Jr. 20.00 50.00
2 Eloy Jimenez 15.00 40.00
3 Kyle Tucker 10.00 25.00
4 Michael Kopech 10.00 25.00
5 Fernando Tatis Jr. 100.00 250.00
6 Bo Bichette 30.00 80.00
8 Justus Sheffield 5.00 12.00
10 Jonathan Loaisiga 5.00 12.00
11 Kyle Wright 5.00 12.00
12 Garrett Hampson 5.00 12.00
13 Christin Stewart 4.00 10.00
14 Kevin Newman 5.00 12.00
15 Kevin Kramer 4.00 10.00
16 Dakota Hudson 4.00 10.00
17 Keston Hiura 12.00 30.00
18 Jo Adell 40.00 100.00
19 Cavan Biggio 20.00 50.00
20 Leody Taveras 5.00 12.00

2019 Panini National Treasures Treasured Material Signatures

RANDOM INSERTS IN PACKS
PRINT RUNS B/WN 5-49 COPIES PER
NO PRICING ON QTY 15 OR LESS
EXCHANGE DEADLINE 3/25/21
*GOLD: .5X TO 1.2X p/r 49
1 Corey Kluber/25 6.00 15.00
2 Kerry Wood/25 5.00 12.00
3 Ronald Acuna Jr./25 60.00 150.00
4 Whit Merrifield/35 6.00 15.00
5 Yoshihisa Hirano/25
6 J.T. Realmuto/25 10.00 25.00
7 Rhys Hoskins/25 15.00 40.00
8 Jordan Hicks/49 EXCH 10.00 25.00
9 Keith Hernandez/25 10.00 25.00
10 Nolan Arenado/25 30.00 80.00
15 Andres Galarraga/25 6.00 15.00
16 Omar Vizquel/25 EXCH 6.00 15.00
18 Xander Bogaerts/25
21 Francisco Lindor/25 EXCH
22 Darryl Strawberry/25 5.00 12.00
23 Jose Abreu/25 8.00 20.00
24 Carlton Fisk/25
27 David Wright/49 12.00 30.00
28 Max Muncy/25 6.00 15.00
30 Charlie Blackmon/25 8.00 20.00
31 Reggie Jackson/49 12.00 30.00
33 Larry Walker/25
34 Mitch Moreland/25 5.00 12.00
35 Vladimir Guerrero/25
36 Yadier Molina/49 50.00 120.00
38 Mitch Haniger/25 6.00 15.00
39 David Bote/25 6.00 15.00
40 Jose Ramirez/25 6.00 15.00
43 Joe Carter/25 EXCH 5.00 12.00
44 Gleyber Torres/25 EXCH 30.00 80.00
45 Dennis Eckersley/25 12.00 30.00
46 Rod Carew/25 12.00 30.00
49 Jose Berrios/25 6.00 15.00
50 Nomar Mazara/25 5.00 12.00
51 Jason Giambi/20 5.00 12.00
53 John Smoltz/25 20.00 50.00
55 Chris Sale/25
56 Scooter Gennett/49 5.00 12.00
57 Tom Glavine/25 20.00 50.00
59 Craig Biggio/20 EXCH 15.00 40.00
60 Fergie Jenkins/25 6.00 15.00
61 Miguel Cabrera/20 25.00 60.00
63 Alex Wood/49 4.00 10.00
64 Charles Johnson/25 5.00 12.00
67 Trey Mancini/25 10.00 25.00
68 Ozzie Albies/25 EXCH 15.00 40.00
70 Yandy Diaz/49 5.00 12.00
71 Adrian Beltre/25
72 Mike Soroka/49 15.00 40.00
73 Rafael Devers/25 EXCH 20.00 50.00
75 Walker Buehler/25 20.00 50.00
76 Joey Votto/25 EXCH 25.00 60.00
77 Dale Murphy/20

2019 Panini National Treasures Treasured Signatures

RANDOM INSERTS IN PACKS
PRINT RUNS B/WN 25-49 COPIES PER
EXCHANGE DEADLINE 3/25/21
1 Rod Carew/25 12.00 30.00
2 Reggie Jackson/25 EXCH 12.00 30.00
3 Rickey Henderson/25 20.00 50.00
4 Ken Griffey Jr./49 100.00 250.00
5 Pedro Martinez/25 30.00 80.00
7 Clayton Kershaw/49 30.00 80.00
8 Cal Ripken/25 40.00 100.00
9 George Brett/25 40.00 100.00
10 Alan Trammell/49 5.00 12.00

2019 Panini National Treasures Treasured Threads Autographs

RANDOM INSERTS IN PACKS
PRINT RUNS B/WN 10-20 COPIES PER
NO PRICING ON QTY 15 OR LESS
EXCHANGE DEADLINE 3/25/21
6 Rickey Henderson/20 40.00 100.00
9 Jose Ramirez/20
10 Roger Clemens/20 40.00 100.00

2019 Panini National Treasures Triple Legend Duos Material Booklets

RANDOM INSERTS IN PACKS
PRINT RUNS B/WN 10-25 COPIES PER
NO PRICING ON QTY 15 OR LESS
2 Vaughan/Lombardi/O'Doul/25 25.00 60.00
3 Heilmann/Rice/Kamm/25 20.00 50.00
4 Frisch/Brecheen/Groh/25 15.00 40.00
6 Pujols/Cabrera/Trout/25 40.00 100.00
7 Drysdale/Pennock/Ryan/25
8 Stanky/Hodges/Campanella/25
9 Suttles/Henrich/Keeler/25 20.00 50.00
10 Robinson/Gehrig/Clemente/25

2019 Panini National Treasures Triple Legend Trios Material Booklets

RANDOM INSERTS IN PACKS
STATED PRINT RUN 25 SER.#'d SETS
1 Griffey Jr./Puckett/Mantle
2 Brett/Boyer/Santo 40.00 100.00
3 Alomar/Carew/Hornsby 25.00 60.00
4 Pujols/Mize/Gehrig
5 Ryan/Martinez/Johnson 30.00 80.00
6 Ripken/Cronin/Smith 15.00 40.00
7 Fisk/Rodriguez/Bench 30.00 80.00
8 Keller/Kiner/Musial 30.00 80.00
9 Waner/Jackson/Gwynn 60.00 150.00
10 Beltre/Rodriguez/Suzuki 15.00 40.00
11 Jackson/Winfield/Sanders 40.00 100.00

2019 Panini National Treasures Twelve Signature Booklets

RANDOM INSERTS IN PACKS
STATED PRINT RUN 25 SER.#'d SETS
EXCHANGE DEADLINE 3/25/21
1 AR/BR/CQ/CP/EJ/FTJ/GC
MC/MK/PA/VGJ/YK 500.00 1200.00
2 BR/CK/CB/EJ/FTJ/JS/KH/KT
MK/NS/TE/VGJ EXCH 600.00 1500.00

2020 Panini National Treasures

PRINT RUNS B/WN 5-99 COPIES PER
NO PRICING ON QTY 15 OR LESS
EXCHANGE DEADLINE 5/4/22
2 Aaron Judge JSY/99 12.00 30.00
3 Giancarlo Stanton JSY/99 3.00 8.00
4 Gleyber Torres JSY/99 6.00 15.00
6 Xander Bogaerts JSY/99 3.00 8.00
7 Rafael Devers JSY/99 4.00 10.00
8 Wade Boggs JSY/26 8.00 20.00
9 Chris Sale JSY/99 3.00 8.00
10 Rowdy Tellez JSY/99 2.50 6.00
11 Vladimir Guerrero Jr. JSY/99 5.00 12.00
12 Cavan Biggio JSY/99 12.00 30.00
13 Austin Meadows JSY/99 3.00 8.00
14 Willy Adames JSY/99 2.00 5.00
15 Cal Ripken JSY/49 10.00 25.00
16 Austin Hays JSY/99 3.00 8.00
17 Eddie Murray JSY/49 3.00 8.00
18 Kirby Puckett JSY/34 12.00 30.00
19 Josh Donaldson JSY/99 2.50 6.00
20 Miguel Sano JSY/99 2.50 6.00
21 Nelson Cruz JSY/99 3.00 8.00
22 Jose Ramirez JSY/99 2.50 6.00
23 Frank Thomas JSY/99 6.00 15.00
24 Tim Anderson JSY/99 3.00 8.00
25 Yoan Moncada JSY/99 3.00 8.00
26 Eloy Jimenez JSY/99 6.00 15.00
27 Harold Baines JSY/99 2.50 6.00
28 George Brett JSY/99 8.00 20.00
29 Whit Merrifield JSY/99 3.00 8.00
30 Alex Gordon JSY/99 2.50 6.00
31 Jorge Soler JSY/99 3.00 8.00
32 Miguel Cabrera JSY/99 3.00 8.00
33 Alan Trammell JSY/99 4.00 10.00
34 Al Kaline JSY/49 8.00 20.00
35 Jose Altuve JSY/49 3.00 8.00
36 George Springer JSY/99 2.50 6.00
37 Alex Bregman JSY/99 3.00 8.00
38 Carlos Correa JSY/99 3.00 8.00
39 Nolan Ryan JSY/34 15.00 40.00
40 Mark McGwire JSY/70 5.00 12.00
41 Jose Canseco JSY/33 6.00 15.00
42 Matt Chapman JSY/99 3.00 8.00
43 Corey Kluber JSY/99 2.50 6.00
44 Mike Trout JSY/27 30.00 80.00
45 Albert Pujols JSY/99 6.00 15.00
46 Shohei Ohtani JSY/99 5.00 12.00
47 Ichiro JSY/99 8.00 20.00
48 Ken Griffey Jr. JSY/99 15.00 40.00
49 Kyle Seager JSY/99 2.00 5.00
50 Dan Vogelbach JSY/99 2.00 5.00
51 Greg Maddux JSY/49 10.00 25.00
52 Chipper Jones JSY/99 6.00 15.00
53 Ronald Acuna Jr. JSY/99 10.00 25.00
54 Freddie Freeman JSY/49 5.00 12.00
55 Juan Soto JSY/99 6.00 15.00
56 Max Scherzer JSY/25 5.00 12.00
57 Stephen Strasburg JSY/99 3.00 8.00
58 Pete Alonso JSY/99 8.00 20.00
59 Noah Syndergaard JSY/99 2.50 6.00
60 Dwight Gooden JSY/49 2.50 6.00
62 Bryce Harper JSY/99 5.00 12.00
63 Mike Schmidt JSY/99 8.00 20.00
64 Rhys Hoskins JSY/99 4.00 10.00
65 Brian Anderson JSY/99 2.00 5.00
67 Ozzie Smith JSY/99 4.00 10.00
68 Matt Carpenter JSY/99 3.00 8.00
69 Yadier Molina JSY/99 8.00 20.00
70 Paul Goldschmidt JSY/99 8.00 20.00
71 Robin Yount JSY/99 3.00 8.00
72 Paul Molitor JSY/99 6.00 15.00
73 Christian Yelich JSY/99 4.00 10.00
74 Anthony Rizzo JSY/99 4.00 10.00
75 Kris Bryant JSY/99 4.00 10.00
76 Javier Baez JSY/99 4.00 10.00
77 Ryne Sandberg JSY/99 6.00 15.00
78 Joey Votto JSY/99 3.00 8.00
79 Pete Rose JSY/99 10.00 25.00
80 Johnny Bench JSY/49 10.00 25.00
81 Josh Bell JSY/99 2.50 6.00
82 Gregory Polanco JSY/99 2.50 6.00
83 Cody Bellinger JSY/99 5.00 12.00
84 Corey Seager JSY/99 8.00 20.00
85 Clayton Kershaw JSY/99 5.00 12.00
87 Randy Johnson JSY/99 3.00 8.00
88 Curt Schilling JSY/99 2.50 6.00
89 Madison Bumgarner JSY/99 2.50 6.00
90 Ketel Marte JSY/99 2.50 6.00
91 Starling Marte JSY/99 2.50 6.00
92 Buster Posey JSY/99 4.00 10.00
93 Brandon Belt JSY/99 2.50 6.00
94 Brandon Crawford JSY/99 2.50 6.00
95 Larry Walker JSY/50 3.00 8.00
96 Andres Galarraga JSY/99 2.50 6.00
97 Nolan Arenado JSY/99 5.00 12.00
98 Trevor Story JSY/25 5.00 12.00
99 Manny Machado JSY/99 3.00 8.00
100 Fernando Tatis Jr. JSY/99 15.00 40.00
101 Satchel Paige BW JSY/29 40.00 100.00
102 Shohei Ohtani BW JSY/99 5.00 12.00
103 Pete Alonso BW JSY/99 8.00 20.00
104 Vladimir Guerrero Jr. BW JSY/99 5.00 12.00
105 Lefty Williams BW JSY/49 6.00 15.00
106 Roy Campanella BW JSY/39 12.00 30.00
107 Xander Bogaerts BW JSY/99 3.00 8.00
108 Pete Rose BW JSY/99 10.00 25.00
109 Juan Soto BW JSY/99 6.00 15.00
110 Cool Papa Bell BW JSY/49 30.00 80.00
111 Hank Greenberg BW MEM/25 25.00 60.00
112 Alex Bregman BW JSY/99 3.00 8.00
113 Cody Bellinger BW JSY/49 6.00 15.00
114 Frankie Frisch BW JSY/25 12.00 30.00
116 Stan Musial BW JSY/25 12.00 30.00
117 Babe Ruth BW JSY/25 200.00 500.00
118 Aaron Judge BW JSY/99 12.00 30.00
119 Jose Abreu BW JSY/99 3.00 8.00
120 Freddie Freeman BW JSY/49 10.00 25.00
121 Anthony Rizzo BW JSY/99 4.00 10.00
122 Mookie Betts BW JSY/99 10.00 25.00
123 Heinie Groh BW JSY/99 10.00 25.00
124 Mike Trout BW JSY/27 30.00 80.00
125 Max Scherzer BW JSY/25 5.00 12.00
127 Casey Stengel BW JSY/25 10.00 25.00
128 Harry Hooper BW JSY/25 15.00 40.00
131 Gabby Hartnett BW JSY/49 12.00 30.00
132 Al Simmons BW JSY/25 15.00 40.00
133 Frankie Crosetti BW JSY/25 12.00 30.00
134 Ken Boyer BW JSY/99 6.00 15.00
135 Ronald Acuna Jr. BW JSY/99 10.00 25.00
136 Joe Jackson BW JSY/25 40.00 100.00
137 Charlie Keller BW JSY/99 6.00 15.00
138 Sam Rice BW JSY/49 12.00 30.00
139 Joe Sewell BW JSY/49 8.00 20.00
140 Ozzie Albies BW JSY/99 3.00 8.00
141 Walker Buehler BW JSY/99 4.00 10.00
142 Ted Williams BW JSY/99 20.00 50.00
143 Rafael Devers BW JSY/99 4.00 10.00
144 Bryce Harper BW JSY/99 5.00 12.00
145 Joe Medwick BW JSY/25 10.00 25.00
146 Goose Goslin BW JSY/25 10.00 25.00
147 Fernando Tatis Jr. BW JSY/99 15.00 40.00
148 Gil Hodges BW JSY/49 8.00 20.00
149 Yogi Berra BW JSY/99 20.00 50.00
151 Logan Allen JSY AU/99 RC 6.00 15.00
152 Aristides Aquino JSY AU/99 RC 20.00 50.00
154 Brendan McKay JSY AU/99 RC 12.00 30.00
155 Adbert Alzolay JSY AU/99 RC 10.00 25.00
156 Edwin Rios JSY AU/99 RC 10.00 25.00
157 Gavin Lux JSY AU/99 RC 40.00 100.00
158 Yu Chang JSY AU/99 RC 15.00 40.00
159 Trent Grisham JSY AU/99 RC 15.00 40.00
160 Abraham Toro JSY AU/99 RC 5.00 12.00
161 Dustin May JSY AU/99 RC 25.00 60.00
162 Adrian Morejon JSY AU/99 RC 8.00 20.00
163 Jake Rogers JSY AU/99 RC 6.00 15.00
164 Patrick Sandoval JSY AU/99 RC 6.00 15.00
165 Justin Dunn JSY AU/99 RC 8.00 20.00
166 Mauricio Dubon JSY AU/99 RC 10.00 25.00
167 Sam Hilliard JSY AU/99 RC 10.00 25.00
168 Jesus Luzardo JSY AU/99 RC 12.00 30.00
169 Bobby Bradley JSY AU/99 RC 8.00 20.00
170 Nico Hoerner JSY AU/99 RC 20.00 50.00
171 A.J. Puk JSY AU/99 RC 6.00 15.00
172 Zack Collins JSY AU/99 RC 8.00 20.00
173 Randy Arozarena JSY AU/99 RC 125.00 300.00
174 Anthony Kay JSY AU/99 RC 4.00 10.00
175 Brusdar Graterol JSY AU/99 RC 6.00 15.00
176 Willi Castro JSY AU/99 RC 12.00 30.00
177 Dylan Cease JSY AU/99 RC 6.00 15.00
178 Yordan Alvarez JSY AU/99 RC 75.00 200.00
179 Brock Burke JSY AU/99 RC 4.00 10.00
180 Nick Solak JSY AU/99 RC 10.00 25.00
181 Jordan Yamamoto JSY AU/99 RC 15.00 40.00
183 Kyle Lewis JSY AU/99 RC 100.00 250.00
184 Sean Murphy JSY AU/99 RC 6.00 15.00
185 Tony Gonsolin JSY AU/99 RC 8.00 20.00
186 Aaron Civale JSY AU/99 RC 10.00 25.00
187 Jaylin Davis JSY AU/99 RC 6.00 15.00
188 Bo Bichette JSY AU/99 RC 75.00 200.00
189 Logan Webb JSY AU/99 RC 6.00 15.00
190 Zac Gallen JSY AU/99 RC 12.00 30.00
191 Donnie Walton JSY AU/99 RC 8.00 20.00
192 Michael King JSY AU/99 RC 20.00 50.00
193 Tyrone Taylor JSY AU/99 RC 10.00 25.00
194 Bryan Abreu JSY AU/99 RC 4.00 10.00
195 Michel Baez JSY AU/99 RC 4.00 10.00
196 Travis Demeritte JSY AU/99 RC 6.00 15.00
197 Ronald Bolanos JSY AU/99 RC 4.00 10.00
198 Jake Fraley JSY AU/99 RC 5.00 12.00
199 Lewis Thorpe JSY AU/99 RC 4.00 10.00
200 Yonathan Daza JSY AU/99 RC 12.00 30.00
201 Joe Palumbo JSY AU/99 RC 4.00 10.00
202 Andres Munoz JSY AU/99 RC 6.00 15.00
203 Deivy Grullon JSY AU/99 RC 4.00 10.00
204 Danny Mendick JSY AU/99 RC 12.00 30.00
205 T.J. Zeuch JSY AU/99 RC 4.00 10.00
206 Josh Rojas JSY AU/99 RC 4.00 10.00
207 Tres Barrera JSY AU/99 RC 8.00 20.00
208 Sheldon Neuse JSY AU/99 RC 5.00 12.00
209 Rico Garcia JSY AU/99 RC 6.00 15.00
210 Matt Thaiss JSY AU/99 RC 5.00 12.00
211 Jonathan Hernandez JSY AU/99 RC 4.00 10.00
212 Luis Robert JSY AU/99 RC 200.00 500.00
213 Shun Yamaguchi JSY AU/99 RC 8.00 20.00
214 Kwang-Hyun Kim JSY AU/99 RC 40.00 100.00
215 Shogo Akiyama JSY AU/99 RC 25.00 60.00
216 Yoshitomo Tsutsugo JSY AU/99 RC 10.00 25.00

2020 Panini National Treasures Holo Gold

*HOLO GOLD JSY/21-25: .6X TO 1.5X p/r 70-99
*HOLO GOLD JSY/21-25: .5X TO 1.2X p/r 26-50
*HOLO GOLD JSY AU/25: .6X TO 1.5X p/r 99
RANDOM INSERTS IN PACKS
PRINT RUNS B/WN 5-25 COPIES PER
NO PRICING ON QTY 15 OR LESS
EXCHANGE DEADLINE 5/4/22
158 Yu Chang JSY AU/25 30.00 80.00
159 Trent Grisham JSY AU/25 40.00 100.00
165 Justin Dunn JSY AU/25 20.00 50.00
212 Luis Robert JSY AU/25 500.00 1000.00

2020 Panini National Treasures 12 Player Signature Booklets

RANDOM INSERTS IN PACKS
STATED PRINT RUN 25 SER.#'d SETS
EXCHANGE DEADLINE 5/4/22
1 AP/AC/AA/AM/BM/DT/DC/JYJD
KHK/SY/ZG 100.00 250.00
2 BB/DL/DL/KL/LR/NH/RA/SM
SA/YA/YT/YC 200.00 500.00

2020 Panini National Treasures 16 Player Material Booklets

RANDOM INSERTS IN PACKS
PRINT RUNS B/WN 25-49 COPIES PER
1 AR/AV/BWJ/CM/DC/EW/FW/JK/JA/JB/JR
NP/RL/RM/SS/WF/25 75.00 200.00
2 AA/BB/BM/DM/DC/GL/ID/JL/KL/LR/NS
NH/SM/YA/YT/ZG/25 100.00 250.00
3 AB/CV/CY/CB/ES/FF/JM/JR/JA/JS/MT
OA/PA/SM/TS/XB/25 100.00 250.00
4 AK/BF/BL/BM/CPB/DD/EL/FC/GH/HG/HG
MS/PW/PWR/SP/TW/49 150.00 400.00

2020 Panini National Treasures American Autographs

RANDOM INSERTS IN PACKS
PRINT RUNS B/WN 10-99 COPIES PER
NO PRICING ON QTY 15 OR LESS
EXCHANGE DEADLINE 5/4/22
*HOLO GOLD/25: .6X TO 1.5X p/r 99
*HOLO GOLD/25: .5X TO 1.2X p/r 49-50
2 Sandy Koufax/25 200.00 500.00
3 Dave Stewart/99 3.00 8.00
4 Ryne Sandberg/49 40.00 100.00
5 Jose Canseco/25 20.00 50.00
7 Alek Thomas/99 4.00 10.00
8 Josh Donaldson/50 15.00 40.00
9 Tony Oliva/25 12.00 30.00
11 Evan White/99 8.00 20.00
14 Sammy Sosa/25 50.00 120.00
15 Ryan Zimmerman/25 20.00 50.00
16 Troy Glaus/99 6.00 15.00
19 David Wright/50 25.00 60.00
21 Aaron Judge/25

22 Alex Bregman/99 15.00 40.00
24 Andre Dawson/25 20.00 50.00
25 Anthony Rizzo/25 25.00 60.00

2020 Panini National Treasures Clearly Jumbo Swatch Signatures

RANDOM INSERTS IN PACKS
PRINT RUNS B/WN 7-99 COPIES PER
NO PRICING ON QTY 15 OR LESS
EXCHANGE DEADLINE 5/4/22
4 Andres Gimenez/75 10.00 25.00
5 Alex Kirilloff/49 12.00 30.00
7 Casey Mize/50 12.00 30.00
10 Kwang-Hyun Kim/99 12.00 30.00
11 Shun Yamaguchi/99 6.00 15.00
12 Shogo Akiyama/99 15.00 40.00
13 Yoshitomo Tsutsugo/99 10.00 25.00
15 Evan White/99 8.00 20.00
17 David Ortiz/25 40.00 100.00
19 Alex Bregman/99 15.00 40.00
23 J.D. Martinez/25 10.00 25.00
24 Juan Soto/99 EXCH 40.00 100.00
25 Kenny Lofton/25 5.00 12.00

2020 Panini National Treasures Clearly Jumbo Swatch Signatures Holo Gold

*HOLO GOLD/25: .6X TO 1.5X p/r 99
*HOLO GOLD/25: .5X TO 1.2X p/r 49-75
RANDOM INSERTS IN PACKS
PRINT RUNS B/WN 5-25 COPIES PER
NO PRICING ON QTY 15 OR LESS
EXCHANGE DEADLINE 5/4/22
5 Alex Kirilloff/25 30.00 80.00
24 Juan Soto/25 EXCH 125.00 300.00

2020 Panini National Treasures Colossal Material Signatures

RANDOM INSERTS IN PACKS
PRINT RUNS B/WN 5-99 COPIES PER
NO PRICING ON QTY 15 OR LESS
*HOLO GOLD/25: .5X TO 1.2X p/r 50-75
3 Bobby Dalbec/99 20.00 50.00
4 Brandon Nimmo/75 5.00 12.00
5 Brent Honeywell/25 6.00 15.00
6 David Fletcher/99 5.00 12.00
9 Hunter Pence/25 6.00 15.00
11 J.D. Davis/99 3.00 8.00
12 Jason Kipnis/25 6.00 15.00
14 Josh Naylor/50 4.00 10.00
15 Kevin Newman/99 5.00 12.00
18 Luke Weaver/25 5.00 12.00
19 Matt Olson/50 6.00 15.00
21 Mitch Moreland/50 4.00 10.00
22 Nicky Lopez/50 4.00 10.00
24 Robert Gsellman/75 4.00 10.00
25 Thyago Vieira/99 3.00 8.00
27 Tyler Mahle/99 3.00 8.00
28 Victor Caratini/99 3.00 8.00

2020 Panini National Treasures Colossal Materials

RANDOM INSERTS IN PACKS
PRINT RUNS B/WN 25-99 COPIES PER
*HOLO GOLD/18-25: .6X TO 1.5X p/r 72-99
*HOLO GOLD/18-25: .5X TO 1.2X p/r 49
1 Ronald Acuna Jr./99 10.00 25.00
2 Chris Paddack/99 3.00 8.00
3 Vladimir Guerrero Jr./99 5.00 12.00
4 Fernando Tatis Jr./99 15.00 40.00
5 Mike Soroka/99 3.00 8.00
6 Rafael Devers/99 4.00 10.00
7 Xander Bogaerts/72 3.00 8.00
8 Albert Pujols/49 5.00 12.00
9 Jasson Dominguez/99 40.00 100.00
10 Dylan Carlson/99 8.00 20.00
11 Nate Pearson/99 6.00 15.00
12 Evan White/99 5.00 12.00
13 Kwang-Hyun Kim/99 4.00 10.00
14 Shun Yamaguchi/99 2.50 6.00
15 Kyle Schwarber/99 3.00 8.00
16 Cody Bellinger/49 8.00 20.00
17 Alex Bregman/75 3.00 8.00
18 Alec Bohm/49 15.00 40.00
19 Ryan Mountcastle/99 10.00 25.00
20 Estevan Florial/99 3.00 8.00
21 Brandon Lowe/99 2.50 6.00
22 Eloy Jimenez/99 6.00 15.00
23 Cavan Biggio/99 4.00 10.00
24 Victor Robles/99 4.00 10.00
25 Gleyber Torres/99 6.00 15.00
26 Greg Maddux/25 8.00 20.00
27 Masahiro Tanaka/99 3.00 8.00
28 Chipper Jones/99 3.00 8.00
29 Barry Larkin/49 5.00 12.00
30 Bubba Starling/99 4.00 10.00
31 Carlos Martinez/99 2.50 6.00
32 CC Sabathia/99 2.50 6.00
33 Chris Davis/49 2.50 6.00
34 Christian Vazquez/99 2.50 6.00
35 David Wright/99 2.50 6.00
36 Eduardo Rodriguez/99 2.00 5.00
37 Hunter Harvey/99 3.00 8.00
38 Jorge Polanco/99 2.50 6.00
39 Luis Tiant/49 2.50 6.00
40 Mitch Haniger/99 2.50 6.00

2020 Panini National Treasures Cut Signature Booklets

RANDOM INSERTS IN PACKS
PRINT RUNS B/WN 7-25 COPIES PER
NO PRICING ON QTY 15 OR LESS
EXCHANGE DEADLINE 5/4/22
*NAMES/20-25: .4X TO 1X p/r 20-25
*STATLINE/20-25: .4X TO 1X p/r 20-25
*STAT.VAR./20-25: .4X TO 1X p/r 20-25
3 Stan Musial/25 40.00 100.00
5 Gary Carter/20 25.00 60.00
8 Harmon Killebrew/25 30.00 80.00
12 Gary Carter/20 25.00 60.00
15 Bobby Thomson/25 15.00 40.00
22 Bob Gibson/25 60.00 150.00

2020 Panini National Treasures Cut Signature Material Booklets

RANDOM INSERTS IN PACKS
PRINT RUNS B/WN 3-25 COPIES PER
NO PRICING ON QTY 15 OR LESS
EXCHANGE DEADLINE 5/4/22
17 Gary Carter/25 25.00 60.00

2020 Panini National Treasures Decades Autograph Booklets

RANDOM INSERTS IN PACKS
PRINT RUNS B/WN 10-25 COPIES PER
NO PRICING ON QTY 15 OR LESS
EXCHANGE DEADLINE 5/4/22
1 Aquino/Bichette/McKay
Lux/Robert/Alvarez/25 EXCH 200.00 500.00
2 Biggio/Seager/Bell/Soto
Alonso/Vlad Jr/25 EXCH 150.00 400.00
8 Rutschman/Witt Jr/Bleday
Bart/Mesa/Franco/25 100.00 250.00

2020 Panini National Treasures Dual Material Signature Booklets

RANDOM INSERTS IN PACKS
STATED PRINT RUN 25 SER.#'d SETS
EXCHANGE DEADLINE 5/4/22
1 Alex Bregman 30.00 80.00
George Springer
2 Bichette/Biggio EXCH 80.00 200.00
3 Nola/Arrieta EXCH 40.00 100.00
4 A.Chapman/Hicks 30.00 80.00
5 Galarraga/Vizquel 60.00 150.00
6 Carpenter/DeJong EXCH 25.00 60.00
7 Alonso/Alvarez 100.00 250.00
8 M.Chapman/Piscotty 25.00 60.00
9 Robert/Franco 500.00 1000.00
10 Reynolds/Bell 20.00 50.00

2020 Panini National Treasures Dual Signature Material Booklets

RANDOM INSERTS IN PACKS
PRINT RUNS B/WN 49-99 COPIES PER
EXCHANGE DEADLINE 5/4/22
1 Puk/Luzardo/99 EXCH 15.00 40.00
2 Aquino/Alvarez/99 40.00 100.00
3 Murphy/Collins/99 8.00 20.00
4 May/Cease/49 15.00 40.00
5 Bichette/Lux/99 50.00 120.00
6 Grisham/Taylor/99 EXCH 10.00 25.00
7 McKay/Luzardo/99 15.00 40.00
8 Alzolay/Hoerner/99 20.00 50.00
9 Bradley/Thaiss/99 10.00 25.00
10 Bichette/Diaz/99 50.00 120.00
11 Bichette/Alvarez/99 75.00 200.00
12 Lux/Dubon/99 20.00 50.00

2020 Panini National Treasures Dual Signatures

RANDOM INSERTS IN PACKS
PRINT RUNS B/WN 5-99 COPIES PER
NO PRICING ON QTY 15 OR LESS
EXCHANGE DEADLINE 5/4/22
*HOLO GOLD/25: .6X TO 1.5X p/r 99
*HOLO GOLD/25: .5X TO 1.2X p/r 49-50
1 Bichette/Alvarez/25 EXCH 80.00 200.00
2 Akiyama/Chang/99 15.00 40.00
3 Kim/Yamaguchi/49 12.00 30.00
4 Morejon/Baez/50 6.00 15.00
6 McKay/Tsutsugo/25 20.00 50.00
7 Cease/Hoerner/50 15.00 40.00
9 Toro/Abreu/99 6.00 15.00
10 Rios/Thaiss/99 8.00 20.00
12 Chapman/Laureano/49 15.00 40.00
15 Turner/Muncy/25 30.00 80.00
18 Civale/Bradley/99 10.00 25.00
19 Rodon/Fedde/25 12.00 30.00
20 Gordon/Perez/25 40.00 100.00

2020 Panini National Treasures Fantasy Lineups Material Booklets

RANDOM INSERTS IN PACKS
STATED PRINT RUN 25 SER.#'d SETS
1 AJ/AB/GR/JB/JB/JS/RAJ/WB/WC 60.00 150.00
2 CB/GS/GS/GS/JV/MM/OA/SM/XB 40.00 100.00

2020 Panini National Treasures Game Gear Dual Material Signatures

RANDOM INSERTS IN PACKS
PRINT RUNS B/WN 5-99 COPIES PER
NO PRICING ON QTY 15 OR LESS
EXCHANGE DEADLINE 5/4/22
*HOLO GOLD/25: .6X TO 1.5X p/r 99
*HOLO GOLD/25: .5X TO 1.2X p/r 50
5 Adrian Morejon/25 5.00 12.00
10 Andres Munoz/99 5.00 12.00
15 Brock Burke/25 5.00 12.00
17 Cavan Biggio/99 10.00 25.00
22 David Fletcher/25 8.00 20.00
24 Deivy Grullon/99 3.00 8.00
25 Domingo Leyba/25 6.00 15.00
32 Jake Marisnick/25 5.00 12.00
33 Jaylin Davis/25 8.00 20.00
34 Jordan Hicks/25 6.00 15.00
40 Lewis Thorpe/99 3.00 8.00
41 Logan Allen/25 5.00 12.00
42 Logan Webb/50 6.00 15.00
43 Luis Robert/99 EXCH 100.00 250.00
46 Patrick Sandoval/50 6.00 15.00
47 Randy Arozarena/50 75.00 200.00
48 Rico Garcia/99 5.00 12.00
49 Tres Barrera/50 8.00 20.00
50 Yoshitomo Tsutsugo/99 10.00 25.00

2020 Panini National Treasures Game Gear Dual Materials

RANDOM INSERTS IN PACKS
PRINT RUNS B/WN 5-99 COPIES PER
NO PRICING ON QTY 15 OR LESS
*HOLO GOLD/21-25: .6X TO 1.5X p/r 99
*HOLO GOLD/21-25: .5X TO 1.2X p/r 27-49
1 Ken Griffey Jr./49 20.00 50.00
2 George Brett/49 10.00 25.00
3 Cal Ripken/49 10.00 25.00
4 Albert Pujols/25 6.00 15.00
5 Juan Soto/99 10.00 25.00
6 George Springer/99 2.50 6.00
7 Kyle Schwarber/99 3.00 8.00
8 Ted Williams/25 30.00 80.00
12 Roger Maris/25 25.00 60.00
14 Mike Trout/27 30.00 80.00
15 Joey Bart/99 6.00 15.00
16 Bobby Witt Jr./99 12.00 30.00
17 Pee Wee Reese/25 10.00 25.00
18 Nolan Ryan/34 15.00 40.00
19 Alex Kirilloff/99 4.00 10.00
20 Walker Buehler/49 5.00 12.00
21 Jack Flaherty/99 3.00 8.00
22 Casey Mize/99 6.00 15.00
23 Tommy Henrich/25 8.00 20.00

2020 Panini National Treasures Game Gear Material Signatures

RANDOM INSERTS IN PACKS
PRINT RUNS B/WN 5-99 COPIES PER
NO PRICING ON QTY 15 OR LESS
EXCHANGE DEADLINE 5/4/22
*HOLO GOLD/25: .6X TO 1.5X p/r 99
*HOLO GOLD/25: .5X TO 1.2X p/r 50
5 Adrian Morejon/25 5.00 12.00
10 Andres Munoz/99 5.00 12.00
15 Brock Burke/25 5.00 12.00
17 Cavan Biggio/99 10.00 25.00
22 David Fletcher/25 8.00 20.00
24 Deivy Grullon/99 3.00 8.00
25 Domingo Leyba/25 6.00 15.00
32 Jake Marisnick/25 5.00 12.00
33 Jaylin Davis/25 8.00 20.00
34 Jordan Hicks/25 6.00 15.00
40 Lewis Thorpe/99 3.00 8.00
41 Logan Allen/25 5.00 12.00
42 Logan Webb/25 8.00 20.00
43 Luis Robert/99 EXCH 100.00 250.00
46 Patrick Sandoval/50 6.00 15.00
47 Randy Arozarena/50 75.00 200.00
48 Rico Garcia/99 5.00 12.00
49 Tres Barrera/50 8.00 20.00
50 Yoshitomo Tsutsugo/99 10.00 25.00

2020 Panini National Treasures Game Gear Materials

RANDOM INSERTS IN PACKS
PRINT RUNS B/WN 10-99 COPIES PER
NO PRICING ON QTY 15 OR LESS
*HOLO GOLD/21-25: .6X TO 1.5X p/r 99
*HOLO GOLD/21-25: .5X TO 1.2X p/r 27-49
1 Ken Griffey Jr./99 15.00 40.00
2 George Brett/99 8.00 20.00
3 Cal Ripken/99 8.00 20.00
4 Albert Pujols/49 5.00 12.00
5 Juan Soto/99 10.00 25.00
6 George Springer/99 2.50 6.00
7 Kyle Schwarber/99 3.00 8.00
8 Ted Williams/25 30.00 80.00
9 Babe Ruth/25 200.00 500.00
12 Roger Maris/49 15.00 40.00
14 Mike Trout/27 30.00 80.00
15 Joey Bart/99 6.00 15.00
16 Bobby Witt Jr./99 12.00 30.00
17 Pee Wee Reese/99 6.00 15.00
18 Nolan Ryan/34 15.00 40.00
19 Alex Kirilloff/99 4.00 10.00
20 Walker Buehler/99 4.00 10.00
21 Jack Flaherty/99 3.00 8.00
22 Casey Mize/99 6.00 15.00
23 Tommy Henrich/99 5.00 12.00
25 Joe Jackson/25 40.00 100.00

2020 Panini National Treasures Game Gear Materials Eights

RANDOM INSERTS IN PACKS
PRINT RUNS B/WN 25-99 COPIES PER
*HOLO GOLD/25: .6X TO 1.5X p/r 72-99
*HOLO GOLD/25: .5X TO 1.2X p/r 44-49
1 Yordan Alvarez/44 25.00 60.00
2 Bo Bichette/99 8.00 20.00
3 Aristides Aquino/99 5.00 12.00
4 Luis Robert/99 12.00 30.00
5 A.J. Puk/99 3.00 8.00
6 Dylan Cease/99 3.00 8.00
7 Nico Hoerner/99 8.00 20.00
8 Brendan McKay/99 3.00 8.00
9 Gavin Lux/99 10.00 25.00
10 Chris Paddack/99 3.00 8.00
11 Xander Bogaerts/72 3.00 8.00
12 Alex Rodriguez/25 12.00 30.00
13 Dylan Carlson/99 8.00 20.00
14 Kyle Lewis/99 15.00 40.00
15 Jo Adell/99 8.00 20.00
16 Jasson Dominguez/99 40.00 100.00
17 Shun Yamaguchi/49 3.00 8.00
18 Forrest Whitley/99 3.00 8.00
19 Fernando Tatis Jr./99 15.00 40.00
20 Evan White/99 5.00 12.00
21 Alec Bohm/99 12.00 30.00
22 Kwang-Hyun Kim/99 4.00 10.00
23 Ryan Mountcastle/99 10.00 25.00
24 Ronald Acuna Jr./99 10.00 25.00
25 Vladimir Guerrero Jr./99 5.00 12.00

2020 Panini National Treasures Game Gear Materials Sevens

RANDOM INSERTS IN PACKS
PRINT RUNS B/WN 44-99 COPIES PER
*HOLO GOLD/25: .6X TO 1.5X p/r 72-99
*HOLO GOLD/25: .5X TO 1.2X p/r 44-49
1 Yordan Alvarez/44 25.00 60.00
2 Bo Bichette/99 8.00 20.00
3 Aristides Aquino/99 5.00 12.00
4 Luis Robert/99 12.00 30.00
5 A.J. Puk/99 3.00 8.00
6 Dylan Cease/99 3.00 8.00
7 Nico Hoerner/99 8.00 20.00
8 Brendan McKay/99 3.00 8.00
9 Gavin Lux/99 10.00 25.00
10 Chris Paddack/99 3.00 8.00
11 Xander Bogaerts/72 3.00 8.00
12 Alex Rodriguez/49 10.00 25.00
13 Dylan Carlson/99 8.00 20.00
14 Kyle Lewis/99 15.00 40.00
15 Jo Adell/99 8.00 20.00
16 Jasson Dominguez/99 40.00 100.00
17 Shun Yamaguchi/49 3.00 8.00
18 Forrest Whitley/99 3.00 8.00
19 Fernando Tatis Jr./99 15.00 40.00
20 Evan White/99 5.00 12.00
21 Alec Bohm/99 12.00 30.00
22 Kwang-Hyun Kim/99 4.00 10.00
23 Ryan Mountcastle/99 10.00 25.00
24 Ronald Acuna Jr./99 10.00 25.00
25 Vladimir Guerrero Jr./99 5.00 12.00

2020 Panini National Treasures Game Gear Materials Sixes

RANDOM INSERTS IN PACKS
PRINT RUNS B/WN 44-99 COPIES PER
*HOLO GOLD/25: .6X TO 1.5X p/r 72-99
*HOLO GOLD/25: .5X TO 1.2X p/r 44-49
1 Yordan Alvarez/44 25.00 60.00
2 Bo Bichette/99 8.00 20.00
3 Aristides Aquino/99 5.00 12.00
4 Luis Robert/99 12.00 30.00
5 A.J. Puk/99 3.00 8.00
6 Dylan Cease/99 3.00 8.00
7 Nico Hoerner/99 8.00 20.00
8 Brendan McKay/99 3.00 8.00
9 Gavin Lux/99 10.00 25.00
10 Chris Paddack/99 3.00 8.00
11 Xander Bogaerts/72 3.00 8.00
12 Alex Rodriguez/49 10.00 25.00
13 Dylan Carlson/99 8.00 20.00
14 Kyle Lewis/99 15.00 40.00
15 Jo Adell/99 8.00 20.00
16 Jasson Dominguez/99 40.00 100.00
17 Shun Yamaguchi/49 3.00 8.00
18 Forrest Whitley/99 3.00 8.00
19 Fernando Tatis Jr./99 15.00 40.00
20 Evan White/99 5.00 12.00
21 Alec Bohm/99 12.00 30.00
22 Kwang-Hyun Kim/99 4.00 10.00
23 Ryan Mountcastle/99 10.00 25.00
24 Ronald Acuna Jr./99 10.00 25.00
25 Vladimir Guerrero Jr./99 5.00 12.00

2020 Panini National Treasures Game Gear Triple Material Signatures

RANDOM INSERTS IN PACKS
PRINT RUNS B/WN 5-99 COPIES PER
NO PRICING ON QTY 15 OR LESS
EXCHANGE DEADLINE 5/4/22
*HOLO GOLD/25: .6X TO 1.5X p/r 99
*HOLO GOLD/25: .5X TO 1.2X p/r 50
5 Adrian Morejon/25 5.00 12.00
10 Andres Munoz/99 5.00 12.00
15 Brock Burke/25 5.00 12.00
17 Cavan Biggio/99 10.00 25.00
22 David Fletcher/25 8.00 20.00
24 Deivy Grullon/99 3.00 8.00
25 Domingo Leyba/25 6.00 15.00
33 Jaylin Davis/25 8.00 20.00
34 Jordan Hicks/25 6.00 15.00
40 Lewis Thorpe/99 3.00 8.00
41 Logan Allen/25 5.00 12.00
42 Logan Webb/50 6.00 15.00
43 Luis Robert/99 EXCH 100.00 250.00
46 Patrick Sandoval/50 6.00 15.00
47 Randy Arozarena/50 75.00 200.00
48 Rico Garcia/99 5.00 12.00
49 Tres Barrera/99 6.00 15.00
50 Yoshitomo Tsutsugo/99 10.00 25.00

2020 Panini National Treasures Game Gear Triple Materials

RANDOM INSERTS IN PACKS
PRINT RUNS B/WN 3-99 COPIES PER
NO PRICING ON QTY 15 OR LESS
*HOLO GOLD/21-25: .6X TO 1.5X p/r 99
*HOLO GOLD/21-25: .5X TO 1.2X p/r 27-49
1 Ken Griffey Jr./49 20.00 50.00
2 George Brett/25 12.00 30.00
3 Cal Ripken/25 12.00 30.00
4 Albert Pujols/25 6.00 15.00
5 Juan Soto/99 10.00 25.00
6 George Springer/99 2.50 6.00
7 Kyle Schwarber/99 3.00 8.00
8 Ted Williams/25 30.00 80.00
14 Mike Trout/27 30.00 80.00
15 Joey Bart/99 6.00 15.00
16 Bobby Witt Jr./99 12.00 30.00
17 Pee Wee Reese/25 10.00 25.00
18 Nolan Ryan/34 15.00 40.00
19 Alex Kirilloff/99 4.00 10.00
20 Walker Buehler/49 5.00 12.00
21 Jack Flaherty/99 3.00 8.00
22 Casey Mize/99 6.00 15.00
23 Tommy Henrich/25 8.00 20.00
24 Herb Pennock/25 12.00 30.00

2020 Panini National Treasures Hall of Fame Material Signatures

PRINT RUNS B/WN 11-50 COPIES PER
NO PRICING ON QTY 15 OR LESS
EXCHANGE DEADLINE 5/4/22
*HOLO GOLD/25: .5X TO 1.2X p/r 49-50
2 Alan Trammell/50 30.00 80.00
3 Cal Ripken/50 40.00 100.00
4 Chipper Jones/25 40.00 100.00
5 Dennis Eckersley/25 10.00 25.00
7 Andre Dawson/25 20.00 50.00
10 Tony Perez/50 5.00 12.00
13 Rickey Henderson/49 50.00 120.00
14 Rod Carew/27 20.00 50.00

2020 Panini National Treasures Hall of Fame Materials

RANDOM INSERTS IN PACKS
PRINT RUNS B/WN 5-99 COPIES PER
NO PRICING ON QTY 15 OR LESS
*HOLO GOLD/25: .6X TO 1.5X p/r 99
*HOLO GOLD/25: .5X TO 1.2X p/r 30-49
1 Tris Speaker/49 15.00 40.00
2 Tim Raines/99 2.50 6.00
3 Gary Carter/99 2.50 6.00
4 Pedro Martinez/99 6.00 15.00
5 Tommy Lasorda/99 12.00 30.00
6 Al Kaline/49 4.00 10.00
7 Ryne Sandberg/99 6.00 15.00
8 Tony Gwynn/99 6.00 15.00
9 Larry Walker/99 2.50 6.00
10 Johnny Bench/49 8.00 20.00
11 Mike Schmidt/49 6.00 15.00
12 Luis Aparicio/99 2.50 6.00
13 Roberto Clemente/21 75.00 200.00
14 Cal Ripken/49 10.00 25.00
15 Ken Griffey Jr./99 15.00 40.00
16 Herb Pennock/49 10.00 25.00
17 Wade Boggs/99 5.00 12.00
18 Richie Ashburn/49 3.00 8.00
19 Eddie Murray/99 2.50 6.00
20 Don Drysdale/49 6.00 15.00
21 Nolan Ryan/30 15.00 40.00
23 Rickey Henderson/99 3.00 8.00
24 Ivan Rodriguez/99 2.50 6.00
25 Jim Thome/99 2.50 6.00
26 Bobby Doerr/99 6.00 15.00
27 Joe Morgan/99 2.50 6.00
28 Frank Thomas/99 3.00 8.00
29 Larry Doby/49 12.00 30.00
30 Orlando Cepeda/99 2.50 6.00
31 George Brett/99 8.00 20.00
32 Mike Piazza/49 4.00 10.00
33 Duke Snider/99 8.00 20.00
34 Craig Biggio/99 2.50 6.00
35 Bill Mazeroski/99 6.00 15.00
36 Joe Torre/99 2.50 6.00
37 Vladimir Guerrero/25 4.00 10.00
38 Harold Baines/99 2.50 6.00
39 Fergie Jenkins/99 2.50 6.00
40 Greg Maddux/99 5.00 12.00
41 Alan Trammell/49 3.00 8.00
42 Mel Ott/25 20.00 50.00
43 Bill Dickey/49 12.00 30.00
44 Kirby Puckett/49 12.00 30.00
45 Jack Morris/49 3.00 8.00
46 Ozzie Smith/99 4.00 10.00
47 Billy Williams/49 3.00 8.00
48 Jeff Bagwell/99 2.50 6.00
49 Lou Brock/49 5.00 12.00
50 Mickey Mantle/25 75.00 200.00

2020 Panini National Treasures Hall of Fame Signatures

RANDOM INSERTS IN PACKS
PRINT RUNS B/WN 10-99 COPIES PER
NO PRICING ON QTY 15 OR LESS
EXCHANGE DEADLINE 5/4/22
*GOLD/49: .5X TO 1.2X p/r 99
*GOLD/25: .5X TO 1.2X p/r 49-50
*HOLO GOLD/25: .6X TO 1.5X p/r 99
2 Sandy Koufax/25 200.00 500.00
4 Ryne Sandberg/49 40.00 100.00
5 Rickey Henderson/49 50.00 120.00
6 Rod Carew/25 20.00 50.00
7 Alan Trammell/25 40.00 100.00
9 Barry Larkin/50 20.00 50.00
10 Goose Gossage/50 10.00 25.00
14 Trevor Hoffman/25 15.00 40.00
17 Cal Ripken/49 40.00 100.00
18 Chipper Jones/25 40.00 100.00
19 Tony Perez/49 20.00 50.00
20 Tom Glavine/99 12.00 30.00
26 Paul Molitor/25 15.00 40.00
27 Dennis Eckersley/25 10.00 25.00
29 Andre Dawson/25 20.00 50.00

2020 Panini National Treasures International Treasures Autographs

RANDOM INSERTS IN PACKS
PRINT RUNS B/WN 10-99 COPIES PER
NO PRICING ON QTY 15 OR LESS
EXCHANGE DEADLINE 5/4/22
1 Fernando Tatis Jr./99 75.00 200.00
2 Vladimir Guerrero Jr./99 30.00 80.00
3 Xander Bogaerts/25 8.00 20.00
5 Rafael Devers/49 15.00 40.00
7 Tony Perez/25 25.00 60.00
8 Eloy Jimenez/49 15.00 40.00
10 Jasson Dominguez/49 200.00 500.00
11 Jose Canseco/25 20.00 50.00
12 Juan Soto/49 50.00 120.00
13 Luis Severino/49 5.00 12.00
14 Max Kepler/25 6.00 15.00
15 Yordan Alvarez/25 30.00 80.00
16 Aristides Aquino/49 12.00 30.00
17 Shohei Ohtani/25 60.00 150.00
18 Ronald Acuna Jr./49 60.00 150.00
19 Yu Chang/25 25.00 60.00
21 Juan Marichal/25 12.00 30.00
22 Joey Votto/25 20.00 50.00
23 Gleyber Torres/25 25.00 60.00
24 Sammy Sosa/25 50.00 120.00
25 Miguel Tejada/25 10.00 25.00

2020 Panini National Treasures Legendary Jumbo Material Booklets

RANDOM INSERTS IN PACKS
STATED PRINT RUN 25 SER.#'d SETS
1 Ted Williams 30.00 80.00
2 Babe Ruth 200.00 500.00
3 Duke Snider 12.00 30.00
4 George Sisler 25.00 60.00
5 Hoyt Wilhelm 15.00 40.00
6 Joe Cronin 15.00 40.00
7 Mickey Mantle 75.00 200.00
8 Larry Doby 15.00 40.00
9 Pee Wee Reese 10.00 25.00
10 Cool Papa Bell 40.00 100.00

2020 Panini National Treasures Legendary Material Booklets

RANDOM INSERTS IN PACKS
PRINT RUNS B/WN 10-99 COPIES PER
NO PRICING ON QTY 15 OR LESS
*HOLO GOLD/25: .6X TO 1.5X p/r 99
*HOLO GOLD/25: .5X TO 1.2X p/r 49
1 Babe Ruth/25 200.00 500.00
2 Ted Williams/99 30.00 80.00
3 Lou Gehrig/25 75.00 200.00
4 Mickey Mantle/99 75.00 200.00
5 Cool Papa Bell/99 25.00 60.00
6 Harmon Killebrew/25 12.00 30.00
7 Frank Chance/99 10.00 25.00
9 Ty Cobb/25 50.00 120.00
10 Hank Greenberg/25 25.00 60.00
12 Lefty O'Doul/99 10.00 25.00
13 Miller Huggins/49 12.00 30.00
14 Sam Rice/25 15.00 40.00
15 Nolan Ryan/99 12.00 30.00
16 Warren Spahn/99 12.00 30.00

2020 Panini National Treasures Legendary Silhouette Duals Booklets

RANDOM INSERTS IN PACKS
PRINT RUNS B/WN 10-99 COPIES PER
NO PRICING ON QTY 15 OR LESS
EXCHANGE DEADLINE 5/4/22
*HOLO GOLD/25: .6X TO 1.5X p/r 99
7 M.Mantle/R.Maris/25 125.00 300.00
14 C.Furillo/J.Gilliam/25 15.00 40.00
15 E.Howard/G.McDougald/99 10.00 25.00
16 J.Pesky/T.Yawkey/25 15.00 40.00

2020 Panini National Treasures Midnight Signatures

RANDOM INSERTS IN PACKS
PRINT RUNS B/WN 10-99 COPIES PER
NO PRICING ON QTY 15 OR LESS
EXCHANGE DEADLINE 5/4/22
2 Austin Meadows/50 6.00 15.00
4 Rickey Henderson/25 60.00 150.00
5 Ronald Acuna Jr./50 60.00 150.00
12 Ketel Marte/50 5.00 12.00
13 Luis Tiant/99 6.00 15.00
14 Andres Gimenez/99 8.00 20.00
15 Fernando Tatis Jr./49 EXCH 100.00 250.00
16 Tony Oliva/25 12.00 30.00
18 Ryan Zimmerman/25 12.00 30.00
20 Sammy Sosa/25 50.00 120.00
22 Adrian Beltre/25 15.00 40.00
25 Corey Seager/49 25.00 60.00

2020 Panini National Treasures Midnight Signatures Holo Gold

*HOLO GOLD/25: .6X TO 1.5X p/r 99
*HOLO GOLD/25: .5X TO 1.2X p/r 49-50
RANDOM INSERTS IN PACKS
PRINT RUNS B/WN 5-25 COPIES PER
NO PRICING ON QTY 15 OR LESS
EXCHANGE DEADLINE 5/4/22
15 Fernando Tatis Jr./25 150.00 400.00

2020 Panini National Treasures Player's Weekend Signatures

RANDOM INSERTS IN PACKS
PRINT RUNS B/WN 10-99 COPIES PER
NO PRICING ON QTY 15 OR LESS
EXCHANGE DEADLINE 5/4/22
2 Aristides Aquino/99 10.00 25.00
3 Bo Bichette/99 40.00 100.00
4 Brendan McKay/25 8.00 20.00
5 Dustin May/25 15.00 40.00
6 Dylan Cease/99 6.00 15.00
7 Isan Diaz/99 5.00 12.00
8 Ryan Zimmerman/49 8.00 20.00
9 Nolan Arenado/25 30.00 80.00
10 Pete Alonso/49 40.00 100.00

2020 Panini National Treasures Retro Materials

RANDOM INSERTS IN PACKS
PRINT RUNS B/WN 4-99 COPIES PER
NO PRICING ON QTY 15 OR LESS
*HOLO GOLD/25: .6X TO 1.5X p/r 99
*HOLO GOLD/25: .5X TO 1.2X p/r 49
1 Harold Baines/49 3.00 8.00
2 Tommy Lasorda/25 20.00 50.00
3 Al Kaline/25 5.00 12.00
4 Red Schoendienst/49 3.00 8.00
5 Randy Johnson/49 4.00 10.00
6 Craig Biggio/49 8.00 20.00
7 Jeff Bagwell/99 2.50 6.00
8 Ted Williams/25 30.00 80.00
10 Roger Maris/25 25.00 60.00
11 Mickey Mantle/25 75.00 200.00
12 George Brett/25 20.00 50.00
13 Tommy Henrich/25 8.00 20.00
14 Herb Pennock/25 12.00 30.00
15 Luke Appling/99 2.50 6.00
16 Eddie Stanky/49 6.00 15.00
17 Ken Griffey Jr./49 20.00 50.00
18 Sammy Sosa/99 6.00 15.00
19 Mariano Rivera/99 8.00 20.00
20 Andy Pettitte/99 2.50 6.00

2020 Panini National Treasures Retro Signatures

PRINT RUNS B/WN 15-49 COPIES PER
NO PRICING ON QTY 15 OR LESS
EXCHANGE DEADLINE 5/4/22
3 Anthony Rizzo/25 25.00 60.00
4 Bo Jackson/25 60.00 150.00
6 Jason Giambi/25 6.00 15.00
7 Lou Brock/25 30.00 80.00
8 Troy Glaus/49 8.00 20.00
9 Bert Blyleven/25 10.00 25.00
11 Willie McGee/49 12.00 30.00
12 Paul Konerko/25 15.00 40.00
13 Tim Wakefield/25 12.00 30.00
14 Steve Garvey/25 25.00 60.00
15 Tony Perez/25 25.00 60.00
16 Barry Larkin/25 25.00 60.00
18 Andy Pettitte/25 12.00 30.00
19 Trevor Hoffman/25 15.00 40.00
20 Wade Boggs/25 15.00 40.00
21 Paul Molitor/25 15.00 40.00
22 Pete Rose/25 25.00 60.00
23 Nolan Ryan/25 50.00 120.00
24 Juan Marichal/25 12.00 30.00
25 Goose Gossage/25 12.00 30.00

2020 Panini National Treasures Rookie Colossal Materials

RANDOM INSERTS IN PACKS
STATED PRINT RUN 99 SER.#'d SETS
*HOLO GOLD/25: .6X TO 1.5X BASIC
1 Logan Allen 2.00 5.00
2 Aristides Aquino 5.00 12.00
3 Brendan McKay 3.00 8.00
4 Adbert Alzolay 2.50 6.00
5 Edwin Rios 5.00 12.00
6 Gavin Lux 10.00 25.00
7 Yu Chang 3.00 8.00
8 Trent Grisham 8.00 20.00
9 Dustin May 6.00 15.00
10 Adrian Morejon 2.00 5.00
11 Justin Dunn 2.50 6.00
12 Mauricio Dubon 2.50 6.00
13 Sam Hilliard 3.00 8.00
14 Jesus Luzardo 4.00 10.00
15 Nico Hoerner 8.00 20.00
16 A.J. Puk 3.00 8.00
17 Zack Collins 2.50 6.00
18 Anthony Kay 2.00 5.00
19 Brusdar Graterol 3.00 8.00
20 Willi Castro 3.00 8.00
21 Dylan Cease 3.00 8.00
22 Yordan Alvarez 20.00 50.00
23 Nick Solak 8.00 20.00
24 Jordan Yamamoto 2.00 5.00
25 Isan Diaz 3.00 8.00
26 Kyle Lewis 15.00 40.00
27 Sean Murphy 3.00 8.00
28 Tony Gonsolin 8.00 20.00
29 Aaron Civale 4.00 10.00
30 Bo Bichette 15.00 40.00
31 Logan Webb 3.00 8.00
32 Zac Gallen 5.00 12.00
33 Tyrone Taylor 2.00 5.00
34 Jake Fraley 2.50 6.00
35 Lewis Thorpe 2.00 5.00
36 Yonathan Daza 2.50 6.00
37 Josh Rojas 2.00 5.00
38 Sheldon Neuse 2.50 6.00
39 Matt Thaiss 2.50 6.00
40 Luis Robert 12.00 30.00

2020 Panini National Treasures Rookie Material Signatures Gold

*GOLD/49: .5X TO 1.2X p/r 99
RANDOM INSERTS IN PACKS
STATED PRINT RUN 49 SER.#'d SETS
EXCHANGE DEADLINE 5/4/22
158 Yu Chang 25.00 60.00
212 Luis Robert 400.00 800.00

2020 Panini National Treasures Rookie Material Signatures Midnight

158 Yu Chang/25 30.00 80.00
159 Trent Grisham/25 40.00 100.00
165 Justin Dunn/25 20.00 50.00

2020 Panini National Treasures Rookie Material Signatures Stars and Stripes

*STARS STRIPES/25: .6X TO 1.5X p/r 99
RANDOM INSERTS IN PACKS
PRINT RUNS B/WN 10-25 COPIES PER
NO PRICING ON QTY 15 OR LESS
EXCHANGE DEADLINE 5/4/22
158 Yu Chang/25 30.00 80.00
159 Trent Grisham/25 40.00 100.00
165 Justin Dunn/25 20.00 50.00

2020 Panini National Treasures Rookie Signature Jumbo Material Booklets

RANDOM INSERTS IN PACKS
STATED PRINT RUN 99 SER.#'d SETS
EXCHANGE DEADLINE 5/4/22
1 Domingo Leyba 4.00 10.00
2 Josh Rojas 3.00 8.00
3 Nico Hoerner 12.00 30.00
4 Danny Mendick 4.00 10.00
5 Aristides Aquino 10.00 25.00
6 Bobby Bradley 3.00 8.00
7 Yu Chang 10.00 25.00
8 Sam Hilliard 5.00 12.00
9 Jake Rogers 3.00 8.00
10 Willi Castro 5.00 12.00
11 Abraham Toro 4.00 10.00
12 Matt Thaiss 4.00 10.00
13 Edwin Rios 8.00 20.00
14 Isan Diaz 5.00 12.00
15 Jordan Yamamoto 3.00 8.00
16 Tyrone Taylor 3.00 8.00
17 Sheldon Neuse 4.00 10.00
18 Adrian Morejon 3.00 8.00
19 Mauricio Dubon 4.00 10.00
20 Donnie Walton 8.00 20.00
21 Jake Fraley 4.00 10.00
22 Randy Arozarena 60.00 150.00
23 Brendan McKay 5.00 12.00
24 Nick Solak 8.00 20.00

2020 Panini National Treasures Rookie Signatures

PRINT RUNS B/WN 5-99 COPIES PER
NO PRICING ON QTY 15 OR LESS
EXCHANGE DEADLINE 5/4/22
1 Anthony Kay/99 3.00 8.00
2 Aristides Aquino/99 10.00 25.00
3 Bo Bichette/99 40.00 100.00
4 Brendan McKay/25 8.00 20.00
5 Bobby Bradley/99 3.00 8.00
6 Brock Burke/99 3.00 8.00
7 Dustin May/25 15.00 40.00
8 Gavin Lux/99 15.00 40.00
9 Dylan Cease/99 6.00 15.00
11 Jesus Luzardo/99 10.00 25.00
12 A.J. Puk/99 5.00 12.00
13 Kyle Lewis/99 50.00 120.00
14 Brusdar Graterol/99 5.00 12.00
15 Mauricio Dubon/99 4.00 10.00
16 Nick Solak/99 8.00 20.00
17 Nico Hoerner/99 12.00 30.00
18 Randy Arozarena/99 60.00 150.00
19 Sam Hilliard/99 5.00 12.00
21 Tony Gonsolin/99 12.00 30.00
22 Trent Grisham/99 12.00 30.00
23 Zac Gallen/99 8.00 20.00
24 Zack Collins/25 6.00 15.00

2020 Panini National Treasures Rookie Silhouette Signatures

PRINT RUNS B/WN 49-99 COPIES PER
EXCHANGE DEADLINE 5/4/22
*HOLO GOLD/25: .6X TO 1.5X p/r 99
*HOLO GOLD/25: .5X TO 1.2X p/r 49
1 Bo Bichette/99 40.00 100.00
2 Yordan Alvarez/99 40.00 100.00
3 Aristides Aquino/49 12.00 30.00
4 Nico Hoerner/49 15.00 40.00
6 Gavin Lux/49 20.00 50.00
7 Brock Burke/99 3.00 8.00
8 Dylan Cease/49 8.00 20.00
9 Zac Gallen/49 10.00 25.00
12 Kyle Lewis/49 60.00 150.00
15 Bobby Bradley/99 3.00 8.00
16 Adbert Alzolay/99 4.00 10.00
17 Brusdar Graterol/99 5.00 12.00
19 Nick Solak/99 8.00 20.00
20 Tres Barrera/99 6.00 15.00
22 Jake Fraley/99 4.00 10.00
23 Logan Webb/99 5.00 12.00
24 Jake Rogers/99 3.00 8.00

2020 Panini National Treasures Signature Names

RANDOM INSERTS IN PACKS
STATED PRINT RUN 99 SER.#'d SETS
EXCHANGE DEADLINE 5/4/22

1 Aristides Aquino 10.00 25.00
2 Brendan McKay 5.00 12.00
3 Adbert Alzolay 4.00 10.00
4 Gavin Lux 15.00 40.00
5 Abraham Toro 4.00 10.00
7 Patrick Sandoval 5.00 12.00
8 Sam Hilliard 5.00 12.00
9 Bobby Bradley 3.00 8.00
10 Zack Collins 4.00 10.00
11 Randy Arozarena 60.00 150.00
12 Willi Castro 5.00 12.00
13 Yordan Alvarez 40.00 100.00
14 Nick Solak 8.00 20.00
16 Jaylin Davis 5.00 12.00
17 Bo Bichette 40.00 100.00
18 Bryan Abreu 3.00 8.00
19 Jake Fraley 4.00 10.00
20 Lewis Thorpe 3.00 8.00
21 Yonathan Daza 4.00 10.00
22 Deivy Grullon 3.00 8.00
23 Donnie Walton 8.00 20.00
24 T.J. Zeuch 3.00 8.00
25 Tres Barrera 6.00 15.00

2020 Panini National Treasures Signature Names Gold

*GOLD/49: .5X TO 1.2X BASIC
RANDOM INSERTS IN PACKS
STATED PRINT RUN 49 SER.#'d SETS
EXCHANGE DEADLINE 5/4/22
6 Dustin May 12.00 30.00

2020 Panini National Treasures Signature Names Holo Gold

*HOLO GOLD/25: .6X TO 1.5X BASIC
RANDOM INSERTS IN PACKS
STATED PRINT RUN 25 SER.#'d SETS
EXCHANGE DEADLINE 5/4/22
6 Dustin May 15.00 40.00

2020 Panini National Treasures Signature Numbers

RANDOM INSERTS IN PACKS
PRINT RUNS B/WN 75-99 COPIES PER
EXCHANGE DEADLINE 5/4/22
*GOLD/49: .5X TO 1.2X BASIC
*HOLO GOLD/25: .6X TO 1.5X BASIC
1 Edwin Rios/99 8.00 20.00
2 Danny Mendick/99 4.00 10.00
4 Tyrone Taylor/99 3.00 8.00
5 Jake Rogers/99 3.00 8.00
6 Mauricio Dubon/99 4.00 10.00
7 A.J. Puk/99 5.00 12.00
8 Anthony Kay/99 3.00 8.00
9 Brusdar Graterol/99 5.00 12.00
10 Jordan Yamamoto /99 3.00 8.00
11 Kyle Lewis/99 50.00 120.00
12 Zac Gallen/99 8.00 20.00
13 Travis Demeritte/99 5.00 12.00
14 Sheldon Neuse/99 4.00 10.00
15 Matt Thaiss/75 4.00 10.00

2020 Panini National Treasures Signatures

RANDOM INSERTS IN PACKS
PRINT RUNS B/WN 7-99 COPIES PER
NO PRICING ON QTY 15 OR LESS
EXCHANGE DEADLINE 5/4/22
*HOLO GOLD/25: .6X TO 1.5X p/r 99
*HOLO GOLD/25: .5X TO 1.2X p/r 35-50
1 Ryan Mountcastle/25 20.00 50.00
2 Aaron Sanchez/25 6.00 15.00
3 Adam Duvall/50 12.00 30.00
4 Aledmys Diaz/99 3.00 8.00
5 Amir Garrett/99 3.00 8.00
6 Billy Williams/25 15.00 40.00
7 Brandon Lowe/99 4.00 10.00
9 Carlos Martinez/50 5.00 12.00
10 Craig Kimbrel/49 5.00 12.00
11 Daniel Norris/99 3.00 8.00
12 Daniel Robertson/99 3.00 8.00
13 Dustin Pedroia/25 12.00 30.00
14 Fergie Jenkins/25 10.00 25.00
15 Garrett Hampson/99 3.00 8.00
16 Harold Baines/25 10.00 25.00
17 Jake Cave/99 4.00 10.00
18 Jim Bunning/25 10.00 25.00
20 Kyle Tucker/50 6.00 15.00
21 Matt Davidson/99 4.00 10.00
22 Michael Chavis/99 4.00 10.00
25 Nick Senzel/25 8.00 20.00
26 Paul Goldschmidt/25 8.00 20.00
27 Roberto Alomar/25 20.00 50.00
28 Ronald Guzman/35 4.00 10.00
29 Stephen Strasburg/25 25.00 60.00
30 Tony La Russa/25 6.00 15.00
31 Touki Toussaint/99 4.00 10.00
34 Tyler Glasnow/25 8.00 20.00
35 Whit Merrifield/25 8.00 20.00
36 Wil Myers/25 6.00 15.00
37 Yasmany Tomas/25 5.00 12.00
38 Yusei Kikuchi/25
39 Zach Davies/99 3.00 8.00
40 Amed Rosario/50 5.00 12.00

2020 Panini National Treasures Six Pack Material Signatures Booklets

RANDOM INSERTS IN PACKS
STATED PRINT RUN 99 SER.#'d SETS
EXCHANGE DEADLINE 5/4/22
1 Yordan Alvarez 40.00 100.00
2 Bo Bichette 40.00 100.00
3 Dylan Cease 6.00 15.00
4 Gavin Lux 15.00 40.00
5 Brendan McKay 5.00 12.00
6 Aristides Aquino 10.00 25.00

2020 Panini National Treasures Social Signatures

RANDOM INSERTS IN PACKS 8.00 20.00
PRINT RUNS B/WN 25-99 COPIES PER
EXCHANGE DEADLINE 5/4/22
1 Adbert Alzolay 4.00 10.00
2 Bobby Bradley 3.00 8.00
3 Jesus Luzardo 10.00 25.00
4 Kyle Lewis 50.00 120.00
5 Tony Gonsolin 12.00 30.00
6 Bryan Abreu 3.00 8.00
7 Edwin Rios 8.00 20.00
8 Jake Fraley 4.00 10.00
9 Jake Rogers 5.00 12.00
10 Jaylin Davis 5.00 12.00
11 Justin Dunn 4.00 10.00
12 Rico Garcia 5.00 12.00
13 Travis Demeritte 5.00 12.00
14 Tyrone Taylor 3.00 8.00
15 Willi Castro 5.00 12.00

2020 Panini National Treasures Teammates Autograph Booklets

RANDOM INSERTS IN PACKS
PRINT RUNS B/WN 5-25 COPIES PER
NO PRICING ON QTY 15 OR LESS
EXCHANGE DEADLINE 5/4/22
3 AC/BB/FL/JB/JR/LA/TN/YC/25 40.00 100.00
6 AM/AM/CP/FTJ/FM/IK/JN/TG/25 100.00 250.00
8 AK/BB/CB/JW/RM/SY/TJZ/VGJ/25 125.00 300.00

2020 Panini National Treasures The Future Autographs

RANDOM INSERTS IN PACKS
STATED PRINT RUN 25 SER.#'d SETS
EXCHANGE DEADLINE 5/4/22
1 Jasson Dominguez 400.00 800.00
2 Royce Lewis 15.00 40.00
3 Bo Bichette 75.00 200.00
5 Eloy Jimenez 15.00 40.00
6 Wander Franco 200.00 500.00
7 Vladimir Guerrero Jr. 50.00 120.00
8 Brendan McKay 8.00 20.00
9 Aristides Aquino 15.00 40.00
10 Luis Robert 200.00 500.00
11 Yordan Alvarez 30.00 80.00
12 Alex Kirilloff 20.00 50.00
13 Alec Bohm 40.00 100.00
14 Joey Bart 25.00 60.00
15 Fernando Tatis Jr. 150.00 400.00
16 Keston Hiura 15.00 40.00
17 Jo Adell 75.00 200.00
18 Pete Alonso 40.00 100.00
19 Julio Rodriguez 60.00 150.00
20 Dylan Carlson 40.00 100.00

2020 Panini National Treasures Treasured Material Signatures

RANDOM INSERTS IN PACKS
PRINT RUNS B/WN 10-99 COPIES PER
NO PRICING ON QTY 16 OR LESS
EXCHANGE DEADLINE 5/4/22
1 David Wright/52 15.00 40.00
5 Jose Canseco/50 15.00 40.00
6 Don Mattingly/50 30.00 80.00
7 Kenny Lofton/22 5.00 12.00
8 Keith Hernandez/99 12.00 30.00
9 Ketel Marte/49 5.00 12.00
11 Austin Meadows/52 6.00 15.00
13 Sammy Sosa/21 8.00 20.00
14 Ryan Zimmerman/25 12.00 30.00
15 Max Kepler/99 4.00 10.00
18 Ronald Acuna Jr./52 60.00 150.00
20 Alex Bregman/99 15.00 40.00
24 Jose Ramirez/99 4.00 10.00
25 Walker Buehler/99 20.00 50.00
27 Fernando Tatis Jr./49 100.00 250.00
29 Pete Alonso/49 25.00 60.00
30 Adrian Beltre/26 15.00 40.00
32 Pete Rose/26 40.00 100.00
33 Luis Severino/99 4.00 10.00
34 Anthony Rizzo/26 25.00 60.00
35 Keston Hiura/49 10.00 25.00
37 Juan Soto/76 EXCH 50.00 120.00
38 Austin Riley/49 8.00 20.00
39 Jasson Dominguez/25 EXCH 200.00 500.00
41 Nolan Ryan/25 50.00 120.00
42 Juan Marichal/25 12.00 30.00
43 Elroy Face/99 8.00 20.00
45 Taylor Trammell/99 8.00 20.00
46 Matt Manning/49 5.00 12.00

2020 Panini National Treasures Treasured Material Signatures Gold

*GOLD/49: .5X TO 1.2X p/r 99
*GOLD/25: .5X TO 1.2X p/r 49-76
RANDOM INSERTS IN PACKS
PRINT RUNS B/WN 10-49 COPIES PER
NO PRICING ON QTY 15 OR LESS
EXCHANGE DEADLINE 5/4/22
27 Fernando Tatis Jr./25 150.00 400.00

2020 Panini National Treasures Treasured Material Signatures Holo Gold

*HOLO GOLD/25: .6X TO 1.5X p/r 99
RANDOM INSERTS IN PACKS
PRINT RUNS B/WN 5-25 COPIES PER
NO PRICING ON QTY 15 OR LESS
EXCHANGE DEADLINE 5/4/22
37 Juan Soto/25 EXCH 125.00 300.00

2020 Panini National Treasures Triple Legend Duos Booklets

RANDOM INSERTS IN PACKS
2 CRJ/Gehrig/Cobb/25 100.00 250.00
3 Vaughan/Clemente/Stargell/20 75.00 200.00
4 Robinson/Durocher/Reese/49 60.00 150.00
5 Mize/Hornsby/Musial/25 50.00 120.00
6 Bell/Suttles/Campanella/49 50.00 120.00
7 Martin/Mantle/Ford/49 60.00 150.00
8 McGwire/Maris/Sosa/99 40.00 100.00
9 Ichiro/Rose/Cobb/25 100.00 250.00
10 Ryan/Johnson/Clemens/99 30.00 80.00

2020 Panini National Treasures Triple Legend Trios Material Booklets

RANDOM INSERTS IN PACKS
NO PRICING ON QTY 15 OR LESS
1 Martin/Torre/Huggins/49 30.00 80.00
2 Drysdale/Hodgers/Reese/49 20.00 50.00
3 Foxx/Ott/P.Waner/49 40.00 100.00
4 Slaughter/Mize/Musial/25 50.00 120.00
5 Pennock/Gehrig/Lazzeri/25 100.00 250.00
7 Furrillo/Robinson/Campanella/25 75.00 200.00
8 Sewell/Paige/Speaker/49 50.00 120.00
9 Bell/Greenberg/Kuenn/49 40.00 100.00
10 Howard/Hooper/Alston/49 30.00 80.00

2020 Panini National Treasures Triple Signatures

RANDOM INSERTS IN PACKS
PRINT RUNS B/WN 5-99 COPIES PER
NO PRICING ON QTY 15 OR LESS
EXCHANGE DEADLINE 5/4/22
*HOLO GOLD/25: .6X TO 1.5X p/r 75-99
*HOLO GOLD/25: .5X TO 1.2X p/r 50
2 King/Bolanos/Zeuch/99 8.00 20.00
3 Murphy/Barrera/Collins/99 10.00 25.00
5 Bradley/McKay/Thaiss/75 12.00 30.00
6 Aquino/Lewis/Alvarez/50 75.00 200.00
7 Leyba/Lux/Solak/75 20.00 50.00
8 Rutschman/Vaughn/Witt Jr/50 100.00 250.00
9 Kirilloff/Dominguez/Franco/25 EXCH 150.00 400.00

2015 Panini National Treasures Collegiate Multisport

4 Alex Gordon 2.50 6.00
10 Anthony Rendon 2.00 5.00
11 Barry Bonds 5.00 12.00
18 Brandon Belt 2.50 6.00
19 Brock Holt 2.00 5.00
20 Buster Posey 5.00 12.00
25 Chase Utley 3.00 8.00
28 Craig Biggio 2.50 6.00
29 Dallas Keuchel 3.00 8.00
38 Dustin Ackley 2.00 5.00
39 Dustin Pedroia 3.00 8.00
44 Frank Howard 2.00 5.00
46 Frank Thomas 3.00 8.00
47 Frank Thomas 3.00 8.00
48 George Springer 3.00 8.00
49 Gerrit Cole 2.50 6.00
65 Josh Donaldson 2.50 6.00
67 Justin Verlander 2.50 6.00
72 Kolten Wong 2.50 6.00
76 Mark McGwire 6.00 15.00
77 Matt Harvey 2.50 6.00
78 Max Scherzer 3.00 8.00
82 Paul Goldschmidt 3.00 8.00
84 Randy Johnson 3.00 8.00
85 Reggie Jackson 2.50 6.00
87 Roger Clemens 4.00 10.00
91 Ryan Braun 2.50 6.00
92 Sonny Gray 2.00 5.00
94 Stephen Strasburg 5.00 12.00
97 Tony Gwynn 3.00 8.00
98 Tony Gwynn 3.00 8.00
100 Will Clark 2.50 6.00
123 Miller Huggins 3.00 8.00
124 George Sisler 2.50 6.00
125 Sam Crawford 2.00 5.00
126 Jackie Robinson 3.00 8.00
127 Jackie Robinson 3.00 8.00
146 Rafael Palmeiro 3.00 8.00
149 Red Badgro 3.00 8.00
151 Chi Chi Gonzalez 3.00 8.00
153 Anthony Ranaudo 2.00 5.00
157 Brandon Finnegan 2.00 5.00
159 Buck Farmer 2.00 5.00
164 Carlos Rodon 2.50 6.00
165 Chris Heston 2.50 6.00
169 Devon Travis 2.00 5.00
178 Kevin Plawecki 3.00 8.00
179 Kris Bryant 10.00 25.00
181 Marco Gonzales 2.50 6.00
185 Matt Barnes 2.00 5.00
189 Preston Tucker 3.00 8.00
196 Taylor Jungmann 2.00 5.00
202 Chi Chi Gonzalez AU 5.00 12.00
204 Andy Wilkins AU 3.00 8.00
206 Anthony Ranaudo AU 3.00 8.00
212 Brandon Finnegan AU 3.00 8.00
214 Buck Farmer AU 3.00 8.00
221 Carlos Rodon AU 4.00 10.00
222 Chris Heston AU 4.00 10.00
223 Christian Walker AU 3.00 8.00
225 Corey Knebel AU 3.00 8.00
233 Devon Travis AU 3.00 8.00
246 Jake Lamb AU 5.00 12.00
248 James McCann AU 3.00 8.00
258 Kendall Graveman AU 3.00 8.00
262 Kevin Plawecki AU 5.00 12.00
263 Kris Bryant AU 100.00 200.00
267 Marco Gonzales AU 4.00 10.00
272 Mark Canha AU 3.00 8.00
273 Matt Barnes AU 3.00 8.00
274 Matt Clark AU 3.00 8.00
275 Matt Szczur AU 3.00 8.00
277 Mikie Mahtook AU 3.00 8.00
280 Nick Ahmed AU 5.00 12.00
284 Preston Tucker AU 5.00 12.00
288 Sean Gilmartin AU 5.00 12.00
293 Taylor Jungmann AU 5.00 12.00
298 Tyler Kroft AU 5.00 12.00
381 Alex Bregman JSY AU 40.00 80.00
382 Thomas Eshelman JSY AU 5.00 12.00
383 Alex Young JSY AU 5.00 12.00
384 Andrew Benintendi JSY AU 50.00 100.00
385 Andrew Suarez JSY AU 5.00 12.00
386 Brett Lilek JSY AU 5.00 12.00
387 Blake Trahan JSY AU 5.00 12.00
388 Brandon Koch JSY AU 5.00 12.00
389 Brandon Lowe JSY AU 8.00 20.00
390 Carson Fulmer JSY AU 20.00 40.00
391 Casey Hughston JSY AU 5.00 12.00
393 Christin Stewart JSY AU 8.00 20.00
394 Kevin Kramer JSY AU 5.00 12.00
395 Dansby Swanson JSY AU 25.00 60.00
397 Dillon Tate JSY AU 6.00 15.00
398 DJ Stewart JSY AU 5.00 12.00
399 Tyler Alexander JSY AU 5.00 12.00
400 Harrison Bader JSY AU 12.00 30.00
401 Ian Happ JSY AU 10.00 25.00
404 A.J. Minter JSY AU 5.00 12.00
405 Tyler Krieger JSY AU 5.00 12.00
406 Kevin Newman JSY AU 5.00 12.00
407 Philip Pfeifer JSY AU 5.00 12.00
408 Michael Matuella JSY AU 6.00 15.00
409 Austin Rei JSY AU 6.00 15.00
410 Mikey White JSY AU 6.00 15.00
411 Nathan Kirby JSY AU 6.00 15.00
412 Phil Bickford JSY AU 8.00 20.00
413 Richie Martin JSY AU 5.00 12.00
414 Riley Ferrell JSY AU 8.00 20.00
416 Scott Kingery JSY AU 8.00 20.00
417 Skye Bolt JSY AU 8.00 20.00
418 Taylor Ward JSY AU 8.00 20.00
419 Drew Smith JSY AU 5.00 12.00
420 Walker Buehler JSY AU 8.00 20.00

2015 Panini National Treasures Collegiate Multisport Colossal Materials Signatures Prime

*PRIME/25: .8X TO 2X BASIC JSY AU/99
*PRIME/25: 1X TO 2.5X BASIC JSY AU/99
384 Andrew Benintendi/25 100.00 200.00

2015 Panini National Treasures Collegiate Multisport Materials

4 Buster Posey/99 4.00 10.00
14 Josh Donaldson/99 2.50 6.00
38 Andrew Cashner/99 3.00 8.00
39 Andy Wilkins/99
54 Christian Walker/99
61 Deven Marrero/99
67 Gordon Beckham/99
84 Luke Weaver/99
87 Michael Conforto/99

2015 Panini National Treasures Collegiate Multisport Materials Signatures

8 Josh Donaldson/99 6.00 15.00
32 Andy Wilkins/99 5.00 12.00
42 Christian Walker/99 5.00 12.00
49 Deven Marrero/99 5.00 12.00
59 Jason Kipnis/49 10.00 25.00
71 Luke Weaver/99
77 Michael Conforto/99 8.00 20.00
83 Peter O'Brien/99 5.00 12.00
85 Robert Refsnyder/99 5.00 12.00
97 Tyler Naquin/99

2015 Panini National Treasures Collegiate Multisport Materials Signatures Silver

*SILVER/25: .6X TO 1.5X BASIC JSY AU/99
*SILVER/25: .5X TO 1.2X BASIC JSY AU/49

2015 Panini National Treasures Collegiate Multisport Signatures

5 Anthony Rendon 10.00 25.00
14 Craig Biggio 8.00 20.00
22 Dustin Ackley
23 Dustin Pedroia 10.00 25.00
27 Frank Howard 6.00 15.00
29 Frank Thomas 15.00 40.00
31 Gerrit Cole 6.00 15.00
47 Max Scherzer 15.00 40.00
52 Reggie Jackson 20.00 50.00
53 Roger Clemens
54 Ryan Braun 10.00 25.00
55 Sonny Gray 10.00 25.00
57 Stephen Strasburg 15.00 40.00
62 Will Clark 10.00 25.00
78 Barry Larkin 15.00 40.00
81 Dick Groat
82 Dave Winfield 10.00 25.00
85 Ozzie Smith 6.00 15.00
86 Paul Molitor 10.00 25.00
87 Rafael Palmeiro

2015 Panini National Treasures Collegiate Multisport Team Combo Materials

1 C.Hughston/M.White/99 4.00 10.00
4 K.Newman/S.Kingery/99 4.00 10.00
6 P.Bickford/T.Eshelman/99 4.00 10.00
8 D.Smith/B.Koch 4.00 10.00
10 R.Martin/H.Bader/99 4.00 10.00
17 A.Bregman/A.Stevenson/99 4.00 10.00
19 A.Suarez/D.Thompson/99 4.00 10.00
26 T.Gwynn/M.Faulk/99 4.00 10.00
31 C.Stewart/J.Richardson/99 4.00 10.00
36 K.Kramer/K.Looney/99 4.00 10.00
39 B.Bishop/A.Rei/99 4.00 10.00

2015 Panini National Treasures Collegiate Multisport Team Quad Materials

5 Jones/Bader/Frazier II/Martin/99 4.00 10.00
7 Judge/Adams/Carr/Ward/99 4.00 10.00
11 Bregman/Martin/Mickey/Stevenson/99 4.00 10.00
15 Conforto/Mannion/Cooks/Browner/99 4.00 10.00
17 Davis/Walker/Shaw/Clowney/99 4.00 10.00
18 Young/Ferrell/Alexander/Cashner/99 4.00 10.00
19 Evans/Minter/Manziel/Naquin/99 4.00 10.00
21 Kramer/Hundley/Looney/Powell/99 4.00 10.00
22 Fulmer/Swanson/Wiseman/Buehler/99 4.00 10.00
23 Bregman/Fulmer/Benintendi/Swanson/99 4.00
10.00

2015 Panini National Treasures Collegiate Multisport Team Trios Materials

2 Marrero/Strong/Lilek/99 4.00 10.00
4 Wilkins/Benintendi/Portis/49 5.00 12.00
5 Donaldson/Coates/Mason/99 4.00 10.00
7 Posey/Weaver/Stewart/99 4.00 10.00
11 Suarez/Thompson/O'Brien/99 4.00 10.00
16 Alexander/Young/Ferrell/99 4.00 10.00
18 Hundley/Looney/Kramer/99 4.00 10.00
22 Buehler/Fulmer/Swanson/99 4.00 10.00
23 Buehler/Fulmer/Beede/99 4.00 10.00
24 Anderson/Kirby/McCarthy/99 4.00 10.00
25 Rei/Bishop/Upshaw/99 4.00 10.00
29 Kaminsky/Mariota/Benintendi/99 4.00 10.00
30 Lilek/Kipnis/Marrero/99 4.00 10.00
31 Newman/Refsnyder/Kingery/99 4.00 10.00
32 Bregman/Stevenson/Nola/99 4.00 10.00
33 Bregman/Hill/Beckham Jr./99 4.00 10.00

2019 Panini Obsidian

RANDOM INSERTS IN PACKS
*PURPLE: 1X TO 2.5X
*ORANGE: 1.2X TO 3X
*RED: 2X TO 5X
1 Yadier Molina .50 1.25
2 Nick Senzel RC .75 2.00
3 Danny Jansen RC .25 .60
4 Blake Snell .30 .75
5 Bryce Harper .60 1.50
6 Aaron Nola .30 .75
7 Vladimir Guerrero Jr. RC 1.50 4.00
8 Ichiro .50 1.25
9 Alex Bregman .40 1.00
10 Cody Bellinger .75 2.00
11 Christian Yelich .50 1.25
12 Jeff McNeil RC .60 1.50
13 Oscar Mercado RC .60 1.50
14 Aaron Judge 1.00 2.50
15 Mike Trout 2.00 5.00
16 Yusei Kikuchi RC .40 1.00
17 Kyle Wright RC .40 1.00
18 Khris Davis .40 1.00
19 Ronald Acuna Jr. 2.00 5.00
20 Juan Soto 1.25 3.00
21 J.D. Martinez .40 1.00
22 Manny Machado .40 1.00
23 Keston Hiura RC .75 2.00
24 Whit Merrifield .40 1.00
25 Jose Ramirez .30 .75
26 Carter Kieboom RC .40 1.00
27 Jon Duplantier RC .25 .60
28 Corbin Burnes RC 2.00 5.00
29 Paul Goldschmidt .40 1.00
30 Gleyber Torres .75 2.00
31 Joey Votto .40 1.00
32 Kris Bryant .50 1.25
33 Javier Baez .50 1.25
34 Brad Keller RC .25 .60
35 Fernando Tatis Jr. RC 4.00 10.00
36 Jose Altuve .30 .75
37 Andrew Benintendi .40 1.00
38 Max Scherzer .40 1.00
39 Brandon Lowe RC .40 1.00
40 Ryan O'Hearn RC .25 .60
41 Justin Verlander .40 1.00
42 Trevor Story .40 1.00
43 Anthony Rizzo .50 1.25
44 Christin Stewart RC .30 .75
45 Pete Alonso RC 2.00 5.00
46 Cavan Biggio RC 1.25 3.00
47 Shohei Ohtani .60 1.50
48 Eloy Jimenez RC 1.00 2.50
49 Rhys Hoskins .50 1.25
50 Francisco Lindor .40 1.00
51 Mookie Betts .75 2.00
52 Jake Bauers RC .40 1.00
53 Freddie Freeman .50 1.25
54 Luis Urias RC .40 1.00
55 Jacob deGrom .75 2.00
56 Nolan Arenado .60 1.50
57 Kyle Tucker RC .60 1.50
58 Justus Sheffield RC .40 1.00
59 Chris Paddack RC .50 1.25
60 Peter Lambert RC .40 1.00

2019 Panini Obsidian Autographs

RANDOM INSERTS IN PACKS
EXCHANGE DEADLINE 2/21/2021
*PURPLE/75-99: .5X TO 1.2X
*PURPLE/35-50: .6X TO 1.5X
*PURPLE/25: .75X TO 2X
*ORANGE/50: .6X TO 1.5X
*ORANGE/25: .75X TO 2X
*RED/25: .75X TO 2X
1 Jonathan Loaisiga 3.00 8.00
3 Yusei Kikuchi 8.00 20.00
4 Chris Paddack 8.00 20.00
5 Luis Urias 4.00 10.00
6 Kyle Wright 4.00 10.00
7 Jake Bauers 4.00 10.00
8 Jon Duplantier 2.50 6.00
10 Cedric Mullins 8.00 20.00
11 Kyle Tucker 6.00 15.00
13 Pete Alonso 40.00 100.00
14 Jeff McNeil 6.00 15.00
15 Yordan Alvarez 40.00 100.00
16 Justus Sheffield 4.00 10.00
17 Danny Jansen 2.50 6.00
18 Eloy Jimenez 10.00 25.00
19 Vladimir Guerrero Jr. 50.00 120.00
20 Fernando Tatis Jr. 75.00 200.00
21 Corbin Burnes 8.00 20.00
22 Nathaniel Lowe 12.00 30.00
23 Michael Chavis 10.00 25.00
24 Keston Hiura 12.00 30.00
25 Ramon Laureano 6.00 15.00
26 Steven Duggar 3.00 8.00
28 Brandon Lowe 10.00 25.00
29 Rowdy Tellez 4.00 10.00
30 Kevin Newman 4.00 10.00
31 Cole Tucker 4.00 10.00
32 Bryan Reynolds 6.00 15.00
33 David Fletcher 8.00 20.00
34 Bryse Wilson 3.00 8.00
35 Shaun Anderson 2.50 6.00
36 Jake Cave 3.00 8.00
37 Carter Kieboom 4.00 10.00
38 Kevin Kramer 3.00 8.00
39 Cal Quantrill 2.50 6.00
40 Ty France 8.00 20.00

2020 Panini Obsidian

RANDOM INSERTS IN PACKS
1 Yordan Alvarez RC 4.00 10.00
2 Jake Rogers RC .40 1.00
3 Gavin Lux RC 2.00 5.00
4 Brendan McKay RC .60 1.50
5 Mauricio Dubon RC .50 1.25
6 Tony Gonsolin RC 1.50 4.00
7 Bryce Harper .60 1.50
8 Randy Arozarena RC 8.00 20.00
9 Sam Hilliard RC .60 1.50
10 Sean Murphy RC .60 1.50
11 Bryan Abreu RC .40 1.00
12 Nick Solak RC 1.50 4.00
13 Kyle Lewis RC 3.00 8.00
14 Jesus Luzardo RC .75 2.00
15 Justin Dunn RC .50 1.25
16 Travis Demeritte RC .60 1.50
17 Bo Bichette RC 3.00 8.00
18 Zack Collins RC .50 1.25
19 Isan Diaz RC .60 1.50
20 Kwang-Hyun Kim RC .75 2.00
21 Yoshitomo Tsutsugo RC 1.00 2.50
22 Luis Robert RC 6.00 15.00
23 Shogo Akiyama RC .60 1.50
24 Shun Yamaguchi RC .50 1.25
25 Jordan Yamamoto RC .40 1.00
26 Brusdar Graterol RC .60 1.50
27 A.J. Puk RC .60 1.50
28 Nico Hoerner RC 1.50 4.00
29 Bobby Bradley RC .40 1.00
30 Dustin May RC 1.25 3.00
31 Aristides Aquino RC 1.00 2.50
32 Dylan Cease RC .60 1.50
33 Zac Gallen RC 1.00 2.50
34 Sheldon Neuse RC .50 1.25
35 Josh Bell .30 .75
36 Eloy Jimenez .75 2.00
37 Francisco Lindor .40 1.00
38 Juan Soto 1.25 3.00
39 Nolan Arenado .60 1.50
40 Shohei Ohtani .60 1.50
41 Ronald Acuna Jr. 1.50 4.00
42 Rafael Devers .50 1.25
43 Aaron Judge 1.00 2.50
44 Vladimir Guerrero Jr. .60 1.50
45 Blake Snell .30 .75
46 Kris Bryant .50 1.25
47 Gleyber Torres .75 2.00
48 Mookie Betts .75 2.00
49 Mike Trout 2.00 5.00
50 Cody Bellinger .75 2.00
51 Alex Bregman .40 1.00
52 Trevor Story .40 1.00
53 Freddie Freeman .50 1.25
54 Rhys Hoskins .50 1.25
55 Pete Alonso 1.00 2.50
56 Javier Baez .50 1.25
57 Fernando Tatis Jr. 2.00 5.00
58 Trea Turner .30 .75
59 Clayton Kershaw .60 1.50
60 Starling Marte .30 .75

2020 Panini Obsidian Electric Etch Orange

*ORANGE VET: 1.5X TO 4X BASIC
*ORANGE RC: 1X TO 2.5X BASIC RC
RANDOM INSERTS IN PACKS
STATED PRINT RUN 50 SER.#'d SETS
8 Randy Arozarena 40.00 100.00
17 Bo Bichette 10.00 25.00
22 Luis Robert 30.00 80.00

2020 Panini Obsidian Electric Etch Purple

*PURPLE VET: 1X TO 2.5X BASIC
*PURPLE RC: .6X TO 1.5X BASIC RC
RANDOM INSERTS IN PACKS
STATED PRINT RUN 99 SER.#'d SETS
8 Randy Arozarena 25.00 60.00
22 Luis Robert 20.00 50.00

2020 Panini Obsidian Electric Etch Red

*RED VET: 2.5X TO 6X BASIC
*RED RC: 1.5X TO 4X BASIC RC
RANDOM INSERTS IN PACKS
STATED PRINT RUN 25 SER.#'d SETS
8 Randy Arozarena 60.00 150.00
17 Bo Bichette 15.00 40.00
22 Luis Robert 50.00 120.00

2020 Panini Obsidian Autographs

RANDOM INSERTS IN PACKS
EXCHANGE DEADLINE 3/18/2022
1 Adbert Alzolay 3.00 8.00
2 Anthony Kay 2.50 6.00
3 Brendan McKay 4.00 10.00
4 Deivy Grullon 2.50 6.00
5 Edwin Rios 6.00 15.00
6 Gavin Lux 12.00 30.00
7 Isan Diaz 4.00 10.00
8 Jaylin Davis 4.00 10.00
10 Kyle Lewis 25.00 60.00
11 Matt Thaiss 3.00 8.00
12 Nick Solak 5.00 12.00
13 Randy Arozarena 40.00 100.00
14 Sean Murphy 4.00 10.00
15 Shogo Akiyama 4.00 10.00
16 T.J. Zeuch 2.50 6.00
17 Travis Demeritte 4.00 10.00
19 Yordan Alvarez 25.00 60.00
20 Yu Chang 4.00 10.00
21 Zac Gallen 6.00 15.00
22 Yoshitomo Tsutsugo 6.00 15.00
23 Willi Castro 4.00 10.00
25 Tony Gonsolin 10.00 25.00
26 Shun Yamaguchi 3.00 8.00
27 Sheldon Neuse 3.00 8.00
30 Michael King 4.00 10.00
31 Luis Robert EXCH 60.00 150.00
32 Kwang-Hyun Kim 12.00 30.00
33 Jonathan Hernandez 2.50 6.00
34 Jake Rogers 2.50 6.00
35 Hunter Greene 4.00 10.00
36 Evan White 6.00 15.00
37 Dylan Carlson 10.00 25.00
39 Aristides Aquino 6.00 15.00
40 Andres Munoz 4.00 10.00

2020 Panini Obsidian Autographs Electric Etch Blue Crystals

RANDOM INSERTS IN PACKS
PRINT RUNS B/WN 21-25 COPIES PER
EXCHANGE DEADLINE 3/18/2022
13 Randy Arozarena/25 125.00 300.00

2020 Panini Obsidian Autographs Electric Etch Purple

*BLUE/75: .5X TO 1.2X
*BLUE/49: .6X TO 1.5X
*BLUE/25: .8X TO 2X
RANDOM INSERTS IN PACKS
PRINT RUNS B/WN 25-75 COPIES PER
EXCHANGE DEADLINE 3/18/2022
13 Randy Arozarena/75 75.00 200.00

2020 Panini Origins Autographs Gold Ink

*GOLD INK/25: .5X TO 1.2X p/r 49
RANDOM INSERTS IN PACKS
PRINT RUNS B/WN 3-25 COPIES PER
NO PRICING QTY 15 OR LESS
EXCHANGE DEADLINE 3/18/2022
18 Jasson Dominguez/25 150.00 400.00

2020 Panini Origins Autographs Silver Ink

RANDOM INSERTS IN PACKS
PRINT RUNS B/WN 5-49 COPIES PER
NO PRICING QTY 15 OR LESS
EXCHANGE DEADLINE 3/18/2022
1 Bo Bichette/49 50.00 120.00
2 Gavin Lux/49 20.00 50.00
3 Yordan Alvarez/25 30.00 80.00
4 A.J. Puk/49 6.00 15.00
5 Nico Hoerner/49 15.00 40.00
7 Isan Diaz/49 6.00 15.00
8 Dustin May/25 15.00 40.00
9 Zac Gallen/49 10.00 25.00
10 Dylan Cease/49 6.00 15.00
11 Brendan McKay/25 8.00 20.00
12 Alec Bohm/25
13 Estevan Florial/49 6.00 15.00
14 Fernando Tatis Jr./49 75.00 200.00
15 Pete Alonso/49 25.00 60.00
16 Forrest Whitley/49 6.00 15.00
17 Luis Robert/49 100.00 250.00
18 Jasson Dominguez/49 75.00 200.00
19 Jo Adell/49 40.00 100.00
20 Vladimir Guerrero Jr./25 12.00 30.00
21 Walker Buehler/49 8.00 20.00
22 Adley Rutschman/25 30.00 80.00
23 Cavan Biggio/49 8.00 20.00
24 Eloy Jimenez/25 15.00 40.00
25 Royce Lewis/25 15.00 40.00
26 Bobby Witt Jr./49 30.00 80.00
27 Austin Riley/25 10.00 25.00
28 Keston Hiura/49 8.00 20.00
29 Bryan Reynolds/49 5.00 12.00
30 Jon Duplantier/49 4.00 10.00
31 Cole Tucker/49 6.00 15.00
33 Joey Bart/25 30.00 80.00
35 Ozzie Smith/25
36 Victor Mesa Jr./49 10.00 25.00
38 Paul Molitor/25 8.00 20.00

2020 Panini Origins Rookie Jumbo Material Autographs

RANDOM INSERTS IN PACKS
PRINT RUNS B/WN 49-99 COPIES PER
EXCHANGE DEADLINE 3/18/2022
*BLUE/25: .6X TO 1.5X p/r 99
*BLUE/25: .5X TO 1.2X p/r 49
1 Yordan Alvarez/99 20.00 50.00
2 Bo Bichette/99 40.00 100.00
3 Gavin Lux/99 15.00 40.00
4 Brendan McKay/99 5.00 12.00
5 Dylan Cease/99 5.00 12.00
6 A.J. Puk/99 5.00 12.00
7 Jesus Luzardo/99 6.00 15.00
8 Nico Hoerner/99 12.00 30.00
9 Sean Murphy/99 5.00 12.00
10 Dustin May/49 12.00 30.00
11 Aristides Aquino/99 12.00 30.00
12 Kyle Lewis/99 40.00 100.00
13 Isan Diaz/99 5.00 12.00
14 Justin Dunn/99 4.00 10.00
15 Brusdar Graterol/99 5.00 12.00
16 Edwin Rios/99 8.00 20.00
17 Jaylin Davis/99 5.00 12.00
18 Josh Rojas/99 3.00 8.00
19 Mauricio Dubon/99 4.00 10.00
20 Yu Chang/99 5.00 12.00
21 Yonathan Daza/99 4.00 10.00

2020 Panini Origins Signatures

RANDOM INSERTS IN PACKS
EXCHANGE DEADLINE 3/18/2022
*RED/99: .5X TO 1.2X
*RED/49: .6X TO 1.5X
*RED/25: .8X TO 2X
*BLUE/25: .8X TO 2X
1 Trent Grisham 10.00 25.00
3 Sean Murphy 4.00 10.00
4 Bobby Bradley 2.50 6.00
5 Zac Gallen 6.00 15.00
6 Tony Gonsolin 10.00 25.00
7 Bryan Abreu 2.50 6.00
8 Gavin Lux 12.00 30.00
9 Sheldon Neuse 3.00 8.00
10 Yordan Alvarez 15.00 40.00
11 Isan Diaz 4.00 10.00
12 Dylan Cease 4.00 10.00
13 Yu Chang 4.00 10.00
14 Brendan McKay 4.00 10.00
15 Logan Allen 2.50 6.00
16 Michael King 4.00 10.00
17 Brusdar Graterol 4.00 10.00
18 Sam Hilliard 4.00 10.00
19 Kyle Lewis 30.00 80.00
20 Mauricio Dubon 3.00 8.00
21 A.J. Puk 4.00 10.00
22 Brock Burke 2.50 6.00
23 Aristides Aquino 10.00 25.00
24 Aaron Civale 5.00 12.00
25 Jesus Luzardo 5.00 12.00
26 Logan Webb 4.00 10.00
27 Jake Rogers 2.50 6.00
28 Jake Fraley 3.00 8.00
29 Willi Castro 4.00 10.00
30 Jordan Yamamoto 2.50 6.00
31 Justin Dunn 3.00 8.00
32 Bo Bichette 30.00 80.00
33 Anthony Kay 2.50 6.00
34 Zack Collins 3.00 8.00
35 Abraham Toro 3.00 8.00
36 Adrian Morejon 2.50 6.00
37 Matt Thaiss 3.00 8.00
38 Nico Hoerner 10.00 25.00
39 Michel Baez 2.50 6.00
40 Yoshitomo Tsutsugo 6.00 15.00

2016 Panini Pantheon

PRINT RUNS B/WN 4-199 COPIES PER
NO PRICING ON QTY 15 OR LESS
1 Barry Bonds/199 10.00 25.00
2 Ken Griffey Jr./199 8.00 20.00
4 Mel Ott/199 10.00 25.00
5 Ken Griffey Jr./199 8.00 20.00
6 Barry Bonds/199 10.00 25.00
7 Frank Robinson/199 6.00 15.00
8 Frank Robinson/199 6.00 15.00
9 Mark McGwire/199 6.00 15.00
10 Harmon Killebrew/99 10.00 25.00
11 Rafael Palmeiro/199 5.00 12.00
12 Reggie Jackson/199 8.00 20.00
13 Mark McGwire/199 6.00 15.00
14 Mike Schmidt/199 12.00 30.00
16 Ted Williams/199 12.00 30.00
17 Willie McCovey/25 10.00 25.00
18 Frank Thomas/199 8.00 20.00
19 Eddie Mathews/99 6.00 15.00
20 Ernie Banks/199 8.00 20.00

21 Gary Sheffield/199 4.00 10.00
22 Ken Griffey Jr./99 8.00 20.00
24 Barry Bonds/199 10.00 25.00
25 Ken Griffey Jr./199 8.00 20.00
26 Barry Bonds/199 10.00 25.00
27 Ken Griffey Jr./25 10.00 25.00
28 Barry Bonds/199 10.00 25.00
29 Barry Bonds/199 10.00 25.00
31 Pete Rose/99 10.00 25.00
33 Rickey Henderson/199 8.00 20.00
34 Stan Musial/99 12.00 30.00
36 Carl Yastrzemski/199 6.00 15.00
38 Paul Molitor/199 6.00 15.00
40 Al Kaline/49 10.00 25.00
41 Eddie Murray/199 5.00 12.00
43 Cal Ripken/199 10.00 25.00
44 George Brett/199 15.00 40.00
45 Paul Waner/199 8.00 20.00
46 Robin Yount/199 6.00 15.00
47 Tony Gwynn/199 12.00 30.00
48 Dave Winfield/199 5.00 12.00
49 Craig Biggio/199 5.00 12.00
50 Rickey Henderson/199 8.00 20.00
51 Rod Carew/99 5.00 12.00
52 Lou Brock/99 8.00 20.00
53 Rafael Palmeiro/199 5.00 12.00
54 Wade Boggs/199 6.00 15.00
57 Greg Maddux/199 6.00 15.00
58 Roger Clemens/199 5.00 12.00
59 Steve Carlton/199 5.00 12.00
60 Nolan Ryan/99 12.00 30.00
61 Don Sutton/199 5.00 12.00
62 Phil Niekro/99 5.00 12.00
63 Gaylord Perry/199 5.00 12.00
65 Tom Glavine/25 6.00 15.00
66 Jose Canseco/25 15.00 40.00
67 Barry Bonds/199 10.00 25.00
68 Tony Perez/99 8.00 20.00
69 Mike Schmidt/199 12.00 25.00
71 Barry Bonds/199 10.00 25.00
73 Stan Musial/49 12.00 30.00
76 Eddie Murray/199 5.00 12.00
77 Chipper Jones/199 8.00 20.00
78 Mel Ott/99 10.00 25.00
79 Carl Yastrzemski/199 6.00 15.00
80 Ted Williams/199 12.00 30.00
81 Ken Griffey Jr./199 8.00 20.00
82 Rafael Palmeiro/199 5.00 12.00
83 Dave Winfield/199 5.00 12.00
84 Harold Baines/199 5.00 12.00
85 Al Simmons/25 12.00 30.00
86 Frank Robinson/99 6.00 15.00
88 Frank Thomas/99 8.00 20.00
89 Reggie Jackson/199 8.00 20.00
90 Reggie Jackson/199 8.00 20.00
91 Cal Ripken/199 10.00 25.00
92 Gary Sheffield/99 4.00 10.00
93 Andre Dawson/199 5.00 12.00
94 Barry Bonds/199 10.00 25.00
95 Pete Rose/25 15.00 40.00
97 Nolan Ryan/199 12.00 30.00
98 Roger Clemens/199 5.00 12.00
99 Steve Carlton/199 5.00 12.00
100 Nolan Ryan/99 12.00 30.00

2016 Panini Pantheon Arena Acclaimed Materials

RANDOM INSERTS IN PACKS
PRINT RUNS B/WN 15-99 COPIES PER
NO PRICING ON QTY 15
*GOLD/25: .5X TO 1.2X p/r 49-99
1 Pedro Martinez/99 5.00 12.00
2 Darryl Strawberry/99 4.00 10.00
3 Jim Rice/99 5.00 12.00
4 Andre Dawson/49 5.00 12.00
6 Gary Sheffield/49 4.00 10.00
7 Ryne Sandberg/99 10.00 25.00
9 Jeff Bagwell/99 5.00 12.00
10 Nolan Ryan/99 12.00 30.00
12 Ivan Rodriguez/99 6.00 15.00
13 Roger Clemens/99 5.00 12.00
14 Mariano Rivera/99 8.00 20.00
15 Roberto Alomar/99 5.00 12.00
16 Dave Winfield/99 5.00 12.00
19 Enos Slaughter/25
20 Greg Maddux/99 6.00 15.00
21 Tony Oliva/49 12.00 30.00
22 Chipper Jones/99 8.00 20.00
23 Stan Musial/25 10.00 25.00
24 Cal Ripken/99 10.00 25.00
25 Manny Ramirez/25 6.00 15.00

2016 Panini Pantheon Chronicled Calligraphy Materials

RANDOM INSERTS IN PACKS
PRINT RUNS B/WN 10-199 COPIES PER
NO PRICING ON QTY 15 OR LESS
EXCHANGE DEADLINE 5/23/2018
*GOLD/25: .6X TO 1.5X BASIC
2 Luis Gonzalez/199 5.00 12.00
4 Juan Gonzalez/199 6.00 15.00
7 Fred McGriff/99 8.00 20.00
8 Juan Gonzalez/199 6.00 15.00
10 Tommy John/199 4.00 10.00
11 Mike Mussina/199 8.00 20.00
12 Don Sutton/99 5.00 12.00
13 Jack Morris/89 6.00 15.00
14 Dennis Eckersley/149 6.00 15.00
15 David Justice/199 8.00 20.00
17 Dale Murphy/149 8.00 20.00
18 Frank Howard/199 6.00 15.00
20 Bruce Sutter/99 6.00 15.00
22 Harold Baines/199 5.00 12.00
23 Dwight Gooden/199 4.00 10.00
24 Bert Campaneris/199 6.00 15.00
25 Omar Vizquel/149 5.00 12.00
26 Paul O'Neill/99 10.00 25.00
27 Edgar Martinez/199 6.00 15.00
28 Mark Grace/199 12.00 30.00
29 Jose Canseco/149 20.00 50.00
34 Jim Palmer/149 8.00 20.00
36 Andruw Jones/199 5.00 12.00
38 Andres Galarraga/199 5.00 12.00
39 Bill Buckner/199 8.00 20.00
40 Steve Garvey/199 4.00 10.00
41 Dave Kingman/199 6.00 15.00
42 Andre Dawson/25 8.00 20.00
43 David Cone/99 4.00 10.00
44 Chan Ho Park/20
47 Lee Smith/149 4.00 10.00
48 Jeff Bagwell/25 40.00 100.00
49 Fergie Jenkins/199 5.00 12.00
51 Robin Ventura/49 5.00 12.00
52 Tommy Lasorda/25
53 Orlando Cepeda/99 10.00 25.00
54 Red Schoendienst/199 8.00 20.00
55 Alan Trammell/49 15.00 40.00
57 Joe Girardi/25
64 Goose Gossage/99 4.00 10.00
65 Tony Perez/99 10.00 25.00

2016 Panini Pantheon Chronicled Cuts

RANDOM INSERTS IN PACKS
PRINT RUNS B/WN 1-99 COPIES PER
NO PRICING ON QTY 10 OR LESS
EXCHANGE DEADLINE 5/23/2018
1 Stan Musial/99 20.00 50.00
5 Bobby Thomson/99 12.00 30.00
9 Johnny Pesky/25
12 Harmon Killebrew/99 10.00 40.00
15 Ralph Kiner/25 10.00 25.00
18 Warren Spahn/25 20.00 50.00

2016 Panini Pantheon Class and Rank Materials

RANDOM INSERTS IN PACKS
PRINT RUNS B/WN 10-99 COPIES PER
NO PRICING ON QTY 15 OR LESS
*GOLD/25: .5X TO 1.2X p/r 49-99
1 Ken Griffey Jr./99 8.00 10.00
2 Cal Ripken/99 10.00 25.00
3 George Brett/99 10.00 25.00
4 Nolan Ryan/49 12.00 30.00
5 Kirby Puckett/99 15.00 40.00
6 Reggie Jackson/99 8.00 20.00
7 Tony Gwynn/99 12.00 30.00
8 Joe Morgan/99 10.00 25.00
9 Lou Brock/99 8.00 20.00
10 Barry Bonds/99 10.00 25.00
13 Willie McCovey/25 10.00 25.00
15 Mariano Rivera/99 8.00 20.00
16 Rickey Henderson/99 8.00 20.00
17 Mark McGwire/99 6.00 15.00
18 Al Kaline/25 15.00 40.00
19 Mike Schmidt/99 12.00 25.00
20 Roger Clemens/99 5.00 12.00
21 Don Mattingly/99 6.00 15.00
30 Stan Musial/25 15.00 40.00
32 Pete Rose/99 12.00 30.00
33 Ted Williams/99 12.00 30.00
34 Carl Yastrzemski/99 6.00 15.00
35 Rogers Hornsby/25 25.00 60.00
36 Ralph Kiner/99 5.00 12.00
37 Orlando Cepeda/99 5.00 12.00
38 Enos Slaughter/25 8.00 20.00
40 Ryne Sandberg/99 10.00 25.00
41 Eddie Mathews/25 8.00 20.00
42 Rick Ferrell/99 4.00 10.00
43 Paul Molitor/99 6.00 15.00
45 Roberto Alomar/99 5.00 12.00
46 Gary Carter/99 6.00 15.00
47 Tom Seaver/99 5.00 12.00
49 Phil Rizzuto/25 6.00 15.00
50 Whitey Ford/99 6.00 15.00

2016 Panini Pantheon Class and Rank Dual Materials

RANDOM INSERTS IN PACKS
PRINT RUNS B/WN 10-99 COPIES PER
NO PRICING ON QTY 15 OR LESS
*GOLD/25: .5X TO 1.2X p/r 49-99
1 Frank Robinson/99 6.00 15.00
2 Nolan Ryan/99 10.00 25.00
3 Rickey Henderson/99 8.00 20.00
4 Pete Rose/99 10.00 25.00
5 F.Thomas/K.Griffey Jr./99 10.00 25.00
6 C.Ripken/G.Brett/99 20.00 50.00
7 K.Puckett/T.Gwynn/99 25.00 60.00
10 N.Lajoie/P.Waner/25 15.00 40.00
11 J.Robinson/P.Reese/49 20.00 50.00
13 H.Greenberg/R.Hornsby/25
15 R.Henderson/P.Rose/99 20.00 50.00
18 Mark McGwire/99 8.00 20.00
19 L.O'Doul/A.Simmons/99 10.00 25.00
20 M.Schmidt/R.Campanella/25 25.00 60.00
23 H.Killebrew/W.McCovey/49 12.00 30.00

2016 Panini Pantheon Decade Deities Materials

RANDOM INSERTS IN PACKS
PRINT RUNS B/WN 10-99 COPIES PER
NO PRICING ON QTY 15 OR LESS
*GOLD/25: .5X TO 1.2X p/r 49-99
9 Bob Feller/25 12.00 30.00
10 Johnny Mize/49 5.00 12.00
12 Stan Musial/25 15.00 40.00
14 Don Drysdale/49 5.00 12.00
15 Pete Rose/99 12.00 30.00
16 Reggie Jackson/99 5.00 12.00
17 Nolan Ryan/99 12.00 30.00
18 Wade Boggs/99 6.00 15.00
19 Ken Griffey Jr./99 8.00 20.00
20 Frank Thomas/99 4.00 10.00
21 Barry Bonds/99 10.00 25.00
22 Manny Ramirez/49 5.00 12.00
23 Mariano Rivera/99 8.00 20.00
24 Chipper Jones/99 4.00 10.00
25 Todd Helton/99 5.00 12.00

2016 Panini Pantheon Gallant Gloves Materials

RANDOM INSERTS IN PACKS
PRINT RUNS B/WN 25-99 COPIES PER
*GOLD/25: .5X TO 1.2X p/r 49-99
1 Gil Hodges/99 12.00 30.00
2 Nellie Fox/99 5.00 12.00
3 Tony Gwynn/99 6.00 15.00
4 Al Kaline/25 15.00 40.00
5 Luis Aparicio/99 12.00 30.00
6 Bob Gibson/25 10.00 25.00
7 Greg Maddux/99 6.00 15.00
8 Ivan Rodriguez/99 6.00 15.00
9 Don Mattingly/99 12.00 30.00
10 Roberto Alomar/99 5.00 12.00
11 Brooks Robinson/99 5.00 12.00
12 Ozzie Smith/99 4.00 10.00
13 Omar Vizquel/99 5.00 12.00
15 Ryne Sandberg/99 10.00 25.00
16 Ken Griffey Jr./99 8.00 20.00
17 Kirby Puckett/99 15.00 40.00
18 Joe Morgan/99 10.00 25.00
19 Johnny Bench/99 6.00 15.00
20 Chipper Jones/99 3.00 8.00

2016 Panini Pantheon Honored and Priveleged Materials

RANDOM INSERTS IN PACKS
PRINT RUNS B/WN 10-99 COPIES PER
NO PRICING ON QTY 10
*GOLD/25: .5X TO 1.2X p/r 49-99
1 Jackie Robinson/25 25.00 60.00
3 Eddie Mathews/25 8.00 20.00
4 Harmon Killebrew/99 10.00 25.00
5 Ernie Banks/99 8.00 20.00
6 Pee Wee Reese/99 5.00 12.00
7 Tony Gwynn/99 12.00 30.00
8 Kirby Puckett/99 12.00 30.00
10 Thurman Munson/99 12.00 30.00
11 Tony Lazzeri/99 8.00 20.00
12 Paul Waner/25 10.00 25.00
13 Nellie Fox/99 12.00 30.00
14 Phil Rizzuto/99 5.00 12.00
15 Mel Ott/49 10.00 25.00
18 Bob Feller/99 10.00 25.00
19 Johnny Pesky/99 4.00 10.00
20 Hank Greenberg/25 25.00 60.00
22 Gary Carter/99 6.00 15.00
23 Al Simmons/25 12.00 30.00
24 Ernie Lombardi/49 10.00 25.00
25 Bobby Doerr/99 6.00 15.00

2016 Panini Pantheon Immortals Materials

RANDOM INSERTS IN PACKS
PRINT RUNS B/WN 10-99 COPIES PER
NO PRICING ON QTY 10
*GOLD/25: .5X TO 1.2X p/r 49-99
4 Ken Griffey Jr./99 8.00 20.00
5 Mike Piazza/99 6.00 15.00
6 Craig Biggio/99 5.00 12.00
7 Pedro Martinez/99 5.00 12.00
8 John Smoltz/99 4.00 10.00
9 Tom Glavine/25 6.00 15.00
10 Greg Maddux/99 6.00 15.00
11 Gary Carter/99 6.00 15.00
12 Nolan Ryan/99 6.00 15.00
13 Frank Thomas/99 4.00 10.00
14 Cal Ripken/99 10.00 25.00
15 George Brett/99 8.00 20.00
16 Kirby Puckett/99 6.00 15.00
17 Wade Boggs/99 6.00 15.00
18 Tony Gwynn/99 12.00 30.00
20 Ted Williams/99 12.00 30.00
22 Hank Greenberg/25 25.00 60.00
24 Roger Bresnahan/99 10.00 25.00

2016 Panini Pantheon Local Lore Materials

RANDOM INSERTS IN PACKS
PRINT RUNS B/WN 15-99 COPIES PER
NO PRICING ON QTY 15
*GOLD/25: .5X TO 1.2X p/r 49-99
1 Todd Helton/99 5.00 12.00
2 Don Mattingly/99 12.00 30.00
3 Mike Schmidt/99 12.00 25.00
4 George Brett/99 15.00 40.00
5 Ernie Banks/99 8.00 20.00
6 Johnny Bench/99 10.00 25.00
7 Jeff Bagwell/99 5.00 12.00
8 Craig Biggio/99 5.00 12.00
12 Bob Feller/99 10.00 25.00
14 Tony Gwynn/99 12.00 30.00
15 Edgar Martinez/25 6.00 15.00
17 Barry Larkin/99 6.00 15.00
19 Cal Ripken/99 10.00 25.00
20 Robin Yount/99 6.00 15.00

2016 Panini Pantheon Metropolis Monuments Materials

RANDOM INSERTS IN PACKS
PRINT RUNS B/WN 5-99 COPIES PER
NO PRICING ON QTY 15 OR LESS
*GOLD/25: .5X TO 1.2X p/r 49-99
1 Ro/Pa/Ro/Ri/99 25.00 60.00
2 Ri/Ma/Wi/Ya/99 60.00 150.00
4 Ca/Al/De/Ha/25 20.00 50.00
5 Ap/Th/Ap/Fo/99 20.00 50.00
6 Fe/Sp/Avi/Vi/49 30.00 80.00
8 Bo/Fi/Fo/Sp/25 20.00 50.00
9 Ca/Ol/Ki/Pu/99 40.00 100.00
10 Bi/Ba/Wy/Ry/99 20.00 50.00
11 Ry/Gu/Ja/Ca/49 25.00 60.00
14 Ro/Go/Ry/Pa/99 20.00 50.00
15 Ma/Ma/Mu/Sp/25
16 Jo/Mu/Sm/Gl/99 20.00 50.00
19 St/Pi/Go/Ca/49
21 Da/Ca/Ra/Ma/99 12.00 30.00
22 Wi/Ba/Sa/Sa/99 25.00 60.00
23 Ha/Da/Je/Sa/99 20.00 50.00
24 Be/Pe/Mo/Ro/99 25.00 60.00
25 La/Ro/Gr/Kl/99 20.00 50.00
26 Br/Gi/Ho/Mu/25
29 Ma/Cl/Mc/Ce/25 40.00 100.00
30 Ga/Gw/Wi/Sm/99 25.00 60.00

2016 Panini Pantheon Metropolis Monuments Materials Milestones

RANDOM INSERTS IN PACKS
PRINT RUNS B/WN 4-99 COPIES PER
NO PRICING ON QTY 15 OR LESS
*GOLD/25: .5X TO 1.2X p/r 49-99
2 Bonds/Griffey Jr./McGwire/Thomas/99 12.00 30.00
3 Killebrew/Schmidt
Robinson/Jackson/25 12.00 30.00
4 Maddux/Niekro/Carlton/Clemens/49 8.00 20.00
7 Rivera/Sutter/Eckersley/Fingers/99 8.00 20.00
8 Martinez/Blyleven/Gibson/Smoltz/25 8.00 20.00
9 Kaline/Brett/Ripken/Carew/25 25.00 60.00

2016 Panini Pantheon Milestone Scripts

RANDOM INSERTS IN PACKS
PRINT RUNS B/WN 10-99 COPIES PER
NO PRICING ON QTY 15 OR LESS
EXCHANGE DEADLINE 5/23/2018
*BRONZE/25: .5X TO 1.2X BASIC
*GOLD/49: .4X TO 1X BASIC
*GOLD/20-25: .5X TO 1.2X BASIC
1 Al Kaline/25 25.00 50.00
4 Craig Biggio/25 6.00 15.00
9 Lou Brock/25 15.00 40.00
10 Paul Molitor/99 8.00 20.00
11 Pete Rose/99 10.00 25.00
12 Rafael Palmeiro/99 5.00 12.00
17 Omar Vizquel/99 5.00 12.00
18 Harold Baines/99 5.00 12.00
19 Brooks Robinson/25 8.00 20.00
22 Al Oliver/99 4.00 10.00
23 Tony Perez/99 5.00 12.00
24 Roberto Alomar/20 20.00 50.00
26 Bill Buckner/99
28 Tim Raines/99
29 Steve Garvey/99 8.00 20.00
30 Luis Gonzalez/49 5.00 12.00
32 Steve Finley/99 4.00 10.00
34 Todd Helton/20 8.00 20.00
36 Buddy Bell/99 4.00 10.00
48 Gary Sheffield/25
49 Fred McGriff/99 6.00 15.00
50 Carlos Delgado/25 5.00 12.00
52 Jose Canseco/99 6.00 15.00
56 Dave Kingman/99 4.00 10.00
57 Jason Giambi/99 6.00 15.00
58 Paul Konerko/99 6.00 15.00
59 Andre Dawson/25 10.00 25.00
60 Andruw Jones/99 4.00 10.00
61 Juan Gonzalez/99 6.00 15.00
63 Billy Williams/20 10.00 25.00
64 Darrell Evans/99 4.00 10.00
70 Don Sutton/99 6.00 15.00
71 Phil Niekro/25
72 Gaylord Perry/99 6.00 15.00
73 Tom Glavine/20 10.00 25.00
74 Tommy John/99 4.00 10.00
75 Bert Blyleven/25 6.00 15.00
76 Fergie Jenkins/99 5.00 12.00
78 Mike Mussina/25 15.00 40.00
79 Jamie Moyer/99 6.00 15.00
80 Jim Palmer/99 6.00 15.00
81 Andy Pettitte/25 12.00 30.00
82 Jack Morris/99 5.00 12.00
85 Curt Schilling/25
87 Jim Bunning/99 6.00 15.00
88 Mickey Lolich/99 6.00 15.00
89 Frank Tanana/99 6.00 15.00
90 David Cone/99 4.00 10.00
91 Chuck Finley/99 4.00 10.00
92 Jerry Koosman/99 6.00 15.00
96 Lee Smith/99 4.00 10.00
97 John Franco/99 4.00 10.00
98 Billy Wagner/99 4.00 10.00
99 Dennis Eckersley/99 5.00 12.00

2016 Panini Pantheon Noble Timber Materials

RANDOM INSERTS IN PACKS
PRINT RUNS B/WN 10-99 COPIES PER
NO PRICING ON QTY 15
*GOLD/25: .5X TO 1.2X p/r 49-99
1 Barry Bonds/99 10.00 25.00
2 Todd Helton/99 5.00 12.00
3 Mike Piazza/99 6.00 15.00
4 Ryne Sandberg/99 12.00 30.00
5 Wade Boggs/99 6.00 15.00
6 Barry Larkin/99 6.00 15.00
8 Gary Carter/99 6.00 15.00
9 Mark McGwire/99 6.00 15.00
10 Eddie Murray/99 5.00 12.00
11 Cal Ripken/99 10.00 25.00
12 Manny Ramirez/49 5.00 12.00
13 Vladimir Guerrero/99 5.00 12.00
14 Juan Gonzalez/99 5.00 12.00
15 Carlos Delgado/25 5.00 12.00
16 Frank Thomas/99 8.00 20.00
18 Kirby Puckett/99 12.00 30.00
19 Roberto Alomar/99 5.00 12.00
20 Mike Schmidt/99 12.00 25.00

2016 Panini Pantheon Scripts Materials

RANDOM INSERTS IN PACKS
PRINT RUNS B/WN 10-99 COPIES PER
NO PRICING ON QTY 15 OR LESS
EXCHANGE DEADLINE 5/23/2018
*GOLD/25: .6X TO 1.5X BASIC
1 Al Kaline/25 20.00 50.00
3 Andre Dawson/25 8.00 20.00
9 Dale Murphy/99 8.00 20.00
10 Darryl Strawberry/99 10.00 25.00
11 Dave Kingman/99 6.00 15.00
12 David Justice/99 8.00 20.00
13 David Wells/99 6.00 15.00
18 Frank Howard/99 6.00 15.00
19 Fred McGriff/99 8.00 20.00
20 Fred Lynn/99 4.00 10.00
22 Gaylord Perry/99 6.00 15.00
31 Jason Giambi/99 4.00 10.00
34 Jorge Posada/25 20.00 50.00
35 Jose Canseco/99 20.00 50.00
38 Lee Smith/99 4.00 10.00
40 Luis Gonzalez/99 5.00 12.00
42 Mark Grace/99 8.00 20.00
43 Mark Grace/99 8.00 20.00
47 Omar Vizquel/99 5.00 12.00
48 Paul Molitor/49 6.00 15.00
50 Red Schoendienst/99 8.00 20.00

2016 Panini Pantheon Scripts Dual Materials

RANDOM INSERTS IN PACKS
PRINT RUNS B/WN 10-99 COPIES PER
NO PRICING ON QTY 15 OR LESS
EXCHANGE DEADLINE 5/23/2018
*GOLD/25: .6X TO 1.5X BASIC
3 Bert Campaneris/99 8.00 20.00
7 Dennis Eckersley/99 6.00 15.00
8 Dwight Gooden/99 8.00 20.00
9 Edgar Martinez/99 6.00 15.00
10 Fergie Jenkins/99 5.00 12.00
11 Fred McGriff/99 8.00 20.00
12 Gary Sheffield/20 12.00 30.00
14 Harold Baines/99 5.00 12.00
15 Jeff Bagwell/20 40.00 100.00
16 Juan Gonzalez/99 6.00 15.00
17 Mike Mussina/20 12.00 30.00

2016 Panini Pantheon Scripts Quad Materials

9 Pete Rose/49 25.00 60.00

2016 Panini Pantheon Scripts Quad Materials Gold

RANDOM INSERTS IN PACKS
PRINT RUNS B/WN 10-25 COPIES PER
NO PRICING ON QTY 10
EXCHANGE DEADLINE 5/23/2018
9 Pete Rose/25 40.00 100.00

2016 Panini Pantheon Scripts Triple Materials

RANDOM INSERTS IN PACKS
PRINT RUNS B/WN 10-99 COPIES PER
NO PRICING ON QTY 15 OR LESS
EXCHANGE DEADLINE 5/23/2018
*GOLD/25: .6X TO 1.5X BASIC
1 Andres Galarraga/99 5.00 12.00
3 Bert Blyleven/25 12.00 30.00
5 Boog Powell/99 10.00 25.00
6 Bruce Sutter/99 6.00 15.00

2016 Panini Pantheon Rudiarius Materials

RANDOM INSERTS IN PACKS
PRINT RUNS B/WN 10-99 COPIES PER
NO PRICING ON QTY 10
*GOLD/25: .5X TO 1.2X p/r 49-99
1 Jackie Robinson/25 25.00 60.00
2 Dale Murphy/99 6.00 15.00
4 Johnny Pesky/99 4.00 10.00
5 Carl Yastrzemski/99 6.00 15.00
6 Ted Williams/99 12.00 30.00
7 Phil Rizzuto/99 5.00 12.00
8 Paul Waner/25 10.00 25.00
9 Roberto Alomar/99 5.00 12.00
10 Jim Rice/99 5.00 12.00
11 Thurman Munson/99 8.00 20.00
12 Ted Kluszewski/99 4.00 10.00
13 Jim Gilliam/99 4.00 10.00
14 Luis Gonzalez/99 5.00 12.00
15 Tony Perez/99 8.00 20.00
17 Andy Pettitte/99 5.00 12.00
18 Bernie Williams/99 5.00 12.00
19 Pedro Martinez/99 5.00 12.00
20 Eddie Mathews/25 8.00 20.00
21 Dave Winfield/99 5.00 12.00
23 Eddie Murray/99 5.00 12.00
24 Rod Carew/99 5.00 12.00
25 Ken Griffey Jr./99 8.00 20.00

2016 Panini Pantheon Sacred Deployments Materials

RANDOM INSERTS IN PACKS
PRINT RUNS B/WN 3-99 COPIES PER
NO PRICING ON QTY 15 OR LESS
*BRONZE/25: .5X TO 1.2X p/r 49-99
2 Morgan/Bench/Rose/99 25.00 60.00
5 Fisk/Yastrzemski/Rice/99 30.00 80.00
6 Jones/Jones/Sheffield/49
10 Gonzalez/Palmeiro/Rodriguez/49 20.00 50.00

2016 Panini Pantheon Script 1 Materials

RANDOM INSERTS IN PACKS
PRINT RUNS B/WN 10-199 COPIES PER
NO PRICING ON QTY 15 OR LESS
EXCHANGE DEADLINE 5/23/2018
*GOLD/25: .6X TO 1.5X BASIC
12 Ron Guidry/199 4.00 10.00
13 Edgar Martinez/99 6.00 15.00
15 Tony Oliva/99 12.00 30.00
17 Jim Rice/99 8.00 20.00
21 Jim Palmer/49 10.00 25.00

2016 Panini Pantheon Script 20 Materials

RANDOM INSERTS IN PACKS
PRINT RUNS B/WN 10-199 COPIES PER
NO PRICING ON QTY 15 OR LESS
EXCHANGE DEADLINE 5/23/2018
*GOLD/49: .4X TO 1X BASIC
*GOLD/25: .6X TO 1.5X BASIC
5 Ron Guidry/199 8.00 20.00
8 David Cone/79 4.00 10.00
9 Jim Palmer/25 12.00 30.00
16 Fergie Jenkins/199 5.00 12.00
18 Whitey Ford/99 20.00 50.00
20 Dennis Eckersley/99 6.00 15.00
21 Tommy John/199 4.00 10.00
22 Jack Morris/25 10.00 25.00
23 David Wells/35 10.00 25.00

2016 Panini Pantheon Script 30/30 Materials

RANDOM INSERTS IN PACKS
PRINT RUNS B/WN 15-199 COPIES PER
NO PRICING ON QTY 15
EXCHANGE DEADLINE 5/23/2018
*GOLD/25: .6X TO 1.5X BASIC
5 Dale Murphy/149 8.00 20.00
8 Jose Canseco/49 12.00 30.00
9 Darryl Strawberry/199 10.00 25.00
13 Jeff Bagwell/25 25.00 60.00
14 Shawn Green/149 8.00 20.00

2016 Panini Pantheon Script 300 Materials

RANDOM INSERTS IN PACKS
PRINT RUNS B/WN 10-199 COPIES PER
NO PRICING ON QTY 15 OR LESS
EXCHANGE DEADLINE 5/23/2018
*GOLD/25: .6X TO 1.5X BASIC
3 Gaylord Perry/199 6.00 15.00
8 Don Sutton/99 5.00 12.00

2016 Panini Pantheon Script 3000 Materials

RANDOM INSERTS IN PACKS
PRINT RUNS B/WN 15-99 COPIES PER
NO PRICING ON QTY 15
EXCHANGE DEADLINE 5/23/2018
*GOLD/25: .6X TO 1.5X BASIC
2 Paul Molitor/99 6.00 15.00
8 Rafael Palmeiro/25 8.00 20.00

2016 Panini Pantheon Script 500 Materials

RANDOM INSERTS IN PACKS
PRINT RUNS B/WN 10-25 COPIES PER
NO PRICING ON QTY 15 OR LESS
EXCHANGE DEADLINE 5/23/2018
2 Rafael Palmeiro/25 8.00 20.00
4 Gary Sheffield/20 12.00 30.00
9 Rafael Palmeiro/25 8.00 20.00

2016 Panini Pantheon Scripted Gallant Gloves Materials

RANDOM INSERTS IN PACKS
PRINT RUNS B/WN 10-149 COPIES PER
NO PRICING ON QTY 15 OR LESS
EXCHANGE DEADLINE 5/23/2018
*GOLD/25: .6X TO 1.5X BASIC
3 Jim Palmer/49 8.00 20.00
7 Omar Vizquel/149 5.00 12.00
9 Steve Garvey/70 15.00 40.00

2016 Panini Pantheon Scripted Noble Timber

RANDOM INSERTS IN PACKS
PRINT RUNS B/WN 10-199 COPIES PER
NO PRICING ON QTY 15 OR LESS
EXCHANGE DEADLINE 5/23/2018
*GOLD/25: .6X TO 1.5X BASIC
1 Juan Gonzalez/199 6.00 15.00
3 Dale Murphy/149 8.00 20.00
7 David Justice/40 8.00 20.00
10 Carlos Delgado/20 6.00 15.00

2016 Panini Pantheon Scripted Rudiarius Materials

RANDOM INSERTS IN PACKS
PRINT RUNS B/WN 10-199 COPIES PER
NO PRICING ON QTY 15 OR LESS
EXCHANGE DEADLINE 5/23/2018
*GOLD/25: .6X TO 1.5X BASIC
1 Dale Murphy/149 8.00 20.00
4 Jim Rice/149 8.00 20.00
5 Luis Gonzalez/199 5.00 12.00
6 Tony Perez/99 10.00 25.00
15 Red Schoendienst/199 8.00 20.00
16 Harold Baines/193 5.00 12.00
17 Paul Molitor/99 6.00 15.00
21 Jeff Bagwell/25 40.00 100.00
22 Steve Garvey/99 15.00 40.00
24 Tony Oliva/149 12.00 30.00
34 Rollie Fingers/149 6.00 15.00
35 Paul Konerko/199 8.00 20.00
36 Pete Rose/25 40.00 100.00
40 Jorge Posada/149 12.00 30.00
41 Jim Palmer/49 8.00 20.00
48 Dennis Eckersley/99 6.00 15.00
49 Ron Guidry/199 8.00 20.00
50 Fergie Jenkins/99 5.00 12.00

2016 Panini Pantheon The Enlightened Ones Materials

RANDOM INSERTS IN PACKS
PRINT RUNS B/WN 10-99 COPIES PER
NO PRICING ON QTY 15 OR LESS
*BRONZE/25: .5X TO 1.2X p/r 49-99
3 Brett/Boggs/Schmidt/49
4 Thomas/Griffey/McGwre/99

2016 Panini Pantheon The Great Entertainers Signature Materials

RANDOM INSERTS IN PACKS
PRINT RUNS B/WN 10-199 COPIES PER
NO PRICING ON QTY 10 OR LESS
EXCHANGE DEADLINE 5/23/2018
*GOLD/25: .6X TO 1.5X BASIC
1 Dave Kingman/199 6.00 15.00
2 Tim Raines/99 5.00 12.00
4 Paul Konerko/199 8.00 20.00
6 Jose Canseco/25 30.00 80.00
7 Al Oliver/99 4.00 10.00
8 Steve Finley/35 6.00 15.00
9 Juan Gonzalez/199 6.00 15.00
10 Andruw Jones/199 5.00 12.00
14 Billy Williams/25 8.00 20.00
15 Lee Smith/99 4.00 10.00
17 Jason Giambi/49 4.00 10.00
20 Paul O'Neill/40 10.00 25.00
21 Omar Vizquel/149 5.00 12.00
29 Pete Rose/25 40.00 100.00
30 Andres Galarraga/199 5.00 12.00
34 Darryl Strawberry/199 8.00 20.00
35 Rollie Fingers/99 6.00 15.00

2016 Panini Pantheon The Inner Sanctum Materials

5 Pete Rose/25 15.00 40.00

2018 Panini Phoenix

1 Alex Verdugo RC .40 1.00
2 Clint Frazier RC .50 1.25
3 Miguel Andujar RC 1.00 2.50
4 Max Scherzer .25 .60
5 Rhys Hoskins RC 1.00 2.50
6 Austin Hays RC .40 1.00
7 Mike Trout 1.25 3.00
8 Aaron Judge .60 1.50
9 Carlos Correa .25 .60
10 Kris Bryant .30 .75
11 Ozzie Albies RC .75 2.00
12 Gleyber Torres RC 2.50 6.00
13 Ryan McMahon RC .60 1.50
14 Francisco Lindor .25 .60
15 Amed Rosario RC .30 .75
16 Paul Goldschmidt .25 .60
17 Bryce Harper .40 1.00
18 Cody Bellinger .50 1.25
19 J.P. Crawford RC .25 .60
20 Shohei Ohtani RC 6.00 15.00
21 Ronald Acuna Jr. RC 8.00 20.00
22 Rafael Devers RC .75 2.00
23 Giancarlo Stanton .25 .60
24 Victor Robles RC .60 1.50
25 Dominic Smith RC .30 .75

2018 Panini Phoenix Signatures

RANDOM INSERTS IN PACKS
8 Brian Anderson 3.00 8.00
9 Dillon Peters 2.50 6.00
10 Mitch Garver 2.50 6.00
11 Tomas Nido 2.50 6.00
12 Paul Blackburn 2.50 6.00
13 Christian Walker 3.00 8.00
16 Scott Kingery 4.00 10.00
17 Chris Taylor 3.00 8.00
20 Mark Zagunis 2.50 6.00

2019 Panini Phoenix

RANDOM INSERTS IN PACKS
*HOLO: .75X TO 2X
*HYPER/299: .75X TO 2X
*RUBY/199: 1X TO 2.5X
*BLUE/99: 1.2X TO 3X
*PURPLE/75: 1.2X TO 3X
*GREEN/50: 1.5X TO 4X
*PINK/25: 2.5X TO 6X
1 Pete Alonso RC 3.00 8.00
2 Eloy Jimenez RC .60 1.50
3 Fernando Tatis Jr. RC 4.00 10.00
4 Michael Kopech RC .50 1.25
5 Kyle Tucker RC .40 1.00
6 Yusei Kikuchi RC .25 .60
7 Chris Paddack RC .30 .75
8 Mike Trout 1.25 3.00
9 Bryce Harper .40 1.00
10 Aaron Judge .60 1.50
11 Kris Bryant .30 .75
12 Shohei Ohtani .40 1.00
13 Aaron Nola .20 .50
14 Vladimir Guerrero Jr. RC 2.50 6.00
15 Michael Chavis RC .25 .60
16 Giancarlo Stanton .25 .60
17 Alex Bregman .25 .60
18 Matt Chapman .25 .60
19 Justin Verlander .25 .60
20 Jordan Hicks .20 .50
21 Brandon Lowe RC .25 .60
22 Miguel Andujar .25 .60
23 Whit Merrifield .25 .60
24 Freddie Freeman .30 .75
25 Christian Yelich .30 .75

2019 Panini Prime Swatches

RANDOM INSERTS IN PACKS
*GOLD/99: .5X TO 1.2X
*GOLD/50: .6X TO 1.5X
*GOLD/25-28: .75X TO 2X
*BLUE/25: .75X TO 2X
1 Brett Gardner 2.00 5.00
2 Starling Marte 2.00 5.00
3 Paul DeJong 2.50 6.00
4 Dallas Keuchel 2.00 5.00
5 Max Kepler 2.00 5.00
6 Willson Contreras 2.00 5.00
7 Ender Inciarte 1.50 4.00
8 Tim Anderson 2.50 6.00
9 Trey Mancini 2.00 5.00
10 Jose Peraza 2.00 5.00
11 Buster Posey 3.00 8.00
12 Eloy Jimenez 6.00 15.00
13 Fernando Tatis Jr. 10.00 25.00
14 Vladimir Guerrero Jr. 10.00 25.00
15 Pete Alonso 12.00 30.00
16 Luis Urias 2.50 6.00
17 Gerrit Cole 2.50 6.00
18 Evan Longoria 2.00 5.00
19 Edwin Diaz 2.00 5.00
20 Lorenzo Cain 1.50 4.00
21 Odubel Herrera 2.00 5.00
22 Brandon Belt 2.00 5.00
23 Jacob deGrom 5.00 12.00
24 Mike Trout 12.00 30.00
25 Mookie Betts 5.00 12.00

2020 Panini Phoenix

RANDOM INSERTS IN PACKS
1 Bo Bichette RC 3.00 8.00
2 Yordan Alvarez RC 2.50 6.00
3 Gavin Lux RC 1.25 3.00
4 Brendan McKay RC .40 1.00
5 Aristides Aquino RC .60 1.50
6 Yoshitomo Tsutsugo RC .60 1.50
7 Luis Robert RC 4.00 10.00
8 Aaron Judge .60 1.50
9 Mike Trout 2.00 5.00
10 Cody Bellinger .50 1.25
11 Fernando Tatis Jr. 2.00 5.00
12 Vladimir Guerrero Jr. .40 1.00
13 Corey Kluber .20 .50
14 Dustin May RC .75 2.00
15 Gleyber Torres .50 1.25
16 Freddie Freeman .30 .75
17 Shohei Ohtani .40 1.00
18 Nico Hoerner RC 1.00 2.50
19 Jake Rogers RC .25 .60
20 Jesus Luzardo RC .50 1.25

2020 Panini Playbook Autographs

RANDOM INSERTS IN PACKS
EXCHANGE DEADLINE 3/18/2022
*GOLD/99: .5X TO 1.2X BASIC
*GOLD/50: .6X TO 1.5X BASIC
*RED/50: .6X TO 1.5X BASIC
*RED/25: .8X TO 2X BASIC
*BLUE/25: .8X TO 2X BASIC
2 Enyel De Los Santos 2.50 6.00
3 Ryan O'Hearn 2.50 6.00
5 Kyle Tucker 4.00 10.00
6 Byron Buxton 4.00 10.00
7 Adley Rutschman 15.00 40.00
8 Daniel Ponce de Leon 2.50 6.00
9 Jake Bauers 3.00 8.00
10 Jose Suarez 2.50 6.00
11 Yoan Lopez 2.50 6.00
12 Kolby Allard 2.50 6.00
13 Joey Lucchesi 2.50 6.00
14 Domingo German 3.00 8.00
15 Harold Castro 3.00 8.00
16 Nick Senzel 4.00 10.00
17 Dawel Lugo 2.50 6.00
18 Reese McGuire 3.00 8.00
19 Brandon Lowe 5.00 12.00
21 A.J. Minter 3.00 8.00
22 Thyago Vieira 2.50 6.00
23 Mike Soroka 4.00 10.00
24 Matt Davidson 3.00 8.00
25 Brian O'Grady 2.50 6.00

2012 Panini Prizm

COMPLETE SET (200) 20.00 50.00
1 Buster Posey .50 1.25
2 Cameron Maybin .25 .60
3 Matt Kemp .30 .75
4 Eric Hosmer .30 .75
5 Adrian Beltre .40 1.00
6 Troy Tulowitzki .40 1.00

7 Robinson Cano .30 .75
8 Albert Pujols .50 1.25
9 Blake Beavan .25 .60
10 Evan Longoria .30 .75
11 Jason Heyward .30 .75
12 Pablo Sandoval .30 .75
13 Aroldis Chapman .40 1.00
14 David Price .30 .75
15 Hanley Ramirez .30 .75
16 Jose Bautista .30 .75
17 Matt Wieters .40 1.00
18 Alex Gordon .30 .75
19 Michael Bourn .25 .60
20 David Wright .30 .75
21 Elvis Andrus .30 .75
22 Derek Jeter 10.00 25.00
23 Andrew McCutchen .40 1.00
24 Miguel Cabrera .40 1.00
25 Ichiro Suzuki .50 1.25
26 Dustin Pedroia .40 1.00
27 Gio Gonzalez .30 .75
28 Anthony Rizzo .50 1.25
29 Clayton Kershaw .60 1.50
30 Jacoby Ellsbury .30 .75
31 Prince Fielder .30 .75
32 Mariano Rivera .50 1.25
33 Adam Jones .30 .75
34 James Shields .25 .60
35 R.A. Dickey .30 .75
36 Colby Rasmus .30 .75
37 Hunter Pence .30 .75
38 Paul Konerko .25 .60
39 Adrian Gonzalez .30 .75
40 David Ortiz .40 1.00
41 Starlin Castro .30 .75
42 Dustin Ackley .25 .60
43 Austin Jackson .30 .75
44 David Freese .25 .60
45 Ryan Braun .25 .60
46 Ian Kennedy .25 .60
47 Curtis Granderson .30 .75
48 Josh Hamilton .30 .75
49 Stephen Strasburg .40 1.00
50 Mike Trout 75.00 200.00
51 Felix Hernandez .30 .75
52 Joey Votto .40 1.00
53 Justin Verlander .40 1.00
54 Freddie Freeman .50 1.25
55 Jose Altuve .30 .75
56 Mike Moustakas .30 .75
57 Giancarlo Stanton .40 1.00
58 Jason Kipnis .30 .75
59 Roy Halladay .30 .75
60 Jered Weaver .30 .75
61 Josh Reddick .25 .60
62 Yovani Gallardo .30 .75
63 Carlos Gonzalez .30 .75
64 Jimmy Rollins .30 .75
65 Ryan Howard .30 .75
66 Joe Mauer .30 .75
67 Alex Rodriguez .50 1.25
68 Jon Lester .25 .60
69 Jose Reyes .25 .60
70 Justin Upton .30 .75
71 Doug Fister .25 .60
72 Josh Willingham .30 .75
73 Yadier Molina .50 1.25
74 Edwin Encarnacion .40 1.00
75 Aramis Ramirez .25 .60
76 Ike Davis .25 .60
77 Jim Johnson .25 .60
78 Billy Butler .25 .60
79 Lance Lynn .25 .60
80 Max Scherzer .40 1.00
81 Johnny Cueto .30 .75
82 Zack Greinke .40 1.00
83 Matt Cain .30 .75
84 B.J. Upton .30 .75
85 Kyle Lohse .25 .60
86 Cole Hamels .30 .75
87 Jay Bruce .30 .75
88 Darwin Barney .25 .60
89 Craig Kimbrel .30 .75
90 Matt Holliday .40 1.00
91 Allen Craig .30 .75
92 Jason Motte .25 .60
93 Kris Medlen .25 .60
94 Chris Sale .40 1.00
95 Tony Campana .25 .60
96 Matt Harrison .25 .60
97 Cliff Lee .30 .75
98 Kevin Youkilis .40 1.00
99 Paul Goldschmidt .40 1.00
100 Chipper Jones 1.00 2.50
101 Dayan Viciedo .25 .60
102 Alex Rios .30 .75
103 Shin-Soo Choo .30 .75
104 Brandon Phillips .25 .60
105 Justin Morneau .30 .75
106 Ryan Roberts .25 .60
107 Coco Crisp .25 .60
108 Nelson Cruz .40 1.00
109 Chase Utley .30 .75
110 Andre Ethier .30 .75
111 Ryan Zimmerman .30 .75
112 James Loney .25 .60
113 Carl Crawford .30 .75
114 Mark Trumbo .25 .60
115 Chase Headley .25 .60
116 Jed Lowrie .25 .60
117 Garrett Jones .25 .60
118 Todd Helton .30 .75
119 Michael Young .25 .60
120 Chris Perez .25 .60
121 Frank Thomas .40 1.00
122 Greg Maddux .50 1.25
123 Ozzie Smith .50 1.25
124 Ernie Banks .40 1.00
125 Stan Musial .60 1.50
126 Paul O'Neill .25 .60
127 Ken Griffey Jr. 10.00 25.00
128 Fernando Valenzuela .15 .40
129 Deion Sanders .25 .60
130 Bo Jackson .40 1.00
131 Don Mattingly .75 2.00
132 Al Kaline .40 1.00
133 Nolan Ryan 1.25 3.00
134 Brooks Robinson .25 .60
135 Will Clark .25 .60
136 Frank Robinson .25 .60
137 Bob Gibson .25 .60
138 Carl Yastrzemski .60 1.50
139 Ivan Rodriguez .25 .60
140 Tony Gwynn .40 1.00
141 Johnny Bench .40 1.00
142 Tom Seaver .25 .60
143 Paul Molitor .40 1.00
144 George Brett .75 2.00
145 Pete Rose .75 2.00
146 Reggie Jackson .25 .60
147 Robin Yount .40 1.00
148 Cal Ripken Jr. 1.25 3.00
149 Rickey Henderson .40 1.00
150 Ryne Sandberg .75 2.00
151 Yu Darvish RC 1.50 4.00
152 Bryce Harper RC 12.00 30.00
153 Wei-Yin Chen RC 1.50 4.00
154 Jarrod Parker RC .75 2.00
155 Brett Lawrie RC .75 2.00
156 Matt Moore RC 1.00 2.50
157 Wade Miley RC .75 2.00
158 Jesus Montero RC .60 1.50
159 Yoenis Cespedes RC 1.50 4.00
160 Sergio Romo RC .75 2.00
161 Scott Diamond RC .60 1.50
162 Jordan Pacheco RC .60 1.50
163 Tom Milone RC .60 1.50
164 Tyler Pastornicky RC .60 1.50
165 Dellin Betances RC 1.00 2.50
166 Trevor Bauer RC 3.00 8.00
167 Quintin Berry RC 1.00 2.50
168 Will Middlebrooks RC .75 2.00
169 Liam Hendriks RC .60 1.50
170 Drew Pomeranz RC .60 1.50
171 David Phelps RC .40 1.00
172 Hector Sanchez RC 1.00 2.50
173 Tyler Moore RC .60 1.50
174 Steve Lombardozzi RC .60 1.50
175 Adron Chambers RC 1.00 2.50
176 Eric Surkamp RC 1.00 2.50
177 Norichika Aoki RC .75 2.00
178 Brett Jackson RC 1.00 2.50
179 Matt Harvey RC 4.00 10.00
180 A.J. Griffin RC .75 2.00
181 Starling Marte RC .75 2.00
182 Andrelton Simmons RC 1.00 2.50
183 Elian Herrera RC 1.00 2.50
184 Drew Smyly RC .60 1.50
185 Hisashi Iwakuma RC 1.25 3.00
186 Matt Adams RC .75 2.00
187 Josh Vitters RC .75 2.00
188 Chris Archer RC .60 1.50
189 Michael Taylor RC .60 1.50
190 Ryan Cook RC .60 1.50
191 Joe Kelly RC 1.00 2.50
192 Zach McAllister RC .75 2.00
193 Jose Quintana RC .60 1.50
194 Addison Reed RC .60 1.50
195 Hector Santiago RC .75 2.00
196 Dale Thayer RC .40 1.00
197 Joe Wieland RC .60 1.50
198 Martin Maldonado RC 1.00 2.50
199 Wilin Rosario RC .60 1.50
200 Kirk Nieuwenhuis RC .60 1.50

2012 Panini Prizm 2013 National Convention Cracked Ice

*CRACKED ICE 1-150: 3X TO 8X BASIC
*CRACKED ICE 151-200: 1.2X TO 3X BASIC
ISSUED AT 2013 NATIONAL CONVENTION
ANNOUNCED PRINT RUN OF 25 COPIES

2012 Panini Prizm Prizms

*PRIZMS: 2X TO 5X BASIC
*PRIZMS RC: .75X TO 2X BASIC RC
22 Derek Jeter 250.00 600.00
50 Mike Trout 750.00 2000.00
127 Ken Griffey Jr. 200.00 500.00
152 Bryce Harper 40.00 100.00

2012 Panini Prizm Prizms Green

*GREEN VET: 2.5X TO 6X BASIC
*GREEN RC: 1X TO 2.5X BASIC RC
22 Derek Jeter 60.00 150.00
50 Mike Trout 1250.00 3000.00
152 Bryce Harper 60.00 150.00

2012 Panini Prizm Prizms Red

*RED VET: 4X TO 10X BASIC
*RED RC: 1.5X TO 4X BASIC RC
22 Derek Jeter 100.00 250.00
50 Mike Trout 2000.00 5000.00
152 Bryce Harper 100.00 200.00

2012 Panini Prizm Autographs

EXCHANGE DEADLINE 10/17/2014
AC Allen Craig 6.00 15.00
AL Adam LaRoche 3.00 8.00
AR Alex Rios 4.00 10.00
BM Brandon McCarthy 3.00 8.00
BO Bo Jackson 40.00 100.00
BW Bernie Williams 15.00 40.00
CP Chris Perez 3.00 8.00
CR Carlos Ruiz 4.00 10.00
CR Clayton Richard 3.00 8.00
CR Cal Ripken Jr. 25.00 60.00
17 Cody Ross 3.00 8.00
CS Chris Sale 6.00 15.00
DB Darwin Barney 4.00 10.00
DF Doug Fister 3.00 8.00
DF Dexter Fowler 3.00 8.00
DH Derek Holland 3.00 8.00
DM Don Mattingly 20.00 50.00
DS Denard Span 3.00 8.00
DS Deion Sanders 15.00 40.00
DW Dave Winfield 10.00 25.00
DW David Wright 12.50 30.00
GB George Brett 40.00 80.00
GB Grant Balfour 3.00 8.00
JB Jonathan Broxton 3.00 8.00
JD Jarrod Dyson 12.00 30.00
JD J.D. Martinez 8.00 20.00
JG Joe Girardi 8.00 20.00
JJ Jim Johnson 5.00 12.00
JK Jason Kipnis 3.00 8.00
JN Joe Nathan 3.00 8.00
JR Ken Griffey Jr. 90.00 150.00
JS Jarrod Saltalamacchia 3.00 8.00
JT Josh Thole 3.00 8.00
JU Julio Teheran 4.00 10.00
JW Josh Willingham 4.00 10.00
KJ Kelly Johnson 3.00 8.00
LD Lucas Duda 5.00 12.00
MH Matt Harrison 3.00 8.00
MM Miguel Montero 3.00 8.00
MR Marc Rzepczynski 4.00 10.00
MR Mark Reynolds 3.00 8.00
MU David Murphy 3.00 8.00
PK Paul Konerko 4.00 10.00
RA R.A. Dickey 3.00 8.00
RH Rickey Henderson 40.00 80.00
RJ Reggie Jackson 20.00 50.00
RR Ryan Roberts 3.00 8.00
RS Ryne Sandberg 15.00 40.00
SS Sergio Santos 3.00 8.00
SS Skip Schumaker 3.00 8.00
TA Jose Tabata 3.00 8.00
TG Tony Gwynn 15.00 40.00
TP Trevor Plouffe 3.00 8.00
WD Wade Davis 3.00 8.00

2012 Panini Prizm Brilliance

*PRIZMS: 1X TO 2.5X BASIC
B1 Felix Hernandez .50 1.25
B2 Miguel Cabrera .60 1.50
B3 Josh Hamilton .50 1.25
B4 Johan Santana .50 1.25
B5 Pablo Sandoval .50 1.25
B6 Mike Trout 20.00 50.00
B7 Ryan Braun .40 1.00
B8 Matt Cain .50 1.25
B9 Adrian Beltre .60 1.50
B10 Philip Humber .40 1.00

2012 Panini Prizm Brilliance Prizms Green

*GREEN: 1.2X TO 3X BASIC

2012 Panini Prizm Dominance

*PRIZMS: 1X TO 2.5X BASIC
D1 Nolan Ryan 2.00 5.00
D2 Bob Gibson .40 1.00
D3 Tom Seaver .40 1.00
D4 Greg Maddux .75 2.00
D5 Justin Verlander .60 1.50
D6 Rickey Henderson .60 1.50
D7 George Brett 1.25 3.00
D8 Derek Jeter 1.50 4.00
D9 Albert Pujols .75 2.00
D10 Miguel Cabrera .60 1.50

2012 Panini Prizm Dominance Prizms

*PRIZMS: 1.5X TO 4X BASIC

2012 Panini Prizm Dominance Prizms Green

*GREEN: 1.2X TO 3X BASIC

2012 Panini Prizm Elite Extra Edition

*PRIZMS: 1X TO 2.5X BASIC
EEE1 Carlos Correa 3.00 8.00
EEE2 Byron Buxton 2.00 5.00
EEE3 Marcus Stroman .60 1.50
EEE4 Max Fried 1.50 4.00
EEE5 Jesse Winker 1.50 4.00
EEE6 Ty Hensley .50 1.25
EEE7 Kevin Plawecki .50 1.25
EEE8 Jeremy Baltz .25 .60
EEE9 Albert Almora 1.00 2.50
EEE10 Damion Carroll .25 .60

2012 Panini Prizm Elite Extra Edition Prizms Green

*GREEN: 1.2X TO 3X BASIC

2012 Panini Prizm Elite Extra Edition Autographs

STATED PRINT RUN 200 SER.#'d SETS
EXCHANGE DEADLINE 10/17/2014
EEEAR Addison Russell/200 12.00 30.00
EEEAS Austin Schotts/200 6.00 15.00
EEEAY Alex Yarbrough/200 3.00 8.00
EEECC Clint Coulter/200 5.00 12.00
EEECH Courtney Hawkins/200 6.00 15.00
EEECS Corey Seager/200 25.00 60.00
EEEDD David Dahl/200 8.00 20.00
EEEGC Gavin Cecchini/200 4.00 10.00
EEEJG Joey Gallo/200 25.00 60.00
EEEJO J.O. Berrios/200 12.00 30.00
EEEKB Keon Barnum/200 3.00 8.00
EEEKZ Kyle Zimmer/200 5.00 12.00
EEELG Lucas Giolito/68 10.00 25.00
EEELM Lance McCullers/200 5.00 12.00
EEEMM Max Muncy/200 12.00 30.00
EEEMO Matt Olson/200 8.00 20.00
EEEMS Matt Smoral/200 3.00 8.00
EEEMZ Mike Zunino/200 8.00 20.00
EEEPB Preston Beck/200 3.00 8.00
EEEPL Pat Light/200 3.00 8.00
EEEPO Peter O'Brien/200 3.00 8.00
EEEST Stryker Trahan/200 4.00 10.00
EEESW Shane Watson/200 6.00 15.00
EEETN Tyler Naquin/200 4.00 10.00
EEEWW Walker Weickel/200 3.00 8.00

2012 Panini Prizm Rookie Autographs

EXCHANGE DEADLINE 10/17/2014
RBJ Brett Jackson 3.00 8.00
RBL Brett Lawrie 6.00 15.00
RDB Dellin Betances 3.00 8.00
RJP Jarrod Parker 3.00 8.00
RMH Matt Harvey 12.00 30.00
RNA Norichika Aoki 12.50 30.00
RQB Quintin Berry 4.00 10.00
RSD Scott Diamond 4.00 10.00
RTB Trevor Bauer 15.00 40.00
RTF Todd Frazier 3.00 8.00
RTM Tom Milone 3.00 8.00
RYC Yoenis Cespedes 12.00 30.00

2012 Panini Prizm Rookie Relevance

COMPLETE SET (12) 8.00 20.00
RR1 Mike Trout 25.00 60.00
RR2 Bryce Harper 6.00 15.00
RR3 Yoenis Cespedes 1.00 2.50
RR4 Wade Miley .50 1.25
RR5 Wilin Rosario .40 1.00
RR6 Yu Darvish 1.00 2.50
RR7 Wei-Yin Chen 1.00 2.50
RR8 Todd Frazier .40 1.00
RR9 Brett Lawrie .50 1.25
RR10 Jesus Montero .40 1.00
RR11 Norichika Aoki .50 1.25
RR12 Jarrod Parker .50 1.25

2012 Panini Prizm Rookie Relevance Prizms

*PRIZMS: 1X TO 2.5X BASIC
RR2 Bryce Harper 4.00 10.00

2012 Panini Prizm Rookie Relevance Prizms Green

*GREEN: 1.2X TO 3X BASIC
RR2 Bryce Harper 5.00 12.00

2012 Panini Prizm Team MVP

MVP1 Craig Kimbrel .50 1.25
MVP2 Aaron Hill .40 1.00
MVP3 Jim Johnson .40 1.00
MVP4 Dustin Pedroia .60 1.50
MVP5 Starlin Castro .50 1.25
MVP6 Paul Konerko .40 1.00
MVP7 Jay Bruce .50 1.25
MVP8 Jason Kipnis .50 1.25
MVP9 Carlos Gonzalez .50 1.25
MVP10 Miguel Cabrera .60 1.50
MVP11 Jose Altuve .50 1.25
MVP12 Billy Butler .40 1.00
MVP13 Mike Trout 30.00 80.00
MVP14 Matt Kemp .50 1.25
MVP15 Giancarlo Stanton .60 1.50
MVP16 Ryan Braun .40 1.00
MVP17 Joe Mauer .50 1.25
MVP18 David Wright .50 1.25
MVP19 Derek Jeter 1.50 4.00
MVP20 Yoenis Cespedes 1.00 2.50
MVP21 Cole Hamels .50 1.25
MVP22 Andrew McCutchen .60 1.50
MVP23 Yadier Molina .75 2.00
MVP24 Chase Headley .40 1.00
MVP25 Buster Posey .75 2.00
MVP26 Felix Hernandez .50 1.25
MVP27 David Price .50 1.25
MVP28 Adrian Beltre .60 1.50
MVP29 Edwin Encarnacion .60 1.50
MVP30 Bryce Harper 6.00 15.00

2012 Panini Prizm Team MVP Prizms

*PRIZMS: 1X TO 2.5X BASIC
MVP30 Bryce Harper 10.00 25.00

2012 Panini Prizm Team MVP Prizms Green

*GREEN: 1.2X TO 3X BASIC

2012 Panini Prizm Top Prospects

*PRIZMS: 1X TO 2.5X BASIC
TP1 Jurickson Profar .50 1.25
TP2 Dylan Bundy .75 2.00
TP3 Shelby Miller .75 2.00
TP4 Gerrit Cole 2.50 6.00
TP5 Wil Myers .60 1.50
TP6 Zach Lee .40 1.00
TP7 Manny Machado 2.50 6.00
TP8 Mike Olt .50 1.25

2012 Panini Prizm Top Prospects Prizms Green

*GREEN: 1.2X TO 3X BASIC
TP7 Manny Machado 8.00 20.00

2012 Panini Prizm USA Baseball

USA1 Mike Trout 30.00 80.00
USA2 Buster Posey .75 2.00
USA3 Justin Verlander .60 1.50
USA4 Stephen Strasburg .60 1.50
USA5 Andrew McCutchen .60 1.50
USA6 Clayton Kershaw 1.00 2.50
USA7 Bryce Harper 6.00 15.00
USA8 Derek Jeter 1.50 4.00
USA9 Justin Upton .50 1.25
USA10 Austin Jackson .50 1.25

2012 Panini Prizm USA Baseball Prizms

*PRIZMS: 1.2X TO 3X BASIC

2013 Panini Prizm

1 Gio Gonzalez .20 .50
2 Alex Gordon .20 .50
3 Clayton Kershaw .40 1.00
4 Desmond Jennings .20 .50
5 Alfonso Soriano .20 .50
6 Tom Milone .15 .40
7 Prince Fielder .20 .50
8 David Freese .15 .40
9 Wellington Castillo .15 .40
10 Josh Reddick .15 .40
11 Dayan Viciedo .15 .40
12 Rickie Weeks .15 .40
13 Martin Prado .15 .40
14 Juan Pierre .15 .40
15 Yadier Molina .30 .75
16 Kris Medlen .20 .50
17 Jed Lowrie .15 .40
18 Zack Cozart .15 .40
19 Paul Goldschmidt .25 .60
20 Michael Bourn .15 .40
21 J.D. Martinez .25 .60
22 Matt Harvey .20 .50
23 Trevor Plouffe .15 .40
24 Victor Martinez .20 .50
25 Miguel Cabrera .25 .60
26 Matt Holliday .25 .60
27 A.J. Burnett .15 .40
28 Max Scherzer .25 .60
29 David Ortiz .25 .60
30 Chris Perez .15 .40
31 Fernando Rodney .15 .40
32 Yoenis Cespedes .25 .60
33 Jeff Samardzija .15 .40
34 Giancarlo Stanton .25 .60
35 James Shields .15 .40
36 Andre Ethier .20 .50
37 Madison Bumgarner .20 .50
38 Jarrod Parker .15 .40
39 Adam Dunn .20 .50
40 Justin Verlander .25 .60
41 Nick Swisher .20 .50
42 Matt Kemp .20 .50
43 Austin Jackson .15 .40
44 Derek Jeter 2.00 5.00
45 Ben Zobrist .20 .50
46 Melky Cabrera .15 .40
47 Hanley Ramirez .20 .50
48 Johan Santana .20 .50
49 Ian Desmond .15 .40
50 Shin-Soo Choo .20 .50
51 Daniel Murphy .20 .50
52 Freddie Freeman .30 .75
53 Coco Crisp .15 .40
54 Lance Berkman .20 .50
55 Carlos Quentin .15 .40
56 Lucas Duda .20 .50
57 Jay Bruce .20 .50
58 Cameron Maybin .15 .40
59 Ian Kinsler .20 .50
60 Jose Reyes .20 .50
61 Wade Miley .15 .40
62 Jordan Zimmermann .20 .50
63 Andy Pettitte .20 .50
64 Aramis Ramirez .15 .40
65 Adam Jones .20 .50
66 Ike Davis .15 .40
67 Cody Ross .15 .40
68 Johnny Cueto .20 .50
69 Scott Diamond .15 .40
70 Andrew McCutchen .25 .60
71 Dexter Fowler .20 .50
72 Michael Morse .15 .40
73 Bryce Harper .40 1.00
74 Evan Longoria .20 .50
75 Neil Walker .15 .40
76 Elvis Andrus .20 .50
77 David Price .20 .50
78 Pedro Alvarez .15 .40
79 Todd Helton .20 .50
80 Craig Kimbrel .20 .50
81 Dustin Pedroia .25 .60
82 Shane Victorino .20 .50
83 Dustin Ackley .15 .40
84 Will Middlebrooks .15 .40
85 Tim Lincecum .20 .50
86 David Wright .20 .50
87 Anthony Rizzo .30 .75
88 Hunter Pence .20 .50
89 Michael Young .15 .40
90 CC Sabathia .20 .50
91 Troy Tulowitzki .25 .60
92 Carlos Santana .20 .50
93 Adam Wainwright .20 .50
94 Carl Crawford .20 .50
95 Joey Votto .25 .60
96 Jesus Montero .15 .40
97 Jason Grilli .15 .40
98 Brett Lawrie .20 .50
99 Adrian Gonzalez .20 .50
100 Yu Darvish .25 .60
101 B.J. Upton .20 .50
102 Curtis Granderson .20 .50
103 Jose Bautista .20 .50
104 Adrian Beltre .25 .60
105 Chris Sale .25 .60
106 Ichiro .30 .75
107 Nelson Cruz .25 .60
108 Norichika Aoki .15 .40
109 Justin Morneau .20 .50
110 Jered Weaver .20 .50
111 Brandon Phillips .15 .40
112 Ryan Braun .20 .50
113 Jose Altuve .20 .50
114 Yonder Alonso .15 .40
115 Ryan Howard .20 .50
116 Justin Upton .20 .50
117 Jeff Francoeur .20 .50
118 Felix Hernandez .20 .50
119 Chase Utley .20 .50
120 Jason Motte .15 .40
121 Robinson Cano .20 .50
122 Huston Street .15 .40
123 Josh Willingham .20 .50
124 Edwin Encarnacion .25 .60
125 Jason Heyward .20 .50
126 Jimmy Rollins .20 .50
127 Trevor Cahill .15 .40
128 Carlos Gonzalez .20 .50
129 Ryan Zimmerman .20 .50
130 Alex Rodriguez .30 .75
131 Billy Butler .15 .40
132 Nick Markakis .20 .50
133 Yovani Gallardo .15 .40
134 Stephen Strasburg .25 .60
135 Zack Greinke .25 .60
136 Wilin Rosario .15 .40
137 Pablo Sandoval .20 .50
138 Vinnie Pestano .15 .40
139 Mike Moustakas .20 .50
140 Torii Hunter .15 .40
141 Jacoby Ellsbury .20 .50
142 Logan Morrison .15 .40
143 Justin Ruggiano .15 .40
144 Matt Garza .15 .40
145 R.A. Dickey .20 .50
146 Starling Marte .20 .50
147 Chase Headley .15 .40
148 Marco Scutaro .20 .50
149 Roy Halladay .20 .50
150 Mark Trumbo .15 .40
151 Josh Hamilton .20 .50
152 Aroldis Chapman .25 .60
153 Wei-Yin Chen .15 .40
154 Asdrubal Cabrera .20 .50
155 Starlin Castro .15 .40
156 Carlos Beltran .20 .50
157 C.J. Wilson .15 .40
158 Mike Napoli .15 .40
159 Mike Trout 3.00 8.00
160 Cole Hamels .20 .50
161 Mariano Rivera .30 .75
162 Allen Craig .20 .50
163 Matt Moore .20 .50
164 Hisashi Iwakuma .20 .50
165 Ian Kennedy .15 .40
166 Buster Posey .30 .75
167 Albert Pujols .30 .75
168 Matt Cain .20 .50
169 Eric Hosmer .20 .50
170 Paul Konerko .20 .50
171 Matt Wieters .25 .60
172 Josh Johnson .20 .50
173 Joe Mauer .20 .50
174 Jim Johnson .15 .40
175 Alex Rios .20 .50
176 Tony Gwynn .25 .60
177 George Brett .50 1.25
178 Jeff Bagwell .20 .50
179 Bernie Williams .20 .50
180 Yogi Berra .25 .60
181 Craig Biggio .20 .50
182 Whitey Ford .20 .50
183 Ken Griffey Jr. 2.00 5.00
184 Pedro Martinez .20 .50
185 Will Clark .20 .50
186 Ryne Sandberg .50 1.25
187 Rickey Henderson .25 .60
188 Carlton Fisk .20 .50
189 Barry Larkin .20 .50
190 Don Mattingly .50 1.25
191 Andre Dawson .20 .50
192 Mike Piazza .25 .60
193 Nomar Garciaparra .20 .50
194 Pete Rose .50 1.25
195 Joe Carter .15 .40
196 Nolan Ryan .75 2.00
197 Willie McCovey .20 .50
198 Bo Jackson .25 .60
199 Cal Ripken Jr. .75 2.00
200 Chipper Jones .25 .60
201 Alfredo Marte RC .25 .60
202 Hyun-Jin Ryu RC .60 1.50
203 Evan Gattis RC .50 1.25
204 Hector Rondon RC .30 .75
205 Nate Freiman RC .25 .60
206 Nick Noonan RC .30 .75
207 Brandon Maurer RC .30 .75
208 Ryan Pressly RC .30 .75
209 Derrick Robinson RC .25 .60
210 Josh Prince RC .25 .60
211 Leury Garcia RC .25 .60
212 T.J. McFarland RC .25 .60
213 Paul Clemens RC .25 .60
214 Alex Wilson RC .25 .60
215 Luis D. Jimenez RC .25 .60
216 Zack Wheeler RC .50 1.25
217 Collin McHugh RC .25 .60
218 Chad Jenkins RC .25 .60
219 Melky Mesa RC .30 .75
220 Nolan Arenado RC 10.00 25.00
221 Khris Davis RC .75 2.00
222 Rob Scahill RC .25 .60
223 Kyuji Fujikawa RC .40 1.00
224 Mike Zunino RC .40 1.00
225 Andrew Taylor RC .25 .60
226 Joe Ortiz RC .25 .60
227 Anthony Rendon RC 1.50 4.00
228 Bruce Rondon RC .25 .60
229 Michael Wacha RC .30 .75
230 Andrew Werner RC .25 .60
231 Justin Grimm RC .25 .60
232 Dylan Bundy RC .60 1.50
233 Manny Machado RC 1.50 4.00
234 Carter Capps RC .25 .60
235 Kyle Gibson RC .40 1.00
236 Tom Koehler RC .25 .60
237 Jaye Chapman RC .25 .60
238 Ryan Jackson RC .25 .60
239 Gerrit Cole RC 1.50 4.00
240 Pedro Villarreal RC .25 .60
241 Zoilo Almonte RC .30 .75
242 Didi Gregorius RC 1.00 2.50
243 David Lough RC .25 .60
244 Chris Herrmann RC .25 .60
245 Rafael Ortega RC .25 .60
246 Bryan Morris RC .25 .60
247 Munenori Kawasaki RC .40 1.00
248 Tyler Cloyd RC .30 .75
249 Adam Eaton RC .40 1.00
250 Hiram Burgos RC .25 .60
251 Mickey Storey RC .25 .60
252 Nathan Karns RC .25 .60
253 Jackie Bradley Jr. RC .60 1.50
254 Brandon Barnes RC .25 .60
255 Yan Gomes RC .30 .75
256 Rob Brantly RC .25 .60
257 Aaron Hicks RC .40 1.00
258 Aaron Loup RC .25 .60
259 Nick Maronde RC .30 .75
260 Yasiel Puig RC 1.00 2.50
261 Brooks Raley RC .25 .60
262 Brock Holt RC .30 .75
263 Francisco Peguero RC .25 .60
264 Paco Rodriguez RC .40 1.00
265 Tyler Skaggs RC .40 1.00
266 Scott Rice RC .40 1.00
267 Wil Myers RC .40 1.00
268 Jake Odorizzi RC .30 .75
269 Mike Olt RC .30 .75
270 Neftali Soto RC .30 .75
271 Tony Cingrani RC .50 1.25
272 Steven Lerud RC .25 .60
273 Deunte Heath RC .25 .60
274 Avisail Garcia RC .30 .75
275 Jurickson Profar RC .30 .75
276 Shelby Miller RC .60 1.50
277 Kevin Gausman RC .75 2.00
278 Carlos Martinez RC .40 1.00
279 L.J. Hoes RC .30 .75
280 Phillippe Aumont RC .25 .60
281 Sean Doolittle RC .25 .60
282 Nick Tepesch RC .30 .75
283 Jose Fernandez RC .60 1.50
284 Marcell Ozuna RC .60 1.50
285 Henry M. Rodriguez RC .25 .60
286 Eury Perez RC .30 .75
287 Matt Magill RC .25 .60
288 Adam Warren RC .25 .60
289 Jake Elmore RC .25 .60
290 Darin Ruf RC .50 1.25
291 Oswaldo Arcia RC .25 .60
292 Robbie Grossman RC .25 .60
293 A.J. Ramos RC .30 .75
294 Casey Kelly RC .30 .75
295 Jedd Gyorko RC .30 .75
296 Jean Machi RC .25 .60
297 Justin Wilson RC .25 .60
298 Jeurys Familia RC .40 1.00
299 Nick Franklin RC .30 .75
300 Allen Webster RC .30 .75
301 Mike Trout SP 12.00 30.00
302 Bryce Harper SP 2.00 5.00
303 Derek Jeter SP 3.00 8.00
304 Stephen Strasburg SP 1.25 3.00
305 Miguel Cabrera SP 1.25 3.00

2013 Panini Prizm Prizms

*PRIZMS 1-200: 1.2X TO 3X BASIC
*PRIZMS 201-300: .75X TO 2X BASIC RC
*PRIZMS 301-305: .4X TO 1X BASIC SP

2013 Panini Prizm Prizms Blue

*BLUE 1-200: 3X TO 8X BASIC
*BLUE 201-300: 2X TO 5X BASIC RC
*BLUE 301-305: .75X TO 2X BASIC SP
159 Mike Trout 60.00 150.00
301 Mike Trout 60.00 150.00

2013 Panini Prizm Prizms Blue Pulsar

*BLUE PULSAR 1-200: 3X TO 8X BASIC
*BLUE PULSAR 201-300: 2X TO 5X BASIC RC
*BLUE PULSAR 301-305: .75X TO 2X BASIC SP
159 Mike Trout 60.00 150.00
301 Mike Trout 60.00 150.00

2013 Panini Prizm Prizms Green

*GREEN 1-200: 4X TO 10X BASIC
*GREEN 201-300: 2.5X TO 6X BASIC RC
*GREEN 301-305: 1X TO 2.5X BASIC SP

2013 Panini Prizm Prizms Orange Die-Cut

*ORANGE 1-200: 8X TO 20X BASIC
*ORANGE 201-300: 5X TO 12X BASIC RC
STATED PRINT RUN 60 SER.#'d SETS
44 Derek Jeter 60.00 150.00
159 Mike Trout 100.00 250.00

2013 Panini Prizm Prizms Red

*RED 1-200: 2.5X TO 6X BASIC
*RED 201-300: 1.5X TO 4X BASIC RC
*RED 301-305: .6X TO 1.5X BASIC SP
159 Mike Trout 50.00 120.00
301 Mike Trout 50.00 120.00

2013 Panini Prizm Prizms Red Pulsar

*RED PULSAR 1-200: 3X TO 8X BASIC
*RED PULSAR 201-300: 2X TO 5X BASIC RC
*RED PULSAR 301-305: .75X TO 2X BASIC SP
159 Mike Trout 60.00 150.00
301 Mike Trout 60.00 150.00

2013 Panini Prizm Autographs

EXCHANGE DEADLNE 03/18/2015
AB Adrian Beltre 12.00 30.00
AC Asdrubal Cabrera 3.00 8.00
AR Andre Ethier 5.00 12.00
AR Aramis Ramirez 3.00 8.00
AT Alan Trammell 6.00 15.00
AZ Anthony Rizzo 10.00 25.00
BM Brandon McCarthy 3.00 8.00
74 Brian Matusz 3.00 8.00
BZ Ben Zobrist 5.00 12.00
CB Craig Biggio 6.00 15.00
CC Carl Crawford 6.00 15.00
CJ Cal Ripken Jr. 20.00 50.00
CL Cliff Lee 3.00 8.00
CR Carlos Ruiz 3.00 8.00
CS Chris Sale 5.00 12.00
DW David Wright 4.00 10.00
FT Frank Thomas 20.00 50.00
GP Glen Perkins 3.00 8.00
GS Gary Sheffield 4.00 10.00
HR Henry A. Rodriguez 3.00 8.00
ID Ike Davis 3.00 8.00
IN Ivan Nova 3.00 8.00
IR Ivan Rodriguez 8.00 20.00
JB Jay Bruce 3.00 8.00
JH J.J. Hardy 3.00 8.00
JJ Josh Johnson 4.00 10.00
JK Jason Kipnis 3.00 8.00
JM Jason Motte 3.00 8.00
JN Joe Nathan 3.00 8.00
JT Julio Teheran 5.00 12.00
JW Josh Willingham 3.00 8.00
JZ Jordan Zimmermann 3.00 8.00
KM Kris Medlen 3.00 8.00
MC James McDonald 3.00 8.00
MM Miguel Montero 3.00 8.00
MP Mike Piazza 20.00 50.00
MR Mariano Rivera 50.00 100.00
MT Mike Trout 60.00 120.00
PB Peter Bourjos 3.00 8.00
PK Pete Kozma 3.00 8.00
PO Paul O'Neill 5.00 12.00
RAE Adam Eaton 3.00 8.00
RAG Avisail Garcia 6.00 15.00
RAH Adeiny Hechavarria 3.00 8.00
RBC Billy Hamilton 3.00 8.00
RBH Brock Holt 3.00 8.00
RCK Casey Kelly 3.00 8.00
RCM Collin McHugh 3.00 8.00
RDB Dylan Bundy 3.00 8.00
RDG Didi Gregorius 3.00 8.00
RDL David Lough 3.00 8.00
RDR Darin Ruf 5.00 12.00
REP Eury Perez 3.00 8.00
RHR Henry M. Rodriguez 3.00 8.00
RJC Jaye Chapman 3.00 8.00
RJF Jeurys Familia 3.00 8.00
RJO Jake Odorizzi 3.00 8.00
RJP Jurickson Profar 4.00 10.00
RK Roger Clemens 15.00 40.00
RLJ L.J. Hoes 5.00 12.00
RMH Mike Olt 4.00 10.00
RMM Manny Machado 15.00 40.00
RMM Melky Mesa 3.00 8.00
RNM Nick Maronde 3.00 8.00
ROS Oscar Taveras 4.00 10.00
RPR Paco Rodriguez 3.00 8.00
RRB Rob Brantly 3.00 8.00
RRS Rob Scahill 3.00 8.00
RS Ryne Sandberg 12.00 30.00
RSM Shelby Miller 4.00 25.00
RST Shawn Tolleson 3.00 8.00
RTB Trevor Bauer 10.00 25.00
RTC Tony Cingrani 8.00 20.00

RTS Tyler Skaggs 3.00 8.00
RTY Tyler Cloyd 10.00 25.00
RWM Wil Myers 4.00 10.00
SM Sean Marshall 3.00 8.00
SR Sergio Romo 5.00 12.00
SS Stephen Strasburg 15.00 40.00
TC Tyler Clippard 3.00 8.00
TF Tyler Flowers 3.00 8.00
TM Tom Milone 3.00 8.00
WC Wei-Yin Chen 20.00 50.00
WE Willie Randolph 3.00 8.00
WI Wilin Rosario 3.00 8.00
WR Wandy Rodriguez 3.00 8.00
ZM Zach McAllister 3.00 8.00

2013 Panini Prizm Band of Brothers

1 Pjols/Hmltn/Trout 10.00 25.00
2 A.Burnett/A.McCutchen 1.25 3.00
3 Gnzlz/Ethier/Kemp 1.00 2.50
4 G.Stanton/L.Morrison 1.25 3.00
5 Hill/Gldschmdt/Mley 1.25 3.00
6 A.Soriano/A.Rizzo 1.50 4.00
7 Gnzlz/Tlwtzki/Rsrio 1.25 3.00
8 Cabrera/Bourn/Swisher 1.00 2.50
9 Ortz/Pdria/Ellsbry 1.25 3.00
10 A.Dunn/P.Konerko 1.00 2.50
11 Btler/Hsmr/Shlds 1.00 2.50
12 Rmrez/Braun/Gllrdo 1.00 2.50
13 D.Wright/I.Davis 1.00 2.50
14 Utly/Hlldy/Hwrd 1.00 2.50
15 C.Quentin/C.Headley .75 2.00
16 J.Mauer/J.Willingham 1.00 2.50
17 F.Hernandez/M.Morse 1.00 2.50
18 Lwrie/Encrncn/Btsta 1.25 3.00
19 Zbrst/Prce/Lngria 1.00 2.50
20 J.Castro/J.Altuve 1.00 2.50
21 C.Beltran/D.Freese SP 1.25 3.00
22 Jnes/Jhnsn/Mrkkis SP 1.25 3.00
23 Bltre/Knsler/Drvsh SP 1.50 4.00
24 Uptn/Hywrd/Uptn SP 1.25 3.00
25 Hrper/Gnzlez/Strsbrg SP 2.50 6.00
26 Philps/Vtto/Cueto SP 1.50 4.00
27 Psey/Cain/Lnccm SP 2.00 5.00
28 Sbthia/Jter/Cano SP 4.00 10.00
29 Prkr/Rddck/Cspdes SP 1.50 4.00
30 Vrlndr/Cbrra/Flder SP 1.50 4.00

2013 Panini Prizm Band of Brothers Prizms

*PRIZMS 1-20: .6X TO 1.5X BASIC
*PRIZMS 21-30: .5X TO 1.2X BASIC

2013 Panini Prizm Band of Brothers Prizms Blue

*BLUE 1-20: .75X TO 2X BASIC

2013 Panini Prizm Band of Brothers Prizms Blue Pulsar

*BLUE PULSAR: 1.2X TO 3X BASIC

2013 Panini Prizm Band of Brothers Prizms Green

*GREEN 1-20: .75X TO 2X BASIC
*GREEN 21-30: .6X TO 1.5X BASIC

2013 Panini Prizm Band of Brothers Prizms Red

*RED 1-20: .75X TO 2X BASIC
*RED 21-30: .6X TO 1.5X BASIC

2013 Panini Prizm Band of Brothers Prizms Red Pulsar

*RED PULSAR: 1.2X TO 3X BASIC

2013 Panini Prizm Father's Day

B6 Mike Trout BRIL 8.00 20.00
127 Ken Griffey Jr. (Rainbow Parallel) 2.00 5.00
149 Rickey Henderson (Rainbow Parallel) 1.00 2.50
152 Bryce Harper (Rainbow Parallel) 1.50 4.00
156 Matt Moore (Rainbowm Parallel) .75 2.00
159 Yoenis Cespedes (Rainbow Parallel) 1.00 2.50
179 Matt Harvey (Rainbow Parallel) .75 2.00
181 Starling Marte (Rainbow Parallel) .75 2.00
RR6 Yu Darvish RR 1.00 2.50
TP4 Gerrit Cole TP 4.00 10.00
MVP13 Mike Trout MVP 8.00 20.00

2013 Panini Prizm Fearless

1 Buster Posey 1.25 3.00
2 Yadier Molina 1.25 3.00
3 Derek Jeter 2.50 6.00
4 Mike Trout 8.00 20.00
5 Bryce Harper 1.50 4.00
6 Justin Verlander 1.00 2.50
7 Adrian Beltre 1.00 2.50
8 Jose Altuve .75 2.00
9 Felix Hernandez .75 2.00
10 Matt Cain .75 2.00
11 Giancarlo Stanton 1.00 2.50
12 Troy Tulowitzki 1.00 2.50
13 Michael Bourn .60 1.50
14 Dustin Pedroia 1.00 2.50
15 Brian McCann .75 2.00
16 Adam Jones .75 2.00
17 Stephen Strasburg 1.00 2.50
18 Michael Young .60 1.50
19 Brandon Phillips .60 1.50
20 Jose Bautista .75 2.00

2013 Panini Prizm Fearless Prizms

*PRIZMS: .75X TO 2X BASIC

2013 Panini Prizm Fearless Prizms Blue

*BLUE: 1X TO 2.5X BASIC

2013 Panini Prizm Fearless Prizms Blue Pulsar

*BLUE PULSAR: 1.2X TO 3X BASIC

2013 Panini Prizm Fearless Prizms Green

*GREEN: 1X TO 2.5X BASIC

2013 Panini Prizm Fearless Prizms Red

*RED: 1X TO 2.5X BASIC

2013 Panini Prizm Fearless Prizms Red Pulsar

*RED PULSAR: 1.2X TO 3X BASIC

2013 Panini Prizm Rookie Challengers

1 Yasiel Puig 2.00 5.00
2 Dylan Bundy 1.25 3.00
3 Evan Gattis 1.00 2.50
4 Jurickson Profar .60 1.50
5 Darin Ruf 1.00 2.50
6 Manny Machado 3.00 8.00
7 Tyler Skaggs .75 2.00
8 Shelby Miller 1.25 3.00
9 Gerrit Cole 3.00 8.00
10 Jake Odorizzi .60 1.50
11 Anthony Rendon 3.00 8.00
12 Michael Wacha .60 1.50
13 Nick Franklin .60 1.50
14 Zack Wheeler 1.00 2.50
15 Jedd Gyorko .60 1.50
16 Kevin Gausman 1.50 4.00
17 Didi Gregorius 2.00 5.00
18 Hyun-Jin Ryu 1.25 3.00

2013 Panini Prizm Rookie Challengers Prizms

*PRIZMS: .75X TO 2X BASIC
1 Yasiel Puig 15.00 40.00

2013 Panini Prizm Rookie Challengers Prizms Blue

*BLUE: 1.2X TO 3X BASIC

2013 Panini Prizm Rookie Challengers Prizms Green

*GREEN: 1.2X TO 3X BASIC

2013 Panini Prizm Rookie Challengers Prizms Red

*RED: 1.2X TO 3X BASIC

2013 Panini Prizm Superstar Spotlight

1 Albert Pujols 1.25 3.00
2 Matt Cain .75 2.00
3 Andrew McCutchen 1.00 2.50
4 Ryan Braun .75 2.00
5 Justin Verlander 1.00 2.50
6 David Wright .75 2.00
7 Giancarlo Stanton 1.00 2.50
8 Clayton Kershaw 1.50 4.00
9 Stephen Strasburg 1.00 2.50
10 Matt Kemp .75 2.00
11 Robinson Cano .75 2.00
12 Joey Votto 1.00 2.50
13 Felix Hernandez .75 2.00
14 Miguel Cabrera 1.00 2.50
15 Joe Mauer .75 2.00

2013 Panini Prizm Superstar Spotlight Prizms

*PRIZMS: .75X TO 2X BASIC

2013 Panini Prizm Superstar Spotlight Prizms Blue

*BLUE: 1X TO 2.5X BASIC

2013 Panini Prizm Superstar Spotlight Prizms Blue Pulsar

*BLUE PULSAR: 1.2X TO 3X BASIC

2013 Panini Prizm Superstar Spotlight Prizms Green

*GREEN: 1X TO 2.5X BASIC

2013 Panini Prizm Superstar Spotlight Prizms Red

*RED: 1X TO 2.5X BASIC

2013 Panini Prizm Top Prospects

1 Carlos Correa 6.00 15.00
2 Nick Castellanos 1.50 4.00
3 Bubba Starling .60 1.50
4 Jameson Taillon .60 1.50
5 Oscar Taveras .60 1.50
6 Miguel Sano .60 1.50
7 Billy Hamilton .60 1.50
8 Addison Russell .75 2.00
9 Javier Baez 2.00 5.00
10 Taijuan Walker .60 1.50
11 Travis d'Arnaud .60 1.50
12 Francisco Lindor 4.00 10.00

2013 Panini Prizm Top Prospects Prizms

*PRIZMS: .75X TO 2X BASIC

2013 Panini Prizm Top Prospects Prizms Blue

*BLUE: 1.2X TO 3X BASIC

2013 Panini Prizm Top Prospects Prizms Green

*GREEN: 1.2X TO 3X BASIC

2013 Panini Prizm Top Prospects Prizms Red

*RED: 1.2X TO 3X BASIC

2013 Panini Prizm USA Baseball

1 Dustin Pedroia 1.00 2.50
2 Joe Mauer .75 2.00
3 Troy Tulowitzki 1.00 2.50
4 Stephen Strasburg 1.00 2.50
5 Matt Harvey .75 2.00
6 R.A. Dickey .75 2.00
7 Alex Gordon .75 2.00
8 David Price .75 2.00
9 Jered Weaver .75 2.00
10 Mike Trout 8.00 20.00

2013 Panini Prizm USA Baseball Prizms

*PRIZMS: .75X TO 2X BASIC

2013 Panini Prizm USA Baseball Prizms Signatures

STATED PRINT RUN 25 SER.#'d SETS
EXCHANGE DEADLNE 03/18/2015
1 Dustin Pedroia 30.00 60.00
3 Troy Tulowitzki 40.00 80.00
4 Stephen Strasburg 60.00 120.00
7 Alex Gordon 15.00 40.00
10 Mike Trout 100.00 200.00

2014 Panini Prizm

COMP.SET w/o SP's (200) 20.00 50.00
1 Stephen Strasburg .25 .60
2 Starling Marte .20 .50
3 Mike Trout 1.25 3.00
4 Shin-Soo Choo .20 .50
5 Miguel Cabrera .25 .60
6 Yoenis Cespedes .25 .60
7 Michael Wacha .20 .50
8 Michael Cuddyer .15 .40
9 Max Scherzer .25 .60
10 Matt Wieters .25 .60
11 Matt Moore .20 .50
12 Robinson Cano .20 .50
13 Miguel Montero .15 .40
14 Shane Victorino .20 .50
15 Salvador Perez .20 .50
16 Ryan Zimmerman .20 .50
17 Ryan Howard .20 .50
18 Ryan Braun .20 .50
19 Matt Kemp .20 .50
20 Matt Holliday .25 .60
21 Matt Harvey .20 .50
22 Matt Carpenter .25 .60
23 Mat Latos .20 .50
24 Zack Greinke .25 .60
25 Yunel Escobar .15 .40
26 Yu Darvish .25 .60
27 Hyun-Jin Ryu .20 .50
28 Yasiel Puig .25 .60
29 Yadier Molina .30 .75
30 Will Venable .15 .40
31 Troy Tulowitzki .25 .60
32 Kris Medlen .20 .50
33 Koji Uehara .15 .40
34 Justin Verlander .25 .60
35 Justin Upton .20 .50
36 Justin Ruggiano .15 .40
37 Victor Martinez .20 .50
38 Justin Masterson .15 .40
39 Jurickson Profar .20 .50
40 Felix Hernandez .20 .50
41 Everth Cabrera .15 .40
42 Alex Gordon .20 .50
43 Albert Pujols .30 .75
44 Manny Machado .25 .60
45 Adrian Beltre .25 .60
46 Adam Wainwright .20 .50
47 Wil Myers .15 .40
48 Adam Dunn .20 .50
49 A.J. Burnett .15 .40
50 Martin Prado .15 .40
51 Marlon Byrd .15 .40
52 Mark Trumbo .15 .40
53 Mark Teixeira .20 .50
54 Adrian Gonzalez .20 .50
55 Justin Morneau .20 .50
56 Adam Jones .20 .50
57 Matt Cain .20 .50
58 Torii Hunter .15 .40
59 Tim Lincecum .20 .50
60 Andrew McCutchen .25 .60
61 Andrelton Simmons .15 .40
62 Allen Craig .20 .50
63 Alfonso Soriano .20 .50
64 Alex Rios .20 .50
65 Evan Longoria .20 .50
66 Eric Hosmer .20 .50
67 Elvis Andrus .20 .50
68 Edwin Encarnacion .25 .60
69 Dustin Pedroia .25 .60
70 David Wright .20 .50
71 Derek Holland .15 .40
72 Chase Headley .15 .40
73 David Price .20 .50
74 David Ortiz .25 .60
75 Chase Utley .20 .50
76 Derek Jeter .60 1.50
77 CC Sabathia .20 .50
78 Carlos Santana .20 .50
79 Bryce Harper .40 1.00
80 Carlos Gomez .15 .40
81 Austin Jackson .15 .40
82 Carl Crawford .20 .50
83 C.J. Wilson .15 .40
84 Buster Posey .30 .75
85 Carlos Gonzalez .20 .50
86 Brian Dozier .20 .50
87 Brandon Phillips .15 .40
88 Billy Butler .15 .40
89 Ben Zobrist .20 .50
90 B.J. Upton .20 .50
91 Carlos Beltran .20 .50
92 Anthony Rizzo .30 .75
93 Francisco Liriano .15 .40
94 Josh Hamilton .20 .50
95 Josh Donaldson .20 .50
96 Jose Reyes .20 .50
97 David DeJesus .15 .40
98 Jose Bautista .20 .50
99 Clayton Kershaw .40 1.00
100 Jorge De La Rosa .15 .40
101 Jordan Zimmerman .20 .50
102 Jon Lester .20 .50
103 Joey Votto .25 .60
104 Joe Mauer .20 .50
105 Jimmy Rollins .20 .50
106 Jim Johnson .15 .40
107 Jose Fernandez .25 .60
108 Curtis Granderson .20 .50
109 Craig Kimbrel .20 .50
110 Colby Rasmus .20 .50
111 Coco Crisp .15 .40
112 Cliff Lee .20 .50
113 Jose Altuve .20 .50
114 Chris Tillman .15 .40
115 Chris Sale .25 .60
116 Jay Bruce .20 .50
117 Chris Davis .15 .40
118 Ichiro Suzuki .40 1.00
119 Jedd Gyorko .15 .40
120 Jean Segura .20 .50
121 Chris Johnson .15 .40
122 Jason Kipnis .20 .50
123 Hanley Ramirez .20 .50
124 Mike Napoli .15 .40
125 Jarrod Parker .15 .40
126 Paul Goldschmidt .25 .60
127 James Shields .15 .40
128 Jacoby Ellsbury .20 .50
129 J.J. Hardy .15 .40
130 Chris Carter .15 .40
131 Hunter Pence .20 .50
132 Hisashi Iwakuma .20 .50
133 Hiroki Kuroda .15 .40
134 Jason Grilli .15 .40
135 Greg Holland .15 .40
136 Giancarlo Stanton .25 .60
137 Freddie Freeman .30 .75
138 Jered Weaver .20 .50
139 Prince Fielder .20 .50
140 Pedro Alvarez .15 .40
141 Paul Konerko .20 .50
142 R.A. Dickey .20 .50
143 Pablo Sandoval .20 .50
144 Nick Swisher .20 .50
145 Nate Schierholtz .15 .40
146 Mitch Moreland .15 .40
147 Starlin Castro .15 .40
148 Gerrit Cole .25 .60
149 Chris Archer .15 .40
150 Julio Teheran .20 .50
151 Rickey Henderson .25 .60
152 Reggie Jackson .20 .50
153 Mike Schmidt .40 1.00
154 Ryne Sandberg .50 1.25
155 Ken Griffey Jr. .50 1.25
156 Alan Trammell .20 .50
157 Tony Gwynn .25 .60
158 Eddie Murray .20 .50
159 Cal Ripken Jr. .75 2.00
160 Bill Mazeroski .20 .50
161 Mariano Rivera .30 .75
162 Frank Thomas .25 .60
163 Don Mattingly .50 1.25
164 Chipper Jones .25 .60
165 Jeff Bagwell .20 .50
166 George Brett .50 1.25
167 Pete Rose .50 1.25
168 Pedro Martinez .20 .50
169 Ozzie Smith .30 .75
170 Nolan Ryan .75 2.00
171 Chad Bettis RC .25 .60
172 Xander Bogaerts RC .75 2.00
173 Ethan Martin RC .25 .60
174 Tim Beckham RC .40 1.00
175 Reymond Fuentes RC .25 .60
176 Taijuan Walker RC .25 .60
177 J.R. Murphy RC .25 .60
178 Chris Owings RC .25 .60
179 James Paxton RC .40 1.00
180 Cameron Rupp RC .25 .60
181 Wilmer Flores RC .30 .75
182 Travis D'Arnaud RC .30 .75
183 Kolten Wong RC .30 .75
184 Michael Choice RC .25 .60
185 Masahiro Tanaka RC .75 2.00
186 Ehire Adrianza RC .25 .60
187 Jimmy Nelson RC .25 .60
188 Charlie Leesman RC .25 .60
189 Brian Flynn RC .25 .60
190 Matt Davidson RC .30 .75
191 Logan Watkins RC .25 .60
192 Ryan Goins RC .30 .75
193 Max Stassi RC .25 .60
194 Marcus Semien RC 1.25 3.00
195 Andrew Lambo RC .25 .60
196 David Holmberg RC .25 .60
197 Matt Den Dekker RC .30 .75
198 Kevin Pillar RC .25 .60
199 Jose Abreu RC 2.00 5.00
200 Billy Hamilton RC .30 .75
201 Miguel Cabrera SP 2.00 5.00
202 Andrew McCutchen SP 2.00 5.00
203 Wil Myers SP 1.25 3.00
204 Jose Fernandez SP 2.00 5.00
205 Max Scherzer SP 2.00 5.00
206 Clayton Kershaw SP 3.00 8.00
207 David Ortiz SP 2.00 5.00
208 Mariano Rivera SP 2.50 6.00
209 Yadier Molina SP 2.50 6.00
210 Chris Davis SP 1.25 3.00

2014 Panini Prizm Prizms

*PRIZMS 1-170: 1.5X TO 4X BASIC
*PRIZMS 171-200: 1X TO 2.5X BASIC RC
*PRIZMS 201-210: .4X TO 1X BASIC SP

2014 Panini Prizm Prizms Blue 42

*BLUE 42 1-170: 8X TO 20X BASIC
*BLUE 42 171-200: 5X TO 12X BASIC RC
STATED PRINT RUN 42 SER.#'d SETS
3 Mike Trout 30.00 80.00
5 Miguel Cabrera 15.00 40.00
28 Yasiel Puig 30.00 80.00
76 Derek Jeter 30.00 80.00
155 Ken Griffey Jr. 25.00 60.00
169 Ozzie Smith 12.00 30.00
199 Jose Abreu 60.00 120.00

2014 Panini Prizm Prizms Blue Mojo

*BLUE MOJO 1-170: 5X TO 12X BASIC
*BLUE MOJO 171-200: 3X TO 8X BASIC RC
*BLUE MOJO 201-210: .6X TO 1.5X BASIC SP
STATED PRINT RUN 75 SER.#'d SETS
76 Derek Jeter 12.00 30.00
199 Jose Abreu 12.00 30.00

2014 Panini Prizm Prizms Camo

*CAMO 1-170: 5X TO 12X BASIC
*CAMO 171-200: 3X TO 8X BASIC RC
199 Jose Abreu 12.00 30.00

2014 Panini Prizm Prizms Orange Die Cut

*ORANGE 1-170: 6X TO 15X BASIC
*ORANGE 171-200: 4X TO 10X BASIC RC
STATED PRINT RUN 60 SER.#'d SETS
3 Mike Trout 25.00 60.00
5 Miguel Cabrera 12.00 30.00
28 Yasiel Puig 25.00 60.00
76 Derek Jeter 25.00 60.00
155 Ken Griffey Jr. 20.00 50.00
169 Ozzie Smith 10.00 25.00
170 Nolan Ryan 20.00 50.00
199 Jose Abreu 30.00 80.00

2014 Panini Prizm Prizms Purple

*PURPLE 1-170: 4X TO 10X BASIC
*PURPLE 171-200: 2.5X TO 6X BASIC RC
*PURPLE 201-210: .5X TO 1.2X BASIC SP
STATED PRINT RUN 99 SER.#'d SETS
76 Derek Jeter 10.00 25.00
199 Jose Abreu 25.00 60.00

2014 Panini Prizm Prizms Red

*RED 1-170: 10X TO 25X BASIC
*RED 171-200: 6X TO 15X BASIC RC
*RED 201-210: 1.2X TO 3X BASIC SP
STATED PRINT RUN 25 SER.#'d SETS
5 Miguel Cabrera 20.00 50.00
28 Yasiel Puig 40.00 100.00
76 Derek Jeter 40.00 100.00
155 Ken Griffey Jr. 30.00 80.00
169 Ozzie Smith 15.00 40.00
170 Nolan Ryan 30.00 80.00
199 Jose Abreu 75.00 200.00

2014 Panini Prizm Prizms Red White and Blue Pulsar

*RWB 1-170: 6X TO 15X BASIC
*RWB 171-200: 4X TO 10X BASIC RC
162 Frank Thomas 8.00 20.00
199 Jose Abreu 12.00 30.00

2014 Panini Prizm Autographs Prizms

EXCHANGE DEADLINE 11/21/2015
AB Archie Bradley 2.50 6.00
BY Byron Buxton 5.00 12.00
CF Clint Frazier 10.00 25.00
DN Daniel Nava 2.50 6.00
JA Jose Abreu 30.00 60.00
JG Jonathan Gray 3.00 8.00
JS Jean Segura 3.00 8.00
JT Jameson Taillon *3.00 8.00
KB Kris Bryant 50.00 120.00
MC Matt Carpenter 6.00 15.00
MN Mike Napoli 5.00 12.00
MO Mitch Moreland 2.50 6.00
MS Miguel Sano 3.00 8.00
NS Noah Syndergaard 6.00 15.00
OT Oscar Taveras 12.00 30.00
SM Starling Marte 6.00 15.00
SV Shane Victorino 6.00 15.00

2014 Panini Prizm Autographs Prizms Mojo

*MOJO: .6X TO 1.5X BASIC
STATED PRINT RUN 75 SER.#'d SETS
EXCHANGE DEADLINE 11/21/2015
BP Brandon Phillips 5.00 12.00
CB Craig Biggio 15.00 40.00
CD Chris Davis 12.00 30.00
CK Clayton Kershaw 25.00 60.00
CM Carlos Martinez 5.00 12.00
DO David Ortiz 20.00 50.00
DS Darryl Strawberry 12.00 30.00
EM Edgar Martinez 12.00 30.00
JB Jeff Bagwell 12.00 30.00
JD Josh Donaldson 10.00 25.00
JF Jose Fernandez 25.00 60.00
JO Jose Bautista 10.00 25.00
JP Jarrod Parker 4.00 10.00
MG Mark Grace 15.00 40.00
MM Manny Machado 20.00 50.00
MT Mike Trout/25 150.00 250.00
PK Paul Konerko 8.00 20.00
PO Paul O'Neill 10.00 25.00
PR Pete Rose 90.00 150.00
TG Tom Glavine 12.00 30.00
TR Mark Trumbo 4.00 10.00
YC Yoenis Cespedes 12.00 30.00

2014 Panini Prizm Autographs Prizms Purple

*PURPLE: .5X TO 1.2X BASIC
STATED PRINT RUN 99 SER.#'d SETS
EXCHANGE DEADLINE 11/21/2015
BP Brandon Phillips 4.00 10.00
DS Darryl Strawberry 10.00 25.00
EM Edgar Martinez 10.00 25.00
GS George Springer 20.00 50.00
JD Josh Donaldson 8.00 20.00
JF Jose Fernandez 20.00 50.00
JP Jarrod Parker 3.00 8.00
PK Paul Konerko 10.00 25.00
TG Tom Glavine 10.00 25.00
TR Mark Trumbo 3.00 8.00

2014 Panini Prizm Chasing the Hall

1 Derek Jeter 2.50 6.00
2 Ichiro Suzuki 1.50 4.00
3 Albert Pujols 1.25 3.00
4 Dustin Pedroia 1.00 2.50
5 Paul Konerko .75 2.00
6 David Ortiz 1.00 2.50
7 Prince Fielder .75 2.00
8 Robinson Cano .75 2.00
9 Adam Dunn .75 2.00
10 Miguel Cabrera 1.00 2.50
11 Adrian Beltre 1.00 2.50
12 Carlos Beltran .75 2.00
13 Roy Halladay .75 2.00
14 Todd Helton .75 2.00
15 Felix Hernandez .75 2.00
16 Joe Mauer .75 2.00
17 Justin Verlander 1.00 2.50
18 CC Sabathia .75 2.00
19 Joey Votto 1.00 2.50
20 David Wright .75 2.00

2014 Panini Prizm Chasing the Hall Prizms

*PRIZMS: .5X TO 1.2X BASIC

2014 Panini Prizm Chasing the Hall Prizms Blue Mojo

*BLUE MOJO: 1.2X TO 3X BASIC
STATED PRINT RUN 75 SER.#'d SETS

2014 Panini Prizm Chasing the Hall Prizms Purple

*PURPLE: 1X TO 2.5X BASIC
STATED PRINT RUN 99 SER.#'d SETS

2014 Panini Prizm Chasing the Hall Prizms Red

*RED: 2.5X TO 6X BASIC
STATED PRINT RUN 25 SER.#'d SETS
1 Derek Jeter 40.00 100.00

2014 Panini Prizm Diamond Dominance

1 Andrew McCutchen 1.00 2.50
2 Mike Trout 5.00 12.00
3 Miguel Cabrera 1.00 2.50
4 Yadier Molina 1.25 3.00
5 Evan Longoria .75 2.00
6 Joey Votto 1.00 2.50
7 Robinson Cano .75 2.00
8 Chris Davis .60 1.50
9 Paul Goldschmidt 1.00 2.50
10 Clayton Kershaw 1.50 4.00
11 Josh Donaldson .75 2.00
12 Carlos Gomez .60 1.50
13 Matt Carpenter 1.00 2.50
14 Max Scherzer 1.00 2.50
15 Manny Machado 1.00 2.50
16 Dustin Pedroia 1.00 2.50
17 David Wright .75 2.00
18 Felix Hernandez .75 2.00
19 Freddie Freeman 1.25 3.00
20 Wil Myers .60 1.50
21 Bryce Harper 1.50 4.00
22.Albert Pujols 1.25 3.00
23 Adrian Beltre 1.00 2.50
24 Buster Posey 1.25 3.00
25 Troy Tulowitzki 1.00 2.50
26 Pete Rose 2.00 5.00
27 Mike Piazza 1.00 2.50
28 George Brett 2.00 5.00
29 Ken Griffey Jr 2.00 5.00
30 Cal Ripken Jr 3.00 8.00

2014 Panini Prizm Diamond Dominance Prizms

*PRIZMS: .5X TO 1.2X BASIC

2014 Panini Prizm Diamond Dominance Prizms Blue Mojo

*BLUE MOJO: 1.2X TO 3X BASIC
STATED PRINT RUN 75 SER.#'d SETS

2014 Panini Prizm Diamond Dominance Prizms Purple

*PURPLE: 1X TO 2.5X BASIC
STATED PRINT RUN 99 SER.#'d SETS

2014 Panini Prizm Diamond Dominance Prizms Red

*RED: 2.5X TO 6X BASIC
STATED PRINT RUN 25 SER.#'d SETS

2014 Panini Prizm Fearless

1 Yasiel Puig 1.00 2.50
2 Buster Posey 1.25 3.00
3 Yadier Molina 1.25 3.00
4 Chris Davis .60 1.50
5 David Ortiz 1.00 2.50
6 Mike Trout 5.00 12.00
7 Andrew McCutchen 1.00 2.50
8 Michael Cuddyer .60 1.50
9 Adrian Beltre 1.00 2.50
10 Jason Kipnis .75 2.00
11 Xander Bogaerts 2.00 5.00
12 Edwin Encarnacion 1.00 2.50
13 Josh Donaldson .75 2.00
14 Jay Bruce .75 2.00
15 Bryce Harper 1.50 4.00
16 Paul Goldschmidt 1.00 2.50
17 Torii Hunter .60 1.50
18 Pedro Alvarez .60 1.50
19 Josh Hamilton .75 2.00
20 Hisashi Iwakuma .75 2.00
21 Cliff Lee .75 2.00
22 Yu Darvish 1.00 2.50
23 Jose Fernandez 1.00 2.50
24 David Price .75 2.00

2014 Panini Prizm Fearless Prizms

*PRIZMS: .5X TO 1.2X BASIC

2014 Panini Prizm Fearless Prizms Blue Mojo

*BLUE MOJO: 1.2X TO 3X BASIC
STATED PRINT RUN 75 SER.#'d SETS

2014 Panini Prizm Fearless Prizms Purple

*PURPLE: 1X TO 2.5X BASIC
STATED PRINT RUN 99 SER.#'d SETS

2014 Panini Prizm Fearless Prizms Red

*RED: 2.5X TO 6X BASIC
STATED PRINT RUN 25 SER.#'d SETS

2014 Panini Prizm Gold Leather Die Cut

1 Yadier Molina 1.25 3.00
2 Paul Goldschmidt 1.00 2.50
3 Brandon Phillips .60 1.50
4 Carlos Gonzalez .75 2.00
5 Carlos Gomez .60 1.50
6 Adam Wainwright .75 2.00
7 R.A. Dickey .75 2.00
8 Shane Victorino .75 2.00
9 Adam Jones .75 2.00
10 Alex Gordon .75 2.00
11 Eric Hosmer .75 2.00
12 Dustin Pedroia 1.00 2.50
13 Manny Machado 1.00 2.50
14 J.J. Hardy .60 1.50
15 Andrelton Simmons .60 1.50

2014 Panini Prizm Gold Leather Die Cut Prizms

*PRIZMS: .5X TO 1.2X BASIC

2014 Panini Prizm Gold Leather Die Cut Prizms Blue Mojo

*BLUE MOJO: 1.2X TO 3X BASIC
STATED PRINT RUN 75 SER.#'d SETS

2014 Panini Prizm Gold Leather Die Cut Prizms Purple

*PURPLE: 1X TO 2.5X BASIC
STATED PRINT RUN 99 SER.#'d SETS

2014 Panini Prizm Gold Leather Die Cut Prizms Red

*RED: 2.5X TO 6X BASIC
STATED PRINT RUN 25 SER.#'d SETS

2014 Panini Prizm Intuition

1 Clayton Kershaw 1.50 4.00
2 Max Scherzer 1.00 2.50
3 Yu Darvish 1.00 2.50
4 Jose Fernandez 1.00 2.50
5 Chris Sale 1.00 2.50
6 Hyun-Jin Ryu .75 2.00
7 Kris Medlen .75 2.00
8 Justin Verlander 1.00 2.50
9 Matt Moore .75 2.00
10 R.A. Dickey .75 2.00
11 Craig Kimbrel .75 2.00
12 Felix Hernandez .75 2.00
13 Stephen Strasburg 1.00 2.50
14 Tim Lincecum .75 2.00
15 Bartolo Colon .60 1.50
16 Matt Harvey .75 2.00
17 Zack Greinke 1.00 2.50
18 Adam Wainwright .75 2.00
19 Shelby Miller .75 2.00
20 Jordan Zimmerman .75 2.00

2014 Panini Prizm Intuition Prizms

*PRIZMS: .5X TO 1.2X BASIC

2014 Panini Prizm Intuition Prizms Blue Mojo

*BLUE MOJO: 1.2X TO 3X BASIC
STATED PRINT RUN 75 SER.#'d SETS

2014 Panini Prizm Intuition Prizms Purple

*PURPLE: 1X TO 2.5X BASIC
STATED PRINT RUN 99 SER.#'d SETS

2014 Panini Prizm Intuition Prizms Red

*RED: 2.5X TO 6X BASIC
STATED PRINT RUN 25 SER.#'d SETS

2014 Panini Prizm Next Era

1 George Springer 2.50 6.00
2 Kris Bryant 4.00 10.00
3 Clint Frazier 2.50 6.00
4 Byron Buxton 3.00 8.00
5 Miguel Sano .75 2.00
6 Carlos Correa 3.00 8.00
7 Oscar Taveras .75 2.00
8 Archie Bradley .60 1.50
9 Noah Syndergaard .75 2.00
10 Gregory Polanco 1.00 2.50
11 Gosuke Katoh 1.00 2.50
12 Kyle Zimmer .60 1.50
13 Javier Baez 2.50 6.00
14 Jameson Taillon .75 2.00
15 Mark Appel .75 2.00
16 Jose Abreu 5.00 12.00
17 Robert Stephsenson .60 1.50
18 Addison Russell 1.00 2.50
19 Masahiro Tanaka 5.00 12.00
20 Fransisco Lindor 5.00 12.00

2014 Panini Prizm Next Era Prizms

*PRIZM: .5X TO 1.2X BASIC

2014 Panini Prizm Next Era Prizms Blue Mojo

*BLUE MOJO: 1.2X TO 3X BASIC
STATED PRINT RUN 75 SER.#'d SETS

2014 Panini Prizm Next Era Prizms Purple

*PURPLE: 1X TO 2.5X BASIC
STATED PRINT RUN 99 SER.#'d SETS

2014 Panini Prizm Next Era Prizms Red

*RED: 2.5X TO 6X BASIC
STATED PRINT RUN 25 SER.#'d SETS
2 Kris Bryant 25.00 60.00
16 Jose Abreu 30.00 80.00

2014 Panini Prizm Rookie Autographs Prizms

EXCHANGE DEADLINE 11/21/2015
BF Brian Flynn 2.50 6.00
BH Billy Hamilton 3.00 8.00
CB Chad Bettis 2.50 6.00
CL Charlie Leesman 2.50 6.00
CO Chris Owings 2.50 6.00
CR Cameron Rupp 2.50 6.00
DH David Hale 2.50 6.00
EA Ehire Adrianza 2.50 6.00
EM Ethan Martin 2.50 6.00
ER Enny Romero 2.50 6.00
JN Jimmy Nelson 2.50 6.00
JP James Paxton 4.00 10.00
JR J.R. Murphy 3.00 8.00
JS Jonathan Schoop 2.50 6.00
KW Kolten Wong 6.00 15.00
MA Marcus Semien 12.00 30.00
MC Michael Choice 2.50 6.00
MD Matt Davidson 3.00 8.00
MS Max Stassi 2.50 6.00
RF Reymond Fuentes 2.50 6.00
TB Tim Beckham 4.00 10.00
TD Travis D'Arnaud 3.00 8.00
TR Tanner Roark 6.00 15.00
TW Taijuan Walker 5.00 12.00
WF Wilmer Flores 3.00 8.00
XB Xander Bogaerts 15.00 40.00
YV Yordano Ventura 12.00 30.00

2014 Panini Prizm Rookie Autographs Prizms Mojo

*MOJO: .6X TO 1.5X BASIC
STATED PRINT RUN 75 SER.#'d SETS
EXCHANGE DEADLINE 11/21/2015

2014 Panini Prizm Rookie Autographs Prizms Purple

*PURPLE: .5X TO 1.2X BASIC
STATED PRINT RUN 99 SER.#'d SETS
EXCHANGE DEADLINE 11/21/2015

2014 Panini Prizm Rookie Reign

1 Travis D'Arnaud .75 2.00
2 Kolten Wong .75 2.00
3 Nick Castellanos 2.00 5.00
4 Billy Hamilton .75 2.00
5 Chris Owings .60 1.50
6 Xander Bogaerts 2.00 5.00
7 Matt Davidson .75 2.00

8 Taijuan Walker .60 1.50
9 Michael Choice .60 1.50
10 Reymond Fuentes .60 1.50
11 J.R. Murphy .60 1.50
12 Cameron Rupp .60 1.50
13 Masahiro Tanaka 5.00 12.00
14 Yordano Ventura .75 2.00
15 James Paxton 1.00 2.50
16 Wilmer Flores .75 2.00
17 Tim Beckham 1.00 2.50
18 Kris Johnson .60 1.50
19 Jose Abreu 5.00 12.00
20 Logan Watkins .60 1.50

2014 Panini Prizm Rookie Reign Prizms

*PRIZM: .5X TO 1.2X BASIC

2014 Panini Prizm Rookie Reign Prizms Blue Mojo

*BLUE MOJO: 1.2X TO 3X BASIC
STATED PRINT RUN 75 SER.#'d SETS

2014 Panini Prizm Rookie Reign Prizms Purple

*PURPLE: 1X TO 2.5X BASIC
STATED PRINT RUN 99 SER.#'d SETS

2014 Panini Prizm Rookie Reign Prizms Red

*RED: 2.5X TO 6X BASIC
STATED PRINT RUN 25 SER.#'d SETS
19 Jose Abreu 40.00 100.00

2014 Panini Prizm Signature Distinctions Die Cut Prizms Purple

STATED PRINT RUN 99 SER.#'d SETS
EXCHANGE DEADLINE 11/21/2015
4 Bo Jackson 30.00 80.00
6 Nolan Ryan 50.00 120.00

2014 Panini Prizm Signature Distinctions Die Cut Prizms Mojo

STATED PRINT RUN 25 SER.#'d SETS
EXCHANGE DEADLINE 11/21/2015
1 George Brett 75.00 200.00
2 Ken Griffey Jr. 125.00 250.00
3 Cal Ripken Jr. 100.00 200.00
4 Bo Jackson 50.00 120.00
5 Frank Thomas 150.00 250.00
6 Nolan Ryan 100.00 200.00
7 Pedro Martinez 50.00 120.00
8 Mariano Rivera 125.00 250.00
9 Greg Maddux 100.00 200.00
10 Chipper Jones 100.00 200.00

2014 Panini Prizm Signatures

EXCHANGE DEADLINE 11/21/2015
1 Rusty Greer 2.50 6.00
2 Jason Grilli 2.50 6.00
3 Brandon Phillips 2.50 6.00
4 Steve Finley 2.50 6.00
5 Ike Davis 2.50 6.00
6 Archie Bradley 2.50 6.00
7 Glen Perkins 2.50 6.00
8 Zach McAllister 2.50 6.00
9 Rick Monday 2.50 6.00
10 Kevin Seitzer 2.50 6.00
11 Kevin Millar 2.50 6.00
12 Steve Sax 2.50 6.00
13 Lee Smith 6.00 15.00
14 Alex Avila 3.00 8.00
15 Adeiny Hechavarria 2.50 6.00
16 Alex Wood 6.00 15.00
17 Scott Diamond 2.50 6.00
18 Rick Dempsey 2.50 6.00
19 Dexter Fowler 5.00 12.00
20 Ron Darling 4.00 10.00
21 Dwayne Murphy 2.50 6.00
22 Lee Mazzilli 2.50 6.00
23 Ron Gant 2.50 6.00
24 Fred Lynn 4.00 10.00
25 Allen Craig 3.00 8.00
27 Shawn Green 2.50 6.00
28 Logan Morrison 2.50 6.00
29 Jose Altuve 20.00 50.00
30 Jon Jay 2.50 6.00
31 Wei-Yin Chen 15.00 40.00
32 Yovani Gallardo 2.50 6.00
33 Evan Longoria 6.00 15.00
34 Troy Tulowitzki 4.00 10.00
35 Stephen Strasburg 15.00 40.00
36 Dave Stieb 4.00 10.00
37 Evan Gattis 2.50 6.00
38 Tony Pena 2.50 6.00
39 Chris Perez 2.50 6.00
41 Chad Billingsley 3.00 8.00
42 Adam Eaton 2.50 6.00
43 Darin Ruf 3.00 8.00
44 Zoilo Almonte 3.00 8.00
45 Elvis Andrus 3.00 8.00
46 Dave Righetti 4.00 10.00
47 Ellis Burks 2.50 6.00
50 Frank White 2.50 6.00

2014 Panini Prizm Top of the Order

1 Shin-Soo Choo 1.00 2.50
2 Matt Carpenter 1.25 3.00
3 Dexter Fowler 1.00 2.50
4 Norichika Aoki .75 2.00
5 Carl Crawford 1.00 2.50
6 Jacoby Ellsbury 1.00 2.50
7 David DeJesus .75 2.00
8 Jose Reyes 1.00 2.50
9 Mike Trout 6.00 15.00
10 Derek Jeter 3.00 8.00
11 Austin Jackson .75 2.00
12 Alex Gordon 1.00 2.50
13 Coco Crisp .75 2.00
14 Jean Segura 1.00 2.50
15 Nick Swisher 1.00 2.50
16 Carlos Beltran 1.00 2.50
17 Shane Victorino 1.00 2.50
18 Starling Marte 1.00 2.50
19 Jose Bautista 1.00 2.50
20 Manny Machado 1.25 3.00

2014 Panini Prizm Top of the Order Prizms

*PRIZMS: .5X TO 1.2X BASIC

2014 Panini Prizm Top of the Order Prizms Blue Mojo

*BLUE MOJO: 1X TO 2.5X BASIC
STATED PRINT RUN 75 SER.#'d SETS
10 Derek Jeter 12.00 30.00

2014 Panini Prizm Top of the Order Prizms Purple

*PURPLE: .75X TO 2X BASIC
STATED PRINT RUN 99 SER.#'d SETS

2014 Panini Prizm Top of the Order Prizms Red

*RED: 2X TO 5X BASIC
STATED PRINT RUN 25 SER.#'d SETS
10 Derek Jeter 40.00 100.00

2014 Panini Prizm USA Baseball

1 Max Scherzer .75 2.00
2 Manny Machado .75 2.00
3 Eric Hosmer .60 1.50
4 Evan Longoria .60 1.50
5 Dustin Pedroia .75 2.00
6 Pedro Alvarez .50 1.25
7 Michael Wacha .60 1.50
8 Paul Konerko .60 1.50
9 Clayton Kershaw 1.25 3.00
10 Buster Posey 1.00 2.50

2014 Panini Prizm USA Baseball Prizms

*PRIZMS: .5X TO 1.2X BASIC

2014 Panini Prizm USA Baseball Prizms Blue Mojo

*BLUE MOJO: 1.2X TO 3X BASIC
STATED PRINT RUN 75 SER.#'d SETS

2014 Panini Prizm USA Baseball Autographs Prizms

EXCHANGE DEADLINE 11/21/2015
1 Max Scherzer 15.00 40.00
2 Manny Machado 15.00 40.00
3 Eric Hosmer 20.00 50.00
4 Evan Longoria 20.00 50.00
5 Dustin Pedroia 20.00 50.00
6 Pedro Alvarez EXCH 15.00 40.00
7 Michael Wacha 30.00 60.00
9 Clayton Kershaw 30.00 80.00

2015 Panini Prizm

COMPLETE SET (200) 20.00 50.00
1 Buster Posey .30 .75
2 Hunter Pence .20 .50
3 Madison Bumgarner .20 .50
4 Tim Lincecum .20 .50
5 Brandon Belt .20 .50
6 Michael Morse .15 .40
7 Tim Hudson .20 .50
8 Lorenzo Cain .15 .40
9 Eric Hosmer .20 .50
10 Greg Holland .15 .40
11 Alex Gordon .20 .50
12 Yordano Ventura .20 .50
13 Salvador Perez .20 .50
14 Mike Moustakas .20 .50
15 Adam Eaton .15 .40
16 Adam Jones .20 .50
17 Adam Wainwright .20 .50
18 Adrian Beltre .25 .60
19 Adrian Gonzalez .20 .50
20 Albert Pujols .30 .75
21 Alex Cobb .15 .40
22 Alex Wood .15 .40
23 Alexei Ramirez .20 .50
24 Andrew Cashner .15 .40
25 Andrew McCutchen .25 .60
26 Anthony Rendon .25 .60
27 Anthony Rizzo .30 .75
28 Arismendy Alcantara .15 .40
29 Aroldis Chapman .25 .60
30 Melvin Upton Jr. .20 .50
31 Bartolo Colon .15 .40
32 Ben Zobrist .20 .50
33 Billy Butler .15 .40
34 Billy Hamilton .20 .50
35 Brett Gardner .20 .50
36 Brian Dozier .20 .50
37 Bryce Harper .40 1.00
38 Carlos Gomez .15 .40
39 Carlos Santana .20 .50
40 Charlie Blackmon .25 .60
41 Chase Utley .20 .50
42 Chris Carter .15 .40
43 Chris Davis .15 .40
44 Chris Sale .25 .60
45 Chris Tillman .15 .40
46 Clayton Kershaw .40 1.00
47 Cliff Lee .20 .50
48 Cole Hamels .20 .50
49 Corey Dickerson .15 .40
50 Corey Kluber .20 .50
51 Dallas Keuchel .20 .50
52 Danny Santana .15 .40
53 David Ortiz .25 .60
54 David Price .20 .50
55 David Robertson .20 .50
56 David Wright .20 .50
57 Dee Gordon .15 .40
58 Devin Mesoraco .15 .40
59 Didi Gregorius .20 .50
60 Doug Fister .15 .40
61 Dustin Pedroia .25 .60
62 Edwin Encarnacion .25 .60
63 Evan Gattis .15 .40
64 Evan Longoria .20 .50
65 Everth Cabrera .15 .40
66 Felix Hernandez .20 .50
67 Francisco Rodriguez .20 .50
68 Freddie Freeman .30 .75
69 George Springer .20 .50
70 Gerrit Cole .25 .60
71 Giancarlo Stanton .25 .60
72 Gregory Polanco .20 .50
73 Hanley Ramirez .20 .50
74 Henderson Alvarez .15 .40
75 Hisashi Iwakuma .20 .50
76 Hyun-Jin Ryu .20 .50
77 Ichiro Suzuki .30 .75
78 Jacob deGrom .50 1.25
79 Jacoby Ellsbury .20 .50
80 Jake Arrieta .20 .50
81 James Loney .15 .40
82 Jason Heyward .20 .50
83 Jered Weaver .20 .50
84 Jimmy Rollins .20 .50
85 Joe Mauer .20 .50
86 Joey Votto .25 .60
87 John Lackey .20 .50
88 Johnny Cueto .20 .50
89 Jon Lester .20 .50
90 Jonathan Lucroy .20 .50
91 Jordan Zimmermann .20 .50
92 Jose Abreu .25 .60
93 Jose Altuve .20 .50
94 Jose Bautista .20 .50
95 Jose Fernandez .25 .60
96 Jose Reyes .20 .50
97 Josh Donaldson .20 .50
98 Julio Teheran .20 .50
99 Junior Lake .15 .40
100 Justin Morneau .20 .50
101 Justin Upton .20 .50
102 Justin Verlander .25 .60
103 Kevin Kiermaier .20 .50
104 Kolten Wong .20 .50
105 Kyle Seager .15 .40
106 Manny Machado .25 .60
107 Marcell Ozuna .25 .60
108 Mark Trumbo .15 .40
109 Masahiro Tanaka .20 .50
110 Matt Adams .15 .40
111 Matt Carpenter .25 .60
112 Matt Harvey .20 .50
113 Matt Holliday .25 .60
114 Matt Kemp .20 .50
115 Matt Shoemaker .20 .50
116 Max Scherzer .25 .60
117 Melky Cabrera .15 .40
118 Michael Brantley .20 .50
119 Miguel Cabrera .25 .60
120 Mike Trout 1.25 3.00
121 Mike Zunino .15 .40
122 Mookie Betts .50 1.25
123 Neil Walker .15 .40
124 Nelson Cruz .25 .60
125 Nolan Arenado .40 1.00
126 Pablo Sandoval .20 .50
127 Patrick Corbin .20 .50
128 Paul Goldschmidt .25 .60
129 Phil Hughes .15 .40
130 Prince Fielder .20 .50
131 R.A. Dickey .20 .50
132 Robinson Cano .20 .50
133 Ryan Braun .20 .50
134 Ryan Howard .20 .50
135 Scott Kazmir .15 .40
136 Shelby Miller .20 .50
137 Shin-Soo Choo .20 .50
138 Sonny Gray .20 .50
139 Starlin Castro .15 .40
140 Starling Marte .20 .50
141 Stephen Strasburg .25 .60
142 Todd Frazier .15 .40
143 Troy Tulowitzki .25 .60
144 Victor Martinez .20 .50
145 Wei-Yin Chen .15 .40
146 Wil Myers .20 .50
147 Xander Bogaerts .25 .60
148 Yadier Molina .30 .75
149 Yan Gomes .15 .40
150 Yasiel Puig .25 .60
151 Yoenis Cespedes .20 .50
152 Yu Darvish .25 .60
153 Zack Greinke .25 .60
154 Ken Griffey Jr. .50 1.25
155 Cal Ripken .75 2.00
156 Pedro Martinez .20 .50
157 Randy Johnson .25 .60
158 Craig Biggio .20 .50
159 Rickey Henderson .25 .60
160 Mike Piazza .25 .60
161 Mark McGwire .40 1.00
162 Frank Thomas .25 .60
163 Kirby Puckett .25 .60
164 Mariano Rivera .30 .75
165 George Brett .50 1.25
166 Ryne Sandberg .50 1.25
167 Barry Bonds .40 1.00
168 Tony Gwynn .25 .60
169 Brandon Finnegan RC .25 .60
170 Rusney Castillo RC .30 .75
171 Dalton Pompey RC .30 .75
172 Javier Baez RC 2.00 5.00
173 Kennys Vargas RC .25 .60
174 Joc Pederson RC 1.00 2.50
175 Jorge Soler RC .40 1.00
176 Michael Taylor RC .25 .60
177 Mike Foltynewicz RC .25 .60
178 Maikel Franco RC .30 .75
179 Yorman Rodriguez RC .25 .60
180 Christian Walker RC .50 1.25
181 Jake Lamb RC .40 1.00
182 Rymer Liriano RC .25 .60
183 Daniel Norris RC .25 .60
184 Andy Wilkins RC .25 .60
185 Anthony Ranaudo RC .25 .60
186 Buck Farmer RC .25 .60
187 Cory Spangenberg RC .25 .60
188 Dilson Herrera RC .30 .75
189 Edwin Escobar RC .25 .60
190 Gary Brown RC .25 .60
191 James McCann RC .40 1.00
192 Kendall Graveman RC .25 .60
193 Lane Adams RC .25 .60
194 Matt Barnes RC .25 .60
195 Matt Szczur RC .30 .75
196 Steven Moya RC .30 .75
197 Terrance Gore RC .25 .60
198 Trevor May RC .25 .60
199 R.J. Alvarez RC .25 .60
200 Ryan Rua RC .25 .60

2015 Panini Prizm Prizms

*PRIZMS: 1.5X TO 4X BASIC
*PRIZMS RC: 1X TO 2.5X BASIC RC
RANDOM INSERTS IN PACKS

2015 Panini Prizm Prizms Black and White Checker

*BW CHECK: 3X TO 8X BASIC
*BW CHECK RC: 2X TO 5X BASIC
RANDOM INSERTS IN PACKS
STATED PRINT RUN 149 SER.#'d SETS
77 Ichiro Suzuki 4.00 10.00
120 Mike Trout 10.00 25.00
154 Ken Griffey Jr. 4.00 10.00
162 Frank Thomas 5.00 12.00
167 Barry Bonds 10.00 25.00
174 Joc Pederson 4.00 10.00

2015 Panini Prizm Prizms Blue

*BLUE: 4X TO 10X BASIC
*BLUE RC: 2.5X TO 6X BASIC
RANDOM INSERTS IN PACKS
STATED PRINT RUN 75 SER.#'d SETS
77 Ichiro Suzuki 5.00 12.00
120 Mike Trout 12.00 30.00
154 Ken Griffey Jr. 5.00 12.00
162 Frank Thomas 6.00 15.00
167 Barry Bonds 12.00 30.00
174 Joc Pederson 5.00 12.00

2015 Panini Prizm Prizms Blue Baseball

*BLUE BSBLL: 2.5X TO 6X BASIC
*BLUE BSBLL RC: 1.5X TO 4X BASIC RC
RANDOM INSERTS IN PACKS

2015 Panini Prizm Prizms Camo

*CAMO: 3X TO 8X BASIC
*CAMO RC: 2X TO 5X BASIC
RANDOM INSERTS IN PACKS
STATED PRINT RUN 199 SER.#'d SETS
77 Ichiro Suzuki 4.00 10.00
120 Mike Trout 10.00 25.00
154 Ken Griffey Jr. 4.00 10.00
162 Frank Thomas 5.00 12.00
167 Barry Bonds 10.00 25.00
174 Joc Pederson 4.00 10.00

2015 Panini Prizm Prizms Jackie Robinson

*ROBINSON: 6X TO 15X BASIC
*ROBINSON RC: 4X TO 10X BASIC
RANDOM INSERTS IN PACKS
STATED PRINT RUN 42 SER.#'d SETS
77 Ichiro Suzuki 8.00 20.00
120 Mike Trout 20.00 50.00
154 Ken Griffey Jr. 8.00 20.00
162 Frank Thomas 10.00 25.00
167 Barry Bonds 20.00 50.00

2015 Panini Prizm Prizms Orange

*ORANGE: 5X TO 12X BASIC
*ORANGE RC: 3X TO 8X BASIC
RANDOM INSERTS IN PACKS
STATED PRINT RUN 60 SER.#'d SETS
77 Ichiro Suzuki 6.00 15.00
120 Mike Trout 15.00 40.00
154 Ken Griffey Jr. 6.00 15.00
162 Frank Thomas 8.00 20.00
167 Barry Bonds 15.00 40.00
174 Joc Pederson 6.00 15.00

2015 Panini Prizm Prizms Purple Flash

*PRPLE FLSH: 4X TO 10X BASIC
*PRPLE FLSH RC: 2.5X TO 6X BASIC
RANDOM INSERTS IN PACKS
STATED PRINT RUN 99 SER.#'d SETS
77 Ichiro Suzuki 5.00 121.00
120 Mike Trout 12.00 30.00
154 Ken Griffey Jr. 5.00 12.00
162 Frank Thomas 6.00 15.00
167 Barry Bonds 12.00 30.00
174 Joc Pederson 5.00 12.00

2015 Panini Prizm Prizms Red Baseball

*RED BSBLL: 2.5X TO 6X BASIC
*RED BSBLL RC: 1.5X TO 4X BASIC RC
RANDOM INSERTS IN PACKS

2015 Panini Prizm Prizms Red Power

*RED POWER: 4X TO 10X BASIC
*RED POWER RC: 2.5X TO 6X BASIC
RANDOM INSERTS IN PACKS
STATED PRINT RUN 125 SER.#'d SETS
77 Ichiro Suzuki 5.00 12.00
120 Mike Trout 12.00 30.00
154 Ken Griffey Jr. 5.00 12.00
162 Frank Thomas 6.00 15.00
167 Barry Bonds 12.00 30.00
174 Joc Pederson 5.00 12.00

2015 Panini Prizm Prizms Red White and Blue Mojo

*RWB MOJO: 2.5X TO 6X BASIC
*RWB MOJO RC: 1.5X TO 4X BASIC RC
RANDOM INSERTS IN PACKS

2015 Panini Prizm Prizms Tie Dyed

*TIE DYE: 6X TO 15X BASIC
*TIE DYE RC: 4X TO 10X BASIC
RANDOM INSERTS IN PACKS
STATED PRINT RUN 50 SER.#'d SETS
77 Ichiro Suzuki 8.00 20.00
120 Mike Trout 20.00 50.00
162 Frank Thomas 10.00 25.00
167 Barry Bonds 10.00 25.00
174 Joc Pederson 8.00 20.00

2015 Panini Prizm Autograph Prizms

RANDOM INSERTS IN PACKS
3 Carlos Gomez 3.00 8.00
9 Wei-Chung Wang 3.00 8.00
11 Tommy La Stella 3.00 8.00
12 Matt Shoemaker 4.00 10.00
13 Kolten Wong 4.00 10.00
18 Matt den Dekker 3.00 8.00
20 Norichika Aoki 3.00 8.00
21 Fernando Rodney 3.00 8.00
22 Jedd Gyorko 3.00 8.00
27 Tim Raines 4.00 10.00
28 Aaron Judge 100.00 250.00
29 Luis Severino 8.00 20.00
30 Corey Seager 15.00 40.00
31 Addison Russell 10.00 25.00
32 Miguel Sano 5.00 12.00
35 Kris Bryant 75.00 150.00
37 Yasmany Tomas 4.00 10.00
38 Brandon Finnegan 3.00 8.00
39 Rusney Castillo 4.00 10.00
40 Dalton Pompey 4.00 10.00
41 Javier Baez 12.00 30.00
42 Kennys Vargas 3.00 8.00
43 Joc Pederson 4.00 10.00
44 Jorge Soler 8.00 20.00
45 Michael Taylor 3.00 8.00
46 Mike Foltynewicz 3.00 8.00
47 Maikel Franco 4.00 10.00
48 Yorman Rodriguez 3.00 8.00
49 Christian Walker 6.00 15.00
50 Jake Lamb 5.00 12.00
51 Rymer Liriano 3.00 8.00
52 Daniel Norris 3.00 8.00
53 Andy Wilkins 3.00 8.00
54 Anthony Ranaudo 3.00 8.00
55 Buck Farmer 3.00 8.00
56 Cory Spangenberg 3.00 8.00
57 Dilson Herrera 4.00 10.00
58 Edwin Escobar 3.00 8.00
60 James McCann 5.00 12.00
61 Kendall Graveman 3.00 8.00
63 Matt Barnes 3.00 8.00
64 Matt Szczur 4.00 10.00
65 Steven Moya 4.00 10.00
66 Terrance Gore 3.00 8.00
67 Trevor May 3.00 8.00
68 R.J. Alvarez 3.00 8.00
69 Ryan Rua 3.00 8.00
70 Matt Clark 3.00 8.00

2015 Panini Prizm Autograph Prizms Blue

*BLUE p/r 75: .5X TO 1.2X BASIC
*BLUE p/r 20-49: .6X TO 1.5X BASIC
RANDOM INSERTS IN PACKS
PRINT RUNS B/WN 20-75 COPIES PER
1 Alex Gordon/25 12.00 30.00
2 Gregory Polanco/75 5.00 12.00
4 Anthony Rizzo/25 15.00 40.00
5 Jose Fernandez/25 25.00 60.00
6 Jacob deGrom/75 25.00 60.00
10 Matt Adams/75 3.00 8.00
14 Xander Bogaerts/49 12.00 30.00
15 Chris Sale/49 15.00 40.00
16 Felix Hernandez/20 12.00 30.00
19 Corey Kluber/75 10.00 25.00
23 Raul Ibanez/49 6.00 15.00
24 Starling Marte/75 8.00 20.00
25 Jim Rice/25 6.00 15.00
26 Andy Pettitte/20 20.00 50.00
34 Byron Buxton/75 20.00 50.00
36 Francisco Lindor/75 15.00 40.00

2015 Panini Prizm Autograph Prizms Purple Flash

*PURPLE p/r 75-99: .5X TO 1.2X BASIC
*PURPLE p/r 25-49: .6X TO 1.5X BASIC
RANDOM INSERTS IN PACKS
PRINT RUNS B/WN 25-99 COPIES PER
1 Alex Gordon/49 12.00 30.00
2 Gregory Polanco/99 5.00 12.00
4 Anthony Rizzo/49 15.00 40.00
5 Jose Fernandez/49 25.00 60.00
6 Jacob deGrom/99 25.00 60.00
10 Matt Adams/99 3.00 8.00
14 Xander Bogaerts/75 10.00 25.00
16 Felix Hernandez/25 12.00 30.00
19 Corey Kluber/99 10.00 25.00
23 Raul Ibanez/75 5.00 12.00
24 Starling Marte/99 8.00 20.00
25 Jim Rice/49 6.00 15.00
26 Andy Pettitte/25 20.00 50.00
34 Byron Buxton/99 20.00 50.00
36 Francisco Lindor/99 15.00 40.00

2015 Panini Prizm Autograph Prizms Red Power

*PURPLE p/r 75-125: .5X TO 1.2X BASIC
*PURPLE p/r 49: .6X TO 1.5X BASIC
RANDOM INSERTS IN PACKS
PRINT RUNS B/WN 49-125 COPIES PER
1 Alex Gordon/75 10.00 25.00
2 Gregory Polanco/125 5.00 12.00
14 Xander Bogaerts/99 10.00 25.00
16 Felix Hernandez/49 12.00 30.00
17 Hisashi Iwakuma/125 6.00 15.00
19 Corey Kluber/125 10.00 25.00
24 Starling Marte/125 8.00 20.00
25 Jim Rice/75 5.00 12.00
26 Andy Pettitte/49 20.00 50.00
34 Byron Buxton/125 20.00 50.00
36 Francisco Lindor/125 15.00 40.00

2015 Panini Prizm Autograph Prizms Tie Dyed

*PURPLE p/r 25-50: .6X TO 1.5X BASIC
RANDOM INSERTS IN PACKS
PRINT RUNS B/WN 15-50 COPIES PER
NO PRICING ON QTY 15
2 Gregory Polanco/50 6.00 15.00
6 Jacob deGrom/50 30.00 80.00
10 Matt Adams/50 4.00 10.00
14 Xander Bogaerts/25 12.00 30.00
15 Chris Sale/25 15.00 40.00
19 Corey Kluber/50 12.00 30.00
23 Raul Ibanez/25 6.00 15.00
24 Starling Marte/50 10.00 25.00
34 Byron Buxton/50 25.00 60.00
36 Francisco Lindor/50 20.00 50.00

2015 Panini Prizm Diamond Marshals

COMPLETE SET (20) 10.00 25.00
RANDOM INSERTS IN PACKS
*PRIZMS: .6X TO 1.5X BASIC
*PRZMS FLSH/100: 2X TO 5X BASIC
1 Mike Trout 4.00 10.00
2 Buster Posey 1.00 2.50
3 Clayton Kershaw 1.25 3.00
4 Jose Abreu .75 2.00
5 Giancarlo Stanton .60 1.50
6 Masahiro Tanaka .60 1.50
7 Andrew McCutchen .75 2.00
8 Albert Pujols 1.00 2.50
9 Yasiel Puig .75 2.00
10 Anthony Rizzo 1.00 2.50
11 Adam Wainwright .60 1.50
12 Yu Darvish .75 2.00
13 Alex Gordon .60 1.50
14 Madison Bumgarner .60 1.50
15 Cal Ripken 2.50 6.00
16 Randy Johnson .75 2.00
17 Pedro Martinez .60 1.50
18 Ken Griffey Jr. 1.50 4.00
19 Roger Clemens 1.00 2.50
20 George Brett 1.50 4.00

2015 Panini Prizm Field Pass

COMPLETE SET (15) 10.00 25.00
RANDOM INSERTS IN PACKS
*PRIZMS: .6X TO 1.5X BASIC
*PRZMS FLSH/100: 2X TO 5X BASIC
1 David Ortiz .75 2.00
2 Albert Pujols 1.00 2.50
3 Carlos Santana .60 1.50
4 Evan Longoria .60 1.50
5 Troy Tulowitzki .75 2.00
6 David Price .60 1.50
7 Kennys Vargas .50 1.25
8 Miguel Cabrera .75 2.00
9 Jose Altuve .60 1.50
10 Jose Abreu .75 2.00
11 Freddie Freeman 1.00 2.50
12 Don Mattingly 1.50 4.00
13 Frank Thomas .75 2.00
14 Dante Bichette .50 1.25
15 Will Clark .60 1.50

2015 Panini Prizm Fireworks

RANDOM INSERTS IN PACKS
*PRIZMS: .6X TO 1.5X BASIC
*PRZMS FLSH/100: 2X TO 5X BASIC
1 Giancarlo Stanton .75 2.00
2 Jose Bautista .60 1.50
3 Miguel Cabrera .75 2.00
4 Mike Trout 4.00 10.00
5 Nelson Cruz .75 2.00
6 Albert Pujols 1.00 2.50
7 Yasiel Puig .75 2.00
8 Bryce Harper 1.25 3.00
9 David Ortiz .75 2.00
10 Jose Abreu .75 2.00
11 Andrew McCutchen .75 2.00
12 Paul Goldschmidt .75 2.00
13 Manny Machado .75 2.00
14 Adrian Beltre .75 2.00
15 David Wright .60 1.50
16 George Brett 1.50 4.00
17 Frank Thomas .75 2.00
18 Ken Griffey Jr. 1.50 4.00
19 Barry Bonds 1.25 3.00
20 Mark McGwire 1.25 3.00

2015 Panini Prizm Fresh Faces

COMPLETE SET (15) 10.00 25.00
RANDOM INSERTS IN PACKS
*PRIZMS: .6X TO 1.5X BASIC
*PRZMS FLSH/100: 2X TO 5X BASIC
1 Rusney Castillo .50 1.25
2 Dalton Pompey .50 1.25
3 Brandon Finnegan .40 1.00
4 Daniel Norris .40 1.00
5 Joc Pederson 1.50 4.00
6 Jorge Soler .60 1.50
7 Javier Baez 3.00 8.00
8 Dilson Herrera .50 1.25
9 Maikel Franco .50 1.25
10 Edwin Escobar .40 1.00
11 Byron Buxton 2.00 5.00
12 Jung-Ho Kang .40 1.00
13 Carlos Rodon 1.00 2.50
14 Kris Bryant 4.00 10.00
15 Yasmany Tomas .50 1.25

2015 Panini Prizm Fresh Faces Signature Prizms

RANDOM INSERTS IN PACKS
1 Mookie Betts 25.00 60.00
5 Robert Stephenson 3.00 8.00
8 Heath Hembree 3.00 8.00
11 C.C. Lee 12.00 30.00
18 Matt den Dekker 3.00 8.00
23 Jung-Ho Kang 20.00 50.00
25 Nick Martinez 5.00 12.00

2015 Panini Prizm Fresh Faces Signature Prizms Black and White Checker

*BW p/r 75-149: .5X TO 1.2X BASIC
RANDOM INSERTS IN PACKS
PRINT RUNS B/WN 75-149 COPIES PER
2 Clint Frazier/75 10.00 25.00
3 Matt Shoemaker/75 5.00 12.00
24 Jacob deGrom/75 25.00 60.00

2015 Panini Prizm Fresh Faces Signature Prizms Camo

*CAMO: .5X TO 1.2X BASIC
RANDOM INSERTS IN PACKS
PRINT RUNS B/WN 99-199 COPIES PER
24 Jacob deGrom/99 25.00 60.00

2015 Panini Prizm Fresh Faces Signature Prizms Red White and Blue

*RWB: .6X TO 1.5X BASIC
RANDOM INSERTS IN PACKS
STATED PRINT RUN 25 SER.#'d SETS
2 Clint Frazier 12.00 30.00
3 Matt Shoemaker 6.00 15.00
24 Jacob deGrom 30.00 80.00

2015 Panini Prizm Fresh Faces Signature Prizms Tie Dyed

*TIE DYED: .6X TO 1.5X BASIC
RANDOM INSERTS IN PACKS
STATED PRINT RUN 50 SER.#'d SETS
2 Clint Frazier 12.00 30.00
3 Matt Shoemaker 6.00 15.00
24 Jacob deGrom 30.00 80.00

2015 Panini Prizm Passion

COMPLETE SET (15) 5.00 12.00
RANDOM INSERTS IN PACKS
*PRIZMS: .6X TO 1.5X BASIC
*PRZMS FLSH/100: 2X TO 5X BASIC
1 Jason Heyward .60 1.50
2 Joe Mauer .60 1.50
3 Joe Panik .60 1.50
4 Dustin Pedroia .75 2.00
5 Jose Reyes .60 1.50
6 Troy Tulowitzki .75 2.00
7 Jackie Bradley Jr. .75 2.00
8 Adam Eaton .50 1.25
9 Miguel Cabrera .75 2.00
10 Brian Dozier .60 1.50
11 Buster Posey 1.00 2.50
12 Rougned Odor .60 1.50
13 Ian Kinsler .60 1.50
14 J.J. Hardy .50 1.25
15 Ichiro Suzuki 1.00 2.50

2015 Panini Prizm Pink Ribbon Ink Prizms

RANDOM INSERTS IN PACKS
PRINT RUNS B/WN 13-100 COPIES PER
NO PRICING ON QTY 13
1 Eric Hosmer/25 10.00 25.00
2 Carlos Gomez/25 8.00 20.00
3 Adam Jones/25 10.00 25.00
4 George Springer/24 10.00 25.00
5 Wil Myers/49 10.00 25.00
8 Justin Upton/25 20.00 50.00
10 Javier Baez/100 60.00 150.00

2015 Panini Prizm Signature Distinctions Prizms Die Cut Red Power

RANDOM INSERTS IN PACKS
STATED PRINT RUN 49 SER.#'d SETS
*PRPLE FLSH/25: .5X TO 1.2X BASIC
2 Jose Canseco 15.00 40.00
3 Paul Goldschmidt 12.00 30.00
4 Manny Machado 15.00 40.00
5 Freddie Freeman 12.00 30.00
7 Jim Palmer 10.00 25.00
8 Paul Molitor 12.00 30.00
9 Orlando Cepeda 12.00 30.00
10 Goose Gossage 15.00 40.00

2015 Panini Prizm Baseball Signature Prizms

RANDOM INSERTS IN PACKS
3 Edgar Martinez 4.00 10.00
4 Andres Galarraga 4.00 10.00
5 Jose Canseco 10.00 25.00
9 Luis Tiant 5.00 12.00
10 Brock Holt 6.00 15.00
19 Alexi Ogando 3.00 8.00
20 Dante Bichette 3.00 8.00
21 Carlos Martinez 4.00 10.00
22 David Justice 6.00 15.00

2015 Panini Prizm Baseball Signature Prizms Black and White Checker

*BW p/r 99-149: .5X TO 1.2X BASIC
*BW p/r 49: .6X TO 1.5X BASIC
RANDOM INSERTS IN PACKS
PRINT RUNS B/WN 49-149 COPIES PER
1 Salvador Perez/49 10.00 25.00
2 Willie McGee/49 8.00 20.00
12 Ozzie Guillen/99 4.00 10.00
16 Gary Gaetti/149 6.00 15.00
17 Jay Buhner/99 5.00 12.00

2015 Panini Prizm Baseball Signature Prizms Camo

*CAMO: .5X TO 1.2X BASIC
RANDOM INSERTS IN PACKS
PRINT RUNS B/WN 99-199 COPIES PER
2 Willie McGee/99 6.00 15.00
16 Gary Gaetti/149 6.00 15.00

2015 Panini Prizm Baseball Signature Prizms Red White and Blue

*RWB p/r 25: .6X TO 1.5X BASIC
RANDOM INSERTS IN PACKS
PRINT RUNS B/WN 10-25 COPIES PER
NO PRICING ON QTY 15 OR LESS
12 Ozzie Guillen/25 5.00 12.00
16 Gary Gaetti/25 8.00 20.00
17 Jay Buhner/25 6.00 15.00

2015 Panini Prizm Baseball Signature Prizms Tie Dyed

*TIE DYED p/r 25-50: .6X TO 1.5X BASIC
RANDOM INSERTS IN PACKS
PRINT RUNS B/WN 25-50 COPIES PER
1 Salvador Perez/25 10.00 25.00
2 Willie McGee/25 8.00 20.00
6 Nolan Ryan/25 40.00 100.00
12 Ozzie Guillen/50 5.00 12.00
15 Josh Donaldson/47 6.00 15.00
16 Gary Gaetti/50 8.00 20.00
17 Jay Buhner/50 6.00 15.00

2015 Panini Prizm USA Baseball

COMPLETE SET (10) 6.00 15.00
RANDOM INSERTS IN PACKS
*CAMO/199: 2X TO 5X BASIC
*PRIZM RWB/50: 2.5X TO 6X BASIC
1 Brandon Finnegan .50 1.25
2 David Price .60 1.50
3 Kolten Wong .60 1.50
4 George Springer .60 1.50
5 Billy Butler .50 1.25
6 Nick Swisher .60 1.50
7 Alex Gordon .60 1.50
8 Todd Frazier .50 1.25
9 Will Clark .60 1.50
10 Freddie Freeman 1.00 2.50

2015 Panini Prizm USA Baseball Signature Prizms Camo

RANDOM INSERTS IN PACKS
STATED PRINT RUN 25 SER.#'d SETS
1 Brandon Finnegan 8.00 20.00
2 David Price 15.00 40.00
8 Todd Frazier 20.00 50.00
9 Will Clark 150.00 250.00
10 Freddie Freeman 15.00 40.00

2017 Panini Prizm

INSERTED IN '17 CHRONICLES PACKS
1 Aaron Judge RC 15.00 40.00
2 Cody Bellinger RC 8.00 20.00
3 Yoan Moncada RC 1.50 4.00
4 Andrew Benintendi RC 1.50 4.00

5 Christian Arroyo RC .75 2.00
6 Dansby Swanson RC 1.25 3.00
7 Mickey Mantle 1.25 3.00
8 Ryon Healy RC .60 1.50
9 Mitch Haniger RC .75 2.00
10 Antonio Senzatela RC .50 1.25
11 Ian Happ RC 1.00 2.50
12 Trey Mancini RC 1.00 2.50
13 Jordan Montgomery RC .75 2.00
14 Bradley Zimmer RC .60 1.50
15 Hunter Renfroe RC .60 1.50
16 Jorge Bonifacio RC .50 1.25
17 Lewis Brinson RC .75 2.00
18 Jacoby Jones RC .60 1.50
19 Alex Bregman RC 2.50 6.00
20 Josh Bell RC 1.25 3.00
21 Derek Fisher RC .60 1.50
22 Austin Slater RC .50 1.25
23 Paul DeJong RC 1.50 4.00
24 K.Bryant/A.Rizzo .50 1.25
25 Sam Travis RC .60 1.50
26 Mike Trout 2.00 5.00
27 Ken Griffey Jr. .75 2.00
28 Bryce Harper .60 1.50
29 Eric Thames .30 .75
30 Manny Machado .40 1.00
31 Kris Bryant .50 1.25
32 Clayton Kershaw .60 1.50
33 Carlos Correa .40 1.00
34 Anthony Rizzo .50 1.25
35 Buster Posey .50 1.25
36 Mookie Betts .75 2.00
37 Paul Goldschmidt .40 1.00
38 Ryan Zimmerman .30 .75
39 Max Scherzer .40 1.00
40 George Brett .75 2.00
41 Joey Votto .40 1.00
42 Dallas Keuchel .30 .75
43 Franklin Barreto RC .50 1.25
44 Noah Syndergaard .30 .75
45 Nolan Arenado .60 1.50
46 Marcell Ozuna .40 1.00
47 Miguel Cabrera .40 1.00
48 Adrian Beltre .40 1.00
49 Francisco Lindor .40 1.00
50 Gary Sanchez .40 1.00

2017 Panini Prizm Blue Wave

*BLUE WAVE: .75X TO 2X BASIC
*BLUE WAVE RC: .75X TO 2X BASIC RC
INSERTED IN '17 CHRONICLES PACKS
STATED PRINT RUN 199 SER.#'d SETS
40 George Brett 8.00 20.00

2017 Panini Prizm Camo

*CAMO: 2.5X TO 6X BASIC
*CAMO RC: 2.5X TO 6X BASIC
INSERTED IN '17 CHRONICLES PACKS
STATED PRINT RUN 25 SER.#'d SETS
24 K.Bryant/A.Rizzo 10.00 25.00
26 Mike Trout 15.00 40.00
27 Ken Griffey Jr. 10.00 2.00
31 Kris Bryant 10.00 25.00
40 George Brett 40.00 100.00

2017 Panini Prizm Flash

*FLASH: .6X TO 1.5X BASIC
*FLASH RC: .6X TO 1.5X BASIC RC
INSERTED IN '17 CHRONICLES PACKS

2017 Panini Prizm Green Power

*GRN POWER: 2X TO 5X BASIC
*GRN POWER RC: 2X TO 5X BASIC
INSERTED IN '17 CHRONICLES PACKS
STATED PRINT RUN 49 SER.#'d SETS
24 K.Bryant/A.Rizzo 8.00 20.00
26 Mike Trout 12.00 30.00
27 Ken Griffey Jr. 8.00 20.00
31 Kris Bryant 8.00 20.00
40 George Brett 30.00 80.00

2017 Panini Prizm Light Blue

*LIGHT BLUE: .75X TO 2X BASIC
*LIGHT BLUE RC: .75X TO 2X BASIC RC
INSERTED IN '17 CHRONICLES PACKS
STATED PRINT RUN 299 SER.#'d SETS
40 George Brett 4.00 10.00

2017 Panini Prizm Orange

*ORANGE: .75X TO 2X BASIC
*ORANGE RC: .75X TO 2X BASIC RC
INSERTED IN '17 CHRONICLES PACKS
STATED PRINT RUN 399 SER.#'d SETS
40 George Brett 4.00 10.00

2017 Panini Prizm Purple Scope

*PURPLE: 1.2X TO 3X BASIC
*PURPLE RC: 1.2X TO 3X BASIC RC
INSERTED IN '17 CHRONICLES PACKS
STATED PRINT RUN 99 SER.#'d SETS
24 K.Bryant/A.Rizzo 5.00 12.00
26 Mike Trout 8.00 20.00
27 Ken Griffey Jr. 5.00 12.00
31 Kris Bryant 5.00 12.00
40 George Brett 10.00 25.00

2017 Panini Prizm Red Crystals

*RED CRSTLS: 1.5X TO 4X BASIC
*RED CRSTLS RC: 1.5X TO 4X BASIC RC
INSERTED IN '17 CHRONICLES PACKS
STATED PRINT RUN 75 SER.#'d SETS
24 K.Bryant/A.Rizzo 6.00 15.00
26 Mike Trout 10.00 25.00
27 Ken Griffey Jr. 6.00 15.00
31 Kris Bryant 6.00 15.00
40 George Brett 25.00 60.00

2017 Panini Prizm Autographs

INSERTED IN '17 CHRONICLES PACKS
EXCHANGE DEADLINE 5/22/2019
1 Andrew Benintendi 15.00 40.00
3 Alex Bregman 12.00 30.00
4 Dansby Swanson
5 Ian Happ 6.00 15.00
6 Cody Bellinger
7 Aaron Judge 75.00 200.00
8 Trey Mancini 5.00 12.00
11 Mitch Haniger 5.00 12.00
12 Theo Epstein
13 Alex Reyes 4.00 10.00
14 Tyler Glasnow 8.00 20.00
15 Manuel Margot 2.50 6.00
16 Hunter Renfroe 3.00 8.00
17 Jorge Bonifacio 2.50 6.00
18 Antonio Senzatela 2.50 6.00
19 Amir Garrett 2.50 6.00
20 David Dahl 3.00 8.00
21 Sam Travis 3.00 8.00
22 Ryon Healy 3.00 8.00
23 Magneuris Sierra 2.50 6.00
24 Lewis Brinson 4.00 10.00
25 Jacoby Jones 3.00 8.00
26 Adam Frazier 2.50 6.00
27 Brock Stewart 2.50 6.00
28 Hunter Dozier 2.50 6.00
29 Daniel Robertson 2.50 6.00
30 Kyle Freeland
31 Anthony Alford 2.50 6.00
32 Dinelson Lamet 2.50 6.00
33 Yandy Diaz 5.00 12.00
34 Derek Fisher 3.00 8.00
35 Francis Martes 2.50 6.00
36 Carson Fulmer 2.50 6.00
37 Anthony Rizzo 12.00 30.00
38 Jose Abreu 6.00 15.00
39 Yasmany Tomas
40 Wade Boggs 10.00 25.00
41 Ivan Rodriguez 3.00 8.00
42 Bob Gibson
43 Tom Glavine
44 Joey Votto 20.00 50.00
45 Francisco Lindor 8.00 20.00
46 Corey Seager
47 Gary Sanchez 20.00 50.00
48 Andrew McCutchen 40.00 100.00
49 Josh Donaldson 15.00 40.00
50 Willie McCovey 15.00 40.00

2017 Panini Prizm Autographs Blue Wave

*BLUE WAVE: .6X TO 1.5X BASIC
INSERTED IN '17 CHRONICLES PACKS
PRINT RUNS B/WN 40-49 COPIES PER
EXCHANGE DEADLINE 5/22/2019
9 Jordan Montgomery/49 10.00 25.00
10 Bradley Zimmer/49 8.00 20.00

2017 Panini Prizm Autographs Green Power

*GREEN POWER/20: .75X TO 2X BASIC
INSERTED IN '17 CHRONICLES PACKS
PRINT RUNS B/WN 15-20 COPIES PER
NO PRICING ON QTY 15
EXCHANGE DEADLINE 5/22/2019
9 Jordan Montgomery/20 12.00 30.00
10 Bradley Zimmer/20 10.00 25.00

2017 Panini Prizm Autographs Purple Scope

*PURPLE SCOPE: .6X TO 1.5X BASIC
INSERTED IN '17 CHRONICLES PACKS
PRINT RUNS B/WN 30-35 COPIES PER
EXCHANGE DEADLINE 5/22/2019
9 Jordan Montgomery/35 10.00 25.00
10 Bradley Zimmer/35 8.00 20.00

2017 Panini Prizm Autographs Red Crystals

*RED CRYSTALS: .75X TO 2X BASIC
INSERTED IN '17 CHRONICLES PACKS
PRINT RUNS B/WN 20-25 COPIES PER
EXCHANGE DEADLINE 5/22/2019
9 Jordan Montgomery/25 12.00 30.00
10 Bradley Zimmer/25 10.00 25.00

2018 Panini Prizm

INSERTED IN '18 CHRONICLES PACKS
1 Aaron Judge 1.00 2.50
2 Ozzie Albies RC 1.25 3.00
3 Ryan McMahon RC 1.00 2.50
4 Clint Frazier RC .75 2.00
5 Mike Trout 2.00 5.00
6 Ronald Acuna Jr. RC 12.00 30.00
7 Bryce Harper .60 1.50
8 Gary Sanchez .40 1.00
9 Miguel Andujar RC 1.50 4.00
10 Austin Hays RC .60 1.50
11 Nicky Delmonico RC .40 1.00
12 Rhys Hoskins RC 1.50 4.00
13 Alex Verdugo RC .60 1.50
14 Juan Soto RC 10.00 25.00
15 Paul Goldschmidt .40 1.00
16 Gleyber Torres RC 4.00 10.00
17 J.P. Crawford RC .40 1.00
18 Rafael Devers RC 1.25 3.00
19 Buster Posey .50 1.25
20 Victor Robles RC 1.00 2.50
21 Anthony Rizzo .50 1.25
22 Jose Altuve .30 .75
23 Shohei Ohtani RC 10.00 25.00
24 Amed Rosario RC .50 1.25
25 Corey Seager .25 .60

2018 Panini Prizm Blue Ice

*BLUE ICE: 1X TO 2.5X BASIC
*BLUE ICE RC: .6X TO 1.5X BASIC
INSERTED IN '18 CHRONICLES PACKS
STATED PRINT RUN 149 SER.#'d SETS
23 Shohei Ohtani 8.00 20.00

2018 Panini Prizm Green

*GREEN: 1.5X TO 4X BASIC
*GREEN RC: 1X TO 2.5X BASIC
INSERTED IN '18 CHRONICLES PACKS
STATED PRINT RUN 50 SER.#'d SETS
23 Shohei Ohtani 12.00 30.00

2018 Panini Prizm Holo

*HOLO: .75X TO 2X BASIC
*HOLO RC: .5X TO 1.2X BASIC
INSERTED IN '18 CHRONICLES PACKS
23 Shohei Ohtani 6.00 15.00

2018 Panini Prizm Hyper

*HYPER: .75X TO 2X BASIC
*HYPER RC: .5X TO 1.2X BASIC
INSERTED IN '18 CHRONICLES PACKS
STATED PRINT RUN 299 SER.#'d SETS
23 Shohei Ohtani 6.00 15.00

2018 Panini Prizm Pink

*PINK: 2.5X TO 6X BASIC
*PINK RC: 1.5X TO 4X BASIC
INSERTED IN '18 CHRONICLES PACKS
STATED PRINT RUN 25 SER.#'d SETS
5 Mike Trout 15.00 40.00
23 Shohei Ohtani 20.00 50.00

2018 Panini Prizm Purple Mojo

*PURPLE: 1.2X TO 3X BASIC
*PURPLE RC: .75X TO 2X BASIC
INSERTED IN '18 CHRONICLES PACKS
STATED PRINT RUN 99 SER.#'d SETS
23 Shohei Ohtani 10.00 25.00

2018 Panini Prizm Ruby Wave

*RUBY: 1X TO 2.5X BASIC
*RUBY RC: .6X TO 1.5X BASIC
INSERTED IN '18 CHRONICLES PACKS
STATED PRINT RUN 199 SER.#'d SETS
23 Shohei Ohtani 8.00 20.00

2018 Panini Prizm Signatures

RANDOM INSERTS IN PACKS
3 Miguel Andujar 10.00 25.00
4 Brandon Woodruff 8.00 20.00
6 Kyle Farmer 2.50 6.00
8 Zack Granite 2.50 6.00
9 Chris Flexen 2.50 6.00
10 Thyago Vieira 2.50 6.00
11 Reyes Moronta 2.50 6.00
13 Brent Honeywell 4.00 10.00
16 Juan Soto 60.00 150.00
19 Matt Barnes 2.50 6.00

2019 Panini Prizm

1 Adam Jones .25 .60
2 Jake Cave RC .40 1.00
3 Danny Jansen RC .30 .75
4 Matt Olson .30 .75
5 Sean Newcomb .20 .50
6 David Wright .25 .60
7 Justus Sheffield RC .50 1.25
8 Yadier Molina .40 1.00
9 Edwin Diaz .25 .60
10 Rowdy Tellez RC .50 1.25
11 Justin Smoak .20 .50
12 Miguel Cabrera .30 .75
13 Manny Machado .30 .75
14 Kyle Schwarber .30 .75
15 George Springer .25 .60
16 Justin Turner .30 .75
17 Robinson Cano .25 .60
18 A.J. Pollock .20 .50
19 Joey Gallo .25 .60
20 Jacob deGrom .60 1.50
21 Jose Ramirez .25 .60
22 Stephen Strasburg .30 .75
23 Kevin Newman RC .50 1.25
24 Nomar Mazara .20 .50
25 Kolby Allard RC .50 1.25
26 Miles Mikolas .30 .75
27 Albert Pujols .40 1.00
28 Hunter Renfroe .20 .50
29 Mallex Smith .20 .50
30 Miguel Sano .25 .60
31 Chris Sale .30 .75
32 Cedric Mullins RC .60 1.50
33 Brandon Belt .25 .60
34 Wade Davis .20 .50
35 Adrian Beltre .30 .75
36 Sean Reid-Foley RC .30 .75
37 Andrew Benintendi .30 .75
38 Bryse Wilson RC .40 1.00
39 Corey Kluber .25 .60
40 Jose Altuve .25 .60
41 Jaime Barria .20 .50
42 Trevor Williams .20 .50
43 Franmil Reyes .20 .50
44 Daniel Ponce de Leon RC .50 1.25
45 Chris Archer .20 .50
46 Michael Kopech RC 1.00 2.50
47 Adalberto Mondesi .40 1.00
48 Luis Ortiz RC .30 .75
49 Jose Urena .20 .50
50 Kyle Wright RC .50 1.25
51 Michael Brantley .25 .60
52 Steven Duggar RC .40 1.00
53 Dakota Hudson RC .40 1.00
54 Kris Bryant .40 1.00
55 Eddie Rosario .25 .60
56 Yoan Moncada .30 .75
57 David Peralta .20 .50
58 Jon Lester .25 .60
59 Luis Castillo .25 .60
60 Trey Mancini .25 .60
61 Francisco Lindor .30 .75
62 Ryan Yarbrough .20 .50
63 Chris Shaw RC .30 .75
64 Brandon Lowe RC .50 1.25
65 Reese McGuire RC .50 1.25
66 Brandon Nimmo .25 .60
67 Cody Bellinger .60 1.50
68 Max Scherzer .30 .75
69 Mike Minor .20 .50
70 Francisco Mejia RC .40 1.00
71 Josh Donaldson .25 .60
72 Patrick Wisdom RC .30 .75
73 Starling Marte .25 .60
74 Shane Bieber .30 .75
75 Scooter Gennett .25 .60
76 Sean Manaea .20 .50
77 Joey Wendle .25 .60
78 Felix Hernandez .25 .60
79 Eugenio Suarez .25 .60
80 Enyel De Los Santos RC .30 .75
81 Austin Meadows .30 .75
82 Framber Valdez RC .30 .75
83 Andrelton Simmons .20 .50
84 Luis Severino .25 .60
85 Carlos Correa .30 .75
86 Jeremy Jeffress .20 .50
87 Whit Merrifield .30 .75
88 Dereck Rodriguez .20 .50
89 J.T. Realmuto .30 .75
90 Jose Abreu .30 .75
91 J.D. Martinez .30 .75
92 Nick Williams .20 .50
93 Nicholas Castellanos .30 .75
94 Kevin Pillar .20 .50
95 Taylor Ward RC .30 .75
96 Myles Straw RC .50 1.25
97 Luis Urias RC .50 1.25
98 Clayton Kershaw .50 1.25
99 Odubel Herrera .25 .60
100 Blake Treinen RC .30 .75
101 Victor Robles .40 1.00
102 Khris Davis .30 .75
103 Corbin Burnes RC 2.50 6.00
104 Stephen Gonsalves RC .30 .75
105 Gleyber Torres .60 1.50
106 Charlie Blackmon .30 .75
107 David Fletcher RC 1.00 2.50
108 Wilson Ramos .20 .50
109 Gerrit Cole .30 .75
110 Miguel Andujar .30 .75
111 Nelson Cruz .30 .75
112 Sandy Alcantara .20 .50
113 Trevor Story .30 .75
114 Alex Bregman .30 .75
115 Corey Dickerson .20 .50
116 Christian Yelich .40 1.00
117 Jeimer Candelario .20 .50
118 Rafael Devers .40 1.00
119 Ji-Man Choi .20 .50
120 Madison Bumgarner .25 .60
121 Touki Toussaint RC .40 1.00
122 Christin Stewart RC .40 1.00
123 German Marquez .20 .50
124 Mike Moustakas .25 .60
125 Mitch Haniger .25 .60
126 Brad Keller RC .30 .75
127 Tyler O'Neill .25 .60
128 Caleb Ferguson RC .40 1.00
129 Brandon Crawford .25 .60
130 Jameson Taillon .25 .60
131 Michael Conforto .25 .60
132 Trea Turner .25 .60
133 Freddy Peralta .30 .75
134 Willie Calhoun .20 .50
135 Aaron Judge .75 2.00
136 Eric Hosmer .25 .60
137 Noah Syndergaard .25 .60
138 Anthony Rendon .30 .75
139 Teoscar Hernandez .30 .75
140 Matt Chapman .30 .75
141 Kyle Tucker RC .75 2.00
142 Amed Rosario .25 .60
143 Harrison Bader .25 .60
144 Edwin Encarnacion .30 .75
145 Jeff McNeil RC .75 2.00
146 Juan Soto 1.00 2.50
147 Carlos Carrasco .20 .50
148 Bryce Harper .50 1.25
149 James Paxton .25 .60
150 Rhys Hoskins .40 1.00
151 Andrew Heaney .20 .50
152 Willy Adames .20 .50
153 Shohei Ohtani .50 1.25
154 Giancarlo Stanton .30 .75
155 Carlos Rodon .30 .75
156 Ramon Laureano RC .60 1.50
157 Nolan Arenado .50 1.25
158 David Bote .25 .60
159 Jake Bauers RC .50 1.25
160 Josh James RC .50 1.25
161 Ozzie Albies .30 .75
162 Jonathan Davis RC .40 1.00
163 Joey Votto .30 .75
164 Justin Verlander .30 .75
165 Kyle Freeland .25 .60
166 Tim Anderson .30 .75
167 Walker Buehler .40 1.00
168 Ryan Borucki RC .30 .75
169 Ronald Acuna Jr. 1.50 4.00
170 Jose Martinez .20 .50
171 Blake Snell .25 .60
172 Javier Baez .40 1.00
173 Hunter Pence .25 .60
174 Matt Carpenter .30 .75
175 Jose Berrios .25 .60
176 Kevin Kramer RC .40 1.00
177 Nick Markakis .25 .60
178 Jacob Nix RC .40 1.00
179 Ryan O'Hearn RC .30 .75
180 Mookie Betts .60 1.50
181 Dennis Santana RC .30 .75
182 Jack Flaherty .30 .75
183 Xander Bogaerts .30 .75
184 Zack Greinke .30 .75
185 Cionel Perez RC .30 .75
186 Mike Foltynewicz .30 .75
187 Jackie Bradley Jr. .30 .75
188 Jonathan Loaisiga RC .40 1.00
189 Paul Goldschmidt .30 .75
190 Brian Anderson .20 .50
191 Aaron Nola .25 .60
192 Mike Trout 1.50 4.00
193 Lorenzo Cain .20 .50
194 Freddie Freeman .40 1.00
195 Jesus Aguilar .25 .60
196 Garrett Hampson RC .50 1.25
197 Travis Shaw .20 .50
198 Chance Adams RC .30 .75
199 Anthony Rizzo .40 1.00
200 Salvador Perez .25 .60
201 Chipper Jones .30 .75
202 Isaac Galloway RC .30 .75
203 Willians Astudillo RC .30 .75
204 Wade Boggs .25 .60
205 Juan Gonzalez .20 .50
206 Meibrys Viloria RC .30 .75
207 Ketel Marte .25 .60
208 Ranger Suarez RC .30 .75
209 Heath Fillmyer RC .30 .75
210 Rosell Herrera .20 .50
211 Miguel Tejada .20 .50
212 Nick Ciuffo RC .30 .75
213 Dwight Gooden .20 .50
214 Andre Dawson .25 .60
215 Brett Kennedy RC .30 .75
216 Robin Yount .30 .75
217 Marcus Semien .30 .75
218 Max Muncy .25 .60
219 Mike Piazza .30 .75
220 Jalen Beeks RC .30 .75
221 Ryan Meisinger RC .30 .75
222 David Ortiz .30 .75
223 Barry Larkin .25 .60
224 Starlin Castro .20 .50
225 C.D. Pelham RC .30 .75
226 Adam Kolarek RC .30 .75
227 Fernando Romero .20 .50
228 Tom Seaver .25 .60
229 Jefry Rodriguez RC .30 .75
230 Pablo Lopez RC .30 .75
231 Abiatal Avelino RC .30 .75
232 Alex Rodriguez .40 1.00
233 Ryne Sandberg .60 1.50
234 Harold Castro RC .40 1.00
235 Scott Barlow RC .30 .75
236 Aaron Hicks .25 .60
237 Thomas Pannone RC .50 1.25
238 Victor Reyes RC .30 .75
239 Dean Deetz RC .30 .75
240 Diego Castillo RC .30 .75
241 Rickey Henderson .30 .75
242 Javier Guerra RC .30 .75
243 Daniel Murphy .25 .60
244 Justin Verlander .30 .75
245 James Norwood RC .30 .75
246 Randy Johnson .30 .75
247 DJ Stewart RC .40 1.00
248 Roger Clemens .40 1.00
249 Jose Peraza .25 .60
250 Ozzie Smith .40 1.00
251 Kirby Puckett .30 .75
252 Gary Carter .25 .60
253 Andrew Velazquez .20 .50
254 Cal Ripken 1.00 2.50
255 Troy Tulowitzki .30 .75
256 Mariano Rivera .40 1.00
257 Yasiel Puig .30 .75
258 Tyler Mahle .20 .50
259 Justin Williams RC .30 .75
260 Michael Perez RC .30 .75
261 Nolan Ryan 1.00 2.50
262 Gabriel Guerrero RC .30 .75
263 Duane Underwood RC .30 .75
264 Trevor Richards RC .30 .75
265 Austin Voth RC .30 .75
266 Albert Pujols .40 1.00
267 Dawel Lugo RC .50 1.25
268 Luke Voit .50 1.25
269 Kevin Mitchell .20 .50
270 Ty Buttrey RC .30 .75
271 Roberto Alomar .25 .60
272 Pablo Reyes RC .30 .75
273 Johan Camargo .20 .50
274 Yency Almonte RC .30 .75
275 Austin Dean RC .30 .75
276 Vladimir Guerrero .25 .60
277 Manny Machado .30 .75
278 Austin Wynns RC .30 .75
279 George Brett .60 1.50
280 Nick Martini RC .30 .75
281 Andrew McCutchen .30 .75
282 Yusei Kikuchi RC .50 1.25
283 Chad Sobotka RC .30 .75
284 Tanner Rainey RC .30 .75
285 Eric Hosmer .25 .60
286 Edmundo Sosa RC .40 1.00
287 Pedro Martinez .25 .60
288 Dontrelle Willis .20 .50
289 Kohl Stewart RC .40 1.00
290 Tony Gwynn .30 .75
291 Evan Longoria .25 .60
292 Connor Sadzeck RC .30 .75
293 Patrick Corbin .25 .60
294 Eric Haase RC .30 .75
295 Craig Biggio .25 .60
296 Larry Walker .25 .60
297 Tim Lincecum .25 .60
298 Dale Murphy .30 .75
299 Frank Thomas .30 .75
300 Ken Griffey Jr. .60 1.50

2019 Panini Prizm Prizms Blue

*BLUE: 1X TO 2.5X BASIC
*BLUE RC: .6X TO 1.5X BASIC
RANDOM INSERTS IN PACKS

2019 Panini Prizm Prizms Blue Mojo

*BLUE MOJO: 2X TO 5X
*BLUE MOJO RC: 1.2X TO 3X
RANDOM INSERTS IN PACKS
STATED PRINT RUN 399 SER.#'d SETS
192 Mike Trout 10.00 25.00
290 Tony Gwynn 4.00 10.00
300 Ken Griffey Jr. 8.00 20.00

2019 Panini Prizm Prizms Blue Wave

*BLUE WAVE: 3X TO 8X
*BLUE WAVE RC: 2X TO 5X
RANDOM INSERTS IN PACKS
STATED PRINT RUN 60 SER.#'d SETS
192 Mike Trout 25.00 60.00
251 Kirby Puckett 15.00 40.00
261 Nolan Ryan 10.00 25.00
279 George Brett 8.00 20.00
290 Tony Gwynn 6.00 15.00
299 Frank Thomas 5.00 12.00
300 Ken Griffey Jr. 12.00 30.00

2019 Panini Prizm Prizms Burgandy Shimmer

*BURGUNDY: 5X TO 12X
*BURGUNDY RC: 3X TO 8X
RANDOM INSERTS IN PACKS
STATED PRINT RUN 25 SER.#'d SETS
192 Mike Trout 75.00 200.00
251 Kirby Puckett 25.00 60.00
261 Nolan Ryan 15.00 40.00
279 George Brett 12.00 30.00
290 Tony Gwynn 10.00 25.00
299 Frank Thomas 8.00 20.00
300 Ken Griffey Jr. 20.00 50.00

2019 Panini Prizm Prizms Carolina Blue

*CAR BLUE: 1.2X TO 3X BASIC
*CAR BLUE RC: .75X TO 2X BASIC
RANDOM INSERTS IN PACKS

2019 Panini Prizm Prizms Cosmic Haze

*COSMIC: 1.2X TO 3X BASIC
*COSMIC RC: .75X TO 2X BASIC
RANDOM INSERTS IN PACKS

2019 Panini Prizm Prizms Green

*GREEN: 1.2X TO 3X BASIC
*GREEN RC: .75X TO 2X BASIC
RANDOM INSERTS IN PACKS

2019 Panini Prizm Prizms Hyper Blue

*HYPER BLUE: 1.2X TO 3X BASIC
*HYPER BLUE RC: .75X TO 2X BASIC
RANDOM INSERTS IN PACKS

2019 Panini Prizm Prizms Hyper Green and Yellow

*HYPER GY: 1.2X TO 3X BASIC
*HYPER GY RC: .75X TO 2X BASIC
RANDOM INSERTS IN PACKS

2019 Panini Prizm Prizms Hyper Purple and Green

*HYPER PG: 1.2X TO 3X BASIC
*HYPER PG RC: .75X TO 2X BASIC
RANDOM INSERTS IN PACKS

2019 Panini Prizm Prizms Lime Green Donut Circles

*LIME GREEN: 2X TO 5X
*LIME GREEN RC: 1.2X TO 3X
RANDOM INSERTS IN PACKS
STATED PRINT RUN 199 SER.#'d SETS
192 Mike Trout 10.00 25.00
290 Tony Gwynn 4.00 10.00
300 Ken Griffey Jr. 8.00 20.00

2019 Panini Prizm Prizms Navy Blue Kaleidoscope

*NAVY BLUE: 4X TO 10X
*NAVY BLUE RC: 2.5X TO 6X
RANDOM INSERTS IN PACKS
STATED PRINT RUN 35 SER.#'d SETS
192 Mike Trout 60.00 150.00
251 Kirby Puckett 20.00 50.00
261 Nolan Ryan 12.00 30.00
279 George Brett 10.00 25.00
290 Tony Gwynn 8.00 20.00
299 Frank Thomas 6.00 15.00
300 Ken Griffey Jr. 15.00 40.00

2019 Panini Prizm Prizms Neon Orange Donut Circles

*NEON ORANGE: 2.5X TO 6X
*NEON ORANGE RC: 1.5X TO 4X
RANDOM INSERTS IN PACKS
STATED PRINT RUN 150 SER.#'d SETS
192 Mike Trout 15.00 40.00
251 Kirby Puckett 12.00 30.00
279 George Brett 6.00 15.00
290 Tony Gwynn 5.00 12.00
300 Ken Griffey Jr. 10.00 25.00

2019 Panini Prizm Prizms Pink

*PINK: 1.2X TO 3X BASIC
*PINK RC: .75X TO 2X BASIC
RANDOM INSERTS IN PACKS

2019 Panini Prizm Prizms Power Plaid

*PLAID: 3X TO 8X
*PLAID RC: 2X TO 5X
RANDOM INSERTS IN PACKS
STATED PRINT RUN 75 SER.#'d SETS
192 Mike Trout 25.00 60.00
251 Kirby Puckett 15.00 40.00
261 Nolan Ryan 10.00 25.00
279 George Brett 8.00 20.00
290 Tony Gwynn 6.00 15.00
299 Frank Thomas 5.00 12.00
300 Ken Griffey Jr. 12.00 30.00

2019 Panini Prizm Prizms Purple

*PURPLE: 1.2X TO 3X BASIC
*PURPLE RC: .75X TO 2X BASIC
RANDOM INSERTS IN PACKS

2019 Panini Prizm Prizms Red

*RED: 1X TO 2.5X BASIC
*RED RC: .6X TO 1.5X BASIC
RANDOM INSERTS IN PACKS

2019 Panini Prizm Prizms Red Mojo

*RED MOJO: 2X TO 5X
*RED MOJO RC: 1.2X TO 3X
RANDOM INSERTS IN PACKS
STATED PRINT RUN 299 SER.#'d SETS
192 Mike Trout 10.00 25.00
290 Tony Gwynn 4.00 10.00
300 Ken Griffey Jr. 8.00 20.00

2019 Panini Prizm Prizms Red White and Blue

*RED WHT BLUE: 1.2X TO 3X BASIC
*RED WHT BLUE RC: .75X TO 2X BASIC
RANDOM INSERTS IN PACKS

2019 Panini Prizm Prizms Silver

*SILVER: 1.5X TO 4X BASIC
*SILVER RC: 1X TO 2.5X BASIC
RANDOM INSERTS IN PACKS
192 Mike Trout 8.00 20.00

2019 Panini Prizm Prizms Snake Skin

*SNAKE SKIN: 4X TO 10X
*SNAKE SKIN RC: 2.5X TO 6X
RANDOM INSERTS IN PACKS
STATED PRINT RUN 50 SER.#'d SETS
192 Mike Trout 30.00 80.00
251 Kirby Puckett 20.00 50.00
261 Nolan Ryan 12.00 30.00
279 George Brett 10.00 25.00
290 Tony Gwynn 8.00 20.00
299 Frank Thomas 6.00 15.00
300 Ken Griffey Jr. 15.00 40.00

2019 Panini Prizm Prizms Zebra Stripes

*ZEBRA: 3X TO 8X
*ZEBRA RC: 2X TO 5X
RANDOM INSERTS IN PACKS
STATED PRINT RUN 99 SER.#'d SETS
192 Mike Trout 60.00 150.00
251 Kirby Puckett 15.00 40.00
261 Nolan Ryan 10.00 25.00
279 George Brett 8.00 20.00
290 Tony Gwynn 6.00 15.00
299 Frank Thomas 5.00 12.00
300 Ken Griffey Jr. 12.00 30.00

2019 Panini Prizm Brilliance

RANDOM INSERTS IN PACKS
*PRIZMS: .75X TO 2X BASIC
1 Blake Snell .40 1.00
2 Justin Verlander .50 1.25
3 Jacob deGrom 1.00 2.50
4 Corey Kluber .40 1.00
5 Aaron Nola .40 1.00
6 Chris Sale .50 1.25
7 Kyle Freeland .40 1.00
8 Max Scherzer .50 1.25
9 Luis Severino .40 1.00
10 Miles Mikolas .50 1.25

2019 Panini Prizm Color Blast

RANDOM INSERTS IN PACKS
1 Bryce Harper 75.00 200.00
2 Shohei Ohtani 75.00 200.00
3 Kris Bryant 30.00 80.00
4 Aaron Judge 100.00 250.00
5 Mike Trout 100.00 250.00
6 Ronald Acuna Jr. 75.00 200.00
7 Mookie Betts 50.00 120.00
8 Manny Machado 30.00 80.00
9 Javier Baez 40.00 100.00
10 Christian Yelich 40.00 100.00

2019 Panini Prizm Fireworks

RANDOM INSERTS IN PACKS
*PRIZMS: .75X TO 2X BASIC
1 Mike Trout 2.50 6.00
2 Mookie Betts 1.00 2.50
3 Jose Ramirez .40 1.00
4 Christian Yelich .60 1.50
5 Javier Baez .60 1.50
6 Nolan Arenado .75 2.00
7 J.D. Martinez .50 1.25
8 Alex Bregman .50 1.25
9 Freddie Freeman .60 1.50
10 Paul Goldschmidt .50 1.25
11 Francisco Lindor .50 1.25
12 Trevor Story .50 1.25
13 Aaron Judge 1.25 3.00
14 Jose Altuve .40 1.00
15 Shohei Ohtani .75 2.00

2019 Panini Prizm Game Ball Graphs

RANDOM INSERTS IN PACKS
EXCHANGE DEADLINE 11/15/2020
1 Anthony Banda 2.50 6.00
2 Stephen Piscotty 2.50 6.00
3 Shane Bieber 15.00 40.00
4 David Dahl 2.50 6.00
5 Josh Bell 10.00 25.00
6 Reynaldo Lopez 3.00 8.00
7 Raimel Tapia 2.50 6.00
8 Franmil Reyes 2.50 6.00
9 Jordan Luplow 2.50 6.00
10 Renato Nunez 3.00 8.00
11 Merandy Gonzalez 2.50 6.00
12 Max Fried 4.00 10.00
13 Aaron Judge EXCH 40.00 100.00
14 Richard Urena 2.50 6.00
15 Austin Slater 2.50 6.00
16 Jacoby Jones 3.00 8.00
17 Luke Weaver 2.50 6.00
19 Luiz Gohara 2.50 6.00
20 Brandon Belt 3.00 8.00
21 Teoscar Hernandez 4.00 10.00
22 Jeimer Candelario 2.50 6.00
23 Eduardo Nunez 2.50 6.00
24 Alex Verdugo 6.00 15.00
25 David Bote 10.00 25.00

2019 Panini Prizm Illumination

RANDOM INSERTS IN PACKS
*PRIZMS: .75X TO 2X BASIC
1 Aaron Judge 1.25 3.00
2 Bryce Harper .75 2.00
3 Kris Bryant .60 1.50
4 Manny Machado .50 1.25
5 Charlie Blackmon .50 1.25
6 Scooter Gennett .40 1.00
7 Clayton Kershaw .75 2.00
8 Giancarlo Stanton .50 1.25
9 Rhys Hoskins .60 1.50
10 Mike Trout 2.50 6.00
11 Whit Merrifield .50 1.25
12 Khris Davis .50 1.25

2019 Panini Prizm Instant Impact

RANDOM INSERTS IN PACKS
*PRIZMS: .75X TO 2X BASIC
1 Gleyber Torres 1.00 2.50
2 Ronald Acuna Jr. 2.50 6.00
3 Walker Buehler .60 1.50
4 Shohei Ohtani .75 2.00
5 Miguel Andujar .50 1.25
6 Ozzie Albies .50 1.25
7 Juan Soto 1.50 4.00
8 Harrison Bader .40 1.00
9 Jack Flaherty .50 1.25
10 Joey Wendle .40 1.00

2019 Panini Prizm Lumber Inc.

RANDOM INSERTS IN PACKS
*PRIZMS: .75X TO 2X BASIC
1 Khris Davis .50 1.25
2 Joey Gallo .40 1.00
3 J.D. Martinez .50 1.25
4 Giancarlo Stanton .50 1.25
5 Bryce Harper .75 2.00
6 Aaron Judge 1.25 3.00
7 Trevor Story .50 1.25
8 Matt Olson .50 1.25
9 Mike Trout 2.50 6.00
10 Gary Sanchez .50 1.25

2019 Panini Prizm Machines

RANDOM INSERTS IN PACKS
*PRIZMS: .75X TO 2X BASIC
1 Mike Trout 2.50 6.00
2 Mookie Betts 1.00 2.50
3 Jose Altuve .40 1.00
4 Aaron Judge 1.25 3.00
5 Javier Baez .60 1.50
6 Alex Bregman .50 1.25
7 Nolan Arenado .75 2.00
8 Christian Yelich .60 1.50
9 Jose Ramirez .40 1.00
10 Paul Goldschmidt .50 1.25

2019 Panini Prizm Numbers Game
RANDOM INSERTS IN PACKS
*PRIZMS: .75X TO 2X BASIC
1 Juan Soto 1.50 4.00
2 Mookie Betts 1.00 2.50
3 Ronald Acuna Jr. 2.50 6.00
4 Miguel Andujar .50 1.25
5 Mike Trout 2.50 6.00
6 J.D. Martinez .50 1.25
7 Christian Yelich .60 1.50
8 Javier Baez .60 1.50

2019 Panini Prizm Pro Penmanship
RANDOM INSERTS IN PACKS
EXCHANGE DEADLINE 11/15/2020
1 Carson Kelly 2.50 6.00
2 Jharel Cotton 2.50 6.00
3 J.D. Davis 2.50 6.00
4 Roman Quinn 2.50 6.00
5 Adalberto Mondesi 6.00 15.00
6 Matt Barnes 2.50 6.00
7 Luis Perdomo 2.50 6.00
8 Jake Thompson 2.50 6.00
9 Trevor May 2.50 6.00
10 Brian Anderson 2.50 6.00
11 Carson Fulmer 2.50 6.00
12 Austin Barnes 2.50 6.00
13 Hunter Dozier 2.50 6.00
14 David Paulino 2.50 6.00
15 Andrew Suarez 2.50 6.00
16 Ryan McMahon 4.00 10.00
17 Jose De Leon 2.50 6.00
18 Kendall Graveman 2.50 6.00
19 Chance Sisco 2.50 6.00
20 Tim Beckham 3.00 8.00
21 Ji-Man Choi 2.50 6.00
22 Freddy Peralta 4.00 10.00
23 Odubel Herrera 3.00 8.00
25 Joe Musgrove 4.00 10.00

2019 Panini Prizm Profiles
RANDOM INSERTS IN PACKS
1 Mike Trout 25.00 60.00
2 Miguel Cabrera 4.00 10.00
3 David Ortiz 4.00 10.00
4 Yasiel Puig 4.00 10.00
5 Jose Altuve 3.00 8.00
6 Nolan Arenado 6.00 15.00
7 Francisco Lindor 4.00 10.00
8 Matt Carpenter 4.00 10.00
9 Max Scherzer 4.00 10.00
10 Clayton Kershaw 6.00 15.00
11 Jacob deGrom 8.00 20.00
12 Rickey Henderson 4.00 10.00
13 Ken Griffey Jr. 8.00 20.00
14 Juan Soto 12.00 30.00
15 Alex Bregman 4.00 10.00

2019 Panini Prizm Rookie Autographs
RANDOM INSERTS IN PACKS
EXCHANGE DEADLINE 11/15/2020
*PRIZM: .5X TO 1.2X
*PRIZM BLUE: .5X TO 1.2X
*PRIZM RED: .5X TO 1.2X
1 Kyle Wright 4.00 10.00
2 Justus Sheffield 4.00 10.00
3 Steven Duggar 3.00 8.00
4 Michael Kopech 8.00 20.00
5 Kolby Allard 4.00 10.00
7 Sean Reid-Foley 2.50 6.00
8 Jake Cave 3.00 8.00
9 Patrick Wisdom 2.50 6.00
10 Myles Straw 4.00 10.00
11 Luis Ortiz 2.50 6.00
12 Dakota Hudson 3.00 8.00
13 Brandon Lowe 12.00 30.00
14 Cedric Mullins 8.00 20.00
15 Framber Valdez 2.50 6.00
16 Reese McGuire 4.00 10.00
17 Taylor Ward 2.50 6.00
18 Chris Shaw 2.50 6.00
19 Rowdy Tellez 4.00 10.00
20 Danny Jansen 2.50 6.00
21 Enyel De Los Santos 2.50 6.00
22 Kevin Newman 4.00 10.00
23 Luis Urias 4.00 10.00
24 Bryse Wilson 3.00 8.00
25 Daniel Ponce de Leon 4.00 10.00
26 Jonathan Loaisiga 3.00 8.00
27 Josh James 4.00 10.00
28 Kyle Tucker 6.00 15.00
29 David Fletcher 8.00 20.00
30 Jacob Nix 3.00 8.00
31 Stephen Gonsalves 2.50 6.00
32 Ramon Laureano 6.00 15.00
33 Fernando Tatis Jr. 60.00 150.00
34 Chance Adams 2.50 6.00
35 Jonathan Davis 3.00 8.00
36 Garrett Hampson 4.00 10.00
37 Caleb Ferguson 3.00 8.00
38 Jake Bauers 4.00 10.00
39 Christin Stewart 3.00 8.00
40 Corbin Burnes 8.00 20.00
41 Cionel Perez 2.50 6.00
42 Eloy Jimenez 20.00 50.00
43 Touki Toussaint 3.00 8.00
44 Kevin Kramer 3.00 8.00
45 Vladimir Guerrero Jr. 30.00 80.00
46 Ryan O'Hearn 2.50 6.00
47 Dennis Santana 2.50 6.00
48 Ryan Borucki 2.50 6.00
49 Brad Keller 2.50 6.00
50 Jeff McNeil 6.00 15.00
51 Trevor Richards 2.50 6.00
53 Javier Guerra 2.50 6.00
54 Ryan Meisinger 2.50 6.00
55 Brett Kennedy 2.50 6.00
56 Eric Haase 2.50 6.00
57 Scott Barlow 2.50 6.00
58 James Norwood 2.50 6.00
59 Victor Reyes 2.50 6.00
60 Andrew Velazquez 2.50 6.00
61 Chad Sobotka 2.50 6.00
62 Duane Underwood 2.50 6.00
63 Austin Voth 2.50 6.00
64 Kohl Stewart 3.00 8.00
65 Nick Ciuffo 2.50 6.00
66 Pablo Lopez 2.50 6.00
67 Edmundo Sosa 3.00 8.00
68 Justin Williams 2.50 6.00
72 Ranger Suarez 2.50 6.00
75 Dean Deetz 2.50 6.00
76 Yusei Kikuchi 6.00 15.00
77 Austin Wynns 2.50 6.00
78 C.D. Pelham 2.50 6.00
81 Adam Kolarek 2.50 6.00
82 Abiatal Avelino 2.50 6.00
83 Thomas Pannone 4.00 10.00
88 Yency Almonte 2.50 6.00
89 Meibrys Viloria 2.50 6.00
90 Jefry Rodriguez 2.50 6.00
91 Tanner Rainey 2.50 6.00
92 Ty Buttrey 2.50 6.00
93 Gabriel Guerrero 2.50 6.00
94 Jalen Beeks 2.50 6.00
95 Connor Joe 2.50 6.00
96 Riley Ferrell 2.50 6.00
97 Richie Martin 2.50 6.00
99 Chris Ellis 2.50 6.00
100 Rosell Herrera 2.50 6.00

2019 Panini Prizm Rookie Autographs Prizms Blue Wave
*BLUE WAVE p/r 60: .6X TO 1.5X
*BLUE WAVE p/r 25: .75X TO 2X
RANDOM INSERTS IN PACKS
PRINT RUNS B/WN 5-60 COPIES PER
NO PRICING ON QTY 5 OR LESS
EXCHANGE DEADLINE 11/15/2020
85 Harold Castro/60 5.00 12.00

2019 Panini Prizm Rookie Autographs Prizms Burgandy Shimmer
*BURGANDY p/r 25: .75X TO 2X
RANDOM INSERTS IN PACKS
PRINT RUNS B/WN 5-25 COPIES PER
NO PRICING ON QTY 5
EXCHANGE DEADLINE 11/15/2020
85 Harold Castro/25 6.00 15.00

2019 Panini Prizm Rookie Autographs Prizms Carolina Blue
*CAR.BLUE p/r 50-100: .6X TO 1.5X
*CAR.BLUE p/r 25: .75X TO 2X
RANDOM INSERTS IN PACKS
PRINT RUNS B/WN 5-100 COPIES PER
NO PRICING ON QTY 5
EXCHANGE DEADLINE 11/15/2020
70 Nick Martini/100 4.00 10.00
74 Michael Perez/100 4.00 10.00
80 Isaac Galloway/100 4.00 10.00
84 Austin Dean/100 4.00 10.00
85 Harold Castro/100 5.00 12.00
86 Connor Sadzeck/100 4.00 10.00

2019 Panini Prizm Rookie Autographs Prizms Navy Blue Kaleidoscope
*NAVY p/r 35: .75X TO 2X
RANDOM INSERTS IN PACKS
PRINT RUNS B/WN 5-35 COPIES PER
NO PRICING ON QTY 5
EXCHANGE DEADLINE 11/15/2020
85 Harold Castro/35 6.00 15.00

2019 Panini Prizm Rookie Autographs Prizms Power Plaid
*PLAID p/r 75: .6X TO 1.5X
*PLAID p/r 25: .75X TO 2X
RANDOM INSERTS IN PACKS
PRINT RUNS B/WN 5-75 COPIES PER
NO PRICING ON QTY 5 OR LESS
EXCHANGE DEADLINE 11/15/2020
85 Harold Castro/75 5.00 12.00

2019 Panini Prizm Rookie Autographs Prizms Purple
*PURPLE p/r 50: .6X TO 1.5X
RANDOM INSERTS IN PACKS
PRINT RUNS B/WN 5-50 COPIES PER
NO PRICING ON QTY 5 OR LESS
EXCHANGE DEADLINE 11/15/2020
85 Harold Castro/50 5.00 12.00

2019 Panini Prizm Rookie Autographs Prizms Red White and Blue
*RWB p/r 50: .6X TO 1.5X
*RWB p/r 25: .75X TO 2X
RANDOM INSERTS IN PACKS
PRINT RUNS B/WN 5-50 COPIES PER
NO PRICING ON QTY 5 OR LESS
EXCHANGE DEADLINE 11/15/2020
85 Harold Castro/50 5.00 12.00

2019 Panini Prizm Rookie Autographs Prizms Snake Skin
*SNAKE p/r 50: .6X TO 1.5X
*SNAKE p/r 25: .75X TO 2X
RANDOM INSERTS IN PACKS
PRINT RUNS B/WN 5-50 COPIES PER
NO PRICING ON QTY 5 OR LESS
EXCHANGE DEADLINE 11/15/2020
85 Harold Castro/50 5.00 12.00

2019 Panini Prizm Rookie Autographs Prizms Zebra Stripes
*ZEBRA p/r 50-99: .6X TO 1.5X
*ZEBRA p/r 25: .75X TO 2X
RANDOM INSERTS IN PACKS
PRINT RUNS B/WN 3-99 COPIES PER
NO PRICING ON QTY 5 OR LESS
EXCHANGE DEADLINE 11/15/2020
85 Harold Castro/99 5.00 12.00

2019 Panini Prizm Scorching
RANDOM INSERTS IN PACKS
*PRIZMS: .75X TO 2X BASIC
1 Max Scherzer .50 1.25
2 Justin Verlander .50 1.25
3 Gerrit Cole .50 1.25
4 Jacob deGrom 1.00 2.50
5 Jordan Hicks .40 1.00
6 Aroldis Chapman .50 1.25
7 Trea Turner .40 1.00
8 Whit Merrifield .50 1.25
9 Jose Ramirez .40 1.00
10 Billy Hamilton .40 1.00
11 Luis Severino .40 1.00
12 Blake Snell .40 1.00
13 Michael Kopech 1.00 2.50
14 Shohei Ohtani .75 2.00
15 Walker Buehler .60 1.50

2019 Panini Prizm Signatures
RANDOM INSERTS IN PACKS
EXCHANGE DEADLINE 11/15/2020
1 Matt Olson 4.00 10.00
2 Andres Galarraga 3.00 8.00
3 Mike Foltynewicz 4.00 10.00
4 Jonathan Lucroy 3.00 8.00
5 Trevor Story 4.00 10.00
6 Victor Robles 6.00 15.00
7 Max Muncy 6.00 15.00
8 Lewis Brinson 2.50 6.00
9 Rhys Hoskins 10.00 25.00
10 Shohei Ohtani EXCH 75.00 200.00
11 Garrett Richards 3.00 8.00
12 Byron Buxton 4.00 10.00
13 Aledmys Diaz 3.00 8.00
14 Roberto Osuna 2.50 6.00
15 Fernando Rodney 2.50 6.00
16 Francisco Mejia 3.00 8.00
17 Walker Buehler 12.00 30.00
18 Eric Thames 2.50 6.00
19 Nomar Mazara 2.50 6.00
20 Bert Blyleven 3.00 8.00
22 Brian McCann 6.00 15.00
23 Carlos Gonzalez
24 Carlton Fisk 10.00 25.00
25 Eddie Rosario 6.00 15.00

2019 Panini Prizm Star Gazing
RANDOM INSERTS IN PACKS
*PRIZMS: .75X TO 2X BASIC
1 Mike Trout 2.50 6.00
2 Mookie Betts 1.00 2.50
3 Bryce Harper .75 2.00
4 Kris Bryant .60 1.50
5 Aaron Judge 1.25 3.00
6 Francisco Lindor .50 1.25
7 Nolan Arenado .75 2.00
8 Ronald Acuna Jr. 2.50 6.00
9 Shohei Ohtani .75 2.00
10 Jose Altuve .40 1.00

2020 Panini Prizm
1 Anthony Rendon .30 .75
2 Keston Hiura .40 1.00
3 T.J. Zeuch RC .30 .75
4 Brandon Woodruff .30 .75
5 Willy Adames .20 .50
6 Shin-Soo Choo .25 .60
7 Eddie Rosario .25 .60
8 Jorge Soler .30 .75
9 Kris Bryant .40 1.00
10 Domingo Leyba RC .40 1.00
11 Howie Kendrick .20 .50
12 Yasmani Grandal .20 .50
13 Yonathan Daza RC .40 1.00
14 David Fletcher .30 .75
15 Ramon Laureano .25 .60
16 John Means .30 .75
17 Kyle Seager .20 .50
18 Eduardo Rodriguez .20 .50
19 Jake Fraley RC .40 1.00
20 Austin Meadows .30 .75
21 Kirby Yates .20 .50
22 Niko Goodrum .25 .60
23 Mike Moustakas .25 .60
24 Lourdes Gurriel .25 .60
25 Isan Diaz RC .50 1.25
26 Patrick Sandoval RC .50 1.25
27 Tony Gonsolin RC 1.25 3.00
28 Cody Bellinger .60 1.50
29 Tommy Pham .20 .50
30 Nico Hoerner RC 1.25 3.00
31 Lucas Giolito .25 .60
32 Lorenzo Cain .20 .50
33 Joey Votto .30 .75
34 Buster Posey .40 1.00
35 Jacob deGrom .60 1.50
36 Shane Bieber .30 .75
37 Brandon Lowe .25 .60
38 Cole Hamels .25 .60
39 Bobby Bradley RC .30 .75
40 Zac Gallen RC .75 2.00
41 Starling Marte .25 .60
42 Julio Teheran .25 .60
43 Clayton Kershaw .50 1.25
44 Justin Dunn RC .40 1.00
45 Marco Gonzales .20 .50
46 Sheldon Neuse RC .40 1.00
47 Juan Soto 1.00 2.50
48 Jonathan Gray .20 .50
49 Jake Odorizzi .20 .50
50 Kyle Hendricks .30 .75
51 Marcell Ozuna .30 .75
52 Luke Weaver .20 .50
53 Randy Arozarena RC 2.50 6.00
54 Kolten Wong .25 .60
55 Aaron Nola .25 .60
56 Brusdar Graterol RC .50 1.25
57 Michael Brantley .25 .60
58 Jack Flaherty .30 .75
59 Ken Giles .20 .50
60 Marcus Stroman .25 .60
61 Jose Abreu .30 .75
62 Andres Munoz RC .50 1.25
63 Bryce Harper .50 1.25
64 Aaron Judge .75 2.00
65 Liam Hendriks .30 .75
66 Pete Alonso .75 2.00
67 Michael King RC .50 1.25
68 Matt Thaiss RC .40 1.00
69 Tyrone Taylor RC .30 .75
70 Logan Allen RC .30 .75
71 Bo Bichette RC 2.50 6.00
72 Deivy Grullon RC .30 .75
73 Joe Palumbo RC .30 .75
74 Brad Keller .20 .50
75 Spencer Turnbull .20 .50
76 Manny Machado .30 .75
77 Josh Bell .25 .60
78 Dallas Keuchel .25 .60
79 Evan Longoria .25 .60
80 Trent Grisham RC 1.25 3.00
81 Charlie Blackmon .30 .75
82 Gary Sanchez .30 .75
83 DJ LeMahieu .30 .75
84 Sean Manaea .20 .50
85 Gio Urshela .30 .75
86 George Springer .25 .60
87 James Paxton .25 .60
88 Luis Castillo .25 .60
89 Bryan Abreu RC .30 .75
90 Michael Baez RC .30 .75
91 Michael Chavis .25 .60
92 Hyun-Jin Ryu .25 .60
93 Stephen Strasburg .30 .75
94 Kyle Lewis RC 2.00 5.00
95 Josh Rojas RC .30 .75
96 Jonathan Hernandez RC .30 .75
97 Abraham Toro RC .40 1.00
98 Justin Turner .30 .75
99 Adalberto Mondesi .25 .60
100 Gleyber Torres .60 1.50
101 Adbert Alzolay RC .40 1.00
102 Dakota Hudson .25 .60
103 Nelson Cruz .30 .75
104 Jesus Luzardo RC .60 1.50
105 Jorge Polanco .25 .60
106 Ronald Bolanos RC .25 .60
107 Josh Hader .25 .60
108 Scott Kingery .25 .60
109 Miguel Sano .25 .60
110 Hanser Alberto .20 .50
111 German Marquez .30 .75
112 Kevin Newman .30 .75
113 Willi Castro RC .50 1.25
114 Travis Demeritte RC .50 1.25
115 Mitch Garver .20 .50
116 Jordan Yamamoto RC .30 .75
117 Mookie Betts .60 1.50
118 Omar Narvaez .20 .50
119 Max Fried .30 .75
120 Cavan Biggio .40 1.00
121 Danny Duffy .20 .50
122 Brett Gardner .25 .60
123 Marcus Semien .30 .75
124 Eduardo Escobar .20 .50
125 Avisail Garcia .25 .60
126 Dustin May RC 1.00 2.50
127 Lance Lynn .20 .50
128 Dylan Cease RC .50 1.25
129 Mike Clevinger .25 .60
130 Masahiro Tanaka .30 .75
131 Christian Yelich .40 1.00
132 Yu Darvish .30 .75
133 Sandy Alcantara .20 .50
134 Sean Murphy RC .50 1.25
135 Trent Thornton .20 .50
136 Sonny Gray .25 .60
137 Jake Rogers RC .30 .75
138 Francisco Lindor .30 .75
139 Adrian Morejon RC .30 .75
140 Aristides Aquino RC .75 2.00
141 Danny Mendick RC .40 1.00
142 Ketel Marte .25 .60
143 Xander Bogaerts .30 .75
144 Starlin Castro .20 .50
145 Max Kepler .25 .60
146 Jose Berrios .25 .60
147 Carlos Santana .25 .60
148 Trea Turner .30 .75
149 Matt Chapman .30 .75
150 Yusei Kikuchi .25 .60
151 Justin Verlander .30 .75
152 Yadier Molina .40 1.00
153 Brendan McKay RC .50 1.25
154 Bryan Reynolds .25 .60
155 Mauricio Dubon RC .40 1.00
156 Rico Garcia RC .50 1.25
157 Matt Carpenter .30 .75
158 Jeff McNeil .25 .60
159 Miguel Cabrera .30 .75
160 Eloy Jimenez .60 1.50
161 Tim Anderson .30 .75
162 Shohei Ohtani .50 1.25
163 Noah Syndergaard .25 .60
164 Giancarlo Stanton .30 .75
165 Vladimir Guerrero Jr. .50 1.25
166 Freddie Freeman .40 1.00
167 Corey Kluber .25 .60
168 Logan Webb RC .50 1.25
169 David Dahl .20 .50
170 Mike Soroka .30 .75
171 Yu Chang RC .50 1.25
172 J.T. Realmuto .30 .75
173 Rafael Devers .40 1.00
174 Trevor Bauer .40 1.00
175 Hunter Dozier .20 .50
176 Tyler Glasnow .20 .50
177 Eugenio Suarez .25 .60
178 Michael Conforto .25 .60
179 Nick Ahmed .20 .50
180 Javier Baez .40 1.00
181 Yordan Alvarez RC 3.00 8.00
182 Victor Robles .40 1.00
183 Chris Paddack .30 .75
184 Ronald Acuna Jr. 1.25 3.00
185 Matt Olson .30 .75
186 Paul Goldschmidt .30 .75
187 Patrick Corbin .25 .60
188 Alex Bregman .30 .75
189 Max Muncy .25 .60
190 Chris Sale .30 .75
191 Max Scherzer .30 .75
192 Jaylin Davis RC .50 1.25
193 Fernando Tatis Jr. 1.50 4.00
194 A.J. Puk RC .50 1.25
195 Brock Burke RC .50 1.25
196 Mike Trout 1.50 4.00
197 Gerrit Cole .50 1.25
198 Gavin Lux RC 1.50 4.00
199 Matt Boyd .20 .50
200 Walker Buehler .40 1.00
201 Donnie Walton RC .75 2.00
202 Jonathan Villar .20 .50
203 Anthony Kay RC .30 .75
204 Dan Vogelbach .20 .50
205 Nicholas Castellanos .30 .75
206 Tres Barrera RC .60 1.50
207 Blake Snell .25 .60
208 Yoan Moncada .30 .75
209 Lewis Thorpe RC .30 .75
210 Rhys Hoskins .40 1.00
211 Aaron Civale RC .60 1.50
212 Trevor Story .30 .75
213 Tommy Edman .30 .75
214 Albert Pujols .40 1.00
215 Joey Gallo .30 .75
216 Christian Vazquez .25 .60
217 Charlie Morton .30 .75
218 Jose Ramirez .25 .60
219 Mike Fiers .20 .50
220 Corey Seager .30 .75
221 Jose Altuve .25 .60
222 Merrill Kelly .20 .50
223 Mike Yastrzemski .50 1.25
224 Anthony Rizzo .40 1.00
225 Paul DeJong .30 .75
226 Brian Anderson .20 .50
227 Robbie Ray .20 .50
228 J.D. Davis .20 .50
229 Josh Donaldson .25 .60
230 Nolan Arenado .50 1.25
231 Ozzie Albies .30 .75
232 Nick Solak RC 1.25 3.00
233 Zack Collins RC .40 1.00
234 Mike Minor .20 .50
235 Will Smith .30 .75
236 Caleb Smith .20 .50
237 Carlos Correa .30 .75
238 Willson Contreras .20 .50
239 Zack Greinke .30 .75
240 Sam Hilliard RC .50 1.25
241 Edwin Rios RC .75 2.00
242 Kyle Schwarber .30 .75
243 Danny Santana .20 .50
244 J.D. Martinez .30 .75
245 James McCann .25 .60
246 Whit Merrifield .30 .75
247 Madison Bumgarner .25 .60
248 Zack Wheeler .25 .60
249 Trey Mancini .30 .75
250 Mitch Haniger .25 .60

2020 Panini Prizm Prizms Blue
*BLUE: 1X TO 2.5X BASIC
*BLUE RC: .6X TO 1.5X BASIC
RANDOM INSERTS IN PACKS
71 Bo Bichette 6.00 15.00

2020 Panini Prizm Prizms Blue Donut Circles
*BLUE DONUT: 2X TO 5X BASIC
*BLUE DONUT RC: 1.2X TO 3X BASIC
RANDOM INSERTS IN PACKS
STATED PRINT RUN 199 SER.#'d SETS
15 Ramon Laureano 2.50 6.00
71 Bo Bichette 12.00 30.00
94 Kyle Lewis 12.00 30.00

2020 Panini Prizm Prizms Blue Mojo
*BLUE MOJO: 2X TO 5X BASIC
*BLUE MOJO RC: 1.2X TO 3X BASIC
RANDOM INSERTS IN PACKS
STATED PRINT RUN 175 SER.#'d SETS
15 Ramon Laureano 2.50 6.00
71 Bo Bichette 12.00 30.00
94 Kyle Lewis 12.00 30.00

2020 Panini Prizm Prizms Blue Wave
*BLUE WAVE: 3X TO 8X
*BLUE WAVE RC: 2X TO 5X
RANDOM INSERTS IN PACKS
STATED PRINT RUN 60 SER.#'d SETS
15 Ramon Laureano 4.00 10.00
30 Nico Hoerner 10.00 25.00
71 Bo Bichette 20.00 50.00
94 Kyle Lewis 30.00 80.00
126 Dustin May 8.00 20.00
138 Francisco Lindor 5.00 12.00
198 Gavin Lux 15.00 40.00

2020 Panini Prizm Prizms Bronze Donut Circles
*BRNZ DONUT: 5X TO 12X
*BRNZ DONUT RC: 3X TO 8X
RANDOM INSERTS IN PACKS
STATED PRINT RUN 25 SER.#'d SETS
15 Ramon Laureano 6.00 15.00
30 Nico Hoerner 20.00 50.00
47 Juan Soto 20.00 50.00
63 Bryce Harper 12.00 30.00
64 Aaron Judge 15.00 40.00
71 Bo Bichette 40.00 100.00
86 George Springer 10.00 25.00
94 Kyle Lewis 50.00 120.00
100 Gleyber Torres 12.00 30.00
126 Dustin May 12.00 30.00
138 Francisco Lindor 8.00 20.00
181 Yordan Alvarez 30.00 80.00
184 Ronald Acuna Jr. 30.00 80.00
198 Gavin Lux 40.00 100.00

2020 Panini Prizm Prizms Burgundy Cracked Ice
*BUR.CRKD ICE: 5X TO 12X
*BUR.CRKD ICE RC: 3X TO 8X
RANDOM INSERTS IN PACKS
STATED PRINT RUN 25 SER.#'d SETS
15 Ramon Laureano 6.00 15.00
30 Nico Hoerner 20.00 50.00
47 Juan Soto 20.00 50.00
63 Bryce Harper 12.00 30.00
64 Aaron Judge 15.00 40.00
71 Bo Bichette 40.00 100.00
86 George Springer 10.00 25.00
94 Kyle Lewis 50.00 120.00
100 Gleyber Torres 12.00 30.00
126 Dustin May 12.00 30.00
138 Francisco Lindor 8.00 20.00
181 Yordan Alvarez 30.00 80.00
184 Ronald Acuna Jr. 30.00 80.00
198 Gavin Lux 40.00 100.00

2020 Panini Prizm Prizms Carolina Blue
*CAR.BLUE: 1.2X TO 3X BASIC
*CAR.BLUE RC: .8X TO 2X BASIC
RANDOM INSERTS IN PACKS
71 Bo Bichette 8.00 20.00
94 Kyle Lewis 6.00 15.00

2020 Panini Prizm Prizms Cosmic Haze
*COSMIC: 1.2X TO 3X BASIC
*COSMIC RC: .8X TO 2X BASIC
RANDOM INSERTS IN PACKS
71 Bo Bichette 8.00 20.00
94 Kyle Lewis 6.00 15.00

2020 Panini Prizm Prizms Green
*GREEN: 1.2X TO 3X BASIC
*GREEN RC: .8X TO 2X BASIC
RANDOM INSERTS IN PACKS
71 Bo Bichette 8.00 20.00
94 Kyle Lewis 6.00 15.00

2020 Panini Prizm Prizms Lime Green
*LIME GRN: 2.5X TO 6X BASIC
*LIME GRN RC: 1.5X TO 4X BASIC
RANDOM INSERTS IN PACKS
STATED PRINT RUN 125 SER.#'d SETS
15 Ramon Laureano 3.00 8.00
71 Bo Bichette 15.00 40.00
94 Kyle Lewis 15.00 40.00
126 Dustin May 6.00 15.00

2020 Panini Prizm Prizms Navy Blue Kaleidoscope
*NVY.BL.KAL: 4X TO 10X
*NVY.BL.KAL RC: 2.5X TO 6X
RANDOM INSERTS IN PACKS
STATED PRINT RUN 35 SER.#'d SETS
15 Ramon Laureano 5.00 12.00
30 Nico Hoerner 15.00 40.00
63 Bryce Harper 10.00 25.00
64 Aaron Judge 12.00 30.00
71 Bo Bichette 30.00 80.00
86 George Springer 8.00 20.00
94 Kyle Lewis 40.00 100.00
100 Gleyber Torres 10.00 25.00
126 Dustin May 10.00 25.00
138 Francisco Lindor 6.00 15.00
181 Yordan Alvarez 25.00 60.00
184 Ronald Acuna Jr. 25.00 60.00
198 Gavin Lux 30.00 80.00

2020 Panini Prizm Prizms Neon Orange
*NEON ORNG: 3X TO 8X BASIC
*NEON ORNG RC: 2X TO 5X BASIC
RANDOM INSERTS IN PACKS
STATED PRINT RUN 100 SER.#'d SETS
15 Ramon Laureano 4.00 10.00
30 Nico Hoerner 10.00 25.00
71 Bo Bichette 20.00 50.00
94 Kyle Lewis 30.00 80.00
126 Dustin May 8.00 20.00
138 Francisco Lindor 5.00 12.00

2020 Panini Prizm Prizms Pink
*PINK: 1.2X TO 3X BASIC
*PINK RC: .8X TO 2X BASIC
RANDOM INSERTS IN PACKS
71 Bo Bichette 8.00 20.00
94 Kyle Lewis 6.00 15.00

2020 Panini Prizm Prizms Power Plaid
*PLAID: 3X TO 8X
*PLAID RC: 2X TO 5X
RANDOM INSERTS IN PACKS
STATED PRINT RUN 75 SER.#'d SETS
15 Ramon Laureano 4.00 10.00
30 Nico Hoerner 10.00 25.00
71 Bo Bichette 20.00 50.00
94 Kyle Lewis 30.00 80.00
126 Dustin May 8.00 20.00
138 Francisco Lindor 5.00 12.00
198 Gavin Lux 15.00 40.00

2020 Panini Prizm Prizms Purple
*PURPLE: 1.2X TO 3X BASIC
*PURPLE RC: .8X TO 2X BASIC
RANDOM INSERTS IN PACKS
71 Bo Bichette 8.00 20.00
94 Kyle Lewis 6.00 15.00

2020 Panini Prizm Prizms Red
*RED: 1X TO 2.5X BASIC
*RED RC: .6X TO 1.5X BASIC
RANDOM INSERTS IN PACKS
71 Bo Bichette 6.00 15.00

2020 Panini Prizm Prizms Red Donut Circles
*RED DONUT: 3X TO 8X BASIC
*RED DONUT RC: 2X TO 5X BASIC
RANDOM INSERTS IN PACKS
STATED PRINT RUN 99 SER.#'d SETS
15 Ramon Laureano 4.00 10.00
30 Nico Hoerner 10.00 25.00
71 Bo Bichette 20.00 50.00
94 Kyle Lewis 30.00 80.00
126 Dustin May 8.00 20.00
138 Francisco Lindor 5.00 12.00
198 Gavin Lux 12.00 30.00

2020 Panini Prizm Prizms Red Mojo
*RED MOJO: 2.5X TO 6X BASIC
*RED MOJO RC: 1.5X TO 4X BASIC
RANDOM INSERTS IN PACKS
STATED PRINT RUN 149 SER.#'d SETS
15 Ramon Laureano 3.00 8.00
71 Bo Bichette 15.00 40.00
94 Kyle Lewis 15.00 40.00
126 Dustin May 6.00 15.00

2020 Panini Prizm Prizms Red Orange
*RED ORNG: 1.2X TO 3X BASIC
*RED ORNG RC: .8X TO 2X BASIC
RANDOM INSERTS IN PACKS
71 Bo Bichette 8.00 20.00
94 Kyle Lewis 6.00 15.00

2020 Panini Prizm Prizms Red Wave
*RED WAVE: 3X TO 8X BASIC
*RED WAVE RC: 2X TO 5X BASIC
RANDOM INSERTS IN PACKS
STATED PRINT RUN 99 SER.#'d SETS
15 Ramon Laureano 4.00 10.00
30 Nico Hoerner 10.00 25.00
71 Bo Bichette 20.00 50.00
94 Kyle Lewis 30.00 80.00
126 Dustin May 8.00 20.00
138 Francisco Lindor 5.00 12.00
198 Gavin Lux 12.00 30.00

2020 Panini Prizm Prizms Red White and Blue
*RWB: 1.2X TO 3X BASIC
*RWB RC: .8X TO 2X BASIC
RANDOM INSERTS IN PACKS
71 Bo Bichette 8.00 20.00
94 Kyle Lewis 6.00 15.00

2020 Panini Prizm Prizms Silver
*SILVER: 1.5X TO 4X BASIC
*SILVER RC: 1X TO 2.5X BASIC
RANDOM INSERTS IN PACKS
71 Bo Bichette 10.00 25.00
94 Kyle Lewis 8.00 20.00

2020 Panini Prizm Prizms Snake Skin
*SNAKE SKIN: 4X TO 10X
*SNAKE SKIN RC: 2.5X TO 6X
RANDOM INSERTS IN PACKS
STATED PRINT RUN 50 SER.#'d SETS
15 Ramon Laureano 5.00 12.00
30 Nico Hoerner 15.00 40.00
63 Bryce Harper 10.00 25.00
64 Aaron Judge 12.00 30.00
71 Bo Bichette 30.00 80.00
86 George Springer 8.00 20.00
94 Kyle Lewis 40.00 100.00
100 Gleyber Torres 10.00 25.00
126 Dustin May 10.00 25.00
138 Francisco Lindor 6.00 15.00
181 Yordan Alvarez 25.00 60.00
184 Ronald Acuna Jr. 25.00 60.00
198 Gavin Lux 30.00 80.00

2020 Panini Prizm Prizms Teal Wave
*TEAL WAVE: 1.2X TO 3X BASIC
*TEAL WAVE RC: .8X TO 2X BASIC
RANDOM INSERTS IN PACKS
71 Bo Bichette 8.00 20.00
94 Kyle Lewis 6.00 15.00

2020 Panini Prizm Brilliance
RANDOM INSERTS IN PACKS
*BLUE: .6X TO 1.5X BASIC
*CAR.BLUE: .6X TO 1.5X BASIC
*COSMIC: .6X TO 1.5X BASIC
*GREEN: .6X TO 1.5X BASIC
*PINK: .6X TO 1.5X BASIC
*PURPLE: .6X TO 1.5X BASIC
*RED: .6X TO 1.5X BASIC
*RED ORNG: .6X TO 1.5X BASIC
*RWB: .6X TO 1.5X BASIC
*SILVER: .6X TO 1.5X BASIC
*TEAL WAVE: .6X TO 1.5X BASIC
*WHITE WAVE: .6X TO 1.5X BASIC
*BLUE DONUT/199: .8X TO 2X BASIC
*BLUE MOJO/175: .8X TO 2X BASIC
*RED MOJO/149: 1X TO 2.5X BASIC
*LIME GRN/125: 1X TO 2.5X BASIC
1 Jacob deGrom 1.00 2.50
2 Gerrit Cole .75 2.00
3 Pete Alonso 1.25 3.00
4 Vladimir Guerrero Jr. .75 2.00
5 Javier Baez .60 1.50
6 Christian Yelich .60 1.50
7 Jose Altuve .40 1.00
8 Rafael Devers .60 1.50
9 Manny Machado .50 1.25
10 Charlie Blackmon .50 1.25

2020 Panini Prizm Brilliance Prizms Blue Wave
*BLUE WAVE: 1.2X TO 3X BASIC
RANDOM INSERTS IN PACKS
STATED PRINT RUN 60 SER.#'d SETS
4 Vladimir Guerrero Jr. 5.00 12.00

2020 Panini Prizm Brilliance Prizms Bronze Donut Circles
*BRNZ DONUT: 2X TO 5X BASIC
RANDOM INSERTS IN PACKS
STATED PRINT RUN 25 SER.#'d SETS
4 Vladimir Guerrero Jr. 8.00 20.00

2020 Panini Prizm Brilliance Prizms Burgundy Cracked Ice
*BUR.CRKD ICE: 2X TO 5X BASIC
RANDOM INSERTS IN PACKS
STATED PRINT RUN 25 SER.#'d SETS
4 Vladimir Guerrero Jr. 8.00 20.00

2020 Panini Prizm Brilliance Prizms Navy Blue Kaleidoscope
*NVY BLU.KAL: 1.5X TO 4X BASIC
RANDOM INSERTS IN PACKS
STATED PRINT RUN 35 SER.#'d SETS
4 Vladimir Guerrero Jr. 6.00 15.00

2020 Panini Prizm Brilliance Prizms Neon Orange
*NEON ORNG: 1.2X TO 3X BASIC
RANDOM INSERTS IN PACKS
STATED PRINT RUN 100 SER.#'d SETS
4 Vladimir Guerrero Jr. 5.00 12.00

2020 Panini Prizm Brilliance Prizms Power Plaid
*PLAID: 1.2X TO 3X BASIC
RANDOM INSERTS IN PACKS
STATED PRINT RUN 75 SER.#'d SETS
4 Vladimir Guerrero Jr. 5.00 12.00

2020 Panini Prizm Brilliance Prizms Red Donut Circles
*RED DONUT: 1.2X TO 3X BASIC
RANDOM INSERTS IN PACKS
STATED PRINT RUN 99 SER.#'d SETS
4 Vladimir Guerrero Jr. 5.00 12.00

2020 Panini Prizm Brilliance Prizms Red Wave
*RED WAVE: 1.2X TO 3X BASIC
RANDOM INSERTS IN PACKS
STATED PRINT RUN 99 SER.#'d SETS
4 Vladimir Guerrero Jr. 5.00 12.00

2020 Panini Prizm Brilliance Prizms Snake Skin
*SNAKE SKIN: 1.5X TO 4X BASIC
RANDOM INSERTS IN PACKS
STATED PRINT RUN 50 SER.#'d SETS
4 Vladimir Guerrero Jr. 6.00 15.00

2020 Panini Prizm Color Blast
RANDOM INSERTS IN PACKS
1 Fernando Tatis Jr. 125.00 300.00
2 Vladimir Guerrero Jr. 125.00 300.00
3 Pete Alonso 100.00 250.00
4 Ken Griffey Jr. 150.00 400.00
5 Yordan Alvarez 150.00 400.00
6 Cody Bellinger 100.00 250.00
7 Juan Soto 150.00 400.00
8 Rafael Devers 30.00 80.00
9 Alex Bregman 50.00 120.00
10 Francisco Lindor 50.00 120.00

2020 Panini Prizm Fireworks
RANDOM INSERTS IN PACKS
1 Christian Yelich .60 1.50
2 Pete Alonso 1.25 3.00
3 Nolan Arenado .75 2.00
4 Mookie Betts 1.00 2.50
5 Cody Bellinger 1.00 2.50
6 Mike Trout 2.50 6.00
7 Ronald Acuna Jr. 3.00 8.00
8 Juan Soto 1.50 4.00
9 Jose Altuve .40 1.00
10 Aaron Judge 1.25 3.00

2020 Panini Prizm Fireworks Prizms Silver
*SILVER: .6X TO 1.5X BASIC
RANDOM INSERTS IN PACKS
2 Pete Alonso 3.00 8.00

2020 Panini Prizm Game Ball Graphs Prizms Silver
*SILVER: .5X TO 1.2X BASIC
RANDOM INSERTS IN PACKS
EXCHANGE DEADLINE 12/17/2021
2 Manny Machado 15.00 40.00
3 Gleyber Torres 30.00 80.00

2020 Panini Prizm Gems
RANDOM INSERTS IN PACKS
1 Bryce Harper 25.00 60.00
2 Christian Yelich 15.00 40.00
3 Shohei Ohtani 15.00 40.00
4 Javier Baez 12.00 30.00
5 Kris Bryant 20.00 50.00
6 Manny Machado 12.00 30.00
7 Mookie Betts 15.00 40.00
8 Mike Trout 60.00 150.00
9 Ronald Acuna Jr. 40.00 100.00
10 Aaron Judge 20.00 50.00

2020 Panini Prizm Illumination
RANDOM INSERTS IN PACKS
*BLUE: .6X TO 1.5X BASIC
*CAR.BLUE: .6X TO 1.5X BASIC
*COSMIC: .6X TO 1.5X BASIC
*GREEN: .6X TO 1.5X BASIC
*PINK: .6X TO 1.5X BASIC
*PURPLE: .6X TO 1.5X BASIC
*RED: .6X TO 1.5X BASIC
*RED ORNG: .6X TO 1.5X BASIC
*RWB: .6X TO 1.5X BASIC
*SILVER: .6X TO 1.5X BASIC
*TEAL WAVE: .6X TO 1.5X BASIC
*WHITE WAVE: .6X TO 1.5X BASIC
*BLUE DONUT/199: .8X TO 2X BASIC
*BLUE MOJO/175: .8X TO 2X BASIC
*RED MOJO/149: 1X TO 2.5X BASIC
*LIME GRN/125: 1X TO 2.5X BASIC
1 Stephen Strasburg .50 1.25
2 Justin Verlander .50 1.25
3 Fernando Tatis Jr. 2.50 6.00
4 Nolan Arenado .75 2.00
5 Bryce Harper .75 2.00
6 Yordan Alvarez 3.00 8.00
7 Freddie Freeman .60 1.50
8 Yoan Moncada .50 1.25
9 Kris Bryant .60 1.50
10 Ketel Marte .40 1.00
11 Shohei Ohtani .75 2.00
12 Anthony Rendon .50 1.25

2020 Panini Prizm Illumination Prizms Blue Wave
*BLUE WAVE/60: 1.2X TO 3X BASIC
RANDOM INSERTS IN PACKS
STATED PRINT RUN 60 SER.#'d SETS
3 Fernando Tatis Jr. 6.00 15.00

2020 Panini Prizm Illumination Prizms Bronze Donut Circles
*BRNZ DONUT/25: 2X TO 5X BASIC
RANDOM INSERTS IN PACKS
STATED PRINT RUN 25 SER.#'d SETS
3 Fernando Tatis Jr. 25.00 60.00

2020 Panini Prizm Illumination Prizms Burgundy Cracked Ice
*BUR.CRKD ICE/25: 2X TO 5X BASIC
RANDOM INSERTS IN PACKS
STATED PRINT RUN 25 SER.#'d SETS
3 Fernando Tatis Jr. 25.00 60.00

2020 Panini Prizm Illumination Prizms Navy Blue Kaleidoscope
*NVY BLU.KAL./35: 1.5X TO 4X BASIC
RANDOM INSERTS IN PACKS
STATED PRINT RUN 35 SER.#'d SETS
3 Fernando Tatis Jr. 15.00 40.00

2020 Panini Prizm Illumination Prizms Neon Orange
*NEON ORNG/100: 1.2X TO 3X BASIC
RANDOM INSERTS IN PACKS
STATED PRINT RUN 100 SER.#'d SETS
3 Fernando Tatis Jr. 6.00 15.00

2020 Panini Prizm Illumination Prizms Power Plaid
*PLAID/75: 1.2X TO 3X BASIC
RANDOM INSERTS IN PACKS
STATED PRINT RUN 75 SER.#'d SETS
3 Fernando Tatis Jr. 6.00 15.00

2020 Panini Prizm Illumination Prizms Red Donut Circles
*RED DONUT/99: 1.2X TO 3X BASIC
RANDOM INSERTS IN PACKS
STATED PRINT RUN 99 SER.#'d SETS
3 Fernando Tatis Jr. 6.00 15.00

2020 Panini Prizm Illumination Prizms Red Wave
*RED WAVE/99: 1.2X TO 3X BASIC
RANDOM INSERTS IN PACKS
STATED PRINT RUN 99 SER.#'d SETS
3 Fernando Tatis Jr. 6.00 15.00

2020 Panini Prizm Illumination Prizms Snake Skin
*SNAKE SKIN/50: 1.5X TO 4X BASIC
RANDOM INSERTS IN PACKS
STATED PRINT RUN 50 SER.#'d SETS
3 Fernando Tatis Jr. 15.00 40.00

2020 Panini Prizm Instant Impact
RANDOM INSERTS IN PACKS
*BLUE: .6X TO 1.5X BASIC
*CAR.BLUE: .6X TO 1.5X BASIC
*COSMIC: .6X TO 1.5X BASIC
*GREEN: .6X TO 1.5X BASIC
*PINK: .6X TO 1.5X BASIC
*PURPLE: .6X TO 1.5X BASIC
*RED: .6X TO 1.5X BASIC
*RED ORNG: .6X TO 1.5X BASIC
*RWB: .6X TO 1.5X BASIC
*SILVER: .6X TO 1.5X BASIC
*TEAL WAVE: .6X TO 1.5X BASIC
*WHITE WAVE: .6X TO 1.5X BASIC
1 Ronald Acuna Jr. 2.00 5.00
2 Bryce Harper .75 2.00
3 Javier Baez .60 1.50
4 Mike Trout 2.50 6.00
5 Christian Yelich .60 1.50
6 Josh Bell .40 1.00
7 Juan Soto 1.50 4.00
8 Cody Bellinger 1.00 2.50
9 Whit Merrifield .50 1.25
10 Xander Bogaerts .50 1.25

2020 Panini Prizm Instant Impact Prizms Blue Donut Circles
*BLUE DONUT/199: .8X TO 2X BASIC
RANDOM INSERTS IN PACKS
STATED PRINT RUN 199 SER.#'d SETS
2 Bryce Harper 4.00 10.00
4 Mike Trout 10.00 25.00
7 Juan Soto 3.00 8.00

2020 Panini Prizm Instant Impact Prizms Blue Mojo
*BLUE MOJO/175: .8X TO 2X BASIC
RANDOM INSERTS IN PACKS
STATED PRINT RUN 175 SER.#'d SETS
2 Bryce Harper 4.00
4 Mike Trout 10.00 25.00
7 Juan Soto 3.00 8.00

2020 Panini Prizm Instant Impact Prizms Blue Wave
*BLUE WAVE/60: 1.2X TO 3X BASIC
RANDOM INSERTS IN PACKS
STATED PRINT RUN 60 SER.#'d SETS
2 Bryce Harper 6.00 15.00
4 Mike Trout 15.00 40.00
7 Juan Soto 5.00 12.00

2020 Panini Prizm Instant Impact Prizms Bronze Donut Circles
*BRNZ DONUT/25: 2X TO 5X BASIC
RANDOM INSERTS IN PACKS
STATED PRINT RUN 25 SER.#'d SETS
2 Bryce Harper 10.00 25.00
4 Mike Trout 30.00 80.00
7 Juan Soto 8.00 20.00

2020 Panini Prizm Instant Impact Prizms Burgundy Cracked Ice
*BUR.CRKD ICE/25: 2X TO 5X BASIC
RANDOM INSERTS IN PACKS
STATED PRINT RUN 25 SER.#'d SETS
2 Bryce Harper 10.00 25.00
4 Mike Trout 30.00 80.00
7 Juan Soto 8.00 20.00

2020 Panini Prizm Instant Impact Prizms Lime Green
*LIME GRN/125: 1X TO 2.5X BASIC
RANDOM INSERTS IN PACKS
STATED PRINT RUN 125 SER.#'d SETS
2 Bryce Harper 5.00 12.00
4 Mike Trout 12.00 30.00
7 Juan Soto 4.00 10.00

2020 Panini Prizm Instant Impact Prizms Navy Blue Kaleidoscope
*NVY BLU.KAL./35: 1.5X TO 4X BASIC
RANDOM INSERTS IN PACKS
STATED PRINT RUN 35 SER.#'d SETS
2 Bryce Harper 8.00 20.00
4 Mike Trout 25.00 60.00
7 Juan Soto 6.00 15.00

2020 Panini Prizm Instant Impact Prizms Neon Orange
*NEON ORNG/100: 1.2X TO 3X BASIC
RANDOM INSERTS IN PACKS
STATED PRINT RUN 100 SER.#'d SETS
2 Bryce Harper 6.00 15.00
4 Mike Trout 15.00 40.00
7 Juan Soto 5.00 12.00

2020 Panini Prizm Instant Impact Prizms Power Plaid
*PLAID/75: 1.2X TO 3X BASIC
RANDOM INSERTS IN PACKS
STATED PRINT RUN 75 SER.#'d SETS
2 Bryce Harper 6.00 15.00
4 Mike Trout 15.00 40.00
7 Juan Soto 5.00 12.00

2020 Panini Prizm Instant Impact Prizms Red Donut Circles
*RED DONUT/99: 1.2X TO 3X BASIC
RANDOM INSERTS IN PACKS
STATED PRINT RUN 99 SER.#'d SETS
2 Bryce Harper 6.00 15.00
4 Mike Trout 15.00 40.00
7 Juan Soto 5.00 12.00

2020 Panini Prizm Instant Impact Prizms Red Mojo
*RED MOJO/149: 1X TO 2.5X BASIC
RANDOM INSERTS IN PACKS
STATED PRINT RUN 149 SER.#'d SETS
2 Bryce Harper 5.00 12.00
4 Mike Trout 12.00 30.00
7 Juan Soto 4.00 10.00

2020 Panini Prizm Instant Impact Prizms Red Wave
*RED WAVE/99: 1.2X TO 3X BASIC
RANDOM INSERTS IN PACKS
STATED PRINT RUN 99 SER.#'d SETS
2 Bryce Harper 6.00 15.00
4 Mike Trout 15.00 40.00
7 Juan Soto 5.00 12.00

2020 Panini Prizm Instant Impact Prizms Snake Skin
*SNAKE SKIN/50: 1.5X TO 4X BASIC
RANDOM INSERTS IN PACKS
STATED PRINT RUN 50 SER.#'d SETS
2 Bryce Harper 8.00 20.00
4 Mike Trout 25.00 60.00
7 Juan Soto 6.00 15.00

2020 Panini Prizm Lumber Inc
RANDOM INSERTS IN PACKS
1 Vladimir Guerrero Jr. .75 2.00
2 Nelson Cruz .50 1.25
3 Alex Bregman .50 1.25
4 Gleyber Torres 1.00 2.50
5 J.D. Martinez .50 1.25
6 Matt Olson .50 1.25
7 Trey Mancini .50 1.25
8 Bryce Harper .75 2.00
9 Eugenio Suarez .40 1.00
10 Kyle Schwarber .50 1.25

2020 Panini Prizm Lumber Inc Prizms Silver
*SILVER: .6X TO 1.5X BASIC
RANDOM INSERTS IN PACKS
8 Bryce Harper 4.00 10.00

2020 Panini Prizm Machines
RANDOM INSERTS IN PACKS
*SILVER: .6X TO 1.5X BASIC
1 George Springer .40 1.00
2 Freddie Freeman .60 1.50
3 Ronald Acuna Jr. 2.00 5.00
4 Mike Trout 3.00 8.00
5 Tim Anderson .50 1.25
6 Ketel Marte .40 1.00
7 DJ LeMahieu .50 1.25
8 Jeff McNeil .40 1.00
9 Whit Merrifield .50 1.25
10 Rafael Devers 1.00 2.50

2020 Panini Prizm Now On Deck
RANDOM INSERTS IN PACKS
*SILVER: .6X TO 1.5X BASIC
1 Wander Franco 5.00 12.00
2 Luis Robert 2.50 6.00
3 Jo Adell 1.25 3.00
4 Royce Lewis .75 2.00
5 Cristian Pache 1.00 2.50
6 Alex Kirilloff .60 1.50
7 Joey Bart 1.00 2.50
8 Drew Waters .75 2.00
9 Dylan Carlson 1.25 3.00
10 Julio Rodriguez 2.00 5.00
11 Taylor Trammell .50 1.25
12 Keibert Ruiz 1.50 4.00
13 Alec Bohm 2.00 5.00
14 Ke'Bryan Hayes 1.50 4.00
15 Nolan Jones .50 1.25

2020 Panini Prizm Numbers Game
RANDOM INSERTS IN PACKS
*BLUE: .6X TO 1.5X BASIC
*CAR.BLUE: .6X TO 1.5X BASIC
*COSMIC: .6X TO 1.5X BASIC
*GREEN: .6X TO 1.5X BASIC
*PINK: .6X TO 1.5X BASIC
*PURPLE: .6X TO 1.5X BASIC
*RED: .6X TO 1.5X BASIC
*RED ORNG: .6X TO 1.5X BASIC
*RWB: .6X TO 1.5X BASIC
*SILVER: .6X TO 1.5X BASIC
*TEAL WAVE: .6X TO 1.5X BASIC
*WHITE WAVE: .6X TO 1.5X BASIC
1 Juan Soto 1.50 4.00
2 Kris Bryant .60 1.50
3 Cody Bellinger 1.00 2.50
4 Alex Bregman .50 1.25
5 Mookie Betts 1.00 2.50
6 Jose Abreu .50 1.25
7 Nelson Cruz .50 1.25
8 Shohei Ohtani .75 2.00

2020 Panini Prizm Numbers Game Prizms Blue Donut Circles
*BLUE DONUT/199: .8X TO 2X BASIC
RANDOM INSERTS IN PACKS
STATED PRINT RUN 199 SER.#'d SETS
5 Mookie Betts 6.00 15.00

2020 Panini Prizm Numbers Game Prizms Blue Mojo
*BLUE MOJO/175: .8X TO 2X BASIC
RANDOM INSERTS IN PACKS
STATED PRINT RUN 175 SER.#'d SETS
5 Mookie Betts 6.00 15.00

2020 Panini Prizm Numbers Game Prizms Blue Wave
*BLUE WAVE/60: 1.2X TO 3X BASIC
RANDOM INSERTS IN PACKS
STATED PRINT RUN 60 SER.#'d SETS
1 Juan Soto 4.00 10.00
5 Mookie Betts 10.00 25.00

2020 Panini Prizm Numbers Game Prizms Bronze Donut Circles
*BRNZ DONUT/25: 2X TO 5X BASIC
RANDOM INSERTS IN PACKS
STATED PRINT RUN 25 SER.#'d SETS
1 Juan Soto 8.00 20.00
5 Mookie Betts 15.00 40.00

2020 Panini Prizm Numbers Game Prizms Burgundy Cracked Ice
*BUR.CRKD ICE/25: 2X TO 5X BASIC
RANDOM INSERTS IN PACKS
STATED PRINT RUN 25 SER.#'d SETS
1 Juan Soto 8.00 20.00
5 Mookie Betts 15.00 40.00

2020 Panini Prizm Numbers Game Prizms Lime Green
*LIME GRN/125: 1X TO 2.5X BASIC
RANDOM INSERTS IN PACKS
STATED PRINT RUN 125 SER.#'d SETS
5 Mookie Betts 8.00 20.00

2020 Panini Prizm Numbers Game Prizms Navy Blue Kaleidoscope
*NVY BLU.KAL./35: 1.5X TO 4X BASIC
RANDOM INSERTS IN PACKS
STATED PRINT RUN 35 SER.#'d SETS
1 Juan Soto 6.00 15.00
5 Mookie Betts 12.00 30.00

2020 Panini Prizm Numbers Game Prizms Neon Orange
*NEON ORNG/100: 1.2X TO 3X BASIC
RANDOM INSERTS IN PACKS
STATED PRINT RUN 100 SER.#'d SETS
1 Juan Soto 4.00 10.00
5 Mookie Betts 10.00 25.00

2020 Panini Prizm Numbers Game Prizms Power Plaid
*PLAID/75: 1.2X TO 3X BASIC
RANDOM INSERTS IN PACKS
STATED PRINT RUN 75 SER.#'d SETS
1 Juan Soto 4.00 10.00
5 Mookie Betts 10.00 25.00

2020 Panini Prizm Numbers Game Prizms Red Donut Circles
*RED DONUT/99: 1.2X TO 3X BASIC
RANDOM INSERTS IN PACKS
STATED PRINT RUN 99 SER.#'d SETS
1 Juan Soto 4.00 10.00
5 Mookie Betts 10.00 25.00

2020 Panini Prizm Numbers Game Prizms Red Mojo
*RED MOJO/149: 1X TO 2.5X BASIC
RANDOM INSERTS IN PACKS
STATED PRINT RUN 149 SER.#'d SETS
5 Mookie Betts 8.00 20.00

2020 Panini Prizm Numbers Game Prizms Red Wave
*RED WAVE/99: 1.2X TO 3X BASIC
RANDOM INSERTS IN PACKS
STATED PRINT RUN 99 SER.#'d SETS
1 Juan Soto 4.00 10.00
5 Mookie Betts 10.00 25.00

2020 Panini Prizm Numbers Game Prizms Snake Skin
*SNAKE SKIN/50: 1.5X TO 4X BASIC
RANDOM INSERTS IN PACKS
STATED PRINT RUN 50 SER.#'d SETS
1 Juan Soto 6.00 15.00
5 Mookie Betts 12.00 30.00

2020 Panini Prizm Pro Penmanship
RANDOM INSERTS IN PACKS
EXCHANGE DEADLINE 12/17/2021
1 Aaron Judge EXCH 60.00 150.00
2 Shohei Ohtani EXCH
3 Juan Soto EXCH 30.00 80.00
4 Eloy Jimenez EXCH 12.00 30.00
5 Vladimir Guerrero Jr. 25.00 60.00
6 Fernando Tatis Jr. 60.00 150.00
7 Michael Chavis 3.00 8.00
8 Mike Soroka 8.00 20.00
9 Xander Bogaerts 20.00 50.00
10 Nolan Arenado 25.00 60.00
11 Jaime Barria 2.50 6.00
12 Ryan O'Hearn 2.50 6.00
13 Adam Haseley 3.00 8.00
14 Patrick Wisdom 2.50 6.00
15 Austin Barnes 2.50 6.00
16 Willy Adames 2.50 6.00
17 Justin Williams 2.50 6.00
18 Austin Dean 2.50 6.00
19 Trevor Richards 2.50 6.00
20 Taylor Clarke 2.50 6.00

2020 Panini Prizm Pro Penmanship Prizms Silver
*SILVER: .5X TO 1.2X BASIC
RANDOM INSERTS IN PACKS
EXCHANGE DEADLINE 12/17/2021
2 Shohei Ohtani EXCH 50.00 120.00

2020 Panini Prizm Prospect Signatures
RANDOM INSERTS IN PACKS
EXCHANGE DEADLINE 12/17/2021
1 Drew Waters 10.00 25.00
2 Bobby Dalbec 5.00 12.00
3 Nick Madrigal 8.00 20.00
4 Jo Adell 20.00 50.00
5 Alex Kirilloff 5.00 12.00
6 Jasson Dominguez EXCH 125.00 300.00
7 Joey Bart 12.00 30.00
8 Wander Franco EXCH 50.00 120.00
9 Nate Pearson 10.00 25.00
10 Taylor Trammell 8.00 20.00
11 Vidal Brujan 10.00 25.00
12 Marco Luciano 10.00 25.00
13 Dylan Carlson 15.00 40.00
14 Alec Bohm 15.00 40.00
15 Royce Lewis 8.00 20.00
16 Sixto Sanchez 6.00 15.00
18 Luis Robert 75.00 200.00
19 Ryan Mountcastle 12.00 30.00

2020 Panini Prizm Prospect Signatures Prizms Silver
*SILVER: .5X TO 1.2X BASIC
RANDOM INSERTS IN PACKS
EXCHANGE DEADLINE 12/17/2021
3 Nick Madrigal 15.00 40.00
6 Jasson Dominguez EXCH 200.00 500.00

2020 Panini Prizm Rookie Autographs
RANDOM INSERTS IN PACKS
EXCHANGE DEADLINE 12/17/2021
1 Abraham Toro 3.00 8.00
2 Adrian Morejon 2.50 6.00
3 Kyle Lewis 30.00 80.00
4 Aaron Civale 5.00 12.00
5 Tony Gonsolin 10.00 25.00
6 Jake Fraley 3.00 8.00
7 Jake Rogers 2.50 6.00
8 Isan Diaz 4.00 10.00
9 Michael King 4.00 10.00
10 Brock Burke 2.50 6.00
11 Zac Gallen 6.00 15.00
12 T.J. Zeuch 2.50 6.00
13 Yu Chang 4.00 10.00
14 Gavin Lux 20.00 50.00
15 Logan Webb 4.00 10.00
16 Sam Hilliard 4.00 10.00
17 Brendan McKay 4.00 10.00
18 Sean Murphy 4.00 10.00
19 Danny Mendick 3.00 8.00
20 Jaylin Davis 4.00 10.00
21 Dustin May 25.00 60.00
22 Travis Demeritte 4.00 10.00
23 Sheldon Neuse 3.00 8.00
24 Anthony Kay 2.50 6.00
25 A.J. Puk 4.00 10.00
26 Ronald Bolanos 2.50 6.00
27 Jesus Luzardo 12.00 30.00
28 Andres Munoz 4.00 10.00
29 Jordan Yamamoto 2.50 6.00
30 Lewis Thorpe 2.50 6.00
31 Trent Grisham 10.00 25.00
32 Domingo Leyba 3.00 8.00
33 Donnie Walton 6.00 15.00
34 Patrick Sandoval 4.00 10.00
35 Deivy Grullon 2.50 6.00
36 Yonathan Daza 3.00 8.00
37 Justin Dunn 3.00 8.00
38 Joe Palumbo 2.50 6.00
39 Michel Baez 2.50 6.00
40 Brusdar Graterol 4.00 10.00
41 Nico Hoerner 6.00 15.00
42 Rico Garcia 4.00 10.00
43 Mauricio Dubon 6.00 15.00
44 Zack Collins 3.00 8.00
45 Bo Bichette 30.00 80.00
46 Bryan Abreu 2.50 6.00
47 Edwin Rios 6.00 15.00
48 Matt Thaiss 3.00 8.00
49 Yordan Alvarez EXCH 25.00 60.00
50 Willi Castro 4.00 10.00
51 Jonathan Hernandez 2.50 6.00
52 Bobby Bradley 2.50 6.00
53 Randy Arozarena 40.00 100.00
54 Logan Allen 2.50 6.00
55 Nick Solak 5.00 12.00
56 Adbert Alzolay 3.00 8.00
57 Dylan Cease 4.00 10.00
58 Tyrone Taylor 2.50 6.00
59 Tres Barrera 5.00 12.00
60 Josh Rojas 2.50 6.00
61 Aristides Aquino 8.00 20.00
62 Scott Heineman 2.50 6.00
63 Edgar Garcia 2.50 6.00
64 Kyle Garlick 4.00 10.00
66 Alex Young 2.50 6.00
67 Tyler Alexander 4.00 10.00
69 Huascar Ynoa 4.00 10.00
70 Bubba Starling 5.00 12.00
73 Nick Dini 3.00 8.00
74 Yoshitomo Tsutsugo EXCH 15.00 40.00
75 Hunter Harvey 4.00 10.00
76 Dom Nunez 3.00 8.00
78 Zach Green 2.50 6.00
79 Kwang-Hyun Kim 12.00 30.00
80 LaMonte Wade Jr. 4.00 10.00
81 Jacob Waguespack 3.00 8.00
82 Shun Yamaguchi 5.00 12.00
83 Robel Garcia 2.50 6.00
84 Jose Urquidy 3.00 8.00
85 Randy Dobnak 5.00 12.00
86 Mike Brosseau 5.00 12.00
88 Seth Brown 2.50 6.00
89 Jorge Alcala 2.50 6.00
90 Shogo Akiyama EXCH 25.00 60.00
91 Ryan McBroom 3.00 8.00
92 Brian O'Grady 2.50 6.00
93 Kevin Ginkel 2.50 6.00
94 Luis Robert 60.00 150.00

2020 Panini Prizm Rookie Autographs Prizms Blue
*BLUE/50-99: .6X TO 1.5X BASIC
*BLUE/35: .8X TO 2X BASIC
RANDOM INSERTS IN PACKS
PRINT RUNS B/WN 15-99 COPIES PER
NO PRICING ON QTY 15 OR LESS
EXCHANGE DEADLINE 12/17/2021
13 Yu Chang/99 8.00 20.00
49 Yordan Alvarez/75 EXCH 50.00 120.00

2020 Panini Prizm Rookie Autographs Prizms Blue Donut Circles
*BLUE DONUT/50: .6X TO 1.5X BASIC
*BLUE DONUT/40: .8X TO 2X BASIC
RANDOM INSERTS IN PACKS
PRINT RUNS B/WN 5-50 COPIES PER
NO PRICING ON QTY 15 OR LESS
EXCHANGE DEADLINE 12/17/2021
13 Yu Chang/50 10.00 25.00
49 Yordan Alvarez/40 EXCH 60.00 150.00
94 Luis Robert/40 150.00 400.00

2020 Panini Prizm Rookie Autographs Prizms Blue Wave
*BLUE WAVE/50: .6X TO 1.5X BASIC
*BLUE WAVE/35: .8X TO 2X BASIC
RANDOM INSERTS IN PACKS
PRINT RUNS B/WN 10-50 COPIES PER
NO PRICING ON QTY 15 OR LESS
EXCHANGE DEADLINE 12/17/2021
13 Yu Chang/50 10.00 25.00
49 Yordan Alvarez/35 EXCH 60.00 150.00
94 Luis Robert/50 125.00 300.00

2020 Panini Prizm Rookie Autographs Prizms Bronze Donut Circles
*BRNZ DONUT/25: .8X TO 2X BASIC
RANDOM INSERTS IN PACKS
PRINT RUNS B/WN 5-25 COPIES PER
NO PRICING ON QTY 15 OR LESS
EXCHANGE DEADLINE 12/17/2021
13 Yu Chang/25 15.00 40.00
14 Gavin Lux/25 50.00 120.00
49 Yordan Alvarez/25 EXCH 75.00 200.00
94 Luis Robert/25 150.00 400.00

2020 Panini Prizm Rookie Autographs Prizms Burgundy Cracked Ice
*BUR.CRKD ICE/25: .8X TO 2X BASIC
RANDOM INSERTS IN PACKS
PRINT RUNS B/WN 10-25 COPIES PER
NO PRICING ON QTY 15 OR LESS
EXCHANGE DEADLINE 12/17/2021
13 Yu Chang/25 15.00 40.00
14 Gavin Lux/25 50.00 120.00
77 Kean Wong/25 10.00 25.00
94 Luis Robert/25 150.00 400.00

2020 Panini Prizm Rookie Autographs Prizms Cosmic Haze
*COSMIC/50: .6X TO 1.5X BASIC
*COSMIC/25-30: .8X TO 2X BASIC
RANDOM INSERTS IN PACKS
PRINT RUNS B/WN 15-50 COPIES PER
NO PRICING ON QTY 15 OR LESS
EXCHANGE DEADLINE 12/17/2021
13 Yu Chang/50 10.00 25.00
49 Yordan Alvarez/25 EXCH 75.00 200.00
65 Genesis Cabrera/50 6.00 15.00
68 Austin Nola/50 6.00 15.00
71 Tim Lopes/50 5.00 12.00
72 Dillon Tate/50 4.00 10.00
77 Kean Wong/50 8.00 20.00
94 Luis Robert/50 125.00 300.00

2020 Panini Prizm Rookie Autographs Prizms Pink
*PINK/50: .6X TO 1.5X BASIC
*PINK/25-30: .8X TO 2X BASIC
RANDOM INSERTS IN PACKS
PRINT RUNS B/WN 15-50 COPIES PER
NO PRICING ON QTY 15 OR LESS
EXCHANGE DEADLINE 12/17/2021
13 Yu Chang/50 10.00 25.00
49 Yordan Alvarez/25 EXCH 75.00 200.00
65 Genesis Cabrera/50 6.00 15.00
68 Austin Nola/50 6.00 15.00
71 Tim Lopes/50 5.00 12.00
72 Dillon Tate/50 4.00 10.00
77 Kean Wong/50 8.00 20.00
94 Luis Robert/50 125.00 300.00

2020 Panini Prizm Rookie Autographs Prizms Purple
*PURPLE/50: .6X TO 1.5X BASIC
*PURPLE/25: .8X TO 2X BASIC
RANDOM INSERTS IN PACKS
PRINT RUNS B/WN 15-50 COPIES PER
NO PRICING ON QTY 15 OR LESS
EXCHANGE DEADLINE 12/17/2021
13 Yu Chang/50 10.00 25.00
49 Yordan Alvarez/25 EXCH 75.00 200.00
65 Genesis Cabrera/50 6.00 15.00
68 Austin Nola/50 6.00 15.00
71 Tim Lopes/50 5.00 12.00
72 Dillon Tate/50 4.00 10.00
77 Kean Wong/50 8.00 20.00
94 Luis Robert/50 125.00 300.00

2020 Panini Prizm Rookie Autographs Prizms Red
*RED/50-75: .6X TO 1.5X BASIC
*RED/25-35: .8X TO 2X BASIC
RANDOM INSERTS IN PACKS
PRINT RUNS B/WN 8-75 COPIES PER
NO PRICING ON QTY 15 OR LESS
EXCHANGE DEADLINE 12/17/2021
13 Yu Chang/75 8.00 20.00
49 Yordan Alvarez/50 EXCH 50.00 120.00

2020 Panini Prizm Rookie Autographs Prizms Red Donut Circles
*RED DONUT/35: .8X TO 2X BASIC
RANDOM INSERTS IN PACKS
PRINT RUNS B/WN 5-35 COPIES PER
NO PRICING ON QTY 15 OR LESS
EXCHANGE DEADLINE 12/17/2021
13 Yu Chang/35 12.00 30.00
14 Gavin Lux/35 50.00 120.00
49 Yordan Alvarez/35 EXCH 60.00 150.00
94 Luis Robert/35 150.00 400.00

2020 Panini Prizm Rookie Autographs Prizms Red Orange
*RED ORNG/25: .8X TO 2X BASIC
RANDOM INSERTS IN PACKS
PRINT RUNS B/WN 5-25 COPIES PER
NO PRICING ON QTY 15 OR LESS
EXCHANGE DEADLINE 12/17/2021
13 Yu Chang/25 15.00 40.00
14 Gavin Lux/25 50.00 120.00
94 Luis Robert/25 150.00 400.00

2020 Panini Prizm Rookie Autographs Prizms Red Wave
*RED WAVE/49-75: .6X TO 1.5X BASIC
RANDOM INSERTS IN PACKS
PRINT RUNS B/WN 10-75 COPIES PER
NO PRICING ON QTY 15 OR LESS
EXCHANGE DEADLINE 12/17/2021
13 Yu Chang/75 8.00 20.00
49 Yordan Alvarez/60 EXCH 50.00 120.00

2020 Panini Prizm Rookie Autographs Prizms Red White and Blue
*RWB/50: .6X TO 1.5X BASIC
*RWB/25: .8X TO 2X BASIC
RANDOM INSERTS IN PACKS
PRINT RUNS B/WN 15-50 COPIES PER
NO PRICING ON QTY 15 OR LESS
EXCHANGE DEADLINE 12/17/2021
13 Yu Chang/50 10.00 25.00
94 Luis Robert/50 125.00 300.00

2020 Panini Prizm Rookie Autographs Prizms Silver
*SILVER: .5X TO 1.2X BASIC
RANDOM INSERTS IN PACKS
EXCHANGE DEADLINE 12/17/2021
49 Yordan Alvarez EXCH 40.00 100.00

2020 Panini Prizm Rookie Autographs Prizms Snake Skin
*SNAKE SKIN/25-35: .8X TO 2X BASIC
RANDOM INSERTS IN PACKS
PRINT RUNS B/WN 10-35 COPIES PER
NO PRICING ON QTY 15 OR LESS
EXCHANGE DEADLINE 12/17/2021
13 Yu Chang/35 12.00 30.00
14 Gavin Lux/35 50.00 120.00
49 Yordan Alvarez/20 EXCH 75.00 200.00
94 Luis Robert/35 150.00 400.00

2020 Panini Prizm Scorching
RANDOM INSERTS IN PACKS
*SILVER: .6X TO 1.5X BASIC
1 Adalberto Mondesi .40 1.00
2 Trea Turner .40 1.00
3 Christian Yelich .60 1.50
4 Xander Bogaerts .50 1.25
5 Anthony Rendon .50 1.25
6 Marcus Semien .50 1.25
7 Juan Soto 1.50 4.00
8 Manny Machado .50 1.25
9 Javier Baez .60 1.50
10 Fernando Tatis Jr. 2.50 6.00

2020 Panini Prizm Signatures
RANDOM INSERTS IN PACKS
EXCHANGE DEADLINE 12/17/2021
*SILVER: .5X TO 1.2X BASIC
1 Cody Bellinger 40.00 100.00
2 Ronald Acuna Jr. 40.00 100.00
3 Gleyber Torres 20.00 50.00
4 Rickey Henderson 25.00 60.00
5 Chipper Jones 40.00 100.00
6 Jorge Polanco 3.00 8.00
7 Rafael Palmeiro 5.00 12.00
8 Adalberto Mondesi 3.00 8.00
9 Don Mattingly 20.00 50.00
10 Gary Sanchez 4.00 10.00
11 Luis Perdomo 2.50 6.00
12 Reynaldo Lopez 2.50 6.00
13 Jason Martin 3.00 8.00
14 Terrance Gore 2.50 6.00
15 Scooter Gennett 3.00 8.00
16 Pablo Lopez 2.50 6.00
17 Jarlin Garcia 2.50 6.00
18 Christian Walker 3.00 8.00
19 Nick Martini 2.50 6.00
20 Meibrys Viloria 2.50 6.00

2020 Panini Prizm Star Gazing
RANDOM INSERTS IN PACKS
*BLUE: .6X TO 1.5X BASIC
*CAR.BLUE: .6X TO 1.5X BASIC
*COSMIC: .6X TO 1.5X BASIC
*GREEN: .6X TO 1.5X BASIC
*PINK: .6X TO 1.5X BASIC
*PURPLE: .6X TO 1.5X BASIC
*RED: .6X TO 1.5X BASIC
*RED ORNG: .6X TO 1.5X BASIC
*RWB: .6X TO 1.5X BASIC
*SILVER: .6X TO 1.5X BASIC
*TEAL WAVE: .6X TO 1.5X BASIC
*WHITE WAVE: .6X TO 1.5X BASIC
SG1 Mike Trout 2.50 6.00
SG2 Max Scherzer .50 1.25
SG3 Ronald Acuna Jr. 2.00 5.00
SG4 Fernando Tatis Jr. 2.50 6.00
SG5 Jose Altuve .40 1.00
SG6 Bo Bichette 2.50 6.00
SG7 Paul Goldschmidt .50 1.25
SG8 Anthony Rizzo .60 1.50
SG9 Aaron Judge 1.25 3.00
SG10 Clayton Kershaw .75 2.00

2020 Panini Prizm Star Gazing Prizms Blue Donut Circles
*BLUE DONUT/199: .8X TO 2X BASIC
RANDOM INSERTS IN PACKS
STATED PRINT RUN 199 SER.#'d SETS
SG1 Mike Trout 10.00 25.00
SG4 Fernando Tatis Jr. 4.00 10.00
SG9 Aaron Judge 6.00 15.00

2020 Panini Prizm Star Gazing Prizms Blue Mojo
*BLUE MOJO/175: .8X TO 2X BASIC
RANDOM INSERTS IN PACKS
STATED PRINT RUN 175 SER.#'d SETS
SG1 Mike Trout 10.00 25.00
SG4 Fernando Tatis Jr. 4.00 10.00
SG9 Aaron Judge 6.00 15.00

2020 Panini Prizm Star Gazing Prizms Blue Wave
*BLUE WAVE/60: 1.2X TO 3X BASIC
RANDOM INSERTS IN PACKS
STATED PRINT RUN 60 SER.#'d SETS
SG1 Mike Trout 30.00 80.00
SG4 Fernando Tatis Jr. 6.00 15.00
SG9 Aaron Judge 10.00 25.00

2020 Panini Prizm Star Gazing Prizms Bronze Donut Circles
*BRNZ DONUT/25: 2X TO 5X BASIC
RANDOM INSERTS IN PACKS
STATED PRINT RUN 25 SER.#'d SETS
SG1 Mike Trout 50.00 120.00
SG4 Fernando Tatis Jr. 10.00 25.00
SG6 Bo Bichette 20.00 50.00
SG9 Aaron Judge 15.00 40.00

2020 Panini Prizm Star Gazing Prizms Burgundy Cracked Ice
*BUR.CRKD ICE/25: 2X TO 5X BASIC
RANDOM INSERTS IN PACKS
STATED PRINT RUN 25 SER.#'d SETS

SG1 Mike Trout 50.00 120.00
SG4 Fernando Tatis Jr. 10.00 25.00
SG6 Bo Bichette 20.00 50.00
SG9 Aaron Judge 15.00 40.00

2020 Panini Prizm Star Gazing Prizms Lime Green

*LIME GRN/125: 1X TO 2.5X BASIC
RANDOM INSERTS IN PACKS
STATED PRINT RUN 125 SER.#'d SETS
SG1 Mike Trout 12.00 30.00
SG4 Fernando Tatis Jr. 5.00 12.00
SG9 Aaron Judge 8.00 20.00

2020 Panini Prizm Star Gazing Prizms Navy Blue Kaleidoscope

*NVY BLU.KAL./35: 1.5X TO 4X BASIC
RANDOM INSERTS IN PACKS
STATED PRINT RUN 35 SER.#'d SETS
SG1 Mike Trout 40.00 100.00
SG4 Fernando Tatis Jr. 8.00 20.00
SG6 Bo Bichette 15.00 40.00
SG9 Aaron Judge 12.00 30.00

2020 Panini Prizm Star Gazing Prizms Neon Orange

*NEON ORNG/100: 1.2X TO 3X BASIC
RANDOM INSERTS IN PACKS
STATED PRINT RUN 100 SER.#'d SETS
SG1 Mike Trout 15.00 40.00
SG4 Fernando Tatis Jr. 6.00 15.00
SG9 Aaron Judge 10.00 25.00

2020 Panini Prizm Star Gazing Prizms Power Plaid

*PLAID/75: 1.2X TO 3X BASIC
RANDOM INSERTS IN PACKS
STATED PRINT RUN 75 SER.#'d SETS
SG1 Mike Trout 30.00 80.00
SG4 Fernando Tatis Jr. 6.00 15.00
SG9 Aaron Judge 10.00 25.00

2020 Panini Prizm Star Gazing Prizms Red Donut Circles

*RED DONUT/99: 1.2X TO 3X BASIC
RANDOM INSERTS IN PACKS
STATED PRINT RUN 99 SER.#'d SETS
SG1 Mike Trout 15.00 40.00
SG4 Fernando Tatis Jr. 6.00 15.00
SG9 Aaron Judge 10.00 25.00

2020 Panini Prizm Star Gazing Prizms Red Mojo

*RED MOJO/149: 1X TO 2.5X BASIC
RANDOM INSERTS IN PACKS
STATED PRINT RUN 149 SER.#'d SETS
SG1 Mike Trout 12.00 30.00
SG4 Fernando Tatis Jr. 5.00 12.00
SG9 Aaron Judge 8.00 20.00

2020 Panini Prizm Star Gazing Prizms Red Wave

*RED WAVE/99: 1.2X TO 3X BASIC
RANDOM INSERTS IN PACKS
STATED PRINT RUN 99 SER.#'d SETS
SG1 Mike Trout 15.00 40.00
SG4 Fernando Tatis Jr. 6.00 15.00
SG9 Aaron Judge 10.00 25.00

2020 Panini Prizm Star Gazing Prizms Snake Skin

*SNAKE SKIN/50: 1.5X TO 4X BASIC
RANDOM INSERTS IN PACKS
STATED PRINT RUN 50 SER.#'d SETS
SG1 Mike Trout 40.00 100.00
SG4 Fernando Tatis Jr. 8.00 20.00
SG6 Bo Bichette 15.00 40.00
SG9 Aaron Judge 12.00 30.00

2020 Panini Prizm Top of the Class

RANDOM INSERTS IN PACKS
*SILVER: .6X TO 1.5X BASIC
1 Adley Rutschman 2.00 5.00
2 Bobby Witt Jr. 4.00 10.00
3 Andrew Vaughn 1.25 3.00
4 JJ Bleday 1.00 2.50
5 Riley Greene 1.25 3.00
6 CJ Abrams 1.00 2.50
7 Nick Lodolo .50 1.25
8 Josh Jung .75 2.00
9 Shea Langeliers .60 1.50
10 Hunter Bishop .60 1.50
11 Alek Manoah .40 1.00
12 Brett Baty 1.00 2.50
13 Keoni Cavaco .30 .75
14 Bryson Stott .75 2.00
15 Will Wilson .40 1.00
16 Corbin Carroll .50 1.25
17 Jackson Rutledge .50 1.25
18 Quinn Priester .40 1.00
19 Zack Thompson .30 .75
20 George Kirby .50 1.25
21 Braden Shewmake .50 1.25
22 Greg Jones .40 1.00
23 Michael Toglia .30 .75
24 Daniel Espino .40 1.00
25 Kody Hoese 1.00 2.50
26 Blake Walston .50 1.25
27 Ryan Jensen .40 1.00
28 Ethan Small .40 1.00
29 Logan Davidson .40 1.00
30 Anthony Volpe 1.25 3.00

2020 Panini Prizm Warming in the Pen

RANDOM INSERTS IN PACKS
*SILVER: .6X TO 1.5X BASIC
1 Nate Pearson 1.00 2.50
2 Forrest Whitley .50 1.25
3 Sixto Sanchez 1.00 2.50
4 Matt Manning .40 1.00
5 Ian Anderson 1.00 2.50
6 Deivi Garcia 1.50 4.00
7 Brent Honeywell .40 1.00
8 Tarik Skubal 1.50 4.00
9 Triston McKenzie 1.00 2.50
10 Casey Mize 1.00 2.50
11 Matthew Liberatore .40 1.00
12 Logan Gilbert .40 1.00
13 Brady Singer 1.50 4.00
14 MacKenzie Gore .60 1.50
15 Daniel Lynch .30 .75

2019 Panini Prizm Draft Picks

COMPLETE SET (100) 30.00 80.00
1 Adley Rutschman 1.50 4.00
2 Bobby Witt Jr. 1.50 4.00
3 Andrew Vaughn .75 2.00
4 CJ Abrams 1.25 3.00
5 Riley Greene 1.50 4.00
6 Matt Wallner .50 1.25
7 Shea Langeliers .50 1.25
8 Zack Thompson .40 1.00
9 Corbin Carroll .40 1.00
10 Josh Jung .75 2.00
11 Ethan Small .30 .75
12 Hunter Bishop .75 2.00
13 Kameron Misner .60 1.50
14 Bryson Stott .75 2.00
15 Adley Rutschman 1.50 4.00
16 Brett Baty .50 1.25
17 Will Wilson .40 1.00
18 Nick Lodolo .50 1.25
19 JJ Bleday 1.25 3.00
20 Alek Manoah .50 1.25
21 Will Wilson .40 1.00
22 Kody Hoese .75 2.00
23 Logan Davidson .25 .60
24 Daniel Espino .30 .75
25 Bobby Witt Jr. 1.50 4.00
26 Shea Langeliers .50 1.25
27 Zack Thompson .40 1.00
28 Brennan Malone .25 .60
29 Jackson Rutledge .50 1.25
30 Andrew Vaughn .75 2.00
31 George Kirby .40 1.00
32 Michael Busch .75 2.00
33 Will Wilson .40 1.00
34 Rece Hinds .30 .75
35 Matt Wallner .50 1.25
36 Logan Wyatt .40 1.00
37 Bobby Witt Jr. 1.50 4.00
38 Seth Johnson .25 .60
39 Brandon Williamson
40 Braden Shewmake .75 2.00
41 J.J. Goss .30 .75
42 Matt Canterino .30 .75
43 Josh Jung .75 2.00
44 Brett Baty .50 1.25
45 JJ Bleday 1.25 3.00
46 Drey Jameson .25 .60
47 Trejyn Fletcher .40 1.00
48 Andrew Vaughn .75 2.00
49 Chase Strumpf .50 1.25
50 Keoni Cavaco .60 1.50
51 Quinn Priester .30 .75
52 Gunnar Henderson .50 1.25
53 Corbin Carroll .40 1.00
54 Kyle Stowers .40 1.00
55 Alek Manoah .50 1.25
56 Kendall Williams .40 1.00
57 Nasim Nunez .25 .60
58 Aaron Schunk .50 1.25
59 Sammy Siani .30 .75
60 Riley Greene 1.50 4.00
61 Ethan Small .30 .75
62 CJ Abrams 1.25 3.00
63 Josh Wolf .30 .75
64 Matthew Thompson .30 .75
65 Cameron Cannon .50 1.25
66 Hunter Bishop .75 2.00
67 T.J. Sikkema .40 1.00
68 Ryan Jensen .40 1.00
69 Anthony Volpe 1.00 2.50
70 Bryson Stott .75 2.00
71 Michael Toglia .40 1.00
72 Korey Lee .50 1.25
73 Kody Hoese .75 2.00
74 Davis Wendzel .40 1.00
75 CJ Abrams 1.25 3.00
76 John Doxakis .30 .75
77 CJ Abrams 1.25 3.00
78 Cameron Cannon .50 1.25
79 Brennan Malone .25 .60
80 Matt Wallner .50 1.25
81 Ryan Garcia .25 .60
82 Adley Rutschman 1.50 4.00
83 Brady McConnell .40 1.00
84 Braden Shewmake .75 2.00
85 Greg Jones .30 .75
86 Riley Greene 1.50 4.00
87 Bobby Witt Jr. 1.50 4.00
88 Riley Greene 1.50 4.00
89 Andrew Vaughn .75 2.00
90 Hunter Bishop .75 2.00
91 Zach Watson .40 1.00
92 Tyler Callihan .30 .75
93 Adley Rutschman 1.50 4.00
94 Bobby Witt Jr. 1.50 4.00
95 Andrew Vaughn .75 2.00
96 JJ Bleday 1.25 3.00
97 Anthony Volpe 1.00 2.50
98 Josh Jung .75 2.00
99 JJ Bleday 1.25 3.00
100 Adley Rutschman 1.50 4.00

2019 Panini Prizm Draft Picks Prizms Blue

*PRIZMS BLUE: 5X TO 1.2X BASIC
RANDOM INSERTS IN PACKS

2019 Panini Prizm Draft Picks Prizms Camo

*PRIZMS CAMO: 2.5X TO 6X BASIC
RANDOM INSERTS IN PACKS
STATED PRINT RUN 25 SER.#'d SETS

2019 Panini Prizm Draft Picks Prizms Carolina Blue

*PRIZMS CAR.BLUE: 2X TO 5X BASIC
RANDOM INSERTS IN PACKS
STATED PRINT RUN 30 SER.#'d SETS

2019 Panini Prizm Draft Picks Prizms Green

*PRIZMS GRN: .5X TO 1.2X BASIC
RANDOM INSERTS IN PACKS

2019 Panini Prizm Draft Picks Prizms Hyper

*PRIZMS HYPER: 1.2X TO 3X BASIC
RANDOM INSERTS IN PACKS
STATED PRINT RUN 75 SER.#'d SETS

2019 Panini Prizm Draft Picks Prizms Mojo

*PRIZMS MOJO: 1.5X TO 4X BASIC
RANDOM INSERTS IN PACKS
STATED PRINT RUN 49 SER.#'d SETS

2019 Panini Prizm Draft Picks Prizms Orange

*PRIZMS ORNG: .5X TO 1.2X BASIC
RANDOM INSERTS IN PACKS

2019 Panini Prizm Draft Picks Prizms Red

*PRIZMS RED: .5X TO 1.2X BASIC
RANDOM INSERTS IN PACKS

2019 Panini Prizm Draft Picks Prizms Red and Black Snake Skin

*PRIZMS SNAKE SKN: 1X TO 2.5X BASIC
RANDOM INSERTS IN PACKS

2019 Panini Prizm Draft Picks Prizms Red White and Blue

*PRIZMS RWB: 1.2X TO 3X BASIC
RANDOM INSERTS IN PACKS
STATED PRINT RUN 99 SER.#'d SETS

2019 Panini Prizm Draft Picks Prizms Silver

*PRIZMS SLVR: .5X TO 1.2X BASIC
RANDOM INSERTS IN PACKS

2019 Panini Prizm Draft Picks Autographs Prizms

RANDOM INSERTS IN PACKS
EXCHANGE DEADLINE 4/16/2021
*GREEN: .5X TO 1.2X
*RWB p/r 75-99: .5X TO 1.2X
*HYPER p/r 49-75: .5X TO 1.2X
*MOJO p/r 49: .5X TO 1.2X
*MOJO p/r 30: .6X TO 1.5X
*CAR BLUE p/r 30: .6X TO 1.5X
*CAR BLUE p/r 25: .75X TO 2X
*CAMO p/r 20-25: .75X TO 2X
*RB SNK SKN: 1X TO 2.5X BASIC
1 Adley Rutschman 20.00 50.00
2 Adley Rutschman 20.00 50.00
3 Bobby Witt Jr. 20.00 50.00
4 Bobby Witt Jr. 20.00 50.00
5 Andrew Vaughn 10.00 25.00
6 Andrew Vaughn 10.00 25.00
7 CJ Abrams 10.00 25.00
8 CJ Abrams 10.00 25.00
9 Riley Greene 10.00 25.00
10 Riley Greene 10.00 25.00
11 Shea Langeliers 6.00 15.00
12 Shea Langeliers 6.00 15.00
13 Corbin Carroll 3.00 8.00
14 Corbin Carroll 3.00 8.00
15 Josh Jung 6.00 15.00
16 Josh Jung 6.00 15.00
17 Hunter Bishop 6.00 15.00
18 Kameron Misner 5.00 12.00
19 Bryson Stott 6.00 15.00
20 Bryson Stott 6.00 15.00
21 Brett Baty 8.00 20.00
22 Nick Lodolo 4.00 10.00
23 JJ Bleday 10.00 25.00
24 Alek Manoah 4.00 10.00
25 Will Wilson 3.00 8.00
26 Will Wilson 3.00 8.00
27 Logan Davidson 2.00 5.00
28 Daniel Espino 2.50 6.00
29 Zack Thompson 3.00 8.00
30 Zack Thompson 3.00 8.00
31 Brennan Malone 2.00 5.00
32 Brennan Malone 2.00 5.00
33 Jackson Rutledge 4.00 10.00
34 George Kirby 3.00 8.00
35 Michael Busch 6.00 15.00
36 Rece Hinds 2.50 6.00
37 Logan Wyatt 3.00 8.00
38 Seth Johnson 2.00 5.00
40 Braden Shewmake EXCH 6.00 15.00
41 J.J. Goss 2.50 6.00
42 Matt Canterino 2.50 6.00
43 Drey Jameson 2.00 5.00
44 Trejyn Fletcher 3.00 8.00
45 Chase Strumpf 4.00 10.00
46 Keoni Cavaco 6.00 15.00
48 Gunnar Henderson 4.00 10.00
49 Kyle Stowers 3.00 8.00
50 Kendall Williams 3.00 8.00
51 Nasim Nunez 2.00 5.00
52 Will Holland 3.00 8.00
53 Sammy Siani 2.50 6.00
54 Ethan Small 2.50 6.00
55 Josh Wolf 2.50 6.00
57 Fidel Montero 3.00 8.00
58 T.J. Sikkema 3.00 8.00
59 Ryan Jensen 3.00 8.00
60 Anthony Volpe 8.00 20.00
61 Anthony Volpe 8.00 20.00
62 Michael Toglia 3.00 8.00
63 Korey Lee 4.00 10.00
64 Kody Hoese 6.00 15.00
65 Davis Wendzel 3.00 8.00
66 John Doxakis 2.50 6.00
67 Cameron Cannon 4.00 10.00
68 Matt Wallner 4.00 10.00
69 Matt Wallner 4.00 10.00
70 Joshua Mears 4.00 10.00
71 Ryan Garcia 2.00 5.00
72 Brady McConnell 3.00 8.00
73 Tommy Henry 2.50 6.00
74 Matt Gorski 3.00 8.00
75 Beau Philip 3.00 8.00
76 Greg Jones 2.50 6.00
77 Aaron Schunk 4.00 10.00
78 Nick Quintana 4.00 10.00
79 Jimmy Lewis 2.00 5.00
80 Isaiah Campbell 4.00 10.00
81 Josh Smith 4.00 10.00
82 Bayron Lora EXCH 40.00 100.00
83 Kyren Paris 2.00 5.00
85 Yordys Valdes 4.00 10.00
86 Matthew Lugo 3.00 8.00
87 Alec Marsh 2.50 6.00
88 Dominic Fletcher 2.00 5.00
89 Jared Triolo 3.00 8.00
90 Tyler Baum 2.50 6.00
91 Logan Driscoll 3.00 8.00
92 Karl Kauffmann 2.00 5.00
93 Zach Watson 3.00 8.00
94 Tyler Callihan 2.50 6.00
95 Andrew Abbott 2.00 5.00
96 Logan Allen 2.00 5.00
97 Tanner Allen 2.00 5.00
98 Patrick Bailey 4.00 10.00
99 Tyler Brown 12.00 30.00
100 Alec Burleson 3.00 8.00
101 Burl Carraway 4.00 10.00
102 Cade Cavalli 4.00 10.00
103 Colton Cowser 2.50 6.00
104 Jeff Criswell 3.00 8.00
105 Reid Detmers 6.00 15.00
106 Lucas Dunn 2.00 5.00
107 Justin Foscue 5.00 12.00
108 Nick Frasso 2.00 5.00
109 Heston Kjerstad 40.00 100.00
110 Asa Lacy 5.00 12.00
111 Nick Loftin 2.00 5.00
112 Austin Martin 20.00 50.00
113 Chris McMahon 2.00 5.00
114 Max Meyer 10.00 25.00
115 Garrett Mitchell 10.00 25.00
116 Doug Nikhazy 2.00 5.00
117 Casey Opitz 3.00 8.00
118 Spencer Torkelson 100.00 250.00
119 Luke Waddell 6.00 15.00
120 Cole Wilcox 2.50 6.00
121 Alika Williams 3.00 8.00
122 Jasson Dominguez 150.00 400.00
123 Robert Puason 10.00 25.00

2019 Panini Prizm Draft Picks College Ties Autographs Prizms

RANDOM INSERTS IN PACKS
EXCHANGE DEADLINE 4/16/2021
*ORNGE PLSR/20: .6X TO 1.5X
2 Vaughn/Lee 25.00 60.00
3 Misner/Sikkema 20.00 50.00
4 Wendzel/Langeliers 10.00 25.00
5 Rutschman/Philip 40.00 100.00

2019 Panini Prizm Draft Picks Color Blast

RANDOM INSERTS IN PACKS
1 Adley Rutschman 50.00 120.00
2 Bobby Witt Jr. 40.00 100.00
3 Andrew Vaughn 40.00 100.00
4 JJ Bleday 25.00 60.00
5 Riley Greene 50.00 120.00
6 CJ Abrams 20.00 50.00
7 Adley Rutschman 50.00 120.00
8 Josh Jung
9 Shea Langeliers
10 Hunter Bishop 20.00 50.00
11 Bobby Witt Jr. 40.00 100.00
12 Brett Baty
13 Andrew Vaughn 40.00 100.00
14 CJ Abrams 20.00 50.00
15 Josh Jung
16 Riley Greene 50.00 120.00

2020 Panini Prizm Draft Picks

1 Spencer Torkelson 3.00 8.00
2 Heston Kjerstad 1.50 4.00
3 Max Meyer .75 2.00
4 Asa Lacy 1.25 3.00
5 Austin Martin .60 1.50
6 Emerson Hancock .75 2.00
7 Nick Gonzales 1.00 2.50
8 Robert Hassell 1.50 4.00
9 Zac Veen 1.00 2.50
10 Reid Detmers .50 1.25
11 Garrett Crochet .50 1.25
12 Austin Hendrick 2.00 5.00
13 Patrick Bailey .60 1.50
14 Justin Foscue .75 2.00
15 Mick Abel .30 .75
16 Ed Howard 1.50 4.00
17 Nick Yorke 1.00 2.50
18 Bryce Jarvis .25 .60
19 Pete Crow-Armstrong .60 1.50
20 Garrett Mitchell 1.50 4.00
21 Jordan Walker .60 1.50
22 Cade Cavalli .40 1.00
23 Carson Tucker .60 1.50
24 Nick Bitsko .60 1.50
25 Jared Shuster .40 1.00
26 Tyler Soderstrom .75 2.00
27 Aaron Sabato .40 1.00
28 Austin Wells .75 2.00
29 Bobby Miller .75 2.00
30 Jordan Westburg .50 1.25
31 Carmen Mlodzinski .25 .60
32 Nick Loftin .30 .75
33 Slade Cecconi .25 .60
34 Justin Lange .20 .50
35 Drew Romo .50 1.25
36 Tanner Burns .20 .50
37 Alika Williams .25 .60
38 Dillon Dingler .60 1.50
39 Hudson Haskin .75 2.00
40 Dax Fulton .30 .75
41 Ben Hernandez .30 .75
42 CJ Van Eyk .30 .75
43 Zach DeLoach .75 2.00
44 Jared Jones .30 .75
45 Owen Caissie .40 1.00
46 Bradlee Beesley .30 .75
47 Jared Kelley .20 .50
48 Christian Roa .25 .60
49 Casey Schmitt .50 1.25
50 Evan Carter .50 1.25
51 Burl Carraway .40 1.00
52 Brady Singer 1.00 2.50
53 Freddy Zamora .30 .75
54 Masyn Winn .75 2.00
55 Cole Henry .25 .60
56 Logan T. Allen .20 .50
57 Ian Seymour .20 .50
58 Jeff Criswell .25 .60
59 Alerick Soularie .25 .60
60 Landon Knack .50 1.25
61 Kyle Nicolas .30 .75
62 Daniel Cabrera .75 2.00
63 Markevian Hence .20 .50
64 Connor Phillips .30 .75
65 Jackson Miller .50 1.25
66 Clayton Beeter .50 1.25
67 Nick Swiney .40 1.00
68 Jimmy Glowenke .40 1.00
69 Isaiah Greene .75 2.00
70 Alec Burleson .30 .75
71 Sammy Infante .75 2.00
72 Alex Santos .60 1.50
73 Trei Cruz .75 2.00
74 Anthony Servideo .25 .60
75 Zach McCambley .20 .50
76 Tyler Gentry .40 1.00
77 Trent Palmer .25 .60
78 Kaden Polcovich .30 .75
79 Nick Garcia .30 .75
80 Joey Bart .60 1.50
81 Sam Weatherly .20 .50
82 David Calabrese .40 1.00
83 Adisyn Coffey .20 .50
84 Bryce Bonnin .30 .75
85 Dane Dunning .60 1.50
86 Tekoah Roby .20 .50
87 Casey Martin .60 1.50
88 Jordan Nwogu .75 2.00
89 Jordan DiValerio .20 .50
90 Liam Norris .20 .50
91 Anthony Walters .25 .60
92 Zavier Warren .25 .60
93 Levi Prater .25 .60
94 Holden Powell .25 .60
95 Petey Halpin .50 1.25
96 Hunter Barnhart .20 .50
97 Jesse Franklin .75 2.00
98 Michael Guldberg .25 .60
99 Trevor Hauver .30 .75
100 Jake Vogel .25 .60
101 Tyler Brown .25 .60
102 Gage Workman .75 2.00
103 Justin Lavey .25 .60
104 Jake Eder .20 .50
105 Matt Scheffler .20 .50
106 Nick Frasso .20 .50
107 Tyler Keenan .20 .50
108 Jack Hartman .20 .50
109 Levi Thomas .20 .50
110 Case Williams .25 .60
111 Werner Blakely .25 .60
112 Kade Mechals .25 .60
113 Mac Wainwright .25 .60
114 R.J. Dabovich .20 .50
115 Dylan MacLean .30 .75
116 Wander Franco 2.00 5.00
117 Luke Little .30 .75
118 Jeremy Wu-Yelland .30 .75
119 A.J. Vukovich .40 1.00
120 Matthew Dyer .30 .75
121 Joey Wiemer .30 .75
122 Ian Bedell .25 .60
123 Brady Lindsly .30 .75
124 Milan Tolentino .30 .75
125 Tanner Murray .25 .60
126 Spencer Strider .30 .75
127 Dane Acker .30 .75
128 Marco Raya .40 1.00
129 Beck Way .20 .50
130 Carson Taylor .30 .75
131 Zach Daniels .30 .75
132 Colten Keith 1.00 2.50
133 Carter Baumler .30 .75
134 Kyle Hurt .30 .75
135 Will Klein .25 .60
136 Zach Britton .25 .60
137 Taylor Dollard .20 .50
138 Logan Hofmann .20 .50
139 Ian Anderson .60 1.50
140 Jack Blomgren .30 .75
141 Adam Seminaris .25 .60
142 Bailey Horn .25 .60
143 Joe Boyle .30 .75
144 Matt Manning .25 .60
145 Triston McKenzie .60 1.50
146 Baron Radcliff .25 .60
147 Gus Steiger .20 .50
148 Shane Drohan .25 .60
149 Brandon Pfaadt .20 .50
150 Eric Orze .20 .50
151 Hayden Cantrelle .25 .60
152 LJ Jones IV .30 .75
153 Mitchell Parker .20 .50
154 Mason Hickman .25 .60
155 Jeff Hakanson .20 .50
156 Jackson Coutts .20 .50
157 Stevie Emanuels .20 .50
158 Kala'i Rosario .50 1.25
159 Gavin Stone .40 1.00
160 Brett Auerbach .30 .75
161 Jordan Mikel .25 .60
162 Thomas Girard .20 .50
163 Chase Antle .20 .50
164 Kale Emshoff .50 1.25

2020 Panini Prizm Draft Picks Prizms Blue Donut Circles

*BLUE DONUT: 3X TO 8X BASIC
RANDOM INSERTS IN PACKS
STATED PRINT RUN 25 SER.#'d SETS
1 Spencer Torkelson 40.00 100.00
116 Wander Franco 20.00 50.00

2020 Panini Prizm Draft Picks Prizms Burgundy Cracked Ice

*BRGNDY ICE: 3X TO 8X BASIC
RANDOM INSERTS IN PACKS
STATED PRINT RUN 23 SER.#'d SETS
1 Spencer Torkelson 40.00 100.00
116 Wander Franco 20.00 50.00

2020 Panini Prizm Draft Picks Prizms Lime Green

*LIME GRN: 1.5X TO 4X BASIC
RANDOM INSERTS IN PACKS
STATED PRINT RUN 75 SER.#'d SETS
1 Spencer Torkelson 20.00 50.00

2020 Panini Prizm Draft Picks Prizms Neon Orange

*NEON ORNG: 2X TO 5X BASIC
RANDOM INSERTS IN PACKS
STATED PRINT RUN 50 SER.#'d SETS
1 Spencer Torkelson 25.00 60.00

2020 Panini Prizm Draft Picks Prizms Power Plaid

*PLAID: 2.5X TO 6X BASIC
RANDOM INSERTS IN PACKS
STATED PRINT RUN 35 SER.#'d SETS
1 Spencer Torkelson 30.00 80.00

2020 Panini Prizm Draft Picks Prizms Red Donut Circles

*RED DONUT: 1.5X TO 4X BASIC
RANDOM INSERTS IN PACKS
STATED PRINT RUN 99 SER.#'d SETS
1 Spencer Torkelson 20.00 50.00

2020 Panini Prizm Draft Picks Prizms Snake Skin

*SNAKE SKN: 3X TO 8X BASIC
RANDOM INSERTS IN PACKS
STATED PRINT RUN 25 SER.#'d SETS
1 Spencer Torkelson 40.00 100.00
116 Wander Franco 20.00 50.00

2020 Panini Prizm Draft Picks Prizms Tiger Stripes

*TIGER: 1.5X TO 4X BASIC
RANDOM INSERTS IN PACKS
STATED PRINT RUN 99 SER.#'d SETS
1 Spencer Torkelson 20.00 50.00

2020 Panini Prizm Draft Picks Prizms White Donut Circles

*WHT DONUT: 2X TO 5X BASIC
RANDOM INSERTS IN PACKS
STATED PRINT RUN 50 SER.#'d SETS
1 Spencer Torkelson 25.00 60.00

2020 Panini Prizm Draft Picks Autographs

RANDOM INSERTS IN PACKS
EXCHANGE DEADLINE 6/2/22
2 Miguel Amaya 2.50 6.00
3 Riley Greene 12.00 30.00
4 Jarred Kelenic 30.00 80.00
5 Evan White 6.00 15.00
6 Drew Rasmussen 6.00 15.00
7 Clay Aguilar 4.00 10.00
8 Triston Casas 8.00 20.00
9 Tarik Skubal 12.00 30.00
10 Luis V. Garcia 10.00 25.00
11 Erick Pena 12.00 30.00
12 Nate Pearson 8.00 20.00
13 Ryan Mountcastle 8.00 20.00
14 Shane Baz 2.50 6.00
15 Heliot Ramos 30.00 80.00
16 Hunter Greene 4.00 10.00
17 Josh Jung 10.00 25.00
19 Bobby Witt Jr. 25.00 60.00
20 A.J. Block 2.50 6.00
21 Ji-Hwan Bae 8.00 20.00
22 Andres Gimenez 6.00 15.00
23 CJ Abrams 8.00 20.00
24 Matthew Liberatore 5.00 12.00
25 Luisangel Acuna 15.00 40.00
26 Brice Turang 4.00 10.00
27 Corbin Carroll 4.00 10.00
28 Bobby Dalbec 15.00 40.00
29 Oneil Cruz 6.00 15.00
30 Drew Waters 8.00 20.00
31 JJ Bleday 8.00 20.00
33 Jesus Sanchez 4.00 10.00
34 Andrew Vaughn 10.00 25.00
35 Estevan Florial 4.00 10.00
37 Bryan Mata 2.50 6.00
38 Cristian Pache 12.00 30.00
39 Daniel Lynch 2.50 6.00
40 MacKenzie Gore 12.00 30.00
41 Noelvi Marte 12.00 30.00
42 Nolan Gorman 10.00 25.00
43 Spencer Howard 5.00 12.00
44 Travis Blankenhorn 5.00 12.00
46 Freudis Nova 2.50 6.00
47 Johan Rojas 5.00 12.00
48 Isaac Paredes 6.00 15.00
49 Jose Salas 6.00 15.00
50 Tyler Freeman 3.00 8.00
51 Kristian Robinson 12.00 30.00
52 Luis Rodriguez 15.00 40.00
53 Alex Kirilloff 10.00 25.00
54 Tanner Houck 10.00 25.00
55 Mason Martin 5.00 12.00
57 Julio Rodriguez 40.00 100.00
58 Luis Garcia 10.00 25.00
61 Nolan Jones 10.00 25.00
62 Rylan Bannon 3.00 8.00
63 Yoelqui Cespedes 50.00 120.00
64 Yiddi Cappe 10.00 25.00
65 Dylan Carlson 12.00 30.00
66 Norge Vera 8.00 20.00
67 Zion Bannister 3.00 8.00
68 Tristen Lutz 3.00 8.00
69 Hyun-il Choi 4.00 10.00
70 Oscar Colas 20.00 50.00

2020 Panini Prizm Draft Picks Base Autographs Prizms Silver

RANDOM INSERTS IN PACKS
EXCHANGE DEADLINE 6/2/22
1 Spencer Torkelson 50.00 120.00
2 Heston Kjerstad 20.00 50.00
3 Max Meyer 8.00 20.00
4 Asa Lacy 10.00 25.00
5 Austin Martin 20.00 50.00
6 Emerson Hancock 8.00 20.00
7 Nick Gonzales 10.00 25.00
8 Robert Hassell 10.00 25.00
9 Zac Veen 15.00 40.00
10 Reid Detmers 6.00 15.00
11 Garrett Crochet 15.00 40.00
12 Austin Hendrick 12.00 30.00
13 Patrick Bailey 8.00 20.00
14 Justin Foscue 6.00 15.00
15 Mick Abel 8.00 20.00
16 Ed Howard 12.00 30.00
17 Nick Yorke 10.00 25.00
18 Bryce Jarvis 2.50 6.00
19 Pete Crow-Armstrong 10.00 25.00
20 Garrett Mitchell 12.00 30.00
21 Jordan Walker 6.00 15.00
22 Cade Cavalli 5.00 12.00
23 Carson Tucker 6.00 15.00
24 Nick Bitsko 5.00 12.00
25 Jared Shuster 4.00 10.00
26 Tyler Soderstrom 8.00 20.00
27 Aaron Sabato 10.00 25.00
28 Austin Wells 8.00 20.00
30 Jordan Westburg 4.00 10.00
31 Carmen Mlodzinski 2.50 6.00
32 Nick Loftin 3.00 8.00
33 Slade Cecconi 2.50 6.00
34 Justin Lange 2.00 5.00
35 Drew Romo 3.00 8.00
36 Tanner Burns 4.00 10.00
37 Alika Williams 2.50 6.00
38 Dillon Dingler 6.00 15.00
39 Hudson Haskin 3.00 8.00
40 Dax Fulton 4.00 10.00
41 Ben Hernandez 3.00 8.00
42 CJ Van Eyk 3.00 8.00
43 Zach DeLoach 6.00 15.00
44 Jared Jones 3.00 8.00
45 Owen Caissie 5.00 12.00
46 Bradlee Beesley 3.00 8.00
47 Jared Kelley 2.00 5.00
49 Casey Schmitt 5.00 12.00
50 Evan Carter 4.00 10.00
51 Burl Carraway 4.00 10.00
53 Freddy Zamora 3.00 8.00
54 Masyn Winn 8.00 20.00
55 Cole Henry 2.50 6.00
56 Logan T. Allen 3.00 8.00
57 Ian Seymour 2.00 5.00
58 Jeff Criswell 4.00 10.00
59 Alerick Soularie 2.50 6.00
60 Landon Knack 4.00 10.00
61 Kyle Nicolas 3.00 8.00
62 Daniel Cabrera 6.00 15.00
63 Markevian Hence 2.00 5.00
64 Connor Phillips 3.00 8.00
65 Jackson Miller 3.00 8.00
66 Clayton Beeter 3.00 8.00
67 Nick Swiney 4.00 10.00
68 Jimmy Glowenke 2.50 6.00
69 Isaiah Greene 5.00 12.00
70 Alec Burleson 3.00 8.00
71 Sammy Infante 5.00 12.00
72 Alex Santos 6.00 15.00
73 Trei Cruz 5.00 12.00
75 Zach McCambley 2.00 5.00
76 Tyler Gentry 4.00 10.00
77 Trent Palmer 2.50 6.00
78 Kaden Polcovich 3.00 8.00
79 Nick Garcia 3.00 8.00
80 Joey Bart 8.00 20.00
81 Sam Weatherly 2.00 5.00
82 David Calabrese 3.00 8.00
83 Adisyn Coffey 2.00 5.00
84 Bryce Bonnin 3.00 8.00
85 Dane Dunning 4.00 10.00
87 Casey Martin 10.00 25.00
88 Jordan Nwogu 8.00 20.00
89 Jordan DiValerio 2.00 5.00
90 Liam Norris 2.00 5.00
91 Anthony Walters 2.50 6.00
92 Zavier Warren 2.00 5.00
93 Levi Prater 2.50 6.00
94 Holden Powell 2.50 6.00
96 Hunter Barnhart 2.00 5.00
97 Jesse Franklin 5.00 12.00
98 Michael Guldberg 2.50 6.00
100 Jake Vogel 2.50 6.00
101 Tyler Brown 3.00 8.00
102 Gage Workman 4.00 10.00
103 Justin Lavey 2.50 6.00
104 Jake Eder 2.00 5.00
105 Matt Scheffler 2.00 5.00
106 Nick Frasso 2.00 5.00
107 Tyler Keenan 3.00 8.00
108 Jack Hartman 2.00 5.00
109 Levi Thomas 2.00 5.00
110 Case Williams 2.50 6.00
111 Werner Blakely 2.50 6.00
112 Kade Mechals 2.00 5.00
114 R.J. Dabovich 2.00 5.00
115 Dylan MacLean 2.00 5.00
116 Wander Franco EXCH 40.00 100.00
118 Jeremy Wu-Yelland 3.00 8.00
119 A.J. Vukovich
120 Matthew Dyer 3.00 8.00
122 Ian Bedell 2.50 6.00
123 Brady Lindsly 3.00 8.00
125 Tanner Murray 3.00 8.00
126 Spencer Strider 3.00 8.00
127 Dane Acker 5.00 12.00
128 Marco Raya 3.00 8.00
129 Beck Way 2.00 5.00
130 Carson Taylor 2.00 5.00
132 Colten Keith 4.00 10.00
133 Carter Baumler 2.00 5.00
134 Kyle Hurt 2.00 5.00
135 Will Klein 2.00 5.00
136 Zach Britton 4.00 10.00
137 Taylor Dollard 2.00 5.00
138 Logan Hofmann 2.00 5.00
139 Ian Anderson 8.00 20.00
140 Jack Blomgren 4.00 10.00
141 Adam Seminaris 2.50 6.00
142 Bailey Horn 2.50 6.00
143 Joe Boyle 3.00 8.00
144 Matt Manning 5.00 12.00
145 Triston McKenzie 8.00 20.00
146 Baron Radcliff 2.50 6.00
147 Gus Steiger 2.00 5.00
148 Shane Drohan 2.50 6.00
149 Brandon Pfaadt 2.00 5.00
151 Hayden Cantrelle 2.00 5.00
153 Mitchell Parker 2.00 5.00
154 Mason Hickman 2.50 6.00
155 Jeff Hakanson 2.00 5.00
156 Jackson Coutts 2.50 6.00
157 Stevie Emanuels 2.00 5.00
158 Kala'i Rosario 2.50 6.00
159 Gavin Stone 15.00 40.00
160 Brett Auerbach 3.00 8.00
161 Jordan Mikel 2.00 5.00
162 Thomas Girard 2.00 5.00
163 Chase Antle 2.00 5.00
164 Kale Emshoff 2.00 5.00

2020 Panini Prizm Draft Picks Base Autographs Prizms Blue

*BLUE/60: .5X TO 1.2X BASIC

*BLUE/35-50: .6X TO 1.5X BASIC
RANDOM INSERTS IN PACKS
PRINT RUNS B/WN 35-60 COPIES PER
EXCHANGE DEADLINE 6/2/22
1 Spencer Torkelson/60 75.00 200.00
2 Heston Kjerstad/60 50.00 120.00
7 Nick Gonzales/60 20.00 50.00
22 Cade Cavalli/60 8.00 20.00
140 Jack Blomgren/60 8.00 20.00

2020 Panini Prizm Draft Picks Base Autographs Prizms Blue Donut Circles
*BLUE DONUT: .8X TO 2X BASIC
RANDOM INSERTS IN PACKS
STATED PRINT RUN 25 SER.#'d SETS
EXCHANGE DEADLINE 6/2/22
1 Spencer Torkelson 125.00 300.00
2 Heston Kjerstad 75.00 200.00
7 Nick Gonzales 30.00 80.00
12 Austin Hendrick 30.00 80.00
21 Jordan Walker 15.00 40.00
22 Cade Cavalli 12.00 30.00
27 Aaron Sabato 25.00 60.00
29 Bobby Miller 25.00 60.00
51 Burl Carraway 12.00 30.00
131 Zach Daniels 12.00 30.00
140 Jack Blomgren 12.00 30.00

2020 Panini Prizm Draft Picks Base Autographs Prizms Lime Green
*LIME GRN: .8X TO 2X BASIC
RANDOM INSERTS IN PACKS
STATED PRINT RUN 23 SER.#'d SETS
EXCHANGE DEADLINE 6/2/22
1 Spencer Torkelson 125.00 300.00
2 Heston Kjerstad 75.00 200.00
7 Nick Gonzales 30.00 80.00
12 Austin Hendrick 30.00 80.00
21 Jordan Walker 15.00 40.00
22 Cade Cavalli 12.00 30.00
27 Aaron Sabato 25.00 60.00
39 Hudson Haskin 8.00 20.00
51 Burl Carraway 12.00 30.00
131 Zach Daniels 12.00 30.00
140 Jack Blomgren 12.00 30.00

2020 Panini Prizm Draft Picks Base Autographs Prizms Neon Orange
*NEON ORNG: .8X TO 2X BASIC
RANDOM INSERTS IN PACKS
STATED PRINT RUN 20 SER.#'d SETS
EXCHANGE DEADLINE 6/2/22
1 Spencer Torkelson 125.00 300.00
2 Heston Kjerstad 75.00 200.00
7 Nick Gonzales 30.00 80.00
12 Austin Hendrick 30.00 80.00
21 Jordan Walker 15.00 40.00
22 Cade Cavalli 12.00 30.00
27 Aaron Sabato 25.00 60.00
39 Hudson Haskin 8.00 20.00
51 Burl Carraway 12.00 30.00
131 Zach Daniels 12.00 30.00
140 Jack Blomgren 12.00 30.00

2020 Panini Prizm Draft Picks Base Autographs Prizms Red
*RED/30-50: .6X TO 1.5X BASIC
RANDOM INSERTS IN PACKS
PRINT RUNS B/WN 30-50 COPIES PER
EXCHANGE DEADLINE 6/2/22
1 Spencer Torkelson/50 100.00 250.00
2 Heston Kjerstad/50 60.00 150.00
7 Nick Gonzales/50 25.00 60.00
22 Cade Cavalli/50 10.00 25.00
27 Aaron Sabato/50 20.00 50.00
51 Burl Carraway/50 8.00 20.00
52 Brady Singer/50 10.00 25.00
131 Zach Daniels/50 5.00 12.00
140 Jack Blomgren/50 10.00 25.00

2020 Panini Prizm Draft Picks Base Autographs Prizms Red Donut Circles
*RED DONUT/75-99: .5X TO 1.2X BASIC
*RED DONUT/35-50: .6X TO 1.5X BASIC
*RED DONUT/25: .8X TO 2X BASIC
RANDOM INSERTS IN PACKS
PRINT RUNS B/WN 25-99 COPIES PER
EXCHANGE DEADLINE 6/2/22
1 Spencer Torkelson/99 75.00 200.00
2 Heston Kjerstad/99 50.00 120.00
7 Nick Gonzales/75 20.00 50.00
22 Cade Cavalli/99 8.00 20.00
95 Petey Halpin/99 6.00 15.00
99 Trevor Hauver/99 4.00 10.00
117 Luke Little/99 4.00 10.00
121 Joey Wiemer/99 4.00 10.00
124 Milan Tolentino/75 4.00 10.00
131 Zach Daniels/99 4.00 10.00
152 LJ Jones IV/75 4.00 10.00

2020 Panini Prizm Draft Picks Base Autographs Prizms Tiger Stripes
*TIGER .8X TO 2X BASIC
RANDOM INSERTS IN PACKS
STATED PRINT RUN 25 SER.#'d SETS
EXCHANGE DEADLINE 6/2/22
1 Spencer Torkelson 125.00 300.00
2 Heston Kjerstad 75.00 200.00
7 Nick Gonzales 30.00 80.00
12 Austin Hendrick 30.00 80.00
21 Jordan Walker 15.00 40.00
22 Cade Cavalli 12.00 30.00
27 Aaron Sabato 25.00 60.00
29 Bobby Miller 25.00 60.00
51 Burl Carraway 12.00 30.00
131 Zach Daniels 12.00 30.00
140 Jack Blomgren 12.00 30.00

2020 Panini Prizm Draft Picks Base Autographs Prizms White Donut Circles
*WHT DONUT/35-50: .6X TO 1.5X BASIC
RANDOM INSERTS IN PACKS
PRINT RUNS B/WN 35-50 COPIES PER
EXCHANGE DEADLINE 6/2/22
1 Spencer Torkelson/50 100.00 250.00
2 Heston Kjerstad/50 60.00 150.00
7 Nick Gonzales/50 25.00 60.00
22 Cade Cavalli/50 10.00 25.00
27 Aaron Sabato/50 20.00 50.00
51 Burl Carraway/50 8.00 20.00
52 Brady Singer/50 10.00 25.00
131 Zach Daniels/50 5.00 12.00
140 Jack Blomgren/50 10.00 25.00

2020 Panini Prizm Draft Picks College Ties Autographs
RANDOM INSERTS IN PACKS
EXCHANGE DEADLINE 6/2/22
1 H.Haskin/K.Hoese 12.00 30.00
2 H.Bishop/S.Torkelson 60.00 150.00
4 A.Lacy/B.Shewmake 20.00 50.00
5 A.Martin/J.Bleday 40.00 100.00
6 A.Wells/N.Quintana 10.00 25.00
7 A.Sabato/M.Busch 25.00 60.00
8 P.Bailey/W.Wilson 15.00 40.00
9 G.Mitchell/M.Togila 15.00 40.00
10 C.Mize/T.Burns 15.00 40.00

2020 Panini Prizm Draft Picks Color Blast
RANDOM INSERTS IN PACKS
1 Spencer Torkelson 300.00 600.00
2 Heston Kjerstad 125.00 300.00
3 Austin Martin 300.00 600.00
4 Nick Gonzales
5 Robert Hassell 75.00 200.00
6 Zac Veen 100.00 250.00
7 Oscar Colas 60.00 150.00
8 Jasson Dominguez 400.00 800.00

2020 Panini Prizm Draft Picks Electric College Stars
RANDOM INSERTS IN PACKS
1 Spencer Torkelson 50.00 120.00
2 Heston Kjerstad 20.00 50.00
3 Austin Martin 15.00 40.00
4 Nick Gonzales 20.00 50.00
5 Asa Lacy 8.00 20.00
6 Max Meyer 15.00 40.00

2020 Panini Prizm Draft Picks Electric Dominican Prospect League Stars
RANDOM INSERTS IN PACKS
1 Victor Acosta 10.00 25.00
2 Cristian Santana 8.00 20.00
3 Willy Fanas 8.00 20.00
4 Shalin Polanco 8.00 20.00
5 Ambioris Tavarez 10.00 25.00
6 Danny De Andrande 5.00 12.00

2020 Panini Prizm Draft Picks Fireworks
RANDOM INSERTS IN PACKS
*BLUE: .5X TO 1.2X BASIC
*BLUE MOJO: .5X TO 1.2X BASIC
*BLUE WAVE: .5X TO 1.2X BASIC
*RED: .5X TO 1.2X BASIC
*RED MOJO: .5X TO 1.2X BASIC
*RED WAVE: .5X TO 1.2X BASIC
*BL.CAR.BL.HYP.: .5X TO 1.2X BASIC
*GRN YLW HYP.: .5X TO 1.2X BASIC
*PRPL RED HYP.: .5X TO 1.2X BASIC
*GRN PLSR.: .5X TO 1.2X BASIC
*SILVER.: .5X TO 1.2X BASIC
*RED DONUT: 1.2X TO 3X BASIC
*TIGER: 1.2X TO 3X BASIC
*LIME GRN: 1.2X TO 3X BASIC
*NEON ORNG: 1.5X TO 4X BASIC
*WHT DONUT: 1.5X TO 4X BASIC
1 Heston Kjerstad 2.00 5.00
2 Austin Martin .75 2.00
3 Zac Veen 1.25 3.00
4 Zach Daniels .40 1.00
5 Ed Howard 2.00 5.00
6 Pete Crow-Armstrong .75 2.00
7 David Calabrese .50 1.25
8 Daniel Cabrera 1.00 2.50
9 Gus Steiger .25 .60
10 Petey Halpin .60 1.50
11 Masyn Winn 1.00 2.50
12 Luke Little .40 1.00

2020 Panini Prizm Draft Picks Fireworks Prizms Blue Donut Circles
1 Heston Kjerstad 12.00 30.00
3 Zac Veen 10.00 25.00

2020 Panini Prizm Draft Picks Fireworks Prizms Burgundy Cracked Ice
*BRGNDY ICE: 2.5X TO 6X BASIC
RANDOM INSERTS IN PACKS
STATED PRINT RUN 23 SER.#'d SETS
1 Heston Kjerstad 12.00 30.00
3 Zac Veen 10.00 25.00

2020 Panini Prizm Draft Picks Fireworks Prizms Neon Orange
1 Heston Kjerstad 8.00 20.00

2020 Panini Prizm Draft Picks Fireworks Prizms Power Plaid
1 Heston Kjerstad 10.00 25.00

2020 Panini Prizm Draft Picks Fireworks Prizms Snake Skin
*SNAKE SKN: 2.5X TO 6X BASIC
RANDOM INSERTS IN PACKS
STATED PRINT RUN 25 SER.#'d SETS
1 Heston Kjerstad 12.00 30.00
3 Zac Veen 10.00 25.00

2020 Panini Prizm Draft Picks Fireworks Prizms White Donut Circles
1 Heston Kjerstad 8.00 20.00

2020 Panini Prizm Draft Picks Fireworks Autographs Prizms Silver
RANDOM INSERTS IN PACKS
EXCHANGE DEADLINE 6/2/22
*BLUE/60: .5X TO 1.2X BASIC
*BLUE/35: .6X TO 1.5X BASIC
*RED/30-50: .6X TO 1.5X BASIC
*WHT DONUT/30-50: .6X TO 1.5X BASIC
1 Heston Kjerstad 12.00 30.00
2 Austin Martin 20.00 50.00
3 Zac Veen 15.00 40.00
5 Ed Howard 12.00 30.00
6 Pete Crow-Armstrong 10.00 25.00
7 David Calabrese 3.00 8.00
8 Daniel Cabrera 6.00 15.00
9 Gus Steiger 2.00 5.00
11 Masyn Winn 8.00 20.00

2020 Panini Prizm Draft Picks Fireworks Autographs Prizms Blue Donut Circles
*BLUE DONUT: .8X TO 2X BASIC
RANDOM INSERTS IN PACKS
STATED PRINT RUN 25 SER.#'d SETS
EXCHANGE DEADLINE 6/2/22
4 Zach Daniels 12.00 30.00

2020 Panini Prizm Draft Picks Fireworks Autographs Prizms Lime Green
*LIME GRN: .8X TO 2X BASIC
RANDOM INSERTS IN PACKS
STATED PRINT RUN 23 SER.#'d SETS
EXCHANGE DEADLINE 6/2/22
4 Zach Daniels 12.00 30.00

2020 Panini Prizm Draft Picks Fireworks Autographs Prizms Neon Orange
*NEON ORNG: .8X TO 2X BASIC
RANDOM INSERTS IN PACKS
STATED PRINT RUN 20 SER.#'d SETS
EXCHANGE DEADLINE 6/2/22
4 Zach Daniels 12.00 30.00

2020 Panini Prizm Draft Picks Fireworks Autographs Prizms Red Donut Circles
*RED DONUT/75-99: .5X TO 1.2X BASIC
*RED DONUT/35: .6X TO 1.5X BASIC
RANDOM INSERTS IN PACKS
PRINT RUNS B/WN 35-99 COPIES PER
EXCHANGE DEADLINE 6/2/22
10 Petey Halpin/99 6.00 15.00
12 Luke Little/99 4.00 10.00

2020 Panini Prizm Draft Picks Fireworks Autographs Prizms Tiger Stripes
4 Zach Daniels 12.00 30.00

2020 Panini Prizm Draft Picks Power Surge
RANDOM INSERTS IN PACKS
*BLUE: .5X TO 1.2X BASIC
*BLUE MOJO: .5X TO 1.2X BASIC
*BLUE WAVE: .5X TO 1.2X BASIC
*RED: .5X TO 1.2X BASIC
*RED MOJO: .5X TO 1.2X BASIC
*RED WAVE: .5X TO 1.2X BASIC
*BL.CAR.BL.HYP.: .5X TO 1.2X BASIC
*GRN YLW HYP.: .5X TO 1.2X BASIC
*PRPL RED HYP.: .5X TO 1.2X BASIC
*GRN PLSR.: .5X TO 1.2X BASIC
*SILVER.: .5X TO 1.2X BASIC
1 Spencer Torkelson 2.50 6.00
2 Nick Gonzales 1.25 3.00
3 Austin Hendrick 2.50 6.00
4 A.J. Vukovich .50 1.25
5 Jordan Walker .75 2.00
6 Garrett Mitchell 2.00 5.00
7 Aaron Sabato .50 1.25
8 Jordan Westburg .60 1.50
9 Alerick Soularie .30 .75
10 Alec Burleson .40 1.00
11 Casey Martin .75 2.00
12 Austin Wells 1.00 2.50

2020 Panini Prizm Draft Picks Power Surge Prizms Blue Donut Circles
*BLUE DONUT: 2.5X TO 6X BASIC
RANDOM INSERTS IN PACKS
STATED PRINT RUN 25 SER.#'d SETS
1 Spencer Torkelson 20.00 50.00
2 Nick Gonzales 10.00 25.00

2020 Panini Prizm Draft Picks Power Surge Prizms Burgundy Cracked Ice
*BRGNDY ICE: 2.5X TO 6X BASIC
RANDOM INSERTS IN PACKS
STATED PRINT RUN 23 SER.#'d SETS
1 Spencer Torkelson 25.00 60.00
2 Nick Gonzales 10.00 25.00

2020 Panini Prizm Draft Picks Power Surge Prizms Lime Green
*LIME GRN: 1.2X TO 3X BASIC
RANDOM INSERTS IN PACKS
STATED PRINT RUN 75 SER.#'d SETS
1 Spencer Torkelson 10.00 25.00

2020 Panini Prizm Draft Picks Power Surge Prizms Neon Orange
*NEON ORNG: 1.5X TO 4X BASIC
RANDOM INSERTS IN PACKS
STATED PRINT RUN 50 SER.#'d SETS
1 Spencer Torkelson 12.00 30.00

2020 Panini Prizm Draft Picks Power Surge Prizms Power Plaid
*PLAID: 2X TO 5X BASIC
RANDOM INSERTS IN PACKS
STATED PRINT RUN 35 SER.#'d SETS
1 Spencer Torkelson 15.00 40.00
2 Nick Gonzales 8.00 20.00

2020 Panini Prizm Draft Picks Power Surge Prizms Red Donut Circles
*RED DONUT: 1.2X TO 3X BASIC
RANDOM INSERTS IN PACKS
STATED PRINT RUN 99 SER.#'d SETS
1 Spencer Torkelson 10.00 25.00

2020 Panini Prizm Draft Picks Power Surge Prizms Snake Skin
*SNAKE SKN: 2.5X TO 6X BASIC
RANDOM INSERTS IN PACKS
STATED PRINT RUN 25 SER.#'d SETS
1 Spencer Torkelson 20.00 50.00
2 Nick Gonzales 10.00 25.00

2020 Panini Prizm Draft Picks Power Surge Prizms Tiger Stripes
*TIGER: 1.2X TO 3X BASIC
RANDOM INSERTS IN PACKS
STATED PRINT RUN 99 SER.#'d SETS
1 Spencer Torkelson 10.00 25.00
2 Nick Gonzales 15.00 40.00

2020 Panini Prizm Draft Picks Power Surge Prizms White Donut Circles
*WHT DONUT: 1.5X TO 4X BASIC
RANDOM INSERTS IN PACKS
STATED PRINT RUN 50 SER.#'d SETS
1 Spencer Torkelson 12.00 30.00

2020 Panini Prizm Draft Picks Power Surge Autographs Prizms Silver
RANDOM INSERTS IN PACKS
EXCHANGE DEADLINE 6/2/22
1 Spencer Torkelson 40.00 100.00
2 Nick Gonzales 10.00 25.00
3 Austin Hendrick 12.00 30.00
4 A.J. Vukovich
5 Jordan Walker 6.00 15.00
6 Garrett Mitchell 12.00 30.00
7 Aaron Sabato 10.00 25.00
8 Jordan Westburg 4.00 10.00
9 Alerick Soularie 2.50 6.00
10 Alec Burleson 3.00 8.00
11 Casey Martin 10.00 25.00
12 Austin Wells 8.00 20.00

2020 Panini Prizm Draft Picks Power Surge Autographs Prizms Blue
*BLUE: .5X TO 1.2X BASIC
RANDOM INSERTS IN PACKS
STATED PRINT RUN 60 SER.#'d SETS
EXCHANGE DEADLINE 6/2/22
1 Spencer Torkelson 75.00 200.00
2 Nick Gonzales 20.00 50.00

2020 Panini Prizm Draft Picks Power Surge Autographs Prizms Blue Donut Circles
*BLUE DONUT: .8X TO 2X BASIC
RANDOM INSERTS IN PACKS
STATED PRINT RUN 25 SER.#'d SETS
EXCHANGE DEADLINE 6/2/22
1 Spencer Torkelson 125.00 300.00
2 Nick Gonzales 30.00 80.00

2020 Panini Prizm Draft Picks Power Surge Autographs Prizms Lime Green
*LIME GRN: .8X TO 2X BASIC
RANDOM INSERTS IN PACKS
STATED PRINT RUN 23 SER.#'d SETS
EXCHANGE DEADLINE 6/2/22
1 Spencer Torkelson 125.00 300.00
2 Nick Gonzales 30.00 80.00
5 Jordan Walker 15.00 40.00

2020 Panini Prizm Draft Picks Power Surge Autographs Prizms Neon Orange
*NEON ORNG: .8X TO 2X BASIC
RANDOM INSERTS IN PACKS
STATED PRINT RUN 20 SER.#'d SETS
EXCHANGE DEADLINE 6/2/22
1 Spencer Torkelson 125.00 300.00
2 Nick Gonzales 30.00 80.00
5 Jordan Walker 15.00 40.00

2020 Panini Prizm Draft Picks Power Surge Autographs Prizms Red
*RED: .6X TO 1.5X BASIC
RANDOM INSERTS IN PACKS
STATED PRINT RUN 50 SER.#'d SETS
EXCHANGE DEADLINE 6/2/22
1 Spencer Torkelson 100.00 250.00
2 Nick Gonzales 25.00 60.00

2020 Panini Prizm Draft Picks Power Surge Autographs Prizms Red Donut Circles
1 Spencer Torkelson/99 75.00 200.00
2 Nick Gonzales/75 20.00 50.00

2020 Panini Prizm Draft Picks Power Surge Autographs Prizms Tiger Stripes
*TIGER .8X TO 2X BASIC
RANDOM INSERTS IN PACKS
STATED PRINT RUN 25 SER.#'d SETS
EXCHANGE DEADLINE 6/2/22
1 Spencer Torkelson 125.00 300.00
2 Nick Gonzales 30.00 80.00
5 Jordan Walker 15.00 40.00

2020 Panini Prizm Draft Picks Power Surge Autographs Prizms White Donut Circles
*WHT DONUT: .6X TO 1.5X BASIC
RANDOM INSERTS IN PACKS
STATED PRINT RUN 50 SER.#'d SETS
EXCHANGE DEADLINE 6/2/22
1 Spencer Torkelson 100.00 250.00
2 Nick Gonzales 25.00 60.00

2020 Panini Prizm Draft Picks Thunderstruck
RANDOM INSERTS IN PACKS
*BLUE: .5X TO 1.2X BASIC
*BLUE MOJO: .5X TO 1.2X BASIC
*BLUE WAVE: .5X TO 1.2X BASIC
*RED: .5X TO 1.2X BASIC
*RED MOJO: .5X TO 1.2X BASIC
*RED WAVE: .5X TO 1.2X BASIC
*BL.CAR.BL.HYP.: .5X TO 1.2X BASIC
*GRN YLW HYP.: .5X TO 1.2X BASIC
*PRPL RED HYP.: .5X TO 1.2X BASIC
*GRN PLSR.: .5X TO 1.2X BASIC
*SILVER.: .5X TO 1.2X BASIC
*RED DONUT: 1.2X TO 3X BASIC
*TIGER: 1.2X TO 3X BASIC
*LIME GRN: 1.2X TO 3X BASIC
1 Max Meyer 1.00 2.50
2 Asa Lacy 1.50 4.00
3 LJ Jones IV .40 1.00
4 Robert Hassell 2.00 5.00
5 Nick Yorke 1.25 3.00
6 Hayden Cantrelle .25 .60
7 Joey Wiemer .40 1.00
8 Milan Tolentino .40 1.00
9 Nick Loftin .40 1.00
10 Alika Williams .30 .75
11 Trevor Hauver .40 1.00
12 Hudson Haskin 1.00 2.50

2020 Panini Prizm Draft Picks Thunderstruck Prizms Blue Donut Circles
*BLUE DONUT: 2.5X TO 6X BASIC
RANDOM INSERTS IN PACKS
STATED PRINT RUN 25 SER.#'d SETS
2 Asa Lacy 12.00 30.00

2020 Panini Prizm Draft Picks Thunderstruck Prizms Burgundy Cracked Ice
*BRGNDY ICE: 2.5X TO 6X BASIC
RANDOM INSERTS IN PACKS
STATED PRINT RUN 23 SER.#'d SETS
2 Asa Lacy 12.00 30.00

2020 Panini Prizm Draft Picks Thunderstruck Prizms Power Plaid
*PLAID: 2X TO 5X BASIC
RANDOM INSERTS IN PACKS
STATED PRINT RUN 35 SER.#'d SETS
2 Asa Lacy 10.00 25.00

2020 Panini Prizm Draft Picks Thunderstruck Prizms Snake Skin
*SNAKE SKN: 2.5X TO 6X BASIC
RANDOM INSERTS IN PACKS
STATED PRINT RUN 25 SER.#'d SETS
2 Asa Lacy 12.00 30.00

2020 Panini Prizm Draft Picks Thunderstruck Autographs Prizms Silver
RANDOM INSERTS IN PACKS
EXCHANGE DEADLINE 6/2/22
*RED DONUT/75-99: .5X TO 1.2X BASIC
*RED DONUT/25: .8X TO 2X BASIC
*BLUE/60: .5X TO 1.2X BASIC
*BLUE/50: .6X TO 1.5X BASIC
*RED/35-50: .6X TO 1.5X BASIC
*WHT DONUT/35-50: .6X TO 1.5X BASIC
*WHT DONUT/25: .8X TO 2X BASIC
*BLUE DONUT/25: .8X TO 2X BASIC
*TIGER/25 .8X TO 2X BASIC
*LIME GRN/23: .8X TO 2X BASIC
*NEON ORNG/20: .8X TO 2X BASIC
1 Max Meyer 8.00 20.00
2 Asa Lacy 10.00 25.00
4 Robert Hassell 10.00 25.00
5 Nick Yorke 10.00 25.00
6 Hayden Cantrelle 2.00 5.00
7 Joey Wiemer 3.00 8.00
8 Milan Tolentino 3.00 8.00
9 Nick Loftin 3.00 8.00
10 Alika Williams 2.50 6.00
12 Hudson Haskin 3.00 8.00

2013 Panini Prizm Perennial Draft Picks
1 Adalberto Mondesi .30 .75
2 Amed Rosario .30 .75
3 Alen Hanson .25 .60
4 Alex Yarbrough .20 .50
5 Andy Burns .20 .50
6 Anthony DeSclafani .20 .50
7 Anthony Garcia .30 .75
8 Archie Bradley .20 .50
9 Cameron Flynn .20 .50
10 Cameron Perkins .20 .50
11 Carlos Correa 2.50 6.00
12 Chad Rogers .20 .50
13 Chris Taylor .30 .75
14 Clint Coulter .20 .50
16 Cory Vaughn .20 .50
17 D.J. Baxendale .20 .50
18 Daniel Fields .20 .50
19 Daniel Winkler .20 .50
20 Devon Travis .30 .75
21 Dixon Machado .20 .50
22 Drew VerHagen .25 .60
23 Eugenio Suarez .40 1.00
24 Francisco Sosa .20 .50
25 Garin Cecchini .20 .50
26 Gregory Polanco .40 1.00
27 Trey Michalczewski .20 .50
28 Jason Coats .20 .50
29 Jayce Boyd .20 .50
30 Jeremy Rathjen .20 .50
31 Jesus Solorzano .20 .50
32 Jose Abreu 1.50 4.00
33 Joey Gallo .60 1.50
34 Jorge Alfaro .40 1.00
35 Kaleb Cowart .25 .60
36 Kyle Zimmer .25 .60
37 Luis Torrens .30 .75
38 Maikel Franco .30 .75
39 Matt Duffy .30 .75
40 Matt Lipka .20 .50
41 Max Muncy .75 2.00
42 Micah Johnson .25 .60
43 Miguel Almonte .20 .50
44 Mike Foltynewicz .20 .50
45 Mike O'Neill .20 .50
46 Mookie Betts 10.00 25.00
47 Orlando Castro .20 .50
48 Preston Beck .20 .50
49 Rainy Lara .20 .50
50 Richie Shaffer .20 .50
51 Roberto Osuna .20 .50
52 Rock Shoulders .20 .50
53 Ronny Carvajal .20 .50
54 Rosell Herrera .25 .60
55 Stetson Allie .30 .75
56 Tyler Heineman .20 .50
57 Vincent Velasquez .30 .75
58 Walker Gourley .20 .50
59 Yancarlos Baez .20 .50
60 Zach Borenstein .30 .75
61 Austin Wilson .25 .60
62 Andrew Thurman .25 .60
63 Ivan Wilson .20 .50
64 Stuart Turner .20 .50
65 Cord Sandberg .25 .60
66 Brandon Dixon .25 .60
67 Carter Hope .25 .60
68 Dace Kime .20 .50
69 Daniel Palka .20 .50
70 Ryan Walker .20 .50
71 Jacob May .20 .50
72 Trevor Williams .20 .50
73 Gosuke Katoh .25 .60
74 Dillon Overton .20 .50
75 Stephen Gonsalves .20 .50
76 Colby Suggs .25 .60
77 Tom Windle .20 .50
78 K.J. Woods .20 .50
79 Luke Farrell .20 .50
80 Brian Navarreto .20 .50
81 Brian Ragira .20 .50
82 Ryan Boldt .20 .50
83 Cory Thompson .20 .50
84 Ryan Aper .20 .50
85 Kevin Franklin .20 .50
86 Jonah Heim .20 .50
87 Johnny Field .20 .50
88 Blake Taylor .20 .50
89 Chance Sisco .40 1.00
90 Sam Moll .25 .60
91 Jake Sweaney .20 .50
92 Tyler Wade .30 .75
93 Trae Arbet .20 .50
94 Chris Kohler .25 .60
95 Brandon Diaz .20 .50
96 Kean Wong .20 .50
97 Ben Verlander .25 .60
98 Rob Zastryzny .30 .75
99 Andrew Church .20 .50
100 Oscar Mercado .30 .75
101 Mark Appel DC .60 1.50
102 Kris Bryant DC 2.50 6.00
103 Jonathan Gray DC .50 1.25
104 Kohl Stewart DC .50 1.25
105 Clint Frazier DC 2.00 5.00
106 Colin Moran DC .50 1.25
107 Trey Ball DC .60 1.50
108 Hunter Dozier DC .40 1.00
109 Austin Meadows DC 1.00 2.50
110 Kyle Crockett DC .40 1.00
111 Dominic Smith DC .60 1.50
112 D.J. Peterson DC .40 1.00
113 Hunter Renfroe DC .60 1.50
114 Reese McGuire DC .50 1.25
115 Braden Shipley DC .40 1.00
116 J.P. Crawford DC .60 1.50
117 Tim Anderson DC 1.50 4.00
118 Chris Anderson DC .50 1.25
119 Marco Gonzales DC .60 1.50
120 Jonathon Crawford DC .40 1.00
121 Nick Ciuffo DC .40 1.00
122 Hunter Harvey DC .50 1.25
123 Alex Gonzalez DC .60 1.50
124 Billy McKinney DC .50 1.25
126 Eric Jagielo DC .50 1.25
127 Phillip Ervin DC .40 1.00
128 Rob Kaminsky DC .50 1.25
129 Ryne Stanek DC .75 2.00
130 Travis Demeritte DC .50 1.25
131 Jason Hursh DC .40 1.00
132 Aaron Judge DC 10.00 25.00
133 Ian Clarkin DC .40 1.00
134 Sean Manaea DC .40 1.00
135 Cody Stubbs DC .40 1.00
136 Aaron Blair DC .40 1.00
137 Josh Hart DC .40 1.00
138 Michael Lorenzen DC .50 1.25
139 Corey Knebel DC .40 1.00
140 Ryan McMahon DC 1.00 2.50
141 Dustin Peterson DC .40 1.00
142 Andrew Knapp DC .40 1.00
143 Riley Unroe DC .40 1.00
144 Teddy Stankiewicz DC .50 1.25
145 Ryder Jones DC .60 1.50
146 Victor Caratini DC 1.25 3.00
147 Jonathan Denney DC .50 1.25
148 Tucker Neuhaus DC .40 1.00
149 Michael O'Neill DC .40 1.00
150 Drew Ward DC .50 1.25

2013 Panini Prizm Perennial Draft Picks Blue Prizms
*BLUE 1-100: 1.5X TO 4X BASIC
*BLUE 101-150: .75X TO 2X BASIC
STATED PRINT RUN 75 SER.#'d SETS

2013 Panini Prizm Perennial Draft Picks Green Prizms
*GREEN PRIZMS 1-100: 1.2X TO 3X BASIC
*GREEN PRIZMS 101-150: .6X TO 1.5X BASIC

2013 Panini Prizm Perennial Draft Picks Prizms
*PRIZMS 1-100: 1X TO 2.5X BASIC
*PRIZMS 101-150: .5X TO 1.2X BASIC

2013 Panini Prizm Perennial Draft Picks Red Prizms
*RED 1-100: 1.5X TO 4X BASIC
*RED 101-150: .75X TO 2X BASIC
STATED PRINT RUN 100 SER.#'d SETS

2013 Panini Prizm Perennial Draft Picks Draft Hits
*PRIZMS: .6X TO 1.5X BASIC
1 Carson Kelly .60 1.50
2 Rio Ruiz .50 1.25
3 Nick Williams .60 1.50
4 Max Muncy 2.00 5.00
5 Tom Murphy .50 1.25
6 Jake Thompson .50 1.25
7 Chase DeJong .30 .75
8 Jairo Beras .75 2.00
9 Alex Yarbrough .50 1.25
10 Brady Rodgers .30 .75
11 Preston Beck .50 1.25
12 Zach Green .30 .75
13 Ross Stripling .50 1.25
14 Josh Turley .30 .75
15 Steve Bean .75 2.00
16 James Ramsey .30 .75
17 Austin Wilson .60 1.50
18 Dustin Peterson .50 1.25
19 Michael O'Neill .50 1.25
20 Brian Ragira .50 1.25
21 Austin Schotts .60 1.50
22 Micah Johnson .60 1.50
23 Stetson Allie .75 2.00
24 Garin Cecchini .50 1.25
25 Joc Pederson 1.25 3.00

2013 Panini Prizm Perennial Draft Picks Draft Hits Green Prizms
*GREEN: .75X TO 2X BASIC

2013 Panini Prizm Perennial Draft Picks First Overall Picks
STATED PRINT RUN 50 SER.#'d SETS
1 Rick Monday 2.50 6.00
2 Ron Blomberg 2.50 6.00
3 Harold Baines 3.00 8.00
4 Bob Horner 2.50 6.00
5 Jeff King 1.50 4.00
6 Ken Griffey Jr. 40.00 100.00
7 Ben McDonald 2.50 6.00
8 Chipper Jones 4.00 10.00
9 Pat Burrell 2.50 6.00
10 Carlos Correa 30.00 80.00

2013 Panini Prizm Perennial Draft Picks High School All-America
STATED PRINT RUN 100 SER.#'d SETS
1 Tyler Danish 2.00 5.00
2 Reese McGuire 1.25 3.00
4 Ian Clarkin 1.00 2.50
5 Clint Frazier 5.00 12.00
6 Billy McKinney 1.25 3.00
7 J.P. Crawford 1.50 4.00
8 Kohl Stewart 1.25 3.00
9 Ryan McMahon 2.50 6.00
10 Nick Ciuffo 1.00 2.50
11 Kevin Franklin 1.00 2.50
12 Trey Ball 1.50 4.00
13 Austin Meadows 2.50 6.00
14 Riley Unroe 1.00 2.50
15 Rob Kaminsky 1.25 3.00
16 Dominic Smith 1.50 4.00
17 Hunter Green 1.00 2.50
18 Gosuke Katoh 1.25 3.00
19 Dustin Peterson 1.00 2.50
20 Jonathan Denney 1.25 3.00

2013 Panini Prizm Perennial Draft Picks High School All-America Green Prizms
*GREEN: .5X TO 1.2X BASIC

2013 Panini Prizm Perennial Draft Picks Minors
1 Courtney Hawkins .50 1.25
2 Kaleb Cowart .60 1.50
3 Archie Bradley .50 1.25
4 Bubba Starling .60 1.50
5 Byron Buxton 2.50 6.00
6 Carlos Correa 6.00 15.00
7 Maikel Franco .75 2.00
8 Lucas Giolito .75 2.00
9 Addison Russell .75 2.00
10 Rio Ruiz .50 1.25
11 J.O. Berrios .75 2.00
12 Tom Murphy .50 1.25
13 Nick Williams .60 1.50
14 Sean Gilmartin .50 1.25
15 Stefen Romero .50 1.25
16 Max Fried 2.00 5.00
17 Dylan Bundy 1.25 3.00
18 Kris Bryant 3.00 8.00
19 Austin Meadows 1.25 3.00
20 Michael Kelly .30 .75
21 Reese McGuire .60 1.50
22 Kohl Stewart .60 1.50
23 D.J. Peterson .50 1.25
24 Mark Appel .75 2.00
25 Jonathan Gray .60 1.50

2013 Panini Prizm Perennial Draft Picks Minors Green Prizms
*GREEN: .75X TO 2X BASIC

2013 Panini Prizm Perennial Draft Picks Minors Prizms
*PRIZMS: .6X TO 1.5X BASIC

2013 Panini Prizm Perennial Draft Picks Press Clippings
STATED PRINT RUN 100 SER.#'d SETS
1 Micah Johnson 1.25 3.00
2 Joey Gallo 3.00 8.00
3 Bubba Starling 1.25 3.00
4 Alen Hanson 1.25 3.00
5 Mark Appel 1.50 4.00
6 Kris Bryant 6.00 15.00
7 Mark Appel 1.50 4.00
8 Carlos Correa 12.00 30.00
9 Travis Demeritte 1.25 3.00
10 Max Muncy 4.00 10.00
11 Alex Yarbrough 1.00 2.50
12 Cory Vaughn 1.00 2.50
13 Rosell Herrera 1.25 3.00
14 Joc Pederson 2.50 6.00
15 Andy Burns 1.00 2.50
16 Jacob May 1.00 2.50
17 Carlos Correa 12.00 30.00
18 D.J. Peterson 1.00 2.50
19 Robert Refsnyder 1.25 3.00
20 Andrew Heaney 1.25 3.00

2013 Panini Prizm Perennial Draft Picks Press Clippings Green Prizms
*GREEN: .5X TO 1.2X BASIC

2013 Panini Prizm Perennial Draft Picks Prospect Signatures
EXCHANGE DEADLINE 4/30/2015
1 Mark Appel 5.00 12.00
2 Austin Wilson 3.00 8.00
3 Clint Frazier 8.00 20.00
4 Kohl Stewart 5.00 12.00
5 Colin Moran 3.00 8.00
6 Kris Bryant 40.00 100.00
7 Trey Ball 6.00 15.00

8 Hunter Dozier 4.00 10.00
9 Austin Meadows 6.00 15.00
10 Cody Stubbs 3.00 8.00
11 Dominic Smith 6.00 15.00
12 D.J. Peterson 5.00 12.00
13 Dustin Peterson 3.00 8.00
14 Hunter Renfroe 3.00 8.00
15 Reese McGuire 3.00 8.00
16 Braden Shipley 3.00 8.00
17 J.P. Crawford 3.00 8.00
18 Tim Anderson 3.00 8.00
19 Chris Anderson 3.00 8.00
20 Marco Gonzales 3.00 8.00
21 Jonathon Crawford 3.00 8.00
22 Nick Ciuffo 3.00 8.00
23 Hunter Harvey 4.00 10.00
24 Alex Gonzalez 6.00 15.00
25 Billy McKinney 3.00 8.00
26 Eric Jagielo 3.00 8.00
27 Phillip Ervin 3.00 8.00
29 Rob Kaminsky 4.00 10.00
30 Travis Demeritte 3.00 8.00
31 Ryne Stanek 3.00 8.00
32 Jason Hursh 3.00 8.00
33 Aaron Judge 60.00 150.00
34 Ian Clarkin 3.00 8.00
35 Sean Manaea 3.00 8.00
36 Andrew Knapp 3.00 8.00
37 Ryan McMahon 6.00 15.00
38 Corey Knebel 3.00 8.00
39 Josh Hart 3.00 8.00
40 Aaron Blair 3.00 8.00
41 Maikel Franco 10.00 25.00
42 Riley Unroe 3.00 8.00
43 Jonathan Denney 4.00 10.00
44 Ryder Jones 3.00 8.00
45 Victor Caratini 3.00 8.00
46 Tucker Neuhaus 3.00 8.00
47 Michael O'Neill 4.00 10.00
48 Jose Abreu 15.00 40.00
49 Byron Buxton 8.00 20.00
50 Kevin Franklin 3.00 8.00
51 Jacob May 3.00 8.00
52 Ivan Wilson 3.00 8.00
53 Gosuke Katoh 3.00 8.00
54 Rob Zastryzny 3.00 8.00
55 Oscar Mercado 3.00 8.00
56 Adalberto Mondesi 6.00 15.00
57 Luis Torrens 3.00 8.00
58 Jayce Boyd 3.00 8.00
59 Archie Bradley 6.00 15.00
60 Cory Vaughn 3.00 8.00
61 D.J. Baxendale 3.00 8.00
62 Dixon Machado 3.00 8.00
63 Rosell Herrera 3.00 8.00
64 Stetson Allie 6.00 15.00
65 Roberto Osuna 3.00 8.00
66 Amed Rosario 4.00 10.00
67 Chad Rogers 3.00 8.00
68 Kaleb Cowart 3.00 8.00
69 Francisco Sosa EXCH 3.00 8.00
70 Alex Yarbrough 3.00 8.00
71 Matt Duffy 3.00 8.00
72 Rock Shoulders 3.00 8.00
73 Rainy Lara 3.00 8.00
74 Yancarlos Baez 3.00 8.00
76 Max Muncy 6.00 15.00
77 Anthony DeSclafani 3.00 8.00
78 Jorge Alfaro 3.00 8.00
79 Ben Verlander 3.00 8.00
80 Alen Hanson 3.00 8.00
81 Jeremy Rathjen 3.00 8.00
82 Miguel Almonte 3.00 8.00
83 Vincent Velasquez 5.00 12.00
84 Tyler Heineman 3.00 8.00
85 Micah Johnson 3.00 8.00
86 Chris Taylor 8.00 20.00
87 Andy Burns 3.00 8.00
88 Daniel Winkler 3.00 8.00
89 Eugenio Suarez 6.00 15.00
91 Anthony Garcia 3.00 8.00
92 Joc Pederson 8.00 20.00
94 Cameron Perkins 3.00 8.00
95 Mike Foltynewicz 4.00 10.00
96 Austin Kubitza 3.00 8.00
97 Mookie Betts 100.00 250.00
98 Devon Travis 3.00 8.00
99 Trey Michalczewski 3.00 8.00
100 Mike O'Neill 3.00 8.00

2013 Panini Prizm Perennial Draft Picks Prospect Signatures Blue Prizms

*BLUE: .6X TO 1.5X BASIC
STATED PRINT RUN 75 SER.#'d SETS
NO PRICING DUE TO SCARCITY

2013 Panini Prizm Perennial Draft Picks Prospect Signatures Green Prizms

*GREEN PRIZMS: .5X TO 1.2X BASIC

2013 Panini Prizm Perennial Draft Picks Prospect Signatures Prizms

*PRIZMS: .5X TO 1.2X BASIC
EXCHANGE DEADLINE 4/30/2015

2013 Panini Prizm Perennial Draft Picks Prospect Signatures Red Prizms

*RED: .6X TO 1.5X BASIC
STATED PRINT RUN 100 SER.#'d SETS
NO PRICING DUE TO SCARCITY

2013 Panini Prizm Perennial Draft Picks Stat Leaders

STATED PRINT RUN 100 SER.#'d SETS
1 Joey Gallo 3.00 8.00
2 Joey Gallo 3.00 8.00
3 Joey Gallo 3.00 8.00
4 Alex Yarbrough 1.00 2.50
5 Alex Yarbrough 1.00 2.50
6 Francisco Sosa 1.00 2.50
7 Rosell Herrera 1.25 3.00
8 Archie Bradley 1.00 2.50
9 Javier Baez 4.00 10.00
10 J.P. Crawford 1.50 4.00
11 J.P. Crawford 1.50 4.00
15 Riley Unroe 1.00 2.50
16 Ty Blach 1.00 2.50
17 Zach Borenstein 1.50 4.00
18 Zach Borenstein 1.50 4.00
19 Zach Borenstein 1.25 3.00
20 Zach Borenstein 1.50 4.00

2013 Panini Prizm Perennial Draft Picks Stat Leaders Green Prizms

*GREEN: .5X TO 1.2X BASIC

2013 Panini Prizm Perennial Draft Picks Top 10

STATED PRINT RUN 100 SER.#'d SETS
1 Carlos Correa 12.00 30.00
2 Byron Buxton 5.00 12.00
3 Mark Appel 1.50 4.00
4 Clint Frazier 5.00 12.00
5 Corey Seager 5.00 12.00
6 Jameson Taillon 1.25 3.00
7 Zach Lee 1.25 3.00
8 Kris Bryant 6.00 15.00
9 Joey Gallo 3.00 8.00
10 Nick Castellanos 3.00 8.00

2014 Panini Prizm Perennial Draft Picks

1 Carson Sands .25 .60
2 Dalton Pompey .40 1.00
3 Mark Zagunis .25 .60
4 Michael Cederoth .30 .75
5 Lane Thomas .40 1.00
6 Joe Gatto .25 .60
7 Aaron Brown .25 .60
8 Brett Graves .25 .60
9 Jake Cosart .30 .75
10 Jordan Luplow .25 .60
11 Grayson Greiner .25 .60
12 Eric Skoglund .25 .60
13 Sam Howard .25 .60
14 Michael Mader .25 .60
15 Cy Sneed .25 .60
16 Matt Railey .25 .60
17 Nick Wells .25 .60
18 Logan Webb .40 1.00
19 Jakson Reetz .25 .60
20 Spencer Turnbull .25 .60
21 Milton Ramos .25 .60
22 Chris Ellis .25 .60
23 Nick Torres .25 .60
24 Daniel Mengden .25 .60
25 Wyatt Strahan .25 .60
26 Brian Anderson .25 .60
27 Jake Peter .25 .60
28 Brett Austin .25 .60
29 Austin Cousino .25 .60
30 Jace Fry .25 .60
31 Chris Oliver .25 .60
32 Matt Morgan .25 .60
33 Taylor Sparks .25 .60
34 Troy Stokes .25 .60
35 Jeremy Rhoades .25 .60
36 Cameron Varga .25 .60
37 Jordan Montgomery .50 1.25
38 Gavin LaValley .25 .60
39 Grant Hockin .25 .60
40 Jordan Schwartz .25 .60
41 Alex Verdugo .50 1.25
42 Kevin McAvoy .25 .60
43 Austin Gomber .30 .75
44 Casey Soltis .25 .60
45 Zach Thompson .25 .60
46 Justin Steele .25 .60
47 Jake Reed .25 .60
48 Dan Altavilla .25 .60
49 Kevin Padlo .25 .60
50 J.D. Davis .40 1.00
51 Mitch Keller .40 1.00
52 Dustin DeMuth .25 .60
53 Auston Bousfield .25 .60
54 Jake Jewell .25 .60
55 Corey Ray .25 .60
56 Drew Van Orden .25 .60
57 Tejay Antone .25 .60
58 Sam Travis .30 .75
59 Jared Walker .25 .60
60 Michael Suchy .25 .60
61 Lane Ratliff .25 .60
62 Skyler Ewing .30 .75
63 Isan Diaz .60 1.50
64 Trace Loehr .25 .60
65 James Norwood .25 .60
66 Brandon Downes .30 .75
67 Reed Reilly .25 .60
68 Ryan O'Hearn .50 1.25
69 Jordan Brink .30 .75
70 Cole Lankford .25 .60
71 Gilbert Lara .25 .60
72 Adrian Rondon .30 .75
73 Raisel Iglesias .30 .75
74 Jhoandro Alfaro .25 .60
75 Luis Severino .40 1.00
76 Jacob Lindgren .30 .75
77 Scott Blewett .25 .60
78 Nelson Gomez .30 .75
79 Dermis Garcia .40 1.00
80 Jose Pujols .25 .60
81 Victor Arano .25 .60
82 Jorge Soler .50 1.25
83 Rusney Castillo .30 .75
84 Dariel Alvarez .25 .60
85 Malik Collymore .25 .60
86 Wes Rogers .25 .60
87 Joey Pankake .25 .60
88 Luke Dykstra .50 1.25
89 Logan Moon .30 .75
90 Mark Payton .25 .60
91 Jonathan Holder .25 .60
92 Deivi Grullon .25 .60
93 Jared Robinson .25 .60
94 John Richy .25 .60
95 Ross Kivett .25 .60
96 Trey Supak .25 .60
97 Derek Campbell .25 .60
98 Andy Ferguson .25 .60
99 Max George .25 .60
100 Marcus Wilson .25 .60

2014 Panini Prizm Perennial Draft Picks Prizms

*PRIZMS: .6X TO 1.5X BASIC
RANDOM INSERTS IN PACKS

2014 Panini Prizm Perennial Draft Picks Prizms Blue Mojo

*BLUE MOJO: 1.5X TO 4X BASIC
RANDOM INSERTS IN PACKS
STATED PRINT RUN 75 SER.#'d SETS

2014 Panini Prizm Perennial Draft Picks Prizms Green

*GREEN: 2.5X TO 6X BASIC
RANDOM INSERTS IN PACKS
STATED PRINT RUN 35 SER.#'d SETS

2014 Panini Prizm Perennial Draft Picks Prizms Orange

*ORANGE: 2X TO 5X BASIC
RANDOM INSERTS IN PACKS
STATED PRINT RUN 60 SER.#'d SETS

2014 Panini Prizm Perennial Draft Picks Prizms Powder Blue

*POWDER BLUE: 1X TO 2.5X BASIC
RANDOM INSERTS IN PACKS
STATED PRINT RUN 199 SER.#'d SETS

2014 Panini Prizm Perennial Draft Picks Prizms Purple

*PURPLE: 1.2X TO 3X BASIC
RANDOM INSERTS IN PACKS
STATED PRINT RUN 149 SER.#'d SETS

2014 Panini Prizm Perennial Draft Picks Prizms Red

*RED: 1.2X TO 3X BASIC
RANDOM INSERTS IN PACKS
STATED PRINT RUN 100 SER.#'d SETS

2014 Panini Prizm Perennial Draft Picks All-America Team Prizms

RANDOM INSERTS IN PACKS
STATED PRINT RUN 100 SER.#'d SETS
1 Braxton Davidson 1.00 2.50
2 Alex Jackson 1.25 3.00
3 Jacob Gatewood 1.00 2.50
4 Jack Flaherty 6.00 15.00
5 Grant Holmes 1.00 2.50
6 Justus Sheffield 2.00 5.00
7 Forrest Wall 1.50 4.00
8 Gareth Morgan 1.00 2.50
9 Cole Tucker 1.00 2.50
10 Alex Verdugo 2.00 5.00

2014 Panini Prizm Perennial Draft Picks Draft Class

COMPLETE SET (50) 20.00 50.00
RANDOM INSERTS IN PACKS
*PRIZMS: .6X TO 1.5X BASIC
*POWD.BLUE/199: 1X TO 2.5X BASIC
*PURPLE/149: 1.2X TO 3X BASIC
*RED/100: 1.2X TO 3X BASIC
*BLUE MOJO/75: 1.5X TO 4X BASIC
*ORANGE/60: 2X TO 5X BASIC
*GREEN/35: 2.5X TO 6X BASIC
1 Tyler Kolek .40 1.00
2 Carlos Rodon 1.00 2.50
3 Kyle Schwarber 1.50 4.00
4 Ti'Quan Forbes .40 1.00
5 Alex Jackson .50 1.25
6 Aaron Nola 2.50 6.00
7 Kyle Freeland .75 2.00
8 Jeff Hoffman .60 1.50
9 Michael Conforto .75 2.00
10 Max Pentecost .40 1.00
11 Kodi Medeiros .40 1.00
12 Trea Turner 1.25 3.00
13 Tyler Beede .60 1.50
14 Sean Newcomb .60 1.50
15 Brandon Finnegan .40 1.00
16 Erick Fedde .40 1.00
17 Nick Howard .40 1.00
18 Casey Gillaspie .60 1.50
19 Bradley Zimmer .60 1.50
20 Grant Holmes .40 1.00
21 Derek Hill .40 1.00
22 Cole Tucker .40 1.00
23 Matt Chapman 2.50 6.00
24 Michael Chavis 2.00 5.00
25 Luke Weaver 1.25 3.00
26 Foster Griffin .40 1.00
27 Alex Blandino .40 1.00
28 Luis Ortiz .40 1.00
29 Justus Sheffield .75 2.00
30 Braxton Davidson .40 1.00
31 Michael Kopech 2.50 6.00
32 Jack Flaherty 2.50 6.00
33 Forrest Wall .60 1.50
34 Scott Blewett .40 1.00
35 Derek Fisher .60 1.50
36 Isan Diaz 1.00 2.50
37 Connor Joe .40 1.00
38 Chase Vallot .40 1.00
39 Jacob Gatewood .40 1.00
40 A.J. Reed .75 2.00
41 Justin Twine .40 1.00
42 Spencer Adams .50 1.25
43 Jake Stinnett .40 1.00
44 Nick Burdi .40 1.00
45 Matt Imhof .40 1.00
46 Ryan Castellani .40 1.00
47 Sean Reid-Foley .40 1.00
48 Monte Harrison .75 2.00
49 Michael Gettys .50 1.25
50 Aramis Garcia .40 1.00

2014 Panini Prizm Perennial Draft Picks First Overall Prizms

RANDOM INSERTS IN PACKS
STATED PRINT RUN 100 SER.#'d SETS
1 Ken Griffey Jr. 10.00 25.00
2 Chipper Jones 8.00 20.00
3 Darryl Strawberry 8.00 20.00
4 Carlos Correa 8.00 20.00
5 Mark Appel 3.00 8.00
6 Rick Monday 8.00 20.00
7 Shawon Dunston 8.00 20.00
8 Bob Horner 8.00 20.00

2014 Panini Prizm Perennial Draft Picks Midnight Ink Die-Cut Autographs Mojo

RANDOM INSERTS IN PACKS
STATED PRINT RUN 50 SER.#'d SETS
MOST NOT PRICED DUE TO LACK OF INFO
EXCHANGE DEADLINE 5/12/2016
1 Alex Jackson 20.00 50.00
4 Trea Turner 20.00 50.00
5 Tyler Beede 20.00 50.00
8 Aaron Nola 30.00 80.00

2014 Panini Prizm Perennial Draft Picks Minors Gold Prizms

RANDOM INSERTS IN PACKS
1 Carlos Rodon 1.50 4.00
2 Tyler Kolek .60 1.50
3 Luis Severino 1.00 2.50
4 Alex Jackson .75 2.00
5 Jorge Alfaro .75 2.00
6 Sean Newcomb 1.00 2.50
7 Michael Conforto 1.25 3.00
8 Dalton Pompey 1.00 2.50
9 Kris Bryant 4.00 10.00
10 Aaron Nola 4.00 10.00
11 Byron Buxton 3.00 8.00
12 Kyle Schwarber 2.50 6.00
13 Kyle Freeland 1.25 3.00
14 Derek Hill .60 1.50
15 Jose Pujols .60 1.50
16 Trea Turner 2.00 5.00
17 Jorge Soler 1.25 3.00
18 Clint Frazier 2.50 6.00
19 Joey Gallo 1.25 3.00
20 David Dahl .75 2.00
21 Michael Chavis 3.00 8.00
22 Miguel Sano .75 2.00
23 Joey Pankake .60 1.50
24 Kohl Stewart .60 1.50
25 Miguel Almonte .60 1.50
26 Brandon Finnegan .60 1.50
27 Joc Pederson 1.50 4.00
28 Carlos Correa 3.00 8.00
29 Dominic Smith .60 1.50

2014 Panini Prizm Perennial Draft Picks Next Era Dual Autograph Prizms

RANDOM INSERTS IN PACKS
STATED PRINT RUN 25 SER.#'d SETS
MOST NOT PRICED DUE TO LACK OF INFO
EXCHANGE DEADLINE 5/12/2016
1 Hill/Ortiz 6.00 15.00
2 Pentecost/Chavis 15.00 40.00
6 Rondon/Lara EXCH 12.00 30.00

2014 Panini Prizm Perennial Draft Picks Prospect Ranker Prizms

RANDOM INSERTS IN PACKS
STATED PRINT RUN 100 SER.#'d SETS
1 Byron Buxton 5.00 12.00
2 Jonathan Gray 1.25 3.00
3 Jameson Taillon 1.25 3.00
4 Addison Russell 1.50 4.00
5 Kyle Zimmer 1.00 2.50
6 Dalton Pompey 1.50 4.00
7 Joey Gallo 2.00 5.00
8 Carlos Rodon 2.50 6.00
9 Tyler Kolek 1.00 2.50
10 Alex Jackson 1.25 3.00
11 Jorge Alfaro 1.25 3.00
12 Aaron Nola 6.00 15.00
13 Derek Hill 1.00 2.50
14 Michael Chavis 5.00 12.00
15 Monte Harrison 2.00 5.00
16 Casey Gillaspie 1.50 4.00
17 Foster Griffin 1.00 2.50
18 Nick Burdi 1.00 2.50
19 Dermis Garcia 1.50 4.00
20 Michael Gettys 1.25 3.00

2014 Panini Prizm Perennial Draft Picks Prospect Signatures Prizms

RANDOM INSERTS IN PACKS
*PRESS PROOF/199: .4X TO 1X BASIC
*PURPLE/149: .5X TO 1.2X BASIC
*RED/100: .5X TO 1.2X BASIC
*BLUE MOJO/75: .5X TO 1.2X BASIC
*ORANGE/60: .5X TO 1.2X BASIC
*GREEN/35: .6X TO 1.5X BASIC
EXCHANGE DEADLINE 5/12/2016
1 Tyler Kolek 3.00 8.00
2 Carlos Rodon 8.00 20.00
3 Kyle Schwarber 15.00 40.00
4 Jorge Soler 8.00 20.00
6 Alex Jackson 4.00 10.00
7 Aaron Nola 6.00 15.00
8 Kyle Freeland 6.00 15.00
9 Jeff Hoffman 5.00 12.00
10 Michael Conforto 10.00 25.00
11 Max Pentecost 3.00 8.00
12 Kodi Medeiros 3.00 8.00
13 Trea Turner 10.00 25.00
14 Tyler Beede 5.00 12.00
15 Sean Newcomb 5.00 12.00
16 Grayson Greiner 3.00 8.00
17 Brandon Finnegan 3.00 8.00
18 Erick Fedde 3.00 8.00
19 Nick Howard 3.00 8.00
20 Casey Gillaspie 5.00 12.00
21 Bradley Zimmer 5.00 12.00
22 Grant Holmes 3.00 8.00
23 Derek Hill 3.00 8.00
24 Cole Tucker 3.00 8.00
25 Matt Chapman 6.00 15.00
26 Michael Chavis 15.00 40.00
27 Luke Weaver 6.00 15.00
28 Foster Griffin 3.00 8.00
30 Luis Ortiz 3.00 8.00
31 Justus Sheffield 3.00 8.00
32 Braxton Davidson 3.00 8.00
34 Jack Flaherty 8.00 20.00
35 Forrest Wall 5.00 12.00
36 Eric Skoglund 3.00 8.00
37 Derek Fisher 5.00 12.00
38 Wyatt Strahan 3.00 8.00
39 Connor Joe 3.00 8.00
40 Chase Vallot 3.00 8.00
41 Jacob Gatewood 3.00 8.00
42 A.J. Reed 6.00 15.00
43 Justin Twine 3.00 8.00
44 Spencer Adams 4.00 10.00
45 Jake Stinnett 3.00 8.00
46 Nick Burdi 3.00 8.00
47 Matt Imhof 3.00 8.00
48 Ryan Castellani 3.00 8.00
49 Sean Reid-Foley 3.00 8.00
50 Josh Morgan 3.00 8.00
51 Troy Stokes 3.00 8.00
52 Aramis Garcia 3.00 8.00
53 Joe Gatto 3.00 8.00
55 Jacob Lindgren 4.00 10.00
56 Scott Blewett 3.00 8.00
57 Brian Schales 3.00 8.00
58 Taylor Sparks 3.00 8.00
59 Ti'Quan Forbes 3.00 8.00
60 Cameron Varga 3.00 8.00
61 Grant Hockin 3.00 8.00
64 Mitch Keller 5.00 12.00
65 Daniel Gossett 3.00 8.00
66 Nick Torres 3.00 8.00
67 Sam Travis 4.00 10.00
69 Marcus Wilson 3.00 8.00
70 Isan Diaz 8.00 20.00
71 Andrew Morales 3.00 8.00
72 Matt Morgan 3.00 8.00
73 Trey Supak 3.00 8.00
74 Gareth Morgan 3.00 8.00
75 Cy Sneed 3.00 8.00
76 Jeremy Rhoades 3.00 8.00
77 Jakson Reetz 3.00 8.00
78 Carson Sands 3.00 8.00
79 Lane Thomas 5.00 12.00
80 Raisel Iglesias 4.00 10.00
81 Dalton Pompey 5.00 12.00
84 Chris Ellis 3.00 8.00
86 Nelson Gomez 4.00 10.00
88 Brett Austin 3.00 8.00
89 Gavin LaValley 3.00 8.00
90 Luis Severino 5.00 12.00
91 Rusney Castillo 4.00 10.00

2014 Panini Prizm Perennial Draft Picks Top 10 Prizms

RANDOM INSERTS IN PACKS
STATED PRINT RUN 100 SER.#'d SETS
1 Carlos Rodon 2.50 6.00
2 Jorge Soler 2.00 5.00
3 Bradley Zimmer 1.50 4.00
4 J.P. Crawford 1.00 2.50
5 David Dahl 1.25 3.00
6 Rusney Castillo 1.25 3.00
7 Aaron Nola 6.00 15.00
8 Luis Severino 1.50 4.00
9 Kris Bryant 6.00 15.00
10 Dalton Pompey 1.50 4.00

2018 Panini Revolution

1 Ken Griffey Jr. .50 1.25
2 Mike Trout 1.25 3.00
3 Giancarlo Stanton .25 .60
4 Rafael Devers RC .75 2.00
5 Anthony Rizzo .30 .75
6 Shohei Ohtani RC 6.00 15.00
7 Mickey Mantle .75 2.00
8 Victor Robles RC .60 1.50
9 Miguel Andujar RC 1.00 2.50
10 Scott Kingery RC .40 1.00
11 J.P. Crawford RC .25 .60
12 Gleyber Torres RC 2.50 6.00
13 Kris Bryant .30 .75
14 Cal Ripken .75 2.00
15 Aaron Judge .60 1.50
16 Amed Rosario RC .30 .75
17 Mookie Betts .50 1.25
18 Clint Frazier RC .50 1.25
19 Jose Altuve .20 .50
20 Austin Hays RC .40 1.00
21 Bryce Harper .40 1.00
22 Ronald Acuna Jr. RC 8.00 20.00
23 Ozzie Albies RC .75 2.00
24 Rhys Hoskins RC 1.00 2.50
25 Cody Bellinger .50 1.25

2018 Panini Signatures

RANDOM INSERTS IN PACKS
*RED/199: .5X TO 1.2X BASIC
*PRPLE/99: .5X TO 1.2X
*HOLO SLVR/25: .75X TO 2X
*RED/25: .75X TO 2X BASIC
7 Brian Anderson 3.00 8.00
10 Nicky Delmonico 2.50 6.00
11 Zack Granite 2.50 6.00
12 Felix Jorge 2.50 6.00
13 Tomas Nido 2.50 6.00
14 Chris Flexen 2.50 6.00
15 Paul Blackburn 2.50 6.00
16 DJ Peters 6.00 15.00
19 Lane Adams 2.50 6.00
20 Freddy Peralta 2.50 6.00

2012 Panini Signature Series

101-150 AU PRINT RUN 299 SER.#'d SETS
151-175 PRINT RUN B/WN 49-99 COPIES PER
151-175 ISSUED IN NATIONAL TREASURES
EXCHANGE DEADLINE 05/07/2014
1 Adam Jones .75 2.00
2 Adrian Beltre 1.00 2.50
3 Adrian Gonzalez .75 2.00
4 Albert Pujols 1.25 3.00
5 Alcides Escobar .75 2.00
6 Alex Avila .60 1.50
7 Alex Gordon .75 2.00
8 Alex Rodriguez 1.25 3.00
9 Alfonso Soriano .75 2.00
10 Andre Ethier .75 2.00
11 Andrew McCutchen 1.00 2.50
12 Aramis Ramirez .60 1.50
13 Aroldis Chapman 1.00 2.50
14 Austin Jackson .75 2.00
15 Bill Bray .40 1.00
16 Billy Butler .60 1.50
17 Brett Gardner .75 2.00
18 Bryce Harper RC 10.00 25.00
19 Buster Posey 1.25 3.00
20 CC Sabathia .75 2.00
21 C.J. Wilson .60 1.50
22 Cameron Maybin .60 1.50
23 Carl Crawford .75 2.00
24 Carlos Santana .75 2.00
25 Chase Utley .75 2.00
26 Chipper Jones 1.00 2.50
27 Clayton Kershaw 1.50 4.00
28 Cliff Lee .75 2.00
29 Colby Rasmus .75 2.00
30 Curtis Granderson .75 2.00
31 David Freese .60 1.50
32 David Ortiz 1.00 2.50
33 David Price .75 2.00
34 David Wright .75 2.00
35 Derek Jeter 2.50 6.00
36 Drew Stubbs .60 1.50
37 Dustin Ackley .60 1.50
38 Dustin Pedroia 1.00 2.50
39 Edwin Encarnacion 1.00 2.50
40 Elvis Andrus .75 2.00
41 Eric Hosmer .75 2.00
42 Evan Longoria .75 2.00
43 Felix Hernandez .75 2.00
44 Freddie Freeman 1.25 3.00
45 Giancarlo Stanton 1.00 2.50
46 Hanley Ramirez .75 2.00
47 Hunter Pence .75 2.00
48 Ian Kennedy .60 1.50
49 Ian Kinsler .75 2.00
50 Ichiro Suzuki 1.25 3.00
51 Jacoby Ellsbury .75 2.00
52 Jake Peavy .60 1.50
53 James Shields .60 1.50
54 Jason Heyward .75 2.00
55 Jered Weaver .75 2.00
56 Jeremy Hellickson .60 1.50
57 Jimmy Rollins .75 2.00
58 Joe Mauer .75 2.00
59 Joey Votto 1.00 2.50
60 Jon Lester .60 1.50
61 Jose Altuve .75 2.00
62 Jose Bautista .75 2.00
63 Jose Reyes .60 1.50
64 Josh Beckett .60 1.50
65 Josh Hamilton .75 2.00
66 Josh Reddick .60 1.50
67 Justin Upton .75 2.00
68 Justin Verlander 1.00 2.50
69 Logan Morrison .60 1.50
70 Mariano Rivera 1.25 3.00
71 Mark Teixeira .75 2.00
72 Matt Joyce .60 1.50
73 Matt Kemp .75 2.00
74 Matt Wieters 1.00 2.50
75 Michael Bourn .60 1.50
76 Michael Young .60 1.50
77 Miguel Cabrera 1.00 2.50
78 Mike Moustakas .75 2.00
79 Mike Napoli .60 1.50
80 Mike Trout 30.00 80.00
81 Neftali Feliz .60 1.50
82 Nelson Cruz 1.00 2.50
83 Nick Swisher .75 2.00
84 Pablo Sandoval .75 2.00
85 Paul Konerko .60 1.50
86 Prince Fielder .75 2.00
87 Robinson Cano .75 2.00
88 Roy Halladay .75 2.00
89 Ryan Braun .60 1.50
90 Ryan Howard .75 2.00
91 Starlin Castro .75 2.00
92 Stephen Strasburg 1.00 2.50
94 Todd Helton .75 2.00
95 Travis Hafner .60 1.50
96 Troy Tulowitzki 1.00 2.50
97 Ubaldo Jimenez .60 1.50
98 Yadier Molina 1.25 3.00
99 Yovani Gallardo .75 2.00
100 Yu Darvish RC 1.50 4.00
101 A.J. Pollock AU RC 4.00 10.00
102 Addison Reed AU RC 4.00 10.00
103 Alex Liddi AU RC 4.00 10.00
104 Austin Romine AU RC 4.00 10.00
105 Brad Peacock AU RC 4.00 10.00
106 Brett Lawrie AU RC 10.00 25.00
107 Chris Marrero AU RC 4.00 10.00
108 Yasmani Grandal AU RC 5.00 12.00
109 Chris Schwinden AU RC 4.00 10.00
110 David Phelps AU RC 4.00 10.00
111 Dellin Betances AU RC 4.00 10.00
112 Devin Mesoraco AU RC 5.00 12.00
113 Drew Hutchison AU RC 4.00 10.00
114 Drew Pomeranz AU RC 6.00 15.00
115 Drew Smyly AU RC 6.00 15.00
116 Eric Surkamp AU RC 4.00 10.00
117 Freddy Galvis AU RC 5.00 12.00
118 Garrett Richards AU RC 10.00 25.00
119 Hector Sanchez AU RC 8.00 20.00
120 Jarrod Parker AU RC 8.00 20.00
121 Jemile Weeks AU RC 4.00 10.00
122 Jesus Montero AU RC 4.00 10.00
123 Joe Benson AU RC 4.00 10.00
124 Joe Wieland AU RC 4.00 10.00
125 Jordan Lyles AU 4.00 10.00
126 Jordany Valdespin AU RC 4.00 10.00
127 Jose Iglesias AU 6.00 15.00
128 Will Middlebrooks AU RC 12.00 30.00
129 Justin De Fratus AU RC 8.00 20.00
130 Kelvin Herrera AU RC 4.00 10.00
131 Kirk Nieuwenhuis AU RC 5.00 12.00
132 Liam Hendriks AU RC 4.00 10.00
133 Lucas Luetge AU RC 4.00 10.00
134 Marwin Gonzalez AU RC 4.00 10.00
135 Matt Dominguez AU RC 4.00 10.00
136 Matt Moore AU RC 6.00 15.00
137 Nick Hagadone AU RC 4.00 10.00
138 Pat Corbin AU RC 4.00 10.00
139 Robbie Ross AU RC 4.00 10.00
140 Ryan Cook AU RC 4.00 10.00
141 Steve Lombardozzi AU RC 6.00 15.00
142 Taylor Green AU RC 4.00 10.00
143 Tim Federowicz AU RC 4.00 10.00
144 Tom Milone AU RC 4.00 10.00
145 Tyler Moore AU RC 8.00 20.00
146 Tyler Pastornicky AU RC 4.00 10.00
147 Martin Perez AU RC 6.00 15.00
148 Wellington Castillo AU 4.00 10.00
149 Wilin Rosario AU RC 8.00 20.00
150 Yoenis Cespedes AU RC 6.00 15.00
151 Adeiny Hechavarria AU/99 RC 4.00 10.00
152 Andrelton Simmons AU/99 RC 8.00 20.00
153 Anthony Gose AU/99 RC 4.00 10.00
154 Brett Jackson AU/99 RC 6.00 15.00
155 Casey Crosby AU/99 RC 4.00 10.00
156 Chris Archer AU/99 RC 5.00 12.00
157 Chris Parmelee AU/99 RC 4.00 10.00
158 Dan Straily AU/99 RC 4.00 10.00
159 Derek Norris AU/99 RC 4.00 10.00
160 Jean Segura AU/99 RC 6.00 15.00
161 Jeff Locke AU/99 RC 4.00 10.00
162 Josh Rutledge AU/99 RC 5.00 12.00
163 Josh Vitters AU/99 RC 4.00 10.00
164 Leonys Martin AU/99 RC 6.00 15.00
165 Matt Adams AU/99 RC 4.00 10.00
166 Matt Harvey AU/99 RC 30.00 80.00
167 Rafael Dolis AU/99 RC 4.00 10.00
168 Scott Barnes AU/99 RC 4.00 10.00
169 Starling Marte AU/99 RC 10.00 25.00
170 Trevor Bauer AU/99 RC 10.00 25.00
171 Trevor Rosenthal AU/99 RC
172 Tyler Thornburg AU/99 RC 5.00 12.00
174 Wei-Yin Chen AU/49 RC 75.00 150.00
175 Zach McAllister AU/99 RC 4.00 10.00

2012 Panini Signature Series MLBPA Logo Signatures

PRINT RUNS B/WN 25-49 COPIES PER
NO PRICING ON MOST DUE TO SCARCITY
EXCHANGE DEADLINE 05/07/2014
7 Andrew McCutchen/49 15.00 40.00
39 Logan Morrison/49 4.00 10.00
49 Ubaldo Jimenez/49 4.00 10.00

2012 Panini Signature Series Rookie MLBPA Logo

101-150 PRINT RUN 299 SER.#'d SETS
151-175 PRINT RUN B/WN 49-99 PER
151-175 ISSUED IN NATIONAL TREASURES
EXCHANGE DEADLINE 05/07/2014
101 A.J. Pollock/299 4.00 10.00
102 Addison Reed/299 4.00 10.00
103 Alex Liddi/299 4.00 10.00
104 Austin Romine/299 4.00 10.00
105 Brad Peacock/299 4.00 10.00
106 Scott Barnes/299 4.00 10.00
107 Chris Marrero/299 4.00 10.00
108 Casey Crosby/299 4.00 10.00
109 Chris Schwinden/299 4.00 10.00
110 David Phelps/299 4.00 10.00
111 Dellin Betances/299 4.00 10.00
112 Devin Mesoraco/299 5.00 12.00
113 Drew Hutchison/299 4.00 10.00
114 Drew Pomeranz/299 6.00 15.00
115 Drew Smyly/299 6.00 15.00
116 Eric Surkamp/299 4.00 10.00
117 Freddy Galvis/299 5.00 12.00
118 Garrett Richards/299 10.00 25.00
119 Hector Sanchez/299 8.00 20.00
120 Jarrod Parker/299 8.00 20.00
121 Jemile Weeks/299 4.00 10.00
122 Rafael Dolis/299 4.00 10.00
123 Joe Benson/299 4.00 10.00
124 Joe Wieland/299 4.00 10.00
125 Jordan Lyles/299 4.00 10.00
126 Jordany Valdespin/299 4.00 10.00
127 Jose Iglesias/299 6.00 15.00
128 Will Middlebrooks/299 12.00 30.00
129 Justin De Fratus/299 8.00 20.00
130 Kelvin Herrera/299 4.00 10.00
131 Kirk Nieuwenhuis/299 5.00 12.00
132 Liam Hendriks/299 4.00 10.00
133 Lucas Luetge/299 4.00 10.00
134 Marwin Gonzalez/299 4.00 10.00
135 Matt Dominguez/299 4.00 10.00
136 Matt Moore/299 6.00 15.00
137 Nick Hagadone/299 4.00 10.00
138 Pat Corbin/299 4.00 10.00
139 Robbie Ross/299 4.00 10.00
140 Ryan Cook/299 4.00 10.00
141 Steve Lombardozzi/299 6.00 15.00
142 Taylor Green/299 4.00 10.00
143 Tim Federowicz/299 4.00 10.00
144 Tom Milone/299 4.00 10.00
145 Tyler Moore/299 8.00 20.00
146 Tyler Pastornicky/299 4.00 10.00
147 Matt Adams/299 6.00 15.00
148 Wellington Castillo/299 4.00 10.00
149 Wilin Rosario/299 8.00 20.00
150 Yoenis Cespedes/299 6.00 15.00
151 Adeiny Hechavarria/99 4.00 10.00
152 Andrelton Simmons/99 8.00 20.00
153 Anthony Gose/99 4.00 10.00
154 Brett Jackson/99 6.00 15.00
156 Chris Archer/99 5.00 12.00
157 Chris Parmelee/99 4.00 10.00
158 Dan Straily/99 4.00 10.00
159 Derek Norris/99 4.00 10.00
160 Jean Segura/99 6.00 15.00
161 Jeff Locke/99 4.00 10.00
162 Josh Rutledge/99 5.00 12.00
163 Josh Vitters/99 4.00 10.00
164 Leonys Martin/99 6.00 15.00
166 Matt Harvey/99 30.00 80.00
169 Starling Marte/99 10.00 25.00
170 Trevor Bauer/99 4.00 10.00
172 Tyler Thornburg/99 5.00 12.00
174 Wei-Yin Chen/49 75.00 150.00
175 Zach McAllister/99 4.00 10.00

2012 Panini Signature Series Rookies Game Ball Signatures

STATED PRINT RUN 299 SER.#'d SETS
EXCHANGE DEADLINE 05/07/2014
101 A.J. Pollock 4.00 10.00
102 Addison Reed 4.00 10.00
103 Alex Liddi 4.00 10.00
104 Austin Romine 4.00 10.00
105 Brad Peacock 4.00 10.00
107 Chris Marrero 4.00 10.00
108 Scott Barnes 4.00 10.00
109 Chris Schwinden 4.00 10.00
110 David Phelps 8.00 20.00
111 Dellin Betances 4.00 10.00
112 Devin Mesoraco 5.00 12.00
113 Drew Hutchison 8.00 20.00
114 Drew Pomeranz 6.00 15.00
115 Drew Smyly 6.00 15.00
116 Eric Surkamp 8.00 20.00
117 Freddy Galvis 5.00 12.00
118 Garrett Richards 10.00 25.00

119 Hector Sanchez 20.00 50.00
120 Jarrod Parker 8.00 20.00
121 Jemile Weeks 4.00 10.00
122 Matt Adams 4.00 10.00
123 Joe Benson 4.00 10.00
124 Joe Wieland 4.00 10.00
125 Jordan Lyles 5.00 12.00
126 Jordany Valdespin 4.00 10.00
127 Jose Iglesias 5.00 12.00
128 Will Middlebrooks 12.50 30.00
129 Justin De Fratus 8.00 20.00
130 Kelvin Herrera 4.00 10.00
131 Kirk Nieuwenhuis 5.00 12.00
132 Liam Hendriks 4.00 10.00
133 Lucas Luetge 4.00 10.00
134 Marwin Gonzalez 4.00 10.00
135 Matt Dominguez 4.00 10.00
136 Matt Moore 6.00 15.00
137 Nick Hagadone 4.00 10.00
138 Pat Corbin 4.00 10.00
139 Robbie Ross 4.00 10.00
140 Ryan Cook 4.00 10.00
141 Steve Lombardozzi 6.00 15.00
142 Taylor Green 4.00 10.00
143 Tim Federowicz 4.00 10.00
144 Tom Milone 4.00 10.00
145 Tyler Moore 8.00 20.00
146 Tyler Pastornicky 4.00 10.00
147 Zach McAllister 4.00 10.00
148 Wellington Castillo 4.00 10.00
149 Wilin Rosario 8.00 20.00
150 Trevor Bauer 12.00 30.00

2012 Panini Signature Series Signature Stamps

PRINT RUNS B/WN 3-50 COPIES PER
NO PRICING ON MOST DUE TO SCARCITY
EXCHANGE DEADLINE 05/07/2014
10 George Brett/50 30.00 60.00
17 Reggie Jackson/50 30.00 60.00
23 Whitey Ford/50 30.00 60.00

2012 Panini Signature Series Signatures

PRINT RUN B/WN 49-99 COPIES PER
NO PRICING ON MOST DUE TO LACK OF INFO
EXCHANGE DEADLINE 05/07/2014
2 Adrian Beltre/99 10.00 25.00
3 Adrian Gonzalez/99 8.00 20.00
4 Alex Avila/99 10.00 25.00
7 Andrew McCutchen/99 12.50 30.00
9 Austin Jackson/99 5.00 12.00
11 Brett Gardner/99 8.00 20.00
12 Buster Posey/49 50.00 100.00
13 CC Sabathia/99 4.00 10.00
16 Clayton Kershaw/99 40.00 100.00
21 David Ortiz/99 20.00 50.00
22 David Wright/49 20.00 50.00
23 Drew Stubbs/99 8.00 20.00
28 Felix Hernandez/99 12.50 30.00
32 Ian Kennedy/99 4.00 10.00
37 Josh Reddick/99 4.00 10.00
38 Justin Upton/99 10.00 25.00
39 Logan Morrison/99 6.00 15.00
40 Mariano Rivera/49 60.00 120.00
41 Matt Kemp/99 10.00 25.00
42 Miguel Cabrera/49 30.00 60.00
44 Neftali Feliz/99 4.00 10.00
45 Pablo Sandoval/49 15.00 40.00
48 Todd Helton/49 10.00 25.00
50 Yovani Gallardo/99 4.00 10.00

2019 Panini Signatures

RANDOM INSERTS IN PACKS
EXCHANGE DEADLINE 2/21/2021
*GOLD/99: .5X TO 1.2X
*GOLD/49: .6X TO 1.5X
*RED/50: .6X TO 1.5X
*RED/25: .75X TO 2X
*HOLO SLVR/23: .75X TO 2X
1 Yusniel Diaz 4.00 10.00
2 Darwinzon Hernandez 2.50 6.00
3 Dylan Cease 4.00 10.00
5 Keston Hiura 10.00 25.00
6 Carter Kieboom 4.00 10.00
7 Mitch Keller 3.00 8.00
8 Forrest Whitley 4.00 10.00
9 Brendan Rodgers 4.00 10.00
10 Jesus Luzardo 4.00 10.00

2017 Panini Spectra Rookie Jersey Autographs

INSERTED IN '17 CHRONICLES PACKS
EXCHANGE DEADLINE 5/22/2019
*NEON BLUE/99: .5X TO 1.2X BASIC
*PINK/49: .6X TO 1.5X BASIC
*NEON GREEN: .75X TO 2X BASIC
1 Andrew Benintendi 20.00 50.00
2 Yoan Moncada 10.00 25.00
3 Alex Bregman 25.00 60.00
4 Dansby Swanson 10.00 25.00
5 Ian Happ 5.00 12.00
6 Cody Bellinger 50.00 120.00
7 Aaron Judge 60.00 150.00
8 Trey Mancini 6.00 15.00
9 Jordan Montgomery 8.00 20.00
10 Bradley Zimmer 6.00 15.00
11 Mitch Haniger 6.00 15.00
12 Orlando Arcia 4.00 10.00
13 Alex Reyes 6.00 15.00
14 Tyler Glasnow 8.00 20.00
15 Manuel Margot 2.50 6.00
16 Hunter Renfroe 3.00 8.00
17 Jorge Bonifacio 2.50 6.00
18 Antonio Senzatela 2.50 6.00
19 Amir Garrett 4.00 10.00
20 David Dahl 3.00 8.00
21 Jorge Alfaro
22 Ryon Healy 5.00 12.00
23 Josh Bell 15.00 40.00
24 Lewis Brinson 5.00 12.00
25 Jacoby Jones 3.00 8.00

2017 Panini Spectra Signatures

INSERTED IN '17 CHRONICLES PACKS
PRINT RUNS B/WN 10-199 COPIES PER
NO PRICING ON QTY 15 OR LESS
EXCHANGE DEADLINE 5/22/2019
*NEON BLUE/35-60: .5X TO 1.2X p/r 199
*NEON BLUE/35-60: .4X TO 1X p/r 49-96
*NEON BLUE/20-25: .5X TO 1.2X p/r 49-96
*NEON GREEN/25: .6X TO 1.5X p/r 199
2 Brandon Belt/199 4.00 10.00
3 Ian Kinsler/49 5.00 12.00
4 Aaron Judge/199 60.00 150.00
5 Edwin Encarnacion/49 6.00 15.00
6 Mike Napoli/49 4.00 10.00
7 Byron Buxton/49 10.00 25.00
8 Alfonso Soriano/49 6.00 15.00
9 Wil Myers/25 6.00 15.00
10 Adam Duvall/96 5.00 12.00
13 Manny Machado/25 20.00 50.00
16 Mark Grace/49 10.00 25.00
17 Paul Goldschmidt/25 12.00 30.00
18 Nomar Mazara/199 3.00 8.00
19 Francisco Lindor/25 12.00 30.00
20 Nolan Arenado/25
21 Marcus Stroman/199 4.00 10.00
22 Xander Bogaerts/25 15.00 40.00
23 Yasmany Tomas/25 5.00 12.00
24 Jose Abreu/20

2017 Panini Spectra Signatures Neon Pink

*NEON PINK/35: .5X TO 1.2X p/r 199
*NEON PINK/35: .4X TO 1X p/r 49-96
*NEON PINK/20-25: .5X TO 1.2X p/r 49-96
INSERTED IN '17 CHRONICLES PACKS
PRINT RUNS B/WN 10-35 COPIES PER
NO PRICING ON QTY 15 OR LESS
EXCHANGE DEADLINE 5/22/2019
1 Hunter Pence/25 15.00 40.00

2017 Panini Spectra Triple Threat Materials

INSERTED IN '17 CHRONICLES PACKS
*NEON BLUE/49-99: .5X TO 1.2X p/r 149
*NEON BLUE/49-99: .4X TO 1X p/r 49-99
*PINK/49: .5X TO 1.2X p/r 149
*PINK/49: .4X TO 1X p/r 49-99
*PINK/25: .5X TO 1.2X p/r 49-99
*NEON GREEN/25: .6X TO 1.5X p/r 149
*NEON GREEN/25: .5X TO 1.2X p/r 49-99
1 Yoan Moncada/149 4.00 10.00
2 Andrew Benintendi/149 5.00 12.00
3 Cody Bellinger/149 5.00 12.00
4 Ian Happ/149 3.00 8.00
5 Dansby Swanson/149 4.00 10.00
6 Aaron Judge/149 20.00 50.00
7 Mickey Mantle/25 60.00 150.00
8 Alex Bregman/149 6.00 15.00
9 Mitch Haniger/149 4.00 10.00
10 Trey Mancini/149 3.00 8.00
12 Anthony Alford/149 1.50 4.00
13 Jordan Montgomery/149 2.50 6.00
14 Alex Reyes/149 2.00 5.00
15 David Dahl/149 2.00 5.00
16 Hunter Renfroe/149 2.00 5.00
17 Carson Fulmer/149 1.50 4.00
18 Antonio Senzatela/149 1.50 4.00
19 Tyler Glasnow/149 6.00 15.00
20 Jacoby Jones/149 2.00 5.00
21 Josh Bell/99 5.00 12.00
22 Starlin Castro/149 1.50 4.00
23 Jorge Bonifacio/149 1.50 4.00
24 Javier Baez/149 3.00 8.00
25 Clayton Kershaw/99 5.00 12.00
26 Gleyber Torres/149 6.00 15.00
27 Manny Machado/99 6.00 15.00
28 Justin Turner/99 3.00 8.00
29 Michael Conforto/149 2.00 5.00
30 Freddie Freeman/149 3.00 8.00
31 Marcell Ozuna/149 2.50 6.00
TTMJG Joey Gallo/149 2.50 6.00
33 Miguel Sano/149 2.00 5.00
34 Chris Davis/149 1.50 4.00
35 Giancarlo Stanton/49 8.00 20.00
36 Jose Abreu/149 2.50 6.00
TTMCS Chris Sale/99 3.00 8.00
38 Daniel Murphy/49 2.50 6.00
39 George Springer/149 4.00 10.00
40 Jacob deGrom/149 5.00 12.00
41 Yu Darvish/49 3.00 8.00
42 Dallas Keuchel/149 2.00 5.00
43 Andrew McCutchen/149 5.00 12.00
44 Billy Hamilton/149 2.00 5.00
45 Trea Turner/99 2.50 6.00
46 Jose Bautista/49 2.50 6.00
47 Brian Dozier/99 3.00 8.00
48 Jon Lester/149 2.00 5.00
49 Todd Frazier/149 1.50 4.00
50 Madison Bumgarner/49 2.50 6.00

2018 Panini Spectra Holo

INSERTED IN '18 CHRONICLES PACKS
1 Nolan Arenado .60 1.50
2 Carlos Correa .40 1.00
3 Cody Bellinger .75 2.00
4 Manny Machado .40 1.00
5 Noah Syndergaard .30 .75
6 Eric Hosmer .30 .75
7 Mickey Mantle 1.00 2.50
8 Max Scherzer .40 1.00
9 Nolan Ryan 1.25 3.00
10 Francisco Mejia RC .50 1.25
11 Yadier Molina .50 1.25
12 Ryan Braun .30 .75
13 Albert Pujols .50 1.25
14 Khris Davis .40 1.00
15 Gary Sanchez .40 1.00
16 Corey Kluber .30 .75
17 Whit Merrifield .40 1.00
18 Mitch Garver .25 .60
19 Aaron Judge 1.00 2.50
20 Gerrit Cole .40 1.00
21 Nicky Delmonico RC .40 1.00
22 Alex Gordon .30 .75
23 Jose Altuve .30 .75
24 Anthony Rizzo .50 1.25
25 Adrian Beltre .40 1.00
26 Carlos Gonzalez .30 .75
27 Jose Abreu .40 1.00
28 Nelson Cruz .40 1.00
29 Josh Bell .30 .75
30 Willie Calhoun RC .60 1.50
31 J.P. Crawford RC .40 1.00
32 Clayton Kershaw .60 1.50
33 Alex Verdugo RC .60 1.50
34 Mike Trout 2.00 5.00
35 Shohei Ohtani RC 10.00 25.00
36 Brandon Woodruff RC 1.25 3.00
37 Walker Buehler RC 1.25 3.00
38 Ryan McMahon RC 1.00 2.50
39 Jake Arrieta .30 .75
40 Giancarlo Stanton .40 1.00
41 Brian Dozier .30 .75
42 Yoenis Cespedes .40 1.00
43 Justin Bour .25 .60
44 Thyago Vieira RC .40 1.00
45 Kyle Farmer RC .40 1.00
46 Tyler Mahle RC .50 1.25
47 Max Fried RC 1.50 4.00
48 Freddie Freeman .50 1.25
49 Ozzie Albies RC 1.25 3.00
50 Andrew McCutchen .40 1.00
51 Wil Myers .30 .75
52 Bryce Harper .60 1.50
53 Paul Blackburn RC .40 1.00
54 Matt Carpenter .40 1.00
55 Rafael Devers RC 1.25 3.00
56 Joey Votto .40 1.00
57 Dominic Smith RC .50 1.25
58 Reggie Jackson .30 .75
59 Alex Rodriguez .50 1.25
60 Victor Caratini RC .50 1.25
61 Rhys Hoskins RC 1.50 4.00
62 Mookie Betts .75 2.00
63 Greg Allen RC .40 1.00
64 Miguel Cabrera .40 1.00
65 Paul Goldschmidt .40 1.00
66 Ken Griffey Jr. .75 2.00
67 Nick Williams RC .50 1.25
68 Chance Sisco RC .50 1.25
69 Jack Flaherty RC 1.50 4.00
70 Buster Posey .50 1.25
71 Cameron Gallagher RC .40 1.00
72 Francisco Lindor .40 1.00
73 Zack Granite RC .40 1.00
74 Victor Robles RC 1.00 2.50
75 Austin Hays RC .60 1.50
76 Shohei Ohtani RC 10.00 25.00
77 George Brett .75 2.00
78 Ronald Acuna Jr. RC 3.00 8.00
79 Harrison Bader RC .60 1.50
80 Luiz Gohara RC .40 1.00
81 Clint Frazier RC .75 2.00
82 Tomas Nido RC .40 1.00
83 Richard Urena RC .40 1.00
84 Amed Rosario RC .50 1.25
85 Cal Ripken 1.25 3.00
86 Javier Baez .50 1.25
87 Juan Soto RC 3.00 8.00
88 Dustin Pedroia .40 1.00
89 Gleyber Torres RC 2.00 5.00
90 Justin Verlander .40 1.00
91 Kris Bryant .50 1.25
92 Scott Kingery RC .60 1.50
93 Shane Bieber RC 8.00 20.00
94 Josh Donaldson .30 .75
95 Dustin Fowler RC .40 1.00
96 Robinson Cano .30 .75
97 Ryne Sandberg .75 2.00
98 Brian Anderson RC .50 1.25
99 Ichiro .50 1.25
100 Miguel Andujar RC 1.50 4.00

2018 Panini Spectra Green Mosiac

*MOSIAC: 4X TO 10X BASIC
*MOSIAC RC: 2.5X TO 6X BASIC
INSERTED IN '18 CHRONICLES PACKS
STATED PRINT RUN 25 SER.#'d SETS
9 Nolan Ryan 20.00 50.00
66 Ken Griffey Jr. 15.00 40.00
85 Cal Ripken 20.00 50.00

2018 Panini Spectra Neon Blue

*BLUE: 2X TO 5X BASIC
*BLUE RC: 1.2X TO 3X BASIC
INSERTED IN '18 CHRONICLES PACKS
STATED PRINT RUN 99 SER.#'d SETS
66 Ken Griffey Jr. 8.00 20.00

2018 Panini Spectra Neon Green

*GREEN: 2.5X TO 6X BASIC
*GREEN RC: 1.5X TO 4X BASIC
INSERTED IN '18 CHRONICLES PACKS
STATED PRINT RUN 49 SER.#'d SETS
66 Ken Griffey Jr. 10.00 25.00
85 Cal Ripken 12.00 30.00

2018 Panini Spectra Neon Pink

*PINK: 2X TO 5X BASIC
*PINK RC: 1.2X TO 3X BASIC
INSERTED IN '18 CHRONICLES PACKS
STATED PRINT RUN 75 SER.#'d SETS
66 Ken Griffey Jr. 8.00 20.00

2018 Panini Spectra Rookie Jersey Autographs

RANDOM INSERTS IN PACKS
RJAAH Austin Hays 4.00 10.00
RJAAR Amed Rosario 3.00 8.00
RJAAV Alex Verdugo 4.00 10.00
RJACF Clint Frazier 6.00 15.00
RJACS Chance Sisco 3.00 8.00
RJAEF Erick Fedde 2.50 6.00
RJAFM Francisco Mejia 6.00 15.00
RJAHB Harrison Bader 4.00 10.00
RJAJC J.P. Crawford 2.50 6.00
RJALS Lucas Sims 2.50 6.00
RJAMA Miguel Andujar 10.00 25.00
RJAMF Max Fried 10.00 25.00
RJANW Nick Williams 3.00 8.00
RJAOA Ozzie Albies 10.00 25.00
RJARD Rafael Devers 12.00 30.00
RJARH Rhys Hoskins 15.00 40.00
RJASO Shohei Ohtani 75.00 200.00
RJATW Tyler Wade 3.00 8.00
RJAVC Victor Caratini 3.00 8.00
RJAVR Victor Robles 8.00 20.00
RJAWB Walker Buehler 20.00 50.00
RJAWC Willie Calhoun 4.00 10.00
RJAZG Zack Granite 2.50 6.00

2018 Panini Spectra Rookie Jersey Autographs Neon Blue

*BLUE: .5X TO 1.2X BASIC
RANDOM INSERTS IN PACKS
PRINT RUNS B/WN 75-99 COPIES PER
RJAKF Kyle Farmer/99 3.00 8.00
RJARM Ryan McMahon/99 8.00 20.00
RJASO Shohei Ohtani/75 100.00 250.00

2018 Panini Spectra Rookie Jersey Autographs Neon Green

*GREEN: .75X TO 2X BASIC
RANDOM INSERTS IN PACKS
STATED PRINT RUN 25 SER.#'d SETS
RJAKF Kyle Farmer 5.00 12.00
RJASO Shohei Ohtani 200.00 400.00

2018 Panini Spectra Rookie Jersey Autographs Neon Pink

*PINK: .6X TO 1.5X BASIC
RANDOM INSERTS IN PACKS
STATED PRINT RUN 49 SER.#'d SETS
RJAKF Kyle Farmer 4.00 10.00
RJASO Shohei Ohtani 150.00 300.00

2018 Panini Spectra Signatures

RANDOM INSERTS IN PACKS
PRINT RUNS B/WN 15-199 COPIES PER
NO PRICING ON QTY 15
*PINK/35: .75X TO 2X p/r 99-199
1 Charles Johnson/99 3.00 8.00
2 Juan Gonzalez/199 3.00 8.00
3 Rhys Hoskins/49 15.00 40.00
4 Clint Frazier/49 8.00 20.00
6 Kevin Maitan/149 4.00 10.00
7 David Wright/25 6.00 15.00
8 Marcus Stroman/99 4.00 10.00
9 Starling Marte/99 4.00 10.00
10 Trea Turner/49 5.00 12.00
11 Jackie Bradley Jr./49 6.00 15.00
12 Gary Sanchez/25 8.00 20.00
13 Jason Kipnis/25 6.00 15.00
16 Jose Altuve/49 10.00 25.00
17 Yadier Molina/25 25.00 60.00
18 Freddie Freeman/25 20.00 50.00
21 Gleyber Torres/99 25.00 60.00
22 Kyle Schwarber/49 10.00 25.00
23 Josh Tomlin/49 4.00 10.00
24 Yoan Moncada/20
25 Lewis Brinson/199 3.00 8.00

2018 Panini Spectra Signatures Neon Blue

*BLUE/60: .4X TO 1X p/r 99-199
*BLUE/25: .6X TO 1.5X p/r 99-199
*BLUE/25: .5X TO 1.2X p/r 49
RANDOM INSERTS IN PACKS
PRINT RUNS B/WN 10-60 COPIES PER
NO PRICING ON QTY 15 OR LESS
5 Carlos Delgado/20 5.00 12.00

2018 Panini Spectra Triple Threat Materials

INSERTED IN '18 CHRONICLES PACKS
PRINT RUNS B/WN 75-199 COPIES PER
*GREEN/25: .75X TO 2X p/r 149-199
1 Ryan McMahon/199 5.00 12.00
2 Rhys Hoskins/199 4.00 10.00
3 Ozzie Albies/199 4.00 10.00
4 Miguel Andujar/199 5.00 12.00
5 Rafael Devers/199 6.00 15.00
6 Chance Sisco/199 2.50 6.00
7 Victor Caratini/199 2.50 6.00
8 Francisco Mejia/199 2.50 6.00
9 Kyle Farmer/199 2.00 5.00
10 Austin Hays/199 3.00 8.00
11 Alex Verdugo/199 3.00 8.00
12 Zack Granite/199 2.00 5.00
13 Clint Frazier/199 4.00 10.00
14 Nick Williams/199 2.50 6.00
15 Harrison Bader/199 3.00 8.00
16 Willie Calhoun/199 3.00 8.00
17 Victor Robles/199 4.00 10.00
18 Max Fried/199 8.00 20.00
19 Lucas Sims/199 2.00 5.00
20 Walker Buehler/199 4.00 10.00
21 Erick Fedde/199 2.00 5.00
22 Amed Rosario/199 2.50 6.00
23 Tyler Wade/199 2.50 6.00
24 J.P. Crawford/199 2.00 5.00
25 Richard Urena/199 2.00 5.00
26 Cameron Gallagher/199 2.00 5.00
27 Nicky Delmonico/199 2.00 5.00
28 Mitch Garver/199 2.00 5.00
29 Brian Anderson/199 2.50 6.00
30 Anthony Santander/199 2.00 5.00
31 Dustin Fowler/199 2.00 5.00
32 Tyler Mahle/199 2.50 6.00
33 Anthony Banda/199 2.00 5.00
34 Felix Jorge/199 2.00 5.00
35 Mike Trout/75 20.00 50.00
36 Manny Machado/99 4.00 10.00
37 Dustin Pedroia/99 4.00 10.00
38 Kris Bryant/75 5.00 12.00
39 Aaron Judge/99 10.00 25.00
40 Joey Gallo/149 2.50 6.00
41 Joey Votto/99 4.00 10.00
42 Edwin Encarnacion/99 4.00 10.00
43 Mookie Betts/99 8.00 20.00
44 Shohei Ohtani/199 12.00 30.00
45 Andrew McCutchen/99 4.00 10.00
46 Didi Gregorius/99 3.00 8.00
47 Evan Longoria/199 2.50 6.00
48 Dee Gordon/199 2.00 5.00
49 Jose Ramirez/199 2.50 6.00

2018 Panini Spectra Triple Threat Materials Neon Blue

*BLUE/75-99: .5X TO 1.2X p/r 149-199
*BLUE/75-99: .4X TO 1X p/r 75-99
*BLUE/49: .5X TO 1.2X p/r 75-99
INSERTED IN '18 CHRONICLES PACKS
PRINT RUNS B/WN 49-99 COPIES PER
50 Jonathan Schoop/99 2.50 6.00

2018 Panini Spectra Triple Threat Materials Neon Pink

*PINK/49: .6X TO 1.5X p/r 149-199
*PINK/49: .5X TO 1.2X p/r 75-99
INSERTED IN '18 CHRONICLES PACKS
STATED PRINT RUN 49 SER.#'d SETS
50 Jonathan Schoop 3.00 8.00

2019 Panini Spectra

INSERTED IN '19 CHRONICLES PACKS
JSY AU (101-150) PRINT RUN 199 SER.#'d SETS
EXCHANGE DEADLINE 2/21/2021
1 Alex Bregman .40 1.00
2 Ichiro .50 1.25
3 Dakota Hudson RC .30 .75
4 Cavan Biggio RC 1.25 3.00
5 Bryce Harper .60 1.50
6 Keston Hiura RC .75 2.00
7 Danny Jansen RC .25 .60
8 Robinson Cano .30 .75
9 Yadier Molina .50 1.25
10 Ronald Acuna Jr. 2.00 5.00
11 Khris Davis .40 1.00
12 Kyle Wright RC .40 1.00
13 Yusei Kikuchi RC .40 1.00
14 Mike Trout 2.00 5.00
15 Aaron Judge 1.00 2.50
16 Peter Lambert RC .40 1.00
17 Jeff McNeil RC .60 1.50
18 Christian Yelich .50 1.25
19 Cody Bellinger .75 2.00
20 Paul Goldschmidt .40 1.00
21 Corbin Burnes RC 2.00 5.00
22 Jon Duplantier RC .25 .60
23 Jonathan Loaisiga RC .30 .75
24 Jose Ramirez .30 .75
25 Whit Merrifield .40 1.00
26 Matt Chapman .40 1.00
27 Manny Machado .40 1.00
28 J.D. Martinez .40 1.00
29 Juan Soto 1.25 3.00
30 Charlie Blackmon .40 1.00
31 Max Scherzer .40 1.00
32 Andrew Benintendi .40 1.00
33 Jose Altuve .40 1.00
34 Fernando Tatis Jr. RC 3.00 8.00
35 Brad Keller RC .25 .60
36 Javier Baez .50 1.25
37 Kris Bryant .50 1.25
38 Joey Votto .40 1.00
39 Gleyber Torres .75 2.00
40 Rhys Hoskins .50 1.25
41 Eloy Jimenez RC 1.50 4.00
42 Shohei Ohtani .60 1.50
43 Austin Riley RC 1.25 3.00
44 Christian Stewart RC .40 1.00
45 Pete Alonso RC 1.50 4.00
46 Anthony Rizzo .50 1.25
47 Trevor Story .40 1.00
48 Justin Verlander .40 1.00
49 Ryan O'Hearn RC .25 .60
50 Luis Urias RC .40 1.00
51 Chris Paddack RC .50 1.25
52 Justus Sheffield RC .30 .75
53 Kyle Tucker RC .60 1.50
54 Nolan Arenado .60 1.50
55 Cedric Mullins RC .50 1.25
56 Jacob deGrom .75 2.00
57 Corbin Martin RC .40 1.00
58 Jake Bauers RC .40 1.00
59 Mookie Betts .75 2.00
60 Francisco Lindor .40 1.00
61 Ramon Laureano RC .50 1.25
62 Chris Shaw RC .25 .60
63 Ozzie Albies .40 1.00
64 Garrett Hampson RC .40 1.00
65 Kolby Allard RC .40 1.00
66 Cole Tucker RC .40 1.00
67 Kevin Newman RC .40 1.00
68 Steven Duggar RC .30 .75
69 Bryan Reynolds RC .40 1.00
70 Michael Chavis RC .40 1.00
71 Daniel Ponce de Leon RC .40 1.00
72 Jonathan Davis RC .30 .75
73 Noah Syndergaard .30 .75
74 Chance Adams RC .25 .60
75 Kyle Freeland .30 .75
76 Starling Marte .30 .75
77 Griffin Canning RC .40 1.00
78 Michael Kopech RC .75 2.00
79 Enyel De Los Santos RC .25 .60
80 Brandon Lowe RC .40 1.00
81 Josh James RC .40 1.00
82 Luis Ortiz RC .25 .60
83 David Fletcher RC .75 2.00
84 Cal Quantrill RC .25 .60
85 Nathaniel Lowe RC 1.25 3.00
86 Luis Arraez RC 2.00 5.00
87 Reese McGuire RC .40 1.00
88 Jake Cave RC .30 .75
89 Carter Kieboom RC .40 1.00
90 Brendan Rodgers RC .40 1.00
91 Buster Posey .50 1.25
92 Myles Straw RC .40 1.00
93 Nick Margevicius .25 .60
94 Kevin Kramer RC .25 .60
95 Vladimir Guerrero Jr. RC 4.00 10.00
96 Nick Senzel RC .75 2.00
97 Lorenzo Cain .25 .60
98 Bryse Wilson RC .30 .75
99 Rowdy Tellez RC .40 1.00
100 Miguel Andujar .40 1.00
101 Taylor Ward JSY AU/199 RC 2.50 6.00
102 Kevin Newman JSY AU/199 4.00 10.00
103 Jeff McNeil JSY AU/199 10.00 25.00
104 Michael Kopech JSY AU/199 6.00 15.00
105 Jake Bauers JSY AU/199 4.00 10.00
106 Stephen Gonsalves JSY AU/199 RC 2.50 6.00
107 Dennis Santana JSY AU/199 RC 2.50 6.00
108 Ryan O'Hearn JSY AU/199 2.50 6.00
109 Sean Reid-Foley JSY AU/199 RC 2.50 6.00
110 Kevin Kramer JSY AU/199 3.00 8.00
111 Caleb Ferguson JSY AU/199 RC 3.00 8.00
112 Jonathan Davis JSY AU/199 3.00 8.00
113 Daniel Ponce de Leon JSY AU/199 4.00 10.00
114 Kyle Tucker JSY AU/199 6.00 15.00
115 Josh James JSY AU/199 4.00 10.00
116 Garrett Hampson JSY AU/199 4.00 10.00
117 Danny Jansen JSY AU/199 2.50 6.00
118 Luis Urias JSY AU/199 4.00 10.00
119 Jacob Nix JSY AU/199 RC 3.00 8.00
120 Patrick Wisdom JSY AU/199 RC 2.50 6.00
121 Justus Sheffield JSY AU/199 4.00 10.00
122 Corbin Burnes JSY AU/199 8.00 20.00
123 Brad Keller JSY AU/199 2.50 6.00
125 Ryan Borucki JSY AU/199 2.50 6.00
126 Luis Ortiz JSY AU/199 2.50 6.00
127 Jake Cave JSY AU/199 5.00 12.00
128 Chance Adams JSY AU/199 2.50 6.00
129 Touki Toussaint JSY AU/199 RC 3.00 8.00
130 Kyle Wright JSY AU/199 4.00 10.00
131 Kolby Allard JSY AU/199 4.00 10.00
132 Dakota Hudson JSY AU/199 6.00 15.00
133 Framber Valdez JSY AU/199 RC 2.50 6.00
134 David Fletcher JSY AU/199 8.00 20.00
135 Brandon Lowe JSY AU/199 6.00 15.00
136 Ramon Laureano JSY AU/199 6.00 15.00
137 Jonathan Loaisiga JSY AU/199 3.00 8.00
138 Cionel Perez JSY AU/199 RC 2.50 6.00
139 Myles Straw JSY AU/199 4.00 10.00
140 Reese McGuire JSY AU/199 4.00 10.00
141 Enyel De Los Santos JSY AU/199 2.50 6.00
142 Chris Shaw JSY AU/199 2.50 6.00
143 Cedric Mullins JSY AU/199 8.00 20.00
144 Bryse Wilson JSY AU/199 3.00 8.00
145 Rowdy Tellez JSY AU/199 5.00 12.00
146 Christin Stewart JSY AU/199 3.00 8.00
147 Vladimir Guerrero Jr. JSY AU/199 50.00 120.00
148 Eloy Jimenez JSY AU/199 15.00 40.00
149 Fernando Tatis Jr. JSY AU/199 50.00 120.00
150 Nick Senzel JSY AU/199 8.00 20.00

2020 Panini Spectra Neon Blue

*NEON BLUE 1-100: 1.5X TO 4X
*NEON BLUE JSY AU: .5X TO 1.2X
RANDOM INSERTS IN PACKS
STATED PRINT RUN 99 SER.#'d SETS
EXCHANGE DEADLINE 2/21/2021
38 Luis Robert 20.00 50.00
128 Randy Arozarena AU JSY 75.00 200.00
140 Aristides Aquino AU JSY 15.00 40.00
149 Kyle Lewis AU JSY 40.00 100.00

2020 Panini Spectra Neon Green

38 Luis Robert 25.00 60.00
114 Bo Bichette AU JSY 60.00 150.00
115 Brendan McKay AU JSY 12.00 30.00
117 Nico Hoerner AU JSY 30.00 80.00
128 Randy Arozarena AU JSY 125.00 300.00
140 Aristides Aquino AU JSY 25.00 60.00
142 Edwin Rios AU JSY 6.00 15.00
149 Kyle Lewis AU JSY 60.00 150.00

2020 Panini Spectra Neon Pink

*NEON PNK 1-100: 1.5X TO 4X
*NEON PNK JSY AU: .6X TO 1.5X
1-100 STATED PRINT RUN 75 SER.#'d SETS
JSY AU STATED PRINT RUN 49 SER.#'d SETS
EXCHANGE DEADLINE 2/21/2021
38 Luis Robert 20.00 50.00
114 Bo Bichette AU JSY 50.00 120.00
115 Brendan McKay AU JSY 10.00 25.00
117 Nico Hoerner AU JSY 15.00 40.00
128 Randy Arozarena AU JSY 100.00 250.00
140 Aristides Aquino AU JSY 20.00 50.00
146 Dustin May AU JSY 25.00 60.00
149 Kyle Lewis AU JSY 50.00 120.00

2020 Panini Spectra Red

38 Luis Robert 40.00 100.00

2020 Panini Spectra Prospect Jersey Autographs

RANDOM INSERTS IN PACKS
STATED PRINT RUN 199 SER.#'d SETS
EXCHANGE DEADLINE 7/31/22
1 Andres Gimenez 8.00 20.00
3 Tristen Lutz 3.00 8.00
7 Jonathan India 40.00 100.00
8 Alex Kirilloff 8.00 20.00
9 Jo Adell 12.00 30.00
11 Tyler Stephenson 6.00 15.00
12 Forrest Whitley 4.00 10.00
13 Nick Neidert 2.50 6.00
14 Luis Robert 75.00 200.00
15 Colton Welker 2.50 6.00

2020 Panini Spectra Prospect Jersey Autographs Neon Blue

*N.BLUE/99: .5X TO 1.2X BASIC
*N.BLUE/49: .6X TO 1.5X BASIC
RANDOM INSERTS IN PACKS
PRINT RUN B/WN 25-60 COPIES PER
EXCHANGE DEADLINE 7/31/22
6 Alec Bohm 30.00 80.00
9 Jo Adell 25.00 60.00

2020 Panini Spectra Prospect Jersey Autographs Neon Green

*N.GREEN/25: .8X TO 2X BASIC
RANDOM INSERTS IN PACKS
PRINT RUN B/WN 10-25 COPIES PER
NO PRICING QTY 15 OR LESS
EXCHANGE DEADLINE 7/31/22
9 Jo Adell 40.00 100.00

2020 Panini Spectra Prospect Jersey Autographs Neon Pink

*N.PINK/49: .6X TO 1.5X BASIC
*N.PINK/25: .8X TO 2X BASIC
RANDOM INSERTS IN PACKS
PRINT RUN B/WN 25-49 COPIES PER
EXCHANGE DEADLINE 7/31/22
6 Alec Bohm 50.00 120.00
9 Jo Adell 30.00 80.00

2020 Panini Spectra Signatures

RANDOM INSERTS IN PACKS
PRINT RUN B/WN 49-199 COPIES PER
EXCHANGE DEADLINE 7/31/22
1 Garrett Hampson 2.50 6.00
2 Enyel De Los Santos 2.50 6.00
4 Yoshitomo Tsutsugo 8.00 20.00
5 Jonathan Davis 3.00 8.00
6 Michael Chavis 5.00 12.00
7 Myles Straw 3.00 8.00
10 Rowdy Tellez 3.00 8.00
11 Sean Reid-Foley 2.50 6.00
12 Taylor Hearn 2.50 6.00
13 Brad Keller 2.50 6.00
14 Bryse Wilson 5.00 12.00
15 Caleb Ferguson 2.50 6.00
16 Chris Paddack 5.00 12.00
17 Cole Tucker 4.00 10.00
18 Corbin Burnes 8.00 20.00
19 David Fletcher 4.00 10.00
20 Eloy Jimenez 12.00 30.00
23 Ty France 6.00 15.00
24 Stephen Gonsalves 2.50 6.00

2020 Panini Spectra Signatures Neon Blue

*N.BLUE/60: .5X TO 1.2X p/r 199
*N.BLUE/4-25: .5X TO 1.2X p/r 4-25
RANDOM INSERTS IN PACKS
PRINT RUN B/WN 25-60 COPIES PER
EXCHANGE DEADLINE 7/31/22
4 Yoshitomo Tsutsugo 12.00 30.00
6 Michael Chavis 8.00 20.00
16 Chris Paddack 8.00 20.00

2020 Panini Spectra Signatures Neon Green

*N.GRN/25: .6X TO 1.5X BASIC
RANDOM INSERTS IN PACKS
PRINT RUN B/WN 5-25 COPIES PER
NO PRICING QTY 15 OR LESS
EXCHANGE DEADLINE 7/31/22
4 Yoshitomo Tsutsugo 15.00 40.00
6 Michael Chavis 10.00 25.00
16 Chris Paddack 12.00 30.00
19 David Fletcher 10.00 25.00
23 Ty France 12.00 30.00

2020 Panini Spectra Signatures Neon Pink

*N.PNK/35: .5X TO 1.2X BASIC
RANDOM INSERTS IN PACKS
PRINT RUN B/WN 10-35 COPIES PER
NO PRICING QTY 15 OR LESS
EXCHANGE DEADLINE 7/31/22
4 Yoshitomo Tsutsugo 12.00 30.00
6 Michael Chavis 8.00 20.00
16 Chris Paddack 8.00 20.00
19 David Fletcher 8.00 20.00

2020 Panini Spectra Silhouettes

RANDOM INSERTS IN PACKS
1 Nelson Cruz 2.50 6.00
2 Eloy Jimenez 3.00 8.00
3 Alex Gordon 2.00 5.00
4 Brandon Belt 2.00 5.00
8 Trey Mancini 2.50 6.00
9 Dustin May 4.00 10.00
10 Alex Bregman 2.50 6.00
11 Yadier Molina 3.00 8.00
12 Albert Pujols 4.00 10.00
13 Rafael Devers 3.00 8.00
14 Jose Abreu 2.50 6.00
15 Mike Trout 12.00 30.00
16 Fernando Tatis Jr. 8.00 20.00
17 Robinson Cano 2.00 5.00
18 Stephen Strasburg 2.50 6.00
19 Shun Yamaguchi 2.00 5.00
20 Corey Seager 6.00 15.00
21 Justin Verlander 2.50 6.00
22 Jorge Soler 2.50 6.00
23 Aaron Nola 2.00 5.00
26 Freddie Freeman 3.00 8.00
27 Gerrit Cole 4.00 10.00
28 George Springer 2.00 5.00
29 Hunter Renfroe 1.50 4.00
30 J.P. Crawford 1.50 4.00
31 Javier Baez 3.00 8.00
33 Evan Longoria 2.00 5.00
35 Trevor Story 2.50 6.00
36 Tim Anderson 2.50 6.00
37 Gary Sanchez 4.00 10.00
38 Luis Robert 8.00 20.00
39 J.D. Martinez 2.50 6.00
42 Marcell Ozuna 2.50 6.00
43 Dan Vogelbach 1.50 4.00
44 Keston Hiura 3.00 8.00
45 Josh Bell 2.00 5.00
46 Buster Posey 3.00 8.00
47 Joey Votto 2.50 6.00
48 Elvis Andrus 2.00 5.00
49 Ozzie Albies 2.50 6.00
50 Cavan Biggio 3.00 8.00
51 Gleyber Torres 4.00 10.00
52 Juan Soto 5.00 12.00
54 Josh Donaldson 2.00 5.00
55 Jonathan Schoop 1.50 4.00
56 Byron Buxton 2.00 5.00
57 Stephen Piscotty 1.50 4.00
58 Giancarlo Stanton 2.50 6.00
59 Vladimir Guerrero Jr. 4.00 10.00
60 Jonathan Villar 1.50 4.00
61 Andrew Benintendi 2.50 6.00
62 Aaron Judge 6.00 15.00
63 Nick Senzel 2.50 6.00
65 Cody Bellinger 5.00 12.00
66 Max Scherzer 2.50 6.00
70 Austin Meadows 2.50 6.00
71 Clayton Kershaw 4.00 10.00
72 Mookie Betts 10.00 25.00
73 Nolan Arenado 4.00 10.00
74 Eugenio Suarez 2.00 5.00
76 Brian Anderson 1.50 4.00
77 Madison Bumgarner 2.00 5.00
78 Kyle Schwarber 2.00 5.00
79 Eric Hosmer 2.00 5.00
81 Whit Merrifield 2.50 6.00
82 Anthony Rizzo 3.00 8.00
83 Austin Hays 2.50 6.00
84 Miguel Cabrera 2.50 6.00
85 Starling Marte 2.00 5.00
86 Matt Chapman 2.50 6.00
87 Joey Gallo 2.50 6.00
88 Rougned Odor 2.00 5.00
89 Christian Yelich 3.00 8.00
92 Max Kepler 2.00 5.00
93 Bryan Reynolds 2.00 5.00
94 Justin Upton 2.00 5.00
95 Lorenzo Cain 1.50 4.00
96 Ronald Acuna Jr. 6.00 15.00
98 Ketel Marte 2.00 5.00

2020 Panini Spectra Silhouettes Neon Blue

*N.BLUE/49-99: .5X TO 1.2X BASIC
*N.BLUE/20-25: .6X TO 1.5X BASIC
RANDOM INSERTS IN PACKS
PRINT RUN B/WN 6-99 COPIES PER
NO PRICING QTY 15 OR LESS
16 Fernando Tatis Jr. 15.00 40.00
38 Luis Robert 15.00 40.00
52 Juan Soto 8.00 20.00
72 Mookie Betts 20.00 50.00

2020 Panini Spectra Silhouettes Red

*RED/25: .6X TO 1.5X BASIC
RANDOM INSERTS IN PACKS
PRINT RUN B/WN 4-25 COPIES PER
NO PRICING QTY 15 OR LESS
16 Fernando Tatis Jr. 20.00 50.00

38 Luis Robert 30.00 80.00
52 Juan Soto 12.00 30.00
96 Ronald Acuna Jr. 40.00 100.00

2020 Panini Spectra Swatches

RANDOM INSERTS IN PACKS
1 Nelson Cruz 2.50 6.00
2 Eloy Jimenez 3.00 8.00
3 Alex Gordon 2.00 5.00
4 Brandon Belt 2.00 5.00
8 Trey Mancini 2.50 6.00
9 Dustin May 4.00 10.00
10 Alex Bregman 2.50 6.00
11 Yadier Molina 3.00 8.00
12 Albert Pujols 4.00 10.00
13 Rafael Devers 3.00 8.00
14 Jose Abreu 2.50 6.00
15 Mike Trout 12.00 30.00
16 Fernando Tatis Jr. 8.00 20.00
17 Robinson Cano 2.00 5.00
18 Stephen Strasburg 2.50 6.00
19 Shun Yamaguchi 2.00 5.00
20 Corey Seager 6.00 15.00
21 Justin Verlander 2.50 6.00
22 Jorge Soler 2.50 6.00
23 Aaron Nola 2.00 5.00
24 Manny Machado 2.50 6.00
26 Freddie Freeman 3.00 8.00
27 Gerrit Cole 4.00 10.00
28 George Springer 2.00 5.00
29 Hunter Renfroe 1.50 4.00
30 J.P. Crawford 1.50 4.00
31 Javier Baez 3.00 8.00
32 Pete Alonso 5.00 12.00
33 Evan Longoria 2.00 5.00
35 Trevor Story 2.50 6.00
36 Tim Anderson 2.50 6.00
37 Gary Sanchez 4.00 10.00
38 Luis Robert 8.00 20.00
39 J.D. Martinez 2.50 6.00
40 Nicholas Castellanos 2.50 6.00
41 Jacob deGrom 5.00 12.00
42 Marcell Ozuna 2.50 6.00
43 Dan Vogelbach 1.50 4.00
44 Keston Hiura 3.00 8.00
45 Josh Bell 2.00 5.00
46 Buster Posey 3.00 8.00
47 Joey Votto 2.50 6.00
48 Elvis Andrus 2.00 5.00
49 Ozzie Albies 2.50 6.00
50 Cavan Biggio 3.00 8.00
51 Gleyber Torres 4.00 10.00
52 Juan Soto 5.00 12.00
54 Josh Donaldson 2.00 5.00
55 Jonathan Schoop 1.50 4.00
56 Byron Buxton 2.50 6.00
57 Stephen Piscotty 1.50 4.00
58 Giancarlo Stanton 2.50 6.00
59 Vladimir Guerrero Jr. 4.00 10.00
60 Jonathan Villar 1.50 4.00
61 Andrew Benintendi 2.50 6.00
62 Aaron Judge 6.00 15.00
63 Nick Senzel 2.50 6.00
65 Cody Bellinger 5.00 12.00
66 Max Scherzer 2.50 6.00
70 Austin Meadows 2.50 6.00
71 Clayton Kershaw 4.00 10.00
72 Mookie Betts 10.00 25.00
73 Nolan Arenado 4.00 10.00
74 Eugenio Suarez 2.00 5.00
76 Brian Anderson 1.50 4.00
77 Madison Bumgarner 2.00 5.00
78 Kyle Schwarber 2.50 6.00
79 Eric Hosmer 2.00 5.00
80 Todd Frazier 1.50 4.00
81 Whit Merrifield 2.50 6.00
82 Anthony Rizzo 3.00 8.00
83 Austin Hays 2.50 6.00
84 Miguel Cabrera 2.50 6.00
85 Starling Marte 2.00 5.00
86 Matt Chapman 2.50 6.00
87 Joey Gallo 2.50 6.00
88 Rougned Odor 2.00 5.00
89 Christian Yelich 3.00 8.00
92 Max Kepler 2.00 5.00
93 Bryan Reynolds 2.00 5.00
94 Justin Upton 2.00 5.00
95 Lorenzo Cain 1.50 4.00
96 Ronald Acuna Jr. 6.00 15.00
98 Ketel Marte 2.00 5.00

2020 Panini Spectra Swatches Neon Blue

*N.BLUE/49-99: .5X TO 1.2X BASIC
*N.BLUE/25: .6X TO 1.5X BASIC
RANDOM INSERTS IN PACKS
PRINT RUN B/WN 10-99 COPIES PER
NO PRICING QTY 15 OR LESS
16 Fernando Tatis Jr. 15.00 40.00
32 Pete Alonso 10.00 25.00
38 Luis Robert 15.00 40.00
52 Juan Soto 8.00 20.00
72 Mookie Betts 15.00 40.00

2020 Panini Spectra Swatches Red

*RED/25: .6X TO 1.5X BASIC
RANDOM INSERTS IN PACKS
PRINT RUN B/WN 5-25 COPIES PER
NO PRICING QTY 15 OR LESS
16 Fernando Tatis Jr. 20.00 50.00
32 Pete Alonso 15.00 40.00
38 Luis Robert 30.00 80.00
52 Juan Soto 15.00 40.00
72 Mookie Betts 20.00 50.00
96 Ronald Acuna Jr. 40.00 100.00

2018 Panini Status

1 Shohei Ohtani RC 6.00 15.00
2 Clint Frazier RC .50 1.25
3 Rafael Devers RC .75 2.00
4 Rhys Hoskins RC 1.00 2.50
5 Austin Hays RC .40 1.00
6 Amed Rosario RC .30 .75
7 Victor Robles RC .60 1.50
8 Nick Williams RC .30 .75
9 Ozzie Albies RC .75 2.00
10 Ryan McMahon RC .60 1.50
11 Victor Caratini RC .30 .75
12 Scott Kingery RC .40 1.00
13 Greg Allen RC .25 .60
14 Jack Flaherty RC 1.00 2.50
15 Andrew Stevenson .15 .40
16 Anthony Rizzo .30 .75
17 Francisco Lindor .25 .60
18 Ronald Guzman RC .25 .60
19 Willy Adames RC .30 .75
20 Paul Goldschmidt .25 .60
21 Ronald Acuna Jr. RC 8.00 20.00
22 Corey Seager .25 .60
23 Gleyber Torres RC 2.50 6.00
24 Erick Fedde RC .25 .60
25 Jimmie Sherfy RC .25 .60

2018 Panini Status Autographs

RANDOM INSERTS IN PACKS
12 Scott Kingery 4.00 10.00
15 Andrew Stevenson 2.50 6.00
19 Willy Adames 3.00 8.00
25 Jimmie Sherfy 2.50 6.00

2018 Panini Status Autographs Gold

*GOLD/25: .75X TO 2X BASIC
RANDOM INSERTS IN PACKS
PRINT RUNS B/WN 3-25 COPIES PER
NO PRICING ON QTY 10 OR LESS
5 Austin Hays/25 8.00 20.00
13 Greg Allen/25 5.00 12.00

2019 Panini Status

RANDOM INSERTS IN PACKS
*GREEN: 1X TO 2.5X
*BLUE/99: 1.2X TO 3X
*RED/25: 2.5X TO 6X
1 Keston Hiura RC .50 1.25
2 Chris Paddack RC .30 .75
3 Corey Kluber .20 .50
4 Trevor Story .25 .60
5 Ramon Laureano RC .30 .75
6 Yusei Kikuchi RC .25 .60
7 Pete Alonso RC 4.00 10.00
8 Aaron Judge .60 1.50
9 Ty France RC .50 1.25
10 Javier Baez .30 .75
11 Eloy Jimenez RC .60 1.50
12 Michael Kopech RC .50 1.25
13 Mike Trout 1.25 3.00
14 Shohei Ohtani .40 1.00
15 Mookie Betts .50 1.25
16 Ryan O'Hearn RC .15 .40
17 Ichiro .30 .75
18 Joey Votto .25 .60
19 Jeff McNeil RC .40 1.00
20 Brandon Lowe RC .25 .60
21 Albert Pujols .30 .75
22 Fernando Tatis Jr. RC 2.00 5.00
23 Kris Bryant .30 .75
24 Yadier Molina .30 .75
25 Kyle Tucker RC .40 1.00
26 Nathaniel Lowe RC .75 2.00
27 Bryce Harper .40 1.00
28 Justus Sheffield RC .25 .60
29 Jason Martin RC .20 .50
30 Bryan Reynolds RC .50 1.25
31 Michael Chavis RC .25 .60
32 Cole Tucker RC .25 .60
33 Darwinzon Hernandez RC .15 .40
34 Vladimir Guerrero Jr. RC 2.50 6.00
35 Carter Kieboom RC .25 .60

2020 Panini Status

RANDOM INSERTS IN PACKS
1 Sean Murphy RC .40 1.00
2 Aristides Aquino RC .60 1.50
3 Gavin Lux RC 1.25 3.00
4 Mike Trout 2.00 5.00
5 Shogo Akiyama RC .40 1.00
6 Bo Bichette RC 3.00 8.00
7 Danny Mendick RC .30 .75
8 Khris Davis .25 .60
9 Shun Yamaguchi RC .30 .75
10 Bryce Harper .40 1.00
11 Yordan Alvarez RC 2.50 6.00
12 Brendan McKay RC .40 1.00
13 Aaron Judge .60 1.50
14 Nico Hoerner RC 1.00 2.50
15 Michel Baez RC .25 .60
16 Bobby Bradley RC .25 .60
17 Yoshitomo Tsutsugo RC .60 1.50
18 Kwang-Hyun Kim RC .50 1.25
19 A.J. Puk RC .40 1.00
20 Luis Robert RC 4.00 10.00

1988 Panini Stickers

These 480 stickers measure approximately 1 15/16" by 2 11/16" (regular) and 2 1/8" by 2 11/16" (foils). There are 80 foil stickers in the set; these foils are essentially the non-player stickers. A 64-page album onto which the stickers could be affixed was available at retail stores (for 59 cents) and was also given away to Little Leaguers as part of a national promotion. The album features Don Mattingly on the front and a photo of a gold glove on the back. The album and the sticker numbering are organized alphabetically by team with AL teams preceding NL teams. The last 26 stickers in the album are actually lettered rather than numbered but are listed below as numbers 455-480. The stickers were also sold at retail outlets packed with the album as a "Complete Collectors Set." The 1988 Panini Sticker set was heavily promoted as Panini entered the baseball sticker market under its own label after producing Topps' stickers for the previous seven years.

COMPLETE SET (480) 15.00 40.00
1 1987 WS Trophy .01 .05
2 Orioles Emblem .01 .05
3 Orioles Uniform .01 .05
4 Eric Bell .01 .05
5 Mike Boddicker .01 .05
6 Dave Schmidt .01 .05
7 Terry Kennedy .01 .05
8 Eddie Murray .60 1.50
9 Bill Ripken .01 .05
10 Orioles TL .01 .05
Action photo
11 Orioles W-L Breakdown .75 2.00
Cal Ripken IA
12 Ray Knight .01 .05
13 Jim Traber .01 .05
14 Ken Gerhart .01 .05
15 Fred Lynn .05 .15
16 Larry Sheets .01 .05
17 Mike Young .01 .05
18 Red Sox Emblem .01 .05
19 Red Sox Uniform .01 .05
20 Oil Can Boyd .01 .05
21 Roger Clemens 1.00 2.50
22 Bruce Hurst .01 .05
23 Bob Stanley .01 .05
24 Rich Gedman .01 .05
25 Dwight Evans .05 .15
26 Red Sox TL .01 .05
Action photo
27 Red Sox W-L Breakdown .01 .05
Action photo
28 Marty Barrett .01 .05
29 Wade Boggs .60 1.50
30 Spike Owen .01 .05
31 Ellis Burks .40 1.00
32 Mike Greenwell .01 .05
33 Jim Rice .05 .15
34 Angels Emblem .01 .05
35 Angels Uniform .01 .05
36 Kirk McCaskill .01 .05
37 Don Sutton .30 .75
38 Mike Witt .01 .05
39 Bob Boone .05 .15
40 Wally Joyner .05 .15
41 Mark McLemore .08 .25
42 Angels TL .01 .05
Action photo
43 Angels W-L Breakdown .05 .15
Devon White IA
44 Jack Howell .01 .05
45 Dick Schofield .01 .05
46 Brian Downing .05 .15
47 Ruppert Jones .01 .05
48 Gary Pettis .01 .05
49 Devon White .05 .15
50 White Sox Emblem .01 .05
51 White Sox Uniform .01 .05
52 Floyd Bannister .01 .05
53 Richard Dotson .01 .05
54 Bob James .01 .05
55 Carlton Fisk .40 1.00
56 Greg Walker .01 .05
57 Fred Manrique .01 .05
58 White Sox TL .01 .05
Action photo
59 White Sox W-L .01 .05
Breakdown/(Action photo)
60 Steve Lyons .05 .15
61 Ozzie Guillen .08 .25
62 Harold Baines .08 .25
63 Ivan Calderon .01 .05
64 Gary Redus .01 .05
65 Ken Williams .15 .40
66 Indians Emblem .01 .05
67 Indians Uniform .01 .05
68 Scott Bailes .01 .05
69 Tom Candiotti .01 .05
70 Greg Swindell .01 .05
71 Chris Bando .01 .05
72 Joe Carter .15 .40
73 Tommy Hinzo .01 .05
74 Indians TL .01 .05
Action photo
75 Indians W-L Breakdown .01 .05
Juan Bonilla IA
76 Brook Jacoby .01 .05
77 Julio Franco .05 .15
78 Brett Butler .05 .15
79 Mel Hall .01 .05
80 Cory Snyder .01 .05
81 Pat Tabler .01 .05
82 Tigers Emblem .01 .05
83 Tigers Uniform .01 .05
84 Willie Hernandez .01 .05
85 Jack Morris .05 .15
86 Frank Tanana .01 .05
87 Walt Terrell .01 .05
88 Matt Nokes .01 .05
89 Darrell Evans .05 .15
90 Tigers TL .05 .15
Darrell Evans IA
91 Tigers W-L Breakdown .08 .25
Carlton Fisk IA
92 Lou Whitaker .05 .15
93 Tom Brookens .01 .05
94 Alan Trammell .08 .25
95 Kirk Gibson .05 .15
96 Chet Lemon .01 .05
97 Pat Sheridan .01 .05
98 Royals Emblem .01 .05
99 Royals Uniform .01 .05
100 Charlie Leibrandt .01 .05
101 Dan Quisenberry .01 .05
102 Bret Saberhagen .05 .15
103 Jamie Quirk .01 .05
104 George Brett 1.00 2.50
105 Frank White .05 .15
106 Royals TL .05 .15
Bret Saberhagen IA
107 Royals W-L Breakdown .05 .15
Bret Saberhagen IA
108 Kevin Seitzer .05 .15
109 Angel Salazar .01 .05
110 Bo Jackson .40 1.00
111 Lonnie Smith .01 .05
112 Danny Tartabull .01 .05
113 Willie Wilson .01 .05
114 Brewers Emblem .01 .05
115 Brewers Uniform .01 .05
116 Ted Higuera .01 .05
117 Juan Nieves .01 .05
118 Dan Plesac .01 .05
119 Bill Wegman .01 .05
120 B.J. Surhoff .08 .25
121 Greg Brock .01 .05
122 Brewers TL .05 .15
Lou Whitaker IA
123 Brewers W-L Breakdown .01 .05
Jim Gantner IA
124 Jim Gantner .01 .05
125 Paul Molitor .40 1.00
126 Dale Sveum .01 .05
127 Glenn Braggs .01 .05
128 Rob Deer .01 .05
129 Robin Yount .40 1.00
130 Twins Emblem .01 .05
131 Twins Uniform .02 .05
132 Bert Blyleven .05 .15
133 Jeff Reardon .05 .15
134 Frank Viola .05 .15
135 Tim Laudner .01 .05
136 Kent Hrbek .05 .15
137 Steve Lombardozzi .01 .05
138 Twins TL .01 .05
Action photo
139 Twins W-L Breakdown .01 .05
Action photo
140 Gary Gaetti .05 .15
141 Greg Gagne .01 .05
142 Tom Brunansky .01 .05
143 Dan Gladden .01 .05
144 Kirby Puckett .50 1.25
145 Gene Larkin .05 .15
146 Team Emblem .01 .05
New York Yankees
147 Team Uniform .01 .05
New York Yankees
148 Tommy John .05 .15
149 Rick Rhoden .01 .05
150 Dave Righetti .05 .15
151 Rick Cerone .01 .05
152 Don Mattingly 1.00 2.50
153 Willie Randolph .05 .15
154 1987 Team Leaders .01 .05
Scott Fletcher IA
155 1987 W-L Breakdown .30 .75
Don Mattingly IA
156 Mike Pagliarulo .01 .05
157 Wayne Tolleson .01 .05
158 Rickey Henderson .60 1.50
159 Dan Pasqua .01 .05
160 Gary Ward .01 .05
161 Dave Winfield .40 1.00
162 Team Emblem .01 .05
Oakland A's
163 Team Uniform .01 .05
Oakland A's
164 Dave Stewart .05 .15
165 Curt Young .01 .05
166 Terry Steinbach .01 .05
167 Mark McGwire 1.00 2.50
168 Tony Phillips .01 .05
169 Carney Lansford .05 .15
170 1987 Team Leaders .01 .05
Action photo
171 1987 W-L Breakdown .01 .05
Action photo
172 Alfredo Griffin .01 .05
173 Jose Canseco .50 1.25
174 Mike Davis .01 .05
175 Reggie Jackson .40 1.00
176 Dwayne Murphy .01 .05
177 Luis Polonia .01 .05
178 Team Emblem .01 .05
Seattle Mariners
179 Team Uniform .01 .05
Seattle Mariners
180 Scott Bankhead .01 .05
181 Mark Langston .01 .05
182 Edwin Nunez .01 .05
183 Scott Bradley .01 .05
184 Dave Valle .01 .05
185 Alvin Davis .01 .05
186 1987 Team Leaders .01 .05
Rey Quinones IA
187 1987 W-L Breakdown .01 .05
Jack Howell IA
188 Harold Reynolds .05 .15
189 Jim Presley .01 .05
190 Rey Quinones .01 .05
191 Phil Bradley .01 .05
192 Mickey Brantley .01 .05
193 Mike Kingery .01 .05
194 Team Emblem .01 .05
Texas Rangers
195 Team Uniform .01 .05
Texas Rangers
196 Edwin Correa .01 .05
197 Charlie Hough .05 .15
198 Bobby Witt .01 .05
199 Mike Stanley .01 .05
200 Pete O'Brien .01 .05
201 Jerry Browne .01 .05
202 1987 Team Leaders .01 .05
Action photo
203 1987 W-L Breakdown .15 .40
Steve Buechele and
Eddie Murray IA
204 Steve Buechele .01 .05
205 Larry Parrish .01 .05
206 Scott Fletcher .01 .05
207 Pete Incaviglia .01 .05
208 Oddibe McDowell .01 .05
209 Ruben Sierra .05 .15
210 Team Emblem .01 .05
Toronto Blue Jays
211 Team Uniform .01 .05
Toronto Blue Jays
212 Mark Eichhorn .01 .05
213 Tom Henke .01 .05
214 Jimmy Key .05 .15
215 Dave Stieb .01 .05
216 Ernie Whitt .01 .05
217 Willie Upshaw .01 .05
218 1987 Team Leaders .01 .05
Willie Upshaw IA
219 1987 W-L Breakdown .01 .05
Harold Reynolds IA
220 Garth Iorg .01 .05
221 Kelly Gruber .01 .05
222 Tony Fernandez .05 .15
223 Jesse Barfield .01 .05
224 George Bell .01 .05
225 Lloyd Moseby .01 .05
226A AL Logo .01 .05
226B NL Logo .01 .05
227 Terry Kennedy and .40 1.00
Don Mattingly
228 Willie Randolph and .15 .40
Wade Boggs
229 Bret Saberhagen .05 .15
230 Cal Ripken and 1.00 2.50
George Bell
231 Rickey Henderson and .15 .40
Dave Winfield
232 Gary Carter and .05 .15
Jack Clark
233 Mike Scott .01 .05
234 Ryne Sandberg and .40 1.00
Mike Schmidt
235 Ozzie Smith and .15 .40
Eric Davis
236 Andre Dawson and .05 .15
Darryl Strawberry
237 Team Emblem .01 .05
Atlanta Braves
238 Team Uniform .01 .05
Atlanta Braves
239 Rick Mahler .01 .05
240 Zane Smith .01 .05
241 Ozzie Virgil .01 .05
242 Gerald Perry .01 .05
243 Glenn Hubbard .01 .05
244 Ken Oberkfell .01 .05
245 1987 Team Leaders .01 .05
Action photo
246 1987 W-L Breakdown .01 .05
Jeffrey Leonard IA
247 Rafael Ramirez .01 .05
248 Ken Griffey .05 .15
249 Albert Hall .01 .05
250 Dion James .01 .05
251 Dale Murphy .15 .40
252 Gary Roenicke .01 .05
253 Team Emblem .01 .05
Chicago Cubs
254 Team Uniform .01 .05
Chicago Cubs
255 Jamie Moyer .15 .40
256 Lee Smith .05 .15
257 Rick Sutcliffe .05 .15
258 Jody Davis .01 .05
259 Leon Durham .01 .05
260 Ryne Sandberg .60 1.50
261 1987 Team Leaders .01 .05
Action photo
262 1987 W-L Breakdown .01 .05
Jody Davis IA
263 Keith Moreland .01 .05
264 Shawon Dunston .01 .05
265 Andre Dawson .15 .40
266 Dave Martinez .01 .05
267 Jerry Mumphrey .01 .05
268 Rafael Palmeiro .60 1.50
269 Team Emblem .01 .05
Cincinnati Reds
270 Team Uniform .01 .05
Cincinnati Reds
271 John Franco .05 .15
272 Ted Power .01 .05
273 Bo Diaz .01 .05
274 Nick Esasky .01 .05
275 Dave Concepcion .05 .15
276 Kurt Stillwell .01 .05
277 1987 Team Leaders .05 .15
Dave Parker IA
278 1987 W-L Breakdown .01 .05
Action photo
279 Buddy Bell .05 .15
280 Barry Larkin .50 1.25
281 Kal Daniels .01 .05
282 Eric Davis .05 .15
283 Tracy Jones .01 .05
284 Dave Parker .05 .15
285 Team Emblem .01 .05
Houston Astros
286 Team Uniform .01 .05
Houston Astros
287 Jim Deshaies .01 .05
288 Nolan Ryan 2.00 5.00
289 Mike Scott .01 .05
290 Dave Smith .01 .05
291 Alan Ashby .01 .05
292 Glenn Davis .01 .05
293 1987 Team Leaders .01 .05
Action photo
294 1987 W-L Breakdown .01 .05
Action photo
295 Bill Doran .01 .05
296 Denny Walling .01 .05
297 Craig Reynolds .01 .05
298 Kevin Bass .01 .05
299 Jose Cruz .05 .15
300 Billy Hatcher .01 .05
301 Team Emblem .01 .05
Los Angeles Dodgers
302 Team Uniform .01 .05
Los Angeles Dodgers
303 Orel Hershiser .05 .15
304 Fernando Valenzuela .05 .15
305 Bob Welch .05 .15
306 Matt Young .01 .05
307 Mike Scioscia .05 .15
308 Franklin Stubbs .01 .05
309 1987 Team Leaders .01 .05
Action photo
310 1987 W-L Breakdown .01 .05
Action photo
311 Steve Sax .05 .15
312 Jeff Hamilton .01 .05
313 Dave Anderson .01 .05
314 Pedro Guerrero .05 .15
315 Mike Marshall .01 .05
316 John Shelby .01 .05
317 Team Emblem .01 .05
Montreal Expos
318 Team Uniform .01 .05
Montreal Expos
319 Neal Heaton .01 .05
320 Bryn Smith .01 .05
321 Floyd Youmans .01 .05
322 Mike Fitzgerald .01 .05
323 Andres Galarraga .15 .40
324 Vance Law .01 .05
325 1987 Team Leaders .05 .15
Tim Raines IA
326 1987 W-L Breakdown .05 .15
John Kruk IA
327 Tim Wallach .01 .05
328 Hubie Brooks .01 .05
329 Casey Candaele .01 .05
330 Tim Raines .08 .25
331 Mitch Webster .01 .05
332 Herm Winningham .01 .05
333 Team Emblem .01 .05
New York Mets
334 Team Uniform .01 .05
New York Mets
335 Ron Darling .01 .05
336 Sid Fernandez .01 .05
337 Dwight Gooden .05 .15
338 Gary Carter .40 1.00
339 Keith Hernandez .05 .15
340 Wally Backman .01 .05
341 1987 Team Leaders .01 .05
Junior Ortiz IA
342 1987 W-L Breakdown .05 .15
Mookie Wilson
Darryl Strawberry
Tim Teufel IA
343 Howard Johnson .01 .05
344 Rafael Santana .01 .05
345 Lenny Dykstra .05 .15
346 Kevin McReynolds .01 .05
347 Darryl Strawberry .05 .15
348 Mookie Wilson .05 .15
349 Team Emblem .01 .05
Philadelphia Phillies
350 Team Uniform .01 .05
Philadelphia Phillies
351 Steve Bedrosian .01 .05
352 Shane Rawley .01 .05
353 Bruce Ruffin .01 .05
354 Kent Tekulve .01 .05
355 Lance Parrish .05 .15
356 Von Hayes .01 .05
357 1987 Team Leaders .01 .05
Action photo
358 1987 W-L Breakdown .01 .05
Glenn Wilson IA
359 Juan Samuel .01 .05
360 Mike Schmidt .60 1.50
361 Steve Jeltz .01 .05
362 Chris James .01 .05
363 Milt Thompson .01 .05
364 Glenn Wilson .01 .05
365 Team Emblem .01 .05
Pittsburgh Pirates
366 Team Uniform .01 .05
Pittsburgh Pirates
367 Mike Dunne .01 .05
368 Brian Fisher .01 .05
369 Mike LaValliere .01 .05
370 Sid Bream .01 .05
371 Jose Lind .01 .05
372 Bobby Bonilla .05 .15
373 1987 Team Leaders .05 .15
Bobby Bonilla IA
374 1987 W-L Breakdown .01 .05
Action photo
375 Al Pedrique .01 .05
376 Barry Bonds 1.00 2.50
377 John Cangelosi .01 .05
378 Mike Diaz .01 .05
379 R.J. Reynolds .05 .15
380 Andy Van Slyke .05 .15
381 Team Emblem .01 .05
St. Louis Cardinals
382 Team Uniform .01 .05
St. Louis Cardinals
383 Danny Cox .01 .05
384 Bob Forsch .01 .05
385 Joe Magrane .01 .05
386 Todd Worrell .05 .15
387 Tony Pena .01 .05
388 Jack Clark .05 .15
389 1987 Team Leaders .01 .05
Tommy Herr IA
390 1987 W-L Breakdown .01 .05
Action photo
391 Tom Herr .01 .05
392 Terry Pendleton .05 .15
393 Ozzie Smith .50 1.25
394 Vince Coleman .01 .05
395 Curt Ford .01 .05
396 Willie McGee .05 .15
397 Team Emblem .01 .05
San Diego Padres
398 Team Uniform .01 .05
San Diego Padres
399 Lance McCullers .01 .05
400 Eric Show .01 .05
401 Ed Whitson .01 .05
402 Benito Santiago .05 .15
403 John Kruk .05 .15
404 Tim Flannery .01 .05
405 1987 Team Leaders .01 .05
Benito Santiago IA
406 1987 W-L Breakdown .01 .05
Action photo
407 Randy Ready .01 .05
408 Chris Brown .01 .05
409 Garry Templeton .01 .05
410 Tony Gwynn .75 2.00
411 Stan Jefferson .01 .05
412 Carmelo Martinez .01 .05
413 Team Emblem .01 .05
San Francisco Giants
414 Team Uniform .01 .05
San Francisco Giants
415 Kelly Downs .01 .05
416 Scott Garrelts .01 .05
417 Mike Krukow .01 .05
418 Mike LaCoss .01 .05
419 Bob Brenly .01 .05
420 Will Clark .60 1.50
421 1987 Team Leaders .08 .25
Will Clark IA
422 1987 W-L Breakdown .01 .05
Action photo
423 Robby Thompson .01 .05
424 Kevin Mitchell .05 .15
425 Jose Uribe .01 .05
426 Mike Aldrete .01 .05
427 Jeffrey Leonard .01 .05
428 Candy Maldonado .01 .05
429 Mike Schmidt .60 1.50
430 Don Mattingly 1.00 2.50
431 Juan Nieves .01 .05
432 Paul Molitor .40 1.00
433 Benito Santiago .01 .05
434 Rickey Henderson .50 1.25
435 Nolan Ryan 2.00 5.00
436 Kevin Seitzer .05 .15
437 Tony Gwynn .75 2.00
438 Mark McGwire 1.00 2.50
439 Howard Johnson .01 .05
switch-hitting
440 Steve Bedrosian .01 .05
441 Darrell Evans .05 .15
442 Eddie Murray .50 1.25
switch-hitting
443 Lou Whitaker IA .05 .15
444 Kirby Puckett and .30 .75
Alan Trammell IA
445 Gary Gaetti .05 .15
446 Jeffrey Leonard .01 .05
447 Tony Pena IA .01 .05
448 Kevin Mitchell IA .05 .15
449 Tony Pena IA .01 .05
450 Randy Bush IA .01 .05
451 Minnesota Twins UL .01 .05
celebrating
452 Minnesota Twins UR .01 .05
celebrating
453 Minnesota Twins LL .01 .05
celebrating
454 Minnesota Twins LR .01 .05
celebrating
455 Baltimore Orioles A .01 .05
Pennant and Logo
456 Boston Red Sox B .01 .05
Pennant and Logo
457 California Angels C .01 .05
Pennant and Logo
458 Chicago White Sox D .01 .05
Pennant and Logo
459 Cleveland Indians E .01 .05
Pennant and Logo
460 Detroit Tigers F .01 .05
Pennant and Logo
461 Kansas City Royals G .01 .05
Pennant and Logo
462 Milwaukee Brewers H .01 .05
Pennant and Logo
463 Minnesota Twins I .01 .05
Pennant and Logo
464 New York Yankees J .01 .05
Pennant and Logo
465 Oakland A's K .01 .05
Pennant and Logo
466 Seattle Mariners L .01 .05
Pennant and Logo
467 Texas Rangers M .01 .05
Pennant and Logo
468 Toronto Blue Jays N .01 .05
Pennant and Logo
469 Atlanta Braves O .01 .05
Pennant and Logo
470 Chicago Cubs P .01 .05
Pennant and Logo
471 Cincinnati Reds Q .01 .05
Pennant and Logo
472 Houston Astros R .01 .05
Pennant and Logo
473 Los Angeles Dodgers S .01 .05
Pennant and Logo
474 Montreal Expos T .01 .05
Pennant and Logo
475 New York Mets U .01 .05
Pennant and Logo
476 Phila. Phillies V .01 .05
Pennant and Logo
477 Pittsburgh Pirates W .01 .05
Pennant and Logo
478 St. Louis Cardinals X .01 .05
Pennant and Logo
479 San Diego Padres Y .01 .05
Pennant and Logo
480 San Fran. Giants Z .01 .05
Pennant and Logo
xx Sticker Album .40 1.00
Don Mattingly on front

1989 Panini Stickers

These 480 stickers measure approximately 1 7/8" by 2 11/16" and feature white-bordered color player action shots. Sticker packets contained six stickers (five paper, one foil) and sold for 30 cents. The set includes 80 foil stickers; the first two stickers are foil, then each of the 26 teams has three foils out of its full complement of 16 stickers. An album onto which the stickers could be affixed was available at retail stores. The album featured Jose Canseco on the front cover and an ad for Oscar Mayer on the back. The stickers are organized alphabetically by city with NL teams preceding AL teams. The following subsets are also included: 1988 World Series Trophy (Foil, 1-2), 1988 Highlights (3-9), 1988 League Championship Series (10-15), 1988 World Series (16-29), 1988 NL Stat Leaders (222-226), 1988 All-Stars (227-244), 1988 AL Stat Leaders (245-249) and 1988 Award Winners (474-480). A rookie year sticker of Randy Johnson is a highlight of this set.

COMPLETE SET (480) 8.00 20.00
1 World Series Trophy .01 .05
2 World Series Trophy .01 .05
3 Mike Schmidt .30 .75
4 Tom Browning .01 .05
5 Doug Jones .01 .05
6 Wrigley Field .01 .05
7 Wade Boggs .30 .75
8 Jose Canseco .30 .75
9 Orel Hershiser .02 .10
10 Oakland wins ALCS .01 .05

11 Oakland wins ALCS .01 .05
12 Dennis Eckersley ALCS .02 .10
13 Orel Hershiser NLCS .02 .10
14 Dodgers win NLCS .01 .05
15 Dodgers win NLCS .01 .05
16 Kirk Gibson .02 .10
17 Kirk Gibson .02 .10
18 Orel Hershiser .02 .10
19 Orel Hershiser .02 .10
20 Mark McGwire .60 1.50
21 Tim Belcher .01 .05
22 Jay Howell .01 .05
23 Mickey Hatcher .01 .05
24 Mike Davis .01 .05
25 Orel Hershiser WS MVP .02 .10
26 Dodgers win AS .01 .05
27 Dodgers win AS .01 .05
28 Dodgers win AS .01 .05
29 Dodgers win AS .01 .05
30 Atlanta team logo .01 .05
31 Jose Alvarez .01 .05
32 Tommy Gregg .01 .05
33 Paul Assenmacher .01 .05
34 Tom Glavine .40 1.00
35 Rick Mahler .01 .05
36 Pete Smith .01 .05
37 Atlanta-Fulton County Stadium .01 .05
38 Atlanta team lettering .01 .05
39 Bruce Sutter .40 1.00
40 Gerald Perry .01 .05
41 Jeff Blauser .01 .05
42 Ron Gant .10 .30
43 Andres Thomas .01 .05
44 Dion James .01 .05
45 Dale Murphy .10 .30
46 Cubs team logo .01 .05
47 Doug Dascenzo .01 .05
48 Mike Harkey .01 .05
49 Greg Maddux 1.00 2.50
50 Jeff Pico .01 .05
51 Rick Sutcliffe .02 .10
52 Damon Berryhill .01 .05
53 Wrigley Field .01 .05
54 Cubs lettering .01 .05
55 Mark Grace .50 1.25
56 Ryne Sandberg .50 1.25
57 Vance Law .01 .05
58 Shawon Dunston .01 .05
59 Andre Dawson .10 .30
60 Rafael Palmeiro .25 .60
61 Mitch Webster .01 .05
62 Reds team logo .01 .05
63 Jack Armstrong .01 .05
64 Chris Sabo .01 .05
65 Tom Browning .01 .05
66 John Franco .02 .10
67 Danny Jackson .01 .05
68 Jose Rijo .01 .05
69 Riverfront Stadium .01 .05
70 Reds team lettering .01 .05
71 Bo Diaz .01 .05
72 Nick Esasky .01 .05
73 Jeff Treadway .01 .05
74 Barry Larkin .30 .75
75 Kal Daniels .01 .05
76 Eric Davis .02 .10
77 Paul O'Neill .07 .20
78 Astros team logo .01 .05
79 Craig Biggio .75 2.00
80 John Fishel .01 .05
81 Juan Agosto .01 .05
82 Bob Knepper .01 .05
83 Nolan Ryan 1.50 4.00
84 Mike Scott .01 .05
85 The Astrodome .01 .05
86 Astros team lettering .01 .05
87 Dave Smith .01 .05
88 Glenn Davis .01 .05
89 Bill Doran .01 .05
90 Rafael Ramirez .01 .05
91 Kevin Bass .01 .05
92 Billy Hatcher .01 .05
93 Gerald Young .01 .05
94 Dodgers team logo .01 .05
95 Tim Belcher .01 .05
96 Tim Crews .01 .05
97 Orel Hershiser .02 .10
98 Jay Howell .01 .05
99 Tim Leary .01 .05
100 John Tudor .01 .05
101 Dodger Stadium .01 .05
102 Dodgers team lettering .01 .05
103 Fernando Valenzuela .02 .10
104 Mike Scioscia .02 .10
105 Mickey Hatcher .01 .05
106 Steve Sax .01 .05
107 Kirk Gibson .02 .10
108 Mike Marshall .01 .05
109 John Shelby .01 .05
110 Expos team logo .01 .05
111 Randy Johnson 2.50 6.00
112 Nelson Santovenia .01 .05
113 Tim Burke .01 .05
114 Dennis Martinez .02 .10
115 Pascual Perez .01 .05
116 Bryn Smith .01 .05
117 Olympic Stadium .01 .05
118 Expos team lettering .01 .05
119 Andres Galarraga .10 .30
120 Wallace Johnson .01 .05
121 Tom Foley .01 .05
122 Tim Wallach .01 .05
123 Hubie Brooks .01 .05
124 Tracy Jones .01 .05
125 Tim Raines .02 .10
126 Mets team logo .01 .05
127 Kevin Elster .01 .05
128 Gregg Jefferies .01 .05
129 David Cone .10 .30
130 Ron Darling .01 .05
131 Dwight Gooden .02 .10
132 Roger McDowell .01 .05
133 Shea Stadium .01 .05
134 Mets team lettering .01 .05
135 Randy Myers .02 .10
136 Gary Carter .30 .75
137 Keith Hernandez .02 .10
138 Lenny Dykstra .02 .10
139 Kevin McReynolds .01 .05
140 Darryl Strawberry .02 .10
141 Mookie Wilson .02 .10
142 Phillies team logo .01 .05
143 Ron Jones .01 .05
144 Ricky Jordan .01 .05
145 Steve Bedrosian .01 .05
146 Don Carman .01 .05
147 Kevin Gross .01 .05
148 Bruce Ruffin .01 .05
149 Veterans Stadium .01 .05
150 Phillies team lettering .01 .05
151 Von Hayes .01 .05
152 Juan Samuel .01 .05
153 Mike Schmidt .40 1.00
154 Phil Bradley .01 .05
155 Bob Dernier .01 .05
156 Chris James .01 .05
157 Milt Thompson .01 .05
158 Pirates team logo .01 .05
159 Randy Kramer .01 .05
160 Scott Medvin .01 .05
161 Doug Drabek .01 .05
162 Mike Dunne .01 .05
163 Jim Gott .01 .05
164 Jeff D. Robinson .01 .05
165 Three Rivers Stadium .01 .05
166 Pirates team lettering .01 .05
167 John Smiley .01 .05
168 Mike LaValliere .01 .05
169 Sid Bream .01 .05
170 Jose Lind .01 .05
171 Bobby Bonilla .02 .10
172 Barry Bonds .75 2.00
173 Andy Van Slyke .02 .10
174 Cardinals team logo .01 .05
175 Luis Alicea .01 .05
176 John Costello .01 .05
177 Jose DeLeon .01 .05
178 Joe Magrane .01 .05
179 Todd Worrell .01 .05
180 Tony Pena .01 .05
181 Busch Stadium .01 .05
182 Cardinals team lettering .01 .05
183 Pedro Guerrero .01 .05
184 Jose Oquendo .01 .05
185 Terry Pendleton .02 .10
186 Ozzie Smith .40 1.00
187 Tom Brunansky .01 .05
188 Vince Coleman .01 .05
189 Willie McGee .02 .10
190 Padres team logo .01 .05
191 Roberto Alomar .40 1.00
192 Sandy Alomar Jr. .20 .50
193 Mark Davis .01 .05
194 Andy Hawkins .01 .05
195 Dennis Rasmussen .01 .05
196 Eric Show .01 .05
197 Jack Murphy Stadium .01 .05
198 Padres team lettering .01 .05
199 Benito Santiago .02 .10
200 John Kruk .02 .10
201 Randy Ready .01 .05
202 Garry Templeton .01 .05
203 Tony Gwynn .75 2.00
204 Carmelo Martinez .01 .05
205 Marvell Wynne .01 .05
206 Giants Team Logo .01 .05
207 Dennis Cook .01 .05
208 Kirt Manwaring .01 .05
209 Kelly Downs .01 .05
210 Rick Reuschel .02 .10
211 Don Robinson .01 .05
212 Will Clark .30 .75
213 Candlestick Park .01 .05
214 Giants team lettering .01 .05
215 Robby Thompson .01 .05
216 Kevin Mitchell .02 .10
217 Jose Uribe .01 .05
218 Matt Williams .40 1.00
219 Mike Aldrete .01 .05
220 Brett Butler .02 .10
221 Candy Maldonado .01 .05
222 Tony Gwynn .75 2.00
223 Darryl Strawberry .01 .05
224 Andres Galarraga .10 .30
225 Orel Hershiser Danny Jackson .02 .10
226 Nolan Ryan 1.50 4.00
227 Dwight Gooden AS .02 .10
228 Gary Carter AS .02 .10
229 Vince Coleman AS .01 .05
230 Andre Dawson AS .02 .10
231 Darryl Strawberry AS .01 .05
232 Will Clark AS .02 .10
233 Ryne Sandberg AS .20 .50
234 Bobby Bonilla AS .02 .10
235 Ozzie Smith AS .20 .50
236 Terry Steinbach AS .01 .05
237 Frank Viola AS .01 .05
238 Jose Canseco AS .02 .10
239 Rickey Henderson AS .20 .50
240 Dave Winfield AS .20 .50
241 Cal Ripken Jr. AS .75 2.00
242 Wade Boggs AS .20 .50
243 Paul Molitor AS .20 .50
244 Mark McGwire AS .30 .75
245 Wade Boggs AS .20 .50
246 Jose Canseco .30 .75
247 Kirby Puckett .40 1.00
248 Frank Viola .01 .05
249 Roger Clemens .40 1.00
250 Orioles team logo .01 .05
251 Bob Milacki .01 .05
252 Craig Worthington .01 .05
253 Jeff Ballard .01 .05
254 Tom Niedenfeuer .01 .05
255 Dave Schmidt .01 .05
256 Terry Kennedy .01 .05
257 Memorial Stadium .01 .05
258 Orioles team lettering .01 .05
259 Mickey Tettleton .02 .10
260 Eddie Murray .40 1.00
261 Bill Ripken .01 .05
262 Cal Ripken Jr. 1.50 4.00
263 Joe Orsulak .01 .05
264 Larry Sheets .01 .05
265 Pete Stanicek .01 .05
266 Red Sox team logo .01 .05
267 Steve Curry .01 .05
268 Jody Reed .01 .05
269 Oil Can Boyd .01 .05
270 Roger Clemens .75 2.00
271 Bruce Hurst .01 .05
272 Lee Smith .02 .10
273 Fenway Park .01 .05
274 Red Sox team lettering .01 .05
275 Todd Benzinger .01 .05
276 Marty Barrett .01 .05
277 Wade Boggs .40 1.00
278 Ellis Burks .10 .30
279 Dwight Evans .02 .10
280 Mike Greenwell .01 .05
281 Jim Rice .02 .10
282 Angels team logo .01 .05
283 Dante Bichette .40 1.00
284 Bryan Harvey .01 .05
285 Kirk McCaskill .01 .05
286 Mike Witt .01 .05
287 Bob Boone .02 .10
288 Brian Downing .02 .10
289 Anaheim Stadium .01 .05
290 Angels team lettering .01 .05
291 Wally Joyner .02 .10
292 Johnny Ray .01 .05
293 Jack Howell .01 .05
294 Dick Schofield .01 .05
295 Tony Armas .01 .05
296 Chili Davis .02 .10
297 Devon White .02 .10
298 White Sox team logo .01 .05
299 Dave Gallagher .01 .05
300 Melido Perez .01 .05
301 Shawn Hillegas .01 .05
302 Jack McDowell .02 .10
303 Bobby Thigpen .01 .05
304 Carlton Fisk .40 1.00
305 Comiskey Park .01 .05
306 White Sox team lettering .01 .05
307 Greg Walker .01 .05
308 Steve Lyons .02 .10
309 Ozzie Guillen .07 .20
310 Harold Baines .07 .20
311 Daryl Boston .01 .05
312 Lance Johnson .01 .05
313 Dan Pasqua .01 .05
314 Indians team logo .01 .05
315 Luis Medina .01 .05
316 Ron Tingley .01 .05
317 Tom Candiotti .01 .05
318 John Farrell .01 .05
319 Doug Jones .01 .05
320 Greg Swindell .01 .05
321 Cleveland Stadium .01 .05
322 Indians team lettering .01 .05
323 Andy Allanson .01 .05
324 Willie Upshaw .01 .05
325 Julio Franco .02 .10
326 Brook Jacoby .01 .05
327 Joe Carter .07 .20
328 Mel Hall .01 .05
329 Cory Snyder .01 .05
330 Tigers team logo .01 .05
331 Paul Gibson .01 .05
332 Torey Lovullo .01 .05
333 Mike Henneman .01 .05
334 Jack Morris .02 .10
335 Jeff M. Robinson .01 .05
336 Frank Tanana .01 .05
337 Tiger Stadium .01 .05
338 Tigers team lettering .01 .05
339 Matt Nokes .01 .05
340 Tom Brookens .01 .05
341 Lou Whitaker .02 .10
342 Luis Salazar .01 .05
343 Alan Trammell .07 .20
344 Chet Lemon .01 .05
345 Gary Pettis .01 .05
346 Royals team logo .01 .05
347 Luis de los Santos .01 .05
348 Gary Thurman .01 .05
349 Steve Farr .01 .05
350 Mark Gubicza .01 .05
351 Charlie Leibrandt .01 .05
352 Bret Saberhagen .02 .10
353 Royals Stadium .01 .05
354 Royals team lettering .01 .05
355 George Brett .60 1.50
356 Frank White .02 .10
357 Kevin Seitzer .01 .05
358 Bo Jackson .20 .50
359 Pat Tabler .01 .05
360 Danny Tartabull .01 .05
361 Willie Wilson .01 .05
362 Brewers team logo .01 .05
363 Joey Meyer .01 .05
364 Gary Sheffield 1.00 2.50
365 Don August .01 .05
366 Ted Higuera .01 .05
367 Dan Plesac .01 .05
368 B.J. Surhoff .02 .10
369 Milwaukee County Stadium .01 .05
370 Brewers team lettering .01 .05
371 Greg Brock .01 .05
372 Jim Gantner .01 .05
373 Paul Molitor .40 1.00
374 Dale Sveum .01 .05
375 Glenn Braggs .01 .05
376 Rob Deer .01 .05
377 Robin Yount .40 1.00
378 Twins team logo .01 .05
379 German Gonzalez .01 .05
380 Kelvin Torve .01 .05
381 Allan Anderson .01 .05
382 Jeff Reardon .02 .10
383 Frank Viola .01 .05
384 Tim Laudner .01 .05
385 Hubert H. Humphrey Metrodome .01 .05
386 Twins team lettering .01 .05
387 Kent Hrbek .02 .10
388 Gene Larkin .01 .05
389 Gary Gaetti .02 .10
390 Greg Gagne .01 .05
391 Randy Bush .01 .05
392 Dan Gladden .01 .05
393 Kirby Puckett .50 1.25
394 Yankees team logo .01 .05
395 Roberto Kelly .02 .10
396 Al Leiter .10 .30
397 John Candelaria .01 .05
398 Rich Dotson .01 .05
399 Rick Rhoden .01 .05
400 Dave Righetti .01 .05
401 Yankee Stadium .01 .05
402 Yankees team lettering .01 .05
403 Don Slaught .01 .05
404 Don Mattingly .75 2.00
405 Willie Randolph .02 .10
406 Mike Pagliarulo .01 .05
407 Rafael Santana .01 .05
408 Rickey Henderson .60 1.50
409 Dave Winfield .40 1.00
410 Athletics team logo .01 .05
411 Todd Burns .01 .05
412 Walt Weiss .02 .10
413 Storm Davis .01 .05
414 Dennis Eckersley .40 1.00
415 Dave Stewart .02 .10
416 Bob Welch .01 .05
417 Oakland Alameda County Coliseum .01 .05
418 Athletics team lettering .01 .05
419 Terry Steinbach .01 .05
420 Mark McGwire .60 1.50
421 Carney Lansford .02 .10
422 Jose Canseco .30 .75
423 Dave Henderson .01 .05
424 Dave Parker .02 .10
425 Luis Polonia .01 .05
426 Mariners team logo .01 .05
427 Mario Diaz .01 .05
428 Edgar Martinez .07 .20
429 Scott Bankhead .01 .05
430 Mark Langston .01 .05
431 Mike Moore .01 .05
432 Scott Bradley .01 .05
433 The Kingdome .01 .05
434 Mariners team lettering .01 .05
435 Alvin Davis .01 .05
436 Harold Reynolds .02 .10
437 Jim Presley .01 .05
438 Rey Quinones .01 .05
439 Mickey Brantley .01 .05
440 Jay Buhner .20 .50
441 Henry Cotto .01 .05
442 Rangers team logo .01 .05
443 Cecil Espy .01 .05
444 Chad Kreuter .01 .05
445 Jose Guzman .01 .05
446 Charlie Hough .02 .10
447 Jeff Russell .01 .05
448 Bobby Witt .01 .05
449 Arlington Stadium .01 .05
450 Rangers team lettering .01 .05
451 Geno Petralli .01 .05
452 Pete O'Brien .01 .05
453 Steve Buechele .01 .05
454 Scott Fletcher .01 .05
455 Pete Incaviglia .01 .05
456 Oddibe McDowell .01 .05
457 Ruben Sierra .02 .10
458 Blue Jays team logo .01 .05
459 Rob Ducey .01 .05
460 Todd Stottlemyre .01 .05
461 Tom Henke .01 .05
462 Jimmy Key .01 .05
463 Dave Stieb .02 .10
464 Pat Borders .01 .05
465 Exhibition Stadium .01 .05
466 Blue Jays team lettering .01 .05
467 Fred McGriff .10 .30
468 Manny Lee .01 .05
469 Kelly Gruber .01 .05
470 Tony Fernandez .02 .10
471 Jesse Barfield .01 .05
472 George Bell .01 .05
473 Lloyd Moseby .01 .05
474 Orel Hershiser .02 .10
475 Frank Viola .01 .05
476 Chris Sabo .01 .05
477 Jose Canseco .30 .75
478 Walt Weiss .01 .05
479 Kirk Gibson .02 .10
480 Jose Canseco .30 .75
xx Sticker Album/(Jose Canseco on front).30 .75

1990 Panini Stickers

These 388 stickers measure approximately 2 1/8" by 3" and feature on their fronts white-bordered color player action shots. Stickers 186-197 are foils. An album onto which the stickers could be affixed was available at retail stores. The album featured Nolan Ryan on the front and an ad for the Panini 1990 Fan Club Pop Star Sticker Collection on the back. The album also featured a four-page insert without stickers on the 1989 post-season. The album and the sticker numbering are organized by team alphabetically by city with AL teams preceding NL teams. Subsets include 1989 AL Stat Leaders (183-185), 1989 League Championship Series (Foil, 186-187), Excellence in the '80s (Foil, 188-197), 1989 All-Stars (198-213), 1989 NL Stat Leaders (214-216), Tomorrow's Headliners (373-382) and 1989 Highlights (383-388).

COMPLETE SET (388) 6.00 15.00
1 Randy Milligan .01 .05
2 Gregg Olson .02 .10
3 Bill Ripken .01 .05
4 Phil Bradley .01 .05
5 Joe Orsulak .01 .05
6 Bob Milacki .01 .05
7 Cal Ripken 1.25 3.00
8 Mickey Tettleton .02 .10
9 Orioles Logo .01 .05
10 Orioles Helmet .01 .05
11 Craig Worthington .01 .05
12 Mike Devereaux .01 .05
13 Jeff Ballard .01 .05
14 Lee Smith .02 .10
15 Marty Barrett .01 .05
16 Mike Greenwell .01 .05
17 Dwight Evans .02 .10
18 John Dopson .01 .05
19 Wade Boggs .30 .75
20 Mike Boddicker .01 .05
21 Ellis Burks .08 .25
22 Red Sox Logo .01 .05
23 Red Sox Helmet .01 .05
24 Roger Clemens .60 1.50
25 Jody Reed .01 .05
26 Nick Esasky .01 .05
27 Brian Downing .01 .05
28 Bert Blyleven .02 .10
29 Devon White .02 .10
30 Claudell Washington .01 .05
31 Wally Joyner .02 .10
32 Chuck Finley .02 .10
33 Johnny Ray .01 .05
34 Jim Abbott .05 .15
35 Angels Logo .01 .05
36 Angels Helmet .01 .05
37 Kirk McCaskill .01 .05
38 Lance Parrish .01 .05
39 Chili Davis .02 .10
40 Steve Lyons .02 .10
41 Ozzie Guillen .05 .15
42 Melido Perez .01 .05
43 Scott Fletcher .01 .05
44 Carlton Fisk .30 .75
45 Greg Walker .01 .05
46 Dave Gallagher .01 .05
47 Ivan Calderon .01 .05
48 White Sox Logo .01 .05
49 White Sox Helmet .01 .05
50 Bobby Thigpen .01 .05
51 Ron Kittle .01 .05
52 Daryl Boston .01 .05
53 John Farrell .01 .05
54 Jerry Browne .01 .05
55 Pete O'Brien .01 .05
56 Cory Snyder .01 .05
57 Tom Candiotti .01 .05
58 Brook Jacoby .01 .05
59 Greg Swindell .01 .05
60 Felix Fermin .01 .05
61 Indians Logo .01 .05
62 Indians Helmet .01 .05
63 Doug Jones .01 .05
64 Dion James .01 .05
65 Joe Carter .02 .10
66 Mike Heath .01 .05
67 Dave Bergman .01 .05
68 Gary Ward .01 .05
69 Mike Henneman .01 .05
70 Alan Trammell .05 .15
71 Lou Whitaker .02 .10
72 Frank Tanana .01 .05
73 Fred Lynn .01 .05
74 Tigers Logo .01 .05
75 Tigers Helmet .01 .05
76 Jack Morris .02 .10
77 Chet Lemon .01 .05
78 Gary Pettis .01 .05
79 Kurt Stillwell .01 .05
80 Jim Eisenreich .01 .05
81 Bret Saberhagen .02 .10
82 Mark Gubicza .01 .05
83 Frank White .02 .10
84 Bo Jackson .08 .25
85 Jeff Montgomery .02 .10
86 Kevin Seitzer .01 .05
87 Royals Logo .01 .05
88 Royals Helmet .01 .05
89 Tom Gordon .05 .15
90 Danny Tartabull .01 .05
91 George Brett .60 1.50
92 Robin Yount .30 .75
93 B.J. Surhoff .02 .10
94 Jim Gantner .01 .05
95 Dan Plesac .01 .05
96 Ted Higuera .01 .05
97 Glenn Braggs .01 .05
98 Paul Molitor .40 1.00
99 Chris Bosio .01 .05
100 Brewers Logo .01 .05
101 Brewers Helmet .01 .05
102 Rob Deer .01 .05
103 Chuck Crim .01 .05
104 Greg Brock .01 .05
105 Kirby Puckett .40 1.00
106 Gary Gaetti .02 .10
107 Roy Smith .01 .05
108 Jeff Reardon .02 .10
109 Randy Bush .01 .05
110 Al Newman .01 .05
111 Dan Gladden .01 .05
112 Kent Hrbek .02 .10
113 Twins Logo .01 .05
114 Twins Helmet .01 .05
115 Greg Gagne .01 .05
116 Brian Harper .01 .05
117 Allan Anderson .01 .05
118 Lee Guetterman .01 .05
119 Roberto Kelly .01 .05
120 Jesse Barfield .01 .05
121 Alvaro Espinoza .01 .05
122 Mel Hall .01 .05
123 Chuck Cary .01 .05
124 Dave Righetti .01 .05
125 Don Mattingly .60 1.50
126 Yankees Logo .01 .05
127 Yankees Helmet .01 .05
128 Bob Geren .01 .05
129 Steve Sax .01 .05
130 Andy Hawkins .01 .05
131 Bob Welch .01 .05
132 Mark McGwire .60 1.50
133 Dave Henderson .01 .05
134 Carney Lansford .02 .10
135 Walt Weiss .01 .05
136 Mike Moore .01 .05
137 Dennis Eckersley .30 .75
138 Rickey Henderson .40 1.00
139 Athletics Logo .01 .05
140 Athletics Helmet .01 .05
141 Dave Stewart .02 .10
142 Jose Canseco .30 .75
143 Terry Steinbach .01 .05
144 Harold Reynolds .02 .10
145 Darnell Coles .01 .05
146 Brian Holman .01 .05
147 Scott Bankhead .01 .05
148 Greg Briley .01 .05
149 Alvin Davis .01 .05
150 Jeffrey Leonard .01 .05
151 Mike Schooler .01 .05
152 Mariners Logo .01 .05
153 Mariners Helmet .01 .05
154 Randy Johnson .50 1.25
155 Ken Griffey Jr. .75 2.00
156 Dave Valle .01 .05
157 Pete Incaviglia .01 .05
158 Fred Manrique .01 .05
159 Jeff Russell .01 .05
160 Nolan Ryan 1.25 3.00
161 Geno Petralli .01 .05
162 Ruben Sierra .02 .10
163 Julio Franco .05 .15
164 Rafael Palmeiro .15 .40
165 Rangers Logo .01 .05
166 Rangers Helmet .01 .05
167 Harold Baines .02 .10
168 Kevin Brown .08 .25
169 Steve Buechele .01 .05
170 Fred McGriff .08 .25
171 Kelly Gruber .01 .05
172 Todd Stottlemyre .01 .05
173 Dave Stieb .02 .10
174 Mookie Wilson .02 .10
175 Pat Borders .01 .05
176 Tony Fernandez .02 .10
177 John Cerutti .01 .05
178 Blue Jays Logo .01 .05
179 Blue Jays Helmet .01 .05
180 George Bell .01 .05
181 Jimmy Key .01 .05
182 Nelson Liriano .01 .05
183 Kirby Puckett .40 1.00
184 Carney Lansford .02 .10
185 Nolan Ryan 1.25 3.00
186 AL Logo .01 .05
187 NL Logo .01 .05
188 World Championship Trophy .01 .05
189 '88 World Championship LA Dodgers Ring .01 .05
190 '87 World Championship Minnesota Twins Ring .01 .05
191 '86 World Championship NY Mets Ring .01 .05
192 '85 World Championship KC Royals Ring .01 .05
193 '84 World Championship Detroit Tigers Ring .01 .05
194 '83 World Championship Baltimore Orioles Ring .01 .05
195 '82 World Championship St.Louis Cardinals Ring .01 .05
196 '81 World Championship LA Dodgers Ring .01 .05
197 '80 World Championship Philadelphia Phillies Rin .01 .05
198 Dave Stewart Bo Jackson .02 .10
199 Wade Boggs Kirby Puckett .08 .25
200 Harold Baines .02 .10
201 Julio Franco .01 .05
202 Cal Ripken 1.25 3.00
203 Ruben Sierra .01 .05
204 Mark McGwire .75 2.00
205 Terry Steinbach .01 .05
206 Rick Reuschel Ozzie Smith .08 .25
207 Tony Gwynn Will Clark .30 .75
208 Kevin Mitchell .01 .05
209 Eric Davis .02 .10
210 Howard Johnson .01 .05
211 Pedro Guerrero .01 .05
212 Ryne Sandberg .40 1.00
213 Benito Santiago .01 .05
214 Kevin Mitchell .01 .05
215 Mark Davis .01 .05
216 Vince Coleman .01 .05
217 Jeff Blauser .01 .05
218 Jeff Treadway .01 .05
219 Tom Glavine .30 .75
220 Joe Boever .01 .05
221 Oddibe McDowell .01 .05
222 Dale Murphy .08 .25
223 Derek Lilliquist .01 .05
224 Tommy Gregg .01 .05
225 Braves Logo .01 .05
226 Braves Helmet .01 .05
227 Lonnie Smith .01 .05
228 John Smoltz .40 1.00
229 Andres Thomas .01 .05
230 Jerome Walton .01 .05
231 Ryne Sandberg .40 1.00
232 Mitch Williams .01 .05
233 Rick Sutcliffe .01 .05
234 Damon Berryhill .01 .05
235 Dwight Smith .01 .05
236 Shawon Dunston .01 .05
237 Greg Maddux .75 2.00
238 Cubs Logo .01 .05
239 Cubs Helmet .01 .05
240 Andre Dawson .08 .25
241 Mark Grace .20 .50
242 Mike Bielecki .01 .05
243 Jose Rijo .01 .05
244 John Franco .02 .10
245 Paul O'Neill .05 .15
246 Eric Davis .02 .10
247 Tom Browning .01 .05
248 Chris Sabo .01 .05
249 Rob Dibble .02 .10
250 Todd Benzinger .01 .05
251 Reds Logo .01 .05
252 Reds Helmet .01 .05
253 Barry Larkin .08 .25
254 Rolando Roomes .01 .05
255 Danny Jackson .01 .05
256 Terry Puhl .01 .05
257 Dave Smith .01 .05
258 Glenn Davis .01 .05
259 Craig Biggio .30 .75
260 Ken Caminiti .30 .75
261 Kevin Bass .01 .05
262 Mike Scott .02 .10
263 Gerald Young .01 .05
264 Astros Logo .01 .05
265 Astros Helmet .01 .05
266 Rafael Ramirez .01 .05
267 Jim Deshaies .01 .05
268 Bill Doran .01 .05
269 Fernando Valenzuela .02 .10
270 Alfredo Griffin .01 .05
271 Kirk Gibson .02 .10
272 Mike Marshall .01 .05
273 Eddie Murray .30 .75
274 Jay Howell .01 .05
275 Orel Hershiser .02 .10
276 Mike Scioscia .02 .10
277 Dodgers Logo .01 .05
278 Dodgers Helmet .01 .05
279 Willie Randolph .02 .10
280 Kal Daniels .01 .05
281 Tim Belcher .01 .05
282 Pascual Perez .01 .05
283 Tim Raines .05 .15
284 Andres Galarraga .08 .25
285 Spike Owen .01 .05
286 Tim Wallach .01 .05
287 Mark Langston .01 .05
288 Dennis Martinez .02 .10
289 Nelson Santovenia .01 .05
290 Expos Logo .01 .05
291 Expos Helmet .01 .05
292 Tom Foley .01 .05
293 Dave Martinez .01 .05
294 Tim Burke .01 .05
295 Ron Darling .01 .05
296 Kevin Elster .01 .05
297 Dwight Gooden .02 .10
298 Gregg Jefferies .01 .05
299 Sid Fernandez .01 .05
300 Dave Magadan .01 .05
301 David Cone .08 .25
302 Darryl Strawberry .02 .10
303 Mets Logo .01 .05
304 Mets Helmet .01 .05
305 Kevin McReynolds .01 .05
306 Howard Johnson .01 .05
307 Randy Myers .02 .10
308 Roger McDowell .01 .05
309 Tom Herr .01 .05
310 John Kruk .02 .10
311 Randy Ready .01 .05
312 Jeff Parrett .01 .05
313 Lenny Dykstra .02 .10
314 Ken Howell .01 .05
315 Ricky Jordan .01 .05
316 Phillies Logo .01 .05
317 Phillies Helmet .01 .05
318 Dickie Thon .01 .05
319 Von Hayes .01 .05
320 Dennis Cook .01 .05
321 Jay Bell .01 .05
322 Barry Bonds .60 1.50
323 John Smiley .01 .05
324 Andy Van Slyke .01 .05
325 Bobby Bonilla .02 .10
326 Bill Landrum .01 .05
327 Randy Kramer .01 .05
328 Jose Lind .01 .05
329 Pirates Logo .01 .05
330 Pirates Helmet .01 .05
331 Gary Redus .01 .05
332 Doug Drabek .01 .05
333 Mike LaValliere .01 .05
334 Jose DeLeon .01 .05
335 Pedro Guerrero .01 .05
336 Vince Coleman .01 .05
337 Terry Pendleton .02 .10
338 Ozzie Smith .50 1.25
339 Willie McGee .02 .10
340 Todd Worrell .01 .05
341 Jose Oquendo .01 .05
342 Cardinals Logo .01 .05
343 Cardinals Helmet .01 .05
344 Tom Brunansky .01 .05
345 Milt Thompson .01 .05
346 Joe Magrane .01 .05
347 Ed Whitson .01 .05
348 Jack Clark .02 .10
349 Roberto Alomar .30 .75
350 Chris James .01 .05
351 Tony Gwynn .60 1.50
352 Mark Davis .01 .05
353 Greg W. Harris .01 .05
354 Garry Templeton .01 .05
355 Padres Logo .01 .05
356 Padres Helmet .01 .05
357 Bruce Hurst .01 .05
358 Benito Santiago .02 .10
359 Bip Roberts .01 .05

360 Dave Dravecky .02 .10
361 Kevin Mitchell .01 .05
362 Craig Lefferts .01 .05
363 Will Clark .08 .25
364 Steve Bedrosian .01 .05
365 Brett Butler .02 .10
366 Matt Williams .05 .15
367 Scott Garrelts .01 .05
368 Giants Logo .01 .05
369 Giants Helmet .01 .05
370 Rick Reuschel .02 .10
371 Robby Thompson .01 .05
372 Jose Uribe .01 .05
373 Ben McDonald .01 .05
374 Carlos Martinez .01 .05
375 Steve Olin .02 .10
376 Bill Spiers .01 .05
377 Junior Felix .01 .05
378 Joe Oliver .01 .05
379 Eric Anthony .01 .05
380 Ramon Martinez .01 .05
381 Todd Zeile .02 .10
382 Andy Benes .01 .05
383 Vince Coleman .01 .05
384 Bo Jackson .08 .25
385 Howard Johnson .01 .05
386 Dave Dravecky .02 .10
387 Nolan Ryan 1.25 3.00
388 Cal Ripken 1.25 3.00
xx Sticker Album/(Nolan Ryan on front) .60 1.50

1991 Panini Stickers

The 1991 Panini baseball set contains 271 stickers measuring 1 1/2" by 2 1/2". The stickers may be pasted in a collectible sticker album that measures 8 1/4" by 10 1/2". After a "Year of the No-Hitter 1990" (1-9) subset, the stickers are checklisted alphabetically according to teams within the NL and then the AL.

COMPLETE SET (271) 6.00 15.00
1 Mark Langston .01 .05
2 Randy Johnson .20 .50
3 Nolan Ryan 1.25 3.00
4 Dave Stewart .02 .10
5 Fernando Valenzuela .02 .10
6 Andy Hawkins .01 .05
7 Melido Perez .01 .05
8 Terry Mulholland .01 .05
9 Dave Stieb .02 .10
10 Craig Biggio .30 .75
11 Jim Deshaies .01 .05
12 Dave Smith .01 .05
13 Eric Yelding .01 .05
14 Astros Pennant .01 .05
15 Astros Logo .01 .05
16 Mike Scott .01 .05
17 Ken Caminiti .30 .75
18 Danny Darwin .01 .05
19 Glenn Davis .01 .05
20 Braves Pennant .01 .05
21 Braves Logo .01 .05
22 Lonnie Smith .01 .05
23 Charlie Leibrandt .01 .05
24 Jim Presley .01 .05
25 Greg Olson .01 .05
26 John Smoltz .08 .25
27 Ron Gant .02 .10
28 Jeff Treadway .01 .05
29 Dave Justice .08 .25
30 Jose Oquendo .01 .05
31 Joe Magrane .01 .05
32 Cardinals Pennant .01 .05
33 Cardinals Logo .01 .05
34 Todd Zeile .02 .10
35 Vince Coleman .01 .05
36 Bob Tewksbury .01 .05
37 Pedro Guerrero .01 .05
38 Lee Smith .02 .10
39 Ozzie Smith .40 1.00
40 Ryne Sandberg .40 1.00
41 Andre Dawson .08 .25
42 Cubs Pennant .01 .05
43 Greg Maddux .75 2.00
44 Jerome Walton .01 .05
45 Cubs Logo .01 .05
46 Mike Harkey .01 .05
47 Shawon Dunston .01 .05
48 Mark Grace .20 .50
49 Joe Girardi .02 .10
50 Ramon Martinez .01 .05
51 Lenny Harris .01 .05
52 Mike Morgan .01 .05
53 Eddie Murray .30 .75
54 Dodgers Pennant .01 .05
55 Dodgers Logo .01 .05
56 Hubie Brooks .01 .05
57 Mike Scioscia .02 .10
58 Kal Daniels .01 .05
59 Fernando Valenzuela .02 .10
60 Expos Pennant .01 .05
61 Expos Logo .01 .05
62 Spike Owen .01 .05
63 Tim Raines .02 .10
64 Tim Wallach .01 .05
65 Larry Walker .20 .50
66 Dave Martinez .01 .05
67 Mark Gardner .01 .05
68 Dennis Martinez .02 .10
69 Delino DeShields .02 .10
70 Jeff Brantley .02 .10
71 Kevin Mitchell .01 .05
72 Giants Pennant .01 .05
73 Giants Logo .01 .05
74 Don Robinson .01 .05
75 Brett Butler .02 .10
76 Matt Williams .05 .15
77 Robby Thompson .01 .05
78 John Burkett .01 .05
79 Will Clark .08 .25
80 David Cone .02 .10
81 Dave Magadan .01 .05
82 Mets Pennant .01 .05
83 Gregg Jefferies .01 .05
84 Frank Viola .01 .05
85 Mets Logo .01 .05
86 Howard Johnson .01 .05
87 John Franco .02 .10
88 Darryl Strawberry .02 .10
89 Dwight Gooden .02 .10
90 Joe Carter .02 .10
91 Ed Whitson .01 .05
92 Andy Benes .01 .05
93 Benito Santiago .02 .10
94 Padres Pennant .01 .05
95 Padres Logo .01 .05
96 Roberto Alomar .30 .75
97 Bip Roberts .01 .05
98 Jack Clark .02 .10
99 Tony Gwynn .75 2.00
100 Phillies Pennant .01 .05
101 Phillies Logo .01 .05
102 Charlie Hayes .01 .05
103 Len Dykstra .02 .10
104 Dale Murphy .08 .25
105 Von Hayes .01 .05
106 Dickie Thon .01 .05
107 John Kruk .02 .10
108 Ken Howell .01 .05
109 Darren Daulton .02 .10
110 Jay Bell .01 .05
111 Bobby Bonilla .02 .10
112 Pirates Pennant .01 .05
113 Pirates Logo .01 .05
114 Barry Bonds .60 1.50
115 Neal Heaton .01 .05
116 Doug Drabek .01 .05
117 Jose Lind .01 .05
118 Andy Van Slyke .01 .05
119 Sid Bream .01 .05
120 Paul O'Neill .02 .10
121 Randy Myers .02 .10
122 Reds Pennant .01 .05
123 Mariano Duncan .01 .05
124 Eric Davis .02 .10
125 Reds Logo .01 .05
126 Jack Armstrong .01 .05
127 Chris Sabo .02 .05
128 Rob Dibble .01 .05
129 Barry Larkin .08 .25
130 National League Logo .01 .05
131 American League Logo .01 .05
132 Dave Winfield .20 .50
133 Lance Parrish .01 .05
134 Chili Davis .02 .10
135 Chuck Finley .02 .10
136 Angels Pennant .01 .05
137 Angels Logo .01 .05
138 Johnny Ray .01 .05
139 Dante Bichette .20 .50
140 Jim Abbott .02 .10
141 Wally Joyner .02 .10
142 Athletics Pennant .01 .05
143 Athletics Logo .01 .05
144 Dave Stewart .02 .10
145 Mark McGwire .60 1.50
146 Rickey Henderson .40 1.00
147 Walt Weiss .01 .05
148 Dennis Eckersley .30 .75
149 Jose Canseco .30 .75
150 Dave Henderson .01 .05
151 Bob Welch .01 .05
152 Tony Fernandez .02 .10
153 David Wells .05 .15
154 Blue Jays Pennant .01 .05
155 Blue Jays Logo .01 .05
156 Pat Borders .01 .05
157 Fred McGriff .08 .25
158 George Bell .01 .05
159 John Olerud .05 .15
160 Dave Stieb .01 .05
161 Kelly Gruber .01 .05
162 Bill Spiers .01 .05
163 Dan Plesac .01 .05
164 Brewers Pennant .01 .05
165 Mark Knudson .01 .05
166 Robin Yount .30 .75
167 Brewers Logo .01 .05
168 Paul Molitor .30 .75
169 B.J. Surhoff .02 .10
170 Gary Sheffield .30 .75
171 Dave Parker .02 .10
172 Sandy Alomar Jr. .02 .10
173 Doug Jones .01 .05
174 Tom Candiotti .01 .05
175 Mitch Webster .01 .05
176 Indians Pennant .01 .05
177 Indians Logo .01 .05
178 Brook Jacoby .01 .05
179 Candy Maldonado .01 .05
180 Carlos Baerga .01 .05
181 Chris James .01 .05
182 Mariners Pennant .01 .05
183 Mariners Logo .01 .05
184 Mike Schooler .01 .05
185 Alvin Davis .01 .05
186 Erik Hanson .01 .05
187 Edgar Martinez .05 .15
188 Randy Johnson .50 1.25
189 Ken Griffey Jr. .75 2.00
190 Jay Buhner .08 .25
191 Harold Reynolds .02 .10
192 Cal Ripken 1.25 3.00
193 Gregg Olson .02 .10
194 Orioles Pennant .01 .05
195 Orioles Logo .01 .05
196 Mike Devereaux .01 .05
197 Ben McDonald .01 .05
198 Craig Worthington .01 .05
199 Dave Johnson .01 .05
200 Joe Orsulak .01 .05
201 Randy Milligan .01 .05
202 Ruben Sierra .02 .10
203 Bobby Witt .01 .05
204 Rangers Pennant .01 .05
205 Nolan Ryan 1.25 3.00
206 Jeff Huson .01 .05
207 Rangers Logo .01 .05
208 Kevin Brown .05 .15
209 Steve Buechele .01 .05
210 Julio Franco .02 .10
211 Rafael Palmeiro .20 .50
212 Ellis Burks .05 .15
213 Dwight Evans .02 .10
214 Wade Boggs .30 .75
215 Roger Clemens .60 1.50
216 Red Sox Pennant .01 .05
217 Red Sox Logo .01 .05
218 Jeff Reardon .02 .10
219 Tony Pena .01 .05
220 Jody Reed .01 .05
221 Carlos Quintana .01 .05
222 Royals Pennant .01 .05
223 Royals Logo .01 .05
224 George Brett .60 1.50
225 Bret Saberhagen .02 .10
226 Bo Jackson .08 .25
227 Kevin Seitzer .01 .05
228 Mark Gubicza .01 .05
229 Jim Eisenreich .01 .05
230 Gerald Perry .01 .05
231 Tom Gordon .02 .10
232 Cecil Fielder .02 .10
233 Lou Whitaker .02 .10
234 Tigers Pennant .01 .05
235 Tigers Logo .01 .05
236 Mike Henneman .01 .05
237 Mike Heath .01 .05
238 Alan Trammell .05 .15
239 Lloyd Moseby .01 .05
240 Dan Petry .01 .05
241 Dave Bergman .01 .05
242 Brian Harper .01 .05
243 Rick Aguilera .02 .10
244 Twins Pennant .01 .05
245 Greg Gagne .01 .05
246 Gene Larkin .01 .05
247 Twins Logo .01 .05
248 Kirby Puckett .40 1.00
249 Kevin Tapani .01 .05
250 Gary Gaetti .02 .10
251 Kent Hrbek .02 .10
252 Bobby Thigpen .01 .05
253 Lance Johnson .01 .05
254 Greg Hibbard .01 .05
255 Carlton Fisk .30 .75
256 White Sox Pennant .01 .05
257 White Sox Logo .01 .05
258 Ivan Calderon .01 .05
259 Barry Jones .01 .05
260 Robin Ventura .08 .25
261 Ozzie Guillen .05 .15
262 Yankees Pennant .01 .05
263 Yankees Logo .01 .05
264 Kevin Maas .01 .05
265 Bob Geren .01 .05
266 Dave Righetti .01 .05
267 Don Mattingly .60 1.50
268 Roberto Kelly .01 .05
269 Alvaro Espinoza .01 .05
270 Oscar Azocar .01 .05
271 Steve Sax .01 .05

1991 Panini Canadian Top 15

The 1991 Panini Top 15 sticker set consists of 136 stickers and features Major League's best players and teams in various statistical categories. An American and a Canadian version were issued. The player's name, team and statistical category (the last item in French and English in the Canadian version) appear below the picture. Moreover, the front also has a number (1-4) indicating the player's finish in that category, the statistic and different color emblems for the National League (blue) and the American League (red). The Gold glove winners have a gold emblem, irrespective of league. The set is subdivided according to the following statistical categories, with National League winners listed first (e.g., 1-4) and then American League winners (e.g., 5-8): batting average (1-8); home runs (9-16); runs batted in (17-24); hits (25-32); slugging average (33-40); stolen bases (41-48); runs (49-56); wins (57-64); earned run average (65-72); strikeouts (73-80); saves (81-88); shutouts (89-96); National League logo (97) and gold glove (98-106); American League logo (107) and gold glove (108-16); and team statistical leaders (117-36). The NL logo (97), AL logo (107) and all the team stickers (117-36) are foil.

COMPLETE SET (136) 12.50 30.00
1 Willie McGee .02 .10
2 Eddie Murray .40 1.00
3 Dave Magadan .01 .05
4 Lenny Dykstra .02 .10
5 George Brett .75 2.00
6 Rickey Henderson .40 1.00
7 Rafael Palmeiro .20 .50
8 Alan Trammell .07 .20
9 Ryne Sandberg .60 1.50
10 Darryl Strawberry .02 .10
11 Kevin Mitchell .01 .05
12 Barry Bonds .75 2.00
13 Cecil Fielder .02 .10
14 Mark McGwire .75 2.00
15 Jose Canseco .30 .75
16 Fred McGriff .30 .75
17 Matt Williams .07 .20
18 Bobby Bonilla .01 .05
19 Joe Carter .02 .10
20 Barry Bonds .60 1.50
21 Cecil Fielder .02 .10
22 Kelly Gruber .01 .05
23 Mark McGwire .75 2.00
24 Jose Canseco .40 1.00
25 Brett Butler .02 .10
26 Lenny Dykstra .02 .10
27 Ryne Sandberg .60 1.50
28 Barry Larkin .10 .30
29 Rafael Palmeiro .25 .60
30 Wade Boggs .40 1.00
31 Roberto Kelly .01 .05
32 Mike Greenwell .01 .05
33 Barry Bonds .60 1.50
34 Ryne Sandberg .60 1.50
35 Kevin Mitchell .01 .05
36 Ron Gant .02 .10
37 Cecil Fielder .02 .10
38 Rickey Henderson .40 1.00
39 Jose Canseco .30 .75
40 Fred McGriff .30 .75
41 Vince Coleman .01 .05
42 Eric Yelding .01 .05
43 Barry Bonds .60 1.50
44 Brett Butler .02 .10
45 Rickey Henderson .40 1.00
46 Steve Sax .01 .05
47 Roberto Kelly .01 .05
48 Alex Cole .01 .05
49 Ryne Sandberg .60 1.50
50 Bobby Bonilla .01 .05
51 Brett Butler .02 .10
52 Ron Gant .02 .10
53 Rickey Henderson .40 1.00
54 Cecil Fielder .02 .10
55 Harold Reynolds .02 .10
56 Robin Yount .30 .75
57 Doug Drabek .01 .05
58 Ramon Martinez .01 .05
59 Frank Viola .01 .05
60 Dwight Gooden .02 .10
61 Bob Welch .01 .05
62 Dave Stewart .02 .10
63 Roger Clemens .75 2.00
64 Dave Stieb .02 .10
65 Danny Darwin .01 .05
66 Zane Smith .01 .05
67 Ed Whitson .01 .05
68 Frank Viola .01 .05
69 Roger Clemens .75 2.00
70 Chuck Finley .02 .10
71 Dave Stewart .02 .10
72 Kevin Appier .02 .10
73 David Cone .02 .10
74 Dwight Gooden .02 .10
75 Ramon Martinez .01 .05
76 Frank Viola .01 .05
77 Nolan Ryan 1.50 4.00
78 Bobby Witt .01 .05
79 Erik Hanson .01 .05
80 Roger Clemens .75 2.00
81 John Franco .02 .10
82 Randy Myers .02 .10
83 Lee Smith .02 .10
84 Craig Lefferts .01 .05
85 Bobby Thigpen .01 .05
86 Dennis Eckersley .20 .50
87 Doug Jones .01 .05
88 Gregg Olson .01 .05
89 Mike Morgan .01 .05
90 Bruce Hurst .01 .05
91 Mark Gardner .01 .05
92 Doug Drabek .01 .05
93 Dave Stewart .02 .10
94 Roger Clemens .75 2.00
95 Kevin Appier .02 .10
96 Melido Perez .01 .05
97 National League .01 .05
98 Greg Maddux 1.00 2.50
99 Benito Santiago .02 .10
100 Andres Galarraga .10 .30
101 Ryne Sandberg .60 1.50
102 Tim Wallach .01 .05
103 Ozzie Smith .60 1.50
104 Tony Gwynn .75 2.00
105 Barry Bonds .75 2.00
106 Andy Van Slyke .02 .10
107 American League .01 .05
108 Mike Boddicker .01 .05
109 Sandy Alomar Jr. .02 .10
110 Mark McGwire 1.00 2.50
111 Harold Reynolds .02 .10
112 Kelly Gruber .01 .05
113 Ozzie Guillen .07 .20
114 Ellis Burks .02 .10
115 Gary Pettis .01 .05
116 Ken Griffey Jr. 1.00 2.50
117 Cincinnati Reds .01 .05
Highest Batting Average
118 New York Mets .01 .05
Most Home Runs
119 New York Mets .01 .05
Most Runs Scored
120 Chicago Cubs .01 .05
Most Hits
121 Montreal Expos .01 .05
Most Stolen Bases
122 Boston Red Sox .01 .05
Highest Batting Average
123 Detroit Tigers .01 .05
Most Home Runs
124 Toronto Blue Jays .01 .05
Most Runs Scored
125 Boston Red Sox .01 .05
Most Hits
126 Milwaukee Brewers .01 .05
Most Stolen Bases
127 Philadelphia Phillies .01 .05
Most Double Plays
128 Cincinnati Reds .01 .05
Fewest Errors
129 Montreal Expos .01 .05
Best ERA
130 New York Mets .01 .05
Most Shutouts
131 Cincinnati Reds .01 .05
Most Saves
132 California Angels .01 .05
Most Double Plays
133 Toronto Blue Jays .01 .05
Fewest Errors
134 Oakland Athletics .01 .05
Best ERA
135 Oakland Athletics .01 .05
Most Shutouts
136 Chicago White Sox .01 .05
Most Saves

1991 Panini French Stickers

The French version of the 1991 Panini baseball set contains 360 stickers measuring approximately 2 1/8" by 3". The stickers may be pasted in a collectible sticker album that measures 8 1/4" by 10 1/2". The stickers are checklisted alphabetically according to teams within the NL and then the AL, with the Canadian teams listed after each league. A special Year of the No-Hitter (352-360) subset is included at the end of the set.

COMPLETE SET (360) 10.00 25.00
1 MLB Logo .01 .05
2 MLBPA Logo .01 .05
3 Panini Baseball/=1991 Logo .01 .05
4 Astros Pennant .01 .05
5 Astros Logo .01 .05
6 Craig Biggio .30 .75
7 Glenn Davis .01 .05
8 Casey Candaele .01 .05
9 Ken Caminiti .20 .50
10 Rafael Ramirez .01 .05
11 Glenn Wilson .01 .05
12 Eric Yelding .01 .05
13 Franklin Stubbs .01 .05
14 Mike Scott .02 .10
15 Danny Darwin .01 .05
16 Braves Pennant .01 .05
17 Braves Logo .01 .05
18 Greg Olson .01 .05
19 Tommy Gregg .01 .05
20 Jeff Treadway .01 .05
21 Jim Presley .01 .05
22 Jeff Blauser .01 .05
23 Ron Gant .02 .10
24 Lonnie Smith .01 .05
25 Dave Justice .30 .75
26 John Smoltz .15 .40
27 Charlie Leibrandt .01 .05
28 Cardinals Pennant .01 .05
29 Cardinals Logo .01 .05
30 Tom Pagnozzi .01 .05
31 Pedro Guerrero .01 .05
32 Jose Oquendo .01 .05
33 Todd Zeile .02 .10
34 Ozzie Smith .40 1.00
35 Vince Coleman .01 .05
36 Milt Thompson .01 .05
37 Rex Hudler .02 .10
38 Joe Magrane .01 .05
39 Lee Smith .08 .25
40 Cubs Pennant .01 .05
41 Cubs Logo .01 .05
42 Joe Girardi .02 .10
43 Mark Grace .20 .50
44 Ryne Sandberg .40 1.00
45 Luis Salazar .01 .05
46 Shawon Dunston .01 .05
47 Dwight Smith .01 .05
48 Jerome Walton .01 .05
49 Andre Dawson .08 .25
50 Greg Maddux .75 2.00
51 Mike Harkey .01 .05
52 Dodgers Pennant .01 .05
53 Dodgers Logo .01 .05
54 Mike Scioscia .02 .10
55 Eddie Murray .40 1.00
56 Juan Samuel .01 .05
57 Lenny Harris .01 .05
58 Alfredo Griffin .01 .05
59 Hubie Brooks .01 .05
60 Kal Daniels .01 .05
61 Stan Javier .01 .05
62 Ramon Martinez .01 .05
63 Mike Morgan .01 .05
64 Giants Pennant .01 .05
65 Giants Logo .01 .05
66 Terry Kennedy .01 .05
67 Will Clark .08 .25
68 Robby Thompson .01 .05
69 Matt Williams .05 .15
70 Jose Uribe .01 .05
71 Kevin Mitchell .01 .05
72 Brett Butler .02 .10
73 Don Robinson .01 .05
74 John Burkett .01 .05
75 Jeff Brantley .02 .10
76 Mets Pennant .01 .05
77 Mets Logo .01 .05
78 Mackey Sasser .01 .05
79 Dave Magadan .01 .05
80 Gregg Jefferies .01 .05
81 Howard Johnson .01 .05
82 Kevin Elster .01 .05
83 Kevin McReynolds .01 .05
84 Daryl Boston .01 .05
85 Darryl Strawberry .02 .10
86 Dwight Gooden .02 .10
87 Frank Viola .01 .05
88 Padres Pennant .01 .05
89 Padres Logo .01 .05
90 Benito Santiago .05 .15
91 Jack Clark .02 .10
92 Roberto Alomar .30 .75
93 Mike Pagliarulo .01 .05
94 Garry Templeton .01 .05
95 Joe Carter .02 .10
96 Bip Roberts .01 .05
97 Tony Gwynn .60 1.50
98 Ed Whitson .01 .05
99 Andy Benes .01 .05
100 Phillies Pennant .01 .05
101 Phillies Logo .01 .05
102 Darren Daulton .02 .10
103 Ricky Jordan .01 .05
104 Randy Ready .01 .05
105 Charlie Hayes .01 .05
106 Dickie Thon .01 .05
107 Von Hayes .01 .05
108 Len Dykstra .02 .10
109 Dale Murphy .08 .25
110 Ken Howell .01 .05
111 Roger McDowell .01 .05
112 Pirates Pennant .01 .05
113 Pirates Logo .01 .05
114 Mike LaValliere .01 .05
115 Sid Bream .01 .05
116 Jose Lind .01 .05
117 Jeff King .01 .05
118 Jay Bell .01 .05
119 Barry Bonds .60 1.50
120 Bobby Bonilla .01 .05
121 Andy Van Slyke .02 .10
122 Doug Drabek .01 .05
123 Neal Heaton .01 .05
124 Reds Pennant .01 .05
125 Reds Logo .01 .05
126 Joe Oliver .01 .05
127 Todd Benzinger .01 .05
128 Mariano Duncan .01 .05
129 Chris Sabo .01 .05
130 Barry Larkin .08 .25
131 Eric Davis .02 .10
132 Billy Hatcher .01 .05
133 Paul O'Neill .02 .10
134 Jose Rijo .01 .05
135 Randy Myers .02 .10
136 Expos Pennant .01 .05
137 Expos Logo .01 .05
138 Mike Fitzgerald .01 .05
139 Andres Galarraga .08 .25
140 Delino DeShields .02 .10
141 Tim Wallach .01 .05
142 Spike Owen .01 .05
143 Tim Raines .02 .10
144 Dave Martinez .01 .05
145 Larry Walker .20 .50
146 Expos Helmet .01 .05
147 Dennis Boyd .01 .05
148 Tim Burke .01 .05
149 Bill Sampen .01 .05
150 Dennis Martinez .02 .10
151 Marquis Grissom .08 .25
152 Otis Nixon .02 .10
153 Jerry Goff .01 .05
154 Steve Frey .01 .05
155 NL Emblem .01 .05
156 AL Emblem .01 .05
157 Benito Santiago .02 .10
158 Will Clark .08 .25
159 Ryne Sandberg .40 1.00
160 Chris Sabo .01 .05
161 Ozzie Smith .40 1.00
162 Kevin Mitchell .01 .05
163 Len Dykstra .02 .10
164 Darryl Strawberry .02 .10
165 Jack Armstrong .01 .05
166 Sandy Alomar Jr. .02 .10
167 Mark McGwire .60 1.50
168 Steve Sax .01 .05
169 Wade Boggs .30 .75
170 Cal Ripken 1.25 3.00
171 Rickey Henderson .30 .75
172 Ken Griffey Jr. .75 2.00
173 Jose Canseco .30 .75
174 Bob Welch .01 .05
175 Wrigley Field .01 .05
176 World Series Trophy .01 .05
177 Angels Pennant .01 .05
178 Angels Logo .01 .05
179 Lance Parrish .01 .05
180 Wally Joyner .02 .10
181 Johnny Ray .01 .05
182 Jack Howell .01 .05
183 Dick Schofield .01 .05
184 Dave Winfield .30 .75
185 Devon White .02 .10
186 Dante Bichette .02 .10
187 Chuck Finley .02 .10
188 Jim Abbott .02 .10
189 Athletics Pennant .01 .05
190 Athletics Logo .01 .05
191 Terry Steinbach .01 .05
192 Mark McGwire .60 1.50
193 Willie Randolph .02 .10
194 Carney Lansford .02 .10
195 Walt Weiss .01 .05
196 Rickey Henderson .30 .75
197 Dave Henderson .01 .05
198 Jose Canseco .25 .60
199 Dave Stewart .02 .10
200 Dennis Eckersley .20 .50
201 Brewers Pennant .01 .05
202 Brewers Logo .01 .05
203 B.J. Surhoff .02 .10
204 Greg Brock .01 .05
205 Paul Molitor .40 1.00
206 Gary Sheffield .30 .75
207 Bill Spiers .01 .05
208 Robin Yount .40 1.00
209 Rob Deer .01 .05
210 Dave Parker .02 .10
211 Mark Knudson .01 .05
212 Dan Plesac .01 .05
213 Indians Pennant .01 .05
214 Indians Logo .01 .05
215 Sandy Alomar Jr. .02 .10
216 Brook Jacoby .01 .05
217 Jerry Browne .01 .05
218 Carlos Baerga .01 .05
219 Felix Fermin .01 .05
220 Candy Maldonado .01 .05
221 Cory Snyder .01 .05
222 Alex Cole .01 .05
223 Tom Candiotti .01 .05
224 Doug Jones .01 .05
225 Mariners Pennant .01 .05
226 Mariners Logo .01 .05
227 Dave Valle .01 .05
228 Pete O'Brien .01 .05
229 Harold Reynolds .02 .10
230 Edgar Martinez .05 .15
231 Omar Vizquel .08 .25
232 Henry Cotto .01 .05
233 Ken Griffey Jr. .75 2.00
234 Jay Buhner .08 .25
235 Erik Hanson .01 .05
236 Mike Schooler .01 .05
237 Orioles Pennant .01 .05
238 Orioles Logo .01 .05
239 Mickey Tettleton .02 .10
240 Randy Milligan .01 .05
241 Bill Ripken .01 .05
242 Craig Worthington .01 .05
243 Cal Ripken 1.25 3.00
244 Steve Finley .08 .25
245 Mike Devereaux .01 .05
246 Joe Orsulak .01 .05
247 Ben McDonald .01 .05
248 Gregg Olson .02 .10
249 Rangers Pennant .01 .05
250 Rangers Logo .01 .05
251 Geno Petralli .01 .05
252 Rafael Palmeiro .15 .40
253 Julio Franco .02 .10
254 Steve Buechele .01 .05
255 Jeff Huson .01 .05
256 Gary Pettis .01 .05
257 Ruben Sierra .02 .10
258 Pete Incaviglia .01 .05
259 Nolan Ryan 1.25 3.00
260 Bobby Witt .01 .05
261 Red Sox Pennant .01 .05
262 Red Sox Logo .01 .05
263 Tony Pena .01 .05
264 Carlos Quintana .01 .05
265 Jody Reed .01 .05
266 Wade Boggs .30 .75
267 Luis Rivera .01 .05
268 Mike Greenwell .01 .05
269 Ellis Burks .05 .15
270 Tom Brunansky .01 .05
271 Roger Clemens .60 1.50
272 Jeff Reardon .02 .10
273 Royals Pennant .01 .05
274 Royals Logo .01 .05
275 Mike Macfarlane .01 .05
276 George Brett .60 1.50
277 Bill Pecota .01 .05
278 Kevin Seitzer .01 .05
279 Kurt Stillwell .01 .05
280 Jim Eisenreich .01 .05
281 Bo Jackson .08 .25
282 Danny Tartabull .01 .05
283 Bret Saberhagen .02 .10
284 Tom Gordon .02 .10
285 Tigers Pennant .01 .05
286 Tigers Logo .01 .05
287 Mike Heath .01 .05
288 Cecil Fielder .01 .05
289 Lou Whitaker .02 .10
290 Tony Phillips .01 .05
291 Alan Trammell .05 .15
292 Chet Lemon .01 .05
293 Lloyd Moseby .01 .05
294 Gary Ward .01 .05
295 Dan Petry .01 .05
296 Jack Morris .02 .10
297 Twins Pennant .01 .05
298 Twins Logo .01 .05
299 Brian Harper .01 .05
300 Kent Hrbek .02 .10
301 Al Newman .01 .05
302 Gary Gaetti .02 .10
303 Greg Gagne .01 .05
304 Dan Gladden .01 .05
305 Kirby Puckett .40 1.00
306 Gene Larkin .02 .10
307 Kevin Tapani .01 .05
308 Rick Aguilera .02 .10
309 White Sox Pennant .01 .05
310 White Sox Logo .01 .05
311 Carlton Fisk .30 .75
312 Carlos Martinez .01 .05
313 Scott Fletcher .01 .05
314 Robin Ventura .08 .25
315 Ozzie Guillen .05 .15
316 Sammy Sosa .50 1.25
317 Lance Johnson .01 .05
318 Ivan Calderon .01 .05
319 Greg Hibbard .01 .05
320 Bobby Thigpen .01 .05
321 Yankees Pennant .01 .05
322 Yankees Logo .01 .05
323 Bob Geren .01 .05
324 Don Mattingly .60 1.50
325 Steve Sax .01 .05
326 Jim Leyritz .02 .10
327 Alvaro Espinoza .01 .05
328 Roberto Kelly .01 .05
329 Oscar Azocar .01 .05
330 Jesse Barfield .01 .05
331 Chuck Cary .01 .05
332 Dave Righetti .01 .05
333 Blue Jays Pennant .01 .05
334 Blue Jays Logo .01 .05
335 Pat Borders .01 .05
336 Fred McGriff .08 .25
337 Manny Lee .01 .05
338 Kelly Gruber .01 .05
339 Tony Fernandez .02 .10
340 George Bell .01 .05
341 Mookie Wilson .02 .10
342 Junior Felix .01 .05
343 Blue Jays Helmet .01 .05
344 Dave Stieb .02 .10
345 Tom Henke .01 .05
346 Greg Myers .01 .05
347 Glenallen Hill .01 .05
348 John Olerud .05 .15
349 Todd Stottlemyre .01 .05
350 David Wells .05 .15
351 Jimmy Key .02 .10
352 Mark Langston .01 .05
353 Randy Johnson .30 .75
354 Nolan Ryan 1.25 3.00
355 Dave Stewart .02 .10
356 Fernando Valenzuela .02 .10
357 Andy Hawkins .01 .05
358 Melido Perez .01 .05
359 Terry Mulholland .01 .05
360 Dave Stieb .01 .05

1992 Panini Stickers

These 288 stickers measure approximately 2 1/8" by 3" and feature on their fronts white-bordered color player action shots that are serrated on their left sides and are framed by a colored line on the remaining three sides. The stickers and album used to store them are organized by team. The Best of the Best AL (144-146), The Best of the Best NL (147-149) and 1991 All-Stars (270-288) are the subsets included within the set. A french version of these stickers were made. They are valued at twice the values listed in our checklist.

COMPLETE SET (288) 12.50 30.00
1 Panini Baseball/1992 Logo .01 .05
2 MLB Logo .01 .05
3 MLBPA Logo .01 .05
4 Lance Parrish .01 .05
5 Wally Joyner .02 .10
6 Luis Sojo .01 .05
7 Gary Gaetti .02 .10
8 Dick Schofield .01 .05
9 Junior Felix .01 .05
10 Luis Polonia .01 .05
11 Mark Langston .01 .05
12 Jim Abbott .02 .10
13 Angels Team Logo .01 .05
14 Terry Steinbach .01 .05
15 Mark McGwire .50 1.25
16 Mike Gallego .01 .05
17 Carney Lansford .02 .10
18 Walt Weiss .01 .05
19 Jose Canseco .25 .60
20 Dave Henderson .01 .05
21 Rickey Henderson .30 .75
22 Dennis Eckersley .25 .60

23 Athletics Team Logo .01 .05
24 Pat Borders .01 .05
25 John Olerud .05 .15
26 Roberto Alomar .08 .25
27 Kelly Gruber .01 .05
28 Manuel Lee .01 .05
29 Joe Carter .02 .10
30 Devon White .01 .05
31 Candy Maldonado .01 .05
32 Dave Stieb .01 .05
33 Blue Jays Team Logo .01 .05
34 B.J. Surhoff .02 .10
35 Franklin Stubbs .01 .05
36 Willie Randolph .02 .10
37 Jim Gantner .01 .05
38 Bill Spiers .01 .05
39 Dante Bichette .02 .10
40 Robin Yount .30 .75
41 Greg Vaughn .05 .15
42 Chris Bosio .01 .05
43 Brewers Team Logo .01 .05
44 Sandy Alomar Jr. .02 .10
45 Mike Aldrete .01 .05
46 Mark Lewis .01 .05
47 Carlos Baerga .01 .05
48 Felix Fermin .01 .05
49 Mark Whiten .01 .05
50 Alex Cole .01 .05
51 Albert Belle .02 .10
52 Greg Swindell .01 .05
53 Indians Team Logo .01 .05
54 Dave Valle .01 .05
55 Pete O'Brien .01 .05
56 Harold Reynolds .02 .10
57 Edgar Martinez .05 .15
58 Omar Vizquel .05 .15
59 Jay Buhner .08 .25
60 Ken Griffey Jr. .60 1.50
61 Greg Briley .01 .05
62 Randy Johnson .40 1.00
63 Mariners Team Logo .01 .05
64 Chris Hoiles .01 .05
65 Randy Milligan .01 .05
66 Bill Ripken .01 .05
67 Leo Gomez .01 .05
68 Cal Ripken 1.00 2.50
69 Dwight Evans .02 .10
70 Mike Devereaux .01 .05
71 Joe Orsulak .01 .05
72 Gregg Olson .02 .10
73 Orioles Team Logo .01 .05
74 Ivan Rodriguez .40 1.00
75 Rafael Palmeiro .15 .40
76 Julio Franco .01 .05
77 Dean Palmer .02 .10
78 Jeff Huson .01 .05
79 Ruben Sierra .02 .10
80 Gary Pettis .01 .05
81 Juan Gonzalez .25 .60
82 Nolan Ryan 1.00 2.50
83 Rangers Team Logo .01 .05
84 Tony Pena .01 .05
85 Carlos Quintana .01 .05
86 Jody Reed .01 .05
87 Wade Boggs .30 .75
88 Luis Rivera .01 .05
89 Tom Brunansky .01 .05
90 Ellis Burks .05 .15
91 Mike Greenwell .01 .05
92 Roger Clemens .50 1.25
93 Red Sox Team Logo .01 .05
94 Todd Benzinger .01 .05
95 Terry Shumpert .01 .05
96 Bill Pecota .01 .05
97 Kurt Stillwell .01 .05
98 Danny Tartabull .01 .05
99 Brian McRae .01 .05
100 Kirk Gibson .02 .10
101 Bret Saberhagen .02 .10
102 George Brett .50 1.25
103 Royals Team Logo .01 .05
104 Mickey Tettleton .01 .05
105 Cecil Fielder .02 .10
106 Lou Whitaker .02 .10
107 Travis Fryman .02 .10
108 Alan Trammell .05 .15
109 Rob Deer .01 .05
110 Milt Cuyler .01 .05
111 Lloyd Moseby .01 .05
112 Bill Gullickson .01 .05
113 Tigers Team Logo .01 .05
114 Brian Harper .01 .05
115 Kent Hrbek .02 .10
116 Chuck Knoblauch .08 .25
117 Mike Pagliarulo .01 .05
118 Greg Gagne .01 .05
119 Shane Mack .01 .05
120 Kirby Puckett .40 1.00
121 Dan Gladden .01 .05
122 Jack Morris .02 .10
123 Twins Team Logo .01 .05
124 Carlton Fisk .30 .75
125 Frank Thomas .30 .75
126 Joey Cora .01 .05
127 Robin Ventura .05 .15
128 Ozzie Guillen .05 .15
129 Sammy Sosa .40 1.00
130 Lance Johnson .01 .05
131 Tim Raines .02 .10
132 Bobby Thigpen .01 .05
133 White Sox Team Logo .01 .05
134 Matt Nokes .01 .05
135 Don Mattingly .60 1.50
136 Steve Sax .01 .05
137 Pat Kelly .01 .05
138 Alvaro Espinoza .01 .05
139 Jesse Barfield .01 .05
140 Roberto Kelly .01 .05
141 Mel Hall .01 .05
142 Scott Sanderson .01 .05
143 Yankees Team Logo .01 .05
144 Cecil Fielder .05 .15
Jose Canseco
145 Julio Franco .02 .10
146 Roger Clemens .60 1.50
147 Howard Johnson .01 .05
148 Terry Pendleton .01 .05
149 Dennis Martinez .02 .10
150 Astros Team Logo .01 .05
151 Craig Biggio .25 .60
152 Jeff Bagwell .30 .75
153 Casey Candaele .01 .05
154 Ken Caminiti .20 .50
155 Andujar Cedeno .01 .05
156 Mike Simms .01 .05
157 Steve Finley .05 .15
158 Luis Gonzalez .08 .25
159 Pete Harnisch .01 .05
160 Braves Team Logo .01 .05
161 Greg Olson .01 .05
162 Sid Bream .01 .05
163 Mark Lemke .01 .05
164 Terry Pendleton .01 .05
165 Rafael Belliard .01 .05
166 Dave Justice .08 .25
167 Ron Gant .02 .10
168 Lonnie Smith .01 .05
169 Steve Avery .01 .05
170 Cardinals Team Logo .01 .05
171 Tom Pagnozzi .01 .05
172 Pedro Guerrero .02 .10
173 Jose Oquendo .01 .05
174 Todd Zeile .02 .10
175 Ozzie Smith .40 1.00
176 Felix Jose .01 .05
177 Ray Lankford .08 .25
178 Jose DeLeon .01 .05
179 Lee Smith .02 .10
180 Cubs Team Logo .01 .05
181 Hector Villanueva .01 .05
182 Mark Grace .08 .25
183 Ryne Sandberg .30 .75
184 Luis Salazar .01 .05
185 Shawon Dunston .01 .05
186 Andre Dawson .08 .25
187 Jerome Walton .01 .05
188 George Bell .01 .05
189 Greg Maddux .60 1.50
190 Dodgers Team Logo .01 .05
191 Mike Scioscia .02 .10
192 Eddie Murray .30 .75
193 Juan Samuel .01 .05
194 Lenny Harris .01 .05
195 Alfredo Griffin .01 .05
196 Darryl Strawberry .02 .10
197 Brett Butler .02 .10
198 Kal Daniels .01 .05
199 Orel Hershiser .02 .10
200 Expos Team Logo .01 .05
201 Gilberto Reyes .01 .05
202 Andres Galarraga .08 .25
203 Delino DeShields .02 .10
204 Tim Wallach .01 .05
205 Spike Owen .01 .05
206 Larry Walker .20 .50
207 Marquis Grissom .02 .10
208 Ivan Calderon .01 .05
209 Dennis Martinez .02 .10
210 Giants Team Logo .01 .05
211 Steve Decker .01 .05
212 Will Clark .08 .25
213 Robby Thompson .01 .05
214 Matt Williams .05 .15
215 Jose Uribe .01 .05
216 Kevin Bass .01 .05
217 Willie McGee .02 .10
218 Kevin Mitchell .02 .10
219 Dave Righetti .01 .05
220 Mets Team Logo .01 .05
221 Rick Cerone .01 .05
222 Dave Magadan .01 .05
223 Gregg Jefferies .01 .05
224 Howard Johnson .01 .05
225 Kevin Elster .01 .05
226 Hubie Brooks .01 .05
227 Vince Coleman .01 .05
228 Kevin McReynolds .01 .05
229 Frank Viola .01 .05
230 Padres Team Logo .01 .05
231 Benito Santiago .02 .10
232 Fred McGriff .08 .25
233 Bip Roberts .01 .05
234 Jack Howell .01 .05
235 Tony Fernandez .02 .10
236 Tony Gwynn .60 1.50
237 Darrin Jackson .01 .05
238 Bruce Hurst .01 .05
239 Craig Lefferts .01 .05
240 Phillies Team Logo .01 .05
241 Darren Daulton .02 .10
242 John Kruk .02 .10
243 Mickey Morandini .01 .05
244 Charlie Hayes .01 .05
245 Dickie Thon .01 .05
246 Dale Murphy .08 .25
247 Lenny Dykstra .02 .10
248 Von Hayes .01 .05
249 Terry Mulholland .01 .05
250 Pirates Team Logo .01 .05
251 Mike LaValliere .01 .05
252 Orlando Merced .01 .05
253 Jose Lind .01 .05
254 Steve Buechele .01 .05
255 Jay Bell .01 .05
256 Bobby Bonilla .02 .10
257 Andy Van Slyke .02 .10
258 Barry Bonds .50 1.25
259 Doug Drabek .01 .05
260 Reds Team Logo .01 .05
261 Joe Oliver .01 .05
262 Hal Morris .01 .05
263 Bill Doran .01 .05
264 Chris Sabo .01 .05
265 Barry Larkin .08 .25
266 Paul O'Neill .05 .15
267 Eric Davis .02 .10
268 Glenn Braggs .01 .05
269 Jose Rijo .01 .05
270 Toronto Skydome .01 .05
271 Sandy Alomar Jr. AS .02 .10
272 Cecil Fielder AS .02 .10
273 Roberto Alomar AS .08 .25
274 Wade Boggs AS .30 .75
275 Cal Ripken AS .60 1.50
276 Dave Henderson AS .01 .05
277 Ken Griffey Jr. AS .50 1.25
278 Rickey Henderson AS .30 .75
279 Jack Morris AS .02 .10
280 Benito Santiago AS .01 .05
281 Will Clark AS .08 .25
282 Ryne Sandberg AS .08 .25
283 Chris Sabo AS .01 .05
284 Ozzie Smith AS .08 .25
285 Andre Dawson AS .05 .15
286 Tony Gwynn AS .30 .75
287 Ivan Calderon AS .01 .05
288 Tom Glavine AS .02 .10

1993 Panini Stickers

The 300 stickers in this set measure approximately 2 3/8" by 3 3/8" and were to be pasted in a 9" by 11" album. Six stickers were distributed in each 49-cent foil pack. Ten players from each of the American and National League teams are featured, including one glitter sticker of Panini's Future Stars. One card for each team displays the team's logo on the front. The stickers are numbered on the back and checklisted below according to special subsets and teams.

COMPLETE SET (300) 6.00 15.00
1 Angels Logo .01 .05
2 Mark Langston .01 .05
3 Ron Tingley .01 .05
4 Gary Gaetti .02 .10
5 Kelly Gruber .01 .05
6 Gary DiSarcina .01 .05
7 Damion Easley .01 .05
8 Luis Polonia .01 .05
9 Lee Stevens .01 .05
10 Chad Curtis .01 .05
11 Rene Gonzales .01 .05
12 Athletics Logo .01 .05
13 Dennis Eckersley .20 .50
14 Terry Steinbach .01 .05
15 Mark McGwire .60 1.50
16 Mike Bordick .01 .05
17 Carney Lansford .01 .05
18 Jerry Browne .01 .05
19 Rickey Henderson .40 1.00
20 Dave Henderson .01 .05
21 Ruben Sierra .02 .10
22 Ron Darling .01 .05
23 Blue Jays Logo .01 .05
24 Jack Morris .02 .10
25 Pat Borders .01 .05
26 John Olerud .05 .15
27 Roberto Alomar .08 .25
28 Luis Sojo .01 .05
29 Dave Stewart .02 .10
30 Devon White .01 .05
31 Joe Carter .02 .10
32 Derek Bell .01 .05
33 Juan Guzman .01 .05
34 Brewers Logo .01 .05
35 Jaime Navarro .01 .05
36 B.J. Surhoff .02 .10
37 Franklin Stubbs .01 .05
38 Bill Spiers .01 .05
39 Pat Listach .01 .05
40 Kevin Seitzer .01 .05
41 Darryl Hamilton .01 .05
42 Robin Yount .30 .75
43 Kevin Reimer .01 .05
44 Greg Vaughn .02 .10
45 Indians Logo .01 .05
46 Charles Nagy .01 .05
47 Sandy Alomar Jr. .01 .05
48 Reggie Jefferson .01 .05
49 Mark Lewis .01 .05
50 Felix Fermin .01 .05
51 Carlos Baerga .01 .05
52 Albert Belle .02 .10
53 Kenny Lofton .20 .50
54 Mark Whiten .01 .05
55 Paul Sorrento .01 .05
56 Mariners Logo .01 .05
57 Dave Fleming .01 .05
58 Dave Valle .01 .05
59 Pete O'Brien .01 .05
60 Randy Johnson .40 1.00
61 Omar Vizquel .05 .15
62 Edgar Martinez .05 .15
63 Ken Griffey Jr. .75 2.00
64 Henry Cotto .01 .05
65 Jay Buhner .08 .25
66 Tino Martinez .08 .25
67 Orioles Logo .01 .05
68 Ben McDonald .01 .05
69 Mike Mussina .08 .25
70 Chris Hoiles .01 .05
71 Randy Milligan .01 .05
72 Billy Ripken .01 .05
73 Cal Ripken 1.25 3.00
74 Leo Gomez .01 .05
75 Mike Devereaux .01 .05
76 Brady Anderson .02 .10
77 Joe Orsulak .01 .05
78 Rangers Logo .01 .05
79 Kevin Brown .05 .15
80 Ivan Rodriguez .30 .75
81 Rafael Palmeiro .20 .50
82 Julio Franco .02 .10
83 Jeff Huson .01 .05
84 Dean Palmer .02 .10
85 Jose Canseco .25 .60
86 Juan Gonzalez .20 .50
87 Nolan Ryan 1.25 3.00
88 Brian Downing .01 .05
89 Red Sox Logo .01 .05
90 Roger Clemens .60 1.50
91 Tony Pena .01 .05
92 Mo Vaughn .02 .10
93 Scott Cooper .01 .05
94 Luis Rivera .01 .05
95 Ellis Burks .02 .10
96 Mike Greenwell .01 .05
97 Andre Dawson .05 .15
98 Ivan Calderon .01 .05
99 Phil Plantier .01 .05
100 Royals Logo .01 .05
101 Kevin Appier .02 .10
102 Mike Macfarlane .01 .05
103 Wally Joyner .02 .10
104 Jim Eisenreich .02 .10
105 Greg Gagne .01 .05
106 Gregg Jefferies .01 .05
107 Kevin McReynolds .01 .05
108 Brian McRae .01 .05
109 Keith Miller .01 .05
110 George Brett .60 1.50
111 Tigers Logo .01 .05
112 Bill Gullickson .01 .05
113 Mickey Tettleton .01 .05
114 Cecil Fielder .01 .05
115 Tony Phillips .01 .05
116 Scott Livingstone .01 .05
117 Travis Fryman .02 .10
118 Dan Gladden .01 .05
119 Rob Deer .01 .05
120 Frank Tanana .01 .05
121 Skeeter Barnes .01 .05
122 Twins Logo .01 .05
123 Scott Erickson .01 .05
124 Brian Harper .01 .05
125 Kent Hrbek .02 .10
126 Chuck Knoblauch .08 .25
127 Willie Banks .01 .05
128 Scott Leius .01 .05
129 Shane Mack .01 .05
130 Kirby Puckett .40 1.00
131 Chili Davis .02 .10
132 Pedro Munoz .01 .05
133 White Sox Logo .01 .05
134 Jack McDowell .01 .05
135 Carlton Fisk .30 .75
136 Frank Thomas .30 .75
137 Steve Sax .01 .05
138 Ozzie Guillen .05 .15
139 Robin Ventura .05 .15
140 Tim Raines .02 .10
141 Lance Johnson .01 .05
142 Ron Karkovice .01 .05
143 George Bell .01 .05
144 Yankees Logo .01 .05
145 Scott Sanderson .01 .05
146 Matt Nokes .01 .05
147 Kevin Maas .01 .05
148 Randy Velarde .01 .05
149 Andy Stankiewicz .01 .05
150 Pat Kelly .01 .05
151 Paul O'Neill .05 .15
152 Wade Boggs .30 .75
153 Danny Tartabull .01 .05
154 Don Mattingly .60 1.50
155 Edgar Martinez LL .05 .15
156 Kevin Brown LL .05 .15
157 Dennis Eckersley LL .02 .10
158 Gary Sheffield LL .08 .25
159 Tom Glavine LL .25 .60
Greg Maddux
160 Lee Smith LL .02 .10
161 Dennis Eckersley CY .02 .10
162 Dennis Eckersley MVP .02 .10
163 Pat Listach ROY .01 .05
164 Greg Maddux CY .40 1.00
165 Barry Bonds MVP .40 1.00
166 Eric Karros ROY .05 .15
167 Astros Logo .01 .05
168 Pete Harnisch .01 .05
169 Eddie Taubensee .01 .05
170 Jeff Bagwell .60 1.50
171 Craig Biggio .25 .60
172 Andujar Cedeno .01 .05
173 Ken Caminiti .20 .50
174 Steve Finley .05 .15
175 Luis Gonzalez .08 .25
176 Eric Anthony .01 .05
177 Casey Candaele .01 .05
178 Braves Logo .01 .05
179 Tom Glavine .20 .50
180 Greg Olson .01 .05
181 Sid Bream .01 .05
182 Mark Lemke .01 .05
183 Jeff Blauser .01 .05
184 Terry Pendleton .01 .05
185 Ron Gant .02 .10
186 Otis Nixon .01 .05
187 Dave Justice .08 .25
188 Deion Sanders .08 .25
189 Cardinals Logo .01 .05
190 Bob Tewksbury .01 .05
191 Tom Pagnozzi .01 .05
192 Lee Smith .08 .25
193 Geronimo Pena .01 .05
194 Ozzie Smith .30 .75
195 Todd Zeile .02 .10
196 Ray Lankford .02 .10
197 Bernard Gilkey .01 .05
198 Felix Jose .01 .05
199 Donovan Osborne .01 .05
200 Cubs Logo .01 .05
201 Mike Morgan .01 .05
202 Rick Wilkins .01 .05
203 Mark Grace .08 .25
204 Ryne Sandberg .30 .75
205 Shawon Dunston .01 .05
206 Steve Buechele .01 .05
207 Kal Daniels .01 .05
208 Sammy Sosa .50 1.25
209 Derrick May .01 .05
210 Doug Dascenzo .01 .05
211 Dodgers Logo .01 .05
212 Ramon Martinez .01 .05
213 Mike Scioscia .02 .10
214 Eric Karros .05 .15
215 Tim Wallach .01 .05
216 Jose Offerman .01 .05
217 Mike Sharperson .01 .05
218 Brett Butler .02 .10
219 Darryl Strawberry .02 .10
220 Lenny Harris .01 .05
221 Eric Davis .02 .10
222 Expos Logo .01 .05
223 Ken Hill .01 .05
224 Darrin Fletcher .01 .05
225 Greg Colbrunn .01 .05
226 Delino DeShields .01 .05
227 Wil Cordero .01 .05
228 Dennis Martinez .02 .10
229 John Vander Wal .01 .05
230 Marquis Grissom .02 .10
231 Larry Walker .20 .50
232 Moises Alou .02 .10
233 Giants Logo .01 .05
234 Bill Swift .01 .05
235 Kirt Manwaring .01 .05
236 Will Clark .08 .25
237 Robby Thompson .01 .05
238 Royce Clayton .01 .05
239 Matt Williams .05 .15
240 Willie McGee .02 .10
241 Mark Leonard .01 .05
242 Cory Snyder .01 .05
243 Barry Bonds .60 1.50
244 Mets Logo .01 .05
245 Dwight Gooden .02 .10
246 Todd Hundley .02 .10
247 Eddie Murray .30 .75
248 Sid Fernandez .01 .05
249 Tony Fernandez .02 .10
250 Dave Magadan .01 .05
251 Howard Johnson .01 .05
252 Vince Coleman .01 .05
253 Bobby Bonilla .02 .10
254 Daryl Boston .01 .05
255 Padres Logo .01 .05
256 Bruce Hurst .01 .05
257 Dan Walters .01 .05
258 Fred McGriff .05 .15
259 Kurt Stillwell .02 .05
260 Craig Shipley .01 .05
261 Gary Sheffield .25 .60
262 Tony Gwynn .60 1.50
263 Oscar Azocar .01 .05
264 Darrin Jackson .01 .05
265 Andy Benes .01 .05
266 Phillies Logo .01 .05
267 Terry Mulholland .01 .05
268 Curt Schilling .25 .60
269 Darren Daulton .02 .10
270 John Kruk .02 .10
271 Mickey Morandini .01 .05
272 Mariano Duncan .01 .05
273 Dave Hollins .01 .05
274 Lenny Dykstra .02 .10
275 Wes Chamberlain .01 .05
276 Stan Javier .01 .05
277 Pirates Logo .01 .05
278 Zane Smith .01 .05
279 Tim Wakefield .08 .25
280 Mike LaValliere .01 .05
281 Orlando Merced .01 .05
282 Stan Belinda .01 .05
283 Jay Bell .01 .05
284 Jeff King .01 .05
285 Andy Van Slyke .02 .10
286 Bob Walk .01 .05
287 Gary Varsho .01 .05
288 Reds Logo .01 .05
289 Jose Rijo .01 .05
290 Joe Oliver .01 .05
291 Hal Morris .01 .05
292 Bip Roberts .01 .05
293 Barry Larkin .08 .25
294 Chris Sabo .01 .05
295 Roberto Kelly .01 .05
296 Kevin Mitchell .01 .05
297 Rob Dibble .01 .05
298 Reggie Sanders .02 .10
299 Marlins Logo .01 .05
300 Rockies Logo .02 .10

1994 Panini Stickers

This set of 1994 Panini Baseball consists of 268 stickers measuring approximately 2 3/8" by 3 3/8". The stickers were sold in Panini packets of six, with 50 packets (suggested retail price of 49 cents each) per box. The collectible sticker album measures 9 1/8" by 10 5/8" (suggested retail price of 99 cents) and features eight baseball players on the bright yellow, UV coated cover. The album's inside front cover carries 1993 Team Statistics for the American and National Leagues and also lists the 1993 League Standings. The back inside cover provides information on how to order missing stickers and take advantage of the mail in offer of 30 stickers for $4.00, plus ten '94 Panini wrappers. After presenting the American (5-10) and National League Leaders (11-16), the set is arranged grouped alphabetically within teams and checklisted below alphabetically according to teams for each league.

COMPLETE SET (268) 6.00 15.00
1 WS Opening Ceremony/(Upper left) .01 .05
2 WS Opening Ceremony/(Upper right) .01 .05
3 WS Opening Ceremony/(Lower left) .01 .05
4 WS Opening Ceremony/(Lower right) .01 .05
5 John Olerud .02 .10
Highest Batting Average
6 Juan Gonzalez .02 .10
Most Home Runs
7 Albert Belle .02 .10
Most Runs Batted In
8 Jack McDowell .01 .05
Most Wins
9 Randy Johnson .20 .50
Most Strikeouts
10 Jeff Montgomery .01 .05
Duane Ward
Most Saves (tie)
11 Andres Galarraga .20 .50
Highest Batting Average
12 Barry Bonds .20 .50
Most Home Runs
13 Barry Bonds .20 .50
Most Runs Batted In
14 Tom Glavine .02 .10
John Burkett
Most Wins (tie)
15 Jose Rijo .01 .05
Most Strikeouts
16 Randy Myers .01 .05
Most Saves
17 Brady Anderson .02 .10
18 Harold Baines .02 .10
19 Mike Devereaux .01 .05
20 Chris Hoiles .01 .05
21 Mike Mussina .08 .25
22 Harold Reynolds .02 .10
23 Cal Ripken Jr. .75 2.00
24 David Segui .01 .05
25 Fernando Valenzuela .02 .10
26 Roger Clemens .40 1.00
27 Scott Cooper .01 .05
28 Andre Dawson .08 .25
29 Scott Fletcher .01 .05
30 Mike Greenwell .01 .05
31 Billy Hatcher .01 .05
32 Tony Pena .01 .05
33 John Valentin .01 .05
34 Mo Vaughn .02 .10
35 Chad Curtis .01 .05
36 Gary DiSarcina .01 .05
37 Damion Easley .01 .05
38 Mark Langston .01 .05
39 Torey Lovullo .01 .05
40 Greg Myers .01 .05
41 Luis Polonia .01 .05
42 Tim Salmon .08 .25
43 J.T. Snow .02 .10
44 George Bell .01 .05
45 Ellis Burks .02 .10
46 Joey Cora .01 .05
47 Ozzie Guillen .05 .15
48 Roberto Hernandez .01 .05
49 Bo Jackson .08 .25
50 Jack McDowell .01 .05
51 Frank Thomas .20 .50
52 Robin Ventura .02 .10
53 Sandy Alomar Jr. .02 .10
54 Carlos Baerga .01 .05
55 Albert Belle .02 .10
56 Felix Fermin .01 .05
57 Wayne Kirby .01 .05
58 Kenny Lofton .15 .40
59 Charles Nagy .01 .05
60 Paul Sorrento .01 .05
61 Jeff Treadway .01 .05
62 Eric Davis .02 .10
63 Cecil Fielder .02 .10
64 Travis Fryman .02 .10
65 Bill Gullickson .01 .05
66 Mike Moore .01 .05
67 Tony Phillips .01 .05
68 Mickey Tettleton .02 .10
69 Alan Trammell .05 .15
70 Lou Whitaker .02 .10
71 Kevin Appier .02 .10
72 Greg Gagne .01 .05
73 Tom Gordon .02 .10
74 Felix Jose .01 .05
75 Wally Joyner .02 .10
76 Jose Lind .01 .05
77 Mike Macfarlane .01 .05
78 Brian McRae .01 .05
79 Kevin McReynolds .01 .05
80 Darryl Hamilton .01 .05
81 Teddy Higuera .01 .05
82 John Jaha .01 .05
83 Pat Listach .01 .05
84 Dave Nilsson .01 .05
85 Kevin Reimer .01 .05
86 Kevin Seitzer .01 .05
87 B.J. Surhoff .02 .10
88 Greg Vaughn .05 .15
89 Willie Banks .01 .05
90 Brian Harper .01 .05
91 Kent Hrbek .02 .10
92 Chuck Knoblauch .08 .25
93 Shane Mack .01 .05
94 Pat Meares .01 .05
95 Pedro Munoz .01 .05
96 Kirby Puckett .20 .50
97 Dave Winfield .20 .50
98 Jim Abbott .02 .10
99 Wade Boggs .20 .50
100 Mike Gallego .01 .05
101 Pat Kelly .01 .05
102 Don Mattingly .40 1.00
103 Paul O'Neill .02 .10
104 Mike Stanley .01 .05
105 Danny Tartabull .01 .05
106 Bernie Williams .08 .25
107 Mike Bordick .01 .05
108 Dennis Eckersley .15 .40
109 Dave Henderson .01 .05
110 Mark McGwire .40 1.00
111 Troy Neel .01 .05
112 Ruben Sierra .02 .10
113 Terry Steinbach .01 .05
114 Todd Van Poppel .01 .05
115 Bob Welch .01 .05
116 Bret Boone .05 .15
117 Jay Buhner .02 .10
118 Ken Griffey Jr. .50 1.25
119 Randy Johnson .30 .75
120 Rich Amaral .01 .05
121 Edgar Martinez .05 .15
122 Tino Martinez .08 .25
123 Dave Valle .01 .05
124 Omar Vizquel .02 .10
125 Jose Canseco .25 .60
126 Julio Franco .01 .05
127 Juan Gonzalez .25 .60
128 Tom Henke .01 .05
129 Manuel Lee .01 .05
130 Rafael Palmeiro .08 .25
131 Dean Palmer .02 .10
132 Ivan Rodriguez .20 .50
133 Doug Strange .01 .05
134 Roberto Alomar .08 .25
135 Pat Borders .01 .05
136 Joe Carter .02 .10
137 Tony Fernandez .02 .10
138 Juan Guzman .01 .05
139 Rickey Henderson .25 .60
140 Paul Molitor .15 .40
141 John Olerud .02 .10
142 Devon White .02 .10
143 Jeff Blauser .01 .05
144 Ron Gant .02 .10
145 Tom Glavine .15 .40
146 Dave Justice .08 .25
147 Greg Maddux .50 1.25
148 Fred McGriff .05 .15
149 Terry Pendleton .01 .05
150 Deion Sanders .08 .25
151 John Smoltz .15 .40
152 Shawon Dunston .01 .05
153 Mark Grace .08 .25
154 Derrick May .01 .05
155 Randy Myers .01 .05
156 Ryne Sandberg .20 .50
157 Dwight Smith .01 .05
158 Sammy Sosa .30 .75
159 Jose Vizcaino .01 .05
160 Rick Wilkins .01 .05
161 Tom Browning .01 .05
162 Roberto Kelly .01 .05
163 Barry Larkin .05 .15
164 Kevin Mitchell .01 .05
165 Hal Morris .01 .05
166 Joe Oliver .01 .05
167 Jose Rijo .01 .05
168 Chris Sabo .01 .05
169 Reggie Sanders .02 .10
170 Freddie Benavides .01 .05
171 Dante Bichette .02 .10
172 Vinny Castilla .02 .10
173 Jerald Clark .01 .05
174 Andres Galarraga .08 .25
175 Charlie Hayes .01 .05
176 Chris Jones .01 .05
177 Roberto Mejia .01 .05
178 Eric Young .01 .05
179 Bret Barberie .01 .05
180 Chuck Carr .01 .05
181 Jeff Conine .01 .05
182 Orestes Destrade .01 .05
183 Bryan Harvey .01 .05
184 Rich Renteria .01 .05
185 Benito Santiago .02 .10
186 Gary Sheffield .20 .50
187 Walt Weiss .01 .05
188 Eric Anthony .01 .05
189 Jeff Bagwell .30 .75
190 Craig Biggio .20 .50
191 Ken Caminiti .15 .40
192 Andujar Cedeno .01 .05
193 Doug Drabek .01 .05
194 Steve Finley .02 .10
195 Doug Jones .01 .05
196 Darryl Kile .01 .05
197 Brett Butler .02 .10
198 Tom Candiotti .02 .10
199 Dave Hansen .01 .05
200 Orel Hershiser .02 .10
201 Eric Karros .02 .10
202 Jose Offerman .01 .05
203 Mike Piazza .60 1.50
204 Cory Snyder .01 .05
205 Darryl Strawberry .02 .10
206 Moises Alou .05 .15
207 Sean Berry .01 .05
208 Wil Cordero .01 .05
209 Delino DeShields .01 .05
210 Marquis Grissom .02 .10
211 Ken Hill .01 .05
212 Mike Lansing .01 .05
213 Larry Walker .15 .40
214 John Wetteland .02 .10
215 Bobby Bonilla .01 .05
216 Jeromy Burnitz .05 .15
217 Dwight Gooden .02 .10
218 Todd Hundley .02 .10
219 Howard Johnson .01 .05
220 Jeff Kent .08 .25
221 Eddie Murray .15 .40
222 Bret Saberhagen .02 .10
223 Ryan Thompson .01 .05
224 Darren Daulton .02 .10
225 Mariano Duncan .01 .05
226 Lenny Dykstra .02 .10
227 Jim Eisenreich .02 .10
228 Dave Hollins .01 .05
229 John Kruk .02 .10
230 Curt Schilling .15 .40
231 Kevin Stocker .01 .05
232 Mitch Williams .01 .05
233 Jay Bell .01 .05
234 Steve Cooke .01 .05
235 Carlos Garcia .01 .05
236 Jeff King .01 .05
237 Orlando Merced .01 .05
238 Don Slaught .01 .05
239 Zane Smith .01 .05
240 Andy Van Slyke .01 .05
241 Kevin Young .01 .05
242 Bernard Gilkey .01 .05
243 Gregg Jefferies .01 .05
244 Brian Jordan .02 .10
245 Ray Lankford .02 .10
246 Tom Pagnozzi .01 .05
247 Geronimo Perez .01 .05
248 Ozzie Smith .20 .50
249 Bob Tewksbury .01 .05
250 Mark Whiten .01 .05
251 Brad Ausmus .01 .05
252 Derek Bell .01 .05
253 Andy Benes .01 .05
254 Phil Clark .01 .05
255 Jeff Gardner .01 .05
256 Tony Gwynn .40 1.00
257 Trevor Hoffman .05 .15
258 Phil Plantier .01 .05
259 Craig Shipley .01 .05
260 Rod Beck .02 .10
261 Barry Bonds .40 1.00
262 John Burkett .01 .05
263 Will Clark .08 .25
264 Royce Clayton .01 .05
265 Willie McGee .02 .10
266 Bill Swift .01 .05
267 Robby Thompson .01 .05
268 Matt Williams .05 .15

1995 Panini Stickers

This 156-sticker set measures approximately 1 15/16" by 3" and was distributed by Fleer. The fronts feature

color action player photos framed in different colors on a white background. The player's name and team logo appear in a bar at the bottom. The backs carry the sponsor logos. The set closes with team logos (129-156).
COMPLETE SET (156) 8.00 20.00
1 Tom Glavine .20 .50
2 Doug Drabek .01 .05
3 Rod Beck .02 .10
4 Pedro Martinez .30 .75
5 Danny Jackson .01 .05
6 Greg Maddux 1.00 2.50
7 Bret Saberhagen .02 .10
8 Ken Hill .01 .05
9 Marvin Freeman .01 .05
10 Andy Benes .01 .05
11 Wilson Alvarez .01 .05
12 Jimmy Key .02 .10
13 Mike Mussina .08 .25
14 Roger Clemens .75 2.00
15 Pat Hentgen .02 .10
16 Randy Johnson .40 1.00
17 Lee Smith .02 .10
18 David Cone .02 .10
19 Jason Bere .01 .05
20 Dennis Martinez .02 .10
21 Darren Daulton .02 .10
22 Darrin Fletcher .01 .05
23 Tom Pagnozzi .01 .05
24 Mike Piazza 1.00 2.50
25 Benito Santiago .02 .10
26 Sandy Alomar Jr. .02 .10
27 Chris Hoiles .01 .05
28 Ivan Rodriguez .40 1.00
29 Mike Stanley .01 .05
30 Dave Nilsson .01 .05
31 Jeff Bagwell .40 1.00
32 Mark Grace .08 .25
33 Gregg Jefferies .01 .05
34 Andres Galarraga .08 .25
35 Fred McGriff .08 .25
36 Will Clark .08 .25
37 Mo Vaughn .02 .10
38 Don Mattingly .75 2.00
39 Frank Thomas .25 .60
40 Cecil Fielder .02 .10
41 Robby Thompson .01 .05
42 Delino DeShields .02 .10
43 Carlos Garcia .01 .05
44 Bret Boone .05 .15
45 Craig Biggio .05 .15
46 Roberto Alomar .08 .25
47 Chuck Knoblauch .08 .25
48 Jose Lind .01 .05
49 Carlos Baerga .02 .10
50 Lou Whitaker .02 .10
51 Bobby Bonilla .01 .05
52 Tim Wallach .01 .05
53 Todd Zeile .02 .10
54 Matt Williams .05 .15
55 Ken Caminiti .30 .75
56 Robin Ventura .02 .10
57 Wade Boggs .30 .75
58 Scott Cooper .01 .05
59 Travis Fryman .02 .10
60 Dean Palmer .02 .10
61 Jay Bell .01 .05
62 Barry Larkin .08 .25
63 Ozzie Smith .40 1.00
64 Wil Cordero .01 .05
65 Royce Clayton .01 .05
66 Chris Gomez .01 .05
67 Ozzie Guillen .05 .15
68 Cal Ripken Jr. 1.50 4.00
69 Omar Vizquel .02 .10
70 Gary DiSarcina .01 .05
71 Dante Bichette .02 .10
72 Lenny Dykstra .02 .10
73 Barry Bonds .75 2.00
74 Gary Sheffield .30 .75
75 Larry Walker .15 .40
76 Raul Mondesi .02 .10
77 Dave Justice .08 .25
78 Moises Alou .02 .10
79 Tony Gwynn .75 2.00
80 Deion Sanders .08 .25
81 Kenny Lofton .05 .15
82 Kirby Puckett .40 1.00
83 Juan Gonzalez .15 .40
84 Jay Buhner .02 .10
85 Joe Carter .02 .10
86 Ken Griffey Jr. 1.00 2.50
87 Ruben Sierra .02 .10
88 Tim Salmon .08 .25
89 Paul O'Neill .02 .10
90 Albert Belle .02 .10
91 Danny Tartabull .01 .05
92 Jose Canseco .25 .60
93 Harold Baines .02 .10
94 Kirk Gibson .02 .10
95 Chili Davis .02 .10
96 Eddie Murray .20 .50
97 Bob Hamelin .01 .05
98 Paul Molitor .20 .50
99 Raul Mondesi .05 .15
100 Ryan Klesko .02 .10
101 Cliff Floyd .02 .10
102 William VanLandingham .01 .05
103 Joey Hamilton .01 .05
104 John Hudek .01 .05
105 Manny Ramirez .50 1.25
106 Bob Hamelin .01 .05
107 Rusty Greer .08 .25
108 Chris Gomez .01 .05
109 Greg Maddux 1.00 2.50
110 Jeff Bagwell .40 1.00
111 Raul Mondesi .05 .15
112 David Cone .05 .15
113 Frank Thomas .40 1.00
114 Bob Hamelin .01 .05
115 Tony Gwynn .75 2.00
116 Matt Williams .05 .15
117 Jeff Bagwell .40 1.00
118 Craig Biggio .15 .40
119 Andy Benes .01 .05
120 Greg Maddux 1.00 2.50
121 John Franco .02 .10
122 Paul O'Neill .02 .10
123 Ken Griffey Jr. 1.00 2.50
124 Kirby Puckett .40 1.00
125 Kenny Lofton .02 .10
126 Randy Johnson .40 1.00
127 Jimmy Key .02 .10
128 Lee Smith .02 .10
129 San Francisco Giants .01 .05
130 Montreal Expos .01 .05
131 Cincinnati Reds .01 .05
132 Los Angeles Dodgers .01 .05
133 New York Mets .01 .05
134 San Diego Padres .01 .05
135 Colorado Rockies .01 .05
136 Pittsburgh Pirates .01 .05
137 Florida Marlins .01 .05
138 Philadelphia Phillies .01 .05
139 Atlanta Braves .01 .05
140 Houston Astros .01 .05
141 St. Louis Cardinals .01 .05
142 Chicago Cubs .01 .05
143 Cleveland Indians .01 .05
144 New York Yankees .01 .05
145 Kansas City Royals .01 .05
146 Chicago White Sox .01 .05
147 Baltimore Orioles .01 .05
148 Seattle Mariners .01 .05
149 Boston Red Sox .01 .05
150 California Angels .01 .05
151 Toronto Blue Jays .01 .05
152 Detroit Tigers .01 .05
153 Texas Rangers .01 .05
154 Oakland Athletics .01 .05
155 Milwaukee Brewers .01 .05
156 Minnesota Twins .01 .05

1996 Panini Stickers

This 246-sticker set was distributed as a complete set in a cellophane wrapper with a suggested retail price of $8. A 60-page album to hold the stickers was included with the set. Stickers to finish ones set were available from the Panini Missing Sticker Club at a cost of $4 for 20 different stickers or $4 for 30 stickers as long as 10 wrappers were sent as well.
COMPLETE SET (246) 5.00 12.00
1 David Justice .08 .25
2 Tom Glavine .20 .50
3 Javier Lopez .02 .10
4 Greg Maddux .60 1.50
5 Marquis Grissom .01 .05
6 Atlanta Braves Team Logo .01 .05
7 Ryan Klesko .02 .10
8 Chipper Jones .60 1.50
9 Quilvio Veras .01 .05
10 Chris Hammond .01 .05
11 Charles Johnson .01 .05
12 John Burkett .01 .05
13 Florida Marlins Team Logo .01 .05
14 Jeff Conine .01 .05
15 Gary Sheffield .25 .60
16 Greg Colbrunn .01 .05
17 Moises Alou .05 .15
18 Pedro Martinez .40 1.00
19 Rondell White .02 .10
20 Tony Tarasco .01 .05
21 Montreal Expos Team Logo .01 .05
22 Carlos Perez .01 .05
23 David Segui .01 .05
24 Wil Cordero .01 .05
25 Jason Isringhausen .08 .25
26 Rico Brogna .01 .05
27 Edgardo Alfonzo .08 .25
28 Todd Hundley .02 .10
29 New York Mets Team Logo .01 .05
30 Bill Pulsipher .01 .05
31 Carl Everett .02 .10
32 Jose Vizcaino .01 .05
33 Lenny Dykstra .02 .10
34 Charlie Hayes .01 .05
35 Heathcliff Slocumb .01 .05
36 Darren Daulton .02 .10
37 Philadelphia Phillies Team Logo .01 .05
38 Mickey Morandini .01 .05
39 Gregg Jefferies .01 .05
40 Jim Eisenreich .01 .05
41 Brian McRae .01 .05
42 Luis Gonzalez .08 .25
43 Randy Myers .02 .10
44 Shawon Dunston .01 .05
45 Chicago Cubs Team Logo .01 .05
46 Jaime Navarro .01 .05
47 Mark Grace .08 .25
48 Sammy Sosa .40 1.00
49 Barry Larkin .08 .25
50 Pete Schourek .01 .05
51 John Smiley .01 .05
52 Reggie Sanders .01 .05
53 Cincinnati Reds Team Logo .01 .05
54 Hal Morris .01 .05
55 Ron Gant .01 .05
56 Bret Boone .05 .15
57 Craig Biggio .15 .40
58 Brian Hunter .01 .05
59 Jeff Bagwell .30 .75
60 Shane Reynolds .01 .05
61 Houston Astros Team Logo .01 .05
62 Derek Bell .01 .05
63 Doug Drabek .01 .05
64 Orlando Miller .01 .05
65 Jay Bell .01 .05
66 Dan Miceli .01 .05
67 Orlando Merced .01 .05
68 Jeff King .01 .05
69 Carlos Garcia .01 .05
70 Pittsburgh Pirates Team Logo .01 .05
71 Al Martin .01 .05
72 Denny Neagle .01 .05
73 Ray Lankford .02 .10
74 Ozzie Smith .40 1.00
75 Bernard Gilkey .01 .05
76 John Mabry .01 .05
77 St. Louis Cardinals Team Logo .01 .05
78 Brian Jordan .02 .10
79 Scott Cooper .01 .05
80 Allen Watson .01 .05
81 Dante Bichette .01 .05
82 Bret Saberhagen .02 .10
83 Walt Weiss .01 .05
84 Andres Galarraga .08 .25
85 Colorado Rockies Team Logo .01 .05
86 Larry Walker .15 .40
87 Bill Swift .01 .05
88 Vinny Castilla .05 .15
89 Raul Mondesi .02 .10
90 Roger Cedeno .02 .10
91 Chad Fonville .01 .05
92 Hideo Nomo .30 .75
93 Los Angeles Dodgers Team Logo .01 .05
94 Ramon Martinez .01 .05
95 Mike Piazza .60 1.50
96 Eric Karros .02 .10
97 Tony Gwynn .60 1.50
98 Brad Ausmus .01 .05
99 Trevor Hoffman .05 .15
100 Ken Caminiti .20 .50
101 San Diego Padres Team Logo .01 .05
102 Andy Ashby .01 .05
103 Steve Finley .02 .10
104 Joey Hamilton .01 .05
105 Matt Williams .05 .15
106 Rod Beck .01 .05
107 Barry Bonds .50 1.25
108 William VanLandingham .01 .05
109 San Francisco Giants Team Logo .01 .05
110 Deion Sanders .08 .25
111 Royce Clayton .01 .05
112 Glenallen Hill .01 .05
113 Tony Gwynn .60 1.50
114 Dante Bichette .01 .05
115 Dante Bichette .01 .05
116 Quilvio Veras .01 .05
117 Hideo Nomo .25 .60
118 Greg Maddux .50 1.25
119 Randy Myers .01 .05
120 Edgar Martinez .05 .15
121 Albert Belle .02 .10
122 Mo Vaughn .02 .10
123 Kenny Lofton .02 .10
124 Randy Johnson .30 .75
125 Mike Mussina .20 .50
126 Jose Mesa .02 .05
127 Mike Mussina .20 .50
128 Cal Ripken Jr. 1.00 2.50
129 Rafael Palmeiro .20 .50
130 Ben McDonald .01 .05
131 Baltimore Orioles Team Logo .01 .05
132 Chris Hoiles .01 .05
133 Bobby Bonilla .01 .05
134 Brady Anderson .02 .10
135 Jose Canseco .25 .60
136 Roger Clemens .50 1.25
137 Mo Vaughn .02 .10
138 Mike Greenwell .01 .05
139 Boston Red Sox Team Logo .01 .05
140 Tim Wakefield .05 .15
141 John Valentin .01 .05
142 Tim Naehring .01 .05
143 Travis Fryman .02 .10
144 Chad Curtis .01 .05
145 Felipe Lira .01 .05
146 Cecil Fielder .02 .10
147 Detroit Tigers Team Logo .01 .05
148 John Flaherty .01 .05
149 Chris Gomez .01 .05
150 Sean Bergman .01 .05
151 Don Mattingly .60 1.50
152 Andy Pettitte .02 .10
153 Wade Boggs .30 .75
154 Paul O'Neill .02 .10
155 New York Yankees Team Logo .01 .05
156 Bernie Williams .20 .50
157 Jack McDowell .01 .05
158 David Cone .02 .10
159 Roberto Alomar .08 .25
160 Paul Molitor .20 .50
161 Shawn Green .20 .50
162 Joe Carter .02 .10
163 Toronto Blue Jays Team Logo .01 .05
164 Alex Gonzalez .01 .05
165 Al Leiter .02 .10
166 John Olerud .02 .10
167 Alex Fernandez .01 .05
168 Ray Durham .05 .15
169 Lance Johnson .01 .05
170 Ozzie Guillen .05 .15
171 Chicago White Sox Team Logo .01 .05
172 Robin Ventura .08 .25
173 Frank Thomas .30 .75
174 Tim Raines .02 .10
175 Albert Belle .02 .10
176 Manny Ramirez .30 .75
177 Eddie Murray .20 .50
178 Orel Hershiser .02 .10
179 Cleveland Indians Team Logo .01 .05
180 Kenny Lofton .05 .15
181 Carlos Baerga .02 .10
182 Jose Mesa .02 .10
183 Gary Gaetti .02 .10
184 Tom Goodwin .01 .05
185 Kevin Appier .02 .10
186 Jon Nunnally .01 .05
187 Kansas City Royals Team Logo .01 .05
188 Wally Joyner .02 .10
189 Jeff Montgomery .01 .05
190 Johnny Damon .30 .75
191 B.J. Surhoff .02 .10
192 Ricky Bones .01 .05
193 John Jaha .01 .05
194 Dave Nilsson .01 .05
195 Milwaukee Brewers Team Logo .01 .05
196 Greg Vaughn .02 .10
197 Kevin Seitzer .01 .05
198 Joe Oliver .01 .05
199 Chuck Knoblauch .08 .25
200 Kirby Puckett .25 .60
201 Marty Cordova .01 .05
202 Pat Meares .01 .05
203 Minnesota Twins Team Logo .01 .05
204 Scott Stahoviak .01 .05
205 Matt Walbeck .01 .05
206 Pedro Munoz .01 .05
207 Garret Anderson .02 .10
208 Chili Davis .02 .10
209 Tim Salmon .08 .25
210 J.T. Snow .02 .10
211 California Angels Team Logo .01 .05
212 Jim Edmonds .08 .25
213 Chuck Finley .02 .10
214 Mark Langston .01 .05
215 Dennis Eckersley .20 .50
216 Todd Stottlemyre .01 .05
217 Geronimo Berroa .01 .05
218 Mark McGwire .50 1.25
219 Oakland A's Team Logo .01 .05
220 Brent Gates .01 .05
221 Terry Steinbach .01 .05
222 Rickey Henderson .30 .75
223 Ken Griffey Jr. .60 1.50
224 Alex Rodriguez .60 1.50
225 Tino Martinez .08 .25
226 Randy Johnson .30 .75
227 Seattle Mariners Team Logo .01 .05
228 Jay Buhner .02 .10
229 Vince Coleman .01 .05
230 Edgar Martinez .05 .15
231 Will Clark .08 .25
232 Juan Gonzalez .20 .50
233 Kenny Rogers .01 .05
234 Ivan Rodriguez .20 .50
235 Texas Rangers Team Logo .01 .05
236 Mickey Tettleton .01 .05
237 Dean Palmer .02 .10
238 Otis Nixon .01 .05
239 Hideo Nomo .10 .30
240 Quilvio Veras .01 .05
241 Jason Isringhausen .08 .25
242 Andy Pettitte .08 .25
243 Chipper Jones .60 1.50
244 Garret Anderson .02 .10
245 Charles Johnson .01 .05
246 Marty Cordova .01 .05

2019 Panini Titan

RANDOM INSERTS IN PACKS
*HOLO: .75X TO 2X
*HYPER/299: .75X TO 2X
*RUBY/199: 1X TO 2.5X
*BLUE/99: 1.2X TO 3X
*PURPLE/75: 1.2X TO 3X
*GREEN/50: 1.5X TO 4X
*PINK/25: 2.5X TO 6X
1 Pete Alonso RC 2.00 5.00
2 Eloy Jimenez RC .60 1.50
3 Fernando Tatis Jr. RC 4.00 10.00
4 Michael Kopech RC .50 1.25
5 Kyle Tucker RC .40 1.00
6 Yusei Kikuchi RC .25 .60
7 Chris Paddack RC .30 .75
8 Mike Trout 3.00 8.00
9 Bryce Harper .40 1.00
10 Aaron Judge 2.00 5.00
11 Kris Bryant .30 .75
12 Shohei Ohtani .40 1.00
13 Clayton Kershaw .40 1.00
14 Mookie Betts .50 1.25
15 Jose Altuve .20 .50
16 Francisco Lindor .25 .60
17 Javier Baez .30 .75
18 Ichiro .30 .75
19 Ronald Acuna Jr. .75 2.00
20 Paul Goldschmidt .25 .60
21 Cavan Biggio RC .75 2.00
22 Nolan Arenado .40 1.00
23 Yadier Molina .30 .75
24 Vladimir Guerrero Jr. RC 2.50 6.00
25 Manny Machado .25 .60

2020 Panini Titan

RANDOM INSERTS IN PACKS
1 Bo Bichette RC 3.00 8.00
2 Yordan Alvarez RC 2.50 6.00
3 Gavin Lux RC 1.25 3.00
4 Brendan McKay RC .40 1.00
5 Aristides Aquino RC .60 1.50
6 Yoshitomo Tsutsugo RC .60 1.50
7 Luis Robert RC 6.00 15.00
8 Aaron Judge .60 1.50
9 Mike Trout 2.00 5.00
10 Cody Bellinger .50 1.25
11 Fernando Tatis Jr. 2.00 5.00
12 Vladimir Guerrero Jr. .40 1.00
13 Shun Yamaguchi RC .40 1.00
14 Eloy Jimenez .50 1.25
15 Nolan Arenado .40 1.00
16 Zac Gallen RC .60 1.50
17 Starling Marte .20 .50
18 Ronald Acuna Jr. 1.50 4.00
19 Juan Soto .75 2.00
20 Anthony Rizzo .30 .75
21 Trea Turner .20 .50
22 Tony Gonsolin RC 1.00 2.50
23 Mauricio Dubon RC .30 .75
24 Willi Castro RC .40 1.00
25 Dylan Cease RC .40 1.00
26 Gerrit Cole .40 1.00
27 Jorge Soler .25 .60
28 Christian Yelich .30 .75
29 Javier Baez .30 .75
30 Mookie Betts .50 1.25

2020 Panini Titanium

RANDOM INSERTS IN PACKS
1 Mike Trout 2.00 5.00
2 Javier Baez .30 .75
3 Bryce Harper .40 1.00
4 Aaron Judge .60 1.50
5 Cody Bellinger .50 1.25
6 Michel Baez RC .25 .60
7 Shogo Akiyama RC .40 1.00
8 A.J. Puk RC .40 1.00
9 Adbert Alzolay RC .30 .75
10 Aristides Aquino RC .60 1.50
11 Bo Bichette RC 3.00 8.00
12 Shun Yamaguchi RC .30 .75
13 Brendan McKay RC .40 1.00
14 Yoshitomo Tsutsugo RC .60 1.50
15 Yordan Alvarez RC 2.50 6.00
16 Dylan Cease RC .40 1.00
17 Gavin Lux RC 1.25 3.00
18 Jordan Yamamoto RC .25 .60
19 Kwang-Hyun Kim RC .50 1.25
20 Luis Robert RC 4.00 10.00

2019 Panini Unparalleled

RANDOM INSERTS IN PACKS
*ASTRAL: 1X TO 2.5X
*DIAMOND/99: 1.2X TO 3X
*SQUARED/25: 2.5X TO 6X
1 Yusei Kikuchi RC .25 .60
2 Mitch Keller RC .20 .50
3 Javier Baez .30 .75
4 Keston Hiura RC .50 1.25
5 Rafael Devers .30 .75
6 Bryce Harper .40 1.00
7 Pete Alonso RC 2.00 5.00
8 Michael Kopech RC .50 1.25
9 Cody Bellinger .50 1.25
10 Ryan O'Hearn RC .15 .40
11 Austin Riley RC .75 2.00
12 Alex Bregman .25 .60
13 Eloy Jimenez RC .60 1.50
14 Aaron Judge .60 1.50
15 Brendan Rodgers .25 .60
16 Cavan Biggio RC .75 2.00
17 Corbin Martin RC .25 .60
18 Francisco Lindor .25 .60
19 Jake Bauers RC .25 .60
20 Fernando Tatis Jr. RC 4.00 10.00
21 Kyle Tucker RC .40 1.00
22 Chris Paddack RC .30 .75
23 Shohei Ohtani .40 1.00
24 Mike Trout 1.25 3.00
25 Kris Bryant .30 .75
26 Brandon Lowe RC .25 .60
27 Vladimir Guerrero Jr. RC 2.50 6.00
28 Cole Tucker RC .25 .60
29 Michael Chavis RC .25 .60
30 Jon Duplantier RC .15 .40

2020 Panini Unparalleled

RANDOM INSERTS IN PACKS
1 Yoshitomo Tsutsugo RC .60 1.50
2 Ronald Acuna Jr. 1.50 4.00
3 Gavin Lux RC 1.25 3.00
4 Luis Robert RC 4.00 10.00
5 Shun Yamaguchi RC .30 .75
6 Nolan Arenado .40 1.00
7 Aaron Judge .60 1.50
8 Bobby Bradley RC .25 .60
9 Pete Alonso .60 1.50
10 Brendan McKay RC .40 1.00
11 Aristides Aquino RC .60 1.50
12 Shogo Akiyama RC .40 1.00
13 Kwang-Hyun Kim RC .50 1.25
14 Bryce Harper .40 1.00
15 Nico Hoerner RC 1.00 2.50
16 Vladimir Guerrero Jr. .40 1.00
17 Juan Soto .75 2.00
18 Christian Yelich .30 .75
19 Bo Bichette RC 3.00 8.00
20 A.J. Puk RC .40 1.00
21 Anthony Rizzo .30 .75
22 Sean Murphy RC .40 1.00
23 Yordan Alvarez RC 2.50 6.00
24 Mike Trout 2.00 5.00
25 Cody Bellinger .50 1.25
26 Alex Bregman .25 .60
27 Rafael Devers .30 .75
28 Dylan Cease RC .40 1.00
29 Mookie Betts .50 1.25
30 Jordan Yamamoto RC .25 .60

1989 PAO Religious Tracts

This five-card set features color player photos on a 4 1/8" by 7 5/8" tri-fold card and was distributed by Pro Athletes Outreach, a Christian leadership training ministry to pro players and their families. The cards are unnumbered and checklisted below in alphabetical order.
COMPLETE SET (5) 2.50 6.00
1 Gary Carter 1.00 2.50
2 Alvin Davis .60 1.50
3 Mike Moore .40 1.00
4 Frank Pastore .40 1.00
5 Craig Reynolds .40 1.00

1978 Papa Gino's Discs

This 40-disc set consists of all American League players with more than half the set being Boston Red Sox players. Papa Gino's was a chain of restaurants located throughout central New England. The discs are 3 3/8" in diameter and have a distinctive thick dark blue border on the front with orange printing. The set was approved by the Major League Baseball Players Association under the auspices of Mike Schechter Associates (MSA) and as such has team logos airbrushed away. The discs are numbered on the back at the bottom; the uniform number is also given at the top of the reverse. The first 25 players in the set are members of the Boston Red Sox. Supposedly eight discs were printed in smaller quantities; these short printed discs are marked SP in the checklist below.
COMPLETE SET (40) 20.00 50.00
COMMON PLAYER (1-40) .20 .50
COMMON SP .40 1.00
1 Allen Ripley .20 .50
2 Jerry Remy .20 .50
3 Jack Brohamer .20 .50
4 Butch Hobson .20 .50
5 Dennis Eckersley 1.25 3.00
6 Sam Bowen SP .40 1.00
7 Rick Burleson .20 .50
8 Carl Yastrzemski 1.50 4.00
9 Bill Lee .40 1.00
10 Bob Montgomery .20 .50
11 Dick Drago SP .40 1.00
12 Bob Stanley SP .40 1.00
13 Fred Kendall SP .40 1.00
14 Jim Rice SP .75 2.00
15 George Scott .40 1.00
16 Tom Burgmeier .20 .50
17 Frank Duffy SP .40 1.00
18 Jim Wright .20 .50
19 Fred Lynn .60 1.50
20 Bob Bailey SP .40 1.00
21 Mike Torrez .20 .50
22 Bill Campbell SP .40 1.00
23 Luis Tiant .60 1.50
24 Dwight Evans .75 2.00
25 Carlton Fisk 1.50 4.00
26 Reggie Jackson 2.00 5.00
27 Thurman Munson 1.25 3.00
28 Ron Guidry .75 2.00
29 Bruce Bochte .20 .50
30 Richie Zisk .20 .50
31 Jim Palmer 1.25 3.00
32 Mark Fidrych 1.25 3.00
33 Frank Tanana .40 1.00
34 Buddy Bell .60 1.50
35 Rod Carew 1.25 3.00
36 George Brett 3.00 8.00
37 Ralph Garr .20 .50
38 Larry Hisle .20 .50
39 Mitchell Page .20 .50
40 John Mayberry .20 .50

1943-48 Parade Sportive

These blank-backed photo sheets of sports figures from the Montreal area around 1945 measure approximately 5" by 8 1/4". They were issued to promote a couple of Montreal radio stations that used to broadcast interviews with some of the pictured athletes. The sheets feature white-bordered black-and-white player photos, some of them crudely retouched. The player's name appears in the bottom white margin and also as a facsimile autograph across the photo. The sheets are unnumbered and are checklisted below in alphabetical order within sport as follows: hockey (1-75), baseball (76-95) and various other sports (96-101). Additions to this checklist are appreciated. Many players are known to appear with two different poses. Since the values are the same for both poses, we have put a (2) next to the players name but have placed a value on only one of the photos.
COMPLETE SET 1250.00 2500.00
77 Jack Banta 15.00 30.00
78 Stan Breard 12.50 25.00
79 Les Burge 12.50 25.00
80 Al Campanis 15.00 30.00
81 Red Durrett 12.50 25.00
82 Herman Franks 15.00 30.00
83 John Gabbard 12.50 25.00
84 Roland Gladu 12.50 25.00
85 Ray Hathaway 12.50 25.00
86 John Jorgensen 12.50 25.00
87 Paul Pepper Martin 12.50 25.00
88 Steve Nagy 12.50 25.00
89 Jackie Robinson 100.00 200.00
90 Marvin Rackley 12.50 25.00
91 Jean-Pierre Roy 12.50 25.00
92 Roland Gaddy 12.50 25.00
Jean-Pierre Roy
Stan Breard
93 Montreal Royals 1944 25.00 50.00
94 Montreal Royals 1945 12.50 25.00
95 Montreal Royals 1946 25.00 50.00

1998 Paramount

The 1998 Paramount set (issued by Pacific) consists of 250 standard-size cards issued in six-card packs with an SRP of $1.49. The fronts feature color action photos with silver foil showcasing today's top players and tomorrow's rising stars. The backs offer a second color photo, along with complete year-by-year career stats.
COMPLETE SET (250) 12.50 30.00
1 Garret Anderson .07 .20
2 Gary DiSarcina .07 .20
3 Jim Edmonds .07 .20
4 Darin Erstad .07 .20
5 Cecil Fielder .07 .20
6 Chuck Finley .07 .20
7 Todd Greene .07 .20
8 Shigetoshi Hasegawa .07 .20
9 Tim Salmon .10 .30
10 Roberto Alomar .10 .30
11 Brady Anderson .07 .20
12 Joe Carter .07 .20
13 Eric Davis .07 .20
14 Ozzie Guillen .07 .20
15 Mike Mussina .10 .30
16 Rafael Palmeiro .10 .30
17 Cal Ripken .60 1.50
18 B.J. Surhoff .07 .20
19 Steve Avery .07 .20
20 Nomar Garciaparra .30 .75
21 Reggie Jefferson .07 .20
22 Pedro Martinez .10 .30
23 Tim Naehring .07 .20
24 John Valentin .07 .20
25 Mo Vaughn .07 .20
26 James Baldwin .07 .20
27 Albert Belle .07 .20
28 Ray Durham .07 .20
29 Benji Gil .07 .20
30 Jaime Navarro .07 .20
31 Magglio Ordonez RC .60 1.50
32 Frank Thomas .20 .50
33 Robin Ventura .07 .20
34 Sandy Alomar Jr. .07 .20
35 Geronimo Berroa .07 .20
36 Travis Fryman .07 .20
37 David Justice .07 .20
38 Kenny Lofton .07 .20
39 Charles Nagy .07 .20
40 Manny Ramirez .10 .30
41 Jim Thome .10 .30
42 Omar Vizquel .10 .30
43 Jaret Wright .07 .20
44 Raul Casanova .07 .20
45 Frank Catalanotto RC .10 .30
46 Tony Clark .07 .20
47 Bobby Higginson .07 .20
48 Brian Hunter .07 .20
49 Todd Jones .07 .20
50 Bip Roberts .07 .20
51 Justin Thompson .07 .20
52 Kevin Appier .07 .20
53 Johnny Damon .10 .30
54 Jermaine Dye .07 .20
55 Jeff King .07 .20
56 Jeff Montgomery .07 .20
57 Dean Palmer .07 .20
58 Jose Rosado .07 .20
59 Larry Sutton .07 .20
60 Rick Aguilera .07 .20
61 Marty Cordova .07 .20
62 Pat Meares .07 .20
63 Paul Molitor .07 .20
64 Otis Nixon .07 .20
65 Brad Radke .07 .20
66 Terry Steinbach .07 .20
67 Todd Walker .07 .20
68 Hideki Irabu .07 .20
69 Derek Jeter .50 1.25
70 Chuck Knoblauch .07 .20
71 Tino Martinez .10 .30
72 Paul O'Neill .10 .30
73 Andy Pettitte .10 .30
74 Mariano Rivera .20 .50
75 Bernie Williams .10 .30
76 Mark Bellhorn .07 .20
77 Tom Candiotti .07 .20
78 Jason Giambi .07 .20
79 Ben Grieve .07 .20
80 Rickey Henderson .20 .50
81 Jason McDonald .07 .20
82 Kevin Small .07 .20
83 Miguel Tejada .20 .50
84 Jay Buhner .07 .20
85 Joey Cora .07 .20
86 Jeff Fassero .07 .20
87 Ken Griffey Jr. .40 1.00
88 Randy Johnson .20 .50
89 Edgar Martinez .10 .30
90 Alex Rodriguez .30 .75
91 David Segui .07 .20
92 Dan Wilson .07 .20
93 Wilson Alvarez .07 .20
94 Wade Boggs .10 .30
95 Miguel Cairo .07 .20
96 John Flaherty .07 .20
97 Dave Martinez .07 .20
98 Quinton McCracken .07 .20
99 Fred McGriff .10 .30
100 Paul Sorrento .07 .20
101 Kevin Stocker .07 .20
102 John Burkett .07 .20
103 Will Clark .10 .30
104 Juan Gonzalez .07 .20
105 Rusty Greer .07 .20
106 Roberto Kelly .07 .20
107 Ivan Rodriguez .10 .30
108 Fernando Tatis .07 .20
109 John Wetteland .07 .20
110 Jose Canseco .10 .30
111 Roger Clemens .40 1.00
112 Jose Cruz Jr. .07 .20
113 Carlos Delgado .07 .20
114 Alex Gonzalez .07 .20
115 Pat Hentgen .07 .20
116 Ed Sprague .07 .20
117 Shannon Stewart .07 .20
118 Brian Anderson .07 .20
119 Jay Bell .07 .20
120 Andy Benes .07 .20
121 Yamil Benitez .07 .20
122 Jorge Fabregas .07 .20
123 Travis Lee .07 .20
124 Devon White .07 .20
125 Matt Williams .07 .20
126 Bob Wolcott .07 .20
127 Andres Galarraga .07 .20
128 Tom Glavine .10 .30
129 Andruw Jones .10 .30
130 Chipper Jones .20 .50
131 Ryan Klesko .07 .20
132 Javy Lopez .07 .20
133 Greg Maddux .30 .75
134 Denny Neagle .07 .20
135 John Smoltz .10 .30
136 Rod Beck .07 .20
137 Jeff Blauser .07 .20
138 Mark Grace .10 .30
139 Lance Johnson .07 .20
140 Mickey Morandini .07 .20
141 Kevin Orie .07 .20
142 Sammy Sosa .20 .50
143 Aaron Boone .07 .20
144 Bret Boone .07 .20
145 Dave Burba .07 .20
146 Lenny Harris .07 .20
147 Barry Larkin .10 .30
148 Reggie Sanders .07 .20
149 Brett Tomko .07 .20
150 Pedro Astacio .07 .20
151 Dante Bichette .07 .20
152 Ellis Burks .07 .20
153 Vinny Castilla .07 .20
154 Todd Helton .10 .30
155 Darryl Kile .07 .20
156 Jeff Reed .07 .20
157 Larry Walker .07 .20
158 Bobby Bonilla .07 .20
159 Todd Dunwoody .07 .20
160 Livan Hernandez .07 .20
161 Charles Johnson .07 .20
162 Mark Kotsay .07 .20
163 Derrek Lee .10 .30
164 Edgar Renteria .07 .20
165 Gary Sheffield .07 .20
166 Moises Alou .07 .20
167 Jeff Bagwell .10 .30
168 Derek Bell .07 .20
169 Craig Biggio .10 .30
170 Mike Hampton .07 .20
171 Richard Hidalgo .07 .20
172 Chris Holt .07 .20
173 Shane Reynolds .07 .20
174 Wilton Guerrero .07 .20
175 Eric Karros .07 .20
176 Paul Konerko .07 .20
177 Ramon Martinez .07 .20
178 Raul Mondesi .07 .20
179 Hideo Nomo .20 .50
180 Chan Ho Park .07 .20
181 Mike Piazza .30 .75
182 Ismael Valdes .07 .20
183 Jeromy Burnitz .07 .20
184 Jeff Cirillo .07 .20
185 Todd Dunn .07 .20
186 Marquis Grissom .07 .20
187 John Jaha .07 .20

188 Doug Jones .07 .20
189 Dave Nilsson .07 .20
190 Jose Valentin .07 .20
191 Fernando Vina .07 .20
192 Orlando Cabrera .07 .20
193 Steve Falteisek RC .07 .20
194 Mark Grudzielanek .07 .20
195 Vladimir Guerrero .20 .50
196 Carlos Perez .07 .20
197 F.P. Santangelo .07 .20
198 Jose Vidro .07 .20
199 Rondell White .07 .20
200 Edgardo Alfonzo .07 .20
201 Carlos Baerga .07 .20
202 John Franco .07 .20
203 Bernard Gilkey .07 .20
204 Todd Hundley .07 .20
205 Butch Huskey .07 .20
206 Bobby Jones .07 .20
207 Brian McRae .07 .20
208 John Olerud .07 .20
209 Rey Ordonez .07 .20
210 Ricky Bottalico .07 .20
211 Bobby Estalella .07 .20
212 Doug Glanville .07 .20
213 Gregg Jefferies .07 .20
214 Mike Lieberthal .07 .20
215 Desi Relaford .07 .20
216 Scott Rolen .10 .30
217 Curt Schilling .07 .20
218 Adrian Brown .07 .20
219 Emil Brown .07 .20
220 Francisco Cordova .07 .20
221 Jose Guillen .07 .20
222 Al Martin .07 .20
223 Abraham Nunez .07 .20
224 Tony Womack .07 .20
225 Kevin Young .07 .20
226 Alan Benes .07 .20
227 Royce Clayton .07 .20
228 Gary Gaetti .07 .20
229 Ron Gant .07 .20
230 Brian Jordan .07 .20
231 Ray Lankford .07 .20
232 Mark McGwire .50 1.25
233 Todd Stottlemyre .07 .20
234 Kevin Brown .10 .30
235 Ken Caminiti .07 .20
236 Steve Finley .07 .20
237 Tony Gwynn .25 .60
238 Wally Joyner .07 .20
239 Ruben Rivera .07 .20
240 Greg Vaughn .07 .20
241 Quilvio Veras .07 .20
242 Barry Bonds .50 1.25
243 Jacob Cruz .07 .20
244 Shawn Estes .07 .20
245 Orel Hershiser .07 .20
246 Stan Javier .07 .20
247 Brian Johnson .07 .20
248 Jeff Kent .07 .20
249 Robb Nen .07 .20
250 J.T. Snow .07 .20

1998 Paramount Copper

COMPLETE SET (250) 60.00 120.00
*STARS: 1.25X TO 3X BASIC CARDS
*ROOKIES: 1X TO 2.5X BASIC CARDS
ONE PER HOBBY PACK

1998 Paramount Gold

COMPLETE SET (250) 75.00 150.00
*STARS: 1.5X TO 4X BASIC CARDS
*ROOKIES: 1.25X TO 3X BASIC CARDS
ONE PER RETAIL PACK

1998 Paramount Holographic Silver

*STARS: 15X TO 40X BASIC CARDS
*ROOKIES: 10X TO 25X BASIC CARDS
RANDOM INSERTS IN HOBBY PACKS
STATED PRINT RUN 99 SERIAL #'d SETS

1998 Paramount Platinum Blue

*STARS: 15X TO 40X BASIC CARDS
*ROOKIES: 10X TO 25X BASIC CARDS
STATED ODDS 1:73 HOBBY/RETAIL

1998 Paramount Red

COMPLETE SET (250) 100.00 200.00
*STARS: 2X TO 5X BASIC CARDS
*ROOKIES: 1.5X TO 4X BASIC CARDS
ONE PER ANCO PACK

1998 Paramount Cooperstown Bound

COMPLETE SET (10) 40.00 80.00
STATED ODDS 1:361
*PROOF: 1.5X TO 4X BASIC COOPERSTOWN
PROOF: RANDOM INSERTS IN HOBBY
PAC.PROOF PRINT RUN 20 SERIAL #'d SETS
1 Greg Maddux 4.00 10.00
2 Cal Ripken 10.00 25.00
3 Frank Thomas 3.00 8.00
4 Mike Piazza 3.00 8.00
5 Paul Molitor 3.00 8.00
6 Mark McGwire 5.00 12.00
7 Tony Gwynn 3.00 8.00
8 Barry Bonds 5.00 12.00
9 Ken Griffey Jr. 6.00 15.00
10 Wade Boggs 2.00 5.00

1998 Paramount Fielder's Choice

COMPLETE SET (20) 50.00 120.00
STATED ODDS 1:73
1 Chipper Jones 3.00 8.00
2 Greg Maddux 4.00 10.00
3 Cal Ripken 10.00 25.00
4 Nomar Garciaparra 2.00 5.00
5 Frank Thomas 3.00 8.00
6 David Justice 1.25 3.00
7 Larry Walker 2.00 5.00
8 Jeff Bagwell 2.00 5.00
9 Hideo Nomo 3.00 8.00
10 Mike Piazza 3.00 8.00
11 Derek Jeter 8.00 20.00
12 Ben Grieve 1.25 3.00
13 Mark McGwire 5.00 12.00
14 Tony Gwynn 3.00 8.00
15 Barry Bonds 5.00 12.00
16 Ken Griffey Jr. 6.00 15.00
17 Alex Rodriguez 4.00 10.00
18 Wade Boggs 2.00 5.00
19 Ivan Rodriguez 2.00 5.00
20 Jose Cruz Jr. 1.25 3.00

1998 Paramount Special Delivery

COMPLETE SET (20) 15.00 40.00
STATED ODDS 1:37
1 Chipper Jones 1.00 2.50
2 Greg Maddux 1.25 3.00
3 Cal Ripken 3.00 8.00
4 Nomar Garciaparra .60 1.50
5 Pedro Martinez .60 1.50
6 Frank Thomas 1.00 2.50
7 David Justice .40 1.00
8 Larry Walker .60 1.50
9 Jeff Bagwell .60 1.50
10 Hideo Nomo 1.00 2.50
11 Mike Piazza 1.00 2.50
12 Vladimir Guerrero .60 1.50
13 Derek Jeter 2.50 6.00
14 Ben Grieve .40 1.00
15 Mark McGwire 1.50 4.00
16 Tony Gwynn 1.00 2.50
17 Barry Bonds 1.50 4.00
18 Ken Griffey Jr. 2.00 5.00
19 Alex Rodriguez 1.25 3.00
20 Jose Cruz Jr. .40 1.00

1998 Paramount Team Checklists

COMPLETE SET (30) 40.00 100.00
STATED ODDS 2:37
1 Tim Salmon 1.25 3.00
2 Cal Ripken 6.00 15.00
3 Nomar Garciaparra 3.00 8.00
4 Frank Thomas 2.00 5.00
5 Manny Ramirez 1.25 3.00
6 Tony Clark .75 2.00
7 Dean Palmer .75 2.00
8 Paul Molitor .75 2.00
9 Derek Jeter 5.00 12.00
10 Ben Grieve .75 2.00
11 Ken Griffey Jr. 4.00 10.00
12 Wade Boggs 1.25 3.00
13 Ivan Rodriguez 1.25 3.00
14 Roger Clemens 4.00 10.00
15 Matt Williams .75 2.00
16 Chipper Jones 2.00 5.00
17 Sammy Sosa 2.00 5.00
18 Barry Larkin 1.25 3.00
19 Larry Walker .75 2.00
20 Livan Hernandez .75 2.00
21 Jeff Bagwell 1.25 3.00
22 Mike Piazza 3.00 8.00
23 John Jaha .75 2.00
24 Vladimir Guerrero 2.00 5.00
25 Todd Hundley .75 2.00
26 Scott Rolen 1.25 3.00
27 Kevin Young .75 2.00
28 Mark McGwire 5.00 12.00
29 Tony Gwynn 2.50 6.00
30 Barry Bonds 5.00 12.00

1999 Paramount

The 1999 Paramount set was issued in one series for a total of 250 cards and distributed in six-card packs with a suggested retail price of $1.49. The set features color action photos of some of today's biggest superstars and tomorrow's up-and-comers in their 1999 uniforms. As was typical with 1999 Pacific products, a Tony Gwynn Sample card was produced and distributed to dealers and hobby media several weeks prior to the product's release. The large "SAMPLE" text running across the back, and lack of a card number make this an easy card to distinguish.

COMPLETE SET (250) 15.00 40.00
1 Garret Anderson .07 .20
2 Gary DiSarcina .07 .20
3 Jim Edmonds .07 .20
4 Darin Erstad .07 .20
5 Chuck Finley .07 .20
6 Troy Glaus .10 .30
7 Troy Percival .07 .20
8 Tim Salmon .10 .30
9 Mo Vaughn .07 .20
10 Tony Batista .07 .20
11 Jay Bell .07 .20
12 Andy Benes .07 .20
13 Steve Finley .07 .20
14 Luis Gonzalez .07 .20
15 Randy Johnson .20 .50
16 Travis Lee .07 .20
17 Todd Stottlemyre .07 .20
18 Matt Williams .07 .20
19 David Dellucci .07 .20
20 Bret Boone .07 .20
21 Andres Galarraga .07 .20
22 Tom Glavine .10 .30
23 Andruw Jones .10 .30
24 Chipper Jones .20 .50
25 Brian Jordan .07 .20
26 Ryan Klesko .07 .20
27 Javy Lopez .07 .20
28 Greg Maddux .30 .75
29 John Smoltz .10 .30
30 Brady Anderson .07 .20
31 Albert Belle .07 .20
32 Will Clark .10 .30
33 Delino DeShields .07 .20
34 Charles Johnson .07 .20
35 Mike Mussina .10 .30
36 Cal Ripken .60 1.50
37 B.J. Surhoff .07 .20
38 Nomar Garciaparra .30 .75
39 Reggie Jefferson .07 .20
40 Darren Lewis .07 .20
41 Pedro Martinez .10 .30
42 Troy O'Leary .07 .20
43 Jose Offerman .07 .20
44 Donnie Sadler .07 .20
45 John Valentin .07 .20
46 Rod Beck .07 .20
47 Gary Gaetti .07 .20
48 Mark Grace .10 .30
49 Lance Johnson .07 .20
50 Mickey Morandini .07 .20
51 Henry Rodriguez .07 .20
52 Sammy Sosa .20 .50
53 Kerry Wood .07 .20
54 Mike Caruso .07 .20
55 Ray Durham .07 .20
56 Paul Konerko .07 .20
57 Jaime Navarro .07 .20
58 Greg Norton .07 .20
59 Magglio Ordonez .07 .20
60 Frank Thomas .20 .50
61 Aaron Boone .07 .20
62 Mike Cameron .07 .20
63 Barry Larkin .10 .30
64 Hal Morris .07 .20
65 Pokey Reese .07 .20
66 Brett Tomko .07 .20
67 Greg Vaughn .07 .20
68 Dmitri Young .07 .20
69 Roberto Alomar .10 .30
70 Sandy Alomar Jr. .07 .20
71 Bartolo Colon .07 .20
72 Travis Fryman .07 .20
73 David Justice .07 .20
74 Kenny Lofton .07 .20
75 Manny Ramirez .10 .30
76 Richie Sexson .07 .20
77 Jim Thome .10 .30
78 Omar Vizquel .10 .30
79 Dante Bichette .07 .20
80 Vinny Castilla .07 .20
81 Darryl Hamilton .07 .20
82 Todd Helton .10 .30
83 Darryl Kile .07 .20
84 Mike Lansing .07 .20
85 Neifi Perez .07 .20
86 Larry Walker .07 .20
87 Tony Clark .07 .20
88 Damion Easley .07 .20
89 Bob Higginson .07 .20
90 Brian Hunter .07 .20
91 Dean Palmer .07 .20
92 Justin Thompson .07 .20
93 Todd Dunwoody .07 .20
94 Cliff Floyd .07 .20
95 Alex Gonzalez .07 .20
96 Livan Hernandez .07 .20
97 Mark Kotsay .07 .20
98 Derrek Lee .10 .30
99 Kevin Orie .07 .20
100 Moises Alou .07 .20
101 Jeff Bagwell .10 .30
102 Derek Bell .07 .20
103 Craig Biggio .10 .30
104 Ken Caminiti .07 .20
105 Ricky Gutierrez .07 .20
106 Richard Hidalgo .07 .20
107 Billy Wagner .07 .20
108 Jeff Conine .07 .20
109 Johnny Damon .10 .30
110 Carlos Febles .07 .20
111 Jeremy Giambi .07 .20
112 Jeff King .07 .20
113 Jeff Montgomery .07 .20
114 Joe Randa .07 .20
115 Kevin Brown .10 .30
116 Mark Grudzielanek .07 .20
117 Todd Hundley .07 .20
118 Eric Karros .07 .20
119 Raul Mondesi .07 .20
120 Chan Ho Park .07 .20
121 Gary Sheffield .07 .20
122 Devon White .07 .20
123 Eric Young .07 .20
124 Jeromy Burnitz .07 .20
125 Jeff Cirillo .07 .20
126 Marquis Grissom .07 .20
127 Geoff Jenkins .07 .20
128 Dave Nilsson .07 .20
129 Jose Valentin .07 .20
130 Fernando Vina .07 .20
131 Rick Aguilera .07 .20
132 Ron Coomer .07 .20
133 Marty Cordova .07 .20
134 Matt Lawton .07 .20
135 David Ortiz .20 .50
136 Brad Radke .07 .20
137 Terry Steinbach .07 .20
138 Javier Valentin .07 .20
139 Todd Walker .07 .20
140 Orlando Cabrera .07 .20
141 Brad Fullmer .07 .20
142 Vladimir Guerrero .20 .50
143 Wilton Guerrero .07 .20
144 Carl Pavano .07 .20
145 Ugueth Urbina .07 .20
146 Rondell White .07 .20
147 Chris Widger .07 .20
148 Edgardo Alfonzo .07 .20
149 Bobby Bonilla .07 .20
150 Rickey Henderson .20 .50
151 Brian McRae .07 .20
152 Hideo Nomo .20 .50
153 John Olerud .07 .20
154 Rey Ordonez .07 .20
155 Mike Piazza .30 .75
156 Robin Ventura .07 .20
157 Masato Yoshii .07 .20
158 Roger Clemens .40 1.00
159 David Cone .07 .20
160 Orlando Hernandez .07 .20
161 Hideki Irabu .07 .20
162 Derek Jeter .50 1.25
163 Chuck Knoblauch .07 .20
164 Tino Martinez .10 .30
165 Paul O'Neill .10 .30
166 Darryl Strawberry .07 .20
167 Bernie Williams .10 .30
168 Eric Chavez .07 .20
169 Ryan Christenson .07 .20
170 Jason Giambi .07 .20
171 Ben Grieve .07 .20
172 Tony Phillips .07 .20
173 Tim Raines .07 .20
174 Scott Spiezio .07 .20
175 Miguel Tejada .07 .20
176 Bobby Abreu .07 .20
177 Rico Brogna .07 .20
178 Ron Gant .07 .20
179 Doug Glanville .07 .20
180 Desi Relaford .07 .20
181 Scott Rolen .10 .30
182 Curt Schilling .07 .20
183 Brant Brown .07 .20
184 Brian Giles .07 .20
185 Jose Guillen .07 .20
186 Jason Kendall .07 .20
187 Al Martin .07 .20
188 Ed Sprague .07 .20
189 Kevin Young .07 .20
190 Eric Davis .07 .20
191 J.D. Drew .07 .20
192 Ray Lankford .07 .20
193 Eli Marrero .07 .20
194 Mark McGwire .50 1.25
195 Edgar Renteria .07 .20
196 Fernando Tatis .07 .20
197 Andy Ashby .07 .20
198 Tony Gwynn .25 .60
199 Carlos Hernandez .07 .20
200 Trevor Hoffman .07 .20
201 Wally Joyner .07 .20
202 Jim Leyritz .07 .20
203 Ruben Rivera .07 .20
204 Matt Clement .07 .20
205 Quilvio Veras .07 .20
206 Rich Aurilia .07 .20
207 Marvin Benard .07 .20
208 Barry Bonds .60 1.50
209 Ellis Burks .07 .20
210 Jeff Kent .07 .20
211 Bill Mueller .07 .20
212 Robb Nen .07 .20
213 J.T. Snow .07 .20
214 Jay Buhner .07 .20
215 Jeff Fassero .07 .20
216 Ken Griffey Jr. .40 1.00
217 Carlos Guillen .07 .20
218 Butch Huskey .07 .20
219 Edgar Martinez .10 .30
220 Alex Rodriguez .30 .75
221 David Segui .07 .20
222 Dan Wilson .07 .20
223 Rolando Arrojo .07 .20
224 Wade Boggs .10 .30
225 Jose Canseco .10 .30
226 Roberto Hernandez .07 .20
227 Dave Martinez .07 .20
228 Quinton McCracken .07 .20
229 Fred McGriff .10 .30
230 Kevin Stocker .07 .20
231 Randy Winn .07 .20
232 Royce Clayton .07 .20
233 Juan Gonzalez .07 .20
234 Tom Goodwin .07 .20
235 Rusty Greer .07 .20
236 Rick Helling .07 .20
237 Rafael Palmeiro .10 .30
238 Ivan Rodriguez .10 .30
239 Aaron Sele .07 .20
240 John Wetteland .07 .20
241 Todd Zeile .07 .20
242 Jose Cruz Jr. .07 .20
243 Carlos Delgado .07 .20
244 Tony Fernandez .07 .20
245 Cecil Fielder .07 .20
246 Alex Gonzalez .07 .20
247 Shawn Green .07 .20
248 Roy Halladay .20 .50
249 Shannon Stewart .07 .20
250 David Wells .07 .20
NNO Tony Gwynn Sample .40 1.00

1999 Paramount Copper

COMPLETE SET (250) 40.00 100.00
*STARS: 1.5X TO 4X BASIC CARDS
ONE PER HOBBY PACK

1999 Paramount Gold

COMPLETE SET (250) 40.00 100.00
*STARS: 1X TO 2.5X BASIC CARDS
ONE PER RETAIL PACK

1999 Paramount Holo-Gold

*STARS: 10X TO 25X BASIC CARDS
RANDOM INSERTS IN PACKS
STATED PRINT RUN 199 SERIAL #'d SETS

1999 Paramount Holo-Silver

*STARS: 15X TO 40X BASIC CARDS
RANDOM INSERTS IN HOBBY PACKS
STATED PRINT RUN 99 SERIAL #'d SETS

1999 Paramount Opening Day

COMMON CARD (1-250) 2.00 5.00
*STARS: 20X TO 50X BASIC CARDS
STATED ODDS 1:36 HOBBY
STATED PRINT RUN 74 SERIAL #'D SETS

1999 Paramount Platinum Blue

*STARS: 15X TO 40X BASIC CARDS
STATED ODDS 1:73 HOB/RET

1999 Paramount Red

COMPLETE SET (250) 40.00 100.00
*STARS: 1.5X TO 4X BASIC CARDS
ONE PER RETAIL PACK

1999 Paramount Cooperstown Bound

STATED ODDS 1:361
*PROOFS: 1.5X TO 4X BASIC COOP
PROOFS: RANDOM INSERTS IN HOBBY
PAC.PROOFS PRINT RUN 20 SERIAL #'d SETS
1 Greg Maddux 12.50 30.00
2 Cal Ripken 25.00 60.00
3 Nomar Garciaparra 12.50 30.00
4 Sammy Sosa 8.00 20.00
5 Frank Thomas 8.00 20.00
6 Mike Piazza 12.50 30.00
7 Mark McGwire 20.00 50.00
8 Tony Gwynn 10.00 25.00
9 Ken Griffey Jr. 15.00 40.00
10 Alex Rodriguez 12.50 30.00

1999 Paramount Fielder's Choice

COMPLETE SET (20) 100.00 200.00
STATED ODDS 1:73
1 Chipper Jones 5.00 12.00
2 Greg Maddux 8.00 20.00
3 Cal Ripken 15.00 40.00
4 Nomar Garciaparra 8.00 20.00
5 Sammy Sosa 5.00 12.00
6 Kerry Wood 2.00 5.00
7 Frank Thomas 5.00 12.00
8 Manny Ramirez 3.00 8.00
9 Todd Helton 3.00 8.00
10 Jeff Bagwell 3.00 8.00
11 Mike Piazza 8.00 20.00
12 Derek Jeter 12.50 30.00
13 Bernie Williams 3.00 8.00
14 J.D. Drew 2.00 5.00
15 Mark McGwire 12.50 30.00
16 Tony Gwynn 6.00 15.00
17 Ken Griffey Jr. 10.00 25.00
18 Alex Rodriguez 8.00 20.00
19 Juan Gonzalez 2.00 5.00
20 Ivan Rodriguez 3.00 8.00

1999 Paramount Personal Bests

COMPLETE SET (36) 125.00 250.00
STATED ODDS 1:37
1 Darin Erstad 1.50 4.00
2 Mo Vaughn 1.50 4.00
3 Travis Lee 1.50 4.00
4 Chipper Jones 4.00 10.00
5 Greg Maddux 6.00 15.00
6 Albert Belle 1.50 4.00
7 Cal Ripken 12.50 30.00
8 Nomar Garciaparra 6.00 15.00
9 Sammy Sosa 4.00 10.00
10 Andruw Jones 2.50 6.00
11 Frank Thomas 4.00 10.00
12 Roberto Alomar 2.50 6.00
13 Manny Ramirez 2.50 6.00
14 Todd Helton 2.50 6.00
15 Larry Walker 1.50 4.00
16 Jeff Bagwell 2.50 6.00
17 Craig Biggio 2.50 6.00
18 Raul Mondesi 1.50 4.00
19 Vladimir Guerrero 4.00 10.00
20 Hideo Nomo 4.00 10.00
21 Mike Piazza 6.00 15.00
22 Roger Clemens 8.00 20.00
23 Derek Jeter 10.00 25.00
24 Bernie Williams 2.50 6.00
25 Eric Chavez 1.50 4.00
26 Ben Grieve 1.50 4.00
27 Scott Rolen 2.50 6.00
28 J.D. Drew 1.50 4.00
29 Mark McGwire 10.00 25.00
30 Tony Gwynn 5.00 12.00
31 Barry Bonds 12.50 30.00
32 Ken Griffey Jr. 8.00 20.00
33 Alex Rodriguez 6.00 15.00
34 Wade Boggs 2.50 6.00
35 Juan Gonzalez 1.50 4.00
36 Ivan Rodriguez 2.50 6.00

1999 Paramount Team Checklists

COMPLETE SET (30) 40.00 100.00
STATED ODDS 2:37
1 Mo Vaughn .75 2.00
2 Travis Lee .75 2.00
3 Chipper Jones 2.00 5.00
4 Cal Ripken 6.00 15.00
5 Nomar Garciaparra 3.00 8.00
6 Sammy Sosa 2.00 5.00
7 Frank Thomas 2.00 5.00
8 Barry Larkin 1.25 3.00
9 Manny Ramirez 1.25 3.00
10 Larry Walker .75 2.00
11 Damion Easley .75 2.00
12 Mark Kotsay .75 2.00
13 Jeff Bagwell 1.25 3.00
14 Jeremy Giambi .75 2.00
15 Raul Mondesi .75 2.00
16 Marquis Grissom .75 2.00
17 Brad Radke .75 2.00
18 Vladimir Guerrero 2.00 5.00
19 Mike Piazza 3.00 8.00
20 Roger Clemens 4.00 10.00
21 Ben Grieve .75 2.00
22 Scott Rolen 1.25 3.00
23 Jason Kendall .75 2.00
24 Mark McGwire 5.00 12.00
25 Tony Gwynn 2.50 6.00
26 Barry Bonds 6.00 15.00
27 Ken Griffey Jr. 4.00 10.00
28 Wade Boggs 1.25 3.00
29 Juan Gonzalez .75 2.00
30 Jose Cruz Jr. .75 2.00

1999 Paramount Players Choice

These cards, which parallel the regular Paramount cards, were distributed at the 1999 Players Choice award ceremony. The cards, are the same as the regular Paramount cards except they have a "Players Choice" stamped on the front. The cards are skip numbered since they share the same number as the regular cards. Each card was issued in different quantities so we have put the print run next to the players name.

COMPLETE SET 150.00 300.00
8 Mike Hampton/75 3.00 8.00
Uses 1998 Paramount card
No 1999
15 Randy Johnson/133 6.00 15.00
18 Matt Williams/108 3.00 8.00
24 Chipper Jones/117 12.50 30.00
28 Greg Maddux/118 12.50 30.00
36 Cal Ripken Jr./60 30.00 80.00
41 Pedro Martinez/118 6.00 15.00
52 Sammy Sosa/98 10.00 25.00
69 Roberto Alomar/133 5.00 12.00
75 Manny Ramirez/139 6.00 15.00
101 Jeff Bagwell/100 6.00 15.00
150 Rickey Henderson/133 8.00 20.00
208 Barry Bonds/53 16.00 40.00
216 Ken Griffey Jr./97 20.00 50.00
237 Rafael Palmeiro/133 4.00 10.00

2000 Paramount

COMPLETE SET (250) 15.00 40.00
COMMON CARD (1-250) .08 .20
1 Garret Anderson .07 .20
2 Jim Edmonds .07 .20
3 Darin Erstad .07 .20
4 Chuck Finley .07 .20
5 Troy Glaus .07 .20
6 Troy Percival .07 .20
7 Tim Salmon .07 .20
8 Mo Vaughn .07 .20
9 Jay Bell .07 .20
10 Erubiel Durazo .07 .20
11 Steve Finley .07 .20
12 Luis Gonzalez .07 .20
13 Randy Johnson .20 .50
14 Travis Lee .07 .20
15 Matt Mantei .07 .20
16 Matt Williams .07 .20
17 Tony Womack .07 .20
18 Bret Boone .07 .20
19 Tom Glavine .12 .30
20 Andruw Jones .07 .20
21 Chipper Jones .20 .50
22 Brian Jordan .07 .20
23 Javy Lopez .07 .20
24 Greg Maddux .25 .60
25 Kevin Millwood .07 .20
26 John Rocker .07 .20
27 John Smoltz .20 .50
28 Brady Anderson .07 .20
29 Albert Belle .07 .20
30 Will Clark .12 .30
31 Charles Johnson .07 .20
32 Mike Mussina .12 .30
33 Cal Ripken .60 1.50
34 B.J. Surhoff .07 .20
35 Nomar Garciaparra .12 .30
36 Derek Lowe .07 .20
37 Pedro Martinez .12 .30
38 Trot Nixon .07 .20
39 Troy O'Leary .07 .20
40 Jose Offerman .07 .20
41 John Valentin .07 .20
42 Jason Varitek .20 .50
43 Mark Grace .12 .30
44 Glenallen Hill .07 .20
45 Jon Lieber .07 .20
46 Cole Liniak .07 .20
47 Jose Nieves .07 .20
48 Henry Rodriguez .07 .20
49 Sammy Sosa .20 .50
50 Kerry Wood .07 .20
51 Jason Dellaero .07 .20
52 Ray Durham .07 .20
53 Paul Konerko .07 .20
54 Carlos Lee .07 .20
55 Greg Norton .07 .20
56 Magglio Ordonez .12 .30
57 Chris Singleton .07 .20
58 Frank Thomas .20 .50
59 Aaron Boone .07 .20
60 Mike Cameron .07 .20
61 Sean Casey .07 .20
62 Pete Harnisch .07 .20
63 Barry Larkin .12 .30
64 Pokey Reese .07 .20
65 Greg Vaughn .07 .20
66 Scott Williamson .07 .20
67 Roberto Alomar .12 .30
68 Sean DePaula RC .07 .20
69 Travis Fryman .07 .20
70 David Justice .07 .20
71 Kenny Lofton .07 .20
72 Manny Ramirez .20 .50
73 Richie Sexson .07 .20
74 Jim Thome .12 .30
75 Omar Vizquel .12 .30
76 Pedro Astacio .07 .20
77 Vinny Castilla .07 .20
78 Derrick Gibson .07 .20
79 Todd Helton .12 .30
80 Neifi Perez .07 .20
81 Ben Petrick .07 .20
82 Larry Walker .12 .30
83 Brad Ausmus .07 .20
84 Tony Clark .07 .20
85 Deivi Cruz .07 .20
86 Damion Easley .07 .20
87 Juan Encarnacion .07 .20
88 Juan Gonzalez .07 .20
89 Bobby Higginson .07 .20
90 Dave Mlicki .07 .20
91 Dean Palmer .07 .20
92 Bruce Aven .07 .20
93 Luis Castillo .07 .20
94 Ramon Castro .07 .20
95 Cliff Floyd .07 .20
96 Alex Gonzalez .07 .20
97 Mike Lowell .07 .20
98 Preston Wilson .07 .20
99 Jeff Bagwell .12 .30
100 Derek Bell .07 .20
101 Craig Biggio .12 .30
102 Ken Caminiti .07 .20
103 Carl Everett .07 .20
104 Mike Hampton .07 .20
105 Jose Lima .07 .20
106 Billy Wagner .07 .20
107 Daryle Ward .07 .20
108 Carlos Beltran .12 .30
109 Johnny Damon .12 .30
110 Jermaine Dye .07 .20
111 Carlos Febles .07 .20
112 Mark Quinn .07 .20
113 Joe Randa .07 .20
114 Jose Rosado .07 .20
115 Mike Sweeney .07 .20
116 Kevin Brown .07 .20
117 Shawn Green .07 .20
118 Mark Grudzielanek .07 .20
119 Todd Hollandsworth .07 .20
120 Eric Karros .07 .20
121 Chan Ho Park .07 .20
122 Gary Sheffield .07 .20
123 Devon White .07 .20
124 Eric Young .07 .20
125 Kevin Barker .07 .20
126 Ron Belliard .07 .20
127 Jeromy Burnitz .07 .20
128 Jeff Cirillo .07 .20
129 Marquis Grissom .07 .20
130 Geoff Jenkins .07 .20
131 David Nilsson .07 .20
132 Chad Allen .07 .20
133 Ron Coomer .07 .20
134 Jacque Jones .07 .20
135 Corey Koskie .07 .20
136 Matt Lawton .07 .20
137 Brad Radke .07 .20
138 Todd Walker .07 .20
139 Michael Barrett .07 .20
140 Peter Bergeron .07 .20
141 Brad Fullmer .07 .20
142 Vladimir Guerrero .12 .30
143 Ugueth Urbina .07 .20
144 Jose Vidro .07 .20
145 Rondell White .07 .20
146 Edgardo Alfonzo .07 .20
147 Armando Benitez .07 .20
148 Roger Cedeno .07 .20
149 Rickey Henderson .20 .50
150 Melvin Mora .07 .20
151 John Olerud .07 .20
152 Rey Ordonez .07 .20
153 Mike Piazza .20 .50
154 Jorge Toca .07 .20
155 Robin Ventura .07 .20
156 Roger Clemens .25 .60
157 David Cone .07 .20
158 Orlando Hernandez .07 .20
159 Derek Jeter .50 1.25
160 Chuck Knoblauch .07 .20
161 Ricky Ledee .07 .20
162 Tino Martinez .07 .20
163 Paul O'Neill .12 .30
164 Mariano Rivera .25 .60
165 Alfonso Soriano .20 .50
166 Bernie Williams .12 .30
167 Eric Chavez .07 .20
168 Jason Giambi .07 .20
169 Ben Grieve .07 .20
170 Tim Hudson .12 .30
171 John Jaha .07 .20
172 Matt Stairs .07 .20
173 Miguel Tejada .12 .30
174 Randy Velarde .07 .20
175 Bobby Abreu .07 .20
176 Marlon Anderson .07 .20
177 Rico Brogna .07 .20
178 Ron Gant .07 .20
179 Doug Glanville .07 .20
180 Mike Lieberthal .07 .20
181 Scott Rolen .12 .30
182 Curt Schilling .12 .30
183 Brian Giles .07 .20
184 Chad Hermansen .07 .20
185 Jason Kendall .07 .20
186 Al Martin .07 .20
187 Pat Meares .07 .20
188 Warren Morris .07 .20
189 Ed Sprague .07 .20
190 Kevin Young .07 .20
191 Rick Ankiel .12 .30
192 Kent Bottenfield .07 .20
193 Eric Davis .07 .20
194 J.D. Drew .07 .20
195 Adam Kennedy .07 .20
196 Ray Lankford .07 .20
197 Joe McEwing .07 .20
198 Mark McGwire .30 .75
199 Edgar Renteria .07 .20
200 Fernando Tatis .07 .20
201 Mike Darr .07 .20
202 Ben Davis .07 .20
203 Tony Gwynn .20 .50
204 Trevor Hoffman .12 .30
205 Damian Jackson .07 .20
206 Phil Nevin .07 .20
207 Reggie Sanders .07 .20
208 Quilvio Veras .07 .20
209 Rich Aurilia .07 .20
210 Marvin Benard .07 .20
211 Barry Bonds .30 .75
212 Ellis Burks .07 .20
213 Livan Hernandez .07 .20
214 Jeff Kent .07 .20
215 Russ Ortiz .07 .20
216 J.T. Snow .07 .20
217 Paul Abbott .07 .20
218 David Bell .07 .20
219 Freddy Garcia .07 .20
220 Ken Griffey Jr. .40 1.00
221 Carlos Guillen .07 .20
222 Brian Hunter .07 .20
223 Edgar Martinez .12 .30
224 Jamie Moyer .07 .20
225 Alex Rodriguez .25 .60
226 Wade Boggs .12 .30
227 Miguel Cairo .07 .20
228 Jose Canseco .12 .30
229 Roberto Hernandez .07 .20
230 Dave Martinez .07 .20
231 Quinton McCracken .07 .20
232 Fred McGriff .12 .30
233 Kevin Stocker .07 .20
234 Royce Clayton .07 .20
235 Rusty Greer .07 .20
236 Ruben Mateo .07 .20
237 Rafael Palmeiro .12 .30
238 Ivan Rodriguez .12 .30
239 Aaron Sele .07 .20
240 John Wetteland .07 .20
241 Todd Zeile .07 .20
242 Tony Batista .07 .20
243 Homer Bush .07 .20
244 Carlos Delgado .07 .20
245 Tony Fernandez .07 .20
246 Billy Koch .07 .20
247 Raul Mondesi .07 .20
248 Shannon Stewart .07 .20
249 David Wells .07 .20
250 Vernon Wells .07 .20

2000 Paramount Copper
COMPLETE SET (250) 50.00 100.00
*COPPER: 1.5X TO 4X BASIC
ONE PER HOBBY PACK

2000 Paramount Gold
COMPLETE SET (250) 40.00 100.00
*GOLD: 1.5X TO 4X BASIC CARDS
ONE PER RETAIL PACK

2000 Paramount Green
COMPLETE SET (250) 40.00 100.00
*GREEN: 2X TO 5X BASIC CARDS
ONE PER 7-11 PACK

2000 Paramount Holographic Gold
*HOLO.GOLD: 8X TO 20X BASIC
STATED PRINT RUN 199 SERIAL #'d SETS

2000 Paramount Holographic Green
*HOLO.GREEN: 12.5X TO 30X BASIC
STATED PRINT RUN 99 SERIAL #'d SETS

2000 Paramount Holographic Silver
*HOLO.SILVER: 12.5X TO 30X BASIC
STATED PRINT RUN 99 SERIAL #'d SETS

2000 Paramount Platinum Blue
*PLAT.BLUE: 15X TO 40X BASIC
STATED PRINT RUN 67 SERIAL #'d SETS

2000 Paramount Premiere Date
*PREM.DATE: 20X TO 50X BASIC
STATED ODDS 1:36 HOBBY
STATED PRINT RUN 50 SERIAL #'d SETS

2000 Paramount Ruby
COMPLETE SET (250) 30.00 60.00
*RUBY: 1.25X TO 3X BASIC CARDS
NINE CARDS PER 7-11 PACK

2000 Paramount Cooperstown Bound
COMPLETE SET (10) 40.00 80.00
STATED ODDS 1:361
*PROOF: 1.5X TO 4X BASIC COOPERSTOWN
PROOF PRINT RUN 20 SERIAL #'d SETS
CANVAS PROOF RANDOM IN HOBBY PACKS
CANVAS PROOF PR.RUN 1 SERIAL #'d SET
CANVAS PROOF TOO SCARCE TO PRICE
1 Greg Maddux 4.00 10.00
2 Cal Ripken 10.00 25.00
3 Nomar Garciaparra 2.00 5.00
4 Sammy Sosa 3.00 8.00
5 Roger Clemens 4.00 10.00
6 Derek Jeter 8.00 20.00
7 Mark McGwire 5.00 12.00
8 Tony Gwynn 3.00 8.00
9 Ken Griffey Jr. 6.00 15.00
10 Alex Rodriguez 4.00 10.00

2000 Paramount Cooperstown Bound Proofs
*PROOFS: 1.5X TO 4X BASIC COOP.BOUND
STATED PRINT RUN 20 SERIAL #'d SETS

2000 Paramount Double Vision
COMPLETE SET (36) 50.00 100.00
STATED ODDS 1:37
EACH PLAYER HAS TWO CARDS
BOTH VERSIONS EQUALLY VALUED
CARDS 1-18 ARE SAME PLAYERS AS 19-36
1 Chipper Jones 1.25 3.00
2 Cal Ripken 4.00 10.00
3 Nomar Garciaparra .75 2.00
4 Pedro Martinez .75 2.00
5 Sammy Sosa 1.25 3.00
6 Manny Ramirez 1.25 3.00
7 Jeff Bagwell .75 2.00
8 Craig Biggio .75 2.00
9 Vladimir Guerrero .75 2.00
10 Mike Piazza 1.25 3.00
11 Roger Clemens 1.50 4.00
12 Derek Jeter 3.00 8.00
13 Mark McGwire 2.00 5.00
14 Tony Gwynn 1.25 3.00
15 Ken Griffey Jr. 2.50 6.00
16 Alex Rodriguez 1.50 4.00
17 Rafael Palmeiro .75 2.00
18 Ivan Rodriguez .75 2.00
19 Chipper Jones 1.25 3.00
20 Cal Ripken 4.00 10.00
21 Nomar Garciaparra .75 2.00
22 Pedro Martinez .75 2.00
23 Sammy Sosa 1.25 3.00
24 Manny Ramirez 1.25 3.00
25 Jeff Bagwell .75 2.00
26 Craig Biggio .75 2.00
27 Vladimir Guerrero .75 2.00
28 Mike Piazza 1.25 3.00
29 Roger Clemens 1.50 4.00
30 Derek Jeter 3.00 8.00
31 Mark McGwire 2.00 5.00
32 Tony Gwynn 1.25 3.00
33 Ken Griffey Jr. 2.50 6.00
34 Alex Rodriguez 1.50 4.00
35 Rafael Palmeiro .75 2.00
36 Ivan Rodriguez .75 2.00

2000 Paramount Fielder's Choice
STATED ODDS 1:73
GOLD GLOVE RANDOM INS.IN HOB/RET
GOLD GLOVE PRINT RUN 10 SERIAL #'d SETS
GOLD GLOVE TOO SCARCE TO PRICE
1 Andruw Jones .60 1.50
2 Chipper Jones 1.50 4.00
3 Greg Maddux 2.00 5.00
4 Cal Ripken 5.00 12.00
5 Nomar Garciaparra 1.00 2.50
6 Sammy Sosa 1.50 4.00
7 Sean Casey .60 1.50
8 Manny Ramirez 1.50 4.00
9 Larry Walker 1.00 2.50
10 Jeff Bagwell 1.00 2.50
11 Mike Piazza 1.50 4.00
12 Derek Jeter 8.00 20.00
13 Bernie Williams 1.00 2.50
14 Scott Rolen 1.00 2.50
15 Mark McGwire 2.50 6.00
16 Tony Gwynn 1.50 4.00
17 Barry Bonds 2.50 6.00
18 Ken Griffey Jr. 3.00 8.00
19 Alex Rodriguez 2.00 5.00
20 Ivan Rodriguez 1.00 2.50

2000 Paramount Maximum Impact
COMPLETE SET (20) 15.00 40.00
STATED ODDS 2:25 RETAIL 7-11
1 Chipper Jones 1.00 2.50
2 Cal Ripken 3.00 8.00
3 Nomar Garciaparra .60 1.50
4 Pedro Martinez .60 1.50
5 Sammy Sosa 1.00 2.50
6 Manny Ramirez 1.00 2.50
7 Larry Walker .60 1.50
8 Jeff Bagwell .60 1.50
9 Carlos Beltran .60 1.50
10 Vladimir Guerrero .60 1.50
11 Mike Piazza 1.00 2.50
12 Derek Jeter 2.50 6.00
13 Roger Clemens 1.25 3.00
14 Mark McGwire 1.50 4.00
15 Tony Gwynn 1.00 2.50
16 Barry Bonds 1.50 4.00
17 Ken Griffey Jr. 2.00 5.00
18 Alex Rodriguez 1.25 3.00
19 Ivan Rodriguez .60 1.50
20 Carlos Delgado .40 1.00

2000 Paramount Season in Review
COMPLETE SET (30) 15.00 40.00
STATED ODDS 2:37
1 Randy Johnson .75 2.00
2 Matt Williams .30 .75
3 Chipper Jones .75 2.00
4 Greg Maddux 1.00 2.50
5 Cal Ripken 2.50 6.00
6 Nomar Garciaparra .50 1.25
7 Pedro Martinez .50 1.25
8 Sammy Sosa .75 2.00
9 Manny Ramirez .75 2.00
10 Larry Walker .50 1.25
11 Jeff Bagwell .50 1.25
12 Craig Biggio .50 1.25
13 Carlos Beltran .50 1.25
14 Mark Quinn .30 .75
15 Vladimir Guerrero .50 1.25
16 Mike Piazza .75 2.00
17 Robin Ventura .30 .75
18 Roger Clemens 1.00 2.50
19 David Cone .30 .75
20 Derek Jeter 2.00 5.00
21 Mark McGwire 1.25 3.00
22 Fernando Tatis .30 .75
23 Tony Gwynn .75 2.00
24 Barry Bonds 1.25 3.00
25 Ken Griffey Jr. 1.50 4.00
26 Alex Rodriguez 1.00 2.50
27 Wade Boggs .50 1.25
28 Jose Canseco .50 1.25
29 Rafael Palmeiro .50 1.25
30 Ivan Rodriguez .50 1.25

2000 Paramount Update
COMP.FACT.SET (100) 12.50 30.00
COMMON CARD (U1-U100) .12 .30
COMMON RC .25 .60
DISTRIBUTED THROUGH J.C. PENNEY
STATED PRINT RUN 12,500 SETS
U1 Adam Kennedy .12 .30
U2 Bengie Molina .12 .30
U3 Derrick Turnbow RC .25 .60
U4 Randy Johnson .30 .75
U5 Danny Klassen .12 .30
U6 Vicente Padilla RC .60 1.50
U7 Rafael Furcal .20 .50
U8 Andres Galarraga .20 .50
U9 Chipper Jones .30 .75
U10 Fernando Lunar .12 .30
U11 Willie Morales RC .25 .60
U12 Cal Ripken 1.00 2.50
U13 B.J. Ryan .12 .30
U14 Carl Everett .12 .30
U15 Nomar Garciaparra .20 .50
U16 Pedro Martinez .20 .50
U17 Wilton Veras .12 .30
U18 Scott Downs RC .25 .60
U19 Daniel Garibay RC .25 .60
U20 Sammy Sosa .30 .75
U21 Julio Zuleta RC .25 .60
U22 Josh Paul .12 .30
U23 Frank Thomas .30 .75
U24 Rob Bell .12 .30
U25 Dante Bichette .12 .30
U26 Travis Dawkins .12 .30
U27 Ken Griffey Jr. .60 1.50
U28 Chuck Finley .12 .30
U29 Manny Ramirez .30 .75
U30 Paul Rigdon RC .25 .60
U31 Jeff Cirillo .12 .30
U32 Larry Walker .20 .50
U33 Masato Yoshii .12 .30
U34 Robert Fick .12 .30
U35 Jose Macias .12 .30
U36 Juan Gonzalez .12 .30
U37 Hideo Nomo .30 .75
U38 Jason Grilli .12 .30
U39 Pablo Ozuna .12 .30
U40 Brad Penny .12 .30
U41 Jeff Bagwell .20 .50
U42 Lance Berkman .20 .50
U43 Roger Cedeno .12 .30
U44 Octavio Dotel .12 .30
U45 Chad Durbin RC .25 .60
U46 Eric Gagne .12 .30
U47 Shawn Green .12 .30
U48 Jose Hernandez .12 .30
U49 Matt LeCroy .12 .30
U50 Johan Santana RC 4.00 10.00
U51 Vladimir Guerrero .20 .50
U52 Hideki Irabu .12 .30
U53 Andy Tracy RC .25 .60
U54 Derek Bell .12 .30
U55 Eric Cammack RC .25 .60
U56 Mike Hampton .12 .30
U57 Jay Payton .12 .30
U58 Mike Piazza .30 .75
U59 Todd Zeile .12 .30
U60 Roger Clemens .40 1.00
U61 Darrell Einertson RC .25 .60
U62 Derek Jeter .75 2.00
U63 Jeremy Giambi .12 .30
U64 Terrence Long .12 .30
U65 Mark Mulder .12 .30
U66 Adam Piatt .12 .30
U67 Luis Vizcaino .12 .30
U68 Pat Burrell .12 .30
U69 Scott Rolen .20 .50
U70 Chad Hermansen .12 .30
U71 Rick Ankiel .20 .50
U72 Jim Edmonds Cards .12 .30
U73 Mark McGwire .50 1.25
U74 Gene Stechschulte RC .25 .60
U75 Fernando Vina .12 .30
U76 Bret Boone .12 .30
U77 Tony Gwynn .30 .75
U78 Ryan Klesko .12 .30
U79 David Newhan .12 .30
U80 Kevin Walker RC .25 .60
U81 Barry Bonds .50 1.25
U82 Aaron Fultz RC .25 .60
U83 Ben Weber RC .25 .60
U84 Rickey Henderson .30 .75
U85 Kevin Hodges RC .25 .60
U86 John Olerud .12 .30
U87 Rob Ramsay .12 .30
U88 Alex Rodriguez .40 1.00
U89 Kazuhiro Sasaki RC .60 1.50
U90 Vinny Castilla .12 .30
U91 Jeff Sparks RC .25 .60
U92 Greg Vaughn .12 .30
U93 Francisco Cordero .12 .30
U94 Gabe Kapler .12 .30
U95 Mike Lamb RC .25 .60
U96 Ivan Rodriguez .20 .50
U97 Clayton Andrews .12 .30
U98 Brad Fullmer .12 .30
U99 Raul Mondesi .12 .30
U100 Dewayne Wise .12 .30

1977-81 Bob Parker Hall of Fame
These 103 cards measure 3 1/2" by 5 1/2". The cards are checklisted in alphabetical order. Noted sports artist Bob Parker drew these pictures of Hall of Famers. Between 1977 and 1981 two different continuation series of 23 postcards were issued. They are each entered in order of issue. A couple of other notes. All three series have unnumbered header cards. The first series header does list the cards in numerical order while the other header cards do not. Also the first and third series card are made of similar stock while the middle series consists of a darker tan paper stock.
COMPLETE SET (103) 100.00 200.00
1 Grover C. Alexander .60 1.50
2 Cap Anson .60 1.50
3 Luke Appling .30 .75
4 Ernie Banks 10.00 25.00
5 Chief Bender .30 .75
6 Jim Bottomley .20 .50
7 Dan Brouthers .20 .50
8 Morgan Bulkeley .10 .25
9 Roy Campanella .40 1.00
10 Alex Cartwright .10 .25
11 Henry Chadwick .10 .25
12 John Clarkson .20 .50
13 Ty Cobb 2.00 5.00
14 Eddie Collins .40 1.00
15 Jimmy Collins .20 .50
16 Charles Comiskey .40 1.00
17 Sam Crawford .30 .75
18 Dizzy Dean .40 1.00
19 Joe DiMaggio 2.00 5.00
20 Buck Ewing .30 .75
21 Bob Feller .60 1.50
22 Lou Gehrig 2.00 5.00
23 Goose Goslin .30 .75
24 Burleigh Grimes .30 .75
25 Chick Hafey .20 .50
26 Rogers Hornsby .60 1.50
27 Carl Hubbell .40 1.00
28 Miller Huggins .20 .50
29 Tim Keefe .20 .50
30 Mike Kelly .30 .75
31 Nap Lajoie .40 1.00
32 Fred Lindstrom .20 .50
33 Connie Mack .40 1.00
34 Mickey Mantle 30.00 60.00
35 Heine Manush .30 .75
36 Joe McGinnity .20 .50
37 John McGraw .40 1.00
38 Eddie Plank .30 .75
39 Eppa Rixey .20 .50
40 Jackie Robinson 1.50 4.00
41 Eddie Roush .30 .75
42 Babe Ruth 3.00 8.00
43 Al Simmons .30 .75
44 Albert Spalding .20 .50
45 Tris Speaker .60 1.50
46 Casey Stengel .40 1.00
47 Bill Terry .30 .75
48 Rube Waddell .20 .50
49 Hans Wagner .75 2.00
50 Paul Waner .30 .75
51 John M. Ward .20 .50
52 Ted Williams 8.00 20.00
53 George Wright .20 .50
54 Harry Wright .20 .50
55 Mordecai Brown .20 .50
56 Frank Chance .30 .75
57 Candy Cummings .20 .50
58 Frank Frisch .20 .50
59 Gabby Hartnett .20 .50
60 Billy Herman .20 .50
61 Waite Hoyt .20 .50
62 Walter Johnson .60 1.50
63 Kenesaw Landis .10 .25
64 Rube Marquard .20 .50
65 Christy Mathewson .60 1.50
66 Eddie Mathews .30 .75
67 Willie Mays 1.50 4.00
68 Bill McKechnie .10 .25
69 Stan Musial 6.00 15.00
70 Mel Ott .40 1.00
71 Satchel Paige .40 1.00
72 Robin Roberts .30 .75
73 George Sisler .20 .50
74 Warren Spahn .30 .75
75 Joe Tinker .10 .25
76 Dazzy Vance .10 .25
77 Cy Young .40 1.00
78 Home Run Baker .30 .75
79 Yogi Berra .40 1.00
80 Max Carey .10 .25
81 Roberto Clemente 15.00 40.00
82 Mickey Cochrane .20 .50
83 Roger Connor .10 .25
84 Joe Cronin .30 .75
85 Kiki Cuyler .20 .50
86 Johnny Evers .30 .75
87 Jimmy Foxx .40 1.00
(Jimmie)
88 Charlie Gehringer .30 .75
89 Lefty Gomez .30 .75
90 Jesse Haines .10 .25
91 Will Harridge .10 .25
92 Monte Irvin .20 .50
93 Addie Joss .20 .50
94 Al Kaline 6.00 15.00
95 Sandy Koufax 8.00 20.00
96 Rabbit Maranville .10 .25
97 Jim O'Rourke .10 .25
98 Wilbert Robinson .20 .50
99 Pie Traynor .20 .50
100 Zach Wheat .10 .25
NNO 3rd series Header .10 .25
NNO 1st series Header .10 .25
NNO 2nd series Header .10 .25

1977 Bob Parker More Baseball Cartoons
These 24 cartoons feature imporant players in Baseball History as drawn by noted sports artist Bob Parker. These cards feature drawings on the front and are blank-backed
COMPLETE SET (24) 15.00 40.00
1 Hank Aaron 2.00 5.00
Babe Ruth
2 Ernie Banks .60 1.50
3 Rod Carew .40 1.00
4 Joe DiMaggio 2.00 5.00
5 Doug Flynn .10 .25
6 Mike Garcia .10 .25
7 Steve Garvey .20 .50
Greg Luzinski
8 Lou Gehrig 2.00 5.00
9 Chuck Klein .20 .50
Hack Wilson
10 Don Larsen .20 .50
11 Fred Lynn .20 .50
12 Roy Majtyka .10 .25
13 Pepper Martin .20 .50
14 Christy Mathewson .40 1.00
15 Cal McVey .30 .75
16 Tony Perez .30 .75
17 Babe Ruth 2.00 5.00
Lou Gehrig
18 Everett Scott .10 .25
19 Bobby Thomson .20 .50
20 Ted Williams/1939 Version of Williams 2.00 5.00
Drawn in 7
21 Ted Williams 2.00 5.00
Last .400 Hitter
Drawn in 76
22 Bill Madlock .20 .50
23 Honus Wagner .30 .75
Al Spalding
Buck Ewing
Henry Chadw
24 Checklist .10 .25

1968-70 Partridge Meats
These black and white (with some red trim and text) photo-like cards feature players from all three Cincinnati major league sports teams of that time: Cincinnati Reds baseball (BB1-BB20), Cincinnati Bengals football (FB1-FB5), and Cincinnati Royals basketball (BK1-BK2). The cards measure approximately 4" by 5" or 3-3/4" by 5-1/2" and were issued over a period of years. The cards are blank backed and a "Mr. Whopper" card was also issued in honor of the 7'-3" company spokesperson. The Tom Rhoads football card was only recently discovered, in 2012, adding to the prevailing thought that these cards were issued over a period of years since its format matches some of the baseball cards and not the other four more well-known football cards in the set. Joe Morgan was also recently added to the checklist indicating that more cards could turn up in the future. This card follows the same format as Gullett, May, Perez, and Tolan (all measuring 3-3/4" by 5-1/2") missing the team's logo on the cap, missing the team's nickname in the text, and missing the company's slogan below the image. Some collectors believe this style to be consistent with a 1972 release.
COMPLETE SET (14) 400.00 800.00
BB1 Ted Abernathy SP 25.00 50.00
BB2 Johnny Bench 60.00 120.00
(measures 4" x 5")
BB3 Jimmy Bragan CO 12.50 25.00
(measures 4" x 5")
BB4 Dave Bristol MG SP 25.00 50.00
BB5 Don Gullett 15.00 30.00
(measures 3 3/4" x 5 1/2")
BB6 Tommy Harper SP 25.00 50.00
BB7 Tommy Helms 12.50 25.00
(measures 4" x 5")
BB8 Lee May 20.00 40.00
(measures 3 3/4" x 5 1/2")
BB9 Denis Menke SP 25.00 50.00
BB10 Jim Merritt SP 25.00 50.00
BB11 Joe Morgan SP 75.00 150.00
(measures 3 3/4" x 5 1/2")
BB12 Gary Nolan 12.50 25.00
(measures 4" x 5")
BB13 Gary Nolan
(measures 3 3/4" x 5 1/2")
BB14 Milt Pappas SP 25.00 50.00
BB15 Don Pavletich SP 25.00 50.00
BB16 Tony Perez 40.00 80.00
(measures 3 3/4" x 5 1/2")
BB17 Mel Queen 12.50 25.00
(measures 4" x 5")
BB18 Pete Rose 75.00 150.00
(measures 4" x 5")
BB19 Jim Stewart SP 25.00 50.00
BB20 Bob Tolan 12.50 25.00
(measures 3 3/4" x 5 1/2")

1914 Pastime Novelty Postcard
This postcard, issued by the Pastime Novelty company featured Christy Mathewson in a photo taken during the 1913 World Series. Little else is known about ths postcard so all additional information is appreciated.
1 Christy Mathewson 400.00 800.00

1868-71 Peck and Snyder Trade Cards
Issued over a period of years, these cards feature rare photos of some of the earliest professional teams. The Lowells card is currently known as only a photocopy.
COMPLETE SET 50000.00 100000.00
1 Lowells/1868 20000.00 40000.00
2 Atlantics/1868 12500.00 25000.00
3 Chicago White Sox 1870 12500.00 25000.00
4 Mutuals/1870 12500.00 25000.00
5 Philadelphia Athletics 1870 12500.00 25000.00

1914 People's Tobacco Kotton T216
The cards in this 59-player set measure 1 1/2" by 2 5/8" and contains unnumbered cards. The players have been alphabetized and numbered for reference in the checklist below. Back variations, listed in order of scarcity from hardest to easiest, within this set include Kotton, Mino and Virginia Brights Cigarettes.
COMPLETE SET 30000.00 60000.00
1A Jack Barry 400.00 800.00
Batting
1B Jack Barry 400.00 800.00
Fielding
2 Harry Bemis 400.00 800.00
3A Chief Bender 750.00 1500.00
Striped Cap
Phila Am.
3B Chief Bender 750.00 1500.00
Striped Cap
Baltimore Fed
3C Chief Bender 750.00 1500.00
White Cap
Phila Am.
3D Chief Bender 750.00 1500.00
White Cap
Baltimore Fed
4 Bill Bergen 400.00 800.00
5A Bob Bescher 400.00 800.00
Cincinnati
5B Bob Bescher 400.00 800.00
St. Louis Fed
6 Roger Bresnahan 750.00 1500.00
7A Al Bridwell 400.00 800.00
batting
7B Al Bridwell 400.00 800.00
Sliding
New York Nat'l
7C Al Bridwell 400.00 800.00
Sliding
St. Louis Feds
8 Donie Bush 450.00 900.00
9 Doc Casey 400.00 800.00
10 Frank Chance 900.00 1800.00
11A Hal Chase 750.00 1500.00
Portrait
11B Hal Chase 750.00 1500.00
Fielding
New York Am.
11C Hal Chase 750.00 1500.00
Fielding
Buffalo
12A Ty Cobb Standing Detroit Am. 7500.00 15000.00
12B Ty Cobb Standing Detroit
Americans 7500.00 15000.00
12C Ty Cobb Batting 7500.00 15000.00
13 Sam Crawford 750.00 1500.00
13A Eddie Collins 750.00 1500.00
Philadelphia Amer.
13B Eddie Collins 750.00 1500.00
Phila Am.
13C Eddie Collins 750.00 1500.00
Chicago Americans
14 Harry Davis 400.00 800.00
15 Ray Demmitt 400.00 800.00
17A Bill Donovan 400.00 800.00
Detroit Amer.
17B Bill Donovan 400.00 800.00
N.Y. Americans
18A Red Dooin 400.00 800.00
Phila Nat.
18B Red Dooin 400.00 800.00
Cincinnati
19A Mickey Doolan 400.00 800.00
Phila Nat.
19B Mickey Doolan 400.00 800.00
Baltimore Fed.
20 Patsy Dougherty 400.00 800.00
21A Larry Doyle 450.00 900.00
N.Y. Nat'l
21B Larry Doyle 450.00 900.00
New York Nat'l
21C Larry Doyle 450.00 900.00
Throwing
22 Clyde Engle 400.00 800.00
23A Johnny Evers 750.00 1500.00
Chicago Nat'l
23B Johnny Evers 750.00 1500.00
Boston National
24 Art Fromme 400.00 800.00
25A George Gibson 400.00 800.00
Back
Pittsburg Nat'l
25B George Gibson 400.00 800.00
Back
Pittsburgh Nat'l.
25C George Gibson 400.00 800.00
Front
Pittsburg Nat'l
25D George Gibson 400.00 800.00
Front
Pittsburgh Nat'l
26A Topsy Hartsel 400.00 800.00
Phila Am.
26B Topsy Hartsel 400.00 800.00
Philadelphia Amer.
27A Roy Hartzell 400.00 800.00
Catching
27B Roy Hartzell 400.00 800.00
Batting
28A Fred Jacklitsch 400.00 800.00
Phila Nat.
28B Fred Jacklitsch 400.00 800.00
Baltimore Feds
29A Hugh Jennings 750.00 1500.00
Dance: Red
29B Hugh Jennings 750.00 1500.00
Dance; Orange
30 Red Kleinow 400.00 800.00
31A Otto Knabe 400.00 800.00
Phila Nat.
31B Otto Knabe 400.00 800.00
Baltimore Fed.
32 John Knight 400.00 800.00
33A Nap Lajoie 1750.00 3500.00
Portrait
33B Nap Lajoie 1750.00 3500.00
Fielding
Cleveland
33C Nap Lajoie 1750.00 3500.00
Fielding
Phila Amer.
34A Hans Lobert 400.00 800.00
Cincinnati
34B Hans Lobert 400.00 800.00
New York Nat'l
35 Sherry Magee 450.00 900.00
36 Rube Marquard 750.00 1500.00
37A Christy Mathewson 1500.00 3000.00
Small Print
37B Christy Mathewson 1500.00 3000.00
Large Print
38A John McGraw MG 750.00 1500.00
Small Print
38B John McGraw MG 750.00 1500.00
Large Print
39 Larry McLean 400.00 800.00
40 George McQuillan 400.00 800.00
41A Dots Miller 400.00 800.00
Batting
41B Dots Miller 400.00 800.00
Fielding
Pittsburg
41C Dots Miller 400.00 800.00
Fielding
St. Louis Nat'l
42A Danny Murphy 400.00 800.00
Phila Amer.
42B Danny Murphy 400.00 800.00
Brooklyn Feds.
43 Rebel Oakes 400.00 800.00
44 Bill O'Hara 400.00 800.00
45 Eddie Plank 750.00 1500.00
46A Germany Schaefer 450.00 900.00
Washington
46B Germany Schaefer 450.00 900.00
Newark Fed.
47 Admiral Schlei 400.00 800.00
48 Boss Schmidt 400.00 800.00
49 Dave Shean 400.00 800.00
50 Johnny Siegle 400.00 800.00
51 Tris Speaker 1750.00 3500.00
52 Oscar Stanage 400.00 800.00
53 George Stovall 400.00 800.00
54 Ed Sweeney 400.00 800.00
55A Joe Tinker 750.00 1500.00
Portrait
55B Joe Tinker 750.00 1500.00
Batting
Chicago Nat'l
55C Joe Tinker 750.00 1500.00
Batting
Chicago Feds
56A Honus Wagner 4000.00 8000.00
Batting
Pittsburg Nat'l
56B Honus Wagner 4000.00 8000.00
Batting
Pittsburgh Nat'l
56C Honus Wagner 4000.00 8000.00
Throwing
S.S
56D Honus Wagner 4000.00 8000.00
Throwing/#2b
57 Hooks Wiltse 400.00 800.00
58 Cy Young 1750.00 3500.00
59A Heinie Zimmerman/2B 400.00 800.00
59B Heinie Zimmerman/3B 400.00 800.00

1977 Pepsi Glove Discs
These discs actually form the middle of a glove-shaped tab which was inserted in cartons of Pepsi-Cola during a baseball related promotion. The disc itself measures 3 3/8" in diameter whereas the glove tab is approximately 9" tall. The backs of the discs and the tab tell how you can get a personalized superstar shirt of Pete Rose, Rico Carty, Joe Morgan, or Rick Manning by sending in Pepsi cap liners. The players are shown in "generic" hats, i.e., the team logos have been airbrushed. This set was sanctioned by the Major League Baseball Players Association. The set is quite heavy in Cleveland Indians and Cincinnati Reds.
COMPLETE SET (72) 40.00 80.00
1 Robin Yount 2.00 5.00
2 Rod Carew 2.00 5.00
3 Butch Wynegar .20 .50
4 Manny Sanguillen .10 .25
5 Mike Hargrove .20 .50
6 Larvell Blanks .10 .25
7 Jim Kern .10 .25
8 Pat Dobson .10 .25
9 Rico Carty .10 .25
10 John Grubb .10 .25
11 Buddy Bell .20 .50
12 Rick Manning .10 .25
13 Dennis Eckersley 2.00 5.00
14 Wayne Garland .10 .25
15 Dave Laroche .10 .25
16 Rick Waits .10 .25
17 Ray Fosse .10 .25
18 Frank Duffy .10 .25
19 Duane Kuiper .10 .25
20 Jim Palmer 2.00 5.00
21 Fred Lynn .20 .50
22 Carlton Fisk 2.00 5.00
23 Carl Yastrzemski 2.00 5.00
24 Nolan Ryan 4.00 10.00
25 Bobby Grich .20 .50
26 Ralph Garr .10 .25
27 Richie Zisk .10 .25
28 Ron LeFlore .10 .25
29 Rusty Staub .40 1.00
30 Mark Fidrych 1.50 4.00
31 Willie Horton .20 .50
32 George Brett 4.00 10.00
33 Amos Otis .10 .25
34 Reggie Jackson 2.00 5.00
35 Don Gullett .10 .25
36 Thurman Munson .60 1.50
37 Al Hrabosky .10 .25
38 Mike Tyson .10 .25
39 Gene Tenace .20 .50
40 George Hendrick .10 .25
41 Chris Speier .10 .25
42 John Montefusco .10 .25
43 Pete Rose 2.00 5.00
44 Johnny Bench 2.00 5.00
45 Dan Driessen .10 .25
46 Joe Morgan 1.25 3.00
47 Dave Concepcion .40 1.00
48 George Foster .40 1.00
49 Cesar Geronimo .10 .25
50 Ken Griffey .40 1.00
51 Gary Nolan .10 .25
52 Santo Alcala .10 .25
53 Jack Billingham .10 .25
54 Pedro Borbon .10 .25
55 Rawly Eastwick .10 .25
56 Fred Norman .10 .25
57 Pat Zachry .10 .25
58 Jeff Burroughs .10 .25
59 Manny Trillo .10 .25
60 Bob Watson .20 .50
61 Steve Garvey .60 1.50
62 Don Sutton 1.25 3.00
63 John Candelaria .10 .25
64 Willie Stargell 1.25 3.00
65 Jerry Reuss .10 .25
66 Dave Cash .10 .25
67 Tom Seaver 2.00 5.00
68 Jon Matlack .10 .25
69 Dave Kingman .60 1.50
70 Mike Schmidt 2.00 5.00
71 Jay Johnstone .20 .50
72 Greg Luzinski .40 1.00

1978 Pepsi
Sponsored by Pepsi-Cola and produced by MSA, this set of 40 collector cards measures approximately 2 1/8" by 9 1/2" and features members of the Cincinnati Reds and 15 national players. A checklist for the Cincinnati Reds (1-25) and for the 15 National players (26-40) is printed. The bottom part of the front has information on how to get a deck of Superstar playing cards free for 250 Pepsi capliners. The backs carry an order form and more detailed information. The cards are unnumbered and checklisted below in alphabetical order by grouping.
COMPLETE SET (40) 50.00 100.00
1 Sparky Anderson MG 1.00 2.50
2 Rick Auerbach .40 1.00
3 Doug Bair UER .40 1.00
Name is spelled Blair
4 Johnny Bench 3.00 8.00
5 Bill Bonham .40 1.00
6 Pedro Borbon .40 1.00
7 Dave Collins .40 1.00
8 Dave Concepcion 1.00 2.50
9 Dan Driessen .60 1.50
10 George Foster .75 2.00
11 Cesar Geronimo .40 1.00
12 Ken Griffey 1.00 2.50
13 Ken Henderson .40 1.00
14 Tom Hume .40 1.00
15 Junior Kennedy .40 1.00
16 Ray Knight .75 2.00
17 Mike Lum .40 1.00
18 Joe Morgan 2.00 5.00
19 Paul Moskau UER .40 1.00
Name is spelled Moscau
20 Fred Norman .40 1.00
21 Pete Rose 3.00 8.00
22 Manny Sarmiento .40 1.00
23 Tom Seaver 3.00 8.00
24 Dave Tomlin .40 1.00
25 Don Werner .40 1.00
26 Buddy Bell .75 2.00
27 Larry Bowa .60 1.50
28 George Brett 6.00 15.00
29 Jeff Burroughs .40 1.00
30 Rod Carew 2.00 5.00
31 Steve Garvey 1.00 2.50
32 Reggie Jackson 3.00 8.00
33 Dave Kingman .75 2.00
34 Jerry Koosman .60 1.50
35 Bill Madlock .60 1.50
36 Jim Palmer 2.00 5.00
37 Nolan Ryan 8.00 20.00
38 Ted Simmons .75 2.00
39 Carl Yastrzemski 2.00 5.00
40 Richie Zisk .40 1.00

1989 Pepsi McGwire
Each of these 12 standard-size cards depicts Mark McGwire. The cards are printed on rather thin card stock. All the pictures used in the set show McGwire in a generic uniform with a Pepsi patch on his upper arm and his number 25 on his chest; in each case his cap or batting helmet is in the Oakland colors but without their logo. The card backs all contain exactly the same statistical and biographical information, only the card

number is different. Reportedly cards were distributed inside specially marked 12-packs of Pepsi in the Northern California area.

COMPLETE SET (12) 10.00 25.00
COMMON PLAYER (1-12) 1.00 2.00

1990 Pepsi Canseco

This ten-card, standard-size set was issued in conjunction with Pepsi-Cola. These blue-bordered cards do not have the team logos. This set is very similar in style to the Pepsi McGwire set issued the year before. All the pictures used in the set are posed showing Canseco in a generic uniform with a Pepsi patch.

COMPLETE SET (10) 4.00 10.00
COMMON PLAYER (1-10) .40 1.00

1991 Pepsi Sid Fernandez

A local Hawaii Pepsi bottling company issued a two-card set of El Sid. He is depicted wearing a "Pepsi" uniform. Back has Pepsi logo and El Sid statistics through 1990.

COMPLETE SET (2) 1.50 4.00
COMMON CARD (1-2) .80 2.00

1991 Pepsi Griffeys

This eight-card standard-size set was sponsored by Pepsi-Cola, and its company logo appears on the front and back of each card. These cards were inserted one per special 12-pack of Pepsi. A ninth card was issued on a very limited basis as only 150 were produced.

COMPLETE SET (8) 4.00 10.00
COMMON PLAYER (1-6) .60 1.50
COMMON PLAYER (7-8) .20 .50
5 Ken Griffey Jr. .75 2.00
Ken Griffey Sr.
Dad seated)
6 Ken Griffey Jr. .75 2.00
Ken Griffey Sr.
Dad standing

1991 Pepsi Rickey Henderson

These ten standard-size cards were sponsored by Pepsi and feature Rickey Henderson. In a horizontal format, the backs have the same career performance statistics but differing career highlights.

COMPLETE SET (10) 4.00 10.00
COMMON PLAYER (1-10) .40 1.00

1991 Pepsi Rickey Henderson Discs

This four-disc set was issued by Pepsi in honor of Rickey Henderson. The discs measure approximately 2 1/8" in diameter. The fronts feature 3-D color action shots that change to different shots when one holds the discs at a different angle. The discs are unnumbered.

COMPLETE SET (4) 2.50 6.00
COMMON PLAYER (1-4) .60 1.50

1991 Pepsi Superstar

This 17-card set was sponsored by Pepsi-Cola of Florida as part of the "Flavor of Baseball" promotion. The promotion featured a chance to win one of 104 rare, older cards, including one 1952 Mickey Mantle card. The Superstar cards were glued inside specially marked 12 packs of Pepsi-Cola products in Orlando, Tampa, and Miami. It is difficult to remove the cards without creasing them; reportedly area supervisors for Pepsi each received a few sets. The cards measure slightly wider than standard size (2 5/8" by 3 1/2").

COMPLETE SET (17) 10.00 25.00
1 Dwight Gooden .25 .60
2 Andre Dawson .40 1.00
3 Ryne Sandberg 1.50 4.00
4 Dave Stieb .25 .60
5 Jose Rijo .15 .40
6 Roger Clemens 2.00 5.00
7 Barry Bonds 1.50 4.00
8 Cal Ripken 4.00 10.00
9 Dave Justice .40 1.00
10 Cecil Fielder .25 .60
11 Don Mattingly 2.00 5.00
12 Ozzie Smith 1.50 4.00
13 Kirby Puckett 1.00 2.50
14 Rafael Palmeiro .50 1.25
15 Bobby Bonilla .15 .40
16 Len Dykstra .25 .60
17 Jose Canseco .75 2.00

1992 Pepsi Diet MSA

Issued in two different types of three-card packs, (a clear cello and a white cello with bilingual printing) this 30-card standard-size set was issued by MSA (Michael Schechter Associates) for Diet Pepsi in Canada. The packs were given away free with the purchase of Diet Pepsi or Diet Caffeine Free Pepsi. As is typical of MSA sets, the team logos have been airbrushed out. A red and blue trim poster which measures approximately 11" by 14" was also issued. A little mini picture of each player is on the poster.

COMPLETE SET (30) 8.00 20.00
1A Roger Clemens .75 2.00
1B Roger Clemens (FL version) .75 2.00
1C Roger Clemens (CDN version) .75 2.00
2 Dwight Gooden .20 .50
3 Tom Henke .08 .25
4 Dennis Martinez .20 .50
5A Tom Glavine ERR .40 1.00
Pitching Righthanded
5B Tom Glavine COR .75 2.00
Pitching lefthanded
6 Jack Morris .20 .50
7 Dennis Eckersley .50 1.25
8 Jeff Reardon .20 .50
9 Bryan Harvey .08 .25
10 Sandy Alomar Jr. .20 .50
11 Carlton Fisk .50 1.25
12 Gary Carter .50 1.25
13 Cecil Fielder .20 .50
14 Will Clark .40 1.00
15 Roberto Alomar .40 1.00
16 Ryne Sandberg .75 2.00
17 Cal Ripken 1.50 4.00
18 Barry Larkin .40 1.00
19 Ozzie Smith .60 1.50
20 Kelly Gruber .08 .25
21 Wade Boggs .50 1.25
22 Tim Wallach .08 .25
23 Howard Johnson .08 .25
24 Jose Canseco .50 1.25
25 Joe Carter .20 .50
26 Ken Griffey Jr. 1.00 2.50
27 Kirby Puckett .50 1.25
28 Rickey Henderson .60 1.50
29 Barry Bonds .75 2.00
30 Dave Winfield .50 1.25
XX Poster 2.00 5.00
All Players in Set Pictured

2003 Pepsi

COMPLETE SET 30.00
1 Troy Glaus .20 .50
2 Chipper Jones 1.00 2.50
3 Randy Johnson 1.00 2.50
4 Tony Batista .10 .25
5 Magglio Ordonez .20 .50
6 Ken Griffey Jr. 1.25 3.00
7 Omar Vizquel .20 .50
8 Todd Helton .40 1.00
9 Bobby Higginson .10 .25
10 Luis Castillo .20 .50
11 Jeff Bagwell .50 1.25
12 Mike Sweeney .30 .75
13 Shawn Green .40 1.00
14 Richie Sexson .20 .50
15 Torii Hunter .20 .50
16 Vladimir Guerrero .50 1.25
17 Mike Piazza 1.25 3.00
18 Jason Giambi .30 .75
19 Barry Zito .40 1.00
20 Pat Burrell .40 1.00
21 Brian Giles .30 .75
22 Trevor Hoffman .40 1.00
23 Barry Bonds 1.00 2.50
24 Ichiro Suzuki 1.25 3.00
25 Albert Pujols 1.50 4.00
26 Ben Grieve .10 .25
27 Alex Rodriguez 1.00 2.50
28 Carlos Delgado .40 1.00
29 Kerry Wood .40 1.00
30 Pedro Martinez .50 1.25

2007 Pepsi

COMPLETE SET (220) 75.00 200.00
P1 Garret Anderson .50 1.25
P2 Nick Swisher .75 2.00
P3 Mark Kotsay .50 1.25
P4 A.J. Burnett .50 1.25
P5 Brian McCann .50 1.25
P6 Bobby Abreu .50 1.25
P7 Mickey Mantle 6.00 15.00
P8 Edgar Renteria .50 1.25
P9 Juan Pierre .50 1.25
P10 Preston Wilson .50 1.25
P11 C.C. Sabathia .75 2.00
P12 Chad Billingsley .75 2.00
P13 J.D. Drew .50 1.25
P14 Kenji Johjima 1.25 3.00
P15 Shawn Green .50 1.25
P16 Ryan Zimmerman .75 2.00
P17 Orlando Hernandez .50 1.25
P18 Brian Giles .50 1.25
P19 Chase Utley .75 2.00
P20 Corey Patterson .50 1.25
P21 David Ortiz 1.25 3.00
P22 Gary Matthews .50 1.25
P23 Curtis Granderson 1.00 2.50
P24 Brandon Inge .50 1.25
P25 Jon Garland .50 1.25
P26 Bronson Arroyo .50 1.25
P27 Andy Pettitte .75 2.00
P28 Ervin Santana .50 1.25
P29 Paul Konerko .75 2.00
P30 Troy Glaus .50 1.25
P31 Tim Hudson .75 2.00
P32 Rickie Weeks .50 1.25
P33 Jim Edmonds .75 2.00
P34 Conor Jackson .50 1.25
P35 Derek Jeter 3.00 8.00
P36 Jason Schmidt .50 1.25
P37 Livan Hernandez .50 1.25
P38 Cliff Lee .75 2.00
P39 Aubrey Huff .50 1.25
P40 Adrian Beltre 1.25 3.00
P41 Andre Ethier .75 2.00
P42 Jeremy Sowers .50 1.25
P43 Ramon Hernandez .50 1.25
P44 Chris Young .50 1.25
P45 Miguel Cabrera 1.25 3.00
P46 Carlos Lee .50 1.25
P47 Jose Castillo .50 1.25
P48 Kevin Millwood .50 1.25
P49 Mike Piazza 1.25 3.00
P50 Cole Hamels 1.00 2.50
P51 Mark Loretta .50 1.25
P52 Torii Hunter .50 1.25
P53 John Smoltz 1.25 3.00
P54 Roy Oswalt .75 2.00
P55 Milton Bradley .50 1.25
P56 Dan Uggla .50 1.25
P57 Chris Capuano .50 1.25
P58 Lyle Overbay .50 1.25
P59 Michael Barrett .50 1.25
P60 Ivan Rodriguez .75 2.00
P61 Jake Westbrook .50 1.25
P62 Matt Morris .50 1.25
P63 Moises Alou .50 1.25
P64 Ichiro 1.50 4.00
P65 Jered Weaver .75 2.00
P66 Tom Glavine .75 2.00
P67 Austin Kearns .50 1.25
P68 Nick Johnson .50 1.25
P69 Josh Barfield .50 1.25
P70 Johan Santana .75 2.00
P71 Jason Bay .75 2.00
P72 Ian Kinsler .75 2.00
P73 Mike Lowell .50 1.25
P74 Brandon Phillips .50 1.25
P75 Scott Rolen .75 2.00
P76 Mark Redman .50 1.25
P77 Justin Morneau .75 2.00
P78 Tadahito Iguchi .50 1.25
P79 Chipper Jones 1.25 3.00
P80 Carlos Silva .50 1.25
P81 Francisco Rodriguez .75 2.00
P82 Joe Crede .50 1.25
P83 Willy Taveras .50 1.25
P84 Dan Haren .50 1.25
P85 Rafael Furcal .50 1.25
P86 Jeff Francoeur 1.25 3.00
P87 Randy Wolf .50 1.25
P88 Marcus Giles .50 1.25
P89 Carlos Zambrano .75 2.00
P90 Joe Blanton .50 1.25
P91 Dontrelle Willis .50 1.25
P92 Jorge Cantu .50 1.25
P93 Luis Gonzalez .50 1.25
P94 Scott Kazmir .75 2.00
P95 Jeff Kent .50 1.25
P96 Victor Martinez .75 2.00
P97 Johnny Estrada .50 1.25
P98 Travis Hafner .50 1.25
P99 Felix Hernandez .75 2.00
P100 Paul Lo Duca .50 1.25
P101 Miguel Tejada .75 2.00
P102 Mike Cameron .50 1.25
P103 Pat Burrell .50 1.25
P104 Nick Markakis 1.00 2.50
P105 Mark Teixeira .75 2.00
P106 Josh Beckett .50 1.25
P107 Ken Griffey 2.50 6.00
P108 Tim Wakefield .75 2.00
P109 Francisco Liriano .50 1.25
P110 Jason Giambi .50 1.25
P111 Mike Mussina .75 2.00
P112 Chone Figgins .50 1.25
P113 Lance Berkman .75 2.00
P114 Huston Street .50 1.25
P115 Carlos Delgado .50 1.25
P116 Ted Lilly .50 1.25
P117 Aramis Ramirez .50 1.25
P118 Albert Pujols 1.50 4.00
P119 Ray Durham .50 1.25
P120 Russell Martin .50 1.25
P121 Gary Sheffield .50 1.25
P122 Jhonny Peralta .50 1.25
P123 Raul Ibanez .75 2.00
P124 Jay Gibbons .50 1.25
P125 Hanley Ramirez .75 2.00
P126 Adrian Gonzalez 1.00 2.50
P127 Jose Reyes .75 2.00
P128 Prince Fielder .75 2.00
P129 Freddy Sanchez .50 1.25
P130 Xavier Nady .50 1.25
P131 Jack Wilson .50 1.25
P132 Michael Young .50 1.25
P133 Kevin Youkilis .50 1.25
P134 Jake Peavy .50 1.25
P135 Javier Vazquez .50 1.25
P136 Todd Helton .75 2.00
P137 Jim Thome .75 2.00
P138 Jose Contreras .50 1.25
P139 Bill Hall .50 1.25
P140 Aaron Harang .50 1.25
P141 Jeremy Bonderman .50 1.25
P142 Jeff Weaver .50 1.25
P143 Eric Chavez .50 1.25
P144 Rocco Baldelli .50 1.25
P145 Vernon Wells .50 1.25
P146 Andruw Jones .50 1.25
P147 Justin Verlander 1.25 3.00
P148 David Eckstein .50 1.25
P149 Orlando Hudson .50 1.25
P150 Zach Duke .50 1.25
P151 Mark Buehrle .75 2.00
P152 Hank Blalock .50 1.25
P153 Mark Teahen .50 1.25
P154 Pedro Martinez .75 2.00
P155 Chien-Ming Wang .75 2.00
P156 Morgan Ensberg .50 1.25
P157 Brian Roberts .50 1.25
P158 Brett Myers .50 1.25
P159 Adam Dunn .75 2.00
P160 Joe Nathan .50 1.25
P161 Roy Halladay .75 2.00
P162 Kenny Rogers .50 1.25
P163 Melvin Mora .50 1.25
P164 Jermaine Dye .50 1.25
P165 Alex Rodriguez 1.50 4.00
P166 B.J. Upton .50 1.25
P167 Grady Sizemore .75 2.00
P168 Matt Cain .75 2.00
P169 Craig Biggio .75 2.00
P170 Carl Crawford .75 2.00
P171 Alex Rios .50 1.25
P172 Derrek Lee .50 1.25
P173 Brandon Webb .75 2.00
P174 Johnny Damon .75 2.00
P175 Derek Lowe .50 1.25
P176 Freddy Garcia .50 1.25
P177 Ryan Shealy .50 1.25
P178 Jeremy Hermida .50 1.25
P179 Carlos Beltran .75 2.00
P180 Chuck James .50 1.25
P181 Jose Vidro .50 1.25
P182 Erik Bedard .50 1.25
P183 Cory Sullivan .50 1.25
P184 Jon Lieber .50 1.25
P185 Ben Sheets .50 1.25
P186 Mark Mulder .50 1.25
P187 Carlos Quentin .50 1.25
P188 Wily Mo Pena .50 1.25
P189 Kazuo Matsui .50 1.25
P190 David DeJesus .50 1.25
P191 Richie Sexson .50 1.25
P192 Brian Schneider .50 1.25
P193 Craig Monroe .50 1.25
P194 Orlando Cabrera .50 1.25
P195 Jason Kendall .50 1.25
P196 Hideki Matsui 1.25 3.00
P197 Ronnie Belliard .50 1.25
P198 Jeff Francis .50 1.25
P199 Robinson Cano .75 2.00
P200 Barry Zito .75 2.00
P201 Garrett Atkins .50 1.25
P202 Carlos Guillen .50 1.25
P203 Chris Carpenter .75 2.00
P204 Chad Tracy .50 1.25
P205 David Wright 1.00 2.50
P206 Jimmy Rollins .75 2.00
P207 Alfonso Soriano .75 2.00
P208 Greg Maddux 1.50 4.00
P209 Curt Schilling .75 2.00
P210 Randy Johnson 1.25 3.00
P211 Matt Holliday 1.25 3.00
P212 Jorge Posada .75 2.00
P213 Vladimir Guerrero .75 2.00
P214 Frank Thomas 1.25 3.00
P215 Jonathan Papelbon 1.25 3.00
P216 Manny Ramirez 1.25 3.00
P217 Magglio Ordonez .75 2.00
P218 Joe Mauer 1.00 2.50
P219 Ryan Howard 1.00 2.50
P220 Stephen Drew .50 1.25

1980-02 Perez-Steele Hall of Fame Postcards

President Ronald Reagan was given the first numbered set issued on May 27th, 1981 at the White House.The sets were also issued with continuation rights. These rights have been transferable over the years. These 3 1/2" by 5 1/2" cards feature noted sports artist Dick Perez drawings. The cards were distributed through Perez-Steele galleries. According to the producer, many of these cards are sold to art or postcard collectors. Just 10,000 of these sets were produced.

COMPLETE SET (260) 1000.00 1500.00
1 Ty Cobb 15.00 40.00
2 Walter Johnson 4.00 10.00
3 Christy Mathewson 4.00 10.00
4 Babe Ruth 25.00 60.00
5 Honus Wagner 4.00 10.00
6 Morgan Bulkeley .40 1.00
7 Ban Johnson .40 1.00
8 Nap Lajoie 2.00 5.00
9 Connie Mack 2.00 5.00
10 John McGraw 2.00 5.00
11 Tris Speaker 2.00 5.00
12 George Wright .40 1.00
13 Cy Young 2.00 5.00
14 Grover Alexander 2.00 5.00
15 Alex. Cartwright .40 1.00
16 Henry Chadwick .40 1.00
17 Cap Anson 1.00 2.50
18 Eddie Collins 2.00 5.00
19 Candy Cummings .60 1.50
20 Charles Comiskey .40 1.00
21 Buck Ewing .60 1.50
22 Lou Gehrig 15.00 40.00
23 Willie Keeler .60 1.50
24 Hoss Radbourne .60 1.50
25 George Sisler 6.00 15.00
26 A.G. Spalding .60 1.50
27 Rogers Hornsby 2.00 5.00
28 Kenesaw Landis .40 1.00
29 Roger Bresnahan .60 1.50
30 Dan Brouthers .60 1.50
31 Fred Clarke .60 1.50
32 Jimmy Collins .60 1.50
33 Ed Delahanty .60 1.50
34 Hugh Duffy .60 1.50
35 Hughie Jennings .60 1.50
36 King Kelly 1.00 2.50
37 Jim O'Rourke .60 1.50
38 Wilbert Robinson .60 1.50
39 Jesse Burkett .60 1.50
40 Frank Chance 2.00 5.00
41 Jack Chesbro .60 1.50
42 Johnny Evers 2.00 5.00
43 Clark Griffith .60 1.50
44 Thomas McCarthy .60 1.50
45 Joe McGinnity .60 1.50
46 Eddie Plank .60 1.50
47 Joe Tinker 2.00 5.00
48 Rube Waddell .60 1.50
49 Ed Walsh .60 1.50
50 Mickey Cochrane 2.00 5.00
51 Frankie Frisch 2.00 5.00
52 Lefty Grove 2.00 5.00
53 Carl Hubbell 4.00 10.00
54 Herb Pennock .60 1.50
55 Pie Traynor 1.00 2.50
56 Mordecai Brown .60 1.50
57 Charlie Gehringer 1.00 2.50
58 Kid Nichols .60 1.50
59 Jimmy Foxx 6.00 15.00
(Jimmie)
60 Mel Ott 4.00 10.00
61 Harry Heilmann .60 1.50
62 Paul Waner 2.00 5.00
63 Edward Barrow .40 1.00
64 Chief Bender 2.00 5.00
65 Tom Connolly .40 1.00
66 Dizzy Dean 6.00 15.00
67 Bill Klem .40 1.00
68 Al Simmons 2.00 5.00
69 Bobby Wallace .60 1.50
70 Harry Wright .60 1.50
71 Bill Dickey 2.00 5.00
72 Rabbit Maranville .60 1.50
73 Bill Terry 2.00 5.00
74 Frank Baker .60 1.50
75 Joe DiMaggio 25.00 60.00
76 Gabby Hartnett .60 1.50
77 Ted Lyons .60 1.50
78 Ray Schalk .60 1.50
79 Dazzy Vance .60 1.50
80 Joe Cronin 1.00 2.50
81 Hank Greenberg 8.00 20.00
82 Sam Crawford 2.00 5.00
83 Joe McCarthy .40 1.00
84 Zack Wheat .60 1.50
85 Max Carey .60 1.50
86 Billy Hamilton .60 1.50
87 Bob Feller 6.00 15.00
88 Bill McKechnie .40 1.00
89 Jackie Robinson 10.00 25.00
90 Edd Roush 1.00 2.50
91 John Clarkson .60 1.50
92 Elmer Flick .60 1.50
93 Sam Rice 2.00 5.00
94 Eppa Rixey .60 1.50
95 Luke Appling 1.00 2.50
96 Red Faber .60 1.50
97 Burleigh Grimes .60 1.50
98 Miller Huggins .60 1.50
99 Tim Keefe .60 1.50
100 Heinie Manush .60 1.50
101 John Ward .60 1.50
102 Pud Galvin .60 1.50
103 Casey Stengel 4.00 10.00
104 Ted Williams 25.00 60.00
105 Branch Rickey .60 1.50
106 Red Ruffing .60 1.50
107 Lloyd Waner .60 1.50
108 Kiki Cuyler .60 1.50
109 Goose Goslin 2.00 5.00
110 Joe Medwick .60 1.50
111 Roy Campanella 4.00 10.00
112 Stan Coveleski .60 1.50
113 Waite Hoyt .60 1.50
114 Stan Musial 15.00 40.00
115 Lou Boudreau 5.00 12.00
116 Earle Combs .60 1.50
117 Ford Frick .40 1.00
118 Jesse Haines .60 1.50
119 David Bancroft .60 1.50
120 Jake Beckley .60 1.50
121 Chick Hafey .40 1.00
122 Harry Hooper .60 1.50
123 Joe Kelley .60 1.50
124 Rube Marquard 2.00 5.00
125 Satchel Paige 10.00 25.00
126 George Weiss .40 1.00
127 Yogi Berra 6.00 15.00
128 Josh Gibson 2.00 5.00
129 Lefty Gomez 1.00 2.50
130 William Harridge .40 1.00
131 Sandy Koufax 8.00 20.00
132 Buck Leonard 6.00 15.00
133 Early Wynn 2.00 5.00
134 Ross Youngs .60 1.50
135 Roberto Clemente 20.00 50.00
136 Billy Evans .40 1.00
137 Monte Irvin 3.00 8.00
138 George Kelly .60 1.50
139 Warren Spahn 4.00 10.00
140 Mickey Welch .60 1.50
141 Cool Papa Bell 3.00 8.00
142 Jim Bottomley .60 1.50
143 Jocko Conlan .40 1.00
144 Whitey Ford 8.00 20.00
145 Mickey Mantle 25.00 60.00
146 Sam Thompson .60 1.50
147 Earl Averill 1.00 2.50
148 Bucky Harris .60 1.50
149 Billy Herman 1.00 2.50
150 Judy Johnson 4.00 10.00
151 Ralph Kiner 4.00 10.00
152 Oscar Charleston 1.00 2.50
153 Roger Connor .60 1.50
154 Cal Hubbard .40 1.00
155 Bob Lemon 2.00 5.00
156 Fred Lindstrom .60 1.50
157 Robin Roberts 4.00 10.00
158 Ernie Banks 6.00 15.00
159 Martin Dihigo 2.00 5.00
160 John Lloyd 2.00 5.00
161 Al Lopez 5.00 12.00
162 Amos Rusie .60 1.50
163 Joe Sewell .60 1.50
164 Addie Joss .60 1.50
165 Larry MacPhail .40 1.00
166 Eddie Mathews 4.00 10.00
167 Warren Giles .40 1.00
168 Willie Mays 15.00 40.00
169 Hack Wilson .60 1.50
170 Al Kaline 6.00 15.00
171 Chuck Klein .60 1.50
172 Duke Snider 8.00 20.00
173 Tom Yawkey .40 1.00
174 Rube Foster .40 1.00
175 Bob Gibson 4.00 10.00
176 Johnny Mize 1.00 2.50
177 Hank Aaron 8.00 20.00
178 Happy Chandler .40 1.00
179 Travis Jackson .60 1.50
180 Frank Robinson 8.00 20.00
181 Walter Alston 3.00 8.00
182 George Kell 3.00 8.00
183 Juan Marichal 2.00 5.00
184 Brooks Robinson 6.00 15.00
185 Luis Aparicio 4.00 10.00
186 Don Drysdale 2.00 5.00
187 Rick Ferrell .60 1.50
188 Harmon Killebrew 4.00 10.00
189 Pee Wee Reese 6.00 15.00
190 Lou Brock 6.00 15.00
191 Enos Slaughter 3.00 8.00
192 Arky Vaughan .60 1.50
193 Hoyt Wilhelm 3.00 8.00
194 Bobby Doerr 3.00 8.00
195 Ernie Lombardi .60 1.50
196 Willie McCovey 2.00 5.00
197 Ray Dandridge 2.00 5.00
198 Catfish Hunter 2.00 5.00
199 Billy Williams 3.00 8.00
200 Willie Stargell 2.50 6.00
201 Al Barlick 1.00 2.50
202 Johnny Bench 2.00 5.00
203 Red Schoendienst 3.00 8.00
204 Carl Yastrzemski 8.00 20.00
205 Joe Morgan 6.00 15.00
206 Jim Palmer 2.00 5.00
207 Rod Carew 6.00 15.00
208 Ferguson Jenkins 4.00 10.00
209 Tony Lazzeri .60 1.50
210 Gaylord Perry 3.00 8.00
211 Bill Veeck .40 1.00
212 Rollie Fingers 3.00 8.00
213 Bill McGowan .40 1.00
214 Hal Newhouser 4.00 10.00
215 Tom Seaver 8.00 20.00
216 Reggie Jackson 8.00 20.00
217 Steve Carlton 6.00 15.00
218 Leo Durocher 2.00 5.00
219 Phil Rizzuto 8.00 20.00
220 Richie Ashburn 4.00 10.00
221 Leon Day 1.00 2.50
222 William Hulbert .40 1.00
223 Mike Schmidt 8.00 20.00
224 Vic Willis 2.00 5.00
225 Jim Bunning 4.00 10.00
226 Bill Foster 2.00 5.00
227 Ned Hanlon 2.00 5.00
228 Earl Weaver 4.00 10.00
229 Nellie Fox .60 1.50
230 Tom Lasorda 4.00 10.00
231 Phil Niekro 3.00 8.00
232 Willie Wells .60 1.50
233 George Davis .60 1.50
234 Larry Doby 3.00 8.00
235 Lee MacPhail .40 1.00
236 Joe Rogan .60 1.50
237 Don Sutton 3.00 8.00
238 George Brett 8.00 20.00
239 Orlando Cepeda 10.00
240 Nestor Chylak .40 1.00
241 Nolan Ryan 10.00 25.00
242 Frank Selee .40 1.00
243 Joe Williams .40 1.00
244 Robin Yount 4.00 10.00
245 Sparky Anderson 1.00 2.50
246 Carlton Fisk 4.00 10.00
247 Bid McPhee .60 1.50
248 Tony Perez 3.00 8.00
249 Turkey Stearnes 2.00 5.00
250 Bill Mazeroski 2.00 5.00
251 Kirby Puckett 6.00 15.00
252 Hilton Smith .60 1.50
253 Dave Winfield 4.00 10.00
F George H.W. Bush 1.00 2.50
Edward W. Stack
G Franklin A. Steele MEM .40 1.00
A Abner Doubleday 2.00 5.00
B Stephen C. Clark .40 1.00
C Paul S. Kerr .40 1.00
D Edward W. Stack .40 1.00
E Perez-Steele Galleries .40 1.00

1989 Perez-Steele Celebration Postcards

This 44-card set celebrates the 50th Anniversary of the National Baseball Hall of Fame and Museum. The cards measure approximately 3 1/2" by 5 1/2" and feature art work by artist Dick Perez. The backs carry a postcard format.

COMPLETE SET (44) 75.00 150.00
1 Hank Aaron 2.50 6.00
2 Luis Aparicio 1.50 4.00
3 Ernie Banks 2.50 6.00
4 Cool Papa Bell 1.25 3.00
5 Johnny Bench 1.50 4.00
6 Yogi Berra 2.50 6.00
7 Lou Boudreau 1.50 4.00
8 Roy Campanella 1.50 4.00
9 Happy Chandler .75 2.00
10 Jocko Conlan .75 2.00
11 Ray Dandridge 1.25 3.00
12 Bill Dickey 1.50 4.00
13 Bobby Doerr 1.50 4.00
14 Rick Ferrell 1.25 3.00
15 Charlie Gehringer 1.50 4.00
16 Lefty Gomez 1.50 4.00
17 Billy Herman 1.00 2.50
18 Catfish Hunter 1.50 4.00
19 Monte Irvin 1.50 4.00
20 Judy Johnson 1.50 4.00
21 Al Kaline 2.50 6.00
22 George Kell 1.50 4.00
23 Harmon Killebrew 1.50 4.00
24 Ralph Kiner 1.50 4.00
25 Bob Lemon 1.25 3.00
26 Buck Leonard 1.50 4.00
27 Al Lopez 1.00 2.50
28 Mickey Mantle 4.00 10.00
29 Juan Marichal 1.50 4.00
30 Eddie Mathews 1.50 4.00
31 Willie McCovey 1.50 4.00
32 Johnny Mize 1.50 4.00
33 Stan Musial 2.50 6.00
34 Pee Wee Reese 1.50 4.00
35 Brooks Robinson 1.50 4.00
36 Joe Sewell 1.25 3.00
37 Enos Slaughter 1.50 4.00
38 Duke Snider 1.50 4.00
39 Warren Spahn 1.50 4.00
40 Willie Stargell 1.50 4.00
41 Bill Terry 1.50 4.00
42 Billy Williams 1.25 3.00
43 Ted Williams 4.00 10.00
44 Carl Yastrzemski 1.50 4.00
NNO Checklist

1990-92 Perez-Steele Master Work

This 50-card set measures 3 1/2" by 5 1/2" and again features the fine artwork of Dick Perez. The set honors living Hall-of Famers at the time of issue and depicts them as if they might have appeared on several vintage card sets. The sets imitated are the Goodwin Champions of 1888, Rose Postcards of 1908, the T205 Gold Borders, 1909 Ramlys and one original design. The sets are numbered and are limited to 10,000 sets. The original issue price for each series was $135.

COMPLETE SET (50) 125.00 250.00
1 Charlie Gehringer .75 2.00
Ramly
2 Charlie Gehringer .75 2.00
Goodwin
3 Charlie Gehringer .75 2.00
Rose
4 Charlie Gehringer .75 2.00
T205
5 Charlie Gehringer .75 2.00
Original Drawing
6 Mickey Mantle 6.00 15.00
Ramly
7 Mickey Mantle 6.00 15.00
Goodwin
8 Mickey Mantle 6.00 15.00
Rose
9 Mickey Mantle 6.00 15.00
T205
10 Mickey Mantle 6.00 15.00
Original Drawing
11 Willie Mays 5.00 12.00
Ramly
12 Willie Mays 5.00 12.00
Goodwin
13 Willie Mays 5.00 12.00
Rose
14 Willie Mays 5.00 12.00
T205
15 Willie Mays 5.00 12.00
Original Drawing
16 Duke Snider 2.50 6.00
Ramly
17 Duke Snider 2.50 6.00
Goodwin
18 Duke Snider 2.50 6.00
Rose
19 Duke Snider 2.50 6.00
T205
20 Duke Snider 2.50 6.00
Original Drawing
21 Warren Spahn 1.25 3.00
Ramly
22 Warren Spahn 1.25 3.00
Goodwin
23 Warren Sphan 1.25 3.00
Rose
24 Warren Spahn 1.25 3.00
T205
25 Warren Spahn 1.25 3.00
Original Drawing
26 Yogi Berra 2.00 5.00
Ramly
27 Yogi Berra 2.00 5.00
Goodwin
28 Yogi Berra 2.00 5.00
Rose
29 Yogi Berra 2.00 5.00
T205
30 Yogi Berra 2.00 5.00
Original Drawing
31 Johnny Mize .75 2.00
Ramly
32 Johnny Mize .75 2.00
Goodwin
33 Johnny Mize .75 2.00
Rose
34 Johnny Mize .75 2.00
T205
35 Johnny Mize .75 2.00
Original Drawing
36 Willie Stargell 1.25 3.00
Ramly
37 Willie Stargell 1.25 3.00
Goodwin
38 Willie Stargell 1.25 3.00
Rose
39 Willie Stargell 1.25 3.00
T205
40 Willie Stargell 1.25 3.00
Original Drawing
41 Ted Williams 5.00 12.00
Ramly
42 Ted Williams 5.00 12.00
Goodwin
43 Ted Williams 5.00 12.00
Rose
44 Ted Williams 5.00 12.00
T205
45 Ted Williams 5.00 12.00
Original Drawing
46 Carl Yastrzemski 2.00 5.00
Ramly
47 Carl Yastrzemski 2.00 5.00
Goodwin
48 Carl Yastrzemski 2.00 5.00
Rose
49 Carl Yastrzemski 2.00 5.00
T205
50 Carl Yastrzemski 2.00 5.00
Original Drawing

1985-97 Perez-Steele Great Moments

These cards were issued in series of 12 cards each. So far, nine series have been issued. The cards measure 3 1/2" by 5 1/2" and feature leading moments in Hall of Famers careers. These sets are also issued with continuation rights.

COMPLETE SET (108) 125.00 250.00
1 Babe Ruth 8.00 20.00
2 Al Kaline 1.25 3.00
3 Jackie Robinson 6.00 15.00
4 Lou Gehrig 6.00 15.00
5 Whitey Ford 2.00 5.00
6 Christy Mathewson 3.00 8.00
7 Roy Campanella 2.00 5.00
8 Walter Johnson 3.00 8.00
9 Hank Aaron 6.00 15.00
10 Cy Young 3.00 8.00
11 Stan Musial 3.00 8.00
12 Ty Cobb 6.00 15.00
13 Ted Williams 6.00 15.00
14 Warren Spahn 1.25 3.00
15 Paul and Lloyd Waner 1.25 3.00
16 Sandy Koufax 3.00 8.00
17 Robin Roberts 1.25 3.00
18 Dizzy Dean 2.00 5.00
19 Mickey Mantle 8.00 20.00
20 Satchel Paige 4.00 10.00
21 Ernie Banks 3.00 8.00
22 Willie McCovey 1.25 3.00
23 Johnny Mize .75 2.00
24 Honus Wagner 2.00 5.00
25 Willie Keeler .75 2.00
26 Pee Wee Reese 2.00 5.00
27 Monte Irvin .75 2.00
28 Eddie Mathews 2.00 5.00
29 Enos Slaughter 1.25 3.00
30 Rube Marquard .75 2.00
31 Charlie Gehringer 1.25 3.00
32 Roberto Clemente 6.00 15.00
33 Duke Snider 2.00 5.00
34 Ray Dandridge .75 2.00
35 Carl Hubbell 1.25 3.00
36 Bobby Doerr 1.25 3.00
37 Bill Dickey 1.25 3.00
38 Willie Stargell 1.25 3.00
39 Brooks Robinson 2.00 5.00
40 Joe Tinker 2.00 5.00
Johnny Evers
Frank Chance
41 Billy Herman .75 2.00
42 Grover Alexander 2.00 5.00

43 Luis Aparicio	1.25	3.00
44 Lefty Gomez	.75	2.00
45 Eddie Collins	.75	2.00
46 Judy Johnson	1.25	3.00
47 Harry Heilmann	.75	2.00
48 Harmon Killebrew	1.25	3.00
49 Johnny Bench	3.00	8.00
50 Max Carey	.75	2.00
51 Cool Papa Bell	1.25	3.00
52 Rube Waddell	.75	2.00
53 Yogi Berra	3.00	8.00
54 Herb Pennock	.75	2.00
55 Red Schoendienst	1.25	3.00
56 Juan Marichal	2.00	5.00
57 Frankie Frisch	.75	2.00
58 Buck Leonard	1.25	3.00
59 George Kell	1.25	3.00
60 Chuck Klein	.75	2.00
61 King Kelly	.75	2.00
62 Catfish Hunter	2.00	5.00
63 Lou Boudreau	1.25	3.00
64 Al Lopez	1.25	3.00
65 Willie Mays	6.00	15.00
66 Lou Brock	2.00	5.00
67 Bob Lemon	1.25	3.00
68 Joe Sewell	.75	2.00
69 Billy Williams	1.25	3.00
70 Rick Ferrell	.75	2.00
71 Arky Vaughan	.75	2.00
72 Carl Yastrzemski	3.00	8.00
73 Tom Seaver	2.00	5.00
74 Rollie Fingers	1.50	4.00
75 Ralph Kiner	1.50	4.00
76 Frank Baker	1.25	3.00
77 Rod Carew	1.50	4.00
78 Goose Goslin	1.25	3.00
79 Gaylord Perry	1.50	4.00
80 Hack Wilson	1.50	4.00
81 Hal Newhouser	.75	2.00
82 Early Wynn	.75	2.00
83 Bob Feller	2.00	5.00
84 Branch Rickey	.75	2.00
85 Jim Palmer	1.50	4.00
86 Al Barlick	.75	2.00
87 Mickey Mantle Willie Mays Duke Snider	4.00	10.00
88 Hank Greenberg	1.50	4.00
89 Joe Morgan	1.50	4.00
90 Chief Bender	1.25	3.00
91 Pee Wee Reese Jackie Robinson	2.00	5.00
92 Jim Bottomley	1.25	3.00
93 Ferguson Jenkins	1.50	4.00
94 Frank Robinson	2.00	5.00
95 Hoyt Wilhelm	.75	2.00
96 Cap Anson	1.25	3.00
97 Jim Bunning	1.25	3.00
98 Richie Ashburn	1.50	4.00
99 Steve Carlton	2.00	5.00
100 Mike Schmidt	2.00	5.00
101 Nellie Fox	1.25	3.00
102 Tom Lasorda	1.25	3.00
103 Leo Durocher	.75	2.00
104 Reggie Jackson	2.00	5.00
105 Phil Niekro	1.25	3.00
106 Phil Rizzuto	1.50	4.00
107 Willie Wells	.75	2.00
108 Earl Weaver	.75	2.00

1995 Perez-Steele Wagner Promotion

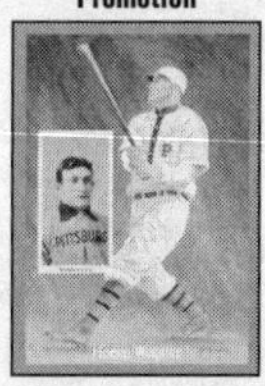

This one card set was issued to go along with the drawing for the T-206 Honus Wagner card run through a promotion at Wal-Mart. The front features a drawing about Honus Wagner while the back has information about the player; the card and the event. This card was given to the first 500 people who visited the exhibit of the famed card at each location.

1 Honus Wagner	2.00	5.00

1981 Perma-Graphic All-Stars

This set commemorates the starters of the 1981 All-Star game. This 18-card set measure 2 1/8" by 3 3/8" and has rounded corners. Because of the players strike of 1981 plenty of time was available to prepare the player's biography with appropriate notes. The set is framed on the front in red for the National League and blue for the American League. This set was originally available from the manufacturer for $21.95

COMPLETE SET (18)	12.00	30.00
1 Gary Carter	3.00	8.00
2 Dave Concepcion	.60	1.50
3 Andre Dawson	1.00	2.50
4 George Foster	.40	1.00
5 Davey Lopes	.60	1.50
6 Dave Parker	.60	1.50
7 Pete Rose	4.00	10.00
8 Mike Schmidt	4.00	10.00
9 Fernando Valenzuela	.60	1.50
10 George Brett	6.00	15.00
11 Rod Carew	3.00	8.00
12 Bucky Dent	.60	1.50
13 Carlton Fisk	3.00	8.00
14 Reggie Jackson	3.00	8.00
15 Jack Morris	.75	2.00
16 Willie Randolph	.60	1.50
17 Ken Singleton	.40	1.00
18 Dave Winfield	3.00	8.00

1981 Perma-Graphic Credit Cards

Perma-Graphic began their three-year foray into card manufacturing with this 32-card set of "credit cards- each measuring approximately 2 1/8" by 3 3/8". The set featured 32 of the leading players of 1981. These sets (made of plastic) were issued with the cooperation of Topps Chewing Gum. This first set of Perma-Graphic cards seems to have been produced in greater quantities than the other five Perma-Graphic sets. These sets were originally available from the manufacturer for $39.95.

COMPLETE SET (32)	12.50	30.00
1 Johnny Bench	1.25	3.00
2 Mike Schmidt	4.00	10.00
3 George Brett	5.00	12.00
4 Carl Yastrzemski	1.00	2.50
5 Pete Rose	2.00	5.00
6 Bob Horner	.40	1.00
7 Reggie Jackson	2.50	6.00
8 Keith Hernandez	.60	1.50
9 George Foster	.40	1.00
10 Garry Templeton	.40	1.00
11 Tom Seaver	2.50	6.00
12 Steve Garvey	.60	1.50
13 Dave Parker	.60	1.50
14 Willie Stargell	1.50	
15 Cecil Cooper	.40	1.00
16 Steve Carlton	1.50	4.00
17 Ted Simmons	.40	1.00
18 Dave Kingman	.60	1.50
19 Rickey Henderson	5.00	12.00
20 Fred Lynn	.60	1.50
21 Dave Winfield	1.50	4.00
22 Rod Carew	1.50	4.00
23 Jim Rice	1.00	2.50
24 Bruce Sutter	1.50	4.00
25 Cesar Cedeno	.40	1.00
26 Nolan Ryan	6.00	12.00
27 Dusty Baker	.40	1.00
28 Jim Palmer	1.50	4.00
29 Gorman Thomas	.40	1.00
30 Ben Oglivie	.40	1.00
31 Willie Wilson	.40	1.00
32 Gary Carter	1.50	4.00

1982 Perma-Graphic All-Stars

For the second time Perma-Graphic issued a special set commemorating the starters of the 1982 All-Star game. This 18-card set measures 2 1/8" by 3 3/8" and features a colorful design framing the players photo on the front The back again feature one line of complete All-Star game statistics including the 1982 game and career highlites. Perma-Graphic also issued the set in a limited (reportedly 1200 sets produced) "gold" edition, i.e., with a gold tint to the cards. The gold edition cards are valued at a multiplte of the regular set. Please refer to the multiplication table below.

COMPLETE SET (18)	25.00	60.00
*GOLD CARDS:2X BASIC CARDS		
1 Dennis Eckersley	3.00	8.00
2 Cecil Cooper	.60	1.50
3 Carlton Fisk	3.00	8.00
4 Robin Yount	3.00	8.00
5 Bobby Grich	.60	1.50
6 Rickey Henderson	4.00	10.00
7 Reggie Jackson	3.00	8.00
8 Fred Lynn	.75	2.00
9 George Brett	5.00	12.00
10 Gary Carter	3.00	8.00
11 Dave Concepcion	.60	1.50
12 Andre Dawson	1.00	2.50
13 Tim Raines	.75	2.00
14 Dale Murphy	1.25	3.00
15 Steve Rogers	.60	1.50
16 Pete Rose	3.00	8.00
17 Mike Schmidt	3.00	8.00
18 Manny Trillo	.60	1.50

1982 Perma-Graphic Credit Cards

For the second year Perma-Graphic, in association with Topps produced a high-quality set on plastic honoring the leading players in baseball of 1982. This 24-card set features plastic cards each measuring approximately 2 1/8" by 3 3/8". On the card back there is one line of career statistics along with career highlights. Perma-Graphic also issued the set in a limited (reportedly 900 sets produced) "gold" edition, i.e., with a gold tint to the cards. The gold edition cards are valued at a mulitple of the regular cards. Please see information in our headers for the multiplication value. Again in 1982 Perma-Graphic issued these sets in conjuction and with the approval of Topps Chewing Gum. This set was originally available from the manufacturer for $29.95. Uncut sheets were also available for this set. The SRP on those sheets were $75. The sheets had three copies of each card printed on it.

COMPLETE SET (24)	25.00	60.00
*GOLD CARDS: .6X TO 1.5X BASIC CARDS		
1 Johnny Bench	2.00	5.00
2 Tom Seaver	2.00	5.00
3 Mike Schmidt	2.00	5.00
4 Gary Carter	2.00	5.00
5 Willie Stargell	1.50	4.00
6 Tim Raines	.50	1.25
7 Bill Madlock	.40	1.00
8 Keith Hernandez	.50	1.25
9 Pete Rose	2.00	5.00
10 Steve Carlton	2.00	5.00
11 Steve Garvey	.50	1.25
12 Fernando Valenzuela	.50	1.25
13 Carl Yastrzemski	1.50	4.00
14 Dave Winfield	2.00	5.00
15 Carney Lansford	.40	1.00
16 Rollie Fingers	1.50	4.00
17 Tony Armas	.40	1.00
18 Cecil Cooper	.40	1.00
19 George Brett	5.00	12.00
20 Reggie Jackson	2.00	5.00
21 Rod Carew	2.00	5.00
22 Eddie Murray	3.00	8.00
23 Rickey Henderson	3.00	8.00
24 Kirk Gibson	.60	1.50

1983 Perma-Graphic All-Stars

The 1983 All-Star Set was the third set Perma-Graphic issued commemorating the starters of the All-Star game. Again, Perma-Graphic used the Topps photos and issued their sets of plastic cards. This 18-card set features cards each measuring approximately 2 1/8" by 3 3/8". Perma-Graphic also issued the set in a limited "gold" edition, i.e., with a gold tint to the cards. The gold edition cards are valued at a multiple of the regular issue cards. Please see information below for values.

COMPLETE SET (18)_	25.00	60.00
*GOLD CARDS:2X BASIC CARDS		
1 George Brett	5.00	12.00
2 Rod Carew	3.00	8.00
3 Fred Lynn	.60	1.50
4 Jim Rice	.60	1.50
5 Ted Simmons	.40	1.00
6 Dave Stieb	.40	1.00
7 Manny Trillo	.40	1.00
8 Dave Winfield	3.00	8.00
9 Robin Yount	3.00	8.00
10 Gary Carter	3.00	8.00
11 Andre Dawson	1.00	2.50
12 Dale Murphy	1.00	2.50
13 Al Oliver	.40	1.00
14 Tim Raines	.60	1.50
15 Steve Sax	.40	1.00
16 Mike Schmidt	3.00	8.00
17 Ozzie Smith	4.00	10.00
18 Mario Soto	.40	1.00

1983 Perma-Graphic Credit Cards

This set was the third straight year Perma-Graphic, with approval from Topps issued their high-quality plastic set. This 36-card set which measures 2 1/8" by 3 3/8" have the players photos framed by colorful backgrounds. The backs again feature one line of career statistics and several informative lines of career highlights. Perma-Graphic also issued the set in a limited (reportedly 1000 sets produced) "gold" edition, i.e., with a gold tint to the cards. The gold edition cards are valued at a multiple of the regular issue cards. Please see information below for values.

COMPLETE SET (36)	30.00	80.00
*GOLD: 2X TO 5X BASIC		
1 Bill Buckner	.40	1.00
2 Steve Carlton	1.50	4.00
3 Gary Carter	1.50	4.00
4 Andre Dawson	1.00	2.50
5 Pedro Guerrero	.40	1.00
6 George Hendrick	.40	1.00
7 Keith Hernandez	.60	1.50
8 Bill Madlock	.40	1.00
9 Dale Murphy	.75	2.00
10 Al Oliver	.40	1.00
11 Dave Parker	.60	1.50
12 Darrell Porter	.40	1.00
13 Pete Rose	3.00	8.00
14 Mike Schmidt	3.00	8.00
15 Lonnie Smith	.40	1.00
16 Ozzie Smith	4.00	10.00
17 Bruce Sutter	1.50	4.00
18 Fernando Valenzuela	.75	2.00
19 George Brett	5.00	12.00
20 Rod Carew	1.50	4.00
21 Cecil Cooper	.40	1.00
22 Doug DeCinces	.40	1.00
23 Rollie Fingers	1.50	4.00
24 Damaso Garcia	.40	1.00
25 Toby Harrah	.40	1.00
26 Rickey Henderson	3.00	8.00
27 Reggie Jackson	2.50	6.00
28 Hal McRae	.40	1.00
29 Eddie Murray	2.50	6.00
30 Lance Parrish	.60	1.50
31 Jim Rice	.60	1.50
32 Gorman Thomas	.40	1.00
33 Willie Wilson	.40	1.00
34 Dave Winfield	1.50	4.00
35 Carl Yastrzemski	1.50	4.00
36 Robin Yount	1.50	4.00

1974 Pete Ward Clinic

These six 5" by 7" blank-back photos feature guest instructors at the Pete Ward Baseball Clinic. These photos, which were issued by the Fred Meyer Company all came in one mailing envelope. Since these photos are unnumbered, we have sequenced them in alphabetical order.

1 Mickey Mantle
2 Billy Martin
3 Pete Rose
4 Harry Walker
5 Pete Ward
6 Maury Wills

1991 Petro-Canada Standups

These 3-D action collector cards consist of three cardboard sheets measuring approximately 2 7/8" by 3 13/16" and joined at one end. The front cover has blue and red stripe borders and features either an American or National league logo inside a baseball diamond. The inside cover has a color photo of the crowd at the game. The middle sheet consists of a 3-D standup of the player. The inside of the last sheet has biographical information, career regular season statistics and All-Star game statistics. The back has career highlights in a sky blue box and "Play the All Star Quiz" questions and answers. The set was first released in Toronto at the All-Star Game in conjunction with the All-Star Fanfest. The cards are numbered on the front.

COMPLETE SET (26)	4.00	10.00
1 Cal Ripken	1.00	2.50
2 Greg Olson	.02	.10
3 Roger Clemens	.50	1.25
4 Ryne Sandberg	.30	.75
5 Dave Winfield	.20	.50
6 Eric Davis	.07	.20
7 Carlton Fisk	.20	.50
8 Mike Scott	.02	.10
9 Sandy Alomar Jr.	.07	.20
10 Tim Wallach	.02	.10
11 Cecil Fielder	.07	.20
12 Dwight Gooden	.07	.20
13 George Brett	.50	1.25
14 Dale Murphy	.10	.30
15 Paul Molitor	.20	.50
16 Barry Bonds	.50	1.25
17 Kirby Puckett	.25	.60
18 Ozzie Smith	.50	1.25
19 Don Mattingly	.50	1.25
20 Will Clark	.15	.40
21 Rickey Henderson	.25	.60
22 Orel Hershiser	.07	.20
23 Ken Griffey Jr.	.75	2.00
24 Tony Gwynn	.50	1.25
25 Nolan Ryan	1.00	2.50
26 Kelly Gruber	.02	.10

1889 Philadelphia Stage

This 14 card set of prints ran in the Stage, a paper issued in Philadelphia late in the 19th century. These prints measure approximately 9" by 12" and filled up an entire newspaper page. Since these were unnumbered, we have sequenced these prints in alphabetical order.

1909 Philadelphia Caramel E95

The cards in this 25-card set measure 1 1/2" by 2 3/4". This set of color drawings was issued by the Philadelphia Caramel Company about 1909. The back is checklisted with its own numbering system (begins with "1. Wagner"), but has been alphabetized for convenience in this listing. Blank backs found in this set are probably cut from advertising panels and should not be considered as proof cards. Of note, our pricing for raw cards is provided in VgEx condition due to the fact that most cards from this set are found in off-grade shape.

COMPLETE SET (25)	15000.00	30000.00
1 Chief Bender	350.00	600.00
2 Bill Carrigan	125.00	200.00
3 Frank Chance	300.00	500.00
4 Ed Cicotte	350.00	600.00
5 Ty Cobb	2500.00	4000.00
6 Eddie Collins	300.00	500.00
7 Sam Crawford	300.00	500.00
8 Art Devlin	125.00	200.00
9 Larry Doyle	125.00	200.00
10 Johnny Evers	300.00	500.00
11 Solly Hoffman	125.00	200.00
12 Harry Krause	125.00	200.00
13 Tommy Leach	125.00	200.00
14 Harry Lord	125.00	200.00
15 Nick Maddox	125.00	200.00
16 Christy Mathewson	900.00	1500.00
17 Matty McIntyre	125.00	200.00
18 Fred Merkle	150.00	250.00
19 Harry (Cy) Morgan	125.00	200.00
20 Eddie Plank	900.00	1500.00
21 Ed Reulbach	125.00	200.00
22 Honus Wagner	1500.00	2500.00
23 Ed Willett	125.00	200.00
24 Vic Willis	300.00	500.00
25 Hooks Wiltse	125.00	200.00

1910 Philadelphia Caramel E96

The cards in this 30-card set measure 1 1/2" by 2 3/4". The red printed backs in this set carry the statement "previous Series 25, making total issue 55 cards", and for this reason it is often referred to as the second series of E95. Issued about 1912, the numbering of the original checklist (starts with "1. Davis") has been rearranged alphabetically below. Some blank backs are known. Listed pricing for raw cards references "VgEx" condition.

COMPLETE SET (30)	2500.00	5000.00
1 Babe Adams	200.00	350.00
2 Red Ames	200.00	350.00
3 Frank Arrelanes	200.00	350.00
4 Frank Baker	350.00	600.00
5 Mordecai Brown	350.00	600.00
6 Fred Clark	300.00	500.00
7 Harry Davis	200.00	350.00
8 Jim Delehanty	200.00	350.00
9 Bill Donovan	200.00	350.00
10 Red Dooin	200.00	350.00
11 George Gibson	200.00	350.00
12 Buck Herzog	200.00	350.00
13 Hugh Jennings MG	300.00	500.00
14 Ed Karger	200.00	350.00
15 Johnny Kling	200.00	350.00
16 Ed Konetchy	200.00	350.00
17 Napoleon Lajoie	600.00	1000.00
18 Connie Mack MG	600.00	1000.00
19 Rube Marquard	300.00	500.00
20 George McQuillan	200.00	350.00
21 Chief Meyers	200.00	350.00
22 Mike Mowrey	200.00	350.00
23 George Mullin	200.00	350.00
24 Red Murray	200.00	350.00
25 Jack Pfeister	200.00	350.00
26 Claude Rossman	200.00	350.00
27 Nap Rucker	200.00	350.00
28 Tubby Spencer	200.00	350.00
29 Ira Thomas	200.00	350.00
30 Joe Tinker	300.00	500.00

1930 Philadelphia Badge Pins

These pins, which measure 1 1/2" in diameter were issued by the Philadelphia Badge company. The fronts have a player photo against a black background with the player's name and team on the bottom

COMPLETE SET (2)	1250.00	2500.00
1 Rogers Hornsby	750.00	1500.00
2 Paul Waner	500.00	1000.00

1949 Philadelphia Bulletin

This 59-card set features black-and-white portraits of the Philadelphia A's and Phillies. Six of the portraits were inserted each week in the "Fun Book" section of the "Philadelphia Sunday Bulletin" from May 22 through July 24, 1949. Only five portraits were inserted in the paper the last Sunday. The cards are unnumbered and checklisted below in alphabetical order.

COMPLETE SET (59)	150.00	300.00
1 Richie Ashburn	12.50	25.00
2 Joe Astroth	2.00	4.00
3 Bennie Bengough CO	2.50	5.00
4 Hank Biasetti	2.00	4.00
5 Charles Bicknell	2.00	4.00
6 Buddy Blattner	2.00	4.00
7 Hank Borowy	2.00	4.00
8 Lou Brissie	2.00	4.00
9 Earle Brucker CO	2.00	4.00
10 Ralph Caballero	2.00	4.00
11 Sam Chapman	2.50	5.00
12 Joe Coleman	2.50	5.00
13 Dusty Cooke CO	2.00	4.00
14 Thomas Davis	2.00	4.00
15 Blix Donnelly	2.00	4.00
16 Jimmy Dykes CO	3.00	6.00
17 Del Ennis	3.00	6.00
18 Ferris Fain	3.00	6.00
19 Dick Fowler	2.00	4.00
20 Nellie Fox	12.50	25.00
21 Mike Guerra	2.00	4.00
22 Granny Hamner	3.00	6.00
23 Charley Harris	2.00	4.00
24 Ken Heintzleman	2.00	4.00
25 Stan Hollmig	2.00	4.00
26 Willie Jones	2.00	4.00
27 Eddie Joost	2.50	5.00
28 Alex Kellner	2.00	4.00
29 Jim Konstanty	3.00	6.00
30 Stan Lopata	2.50	5.00
31 Connie Mack MG	12.50	25.00
32 Earle Mack CO	2.50	5.00
33 Hank Majeskie	2.00	4.00
34 Phil Marchildon	2.00	4.00
35 Jackie Mayo	2.00	4.00
36 Bill McCahan	2.00	4.00
37 Barney McCoskey	2.00	4.00
38 Russ Meyer	2.50	5.00
39 Eddie Miller	2.00	4.00
40 Wally Moses	2.00	4.00
41 Bill Nicholson	2.00	4.00
42 Cy Perkins CO	2.00	4.00
43 Robin Roberts	10.00	20.00
44 Buddy Rosar	2.00	4.00
45 Schoolboy Rowe	3.00	6.00
46 Eddie Sawyer	2.00	4.00
47 Carl Scheib	2.00	4.00
48 Andy Seminick	3.00	6.00
49 Bobby Shantz	4.00	8.00
50 Ken Silvestri	2.00	4.00
51 Al Simmons CO	6.00	12.00
52 Curt Simmons	6.00	12.00
53 Dick Sisler	2.00	4.00
54 Pete Suder	2.00	4.00
55 Ken Trinkle	2.00	4.00
56 Elmer Valo	2.00	4.00
57 Eddie Waitkus	3.00	6.00
58 Don White	2.00	4.00
59 Taft Wright	2.00	4.00

1992 Philadelphia Daily News

This nine-card set, which is aptly subtitled "Great Moments in Philadelphia Sports," was sponsored by the Philadelphia Daily News. The fronts of the standard-size cards have red borders and feature miniature reproductions of newspaper front pages with famous headlines and memorable photos. Each card captures a great moment in the history of Philadelphia sports. Sports represented are baseball, (cards 1 and 7-8) hockey, (2) basketball, (3-4) football, (5-6) and boxing (9). The backs are printed in gray, black and white and provide text relating to the event commemorated on the card.

COMPLETE SET (9)	1.40	3.50
1 We Win Phillies win World Series	.20	.50
7 Mike Schmidt: It's Over/(Schmidt announces retirement	.40	1.00
8 City Wild/(Phillies win National League Championship	.10	.25

1979 Philadelphia Doubleheaders

These 27 cards were issued to promote the EPSCC shows that have been put on in the Philadelphia area since the 1970's The set features two 1950 Philadelphia players on each card along with a back that either promoted the March 1979 EPSCC show or the Philadelphia Phillies checklist book. The two managers are the only people who have cards to themselves.

COMPLETE SET (30)	12.50	30.00
1 Connie Mack MG	1.25	3.00
2 Joe Astroth Dick Fowler	.40	1.00
3 Sam Chapman Lou Brissie	.40	1.00
4 Bob Dillinger Billy Hitchcock	.60	1.50
5 Ben Guintini Joe Tipton	.40	1.00
6 Bob Hooper Barney McCosky	.40	1.00
7 Eddie Joost Kermit Wahl	.40	1.00
8 Ed Klieman Mike Guerra	.40	1.00
9 Paul Lehner Ferris Fain	.60	1.50
10 Earl Mack AMG Mickey Cochrane CO	1.00	2.50
11 Wally Moses Carl Scheib	.40	1.00
12 Pete Suder Alex Kellner	.40	1.00
13 Elmer Valo Bobby Shantz	.60	1.50
14 Hank Wyse Gene Markland	.40	1.00
15 Robert Wellman Joe Coleman	.40	1.00
16 Eddie Sawyer MG	.60	1.50
17 Johnny Blatnik Taffy Wright	.40	1.00
18 Ralph Caballero Bubba Church	.40	1.00
19 Milo Candini Hank Bowory	.40	1.00
20 Blix Donnelly Bill Nicholson	.60	1.50
21 Mike Goliat Dick Whitman	.40	1.00
22 Granny Hamner Richie Ashburn	1.00	2.50
23 Ken Heintzelman Del Ennis	.40	1.00
24 Willie Jones Russ Meyer	.40	1.00
25 Jim Konstanty Ken Silvestri	.40	1.00
26 Stan Lopata Eddie Waitkus	.40	1.00
27 Ed Sanicki Robin Roberts	1.00	2.50
28 Andy Seminick/Ken Trickle	.40	1.00
29 Dick Sisler Stan Hollmig	.40	1.00
30 Jocko Thompson Curt Simmons	.60	1.50

1911 Philadelphia Evening Times Supplements

Issued as a supplement within the Philadelphia Evening Times, these 15 known supplements feature mainly members of the Philadelphia A's and the New York Giants, who squared off against each other in the 1911 World Series.

COMPLETE SET (15)	2000.00	4000.00

1977 Philadelphia Favorites

This 25-card set was used as promotional give-aways for the EPSCC in the Delaware Valley area during the summer of 1977 and measures approximately 3 3/4" by 2 1/4". Some complete sets were also available by mail at the time of issue for $2.75 from the set's producer. The fronts feature a sepia photo of a former Phillies or Athletics player with white borders. The player's name, position, team, and years played are printed in the bottom margin.

COMPLETE SET (25)	20.00	50.00
1 Connie Mack	2.00	5.00
2 Nap Lajoie	2.00	5.00
3 Eddie Collins	2.00	5.00
4 Lefty Grove	2.00	5.00
5 Al Simmons	1.00	2.50
6 Jimmy Foxx (Jimmie)	2.00	5.00
7 Frank Baker	1.00	2.50
8 Ferris Fain	.40	1.00
9 Jimmy Dykes	.40	1.00
10 Willie Jones	.40	1.00
11 Del Ennis	.40	1.00
12 Granny Hamner	.40	1.00
13 Andy Seminick	.40	1.00
14 Robin Roberts	2.00	5.00
15 Ed Delahanty	1.00	2.50
16 Gavvy Cravath	.75	2.00
17 Cy Williams	.40	1.00
18 Chuck Klein	1.00	2.50
19 Richie Ashburn	2.00	5.00
20 Bobby Shantz	.40	1.00
21 Gus Zernial	.40	1.00
22 Eddie Sawyer	.40	1.00
23 G.C. Alexander	1.00	2.50
24 Wally Moses	.40	1.00
25 Connie Mack Stadium (nee Shibe Park)	.40	1.00

1981-82 Philip Morris

This 18-card standard-size set was included in the Champions of American Sport program and features major stars from a variety of sports. The program was issued in conjunction with a traveling exhibition organized by the National Portrait Gallery and the Smithsonian Institution and sponsored by Philip Morris and Miller Brewing Company. The cards are either reproductions of works of art (paintings) or famous photographs of the time. The cards are frequently found with a perforated edge on at least one side. The cards were actually obtained from two perforated pages in the program. There is no notation anywhere on the cards indicating the manufacturer or sponsor.

COMPLETE SET (18)	40.00	100.00
7 Sandy Koufax	3.20	8.00
10 Willie Mays	4.00	10.00
17 Casey Stengel	1.00	2.50

1940 Phillies Team Issue

These 31 5 7/8" by 8 1/2" blank backed photos were issued by the Philadelphia Phillies. They are unnumbered and we have sequenced them in alphabetical order.

COMPLETE SET	90.00	180.00
1 Morrie Arnovich	5.00	10.00
2 Bill Atwood	5.00	10.00
3 Walter Beck	5.00	10.00
4 Stan Benjamin	5.00	10.00
5 Wally Berger	7.50	15.00
6 Cy Blanton	5.00	10.00
7 Bob Bragan	10.00	20.00
8 Lloyd Brown	5.00	10.00
9 Roy Bruner	5.00	10.00
10 Kirby Higbe	6.00	12.00
11 Frank Hoerst	5.00	10.00
12 Si Johnson	5.00	10.00
13 Syl Johnson	5.00	10.00
14 Chuck Klein	15.00	30.00
15 Ed Levy	5.00	10.00
16 Dan Litwhiler	6.00	12.00
17 Hans Lobert CO	6.00	12.00
18 Art Mahan	5.00	10.00
19 Hershel Martin	5.00	10.00
20 Joe Marty	5.00	10.00
21 Merrill May	5.00	10.00
22 Mel Mazzera	5.00	10.00
23 Walt Millies	5.00	10.00
24 Alex Monchak	5.00	10.00
25 Heinie Mueller	5.00	10.00
26 Hugh Mulcahy	5.00	10.00
27 Ike Pearson	5.00	10.00
28 Doc Prothro MG	5.00	10.00
29 John Rizzo	5.00	10.00
30 George Scharein	5.00	10.00
31 Ham Schulte	5.00	10.00
32 Clyde Smoll	5.00	10.00
33 Gus Suhr	6.00	12.00
34 Ben Warren	5.00	10.00
35 Del Young	5.00	10.00
36 Philadelphia Phillies	10.00	20.00

1941 Phillies Team Issue

This 26-card set of the Philadelphia Phillies measuring approximately 6" by 8 1/2" features black-and-white player photos with fascimile autographs. The backs are blank. The cards are unnumbered and checklisted below in alphabetical order.

COMPLETE SET (26)	125.00	250.00
1 Morrie Arnovich	5.00	10.00
2 Bill Atwood	5.00	10.00
3 Walter Beck	5.00	10.00
4 Stan Benjamin	5.00	10.00
5 Bob Bragan	7.50	15.00
6 Roy Bruner	5.00	10.00
7 Kirby Higbe	6.00	12.00
8 Frank Hoerst	5.00	10.00
9 Si Johnson	5.00	10.00
10 Syl Johnson	5.00	10.00
11 Chuck Klein	15.00	30.00
12 Ed Levy	5.00	10.00
13 Dan Litwhiler	6.00	12.00
14 Hans Lobert	6.00	12.00
15 Hershel Martin	5.00	10.00
16 Joe Marty	5.00	10.00
17 Merrill May	5.00	10.00
18 Walt Millies	5.00	10.00
19 Hugh Mulcahy	5.00	10.00
20 Ike Pearson	5.00	10.00
21 Doc Prothro	5.00	10.00
22 George Scharein	5.00	10.00
23 Clyde Smoll	5.00	10.00
24 Gus Suhr	6.00	12.00
25 Ben Warren	5.00	10.00
26 Del Young	5.00	10.00

1943 Phillies Team Issue

This 23-card set of the Philadelphia Phillies measures approximately 6" by 8 1/2" and features black-and-white player photos with white borders. The backs are blank. The cards are unnumbered and checklisted below in alphabetical order. This set is so large as it presumed that the Phillies kept issuing photos during the year as players were shuttling in and out of the majors during World War II.

COMPLETE SET (23)	200.00	400.00
1 Buster Adams	5.00	10.00
2 Walter Beck	5.00	10.00
3 Stan Benjamin	5.00	10.00
4 Cy Blanton	5.00	10.00
5 Bobby Bragan	6.00	12.00
6 Charlie Brewster	5.00	10.00
7 Paul Busby	5.00	10.00
8 Bennie Culp	5.00	10.00
9 Babe Dahlgren	6.00	12.00
10 Lloyd Dietz	5.00	10.00
11 Nick Etten	6.00	12.00
12 George Eyrich	5.00	10.00
13 Charlie Fuchs	5.00	10.00
14 Al Glossop	5.00	10.00
14 Al Gerheauser	5.00	10.00
15 Frank Hoerst	5.00	10.00
16 Si Johnson	5.00	10.00
17 Bill Killefer	5.00	10.00
18 Newell Kimball	5.00	10.00
19 Chuck Klein	20.00	40.00
20 Ernie Koy	6.00	12.00
22 Danny Litwhiler	6.00	12.00
23 Jack Kraus	5.00	10.00
24 Mickey Livingston	5.00	10.00
25 Hans Lobert	5.00	10.00
26 Harry Marnie	5.00	10.00
27 Merrill May	5.00	10.00
28 Rube Melton	5.00	10.00
29 Danny Murtaugh	8.00	20.00
30 Sam Nahem	5.00	10.00
31 Earl Naylor	5.00	10.00
32 Ron Northey	5.00	10.00
33 Tom Padden	5.00	10.00
34 Ike Pearson	5.00	10.00
35 Johnny Podgajny	5.00	10.00
36 Schoolboy Rowe	6.00	12.00
37 Neb Stewart	5.00	10.00
38 Coaker Triplett	5.00	10.00
39 Lloyd Waner	12.50	25.00
40 Ben Warren	5.00	10.00
41 Jimmie Wasdell	5.00	10.00

1949 Phillies Lummis Peanut Butter

The cards in this 12-card set measure 3 1/4" by 4 1/4". The 1949 Lummis set of black and white, unnumbered action poses depicts Philadelphia Phillies only. These "cards" are actually stickers and were distributed locally by Lummis Peanut Butter and Sealtest Dairy Products. The prices listed below are for the Sealtest cards. The harder-to-find Lummis variety are worth double the listed values below. The catalog designation is F343.

COMPLETE SET (12)	5000.00	10000.00
1 Rich Ashburn	2000.00	4000.00
2 Hank Borowy	500.00	1000.00
3 Del Ennis	800.00	1600.00
4 Granny Hamner	500.00	1000.00
5 Puddinhead Jones	500.00	1000.00
6 Russ Meyer	500.00	1000.00
7 Bill Nicholson	500.00	1000.00
8 Robin Roberts	1500.00	3000.00
9 Schoolboy Rowe	600.00	1200.00
10 Andy Seminick	750.00	1500.00
11 Curt Simmons	750.00	1500.00
12 Ed Waitkus	600.00	1200.00

1950 Phillies Philadelphia Inquirer

This set of cards have posed color photos and measure 4 1/4" X 5 3/4". Cards are printed on newsprint and have facsimile autographs. A brief biography of the player is printed underneath his name. The set is titled on the bottom "Inquirer Fightin" Phillies Album".

COMPLETE SET (24)	125.00	250.00
1 Richie Ashburn	12.50	25.00
2 Jimmy Bloodworth	5.00	10.00
3 Putsy Caballero	5.00	10.00
4 Milo Candini	5.00	10.00
5 Bubba Church	5.00	10.00
6 Blix Donnelly	5.00	10.00
7 Del Ennis	7.50	15.00

8 Mike Goliat 5.00 10.00
9 Granny Hamner 6.00 12.00
10 Ken Heintzelman 5.00 10.00
11 Stan Hollmig 5.00 10.00
12 Ken Johnson 5.00 10.00
13 Willie Puddin-Head Jones 6.00 12.00
14 Stan Lopata 5.00 10.00
15 Russ Meyer 5.00 10.00
16 Bob Miller 5.00 10.00
17 Bill Nicholson 6.00 12.00
18 Robin Roberts 12.50 25.00
19 Andy Seminick 5.00 10.00
20 Ken Silvestri 5.00 10.00
21 Curt Simmons 7.50 15.00
22 Dick Sisler 6.00 12.00
23 Eddie Waitkus 6.00 12.00
24 Dick Whitman 5.00 10.00

1955 Phillies Felin's Franks

These horizontal 4" by 3 5/8" cards, with rounded corners, features members of the 1955 Philadelphia Phillies.The red bordered cards have the player photo on the left with biographical information underneath. The right side of the card lists a different players information from the 1954 season and asks the collector to identify who the player is. The back has information about the contest these cards are involved with. While 30 cards were printed for this set, this set is scarce enough that not all cards are known so any additional information on missing cards are appreciated.

COMPLETE SET 30000.00 60000.00
1 Mayo Smith MG 1500.00 3000.00
3 Wally Moses CO 1500.00 3000.00
4 Whit Wyatt CO 1500.00 3000.00
5 Maje McDonell CO 1500.00 3000.00
6 Frank Wiechec TR 1500.00 3000.00
7 Murry Dickson 1500.00 3000.00
8 Earl Torgeson 1500.00 3000.00
9 Bobby Morgan 1500.00 3000.00
10 Jack Meyer 1500.00 3000.00
11 Bob Miller 1500.00 3000.00
12 Jim Owens 1500.00 3000.00
13 Steve Ridzik 1500.00 3000.00
14 Robin Roberts 3000.00 6000.00
16 Herm Wehmeier 1500.00 3000.00
17 Smoky Burgess 2000.00 4000.00
18 Stan Lopata 1500.00 3000.00
19 Gus Niarhos 1500.00 3000.00
20 Floyd Baker 1500.00 3000.00
21 Merv Blaylock 1500.00 3000.00
22 Granny Hamner 2000.00 4000.00
23 Willie Jones 2000.00 4000.00
26 Richie Ashburn 2500.00 5000.00
27 Joe Lonnett 1500.00 3000.00
28 Mel Clark 1500.00 3000.00
29 Bob Greenwood 1500.00 3000.00

1956 Phillies Postcards

These six 3 1/4" by 5 1/2" cards feature white borders, autographs on the picture and were sent by the club in relation to fan requests. These cards are unnumbered and we have sequenced them in alphabetical order.

COMPLETE SET (6) 20.00 40.00
1 Richie Ashburn 5.00 10.00
2 Granny Hammer 2.50 5.00
3 Willie Jones 3.00 6.00
4 Stan Lopata 2.50 5.00
5 Robin Roberts 5.00 10.00
6 Curt Simmons 3.00 6.00

1958 Phillies Jay Publishing

This 12-card set of the Philadelphia Phillies measures approximately 5" by 7" and features black-and-white player photos in a white border. These cards were packaged 12 to a packet. The backs are blank. The cards are unnumbered and checklisted below in alphabetical order.

COMPLETE SET (12) 25.00 50.00
1 Harry Anderson 1.50 3.00
2 Richie Ashburn 6.00 12.00
3 Bob Bowman 1.50 3.00
4 Dick Farrell 1.50 3.00
5 Chico Fernandez 1.50 3.00
6 Granny Hamner 1.50 3.00
7 Stan Lopata 1.50 3.00
8 Rip Repulski 1.50 3.00
9 Robin Roberts 6.00 12.00
10 Jack Sanford UER 1.50 3.00
Sandford
11 Curt Simmons 2.50 5.00
12 Mayo Smith MG 1.50 3.00

1958-60 Phillies Team Issue

This 19-card blank-backed set features black-and-white photos of the Philadelphia Phillies measuring approximately 3 1/4" by 5 1/2". The cards are unnumbered and checklisted below in alphabetical order.

COMPLETE SET (19) 37.50 75.00
1 Harry Anderson 1.50 3.00
2 Richie Ashburn 5.00 10.00
3 Ed Bouchee 1.50 3.00
4 John Buzhardt 1.50 3.00
5 Johnny Callison 3.00 6.00
6 Jim Coker 1.50 3.00
7 Clay Dalrymple 1.50 3.00
8 Tony Gonzalez 1.50 3.00
9 Granny Hamner 1.50 3.00
10 Willie Jones 2.00 4.00
11 Stan Lopata 1.50 3.00
12 Art Mahaffey 2.00 4.00
13 Gene Mauch MG 2.50 5.00
14 Wally Post 1.50 3.00
15 Robin Roberts 4.00 8.00
16 Eddie Sawyer MG 1.50 3.00
17 Ray Semproch 1.50 3.00
18 Chris Short 2.50 5.00
19 Curt Simmons 2.50 5.00

1959 Phillies Jay Publishing

This 12-card set of the Philadelphia Phillies measures approximately 5" by 7" and features black-and-white player photos in a white border. These cards were packaged 12 to a packet. The backs are blank. The cards are unnumbered and checklisted below in alphabetical order.

COMPLETE SET 20.00 50.00
1 Harry Anderson 1.50 4.00
2 Richie Ashburn 5.00 12.00
3 Ed Bouchee 1.50 4.00
4 Dick Farrell 1.50 4.00
5 Chico Fernandez 1.50 4.00
6 Ruben Gomez 1.50 4.00
7 Harry Hanebrink 1.50 4.00
8 Wally Post 1.50 4.00
9 Robin Roberts 5.00 12.00
10 Eddie Sawyer MG 1.50 4.00
11 Roman Semproch 1.50 4.00
12 Curt Simmons 2.00 5.00

1960 Phillies Jay Publishing

This 12-card set of the Philadelphia Phillies measures approximately 5" X 7". The fronts feature black-and-white posed player photos with the player's and team name printed below in the white border. These cards were packaged 12 to a packet and originally sold for 25 cents. The backs are blank. The cards are unnumbered and checklisted below in alphabetical order.

COMPLETE SET (12) 20.00 50.00
1 Ruben Amaro 1.50 4.00
2 Harry Anderson 1.50 4.00
3 Ed Bouchee 1.50 4.00
4 John Callison 2.50 6.00
5 Jim Coker 1.50 4.00
6 Al Dark 2.50 6.00
7 Dick Farrell 1.50 4.00
8 Pancho Herrera 1.50 4.00
9 Jim Owens 1.50 4.00
10 Wally Post 2.50 6.00
11 Robin Roberts 6.00 15.00
12 Eddie Sawyer MG 1.50 4.00

1961 Phillies Jay Publishing

This 12-card set of the Philadelphia Phillies measures approximately 5" X 7". The fronts feature black-and-white posed player photos with the player's and team name printed below in the white border. These cards were packaged 12 to a packet and originally sold for 25 cents. The backs are blank. The cards are unnumbered and checklisted below in alphabetical order.

COMPLETE SET (12) 10.00 25.00
1 Ruben Amaro 1.00 2.50
2 Johnny Callison 1.00 2.50
3 Bobby Del Greco 1.00 2.50
4 Dick Farrell 1.00 2.50
5 Dallas Green 1.25 3.00
6 Pancho Herrera 1.00 2.50
7 Gene Mauch MG 1.00 2.50
8 Bob Malkmus 1.00 2.50
9 Robin Roberts 3.00 8.00
10 Tony Taylor 1.25 3.00
11 Lee Walls 1.00 2.50
12 Ken Walters 1.00 2.50

1962 Phillies Jay Publishing

This 12-card set of the Philadelphia Phillies measures approximately 5" by 7". The fronts feature black-and-white posed player photos with the player's and team name printed below in the white border. These cards were packaged 12 to a packet. The backs are blank. The cards are unnumbered and checklisted below in alphabetical order.

COMPLETE SET (12) 15.00 40.00
1 Jack Baldschun 1.50 4.00
2 John Callison 2.50 6.00
3 Clay Dalrymple 1.50 4.00
4 Don Demeter 1.50 4.00
5 Dallas Green 2.00 5.00
6 Art Mahaffey 1.50 4.00
7 Gene Mauch MG 1.50 4.00
8 Cal McLish 1.50 4.00
9 Roy Sievers 2.00 5.00
10 Frank Sullivan 1.50 4.00
11 Tony Taylor 2.00 5.00
12 Ken Walters 1.50 4.00

1963 Phillies Jay Publishing

This 12-card set of the Philadelphia Phillies measures approximately 5" by 7". The fronts feature black-and-white posed player photos with the player's and team name printed below in the white border. These cards were packaged 12 to a packet. The backs are blank. The cards are unnumbered and checklisted below in alphabetical order.

COMPLETE SET (12) 20.00 50.00
1 Ruben Amaro 1.50 4.00
2 Jack Baldschun 1.50 4.00
3 John Callison 3.00 8.00
4 Clay Dalrymple 1.50 4.00
5 Don Demeter 1.50 4.00
6 Art Mahaffey 1.50 4.00
7 Gene Mauch MG 1.50 4.00
8 Cal McLish 1.50 4.00
9 Chris Short 2.00 5.00
10 Roy Sievers 2.00 5.00
11 Tony Taylor 2.00 5.00
12 Bobby Wine 1.50 4.00

1964 Phillies Jay Publishing

This 12-card set of the Philadelphia Phillies measures approximately 5" by 7". The fronts feature black-and-white posed player photos with the player's and team name printed below in the white border. These cards were packaged 12 to a packet. The backs are blank. The cards are unnumbered and checklisted below in alphabetical order.

COMPLETE SET (12) 8.00 20.00
1 Jack Baldschun .75 2.00
2 John Callison 1.25 3.00
3 Wes Covington .75 2.00
4 Clay Dalrymple .75 2.00
5 Tony Gonzalez .75 2.00
6 Dallas Green 1.00 2.50
7 Don Hoak .75 2.00
8 Art Mahaffey .75 2.00
9 Gene Mauch MG .75 2.00
10 Roy Sievers 1.00 2.50
11 Tony Taylor 1.00 2.50
12 Bob Wine .75 2.00

1964 Phillies Philadelphia Bulletin

This 27-subject set was produced by the Philadelphia Bulletin newspaper. The catalog designation for this set is M130-5. These large, approximately 8" by 10", photo cards are unnumbered and blank backed. The complete set price below includes both Bunning variation cards.

COMPLETE SET (27) 100.00 200.00
1 Richie Allen 10.00 25.00
2 Ruben Amaro 2.50 6.00
3 Jack Baldschun 2.50 6.00
4 Dennis Bennett 2.50 6.00
5 John Boozer 2.50 6.00
6 Johnny Briggs 2.50 6.00
7 Jim Bunning (2) 10.00 25.00
8 Johnny Callison 3.00 8.00
9 Danny Cater 2.50 6.00
10 Wes Covington 2.50 6.00
11 Ray Culp 2.50 6.00
12 Clay Dalrymple 2.50 6.00
13 Tony Gonzalez 2.50 6.00
14 John Herrnstein 2.50 6.00
15 Alex Johnson 2.50 6.00
16 Art Mahaffey 2.50 6.00
17 Gene Mauch MG 3.00 8.00
18 Vic Power 2.50 6.00
19 Ed Roebuck 2.50 6.00
20 Cookie Rojas 3.00 8.00
21 Bobby Shantz 3.00 8.00
22 Chris Short 3.00 8.00
23 Tony Taylor 3.00 8.00
24 Frank Thomas 3.00 8.00
25 Gus Triandos 2.50 6.00
26 Bobby Wine 2.50 6.00
27 Rick Wise 3.00 8.00

1964 Phillies Team Set

This six-card set of the Philadelphia Phillies measures approximately 3 1/4" by 5 1/2" and feature black-and-white player portraits with a facsimile autograph. The backs are blank. The cards are unnumbered and checklisted below in alphabetical order.

COMPLETE SET (7) 8.00 20.00
1 Jim Bunning 3.00 8.00
2 Johnny Callison 1.50 4.00
3 Clay Dalrymple 1.25 3.00
4 Tony Gonzalez 1.25 3.00
5 Cookie Rojas 1.50 4.00
6 Chris Short 1.50 4.00
7 Roy Sievers 1.50 4.00

1965 Phillies Ceramic Tiles

These tiles, which measure 6" square, feature members of the Philadelphia Phillies. The players photo and a fascimile autograph are set against a white background. Since these are unnumbered, we have sequenced them in alphabetical order.

COMPLETE SET 300.00 600.00
1 Richie Allen 100.00 200.00
2 Bo Belinsky 60.00 120.00
3 Jim Bunning 75.00 150.00
4 John Callison 60.00 120.00
5 Clay Dalrymple 50.00 100.00
6 Gene Mauch MG 50.00 100.00
7 Tony Taylor 50.00 100.00

1965 Phillies Jay Publishing

This 12-card set of the Philadelphia Phillies measures approximately 5" X 7". The fronts feature black-and-white posed player photos with the player's and team's names printed below in the white border. These cards were packaged 12 to a packet and originally sold for 25 cents. The backs are blank. The cards are unnumbered and checklisted below in alphabetical order.

COMPLETE SET (12) 20.00 50.00
1 Ruben Amaro 1.50 4.00
2 Jack Baldschun 1.50 4.00
3 Jim Bunning 5.00 12.00
4 John Callison 2.50 6.00
5 Clay Dalrymple 1.50 4.00
6 Dallas Green 2.00 5.00
7 Art Mahaffey 1.50 4.00
8 Gene Mauch MG 2.00 5.00
9 Chris Short 2.00 5.00
10 Tony Taylor 2.00 5.00
11 Gus Triandos 1.50 4.00
12 Bob Wine 1.50 4.00

1966 Phillies Team Issue

This 12-card set features black-and-white photos of the 1966 Philadelphia Phillies. The cards are unnumbered and checklisted below in alphabetical order.

COMMON CARD (1-12) 12.50 30.00
1 Richie Allen 1.50 4.00
2 Jackie Brandt .75 2.00
3 Jim Bunning 2.50 6.00
4 John Callison 1.25 3.00
5 Ray Culp .75 2.00
6 Clay Dalrymple .75 2.00
7 Tony Gonzalez .75 2.00
8 Dick Groat 1.25 3.00
9 Phil Linz .75 2.00
10 Cookie Rojas 1.00 2.50
11 Chris Short .75 2.00
12 Bill White 1.25 3.00

1967 Phillies Police

The 1967 Philadelphia Phillies Police/Safety set contains 13 cards measuring approximately 2 13/16" by 4 7/16". The black and white posed player photos on the fronts are bordered in white and have the player's signature inscribed across the picture. In blue print on white, the backs have biography, player profile, and a "Safe Driving" emblem at the bottom. Cards can be found where the players' pictured on the fronts do not match the card backs. For example, the Jim Bunning card has a Dick Ellsworth back, the John Briggs card has a Dick Groat back, the Johnny Callison card has a Bill White back, the Clay Dalrymple card has a Chris Short back, and the Gene Mauch card has a Tony Gonzalez back. The cards are unnumbered and checklisted below in alphabetical order.

COMPLETE SET (13) 50.00 100.00
1 Richie Allen 4.00 10.00
2 Jim Bunning 12.50 30.00
3 John Briggs 2.00 5.00
4 Johnny Callison 3.00 8.00
5 Clay Dalrymple 2.00 5.00
6 Dick Ellsworth 2.00 5.00
7 Tony Gonzalez 2.00 5.00
8 Dick Groat 3.00 8.00
9 Larry Jackson 2.50 6.00
10 Gene Mauch MG 2.50 6.00
11 Cookie Rojas 2.50 6.00
12 Chris Short 2.50 6.00
13 Bill White 3.00 8.00

1969 Phillies Team Issue

This 12-card set of the Philadelphia Phillies measures approximately 4 1/4" by 7". The fronts freature black-and-white player portraits in a white border. The player's name and team name are printed above. The backs are blank. The cards are unnumbered and checklisted below in alphabetical order.

COMPLETE SET (12) 10.00 25.00
1 Richie Allen 1.50 4.00
2 John Callison 1.25 3.00
3 Woody Fryman .75 2.00
4 Larry Hisle 1.00 2.50
5 Deron Johnson 1.00 2.50
6 Don Money 1.00 2.50
7 Cookie Rojas 1.00 2.50
8 Mike Ryan .75 2.00
9 Chris Short 1.00 2.50
10 Bob Skinner .75 2.00
11 Tony Taylor 1.00 2.50
12 Rick Wise 1.00 2.50

1970 Phillies Team Issue

This 12-card set of the Philadelphia Phillies measures approximately 4 1/4" by 7" and features black-and-white player photos in a white border. Packaged 12 to a packet with blank backs, the cards are unnumbered and checklisted below in alphabetical order.

COMPLETE SET (12) 10.00 25.00
1 Larry Bowa 1.50 4.00
2 John Briggs .75 2.00
3 Denny Doyle .75 2.00
4 Larry Hisle 1.00 2.50
5 Grant Jackson .75 2.00
6 Deron Johnson 1.00 2.50
7 Rick Joseph .75 2.00
8 Tim McCarver 1.50 4.00
9 Don Money 1.00 2.50
10 Chris Short 1.00 2.50
11 Tony Taylor 1.00 2.50
12 Rick Wise 1.00 2.50

1971 Phillies Arco Oil

Sponsored by Arco Oil, these 13 pictures of the 1971 Philadelphia Phillies measure approximately 8" by 10" and feature on their fronts white-bordered posed color player photos. The player's name is shown in black lettering within the white margin below the photo. His facsimile autograph appears across the picture. The white back carries the team's and player's names at the top, followed below by position, biography, career highlights, and statistics. An ad at the bottom for picture frames rounds out the back. The cards are unnumbered and checklisted below in alphabetical order.

COMPLETE SET (13) 15.00 40.00
1 Larry Bowa 2.00 5.00
2 Jim Bunning 3.00 8.00
3 Roger Freed 1.00 2.50
4 Terry Harmon 1.00 2.50
5 Larry Hisle 1.25 3.00
6 Joe Hoerner 1.00 2.50
7 Deron Johnson 1.25 3.00
8 Tim McCarver 2.00 5.00
9 Don Money 1.25 3.00
10 Dick Selma 1.00 2.50
11 Chris Short 1.25 3.00
12 Tony Taylor 1.25 3.00
13 Rick Wise 1.25 3.00

1972 Phillies Ticketron

These cards, featuring members of the 1972 Phillies, were issued in conjunction with Ticketron. Since these cards are unnumbered, we have sequenced them in alphabetical order.

COMPLETE SET 30.00 60.00
1 Mike Anderson 2.00 5.00
2 Larry Bowa 2.50 6.00
3 Steve Carlton 6.00 15.00
4 Deron Johnson 2.00 5.00
5 Frank Lucchesi MG 2.00 5.00
6 Greg Luzinski 4.00 10.00
7 Tim McCarver 4.00 10.00
8 Don Money 2.00 5.00
9 Willie Montanez 2.00 5.00
10 Dick Selma 2.00 5.00

1973 Phillies Team Issue

This 29-card set of the Philadelphia Phillies measures approximately 3 1/4" by 5 1/2" and features black-and-white player photos with white borders. The backs are blank. The cards are unnumbered and checklisted below in alphabetical order. An early card of Mike Schmidt is in this set.

COMPLETE SET (29) 15.00 40.00
1 Mike Anderson .40 1.00
2 Bob Boone 1.25 3.00
3 Larry Bowa 1.25 3.00
4 Darrell Brandon .40 1.00
5 Ken Brett .40 1.00
6 Steve Carlton 2.50 6.00
7 Denny Doyle .40 1.00
8 Terry Harmon .40 1.00
9 Tommy Hutton .40 1.00
10 Barry Lersch .40 1.00
11 Jim Lonborg .75 2.00
12 Greg Luzinski 1.25 3.00
13 Willie Montanez .40 1.00
14 Jose Pagan .40 1.00
15 Bill Robinson .40 1.00
16 Dick Ruthven .40 1.00
17 Mike Ryan .40 1.00
18 Mac Scarce .40 1.00
19 Mike Schmidt 6.00 15.00
20 Cesar Tovar .40 1.00
21 Mike Rogodzinski .40 1.00
22 Wayne Twitchell .40 1.00
23 Del Unser .40 1.00
24 Billy Wilson .40 1.00
25 Danny Ozark MG .40 1.00
26 Ray Rippelmeyer CO .40 1.00
27 Carroll Beringer CO .40 1.00
28 Billy Demars CO .40 1.00
29 Bobby Wine CO .40 1.00

1974 Phillies Johnny Pro

This 12-card set measures approximately 3 3/4" by 7 1/8" and features members of the 1974 Philadelphia Phillies. The most significant player in this series is an early card of Mike Schmidt. The cards are designed to be pushed out and have the players photo against a solid white background. The backs are blank and marked the second straight year that Johnny Pro issued cards of a major league team. The set is checklisted by uniform number. According to informed sources, there were less than 15,000 sets produced.

COMPLETE SET (12) 100.00 200.00
8 Bob Boone 4.00 10.00
10 Larry Bowa 3.00 8.00
16 Dave Cash 2.00 5.00
19 Greg Luzinski 4.00 10.00
20 Mike Schmidt 75.00 150.00
22 Mike Anderson 2.00 5.00
24 Bill Robinson 2.50 6.00
25 Del Unser 2.00 5.00
27 Willie Montanez 2.00 5.00
32 Steve Carlton 12.50 30.00
37 Ron Schueler 2.50 6.00
41 Jim Lonborg 3.00 8.00

1975 Phillies 1950 TCMA

This 31-card set features black-and-white photos of the 1950 Philadelphia Phillies Baseball team with red lettering. The cards are unnumbered and checklisted below alphabetically.

COMPLETE SET (31) 8.00 20.00
1 Richie Ashburn 1.50 4.00
2 Benny Bengough CO .20 .50
3 Jimmy Bloodworth .20 .50
4 Hank Borowy .20 .50
5 Putsy Caballero .20 .50
6 Emory Church .20 .50
7 Dusty Cooke CO .20 .50
8 Blix Donnelly .20 .50
9 Del Ennis .60 1.50
10 Mike Goliat .20 .50
11 Granny Hamner .30 .75
12 Ken Heintzleman .20 .50
13 Stan Hollmig .20 .50
14 Ken Johnson .20 .50
15 Willie Jones .30 .75
16 Jim Konstantly .40 1.00
17 Stan Lopata .20 .50
18 Eddie Mayo .20 .50
19 Russ Meyer .20 .50
20 Bob Miller .20 .50
21 Bill Nicholson .20 .50
22 Cy Perkins CO .20 .50
23 Robin Roberts 1.25 3.00
24 Eddie Sawyer MG .20 .50
25 Andy Seminick .20 .50
26 Ken Silvestri .20 .50
27 Curt Simmons .30 .75
28 Dick Sisler .30 .75
29 Jocko Thompson .20 .50
30 Eddie Waitkus .30 .75
31 Dick Whitman .20 .50

1975 Phillies Photo Album

These seven 6" by 9" photos were issued by the Philadelphia Phillies and feature some of their leading players in 1975. The player photos are surrounded by red borders and have a fascimile signature. The backs look as they are taken from the Phillies Media Guide. The backs have a small photo, biographical information, a brief blurb and career statistics. Since the photos are unnumbered we have sequenced them in alphabetical order.

COMPLETE SET (7) 8.00 20.00
1 Dick Allen 1.25 3.00
2 Larry Bowa 1.00 2.50
3 Dave Cash .40 1.00
4 Jay Johnstone .60 1.50
5 Greg Luzinski .75 2.00
6 Garry Maddox .40 1.00
7 Mike Schmidt 4.00 10.00

1975 Phillies Postcards

This 31-card set of the Philadelphia Phillies features player photos on postcard-size cards. The cards are unnumbered and checklisted below in alphabetical order.

COMPLETE SET (31) 8.00 20.00
1 Dick Allen .60 1.50
2 Mike Anderson .20 .50
3 Alan Bannister .20 .50
4 Carroll Beringer CO .20 .50
5 Bob Boone .60 1.50
6 Larry Bowa .20 .50
7 Ollie Brown .20 .50
8 Steve Carlton 1.25 3.00
9 Dave Cash .20 .50
10 Larry Christenson .20 .50
11 Larry Cox .20 .50
12 Billy DeMars CO .20 .50
13 Gene Garber .30 .75
14 Terry Harmon .20 .50
15 Tom Hilgendorf .20 .50
16 Joe Hoerner .20 .50
17 Tommy Hutton .20 .50
18 Jay Johnstone .40 1.00
19 Jim Lonborg .30 .75
20 Greg Luzinski .60 1.50
21 Garry Maddox .30 .75
22 Tim McCarver .40 1.00
23 Tug McGraw .40 1.00
24 Danny Ozark MG .20 .50
25 Ray Ripplemeyer CO .20 .50
26 Mike Schmidt 2.50 6.00
27 Ron Schueler .20 .50
28 Tony Taylor .30 .75
29 Wayne Twitchell .20 .50
30 Tom Underwood .20 .50
31 Bobby Wine .20 .50

1976 Phillies Photo Album

Issued as a photo album, but with easily perforated photos, which measure approximately 5 1/4" by 8 1/2" when seperated, these pictures feature members of the Eastern Division Champion Philadelphia Phillies. Since the photos were issued in alphabetical order, we have notated these photos in that order as well.

COMPLETE SET , 10.00 25.00
1 Dick Allen .75 2.00
2 Bob Boone .60 1.50
3 Larry Bowa .60 1.50
4 Ollie Brown .30 .75
5 Steve Carlton 1.50 4.00
6 Dave Cash .30 .75
7 Larry Christenson .30 .75
8 Gene Garber .30 .75
9 Terry Harmon .30 .75
10 Tommy Hutton .30 .75
11 Jay Johnstone .30 .75
12 Jim Kaat .75 2.00
13 Jim Lonborg .40 1.00
14 Greg Luzinski .60 1.50
15 Garry Maddox .40 1.00
16 Jerry Martin .30 .75
17 Tim McCarver .75 2.00
18 Tug McGraw .75 2.00
19 Johnny Oates .30 .75
20 Ron Reed .30 .75
21 Mike Schmidt 2.50 6.00
22 Ron Schueler .30 .75
23 Tony Taylor .30 .75
24 Bobby Tolan .30 .75
25 Wayne Twitchell .30 .75
26 Tom Underwood .30 .75
27 Danny Ozark MG .30 .75
28 Billy DeMars CO .30 .75
Ray Ripplemeyer CO
Bobby Wine CO
Carroll Beringer CO

1976 Phillies Postcards

This 31-card set of the Philadelphia Phillies features player photos on postcard-size cards. The cards are unnumbered and checklisted below in alphabetical order.

COMPLETE SET (31) 10.00 25.00
1 Dick Allen .60 1.50
2 Carroll Beringer CO .20 .50
3 Bob Boone .60 1.50
4 Larry Bowa .20 .50
5 Ollie Brown .20 .50
6 Steve Carlton 1.25 3.00
7 Dave Cash .20 .50
8 Larry Christenson .20 .50
9 Billy DeMars CO .20 .50
10 Gene Garber .30 .75
11 Terry Harmon .20 .50
12 Tommy Hutton .20 .50
13 Jay Johnstone .40 1.00
14 Jim Kaat .40 1.00
15 Jim Lonborg .30 .75
16 Greg Luzinski .40 1.00
17 Garry Maddox .20 .50
18 Jerry Martin .20 .50
19 Tim McCarver .60 1.50
20 Tug McGraw .40 1.00
21 Johnny Oates .20 .50
22 Danny Ozark CO .20 .50
23 Ron Reed .20 .50
24 Ray Ripplemeyer CO .20 .50
25 Mike Schmidt 2.00 5.00
26 Ron Schueler .20 .50
27 Tony Taylor .30 .75
28 Bobby Tolan .20 .50
29 Wayne Twitchell .20 .50
30 Tom Underwood .20 .50
31 Bobby Wine .20 .50

1979 Phillies Burger King

The cards in this 23-card set measure 2 1/2" by 3 1/2". The 1979 Burger King Phillies set follows the regular format of 22 player cards and one unnumbered checklist card. The asterisk indicates where the pose differs from the Topps card of that year. The set features the first card of Pete Rose as a member of the Philadelphia Phillies.

COMPLETE SET (23) 4.00 10.00
1 Danny Ozark MG * .08 .20
2 Bob Boone .20 .50
3 Tim McCarver .20 .50
4 Steve Carlton 1.00 2.50
5 Larry Christenson .08 .20
6 Dick Ruthven .08 .20
7 Ron Reed .08 .20
8 Randy Lerch .08 .20
9 Warren Brusstar .08 .20
10 Tug McGraw .12 .30
11 Nino Espinosa * .08 .20
12 Doug Bird * .08 .20
13 Pete Rose */(Shown as Reds in 1979 Topps) 1.50 4.00
14 Manny Trillo * .08 .20
15 Larry Bowa .12 .30
16 Mike Schmidt 1.50 4.00
17 Pete Mackanin * .08 .20
18 Jose Cardenal .08 .20
19 Greg Luzinski .12 .30
20 Garry Maddox .08 .20
21 Bake McBride .08 .20
22 Greg Gross * .08 .20
NNO Checklist Card TP .08 .20

1979 Phillies Postcards

These attractive postcards were issued in black and white and many of them featured facsmile autographs. Since the cards are unnumbered, we have sequenced them in alphabetical order.

COMPLETE SET 12.50 30.00
1 Ramon Aviles .20 .50
2 Doug Bird .20 .50
3 Bob Boone .40 1.00
4 Larry Bowa .60 1.50
5 Warren Brusstar .20 .50
6 Jose Cardenal .20 .50
7 Steve Carlton 1.25 3.00
8 Larry Christenson .20 .50
9 Rawly Eastwick .20 .50
10 Nino Espinosa .20 .50
11 Greg Gross .20 .50
12 Bud Harrelson .20 .50
13 Jim Kaat .60 1.50
14 Randy Lerch .20 .50
15 Jim Lonborg .30 .75
16 Greg Luzinski .40 1.00
17 Pete Mackanin .20 .50
18 Garry Maddox .20 .50
19 Rudy Meoli .20 .50
20 Bake McBride .20 .50
21 Tim McCarver .30 .75
22 Tug McGraw .30 .75
23 Dickie Noles .20 .50
24 Danny Ozark MG .20 .50
25 Dave Rader .20 .50
26 Ron Reed .20 .50
27 Pete Rose 2.00 5.00
28 Dick Ruthven .20 .50
29 Kevin Saucier .20 .50
30 Mike Schmidt 2.00 5.00
31 Lonnie Smith .20 .50
32 Tony Taylor CO .20 .50
33 Bob Tiefenauer CO .20 .50
34 Manny Trillo .30 .75
Batting
35 Manny Trillo .30 .75
Portrait
36 Del Unser .20 .50
37 Bobby Wine CO .20 .50

1979 Phillies Team Issue Drawings

This 10-card set of the Philadelphia Phillies was issued in a clear front envelope and was likely sold at the stadium. The set measures approximately 8 3/4" by 11 5/8" and features art work by Todd Alan Gold. Each card displays two action drawings and a portrait of the same player. The backs are blank. The cards are unnumbered and checklisted below in alphabetical order.

COMPLETE SET (10) 8.00 20.00
1 Rich Ashburn 1.50 4.00
2 Bob Boone 1.25 3.00
3 Larry Bowa .75 2.00
4 Greg Luzinski .75 2.00
5 Garry Maddox .60 1.50
6 Bake McBride .60 1.50
7 Robin Roberts 1.25 3.00
8 Pete Rose 1.50 4.00
9 Mike Schmidt 1.50 4.00
10 Manny Trillo .60 1.50

1980 Phillies Burger King

The cards in this 23-card set measure 2 1/2" by 3 1/2". The 1980 edition of Burger King Phillies follows the established pattern of 22 numbered player cards and one unnumbered checklist. Cards marked with asterisks contain poses different from those found in the regular 1980 Topps cards. This was the first Burger King set to carry the Burger King logo and hence does not generate the same confusion that the three previous years do for collectors trying to distinguish Burger King cards from the very similar Topps cards of the same years.

COMPLETE SET (23) 3.00 8.00
1 Dallas Green MG * .07 .20
2 Bob Boone .10 .30
3 Keith Moreland * .10 .30
4 Pete Rose 1.50 4.00
5 Manny Trillo .07 .20
6 Mike Schmidt 1.50 4.00
7 Larry Bowa .07 .20
8 John Vukovich * .02 .10
9 Bake McBride .02 .10
10 Garry Maddox .07 .20
11 Greg Luzinski .07 .20
12 Greg Gross .02 .10
13 Del Unser .02 .10
14 Lonnie Smith * .07 .20
15 Steve Carlton 1.00 2.50
16 Larry Christenson .02 .10
17 Nino Espinosa .02 .10
18 Randy Lerch .02 .10
19 Dick Ruthven .02 .10
20 Tug McGraw .10 .30
21 Ron Reed .02 .10
22 Kevin Saucier * .02 .10
NNO Checklist Card TP .01 .05

1980 Phillies 1950 TCMA

This 31-card set features black-and-white photos of the 1950 Philadelphia Phillies Baseball team in red borders. The words, "Whiz Kids" are printed in white at the top. The backs carry player information and career statistics. The cards are unnumbered and checklisted below alphabetically.

COMPLETE SET (31) 10.00 25.00
1 Richie Ashburn .40 1.00
2 Benny Bengough CO .20 .50
3 Jimmy Bloodworth .08 .25
4 Hank Borowy .08 .25
5 Putsy Caballero .08 .25
6 Emory Church .08 .25
7 Dusty Cooke .08 .25
8 Blix Donnelly .08 .25
9 Del Ennis .30 .75
10 Mike Goliat .08 .25
11 Granny Hamner .20 .50
12 Ken Heintzleman .08 .25
13 Stan Hollmig .08 .25
14 Ken Johnson .08 .25
15 Willie Jones .20 .50
16 Jim Konstantly .20 .50
17 Stan Lopata .08 .25
18 Jackie Mayo .08 .25
19 Russ Meyer .08 .25
20 Bob Miller .08 .25
21 Bill Nicholson .20 .50
22 Cy Perkins .08 .25
23 Robin Roberts .40 1.00
24 Eddie Sawyer MG .08 .25
25 Andy Seminick .20 .50
26 Ken Silvestri .08 .25
27 Curt Simmons .20 .50
28 Dick Sisler .08 .25
29 Jocko Thompson .08 .25
30 Eddie Waitkus .20 .50
31 Dick Whitman .08 .25

1980 Phillies Postcards

These black and white postcards were issued by the Phillies during their World Championship season. Since the cards are unnumbered we have sequenced them in alphabetical order.

COMPLETE SET 10.00 25.00
1 Ruben Amaro CO .20 .50
2 Luis Aguayo .20 .50
3 Ramon Aviles .20 .50
4 Bob Boone .40 1.00
5 Larry Bowa .60 1.50
6 Warren Brusstar .20 .50
7 Steve Carlton 1.25 3.00

8 Larry Christenson .20 .50
9 Billy DeMars CO .20 .50
10 Lee Elia CO .20 .50
11 Nino Espinosa .20 .50
12 Dallas Green MG .20 .50
13 Greg Gross .20 .50
14 Lerrin LaGrow .20 .50
15 Dan Larson .20 .50
16 Randy Lerch .20 .50
17 Greg Luzinski .40 1.00
18 Bake McBride .30 .75
19 Tug McGraw .40 1.00
20 Keith Moreland .20 .50
21 Scott Munninghoff .20 .50
22 Ron Reed .20 .50
23 Pete Rose 2.00 5.00
24 Dick Ruthven .20 .50
25 Mike Ryan CO .20 .50
26 Kevin Saucier .20 .50
27 Mike Schmidt 2.00 5.00
28 Lonnie Smith .30 .75
29 Herm Starrette CO .20 .50
30 Manny Trillo .30 .75
31 Del Unser .20 .50
32 George Vukovich .20 .50
33 Bob Walk .20 .50
34 Bobby Wine CO .20 .50

1982 Phillies Tastykake

These blank-back postcards, which measure 3 1/4" by 5 1/2" feature members of the 1982 Philadelphia Phillies. There is a "Tastykake" logo on the bottom of the card. Since these cards are unnumbered, we have sequenced them in alphabetical order.

COMPLETE SET (37) 8.00 20.00
1 Luis Aguayo .20 .50
2 Porfirio Altamirano .20 .50
3 Dave Bristol CO .20 .50
4 Warren Brusstar .20 .50
5 Steve Carlton 1.25 3.00
6 Larry Christenson .20 .50
7 Pat Corrales MG .20 .50
8 Dick Davis .20 .50
9 Mark Davis .20 .50
10 Ivan DeJesus .20 .50
11 Bob Dernier .20 .50
12 Bo Diaz .20 .50
Action
13 Bo Diaz .20 .50
Portrait
14 Karen Eberhard .30 .75
Ball Girl
15 Ed Farmer .20 .50
16 Greg Gross .20 .50
17 Deron Johnson CO .20 .50
18 Mike Krukow .20 .50
19 Sparky Lyle .30 .75
20 Garry Maddox .30 .75
21 Gary Matthews .30 .75
22 Len Matusek .20 .50
23 Tug McGraw .40 1.00
24 Sid Monge .20 .50
25 Claude Osteen CO .20 .50
26 Ron Reed .20 .50
27 Dave Roberts .20 .50
28 Pete Rose 1.50 4.00
29 Dick Ruthven .20 .50
30 Mike Ryan .20 .50
31 Mike Schmidt 1.50 4.00
32 Manny Trillo .20 .50
Hat
33 Manny Trillo .20 .50
No Hat
34 Del Unser .20 .50
35 Ossie Virgil Jr .20 .50
36 George Vukovich .20 .50
37 Bobby Wine CO .20 .50

1983 Phillies Postcards Great Moments

On "Nostalgia Nights" during the Philadelphia Phillies 100th Anniversary season, two collectors' art postcards were presented to fans at every Friday night home game. One card commemorated the great Phillies moments and the players involved in these, and the other card honored great Phillies players and managers that were depicted in the Phillies 1983 calendar. The art work on the card front was reproduced from original watercolors by Dick Perez who is the official artist for the National Baseball Hall of Fame in Cooperstown, New York. The backs carry a postcard format. The 13 cards in the Great Moments set along with the 13 cards in the Great Players and Managers set are combined with a checklist card and a title card to make a 28-card set.

COMPLETE SET (14) 15.00 40.00
1 Richie Ashburn 2.00 5.00
2 Dick Sisler .75 2.00
Del Ennis
3 Art Mahaffey .75 2.00
4 Jim Bunning 1.25 3.00
Tony Taylor
5 Mike Schmidt 5.00 12.00
6 Johnny Callison 1.25 3.00
7 Grover Alexander 2.00 5.00
8 Robin Roberts 2.00 5.00
9 Steve Carlton 2.00 5.00
10 Tug McGraw .75 2.00
Del Unser
11 Rick Wise .75 2.00
12 Greg Luzinski .75 2.00
Jim Lonborg
13 Pete Rose 3.00 8.00

1983 Phillies Postcards Great Players and Managers

On "Nostalgia Nights" during the Philadelphia Phillies 100th Anniversary season, two collectors' art postcards were presented to fans at every Friday night home game. One card honored the great Phillies players and managers that were depicted in the Phillies 1983 calendar, and the other card commemorated great Phillies moments and the players involved in these. The art work on the card front is a reproduction fof original watercolors by Dick Perez, the official artist for the National Baseball Hall of Fame in Cooperstown, New York. The backs carry a postcard format. The 13 cards in the Great Players and Managers set along with the 13 cards in the Great Moments set are combined with a checklist card and a title card to make a 28-card set.

COMPLETE SET (14) 15.00 40.00
1 Chuck Klein 1.25 3.00
Johnny Callison
Cy Williams
2 Robin Roberts 4.00 10.00
Steve Carlton
Grover Alexander
3 Bob Boone .75 2.00
Stan Lopata
Andy Seminick
Bo Diaz
4 Ruben Amaro .75 2.00
Larry Bowa
Granny Hamner
Bobby Wine
5 Ed Delahanty 1.50 4.00
Gavvy Cravath
Sherry Magee
6 Gary Matthews 1.25 3.00
Greg Luzinski
Del Ennis
7 Eddie Waitkus 2.00 5.00
Pete Rose
Dick Allen
8 Tony Taylor .75 2.00
Manny Trillo
Cookie Rojas
9 Chris Short 1.25 3.00
Curt Simmons
Jim Bunning
10 Willie Jones 4.00 10.00
Mike Schmidt
Pinky Whitney
11 Eddie Sawyer .75 2.00
Pat Moran
Harry Wright
Dallas Gre
12 Tony Gonzalez 1.50 4.00
Richie Ashburn
Garry Maddox
13 Ron Reed 1.25 3.00
Jim Konstanty
Tug McGraw
14 Checklist .75 2.00

1983 Phillies Tastykake

This 31-card set features the Philadelphia Phillies and was sponosred by Tastykake. The cards measure 3 1/2" by 5 1/4" and are printed on thin card stock. Inside white borders, the fronts display posed color headshots with a blue studio background. The backs carry a short letter or slogan from the player and his facsimile autograph. The cards are unnumbered and checklisted below in alphabetical order.

COMPLETE SET (31) 6.00 15.00
1 Luis Aguayo .08 .25
2 Joe Amalfitano CO .08 .25
3 Marty Bystrom .08 .25
4 Steve Carlton 1.00 2.50
5 Larry Christenson .08 .25
6 Pat Corrales MG .08 .25
7 Ivan DeJesus .08 .25
8 John Denny .20 .50
9 Bob Dernier .08 .25
10 Bo Diaz .08 .25
11 Ed Farmer .08 .25
12 Greg Gross .08 .25
13 Von Hayes .08 .25
14 Al Holland .08 .25
15 Garry Maddox .20 .50
16 Gary Matthews .20 .50
17 Tug McGraw .30 .75
18 Larry Milbourne .08 .25
19 Bob Molinaro .08 .25
20 Sid Monge .08 .25
21 Joe Morgan .75 2.00
22 Tony Perez .40 1.00
23 Ron Reed .08 .25
24 Bill Robinson .08 .25
25 Pete Rose 1.50 4.00
26 Dick Ruthven .08 .25
27 Mike Schmidt 1.50 4.00
28 Ozzie Virgil .08 .25
29 Coaches .08 .25
30 Philly Phanatic .30 .75
Mascot
31 Veterans Stadium .08 .25

1984 Phillies Tastykake

This set features the Philadelphia Phillies and was sponsored by Tastykake. The card fronts feature a colorful picture of the player or subject inside a white border. The cards measure approximately 3 1/2" by 5 1/4". The set was distributed to fans attending a specific game. There were four additional cards which were put out late in the year updating new players (after the first 40 had been out for some time). The update cards are numbered 41-44 after the first group. The card backs contain a brief message (tip) from the player with his facsimile autograph. The cards are unnumbered but the title card gives a numbering system essentially alphabetically within position; that system is used below for the first 40 cards.

COMPLETE SET (44) 6.00 15.00
COMMON CARD (1-40) .10 .25
COMMON CARD (41-44) .30 .75
1 Logo Card .08 .25
Checklist
2 Team Photo .20 .50
3 Phillie Phanatic/(Mascot) .30 .75
4 Veterans Stadium .08 .25
5 Steve Carlton .75 2.00
Hall of Fame
6 Mike Schmidt 1.25 3.00
Hall of Fame
7 Phillies Broadcasters .20 .50
8 Paul Owens MG .08 .25
9 Dave Bristol CO .08 .25
10 John Felske CO .08 .25
11 Deron Johnson CO .08 .25
12 Claude Osteen CO .08 .25
13 Mike Ryan CO .08 .25
14 Larry Andersen .08 .25
15 Marty Bystrom .08 .25
16 Bill Campbell .08 .25
17 Steve Carlton .75 2.00
18 John Denny .20 .50
19 Tony Ghelfi .08 .25
20 Kevin Gross .20 .50
21 Al Holland .08 .25
22 Charles Hudson .08 .25
23 Jerry Koosman .30 .75
24 Tug McGraw .40 1.00
25 Bo Diaz .08 .25
26 Ozzie Virgil .08 .25
27 John Wockenfuss .08 .25
28 Luis Aguayo .08 .25
29 Ivan DeJesus .08 .25
30 Kiko Garcia .08 .25
31 Len Matuszek .08 .25
32 Juan Samuel .40 1.00
33 Mike Schmidt 1.25 3.00
34 Tim Corcoran .08 .25
35 Greg Gross .08 .25
36 Von Hayes .20 .50
37 Joe Lefebvre .08 .25
38 Sixto Lezcano .08 .25
39 Garry Maddox .20 .50
40 Glenn Wilson .08 .25
41 Don Carman .30 .75
42 John Russell .30 .75
43 Jeff Stone .30 .75
44 Dave Wehrmeister .30 .75

1985 Phillies CIGNA

This colorful 16-card set (measuring approximately 2 5/8" by 4 1/8") features the Philadelphia Phillies and was also sponsored by CIGNA Corporation. Cards are numbered on the back and contain a safety tip as such the set is frequently categorized and referenced as a safety set. Cards are also numbered by uniform number on the front.

COMPLETE SET (16) 3.00 8.00
1 Juan Samuel .20 .50
2 Von Hayes .20 .50
3 Ozzie Virgil .08 .25
4 Mike Schmidt 1.50 4.00
5 Greg Gross .08 .25
6 Tim Corcoran .08 .25
7 Jerry Koosman .20 .50
8 Jeff Stone .08 .25
9 Glenn Wilson .08 .25
10 Steve Jeltz .08 .25
11 Garry Maddox .20 .50
12 Steve Carlton .75 2.00
13 John Denny .20 .50
14 Kevin Gross .08 .25
15 Shane Rawley .08 .25
16 Charlie Hudson .08 .25

1985 Phillies Tastykake

The 1985 Tastykake Philadelphia Phillies set consists of 47 cards, each measuring approximately 3 1/2" by 5 1/4". They feature a color photo of the player framed against white borders. The group shots of the various parts of the teams were posed after the other cards were issued so there are stylistic differences between the group shots and the individual shots. The backs feature brief biographies of the players. The cards are arranged below by position and in alphabetical order within these positions. The set features an early card of Darren Daulton.

COMPLETE SET (47) 6.00 15.00
1 Checklist Card .20 .50
2 John Felske MG .08 .25
3 Dave Bristol CO .08 .25
4 Lee Elia CO .08 .25
5 Claude Osteen CO .08 .25
6 Mike Ryan CO .08 .25
7 Del Unser CO .08 .25
8 John Felske MG and .08 .25
Del Unser CO
Dave Bristol CO#
9 Pitching Staff .30 .75
Zachry& Andersen&
Hudson& Rawley&
10 Catchers .60 1.50
Darren Daulton&
Bo Diaz&
Ozzie Virgil
11 Infielders .40 1.00
Schmidt& Jeltz&
Ivan DeJesus& Samuel&
12 Outfielders .08 .25
Corcoran& Gross&
Hayes& Lefebvre&
S
13 Larry Andersen .08 .25
14 Steve Carlton .75 2.00
15 Don Carman .08 .25
16 John Denny .20 .50
17 Tony Ghelfi .08 .25
18 Kevin Gross .08 .25
19 Al Holland .08 .25
20 Charles Hudson .08 .25
21 Jerry Koosman .20 .50
22 Shane Rawley .08 .25
23 Pat Zachry .08 .25
24 Darren Daulton 1.00 2.50
25 Bo Diaz .08 .25
26 Ozzie Virgil .08 .25
27 John Wockenfuss .08 .25
28 Luis Aguayo .08 .25
29 Kiko Garcia .08 .25
30 Steve Jeltz .08 .25
31 John Russell .08 .25
32 Juan Samuel .20 .50
33 Mike Schmidt 1.25 3.00
34 Tim Corcoran .08 .25
35 Greg Gross .08 .25
36 Von Hayes .20 .50
37 Joe Lefebvre .08 .25
38 Garry Maddox .20 .50
39 Jeff Stone .08 .25
40 Glenn Wilson .08 .25
41 Ramon Caraballo .08 .25
and Mike Diaz
42 Mike Maddux .08 .25
and Rodger Cole
43 Rick Schu and .20 .50
Chris James
44 Francisco Melendez .08 .25
and Ken Jackson
45 Randy Salava and .08 .25
Rocky Childress
46 Rich Surhoff and .08 .25
Ralph Citarella
47 Team Photo .20 .50

1986 Phillies CIGNA

This 16-card set was sponsored by CIGNA Corp. and was given away by the Philadelphia area Fire Departments. Cards measure approximately 2 3/4" by 4 1/8" and feature full color fronts. The card backs are printed in maroon and black on white card stock. Although the uniform numbers are given on the front of the card, the cards are numbered on the back in the order listed below.

COMPLETE SET (16) 3.00 8.00
1 Juan Samuel .20 .50
2 Don Carman .08 .25
3 Von Hayes .20 .50
4 Kent Tekulve .20 .50
5 Greg Gross .08 .25
6 Shane Rawley .08 .25
7 Darren Daulton .75 2.00
8 Kevin Gross .08 .25
9 Steve Jeltz .08 .25
10 Mike Schmidt 1.50 4.00
11 Steve Bedrosian .20 .50
12 Gary Redus .08 .25
13 Charles Hudson .08 .25
14 John Russell .08 .25
15 Fred Toliver .08 .25
16 Glenn Wilson .08 .25

1986 Phillies Greats TCMA

This 12-card standard-size set features some all-time great Phillies. The fronts feature a player photo, his name and position. The backs have vital statistics, a biography and career totals.

COMPLETE SET (12) 1.50 4.00
1 Chuck Klein .30 .75
2 Richie Ashburn .40 1.00
3 Del Ennis .20 .50
4 Spud Davis .08 .25
5 Grover Alexander .40 1.00
6 Chris Short .08 .25
7 Jim Konstanty .08 .25
8 Danny Ozark MG .08 .25
9 Larry Bowa .08 .25
10 Richie Allen .20 .50
11 Don Hurst .08 .25
12 Tony Taylor .08 .25

1986 Phillies Keller's

These cards were printed crudely on the boxes of one-pound packages of butter made by Keller's. The cards are approximately 2 1/2" by 2 3/4" and are very similar to the Meadow Gold cards. The same art was used on the Schmidt card which is in both sets. Both Keller's and Meadow Gold are subsidiaries of Beatrice Foods. The set was licensed by Mike Schechter Associates and the Major League Baseball Players' Association. The set contains only Philadelphia Phillies players. The cards are blank backed and are printed in red, dark blue and yellow on white waxed cardboard. Complete boxes would bring double the values listed below. Since the cards are unnumbered they are listed below in alphabetical order.

COMPLETE SET (6) 5.00 12.00
1 Steve Carlton 1.50 4.00
2 Von Hayes .30 .75
3 Gary Redus .30 .75
4 Juan Samuel .40 1.00
5 Mike Schmidt 2.50 6.00
6 Glenn Wilson .30 .75

1986 Phillies Tastykake

The 1986 Tastykake Philadelphia Phillies set consists of 47 cards, which measure approximately 3 1/2" by 5 1/4". This set features members of the 1986 Philadelphia Phillies. The front of the cards features a full-color photo of the player against white borders while the back has brief biographies. The set has been checklisted for reference below in order by uniform number.

COMPLETE SET (47) 5.00 12.00
2 Jim Davenport CO .08 .25
3 Claude Osteen CO .08 .25
4 Lee Elia CO .08 .25
5 Mike Ryan CO .08 .25
6 John Russell .08 .25
7 John Felske MG .08 .25
8 Juan Samuel .20 .50
9 Von Hayes .08 .25
10 Darren Daulton .75 2.00
11 Tom Foley .08 .25
12 Glenn Wilson .08 .25
14 Jeff Stone .08 .25
15 Rick Schu .08 .25
16 Luis Aguayo .08 .25
20 Mike Schmidt 1.25 3.00
21 Greg Gross .08 .25
22 Gary Redus .08 .25
23 Joe Lefebvre .08 .25
24 Milt Thompson .08 .25
25 Del Unser CO .08 .25
26 Chris James .08 .25
27 Kent Tekulve .20 .50
28 Shane Rawley .08 .25
29 Ronn Reynolds .08 .25
30 Steve Jeltz .08 .25
31 Garry Maddox .20 .50
32 Steve Carlton .75 2.00
33 David Shipanoff .08 .25
35 Randy Lerch .08 .25
36 Robin Roberts .40 1.00
39 Dave Rucker .08 .25
40 Steve Bedrosian .20 .50
41 Tom Hume .08 .25
42 Don Carman .08 .25
43 Fred Toliver .08 .25
46 Kevin Gross .08 .25
47 Larry Andersen .08 .25
48 Dave Stewart .30 .75
49 Charles Hudson .08 .25
50 Rocky Childress .08 .25
NNO Future Phillies .08 .25
Ramon Caraballo
Joe Cipolloni
NNO Future Phillies .08 .25
Arturo Gonzalez
Mike Maddux
NNO Future Phillies .20 .50
Francisco Melendez
Ricky Jordan
NNO Future Phillies .08 .25
Kevin Ward
Randy Day
NNO Night to Remember
26-7& June 11& 1985 .20 .50
NNO Pennant Winning Team
1915 Phillies .20 .50
NNO Pennant Winning Team
1950 Phillies .20 .50
NNO Pennant Winning Team
1980 Phillies .20 .50
NNO Pennant Winning Team
1983 Phillies .20 .50

1987 Phillies 1950 TCMA

This nine-card standard-size set honors members of the "Whiz Kids" who won the 1950 National League Pennant. The fronts feature player photos, identification and position. The backs carry some biographical information as well as the 1950 stats.

COMPLETE SET (9) 1.50 4.00
1 Eddie Sawyer MG .08 .25
2 Curt Simmons .20 .50
3 Jim Konstanty .20 .50
4 Eddie Waitkus .08 .25
5 Granny Hamner .08 .25
6 Del Ennis .20 .50
7 Richie Ashburn .40 1.00
8 Dick Sisler .08 .25
9 Robin Roberts .40 1.00

1987 Phillies Champion

This four-card set which measures approximately 3" by 4 3/4" (with scratch-off tab) is unusual in that there is no way to determine the player's identity other than knowing and recognizing whose photo it is. The top part of the card has a color photo of the player surrounded in the upper left hand corner with a Champion spark plug logo. The Philadelphia Phillies logo is in the upper right hand part of the card. A Pep Boys ad is in the lower left hand corner of the photo and the WIP Philadelphia Sports Radio promo is in the lower right hand corner of the photo. The set is checklisted alphabetically by subject since the cards are unnumbered.

COMPLETE SET (4) 8.00 20.00
1 Von Hayes .60 1.50
2 Steve Jeltz .60 1.50
3 Juan Samuel .75 2.00
4 Mike Schmidt 6.00 15.00

1987 Phillies Tastykake

The 1987 Tastykake Philadelphia Phillies set consists of 47 cards which measure approximately 3 1/2" by 5 1/4". The sets again feature full-color photos against a solid white background. There were two number 39s in this set as the Phillies changed personnel during the season, Joe Cowley and Bob Scanlan. For convenience uniform numbers are used below as a basis for numbering and checklisting this set.

COMPLETE SET (47) 5.00 12.00
6 John Russell .08 .25
7 John Felske MG .08 .25
8 Juan Samuel .20 .50
9 Von Hayes .08 .25
10 Darren Daulton .40 1.00
11 Greg Legg .08 .25
12 Glenn Wilson .08 .25
13 Lance Parrish .30 .75
14 Jeff Stone .08 .25
15 Rick Schu .08 .25
16 Luis Aguayo .08 .25
17 Ron Roenicke .08 .25
18 Chris James .08 .25
20 Mike Schmidt 1.50 4.00
21 Greg Gross .08 .25
23 Joe Cipolloni .08 .25
24 Milt Thompson .08 .25
27 Kent Tekulve .20 .50
28 Shane Rawley .08 .25
29 Ronn Reynolds .08 .25
30 Steve Jeltz .08 .25
33 Mike Jackson .40 1.00
34 Mike Easler .08 .25
35 Dan Schatzeder .08 .25
37 Ken Howell .08 .25
38 Jim Olander .08 .25
39A Joe Cowley .08 .25
39B Bob Scanlan .08 .25
40 Steve Bedrosian .20 .50
41 Tom Hume .08 .25
42 Don Carman .08 .25
43 Freddie Toliver .08 .25
44 Mike Maddux .08 .25
45 Greg Jelks .08 .25
46 Kevin Gross .08 .25
47 Bruce Ruffin .08 .25
48 Marvin Freeman .08 .25
49 Len Watts .08 .25
50 Tom Newell .08 .25
51 Ken Jackson .08 .25
52 Todd Frohwirth .08 .25
58 Doug Bair .08 .25
xx Phillie Phanatic/(Mascot) .30 .75
xx Team Photo .20 .50
xx Shawn Barton .08 .25
and Rick Lundblade
xx Jeff Kaye .08 .25
and Darren Loy
xx0 Coaches Card .08 .25
Claude Osteen CO
Del Unser CO
Jim

1988 Phillies Tastykake

The 1988 Tastykake Philadelphia Phillies set is a 30-card set measuring approximately 4 7/8" by 6 1/4". This set is listed below alphabetically by player. The cards have a full-color photo front and complete player history on the back. There was also a nine-card update set issued later in the year which included a Ricky Jordan card; the update cards are numbered as 31-39 and are blank backed.

COMPLETE SET (39) 4.00 10.00
COMMON CARD (1-30) .10 .25
COMMON CARD (31-39) .12 .30
1 Luis Aguayo .08 .25
2 Bill Almon .08 .25
3 Steve Bedrosian .20 .50
4 Phil Bradley .08 .25
5 Jeff Calhoun .08 .25
6 Don Carman .08 .25
7 Darren Daulton .40 1.00
8 Bob Dernier .08 .25
9A Lee Elia MG/(Vertical format) .20 .50
9B Lee Elia MG/(Horizontal format) .20 .50
10 Todd Frohwirth .08 .25
11 Greg Gross .08 .25
12 Kevin Gross .08 .25
13 Von Hayes .20 .50
14 Chris James .08 .25
15 Steve Jeltz .08 .25
16 Mike Maddux .08 .25
17 Dave Palmer .08 .25
18 Lance Parrish .20 .50
19 Shane Rawley .08 .25
20 Wally Ritchie .08 .25
21 Bruce Ruffin .08 .25
22 Juan Samuel .20 .50
23 Mike Schmidt .75 2.00
24 Kent Tekulve .20 .50
25 Milt Thompson .08 .25
26 Mike Young .08 .25
27 Phillies Prospects .08 .25
Tom Barrett
Brad Brink
Steve
28 Team Card .20 .50
29 Phillies Coaches .08 .25
Claude Osteen
Del Unser
John V
30 Phillie Phanatic/(Mascot) .20 .50
31 Larry Bowa CO .15 .40
32 Lee Elia CO .10 .30
33 Jackie Gutierrez .10 .30
34 Greg A. Harris .10 .30
35 Ricky Jordan .10 .30
36 Keith Miller .10 .30
37 John Russell .10 .30
38 John Vukovich CO .10 .30
39 Phillies Announcers .25 .60
Garry Maddox
Richie Ashburn#

1988 Phillies Topps Ashburn Sheet

This 13-card set was issued on one perforated sheet measuring approximately 10" by 14" commemorating Richie Ashburn's 40 years in baseball. Sponsored by Campbell's, the sheet features 12 smaller versions of different Topps cards printed on a sky-blue and flag background with a bigger 5" by 7" portrait card in the middle. The back of this card displayed his complete Major League batting record and accomplishments. The cards are listed below according to the year they appeared in the Topps sets.

COMPLETE SET (13) 4.00 10.00
COMMON CARD (1-13) .40 1.00
13 Richie Ashburn/1988 Richie Ashburn .60 1.50

1989 Phillies Tastykake

This set was a 36-card set of Philadelphia Phillies measuring approximately 4 1/8" by 6" featuring full-color fronts with complete biographical information and career stats on the back. The set is checklisted alphabetically in the list below. The set was a give away to fans attending the Phillies Tastykake Photocard Night on May 13, 1989 and was later available from a mail-away offer. There was also a nine-player extended set issued later during the 1989 season; the extended players are numbered below in alphabetical order, numbers 37-45. Chris James' card lists him as uniform number 26, but his number is 18, while 26 was Ron Jones' number.

COMPLETE SET (45) 4.00 10.00
COMMON CARD (1-36) .10 .25
COMMON CARD (37-45) .20 .50
1 Steve Bedrosian .20 .50
2 Larry Bowa CO .20 .50
3 Don Carman .08 .25
4 Darren Daulton .40 1.00
5 Bob Dernier .08 .25
6 Curt Ford .08 .25
7 Todd Frohwirth .08 .25
8 Greg A. Harris .08 .25
9 Von Hayes .08 .25
10 Tom Herr .08 .25
11 Ken Howell .08 .25
12 Chris James UER/(Wrong uniform .08 .25
number on card)
13 Steve Jeltz .08 .25
14 Ron Jones .08 .25
15 Ricky Jordan .08 .25
16 Darold Knowles CO .08 .25
17 Steve Lake .08 .25
18 Nick Levya MG .08 .25
19 Mike Maddux .08 .25
20 Alex Madrid .08 .25
21 Larry McWilliams .08 .25
22 Denis Menke CO .08 .25
23 Dwayne Murphy .08 .25
24 Tom Nieto .08 .25
25 Randy O'Neal .08 .25
26 Steve Ontiveros .08 .25
27 Jeff Parrett .08 .25
28 Bruce Ruffin .08 .25
29 Mark Ryal .08 .25
30 Mike Ryan CO .08 .25
31 Juan Samuel .20 .50
32 Mike Schmidt 1.00 2.50
33 Tony Taylor CO .08 .25
34 Dickie Thon .08 .25
35 John Vukovich CO .08 .25
36 Floyd Youmans .08 .25
37 Jim Adduci .20 .50
38 Eric Bullock .20 .50
39 Dennis Cook .20 .50
40 Len Dykstra .60 1.50
41 Charlie Hayes .30 .75
42 John Kruk .40 1.00
43 Roger McDowell .30 .75
44 Terry Mulholland .30 .75
45 Randy Ready .20 .50

1990 Phillies Tastykake

The 1990 Tastykake Philadelphia Phillies set is a 36-card set measuring approximately 4 1/8" by 6" which features players, coaches and manager, four players who have had their uniform numbers retired, broadcasters, and even the Phillies Mascot. The set is checklisted alphabetically, with complete biography and complete stats on the back.

COMPLETE SET (36) 4.00 10.00
1 Darrel Akerfelds .08 .25
2 Rod Booker .08 .25
3 Sil Campusano .08 .25
4 Don Carman .08 .25
5 Pat Combs .08 .25
6 Dennis Cook .08 .25
7 Darren Daulton .40 1.00
8 Len Dykstra .40 1.00
9 Curt Ford .08 .25
10 Jason Grimsley .08 .25
11 Charlie Hayes .08 .25
12 Von Hayes .08 .25
13 Tommy Herr .08 .25
14 Dave Hollins .20 .50
15 Ken Howell .08 .25
16 Ron Jones .08 .25
17 Ricky Jordan .08 .25
18 John Kruk .30 .75
19 Steve Lake .08 .25
20 Nick Levya MG .08 .25
21 Carmelo Martinez .08 .25
22 Roger McDowell .08 .25
23 Chuck McElroy .08 .25
24 Terry Mulholland .08 .25
25 Jeff Parrett .08 .25
26 Randy Ready .08 .25
27 Bruce Ruffin .08 .25
28 Dickie Thon .08 .25
29 Richie Ashburn .40 1.00
30 Steve Carlton .40 1.00
31 Robin Roberts .40 1.00
32 Mike Schmidt .75 2.00
33 Phillie Phanatic/(Mascot) .30 .75
34 Phillie Coaches .08 .25
Denis Menke
Mike Ryan
John Vuko
35 Phillies Broadcasters .20 .50
Chris Wheeler
Andy Musser#
36 Phillies Broadcasters .30 .75
Mike Schmidt
Jim Barniak/

1991 Phillies Medford

This 35-card set was sponsored by Medford (rather than by Tastykake as in past years), and its company logo is found on the bottom of the reverse. The oversized cards measure approximately 4 1/8" by 6" and feature borderless glossy color action player photos on the obverse. The player's name is given in a red bar at either the top or bottom of the picture. The backs are printed in red and black on white and present biographical as well as statistical information. The cards are unnumbered and checklisted below in alphabetical order.

COMPLETE SET (35) 3.00 8.00
1 Darrel Akerfelds .02 .10
2 Andy Ashby .08 .25
3 Wally Backman .02 .10
4 Joe Boever .02 .10
5 Rod Booker .02 .10
6 Larry Bowa CO .08 .25
7 Sil Campusano .02 .10
8 Wes Chamberlain .02 .10
9 Pat Combs .02 .10
10 Danny Cox .02 .10
11 Darren Daulton .30 .75
12 Jose DeJesus .02 .10
13 Len Dykstra .20 .50
14 Darrin Fletcher .02 .10
15 Tommy Greene .02 .10
16 Jason Grimsley .02 .10
17 Charlie Hayes .02 .10
18 Von Hayes .02 .10
19 Dave Hollins .02 .10
20 Ken Howell .02 .10
21 Ricky Jordan .02 .10
22 John Kruk .20 .50
23 Steve Lake .02 .10
24 Hal Lanier CO .02 .10
25 Tim Mauser .02 .10
26 Roger McDowell .02 .10
27 Denis Menke CO .02 .10
28 Mickey Morandini .08 .25
29 John Morris .02 .10
30 Terry Mulholland .02 .10
31 Dale Murphy .30 .75
32 Johnny Podres CO .08 .25
33 Randy Ready .02 .10
34 Dickie Thon .02 .10
35 John Vukovich CO .02 .10

1992 Phillies Medford

For the second consecutive year, Medford has sponsored a Phillies set, consisting of a first series of 36 cards measuring approximately 4 1/8" by 6" and an extended update series of another ten cards of the same size. The players featured in the update series were mostly mid-season call-ups from the minor leagues. The cards are unnumbered and checklisted

below alphabetically within series, with the nonplayer cards listed at the end.
COMPLETE SET (46) 5.00 12.00
COMMON CARD (1-36) .10 .25
COMMON CARD (37-46) .20 .50
1 Kyle Abbott .08 .25
2 Ruben Amaro .08 .25
3 Andy Ashby .08 .25
4 Wally Backman .08 .25
5 Kim Batiste .08 .25
6 Larry Bowa CO .20 .50
7 Cliff Brantley .08 .25
8 Wes Chamberlain .08 .25
9 Danny Cox .08 .25
10 Darren Daulton .40 1.00
11 Mariano Duncan .08 .25
12 Len Dykstra .40 1.00
13 Jim Fregosi MG .20 .50
14 Tommy Greene .08 .25
15 Dave Hollins .08 .25
16 Barry Jones .08 .25
17 John Kruk .30 .75
18 Steve Lake .08 .25
19 Jim Lindeman .08 .25
20 Denis Menke CO .08 .25
21 Mickey Morandini .20 .50
22 Terry Mulholland .08 .25
23 Dale Murphy .40 1.00
24 Johnny Podres CO .20 .50
25 Wally Ritchie .08 .25
26 Mel Roberts CO .08 .25
27 Mike Ryan CO .08 .25
28 Curt Schilling 1.25 3.00
29 Steve Searcy .08 .25
30 Dale Sveum .08 .25
31 John Vukovich .08 .25
Dugout Assistant
32 Mitch Williams .20 .50
33 Phillie Phanatic/(Mascot) .30 .75
34 Team Photo .20 .50
35 Veterans Stadium .08 .25
36 Uniforms Through .20 .50
The Years
37 Bob Ayrault .20 .50
38 Brad Brink .20 .50
39 Pat Combs .20 .50
40 Jeff Grotewold .20 .50
41 Mike Hartley .20 .50
42 Ricky Jordan .20 .50
43 Tom Marsh .20 .50
44 Terry Mulholland .20 .50
45 Ben Rivera .20 .50
46 Don Robinson .20 .50

1993 Phillies Medford

This 35-card set was sponsored by Medford, and its company logo is found on the bottom of the reverse. The oversized cards measure approximately 4 1/8" by 6" and feature borderless glossy color player action photos on their fronts. The cards are unnumbered and checklisted below in alphabetical order.

COMPLETE SET (35) 3.00 8.00
1 Kyle Abbott .08 .25
2 Ruben Amaro .08 .25
3 Larry Andersen .08 .25
4 Bob Ayrault .08 .25
5 Kim Batiste .08 .25
6 Juan Bell .08 .25
7 Larry Bowa CO .20 .50
8 Wes Chamberlain .08 .25
9 Darren Daulton .40 1.00
10 Jose DeLeon .08 .25
11 Mariano Duncan .08 .25
12 Len Dykstra .40 1.00
13 Jim Eisenreich .30 .75
14 Jim Fregosi MG .20 .50
15 Tyler Green .08 .25
16 Tommy Greene .08 .25
17 Dave Hollins .08 .25
18 Pete Incaviglia .20 .50
19 Danny Jackson .08 .25
20 Ricky Jordan .08 .25
21 John Kruk .30 .75
22 Denis Menke CO .08 .25
23 Mickey Morandini .08 .25
24 Terry Mulholland .08 .25
25 Phillie Phanatic/(Mascot) .20 .50
26 Johnny Podres CO .20 .50
27 Todd Pratt .08 .25
28 Ben Rivera .08 .25
29 Mel Roberts CO .08 .25
30 Mike Ryan CO .08 .25
31 Curt Schilling 1.00 2.50
32 Milt Thompson .08 .25
33 John Vukovich CO .08 .25
34 David West .08 .25
35 Mitch Williams .20 .50

1993 Phillies Stadium Club

This 30-card standard-size set features the 1993 Philadelphia Phillies. The set was issued in hobby (plastic box) and retail (blister) form.

COMP. FACT SET (30) 1.50 4.00
1 Darren Daulton .08 .25
2 Larry Andersen .02 .10
3 Kyle Abbott .02 .10
4 Chad McConnell .02 .10
5 Danny Jackson .02 .10
6 Kevin Stocker .02 .10
7 Jim Eisenreich .08 .25
8 Mickey Morandini .02 .10
9 Bob Ayrault .02 .10
10 Doug Lindsey .02 .10
11 Dave Hollins .02 .10
12 Dave West .02 .10
13 Wes Chamberlain .02 .10
14 Curt Schilling .60 1.50
15 Len Dykstra .08 .25
16 Trevor Humphry .02 .10
17 Terry Mulholland .04 .10
18 Gene Schall .02 .10
19 Mike Lieberthal .20 .50
20 Ben Rivera .02 .10
21 Mariano Duncan .02 .10
22 Pete Incaviglia .02 .10
23 Ron Blazier .02 .10
24 Jeff Jackson .02 .10
25 Jose DeLeon .02 .10
26 Ron Lockett .02 .10
27 Tommy Greene .02 .10
28 Milt Thompson .02 .10
29 Mitch Williams .08 .25
30 John Kruk .08 .25

1994 Phillies Medford

These 36 cards measure approximately 4" by 6" and feature borderless color player photos on their fronts. The player's name appears in white lettering within a red bar on the card face. The white back carries the player's uniform number, name, position, biography, and statistics in red and black lettering. The Phillies logo at the upper right rounds out the card. The cards are unnumbered and checklisted below in alphabetical order.

COMPLETE SET (36) 4.00 10.00
1 Larry Andersen .08 .25
2 Kim Batiste .08 .25
3 Larry Bowa CO .20 .50
4 Wes Chamberlain .08 .25
5 Norm Charlton .08 .25
6 Darren Daulton .40 1.00
7 Mariano Duncan .08 .25
8 Lenny Dykstra .30 .75
9 Jim Eisenreich .20 .50
10 Jim Fregosi MG .08 .25
11 Tyler Green .08 .25
12 Tommy Greene .08 .25
13 Dave Hollins .20 .50
14 Pete Incaviglia .20 .50
15 Danny Jackson .08 .25
16 Doug Jones .20 .50
17 Ricky Jordan .08 .25
18 Jeff Juden .08 .25
19 John Kruk .30 .75
20 Tony Longmire .08 .25
21 Roger Mason .08 .25
22 Denis Menke CO .08 .25
23 Mickey Morandini .20 .50
24 Bobby Munoz .08 .25
25 Johnny Podres CO .20 .50
26 Todd Pratt .08 .25
27 Ben Rivera .08 .25
28 Mel Roberts CO .08 .25
29 Mike Ryan CO .08 .25
30 Curt Schilling 1.00 2.50
31 Heathcliff Slocumb .08 .25
32 Kevin Stocker .08 .25
33 Milt Thompson .08 .25
34 John Vukovich CO .08 .25
35 David West .08 .25
36 Mike Williams .08 .25

1994 Phillies Mellon

The 1994 Phillies Team Photo/Card Pack was sponsored by Mellon PSFS, "The Official Bank of the Phillies." The set consists of three 12 1/2" by 7" sheets and one 12 1/2" by 3" strip all joined together. The first sheet features a team photo. The second and third sheets consist of two row of five cards each, while the third strip presents one row of five cards. The sheets are perforated and the cards measure the standard-size. The cards are unnumbered and checklisted below in alphabetical order.

COMPLETE SET (26) 3.00 8.00
1 Larry Andersen .08 .25
2 Kim Batiste .08 .25
3 Shawn Boskie .08 .25
4 Darren Daulton .40 1.00
5 Mariano Duncan .08 .25
6 Lenny Dykstra .30 .75
7 Jim Eisenreich .20 .50
8 Tommy Greene .08 .25
9 Dave Hollins .08 .25
10 Pete Incaviglia .20 .50
11 Danny Jackson .20 .50
12 Doug Jones .20 .50
13 Ricky Jordan .08 .25
14 John Kruk .30 .75
15 Tony Longmire .08 .25
16 Mickey Morandini .20 .50
17 Bobby Munoz .08 .25
18 Todd Pratt .08 .25
19 Paul Quantrill .08 .25
Billy Hatcher
20 Curt Schilling 1.00 2.50
21 Heathcliff Slocumb .08 .25
22 Kevin Stocker .08 .25
23 Milt Thompson .08 .25
24 David West .08 .25
25 Mike Williams .08 .25
26 Large Team Photo/(12 1/2-in by 7-in) .75 2.00

1994 Phillies U.S. Playing Cards

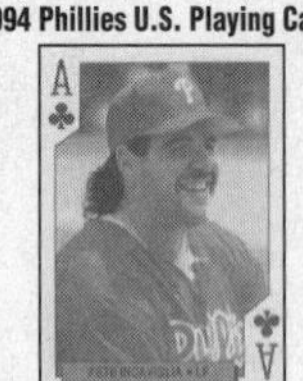

These 56 playing standard-size cards have rounded corners, and feature color posed and action player photos on their white-bordered fronts. The player's name and position appear near the bottom. The blue and gray backs carry the logos for the Phillies, baseball's 125th Anniversary, MLBPA, and Bicycle Sports Collection. The set is checklisted below in playing card order by suits and assigned numbers to aces (1), jacks (11), queens (12), and kings (13).

COMPLETE SET (56) 1.25 3.00
1C Pete Incaviglia .01 .05
1D Terry Mulholland .01 .05
1H Lenny Dykstra .08 .25
1S Dave Hollins .01 .05
2C Lenny Dykstra .08 .25
2D Brad Brink .01 .05
2H Tony Longmire .01 .05
2S Danny Jackson .01 .05
3C Milt Thompson .01 .05
3D Roger Mason .01 .05
3H Kim Batiste .01 .05
3S Todd Pratt .01 .05
4C Mickey Morandini .02 .10
4D Mariano Duncan .01 .05
4H Pete Incaviglia .02 .10
4S David West .01 .05
5C Kevin Stocker .02 .10
5D Danny Jackson .01 .05
5H Ben Rivera .01 .05
5S Lenny Dykstra .08 .25
6C Terry Mulholland .01 .05
6D Jim Eisenreich .02 .10
6H Ricky Jordan .01 .05
6S Wes Chamberlain .01 .05
7C Curt Schilling .40 1.00
7D John Kruk .02 .10
7H Dave Hollins .01 .05
7S Tommy Greene .01 .05
8C Darren Daulton .08 .25
8D David West .01 .05
8H Kevin Foster .01 .05
8S Tony Longmire .01 .05
9C Terry Mulholland .01 .05
9D Todd Pratt .01 .05
9H Kevin Stocker .02 .10
9S Brad Brink .01 .05
10C Roger Mason .01 .05
10D Wes Chamberlain .01 .05
10H Mike Williams .01 .05
10S Ricky Jordan .01 .05
11C Mariano Duncan .01 .05
11D Jim Eisenreich .02 .10
11H Milt Thompson .01 .05
11S Kim Batiste .01 .05
12C Ben Rivera .01 .05
12D Mickey Morandini .01 .05
12H Curt Schilling .40 1.00
12S Tyler Green .01 .05
13C John Kruk .02 .10
13D Tommy Greene .01 .05
13H Darren Daulton .08 .25
13S Jim Eisenreich .02 .10
NNO Featured Players .01 .05

1995 Phillies

This 36-card set measures approximately 4" by 6". The fronts feature borderless color player photos with the player's name printed in white on a red bar. The white backs carry the player's uniform number, name, position, biography, and statistics in red and black lettering with the team logo below. The cards are unnumbered and checklisted below in alphabetical order.

COMPLETE SET (36) 4.00 10.00
1 Kyle Abbott .08 .25
2 Richie Ashburn HOF .40 1.00
3 Toby Borland .08 .25
4 Ricky Bottalico .08 .25
5 Larry Bowa CO .20 .50
6 Norm Charlton .08 .25
7 Darren Daulton .40 1.00
8 Mariano Duncan .08 .25
9 Lenny Dykstra .30 .75
10 Jim Eisenreich .20 .50
11 Jim Fregosi MG .08 .25
12 Dave Gallagher .08 .25
13 Tyler Green .08 .25
14 Gene Harris .08 .25
15 Charlie Hayes .08 .25
16 Dave Hollins .08 .25
17 Gregg Jefferies .08 .25
18 Tony Longmire .08 .25
19 Denis Menke CO .08 .25
20 Michael Mimbs .08 .25
21 Mickey Morandini .08 .25
22 Bobby Munoz .08 .25
23 Johnny Podres CO .20 .50
24 Paul Quantrill .08 .25
25 Randy Ready .08 .25
26 Mel Roberts CO .08 .25
27 Mike Ryan CO .08 .25
28 Curt Schilling .75 2.00
29 Mike Schmidt HOF .40 1.00
30 Heathcliff Slocumb .08 .25
31 Kevin Stocker .08 .25
32 Gary Varsho .08 .25
33 John Vukovich .08 .25
34 Lenny Webster .08 .25
35 David West .08 .25
36 Team Photo .20 .50

1995 Phillies Mellon

This 25-card set of the Phillies measures the standard size and was issued in perforated sheets. The fronts feature color action player photos on white-and-red pinstripe background. The team name appears in a box above the photo with the player's name printed inside a banner on the bottom. The backs carry a short player biography and career records. The team's Silver Season logo and Mellon Bank's logo at the bottom round out the card. The cards are unnumbered and checklisted below in alphabetical order.

COMPLETE SET (25) 2.50 6.00
1 Kyle Abbott .08 .25
2 Toby Borland .08 .25
3 Ricky Bottalico .08 .25
4 Norm Charlton .08 .25
5 Darren Daulton .40 1.00
6 Mariano Duncan .08 .25
7 Lenny Dykstra .30 .75
8 Jim Eisenreich .20 .50
9 Dave Gallagher .08 .25
10 Tyler Green .08 .25
11 Gene Harris .08 .25
12 Charlie Hayes .08 .25
13 Dave Hollins .08 .25
14 Gregg Jefferies .08 .25
15 Tony Longmire .08 .25
16 Michael Mimbs .08 .25
17 Mickey Morandini .08 .25
18 Paul Quantrill .08 .25
19 Randy Ready .08 .25
20 Curt Schilling 1.00 2.50
21 Heathcliff Slocumb .08 .25
22 Kevin Stocker .08 .25
23 Gary Varsho .08 .25
24 Lenny Webster .08 .25
25 David West .08 .25

1996 Phillies Team Issue

These 4" by 6" cards feature members of the 1996 Philadelphia Phillies. The full-bleed fronts feature color player photos with their names in the upper left corner. The backs have vital statistics and a career record. This set is unnumbered and we have checklisted it in alphabetical order.

COMPLETE SET (36) 3.00 8.00
1 Howard Battle .08 .25
2 Mike Benjamin .08 .25
3 Toby Borland .08 .25
4 Ricky Bottalico .08 .25
5 Larry Bowa CO .20 .50
6 Dave Cash CO .20 .50
7 Carlos Crawford .08 .25
8 Darren Daulton .40 1.00
9 Lenny Dykstra .30 .75
10 Jim Eisenreich .20 .50
11 Sid Fernandez .20 .50
12 Jim Fregosi MG .08 .25
13 Steve Frey .08 .25
14 Mike Grace .08 .25
15 Tyler Green .08 .25
16 Pete Incaviglia .08 .25
17 Gregg Jefferies .08 .25
18 Kevin Jordan .08 .25
19 Dave Leiper .08 .25
20 Mike Lieberthal .30 .75
21 Denis Menke CO .08 .25
22 Mike Mimbs .08 .25
23 Mickey Morandini .08 .25
24 Terry Mulholland .08 .25
25 Phillie Phanatic .20 .50
26 Johnny Podres CO .20 .50
27 Joe Rigoli CO .08 .25
28 Ken Ryan .08 .25
29 Benito Santiago .20 .50
30 Russ Springer .08 .25
31 Kevin Stocker .08 .25
32 Lee Tinsley .08 .25
33 John Vukovich CO .08 .25
34 Mark Whiten .08 .25
35 Mike Williams .08 .25
36 Todd Zeile .20 .50

1997 Phillies Copi Quik

This 28-card set was produced by Copi Quik and features borderless color action player photos measuring approximately 8 1/2" by 11". The backs carry player biographical information and career statistics. The set also includes a 50th Anniversary Jackie Robinson Commemorative Card and several pictures of opposing team members representing the interleague series. These players are indicated with "IL" after their names. A limited number of each card was produced and sequentially numbered. The cards are unnumbered and checklisted below in alphabetical order.

COMPLETE SET (28) 4.00 10.00
1 Ruben Amaro .08 .25
2 Matt Beech .08 .25
3 Ricky Bottalico .08 .25
4 Rico Brogna .08 .25
5 Roger Clemens IL 1.00 2.50
6 Darren Daulton .30 .75
7 Terry Francona MG .20 .50
8 Wayne Gomes .08 .25
9 Mike Grace .08 .25
10 Tyler Green .08 .25
11 Rex Hudler .20 .50
12 Gregg Jefferies .08 .25
13 Kevin Jordan .08 .25
14 Mark Leiter .08 .25
15 Mike Lieberthal .40 1.00
16 Wendell Magee Jr. .08 .25
17 Tino Martinez IL .40 1.00
18 Mickey Morandini .08 .25
19 Mark Parent .08 .25
20 Ricky Otero .08 .25
21 Phillie Phanatic(Mascot) .20 .50
22 Mark Portugal .08 .25
23 Jackie Robinson/50th Anniversary .75 2.00
24 Scott Rolen 1.25 3.00
25 Curt Schilling 1.00 2.50
26 Curt Schilling/1997 All-Star 1.00 2.50
27 Garrett Stephenson .08 .25
28 Kevin Stocker .08 .25

1997 Phillies Team Issue

These cards were issued by the Philadelphia Phillies to honor the members of the 1997 Phillies. The cards are unnumbered and we have sequenced them in uniform number order.

COMPLETE SET 6.00 15.00
2 Rico Brogna .20 .50
3 Chuck Cottier CO .20 .50
7 Terry Francona MG .30 .75
8 Mark Parent .20 .50
9 Brad Mills CO .20 .50
10 Darren Daulton .60 1.50
12 Mickey Moradini .20 .50
14 Rex Hudler .30 .75
17 Scott Rolen 1.50 4.00
18 John Vukovich CO .20 .50
19 Kevin Stocker .20 .50
21 Mark Portugal .20 .50
22 Ron Blazier .20 .50
23 Kevin Jordan .20 .50
24 Mike Lieberthal .40 1.00
25 Gregg Jefferies .20 .50
29 Wendell Magee Jr. .20 .50
31A Kevin Sefcik .30 .75
31B Mark Leiter .30 .75
33 Scott Ruffcorn .20 .50
34 Derrick May .20 .50
35 Bobby Munoz .20 .50
37 Ruben Amaro Jr. .20 .50
38 Curt Schilling 1.25 3.00
40 Reggie Harris .20 .50
41 Erik Plantenburg .20 .50
42 Galen Cisco CO .20 .50
45 Danny Tartabull .20 .50
47 Michael Mimbs .20 .50
48 Jerry Spradlin .20 .50
50 Calvin Maduro .20 .50
51 Ken Ryan .20 .50
52 Ricky Bottalico .20 .50
56 Hal McRae CO .20 .50
59 Joe Rigoli .20 .50
NNO Phillie Phanatic .30 .75

1998 Phillies Team Issue

This 36-card set measuring approximately 4" by 6" features borderless color player photos. The backs carry player biographical information and career statistics. The cards are unnumbered and we have checklisted below in alphabetical order.

COMPLETE SET (36) 4.00 10.00
1 Bobby Abreu .60 1.50
2 Ruben Amaro .08 .25
3 Alex Arias .08 .25
4 Matt Beech .08 .25
5 Ricky Bottalico .08 .25
6 Billy Brewer .08 .25
7 Rico Brogna .08 .25
8 Galen Cisco .08 .25
9 Chuck Cottier CO .08 .25
10 Bobby Estalella .08 .25
11 Terry Francona MG .08 .25
12 Doug Glanville .08 .25
13 Wayne Gomes .08 .25
14 Mike Grace .08 .25
15 Tyler Green .08 .25
16 Ramon Henderson CO .08 .25
17 Rex Hudler .20 .50
18 Gregg Jefferies .08 .25
19 Kevin Jordan .08 .25
20 Mark Leiter .08 .25
21 Mark Lewis .08 .25
22 Mike Lieberthal .30 .75
23 Billy McMillon .08 .25
24 Hal McRae .08 .25
25 Brad Mills CO .08 .25
26 Mark Parent .08 .25
27 Mark Portugal .08 .25
28 Desi Relaford .08 .25
29 Scott Rolen 1.00 2.50
30 Kevin Sefcik .08 .25
31 Curt Schilling .75 2.00
32 Jerry Spradlin .08 .25
33 Garrett Stephenson .08 .25
34 John Vukovich CO .08 .25
35 Darrin Winston .08 .25
36 Phillie Phanatic .20 .50

2001 Phillies Modell's

COMPLETE SET (4) 8.00 20.00
1 Marlon Anderson/4000 2.00 5.00
2 Doug Glanville/500 2.40 6.00
3 Jimmy Rollins/3500 4.00 10.00
4 Randy Wolf/4000 2.00 5.00

2002 Phillies Nabisco-Acme

COMPLETE SET 4.00 10.00
1 Bobby Abreu .60 1.50
2 Terry Adams .08 .25
3 Marlon Anderson .08 .25
4 Ricky Bottalico .08 .25
5 Larry Bowa MG .20 .50
6 Pat Burrell .40 1.00
7 David Coggin .08 .25
8 Rheal Cormier .08 .25
9 Brandon Duckworth .08 .25
10 Jeremy Giambi .08 .25
11 Doug Glanville .08 .25
12 Greg Gross CO .08 .25
13 Ramon Henderson .08 .25
14 Dave Hollins .08 .25
15 Ricky Ledee .08 .25
16 Travis Lee .08 .25
17 Mike Lieberthal .30 .75
18 Jose Mesa .20 .50
19 Jason Michaels .08 .25
20 Doug Nickle .08 .25
21 Vicente Padilla .20 .50
22 Tomas Perez .08 .25
23 Robert Person .08 .25
24 Dan Plesac .08 .25
25 Todd Pratt .08 .25
26 Scott Rolen .60 1.50
27 Jimmy Rollins .60 1.50
28 Vern Ruhle CO .08 .25
29 Jose Santiago .08 .25
30 Tony Scott CO .08 .25
31 Carlos Silva .08 .25
32 Gary Varsho CO .08 .25
33 John Vukovich CO .08 .25
34 Turk Wendell .08 .25
35 Randy Wolf .30 .75
XX Oreo Coupon .02 .10

2002 Phillies Team Issue

COMPLETE SET (36) 4.00 10.00
1 Bobby Abreu .60 1.50
2 Terry Adams .08 .25
3 Marlon Anderson .08 .25
4 Ricky Bottalico .08 .25
5 Larry Bowa MG .20 .50
6 Pat Burrell .60 1.50
7 David Coggin .08 .25
8 Rheal Cormier .08 .25
9 Brandon Duckworth .08 .25
10 Doug Glanville .08 .25
11 Greg Gross CO .08 .25
12 Ramon Henderson .08 .25
13 Dave Hollins .08 .25
14 Ricky Ledee .08 .25
15 Travis Lee .08 .25
16 Mike Lieberthal .30 .75
17 John Mabry .08 .25
18 Jose Mesa .20 .50
19 Vicente Padilla .08 .25
20 Tomas Perez .08 .25
21 Robert Person .08 .25
22 Cliff Politte .08 .25
23 Todd Pratt .08 .25
24 Nick Punto .08 .25
25 Scott Rolen .75 2.00
26 Jimmy Rollins .60 1.50
27 Vern Ruhle CO .08 .25
28 Jose Santiago .08 .25
29 Tony Scott CO .08 .25
30 Carlos Silva .08 .25
31 Gary Varsho CO .08 .25
32 John Vukovich CO .08 .25
33 Turk Wendell .08 .25
34 Randy Wolf .30 .75
35 Phillies Broadcasters .08 .25
36 Phillie Phanatic MASCOT .08 .25

2003 Phillies Fleer Veteran's Stadium

COMPLETE SET (12) 3.00 8.00
1 Steve Carlton .40 1.00
2 Darren Daulton .20 .50
3 John Kruk .20 .50
4 Juan Samuel .10 .25
5 Mike Schmidt .60 1.50
6 Larry Bowa .20 .50
7 Greg Luzinski .20 .50
8 Garry Maddox .10 .25
9 Bobby Abreu .40 1.00
10 Tug McGraw .40 1.00
11 Curt Schilling .50 1.25
12 Dallas Green MG .10 .25

2003 Phillies Team Issue

COMPLETE SET 4.00 10.00
1 Bobby Abreu .60 1.50
2 Terry Adams .10 .25
3 David Bell .10 .25
4 Larry Bowa MG .10 .25
5 Pat Burrell .40 1.00
6 Marlon Byrd .20 .50
7 Rheal Cormier .10 .25
8 Brandon Duckworth .10 .25
9 Greg Gross CO .10 .25
10 Ramon Henderson .10 .25
11 Tyler Houston .10 .25
12 Joe Kerrigan CO .10 .25
13 Ricky Ledee .10 .25
14 Mike Lieberthal .30 .75
15 Hector Mercado .10 .25
16 Jose Mesa .20 .50
17 Jason Michaels .10 .25
18 Kevin Millwood .30 .75
19 Brett Myers .40 1.00
20 Vicente Padilla .10 .25
21 Thomas Perez .10 .25
22 Placido Polanco .10 .25
23 Dan Plesac .10 .25
24 Todd Pratt .10 .25
25 Joe Roa .10 .25
26 Jimmy Rollins .60 1.50
27 Tony Scott CO .10 .25
28 Carlos Silva CO .10 .25
29 Jim Thome .60 1.50
30 Gary Varsho CO .10 .25
31 John Vukovich CO .10 .25
32 Turk Wendell .10 .25
33 Phillie Phanatic .10 .25
34 Phillies Annoucers .10 .25

2004 Phillies McDonald's

COMPLETE SET (27) 5.00 10.00
1 Jim Thome .60 1.50
2 Placido Polanco .10 .25
3 Jimmy Rollins .60 1.50
4 David Bell .10 .25
5 Bobby Abreu .50 1.25
6 Pat Burrell .40 1.00
7 Marlon Byrd .20 .50
8 Mike Lieberthal .30 .75
9 Kevin Millwood .40 1.00
10 Randy Wolf .20 .50
11 Vicente Padilla .20 .50
12 Eric Milton .10 .25
13 Brett Myers .30 .75
14 Billy Wagner .40 1.00
15 Tim Worrell .10 .25
16 Rheal Cormier .10 .25
17 Roberto Hernandez .20 .50
18 Ryan Madson .10 .25
19 Amaury Telemaco .10 .25
20 Tomas Perez .10 .25
21 Shawn Wooten .10 .25
22 Doug Glanville .10 .25
23 Ricky Ledee .10 .25
24 Jason Michaels .10 .25
25 Todd Pratt .10 .25
26 Larry Bowa MG .20 .50
27 Citizens Bank Park CL .10 .25

2005 Phillies Team Issue

COMPLETE SET
1 Bobby Abreu .75 2.00
2 Terry Adams .20 .50
3 David Bell .20 .50
4 Mick Billmeyer INS .20 .50
5 Marc Bombard CO .20 .50
6 Pat Burrell .60 1.50
7 Marlon Byrd .20 .50
8 Rheal Cormier .20 .50
9 Bill Dancy CO .20 .50
10 Rich Dubee CO .20 .50
11 Gavin Floyd .30 .75
12 Aaron Fultz .20 .50
13 Ramon Henderson CO .20 .50
14 Cory Lidle .20 .50
15 Jon Lieber .30 .75
16 Mike Lieberthal .40 1.00
17 Pedro Liriano .20 .50
18 Kenny Lofton .30 .75
19 Ryan Madson .20 .50
20 Charlie Manuel MG .20 .50
21 Jason Michaels .30 .75
22 Brett Myers .30 .75
23 Jose Offerman .20 .50
24 Vicente Padilla .30 .75
25 Tomas Perez .20 .50
26 Phillie Phanatic
Mascot .20 .50
27 Placido Polanco .20 .50
28 Todd Pratt .20 .50
29 Jimmy Rollins .75 2.00
30 Jim Thome .75 2.00
31 Milt Thompson CO .20 .50
32 Chase Utley 1.00 2.50
33 Gary Varsho CO .20 .50
34 Billy Wagner .60 1.50
35 Randy Wolf .20 .50
36 Tim Worrell .20 .50

2006 Phillies Topps

COMPLETE SET (14) 3.00 8.00
PHI1 David Bell .12 .30
PHI2 Ryan Howard .25 .60
PHI3 Pat Burrell .12 .30
PHI4 Bobby Abreu .12 .30
PHI5 Mike Lieberthal .12 .30
PHI6 Jason Michaels .12 .30
PHI7 Jimmy Rollins .20 .50
PHI8 Aaron Rowand .12 .30
PHI9 Chase Utley .20 .50
PHI10 Randy Wolf .12 .30
PHI11 Jon Lieber .12 .30
PHI12 Brett Myers .12 .30
PHI13 Tom Gordon .12 .30
PHI14 Ryan Madson .12 .30

2007 Phillies Topps

COMPLETE SET (14) 3.00 8.00
PHI1 Ryan Howard .25 .60
PHI2 Wes Helms .12 .30
PHI3 Freddy Garcia .12 .30
PHI4 Shane Victorino .12 .30
PHI5 Pat Burrell .12 .30
PHI6 Jamie Moyer .12 .30
PHI7 Tom Gordon .12 .30
PHI8 Cole Hamels .25 .60
PHI9 Aaron Rowand .12 .30
PHI10 Chase Utley .20 .50
PHI11 Jimmy Rollins .20 .50
PHI12 Brett Myers .12 .30
PHI13 Ryan Madson .12 .30
PHI14 Rod Barajas .12 .30

2008 Phillies Topps

COMPLETE SET (14) 3.00 8.00
PHI1 Ryan Howard .20 .50
PHI2 Greg Dobbs .12 .30
PHI3 Jayson Werth .20 .50
PHI4 Shane Victorino .20 .50
PHI5 Pat Burrell .12 .30
PHI6 Jamie Moyer .12 .30
PHI7 Kyle Kendrick .12 .30
PHI8 Cole Hamels .25 .60
PHI9 Geoff Jenkins .12 .30
PHI10 Chase Utley .20 .50
PHI11 Jimmy Rollins .20 .50
PHI12 Brett Myers .12 .30
PHI13 Brad Lidge .12 .30
PHI14 Carlos Ruiz .12 .30

2009 Phillies Topps

PHI1 Cole Hamels .30 .75
PHI2 Ryan Howard .30 .75
PHI3 Chase Utley .25 .60
PHI4 Brett Myers .15 .40
PHI5 Jimmy Rollins .25 .60
PHI6 Jamie Moyer .15 .40
PHI7 Raul Ibanez .25 .60
PHI8 Brad Lidge .15 .40
PHI9 Jayson Werth .25 .60
PHI10 Joe Blanton .15 .40
PHI11 Shane Victorino .15 .40
PHI12 Pedro Feliz .15 .40
PHI13 Ryan Madson .15 .40
PHI14 Carlos Ruiz .15 .40
PHI15 Phillie Phanatic .15 .40

2010 Phillies Topps

PHI1 Ryan Howard .30 .75
PHI2 Joe Blanton .15 .40
PHI3 Carlos Ruiz .15 .40
PHI4 Shane Victorino .25 .60
PHI5 J.A. Happ .25 .60
PHI6 Cole Hamels .30 .75
PHI7 Roy Halladay .30 .75
PHI8 Chase Utley .25 .60
PHI9 John Mayberry .15 .40
PHI10 Ben Francisco .15 .40
PHI11 Jayson Werth .25 .60
PHI12 Brad Lidge .15 .40
PHI13 Jimmy Rollins .25 .60
PHI14 Raul Ibanez .25 .60
PHI15 Ryan Madson .15 .40
PHI16 Placido Polanco .15 .40
PHI17 J.C. Romero .15 .40

2011 Phillies Topps

PHI1 Cliff Lee .25 .60
PHI2 Roy Halladay .25 .60
PHI3 Ryan Howard .30 .75
PHI4 Cole Hamels .30 .75
PHI5 Chase Utley .25 .60
PHI6 Domonic Brown .30 .75
PHI7 Roy Oswalt .25 .60
PHI8 Raul Ibanez .25 .60
PHI9 Jimmy Rollins .25 .60
PHI10 Shane Victorino .25 .60
PHI11 Wilson Valdez .15 .40
PHI12 Ben Francisco .15 .40
PHI13 Carlos Ruiz .15 .40
PHI14 Ryan Madson .15 .40
PHI15 Brad Lidge .15 .40
PHI16 Placido Polanco .15 .40
PHI17 Citizens Bank Park .15 .40

2012 Phillies Topps

PHI1 Roy Halladay .30 .75
PHI2 Shane Victorino .30 .75
PHI3 Kyle Kendrick .25 .60
PHI4 Jim Thome .30 .75
PHI5 Jimmy Rollins .30 .75
PHI6 Cliff Lee .30 .75
PHI7 John Mayberry .25 .60
PHI8 Placido Polanco .25 .60
PHI9 Carlos Ruiz .25 .60
PHI10 Ryan Howard .30 .75
PHI11 Cole Hamels .30 .75
PHI12 Hunter Pence .30 .75
PHI13 Chase Utley .30 .75
PHI14 Joe Blanton .25 .60
PHI15 Jonathan Papelbon .30 .75
PHI16 Vance Worley .30 .75
PHI17 Citizens Bank Park .15 .40

2013 Phillies Topps

COMPLETE SET (17) 3.00 8.00
PHI1 Cole Hamels .20 .50
PHI2 Roy Halladay .30 .75
PHI3 Cliff Lee .30 .75
PHI4 Ryan Howard .30 .75
PHI5 Jimmy Rollins .30 .75

PHI6 Chase Utley	.30	.75
PHI7 Kyle Kendrick	.25	.60
PHI8 Jonathan Papelbon	.30	.75
PHI9 Michael Young	.15	.40
PHI10 Delmon Young	.20	.50
PHI11 Carlos Ruiz	.25	.60
PHI12 Darin Ruf	.50	1.25
PHI13 Domonic Brown	.20	.50
PHI14 Ben Revere	.25	.60
PHI15 Erik Kratz	.15	.40
PHI16 John Mayberry	.25	.60
PHI17 Citizens Bank Park	.15	.40

2014 Phillies Topps

COMPLETE SET (17)	3.00	8.00
PHI1 Cole Hamels	.20	.50
PHI2 Marlon Byrd	.15	.40
PHI3 Cliff Lee	.20	.50
PHI4 Ryan Howard	.20	.50
PHI5 Jimmy Rollins	.20	.50
PHI6 Chase Utley	.20	.50
PHI7 Kyle Kendrick	.15	.40
PHI8 Jonathan Papelbon	.20	.50
PHI9 Jonathan Pettibone	.15	.40
PHI10 Cody Asche	.20	.50
PHI11 Carlos Ruiz	.15	.40
PHI12 Darin Ruf	.20	.50
PHI13 Domonic Brown	.20	.50
PHI14 Ben Revere	.15	.40
PHI15 Freddy Galvis	.15	.40
PHI16 John Mayberry	.15	.40
PHI17 Citizens Bank Park	.15	.40

2015 Phillies Pope Francis

266 Pope Francis	6.00	15.00

2016 Phillies Topps

COMPLETE SET (17)	3.00	8.00
PHI1 Maikel Franco	.20	.50
PHI2 Aaron Nola	.30	.75
PHI3 Carlos Ruiz	.15	.40
PHI4 Ryan Howard	.20	.50
PHI5 Cesar Hernandez	.15	.40
PHI6 Freddy Galvis	.15	.40
PHI7 Cody Asche	.15	.40
PHI8 Odubel Herrera	.20	.50
PHI9 Aaron Altherr	.15	.40
PHI10 Darnell Sweeney	.15	.40
PHI11 Adam Morgan	.15	.40
PHI12 Jerad Eickhoff	.25	.60
PHI13 Darin Ruf	.15	.40
PHI14 Cameron Rupp	.15	.40
PHI15 Andres Blanco	.15	.40
PHI16 Jeremy Hellickson	.15	.40
PHI17 Charlie Morton	.25	.60

2017 Phillies Topps

COMPLETE SET (17)	3.00	8.00
PHI1 Maikel Franco	.20	.50
PHI2 Aaron Nola	.20	.50
PHI3 Vince Velasquez	.15	.40
PHI4 Cesar Hernandez	.15	.40
PHI5 Hector Neris	.15	.40
PHI6 Cameron Rupp	.15	.40
PHI7 Jeanmar Gomez	.15	.40
PHI8 Clay Buchholz	.15	.40
PHI9 Roman Quinn	.15	.40
PHI10 Odubel Herrera	.20	.50
PHI11 Jerad Eickhoff	.15	.40
PHI12 Freddy Galvis	.15	.40
PHI13 Andres Blanco	.15	.40
PHI14 Jeremy Hellickson	.15	.40
PHI15 Tommy Joseph	.25	.60
PHI16 Howie Kendrick	.15	.40
PHI17 Aaron Altherr	.15	.40

2018 Phillies Topps

COMPLETE SET (17)	2.50	6.00
PP1 Rhys Hoskins	.60	1.50
PP2 Odubel Herrera	.20	.50
PP3 Pat Neshek	.15	.40
PP4 Cesar Hernandez	.15	.40
PP5 Cameron Rupp	.15	.40
PP6 Luis Garcia	.15	.40
PP7 Maikel Franco	.20	.50
PP8 Aaron Nola	.20	.50
PP9 Jorge Alfaro	.15	.40
PP10 Carlos Santana	.20	.50
PP11 Tommy Joseph	.25	.60
PP12 Jerad Eickhoff	.15	.40
PP13 Hector Neris	.15	.40
PP14 Vince Velasquez	.15	.40
PP15 Aaron Altherr	.15	.40
PP16 Nick Williams	.20	.50
PP17 J.P. Crawford	.15	.40

2019 Phillies Topps

COMPLETE SET (18)	2.50	6.00
PP1 Rhys Hoskins	.30	.75
PP2 Aaron Nola	.20	.50
PP3 Jake Arrieta	.20	.50
PP4 Maikel Franco	.20	.50
PP5 Odubel Herrera	.20	.50
PP6 Nick Williams	.15	.40
PP7 Scott Kingery	.20	.50
PP8 Dylan Cozens	.15	.40
PP9 Jean Segura	.25	.60
PP10 Cesar Hernandez	.15	.40
PP11 Nick Pivetta	.15	.40
PP12 Vince Velasquez	.15	.40
PP13 Jorge Alfaro	.15	.40
PP14 Roman Quinn	.15	.40
PP15 Zach Eflin	.15	.40
PP16 Seranthony Dominguez	.15	.40
PP17 Andrew McCutchen	.25	.60
PP18 Bryce Harper	.40	1.00

2020 Phillies Topps

PHI1 Bryce Harper	.40	1.00
PHI2 Rhys Hoskins	.30	.75
PHI3 Aaron Nola	.20	.50
PHI4 Roman Quinn	.15	.40
PHI5 Vince Velazquez	.15	.40
PHI6 Zack Wheeler	.20	.50
PHI7 Jean Segura	.20	.50
PHI8 Andrew McCutchen	.25	.60
PHI9 Scott Kingery	.20	.50
PHI10 Andrew Knapp	.15	.40
PHI11 Zach Eflin	.15	.40
PHI12 Hector Neris	.15	.40
PHI13 Didi Gregorius	.20	.50
PHI14 Adam Haseley	.20	.50
PHI15 Jake Arrieta	.20	.50
PHI16 Jay Bruce	.20	.50
PHI17 J.T. Realmuto	.25	.60

2017 Phillies Topps National Baseball Card Day

COMPLETE SET (20)	10.00	25.00
1 Robin Roberts	.75	2.00
2 Richie Ashburn	.75	2.00
3 Jim Bunning	.75	2.00
4 Steve Carlton	.75	2.00
5 John Kruk	.60	1.50
6 Mike Schmidt	1.50	4.00
7 Larry Bowa	.60	1.50
8 Dick Allen	.60	1.50
9 Greg Luzinski	.60	1.50
10 Tug McGraw	.60	1.50
11 Tony Taylor	.60	1.50
12 Bob Boone	.60	1.50
13 Dallas Green	.60	1.50
14 Juan Samuel	.60	1.50
15 Darren Daulton	.60	1.50
16 Mike Lieberthal	.60	1.50
17 Charlie Manuel	.60	1.50
18 Pat Burrell	.60	1.50
19 Jim Thome	.75	2.00
20 Garry Maddox	.60	1.50

2015 Phillies Topps

COMPLETE SET (17)	3.00	8.00
PHP1 Chase Utley	.20	.50
PHP2 Domonic Brown	.20	.50
PHP3 David Buchanan	.15	.40
PHP4 Darin Ruf	.15	.40
PHP5 Cole Hamels	.20	.50
PHP6 Ryan Howard	.20	.50
PHP7 Freddy Galvis	.15	.40
PHP8 Jonathan Papelbon	.20	.50
PHP9 Ben Revere	.15	.40
PHP10 Carlos Ruiz	.15	.40
PHP11 Cliff Lee	.20	.50
PHP12 Maikel Franco	.20	.50
PHP13 Cody Asche	.20	.50
PHP14 Jerome Williams	.15	.40
PHP15 Ken Giles	.15	.40
PHP16 Grady Sizemore	.20	.50
PHP17 Jake Diekman	.15	.40

2008 Phillies Upper Deck World Series Champions

COMPLETE SET (50)	8.00	20.00
COMMON CARD	.20	.50
PP1 Jimmy Rollins	.30	.75
PP2 Jayson Werth	.30	.75
PP3 Chase Utley	.30	.75
PP4 Ryan Howard	.30	.75
PP5 Pat Burrell	.20	.50
PP6 Shane Victorino	.20	.50
PP7 Pedro Feliz	.20	.50
PP8 Carlos Ruiz	.20	.50
PP9 Cole Hamels	.40	1.00
PP10 Brad Lidge	.20	.50
PP11 Jamie Moyer	.20	.50
PP12 Brett Myers	.20	.50
PP13 Joe Blanton	.20	.50
PP14 Greg Dobbs	.20	.50
PP15 Chris Coste	.20	.50
PP16 Eric Bruntlett	.20	.50
PP17 Geoff Jenkins	.20	.50
PP18 Matt Stairs	.20	.50
PP19 So Taguchi	.20	.50
PP20 J.C. Romero	.20	.50
PP21 Ryan Madson	.20	.50
PP22 J.A. Happ	.20	.50
PP23 Chad Durbin	.20	.50
PP24 Clay Condrey	.20	.50
PP25 Scott Eyre	.20	.50
PP26 Cole Hamels HL	.40	1.00
PP27 Ryan Howard HL	.30	.75
PP28 Jamie Moyer HL	.20	.50
PP29 Brad Lidge HL	.20	.50
PP30 Brett Myers HL	.20	.50
PP31 Carlos Ruiz HL	.20	.50
PP32 Chris Coste HL	.20	.50
PP33 Pedro Feliz HL	.20	.50
PP34 Jayson Werth HL	.30	.75
PP35 Shane Victorino HL	.20	.50
PP36 Pat Burrell HL	.20	.50
PP37 Jimmy Rollins HL	.30	.75
PP38 Chase Utley HL	.30	.75
PP39 Greg Dobbs HL	.20	.50
PP40 Ryan Madson HL	.20	.50
PP41 Shane Victorino MM	.20	.50
PP42 Pat Burrell MM	.20	.50
PP43 Brad Lidge MM	.20	.50
PP44 Brett Myers MM	.20	.50
PP45 Matt Stairs MM	.20	.50
PP46 Chase Utley MM	.30	.75
PP47 Jamie Moyer MM	.20	.50
PP48 Ryan Howard MM	.30	.75
PP49 Geoff Jenkins MM	.20	.50
PP50 Cole Hamels MVP	.40	1.00

2008 Phillies Upper Deck World Series Champions Jumbo

PHILLY Philadelphia Phillies	.40	1.00

1987-94 Photo File Hall of Fame

These 8" by 10" cards produced by Photo File displays color photos of various Baseball Hall of Fame inductees. The cards commemorate the induction day ceremonies and include player statistics and biographical information. The cards are checklisted below alphabetically by year.

COMPLETE SET	10.00	25.00
1 Ray Dandridge	.75	2.00
2 Bill Veeck	.75	2.00
3 Rollie Fingers	1.00	2.50
4 Hal Newhouser	.75	2.00
5 Tom Seaver Pitching	1.50	4.00
6 Tom Seaver Still photo	1.50	4.00
7 Reggie Jackson Angels Uniform	1.50	4.00
8 Reggie Jackson Orioles Uniform	1.50	4.00
9 Leo Durocher Dodgers Black and White Photo	.75	2.00
10 Steve Carlton	1.25	3.00

1993 Photo File Ryan

This eight-card set measures approximately 8" by 10" and commemorates Nolan Ryan's career record seven no-hitters. Each card features a black-and-white or color photo of Ryan as well as the box score from the game. The cards are checklisted below according to the date of the no-hitter.

COMPLETE SET (8)	8.00	20.00
COMMON CARD (1-8)	1.00	2.50

1914 Piedmont Stamps T330-2

These attractive stamps are approximately 1 7/16" by 2 5/8" and are unnumbered. Unlike most stamps, these have blue printing on the back. On the back there is an offer for an album to house these stamps. This offer expired on June 30, 1915." The front designs are similar to T205.

COMPLETE SET	7500.00	15000.00
1 Leon Ames	60.00	120.00
2 Jimmy Archer	60.00	120.00
3 Jimmy Austin	60.00	120.00
4 Frank Baker	125.00	250.00
5 Cy Barger	60.00	120.00
6 Jack Barry	60.00	120.00
7 Johnny Bates	60.00	120.00
8 Beals Becker	60.00	120.00
9 Chief Bender	125.00	250.00
10 Bob Bescher	60.00	120.00
11 Joe Birmingham	60.00	120.00
12 Walter Blair	60.00	120.00
13 Roger Breshnahan	125.00	250.00
14 Al Bridwell	60.00	120.00
15 Mordecai Brown	125.00	250.00
16 Robert Byrne	60.00	120.00
17 Howie Camnitz	60.00	120.00
18 Bill Carrigan	60.00	120.00
19 Frank Chance	200.00	400.00
20 Hal Chase Identified as Hal Chase	125.00	250.00
21 Hal Chase Indentified only as Chase	100.00	200.00
22 Eddie Cicotte	125.00	250.00
23 Fred Clarke	125.00	250.00
24 Ty Cobb	750.00	1500.00
25 Eddie Collins Mouth Open	150.00	300.00
26 Eddie Collins Mouth Closed	250.00	500.00
27 Doc Crandall	60.00	120.00
28 Bill Dahlen	75.00	150.00
29 Jake Daubert	100.00	200.00
30 Jim Delahanty	60.00	120.00
31 Josh Devore	60.00	120.00
32 Red Dooin	60.00	120.00
33 Mike Doolan	60.00	120.00
34 Tom Downey	60.00	120.00
35 Larry Doyle	75.00	150.00
36 Joe Egan	60.00	120.00
37 Kid Elberfeld	60.00	120.00
38 Clyde Engle	60.00	120.00
39 Steve Evans	60.00	120.00
40 Johnny Evers	200.00	400.00
41 Ray Fisher	60.00	120.00
42 Art Fletcher	60.00	120.00
43 Russ Ford White Cap	60.00	120.00
44 Russ Ford Dark Cap	60.00	120.00
45 Arthur Fromme	60.00	120.00
46 George Gibson	60.00	120.00
47 William Goode	60.00	120.00
48 Eddie Grant	75.00	150.00
49 Clark Griffith	125.00	250.00
50 Bob Groom	60.00	120.00
51 Bob Harmon	60.00	120.00
52 Arnold Hauser	60.00	120.00
53 Buck Herzog	60.00	120.00
54 Doc Hoblitzell	60.00	120.00
55 Miller Huggins	125.00	250.00
56 John Hummel	60.00	120.00
57 Hugh Jennings MG	200.00	400.00
58 Walter Johnson	300.00	600.00
59 Davy Jones	60.00	120.00
60 William Killifer	100.00	200.00
61 Ed Konetchy	60.00	120.00
62 John Knight	60.00	120.00
63 Frank LaPorte	60.00	120.00
64 Tommy Leach	75.00	150.00
65 Ed Lennox	60.00	120.00
66 Hans Lobert	75.00	150.00
67 Bris Lord	60.00	120.00
68 Sherry Magee	75.00	150.00
69 Rube Marquard	125.00	250.00
70 Christy Mathewson	300.00	600.00
71 George McBride	60.00	120.00
72 John McGraw MG	200.00	400.00
73 Larry McLean	60.00	120.00
74 Chief Meyers	75.00	150.00
75 Fred Merkle	75.00	150.00
76 Clyde Milan	75.00	150.00
77 Dots Miller	60.00	120.00
78 Michael Mitchell	60.00	120.00
79 Pat Moran	60.00	120.00
80 George Moriarty	60.00	120.00
81 George Mullin	75.00	150.00
82 Danny Murphy	60.00	120.00
83 Jack Murray	60.00	120.00
84 Tom Needham	60.00	120.00
85 Rebel Oakes	60.00	120.00
86 Rube Oldring	60.00	120.00
87 Freddy Parent	60.00	120.00
88 Dode Paskert	60.00	120.00
89 Jack Quinn	75.00	150.00
90 Ed Reulbach	100.00	200.00
91 Lewis Ritchie	60.00	120.00
92 John A. Rowan	60.00	120.00
93 Nap Rucker	75.00	150.00
94 Germany Schaefer	75.00	150.00
95 Fred Schulte	75.00	150.00
96 Jim Scott	60.00	120.00
97 Fred Snodgrass	60.00	120.00
98 Tris Speaker	200.00	400.00
99 Oscar Stanage	60.00	120.00
100 George Stovall	60.00	120.00
101 George Suggs	60.00	120.00
102 Jeff Sweeney	60.00	120.00
103 Ira Thomas	60.00	120.00
104 Joe Tinker	125.00	250.00
105 Terry Turner	75.00	150.00
106 Hippo Vaughn	60.00	120.00
107 Heinie Wagner	60.00	120.00
108 Bobby Wallace With Cap	125.00	250.00
109 Bobby Wallace No Cap	125.00	250.00
110 Ed Walsh	125.00	250.00
111 Zach Wheat	125.00	250.00
112 Kaiser Wilhelm	60.00	120.00
113 Ed Willett	60.00	120.00
114 J. Owen Wilson	60.00	120.00
115 Hooks Wiltse	60.00	120.00
116 Joe Wood	100.00	200.00

1954 Piersall Colonial Meat Products

These black and white postcards measure 3 1/2" by 5 3/8" and were issued by Colonial Meat Products. Both of these cards feature Jimmy Piersall; however, the cropping and the color of the facsimile autograph on the front of the card are different. The backs of the cards contain a Colonial Meat advertisement and endorsement by Piersall.

COMPLETE SET (2)	15.00	30.00
1 Jimmy Piersall	15.00	30.00
2 Jimmy Piersall	15.00	30.00

1957 Piersall Neptune Sardines

This black and white postcard features a batting photo of Jimmy Piersall on the front and a back message with an ad for Neptune Sardines.

COMPLETE SET		
1 Jimmy Piersall	7.50	15.00

1969 Pilots Post-Intelligencer

This set was originally inserted into copies of the Seattle Post-Intelligencer in 1969. They were drawn by Stu Moldrem, the Post-Intellingencer staff artist. The reprint cards measure approximately 2 3/8" by 4 7/8". The fronts feature drawings; and year by year stats. This set is dated 1969 as that was the only year of the Pilots existence. According to reports, the reprint set was issued with the Post-Intelligencer permission. The original cards measure approximately 7" by 3" but there is considerable variation with these numbers. Card number five was printed in the fashion section, rather than the sports section, making this a much harder item to find in 1969 and years later. Therefore, Card number five was never issued in the reprint set. The set was reprinted as a collectors issue in 1977 and is priced seperately. Card number 34 is larger than the other cards in this set.

COMPLETE SET (38)	200.00	400.00
COMMON CARD (1-39)	4.00	10.00
COMMON SP	15.00	40.00
1 Don Mincher	4.00	10.00
2 Tommy Harper	5.00	12.00
3 Ray Oyler	4.00	10.00
4 Jerry McNertney	4.00	10.00
5 Joe Schultz MG SP	15.00	40.00
6 Tommy Davis	6.00	15.00
7 Gary Bell	4.00	10.00
8 Chico Salmon	5.00	12.00
9 Jack Aker	4.00	10.00
10 Rich Rollins	4.00	10.00
11 Diego Segui	5.00	12.00
12 Steve Barber	5.00	12.00
13 Wayne Comer	4.00	10.00
14 John Kennedy	4.00	10.00
15 Buzz Stephen	4.00	10.00
16 Jim Gosger	4.00	10.00
17 Mike Ferraro	4.00	10.00
18 Marty Pattin	4.00	10.00
19 Gerry Schoen	4.00	10.00
20 Steve Hovely	4.00	10.00
21 Frank Crosetti CO	8.00	20.00
22 Dick Bates	4.00	10.00
23 Jose Vidal	4.00	10.00
24 Bob Richmond	4.00	10.00
25 Lou Piniella	15.00	40.00
26 John Miklos	4.00	10.00
27 John Morris	4.00	10.00
28 Larry Haney	4.00	10.00
29 Mike Marshall	6.00	15.00
30 Marv Staehle	4.00	10.00
31 Gus Gil	4.00	10.00
32 Sal Maglie CO	6.00	15.00
33 Ron Plaza CO	4.00	10.00
34 Ed O'Brien CO	4.00	10.00
35 Jim Bouton	12.50	30.00
36 Bill Stafford	4.00	10.00
37 Darrell Brandon	4.00	10.00
38 Mike Hegan	4.00	10.00
39 Dick Baney	4.00	10.00

1969 Pilots Wheeldon

This eight-card set features color player portraits by artist, John Wheeldon, printed on cards measuring approximately 8 1/2" by 11" in white borders. The fronts carry a facsimile autograph with the player's name printed in the wide bottom margin. The backs display player information, career statistics, and a paragraph about the artist. The cards are unnumbered and checklisted below in alphabetical order.

COMPLETE SET (8)	12.50	30.00
1 Wayne Comer	1.50	4.00
2 Tommy Harper	1.50	4.00
3 Mike Hegan	1.50	4.00
4 Jerry McNertney	1.50	4.00
5 Don Mincher	1.50	4.00
6 Ray Oyler	1.50	4.00
7 Marty Pattin	1.50	4.00
8 Diego Segui	1.50	4.00

1977 Pilots Post-Intelligencer Reprints

These are the reprint cards referenced to in the 1969 write-up. Please note that the 1969 and 1977 sets are different sizes and were issued almost 10 years apart. They were produced by Frank Caruso, who also produced minor league sets during this period. Please note that card number 5 does not exist in this set.The reprint cards measure approximately 2 3/8" by 4 7/8."

COMPLETE SET (38)	50.00	100.00
1 Don Mincher	1.50	4.00
2 Tommy Harper	2.00	5.00
3 Ray Oyler	1.50	4.00
4 Jerry McNertney	1.50	4.00
6 Tommy Davis	2.50	6.00
7 Gary Bell	1.50	4.00
8 Chico Salmon	1.50	4.00
9 Jack Aker	1.50	4.00
10 Rich Rollins	1.50	4.00
11 Diego Segui	2.00	5.00
12 Steve Barber	2.00	5.00
13 Wayne Comer	1.50	4.00
14 John Kennedy	1.50	4.00
15 Buzz Stephen	1.50	4.00
16 Jim Gosger	1.50	4.00
17 Mike Ferraro	1.50	4.00
18 Marty Pattin	1.50	4.00
19 Gerry Schoen	1.50	4.00
20 Steve Hovely	1.50	4.00
21 Frank Crosetti CO	3.00	8.00
22 Dick Bates	1.50	4.00
23 Jose Vidal	1.50	4.00
24 Bob Richmond	1.50	4.00
25 Lou Piniella	8.00	20.00
26 John Miklos	1.50	4.00
27 John Morris	1.50	4.00
28 Larry Haney	1.50	4.00
29 Mike Marshall	2.50	6.00
30 Marv Staehle	1.50	4.00
31 Gus Gil	1.50	4.00
32 Sal Maglie CO	3.00	8.00
33 Ron Plaza CO	1.50	4.00
34 Ed O'Brien CO	1.50	4.00
35 Jim Bouton	3.00	8.00
36 Bill Stafford	1.50	4.00
37 Darrell Brandon	1.50	4.00
38 Mike Hegan	1.50	4.00
39 Dick Baney	1.50	4.00

1983 Pilots 69 Galasso

This 43-card standard-size set features members of the Seattle Pilots. The fronts have a player photo with his name and position located under the photo. All of this is surronded by yellow borders. The backs have a career history along with their stats for the Pilots. Some sets were issued with specially autographed Jim Bouton cards. This set was originally available for $5.50.

COMPLETE SET (43)	4.00	10.00
1 Jim Bouton	.30	.75
1AU Jim Bouton AU	4.00	10.00
2 Joe Schultz MG	.08	.25
3 Bill Edgerton	.08	.25
4 Gary Timberlake	.08	.25
5 Dick Baney	.08	.25
6 Mike Marshall	.20	.50
7 Jim Gosger	.08	.25
8 Mike Hegan	.08	.25
9 Steve Hovley	.08	.25
10 Don Mincher	.08	.25
11 Miguel Fuentes	.08	.25
12 Charlie Bates	.08	.25
13 John O'Donoghue	.08	.25
14 Tommy Davis	.20	.50
15 Jerry McNertney	.08	.25
16 Rich Rollins	.08	.25
17 Fred Talbot	.08	.25
18 John Gelnar	.08	.25
19 Bob Locker	.08	.25
20 Frank Crosetti CO	.30	.75
21 Sal Maglie CO	.20	.50
22 Sibby Sisti CO	.08	.25
23 Ron Plaza CO	.08	.25
24 Federico Velazaquez	.60	1.50
25 Diego Segui	.08	.25
26 Steve Barber	.08	.25
27 Jack Aker	.08	.25
28 Marty Pattin	.08	.25
29 Ray Oyler	.08	.25
30 Danny Walton	.08	.25
31 Merritt Ranew	.08	.25
32 John Donaldson	.08	.25
33 Greg Goossen	.20	.50
34 Gary Bell	.08	.25
35 Jim Pagliaroni	.08	.25
36 Mike Ferraro	.08	.25
37 Tommy Harper	.20	.50
38 John Morris	.08	.25
39 Larry Haney	.08	.25
40 Ron Clark	.08	.25
41 Steve Whitaker	.08	.25
42 Wayne Comer	.08	.25
43 Gene Brabender	.08	.25

1911 Pinkerton T5

This 376-card set is called a true Cabinet card set meaning a player photograph is affixed to a cardboard backing. The set was produced by the Pinkerton Tobacco Company and could be obtained by sending in a certain number of coupons from Pinkerton tobacco products. Cards numbered 101-875 are Major League player cards while cards numbered 901-1115 are Minor League players. This is the original checklist as Pinkerton provided in 1911. No individual cards are priced due to scarcity and it is possible that not all exist. A Joe Jackson in ex/mt condition sold for more than $180,000 in an Mile High Auction while a Jackson in vg/ex sold for more than $40,000 in an Mastro Auction in 2006. A recently discovered card number 1510, indicates that the checklist may be incomplete. Any pricing information or checklist verification is appreciated.

1992 Pinnacle

The 1992 Pinnacle set (issued by Score) consists of two series each with 310 standard-size cards. Cards were distributed in first and second series 16-card foil packs and 27-card cello packs. An anti-counterfeit device appears in the bottom border of each card back. A special ribbed plastic lenticular detector card was made available that allowed the user to view the anti-counterfeit device and unscramble the coding with the word "Pinnacle" appearing. Special subsets featured include '92 Rookie Prospects (52, 55, 168, 247-261, 263-280), Idols (281-286/584-591), Sidelines (287-294/592-596), Draft Picks (295-304), Shades (305-310/601-605), Grips (606-612), and Technicians (614-620). Rookie Cards in the set include Brian Jordan, Jeff Kent and Manny Ramirez.

COMPLETE SET (620)	15.00	40.00
COMPLETE SERIES 1 (310)	10.00	25.00
COMPLETE SERIES 2 (310)	6.00	15.00
1 Frank Thomas	.20	.50
2 Benito Santiago	.07	.20
3 Carlos Baerga	.02	.10
4 Cecil Fielder	.07	.20
5 Barry Larkin	.10	.30
6 Ozzie Smith	.30	.75
7 Willie McGee	.07	.20
8 Paul Molitor	.07	.20
9 Andy Van Slyke	.10	.30
10 Ryne Sandberg	.30	.75
11 Kevin Seitzer	.02	.10
12 Len Dykstra	.07	.20
13 Edgar Martinez	.10	.30
14 Ruben Sierra	.07	.20
15 Howard Johnson	.02	.10
16 Dave Henderson	.02	.10
17 Devon White	.07	.20
18 Terry Pendleton	.07	.20
19 Steve Finley	.07	.20
20 Kirby Puckett	.20	.50
21 Orel Hershiser	.07	.20
22 Hal Morris	.02	.10
23 Don Mattingly	.50	1.25
24 Delino DeShields	.02	.10
25 Dennis Eckersley	.07	.20
26 Ellis Burks	.07	.20
27 Jay Buhner	.07	.20
28 Matt Williams	.07	.20
29 Lou Whitaker	.07	.20
30 Alex Fernandez	.02	.10
31 Albert Belle	.07	.20
32 Todd Zeile	.02	.10
33 Tony Pena	.02	.10
34 Jay Bell	.07	.20
35 Rafael Palmeiro	.10	.30
36 Wes Chamberlain	.02	.10
37 George Bell	.02	.10
38 Robin Yount	.30	.75
39 Vince Coleman	.02	.10
40 Bruce Hurst	.02	.10
41 Harold Baines	.07	.20
42 Chuck Finley	.07	.20
43 Ken Caminiti	.07	.20
44 Ben McDonald	.02	.10
45 Roberto Alomar	.10	.30
46 Chili Davis	.07	.20
47 Bill Doran	.02	.10
48 Jerald Clark	.02	.10
49 Jose Lind	.02	.10
50 Nolan Ryan	.75	2.00
51 Phil Plantier	.02	.10
52 Gary DiSarcina	.02	.10
53 Kevin Bass	.02	.10
54 Pat Kelly	.02	.10
55 Mark Wohlers	.02	.10
56 Walt Weiss	.02	.10
57 Lenny Harris	.02	.10
58 Ivan Calderon	.02	.10
59 Harold Reynolds	.07	.20
60 George Brett	.50	1.25
61 Gregg Olson	.02	.10
62 Orlando Merced	.02	.10
63 Steve Decker	.02	.10
64 John Franco	.07	.20
65 Greg Maddux	.30	.75
66 Alex Cole	.02	.10
67 Dave Hollins	.02	.10
68 Kent Hrbek	.07	.20
69 Tom Pagnozzi	.02	.10
70 Jeff Bagwell	.20	.50
71 Jim Gantner	.02	.10
72 Matt Nokes	.02	.10
73 Brian Harper	.02	.10
74 Andy Benes	.02	.10
75 Tom Glavine	.10	.30
76 Terry Steinbach	.02	.10
77 Dennis Martinez	.07	.20
78 John Olerud	.07	.20
79 Ozzie Guillen	.07	.20
80 Darryl Strawberry	.07	.20
81 Gary Gaetti	.07	.20
82 Dave Righetti	.07	.20
83 Chris Hoiles	.02	.10
84 Andujar Cedeno	.02	.10
85 Jack Clark	.07	.20
86 David Howard	.02	.10
87 Bill Gullickson	.02	.10
88 Bernard Gilkey	.02	.10
89 Kevin Elster	.02	.10
90 Kevin Maas	.02	.10
91 Mark Lewis	.02	.10
92 Greg Vaughn	.02	.10
93 Bret Barberie	.02	.10
94 Dave Smith	.02	.10
95 Roger Clemens	.40	1.00
96 Doug Drabek	.02	.10
97 Omar Vizquel	.10	.30
98 Jose Guzman	.02	.10
99 Juan Samuel	.02	.10
100 David Justice	.07	.20
101 Tom Browning	.02	.10
102 Mark Gubicza	.02	.10
103 Mickey Morandini	.02	.10
104 Ed Whitson	.02	.10
105 Lance Parrish	.07	.20
106 Scott Erickson	.02	.10
107 Jack McDowell	.02	.10
108 Dave Stieb	.02	.10
109 Mike Moore	.02	.10
110 Travis Fryman	.07	.20
111 Dwight Gooden	.07	.20
112 Fred McGriff	.10	.30
113 Alan Trammell	.07	.20
114 Roberto Kelly	.02	.10
115 Andre Dawson	.07	.20
116 Bill Landrum	.02	.10
117 Brian McRae	.02	.10
118 B.J. Surhoff	.07	.20
119 Chuck Knoblauch	.07	.20
120 Steve Olin	.02	.10
121 Robin Ventura	.07	.20
122 Will Clark	.10	.30
123 Tino Martinez	.10	.30
124 Dale Murphy	.10	.30
125 Pete O'Brien	.02	.10
126 Ray Lankford	.07	.20
127 Juan Gonzalez	.10	.30
128 Ron Gant	.07	.20
129 Marquis Grissom	.07	.20
130 Jose Canseco	.10	.30
131 Mike Greenwell	.02	.10
132 Mark Langston	.02	.10
133 Brett Butler	.07	.20
134 Kelly Gruber	.02	.10
135 Chris Sabo	.02	.10
136 Mark Grace	.10	.30
137 Tony Fernandez	.02	.10
138 Glenn Davis	.02	.10
139 Pedro Munoz	.02	.10
140 Craig Biggio	.10	.30
141 Pete Schourek	.02	.10
142 Mike Boddicker	.02	.10
143 Robby Thompson	.02	.10
144 Mel Hall	.02	.10
145 Bryan Harvey	.02	.10
146 Mike LaValliere	.02	.10
147 John Kruk	.07	.20
148 Joe Carter	.07	.20
149 Greg Olson	.02	.10
150 Julio Franco	.07	.20
151 Darryl Hamilton	.02	.10
152 Felix Fermin	.02	.10
153 Jose Offerman	.02	.10
154 Paul O'Neill	.10	.30
155 Tommy Greene	.02	.10
156 Ivan Rodriguez	.20	.50
157 Dave Stewart	.07	.20
158 Jeff Reardon	.07	.20
159 Felix Jose	.02	.10
160 Doug Dascenzo	.02	.10
161 Tim Wallach	.02	.10
162 Dan Plesac	.02	.10
163 Luis Gonzalez	.07	.20
164 Mike Henneman	.02	.10
165 Mike Devereaux	.02	.10
166 Luis Polonia	.02	.10
167 Mike Sharperson	.02	.10
168 Chris Donnels	.02	.10
169 Greg W. Harris	.02	.10
170 Deion Sanders	.10	.30
171 Mike Schooler	.02	.10
172 Jose DeJesus	.02	.10
173 Jeff Montgomery	.02	.10
174 Milt Cuyler	.02	.10
175 Wade Boggs	.10	.30
176 Kevin Tapani	.02	.10
177 Bill Spiers	.02	.10
178 Tim Raines	.07	.20
179 Randy Milligan	.02	.10
180 Rob Dibble	.07	.20
181 Kirt Manwaring	.02	.10
182 Pascual Perez	.02	.10
183 Juan Guzman	.02	.10
184 John Smiley	.02	.10
185 David Segui	.02	.10
186 Omar Olivares	.02	.10
187 Joe Slusarski	.02	.10
188 Erik Hanson	.02	.10
189 Mark Portugal	.02	.10
190 Walt Terrell	.02	.10
191 John Smoltz	.10	.30
192 Wilson Alvarez	.02	.10
193 Jimmy Key	.07	.20
194 Larry Walker	.10	.30
195 Lee Smith	.07	.20
196 Pete Harnisch	.02	.10
197 Mike Harkey	.02	.10
198 Frank Tanana	.02	.10
199 Terry Mulholland	.02	.10
200 Cal Ripken	.60	1.50
201 Dave Magadan	.02	.10
202 Bud Black	.02	.10
203 Terry Shumpert	.02	.10
204 Mike Mussina	.20	.50
205 Mo Vaughn	.07	.20
206 Steve Farr	.02	.10
207 Darrin Jackson	.02	.10
208 Jerry Browne	.02	.10
209 Jeff Russell	.02	.10
210 Mike Scioscia	.02	.10
211 Rick Aguilera	.07	.20
212 Jaime Navarro	.02	.10
213 Randy Tomlin	.02	.10
214 Bobby Thigpen	.02	.10
215 Mark Gardner	.02	.10
216 Norm Charlton	.02	.10
217 Mark McGwire	.50	1.25
218 Skeeter Barnes	.02	.10
219 Bob Tewksbury	.02	.10
220 Junior Felix	.02	.10
221 Sam Horn	.02	.10
222 Jody Reed	.02	.10
223 Luis Sojo	.02	.10
224 Jerome Walton	.02	.10
225 Darryl Kile	.07	.20
226 Mickey Tettleton	.02	.10
227 Dan Pasqua	.02	.10
228 Jim Gott	.02	.10
229 Bernie Williams	.10	.30
230 Shane Mack	.02	.10
231 Steve Avery	.02	.10
232 Dave Valle	.02	.10
233 Mark Leonard	.02	.10
234 Spike Owen	.02	.10
235 Gary Sheffield	.07	.20
236 Steve Chitren	.02	.10
237 Zane Smith	.02	.10
238 Tom Gordon	.02	.10
239 Jose Oquendo	.02	.10
240 Todd Stottlemyre	.02	.10
241 Darren Daulton	.07	.20
242 Tim Naehring	.02	.10
243 Tony Phillips	.02	.10
244 Shawon Dunston	.02	.10
245 Manuel Lee	.02	.10
246 Mike Pagliarulo	.02	.10
247 Jim Thome	.20	.50

248 Luis Mercedes .02 .10
249 Cal Eldred .02 .10
250 Derek Bell .07 .20
251 Arthur Rhodes .02 .10
252 Scott Cooper .02 .10
253 Roberto Hernandez .02 .10
254 Mo Sanford .02 .10
255 Scott Servais .02 .10
256 Eric Karros .07 .20
257 Andy Mota .02 .10
258 Keith Mitchell .02 .10
259 Joel Johnston .02 .10
260 John Wehner .02 .10
261 Gino Minutelli .02 .10
262 Greg Gagne .02 .10
263 Stan Royer .02 .10
264 Carlos Garcia .02 .10
265 Andy Ashby .02 .10
266 Kim Batiste .02 .10
267 Julio Valera .02 .10
268 Royce Clayton .02 .10
269 Gary Scott .02 .10
270 Kirk Dressendorfer .02 .10
271 Sean Berry .02 .10
272 Lance Dickson .02 .10
273 Rob Maurer RC .02 .10
274 Scott Brosius RC .30 .75
275 Dave Fleming .02 .10
276 Lenny Webster .02 .10
277 Mike Humphreys .02 .10
278 Freddie Benavides .02 .10
279 Harvey Pulliam .02 .10
280 Jeff Carter .02 .10
281 Jim Abbott I .20 .50
Nolan Ryan
282 Wade Boggs I .20 .50
George Brett
283 Ken Griffey Jr. I .25 .60
Rickey Henderson
284 Wally Joyner .10 .30
Dale Murphy
285 Chuck Knoblauch I .10 .30
Ozzie Smith
286 Robin Ventura I .20 .50
Lou Gehrig
287 Robin Yount SIDE .20 .50
288 Bob Tewksbury SIDE .02 .10
289 Kirby Puckett SIDE .10 .30
290 Kenny Lofton SIDE .07 .20
291 Jack McDowell SIDE .02 .10
292 John Burkett SIDE .02 .10
293 Dwight Smith SIDE .02 .10
294 Nolan Ryan SIDE .40 1.00
295 Manny Ramirez RC 1.50 4.00
296 Cliff Floyd UER RC .40 1.00
297 Al Shirley RC .05 .15
298 Brian Barber RC .05 .15
299 Jon Farrell RC .05 .15
300 Scott Ruffcorn RC .05 .15
301 Tyrone Hill RC .05 .15
302 Benji Gil RC .15 .40
303 Tyler Green RC .05 .15
304 Allen Watson RC .05 .15
305 Jay Buhner SH .02 .10
306 Roberto Alomar SH .07 .20
307 Chuck Knoblauch SH .02 .10
308 Darryl Strawberry SH .02 .10
309 Danny Tartabull SH .02 .10
310 Bobby Bonilla SH .02 .10
311 Mike Felder .02 .10
312 Storm Davis .02 .10
313 Tim Teufel .02 .10
314 Tom Brunansky .02 .10
315 Rex Hudler .02 .10
316 Dave Otto .02 .10
317 Jeff King .02 .10
318 Dan Gladden .02 .10
319 Bill Pecota .02 .10
320 Franklin Stubbs .02 .10
321 Gary Carter .07 .20
322 Melido Perez .02 .10
323 Eric Davis .07 .20
324 Greg Myers .02 .10
325 Pete Incaviglia .02 .10
326 Von Hayes .02 .10
327 Greg Swindell .02 .10
328 Steve Sax .02 .10
329 Chuck McElroy .02 .10
330 Gregg Jefferies .02 .10
331 Joe Oliver .02 .10
332 Paul Faries .02 .10
333 David West .02 .10
334 Craig Grebeck .02 .10
335 Chris Hammond .02 .10
336 Billy Ripken .02 .10
337 Scott Sanderson .02 .10
338 Dick Schofield .02 .10
339 Bob Milacki .02 .10
340 Kevin Reimer .02 .10
341 Jose DeLeon .02 .10
342 Henry Cotto .02 .10
343 Daryl Boston .02 .10
344 Kevin Gross .02 .10
345 Milt Thompson .02 .10
346 Luis Rivera .02 .10
347 Al Osuna .02 .10
348 Rob Deer .02 .10
349 Tim Leary .02 .10
350 Mike Stanton .02 .10
351 Dean Palmer .07 .20
352 Trevor Wilson .02 .10
353 Mark Eichhorn .02 .10
354 Scott Aldred .02 .10
355 Mark Whiten .02 .10
356 Leo Gomez .02 .10
357 Rafael Belliard .02 .10
358 Carlos Quintana .02 .10
359 Mark Davis .02 .10
360 Chris Nabholz .02 .10
361 Carlton Fisk .10 .30
362 Joe Orsulak .02 .10
363 Eric Anthony .02 .10
364 Greg Hibbard .02 .10
365 Scott Leius .02 .10
366 Hensley Meulens .02 .10
367 Chris Bosio .02 .10
368 Brian Downing .02 .10
369 Sammy Sosa .20 .50
370 Stan Belinda .02 .10
371 Joe Grahe .02 .10
372 Luis Salazar .02 .10
373 Lance Johnson .02 .10
374 Kal Daniels .02 .10
375 Dave Winfield .07 .20
376 Brook Jacoby .02 .10
377 Mariano Duncan .02 .10
378 Ron Darling .02 .10
379 Randy Johnson .20 .50
380 Chito Martinez .02 .10
381 Andres Galarraga .07 .20
382 Willie Randolph .07 .20
383 Charles Nagy .02 .10
384 Tim Belcher .02 .10
385 Duane Ward .02 .10
386 Vicente Palacios .02 .10
387 Mike Gallego .02 .10
388 Rich DeLucia .02 .10
389 Scott Radinsky .02 .10
390 Damon Berryhill. .02 .10
391 Kirk McCaskill .02 .10
392 Pedro Guerrero .07 .20
393 Kevin Mitchell .02 .10
394 Dickie Thon .02 .10
395 Bobby Bonilla .07 .20
396 Bill Wegman .02 .10
397 Dave Martinez .02 .10
398 Rick Sutcliffe .07 .20
399 Larry Andersen .02 .10
400 Tony Gwynn .25 .60
401 Rickey Henderson .20 .50
402 Greg Cadaret .02 .10
403 Keith Miller .02 .10
404 Bip Roberts .02 .10
405 Kevin Brown .07 .20
406 Mitch Williams .02 .10
407 Frank Viola .07 .20
408 Darren Lewis .02 .10
409 Bob Welch .02 .10
410 Bob Walk .02 .10
411 Todd Frohwirth .02 .10
412 Brian Hunter .02 .10
413 Ron Karkovice .02 .10
414 Mike Morgan .02 .10
415 Joe Hesketh .02 .10
416 Don Slaught .02 .10
417 Tom Henke .02 .10
418 Kurt Stillwell .02 .10
419 Hector Villaneuva .02 .10
420 Glenallen Hill .02 .10
421 Pat Borders .02 .10
422 Charlie Hough .07 .20
423 Charlie Leibrandt .02 .10
424 Eddie Murray .20 .50
425 Jesse Barfield .02 .10
426 Mark Lemke .02 .10
427 Kevin McReynolds .02 .10
428 Gilberto Reyes .02 .10
429 Ramon Martinez .02 .10
430 Steve Buechele .02 .10
431 David Wells .07 .20
432 Kyle Abbott .02 .10
433 John Habyan .02 .10
434 Kevin Appier .07 .20
435 Gene Larkin .02 .10
436 Sandy Alomar Jr. .02 .10
437 Mike Jackson .02 .10
438 Todd Benzinger .02 .10
439 Teddy Higuera .02 .10
440 Reggie Sanders .07 .20
441 Mark Carreon .02 .10
442 Bret Saberhagen .07 .20
443 Gene Nelson .02 .10
444 Jay Howell .02 .10
445 Roger McDowell .02 .10
446 Sid Bream .02 .10
447 Mackey Sasser .02 .10
448 Bill Swift .02 .10
449 Hubie Brooks .02 .10
450 David Cone .07 .20
451 Bobby Witt .02 .10
452 Brady Anderson .07 .20
453 Lee Stevens .02 .10
454 Luis Aquino .02 .10
455 Carney Lansford .07 .20
456 Carlos Hernandez .02 .10
457 Danny Jackson .02 .10
458 Gerald Young .02 .10
459 Tom Candiotti .02 .10
460 Billy Hatcher .02 .10
461 John Wetteland .07 .20
462 Mike Bordick .02 .10
463 Don Robinson .02 .10
464 Jeff Johnson .02 .10
465 Lonnie Smith .02 .10
466 Paul Assenmacher .02 .10
467 Alvin Davis .02 .10
468 Jim Eisenreich .02 .10
469 Brent Mayne .02 .10
470 Jeff Brantley .02 .10
471 Tim Burke .02 .10
472 Pat Mahomes RC .15 .40
473 Ryan Bowen .02 .10
474 Bryn Smith .02 .10
475 Mike Flanagan .02 .10
476 Reggie Jefferson .02 .10
477 Jeff Blauser .02 .10
478 Craig Lefferts .02 .10
479 Todd Worrell .02 .10
480 Scott Scudder .02 .10
481 Kirk Gibson .07 .20
482 Kenny Rogers .07 .20
483 Jack Morris .07 .20
484 Russ Swan .02 .10
485 Mike Huff .02 .10
486 Ken Hill .02 .10
487 Geronimo Pena .02 .10
488 Charlie O'Brien .02 .10
489 Mike Maddux .02 .10
490 Scott Livingstone .02 .10
491 Carl Willis .02 .10
492 Kelly Downs .02 .10
493 Dennis Cook .02 .10
494 Joe Magrane .02 .10
495 Bob Kipper .02 .10
496 Jose Mesa .02 .10
497 Charlie Hayes .02 .10
498 Joe Girardi .02 .10
499 Doug Jones .02 .10
500 Barry Bonds .60 1.50
501 Bill Krueger .02 .10
502 Glenn Braggs .02 .10
503 Eric King .02 .10
504 Frank Castillo .02 .10
505 Mike Gardiner .02 .10
506 Cory Snyder .02 .10
507 Steve Howe .02 .10
508 Jose Rijo .02 .10
509 Sid Fernandez .02 .10
510 Archi Cianfrocco RC .05 .15
511 Mark Guthrie .02 .10
512 Bob Ojeda .02 .10
513 John Doherty RC .05 .15
514 Dante Bichette .07 .20
515 Juan Berenguer .02 .10
516 Jeff M. Robinson .02 .10
517 Mike Macfarlane .02 .10
518 Matt Young .02 .10
519 Otis Nixon .02 .10
520 Brian Holman .02 .10
521 Chris Haney .02 .10
522 Jeff Kent RC 1.00 2.50
523 Chad Curtis RC .15 .40
524 Vince Horsman .02 .10
525 Rod Nichols .02 .10
526 Peter Hoy .02 .10
527 Shawn Boskie .02 .10
528 Alejandro Pena .02 .10
529 Dave Burba .02 .10
530 Ricky Jordan .02 .10
531 Dave Silvestri .02 .10
532 John Patterson UER RC .02 .10
533 Jeff Branson .02 .10
534 Derrick May .02 .10
535 Esteban Beltre .02 .10
536 Jose Melendez .02 .10
537 Wally Joyner .07 .20
538 Eddie Taubensee RC .15 .40
539 Jim Abbott .10 .30
540 Brian Williams RC .05 .15
541 Donovan Osborne .02 .10
542 Patrick Lennon .02 .10
543 Mike Groppuso RC .05 .15
544 Jarvis Brown .02 .10
545 Shawn Livsey RC .05 .15
546 Jeff Ware .02 .10
547 Danny Tartabull .02 .10
548 Bobby Jones RC .15 .40
549 Ken Griffey Jr. .40 1.00
550 Rey Sanchez RC .15 .40
551 Pedro Astacio RC .15 .40
552 Juan Guerrero .02 .10
553 Jacob Brumfield .02 .10
554 Ben Rivera .02 .10
555 Brian Jordan RC .30 .75
556 Denny Neagle .07 .20
557 Cliff Brantley .02 .10
558 Anthony Young .02 .10
559 John Vander Wal .02 .10
560 Monty Fariss .02 .10
561 Russ Springer RC .05 .15
562 Pat Listach RC .15 .40
563 Pat Hentgen .02 .10
564 Andy Stankiewicz .02 .10
565 Mike Perez .02 .10
566 Mike Bielecki .02 .10
567 Butch Henry RC .05 .15
568 Dave Nilsson .02 .10
569 Scott Hatteberg RC .15 .40
570 Ruben Amaro .02 .10
571 Todd Hundley .02 .10
572 Moises Alou .07 .20
573 Hector Fajardo RC .05 .15
574 Todd Van Poppel .02 .10
575 Willie Banks .02 .10
576 Bob Zupcic RC .05 .15
577 J.J. Johnson RC .05 .15
578 John Burkett .02 .10
579 Trever Miller RC .05 .15
580 Scott Bankhead .02 .10
581 Rich Amaral .02 .10
582 Kenny Lofton .10 .30
583 Matt Stairs RC .15 .40
584 Don Mattingly .20 .50
Rod Carew IDOLS
585 S.Avery/J.Morris .02 .10
586 Roberto Alomar .07 .20
Sandy Alomar SR. IDOLS
587 Scott Sanderson .07 .20
Catfish Hunter IDOLS
588 Dave Justice .07 .20
Willie Stargell IDOLS
589 Rex Hudler .20 .50
Roger Staubach IDOLS
590 David Cone .07 .20
Jackie Gleason IDOLS
591 T.Gwynn/W.Davis .10 .30
592 Orel Hershiser SIDE .02 .10
593 John Wetteland SIDE .02 .10
594 Tom Glavine SIDE .07 .20
595 Randy Johnson SIDE .10 .30
596 Jim Gott SIDE .02 .10
597 Donald Harris .02 .10
598 Shawn Hare RC .05 .15
599 Chris Gardner .02 .10
600 Rusty Meacham .02 .10
601 Benito Santiago .07 .20
602 Eric Davis SHADE .02 .10
603 Jose Lind SHADE .02 .10
604 David Justice SHADES .02 .10
605 Tim Raines SHADE .02 .10
606 Randy Tomlin GRIP .02 .10
607 Jack McDowell GRIP .02 .10
608 Greg Maddux GRIP .20 .50
609 Charles Nagy GRIP .02 .10
610 Tom Candiotti GRIP .02 .10
611 David Cone GRIP .02 .10
612 Steve Avery GRIP .02 .10
613 Rod Beck GRIP .15 .40
614 Rickey Henderson TECH .10 .30
615 Benito Santiago TECH .02 .10
616 Ruben Sierra TECH .02 .10
617 Ryne Sandberg TECH .20 .50
618 Nolan Ryan TECH .40 1.00
619 Brett Butler TECH .02 .10
620 David Justice TECH .02 .10

1992 Pinnacle Rookie Idols

COMPLETE SET (18) 10.00 25.00
RANDOM INSERTS IN SER.2 FOIL PACKS
1 R.Sanders .50 1.25
E.Davis
2 Hector Fajardo .75 2.00
J.Abbott
3 G.Brett 4.00 10.00
G.Cooper
4 R.Clemens 3.00 8.00
M.Wohlers
5 Luis Mercedes .50 1.25
and Julio Franco
6 Willie Banks .50 1.25
D.Gooden
7 K.Lofton 1.50 4.00
R.Henderson
8 Keith Mitchell .30 .75
and Dave Henderson
9 K.Batiste .75 2.00
B.Larkin
10 T.Munson 1.50 4.00
T.Hundley
11 C.Ripken 5.00 12.00
E.Zosky
12 N.Ryan 6.00 15.00
T.Van Poppel
13 J.Thome 2.50 6.00
R.Sandberg
14 Dave Fleming .50 1.25
B.Murcer
15 O.Smith 2.50 6.00
R.Clayton
16 Don Harris .50 1.25
D.Strawberry
17 Chad Curtis .50 1.25
A.Trammell
18 D.Bell .50 1.25
D.Winfield

1992 Pinnacle Slugfest

COMPLETE SET (15) 12.50 30.00
ONE PER SLUGFEST JUMBO PACK
1 Cecil Fielder .30 .75
2 Mark McGwire 2.00 5.00
3 Jose Canseco .50 1.25
4 Barry Bonds 2.50 6.00
5 David Justice .30 .75
6 Bobby Bonilla .30 .75
7 Ken Griffey Jr. 1.50 4.00
8 Ron Gant .30 .75
9 Ryne Sandberg 1.25 3.00
10 Ruben Sierra .30 .75
11 Frank Thomas .75 2.00
12 Will Clark .50 1.25
13 Kirby Puckett .75 2.00
14 Cal Ripken 2.50 6.00
15 Jeff Bagwell .75 2.00

1992 Pinnacle Team 2000

COMPLETE SET (80) 12.50 30.00
COMPLETE SERIES 1 (40) 8.00 20.00
COMPLETE SERIES 2 (40) 4.00 10.00
THREE PER JUMBO PACK .50 1.25
1 Mike Mussina .50 1.25
2 Phil Plantier .08 .25
3 Frank Thomas .50 1.25
4 Travis Fryman .20 .50
5 Kevin Appier .20 .50
6 Chuck Knoblauch .20 .50
7 Pat Kelly .08 .25
8 Ivan Rodriguez .50 1.25
9 David Justice .20 .50
10 Jeff Bagwell .50 1.25
11 Marquis Grissom .20 .50
12 Andy Benes .08 .25
13 Gregg Olson .08 .25
14 Kevin Morton .08 .25
15 Tim Naehring .08 .25
16 Dave Hollins .08 .25
17 Sandy Alomar Jr. .08 .25
18 Albert Belle .20 .50
19 Charles Nagy .08 .25
20 Brian McRae .08 .25
21 Larry Walker .30 .75
22 Delino DeShields .08 .25
23 Jeff Johnson .08 .25
24 Bernie Williams .30 .75
25 Jose Offerman .08 .25
26 Juan Gonzalez .30 .75
27A Juan Guzman .08 .25
27B Juan Guzman .08 .25
28 Eric Anthony .08 .25
29 Brian Hunter .08 .25
30 John Smoltz .30 .75
31 Deion Sanders .30 .75
32 Greg Maddux .75 2.00
33 Andujar Cedeno .08 .25
34 Royce Clayton .08 .25
35 Kenny Lofton .30 .75
36 Cal Eldred .08 .25
37 Jim Thome .50 1.25
38 Gary DiSarcina .08 .25
39 Brian Jordan .75 2.00
40 Chad Curtis .40 1.00
41 Ben McDonald .08 .25
42 Jim Abbott .30 .75
43 Robin Ventura .20 .50
44 Milt Cuyler .08 .25
45 Gregg Jefferies .08 .25
46 Scott Radinsky .08 .25
47 Ken Griffey Jr. 1.00 2.50
48 Roberto Alomar .30 .75
49 Ramon Martinez .08 .25
50 Bret Barberie .08 .25
51 Ray Lankford .20 .50
52 Leo Gomez .08 .25
53 Tommy Greene .08 .25
54 Mo Vaughn .20 .50
55 Sammy Sosa .50 1.25
56 Carlos Baerga .08 .25
57 Mark Lewis .08 .25
58 Tom Gordon .08 .25
59 Gary Sheffield .20 .50
60 Scott Erickson .08 .25
61 Pedro Munoz .08 .25
62 Tino Martinez .30 .75
63 Darren Lewis .08 .25
64 Dean Palmer .20 .50
65 John Olerud .20 .50
66 Steve Avery .08 .25
67 Pete Harnisch .08 .25
68 Luis Gonzalez .20 .50
69 Kim Batiste .08 .25
70 Reggie Sanders .20 .50
71 Luis Mercedes .08 .25
72 Todd Van Poppel .08 .25
73 Gary Scott .08 .25
74 Monty Fariss .08 .25
75 Kyle Abbott .08 .25
76 Eric Karros .20 .50
77 Mo Sanford .08 .25
78 Todd Hundley .08 .25
79 Reggie Jefferson .08 .25
80 Pat Mahomes .40 1.00

1992 Pinnacle Team Pinnacle

COMPLETE SET (12) 15.00 40.00
RANDOM INSERTS IN SER.1 FOIL PACKS
1 R.Clemens 1.25 3.00
R.Martinez
2 J.Abbott .40 1.00
S.Avery
3 I.Rodriguez 1.00 2.50
B.Santiago
4 F.Thomas 12.00 30.00
W.Clark
5 R.Sandberg 2.00 5.00
R.Alomar
6 R.Ventura .40 1.00
M.Williams
7 C.Ripken 3.00 8.00
B.Larkin
8 B.Bonds 1.50 4.00
D.Tartabull
9 K.Griffey Jr. 2.00 5.00
B.Butler
10 R.Sierra .40 1.00
D.Justice
11 D.Eckersley .60 1.50
R.Dibble
12 S.Radinsky .40 1.00
J.Franco

1992 Pinnacle Rookies

This 30-card boxed set features top rookies of the 1992 season, with at least one player from each team. A total of 180,000 sets were produced.

COMP.FACT.SET (30) 1.50 4.00
1 Luis Mercedes .07 .20
2 Scott Cooper .07 .20
3 Kenny Lofton .20 .50
4 John Doherty .07 .20
5 Pat Listach .10 .30
6 Andy Stankiewicz .07 .20
7 Derek Bell .10 .30
8 Gary DiSarcina .07 .20
9 Roberto Hernandez .07 .20
10 Joel Johnston .07 .20
11 Pat Mahomes .07 .20
12 Todd Van Poppel .07 .20
13 Dave Fleming .07 .20
14 Monty Fariss .07 .20
15 Gary Scott .07 .20
16 Moises Alou .10 .30
17 Todd Hundley .07 .20
18 Kim Batiste .07 .20
19 Denny Neagle .10 .30
20 Donovan Osborne .07 .20
21 Mark Wohlers .07 .20
22 Reggie Sanders .10 .30
23 Brian Williams .07 .20
24 Eric Karros .10 .30
25 Frank Seminara RC .07 .20
26 Royce Clayton .07 .20
27 Dave Nilsson .07 .20
28 Matt Stairs .10 .30
29 Chad Curtis .10 .30
30 Carlos Hernandez .07 .20

1992 Pinnacle Mantle

This 30-card standard-size set commemorates the life and career of Mickey Mantle. A total of 180,000 sets were produced. Each set was packaged in a black and blue box that featured a picture of Mantle and a checklist.

COMPLETE SET (30) 8.00 20.00
COMMON CARD (1-30) .30 .75
1 Father and Son .40 1.00
24 Mick and Stan .60 1.50
Stan Musial
25 Whitey and Yogi .40 1.00
Whitey Ford
Yogi Berra
26 Mick and Billy .40 1.00
Billy Martin
27 Mick and Casey .40 1.00
Casey Stengel

1993 Pinnacle

The 1993 Pinnacle set (by Score) contains 620 standard-size cards issued in two series of 310 cards each. Cards were distributed in hobby and retail foil packs and 27-card jumbo superpacks. The set includes the following topical subsets: Rookies (238-288, 575-620), Now and Then (289-296, 470-476), Idols (297-303, 477-483), Hometown Heroes (304-310, 484-490), and Draft Picks (455-469). Rookie Cards in this set include Derek Jeter, Jason Kendall and Shannon Stewart.

COMPLETE SET (620) 15.00 40.00
COMPLETE SERIES 1 (310) 6.00 15.00
COMPLETE SERIES 2 (310) 10.00 25.00
SUBSET CARDS HALF VALUE OF BASE CARDS
1 Gary Sheffield .10 .30
2 Cal Eldred .05 .15
3 Larry Walker .10 .30
4 Deion Sanders .20 .50
5 Dave Fleming .05 .15
6 Carlos Baerga .05 .15
7 Bernie Williams .20 .50
8 John Kruk .10 .30
9 Jimmy Key .10 .30
10 Jeff Bagwell .20 .50
11 Jim Abbott .20 .50
12 Terry Steinbach .05 .15
13 Bob Tewksbury .05 .15
14 Eric Karros .10 .30
15 Ryne Sandberg .50 1.25
16 Will Clark .20 .50
17 Edgar Martinez .20 .50
18 Eddie Murray .30 .75
19 Andy Van Slyke .20 .50
20 Cal Ripken 1.00 2.50
21 Ivan Rodriguez .20 .50
22 Barry Larkin .20 .50
23 Don Mattingly .75 2.00
24 Gregg Jefferies .05 .15
25 Roger Clemens .60 1.50
26 Cecil Fielder .10 .30
27 Kent Hrbek .10 .30
28 Robin Ventura .10 .30
29 Rickey Henderson .30 .75
30 Roberto Alomar .20 .50
31 Luis Polonia .05 .15
32 Andujar Cedeno .05 .15
33 Pat Listach .05 .15
34 Mark Grace .20 .50
35 Otis Nixon .05 .15
36 Felix Jose .05 .15
37 Mike Sharperson .05 .15
38 Dennis Martinez .10 .30
39 Willie McGee .10 .30
40 Kenny Lofton .10 .30
41 Randy Johnson .30 .75
42 Andy Benes .05 .15
43 Bobby Bonilla .10 .30
44 Mike Mussina .20 .50
45 Len Dykstra .10 .30
46 Ellis Burks .10 .30
47 Chris Sabo .05 .15
48 Jay Bell .10 .30
49 Jose Canseco .20 .50
50 Craig Biggio .20 .50
51 Wally Joyner .10 .30
52 Mickey Tettleton .05 .15
53 Tim Raines .10 .30
54 Brian Harper .05 .15
55 Rene Gonzales .05 .15
56 Mark Langston .05 .15
57 Jack Morris .10 .30
58 Mark McGwire .75 2.00
59 Ken Caminiti .10 .30
60 Terry Pendleton .10 .30
61 Dave Nilsson .05 .15
62 Tom Pagnozzi .05 .15
63 Mike Morgan .05 .15
64 Darryl Strawberry .10 .30
65 Charles Nagy .05 .15
66 Ken Hill .05 .15
67 Matt Williams .10 .30
68 Jay Buhner .10 .30
69 Vince Coleman .05 .15
70 Brady Anderson .10 .30
71 Fred McGriff .20 .50
72 Ben McDonald .05 .15
73 Terry Mulholland .05 .15
74 Randy Tomlin .05 .15
75 Nolan Ryan 1.25 3.00
76 Frank Viola UER .10 .30
77 Jose Rijo .05 .15
78 Shane Mack .05 .15
79 Travis Fryman .10 .30
80 Jack McDowell .05 .15
81 Mark Gubicza .05 .15
82 Matt Nokes .05 .15
83 Bert Blyleven .10 .30
84 Eric Anthony .05 .15
85 Mike Bordick .05 .15
86 John Olerud .10 .30
87 B.J. Surhoff .10 .30
88 Bernard Gilkey .05 .15
89 Shawon Dunston .05 .15
90 Tom Glavine .20 .50
91 Brett Butler .10 .30
92 Moises Alou .10 .30
93 Albert Belle .10 .30
94 Darren Lewis .05 .15
95 Omar Vizquel .20 .50
96 Dwight Gooden .10 .30
97 Gregg Olson .05 .15
98 Tony Gwynn .40 1.00
99 Darren Daulton .10 .30
100 Dennis Eckersley .10 .30
101 Rob Dibble .10 .30
102 Mike Greenwell .05 .15
103 Jose Lind .05 .15
104 Julio Franco .10 .30
105 Tom Gordon .05 .15
106 Scott Livingstone .05 .15
107 Chuck Knoblauch .10 .30
108 Frank Thomas .30 .75
109 Melido Perez .05 .15
110 Ken Griffey Jr. .60 1.50
111 Harold Baines .10 .30
112 Gary Gaetti .10 .30
113 Pete Harnisch .05 .15
114 David Wells .10 .30
115 Charlie Leibrandt .05 .15
116 Ray Lankford .10 .30
117 Kevin Seitzer .05 .15
118 Robin Yount .50 1.25
119 Lenny Harris .05 .15
120 Chris James .05 .15
121 Delino DeShields .05 .15
122 Kirt Manwaring .05 .15
123 Glenallen Hill .05 .15
124 Hensley Meulens .05 .15
125 Darrin Jackson .05 .15
126 Todd Hundley .05 .15
127 Dave Hollins .05 .15
128 Sam Horn .05 .15
129 Roberto Hernandez .05 .15
130 Vicente Palacios .05 .15
131 George Brett .75 2.00
132 Dave Martinez .05 .15
133 Kevin Appier .10 .30
134 Pat Kelly .05 .15
135 Pedro Munoz .05 .15
136 Mark Carreon .05 .15
137 Lance Johnson .05 .15
138 Devon White .10 .30
139 Julio Valera .05 .15
140 Eddie Taubensee .05 .15
141 Willie Wilson .05 .15
142 Stan Belinda .05 .15
143 John Smoltz .20 .50
144 Darryl Hamilton .05 .15
145 Sammy Sosa .30 .75
146 Carlos Hernandez .05 .15
147 Tom Candiotti .05 .15
148 Mike Felder .05 .15
149 Rusty Meacham .05 .15
150 Ivan Calderon .05 .15
151 Pete O'Brien .05 .15
152 Erik Hanson .05 .15
153 Billy Ripken .05 .15
154 Kurt Stillwell .05 .15
155 Jeff Kent .30 .75
156 Mickey Morandini .05 .15
157 Randy Milligan .05 .15
158 Reggie Sanders .10 .30
159 Luis Rivera .05 .15
160 Orlando Merced .05 .15
161 Dean Palmer .10 .30
162 Mike Perez .05 .15
163 Scott Erickson .05 .15
164 Kevin McReynolds .05 .15
165 Kevin Maas .05 .15
166 Ozzie Guillen .10 .30
167 Rob Deer .05 .15
168 Danny Tartabull .05 .15
169 Lee Stevens .05 .15
170 Dave Henderson .05 .15
171 Derek Bell .05 .15
172 Steve Finley .10 .30
173 Greg Olson .05 .15
174 Geronimo Pena .05 .15
175 Paul Quantrill .05 .15
176 Steve Buechele .05 .15
177 Kevin Gross .05 .15
178 Tim Wallach .05 .15
179 Dave Valle .05 .15
180 Dave Silvestri .05 .15
181 Bud Black .05 .15
182 Henry Rodriguez .05 .15
183 Tim Teufel .05 .15
184 Mark McLemore .05 .15
185 Bret Saberhagen .10 .30
186 Chris Hoiles .05 .15
187 Ricky Jordan .05 .15
188 Don Slaught .05 .15
189 Mo Vaughn .10 .30
190 Joe Oliver .05 .15
191 Juan Gonzalez .10 .30
192 Scott Leius .05 .15
193 Milt Cuyler .05 .15
194 Chris Haney .05 .15
195 Ron Karkovice .05 .15
196 Steve Farr .05 .15
197 John Orton .05 .15
198 Kelly Gruber .05 .15
199 Ron Darling .05 .15
200 Ruben Sierra .10 .30
201 Chuck Finley .10 .30
202 Mike Moore .05 .15
203 Pat Borders .05 .15
204 Sid Bream .05 .15
205 Todd Zeile .05 .15
206 Rick Wilkins .05 .15
207 Jim Gantner .05 .15
208 Frank Castillo .05 .15
209 Dave Hansen .05 .15
210 Trevor Wilson .05 .15
211 Sandy Alomar Jr. .05 .15
212 Sean Berry .05 .15
213 Tino Martinez .20 .50
214 Chito Martinez .05 .15
215 Dan Walters .05 .15
216 John Franco .10 .30
217 Glenn Davis .05 .15
218 Mariano Duncan .05 .15
219 Mike LaValliere .05 .15
220 Rafael Palmeiro .20 .50
221 Jack Clark .10 .30
222 Hal Morris .05 .15
223 Ed Sprague .05 .15
224 John Valentin .05 .15
225 Sam Militello .05 .15
226 Bob Wickman .05 .15
227 Damion Easley .05 .15
228 John Jaha .05 .15
229 Bob Ayrault .05 .15
230 Mo Sanford .05 .15
231 Walt Weiss .05 .15
232 Dante Bichette .10 .30
233 Steve Decker .05 .15
234 Jerald Clark .05 .15
235 Bryan Harvey .05 .15
236 Joe Girardi .05 .15
237 Dave Magadan .05 .15
238 David Nied .05 .15
239 Eric Wedge RC .15 .40
240 Rico Brogna .05 .15
241 J.T. Bruett .05 .15
242 Jonathan Hurst .05 .15
243 Bret Boone .10 .30
244 Manny Alexander .05 .15
245 Scooter Tucker .05 .15
246 Troy Neel .05 .15
247 Eddie Zosky .05 .15
248 Melvin Nieves .05 .15
249 Ryan Thompson .05 .15
250 Shawn Barton RC .05 .15
251 Ryan Klesko .10 .30
252 Mike Piazza 1.25 3.00
253 Steve Hosey .05 .15
254 Shane Reynolds .05 .15
255 Dan Wilson .10 .30
256 Tom Marsh .05 .15
257 Barry Manuel .05 .15
258 Paul Miller .05 .15
259 Pedro Martinez .60 1.50

260 Steve Cooke .05 .15
261 Johnny Guzman .05 .15
262 Mike Butcher .05 .15
263 Bien Figueroa .05 .15
264 Rich Rowland .05 .15
265 Shawn Jeter .05 .15
266 Gerald Williams .05 .15
267 Derek Parks .05 .15
268 Henry Mercedes .05 .15
269 David Hulse RC .05 .15
270 Tim Pugh RC .05 .15
271 William Suero .05 .15
272 Ozzie Canseco .05 .15
273 Fernando Ramsey RC .05 .15
274 Bernardo Brito .05 .15
275 Dave Mlicki .05 .15
276 Tim Salmon .20 .50
277 Mike Raczka .05 .15
278 Ken Ryan RC .15 .40
279 Rafael Bournigal .05 .15
280 Wil Cordero .05 .15
281 Billy Ashley .05 .15
282 Paul Wagner .05 .15
283 Blas Minor .05 .15
284 Rick Trlicek .05 .15
285 Willie Greene .05 .15
286 Ted Wood .05 .15
287 Phil Clark .05 .15
288 Jesse Levis .05 .15
289 Tony Gwynn NT .20 .50
290 Nolan Ryan NT .60 1.50
291 Dennis Martinez NT .05 .15
292 Eddie Murray NT .20 .50
293 Robin Yount NT .30 .75
294 George Brett NT .40 1.00
295 Dave Winfield NT .05 .15
296 Bert Blyleven NT .05 .15
297 J.Bagwell .30 .75
C.Yastrzemski
298 J.Smoltz .10 .30
J.Morris
299 L.Walker .10 .30
M.Bossy
300 G.Sheffield .10 .30
B.Larkin
301 I.Rodriguez .10 .30
C.Fisk
302 D.DeShields .30 .75
Malcolm X
303 T.Salmon .20 .50
D.Evans
304 Bernard Gilkey HH .05 .15
305 Cal Ripken HH .50 1.25
306 Barry Larkin HH .10 .30
307 Kent Hrbek HH .05 .15
308 Rickey Henderson HH .20 .50
309 Darryl Strawberry HH .05 .15
310 John Franco HH .05 .15
311 Todd Stottlemyre .05 .15
312 Luis Gonzalez .10 .30
313 Tommy Greene .05 .15
314 Randy Velarde .05 .15
315 Steve Avery .05 .15
316 Jose Oquendo .05 .15
317 Rey Sanchez .05 .15
318 Greg Vaughn .05 .15
319 Orel Hershiser .10 .30
320 Paul Sorrento .05 .15
321 Royce Clayton .05 .15
322 John Vander Wal .05 .15
323 Henry Cotto .05 .15
324 Pete Schourek .05 .15
325 David Segui .05 .15
326 Arthur Rhodes .05 .15
327 Bruce Hurst .05 .15
328 Wes Chamberlain .05 .15
329 Ozzie Smith .50 1.25
330 Scott Cooper .05 .15
331 Felix Fermin .05 .15
332 Mike Macfarlane .05 .15
333 Dan Gladden .05 .15
334 Kevin Tapani .05 .15
335 Steve Sax .05 .15
336 Jeff Montgomery .05 .15
337 Gary DiSarcina .05 .15
338 Lance Blankenship .05 .15
339 Brian Williams .05 .15
340 Duane Ward .05 .15
341 Chuck McElroy .05 .15
342 Joe Magrane .05 .15
343 Jaime Navarro .05 .15
344 David Justice .10 .30
345 Jose Offerman .05 .15
346 Marquis Grissom .10 .30
347 Bill Swift .05 .15
348 Jim Thome .20 .50
349 Archi Cianfrocco .05 .15
350 Anthony Young .05 .15
351 Leo Gomez .05 .15
352 Bill Gullickson .05 .15
353 Alan Trammell .10 .30
354 Dan Pasqua .05 .15
355 Jeff King .05 .15
356 Kevin Brown .10 .30
357 Tim Belcher .05 .15
358 Bip Roberts .05 .15
359 Brent Mayne .05 .15
360 Rheal Cormier .05 .15
361 Mark Guthrie .05 .15
362 Craig Grebeck .05 .15
363 Andy Stankiewicz .05 .15
364 Juan Guzman .05 .15
365 Bobby Witt .05 .15
366 Mark Portugal .05 .15
367 Brian McRae .05 .15
368 Mark Lemke .05 .15
369 Bill Wegman .05 .15
370 Donovan Osborne .05 .15
371 Derrick May .05 .15
372 Carl Willis .05 .15
373 Chris Nabholz .05 .15
374 Mark Lewis .05 .15
375 John Burkett .05 .15
376 Luis Mercedes .05 .15
377 Ramon Martinez .05 .15
378 Kyle Abbott .05 .15
379 Mark Wohlers .05 .15
380 Bob Walk .05 .15
381 Kenny Rogers .10 .30
382 Tim Naehring .05 .15
383 Alex Fernandez .05 .15
384 Keith Miller .05 .15
385 Mike Henneman .05 .15
386 Rick Aguilera .05 .15
387 George Bell .05 .15
388 Mike Gallego .05 .15
389 Howard Johnson .05 .15
390 Kim Batiste .05 .15
391 Jerry Browne .05 .15
392 Damon Berryhill .05 .15
393 Ricky Bones .05 .15
394 Omar Olivares .05 .15
395 Mike Harkey .05 .15
396 Pedro Astacio .05 .15
397 John Wetteland .10 .30
398 Rod Beck .05 .15
399 Thomas Howard .05 .15
400 Mike Devereaux .05 .15
401 Tim Wakefield .30 .75
402 Curt Schilling .10 .30
403 Zane Smith .05 .15
404 Bob Zupcic .05 .15
405 Tom Browning .05 .15
406 Tony Phillips .05 .15
407 John Doherty .05 .15
408 Pat Mahomes .05 .15
409 John Habyan .05 .15
410 Steve Olin .05 .15
411 Chad Curtis .05 .15
412 Joe Grahe .05 .15
413 John Patterson .05 .15
414 Brian Hunter .05 .15
415 Doug Henry .05 .15
416 Lee Smith .10 .30
417 Bob Scanlan .05 .15
418 Kent Mercker .05 .15
419 Mel Rojas .05 .15
420 Mark Whiten .05 .15
421 Carlton Fisk .20 .50
422 Candy Maldonado .05 .15
423 Doug Drabek .05 .15
424 Wade Boggs .20 .50
425 Mark Davis .05 .15
426 Kirby Puckett .30 .75
427 Joe Carter .10 .30
428 Paul Molitor .10 .30
429 Eric Davis .10 .30
430 Darryl Kile .10 .30
431 Jeff Parrett .05 .15
432 Jeff Blauser .05 .15
433 Dan Plesac .05 .15
434 Andres Galarraga .10 .30
435 Jim Gott .05 .15
436 Jose Mesa .05 .15
437 Ben Rivera .05 .15
438 Dave Winfield .10 .30
439 Norm Charlton .05 .15
440 Chris Bosio .05 .15
441 Wilson Alvarez .05 .15
442 Dave Stewart .10 .30
443 Doug Jones .05 .15
444 Jeff Russell .05 .15
445 Ron Gant .10 .30
446 Paul O'Neill .20 .50
447 Charlie Hayes .05 .15
448 Joe Hesketh .05 .15
449 Chris Hammond .05 .15
450 Hipolito Pichardo .05 .15
451 Scott Radinsky .05 .15
452 Bobby Thigpen .05 .15
453 Xavier Hernandez .05 .15
454 Lonnie Smith .05 .15
455 Jamie Arnold RC .05 .15
456 B.J.Wallace .05 .15
457 Derek Jeter RC 20.00 50.00
458 Jason Kendall RC .50 1.25
459 Rick Helling .05 .15
460 Derek Wallace RC .05 .15
461 Sean Lowe RC .05 .15
462 Shannon Stewart RC .40 1.00
463 Benji Grigsby RC .05 .15
464 Todd Steverson RC .05 .15
465 Dan Serafini RC .05 .15
466 Michael Tucker .05 .15
467 Chris Roberts .05 .15
468 Pete Janicki RC .05 .15
469 Jeff Schmidt RC .05 .15
470 Don Mattingly NT .40 1.00
471 Cal Ripken NT .50 1.25
472 Jack Morris NT .05 .15
473 Terry Pendleton NT .05 .15
474 Dennis Eckersley NT .10 .30
475 Carlton Fisk NT .10 .30
476 Wade Boggs NT .10 .30
477 L.Dykstra .10 .30
K.Stabler
478 D.Tartabull .05 .15
J.Tartabull
479 J.Conine .20 .50
D.Murphy
480 G.Jefferies .05 .15
R.Cey
481 P.Molitor .10 .30
H.Killebrew
482 J.Valentin .05 .15
D.Concepcion
483 A.Arias .05 .15
D.Winfield
484 Barry Bonds HH .40 1.00
485 Doug Drabek HH .05 .15
486 Dave Winfield HH .05 .15
487 Brett Butler HH .05 .15
488 Harold Baines HH .05 .15
489 David Cone HH .05 .15
490 Willie McGee HH .05 .15
491 Robby Thompson .05 .15
492 Pete Incaviglia .05 .15
493 Manuel Lee .05 .15
494 Rafael Belliard .05 .15
495 Scott Fletcher .05 .15
496 Jeff Frye .05 .15
497 Andre Dawson .10 .30
498 Mike Scioscia .05 .15
499 Spike Owen .05 .15
500 Sid Fernandez .05 .15
501 Joe Orsulak .05 .15
502 Benito Santiago .10 .30
503 Dale Murphy .20 .50
504 Barry Bonds .75 2.00
505 Jose Guzman .05 .15
506 Tony Pena .05 .15
507 Greg Swindell .05 .15
508 Mike Pagliarulo .05 .15
509 Lou Whitaker .10 .30
510 Greg Gagne .05 .15
511 Butch Henry .05 .15
512 Jeff Brantley .05 .15
513 Jack Armstrong .05 .15
514 Danny Jackson .05 .15
515 Junior Felix .05 .15
516 Milt Thompson .05 .15
517 Greg Maddux .50 1.25
518 Eric Young .05 .15
519 Jody Reed .05 .15
520 Roberto Kelly .05 .15
521 Darren Holmes .05 .15
522 Craig Lefferts .05 .15
523 Charlie Hough .10 .30
524 Bo Jackson .30 .75
525 Bill Spiers .05 .15
526 Orestes Destrade .05 .15
527 Greg Hibbard .05 .15
528 Roger McDowell .05 .15
529 Cory Snyder .05 .15
530 Harold Reynolds .10 .30
531 Kevin Reimer .05 .15
532 Rick Sutcliffe .10 .30
533 Tony Fernandez .05 .15
534 Tom Brunansky .05 .15
535 Jeff Reardon .10 .30
536 Chili Davis .10 .30
537 Bob Ojeda .05 .15
538 Greg Colbrunn .05 .15
539 Phil Plantier .05 .15
540 Brian Jordan .10 .30
541 Pete Smith .05 .15
542 Frank Tanana .05 .15
543 John Smiley .05 .15
544 David Cone .10 .30
545 Daryl Boston .05 .15
546 Tom Henke .05 .15
547 Bill Krueger .05 .15
548 Freddie Benavides .05 .15
549 Randy Myers .05 .15
550 Reggie Jefferson .05 .15
551 Kevin Mitchell .05 .15
552 Dave Stieb .05 .15
553 Bret Barberie .05 .15
554 Tim Crews .05 .15
555 Doug Dascenzo .05 .15
556 Alex Cole .05 .15
557 Jeff Innis .05 .15
558 Carlos Garcia .05 .15
559 Steve Howe .05 .15
560 Kirk McCaskill .05 .15
561 Frank Seminara .05 .15
562 Cris Carpenter .05 .15
563 Mike Stanley .05 .15
564 Carlos Quintana .05 .15
565 Mitch Williams .05 .15
566 Juan Bell .05 .15
567 Eric Fox .05 .15
568 Al Leiter .10 .30
569 Mike Stanton .05 .15
570 Scott Kamieniecki .05 .15
571 Ryan Bowen .05 .15
572 Andy Ashby .05 .15
573 Bob Welch .05 .15
574 Scott Sanderson .05 .15
575 Joe Kmak .05 .15
576 Scott Pose RC .05 .15
577 Ricky Gutierrez .05 .15
578 Mike Trombley .05 .15
579 Sterling Hitchcock RC .15 .40
580 Rodney Bolton .05 .15
581 Tyler Green .05 .15
582 Tim Costo .05 .15
583 Tim Laker RC .05 .15
584 Steve Reed RC .05 .15
585 Tom Kramer RC .05 .15
586 Robb Nen .10 .30
587 Jim Tatum RC .05 .15
588 Frank Bolick .05 .15
589 Kevin Young .10 .30
590 Matt Whiteside RC .05 .15
591 Cesar Hernandez .05 .15
592 Mike Mohler RC .15 .40
593 Alan Embree .05 .15
594 Terry Jorgensen .05 .15
595 John Cummings RC .05 .15
596 Domingo Martinez RC .05 .15
597 Benji Gil .05 .15
598 Todd Pratt RC .15 .40
599 Rene Arocha RC .15 .40
600 Dennis Moeller .05 .15
601 Jeff Conine .10 .30
602 Trevor Hoffman .30 .75
603 Daniel Smith .05 .15
604 Lee Tinsley .05 .15
605 Dan Peltier .05 .15
606 Billy Brewer .05 .15
607 Matt Walbeck RC .15 .40
608 Richie Lewis RC .05 .15
609 J.T.Snow RC .25 .60
610 Pat Gomez RC .05 .15
611 Phil Hiatt .05 .15
612 Alex Arias .05 .15
613 Kevin Rogers .05 .15
614 Al Martin .05 .15
615 Greg Gohr .05 .15
616 Graeme Lloyd RC .15 .40
617 Kent Bottenfield .05 .15
618 Chuck Carr .05 .15
619 Darrell Sherman RC .05 .15
620 Mike Lansing RC .15 .40

1993 Pinnacle Expansion Opening Day

COMPLETE SET (9) 10.00 25.00
ONE CARD PER SEALED SER.2 HOBBY BOX
SETS DISTRIBUTED VIA MAIL-IN OFFER
1 C.Hough 2.00 5.00
D.Nied
2 B.Santiago 2.00 5.00
J.Girardi
3 A.Galarraga 2.00 5.00
O.Destrade
4 B.Barberie 1.00 2.50
E.Young
5 D.Magadan 1.00 2.50
C.Hayes
6 W.Weiss 1.00 2.50
F.Benavides
7 J.Conine 2.00 5.00
J.Clark
8 S.Pose 1.00 2.50
A.Cole
9 J.Felix 2.00 5.00
D.Bichette

1993 Pinnacle Rookie Team Pinnacle

COMPLETE SET (10) 15.00 40.00
SER.2 STATED ODDS 1:90
1 P.Martinez 6.00 15.00
M.Trombley
2 K.Rogers 2.00 5.00
S.Hitchcock
3 M.Piazza 10.00 25.00
J.Levis
4 R.Klesko 3.00 8.00
J.T.Snow
5 J.Patterson 3.00 8.00
B.Boone
6 K.Young 2.00 5.00
D.Martinez
7 W.Cordero 2.00 5.00
M.Alexander
8 T.Salmon 4.00 10.00
S.Hosey
9 R.Thompson 2.00 5.00
G.Williams
10 M.Nieves 2.00 5.00
D.Hulse

1993 Pinnacle Slugfest

COMPLETE SET (30) 25.00 60.00
ONE PER SER.2 JUMBO PACK
1 Juan Gonzalez .60 1.50
2 Mark McGwire 4.00 10.00
3 Cecil Fielder .60 1.50
4 Joe Carter .60 1.50
5 Fred McGriff 1.00 2.50
6 Barry Bonds 4.00 10.00
7 Gary Sheffield .60 1.50
8 Dave Hollins .30 .75
9 Frank Thomas 1.50 4.00
10 Danny Tartabull .30 .75
11 Albert Belle .60 1.50
12 Ruben Sierra .60 1.50
13 Larry Walker .60 1.50
14 Jeff Bagwell 1.00 2.50
15 David Justice .60 1.50
16 Kirby Puckett 1.50 4.00
17 John Kruk .60 1.50
18 Howard Johnson .30 .75
19 Darryl Strawberry .60 1.50
20 Will Clark 1.00 2.50
21 Kevin Mitchell .30 .75
22 Mickey Tettleton .30 .75
23 Don Mattingly 4.00 10.00
24 Jose Canseco 1.00 2.50
25 George Bell .30 .75
26 Andre Dawson .60 1.50
27 Ryne Sandberg 2.50 6.00
28 Ken Griffey Jr. 3.00 8.00
29 Carlos Baerga .30 .75
30 Travis Fryman .60 1.50

1993 Pinnacle Team 2001

COMPLETE SET (30) 15.00 40.00
ONE PER SER.1 JUMBO PACK
1 Wil Cordero .30 .75
2 Cal Eldred .30 .75
3 Mike Mussina 1.00 2.50
4 Chuck Knoblauch .60 1.50
5 Melvin Nieves .30 .75
6 Tim Wakefield 1.50 4.00
7 Carlos Baerga .30 .75
8 Bret Boone .60 1.50
9 Jeff Bagwell 1.00 2.50
10 Travis Fryman .60 1.50
11 Royce Clayton .30 .75
12 Delino DeShields .30 .75
13 Juan Gonzalez .60 1.50
14 Pedro Martinez 3.00 8.00
15 Bernie Williams 1.00 2.50
16 Billy Ashley .30 .75
17 Marquis Grissom .60 1.50
18 Kenny Lofton .60 1.50
19 Ray Lankford .60 1.50
20 Tim Salmon 1.00 2.50
21 Steve Hosey .30 .75
22 Charles Nagy .30 .75
23 Dave Fleming .30 .75
24 Reggie Sanders .60 1.50
25 Sam Militello .30 .75
26 Eric Karros .60 1.50
27 Ryan Klesko .60 1.50
28 Dean Palmer .60 1.50
29 Ivan Rodriguez 1.00 2.50
30 Sterling Hitchcock .75 2.00

1993 Pinnacle Team Pinnacle

COMPLETE SET (10) 30.00 80.00
RANDOM INSERTS IN SER.1 PACKS
B11 DISTRIBUTED ONLY BY MAIL
1 G.Maddux 6.00 15.00
M.Mussina
2 T.Glavine 2.50 6.00
J.Smiley
3 I.Rodriguez 2.50 6.00
D.Daulton
4 F.Thomas 4.00 10.00
F.McGriff
5 D.DeShields .75 2.00
C.Baerga
6 G.Sheffield 1.50 4.00
E.Martinez
7 O.Smith 6.00 15.00
P.Listach
8 J.Gonzalez 10.00 25.00
B.Bonds
9 K.Puckett 4.00 10.00
A.Van Slyke
10 L.Walker 1.50 4.00
Joe Carter
B11 R.Dibble .75 2.00
R.Aguilera

1993 Pinnacle Tribute

COMPLETE SET (10) 25.00 60.00
COMMON BRETT (1-5) 2.00 5.00
COMMON RYAN (6-10) 4.00 10.00
SER.2 STATED ODDS 1:24

1993 Pinnacle Cooperstown Promos

1 Nolan Ryan 125.00 300.00
2 George Brett 80.00 200.00
4 Carlton Fisk 25.00 60.00
5 Dale Murphy 40.00 100.00
10 Dave Winfield 25.00 60.00
11 Andre Dawson 25.00 60.00
12 Kirby Puckett 40.00 100.00
14 Don Mattingly 80.00 200.00
16 Will Clark 30.00 80.00
17 Cal Ripken Jr 125.00 300.00
18 Roger Clemens 50.00 125.00
19 Dwight Gooden 25.00 60.00
20 Tony Gwynn 40.00 100.00
21 Joe Carter 25.00 60.00
22 Ken Griffey Jr. 80.00 200.00
24 Frank Thomas 40.00 100.00
27 Eddie Murray 25.00 60.00
30 Mark McGwire 60.00 150.00

1993 Pinnacle Cooperstown

This 30-card standard-size set features full-bleed color player photos of possible future HOF inductees. Promo cards of Andre Dawson, Mark McGwire and Eddie Murray were issued to preview the series.

COMP.FACT SET (30) 4.00 10.00
DUFEX: 8X TO 20X BASIC CARDS
1 Nolan Ryan 1.25 3.00
2 George Brett .60 1.50
3 Robin Yount .30 .75
4 Carlton Fisk .30 .75
5 Dale Murphy .10 .30
6 Dennis Eckersley .30 .75
7 Rickey Henderson .40 1.00
8 Ryne Sandberg .30 .75
9 Ozzie Smith .30 .75
10 Dave Winfield .30 .75
11 Andre Dawson .20 .50
12 Kirby Puckett .40 1.00
13 Wade Boggs .40 1.00
14 Don Mattingly .75 2.00
15 Barry Bonds .50 1.25
16 Will Clark .15 .40
17 Cal Ripken 1.25 3.00
18 Roger Clemens .60 1.50
19 Dwight Gooden .07 .20
20 Tony Gwynn .60 1.50
21 Joe Carter .07 .20
22 Ken Griffey Jr. .75 2.00
23 Paul Molitor .30 .75
24 Frank Thomas .25 .60
25 Juan Gonzalez .15 .40
26 Barry Larkin .15 .40
27 Eddie Murray .20 .50
28 Cecil Fielder .02 .10
29 Roberto Alomar .15 .40
30 Mark McGwire .60 1.50

1993 Pinnacle DiMaggio

This 30-card standard-size set commemorates the life and career of Joe DiMaggio. Production was limited to 209,000 sets, with each set packaged in a black and gold collector's tin that features a color picture of DiMaggio. A certificate of authenticity card is also included that carries the production number of the set. DiMaggio also signed 9,000 cards for this set. One of 9,000 autographed cards from a special five-card set were randomly inserted into 30-card boxed hobby sets of 1993 Pinnacle Joe DiMaggio.

COMPLETE SET (30) 10.00 25.00
COMMON CARD (1-30) .30 .75
11 Rapid Robert .75 2.00
vs. Joltin' Joe
21 Joe McCarthy .40 1.00

1993 Pinnacle DiMaggio Autographs

ONE PER SPECIALLY MARKED FACT.SET
STATED PRINT RUN 9,000 TOTAL CARDS
1 J.DiMaggio 1936 75.00 200.00
2 J.DiMaggio Joltin' 75.00 200.00
3 J.DiMaggio Streak 75.00 200.00
4 J.DiMaggio Opening 75.00 200.00
5 J.DiMaggio Ebbets 75.00 250.00

1993 Pinnacle Home Run Club

This 48-card boxed standard-size set features players with outstanding home run statistics. Each set contains a certificate of authenticity card that verifies the set is one of 200,000 sets produced and includes the set number printed on a white bar. The checklist is printed on an outer sleeve that encases the black hinged box.

COMPLETE SET (48) 10.00 25.00
1 Juan Gonzalez .40 1.00
2 Fred McGriff .30 .75
3 Cecil Fielder .20 .50
4 Barry Bonds .75 2.00
5 Albert Belle .20 .50
6 Gary Sheffield .50 1.25
7 Joe Carter .20 .50
8 Mark McGwire 1.00 2.50
9 Darren Daulton .20 .50
10 Jose Canseco .50 1.25
11 Dave Hollins .08 .25
12 Ryne Sandberg .75 2.00
13 Ken Griffey Jr. 1.25 3.00
14 Larry Walker .20 .50
15 Rob Deer .08 .25
16 Andre Dawson .30 .75
17 Frank Thomas .50 1.25
18 Mickey Tettleton .08 .25
19 Charlie Hayes .08 .25
20 Ron Gant .08 .25
21 Rickey Henderson .60 1.50
22 Matt Williams .30 .75
23 Kevin Mitchell .20 .50
24 Robin Ventura .40 1.00
25 Dean Palmer .20 .50
26 Mike Piazza 1.25 3.00
27 J.T. Snow .40 1.00
28 Jeff Bagwell .50 1.25
29 John Olerud .30 .75
30 Greg Vaughn .20 .50
31 Dave Justice .40 1.00
32 Dave Winfield .50 1.25
33 Danny Tartabull .08 .25
34 Eric Anthony .08 .25
35 Eddie Murray .50 1.25
36 Jay Buhner .20 .50
37 Derek Bell .08 .25
38 Will Clark .40 1.00
39 Carlos Baerga .08 .25
40 Mo Vaughn .20 .50
41 Bobby Bonilla .08 .25
42 Tim Salmon .30 .75
43 Bo Jackson .40 1.00
44 Howard Johnson .08 .25
45 Kent Hrbek .20 .50
46 Ruben Sierra .20 .50
47 Cal Ripken 2.00 5.00
48 Travis Fryman .20 .50

1994 Pinnacle Samples

COMPLETE SET (12) 3.00 8.00
2 Carlos Baerga .20 .50
3 Sammy Sosa 1.00 2.50
5 John Olerud .20 .50
7 Moises Alou .20 .50
8 Steve Avery .08 .25
10 Cecil Fielder .20 .50
11 Greg Maddux 1.25 3.00
269 Jeff Granger .08 .25
TR1 Paul Molitor .60 1.50
Tribute
NNO Title card .08 .25
Hobby Edition/(Pinnacle ad)
NNO Title card .08 .25
Retail Edition/(Pinnacle ad)
NNO Jeff Granger/1994 Museum Collection .30
.75

1994 Pinnacle

The 540-card 1994 Pinnacle standard-size set was issued in two series of 270. Cards were issued in hobby and retail foil-wrapped packs. The card fronts feature full-bleed color action player photos with a small foil logo and players name at the base. Subsets include Rookie Prospects (224-261) and Draft Picks (262-270/430-438). Notable Rookie Cards include Trot Nixon, Chan Ho Park and Billy Wagner. A Carlos Delgado Super Rookie one shot insert was put into packs at a rate of one in 360. It is labeled SR1 and is listed at the end of the set.

COMPLETE SET (540) 8.00 20.00
COMPLETE SERIES 1 (270) 4.00 10.00
COMPLETE SERIES 2 (270) 4.00 10.00
DELGADO SR STATED ODDS 1:360
1 Frank Thomas .20 .50
2 Carlos Baerga .02 .10
3 Sammy Sosa .20 .50
4 Tony Gwynn .25 .60
5 John Olerud .07 .20
6 Ryne Sandberg .30 .75
7 Moises Alou .07 .20
8 Steve Avery .02 .10
9 Tim Salmon .10 .30
10 Cecil Fielder .07 .20
11 Greg Maddux .30 .75
12 Barry Larkin .10 .30
13 Mike Devereaux .02 .10
14 Charlie Hayes .02 .10
15 Albert Belle .07 .20
16 Andy Van Slyke .10 .30
17 Mo Vaughn .07 .20
18 Brian McRae .02 .10
19 Cal Eldred .02 .10
20 Craig Biggio .10 .30
21 Kirby Puckett .20 .50
22 Derek Bell .02 .10
23 Don Mattingly .50 1.25
24 John Burkett .02 .10
25 Roger Clemens .40 1.00
26 Barry Bonds .60 1.50
27 Paul Molitor .07 .20
28 Mike Piazza .40 1.00
29 Robin Ventura .07 .20
30 Jeff Conine .07 .20
31 Wade Boggs .10 .30
32 Dennis Eckersley .07 .20
33 Bobby Bonilla .07 .20
34 Lenny Dykstra .07 .20
35 Manny Alexander .02 .10
36 Ray Lankford .07 .20
37 Greg Vaughn .02 .10
38 Chuck Finley .07 .20
39 Todd Benzinger .02 .10
40 David Justice .07 .20
41 Rob Dibble .07 .20
42 Tom Henke .02 .10
43 David Nied .02 .10
44 Sandy Alomar Jr. .02 .10
45 Pete Harnisch .02 .10
46 Jeff Russell .02 .10
47 Terry Mulholland .02 .10
48 Kevin Appier .07 .20
49 Randy Tomlin .02 .10
50 Cal Ripken .60 1.50
51 Andy Benes .02 .10
52 Jimmy Key .07 .20
53 Kirt Manwaring .02 .10
54 Kevin Tapani .02 .10
55 Jose Guzman .02 .10
56 Todd Stottlemyre .02 .10
57 Jack McDowell .02 .10
58 Orel Hershiser .07 .20
59 Chris Hammond .02 .10
60 Chris Nabholz .02 .10
61 Ruben Sierra .07 .20
62 Dwight Gooden .07 .20
63 John Kruk .07 .20
64 Omar Vizquel .10 .30
65 Tim Naehring .02 .10
66 Dwight Smith .02 .10
67 Mickey Tettleton .02 .10
68 J.T. Snow .07 .20
69 Greg McMichael .02 .10
70 Kevin Mitchell .02 .10
71 Kevin Brown .07 .20
72 Scott Cooper .02 .10
73 Jim Thome .10 .30
74 Joe Girardi .02 .10
75 Eric Anthony .02 .10
76 Orlando Merced .02 .10
77 Felix Jose .02 .10
78 Tommy Greene .02 .10
79 Bernard Gilkey .02 .10
80 Phil Plantier .02 .10
81 Danny Tartabull .02 .10
82 Trevor Wilson .02 .10
83 Chuck Knoblauch .07 .20
84 Rick Wilkins .02 .10
85 Devon White .07 .20
86 Lance Johnson .02 .10
87 Eric Karros .07 .20
88 Gary Sheffield .07 .20
89 Wil Cordero .02 .10
90 Ron Darling .02 .10
91 Darren Daulton .07 .20
92 Joe Orsulak .02 .10
93 Steve Cooke .02 .10
94 Darryl Hamilton .02 .10
95 Aaron Sele .02 .10
96 John Doherty .02 .10
97 Gary DiSarcina .02 .10
98 Jeff Blauser .02 .10
99 John Smiley .02 .10
100 Ken Griffey Jr. .40 1.00
101 Dean Palmer .07 .20
102 Felix Fermin .02 .10
103 Jerald Clark .02 .10
104 Doug Drabek .02 .10
105 Curt Schilling .07 .20
106 Jeff Montgomery .02 .10
107 Rene Arocha .02 .10
108 Carlos Garcia .02 .10
109 Wally Whitehurst .02 .10
110 Jim Abbott .10 .30
111 Royce Clayton .02 .10
112 Chris Hoiles .02 .10
113 Mike Morgan .02 .10
114 Joe Magrane .02 .10
115 Tom Candiotti .02 .10
116 Ron Karkovice .02 .10
117 Ryan Bowen .02 .10
118 Rod Beck .02 .10
119 John Wetteland .07 .20
120 Terry Steinbach .02 .10
121 Dave Hollins .02 .10
122 Jeff Kent .10 .30
123 Ricky Bones .02 .10
124 Brian Jordan .07 .20
125 Chad Kreuter .02 .10
126 John Valentin .02 .10
127 Hilly Hathaway .02 .10
128 Wilson Alvarez .02 .10
129 Tino Martinez .10 .30
130 Rodney Bolton .02 .10
131 David Segui .02 .10
132 Wayne Kirby .02 .10
133 Eric Young .02 .10
134 Scott Servais .02 .10
135 Scott Radinsky .02 .10
136 Bret Barberie .02 .10
137 John Roper .02 .10
138 Ricky Gutierrez .02 .10
139 Bernie Williams .10 .30
140 Bud Black .02 .10
141 Jose Vizcaino .02 .10
142 Gerald Williams .02 .10
143 Duane Ward .02 .10
144 Danny Jackson .02 .10
145 Allen Watson .02 .10
146 Scott Fletcher .02 .10
147 Delino DeShields .02 .10
148 Shane Mack .02 .10
149 Jim Eisenreich .02 .10
150 Troy Neel .02 .10
151 Jay Bell .07 .20
152 B.J. Surhoff .07 .20
153 Mark Whiten .02 .10
154 Mike Henneman .02 .10
155 Todd Hundley .02 .10
156 Greg Myers .02 .10
157 Ryan Klesko .07 .20
158 Dave Fleming .02 .10
159 Mickey Morandini .02 .10
160 Blas Minor .02 .10
161 Reggie Jefferson .02 .10
162 David Hulse .02 .10
163 Greg Swindell .02 .10
164 Roberto Hernandez .02 .10
165 Brady Anderson .07 .20
166 Jack Armstrong .02 .10
167 Phil Clark .02 .10
168 Melido Perez .02 .10
169 Darren Lewis .02 .10
170 Sam Horn .02 .10
171 Mike Harkey .02 .10
172 Juan Guzman .02 .10
173 Bob Natal .02 .10
174 Deion Sanders .10 .30
175 Carlos Quintana .02 .10
176 Mel Rojas .02 .10
177 Willie Banks .02 .10

178 Ben Rivera .02 .10
179 Kenny Lofton .07 .20
180 Leo Gomez .02 .10
181 Roberto Mejia .02 .10
182 Mike Perez .02 .10
183 Travis Fryman .07 .20
184 Ben McDonald .02 .10
185 Steve Frey .02 .10
186 Kevin Young .02 .10
187 Dave Magadan .02 .10
188 Bobby Munoz .02 .10
189 Pat Rapp .02 .10
190 Jose Offerman .02 .10
191 Vinny Castilla .07 .20
192 Ivan Calderon .02 .10
193 Ken Caminiti .07 .20
194 Benji Gil .02 .10
195 Chuck Carr .02 .10
196 Derrick May .02 .10
197 Pat Kelly .02 .10
198 Jeff Brantley .02 .10
199 Jose Lind .02 .10
200 Steve Buechele .02 .10
201 Wes Chamberlain .02 .10
202 Eduardo Perez .02 .10
203 Bret Saberhagen .07 .20
204 Gregg Jefferies .02 .10
205 Darrin Fletcher .02 .10
206 Kent Hrbek .07 .20
207 Kim Batiste .02 .10
208 Jeff King .02 .10
209 Donovan Osborne .02 .10
210 Dave Nilsson .02 .10
211 Al Martin .02 .10
212 Mike Moore .02 .10
213 Sterling Hitchcock .02 .10
214 Geronimo Pena .02 .10
215 Kevin Higgins .02 .10
216 Norm Charlton .02 .10
217 Don Slaught .02 .10
218 Mitch Williams .02 .10
219 Derek Lilliquist .02 .10
220 Armando Reynoso .02 .10
221 Kenny Rogers .07 .20
222 Doug Jones .02 .10
223 Luis Aquino .02 .10
224 Mike Oquist .02 .10
225 Darryl Scott .02 .10
226 Kurt Abbott RC .02 .10
227 Andy Tomberlin .02 .10
228 Norberto Martin .02 .10
229 Pedro Castellano .02 .10
230 Curtis Pride RC .15 .40
231 Jeff McNeely .02 .10
232 Scott Lydy .02 .10
233 Darren Oliver RC .15 .40
234 Danny Bautista .02 .10
235 Butch Huskey .02 .10
236 Chipper Jones .20 .50
237 Eddie Zambrano RC .02 .10
238 Domingo Jean .02 .10
239 Javier Lopez .07 .20
240 Nigel Wilson .02 .10
241 Drew Denson .02 .10
242 Raul Mondesi .07 .20
243 Luis Ortiz .02 .10
244 Manny Ramirez .20 .50
245 Greg Blosser .02 .10
246 Rondell White .07 .20
247 Steve Karsay .02 .10
248 Scott Stahoviak .02 .10
249 Jose Valentin .02 .10
250 Marc Newfield .02 .10
251 Keith Kessinger .02 .10
252 Carl Everett .07 .20
253 John O'Donoghue .02 .10
254 Turk Wendell .02 .10
255 Scott Ruffcorn .02 .10
256 Tony Tarasco .02 .10
257 Andy Cook .02 .10
258 Matt Mieske .02 .10
259 Luis Lopez .02 .10
260 Ramon Caraballo .02 .10
261 Salomon Torres .02 .10
262 Brooks Kieschnick RC .02 .10
263 Daron Kirkreit .02 .10
264 Billy Wagner RC .75 2.00
265 Matt Drews RC .02 .10
266 Scott Christman RC .02 .10
267 Torii Hunter RC .60 1.50
268 Jamey Wright RC .02 .10
269 Jeff Granger .02 .10
270 Trot Nixon RC .50 1.25
271 Randy Myers .02 .10
272 Trevor Hoffman .10 .30
273 Bob Wickman .02 .10
274 Willie McGee .07 .20
275 Hipolito Pichardo .02 .10
276 Bobby Witt .02 .10
277 Gregg Olson .02 .10
278 Randy Johnson .20 .50
279 Robb Nen .07 .20
280 Paul O'Neill .10 .30
281 Lou Whitaker .07 .20
282 Chad Curtis .02 .10
283 Doug Henry .02 .10
284 Tom Glavine .10 .30
285 Mike Greenwell .02 .10
286 Roberto Kelly .02 .10
287 Roberto Alomar .10 .30
288 Charlie Hough .07 .20
289 Alex Fernandez .02 .10
290 Jeff Bagwell .10 .30
291 Wally Joyner .07 .20
292 Andujar Cedeno .02 .10
293 Rick Aguilera .02 .10
294 Darryl Strawberry .07 .20
295 Mike Mussina .10 .30
296 Jeff Gardner .02 .10
297 Chris Gwynn .02 .10
298 Matt Williams .07 .20
299 Brent Gates .02 .10
300 Mark McGwire .50 1.25
301 Jim Deshaies .02 .10
302 Edgar Martinez .10 .30
303 Danny Darwin .02 .10
304 Pat Meares .02 .10
305 Benito Santiago .02 .10
306 Jose Canseco .10 .30
307 Jim Gott .02 .10
308 Paul Sorrento .02 .10
309 Scott Kamieniecki .02 .10
310 Larry Walker .07 .20
311 Mark Langston .02 .10
312 John Jaha .02 .10
313 Stan Javier .02 .10
314 Hal Morris .02 .10
315 Robby Thompson .02 .10
316 Pat Hentgen .02 .10
317 Tom Gordon .02 .10
318 Joey Cora .02 .10
319 Luis Alicea .02 .10
320 Andre Dawson .07 .20
321 Darryl Kile .07 .20
322 Jose Rijo .02 .10
323 Luis Gonzalez .07 .20
324 Billy Ashley .02 .10
325 David Cone .07 .20
326 Bill Swift .02 .10
327 Phil Hiatt .02 .10
328 Craig Paquette .02 .10
329 Bob Welch .02 .10
330 Tony Phillips .02 .10
331 Archi Cianfrocco .02 .10
332 Dave Winfield .07 .20
333 David McCarty .02 .10
334 Al Leiter .07 .20
335 Tom Browning .02 .10
336 Mark Grace .10 .30
337 Jose Mesa .02 .10
338 Mike Stanley .02 .10
339 Roger McDowell .02 .10
340 Damion Easley .02 .10
341 Angel Miranda .02 .10
342 John Smoltz .10 .30
343 Jay Buhner .07 .20
344 Bryan Harvey .02 .10
345 Joe Carter .07 .20
346 Dante Bichette .07 .20
347 Jason Bere .02 .10
348 Frank Viola .07 .20
349 Ivan Rodriguez .10 .30
350 Juan Gonzalez .07 .20
351 Steve Finley .07 .20
352 Mike Felder .02 .10
353 Ramon Martinez .02 .10
354 Greg Gagne .02 .10
355 Ken Hill .02 .10
356 Pedro Munoz .02 .10
357 Todd Van Poppel .02 .10
358 Marquis Grissom .07 .20
359 Milt Cuyler .02 .10
360 Reggie Sanders .07 .20
361 Scott Erickson .02 .10
362 Billy Hatcher .02 .10
363 Gene Harris .02 .10
364 Rene Gonzales .02 .10
365 Kevin Rogers .02 .10
366 Eric Plunk .02 .10
367 Todd Zeile .02 .10
368 John Franco .07 .20
369 Brett Butler .07 .20
370 Bill Spiers .02 .10
371 Terry Pendleton .07 .20
372 Chris Bosio .02 .10
373 Orestes Destrade .02 .10
374 Dave Stewart .07 .20
375 Darren Holmes .02 .10
376 Doug Strange .02 .10
377 Brian Turang .02 .10
378 Carl Willis .02 .10
379 Mark McLemore .02 .10
380 Bobby Jones .02 .10
381 Scott Sanders .02 .10
382 Kirk Rueter .02 .10
383 Randy Velarde .02 .10
384 Fred McGriff .10 .30
385 Charles Nagy .02 .10
386 Rich Amaral .02 .10
387 Geronimo Berroa .02 .10
388 Eric Davis .07 .20
389 Ozzie Smith .30 .75
390 Alex Arias .02 .10
391 Brad Ausmus .10 .30
392 Cliff Floyd .07 .20
393 Roger Salkeld .02 .10
394 Jim Edmonds .20 .50
395 Jeromy Burnitz .07 .20
396 Dave Staton .02 .10
397 Rob Butler .02 .10
398 Marcos Armas .02 .10
399 Darrell Whitmore .02 .10
400 Ryan Thompson .02 .10
401 Ross Powell RC .02 .10
402 Joe Oliver .02 .10
403 Paul Carey .02 .10
404 Bob Hamelin .02 .10
405 Chris Turner .02 .10
406 Nate Minchey .02 .10
407 Lonnie Maclin RC .02 .10
408 Harold Baines .07 .20
409 Brian Williams .02 .10
410 Johnny Ruffin .02 .10
411 Julian Tavarez RC .10 .30
412 Mark Hutton .02 .10
413 Carlos Delgado .10 .30
414 Chris Gomez .02 .10
415 Mike Hampton .07 .20
416 Alex Diaz RC .02 .10
417 Jeffrey Hammonds .02 .10
418 Jayhawk Owens .02 .10
419 J.R. Phillips .02 .10
420 Cory Bailey RC .02 .10
421 Denny Hocking .02 .10
422 Jon Shave .02 .10
423 Damon Buford .02 .10
424 Troy O'Leary .02 .10
425 Tripp Cromer .02 .10
426 Albie Lopez .02 .10
427 Tony Fernandez .02 .10
428 Ozzie Guillen .07 .20
429 Alan Trammell .07 .20
430 John Wasdin RC .02 .10
431 Marc Valdes .02 .10
432 Brian Anderson RC .15 .40
433 Matt Brunson RC .02 .10
434 Wayne Gomes RC .02 .10
435 Jay Powell RC .02 .10
436 Kirk Presley RC .02 .10
437 Jon Ratliff RC .02 .10
438 Derrek Lee RC 1.25 3.00
439 Tom Pagnozzi .02 .10
440 Kent Mercker .02 .10
441 Phil Leftwich RC .02 .10
442 Jamie Moyer .07 .20
443 John Flaherty .02 .10
444 Mark Wohlers .02 .10
445 Jose Bautista .02 .10
446 Andres Galarraga .07 .20
447 Mark Lemke .02 .10
448 Tim Wakefield .10 .30
449 Pat Listach .02 .10
450 Rickey Henderson .20 .50
451 Mike Gallego .02 .10
452 Bob Tewksbury .02 .10
453 Kirk Gibson .07 .20
454 Pedro Astacio .02 .10
455 Mike Lansing .02 .10
456 Sean Berry .02 .10
457 Bob Walk .02 .10
458 Chili Davis .07 .20
459 Ed Sprague .02 .10
460 Kevin Stocker .02 .10
461 Mike Stanton .02 .10
462 Tim Raines .07 .20
463 Mike Bordick .02 .10
464 David Wells .07 .20
465 Tim Laker .02 .10
466 Cory Snyder .02 .10
467 Alex Cole .02 .10
468 Pete Incaviglia .02 .10
469 Roger Pavlik .02 .10
470 Greg W. Harris .02 .10
471 Xavier Hernandez .02 .10
472 Erik Hanson .02 .10
473 Jesse Orosco .02 .10
474 Greg Colbrunn .02 .10
475 Harold Reynolds .07 .20
476 Greg A. Harris .02 .10
477 Pat Borders .02 .10
478 Melvin Nieves .02 .10
479 Mariano Duncan .02 .10
480 Greg Hibbard .02 .10
481 Tim Pugh .02 .10
482 Bobby Ayala .02 .10
483 Sid Fernandez .02 .10
484 Tim Wallach .02 .10
485 Randy Milligan .02 .10
486 Walt Weiss .02 .10
487 Matt Walbeck .02 .10
488 Mike Macfarlane .02 .10
489 Jerry Browne .02 .10
490 Chris Sabo .02 .10
491 Tim Belcher .02 .10
492 Spike Owen .02 .10
493 Rafael Palmeiro .10 .30
494 Brian Harper .02 .10
495 Eddie Murray .20 .50
496 Ellis Burks .07 .20
497 Karl Rhodes .02 .10
498 Otis Nixon .02 .10
499 Lee Smith .07 .20
500 Bip Roberts .02 .10
501 Pedro Martinez .20 .50
502 Brian Hunter .02 .10
503 Tyler Green .02 .10
504 Bruce Hurst .02 .10
505 Alex Gonzalez .02 .10
506 Mark Portugal .02 .10
507 Bob Ojeda .02 .10
508 Dave Henderson .02 .10
509 Bo Jackson .20 .50
510 Bret Boone .07 .20
511 Mark Eichhorn .02 .10
512 Luis Polonia .02 .10
513 Will Clark .10 .30
514 Dave Valle .02 .10
515 Dan Wilson .02 .10
516 Dennis Martinez .07 .20
517 Jim Leyritz .02 .10
518 Howard Johnson .02 .10
519 Jody Reed .02 .10
520 Julio Franco .07 .20
521 Jeff Reardon .07 .20
522 Willie Greene .02 .10
523 Shawon Dunston .02 .10
524 Keith Mitchell .02 .10
525 Rick Helling .02 .10
526 Mark Kiefer .02 .10
527 Chan Ho Park RC .30 .75
528 Tony Longmire .02 .10
529 Rich Becker .02 .10
530 Tim Hyers RC .02 .10
531 Darrin Jackson .02 .10
532 Jack Morris .07 .20
533 Rick White .02 .10
534 Mike Kelly .02 .10
535 James Mouton .02 .10
536 Steve Trachsel .02 .10
537 Tony Eusebio .02 .10
538 Kelly Stinnett RC .15 .40
539 Paul Spoljaric .02 .10
540 Darren Dreifort .02 .10
SR1 C.Delgado Super Rookie 2.00 5.00

1994 Pinnacle Artist's Proofs

COMPLETE SET (540) 2500.00 3500.00
*STARS: 10X TO 25X BASIC CARDS
*ROOKIES: 5X TO 12X BASIC
STATED ODDS 1:26 HOB, 1:22 RET
STATED PRINT RUN 1000 SETS
438 Derrek Lee 15.00 40.00

1994 Pinnacle Museum Collection

*STARS: 2.5X TO 6X BASIC CARDS
*ROOKIES: 2X TO 5X BASIC
STATED ODDS 1:4 HOB, 1:3 RET, 1:4 JUM
STATED PRINT RUN 6500 SETS
TRADE: 279/313/328/382/387
279 Robb Nen TRADE 15.00 40.00
313 Stan Javier TRADE 6.00 15.00
328 Craig Paquette TRADE 6.00 15.00
382 Kirk Rueter TRADE 6.00 15.00
387 Geronimo Berroa TRADE 6.00 15.00
438 Derrek Lee 6.00 15.00

1994 Pinnacle Rookie Team Pinnacle

COMPLETE SET (9) 25.00 60.00
SER.1 STATED ODDS 1:90 HOB, 1:72 RET
1 C.Delgado J.Lopez 3.00 8.00
2 B.Hamelin J.Phillips 1.50 4.00
3 J.Shave K.Kessinger 1.50 4.00
4 B.Huskey L.Ortiz 1.50 4.00
5 C.Jones K.Abbott 4.00 10.00
6 M.Ramirez R.White 4.00 10.00
7 J.Hammonds C.Floyd 2.50 6.00
8 M.Newfield N.Wilson 1.50 4.00
9 M.Hutton S.Torres 1.50 4.00

1994 Pinnacle Run Creators

COMPLETE SET (44) 30.00 80.00
COMPLETE SERIES 1 (22) 20.00 50.00
COMPLETE SERIES 2 (22) 12.50 30.00
STATED ODDS 1:4 JUMBO
RC1 John Olerud .40 1.00
RC2 Frank Thomas 1.00 2.50
RC3 Ken Griffey Jr. 2.00 5.00
RC4 Paul Molitor .40 1.00
RC5 Rafael Palmeiro .60 1.50
RC6 Roberto Alomar .60 1.50
RC7 Juan Gonzalez .40 1.00
RC8 Albert Belle .40 1.00
RC9 Travis Fryman .40 1.00
RC10 Rickey Henderson 1.00 2.50
RC11 Tony Phillips .20 .50
RC12 Mo Vaughn .40 1.00
RC13 Tim Salmon .60 1.50
RC14 Kenny Lofton .40 1.00
RC15 Carlos Baerga .20 .50
RC16 Greg Vaughn .20 .50
RC17 Jay Buhner .40 1.00
RC18 Chris Hoiles .20 .50
RC19 Mickey Tettleton .20 .50
RC20 Kirby Puckett 1.00 2.50
RC21 Danny Tartabull .20 .50
RC22 Devon White .40 1.00
RC23 Barry Bonds 3.00 8.00
RC24 Lenny Dykstra .40 1.00
RC25 John Kruk .40 1.00
RC26 Fred McGriff .60 1.50
RC27 Gregg Jefferies .20 .50
RC28 Mike Piazza 2.00 5.00
RC29 Jeff Blauser .20 .50
RC30 Andres Galarraga .40 1.00
RC31 Darren Daulton .40 1.00
RC32 David Justice .40 1.00
RC33 Craig Biggio .60 1.50
RC34 Mark Grace .60 1.50
RC35 Tony Gwynn 1.25 3.00
RC36 Jeff Bagwell .60 1.50
RC37 Jay Bell .40 1.00
RC38 Marquis Grissom .40 1.00
RC39 Matt Williams .40 1.00
RC40 Charlie Hayes .20 .50
RC41 Dante Bichette .40 1.00
RC42 Bernard Gilkey .20 .50
RC43 Brett Butler .40 1.00
RC44 Rick Wilkins .20 .50

1994 Pinnacle Team Pinnacle

COMPLETE SET (9) 12.00 30.00
SER.2 STATED ODDS 1:90 HOB/RET
1 F.Thomas J.Bagwell 1.25 3.00
2 R.Thompson C.Baerga .50 1.25
3 M.Williams D.Palmer .50 1.25
4 C.Ripken J.Bell 4.00 10.00
5 M.Piazza I.Rodriguez 1.25 3.00
6 K.Griffey Jr. L.Dykstra 2.50 6.00
7 J.Gonzalez B.Bonds 2.50 6.00
8 D.Justice T.Salmon .50 1.25
9 G.Maddux J.McDowell 2.00 5.00

1994 Pinnacle Tribute

COMPLETE SET (18) 40.00 100.00
COMPLETE SERIES 1 (9) 12.50 30.00
COMPLETE SERIES 2 (9) 30.00 80.00
STATED ODDS 1:18 HOBBY
TR1 Paul Molitor .60 1.50
TR2 Jim Abbott 1.00 2.50
TR3 Dave Winfield .60 1.50
TR4 Bo Jackson 1.50 4.00
TR5 David Justice .60 1.50
TR6 Len Dykstra .60 1.50
TR7 Mike Piazza 3.00 8.00
TR8 Barry Bonds 5.00 12.00
TR9 Randy Johnson 1.50 4.00
TR10 Ozzie Smith 2.50 6.00
TR11 Mark Whiten .30 .75
TR12 Greg Maddux 2.50 6.00
TR13 Cal Ripken 5.00 12.00
TR14 Frank Thomas 1.50 4.00
TR15 Juan Gonzalez .60 1.50
TR16 Roberto Alomar 1.00 2.50
TR17 Ken Griffey Jr. 3.00 8.00
TR18 Lee Smith .60 1.50

1994 Pinnacle The Naturals

These 25 standard-size cards were issued as a boxed set and were printed with Pinnacle's Dufex process, which imparts a metallic appearance to the cards. A certificate of authenticity that carries the set's production number out of 100,000 produced was included with every boxed set.

COMP. FACT SET (25) 4.00 10.00
1 Frank Thomas .30 .75
2 Barry Bonds .50 1.25
3 Ken Griffey Jr. .75 2.00
4 Juan Gonzalez .15 .40
5 David Justice .15 .40
6 Albert Belle .07 .20
7 Kenny Lofton .10 .30
8 Roberto Alomar .15 .40
9 Tim Salmon .15 .40
10 Randy Johnson .30 .75
11 Kirby Puckett .40 1.00
12 Tony Gwynn .60 1.50
13 Fred McGriff .10 .30
14 Ryne Sandberg .50 1.25
15 Greg Maddux .75 2.00
16 Matt Williams .10 .30
17 Lenny Dykstra .07 .20
18 Gary Sheffield .30 .75
19 Mike Piazza 1.00 2.50
20 Dean Palmer .07 .20
21 Travis Fryman .07 .20
22 Carlos Baerga .07 .20
23 Cal Ripken 1.25 3.00
24 John Olerud .10 .30
25 Roger Clemens .60 1.50
P18 Gary Sheffield Promo .60 1.50

1994 Pinnacle New Generation

This 25-card standard-size set spotlights 25 of the most prominent prospects to hit the major leagues. Just 100,000 sets were produced, and a certificate of authenticity carrying the set serial number was printed on the back of the display box. A Cliff Floyd promo card was distributed to dealers and hobby media to preview the set.

COMP. FACT SET (25) 2.00 5.00
NG1 Tim Salmon .07 .20
NG2 Mike Piazza .75 2.00
NG3 Jason Bere .01 .05
NG4 Jeffrey Hammonds .01 .05
NG5 Aaron Sele .01 .05
NG6 Salomon Torres .01 .05
NG7 Wilfredo Cordero .01 .05
NG8 Allen Watson .01 .05
NG9 J.T. Snow .02 .10
NG10 Cliff Floyd .05 .15
NG11 Jeff McNeely .01 .05
NG12 Butch Huskey .01 .05
NG13 J.R. Phillips .01 .05
NG14 Bobby Jones .01 .05
NG15 Javier Lopez .15 .40
NG16 Scott Ruffcorn .01 .05
NG17 Manny Ramirez .40 1.00
NG18 Carlos Delgado .20 .50
NG19 Rondell White .02 .10
NG20 Chipper Jones .60 1.50
NG21 Billy Ashley .01 .05
NG22 Nigel Wilson .01 .05
NG23 Jeromy Burnitz .02 .10
NG24 Danny Bautista .01 .05
NG25 Darrell Whitmore .01 .05
PNG10 Cliff Floyd Promo .60 1.50

1994 Pinnacle Power Surge

These 25 standard-size cards came in a boxed set from Pinnacle and feature on their fronts borderless color action shots. A Carlos Baerga promo card was distributed to dealers and hobby media to preview the set.

COMP. FACT SET (25) 2.00 5.00
PS1 David Justice .07 .20
PS2 Chris Hoiles .01 .05
PS3 Mo Vaughn .02 .10
PS4 Tim Salmon .07 .20
PS5 J.T. Snow .02 .10
PS6 Frank Thomas .20 .50
PS7 Sammy Sosa .40 1.00
PS8 Rick Wilkins .01 .05
PS9 Robin Ventura .07 .20
PS10 Reggie Sanders .01 .05
PS11 Albert Belle .02 .10
PS12 Carlos Baerga .01 .05
PS13 Manny Ramirez .20 .50
PS14 Travis Fryman .02 .10
PS15 Gary Sheffield .20 .50
PS16 Jeff Bagwell .20 .50
PS17 Mike Piazza .50 1.25
PS18 Eric Karros .02 .10
PS19 Cliff Floyd .05 .15
PS20 Mark Whiten .01 .05
PS21 Phil Plantier .01 .05
PS22 Derek Bell .01 .05
PS23 Ken Griffey Jr. .50 1.25
PS24 Juan Gonzalez .07 .20
PS25 Dean Palmer .02 .10
PS12P Carlos Baerga Promo .30 .75

1995 Pinnacle Samples

COMPLETE SET (9) 4.00 10.00
16 Mickey Morandini .20 .50
119 Gary Sheffield .75 2.00
122 Ivan Rodriguez .75 2.00
132 Alex Rodriguez 2.50 6.00
208 Bo Jackson .60 1.50
223 Jose Rijo .20 .50
224 Ryan Klesko .30 .75
US22 Wil Cordero .20 .50
NNO Title Card .20 .50

1995 Pinnacle

This 450-card standard-size set was issued in two series of 225 cards. They were released in 12-card packs, 24 packs to a box and 18 boxes in a case. The full-bleed fronts feature action photos. The player's last name is printed in black ink against a dramatic gold foil background at the base of the card. There are no notable Rookie Cards in this set.

COMPLETE SET (450) 15.00 40.00
COMPLETE SERIES 1 (225) 6.00 15.00
COMPLETE SERIES 2 (225) 6.00 15.00
SUBSET CARDS HALF VALUE OF BASE CARDS
1 Jeff Bagwell .10 .30
2 Roger Clemens .40 1.00
3 Mark Whiten .02 .10
4 Shawon Dunston .02 .10
5 Bobby Bonilla .07 .20
6 Kevin Tapani .02 .10
7 Eric Karros .07 .20
8 Cliff Floyd .07 .20
9 Pat Kelly .02 .10
10 Jeffrey Hammonds .02 .10
11 Jeff Conine .07 .20
12 Fred McGriff .10 .30
13 Chris Bosio .02 .10
14 Mike Mussina .10 .30
15 Danny Bautista .02 .10
16 Mickey Morandini .02 .10
17 Chuck Finley .07 .20
18 Jim Thome .10 .30
19 Luis Ortiz .02 .10
20 Walt Weiss .02 .10
21 Don Mattingly .50 1.25
22 Bob Hamelin .02 .10
23 Melido Perez .02 .10
24 Keith Mitchell .02 .10
25 John Smoltz .10 .30
26 Hector Carrasco .02 .10
27 Pat Hentgen .02 .10
28 Derrick May .02 .10
29 Mike Kingery .02 .10
30 Chuck Carr .02 .10
31 Billy Ashley .02 .10
32 Todd Hundley .02 .10
33 Luis Gonzalez .07 .20
34 Marquis Grissom .07 .20
35 Jeff King .02 .10
36 Eddie Williams .02 .10
37 Tom Pagnozzi .02 .10
38 Chris Hoiles .02 .10
39 Sandy Alomar Jr. .02 .10
40 Mike Greenwell .02 .10
41 Lance Johnson .02 .10
42 Junior Felix .02 .10
43 Felix Jose .02 .10
44 Scott Leius .02 .10
45 Ruben Sierra .07 .20
46 Kevin Seitzer .02 .10
47 Wade Boggs .10 .30
48 Reggie Jefferson .02 .10
49 Jose Canseco .10 .30
50 David Justice .07 .20
51 John Smiley .02 .10
52 Joe Carter .07 .20
53 Rick Wilkins .02 .10
54 Ellis Burks .07 .20
55 Dave Weathers .02 .10
56 Pedro Astacio .02 .10
57 Ryan Thompson .02 .10
58 James Mouton .02 .10
59 Mel Rojas .02 .10
60 Orlando Merced .02 .10
61 Matt Williams .07 .20
62 Bernard Gilkey .02 .10
63 J.R. Phillips .02 .10
64 Lee Smith .07 .20
65 Jim Edmonds .10 .30
66 Darrin Jackson .02 .10
67 Scott Cooper .02 .10
68 Ron Karkovice .02 .10
69 Chris Gomez .02 .10
70 Kevin Appier .07 .20
71 Bobby Jones .02 .10
72 Doug Drabek .02 .10
73 Matt Mieske .02 .10
74 Sterling Hitchcock .02 .10
75 John Valentin .02 .10
76 Reggie Sanders .07 .20
77 Wally Joyner .07 .20
78 Turk Wendell .02 .10
79 Charlie Hayes .02 .10
80 Bret Barberie .02 .10
81 Troy Neel .02 .10
82 Ken Caminiti .07 .20
83 Milt Thompson .02 .10
84 Paul Sorrento .02 .10
85 Trevor Hoffman .07 .20
86 Jay Bell .07 .20
87 Mark Portugal .02 .10
88 Sid Fernandez .02 .10
89 Charles Nagy .02 .10
90 Jeff Montgomery .02 .10
91 Chuck Knoblauch .07 .20
92 Jeff Frye .02 .10
93 Tony Gwynn .25 .60
94 John Olerud .07 .20
95 David Nied .02 .10
96 Chris Hammond .02 .10
97 Edgar Martinez .10 .30
98 Kevin Stocker .02 .10
99 Jeff Fassero .02 .10
100 Curt Schilling .07 .20
101 Dave Clark .02 .10
102 Delino DeShields .02 .10
103 Leo Gomez .02 .10
104 Dave Hollins .02 .10
105 Tim Naehring .02 .10
106 Otis Nixon .02 .10
107 Ozzie Guillen .07 .20
108 Jose Lind .02 .10
109 Stan Javier .02 .10
110 Greg Vaughn .02 .10
111 Chipper Jones .20 .50
112 Ed Sprague .02 .10
113 Mike Macfarlane .02 .10
114 Steve Finley .07 .20
115 Ken Hill .02 .10
116 Carlos Garcia .02 .10
117 Lou Whitaker .07 .20
118 Todd Zeile .02 .10
119 Gary Sheffield .07 .20
120 Ben McDonald .02 .10
121 Pete Harnisch .02 .10
122 Ivan Rodriguez .10 .30
123 Wilson Alvarez .02 .10
124 Travis Fryman .07 .20
125 Pedro Munoz .02 .10
126 Mark Lemke .02 .10
127 Jose Valentin .02 .10
128 Ken Griffey Jr. .40 1.00
129 Omar Vizquel .10 .30
130 Milt Cuyler .04 .10
131 Steve Trachsel .02 .10
132 Alex Rodriguez .50 1.25
133 Garret Anderson .07 .20
134 Armando Benitez .02 .10
135 Shawn Green .07 .20
136 Jorge Fabregas .02 .10
137 Orlando Miller .02 .10
138 Rikkert Faneyte .02 .10
139 Ismael Valdes .02 .10
140 Jose Oliva .02 .10
141 Aaron Small .02 .10
142 Tim Davis .02 .10
143 Ricky Bottalico .02 .10
144 Mike Matheny .02 .10
145 Roberto Petagine .02 .10
146 Fausto Cruz .02 .10
147 Bryce Florie .02 .10
148 Jose Lima .02 .10
149 John Hudek .02 .10
150 Duane Singleton .02 .10
151 John Mabry .02 .10
152 Robert Eenhoorn .02 .10
153 Jon Lieber .02 .10
154 Garey Ingram .02 .10
155 Paul Shuey .02 .10
156 Mike Lieberthal .07 .20
157 Steve Dunn .02 .10
158 Charles Johnson .07 .20
159 Ernie Young .02 .10
160 Jose Martinez .02 .10
161 Kurt Miller .02 .10
162 Joey Eischen .02 .10
163 Dave Stevens .02 .10
164 Brian L.Hunter .02 .10
165 Jeff Cirillo .02 .10
166 Mark Smith .02 .10
167 McKay Christensen RC .02 .10
168 C.J. Nitkowski .02 .10
169 Antone Williamson RC .02 .10
170 Paul Konerko .40 1.00
171 Scott Elarton RC .08 .25
172 Jacob Shumate .02 .10
173 Terrence Long .02 .10
174 Mark Johnson RC .08 .25
175 Ben Grieve .07 .20
176 Jayson Peterson RC .02 .10
177 Checklist .02 .10
178 Checklist .02 .10
179 Checklist .02 .10
180 Checklist .02 .10
181 Brian Anderson .02 .10
182 Steve Buechele .02 .10
183 Mark Clark .02 .10
184 Cecil Fielder .07 .20
185 Steve Avery .02 .10
186 Devon White .07 .20
187 Craig Shipley .02 .10
188 Brady Anderson .07 .20
189 Kenny Lofton .07 .20
190 Alex Cole .02 .10
191 Brent Gates .02 .10
192 Dean Palmer .07 .20
193 Alex Gonzalez .02 .10
194 Steve Cooke .02 .10
195 Ray Lankford .07 .20
196 Mark McGwire .50 1.25
197 Marc Newfield .02 .10
198 Pat Rapp .02 .10
199 Darren Lewis .02 .10
200 Carlos Baerga .02 .10
201 Rickey Henderson .20 .50
202 Kurt Abbott .02 .10
203 Kirt Manwaring .02 .10
204 Cal Ripken .60 1.50
205 Darren Daulton .07 .20
206 Greg Colbrunn .02 .10
207 Darryl Hamilton .02 .10
208 Bo Jackson .20 .50
209 Tony Phillips .02 .10
210 Geronimo Berroa .02 .10
211 Rich Becker .02 .10
212 Tony Tarasco .02 .10
213 Karl Rhodes .02 .10
214 Phil Plantier .02 .10
215 J.T. Snow .07 .20
216 Mo Vaughn .07 .20
217 Greg Gagne .02 .10
218 Ricky Bones .02 .10
219 Mike Bordick .02 .10
220 Chad Curtis .02 .10
221 Royce Clayton .02 .10
222 Roberto Alomar .10 .30
223 Jose Rijo .02 .10
224 Ryan Klesko .07 .20
225 Mark Langston .02 .10
226 Frank Thomas .20 .50
227 Juan Gonzalez .07 .20
228 Ron Gant .07 .20
229 Javier Lopez .07 .20
230 Sammy Sosa .20 .50
231 Kevin Brown .07 .20
232 Gary DiSarcina .02 .10
233 Albert Belle .07 .20
234 Jay Buhner .07 .20
235 Pedro Martinez .10 .30
236 Bob Tewksbury .02 .10
237 Mike Piazza .30 .75
238 Darryl Kile .07 .20
239 Bryan Harvey .02 .10
240 Andres Galarraga .07 .20
241 Jeff Blauser .02 .10
242 Jeff Kent .07 .20
243 Bobby Munoz .02 .10
244 Greg Maddux .30 .75
245 Paul O'Neill .10 .30
246 Lenny Dykstra .07 .20
247 Todd Van Poppel .02 .10
248 Bernie Williams .10 .30
249 Glenallen Hill .02 .10
250 Duane Ward .02 .10
251 Dennis Eckersley .07 .20
252 Pat Mahomes .02 .10
253 Rusty Greer .07 .20
254 Roberto Kelly .02 .10
255 Randy Myers .02 .10

256 Scott Ruffcorn .02 .10
257 Robin Ventura .07 .20
258 Eduardo Perez .02 .10
259 Aaron Sele .02 .10
260 Paul Molitor .07 .20
261 Juan Guzman .02 .10
262 Darren Oliver .02 .10
263 Mike Stanley .02 .10
264 Tom Glavine .10 .30
265 Rico Brogna .02 .10
266 Craig Biggio .10 .30
267 Darrell Whitmore .02 .10
268 Jimmy Key .07 .20
269 Will Clark .10 .30
270 David Cone .07 .20
271 Brian Jordan .07 .20
272 Barry Bonds .60 1.50
273 Danny Tartabull .02 .10
274 Ramon J.Martinez .02 .10
275 Al Martin .02 .10
276 Fred McGriff SM .07 .20
277 Carlos Delgado SM .02 .10
278 Juan Gonzalez SM .02 .10
279 Shawn Green SM .02 .10
280 Carlos Baerga SM .02 .10
281 Cliff Floyd SM .02 .10
282 Ozzie Smith SM .20 .50
283 Alex Rodriguez SM .20 .50
284 Kenny Lofton SM .02 .10
285 David Justice SM .02 .10
286 Tim Salmon SM .07 .20
287 Manny Ramirez SM .07 .20
288 Will Clark SM .07 .20
289 Garret Anderson SM .02 .10
290 Billy Ashley SM .02 .10
291 Tony Gwynn SM .10 .30
292 Raul Mondesi SM .02 .10
293 Rafael Palmeiro SM .07 .20
294 Matt Williams SM .02 .10
295 Don Mattingly SM .25 .60
296 Kirby Puckett SM .10 .30
297 Paul Molitor SM .02 .10
298 Albert Belle SM .02 .10
299 Barry Bonds SM .30 .75
300 Mike Piazza SM .20 .50
301 Jeff Bagwell SM .07 .20
302 Frank Thomas SM .10 .30
303 Chipper Jones SM .10 .30
304 Ken Griffey Jr. SM .25 .60
305 Cal Ripken SM .30 .75
306 Eric Anthony .02 .10
307 Todd Benzinger .02 .10
308 Jacob Brumfield .02 .10
309 Wes Chamberlain .02 .10
310 Tino Martinez .10 .30
311 Roberto Mejia .02 .10
312 Jose Offerman .02 .10
313 David Segui .02 .10
314 Eric Young .02 .10
315 Rey Sanchez .02 .10
316 Raul Mondesi .07 .20
317 Bret Boone .07 .20
318 Andre Dawson .07 .20
319 Brian McRae .02 .10
320 Dave Nilsson .02 .10
321 Moises Alou .07 .20
322 Don Slaught .02 .10
323 Dave McCarty .02 .10
324 Mike Huff .02 .10
325 Rick Aguilera .02 .10
326 Rod Beck .02 .10
327 Kenny Rogers .07 .20
328 Andy Benes .02 .10
329 Allen Watson .02 .10
330 Randy Johnson .20 .50
331 Willie Greene .02 .10
332 Hal Morris .02 .40
333 Ozzie Smith .30 .75
334 Jason Bere .02 .10
335 Scott Erickson .02 .10
336 Dante Bichette .07 .20
337 Willie Banks .02 .10
338 Eric Davis .07 .20
339 Rondell White .07 .20
340 Kirby Puckett .20 .50
341 Deion Sanders .10 .30
342 Eddie Murray .20 .50
343 Mike Harkey .02 .10
344 Joey Hamilton .02 .10
345 Roger Salkeld .02 .10
346 Wil Cordero .02 .10
347 John Wetteland .07 .20
348 Geronimo Pena .02 .10
349 Kirk Gibson .07 .20
350 Manny Ramirez .10 .30
351 Wm.VanLandingham .02 .10
352 B.J. Surhoff .07 .20
353 Ken Ryan .02 .10
354 Terry Steinbach .02 .10
355 Bret Saberhagen .07 .20
356 John Jaha .02 .10
357 Joe Girardi .02 .10
358 Steve Karsay .02 .10
359 Alex Fernandez .02 .10
360 Salomon Torres .02 .10
361 John Burkett .02 .10
362 Derek Bell .02 .10
363 Tom Henke .02 .10
364 Gregg Jefferies .02 .10
365 Jack McDowell .02 .10
366 Andujar Cedeno .02 .10
367 Dave Winfield .07 .20
368 Carl Everett .07 .20
369 Danny Jackson .02 .10
370 Jeromy Burnitz .07 .20
371 Mark Grace .10 .30
372 Larry Walker .07 .20
373 Bill Swift .02 .10
374 Dennis Martinez .07 .20
375 Mickey Tettleton .02 .10
376 Mel Nieves .02 .10
377 Cal Eldred .02 .10
378 Orel Hershiser .07 .20
379 David Wells .07 .20
380 Gary Gaetti .07 .20
381 Tim Raines .07 .20
382 Barry Larkin .10 .30
383 Jason Jacome .02 .10
384 Tim Wallach .02 .10
385 Robby Thompson .02 .10
386 Frank Viola .07 .20
387 Dave Stewart .07 .20
388 Bip Roberts .02 .10
389 Ron Darling .02 .10
390 Carlos Delgado .07 .20
391 Tim Salmon .10 .30
392 Alan Trammell .07 .20
393 Kevin Foster .02 .10
394 Jim Abbott .10 .30
395 John Kruk .07 .20
396 Andy Van Slyke .10 .30
397 Dave Magadan .02 .10
398 Rafael Palmeiro .10 .30
399 Mike Devereaux .02 .10
400 Benito Santiago .07 .20
401 Brett Butler .07 .20
402 John Franco .07 .20
403 Matt Walbeck .02 .10
404 Terry Pendleton .07 .20
405 Chris Sabo .02 .10
406 Andrew Lorraine .02 .10
407 Dan Wilson .02 .10
408 Mike Lansing .02 .10
409 Ray McDavid .02 .10
410 Shane Andrews .02 .10
411 Tom Gordon .02 .10
412 Chad Ogea .02 .10
413 James Baldwin .02 .10
414 Russ Davis .02 .10
415 Ray Holbert .02 .10
416 Ray Durham .07 .20
417 Matt Nokes .02 .10
418 Rod Henderson .02 .10
419 Gabe White .02 .10
420 Todd Hollandsworth .02 .10
421 Midre Cummings .02 .10
422 Harold Baines .07 .20
423 Troy Percival .07 .20
424 Joe Vitiello .02 .10
425 Andy Ashby .02 .10
426 Michael Tucker .02 .10
427 Mark Gubicza .02 .10
428 Jim Bullinger .02 .10
429 Jose Malave .02 .10
430 Pete Schourek .02 .10
431 Bobby Ayala .02 .10
432 Marvin Freeman .02 .10
433 Pat Listach .02 .10
434 Eddie Taubensee .02 .10
435 Steve Howe .02 .10
436 Kent Mercker .02 .10
437 Hector Fajardo .02 .10
438 Scott Kamieniecki .02 .10
439 Robb Nen .07 .20
440 Mike Kelly .02 .10
441 Tom Candiotti .02 .10
442 Albie Lopez .02 .10
443 Jeff Granger .02 .10
444 Rich Aude .02 .10
445 Luis Polonia .02 .10
446 Frank Thomas CL .10 .30
447 Ken Griffey Jr. CL .25 .60
448 Mike Piazza CL .20 .50
449 Jeff Bagwell CL .07 .20
450 Bag .25 .60
Thom
Grif
Piaz CL

1995 Pinnacle Artist's Proofs

COMPLETE SET (450) 1200.00 1600.00
*STARS: 10X TO 25X BASIC CARDS
*ROOKIES: 6X TO 15X BASIC
SER.1 STATED ODDS 1:36 H/R
SER.2 STATED ODDS 1:26 H/R

1995 Pinnacle Museum Collection

COMMON CARD (1-450) .50 1.25
*STARS: 4X TO 10X BASIC CARDS
*ROOKIES: 2.5X TO 6X BASIC
STATED ODDS 1:4 H/R/J, 1:3 ANCO
TRADE: 410/413/416/420/423/426/444
TRADE CARD EXCH.DEADLINE 12/31/95
132 Alex Rodriguez 10.00 25.00
410 Shane Andrews TRADE 2.00 5.00
413 James Baldwin TRADE 2.00 5.00
416 Ray Durham TRADE 4.00 10.00
420 Todd Hollandsworth TRADE 2.00 5.00
423 Troy Percival TRADE 4.00 10.00
426 Michael Tucker TRADE 2.00 5.00
444 Rich Aude TRADE 2.00 5.00

1995 Pinnacle ETA

COMPLETE SET (6) 6.00 15.00
SER.1 STATED ODDS 1:24 HOBBY
ETA1 Ben Grieve .75 2.00
ETA2 Alex Ochoa .75 2.00
ETA3 Joe Vitiello .75 2.00
ETA4 Johnny Damon 1.25 3.00
ETA5 Trey Beamon .75 2.00
ETA6 Brooks Kieschnick .75 2.00

1995 Pinnacle Gate Attractions

COMPLETE SET (18) 12.00 30.00
SER.2 STATED ODDS 1:12 JUMBO
GA1 Ken Griffey Jr. 2.00 5.00
GA2 Frank Thomas 1.00 2.50
GA3 Cal Ripken 3.00 8.00
GA4 Jeff Bagwell .60 1.50
GA5 Mike Piazza 1.00 2.50
GA6 Barry Bonds 1.50 4.00
GA7 Kirby Puckett 1.00 2.50
GA8 Albert Belle .40 1.00
GA9 Tony Gwynn 1.00 2.50
GA10 Raul Mondesi .40 1.00
GA11 Will Clark .40 1.00
GA12 Don Mattingly 2.00 5.00
GA13 Roger Clemens 1.50 4.00
GA14 Paul Molitor 1.00 2.50
GA15 Matt Williams .40 1.00
GA16 Greg Maddux 1.50 4.00
GA17 Kenny Lofton .40 1.00
GA18 Cliff Floyd .40 1.00

1995 Pinnacle New Blood

COMPLETE SET (9) 25.00 60.00
SER.2 ODDS 1:90 HOB/RET, 1:72 ANCO
NB1 Alex Rodriguez 8.00 20.00
NB2 Shawn Green 1.50 4.00
NB3 Brian L.Hunter 1.00 2.50
NB4 Garret Anderson 1.50 4.00
NB5 Charles Johnson 1.50 4.00
NB6 Chipper Jones 3.00 8.00
NB7 Carlos Delgado 1.50 4.00
NB8 Billy Ashley 1.00 2.50
NB9 J.R. Phillips 1.00 2.50

1995 Pinnacle Performers

COMPLETE SET (18) 40.00 100.00
SER.1 STATED ODDS 1:12 JUMBO
PP1 Frank Thomas 2.50 6.00
PP2 Albert Belle 1.00 2.50
PP3 Barry Bonds 8.00 20.00
PP4 Juan Gonzalez 1.00 2.50
PP5 Andres Galarraga 1.00 2.50
PP6 Raul Mondesi 1.00 2.50
PP7 Paul Molitor 1.00 2.50
PP8 Tim Salmon 1.50 4.00
PP9 Mike Piazza 4.00 10.00
PP10 Gregg Jefferies .50 1.25
PP11 Will Clark 1.50 4.00
PP12 Greg Maddux 4.00 10.00
PP13 Manny Ramirez 1.50 4.00
PP14 Kirby Puckett 2.50 6.00
PP15 Shawn Green 1.00 2.50
PP16 Rafael Palmeiro 1.50 4.00
PP17 Paul O'Neill 1.50 4.00
PP18 Jason Bere .50 1.25

1995 Pinnacle Pin Redemption

COMPLETE SET (18) 25.00 60.00
SER.2 ODDS 1:48 H/R, 1:36 JUM/ANCO
*PINS: .75X TO 1.5X BASIC PIN REDEMPTION
ONE PIN VIA MAIL PER REDEMPTION CARD
1 Greg Maddux 1.50 4.00
2 Mike Mussina .60 1.50
3 Mike Piazza 1.50 4.00
4 Carlos Delgado .40 1.00
5 Jeff Bagwell .60 1.50
6 Frank Thomas 1.00 2.50
7 Craig Biggio .60 1.50
8 Roberto Alomar .60 1.50
9 Ozzie Smith 1.50 4.00
10 Cal Ripken 3.00 8.00
11 Matt Williams .40 1.00
12 Travis Fryman .40 1.00
13 Barry Bonds 3.00 8.00
14 Ken Griffey Jr. 2.00 5.00
15 David Justice .40 1.00
16 Albert Belle .40 1.00
17 Tony Gwynn 1.25 3.00
18 Kirby Puckett 1.00 2.50

1995 Pinnacle Red Hot

COMPLETE SET (25) 30.00 80.00
SER.2 STAT.ODDS 1:16 HOB/RET, 1:12 ANCO
*WHITE HOT: 1.5X TO 4X RED HOTS
WHITE HOT SER.2 ODDS 1:36 HOBBY
RH1 Cal Ripken 3.00 8.00
RH2 Ken Griffey Jr. 6.00 15.00
RH3 Frank Thomas 1.00 2.50
RH4 Jeff Bagwell .60 1.50
RH5 Mike Piazza 1.50 4.00
RH6 Barry Bonds 3.00 8.00
RH7 Albert Belle .40 1.00
RH8 Tony Gwynn 1.25 3.00
RH9 Kirby Puckett 1.00 2.50
RH10 Don Mattingly 2.50 6.00
RH11 Matt Williams .40 1.00
RH12 Greg Maddux 1.50 4.00
RH13 Raul Mondesi .40 1.00
RH14 Paul Molitor .40 1.00
RH15 Manny Ramirez .60 1.50
RH16 Joe Carter .40 1.00
RH17 Will Clark .60 1.50
RH18 Roger Clemens 2.00 5.00
RH19 Tim Salmon .60 1.50
RH20 David Justice .40 1.00
RH21 Kenny Lofton .40 1.00
RH22 Deion Sanders .60 1.50
RH23 Roberto Alomar .60 1.50
RH24 Cliff Floyd .40 1.00
RH25 Carlos Baerga .20 .50

1995 Pinnacle Team Pinnacle

COMPLETE SET (9) 25.00 60.00
SER.1 ODDS 1:90 HOB/RET, 1:72 ANCO
TP1 G.Maddux 4.00 10.00
M.Mussina
TP2 M.Piazza 2.50 6.00
C.Delgado
TP3 F.Thomas 2.50 6.00
J.Bagwell
TP4 R.Alomar 1.50 4.00
C.Biggio
TP5 C.Ripken 8.00 20.00
O.Smith
TP6 T.Fryman 1.00 2.50
M.Williams
TP7 K.Griffey 5.00 12.00
B.Bonds
TP8 A.Belle 1.00 2.50
D.Justice
TP9 T.Gwynn 2.50 6.00
K.Puckett

1995 Pinnacle Team Pinnacle Dufex Back

*DUFEX BACK: .4X TO 1X BASIC

1995 Pinnacle Upstarts

COMPLETE SET (30) 20.00 50.00
SER.1 ODDS 1:8 HOB/RET, 1:6 ANCO
US1 Frank Thomas 1.25 3.00
US2 Roberto Alomar .75 2.00
US3 Mike Piazza 2.00 5.00
US4 Javier Lopez .50 1.25
US5 Albert Belle .50 1.25
US6 Carlos Delgado .50 1.25
US7 Brent Gates .25 .60
US8 Tim Salmon .75 2.00
US9 Raul Mondesi .50 1.25
US10 Juan Gonzalez .50 1.25
US11 Manny Ramirez .75 2.00
US12 Sammy Sosa 1.25 3.00
US13 Jeff Kent .50 1.25
US14 Melvin Nieves .25 .60
US15 Rondell White .50 1.25
US16 Shawn Green .50 1.25
US17 Bernie Williams .75 2.00
US18 Aaron Sele .25 .60
US19 Jason Bere .25 .60
US20 Joey Hamilton .25 .60
US21 Mike Kelly .25 .60
US22 Wil Cordero .25 .60
US23 Moises Alou .50 1.25
US24 Roberto Kelly .25 .60
US25 Deion Sanders .75 2.00
US26 Steve Karsay .25 .60
US27 Bret Boone .50 1.25
US28 Willie Greene .25 .60
US29 Billy Ashley .25 .60
US30 Brian Anderson .25 .60

1995 Pinnacle FanFest

Available in two-card cello packs, this 30-card standard-size set was issued to commemorate the Pinnacle All-Star FanFest July 7-11 in Arlington, Texas.

COMPLETE SET (30) 15.00 40.00
1 Cal Ripken 2.00 5.00
2 Roger Clemens 1.00 2.50
3 Don Mattingly 1.00 2.50
4 Albert Belle .20 .50
5 Kirby Puckett .60 1.50
6 Cecil Fielder .20 .50
7 Kevin Appier .20 .50
8 Will Clark .40 1.00
9 Juan Gonzalez .40 1.00
10 Ivan Rodriguez .50 1.25
11 Ken Griffey Jr. 1.25 3.00
12 Tim Salmon .40 1.00
13 Frank Thomas .50 1.25
14 Roberto Alomar .40 1.00
15 Rickey Henderson .60 1.50
16 Raul Mondesi .30 .75
17 Matt Williams .30 .75
18 Ozzie Smith 1.00 2.50
19 Deion Sanders .20 .50
20 Tony Gwynn 1.00 2.50
21 Greg Maddux 1.25 3.00
22 Sammy Sosa .75 2.00
23 Mike Piazza 1.25 3.00
24 Barry Bonds 1.00 2.50
25 Jeff Bagwell .50 1.25
26 Lenny Dykstra .20 .50
27 Rico Brogna .08 .25
28 Larry Walker .30 .75
29 Gary Sheffield .50 1.25
30 Wil Cordero .08 .25

1996 Pinnacle Samples

COMPLETE SET (9) 3.00 8.00
1 Greg Maddux 1.25 3.00
2 Bill Pulsipher .08 .25
3 Dante Bichette .08 .25
4 Mike Piazza 1.25 3.00
5 Garret Anderson .15 .40
165 Ruben Rivera .08 .25
166 Tony Clark .08 .25
PP2 Mo Vaughn 1.00 2.50
Pinnacle Power
NNO Title Card .08 .25

1996 Pinnacle

The 1996 Pinnacle set was issued in two separate series of 200 cards each. The 10-card packs retailed for $2.49. On 20-point card stock, the fronts feature full-bleed color action photos, bordered at the bottom by a gold foil triangle. The Series I set features the following topical subsets: The Naturals (134-163), '95 Rookies (164-193) and Checklists (194-200). Series II set features these subsets: Hardball Heroes (30 cards), 300 Series (17 cards), Rookies (25 cards), and Checklists (7 cards). Numbering for the 300 Series subset was based on player's career batting average. At that time, both Paul Molitor and Jeff Bagwell had identical career batting averages of .305, thus Pinnacle numbered both of their 300 Series subset cards as 305. Due to this quirky numbering, the set only runs through card 399, but actually contains 400 cards. A special Cal Ripken Jr. Tribute card was inserted in first series packs at the rate of one in 150. Please note that the Ripken Tribute card does not carry a CR prefix. That was added in order to differentiate it from card number 1 in the base set.

COMPLETE SET (400) 12.50 30.00
COMPLETE SERIES 1 (200) 6.00 15.00
COMPLETE SERIES 2 (200) 6.00 15.00
RIPKEN TRIB.SER.1 STATED ODDS 1:150
1 Greg Maddux .30 .75
2 Bill Pulsipher .07 .20
3 Dante Bichette .07 .20
4 Mike Piazza .30 .75
5 Garret Anderson .07 .20
6 Steve Finley .07 .20
7 Andy Benes .07 .20
8 Chuck Knoblauch .07 .20
9 Tom Gordon .07 .20
10 Jeff Bagwell .10 .30
11 Wil Cordero .07 .20
12 John Mabry .07 .20
13 Jeff Frye .07 .20
14 Travis Fryman .07 .20
15 John Wetteland .07 .20
16 Jason Bates .07 .20
17 Danny Tartabull .07 .20
18 Charles Nagy .07 .20
19 Robin Ventura .07 .20
20 Reggie Sanders .07 .20
21 Dave Clark .07 .20
22 Jaime Navarro .07 .20
23 Joey Hamilton .07 .20
24 Al Leiter .07 .20
25 Deion Sanders .10 .30
26 Tim Salmon .10 .30
27 Tino Martinez .10 .30
28 Mike Greenwell .07 .20
29 Phil Plantier .07 .20
30 Bobby Bonilla .07 .20
31 Kenny Rogers .07 .20
32 Chili Davis .07 .20
33 Joe Carter .07 .20
34 Mike Mussina .10 .30
35 Matt Mieske .07 .20
36 Jose Canseco .10 .30
37 Brad Radke .07 .20
38 Juan Gonzalez .07 .20
39 David Segui .07 .20
40 Alex Fernandez .07 .20
41 Jeff Kent .07 .20
42 Todd Zeile .07 .20
43 Darryl Strawberry .07 .20
44 Jose Rijo .07 .20
45 Ramon Martinez .07 .20
46 Manny Ramirez .10 .30
47 Gregg Jefferies .07 .20
48 Bryan Rekar .07 .20
49 Jeff King .07 .20
50 John Olerud .07 .20
51 Marc Newfield .07 .20
52 Charles Johnson .07 .20
53 Robby Thompson .07 .20
54 Brian L. Hunter .07 .20
55 Mike Blowers .07 .20
56 Keith Lockhart .07 .20
57 Ray Lankford .07 .20
58 Tim Wallach .07 .20
59 Ivan Rodriguez .10 .30
60 Ed Sprague .07 .20
61 Paul Molitor .07 .20
62 Eric Karros .07 .20
63 Glenallen Hill .07 .20
64 Jay Bell .07 .20
65 Tom Pagnozzi .07 .20
66 Greg Colbrunn .07 .20
67 Edgar Martinez .10 .30
68 Paul Sorrento .07 .20
69 Kirt Manwaring .07 .20
70 Pete Schourek .07 .20
71 Orlando Merced .07 .20
72 Shawon Dunston .07 .20
73 Ricky Bottalico .07 .20
74 Brady Anderson .07 .20
75 Steve Ontiveros .07 .20
76 Jim Abbott .10 .30
77 Carl Everett .07 .20
78 Mo Vaughn .07 .20
79 Pedro Martinez .10 .30
80 Harold Baines .07 .20
81 Alan Trammell .07 .20
82 Steve Avery .07 .20
83 Jeff Cirillo .07 .20
84 John Valentin .07 .20
85 Bernie Williams .10 .30
86 Andre Dawson .07 .20
87 Dave Winfield .07 .20
88 B.J. Surhoff .07 .20
89 Jeff Blauser .07 .20
90 Barry Larkin .10 .30
91 Cliff Floyd .07 .20
92 Sammy Sosa .20 .50
93 Andres Galarraga .07 .20
94 Dave Nilsson .07 .20
95 James Mouton .07 .20
96 Marquis Grissom .07 .20
97 Matt Williams .07 .20
98 John Jaha .07 .20
99 Don Mattingly .50 1.25
100 Tim Naehring .07 .20
101 Kevin Appier .07 .20
102 Bobby Higginson .07 .20
103 Andy Pettitte .10 .30
104 Ozzie Smith .30 .75
105 Kenny Lofton .07 .20
106 Ken Caminiti .07 .20
107 Walt Weiss .07 .20
108 Jack McDowell .07 .20
109 Brian McRae .07 .20
110 Gary Gaetti .07 .20
111 Curtis Goodwin .07 .20
112 Dennis Martinez .07 .20
113 Omar Vizquel .10 .30
114 Chipper Jones .20 .50
115 Mark Gubicza .07 .20
116 Ruben Sierra .07 .20
117 Eddie Murray .20 .50
118 Chad Curtis .07 .20
119 Hal Morris .07 .20
120 Ben McDonald .07 .20
121 Marty Cordova .07 .20
122 Ken Griffey Jr. .40 1.00
123 Gary Sheffield .07 .20
124 Charlie Hayes .07 .20
125 Shawn Green .07 .20
126 Jason Giambi .07 .20
127 Mark Langston .07 .20
128 Mark Whiten .07 .20
129 Greg Vaughn .07 .20
130 Mark McGwire .50 1.25
131 Hideo Nomo .20 .50
132 Dodger ROY's .20 .50
133 Jason Bere .07 .20
134 Ken Griffey Jr. NAT .25 .60
135 Frank Thomas NAT .10 .30
136 Cal Ripken NAT .30 .75
137 Albert Belle NAT .07 .20
138 Mike Piazza NAT .20 .50
139 Dante Bichette NAT .07 .20
140 Sammy Sosa NAT .10 .30
141 Mo Vaughn NAT .07 .20
142 Tim Salmon NAT .07 .20
143 Reggie Sanders NAT .07 .20
144 Cecil Fielder NAT .07 .20
145 Jim Edmonds NAT .07 .20
146 Rafael Palmeiro NAT .07 .20
147 Edgar Martinez NAT .07 .20
148 Barry Bonds NAT .30 .75
149 Manny Ramirez NAT .07 .20
150 Larry Walker NAT .07 .20
151 Jeff Bagwell NAT .07 .20
152 Ron Gant NAT .07 .20
153 Andres Galarraga NAT .07 .20
154 Eddie Murray NAT .10 .30
155 Kirby Puckett NAT .10 .30
156 Will Clark NAT .07 .20
157 Don Mattingly NAT .25 .60
158 Mark McGwire NAT .25 .60
159 Dean Palmer NAT .07 .20
160 Matt Williams NAT .07 .20
161 Fred McGriff NAT .07 .20
162 Joe Carter NAT .07 .20
163 Juan Gonzalez NAT .07 .20
164 Alex Ochoa .07 .20
165 Ruben Rivera .07 .20
166 Tony Clark .07 .20
167 Brian Barber .07 .20
168 Matt Lawton RC .15 .40
169 Terrell Wade .07 .20
170 Johnny Damon .10 .30
171 Derek Jeter .50 1.25
172 Phil Nevin .07 .20
173 Robert Perez .07 .20
174 C.J. Nitkowski .07 .20
175 Joe Vitiello .07 .20
176 Roger Cedeno .07 .20
177 Ron Coomer .07 .20
178 Chris Widger .07 .20
179 Jimmy Haynes .07 .20
180 Mike Sweeney RC .40 1.00
181 Howard Battle .07 .20
182 John Wasdin .07 .20
183 Jim Pittsley .07 .20
184 Bob Wolcott .07 .20
185 LaTroy Hawkins .07 .20
186 Nigel Wilson .07 .20
187 Dustin Hermanson .07 .20
188 Chris Snopek .07 .20
189 Mariano Rivera .40 1.00
190 Jose Herrera .07 .20
191 Chris Stynes .07 .20
192 Larry Thomas .07 .20
193 David Bell .07 .20
194 Frank Thomas CL .10 .30
195 Ken Griffey Jr. CL .25 .60
196 Cal Ripken CL .30 .75
197 Jeff Bagwell CL .07 .20
198 Mike Piazza CL .20 .50
199 Barry Bonds CL .30 .75
200 G.Anderson .10 .30
C.Jones CL
201 Frank Thomas .20 .50
202 Michael Tucker .07 .20
203 Kirby Puckett .20 .50
204 Alex Gonzalez .07 .20
205 Tony Gwynn .25 .60
206 Moises Alou .07 .20
207 Albert Belle .07 .20
208 Barry Bonds .60 1.50
209 Fred McGriff .10 .30
210 Dennis Eckersley .07 .20
211 Craig Biggio .10 .30
212 David Cone .07 .20
213 Will Clark .10 .30
214 Cal Ripken .60 1.50
215 Wade Boggs .10 .30
216 Pete Schourek .07 .20
217 Darren Daulton .07 .20
218 Carlos Baerga .07 .20
219 Larry Walker .07 .20
220 Denny Neagle .07 .20
221 Jim Edmonds .07 .20
222 Lee Smith .07 .20
223 Jason Isringhausen .07 .20
224 Jay Buhner .07 .20
225 John Olerud .07 .20
226 Jeff Conine .07 .20
227 Dean Palmer .07 .20
228 Jim Abbott .10 .30
229 Raul Mondesi .07 .20
230 Tom Glavine .10 .30
231 Kevin Seitzer .07 .20
232 Lenny Dykstra .07 .20
233 Brian Jordan .07 .20
234 Rondell White .07 .20
235 Bret Boone .07 .20
236 Randy Johnson .20 .50
237 Paul O'Neill .10 .30
238 Jim Thome .10 .30
239 Edgardo Alfonzo .07 .20
240 Terry Pendleton .07 .20
241 Harold Baines .07 .20
242 Roberto Alomar .10 .30
243 Mark Grace .10 .30
244 Derek Bell .07 .20
245 Vinny Castilla .07 .20
246 Cecil Fielder .07 .20
247 Roger Clemens .40 1.00
248 Orel Hershiser .07 .20
249 J.T. Snow .07 .20
250 Rafael Palmeiro .10 .30
251 Bret Saberhagen .07 .20
252 Todd Hollandsworth .07 .20
253 Ryan Klesko .07 .20
254 Greg Maddux HH .20 .50
255 Ken Griffey Jr. HH .25 .60
256 Hideo Nomo HH .10 .30
257 Frank Thomas HH .10 .30
258 Cal Ripken HH .30 .75
259 Jeff Bagwell HH .07 .20
260 Barry Bonds HH .30 .75
261 Mo Vaughn HH .07 .20
262 Albert Belle HH .07 .20
263 Sammy Sosa HH .10 .30
264 Reggie Sanders HH .07 .20
265 Mike Piazza HH .20 .50
266 Chipper Jones HH .10 .30
267 Tony Gwynn HH .10 .30
268 Kirby Puckett HH .10 .30
269 Wade Boggs HH .07 .20
270 Will Clark HH .07 .20
271 Gary Sheffield HH .07 .20
272 Dante Bichette HH .07 .20
273 Randy Johnson HH .10 .30
274 Matt Williams HH .07 .20
275 Alex Rodriguez HH .40 1.00
276 Tim Salmon HH .07 .20
277 Johnny Damon HH .07 .20
278 Manny Ramirez HH .07 .20
279 Derek Jeter HH .25 .60
280 Eddie Murray HH .10 .30
281 Ozzie Smith HH .20 .50
282 Garret Anderson HH .07 .20
283 Raul Mondesi HH .07 .20
284 Terry Steinbach .07 .20
285 Carlos Garcia .07 .20
286 Dave Justice .07 .20
287 Eric Anthony .07 .20
288 Benji Gil .07 .20
289 Bob Hamelin .07 .20
290 Dwayne Hosey .07 .20
291 Andy Pettitte HH .07 .20
292 Rod Beck .07 .20
293 Shane Andrews .07 .20
294 Julian Tavarez .07 .20
295 Willie Greene .07 .20
296 Ismael Valdes .07 .20
297 Glenallen Hill .07 .20
298 Troy Percival .07 .20
299 Ray Durham .07 .20
300 Jeff Conine 300 .07 .20
301 Ken Griffey Jr. 300 .25 .60
302 Will Clark 300 .07 .20
303 Mike Greenwell 300 .07 .20
304 Carlos Baerga 300 .07 .20
305A Paul Molitor 300 .07 .20
305B Jeff Bagwell 300 .07 .20
306 Mark Grace 300 .07 .20
307 Don Mattingly 300 .25 .60
308 Hal Morris 300 .07 .20
309 Butch Huskey .07 .20
310 Ozzie Guillen .07 .20
311 Erik Hanson .07 .20
312 Kenny Lofton 300 .07 .20
313 Edgar Martinez 300 .07 .20
314 Kurt Abbott .07 .20
315 John Smoltz .10 .30
316 Ariel Prieto .07 .20
317 Mark Carreon .07 .20
318 Kirby Puckett 300 .10 .30
319 Carlos Perez .07 .20
320 Gary DiSarcina .07 .20
321 Trevor Hoffman .07 .20
322 Mike Piazza 300 .20 .50
323 Frank Thomas 300 .10 .30
324 Juan Acevedo .07 .20
325 Bip Roberts .07 .20
326 Javier Lopez .07 .20
327 Benito Santiago .07 .20
328 Mark Lewis .07 .20
329 Royce Clayton .07 .20
330 Tom Gordon .07 .20
331 Ben McDonald .07 .20
332 Dan Wilson .07 .20
333 Ron Gant .07 .20
334 Wade Boggs 300 .07 .20
335 Paul Molitor .07 .20
336 Tony Gwynn 300 .10 .30
337 Sean Berry .07 .20
338 Rickey Henderson .20 .50
339 Wil Cordero .07 .20
340 Kent Mercker .07 .20
341 Kenny Rogers .07 .20
342 Ryne Sandberg .30 .75
343 Charlie Hayes .07 .20
344 Andy Benes .07 .20
345 Sterling Hitchcock .07 .20
346 Bernard Gilkey .07 .20
347 Julio Franco .07 .20
348 Ken Hill .07 .20
349 Russ Davis .07 .20
350 Mike Blowers .07 .20
351 B.J. Surhoff .07 .20
352 Lance Johnson .07 .20
353 Darryl Hamilton .07 .20
354 Shawon Dunston .07 .20
355 Rick Aguilera .07 .20
356 Danny Tartabull .07 .20
357 Todd Stottlemyre .07 .20
358 Mike Bordick .07 .20
359 Jack McDowell .07 .20
360 Todd Zeile .07 .20
361 Tino Martinez .10 .30
362 Greg Gagne .07 .20
363 Mike Kelly .07 .20
364 Tim Raines .07 .20
365 Ernie Young .07 .20
366 Mike Stanley .07 .20
367 Wally Joyner .07 .20
368 Karim Garcia .07 .20
369 Paul Wilson .07 .20
370 Sal Fasano .07 .20
371 Jason Schmidt .10 .30
372 Livan Hernandez RC .40 1.00
373 George Arias .07 .20
374 Steve Gibralter .07 .20
375 Jermaine Dye .07 .20
376 Jason Kendall .07 .20
377 Brooks Kieschnick .07 .20
378 Jeff Ware .07 .20
379 Alan Benes .07 .20
380 Rey Ordonez .07 .20
381 Jay Powell .07 .20
382 Osvaldo Fernandez RC .08 .25
383 Wilton Guerrero RC .08 .25
384 Eric Owens .07 .20
385 George Williams RC .08 .25
386 Chan Ho Park .07 .20
387 Jeff Suppan .07 .20
388 F.P. Santangelo RC .15 .40
389 Terry Adams .07 .20
390 Bob Abreu .20 .50
391 Quinton McCracken .07 .20
392 Mike Busby RC .08 .25
393 Cal Ripken CL .30 .75
394 Ken Griffey Jr. CL .25 .60
395 Frank Thomas CL .10 .30
396 Chipper Jones CL .10 .30
397 Greg Maddux CL .20 .50
398 Mike Piazza CL .20 .50
399 Superstar CL .25 .60
CR1 Cal Ripken Tribute 6.00 15.00

1996 Pinnacle Foil

COMPLETE SET (200) 12.50 30.00
*STARS: .75X TO 2X BASIC CARDS
DISTRIBUTED IN FOIL RETAIL SUPER PACKS

1996 Pinnacle Starburst

*STARS: 1.5X TO 4X BASIC CARDS
STATED ODDS 1:7 H/R, 1:6 JUM, 1:10 MAG
97 Derek Jeter 8.00 20.00

1996 Pinnacle Starburst Artist's Proofs
*STARS: 8X TO 20X BASIC CARDS
STATED ODDS 1:47 H/R, 1:39 JUM, 1:67 MAG
97 Derek Jeter 25.00 60.00
168 Kirby Puckett HH 10.00 25.00

1996 Pinnacle Christie Brinkley Collection
COMPLETE SET (16) 25.00 60.00
SER.2 STATED ODDS 1:23H/R, 1:19J, 1:32 M
1 Greg Maddux 5.00 12.00
2 Ryan Klesko 1.25 3.00
3 Dave Justice 1.25 3.00
4 Tom Glavine 2.00 5.00
5 Chipper Jones 3.00 8.00
6 Fred McGriff 2.00 5.00
7 Javier Lopez 1.25 3.00
8 Marquis Grissom 1.25 3.00
9 Jason Schmidt 2.00 5.00
10 Albert Belle 1.25 3.00
11 Manny Ramirez 2.00 5.00
12 Carlos Baerga 1.25 3.00
13 Sandy Alomar Jr. 1.25 3.00
14 Jim Thome 2.00 5.00
15 Julio Franco 1.25 3.00
16 Kenny Lofton 1.25 3.00
PCB Christie Brinkley Promo 1.25 3.00

1996 Pinnacle Essence of the Game
COMPLETE SET (18) 25.00 60.00
SER.1 STATED ODDS 1:23 HOBBY
1 Cal Ripken 6.00 15.00
2 Greg Maddux 3.00 8.00
3 Frank Thomas 2.00 5.00
4 Matt Williams .75 2.00
5 Chipper Jones 2.00 5.00
6 Reggie Sanders .75 2.00
7 Ken Griffey Jr. 4.00 10.00
8 Kirby Puckett 2.00 5.00
9 Hideo Nomo 2.00 5.00
10 Mike Piazza 2.00 5.00
11 Jeff Bagwell 1.25 3.00
12 Mo Vaughn .75 2.00
13 Albert Belle .75 2.00
14 Tim Salmon .75 2.00
15 Don Mattingly 4.00 10.00
16 Will Clark 1.25 3.00
17 Eddie Murray 1.25 3.00
18 Barry Bonds 3.00 8.00

1996 Pinnacle First Rate
COMPLETE SET (18) 60.00 120.00
SER.1 STATED ODDS 1:23 RETAIL
UNINTENTIONALLY INSERTED IN SOME HOBBY
1 Ken Griffey Jr. 6.00 15.00
2 Frank Thomas 3.00 8.00
3 Mo Vaughn 1.25 3.00
4 Chipper Jones 3.00 8.00
5 Alex Rodriguez 6.00 15.00
6 Kirby Puckett 4.00 10.00
7 Gary Sheffield 1.25 3.00
8 Matt Williams 1.25 3.00
9 Barry Bonds 10.00 25.00
10 Craig Biggio 2.00 5.00
11 Robin Ventura 1.25 3.00
12 Michael Tucker 1.25 3.00
13 Derek Jeter 15.00 40.00
14 Manny Ramirez 2.00 5.00
15 Barry Larkin 2.00 5.00
16 Shawn Green 1.25 3.00
17 Will Clark 2.00 5.00
18 Mark McGwire 8.00 20.00

1996 Pinnacle Power
COMPLETE SET (20) 15.00 40.00
SER.1 STATED ODDS 1:35
1 Frank Thomas 1.50 4.00
2 Mo Vaughn .60 1.50
3 Ken Griffey Jr. 3.00 8.00
4 Matt Williams .60 1.50
5 Barry Bonds 2.50 6.00
6 Reggie Sanders .60 1.50
7 Mike Piazza 1.50 4.00
8 Jim Edmonds .60 1.50
9 Dante Bichette .60 1.50
10 Sammy Sosa 1.50 4.00
11 Jeff Bagwell 1.00 2.50
12 Fred McGriff 1.00 2.50
13 Albert Belle .60 1.50
14 Tim Salmon .60 1.50
15 Joe Carter .60 1.50
16 Manny Ramirez 1.00 2.50
17 Eddie Murray 1.00 2.50
18 Cecil Fielder .60 1.50
19 Larry Walker 1.00 2.50
20 Juan Gonzalez .60 1.50

1996 Pinnacle Project Stardom
COMPLETE SET (18) 60.00 120.00
SER.2 STATED ODDS 1:35
1 Paul Wilson 1.50 4.00
2 Derek Jeter 15.00 40.00
3 Karim Garcia 1.50 4.00
4 Johnny Damon 2.50 6.00
5 Alex Rodriguez 8.00 20.00
6 Chipper Jones 4.00 10.00
7 Charles Johnson 1.50 4.00
8 Bob Abreu 4.00 10.00
9 Alan Benes 1.50 4.00
10 Richard Hidalgo 1.50 4.00
11 Brooks Kieschnick 1.50 4.00
12 Garret Anderson 1.50 4.00
13 Livan Hernandez 8.00 20.00
14 Manny Ramirez 2.50 6.00
15 Jermaine Dye 1.50 4.00
16 Todd Hollandsworth 1.50 4.00
17 Raul Mondesi 1.50 4.00
18 Ryan Klesko 1.50 4.00

1996 Pinnacle Skylines
SER.2 STATED ODDS 1:29 JUM, 1:50 MAG
1 Ken Griffey Jr. 150.00 250.00
2 Frank Thomas 60.00 150.00
3 Greg Maddux 25.00 60.00
4 Cal Ripken 30.00 80.00
5 Albert Belle 10.00 25.00
6 Mo Vaughn 10.00 25.00
7 Mike Piazza 15.00 40.00
8 Wade Boggs 20.00 50.00
9 Will Clark 50.00 120.00
10 Barry Bonds 40.00 100.00
11 Gary Sheffield 15.00 40.00
12 Hideo Nomo 15.00 40.00
13 Tony Gwynn 15.00 40.00
14 Kirby Puckett 125.00 250.00
15 Chipper Jones 60.00 150.00
16 Jeff Bagwell 30.00 80.00
17 Manny Ramirez 20.00 50.00
18 Raul Mondesi 6.00 15.00

1996 Pinnacle Slugfest
COMPLETE SET (18) 15.00 40.00
SER.2 RETAIL STATED ODDS 1:35
1 Frank Thomas 2.00 5.00
2 Ken Griffey Jr. 4.00 10.00
3 Jeff Bagwell 1.25 3.00
4 Barry Bonds 3.00 8.00
5 Mo.Vaughn .75 2.00
6 Albert Belle .75 2.00
7 Mike Piazza 2.00 5.00
8 Matt Williams .75 2.00
9 Dante Bichette .75 2.00
10 Sammy Sosa 2.00 5.00
11 Gary Sheffield .75 2.00
12 Reggie Sanders .75 2.00
13 Manny Ramirez 1.25 3.00
14 Eddie Murray 1.25 3.00
15 Juan Gonzalez .75 2.00
16 Dean Palmer .75 2.00
17 Rafael Palmeiro 1.25 3.00
18 Cecil Fielder .75 2.00

1996 Pinnacle Team Pinnacle
COMPLETE SET (9) 12.50 30.00
SER.1 STATED ODDS 1:72
ONE SIDE OF EACH CARD IS DUFEX
1 F.Thomas 1.50 4.00
J.Bagwell
2 C.Knoblauch 1.00 2.50
C.Biggio
3 J.Thome 1.00 2.50
M.Williams
4 C.Ripken 5.00 12.00
B.Larkin
5 B.Bonds 2.50 6.00
T.Salmon
6 K.Griffey Jr. 3.00 8.00
R.Sanders
7 S.Sosa 1.50 4.00
A.Belle
8 M.Piazza 1.50 4.00
I.Rodriguez
9 G.Maddux 2.50 6.00
R.Johnson

1996 Pinnacle Team Spirit
COMPLETE SET (12) 30.00 60.00
SER.2 ODDS 1:72 H/R, 1:60 J, 1:103 M
1 Greg Maddux 3.00 8.00
2 Ken Griffey Jr. 4.00 10.00
3 Derek Jeter 5.00 12.00
4 Mike Piazza 2.00 5.00
5 Cal Ripken 6.00 15.00
6 Frank Thomas 2.00 5.00
7 Jeff Bagwell 1.25 3.00
8 Mo Vaughn .75 2.00
9 Albert Belle .75 2.00
10 Chipper Jones 2.00 5.00
11 Johnny Damon 1.25 3.00
12 Barry Bonds 3.00 8.00

1996 Pinnacle Team Tomorrow
COMPLETE SET (10) 12.50 30.00
SER.1 STATED ODDS 1:19 JUMBO
1 Ruben Rivera 1.25 3.00
2 Johnny Damon 2.00 5.00
3 Raul Mondesi 1.25 3.00
4 Manny Ramirez 2.00 5.00
5 Hideo Nomo 3.00 8.00
6 Chipper Jones 3.00 8.00
7 Garret Anderson 1.25 3.00
8 Alex Rodriguez 4.00 10.00
9 Derek Jeter 8.00 20.00
10 Karim Garcia 1.25 3.00

1996 Pinnacle FanFest
This standard-size set was issued by Pinnacle in conjunction with the 1996 Pinnacle All-Star FanFest held in Philadelphia and was distributed in two-card poly packs. The Daulton card (number 30) features Sportflics technology and was inserted at a rate of about 1:60 packs. The Carlton card (number 31) was used for the official FanFest badges; apparently, some loose cards also were given to FanFest volunteers. The Carlton card is not considered part of the complete set. Five other cards (with the same design but no foil stamping or UV coating) were also issued by Pinnacle as part of the celebration. These five cards feature different personalities (most of whom are non-baseball related) involved in the show. The set is considered complete at 30 cards with the Daulton SP.

COMPLETE SET (30) 12.50 30.00
COMMON CARD (1-30) .06 .15
COMMON SP 2.00 5.00
1 Cal Ripken 1.25 3.00
2 Greg Maddux .75 2.00
3 Ken Griffey Jr. .75 2.00
4 Frank Thomas .30 .75
5 Jeff Bagwell .30 .75
6 Hideo Nomo .25 .60
7 Tony Gwynn .60 1.50
8 Albert Belle .08 .25
9 Mo Vaughn .08 .25
10 Mike Piazza .75 2.00
11 Dante Bichette .05 .15
12 Ryne Sandberg .30 .75
13 Wade Boggs .30 .75
14 Kirby Puckett .40 1.00
15 Ozzie Smith .40 1.00
16 Barry Bonds .50 1.25
17 Gary Sheffield .30 .75
18 Barry Larkin .25 .60
19 Kevin Seitzer .05 .15
20 Jay Bell .05 .15
21 Chipper Jones .60 1.50
22 Ivan Rodriguez .30 .75
23 Cecil Fielder .08 .25
24 Manny Ramirez .30 .75
25 Randy Johnson .40 1.00
26 Moises Alou .15 .40
27 Mark McGwire .60 1.50
28 Jason Isringhausen .15 .40
29 Joe Carter .08 .25
30 Darren Daulton SP 2.00 5.00
31 Steve Carlton 4.00 10.00
AC1 Amtrak Conductors 1.25 3.00
BF1 Ben Franklin 1.25 3.00
BS1 Bud Selig COMM 2.00 5.00
ER1 Ed Rendell 1.50 4.00
Mayor of Philadelphia
JS1 John Street 1.25 3.00
City Councilman
PP1 Phillie Phanatic 2.00 5.00

1997 Pinnacle
The 1997 Pinnacle set was issued as one series of 200 cards. Cards were distributed in 10-card hobby and retail packs (SRP $2.49) and seven-card magazine packs. This set was released in February, 1997. The set contains the following subsets: Rookies (156-185), Clout (186-197) and Checklists (198-200).

COMPLETE SET (200) 8.00 20.00
1 Cecil Fielder .10 .30
2 Garret Anderson .10 .30
3 Charles Nagy .10 .30
4 Darryl Hamilton .10 .30
5 Greg Myers .10 .30
6 Eric Davis .10 .30
7 Jeff Frye .10 .30
8 Marquis Grissom .10 .30
9 Curt Schilling .10 .30
10 Jeff Fassero .10 .30
11 Alan Benes .10 .30
12 Orlando Miller .10 .30
13 Alex Fernandez .10 .30
14 Andy Pettitte .20 .50
15 Andre Dawson .10 .30
16 Mark Grudzielanek .10 .30
17 Joe Vitiello .10 .30
18 Juan Gonzalez .10 .30
19 Mark Whiten .10 .30
20 Lance Johnson .10 .30
21 Trevor Hoffman .10 .30
22 Marc Newfield .10 .30
23 Jim Eisenreich .10 .30
24 Joe Carter .10 .30
25 Jose Canseco .20 .50
26 Bill Swift .10 .30
27 Ellis Burks .10 .30
28 Ben McDonald .10 .30
29 Edgar Martinez .20 .50
30 Jamie Moyer .10 .30
31 Chan Ho Park .10 .30
32 Carlos Delgado .10 .30
33 Kevin Mitchell .10 .30
34 Carlos Garcia .10 .30
35 Darryl Strawberry .10 .30
36 Jim Thome .20 .50
37 Jose Offerman .10 .30
38 Ryan Klesko .10 .30
39 Ruben Sierra .10 .30
40 Devon White .10 .30
41 Brian Jordan .10 .30
42 Tony Gwynn .40 1.00
43 Rafael Palmeiro .20 .50
44 Dante Bichette .10 .30
45 Scott Stahoviak .10 .30
46 Roger Cedeno .10 .30
47 Ivan Rodriguez .20 .50
48 Bob Abreu .20 .50
49 Darryl Kile .10 .30
50 Darren Dreifort .10 .30
51 Shawon Dunston .10 .30
52 Mark McGwire .75 2.00
53 Tim Salmon .20 .50
54 Gene Schall .10 .30
55 Roger Clemens .60 1.50
56 Rondell White .10 .30
57 Ed Sprague .10 .30
58 Craig Paquette .10 .30
59 David Segui .10 .30
60 Jaime Navarro .10 .30
61 Tom Glavine .20 .50
62 Jeff Brantley .10 .30
63 Kimera Bartee .10 .30
64 Fernando Vina .10 .30
65 Eddie Murray .30 .75
66 Lenny Dykstra .10 .30
67 Kevin Elster .10 .30
68 Vinny Castilla .10 .30
69 Mike Fetters .10 .30
70 Brett Butler .10 .30
71 Robby Thompson .10 .30
72 Reggie Jefferson .10 .30
73 Todd Hundley .10 .30
74 Jeff King .10 .30
75 Ernie Young .10 .30
76 Jeff Bagwell .20 .50
77 Dan Wilson .10 .30
78 Paul Molitor .10 .30
79 Kevin Seitzer .10 .30
80 Kevin Brown .10 .30
81 Ron Gant .10 .30
82 Dwight Gooden .10 .30
83 Todd Stottlemyre .10 .30
84 Ken Caminiti .10 .30
85 James Baldwin .10 .30
86 Jermaine Dye .10 .30
87 Harold Baines .10 .30
88 Pat Hentgen .10 .30
89 Frank Rodriguez .10 .30
90 Mark Johnson .10 .30
91 Jason Kendall .10 .30
92 Alex Rodriguez .50 1.25
93 Alan Trammell .10 .30
94 Scott Brosius .10 .30
95 Delino DeShields .10 .30
96 Chipper Jones .30 .75
97 Barry Bonds .75 2.00
98 Brady Anderson .10 .30
99 Ryne Sandberg .50 1.25
100 Albert Belle .10 .30
101 Jeff Cirillo .10 .30
102 Frank Thomas .30 .75
103 Mike Piazza .50 1.25
104 Rickey Henderson .30 .75
105 Rey Ordonez .10 .30
106 Mark Grace .20 .50
107 Terry Steinbach .10 .30
108 Ray Durham .10 .30
109 Barry Larkin .20 .50
110 Tony Clark .10 .30
111 Bernie Williams .20 .50
112 John Smoltz .20 .50
113 Moises Alou .10 .30
114 Alex Gonzalez .10 .30
115 Rico Brogna .10 .30
116 Eric Karros .10 .30
117 Jeff Conine .10 .30
118 Todd Hollandsworth .10 .30
119 Troy Percival .10 .30
120 Paul Wilson .10 .30
121 Orel Hershiser .10 .30
122 Ozzie Smith .50 1.25
123 Dave Hollins .10 .30
124 Ken Hill .10 .30
125 Rick Wilkins .10 .30
126 Scott Servais .10 .30
127 Fernando Valenzuela .10 .30
128 Mariano Rivera .30 .75
129 Mark Loretta .10 .30
130 Shane Reynolds .10 .30
131 Darren Oliver .10 .30
132 Steve Trachsel .10 .30
133 Darren Bragg .10 .30
134 Jason Dickson .10 .30
135 Darrin Fletcher .10 .30
136 Gary Gaetti .10 .30
137 Joey Cora .10 .30
138 Terry Pendleton .10 .30
139 Derek Jeter .75 2.00
140 Danny Tartabull .10 .30
141 John Flaherty .10 .30
142 B.J. Surhoff .10 .30
143 Mike Sweeney .10 .30
144 Chad Mottola .10 .30
145 Andujar Cedeno .10 .30
146 Tim Belcher .10 .30
147 Mark Thompson .10 .30
148 Rafael Bournigal .10 .30
149 Marty Cordova .10 .30
150 Osvaldo Fernandez .10 .30
151 Mike Stanley .10 .30
152 Ricky Bottalico .10 .30
153 Donne Wall .10 .30
154 Omar Vizquel .20 .50
155 Mike Mussina .20 .50
156 Brant Brown .10 .30
157 F.P. Santangelo .10 .30
158 Ryan Hancock .10 .30
159 Jeff D'Amico .10 .30
160 Luis Castillo .10 .30
161 Darin Erstad .10 .30
162 Ugueth Urbina .10 .30
163 Andruw Jones .20 .50
164 Steve Gibralter .10 .30
165 Robin Jennings .10 .30
166 Mike Cameron .10 .30
167 George Arias .10 .30
168 Chris Stynes .10 .30
169 Justin Thompson .10 .30
170 Jamey Wright .10 .30
171 Todd Walker .10 .30
172 Nomar Garciaparra .50 1.25
173 Jose Paniagua .10 .30
174 Marvin Benard .10 .30
175 Rocky Coppinger .10 .30
176 Quinton McCracken .10 .30
177 Amaury Telemaco .10 .30
178 Neifi Perez .10 .30
179 Todd Greene .10 .30
180 Jason Thompson .10 .30
181 Wilton Guerrero .10 .30
182 Edgar Renteria .10 .30
183 Billy Wagner .10 .30
184 Alex Ochoa .10 .30
185 Dmitri Young .10 .30
186 Kenny Lofton CT .10 .30
187 Andres Galarraga CT .10 .30
188 Chuck Knoblauch CT .10 .30
189 Greg Maddux CT .50 1.25
190 Mo Vaughn CT .10 .30
191 Cal Ripken CT 1.00 2.50
192 Hideo Nomo CT .30 .75
193 Ken Griffey Jr. CT .60 1.50
194 Sammy Sosa CT .20 .50
195 Jay Buhner CT .10 .30
196 Manny Ramirez CT .10 .30
197 Matt Williams CT .10 .30
198 Andruw Jones CL .10 .30
199 Darin Erstad CL .10 .30
200 Trey Beamon CL .10 .30

1997 Pinnacle Artist's Proofs
*BRONZE CARDS: 8X TO 20X BASE CARD HI
*SILVER CARDS: 10X TO 25X BASE CARD HI
*GOLD CARDS: 12.5X TO 30X BASE CARD HI
STATED ODDS 1:47 HOB/RET, 1:55 MAG

1997 Pinnacle Museum Collection
*STARS: 5X TO 12X BASIC CARDS
STATED ODDS 1:9 HOB/RET, 1:13 MAG

1997 Pinnacle Press Plate Previews
ONE PER SEALED CASE OF NEW PINNACLE
NO PRICING DUE TO SCARCITY

1997 Pinnacle Cardfrontations
COMPLETE SET (20) 50.00 120.00
SER.1 STATED ODDS 1:23 HOBBY
1 G.Maddux 5.00 12.00
M.Piazza
2 T.Glavine 2.00 5.00
K.Caminiti
3 C.Ripken 10.00 25.00
R.Johnson
4 M.McGwire 5.00 12.00
K.Appier
5 J.Gonzalez 2.00 5.00
A.Pettitte
6 A.Belle 1.25 3.00
P.Hentgen
7 C.Jones 3.00 8.00
H.Nomo
8 S.Sosa 2.00 5.00
I.Valdes
9 M.Mussina 2.00 5.00
M.Ramirez
10 D.Cone 1.25 3.00
J.Buhner
11 M.Wohlers 1.25 3.00
G.Sheffield
12 B.Bonds 5.00 12.00
A.Benes
13 R.Clemens 4.00 10.00
I.Rodriguez
14 K.Griffey Jr. 10.00 25.00
M.Rivera
15 F.Thomas 3.00 8.00
D.Gooden
16 D.Erstad 1.25 3.00
J.Wetteland
17 J.Smoltz 2.00 5.00
B.Jordan
18 J.Bagwell 2.00 5.00
K.Brown
19 A.Rodriguez 4.00 10.00
J.McDowell
20 C.Nagy 2.00 5.00
B.Williams

1997 Pinnacle Home/Away
SER.1 STATED ODDS 1:33 JUMBO
1A Chipper Jones 4.00 10.00
2A Ken Griffey Jr. 8.00 20.00
2B K.Griffey Jr. HOME 75.00 200.00
3A Mike Piazza 4.00 10.00
4A Frank Thomas 4.00 10.00
4B F.Thomas HOME 75.00 200.00
5A Jeff Bagwell 2.50 6.00
6A Alex Rodriguez 5.00 12.00
6B A.Rodriguez HOME 10.00 25.00
7A Barry Bonds 6.00 15.00
7B B.Bonds HOME 12.00 30.00
8A Mo Vaughn 1.50 4.00
9A Derek Jeter 10.00 25.00
9B D.Jeter HOME 125.00 250.00
10A Mark McGwire 6.00 15.00
10B M.McGwire HOME 12.00 30.00
11A Cal Ripken 8.00 20.00
11B C.Ripken HOME 25.00 60.00
12A Albert Belle 1.50 4.00

1997 Pinnacle Passport to the Majors
COMPLETE SET (25) 30.00 80.00
SER.1 STAT.ODDS 1:36 HOB/RET, 1:51 MAG
1 Greg Maddux 3.00 8.00
2 Ken Griffey Jr. 8.00 20.00
3 Frank Thomas 2.00 5.00
4 Cal Ripken 6.00 15.00
5 Mike Piazza 2.00 5.00
6 Alex Rodriguez 2.50 6.00
7 Mo Vaughn .75 2.00
8 Chipper Jones 2.00 5.00
9 Roberto Alomar 1.25 3.00
10 Edgar Martinez 1.25 3.00
11 Javier Lopez .75 2.00
12 Ivan Rodriguez 1.25 3.00
13 Juan Gonzalez .75 2.00
14 Carlos Baerga .75 2.00
15 Sammy Sosa 1.25 3.00
16 Manny Ramirez 1.25 3.00
17 Raul Mondesi .75 2.00
18 Henry Rodriguez .75 2.00
19 Rafael Palmeiro .75 2.00
20 Rey Ordonez .75 2.00
21 Hideo Nomo 1.25 3.00
22 Mac Suzuki .75 2.00
23 Chan Ho Park .75 2.00
24 Larry Walker 1.25 3.00
25 Ruben Rivera .75 2.00

1997 Pinnacle Shades
COMPLETE SET (10) 25.00 60.00
SER.1 STATED ODDS 1:23 MAGAZINE
1 Ken Griffey Jr. 2.00 5.00
2 Juan Gonzalez .40 1.00
3 John Smoltz .60 1.50
4 Gary Sheffield .40 1.00
5 Cal Ripken 3.00 8.00
6 Mo Vaughn .40 1.00
7 Brian Jordan .40 1.00
8 Mike Piazza 1.50 4.00
9 Frank Thomas 1.00 2.50
10 Alex Rodriguez 1.50 4.00

1997 Pinnacle Team Pinnacle
COMPLETE SET (10) 60.00 120.00
SER.1 STAT.ODDS 1:90 HOB/RET, 1:107 MAG
1 F.Thomas 5.00 12.00
J.Bagwell
2 C.Knoblauch 2.00 5.00
E.Young
3 K.Caminiti 2.00 5.00
J.Thome
4 A.Rodriguez 8.00 20.00
C.Jones
5 M.Piazza 8.00 20.00
I.Rodriguez
6 B.Bonds 12.50 30.00
A.Belle
7 K.Griffey Jr. 10.00 25.00
E.Burks
8 J.Gonzalez 2.00 5.00
G.Sheffield
9 J.Smoltz 3.00 8.00
A.Pettitte
10 Full Team Picture 5.00 12.00

1997 Pinnacle All-Star FanFest Promos
This set of seven cards was issued at the Pinnacle all-Star Fanfest held in Cleveland, Ohio, on July 4-8, 1997. The cards feature the same design as the Pinnacle FanFest set. The fronts display color action player photos with gold foil enhancements. The backs carry a schedule of the times for FanFest. Card number 2 differs in that the player photo is in black and White, and the back displays information about the player. The cards are unnumbered and checklisted below alphabetically.

COMPLETE SET (7) 6.00 15.00
1 Roger Clemens 1.25 3.00
2 Larry Doby .60 1.50
3 Greg Maddux 1.50 4.00
4 Hideo Nomo .40 1.00
5 Andy Pettitte .40 1.00
6 Mike Piazza 1.50 4.00
7 Ivan Rodriguez .50 1.25

1997 Pinnacle FanFest
This 21-card set was issued by Pinnacle in conjunction with the 1997 Pinnacle All-Star FanFest held in Cleveland, Ohio, July 4-8, 1997 at the Convention Center. The set was issued in three-card packs and features borderless color action player photos with gold foil stamping. The backs carry a player portrait in a star with player information and statistics printed on a black-and-gray city silhouetted background. Card number 21 could only be obtained with a redemption card at the locations listed on the card's back. The Alomar card is not considered part of the complete set. Twelve other cards with the same design were also issued by Pinnacle as part of the celebration. These twelve cards feature different personalities involved in the show or with the Cleveland Indians. These 12 cards are not considered part of the Fan Fest set and are not included in the complete set price.

COMPLETE SET (20) 10.00 25.00
COMMON CARD (FF1-FF20) .20 .25
COMMON SP 4.00 10.00
COMMON PC CARD 2.00 5.00
FF1 Frank Thomas .50 1.25
FF2 Jeff Bagwell .50 1.25
FF3 Chuck Knoblauch .40 1.00
FF4 Craig Biggio .40 1.00
FF5 Alex Rodriguez 1.00 2.50
FF6 Chipper Jones 1.00 2.50
FF7 Cal Ripken 2.00 5.00
FF8 Ken Caminiti .08 .25
FF9 Juan Gonzalez .40 1.00
FF10 Barry Bonds .75 2.00
FF11 Ken Griffey Jr. 1.25 3.00
FF12 Andruw Jones 1.00 2.50
FF13 Manny Ramirez .50 1.25
FF14 Tony Gwynn 1.00 2.50
FF15 Ivan Rodriguez .50 1.25
FF16 Mike Piazza 1.25 3.00
FF17 Andy Pettitte .40 1.00
FF18 Hideo Nomo .40 1.00
FF19 Roger Clemens 1.00 2.50
FF20 Greg Maddux 1.25 3.00
FF21 Sandy Alomar SP 4.00 10.00
PC1 Macie McInnis 2.00 5.00
PC2 Bill Martin 2.00 5.00
PC3 Dick Goddard 2.00 5.00
PC4 Jack Corrigan ANN 2.00 5.00
PC5 Mike Hegan ANN 3.00 8.00
PC6 Rick Manning ANN 4.00 10.00
PC7 John Sanders ANN 2.00 5.00
PC8 Michael R. White 2.00 5.00
Mayor
PC9 Wilma Smith 2.00 5.00
PC10 Tim Taylor 2.00 5.00
PC11 Robin Swoboda 2.00 5.00
PC12 Slider 3.00 8.00

1998 Pinnacle
The 1998 Pinnacle set was issued in one series totalling 200 cards and was distributed in 10-card packs with a suggested retail price of $2.99. The fronts feature borderless color player photos with player information on the backs. The set contains the following subsets: Rookies (158-181), Field of Vision (182-187), Goin' Jake (188-197) and Checklists (198-200). Three variations of each card 1-157 were issued. The cards have home, away or seasonal stats on the back and were all produced in equal quantities. This concept of variations on the statistics was met with a lack of interest and all three versions trade for equal values. In fact, complete sets typically carry a mix of all three stat variations.

COMPLETE SET (200) 10.00 25.00
1 Tony Gwynn .40 1.00
2 Pedro Martinez .20 .50
3 Kenny Lofton .10 .30
4 Curt Schilling .10 .30
5 Shawn Estes .10 .30
6 Tom Glavine .20 .50
7 Mike Piazza .50 1.25
8 Ray Lankford .10 .30
9 Barry Larkin .20 .50
10 Tony Womack .10 .30
11 Jeff Blauser .10 .30
12 Rod Beck .10 .30
13 Larry Walker .10 .30
14 Greg Maddux .50 1.25
15 Mark Grace .20 .50
16 Ken Caminiti .10 .30
17 Bobby Jones .10 .30
18 Chipper Jones .30 .75
19 Javier Lopez .10 .30
20 Moises Alou .10 .30
21 Royce Clayton .10 .30
22 Darryl Kile .10 .30
23 Barry Bonds .75 2.00
24 Steve Finley .10 .30
25 Andres Galarraga .10 .30
26 Denny Neagle .10 .30
27 Todd Hundley .10 .30
28 Jeff Bagwell .20 .50
29 Andy Pettitte .20 .50
30 Darin Erstad .10 .30
31 Carlos Delgado .10 .30
32 Matt Williams .10 .30
33 Will Clark .20 .50
34 Vinny Castilla .10 .30
35 Brad Radke .10 .30
36 John Olerud .10 .30
37 Andruw Jones .20 .50
38 Jason Giambi .10 .30
39 Scott Rolen .20 .50
40 Gary Sheffield .10 .30
41 Jimmy Key .10 .30
42 Kevin Appier .10 .30
43 Wade Boggs .20 .50
44 Hideo Nomo .30 .75
45 Manny Ramirez .20 .50
46 Wilton Guerrero .10 .30
47 Travis Fryman .10 .30
48 Chili Davis .10 .30
49 Jeromy Burnitz .10 .30
50 Craig Biggio .20 .50
51 Tim Salmon .10 .30
52 Jose Cruz Jr. .10 .30
53 Sammy Sosa .30 .75
54 Hideki Irabu .10 .30
55 Chan Ho Park .10 .30
56 Robin Ventura .10 .30
57 Jose Guillen .10 .30
58 Deion Sanders .20 .50
59 Jose Canseco .20 .50
60 Jay Buhner .10 .30
61 Rafael Palmeiro .20 .50
62 Vladimir Guerrero .30 .75
63 Mark McGwire .75 2.00
64 Derek Jeter .75 2.00
65 Bobby Bonilla .10 .30
66 Raul Mondesi .10 .30
67 Paul Molitor .10 .30
68 Joe Carter .10 .30
69 Marquis Grissom .10 .30
70 Juan Gonzalez .10 .30
71 Kevin Orie .10 .30
72 Rusty Greer .10 .30
73 Henry Rodriguez .10 .30
74 Fernando Tatis .10 .30
75 John Valentin .10 .30
76 Matt Morris .10 .30
77 Ray Durham .10 .30
78 Geronimo Berroa .10 .30
79 Scott Brosius .10 .30
80 Willie Greene .10 .30
81 Rondell White .10 .30
82 Doug Drabek .10 .30
83 Derek Bell .10 .30
84 Butch Huskey .10 .30
85 Doug Jones .10 .30
86 Jeff Kent .10 .30
87 Jim Edmonds .10 .30
88 Mark McLemore .10 .30
89 Todd Zeile .10 .30
90 Edgardo Alfonzo .10 .30
91 Carlos Baerga .10 .30
92 Jorge Fabregas .10 .30
93 Alan Benes .10 .30
94 Troy Percival .10 .30
95 Edgar Renteria .10 .30
96 Jeff Fassero .10 .30
97 Reggie Sanders .10 .30
98 Dean Palmer .10 .30
99 J.T. Snow .10 .30
100 Dave Nilsson .10 .30
101 Dan Wilson .10 .30
102 Robb Nen .10 .30
103 Damion Easley .10 .30
104 Kevin Foster .10 .30
105 Jose Offerman .10 .30
106 Steve Cooke .10 .30
107 Matt Stairs .10 .30
108 Darryl Hamilton .10 .30
109 Steve Karsay .10 .30
110 Gary DiSarcina .10 .30
111 Dante Bichette .10 .30
112 Billy Wagner .10 .30
113 David Segui .10 .30
114 Bobby Higginson .10 .30
115 Jeffrey Hammonds .10 .30
116 Kevin Brown .10 .30
117 Paul Sorrento .10 .30
118 Mark Leiter .10 .30
119 Charles Nagy .10 .30
120 Danny Patterson .10 .30
121 Brian McRae .10 .30
122 Jay Bell .10 .30
123 Jamie Moyer .10 .30
124 Carl Everett .10 .30
125 Greg Colbrunn .10 .30
126 Jason Kendall .10 .30
127 Luis Sojo .10 .30
128 Mike Lieberthal .10 .30
129 Reggie Jefferson .10 .30
130 Cal Eldred .10 .30
131 Orel Hershiser .10 .30
132 Doug Glanville .10 .30
133 Willie Blair .10 .30
134 Neifi Perez .10 .30
135 Sean Berry .10 .30
136 Chuck Finley .10 .30
137 Alex Gonzalez .10 .30
138 Dennis Eckersley .10 .30
139 Kenny Rogers .10 .30
140 Troy O'Leary .10 .30
141 Roger Bailey .10 .30
142 Yamil Benitez .10 .30
143 Wally Joyner .10 .30
144 Bobby Witt .10 .30
145 Pete Schourek .10 .30
146 Terry Steinbach .10 .30
147 B.J. Surhoff .10 .30
148 Esteban Loaiza .10 .30
149 Heathcliff Slocumb .10 .30
150 Ed Sprague .10 .30
151 Gregg Jefferies .10 .30
152 Scott Erickson .10 .30
153 Jaime Navarro .10 .30
154 David Wells .10 .30
155 Alex Fernandez .10 .30
156 Tim Belcher .10 .30
157 Mark Grudzielanek .10 .30
158 Scott Hatteberg .10 .30
159 Paul Konerko .10 .30
160 Ben Grieve .10 .30
161 Abraham Nunez .10 .30
162 Shannon Stewart .10 .30
163 Jaret Wright .10 .30
164 Derrek Lee .20 .50
165 Todd Dunwoody .10 .30
166 Steve Woodard .10 .30
167 Ryan McGuire .10 .30
168 Jeremi Gonzalez .10 .30
169 Mark Kotsay .10 .30

170 Brett Tomko .10 .30
171 Bobby Estalella .10 .30
172 Livan Hernandez .10 .30
173 Todd Helton .20 .50
174 Garrett Stephenson .10 .30
175 Pokey Reese .10 .30
176 Tony Saunders .10 .30
177 Antone Williamson .10 .30
178 Bartolo Colon .10 .30
179 Karim Garcia .10 .30
180 Juan Encarnacion .10 .30
181 Jacob Cruz .10 .30
182 Alex Rodriguez FV .50 1.25
183 C.Ripken R.Alomar FV .75 2.00
184 Roger Clemens FV .60 1.50
185 Derek Jeter FV .75 2.00
186 Frank Thomas FV .30 .75
187 Ken Griffey Jr. FV .60 1.50
188 Mark McGwire GJ .75 2.00
189 Tino Martinez GJ .20 .50
190 Larry Walker GJ .10 .30
191 Brady Anderson GJ .10 .30
192 Jeff Bagwell GJ .20 .50
193 Ken Griffey Jr. GJ .60 1.50
194 Chipper Jones GJ .20 .50
195 Ray Lankford GJ .10 .30
196 Jim Thome GJ .20 .50
197 Nomar Garciaparra GJ .50 1.25
198 AS HR Contestants CL .25 .60
199 Tino Martinez CL .20 .50
200 Jacob's Field CL .10 .30

1998 Pinnacle Artist's Proofs

*STARS: 10X TO 25X BASIC CARDS
STATED ODDS 1:39
AP NUMBERS DON'T MATCH BASIC CARDS

1998 Pinnacle Away Statistics Back

*AWAY: .4X TO 1X BASIC
BASE/AWAY/HOME ALL EQUAL QUANTITY

1998 Pinnacle Home Statistics Back

*HOME: .4X TO 1X BASIC
BASE/AWAY/HOME ALL EQUAL QUANTITY

1998 Pinnacle Museum Collection

*STARS: 4X TO 10X BASIC CARDS
STATED ODDS 1:9
MC NUMBERS DON'T MATCH BASIC CARDS

1998 Pinnacle Press Plates

COMMON FRONT 20.00 50.00
COMMON BACK 12.50 30.00
STATED ODDS 1:1250
STATED PRINT RUN 4 SETS
NO STAR PRICING DUE TO SCARCITY

1998 Pinnacle Hit It Here

COMPLETE SET (10) 12.50 30.00
STATED ODDS 1:17
1 Larry Walker .40 1.00
2 Ken Griffey Jr. 2.00 5.00
3 Mike Piazza 1.50 4.00
4 Frank Thomas 1.00 2.50
5 Barry Bonds 2.50 6.00
6 Albert Belle .40 1.00
7 Tino Martinez .40 1.00
8 Mark McGwire 2.50 6.00
9 Juan Gonzalez .40 1.00
10 Jeff Bagwell .60 1.50

1998 Pinnacle Power Pack Jumbos

COMPLETE SET (24) 10.00 25.00
ONE PER POWER PACK
1 Alex Rodriguez FV .60 1.50
2 C.Ripken R.Alomar FV 1.00 2.50
3 Roger Clemens FV .75 2.00
4 Derek Jeter FV 1.00 2.50
5 Frank Thomas FV .40 1.00
6 Ken Griffey Jr. FV .75 2.00
7 Mark McGwire GJ 1.00 2.50
8 Tino Martinez GJ .25 .60
9 Larry Walker GJ .15 .40
10 Brady Anderson GJ .15 .40
11 Jeff Bagwell GJ .25 .60
12 Ken Griffey Jr. GJ .75 2.00
13 Chipper Jones GJ .25 .60
14 Ray Lankford GJ .15 .40
15 Jim Thome GJ .25 .60
16 Nomar Garciaparra GJ .60 1.50
17 Mike Piazza .60 1.50
18 Andruw Jones .25 .60
19 Greg Maddux .60 1.50
20 Tony Gwynn .50 1.25
21 Larry Walker .15 .40
22 Jeff Bagwell .25 .60
23 Chipper Jones .40 1.00
24 Scott Rolen .25 .60

1998 Pinnacle Spellbound

COMPLETE SET (50) 75.00 200.00
COMMON M.MCGWIRE 4.00 10.00
COMMON R.CLEMENS 2.50 6.00
COMMON F.THOMAS 2.00 5.00
COMMON S.ROLEN 1.25 3.00
COMMON K.GRIFFEY 4.00 10.00
COMMON L.WALKER 1.25 3.00
COMMON N.GARCIAPARRA 1.25 3.00
COMMON C.RIPKEN 6.00 15.00
COMMON T.GWYNN 2.00 5.00
STATED ODDS 1:17

1998 Pinnacle Epix Game Orange

*GAME EMERALD: 1.25X TO 3X ORANGE
*GAME PURPLE: .6X TO 1.5X ORANGE
PINNACLE STATED ODDS 1:21
SCORE STATED ODDS 1:61
ZENITH STATED ODDS 1:11
E1 Ken Griffey Jr. 2.50 6.00
E2 Juan Gonzalez .50 1.25
E3 Jeff Bagwell .75 2.00
E4 Ivan Rodriguez 1.25 3.00
E5 Nomar Garciaparra 2.00 5.00
E6 Ryne Sandberg 1.25 3.00
E7 Frank Thomas 1.25 3.00
E8 Derek Jeter 3.00 8.00
E9 Tony Gwynn 1.50 4.00
E10 Albert Belle .75 2.00
E11 Scott Rolen .75 2.00
E12 Barry Larkin .75 2.00
E19 Mike Piazza 2.00 5.00
E20 Andruw Jones .75 2.00
E21 Greg Maddux 2.00 5.00
E22 Barry Bonds 3.00 8.00
E23 Paul Molitor .50 1.25
E24 Eddie Murray 1.25 3.00

1998 Pinnacle Epix Moment Orange

*MOMENT EMERALD: 1.25X TO 3X ORANGE
MOMENT EMERALD PRINT RUN 30 SETS
*MOMENT PURPLE: .6X TO 1.5X ORANGE
PINNACLE STATED ODDS 1:21
SCORE STATED ODDS 1:61
ZENITH STATED ODDS 1:11
E7 Frank Thomas 1.50 4.00
E8 Derek Jeter 4.00 10.00
E9 Tony Gwynn 2.00 5.00
E10 Albert Belle 1.00 2.50
E11 Scott Rolen 1.00 2.50
E12 Barry Larkin 1.00 2.50
E13 Alex Rodriguez 2.50 6.00
E14 Cal Ripken 4.00 10.00
E15 Chipper Jones 1.50 4.00
E16 Mo Vaughn .60 1.50
E17 Roger Clemens 3.00 8.00
E18 Mark McGwire 4.00 10.00
E19 Mike Piazza 2.50 6.00
E20 Andruw Jones 1.00 2.50
E21 Greg Maddux 2.50 6.00
E22 Barry Bonds 4.00 10.00
E23 Paul Molitor .60 1.50
E24 Eddie Murray 1.50 4.00

1998 Pinnacle Epix Play Orange

*PLAY EMERALD: 1.25X TO 3X ORANGE
*PLAY PURPLE: .6X TO 1.5X ORANGE
PINNACLE STATED ODDS 1:21
SCORE STATED ODDS 1:61
ZENITH STATED ODDS 1:11
E1 Ken Griffey Jr. 1.50 4.00
E2 Juan Gonzalez .30 .75
E3 Jeff Bagwell .50 1.25
E4 Ivan Rodriguez .75 2.00
E5 Nomar Garciaparra 1.25 3.00
E6 Ryne Sandberg .75 2.00
E13 Alex Rodriguez 1.25 3.00
E14 Cal Ripken 2.00 5.00
E15 Chipper Jones .75 2.00
E16 Mo Vaughn .30 .75
E17 Roger Clemens 1.50 4.00
E18 Mark McGwire 2.00 5.00
E19 Mike Piazza 1.25 3.00
E20 Andruw Jones .50 1.25
E21 Greg Maddux 1.25 3.00
E22 Barry Bonds 2.00 5.00
E23 Paul Molitor .30 .75
E24 Eddie Murray .75 2.00

1998 Pinnacle Epix Season Orange

*SEASON EMERALD: 1.25X TO 3X ORANGE
*SEASON PURPLE: .6X TO 1.5X ORANGE
PINNACLE STATED ODDS 1:21
SCORE STATED ODDS 1:61
ZENITH STATED ODDS 1:11
E1 Ken Griffey Jr. 5.00 12.00
E2 Juan Gonzalez 1.00 2.50
E3 Jeff Bagwell 1.50 4.00
E4 Ivan Rodriguez 2.50 6.00
E5 Nomar Garciaparra 4.00 10.00
E6 Ryne Sandberg 2.50 6.00
E7 Frank Thomas 2.50 6.00
E8 Derek Jeter 6.00 15.00
E9 Tony Gwynn 3.00 8.00
E10 Albert Belle 1.50 4.00
E11 Scott Rolen 1.50 4.00
E12 Barry Larkin 1.50 4.00
E13 Alex Rodriguez 4.00 10.00
E14 Cal Ripken 6.00 15.00
E15 Chipper Jones 2.50 6.00
E16 Mo Vaughn 1.00 2.50
E17 Roger Clemens 5.00 12.00
E18 Mark McGwire 6.00 15.00

1998 Pinnacle Fanfest Elway

This one card set, issued at the All-Star FanFest in Denver in 1998 honored long time Denver Bronco hero, John Elway. The front of the card features him in an Oneonta Yankee uniform while the back has a brief biography; a ghosted photo of Elway as a Bronco and his career minor league stats. The card was available for a small charity donation at the Pinnacle Booth.
NNO John Elway 8.00 20.00

1998 Pinnacle Team Pinnacle Collector's Club Promos

This four-card set originally to have been issued to members of the Pinnacle Collector's Club. Ultimately the cards were released after the company's bankruptcy. Each card reads "Team Pinnacle" at the bottom of the cardfront with the player's name above the image on the front.
COMPLETE SET (4) 15.00 30.00
2 Ken Griffey Jr. 4.00 10.00
3 Derek Jeter 5.00 12.00

2013 Pinnacle

COMPLETE SET (200) 12.50 30.00
1 Aroldis Chapman .20 .50
2 Jesus Montero .12 .30
3 Ian Kennedy .12 .30
4 Anthony Rizzo .25 .60
5 Mike Moustakas .15 .40
6 Mike Napoli .12 .30
7 Chase Utley .15 .40
8 Curtis Granderson .15 .40
9 Chris Perez .12 .30
10 Tommy Hanson .12 .30
11 David Price .15 .40
12 Eric Hosmer .15 .40
13 Asdrubal Cabrera .15 .40
14 Miguel Cabrera .20 .50
15 Kevin Youkilis .12 .30
16 Bo Jackson .20 .50
17 Jeff Samardzija .12 .30
18 Jason Heyward .15 .40
19 Tim Lincecum .15 .40
20 Justin Verlander .20 .50
21 Starling Marte .15 .40
22 Clayton Kershaw .30 .75
23 Matt Harvey .15 .40
24 Dustin Pedroia .20 .50
25 Johnny Cueto .15 .40
26 R.A. Dickey .15 .40
27 Paul Konerko .15 .40
28 Matt Cain .15 .40
29 Jason Kipnis .15 .40
30 Giancarlo Stanton .20 .50
31 Andy Pettitte .15 .40
32 Mark Trumbo .12 .30
33 Ryan Zimmerman .15 .40
34 Matt Moore .15 .40
35 Logan Morrison .12 .30
36 Chris Davis .15 .40
37 Joe Mauer .15 .40
38 Derek Jeter .50 1.25
39 Yoenis Cespedes .20 .50
40 Allen Craig .15 .40
41 David Freese .12 .30
42 C.J. Wilson .12 .30
43 Michael Morse .12 .30
44 Rickey Henderson .20 .50
45 Mike Trout 1.50 4.00
46 Trevor Bauer .25 .60
47 James Shields .12 .30
48 Ryne Sandberg .40 1.00
49 Hisashi Iwakuma .15 .40
50 Justin Morneau .15 .40
51 Stephen Strasburg .20 .50
52 Nick Swisher .15 .40
53 Jarrod Parker .12 .30
54 Adrian Gonzalez .15 .40
55 Roy Halladay .15 .40
56 Josh Hamilton .15 .40
57 Billy Butler .12 .30
58 B.J. Upton .15 .40
59 Matt Wieters .20 .50
60 Craig Kimbrel .15 .40
61 CC Sabathia .15 .40
62 Hunter Pence .15 .40
63 Ike Davis .12 .30
64 Carl Crawford .15 .40
65 Carlos Gonzalez .15 .40
66 Jay Bruce .15 .40
67 Carlos Quentin .12 .30
68 Evan Longoria .15 .40
69 Adam Wainwright .15 .40
70 J.D. Martinez .20 .50
71 Carlos Pena .15 .40
72 Ichiro Suzuki .25 .60
73 Justin Upton .15 .40
74 Jim Johnson .12 .30
75 Josh Willingham .15 .40
76 Shin-Soo Choo .15 .40
77 Wei-Yin Chen .12 .30
78 Chase Headley .12 .30
79 Martin Prado .12 .30
80 Elvis Andrus .15 .40
81 Gio Gonzalez .15 .40
82 Ricky Nolasco .12 .30
83 Jon Lester .15 .40
84 Paul Goldschmidt .20 .50
85 Kendrys Morales .12 .30
86 Troy Tulowitzki .20 .50
87 Ryan Braun .15 .40
88 Yu Darvish .20 .50
89 Shane Victorino .15 .40
90 Jason Kubel .12 .30
91 Alex Gordon .15 .40
92 Yadier Molina .25 .60
93 Aramis Ramirez .12 .30
94 Alex Rios .15 .40
95 Lance Berkman .15 .40
96 Lucas Duda .15 .40
97 Yonder Alonso .12 .30
98 Dan Haren .12 .30
99 Dayan Viciedo .12 .30
100 Prince Fielder .15 .40
101 Felix Hernandez .15 .40
102 Nolan Ryan .60 1.50
103 Josh Johnson .15 .40
104 Ken Griffey Jr. .40 1.00
105 Starlin Castro .12 .30
106 Adrian Beltre .20 .50
107 Pedro Alvarez .12 .30
108 Chris Sale .20 .50
109 Huston Street .12 .30
110 Pablo Sandoval .15 .40
111 Grant Balfour .12 .30
112 Cole Hamels .15 .40
113 Jose Reyes .15 .40
114 Jose Bautista .15 .40
115 David Wright .15 .40
116 Brett Anderson .12 .30
117 Mariano Rivera .25 .60
118 Alex Rodriguez .25 .60
119 Hanley Ramirez .15 .40
120 Jose Altuve .15 .40
121 David Ortiz .20 .50
122 Adam Dunn .15 .40
123 Freddie Freeman .25 .60
124 George Brett .40 1.00
125 Brandon Phillips .12 .30
126 Jered Weaver .15 .40
127 Yovani Gallardo .12 .30
128 Zack Greinke .20 .50
129 Matt Holliday .20 .50
130 Norichika Aoki .12 .30
131 Brett Lawrie .15 .40
132 Josh Reddick .12 .30
133 Cal Ripken Jr. .60 1.50
134 Austin Jackson .12 .30
135 Michael Bourn .12 .30
136 Andrew McCutchen .20 .50
137 Matt Kemp .15 .40
138 Michael Young .12 .30
139 Ryan Howard .15 .40
140 Carlos Beltran .15 .40
141 Bryce Harper .30 .75
142 Robinson Cano .15 .40
143 Todd Helton .15 .40
144 Buster Posey .25 .60
145 Johan Santana .15 .40
146 Jacob Turner .15 .40
147 Joey Votto .20 .50
148 Adam Jones .15 .40
149 Albert Pujols .25 .60
150 Ian Kinsler .15 .40
151 Jeurys Familia RC .40 1.00
152 Adam Eaton RC .40 1.00
153 Wil Myers RC .40 1.00
154 Justin Grimm RC .25 .60
155 Jose Fernandez RC .60 1.50
156 L.J. Hoes RC .30 .75
157 Jake Odorizzi RC .30 .75
158 Dylan Bundy RC .60 1.50
159 Melky Mesa RC .30 .75
160 Kyuji Fujikawa RC .40 1.00
161 Darin Ruf RC .50 1.25
162 Jurickson Profar RC .30 .75
163 Manny Machado RC 1.50 4.00
164 Tyler Skaggs RC .40 1.00
165 Zack Wheeler RC .50 1.25
166 Evan Gattis RC .50 1.25
167 Bryan Morris RC .25 .60
168 Rob Scahill RC .25 .60
169 Didi Gregorius RC 1.00 2.50
170 Hyun-Jin Ryu RC .60 1.50
171 Rob Brantly RC .25 .60
172 Thomas Neal RC .25 .60
173 Aaron Hicks RC .40 1.00
174 Mike Olt RC .30 .75
175 Jean Machi RC .25 .60
176 Henry Rodriguez RC .25 .60
177 Denis Phipps RC .25 .60
178 Shelby Miller RC .60 1.50
179 Jackie Bradley Jr. RC .60 1.50
180 Chris Rusin RC .25 .60
181 Andrew Werner RC .25 .60
182 Gerrit Cole RC 1.50 4.00
183 Brock Holt RC .30 .75
184 Paco Rodriguez RC .40 1.00
185 Tony Cingrani RC .50 1.25
186 Carlos Triunfel RC .30 .75
187 Jedd Gyorko RC .30 .75
188 A.J. Ramos RC .30 .75
189 Mike Zunino RC .40 1.00
190 Jaye Chapman RC .25 .60
191 Nick Maronde RC .30 .75
192 Eury Perez RC .30 .75
193 Yasiel Puig RC 1.00 2.50
194 Casey Kelly RC .30 .75
195 Justin Wilson RC .25 .60
196 Collin McHugh RC .25 .60
197 Luis Jimenez RC .25 .60
198 David Lough RC .25 .60
199 Avisail Garcia RC .30 .75
200 Tyler Cloyd RC .30 .75

2013 Pinnacle Artists Proof

*AP VET: 3X TO 8X BASIC
*AP RC: 1.5X TO 4X BASIC
133 Cal Ripken Jr. 20.00 50.00

2013 Pinnacle Artists Proof Blue

*AP BLUE VET: 4X TO 10X BASIC
*AP BLUE RC: 2X TO 5X BASIC
133 Cal Ripken Jr. 25.00 60.00

2013 Pinnacle Museum Collection

*MUSEUM VET: 2X TO 5X BASIC
*MUSEUM RC: 1X TO 2.5X BASIC

2013 Pinnacle Aces

1 Justin Verlander 1.00 2.50
2 Jered Weaver .75 2.00
3 Stephen Strasburg 1.00 2.50
4 Clayton Kershaw 1.50 4.00
5 David Price .75 2.00
6 R.A. Dickey .75 2.00
7 Gio Gonzalez .75 2.00
8 Felix Hernandez .75 2.00
9 Matt Cain .75 2.00
10 Cole Hamels .75 2.00

2013 Pinnacle Autographs

EXCHANGE DEADLINE 02/14/2015
AC Asdrubal Cabrera 3.00 8.00
AH Adeiny Hechavarria 3.00 8.00
ARA Aramis Ramirez
ARI Anthony Rizzo 12.00 30.00
AT Alan Trammell
BL Boone Logan 3.00 8.00
BZ Ben Zobrist 6.00 15.00
BZ Brad Ziegler
CH Chris Heisey 4.00 10.00
CL Cory Luebke 3.00 8.00
CP Chris Perez
CR Cody Ross 3.00 8.00
CR Cal Ripken Jr. 25.00 60.00
CS Chris Sale 4.00 10.00
DB Darwin Barney 3.00 8.00
DF Dexter Fowler 3.00 8.00
DG Dwight Gooden 10.00 25.00
DH Derek Holland 3.00 8.00
DM David Murphy 3.00 8.00
DMA Don Mattingly 25.00 60.00
DS Denard Span 3.00 8.00
EH Eric Hosmer
FT Frank Thomas 20.00 50.00
FV Fernando Valenzuela 20.00 50.00
ID Ike Davis 4.00 10.00
JA John Axford 3.00 8.00
JB Jose Bautista 8.00 20.00
JB Jay Bruce 6.00 15.00
JG Jeremy Guthrie 3.00 8.00
JH Josh Hamilton 15.00 40.00
JJ Josh Johnson 4.00 10.00
JJ Jim Johnson 3.00 8.00
JK Jason Kipnis 6.00 15.00
JM Jason Motte
JN Joe Nathan
JP Justin Upton 10.00 25.00
JS James Shields 4.00 10.00
JT Josh Thole 3.00 8.00
JU Julio Teheran 4.00 10.00
JV Jonny Venters 3.00 8.00
JW Josh Willingham 3.00 8.00
JZ Jordan Zimmermann 4.00 10.00
KG Ken Griffey Jr. 60.00 120.00
KJ Kelly Johnson 3.00 8.00
KM Kris Medlen 30.00 60.00
KN Kirk Nieuwenhuis 3.00 8.00
LD Lucas Duda 3.00 8.00
LW Larry Walker 10.00 25.00
MH Matt Harrison 3.00 8.00
MM Miguel Montero 3.00 8.00
MR Mariano Rivera
MR Marc Rzepczynski 3.00 8.00
MT Mike Trout 60.00 120.00
OI Omar Infante 3.00 8.00
PK Paul Konerko 6.00 15.00
PR Pete Rose 40.00 80.00
RB Ryan Braun 8.00 20.00
RD Ryan Doumit 4.00 10.00
RD Randall Delgado 3.00 8.00
RD R.A. Dickey 8.00 20.00
RR Ryan Roberts 3.00 8.00
SD Scott Diamond 4.00 10.00
SM Sean Marshall 3.00 8.00
SS Stephen Strasburg 30.00 60.00
SSC Skip Schumaker 4.00 10.00
TB Travis Blackley 3.00 8.00
TC Tyler Clippard
TC Tony Campana 3.00 8.00
TF Todd Frazier 4.00 10.00
TM Tom Milone 3.00 8.00
TP Trevor Plouffe 3.00 8.00
WL Wade LeBlanc 3.00 8.00
WR Wilin Rosario 4.00 10.00
WYC Wei-Yin Chen

2013 Pinnacle Awaiting the Call

1 Tim Raines .60 1.50
2 Greg Maddux 1.25 3.00
3 Alan Trammell .75 2.00
4 Randy Johnson 1.00 2.50
5 Edgar Martinez .60 1.50
6 Ivan Rodriguez .60 1.50
7 Fred McGriff .75 2.00
8 Frank Thomas 1.00 2.50
9 Jack Morris .75 2.00
10 Ken Griffey Jr. 2.00 5.00

2013 Pinnacle Awaiting the Call Artists Proof

*AP: 1.5X TO 4X BASIC
10 Ken Griffey Jr. 12.50 30.00

2013 Pinnacle Awaiting the Call Die-Cuts

*DIE CUT: 1.2X TO 3X BASIC

2013 Pinnacle Behind the Numbers

1 Albert Pujols 1.25 3.00
2 Alex Rodriguez 1.25 3.00
3 Jose Bautista .75 2.00
4 Evan Longoria .75 2.00
5 Troy Tulowitzki 1.00 2.50
6 Giancarlo Stanton 1.00 2.50
7 Joe Mauer .75 2.00
8 Justin Upton .75 2.00
9 Yadier Molina 1.25 3.00
10 Prince Fielder .75 2.00

2013 Pinnacle Behind the Numbers Artists Proof

*AP: 1.2X TO 3X BASIC
2 Alex Rodriguez 10.00 25.00

2013 Pinnacle Behind the Numbers Die-Cuts

*DC: 1X TO 2.5X BASIC

2013 Pinnacle Clear Vision Hitting Single

1 Derek Jeter 4.00 10.00
2 Mike Trout 12.00 30.00
3 Miguel Cabrera 1.50 4.00
4 David Wright 1.25 3.00
5 Buster Posey 2.00 5.00
6 Joe Mauer 1.25 3.00
7 Robinson Cano 1.25 3.00
8 Adrian Beltre 1.50 4.00
9 Ryan Braun 1.25 3.00
10 Andrew McCutchen 1.50 4.00
11 Giancarlo Stanton 1.50 4.00
12 Joey Votto 1.50 4.00
13 Josh Hamilton 1.25 3.00
14 Paul Konerko 1.25 3.00
15 Albert Pujols 2.00 5.00
16 Chase Headley 1.00 2.50
17 Matt Kemp 1.25 3.00
18 Jose Bautista 1.25 3.00
19 Starlin Castro 1.00 2.50
20 Evan Longoria 1.25 3.00
21 Bryce Harper 2.50 6.00
22 Adrian Gonzalez 1.25 3.00
23 Adam Jones 1.25 3.00
24 Prince Fielder 1.25 3.00
25 Ryan Howard 1.25 3.00
26 Billy Butler 1.00 2.50
27 Ichiro Suzuki 2.00 5.00
28 Edwin Encarnacion 1.50 4.00
29 Hunter Pence 1.25 3.00
30 Matt Holliday 1.50 4.00
31 Alex Rios 1.25 3.00
32 Jose Altuve 1.25 3.00
33 Yadier Molina 2.00 5.00
34 Carlos Gonzalez 1.25 3.00
35 Yoenis Cespedes 1.50 4.00
36 Jason Heyward 1.25 3.00
37 Dustin Pedroia 1.50 4.00
38 Nick Markakis 1.25 3.00
39 Michael Bourn 1.00 2.50
40 Alex Gordon 1.25 3.00
41 B.J. Upton 1.25 3.00
42 Austin Jackson 1.00 2.50
43 Ian Kinsler 1.25 3.00
44 Troy Tulowitzki 1.50 4.00
45 Todd Frazier 1.00 2.50
46 Justin Upton 1.25 3.00
47 Hanley Ramirez 1.25 3.00
48 Jay Bruce 1.25 3.00
49 Ryan Zimmerman 1.25 3.00
50 Chase Utley 1.25 3.00
51 Aramis Ramirez 1.00 2.50
52 Brandon Phillips 1.00 2.50
53 Paul Goldschmidt 1.50 4.00
54 Mark Teixeira 1.25 3.00
55 Allen Craig 1.25 3.00
56 Jose Reyes 1.25 3.00
57 David Ortiz 1.50 4.00
58 Josh Willingham 1.25 3.00
59 Todd Helton 1.25 3.00
60 Alex Rodriguez 2.00 5.00
61 Michael Morse 1.00 2.50
62 Pete Rose 3.00 8.00
63 Chipper Jones 1.50 4.00
64 Bo Jackson 1.50 4.00
65 Ryne Sandberg 3.00 8.00
66 George Brett 3.00 8.00
67 Ivan Rodriguez 1.00 2.50
68 Tony Gwynn 1.50 4.00
69 Reggie Jackson 1.25 3.00
70 Frank Thomas 1.50 4.00
71 Paul Molitor 1.50 4.00
72 Rickey Henderson 1.50 4.00
73 Don Mattingly 3.00 8.00
74 Cal Ripken Jr. 5.00 12.00
75 Ken Griffey Jr. 3.00 8.00

2013 Pinnacle Clear Vision Hitting Double

*DOUBLE: .5X TO 1.2X SINGLE
62 Pete Rose 8.00 20.00
65 Ryne Sandberg 5.00 12.00
66 George Brett 6.00 15.00
73 Don Mattingly 10.00 25.00
75 Ken Griffey Jr. 12.50 30.00

2013 Pinnacle Clear Vision Hitting Triple

*TRIPLE: .6X TO 1.5X SINGLE
62 Pete Rose 12.50 30.00
65 Ryne Sandberg 6.00 15.00
66 George Brett 10.00 25.00
70 Frank Thomas 10.00 25.00
73 Don Mattingly 12.50 30.00
74 Cal Ripken Jr. 12.50 30.00
75 Ken Griffey Jr. 15.00 40.00

2013 Pinnacle Clear Vision Hitting Home Run

*HOME RUN: 1.5X TO 4X SINGLE
27 Ichiro Suzuki 15.00 40.00
62 Pete Rose 40.00 80.00
65 Ryne Sandberg 15.00 40.00
66 George Brett 75.00 150.00
73 Don Mattingly 50.00 100.00
74 Cal Ripken Jr. 50.00 100.00
75 Ken Griffey Jr. 30.00 80.00

2013 Pinnacle Clear Vision Pitching Complete Game

1 Justin Verlander 1.25 3.00
2 Jered Weaver 1.50 4.00
3 Gio Gonzalez 1.50 4.00
4 Craig Kimbrel 1.50 4.00
5 Jim Johnson 1.25 3.00
6 R.A. Dickey 1.50 4.00
7 Felix Hernandez 1.50 4.00
8 CC Sabathia 1.50 4.00
9 Johnny Cueto 1.50 4.00
10 Mariano Rivera 2.50 6.00
11 Fernando Rodney 1.25 3.00
12 David Price 1.50 4.00
13 Cole Hamels 1.50 4.00
14 Matt Cain 1.50 4.00
15 Stephen Strasburg 2.00 5.00
16 Chris Sale 2.00 5.00
17 Clayton Kershaw 3.00 8.00
18 Yu Darvish 2.00 5.00
19 James Shields 1.25 3.00
20 Hiroki Kuroda 1.25 3.00
21 Nolan Ryan 6.00 15.00
22 Randy Johnson 2.00 5.00
23 Greg Maddux 2.50 6.00
24 Jim Palmer 1.50 4.00
25 Steve Carlton 1.50 4.00

2013 Pinnacle Clear Vision Pitching No Hitter

*NO HIT: 1.2X TO 3X COMPLETE

2013 Pinnacle Clear Vision Pitching Shutout

*SHO: 1X TO 2.5X COMPLETE

2013 Pinnacle Essence of the Game

1 Derek Jeter 5.00 12.00
2 Cal Ripken Jr. 6.00 15.00
3 Ken Griffey Jr. 4.00 10.00
4 Chipper Jones 2.00 5.00
5 Troy Tulowitzki 2.00 5.00
6 Tony Gwynn 2.00 5.00
7 Joe Mauer 1.50 4.00
8 David Wright 1.50 4.00
9 Ryne Sandberg 4.00 10.00
10 Buster Posey 2.50 6.00
11 Joey Votto 2.00 5.00
12 Evan Longoria 1.50 4.00

2013 Pinnacle Looking Back

1 Chase Utley .75 2.00
2 Starlin Castro .60 1.50
3 Mike Trout 8.00 20.00
4 Clayton Kershaw 1.50 4.00
5 Bryce Harper 1.50 4.00

2013 Pinnacle Looking Back Artists Proof

*AP: .75X TO 2X BASIC

2013 Pinnacle Looking Back Die-Cuts

*DC: .6X TO 1.5X BASIC
3 Mike Trout 10.00 25.00

2013 Pinnacle Pinnacle of Success

1 David Wright .75 2.00
2 R.A. Dickey .75 2.00
3 Mike Trout 8.00 20.00
4 Bryce Harper 1.50 4.00
5 Buster Posey 1.25 3.00
6 Miguel Cabrera 1.00 2.50
7 Jim Johnson .60 1.50
8 Craig Kimbrel .75 2.00
9 Albert Pujols 1.25 3.00
10 Jered Weaver .75 2.00
11 Ryan Braun .75 2.00
12 Stephen Strasburg 1.00 2.50
13 Derek Jeter 2.50 6.00
14 Andrew McCutchen 1.00 2.50
15 Justin Verlander 1.00 2.50
16 Clayton Kershaw 1.50 4.00

2013 Pinnacle Position Powers

1 Gio Gonzalez .75 2.00
2 Buster Posey 1.25 3.00
3 Joey Votto 1.00 2.50
4 Chase Utley .75 2.00
5 David Wright .75 2.00
6 Ian Desmond .60 1.50
7 Andrew McCutchen 1.00 2.50
8 Giancarlo Stanton 1.00 2.50
9 Ryan Braun .75 2.00
10 Craig Kimbrel .75 2.00
11 Jered Weaver .75 2.00
12 Joe Mauer .75 2.00
13 Albert Pujols 1.25 3.00
14 Robinson Cano .75 2.00
15 Miguel Cabrera 1.00 2.50
16 Derek Jeter 2.50 6.00
17 Josh Hamilton .75 2.00
18 Mike Trout 8.00 20.00
19 Alex Rios .75 2.00
20 Jim Johnson .60 1.50

2013 Pinnacle Position Powers Artists Proof

*AP: .75X TO 2X BASIC

2013 Pinnacle Position Powers Die-Cuts

*DC: .6X TO 1.5X BASIC

2013 Pinnacle Rookie Autographs

AE Adam Eaton 4.00 10.00
AG Avisail Garcia 4.00 10.00
CM Collin McHugh 4.00 10.00
DR Darin Ruf 6.00 15.00
DG Didi Gregorius 3.00 8.00
DB Dylan Bundy 8.00 20.00
EP Eury Perez 3.00 8.00
JO Jake Odorizzi 3.00 8.00
JC Jaye Chapman 5.00 12.00
JP Jurickson Profar 10.00 25.00
MM Manny Machado 40.00 80.00
MO Mike Olt 3.00 8.00
SM Shelby Miller 4.00 10.00
TS Tyler Skaggs 3.00 8.00
PR Paco Rodriguez 3.00 8.00
TC Tony Cingrani 5.00 12.00
JF Jeurys Familia 3.00 8.00
CK Casey Kelly 3.00 8.00
BH Brock Holt 3.00 8.00
NM Nick Maronde 3.00 8.00
TC Tyler Cloyd 4.00 10.00
MME Melky Mesa 3.00 8.00
HR Henry Rodriguez 4.00 10.00
RS Rob Scahill 3.00 8.00
DL David Lough 3.00 8.00
RB Rob Brantly 3.00 8.00

2013 Pinnacle Skylines

1 Derek Jeter 8.00 20.00
2 Ryan Braun 1.50 4.00
3 David Wright 1.50 4.00
4 Mike Trout 15.00 40.00
5 Miguel Cabrera 2.00 5.00
6 Joe Mauer 1.50 4.00
7 Buster Posey 2.50 6.00
8 Bryce Harper 3.00 8.00

2013 Pinnacle Slugfest

1 Albert Pujols 1.50 4.00
2 Prince Fielder 1.00 2.50
3 Giancarlo Stanton 1.25 3.00
4 Miguel Cabrera 1.25 3.00
5 Curtis Granderson 1.00 2.50
6 Josh Hamilton 1.00 2.50
7 Ryan Braun 1.00 2.50
8 Adrian Beltre 1.25 3.00
9 Edwin Encarnacion 1.25 3.00
10 Jay Bruce 1.00 2.50
11 Josh Willingham 1.00 2.50
12 Carlos Beltran 1.00 2.50
13 Adam Dunn 1.00 2.50
14 Adam LaRoche .75 2.00
15 Robinson Cano 1.00 2.50

2013 Pinnacle Swing for the Fences

1 Reggie Jackson 1.00 2.50
2 Prince Fielder 1.00 2.50
3 Mark Reynolds .75 2.00
4 Ken Griffey Jr. 2.50 6.00
5 Adam Dunn 1.00 2.50
6 Nelson Cruz 1.25 3.00
7 Edwin Encarnacion 1.25 3.00
8 Aramis Ramirez .75 2.00
9 Josh Hamilton 1.00 2.50
10 Miguel Cabrera 1.25 3.00
11 Ryan Braun 1.00 2.50
12 Adrian Beltre 1.25 3.00
13 Giancarlo Stanton 1.25 3.00
14 Matt Kemp 1.00 2.50
15 Jose Bautista 1.00 2.50
16 Albert Pujols 1.50 4.00

2013 Pinnacle Team 2020

1 Jurickson Profar .75 2.00
2 Manny Machado 4.00 10.00
3 Bryce Harper 1.50 4.00
4 Stephen Strasburg 1.00 2.50
5 Mike Trout 8.00 20.00
6 Shelby Miller 1.50 4.00
7 Yoenis Cespedes 1.00 2.50
8 Dylan Bundy 1.50 4.00
9 Jarrod Parker .60 1.50
10 Yu Darvish 1.00 2.50

2013 Pinnacle Team 2020 Artists Proof

*AP: .75X TO 2X BASIC

2013 Pinnacle Team 2020 Die-Cuts

*DC: .6X TO 1.5X BASIC

2013 Pinnacle Team Pinnacle

ALL VERSIONS EQUALLY PRICED
1A J.Hamilton/R.Jackson .75 2.00
1B R.Jackson/J.Hamilton .75 2.00
2A C.Ripken Jr./D.Jeter 5.00 12.00
2B D.Jeter/C.Ripken Jr. 5.00 12.00
3A K.Griffey Jr./M.Trout 8.00 20.00
3B M.Trout/K.Griffey Jr. 8.00 20.00

4A G.Brett/M.Cabrera 2.00 5.00
4B M.Cabrera/G.Brett 2.00 5.00
5A A.Pujols/F.Thomas 1.25 3.00
5B F.Thomas/A.Pujols 1.25 3.00
6A J.Verlander/R.Johnson 1.00 2.50
6B R.Johnson/J.Verlander 1.00 2.50
7A B.Harper/M.Trout 8.00 20.00
7B M.Trout/B.Harper 8.00 20.00
8A B.Jackson/B.Harper 1.50 4.00
8B B.Harper/B.Jackson 1.50 4.00
9A B.Posey/I.Rodriguez 1.25 3.00
9B I.Rodriguez/B.Posey 1.25 3.00
10A G.Maddux/S.Strasburg 1.25 3.00
10B S.Strasburg/G.Maddux 1.25 3.00
11A C.Ripken Jr./T.Tulowitzki 3.00 8.00
11B T.Tulowitzki/C.Ripken Jr. 3.00 8.00
12A G.Stanton/R.Braun 1.00 2.50
12B R.Braun/G.Stanton 1.00 2.50
13A N.Ryan/S.Strasburg 3.00 8.00
13B S.Strasburg/N.Ryan 3.00 8.00
14A A.McCutchen/M.Kemp 1.00 2.50
14B M.Kemp/A.McCutchen 1.00 2.50
15B E.Longoria/D.Wright .75 2.00
15A D.Wright/E.Longoria .75 2.00

2013 Pinnacle The Hit King

1 Pete Rose 5.00 12.00
2 Pete Rose 5.00 12.00
3 Pete Rose 5.00 12.00
4 Pete Rose 5.00 12.00
5 Pete Rose 5.00 12.00

2013 Pinnacle The Hit King Artists Proof

*AP: 1X TO 2.5X BASIC

2013 Pinnacle The Hit King Die-Cuts

*DIE CUT: .75X TO 2X BASIC

2013 Pinnacle The Naturals

1 Derek Jeter 4.00 10.00
2 Joey Votto 1.50 4.00
3 Josh Hamilton 1.25 3.00
4 Albert Pujols 2.00 5.00
5 Miguel Cabrera 1.50 4.00
6 Bryce Harper 2.50 6.00
7 Mike Trout 12.00 30.00
8 Troy Tulowitzki 1.50 4.00
9 Yu Darvish 1.50 4.00
10 Felix Hernandez 1.25 3.00
11 Justin Verlander 1.50 4.00
12 Stephen Strasburg 1.50 4.00

2013 Pinnacle Z Team

1 Bryce Harper 5.00 12.00
2 Albert Pujols 4.00 10.00
3 Joe Mauer 2.50 6.00
4 Mike Trout 25.00 60.00
5 Derek Jeter 12.50 30.00
6 David Wright 2.50 6.00
7 Stephen Strasburg 3.00 8.00
8 Yu Darvish 3.00 8.00

1996 Pinnacle Aficionado Promos

COMPLETE SET (3) 2.00 5.00
9 Roger Clemens 1.25 3.00
107 Ryan Klesko .40 1.00
MN7 Albert Belle .40 1.00
Magic Number

1996 Pinnacle Aficionado

The 1996 Aficionado set was issued in one series totalling 200 cards. The five-card packs retailed for $3.99 and had a special bubble gum scent which was released when the packs were opened. Cards numbered 151-160 are a subset titled "Global Reach" and feature color action player cut-outs of international players on a background of a map, a global baseball, and their country's flag.

COMPLETE SET (200) 12.50 30.00
1 Jack McDowell .15 .40
2 Jay Bell .15 .40
3 Rafael Palmeiro .25 .60
4 Wally Joyner .15 .40
5 Ozzie Smith .60 1.50
6 Mark McGwire 1.00 2.50
7 Kevin Seitzer .15 .40
8 Fred McGriff .25 .60
9 Roger Clemens .75 2.00
10 Randy Johnson .40 1.00
11 Cecil Fielder .15 .40
12 David Cone .15 .40
13 Chili Davis .15 .40
14 Andres Galarraga .15 .40
15 Joe Carter .15 .40
16 Ryne Sandberg .60 1.50
17 Paul O'Neill .25 .60
18 Cal Ripken 1.25 3.00
19 Wade Boggs .25 .60
20 Greg Gagne .15 .40
21 Edgar Martinez .25 .60
22 Greg Maddux .60 1.50
23 Ken Caminiti .15 .40
24 Kirby Puckett .40 1.00
25 Craig Biggio .25 .60
26 Will Clark .25 .60
27 Ron Gant .15 .40
28 Eddie Murray .40 1.00
29 Lance Johnson .15 .40
30 Tony Gwynn .50 1.25
31 Dante Bichette .15 .40
32 Darren Daulton .15 .40
33 Danny Tartabull .15 .40
34 Jeff King .15 .40
35 Tom Glavine .25 .60
36 Rickey Henderson .40 1.00
37 Jose Canseco .25 .60
38 Barry Larkin .25 .60
39 Dennis Martinez .15 .40
40 Ruben Sierra .15 .40
41 Bobby Bonilla .15 .40
42 Jeff Conine .15 .40
43 Lee Smith .15 .40
44 Charlie Hayes .15 .40
45 Walt Weiss .15 .40
46 Jay Buhner .15 .40
47 Kenny Rogers .15 .40
48 Paul Molitor .15 .40
49 Hal Morris .15 .40
50 Todd Stottlemyre .15 .40
51 Mike Stanley .15 .40
52 Mark Grace .25 .60
53 Lenny Dykstra .15 .40
54 Andre Dawson .15 .40
55 Dennis Eckersley .15 .40
56 Ben McDonald .15 .40
57 Ray Lankford .15 .40
58 Mo Vaughn .15 .40
59 Frank Thomas .40 1.00
60 Julio Franco .15 .40
61 Jim Abbott .25 .60
62 Greg Vaughn .15 .40
63 Marquis Grissom .15 .40
64 Tino Martinez .25 .60
65 Kevin Appier .15 .40
66 Matt Williams .15 .40
67 Sammy Sosa .40 1.00
68 Larry Walker .15 .40
69 Ivan Rodriguez .25 .60
70 Eric Karros .15 .40
71 Bernie Williams .25 .60
72 Carlos Baerga .15 .40
73 Jeff Bagwell .25 .60
74 Pete Schourek .15 .40
75 Ken Griffey Jr. .75 2.00
76 Bernard Gilkey .15 .40
77 Albert Belle .15 .40
78 Chuck Knoblauch .15 .40
79 John Smoltz .25 .60
80 Barry Bonds 1.00 2.50
81 Vinny Castilla .15 .40
82 John Olerud .15 .40
83 Mike Mussina .25 .60
84 Alex Fernandez .15 .40
85 Shawon Dunston .15 .40
86 Travis Fryman .15 .40
87 Moises Alou .15 .40
88 Dean Palmer .15 .40
89 Gregg Jefferies .15 .40
90 Jim Thome .25 .60
91 Dave Justice .15 .40
92 B.J. Surhoff .15 .40
93 Ramon Martinez .15 .40
94 Gary Sheffield .15 .40
95 Andy Benes .15 .40
96 Reggie Sanders .15 .40
97 Roberto Alomar .25 .60
98 Omar Vizquel .25 .60
99 Juan Gonzalez .15 .40
100 Robin Ventura .15 .40
101 Jason Isringhausen .15 .40
102 Greg Colbrunn .15 .40
103 Brian Jordan .15 .40
104 Shawn Green .15 .40
105 Brian Hunter .15 .40
106 Rondell White .15 .40
107 Ryan Klesko .15 .40
108 Sterling Hitchcock .15 .40
109 Manny Ramirez .25 .60
110 Bret Boone .15 .40
111 Michael Tucker .15 .40
112 Julian Tavarez .15 .40
113 Benji Gil .15 .40
114 Kenny Lofton .15 .40
115 Mike Kelly .15 .40
116 Ray Durham .15 .40
117 Trevor Hoffman .15 .40
118 Butch Huskey .15 .40
119 Phil Nevin .15 .40
120 Pedro Martinez .25 .60
121 Wil Cordero .15 .40
122 Tim Salmon .25 .60
123 Jim Edmonds .15 .40
124 Mike Piazza .60 1.50
125 Rico Brogna .15 .40
126 John Mabry .15 .40
127 Chipper Jones .40 1.00
128 Johnny Damon .25 .60
129 Raul Mondesi .15 .40
130 Denny Neagle .15 .40
131 Marc Newfield .15 .40
132 Hideo Nomo .40 1.00
133 Joe Vitiello .15 .40
134 Garret Anderson .15 .40
135 Dave Nilsson .15 .40
136 Alex Rodriguez .75 2.00
137 Russ Davis .15 .40
138 Frank Rodriguez .15 .40
139 Royce Clayton .15 .40
140 John Valentin .15 .40
141 Marty Cordova .15 .40
142 Alex Gonzalez .15 .40
143 Carlos Delgado .15 .40
144 Willie Greene .15 .40
145 Cliff Floyd .15 .40
146 Bobby Higginson .15 .40
147 J.T. Snow .15 .40
148 Derek Bell .15 .40
149 Edgardo Alfonzo .15 .40
150 Charles Johnson .15 .40
151 Hideo Nomo GR .25 .60
152 Larry Walker GR .15 .40
153 Bob Abreu GR .25 .60
154 Karim Garcia GR .15 .40
155 Dave Nilsson GR .15 .40
156 Chan Ho Park GR .15 .40
157 Dennis Martinez GR .15 .40
158 Sammy Sosa GR .25 .60
159 Rey Ordonez GR .15 .40
160 Roberto Alomar GR .15 .40
161 George Arias .15 .40
162 Jason Schmidt .25 .60
163 Derek Jeter 1.00 2.50
164 Chris Snopek .15 .40
165 Todd Hollandsworth .15 .40
166 Sal Fasano .15 .40
167 Jay Powell .15 .40
168 Paul Wilson .15 .40
169 Jim Pittsley .15 .40
170 LaTroy Hawkins .15 .40
171 Bob Abreu .40 1.00
172 Mike Grace RC .15 .40
173 Karim Garcia .15 .40
174 Richard Hidalgo .15 .40
175 Felipe Crespo .15 .40
176 Terrell Wade .15 .40
177 Steve Gibralter .15 .40
178 Jermaine Dye .15 .40
179 Alan Benes .15 .40
180 Wilton Guerrero RC .15 .40
181 Brooks Kieschnick .15 .40
182 Roger Cedeno .15 .40
183 Osvaldo Fernandez RC .15 .40
184 Matt Lawton RC .15 .40
185 George Williams .15 .40
186 Jimmy Haynes .15 .40
187 Mike Busby RC .15 .40
188 Chan Ho Park .15 .40
189 Marc Barcelo .15 .40
190 Jason Kendall .15 .40
191 Rey Ordonez .15 .40
192 Tyler Houston .15 .40
193 John Wasdin .15 .40
194 Jeff Suppan .15 .40
195 Jeff Ware .15 .40
196 Ken Griffey Jr. CL .50 1.25
197 Albert Belle CL .15 .40
198 Mike Piazza CL .40 1.00
199 Greg Maddux CL .40 1.00
200 Frank Thomas CL .25 .60

1996 Pinnacle Aficionado Artist's Proofs

*STARS:8X TO 20X BASIC CARDS
*ROOKIES: 5X TO 12X BASIC CARDS
STATED ODDS 1:35

1996 Pinnacle Aficionado Magic Numbers

COMPLETE SET (10) 60.00 120.00
STATED ODDS 1:72
1 Ken Griffey Jr. 10.00 25.00
2 Greg Maddux 6.00 15.00
3 Frank Thomas 4.00 10.00
4 Mo Vaughn 1.50 4.00
5 Jeff Bagwell 2.50 6.00
6 Chipper Jones 4.00 10.00
7 Albert Belle 1.50 4.00
8 Cal Ripken 12.50 30.00
9 Matt Williams 1.50 4.00
10 Sammy Sosa 4.00 10.00

1996 Pinnacle Aficionado Rivals

COMPLETE SET (24) 100.00 200.00
STATED ODDS 1:24
1 K.Griffey 4.00 10.00
F.Thomas
2 F.Thomas 6.00 15.00
C.Ripken
3 C.Ripken 6.00 15.00
M.Vaughn
4 M.Vaughn 4.00 10.00
K.Griffey Jr.
5 K.Griffey 8.00 20.00
C.Ripken
6 F.Thomas 2.00 5.00
M.Vaughn
7 C.Ripken 8.00 20.00
K.Griffey
8 M.Vaughn 2.00 5.00
F.Thomas
9 K.Griffey 4.00 10.00
M.Vaughn
10 F.Thomas 4.00 10.00
K.Griffey
11 C.Ripken 6.00 15.00
F.Thomas
12 M.Vaughn 6.00 15.00
C.Ripken
13 M.Piazza 3.00 8.00
J.Bagwell
14 J.Bagwell 5.00 12.00
B.Bonds
15 J.Bagwell 3.00 8.00
M.Piazza
16 T.Gwynn 3.00 8.00
M.Piazza
17 M.Piazza 3.00 8.00
B.Bonds
18 J.Bagwell 2.50 6.00
T.Gwynn
19 B.Bonds 3.00 8.00
M.Piazza
20 T.Gwynn 2.50 6.00
J.Bagwell
21 M.Piazza 3.00 8.00
T.Gwynn
22 B.Bonds 5.00 12.00
J.Bagwell
23 T.Gwynn 2.50 6.00
B.Bonds
24 B.Bonds 2.50 6.00
T.Gwynn

1996 Pinnacle Aficionado Slick Picks

COMPLETE SET (32) 20.00 50.00
STATED ODDS 1:10
1 Mike Piazza 1.00 2.50
2 Cal Ripken 3.00 8.00
3 Ken Griffey Jr. 2.00 5.00
4 Paul Wilson .40 1.00
5 Frank Thomas 1.00 2.50
6 Mo Vaughn .40 1.00
7 Barry Bonds 1.50 4.00
8 Albert Belle .40 1.00
9 Jeff Bagwell .60 1.50
10 Dante Bichette .40 1.00
11 Hideo Nomo 1.00 2.50
12 Raul Mondesi .40 1.00
13 Manny Ramirez .60 1.50
14 Greg Maddux 1.50 4.00
15 Tony Gwynn 1.00 2.50
16 Ryne Sandberg 1.50 4.00
17 Reggie Sanders .40 1.00
18 Derek Jeter 2.50 6.00
19 Johnny Damon .60 1.50
20 Alex Rodriguez 1.25 3.00
21 Ryan Klesko .40 1.00
22 Jim Thome .60 1.50
23 Kenny Lofton .40 1.00
24 Tino Martinez .40 1.00
25 Randy Johnson 1.00 2.50
26 Wade Boggs .60 1.50
27 Juan Gonzalez .40 1.00
28 Kirby Puckett 1.00 2.50
29 Tim Salmon .40 1.00
30 Chipper Jones 1.00 2.50
31 Garret Anderson .40 1.00
32 Eddie Murray .60 1.50

1997 Pinnacle Certified

This 150-card set was distributed in six-card hobby only packs with a suggested price of $4.99 and features color action player photos with side triangular silver mylar borders and black-and-white center backgrounds. The backs carry another player photo with player information and statistics. The set is divided into the following subsets: Rookie (106-135) and Certified Stars (136-150) which display a color player image on a background of stars. A Jose Cruz Exchange card was randomly seeded into packs. The deadline to redeem the card was March 31, 1998. Collectors who exchanged this cards received a Cruz card featuring him in a Blue Jay uniform. This number 151 card is not considered part of the complete set.

COMPLETE SET (150) 15.00 40.00
151 CRUZ JR. EXCH RANDOM IN PACKS
COMP.SET EXCLUDES CRUZ JR. 151
1 Barry Bonds 1.00 2.50
2 Mo Vaughn .15 .40
3 Matt Williams .15 .40
4 Ryne Sandberg .60 1.50
5 Jeff Bagwell .25 .60
6 Alan Benes .15 .40
7 John Wetteland .15 .40
8 Fred McGriff .25 .60
9 Craig Biggio .25 .60
10 Bernie Williams .25 .60
11 Brian Hunter .15 .40
12 Sandy Alomar Jr. .15 .40
13 Ray Lankford .15 .40
14 Ryan Klesko .15 .40
15 Jermaine Dye .15 .40
16 Andy Benes .15 .40
17 Albert Belle .15 .40
18 Tony Clark .15 .40
19 Dean Palmer .15 .40
20 Bernard Gilkey .15 .40
21 Ken Caminiti .15 .40
22 Alex Rodriguez .60 1.50
23 Tim Salmon .25 .60
24 Larry Walker .15 .40
25 Barry Larkin .25 .60
26 Mike Piazza .60 1.50
27 Brady Anderson .15 .40
28 Cal Ripken 1.25 3.00
29 Charles Nagy .15 .40
30 Paul Molitor .15 .40
31 Darin Erstad .15 .40
32 Rey Ordonez .15 .40
33 Wally Joyner .15 .40
34 David Cone .15 .40
35 Sammy Sosa .40 1.00
36 Dante Bichette .15 .40
37 Eric Karros .15 .40
38 Omar Vizquel .25 .60
39 Roger Clemens .75 2.00
40 Joe Carter .15 .40
41 Frank Thomas .40 1.00
42 Javy Lopez .15 .40
43 Mike Mussina .25 .60
44 Gary Sheffield .15 .40
45 Tony Gwynn .50 1.25
46 Jason Kendall .15 .40
47 Jim Thome .25 .60
48 Andres Galarraga .15 .40
49 Mark McGwire 1.00 2.50
50 Troy Percival .15 .40
51 Derek Jeter 1.00 2.50
52 Todd Hollandsworth .15 .40
53 Ken Griffey Jr. .75 2.00
54 Randy Johnson .40 1.00
55 Pat Hentgen .15 .40
56 Rusty Greer .15 .40
57 John Jaha .15 .40
58 Kenny Lofton .15 .40
59 Chipper Jones .40 1.00
60 Robb Nen .15 .40
61 Rafael Palmeiro .25 .60
62 Mariano Rivera .40 1.00
63 Hideo Nomo .40 1.00
64 Greg Vaughn .15 .40
65 Ron Gant .15 .40
66 Eddie Murray .40 1.00
67 John Smoltz .25 .60
68 Manny Ramirez .25 .60
69 Juan Gonzalez .15 .40
70 F.P. Santangelo .15 .40
71 Moises Alou .15 .40
72 Alex Ochoa .15 .40
73 Chuck Knoblauch .15 .40
74 Raul Mondesi .15 .40
75 J.T. Snow .15 .40
76 Rickey Henderson .40 1.00
77 Bobby Bonilla .15 .40
78 Wade Boggs .25 .60
79 Ivan Rodriguez .25 .60
80 Brian Jordan .15 .40
81 Al Leiter .15 .40
82 Jay Buhner .15 .40
83 Greg Maddux .60 1.50
84 Edgar Martinez .25 .60
85 Kevin Brown .15 .40
86 Eric Young .15 .40
87 Todd Hundley .15 .40
88 Ellis Burks .15 .40
89 Marquis Grissom .15 .40
90 Jose Canseco .25 .60
91 Henry Rodriguez .15 .40
92 Andy Pettitte .25 .60
93 Mark Grudzielanek .15 .40
94 Dwight Gooden .15 .40
95 Roberto Alomar .25 .60
96 Paul Wilson .15 .40
97 Will Clark .25 .60
98 Rondell White .15 .40
99 Charles Johnson .15 .40
100 Jim Edmonds .15 .40
101 Jason Giambi .15 .40
102 Billy Wagner .15 .40
103 Edgar Renteria .15 .40
104 Johnny Damon .25 .60
105 Jason Isringhausen .15 .40
106 Andruw Jones .25 .60
107 Jose Guillen .15 .40
108 Kevin Orie .15 .40
109 Brian Giles RC 1.25 3.00
110 Danny Patterson .15 .40
111 Vladimir Guerrero .40 1.00
112 Scott Rolen .25 .60
113 Damon Mashore .15 .40
114 Nomar Garciaparra .60 1.50
115 Todd Walker .15 .40
116 Wilton Guerrero .15 .40
117 Bob Abreu .25 .60
118 Brooks Kieschnick .15 .40
119 Pokey Reese .15 .40
120 Todd Greene .15 .40
121 Dmitri Young .15 .40
122 Raul Casanova .15 .40
123 Glendon Rusch .15 .40
124 Jason Dickson .15 .40
125 Jorge Posada .25 .60
126 Rod Myers .15 .40
127 Bubba Trammell RC .20 .50
128 Scott Spiezio .15 .40
129 Hideki Irabu RC .20 .50
130 Wendell Magee .15 .40
131 Bartolo Colon .15 .40
132 Chris Holt .15 .40
133 Calvin Maduro .15 .40
134 Ray Montgomery RC .20 .50
135 Shannon Stewart .15 .40
136 Ken Griffey Jr. CERT .50 1.25
137 Vladimir Guerrero CERT .25 .60
138 Roger Clemens CERT .40 1.00
139 Mark McGwire CERT .50 1.25
140 Albert Belle CERT .15 .40
141 Derek Jeter CERT .50 1.25
142 Juan Gonzalez CERT .15 .40
143 Greg Maddux CERT .40 1.00
144 Alex Rodriguez CERT .40 1.00
145 Jeff Bagwell CERT .15 .40
146 Cal Ripken CERT .60 1.50
147 Tony Gwynn CERT .25 .60
148 Frank Thomas CERT .25 .60
149 Hideo Nomo CERT .15 .40
150 Andruw Jones CERT .15 .40
151 Jose Cruz Jr. Blue Jays .20 .50
NNO Checklist 1-75 .15 .40
NNO Checklist 76-150 .15 .40
NNO Checklist Inserts .15 .40

1997 Pinnacle Certified Mirror Black

UNNANOUNCED RANDOM INSERTS IN PACKS

1997 Pinnacle Certified Mirror Blue

*STARS: 12.5X TO 30X BASIC CARDS
*ROOKIES: 4X TO 10X BASIC CARDS
STATED ODDS 1:199

1997 Pinnacle Certified Mirror Gold

*STARS: 20X TO 50X BASIC CARDS
*ROOKIES: 6X TO 15X BASIC CARDS
STATED ODDS 1:299

1997 Pinnacle Certified Mirror Red

*STARS: 6X TO 15X BASIC CARDS
*ROOKIES: 2X TO 5X BASIC CARDS
STATED ODDS 1:99

1997 Pinnacle Certified Red

*STARS: 1.5X TO 4X BASIC CARDS
*ROOKIES: .6X TO 1.5X BASIC CARDS
STATED ODDS 1:5 HOBBY

1997 Pinnacle Certified Certified Team

COMPLETE SET (20) 40.00 100.00
STATED ODDS 1:19 HOBBY
GOLD TEAM STATED ODDS 1:119 HOBBY
GOLD TEAM PRINT RUN 475 SERIAL #'d SETS
MIR.GOLD: RANDOM INSERTS IN PACKS
MIR.GOLD PRINT RUN 25 SETS
1 Frank Thomas 2.50 6.00
2 Jeff Bagwell 1.50 4.00
3 Derek Jeter 6.00 15.00
4 Chipper Jones 2.50 6.00
5 Alex Rodriguez 4.00 10.00
6 Ken Caminiti 1.00 2.50
7 Cal Ripken 8.00 20.00
8 Mo Vaughn 1.00 2.50
9 Ivan Rodriguez 1.50 4.00
10 Mike Piazza 4.00 10.00
11 Juan Gonzalez 1.00 2.50
12 Barry Bonds 6.00 15.00
13 Ken Griffey Jr. 5.00 12.00
14 Andruw Jones 1.50 4.00
15 Albert Belle 1.00 2.50
16 Gary Sheffield 1.00 2.50
17 Andy Pettitte 1.50 4.00
18 Hideo Nomo 2.50 6.00
19 Greg Maddux 4.00 10.00
20 John Smoltz 1.50 4.00

1997 Pinnacle Certified Lasting Impressions

COMPLETE SET (20) 30.00 80.00
STATED ODDS 1:19 HOBBY
1 Cal Ripken 5.00 12.00
2 Ken Griffey Jr. 3.00 8.00
3 Mo Vaughn .60 1.50
4 Brian Jordan .60 1.50
5 Mark McGwire 4.00 10.00
6 Chuck Knoblauch .60 1.50
7 Sammy Sosa 1.50 4.00
8 Brady Anderson .60 1.50
9 Frank Thomas 1.50 4.00
10 Tony Gwynn 2.00 5.00
11 Roger Clemens 3.00 8.00
12 Alex Rodriguez 2.50 6.00
13 Paul Molitor .60 1.50
14 Kenny Lofton .60 1.50
15 John Smoltz 1.00 2.50
16 Roberto Alomar 1.00 2.50
17 Randy Johnson 1.50 4.00
18 Ryne Sandberg 2.50 6.00
19 Manny Ramirez 1.00 2.50
20 Mike Mussina 1.00 2.50

1997 Pinnacle Inside

The 1997 Pinnacle Inside set was issued in one series totalling 150 cards and was distributed inside 24 different collectible player cans with a suggested retail price of $2.99 for a 10-card can. Printed on 14 pt. stock, the fronts feature a color player photo with a thin black-and-white photo as a side border. The set contains a Rookie subset (128-147) and a checklist subset (148-150). The three checklists display black-and-white player photos of American and National League pairings of the 1996 Rookies of the Year, Cy Young winners, and MVPs.

COMPLETE SET (150) 10.00 25.00
1 David Cone .15 .40
2 Sammy Sosa .40 1.00
3 Joe Carter .15 .40
4 Juan Gonzalez .15 .40
5 Hideo Nomo .40 1.00
6 Moises Alou .15 .40
7 Marc Newfield .15 .40
8 Alex Rodriguez .60 1.50
9 Kimera Bartee .15 .40
10 Chuck Knoblauch .15 .40
11 Jason Isringhausen .15 .40
12 Jermaine Allensworth .15 .40
13 Frank Thomas .40 1.00
14 Paul Molitor .15 .40
15 John Mabry .15 .40
16 Greg Maddux .60 1.50
17 Rafael Palmeiro .25 .60
18 Brian Jordan .15 .40
19 Ken Griffey Jr. .75 2.00
20 Brady Anderson .15 .40
21 Ruben Sierra .15 .40
22 Travis Fryman .15 .40
23 Cal Ripken 1.25 3.00
24 Will Clark .25 .60
25 Todd Hollandsworth .15 .40
26 Kevin Brown .15 .40
27 Mike Piazza .60 1.50
28 Craig Biggio .25 .60
29 Paul Wilson .15 .40
30 Andres Galarraga .15 .40
31 Chipper Jones .40 1.00
32 Jason Giambi .15 .40
33 Ernie Young .15 .40
34 Marty Cordova .15 .40
35 Albert Belle .15 .40
36 Roger Clemens .75 2.00
37 Ryne Sandberg .60 1.50
38 Henry Rodriguez .15 .40
39 Jay Buhner .15 .40
40 Raul Mondesi .15 .40
41 Jeff Fassero .15 .40
42 Edgar Martinez .25 .60
43 Trey Beamon .15 .40
44 Mo Vaughn .15 .40
45 Gary Sheffield .15 .40
46 Ray Durham .15 .40
47 Brett Butler .15 .40
48 Ivan Rodriguez .25 .60
49 Fred McGriff .25 .60
50 Dean Palmer .15 .40
51 Rickey Henderson .40 1.00
52 Andy Pettitte .25 .60
53 Bobby Bonilla .15 .40
54 Shawn Green .15 .40
55 Tino Martinez .25 .60
56 Tony Gwynn .50 1.25
57 Tom Glavine .25 .60
58 Eric Young .15 .40
59 Kevin Appier .15 .40
60 Barry Bonds 1.00 2.50
61 Wade Boggs .25 .60
62 Jason Kendall .15 .40
63 Jeff Bagwell .25 .60
64 Jeff Conine .15 .40
65 Greg Vaughn .15 .40
66 Eric Karros .15 .40
67 Manny Ramirez .25 .60
68 John Smoltz .25 .60
69 Terrell Wade .15 .40
70 John Wetteland .15 .40
71 Kenny Lofton .15 .40
72 Jim Thome .25 .60
73 Bill Pulsipher .15 .40
74 Darryl Strawberry .15 .40
75 Roberto Alomar .25 .60
76 Bobby Higginson .15 .40
77 James Baldwin .15 .40
78 Mark McGwire 1.00 2.50
79 Jose Canseco .25 .60
80 Mark Grudzielanek .15 .40
81 Ryan Klesko .15 .40
82 Javy Lopez .15 .40
83 Ken Caminiti .15 .40
84 Dave Nilsson .15 .40
85 Tim Salmon .25 .60
86 Cecil Fielder .15 .40
87 Derek Jeter 1.00 2.50
88 Garret Anderson .15 .40
89 Dwight Gooden .15 .40
90 Carlos Delgado .15 .40
91 Ugueth Urbina .15 .40
92 Chan Ho Park .15 .40
93 Eddie Murray .40 1.00
94 Alex Ochoa .15 .40
95 Rusty Greer .15 .40
96 Mark Grace .25 .60
97 Pat Hentgen .15 .40
98 John Jaha .15 .40
99 Charles Johnson .15 .40
100 Jermaine Dye .15 .40
101 Quinton McCracken .15 .40
102 Troy Percival .15 .40
103 Shane Reynolds .15 .40
104 Rondell White .15 .40
105 Charles Nagy .15 .40
106 Alan Benes .15 .40
107 Tom Goodwin .15 .40
108 Ron Gant .15 .40
109 Dan Wilson .15 .40
110 Darin Erstad .15 .40
111 Matt Williams .15 .40
112 Barry Larkin .25 .60
113 Mariano Rivera .40 1.00
114 Larry Walker .15 .40
115 Jim Edmonds .15 .40
116 Michael Tucker .15 .40
117 Todd Hundley .15 .40
118 Alex Fernandez .15 .40
119 J.T. Snow .15 .40
120 Ellis Burks .15 .40
121 Steve Finley .15 .40
122 Mike Mussina .25 .60
123 Curtis Pride .15 .40
124 Derek Bell .15 .40
125 Dante Bichette .15 .40
126 Terry Steinbach .15 .40
127 Randy Johnson .40 1.00
128 Andruw Jones .25 .60
129 Vladimir Guerrero .40 1.00
130 Ruben Rivera .15 .40
131 Billy Wagner .15 .40
132 Scott Rolen .25 .60
133 Rey Ordonez .15 .40
134 Karim Garcia .15 .40
135 George Arias .15 .40
136 Todd Greene .15 .40
137 Robin Jennings .15 .40
138 Raul Casanova .15 .40
139 Steve Gibralter .15 .40
140 Edgar Renteria .15 .40
141 Chad Mottola .15 .40
142 Dmitri Young .15 .40
143 Tony Clark .15 .40
144 Todd Walker .15 .40
145 Kevin Brown .15 .40
146 Nomar Garciaparra .60 1.50
147 Neifi Perez .15 .40
148 D.Jeter .40 1.00
T.Hollandsworth CL
149 P.Hentgen .15 .40
J.Smoltz CL
150 J.Gonzalez .15 .40
K.Caminiti CL

1997 Pinnacle Inside Club Edition

*STARS: 2X TO 5X BASIC CARDS
STATED ODDS 1:7

1997 Pinnacle Inside Diamond Edition

*STARS: 10X TO 25X BASIC CARDS
STATED ODDS 1:63

1997 Pinnacle Inside 40 Something

COMPLETE SET (16) 75.00 150.00
STATED ODDS 1:47
1 Juan Gonzalez 2.00 5.00
2 Barry Bonds 12.50 30.00
3 Ken Caminiti 2.00 5.00
4 Mark McGwire 12.50 30.00
5 Todd Hundley 2.00 5.00
6 Albert Belle 2.00 5.00
7 Ellis Burks 2.00 5.00
8 Jay Buhner 2.00 5.00
9 Brady Anderson 2.00 5.00
10 Vinny Castilla 2.00 5.00
11 Mo Vaughn 2.00 5.00
12 Ken Griffey Jr. 10.00 25.00
13 Sammy Sosa 5.00 12.00
14 Andres Galarraga 2.00 5.00
15 Gary Sheffield 2.00 5.00
16 Frank Thomas 5.00 12.00

1997 Pinnacle Inside Cans

COMPLETE SET (24) 10.00 25.00
DISTRIBUTED AS COLLECTIBLE PACKAGE
1 Kenny Lofton .10 .30
2 Frank Thomas .30 .75
3 John Smoltz .20 .50
4 Manny Ramirez .20 .50
5 Alex Rodriguez .50 1.25
6 Barry Bonds .75 2.00
7 Mo Vaughn .10 .30
8 Ken Griffey Jr. .60 1.50
9 Albert Belle .10 .30
10 Greg Maddux .50 1.25
11 Juan Gonzalez .10 .30
12 Andy Pettitte .20 .50
13 Jeff Bagwell .20 .50
14 Ryan Klesko .10 .30
15 Chipper Jones .30 .75
16 Derek Jeter .75 2.00
17 Ivan Rodriguez .20 .50
18 Andruw Jones .20 .50
19 Mike Piazza .50 1.25
20 Hideo Nomo .30 .75
21 Ken Caminiti .10 .30
22 Cal Ripken 1.00 2.50
23 Mark McGwire .75 2.00
24 Tony Gwynn .40 1.00

1997 Pinnacle Inside Dueling Dugouts

STATED ODDS 1:23
1 C.Ripken 15.00 40.00
A.Rodriguez
2 J.Bagwell 3.00 8.00
K.Caminiti
3 B.Bonds 12.50 30.00
A.Belle
4 M.Piazza 8.00 20.00
I.Rodriguez
5 C.Knoblauch 3.00 8.00
R.Alomar
6 K.Griffey Jr. 10.00 25.00
A.Jones
7 C.Jones 5.00 12.00
J.Thome
8 F.Thomas 5.00 12.00
M.Vaughn
9 M.McGwire 12.50 30.00

F.McGriff
10 T.Gwynn 6.00 15.00
B.Jordan
11 D.Jeter 12.50 30.00
B.Larkin
12 K.Lofton 5.00 12.00
B.Williams
13 J.Gonzalez 3.00 8.00
M.Ramirez
14 W.Clark 3.00 8.00
R.Palmeiro
15 G.Maddux 8.00 20.00
R.Clemens
16 J.Smoltz 3.00 8.00
A.Pettitte
17 M.Rivera 5.00 12.00
J.Wetteland
18 H.Nomo 5.00 12.00
M.Mussina
19 D.Erstad 2.00 5.00
T.Hollandsworth
20 V.Guerrero 5.00 12.00
K.Garcia

1998 Pinnacle Inside

The 1998 Pinnacle Inside set was issued in one series totalling 150 cards and distributed in packs inside 23 different collectible player cans. The fronts feature color player photos while the backs carry player information. The set contains the topical subset: Inside Tips (133-147) and three checklists (148-150).

COMPLETE SET (150) 10.00 25.00
1 Darin Erstad .15 .40
2 Derek Jeter 1.00 2.50
3 Alex Rodriguez .60 1.50
4 Bobby Higginson .15 .40
5 Nomar Garciaparra .60 1.50
6 Kenny Lofton .15 .40
7 Ivan Rodriguez .25 .60
8 Cal Ripken 1.25 3.00
9 Todd Hundley .15 .40
10 Chipper Jones .40 1.00
11 Barry Larkin .25 .60
12 Roberto Alomar .25 .60
13 Mo Vaughn .15 .40
14 Sammy Sosa .40 1.00
15 Sandy Alomar Jr. .15 .40
16 Albert Belle .15 .40
17 Scott Rolen .25 .60
18 Pokey Reese .15 .40
19 Ryan Klesko .15 .40
20 Andres Galarraga .15 .40
21 Justin Thompson .15 .40
22 Gary Sheffield .15 .40
23 David Justice .15 .40
24 Ken Griffey Jr. .75 2.00
25 Andruw Jones .25 .60
26 Jeff Bagwell .25 .60
27 Vladimir Guerrero .40 1.00
28 Mike Piazza .60 1.50
29 Chuck Knoblauch .15 .40
30 Rondell White .15 .40
31 Greg Maddux .60 1.50
32 Andy Pettitte .25 .60
33 Larry Walker .15 .40
34 Bobby Estalella .15 .40
35 Frank Thomas .40 1.00
36 Tony Womack .15 .40
37 Tony Gwynn .50 1.25
38 Barry Bonds 1.00 2.50
39 Randy Johnson .40 1.00
40 Mark McGwire 1.00 2.50
41 Juan Gonzalez .15 .40
42 Tim Salmon .25 .60
43 John Smoltz .25 .60
44 Rafael Palmeiro .25 .60
45 Mark Grace .25 .60
46 Mike Cameron .15 .40
47 Jim Thome .25 .60
48 Neifi Perez .15 .40
49 Kevin Brown .25 .60
50 Craig Biggio .25 .60
51 Bernie Williams .25 .60
52 Hideo Nomo .40 1.00
53 Bob Abreu .15 .40
54 Edgardo Alfonzo .15 .40
55 Wade Boggs .25 .60
56 Jose Guillen .15 .40
57 Ken Caminiti .15 .40
58 Paul Molitor .15 .40
59 Shawn Estes .15 .40
60 Edgar Martinez .25 .60
61 Livan Hernandez .15 .40
62 Ray Lankford .15 .40
63 Rusty Greer .15 .40
64 Jim Edmonds .15 .40
65 Tom Glavine .25 .60
66 Alan Benes .15 .40
67 Will Clark .25 .60
68 Garret Anderson .15 .40
69 Javier Lopez .15 .40
70 Mike Mussina .25 .60
71 Kevin Orie .15 .40
72 Matt Williams .15 .40
73 Bobby Bonilla .15 .40
74 Ruben Rivera .15 .40
75 Jason Giambi .15 .40
76 Todd Walker .15 .40
77 Tino Martinez .25 .60
78 Matt Morris .15 .40
79 Fernando Tatis .15 .40
80 Todd Greene .15 .40
81 Fred McGriff .25 .60
82 Brady Anderson .15 .40
83 Mark Kotsay .15 .40
84 Raul Mondesi .15 .40
85 Moises Alou .15 .40
86 Roger Clemens .75 2.00
87 Wilton Guerrero .15 .40
88 Shannon Stewart .15 .40
89 Chan Ho Park .15 .40
90 Carlos Delgado .15 .40
91 Jose Cruz Jr. .15 .40
92 Shawn Green .15 .40
93 Robin Ventura .15 .40
94 Reggie Sanders .15 .40
95 Orel Hershiser .15 .40
96 Dante Bichette .15 .40
97 Charles Johnson .15 .40
98 Pedro Martinez .25 .60
99 Mariano Rivera .40 1.00
100 Joe Randa .15 .40
101 Jeff Kent .15 .40
102 Jay Buhner .15 .40
103 Brian Jordan .15 .40
104 Jason Kendall .15 .40
105 Scott Spiezio .15 .40
106 Desi Relaford .15 .40
107 Bernard Gilkey .15 .40
108 Manny Ramirez .25 .60
109 Tony Clark .15 .40
110 Eric Young .15 .40
111 Johnny Damon .25 .60
112 Glendon Rusch .15 .40
113 Ben Grieve .15 .40
114 Homer Bush .15 .40
115 Miguel Tejada .40 1.00
116 Lou Collier .15 .40
117 Derrek Lee .25 .60
118 Jacob Cruz .15 .40
119 Raul Ibanez .15 .40
120 Ryan McGuire .15 .40
121 Antone Williamson .15 .40
122 Abraham Nunez .15 .40
123 Jeff Abbott .15 .40
124 Brett Tomko .15 .40
125 Richie Sexson .15 .40
126 Todd Helton .25 .60
127 Juan Encarnacion .15 .40
128 Richard Hidalgo .15 .40
129 Paul Konerko .15 .40
130 Brad Fullmer .15 .40
131 Jeremi Gonzalez .15 .40
132 Jaret Wright .15 .40
133 Derek Jeter IT .50 1.25
134 Frank Thomas IT .25 .60
135 Nomar Garciaparra IT .40 1.00
136 Kenny Lofton IT .15 .40
137 Jeff Bagwell IT .15 .40
138 Todd Hundley IT .15 .40
139 Alex Rodriguez IT .40 1.00
140 Ken Griffey Jr. IT .50 1.25
141 Sammy Sosa IT .25 .60
142 Greg Maddux IT .40 1.00
143 Albert Belle IT .15 .40
144 Cal Ripken IT .60 1.50
145 Mark McGwire IT .50 1.25
146 Chipper Jones IT .25 .60
147 Charles Johnson IT .15 .40
148 Ken Griffey Jr. CL .50 1.25
149 Jose Cruz Jr. CL .15 .40
150 Larry Walker CL .15 .40

1998 Pinnacle Inside Club Edition

*STARS: 2.5X TO 6X BASIC CARDS
STATED ODDS 1:7

1998 Pinnacle Inside Diamond Edition

*STARS: 8X TO 20X BASIC CARDS
STATED ODDS 1:67

1998 Pinnacle Inside Behind the Numbers

COMPLETE SET (20) 40.00 100.00
STATED ODDS 1:23
1 Ken Griffey Jr. 5.00 12.00
2 Cal Ripken 8.00 20.00
3 Alex Rodriguez 3.00 8.00
4 Jose Cruz Jr. 1.00 2.50
5 Mike Piazza 2.50 6.00
6 Nomar Garciaparra 1.50 4.00
7 Scott Rolen 1.50 4.00
8 Andruw Jones 1.00 2.50
9 Frank Thomas 2.50 6.00
10 Mark McGwire 4.00 10.00
11 Ivan Rodriguez 1.50 4.00
12 Greg Maddux 3.00 8.00
13 Roger Clemens 3.00 8.00
14 Derek Jeter 6.00 15.00
15 Tony Gwynn 2.50 6.00
16 Ben Grieve 1.00 2.50
17 Jeff Bagwell 1.50 4.00
18 Chipper Jones 2.50 6.00
19 Hideo Nomo 2.50 6.00
20 Sandy Alomar Jr. 1.00 2.50

1998 Pinnacle Inside Cans

COMPLETE SET (23) 10.00 25.00
*GOLD CANS: 2.5X TO 6X BASIC CAN
GOLD CAN STATED ODDS 1:24 HOBBY
1 Roger Clemens .75 2.00
2 Jose Cruz Jr. .15 .40
3 Nomar Garciaparra ROY .60 1.50
4 Juan Gonzalez .15 .40
5 Ben Grieve .15 .40
6 Ken Griffey Jr. .75 2.00
7 Vladimir Guerrero .40 1.00
8 Tony Gwynn .50 1.25
9 Derek Jeter 1.00 2.50
10 Andruw Jones .25 .60
11 Chipper Jones .40 1.00
12 Greg Maddux .60 1.50
13 Mark McGwire 1.00 2.50
14 Hideo Nomo .40 1.00
15 Mike Piazza .60 1.50
16 Cal Ripken 1.25 3.00
17 Alex Rodriguez .60 1.50
18 Scott Rolen ROY .25 .60
19 Frank Thomas .40 1.00
20 Larry Walker MVP .15 .40
21 Arizona Diamondbacks .15 .40
22 Florida Marlins Champs .15 .40
23 Tampa Bay Devil Rays .15 .40

1998 Pinnacle Inside Stand-Up Guys Samples

1AB Piazza 12.00 30.00
Griffey
Gwynn
Ripken
1CD Griffey 12.00 30.00
Gwynn
Ripken
Piazza
2AB Nomar 5.00 12.00
Andruw
Rolen
A.Rod
2CD Andruw 5.00 12.00
Rolen
A.Rod
Nomar
3AB Chipper 5.00 12.00
Andruw
Lopez
Maddux
3CD Andruw 5.00 12.00
Lopez
Maddux
Chipper
4AB A.Rod 8.00 20.00
Buhner
Griffey
R.John
4CD Buhner 8.00 20.00
Griffey
R.John
A.Rod
5AB Mo 6.00 15.00
F.Thomas
McGw
Bagw
5CD F.Thomas 6.00 15.00
McGw
Bagw
Mo
6AB Larkin 10.00 25.00
Nomar
A.Rod
Jeter
6CD Nomar 10.00 25.00
A.Rod
Jeter
Larkin
7AB Lopez 4.00 10.00
Piazza
C.John
I.Rod
7CD Piazza 4.00 10.00
C.John
I.Rod
Lopez
8AB Rolen 12.00 30.00
Ripken
K.Cam
Chipper
8CD Ripken 12.00 30.00
K.Cam
Chipper
Rolen
9AB Guillen 2.50 6.00
Cruz
Andruw
V.Guer
9CD Cruz 2.50 6.00
Andruw
V.Guer
Guillen
10AB Neifi 2.50 6.00
L.Walker
Burks
Bichette
10CD L.Walker 2.50 6.00
Burks
Bichette
Neifi
11AB M.Ram 4.00 10.00
J.Gonz
V.Guer
Sosa
11CD J.Gonz 4.00 10.00
V.Guer
Sosa
M.Ram
12AB R.John 5.00 12.00
Maddux
Nomo
Clemens
12CD Maddux 5.00 12.00
Nomo
Clemens
R.John
13AB Tatis 1.50 4.00
Grieve
Cruz
Konerko
13CD Grieve 1.50 4.00
Cruz
Konerko
Tatis
14AB Biggio 6.00 15.00
Ryno
Alomar
Knob
14CD Ryno 6.00 15.00
Alomar
Knob
Biggio
15AB Alomar 12.00 30.00
Ripken
Palm
Brady
15CD Ripken 12.00 30.00
Palm
Brady
Alomar
16AB G.And 2.50 6.00
Erstad
Salmon
Edmonds
16CD Erstad 2.50 6.00
Salmon
Edmonds
G.And
17AB Karros 4.00 10.00
Piazza
Mond
Nomo
17CD Piazza 4.00 10.00
Mond
Nomo
Karros
18AB Greer 2.50 6.00
I.Rod
W.Clark
J.Gonz
18CD I.Rod 2.50 6.00
W.Clark
J.Gonz
Greer
19AB Pettitte 10.00 25.00
Jeter
T.Mart
B.Will
19CD Jeter 10.00 25.00
T.Mart
B.Will
Pettitte
20AB B.Will 8.00 20.00
Lofton
Brady
Griffey
20CD Lofton 8.00 20.00
Brady
Griffey
B.Will
21AB R.Hend 6.00 15.00
Molitor
Ryno
Murray
21CD Molitor 6.00 15.00
Ryno
Murray
R.Hend
22AB McGw 6.00 15.00
T.Clark
Bagw
F.Thomas
22CD T.Clark 6.00 15.00
Bagw
F.Thomas
McGw
23AB S.Alom 4.00 10.00
M.Ram
Justice
Thome
23CD M.Ram 4.00 10.00
Justice
Thome
S.Alom
24AB Bichette 6.00 15.00
Bonds
Bagw
Belle
24CD Bonds 6.00 15.00
Bagw
Belle
Bichette
25AB Andruw 8.00 20.00
Griffey
A.Rod
Thomas
25CD Griffey 8.00 20.00
A.Rod
Thomas
Andruw

1998 Pinnacle Inside Stand-Up Guys

COMPLETE SET (50) 12.50 30.00
1AB Piazza .60 1.50
Grif
Gwynn
Ripken
1CD Griff .60 1.50
Gwynn
Rip
Piazza
2AB Nomar .50 1.25
And
Rolen
A.Rod
2CD Andruw .50 1.25
Rolen
ARod
Nomar
3AB Chip .50 1.25
Andruw
Lopez
Madd
3CD Andruw .50 1.25
Lopez
Madd
Chip
4AB A.Rod .60 1.50
Buhner
Grif
R.John
4CD Buhner .60 1.50
Grif
R.John
A.Rod
5AB Mo .75 2.00
Thomas
McGw
Bag
5CD F.Thomas .75 2.00
McGw
Bagw
Mo
6AB Larkin .75 2.00
Nomar
A.Rod
Jeter
6CD Nomar .75 2.00
A.Rod
Jeter
Larkin
7AB Lopez .50 1.25
Piazza
C.John
I.Rod
7CD Piazza .50 1.25
C.John
I.Rod
Lopez
8AB Rolen 1.00 2.50
Ripken
K.Cam
Chip
8CD Ripken 1.00 2.50
K.Cam
Chip
Rolen
9AB Guillen .30 .75
Cruz
Andruw
Vlad
9CD Cruz .30 .75
Andruw
Vlad
Guillen
10AB Neifi .10 .30
L.Walker
Burks
Bich
10CD L.Walker .10 .30
Burks
Bich
Neifi
11AB M.Ram .30 .75
J.Gonz
Vlad
Sosa
11CD J.Gonz .30 .75
Vlad
Sosa
M.Ram
12AB R.John .50 1.25
Madd
Nomo
Clem
12CD Madd .50 1.25
Nomo
Clem
R.John
13AB Tatis .10 .30
Grieve
Cruz
Konerko
13CD Grieve .10 .30
Cruz
Konerko
Tatis
14AB Biggio .20 .50
Ryno
Alomar
Knob
14CD Ryno .20 .50
Alomar
Knob
Biggio
15AB R.Alom 1.00 2.50
Rip
Palm
Brady
15CD Ripken 1.00 2.50
Palm
Brady
Alomar
16AB G.And .10 .30
Erst
Salm
Edmonds
16CD Erstad .10 .30
Salm
Edm
G.And
17AB Karros .50 1.25
Piazza
Mond
Nomo
17CD Piazza .50 1.25
Mond
Nomo
Karros
18AB Greer .20 .50
I.Rod
Clark
J.Gonz
18CD I.Rod .20 .50
Clark
J.Gonz
Greer
19AB Pettitte .75 2.00
Jeter
T.Mart
B.Will
19CD Jeter .75 2.00
T.Mart
B.Will
Pettitte
20AB B.Will .60 1.50
Loft
Brady
Griffey
20CD Lofton .60 1.50
Brady
Griffey
B.Will
21AB R.Hend .10 .30
Molit
Ryno
Murray
21CD Molit .10 .30
Ryno
Murr
Hend
22AB McGw .75 2.00
Clark
Bag
Thomas
22CD Clark .75 2.00
Bag
Thom
McGw
23AB S.Alom .20 .50
Ram
Just
Thome
23CD Manny .20 .50
Just
Thome
Alom
24AB Bich .75 2.00
Bonds
Bagw
Belle
24CD Bonds .75 2.00
Bagw
Belle
Bichette
25AB Andruw .60 1.50
Grif
ARod
Thomas
25CD Grif .60 1.50
ARod
Thomas
And

1997 Pinnacle Mint

The 1997 Pinnacle Mint set was issued in one series totalling 30 cards and was distributed in packs of three cards and two coins for a suggested retail price of $3.99. The challenge was to fit the coins with the die-cut cards that pictured the same player on the minted coin. Two die-cut cards were inserted in each pack. Either one bronze, silver or gold card was also included in each pack. The fronts featured color action player images on a sepia player portrait background and a cut-out area for the matching coin. Ryan Klesko's die cut card was distributed to dealers as a promo. Die cut cards are listed below.

COMP.DIE CUT SET (30) 4.00 10.00
TWO DIE CUTS PER PACK
*BRONZE: .75X TO 2X HI COLUMN
*SILVER: 5X TO 12X HI COLUMN
*GOLD: 10X TO 25X HI COLUMN
1 Ken Griffey Jr. .40 1.00
2 Frank Thomas .20 .50
3 Alex Rodriguez .30 .75
4 Cal Ripken .60 1.50
5 Mo Vaughn .07 .20
6 Juan Gonzalez .07 .20
7 Mike Piazza .30 .75
8 Albert Belle .07 .20
9 Chipper Jones .20 .50
10 Andruw Jones .10 .30
11 Greg Maddux .30 .75
12 Hideo Nomo .20 .50
13 Jeff Bagwell .10 .30
14 Manny Ramirez .10 .30
15 Mark McGwire .50 1.25
16 Derek Jeter .50 1.25
17 Sammy Sosa .20 .50
18 Barry Bonds .60 1.50
19 Chuck Knoblauch .07 .20
20 Dante Bichette .07 .20
21 Tony Gwynn .25 .60
22 Ken Caminiti .07 .20
23 Gary Sheffield .07 .20
24 Tim Salmon .10 .30
25 Ivan Rodriguez .10 .30
26 Henry Rodriguez .07 .20
27 Barry Larkin .10 .30
28 Ryan Klesko .07 .20
29 Brian Jordan .07 .20
30 Jay Buhner .07 .20
P28 Ryan Klesko Promo .40 1.00

1997 Pinnacle Mint Gold

*GOLD: 10X TO 25X BASIC CARDS
STATED ODDS 1:48

1997 Pinnacle Mint Silver

COMPLETE SET (30) 100.00 200.00
*SILVER: 5X TO 12X BASIC CARDS
STATED ODDS 1:15

1997 Pinnacle Mint Coins Brass

COMPLETE SET (30) 20.00 50.00
TWO BRASS COINS PER PACK
*NICKEL: 3X TO 8X BASIC BRASS
NICKEL STATED ODDS 1:20
*GOLD PLATED: 8X TO 20X BASIC BRASS
GOLD PLATED STATED ODDS 1:48
*SILVER: 40X TO 100X BASIC BRASS
SILVER STATED ODDS 1:2300
BRASS COINS LISTED BELOW
RAMIREZ ERROR NOT PART OF BASIC SET
1 Ken Griffey Jr. 1.25 3.00
2 Frank Thomas .60 1.50
3 Alex Rodriguez 1.00 2.50
4 Cal Ripken 2.00 5.00
5 Mo Vaughn .25 .60
6 Juan Gonzalez .25 .60
7 Mike Piazza 1.00 2.50
8 Albert Belle .25 .60
9 Chipper Jones .60 1.50
10 Andruw Jones .40 1.00
11 Greg Maddux 1.00 2.50
12 Hideo Nomo .60 1.50
13 Jeff Bagwell .40 1.00
14A Manny Ramirez COR .40 1.00
14B Manny Ramirez ERR .40 1.00
15 Mark McGwire 1.50 4.00
16 Derek Jeter 1.50 4.00
17 Sammy Sosa .60 1.50
18 Barry Bonds 2.00 5.00
19 Chuck Knoblauch .25 .60
20 Dante Bichette .25 .60
21 Tony Gwynn .75 2.00
22 Ken Caminiti .25 .60
23 Gary Sheffield .25 .60
24 Tim Salmon .40 1.00
25 Ivan Rodriguez .40 1.00
26 Henry Rodriguez .25 .60
27 Barry Larkin .40 1.00
28 Ryan Klesko .25 .60
29 Brian Jordan .25 .60
30 Jay Buhner .25 .60
P28 Ryan Klesko Promo 1.25 3.00

1998 Pinnacle Mint Samples

COMPLETE SET (6) 6.00 15.00
12 Greg Maddux 1.00 2.50
14 Mark McGwire 1.25 3.00
17 Mike Piazza 1.00 2.50
18 Cal Ripken 1.50 4.00
22 Frank Thomas .60 1.50
24 Larry Walker .30 .75

1998 Pinnacle Mint

The 1998 Pinnacle Mint set was issued in one series totalling 30 cards and was distributed in packs of three cards and two coins with a suggest retail price of $3.99. The challenge was to fit the coins with the die-cut cards that pictured the same player on the minted coin. Two die-cut cards were inserted one in every hobby pack and one die-cut card in every retail pack. The fronts feature color action player photos with a cut-out area for the matching coin.

COMP.DIE CUT SET (30) 4.00 10.00
STATED 2:1 HOBBY, 1:1 RETAIL
1 Jeff Bagwell .10 .30
2 Albert Belle .07 .20
3 Barry Bonds .60 1.50
4 Tony Clark .07 .20
5 Roger Clemens .40 1.00
6 Juan Gonzalez .07 .20
7 Ken Griffey Jr. .40 1.00
8 Tony Gwynn .25 .60
9 Derek Jeter .50 1.25
10 Randy Johnson .20 .50
11 Chipper Jones .20 .50
12 Greg Maddux .30 .75
13 Tino Martinez .10 .30
14 Mark McGwire .50 1.25
15 Hideo Nomo .20 .50
16 Andy Pettitte .10 .30
17 Mike Piazza .30 .75
18 Cal Ripken .60 1.50
19 Alex Rodriguez .30 .75
20 Ivan Rodriguez .10 .30
21 Sammy Sosa .20 .50
22 Frank Thomas .20 .50
23 Mo Vaughn .07 .20
24 Larry Walker .07 .20
25 Jose Cruz Jr. .07 .20
26 Nomar Garciaparra .30 .75
27 Vladimir Guerrero .20 .50
28 Livan Hernandez .07 .20
29 Andruw Jones .10 .30
30 Scott Rolen .10 .30

1998 Pinnacle Mint Bronze

*BRONZE: .75X TO 2X DIE CUTS
TWO PER HOBBY, ONE PER RETAIL PACK

1998 Pinnacle Mint Gold

*GOLD: 6X TO 15X DIE CUT
STATED ODDS 1:47 HOBBY, 1:71 RETAIL

1998 Pinnacle Mint Silver

*SILVER: 3X TO 8X DIE CUT
STATED ODDS 1:15 HOBBY, 1:23 RETAIL

1998 Pinnacle Mint Coins Brass

COMPLETE SET (30) 25.00 60.00
STATED ODDS 2:1 HOBBY, 1:1 RETAIL
*BRASS AP's: 5X TO 12X BASIC BRASS
BRASS AP RANDOM INSERTS IN PACKS
BRASS AP PRINT RUN 500 SETS
*GOLD PLATE: 10X TO 25X BASIC BRASS
GOLD PLATED ODDS 1:199 HOBBY/RETAIL
*GOLD PLATED AP's: 15X TO 40X BRASS
GOLD PLATED AP RAND.INS.IN PACKS
GOLD PLATED AP PRINT RUN 100 SETS
*NICKEL: 3X TO 8X BASIC BRASS
NICKEL ODDS 1:41 HOBBY/RETAIL
*NICKEL AP: 8X TO 20X BASIC BRASS
NICKEL AP ODDS 1:48 HOBBY, 1:97 RETAIL
NICKEL AP PRINT RUN 250 SETS
*SOLID SILVER: 12.5X TO 30X BASIC BRASS
SOLID SILVER 1:288 HOBBY, 1:960 RETAIL
1 Jeff Bagwell .50 1.25
2 Albert Belle .30 .75
3 Barry Bonds 1.50 4.00
4 Tony Clark .30 .75
5 Roger Clemens 1.50 4.00
6 Juan Gonzalez .30 .75
7 Ken Griffey Jr. 1.50 4.00
8 Tony Gwynn 1.00 2.50
9 Derek Jeter 2.00 5.00
10 Randy Johnson .75 2.00
11 Chipper Jones .75 2.00
12 Greg Maddux 1.25 3.00
13 Tino Martinez .50 1.25
14 Mark McGwire 2.00 5.00
15 Hideo Nomo .75 2.00
16 Andy Pettitte .50 1.25
17 Mike Piazza 1.25 3.00
18 Cal Ripken 2.50 6.00
19 Alex Rodriguez 1.25 3.00
20 Ivan Rodriguez .50 1.25
21 Sammy Sosa .75 2.00
22 Frank Thomas .75 2.00
23 Mo Vaughn .30 .75
24 Larry Walker .30 .75
25 Jose Cruz Jr. .30 .75
26 Nomar Garciaparra 1.25 3.00
27 Vladimir Guerrero .75 2.00
28 Livan Hernandez .30 .75
29 Andruw Jones .50 1.25
30 Scott Rolen .50 1.25

1998 Pinnacle Mint Coins Brass Samples

COMPLETE SET (3) 4.00 10.00
12 Greg Maddux 1.25 3.00
14 Mark McGwire 2.00 5.00
22 Frank Thomas 1.25 3.00

1998 Pinnacle Mint Gems

COMPLETE SET (6) 10.00 25.00
STATED ODDS 1:31 HOBBY, 1:47 RETAIL
GEM COINS ODDS 1:31 HOBBY
1 Ken Griffey Jr. 3.00 8.00
2 Larry Walker .60 1.50
3 Roger Clemens 3.00 8.00
4 Pedro Martinez 1.50 4.00
5 Nomar Garciaparra 2.50 6.00
6 Scott Rolen 1.00 2.50

1998 Pinnacle Mint Benefactor Mail-Away

This one card set was available through a mail-order offer on 1998 Pinnacle Mint packs. The card could be ordered for $9.95 plus a $4 shipping and handling charge.

1 Chipper Jones 8.00 20.00

1998 Pinnacle Performers

The 1998 Pinnacle Performers set was issued in one series totalling 150 cards. The eight-card packs retailed for $1.99 each. The set contains the topical subset: Far and Away (138-147) and Checklists (148-150).

COMPLETE SET (150) 8.00 20.00
1 Ken Griffey Jr. .40 1.00
2 Frank Thomas .20 .50
3 Cal Ripken .60 1.50
4 Alex Rodriguez .30 .75
5 Greg Maddux .30 .75
6 Mike Piazza .30 .75
7 Chipper Jones .20 .50
8 Tony Gwynn .25 .60

9 Derek Jeter .50 1.25
10 Jeff Bagwell .10 .30
11 Juan Gonzalez .07 .20
12 Nomar Garciaparra .30 .75
13 Andruw Jones .10 .30
14 Hideo Nomo .20 .50
15 Roger Clemens .40 1.00
16 Mark McGwire .50 1.25
17 Scott Rolen .10 .30
18 Vladimir Guerrero .20 .50
19 Barry Bonds .60 1.50
20 Darin Erstad .07 .20
21 Albert Belle .07 .20
22 Kenny Lofton .07 .20
23 Mo Vaughn .07 .20
24 Tony Clark .07 .20
25 Ivan Rodriguez .10 .30
26 Jose Cruz Jr. .07 .20
27 Larry Walker .07 .20
28 Jaret Wright .07 .20
29 Andy Pettitte .10 .30
30 Roberto Alomar .10 .30
31 Randy Johnson .20 .50
32 Manny Ramirez .10 .30
33 Paul Molitor .07 .20
34 Mike Mussina .10 .30
35 Jim Thome .10 .30
36 Tino Martinez .10 .30
37 Gary Sheffield .07 .20
38 Chuck Knoblauch .07 .20
39 Bernie Williams .10 .30
40 Tim Salmon .10 .30
41 Sammy Sosa .20 .50
42 Wade Boggs .10 .30
43 Will Clark .10 .30
44 Andres Galarraga .07 .20
45 Raul Mondesi .07 .20
46 Rickey Henderson .20 .50
47 Jose Canseco .10 .30
48 Pedro Martinez .10 .30
49 Jay Buhner .07 .20
50 Ryan Klesko .07 .20
51 Barry Larkin .10 .30
52 Charles Johnson .07 .20
53 Tom Glavine .10 .30
54 Edgar Martinez .10 .30
55 Fred McGriff .10 .30
56 Moises Alou .07 .20
57 Dante Bichette .07 .20
58 Jim Edmonds .07 .20
59 Mark Grace .10 .30
60 Chan Ho Park .07 .20
61 Justin Thompson .07 .20
62 John Smoltz .10 .30
63 Craig Biggio .10 .30
64 Ken Caminiti .07 .20
65 Richard Hidalgo .07 .20
66 Carlos Delgado .07 .20
67 David Justice .07 .20
68 J.T. Snow .07 .20
69 Jason Giambi .07 .20
70 Garret Anderson .07 .20
71 Rondell White .07 .20
72 Matt Williams .07 .20
73 Brady Anderson .07 .20
74 Eric Karros .07 .20
75 Javier Lopez .07 .20
76 Pat Hentgen .07 .20
77 Todd Hundley .07 .20
78 Ray Lankford .07 .20
79 Denny Neagle .07 .20
80 Sandy Alomar Jr. .07 .20
81 Jason Kendall .07 .20
82 Omar Vizquel .10 .30
83 Kevin Brown .10 .30
84 Kevin Appier .07 .20
85 Al Martin .07 .20
86 Rusty Greer .07 .20
87 Bobby Bonilla .07 .20
88 Shawn Estes .07 .20
89 Rafael Palmeiro .10 .30
90 Edgar Renteria .07 .20
91 Alan Benes .07 .20
92 Bobby Higginson .07 .20
93 Mark Grudzielanek .07 .20
94 Jose Guillen .07 .20
95 Neifi Perez .07 .20
96 Jeff Abbott .07 .20
97 Todd Walker .07 .20
98 Eric Young .07 .20
99 Brett Tomko .07 .20
100 Mike Cameron .07 .20
101 Karim Garcia .07 .20
102 Brian Jordan .07 .20
103 Jeff Suppan .07 .20
104 Robin Ventura .07 .20
105 Henry Rodriguez .07 .20
106 Shannon Stewart .07 .20
107 Kevin Orie .07 .20
108 Bartolo Colon .07 .20
109 Bob Abreu .07 .20
110 Vinny Castilla .07 .20
111 Livan Hernandez .07 .20
112 Derrek Lee .10 .30
113 Mark Kotsay .07 .20
114 Todd Greene .07 .20
115 Edgardo Alfonzo .07 .20
116 A.J. Hinch .07 .20
117 Paul Konerko .07 .20
118 Todd Helton .10 .30
119 Miguel Tejada .20 .50
120 Fernando Tatis .07 .20
121 Ben Grieve .07 .20
122 Travis Lee .07 .20
123 Kerry Wood .08 .25
124 Eli Marrero .07 .20
125 David Ortiz .25 .60
126 Juan Encarnacion .07 .20
127 Brad Fullmer .07 .20
128 Richie Sexson .07 .20
129 Aaron Boone .07 .20
130 Enrique Wilson .07 .20
131 Javier Valentin .07 .20
132 Abraham Nunez .07 .20
133 Ricky Ledee .07 .20
134 Carl Pavano .07 .20
135 Bobby Estalella .07 .20
136 Homer Bush .07 .20
137 Brian Rose .07 .20
138 Ken Griffey Jr. FA .25 .60
139 Frank Thomas FA .10 .30
140 Cal Ripken FA .30 .75
141 Alex Rodriguez FA .20 .50
142 Greg Maddux FA .20 .50
143 Chipper Jones FA .10 .30
144 Mike Piazza FA .20 .50
145 Tony Gwynn FA .10 .30
146 Derek Jeter FA .25 .60
147 Jeff Bagwell FA .07 .20
148 Checklist .07 .20
149 Checklist .07 .20
150 Checklist .07 .20

1998 Pinnacle Performers Peak Performers

COMPLETE SET (150) 100.00 200.00
*STARS: 3X TO 8X BASIC CARDS
STATED ODDS 1:7

1998 Pinnacle Performers Big Bang Samples

COMPLETE SET (20) 75.00 150.00
1 Ken Griffey Jr. 10.00 25.00
2 Frank Thomas 4.00 8.00
3 Mike Piazza 6.00 15.00
4 Chipper Jones 5.00 12.00
5 Alex Rodriguez 6.00 15.00
6 Nomar Garciaparra 6.00 15.00
7 Jeff Bagwell 2.50 6.00
8 Cal Ripken 10.00 25.00
9 Albert Belle 1.25 3.00
10 Mark McGwire 8.00 20.00
11 Juan Gonzalez 2.00 5.00
12 Larry Walker 1.25 3.00
13 Tino Martinez 1.25 3.00
14 Jim Thome 2.00 5.00
15 Manny Ramirez 2.50 6.00
16 Barry Bonds 5.00 12.00
17 Mo Vaughn 1.25 3.00
18 Jose Cruz Jr. 1.25 3.00
19 Tony Clark 1.25 3.00
20 Andruw Jones 2.00 5.00

1998 Pinnacle Performers Big Bang

COMPLETE SET (20) 75.00 150.00
STATED ODDS 1:45
1 Ken Griffey Jr. 6.00 15.00
2 Frank Thomas 3.00 8.00
3 Mike Piazza 5.00 12.00
4 Chipper Jones 3.00 8.00
5 Alex Rodriguez 5.00 12.00
6 Nomar Garciaparra 5.00 12.00
7 Jeff Bagwell 2.00 5.00
8 Cal Ripken 10.00 25.00
9 Albert Belle 1.25 3.00
10 Mark McGwire 8.00 20.00
11 Juan Gonzalez 1.25 3.00
12 Larry Walker 1.25 3.00
13 Tino Martinez 2.00 5.00
14 Jim Thome 2.00 5.00
15 Manny Ramirez 2.00 5.00
16 Barry Bonds 10.00 25.00
17 Mo Vaughn 1.25 3.00
18 Jose Cruz Jr. 1.25 3.00
19 Tony Clark 1.25 3.00
20 Andruw Jones 2.00 5.00

1998 Pinnacle Performers Big Bang Seasonal Outburst

RANDOM INSERTS IN PACKS
PRINT RUNS B/WN 17-56 COPIES PER
*NON-SERIAL #'d: .2X TO .5X OUTBURST
NNO CARDS NOT INTENDED FOR PUBLIC
NO PRICING ON QTY OF 25 OR LESS
1 Ken Griffey Jr./56 15.00 40.00
2 Frank Thomas/35 8.00 20.00
3 Mike Piazza/40 12.50 30.00
4 Chipper Jones/21
5 Alex Rodriguez/23
6 Nomar Garciaparra/30 12.50 30.00
7 Jeff Bagwell/43 5.00 12.00
8 Cal Ripken/17
9 Albert Belle/30 4.00 10.00
10 Mark McGwire/58 20.00 50.00
11 Juan Gonzalez/42 4.00 10.00
12 Larry Walker/49 4.00 10.00
13 Tino Martinez/44 5.00 12.00
14 Jim Thome/40 5.00 12.00
15 Manny Ramirez/26 5.00 12.00
16 Barry Bonds/40 20.00 50.00
17 Mo Vaughn/35 4.00 10.00
18 Jose Cruz Jr./26 4.00 10.00
19 Tony Clark/32 4.00 10.00
20 Andruw Jones/18

1998 Pinnacle Performers Launching Pad

COMPLETE SET (20) 25.00 60.00
STATED ODDS 1:9
1 Ben Grieve .40 1.00
2 Ken Griffey Jr. 2.00 5.00
3 Derek Jeter 2.50 6.00
4 Frank Thomas 1.00 2.50
5 Travis Lee .40 1.00
6 Vladimir Guerrero 1.00 2.50
7 Tony Gwynn 1.25 3.00
8 Jose Cruz Jr. .40 1.00
9 Cal Ripken 3.00 8.00
10 Chipper Jones 1.00 2.50
11 Scott Rolen .60 1.50
12 Andruw Jones .60 1.50
13 Ivan Rodriguez .60 1.50
14 Todd Helton .60 1.50
15 Nomar Garciaparra 1.50 4.00
16 Mark McGwire 2.50 6.00
17 Gary Sheffield .40 1.00
18 Bernie Williams .60 1.50
19 Alex Rodriguez 1.50 4.00
20 Mike Piazza 1.50 4.00

1998 Pinnacle Performers Power Trip

COMPLETE SET (10) 15.00 40.00
STATED ODDS 1:21
1 Frank Thomas 1.25 3.00
2 Alex Rodriguez 2.00 5.00
3 Nomar Garciaparra 2.00 5.00
4 Jeff Bagwell .75 2.00
5 Cal Ripken 4.00 10.00
6 Mike Piazza 2.00 5.00
7 Chipper Jones 1.25 3.00
8 Ken Griffey Jr. 2.50 6.00
9 Mark McGwire 3.00 8.00
10 Juan Gonzalez .50 1.25

1998 Pinnacle Performers Swing for the Fences

COMPLETE SET (50) 15.00 40.00
STATED ODDS 1:2
1 Brady Anderson .20 .50
2 Albert Belle .20 .50
3 Jay Buhner .20 .50
4 Jose Canseco .30 .75
5 Tony Clark .20 .50
6 Jose Cruz Jr. .20 .50
7 Jim Edmonds .20 .50
8 Cecil Fielder .20 .50
9 Travis Fryman .20 .50
10 Nomar Garciaparra .75 2.00
11 Juan Gonzalez .20 .50
12 Ken Griffey Jr. 1.00 2.50
13 David Justice .20 .50
14 Travis Lee .20 .50
15 Edgar Martinez .30 .75
16 Tino Martinez .30 .75
17 Rafael Palmeiro .30 .75
18 Manny Ramirez .30 .75
19 Cal Ripken 1.50 4.00
20 Alex Rodriguez .75 2.00
21 Tim Salmon .30 .75
22 Frank Thomas .50 1.25
23 Jim Thome .30 .75
24 Mo Vaughn .20 .50
25 Bernie Williams .30 .75
26 Fred McGriff .30 .75
27 Jeff Bagwell .30 .75
28 Dante Bichette .20 .50
29 Barry Bonds 1.50 4.00
30 Ellis Burks .20 .50
31 Ken Caminiti .20 .50
32 Vinny Castilla .20 .50
33 Andres Galarraga .20 .50
34 Vladimir Guerrero .50 1.25
35 Todd Helton .30 .75
36 Todd Hundley .20 .50
37 Andruw Jones .30 .75
38 Chipper Jones .50 1.25
39 Eric Karros .20 .50
40 Ryan Klesko .20 .50
41 Ray Lankford .20 .50
42 Mark McGwire 1.25 3.00
43 Raul Mondesi .20 .50
44 Mike Piazza .75 2.00
45 Scott Rolen .30 .75
46 Gary Sheffield .20 .50
47 Sammy Sosa .50 1.25
48 Larry Walker .20 .50
49 Matt Williams .20 .50
50 Wild Card .20 .50

1998 Pinnacle Performers Swing for the Fences Shop Exchange

COMPLETE SET (12) 3.00 8.00
1 Jeff Bagwell .20 .50
2 Barry Bonds .40 1.00
3 Nomar Garciaparra .40 1.00
4 Juan Gonzalez .30 .75
5 Ken Griffey Jr. .60 1.50
6 Chipper Jones .30 .75
7 Mark McGwire .60 1.50
8 Mike Piazza .40 1.00
9 Cal Ripken .75 2.00
10 Alex Rodriguez .40 1.00
11 Scott Rolen .15 .40
12 Frank Thomas .25 .60

1998 Pinnacle Plus Samples

COMPLETE SET (6) 5.00 12.00
8 Nomar Garciaparra 1.25 3.00
9 Ken Griffey Jr. 1.50 4.00
24 Frank Thomas .75 2.00
33 Mike Piazza 1.25 3.00
56 Chipper Jones 1.00 2.50
72 Larry Walker .40 1.00

1998 Pinnacle Plus

The 1998 Pinnacle Plus set was issued in one series totalling 200 standard size cards. The 10-card packs retailed for $2.99 each. The set contains the subsets: The Naturals (183-194) and Field of Vision (195-200). The Nolan Ryan AU Ball is supposed to not have been redeemed.

COMPLETE SET (200) 10.00 25.00
RYAN BALL ISSUED AFTER BANKRUPTCY
1 Roberto Alomar .15 .40
2 Sandy Alomar Jr. .08 .25
3 Brady Anderson .08 .25
4 Albert Belle .08 .25
5 Jeff Cirillo .08 .25
6 Roger Clemens .50 1.25
7 David Cone .08 .25
8 Nomar Garciaparra .40 1.00
9 Ken Griffey Jr. .50 1.25
10 Jason Dickson .08 .25
11 Edgar Martinez .15 .40
12 Tino Martinez .15 .40
13 Randy Johnson .25 .60
14 Mark McGwire .60 1.50
15 David Justice .08 .25
16 Mike Mussina .15 .40
17 Chuck Knoblauch .08 .25
18 Joey Cora .08 .25
19 Pat Hentgen .08 .25
20 Randy Myers .08 .25
21 Cal Ripken .75 2.00
22 Mariano Rivera .25 .60
23 Jose Rosado .08 .25
24 Frank Thomas .25 .60
25 Alex Rodriguez .40 1.00
26 Justin Thompson .08 .25
27 Ivan Rodriguez .15 .40
28 Bernie Williams .15 .40
29 Pedro Martinez .15 .40
30 Tony Clark .08 .25
31 Garret Anderson .08 .25
32 Travis Fryman .08 .25
33 Mike Piazza .40 1.00
34 Carl Pavano .08 .25
35 Kevin Millwood RC .40 1.00
36 Miguel Tejada .25 .60
37 Willie Blair .08 .25
38 Devon White .08 .25
39 Andres Galarraga .08 .25
40 Barry Larkin .15 .40
41 Al Leiter .08 .25
42 Moises Alou .08 .25
43 Eric Young .08 .25
44 John Jaha .08 .25
45 Bernard Gilkey .08 .25
46 Freddy Garcia .08 .25
47 Ruben Rivera .08 .25
48 Robb Nen .08 .25
49 Ray Lankford .08 .25
50 Kenny Lofton .08 .25
51 Joe Carter .08 .25
52 Jason McDonald .08 .25
53 Quinton McCracken .08 .25
54 Kerry Wood .10 .30
55 Mike Lansing .08 .25
56 Chipper Jones .25 .60
57 Barry Bonds .60 1.50
58 Brad Fullmer .08 .25
59 Jeff Bagwell .15 .40
60 Rondell White .08 .25
61 Geronimo Berroa .08 .25
62 Magglio Ordonez RC .60 1.50
63 Dwight Gooden .08 .25
64 Brian Hunter .08 .25
65 Todd Walker .08 .25
66 Frank Catalanotto RC .25 .60
67 Tony Saunders .08 .25
68 Travis Lee .08 .25
69 Michael Tucker .08 .25
70 Reggie Sanders .08 .25
71 Derrek Lee .15 .40
72 Larry Walker .08 .25
73 Marquis Grissom .08 .25
74 Craig Biggio .15 .40
75 Kevin Brown .15 .40
76 J.T. Snow .08 .25
77 Eric Davis .08 .25
78 Jeff Abbott .08 .25
79 Jermaine Dye .08 .25
80 Otis Nixon .08 .25
81 Curt Schilling .08 .25
82 Enrique Wilson .08 .25
83 Tony Gwynn .30 .75
84 Orlando Cabrera .08 .25
85 Ramon Martinez .08 .25
86 Greg Vaughn .08 .25
87 Alan Benes .08 .25
88 Dennis Eckersley .08 .25
89 Jim Thome .15 .40
90 Juan Encarnacion .08 .25
91 Jeff King .08 .25
92 Shannon Stewart .08 .25
93 Roberto Hernandez .08 .25
94 Raul Ibanez .08 .25
95 Darryl Kile .08 .25
96 Charles Johnson .08 .25
97 Rich Becker .08 .25
98 Hal Morris .08 .25
99 Ismael Valdes .08 .25
100 Orel Hershiser .08 .25
101 Mo Vaughn .08 .25
102 Aaron Boone .08 .25
103 Jeff Conine .08 .25
104 Paul O'Neill .15 .40
105 Tom Candiotti .08 .25
106 Wilson Alvarez .08 .25
107 Mike Stanley .08 .25
108 Carlos Delgado .08 .25
109 Tony Batista .08 .25
110 Dante Bichette .08 .25
111 Henry Rodriguez .08 .25
112 Karim Garcia .08 .25
113 Shane Reynolds .08 .25
114 Ken Caminiti .08 .25
115 Jose Silva .08 .25
116 Juan Gonzalez .08 .25
117 Brian Jordan .08 .25
118 Jim Leyritz .08 .25
119 Manny Ramirez .15 .40
120 Fred McGriff .15 .40
121 Brooks Kieschnick .08 .25
122 Sean Casey .08 .25
123 John Smoltz .15 .40
124 Rusty Greer .08 .25
125 Cecil Fielder .08 .25
126 Mike Cameron .08 .25
127 Reggie Jefferson .08 .25
128 Bobby Higginson .08 .25
129 Kevin Appier .08 .25
130 Robin Ventura .08 .25
131 Ben Grieve .08 .25
132 Wade Boggs .15 .40
133 Jose Cruz Jr. .08 .25
134 Jeff Suppan .08 .25
135 Vinny Castilla .08 .25
136 Sammy Sosa .25 .60
137 Mark Wohlers .08 .25
138 Jay Bell .08 .25
139 Brett Tomko .08 .25
140 Gary Sheffield .08 .25
141 Tim Salmon .15 .40
142 Jaret Wright .08 .25
143 Kenny Rogers .08 .25
144 Brian Anderson .08 .25
145 Darrin Fletcher .08 .25
146 John Flaherty .08 .25
147 Dmitri Young .08 .25
148 Andruw Jones .15 .40
149 Matt Williams .08 .25
150 Bobby Bonilla .08 .25
151 Mike Hampton .08 .25
152 Al Martin .08 .25
153 Mark Grudzielanek .08 .25
154 Dave Nilsson .08 .25
155 Roger Cedeno .08 .25
156 Greg Maddux .40 1.00
157 Mark Kotsay .08 .25
158 Steve Finley .08 .25
159 Wilson Delgado .08 .25
160 Ron Gant .08 .25
161 Jim Edmonds .08 .25
162 Jeff Blauser .08 .25
163 Dave Burba .08 .25
164 Pedro Astacio .08 .25
165 Livan Hernandez .08 .25
166 Neifi Perez .08 .25
167 Ryan Klesko .08 .25
168 Fernando Tatis .08 .25
169 Richard Hidalgo .08 .25
170 Carlos Perez .08 .25
171 Bob Abreu .08 .25
172 Francisco Cordova .08 .25
173 Todd Helton .15 .40
174 Doug Glanville .08 .25
175 Brian Rose .08 .25
176 Yamil Benitez .08 .25
177 Darin Erstad .08 .25
178 Scott Rolen .15 .40
179 John Wetteland .08 .25
180 Paul Sorrento .08 .25
181 Walt Weiss .08 .25
182 Vladimir Guerrero .25 .60
183 Ken Griffey Jr. NAT .30 .75
184 Alex Rodriguez NAT .25 .60
185 Cal Ripken NAT .40 1.00
186 Frank Thomas NAT .15 .40
187 Chipper Jones NAT .15 .40
188 Hideo Nomo NAT .15 .40
189 Nomar Garciaparra NAT .25 .60
190 Mike Piazza NAT .25 .60
191 Greg Maddux NAT .25 .60
192 Tony Gwynn NAT .15 .40
193 Mark McGwire NAT .30 .75
194 Roger Clemens NAT .25 .60
195 Mike Piazza FV .25 .60
196 Mark McGwire FV .30 .75
197 Chipper Jones FV .15 .40
198 Larry Walker FV .08 .25
199 Hideo Nomo FV .15 .40
200 Barry Bonds FV .30 .75

1998 Pinnacle Plus Artist's Proofs

COMPLETE SET (60) 300.00 600.00
STATED ODDS 1:35
AP1 Roberto Alomar 3.00 8.00
AP2 Albert Belle 2.00 5.00
AP3 Roger Clemens 10.00 25.00
AP4 Nomar Garciaparra 8.00 20.00
AP5 Ken Griffey Jr. 10.00 25.00
AP6 Tino Martinez 3.00 8.00
AP7 Randy Johnson 5.00 12.00
AP8 Mark McGwire 12.50 30.00
AP9 David Justice 2.00 5.00
AP10 Chuck Knoblauch 2.00 5.00
AP11 Cal Ripken 15.00 40.00
AP12 Frank Thomas 5.00 12.00
AP13 Alex Rodriguez 8.00 20.00
AP14 Ivan Rodriguez 3.00 8.00
AP15 Bernie Williams 3.00 8.00
AP16 Pedro Martinez 3.00 8.00
AP17 Tony Clark 2.00 5.00
AP18 Mike Piazza 8.00 20.00
AP19 Miguel Tejada 4.00 10.00
AP20 Andres Galarraga 2.00 5.00
AP21 Barry Larkin 3.00 8.00
AP22 Kenny Lofton 2.00 5.00
AP23 Chipper Jones 5.00 12.00
AP24 Barry Bonds 12.50 30.00
AP25 Brad Fullmer 2.00 5.00
AP26 Jeff Bagwell 3.00 8.00
AP27 Todd Walker 2.00 5.00
AP28 Travis Lee 1.50 4.00
AP29 Larry Walker 2.00 5.00
AP30 Craig Biggio 3.00 8.00
AP31 Tony Gwynn 6.00 15.00
AP32 Jim Thome 3.00 8.00
AP33 Juan Encarnacion 2.00 5.00
AP34 Mo Vaughn 2.00 5.00
AP35 Karim Garcia 2.00 5.00
AP36 Ken Caminiti 2.00 5.00
AP37 Juan Gonzalez 2.00 5.00
AP38 Manny Ramirez 3.00 8.00
AP39 Fred McGriff 3.00 8.00
AP40 Rusty Greer 2.00 5.00
AP41 Bobby Higginson 2.00 5.00
AP42 Ben Grieve 2.00 5.00
AP43 Wade Boggs 3.00 8.00
AP44 Jose Cruz Jr. 1.50 4.00
AP45 Sammy Sosa 5.00 12.00
AP46 Gary Sheffield 2.00 5.00
AP47 Tim Salmon 3.00 8.00
AP48 Jaret Wright 2.00 5.00
AP49 Andruw Jones 3.00 8.00
AP50 Matt Williams 2.00 5.00
AP51 Greg Maddux 8.00 20.00
AP52 Jim Edmonds 2.00 5.00
AP53 Livan Hernandez 2.00 5.00
AP54 Neifi Perez 2.00 5.00
AP55 Fernando Tatis 1.50 4.00
AP56 Richard Hidalgo 2.00 5.00
AP57 Todd Helton 3.00 8.00
AP58 Darin Erstad 2.00 5.00
AP59 Scott Rolen 3.00 8.00
AP60 Vladimir Guerrero 5.00 12.00

1998 Pinnacle Plus Gold Artist's Proofs

*STARS: 12.5X TO 30X BASIC CARDS
RANDOM INSERTS IN PACKS
STATED PRINT RUN 100 SERIAL #'d SETS

1998 Pinnacle Plus All-Star Epix

COMPLETE SET (24) 30.00 80.00
STATED ODDS 1:21
CARDS 1-12 DISTRIBUTED IN SCORE R/T
CARDS 13-24 DISTRIBUTED IN PIN.PLUS
ONLY ORANGE CARDS LISTED BELOW!
USE MULTIPLIERS FOR EMERALD/PURPLE
1 Ken Griffey Jr. MOM 2.50 6.00
2 Juan Gonzalez MOM .50 1.25
3 Jeff Bagwell MOM .75 2.00
4 Ivan Rodriguez MOM .75 2.00
5 Nomar Garciaparra MOM 2.00 5.00
6 Ryne Sandberg MOM 2.50 6.00
7 Frank Thomas MOM 1.25 3.00
8 Derek Jeter MOM 4.00 10.00
9 Tony Gwynn MOM 1.50 4.00
10 Albert Belle MOM .50 1.25
11 Scott Rolen MOM .75 2.00
12 Barry Larkin MOM .75 2.00
13 Alex Rodriguez MOM 2.00 5.00
14 Cal Ripken MOM 4.00 10.00
15 Chipper Jones MOM 1.25 3.00
16 Roger Clemens MOM 2.50 6.00
17 Mo Vaughn MOM .50 1.25
18 Mark McGwire MOM 3.00 8.00
19 Mike Piazza MOM 2.00 5.00
20 Andruw Jones MOM .75 2.00
21 Greg Maddux MOM 2.00 5.00
22 Barry Bonds MOM 3.00 8.00
23 Paul Molitor MOM 1.25 3.00
24 Hideo Nomo MOM 1.25 3.00

1998 Pinnacle Plus Lasting Memories

COMPLETE SET (30) 20.00 50.00
STATED ODDS 1:5
1 Nomar Garciaparra 1.00 2.50
2 Ken Griffey Jr. 1.25 3.00
3 Livan Hernandez .25 .60
4 Hideo Nomo .60 1.50
5 Ben Grieve .25 .60
6 Scott Rolen .40 1.00
7 Roger Clemens 1.25 3.00
8 Cal Ripken 2.00 5.00
9 Mo Vaughn .25 .60
10 Frank Thomas .60 1.50
11 Mark McGwire 1.50 4.00
12 Barry Larkin .40 1.00
13 Matt Williams .25 .60
14 Jose Cruz Jr. .25 .60
15 Andruw Jones .40 1.00
16 Mike Piazza 1.00 2.50
17 Jeff Bagwell .40 1.00
18 Chipper Jones .60 1.50
19 Juan Gonzalez .25 .60
20 Kenny Lofton .25 .60
21 Greg Maddux 1.00 2.50
22 Ivan Rodriguez .40 1.00
23 Alex Rodriguez 1.00 2.50
24 Derek Jeter 2.00 5.00
25 Albert Belle .25 .60
26 Barry Bonds 1.50 4.00
27 Larry Walker .25 .60
28 Sammy Sosa .60 1.50
29 Tony Gwynn .75 2.00
30 Randy Johnson .60 1.50

1998 Pinnacle Plus Piece of the Game

COMPLETE SET (10) 25.00 60.00
STATED ODDS 1:19
1 Ken Griffey Jr. 4.00 10.00
2 Frank Thomas 2.00 5.00
3 Alex Rodriguez 3.00 8.00
4 Chipper Jones 2.00 5.00
5 Cal Ripken 6.00 15.00
6 Mike Piazza 3.00 8.00
7 Greg Maddux 3.00 8.00
8 Juan Gonzalez .75 2.00
9 Nomar Garciaparra 3.00 8.00
10 Larry Walker .75 2.00

1998 Pinnacle Plus Team Pinnacle

COMPLETE SET (15) 125.00 250.00
STATED ODDS 1:71
*GOLD: .75X TO 2X BASIC TEAM PINNACLE
GOLD STATED ODDS 1:199 HOBBY
MIRROR: RANDOM INSERTS IN PACKS
MIRROR STATED PRINT RUN 25 SETS
1 M.Piazza 6.00 15.00
I.Rodriguez
2 M.McGwire 10.00 25.00
M.Vaughn
3 R.Alomar 2.50 6.00
C.Biggio
4 A.Rodriguez 6.00 15.00
B.Larkin
5 C.Ripken 12.50 30.00
C.Jones
6 K.Griffey Jr. 10.00 25.00
L.Walker
7 J.Gonzalez 5.00 12.00
T.Gwynn
8 B.Bonds 10.00 25.00
A.Belle
9 K.Lofton 2.50 6.00
A.Jones
10 T.Martinez 2.50 6.00
J.Bagwell
11 F.Thomas 4.00 10.00
A.Galarraga
12 R.Clemens 6.00 15.00
G.Maddux
13 P.Martinez 2.50 6.00
H.Nomo
14 N.Garciaparra 6.00 15.00
S.Rolen
15 B.Grieve 1.50 4.00
P.Konerko

1998 Pinnacle Plus Yardwork

COMPLETE SET (15) 10.00 25.00
STATED ODDS 1:7
1 Mo Vaughn .30 .75
2 Frank Thomas .75 2.00
3 Albert Belle .30 .75
4 Nomar Garciaparra 1.25 3.00
5 Tony Clark .30 .75
6 Tino Martinez .50 1.25
7 Ken Griffey Jr. 1.50 4.00
8 Juan Gonzalez .30 .75
9 Sammy Sosa .75 2.00
10 Jose Cruz Jr. .30 .75
11 Jeff Bagwell .50 1.25
12 Mike Piazza 1.25 3.00
13 Larry Walker .30 .75
14 Mark McGwire 2.00 5.00
15 Barry Bonds 2.00 5.00

1998 Pinnacle Snapshots Samples

COMPLETE SET (9) 10.00 25.00
1 Greg Maddux 2.00 5.00
2 Cal Ripken 3.00 8.00
3 Travis Lee .50 1.25
4 Brian Jordan .40 1.00
5 Mike Piazza 2.00 5.00
6 Alex Rodriguez 2.00 5.00
7 Edgar Martinez .50 1.25
8 Joey Cora .40 1.00
9 Alvaro Espinoza .40 1.00

1998 Pinnacle Snapshots

These 4" by 6" cards were issued by Pinnacle in eight-card packs which retailed for $1.99. These cards feature a mix of pre-season and early regular season photos and were designed to be sold like "photos" rather than cards. These cards are entered below the way they appear on the original checklist. Please note there are duplications on the various teams. The cards are sequenced by teams using their initials (I.e. Atlanta Braves are AB,)

COMP.ANGELS (18) 3.00 8.00
COMP.BRAVES (18) 6.00 15.00
COMP.D'BACKS (18) 4.00 10.00
COMP.ORIOLES (18) 4.00 10.00
COMP.CUBS (18) 2.50 6.00
COMP.INDIANS (18) 4.00 10.00
COMP.ROCKIES (18) 3.00 8.00
COMP.MARINERS (18) 5.00 12.00
COMP.RANGERS (18) 3.00 8.00
COMP.RED SOX (18) 4.00 10.00
COMP.DODGERS (18) 4.00 10.00
COMP.METS (18) 2.50 5.00
COMP.YANKEES (18) 4.00 10.00
COMP.CARDINALS (18) 4.00 10.00
COMP.DEVIL RAYS (18) 2.50 6.00
AA1 Jason Dickson .08 .25
AA2 Gary DiSarcina .08 .25
AA3 Garret Anderson .30 .75
AA4 Shigetoshi Hasegawa .08 .25
AA5 Ken Hill .08 .25
AA6 Todd Greene .08 .25
AA7 Tim Salmon .20 .50
AA8 Jim Edmonds .40 1.00
AA9 Garret Anderson .30 .75
AA10 Dave Hollins .08 .25
AA11 Todd Greene .08 .25
AA12 Troy Percival .20 .50
AA13 Gary DiSarcina .08 .25
AA14 Cecil Fielder .20 .50
AA15 Darin Erstad .30 .75
AA16 Chuck Finley .20 .50
AA17 Jim Edmonds .40 1.00
AA18 Jason Dickson .08 .25
AB1 Ryan Klesko .20 .50
AB2 Walt Weiss .08 .25
AB3 Tom Glavine .40 1.00
AB4 Randall Simon .08 .25
AB5 John Smoltz .40 1.00
AB6 Chipper Jones 1.00 2.50
AB7 Javier Lopez .20 .50
AB8 Greg Maddux 1.25 3.00
AB9 Andruw Jones .50 1.25
AB10 Michael Tucker .08 .25
AB11 Andres Galarraga .40 1.00
AB12 Andres Galarraga .40 1.00
AB13 Greg Maddux 1.25 3.00
AB14 Wes Helms .08 .25
AB15 Bruce Chen .20 .50
AB16 Denny Neagle .08 .25
AB17 Mark Wohlers .08 .25
AB18 Kevin Millwood 1.50 4.00
AD1 Travis Lee .20 .50
AD2 Matt Williams .30 .75
AD3 Jay Bell .08 .25
AD4 Devon White .20 .50
AD5 Andy Benes .08 .25
AD6 Tony Batista .08 .25
AD7 Jay Bell .08 .25
AD8 Edwin Diaz .08 .25
AD9 Devon White .08 .25
AD10 Bob Wolcott .08 .25
AD11 Karim Garcia .08 .25
AD12 Yamil Benitez .08 .25
AD13 Jorge Fabregas .08 .25
AD14 Jeff Suppan .08 .25
AD15 Ben Ford .08 .25
AD16 Brian Anderson .08 .25
AD17 Travis Lee .20 .50
AD18 Matt Williams .30 .75
BO1 Cal Ripken 2.00 5.00
BO2 Rocky Coppinger .08 .25
BO3 Eric Davis .20 .50
BO4 Chris Hoiles .08 .25
BO5 Mike Mussina .40 1.00
BO6 Joe Carter .20 .50
BO7 Rafael Palmeiro .50 1.25
BO8 B.J. Surhoff .20 .50
BO9 Jimmy Key .20 .50
BO10 Scott Erickson .08 .25
BO11 Armando Benitez .20 .50
BO12 Roberto Alomar .40 1.00
BO13 Cal Ripken 2.00 5.00
BO14 Mike Bordick .08 .25
BO15 Roberto Alomar .40 1.00
BO16 Jeffrey Hammonds .08 .25
BO17 Rafael Palmeiro .40 1.00
BO18 Brady Anderson .20 .50
CC1 Mark Grace .30 .75
CC2 Manny Alexander .08 .25
CC3 Jeremi Gonzalez .08 .25
CC4 Brant Brown .08 .25

CC5 Mark Grace .30 .75
CC6 Lance Johnson .08 .25
CC7 Mark Clark .08 .25
CC8 Kevin Foster .08 .25
CC9 Brant Brown .08 .25
CC10 Kevin Foster .08 .25
CC11 Kevin Tapani .08 .25
CC12 Sammy Sosa .60 1.50
CC13 Sammy Sosa .60 1.50
CC14 Pat Cline .08 .25
CC15 Kevin Orie .08 .25
CC16 Steve Trachsel .08 .25
CC17 Lance Johnson .08 .25
CC18 Robin Jennings .08 .25
CI1 Manny Ramirez .50 1.25
CI2 Travis Fryman .20 .50
CI3 Jaret Wright .08 .25
CI4 Brian Giles .40 1.00
CI5 Bartolo Colon .40 1.00
CI6 Kenny Lofton .30 .75
CI7 David Justice .20 .50
CI8 Brian Giles .40 1.00
CI9 Sandy Alomar Jr. .20 .50
CI10 Jose Mesa .08 .25
CI11 Jim Thome .40 1.00
CI12 Sandy Alomar Jr. .20 .50
CI13 Omar Vizquel .20 .50
CI14 Geronimo Berroa .08 .25
CI15 John Smiley .08 .25
CI16 Chad Ogea .08 .25
CI17 Charles Nagy .08 .25
CI18 Enrique Wilson .08 .25
CR1 Larry Walker .40 1.00
CR2 Pedro Astacio .08 .25
CR3 Jamey Wright .08 .25
CR4 Darryl Kile .20 .50
CR5 Kirt Manwaring .08 .25
CR6 Todd Helton .60 1.50
CR7 Mike Lansing .08 .25
CR8 Neifi Perez .08 .25
CR9 Dante Bichette .20 .50
CR10 Derrick Gibson .08 .25
CR11 Neifi Perez .08 .25
CR12 Darryl Kile .20 .50
CR13 Larry Walker .40 1.00
CR14 Roger Bailey .08 .25
CR15 Ellis Burks .20 .50
CR16 Dante Bichette .20 .50
CR17 Derrick Gibson .08 .25
CR18 Ellis Burks .20 .50
SM1 Alex Rodriguez 1.00 2.50
SM2 Jay Buhner .20 .50
SM3 Russ Davis .08 .25
SM4 Joey Cora .08 .25
SM5 Joey Cora .08 .25
SM6 Jay Buhner .20 .50
SM7 Ken Griffey Jr. 1.25 3.00
SM8 Raul Ibanez .20 .50
SM9 Rich Amaral .08 .25
SM10 Shane Monahan .08 .25
SM11 Alex Rodriguez 1.25 3.00
SM12 Dan Wilson .08 .25
SM13 Bob Wells .08 .25
SM14 Randy Johnson .50 1.25
SM15 Randy Johnson .50 1.25
SM16 Jeff Fassero .08 .25
SM17 Ken Cloude .08 .25
SM18 Edgar Martinez .30 .75
TR1 Ivan Rodriguez .50 1.25
TR2 Fernando Tatis .08 .25
TR3 Danny Patterson .08 .25
TR4 Will Clark .40 1.00
TR5 Kevin Elster .08 .25
TR6 Rusty Greer .20 .50
TR7 Darren Oliver .08 .25
TR8 John Burkett .08 .25
TR9 Tom Goodwin .08 .25
TR10 Roberto Kelly .08 .25
TR11 Aaron Sele .08 .25
TR12 Rick Helling .08 .25
TR13 Mark McLemore .08 .25
TR14 Lee Stevens .08 .25
TR15 John Wetteland .20 .50
TR16 Will Clark .40 1.00
TR17 Juan Gonzalez .40 1.00
TR18 Roger Pavlik .08 .25
BRS1 Tim Naehring .08 .25
BRS2 Brian Rose .08 .25
BRS3 Darren Bragg .08 .25
BRS4 Pedro Martinez .50 1.25
BRS5 Mo Vaughn .20 .50
BRS6 Jim Leyritz .08 .25
BRS7 Troy O'Leary .08 .25
BRS8 Mo Vaughn .20 .50
BRS9 Nomar Garciaparra 1.00 2.50
BRS10 Michael Coleman .08 .25
BRS11 Tom Gordon .20 .50
BRS12 Tim Naehring .08 .25
BRS13 Nomar Garciaparra 1.00 2.50
BRS14 John Valentin .08 .25
BRS15 Steve Avery .08 .25
BRS16 Damon Buford .08 .25
BRS17 Troy O'Leary .08 .25
BRS18 Bret Saberhagen .20 .50
LAD1 Mike Piazza 1.25 3.00
LAD2 Eric Karros .20 .50
LAD3 Raul Mondesi .08 .25
LAD4 Wilton Guerrero .08 .25
LAD5 Darren Dreifort .08 .25
LAD6 Roger Cedeno .08 .25
LAD7 Todd Zeile .20 .50
LAD8 Paul Konerko .40 1.00
LAD9 Todd Hollandsworth .08 .25
LAD10 Ismael Valdes .08 .25
LAD11 Hideo Nomo .40 1.00
LAD12 Ramon Martinez .08 .25
LAD13 Chan Ho Park .08 .25
LAD14 Eric Young .08 .25
LAD15 Dennis Reyes .08 .25
LAD16 Eric Karros .20 .50
LAD17 Mike Piazza 1.25 3.00
LAD18 Raul Mondesi .20 .50
NYM1 Rey Ordonez .08 .25
NYM2 Todd Hundley .20 .50
NYM3 Preston Wilson .20 .50
NYM4 Rich Becker .08 .25
NYM5 Bernard Gilkey .08 .25
NYM6 Rey Ordonez .08 .25
NYM7 Butch Huskey .08 .25
NYM8 Carlos Baerga .20 .50
NYM9 Edgardo Alfonzo .20 .50
NYM10 Bill Pulsipher .08 .25
NYM11 John Franco .20 .50
NYM12 Todd Pratt .08 .25
NYM13 Brian McRae .08 .25
NYM14 Bobby Jones .08 .25
NYM15 John Olerud .20 .50
NYM16 Todd Hundley .20 .50
NYM17 Jay Payton .20 .50
NYM18 Paul Wilson .08 .25
NYY1 Andy Pettitte .40 1.00
NYY2 Darryl Strawberry .20 .50
NYY3 Joe Girardi .08 .25
NYY4 Derek Jeter 2.00 5.00
NYY5 Andy Pettitte .40 1.00
NYY6 Tim Raines .20 .50
NYY7 Mariano Rivera .40 1.00
NYY8 Tino Martinez .20 .50
NYY9 Derek Jeter 2.00 5.00
NYY10 Hideki Irabu .08 .25
NYY11 Tino Martinez .20 .50
NYY12 David Cone .40 1.00
NYY13 Bernie Williams .40 1.00
NYY14 David Cone .40 1.00
NYY15 Bernie Williams .40 1.00
NYY16 Chuck Knoblauch .20 .50
NYY17 Paul O'Neill .20 .50
NYY18 David Wells .20 .50
SLC1 Alan Benes .08 .25
SLC2 Ron Gant .08 .25
SLC3 Donovan Osborne .08 .25
SLC4 Eli Marrero .08 .25
SLC5 Mark McGwire 1.00 2.50
SLC6 Delino DeShields .08 .25
SLC7 Tom Pagnozzi .08 .25
SLC8 Delino DeShields .08 .25
SLC9 Mark McGwire 1.00 2.50
SLC10 Royce Clayton .08 .25
SLC11 Brian Jordan .20 .50
SLC12 Ray Lankford .20 .50
SLC13 Brian Jordan .20 .50
SLC14 Matt Morris .30 .75
SLC15 John Mabry .08 .25
SLC16 Luis Ordaz .08 .25
SLC17 Ron Gant .08 .25
SLC18 Todd Stottlemyre .08 .25
TBDR1 Kevin Stocker .08 .25
TBDR2 Paul Sorrento .08 .25
TBDR3 John Flaherty .08 .25
TBDR4 Wade Boggs .50 1.25
TBDR5 Rich Butler .08 .25
TBDR6 Wilson Alvarez .08 .25
TBDR7 Bubba Trammell .08 .25
TBDR8 Dave Martinez .08 .25
TBDR9 Brooks Kieschnick .08 .25
TBDR10 Tony Saunders .08 .25
TBDR11 Esteban Yan .08 .25
TBDR12 Quinton McCracken .08 .25
TBDR13 Albie Lopez .08 .25
TBDR14 Roberto Hernandez .20 .50
TBDR15 Fred McGriff .30 .75
TBDR16 Bubba Trammell .08 .25
TBDR17 Brooks Kieschnick .08 .25
TBDR18 Fred McGriff .30 .75

1997 Pinnacle Totally Certified Samples

COMPLETE SET (5) 4.00 10.00
5 Jeff Bagwell RED .60 1.50
18 Tony Clark RED .40 1.00
24 Larry Walker BLUE .40 1.00
39 Roger Clemens BLUE .75 2.00
41 Frank Thomas GOLD .60 1.50
53 Ken Griffey Jr. GOLD 2.50 6.00

1997 Pinnacle Totally Certified Platinum Blue

*STARS: .6X TO 1.5X PLAT.RED
*ROOKIES: .4X TO 1X PLAT.RED
STATED ODDS ONE PER PACK
STATED PRINT RUN 1999 SERIAL #'d SETS

1997 Pinnacle Totally Certified Platinum Gold

*STARS: 8X TO 20X PLAT. RED
*ROOKIES: 2.5X TO 6X PLAT.RED
STATED ODDS 1:79 PACKS
STATED PRINT RUN SERIAL #'d 30 SETS

1997 Pinnacle Totally Certified Platinum Red

COMPLETE SET (150) 75.00 150.00
1 Barry Bonds 4.00 10.00
2 Mo Vaughn .60 1.50
3 Matt Williams .60 1.50
4 Ryne Sandberg 2.50 6.00
5 Jeff Bagwell 1.00 2.50
6 Alan Benes .60 1.50
7 John Wetteland .60 1.50
8 Fred McGriff 1.00 2.50
9 Craig Biggio 1.00 2.50
10 Bernie Williams 1.00 2.50
11 Brian Hunter .60 1.50
12 Sandy Alomar Jr. .60 1.50
13 Ray Lankford .60 1.50
14 Ryan Klesko .60 1.50
15 Jermaine Dye .60 1.50
16 Andy Benes .60 1.50
17 Albert Belle .60 1.50
18 Tony Clark .60 1.50
19 Dean Palmer .60 1.50
20 Bernard Gilkey .60 1.50
21 Ken Caminiti .60 1.50
22 Alex Rodriguez 2.50 6.00
23 Tim Salmon 1.00 2.50
24 Larry Walker .60 1.50
25 Barry Larkin 1.00 2.50
26 Mike Piazza 2.50 6.00
27 Brady Anderson .60 1.50
28 Cal Ripken 5.00 12.00
29 Charles Nagy .60 1.50
30 Paul Molitor .60 1.50
31 Darin Erstad .60 1.50
32 Rey Ordonez .60 1.50
33 Wally Joyner .60 1.50
34 David Cone .60 1.50
35 Sammy Sosa 1.50 4.00
36 Dante Bichette .60 1.50
37 Eric Karros .60 1.50
38 Omar Vizquel 1.00 2.50
39 Roger Clemens 3.00 8.00
40 Joe Carter .60 1.50
41 Frank Thomas 1.50 4.00
42 Javy Lopez .60 1.50
43 Mike Mussina 1.00 2.50
44 Gary Sheffield .60 1.50
45 Tony Gwynn 2.00 5.00
46 Jason Kendall .60 1.50
47 Jim Thome 1.00 2.50
48 Andres Galarraga .60 1.50
49 Mark McGwire 4.00 10.00
50 Troy Percival .60 1.50
51 Derek Jeter 4.00 10.00
52 Todd Hollandsworth .60 1.50
53 Ken Griffey Jr. 3.00 8.00
54 Randy Johnson 1.50 4.00
55 Pat Hentgen .60 1.50
56 Rusty Greer .60 1.50
57 John Jaha .60 1.50
58 Kenny Lofton .60 1.50
59 Chipper Jones 1.50 4.00
60 Robb Nen .60 1.50
61 Rafael Palmeiro 1.00 2.50
62 Mariano Rivera 1.50 4.00
63 Hideo Nomo 1.50 4.00
64 Greg Vaughn .60 1.50
65 Ron Gant .60 1.50
66 Eddie Murray 1.50 4.00
67 John Smoltz 1.00 2.50
68 Manny Ramirez 1.00 2.50
69 Juan Gonzalez .60 1.50
70 F.P. Santangelo .60 1.50
71 Moises Alou .60 1.50
72 Alex Ochoa .60 1.50
73 Chuck Knoblauch .60 1.50
74 Raul Mondesi .60 1.50
75 J.T. Snow .60 1.50
76 Rickey Henderson 1.50 4.00
77 Bobby Bonilla .60 1.50
78 Wade Boggs 1.00 2.50
79 Ivan Rodriguez 1.00 2.50
80 Brian Jordan .60 1.50
81 Al Leiter .60 1.50
82 Jay Buhner .60 1.50
83 Greg Maddux 2.50 6.00
84 Edgar Martinez 1.00 2.50
85 Kevin Brown .60 1.50
86 Eric Young .60 1.50
87 Todd Hundley .60 1.50
88 Ellis Burks .60 1.50
89 Marquis Grissom .60 1.50
90 Jose Canseco 1.00 2.50
91 Henry Rodriguez .60 1.50
92 Andy Pettitte 1.00 2.50
93 Mark Grudzielanek .60 1.50
94 Dwight Gooden .60 1.50
95 Roberto Alomar 1.00 2.50
96 Paul Wilson .60 1.50
97 Will Clark 1.00 2.50
98 Rondell White .60 1.50
99 Charles Johnson .60 1.50
100 Jim Edmonds .60 1.50
101 Jason Giambi .60 1.50
102 Billy Wagner .60 1.50
103 Edgar Renteria .60 1.50
104 Johnny Damon 1.00 2.50
105 Jason Isringhausen .60 1.50
106 Andruw Jones 1.00 2.50
107 Jose Guillen .60 1.50
108 Kevin Orie .60 1.50
109 Brian Giles RC 4.00 10.00
110 Danny Patterson .60 1.50
111 Vladimir Guerrero 1.50 4.00
112 Scott Rolen 1.00 2.50
113 Damon Mashore .60 1.50
114 Nomar Garciaparra 2.50 6.00
115 Todd Walker .60 1.50
116 Wilton Guerrero .60 1.50
117 Bob Abreu 1.00 2.50
118 Brooks Kieschnick .60 1.50
119 Pokey Reese .60 1.50
120 Todd Greene .60 1.50
121 Dmitri Young .60 1.50
122 Raul Casanova .60 1.50
123 Glendon Rusch .60 1.50
124 Jason Dickson .60 1.50
125 Jorge Posada 1.00 2.50
126 Rod Myers .60 1.50
127 Bubba Trammell RC .60 1.50
128 Scott Spiezio .60 1.50
129 Hideki Irabu RC .60 1.50
130 Wendell Magee .60 1.50
131 Bartolo Colon .60 1.50
132 Chris Holt .60 1.50
133 Calvin Maduro .60 1.50
134 Ray Montgomery .60 1.50
135 Shannon Stewart .60 1.50
136 Ken Griffey Jr. CERT 2.00 5.00
137 Vladimir Guerrero CERT 1.00 2.50
138 Roger Clemens CERT 1.50 4.00
139 Mark McGwire CERT 2.00 5.00
140 Albert Belle CERT .60 1.50
141 Derek Jeter CERT 2.00 5.00
142 Juan Gonzalez CERT .60 1.50
143 Greg Maddux CERT 1.50 4.00
144 Alex Rodriguez CERT 1.50 4.00
145 Jeff Bagwell CERT .60 1.50
146 Cal Ripken CERT 2.50 6.00
147 Tony Gwynn CERT 1.00 2.50
148 Frank Thomas CERT 1.00 2.50
149 Hideo Nomo CERT .60 1.50
150 Andruw Jones CERT .60 1.50

1997 Pinnacle X-Press

The 1997 Pinnacle X-Press set was issued in one series totalling 150 cards and was distributed in two different kinds of packs. The eight-card packs retailed for $1.99. X-Press Metal Works home plate-shaped retail boxes carried a suggested retail price of $14.99 and contained an eight-card regular pack along with a master deck that had eight more cards, plus one Metal Works card. The set contains the topical subsets: Rookies (116-137), Peak Performers (138-147), and Checklists (148-150).

COMPLETE SET (150) 6.00 15.00
1 Larry Walker .07 .20
2 Andy Pettitte .10 .30
3 Matt Williams .07 .20
4 Juan Gonzalez .07 .20
5 Frank Thomas .20 .50
6 Kenny Lofton .07 .20
7 Ken Griffey Jr. .40 1.00
8 Andres Galarraga .07 .20
9 Greg Maddux .30 .75
10 Hideo Nomo .20 .50
11 Cecil Fielder .07 .20
12 Jose Canseco .10 .30
13 Tony Gwynn .25 .60
14 Eddie Murray .20 .50
15 Alex Rodriguez .30 .75
16 Mike Piazza .30 .75
17 Ken Hill .07 .20
18 Chuck Knoblauch .07 .20
19 Ellis Burks .07 .20
20 Rafael Palmeiro .10 .30
21 Vinny Castilla .07 .20
22 Rusty Greer .07 .20
23 Chipper Jones .20 .50
24 Rey Ordonez .07 .20
25 Mariano Rivera .20 .50
26 Garret Anderson .07 .20
27 Edgar Martinez .10 .30
28 Dante Bichette .07 .20
29 Todd Hundley .07 .20
30 Barry Bonds .60 1.50
31 Barry Larkin .10 .30
32 Derek Jeter .50 1.25
33 Marquis Grissom .07 .20
34 Dave Justice .07 .20
35 Ivan Rodriguez .10 .30
36 Jay Buhner .07 .20
37 Fred McGriff .10 .30
38 Brady Anderson .07 .20
39 Tony Clark .07 .20
40 Eric Young .07 .20
41 Charles Nagy .07 .20
42 Mark McGwire .50 1.25
43 Paul O'Neill .10 .30
44 Tino Martinez .10 .30
45 Ryne Sandberg .30 .75
46 Bernie Williams .10 .30
47 Albert Belle .07 .20
48 Jeff Cirillo .07 .20
49 Tim Salmon .10 .30
50 Steve Finley .07 .20
51 Lance Johnson .07 .20
52 John Smoltz .10 .30
53 Javier Lopez .07 .20
54 Roger Clemens .40 1.00
55 Kevin Appier .07 .20
56 Ken Caminiti .07 .20
57 Cal Ripken .60 1.50
58 Moises Alou .07 .20
59 Marty Cordova .07 .20
60 David Cone .07 .20
61 Manny Ramirez .10 .30
62 Ray Durham .07 .20
63 Jermaine Dye .07 .20
64 Craig Biggio .10 .30
65 Will Clark .10 .30
66 Omar Vizquel .10 .30
67 Bernard Gilkey .07 .20
68 Greg Vaughn .07 .20
69 Wade Boggs .10 .30
70 Dave Nilsson .07 .20
71 Mark Grace .10 .30
72 Dean Palmer .07 .20
73 Sammy Sosa .20 .50
74 Mike Mussina .10 .30
75 Alex Fernandez .07 .20
76 Henry Rodriguez .07 .20
77 Travis Fryman .07 .20
78 Jeff Bagwell .10 .30
79 Pat Hentgen .07 .20
80 Gary Sheffield .07 .20
81 Jim Edmonds .07 .20
82 Darin Erstad .07 .20
83 Mark Grudzielanek .07 .20
84 Jim Thome .10 .30
85 Bobby Higginson .07 .20
86 Al Martin .07 .20
87 Jason Giambi .07 .20
88 Mo Vaughn .07 .20
89 Jeff Conine .07 .20
90 Edgar Renteria .07 .20
91 Andy Ashby .07 .20
92 Ryan Klesko .07 .20
93 John Jaha .07 .20
94 Paul Molitor .07 .20
95 Brian Hunter .07 .20
96 Randy Johnson .20 .50
97 Joey Hamilton .07 .20
98 Billy Wagner .07 .20
99 John Wetteland .07 .20
100 Jeff Fassero .07 .20
101 Rondell White .07 .20
102 Kevin Brown .07 .20
103 Andy Benes .07 .20
104 Raul Mondesi .07 .20
105 Todd Hollandsworth .07 .20
106 Alex Ochoa .07 .20
107 Bobby Bonilla .07 .20
108 Brian Jordan .07 .20
109 Tom Glavine .10 .30
110 Ron Gant .07 .20
111 Jason Kendall .07 .20
112 Roberto Alomar .10 .30
113 Troy Percival .07 .20
114 Michael Tucker .07 .20
115 Joe Carter .07 .20
116 Andruw Jones .10 .30
117 Nomar Garciaparra .30 .75
118 Todd Walker .07 .20
119 Jose Guillen .07 .20
120 Bubba Trammell RC .07 .20
121 Wilton Guerrero .07 .20
122 Bob Abreu .10 .30
123 Vladimir Guerrero .20 .50
124 Dmitri Young .07 .20
125 Kevin Orie .07 .20
126 Jose Cruz Jr. RC .07 .20
127 Brooks Kieschnick .07 .20
128 Scott Spiezio .07 .20
129 Brian Giles RC .40 1.00
130 Jason Dickson .07 .20
131 Damon Mashore .07 .20
132 Wendell Magee .07 .20
133 Matt Morris .07 .20
134 Scott Rolen .10 .30
135 Shannon Stewart .07 .20
136 Deivi Cruz RC .07 .20
137 Hideki Irabu RC .07 .20
138 Larry Walker PP .07 .20
139 Ken Griffey Jr. PP .25 .60
140 Frank Thomas PP .10 .30
141 Ivan Rodriguez PP .07 .20
142 Randy Johnson PP .10 .30
143 Mark McGwire PP .25 .60
144 Tino Martinez PP .07 .20
145 Tony Clark PP .07 .20
146 Mike Piazza PP .20 .50
147 Alex Rodriguez PP .20 .50
148 Roger Clemens CL .20 .50
149 Greg Maddux CL .20 .50
150 Hideo Nomo CL .07 .20

1997 Pinnacle X-Press Men of Summer

*STARS: 4X TO 10X BASIC CARDS
*ROOKIES: 2X TO 5X BASIC CARDS
STATED ODDS 1:7, 1 PER MASTER PACK

1997 Pinnacle X-Press Far and Away

COMPLETE SET (18) 30.00 80.00
STAT.ODDS 1:19 HOB, 1:5 MAST.DECK
1 Albert Belle .75 2.00
2 Mark McGwire 5.00 12.00
3 Frank Thomas 2.00 5.00
4 Mo Vaughn .75 2.00
5 Jeff Bagwell 1.25 3.00
6 Juan Gonzalez .75 2.00
7 Mike Piazza 3.00 8.00
8 Andruw Jones 1.25 3.00
9 Chipper Jones 2.00 5.00
10 Gary Sheffield .75 2.00
11 Sammy Sosa 2.00 5.00
12 Darin Erstad .75 2.00
13 Jay Buhner .75 2.00
14 Ken Griffey Jr. 4.00 10.00
15 Ken Caminiti .75 2.00
16 Brady Anderson .75 2.00
17 Manny Ramirez 1.25 3.00
18 Alex Rodriguez 3.00 8.00

1997 Pinnacle X-Press Melting Pot

1 Jose Guillen 1.00 2.50
2 Vladimir Guerrero 1.50 4.00
3 Andruw Jones 1.00 2.50
4 Larry Walker 1.50 4.00
5 Manny Ramirez 1.50 4.00
6 Ken Griffey Jr. 5.00 12.00
7 Alex Rodriguez 3.00 8.00
8 Frank Thomas 2.50 6.00
9 Juan Gonzalez 1.00 2.50
10 Ivan Rodriguez 1.50 4.00
11 Hideo Nomo 1.50 4.00
12 Rafael Palmeiro 1.00 2.50
13 Dave Nilsson 1.00 2.50
14 Nomar Garciaparra 1.50 4.00
15 Wilton Guerrero 1.00 2.50
16 Sammy Sosa 1.50 4.00
17 Edgar Renteria 1.00 2.50
18 Cal Ripken 8.00 20.00
19 Derek Jeter 6.00 15.00
20 Rey Ordonez 1.00 2.50

1997 Pinnacle X-Press Metal Works

COMPLETE SET (20) 20.00 50.00
*SILVER: 1.25X TO 3X BRONZE METAL WORKS
SILVER ODDS 1:54 MASTER DECKS
SILVER REDEMPTION ODDS 1:470 HOBBY
SILVER PRINT RUN 400 SERIAL #'d SETS
*GOLD: 2X TO 5X BRONZE METAL WORKS
GOLD ODDS 1:108 MASTER DECKS
GOLD REDEMPTION ODDS 1:950 HOBBY
GOLD PRINT RUN 200 SERIAL #'d SETS
1 Ken Griffey Jr. 3.00 8.00
2 Frank Thomas 1.50 4.00
3 Andruw Jones .60 1.50
4 Alex Rodriguez 2.00 5.00
5 Derek Jeter 4.00 10.00
6 Cal Ripken 5.00 12.00
7 Mike Piazza 1.50 4.00
8 Chipper Jones 1.50 4.00
9 Juan Gonzalez .60 1.50
10 Greg Maddux 2.50 6.00
11 Tony Gwynn 1.50 4.00
12 Jeff Bagwell 1.00 2.50
13 Albert Belle .60 1.50
14 Mark McGwire 2.50 6.00
15 Nomar Garciaparra 1.00 2.50
16 Mo Vaughn .60 1.50
17 Andy Pettitte 1.00 2.50
18 Manny Ramirez 1.00 2.50
19 Kenny Lofton .60 1.50
20 Roger Clemens 2.00 5.00
NNO Gold Redemption Card .40 1.00
NNO Silver Redemption Card .40 1.00

1997 Pinnacle X-Press Swing for the Fences

COMPLETE SET (60) 25.00 60.00
STATED ODDS 1:2
*UPGRADES: 2.5X TO 6X BASIC SWING
TEN UPGRADES VIA MAIL PER SWING WIN
UPGRADE EXCH.DEADLINE: 3/1/98
NNO CARDS LISTED IN ALPH.ORDER .50 1.25
1 Sandy Alomar Jr. .20 .50
2 Moises Alou .20 .50
3 Brady Anderson .20 .50
4 Jeff Bagwell .30 .75
5 Derek Bell .20 .50
6 Jay Bell .20 .50
7 Albert Belle .20 .50
8 Geronimo Berroa .20 .50
9 Dante Bichette .20 .50
10 Barry Bonds 1.50 4.00
11 Bobby Bonilla .20 .50
12 Jay Buhner .20 .50
13 Ellis Burks .20 .50
14 Ken Caminiti .20 .50
15 Jose Canseco .30 .75
16 Joe Carter .20 .50
17 Vinny Castilla .20 .50
18 Tony Clark .20 .50
19 Carlos Delgado .50 1.25
20 Jim Edmonds .20 .50
21 Cecil Fielder .20 .50
22 Andres Galarraga .20 .50
23 Ron Gant .20 .50
24 Bernard Gilkey .20 .50
25 Juan Gonzalez .20 .50
26 Ken Griffey Jr. W 2.00 5.00
27 Vladimir Guerrero .50 1.25
28 Todd Hundley .20 .50
29 John Jaha .20 .50
30 Andruw Jones .30 .75
31 Chipper Jones .50 1.25
32 David Justice .20 .50
33 Jeff Kent .20 .50
34 Ryan Klesko .20 .50
35 Barry Larkin .30 .75
36 Mike Lieberthal .20 .50
37 Javier Lopez .20 .50
38 Edgar Martinez .30 .75
39 Tino Martinez .30 .75
40 Fred McGriff .30 .75
41 Mark McGwire W 2.50 6.00
42 Raul Mondesi .20 .50
43 Tim Naehring .20 .50
44 Dave Nilsson .20 .50
45 Rafael Palmeiro .30 .75
46 Dean Palmer .20 .50
47 Mike Piazza .75 2.00
48 Cal Ripken 1.50 4.00
49 Henry Rodriguez .20 .50
50 Tim Salmon .30 .75
51 Gary Sheffield .20 .50
52 Sammy Sosa .50 1.25
53 Terry Steinbach .20 .50
54 Frank Thomas .50 1.25
55 Jim Thome .30 .75
56 Mo Vaughn .20 .50
57 Larry Walker W .60 1.50
58 Rondell White .20 .50
59 Matt Williams .20 .50
60 Todd Zeile .20 .50
NNO A.Jones AU 10.00 25.00

1910 American Caramel Pirates E90-2

The cards in this 11-card set measure 1 1/2" by 2 3/4". The 1910 E90-2 American Caramels Baseball Star set contains unnumbered cards featuring players from the 1909 Pittsburgh Pirates. The backs of these cards are exactly like the E90-1 cards; however, blue print is used for the names of the players and the teams on the fronts of the cards. Listed pricing for raw cards references "VgEx" conditon.

COMPLETE SET (11) 7500.00 15000.00
1 Babe Adams 300.00 500.00
2 Fred Clarke 600.00 1000.00
3 George Gibson 300.00 500.00
4 Ham Hyatt 300.00 500.00
5 Tommy Leach 300.00 500.00
6 Sam Leever 300.00 500.00
7 Nick Maddox 300.00 500.00
8 Dots Miller 300.00 500.00
9 Deacon Phillippe 300.00 500.00
10 Honus Wagner 7000.00 10000.00
11 Chief Wilson 300.00 500.00

1910 Pirates Tip-Top D322

This 25-card set of the Pittsburgh Pirates was distributed by Tip-Top Bread at a rate of one per bread loaf and measures approximately 1 13/15" by 2 3/8". The fronts feature pastel paintings of the World Champion Team. The backs carry a checklist, ad for the bakery, and offer to send the complete set for 50 bread labels.

COMPLETE SET (25) 60000.00 120000.00
1 Barney Dreyfuss 2500.00 5000.00
2 William Locke 2000.00 4000.00
3 Fred Clarke 4000.00 8000.00
4 Honus Wagner 12500.00 25000.00
5 Tom Leach 2000.00 4000.00
6 George Gibson 2000.00 4000.00
7 Dots Miller 2000.00 4000.00
8 Howie Camnitz 2000.00 4000.00
9 Babe Adams 2500.00 5000.00
10 Lefty Leifield 2000.00 4000.00
11 Nick Maddox 2000.00 4000.00
12 Deacon Phillippe 2500.00 5000.00
13 Bobby Byrne 2000.00 4000.00
14 Ed Abbaticchio 2000.00 4000.00
15 Lefty Webb 2000.00 4000.00
16 Vin Campbell 2000.00 4000.00
17 Owen Wilson 2500.00 5000.00
18 Sam Leever 2000.00 4000.00
19 Mike Simon 2000.00 4000.00
20 Ham Hyatt 2000.00 4000.00
21 Paddy O'Connor 2000.00 4000.00
22 John Flynn 2000.00 4000.00
23 Kirby White 2000.00 4000.00
24 Boy Mascot 2000.00 4000.00
25 Forbes Field 2000.00 4000.00

1913 Pirates Voskamps

These cards, which measure approximately 3 5/8" by 2 1/4" feature members of the 1913 Pittsburgh Pirates. Both Hoffman and O'Toole are known to exist in two different versions. Since these cards were unnumbered, we have sequenced them in alphabetical order.

COMPLETE SET 6000.00 12000.00
1 Babe Adams 600.00 1200.00
2 Everitt Booe 500.00 1000.00
3 Bobby Byrne 500.00 1000.00
4 Howie Camnitz 500.00 1000.00
5 Max Carey 1500.00 3000.00
6 Joe Conzelman 500.00 1000.00
7 Jack Ferry 500.00 1000.00
8 George Gibson 500.00 1000.00
9 Claude Hendrix 500.00 1000.00
10 Solly Hofman 500.00 1000.00
11 Ham Hyatt 500.00 1000.00
12 Bill Kelly 500.00 1000.00
13 Ed Mensor 500.00 1000.00
14 Dots Miller 500.00 1000.00
15 Marty O'Toole 500.00 1000.00
16 Hank Robinson 500.00 1000.00
17 Mike Simon 500.00 1000.00
18 Jim Viox 500.00 1000.00
19 Honus Wagner 5000.00 10000.00
20 Chief Wilson 600.00 1200.00

1950 Pirates Team Issue

This set of the Pittsburgh Pirates measures approximately 6 1/2" by 9" and features black-and-white player photos. The backs are blank. The cards are unnumbered and checklisted below in alphabetical order.

COMPLETE SET (25) 75.00 150.00
1 Ted Beard 2.50 5.00
2 Gus Bell 4.00 8.00
3 Pete Castiglione 2.50 5.00
4 Cliff Chambers 2.50 5.00
5 Dale Coogan 2.50 5.00
6 Murry Dickson 3.00 6.00
7 Froilan Fernandez 2.50 5.00
8 Johnny Hopp 3.00 6.00
9 Ralph Kiner 10.00 20.00
10 Vernon Law 5.00 10.00
11 Vic Lombardi 2.50 5.00
12 William MacDonald 2.50 5.00
13 Clyde McCullough 2.50 5.00
14 Bill Meyer MG 2.50 5.00
15 Ray Mueller 2.50 5.00
16 Danny Murtaugh 4.00 8.00
17 Jack Phillips 2.50 5.00
18 Mel Queen 2.50 5.00
19 Stan Rojek 2.50 5.00
20 Henry Schenz 2.50 5.00
21 George Strickland 2.50 5.00
22 Earl Turner 2.50 5.00
23 Jim Walsh 2.50 5.00
24 Bill Werle 2.50 5.00
25 Wally Westlake 2.50 5.00

1956 Pirates Team Issue

This 24-card set of the Pittsburgh Pirates features black-and-white player photos with white borders and was sold by the club for 15 cents each. The backs are blank. The cards are unnumbered and checklisted below in alphabetical order. The Bill Mazeroski card in this set predates his Rookie Card.

COMPLETE SET (24) 100.00 200.00
1 Luis Arroyo 2.00 4.00
2 Bobby Bragan MG 3.00 6.00
3 Roberto Clemente 50.00 100.00
4 Dick Cole 2.00 4.00
5 Roy Face 3.00 6.00
6 Hank Foiles 2.00 4.00
7 Gene Freese 2.00 4.00
8 Bob Friend 3.00 6.00
9 Dick Groat 3.00 6.00
10 Dick Hall 2.00 4.00
11 Nelson King 2.00 4.00
12 Ronnie Kline 2.00 4.00
13 Danny Kravitz 2.00 4.00
14 Vernon Law 3.00 6.00
15 Dale Long 2.00 4.00
16 Jerry Lynch 2.00 4.00
17 Bill Mazeroski 20.00 40.00
18 Johnny O'Brien 2.00 4.00
19 Curt Roberts 2.00 4.00
20 Jack Shepard 2.00 4.00
21 Bob Skinner 2.00 4.00
22 Frank Thomas 3.00 6.00
23 Bill Virdon 3.00 6.00
24 Lee Walls 2.00 4.00

1957 Pirates Team Issue

This 10-card set of the Pittsburgh Pirates features black-and-white player photos with white borders. The backs are blank. The cards are unnumbered and checklisted below in alphabetical order. The checklist might be incomplete and any confirmed addtions are welcomed. Bill Mazerosi appears in his Rookie Card year.

COMPLETE SET (10) 30.00 60.00
1 Roberto Clemente 12.50 25.00
2 Dick Groat 2.50 5.00
3 Danny Kravitz 1.50 3.00
4 Vernon Law 2.00 4.00
5 Dale Long 1.50 3.00
6 Bill Mazeroski 6.00 12.00
7 Johnny O'Brien 1.50 3.00
8 Bob Skinner 1.50 3.00
9 Frank Thomas 2.00 4.00
10 Bill Virdon 2.50 5.00

1958 Pirates Team Issue

This set of the Pittsburgh Pirates measures approximately 5" by 7" and features black-and-white player portraits with white borders. The set was sold by the club through the mail for 50 cents. The cards are unnumbered and checklisted below in alphabetical order. An 8 1/2" by 11" team photo was added to the set along with an 8 1/4" by 10 1/4" glossy photo of Dick Groat (card number 13) with a printed autograph and name in the white border.

COMPLETE SET (12) 40.00 80.00
1 Roberto Clemente 12.50 25.00
2 Hank Foiles 1.50 3.00
3 Bob Friend 1.50 3.00
4 Dick Groat 2.50 5.00
5 Ronald Kline 1.50 3.00
6 Bill Mazeroski 6.00 12.00
7 Roman Mejias 1.50 3.00
8 Danny Murtaugh 2.50 5.00
9 Bob Skinner 1.50 3.00
10 Dick Stuart 1.50 3.00
11 Frank Thomas 1.50 3.00
12 Bill Virdon 2.50 5.00
13 Dick Groat 3.00 6.00
14 Team Picture 7.50 15.00

1959 Pirates Jay Publishing

This 12-card set of the Pittsburgh Pirates measures approximately 5" by 7" and features black-and-white player photos in a white border. These cards were packaged 12 to a packet. The backs are blank. The cards are unnumbered and checklisted below in alphabetical order.

COMPLETE SET 40.00 80.00
1 Roberto Clemente 12.50 25.00
2 Hank Foiles 2.50 6.00
3 Bob Friend 2.50 6.00
4 Dick Groat 4.00 10.00
5 Don Hoak 2.50 6.00
6 Ron Kline 2.50 6.00
7 Ted Kluszewski 5.00 12.00
8 Bill Mazeroski 5.00 12.00

9 Danny Murtaugh MG 2.50 6.00
10 Bob Skinner 2.50 6.00
11 Dick Stuart 2.50 6.00
12 Bill Virdon 3.00 8.00

1960 Pirates Jay Publishing

This 12-card set of the Pittsburgh Pirates measures approximately 5" by 7". The fronts feature black-and-white posed player photos with the player's and team name printed below in the white border. These cards were packaged 12 to a packet and originally sold for 50 cents. The backs are blank. The cards are unnumbered and checklisted below in alphabetical order.

COMPLETE SET (12) 30.00 60.00
1 Smoky Burgess 1.50 4.00
2 Gino Cimoli 1.00 2.50
3 Roberto Clemente 10.00 25.00
4 Roy Face 1.50 4.00
5 Bob Friend 1.25 3.00
6 Dick Groat 2.00 5.00
7 Harvey Haddix 1.25 3.00
8 Don Hoak 1.25 3.00
9 Bill Mazeroski 3.00 8.00
10 Danny Murtaugh MG 1.50 4.00
11 Bob Skinner 1.00 2.50
12 Dick Stuart 1.25 3.00

1960 Pirates Tag-Ons

This 10-card set originally sold for $1.98 and features individually die-cut self-sticking figures in full color on one large sheet measuring approximately 10" by 15 1/2". These flexible color-fast Tag-ons are weatherproof and can be applied to any surface. The figures are checklisted below according to the small black numbers printed on their shoulders.

COMPLETE SET (10) 40.00 80.00
4 Robert Skinner 2.00 5.00
6 Forrest Burgess 2.00 5.00
7 Dick Stuart 2.50 6.00
9 Bill Mazeroski 4.00 10.00
12 Don Hoak 2.00 5.00
18 Bill Virdon 2.50 6.00
19 Bob Friend 2.00 5.00
21 Roberto Clemente 10.00 25.00
24 Dick Groat 3.00 8.00
26 Roy Face 2.50 6.00
XX Complete Sheet 40.00 80.00

1961 Pirates Riger Ford

This six-card set was distributed by Ford Motor Company and measures approximately 11" by 14". The fronts feature pencil drawings by Robert Riger of six of the 1960 World Champion Pittsburgh Pirates. The cards are unnumbered and checklisted below in alphabetical order.

COMPLETE SET (6) 40.00 80.00
1 Roberto Clemente 20.00 50.00
2 Bob Friend 4.00 10.00
3 Dick Groat 8.00 20.00
4 Don Hoak 4.00 10.00
5 Vernon Law 6.00 15.00
6 Bill Mazeroski 10.00 25.00

1962 Pirates Jay Publishing

This 12-card set of the Pittsburgh Pirates measures approximately 5" by 7". The fronts feature black-and-white posed player photos with the player's and team name printed below in the white border. These cards were packaged 12 to a packet. The backs are blank. The cards are unnumbered and checklisted below in alphabetical order.

COMPLETE SET (12) 30.00 60.00
1 Smoky Burgess 1.25 3.00
2 Roberto Clemente 10.00 25.00
3 Roy Face 1.50 4.00
4 Bob Friend 1.25 3.00
5 Dick Groat 1.50 4.00
6 Don Hoak 1.00 2.50
7 Vern Law 1.25 3.00
8 Bill Mazeroski 3.00 8.00
9 Danny Murtaugh MG 1.25 3.00
10 Bob Skinner 1.00 2.50
11 Dick Stuart 1.25 3.00
12 Bill Virdon 1.25 3.00

1963 Pirates IDL

This 26-card set measures approximately 4" by 5" and is blank-backed. The fronts have black and white photos on the top of the card along with the IDL Drug Store logo in the lower left corner of the card and the players name printed in block letters underneath the picture. The only card which has any designation as to position is the manager card of Danny Murtaugh. These cards are unnumbered and feature members of the Pittsburgh Pirates. The catalog designation for the set is H801-13 although it is infrequently referenced. The Stargell card is one of his few cards from 1963, his rookie year for cards.

COMPLETE SET (26) 150.00 300.00
1 Bob Bailey 3.00 8.00
2 Smoky Burgess 4.00 10.00
3 Don Cardwell 3.00 8.00
4 Roberto Clemente 75.00 150.00
5 Donn Clendenon 4.00 10.00
6 Roy Face 5.00 12.00
7 Earl Francis 3.00 8.00
8 Bob Friend 4.00 10.00
9 Joe Gibbon 3.00 8.00
10 Julio Gotay 3.00 8.00
11 Harvey Haddix 4.00 10.00
12 Johnny Logan 3.00 8.00
13 Bill Mazeroski 10.00 25.00
14 Al McBean 3.00 8.00
15 Danny Murtaugh MG 4.00 10.00
16 Sam Narron CO 3.00 8.00
17 Ron Northey CO 3.00 8.00
18 Frank Oceak CO 3.00 8.00
19 Jim Pagliaroni 3.00 8.00
20 Ted Savage 3.00 8.00
21 Dick Schofield 3.00 8.00
22 Willie Stargell 15.00 40.00
23 Tom Sturdivant 3.00 8.00
24 Virgil Trucks CO 3.00 8.00
25 Bob Veale 3.00 8.00
26 Bill Virdon 4.00 10.00

1963 Pirates Jay Publishing

This 12-card set of the Pittsburgh Pirates measures approximately 5" by 7". The fronts feature black-and-white posed player photos with the player's and team name printed below in the white border. These cards were packaged 12 to a packet. The backs are blank. The cards are unnumbered and checklisted below in alphabetical order.

COMPLETE SET (12) 20.00 50.00
1 Bob Bailey 1.00 2.50
2 Smoky Burgess 1.25 3.00
3 Roberto Clemente 10.00 25.00
4 Donn Clendenon 1.00 2.50
5 Roy Face 1.50 4.00
6 Bob Friend 1.25 3.00
7 Harvey Haddix 1.25 3.00
8 Vern Law 1.25 3.00
9 Bill Mazeroski 3.00 8.00
10 Danny Murtaugh MG 1.25 3.00
11 Bob Skinner 1.00 2.50
12 Bill Virdon 1.25 3.00

1964 Pirates Jay Publishing

This 12-card set of the Pittsburgh Pirates measures approximately 5" by 7". The fronts feature black-and-white posed player photos with the player's and team name printed below in the white border. These cards were packaged 12 to a packet. The backs are blank. The cards are unnumbered and checklisted below in alphabetical order.

COMPLETE SET (12) 20.00 50.00
1 Bob Bailey .75 2.00
2 Smoky Burgess 1.00 2.50
3 Roberto Clemente 10.00 25.00
4 Donn Clendenon 1.00 2.50
5 Roy Face 1.25 3.00
6 Bob Friend 1.00 2.50
7 Bill Mazeroski 3.00 8.00
8 Danny Murtaugh MG 1.00 2.50
9 Dick Schofield .75 2.00
10 Willie Stargell 5.00 12.00
11 Bob Veale .75 2.00
12 Bill Virdon 1.00 2.50

1964 Pirates KDKA

This set featured members of the 1964 Pittsburgh Pirates. It was issued by radio station KDKA. The set can be dated to 1964 by the card of Rex Johnston, who only played for the Pirates in that season.

COMPLETE SET (28) 1500.00 3000.00
1 Gene Alley 40.00 80.00
2 Bob Bailey 40.00 80.00
3 Frank Bork 40.00 80.00
4 Smoky Burgess 50.00 100.00
5 Tom Butters 40.00 80.00
6 Don Cardwell 40.00 80.00
7 Roberto Clemente 500.00 1000.00
8 Donn Clendenon 50.00 100.00
9 Roy Face 60.00 120.00
10 Gene Freese 40.00 80.00
11 Bob Friend 50.00 100.00
12 Joe Gibbon 40.00 80.00
13 Julio Gotay 40.00 80.00
14 Rex Johnston 40.00 80.00
15 Vernon Law 60.00 120.00
16 Jerry Lynch 40.00 80.00
17 Bill Mazeroski 200.00 400.00
18 Al McBean 40.00 80.00
19 Orlando McFarlane 40.00 80.00
20 Manny Mota 60.00 120.00
21 Danny Murtaugh MG 50.00 100.00
22 Jim Pagliaroni 60.00 120.00
23 Dick Schofield 40.00 80.00
24 Don Schwall 40.00 80.00
25 Tommie Sisk 40.00 80.00
26 Willie Stargell 200.00 400.00
27 Bob Veale 40.00 80.00
28 Bill Virdon 50.00 100.00

1965 Pirates Jay Publishing

This 12-card set of the Pittsburgh Pirates measures approximately 5" by 7". The fronts feature black-and-white posed player photos with the player's and team name printed below in the white border. These cards were packaged 12 to a packet. The backs are blank. The cards are unnumbered and checklisted below in alphabetical order.

COMPLETE SET (12) 40.00 80.00
1 Bob Bailey 1.50 4.00
2 Roberto Clemente 15.00 40.00
3 Donn Clendenon 2.00 5.00
4 Del Crandall 2.00 5.00
5 Vern Law 2.50 6.00
6 Bill Mazeroski 6.00 15.00
7 Manny Mota 2.00 5.00
8 Jim Pagliaroni 1.50 4.00
9 Dick Schofield 1.50 4.00
10 Willie Stargell 8.00 20.00
11 Bill Virdon 2.00 5.00
12 Harry Walker MG 1.50 4.00

1965 Pirates KDKA Posters

These posters, which measure approximately 8" by 12" feature members of the 1965 Pirates and give the collector a chance to win an Emenee Electric Guitar. The top of the poster has the player's photo as well as his name while the bottom half is dedicated to information about the contest. We have sequenced the known players in alphabetical order but it would be suspected that there would be additions to this checklist.

COMPLETE SET 75.00 150.00
1 Tom Butters 20.00 50.00
2 Joe Gibbon 75.00 150.00

1966 Pirates East Hills

The 1966 East Hills Pirates set consists of 25 large (approximately 3 1/4" by 4 1/4"), full color photos of Pittsburgh Pirate ballplayers. These blank-backed cards are numbered in the lower right corner according to the uniform number of the individual depicted. The set was distributed by various stores located in the East Hills Shopping Center. The catalog number for this set is F405.

COMPLETE SET (25) 40.00 80.00
3 Harry Walker MG .30 .75
7 Bob Bailey .20 .50
8 Willie Stargell 10.00 25.00
9 Bill Mazeroski 2.00 5.00
10 Jim Pagliaroni .20 .50
11 Jose Pagan .20 .50
12 Jerry May .20 .50
14 Gene Alley .40 1.00
15 Manny Mota .40 1.00
16 Andre Rodgers UER/(Andy on card) .20 .50
17 Donn Clendenon .40 1.00
18 Matty Alou 1.25 3.00
19 Pete Mikkelsen .20 .50
20 Jesse Gonder .20 .50
21 Roberto Clemente 20.00 50.00
22 Woody Fryman .30 .75
24 Jerry Lynch .20 .50
25 Tommie Sisk .20 .50
26 Roy Face .40 1.00
28 Steve Blass .40 1.00
32 Vernon Law .40 1.00
34 Al McBean .20 .50
39 Bob Veale .30 .75
43 Don Cardwell .20 .50
45 Gene Michael .30 .75

1967 Pirates Stickers Topps

This was a limited production "test" issue for Topps. It is very similar to the Red Sox "test" issue following. The stickers are blank backed and measure 2 1/2" by 3 1/2". The stickers look like cards from the front and are somewhat attractive in spite of the "no neck" presentation of many of the players' photos. The cards are numbered on the front.

COMPLETE SET (33) 500.00 1000.00
WRAPPERS 20.00 50.00
1 Gene Alley 10.00 25.00
2 Matty Alou 10.00 25.00
3 Dennis Ribant 8.00 20.00
4 Steve Blass 10.00 25.00
5 Juan Pizarro 8.00 20.00
6 Roberto Clemente 250.00 500.00
7 Donn Clendenon 10.00 25.00
8 Roy Face 12.50 30.00
9 Woodie Fryman 8.00 20.00
10 Jesse Gonder 8.00 20.00
11 Vern Law 10.00 25.00
12 Al McBean 8.00 20.00
13 Jerry May 8.00 20.00
14 Bill Mazeroski 30.00 60.00
15 Pete Mikkelsen 8.00 20.00
16 Manny Mota 10.00 25.00
17 Bill O'Dell 8.00 20.00
18 Jose Pagan 8.00 20.00
19 Jim Pagliaroni 8.00 20.00
20 Johnny Pesky CO 10.00 25.00
21 Tommie Sisk 8.00 20.00
22 Willie Stargell 75.00 150.00
23 Bob Veale 10.00 25.00
24 Harry Walker MG 8.00 20.00
25 I Love the Pirates 8.00 20.00
26 Let's Go Pirates 8.00 20.00
27 Roberto Clemente for Mayor 125.00 250.00
28 Matty Alou NL Batting Champ 10.00 25.00
29 Happiness is a Pirate Win 8.00 20.00
30 Donn Clendenon is my Hero 10.00 25.00
31 Willie Stargell Pirates HR Champ 50.00 100.00
32 Pirates Logo 8.00 20.00
33 Pirates Pennant 8.00 20.00

1967 Pirates Team Issue

This 24-card set of the Pittsburgh Pirates features color player photos with white borders and measures approximately 3 1/4" by 4 1/4". A facsimile autograph is printed in the wide bottom border. The backs are blank. The cards are unnumbered and checklisted below in alphabetical order. The complete set of 24 was available for $1 from Pitt Sportservice at time of issue.

COMPLETE SET (24) 50.00 100.00
1 Gene Alley 1.25 3.00
2 Matty Alou 1.50 4.00
3 Steve Blass 1.25 3.00
4 Roberto Clemente 8.00 20.00
5 Donn Clendenon 1.50 4.00
6 Roy Face 2.00 5.00
7 Woody Fryman 1.25 3.00
8 Jesse Gonder 1.25 3.00
9 Vernon Law 2.00 5.00
10 Jerry May 1.25 3.00
11 Bill Mazeroski 3.00 8.00
12 Al McBean 1.25 3.00
13 Pete Mikkelsen 1.25 3.00
14 Manny Mota 1.50 4.00
15 Jose Pagan 1.25 3.00
16 Jim Pagliaroni 1.25 3.00
17 Juan Pizarro 1.25 3.00
18 Dennis Ribant 1.25 3.00
19 Andy Rodgers 1.25 3.00
20 Tommie Sisk 1.25 3.00
21 Willie Stargell 4.00 10.00
22 Bob Veale 1.25 3.00
23 Harry Walker 1.50 4.00
24 Maury Wills 2.50 6.00

1967 Pirates Team Issue 8 by 10

These 24 blank-backed photos, which measure approximately 8" by 10", feature members of the 1967 Pittsburgh Pirates. From the description given, these were promotional shots mailed out to members of the press at the start of the 1967 season. Since these photos are unnumbered, we have sequenced them in alphabetical order.

COMPLETE SET (24) 75.00 150.00
1 Gene Alley 2.00 5.00
2 Matty Alou 2.50 6.00
3 Steve Blass 2.00 5.00
4 Roberto Clemente 15.00 40.00
5 Donn Clendenon 2.00 5.00
6 Roy Face 2.50 6.00
7 Woodie Fryman 2.00 5.00
8 Jesse Gonder 2.00 5.00
9 Vern Law 2.50 6.00
10 Jerry May 2.00 5.00
11 Bill Mazeroski 6.00 15.00
12 Al McBean 2.00 5.00
13 Pete Mikkelsen 2.00 5.00
14 Manny Mota 2.50 6.00
15 Billy O'Dell 2.00 5.00
16 Jose Pagan 2.00 5.00
17 Jim Pagliaroni 2.00 5.00
18 Juan Pizarro 2.00 5.00
19 Dennis Ribant 2.00 5.00
20 Tommie Sisk 2.00 5.00
21 Willie Stargell 6.00 15.00
22 Bob Veale 2.00 5.00
23 Harry Walker MG 2.00 5.00
24 Maury Wills 4.00 10.00

1968 Pirates KDKA

This 23-card set measures approximately 2 3/8" by 4" and was issued by radio and television station KDKA to promote the Pittsburgh Pirates, whom they were covering at the time. The fronts have the players' photo on the top 2/3 of the card and a facsimile autograph, the players name and position and uniform number on the lower left hand corner and an ad for KDKA on the lower right corner of the card. The back has an advertisment for both KDKA radio and television. The set is checklisted below by uniform number.

COMPLETE SET (23) 40.00 80.00
7 Larry Shepard MG .60 1.50
8 Willie Stargell 6.00 15.00
9 Bill Mazeroski 3.00 8.00
10 Gary Kolb .60 1.50
11 Jose Pagan .60 1.50
12 Jerry May .60 1.50
14 Jim Bunning 2.50 6.00
15 Manny Mota .75 2.00
17 Donn Clendenon .75 2.00
18 Matty Alou .75 2.00
21 Roberto Clemente 12.50 30.00
22 Gene Alley .75 2.00
25 Tommy Sisk .60 1.50
26 Roy Face 1.25 3.00
27 Ron Kline .60 1.50
28 Steve Blass .75 2.00
29 Juan Pizzaro .60 1.50
30 Maury Wills 1.50 4.00
34 Al McBean .60 1.50
35 Manny Sanguillen 1.25 3.00
38 Bob Moose .75 2.00
39 Bob Veale .60 1.50
40 Dave Wickersham .60 1.50

1968 Pirates Team Issue

This 24-card set of the Pittsburgh Pirates features color player photos with white borders and measures approximately 3 1/4" by 4 1/4". A facsimile autograph is printed in the wide bottom border. The backs are blank. The cards are unnumbered and checklisted below in alphabetical order.

COMPLETE SET (24) 50.00 100.00
1 Gene Alley 1.25 3.00
2 Matty Alou 2.00 5.00
3 Steve Blass 1.25 3.00
4 Jim Bunning 3.00 8.00
5 Roberto Clemente 8.00 20.00
6 Donn Clendenon 1.50 4.00
7 Roy Face 2.00 5.00
8 Ronnie Kline 1.25 3.00
9 Gary Kolb 1.25 3.00
10 Jerry May 1.25 3.00
11 Bill Mazeroski 3.00 8.00
12 Al McBean 1.25 3.00
13 Bob Moose 1.25 3.00
14 Manny Mota 1.50 4.00
15 Jose Pagan 1.25 3.00
16 Juan Pizarro 1.25 3.00
17 Manny Sanguillen 1.50 4.00
18 Jim Shellenback 1.25 3.00
19 Larry Shepard 1.25 3.00
20 Tommie Sisk 1.25 3.00
21 Willie Stargell 4.00 10.00
22 Bob Veale 1.25 3.00
23 Dave Wickersham 1.25 3.00
24 Maury Wills 2.50 6.00

1969 Pirates Jack in the Box

This 12-card set measures approximately 2 1/16" by 3 5/8" and features black-and-white player photos on a white card face. The player's name, team name, position, and batting or pitching record appear below the photo. The backs are blank. The cards are unnumbered and checklisted below in alphabetical order. Pittsburgh is misspelled Pittsburg on the front of the cards.

COMPLETE SET (12) 20.00 50.00
1 Gene Alley 1.25 3.00
2 Dave Cash 1.50 4.00
3 Dock Ellis 1.25 3.00
4 Dave Giusti .75 2.00
5 Jerry May .75 2.00
6 Bill Mazeroski 3.00 8.00
7 Al Oliver 2.50 6.00
8 Jose Pagan .75 2.00
9 Fred Patek 1.25 3.00
10 Bob Robertson .75 2.00
11 Manny Sanguillen 1.25 3.00
12 Willie Stargell 8.00 20.00

1969 Pirates Greiner

This eight-card set of the Pittsburgh Pirates, sponsored by Greiner Tire Service, measures approximately 5 1/2" by 8 1/2" and features black-and-white player portraits inside a white border. The player's name and team is printed with a "good luck" message in the wide bottom margin along with the sponsor name, address and phone number. The backs are blank. The cards are unnumbered and checklisted below in alphabetical order.

COMPLETE SET (8) 20.00 50.00
1 Gene Alley 2.00 5.00
2 Matty Alou 2.50 6.00
3 Steve Blass 1.50 4.00
4 Roberto Clemente 15.00 40.00
5 Jerry May 1.50 4.00
6 Bill Mazeroski 4.00 10.00
7 Larry Shepard MG 1.50 4.00
8 Willie Stargell 5.00 12.00

1969 Pirates Team Issue

This 26-card set of the Pittsburgh Pirates was issued in two series and measures approximately 3 1/4" by 4 1/4". The fronts feature color player photos in white borders with a facsimile autograph printed in the wide bottom margin. The backs are blank. The cards are unnumbered and checklisted below in alphabetical order.

COMPLETE SET (24) 40.00 80.00
1 Gene Alley .75 2.00
2 Matty Alou 1.25 3.00
3 Steve Blass .75 2.00
4 Jim Bunning 2.00 5.00
5 Roberto Clemente 8.00 20.00
6 Bruce Dal Canton .75 2.00
7 Doc Ellis 1.00 2.50
8 Chuck Hartenstein .75 2.00
9 Richie Hebner 1.00 2.50
10 Ronnie Kline .75 2.00
11 Gary Kolb .75 2.00
12 Vernon Law CO 1.00 2.50
13 Jose Martinez .75 2.00
14 Jerry May .75 2.00
15 Bill Mazeroski 2.50 6.00
16 Bob Moose .75 2.00
17 Al Oliver 1.50 4.00
18 Jose Pagan .75 2.00
19 Fred Patek 1.00 2.50
20 Manny Sanguillen 1.00 2.50
21 Larry Shepard MG .75 2.00
22 Willie Stargell 4.00 10.00
23 Carl Taylor .75 2.00
24 Bob Veale .75 2.00
25 Bill Virdon CO 1.00 2.50
26 Luke Walker .75 2.00

1970 Pirates Team Issue

This 20-card set of the Pittsburgh Pirates was issued in two series of 10 cards each measuring approximately 3 1/4" by 4 1/4". The fronts feature color player portraits in white borders. A facsimile autograph is printed in the wide bottom margin. The backs are blank. The cards are unnumbered and checklisted below in alphabetical order.

COMPLETE SET (20) 100.00 175.00
1 Gene Alley 2.00 5.00
2 Matty Alou 3.00 8.00
3 Steve Blass 2.00 5.00
4 Bob Clemente 15.00 40.00
5 Bruce Dal Canton 2.00 5.00
6 Dock Ellis 2.00 5.00
7 Chuck Hartenstein 2.00 5.00
8 Richie Hebner 2.50 6.00
9 Gary Kolb 2.00 5.00
10 Jerry May 2.00 5.00
11 Bill Mazeroski 6.00 15.00
12 Bob Moose 2.00 5.00
13 Al Oliver 4.00 10.00
14 Jose Pagan 2.00 5.00
15 Fred Patek 2.50 6.00
16 Manny Sanguillen 2.50 6.00
17 Willie Stargell 8.00 20.00
18 Bob Veale 2.00 5.00
19 Bill Virdon CO 2.50 6.00
20 Luke Walker 2.00 5.00

1971 Pirates

The six blank-backed photos comprising this Set "A" of the '71 Pirates measure approximately 7" by 8 3/4" and feature white-bordered posed color player shots. The player's name appears in black lettering within the bottom white margin. The pictures are unnumbered and checklisted below in alphabetical order.

COMPLETE SET (6) 12.50 30.00
1 Nelson Briles 2.00 5.00
2 Dave Cash 1.50 4.00
3 Roberto Clemente 50.00 100.00
4 Richie Hebner 2.00 5.00
5 Bob Robertson 1.50 4.00
6 Luke Walker 1.50 4.00

1971 Pirates Action Photos

These unnumbered cards feature members of the World Champion Pittsburgh Pirates. These cards were issued in two series (1-12, 13-24) and each group is sequenced into alphabetical order.

COMPLETE SET (24) 100.00 200.00
1 Gene Alley 1.50 4.00
2 Nelson Briles 1.00 2.50
3 Dave Cash 1.00 2.50
4 Roberto Clemente 50.00 100.00
5 Dock Ellis 2.00 5.00
6 Mudcat Grant 1.00 2.50
7 Bob Johnson 1.00 2.50
8 Milt May 1.00 2.50
9 Jose Pagan 1.00 2.50
10 Manny Sanguillen 2.00 5.00
11 Bob Veale 1.00 2.50
12 Luke Walker 1.00 2.50
13 Steve Blass 1.50 4.00
14 Gene Clines 1.00 2.50
15 Vic Davalillo 1.00 2.50
16 Dave Giusti 1.00 2.50
17 Richie Hebner 1.50 4.00
18 Jackie Hernandez 1.00 2.50
19 Bill Mazeroski 10.00 25.00
20 Bob Moose 1.00 2.50
21 Al Oliver 2.50 6.00
22 Bob Robertson 1.00 2.50
23 Charlie Sands 1.00 2.50
24 Willie Stargell 6.00 15.00

1971 Pirates Arco Oil

Sponsored by Arco Oil, this 12-card set features photos of the 1971 Pittsburgh Pirates. The cards are unnumbered and checklisted below in alphabetical order.

COMPLETE SET (12) 40.00 80.00
1 Gene Alley 2.00 5.00
2 Steve Blass 2.50 6.00
3 Roberto Clemente 10.00 25.00
4 Dave Giusti 2.00 5.00
5 Richie Hebner 2.00 5.00
6 Bill Mazeroski 5.00 12.00
7 Bob Moose 2.00 5.00
8 Al Oliver 3.00 8.00
9 Bob Robertson 2.00 5.00
10 Manny Sanguillen 3.00 8.00
11 Willie Stargell 6.00 15.00
12 Luke Walker 2.00 5.00

1971 Pirates Post-Gazette Inserts

These inserts, which feature members of the 1971 Pittsburgh Pirates, were inserted daily into the Post-Gazette newspaper. These inserts are numbered and this list may be incomplete so any further information is appreciated.

COMPLETE SET 50.00 100.00
5 Dave Cash 5.00 12.00
7 Bob Johnson 4.00 10.00
8 Nelson Briles 4.00 10.00
11 Dave Giusti 4.00 10.00
12 Luke Walker 4.00 10.00
13 Gene Clines 4.00 10.00
14 Milt May 4.00 10.00
15 Bob Robertson 4.00 10.00
17 Gene Alley 4.00 10.00
18 Bruce Kison 4.00 10.00
19 Jose Pagan 4.00 10.00
20 Dock Ellis 4.00 10.00
22 Bob Miller 4.00 10.00
23 Jackie Hernandez 4.00 10.00

1972 Pirates Team Issue

This eight-card set of the Pittsburgh Pirates measures approximately 3 1/4" by 4 1/4" and features color player portraits with a facsimile autograph in the wide bottom margin. The cards are unnumbered and checklisted below in alphabetical order.

COMPLETE SET 30.00 60.00
1 Steve Blass 1.25 3.00
2 Roberto Clemente 8.00 20.00
3 Dock Ellis 1.50 4.00
4 Richie Hebner 1.25 3.00
5 Dave Giusti 1.25 3.00
6 Bob Johnson 1.25 3.00
7 Bob Moose 1.25 3.00
8 Al Oliver 2.50 6.00
9 Jose Pagan 1.25 3.00
10 Bob Robertson 1.25 3.00
11 Manny Sanguillen 1.50 4.00
12 Willie Stargell 3.00 8.00

1973 Pirates Post/Gazette Inserts

These photos were inserted each day into the Pittsburgh Post Gazette. This listing is incomplete and any further information is appreciated. There may be other photos so all additional information is appreciated.

COMPLETE SET 20.00 50.00
6 Vic Davallilo 2.00 5.00
10 Ramon Hernandez 2.00 5.00
12 Bob Johnson 2.00 5.00
14 Milt May 2.00 5.00
15 Bob Miller 2.00 5.00
19 Charlie Sands 2.00 5.00
23 Luke Walker 2.00 5.00
24 Bill Virdon MG 2.00 5.00
NNO Gene Alley 2.00 5.00
NNO Steve Blass 2.00 5.00
NNO Nelson Briles 2.00 5.00
NNO Dave Cash 2.00 5.00

1974 Pirates 1938 Bra-Mac

These 26 photos, which measure 3 1/2" by 5" feature members of the 1938 Pittsburgh Pirates who lost the battle for the NL pennant very late in that season.

COMPLETE SET 6.00 15.00
1 Paul Waner .75 2.00
2 Lloyd Waner .60 1.50
3 Bill Swift .20 .50
4 Woody Jensen .20 .50
5 Jim Tobin .20 .50
6 Ray Berres .20 .50
7 Tommy Thevenow .20 .50
8 Bob Klinger .20 .50
9 Arky Vaughan .60 1.50
10 Pep Young .20 .50
11 Heinie Manush .60 1.50
12 Bill Brubaker .20 .50
13 Pie Traynor .75 2.00
14 Lee Handley .20 .50
15 Rip Sewell .20 .50
16 Johnny Dickshot .20 .50
17 Cy Blanton .20 .50
18 Gus Suhr .30 .75
19 Mace Brown .20 .50
20 Johnny Rizzo .20 .50
21 Al Todd .20 .50
22 Russ Bauers .20 .50
23 Ed Brandt .20 .50
24 Red Lucas .20 .50
25 Joe Bowman .20 .50
26 Ken Heintzleman .20 .50

1975 Pirates Postcards

This 29-card set of the Pittsburgh Pirates features player photos on postcard-size cards. The average size is 3 3/4" by 5 1/4". The fronts feature white-bordered black and white portraits. The player's name is printed in the wider bottom margin. Also a fascimile autograph in blue ink is inscribed across each picture. The backs are blank. The cards are unnumbered and checklisted below in alphabetical order.

COMPLETE SET (29) 8.00 20.00
1 Ken Brett .20 .50
2 John Candelaria .60 1.50
3 Larry Demery .20 .50
4 Duffy Dyer .20 .50
5 Dock Ellis .20 .50
6 Dave Giusti .20 .50
7 Richie Hebner .30 .75
8 Ramon Hernandez .20 .50
9 Art Howe .60 1.50
10 Ed Kirkpatrick .20 .50
11 Bruce Kison .20 .50
12 Don Leppert CO .20 .50
13 Mario Mendoza .20 .50
14 Bob Moose .20 .50
15 Danny Murtaugh MG .20 .50
16 Al Oliver .60 1.50
17 Don Osborne CO .20 .50
18 Jose Pagan CO .20 .50
19 Dave Parker 1.00 2.50
20 Paul Popovich .20 .50
21 Jerry Reuss .40 1.00
22 Bill Robinson .20 .50
23 Bob Robertson .20 .50
24 Jim Rooker .30 .75
25 Manny Sanguillen .30 .75
26 Willie Stargell 1.50 4.00
27 Rennie Stennett .20 .50
28 Frank Taveras .20 .50
29 Richie Zisk .20 .50

1976 Pirates Postcards

This 27-card set of the Pittsburgh Pirates features player photos on postcard-size cards. The cards are unnumbered and checklisted below in alphabetical order.

COMPLETE SET (27) 10.00 25.00
1 John Candelaria 1.25 3.00
2 Larry Demery .40 1.00
3 Dave Giusti .40 1.00
4 Richie Hebner .60 1.50
5 Tommy Helms .40 1.00
6 Ramon Hernandez .40 1.00
7 Ed Kirkpatrick .40 1.00
8 Bruce Kison .40 1.00
9 Don Leppert CO .40 1.00
10 George Medich .40 1.00
11 Mario Mendoza .40 1.00
12 Bob Moose .40 1.00
13 Danny Murtaugh MG .40 1.00
14 Al Oliver 1.25 3.00
15 Ed Ott .40 1.00
16 Dave Parker 1.25 3.00
17 Jerry Reuss .60 1.50
18 Bob Robertson .40 1.00
19 Bill Robinson .40 1.00
20 Jim Rooker .40 1.00
21 Manny Sanguillen .40 1.00
22 Bob Skinner CO .40 1.00
23 Willie Stargell 2.50 6.00
24 Rennie Stennett .40 1.00
25 Frank Taveras .40 1.00
26 Kent Tekulve .75 2.00
27 Richie Zisk .40 1.00

1977 Pirates Post-Gazette Portraits

This 30-card set was distributed in an 8 1/2" by 11" book from the Pittsburgh Post-Gazette. The black-and-white player portraits were detachable and measured approximately 8" by 11". The backs are blank. The cards are unnumbered and checklisted below in alphabetical order.

COMPLETE SET (30) 40.00 80.00
1 John Candelaria 1.50 4.00
2 Larry Demery 1.00 2.50
3 Miguel Dilone 1.00 2.50
4 Duffy Dyer 1.00 2.50
5 Terry Forster 1.00 2.50
6 Jim Fregosi 1.00 2.50
7 Phil Garner 1.50 4.00
8 Fernando Gonzalez 1.00 2.50
9 Goose Gossage 3.00 8.00
10 Grant Jackson 1.00 2.50
11 Odell Jones 1.00 2.50
12 Bruce Kison 1.00 2.50
13 Joe Lonnett CO 1.00 2.50
14 Mario Mendoza 1.00 2.50
15 Al Monchak CO 1.00 2.50
16 Omar Moreno 1.50 4.00
17 Al Oliver 3.00 8.00
18 Ed Ott 1.00 2.50
19 Jose Pagan CO 1.00 2.50
20 Dave Parker 3.00 8.00
21 Jerry Reuss 1.50 4.00
22 Bill Robinson 1.00 2.50
23 Jim Rooker 1.00 2.50
24 Larry Sherry CO 1.00 2.50
25 Willie Stargell 6.00 15.00
26 Rennie Stennett 1.00 2.50
27 Chuck Tanner MG 1.00 2.50
28 Frank Taveras 1.00 2.50
29 Kent Tekulve 1.50 4.00
30 Bobby Tolan 1.00 2.50

1977 Pirates 1960 World Champions TCMA

This 41-card set features black-and-white photos of the 1960 World Champion Pittsburgh Pirates in orange borders. The backs carry player information and statistics. (There is no card number 35 in the checklist.)

COMPLETE SET (41) 30.00 60.00
1 Danny Murtaugh MG .60 1.50
2 Dick Stuart .60 1.50
3 Bill Mazeroski 2.50 6.00
4 Dick Groat 1.00 2.50
5 Don Hoak .60 1.50
6 Roberto Clemente 6.00 15.00
7 Bill Virdon 1.00 2.50
8 Bob Skinner .60 1.50
9 Smoky Burgess 1.00 2.50
10 Gino Cimoli .60 1.50
11 Rocky Nelson .60 1.50
12 Hal Smith .60 1.50
13 Dick Schofield .60 1.50
14 Joe Christopher .60 1.50
15 Gene Baker .60 1.50
16 Bob Oldis .60 1.50
17 Vern Law 1.00 2.50
18 Bob Friend .60 1.50
19 Vinegar Bend Mizell .60 1.50
20 Havey Haddix .60 1.50
21 Roy Face 1.00 2.50
22 Freddie Green .60 1.50
23 Joe Gibbon .60 1.50
24 Clem Labine .60 1.50
25 Paul Giel .60 1.50
26 Tom Chaney .60 1.50
27 Earl Francis .60 1.50
28 Jim Umbricht .60 1.50
29 George Witt .60 1.50
30 Bennie Daniels .60 1.50
31 Don Gross .60 1.50
32 Diomedes Olivo .60 1.50
33 Ramon Mejias .60 1.50
34 Mickey Vernon 1.00 2.50

36 Danny Kravitz .60 1.50
37 Harry Bright .60 1.50
38 Dick Barone .60 1.50
39 Bill Burwell CO .60 1.50
40 Lenny Levy .60 1.50
41 Sam Narron CO .60 1.50
42 Bob Friend 1.00 2.50

1980 Pirates 1960 TCMA

This 41 card set was issued in 1980 and can be differentiated from the earlier TCMA 1960 Pirates set as the photos are clearer and the 1960 Pirates and player's name are on the front.

COMPLETE SET 8.00 20.00
1 Clem Labine .20 .50
2 Bob Friend .20 .50
3 Roy Face .30 .75
4 Vern Law .30 .75
5 Harvey Haddix .20 .50
6 Wilmer Mizell .08 .25
7 Bill Burwell .08 .25
8 Diomedes Olivo .08 .25
9 Don Gross .08 .25
10 Fred Green .08 .25
11 Jim Umbricht .08 .25
12 George Witt .08 .25
13 Tom Cheney .08 .25
14 Bennie Daniels .08 .25
15 Earl Francis .08 .25
16 Joe Gibbon .08 .25
17 Paul Giel .08 .25
18 Danny Kravitz .08 .25
19 R.C. Stevens .08 .25
20 Roman Mejias .08 .25
21 Dick Barone .08 .25
22 Sam Narron .08 .25
23 Harry Bright .08 .25
24 Mickey Vernon .20 .50
25 Bob Skinner .08 .25
26 Smoky Burgess .08 .25
27 Bill Virdon .08 .25
28 Roberto Clemente 2.00 5.00
No Number on back
29 Don Hoak .20 .50
30 Bill Mazeroski 1.00 2.50
31 Dick Stuart .30 .75
32 Dick Groat .40 1.00
33 Bob Oldis .08 .25
34 Gene Baker .08 .25
35 Joe Christopher .08 .25
36 Dick Schofield .08 .25
37 Hal W. Smith .08 .25
38 Rocky Nelson .08 .25
39 Gino Cimoli .08 .25
40 Danny Murtaugh MG .08 .25
41 Leo Levy .08 .25

1983 Pirates All-Time TCMA

1 Willie Stargell .40 1.00
2 Bill Mazeroski .40 1.00
3 Pie Traynor .30 .75
4 Honus Wagner .40 1.00
5 Roberto Clemente .75 2.00
6 Paul Waner .40 1.00
Lloyd Waner
7 Ralph Kiner .40 1.00
8 Manny Sanguillen .08 .25
9 Deacon Phillippe .08 .25
10 Bob Veale .08 .25
11 Roy Face .08 .25
12 Danny Murtaugh .08 .25

1983 Pirates Greats TCMA

This 12-card set features various all-time Pittsburgh Pirates greats. The fronts display a black-and-white player photo with blue borders. The backs carry player information.

COMPLETE SET (12) 3.00 8.00
1 Willie Stargell .40 1.00
2 Bill Mazeroski .40 1.00
3 Pie Traynor .30 .75
4 Honus Wagner .40 1.00
5 Roberto Clemente .75 2.00
6 Paul Waner .40 1.00
Lloyd Waner
7 Ralph Kiner .40 1.00
8 Manny Sanguillen .08 .25
9 Deacon Phillippe .08 .25
10 Bob Veale .08 .25
11 Roy Face .08 .25
12 Danny Murtaugh .08 .25

1984 Pirates

This 27-card set of the Pittsburgh Pirates measures approximately 3 3/8" by 5 1/4" and features white-bordered color player portraits with the player's name, jersey number, and position printed in the wide bottom margin. A facsimile autograph rounds out the front. The backs carry the dates of different games and name of the game sponsor. The cards are unnumbered and checklisted below in alphabetical order.

COMPLETE SET (27) 3.00 8.00
1 Rafael Belliard .08 .25
2 Dale Berra .08 .25
3 John Candelaria .20 .50
4 Jose DeLeon .08 .25
5 Doug Frobel .08 .25
6 Cecilio Guante .08 .25
7 Brian Harper .08 .25
8 Lee Lacy .08 .25
9 Bill Madlock .20 .50
10 Milt May .08 .25
11 Lee Mazzilli .20 .50
12 Larry McWilliams .08 .25
13 Jim Morrison .08 .25
14 Amos Otis .08 .25
15 Tony Pena .20 .50
16 Johnny Ray .08 .25
17 Rick Rhoden .08 .25
18 Don Robinson .08 .25
19 Manny Sarmiento .08 .25
20 Rod Scurry .08 .25
21 Chuck Tanner .20 .50
22 Kent Tekulve .20 .50
23 Jason Thompson .08 .25
24 John Tudor .20 .50
25 Lee Tunnell .08 .25
26 Hedi Vargas .08 .25
27 Marvell Wynne .08 .25

1985 Pirates

This 23-card set of the Pittsburgh Pirates measures approximately 3 3/8" by 5 1/4" and features white-bordered color player portraits with the player's name, jersey number, and position printed in the wide bottom margin. A facsimile autograph rounds out the front. The backs carry the dates of different games and name of the game sponsor. The cards are unnumbered and checklisted below in alphabetical order.

COMPLETE SET (23) 2.50 6.00
1 Bill Almon .08 .25
2 Rafael Belliard .08 .25
3 Mike Bielecki .08 .25
4 John Candelaria .20 .50
5 Jose DeLeon .08 .25
6 Tim Foli .08 .25
7 George Hendrick .08 .25
8 Steve Kemp .08 .25
9 Sixto Lezcano .08 .25
10 Bill Madlock .20 .50
11 Lee Mazzilli .08 .25
12 Larry McWilliams .08 .25
13 Jim Morrison .08 .25
14 Junior Ortiz .08 .25
15 Tony Pena .20 .50
16 Johnny Ray .08 .25
17 Rick Rhoden .08 .25
18 Don Robinson .08 .25
19 Rod Scurry .08 .25
20 Chuck Tanner .20 .50
21 Jason Thompson .08 .25
22 Lee Tunnell .08 .25
23 Marvell Wynne .08 .25

1986 Pirates Greats TCMA

This 12-card standard-size set features all-time leading Pittsburgh Pirates. The player's photo and his name are featured on the front. The back gives more information about that player.

COMPLETE SET (12) 3.00 8.00
1 Willie Stargell .40 1.00
2 Bill Mazeroski .30 .75
3 Honus Wagner .40 1.00
4 Pie Traynor .40 1.00
5 Ralph Kiner .30 .75
6 Paul Waner .30 .75
7 Roberto Clemente 1.00 2.50
8 Manny Sanguillen .08 .25
9 Vic Willis .20 .50
10 Wilbur Cooper .08 .25
11 Roy Face .08 .25
12 Danny Murtaugh MG .08 .25

1987 Pirates 1960 TCMA

This nine-card standard-size set features members of the 1960 Pittsburgh Pirates. The player photo takes up most of the front with his name noted underneath. The backs give more information about the player as well as their 1960 stats.

COMPLETE SET (9) 1.50 4.00
1 Dick Stuart .08 .25
2 Bill Mazeroski .40 1.00
3 Dick Groat .20 .50
4 Roberto Clemente 1.00 2.50
5 Bob Skinner .08 .25
6 Smoky Burgess .08 .25
7 Roy Face .20 .50
8 Bob Friend .08 .25
9 Vernon Law .20 .50

1988 Pirates Schedule Postcards

This 33-card set features color photos of the Pittsburgh Pirates measuring approximately 3 1/2" by 5 1/2". The cards are unnumbered and checklisted below in alphabetical order. The backs of these cards have basic player information and the Pirated 1988 home schedule.

COMPLETE SET (33) 8.00 20.00
1 Rafael Belliard .08 .25
2 Barry Bonds 4.00 10.00
3 Bobby Bonilla .20 .50
4 Sid Bream .08 .25
5 John Cangelosi .08 .25
6 Darnell Coles .08 .25
7 Mike Diaz .08 .25
8 Rich Donnelly CO .08 .25
9 Doug Drabek .20 .50
10 Mike Dunne .08 .25
11 Felix Fermin .08 .25
12 Brian Fisher .08 .25
13 Lanny Frattare ANN .08 .25
14 Jim Gott .08 .25
15 Barry Jones .08 .25
16 Bob Kipper .08 .25
17 Gene Lamont CO .08 .25
18 Mike LaValliere .08 .25
19 Jim Leyland MG .20 .50
20 Jose Lind .08 .25
21 Milt May CO .08 .25
22 Ray Miller CO .08 .25
23 Randy Milligan .08 .25
24 Junior Ortiz .08 .25
25 Al Pedrique .08 .25
26 Pirate Parrot(Mascot) .20 .50
27 R.J. Reynolds .08 .25
28 Jeff Robinson .08 .25
29 Jim Rooker ANN .08 .25
30 Tommy Sandt CO .08 .25
31 John Smiley .08 .25
32 Andy Van Slyke .20 .50
33 Bob Walk .08 .25

1989 Pirates Very Fine Juice

The 1989 Very Fine Juice Pittsburgh Pirates set is a 30-card set with cards measuring approximately 2 1/2" by 3 1/2" featuring the members of the 1989 Pittsburgh Pirates. This set was issued on three separate perforated sheets: two panels contain 15 player cards each, while the third panel serves as a cover for the set and displays color action photos of the Pirates. These panels were given away to fans attending the Pirates home game on April 23, 1989. There was a coupon (expiring on 10/31/89) on the back that could be redeemed for a free can of juice. The cards are numbered by uniform number in the list below. The cards are very colorful.

COMPLETE SET (30) 8.00 20.00
NNO Jumior Ortiz .20 .50
2 Gary Redus .20 .50
3 Jay Bell .20 .50
5 Sid Bream .20 .50
6 Rafael Belliard .20 .50
10 Jim Leyland MG .30 .75
11 Glenn Wilson .20 .50
12 Mike LaValliere .20 .50
13 Jose Lind .20 .50
14 Ken Oberkfell .20 .50
15 Doug Drabek .30 .75
16 Bob Kipper .20 .50
17 Bob Walk .20 .50
18 Andy Van Slyke .30 .75
23 R.J. Reynolds .20 .50
24 Barry Bonds 2.50 6.00
25 Bobby Bonilla .30 .75
26 Neal Heaton .20 .50
30 Benny Distefano .20 .50
31 Ray Miller CO and .20 .50
37 Tommy Sandt CO
35 Jim Gott .20 .50
36 Bruce Kimm CO and .20 .50
32 Gene Lamont CO
39 Milt May CO and .20 .50
45 Rich Donnelly CO
41 Mike Dunne .20 .50
43 Bill Landrum .20 .50
44 John Cangelosi .20 .50
49 Jeff D. Robinson .20 .50
52 Dorn Taylor .20 .50
54 Brian Fisher .20 .50
57 John Smiley .20 .50

1990 Pirates Homers Cookies

The 1990 Homers Cookies Pittsburgh Pirates set is an attractive 31-card set measuring approximately 4" by 6", used as a giveaway at a Pirates home game. It has been reported that 25,000 of these sets were produced. Four Homers Baseball trivia question cards were also included with the complete set. The fronts are full-color action photos with the backs containing complete statistical information. The set has been checklisted alphabetically below.

COMPLETE SET (31) 6.00 15.00
1 Wally Backman .08 .25
2 Doug Bair .08 .25
3 Rafael Belliard .08 .25
4 Jay Bell .08 .25
5 Barry Bonds 4.00 10.00
6 Bobby Bonilla .20 .50
7 Sid Bream .08 .25
8 John Cangelosi .08 .25
9 Rich Donnelly CO .08 .25
10 Doug Drabek .20 .50
11 Billy Hatcher .08 .25
12 Neal Heaton .08 .25
13 Jeff King .08 .25
14 Bob Kipper .08 .25
15 Randy Kramer .08 .25
16 Gene Lamont CO .08 .25
17 Bill Landrum .08 .25
18 Mike LaValliere .08 .25
19 Jim Leyland MG .20 .50
20 Jose Lind .08 .25
21 Milt May .08 .25
22 Ray Miller CO .08 .25
23 Ted Power .08 .25
24 Gary Redus .08 .25
25 R.J. Reynolds .08 .25
26 Tommy Sandt CO .08 .25
27 Don Slaught .08 .25
28 Walt Terrell .08 .25
29 Andy Van Slyke .20 .50
30 John Smiley .08 .25
31 Bob Walk .08 .25

1992 Pirates Nationwide Insurance

This 25-card set was sponsored by Nationwide Insurance, the Pittsburgh Bureau of Fire, and West Penn Hospital. The cards are oversized and measure 3 1/2" by 5 3/4". The color action player photos on the front are edged by a thin red and a wider white border. Superimposed at the bottom of the picture are the team logo, the player's name in a yellow banner, and his jersey number in a baseball icon. The backs feature statistical information about the player and fire safety tips. The cards are unnumbered and checklisted below in alphabetical order.

COMPLETE SET (25) 6.00 15.00
1 Stan Belinda .20 .50
2 Jay Bell .30 .75
3 Barry Bonds 3.00 8.00
4 Steve Buechele .20 .50
5 Terry Collins CO .20 .50
6 Rich Donnelly CO .20 .50
7 Doug Drabek .40 1.00
8 Cecil Espy .20 .50
9 Jeff King .20 .50
10 Mike LaValliere .20 .50
11 Jim Leyland MG .30 .75
12 Jose Lind .20 .50
13 Roger Mason .20 .50
14 Milt May CO .20 .50
15 Lloyd McClendon .20 .50
16 Orlando Merced .20 .50
17 Denny Neagle .60 1.50
18 Bob Patterson .20 .50
19 Gary Redus .20 .50
20 Don Slaught .20 .50
21 Zane Smith .20 .50
22 Randy Tomlin .20 .50
23 Andy Van Slyke .30 .75
24 Gary Varsho .20 .50
25 Bob Walk .20 .50

1993 Pirates Hills

Originally issued in perforated sheet form , these 24 standard-size cards feature on their fronts color player action shots with white outer borders and yellow inner borders. The cards are unnumbered and checklisted below in alphabetical order.

COMPLETE SET 8.00 20.00
1 Stan Belinda .30 .75
2 Jay Bell .30 .75
3 John Candelaria .40 1.00
4 Dave Clark .30 .75
5 Steve Cooke .30 .75
6 Tom Foley .30 .75
7 Carlos Garcia .30 .75
8 Jeff King .30 .75
9 Jim Leyland MG .40 1.00
10 Al Martin .30 .75
11 Lloyd McClendon .30 .75
12 Orlando Merced .30 .75
13 Blas Minor .30 .75
14 Denny Neagle .30 .75
15 Tom Prince .30 .75
16 Don Slaught .30 .75
17 Lonnie Smith .30 .75
18 Zane Smith .30 .75
19 Randy Tomlin .30 .75
20 Andy Van Slyke .40 1.00
21 Paul Wagner .30 .75
22 Tim Wakefield 1.00 2.50
23 Bob Walk .30 .75
24 Kevin Young .30 .75

1993 Pirates Nationwide Insurance

These 40 oversized cards measure approximately 3 3/8" by 5 5/8". The color action player photos on the front are edged by a thin black line and a wide white border. The top of the card has a thin red border, and a red block carries the player's name printed in white and the Bucs' Three-Peat logo. The backs include biography and how the player was obtained. The Nationwide Insurance logo at the bottom rounds out the back. On Sunday June 27, children 14 and under were given a set at the Pirates-Phillies game at Three Rivers Stadium. Quintex Mobile Communications/Bell Atlantic is listed as the sponsor on the backs of the giveaway sets. The Parrot card and the Three Rivers card are not included in the Quintex sets.

COMPLETE SET (40) 4.00 10.00
1 Stan Belinda .08 .25
2 Jay Bell .08 .25
3 Steve Blass ANN .08 .25
4 John Candelaria .20 .50
5 Dave Clark .08 .25
6 Terry Collins CO .08 .25
7 Steve Cooke .08 .25
8 Kent Derdivannis ANN .08 .25
9 Rich Donnelly CO .08 .25
10 Tom Foley .08 .25
11 Lanny Frattare ANN .08 .25
12 Carlos Garcia .08 .25
13 Jeff King .08 .25
14 Jim Leyland MG .20 .50
15 Al Martin .08 .25
16 Milt May CO .08 .25
17 Lloyd McClendon .08 .25
18 Orlando Merced .08 .25
19 Ray Miller CO .08 .25
20 Blas Minor .08 .25
21 Dennis Moeller .08 .25
22 Denny Neagle .40 1.00
23 Dave Otto .08 .25
24 Pirate Parrot(Mascot) .20 .50
25 Tom Prince .08 .25
26 Jim Rooker ANN .08 .25
27 Tommy Sandt CO .08 .25
28 Ted Simmons XGM .30 .75
29 Don Slaught .08 .25
30 Lonnie Smith .08 .25
31 Zane Smith .08 .25
32 Randy Tomlin .08 .25
33 Andy Van Slyke .20 .50
34 Bill Virdon CO .20 .50
35 Paul Wagner .08 .25
36 Tim Wakefield .60 1.50
37 Bob Walk .08 .25
38 John Wehner .08 .25
39 Kevin Young .08 .25
40 Three Rivers Stadium .08 .25

1994 Pirates Quintex

These 29 oversized cards measure approximately 3 1/2" by 5 3/4". This set was passed out on July 31, 1994 at the Pirates' home game. A coupon for a cellular transportable bag phone at no charge came with it. The cards are unnumbered and checklisted below in alphabetical order. Cards are also known which say Nationwide Insurance. These cards have the same value as the Quintex cards. The Jon Lieber card was issued later and is considered a Short Print since it was not included in the regular set.

COMPLETE SET (30 5.00 12.00
COMMON CARD (1-30 .10 .25
COMMON SP 2.00 5.00
1 Jay Bell .08 .25
2 Dave Clark .08 .25
3 Steve Cooke .08 .25
4 Mark Dewey .08 .25
5 Rich Donnelly CO .08 .25
6 Tom Foley .08 .25
7 Carlos Garcia .08 .25
8 Brian Hunter .08 .25
9 Jeff King .08 .25
10 Jim Leyland MG .20 .50
11 Jon Lieber SP
12 Ravelo Manzanillo .08 .25
13 Al Martin .08 .25
14 Milt May CO .08 .25
15 Lloyd McClendon .08 .25
16 Orlando Merced .08 .25
17 Dan Miceli .08 .25
18 Ray Miller CO .08 .25
19 Denny Neagle .30 .75
20 Pirate Parrot (Mascot) .20 .50
21 Tommy Sandt CO .08 .25
22 Don Slaught .08 .25
23 Zane Smith .08 .25
24 Andy Van Slyke .20 .50
25 Bill Virdon CO .20 .50
26 Paul Wagner .08 .25
27 Rick White .08 .25
28 Spin Williams CO .08 .25
29 Kevin Young .08 .25
30 Three Rivers Stadium .08 .25

1995 Pirates Coca-Cola Pogs

This set of 27 pogs commemorates the 25th anniversary of Three River Stadium where the Pirates play and was issued in three sheets of nine pogs each. The pogs measure approximately 11/16" in diameter. The fronts feature color and black-and-white photos of great moments that happened at the stadium. The backs carry the significance of the moment and the date it occurred along with either the Coke, Sprite, or Fruitopia logo.

COMPLETE SET (25) 6.00 15.00
1 1994 All-Star Game 7/12/94 .08 .25
2 Roberto Clemente 1.25 3.00
3,000th Career Hit 9/30/72
3 Roberto Clemente 1.25 3.00
Uniform #21 Retired 4/6/73
4 We Are Family Logo .08 .25
Pirates win NL Pennant 10/5/79
5 John Candelaria .08 .25
No-Hits the Dodgers 8/9/76
6 Willie Stargell .40 1.00
Uniform #8 Retired 9/6/82
7 Mike Schmidt/500th Home Run 4/18/87.75 2.00
8 A Pirates' Pitcher .08 .25
First Game Played at Three Rivers 7/16/70
9 1971 World Series Game 4 .08 .25
First Ever Played at Night 10/13/71
10 Nellie Briles .08 .25
World Series Game Five 10/14/71
11 Pirates Win 1971 NL Pennant .08 .25
Pirates beat Giants 10/6/71
12 Pirates Clinch NL East .08 .25
10/30/1979
13 Pirates Three-Peat .08 .25
Clinch NL East 9/27/92
14 Bob Gibson .40 1.00
No-Hits the Pirates 8/14/71
15 1979 World Series Game 5 .08 .25
Bucs Battle Back vs Baltimore 10/14/79
16 Pirates Clinch NL East 9/27/70 .08 .25
17 Bob Walk .08 .25
Beats Braves
NLCS Game Five 10/10/92
18 John Milner .08 .25
9th Inning Grand Slam Beats Phillies 8/5/79
19 Barry Bonds 1.25 3.00
11th Inning Homer Beats St. Louis 8/12/91
20 Pirates Score 5 Runs in 9th .08 .25
Beat Dodgers 5/28/90
21 Danny Murtaugh MG .08 .25
Joe Brown GM
Retire 10/3/76
22 The Gunner .08 .25
Returns to Broadcast Booth 5/3/85
23 Pirates Sweep Phillies .08 .25
Doubleheader 9/29/78
24 Jim Leyland MG .08 .25
Makes Pittsburgh Debut 4/8/86
25 1974 All-Star Game 7/23/74 .08 .25
NNO Coke Logo .08 .25
NNO Coke Logo .08 .25
Fruitopia Logo

1995 Pirates Filmet

This 30-card set of the Pittsburgh Pirates was distributed on Picture Card Night as a perforated sheet measuring approximately 20 1/4" by 13 1/2". The cards themselves measure 2 1/4" by 3 1/4" and feature a color action player photo in a white border. The player's name is printed in yellow in a red banner at the top with the team name in gold running down the side margins. The white backs carry the player's name, position, biography and career information. The cards were created using Kodak Photo CD technology, output, and printed by Filmet Commercial Services. A coupon at the bottom could be used at Filmet locations for film processing. The cards are unnumbered and checklisted below in alphabetical order.

COMPLETE SET (30) 3.00 8.00
1 Rich Aude .08 .25
2 Jay Bell .08 .25
3 Jacob Brumfield .08 .25
4 Jason Christiansen .08 .25
5 Dave Clark .08 .25
6 Steve Cooke .08 .25
7 Midre Cummings .08 .25
8 Mike Dyer .08 .25
9 Angelo Encarnacion .08 .25
10 Carlos Garcia .08 .25
11 Freddy Adrian Garcia .08 .25
12 Jim Gott .08 .25
13 Mark Johnson .08 .25
14 Jeff King .08 .25
15 Jim Leyland MG .20 .50
16 Jon Lieber .20 .50
17 Nelson Liriano .08 .25
18 Esteban Loaiza .40 1.00
19 Al Martin .08 .25
20 Jeff McCurry .08 .25
21 Orlando Merced .08 .25
22 Dan Miceli .08 .25
23 Denny Neagle .08 .25
24 Mark Parent .08 .25
25 Steve Pegues .08 .25
26 Dan Plesac .08 .25
27 Don Slaught .08 .25
28 Paul Wagner .08 .25
29 Rick White .08 .25
30 Gary Wilson .08 .25

1997 Pirates Post-Gazette

This one-card set measures approximately 3 1/2" by 5 3/4" and features a color photo of Pittsburgh Pirates catcher Jason Kendall in a paint-splashed border with a simulated autograph on the front. The back contains player information in a ticket format.

1 Jason Kendall 2.00 5.00

1997 Pirates Postcards

This 45-card set of the 1997 Pittsburgh Pirates features color player portraits with the player's name, position, and jersey number printed on the front. The backs carry the team logo and player information. The cards are unnumbered and checklisted below in alphabetical order.

COMPLETE SET (45) 5.00 12.00
1 Jermaine Allensworth .08 .25
2 Steve Blass ANN .20 .50
3 Adrian Brown .08 .25
4 Emil Brown .20 .50
5 Greg Brown ANN .08 .25
6 Jason Christiansen .08 .25
7 Lou Collier .08 .25
8 Steve Cooke .08 .25
9 Francisco Cordova .08 .25
10 Midre Cummings .08 .25
11 Kevin Elster .08 .25
12 John Ericks .08 .25
13 Lanny Frattare ANN .08 .25
13 Spin Williams CO .08 .25
14 Jeff Granger .08 .25
15 Jose Guillen .75 2.00
16 Mark Johnson .08 .25
17 Joe Jones CO .08 .25
18 Jason Kendall .60 1.50
19 Gene Lamont MG .08 .25
20 Jon Lieber .30 .75
21 Jack Lind CO .08 .25
22 Esteban Loaiza .30 .75
23 Rich Loiselle .08 .25
24 Al Martin .08 .25
25 Lloyd McClendon CO .08 .25
26 Keith Osik .08 .25
27 Chris Peters .08 .25
28 Kevin Polcovich .08 .25
29 Joe Randa .20 .50
30 Rick Renick CO .08 .25
31 Ricardo Rincon .08 .25
32 Matt Ruebel .08 .25
33 Jason Schmidt .75 2.00
34 Jose Silva .08 .25
35 Mark Smith .08 .25
36 Clint Sodowsky .08 .25
37 Dale Sveum .08 .25
38 Pete Vuckovich CO .08 .25
39 Dave Wainhouse .08 .25
40 Bob Walk ANN .08 .25
41 Turner Ward .08 .25
42 Marc Wilkins .08 .25
44 Tony Womack .08 .25
45 Kevin Young .08 .25

1998 Pirates Postcards

These 3 5/8" by 4 3/4" color postcards feature members of the 1998 Pittsburgh Pirates. The fronts have the player photo, his name and position. The backs can have the Pirates logo, a brief bio and and an "Advance Auto Parts" logo. Since the cards are unnumbered we have sequenced them in alphabetical order.

COMPLETE SET 6.00 15.00
1 Jermaine Allensworth .20 .50
2 Steve Blass ANN .30 .75
3 Greg Brown ANN .20 .50
4 Jason Christianson .20 .50
5 Lou Collier .20 .50
6 Francisco Cordova .20 .50
7 Elmer Dessens .20 .50
8 Lanny Frattare ANN .20 .50
9 Jose Guillen .75 2.00
10 Jason Kendall .60 1.50
11 Gene Lamont MG .20 .50
12 Jon Lieber .40 1.00
13 Jack Lind CO .20 .50
14 Scott Little CO .20 .50
15 Esteban Loaiza .40 1.00
16 Rich Loiselle .20 .50
17 Al Martin .20 .50
18 Javier Martinez .20 .50
19 Manny Martinez .20 .50
20 Keith Osik .20 .50
21 Chris Peters .20 .50
22 Kevin Polcovich .20 .50
23 Aramis Ramirez 1.50 4.00
24 Ricardo Rincon .20 .50
25 Chance Sanford .20 .50
26 Jason Schmidt .75 2.00
27 Jose Silva .20 .50
28 Jeff Tabaka .20 .50
29 Turner Ward .20 .50
30 Marc Wilkins .20 .50
31 Mike Williams .20 .50
32 Tony Womack .20 .50
32 Kevin Young .20 .50

1999 Pirates Postcards Advance

This 36 card set measures 3 5/8" by 4 3/4" and features members of the 1999 Pittsburgh Pirates. The set was sponsored by Advance Auto Parts. The cards are unnumbered so we have sequenced them in alphabetical order

COMPLETE SET 4.00 10.00
1 Jeff Banister .08 .25
2 Mike Benjamin .08 .25
3 Kris Benson .60 1.50
4 Adrian Brown .08 .25
5 Brant Brown .08 .25
6 Jason Christiansen .08 .25
7 Brad Clontz .08 .25
8 Francisco Cordova .08 .25
9 Freddy Garcia .08 .25
10 Brian Giles .40 1.00
11 Jose Guillen .40 1.00
12 Joe Jones .08 .25
13 Jason Kendall .40 1.00
14 Gene Lamont MG .08 .25
15 Jack Lind .08 .25
16 Rich Loiselle .08 .25
17 Al Martin .08 .25
18 Lloyd McClendon CO .08 .25
19 Pat Meares .08 .25
20 Warren Morris .08 .25
21 Abraham Nunez .08 .25
22 Keith Osik .08 .25
23 Chris Peters .08 .25
24 Rich Renick CO .08 .25
25 Todd Ritchie .08 .25
26 Scott Sauerbeck .08 .25
27 Pete Schourek .08 .25
28 Jason Schmidt .40 1.00
29 Jose Silva .08 .25
30 Ed Sprague .08 .25
31 Chris Tremie .08 .25
32 Pete Vuckovich CO .08 .25
33 Jeff Wallace .08 .25
34 Turner Ward .08 .25
35 John Werner .08 .25
36 Marc Wilkins .08 .25
37 Mike Williams .08 .25
38 Spin Williams .08 .25
39 Kevin Young .08 .25

1999 Pirates Postcards Post-Gazette

These seven postcards measure 3 1/2" by 5 3/4" and are numbered by the uniform numbers. The backs feature the stats of the players featured.

COMPLETE SET 4.00 10.00
1 Brian Giles 1.00 2.50
2 Jason Kendall 1.00 2.50
3 Pat Meares .40 1.00
4 Warren Morris .40 1.00
5 Jason Schmidt 1.00 2.50
6 Ed Sprague .40 1.00
7 Kevin Young .40 1.00

2000 Pirates Postcards

COMPLETE SET 6.00 15.00
1 Jimmy Anderson .20 .50
2 Bruce Aven .20 .50
3 Jeff Banister .20 .50
4 Mike Benjamin .20 .50
5 Kris Benson .60 1.50
6 Adrian Brown .20 .50
7 Jason Christensen .20 .50
8 Wil Cordero .20 .50
9 Francisco Cordova .20 .50
10 Brian Giles .60 1.50
11 Jason Kendall .60 1.50
12 Gene Lamont MG .20 .50
13 Rich Loiselle .20 .50
14 Lloyd McClendon CO .20 .50
15 Pat Meares .20 .50
16 Warren Morris .20 .50
17 Abraham Nunez .20 .50
18 Keith Osik .20 .50
19 Rick Renick CO .20 .50
20 Todd Richie .20 .50
21 Scott Sauerbeck .20 .50
22 Jason Schmidt .60 1.50
23 Jose Silva .20 .50
24 Luis Sojo .20 .50
25 John Vander Wal .20 .50
26 Pete Vuckovich CO .20 .50
27 Mike Williams .20 .50
28 Spin Williams CO .20 .50
29 Kevin Young .20 .50

2002 Pirates Outback

COMPLETE SET 10.00 20.00
1 Jimmy Anderson .20 .50
2 Jeff Banister .20 .50
3 Joe Beimel .20 .50
4 Mike Benjamin .20 .50
5 Steve Blass ANN .30 .75
6 Brian Boehringer .20 .50
7 Adrian Brown .20 .50
8 Greg Brown ANN .20 .50
9 Dave Clark .20 .50
10 Mike Fetters .20 .50
11 Josh Fogg .30 .75
12 Lanny Frattare ANN .20 .50
13 Brian Giles .60 1.50
14 Chad Hermansen .20 .50
15 Trent Jewett .20 .50
16 Jason Kendall .60 1.50
17 Sean Lowe .20 .50
18 Rob Mackowiak .20 .50
19 Josias Manzanillo .20 .50
20 Lloyd McClendon MG .20 .50
21 Russ Nixon CO .20 .50
22 Abraham Nunez .20 .50
23 Keith Osik .20 .50
24 Aramis Ramirez .75 2.00
25 Pokey Reese .20 .50
26 Armando Rios .20 .50
27 Tommy Sandt CO .20 .50
28 Scott Sauerbeck .20 .50
29 Bruce Tanner CO .20 .50
30 Ron Villone .20 .50
31 Bill Virdon CO .20 .50
32 Ryan Vogelsong .20 .50
33 Bob Walk ANN .20 .50
34 Dave Williams .20 .50
35 Mike Williams .20 .50
36 Spin Williams .20 .50
37 Craig Wilson .60 1.50
38 Jack Wilson .60 1.50
39 Kip Wells .20 .50
40 Kevin Young .20 .50
41 Pirate Parrot .20 .50
Mascot

2003 Pirates Outback

COMPLETE SET 10.00 20.00
1 Joe Beimel .20 .50
2 Kris Benson .60 1.50
3 Brian Boehringer .20 .50
4 Humberto Cota .20 .50
5 Jeff D'Amico .20 .50
6 Alvaro Espinoza CO .20 .50
7 Josh Fogg .20 .50
8 Lanny Frattare ANN .20 .50
9 Brian Giles .60 1.50
10 Adam Hyzdu .20 .50
11 Jason Kendall .60 1.50
12 Rusty Kuntz CO .20 .50
13 Mike Lincoln .20 .50
14 Dave Littlefield .20 .50
15 Kenny Lofton .40 1.00
16 Pete Mackanin CO .20 .50
17 Rob Mackowiak .20 .50
18 Kevin McClatchy OWN .20 .50
19 Lloyd McClendon MG .20 .50
Outback Logo
20 Lloyd McClendon MG .20 .50
No Outback Logo
21 Brian Meadows .20 .50
22 Gerald Perry CO .20 .50
23 Aramis Ramirez .75 2.00
24 Jeff Reboulet .20 .50
25 Pokey Reese .20 .50
26 Dennys Reyes .20 .50
27 Carlos Rivera .20 .50
28 John Russell .20 .50
29 Reggie Sanders .30 .75

30 Scott Sauerbeck .20 .50
31 Randall Simon .20 .50
32 Matt Stairs .20 .50
33 Jeff Suppan .20 .50
34 Bruce Tanner CO .20 .50
35 Julian Tavarez .20 .50
36 Salomon Torres .20 .50
37 Bob Walk ANN .20 .50
38 Kip Wells .20 .50
39 Dave Williams .20 .50
40 Mike Williams .20 .50
41 Spin Williams .20 .50
42 Craig Wilson .60 1.50
43 Jack Wilson .60 1.50
44 Kevin Young .20 .50
45 Pirate Parrot Mascot .20 .50

2006 Pirates Topps

COMPLETE SET (14) 3.00 8.00
PIT1 Jason Bay .12 .30
PIT2 Zach Duke .12 .30
PIT3 Oliver Perez .12 .30
PIT4 Kip Wells .12 .30
PIT5 Jack Wilson .12 .30
PIT6 Jose Castillo .12 .30
PIT7 Freddy Sanchez .12 .30
PIT8 Jody Gerut .12 .30
PIT9 Chris Duffy .12 .30
PIT10 Joe Randa .12 .30
PIT11 Daryle Ward .12 .30
PIT12 Sean Casey .12 .30
PIT13 Jeromy Burnitz .12 .30
PIT14 Ryan Doumit .12 .30

2007 Pirates Topps

COMPLETE SET (14) 3.00 8.00
PIT1 Jason Bay .20 .50
PIT2 Ronny Paulino .12 .30
PIT3 Matt Capps .12 .30
PIT4 Jose Castillo .12 .30
PIT5 Ian Snell .12 .30
PIT6 Freddy Sanchez .12 .30
PIT7 Adam LaRoche .12 .30
PIT8 Tom Gorzelanny .12 .30
PIT9 Jack Wilson .12 .30
PIT10 Chris Duffy .12 .30
PIT11 Jose Bautista .20 .50
PIT12 Xavier Nady .12 .30
PIT13 Paul Maholm .12 .30
PIT14 Zach Duke .12 .30

2008 Pirates Topps

COMPLETE SET (14) 3.00 8.00
PIT1 Jason Bay .20 .50
PIT2 Ronny Paulino .12 .30
PIT3 Matt Capps .12 .30
PIT4 Nate McLouth .12 .30
PIT5 Ian Snell .12 .30
PIT6 Freddy Sanchez .12 .30
PIT7 Adam LaRoche .12 .30
PIT8 Tom Gorzelanny .12 .30
PIT9 Jack Wilson .12 .30
PIT10 Chris Duffy .12 .30
PIT11 Jose Bautista .20 .50
PIT12 Xavier Nady .12 .30
PIT13 Paul Maholm .12 .30
PIT14 Zach Duke .12 .30

2009 Pirates Topps

PIT1 Nate McLouth .15 .40
PIT2 Tom Gorzelanny .15 .40
PIT3 Ryan Doumit .15 .40
PIT4 Paul Maholm .15 .40
PIT5 Freddy Sanchez .15 .40
PIT6 Zach Duke .15 .40
PIT7 Adam LaRoche .15 .40
PIT8 Matt Capps .15 .40
PIT9 Jack Wilson .15 .40
PIT10 Ian Snell .15 .40
PIT11 Jeff Karstens .15 .40
PIT12 Nyjer Morgan .15 .40
PIT13 Steve Pearce .40 1.00
PIT14 Andy LaRoche .15 .40
PIT15 PNC BallPark .15 .40

2010 Pirates Topps

PIT1 Andrew McCutchen .40 1.00
PIT2 Ryan Doumit .15 .40
PIT3 Garrett Jones .15 .40
PIT4 Neil Walker .25 .60
PIT5 Ross Ohlendorf .15 .40
PIT6 Bobby Crosby .15 .40
PIT7 Zach Duke .15 .40
PIT8 Kevin Hart .15 .40
PIT9 Ronny Cedeno .15 .40
PIT10 Daniel McCutchen .25 .60
PIT11 Lastings Milledge .15 .40
PIT12 Jason Jaramillo .15 .40
PIT13 Andy LaRoche .15 .40
PIT14 Delwyn Young .15 .40
PIT15 Akinori Iwamura .15 .40
PIT16 Steve Pearce .40 1.00
PIT17 Paul Maholm .15 .40

2011 Pirates Topps

PIT1 Pedro Alvarez .30 .75
PIT2 Andrew McCutchen .40 1.00
PIT3 Matt Diaz .15 .40
PIT4 Chris Snyder .15 .40
PIT5 Jose Tabata .15 .40
PIT6 Neil Walker .25 .60
PIT7 James McDonald .15 .40
PIT8 Joel Hanrahan .25 .60
PIT9 Evan Meek .15 .40
PIT10 Lyle Overbay .15 .40
PIT11 Ross Ohlendorf .15 .40
PIT12 Jason Jaramillo .15 .40
PIT13 Daniel McCutchen .15 .40
PIT14 Garrett Jones .15 .40
PIT15 Kevin Correia .15 .40
PIT16 Paul Maholm .15 .40
PIT17 PNC Park .15 .40

2012 Pirates Topps

PIT1 Andrew McCutchen .40 1.00
PIT2 Alex Presley .25 .60
PIT3 Clint Barmes .25 .60
PIT4 Neil Walker .25 .60
PIT5 Garrett Jones .25 .60
PIT6 Casey McGehee .25 .60
PIT7 Michael McKenry .25 .60
PIT8 Jose Tabata .25 .60
PIT9 Chase d'Arnaud .25 .60
PIT10 Erik Bedard .25 .60
PIT11 Charlie Morton .40 1.00
PIT12 Kevin Correia .25 .60
PIT13 Pedro Alvarez .25 .60
PIT14 James McDonald .25 .60
PIT15 Jeff Karstens .25 .60
PIT16 Joel Hanrahan .25 .60
PIT17 PNC Park .15 .40

2013 Pirates Topps

COMPLETE SET (17) 3.00 8.00
PIT1 Andrew McCutchen .25 .60
PIT2 Starling Marte .20 .50
PIT3 Travis Snider .25 .60
PIT4 Jose Tabata .15 .40
PIT5 Pedro Alvarez .15 .40
PIT6 Neil Walker .15 .40
PIT7 Garrett Jones .15 .40
PIT8 Clint Barmes .15 .40
PIT9 A.J. Burnett .15 .40
PIT10 James McDonald .15 .40
PIT11 Wandy Rodriguez .25 .60
PIT12 Russell Martin .25 .60
PIT13 Alex Presley .15 .40
PIT14 Jason Grilli .15 .40
PIT15 Josh Harrison .25 .60
PIT16 Jeff Locke .25 .60
PIT17 PNC Park .15 .40

2014 Pirates Topps

COMPLETE SET (18) 3.00 8.00
PIT1 Andrew McCutchen .25 .60
PIT2 Starling Marte .20 .50
PIT3 Travis Snider .15 .40
PIT4 Jose Tabata .15 .40
PIT5 Pedro Alvarez .15 .40
PIT6 Neil Walker .15 .40
PIT7 Jeff Locke .15 .40
PIT8 Francisco Liriano .15 .40
PIT9 Jordy Mercer .15 .40
PIT10 Gerrit Cole .25 .60
PIT11 Wandy Rodriguez .15 .40
PIT12 Russell Martin .15 .40
PIT13 Mark Melancon .15 .40
PIT14 Jason Grilli .15 .40
PIT15 Andrew Lambo .15 .40
PIT16 Gaby Sanchez .15 .40
PIT17 PNC Park .15 .40
PIT18 Gregory Polanco .25 .60

2015 Pirates Topps

COMPLETE SET (17) 3.00 8.00
PIP1 Andrew McCutchen .25 .60
PIP2 A.J. Burnett .15 .40
PIP3 Gregory Polanco .20 .50
PIP4 Josh Harrison .15 .40
PIP5 Starling Marte .20 .50
PIP6 Mark Melancon .15 .40
PIP7 Jordy Mercer .15 .40
PIP8 Charlie Morton .25 .60
PIP9 Neil Walker .15 .40
PIP10 Tony Watson .15 .40
PIP11 Vance Worley .15 .40
PIP12 Jeff Locke .15 .40
PIP13 Antonio Bastardo .15 .40
PIP14 Pedro Alvarez .15 .40
PIP15 Gerrit Cole .25 .60
PIP16 Francisco Cervelli .15 .40
PIP17 Francisco Liriano .15 .40

2016 Pirates Topps

COMPLETE SET (17) 3.00 8.00
PIT1 Andrew McCutchen .25 .60
PIT2 Francisco Cervelli .15 .40
PIT3 Jon Niese .15 .40
PIT4 Jordy Mercer .15 .40
PIT5 Jung-Ho Kang .15 .40
PIT6 Josh Harrison .15 .40
PIT7 Starling Marte .20 .50
PIT8 Gregory Polanco .20 .50
PIT9 Gerrit Cole .25 .60
PIT10 Francisco Liriano .15 .40
PIT11 Tony Watson .15 .40
PIT12 Mark Melancon .15 .40
PIT13 Jeff Locke .15 .40
PIT14 Michael Morse .15 .40
PIT15 Chris Stewart .15 .40
PIT16 Neftali Feliz .15 .40
PIT17 Jared Hughes .15 .40

2017 Pirates Topps

COMPLETE SET (17) 3.00 8.00
PIT1 Starling Marte .20 .50
PIT2 David Freese .15 .40
PIT3 Tyler Glasnow .60 1.50
PIT4 Josh Bell .40 1.00
PIT5 Gerrit Cole .25 .60
PIT6 Felipe Rivero .20 .50
PIT7 Ivan Nova .20 .50
PIT8 Jordy Mercer .15 .40
PIT9 Gregory Polanco .20 .50
PIT10 Jameson Taillon .20 .50
PIT11 Francisco Cervelli .15 .40
PIT12 Andrew McCutchen .25 .60
PIT13 John Jaso .15 .40
PIT14 Josh Harrison .15 .40
PIT15 Jung Ho Kang .15 .40
PIT16 Tony Watson .15 .40
PIT17 Adam Frazier .15 .40

2018 Pirates Topps

COMPLETE SET (17) 2.00 5.00
PI1 Josh Harrison .15 .40
PI2 Felipe Rivero .20 .50
PI3 Trevor Williams .15 .40
PI4 Chad Kuhl .15 .40
PI5 Ivan Nova .20 .50
PI6 Starling Marte .20 .50
PI7 Gregory Polanco .20 .50
PI8 Jordy Mercer .15 .40
PI9 Sean Rodriguez .15 .40
PI10 Tyler Glasnow .25 .60
PI11 Francisco Cervelli .15 .40
PI12 Daniel Hudson .15 .40
PI13 Josh Bell .20 .50
PI14 David Freese .15 .40
PI15 Adam Frazier .15 .40
PI16 Jameson Taillon .20 .50
PI17 Jose Osuna .15 .40

2019 Pirates Topps

COMPLETE SET (17) 2.00 5.00
PI1 Starling Marte .20 .50
PI2 Chris Archer .15 .40
PI3 Corey Dickerson .15 .40
PI4 Gregory Polanco .20 .50
PI5 Josh Bell .20 .50
PI6 Jameson Taillon .20 .50
PI7 Trevor Williams .15 .40
PI8 Francisco Cervelli .15 .40
PI9 Felipe Vazquez .15 .40
PI10 Kevin Kramer .20 .50
PI11 Joe Musgrove .25 .60
PI12 Kevin Newman .25 .60
PI13 Adam Frazier .15 .40
PI14 Colin Moran .15 .40
PI15 Nick Kingham .15 .40
PI16 Erik Gonzalez .15 .40
PI17 Keone Kela .15 .40

2020 Pirates Topps

PIT1 Chris Archer .15 .40
PIT2 Starling Marte .20 .50
PIT3 James Marvel .15 .40
PIT4 Bryan Reynolds .20 .50
PIT5 Colin Moran .15 .40
PIT6 Kevin Newman .25 .60
PIT7 Adam Frazier .15 .40
PIT8 Trevor Williams .15 .40
PIT9 Joe Musgrove .25 .60
PIT10 Josh Bell .20 .50
PIT11 Keone Kela .15 .40
PIT12 Mitch Keller .25 .60
PIT13 Jameson Taillon .20 .50
PIT14 Jacob Stallings .20 .50
PIT15 Jose Osuna .15 .40
PIT16 Cole Tucker .25 .60
PIT17 Kevin Kramer .15 .40

2017 Pirates Topps National Baseball Card Day

COMPLETE SET (10) 6.00 15.00
PIT1 Josh Bell 1.50 4.00
PIT2 Gerrit Cole 1.00 2.50
PIT3 Francisco Cervelli .60 1.50
PIT4 Josh Harrison .60 1.50
PIT5 Ivan Nova .75 2.00
PIT6 Andrew McCutchen 1.00 2.50
PIT7 Jordy Mercer .60 1.50
PIT8 Gregory Polanco .75 2.00
PIT9 Jameson Taillon .75 2.00
PIT10 Roberto Clemente 2.50 6.00

1996 Pitch Postcards HOF

This 12-card set measures approximately 6" by 4" and features black-and-white player drawings. The backs carry player career stats. The cards are unnumbered and checklisted below in alphabetical order.

COMPLETE SET (12) 2.50 6.00
1 Frank Baker .20 .50
2 Frank Chance .30 .75
3 Fred Clarke .20 .50
4 Eddie Collins .40 1.00
5 Sam Crawford .20 .50
6 Johnny Evers .20 .50
7 Willie Keeler .20 .50
8 Nap Lajoie .40 1.00
9 Rube Marquard .20 .50
10 Eddie Plank .30 .75
11 Joe Tinker .30 .75
12 Rube Waddell .20 .50

1996 Pizza Hut

This four card set was issued by Pizza Hut as a premium for ordering a special pizza. A person would receive a bat as well as a card for ordering this deal. The cards are unnumbered and each features a hitter and a pitcher. We have sequenced the cards in alphabetical order of the hitter. We are pricing just the cards.

COMPLETE SET (4) 3.00 8.00
1 Jeff Bagwell / Orel Hershiser .50 1.25
2 Ken Griffey Jr. / Greg Maddux 2.00 5.00
3 Mike Piazza / David Cone 1.25 3.00
4 Mo Vaughn / Randy Johnson .20 .50

1995 PKK Griffey National Promo

This card was given out at the 1995 National Sports Collectors Convention in St. Louis, Missouri and features a borderless color action photo of Ken Griffey Jr. The back displays the sponsor's and Convention's logos.

1 Ken Griffey Jr. .50 1.25

1995 PKK Griffey

This 10 card standard-size borderless set was issued by card supply manufacturer PKK and featured photos and highlights of Ken Griffey Jr.'s career.

COMPLETE SET (10) 4.00 10.00
COMMON CARD (1-10) .40 1.00

1939 Play Ball

The cards in this 161-card set measure approximately 2 1/2" by 3 1/8". Gum Incorporated introduced a brief (war-shortened) but innovative era of baseball card production with its set of 1939. The combination of actual player photos (black and white), large card size, and extensive biography proved extremely popular. Player names are found either entirely capitalized or with initial caps only, and a "sample card" overprint is not uncommon. The "sample card" overprint variations are valued at double the prices below. Card number 126 was never issued, and cards 116-162 were produced in lesser quantities than cards 1-115. A card of Ted Williams in his rookie season as well as an early card of Joe DiMaggio are the key cards in the set.

COMPLETE SET (161) 5000.00 12000.00
COMMON CARD (1-115) 6.00 15.00
COMMON CARD (116-162) 30.00 80.00
WRAPPER (1-CENT) 150.00 200.00
1 Jake Powell RC 15.00 40.00
2 Lee Grissom RC 6.00 15.00
3 Red Ruffing 50.00 120.00
4 Eldon Auker RC 15.00 40.00
5 Luke Sewell 6.00 15.00
6 Leo Durocher 40.00 100.00
7 Bobby Doerr RC 50.00 150.00
8 Henry Pippen RC 6.00 15.00
9 James Tobin RC 6.00 15.00
10 James DeShong 8.00 20.00
11 Johnny Rizzo RC 6.00 15.00
12 Hershel Martin RC 6.00 15.00
13 Luke Hamlin RC 8.00 20.00
14 Jim Tabor RC 8.00 20.00
15 Paul Derringer 8.00 20.00
16 John Peacock RC 6.00 15.00
17 Emerson Dickman RC 6.00 15.00
18 Harry Danning RC 6.00 15.00
19 Paul Dean RC 12.00 30.00
20 Joe Heving RC 8.00 20.00
21 Dutch Leonard RC 10.00 25.00
22 Bucky Walters RC 8.00 20.00
23 Burgess Whitehead RC 8.00 20.00
24 Richard Coffman 6.00 15.00
25 George Selkirk RC 20.00 50.00
26 Joe DiMaggio RC 1500.00 4000.00
27 Fred Ostermueller 6.00 15.00
28 Sylvester Johnson RC 8.00 20.00
29 John(Jack) Wilson RC 8.00 20.00
30 Bill Dickey 40.00 100.00
31 Sam West 10.00 25.00
32 Bob Seeds RC 12.00 30.00
33 Del Young RC 6.00 15.00
34 Frank Demaree 6.00 15.00
35 Bill Jurges 6.00 15.00
36 Frank McCormick RC 6.00 15.00
37 Virgil Davis 6.00 15.00
38 Billy Myers RC 6.00 15.00
39 Rick Ferrell 25.00 60.00
40 James Bagby Jr. RC 6.00 15.00
41 Lon Warneke 6.00 15.00
42 Arndt Jorgens 6.00 15.00
43 Melo Almada RC 6.00 15.00
44 Don Heffner RC 6.00 15.00
45 Merrill May RC 6.00 15.00
46 Morris Arnovich RC 6.00 15.00
47 Buddy Lewis RC 15.00 40.00
48 Lefty Gomez 50.00 120.00
49 Eddie Miller RC 8.00 20.00
50 Charley Gehringer 100.00 250.00
51 Mel Ott 50.00 150.00
52 Tommy Henrich RC 12.00 30.00
53 Carl Hubbell 100.00 250.00
54 Harry Gumpert RC 10.00 25.00
55 Arky Vaughan 25.00 60.00
56 Hank Greenberg 150.00 400.00
57 Buddy Hassett RC 6.00 15.00
58 Lou Chiozza RC 6.00 15.00
59 Ken Chase RC 6.00 15.00
60 Schoolboy Rowe RC 15.00 40.00
61 Tony Cuccinello 10.00 25.00
62 Tom Carey RC 8.00 20.00
63 Emmett Mueller RC 8.00 20.00
64 Wally Moses RC 6.00 15.00
65 Harry Craft RC 8.00 20.00
66 Jimmy Ripple RC 6.00 15.00
67 Ed Joost RC 12.00 30.00
68 Fred Sington RC 10.00 25.00
69 Elbie Fletcher RC 6.00 15.00
70 Fred Frankhouse 8.00 20.00
71 Monte Pearson RC 8.00 20.00
72 Debs Garms RC 8.00 20.00
73 Hal Schumacher 6.00 15.00
74 Cookie Lavagetto RC 12.00 30.00
75 Stan Bordagaray RC 10.00 25.00
76 Goody Rosen RC 12.00 30.00
77 Lew Riggs RC 8.00 20.00
78 Julius Solters 6.00 15.00
79 Jo Jo Moore 10.00 25.00
80 Pete Fox 8.00 20.00
81 Babe Dahlgren RC 8.00 20.00
82 Chuck Klein 30.00 80.00
83 Gus Suhr 6.00 15.00
84 Skeeter Newsom RC 6.00 15.00
85 Johnny Cooney RC 6.00 15.00
86 Dolph Camilli 6.00 15.00
87 Milburn Shoffner RC 6.00 15.00
88 Charlie Keller RC 12.00 30.00
89 Lloyd Waner 50.00 150.00
90 Robert Klinger RC 10.00 25.00
91 John Knott RC 10.00 25.00
92 Ted Williams RC 4000.00 10000.00
93 Charles Gelbert RC 6.00 15.00
94 Heinie Manush 30.00 80.00
95 Whit Wyatt RC 8.00 20.00
96 Babe Phelps RC 10.00 25.00
97 Bob Johnson 12.00 30.00
98 Pinky Whitney RC 12.00 30.00
99 Wally Berger 12.00 30.00
100 Buddy Myer 12.00 30.00
101 Roger Cramer 15.00 40.00
102 Lem (Pep) Young RC 12.00 30.00
103 Moe Berg 100.00 250.00
104 Tom Bridges 6.00 15.00
105 Rabbit McNair RC 8.00 20.00
106 Dolly Stark UMP 12.00 30.00
107 Joe Vosmik 12.00 30.00
108 Frank Hayes 6.00 15.00
109 Myril Hoag 10.00 25.00
110 Fred Fitzsimmons 12.00 30.00
111 Van Lingle Mungo RC 8.00 20.00
112 Paul Waner 25.00 60.00
113 Al Schacht 10.00 25.00
114 Cecil Travis RC 10.00 25.00
115 Ralph Kress 6.00 15.00
116 Gene Desautels RC 20.00 50.00
117 Wayne Ambler RC 15.00 40.00
118 Lynn Nelson 15.00 40.00
119 Will Hershberger RC 25.00 60.00
120 Rabbit Warstler RC 20.00 50.00
121 Bill Posedel RC 15.00 40.00
122 George McQuinn RC 15.00 40.00
123 Ray T. Davis RC 15.00 40.00
124 Walter Brown 15.00 40.00
125 Cliff Melton RC 25.00 60.00
127 Gil Brack RC 15.00 40.00
128 Joe Bowman RC 15.00 40.00
129 Bill Swift 15.00 40.00
130 Bill Brubaker RC 20.00 50.00
131 Mort Cooper RC 20.00 50.00
132 Jim Brown RC 20.00 50.00
133 Lynn Myers RC 15.00 40.00
134 Tot Presnell RC 15.00 40.00
135 Mickey Owen RC 25.00 60.00
136 Roy Bell RC 15.00 40.00
137 Pete Appleton 15.00 40.00
138 George Case RC 20.00 50.00
139 Vito Tamulis RC 20.00 50.00
140 Ray Hayworth RC 15.00 40.00
141 Pete Coscarart RC 15.00 40.00
142 Ira Hutchinson RC 15.00 40.00
143 Earl Averill 50.00 120.00
144 Zeke Bonura RC 15.00 40.00
145 Hugh Mulcahy RC 25.00 60.00
146 Tom Sunkel RC 20.00 50.00
147 George Coffman RC 15.00 40.00
148 Bill Trotter RC 15.00 40.00
149 Max West RC 15.00 40.00
150 James Walkup RC 15.00 40.00
151 Hugh Casey RC 15.00 40.00
152 Roy Weatherly RC 15.00 40.00
153 Dizzy Trout RC 20.00 50.00
154 Johnny Hudson RC 25.00 60.00
155 Jimmy Outlaw RC 15.00 40.00
156 Ray Berres RC 15.00 40.00
157 Don Padgett RC 20.00 50.00
158 Bud Thomas RC 20.00 50.00
159 Red Evans RC 15.00 40.00
160 Gene Moore RC 15.00 40.00
161 Lonnie Frey 15.00 40.00
162 Whitey Moore RC 50.00 120.00

1940 Play Ball

The cards in this 240-card series measure approximately 2 1/2" by 3 1/8". Gum Inc. improved upon its 1939 design by enclosing the 1940 black and white player photo with a frame line and printing the player's name in a panel below the picture (often using a nickname). The set included many Hall of Famers and Old Timers. Cards 1-114 are numbered in team groupings. Cards 181-240 are scarcer than cards 1-180. The backs contain an extensive biography and a dated copyright line. The key cards in the set are the cards of Joe DiMaggio, Shoeless Joe Jackson, and Ted Williams.

COMPLETE SET (240) 5000.00 12000.00
COMMON CARD (1-120) 8.00 20.00
COMMON CARD (121-180) 8.00 20.00
COMMON CARD (181-240) 30.00 80.00
WRAP.(1-CENT, DIFF. COL.) 700.00 800.00
1 Joe DiMaggio 1250.00 3000.00
2 Art Jorgens 8.00 20.00
3 Babe Dahlgren 8.00 20.00
4 Tommy Henrich 10.00 25.00
5 Monte Pearson 8.00 20.00
6 Lefty Gomez 50.00 120.00
7 Bill Dickey 60.00 150.00
8 George Selkirk 8.00 20.00
9 Charlie Keller 10.00 25.00
10 Red Ruffing 30.00 80.00
11 Jake Powell 8.00 20.00
12 Johnny Schulte 8.00 20.00
13 Jack Knott 10.00 25.00
14 Rabbit McNair 12.00 30.00
15 George Case 8.00 20.00
16 Cecil Travis 8.00 20.00
17 Buddy Myer 10.00 25.00
18 Charlie Gelbert 12.00 30.00
19 Ken Chase 8.00 20.00
20 Buddy Lewis 8.00 20.00
21 Rick Ferrell 30.00 80.00
22 Sammy West 8.00 20.00
23 Dutch Leonard 12.00 30.00
24 Frank Hayes 8.00 20.00
25 Bob Johnson 10.00 25.00
26 Wally Moses 12.00 30.00
27 Ted Williams 1000.00 2500.00
28 Gene Desautels 8.00 20.00
29 Doc Cramer 8.00 20.00
30 Moe Berg 75.00 200.00
31 Jack Wilson 10.00 25.00
32 Jim Bagby 8.00 20.00
33 Fritz Ostermueller 8.00 20.00
34 John Peacock 8.00 20.00
35 Joe Heving 8.00 20.00
36 Jim Tabor 8.00 20.00
37 Emerson Dickman 8.00 20.00
38 Bobby Doerr 25.00 60.00
39 Tom Carey 8.00 20.00
40 Hank Greenberg 150.00 400.00
41 Charley Gehringer 125.00 300.00
42 Bud Thomas 8.00 20.00
43 Pete Fox 8.00 20.00
44 Dizzy Trout 12.00 30.00
45 Red Kress 8.00 20.00
46 Earl Averill 30.00 80.00
47 Oscar Vitt RC 8.00 20.00
48 Luke Sewell 8.00 20.00
49 Stormy Weatherly 8.00 20.00
50 Hal Trosky 8.00 20.00
51 Don Heffner 8.00 20.00
52 Myril Hoag 8.00 20.00
53 George McQuinn 8.00 20.00
54 Bill Trotter 8.00 20.00
55 Slick Coffman 8.00 20.00
56 Eddie Miller RC 8.00 20.00
57 Max West 8.00 20.00
58 Bill Posedel 8.00 20.00
59 Rabbit Warstler 8.00 20.00
60 John Cooney 12.00 30.00
61 Tony Cuccinello 8.00 20.00
62 Buddy Hassett 8.00 20.00
63 Pete Coscarart 8.00 20.00
64 Van Lingle Mungo 8.00 20.00
65 Fred Fitzsimmons 12.00 30.00
66 Babe Phelps 8.00 20.00
67 Whit Wyatt 8.00 20.00
68 Dolph Camilli 10.00 25.00
69 Cookie Lavagetto 8.00 20.00
70 Luke Hamlin/(Hot Potato) 8.00 20.00
71 Mel Almada 8.00 20.00
72 Chuck Dressen RC 8.00 20.00
73 Bucky Walters 10.00 25.00
74 Paul(Duke) Derringer 8.00 20.00
75 Frank (Buck) McCormick 8.00 20.00
76 Lonny Frey 8.00 20.00
77 Willard Hershberger 12.00 30.00
78 Lew Riggs 8.00 20.00
79 Harry Craft 8.00 20.00
80 Billy Myers 8.00 20.00
81 Wally Berger 8.00 20.00
82 Hank Gowdy CO 8.00 20.00
83 Cliff Melton 8.00 20.00
84 Jo Jo Moore 8.00 20.00
85 Hal Schumacher 8.00 20.00
86 Harry Gumbert 8.00 20.00
87 Carl Hubbell 75.00 200.00
88 Mel Ott 150.00 400.00
89 Bill Jurges 8.00 20.00
90 Frank Demaree 8.00 20.00
91 Bob Seeds 8.00 20.00
92 Whitey Whitehead 10.00 25.00
93 Harry Danning 8.00 20.00
94 Gus Suhr 8.00 20.00
95 Hugh Mulcahy 8.00 20.00
96 Heinie Mueller 8.00 20.00
97 Morry Arnovich 8.00 20.00
98 Pinky May 8.00 20.00
99 Syl Johnson 15.00 40.00
100 Hersh Martin 8.00 20.00
101 Del Young 10.00 25.00
102 Chuck Klein 30.00 80.00
103 Elbie Fletcher 8.00 20.00
104 Paul Waner 60.00 150.00
105 Lloyd Waner 40.00 100.00
106 Pep Young 8.00 20.00
107 Arky Vaughan 15.00 40.00
108 Johnny Rizzo 8.00 20.00
109 Don Padgett 8.00 20.00
110 Tom Sunkel 8.00 20.00
111 Mickey Owen 20.00 50.00
112 Jimmy Brown 8.00 20.00
113 Mort Cooper 8.00 20.00
114 Lon Warneke 8.00 20.00
115 Mike Gonzalez CO 8.00 20.00
116 Al Schacht 10.00 25.00
117 Dolly Stark UMP 15.00 40.00
118 Waite Hoyt 30.00 80.00
119 Grover C. Alexander 125.00 300.00
120 Walter Johnson 150.00 400.00
121 Atley Donald RC 8.00 20.00
122 Sandy Sundra RC 8.00 20.00
123 Hildy Hildebrand 8.00 20.00
124 Earle Combs 25.00 60.00
125 Art Fletcher RC 8.00 20.00
126 Jake Solters 8.00 20.00
127 Muddy Ruel 8.00 20.00
128 Pete Appleton 12.00 30.00
129 Bucky Harris MG RC 15.00 40.00
130 Clyde Milan RC 8.00 20.00
131 Zeke Bonura 12.00 30.00
132 Connie Mack MG RC 60.00 150.00
133 Jimmie Foxx 150.00 400.00
134 Joe Cronin 50.00 120.00
135 Line Drive Nelson 8.00 20.00
136 Cotton Pippen 8.00 20.00
137 Bing Miller 8.00 20.00
138 Beau Bell 8.00 20.00
139 Elden Auker 8.00 20.00
140 Dick Coffman 8.00 20.00
141 Casey Stengel MG RC 100.00 250.00
142 George Kelly RC 15.00 40.00
143 Gene Moore 8.00 20.00
144 Joe Vosmik 8.00 20.00
145 Vito Tamulis 8.00 20.00
146 Tot Pressnell 8.00 20.00
147 Johnny Hudson 8.00 20.00
148 Hugh Casey 8.00 20.00
149 Pinky Shoffner 10.00 25.00
150 Whitey Moore 12.00 30.00
151 Edwin Joost 12.00 30.00
152 Jimmy Wilson 10.00 25.00
153 Bill McKechnie MG RC 15.00 40.00
154 Jumbo Brown 8.00 20.00
155 Ray Hayworth 8.00 20.00
156 Daffy Dean 20.00 50.00
157 Lou Chiozza 10.00 25.00
158 Travis Jackson 25.00 60.00
159 Pancho Snyder RC 8.00 20.00
160 Hans Lobert CO 8.00 20.00
161 Debs Garms 8.00 20.00
162 Joe Bowman 8.00 20.00
163 Spud Davis 8.00 20.00
164 Ray Berres 8.00 20.00
165 Bob Klinger 8.00 20.00
166 Bill Brubaker 12.00 30.00
167 Frankie Frisch MG 40.00 100.00
168 Honus Wagner CO 125.00 300.00
169 Gabby Street 10.00 25.00
170 Tris Speaker 60.00 150.00
171 Harry Heilmann 30.00 80.00
172 Chief Bender 20.00 50.00
173 Napoleon Lajoie 125.00 300.00
174 Johnny Evers 25.00 60.00
175 Christy Mathewson 125.00 300.00
176 Heinie Manush 25.00 60.00
177 Frank Baker 40.00 100.00
178 Max Carey 20.00 50.00
179 George Sisler 40.00 100.00
180 Mickey Cochrane 50.00 120.00
181 Spud Chandler RC 10.00 25.00
182 Knick Knickerbocker RC 10.00 25.00
183 Marvin Breuer RC 10.00 25.00
184 Mule Haas 10.00 25.00
185 Joe Kuhel 12.00 30.00
186 Taft Wright RC 10.00 25.00
187 Jimmy Dykes MG 10.00 25.00
188 Joe Krakauskas RC 20.00 50.00
189 Jim Bloodworth RC 10.00 25.00
190 Charley Berry 20.00 50.00
191 John Babich RC 10.00 25.00
192 Dick Siebert RC 10.00 25.00
193 Chubby Dean RC 20.00 50.00
194 Sam Chapman RC 10.00 25.00
195 Dee Miles RC 10.00 25.00
196 Red (Nonny) Nonnenkamp RC 15.00 40.00
197 Lou Finney RC 10.00 25.00
198 Denny Galehouse RC 10.00 25.00
199 Pinky Higgins 10.00 25.00
200 Soup Campbell RC 10.00 25.00
201 Barney McCosky RC 10.00 25.00
202 Al Milnar RC 10.00 25.00
203 Bad News Hale RC 15.00 40.00
204 Harry Eisenstat RC 30.00 80.00
205 Rollie Hemsley RC 10.00 25.00
206 Chet Laabs RC 10.00 25.00
207 Gus Mancuso 10.00 25.00
208 Lee Gamble RC 15.00 40.00
209 Hy Vandenberg RC 10.00 25.00
210 Bill Lohrman RC 10.00 25.00
211 Pop Joiner RC 10.00 25.00
212 Babe Young RC 12.00 30.00
213 John Rucker RC 15.00 40.00
214 Ken O'Dea RC 10.00 25.00
215 Johnnie McCarthy RC 10.00 25.00
216 Joe Marty RC 15.00 40.00
217 Walter Beck 12.00 30.00
218 Wally Millies RC 10.00 25.00
219 Russ Bauers RC 10.00 25.00
220 Mace Brown RC 15.00 40.00
221 Lee Handley RC 10.00 25.00
222 Max Butcher RC 10.00 25.00
223 Hughie Jennings 30.00 80.00
224 Pie Traynor 30.00 80.00
225 Joe Jackson 1000.00 2500.00
226 Harry Hooper 40.00 100.00
227 Jesse Haines 40.00 100.00
228 Charlie Grimm 10.00 25.00
229 Buck Herzog 10.00 25.00
230 Red Faber 25.00 60.00
231 Dolf Luque 20.00 50.00
232 Goose Goslin 25.00 60.00
233 George Earnshaw 10.00 25.00
234 Frank Chance 40.00 100.00
235 John McGraw 50.00 120.00
236 Jim Bottomley 30.00 80.00
237 Willie Keeler 50.00 120.00
238 Tony Lazzeri 50.00 120.00
239 George Uhle 10.00 25.00
240 Bill Atwood RC 25.00 60.00

1941 Play Ball

The cards in this 72-card set measure approximately 2 1/2" by 3 1/8". Many of the cards in the 1941 Play Ball series are simply color versions of pictures appearing in the 1940 set. This was the only color baseball card set produced by Gum, Inc.. Card numbers 49-72 are slightly more difficult to obtain as they were not issued until 1942. In 1942, numbers 1-48 were also reissued but without the copyright date. The cards were also printed on paper without a cardboard backing; these are generally encountered in sheets or strips. The set features a card of Pee Wee Reese in his rookie year.

COMPLETE SET (72) 5000.00 12000.00
COMMON CARD (1-48) 15.00 40.00
COMMON CARD (49-72) 25.00 60.00
WRAPPER (1-CENT) 700.00 800.00
1 Eddie Miller 50.00 120.00
2 Max West 20.00 50.00
3 Bucky Walters 25.00 60.00
4 Paul Derringer 30.00 80.00
5 Frank (Buck) McCormick 25.00 60.00
6 Carl Hubbell 100.00 250.00
7 Harry Danning 30.00 80.00
8 Mel Ott 200.00 500.00
9 Pinky May 15.00 40.00
10 Arky Vaughan 50.00 120.00
11 Debs Garms 15.00 40.00
12 Jimmy Brown 20.00 50.00
13 Jimmie Foxx 300.00 800.00
14 Ted Williams 1000.00 2500.00
15 Joe Cronin 75.00 200.00
16 Hal Trosky 30.00 80.00
17 Roy Weatherly 20.00 50.00
18 Hank Greenberg 125.00 300.00
19 Charley Gehringer 100.00 250.00
20 Red Ruffing 75.00 200.00
21 Charlie Keller 25.00 60.00
22 Bob Johnson 30.00 80.00
23 George McQuinn 30.00 80.00
24 Dutch Leonard 25.00 60.00
25 Gene Moore 15.00 40.00
26 Harry Gumpert 15.00 40.00
27 Babe Young 25.00 60.00
28 Joe Marty 15.00 40.00
29 Jack Wilson 20.00 50.00
30 Lou Finney 30.00 80.00
31 Joe Kuhel 15.00 40.00
32 Taft Wright 15.00 40.00
33 Al Milnar 15.00 40.00
34 Rollie Hemsley 20.00 50.00
35 Pinky Higgins 20.00 50.00
36 Barney McCosky 15.00 30.00
37 Bruce Campbell RC 15.00 40.00
38 Atley Donald 15.00 40.00
39 Tommy Henrich 40.00 100.00
40 John Babich 15.00 40.00
41 Frank (Blimp) Hayes 20.00 50.00
42 Wally Moses 15.00 40.00
43 Al Brancato RC 20.00 50.00
44 Sam Chapman 15.00 30.00
45 Eldon Auker 15.00 40.00
46 Sid Hudson RC 15.00 40.00
47 Buddy Lewis 15.00 30.00
48 Cecil Travis 25.00 60.00
49 Babe Dahlgren 15.00 40.00
50 Johnny Cooney 15.00 40.00
51 Dolph Camilli 30.00 80.00
52 Kirby Higbe RC 20.00 50.00
53 Luke Hamlin 20.00 50.00
54 Pee Wee Reese RC 500.00 1200.00
55 Whit Wyatt 25.00 60.00
56 Johnny VanderMeer RC 75.00 200.00
57 Moe Arnovich 20.00 50.00
58 Frank Demaree 15.00 40.00
59 Bill Jurges 15.00 40.00
60 Chuck Klein 60.00 150.00
61 Vince DiMaggio RC 75.00 200.00
62 Elbie Fletcher 15.00 40.00
63 Dom DiMaggio RC 75.00 200.00
64 Bobby Doerr 100.00 250.00
65 Tommy Bridges 20.00 50.00
66 Harland Clift RC 15.00 40.00
67 Walt Judnich RC 20.00 50.00
68 John Knott 15.00 40.00
69 George Case 15.00 40.00
70 Bill Dickey 125.00 300.00
71 Joe DiMaggio 2500.00 6000.00
72 Lefty Gomez 150.00 400.00

1991 Playball Will Clark

The numbering and card design indicates that this ten-card standard-size set is made up of two five-card sets. These single-player Playball sets were important as they were issued by Rob Broder, who had been associated with unliscenced cards in the 1980's and all of the variants had been given the "Broder" label. These cards were all given the OK by Major League Baseball as well as the player's team.

COMPLETE SET (10) 2.50 6.00
COMMON CARD (21-25/39-43) .30 .75

1991 Playball Griffey Jr.

The glossy color player photos on the first five cards are full bleed without any border stripes. The glossy player photos on card numbers 1 and 49 bleed to the sides of the card but are bordered above and below by different color stripes. The photo on card number 50 is full bleed, while the unnumbered card has a gold-patterned border.

COMPLETE SET 6.00 15.00
COMMON CARD .40 1.00

1991 Playball Mattingly

The numbering and card design indicates that this ten-card standard-size set is made up of two five-card sets. The glossy player photos on the first five cards bleed to the sides of the card but are bordered above by a dark blue stripe and below by silver and dark blue stripes. The glossy color player photos on the second five cards are full bleed without any border stripes.

COMPLETE SET (10) 2.00 5.00
COMMON PLAYER .20 .50

1991 Playball Mattingly Gold

This two-card standard-size set features color action photos framed by gold foil borders. The team logo appears in the upper left corner, while the player's name and team name appear in white lettering at the lower left. The horizontal backs have the player's name, team name, serial number and card number ("91G-X") on the upper portion and MLB and team logos on the lower portion.

COMPLETE SET 1.50 4.00
COMMON CARD .80 2.00

1991 Playball Strawberry

As with the other 1991 Playball sets, this seven-card standard-size set exhibits two different front designs. A blue border stripe above and silver and blue border stripes below frame the glossy color player photos on the first three cards, while the player photos on the last four cards are without any border stripes. The back design of all cards is horizontally oriented and features the player's name, team name, logo, year and MLB logo in black on a white card stock.

COMPLETE SET (7) 1.25 3.00
COMMON PLAYER (53-58/60) .20 .50

1992 Playball Griffey Jr.

This four-card standard-size set features color action shots of Ken Griffey Jr. These photos are edged in blue and bordered in prismatic gold foil. The cards are unnumbered.

COMPLETE SET (4) 1.50 4.00
COMMON PLAYER (1-4) .40 1.00

2019 Playoff

RANDOM INSERTS IN PACKS
*GOLD/199: 1.2X TO 3X
*BLUE/99: 1.5X TO 4X
*RED/50: 2X TO 5X
*HOLO SLVR/25: 3X TO 8X
1 Pete Alonso RC 2.00 5.00
2 Eloy Jimenez RC .60 1.50
3 Fernando Tatis Jr. RC 4.00 10.00
4 Michael Kopech RC .50 1.25
5 Kyle Tucker RC .40 1.00
6 Yusei Kikuchi RC .25 .60
7 Chris Paddack RC .30 .75
8 Nick Senzel RC .50 1.25
9 Bryce Harper .40 1.00
10 Cal Quantrill RC .15 .40
11 Kris Bryant .30 .75
12 Shohei Ohtani .40 1.00
13 Griffin Canning RC .25 .60
14 Jon Duplantier RC .15 .40
15 Adalberto Mondesi .20 .50
16 Vladimir Guerrero Jr. RC 2.50 6.00
17 Scooter Gennett .20 .50
18 Jose Abreu .25 .60
19 Brendan Rodgers .25 .60
20 Tommy Pham .15 .40

2008 Playoff Contenders

COMP.SET w/o AU's (50) 8.00 20.00
COMMON CARD (1-50) .25 .60
COMMON AU (51-130) 3.00 8.00
OVERALL AUTO ODDS 5 PER BOX
EXCHANGE DEADLINE 8/4/2010
1 Aaron Shafer .25 .60
2 Adrian Nieto .25 .60
3 Andrew Liebel .25 .60
4 Blake Tekotte .40 1.00
5 Brad Mills .25 .60
6 Brandon Waring .40 1.00
7 Brett Hunter .25 .60
8 Byron Wiley .25 .60
9 Caleb Gindl .25 .60
10 Carlos Peguero .40 1.00
11 Carson Blair .25 .60
12 Charlie Blackmon 2.00 5.00
13 Chris Johnson .40 1.00
14 Cody Adams .40 1.00
15 Cody Satterwhite .40 1.00
16 Cole Rohrbough .25 .60
17 Cole St. Clair .25 .60
18 Daniel Thomas .25 .60
19 Dennis Raben .40 1.00
20 Derek Norris .40 1.00
21 Dominic Brown 1.50 4.00
22 Dusty Coleman .25 .60
23 Gerardo Parra .25 .60
24 Greg Halman .40 1.00
25 J.P. Ramirez .25 .60
26 James Darnell .40 1.00
27 Jason Knapp .25 .60
28 Jay Austin .25 .60
29 Jesus Montero .40 1.00
30 Jharmidy De Jesus .25 .60
31 Jose Duran .40 1.00
32 Josh Vitters .25 .60
33 Kenn Kasparek .60 1.50
34 L. J. Hoes .25 .60
35 Logan Schafer .25 .60
36 Matt Harrison .40 1.00
37 Matt Mitchell .25 .60
38 Max Ramirez .25 .60
39 Mike Cisco .25 .60
40 Niko Vasquez .60 1.50
41 Rolando Gomez .40 1.00
42 Ryan Kalish .60 1.50
43 Stolmy Pimentel .25 .60
44 T.J. Steele .40 1.00
45 Tim Murphy .25 .60
46 Tony Delmonico .40 1.00
47 Tyler Ladendorf .40 1.00
48 Tyler Sample .25 .60
49 Vance Worley 1.25 3.00
50 Xavier Avery .60 1.50
51 A.Cunningham AU/283 * 5.00 12.00
52 Alex Buchholz AU 3.00 8.00
53 Allan Dykstra AU 3.00 8.00
54 A.Cashner AU/216 * 5.00 12.00
55 A.Walker AU/288 * 8.00 20.00
56 Angel Morales AU 3.00 8.00
57 Angel Villalona AU 8.00 20.00
58 Anthony Hewitt AU 4.00 10.00
59 B.Hand AU/274 * 4.00 10.00
60 B.Holt AU/236 * 4.00 10.00
61 B.Crawford AU/339 * 12.00 30.00
62 B.Price AU/165 * 10.00 25.00
63 Buster Posey AU 40.00 100.00
64 C.Gutierrez AU/87 * 15.00 40.00
65 C.D'Arnaud AU/304 * 3.00 8.00
66 Chris Davis AU 6.00 15.00
67 C.Hicks AU/230 * 3.00 8.00
68 Christian Friedrich AU 6.00 15.00
69 Clark Murphy AU 3.00 8.00
70 C.Phelps AU/244 * 3.00 8.00
71 Curtis Petersen AU/244 * 3.00 8.00
72 D.Cortes AU/292 * 4.00 10.00
73 D.Schlereth AU/317 * 4.00 10.00
74 Danny Carroll AU 3.00 8.00
75 Danny Espinosa AU/395 * 3.00 8.00
76 D.Viciedo AU/395 * 10.00 25.00
77 Derek Holland AU 5.00 12.00
78 D.Rose AU/88 * 150.00 300.00
79 Devaris Gordon AU 5.00 12.00
80 Engel Beltre AU 5.00 12.00
81 E.Frederickson AU/177 * 5.00 12.00
82 Gordon Beckham AU 6.00 15.00
83 G.Veloz AU/339 * 3.00 8.00
84 Ike Davis AU 6.00 15.00
85 Isaac Galloway AU 3.00 8.00
86 Jared Bolden AU 3.00 8.00
87 J.Cunningham AU/229 * 3.00 8.00
88 Jhoulys Chacin AU 3.00 8.00
89 Jon Jay AU 6.00 15.00
90 J.Danks AU/354 * 10.00 25.00
91 J.Lindblom AU/288 * 4.00 10.00
92 Juan Carlos Sulbaran AU 3.00 8.00
93 J.Ramirez AU/267 * 4.00 10.00
94 J.Parker AU/229 * 6.00 15.00
95 Kirk Nieuwenhuis AU 4.00 10.00
96 Pat Venditte AU 8.00 20.00
97 Lance Lynn AU 4.00 10.00
98 L.Forsythe AU/262 * 6.00 15.00
99 L.Morrison AU/314 * 6.00 15.00
100 Marcus Lemon AU 3.00 8.00
101 M.Sobolewski AU/277 * 3.00 8.00
102 Mat Gamel AU 5.00 12.00
103 M.Beasley AU/88 * 30.00 60.00
104 Michael Kohn AU 3.00 8.00
105 M.Taylor AU/362 * 10.00 25.00
106 Michel Inoa AU 5.00 12.00
107 Mike Jones AU 3.00 8.00
108 Mike Montgomery AU 6.00 15.00
109 M.Stanton AU/149 * 250.00 500.00
110 N.Feliz AU/246 * 3.00 8.00
111 N.Soto AU/249 * 8.00 20.00
112 O.Mayo AU/88 * 40.00 80.00
113 Pedro Baez AU 3.00 8.00
114 Petey Paramore AU 3.00 8.00
115 Rafael Rodriguez AU 3.00 8.00
116 Rashun Dixon AU 6.00 15.00
117 Rick Porcello AU 6.00 15.00
118 R.Grossman AU/227 * 6.00 15.00
119 R.Kieschnick AU/289 * 5.00 12.00
120 Ryan Perry AU 3.00 8.00
121 S.Peterson AU/399 * 3.00 8.00
122 Shooter Hunt AU/52 * 50.00 100.00
123 T.Haley AU/309 * 4.00 10.00
124 Tyler Chatwood AU 5.00 12.00
125 Tyson Ross AU 3.00 8.00
126 Wilin Rosario AU 6.00 15.00
127 W.Flores AU/75 * EXCH 30.00 80.00
128 Yamaico Navarro AU 3.00 8.00
129 Z.Collier AU/200 * 5.00 12.00
130 Zach Putnam AU 3.00 8.00

2008 Playoff Contenders Playoff Ticket

COMMON CARD (51-130) 1.00 2.50
OVERALL INSERT ODDS 1:3

2008 Playoff Contenders Season Ticket Autographs

OVERALL AUTO ODDS 5 PER BOX
CARDS ARE NOT SERIAL NUMBERED
PRINT RUN INFO PROVIDED BY DLP
EXCHANGE DEADLINE 8/4/2010
1 Aaron Shafer/35 5.00 12.00
2 Adrian Nieto 3.00 8.00
3 Andrew Liebel/141 3.00 8.00
4 Blake Tekotte 5.00 12.00
5 Brad Mills/127 3.00 8.00
6 Brandon Waring/149 6.00 15.00
7 Brett Hunter/121 5.00 12.00
8 Byron Wiley 4.00 10.00
9 Caleb Gindl/134 12.50 30.00
10 Carlos Peguero/72 10.00 25.00
11 Carson Blair 4.00 10.00
12 Charlie Blackmon 15.00 40.00
14 Cody Adams 4.00 10.00
15 Cody Satterwhite/90 6.00 15.00
16 Cole Rohrbough 3.00 8.00
17 Cole St. Clair 3.00 8.00
18 Daniel Thomas 3.00 8.00
19 Dennis Raben/38 10.00 25.00
20 Derek Norris/39 15.00 40.00
21 Dominic Brown/98 30.00 60.00
22 Dusty Coleman 3.00 8.00
23 Gerardo Parra 5.00 12.00
24 Greg Halman/88 30.00 60.00
25 J.P. Ramirez 5.00 12.00
26 James Darnell 12.50 30.00
27 Jason Knapp/124 5.00 12.00
28 Jay Austin 4.00 10.00
29 Jesus Montero/39 100.00 200.00
30 Jharmidy De Jesus/53 4.00 10.00
31 Jose Duran 4.00 10.00
32 Josh Vitters 6.00 15.00
33 Kenn Kasparek 4.00 10.00
34 L. J. Hoes 8.00 20.00
35 Logan Schafer 3.00 8.00
36 Matt Harrison/114 5.00 12.00
37 Matt Mitchell 3.00 8.00
38 Max Ramirez/39 6.00 15.00
39 Mike Cisco/123 15.00 40.00
40 Niko Vasquez 6.00 15.00
41 Rolando Gomez/113 20.00 50.00
42 Ryan Kalish/55 15.00 40.00
43 Stolmy Pimentel/39 10.00 25.00
44 T.J. Steele 5.00 12.00
45 Tim Murphy/55 5.00 12.00
46 Tony Delmonico 3.00 8.00
47 Tyler Ladendorf 3.00 8.00
48 Tyler Sample 4.00 10.00
49 Vance Worley 10.00 25.00
50 Xavier Avery 8.00 20.00

2008 Playoff Contenders Draft Class

OVERALL INSERT ODDS 1:3
STATED PRINT RUN 1500 SER.#'d SETS
*BLACK: .75X TO 2X BASIC
BLACK PRINT RUN 100 SER.#'d SETS
*GOLD: .6X TO 1.5X BASIC
GOLD PRINT RUN 250 SER.#'d SETS
1 Davis/Nieuwenhuis 1.50 4.00
2 Curtis Petersen/Isaac Galloway 1.25 3.00
3 Jon Jay/Lance Lynn 2.00 5.00
4 Clark Murphy/Chris Davis 1.50 4.00
5 Trey Haley/Zach Putnam .75 2.00

2008 Playoff Contenders Draft Class Autographs

RANDOM INSERTS IN PACKS
OVERALL AUTO ODDS 5 PER BOX
STATED PRINT RUN 25 SER.#'d SETS
NO PRICING DUE TO SCARCITY
EXCHANGE DEADLINE 8/4/2010

2008 Playoff Contenders Legendary Rookies

OVERALL INSERT ODDS 1:3
STATED PRINT RUN 1500 SER.#'d SETS
*BLACK: .75X TO 2X BASIC
BLACK PRINT RUN 100 SER.#'d SETS
*GOLD: .6X TO 1.5X BASIC
GOLD PRINT RUN 250 SER.#'d SETS
1 Willie Mays 2.00 5.00
2 Pete Rose 2.00 5.00
3 Cal Ripken Jr. 3.00 8.00
4 Mike Schmidt 1.50 4.00
5 Robin Yount 1.00 2.50

2008 Playoff Contenders Rookie Roll Call

OVERALL INSERT ODDS 1:3
STATED PRINT RUN 1500 SER.#'d SETS
*BLACK: .75X TO 2X BASIC
BLACK PRINT RUN 100 SER.#'d SETS
*GOLD: .6X TO 1.5X BASIC
GOLD PRINT RUN 250 SER.#'d SETS
1 Mat Gamel 2.00 5.00
2 Michel Inoa 2.00 5.00
3 Rafael Rodriguez .75 2.00
4 Isaac Galloway 1.25 3.00
5 Angel Villalona 2.00 5.00

2008 Playoff Contenders Round Numbers

OVERALL INSERT ODDS 1:3
STATED PRINT RUN 1500 SER.#'d SETS
*BLACK: .75X TO 2X BASIC
BLACK PRINT RUN 100 SER.#'d SETS
*GOLD: .6X TO 1.5X BASIC
GOLD PRINT RUN 250 SER.#'d SETS
1 B.Posey/G.Beckham 3.00 8.00
2 Daniel Schlereth/Ryan Perry 1.25 3.00
3 Allan Dykstra/Anthony Hewitt .75 2.00
4 Tyson Ross/Tyler Chatwood 1.25 3.00
5 Chase D'Arnaud/Brandon Crawford 2.00 5.00

2011 Playoff Contenders

COMPLETE SET (50) 6.00 15.00
COMMON CARD .20 .50
COMMON RC .20 .50
PRINTING PLATES RANDOMLY INSERTED
PLATE PRINT RUN 1 SET PER COLOR
BLACK-CYAN-MAGENTA-YELLOW ISSUED
NO PLATE PRICING DUE TO SCARCITY
1 Josh Hamilton .30 .75
2 Jimmy Rollins .30 .75
3 David Ortiz .50 1.25
4 Robinson Cano .30 .75
5 Ryan Howard .40 1.00
6 Starlin Castro .30 .75
7 Andrew McCutchen .50 1.25
8 Jordan Walden .20 .50
9 Carlos Gonzalez .30 .75
10 Clayton Kershaw .75 2.00
11 Justin Verlander .50 1.25
12 Albert Pujols .60 1.50
13 Nick Swisher .30 .75
14 Freddie Freeman 3.00 8.00
15 Jordan Lyles .20 .50
16 Adam Jones .30 .75
17 Mike Trout RC 60.00 150.00
18 Jose Reyes .30 .75
19 Craig Kimbrel .50 1.25
20 Jay Bruce .30 .75
21 Ian Kennedy .20 .50
22 Mat Latos .30 .75
23 Paul Konerko .30 .75
24 Neftali Feliz .20 .50
25 Johnny Damon .30 .75
26 Josh Beckett .20 .50
27 Prince Fielder .30 .75
28 Cliff Lee .30 .75
29 David Freese .20 .50
30 Troy Tulowitzki .50 1.25
31 Jacoby Ellsbury .40 1.00
32 Matt Kemp .40 1.00
33 Heath Bell .20 .50
34 Justin Upton .30 .75
35 Mariano Rivera .60 1.50
36 Alex Presley .30 .75
37 Gordon Beckham .20 .50
38 Ichiro Suzuki .60 1.50
39 Andy Dirks .50 1.25
40 Felix Hernandez .30 .75
41 Curtis Granderson .40 1.00
42 Michael Bourn .20 .50
43 Nelson Cruz .50 1.25
44 Jason Kipnis .60 1.50
45 Mark Trumbo .50 1.25
46 Yovani Gallardo .20 .50
47 Matt Holliday .50 1.25
48 Brian McCann .30 .75
49 J.P. Arencibia .20 .50
50 Chris Carpenter .30 .75

2011 Playoff Contenders Artist's Proof

*ARTIST PROOF: 2X TO 5X BASIC
RANDOM INSERTS IN PACKS
STATED PRINT RUN 49 SER.#'d SETS
18 Jose Reyes 10.00 25.00
38 Ichiro Suzuki 50.00 100.00

2011 Playoff Contenders Crystal Collection

*CRYSTAL: .6X TO 1.5X BASIC
RANDOM INSERTS IN PACKS
STATED PRINT RUN 299 SER.#'d SETS

2011 Playoff Contenders Playoff Ticket

*PLAYOFF TICKET: 1.5X TO 4X BASIC
RANDOM INSERTS IN PACKS
STATED PRINT RUN 99 SER.#'d SETS

2011 Playoff Contenders Award Winners

APPX.ODDS 1:6 HOBBY
1 Trevor Bauer 4.00 10.00
2 Taylor Jungmann .60 1.50
3 Jake Lowery .40 1.00
4 Brad Miller .40 1.00
5 Tyler Collins .40 1.00
6 Trevor Bauer 4.00 10.00
7 Dylan Bundy 1.25 3.00
8 Matt Purke 1.00 2.50
9 Anthony Rendon 4.00 10.00
10 Alex Wimmers .40 1.00
11 Bryan Holaday .40 1.00
12 Anthony Rendon 4.00 10.00
13 Stephen Strasburg 1.00 2.50
14 Curtis Granderson .75 2.00
15 Matt Kemp .75 2.00
16 Justin Verlander 1.00 2.50
17 Clayton Kershaw 1.50 4.00
18 Rickie Weeks .40 1.00
19 Neftali Feliz .40 1.00
20 Buster Posey 1.25 3.00
21 Albert Pujols 1.25 3.00
22 Joe Mauer .75 2.00
23 Michael Young .40 1.00
24 Chris Coghlan .40 1.00
25 Andrew Bailey .40 1.00
26 Evan Longoria .60 1.50
27 Geovany Soto .60 1.50
28 Alex Gordon .60 1.50
29 Dustin Pedroia 1.00 2.50
30 Albert Pujols 1.25 3.00
31 Mark Trumbo 1.00 2.50
32 Craig Kimbrel 1.00 2.50
33 Alex Rodriguez 1.25 3.00
34 Jimmy Rollins .60 1.50
35 Ryan Braun .60 1.50
36 Dustin Pedroia 1.00 2.50
37 Justin Verlander 1.00 2.50
38 Ryan Howard .75 2.00
39 Justin Morneau .60 1.50
40 Hanley Ramirez .60 1.50
41 Justin Verlander 1.00 2.50
42 Jacoby Ellsbury .75 2.00
43 Ryan Howard .75 2.00
44 Huston Street .40 1.00
45 Jered Weaver .60 1.50
46 Lance Berkman .60 1.50
47 Ichiro Suzuki 1.25 3.00
48 Derek Jeter 2.50 6.00
49 Francisco Liriano .40 1.00
50 Tim Hudson .60 1.50

2011 Playoff Contenders Award Winners Autographs

OVERALL AUTO ODDS 1:4
PRINT RUNS B/WN 10-149 COPIES PER
NO PRICING ON QTY 10
EXCHANGE DEADLINE 08/22/2013
1 Trevor Bauer/49 15.00 40.00
2 Taylor Jungmann/50 10.00 25.00
3 Jake Lowery/149 4.00 10.00
4 Brad Miller/141 4.00 10.00
5 Tyler Collins/99 6.00 15.00
6 Trevor Bauer/44 15.00 40.00
7 Dylan Bundy/99 20.00 50.00
8 Matt Purke/49 4.00 10.00
9 Anthony Rendon/49 15.00 40.00
10 Alex Wimmers/149 4.00 10.00
11 Bryan Holaday/94 10.00 25.00
12 Anthony Rendon/49 15.00 40.00

2011 Playoff Contenders Draft Ticket

PRINTING PLATES RANDOMLY INSERTED
PLATE PRINT RUN 1 SET PER COLOR
BLACK-CYAN-MAGENTA-YELLOW ISSUED
NO PLATE PRICING DUE TO SCARCITY
DT1 Travis Harrison .40 1.00
DT2 Matt Duran .40 1.00
DT3 Lenny Linsky .40 1.00
DT4 Burch Smith .25 .60
DT5 Jack Leathersich .25 .60
DT6 Ronald Guzman .60 1.50
DT7 Shane Opitz .40 1.00
DT8 Nicky Delmonico .25 .60
DT9 Eric Arce .60 1.50
DT10 Anthony Meo .25 .60
DT11 Keenyn Walker .25 .60
DT12 Anderson Feliz .25 .60
DT13 Robert Stephenson .50 1.25
DT14 Alex Hassan .25 .60
DT15 Heath Hembree .25 .60
DT16 Sean Halton .25 .60
DT17 Abel Baker .25 .60
DT18 Scott Snodgress .25 .60
DT19 Nick Fleece .25 .60
DT20 Andrew Susac .40 1.00
DT21 Tony Zych .25 .60
DT22 B.A. Vollmuth .25 .60
DT23 Logan Verrett .50 1.25
DT24 Carl Thomore .25 .60
DT25 Alex Santana .40 1.00
DT26 Blake Snell 1.00 2.50
DT27 Hudson Boyd .25 .60
DT28 Kylin Turnbull .25 .60
DT29 Jake Lowery .25 .60
DT30 Evan Marshall .25 .60
DT31 Jordan Cole .60 1.50
DT32 Aaron Westlake .25 .60
DT33 Scott Woodward .40 1.00
DT34 Travis Shaw .60 1.50
DT35 Phillip Evans .25 .60
DT36 Parker Markel .25 .60
DT37 Jordan Akins .25 .60
DT38 Sean Gilmartin .25 .60
DT39 Jacob Anderson .75 2.00
DT40 Kyle Crick .60 1.50
DT41 Roman Quinn .60 1.50
DT42 Tommy La Stella .60 1.50
DT43 Tyler Grimes .25 .60
DT44 Lee Orr .25 .60
DT45 Cole Green .25 .60
DT46 Matt Szczur .60 1.50
DT47 Steven Ames .25 .60
DT48 Dwight Smith Jr. .25 .60
DT49 Kes Carter .40 1.00
DT50 Chad Comer .25 .60
DT51 Corey Williams .25 .60
DT52 John Hicks .40 1.00
DT53 Adam Morgan .40 1.00
DT54 James Allen .25 .60
DT55 Cristhian Adames .25 .60
DT56 Forrest Snow .40 1.00
DT57 Tyler Gibson .25 .60
DT58 James Baldwin .25 .60
DT59 Kendrick Perkins .25 .60
DT60 Josh Osich .40 1.00
DT61 Nick Ramirez .40 1.00
DT62 Jason Krizan .25 .60
DT63 Michael Goodnight .25 .60
DT64 Zach Good .25 .60
DT65 Mitch Walding .25 .60
DT66 Bobby Crocker .25 .60
DT67 Shawon Dunston Jr. .25 .60
DT68 Jason King .25 .60
DT69 Kyle Winkler .25 .60
DT70 Miles Hamblin .25 .60
DT71 Madison Boer .25 .60
DT72 Johnny Eierman .25 .60
DT73 Kevin Comer .40 1.00
DT74 Jason Esposito .60 1.50
DT75 Dan Vogelbach .75 2.00
DT76 James Harris .25 .60
DT77 Cameron Gallagher .60 1.50
DT78 Mark Montgomery 1.25 3.00
DT79 Christian Lopes .60 1.50
DT80 J.R. Graham .25 .60
DT81 Brian Flynn .25 .60
DT82 Bryan Brickhouse .60 1.50
DT83 Greg Bird .50 1.25
DT84 Nick Tropeano .25 .60
DT85 Kevin Quackenbush .40 1.00
DT86 Kyle Kubitza .25 .60
DT87 Jordan Swagerty .40 1.00
DT88 Brian Dupra .25 .60
DT89 Zeke DeVoss .40 1.00
DT90 Brandon Loy .25 .60
DT91 Kyle McMyne .25 .60
DT92 Taylor Hill .25 .60
DT93 Cory Mazzoni .25 .60
DT94 Leonys Martin .75 2.00
DT95 Danry Vasquez .25 .60
DT96 Jake Floethe .25 .60
DT97 Taylor Featherston .25 .60
DT98 Matt Skole .40 1.00
DT99 Joseph Musgrove 1.25 3.00
DT100 Carson Smith .25 .60

2011 Playoff Contenders Draft Ticket Artist's Proof

*ARTIST PROOF: 2X TO 5X BASIC
RANDOM INSERTS IN PACKS
STATED PRINT RUN 49 SER.#'d SETS

2011 Playoff Contenders Draft Ticket Crystal Collection

*CRYSTAL: 1X TO 2.5X BASIC
RANDOM INSERTS IN PACKS
STATED PRINT RUN 299 SER.#'d SETS

2011 Playoff Contenders Draft Ticket Playoff Tickets

*PLAYOFF TICKET: 1.5X TO 4X BASIC
RANDOM INSERTS IN PACKS
STATED PRINT RUN 99 SER.#'d SETS

2011 Playoff Contenders Draft Ticket Autographs

OVERALL AUTO ODDS 1:4 HOBBY
ANNCD PRINT RUNS OF 90-299 COPIES PER
ASTERISK DENOTES ANND PRINT RUN
EXCHANGE DEADLINE 08/22/2013
DT1 Travis Harrison 5.00 12.00
DT2 Matt Duran 5.00 12.00
DT3 Lenny Linsky 3.00 8.00
DT4 Burch Smith 3.00 8.00
DT5 Jack Leathersich 3.00 8.00
DT6 Ronald Guzman 3.00 8.00
DT7 Shane Opitz/295 * 3.00 8.00
DT8 Nicky Delmonico 5.00 12.00
DT9 Eric Arce 6.00 15.00
DT10 Anthony Meo/299 * 8.00 20.00
DT11 Keenyn Walker/269 * 3.00 8.00
DT12 Anderson Feliz 3.00 8.00
DT13 Robert Stephenson/271 * 4.00 10.00
DT14 Alex Hassan/299 * 3.00 8.00
DT15 Heath Hembree 3.00 8.00
DT16 Sean Halton 3.00 8.00
DT17 Abel Baker 5.00 12.00
DT18 Scott Snodgress 3.00 8.00
DT19 Nick Fleece 3.00 8.00
DT20 Andrew Susac/259 * 10.00 25.00
DT21 Tony Zych/110 * 5.00 12.00
DT22 B.A. Vollmuth 3.00 8.00
DT23 Logan Verrett 6.00 15.00
DT24 Carl Thomore 3.00 8.00
DT25 Alex Santana 5.00 12.00
DT26 Blake Snell 3.00 8.00
DT27 Hudson Boyd/229 * 3.00 8.00
DT28 Kylin Turnbull 3.00 8.00
DT29 Jake Lowery 3.00 8.00
DT30 Evan Marshall 3.00 8.00
DT31 Jordan Cote 5.00 12.00
DT32 Aaron Westlake 3.00 8.00
DT33 Scott Woodward 3.00 8.00
DT34 Travis Shaw 6.00 15.00
DT35 Phillip Evans/298 * 3.00 8.00
DT36 Parker Markel 3.00 8.00
DT37 Jordan Akins 3.00 8.00
DT38 Sean Gilmartin/99 * 6.00 15.00
DT39 Jacob Anderson/169 * 15.00 40.00
DT40 Kyle Crick 3.00 8.00
DT41 Roman Quinn 5.00 12.00
DT42 Tommy La Stella 5.00 12.00
DT43 Tyler Grimes 3.00 8.00
DT44 Lee Orr 3.00 8.00
DT45 Cole Green 3.00 8.00
DT46 Matt Szczur/299 * 5.00 12.00
DT47 Steven Ames 3.00 8.00
DT48 Dwight Smith Jr. 3.00 8.00
DT49 Kes Carter 3.00 8.00
DT50 Chad Comer 3.00 8.00
DT51 Corey Williams/184 * 3.00 8.00
DT52 John Hicks 4.00 10.00
DT53 Adam Morgan 3.00 8.00
DT54 James Allen 3.00 8.00
DT55 Cristhian Adames 3.00 8.00
DT56 Forrest Snow 4.00 10.00
DT57 Tyler Gibson 5.00 12.00
DT58 James Baldwin 4.00 10.00
DT59 Kendrick Perkins 3.00 8.00
DT60 Josh Osich/271 * 4.00 10.00
DT61 Nick Ramirez 3.00 8.00
DT62 Jason Krizan/261 * 3.00 8.00
DT63 Michael Goodnight/99 * 3.00 8.00
DT64 Zach Good/246 * 5.00 12.00
DT65 Mitch Walding 3.00 8.00
DT66 Bobby Crocker/290 * 6.00 15.00
DT67 Shawon Dunston Jr. 6.00 15.00
DT68 Jason King/258 * 3.00 8.00
DT69 Kyle Winkler 3.00 8.00
DT70 Miles Hamblin 5.00 12.00
DT71 Madison Boer/288 * 3.00 8.00
DT72 Johnny Eierman 3.00 8.00
DT73 Kevin Comer 3.00 8.00
DT74 Jason Esposito 3.00 8.00
DT75 Dan Vogelbach 3.00 8.00
DT76 James Harris/218 * 5.00 12.00
DT77 Cameron Gallagher/195 * 6.00 15.00
DT78 Mark Montgomery 5.00 12.00
DT79 Christian Lopes 3.00 8.00
DT80 J.R. Graham/299 * 3.00 8.00
DT81 Brian Flynn 3.00 8.00
DT82 Bryan Brickhouse/290 * 3.00 8.00
DT83 Greg Bird 25.00 60.00
DT84 Nick Tropeano 3.00 8.00
DT85 Kevin Quackenbush 3.00 8.00
DT86 Kyle Kubitza 4.00 10.00
DT87 Jordan Swagerty 3.00 8.00
DT88 Brian Dupra 3.00 8.00
DT89 Zeke DeVoss/260 * 3.00 8.00
DT90 Brandon Loy 5.00 12.00
DT91 Kyle McMyne 3.00 8.00
DT92 Taylor Hill 3.00 8.00
DT93 Cory Mazzoni/249 * 4.00 10.00
DT94 Leonys Martin/90 * 5.00 12.00
DT95 Danry Vasquez 3.00 8.00
DT96 Jake Floethe 3.00 8.00
DT97 Taylor Featherston 3.00 8.00
DT98 Matt Skole 5.00 12.00
DT99 Joseph Musgrove 8.00 20.00
DT100 Carson Smith 3.00 8.00

2011 Playoff Contenders First Overall

APPX.ODDS 1:12 HOBBY
1 Gerrit Cole 4.00 10.00
2 Stephen Strasburg 1.00 2.50
3 David Price .75 2.00
4 Luke Hochevar .40 1.00
5 Justin Upton .60 1.50
6 Delmon Young .60 1.50
7 Joe Mauer .75 2.00
8 Adrian Gonzalez .75 2.00
9 Josh Hamilton .60 1.50
10 Chipper Jones 1.00 2.50

2011 Playoff Contenders Future Stars

APPX.ODDS 1:8 HOBBY
1 Brian Goodwin 1.00 2.50
2 John Hicks .60 1.50
3 Jason Krizan .40 1.00
4 Kevin Matthews .40 1.00
5 Dante Bichette Jr. .60 1.50
6 Keenyn Walker .40 1.00
7 Hudson Boyd .40 1.00
8 Austin Hedges .40 1.00
9 Jeff Ames .40 1.00
10 Matt Dean .60 1.50
11 Tyler Gibson .40 1.00
12 Matt Szczur 1.00 2.50
13 Logan Verrett .75 2.00
14 Josh Osich .60 1.50
15 Dillon Maples .40 1.00
16 Jason Esposito 1.00 2.50
17 Aaron Westlake .40 1.00
18 Bryson Myles .60 1.50
19 Matt Barnes .60 1.50

2011 Playoff Contenders Future Stars Autographs

OVERALL AUTO ODDS 1:4
PRINT RUNS B/WN 1-199 COPIES PER
NO PRICING ON QTY 25 OR LESS
EXCHANGE DEADLINE 08/22/2013
2 John Hicks/199 4.00 10.00
3 Jason Krizan/199 4.00 10.00
4 Kevin Matthews/199 4.00 10.00
5 Dante Bichette Jr./199 10.00 25.00
6 Keenyn Walker/140 6.00 15.00
7 Hudson Boyd/199 4.00 10.00
8 Austin Hedges/199 3.00 8.00
10 Matt Dean/199 5.00 12.00
11 Tyler Gibson/199 4.00 10.00
12 Matt Szczur/199 4.00 10.00
13 Logan Verrett/199 6.00 15.00
14 Josh Osich/199 4.00 10.00
15 Dillon Maples/199 3.00 38.00
16 Jason Esposito/199 6.00 15.00
17 Aaron Westlake/199 5.00 12.00
18 Bryson Myles/170 5.00 12.00

2011 Playoff Contenders Legendary Debuts

APPX.ODDS 1:24 HOBBY
1 Dwight Gooden .60 1.50
2 Fred Lynn .60 1.50
3 Al Kaline 1.50 4.00
4 Bruce Sutter 1.00 2.50
5 Gaylord Perry 1.00 2.50
6 Bobby Doerr 1.00 2.50
7 Bob Gibson 1.00 2.50
8 Pete Rose 3.00 8.00
9 Denny McLain .60 1.50
10 Lou Brock 1.00 2.50
11 Gary Carter 1.00 2.50
12 Bob Feller 1.00 2.50
13 Carl Erskine .60 1.50
14 Ernie Banks 1.50 4.00
15 Jim Rice 1.00 2.50

2011 Playoff Contenders Legendary Debuts Autographs

OVERALL AUTO ODDS 1:4
PRINT RUNS B/WN 6-99 COPIES PER
NO PRICING ON QTY 25 OR LESS
EXCHANGE DEADLINE 08/22/2013
1 Dwight Gooden/99 8.00 20.00
4 Bruce Sutter/49 8.00 20.00
5 Gaylord Perry/60 6.00 15.00
6 Bobby Doerr/99 8.00 20.00
9 Denny McLain/31 10.00 25.00
11 Gary Carter/49 12.50 30.00
13 Carl Erskine/99 8.00 20.00
15 Jim Rice/99 8.00 20.00

2011 Playoff Contenders Prospect Ticket

PRINTING PLATES RANDOMLY INSERTED
PLATE PRINT RUN 1 SET PER COLOR
BLACK-CYAN-MAGENTA-YELLOW ISSUED
NO PLATE PRICING DUE TO SCARCITY
RT1 Gerrit Cole 2.50 6.00
RT2 Danny Hultzen 1.25 3.00
RT3 Larry Greene .40 1.00
RT4 Matt Barnes .40 1.00
RT5 Bubba Starling .40 1.00
RT6 Alex Meyer .25 .60
RT7 Francisco Lindor 3.00 8.00
RT8 Trevor Bauer 2.50 6.00
RT9 Dylan Bundy .75 2.00
RT10 Anthony Rendon 2.50 6.00
RT11 Henry Owens .40 1.00
RT12 Brandon Nimmo 1.25 3.00
RT13 Javier Baez 3.00 8.00
RT14 Zach Cone .40 1.00
RT15 Archie Bradley .75 2.00
RT16 Sonny Gray .60 1.50
RT17 Tyler Collins .25 .60
RT18 Cory Spangenberg .40 1.00
RT19 George Springer 1.50 4.00
RT20 Jackie Bradley Jr. 1.00 2.50
RT21 Nick Ahmed .25 .60
RT22 Taylor Jungmann .40 1.00
RT23 Josh Bell 1.50 4.00
RT24 Austin Hedges .25 .60
RT25 C.J. Cron .75 2.00
RT26 Joe Ross .60 1.50
RT27 Trevor Story 4.00 10.00
RT28 Kolten Wong .40 1.00
RT29 Tyler Anderson .25 .60
RT30 Blake Swihart .40 1.00
RT31 Matt Purke .60 1.50
RT32 Bryson Myles .40 1.00
RT33 Tyler Goeddel .25 .60
RT34 Dean Green .25 .60
RT35 Mikie Mahtook .60 1.50
RT36 Brian Goodwin .60 1.50
RT37 Jed Bradley .40 1.00
RT38 Granden Goetzman .25 .60
RT39 Dante Bichette Jr. .40 1.00
RT40 Levi Michael .40 1.00
RT41 Andrew Chafin .25 .60
RT42 Taylor Guerrieri .25 .60
RT43 Dillon Maples .25 .60
RT44 Brandon Martin .40 1.00
RT45 Chris Reed .40 1.00
RT46 Michael Fulmer .60 1.50
RT47 Jace Peterson .25 .60
RT48 Dillon Howard .40 1.00
RT49 Alex Dickerson .40 1.00
RT50 Michael Kelly .25 .60

2011 Playoff Contenders Prospect Ticket 1st Day Proof

RANDOM INSERTS IN PACKS
STATED PRINT RUN 10 SER.#'d SETS
NO PRICING DUE TO SCARCITY

2011 Playoff Contenders Prospect Ticket Artist's Proof

*ARTIST PROOF: 2X TO 5X BASIC
RANDOM INSERTS IN PACKS
STATED PRINT RUN 49 SER.#'d SETS

2011 Playoff Contenders Prospect Ticket Crystal Collection

*CRYSTAL: 1X TO 2.5X BASIC
RANDOM INSERTS IN PACKS
STATED PRINT RUN 299 SER.#'d SETS

2011 Playoff Contenders Prospect Ticket Playoff Tickets

*PLAYOFF TICKET: 1.5X TO 4X BASIC
RANDOM INSERTS IN PACKS
STATED PRINT RUN 99 SER.#'d SETS

2011 Playoff Contenders Rookie Ticket Autographs

OVERALL AUTO ODDS 1:4 HOBBY
ANNCD PRINT RUNS OF 87-299 COPIES PER
ASTERISK DENOTES ANND PRINT RUN
EXCHANGE DEADLINE 08/22/2013
RT1 Gerrit Cole/297 * 15.00 40.00
RT2 Danny Hultzen/87 * 20.00 50.00
RT3 Larry Greene 6.00 15.00
RT4 Matt Barnes 3.00 8.00
RT5 Bubba Starling 3.00 8.00
RT6 Alex Meyer 6.00 15.00
RT7 Francisco Lindor 12.00 30.00
RT8 Trevor Bauer 15.00 40.00
RT9 Dylan Bundy/245 * 4.00 10.00
RT10 Anthony Rendon 10.00 25.00
RT11 Henry Owens 3.00 8.00
RT12 Brandon Nimmo 3.00 8.00
RT13 Javier Baez/299 * 12.00 30.00
RT14 Zach Cone 3.00 8.00
RT15 Archie Bradley 3.00 8.00
RT16 Sonny Gray 5.00 12.00
RT17 Tyler Collins 4.00 10.00
RT18 Cory Spangenberg 5.00 12.00
RT19 George Springer/199 * 15.00 40.00
RT20 Jackie Bradley Jr. 10.00 25.00
RT21 Nick Ahmed 3.00 8.00
RT22 Taylor Jungmann 3.00 8.00
RT23 Josh Bell 15.00 40.00
RT24 Austin Hedges 3.00 8.00
RT25 C.J. Cron 3.00 8.00
RT26 Joe Ross 4.00 10.00
RT27 Trevor Story 12.00 30.00
RT28 Kolten Wong 4.00 10.00
RT29 Tyler Anderson 4.00 10.00
RT30 Blake Swihart 6.00 15.00
RT31 Matt Purke 4.00 10.00
RT32 Bryson Myles 5.00 12.00
RT33 Tyler Goeddel 3.00 8.00
RT34 Dean Green 3.00 8.00
RT35 Mikie Mahtook 5.00 12.00
RT36 Brian Goodwin 6.00 15.00
RT37 Jed Bradley 5.00 12.00
RT38 Granden Goetzman 3.00 8.00
RT39 Dante Bichette Jr. 12.00 30.00
RT40 Levi Michael 5.00 12.00
RT41 Andrew Chafin 3.00 8.00
RT42 Taylor Guerrieri 5.00 12.00
RT43 Dillon Maples 5.00 12.00
RT44 Brandon Martin 3.00 8.00
RT45 Chris Reed 3.00 8.00
RT46 Michael Fulmer 8.00 20.00
RT47 Jace Peterson 5.00 12.00
RT48 Dillon Howard 5.00 12.00
RT49 Alex Dickerson 4.00 10.00
RT50 Michael Kelly/255 * 4.00 10.00

2011 Playoff Contenders Season Ticket Autographs

OVERALL AUTO ODDS 1:4
PRINT RUNS B/WN 50-224 COPIES PER
EXCHANGE DEADLINE 08/22/2013
1 Josh Hamilton/50 * EXCH 6.00 15.00
7 Andrew McCutchen /99 * 20.00 50.00
10 Clayton Kershaw/50 * EXCH 20.00 50.00
15 Jordan Lyles/200 * 5.00 12.00
24 Neftali Feliz/224 * 5.00 12.00
29 David Freese/50 * 10.00 25.00
32 Matt Kemp/99 * 5.00 12.00
36 Alex Presley/224 * 6.00 15.00
39 Andy Dirks/224 * EXCH 8.00 20.00
46 Yovani Gallardo/99 * 5.00 12.00

2011 Playoff Contenders Sweet Signs Autographs

OVERALL AUTO ODDS 1:4
PRINT RUNS B/WN 5-99 COPIES PER
NO PRICING ON QTY 25 OR LESS
EXCHANGE DEADLINE 08/22/2013
4 Kendrick Perkins /99 5.00 12.00
6 Forrest Snow/99 5.00 12.00
7 Logan Bawcom/99 5.00 12.00
8 Brandon Loy/50 6.00 15.00
10 Nicky Delmonico/99 8.00 20.00
11 James Baldwin/99 8.00 20.00
13 James Allen/99 12.00 30.00
14 Gerrit Cole/99 12.00 30.00
15 B.A. Vollmuth/99 8.00 20.00
16 Abel Baker/99 5.00 12.00
17 Brian Flynn/50 12.00 30.00
18 Williams Jerez/99 6.00 15.00
21 Dylan Bundy/99 6.00 15.00
22 Aaron Westlake/99 6.00 15.00
23 Blake Swihart/99 15.00 40.00
24 Delino DeShields Jr./99 8.00 20.00
25 Bubba Starling/99 8.00 20.00
26 Dwight Gooden/49 8.00 20.00
29 Chris Wallace/99 8.00 20.00
30 Brian Goodwin/99 6.00 15.00
32 Shawon Dunston Jr./99 6.00 15.00
34 Bryson Myles/99 5.00 12.00
35 Lee Orr/99 6.00 15.00
36 Jack Morris/35 6.00 15.00
39 Tyler Collins/99 5.00 12.00
40 Greg Bird/50 30.00 80.00
41 Carson Smith/99 8.00 20.00
43 Red Schoendienst/35 10.00 25.00
44 Jackie Bradley Jr./50 30.00 80.00
46 Eric Arce/99 8.00 20.00
47 Tommy La Stella/99 12.00 30.00
48 Matt Szczur/99 5.00 12.00
50 Joseph Musgrove/99 40.00 100.00

2011 Playoff Contenders Winning Combos

COMPLETE SET (25) 12.50 30.00
APPX.ODDS 1:4 HOBBY
1 Zeke DeVoss .60 1.50
Harold Martinez
2 Josh Osich .60 1.50
Andrew Susac
3 Abel Baker .40 1.00
Tyler Collins
4 Springer/Barnes 2.50 6.00
5 Dan Vogelbach 1.25 3.00
Hudson Boyd
6 Brad Miller .40 1.00
Will Lamb
7 Chad Comer .40 1.00
Jason Krizan
8 J.Bell/G.Cole 4.00 10.00
9 C.Mazzoni/P.Maynard .40 1.00
10 D.Hultzen/J.Hicks 2.00 5.00
11 Brian Flynn .40 1.00
Tyler Grimes
12 Travis Shaw 1.00 2.50
Andrew Chafin
13 Taylor Jungmann .60 1.50
Jed Bradley
14 Jason King .40 1.00
Evan Marshall
15 Taylor Featherston .40 1.00
Kyle Winkler
16 Tyler Anderson .40 1.00
Madison Boer
17 Cristhian Adames .40 1.00
Anderson Feliz
18 Scott Snodgress .60 1.50
Chris Reed
19 D.Jeter/R.Cano 2.50 6.00
20 Roy Halladay .60 1.50
Cliff Lee
21 M.Kemp/C.Kershaw 1.50 4.00
22 R.Braun/P.Fielder .60 1.50
23 Ian Kinsler .60 1.50
Josh Hamilton
24 A.Avila/J.Verlander 1.00 2.50
25 Justin Upton .60 1.50
Ian Kennedy

2011 Playoff Contenders Winning Combos Autographs

OVERALL AUTO ODDS 1:4
PRINT RUNS B/WN 10-149 COPIES PER
NO PRICING ON QTY 25 OR LESS
EXCHANGE DEADLINE 08/22/2013
1 DeVoss/Martinez/149 6.00 15.00
2 Osich/Susac/149 10.00 25.00
3 Abel Baker/Tyler Collins/149 4.00 10.00
4 Barnes/Springer/94 8.00 20.00
5 Vogelbach/Boyd/149 6.00 15.00
6 Miller/Lamb/49 5.00 12.00
7 Chad Comer/Jason Krizan/149 4.00 10.00
9 Mazzoni/Maynard/99 8.00 20.00
11 Flynn/Grimes/149 10.00 25.00
12 Shaw/Chafin/149 10.00 25.00
14 Jason King/Evan Marshall/149 4.00 10.00
15 Taylor Featherston/Kyle Winkler/149 4.00 10.00
16 Anderson/Boer/99 6.00 15.00
17 Adames/Feliz/149 5.00 12.00
18 Snodgress/Reed/149 4.00 10.00

2004 Playoff Honors

COMP.SET w/o SP's (200) 10.00 25.00
COMMON ACTIVE (1-200) .15 .40
COMMON RETIRED (1-200) .15 .40
COMMON RC/1999 (201-250) .60 1.50
RC/1999 PRINT RUN 1999 SERIAL #'d SETS
COMMON AUTO (201-250) 3.00 8.00
AUTO PRINT RUNS B/WN 675-1000 PER
201-250 RANDOM INSERTS IN PACKS
1 Bartolo Colon .15 .40
2 Garret Anderson .15 .40
3 Tim Salmon .15 .40
4 Troy Glaus .15 .40
5 Vladimir Guerrero .25 .60
6 Brandon Webb .15 .40
7 Brian Bruney .15 .40
8 Luis Gonzalez .15 .40
9 Randy Johnson .40 1.00
10 Richie Sexson .15 .40
11 Robby Hammock .15 .40
12 Roberto Alomar .25 .60
13 Shea Hillenbrand .15 .40
14 Steve Finley .15 .40
15 Adam LaRoche .15 .40
16 Andruw Jones .15 .40
17 Bubba Nelson .15 .40
18 Chipper Jones .40 1.00
19 Dale Murphy .40 1.00
20 J.D. Drew .15 .40
21 John Smoltz .40 1.00
22 Marcus Giles .15 .40
23 Rafael Furcal .15 .40
24 Warren Spahn .25 .60
25 Greg Maddux .50 1.25
26 Adam Loewen .15 .40
27 Cal Ripken 1.25 3.00
28 Javy Lopez .15 .40
29 Jay Gibbons .15 .40
30 Luis Matos .15 .40
31 Miguel Tejada .25 .60
32 Rafael Palmeiro .25 .60
33 Bobby Doerr .25 .60
34 Curt Schilling .25 .60
35 Edwin Almonte .15 .40
36 Jason Varitek .40 1.00
37 Kevin Youkilis .15 .40
38 Manny Ramirez .40 1.00
39 Nomar Garciaparra .25 .60
40 Pedro Martinez .25 .60
41 Trot Nixon .15 .40
42 Andre Dawson .25 .60
43 Aramis Ramirez .15 .40
44 Brendan Harris .15 .40
45 Derrek Lee .15 .40
46 Ernie Banks .40 1.00
47 Kerry Wood .15 .40
48 Mark Prior .25 .60
49 Ryne Sandberg .75 2.00
50 Sammy Sosa .40 1.00
51 Carlos Lee .15 .40
52 Frank Thomas .40 1.00
53 Joe Borchard .15 .40
54 Joe Crede .15 .40
55 Magglio Ordonez .25 .60
56 Adam Dunn .25 .60
57 Austin Kearns .15 .40
58 Barry Larkin .25 .60
59 Brandon Larson .15 .40
60 Ken Griffey Jr. .75 2.00
61 Ryan Wagner .15 .40
62 Sean Casey .15 .40
63 Bob Feller .25 .60
64 Brian Tallet .15 .40
65 C.C. Sabathia .25 .60
66 Jeremy Guthrie .15 .40
67 Jody Gerut .15 .40
68 Clint Barmes .25 .60
69 Jeff Baker .15 .40
70 Joe Kennedy .15 .40
71 Larry Walker .25 .60
72 Preston Wilson .15 .40
73 Todd Helton .25 .60
74 Alan Trammell .25 .60
75 Dmitri Young .15 .40
76 Ivan Rodriguez .25 .60
77 Jeremy Bonderman .15 .40
78 Preston Larrison .15 .40
79 Dontrelle Willis .15 .40
80 Josh Beckett .15 .40
81 Juan Pierre .15 .40
82 Luis Castillo .15 .40
83 Miguel Cabrera .40 1.00
84 Mike Lowell .15 .40
85 Andy Pettitte .25 .60
86 Chris Burke .15 .40
87 Craig Biggio .25 .60
88 Jeff Bagwell .25 .60
89 Jeff Kent .15 .40
90 Lance Berkman .25 .60
91 Morgan Ensberg .15 .40
92 Richard Hidalgo .15 .40
93 Roger Clemens .50 1.25
94 Roy Oswalt .25 .60
95 Angel Berroa .15 .40
96 Byron Gettis .15 .40
97 Carlos Beltran .25 .60
98 George Brett .75 2.00
99 Juan Gonzalez .15 .40
100 Mike Sweeney .15 .40
101 Duke Snider .25 .60
102 Edwin Jackson .15 .40
103 Eric Gagne .15 .40
104 Hideo Nomo .40 1.00
105 Hong-Chih Kuo .15 .40
106 Kazuhisa Ishii .15 .40
107 Paul Lo Duca .15 .40
108 Robin Ventura .15 .40
109 Shawn Green .15 .40
110 Junior Spivey .15 .40
111 Rickie Weeks .15 .40
112 Scott Podsednik .15 .40
113 J.D. Durbin .15 .40
114 Jacque Jones .15 .40
115 Jason Kubel .15 .40
116 Johan Santana .25 .60
117 Shannon Stewart .15 .40
118 Torii Hunter .15 .40
119 Brad Wilkerson .15 .40
120 Jose Vidro .15 .40
121 Nick Johnson .15 .40
122 Orlando Cabrera .15 .40
123 Gary Carter .25 .60
124 Jae Weong Seo .15 .40
125 Lenny Dykstra .15 .40
126 Mike Piazza .40 1.00
127 Tom Glavine .25 .60
128 Alex Rodriguez .50 1.25
129 Bernie Williams .25 .60
130 Chien-Ming Wang .60 1.50
131 Derek Jeter 1.00 2.50
132 Don Mattingly .75 2.00
133 Gary Sheffield .15 .40
134 Hideki Matsui .60 1.50
135 Jason Giambi .15 .40
136 Javier Vazquez .15 .40
137 Jorge Posada .25 .60
138 Jose Contreras .15 .40
139 Kevin Brown .15 .40
140 Mariano Rivera .50 1.25
141 Mike Mussina .25 .60
142 Whitey Ford .25 .60
143 Barry Zito .25 .60
144 Eric Chavez .15 .40
145 Mark Mulder .15 .40
146 Rich Harden .15 .40
147 Tim Hudson .25 .60
148 Reggie Jackson .25 .60
149 Rickey Henderson .40 1.00
150 Brett Myers .15 .40
151 Bobby Abreu .15 .40
152 Jim Thome .25 .60
153 Kevin Millwood .15 .40
154 Marlon Byrd .15 .40
155 Mike Schmidt .60 1.50
156 Ryan Howard .30 .75
157 Jack Wilson .15 .40
158 Jason Kendall .15 .40
159 Brian Giles .15 .40
160 David Wells .15 .40
161 Jay Payton .15 .40
162 Phil Nevin .15 .40
163 Ryan Klesko .15 .40
164 Sean Burroughs .15 .40
165 A.J. Pierzynski .15 .40
166 J.T. Snow .15 .40
167 Jason Schmidt .15 .40
168 Jerome Williams .15 .40
169 Will Clark .25 .60
170 Bret Boone .15 .40
171 Chris Snelling .15 .40
172 Edgar Martinez .25 .60
173 Ichiro Suzuki .50 1.25
174 Randy Winn .15 .40
175 Rich Aurilia .15 .40
176 Shigetoshi Hasegawa .15 .40
177 Albert Pujols .50 1.25
178 Dan Haren .15 .40
179 Edgar Renteria .15 .40
180 Jim Edmonds .25 .60
181 Matt Morris .15 .40
182 Scott Rolen .25 .60
183 Stan Musial .60 1.50
184 Aubrey Huff .15 .40
185 Chad Gaudin .15 .40
186 Delmon Young .25 .60
187 Fred McGriff .15 .40
188 Rocco Baldelli .15 .40
189 Alfonso Soriano .25 .60
190 Hank Blalock .15 .40
191 Mark Teixeira .25 .60
192 Nolan Ryan 1.25 3.00
193 Alexis Rios .15 .40
194 Carlos Delgado .15 .40
195 Dustin McGowan .15 .40
196 Guillermo Quiroz .15 .40
197 Josh Phelps .15 .40
198 Roy Halladay .25 .60
199 Vernon Wells .15 .40
200 Vinnie Chulk .15 .40
201 Jose Capellan/1999 RC .60 1.50
202 Kazuo Matsui/1999 RC 1.00 2.50
203 Dave Crouthers/1999 RC .60 1.50
204 Akinori Otsuka/1999 RC .60 1.50
205 Nick Regilio/1999 RC .60 1.50
206 Justin Hampson/1999 RC .60 1.50
207 Lincoln Holdzkom/1999 RC .60 1.50
208 Jorge Sequea/1999 RC .60 1.50
209 Justin Leone/1999 RC .60 1.50
210 Renyel Pinto/1999 RC .60 1.50
211 Mariano Gomez/1999 RC .60 1.50
212 Onil Joseph AU/1000 RC 3.00 8.00
213 J.Labandeira AU/1000 RC 3.00 8.00
214 Cory Sullivan/1999 RC .60 1.50
215 Carlos Vasquez AU/675 RC 4.00 10.00
216 Chris Shelton/1999 RC .60 1.50
217 Willy Taveras/1999 RC 1.50 4.00
218 John Gall/1999 RC .60 1.50
219 Jerry Gil/1999 RC .60 1.50
220 Jason Frasor/1999 RC .60 1.50
221 Justin Knoedler/1999 RC .60 1.50
222 Ronald Belisario/1999 RC .60 1.50
223 Mike Rouse/1999 RC .60 1.50
224 Dennis Sarfate/1999 RC .60 1.50
225 Casey Daigle/1999 RC .60 1.50
226 S.Takatsu AU/800 RC 6.00 15.00
227 Jason Bartlett AU/800 RC 4.00 10.00
228 Alfredo Simon AU/1000 RC 3.00 8.00
229 Chris Oxspring/1999 RC .60 1.50
230 Fern Nieve AU/1000 RC 3.00 8.00
231 Ruddy Yan AU/800 3.00 8.00
232 Ryan Wing/1999 RC .60 1.50
233 Tim Bittner AU/1000 RC 3.00 8.00
234 Ram Ramirez AU/1000 RC 3.00 8.00
235 Sean Henn AU/1000 RC 3.00 8.00
236 Roberto Novoa AU/800 RC 3.00 8.00
237 Jerome Gamble AU/800 RC 3.00 8.00
238 Jamie Brown AU/800 RC 3.00 8.00
239 Ian Snell AU/800 RC 6.00 15.00
240 Freddy Guzman AU/800 RC 3.00 8.00
241 Aarom Baldiris AU/1000 RC 3.00 8.00
242 Greg Dobbs/1999 RC .60 1.50
243 Ivan Ochoa/1999 RC .60 1.50
244 Angel Chavez AU/800 RC 3.00 8.00
245 Merkin Valdez AU/800 RC 3.00 8.00
246 Mike Gosling AU/800 RC 3.00 8.00
247 Carlos Hines AU/800 RC 3.00 8.00
248 Graham Koonce AU/1000 3.00 8.00
249 Will Bergolla AU/1000 RC 3.00 8.00
250 Hect Gimenez AU/1000 RC 3.00 8.00

2004 Playoff Honors Credits Bronze

*BRONZE ACTIVE 1-200: 3X TO 8X BASIC
*BRONZE RETIRED 1-200: 3X TO 8X BASIC
RANDOM INSERTS IN PACKS
STATED PRINT RUN 100 SERIAL #'d SETS
201 Jose Capellan 1.25 3.00
202 Kazuo Matsui 2.00 5.00
203 Dave Crouthers 1.25 3.00
204 Akinori Otsuka 1.25 3.00
205 Nick Regilio 1.25 3.00
206 Justin Hampson 1.25 3.00
207 Lincoln Holdzkom 1.25 3.00
208 Jorge Sequea 1.25 3.00
209 Justin Leone 1.25 3.00
210 Renyel Pinto 1.25 3.00
211 Mariano Gomez 1.25 3.00
212 Onil Joseph 1.25 3.00
213 Josh Labandeira 1.25 3.00
214 Cory Sullivan 1.25 3.00
215 Carlos Vasquez 1.25 3.00
216 Chris Shelton 1.25 3.00
217 Willy Taveras 3.00 8.00
218 John Gall 1.25 3.00
219 Jerry Gil 1.25 3.00
220 Jason Frasor 1.25 3.00
221 Justin Knoedler 1.25 3.00
222 Ronald Belisario 1.25 3.00
223 Mike Rouse 1.25 3.00
224 Dennis Sarfate 1.25 3.00
225 Casey Daigle 1.25 3.00
226 Shingo Takatsu 1.25 3.00
227 Jason Bartlett 4.00 10.00
228 Alfredo Simon 2.00 5.00
229 Chris Oxspring 1.25 3.00
230 Fernando Nieve 1.25 3.00
231 Ruddy Yan 1.25 3.00
232 Ryan Wing 1.25 3.00
233 Tim Bittner 1.25 3.00
234 Ramon Ramirez 1.25 3.00
235 Sean Henn 1.25 3.00
236 Roberto Novoa 1.25 3.00
237 Jerome Gamble 1.25 3.00
238 Jamie Brown 1.25 3.00
239 Ian Snell 1.25 3.00
240 Freddy Guzman 1.25 3.00
241 Aarom Baldiris 1.25 3.00
242 Greg Dobbs 1.25 3.00
243 Ivan Ochoa 1.25 3.00
244 Angel Chavez 1.25 3.00
245 Merkin Valdez 1.25 3.00
246 Mike Gosling 1.25 3.00
247 Carlos Hines 1.25 3.00
248 Graham Koonce 1.25 3.00
249 William Bergolla 1.25 3.00
250 Hector Gimenez 1.25 3.00

2004 Playoff Honors Credits Gold

*GOLD ACTIVE 1-200: 6X TO 15X BASIC
*GOLD RETIRED 1-200: 6X TO 15X BASIC
RANDOM INSERTS IN PACKS
STATED PRINT RUN 25 SERIAL #'d SETS
NO PRICING ON 201-250 DUE TO SCARCITY

2004 Playoff Honors Credits Silver

*SILVER ACTIVE 1-200: 5X TO 12X BASIC
*SILVER RETIRED 1-200: 5X TO 12X BASIC
RANDOM INSERTS IN PACKS
STATED PRINT RUN 50 SERIAL #'d SETS
201 Jose Capellan 2.00 5.00
202 Kazuo Matsui 3.00 8.00
203 Dave Crouthers 2.00 5.00
204 Akinori Otsuka 2.00 5.00
205 Nick Regilio 2.00 5.00
206 Justin Hampson 2.00 5.00
207 Lincoln Holdzkom 2.00 5.00
208 Jorge Sequea 2.00 5.00
209 Justin Leone 2.00 5.00
210 Renyel Pinto 2.00 5.00
211 Mariano Gomez 2.00 5.00
212 Onil Joseph 2.00 5.00
213 Josh Labandeira 2.00 5.00
214 Cory Sullivan 2.00 5.00
215 Carlos Vasquez 2.00 5.00
216 Chris Shelton 2.00 5.00
217 Willy Taveras 5.00 12.00
218 John Gall 2.00 5.00
219 Jerry Gil 2.00 5.00
220 Jason Frasor 2.00 5.00
221 Justin Knoedler 2.00 5.00
222 Ronald Belisario 2.00 5.00
223 Mike Rouse 2.00 5.00
224 Dennis Sarfate 2.00 5.00
225 Casey Daigle 2.00 5.00
226 Shingo Takatsu 2.00 5.00
227 Jason Bartlett 6.00 15.00
228 Alfredo Simon 3.00 8.00
229 Chris Oxspring 2.00 5.00
230 Fernando Nieve 2.00 5.00
231 Ruddy Yan 2.00 5.00
232 Ryan Wing 2.00 5.00
233 Tim Bittner 2.00 5.00
234 Ramon Ramirez 2.00 5.00
235 Sean Henn 2.00 5.00
236 Roberto Novoa 2.00 5.00
237 Jerome Gamble 2.00 5.00
238 Jamie Brown 2.00 5.00
239 Ian Snell 2.00 5.00
240 Freddy Guzman 2.00 5.00
241 Aarom Baldiris 2.00 5.00
242 Greg Dobbs 2.00 5.00
243 Ivan Ochoa 2.00 5.00
244 Angel Chavez 2.00 5.00
245 Merkin Valdez 2.00 5.00
246 Mike Gosling 2.00 5.00
247 Carlos Hines 2.00 5.00
248 Graham Koonce 2.00 5.00
249 William Bergolla 2.00 5.00
250 Hector Gimenez 2.00 5.00

2004 Playoff Honors Signature Bronze

PRINT RUNS B/WN 1-100 COPIES PER
NO PRICING ON QTY OF 10 OR LESS
NO RC PRICING ON QTY OF 25 OR LESS
2 Garret Anderson/100 6.00 15.00
5 Vladimir Guerrero/50 6.00 15.00
6 Brandon Webb/100 4.00 10.00
7 Brian Bruney/96 4.00 10.00
11 Robby Hammock/100 4.00 10.00
13 Shea Hillenbrand/100 6.00 15.00
15 Adam LaRoche/100 4.00 10.00
16 Andruw Jones/25 20.00 50.00
17 Bubba Nelson/100 4.00 10.00
22 Marcus Giles/100 6.00 15.00
23 Rafael Furcal/50 8.00 20.00
26 Adam Loewen/100 4.00 10.00
27 Cal Ripken/25 30.00 80.00
29 Jay Gibbons/100 4.00 10.00
30 Luis Matos/100 4.00 10.00
33 Bobby Doerr/100 6.00 15.00
35 Edwin Almonte/99 4.00 10.00
37 Kevin Youkilis/100 5.00 12.00
41 Trot Nixon/50 8.00 20.00
42 Andre Dawson/100 6.00 15.00
43 Aramis Ramirez/25 12.50 30.00
44 Brendan Harris/100 4.00 10.00
45 Derrek Lee/100 6.00 15.00
46 Ernie Banks/25 30.00 60.00
47 Kerry Wood/25 20.00 50.00
48 Mark Prior/50 12.50 30.00
50 Sammy Sosa/50 50.00 100.00
51 Carlos Lee/100 6.00 15.00
52 Frank Thomas/25 30.00 60.00
53 Joe Borchard/100 4.00 10.00
54 Joe Crede/50 8.00 20.00
55 Magglio Ordonez/50 8.00 20.00
58 Barry Larkin/25 30.00 60.00
59 Brandon Larson/100 4.00 10.00
61 Ryan Wagner/100 4.00 10.00
63 Bob Feller/100 10.00 25.00
64 Brian Tallet/100 4.00 10.00
66 Jeremy Guthrie/100 4.00 10.00
67 Jody Gerut/100 4.00 10.00
68 Clint Barmes/100 6.00 15.00
69 Jeff Baker/25 8.00 20.00
72 Preston Wilson/100 6.00 15.00
74 Alan Trammell/100 6.00 15.00
78 Preston Larrison/100 4.00 10.00
79 Dontrelle Willis/25 20.00 50.00
83 Miguel Cabrera/100 30.00 60.00
85 Andy Pettitte/25 10.00 25.00
86 Chris Burke/100 6.00 15.00
88 Jeff Bagwell/25 30.00 60.00
91 Morgan Ensberg/100 6.00 15.00
96 Byron Gettis/100 4.00 10.00
97 Carlos Beltran/100 6.00 15.00
98 George Brett/25 50.00 100.00
101 Duke Snider/100 10.00 25.00
102 Edwin Jackson/100 5.00 12.00
105 Hong-Chih Kuo/100 10.00 25.00
106 Kazuhisa Ishii/25 12.50 30.00
107 Paul Lo Duca/100 6.00 15.00
108 Robin Ventura/50 8.00 20.00
110 Junior Spivey/50 5.00 12.00
112 Scott Podsednik/100 10.00 25.00
113 J.D. Durbin/100 4.00 10.00
114 Jacque Jones/100 6.00 15.00
115 Jason Kubel/50 4.00 10.00
116 Johan Santana/100 12.50 30.00
117 Shannon Stewart/50 5.00 12.00
123 Gary Carter/100 10.00 25.00
125 Lenny Dykstra/100 6.00 15.00
130 Chien-Ming Wang/100 75.00 150.00
132 Don Mattingly/25 30.00 60.00
133 Gary Sheffield/50 12.50 30.00
137 Jorge Posada/50 30.00 60.00
142 Whitey Ford/50 12.50 30.00
145 Mark Mulder/100 6.00 15.00
146 Rich Harden/100 6.00 15.00
147 Tim Hudson/25 6.00 15.00
148 Reggie Jackson/25 30.00 60.00
149 Rickey Henderson/25 60.00 120.00
150 Brett Myers/100 6.00 15.00
154 Marlon Byrd/100 4.00 10.00
155 Mike Schmidt/50 40.00 80.00
156 Ryan Howard/100 12.00 30.00
161 Jay Payton/100 4.00 10.00
168 Jerome Williams/50 5.00 12.00
169 Will Clark/50 30.00 60.00
171 Chris Snelling/100 4.00 10.00
176 Shigetoshi Hasegawa/100 30.00 60.00
178 Dan Haren/100 4.00 10.00
180 Jim Edmonds/25 10.00 25.00
182 Scott Rolen/50 12.50 30.00
183 Stan Musial/50 30.00 60.00
184 Aubrey Huff/100 6.00 15.00
185 Chad Gaudin/100 4.00 10.00
186 Delmon Young/50 12.50 30.00
191 Mark Teixeira/50 6.00 15.00
192 Nolan Ryan/50 30.00 80.00
193 Alexis Rios/100 6.00 15.00
195 Dustin McGowan/100 4.00 10.00
196 Guillermo Quiroz/50 5.00 12.00
197 Josh Phelps/25 8.00 20.00
198 Roy Halladay/25 12.50 30.00
200 Vinnie Chulk/25 8.00 20.00
201 Jose Capellan/100 5.00 12.00
203 Dave Crouthers/100 4.00 10.00
204 Akinori Otsuka/100 12.50 30.00
205 Nick Regilio/100 4.00 10.00
206 Justin Hampson/100 4.00 10.00
207 Lincoln Holdzkom/100 4.00 10.00
208 Jorge Sequea/100 4.00 10.00
209 Justin Leone/100 6.00 15.00
210 Renyel Pinto/100 5.00 12.00
211 Mariano Gomez/100 4.00 10.00
214 Cory Sullivan/100 4.00 10.00
216 Chris Shelton/100 10.00 25.00
218 John Gall/100 6.00 15.00
222 Ronald Belisario/100 4.00 10.00
223 Mike Rouse/100 4.00 10.00
224 Dennis Sarfate/100 4.00 10.00

2004 Playoff Honors Signature Gold

*GOLD p/r 50: .5X TO 1.2X BRONZE p/r 100
*GOLD p/r 50: .4X TO 1X BRONZE p/r 50
*GOLD p/r 25: .75 TO 2X BRONZE p/r 100
*GOLD p/r 25: .5X TO 1.2X BRONZE p/r 50
RANDOM INSERTS IN PACKS
PRINT RUNS B/WN 1-50 COPIES PER
NO PRICING ON QTY OF 11 OR LESS
NO RC PRICING ON QTY OF 25 OR LESS
6 Brandon Webb/50 5.00 12.00
13 Shea Hillenbrand/50 8.00 20.00
14 Steve Finley/25 10.00 25.00
15 Adam LaRoche/50 5.00 12.00
17 Bubba Nelson/50 5.00 12.00
22 Marcus Giles/50 8.00 20.00
23 Rafael Furcal/25 10.00 25.00
26 Adam Loewen/50 5.00 12.00
29 Jay Gibbons/50 5.00 12.00
30 Luis Matos/50 5.00 12.00
33 Bobby Doerr/50 8.00 20.00
35 Edwin Almonte/50 5.00 12.00
36 Jason Varitek/25 20.00 50.00
37 Kevin Youkilis/50 6.00 15.00
41 Trot Nixon/25 10.00 25.00
42 Andre Dawson/50 8.00 20.00
44 Brendan Harris/50 5.00 12.00
50 Sammy Sosa/25 50.00 120.00
51 Carlos Lee/50 8.00 20.00
57 Austin Kearns/25 6.00 15.00
59 Brandon Larson/50 5.00 12.00
61 Ryan Wagner/50 5.00 12.00
63 Bob Feller/50 12.50 30.00
64 Brian Tallet/50 5.00 12.00
66 Jeremy Guthrie/25 8.00 20.00
67 Jody Gerut/50 5.00 12.00
68 Clint Barmes/50 8.00 20.00
72 Preston Wilson/50 8.00 20.00
74 Alan Trammell/50 8.00 20.00
83 Miguel Cabrera/50 40.00 80.00
86 Chris Burke/50 8.00 20.00
91 Morgan Ensberg/50 8.00 20.00
96 Byron Gettis/50 5.00 12.00
97 Carlos Beltran/25 12.50 30.00
101 Duke Snider/50 12.50 30.00
102 Edwin Jackson/50 6.00 15.00
105 Hong-Chih Kuo/50 25.00 60.00
107 Paul Lo Duca/25 12.50 30.00
108 Robin Ventura/25 10.00 25.00
110 Junior Spivey/25 6.00 15.00
112 Scott Podsednik/50 12.50 30.00
113 J.D. Durbin/50 5.00 12.00
114 Jacque Jones/50 8.00 20.00
115 Jason Kubel/50 4.00 10.00
116 Johan Santana/50 15.00 40.00
123 Gary Carter/50 8.00 20.00
124 Jae Weong Seo/25 10.00 25.00
125 Lenny Dykstra/50 8.00 20.00
133 Gary Sheffield/25 15.00 40.00
145 Mark Mulder/25 12.50 30.00
146 Rich Harden/50 8.00 20.00
150 Brett Myers/50 8.00 20.00
154 Marlon Byrd/50 5.00 12.00
156 Ryan Howard/50 15.00 40.00
161 Jay Payton/50 5.00 12.00
176 Shigetoshi Hasegawa/50 30.00 80.00
178 Dan Haren/50 5.00 12.00
182 Scott Rolen/25 15.00 40.00
184 Aubrey Huff/50 8.00 20.00
185 Chad Gaudin/50 5.00 12.00
193 Alexis Rios/50 8.00 20.00
196 Guillermo Quiroz/25 6.00 15.00
203 Dave Crouthers/50 5.00 12.00
204 Akinori Otsuka/50 15.00 40.00
205 Nick Regilio/50 5.00 12.00
206 Justin Hampson/50 5.00 12.00
207 Lincoln Holdzkom/50 5.00 12.00
208 Jorge Sequea/50 5.00 12.00
209 Justin Leone/50 8.00 20.00
210 Renyel Pinto/50 6.00 15.00
214 Cory Sullivan/50 5.00 12.00
216 Chris Shelton/50 12.50 30.00
218 John Gall/50 8.00 20.00
222 Ronald Belisario/50 5.00 12.00
224 Dennis Sarfate/50 5.00 12.00

2004 Playoff Honors Signature Silver

*SILVER p/r 85-100: .4X TO 1X BRZ p/r 100
*SILVER p/r 95-100: .3X TO .8X BRZ p/r 50
*SILVER p/r 50-59: .5X TO 1.2X BRZ p/r 100
*SILVER p/r 50-59: .4X TO 1X BRZ p/r 50
*SILVER p/r 27-34: .5X TO 1.2X BRZ p/r 50
*SILVER p/r 20-25: .75X TO 2X BRZ p/r 100
*SILVER p/r 20-25: .5X TO 1.2X BRZ p/r 50
*SILVER p/r 20-25: .4X TO 1X BRZ p/r 25
RANDOM INSERTS IN PACKS
PRINT RUNS B/WN 5-100 COPIES PER
NO PRICING ON QTY OF 11 OR LESS
2 Garret Anderson/100 6.00 15.00
5 Vladimir Guerrero/27 8.00 20.00
6 Brandon Webb/100 4.00 10.00
7 Brian Bruney/100 4.00 10.00
11 Robby Hammock/51 5.00 12.00
13 Shea Hillenbrand/100 6.00 15.00
14 Steve Finley/25 10.00 25.00
15 Adam LaRoche/100 4.00 10.00
17 Bubba Nelson/100 4.00 10.00
22 Marcus Giles/100 6.00 15.00
23 Rafael Furcal/50 8.00 20.00
26 Adam Loewen/100 4.00 10.00
29 Jay Gibbons/100 4.00 10.00
30 Luis Matos/100 4.00 10.00
33 Bobby Doerr/100 6.00 15.00
35 Edwin Almonte/100 4.00 10.00
36 Jason Varitek/25 30.00 60.00
37 Kevin Youkilis/100 5.00 12.00
41 Trot Nixon/25 10.00 25.00
42 Andre Dawson/100 6.00 15.00
43 Aramis Ramirez/25 12.50 30.00
44 Brendan Harris/85 4.00 10.00
45 Derrek Lee/25 12.50 30.00
46 Ernie Banks/20 25.00 60.00
48 Mark Prior/25 25.00 60.00
50 Sammy Sosa/25 50.00 120.00
51 Carlos Lee/100 6.00 15.00
52 Frank Thomas/25 25.00 60.00
53 Joe Borchard/100 4.00 10.00
55 Magglio Ordonez/25 10.00 25.00
59 Brandon Larson/100 4.00 10.00
61 Ryan Wagner/100 4.00 10.00
63 Bob Feller/100 10.00 25.00
64 Brian Tallet/100 4.00 10.00
66 Jeremy Guthrie/100 4.00 10.00
67 Jody Gerut/100 4.00 10.00
68 Clint Barmes/50 8.00 20.00
72 Preston Wilson/100 6.00 15.00
74 Alan Trammell/100 6.00 15.00
78 Preston Larrison/50 5.00 12.00
83 Miguel Cabrera/100 30.00 60.00
86 Chris Burke/100 6.00 15.00
96 Byron Gettis/100 4.00 10.00
97 Carlos Beltran/50 8.00 20.00
98 George Brett/25 40.00 100.00
101 Duke Snider/100 10.00 25.00
102 Edwin Jackson/100 5.00 12.00
105 Hong-Chih Kuo/100 20.00 50.00
107 Paul Lo Duca/50 8.00 20.00
108 Robin Ventura/25 10.00 25.00
110 Junior Spivey/25 6.00 15.00
112 Scott Podsednik/100 10.00 25.00
113 J.D. Durbin/100 4.00 10.00
114 Jacque Jones/100 6.00 15.00
115 Jason Kubel/100 3.00 8.00
116 Johan Santana/100 12.50 30.00
117 Shannon Stewart/50 5.00 12.00
123 Gary Carter/100 6.00 15.00
125 Lenny Dykstra/100 6.00 15.00
130 Chien-Ming Wang/100 75.00 150.00
132 Don Mattingly/25 25.00 60.00
133 Gary Sheffield/25 15.00 40.00
137 Jorge Posada/25 75.00 150.00
145 Mark Mulder/50 8.00 20.00
146 Rich Harden/100 6.00 15.00
150 Brett Myers/25 12.50 30.00
155 Mike Schmidt/20 40.00 100.00
156 Ryan Howard/100 15.00 40.00
161 Jay Payton/100 4.00 10.00
168 Jerome Williams/50 5.00 12.00
169 Will Clark/25 40.00 80.00
171 Chris Snelling/100 4.00 10.00
176 Shigetoshi Hasegawa/50 30.00 80.00

178 Dan Haren/100 4.00 10.00
180 Jim Edmonds/25 10.00 25.00
182 Scott Rolen/50 12.50 30.00
183 Stan Musial/25 30.00 80.00
184 Aubrey Huff/100 6.00 15.00
185 Chad Gaudin/100 4.00 10.00
186 Delmon Young/25 15.00 40.00
191 Mark Teixeira/25 15.00 40.00
192 Nolan Ryan/34 30.00 80.00
193 Alexis Rios/100 6.00 15.00
195 Dustin McGowan/59 5.00 12.00
196 Guillermo Quiroz/59 5.00 12.00
197 Josh Phelps/25 8.00 20.00
198 Roy Halladay/25 12.50 30.00
200 Vinnie Chulk/25 8.00 20.00
201 Jose Capellan/100 5.00 12.00
203 Dave Crouthers/100 4.00 10.00
204 Akinori Otsuka/100 12.50 30.00
205 Nick Regilio/100 4.00 10.00
206 Justin Hampson/100 4.00 10.00
207 Lincoln Holdzkom/100 4.00 10.00
208 Jorge Sequea/100 4.00 10.00
209 Justin Leone/100 6.00 15.00
210 Renyel Pinto/100 5.00 12.00
214 Cory Sullivan/100 4.00 10.00
216 Chris Shelton/100 10.00 25.00
218 John Gall/100 6.00 15.00
222 Ronald Belisario/100 4.00 10.00
223 Mike Rouse/100 4.00 10.00
224 Dennis Sarfate/100 4.00 10.00

2004 Playoff Honors Awards

ANDOM INSERTS IN PACKS
PRINT RUNS B/WN 1940-2003 COPIES PER
1 Phil Rizzuto/1950 1.00 2.50
2 Fred Lynn/1975 .60 1.50
3 George Brett/1980 3.00 8.00
4 Cal Ripken/1983 5.00 12.00
5 Don Mattingly/1985 3.00 8.00
6 Rickey Henderson/1990 1.50 4.00
7 Stan Musial/1943 2.50 6.00
8 Marty Marion/1944 .60 1.50
9 Ernie Banks/1958 1.50 4.00
10 Sammy Sosa/1998 1.50 4.00
11 Terry Pendleton/1991 .60 1.50
12 Ryne Sandberg/1984 3.00 8.00
13 Andre Dawson/1987 1.00 2.50
14 George Foster/1977 .60 1.50
15 Dave Parker/1978 .60 1.50
16 Keith Hernandez/1979 .60 1.50
17 Mike Schmidt/1980 2.50 6.00
18 Dale Murphy/1982 1.50 4.00
19 Whitey Ford/1961 1.00 2.50
20 Roy Halladay/2003 1.00 2.50
21 Orel Hershiser/1988 .60 1.50
22 Bob Feller/1940 1.00 2.50
23 Dwight Gooden/1985 .60 1.50
24 Steve Carlton/1972 1.00 2.50
25 Randy Johnson/2002 1.50 4.00

2004 Playoff Honors Awards Signature

PRINT RUNS B/WN 1-100 COPIES PER
NO PRICING ON QTY OF 10 OR LESS
1 Phil Rizzuto/50 12.50 30.00
2 Fred Lynn/100 6.00 15.00
8 Marty Marion/50 5.00 12.00
10 Sammy Sosa/21 50.00 100.00
11 Terry Pendleton/100 4.00 10.00
13 Andre Dawson/100 6.00 15.00
14 George Foster/100 4.00 10.00
15 Dave Parker/88 6.00 15.00
16 Keith Hernandez/100 6.00 15.00
19 Whitey Ford/50 12.50 30.00
20 Roy Halladay/25 12.50 30.00
21 Orel Hershiser/25 20.00 50.00
22 Bob Feller/100 10.00 25.00
23 Dwight Gooden/100 6.00 15.00

2004 Playoff Honors Champions

RANDOM INSERTS IN PACKS
PRINT RUNS B/WN 1951-2002 COPIES PER
1 Stan Musial/1951 2.50 6.00
2 Warren Spahn/1958 1.00 2.50
3 Bob Gibson/1968 1.00 2.50
4 Mike Schmidt/1980 2.50 6.00
5 Dale Murphy/1982 1.50 4.00
6 Steve Carlton/1983 1.00 2.50
7 Will Clark/1988 1.00 2.50
8 Nolan Ryan/1990 5.00 12.00
9 Ryne Sandberg/1990 3.00 8.00
10 Roger Clemens/1990 2.00 5.00
11 George Brett/1990 3.00 8.00
12 Tony Gwynn/1997 1.50 4.00
13 Todd Helton/2000 1.00 2.50
14 Troy Glaus/2000 .60 1.50
15 Sammy Sosa/2000 1.50 4.00
16 Pedro Martinez/2000 1.00 2.50
17 Mark Mulder/2001 .60 1.50
18 Manny Ramirez/2002 1.50 4.00
19 Lance Berkman/2002 1.00 2.50
20 Alex Rodriguez Rgr/2002 2.00 5.00

2004 Playoff Honors Champions Jersey

PRINT RUNS B/WN 82-250 COPIES PER
PRIME PRINT RUNS B/WN 1-10 COPIES PER
NO PRIME PRICING DUE TO SCARCITY
1 Stan Musial/100 10.00 25.00
2 Warren Spahn/100 6.00 15.00
3 Bob Gibson/100 6.00 15.00
4 Mike Schmidt/100 10.00 25.00
6 Steve Carlton/100 4.00 10.00
7 Will Clark/100 6.00 15.00
8 Nolan Ryan/100 12.50 30.00
9 Ryne Sandberg/100 10.00 25.00
10 Roger Clemens/100 6.00 15.00
11 George Brett/100 10.00 25.00
12 Tony Gwynn/250 6.00 15.00
13 Todd Helton/250 3.00 8.00
14 Troy Glaus/250 2.00 5.00
15 Sammy Sosa/250 3.00 8.00
16 Pedro Martinez/250 3.00 8.00
17 Mark Mulder/250 2.00 5.00
18 Manny Ramirez/250 3.00 8.00
19 Lance Berkman/250 2.00 5.00
20 Alex Rodriguez Rgr/250 4.00 10.00

2004 Playoff Honors Champions Signature

RANDOM INSERTS IN PACKS
PRINT RUNS B/WN 1-50 COPIES PER
NO PRICING ON QTY OF 10 OR LESS
1 Stan Musial/50 40.00 80.00
3 Bob Gibson/50 12.50 30.00
7 Will Clark/50 12.50 30.00
8 Nolan Ryan/34 75.00 150.00

2004 Playoff Honors Class Reunion

RANDOM INSERTS IN PACKS
PRINT RUNS B/WN 1973-2003 COPIES PER
1 E.Murray 1.00 2.50
G.Carter/2003
2 C.Fisk 1.00 2.50
T.Perez/2000
3 N.Ryan 5.00 12.00
G.Brett/1999
4 R.Carew 1.00 2.50
F.Jenkins/1991
5 J.Morgan 1.00 2.50
J.Palmer/1990
6 C.Yastrzemski 1.50 4.00
J.Bench/1989
7 H.Killebrew 1.50 4.00
L.Aparicio/1984
8 B.Robinson 1.00 2.50
J.Marichal/1983
9 A.Kaline 1.50 4.00
D.Snider/1980
10 R.Clemente 4.00 10.00
W.Spahn/1973
11 M.Prior 1.00 2.50
M.Teixeira/2001
12 J.Beckett 1.00 2.50
B.Zito/1999
13 M.Mulder 1.00 2.50
A.Dunn/1998
14 V.Wells 1.00 2.50
L.Berkman/1997
15 E.Chavez .60 1.50
N.Johnson/1996
16 K.Wood 1.00 2.50
R.Halladay/1995
17 T.Helton 1.00 2.50
C.Beltran/1995
18 D.Jeter 4.00 10.00
J.Giambi/1992
19 M.Ramirez 1.50 4.00
S.Green/1991
20 C.Jones 1.50 4.00
M.Mussina/1990

2004 Playoff Honors Class Reunion Material

RANDOM INSERTS IN PACKS
PRINT RUNS B/WN 25-250 COPIES PER
1 Murray Jsy/Carter Jsy/100 8.00 20.00
2 Fisk Jsy/Perez Bat/250 10.00 25.00
3 Ryan Jsy/Brett Jsy/100 30.00 60.00
4 Carew Jsy/Fergie Pants/250 6.00 15.00
5 Morgan Jsy/Palmer Jsy/100 5.00 12.00
6 Yaz Jsy/Bench Jsy/250 15.00 40.00
7 Killebrew Jsy/Aparic Jsy/250 6.00 15.00
8 B.Rob Jsy/Marichal Jsy/100 8.00 20.00
9 Kaline Jsy/Snider Jsy/25 15.00 40.00
10 R.Clem Jsy/Spahn Jsy/100 50.00 100.00
11 Prior Jsy/Teixeira Jsy/250 6.00 15.00
12 Beckett Jsy/Zito Jsy/250 3.00 8.00
13 Mulder Jsy/Dunn Jsy/250 3.00 8.00
14 Wells Jsy/Berkman Jsy/250 3.00 8.00
15 Chavez Jsy/N.John Jsy/250 3.00 8.00
16 Wood Jsy/Halladay Jsy/250 3.00 8.00
17 Helton Jsy/Beltran Jsy/250 4.00 10.00
18 Jeter Jsy/Giambi Jsy/250 10.00 25.00
19 Manny Jsy/S.Green Jsy/50 8.00 20.00
20 Chipper Jsy/Mussina Jsy/250 4.00 10.00

2004 Playoff Honors Fans of the Game

RANDOM INSERTS IN PACKS
251 Charlie Sheen 1.25 3.00
252 Corbin Bernsen .75 2.00
253 Peter Gammons 1.25 3.00
254 Jeff Garlin .75 2.00
255 Larry King 1.25 3.00

2004 Playoff Honors Fans of the Game Autographs

RANDOM INSERTS IN PACKS
SP PRINT RUNS PROVIDED BY DONRUSS
SP'S ARE NOT SERIAL-NUMBERED
251 Charlie Sheen SP/250 75.00 200.00
252 Corbin Bernsen 8.00 20.00
253 Peter Gammons 10.00 25.00
254 Jeff Garlin SP/200 12.00 30.00
255 Larry King 25.00 60.00

2004 Playoff Honors Game Day Souvenir

RANDOM INSERTS IN PACKS
PRINT RUNS B/WN 9-100 COPIES PER
NO PRICING ON QTY OF 9 OR LESS
2 Bob Gibson Jsy/75 6.00 15.00
3 Frank Robinson Bat/61 5.00 12.00
4 Tony Gwynn Pants/99 10.00 25.00
5 Warren Spahn Jsy/53 8.00 20.00
6 George Brett Bat/77 12.50 30.00
7 Cal Ripken Hat/19 75.00 150.00
8 Frank Thomas Bat/93 4.00 10.00
9 Sammy Sosa Jsy/100 4.00 10.00
10 Harmon Killebrew Bat/75 6.00 15.00

2004 Playoff Honors Piece of the Game Bat

*BAT p/r 250: .4X TO 1X JSY p/r 250
*BAT p/r 250: .3X TO .8X JSY p/r 100
*BAT p/r 250: .2X TO .5X JSY p/r 50
*BAT p/r 150: .4X TO 1X JSY p/r 250
*BAT p/r 100: .5X TO 1.2X JSY p/r 250
*BAT p/r 50: .5X TO 1.2X JSY p/r 100
RANDOM INSERTS IN PACKS
PRINT RUNS B/WN 50-250 COPIES PER
11 Gary Sheffield/250 2.00 5.00

2004 Playoff Honors Piece of the Game Jersey

PRINT RUNS B/WN 50-250 COPIES PER
BAT PRINT RUNS B/WN 50-250 COPIES PER
*COMBO p/r 100: 1X TO 2.5X JSY p/r 250
*COMBO p/r 100: .6X TO 1.5X JSY p/r 100
*COMBO p/r 100: .5X TO 1.2X JSY p/r 50
*COMBO p/r 50: 1.25X TO 3X JSY p/r 250
*COMBO p/r 50: .6X TO 1.5X JSY p/r 50
*COMBO p/r 25: 1.25X TO 3X JSY p/r 100
COMBO PRINT RUNS B/WN 25-100 PER
*NBR p/r 250: .4X TO 1X JSY p/r 250
*NBR p/r 100: .5X TO 1.2X JSY p/r 250
*NBR p/r 100: .4X TO 1X JSY p/r 100
*NBR p/r 75: .6X TO 1.5X JSY p/r 250
*NBR p/r 50: .75X TO 2X JSY p/r 250
*NBR p/r 50: .4X TO 1X JSY p/r 50
*NBR p/r 20: .75X TO 2X JSY p/r 100
*NBR p/r 20: .6X TO 1.5X JSY p/r 50
NUMBER PRINTS B/WN 11-250 COPIES PER
NO NBR PRICING ON QTY OF 11 OR LESS
*POS p/r 250: .4X TO 1X JSY p/r 250
*POS p/r 250: .3X TO .8X JSY p/r 100
*POS p/r 100: .5X TO 1.2X JSY p/r 250
*POS p/r 100: .4X TO 1X JSY p/r 100
*POS p/r 50: .4X TO 1X JSY p/r 50
*POS p/r 20: .75X TO 2X JSY p/r 100
*POS p/r 20: .6X TO 1.5X JSY p/r 50
POSITION PRINTS B/WN 20-250 COPIES PER
1 Albert Pujols/250 6.00 15.00
2 Angel Berroa/250 2.00 5.00
3 Aubrey Huff/250 2.00 5.00
4 Barry Zito/250 2.00 5.00
5 Bobby Abreu/250 2.00 5.00
6 Carlos Beltran/250 2.00 5.00
7 Chipper Jones/250 3.00 8.00
8 Derek Jeter/50 15.00 40.00
9 Eric Chavez/250 2.00 5.00
10 Eric Hinske/100 3.00 8.00
12 George Brett/250 6.00 15.00
13 Jay Gibbons/250 2.00 5.00
14 Jim Edmonds/250 2.00 5.00
15 Josh Beckett/250 2.00 5.00
16 Manny Ramirez/250 3.00 8.00
17 Mark Mulder/100 3.00 8.00
18 Marlon Byrd/250 2.00 5.00
19 Mike Lowell/250 2.00 5.00
20 Mike Schmidt/50 8.00 20.00
21 Nolan Ryan/100 8.00 20.00
22 Rafael Furcal/250 2.00 5.00
23 Randy Johnson/250 3.00 8.00
24 Rod Carew/100 4.00 10.00
25 Torii Hunter/250 2.00 5.00

2004 Playoff Honors Players Collection Jersey Blue Number

*HNR.NBR.BLUE: .4X TO 1X PRESTIGE PC
STATED PRINT RUN 250 SERIAL #'d SETS
*HNR BLUE: .4X TO 1X PRESTIGE PC
HONORS BLUE PRINT RUN 250 #'d SETS
HONORS GOLD PRINT RUN 10 #'d SETS
NO GOLD PRICING DUE TO SCARCITY
*HNR.PLAT: 1X TO 2.5X PRESTIGE PC
HONORS PLAT.PRINT RUN 25 #'d SETS
*HNR.NBR.PLAT: .75X TO 2X PRESTIGE PC
HONORS NBR.PLAT.PRINT RUN 50 #'d SETS

2004 Playoff Honors Prime Signature Insert

RANDOM INSERTS IN PACKS
STATED PRINT RUN 2500 SERIAL #'d SETS
1 Garret Anderson 1.25 3.00
2 Rafael Palmeiro 1.50 4.00
3 Vladimir Guerrero 1.50 4.00
4 Alex Rodriguez 2.00 5.00
5 Dontrelle Willis 1.50 4.00
6 Miguel Cabrera 1.50 4.00
7 Shannon Stewart 1.25 3.00
8 Mike Piazza 2.00 5.00
9 Gary Sheffield 1.25 3.00
10 Ivan Rodriguez 1.50 4.00
11 Randy Johnson 1.50 4.00
12 Tom Glavine 1.25 3.00
13 Brandon Webb 1.25 3.00
14 Carlos Lee 1.25 3.00
15 Hideo Nomo 1.50 4.00
16 Mike Mussina 1.50 4.00
17 Magglio Ordonez 1.25 3.00
18 Austin Kearns 1.25 3.00
19 Andruw Jones 1.50 4.00
20 Mariano Rivera 1.50 4.00
21 Sammy Sosa 1.50 4.00
22 Juan Gonzalez 1.25 3.00
23 Jeff Bagwell 1.50 4.00
24 Rickey Henderson 1.50 4.00
25 Mike Schmidt 3.00 8.00
26 Jim Rice 1.25 3.00
27 Billy Williams 1.25 3.00
28 Lou Brock 1.50 4.00
29 Robin Yount 1.50 4.00
30 Nolan Ryan 4.00 10.00
31 Darryl Strawberry 1.25 3.00
32 Cal Ripken 6.00 15.00
33 Andre Dawson 1.25 3.00
34 Don Mattingly 3.00 8.00
35 Paul Molitor 1.25 3.00
36 Bo Jackson 1.50 4.00
37 Ernie Banks 1.50 4.00
38 Orel Hershiser 1.50 4.00
39 Mark Grace 1.50 4.00
40 Carlton Fisk 1.50 4.00

2004 Playoff Honors Prime Signature Autograph

PRINT RUNS B/WN 5-100 COPIES PER
NO PRICING ON QTY OF 10 OR LESS
AU BAT PRINT RUN B/WN 1-10 COPIES PER
NO AU BAT PRICING DUE TO SCARCITY
*AU JSY p/r 20-25: 1X TO 2.5X AU p/r 100
*AU JSY p/r 20-25: .75X TO 2X AU p/r 50
*AU JSY p/r 19: .6X TO 1.5X AU p/r 25
*AU JSY p/r 17: 1X TO 2.5X AU p/r 50
*AU JSY p/r 16: 1.25X TO 3X AU p/r 100
AU JSY PRINT RUN B/WN 1-25 COPIES PER
NO AU JSY PRICING ON QTY OF 14 OR LESS
1 Garret Anderson/100 6.00 15.00
2 Rafael Palmeiro/50 10.00 25.00
3 Vladimir Guerrero/50 20.00 50.00
5 Dontrelle Willis/50 12.50 30.00
6 Miguel Cabrera/100 20.00 50.00
7 Shannon Stewart/100 4.00 10.00
9 Gary Sheffield/100 10.00 25.00
12 Tom Glavine/25 20.00 50.00
13 Brandon Webb/100 4.00 10.00
14 Carlos Lee/100 6.00 15.00
17 Magglio Ordonez/100 6.00 15.00
19 Andruw Jones/50 12.50 30.00
21 Sammy Sosa/50 50.00 100.00
22 Juan Gonzalez/50 8.00 20.00
23 Jeff Bagwell/25 30.00 60.00
24 Rickey Henderson/25 30.00 80.00
25 Mike Schmidt/50 20.00 50.00
26 Jim Rice/100 6.00 15.00
27 Billy Williams/100 6.00 15.00
28 Lou Brock/100 10.00 25.00
29 Robin Yount/25 40.00 80.00
30 Nolan Ryan/50 60.00 120.00
31 Darryl Strawberry/100 10.00 25.00
32 Cal Ripken/25 125.00 200.00
33 Andre Dawson/100 6.00 15.00
34 Don Mattingly/50 20.00 50.00
35 Paul Molitor/25 12.50 30.00
36 Bo Jackson/50 20.00 50.00
37 Ernie Banks/50 20.00 50.00
38 Orel Hershiser/100 10.00 25.00
39 Mark Grace/50 20.00 50.00
40 Carlton Fisk/50 12.50 30.00

2004 Playoff Honors Quad Material

PRINT RUNS B/WN 10-100 COPIES PER
NO PRICING ON QTY OF 10 OR LESS
ALL ARE FOUR JSY SWATCH UNLESS NOTED
FERGIE JENKINS SWATCH IS PANTS
COMBO PRINT RUNS B/WN 1-10 COPIES PER
NO COMBO PRICING DUE TO SCARCITY
ALL COMBO ARE BAT-JSY FOR EACH PLAYER
1 Matt/Grace/Clark/Hern/100 30.00 60.00
2 Giam/Thome/Delg/Raffy/100 10.00 25.00
3 Pujols/Banks/Bag/Thom/100 30.00 60.00
4 Molitor/Morg/Ryno/Sor/50 30.00 60.00
5 Rip/Jeter/A.Rod/Nomar/100 20.00 50.00
6 Ozzie/Yount/Tram/Conc/50 15.00 40.00
8 Bench/Fisk/Carter/Piaz/100 15.00 40.00
9 Helton/Giles/Rent/Rolen/25 20.00 50.00
10 Delg/Sor/A.Rod/Glaus/100 10.00 25.00
11 Kill/Reg/Schmidt/Sosa/100 10.00 25.00
12 Musial/Hend/Gwy/Brock/25 50.00 100.00
13 Rip/Brett/Molit/Carew/100 15.00 40.00
14 Sosa/Vlad/Manny/Mag/100 10.00 25.00
15 Andruw/Edm/Torii/Wells/100 10.00 25.00
16 Chip/Shawn/And/Berk/100 10.00 25.00
17 Gwy/Dale/Puck/Andre/100 20.00 50.00
19 Ryan/Clem/Wood/Beck/100 40.00 80.00
21 Eck/Smoltz/Riv/Smith/100 10.00 25.00
22 Muss/Maddux/Morr/Bly/100 15.00 40.00
23 Carlton/Glav/Zito/Pett/100 10.00 25.00
24 Ford/Spahn/Feller/Mari/25 20.00 50.00
25 Ryan/Clem/Carlt/Randy/100 10.00 25.00

2004 Playoff Honors Rookie Year Jersey Number

RANDOM INSERTS IN PACKS
PRINT RUNS B/WN 25-100 COPIES PER
1 Gary Carter/50 5.00 12.00
2 Robin Yount/50 8.00 20.00
3 Roger Clemens/25 20.00 50.00
4 Gary Sheffield/50 4.00 10.00
5 Mike Piazza/25 15.00 40.00
6 Hideo Nomo/25 15.00 40.00
7 Alex Rodriguez/25 15.00 40.00
8 Mark Prior/25 10.00 25.00
9 Dontrelle Willis/100 4.00 10.00
10 Angel Berroa/100 3.00 8.00

2004 Playoff Honors Signs of Greatness

RANDOM INSERTS IN PACKS
PRINT RUNS B/WN 20-25 COPIES PER
1 Mark Prior/25 15.00 40.00
2 Scott Podsednik/25 20.00 50.00
4 Dontrelle Willis/25 20.00 50.00
5 Rocco Baldelli/20 12.50 30.00
6 Brandon Webb/25 6.00 15.00
7 Rich Harden/25 12.50 30.00
8 Miguel Cabrera/25 30.00 60.00
9 Josh Beckett/25 20.00 50.00
10 Mark Teixeira/25 20.00 50.00

2004 Playoff Honors Tandem Material

PRINT RUNS B/WN 5-250 COPIES PER
NO PRICING ON QTY OF 5 OR LESS
ALL ARE DUAL JSY SWATCH UNLESS NOTED
*COMBO p/r 25: 1.5X TO 4X TANDEM p/r 250
*COMBO p/r 25: .75X TO 2X TANDEM p/r 100
COMBO PRINTS B/WN 1-25 COPIES PER
NO COMBO PRICING ON QTY OF 10 OR LESS
ALL COMBO ARE BAT-JSY FOR EACH PLAYER
1 B.Jackson/D.Sanders/100 15.00 40.00
2 E.Murray/R.Palmeiro/250 6.00 15.00
3 A.Rod Rgr/D.Murphy/250 6.00 15.00
4 C.Fisk/I.Rodriguez/250 6.00 15.00
5 R.Henderson/L.Brock/50 15.00 40.00
6 S.Sosa/E.Banks/250 10.00 25.00
7 W.Spahn/S.Carlton/100 6.00 15.00
8 C.Yastrzemski/D.Evans/250 10.00 25.00
9 K.Hernandez/L.Dykstra/250 4.00 10.00
10 P.Reese/M.Marion/100 6.00 15.00
11 H.Nomo/C.Jones/250 6.00 15.00
12 W.McCov/R.Jackson/100 10.00 25.00
13 M.Prior/B.Zito/250 6.00 15.00
14 C.Ripken/M.Tejada Bat/100 20.00 50.00
15 R.Clemente/V.Guer Bat/100 40.00 80.00
16 G.Carter/M.Piazza/250 6.00 15.00
17 J.Rice/F.Lynn/50 10.00 25.00
18 W.Stargell/K.Hern/250 6.00 15.00
19 N.Garc/M.Teixeira/100 10.00 25.00
20 D.Jeter/P.Rizzuto/50 12.50 30.00
21 E.Chavez/H.Blalock/100 4.00 10.00
22 E.Davis/D.Strawberry/100 8.00 20.00
23 R.Hend/D.Sanders/100 15.00 40.00
24 D.Parker/A.Kearns/250 4.00 10.00
25 L.Aparicio/D.Conc/100 8.00 20.00
26 R.Palmeiro/W.Clark/100 10.00 25.00
27 R.Sandberg/O.Smith/250 10.00 25.00
28 A.Rod M's/J.Canseco/250 6.00 15.00
29 S.Sosa/J.Gonzalez/250 6.00 15.00
30 P.Martinez/J.Marichal/50 10.00 25.00
32 D.Gooden/G.Sheffield/250 4.00 10.00
33 L.Boudreau/O.Vizquel/100 8.00 20.00
34 M.Prior Hat/R.Santo Bat/100 15.00 40.00
35 A.Pujols/K.Boyer/250 10.00 25.00
36 T.Seaver/C.Schilling/250 6.00 15.00
37 J.Morgan/J.Kent/250 4.00 10.00
38 S.Garvey/D.Smith/250 10.00 25.00
39 M.Piazza/I.Rodriguez/250 6.00 15.00
40 M.Schmidt/J.Thome/100 12.50 30.00

2002 Playoff Piece of the Game

COMP.SET w/o SP's (50) 15.00 40.00
COMMON CARD (1-50) .30 .75
COMMON CARD (51-100) 2.00 5.00
51-100 RANDOM INSERTS IN PACKS
51-100 PRINT RUN 500 SERIAL #'d SETS
1 Vladimir Guerrero .75 2.00
2 Troy Glaus .30 .75
3 Ichiro Suzuki 1.50 4.00
4 Chipper Jones .75 2.00
5 Roberto Alomar .50 1.25
6 Scott Rolen .50 1.25
7 Randy Johnson .75 2.00
8 Roger Clemens 1.50 4.00
9 Nomar Garciaparra 1.25 3.00
10 Greg Maddux 1.25 3.00
11 Barry Bonds 2.00 5.00
12 Derek Jeter 2.00 5.00
13 Albert Pujols 1.50 4.00
14 Kerry Wood .30 .75
15 Jim Thome .50 1.25
16 Manny Ramirez .50 1.25
17 Carlos Delgado .30 .75
18 Magglio Ordonez .30 .75
19 Torii Hunter .30 .75
20 Garret Anderson .30 .75
21 Eric Chavez .30 .75
22 Rafael Palmeiro .50 1.25
23 Andruw Jones .50 1.25
24 Cliff Floyd .30 .75
25 Sammy Sosa .75 2.00
26 Mike Mussina .50 1.25
27 Jeff Bagwell .50 1.25
28 Miguel Tejada .30 .75
29 Curt Schilling .30 .75
30 Tom Glavine .50 1.25
31 Frank Thomas .75 2.00
32 Jim Edmonds .30 .75
33 Juan Gonzalez .30 .75
34 Todd Helton .50 1.25
35 Shawn Green .30 .75
36 Alfonso Soriano .30 .75
37 Lance Berkman .30 .75
38 Barry Zito .30 .75
39 Ryan Klesko .30 .75
40 Larry Walker .30 .75
41 Craig Biggio .50 1.25
42 Luis Gonzalez .30 .75
43 Ivan Rodriguez .50 1.25
44 J.D. Drew .30 .75
45 Roy Oswalt .30 .75
46 Jason Giambi .30 .75
47 Brian Giles .30 .75
48 Richie Sexson .30 .75
49 Pat Burrell .30 .75
50 Alex Rodriguez 1.00 2.50
51 So Taguchi ROO RC 3.00 8.00
52 Allan Simpson ROO RC 2.00 5.00
53 Oliver Perez ROO RC 3.00 8.00
54 Ben Howard ROO RC 2.00 5.00
55 Kirk Saarloos ROO RC 2.00 5.00
56 Francis Beltran ROO RC 2.00 5.00
57 Jorge Padilla ROO RC 2.00 5.00
58 Brandon Puffer ROO RC 2.00 5.00
59 Brian Mallette ROO RC 2.00 5.00
60 Kyle Kane ROO RC 2.00 5.00
61 Travis Driskill ROO RC 2.00 5.00
62 Jeremy Lambert ROO RC 2.00 5.00
63 Steve Kent ROO RC 2.00 5.00
64 Julius Matos ROO RC 2.00 5.00
65 Julio Mateo ROO RC 2.00 5.00
66 Kazuhisa Ishii ROO RC 3.00 8.00
67 Franklyn German ROO RC 2.00 5.00
68 John Foster ROO RC 2.00 5.00
69 Luis Ugueto ROO RC 2.00 5.00
70 Shawn Sedlacek ROO RC 2.00 5.00
71 Earl Snyder ROO RC 2.00 5.00
72 Jason Simontacchi ROO RC 2.00 5.00
73 Victor Alvarez ROO RC 2.00 5.00
74 Tom Shearn ROO RC 2.00 5.00
75 Corey Thurman ROO RC 2.00 5.00
76 Eric Junge ROO RC 2.00 5.00
77 Hansel Izquierdo ROO RC 2.00 5.00
78 Elio Serrano ROO RC 2.00 5.00
79 J.J. Trujillo ROO RC 2.00 5.00
80 Chris Snelling ROO RC 2.50 6.00
81 Satoru Komiyama ROO RC 2.00 5.00
82 Brandon Backe ROO RC 3.00 8.00
83 Anderson Machado ROO RC 2.00 5.00
84 Doug Devore ROO RC 2.00 5.00
85 Steve Bechler ROO RC 2.00 5.00
86 John Ennis ROO RC 2.00 5.00
87 Rodrigo Rosario ROO RC 2.00 5.00
88 Jorge Sosa ROO RC 3.00 8.00
89 Ken Huckaby ROO RC 2.00 5.00
90 Mike Moriarty ROO RC 2.00 5.00
91 Mike Crudale ROO RC 2.00 5.00
92 Kevin Frederick ROO RC 2.00 5.00
93 Aaron Guiel ROO RC 2.00 5.00
94 Jose Rodriguez ROO RC 2.00 5.00
95 Andy Shibilo ROO RC 2.00 5.00
96 Deivis Santos ROO 2.00 5.00
97 Felix Escalona ROO RC 2.00 5.00
98 Miguel Asencio ROO RC 2.00 5.00
99 Takahito Nomura ROO RC 2.00 5.00
100 Cam Esslinger ROO RC 2.00 5.00

2002 Playoff Piece of the Game Materials

1-90 SP PRINT RUNS LISTED BELOW
91-95 PRINT RUN 500 SERIAL #'d SETS
96-100 PRINT RUN 250 SERIAL #'d SETS
1A Adam Dunn Bat 3.00 8.00
1B Adam Dunn Jsy/50 * 6.00 15.00
1C Adam Dunn Btg Glv/50 * 6.00 15.00
2A Adrian Beltre Bat 3.00 8.00
2B Adrian Beltre Jsy/100 * 4.00 10.00
3A Albert Pujols Base 6.00 15.00
3B Albert Pujols Ball/50 * 15.00 40.00
4A Alex Rodriguez Jsy 6.00 15.00
5A Alex Rodriguez Bat 6.00 15.00
5B Alex Rodriguez Fld Glv/50 * 30.00 60.00
6A Andruw Jones Jsy 4.00 10.00
6B Andruw Jones Fld Glv/50 * 10.00 25.00
6C Andruw Jones Hat/50 * 10.00 25.00
7A Andruw Jones Bat 4.00 10.00
7B Andruw Jones Shoe/50 * 10.00 25.00
7C Andruw Jones Btg Glv/50 * 10.00 25.00
8A Barry Bonds Base 8.00 20.00
8B Barry Bonds Ball/50 * 20.00 50.00
9A Barry Larkin Bat 4.00 10.00
9B Barry Larkin Jsy/100 * 6.00 15.00
10A Juan Gonzalez Jsy 3.00 8.00
11A Bernie Williams Bat 4.00 10.00
11C Bernie Williams Jsy/50 * 10.00 25.00
12A Carlos Delgado Jsy 3.00 8.00
12B Carlos Delgado Bat/100 * 4.00 10.00
13A Chipper Jones Jsy 4.00 10.00
14A Chipper Jones Bat 4.00 10.00
14B Chipper Jones Fld Glv/50 * 10.00 25.00
15A Craig Biggio Jsy 4.00 10.00
15B Craig Biggio Btg Glv/50 * 10.00 25.00
16A Craig Biggio Bat 4.00 10.00
16B Craig Biggio Shoe/100 * 6.00 15.00
17A Cristian Guzman Jsy 3.00 8.00
18A Curt Schilling Jsy 3.00 8.00
19A Derek Jeter Base 8.00 20.00
19B Derek Jeter Ball/50 * 20.00 50.00
20A Edgar Martinez Jsy 4.00 10.00
20B Edgar Martinez Bat/100 * 6.00 15.00
21A Edgardo Alfonzo Jsy 3.00 8.00
21B Edgardo Alfonzo Bat/100 * 4.00 10.00
22A Ellis Burks Jsy 3.00 8.00
23A Frank Thomas Bat 4.00 10.00
23B Frank Thomas Jsy/100 * 6.00 15.00
24A Freddy Garcia Jsy 3.00 8.00
25A Greg Maddux Jsy 6.00 15.00
25B Greg Maddux Bat/50 * 30.00 60.00
25B Greg Maddux Shoe/50 * 30.00 60.00
26A Harmon Killebrew Bat 4.00 10.00
26B Harmon Killebrew Bat/50 * 10.00 25.00
26C Harmon Killebrew Jsy/50 * 10.00 25.00
27A Hideo Nomo Jsy 8.00 20.00
27B Hideo Nomo Bat/50 * 50.00 100.00
28A Ichiro Suzuki Base 8.00 20.00
28B Ichiro Suzuki Ball/50 * 30.00 60.00
29A Ivan Rodriguez Jsy 4.00 10.00
29B Ivan Rodriguez Fld Glv/50 * 10.00 25.00
29C Ivan Rodriguez Btg Glv/50 * 10.00 25.00
30A Ivan Rodriguez Bat 4.00 10.00
30B Ivan Rodriguez Hat/50 * 10.00 25.00
30C Ivan Rodriguez Shoe/50 * 10.00 25.00
31A J.D. Drew Bat 3.00 8.00
31B J.D. Drew Shoe/100 * 4.00 10.00
32A J.D. Drew Jsy 3.00 8.00
33A Javy Lopez Jsy 3.00 8.00
33B Javy Lopez Bat/100 * 4.00 10.00
34A Jeff Bagwell Jsy 4.00 10.00
35A Jim Edmonds Jsy 3.00 8.00
35B Jim Edmonds Btg Glv/50 * 6.00 15.00
36A Jim Edmonds Bat 3.00 8.00
36B Jim Edmonds Shoe/50 * 6.00 15.00
36C Jim Edmonds Wristband/50 * 6.00 15.00
37A John Olerud Jsy 3.00 8.00
37B John Olerud Bat/100 * 4.00 10.00
38A John Smoltz Jsy 4.00 10.00
39A Jose Cruz Jr. Jsy 3.00 8.00
39B Jose Cruz Jr. Bat/100 * 4.00 10.00
40A Jose Vidro Jsy 3.00 8.00
40B Jose Vidro Bat/100 * 4.00 10.00
41A Juan Gonzalez Bat 3.00 8.00
42A Juan Pierre Jsy 3.00 8.00
42B Juan Pierre Shoe/50 * 6.00 15.00
42C Juan Pierre Btg Glv/50 * 6.00 15.00
43A Ken Griffey Jr. Base 6.00 15.00
44A Kenny Lofton Bat 3.00 8.00
44B Kenny Lofton Shoe/50 * 10.00 25.00
44C Kenny Lofton Btg Glv/50 * 10.00 25.00
45A Kerry Wood Bat 3.00 8.00
45C Kerry Wood Btg Glv/50 * 6.00 15.00
46A Kevin Brown Jsy 3.00 8.00
47A Lance Berkman Jsy 3.00 8.00
47B Lance Berkman Btg Glv/50 * 6.00 15.00
48A Lance Berkman Bat 3.00 8.00
48C Lance Berkman Fld Glv/50 * 6.00 15.00
49A Larry Walker Jsy 3.00 8.00
49B Larry Walker Bat/50 * 6.00 15.00
50A Luis Gonzalez Jsy 3.00 8.00
50B Luis Gonzalez Bat/100 * 4.00 10.00
51A Magglio Ordonez Jsy 3.00 8.00
51B Magglio Ordonez Btg Glv/50 * 6.00 15.00
52A Magglio Ordonez Bat 3.00 8.00
52B Magglio Ordonez Shoe/50 * 6.00 15.00
52C Magglio Ordonez Hat/50 * 6.00 15.00
53A Manny Ramirez Jsy 4.00 10.00
54A Manny Ramirez Bat 4.00 10.00
54B Manny Ramirez Hat/50 * 10.00 25.00
54C Manny Ramirez Fld Glv/50 * 10.00 25.00
55A Vladimir Guerrero White Jsy 4.00 10.00
56A Mark Grace Bat 4.00 10.00
56B Mark Grace Fld Glv/50 * 10.00 25.00
57A Michael Barrett Jsy 3.00 8.00
58A Miguel Tejada Jsy 3.00 8.00
58B Miguel Tejada Hat/50 * 6.00 15.00
58C Miguel Tejada Bat/50 * 6.00 15.00
59A Mike Piazza Jsy 6.00 15.00
60A Mike Piazza Bat 6.00 15.00
60B Mike Piazza Shoe/100 * 20.00 50.00
61A Mike Schmidt Bat 8.00 20.00
62A Mike Sweeney Jsy 3.00 8.00
63A Nolan Ryan Jsy 10.00 25.00
64A Nomar Garciaparra Jsy 6.00 15.00
64B Nomar Garciaparra Bat/50 * 20.00 50.00
65A Paul Lo Duca Jsy 3.00 8.00
65C Paul Lo Duca Fld Glv/50 * 6.00 15.00
66A Rafael Palmeiro Jsy 4.00 10.00
67A Rafael Palmeiro Bat 4.00 10.00
67B Rafael Palmeiro Shoe/50 * 10.00 25.00
67C Rafael Palmeiro Fld Glv/50 * 10.00 25.00
68A Jose Canseco Bat 4.00 10.00
68B Jose Canseco Jsy/50 * 10.00 25.00
69A Raul Mondesi Jsy 3.00 8.00
70A Reggie Jackson Bat 4.00 10.00
70B Reggie Jackson Jsy/50 * 10.00 25.00
71A Rickey Henderson Bat 4.00 10.00
71B Rickey Henderson Jsy/100 * 6.00 15.00
72A Roberto Alomar Bat 4.00 10.00
73A Robin Ventura Jsy 3.00 8.00
74A Rod Carew Bat 4.00 10.00
74C Rod Carew Jsy/50 * 10.00 25.00
75A Roger Clemens Jsy 6.00 15.00
75B Roger Clemens Fld Glv/50 * 30.00 60.00
76A Sammy Sosa Base 4.00 10.00
76B Sammy Sosa Ball/50 * 10.00 25.00
77A Sean Casey Jsy 3.00 8.00
77B Sean Casey Bat/100 * 4.00 10.00
78A Shannon Stewart Jsy 3.00 8.00
78B Shannon Stewart Hat/100 * 4.00 10.00
79A Shawn Green Jsy 3.00 8.00
80A Shawn Green Bat 3.00 8.00
81A Tim Hudson Jsy 3.00 8.00
81B Tim Hudson Shoe/50 * 6.00 15.00
81C Tim Hudson Fld Glv/50 * 6.00 15.00
82A Todd Helton Bat 4.00 10.00
82B Todd Helton Jsy/100 * 6.00 15.00
83A Tom Glavine Jsy 4.00 10.00
83B Tom Glavine Btg Glv/50 * 10.00 25.00
84A Tony Gwynn Grey Jsy 6.00 15.00
84B Tony Gwynn Fld Glv/50 * 40.00 80.00
85A Tony Gwynn Blue Jsy 6.00 15.00
85B Tony Gwynn Hat/100 * 20.00 50.00
86A Tony Gwynn Bat 6.00 15.00
86B Tony Gwynn Shoe/50 * 40.00 80.00
87A Troy Glaus Jsy 3.00 8.00
87B Troy Glaus Bat/50 * 6.00 15.00
87C Troy Glaus Shoe/50 * 6.00 15.00
88A Tsuyoshi Shinjo Bat 3.00 8.00
88B Tsuyoshi Shinjo Hat/50 * 6.00 15.00
88C Tsuyoshi Shinjo Btg Glv/50 * 6.00 15.00
89A Vladimir Guerrero Grey Jsy 4.00 10.00
90A Vladimir Guerrero Bat 4.00 10.00
91 Garciaparra Jsy/Martinez Jsy 15.00 40.00
92 Johnson Jsy/Schilling Jsy 6.00 15.00
93 A.Jones Jsy/C.Jones Jsy 6.00 15.00
94 Helton Jsy/Walker Jsy 4.00 10.00
95 Bagwell Pants/Biggio Pants 6.00 15.00
96 Alex Rodriguez Bat-Jsy 15.00 40.00
97 Greg Maddux Bat-Jsy 15.00 40.00
98 Mike Piazza Bat-Jsy 15.00 40.00
99 Lance Berkman Bat-Jsy 6.00 15.00
100 Vladimir Guerrero Bat-Jsy 10.00 25.00

2002 Playoff Piece of the Game Materials Bronze

*BRONZE 1-90: .6X TO 1.5X BASIC MATERIAL
STATED PRINT RUN 250 SERIAL #'d SETS
*BRONZE 91-95: .5X TO 1.2X BASIC MATERIAL
91-95 PRINT RUN 100 SERIAL #'d SETS
*BRONZE 96-100: .6X TO 1.5X BASIC MATERIAL
96-100 PRINT RUN 50 SERIAL #'d SETS

2002 Playoff Piece of the Game Materials Gold

*GOLD 1-90: 1.25X TO 3X BASIC MATERIAL
1-90 PRINT RUN 50 SERIAL #'d SETS
91-95 PRINT RUN 25 SERIAL #'d SETS
91-95 NO PRICING DUE TO SCARCITY
96-100 PRINT RUN 10 SERIAL #'d SETS
96-100 NO PRICING DUE TO SCARCITY

2002 Playoff Piece of the Game Materials Silver

*SILVER 1-90: .75X TO 2X BASIC MATERIAL
1-90 PRINT RUN 100 SERIAL #'d SETS
*SILVER 91-95: .75X TO 2X BASIC MATERIAL
91-95 PRINT RUN 25 SERIAL #'d SETS
96-100 PRINT RUN 25 SERIAL #'d SETS
96-100 NO PRICING DUE TO SCARCITY

2003 Playoff Piece of the Game

STATED ODDS 1:1.5
SERIAL #'d PRINTS B/WN 10-200 COPIES PER
NO PRICING ON QTY OF 25 OR LESS
1A Adam Dunn Bat 3.00 8.00
1B Adam Dunn Btg Glv/40 6.00 15.00
2 Adam Dunn Jsy 3.00 8.00
3A Adrian Beltre Bat 3.00 8.00
3B Adrian Beltre Jsy/100 4.00 10.00
3C Adrian Beltre Hat/50 6.00 15.00
3D Adrian Beltre Shoe/50 6.00 15.00
4 Albert Pujols Jsy 8.00 20.00
5 Albert Pujols Bat 8.00 20.00
6 Alex Rodriguez Bat 4.00 10.00
7 Alex Rodriguez Blue Jsy 4.00 10.00
8 Alex Rodriguez White Jsy 4.00 10.00
9 Alfonso Soriano Bat 3.00 8.00
10 Alfonso Soriano Gray Jsy 3.00 8.00
11 Alfonso Soriano White Jsy 3.00 8.00
12 Brett Myers Jsy/50 6.00 15.00
13 Andruw Jones Jsy 4.00 10.00
14A Austin Kearns Jsy 3.00 8.00
14B Austin Kearns Bat/195 3.00 8.00
15A Barry Larkin Bat 4.00 10.00
15B Barry Larkin Bat/200 4.00 10.00
16A Barry Zito Jsy 3.00 8.00
16B Barry Zito Hat/40 6.00 15.00
17A Bernie Williams Jsy 4.00 10.00
17B Bernie Williams Bat/95 6.00 15.00
17C Bernie Williams Shoe/45 10.00 25.00
18A Brian Giles Bat 3.00 8.00
18B Brian Giles Hat/85 4.00 10.00
18C Brian Giles Btg Glv/40 6.00 15.00
18D Brian Giles Shoe/45 6.00 15.00
19 Zach Day Jsy/50 6.00 15.00
20A Carlos Beltran Bat 3.00 8.00
20B Carlos Beltran Jsy/75 4.00 10.00
20C Carlos Beltran Hat/45 6.00 15.00
21 Brandon Phillips Bat/50 6.00 15.00
22 Carlos Lee Bat/50 6.00 15.00
23A Casey Fossum Jsy/75 4.00 10.00
24A Chipper Jones Jsy 4.00 10.00
24B Chipper Jones Bat/195 4.00 10.00
25 Marcus Giles Jsy/50 6.00 15.00
26A Craig Biggio Bat 4.00 10.00
26B Craig Biggio Jsy/100 6.00 15.00
26C Craig Biggio Hat/50 10.00 25.00
26D Craig Biggio Shoe/50 10.00 25.00
27 Curt Schilling Jsy 3.00 8.00
28 Derek Jeter Base 8.00 20.00

29A Edgar Martinez Jsy 4.00 10.00
29B Edgar Martinez Bat/150 4.00 10.00
30A Eric Chavez Jsy 3.00 8.00
30B Eric Chavez Bat/175 3.00 8.00
32A Frank Thomas Jsy 4.00 10.00
32B Frank Thomas Bat/190 4.00 10.00
33 Aubrey Huff Jsy/50 6.00 15.00
34A Gary Carter Jacket 3.00 8.00
34B Gary Carter Fld Glv/40 6.00 15.00
34C Gary Carter Bat/40 6.00 15.00
35 Greg Maddux Gray Jsy 4.00 10.00
36 Greg Maddux White Jsy 4.00 10.00
37 Hideki Matsui Base RC 6.00 15.00
38 Hideo Nomo White Jsy 6.00 15.00
39A Rod Carew Jacket 4.00 10.00
39B Rod Carew Shoe/100 6.00 15.00
39C Rod Carew Hat/50 10.00 25.00
40 Ichiro Suzuki Base 6.00 15.00
41A Ivan Rodriguez Bat 4.00 10.00
42A Jason Giambi A's Bat 3.00 8.00
42B Jason Giambi A's Hat/200 3.00 8.00
43 Jason Giambi Yanks Bat 3.00 8.00
44 J.C. Romero Jsy/50 6.00 15.00
45 Jason Giambi Yanks Jsy 3.00 8.00
46A Jeff Bagwell Jsy 4.00 10.00
46B Jeff Bagwell Bat/195 4.00 10.00
47 Josh Bard Jsy/50 6.00 15.00
48A Jim Thome Jsy 4.00 10.00
48B Jim Thome Bat/200 4.00 10.00
49 Jay Gibbons Jsy/200 3.00 8.00
50A Jorge Posada Jsy 4.00 10.00
50B Jorge Posada Bat/200 4.00 10.00
51A Juan Gonzalez Bat 3.00 8.00
51B Juan Gonzalez Jsy/40 6.00 15.00
52A Kazuhisa Ishii Bat 3.00 8.00
52B Kazuhisa Ishii Jsy/200 3.00 8.00
53 George Brett Bat 6.00 15.00
54A Kenny Lofton Bat 3.00 8.00
54B Kenny Lofton Hat/90 4.00 10.00
54C Kenny Lofton Fld Glv/45 10.00 25.00
54D Kenny Lofton Shoe/45 10.00 25.00
55A Kerry Wood Jsy 3.00 8.00
55B Kerry Wood Hat/90 4.00 10.00
55C Kerry Wood Fld Glv/45 6.00 15.00
55D Kerry Wood Shoe/45 6.00 15.00
56 Kevin Brown Jsy 3.00 8.00
57 Kirk Saarloos Jsy 3.00 8.00
58A Lance Berkman Jsy 3.00 8.00
58B Lance Berkman Bat/90 4.00 10.00
58C Lance Berkman Btg Glv/45 6.00 15.00
58D Lance Berkman Shoe/45 6.00 15.00
59A Larry Walker Jsy 3.00 8.00
59B Larry Walker Bat/200 3.00 8.00
60A Magglio Ordonez Jsy 3.00 8.00
60B Magglio Ordonez Hat/100 4.00 10.00
60C Magglio Ordonez Bat/50 6.00 15.00
60D Magglio Ordonez Shoe/50 6.00 15.00
61A Manny Ramirez Jsy 4.00 10.00
61B Manny Ramirez Bat/200 4.00 10.00
62 Mark Mulder Jsy 3.00 8.00
63A Mark Prior Jsy 4.00 10.00
63B Mark Prior Hat/95 6.00 15.00
63C Mark Prior Fld Glv/45 10.00 25.00
63D Mark Prior Shoe/45 10.00 25.00
64 Matt Williams Jsy/50 6.00 15.00
65A Miguel Tejada Jsy 3.00 8.00
65B Miguel Tejada Bat/100 4.00 10.00
65C Miguel Tejada Hat/50 6.00 15.00
66A Mike Mussina Jsy 4.00 10.00
66B Mike Mussina Fld Glv/45 10.00 25.00
67 Mike Piazza Bat 4.00 10.00
68 Mike Piazza Black Jsy 4.00 10.00
69 Mike Piazza White Jsy 4.00 10.00
70 Nomar Garciaparra Bat 6.00 15.00
71 Nomar Garciaparra Gray Jsy 6.00 15.00
72 Nomar Garciaparra White Jsy 6.00 15.00
73 Paul Lo Duca Jsy/50 6.00 15.00
74 Pedro Martinez Jsy 4.00 10.00
75A Rafael Palmeiro Jsy 4.00 10.00
75B Rafael Palmeiro Hat/95 6.00 15.00
75C Rafael Palmeiro Fld Glv/45 10.00 25.00
75D Rafael Palmeiro Btg Glv/45 10.00 25.00
76 Randy Johnson Gray Jsy 4.00 10.00
77 Randy Johnson White Jsy 4.00 10.00
78A Rickey Henderson Jsy 4.00 10.00
78B Rickey Henderson Bat/195 4.00 10.00
79A Roberto Alomar Jsy 4.00 10.00
79B Roberto Alomar Bat/90 6.00 15.00
79C Roberto Alomar Btg Glv/45 10.00 25.00
80 Rod Carew Pants 4.00 10.00
81 Roger Clemens Gray Jsy 6.00 15.00
82 Roger Clemens White Jsy 6.00 15.00
83 Cal Ripken Jsy 6.00 15.00
84A Roy Oswalt Jsy 3.00 8.00
84B Roy Oswalt Fld Glv/95 4.00 10.00
84C Roy Oswalt Shoe/45 6.00 15.00
85 Jer Bonderman Jsy/50 RC 15.00 40.00
86 Ryne Sandberg Bat 6.00 15.00
87 Sammy Sosa Bat 4.00 10.00
88 Sammy Sosa Gray Jsy 4.00 10.00
89 Sammy Sosa White Jsy 4.00 10.00
90A Scott Rolen Jsy 4.00 10.00
90B Scott Rolen Bat/185 4.00 10.00
91 Frank Catalanotto Jsy/50 6.00 15.00
92A Shawn Green Jsy 3.00 8.00
92B Shawn Green Bat/195 3.00 8.00
93A Tim Hudson Jsy 3.00 8.00
93B Tim Hudson Hat/100 4.00 10.00
93C Tim Hudson Shoe/50 6.00 15.00
94A Todd Helton Jsy 4.00 10.00
94B Todd Helton Bat/195 4.00 10.00
95A Tony Gwynn Pants 4.00 10.00
95B Tony Gwynn Bat/95 6.00 15.00
95C Tony Gwynn Btg Glv/45 12.50 30.00
96A Torii Hunter Jsy 3.00 8.00
96B Torii Hunter Bat/150 3.00 8.00
97A Troy Glaus Jsy 3.00 8.00
97B Troy Glaus Bat/195 3.00 8.00
98 Runelvys Hernandez Jsy/50 6.00 15.00
99 Vernon Wells Jsy 3.00 8.00
100A Vladimir Guerrero Jsy 4.00 10.00
100B Vladimir Guerrero Bat/150 4.00 10.00

2003 Playoff Piece of the Game Bronze

*BRONZE ACTIVE: .4X TO 1X BASIC
*BRONZE RETIRED: .6X TO 1.5X BASIC
*BRONZE: .5X TO 1.2X BASIC RC's
*BRONZE: .4X TO 1X BASIC p/r 200
*BRONZE: .2X TO .5X BASIC p/r 50-75
*BRONZE: .2X TO .5X BASIC p/r 50 RC's
RANDOM INSERTS IN PACKS
STATED PRINT RUN 150 SERIAL #'d SETS
CARDS 21 AND 22 DO NOT EXIST

2003 Playoff Piece of the Game Gold

*GOLD ACTIVE: .75X TO 2X BASIC
*GOLD RETIRED: 1.25X TO 3X BASIC
*GOLD: 1X TO 2.5X BASIC RC's
*GOLD: .75X TO 2X BASIC p/r 200
*GOLD: .4X TO 1X BASIC p/r 50-75
*GOLD: .4X TO 1X BASIC p/r 50 RC's
RANDOM INSERTS IN PACKS
STATED PRINT RUN 50 SERIAL #'d SETS

2003 Playoff Piece of the Game Silver

*SILVER ACTIVE: .6X TO 1.5X BASIC
*SILVER RETIRED: 1X TO 2.5X BASIC
*SILVER: .75X TO 2X BASIC RC's
*SILVER: .6X TO 1.5X BASIC p/r 200
*SILVER: .3X TO .8X BASIC p/r 50-75
*SILVER: .3X TO .8X BASIC p/r 50 RC's
RANDOM INSERTS IN PACKS
STATED PRINT RUN 75 SERIAL #'d SETS

2003 Playoff Piece of the Game Autographs

SERIAL #'d PRINTS B/WN 5-150 COPIES PER
12 Brett Myers Jsy 6.00 15.00
13 Andruw Jones Jsy/50 20.00 50.00
18A Brian Giles Bat/30 10.00 25.00
19 Zach Day Jsy 4.00 10.00
21 Brandon Phillips Bat 6.00 15.00
22 Carlos Lee Bat 6.00 15.00
23A Casey Fossum Jsy 4.00 10.00
23B Casey Fossum Hat/75 8.00 20.00
25 Marcus Giles Jsy 6.00 15.00
29A Edgar Martinez Jsy/100 20.00 50.00
29B Edgar Martinez Bat/50 25.00 60.00
30A Eric Chavez Jsy/75 12.50 30.00
31A Eric Hinske Bat 4.00 10.00
31B Eric Hinske Hat/75 8.00 20.00
31C Eric Hinske Shoe/40 10.00 25.00
33 Aubrey Huff Jsy 6.00 15.00
41A Ivan Rodriguez Bat/75 10.00 25.00
41B Ivan Rodriguez Btg Glv/50 12.50 30.00
44 J.C. Romero Jsy 4.00 10.00
47 Josh Bard Jsy 4.00 10.00
49 Jay Gibbons Jsy 8.00 20.00
51A Juan Gonzalez Bat/50 15.00 40.00
57 Kirk Saarloos Jsy 4.00 10.00
62 Mark Mulder Jsy/100 6.00 15.00
64 Matt Williams Jsy 6.00 15.00
73 Paul Lo Duca Jsy 6.00 15.00
84A Roy Oswalt Jsy/50 4.00 10.00
85 Jeremy Bonderman Jsy 20.00 50.00
86 Ryne Sandberg Bat/40 20.00 50.00
90A Scott Rolen Jsy/50 10.00 25.00
91 Frank Catalanotto Jsy 4.00 10.00
96A Torii Hunter Jsy/140 6.00 15.00
96B Torii Hunter Bat/50 6.00 15.00
98 Runelvys Hernandez Jsy 4.00 10.00
100A Vladimir Guerrero Jsy/150 8.00 20.00
100B Vladimir Guerrero Bat/50 12.50 30.00

2003 Playoff Piece of the Game Player Collection

*PLAY.COLL: .6X TO 1.5X PRESTIGE P.COLL.
RANDOM INSERTS IN PACKS
STATED PRINT RUN 100 SERIAL #'d SETS

2003 Playoff Portraits

COMPLETE SET (144) 20.00 50.00
COMMON CARD (1-144) .30 .75
COMMON RC .30 .75
COMMON RETIRED .30 .75
ORIGINAL ART EXCH. DEADLINE 04/01/05
1 Vladimir Guerrero .50 1.25
2 Luis Gonzalez .30 .75
3 Andruw Jones .30 .75
4 Manny Ramirez .75 2.00
5 Derek Jeter 2.00 5.00
6 Eric Hinske .30 .75
7 Curt Schilling .50 1.25
8 Adam Dunn .50 1.25
9 Jason Jennings .30 .75
10 Mike Piazza Mets .75 2.00
11 Jason Giambi Yanks .30 .75
12 Jeff Bagwell .50 1.25
13 Rickey Henderson Sox .75 2.00
14 Randy Johnson D'backs .75 2.00
15 Roger Clemens Yanks 1.00 2.50
16 Troy Glaus .30 .75
17 Hideo Nomo Dodgers .75 2.00
18 Joe Borchard .30 .75
19 Torii Hunter .30 .75
20 Lance Berkman .50 1.25
21 Todd Helton .50 1.25
22 Mike Mussina .50 1.25
23 Vernon Wells .30 .75
24 Pat Burrell .30 .75
25 Ichiro Suzuki 1.00 2.50
26 Shawn Green .30 .75
27 Frank Thomas .75 2.00
28 Barry Zito .50 1.25
29 Barry Bonds 1.25 3.00
30 Ken Griffey Jr. 1.50 4.00
31 Albert Pujols 1.00 2.50
32 Roberto Alomar .50 1.25
33 Barry Larkin .50 1.25
34 Tony Gwynn .75 2.00
35 Chipper Jones .75 2.00
36 Pedro Martinez Sox .50 1.25
37 Juan Gonzalez .30 .75
38 Greg Maddux 1.00 2.50
39 Tim Hudson .50 1.25
40 Sammy Sosa .75 2.00
41 Victor Martinez .50 1.25
42 Mark Buehrle .50 1.25
43 Austin Kearns .30 .75
44 Kerry Wood .30 .75
45 Nomar Garciaparra .50 1.25
46 Alfonso Soriano .50 1.25
47 Mark Prior .50 1.25
48 Richie Sexson .30 .75
49 Mark Teixeira .50 1.25
50 Craig Biggio .50 1.25
51 Rafael Palmeiro .50 1.25
52 Carlos Beltran .50 1.25
53 Bernie Williams .50 1.25
54 Eric Chavez .30 .75
55 Paul Konerko .50 1.25
56 Nolan Ryan Rgr 2.50 6.00
57 Mark Mulder .30 .75
58 Miguel Tejada .50 1.25
59 Roy Oswalt .50 1.25
60 Jim Edmonds .50 1.25
61 Ryan Klesko .30 .75
62 Cal Ripken 2.50 6.00
63 Josh Beckett .30 .75
64 Kazuhisa Ishii .30 .75
65 Alex Rodriguez Rgr 1.00 2.50
66 Mike Sweeney .30 .75
67 C.C. Sabathia .50 1.25
68 Jose Vidro .30 .75
69 Magglio Ordonez .50 1.25
70 Carlos Delgado .30 .75
71 Jorge Posada .50 1.25
72 Bobby Abreu .30 .75
73 Brian Giles .30 .75
74 Kirby Puckett .75 2.00
75 Yogi Berra .75 2.00
76 Ryne Sandberg 1.50 4.00
77 Tom Glavine .50 1.25
78 Jim Thome .50 1.25
79 Chris Snelling .30 .75
80 Drew Henson .30 .75
81 Junior Spivey .30 .75
82 Mike Schmidt 1.25 3.00
83 Jeff Kent .30 .75
84 Stan Musial 1.25 3.00
85 Garret Anderson .30 .75
86 Jose Contreras RC .75 2.00
87 Ivan Rodriguez .50 1.25
88 Hideki Matsui RC 1.50 4.00
89 Don Mattingly 1.50 4.00
90 Angel Berroa .30 .75
91 George Brett 1.50 4.00
92 Jermaine Dye .30 .75
93 John Olerud .30 .75
94 Josh Phelps .30 .75
95 Sean Casey .30 .75
96 Larry Walker .50 1.25
97 Jason Lane .30 .75
98 Travis Hafner .30 .75
99 Terrence Long .30 .75
100 Shannon Stewart .30 .75
101 Richard Hidalgo .30 .75
102 Joe Thurston .30 .75
103 Ben Sheets .30 .75
104 Orlando Cabrera .30 .75
105 Aramis Ramirez .30 .75
106 So Taguchi .30 .75
107 Frank Robinson .50 1.25
108 Phil Nevin .30 .75
109 Dennis Tankersley .30 .75
110 J.D. Drew .30 .75
111 Paul Lo Duca .30 .75
112 Ozzie Smith 1.00 2.50
113 Carlos Lee .30 .75
114 Nick Johnson .30 .75
115 Edgar Martinez .50 1.25
116 Hank Blalock .30 .75
117 Orlando Hudson .30 .75
118 Corey Patterson .30 .75
119 Steve Carlton .50 1.25
120 Wade Miller .30 .75
121 Adrian Beltre .75 2.00
122 Scott Rolen .50 1.25
123 Brian Lawrence .30 .75
124 Rich Aurilia .30 .75
125 Tsuyoshi Shinjo .30 .75
126 John Buck .30 .75
127 Marlon Byrd .30 .75
128 Michael Cuddyer .30 .75
129 Marshall McDougall .30 .75
130 Travis Chapman .30 .75
131 Jose Morban .30 .75
132 Adam LaRoche .30 .75
133 Jose Castillo .30 .75
134 Walter Young .30 .75
135 Jeff Baker .30 .75
136 Jeremy Guthrie .30 .75
137 Pedro Martinez Expos .50 1.25
138 Randy Johnson M's .75 2.00
139 Alex Rodriguez M's 1.00 2.50
140 Hideo Nomo Mets .75 2.00
141 Roger Clemens Sox 1.00 2.50
142 Rickey Henderson A's .75 2.00
143 Jason Giambi A's .30 .75
144 Mike Piazza Dodgers .75 2.00

2003 Playoff Portraits Beckett Samples

*SAMPLES: 1.5X TO 4X BASIC
1 Vladimir Guerrero 2.00 5.00
2 Luis Gonzalez 1.25 3.00
3 Andruw Jones 1.25 3.00
4 Manny Ramirez 3.00 8.00
5 Derek Jeter 8.00 20.00
6 Eric Hinske 1.25 3.00
7 Curt Schilling 2.00 5.00
8 Adam Dunn 2.00 5.00
9 Jason Jennings 1.25 3.00
10 Mike Piazza Mets 3.00 8.00
11 Jason Giambi Yanks 1.25 3.00
12 Jeff Bagwell 2.00 5.00
13 Rickey Henderson Sox 3.00 8.00
14 Randy Johnson D'backs 3.00 8.00
15 Roger Clemens Yanks 4.00 10.00
16 Troy Glaus 1.25 3.00
17 Hideo Nomo Dodgers 3.00 8.00
18 Joe Borchard 1.25 3.00
19 Torii Hunter 1.25 3.00
20 Lance Berkman 2.00 5.00
21 Todd Helton 2.00 5.00
22 Mike Mussina 2.00 5.00
23 Vernon Wells 1.25 3.00
24 Pat Burrell 1.25 3.00
25 Ichiro Suzuki 4.00 10.00
26 Shawn Green 1.25 3.00
27 Frank Thomas 3.00 8.00
28 Barry Zito 2.00 5.00
29 Barry Bonds 5.00 12.00
30 Ken Griffey Jr. 6.00 15.00
31 Albert Pujols 4.00 10.00
32 Roberto Alomar 2.00 5.00
33 Barry Larkin 2.00 5.00
34 Tony Gwynn 3.00 8.00
35 Chipper Jones 3.00 8.00
36 Pedro Martinez Sox 2.00 5.00
37 Juan Gonzalez 1.25 3.00
38 Greg Maddux 4.00 10.00
39 Tim Hudson 2.00 5.00
40 Sammy Sosa 3.00 8.00
41 Victor Martinez 2.00 5.00
42 Mark Buehrle 2.00 5.00
43 Austin Kearns 1.25 3.00
44 Kerry Wood 1.25 3.00
45 Nomar Garciaparra 2.00 5.00
46 Alfonso Soriano 2.00 5.00
47 Mark Prior 2.00 5.00
48 Richie Sexson 1.25 3.00
49 Mark Teixeira 2.00 5.00
50 Craig Biggio 2.00 5.00
51 Rafael Palmeiro 2.00 5.00
52 Carlos Beltran 2.00 5.00
53 Bernie Williams 2.00 5.00
54 Eric Chavez 1.25 3.00
55 Paul Konerko 2.00 5.00
56 Nolan Ryan Rgr 10.00 25.00
57 Mark Mulder 1.25 3.00
58 Miguel Tejada 2.00 5.00
59 Roy Oswalt 2.00 5.00
60 Jim Edmonds 2.00 5.00
61 Ryan Klesko 1.25 3.00
62 Cal Ripken 10.00 25.00
63 Josh Beckett 1.25 3.00
64 Kazuhisa Ishii 1.25 3.00
65 Alex Rodriguez Rgr 4.00 10.00
66 Mike Sweeney 1.25 3.00
67 C.C. Sabathia 2.00 5.00
68 Jose Vidro 1.25 3.00
69 Magglio Ordonez 2.00 5.00
70 Carlos Delgado 1.25 3.00
71 Jorge Posada 2.00 5.00
72 Bobby Abreu 1.25 3.00
73 Brian Giles 1.25 3.00
74 Kirby Puckett 3.00 8.00
75 Yogi Berra 3.00 8.00
76 Ryne Sandberg 6.00 15.00
77 Tom Glavine 2.00 5.00
78 Jim Thome 2.00 5.00
79 Chris Snelling 1.25 3.00
80 Drew Henson 1.25 3.00
81 Junior Spivey 1.25 3.00
82 Mike Schmidt 5.00 12.00
83 Jeff Kent 1.25 3.00
84 Stan Musial 5.00 12.00
85 Garret Anderson 1.25 3.00
86 Jose Contreras RC 3.00 8.00
87 Ivan Rodriguez 2.00 5.00
88 Hideki Matsui RC 6.00 15.00
89 Don Mattingly 6.00 15.00
90 Angel Berroa 1.25 3.00
91 George Brett 6.00 15.00
92 Jermaine Dye 1.25 3.00
93 John Olerud 1.25 3.00
94 Josh Phelps 1.25 3.00
95 Sean Casey 1.25 3.00
96 Larry Walker 2.00 5.00
97 Jason Lane 1.25 3.00
98 Travis Hafner 1.25 3.00
99 Terrence Long 1.25 3.00
100 Shannon Stewart 1.25 3.00
101 Richard Hidalgo 1.25 3.00
102 Joe Thurston 1.25 3.00
103 Ben Sheets 1.25 3.00
104 Orlando Cabrera 1.25 3.00
105 Aramis Ramirez 1.25 3.00
106 So Taguchi 1.25 3.00
107 Frank Robinson 2.00 5.00
108 Phil Nevin 1.25 3.00
109 Dennis Tankersley 1.25 3.00
110 J.D. Drew 1.25 3.00
111 Paul Lo Duca 1.25 3.00
112 Ozzie Smith 4.00 10.00
113 Carlos Lee 1.25 3.00
114 Nick Johnson 1.25 3.00
115 Edgar Martinez 2.00 5.00
116 Hank Blalock 1.25 3.00
117 Orlando Hudson 1.25 3.00
118 Corey Patterson 1.25 3.00
119 Steve Carlton 2.00 5.00
120 Wade Miller 1.25 3.00
121 Adrian Beltre 3.00 8.00
122 Scott Rolen 2.00 5.00
123 Brian Lawrence 1.25 3.00
124 Rich Aurilia 1.25 3.00
125 Tsuyoshi Shinjo 1.25 3.00
126 John Buck 1.25 3.00
127 Marlon Byrd 1.25 3.00
128 Michael Cuddyer 1.25 3.00
129 Marshall McDougall 1.25 3.00
130 Travis Chapman 1.25 3.00
131 Jose Morban 1.25 3.00
132 Adam LaRoche 1.25 3.00
133 Jose Castillo 1.25 3.00
134 Walter Young 1.25 3.00
135 Jeff Baker 1.25 3.00
136 Jeremy Guthrie 1.25 3.00
137 Pedro Martinez Expos 2.00 5.00
138 Randy Johnson M's 3.00 8.00
139 Alex Rodriguez M's 4.00 10.00
140 Hideo Nomo Mets 3.00 8.00
141 Roger Clemens Sox 4.00 10.00
142 Rickey Henderson A's 3.00 8.00
143 Jason Giambi A's 1.25 3.00
144 Mike Piazza Dodgers 3.00 8.00

2003 Playoff Portraits Beige

*BEIGE: 1X TO 2.5X BASIC
*BEIGE RC'S: 1X TO 2.5X BASIC
RANDOM INSERTS IN PACKS
ONE BEIGE GLUED TO EACH SEALED BOX
STATED PRINT RUN 250 SERIAL #'d SETS

2003 Playoff Portraits Bronze

*BRONZE: 2X TO 5X BASIC
*BRONZE RC'S: 2X TO 5X BASIC
RANDOM INSERTS IN PACKS
STATED PRINT RUN 100 SERIAL #'d SETS

2003 Playoff Portraits National Red

*RED: 2X TO 5X BASIC

2003 Playoff Portraits Silver

*SILVER ACTIVE: 2.5X TO 6X BASIC
*SILVER RETIRED: 2.5X TO 6X BASIC
*SILVER RC'S: 2.5X TO 6X BASIC
RANDOM INSERTS IN PACKS
STATED PRINT RUN 50 SERIAL #'d SETS

2003 Playoff Portraits Autographs Bronze

PRINT RUNS B/WN 2-100 COPIES PER
NO PRICING ON QTY OF 29 OR LESS
1 Vladimir Guerrero/100 6.00 16.00
6 Eric Hinske/100 4.00 10.00
8 Adam Dunn/50 15.00 40.00
9 Jason Jennings/100 4.00 10.00
16 Troy Glaus/60 15.00 40.00
18 Joe Borchard/100 4.00 10.00
32 Roberto Alomar/100 10.00 25.00
33 Barry Larkin/95 12.50 30.00
34 Tony Gwynn/60 15.00 40.00
37 Juan Gonzalez/50 15.00 40.00
41 Victor Martinez/100 5.00 12.00
42 Mark Buehrle/100 6.00 15.00
44 Kerry Wood/40 15.00 40.00
48 Richie Sexson/100 6.00 15.00
57 Mark Mulder/100 6.00 15.00
59 Roy Oswalt/40 10.00 25.00
61 Ryan Klesko/40 10.00 25.00
67 C.C. Sabathia/50 10.00 25.00
72 Bobby Abreu/100 6.00 15.00
73 Brian Giles/50 10.00 25.00
74 Kirby Puckett/50 75.00 150.00
77 Tom Glavine/100 6.00 15.00
79 Chris Snelling/100 4.00 10.00
81 Junior Spivey/100 4.00 10.00
82 Mike Schmidt/50 15.00 40.00
83 Jeff Kent/50 10.00 25.00
84 Stan Musial/50 12.00 30.00
86 Jose Contreras/50 15.00 40.00
89 Don Mattingly/50 30.00 60.00
90 Angel Berroa/100 4.00 10.00
92 Jermaine Dye/100 6.00 15.00
94 Josh Phelps/100 4.00 10.00
97 Jason Lane/100 6.00 15.00
98 Travis Hafner/100 6.00 15.00
99 Terrence Long/100 4.00 10.00
100 Shannon Stewart/100 6.00 15.00
102 Joe Thurston/100 4.00 10.00
103 Ben Sheets/100 6.00 15.00
105 Aramis Ramirez/40 4.00 10.00
108 Phil Nevin/100 6.00 15.00
109 Dennis Tankersley/100 4.00 10.00
111 Paul Lo Duca/100 6.00 15.00
113 Carlos Lee/100 6.00 15.00
114 Nick Johnson/100 6.00 15.00
115 Edgar Martinez/100 10.00 25.00
117 Orlando Hudson/100 4.00 10.00
118 Corey Patterson/100 4.00 10.00
120 Wade Miller/100 4.00 10.00
122 Scott Rolen/100 10.00 25.00
123 Brian Lawrence/100 4.00 10.00
126 John Buck/100 4.00 10.00
127 Marlon Byrd/100 4.00 10.00
128 Michael Cuddyer/100 4.00 10.00
129 Marshall McDougall/100 4.00 10.00
130 Travis Chapman/100 4.00 10.00
131 Jose Morban/100 4.00 10.00
132 Adam LaRoche/100 4.00 10.00
133 Jose Castillo/100 4.00 10.00
134 Walter Young/100 4.00 10.00
135 Jeff Baker/100 4.00 10.00
136 Jeremy Guthrie/100 4.00 10.00

2003 Playoff Portraits Autographs Silver

PRINT RUNS B/WN 2-50 COPIES PER
NO PRICING ON QTY OF 25 OR LESS
1 Vladimir Guerrero/50 10.00 25.00
6 Eric Hinske/50 6.00 15.00
9 Jason Jennings/50 6.00 15.00
18 Joe Borchard/50 6.00 15.00
32 Roberto Alomar/35 8.00 20.00
37 Juan Gonzalez/35 15.00 40.00
41 Victor Martinez/50 15.00 40.00
42 Mark Buehrle/50 10.00 25.00
48 Richie Sexson/35 10.00 25.00
57 Mark Mulder/35 10.00 25.00
72 Bobby Abreu/50 10.00 25.00
73 Brian Giles/35 10.00 25.00
74 Kirby Puckett/35 75.00 150.00
77 Tom Glavine/35 20.00 50.00
79 Chris Snelling/50 6.00 15.00
81 Junior Spivey/50 6.00 15.00
84 Stan Musial/35 40.00 80.00
86 Jose Contreras/35 15.00 40.00
89 Don Mattingly/35 30.00 60.00
90 Angel Berroa/50 6.00 15.00
92 Jermaine Dye/50 10.00 25.00
94 Josh Phelps/50 6.00 15.00
97 Jason Lane/50 10.00 25.00
98 Travis Hafner/50 10.00 25.00
99 Terrence Long/50 6.00 15.00
100 Shannon Stewart/50 10.00 25.00
102 Joe Thurston/50 6.00 15.00
103 Ben Sheets/50 10.00 25.00
108 Phil Nevin/50 10.00 25.00
109 Dennis Tankersley/50 6.00 15.00
111 Paul Lo Duca/35 10.00 25.00
113 Carlos Lee/50 10.00 25.00
114 Nick Johnson/50 10.00 25.00
115 Edgar Martinez/35 15.00 40.00
117 Orlando Hudson/50 6.00 15.00
118 Corey Patterson/50 6.00 15.00
120 Wade Miller/50 6.00 15.00
122 Scott Rolen/35 15.00 40.00
123 Brian Lawrence/50 6.00 15.00
126 John Buck/50 6.00 15.00
127 Marlon Byrd/50 6.00 15.00
128 Michael Cuddyer/50 6.00 15.00
129 Marshall McDougall/50 6.00 15.00
130 Travis Chapman/50 6.00 15.00
132 Adam LaRoche/50 6.00 15.00
133 Jose Castillo/50 6.00 15.00
134 Walter Young/50 6.00 15.00
135 Jeff Baker/50 6.00 15.00
136 Jeremy Guthrie/50 6.00 15.00

2003 Playoff Portraits Materials Bronze

PRINT RUNS B/WN 20-100 COPIES PER
NO PRICING ON QTY OF 25 OR LESS
1 Vladimir Guerrero Jsy/100 6.00 15.00
2 Luis Gonzalez Jsy/100 3.00 8.00
3 Andruw Jones Jsy/100 4.00 10.00
4 Manny Ramirez Jsy/50 6.00 15.00
5B Derek Jeter Base/100 12.50 30.00
6 Eric Hinske Jsy/100 3.00 8.00
7A Curt Schilling Bat/50 4.00 10.00
7B Curt Schilling Jsy/100 3.00 8.00
8A Adam Dunn Bat/50 4.00 10.00
8B Adam Dunn Jsy/50 4.00 10.00
9 Jason Jennings Jsy/100 3.00 8.00
10 Mike Piazza Mets Jsy/100 6.00 15.00
11 Jason Giambi Yanks Jsy/100 3.00 8.00
12A Jeff Bagwell Bat/50 6.00 15.00
12B Jeff Bagwell Jsy/50 6.00 15.00
13A R.Henderson Sox Bat/50 10.00 25.00
13B R.Henderson Sox Jsy/50 10.00 25.00
14 R.Johnson D'backs Jsy/100 6.00 15.00
15A R.Clemens Yanks Bat/50 15.00 40.00
15B R.Clemens Yanks Jsy/100 10.00 25.00
16 Troy Glaus Jsy/100 3.00 8.00
17 H.Nomo Dodgers Jsy/100 10.00 25.00
19 Torii Hunter Jsy/100 3.00 8.00
20 Lance Berkman Jsy/100 3.00 8.00
21A Todd Helton Bat/50 6.00 15.00
21B Todd Helton Jsy/50 6.00 15.00
22A Mike Mussina Bat/50 15.00 40.00
22B Mike Mussina Jsy/100 10.00 25.00
23 Vernon Wells Jsy/100 3.00 8.00
24A Pat Burrell Bat/50 4.00 10.00
24B Pat Burrell Jsy/100 3.00 8.00
25A Ichiro Suzuki Ball/50 15.00 40.00
25B Ichiro Suzuki Base/100 10.00 25.00
26 Shawn Green Jsy/100 3.00 8.00
27 Frank Thomas Jsy/100 6.00 15.00
28 Barry Zito Jsy/100 3.00 8.00
29 Barry Bonds Ball/50 15.00 40.00
29 Barry Bonds Base/100 10.00 25.00
30 Ken Griffey Jr. Base/100 8.00 20.00
31 Albert Pujols Jsy/100 10.00 25.00
32A Roberto Alomar Bat/50 6.00 15.00
32B Roberto Alomar Jsy/50 6.00 15.00
33 Barry Larkin Jsy/50 6.00 15.00
34 Tony Gwynn Jsy/100 10.00 25.00
35 Chipper Jones Jsy/100 6.00 15.00
36A Pedro Martinez Sox Bat/50 6.00 15.00
36B P.Martinez Sox Jsy/100 4.00 10.00
37A Juan Gonzalez Bat/50 4.00 10.00
37B Juan Gonzalez Jsy/50 4.00 10.00
38A Greg Maddux Bat/50 10.00 25.00
38B Greg Maddux Jsy/100 6.00 15.00
39 Tim Hudson Jsy/100 3.00 8.00
40 Sammy Sosa Jsy/100 6.00 15.00
41 Victor Martinez Jsy/100 4.00 10.00
42A Mark Buehrle Bat/50 4.00 10.00
42B Mark Buehrle Jsy/50 4.00 10.00
43A Austin Kearns Bat/50 4.00 10.00
43B Austin Kearns Jsy/100 3.00 8.00
44A Kerry Wood Bat/50 4.00 10.00
44B Kerry Wood Jsy/50 4.00 10.00
45 Nomar Garciaparra Jsy/100 8.00 20.00
46 Alfonso Soriano Jsy/100 3.00 8.00
47 Mark Prior Jsy/100 4.00 10.00
48 Richie Sexson Jsy/100 3.00 8.00
49A Mark Teixeira Bat/50 6.00 15.00
49B Mark Teixeira Jsy/50 6.00 15.00
50A Craig Biggio Bat/50 6.00 15.00
50B Craig Biggio Jsy/50 6.00 15.00
51A Rafael Palmeiro Bat/50 6.00 15.00
52 Carlos Beltran Jsy/50 4.00 10.00
53A Bernie Williams Bat/50 6.00 15.00
53B Bernie Williams Jsy/50 6.00 15.00
54 Eric Chavez Jsy/100 3.00 8.00
55 Paul Konerko Jsy/100 3.00 8.00
56A Nolan Ryan Rgr Bat/50 30.00 80.00
56B Nolan Ryan Rgr Jsy/100 20.00 50.00
57 Mark Mulder Jsy/100 3.00 8.00
58 Miguel Tejada Jsy/100 3.00 8.00
59B Roy Oswalt Jsy/50 4.00 10.00
60B Jim Edmonds Jsy/50 4.00 10.00
61A Ryan Klesko Bat/50 4.00 10.00
61B Ryan Klesko Jsy/100 3.00 8.00
62 Cal Ripken Jsy/100 20.00 50.00
63A Josh Beckett Bat/50 4.00 10.00
63B Josh Beckett Jsy/100 3.00 8.00
64 Kazuhisa Ishii Jsy/50 4.00 10.00
65 Alex Rodriguez Rgr Jsy/100 8.00 20.00
66A Mike Sweeney Bat/50 4.00 10.00
66B Mike Sweeney Jsy/100 3.00 8.00
67 C.C. Sabathia Jsy/100 3.00 8.00
68 Jose Vidro Jsy/100 3.00 8.00
69A Magglio Ordonez Bat/50 4.00 10.00
69B Magglio Ordonez Jsy/50 4.00 10.00
70A Carlos Delgado Bat/50 4.00 10.00
70B Carlos Delgado Jsy/50 4.00 10.00
71 Jorge Posada Jsy/100 4.00 10.00
72 Bobby Abreu Jsy/100 3.00 8.00
74A Kirby Puckett Bat/50 15.00 40.00
74B Kirby Puckett Jsy/50 15.00 40.00
75A Yogi Berra Bat/50 10.00 25.00
75B Yogi Berra Jsy/50 10.00 25.00
76 Ryne Sandberg Jsy/50 25.00 60.00
77A Tom Glavine Bat/50 6.00 15.00
77B Tom Glavine Jsy/50 6.00 15.00
78 Jim Thome Jsy/100 4.00 10.00
79 Chris Snelling Bat/50 4.00 10.00
80 Drew Henson Bat/50 4.00 10.00
81A Junior Spivey Bat/50 4.00 10.00
81B Junior Spivey Jsy/50 4.00 10.00
82A Mike Schmidt Bat/50 20.00 50.00
82B Mike Schmidt Jsy/50 20.00 50.00
83 Jeff Kent Bat/50 4.00 10.00
84 Stan Musial Jsy/100 15.00 40.00
85 Garret Anderson Bat/50 4.00 10.00
85 Garret Anderson Jsy/50 4.00 10.00
86 Jose Contreras Base/50 6.00 15.00
87 Ivan Rodriguez Bat/50 6.00 15.00
88A Hideki Matsui Ball/50 15.00 40.00
88B Hideki Matsui Base/100 10.00 25.00
89 Don Mattingly Jsy/100 15.00 40.00
90 Angel Berroa Pants/100 3.00 8.00
91A George Brett Bat/50 10.00 25.00
91B George Brett Jsy/50 10.00 25.00
92 Jermaine Dye Bat/50 4.00 10.00
93 John Olerud Jsy/100 3.00 8.00
94A Josh Phelps Bat/50 4.00 10.00
94B Josh Phelps Jsy/50 4.00 10.00
95A Sean Casey Bat/50 4.00 10.00
95B Sean Casey Jsy/50 4.00 10.00
96 Larry Walker Jsy/50 4.00 10.00
97 Jason Lane Bat/50 4.00 10.00
98 Travis Hafner Bat/100 3.00 8.00
99A Terrence Long Bat/50 4.00 10.00
99B Terrence Long Jsy/50 4.00 10.00
100A Shannon Stewart Bat/50 4.00 10.00
100B Shannon Stewart Jsy/100 3.00 8.00
101A Richard Hidalgo Bat/50 4.00 10.00
101B Richard Hidalgo Pants/50 4.00 10.00
102 Joe Thurston Bat/100 3.00 8.00
103 Ben Sheets Jsy/100 3.00 8.00
104A Orlando Cabrera Bat/50 4.00 10.00
104B Orlando Cabrera Jsy/50 4.00 10.00
105 Aramis Ramirez Jsy/100 3.00 8.00
106A So Taguchi Bat/50 4.00 10.00
107A Frank Robinson Bat/50 6.00 15.00
107B Frank Robinson Jsy/50 6.00 15.00
109 Dennis Tankersley Jsy/100 3.00 8.00
110 J.D. Drew Jsy/100 3.00 8.00
111A Paul Lo Duca Bat/50 4.00 10.00
111B Paul Lo Duca Jsy/50 4.00 10.00
112A Ozzie Smith Bat/50 20.00 50.00
112B Ozzie Smith Jsy/50 20.00 50.00
113 Carlos Lee Jsy/100 3.00 8.00
114 Nick Johnson Jsy/100 3.00 8.00
115 Edgar Martinez Jsy/100 4.00 10.00
116A Hank Blalock Bat/50 4.00 10.00
116B Hank Blalock Jsy/50 4.00 10.00
117 Orlando Hudson Bat/50 4.00 10.00
118 Corey Patterson Pants/100 3.00 8.00
119 Steve Carlton Bat/50 4.00 10.00
120 Wade Miller Jsy/50 4.00 10.00
121A Adrian Beltre Bat/50 4.00 10.00
121B Adrian Beltre Jsy/50 4.00 10.00
122 Scott Rolen Bat/50 6.00 15.00
123 Brian Lawrence Bat/50 4.00 10.00
124 Rich Aurilia Jsy/50 4.00 10.00
125A Tsuyoshi Shinjo Bat/50 4.00 10.00
125B Tsuyoshi Shinjo Jsy/50 4.00 10.00
126A John Buck Bat/50 4.00 10.00
126B John Buck Jsy/50 4.00 10.00
127 Marlon Byrd Jsy/100 3.00 8.00
128A Michael Cuddyer Bat/50 4.00 10.00
128B Michael Cuddyer Jsy/50 4.00 10.00
130 Travis Chapman Bat/100 3.00 8.00
131 Jose Morban Bat/100 3.00 8.00
132 Adam LaRoche Bat/100 3.00 8.00
133 Jose Castillo Bat/100 3.00 8.00
134 Walter Young Bat/100 3.00 8.00
137 P.Martinez Expos Jsy/100 4.00 10.00
138 R.Johnson M's Jsy/100 6.00 15.00
139 Alex Rodriguez M's Jsy/100 8.00 20.00
140A Hideo Nomo Mets Bat/50 15.00 40.00
140B Hideo Nomo Mets Jsy/50 15.00 40.00
141A R.Clemens Sox Bat/50 15.00 40.00
141B R.Clemens Sox Jsy/100 10.00 25.00
142A R.Henderson A's Bat/50 10.00 25.00
142B R.Henderson A's Jsy/50 10.00 25.00
143 Jason Giambi A's Jsy/100 3.00 8.00
144 Mike Piazza Dodgers Jsy/50 10.00 25.00

2003 Playoff Portraits Materials Gold

PRINT RUNS B/WN 10-25 COPIES PER
NO PRICING DUE TO SCARCITY

2003 Playoff Portraits Materials Silver

RANDOM INSERTS IN PACKS
PRINT RUNS B/WN 10-50 COPIES PER
NO PRICING ON QTY OF 25 OR LESS
1 Vladimir Guerrero Jsy/50 10.00 25.00
2 Luis Gonzalez Jsy/50 4.00 10.00
3 Andruw Jones Jsy/50 6.00 15.00
4 Manny Ramirez Jsy/50 6.00 15.00
5 Derek Jeter Base/50 20.00 50.00
6 Eric Hinske Jsy/50 4.00 10.00
7 Curt Schilling Jsy/50 4.00 10.00
8 Adam Dunn Jsy/50 4.00 10.00
9 Jason Jennings Jsy/50 4.00 10.00
10 Mike Piazza Mets Jsy/50 10.00 25.00
11 Jason Giambi Yanks Jsy/50 4.00 10.00
12 Jeff Bagwell Jsy/50 6.00 15.00
13 R.Henderson Sox Jsy/50 10.00 25.00
14 R.Johnson D'backs Jsy/50 10.00 25.00
15 R.Clemens Yanks Jsy/50 15.00 40.00
16 Troy Glaus Jsy/50 4.00 10.00
17 H.Nomo Dodgers Jsy/50 15.00 40.00
19 Torii Hunter Jsy/50 4.00 10.00
20 Lance Berkman Jsy/50 4.00 10.00
21 Todd Helton Jsy/50 6.00 15.00
22 Mike Mussina Jsy/50 15.00 40.00
23 Vernon Wells Jsy/50 4.00 10.00
24 Pat Burrell Jsy/50 4.00 10.00
25 Ichiro Suzuki Base/50 15.00 40.00
26 Shawn Green Jsy/50 4.00 10.00
27 Frank Thomas Jsy/50 10.00 25.00
28 Barry Zito Jsy/50 4.00 10.00
29 Barry Bonds Base/50 15.00 40.00
30 Ken Griffey Jr. Base/50 12.50 30.00
31 Albert Pujols Jsy/50 15.00 40.00
32 Roberto Alomar Jsy/50 6.00 15.00
33 Barry Larkin Jsy/50 6.00 15.00
34 Tony Gwynn Jsy/50 15.00 40.00
35 Chipper Jones Jsy/50 10.00 25.00
36 P.Martinez Sox Jsy/50 6.00 15.00
37 Juan Gonzalez Jsy/50 4.00 10.00
38 Greg Maddux Jsy/50 10.00 25.00
39 Tim Hudson Jsy/50 4.00 10.00
40 Sammy Sosa Jsy/50 10.00 25.00
41 Victor Martinez Jsy/50 6.00 15.00
42 Mark Buehrle Jsy/50 4.00 10.00
43 Austin Kearns Jsy/50 4.00 10.00
44 Kerry Wood Jsy/50 4.00 10.00
45 Nomar Garciaparra Jsy/50 12.50 30.00
46 Alfonso Soriano Jsy/50 4.00 10.00
47 Mark Prior Jsy/50 6.00 15.00
48 Richie Sexson Jsy/50 4.00 10.00
49 Mark Teixeira Jsy/50 6.00 15.00
50 Craig Biggio Jsy/50 6.00 15.00
51 Rafael Palmeiro Jsy/50 6.00 15.00
52 Carlos Beltran Jsy/50 4.00 10.00
53 Bernie Williams Jsy/50 6.00 15.00
54 Eric Chavez Jsy/50 4.00 10.00

55 Paul Konerko Jsy/50 4.00 10.00
56 Nolan Ryan Rgr Jsy/50 15.00 40.00
57 Mark Mulder Jsy/50 4.00 10.00
58 Miguel Tejada Jsy/50 4.00 10.00
59 Roy Oswalt Jsy/50 4.00 10.00
60 Jim Edmonds Jsy/50 4.00 10.00
61 Ryan Klesko Jsy/50 4.00 10.00
62 Cal Ripken Jsy/50 12.50 30.00
63 Josh Beckett Jsy/50 4.00 10.00
64 Kazuhisa Ishii Jsy/50 4.00 10.00
65 Alex Rodriguez Rgr Jsy/50 12.50 30.00
66 Mike Sweeney Jsy/50 4.00 10.00
67 C.C. Sabathia Jsy/50 4.00 10.00
68 Jose Vidro Jsy/50 4.00 10.00
69 Magglio Ordonez Jsy/50 4.00 10.00
70 Carlos Delgado Jsy/50 4.00 10.00
71 Jorge Posada Jsy/50 6.00 15.00
72 Bobby Abreu Jsy/50 4.00 10.00
75 Yogi Berra Jsy/50 10.00 25.00
76 Ryne Sandberg Jsy/50 25.00 60.00
78 Jim Thome Jsy/50 6.00 15.00
82 Mike Schmidt Jsy/50 20.00 50.00
84 Stan Musial Jsy/50 25.00 60.00
85 Garret Anderson Jsy/50 4.00 10.00
88 Hideki Matsui Base/50 15.00 40.00
89 Don Mattingly Jsy/50 20.00 50.00
90 Angel Berroa Pants/50 4.00 10.00
91 George Brett Jsy/50 20.00 50.00
93 John Olerud Jsy/50 4.00 10.00
94 Josh Phelps Jsy/50 4.00 10.00
95 Sean Casey Jsy/50 4.00 10.00
96 Larry Walker Jsy/50 4.00 10.00
99 Terrence Long Jsy/50 4.00 10.00
100 Shannon Stewart Jsy/50 4.00 10.00
101 Richard Hidalgo Pants/50 4.00 10.00
103 Ben Sheets Jsy/50 4.00 10.00
104 Orlando Cabrera Jsy/50 4.00 10.00
105 Aramis Ramirez Jsy/50 4.00 10.00
106 So Taguchi Jsy/50 4.00 10.00
107 Frank Robinson Jsy/50 6.00 15.00
109 Dennis Tankersley Jsy/50 4.00 10.00
110 J.D. Drew Jsy/50 4.00 10.00
111 Paul Lo Duca Jsy/50 4.00 10.00
112 Ozzie Smith Jsy/50 20.00 50.00
113 Carlos Lee Jsy/50 4.00 10.00
114 Nick Johnson Jsy/50 4.00 10.00
115 Edgar Martinez Jsy/50 6.00 15.00
116 Hank Blalock Jsy/50 4.00 10.00
118 Corey Patterson Pants/50 4.00 10.00
120 Wade Miller Jsy/50 4.00 10.00
121 Adrian Beltre Jsy/50 4.00 10.00
125 Tsuyoshi Shinjo Jsy/50 4.00 10.00
126 John Buck Jsy/50 4.00 10.00
127 Marlon Byrd Jsy/50 4.00 10.00
128 Michael Cuddyer Jsy/50 4.00 10.00
137 P.Martinez Expos Jsy/50 6.00 15.00
138 R.Johnson M's Jsy/50 10.00 25.00
139 Alex Rodriguez M's Jsy/50 12.50 30.00
140 Hideo Nomo Mets Jsy/50 15.00 40.00
141 R.Clemens Sox Jsy/50 15.00 40.00
142 R.Henderson A's Jsy/50 10.00 25.00
143 Jason Giambi A's Jsy/50 4.00 10.00
144 Mike Piazza Dodgers Jsy/50 10.00 25.00

2003 Playoff Portraits Materials Combo Bronze

RANDOM INSERTS IN PACKS
PRINT RUNS B/WN 10-50 COPIES PER
NO PRICING ON QTY OF 25 OR LESS
1 Vladimir Guerrero Bat-Jsy 12.50 30.00
2 Luis Gonzalez Bat-Jsy 6.00 15.00
3 Andruw Jones Bat-Jsy 8.00 20.00
4 Manny Ramirez Bat-Jsy 8.00 20.00
6 Eric Hinske Bat-Jsy 6.00 15.00
7 Curt Schilling Bat-Jsy 6.00 15.00
8 Adam Dunn Bat-Jsy 6.00 15.00
9 Jason Jennings Bat-Jsy 6.00 15.00
10 Mike Piazza Mets Bat-Jsy 15.00 40.00
11 Jason Giambi Yanks Bat-Jsy 6.00 15.00
12 Jeff Bagwell Bat-Jsy 8.00 20.00
13 R.Henderson Sox Bat-Jsy 12.50 30.00
14 R.Johnson D'backs Bat-Jsy 12.50 30.00
15 R.Clemens Yanks Bat-Jsy 20.00 50.00
16 Troy Glaus Bat-Jsy 6.00 15.00
17 H.Nomo Dodgers Bat-Jsy 20.00 50.00
19 Torii Hunter Bat-Jsy 6.00 15.00
20 Lance Berkman Bat-Jsy 6.00 15.00
21 Todd Helton Bat-Jsy 8.00 20.00
22 Mike Mussina Bat-Jsy 20.00 50.00
23 Vernon Wells Bat-Jsy 6.00 15.00
24 Pat Burrell Bat-Jsy 6.00 15.00
25 Ichiro Suzuki Ball-Base 20.00 50.00
26 Shawn Green Bat-Jsy 6.00 15.00
27 Frank Thomas Bat-Jsy 12.50 30.00
28 Barry Zito Bat-Jsy 6.00 15.00
29 Barry Bonds Ball-Base 20.00 50.00
31 Albert Pujols Bat-Jsy 20.00 50.00
32 Roberto Alomar Bat-Jsy 8.00 20.00
33 Barry Larkin Bat-Jsy 8.00 20.00
34 Tony Gwynn Bat-Jsy 20.00 50.00
35 Chipper Jones Bat-Jsy 12.50 30.00
36 P.Martinez Sox Bat-Jsy 8.00 20.00
37 Juan Gonzalez Bat-Jsy 6.00 15.00
38 Greg Maddux Bat-Jsy 15.00 40.00
40 Sammy Sosa Bat-Jsy 12.50 30.00
41 Victor Martinez Bat-Jsy 8.00 20.00
42 Mark Buehrle Bat-Jsy 6.00 15.00
43 Austin Kearns Bat-Jsy 6.00 15.00
44 Kerry Wood Bat-Jsy 6.00 15.00
45 Nomar Garciaparra Bat-Jsy 15.00 40.00
46 Alfonso Soriano Bat-Jsy 6.00 15.00
47 Mark Prior Bat-Jsy 8.00 20.00
48 Richie Sexson Bat-Jsy 6.00 15.00
49 Mark Teixeira Bat-Jsy 8.00 20.00
50 Craig Biggio Bat-Jsy 8.00 20.00
51 Rafael Palmeiro Bat-Jsy 8.00 20.00
52 Carlos Beltran Bat-Jsy 6.00 15.00
53 Bernie Williams Bat-Jsy 8.00 20.00
54 Eric Chavez Bat-Jsy 6.00 15.00
55 Paul Konerko Bat-Jsy 6.00 15.00
56 Nolan Ryan Rgr Bat-Jsy 40.00 100.00
57 Mark Mulder Bat-Jsy 6.00 15.00
58 Miguel Tejada Bat-Jsy 6.00 15.00
59 Roy Oswalt Bat-Jsy 6.00 15.00
60 Jim Edmonds Bat-Jsy 6.00 15.00
61 Ryan Klesko Bat-Jsy 6.00 15.00
62 Cal Ripken Bat-Jsy 40.00 100.00
63 Josh Beckett Bat-Jsy 6.00 15.00
64 Kazuhisa Ishii Bat-Jsy 6.00 15.00
65 Alex Rodriguez Rgr Bat-Jsy 15.00 40.00
66 Mike Sweeney Bat-Jsy 6.00 15.00
68 Jose Vidro Bat-Jsy 6.00 15.00
69 Magglio Ordonez Bat-Jsy 6.00 15.00
70 Carlos Delgado Bat-Jsy 6.00 15.00
71 Jorge Posada Bat-Jsy 8.00 20.00
72 Bobby Abreu Bat-Jsy 6.00 15.00
74 Kirby Puckett Bat-Jsy 20.00 50.00
75 Yogi Berra Bat-Jsy 12.50 30.00
76 Ryne Sandberg Bat-Jsy 30.00 80.00
77 Tom Glavine Bat-Jsy 8.00 20.00
78 Jim Thome Bat-Jsy 8.00 20.00
81 Junior Spivey Bat-Jsy 6.00 15.00
82 Mike Schmidt Bat-Jsy 25.00 60.00
84 Stan Musial Bat-Jsy 30.00 80.00
85 Garret Anderson Bat-Jsy 6.00 15.00
88 Hideki Matsui Ball-Base 20.00 50.00
89 Don Mattingly Bat-Jsy 25.00 60.00
90 Angel Berroa Bat-Pants 6.00 15.00
91 George Brett Bat-Jsy 25.00 60.00
93 John Olerud Bat-Jsy 6.00 15.00
94 Josh Phelps Bat-Jsy 6.00 15.00
95 Sean Casey Bat-Jsy 6.00 15.00
96 Larry Walker Bat-Jsy 6.00 15.00
99 Terrence Long Bat-Jsy 6.00 15.00
100 Shannon Stewart Bat-Jsy 6.00 15.00
101 Richard Hidalgo Bat-Pants 6.00 15.00
103 Ben Sheets Bat-Jsy 6.00 15.00
104 Orlando Cabrera Bat-Jsy 6.00 15.00
105 Aramis Ramirez Bat-Jsy 6.00 15.00
106 So Taguchi Bat-Jsy 6.00 15.00
107 Frank Robinson Bat-Jsy 8.00 20.00
109 Dennis Tankersley Bat-Jsy 6.00 15.00
110 J.D. Drew Bat-Jsy 6.00 15.00
111 Paul Lo Duca Bat Jsy 6.00 15.00
112 Ozzie Smith Bat-Jsy 10.00 25.00
113 Carlos Lee Bat-Jsy 6.00 15.00
114 Nick Johnson Bat-Jsy 6.00 15.00
115 Edgar Martinez Bat-Jsy 8.00 20.00
116 Hank Blalock Bat-Jsy 6.00 15.00
118 Corey Patterson Bat-Pants 6.00 15.00
120 Wade Miller Bat-Jsy 6.00 15.00
121 Adrian Beltre Bat-Jsy 6.00 15.00
122 Scott Rolen Bat-Jsy 8.00 20.00
125 Tsuyoshi Shinjo Bat-Jsy 6.00 15.00
126 John Buck Bat-Jsy 6.00 15.00
127 Marlon Byrd Bat-Jsy 6.00 15.00
128 Michael Cuddyer Bat-Jsy 6.00 15.00
137 P. Martinez Expos Bat-Jsy 8.00 20.00
138 R.Johnson M's Bat-Jsy 12.50 30.00
139 Alex Rodriguez M's Bat-Jsy 15.00 40.00
140 Hideo Nomo Mets Bat-Jsy 20.00 50.00
141 R.Clemens Sox Bat-Jsy 20.00 50.00
142 R.Henderson A's Bat-Jsy 12.50 30.00
143 Jason Giambi A's Bat-Jsy 6.00 15.00
144 M.Piazza Dodgers Bat-Jsy 15.00 40.00

2003 Playoff Prestige Samples

*SAMPLES: 1.5X TO 4X BASIC
INSERTED ONE PER BBCM

2003 Playoff Prestige Samples Gold

*GOLD SAMPLES: 4X TO 10X BASIC
RANDOM INSERTS IN BBCM

2003 Playoff Prestige

COMP.LO SET (200) 15.00 40.00
COMP.LO SET w/o SP's (180) 10.00 25.00
COMP.UPDATE SET (10) 3.00 8.00
COMMON CARD (1-180) .15 .40
COMMON CARD (181-200) .40 1.00
181-200 STATED ODDS 1:3
COMMON CARD (201-210) .20 .50
201-210 ISSUED IN DLP R/T PACKS
1 Darin Erstad .15 .40
2 David Eckstein .15 .40
3 Garret Anderson .15 .40
4 Jarrod Washburn .15 .40
5 Tim Salmon .15 .40
6 Troy Glaus .15 .40
7 Jay Gibbons .15 .40
8 Marty Cordova .15 .40
9 Melvin Mora .15 .40
10 Rodrigo Lopez .15 .40
11 Tony Batista .15 .40
12 Cliff Floyd .15 .40
13 Derek Lowe .15 .40
14 Johnny Damon .25 .60
15 Manny Ramirez .40 1.00
16 Nomar Garciaparra .25 .60
17 Pedro Martinez .25 .60
18 Rickey Henderson .40 1.00
19 Shea Hillenbrand .15 .40
20 Carlos Lee .15 .40
21 Frank Thomas .40 1.00
22 Magglio Ordonez .25 .60
23 Mark Buehrle .25 .60
24 Paul Konerko .25 .60
25 C.C. Sabathia .25 .60
26 Danys Baez .15 .40
27 Ellis Burks .15 .40
28 Travis Hafner .15 .40
29 Omar Vizquel .25 .60
30 Bobby Higginson .15 .40
31 Carlos Pena .25 .60
32 Mark Redman .15 .40
33 Robert Fick .15 .40
34 Steve Sparks .15 .40
35 Carlos Beltran .25 .60
36 Joe Randa .15 .40
37 Mike Sweeney .15 .40
38 Paul Byrd .15 .40
39 Raul Ibanez .25 .60
40 Runelvys Hernandez .15 .40
41 Brad Radke .15 .40
42 Corey Koskie .15 .40
43 Cristian Guzman .15 .40
44 David Ortiz .40 1.00
45 Doug Mientkiewicz .15 .40
46 Dustin Mohr .15 .40
47 Jacque Jones .15 .40
48 Torii Hunter .15 .40
49 Alfonso Soriano .25 .60
50 Andy Pettitte .25 .60
51 Bernie Williams .25 .60
52 David Wells .15 .40
53 Derek Jeter 1.00 2.50
54 Jason Giambi .15 .40
55 Jeff Weaver .15 .40
56 Jorge Posada .25 .60
57 Mike Mussina .25 .60
58 Roger Clemens .50 1.25
59 Barry Zito .25 .60
60 David Justice .15 .40
61 Eric Chavez .15 .40
62 Jermaine Dye .15 .40
63 Mark Mulder .15 .40
64 Miguel Tejada .25 .60
65 Ray Durham .15 .40
66 Tim Hudson .25 .60
67 Bret Boone .15 .40
68 Chris Snelling .15 .40
69 Edgar Martinez .25 .60
70 Freddy Garcia .15 .40
71 Ichiro Suzuki .50 1.25
72 Jamie Moyer .15 .40
73 John Olerud .15 .40
74 Kazuhiro Sasaki .15 .40
75 Aubrey Huff .15 .40
76 Joe Kennedy .15 .40
77 Paul Wilson .15 .40
78 Alex Rodriguez .50 1.25
79 Chan Ho Park .25 .60
80 Hank Blalock .15 .40
81 Ivan Rodriguez .25 .60
82 Juan Gonzalez .15 .40
83 Kevin Mench .15 .40
84 Rafael Palmeiro .25 .60
85 Carlos Delgado .15 .40
86 Eric Hinske .15 .40
87 Jose Cruz Jr. .15 .40
88 Josh Phelps .15 .40
89 Roy Halladay .25 .60
90 Shannon Stewart .15 .40
91 Vernon Wells .15 .40
92 Curt Schilling .25 .60
93 Junior Spivey .15 .40
94 Luis Gonzalez .15 .40
95 Mark Grace .25 .60
96 Randy Johnson .40 1.00
97 Andruw Jones .15 .40
98 Chipper Jones .40 1.00
99 Gary Sheffield .15 .40
100 Greg Maddux .50 1.25
101 John Smoltz .40 1.00
102 Kevin Millwood .15 .40
103 Mike Hampton .15 .40
104 Corey Patterson .15 .40
105 Fred McGriff .25 .60
106 Kerry Wood .15 .40
107 Mark Prior .25 .60
108 Moises Alou .15 .40
109 Sammy Sosa .40 1.00
110 Adam Dunn .25 .60
111 Austin Kearns .15 .40
112 Barry Larkin .25 .60
113 Ken Griffey Jr. .75 2.00
114 Sean Casey .15 .40
115 Jason Jennings .15 .40
116 Jay Payton .15 .40
117 Larry Walker .25 .60
118 Todd Helton .25 .60
119 A.J. Burnett .15 .40
120 Josh Beckett .15 .40
121 Juan Encarnacion .15 .40
122 Mike Lowell .15 .40
123 Craig Biggio .25 .60
124 Daryle Ward .15 .40
125 Jeff Bagwell .25 .60
126 Lance Berkman .25 .60
127 Roy Oswalt .25 .60
128 Adrian Beltre .40 1.00
129 Hideo Nomo .40 1.00
130 Kazuhisa Ishii .15 .40
131 Kevin Brown .15 .40
132 Odalis Perez .15 .40
133 Paul Lo Duca .15 .40
134 Shawn Green .15 .40
135 Jeff Kent .15 .40
136 Ben Sheets .15 .40
137 Jeffrey Hammonds .15 .40
138 Jose Hernandez .15 .40
139 Richie Sexson .15 .40
140 Bartolo Colon .15 .40
141 Brad Wilkerson .15 .40
142 Javier Vazquez .15 .40
143 Jose Vidro .15 .40
144 Michael Barrett .15 .40
145 Vladimir Guerrero .25 .60
146 Al Leiter .15 .40
147 Mike Piazza .40 1.00
148 Mo Vaughn .15 .40
149 Pedro Astacio .15 .40
150 Roberto Alomar .25 .60
151 Roger Cedeno .15 .40
152 Tom Glavine .25 .60
153 Bobby Abreu .15 .40
154 Jimmy Rollins .25 .60
155 Mike Lieberthal .15 .40
156 Pat Burrell .15 .40
157 Vicente Padilla .15 .40
158 Jim Thome .25 .60
159 Aramis Ramirez .15 .40
160 Brian Giles .15 .40
161 Jason Kendall .15 .40
162 Josh Fogg .15 .40
163 Kip Wells .15 .40
164 Mark Kotsay .15 .40
165 Oliver Perez .15 .40
166 Phil Nevin .15 .40
167 Ryan Klesko .15 .40
168 Sean Burroughs .15 .40
169 Trevor Hoffman .25 .60
170 Barry Bonds .60 1.50
171 Benito Santiago .15 .40
172 Reggie Sanders .15 .40
173 Rich Aurilia .15 .40
174 Russ Ortiz .15 .40
175 Albert Pujols .50 1.25
176 J.D. Drew .15 .40
177 Jim Edmonds .25 .60
178 Matt Morris .15 .40
179 Tino Martinez .15 .40
180 Scott Rolen .25 .60
181 Joe Borchard ROO .40 1.00
182 Freddy Sanchez ROO .40 1.00
183 Jose Contreras ROO RC 1.00 2.50
184 Jeff Baker ROO .40 1.00
185 Ryan Church ROO .40 1.00
186 Mario Ramos ROO .40 1.00
187 Corwin Malone ROO .40 1.00
188 Jimmy Gobble ROO .40 1.00
189 Jon Adkins ROO .40 1.00
190 Tim Kalita ROO .40 1.00
191 Nelson Castro ROO .40 1.00
192 Colin Young ROO .40 1.00
193 Luis Martinez ROO .40 1.00
194 Todd Donovan ROO .40 1.00
195 Jeremy Ward ROO .40 1.00
196 Wilson Valdez ROO .40 1.00
197 Hideki Matsui ROO RC 2.00 5.00
198 Mitch Wylie ROO .40 1.00
199 Adam Walker ROO .40 1.00
200 Cliff Bartosh ROO .40 1.00
201 Jeremy Bonderman ROO RC .75 2.00
202 Brandon Webb ROO RC .60 1.50
203 Adam Loewen ROO RC .20 .50
204 Chien-Ming Wang ROO RC .75 2.00
205 Hong-Chih Kuo ROO RC 1.00 2.50
206 Delmon Young ROO RC 1.25 3.00
207 Ryan Wagner ROO RC .20 .50
208 Dan Haren ROO RC 1.00 2.50
209 Rickie Weeks ROO RC .60 1.50
210 Ramon Nivar ROO RC .20 .50

2003 Playoff Prestige Autographs

PRINT RUNS B/WN 10-100 COPIES PER
NO PRICING ON QTY OF 25 OR LESS
201 J.Bonderman ROO/100 20.00 50.00
202 Brandon Webb ROO/100 10.00 25.00
203 Adam Loewen ROO/100 10.00 25.00
204 C.Wang ROO/50 75.00 150.00
205 Hong-Chih Kuo ROO/100 100.00 200.00
207 Ryan Wagner ROO/100 4.00 10.00
208 Dan Haren ROO/100 8.00 20.00
210 Ramon Nivar ROO/100 4.00 10.00

2003 Playoff Prestige Xtra Points Green

*GREEN 1-180: 3X TO 8X BASIC
1-180 PRINT RUN 150 SERIAL #'d SETS
*GREEN 181-200: 1.5X TO 4X BASIC
*GREEN 201-210: 3X TO 8X BASIC
181-210 PRINT RUN 50 SERIAL #'d SETS
1-200 RANDOM INSERTS IN RETAIL PACKS

2003 Playoff Prestige Xtra Points Purple

*PURPLE 1-180: 3X TO 8X BASIC
1-180 PRINT RUN 150 SERIAL #'d SETS
*PURPLE 181-200: 1.5X TO 4X BASIC
*PURPLE 201-210: 3X TO 8X BASIC
181-200 PRINT RUN 50 SERIAL #'d SETS

2003 Playoff Prestige Award Winners

RANDOM INSERTS IN PACKS
SERIAL NUMBERED TO YEAR OF AWARD
1 Barry Zito CY/2002 1.00 2.50
2 Barry Bonds MVP/2001 2.50 6.00
3 Randy Johnson CY/2002 1.50 4.00
4 Roger Clemens CY/2001 2.00 5.00
5 Ichiro Suzuki MVP/2001 2.00 5.00
6 Chipper Jones MVP/1999 1.50 4.00
7 Ken Griffey Jr. MVP/1997 3.00 8.00
8 Miguel Tejada MVP/2002 1.00 2.50
9 Greg Maddux CY/1995 2.00 5.00
10 Jeff Bagwell MVP/1994 1.00 2.50
11 Rickey Henderson MVP/1990 1.50 4.00
12 Tom Glavine CY/1998 1.00 2.50
13 Albert Pujols ROY/2001 2.00 5.00
14 Nomar Garciaparra ROY/1997 1.00 2.50
15 Derek Jeter ROY/1996 4.00 10.00

2003 Playoff Prestige Connections

STATED ODDS 1:8 HOBBY/RETAIL
*PARALLEL 100: 1.5X TO 4X BASIC
PARALLEL 100 PRINT RUN 100 #'d SETS
1 T.Glaus .40 1.00
G.Anderson
2 T.Glaus .40 1.00
T.Salmon
3 R.Johnson 1.00 2.50
C.Schilling
4 M.Williams .40 1.00
L.Gonzalez
5 G.Maddux 1.25 3.00
J.Smoltz
6 A.Jones 1.00 2.50
C.Jones
7 G.Maddux 1.25 3.00
K.Millwood
8 T.Batista .40 1.00
G.Gil
9 P.Martinez .60 1.50
N.Garciaparra
10 M.Ramirez 1.00 2.50
N.Garciaparra
11 N.Garciaparra 1.00 2.50
R.Henderson
12 T.Nixon 1.00 2.50
M.Ramirez
13 K.Wood .60 1.50
M.Prior
14 S.Sosa 1.00 2.50
F.McGriff
15 S.Sosa 1.00 2.50
C.Patterson
16 F.Thomas 1.00 2.50
M.Ordonez
17 J.Borchard .60 1.50
M.Ordonez
18 A.Dunn .60 1.50
A.Kearns
19 B.Larkin 2.00 5.00
K.Griffey Jr.
20 A.Dunn .60 1.50
B.Larkin
21 A.Dunn 2.00 5.00
K.Griffey Jr.
22 V.Martinez .60 1.50
O.Vizquel
23 C.Sabathia .60 1.50
V.Martinez
24 L.Walker .60 1.50
T.Helton
25 C.Pena .60 1.50
R.Fick
26 J.Beckett .40 1.00
J.Encarnacion
27 J.Bagwell .60 1.50
C.Biggio
28 L.Berkman .60 1.50
R.Oswalt
29 L.Berkman .60 1.50
J.Bagwell
30 M.Sweeney .60 1.50
C.Beltran
31 M.Sweeney .40 1.00
A.Berroa
32 K.Ishii .40 1.00
S.Green
33 A.Beltre 1.00 2.50
S.Green
34 K.Ishii 1.00 2.50
H.Nomo
35 R.Sexson .40 1.00
B.Sheets
36 J.Jones .40 1.00
I.Hunter
37 D.Mientkiewicz 1.00 2.50
D.Ortiz
38 V.Guerrero .60 1.50
J.Vidro
39 D.Jeter 2.50 6.00
J.Giambi
40 D.Jeter 2.50 6.00
B.Williams
41 R.Clemens 1.25 3.00
M.Mussina
42 A.Soriano .60 1.50
J.Posada
43 D.Jeter 2.50 6.00
A.Soriano
44 M.Piazza 1.00 2.50
R.Alomar
45 M.Piazza 1.00 2.50
M.Vaughn
46 E.Chavez .60 1.50
M.Tejada
47 M.Mulder .60 1.50
B.Zito
48 T.Hudson .60 1.50
B.Zito
49 P.Burrell .40 1.00
B.Abreu
50 J.Thome .60 1.50
P.Burrell
51 J.Thome .60 1.50
M.Byrd
52 B.Giles .40 1.00
A.Ramirez
53 R.Klesko .40 1.00
P.Nevin
54 B.Bonds 1.50 4.00
B.Santiago
55 J.Kent .40 1.00
R.Aurilia
56 B.Bonds 1.50 4.00
J.Kent
57 I.Suzuki 1.25 3.00
K.Sasaki
58 E.Martinez .60 1.50
J.Olerud
59 A.Pujols 1.25 3.00
S.Rolen
60 J.Edmonds .60 1.50
J.Drew
61 A.Pujols 1.25 3.00
J.Edmonds
62 D.Brazelton .40 1.00
J.Kennedy
63 A.Rodriguez 1.25 3.00
I.Rodriguez
64 J.Gonzalez .60 1.50
R.Palmeiro
65 M.Teixeira .60 1.50
H.Blalock
66 A.Rodriguez 1.25 3.00
R.Palmeiro
67 A.Rodriguez 1.25 3.00
J.Gonzalez
68 S.Stewart .40 1.00
C.Delgado
69 J.Phelps .40 1.00
E.Hinske
70 V.Wells .60 1.50
R.Halladay

2003 Playoff Prestige Connections Materials

RANDOM INSERTS IN PACKS
STATED PRINT RUN 400 SERIAL #'d SETS
1 Glaus Jsy/G.Anderson Bat 1.50 4.00
2 T.Glaus Jsy/T.Salmon Bat 1.50 4.00
4 M.Williams Jsy/L.Gonz Bat 1.50 4.00
5 G.Maddux Jsy/J.Smoltz Jsy 5.00 12.00
6 A.Jones Bat/C.Jones Bat 4.00 10.00
7 Maddux Jsy/Millwood Jsy 5.00 12.00
8 T.Batista Jsy/G.Gil Bat 1.50 4.00
9 P.Martinez Jsy/Nomar Jsy 2.50 6.00
10 M.Ramirez Bat/Nomar Bat 4.00 10.00
11 Nomar Bat/Rickey Bat 4.00 10.00
12 T.Nixon Bat/M.Ramirez Bat 4.00 10.00
13 K.Wood Jsy/M.Prior Jsy 2.50 6.00
14 S.Sosa Base/F.McGriff Base 4.00 10.00
15 Sosa Base/Patterson Base 4.00 10.00
16 F.Thomas Jsy/Magglio Jsy 4.00 10.00
17 J.Borchard Jsy/Magglio Bat 2.50 6.00
18 A.Dunn Bat/A.Kearns Jsy 2.50 6.00
20 A.Dunn Jsy/B.Larkin Bat 2.50 6.00
22 V.Martinez Bat/Vizquel Bat 2.50 6.00
23 C.Sabathia Jsy/V.Mart Bat 2.50 6.00
24 L.Walker Jsy/T.Helton Bat 2.50 6.00
26 J.Beckett Jsy/J.Encarn Bat 1.50 4.00
27 Bagwell Pants/Biggio Pants 2.50 6.00
28 L.Berkman Jsy/R.Oswalt Jsy 2.50 6.00
29 Berkman Jsy/Bagwell Pants 2.50 6.00
30 Sweeney Bat/Beltran Bat 2.50 6.00
31 Sweeney Bat/Berroa Pants 1.50 4.00
32 K.Ishii Jsy/S.Green Bat 1.50 4.00
33 A.Beltre Bat/S.Green Jsy 4.00 10.00
34 K.Ishii Jsy/H.Nomo Jsy 4.00 10.00
35 R.Sexson Jsy/B.Sheets Jsy 1.50 4.00
36 J.Jones Jsy/T.Hunter Bat 1.50 4.00
37 Mientkiewicz Bat/D.Ortiz Jsy 4.00 10.00
38 V.Guerrero Bat/J.Vidro Jsy 2.50 6.00
39 D.Jeter Base/J.Giambi Bat 10.00 25.00
40 Jeter Base/B.Williams Base 10.00 25.00
41 Clemens Jsy/Mussina Jsy 5.00 12.00
42 A.Soriano Jsy/J.Posada Jsy 2.50 6.00
43 Jeter Base/Soriano Base 10.00 25.00
44 M.Piazza Bat/R.Alomar Jsy 4.00 10.00
45 M.Piazza Bat/M.Vaughn Bat 4.00 10.00
46 E.Chavez Jsy/M.Tejada Jsy 2.50 6.00
47 M.Mulder Jsy/B.Zito Jsy 2.50 6.00
48 T.Hudson Jsy/B.Zito Jsy 2.50 6.00
49 P.Burrell Bat/B.Abreu Bat 1.50 4.00
50 J.Thome Bat/P.Burrell Bat 2.50 6.00
51 J.Thome Bat/M.Byrd Jsy 1.50 4.00
52 B.Giles Bat/A.Ramirez Jsy 1.50 4.00
53 R.Klesko Jsy/P.Nevin Jsy 1.50 4.00
54 Bonds Base/Santiago Base 6.00 15.00
55 J.Kent Jsy/R.Aurilia Jsy 1.50 4.00
56 B.Bonds Base/J.Kent Base 6.00 15.00
57 I.Suzuki Base/K.Sasaki Base 5.00 12.00
58 E.Martinez Bat/J.Olerud Jsy 2.50 6.00
59 A.Pujols Base/S.Rolen Base 5.00 12.00
60 J.Edmonds Bat/J.Drew Jsy 2.50 6.00
61 Pujols Base/Edmonds Base 5.00 12.00
62 Brazelton Jsy/Kennedy Jsy 1.50 4.00
63 A.Rod Jsy/I.Rod Bat 5.00 12.00
64 J.Gonz Pants/Raffy Pants 2.50 6.00
65 Teixeira Bat/Blalock Bat 2.50 6.00
66 A.Rod Jsy/Palmeiro Pants 5.00 12.00
67 A.Rod Bat/J.Gonz Pants 5.00 12.00
68 Stewart Bat/Delgado Jsy 1.50 4.00
69 J.Phelps Bat/E.Hinske Bat 1.50 4.00
70 V.Wells Jsy/R.Halladay Jsy 2.50 6.00

2003 Playoff Prestige Diamond Heritage

STATED ODDS 1:21 HOBBY, 1:43 RETAIL
*GOLDEN: 1.25X TO 3X BASIC
GOLDEN PRINT RUN 50 SERIAL #'d SETS
1 Larry Walker .60 1.50
2 Troy Glaus .40 1.00
3 Magglio Ordonez .60 1.50
4 Roy Oswalt .60 1.50
5 Barry Zito .60 1.50
6 Nomar Garciaparra .60 1.50
7 Kerry Wood .40 1.00
8 Roger Clemens 1.25 3.00
9 Pedro Martinez .60 1.50
10 Mark Prior .60 1.50
11 Sammy Sosa 1.00 2.50
12 Randy Johnson 1.00 2.50
13 Greg Maddux 1.25 3.00
14 Manny Ramirez 1.00 2.50
15 Torii Hunter .40 1.00
16 Alex Rodriguez 1.25 3.00
17 Mike Piazza 1.00 2.50
18 Vladimir Guerrero .60 1.50
19 Ivan Rodriguez .60 1.50
20 Lance Berkman .60 1.50
21 Miguel Tejada .60 1.50
22 Chipper Jones 1.00 2.50
23 Todd Helton .60 1.50
24 Shawn Green .40 1.00
25 Scott Rolen .60 1.50
26 Adam Dunn .60 1.50
27 Jim Thome .60 1.50
28 Rafael Palmeiro .60 1.50
29 Eric Chavez .40 1.00
30 Andruw Jones .40 1.00

2003 Playoff Prestige Diamond Heritage Material

*MULTI-COLOR PATCH 1-15: 1X TO 1.5X HI
JERSEY PRINT RUN 200 SERIAL #'d SETS
BAT PRINT RUN 100 SERIAL #'d SETS
1 Larry Walker Jsy 3.00 8.00
2 Troy Glaus Jsy 3.00 8.00
3 Magglio Ordonez Jsy 3.00 8.00
4 Roy Oswalt Jsy 3.00 8.00
5 Barry Zito Jsy 3.00 8.00
6 Nomar Garciaparra Jsy 6.00 15.00
7 Kerry Wood Jsy 3.00 8.00
8 Roger Clemens Jsy 8.00 20.00
9 Pedro Martinez Jsy 4.00 10.00
10 Mark Prior Jsy 4.00 10.00
11 Sammy Sosa Jsy 4.00 10.00
12 Randy Johnson Jsy 4.00 10.00
13 Greg Maddux Jsy 6.00 15.00
14 Manny Ramirez Jsy 4.00 10.00
15 Torii Hunter Jsy 3.00 8.00
16 Alex Rodriguez Bat 8.00 20.00
17 Mike Piazza Bat 6.00 15.00
18 Vladimir Guerrero Bat 6.00 15.00
19 Ivan Rodriguez Bat 6.00 15.00
20 Lance Berkman Bat 4.00 10.00
21 Miguel Tejada Bat 4.00 10.00
22 Chipper Jones Bat 6.00 15.00
23 Todd Helton Bat 6.00 15.00
24 Shawn Green Bat 4.00 10.00
25 Scott Rolen Bat 6.00 15.00
26 Adam Dunn Bat 4.00 10.00
27 Jim Thome Bat 6.00 15.00
28 Rafael Palmeiro Bat 6.00 15.00
29 Eric Chavez Bat 4.00 10.00
30 Andruw Jones Bat 6.00 15.00

2003 Playoff Prestige Draft Class Reunion

STATED ODDS 1:24 HOBBY, 1:42 RETAIL
1 M.Piazza 1.00 2.50
J.Olerud
2 D.Jeter 2.50 6.00
S.Stewart
3 A.Rodriguez 1.25 3.00
T.Hunter
4 N.Garciaparra .60 1.50
P.Konerko
5 K.Wood .60 1.50
T.Helton
6 E.Chavez .40 1.00
B.Koch
7 L.Berkman .60 1.50
T.Glaus
8 P.Burrell .40 1.00
M.Mulder
9 B.Zito .60 1.50
J.Jennings
10 M.Prior .60 1.50
M.Teixeira

2003 Playoff Prestige Infield/Outfield Tandems Materials

RANDOM INSERTS IN PACKS
STATED PRINT RUN 100 SERIAL #'d SETS
1 Glaus Jsy/G.Anderson Bat 4.00 10.00
2 M.Grace Bat/L.Gonz Jsy 6.00 15.00
3 Nomar Jsy/M.Ramirez Jsy 10.00 25.00
4 Soriano Jsy/B.Williams Jsy 6.00 15.00
5 Bagwell Jsy/Berkman Jsy 6.00 15.00
6 A.Rod Jsy/J.Gonz Jsy 10.00 25.00
7 B.Larkin Jsy/A.Dunn Jsy 4.00 10.00
8 Rolen Bat/Edmonds Jsy 10.00 25.00
9 T.Helton Jsy/L.Walker Jsy 6.00 15.00
10 A.Beltre Jsy/S.Green Jsy 4.00 10.00
11 J.Vidro Jsy/V.Guerrero Jsy 6.00 15.00
12 Sweeney Jsy/Beltran Jsy 4.00 10.00
13 J.Phelps Jsy/V.Wells Jsy 4.00 10.00
14 Konerko Jsy/Ordonez Jsy 4.00 10.00
15 P.Nevin Jsy/R.Klesko Jsy 4.00 10.00

2003 Playoff Prestige Inside the Numbers

STATED PRINT RUN 2002 SERIAL #'d SETS
*DIE CUT p/r 45-75: 2X TO 5X BASIC
*DIE CUT p/r 27-38: 2.5X TO 6X BASIC
DIE CUT PRINT RUN BASED ON UNIFORM
NO DIE CUT PRICING ON QTY OF 25 OR LESS
1 Roger Clemens 2.00 5.00
2 Greg Maddux 2.00 5.00
3 Miguel Tejada 1.00 2.50
4 Alex Rodriguez 2.00 5.00
5 Ichiro Suzuki 2.00 5.00
6 Sammy Sosa 1.50 4.00
7 Jim Thome 1.00 2.50
8 Derek Jeter 4.00 10.00
9 Randy Johnson 1.50 4.00
10 Barry Zito 1.00 2.50
11 Jason Giambi .60 1.50
12 Shawn Green .60 1.50
13 Curt Schilling 1.00 2.50
14 Albert Pujols 2.00 5.00
15 Vladimir Guerrero 1.00 2.50
16 Pedro Martinez 1.00 2.50
17 Alfonso Soriano 1.00 2.50
18 Barry Bonds 2.50 6.00
19 Magglio Ordonez 1.00 2.50
20 Chipper Jones 1.50 4.00
21 Pat Burrell .60 1.50
22 Luis Gonzalez .60 1.50
23 Jeff Bagwell 1.00 2.50
24 Garret Anderson .60 1.50
25 Larry Walker 1.00 2.50

2003 Playoff Prestige League Leaders

RANDOM INSERTS IN PACKS
STATED PRINT RUN 2002 SERIAL #'d SETS
1 Manny Ramirez AVG 1.50 4.00
2 Sammy Sosa HR 1.50 4.00
3 Alex Rodriguez RBI 2.00 5.00
4 Alfonso Soriano Runs 1.00 2.50
5 Vladimir Guerrero Hits 1.00 2.50
6 Nomar Garciaparra 2B 1.00 2.50
7 Johnny Damon 3B 1.00 2.50
8 Alfonso Soriano SB 1.00 2.50
9 Barry Bonds Walks 2.50 6.00
10 Barry Zito Wins 1.00 2.50
11 Pedro Martinez ERA 1.00 2.50
12 John Smoltz SV 1.50 4.00
13 Randy Johnson CG 1.50 4.00
14 Lance Berkman RBI 1.00 2.50
15 Randy Johnson SO 1.50 4.00

2003 Playoff Prestige League Leaders Materials

RANDOM INSERTS IN PACKS
STATED PRINT RUN 250 SERIAL #'d SETS
1 Manny Ramirez AVG Jsy 4.00 10.00
2 Sammy Sosa HR Base 4.00 10.00
3 Alex Rodriguez RBI Jsy 6.00 15.00
4 Alfonso Soriano Runs Jsy 3.00 8.00
5 Vladimir Guerrero Hits Jsy 4.00 10.00
6 Nomar Garciaparra 2B Jsy 8.00 20.00
7 Johnny Damon 3B Bat 4.00 10.00
8 Alfonso Soriano SB Jsy 3.00 8.00
9 Barry Bonds Walks Base 6.00 15.00
10 Barry Zito Wins Jsy 3.00 8.00
11 Pedro Martinez ERA Jsy 4.00 10.00
12 John Smoltz SV Jsy 4.00 10.00
13 Randy Johnson CG Jsy 4.00 10.00
14 Lance Berkman RBI Jsy 3.00 8.00
15 Randy Johnson SO Jsy 4.00 10.00

2003 Playoff Prestige Player Collection

*MULTI-COLOR PATCH: 1.25X TO 3X HI
RANDOM INSERTS IN PACKS
STATED PRINT RUN 325 SERIAL #'d SETS
CARDS LISTED ALPHABETICALLY
1 Roberto Alomar Bat 4.00 10.00
2 Jeff Bagwell Bat 4.00 10.00
3 Jeff Bagwell Jsy 4.00 10.00
4 Jeff Bagwell Pants 4.00 10.00
5 Jay Bell Jsy 3.00 8.00
6 Adrian Beltre Jsy 3.00 8.00
7 Lance Berkman Jsy 3.00 8.00
8 Craig Biggio Bat 4.00 10.00
9 Craig Biggio Jsy 4.00 10.00
10 Bret Boone Jsy 3.00 8.00
11 Joe Borchard Jsy 3.00 8.00
12 Kevin Brown Jsy 3.00 8.00
13 Jeromy Burnitz Jsy 3.00 8.00
14 Pat Burrell Bat 3.00 8.00
15 Marlon Byrd Bat 3.00 8.00
16 Marlon Byrd Jsy 3.00 8.00
17 Roger Clemens Stand Jsy 6.00 15.00

18 Roger Clemens Throw Jsy 6.00 15.00
19 Doug Davis Jsy 3.00 8.00
20 Carlos Delgado Jsy 3.00 8.00
21 J.D. Drew Jsy 3.00 8.00
22 Adam Dunn Jsy 3.00 8.00
23 Jim Edmonds Jsy 3.00 8.00
24 Steve Finley Jsy 3.00 8.00
25 Freddy Garcia Jsy 3.00 8.00
26 Nomar Garciaparra Jsy 6.00 15.00
27 Jason Giambi Bat 3.00 8.00
28 Jason Giambi Jsy 3.00 8.00
29 Troy Glaus Jsy 3.00 8.00
30 Juan Gonzalez Bat 3.00 8.00
31 Juan Gonzalez Jsy 3.00 8.00
32 Luis Gonzalez Bat 3.00 8.00
33 Shawn Green Jsy 3.00 8.00
34 Ben Grieve Jsy 3.00 8.00
35 Vladimir Guerrero Jsy 4.00 10.00
36 Tony Gwynn Jsy 8.00 20.00
37 Toby Hall Jsy 3.00 8.00
38 Wes Helms Jsy 3.00 8.00
39 Todd Helton Bat 4.00 10.00
40 Todd Helton Jsy 8.00 20.00
41 Rickey Henderson Bat 8.00 20.00
42 Rickey Henderson Jsy 8.00 20.00
43 Rickey Henderson Pants 8.00 20.00
44 Tim Hudson Jsy 3.00 8.00
45 Jason Jennings Jsy 3.00 8.00
46 Andruw Jones Bat 4.00 10.00
47 Andruw Jones Jsy 4.00 10.00
48 Chipper Jones Jsy 4.00 10.00
49 Ryan Klesko Jsy 3.00 8.00
50 Paul Konerko Jsy 3.00 8.00
51 Barry Larkin Bat 4.00 10.00
52 Barry Larkin Jsy 4.00 10.00
53 Travis Lee Jsy 3.00 8.00
54 Paul Lo Duca Jsy 3.00 8.00
55 Terrence Long Jsy 3.00 8.00
56 Pedro Martinez Jsy 4.00 10.00
57 Joe Mays Jsy 3.00 8.00
58 Mark Mulder Jsy 3.00 8.00
59 John Olerud Jsy 3.00 8.00
60 Magglio Ordonez Bat 3.00 8.00
61 Magglio Ordonez Jsy 3.00 8.00
62 Roy Oswalt Jsy 3.00 8.00
63 Rafael Palmeiro Pants 4.00 10.00
64 Chan Ho Park Jsy 3.00 8.00
65 Jay Payton Jsy 3.00 8.00
66 Robert Person Jsy 3.00 8.00
67 Andy Pettitte Jsy 4.00 10.00
68 Mike Piazza Bat 4.00 10.00
69 Mike Piazza Jsy 4.00 10.00
70 Mark Prior Bat 4.00 10.00
71 Mark Prior Jsy 4.00 10.00
72 Manny Ramirez Bat 4.00 10.00
73 Manny Ramirez Jsy 4.00 10.00
74 Cal Ripken Jsy 10.00 25.00
75 Alex Rodriguez Bat 4.00 10.00
76 Alex Rodriguez M's Jsy 4.00 10.00
77 Alex Rodriguez Rgr Jsy 4.00 10.00
78 Ivan Rodriguez Bat 4.00 10.00
79 Ivan Rodriguez Jsy 4.00 10.00
80 C.C. Sabathia Jsy 3.00 8.00
81 Reggie Sanders Jsy 3.00 8.00
82 Kazuhiro Sasaki Jsy 3.00 8.00
83 Curt Schilling Jsy 3.00 8.00
84 Richie Sexson Jsy 3.00 8.00
85 Tsuyoshi Shinjo Jsy 3.00 8.00
86 Alfonso Soriano Bat 3.00 8.00
87 Alfonso Soriano Jsy 3.00 8.00
88 Sammy Sosa Jsy 4.00 10.00
89 Miguel Tejada Jsy 3.00 8.00
90 Frank Thomas Jsy 4.00 10.00
91 Jim Thome Jsy 6.00 15.00
92 Larry Walker Bat 3.00 8.00
93 Larry Walker Jsy 3.00 8.00
94 David Wells Jsy 3.00 8.00
95 Vernon Wells Jsy 3.00 8.00
96 Bernie Williams Jsy 4.00 10.00
97 Matt Williams Jsy 3.00 8.00
98 Preston Wilson Jsy 3.00 8.00
99 Kerry Wood Jsy 3.00 8.00
100 Barry Zito Jsy 3.00 8.00

2003 Playoff Prestige Signature Impressions

PRINT RUNS B/WN 5-100 COPIES PER CARD
NO PRICING ON QTY OF 25 OR LESS
SEE BECKETT.COM FOR FULL CHECKLIST
1 A.J. Pierzynski/50 10.00 25.00
28 Joe Kennedy/50 6.00 15.00
30 Lenny Dykstra/50 10.00 25.00
39 Toby Hall/50 6.00 15.00
50 Jeremy Bonderman/100 20.00 50.00

2003 Playoff Prestige Stars of MLB Jersey

RANDOM INSERTS IN PACKS
STATED PRINT RUN 150 SERIAL #'d SETS
1 Roger Clemens 8.00 20.00
2 Randy Johnson 4.00 10.00
3 Sammy Sosa 4.00 10.00
4 Vladimir Guerrero 4.00 10.00
5 Lance Berkman 3.00 8.00
6 Alfonso Soriano 3.00 8.00
7 Alex Rodriguez 6.00 15.00
8 Roberto Alomar 4.00 10.00
9 Miguel Tejada 3.00 8.00
10 Pedro Martinez 4.00 10.00
11 Greg Maddux 6.00 15.00
12 Barry Zito 3.00 8.00
13 Magglio Ordonez 3.00 8.00
14 Chipper Jones 4.00 10.00
15 Manny Ramirez 4.00 10.00
16 Troy Glaus 3.00 8.00
17 Pat Burrell 3.00 8.00
18 Roy Oswalt 3.00 8.00
19 Mike Piazza 6.00 15.00
20 Nomar Garciaparra 8.00 20.00

2004 Playoff Prestige

COMPLETE SET (200) 10.00 25.00
COMMON CARD (1-200) .15 .40
COMMON PROSPECT .15 .40
PROSPECTS ARE NOT SHORT-PRINTED
1 Bengie Molina .15 .40
2 Garret Anderson .15 .40
3 Jarrod Washburn .15 .40
4 Scott Spiezio .15 .40
5 Tim Salmon .15 .40
6 Troy Glaus .15 .40
7 Alex Cintron .15 .40
8 Brandon Webb .15 .40
9 Curt Schilling .25 .60
10 Edgar Gonzalez PROS .15 .40
11 Luis Gonzalez .15 .40
12 Randy Johnson .40 1.00
13 Steve Finley .15 .40
14 Andruw Jones .15 .40
15 Bubba Nelson PROS .15 .40
16 Chipper Jones .40 1.00
17 Gary Sheffield .15 .40
18 Greg Maddux .50 1.25
19 Javy Lopez .15 .40
20 John Smoltz .40 1.00
21 Marcus Giles .15 .40
22 Rafael Furcal .15 .40
23 Brian Roberts .15 .40
24 Jason Johnson .15 .40
25 Jay Gibbons .15 .40
26 Luis Matos .15 .40
27 Melvin Mora .15 .40
28 Tony Batista .15 .40
29 Bill Mueller .15 .40
30 David Ortiz .40 1.00
31 Johnny Damon .25 .60
32 Kevin Youkilis PROS .15 .40
33 Manny Ramirez .40 1.00
34 Nomar Garciaparra .25 .60
35 Pedro Martinez .25 .60
36 Trot Nixon .15 .40
37 Aramis Ramirez .15 .40
38 Brendan Harris PROS .15 .40
39 Carlos Zambrano .25 .60
40 Corey Patterson .15 .40
41 Kenny Lofton .15 .40
42 Kerry Wood .15 .40
43 Mark Prior .25 .60
44 Sammy Sosa .40 1.00
45 Bartolo Colon .15 .40
46 Carlos Lee .15 .40
47 Esteban Loaiza .15 .40
48 Frank Thomas .40 1.00
49 Joe Crede .15 .40
50 Magglio Ordonez .25 .60
51 Roberto Alomar .25 .60
52 Adam Dunn .25 .60
53 Austin Kearns .15 .40
54 Josh Hall .15 .40
55 Ken Griffey Jr. .75 2.00
56 Sean Casey .15 .40
57 Mike Nakamura .15 .40
58 C.C. Sabathia .25 .60
59 Casey Blake .15 .40
60 Jody Gerut .15 .40
61 Matt Lawton .15 .40
62 Milton Bradley .15 .40
63 Omar Vizquel .25 .60
64 Jason Jennings .15 .40
65 Jay Payton .15 .40
66 Larry Walker .25 .60
67 Preston Wilson .15 .40
68 Todd Helton .25 .60
69 Bobby Higginson .15 .40
70 Carlos Pena .25 .60
71 Dmitri Young .15 .40
72 Jeremy Bonderman .15 .40
73 Preston Larrison PROS .15 .40
74 Derrek Lee .15 .40
75 Dontrelle Willis .15 .40
76 Ivan Rodriguez .25 .60
77 Josh Beckett .15 .40
78 Juan Pierre .15 .40
79 Miguel Cabrera .40 1.00
80 Mike Lowell .15 .40
81 Chris Burke PROS .15 .40
82 Craig Biggio .25 .60
83 Jeff Bagwell .25 .60
84 Jeff Kent .15 .40
85 Lance Berkman .25 .60
86 Richard Hidalgo .15 .40
87 Roy Oswalt .25 .60
88 Aaron Guiel .15 .40
89 Angel Berroa .15 .40
90 Carlos Beltran .25 .60
91 Jeremy Affeldt .15 .40
92 Mike Sweeney .15 .40
93 Runelvys Hernandez .15 .40
94 Dave Roberts .25 .60
95 Eric Gagne .15 .40
96 Hideo Nomo .40 1.00
97 Kevin Brown .15 .40
98 Paul Lo Duca .15 .40
99 Shawn Green .15 .40
100 Ben Sheets .15 .40
101 Geoff Jenkins .15 .40
102 Richie Sexson .15 .40
103 Rickie Weeks PROS .15 .40
104 Scott Podsednik .15 .40
105 J.D. Durbin PROS .15 .40
106 Jacque Jones .15 .40
107 Jason Kubel PROS .15 .40
108 Shannon Stewart .15 .40
109 Torii Hunter .15 .40
110 Chad Cordero PROS .15 .40
111 Javier Vazquez .15 .40
112 Jose Vidro .15 .40
113 Livan Hernandez .15 .40
114 Orlando Cabrera .15 .40
115 Tony Armas Jr. .15 .40
116 Vladimir Guerrero .25 .60
117 Al Leiter .15 .40
118 Cliff Floyd .15 .40
119 Jae Weong Seo .15 .40
120 Jose Reyes .25 .60
121 Mike Piazza .40 1.00
122 Tom Glavine .25 .60
123 Aaron Boone .15 .40
124 Alfonso Soriano .25 .60
125 Andy Pettitte .25 .60
126 Derek Jeter 1.00 2.50
127 Hideki Matsui .60 1.50
128 Jason Giambi .15 .40
129 Jorge Posada .25 .60
130 Jose Contreras .15 .40
131 Mike Mussina .25 .60
132 Barry Zito .25 .60
133 Eric Byrnes .15 .40
134 Eric Chavez .15 .40
135 Jose Guillen .15 .40
136 Mark Mulder .15 .40
137 Miguel Tejada .25 .60
138 Ramon Hernandez .15 .40
139 Rich Harden .15 .40
140 Tim Hudson .25 .60
141 Bobby Abreu .15 .40
142 Brett Myers .15 .40
143 Jim Thome .25 .60
144 Kevin Millwood .15 .40
145 Mike Lieberthal .15 .40
146 Ryan Howard PROS .30 .75
147 Craig Wilson .15 .40
148 Jack Wilson .15 .40
149 Jason Kendall .15 .40
150 Kip Wells .15 .40
151 Reggie Sanders .15 .40
152 Albert Pujols .50 1.25
153 Edgar Renteria .15 .40
154 Jim Edmonds .25 .60
155 Matt Morris .15 .40
156 Scott Rolen .25 .60
157 Tino Martinez .25 .60
158 Woody Williams .15 .40
159 Brian Giles .15 .40
160 Freddy Guzman PROS RC .15 .40
161 Jake Peavy .15 .40
162 Khalil Greene PROS .25 .60
163 Phil Nevin .15 .40
164 Ryan Klesko .15 .40
165 Ray Durham .15 .40
166 Jason Schmidt .15 .40
167 Jerome Williams PROS .15 .40
168 Jesse Foppert .15 .40
169 Jose Cruz Jr. .15 .40
170 Marquis Grissom .15 .40
171 Merkin Valdez PROS RC .15 .40
172 Rich Aurilia .15 .40
173 Bret Boone .15 .40
174 Freddy Garcia .15 .40
175 Ichiro Suzuki .50 1.25
176 Jamie Moyer .15 .40
177 John Olerud .15 .40
178 Mike Cameron .15 .40
179 Randy Winn .15 .40
180 Aubrey Huff .15 .40
181 Carl Crawford .25 .60
182 Chad Gaudin PROS .15 .40
183 Rocco Baldelli .15 .40
184 Toby Hall .15 .40
185 Travis Lee .15 .40
186 Alex Rodriguez .50 1.25
187 Hank Blalock .15 .40
188 John Thomson .15 .40
189 Juan Gonzalez .15 .40
190 Mark Teixeira .25 .60
191 Michael Young .15 .40
192 Rafael Palmeiro .25 .60
193 Ramon Nivar PROS .15 .40
194 Carlos Delgado .15 .40
195 Dustin McGowan PROS .15 .40
196 Frank Catalanotto .15 .40
197 Vinny Chulk .15 .40
198 Orlando Hudson .15 .40
199 Roy Halladay .25 .60
200 Vernon Wells .15 .40

2004 Playoff Prestige Autographs

RANDOM INSERTS IN PACKS
PRINT RUNS B/WN 4-500 COPIES PER
PRINT RUNS PROVIDED BY DONRUSS
CARDS ARE NOT SERIAL-NUMBERED
SEE BECKETT.COM OPG FOR PRINT RUNS
NO PRICING ON QTY OF 25 OR LESS
8 Brandon Webb/100 4.00 10.00
10 Edgar Gonzalez PROS/150 4.00 10.00
15 Bubba Nelson PROS/250 4.00 10.00
25 Jay Gibbons/50 5.00 12.00
32 Kevin Youkilis PROS/100 6.00 15.00
38 Brendan Harris PROS/400 4.00 10.00
57 Mike Nakamura/250 4.00 10.00
60 Jody Gerut/50 5.00 12.00
73 Preston Larrison PROS/250 4.00 10.00
79 Miguel Cabrera/100 20.00 50.00
81 Chris Burke PROS/250 6.00 15.00
93 Runelvys Hernandez/50 5.00 12.00
105 J.D. Durbin PROS/500 4.00 10.00
106 Jacque Jones/50 5.00 12.00
107 Jason Kubel PROS/400 4.00 10.00
108 Shannon Stewart/50 5.00 12.00
133 Eric Byrnes/50 5.00 12.00
139 Rich Harden/50 8.00 20.00
146 Ryan Howard PROS/400 12.50 30.00
193 Ramon Nivar PROS/100 4.00 10.00
195 Dustin McGowan PROS/100 4.00 10.00
197 Vinny Chulk/112 4.00 10.00
198 Orlando Hudson/100 4.00 10.00

2004 Playoff Prestige Xtra Bases Black

*XB BLACK: 5X TO 12X BASIC
*XB BLACK: 5X TO 12X BASIC PROS
RANDOM INSERTS IN HOBBY PACKS
STATED PRINT RUN 75 SERIAL #'d SETS

2004 Playoff Prestige Xtra Bases Green

*XB GREEN: 3X TO 8X BASIC
*XB GREEN: 3X TO 8X BASIC PROS
RANDOM INSERTS IN RETAIL PACKS
STATED PRINT RUN 150 SERIAL #'d SETS

2004 Playoff Prestige Xtra Bases Green Autographs

RANDOM INSERTS IN RETAIL PACKS
STATED PRINT RUN 100 SERIAL #'d SETS
10 Edgar Gonzalez PROS 4.00 10.00
15 Bubba Nelson PROS 4.00 10.00
38 Brendan Harris PROS 4.00 10.00
57 Mike Nakamura 4.00 10.00
81 Chris Burke PROS 6.00 15.00
105 J.D. Durbin PROS 4.00 10.00
107 Jason Kubel PROS 4.00 10.00
146 Ryan Howard PROS 20.00 50.00
195 Dustin McGowan PROS 4.00 10.00

2004 Playoff Prestige Xtra Bases Purple

*XB PURPLE: 3X TO 8X BASIC
*XB PURPLE: 3X TO 8X BASIC PROS
RANDOM INSERTS IN HOBBY PACKS
STATED PRINT RUN 150 SERIAL #'d SETS

2004 Playoff Prestige Xtra Bases Purple Autographs

RANDOM INSERTS IN HOBBY PACKS
STATED PRINT RUN 100 SERIAL #'d SETS
10 Edgar Gonzalez PROS 4.00 10.00
15 Bubba Nelson PROS 4.00 10.00
32 Kevin Youkilis PROS 4.00 10.00
38 Brendan Harris PROS 4.00 10.00
57 Mike Nakamura 4.00 10.00
73 Preston Larrison PROS 4.00 10.00
79 Miguel Cabrera 12.50 30.00
81 Chris Burke PROS 6.00 15.00
105 J.D. Durbin PROS 4.00 10.00
107 Jason Kubel PROS 4.00 10.00
146 Ryan Howard PROS 20.00 50.00
193 Ramon Nivar PROS 4.00 10.00
195 Dustin McGowan PROS 4.00 10.00
198 Orlando Hudson 4.00 10.00

2004 Playoff Prestige Achievements

STATED ODDS 1:8
1 Hideo Nomo 95 ROY 1.00 2.50
2 Don Mattingly 85 MVP 2.00 5.00
3 Roger Clemens 86 CY MVP 1.25 3.00
4 Greg Maddux 95 CY 1.25 3.00
5 Stan Musial 43 MVP 1.50 4.00
6 Roberto Clemente 66 MVP 2.50 6.00
7 Derek Jeter 96 ROY 2.50 6.00
8 Albert Pujols 01 ROY 1.25 3.00
9 Cal Ripken 91 MVP 3.00 8.00
10 George Brett 80 MVP 2.00 5.00
11 Carl Yastrzemski 67 MVP 1.00 2.50
12 Rickey Henderson 90 MVP 1.00 2.50
13 Sammy Sosa 98 MVP 1.00 2.50
14 Randy Johnson 02 CY 1.00 2.50
15 Bob Gibson 68 CY MVP .60 1.50

2004 Playoff Prestige Changing Stripes

STATED ODDS 1:11
*FOIL: .75X TO 2X BASIC
FOIL PRINT RUN 150 SERIAL #'d SETS
*HOLO-FOIL: 1.5X TO 4X BASIC
HOLO-FOIL PRINT RUN 50 SERIAL #'d SETS
FOIL/HOLO-FOIL RANDOM IN PACKS
1 Rickey Henderson A's-Yanks 1.00 2.50
2 Mike Mussina O's-Yanks .60 1.50
3 Jim Thome Indians-Phils .60 1.50
4 Hideo Nomo Sox-Dodgers 1.00 2.50
5 Scott Rolen Phils-Cards .60 1.50
6 Jason Giambi A's-Yanks .40 1.00
7 R.Johnson Astros-D'backs 1.00 2.50
8 Shawn Green Jays-Dodgers .40 1.00
9 Curt Schilling Phils-D'backs .60 1.50
10 Alex Rodriguez M's-Rangers 1.25 3.00
11 Greg Maddux Cubs-Braves 1.25 3.00
12 Randy Johnson M's-Astros 1.00 2.50
13 Hideo Nomo Dodgers-Mets 1.00 2.50
14 Ivan Rodriguez Rgr-Marlins .60 1.50
15 Juan Gonzalez Indians-Rangers .40 1.00
16 Manny Ramirez Indians-Sox 1.00 2.50
17 Mike Piazza Dodgers-Mets 1.00 2.50
18 Nolan Ryan Angels-Astros 3.00 8.00
19 Nolan Ryan Astros-Rangers 3.00 8.00
20 Pedro Martinez Expos-Sox .60 1.50
21 Reg Jackson Yanks-Angels .60 1.50
22 Roberto Alomar Mets-Sox .60 1.50
23 Rod Carew Twins-Angels .60 1.50
24 Roger Clemens Sox-Yanks 1.25 3.00
25 Sammy Sosa Sox-Cubs 1.00 2.50

2004 Playoff Prestige Changing Stripes Dual Jersey

STATED PRINT RUN 150 SERIAL #'d SETS
PRIME PRINT RUN 25 SERIAL #'d SETS
NO PRIME PRICING DUE TO SCARCITY
1 Rickey Henderson A's-Yanks 6.00 15.00
2 Mike Mussina O's-Yanks 6.00 15.00
3 Jim Thome Indians-Phils 6.00 15.00
4 Hideo Nomo Sox-Dodgers 10.00 25.00
5 Scott Rolen Phils-Cards 6.00 15.00
6 Jason Giambi A's-Yanks 4.00 10.00
7 R.Johnson Astros-D'backs 6.00 15.00
8 Shawn Green Jays-Dodgers 4.00 10.00
9 Curt Schilling Phils-D'backs 4.00 10.00
10 Alex Rodriguez M's-Rangers 6.00 15.00
12 Randy Johnson M's-Astros 6.00 15.00
13 Hideo Nomo Dodgers-Mets 10.00 25.00
14 Ivan Rodriguez Rgr-Marlins 6.00 15.00
15 Juan Gonzalez Indians-Rangers 4.00 10.00
16 Manny Ramirez Indians-Sox 6.00 15.00
17 Mike Piazza Dodgers-Mets 6.00 15.00
18 Nolan Ryan Angels-Astros 10.00 25.00
19 Nolan Ryan Astros-Rangers 10.00 25.00
20 Pedro Martinez Expos-Sox 6.00 15.00
22 Roberto Alomar Mets-Sox 6.00 15.00
23 Rod Carew Twins-Angels 6.00 15.00
24 Roger Clemens Sox-Yanks 8.00 20.00
25 Sammy Sosa Sox-Cubs 6.00 15.00

2004 Playoff Prestige Connections

STATED ODDS 1:9
*FOIL: 1.5X TO 4X BASIC
FOIL PRINT RUN 100 SERIAL #'d SETS
HOLO-FOIL PRINT RUN 21 SERIAL #'d SETS
NO HOLO-FOIL PRICING DUE TO SCARCITY
FOIL/HOLO-FOIL RANDOM IN PACKS
1 D.Jeter A.Soriano 2.50 6.00
2 G.Maddux C.Jones 1.25 3.00
3 A.Pujols S.Rolen 1.25 3.00
4 R.Johnson C.Schilling 1.00 2.50
5 N.Garciaparra M.Ramirez 1.00 2.50
6 A.Rodriguez M.Teixeira 1.25 3.00
7 B.Zito T.Hudson .60 1.50
8 S.Sosa M.Prior 1.00 2.50
9 D.Jeter J.Giambi 2.50 6.00
10 R.Clemens M.Mussina 1.25 3.00
11 M.Prior K.Wood .60 1.50
12 A.Rodriguez H.Blalock 1.25 3.00
13 F.Thomas M.Ordonez 1.00 2.50
14 N.Garciaparra P.Martinez .60 1.50
15 C.Delgado V.Wells .40 1.00
16 M.Tejada E.Chavez .60 1.50
17 J.Bagwell L.Berkman .60 1.50
18 J.Thome B.Abreu .60 1.50
19 T.Helton P.Wilson .60 1.50
20 V.Guerrero J.Vazquez .60 1.50

2004 Playoff Prestige Connections Material

RANDOM INSERTS IN PACKS
STATED PRINT RUN 250 SERIAL #'d SETS
1 Jeter Bat/Soriano Bat 10.00 25.00
2 Maddux Bat/Chipper Jsy 6.00 15.00
3 Pujols Bat/Rolen Bat 8.00 20.00
4 Randy Bat/Schilling Bat 6.00 15.00
5 Nomar Bat/Manny Bat 6.00 15.00
6 A.Rod Bat/Teixeira Bat 6.00 15.00
7 Zito Bat/Hudson Bat 4.00 10.00
8 Sosa Bat/Prior Bat 6.00 15.00
9 Jeter Bat/Giambi Bat 10.00 25.00
10 Clemens Jsy/Mussina Bat 8.00 20.00
11 Prior Bat/Wood Bat 6.00 15.00
12 A.Rod Bat/Blalock Bat 6.00 15.00
13 Thomas Bat/Magglio Bat 6.00 15.00
14 Nomar Bat/Pedro Bat 10.00 25.00
15 Delgado Bat/V.Wells Bat 4.00 10.00
16 Tejada Bat/Chavez Bat 4.00 10.00
17 Bagwell Bat/Berkman Bat 6.00 15.00
18 Thome Jsy/Abreu Bat 6.00 15.00
19 Helton Bat/P.Wilson Bat 6.00 15.00
20 Guerrero Bat/Vazquez Jsy 6.00 15.00

2004 Playoff Prestige Diamond Heritage

STATED ODDS 1:13
1 Mike Piazza 1.00 2.50
2 Greg Maddux 1.25 3.00
3 Nomar Garciaparra .60 1.50
4 Chipper Jones 1.00 2.50
5 Albert Pujols 1.25 3.00
6 Derek Jeter 2.50 6.00
7 Shawn Green .40 1.00
8 Alex Rodriguez 1.25 3.00
9 Jim Thome .60 1.50
10 Jason Giambi .40 1.00
11 Sammy Sosa 1.00 2.50
12 Hank Blalock .40 1.00
13 Garret Anderson .40 1.00
14 Manny Ramirez 1.00 2.50
15 Scott Rolen .60 1.50
16 Jeff Bagwell .60 1.50
17 Randy Johnson 1.00 2.50
18 Ichiro Suzuki 1.25 3.00
19 Ivan Rodriguez .60 1.50
20 Alfonso Soriano .60 1.50

2004 Playoff Prestige Diamond Heritage Material

STATED ODDS 1:92
1 Mike Piazza Bat 6.00 15.00
2 Greg Maddux Bat 6.00 15.00
3 Nomar Garciaparra Bat 6.00 15.00
4 Chipper Jones Jsy 4.00 10.00
5 Albert Pujols Bat 8.00 20.00
6 Derek Jeter Jsy 10.00 25.00
7 Shawn Green Bat 3.00 8.00
8 Alex Rodriguez Bat 6.00 15.00
9 Jim Thome Jsy 4.00 10.00
10 Jason Giambi Bat 3.00 8.00
11 Sammy Sosa Bat 4.00 10.00
12 Hank Blalock Bat 3.00 8.00
13 Garret Anderson Bat 3.00 8.00
14 Manny Ramirez Bat 4.00 10.00
15 Scott Rolen Bat 4.00 10.00
16 Jeff Bagwell Bat 4.00 10.00
17 Randy Johnson Bat 4.00 10.00
19 Ivan Rodriguez Bat 4.00 10.00
20 Alfonso Soriano Bat 3.00 8.00

2004 Playoff Prestige League Leaders Single

STATED ODDS 1:18
*FOIL: 1.5X TO 4X BASIC
FOIL PRINT RUN 100 SERIAL #'d SETS
HOLO-FOIL PRINT RUN 25 SERIAL #'d SETS
NO HOLO-FOIL PRICING DUE TO SCARCITY
FOIL/HOLO-FOIL RANDOM IN PACKS
1 Alex Rodriguez AL HR 1.25 3.00
2 Albert Pujols NL Hit 1.25 3.00
3 Albert Pujols NL Avg 1.25 3.00
4 Nomar Garciaparra AL Hit .60 1.50
5 Mark Prior NL ERA .60 1.50
6 Pedro Martinez AL ERA .60 1.50
7 Kerry Wood NL SO .40 1.00
8 Derek Jeter AL Avg 2.50 6.00
9 Jason Giambi AL BB .40 1.00
10 Roger Clemens AL SO 1.25 3.00

2004 Playoff Prestige League Leaders Single Material

RANDOM INSERTS IN PACKS
STATED PRINT RUN 250 SERIAL #'d SETS
1 Alex Rodriguez AL HR Bat 4.00 10.00
2 Albert Pujols NL Hit Bat 6.00 15.00
3 Albert Pujols NL Avg Bat 6.00 15.00
4 Nomar Garciaparra AL Hit Bat 4.00 10.00
5 Mark Prior NL ERA Jsy 4.00 10.00
6 Pedro Martinez AL ERA Jsy 4.00 10.00
7 Kerry Wood NL SO Jsy 3.00 8.00
8 Derek Jeter AL Avg Jsy 8.00 20.00
9 Jason Giambi AL BB Jsy 3.00 8.00

2004 Playoff Prestige League Leaders Double

STATED PRINT RUN 500 SERIAL #'d SETS
*FOIL: .75X TO 2X BASIC
FOIL PRINT RUN 75 SERIAL #'d SETS
HOLO-FOIL PRINT RUN 10 SERIAL #'d SETS
NO HOLO-FOIL PRICING DUE TO SCARCITY
1 A.Rodriguez J.Thome HR 2.00 5.00
2 M.Prior P.Martinez ERA 1.00 2.50
3 R.Clemens K.Wood SO 2.00 5.00
4 N.Garciaparra A.Pujols Hit 2.00 5.00
5 D.Jeter A.Pujols Avg 4.00 10.00

2004 Playoff Prestige League Leaders Double Material

RANDOM INSERTS IN PACKS
STATED PRINT RUN 100 SERIAL #'d SETS
1 A.Rod Bat/Thome Bat HR 10.00 25.00
2 Prior Jsy/Pedro Jsy ERA 10.00 25.00
3 Clemens Jsy/Wood Jsy SO 12.50 30.00
4 Nomar Bat/Pujols Bat Hits 12.50 30.00
5 Jeter Jsy/Pujols Bat Avg 15.00 40.00

2004 Playoff Prestige League Leaders Quad

STATED PRINT RUN 250 SERIAL #'d SETS
*FOIL: .75X TO 2X BASIC
FOIL PRINT RUN 50 SERIAL #'d SETS
HOLO-FOIL PRINT RUN 5 SERIAL #'d SETS
NO HOLO-FOIL PRICING DUE TO SCARCITY
1 Pujols Helton Renteria Shef 2.00 5.00
2 Jeter Manny Nomar Ichiro 4.00 10.00
3 Prior Schill Nomo K.Brown 1.50 4.00
4 Sexson Sosa Pujols Thome 2.00 5.00
5 A.Rod Thomas Giambi Delg 2.00 5.00

2004 Playoff Prestige League Leaders Quad Material

RANDOM INSERTS IN PACKS
STATED PRINT RUN 50 SERIAL #'d SETS
1 Pujols/Helton/Renteria/Sheff 15.00 40.00
3 Prior/Schill/Nomo/K.Brown 15.00 40.00
4 Sexson/Sosa/Pujols/Thome 20.00 50.00
5 A.Rod/Thomas/Giambi/Delg 15.00 40.00

2004 Playoff Prestige Players Collection Jersey

STATED ODDS 1:79
*PLATINUM: .75X TO 2X BASIC
PLATINUM RANDOM INSERTS IN PACKS
PLATINUM PRINT RUN 50 SERIAL #'d SETS
1 Adam Dunn AS 2.00 5.00
2 Adam Dunn Gray 2.00 5.00
3 Adam Dunn White 2.00 5.00
4 Alex Rodriguez M's 4.00 10.00
5 Alex Rodriguez Rgr AS 4.00 10.00
6 Alex Rodriguez Rgr Blue 4.00 10.00
7 Alex Rodriguez Rgr White 4.00 10.00
8 Andruw Jones Home 3.00 8.00
9 Andruw Jones Road 3.00 8.00
10 Austin Kearns 2.00 5.00
11 Brandon Webb 2.00 5.00
12 C.C. Sabathia 2.00 5.00
13 Cal Ripken 15.00 40.00
14 Carlos Beltran 2.00 5.00
15 Carlos Delgado 2.00 5.00
16 Carlos Lee 2.00 5.00
17 Chipper Jones Home 3.00 8.00
18 Chipper Jones Road 3.00 8.00
19 Craig Biggio 3.00 8.00
20 Curt Schilling 2.00 5.00
21 David Wells 2.00 5.00
22 Don Mattingly 6.00 15.00
23 Dontrelle Willis 3.00 8.00
24 Frank Thomas Black 3.00 8.00
25 Frank Thomas White 3.00 8.00
26 Fred McGriff 3.00 8.00
27 Garret Anderson AS 2.00 5.00
28 Gary Sheffield Braves 2.00 5.00
29 Gary Sheffield Dodgers 2.00 5.00
30 Greg Maddux Gray 4.00 10.00
31 Hank Blalock Home 2.00 5.00
32 Hank Blalock Road 2.00 5.00
33 Hee Seop Choi 2.00 5.00
34 Hideo Nomo Mets 3.00 8.00
35 Hideo Nomo Dodgers Gray 3.00 8.00
36 Hideo Nomo Dodgers White 3.00 8.00
37 Ivan Rodriguez Marlins 3.00 8.00
38 Ivan Rodriguez Rgr 3.00 8.00
39 Jason Giambi Home 2.00 5.00
40 Jim Edmonds 2.00 5.00
41 Jim Thome 3.00 8.00
42 John Olerud 2.00 5.00
43 John Smoltz 3.00 8.00
44 Josh Beckett 2.00 5.00
45 Josh Phelps 2.00 5.00
46 Juan Gonzalez Rgr 2.00 5.00
47 Juan Gonzalez Indians 2.00 5.00
48 Kazuhisa Ishii 2.00 5.00
49 Lance Berkman White 2.00 5.00
50 Larry Walker Home 2.00 5.00
51 Larry Walker Road 2.00 5.00
52 Luis Gonzalez AS 2.00 5.00
53 Magglio Ordonez Home 2.00 5.00
54 Magglio Ordonez Road 2.00 5.00
55 Manny Ramirez 3.00 8.00
56 Manny Ramirez AS 3.00 8.00
57 Mark Prior Home 3.00 8.00
58 Mark Prior Road 3.00 8.00
59 Mark Teixeira 3.00 8.00
60 Mike Mussina 3.00 8.00
61 Mike Piazza AS 4.00 10.00
62 Mike Piazza Black 4.00 10.00
63 Mike Piazza White 4.00 10.00
64 Nomar Garciaparra Gray 4.00 10.00
65 Nomar Garciaparra White 4.00 10.00
66 Pat Burrell 2.00 5.00
67 Paul Konerko 2.00 5.00
68 Paul Lo Duca 2.00 5.00
69 Pedro Martinez 3.00 8.00
70 Rafael Furcal 2.00 5.00
71 Rafael Palmeiro Blue 3.00 8.00
72 Rafael Palmeiro Gray 3.00 8.00
73 Ramon Hernandez 2.00 5.00
74 Rickey Henderson 3.00 8.00
75 Rickey Henderson Black 3.00 8.00
76 Rickey Henderson White 3.00 8.00
77 Roberto Alomar Indians 3.00 8.00
78 Roberto Alomar Mets 3.00 8.00
79 Robin Ventura AS 2.00 5.00
80 Roger Clemens Away 6.00 15.00
81 Roger Clemens Home 6.00 15.00
82 Roy Halladay 2.00 5.00
83 Sammy Sosa AS 3.00 8.00
84 Sammy Sosa Gray 3.00 8.00
85 Sammy Sosa White 3.00 8.00
86 Scott Rolen 3.00 8.00
87 Shannon Stewart 2.00 5.00
88 Shawn Green Blue 2.00 5.00
89 Shawn Green Gray 2.00 5.00
90 Shawn Green White 2.00 5.00
91 Terrence Long 2.00 5.00
92 Tim Hudson 2.00 5.00
93 Todd Helton Away 3.00 8.00
94 Todd Helton Home 3.00 8.00
95 Tom Glavine Braves 3.00 8.00
96 Tom Glavine Mets 3.00 8.00
97 Torii Hunter 2.00 5.00
98 Vernon Wells 2.00 5.00
99 Vladimir Guerrero 3.00 8.00
100 Vladimir Guerrero AS 3.00 8.00

2004 Playoff Prestige Prestigious Pros

STATED ODDS 1:23
1 Mark Prior .60 1.50
2 Derek Jeter 2.50 6.00
3 Mike Mussina .60 1.50
4 Nomar Garciaparra .60 1.50
5 Roger Clemens 1.25 3.00
6 Jason Giambi .40 1.00
7 Randy Johnson 1.00 2.50
8 Rafael Palmeiro .60 1.50
9 Barry Zito .60 1.50
10 Pat Burrell .40 1.00

2004 Playoff Prestige Stars of MLB

STATED ODDS 1:36
*FOIL: .75X TO 2X BASIC
FOIL PRINT RUN 100 SERIAL #'d SETS
HOLO-FOIL PRINT RUN 25 SERIAL #'d SETS
NO HOLO-FOIL PRICING DUE TO SCARCITY
FOIL/HOLO-FOIL RANDOM IN PACKS
1 Albert Pujols 1.25 3.00
2 Derek Jeter 2.50 6.00
3 Mike Piazza 1.00 2.50
4 Greg Maddux 1.25 3.00
5 Ichiro Suzuki 1.25 3.00
6 Nomar Garciaparra .60 1.50
7 Ivan Rodriguez .60 1.50
8 Randy Johnson 1.00 2.50
9 Alex Rodriguez 1.25 3.00
10 Sammy Sosa 1.00 2.50
11 Alfonso Soriano .60 1.50
12 Vladimir Guerrero .60 1.50
13 Jason Giambi .40 1.00
14 Mark Prior .60 1.50
15 Chipper Jones 1.00 2.50

2004 Playoff Prestige Stars of MLB Jersey

STATED PRINT RUN 250 SERIAL #'d SETS
*PRIME: 1X TO 2.5X BASIC
PRIME PRINT RUN 50 SERIAL #'d SETS
RANDOM INSERTS IN PACKS
1 Albert Pujols 6.00 15.00
2 Derek Jeter 8.00 20.00
3 Mike Piazza 4.00 10.00
4 Greg Maddux 4.00 10.00
6 Nomar Garciaparra 4.00 10.00
7 Ivan Rodriguez 4.00 10.00
8 Randy Johnson 4.00 10.00
9 Alex Rodriguez 4.00 10.00
10 Sammy Sosa 4.00 10.00
11 Alfonso Soriano 3.00 8.00
12 Vladimir Guerrero 4.00 10.00
13 Jason Giambi 3.00 8.00
14 Mark Prior 4.00 10.00
15 Chipper Jones 4.00 10.00

2005 Playoff Prestige

COMPLETE SET (200) 15.00 40.00
COMMON CARD (1-185) .15 .40
COMMON RC (1-185) .30 .75
COMMON CARD (186-200) .20 .50
1 Rafael Furcal .15 .40
2 Derek Jeter 1.00 2.50
3 Edgar Renteria .15 .40
4 Jeff Bagwell .25 .60
5 Nomar Garciaparra .25 .60
6 Melvin Mora .15 .40
7 Craig Biggio .25 .60
8 Brad Penny .15 .40
9 Hank Blalock .15 .40
10 Vernon Wells .15 .40
11 Gary Sheffield .15 .40
12 Jeff Kent .15 .40
13 Carl Crawford .25 .60
14 Paul Konerko .25 .60
15 Carlos Beltran .25 .60
16 Garret Anderson .15 .40
17 Todd Helton .25 .60
18 Javy Lopez .15 .40
19 Mike Lowell .15 .40
20 Robb Quinlan .15 .40
21 Andy Pettitte .25 .60
22 Roger Clemens .50 1.25
23 Mark Teixeira .25 .60
24 Miguel Cabrera .40 1.00

25 Andruw Jones .15 .40
26 Josh Beckett .15 .40
27 Scott Rolen .25 .60
28 J.J. Putz .15 .40
29 Adrian Beltre .40 1.00
30 Magglio Ordonez .25 .60
31 Mike Piazza .40 1.00
32 Danny Graves .15 .40
33 Larry Walker .25 .60
34 Kerry Wood .15 .40
35 Mike Mussina .25 .60
36 Joe Nathan .15 .40
37 Chone Figgins .15 .40
38 Curt Schilling .25 .60
39 Brett Myers .15 .40
40 Jae Weong Seo .15 .40
41 Danny Kolb .15 .40
42 Mariano Rivera .50 1.25
43 Francisco Cordero .15 .40
44 Adam Dunn .25 .60
45 Pedro Martinez .25 .60
46 Frank Thomas .40 1.00
47 Tom Glavine .25 .60
48 Torii Hunter .15 .40
49 Ben Sheets .15 .40
50 Shawn Green .15 .40
51 Randy Johnson .40 1.00
52 C.C. Sabathia .25 .60
53 Bobby Abreu .15 .40
54 Octavio Dotel .15 .40
55 Hideki Matsui .60 1.50
56 Mark Buehrle .25 .60
57 Johan Santana .25 .60
58 Brandon Inge .15 .40
59 Dewon Brazelton .15 .40
60 Ryan Wagner .15 .40
61 Kevin Brown .15 .40
62 Laynce Nix .15 .40
63 Jason Bay .15 .40
64 J.D. Drew .15 .40
65 Jacque Jones .15 .40
66 Jason Schmidt .15 .40
67 Joe Kennedy .15 .40
68 Miguel Tejada .25 .60
69 Hideo Nomo .40 1.00
70 Michael Young .15 .40
71 Lyle Overbay .15 .40
72 Omar Vizquel .25 .60
73 Johnny Estrada .15 .40
74 Khalil Greene .15 .40
75 Barry Zito .25 .60
76 Wilson Valdez .15 .40
77 Nick Green .15 .40
78 Bucky Jacobsen .15 .40
79 Keith Foulke .15 .40
80 Sean Burroughs .15 .40
81 Carlos Zambrano .25 .60
82 Orlando Cabrera .15 .40
83 Shigetoshi Hasegawa .15 .40
84 Troy Glaus .15 .40
85 Mike Sweeney .15 .40
86 Jason Giambi .15 .40
87 Derrek Lee .15 .40
88 Carlos Delgado .15 .40
89 Kazuo Matsui .15 .40
90 Lew Ford .15 .40
91 Akinori Otsuka .15 .40
92 Bobby Crosby .15 .40
93 Jose Reyes .25 .60
94 Jose Vidro .15 .40
95 Shingo Takatsu .15 .40
96 Sean Casey .15 .40
97 Tim Olson .15 .40
98 Jeff Suppan .15 .40
99 Rafael Palmeiro .25 .60
100 Esteban Loaiza .15 .40
101 Brian Roberts .15 .40
102 Jack Wilson .15 .40
103 Eric Chavez .15 .40
104 Eric Milton .15 .40
105 Albert Pujols .50 1.25
106 Jake Peavy .15 .40
107 Ivan Rodriguez .25 .60
108 Chad Cordero .15 .40
109 Jody Gerut .15 .40
110 Chipper Jones .40 1.00
111 Barry Larkin .25 .60
112 Alfonso Soriano .25 .60
113 Alex Rodriguez .50 1.25
114 Paul Lo Duca .15 .40
115 Jim Edmonds .25 .60
116 Aramis Ramirez .15 .40
117 Lance Berkman .25 .60
118 Johnny Damon .25 .60
119 Aubrey Huff .15 .40
120 Mark Mulder .15 .40
121 Sammy Sosa .40 1.00
122 Mark Prior .25 .60
123 Shannon Stewart .15 .40
124 Manny Ramirez .40 1.00
125 Jim Thome .25 .60
126 Doug Devore .15 .40
127 Vladimir Guerrero .25 .60
128 Ken Harvey .15 .40
129 Jacob Cruz .15 .40
130 Ken Griffey Jr. .75 2.00
131 Greg Maddux .50 1.25
132 Derek Lowe .15 .40
133 Craig Monroe .15 .40
134 David Ortiz .40 1.00
135 Dontrelle Willis .15 .40
136 Tom Gordon .15 .40
137 David Dellucci .15 .40
138 Vance Wilson .15 .40
139 Milton Bradley .15 .40
140 Ichiro Suzuki .50 1.25
141 Victor Martinez .25 .60
142 Wade Miller .15 .40
143 Francisco Rodriguez .25 .60
144 Roy Oswalt .25 .60
145 Carlos Lee .15 .40
146 Kazuhisa Ishii .15 .40
147 Tim Hudson .25 .60
148 Travis Hafner .15 .40
149 Jermaine Dye .15 .40
150 Steve Finley .15 .40
151 Justin Verlander RC 6.00 15.00
152 Yadier Molina 1.50 4.00
153 Andy Green .15 .40
154 Nick Swisher .25 .60
155 Clint Nageotte .15 .40
156 Grady Sizemore .25 .60
157 Gavin Floyd .15 .40
158 Josh Kroeger .15 .40
159 Russ Adams .15 .40
160 Jeff Baker .15 .40
161 Dioner Navarro .15 .40
162 Shawn Hill .15 .40
163 Ryan Howard .30 .75
164 Scott Proctor .15 .40
165 Jason Kubel .15 .40
166 Jose Lopez .15 .40
167 Ryan Church .15 .40
168 Yhency Brazoban .15 .40
169 Jeff Francis .15 .40
170 Angel Guzman .15 .40
171 John Van Benschoten .15 .40
172 Adrian Gonzalez .30 .75
173 Casey Kotchman .15 .40
174 David Wright .30 .75
175 B.J. Upton .25 .60
176 Dallas McPherson .15 .40
177 Rene Rivera .15 .40
178 Denny Bautista .15 .40
179 Logan Kensing .15 .40
180 Matt Peterson .15 .40
181 Jeremy Reed .15 .40
182 Jairo Garcia .15 .40
183 Val Majewski .15 .40
184 Victor Diaz .15 .40
185 Dave Krynzel .15 .40
186 Ron Cey .20 .50
187 Bill Madlock .20 .50
188 Dave Stewart .20 .50
189 Billy Ripken .20 .50
190 Gary Carter .30 .75
191 Darryl Strawberry .20 .50
192 Dave Parker .20 .50
193 Ron Guidry .20 .50
194 Gaylord Perry .30 .75
195 Fred Lynn .20 .50
196 Jack Morris .30 .75
197 Steve Garvey .20 .50
198 Andre Dawson .30 .75
199 Nolan Ryan 1.50 4.00
200 Paul Molitor .50 1.25

2005 Playoff Prestige Red Foil

*RED FOIL: 8X TO 20X BASIC
RANDOM INSERTS IN RETAIL PACKS
STATED PRINT RUN 25 SERIAL #'d SETS
NO RC PRICING DUE TO SCARCITY

2005 Playoff Prestige Xtra Bases Black

*BLACK: 8X TO 20X BASIC
RANDOM INSERTS IN PACKS
STATED PRINT RUN 25 SERIAL #'d SETS
NO RC PRICING DUE TO SCARCITY

2005 Playoff Prestige Xtra Bases Green

*GREEN: 5X TO 12X BASIC
*GREEN: 3X TO 8X BASIC RC's
RANDOM INSERTS IN PACKS
STATED PRINT RUN 50 SERIAL #'d SETS

2005 Playoff Prestige Xtra Bases Purple

*PURPLE: 4X TO 10X BASIC
*PURPLE: 2.5X TO 6X BASIC RC's
RANDOM INSERTS IN PACKS
STATED PRINT RUN 100 SERIAL #'d SETS

2005 Playoff Prestige Xtra Bases Red

*RED: 3X TO 8X BASIC
*RED: 2X TO 5X BASIC RC's
RANDOM INSERTS IN PACKS
STATED PRINT RUN 150 SERIAL #'d SETS

2005 Playoff Prestige Autographs

OVERALL AU-GU ODDS 1:12
SP INFO PROVIDED BY DONRUSS
SP's APPROXIMATELY 3X TOUGHER
20 Robb Quinlan 4.00 10.00
28 J.J. Putz 4.00 10.00
58 Brandon Inge SP 6.00 15.00
67 Joe Kennedy 4.00 10.00
76 Wilson Valdez 4.00 10.00
77 Nick Green 4.00 10.00
78 Bucky Jacobsen 4.00 10.00
97 Tim Olson 4.00 10.00
98 Jeff Suppan SP 10.00 25.00
126 Doug Devore 4.00 10.00
129 Jacob Cruz 4.00 10.00
133 Craig Monroe 4.00 10.00
138 Vance Wilson 4.00 10.00
153 Andy Green 4.00 10.00
164 Scott Proctor 4.00 10.00

2005 Playoff Prestige Signature Xtra Bases Black

OVERALL AU-GU ODDS 1:12
PRINT RUNS B/WN 3-10 COPIES PER
NO PRICING DUE TO SCARCITY

2005 Playoff Prestige Signature Xtra Bases Purple

*PURPLE p/r 50: .4X TO 1X AUTO
*PURPLE p/r 50: .4X TO 1X AUTO SP
*PURPLE p/r 25: .6X TO 1.5X AUTO
OVERALL AU-GU ODDS 1:12
PRINT RUNS B/WN 5-50 COPIES PER
NO PRICING ON QTY OF 10 OR LESS
6 Melvin Mora/25 10.00 25.00
8 Brad Penny/50 4.00 10.00
13 Carl Crawford/25 10.00 25.00
32 Danny Graves/50 4.00 10.00
36 Joe Nathan/50 10.00 25.00
37 Chone Figgins/50 4.00 10.00
39 Brett Myers/50 6.00 15.00
41 Danny Kolb/50 4.00 10.00
43 Francisco Cordero/50 4.00 10.00
52 C.C. Sabathia/25 10.00 25.00
54 Octavio Dotel/50 6.00 15.00
56 Mark Buehrle/25 20.00 50.00
59 Dewon Brazelton/50 4.00 10.00
60 Ryan Wagner/50 4.00 10.00
62 Laynce Nix/50 4.00 10.00
63 Jason Bay/50 6.00 15.00
65 Jacque Jones/25 10.00 25.00
71 Lyle Overbay/25 6.00 15.00
73 Johnny Estrada/50 4.00 10.00
79 Keith Foulke/50 10.00 25.00
81 Carlos Zambrano/25 15.00 40.00
82 Orlando Cabrera/25 10.00 25.00
90 Lew Ford/50 4.00 10.00
92 Bobby Crosby/50 6.00 15.00
100 Esteban Loaiza/50 6.00 15.00
101 Brian Roberts/50 6.00 15.00
102 Jack Wilson/50 6.00 15.00
106 Jake Peavy/25 5.00 12.00
108 Chad Cordero/50 6.00 15.00
109 Jody Gerut/25 6.00 15.00
128 Ken Harvey/50 4.00 10.00
136 Tom Gordon/50 6.00 15.00
137 David Dellucci/50 10.00 25.00
139 Milton Bradley/50 6.00 15.00
141 Victor Martinez/25 10.00 25.00
142 Wade Miller/50 6.00 15.00
145 Carlos Lee/25 10.00 25.00
148 Travis Hafner/50 6.00 15.00
149 Jermaine Dye/50 6.00 15.00
152 Yadier Molina/25 150.00 400.00
161 Dioner Navarro/50 6.00 15.00
162 Shawn Hill/50 4.00 10.00
165 Jason Kubel/50 4.00 10.00
168 Yhency Brazoban/50 4.00 10.00
170 Angel Guzman/50 4.00 10.00
172 Adrian Gonzalez/50 10.00 25.00
173 Casey Kotchman/50 6.00 15.00
187 Bill Madlock/25 10.00 25.00
189 Billy Ripken/25 6.00 15.00
190 Gary Carter/25 10.00 25.00
191 Darryl Strawberry/25 10.00 25.00
192 Dave Parker/25 15.00 40.00
195 Fred Lynn/25 10.00 25.00
196 Jack Morris/25 10.00 25.00
198 Andre Dawson/25 10.00 25.00

2005 Playoff Prestige Changing Stripes

COMPLETE SET (25) 10.00 25.00
STATED ODDS 1:8
*FOIL: 1.25X TO 3X BASIC
FOIL PRINT RUN 100 SERIAL #'d SETS
*HOLO-FOIL: 2.5X TO 6X BASIC
HOLO-FOIL PRINT RUN 25 SERIAL #'d SETS
FOIL/HOLO-FOIL RANDOM IN PACKS
1 I.Rod Marlins-Tigers .60 1.50
2 Roger Clemens Yanks-Astros 1.25 3.00
3 Curt Schilling D'backs-Sox .60 1.50
4 Alex Rodriguez Rgr-Yanks 1.25 3.00
5 Greg Maddux Braves-Cubs 1.25 3.00
6 Juan Gonzalez Rgr-Royals .40 1.00
7 Pedro Martinez Dgr-Expos .60 1.50
8 Roberto Alomar Indians-Mets .60 1.50
9 Randy Johnson Expos-M's 1.00 2.50
10 Ken Griffey Jr. M's-Reds 2.00 5.00
11 Carlos Beltran Royals-Astros .60 1.50
12 Andy Pettitte Yanks-Astros .60 1.50
13 Tom Glavine Braves-Mets .60 1.50
14 Miguel Tejada A's-O's .60 1.50
15 Alfonso Soriano Yanks-Rgr .60 1.50
16 Shannon Stewart Jays-Twins .40 1.00
17 Nomar Garciaparra Sox-Cubs .60 1.50
18 Jeff Kent Giants-Astros .40 1.00
19 David Ortiz Twins-Sox 1.00 2.50
20 Sean Casey Indians-Reds .40 1.00
21 Rickey Henderson Mets-M's 1.00 2.50
22 Carlton Fisk R.Sox-W.Sox .60 1.50
23 Phil Niekro Braves-Yanks .60 1.50
24 Dale Murphy Braves-Phils 1.00 2.50
25 Reggie Jackson A's-Yanks .60 1.50

2005 Playoff Prestige Changing Stripes Material Dual Jersey

OVERALL AU-GU ODDS 1:12
PRINT RUNS B/WN 12-250 COPIES PER
NO PRICING ON QTY OF 12
1 I.Rod Marlins-Tigers/250 6.00 15.00
2 R.Clemens Yanks-Astros/50 10.00 25.00
3 C.Schilling D'backs-Sox/250 6.00 15.00
6 J.Gonzalez Rgr-Royals/250 4.00 10.00
7 P.Martinez Dgr-Expos/100 8.00 20.00
8 R.Alomar Indians-Mets/250 6.00 15.00
9 R.Johnson Expos-M's/100 8.00 20.00
11 C.Beltran Royals-Astros/100 5.00 12.00
12 A.Pettitte Yanks-Astros/250 6.00 15.00
13 T.Glavine Braves-Mets/50 10.00 25.00
14 M.Tejada A's-O's/250 4.00 10.00
15 A.Soriano Yanks-Rgr/100 5.00 12.00
16 S.Stewart Jays-Twins/100 5.00 12.00
19 D.Ortiz Twins-Sox/100 8.00 20.00
20 S.Casey Indians-Reds/50 6.00 15.00
21 R.Henderson Mets-M's/250 8.00 28.00
22 C.Fisk R.Sox-W.Sox Jkt/250 8.00 20.00
23 P.Niekro Braves-Yanks/250 5.00 12.00
24 D.Murphy Braves-Phils/250 8.00 20.00
25 R.Jack A's Jkt-Yanks/100 10.00 25.00

2005 Playoff Prestige Changing Stripes Material Dual Jersey Prime

*PRIME p/r 25: 1.25X TO 3X JSY p/r 250
*PRIME p/r 25: 1X TO 2.5X JSY p/r 100
*PRIME p/r 25: .75X TO 2X JSY p/r 50
OVERALL AU-GU ODDS 1:12
PRINT RUNS B/WN 10-25 COPIES PER
NO PRICING ON QTY OF 10
5 G.Maddux Braves-Cubs/25 20.00 50.00

2005 Playoff Prestige Connections

COMPLETE SET (25) 10.00 25.00
STATED ODDS 1:8
*FOIL: 1.5X TO 4X BASIC
FOIL PRINT RUN 100 SERIAL #'d SETS
*HOLO-FOIL: 3X TO 8X BASIC
HOLO-FOIL PRINT RUN 25 SERIAL #'d SETS
FOIL/HOLO-FOIL RANDOM IN PACKS
1 J.Beckett .40 1.00
D.Willis
2 A.Jones 1.00 2.50
C.Jones
3 K.Matsui .60 1.50
J.Reyes
4 B.Abreu .60 1.50
J.Thome
5 J.Bagwell .60 1.50
L.Berkman
6 R.Clemens 1.25 3.00
R.Oswalt
7 S.Rolen .60 1.50
L.Walker
8 A.Pujols 1.25 3.00
J.Edmonds
9 G.Maddux 1.25 3.00
S.Sosa
10 M.Prior .60 1.50
N.Garciaparra
11 B.Larkin .60 1.50
S.Casey
12 S.Green 1.00 2.50
A.Beltre
13 A.Rodriguez 2.50 6.00
D.Jeter
14 J.Varitek 1.00 2.50
M.Ramirez
15 M.Tejada .60 1.50
J.Lopez
16 B.Upton .60 1.50
C.Crawford
17 F.Thomas 1.00 2.50
P.Konerko
18 J.Mauer .75 2.00
J.Morneau
19 V.Martinez .60 1.50
J.Gerut
20 B.Crosby .60 1.50
B.Zito
21 M.Teixeira .60 1.50
H.Blalock
22 R.Jackson .60 1.50
R.Carew
23 R.Henderson 1.25 3.00
T.Gwynn
24 T.Seaver 1.00 2.50
J.Bench
25 D.Mattingly 2.00 5.00
D.Righetti

2005 Playoff Prestige Connections Material Dual Bat

*BAT p/r 250: .4X TO 1X JSY p/r 250
*BAT p/r 250: .3X TO .8X JSY p/r 100
*BAT p/r 100: .5X TO 1.2X JSY p/r 250
*BAT p/r 100: .4X TO 1X JSY p/r 100
*BAT p/r 100: .3X TO .8X JSY p/r 50
OVERALL AU-GU ODDS 1:12
PRINT RUNS B/WN 25-250 COPIES PER
10 M.Prior/N.Garciaparra/100 6.00 15.00
19 V.Martinez/J.Gerut/25 6.00 15.00

2005 Playoff Prestige Connections Material Dual Jersey

PRINT RUNS B/WN 10-250 COPIES PER
NO PRICING ON QTY OF 10
*PRIME p/r 25: 1X TO 2.5X JSY p/r 250
*PRIME p/r 25: .75X TO 2X JSY p/r 100
PRIME PRINT RUNS B/WN 10-25 PER
NO PRIME PRICING ON QTY OF 10
OVERALL AU-GU ODDS 1:12
1 J.Beckett/D.Willis 3.00 8.00
2 A.Jones/C.Jones 5.00 12.00
3 K.Matsui/J.Reyes 6.00 15.00
4 B.Abreu/J.Thome 5.00 12.00
5 J.Bagwell/L.Berkman 5.00 12.00
6 R.Clemens/R.Oswalt 6.00 15.00
8 A.Pujols/J.Edmonds 10.00 25.00
11 B.Larkin/S.Casey 8.00 20.00
12 S.Green/A.Beltre 3.00 8.00
14 J.Varitek/M.Ramirez 8.00 20.00
15 M.Tejada/J.Lopez 5.00 12.00
17 F.Thom Pants/Konerko 5.00 12.00
20 B.Crosby/B.Zito 3.00 8.00
21 M.Teixeira/H.Blalock 6.00 15.00
22 R.Jackson/R.Carew Jkt 6.00 15.00
23 T.Gwynn/R.Henderson 10.00 25.00
24 T.Seaver/J.Bench Pants 8.00 20.00
25 D.Mattingly/D.Righetti 12.50 30.00

2005 Playoff Prestige Diamond Heritage

STATED ODDS 1:12
1 Pedro Martinez .60 1.50
2 Mark Teixeira .60 1.50
3 Lance Berkman .60 1.50
4 Vladimir Guerrero .60 1.50
5 Albert Pujols 1.25 3.00
6 Roger Clemens 1.25 3.00
7 Manny Ramirez 1.00 2.50
8 Mike Piazza 1.00 2.50
9 Jim Thome .60 1.50
10 Mark Prior .60 1.50
11 Gary Sheffield .40 1.00
12 Sammy Sosa 1.00 2.50
13 Tim Hudson .60 1.50
14 Hideki Matsui 1.50 4.00
15 Jim Edmonds .60 1.50

2005 Playoff Prestige Diamond Heritage Material Jersey

STATED PRINT RUN 100 SERIAL #'d SETS
*BAT: .4X TO 1X JSY
BAT PRINT RUN 100 SERIAL #'d SETS
OVERALL AU-GU ODDS 1:12
1 Pedro Martinez 4.00 10.00
2 Mark Teixeira 4.00 10.00
3 Lance Berkman 3.00 8.00
4 Vladimir Guerrero 4.00 10.00
5 Albert Pujols 10.00 25.00
6 Roger Clemens 6.00 15.00
7 Manny Ramirez 4.00 10.00
8 Mike Piazza 4.00 10.00
9 Jim Thome 4.00 10.00
10 Mark Prior 4.00 10.00
11 Gary Sheffield 3.00 8.00
12 Sammy Sosa 4.00 10.00
13 Tim Hudson 3.00 8.00
14 Hideki Matsui Pants 10.00 25.00
15 Jim Edmonds 3.00 8.00

2005 Playoff Prestige Fans of the Game

STATED ODDS 1:24
1 Tony Hawk 1.25 3.00
2 Tia Carrere .75 2.00
3 Matthew Modine .75 2.00

2005 Playoff Prestige Fans of the Game Signature Silver

*GOLD: .6X TO 1.2X BASIC
GOLD PRINT RUN 100 SERIAL #'d SETS
*PLATINUM: .75X TO 1.5X BASIC
PLATINUM PRINT RUN 50 SERIAL #'d SETS
OVERALL AU-GU ODDS 1:12
1 Tony Hawk 20.00 50.00
2 Tia Carrere 40.00 80.00
3 Matthew Modine 20.00 50.00

2005 Playoff Prestige League Leaders Single

COMPLETE SET (10) 6.00 15.00
STATED ODDS 1:21
*FOIL: 1.5X TO 4X BASIC
FOIL PRINT RUN 100 SERIAL #'d SETS
*HOLO-FOIL: 3X TO 8X BASIC
HOLO-FOIL PRINT RUN 25 SERIAL #'d SETS
FOIL/HOLO-FOIL RANDOM IN PACKS
1 Gary Sheffield .40 1.00
2 Ben Sheets .40 1.00
3 Adrian Beltre 1.00 2.50
4 Scott Rolen .60 1.50
5 George Brett 2.00 5.00
6 Johan Santana .60 1.50
7 Manny Ramirez 1.00 2.50
8 Cal Ripken 3.00 8.00
9 Carlos Zambrano .60 1.50
10 Tony Gwynn 1.25 3.00

2005 Playoff Prestige League Leaders Single Material Bat

*BAT: .4X TO 1X JSY p/r 250
*BAT: .6X TO 1.5X JSY p/r 50
OVERALL AU-GU ODDS 1:12
STATED PRINT RUN 250 SERIAL #'d SETS

2005 Playoff Prestige League Leaders Single Material Jersey

OVERALL AU-GU ODDS 1:12
PRINT RUNS B/WN 25-250 COPIES PER
1 Gary Sheffield/250 3.00 8.00
2 Ben Sheets/250 3.00 8.00
3 Adrian Beltre/50 4.00 10.00
4 Scott Rolen/250 4.00 10.00
5 George Brett/250 6.00 15.00
6 Johan Santana/25 10.00 25.00
7 Manny Ramirez/250 3.00 8.00
8 Cal Ripken/250 5.00 12.00
9 Carlos Zambrano/250 3.00 8.00
10 Tony Gwynn/250 4.00 10.00

2005 Playoff Prestige League Leaders Double

COMPLETE SET (5) 4.00 10.00
STATED ODDS 1:39
*FOIL: 1.25X TO 3X BASIC
FOIL PRINT RUN 100 SERIAL #'d SETS
*HOLO-FOIL: 2.5X TO 6X BASIC
HOLO-FOIL PRINT RUN 25 SERIAL #'d SETS
FOIL/HOLO-FOIL RANDOM IN PACKS
1 T.Hudson .60 1.50
R.Oswalt
2 I.Rodriguez .60 1.50
T.Helton
3 M.Teixeira .60 1.50
J.Edmonds
4 N.Ryan 3.00 8.00
R.Clemens
5 S.Sosa 1.00 2.50
T.Glaus

2005 Playoff Prestige League Leaders Double Material Bat

OVERALL AU-GU ODDS 1:12
STATED PRINT RUN 250 SERIAL #'d SETS
1 T.Hudson/R.Oswalt 4.00 10.00
2 I.Rodriguez/T.Helton 6.00 15.00
3 M.Teixeira/J.Edmonds 6.00 15.00
4 N.Ryan/R.Clemens 12.50 30.00
5 S.Sosa/T.Glaus 6.00 15.00

2005 Playoff Prestige League Leaders Double Material Jersey

*JSY p/r 250: .4X TO 1X BAT
*JSY p/r 100: .5X TO 1.2X BAT
*JSY p/r 50: .6X TO 1.5X BAT
OVERALL AU-GU ODDS 1:12
PRINT RUNS B/WN 50-250 COPIES PER

2005 Playoff Prestige League Leaders Quad

COMPLETE SET (5) 6.00 15.00
STATED ODDS 1:39
*FOIL: 1X TO 2.5X BASIC
FOIL PRINT RUN 100 SERIAL #'d SETS
*HOLO-FOIL: 2X TO 5X BASIC
HOLO-FOIL PRINT RUN 25 SERIAL #'d SETS
FOIL/HOLO-FOIL RANDOM IN PACKS
1 Boggs 1.00 2.50
Molitor
Tram
Puck
2 Murph 1.50 4.00
Schmidt
Cart
Straw
3 Cans 1.00 2.50
Puck
W.Clark
Straw
4 Pedro 1.25 3.00
K.Brown
Randy
Clem
5 Matt 2.00 5.00
Park
Murray
Murphy

2005 Playoff Prestige League Leaders Quad Material Jersey

STATED PRINT RUN 100 SERIAL #'d SETS
*BAT: .4X TO 1X JSY
BAT PRINT RUN 100 SERIAL #'d SETS
OVERALL AU-GU ODDS 1:12
1 Boggs/Molitor/Tram/Puck 15.00 40.00
2 Mur/Schm/Cart/Straw Pants 15.00 40.00
3 Cans/Puc/Clark/Straw Pants 15.00 40.00
4 Ped/Brow/Randy P/Clem 15.00 40.00
5 Matt/Park/Murray/Murphy 12.00 30.00

2005 Playoff Prestige Playoff Champions Combos Division

*DIVISION: .4X TO 1X WILD CARD
OVERALL PC COMBO ODDS 1:93

2005 Playoff Prestige Playoff Champions Combos Wild Card

WILD CARD STATED ODDS 1:391
*DIVISION COMBO: .4X TO 1X BASIC
*LEAGUE COMBO: .4X TO 1X BASIC
*WORLD SERIES COMBO: .4X TO 1X BASIC
OVERALL PC COMBO ODDS 1:93
EXCHANGE DEADLINE 04/15/06
1 Andruw 2.00 5.00
Chipper
Estrada
2 Cabrera/Beckett/Willis 2.00 5.00
3 Cordero/Wilk/N.Johnson .75 2.00
4 Thome/Abreu/Utley 1.25 3.00
5 Piazza/Matsui/Wright 2.00 5.00
6 Pujols/Rolen/Edmonds 2.50 6.00
7 Wood/Prior/Zambrano 1.25 3.00
8 Sheets/Jenkins/Overbay .75 2.00
9 K.Wells/J.Wilson/Bay .75 2.00
10 Kearns/Dunn/Griffey Jr. 4.00 10.00
11 Bagwell/Berkman/Oswalt 1.25 3.00
12 Jennings/Holliday/Helton 2.00 5.00
13 Gagne/Werth/Bradley 1.25 3.00
14 Cintron/Webb/L.Gonzalez 1.25 3.00
15 J.Schmidt/Alfonzo/Rueter 3.00 8.00
16 Greene/Peavy/Hoffman 1.25 3.00
17 Manny/Schilling/Ortiz 2.00 5.00
18 Tejada/Mora/J.Lopez 1.25 3.00
19 Halladay/Rios/Gross 1.25 3.00
20 A.Rod/Jeter/Matsui 5.00 12.00
21 Upton/Kazmir/Crawford 2.00 5.00
22 Thomas/Takatsu/Rowand 2.00 5.00
23 V.Mart/Sabathia/Hafner 1.25 3.00
24 Torii/Johan/Morneau 1.25 3.00
25 Greinke/Sweeney/Harvey 2.50 6.00
26 I.Rod/Bonderman/C.Guillen 1.25 3.00
27 Harden/Crosby/Zito 1.25 3.00
28 Boone/Ichiro/J.Reed 2.50 6.00
29 M.Young/Teixeira/Blalock 1.25 3.00
30 Guerrero/Erstad/Garret 1.25 3.00

2005 Playoff Prestige Playoff MLB Game-Worn Jersey Collection

STATED ODDS 1:8 EXCEL RETAIL

2005 Playoff Prestige Prestigious Pros Blue

STATED PRINT RUN 900 SERIAL #'d SETS
BLACK PRINT RUN 10 SERIAL #'d SETS
NO BLACK PRICING DUE TO SCARCITY
*BRONZE: 1.25X TO 3X BLUE
BRONZE PRINT RUN 100 SERIAL #'d SETS
*GOLD: 1.5X TO 4X BLUE
GOLD PRINT RUN 50 SERIAL #'d SETS
*GREEN: .75X TO 2X BLUE
GREEN PRINT RUN 350 SERIAL #'d SETS
*ORANGE: .6X TO 1.5X BLUE
ORANGE PRINT RUN 500 SERIAL #'d SETS
*PLATINUM: 2.5X TO 6X BLUE
PLATINUM PRINT RUN 25 SERIAL #'d SETS
*PURPLE: 1X TO 2.5X BLUE
PURPLE PRINT RUN 200 SERIAL #'d SETS
*RED: .5X TO 1.2X BLUE
RED PRINT RUN 700 SERIAL #'d SETS
*SILVER: 1.25X TO 3X BLUE
SILVER PRINT RUN 75 SERIAL #'d SETS
1 Ozzie Smith 1.25 3.00
2 Derek Jeter 2.50 6.00
3 Eric Chavez .40 1.00
4 Paul Molitor 1.00 2.50
5 Jeff Bagwell .60 1.50
6 Melvin Mora .40 1.00
7 Craig Biggio .60 1.50
8 Cal Ripken 3.00 8.00
9 Hank Blalock .40 1.00
10 Miguel Tejada .60 1.50
11 Jacque Jones .40 1.00
12 Alfonso Soriano .60 1.50
13 Omar Vizquel .60 1.50
14 Paul Konerko .60 1.50
15 Tim Hudson .60 1.50
16 Garret Anderson .40 1.00
17 Lance Berkman .60 1.50
18 Randy Johnson 1.00 2.50
19 Robin Yount 1.00 2.50
20 Mark Mulder .40 1.00
21 Sean Casey .40 1.00
22 Jim Palmer .60 1.50
23 Don Mattingly 2.00 5.00
24 Manny Ramirez 1.00 2.50
25 Rafael Palmeiro .60 1.50
26 Vernon Wells .40 1.00
27 Vladimir Guerrero .60 1.50
28 Ken Harvey .40 1.00
29 Rod Carew .60 1.50
30 Nolan Ryan 3.00 8.00
31 Mike Piazza 1.00 2.50
32 Steve Carlton .60 1.50
33 Miguel Cabrera 1.00 2.50
34 Kerry Wood .40 1.00
35 Mike Mussina .60 1.50
36 Gaylord Perry .60 1.50
37 Gary Sheffield .40 1.00
38 Curt Schilling .60 1.50
39 Don Sutton .60 1.50
40 Roger Clemens 1.25 3.00
41 Victor Martinez .60 1.50
42 Jason Giambi .40 1.00
43 Dennis Eckersley .60 1.50
44 Adam Dunn .60 1.50
45 Pedro Martinez .60 1.50
46 Tony Perez .60 1.50
47 Tom Glavine .60 1.50
48 Torii Hunter .40 1.00
49 Hideo Nomo 1.00 2.50
50 Scott Rolen .60 1.50
51 Ichiro Suzuki 1.25 3.00
52 C.C. Sabathia .60 1.50
53 George Brett 2.00 5.00
54 David Ortiz 1.00 2.50
55 Hideki Matsui 1.50 4.00
56 Nomar Garciaparra .60 1.50
57 Johan Santana .60 1.50
58 Phil Niekro .60 1.50
59 Dontrelle Willis .40 1.00
60 Magglio Ordonez .60 1.50
61 Livan Hernandez .40 1.00
62 Edgar Renteria .40 1.00
63 Todd Helton .60 1.50
64 Carlos Beltran .60 1.50
65 Sammy Sosa 1.00 2.50
66 Albert Pujols 1.25 3.00
67 Mike Lowell .40 1.00
68 Mark Prior .60 1.50
69 Ivan Rodriguez .60 1.50
70 Jake Peavy .40 1.00
71 Jim Thome .60 1.50
72 Mark Teixeira .60 1.50
73 Shawn Green .40 1.00
74 Rollie Fingers .60 1.50
75 Barry Zito .60 1.50
76 Jose Vidro .40 1.00
77 Ben Sheets .40 1.00
78 Roy Halladay .60 1.50
79 Frank Thomas 1.00 2.50
80 Chipper Jones 1.00 2.50
81 Jason Bay .40 1.00
82 Tony Gwynn 1.25 3.00
83 Shannon Stewart .40 1.00
84 Carl Crawford .60 1.50
85 Andruw Jones .40 1.00
86 Greg Maddux 1.25 3.00
87 Barry Larkin .60 1.50
88 Alex Rodriguez 1.25 3.00
89 Rickey Henderson 1.00 2.50
90 Troy Glaus .40 1.00
91 Roy Oswalt .60 1.50
92 Michael Young .40 1.00
93 Carlos Lee .40 1.00
94 Jim Edmonds .60 1.50
95 Fergie Jenkins .60 1.50
96 Paul Lo Duca .40 1.00
97 Aubrey Huff .40 1.00
98 Ken Griffey Jr. 2.00 5.00
99 Carlos Delgado .40 1.00
100 Mike Schmidt 1.50 4.00

2005 Playoff Prestige Prestigious Pros Material Bat Silver

*BAT p/r 50: .4X TO 1X JSY p/r 50
*BAT p/r 50: .3X TO .8X JSY p/r 25
*BAT p/r 25: .4X TO 1X JSY p/r 25
OVERALL AU-GU ODDS 1:12
PRINT RUNS B/WN 5-50 COPIES PER
NO PRICING ON QTY OF 10 OR LESS
9 Hank Blalock/25 5.00 12.00
16 Garret Anderson/25 5.00 12.00
25 Rafael Palmeiro/25 8.00 20.00
44 Adam Dunn/25 5.00 12.00
47 Tom Glavine/25 8.00 20.00
48 Torii Hunter/50 4.00 10.00
54 David Ortiz/50 6.00 15.00
56 Nomar Garciaparra/25 10.00 25.00
64 Carlos Beltran/25 5.00 12.00
67 Mike Lowell/25 5.00 12.00
69 Ivan Rodriguez/50 6.00 15.00
76 Jose Vidro/25 5.00 12.00
83 Shannon Stewart/25 5.00 12.00
91 Roy Oswalt/25 5.00 12.00
96 Paul Lo Duca/25 5.00 12.00

2005 Playoff Prestige Prestigious Pros Material Jersey Gold

PRINT RUNS B/WN 5-50 COPIES PER
NO PRICING ON QTY OF 10 OR LESS
PATCH PLATINUM PRINTS B/WN 5-10 PER
NO PATCH PLAT.PRICING AVAILABLE
OVERALL AU-GU ODDS 1:12
1 Ozzie Smith/50 12.50 30.00
3 Eric Chavez/25 5.00 12.00
4 Paul Molitor/50 4.00 10.00
5 Jeff Bagwell/50 6.00 15.00
6 Melvin Mora/25 5.00 12.00
7 Craig Biggio/25 8.00 20.00
8 Cal Ripken/50 30.00 60.00
10 Miguel Tejada/25 5.00 12.00
13 Omar Vizquel/25 8.00 20.00
14 Paul Konerko/25 5.00 12.00
15 Tim Hudson/25 5.00 12.00
17 Lance Berkman/50 4.00 10.00
18 Randy Johnson/25 10.00 25.00
19 Robin Yount/50 10.00 25.00
20 Mark Mulder/20 5.00 12.00
21 Sean Casey/25 5.00 12.00
22 Jim Palmer/50 4.00 10.00
23 Don Mattingly/50 15.00 40.00
26 Vernon Wells/25 5.00 12.00
27 Vladimir Guerrero/25 10.00 25.00
28 Ken Harvey/25 5.00 12.00
29 Rod Carew/50 6.00 15.00
30 Nolan Ryan/50 12.50 30.00
31 Mike Piazza/25 10.00 25.00
32 Steve Carlton/50 4.00 10.00
34 Kerry Wood/25 5.00 12.00
35 Mike Mussina/25 8.00 20.00
36 Gaylord Perry/50 4.00 10.00
37 Gary Sheffield/25 5.00 12.00
38 Curt Schilling/25 8.00 20.00
39 Don Sutton/50 4.00 10.00
40 Roger Clemens/25 12.50 30.00
41 Victor Martinez/25 5.00 12.00
42 Jason Giambi/25 5.00 12.00
43 Dennis Eckersley/50 4.00 10.00
45 Pedro Martinez/25 8.00 20.00
46 Tony Perez/50 4.00 10.00
49 Hideo Nomo/25 10.00 25.00
50 Scott Rolen/25 8.00 20.00

52 C.C. Sabathia/25 5.00 12.00
53 George Brett/50 15.00 40.00
55 Hideki Matsui/25 20.00 50.00
58 Phil Niekro/50 4.00 10.00
59 Dontrelle Willis/25 5.00 12.00
60 Magglio Ordonez/25 5.00 12.00
61 Livan Hernandez/25 5.00 12.00
62 Edgar Renteria/25 5.00 12.00
63 Todd Helton/25 8.00 20.00
65 Sammy Sosa/25 10.00 25.00
66 Albert Pujols/25 15.00 40.00
68 Mark Prior/25 8.00 20.00
71 Jim Thome/25 8.00 20.00
72 Mark Teixeira/25 8.00 20.00
73 Shawn Green/25 5.00 12.00
74 Rollie Fingers/50 4.00 10.00
77 Ben Sheets/25 5.00 12.00
78 Roy Halladay/25 5.00 12.00
79 Frank Thomas/25 10.00 25.00
80 Chipper Jones/25 10.00 25.00
81 Jason Bay/25 5.00 12.00
82 Tony Gwynn/50 10.00 25.00
84 Carl Crawford/25 5.00 12.00
85 Andruw Jones/25 8.00 20.00
86 Greg Maddux/25 12.50 30.00
87 Barry Larkin/25 8.00 20.00
89 Rickey Henderson/50 10.00 25.00
90 Troy Glaus/25 5.00 12.00
92 Michael Young/25 5.00 12.00
93 Carlos Lee/25 5.00 12.00
94 Jim Edmonds/25 5.00 12.00
95 Fergie Jenkins/50 4.00 10.00
97 Aubrey Huff/25 5.00 12.00
99 Carlos Delgado/25 5.00 12.00
100 Mike Schmidt/50 15.00 40.00

2005 Playoff Prestige Prestigious Pros Signature Black

OVERALL AU-GU ODDS 1:12
STATED PRINT RUN 5 SERIAL #'d SETS
NO PRICING DUE TO SCARCITY

2005 Playoff Prestige Stars of MLB

STATED ODDS 1:12
*FOIL: 1.5X TO 4X BASIC
FOIL PRINT RUN 100 SERIAL #'d SETS
*HOLO-FOIL: 3X TO 8X BASIC
HOLO-FOIL PRINT RUN 25 SERIAL #'d SETS
FOIL/HOLO-FOIL RANDOM IN PACKS
1 Randy Johnson 1.00 2.50
2 Adrian Beltre 1.00 2.50
3 Eric Chavez .40 1.00
4 Mike Mussina .60 1.50
5 Todd Helton .60 1.50
6 Curt Schilling .60 1.50
7 Miguel Cabrera 1.00 2.50
8 Kerry Wood .40 1.00
9 David Ortiz 1.00 2.50
10 Michael Young .40 1.00
11 Mark Mulder .40 1.00
12 Victor Martinez .60 1.50
13 Johan Santana .60 1.50
14 Scott Rolen .60 1.50
15 Carlos Beltran .60 1.50

2005 Playoff Prestige Stars of MLB Material Bat

*BAT p/r 100: .4X TO 1X STARS JSY
*BAT p/r 50: .5X TO 1.2X STARS JSY
OVERALL AU-GU ODDS 1:12
PRINT RUNS B/WN 50-100 COPIES PER

2005 Playoff Prestige Stars of MLB Material Jersey

STATED PRINT RUN 100 SERIAL #'d SETS
*PRIME: .75X TO 2X JSY
PRIME PRINT RUN 25 SERIAL #'d SETS
OVERALL AU-GU ODDS 1:12
1 Randy Johnson Pants 5.00 12.00
2 Adrian Beltre 3.00 8.00
3 Eric Chavez 3.00 8.00
4 Mike Mussina 5.00 12.00
5 Todd Helton 5.00 12.00
6 Curt Schilling 5.00 12.00
7 Miguel Cabrera 5.00 12.00
8 Kerry Wood 3.00 8.00
9 David Ortiz 5.00 12.00
10 Michael Young 3.00 8.00
11 Mark Mulder 3.00 8.00
12 Victor Martinez 3.00 8.00
13 Johan Santana 5.00 12.00
14 Scott Rolen 5.00 12.00
15 Carlos Beltran 3.00 8.00

2005 Playoff Prestige Stars of MLB Signature Material Bat

*BAT p/r 50: .4X TO 1X JSY p/r 50
*BAT p/r 25: .4X TO 1X JSY p/r 25
OVERALL AU-GU ODDS 1:12
PRINT RUNS B/WN 10-50 COPIES PER
NO PRICING ON QTY OF 10

2005 Playoff Prestige Stars of MLB Signature Material Jersey

PRINT RUNS B/WN 10-50 COPIES PER
NO PRICING ON QTY OF 10
PRIME PRINT RUN 5 SERIAL #'d SETS
NO PRIME PRICING DUE TO SCARCITY
OVERALL AU-GU ODDS 1:12
2 Adrian Beltre/50 10.00 25.00
3 Eric Chavez/50 10.00 25.00
8 Kerry Wood/25 20.00 50.00
9 David Ortiz/50 20.00 50.00
10 Michael Young/50 10.00 25.00
12 Victor Martinez/50 10.00 25.00
13 Johan Santana/50 15.00 40.00
15 Carlos Beltran/25 12.50 30.00

1912 Plow's Candy E300

The cards in this set measure 3" X 4" with a sepia photograph measuring 2 1/4" X 3 5/16". This set was issued by Plow's Candy Company in 1912 on thin cardboard with wide borders. The subject's name is printed in block letters outside the bottom frame, and his team is listed directly beneath. The title "Plow's Candy Collection" is printed at the top; the cards are unnumbered and blank-backed. A few cards have been discovered with "premium or offer" backs. Those cards do trade at a premium. The cards have been alphabetized and numbered in the checklist below. The Doyle card was just discovered recently, leading many to believe that there might be other additions to this checklist. Any additions are therefore appreciated.
1 Babe Adams 1250.00 2500.00
2 Frank Baker 2000.00 4000.00
3 Cy Barger 1000.00 2000.00
4 Jack Barry 1000.00 2000.00
5 Johnny Bates 1000.00 2000.00
6 Chief Bender 2000.00 4000.00
7 Joe Benz 1000.00 2000.00
8 Bill Bergen 1000.00 2000.00
UER Berger
9 Roger Breshnahan 2000.00 4000.00
10 Mordecai Brown 2000.00 4000.00
11 Donie Bush 1000.00 2000.00
12 Bobby Byrne 1000.00 2000.00
13 Nixey Callahan 1000.00 2000.00
14 Hal Chase 1500.00 3000.00
15 Fred Clarke 2000.00 4000.00
16 Ty Cobb 7500.00 15000.00
17 King Cole 1000.00 2000.00
18 Eddie Collins 2000.00 4000.00
19 Jack Coombs 1000.00 2000.00
20 Bill Dahlen 1000.00 2000.00
21 Bert Daniels 1000.00 2000.00
22 Harry Davis 2000.00 4000.00
23 Jim Delahanty 1000.00 2000.00
24 Josh Devore 1000.00 2000.00
25 Bill Donovan 1250.00 2500.00
26 Red Dooin 1000.00 2000.00
27 Larry Doyle 1250.00 2500.00
28 Johnny Evers 2000.00 4000.00
29 Russ Ford 1000.00 2000.00
30 Del Gainor 1000.00 2000.00
31 Vean Gregg 1000.00 2000.00
32 Robert Harmon 1000.00 2000.00
33 Arnold Hauser 1000.00 2000.00
34 Dick Hoblitzell 1000.00 2000.00
UER Hoblitzelle
35 Solly Hofman 1000.00 2000.00
36 Miller Huggins 2000.00 4000.00
37 John Hummel 1000.00 2000.00
38 Walter Johnson 4000.00 8000.00
39 Johnny Kling 1000.00 2000.00
40 Nap Lajoie 2000.00 4000.00
41 John Lapp 1000.00 2000.00
42 Fred Luderus 1000.00 2000.00
43 Sherry Magee 1250.00 2500.00
44 Rube Marquard 2000.00 4000.00
45 Christy Mathewson 4000.00 8000.00
46 Stuffy McInnis 1250.00 2500.00
UER McInnes
47 Larry McLean 1000.00 2000.00
48 Fred Merkle 1500.00 3000.00
49 Cy Morgan 1000.00 2000.00
50 George Moriarity 1000.00 2000.00
51 Harry Mowrey 1000.00 2000.00
52 Chief Meyers 1250.00 2500.00
UER Myers
53 Rube Oldring 1000.00 2000.00
54 Martin O'Toole 1000.00 2000.00
55 Eddie Plank 2000.00 4000.00
56 Nap Rucker 1250.00 2500.00
57 Slim Sallee 1000.00 2000.00
58 Boss Schmidt 1000.00 2000.00
59 Jimmy Sheckard 1000.00 2000.00
60 Tris Speaker 2000.00 4000.00
61 Billy Sullivan 1000.00 2000.00
62 Ira Thomas 1000.00 2000.00
63 Joe Tinker 2000.00 4000.00
64 John Titus 1000.00 2000.00
65 Hippo Vaughn 1000.00 2000.00
UER Vaughan
66 Honus Wagner 4000.00 8000.00
67 Ed Walsh 2000.00 4000.00
68 Bob Williams 1000.00 2000.00

1910-12 Plow Boy Tobacco

Measuring approximately 5 3/4" by 8", these cards were issued with Large tins of Plow Boy tobacco. These cards feature only members of the Chicago Cubs and Chicago White Sox. Since these cards are unnumbered, we have sequenced them in alphabetical order. In addition, there is a good chance that additions to this checklist may still be found; if so, we appreciate the help to our checklist in advance.
COMPLETE SET 40000.00 80000.00
1 Jimmy Archer 750.00 1500.00
2 Ginger Beaumont 750.00 1500.00
3 Lena Blackburne 750.00 1500.00
4 Bruno Block 750.00 1500.00
5 Ping Bodie 750.00 1500.00
6 Mordecai Brown 2000.00 4000.00
7 Al Carson 750.00 1500.00
8 Frank Chance 2000.00 4000.00
9 Eddie Cicotte 2500.00 5000.00
10 King Cole 750.00 1500.00
11 Shano Collins 750.00 1500.00
12 George Davis 750.00 1500.00
13 Patsy Dougherty 750.00 1500.00
14 Chick Gandil 1500.00 3000.00
15 Ed Hahn 750.00 1500.00
16 George Howard 750.00 1500.00
17 Bill Jones 750.00 1500.00
18 Johnny Kling 1000.00 2000.00
19 Rube Kroh 750.00 1500.00
20 Frank Lange 750.00 1500.00
21 Fred Luderus 750.00 1500.00
22 Harry McIntyre 750.00 1500.00
23 Ward Miller 750.00 1500.00
24 Charlie Mullen 750.00 1500.00
25 Fred Olmstead 750.00 1500.00
26 Orvie Overall 1000.00 2000.00
27 Fred Parent 750.00 1500.00
28 Fred Payne 750.00 1500.00
29 Jeff Pfeffer 750.00 1500.00
30 Jeff Pfeister 750.00 1500.00
31 Billy Purtell 750.00 1500.00
32 Ed Reulbach 1250.00 2500.00
33 Lew Richie 750.00 1500.00
34 Frank Schulte 1250.00 2500.00
35 Jim Scott 750.00 1500.00
Sic, Scotts
36 Jim Scott 750.00 1500.00
37 Frank Smith 750.00 1500.00
38 Jimmy Sheckard 1000.00 2000.00
39 Harry Steinfeldt 1000.00 2000.00
40 Billy Sullivan 750.00 1500.00
41 Lee Tannehill 750.00 1500.00
42 Joe Tinker 2000.00 4000.00
43 Ed Walsh 2000.00 4000.00
44 Doc White 1000.00 2000.00
45 Irv Young 750.00 1500.00
46 Rollie Zeider 750.00 1500.00
47 Heinie Zimmerman 1000.00 2000.00

1991 PM Gold Card Prototype

This standard-size card is a prototype for PM cards. Each card contains one gram of pure 999.9 gold (24 karat) and will feature baseball, basketball, football and hockey players (some promos were also printed that do not contain gold). The front design features a color player photo of a fictional player, with a yellow/orange inner border and a gold outer border. The back has the serial number, player biography and an advertisement for PM cards.
1 Ken Katcher .40 1.00

1992 PM Gold

Distributed by Powell Associates, these PM ("precious metal") cards each contain one gram of pure 24K (999.9 percent) fine gold. These standard-size cards are the product of a technological break through developed by Mitsubishi that makes it possible to put a full color picture on precious metals. Artist Gregory Perillo created the oil paintings of the players reproduced on the card fronts. Production quantities vary for each card. Only 1,000 of card number 1 (a prototype) were produced and distributed to attendees of the Gold Glove charity dinner. The production run of cards number 2 and 3 were 10,000 and 1,200 respectively. The card front also has gold borders and the player's name appears in a gold plaque in the bottom gold border. The back has the serial number and career summary. The cards are numbered on the back by "Rawling Series Card number X."
COMPLETE SET (3) 15.00 40.00
1 Brooks Robinson 8.00 20.00
Defensive posture, Prototype
2 Brooks Robinson 1.25 3.00
Portrait
3 Roberto Clemente 10.00 25.00

1992 PM Gold Ruth Prototype

Distributed by Powell Associates, this Babe Ruth Precious Metal card contains one gram of pure 24K (999.9 percent) fine gold. The card measures the standard size. Artist Gregory Perillo created the oil painting of Ruth that was reproduced on the card front. The card front also has gold borders and the player's name appears in a gold plaque in the bottom gold border. The back has the serial number and career summary. The card is numbered on the back by "Baseball Series Card Number 1."
1 Babe Ruth 1.25 3.00

1993 PM Gold Bench

A one-gram, 24-K gold card featuring former Reds catcher Johnny Bench was given to each attendee at the Third Annual Rawlings Gold Glove Award Charity Dinner held Nov. 18, 1993 at the Sheraton New York. The card was created from an original painting by sports artist Daniel Fruend. The back features a brief biography of the baseball legend.
1 Johnny Bench 20.00 50.00

1901-17 Police Gazette Supplements

These 11" by 16" premiums were issued with copies of the "Police Gazette" magazine. The high quality photos have the police gazette ID on the top and an ID of the athlete as well as some information about him on the bottom. We have just listed the Baseball players here but it is believed many more should exist. Although this list is alphabetical, when 2 or more supplements are confirmed for the same player we have put the supplement number next to the player's name.
COMPLETE SET 15000.00 30000.00
1 Grover C. Alexander 500.00 1000.00
2 Leon Ames 150.00 300.00
3 Jimmy Archer 125.00 250.00
4 Harry Bay 125.00 250.00
5 Frank Baker 300.00 600.00
6 Ping Bodie 125.00 250.00
7 Frank Bowerman 125.00 250.00
8 Roger Bresnahan 250.00 500.00
9 Al Bridwell 125.00 250.00
10 Mordecai Brown 300.00 600.00
11 Al Burch 125.00 250.00
12 Owen Bush 125.00 250.00
13 Ray Caldwell 125.00 250.00
14 Jimmy Casey 125.00 250.00
15 Frank Chance 400.00 800.00
16 Hal Chase 300.00 600.00
17 Hal Chase 250.00 500.00
Charlie Armbruster
18 Jack Chesbro 300.00 600.00
19 Ty Cobb 1250.00 2500.00
20 Eddie Collins 400.00 800.00
21 Jack Coombs 150.00 300.00
22 Harry Coveleski 125.00 250.00
23 Stan Coveleskie 250.00 500.00
24 Sam Crawford 250.00 500.00
25 Birdie Cree 125.00 250.00
26 Jack Cronin 125.00 250.00
27 Nick Cullop 125.00 250.00
28 Bill Dahlen 150.00 300.00
29 Tom Dalton 125.00 250.00
30 Bert Daniels 125.00 250.00
31 Jake Daubert 150.00 300.00
32 George Davis 250.00 500.00
33 Harry Davis 125.00 250.00
34 Josh Devore 125.00 250.00
35 Mike Donlin 150.00 300.00
36 Red Dooin 125.00 250.00
37 Larry Doyle 150.00 300.00
38 Louis Drucke 125.00 250.00
39 Cecil Ferguson 125.00 250.00
40 Dave Fultz 125.00 250.00
41 Russ Ford 125.00 250.00
42 Clark Griffith 250.00 500.00
43 Charley Hemphill 125.00 250.00
44 Dick Hoblitzel 125.00 250.00
45 Danny Hoffman 125.00 250.00
46 Buck Herzog 150.00 300.00
47 Bill Hogg 125.00 250.00
48 Del Howard 125.00 250.00
49 Joe Jackson 1000.00 2000.00
50 Walter Johnson 750.00 1500.00
51 Benny Kauff 125.00 250.00
52 Willie Keeler 300.00 600.00
53 Willie Keeler 250.00 500.00
Jack Kleinow
54 Malachi Kittredge 125.00 250.00
55 Jack Kleinow 125.00 250.00
56 Napoleon Lajoie 400.00 800.00
57 Tommy Leach 125.00 250.00
58 Hans Lobert/1660 125.00 250.00
59 Hans Lobert/1975 125.00 250.00
60 Hans Lobert/2074 125.00 250.00
61 Fred Luderus 125.00 250.00
62 Harry Lumley 125.00 250.00
63 Sherry Magee/1722 150.00 300.00
64 Sherry Magee/1970 150.00 300.00
65 Fritz Maisel 125.00 250.00
66 Rabbit Maranville 250.00 500.00
67 Rube Marquard 250.00 500.00
68 Christy Mathewson/1251 750.00 1500.00
69 Christy Mathewson/1771 750.00 1500.00
70 Dan McGann 125.00 250.00
71 Joe McGinnity 250.00 500.00
72 John McGraw 400.00 800.00
73 Sandow Mertes 125.00 250.00
74 Clarence Mitchell 125.00 250.00
75 George Moriarty 125.00 250.00
76 Dick Morris 125.00 250.00
77 Jack Myers 125.00 250.00
78 Orval Overall 125.00 250.00
79 Pol Perritt 125.00 250.00
80 Philadelphia A's/1914 150.00 300.00
81 Pittsburgh Pirates/1905 150.00 300.00
82 Eddie Plank 300.00 600.00
83 Maurice Powers 125.00 250.00
84 Bugs Raymond 125.00 250.00
85 Dave Robertson 125.00 250.00
86 Nap Rucker 150.00 300.00
87 Dick Rudolph 125.00 250.00
88 Cy Seymour 125.00 250.00
89 Nap Shea 125.00 250.00
90 George Sisler 300.00 600.00
91 Alec Smith 125.00 250.00
92 Jake Stahl 125.00 250.00
93 Sammy Strang 125.00 250.00
94 Roy Thomas 125.00 250.00
95 Jim Thorpe 1000.00 2000.00
96 Honus Wagner 1000.00 2000.00
97 Honus Wagner 1000.00 2000.00
Roger Bresnahan
98 Jack Warhop 125.00 250.00
99 Jack Warner 125.00 250.00
100 Zach Wheat 250.00 500.00
101 Arthur Wilson 125.00 250.00
102 Joe Wood 200.00 400.00
103 Heinie Zimmerman 150.00 300.00

1985 Police Mets/Yankees

This 12-card set was supposedly issued courtesy of the Kiwanis Club, a local law enforcement agency, and the New York Mets and New York Yankees. The cards measure approximately 2 9/16" by 4 1/16". The cards are numbered on the back and are indicated below by a prefix for Mets or Yankees.
COMPLETE SET (12) 2.50 6.00
M1 George Foster and .20 .50
Bill Robinson CO
M2 Davey Johnson MG .40 1.00
and Gary Carter
M3 Dwight Gooden .60 1.50
M4 Mookie Wilson .30 .75
M5 Keith Hernandez .40 1.00
M6 Darryl Strawberry .30 .75
Y1 Willie Randolph .30 .75
Y2 Phil Niekro .60 1.50
Y3 Ron Guidry .30 .75
Y4 Dave Winfield 1.00 2.50
Y5 Dave Righetti .30 .75
Y6 Billy Martin MG .40 1.00

1914 Polo Grounds Game WG4

These cards were distributed as part of a baseball game produced around 1914. The cards each measure approximately 2 1/2" by 3 1/2" and have rounded corners. The card fronts show a photo of the player, his name, his team, and the game outcome associated with that particular card. The card backs are printed in green and white and are all the same each showing a panoramic picture of the Polo Grounds inside an ornate frame with a white outer border. Since the cards are unnumbered, they are listed below in alphabetical order.
COMPLETE SET (30) 1500.00 3000.00
1 Jimmy Archer 15.00 25.00
2 Frank Baker 35.00 60.00
3 Frank Chance 30.00 50.00
4 Larry Cheney 15.00 25.00
5 Ty Cobb 175.00 300.00
6 Eddie Collins 35.00 60.00
7 Larry Doyle 15.00 25.00
8 Art Fletcher 15.00 25.00
9 Claude Hendrix 15.00 25.00
10 Joe Jackson 300.00 500.00
11 Hugh Jennings MG 35.00 60.00
12 Nap Lajoie 50.00 80.00
13 Jimmy Lavender 15.00 25.00
14 Fritz Maisel 15.00 25.00
15 Rabbit Maranville 35.00 60.00
16 Rube Marquard 35.00 60.00
17 Christy Mathewson 90.00 150.00
18 John McGraw MG 35.00 60.00
19 Stuffy McInnis 15.00 25.00
20 Chief Meyers 15.00 25.00
21 Red Murray 15.00 25.00
22 Eddie Plank 35.00 60.00
23 Nap Rucker 15.00 25.00
24 Reb Russell 15.00 25.00
25 Frank Schulte 15.00 25.00
26 Jim Scott 15.00 25.00
27 Tris Speaker 50.00 80.00
28 Honus Wagner 150.00 250.00
29 Ed Walsh 35.00 60.00
30 Joe Wood 35.00 60.00

2013 Pop Century

COMMON CARD 3.00 8.00
*SILVER/25: .5X TO 1.2X BASIC CARDS
*BLUE/10: UNPRICED DUE TO SCARCITY
*RED/5: UNPRICED DUE TO SCARCITY
*GOLD/1: UNPRICED DUE TO SCARCITY
*P.P.BLACK/1: UNPRICED DUE TO SCARCITY
*P.P.CYAN/1: UNPRICED DUE TO SCARCITY
*P.P.MAGENTA/1: UNPRICED DUE TO SCARCITY
*P.P.YELLOW/1: UNPRICED DUE TO SCARCITY
BABG1 Bob Gibson 12.00 30.00
BACRJ Cal Ripken Jr. 40.00 80.00
BAPR1 Pete Rose 8.00 20.00

2013 Pop Century Keeping It Real Autographs

COMMON CARD 3.00 8.00
*SILVER/25: .5X TO 1.2X BASIC CARDS
*BLUE/10: UNPRICED DUE TO SCARCITY
*RED/5: UNPRICED DUE TO SCARCITY
*GOLD/1: UNPRICED DUE TO SCARCITY
*P.P.BLACK/1: UNPRICED DUE TO SCARCITY
*P.P.CYAN/1: UNPRICED DUE TO SCARCITY
*P.P.MAGENTA/1: UNPRICED DUE TO SCARCITY
*P.P.YELLOW/1: UNPRICED DUE TO SCARCITY
KRPR1 Pete Rose 8.00 20.00

2015 Pop Century

COMMON AUTO 5.00 12.00
*SILVER/25: UNPRICED DUE TO SCARCITY
*PURPLE/15: UNPRICED DUE TO SCARCITY
*BLUE/10: UNPRICED DUE TO SCARCITY
*RED/5: UNPRICED DUE TO SCARCITY
*GOLD/1: UNPRICED DUE TO SCARCITY
*P.P.BLACK/1: UNPRICED DUE TO SCARCITY
*P.P.CYAN/1: UNPRICED DUE TO SCARCITY
*P.P.MAGENTA/1: UNPRICED DUE TO SCARCITY
*P.P.YELLOW/1: UNPRICED DUE TO SCARCITY
BACRJ Cal Ripken Jr. 12.00 30.00
BAPR1 Pete Rose 8.00 20.00

1930 Post Famous North Americans

This blank-backed card, which measures approximately 2 3/8" by 3 3/8" was cut from a strip of 4 cards and features a photo of Christy Mathewson on the front. Mathewson is the only sports personage featured in this set of 32 cards.
8 Christy Mathewson 75.00 150.00

1960 Post Cereal

These large cards measure approximately 7" by 8 3/4". The 1960 Post Cereal Sports Stars set contains nine cards depicting current baseball, football and basketball players. Each card comprised the entire back of a Grape Nuts Flakes Box and is blank backed. The color player photos are set on a colored background surrounded by a wooden frame design, and they are unnumbered (assigned numbers below for reference according to sport). The catalog designation is F278-26.
COMPLETE SET (9) 3000.00 5000.00
BB1 Don Drysdale 150.00 300.00
BB2 Al Kaline 200.00 400.00
BB3 Harmon Killebrew 250.00 500.00
BB4 Ed Mathews 200.00 400.00
BB5 Mickey Mantle 1000.00 2000.00

1961 Post

The cards in this 200-card set measure 2 1/2" by 3 1/2". The 1961 Post set was this company's first major set. The cards were available on thick cardbox stock, singly or in various panel sizes from cereal boxes (BOX), or in team sheets, printed on thinner cardboard stock, directly from the Post Cereal Company (COM). It is difficult to differentiate the COM cards from the BOX cards; the thickness of the card stock is the best indicator. Many variations exist and are noted in the checklist below. There are many cards which were produced in lesser quantities; the prices below reflect the relative scarcity of the cards. Cards 10, 23, 70, 73, 94, 113, 135, 163, and 183 are examples of cards printed in limited quantities and hence commanding premium prices. The cards are numbered essentially in team groups, i.e., New York Yankees (1-18), Chicago White Sox (19-34), Detroit (35-46), Boston (47-56), Cleveland (57-67), Baltimore (68-80), Kansas City (81-90), Minnesota (91-100), Milwaukee (101-114), Philadelphia (115-124), Pittsburgh (125-140), San Francisco (141-155), Los Angeles Dodgers (156-170), St. Louis (171-180), Cincinnati (181-190), and Chicago Cubs (191-200). The catalog number is F278-33. The complete set price refers to the set with all variations (357). There was also an album produced by Post to hold the cards.
COMPLETE MASTER SET (357) 1700.00 3400.00
1A Yogi Berra COM 15.00 40.00
1B Yogi Berra BOX 15.00 40.00
2A Elston Howard COM 2.50 6.00
2B Elston Howard BOX 2.50 6.00
3A Bill Skowron COM 2.50 6.00
3B Bill Skowron BOX 2.50 6.00
4A Mickey Mantle COM 100.00 200.00
4B Mickey Mantle BOX 100.00 200.00
5 Bob Turley COM only 10.00 25.00
6A Whitey Ford COM 6.00 15.00
6B Whitey Ford BOX 6.00 15.00
7A Roger Maris COM 15.00 40.00
7B Roger Maris BOX 15.00 40.00
8A Bobby Richardson COM 2.50 6.00
8B Bobby Richardson BOX 2.50 6.00
9A Tony Kubek COM 2.50 6.00
9B Tony Kubek BOX 2.50 6.00
10 G.McDougald BOX only 30.00 60.00
11 Cletis Boyer BOX only 2.50 6.00
12A Hector Lopez COM 1.50 4.00
12B Hector Lopez BOX 1.50 4.00
13 Bob Cerv BOX only 1.50 4.00
14 Ryne Duren BOX only 1.50 4.00
15 Bobby Shantz BOX only 1.50 4.00
16 Art Ditmar BOX only 1.50 4.00
17 Jim Coates BOX only 1.50 4.00
18 Johnny Blanchard BOX only 1.50 4.00
19A Luis Aparicio COM 4.00 10.00
19B Luis Aparicio BOX 4.00 10.00
20A Nellie Fox COM 4.00 10.00
20B Nellie Fox BOX 4.00 10.00
21A Billy Pierce COM 2.50 6.00
21B Billy Pierce BOX 2.50 6.00
22A Early Wynn COM 8.00 20.00
22B Early Wynn BOX 8.00 20.00
23 Bob Shaw BOX only 60.00 120.00
24A Al Smith COM 2.50 6.00
24B Al Smith BOX 2.50 6.00
25A Minnie Minoso COM 3.00 8.00
25B Minnie Minoso BOX 3.00 8.00
26A Roy Sievers COM 1.50 4.00
26B Roy Sievers BOX 1.50 4.00
27A Jim Landis COM 1.50 4.00
27B Jim Landis BOX 1.50 4.00
28A Sherm Lollar COM 1.50 4.00
28B Sherm Lollar BOX 1.50 4.00
29 Gerry Staley BOX only 1.50 4.00
30A G.Freese COM(Reds) 6.00 15.00
30B G.Freese BOX (WS) 1.50 4.00
31 T.Kluszewski BOX only 3.00 8.00
32 Turk Lown BOX only 1.50 4.00
33A Jim Rivera COM 1.50 4.00
33B Jim Rivera BOX 1.50 4.00
34 Frank Baumann BOX only 1.50 4.00
35A Al Kaline COM 10.00 25.00
35B Al Kaline BOX 10.00 25.00
36A Rocky Colavito COM 5.00 12.00
36B Rocky Colavito BOX 5.00 12.00
37A Charlie Maxwell COM 2.50 6.00
37B Charlie Maxwell BOX 2.50 6.00
38A Frank Lary COM 2.50 6.00
38B Frank Lary BOX 2.50 6.00
39A Jim Bunning COM 4.00 10.00
39B Jim Bunning BOX 4.00 10.00
40A Norm Cash COM 2.50 6.00
40B Norm Cash BOX 2.50 6.00
41A F.Bolling COM Braves 2.50 6.00
41B F.Bolling BOX Tigers 4.00 10.00
42A Don Mossi COM 1.50 4.00
42B Don Mossi BOX 1.50 4.00
43A Lou Berberet COM 1.50 4.00
43B Lou Berberet BOX 1.50 4.00
44 Dave Sisler BOX only 1.50 4.00
45 Eddie Yost BOX only 1.50 4.00
46 Pete Burnside BOX only 1.50 4.00
47A Pete Runnels COM 2.50 6.00
47B Pete Runnels BOX 2.50 6.00
48A Frank Malzone COM 1.50 4.00
48B Frank Malzone BOX 1.50 4.00
49A Vic Wertz COM 2.50 6.00
49B Vic Wertz BOX 2.50 6.00
50A Tom Brewer COM 1.50 4.00
50B Tom Brewer BOX 1.50 4.00
51A W.Tasby COM(S Wash.) 4.00 10.00
51B W.Tasby BOX (No sale) 2.50 6.00
52A Russ Nixon COM 1.50 4.00
52B Russ Nixon BOX 1.50 4.00
53A Don Buddin COM 1.50 4.00
53B Don Buddin BOX 1.50 4.00
54A Bill Monbouquette COM 1.50 4.00
54B Bill Monbouquette BOX 1.50 4.00
55A F.Sullivan COM Phillies 5.00 12.00
55B F.Sullivan BOX Red Sox 1.50 4.00
56A Haywood Sullivan COM 1.50 4.00
56B Haywood Sullivan BOX 1.50 4.00
57A H.Kuenn COM Giants 4.00 10.00
57B H.Kuenn BOX Indians 3.00 8.00
58A Gary Bell COM 2.50 6.00
58B Gary Bell BOX 2.50 6.00
59A Jim Perry COM 1.50 4.00
59B Jim Perry BOX 1.50 4.00
60A Jim Grant COM 2.50 6.00
60B Jim Grant BOX 2.50 6.00
61A Johnny Temple COM 2.50 6.00
61B Johnny Temple BOX 2.50 6.00
62A Paul Foytack COM 1.50 4.00
62B Paul Foytack BOX 1.50 4.00
63A Vic Power COM 1.50 4.00
63B Vic Power BOX 1.50 4.00
64A Tito Francona COM 1.50 4.00
64B Tito Francona BOX 1.50 4.00
65A K.Aspromonte COM Sold LA 4.00 10.00
65B K.Aspromonte BOX No sale 4.00 10.00
66 Bob Wilson BOX only 1.50 4.00
67A John Romano COM 1.50 4.00
67B John Romano BOX 1.50 4.00
68A Jim Gentile COM 2.50 6.00
68B Jim Gentile BOX 2.50 6.00
69A Gus Triandos COM 2.50 6.00
69B Gus Triandos BOX 2.50 6.00
70 G.Woodling BOX only 15.00 40.00
71A Milt Pappas COM 2.50 6.00
71B Milt Pappas BOX 2.50 6.00
72A Ron Hansen COM 1.50 4.00
72B Ron Hansen BOX 1.50 4.00
73 C.Estrada COM only 75.00 150.00
74A Steve Barber COM 1.50 4.00
74B Steve Barber BOX 1.50 4.00
75A Brooks Robinson COM 12.50 30.00
75B Brooks Robinson BOX 12.50 30.00
76A Jackie Brandt COM 1.50 4.00
76B Jackie Brandt BOX 1.50 4.00
77A Marv Breeding COM 1.50 4.00
77B Marv Breeding BOX 1.50 4.00
78 Hal Brown BOX only 1.50 4.00
79 Billy Klaus BOX only 1.50 4.00
80A Hoyt Wilhelm COM 4.00 10.00
80B Hoyt Wilhelm BOX 4.00 10.00
81A Jerry Lumpe COM 2.50 6.00
81B Jerry Lumpe BOX 2.50 6.00
82A Norm Siebern COM 1.50 4.00
82B Norm Siebern BOX 1.50 4.00
83A Bud Daley COM 2.50 6.00
83B Bud Daley BOX 2.50 6.00
84A Bill Tuttle COM 1.50 4.00
84B Bill Tuttle BOX 1.50 4.00
85A Marv Throneberry COM 2.50 6.00
85B Marv Throneberry BOX 2.50 6.00
86A Dick Williams COM 2.50 6.00
86B Dick Williams BOX 2.50 6.00
87A Ray Herbert COM 1.50 4.00
87B Ray Herbert BOX 1.50 4.00
88A Whitey Herzog COM 3.00 8.00
88B Whitey Herzog BOX 3.00 8.00
89A K.Hamlin COM Sold LA 10.00 25.00
89B K.Hamlin BOX No sold 1.50 4.00
90A Hank Bauer COM 2.50 6.00
90B Hank Bauer BOX 2.50 6.00
91A B.Allison COM Minnesota 3.00 8.00
91B B.Allison BOX Minneapolis 3.00 8.00
92A H.Killebrew COM Minnesota 30.00 60.00
92B H.Killebrew BOX Minneapolis 20.00 50.00
93A J.Lemon COM Minnesota 12.50 30.00
93B J.Lemon BOX Minneapolis 50.00 100.00
94A C.Stobbs COM only Minnesota 125.00 250.00
95A R.Bertoia COM Minnesota 2.50 6.00
95B R.Bertoia BOX Minneapolis 1.50 4.00
96A B.Gardner COM Minnesota 2.50 6.00
96B B.Gardner BOX Minneapolis 1.50 4.00
97A E.Battey COM Minnesota 2.50 6.00
97B E.Battey BOX Minneapolis 1.50 4.00
98A P.Ramos COM Minnesota 2.50 6.00
98B P.Ramos BOX Minneapolis 1.50 4.00
99A C.Pascual COM Minnesota 2.50 6.00
99B C.Pascual BOX Minneapolis 1.50 4.00
100A B.Consolo COM Minnesota 2.50 6.00
100B B.Consolo BOX Minneapolis 1.50 4.00
101A Warren Spahn COM 12.50 30.00
101B Warren Spahn BOX 12.50 30.00
102A Lew Burdette COM 2.50 6.00
102B Lew Burdette BOX 2.50 6.00
103A Bob Buhl COM 1.50 4.00
103B Bob Buhl BOX 1.50 4.00
104A Joe Adcock COM 2.50 6.00
104B Joe Adcock BOX 2.50 6.00
105A Johnny Logan COM 2.50 6.00
105B Johnny Logan BOX 2.50 6.00
106 E.Mathews COM only 20.00 50.00
107A Hank Aaron COM 15.00 40.00
107B Hank Aaron BOX 15.00 40.00
108A Wes Covington COM 1.50 4.00
108B Wes Covington BOX 1.50 4.00
109A B.Bruton COM Tigers 3.00 8.00
109B B.Bruton BOX Braves 3.00 8.00
110A Del Crandall COM 2.50 6.00
110B Del Crandall BOX 2.50 6.00
111 E.Schoendienst BOX only 3.00 8.00
112 J.Pizarro BOX only 1.50 4.00
113 C.Cottier BOX only 8.00 20.00
114 Al Spangler BOX only 1.50 4.00
115A Dick Farrell COM 2.50 6.00
115B Dick Farrell BOX 2.50 6.00
116A Jim Owens COM 2.50 6.00
116B Jim Owens BOX 2.50 6.00
117A Robin Roberts COM 5.00 12.00
117B Robin Roberts BOX 4.00 10.00
118A Tony Taylor COM 1.50 4.00
118B Tony Taylor BOX 1.50 4.00
119A Lee Walls COM 1.50 4.00
119B Lee Walls BOX 1.50 4.00
120A Tony Curry COM 1.50 4.00
120B Tony Curry BOX 1.50 4.00
121A Pancho Herrera COM 2.50 6.00
121B Pancho Herrera BOX 2.50 6.00
122A Ken Walters COM 2.50 6.00
122B Ken Walters BOX 2.50 6.00
123A John Callison COM 2.50 6.00
123B John Callison BOX 2.50 6.00
124A G.Conley COM Red Sox 6.00 15.00
124B G.Conley BOX Phillies 1.50 4.00
125A Bob Friend COM 2.50 6.00
125B Bob Friend BOX 2.50 6.00
126A Vern Law COM 2.50 6.00
126B Vern Law BOX 2.50 6.00
127A Dick Stuart COM 2.50 6.00
127B Dick Stuart BOX 2.50 6.00
128A Bill Mazeroski COM 3.00 8.00
128B Bill Mazeroski BOX 3.00 8.00
129A Dick Groat COM 2.50 6.00
129B Dick Groat BOX 2.50 6.00
130A Don Hoak COM 1.50 4.00
130B Don Hoak BOX 1.50 4.00
131A Bob Skinner COM 1.50 4.00
131B Bob Skinner BOX 1.50 4.00
132A R.Clemente COM 40.00 80.00
132B R.Clemente BOX 40.00 80.00
133 Roy Face BOX only 2.50 6.00
134 H.Haddix BOX only 1.50 4.00
135 Bill Virdon BOX only 20.00 50.00
136A Gino Cimoli COM 1.50 4.00
136B Gino Cimoli BOX 1.50 4.00
137 R.Nelson BOX only 1.50 4.00
138A Smoky Burgess COM 2.50 6.00
138B Smoky Burgess BOX 2.50 6.00
139 Hal W. Smith BOX only 1.50 4.00
140 Wilmer Mizell BOX only 1.50 4.00
141A Mike McCormick COM 1.50 4.00
141B Mike McCormick BOX 1.50 4.00
142A J. Antonelli COM Cleve 3.00 8.00
142B J.Antonelli BOX S.F. 2.50 6.00
143A Sam Jones COM 2.50 6.00
143B Sam Jones BOX 2.50 6.00
144A Orlando Cepeda COM 5.00 12.00
144B Orlando Cepeda BOX 5.00 12.00
145A Willie Mays COM 20.00 50.00
145B Willie Mays BOX 20.00 50.00
146A W.Kirkland COM Cleve 4.00 10.00
146B W.Kirkland BOX S.F. 3.00 8.00
147A Willie McCovey COM 5.00 12.00
147B Willie McCovey BOX 5.00 12.00
148A Don Blasingame COM 1.50 4.00
148B Don Blasingame BOX 1.50 4.00
149A Jim Davenport COM 2.50 6.00
149B Jim Davenport BOX 2.50 6.00
150A Hobie Landrith COM 1.50 4.00
150B Hobie Landrith BOX 1.50 4.00
151 Bob Schmidt BOX only 1.50 4.00
152A Ed Bressoud COM 1.50 4.00
152B Ed Bressoud BOX 1.50 4.00
153A A.Rodgers BOX no trade 10.00 25.00
153B A.Rodgers BOX Traded 2.50 6.00
154 Jack Sanford BOX only 1.50 4.00
155 Billy O'Dell BOX only 1.50 4.00
156A Norm Larker COM 1.50 4.00
156B Norm Larker BOX 1.50 4.00
157A Charlie Neal COM 2.50 6.00
157B Charlie Neal BOX 2.50 6.00
158A Jim Gilliam COM 4.00 10.00
158B Jim Gilliam BOX 4.00 10.00
159A Wally Moon COM 3.00 8.00
159B Wally Moon BOX 3.00 8.00
160A Don Drysdale COM 8.00 20.00
160B Don Drysdale BOX 8.00 20.00

161A Larry Sherry COM 2.50 6.00
161B Larry Sherry BOX 2.50 6.00
162 S.Williams BOX only 4.00 10.00
163 Mel Roach BOX only 60.00 120.00
164A Maury Wills COM 5.00 12.00
164B Maury Wills BOX 5.00 12.00
165 Tommy Davis BOX only 2.50 6.00
166A John Roseboro COM 1.50 4.00
166B John Roseboro BOX 1.50 4.00
167A Duke Snider COM 4.00 10.00
167B Duke Snider BOX 4.00 10.00
168A Gil Hodges COM 4.00 10.00
168B Gil Hodges BOX 4.00 10.00
169 John Podres BOX only 2.50 6.00
170 Ed Roebuck BOX only 2.50 6.00
171A Ken Boyer COM 5.00 12.00
171B Ken Boyer BOX 5.00 12.00
172A Joe Cunningham COM 1.50 4.00
172B Joe Cunningham BOX 1.50 4.00
173A Daryl Spencer COM 1.50 4.00
173B Daryl Spencer BOX 1.50 4.00
174A Larry Jackson COM 2.50 6.00
174B Larry Jackson BOX 2.50 6.00
175A Lindy McDaniel COM 1.50 4.00
175B Lindy McDaniel BOX 1.50 4.00
176A Bill White COM 2.50 6.00
176B Bill White BOX 2.50 6.00
177A Alex Grammas COM 1.50 4.00
177B Alex Grammas BOX 1.50 4.00
178A Curt Flood COM 3.00 8.00
178B Curt Flood BOX 3.00 8.00
179A Ernie Broglio COM 1.50 4.00
179B Ernie Broglio BOX 1.50 4.00
180A Hal Smith COM 1.50 4.00
180B Hal Smith BOX 1.50 4.00
181A Vada Pinson COM 2.50 6.00
181B Vada Pinson BOX 2.50 6.00
182A Frank Robinson COM 20.00 50.00
182B Frank Robinson BOX 20.00 50.00
183 R.McMillan BOX only 60.00 120.00
184A Bob Purkey COM 1.50 4.00
184B Bob Purkey BOX 1.50 4.00
185A Ed Kasko COM 1.50 4.00
185B Ed Kasko BOX 1.50 4.00
186A Gus Bell COM 1.50 4.00
186B Gus Bell BOX 1.50 4.00
187A Jerry Lynch COM 1.50 4.00
187B Jerry Lynch BOX 1.50 4.00
188A Ed Bailey COM 1.50 4.00
188B Ed Bailey BOX 1.50 4.00
189A Jim O'Toole COM 1.50 4.00
189B Jim O'Toole BOX 1.50 4.00
190A B.Martin COM Sold Milw 5.00 12.00
190B B.Martin BOX No sold 3.00 8.00
191A Ernie Banks COM 15.00 40.00
191B Ernie Banks BOX 15.00 40.00
192A Richie Ashburn COM 5.00 12.00
192B Richie Ashburn BOX 5.00 12.00
193A Frank Thomas COM 30.00 60.00
193B Frank Thomas BOX 30.00 60.00
194A Don Cardwell COM 2.50 6.00
194B Don Cardwell BOX 2.50 6.00
195A George Altman COM 1.50 4.00
195B George Altman BOX 1.50 4.00
196A Ron Santo COM 3.00 8.00
196B Ron Santo BOX 3.00 8.00
197A Glen Hobbie COM 1.50 4.00
197B Glen Hobbie BOX 1.50 4.00
198A Sam Taylor COM 1.50 4.00
198B Sam Taylor BOX 1.50 4.00
199A Jerry Kindall COM 1.50 4.00
199B Jerry Kindall BOX 1.50 4.00
200A Don Elston COM 2.50 6.00
200B Don Elston BOX 2.50 6.00
XX Album

1962 Post

The cards in this 200-player series measure 2 1/2" by 3 1/2" and are oriented horizontally. The 1962 Post set is the easiest of the Post sets to complete. The cards are grouped numerically by team, for example, New York Yankees (1-13), Detroit (14-26), Baltimore (27-36), Cleveland (37-45), Chicago White Sox (46-55), Boston (56-64), Washington (65-73), Los Angeles Angels (74-82), Minnesota (83-91), Kansas City (92-100), Los Angeles Dodgers (101-115), Cincinnati (116-130), San Francisco (131-144), Milwaukee (145-157), St. Louis (158-168), Pittsburgh (169-181), Chicago Cubs (182-191), and Philadelphia (192-200). Cards 5B and 6B were printed on thin stock in a two-card panel and distributed in a Life magazine promotion. The scarce cards are 55, 69, 83, 92, 101, 103, 113, 116, 122, 125, 127, 131, 140, 144, and 158. The checklist for this set is the same as that of 1962 Jello and 1962 Post Canadian, but those sets are considered separate issues. The catalog number for this set is F278-37.

COMPLETE MASTER SET (210) 1300.00 2600.00
1 Bill Skowron 3.00 8.00
2 Bobby Richardson 3.00 8.00
3 Cletis Boyer 2.50 6.00
4 Tony Kubek 3.00 8.00
5A Mickey Mantle 100.00 200.00
5B Mickey Mantle AD 100.00 200.00
6A Roger Maris 12.50 30.00
6B Roger Maris AD 12.50 30.00
7 Yogi Berra 12.50 30.00
8 Elston Howard 2.50 6.00
9 Whitey Ford 5.00 12.00
10 Ralph Terry 2.50 5.00
11 John Blanchard 1.50 4.00
12 Luis Arroyo 2.50 5.00
13 Bill Stafford 1.50 4.00
14A N.Cash ERR(T:right) 10.00 25.00
14B N.Cash COR(T:left) 3.00 8.00
15 Jake Wood 1.50 4.00
16 Steve Boros 1.50 4.00
17 Chico Fernandez 1.50 4.00
18 Bill Bruton 1.50 4.00
19 Rocky Colavito 4.00 10.00
20 Al Kaline 8.00 20.00
21 Dick Brown * 1.50 4.00
22 Frank Lary 1.50 4.00
23 Don Mossi 1.50 4.00
24 Phil Regan 1.50 4.00
25 Charley Maxwell 1.50 4.00
26 Jim Bunning 4.00 10.00
27A J.Gentile H-Baltimore 2.50 5.00
27B J.Gentile H-San Lorenzo 10.00 25.00
28 Marv Breeding 1.50 4.00
29 Brooks Robinson 8.00 20.00
30A Ron Hansen (At-Bats) 2.50 6.00
30B Ron Hansen (At Bats) 2.50 6.00
31 Jackie Brandt 1.50 4.00
32 Dick Williams 2.50 5.00
33 Gus Triandos 1.50 4.00
34 Milt Pappas 2.50 5.00
35 Hoyt Wilhelm 4.00 10.00
36 Chuck Estrada 5.00 12.00
37 Vic Power 1.50 4.00
38 Johnny Temple 1.50 4.00
39 Bubba Phillips 1.50 4.00
40 Tito Francona 1.50 4.00
41 Willie Kirkland 1.50 4.00
42 John Romano 1.50 4.00
43 Jim Perry 1.50 4.00
44 Woodie Held 1.50 4.00
45 Chuck Essegian 1.50 4.00
46 Roy Sievers 1.50 4.00
47 Nellie Fox 4.00 10.00
48 Al Smith 1.50 4.00
49 Luis Aparicio 4.00 10.00
50 Jim Landis 1.50 4.00
51 Minnie Minoso 2.50 6.00
52 Andy Carey 1.50 4.00
53 Sherman Lollar 1.50 4.00
54 Billy Pierce 2.50 5.00
55 Early Wynn 15.00 40.00
56 Chuck Schilling 2.50 5.00
57 Pete Runnels 1.50 4.00
58 Frank Malzone 1.50 4.00
59 Don Buddin 1.50 4.00
60 Gary Geiger 1.50 4.00
61 Carl Yastrzemski 20.00 50.00
62 Jackie Jensen 2.50 5.00
63 Jim Pagliaroni 1.50 4.00
64 Don Schwall 1.50 4.00
65 Dale Long 1.50 4.00
66 Chuck Cottier 1.50 4.00
67 Billy Klaus 1.50 4.00
68 Coot Veal 2.50 5.00
69 Marty Keough 20.00 50.00
70 Willie Tasby 1.50 4.00
71 Gene Woodling 1.50 4.00
72 Gene Green 2.50 5.00
73 Dick Donovan 1.50 4.00
74 Steve Bilko 1.50 4.00
75 Rocky Bridges 1.50 4.00
76 Eddie Yost 1.50 4.00
77 Leon Wagner 1.50 4.00
78 Albie Pearson 2.50 5.00
79 Ken Hunt 1.50 4.00
80 Earl Averill 1.50 4.00
81 Ryne Duren 1.50 4.00
82 Ted Kluszewski 5.00 12.00
83 Bob Allison 15.00 40.00
84 Billy Martin 4.00 10.00
85 Harmon Killebrew 5.00 12.00
86 Zoilo Versalles 1.50 4.00
87 Lenny Green 1.50 4.00
88 Bill Tuttle 1.50 4.00
89 Jim Lemon 1.50 4.00
90 Earl Battey 1.50 4.00
91 Camilo Pascual 1.50 4.00
92 Norm Siebern 50.00 100.00
93 Jerry Lumpe 1.50 4.00
94 Dick Howser 2.50 5.00
95A G.Stephens (BD:Jan. 5) 2.50 6.00
95B G.Stephens(BD:Jan.20) 10.00 25.00
96 Leo Posada 1.50 4.00
97 Joe Pignatano 1.50 4.00
98 Jim Archer 1.50 4.00
99 Haywood Sullivan 1.50 4.00
100 Art Ditmar 1.50 4.00
101 Gil Hodges 60.00 120.00
102 Charlie Neal 1.50 4.00
103 Daryl Spencer 15.00 40.00
104 Maury Wills 5.00 12.00
105 Tommy Davis 2.50 5.00
106 Willie Davis 2.50 5.00
107 John Roseboro 1.50 4.00
108 Johnny Podres 2.50 5.00
109A Sandy Koufax 20.00 50.00
109B S.Koufax(w/blue lines) 100.00 200.00
110 Don Drysdale 6.00 15.00
111 Larry Sherry 2.50 5.00
112 Jim Gilliam 2.50 6.00
113 Norm Larker 20.00 50.00
114 Duke Snider 4.00 10.00
115 Stan Williams 1.50 4.00
116 Gordy Coleman 60.00 120.00
117 Don Blasingame 1.50 4.00
118 Gene Freese 1.50 4.00
119 Ed Kasko 1.50 4.00
120 Gus Bell 1.50 4.00
121 Vada Pinson 2.50 5.00
122 Frank Robinson 15.00 40.00
123 Bob Purkey 1.50 4.00
124A Joey Jay 2.50 5.00
124B Joey Jay(w/blue lines) 10.00 25.00
125 Jim Brosnan 15.00 40.00
126 Jim O'Toole 1.50 4.00
127 Jerry Lynch 50.00 100.00
128 Wally Post 1.50 4.00
129 Ken Hunt 1.50 4.00
130 Jerry Zimmerman 1.50 4.00
131 Willie McCovey 60.00 120.00
132 Jose Pagan 1.50 4.00
133 Felipe Alou UER 2.50 5.00
134 Jim Davenport 1.50 4.00
135 Harvey Kuenn 2.50 5.00
136 Orlando Cepeda 3.00 8.00
137 Ed Bailey 1.50 4.00
138 Sam Jones 1.50 4.00
139 Mike McCormick 2.50 5.00
140 Juan Marichal 75.00 150.00
141 Jack Sanford 1.50 4.00
142 Willie Mays 30.00 60.00
143 Stu Miller 3.00 8.00
144 Joe Amalfitano 12.50 30.00
145A Joe Adock (sic) ERR 50.00 100.00
145B Joe Adcock COR 2.50 6.00
146 Frank Bolling 1.50 4.00
147 Eddie Mathews 6.00 15.00
148 Roy McMillan 1.50 4.00
149 Hank Aaron 30.00 60.00
150 Gino Cimoli 1.50 4.00
151 Frank Thomas 1.50 4.00
152 Joe Torre 3.00 8.00
153 Lew Burdette 2.50 5.00
154 Bob Buhl 1.50 4.00
155 Carlton Willey 1.50 4.00
156 Lee Maye 1.50 4.00
157 Al Spangler 1.50 4.00
158 Bill White 20.00 50.00
159 Ken Boyer 3.00 8.00
160 Joe Cunningham 1.50 4.00
161 Carl Warwick 1.50 4.00
162 Carl Sawatski 1.50 4.00
163 Lindy McDaniel 1.50 4.00
164 Ernie Broglio 1.50 4.00
165 Larry Jackson 1.50 4.00
166 Curt Flood 2.50 5.00
167 Curt Simmons 2.50 5.00
168 Alex Grammas 1.50 4.00
169 Dick Stuart 2.50 6.00
170 Bill Mazeroski UER 3.00 8.00
171 Don Hoak 1.50 4.00
172 Dick Groat 2.50 5.00
173A Roberto Clemente 50.00 100.00
173B Clemente(w/blue lines) 150.00 300.00
174 Bob Skinner 1.50 4.00
175 Bill Virdon 2.50 5.00
176 Smoky Burgess 1.50 4.00
177 Roy Face 2.50 5.00
178 Bob Friend 1.50 4.00
179 Vernon Law 1.50 4.00
180 Harvey Haddix 1.50 4.00
181 Hal Smith 1.50 4.00
182 Ed Bouchee 1.50 4.00
183 Don Zimmer 1.50 4.00
184 Ron Santo 2.50 6.00
185 Andre Rodgers 1.50 4.00
186 Richie Ashburn 4.00 10.00
187 George Altman 1.50 4.00
188 Ernie Banks 8.00 20.00
189 Sam Taylor 2.50 5.00
190 Don Elston 1.50 4.00
191 Jerry Kindall 1.50 4.00
192 Pancho Herrera 2.50 5.00
193 Tony Taylor 1.50 4.00
194 Ruben Amaro 1.50 4.00
195 Don Demeter 1.50 4.00
196 Bobby Gene Smith 1.50 4.00
197 Clay Dalrymple 1.50 4.00
198 Robin Roberts 4.00 10.00
199 Art Mahaffey 2.50 5.00
200 John Buzhardt 5.00 12.00

1962 Post Canadian

The 200 blank-backed cards comprising the 1962 Post Canadian set measure approximately 2 1/2" by 3 1/2". The set is similar in appearance to the Jell-O set released in the U.S. that same year. The fronts feature a posed color player photo at the upper right. To the left of the photo, the player's name appears in blue cursive lettering, followed below by bilingual biography and career highlights. The cards are numbered on the front. The cards are grouped by team as follows: New York Yankees (1-13), Detroit (14-26), Baltimore (27-36), Cleveland (37-45), Chicago White Sox (46-55), Boston (56-64), Washington (65-73), Los Angeles Angels (74-82), Minnesota (83-91), Kansas City (92-100), Los Angeles Dodgers (101-115), Cincinnati (116-130), San Francisco (131-144), Milwaukee (145-157), St. Louis (158-168), Pittsburgh (169-181), Chicago Cubs (182-191) and Philadelphia (192-200). Maris (6) and Mays (142) are somewhat scarce. Whitey Ford is listed incorrectly with the Dodgers and correctly with the Yankees. The complete set price includes both Whitey Ford variations.

COMPLETE SET (201) 1500.00 3000.00
1 Bill Skowron 5.00 12.00
2 Bobby Richardson 5.00 12.00
3 Cletis Boyer 4.00 10.00
4 Tony Kubek 5.00 12.00
5 Mickey Mantle 200.00 400.00
6 Roger Maris 60.00 120.00
7 Yogi Berra 30.00 60.00
8 Elston Howard 5.00 12.00
9A Whitey Ford ERR (Los Angeles Dodgers) 40.00 80.00
9B Whitey Ford COR/(New York Yankees) 40.00 80.00
10 Ralph Terry 3.00 8.00
11 John Blanchard 3.00 8.00
12 Luis Arroyo 2.50 6.00
13 Bill Stafford 2.50 6.00
14 Norm Cash 5.00 12.00
15 Jake Wood 2.50 6.00
16 Steve Boros 2.50 6.00
17 Chico Fernandez 2.50 6.00
18 Bill Bruton 2.50 6.00
19A Rocky Colavito 8.00 20.00
Colavito spelled in Large Letter
19B Rocky Colavito 8.00 20.00
Name is in small letter
20 Al Kaline 15.00 40.00
21 Dick Brown 2.50 6.00
22A Frank Lary 8.00 20.00
The word residence is in his vital sta
22B Frank Lary 8.00 20.00
No word residence in french vital stat
23 Don Mossi 3.00 8.00
24 Phil Regan 2.50 6.00
25 Charlie Maxwell 2.50 6.00
26 Jim Bunning 6.00 15.00
27A Jim Gentile 6.00 15.00
Partie is in third line
27B Jim Gentile 6.00 15.00
Partie in on final line of French tex
28 Marv Breeding 2.50 6.00
29 Brooks Robinson 15.00 40.00
30 Ron Hansen 2.50 6.00
31 Jackie Brandt 2.50 6.00
32 Dick Williams 5.00 12.00
33 Gus Triandos 2.50 6.00
34 Milt Pappas 4.00 10.00
35 Hoyt Wilhelm 20.00 50.00
36 Chuck Estrada 2.50 6.00
37 Vic Power 2.50 6.00
38 Johnny Temple 2.50 6.00
39 Bubba Phillips 2.50 6.00
40 Tito Francona 8.00 20.00
41 Willie Kirkland 2.50 6.00
42 John Romano 2.50 6.00
43 Jim Perry 4.00 10.00
44 Woodie Held 2.50 6.00
45 Chuck Essegian 2.50 6.00
46 Roy Sievers 4.00 10.00
47 Nellie Fox 6.00 15.00
48 Al Smith 2.50 6.00
49 Luis Aparicio 20.00 50.00
50 Jim Landis 2.50 6.00
51 Minnie Minoso 5.00 12.00
52 Andy Carey 2.50 6.00
53 Sherman Lollar 2.50 6.00
54 Bill Pierce 4.00 10.00
55 Early Wynn 6.00 15.00
56 Chuck Schilling 2.50 6.00
57 Pete Runnels 3.00 8.00
58 Frank Malzone 3.00 8.00
59 Don Buddin 2.50 6.00
60 Gary Geiger 2.50 6.00
61 Carl Yastrzemski 30.00 60.00
62 Jackie Jensen 4.00 10.00
63 Jim Pagliaroni 2.50 6.00
64 Don Schwall 8.00 20.00
65 Dale Long 2.50 6.00
66 Chuck Cottier 2.50 6.00
67 Billy Klaus 2.50 6.00
68 Coot Veal 2.50 6.00
69 Marty Keough 2.50 6.00
70 Willie Tasby 2.50 6.00
71 Gene Woodling 3.00 8.00
72 Gene Green 2.50 6.00
73 Dick Donovan 2.50 6.00
74 Steve Bilko 2.50 6.00
75 Rocky Bridges 2.50 6.00
76 Eddie Yost 2.50 6.00
77 Leon Wagner 8.00 20.00
78 Albie Pearson 2.50 6.00
79 Ken L. Hunt 2.50 6.00
80 Earl Averill 2.50 6.00
81 Ryne Duren 3.00 8.00
82 Ted Kluszewski 5.00 12.00
83 Bob Allison 2.50 6.00
84 Billy Martin 5.00 12.00
85 Harmon Killebrew 12.50 30.00
86 Zoilo Versalles 4.00 10.00
87 Lenny Green 8.00 20.00
88 Bill Tuttle 2.50 6.00
89 Jim Lemon 2.50 6.00
90 Earl Battey 2.50 6.00
91 Camilo Pascual 3.00 8.00
92 Norm Siebern 2.50 6.00
93 Jerry Lumpe 2.50 6.00
94 Dick Howser 3.00 8.00
95 Gene Stephens 2.50 6.00
96 Leo Posada 2.50 6.00
97 Joe Pignatano 2.50 6.00
98 Jim Archer 2.50 6.00
99 Haywood Sullivan 2.50 6.00
100 Art Ditmar 2.50 6.00
101 Gil Hodges 12.50 30.00
102 Charlie Neal 2.50 6.00
103 Daryl Spencer 2.50 6.00
104 Maury Wills 6.00 15.00
105 Tommy Davis 10.00 25.00
106 Willie Davis 3.00 8.00
107 John Roseboro 3.00 8.00
108 John Podres 4.00 10.00
109 Sandy Koufax 30.00 60.00
110 Don Drysdale 12.50 30.00
111 Larry Sherry 3.00 8.00
112 Jim Gilliam 10.00 25.00
113 Norm Larker 2.50 6.00
114 Duke Snider 15.00 40.00
115 Stan Williams 2.50 6.00
116 Gordy Coleman 2.50 6.00
117 Don Blasingame 8.00 20.00
118 Gene Freese 2.50 6.00
119 Ed Kasko 2.50 6.00
120 Gus Bell 2.50 6.00
121 Vada Pinson 4.00 10.00
122 Frank Robinson 12.50 30.00
123 Bob Purkey 8.00 20.00
124 Joey Jay 2.50 6.00
125 Jim Brosnan 3.00 8.00
126 Jim O'Toole 2.50 6.00
127 Jerry Lynch 2.50 6.00
128 Wally Post 3.00 8.00
129 Ken R. Hunt 2.50 6.00
130 Jerry Zimmerman 3.00 8.00
131 Willie McCovey 12.50 30.00
132 Jose Pagan 2.50 6.00
133 Felipe Alou 5.00 12.00
134 Jim Davenport 2.50 6.00
135 Harvey Kuenn 3.00 8.00
136 Orlando Cepeda 8.00 20.00
137 Ed Bailey 8.00 20.00
138 Sam Jones 2.50 6.00
139 Mike McCormick 2.50 6.00
140 Juan Marichal 12.50 30.00
141 Jack Sanford 2.50 6.00
142 Willie Mays 50.00 100.00
143 Stu Miller 2.50 6.00
144 Joe Amalfitano 15.00 40.00
145 Joe Adcock 3.00 8.00
146 Frank Bolling 2.50 6.00
147 Eddie Mathews 10.00 25.00
148 Roy McMillan 2.50 6.00
149 Hank Aaron 50.00 100.00
150 Gino Cimoli 2.50 6.00
151 Frank Thomas 3.00 8.00
152 Joe Torre 8.00 20.00
153 Lew Burdette 4.00 10.00
154 Bob Buhl 2.50 6.00
155 Carlton Willey 2.50 6.00
156 Lee Maye 2.50 6.00
157 Al Spangler 2.50 6.00
158 Bill White 4.00 10.00
159 Ken Boyer 5.00 12.00
160 Joe Cunningham 3.00 8.00
161 Carl Warwick 8.00 20.00
162 Carl Sawatski 2.50 6.00
163 Lindy McDaniel 2.50 6.00
164 Ernie Broglio 2.50 6.00
165 Larry Jackson 2.50 6.00
166 Curt Flood 4.00 10.00
167 Curt Simmons 2.50 6.00
168 Alex Grammas 2.50 6.00
169 Dick Stuart 2.50 6.00
170 Bill Mazeroski 6.00 15.00
171 Don Hoak 2.50 6.00
172 Dick Groat 4.00 10.00
173 Roberto Clemente 75.00 150.00
174 Bob Skinner 2.50 6.00
175 Bill Virdon 2.50 6.00
176 Smoky Burgess 8.00 20.00
177 Roy Face 4.00 10.00
178 Bob Friend 2.50 6.00
179 Vernon Law 3.00 8.00
180 Harvey Haddix 2.50 6.00
181 Hal Smith 2.50 6.00
182 Ed Bouchee 8.00 20.00
183 Don Zimmer 3.00 8.00
184 Ron Santo 6.00 15.00
185 Andre Rodgers 2.50 6.00
186 Richie Ashburn 6.00 15.00
187 George Altman 2.50 6.00
188 Ernie Banks 15.00 40.00
189 Sam Taylor 2.50 6.00
190 Don Elston 2.50 6.00
191 Jerry Kindall 2.50 6.00
192 Pancho Herrera 2.50 6.00
193 Tony Taylor 3.00 8.00
194 Ruben Amaro 2.50 6.00
195 Don Demeter 2.50 6.00
196 Bobby Gene Smith 2.50 6.00
197 Clay Dalrymple 2.50 6.00
198 Robin Roberts 10.00 25.00
199 Art Mahaffey 2.50 6.00
200 John Buzhardt 2.50 6.00

1963 Post

The cards in this 200-card set measure 2 1/2" by 3 1/2". The players are grouped by team with American Leaguers comprising 1-100 and National Leaguers 101-200. The ordering of teams is as follows: Minnesota (1-11), New York Yankees (12-23), Los Angeles Angels (24-34), Chicago White Sox (35-45), Detroit (46-56), Baltimore (57-66), Cleveland (67-76), Boston (77-84), Kansas City (85-92), Washington (93-100), San Francisco (101-112), Los Angeles Dodgers (113-124), Cincinnati (125-136), Pittsburgh (137-147), Milwaukee (148-157), St. Louis (158-168), Chicago Cubs (169-176), Philadelphia (177-184), Houston (185-192), and New York Mets (193-200). In contrast to the 1962 issue, the 1963 Post baseball card series is very difficult to complete. There are many card scarcities reflected in the price list below. Cards of the Post set are easily confused with those of the 1963 Jello set, which are 1/4" narrower (a difference which is often eliminated by bad cutting). The catalog designation is F278-38. There was also an album produced by Post to hold the cards. The album could only hold 120 cards.

COMPLETE SET (206) 2400.00 4800.00
1 Vic Power 3.00 8.00
2 Bernie Allen 2.50 5.00
3 Zoilo Versalles 2.50 5.00
4 Rich Rollins 2.50 5.00
5 Harmon Killebrew 10.00 25.00
6 Lenny Green 30.00 60.00
7 Bob Allison 2.50 6.00
8 Earl Battey 2.50 6.00
9 Camilo Pascual 2.50 6.00
10 Jim Kaat 3.00 8.00
11 Jack Kralick 2.50 5.00
12 Bill Skowron 3.00 8.00
13 Bobby Richardson 5.00 12.00
14 Cletis Boyer 2.50 5.00
15 Mickey Mantle 200.00 400.00
16 Roger Maris 125.00 250.00
17 Yogi Berra 12.50 30.00
18 Elston Howard 3.00 8.00
19 Whitey Ford 8.00 20.00
20 Ralph Terry 2.50 5.00
21 John Blanchard 2.50 6.00
22 Bill Stafford 2.50 5.00
23 Tom Tresh 2.50 5.00
24 Steve Bilko 2.50 5.00
25 Bill Moran 2.50 5.00
26A Joe Koppe (BA: .277) 2.50 5.00
26B Joe Koppe (BA: .227) 10.00 25.00
27 Felix Torres 2.50 5.00
28A L.Wagner (BA: .278) 2.50 5.00
28B L.Wagner (BA: .272) 10.00 25.00
29 Albie Pearson 2.50 5.00
30 Lee Thomas UER 75.00 150.00
31 Bob Rodgers 2.50 5.00
32 Dean Chance 2.50 5.00
33 Ken McBride 2.50 5.00
34 George Thomas UER 2.50 5.00
35 Joe Cunningham 2.50 5.00
36 Nellie Fox 5.00 12.00
37 Luis Aparicio 4.00 10.00
38 Al Smith 30.00 60.00
39 Floyd Robinson 75.00 150.00
40 Jim Landis 2.50 5.00
41 Charlie Maxwell 2.50 5.00
42 Sherman Lollar 2.50 5.00
43 Early Wynn 4.00 10.00
44 Juan Pizarro 2.50 6.00
45 Ray Herbert 2.50 6.00
46 Norm Cash 2.50 6.00
47 Steve Boros 2.50 5.00
48 Dick McAuliffe 12.50 30.00
49 Bill Bruton 2.50 6.00
50 Rocky Colavito 2.50 6.00
51 Al Kaline 12.50 30.00
52 Dick Brown 2.50 5.00
53 Jim Bunning 125.00 250.00
54 Hank Aguirre 2.50 5.00
55 Frank Lary 2.50 5.00
56 Don Mossi 2.50 5.00
57 Jim Gentile 2.50 5.00
58 Jackie Brandt 2.50 5.00
59 Brooks Robinson 12.50 30.00
60 Ron Hansen 2.50 6.00
61 Jerry Adair 125.00 250.00
62 Boog Powell 3.00 8.00
63 Russ Snyder 2.50 5.00
64 Steve Barber 2.50 5.00
65 Milt Pappas 2.50 5.00
66 Robin Roberts 4.00 10.00
67 Tito Francona 2.50 5.00
68 Jerry Kindall 2.50 5.00
69 Woody Held 2.50 5.00
70 Bubba Phillips 8.00 20.00
71 Chuck Essegian 2.50 5.00
72 Willie Kirkland 2.50 5.00
73 Al Luplow 2.50 5.00
74 Ty Cline 2.50 5.00
75 Dick Donovan 2.50 5.00
76 John Romano 2.50 5.00
77 Pete Runnels 2.50 5.00
78 Ed Bressoud 2.50 5.00
79 Frank Malzone 2.50 5.00
80 Carl Yastrzemski 175.00 350.00
81 Gary Geiger 2.50 5.00
82 Lou Clinton 2.50 5.00
83 Earl Wilson 2.50 5.00
84 Bill Monbouquette 2.50 5.00
85 Norm Siebern 2.50 5.00
86 Jerry Lumpe 75.00 150.00
87 Manny Jimenez 75.00 150.00
88 Gino Cimoli 2.50 5.00
89 Ed Charles 2.50 5.00
90 Ed Rakow 2.50 5.00
91 Bob Del Greco 2.50 5.00
92 Haywood Sullivan 2.50 5.00
93 Chuck Hinton 2.50 5.00
94 Ken Retzer 2.50 5.00
95 Harry Bright 2.50 5.00
96 Bob Johnson 2.50 5.00
97 Dave Stenhouse 8.00 20.00
98 Chuck Cottier 12.50 30.00
99 Tom Cheney 2.50 5.00
100 Claude Osteen 8.00 20.00
101 Orlando Cepeda 4.00 10.00
102 Chuck Hiller 2.50 5.00
103 Jose Pagan 2.50 5.00
104 Jim Davenport 2.50 5.00
105 Harvey Kuenn 2.50 6.00
106 Willie Mays 30.00 60.00
107 Felipe Alou 2.50 6.00
108 Tom Haller 75.00 150.00
109 Juan Marichal 5.00 12.00
110 Jack Sanford 2.50 5.00
111 Bill O'Dell 2.50 5.00
112 Willie McCovey 5.00 12.00
113 Lee Walls 2.50 5.00
114 Jim Gilliam 3.00 8.00
115 Maury Wills 3.00 8.00
116 Ron Fairly 2.50 6.00
117 Tommy Davis 2.50 6.00
118 Duke Snider 5.00 12.00
119 Willie Davis 125.00 250.00
120 John Roseboro 2.50 5.00
121 Sandy Koufax 30.00 60.00
122 Stan Williams 2.50 5.00
123 Don Drysdale 5.00 12.00
124 Daryl Spencer 2.50 5.00
125 Gordy Coleman 2.50 5.00
126 Don Blasingame 2.50 5.00
127 Leo Cardenas 2.50 5.00
128 Eddie Kasko 125.00 250.00
129 Jerry Lynch 8.00 20.00
130 Vada Pinson 3.00 8.00
131A F.Robinson(No stripes) 12.50 30.00
131B F.Robinson(Stripes/hat) 30.00 60.00
132 John Edwards 2.50 6.00
133 Joey Jay 2.50 5.00
134 Bob Purkey 2.50 5.00
135 Marty Keough 15.00 40.00
136 Jim O'Toole 2.50 5.00
137 Dick Stuart 2.50 5.00
138 Bill Mazeroski 5.00 12.00
139 Dick Groat 2.50 6.00
140 Don Hoak 20.00 50.00
141 Bob Skinner 10.00 25.00
142 Bill Virdon 2.50 6.00
143 Roberto Clemente 60.00 120.00
144 Smoky Burgess 2.50 6.00
145 Bob Friend 2.50 5.00
146 Al McBean 2.50 5.00
147 Roy Face 2.50 6.00
148 Joe Adcock 2.50 6.00
149 Frank Bolling 2.50 5.00
150 Roy McMillan 2.50 5.00
151 Eddie Mathews 10.00 25.00
152 Hank Aaron 100.00 200.00
153 Del Crandall 20.00 50.00
154A Bob Shaw COR 2.50 5.00
154B Bob Shaw ERR (Two in 1959) 8.00 20.00
155 Lew Burdette 3.00 8.00
156 Joe Torre 3.00 8.00
157 Tony Cloninger 2.50 5.00
158A Bill White (Ht. 6'0) 2.50 6.00
158B Bill White (Ht. 6';) 2.50 6.00
159 Julian Javier 2.50 5.00
160 Ken Boyer 4.00 10.00
161 Julio Gotay 2.50 5.00
162 Curt Flood 75.00 150.00
163 Charlie James 2.50 5.00
164 Gene Oliver 2.50 5.00
165 Ernie Broglio 2.50 5.00
166 Bob Gibson 5.00 12.00
167A Lindy McDaniel (No *) 4.00 10.00
167B L.McDaniel (w/*trade) 4.00 10.00
168 Ray Washburn 2.50 5.00
169 Ernie Banks 10.00 25.00
170 Ron Santo 3.00 8.00
171 George Altman 2.50 5.00
172 Billy Williams 125.00 250.00
173 Andre Rodgers 8.00 20.00
174 Ken Hubbs 15.00 40.00
175 Don Landrum 2.50 5.00
176 Dick Bertell 10.00 25.00
177 Roy Sievers 2.50 5.00
178 Tony Taylor 2.50 6.00
179 John Callison 2.50 5.00
180 Don Demeter 2.50 6.00
181 Tony Gonzalez 8.00 20.00
182 Wes Covington 12.50 30.00
183 Art Mahaffey 2.50 5.00
184 Clay Dalrymple 2.50 5.00
185 Al Spangler 2.50 5.00
186 Roman Mejias 2.50 5.00
187 Bob Aspromonte 250.00 500.00
188 Norm Larker 20.00 50.00
189 Johnny Temple 2.50 5.00
190 Carl Warwick 2.50 5.00
191 Bob Lillis 2.50 5.00
192 Dick Farrell 2.50 5.00
193 Gil Hodges 5.00 12.00
194 Marv Throneberry 2.50 6.00
195 Charlie Neal 5.00 12.00
196 Frank Thomas 150.00 300.00
197 Richie Ashburn 15.00 40.00
198 Felix Mantilla 2.50 5.00
199 Rod Kanehl 10.00 25.00
200 Roger Craig 2.50 6.00
XX Album

1979 Post Garvey Tips

These "Baseball Tips" were printed on boxes of Post Raisin Bran cereal in 1979. Cards 1-6 were on 15 oz. boxes and cards 7-12 were on the larger 20 oz. boxes. The cards are blank backed and feature a lime green background color with a red stitching border around the card. The cards measure approximately 7" by 2 1/16" although as with most cereal cards they are frequently found badly cut. The set essentially consists of Steve Garvey's advice or tips on various segments and aspects of the game of baseball. Each card shows a crude line drawing demonstrating the skill discussed in the narrative on the card. Each card contains a color drawing of Steve Garvey in the upper left corner of the card along with his facsimile autograph. Cards on full boxes are worth 3x the listed price.

COMPLETE SET (12) 30.00 60.00
COMMON CARD (1-6) 2.00 5.00
COMMON CARD (7-12) 3.00 8.00

1990 Post

1990 Post Cereal is a 30-card standard-size set issued with the assistance of Mike Schechter Associates. The sets do not have either team logos or other uniform identification on them. There is also a facsimile autograph on the back of the cards. The cards were inserted randomly as a cello pack (with three cards) inside specially marked boxes of Post cereals. The cards feature red, white, and blue fronts with the words, "First Collector Series". Card backs feature a facsimile autograph.

COMPLETE SET (30) 4.00 10.00
1 Don Mattingly .50 1.25
2 Roger Clemens .50 1.25
3 Kirby Puckett .25 .60
4 George Brett .40 1.00
5 Tony Gwynn .50 1.25
6 Ozzie Smith .30 .75
7 Will Clark .10 .30
8 Orel Hershiser .02 .10
9 Ryne Sandberg .30 .75
10 Darryl Strawberry .02 .10
11 Nolan Ryan 1.00 2.50
12 Mark McGwire .50 1.25
13 Jim Abbott .07 .20
14 Bo Jackson .10 .30
15 Kevin Mitchell .01 .05
16 Jose Canseco .25 .60
17 Wade Boggs .20 .50
18 Dale Murphy .10 .30
19 Mark Grace .10 .30
20 Mike Scott .01 .05
21 Cal Ripken 1.00 2.50
22 Pedro Guerrero .01 .05
23 Ken Griffey Jr. .60 1.50
24 Eric Davis .02 .10
25 Rickey Henderson .30 .75
26 Robin Yount .15 .40
27 Von Hayes .01 .05
28 Alan Trammell .10 .30
29 Dwight Gooden .02 .10
30 Joe Carter .02 .10

1991 Post

This 30-card standard-size set was released early in 1991 by Post Cereal in conjunction with Michael Schechter Associates (MSA). The players pictured are some of the star players of baseball entering the 1991 season. The cards were inserted three-at-a-time in boxes of the following cereals: Post Honeycomb, Super Golden Crisp, Cocoa Pebbles, Fruity Pebbles, Alpha-Bits, and Marshmallow Alpha-Bits. Some cards (numbers 1, 6, 25, and 30) have a banner at the top that reads "Rookie Star".

COMPLETE SET (30) 3.00 8.00
1 Dave Justice .10 .30
2 Mark McGwire .50 1.25
3 Will Clark .10 .30
4 Jose Canseco .15 .40
5 Vince Coleman .01 .05
6 Sandy Alomar Jr. .02 .10
7 Darryl Strawberry .02 .10
8 Len Dykstra .02 .10
9 Gregg Jefferies .01 .05
10 Tony Gwynn .50 1.25
11 Ken Griffey Jr. .60 1.50
12 Roger Clemens .50 1.25
13 Chris Sabo .01 .05
14 Bobby Bonilla .01 .05
15 Gary Sheffield .15 .40
16 Ryne Sandberg .30 .75
17 Nolan Ryan 1.00 2.50
18 Barry Larkin .10 .30
19 Cal Ripken 1.00 2.50
20 Jim Abbott .02 .10
21 Barry Bonds .50 1.25
22 Mark Grace .10 .30
23 Cecil Fielder .02 .10
24 Kevin Mitchell .01 .05
25 Todd Zeile .02 .10
26 George Brett .50 1.25
27 Rickey Henderson .20 .50
28 Kirby Puckett .25 .60
29 Don Mattingly .50 1.25
30 Kevin Maas .01 .05

1991 Post Canadian

This 30-card Super Stars set was sponsored by Post and features 14 National League and 16 American League players. Two cards were inserted in specially marked boxes of Post Alpha-Bits, Sugar Crisp and Honeycomb sold in Canada. The cards measure the standard size and are bilingual (French and English) on both sides. While all the cards feature color player photos (action or posed) on the fronts, the NL cards (1-14) are accentuated with red stripes while the AL cards (15-30) have royal blue stripes.

COMPLETE SET (30) 6.00 15.00
1 Delino DeShields .07 .20
2 Tim Wallach .02 .10
3 Andres Galarraga .15 .40
4 Dave Magadan .02 .10
5 Barry Bonds UER/(Career BA .256, should be .265) .50 1.25

6 Len Dykstra .07 .20
7 Andre Dawson .15 .40
8 Ozzie Smith .40 1.00
9 Will Clark .15 .40
10 Chris Sabo .02 .10
11 Eddie Murray .20 .50
12 Dave Justice .15 .40
13 Benito Santiago .07 .20
14 Glenn Davis .02 .10
15 Kelly Gruber .02 .10
16 Dave Stieb .07 .20
17 John Olerud .07 .20
18 Roger Clemens .60 1.50
19 Cecil Fielder .07 .20
20 Kevin Maas .02 .10
21 Robin Yount .20 .50
22 Cal Ripken 1.25 3.00
23 Sandy Alomar Jr. .07 .20
24 Rickey Henderson .30 .75
25 Bobby Thigpen .02 .10
26 Ken Griffey Jr. .75 2.00
27 Nolan Ryan 1.25 3.00
28 Dave Winfield .20 .50
29 George Brett .50 1.25
30 Kirby Puckett .25 .60

1992 Post

This 30-card standard-size set was manufactured by MSA (Michael Schechter Associates) for Post Cereal. Three-card packs were inserted in the following Post cereals: Honeycomb, Super Golden Crisp, Cocoa Pebbles, Fruity Pebbles, Alpha-Bits, Marshmallow Alpha-Bits and, for the first time, Raisin Bran. In the last-mentioned cereal, the cards were protected in cello packs that also had a 50 cent manufacturers coupon good on the next purchase. The other cereals contained tan paper wrapped packs. The complete set could also be obtained via a mail-in offer for 1.00 and five UPC symbols. The Bagwell and Knoblauch cards display the words "Rookie Star" in a yellow banner at the card top.

COMPLETE SET (30) 2.50 6.00
1 Jeff Bagwell .20 .50
2 Ryne Sandberg .25 .60
3 Don Mattingly .40 1.00
4 Wally Joyner .02 .10
5 Dwight Gooden .02 .10
6 Chuck Knoblauch .07 .20
7 Kirby Puckett .20 .50
8 Ozzie Smith .25 .60
9 Cal Ripken .75 2.00
10 Darryl Strawberry .02 .10
11 George Brett .30 .75
12 Joe Carter .02 .10
13 Cecil Fielder .02 .10
14 Will Clark .07 .20
15 Barry Bonds .40 1.00
16 Roger Clemens .40 1.00
17 Paul Molitor .15 .40
18 Scott Erickson .02 .10
19 Wade Boggs .25 .60
20 Ken Griffey Jr. .50 1.25
21 Bobby Bonilla .01 .05
22 Terry Pendleton .01 .05
23 Barry Larkin .07 .20
24 Frank Thomas .20 .50
25 Jose Canseco .15 .40
26 Tony Gwynn .40 1.00
27 Nolan Ryan .75 2.00
28 Howard Johnson .01 .05
29 Dave Justice .07 .20
30 Danny Tartabull .01 .05

1992 Post Canadian

This 18-card Post Super Star II stand-up set was sponsored by Post and measures the standard size. The set features nine American League and nine National League players and is bilingual (French and English) on both sides. The NL cards (1-9) are accented with a red stripe at the top and bottom of the photo and the AL cards (10-18) are accented with blue stripes. A "collector album" was also issued which held the cards in nine-pocket pages. Also included in the album was a guide to player stats.

COMPLETE SET (18) 6.00 15.00
1 Dennis Martinez .15 .40
2 Benito Santiago .15 .40
3 Will Clark .40 1.00
4 Ryne Sandberg .60 1.50
5 Tim Wallach .07 .20
6 Ozzie Smith .60 1.50
7 Darryl Strawberry .15 .40
8 Brett Butler .15 .40
9 Barry Bonds .75 2.00
10 Roger Clemens .75 2.00
11 Sandy Alomar Jr. .15 .40
12 Cecil Fielder .15 .40
13 Roberto Alomar .30 .75
14 Kelly Gruber .07 .20
15 Cal Ripken 1.50 4.00
16 Jose Canseco .40 1.00
17 Kirby Puckett .50 1.25
18 Rickey Henderson .50 1.25

1993 Post

This 30-card standard-size set features full-bleed action color player photos. Three-packs of cards were found in specially marked boxes of Post Cereal during this promotion. In addition, complete sets were available as a mail-in for five proofs of purchase from any Post Cereal plus 1.00.

COMPLETE SET (30) 2.50 6.00
1 Dave Fleming .01 .05
2 Will Clark .10 .30
3 Kirby Puckett .20 .50
4 Roger Clemens .40 1.00
5 Fred McGriff .07 .20
6 Eric Karros .07 .20
7 Ken Griffey Jr. .50 1.25
8 Tony Gwynn .30 .75
9 Cal Ripken .75 2.00
10 Cecil Fielder .02 .10
11 Gary Sheffield .20 .50
12 Don Mattingly .40 1.00
13 Ryne Sandberg .30 .75
14 Frank Thomas .15 .40
15 Barry Bonds .40 1.00
16 Paul Molitor .15 .40
17 Terry Pendleton .01 .05
18 Darren Daulton .02 .10
19 Mark McGwire .40 1.00
20 Nolan Ryan .75 2.00
21 Tom Glavine .15 .40
22 Roberto Alomar .10 .30
23 Juan Gonzalez .10 .30
24 Bobby Bonilla .01 .05
25 George Brett .30 .75
26 Ozzie Smith .30 .75
27 Andy Van Slyke .02 .10
28 Barry Larkin .10 .30
29 John Kruk .02 .10
30 Robin Yount .15 .40

1993 Post Canadian

This 18-card limited edition stand-up set was sponsored by Post and measures the standard size. The set features American League (1-9) and National League (10-18) players and is printed in French and English. The cards are numbered on the front.

COMPLETE SET (18) 8.00 20.00
1 Pat Borders .08 .25
2 Juan Guzman .08 .25
3 Roger Clemens 1.00 2.50
4 Joe Carter .20 .50
5 Roberto Alomar .40 1.00
6 Robin Yount .50 1.25
7 Ken Griffey Jr. 1.25 3.00
8 Kirby Puckett .60 1.50
9 Cal Ripken 2.00 5.00
10 Darren Daulton .20 .50
11 Andy Van Slyke .20 .50
12 Bobby Bonilla .08 .25
13 Larry Walker .40 1.00
14 Ryne Sandberg .60 1.50
15 Barry Larkin .40 1.00
16 Gary Sheffield .50 1.25
17 Ozzie Smith .50 1.25
18 Terry Pendleton .08 .25

1994 Post

This 30-card standard-size set was sponsored by Post and produced by MSA (Michael Schechter Associates). The cards are numbered on the back "X of 30."

COMPLETE SET (30) 2.00 5.00
1 Mike Piazza .50 1.25
2 Don Mattingly .40 1.00
3 Juan Gonzalez .08 .25
4 Kirby Puckett .10 .30
5 Gary Sheffield .15 .40
6 Dave Justice .08 .25
7 Jack McDowell .01 .05
8 Mo Vaughn .02 .10
9 Darren Daulton .02 .10
10 Bobby Bonilla .01 .05
11 Barry Bonds .40 1.00
12 Barry Larkin .08 .25
13 Tony Gwynn .40 1.00
14 Mark Grace .05 .15
15 Ken Griffey Jr. .60 1.50
16 Tom Glavine .10 .30
17 Cecil Fielder .02 .10
18 Roberto Alomar .08 .25
19 Mark Whiten .01 .05
20 Lenny Dykstra .02 .10
21 Frank Thomas .20 .50
22 Will Clark .08 .25
23 Andres Galarraga .08 .25
24 John Olerud .02 .10
25 Cal Ripken .75 2.00
26 Tim Salmon .08 .25
27 Albert Belle .02 .10
28 Gregg Jefferies .01 .05
29 Jeff Bagwell .30 .75
30 Orlando Merced .01 .05

1994 Post Canadian

This 18-card set was distributed as single cello-wrapped cards in Canadian Post Alpha-Bits, Honeycomb, Sugar-Crisp, and Marshmallow Alpha-Bits. The cards are slightly smaller than standard-size, measuring 2 1/2" by 3 3/8". Randomly inserted throughout the boxes were Joe Carter HERO cards; 1,000 of these were personally signed. Odds of finding a HERO card were about 1 in 16; odds for finding a signed HERO card were 1 in 3,000. The entire set was available through a mail-in offer for 7 UPC's and $3.49 for postage and handling. An album to display the cards was offered for 2 UPC's and $5.99, plus $4.50 for postage and handling. The cards are numbered on the back as "X of 18." It is believed that only Joe Carter comes in a gold version.

COMPLETE SET (18) 8.00 20.00
1 Joe Carter .20 .50
1G Joe Carter Gold 2.00 5.00
2 Paul Molitor .50 1.25
3 Roberto Alomar .40 1.00
4 John Olerud .20 .50
5 Dave Stewart .20 .50
6 Juan Guzman .08 .25
7 Pat Borders .08 .25
8 Larry Walker .40 1.00
9 Moises Alou .20 .50
10 Ken Griffey Jr. 1.25 3.00
11 Barry Bonds .75 2.00
12 Frank Thomas .50 1.25
13 Cal Ripken 2.00 5.00
14 Mike Piazza 1.25 3.00
15 Juan Gonzalez .40 1.00
16 Len Dykstra .20 .50
17 David Justice .30 .75
18 Kirby Puckett .50 1.25
NNO Joe Carter AU Hero Card 8.00 20.00

1995 Post

This 16-card standard-size set was distributed solely in limited in-store promotions. Unlike previous years, the cards were not available in cereal boxes nor directly from the company.

COMPLETE SET (16) 4.00 10.00
1 Wade Boggs .30 .75
2 Jeff Bagwell .20 .50
3 Greg Maddux .75 2.00
4 Ken Griffey Jr. .75 2.00
5 Roberto Alomar .15 .40
6 Kirby Puckett .25 .60
7 Tony Gwynn .60 1.50
8 Cal Ripken Jr. 1.25 3.00
9 Matt Williams .10 .30
10 David Justice .15 .40
11 Barry Bonds .50 1.25
12 Mike Piazza .75 2.00
13 Albert Belle .07 .20
14 Frank Thomas .30 .75
15 Len Dykstra .02 .10
16 Will Clark .15 .40

1995 Post Canadian

This 18-card standard-size set was produced by Upper Deck and issued one per box and was also available via mail-order from the company. The cards carry both English and French printing and were designed to fit into a marblized design black book with the words "1995 Anniversary Edition" printed in gold foil in English and French on the front.

COMPLETE SET (18) 12.50 30.00
1 Ken Griffey Jr. 3.00 8.00
2 Roberto Alomar 1.00 2.50
3 Paul Molitor 1.25 3.00
4 Devon White .40 1.00
5 Moises Alou .60 1.50
6 Ken Hill .40 1.00
7 Paul O'Neill .60 1.50
8 Joe Carter .60 1.50
9 Kirby Puckett 1.25 3.00
10 Jimmy Key .60 1.50
11 Frank Thomas 1.25 3.00
12 David Cone .75 2.00
13 Tony Gwynn 2.00 5.00
14 Matt Williams .75 2.00
15 Greg Maddux 2.50 6.00
16 Jeff Bagwell 1.25 3.00
17 Barry Bonds 2.00 5.00
18 Cal Ripken Jr. 4.00 10.00
XX Album 2.00 5.00

2001 Post

COMPLETE SET (18) 8.00 25.00
1 Alex Rodriguez .75 2.00
2 Barry Bonds .75 2.00
3 Bernie Williams .50 1.00
4 Frank Thomas .60 1.25
5 Greg Maddux 1.20 3.00
6 Mark McGwire 1.00 2.50
7 Manny Ramirez .50 1.00
8 Orlando Hernandez .10 .25
9 Pedro Martinez .50 1.25
10 Gary Sheffield .50 1.25
11 Jermaine Dye .10 .25
12 Mike Piazza 1.20 3.00
13 Barry Larkin .50 1.00
14 Brad Radke .20 .50
15 Ivan Rodriguez .50 1.25
16 Moises Alou .20 .50
17 Tony Gwynn 1.00 2.50
18 Todd Helton .60 1.50

2001 Post 500 Club

COMPLETE SET (8) 3.20 8.00
1 Babe Ruth 1.20 3.00
2 Ernie Banks .40 1.00
3 Jimmie Foxx .60 1.50
4 Willie McCovey .30 .75
5 Frank Robinson .40 1.00
6 Harmon Killebrew .30 .75
7 Mike Schmidt .60 1.50
8 Reggie Jackson .60 1.50

2002 Post

COMPLETE SET (30) 8.00 30.00
1 Alex Rodriguez 1.00 2.50
2 Pedro Martinez .50 1.25
3 Bernie Williams .50 1.25
4 Mike Piazza 1.50 4.00
5 Jim Edmonds .30 .75
6 Rich Aurilia .20 .50
7 Sammy Sosa 1.25 3.00
8 Sean Casey .30 .75
9 Ichiro Suzuki 2.00 5.00
10 Jason Giambi .30 .75
11 Todd Helton .50 1.25
12 Chipper Jones .60 1.50
13 Frank Thomas .60 1.50
14 Scott Rolen .60 1.50
15 Carlos Delgado .50 1.25
16 Jeff Bagwell .50 1.25
17 Jim Thome .60 1.50
18 Shawn Green .50 1.25
19 Luis Gonzalez .50 1.25
20 Vladimir Guerrero .60 1.50
21 Troy Glaus .50 1.25
22 Ryan Klesko .30 .75
23 Jeromy Burnitz .20 .50
24 Bobby Higginson .20 .50
25 Jason Kendall .30 .75
26 Cliff Floyd .30 .75
27 Greg Vaughn .30 .75
28 Brad Radke .30 .75
29 Mike Sweeney .30 .75
30 Jeff Conine .20 .50

2003 Post

COMPLETE SET (6) 2.50 6.00
COMMON CARD .20 .50
1 Barry Bonds .75 2.00
2 Miguel Tejada .30 .75
3 Ichiro Suzuki .60 1.50
4 Ken Griffey Jr. 1.00 2.50
5 Jason Giambi .20 .50
6 Sammy Sosa .50 1.25

2003 Post Upper Deck

COMPLETE SET 4.00 10.00
COMMON CARD .10 .25
1 Troy Percival .10 .25
2 Curt Schilling .15 .40
3 John Smoltz .25 .60
4 Tony Batista .10 .25
5 Pedro Martinez .15 .40
6 Sammy Sosa .25 .60
7 Paul Konerko .15 .40
8 Ken Griffey Jr .50 1.25
9 Jim Thome .15 .40
11 Larry Walker .15 .40
12 Luis Castillo .10 .25
13 Craig Biggio .15 .40
14 Mike Sweeney .10 .25
15 Shawn Green .10 .25
16 Richie Sexson .10 .25
17 Torii Hunter .10 .25
18 Vladimir Guerrero .15 .40
19 Mike Piazza .25 .60
20 Jason Giambi .10 .25
21 Miguel Tejada .15 .40
22 Pat Burrell .10 .25
23 Brian Giles .10 .25
24 Trevor Hoffman .15 .40
25 Barry Bonds .40 1.00
26 Ichiro Suzuki .30 .75
27 Albert Pujols .30 .75
28 Randy Winn .10 .25
29 Alex Rodriguez .30 .75
30 Carlos Delgado .10 .25
31 Troy Glaus .10 .25

1997 Premier Concepts

This 30-card set produced and distributed by Premier Concepts, Inc. features color action player photos on lenticular cards with a thin white inner border and black outer border with gold foil lettering. When held, these motion cards show the player swinging the bat with a twist of the wrist. The cards measure approximately 7 1/8" by 6 1/4". The backs carry a checklist of the set. Only 5,000 numbered editions of each framed motion print were made and sequentially numbered on the back. The cards were separated into four divisions: East (1-7), Central (8-14), West (15-21), and Rookies (22-30). The cards are unnumbered and checklisted below alphabetically within each division.

COMPLETE SET (30) 60.00 120.00
1 Roberto Alomar 1.25 3.00
2 Derek Jeter 4.00 10.00
3 Chipper Jones 2.50 6.00
4 Greg Maddux 2.50 6.00
5 Cal Ripken 4.00 10.00
6 Gary Sheffield 1.50 4.00
7 Mo Vaughn .75 2.00
8 Jeff Bagwell 1.50 4.00
9 Albert Belle .75 2.00
10 Brian Jordan .75 2.00
11 Manny Ramirez 1.50 4.00
12 Ryne Sandberg 2.00 5.00
13 Sammy Sosa 1.50 4.00
14 Frank Thomas 1.25 3.00
15 Barry Bonds 1.50 4.00
16 Juan Gonzalez .75 2.00
17 Ken Griffey Jr. 2.50 6.00
18 Tony Gwynn 2.00 5.00
19 Mark McGwire 2.50 6.00
20 Mike Piazza 2.50 6.00
21 Alex Rodriguez 3.00 8.00
22 Tony Clark .60 1.50
23 Darin Erstad 1.25 3.00
24 Nomar Garciaparra 2.00 5.00
25 Vladimir Guerrero 2.00 5.00
26 Todd Hollandsworth .60 1.50
27 Andruw Jones(1) 2.00 5.00
28 Andruw Jones(2) 2.00 5.00
29 Scott Rolen 1.50 4.00
30 Dmitri Young .75 2.00

1998 Premier Concepts

This 20-card set produced and distributed by Premier Concepts, Inc. features color action player photos on lenticular cards set in a plastic black frame with a suggested retail price of $6. When held, these motion cards show the player swinging the bat with a twist of the wrist. The cards measure approximately 6 1/2" by 8" including the frame and were distributed in a blister package which included a tripod to display the Replay card. Twelve of the cards show only single players (1-12), while eight picture two players (13-20). The cards are unnumbered and checklisted below in alphabetical order within the single and by the first player listed in the double divisions.

COMPLETE SET (20) 30.00 80.00
1 Jeff Bagwell 1.00 2.50
2 Barry Bonds 2.00 5.00
3 Nomar Garciaparra 2.00 5.00
4 Ken Griffey Jr.(1) 2.50 6.00
5 Ken Griffey Jr.(2) 2.50 6.00
6 Tony Gwynn 2.00 5.00
7 Chipper Jones 2.00 5.00
8 Mike Piazza 2.50 6.00
9 Cal Ripken 4.00 10.00
10 Alex Rodriguez 2.00 5.00
11 Frank Thomas 1.50 4.00
12 Larry Walker .40 1.00
13 Sandy Alomar Jr. Omar Vizquel .40 1.00
14 Anderson Mike Mussina .75 2.00
15 Juan Gonzalez Ivan Rodriguez 1.50 4.00
16 Johnson Hernandez .40 1.00
17 Dave Justice Jim Thome .75 2.00
18 Tino Martinez Bernie Williams .75 2.00
19 Mark McGwire Lankford 1.50 4.00
20 Andy Pettitte Derek Jeter 4.00 10.00

2009 Press Pass Fusion

COMPLETE SET (90) 15.00 40.00
1 Joba Chamberlain .50 1.25
2 Bob Gibson .30 .75
3 Tony Gwynn .30 .75
4 Orel Hershiser .15 .40
5 Fred Lynn .15 .40
6 Paul Molitor .15 .40
7 Tom Seaver .30 .75
8 Jason Varitek .15 .40
9 Matt Williams .15 .40
10 Carl Yastrzemski .30 .75
11 John Elway .75 2.00
12 Kirk Gibson .15 .40
13 Dustin Pedroia .50 1.25

2009 Press Pass Fusion Bronze

*BRONZE: 1X TO 2.5X BASE
STATED PRINT RUN 150 SER. #'d SETS

2009 Press Pass Fusion Gold

*GOLD: 2X TO 5X BASE
STATED PRINT RUN 50 SER. #'d SETS

2009 Press Pass Fusion Green

*GREEN: 3X TO 8X BASE
STATED PRINT RUN 25 SER. #'d SETS

2009 Press Pass Fusion Silver

*SILVER: 1.25X TO 3X BASE
STATED PRINT RUN 99 SER. #'d SETS

2009 Press Pass Fusion Autographs Gold

STATED PRINT RUN 10-199
EXCHANGE DEADLINE 12/1/10
SSBG Bob Gibson/50 15.00 30.00
SSDP Dustin Pedroia/47 20.00 40.00
SSFL Fred Lynn/146 10.00 20.00
SSJC Joba Chamberlain/25 20.00 40.00
SSJV Jason Varitek/26 10.00 20.00
SSKG Kirk Gibson/25 10.00 20.00
SSMW Matt Williams/75 6.00 15.00
SSTG Tony Gwynn/99 25.00 50.00

2009 Press Pass Fusion Autographs Green

STATED PRINT RUN 5-100
EXCHANGE DEADLINE 12/1/2010
SSDP Dustin Pedroia/21 25.00 50.00
SSFL Fred Lynn/100 8.00 20.00
SSMW Matt Williams/50 8.00 20.00
SSTG Tony Gwynn/50 30.00 60.00

2009 Press Pass Fusion Autographs Silver

RANDOM INSERT IN PACKS
EXCHANGE DEADLINE 12/1/2010
SSBG Bob Gibson 15.00 30.00
SSDP Dustin Pedroia 15.00 30.00
SSFL Fred Lynn 10.00 20.00
SSKG Kirk Gibson 6.00 15.00
SSMW Matt Williams 6.00 15.00
SSTG Tony Gwynn 20.00 40.00

2009 Press Pass Fusion Classic Champions

COMPLETE SET (10) 6.00 15.00
STATED ODDS 1:10
CCH1 Tom Seaver 1.00 2.50

2009 Press Pass Fusion Collegiate Connections

COMPLETE SET (10) 6.00 15.00
STATED ODDS 1:10
CCN1 K.McHale/P.Molitor .60 1.50
CCN2 J.Montana/C.Yastrzemski 2.50 6.00
CCN4 F.Gifford/T.Seaver 1.00 2.50

2009 Press Pass Fusion Cross Training

COMPLETE SET (10) 6.00 15.00
STATED ODDS 1:10
CT1 K.Gibson/O.Hershiser .60 1.50
CT3 D.Rose/D.Sanders 1.00 2.50
CT5 J.Chamberlain/C.Osterman 1.00 2.50
CT8 B.Gibson/R.Petty 1.50 4.00
CT10 T.Gwynn/P.Hellmuth 1.00 2.50

2009 Press Pass Fusion Cross Training Autographs Gold

STATED PRINT RUN 50-100
CTAKGOH Gibson/Hershiser/50 20.00 40.00

2009 Press Pass Fusion Renowned Rivals

COMPLETE SET (10) 6.00 15.00
STATED ODDS 1:10
RR1 T.Gwynn/O.Hershiser 1.00 2.50
RR7 J.Chamberlain/D.Pedroia 1.50 4.00

2009 Press Pass Fusion Timeless Talent

COMPLETE SET (10) 6.00 15.00
STATED ODDS 1:10
TT1 Paul Molitor .60 1.50
TT6 Jason Varitek .60 1.50
TT7 Matt Williams .60 1.50
TT8 Joba Chamberlain 1.50 4.00

2009 Press Pass Fusion Timeless Talent Autographs Gold

STATED PRINT RUN 15-99
TTJC Joba Chamberlain/25 20.00 40.00
TTMW Matt Williams/98 8.00 20.00

2009 Press Pass Fusion Timeless Talent Autographs Green

STATED PRINT RUN 10-50
TTMW Matt Williams/50 15.00 30.00

2009 Press Pass Fusion Timeless Talent Autographs Silver

STATED PRINT RUN 26-193
TTJC Joba Chamberlain/54 20.00 40.00
TTJV Jason Varitek/26 10.00 20.00
TTMW Matt Williams/150 8.00 20.00
TTPM Paul Molitor/28 15.00 30.00

2012 Press Pass Legends Hall of Fame Blue

LGGP Gaylord Perry/35 8.00 20.00
LGJM Juan Marichal/35 10.00 25.00
LGJP Jim Palmer/35 10.00 25.00
LGMI Monte Irvin/35
LGNR Nolan Ryan/35 75.00 150.00
LGOS Ozzie Smith/35 25.00 50.00
LGRH Rickey Henderson/12*
LGRS Red Schoendienst/30* 8.00 20.00
LGRS Ryne Sandberg/27* 25.00 50.00
LGTG Tony Gwynn/33* 12.00 30.00

2012 Press Pass Legends Hall of Fame Blue Red Ink

STATED PRINT RUN 2-35
LGRH Rickey Henderson/23*
LGRK Ralph Kiner/35 8.00 20.00
LGRS Red Schoendienst/5*
LGRS Ryne Sandberg/8*
LGTG Tony Gwynn/2*

2012 Press Pass Legends Hall of Fame Bronze

*BRONZE/95-99: .3X TO .8X RED/50
*BRONZE/50: .4X TO 1X RED/50
*BRONZE/30: .5X TO 1.2X RED/50
PRINT RUN 19-99
LGGP Gaylord Perry/99 6.00 15.00

2012 Press Pass Legends Hall of Fame Bronze Red Ink

STATED PRINT RUN 11-50
LGOS Ozzie Smith/40 15.00 40.00

2012 Press Pass Legends Hall of Fame Champions Blue

STATED PRINT RUN 19-35
CHRH Rickey Henderson/35 50.00 100.00

2012 Press Pass Legends Hall of Fame Champions Purple

STATED PRINT RUN 8-25
CHRH Rickey Henderson/25 50.00 100.00

2012 Press Pass Legends Hall of Fame Fan Favorites Blue

STATED PRINT RUN 12-35
FFMI Monte Irvin/12*
FFRS Red Schoendienst/35 8.00 20.00
FFTG Tony Gwynn/35 12.00 30.00

2012 Press Pass Legends Hall of Fame Fan Favorites Blue Red Ink

STATED PRINT RUN 10-23
FFMI Monte Irvin/23* 15.00 40.00

2012 Press Pass Legends Hall of Fame Fan Favorites Purple

STATED PRINT RUN 10-25
FFMI Monte Irvin/24* 15.00 40.00
FFNR Nolan Ryan/10
FFRS Red Schoendienst/25 8.00 20.00
FFTG Tony Gwynn/25 12.00 30.00

2012 Press Pass Legends Hall of Fame Fan Favorites Red

*RED/43-50: .3X TO .8X PURPLE
STATED PRINT RUN 12-50

2012 Press Pass Legends Hall of Fame Fan Favorites Red Red Ink

STATED PRINT RUN 5-36
NO PRICING ON PRINT RUNS UNDER 20
FFRS Red Schoendienst/36* 8.00 20.00
FFTG Tony Gwynn/8*

2012 Press Pass Legends Hall of Fame Gold

LGGP Gaylord Perry/75 6.00 15.00
LGJM Juan Marichal/63* 8.00 20.00
LGJP Jim Palmer/65 8.00 20.00
LGMI Monte Irvin/20
LGOS Ozzie Smith/65 15.00 40.00
LGRH Rickey Henderson/20 75.00 150.00
LGRK Ralph Kiner/65 6.00 15.00
LGRS Red Schoendienst/35 8.00 20.00
LGRS Ryne Sandberg/47* 15.00 40.00
LGTG Tony Gwynn/15

2012 Press Pass Legends Hall of Fame Gold Red Ink

STATED PRINT RUN 1-65
LGJM Juan Marichal/2*
LGRS Ryne Sandberg/18*

2012 Press Pass Legends Hall of Fame Red

STATED PRINT RUN 1-50
EXCH DEADLINE 12/31/2013
LGJM Juan Marichal/50 8.00 20.00
LGJP Jim Palmer/50 8.00 20.00
LGOS Ozzie Smith/50 15.00 40.00
LGRK Ralph Kiner/50 6.00 15.00
LGRS Red Schoendienst/50 6.00 15.00
LGRS Ryne Sandberg/35* 15.00 40.00
LGTG Tony Gwynn/50 10.00 25.00

2012 Press Pass Legends Hall of Fame Red Red Ink

STATED PRINT RUN 3-50
LGGP Gaylord Perry/47* 8.00 20.00

2012 Press Pass Legends Hall of Fame Silver

STATED PRINT RUN 3-89
LGGP Gaylord Perry/89 6.00 15.00
LGJM Juan Marichal/28* 10.00 25.00
LGJP Jim Palmer/75 8.00 20.00
LGOS Ozzie Smith/7*
LGRK Ralph Kiner/75 6.00 15.00
LGRS Ryne Sandberg/3*

2012 Press Pass Legends Hall of Fame Silver Red Ink

STATED PRINT RUN 1-48
LGJM Juan Marichal/47* 8.00 20.00
LGOS Ozzie Smith/8*
LGRS Ryne Sandberg/1*

2018 Prestige

1 Clint Frazier RC .50 1.25
2 J.P. Crawford RC .25 .60
3 Shohei Ohtani RC 6.00 15.00
4 Carlos Correa .25 .60
5 Joey Votto .25 .60
6 Kris Bryant .30 .75
7 Miguel Andujar RC 1.00 2.50
8 Ronald Acuna Jr. RC 8.00 20.00
9 Austin Hays RC .40 1.00
10 Buster Posey .30 .75
11 Mike Trout 1.25 3.00
12 Anthony Rizzo .30 .75
13 Bryce Harper .40 1.00
14 Nolan Arenado .40 1.00
15 Paul Goldschmidt .25 .60
16 Aaron Judge .60 1.50
17 Ozzie Albies RC .75 2.00
18 Trea Turner .20 .50
19 Gleyber Torres RC 2.50 6.00
20 Cody Bellinger .50 1.25
21 Manny Machado .25 .60
22 Rafael Devers RC .75 2.00
23 Nick Williams RC .30 .75
24 Ryan McMahon RC .60 1.50
25 Alex Verdugo RC .40 1.00
26 Amed Rosario RC .30 .75
27 Victor Robles RC .60 1.50
28 Shohei Ohtani RC 6.00 15.00
29 Jose Altuve .20 .50
30 Rhys Hoskins RC 1.00 2.50

2018 Prestige Autographs

RANDOM INSERTS IN PACKS
1 Erik Gonzalez 2.50 6.00
7 Brandon Woodruff 8.00 20.00
8 Anthony Santander 2.50 6.00
11 Thyago Vieira 2.50 6.00
12 Reyes Moronta 2.50 6.00
15 Andrew Stevenson 2.50 6.00
16 Jimmie Sherfy 2.50 6.00
17 Shane Bieber
18 Bobby Witt 2.50 6.00
19 Christian Villanueva 2.50 6.00

2018 Prestige Autographs Xtra Points Holo Silver

*HOLO SILVR/25: .75X TO 2X BASIC
RANDOM INSERTS IN PACKS
PRINTR RUNS B/WN 5-25 COPIES PER
NO PRICING ON QTY 5
5 Greg Allen/25 5.00 12.00

2018 Prestige Autographs Xtra Points Purple

*PURPLE/99: .5X TO 1.2X BASIC
RANDOM INSERTS IN PACKS
PRINTR RUNS B/WN 10-99 COPIES PER
NO PRICING ON QTY 10
5 Greg Allen/99 3.00 8.00

2018 Prestige Autographs Xtra Points Red

*RED: .5X TO 1.2X BASIC
RANDOM INSERTS IN PACKS
STATED PRINT RUN 199 SER.#'d SETS
5 Greg Allen 3.00 8.00

2019 Prestige Autographs

RANDOM INSERTS IN PACKS
EXCHANGE DEADLINE 2/21/2021
*GOLD/99: .5X TO 1.2X
*GOLD/35: .6X TO 1.5X
*RED/50: .6X TO 1.5X
*RED/25: .75X TO 2X
*HOLO SLVR/23: .75X TO 2X
1 J.T. Realmuto 8.00 20.00
2 Joey Bart 8.00 20.00
3 Patrick Corbin 3.00 8.00
5 German Marquez 2.50 6.00
6 Matt Olson 4.00 10.00
7 Tim Anderson 4.00 10.00
8 Asdrubal Cabrera 3.00 8.00
9 Austin Meadows 4.00 10.00
10 Dan Vogelbach 2.50 6.00
11 Jorge Polanco 3.00 8.00

1950 Prest-o-Lite Postcards

These postcards were issued to promote the "Prest-O-Lite" batteries. The front contains an action photo of the star while the back has a promotion for those batteries. There might be more photos so any additions are appreiciated.

2 Tommy Henrich 10.00 20.00
3 Ted Williams 30.00 60.00

2004 Prime Cuts

COMPLETE SET (50) 100.00 200.00
COMMON CARD (1-50) .75 2.00
STATED PRINT RUN 949 SERIAL #'d SETS
B.RUTH SANTA STATED ODDS 1:15
1 Roger Clemens Yanks 2.50 6.00
2 Nomar Garciaparra 1.25 3.00
3 Albert Pujols 2.50 6.00
4 Sammy Sosa 2.00 5.00
5 Greg Maddux Braves 2.00 5.00
6 Jason Giambi .75 2.00
7 Hideo Nomo Dodgers 2.00 5.00
8 Mike Piazza Mets 2.00 5.00
9 Ichiro Suzuki 2.50 6.00
10 Jeff Bagwell 1.25 3.00
11 Derek Jeter 5.00 12.00
12 Manny Ramirez 2.00 5.00
13 R.Henderson Dodgers 2.00 5.00
14 Alex Rodriguez Rgr 2.50 6.00
15 Troy Glaus .75 2.00
16 Mike Mussina 1.25 3.00
17 Kerry Wood .75 2.00
18 Kazuhisa Ishii .75 2.00
19 Hideki Matsui 3.00 8.00
20 Frank Thomas 2.00 5.00
21 Barry Bonds Giants 3.00 8.00
22 Adam Dunn 1.25 3.00
23 Randy Johnson D'backs 2.00 5.00
24 Alfonso Soriano 1.25 3.00
25 Pedro Martinez Sox 1.25 3.00
26 Andruw Jones .75 2.00
27 Mark Prior 1.25 3.00
28 Vladimir Guerrero 1.25 3.00
29 Chipper Jones 2.00 5.00
30 Todd Helton 1.25 3.00
31 Rafael Palmeiro 1.25 3.00
32 Mark Grace 1.25 3.00
33 Pedro Martinez Dodgers 1.25 3.00
34 Randy Johnson M's 2.00 5.00
35 Randy Johnson Astros 2.00 5.00
36 Roger Clemens Sox 2.50 6.00
37 Roger Clemens Jays 2.50 6.00
38 Alex Rodriguez M's 2.50 6.00
39 Greg Maddux Cubs 2.50 6.00
40 Mike Piazza Dodgers 2.00 5.00
41 Mike Piazza Marlins 2.00 5.00
42 Hideo Nomo Mets 2.00 5.00
43 R.Henderson Yanks 2.00 5.00
44 Rickey Henderson A's 2.00 5.00
45 Barry Bonds Pirates 3.00 8.00
46 Ivan Rodriguez 1.25 3.00
47 George Brett 4.00 10.00
48 Cal Ripken 6.00 15.00
49 Nolan Ryan 6.00 15.00
50 Don Mattingly 4.00 10.00
BRS1 Babe Ruth Santa 5.00 12.00

2004 Prime Cuts Century

*CENTURY 1-46: .75X TO 2X BASIC
*CENTURY MATSUI: .75X TO 2X BASIC
*CENTURY 47-50: .75X TO 2X BASIC
STATED PRINT RUN 100 SERIAL #'d SETS

2004 Prime Cuts Century Proofs

STATED PRINT RUN 1 SERIAL #'d SET
NO PRICING DUE TO SCARCITY

2004 Prime Cuts Material

RANDOM INSERTS IN PACKS
PRINT RUNS B/WN 10-50 COPIES PER
NO PRICING ON QTY OF 10 OR LESS
ALL CARDS FEATURE PRIME SWATCHES
1 Roger Clemens Yanks Jsy/50 15.00 40.00
2 Nomar Garciaparra Jsy/50 15.00 40.00
3 Albert Pujols Jsy/50 20.00 50.00
4 Sammy Sosa Jsy/50 10.00 25.00
5 Greg Maddux Jsy/50 15.00 40.00
6 Jason Giambi Jsy/25 10.00 25.00
7 H.Nomo Dodgers Jsy/50 15.00 40.00
8 Mike Piazza Mets Jsy/50 10.00 25.00
9 Ichiro Suzuki Base/25 40.00 80.00
10 Jeff Bagwell Jsy/25 15.00 40.00
11 Derek Jeter Base/25 40.00 80.00
12 Manny Ramirez Jsy/25 15.00 40.00
13 R.Henderson Dodgers Jsy/50 10.00 25.00
14 Alex Rodriguez Rgr Jsy/25 20.00 50.00
15 Troy Glaus Jsy/25 10.00 25.00
17 Kerry Wood Jsy/25 10.00 25.00
18 Kazuhisa Ishii Jsy/25 10.00 25.00
19 Hideki Matsui Base/25 40.00 80.00
20 Frank Thomas Jsy/25 15.00 40.00
21 Barry Bonds Base/25 40.00 80.00
22 Adam Dunn Jsy/25 10.00 25.00
23 R.Johnson D'backs Jsy/25 15.00 40.00
24 Alfonso Soriano Jsy/35 6.00 15.00
25 Pedro Martinez Sox Jsy/25 15.00 40.00
26 Andruw Jones Jsy/25 15.00 40.00
27 Mark Prior Jsy/50 10.00 25.00
28 Vladimir Guerrero Jsy/25 15.00 40.00
29 Chipper Jones Jsy/25 15.00 40.00
30 Todd Helton Jsy/25 15.00 40.00
31 Rafael Palmeiro Jsy/25 15.00 40.00
32 Mark Grace Jsy/25 15.00 40.00
33 P.Martinez Dodgers Jsy/25 15.00 40.00
34 Randy Johnson M's Jsy/25 15.00 40.00
35 R.Johnson Astros Jsy/25 15.00 40.00
36 Roger Clemens Sox Jsy/50 15.00 40.00
38 Alex Rodriguez M's Jsy/25 30.00 60.00
40 Mike Piazza Dodgers Jsy/50 15.00 40.00
42 Hideo Nomo Mets Jsy/50 15.00 40.00
43 R.Henderson Yanks Jsy/50 10.00 25.00
44 R.Henderson A's Jsy/50 10.00 25.00
46 Ivan Rodriguez Jsy/25 15.00 40.00
47 George Brett Jsy/50 20.00 50.00
48 Cal Ripken Jsy/50 12.00 30.00
49 Nolan Ryan Jsy/50 20.00 50.00
50 Don Mattingly Jsy/50 20.00 50.00

2004 Prime Cuts Material Combos

STATED PRINT RUN 25 SERIAL #'d SETS
ALL CARDS FEATURE PRIME SWATCHES
1 Roger Clemens Yanks Bat-Jsy 30.00 60.00
2 Nomar Garciaparra Bat-Jsy 30.00 60.00
3 Albert Pujols Bat-Jsy 50.00 100.00
4 Sammy Sosa Bat-Jsy 20.00 50.00
5 Greg Maddux Bat-Jsy 30.00 60.00
6 Jason Giambi Bat-Jsy 15.00 40.00
7 Hideo Nomo Dodgers Bat-Jsy 30.00 60.00
8 Mike Piazza Mets Bat-Jsy 15.00 40.00
9 Ichiro Suzuki Ball-Base 40.00 80.00
10 Jeff Bagwell Bat-Jsy 20.00 50.00
11 Derek Jeter Ball-Base 40.00 80.00
12 Manny Ramirez Bat-Jsy 20.00 50.00
13 Rickey Henderson Dodgers Bat-Jsy 20.00 50.00
14 Alex Rodriguez Rgr Bat-Jsy 30.00 60.00
15 Troy Glaus Bat-Jsy 15.00 40.00
16 Mike Mussina Bat-Jsy 20.00 50.00
17 Kerry Wood Bat-Jsy 15.00 40.00
18 Kazuhisa Ishii Bat-Jsy 15.00 40.00
19 Hideki Matsui Ball-Base 50.00 100.00
20 Frank Thomas Bat-Jsy 20.00 50.00
21 Barry Bonds Ball-Base 50.00 100.00
22 Adam Dunn Bat-Jsy 15.00 40.00
23 Randy Johnson D'backs Bat-Jsy 20.00 50.00
24 Alfonso Soriano Bat-Jsy 15.00 40.00
25 Pedro Martinez Sox Bat-Jsy 20.00 50.00
26 Andruw Jones Bat-Jsy 20.00 50.00
27 Mark Prior Bat-Jsy 20.00 50.00
28 Vladimir Guerrero Bat-Jsy 20.00 50.00
29 Chipper Jones Bat-Jsy 20.00 50.00
30 Todd Helton Bat-Jsy 20.00 50.00
31 Rafael Palmeiro Bat-Jsy 20.00 50.00
32 Mark Grace Bat-Jsy 20.00 50.00
33 Pedro Martinez Dodgers Bat-Jsy 20.00 50.00
34 Randy Johnson M's Bat-Jsy 20.00 50.00
35 Randy Johnson Astros Bat-Jsy 20.00 50.00
36 Roger Clemens Sox Bat-Jsy 30.00 60.00
38 Alex Rodriguez M's Bat-Jsy 30.00 60.00
40 Mike Piazza Dodgers Bat-Jsy 30.00 60.00
42 Hideo Nomo Mets Bat-Jsy 30.00 60.00
43 Rickey Henderson Yanks Bat-Jsy 20.00 50.00
44 Rickey Henderson A's Bat-Jsy 20.00 50.00
46 Ivan Rodriguez Bat-Jsy 20.00 50.00
47 George Brett Bat-Jsy 50.00 100.00
48 Cal Ripken Bat-Jsy 60.00 120.00
49 Nolan Ryan Bat-Jsy 50.00 100.00
50 Don Mattingly Bat-Jsy 20.00 50.00

2004 Prime Cuts Material Signature

RANDOM INSERTS IN PACKS
PRINT RUNS B/WN 5-50 COPIES PER
NO PRICING ON QTY OF 10 OR LESS
ALL CARDS FEATURE PRIME SWATCHES
1 R.Clemens Yanks Jsy/25 150.00 250.00
3 Albert Pujols Jsy/25 100.00 250.00
5 Greg Maddux Jsy/25 60.00 150.00
10 Jeff Bagwell Jsy/25 30.00 80.00
12 Manny Ramirez Jsy/25 40.00 100.00
13 R.Hend Dodgers Jsy/25 40.00 100.00
14 Alex Rodriguez Rgr Jsy/25 100.00 200.00
15 Troy Glaus Jsy/50 12.00 30.00
16 Mike Mussina Jsy/25 30.00 80.00
17 Kerry Wood Jsy/25 30.00 80.00
18 Kazuhisa Ishii Jsy/50 12.00 30.00
20 Frank Thomas Jsy/25 40.00 100.00
22 Adam Dunn Jsy/50 12.00 30.00
24 Alfonso Soriano Jsy/25 30.00 80.00
26 Andruw Jones Jsy/25 20.00 50.00
27 Mark Prior Jsy/50 20.00 50.00
28 Vladimir Guerrero Jsy/50 20.00 50.00
29 Chipper Jones Jsy/50 30.00 80.00
30 Todd Helton Jsy/50 30.00 80.00
31 Rafael Palmeiro Jsy/25 40.00 100.00
32 Mark Grace Jsy/50 12.00 30.00
36 Roger Clemens Sox Jsy/25 150.00 250.00
38 Alex Rodriguez M's Jsy/25 30.00 80.00
44 R.Henderson A's Jsy/25 40.00 100.00
46 Ivan Rodriguez Jsy/25 40.00 100.00
47 George Brett Jsy/50 30.00 80.00
48 Cal Ripken Jsy/50 60.00 120.00
49 Nolan Ryan Jsy/50 75.00 150.00
50 Don Mattingly Jsy/50 30.00 80.00

2004 Prime Cuts MLB Icons Material

RANDOM INSERTS IN PACKS
PRINT RUNS B/WN 9-50 COPIES PER
NO PRICING ON QTY OF 9 OR LESS
MLB4 Johnny Bench Jsy/50 20.00 50.00
MLB5 Lefty Grove A's Hat/25 75.00 150.00
MLB6 Carlton Fisk Jsy/50 15.00 40.00
MLB7 Mel Ott Jsy/25 50.00 100.00
MLB8 Bob Feller Jsy/25 15.00 40.00
MLB9 Jackie Robinson Jsy/25 20.00 50.00
MLB10 Ted Williams Jsy/50 20.00 50.00
MLB11 Roy Campanella Pants/50 30.00 60.00
MLB12 Stan Musial Jsy/50 30.00 60.00
MLB13 Yogi Berra Jsy/50 20.00 50.00
MLB14 Babe Ruth Jsy/25 800.00 1200.00
MLB15 Roberto Clemente Jsy/50 50.00 100.00
MLB16 Warren Spahn Jsy/50 20.00 50.00
MLB17 Ernie Banks Jsy/50 20.00 50.00
MLB18 Eddie Mathews Jsy/50 20.00 50.00
MLB19 Ryne Sandberg Jsy/50 30.00 60.00
MLB20 Rod Carew Angels Jsy/50 15.00 40.00
MLB21 Duke Snider Jsy/50 15.00 40.00
MLB22 Jim Palmer Jsy/50 12.00 30.00
MLB24 Frank Robinson Jsy/50 12.00 30.00
MLB25 Brooks Robinson Jsy/50 15.00 40.00
MLB26 Harmon Killebrew Jsy/50 20.00 50.00
MLB27 Carl Yastrzemski Jsy/50 12.00 30.00
MLB28 Reggie Jackson A's Jsy/50 15.00 40.00
MLB29 Mike Schmidt Jsy/50 12.00 30.00
MLB30 Robin Yount Jsy/50 20.00 50.00
MLB31 George Brett Jsy/50 15.00 40.00
MLB32 Nolan Ryan Rgr Jsy/50 30.00 60.00
MLB33 Kirby Puckett Jsy/50 20.00 50.00
MLB34 Cal Ripken Jsy/50 15.00 40.00
MLB35 Don Mattingly Jsy/50 12.00 30.00
MLB36 Tony Gwynn Jsy/19 15.00 40.00
MLB37 Deion Sanders Jsy/19 20.00 50.00
MLB38 Dave Winfield Yanks Jsy/19 15.00 40.00
MLB39 Eddie Murray Jsy/19 30.00 60.00
MLB40 Tom Seaver Jsy/19 20.00 50.00
MLB41 Willie Stargell Jsy/19 20.00 50.00
MLB42 Wade Boggs Yanks Jsy/19 20.00 50.00
MLB43 Ozzie Smith Jsy/19 30.00 60.00
MLB44 Willie McCovey Jsy/19 15.00 40.00
MLB45 R.Jackson Angels Jsy/19 20.00 50.00
MLB46 Whitey Ford Jsy/19 20.00 50.00
MLB47 Lou Brock Jsy/19 20.00 50.00
MLB48 Lou Boudreau Jsy/19 15.00 40.00
MLB49 Steve Carlton Jsy/19 15.00 40.00
MLB50 Rod Carew Twins Jsy/19 20.00 50.00
MLB51 Bob Gibson Jsy/19 20.00 50.00
MLB52 Thurman Munson Jsy/19 30.00 60.00
MLB53 Roger Maris Jsy/19 60.00 120.00
MLB54 Nolan Ryan Astros Jsy/50 30.00 60.00
MLB55 Nolan Ryan Angels Jsy/50 30.00 60.00
MLB56 Bo Jackson Jsy/19 30.00 60.00
MLB57 Joe Morgan Jsy/19 15.00 40.00
MLB58 Phil Rizzuto Jsy/19 20.00 50.00
MLB59 Gary Carter Jsy/19 20.00 50.00
MLB60 Paul Molitor Jsy/19 15.00 40.00
MLB61 Don Drysdale Jsy/19 30.00 60.00
MLB62 Catfish Hunter Jsy/19 20.00 50.00
MLB63 Fergie Jenkins Pants/19 15.00 40.00
MLB64 Pee Wee Reese Jsy/19 20.00 50.00
MLB65 Dave Winfield Padres Jsy/19 15.00 40.00
MLB66 Wade Boggs Sox Jsy/19 20.00 50.00
MLB67 Lefty Grove Sox Hat/19 75.00 150.00
MLB68 Rickey Henderson Jsy/19 20.00 50.00
MLB69 Roger Clemens Sox Jsy/19 30.00 60.00
MLB70 R.Clemens Yanks Jsy/19 30.00 60.00

2004 Prime Cuts MLB Icons Material Combos Prime

PRINT RUNS B/WN 1-25 COPIES PER
NO PRICING ON QTY OF 15 OR LESS
MLB6 Carlton Fisk Bat-Jsy/25 40.00 80.00
MLB11 R.Campanella Bat-Pants/25 50.00 100.00
MLB15 R.Clemente Bat-Jsy/25 100.00 200.00
MLB17 Ernie Banks Bat-Jsy/25 50.00 100.00
MLB18 Eddie Mathews Bat-Jsy/25 50.00 100.00
MLB19 Ryne Sandberg Bat-Jsy/25 30.00 60.00
MLB20 R.Carew Angels Bat-Jsy/25 40.00 80.00
MLB24 Frank Robinson Bat-Jsy/25 30.00 60.00
MLB25 Brooks Robinson Bat-Jsy/25 40.00 80.00
MLB27 Carl Yastrzemski Bat-Jsy/25 75.00 150.00
MLB28 R.Jackson A's Bat-Jsy/25 40.00 80.00
MLB29 Mike Schmidt Bat-Jsy/25 50.00 100.00
MLB30 Robin Yount Bat-Jsy/25 50.00 100.00
MLB31 George Brett Bat-Jsy/25 50.00 100.00
MLB32 Nolan Ryan Rgr Bat-Jsy/25 60.00 120.00
MLB33 Kirby Puckett Bat-Jsy/25 50.00 100.00
MLB34 Cal Ripken Bat-Jsy/25 75.00 150.00
MLB35 Don Mattingly Bat-Jsy/25 50.00 100.00
MLB36 Tony Gwynn Bat-Jsy/19 60.00 120.00
MLB37 Deion Sanders Bat-Jsy/19 40.00 80.00
MLB38 D.Winfield Yanks Bat-Jsy/19 30.00 60.00
MLB39 Eddie Murray Bat-Jsy/19 60.00 120.00
MLB41 Willie Stargell Bat-Jsy/19 40.00 80.00
MLB42 W.Boggs Yanks Bat-Jsy/19 40.00 80.00
MLB43 Ozzie Smith Bat-Jsy/19 75.00 150.00
MLB44 Willie McCovey Bat-Jsy/19 30.00 60.00
MLB45 R.Jackson Angels Bat-Jsy/19 40.00 80.00
MLB46 Whitey Ford Jsy-Pants/19 40.00 80.00
MLB47 Lou Brock Bat-Jsy/19 30.00 60.00
MLB48 Lou Boudreau Jsy-Jsy/19 30.00 60.00
MLB49 Steve Carlton Bat-Jsy/19 30.00 60.00
MLB50 Rod Carew Twins Bat-Jsy/19 40.00 80.00
MLB52 T.Munson Bat-Jsy/19 60.00 120.00
MLB53 Roger Maris Bat-Jsy/19 100.00 200.00
MLB54 N.Ryan Astros Bat-Jsy/19 75.00 150.00
MLB55 N.Ryan Angels Bat-Jsy/19 75.00 150.00
MLB56 Bo Jackson Bat-Jsy/19 50.00 100.00
MLB57 Joe Morgan Bat-Jsy/19 30.00 60.00
MLB58 Phil Rizzuto Bat-Pants/19 40.00 80.00
MLB59 Gary Carter Bat-Jsy/19 40.00 80.00
MLB60 Paul Molitor Bat-Jsy/19 30.00 60.00
MLB63 F.Jenkins Fld Glv-Pants/19 30.00 60.00
MLB64 P.Reese Bat-Jsy/19 50.00 100.00
MLB65 D.Winfield Padres Bat-Jsy/19 30.00 60.00
MLB66 W.Boggs Sox Bat-Jsy/19 40.00 80.00
MLB68 R.Henderson Bat-Jsy/19 50.00 100.00
MLB69 R.Clemens Sox Bat-Jsy/19 50.00 100.00
MLB70 R.Clemens Yanks Bat-Jsy/19 50.00 100.00

2004 Prime Cuts MLB Icons Material Prime

PRINT RUNS B/WN 1-25 COPIES PER
NO PRICING ON QTY OF 9 OR LESS
MLB6 Carlton Fisk Jsy/25 15.00 40.00
MLB7 Mel Ott Jsy/25 100.00 200.00
MLB11 Roy Campanella Pants/25 25.00 60.00
MLB15 Roberto Clemente Jsy/25 100.00 200.00
MLB16 Warren Spahn Jsy/25 60.00 120.00
MLB17 Ernie Banks Jsy/25 25.00 60.00
MLB18 Eddie Mathews Jsy/25 25.00 60.00
MLB19 Ryne Sandberg Jsy/25 50.00 100.00
MLB20 Rod Carew Angels Jsy/25 15.00 40.00
MLB22 Jim Palmer Jsy/25 10.00 25.00
MLB24 Frank Robinson Jsy/25 10.00 25.00
MLB25 Brooks Robinson Jsy/25 15.00 40.00
MLB27 Carl Yastrzemski Jsy/25 50.00 100.00
MLB28 Reggie Jackson A's Jsy/25 15.00 40.00
MLB29 Mike Schmidt Jsy/25 25.00 60.00
MLB30 Robin Yount Jsy/25 25.00 60.00
MLB31 George Brett Jsy/25 15.00 40.00
MLB32 Nolan Ryan Rgr Jsy/25 50.00 100.00
MLB33 Kirby Puckett Jsy/25 25.00 60.00
MLB34 Cal Ripken Jsy/25 60.00 120.00
MLB35 Don Mattingly Jsy/25 25.00 60.00
MLB36 Tony Gwynn Jsy/19 15.00 40.00
MLB37 Deion Sanders Jsy/19 15.00 40.00
MLB38 Dave Winfield Yanks Jsy/19 10.00 25.00
MLB39 Eddie Murray Jsy/19 50.00 100.00
MLB40 Tom Seaver Jsy/19 15.00 40.00
MLB41 Willie Stargell Jsy/19 15.00 40.00
MLB42 Wade Boggs Yanks Jsy/19 15.00 40.00
MLB43 Ozzie Smith Jsy/19 25.00 60.00
MLB44 Willie McCovey Jsy/19 10.00 25.00
MLB45 R.Jackson Angels Jsy/19 15.00 40.00
MLB46 Whitey Ford Jsy/19 15.00 40.00
MLB47 Lou Brock Jsy/19 25.00 60.00
MLB48 Lou Boudreau Jsy/19 10.00 25.00
MLB49 Steve Carlton Jsy/19 10.00 25.00
MLB50 Rod Carew Twins Jsy/19 15.00 40.00
MLB51 Bob Gibson Jsy/19 25.00 60.00
MLB52 Thurman Munson Jsy/19 50.00 100.00
MLB53 Roger Maris Jsy/19 75.00 150.00
MLB54 Nolan Ryan Astros Jsy/19 50.00 100.00
MLB55 Nolan Ryan Angels Jsy/19 50.00 100.00
MLB56 Bo Jackson Jsy/19 25.00 60.00
MLB57 Joe Morgan Jsy/19 10.00 25.00
MLB59 Gary Carter Jsy/19 15.00 40.00
MLB60 Paul Molitor Jsy/19 10.00 25.00
MLB61 Don Drysdale Jsy/19 50.00 100.00
MLB62 Catfish Hunter Jsy/19 15.00 40.00
MLB63 Fergie Jenkins Pants/19 10.00 25.00
MLB64 Pee Wee Reese Jsy/19 15.00 40.00
MLB65 Dave Winfield Padres Jsy/19 10.00 25.00
MLB66 Wade Boggs Sox Jsy/19 15.00 40.00
MLB67 Lefty Grove Sox Hat/19 90.00 180.00
MLB68 Rickey Henderson Jsy/19 25.00 60.00
MLB69 Roger Clemens Sox Jsy/19 25.00 60.00
MLB70 R.Clemens Yanks Jsy/19 25.00 60.00

2004 Prime Cuts MLB Icons Material Signature

RANDOM INSERTS IN PACKS
PRINT RUNS B/WN 16-45 COPIES PER
MLB4 Johnny Bench Jsy/18 75.00 150.00
MLB8 Bob Feller Jsy/45 25.00 60.00
MLB12 Stan Musial Jsy/30 75.00 150.00
MLB13 Yogi Berra Jsy/42 30.00 80.00
MLB21 Duke Snider Jsy/35 50.00 100.00
MLB26 Harmon Killebrew Jsy/30 75.00 150.00
MLB33 Kirby Puckett Jsy/16 75.00 150.00
MLB69 Roger Clemens Sox Jsy/25 125.00 200.00

2004 Prime Cuts MLB Icons Material Signature Prime

RANDOM INSERTS IN PACKS
PRINT RUNS B/WN 1-50 COPIES PER
NO PRICING ON QTY OF 15 OR LESS
MLB6 Carlton Fisk Jsy/50 40.00 80.00
MLB12 Stan Musial Jsy/20 125.00 200.00
MLB16 Warren Spahn Jsy/25 125.00 200.00
MLB17 Ernie Banks Jsy/50 60.00 120.00
MLB19 Ryne Sandberg Jsy/50 25.00 60.00
MLB20 Rod Carew Angels Jsy/50 40.00 80.00
MLB22 Jim Palmer Jsy/50 30.00 60.00
MLB24 Frank Robinson Jsy/50 30.00 60.00
MLB25 Brooks Robinson Jsy/50 40.00 80.00
MLB26 Harmon Killebrew Jsy/20 100.00 200.00
MLB27 Carl Yastrzemski Jsy/50 60.00 120.00
MLB28 Reggie Jackson A's Jsy/50 50.00 100.00
MLB29 Mike Schmidt Jsy/20 125.00 200.00
MLB30 Robin Yount Jsy/50 40.00 80.00
MLB31 George Brett Jsy/50 75.00 150.00
MLB32 Nolan Ryan Rgr Jsy/50 40.00 80.00
MLB33 Kirby Puckett Jsy/34 50.00 100.00
MLB34 Cal Ripken Jsy/50 100.00 200.00
MLB35 Don Mattingly Jsy/50 40.00 80.00
MLB36 Tony Gwynn Jsy/50 50.00 100.00
MLB37 Deion Sanders Jsy/50 50.00 100.00
MLB38 Dave Winfield Yanks Jsy/50 12.00 30.00
MLB39 Eddie Murray Jsy/50 60.00 120.00
MLB42 Wade Boggs Yanks Jsy/50 50.00 100.00
MLB43 Ozzie Smith Jsy/50 75.00 150.00
MLB44 Willie McCovey Jsy/50 40.00 80.00
MLB45 R.Jackson Angels Jsy/50 20.00 50.00
MLB46 Whitey Ford Jsy/50 20.00 50.00
MLB47 Lou Brock Jsy/25 50.00 100.00
MLB48 Lou Boudreau Jsy/50 40.00 80.00
MLB49 Steve Carlton Jsy/50 30.00 60.00
MLB50 Rod Carew Twins Jsy/50 40.00 80.00
MLB51 Bob Gibson Jsy/50 60.00 120.00
MLB54 Nolan Ryan Astros Jsy/50 50.00 100.00
MLB55 Nolan Ryan Angels Jsy/50 50.00 100.00
MLB56 Bo Jackson Jsy/50 40.00 80.00
MLB57 Joe Morgan Jsy/50 30.00 60.00
MLB58 Phil Rizzuto Pants/50 40.00 80.00
MLB59 Gary Carter Jsy/50 30.00 60.00
MLB60 Paul Molitor Jsy/50 30.00 60.00
MLB63 Fergie Jenkins Pants/50 12.00 30.00
MLB65 D.Winfield Padres Jsy/50 40.00 80.00
MLB66 Wade Boggs Sox Jsy/50 50.00 100.00
MLB68 Rickey Henderson Jsy/50 75.00 150.00
MLB69 Roger Clemens Sox Jsy/25 150.00 250.00
MLB70 R.Clemens Yanks Jsy/50 25.00 60.00

2004 Prime Cuts MLB Icons Signature

RANDOM INSERTS IN PACKS
PRINT RUNS B/WN 1-50 COPIES PER
NO PRICING ON QTY OF 12 OR LESS
MLB4 Johnny Bench/50 20.00 50.00
MLB6 Carlton Fisk/50 10.00 25.00
MLB8 Bob Feller/50 10.00 25.00
MLB12 Stan Musial/50 40.00 100.00
MLB13 Yogi Berra/50 25.00 60.00
MLB16 Warren Spahn/25 25.00 60.00
MLB17 Ernie Banks/50 20.00 50.00
MLB19 Ryne Sandberg/50 20.00 50.00
MLB21 Duke Snider/25 40.00 80.00
MLB22 Jim Palmer/25 12.00 30.00
MLB24 Frank Robinson/50 10.00 25.00
MLB25 Brooks Robinson/50 15.00 40.00
MLB26 Harmon Killebrew/25 20.00 50.00
MLB27 Carl Yastrzemski/50 50.00 100.00
MLB28 Reggie Jackson A's/50 20.00 50.00
MLB29 Mike Schmidt/20 60.00 120.00
MLB30 Robin Yount/25 60.00 120.00
MLB31 George Brett/25 60.00 120.00
MLB32 Nolan Ryan Rgr/50 30.00 80.00
MLB33 Kirby Puckett/25 150.00 300.00
MLB34 Cal Ripken/25 150.00 250.00
MLB35 Don Mattingly/50 20.00 50.00
MLB36 Tony Gwynn/25 15.00 40.00
MLB38 Dave Winfield Yanks/25 40.00 80.00
MLB39 Eddie Murray/25 10.00 25.00
MLB42 Wade Boggs Yanks/25 50.00 100.00
MLB43 Ozzie Smith/25 75.00 150.00
MLB44 Willie McCovey/25 10.00 25.00
MLB45 Reggie Jackson Angels/25 50.00 122.00
MLB47 Lou Brock/25 15.00 40.00
MLB48 Lou Boudreau/25 75.00 150.00
MLB51 Bob Gibson/25 20.00 50.00
MLB56 Bo Jackson/25 40.00 100.00
MLB57 Joe Morgan/25 12.00 30.00
MLB59 Gary Carter/25 40.00 80.00
MLB60 Paul Molitor/25 15.00 40.00
MLB65 Dave Winfield Padres/25 40.00 80.00
MLB66 Wade Boggs Sox/25 50.00 100.00

2004 Prime Cuts Signature

PRINT RUNS B/WN 5-25 COPIES PER
NO PRICING ON QTY OF 14 OR LESS
1 Roger Clemens Yanks/25 60.00 120.00
3 Albert Pujols/25 75.00 200.00
10 Jeff Bagwell/25 40.00 80.00
13 R.Henderson Dodgers/25 40.00 80.00
14 Alex Rodriguez Rgr/25 60.00 120.00
15 Troy Glaus/25 30.00 60.00
16 Mike Mussina/25 20.00 50.00
17 Kerry Wood/25 30.00 60.00
18 Kazuhisa Ishii/25 15.00 40.00
20 Frank Thomas/25 40.00 80.00
22 Adam Dunn/25 15.00 40.00
24 Alfonso Soriano/25 10.00 25.00
26 Andruw Jones/25 30.00 60.00
27 Mark Prior/25 10.00 25.00
28 Vladimir Guerrero/25 40.00 80.00
29 Chipper Jones/25 40.00 80.00
30 Todd Helton/17 30.00 60.00
31 Rafael Palmeiro/25 40.00 80.00
32 Mark Grace/25 20.00 50.00
36 Roger Clemens Sox/25 75.00 150.00
37 Roger Clemens Jays/25 75.00 150.00
38 Alex Rodriguez M's/25 60.00 120.00
43 Rick. Henderson Yanks/25 50.00 100.00
44 Rickey Henderson A's/25 50.00 100.00
46 Ivan Rodriguez/25 20.00 50.00
47 George Brett/25 40.00 100.00
48 Cal Ripken/25 100.00 200.00
49 Nolan Ryan/25 40.00 80.00
50 Don Mattingly/25 30.00 60.00

2004 Prime Cuts Timeline Dual Achievements Material

PRINT RUNS B/WN 9-19 COPIES PER
NO PRICING ON QTY OF 9 OR LESS
3 Stan Musial Jsy 125.00 200.00
Ted Williams Jsy/19
4 Mike Schmidt Jsy 60.00 120.00
George Brett Jsy/19
5 Dale Murphy Jsy 60.00 120.00
Cal Ripken Jsy/19
6 Roger Clemens Jsy 50.00 100.00
Mike Schmidt Jsy/19
10 George Brett Jsy 40.00 80.00
Nolan Ryan Jsy/19
12 Al Kaline Pants 40.00 80.00
Duke Snider Jsy/19

2004 Prime Cuts Timeline Dual Achievements Material Combos

PRINT RUNS B/WN 1-19 COPIES PER
NO PRICING ON QTY OF 15 OR LESS
4 M.Schmidt/G.Brett/19 150.00 250.00
5 D.Murphy/C.Ripken/19 100.00 200.00
6 R.Clemens/M.Schmidt/19 75.00 150.00
10 G.Brett/N.Ryan/19 150.00 250.00

2004 Prime Cuts Timeline Dual Achievements Material Prime

PRINT RUNS B/WN 1-19 COPIES PER
NO PRICING ON QTY OF 15 OR LESS
4 Mike Schmidt Jsy 100.00 200.00
George Brett Jsy/19
5 Dale Murphy Jsy 100.00 200.00
Cal Ripken Jsy/19
6 Roger Clemens Jsy 75.00 150.00
Mike Schmidt Jsy/19
10 George Brett Jsy 60.00 120.00
Nolan Ryan Jsy/19

2004 Prime Cuts Timeline Dual Achievements Material Signature

PRINT RUNS B/WN 1-25 COPIES PER
NO PRICING ON QTY OF 15 OR LESS
4 Mike Schmidt Jsy 175.00 300.00
George Brett Jsy/24
5 Dale Murphy Jsy 175.00 300.00
Cal Ripken Jsy/25
6 Roger Clemens Jsy 175.00 300.00
Mike Schmidt Jsy/24
10 George Brett Jsy 200.00 350.00
Nolan Ryan Jsy/25

2004 Prime Cuts Timeline Dual Achievements Signature

PRINT RUNS B/WN 24-25 COPIES PER
4 M.Schmidt 150.00 250.00
G.Brett/24
5 Dale Murphy 60.00 150.00
Cal Ripken/25
6 Roger Clemens 75.00 200.00
Mike Schmidt/24
10 George Brett 75.00 200.00
Nolan Ryan/25
12 Al Kaline 25.00 50.00
Duke Snider/25

2004 Prime Cuts Timeline Dual Achievements Signature Proofs

STATED PRINT RUN 1 SERIAL #'d SET
NO PRICING DUE TO SCARCITY

2004 Prime Cuts Timeline Dual League Leaders Material

PRINT RUNS B/WN 9-19 COPIES PER
NO PRICING ON QTY OF 9 OR LESS
TL4 Steve Carlton Jsy 12.00 30.00
Jim Palmer Jsy/19
TL7 Steve Carlton Jsy 50.00 100.00
Nolan Ryan Jsy/19
TL8 Don Mattingly Jsy 50.00 100.00
Tony Gwynn Jsy/19
TL9 Roger Clemens Jsy 60.00 120.00
Nolan Ryan Jsy/19

2004 Prime Cuts Timeline Dual League Leaders Material Combos

PRINT RUNS B/WN 9-19 COPIES PER
NO PRICING ON QTY OF 9 OR LESS
TL7 Steve Carlton Bat-Jsy 75.00 150.00
Nolan Ryan Bat-Jsy/19
TL8 Don Mattingly Bat-Jsy 20.00 50.00
Tony Gwynn Bat-Jsy/19
TL9 Roger Clemens Bat-Jsy 100.00 200.00
Nolan Ryan Bat-Jsy/19

2004 Prime Cuts Timeline Dual League Leaders Material Prime

PRINT RUNS B/WN 9-19 COPIES PER
NO PRICING DUE TO SCARCITY
TL4 Steve Carlton Jsy 50.00 100.00
Jim Palmer Jsy/19
TL7 Steve Carlton Jsy 75.00 150.00
Nolan Ryan Jsy/19
TL8 Don Mattingly Jsy 75.00 150.00
Tony Gwynn Jsy/19
TL9 Roger Clemens Jsy 100.00 200.00
Nolan Ryan Jsy/19

2004 Prime Cuts Timeline Dual League Leaders Material Signature

PRINT RUNS B/WN 1-50 COPIES PER
NO PRICING ON QTY OF 1
TL4 Steve Carlton Jsy 60.00 120.00
Jim Palmer Jsy/50
TL7 Steve Carlton Jsy 150.00 250.00
Nolan Ryan Jsy/25
TL8 Don Mattingly Jsy 150.00 250.00
Tony Gwynn Jsy/25
TL9 Roger Clemens Jsy 300.00 500.00
Nolan Ryan Jsy/25

2004 Prime Cuts Timeline Dual League Leaders Signature

PRINT RUNS B/WN 25-50 COPIES PER
TL4 Steve Carlton 15.00 40.00
Jim Palmer/50
TL7 Steve Carlton 125.00 200.00
Nolan Ryan/25
TL8 Don Mattingly 50.00 100.00
Tony Gwynn/25
TL9 Roger Clemens 250.00 400.00
Nolan Ryan/25

2004 Prime Cuts Timeline Material

RANDOM INSERTS IN PACKS
NO PRICING ON QTY OF 9 OR LESS
T4 Ted Williams TC Jsy/50 60.00 120.00
T5 Roy Campanella Pants/50 30.00 60.00
T6 Stan Musial MVP Jsy/50 30.00 60.00
T7 Yogi Berra 51M Jsy/50 20.00 50.00
T9 R.Clemente MVP Jsy/50 75.00 150.00
T10 Will Clark Jsy/25 20.00 50.00
T12 Carl Yastrzemski Jsy/50 30.00 60.00
T13 Mike Schmidt Jsy/50 20.00 50.00
T14 George Brett MVP Jsy/50 20.00 50.00
T15 Nolan Ryan WIN Jsy/50 12.00 30.00
T16 Stan Musial BA Jsy/50 30.00 60.00
T17 Ted Williams BA Jsy/50 60.00 120.00
T18 R.Clemente BTG Jsy/50 75.00 150.00
T19 Greg Maddux Jsy/50 20.00 50.00
T21 Robin Yount Jsy/50 20.00 50.00
T22 Nolan Ryan HOF Jsy/50 15.00 40.00
T23 Ted Williams RET Jsy/50 60.00 120.00
T24 George Brett RET Jsy/50 15.00 40.00
T25 Yogi Berra 55M Jsy/50 20.00 50.00
T26 Rod Carew Jsy/50 15.00 40.00
T27 Dale Murphy Jsy/25 20.00 50.00

2004 Prime Cuts Timeline Material Combos

PRINT RUNS B/WN 1-19 COPIES PER
NO PRICING ON QTY OF 9 OR LESS
T10 Will Clark Bat-Jsy/19 75.00 150.00
T12 Carl Yastrzemski Bat-Jsy/19 25.00 60.00
T13 Mike Schmidt Bat-Jsy/19 60.00 120.00
T14 G.Brett MVP Bat-Jsy/19 25.00 60.00
T15 N.Ryan WIN Bat-Jsy/19 75.00 150.00
T19 Greg Maddux Bat-Jsy/19 25.00 60.00
T21 Robin Yount Bat-Jsy/19 25.00 60.00
T22 N.Ryan HOF Bat-Jsy/19 75.00 150.00
T24 G.Brett RET Bat-Jsy/19 25.00 60.00
T26 Rod Carew Bat-Jsy/19 40.00 80.00
T27 Dale Murphy Bat-Jsy/19 40.00 80.00

2004 Prime Cuts Timeline Material Prime

PRINT RUNS B/WN 1-25 COPIES PER
NO PRICING ON QTY OF 9 OR LESS
T5 Roy Campanella Pants/25 40.00 80.00
T9 R.Clemente MVP Jsy/25 75.00 150.00
T10 Will Clark Jsy/25 40.00 80.00
T12 Carl Yastrzemski Jsy/25 60.00 120.00
T13 Mike Schmidt Jsy/25 50.00 100.00
T14 George Brett MVP Jsy/25 50.00 100.00
T15 Nolan Ryan WIN Jsy/25 15.00 40.00
T18 R.Clemente BTG Jsy/25 75.00 150.00
T19 Greg Maddux Jsy/25 40.00 80.00
T21 Robin Yount Jsy/25 40.00 80.00
T22 Nolan Ryan HOF Jsy/25 50.00 100.00
T24 George Brett RET Jsy/25 15.00 40.00
T26 Rod Carew Jsy/25 40.00 80.00
T27 Dale Murphy Jsy/25 20.00 50.00

2004 Prime Cuts Timeline Material Signature

PRINT RUNS B/WN 33-42 COPIES PER
T6 Stan Musial MVP Jsy/33 60.00 120.00
T7 Yogi Berra 51M Jsy/42 60.00 150.00
T16 Stan Musial BA Jsy/38 75.00 150.00
T25 Yogi Berra 55M Jsy/42 60.00 150.00

2004 Prime Cuts Timeline Material Signature Prime

RANDOM INSERTS IN PACKS
PRINT RUNS B/WN 1-50 COPIES PER
NO PRICING ON QTY OF 10 OR LESS
T10 Will Clark Jsy/50 60.00 120.00
T12 Carl Yastrzemski Jsy/50 75.00 150.00
T13 Mike Schmidt Jsy/20 125.00 200.00
T14 George Brett MVP Jsy/25 125.00 200.00
T15 Nolan Ryan WIN Jsy/50 50.00 120.00
T19 Greg Maddux Jsy/50 125.00 200.00
T21 Robin Yount Jsy/50 40.00 80.00
T22 Nolan Ryan HOF Jsy/50 75.00 150.00
T24 George Brett RET Jsy/25 125.00 200.00
T26 Rod Carew Jsy/50 40.00 80.00
T27 Dale Murphy Jsy/50 40.00 80.00

2004 Prime Cuts Timeline Signature

RANDOM INSERTS IN PACKS
PRINT RUNS B/WN 10-50 COPIES PER
NO PRICING ON QTY OF 20 OR LESS
T6 Stan Musial MVP/50 50.00 100.00
T7 Yogi Berra 51M/50 40.00 100.00
T10 Will Clark/25 75.00 150.00
T12 Carl Yastrzemski/50 40.00 80.00
T13 Mike Schmidt/20 30.00 80.00
T14 George Brett MVP/25 50.00 100.00
T15 Nolan Ryan WIN/50 75.00 150.00
T16 Stan Musial BA/50 50.00 100.00
T19 Greg Maddux/31 75.00 150.00
T21 Robin Yount/25 60.00 120.00
T22 Nolan Ryan HOF/50 75.00 150.00
T24 George Brett RET/25 60.00 120.00
T25 Yogi Berra 55M/50 40.00 100.00
T27 Dale Murphy/25 8.00 20.00

2004 Prime Cuts II

COMMON CARD (1-91) .75 2.00
COMMON RC 1-91 .75 2.00
COMMON CARD (92-100) .75 2.00
STATED PRINT RUN 699 SERIAL #'d SETS
1 Mark Prior 1.25 3.00
2 Derek Jeter 5.00 12.00
3 Eric Chavez .75 2.00
4 Carlos Delgado .75 2.00
5 Albert Pujols 2.50 6.00
6 Miguel Cabrera 2.00 5.00
7 Ivan Rodriguez 1.25 3.00
8 Javy Lopez .75 2.00
9 Hank Blalock .75 2.00
10 Chipper Jones 2.00 5.00
11 Gary Sheffield .75 2.00
12 Alfonso Soriano 1.25 3.00
13 Alex Rodriguez Yanks 2.50 6.00
14 Edgar Renteria .75 2.00
15 Jim Edmonds 1.25 3.00
16 Garret Anderson .75 2.00
17 Lance Berkman 1.25 3.00
18 Brandon Webb .75 2.00
19 Mike Lowell .75 2.00
20 Mark Mulder .75 2.00
21 Sammy Sosa 2.00 5.00
22 Roger Clemens Astros 2.50 6.00
23 Mark Teixeira 1.25 3.00
24 Manny Ramirez 2.00 5.00
25 Rafael Palmeiro 1.25 3.00
26 Ichiro Suzuki 2.50 6.00
27 Vladimir Guerrero 1.25 3.00
28 Austin Kearns .75 2.00
29 Troy Glaus .75 2.00
30 Ken Griffey Jr. 4.00 10.00
31 Greg Maddux 2.50 6.00
32 Roy Halladay 1.25 3.00
33 Roy Oswalt 1.25 3.00
34 Kerry Wood .75 2.00
35 Mike Mussina Yanks 1.25 3.00
36 Michael Young .75 2.00
37 Juan Gonzalez .75 2.00
38 Curt Schilling 1.25 3.00
39 Shannon Stewart .75 2.00
40 Todd Helton 1.25 3.00
41 Larry Walker Cards 1.25 3.00
42 Mariano Rivera 2.50 6.00
43 Nomar Garciaparra 1.25 3.00
44 Adam Dunn 1.25 3.00
45 Pedro Martinez Sox 1.25 3.00
46 Bernie Williams 1.25 3.00
47 Tom Glavine 1.25 3.00
48 Torii Hunter .75 2.00
49 David Ortiz 2.00 5.00
50 Frank Thomas 2.00 5.00
51 Randy Johnson D'backs 2.00 5.00
52 Jason Giambi .75 2.00
53 Carlos Lee .75 2.00
54 Mike Sweeney .75 2.00
55 Hideki Matsui 3.00 8.00
56 Dontrelle Willis .75 2.00
57 Tim Hudson 1.25 3.00
58 Jose Vidro .75 2.00
59 Jeff Bagwell 1.25 3.00
60 Rocco Baldelli .75 2.00
61 Craig Biggio 1.25 3.00
62 Mike Piazza Mets 2.00 5.00
63 Magglio Ordonez 1.25 3.00
64 Hideo Nomo 2.00 5.00
65 Miguel Tejada 1.25 3.00
66 Vernon Wells .75 2.00
67 Barry Larkin 1.25 3.00
68 Jacque Jones .75 2.00
69 Scott Rolen 1.25 3.00
70 Jeff Kent .75 2.00
71 Steve Finley .75 2.00
72 Kazuo Matsui RC 1.25 3.00
73 Carlos Beltran 1.25 3.00
74 Shawn Green .75 2.00
75 Barry Zito 1.25 3.00
76 Aramis Ramirez .75 2.00
77 Paul Lo Duca .75 2.00
78 Kazuhisa Ishii .75 2.00
79 Aubrey Huff .75 2.00
80 Jim Thome 1.25 3.00
81 Andy Pettitte Astros 1.25 3.00
82 Andruw Jones .75 2.00
83 Josh Beckett .75 2.00
84 Sean Casey .75 2.00
85 Alex Rodriguez M's 2.50 6.00
86 Roger Clemens Yanks 2.50 6.00
87 Mike Mussina O's 1.25 3.00
88 Pedro Martinez Dgr 1.25 3.00
89 Randy Johnson Astros 2.00 5.00
90 Mike Piazza Dgr 2.00 5.00
91 Andy Pettitte Yanks 1.25 3.00
92 Cal Ripken 6.00 15.00
93 Dale Murphy 2.00 5.00
94 Don Mattingly 4.00 10.00
95 Gary Carter 1.25 3.00
96 George Brett 4.00 10.00
97 Nolan Ryan 6.00 15.00
98 Ozzie Smith 2.50 6.00
99 Steve Carlton 1.25 3.00
100 Tony Gwynn 2.00 5.00

2004 Prime Cuts II Century Gold

*GOLD 1-91: 1X TO 2.5X BASIC
*GOLD 92-100: 1X TO 2.5X BASIC
STATED PRINT RUN 25 SERIAL #'d SETS
NO RC YR PRICING DUE TO SCARCITY

2004 Prime Cuts II Century Silver

*SILVER 1-91: .6X TO 1.5X BASIC
*SILVER 92-100: .6X TO 1.5X BASIC
STATED PRINT RUN 50 SERIAL #'d SETS

2004 Prime Cuts II Material Number

*1-91 p/r 25: .3X TO .8X COMBO p/r 22
*92-100 p/r 25: .3X TO .8X COMBO p/r 25
OVERALL AU-GU ODDS 1:1
PRINT RUNS B/WN 1-25 COPIES PER
NO PRICING ON QTY OF 10 OR LESS

2004 Prime Cuts II Material Prime

OVERALL AU-GU ODDS 1:1
PRINT RUNS B/WN 1-10 COPIES PER
NO PRICING DUE TO SCARCITY

2004 Prime Cuts II Material Combo

OVERALL AU-GU ODDS 1:1
PRINT RUNS B/WN 1-35 COPIES PER
NO PRICING ON QTY OF 10 OR LESS
1 Mark Prior Hat-Jsy/22 10.00 25.00
12 Alfonso Soriano Bat-Jsy/25 6.00 15.00
15 Jim Edmonds Bat-Jsy/15 8.00 20.00
16 Garret Anderson Bat-Jsy/16 8.00 20.00
17 Lance Berkman Hat-Jsy/17 8.00 20.00
21 Sammy Sosa Bat-Jsy/21 12.50 30.00
22 R.Clem Astros Bat-Jsy/22 20.00 50.00
24 Manny Ramirez Bat-Jsy/24 10.00 25.00
25 Rafael Palmeiro Bat-Jsy/25 10.00 25.00
27 Vlad Guerrero Bat-Jsy/27 12.50 30.00
31 Greg Maddux Bat-Jsy/31 12.50 30.00
35 M.Muss Yanks Bat-Jsy/35 10.00 25.00
40 Todd Helton Bat-Jsy/17 12.50 30.00
86 R.Clem Ynk Fld Glv-Jsy/22 20.00 50.00
92 Cal Ripken Bat-Jsy/25 50.00 100.00
93 Dale Murphy Bat-Jsy/25 12.50 30.00
94 Don Mattingly Bat-Jsy/25 30.00 60.00
96 George Brett Bat-Jsy/25 12.50 30.00
97 Nolan Ryan Bat-Jkt/25 30.00 60.00
98 Ozzie Smith Bat-Jsy/25 20.00 50.00

2004 Prime Cuts II Signature Century Gold

*1-91 p/r 15-19: .5X TO 1.2X SILV p/r 25
*92-100 p/r 15-19: .5X TO 1.2X SILV p/r 25
OVERALL AU-GU ODDS 1:1
PRINT RUNS B/WN 1-19 COPIES PER
NO PRICING ON QTY OF 11 OR LESS

2004 Prime Cuts II Signature Century Silver

OVERALL AU-GU ODDS 1:1
PRINT RUNS B/WN 1- COPIES PER
NO PRICING ON QTY OF OR LESS
1 Mark Prior/22 12.50 30.00
6 Miguel Cabrera/24 30.00 60.00
9 Hank Blalock/25 10.00 25.00
11 Gary Sheffield/25 15.00 40.00
15 Jim Edmonds/25 15.00 40.00
16 Garret Anderson/25 10.00 25.00
17 Lance Berkman/25 15.00 40.00
19 Mike Lowell/19 12.50 30.00
20 Mark Mulder/20 10.00 25.00
21 Sammy Sosa/21 50.00 100.00
23 Mark Teixeira/23 15.00 40.00
24 Manny Ramirez/24 40.00 80.00
25 Rafael Palmeiro/25 30.00 60.00
31 Greg Maddux/31 60.00 120.00
34 Kerry Wood/34 15.00 40.00
35 Mike Mussina Yanks/35 15.00 40.00
37 Juan Gonzalez/22 10.00 25.00
40 Todd Helton/17 20.00 50.00
44 Adam Dunn/44 12.50 30.00
49 David Ortiz/34 20.00 50.00
50 Frank Thomas/35 20.00 50.00
57 Tim Hudson/15 20.00 50.00
61 Craig Biggio/25 15.00 40.00
63 Magglio Ordonez/30 10.00 25.00
66 Vernon Wells/25 10.00 25.00
69 Scott Rolen/27 15.00 40.00
73 Carlos Beltran/15 12.50 30.00

74 Shawn Green/15 20.00 50.00
78 Kazuhisa Ishii/17 12.50 30.00
82 Andruw Jones/25 15.00 40.00
83 Josh Beckett/21 15.00 40.00
87 Mike Mussina O's/35 15.00 40.00
92 Cal Ripken/25 100.00 200.00
93 Dale Murphy/25 15.00 40.00
94 Don Mattingly/23 40.00 80.00
95 Gary Carter/25 10.00 25.00
97 Nolan Ryan/34 60.00 120.00
99 Steve Carlton/32 10.00 25.00
100 Tony Gwynn/25 30.00 60.00

2004 Prime Cuts II Signature Material Number

*1-91 p/r 20-35: .5X TO 1.2X SILV p/r 20-35
*1-91 p/r 15-19: .6X TO 1.5X SILV p/r 20-25
*1-91 p/r 15-19: .5X TO 1.2X SILV p/r 15-19
*92-100 p/r 20-35: .5X TO 1.2X SILV p/r 20-35
*92-100 p/r 15-19: .6X TO 1.5X SILV p/r 20-25
OVERALL AU-GU ODDS 1:1
PRINT RUNS B/WN 1- COPIES PER
NO PRICING ON QTY OF OR LESS

2004 Prime Cuts II Signature Material Combo

*1-91 p/r 20-35: .6X TO 1.5X SILV p/r 20-35
*1-91 p/r 15-19: .75X TO 2X SILV p/r 20-35
*1-91 p/r 15-19: .6X TO 1.5X SILV p/r 15-19
*92-100 p/r 20-35: .6X TO 1.5X SILV p/r 20-35
OVERALL AU-GU ODDS 1:1
PRINT RUNS B/WN 1-25 COPIES PER
NO PRICING ON QTY OF 10 OR LESS

2004 Prime Cuts II MLB Icons

RANDOM INSERTS IN PACKS
STATED PRINT RUN 50 SERIAL #'d SETS
MLB1 Dale Murphy 4.00 10.00
MLB2 Eddie Mathews 4.00 10.00
MLB3 Brooks Robinson 2.50 6.00
MLB4 Cal Ripken Right 12.00 30.00
MLB5 Cal Ripken Left 12.00 30.00
MLB6 Eddie Murray 2.50 6.00
MLB7 Frank Robinson 2.50 6.00
MLB8 Jim Palmer 2.50 6.00
MLB9 Bobby Doerr 2.50 6.00
MLB10 Carl Yastrzemski 4.00 10.00
MLB11 Carlton Fisk R.Sox 2.50 6.00
MLB12 Dennis Eckersley 2.50 6.00
MLB13 Luis Aparicio 2.50 6.00
MLB14 Luis Tiant 1.50 4.00
MLB15 Ted Williams 8.00 20.00
MLB16 Wade Boggs Sox 2.50 6.00
MLB17 Duke Snider Dgr 2.50 6.00
MLB18 Jackie Robinson 4.00 10.00
MLB19 Pee Wee Reese 2.50 6.00
MLB20 Burleigh Grimes 2.50 6.00
MLB21 Nolan Ryan Angels 12.00 30.00
MLB22 Reggie Jackson Angels 2.50 6.00
MLB23 Rod Carew White 2.50 6.00
MLB24 Rod Carew Navy 2.50 6.00
MLB25 Billy Williams 2.50 6.00
MLB26 Ernie Banks 4.00 10.00
MLB27 Mark Grace 2.50 6.00
MLB28 Ron Santo 2.50 6.00
MLB29 Paul Molitor Brew 4.00 10.00
MLB30 Bo Jackson Sox 4.00 10.00
MLB31 Carlton Fisk W.Sox 2.50 6.00
MLB32 Johnny Bench 4.00 10.00
MLB33 Tom Seaver Reds 2.50 6.00
MLB34 Tony Perez 2.50 6.00
MLB35 Bob Feller 2.50 6.00
MLB36 Lou Boudreau 2.50 6.00
MLB37 Al Kaline 4.00 10.00
MLB38 Alan Trammell 2.50 6.00
MLB39 Ty Cobb 6.00 15.00
MLB40 Don Sutton 2.50 6.00
MLB41 Nolan Ryan Astros 12.00 30.00
MLB42 Roger Maris A's 4.00 10.00
MLB43 Bo Jackson Royals 4.00 10.00
MLB44 George Brett Gray 8.00 20.00
MLB45 George Brett White 8.00 20.00
MLB46 Maury Wills 1.50 4.00
MLB47 Warren Spahn 2.50 6.00
MLB48 Robin Yount 4.00 10.00
MLB49 Harmon Killebrew Twins 4.00 10.00
MLB50 Kirby Puckett 4.00 10.00
MLB51 Paul Molitor Twins 4.00 10.00
MLB52 Andre Dawson 2.50 6.00
MLB53 Mel Ott Pinstripe 4.00 10.00
MLB54 Mel Ott White 4.00 10.00
MLB55 Duke Snider Mets 2.50 6.00
MLB56 Rickey Henderson Mets 4.00 10.00
MLB57 Tom Seaver Mets 2.50 6.00
MLB58 Babe Ruth w/Bats 10.00 25.00
MLB59 Babe Ruth Gray 10.00 25.00
MLB60 Catfish Hunter 2.50 6.00
MLB61 Dave Righetti 1.50 4.00
MLB62 Dave Winfield Yanks 2.50 6.00
MLB63 Don Mattingly White 8.00 20.00
MLB64 Don Mattingly Navy 8.00 20.00
MLB65 Lou Gehrig w/o Cap 8.00 20.00
MLB66 Lou Gehrig w/Cap 8.00 20.00
MLB67 Phil Niekro 2.50 6.00
MLB68 Phil Rizzuto 2.50 6.00
MLB69 Reggie Jackson Yanks 2.50 6.00
MLB70 Rickey Henderson Yanks 4.00 10.00
MLB71 Roger Maris Yanks 4.00 10.00
MLB72 Thurman Munson w/Bat 4.00 10.00
MLB73 Thurman Munson w/o Bat 4.00 10.00
MLB74 Wade Boggs Yanks 2.50 6.00
MLB75 Whitey Ford 2.50 6.00
MLB76 Yogi Berra 4.00 10.00
MLB77 Lefty Grove 2.50 6.00
MLB78 Mike Schmidt w/Bat 6.00 15.00
MLB79 Mike Schmidt w/o Bat 6.00 15.00
MLB80 Steve Carlton Phils 2.50 6.00
MLB81 Ralph Kiner 2.50 6.00
MLB82 Roberto Clemente w/Bat 10.00 25.00
MLB83 Roberto Clemente w/o Bat 10.00 25.00
MLB84 Dave Winfield Padres 2.50 6.00
MLB85 Rickey Henderson Padres 4.00 10.00
MLB86 Steve Garvey 1.50 4.00
MLB87 Tony Gwynn Gray 4.00 10.00
MLB88 Tony Gwynn White 4.00 10.00
MLB89 Gaylord Perry 2.50 6.00
MLB90 Joe Morgan 2.50 6.00
MLB91 Juan Marichal 2.50 6.00
MLB92 Steve Carlton Giants 2.50 6.00
MLB93 Will Clark 2.50 6.00
MLB94 Willie McCovey 2.50 6.00
MLB95 Bob Gibson 2.50 6.00
MLB96 Lou Brock 2.50 6.00
MLB97 Stan Musial 6.00 15.00
MLB98 Fergie Jenkins 2.50 6.00
MLB99 Nolan Ryan Rgr 12.00 30.00
MLB100 Harmon Killebrew Senators 4.00 10.00

2004 Prime Cuts II MLB Icons Century Silver

*SILVER: .6X TO 1.5X BASIC
STATED PRINT RUN 25 SERIAL #'d SETS

2004 Prime Cuts II MLB Icons Material Number

*RUTH SWATCH W/P'STRIPE: ADD 25%
OVERALL AU-GU ODDS 1:1
PRINT RUNS B/WN 1- COPIES PER
NO PRICING ON QTY OF OR LESS
MLB1 Dale Murphy Jsy/25 10.00 25.00
MLB3 Brooks Robinson Jsy/25 10.00 25.00
MLB4 Cal Ripken Jsy/25 40.00 80.00
MLB5 Cal Ripken Jkt/25 40.00 80.00
MLB6 Eddie Murray Jsy/25 15.00 40.00
MLB7 Frank Robinson Jsy/25 6.00 15.00
MLB8 Jim Palmer Jsy/25 6.00 15.00
MLB9 Bobby Doerr Jsy/25 6.00 15.00
MLB10 Carl Yastrzemski Jsy/25 20.00 50.00
MLB11 Carlton Fisk R.Sox Jsy/25 10.00 25.00
MLB15 Ted Williams Jsy/50 50.00 100.00
MLB17 Duke Snider Dgr Jsy/25 10.00 25.00
MLB18 Jackie Robinson Jkt/50 40.00 80.00
MLB19 Pee Wee Reese Jsy/25 10.00 25.00
MLB20 Burleigh Grimes Pants/25 30.00 60.00
MLB21 Nolan Ryan Angels Jsy/25 20.00 50.00
MLB22 R.Jackson Angels Jsy/25 10.00 25.00
MLB23 Rod Carew Jsy/25 10.00 25.00
MLB24 Rod Carew Jkt/25 10.00 25.00
MLB25 Billy Williams Jsy/25 6.00 15.00
MLB26 Ernie Banks Jsy/25 12.50 30.00
MLB29 Paul Molitor Brew Pants/25 6.00 15.00
MLB31 Carlton Fisk W.Sox Jsy/25 10.00 25.00
MLB32 Johnny Bench Jsy/25 12.50 30.00
MLB33 Tom Seaver Reds Jsy/25 10.00 25.00
MLB35 Bob Feller Jsy/25 6.00 15.00
MLB36 Lou Boudreau Jsy/25 12.50 30.00
MLB39 Ty Cobb Pants/50 60.00 120.00
MLB41 Nolan Ryan Astros Jsy/25 20.00 50.00
MLB42 Roger Maris A's Jsy/25 30.00 60.00
MLB44 George Brett Jsy/25 20.00 50.00
MLB45 George Brett Jsy/25 12.50 30.00
MLB47 Warren Spahn Jsy/25 12.50 30.00
MLB48 Robin Yount Jsy/25 12.50 30.00
MLB49 H.Killebrew Twins Jsy/25 15.00 40.00
MLB50 Kirby Puckett Jsy/25 12.50 30.00
MLB51 Paul Molitor Twins Jsy/25 6.00 15.00
MLB53 Mel Ott Jsy/25 20.00 50.00
MLB54 Mel Ott Pants/25 20.00 50.00
MLB55 Duke Snider Mets Jsy/25 10.00 25.00
MLB58 Babe Ruth Jsy/25 200.00 350.00
MLB59 Babe Ruth Pants/50 150.00 250.00
MLB60 Catfish Hunter Jsy/25 10.00 25.00
MLB63 Don Mattingly Jsy/25 20.00 50.00
MLB64 Don Mattingly Jkt/25 20.00 50.00
MLB65 Lou Gehrig Jsy/25 100.00 200.00
MLB66 Lou Gehrig Pants/50 75.00 150.00
MLB68 Phil Rizzuto Pants/25 10.00 25.00
MLB69 R.Jackson Yanks Jsy/25 10.00 25.00
MLB71 R.Maris Yanks Pants/25 20.00 50.00
MLB72 Thurman Munson Jsy/50 15.00 40.00
MLB73 Thurman Munson Pants/50 15.00 40.00
MLB75 Whitey Ford Pants/16 15.00 40.00
MLB77 Lefty Grove Hat/25 75.00 150.00
MLB78 Mike Schmidt Jsy/20 20.00 50.00
MLB79 Mike Schmidt Jkt/20 20.00 50.00
MLB82 Roberto Clemente Jsy/21 75.00 150.00
MLB83 Roberto Clemente Hat/21 75.00 150.00
MLB91 Juan Marichal Jsy/25 6.00 15.00
MLB93 Will Clark Jsy/22 10.00 25.00
MLB94 Willie McCovey Jsy/25 10.00 25.00
MLB95 Bob Gibson Jsy/25 10.00 25.00
MLB96 Lou Brock Jkt/20 10.00 25.00
MLB99 Nolan Ryan Rgr Pants/25 20.00 50.00
MLB100 H.Killebrew Senators Jsy/25 15.00 40.00

2004 Prime Cuts II MLB Icons Material Combo

*p/r 20-25: .6X TO 1.5X NBR p/r 50
*p/r 20-25: .5X TO 1.2X NBR p/r 25
*p/r 16-19: .6X TO 1.5X NBR p/r 25
*p/r 16-19: .5X TO 1.2X NBR p/r 16
OVERALL AU-GU ODDS 1:1
PRINT RUNS B/WN 1-25 COPIES PER
NO PRICING ON QTY OF 14 OR LESS
MLB39 Ty Cobb Bat-Pants/25 125.00 200.00
MLB58 Babe Ruth Bat-Jsy/25 250.00 400.00
MLB59 Babe Ruth Bat-Pants/25 200.00 350.00
MLB65 Lou Gehrig Bat-Jsy/25 175.00 300.00
MLB66 Lou Gehrig Bat-Pants/25 150.00 250.00

2004 Prime Cuts II MLB Icons Signature Century Gold

*p/r 20-25: .5X TO 1.2X SILV p/r 36-50
*p/r 20-25: .4X TO 1X SILV p/r 20-35
*p/r 16-19: .6X TO 1.5X SILV p/r 36-50
*p/r 16-19: .5X TO 1.2X SILV p/r 20-35
OVERALL AU-GU ODDS 1:1
PRINT RUNS B/WN 1-25 COPIES PER
NO PRICING ON QTY OF 11 OR LESS

2004 Prime Cuts II MLB Icons Signature Century Platinum

OVERALL AU-GU ODDS 1:1
STATED PRINT RUN 1 SERIAL #'d SET
NO PRICING DUE TO SCARCITY

2004 Prime Cuts II MLB Icons Signature Century Silver

OVERALL AU-GU ODDS 1:1
PRINT RUNS B/WN 1-50 COPIES PER
NO PRICING ON QTY OF 12 OR LESS
MLB1 Dale Murphy/25 15.00 40.00
MLB3 Brooks Robinson/50 12.50 30.00
MLB4 Cal Ripken Right/25 100.00 200.00
MLB5 Cal Ripken Left/25 100.00 200.00
MLB6 Eddie Murray/25 30.00 60.00
MLB7 Frank Robinson/50 12.50 30.00
MLB8 Jim Palmer/50 12.50 30.00
MLB9 Bobby Doerr/25 10.00 25.00
MLB10 Carl Yastrzemski/25 40.00 80.00
MLB11 Carlton Fisk R.Sox/27 15.00 40.00
MLB12 Dennis Eckersley/43 12.50 30.00
MLB13 Luis Aparicio/25 10.00 25.00
MLB16 Wade Boggs Sox/26 15.00 40.00
MLB17 Duke Snider Dgr/50 12.50 30.00
MLB21 Nolan Ryan Angels/30 60.00 120.00
MLB22 Reggie Jackson Angels/25 30.00 60.00
MLB23 Rod Carew White/29 15.00 40.00
MLB24 Rod Carew Navy/29 15.00 40.00
MLB25 Billy Williams/26 10.00 25.00
MLB29 Paul Molitor Brew/25 10.00 25.00
MLB30 Bo Jackson Sox/25 30.00 60.00
MLB31 Carlton Fisk W.Sox/25 15.00 40.00
MLB32 Johnny Bench/50 20.00 50.00
MLB33 Tom Seaver Reds/25 20.00 50.00
MLB34 Tony Perez/25 15.00 40.00
MLB35 Bob Feller/25 10.00 25.00
MLB37 Al Kaline/50 25.00 50.00
MLB40 Don Sutton/20 10.00 25.00
MLB41 Nolan Ryan Astros/34 60.00 120.00
MLB43 Bo Jackson Royals/25 30.00 60.00
MLB44 George Brett Gray/25 50.00 100.00
MLB45 George Brett White/25 50.00 100.00
MLB48 Robin Yount/19 40.00 80.00
MLB49 H.Killebrew Twins/50 30.00 60.00
MLB51 Paul Molitor Twins/50 8.00 20.00
MLB55 Duke Snider Mets/50 12.50 30.00
MLB56 Rickey Henderson Mets/24 30.00 60.00
MLB57 Tom Seaver Mets/25 20.00 50.00
MLB62 Dave Winfield Yanks/31 15.00 40.00
MLB63 Don Mattingly White/50 30.00 60.00
MLB64 Don Mattingly Navy/50 30.00 60.00
MLB67 Phil Niekro/35 10.00 25.00
MLB68 Phil Rizzuto/25 15.00 40.00
MLB69 Reggie Jackson Yanks/25 30.00 60.00
MLB70 Rickey Henderson Yanks/24 30.00 60.00
MLB75 Whitey Ford/25 30.00 60.00
MLB76 Yogi Berra/25 30.00 60.00
MLB78 Mike Schmidt w/Bat/20 40.00 80.00
MLB79 Mike Schmidt w/o Bat/20 40.00 80.00
MLB80 Steve Carlton Phils/32 10.00 25.00
MLB81 Ralph Kiner/25 15.00 40.00
MLB84 Dave Winfield Padres/31 15.00 40.00
MLB85 R.Henderson Padres/24 30.00 60.00
MLB87 Tony Gwynn Gray/50 20.00 50.00
MLB88 Tony Gwynn White/50 20.00 50.00
MLB89 Gaylord Perry/36 8.00 20.00
MLB90 Joe Morgan/24 10.00 25.00
MLB91 Juan Marichal/27 10.00 25.00
MLB92 Steve Carlton Giants/32 10.00 25.00
MLB93 Will Clark/22 15.00 40.00
MLB94 Willie McCovey/25 15.00 40.00
MLB95 Bob Gibson/45 12.50 30.00
MLB96 Lou Brock/50 12.50 30.00
MLB97 Stan Musial/50 40.00 80.00
MLB98 Fergie Jenkins/31 10.00 25.00
MLB99 Nolan Ryan Rgr/34 60.00 120.00
MLB100 H.Killebrew Senators/50 15.00 40.00

2004 Prime Cuts II MLB Icons Signature Material Number

*p/r 36-50: .5X TO 1.2X SILV p/r 36-50
*p/r 36-50: .4X TO 1X SILV p/r 20-35
*p/r 20-35: .6X TO 1.5X SILV p/r 36-50
*p/r 20-35: .5X TO 1.2X SILV p/r 20-35
*p/r 20-35: .4X TO 1X SILV p/r 15-19
*p/r 15-19: .75X TO 2X SILV p/r 36-50
*p/r 15-19: .6X TO 1.5X SILV p/r 20-35
OVERALL AU-GU ODDS 1:1
PRINT RUNS B/WN 1-45 COPIES PER
NO PRICING ON QTY OF 12 OR LESS
MLB27 Mark Grace Jsy/17 40.00 80.00

2004 Prime Cuts II MLB Icons Signature Material Combo

*p/r 20-35: .75X TO 2X SILV p/r 36-50
*p/r 20-35: .6X TO 1.5X SILV p/r 20-35
*p/r 15-19: 1X TO 2.5X SILV p/r 36-50
*p/r 15-19: .75X TO 2X SILV p/r 20-35
*p/r 15-19: .6X TO 1.5X SILV p/r 15-19
OVERALL AU-GU ODDS 1:1
PRINT RUNS B/WN 1-32 COPIES PER
NO PRICING ON QTY OF 11 OR LESS

2004 Prime Cuts II MLB Icons Signature Material Combo Prime

OVERALL AU-GU ODDS 1:1
PRINT RUNS B/WN 1-10 COPIES PER
NO PRICING DUE TO SCARCITY

2004 Prime Cuts II Timeline

RANDOM INSERTS IN PACKS
STATED PRINT RUN 50 SERIAL #'d SETS
TL1 Al Kaline 4.00 10.00
TL2 Alex Rodriguez 5.00 12.00
TL3 Andre Dawson 2.50 6.00
TL4 Babe Ruth 10.00 25.00
TL5 Barry Zito 2.50 6.00
TL6 Bob Feller 2.50 6.00
TL7 Bob Gibson 2.50 6.00
TL8 Bobby Doerr 2.50 6.00
TL9 Brooks Robinson 2.50 6.00
TL10 Cal Ripken 12.00 30.00
TL11 Carl Hubbell 2.50 6.00
TL12 Carl Yastrzemski 4.00 10.00
TL13 Carlton Fisk 2.50 6.00
TL14 Catfish Hunter 2.50 6.00
TL15 Chipper Jones 4.00 10.00
TL16 Cy Young 2.50 6.00
TL17 Dale Murphy 4.00 10.00
TL18 Dave Parker 1.50 4.00
TL19 Dennis Eckersley 2.50 6.00
TL20 Don Drysdale 2.50 6.00
TL21 Don Mattingly 8.00 20.00
TL22 Duke Snider 2.50 6.00
TL23 Dwight Gooden 1.50 4.00
TL24 Early Wynn 2.50 6.00
TL25 Eddie Mathews 4.00 10.00
TL26 Eddie Murray 2.50 6.00
TL27 Enos Slaughter 2.50 6.00
TL28 Ernie Banks 4.00 10.00
TL29 Fergie Jenkins 2.50 6.00
TL30 Frank Robinson 2.50 6.00
TL31 Frank Thomas 4.00 10.00
TL32 Frankie Frisch 2.50 6.00
TL33 Fred Lynn 1.50 4.00
TL34 Gary Carter 2.50 6.00
TL35 Gaylord Perry 2.50 6.00
TL36 George Brett 8.00 20.00
TL37 Greg Maddux 5.00 12.00
TL38 Hal Newhouser 2.50 6.00
TL39 Harmon Killebrew 4.00 10.00
TL40 Honus Wagner 4.00 10.00
TL41 Hoyt Wilhelm 2.50 6.00
TL42 Ivan Rodriguez 2.50 6.00
TL43 Jackie Robinson 4.00 10.00
TL44 Jason Giambi 1.50 4.00
TL45 Jeff Bagwell 2.50 6.00
TL46 Jim Palmer 2.50 6.00
TL47 Jimmie Foxx 4.00 10.00
TL48 Joe Morgan 2.50 6.00
TL49 Johnny Bench 4.00 10.00
TL50 Johnny Mize 2.50 6.00
TL51 Jose Canseco 2.50 6.00
TL52 Juan Gonzalez 1.50 4.00
TL53 Juan Marichal 2.50 6.00
TL54 Keith Hernandez 1.50 4.00
TL55 Kirby Puckett 4.00 10.00
TL56 Lefty Grove 2.50 6.00
TL57 Lou Boudreau 2.50 6.00
TL58 Lou Brock 2.50 6.00
TL59 Lou Gehrig 8.00 20.00
TL60 Luis Aparicio 2.50 6.00
TL61 Marty Marion 1.50 4.00
TL62 Mel Ott 4.00 10.00
TL63 Miguel Tejada 2.50 6.00
TL64 Mike Schmidt 6.00 15.00
TL65 Nellie Fox 2.50 6.00
TL66 Nolan Ryan 12.00 30.00
TL67 Orel Hershiser 1.50 4.00
TL68 Orlando Cepeda 2.50 6.00
TL69 Paul Molitor 4.00 10.00
TL70 Pedro Martinez 2.50 6.00
TL71 Pee Wee Reese 2.50 6.00
TL72 Phil Niekro 2.50 6.00
TL73 Phil Rizzuto 2.50 6.00
TL74 Ralph Kiner 2.50 6.00
TL75 Randy Johnson 4.00 10.00
TL76 Red Schoendienst 2.50 6.00
TL77 Reggie Jackson 2.50 6.00
TL78 Rickey Henderson 4.00 10.00
TL79 Roberto Clemente 10.00 25.00
TL80 Robin Yount 4.00 10.00
TL81 Rod Carew 2.50 6.00
TL82 Roger Clemens 5.00 12.00
TL83 Roger Maris 4.00 10.00
TL84 Rogers Hornsby 2.50 6.00
TL85 Roy Campanella 4.00 10.00
TL86 Ozzie Smith 5.00 12.00
TL87 Sammy Sosa 4.00 10.00
TL88 Satchel Paige 4.00 10.00
TL89 Stan Musial 6.00 15.00
TL90 Steve Carlton 2.50 6.00
TL91 Ted Williams 8.00 20.00
TL92 Thurman Munson 4.00 10.00
TL93 Tom Seaver 2.50 6.00
TL94 Ty Cobb 6.00 15.00
TL95 Walter Johnson 2.50 6.00
TL96 Warren Spahn 2.50 6.00
TL97 Whitey Ford 2.50 6.00
TL98 Willie McCovey 2.50 6.00
TL99 Willie Stargell 2.50 6.00
TL100 Yogi Berra 4.00 10.00

2004 Prime Cuts II Timeline Century Silver

*SILVER: .6X TO 1.5X BASIC
STATED PRINT RUN 25 SERIAL #'d SETS

2004 Prime Cuts II Timeline Material Number

*RUTH SWATCH W/P'STRIPE: ADD 25%
OVERALL AU-GU ODDS 1:1
PRINT RUNS B/WN 1-42 COPIES PER
NO PRICING ON QTY OF 11 OR LESS
TL4 Babe Ruth Jsy/25 250.00 400.00
TL6 Bob Feller Pants/19 8.00 20.00
TL7 Bob Gibson Jsy/25 10.00 25.00
TL10 Cal Ripken Jsy/25 40.00 80.00
TL12 Carl Yastrzemski Jsy/25 20.00 50.00
TL13 Carlton Fisk Jsy/27 10.00 25.00
TL14 Catfish Hunter Jsy/27 10.00 25.00
TL20 Don Drysdale Jsy/25 20.00 50.00
TL22 Duke Snider Pants/25 10.00 25.00
TL24 Early Wynn Jsy/24 6.00 15.00
TL25 Eddie Mathews Jsy/25 15.00 40.00
TL26 Eddie Murray Jsy/25 15.00 40.00
TL28 Ernie Banks Jsy/25 12.50 30.00
TL32 Frankie Frisch Jkt/25 15.00 40.00
TL36 George Brett Jsy/25 20.00 50.00
TL38 Hal Newhouser Jsy/16 15.00 40.00
TL39 Harmon Killebrew Jsy/25 15.00 40.00
TL43 Jackie Robinson Jkt/42 40.00 80.00
TL46 Jim Palmer Jsy/22 6.00 15.00
TL47 Jimmie Foxx Fld Glv/25 50.00 100.00
TL49 Johnny Bench Jsy/25 12.50 30.00
TL53 Juan Marichal Jsy/25 6.00 15.00
TL55 Kirby Puckett Jsy/25 12.50 30.00
TL58 Lou Brock Jsy/20 10.00 25.00
TL59 Lou Gehrig Jsy/25 100.00 200.00
TL62 Mel Ott Pants/25 20.00 50.00
TL64 Mike Schmidt Jsy/20 20.00 50.00
TL66 Nolan Ryan Jsy/25 20.00 50.00
TL68 Orlando Cepeda Pants/25 6.00 15.00
TL71 Pee Wee Reese Jsy/25 10.00 25.00
TL74 Ralph Kiner Bat/25 6.00 15.00
TL77 Reggie Jackson Jsy/25 10.00 25.00
TL80 Robin Yount Jsy/19 15.00 40.00
TL81 Rod Carew Jsy/25 10.00 25.00
TL82 Roger Clemens Jsy/21 12.50 30.00
TL83 Roger Maris Jsy/25 30.00 60.00
TL84 Rogers Hornsby Bat/25 40.00 80.00
TL85 Roy Campanella Pants/25 12.50 30.00
TL86 Ozzie Smith Jsy/25 15.00 40.00
TL87 Sammy Sosa Jsy/21 10.00 25.00
TL88 Satchel Paige CO Jsy/25 40.00 80.00
TL90 Steve Carlton Jsy/25 6.00 15.00
TL91 Ted Williams Jsy/25 20.00 50.00
TL92 Thurman Munson Jsy/25 20.00 50.00
TL93 Tom Seaver Pants/25 10.00 25.00
TL94 Ty Cobb Pants/25 75.00 150.00
TL96 Warren Spahn Jsy/21 12.50 30.00
TL97 Whitey Ford Jsy/16 15.00 40.00
TL98 Willie McCovey Jsy/25 10.00 25.00

2004 Prime Cuts II Timeline Material Position

*RET p/r 36-50: .4X TO 1X NBR p/r 36-50
*ACT p/r 20-35: .4X TO 1X NBR p/r 20-35
*RET p/r 20-35: .4X TO 1X NBR p/r 20-35
*RET p/r 15-19: .5X TO 1.2X NBR p/r 20-35
*RET p/r 15-19: .4X TO 1X NBR p/r 15-19
OVERALL AU-GU ODDS 1:1
PRINT RUNS B/WN 1-42 COPIES PER
NO PRICING ON QTY OF 11 OR LESS
TL4 Babe Ruth Jsy/25 250.00 400.00
TL59 Lou Gehrig Jsy/25 100.00 200.00

2004 Prime Cuts II Timeline Material Combo

*RET p/r 36-50: .5X TO 1.2X NBR p/r 36-50
*RET p/r 36-50: .4X TO 1X NBR p/r 20-35
*ACT p/r 20-35: .5X TO 1.2X NBR p/r 20-35
*RET p/r 20-35: .5X TO 1.2X NBR p/r 20-35
*RET p/r 15-19: .6X TO 1.5X NBR p/r 20-35
*RET p/r 15-19: .5X TO 1.2X NBR p/r 15-19
OVERALL AU-GU ODDS 1:1
PRINT RUNS B/WN 1-42 COPIES PER
NO PRICING ON QTY OF 14 OR LESS
TL4 Babe Ruth Jsy-Jsy/25 300.00 500.00
TL17 Dale Murphy Bat-Jsy/25 12.50 30.00
TL21 D.Matt Btg Glv-Pants/25 30.00 60.00
TL59 Lou Gehrig Jsy-Pants/25 175.00 300.00
TL79 R.Clemente Hat-Jsy/21 100.00 200.00

2004 Prime Cuts II Timeline Material Combo CY

*ACT p/r 20-35: .5X TO 1.2X NBR p/r 20-35
*RET p/r 20-35: .5X TO 1.2X NBR p/r 20-35
*RET p/r 15-19: .5X TO 1.2X NBR p/r 15-19
OVERALL AU-GU ODDS 1:1
PRINT RUNS B/WN 1-32 COPIES PER
NO PRICING ON QTY OF 10 OR LESS
TL70 Pedro Martinez Bat-Jsy/25 30.00 60.00

2004 Prime Cuts II Timeline Material Trio

*ACT p/r 20-35: .6X TO 1.5X NBR p/r 20-35
*RET p/r 20-35: .6X TO 1.5X NBR p/r 20-35
*RET p/r 15-19: .75X TO 2X NBR p/r 20-35
*RET p/r 15-19: .6X TO 1.5X NBR p/r 15-19
OVERALL AU-GU ODDS 1:1
PRINT RUNS B/WN 1-25 COPIES PER
NO PRICING ON QTY OF 10 OR LESS
TL17 Dale Murphy Bat-Jsy-Jsy/25 15.00 40.00
TL21 D.Matt Bat-Jkt-Pants/25 40.00 80.00
TL26 E.Murray Bat-Jsy-Shoe/25 60.00 120.00

2004 Prime Cuts II Timeline Material Trio MVP

*RET p/r 15-19: .75X TO 2X NBR p/r 20-35
OVERALL AU-GU ODDS 1:1
PRINT RUNS B/WN 1-15 COPIES PER
NO PRICING ON QTY OF 10 OR LESS

2004 Prime Cuts II Timeline Material Trio Stats

*RET p/r 15-19: .75X TO 2X NBR p/r 20-35
OVERALL AU-GU ODDS 1:1
PRINT RUNS B/WN 1-15 COPIES PER
NO PRICING ON QTY OF 10 OR LESS

2004 Prime Cuts II Timeline Material Quad

OVERALL AU-GU ODDS 1:1
PRINT RUNS B/WN 1-25 COPIES PER
NO PRICING ON QTY OF 10 OR LESS
B ='s Bat, BG ='s Btg Glv, FG ='s Fld Glv
H ='s Hat, J ='s Jsy, JK ='s Jkt, P ='s Pants
TL4 Babe Ruth B-J-J-P/25 600.00 1000.00
TL91 Ted Williams B-JK-J-J/25 175.00 300.00

2004 Prime Cuts II Timeline Signature Material Number

OVERALL AU-GU ODDS 1:1
PRINT RUNS B/WN 1-34 COPIES PER
NO PRICING ON QTY OF 11 OR LESS
6 Bob Feller Pants/19 15.00 40.00
7 Bob Gibson Jsy/25 20.00 50.00
8 Bobby Doerr Jsy/25 12.50 30.00
21 Don Mattingly Pants/23 50.00 100.00
46 Jim Palmer Jsy/22 20.00 50.00
53 Juan Marichal Jsy/27 12.50 30.00
58 Lou Brock Jsy/20 20.00 50.00
66 Nolan Ryan Jsy/34 40.00 80.00
90 Steve Carlton Jsy/32 12.50 30.00

2004 Prime Cuts II Timeline Signature Material Position

*RET p/r 20-35: .4X TO 1X NBR p/r 20-35
*RET p/r 15-19: .4X TO 1X NBR p/r 15-19
OVERALL AU-GU ODDS 1:1
PRINT RUNS B/WN 1-34 COPIES PER
NO PRICING ON QTY OF 10 OR LESS

2004 Prime Cuts II Timeline Signature Material Combo

*RET p/r 20-35: .5X TO 1.2X NBR p/r 20-35
OVERALL AU-GU ODDS 1:1
PRINT RUNS B/WN 1-25 COPIES PER
NO PRICING ON QTY OF 11 OR LESS

2004 Prime Cuts II Timeline Signature Material Combo CY

*RET p/r 20-35: .5X TO 1.2X NBR p/r 20-35
OVERALL AU-GU ODDS 1:1
PRINT RUNS B/WN 1-15 COPIES PER
NO PRICING ON QTY OF 5 OR LESS

2004 Prime Cuts II Timeline Signature Material Quad

OVERALL AU-GU ODDS 1:1
PRINT RUNS B/WN 1-25 COPIES PER
NO PRICING ON QTY OF 11 OR LESS
B ='s Bat, BG ='s Btg Glv, FG ='s Fld Glv
H ='s Hat, J ='s Jsy, JK ='s Jkt, P ='s Pants
17 Dale Murphy B-J-J-J/25 60.00 120.00

2005 Prime Cuts

COMMON CARD (1-91) .75 2.00
COMMON CARD (92-100) .75 2.00
PRINT RUNS B/WN 399-499 COPIES PER
1 Vladimir Guerrero Angels/499 1.25 3.00
2 Roger Clemens Astros/499 2.50 6.00
3 Carlos Beltran/499 1.25 3.00
4 Johan Santana/499 1.25 3.00
5 Alfonso Soriano/499 1.25 3.00
6 Derek Jeter/499 5.00 12.00
7 Chipper Jones/499 2.00 5.00
8 David Ortiz/499 2.00 5.00
9 Josh Beckett/499 .75 2.00
10 Mike Piazza Mets/499 2.00 5.00
11 Alex Rodriguez/449 2.50 6.00
12 Albert Pujols/449 2.50 6.00
13 Mike Sweeney/449 .75 2.00
14 Miguel Tejada/449 1.25 3.00
15 Barry Zito/449 1.25 3.00
16 Mark Mulder/449 .75 2.00
17 Tim Hudson/449 1.25 3.00
18 Troy Glaus/449 .75 2.00
19 Ichiro Suzuki/449 2.50 6.00
20 Ken Griffey Jr./449 4.00 10.00
21 Miguel Cabrera/449 2.00 5.00
22 Jeff Bagwell/449 1.25 3.00
23 Todd Helton/449 1.25 3.00
24 Mark Buehrle/449 1.25 3.00
25 Greg Maddux Cubs/449 2.50 6.00
26 Ivan Rodriguez/449 1.25 3.00
27 Carlos Lee/449 .75 2.00
28 Nick Johnson/449 .75 2.00
29 Mike Mussina/449 1.25 3.00
30 Mark Teixeira/449 1.25 3.00
31 Adrian Beltre/499 2.00 5.00
32 Torii Hunter/499 .75 2.00
33 Jim Edmonds/499 1.25 3.00
34 Manny Ramirez/499 2.00 5.00
35 Pedro Martinez/499 1.25 3.00
36 Jim Thome/499 1.25 3.00
37 Craig Biggio/499 1.25 3.00
38 Garret Anderson/499 .75 2.00
39 Paul Konerko/499 1.25 3.00
40 Adam Dunn/499 1.25 3.00
41 Brian Roberts/449 .75 2.00
42 Derrek Lee/449 .75 2.00
43 Hank Blalock/449 .75 2.00
44 Justin Morneau/449 1.25 3.00
45 David Wright/449 1.50 4.00
46 Richie Sexson/449 .75 2.00
47 Ben Sheets/449 .75 2.00
48 Gary Sheffield/449 .75 2.00
49 Pat Burrell/449 .75 2.00
50 Larry Walker/449 1.25 3.00
51 Johnny Damon/449 1.25 3.00
52 Jeff Kent/449 .75 2.00
53 Aubrey Huff/449 .75 2.00
54 Shawn Green/449 .75 2.00
55 Milton Bradley/449 .75 2.00
56 Magglio Ordonez/449 1.25 3.00
57 J.T. Snow/449 .75 2.00
58 Scott Rolen/449 1.25 3.00
59 Michael Young/449 .75 2.00
60 Roy Oswalt/449 1.25 3.00
61 Carlos Zambrano/449 1.25 3.00
62 Dontrelle Willis/449 .75 2.00
63 Curt Schilling/449 1.25 3.00
64 Roy Halladay/449 1.25 3.00
65 Eric Chavez/449 .75 2.00
66 Randy Johnson Yanks/499 2.00 5.00
67 Mark Prior/499 1.25 3.00
68 Victor Martinez/399 1.25 3.00
69 Sammy Sosa O's/399 2.00 5.00
70 Lance Berkman/399 1.25 3.00
71 Jeremy Bonderman/399 .75 2.00
72 Frank Thomas/399 2.00 5.00
73 Jake Peavy/399 .75 2.00
74 Jason Schmidt/399 .75 2.00
75 Carlos Delgado/399 .75 2.00
76 Andruw Jones/399 .75 2.00
77 Vernon Wells/399 .75 2.00
78 Sean Casey/399 .75 2.00
79 Jason Bay/399 .75 2.00
80 Hideki Matsui/399 3.00 8.00
81 Jason Varitek/399 2.00 5.00
82 Kerry Wood/399 .75 2.00
83 Moises Alou/399 .75 2.00
84 Joe Mauer/399 1.50 4.00
85 Rafael Palmeiro/399 2.00 5.00
86 Mike Piazza Dgr/399 2.00 5.00
87 Sammy Sosa Cubs/399 2.00 5.00
88 Randy Johnson Astros/399 2.00 5.00
89 Vladimir Guerrero Expos/399 1.25 3.00
90 Greg Maddux Braves/399 2.50 6.00
91 Roger Clemens Yanks/399 2.50 6.00
92 Nolan Ryan/399 6.00 15.00
93 Cal Ripken/399 6.00 15.00
94 Tony Gwynn/399 2.50 6.00
95 Wade Boggs/449 1.25 3.00
96 Ryne Sandberg/449 4.00 10.00
97 Dale Murphy/449 2.00 5.00
98 Mike Schmidt/449 3.00 8.00
99 Don Mattingly/449 4.00 10.00
100 Willie Mays/449 4.00 10.00

2005 Prime Cuts Century Gold

*GOLD 1-91: 1X TO 2.5X BASIC
*GOLD 92-100: 1X TO 2.5X BASIC
STATED PRINT RUN 25 SERIAL #'d SETS

2005 Prime Cuts Century Silver

*SILVER 1-91: .6X TO 1.5X BASIC
*SILVER 92-100: .6X TO 1.5X BASIC
STATED PRINT RUN 50 SERIAL #'d SETS

2005 Prime Cuts Material Bat

*1-91 p/r 48-50: .4X TO 1X JSY p/r 50
*92-100 p/r 50: .4X TO 1X JSY p/r 50
OVERALL AU-GU ODDS ONE PER PACK
PRINT RUNS B/WN 1-50 COPIES PER
NO PRICING ON QTY OF 7 OR LESS
1 Vladimir Guerrero Angels/50 5.00 12.00
3 Carlos Beltran/50 3.00 8.00
16 Mark Mulder/50 3.00 8.00
17 Tim Hudson/30 4.00 10.00
18 Troy Glaus/50 3.00 8.00
24 Mark Buehrle/50 3.00 8.00
26 Ivan Rodriguez/50 4.00 10.00
27 Carlos Lee/50 3.00 8.00
28 Nick Johnson/50 3.00 8.00
29 Mike Mussina/48 4.00 10.00
35 Pedro Martinez/50 4.00 10.00
40 Adam Dunn/50 3.00 8.00
46 Richie Sexson/50 3.00 8.00
50 Larry Walker/18 6.00 15.00
52 Jeff Kent/50 3.00 8.00
54 Shawn Green/50 3.00 8.00
56 Magglio Ordonez/50 3.00 8.00
66 Randy Johnson Yanks/50 5.00 12.00
69 Sammy Sosa O's/50 5.00 12.00
81 Jason Varitek/50 5.00 12.00
83 Moises Alou/50 3.00 8.00
95 Wade Boggs/50 5.00 12.00

2005 Prime Cuts Material Jersey

OVERALL AU-GU ODDS ONE PER PACK
PRINT RUNS B/WN 11-50 COPIES PER
NO PRICING ON QTY OF 13 OR LESS
2 Roger Clemens Astros/50 6.00 15.00
4 Johan Santana/50 5.00 12.00
5 Alfonso Soriano/50 3.00 8.00
7 Chipper Jones/50 5.00 12.00
8 David Ortiz/50 4.00 10.00
9 Josh Beckett/50 3.00 8.00
10 Mike Piazza Mets/50 5.00 12.00
12 Albert Pujols/50 8.00 20.00
13 Mike Sweeney/50 3.00 8.00
14 Miguel Tejada/50 3.00 8.00
15 Barry Zito/50 3.00 8.00
21 Miguel Cabrera/50 4.00 10.00
22 Jeff Bagwell/50 4.00 10.00
23 Todd Helton/50 4.00 10.00
25 Greg Maddux Cubs/50 6.00 15.00
26 Ivan Rodriguez/27 5.00 12.00
29 Mike Mussina/50 4.00 10.00
30 Mark Teixeira/50 4.00 10.00
31 Adrian Beltre/50 3.00 8.00
32 Torii Hunter/50 3.00 8.00
33 Jim Edmonds/50 3.00 8.00
34 Manny Ramirez/50 4.00 10.00
36 Jim Thome/50 4.00 10.00
37 Craig Biggio/50 4.00 10.00
38 Garret Anderson/50 3.00 8.00
39 Paul Konerko/50 3.00 8.00
41 Brian Roberts/50 3.00 8.00
42 Derrek Lee/50 4.00 10.00
43 Hank Blalock/50 3.00 8.00
44 Justin Morneau/50 3.00 8.00
45 David Wright/50 6.00 15.00
47 Ben Sheets/50 3.00 8.00
48 Gary Sheffield/50 3.00 8.00
49 Pat Burrell/50 3.00 8.00
50 Larry Walker/50 4.00 10.00
53 Aubrey Huff/50 3.00 8.00
57 J.T. Snow/50 3.00 8.00
58 Scott Rolen/50 4.00 10.00
59 Michael Young/50 3.00 8.00
60 Roy Oswalt/50 3.00 8.00
61 Carlos Zambrano/50 3.00 8.00
62 Dontrelle Willis/50 3.00 8.00
63 Curt Schilling/50 4.00 10.00
64 Roy Halladay/22 4.00 10.00
65 Eric Chavez/50 3.00 8.00
67 Mark Prior/50 4.00 10.00
68 Victor Martinez/50 3.00 8.00
70 Lance Berkman/50 3.00 8.00
72 Frank Thomas/50 5.00 12.00
75 Carlos Delgado/50 3.00 8.00
76 Andruw Jones/50 4.00 10.00
77 Vernon Wells/50 3.00 8.00
78 Sean Casey/50 3.00 8.00
79 Jason Bay/50 3.00 8.00
80 Hideki Matsui/50 12.50 30.00
82 Kerry Wood/50 3.00 8.00
85 Rafael Palmeiro/50 4.00 10.00
86 Mike Piazza Dgr/50 5.00 12.00
87 Sammy Sosa Cubs/50 5.00 12.00
88 Randy Johnson Astros/50 5.00 12.00
89 Vladimir Guerrero Expos/50 5.00 12.00
90 Greg Maddux Braves/50 6.00 15.00
91 Roger Clemens Yanks/50 6.00 15.00
92 Nolan Ryan/38 10.00 25.00
93 Cal Ripken/25 10.00 25.00
94 Tony Gwynn/50 6.00 15.00
96 Ryne Sandberg/50 8.00 20.00
97 Dale Murphy/50 5.00 12.00
98 Mike Schmidt/50 6.00 15.00
99 Don Mattingly/50 6.00 15.00
100 Willie Mays/50 10.00 25.00

2005 Prime Cuts Material Jersey Number

*1-91 p/r 50: .4X TO 1X JSY p/r 50
*1-91 p/r 50: .3X TO .8X JSY p/r 27
*92-100 p/r 50: .4X TO 1X JSY p/r 50
STATED PRINT RUN 50 SERIAL #'d SETS
PRIME PRINT RUN B/WN 5-10 COPIES PER
NO PRIME PRICING DUE TO SCARCITY
OVERALL AU-GU ODDS ONE PER PACK
1 Vladimir Guerrero Angels 5.00 12.00
24 Mark Buehrle 3.00 8.00
40 Adam Dunn 3.00 8.00

2005 Prime Cuts Material Jersey Position

*1-91 p/r 50: .4X TO 1X JSY p/r 50
*1-91 p/r 50: .3X TO .8X JSY p/r 22-27
*1-91 p/r 25: .5X TO 1.2X JSY p/r 50
*92-100 p/r 50: .4X TO 1X JSY p/r 38-50
OVERALL AU-GU ODDS ONE PER PACK
PRINT RUNS B/WN 25-50 COPIES PER
1 Vladimir Guerrero Angels/50 5.00 12.00
24 Mark Buehrle/50 3.00 8.00
40 Adam Dunn/50 3.00 8.00
71 Jeremy Bonderman/50 3.00 8.00

2005 Prime Cuts Material Combo

*1-91 p/r 50: .5X TO 1.2X JSY p/r 50
*1-91 p/r 25: .6X TO 1.5X JSY p/r 50
*1-91 p/r 25: .5X TO 1.2X JSY p/r 22-27
*92-100 p/r 50: .5X TO 1.2X JSY p/r 50
PRINT RUNS B/WN 1-50 COPIES PER
NO PRICING ON QTY OF 10 OR LESS
PRIME PRINT RUN B/WN 1-10 COPIES PER
NO PRIME PRICING DUE TO SCARCITY
OVERALL AU-GU ODDS ONE PER PACK
24 Mark Buehrle Bat-Jsy/50 4.00 10.00
40 Adam Dunn Bat-Jsy/18 6.00 15.00
51 Johnny Damon Bat-Jsy/15 8.00 20.00

2005 Prime Cuts Signature Century Gold

*GOLD p/r 25: .4X TO 1X SILVER p/r 25
OVERALL AU-GU ODDS ONE PER PACK
PRINT RUNS B/WN 1-25 COPIES PER
NO PRICING ON QTY OF 10 OR LESS

2005 Prime Cuts Signature Century Platinum

OVERALL AU-GU ODDS ONE PER PACK
STATED PRINT RUN 1 SERIAL #'d SET
NO PRICING DUE TO SCARCITY

2005 Prime Cuts Signature Century Silver
OVERALL AU-GU ODDS ONE PER PACK
PRINT RUNS B/WN 1-25 COPIES PER
NO PRICING ON QTY OF 10 OR LESS
3 Carlos Beltran/25 10.00 25.00
4 Johan Santana/25 15.00 40.00
5 Alfonso Soriano/25 10.00 25.00
21 Miguel Cabrera/25 20.00 50.00

2005 Prime Cuts MLB Icons
STATED PRINT RUN 100 SERIAL #'d SETS
*GOLD: .75X TO 2X BASIC
GOLD PRINT RUN 25 SERIAL #'d SETS
PLATINUM PRINT RUN 1 SERIAL #'d SET
NO PLATINUM PRICING DUE TO SCARCITY
*SILVER: .5X TO 1.2X BASIC
SILVER PRINT RUN 50 SERIAL #'d SETS
RANDOM INSERTS IN PACKS
MLB1 Andre Dawson 2.00 5.00
MLB2 Babe Ruth 8.00 20.00
MLB3 Billy Williams 2.00 5.00
MLB4 Bob Feller 2.00 5.00
MLB5 Bob Gibson 2.00 5.00
MLB6 Bobby Doerr 2.00 5.00
MLB7 Brooks Robinson 2.00 5.00
MLB8 Burleigh Grimes 2.00 5.00
MLB9 Cal Ripken 10.00 25.00
MLB10 Carlton Fisk 2.00 5.00
MLB11 Dale Murphy 3.00 8.00
MLB12 Don Mattingly 6.00 15.00
MLB13 Don Sutton 2.00 5.00
MLB14 Ted Williams 6.00 15.00
MLB15 Ernie Banks 3.00 8.00
MLB16 Frank Robinson 2.00 5.00
MLB17 Gary Carter 2.00 5.00
MLB18 Gaylord Perry 2.00 5.00
MLB19 Hank Aaron 6.00 15.00
MLB20 Harmon Killebrew 3.00 8.00
MLB21 Jim Palmer 2.00 5.00
MLB22 Jim Thorpe 5.00 12.00
MLB23 Babe Ruth 8.00 20.00
MLB24 Johnny Bench 3.00 8.00
MLB25 Juan Marichal 2.00 5.00
MLB26 Kirby Puckett 3.00 8.00
MLB27 Lou Brock 2.00 5.00
MLB28 Luis Aparicio 2.00 5.00
MLB29 Marty Marion 1.25 3.00
MLB30 Mike Schmidt 5.00 12.00
MLB31 Nolan Ryan 10.00 25.00
MLB32 Red Schoendienst 2.00 5.00
MLB33 Rickey Henderson 3.00 8.00
MLB34 Roberto Clemente 8.00 20.00
MLB35 Rod Carew 2.00 5.00
MLB36 Sandy Koufax 6.00 15.00
MLB37 Stan Musial 5.00 12.00
MLB38 Steve Carlton 2.00 5.00
MLB39 Steve Garvey 1.25 3.00
MLB40 Ted Williams 6.00 15.00
MLB41 Tom Seaver 2.00 5.00
MLB42 Tony Gwynn 4.00 10.00
MLB43 Whitey Ford 2.00 5.00
MLB44 Willie Mays 6.00 15.00
MLB45 Willie McCovey 2.00 5.00

2005 Prime Cuts MLB Icons Material Bat
*BAT p/r 50: .4X TO 1X JSY p/r 50
*BAT p/r 50: .3X TO .8X JSY p/r 24-35
OVERALL AU-GU ODDS ONE PER PACK
PRINT RUNS B/WN 13-50 COPIES PER
NO PRICING ON QTY OF 13
MLB2 Babe Ruth/50 100.00 175.00
MLB7 Brooks Robinson/50 5.00 12.00
MLB23 Babe Ruth/50 100.00 175.00
MLB26 Kirby Puckett/50 6.00 15.00
MLB27 Lou Brock/50 5.00 12.00
MLB28 Luis Aparicio/50 4.00 10.00
MLB32 Red Schoendienst/50 4.00 10.00
MLB34 Roberto Clemente/50 30.00 60.00

2005 Prime Cuts MLB Icons Material Jersey
OVERALL AU-GU ODDS ONE PER PACK
PRINT RUNS B/WN 1-50 COPIES PER
NO PRICING ON QTY OF 12 OR LESS
MLB1 Andre Dawson/50 4.00 10.00
MLB2 Babe Ruth/25 200.00 300.00
MLB3 Billy Williams/50 4.00 10.00
MLB5 Bob Gibson/25 6.00 15.00
MLB6 Bobby Doerr Pants/50 4.00 10.00
MLB8 Burleigh Grimes Pants/50 30.00 60.00
MLB9 Cal Ripken/50 10.00 25.00
MLB10 Carlton Fisk/50 5.00 12.00
MLB11 Dale Murphy/50 5.00 12.00
MLB12 Don Mattingly/50 6.00 15.00
MLB13 Don Sutton/24 5.00 12.00
MLB14 Ted Williams/25 30.00 60.00
MLB15 Ernie Banks/25 8.00 20.00
MLB16 Frank Robinson/25 5.00 12.00
MLB17 Gary Carter/50 4.00 10.00
MLB18 Gaylord Perry/50 4.00 10.00
MLB19 Hank Aaron/25 20.00 50.00
MLB20 Harmon Killebrew/50 6.00 15.00
MLB22 Jim Thorpe/50 100.00 175.00
MLB23 Babe Ruth/25 150.00 300.00
MLB24 Johnny Bench/50 6.00 15.00
MLB25 Juan Marichal/50 4.00 10.00
MLB30 Mike Schmidt/35 8.00 20.00
MLB31 Nolan Ryan Pants/50 10.00 25.00
MLB33 Rickey Henderson/50 6.00 15.00
MLB35 Rod Carew/50 5.00 12.00
MLB37 Stan Musial/50 8.00 20.00
MLB38 Steve Carlton/30 5.00 12.00
MLB39 Steve Garvey/50 4.00 10.00
MLB40 Ted Williams/25 30.00 60.00
MLB41 Tom Seaver/50 5.00 12.00
MLB42 Tony Gwynn/50 6.00 15.00
MLB43 Whitey Ford/50 5.00 12.00
MLB44 Willie Mays/50 10.00 25.00
MLB45 Willie McCovey/50 5.00 12.00

2005 Prime Cuts MLB Icons Material Jersey Number
*NBR p/r 25: .5X TO 1.2X JSY p/r 50
*NBR p/r 25: .4X TO 1X JSY p/r 25
OVERALL AU-GU ODDS ONE PER PACK
PRINT RUNS B/WN 5-25 COPIES PER
NO PRICING ON QTY OF 10 OR LESS
MLB23 Babe Ruth/25 150.00 300.00
MLB36 Sandy Koufax/25 75.00 150.00

2005 Prime Cuts MLB Icons Material Jersey Number Prime
*PRIME p/r 20-25: .75X TO 2X JSY p/r 50
*PRIME p/r 20-25: .6X TO 1.5X JSY p/r 24-35
*PRIME p/r 15: 1X TO 2.5X JSY p/r 50
OVERALL AU-GU ODDS ONE PER PACK
PRINT RUNS B/WN 1-25 COPIES PER
NO PRICING ON QTY OF 10 OR LESS

2005 Prime Cuts MLB Icons Material Jersey Position
*POS p/r 50: .4X TO 1X JSY p/r 50
*POS p/r 50: .3X TO .8X JSY p/r 24-35
OVERALL AU-GU ODDS ONE PER PACK
PRINT RUNS B/WN 25-50 COPIES PER
MLB2 Babe Ruth/50 175.00 300.00
MLB4 Bob Feller Pants/50 4.00 10.00
MLB22 Jim Thorpe/50 100.00 175.00
MLB23 Babe Ruth/50 150.00 300.00
MLB28 Luis Aparicio/25 5.00 12.00
MLB29 Marty Marion/50 4.00 10.00
MLB34 Roberto Clemente/25 40.00 80.00

2005 Prime Cuts MLB Icons Material Combo
*COMBO p/r 25: .6X TO 1.5X JSY p/r 50
*COMBO p/r 25: .5X TO 1.2X JSY p/r 25
PRINT RUNS B/WN 1-25 COPIES PER
NO PRICING ON QTY OF 10 OR LESS
PRIME PRINT RUN B/WN 1-10 COPIES PER
NO PRIME PRICING DUE TO SCARCITY
OVERALL AU-GU ODDS ONE PER PACK

2005 Prime Cuts MLB Icons Material Trio MLB
PRINT RUNS B/WN 1-25 COPIES PER
NO PRICING ON QTY OF 10 OR LESS
PRIME PRINT RUN B/WN 1-10 COPIES PER
NO PRIME PRICING DUE TO SCARCITY
OVERALL AU-GU ODDS ONE PER PACK
B=Bat; BG=Btg Glv; H=Hat; J=Jsy; JK=Jkt
P=Pants; S=Shoe
MLB22 Jim Thorpe J-J-J/25 200.00 300.00
MLB34 Roberto Clemente B-B-H/25 75.00 150.00

2005 Prime Cuts MLB Icons Signature Century Gold
OVERALL AU-GU ODDS ONE PER PACK
PRINT RUNS B/WN 1-15 COPIES PER
NO PRICING ON QTY OF 10 OR LESS
MLB36 Sandy Koufax/15 150.00 400.00

2005 Prime Cuts MLB Icons Signature Century Silver
OVERALL AU-GU ODDS ONE PER BOX
PRINT RUNS B/WN 1-32 COPIES PER
NO PRICING ON QTY OF 10 OR LESS
MLB3 Billy Williams/25 10.00 25.00
MLB4 Bob Feller/25 10.00 25.00
MLB5 Bob Gibson/25 15.00 40.00
MLB6 Bobby Doerr/25 10.00 25.00
MLB7 Brooks Robinson/25 15.00 40.00
MLB10 Carlton Fisk/25 15.00 40.00
MLB12 Don Mattingly/20 30.00 60.00
MLB13 Don Sutton/25 10.00 25.00
MLB15 Ernie Banks/20 20.00 50.00
MLB16 Frank Robinson/25 10.00 25.00
MLB17 Gary Carter/25 10.00 25.00
MLB18 Gaylord Perry/25 10.00 25.00
MLB19 Hank Aaron/15 75.00 150.00
MLB20 Harmon Killebrew/25 30.00 60.00
MLB21 Jim Palmer/25 10.00 25.00
MLB24 Johnny Bench/25 20.00 50.00
MLB25 Juan Marichal/25 10.00 25.00
MLB26 Kirby Puckett/25 50.00 100.00
MLB27 Lou Brock/25 15.00 40.00
MLB28 Luis Aparicio/25 10.00 25.00
MLB29 Marty Marion/25 10.00 25.00
MLB30 Mike Schmidt/25 30.00 60.00
MLB31 Nolan Ryan/25 50.00 100.00
MLB32 Red Schoendienst/25 10.00 25.00
MLB35 Rod Carew/25 15.00 40.00
MLB36 Sandy Koufax/32 125.00 300.00
MLB37 Stan Musial/25 30.00 60.00
MLB38 Steve Carlton/25 10.00 25.00
MLB41 Tom Seaver/25 25.00 60.00
MLB42 Tony Gwynn/25 20.00 50.00
MLB43 Whitey Ford/25 15.00 40.00
MLB45 Willie McCovey/25 15.00 40.00

2005 Prime Cuts MLB Icons Signature Material Jersey Number
OVERALL AU-GU ODDS ONE PER BOX
PRINT RUNS B/WN 1-25 COPIES PER
NO PRICING ON QTY OF 10 OR LESS
MLB9 Cal Ripken/25 75.00 150.00

2005 Prime Cuts MLB Icons Signature Material Jersey Number Prime
*PRIME p/r 20: .6X TO 1.5X SILV p/r 20-32
*PRIME p/r 15: .75X TO 2X SILV p/r 20-32
OVERALL AU-GU ODDS ONE PER PACK
PRINT RUNS B/WN 1-25 COPIES PER
NO PRICING ON QTY OF 10 OR LESS
MLB9 Cal Ripken/25 75.00 150.00

2005 Prime Cuts MLB Icons Signature Material Combo
*COMBO p/r 25: .5X TO 1.2X SILV p/r 20-32
PRINT RUNS B/WN 1-25 COPIES PER
NO PRICING ON QTY OF 10 OR LESS
PRIME PRINT RUN B/WN 1-10 COPIES PER
NO PRIME PRICING DUE TO SCARCITY
OVERALL AU-GU ODDS ONE PER PACK
MLB11 Dale Murphy Bat-Jsy/25 20.00 50.00

2005 Prime Cuts Souvenir Cuts
OVERALL AU-GU ODDS ONE PER PACK
PRINT RUNS B/WN 1-50 COPIES PER
NO PRICING ON QTY OF 12 OR LESS
3 Al Lopez/50 20.00 50.00
4 Bill Terry/50 100.00 175.00
6 Buck Leonard/50 100.00 175.00
8 Cal Hubbard/26 75.00 150.00
9 Carl Hubbell/50 75.00 150.00
10 Charlie Gehringer/50 75.00 150.00
14 Earl Averill/47 60.00 120.00
16 Edd Roush/48 30.00 80.00
18 Sam Rice/27 60.00 150.00
19 Ernie Lombardi/50 40.00 80.00
20 Ford Frick/50 50.00 120.00
21 Gabby Hartnett/50 150.00 250.00
22 George Kelly/50 40.00 80.00
25 Heinie Manush/33 125.00 200.00
27 Joe McCarthy/44 125.00 200.00
28 Joe Medwick/50 125.00 200.00
32 Lefty Gomez/32 100.00 175.00
35 Luke Appling/35 30.00 80.00
43 Waite Hoyt/50 75.00 150.00
44 Walter Alston/22 125.00 200.00
46 Jocko Conlan/35 75.00 150.00
47 Lloyd Waner/50 75.00 150.00
48 Rube Marquard/50 75.00 150.00
49 Hank Greenberg/43 200.00 350.00
50 Travis Jackson/50 20.00 50.00
51 Joe Cronin/50 25.00 60.00
52 Bill Dickey/26 125.00 200.00
53 Red Ruffing/26 175.00 300.00
54 Jesse Haines/50 150.00 250.00
55 Chick Hafey/50 50.00 100.00
102 Hal Newhouser/24 75.00 150.00
104 Lou Boudreau/48 20.00 50.00
105 Pee Wee Reese/28 75.00 150.00
109 Willie Stargell/23 75.00 150.00
111 Buck Leonard/50 100.00 175.00
112 Carl Hubbell/50 75.00 150.00
113 Charlie Gehringer/40 40.00 80.00
115 Joe Medwick/32 40.00 100.00
117 Rube Marquard/37 40.00 80.00
120 Jesse Haines/27 60.00 120.00
121 Chick Hafey/25 125.00 200.00

2005 Prime Cuts Timeline
STATED PRINT RUN 100 SERIAL #'d SETS
*GOLD: .75X TO 2X BASIC
GOLD PRINT RUN 25 SERIAL #'d SETS
PLATINUM PRINT RUN 1 SERIAL #'d SET
NO PLATINUM PRICING DUE TO SCARCITY
*SILVER: .5X TO 1.2X BASIC
SILVER PRINT RUN 50 SERIAL #'d SETS
RANDOM INSERTS IN PACKS
T1 Dale Murphy 3.00 8.00
T2 Dennis Eckersley 2.00 5.00
T3 Fergie Jenkins 2.00 5.00
T4 Greg Maddux 4.00 10.00
T5 Orel Hershiser 1.25 3.00
T6 Stan Musial 5.00 12.00
T7 Don Mattingly 6.00 15.00
T8 Willie Mays NY Giants 6.00 15.00
T9 Ozzie Smith 4.00 10.00
T10 Roger Clemens Yanks 4.00 10.00
T11 Cal Ripken 10.00 25.00
T12 Duke Snider 2.00 5.00
T13 Hank Aaron 6.00 15.00
T14 Lou Brock 2.00 5.00
T15 Paul Molitor 3.00 8.00
T16 Ted Williams 6.00 15.00
T17 Dwight Gooden 1.25 3.00
T18 Frankie Frisch 2.00 5.00
T19 Pedro Martinez 2.00 5.00
T20 Robin Yount 3.00 8.00
T21 Babe Ruth 8.00 20.00
T22 Carl Yastrzemski 4.00 10.00
T23 Rod Carew 2.00 5.00
T24 Willie Mays SF Giants 6.00 15.00
T25 Eddie Murray 2.00 5.00
T26 Ivan Rodriguez 2.00 5.00
T27 Roger Clemens Sox 4.00 10.00
T28 Willie McCovey 2.00 5.00
T29 Bob Feller 2.00 5.00
T30 Catfish Hunter 2.00 5.00
T31 Gaylord Perry 2.00 5.00
T32 Wade Boggs 2.00 5.00
T33 Phil Rizzuto 2.00 5.00
T34 Roger Maris 3.00 8.00
T35 Bob Gibson 2.00 5.00
T36 Chipper Jones 3.00 8.00
T37 Ernie Banks 3.00 8.00
T38 George Brett 6.00 15.00
T39 Keith Hernandez 1.25 3.00
T40 Ryne Sandberg 6.00 15.00
T41 Reggie Jackson 2.00 5.00
T42 Sandy Koufax 6.00 15.00
T43 Warren Spahn 2.00 5.00
T44 Nolan Ryan Mets 10.00 25.00
T45 Yogi Berra 3.00 8.00
T46 Cal Ripken 10.00 25.00
T47 Willie Mays NY Mets 6.00 15.00
T48 Nolan Ryan Angels 10.00 25.00
T49 Stan Musial 5.00 12.00
T50 Roberto Clemente 8.00 20.00

2005 Prime Cuts Timeline Material Bat
*BAT p/r 50: .4X TO 1X JSY p/r 49-50
*BAT p/r 50: .3X TO .8X JSY p/r 24-35
*BAT p/r 22: .4X TO 1X JSY p/r 24-35
*BAT p/r 15: .6X TO 1.5X JSY p/r 49-50
OVERALL AU-GU ODDS ONE PER PACK
PRINT RUNS B/WN 3-50 COPIES PER
NO PRICING ON QTY OF 3
T8 Willie Mays NY Giants/50 10.00 25.00
T14 Lou Brock/50 5.00 12.00
T21 Babe Ruth/50 60.00 150.00
T50 Roberto Clemente/50 30.00 60.00

2005 Prime Cuts Timeline Material Jersey
OVERALL AU-GU ODDS ONE PER PACK
PRINT RUNS B/WN 5-50 COPIES PER
NO PRICING ON QTY OF 5
T1 Dale Murphy/50 5.00 12.00
T2 Dennis Eckersley/50 4.00 10.00
T3 Fergie Jenkins/50 4.00 10.00
T4 Greg Maddux/50 6.00 15.00
T5 Orel Hershiser/50 4.00 10.00
T6 Stan Musial/50 8.00 20.00
T7 Don Mattingly/49 6.00 15.00
T9 Ozzie Smith/17 12.50 30.00
T10 Roger Clemens Yanks/50 6.00 15.00
T11 Cal Ripken/50 10.00 25.00
T12 Duke Snider/24 6.00 15.00
T13 Hank Aaron/50 20.00 50.00
T15 Paul Molitor/50 4.00 10.00
T16 Ted Williams/50 20.00 50.00
T17 Dwight Gooden/50 4.00 10.00
T19 Pedro Martinez/50 5.00 12.00
T20 Robin Yount/50 6.00 15.00
T21 Babe Ruth/25 250.00 350.00
T22 Carl Yastrzemski/50 8.00 20.00
T23 Rod Carew/50 5.00 12.00
T24 Willie Mays SF Giants/50 12.50 30.00
T25 Eddie Murray/50 6.00 15.00
T26 Ivan Rodriguez/50 5.00 12.00
T27 Roger Clemens Sox/50 6.00 15.00
T28 Willie McCovey/50 5.00 12.00
T32 Wade Boggs/50 5.00 12.00
T33 Phil Rizzuto/50 5.00 12.00
T34 Roger Maris/50 15.00 40.00
T35 Bob Gibson/50 5.00 12.00
T36 Chipper Jones/50 6.00 15.00
T37 Ernie Banks/50 6.00 15.00
T38 George Brett/50 6.00 15.00
T40 Ryne Sandberg/50 8.00 20.00
T41 Reggie Jackson/35 6.00 15.00
T43 Warren Spahn/50 5.00 12.00
T44 Nolan Ryan Mets/50 10.00 25.00
T45 Yogi Berra/50 6.00 15.00
T46 Cal Ripken/50 10.00 25.00
T47 Willie Mays NY Mets/50 10.00 25.00
T48 Nolan Ryan Angels/50 10.00 25.00
T49 Stan Musial/25 10.00 25.00

2005 Prime Cuts Timeline Material Jersey Number Prime
*PRIME p/r 25: .75X TO 2X JSY p/r 49-50
*PRIME p/r 15: .6X TO 1.5X JSY p/r 17
PRINT RUNS B/WN 1-25 COPIES PER
NO PRICING ON QTY OF 10 OR LESS
NBR PRINT RUN B/WN 1-10 COPIES PER
NO NUMBER PRICING DUE TO SCARCITY
OVERALL AU-GU ODDS ONE PER PACK
T39 Keith Hernandez/25 8.00 20.00

2005 Prime Cuts Timeline Material Jersey Position
*POS p/r 23-25: .5X TO 1.2X JSY p/r 49-50
*POS p/r 23-25: .4X TO 1X JSY p/r 24-35
OVERALL AU-GU ODDS ONE PER PACK
PRINT RUNS B/WN 10-25 COPIES PER
NO PRICING ON QTY OF 12 OR LESS
T14 Lou Brock Jkt/25 6.00 15.00
T18 Frankie Frisch Jkt/23 8.00 20.00
T21 Babe Ruth/25 200.00 300.00
T30 Catfish Hunter/18 6.00 15.00
T39 Keith Hernandez/25 5.00 12.00

2005 Prime Cuts Timeline Material Combo
*COMBO p/r 25: .6X TO 1.5X JSY p/r 49-50
*COMBO p/r 25: .5X TO 1.2X JSY p/r 24-35
OVERALL AU-GU ODDS ONE PER PACK
PRINT RUNS B/WN 1-25 COPIES PER
NO PRICING ON QTY OF 10 OR LESS
T21 Babe Ruth Bat-Jsy/25 350.00 450.00

2005 Prime Cuts Timeline Material Combo Prime
*PRIME p/r 25: .75X TO 2X JSY p/r 49-50
OVERALL AU-GU ODDS ONE PER PACK
PRINT RUNS B/WN 1-25 COPIES PER
NO PRICING ON QTY OF 10 OR LESS
T14 Lou Brock Bat-Jsy/25 12.50 30.00
T39 Keith Hernandez Bat-Jsy/15 12.50 30.00

2005 Prime Cuts Timeline Material Combo CY HR
*CY HR p/r 25: .6X TO 1.5X JSY p/r 49-50
*CY HR p/r 25: .5X TO 1.2X JSY p/r 24-35
*CY HR p/r 25: .4X TO 1X JSY p/r 17
OVERALL AU-GU ODDS ONE PER PACK
PRINT RUNS B/WN 1-25 COPIES PER
NO PRICING ON QTY OF 10 OR LESS
T8 W.Mays NYG Bat-Jsy/25 15.00 40.00
T14 Lou Brock Bat-Jkt/25 8.00 20.00
T18 Frankie Frisch Jkt-Jkt/25 10.00 25.00
T21 Babe Ruth Bat-Pants/25 250.00 400.00
T42 Sandy Koufax Jsy-Jsy/25 40.00 80.00

2005 Prime Cuts Timeline Material Combo CY HR Prime
*PRIME p/r 25: .75X TO 2X JSY p/r 49-50
OVERALL AU-GU ODDS ONE PER PACK
PRINT RUNS B/WN 1-25 COPIES PER
NO PRICING ON QTY OF 10 OR LESS

2005 Prime Cuts Timeline Material Trio MVP
*MVP p/r 50: .6X TO 1.5X J p/r 49-50
*MVP p/r 50: .5X TO 1.2X J p/r 24-35
*MVP p/r 25: .75X TO 2X J p/r 49-50
PRINT RUNS B/WN 1-50 COPIES PER
NO PRICING ON QTY OF 10 OR LESS
PRIME PRINT RUN B/WN 1-10 COPIES PER
NO PRIME PRICING DUE TO SCARCITY
OVERALL AU-GU ODDS ONE PER PACK
T21 Babe Ruth B-J-P/50 400.00 550.00
T50 Roberto Clemente B-B-B/50 30.00 60.00

2005 Prime Cuts Timeline Material Custom Names
*NAME 3P p/r 50: .2X TO .5X NBR 4P p/r 25
*NAME 4P p/r 50: .5X TO 1.2X NBR 3P p/r 50
*NAME 4P p/r 50: .4X TO 1X NBR 4P p/r 50
*NAME 4P p/r 25: .6X TO 1.5X NBR 4P p/r 50
*NAME 4P p/r 15: .5X TO 1.2X NBR 4P p/r 25
PRINT RUNS B/WN 1-50 COPIES PER
NO PRICING ON QTY OF 1
PRIME PRINT RUN B/WN 1-5 COPIES PER
NO PRIME PRICING DUE TO SCARCITY
OVERALL AU-GU ODDS ONE PER PACK
T16 Ted Williams B-J-J-J/50 125.00 200.00
T21 Babe Ruth B-B-J-P/50 500.00 800.00
T34 Roger Maris B-B-J-P/50 50.00 100.00

2005 Prime Cuts Timeline Material Custom Nicknames
*NICK 3P p/r 50: .4X TO 1X NBR 3P p/r 50
*NICK 4P p/r 50: .4X TO 1X NBR 4P p/r 50
PRINT RUNS B/WN 5-50 COPIES PER
NO PRICING ON QTY OF 10 OR LESS
PRIME PRINT RUN B/WN 1-5 COPIES PER
NO PRIME PRICING DUE TO SCARCITY
OVERALL AU-GU ODDS ONE PER PACK
T6 S.Musial B-B-J-J-P-P/50 60.00 120.00
T21 Babe Ruth B-J-J-P/50 600.00 900.00
T24 W.Mays SF B-B-B-J-J-J/50 75.00 150.00
T37 E.Banks B-B-H-J-J/50 20.00 50.00
T47 W.Mays NY B-B-B-J-J-J/50 40.00 100.00

2005 Prime Cuts Timeline Material Custom Numbers
PRINT RUNS B/WN 1-50 COPIES PER
NO PRICING ON QTY OF 10 OR LESS
PRIME PRINT RUN B/WN 1-10 COPIES PER
NO PRIME PRICING DUE TO SCARCITY
OVERALL AU-GU ODDS ONE PER PACK
T1 D.Murphy B-B-J-J/50 10.00 25.00
T2 D.Eckersley J-P-P/50 6.00 15.00
T4 G.Maddux B-J-J/50 20.00 50.00
T5 O.Hershiser J-J-J/50 6.00 15.00
T6 Stan Musial B-B-J-P/50 30.00 60.00
T7 D.Mattingly B
BG-H-JK-J/25 40.00 80.00
T10 R.Clem Yanks B-B-J-J/50 20.00 50.00
T11 C.Ripken B-H-J-P/50 40.00 80.00
T12 Duke Snider J-J-P-P/50 15.00 40.00
T13 Hank Aaron B-B-J-J/50 40.00 80.00
T14 Lou Brock B-B-J-J/25 15.00 40.00
T15 P.Molitor B-J-P-S/50 8.00 20.00
T16 T.Williams B-JK-J-J/50 60.00 120.00
T17 D.Gooden B-FG-H-J/50 8.00 20.00
T18 F.Frisch JK-JK-JK-JK/50 20.00 50.00
T19 P.Martinez B-B-J-P/50 10.00 25.00
T21 Babe Ruth B-B-J-P/50 500.00 800.00
T22 C.Yaz B-H-J-P/50 30.00 60.00
T23 R.Carew B-J-J-S/25 15.00 40.00
T24 W.Mays SFG B-B-J-J/50 30.00 60.00
T25 E.Murray B-J-P-S/50 15.00 40.00
T26 I.Rod B-FG-J-S/50 10.00 25.00
T27 R.Clem Sox B-B-J-J/50 20.00 50.00
T28 W.McCovey J-J-P-P/50 10.00 25.00
T32 Wade Boggs B-H-J-J/50 10.00 25.00
T34 Roger Maris B-B-J-P/50 50.00 100.00
T36 C.Jones B-FG-J-J/50 20.00 50.00
T37 Ernie Banks B-B-H-J/50 20.00 50.00
T38 G.Brett B-H-J-J/50 30.00 60.00
T40 R.Sandberg B-FG-H-J/50 40.00 80.00
T43 W.Spahn J-J-P-P/50 20.00 50.00
T44 N.Ryan Mets B-B-J-J/25 40.00 80.00
T45 Yogi Berra B-J-P-P/50 30.00 60.00
T46 C.Ripken B-H-J-P/50 20.00 50.00
T47 W.Mays NYM B-B-J-J/50 30.00 60.00
T50 R.Clemente B-B-H-J/25 150.00 250.00

2005 Prime Cuts Timeline Signature Century Silver
OVERALL AU-GU ODDS ONE PER PACK
PRINT RUNS B/WN 1-32 COPIES PER
NO PRICING ON QTY OF 10 OR LESS
T2 Dennis Eckersley/25 10.00 25.00
T3 Fergie Jenkins/25 10.00 25.00
T6 Stan Musial/25 50.00 100.00
T9 Ozzie Smith/25 20.00 50.00
T12 Duke Snider/25 15.00 40.00
T13 Hank Aaron/15 100.00 250.00
T14 Lou Brock/25 15.00 40.00
T15 Paul Molitor/25 10.00 25.00
T23 Rod Carew/25 15.00 40.00
T28 Willie McCovey/25 15.00 40.00
T29 Bob Feller/25 10.00 25.00
T31 Gaylord Perry/25 10.00 25.00
T32 Wade Boggs/25 15.00 40.00
T33 Phil Rizzuto/25 15.00 40.00
T35 Bob Gibson/25 15.00 40.00
T36 Chipper Jones/25 20.00 50.00
T38 George Brett/25 40.00 80.00
T40 Ryne Sandberg/25 30.00 60.00
T42 Sandy Koufax/32 225.00 300.00
T44 Nolan Ryan Mets/25 50.00 100.00
T48 Nolan Ryan Angels/25 50.00 100.00
T49 Stan Musial/25 50.00 100.00

2005 Prime Cuts Timeline Signature Material Combo CY HR
*CY HR: .5X TO 1.2X SILVER
OVERALL AU-GU ODDS ONE PER PACK
PRINT RUNS B/WN 5-25 COPIES PER
NO PRICING ON QTY OF 10 OR LESS
T1 Dale Murphy Bat-Jsy/25 20.00 50.00
T7 Don Mattingly Jsy-Jsy/25 40.00 80.00
T11 Cal Ripken Bat-Jsy/25 75.00 150.00
T13 Hank Aaron Bat-Jsy/25 125.00 200.00
T17 D.Gooden Jsy-Jsy/25 12.50 30.00
T24 W.Mays SFG Bat-Jsy/25 100.00 175.00
T46 Cal Ripken Jsy-Pants/25 75.00 150.00
T47 W.Mays NYM Bat-Jsy/25 100.00 175.00

2005 Prime Cuts Timeline Signature Material Combo CY HR Prime
*PRIME p/r 25: .75X TO 2X SILVER p/r 25
OVERALL AU-GU ODDS ONE PER PACK
PRINT RUNS B/WN 1-25 COPIES PER
NO PRICING ON QTY OF 10 OR LESS
T24 W.Mays SFG Bat-Jsy/25 150.00 250.00
T47 W.Mays NYM Bat-Jsy/25 150.00 250.00

2005 Prime Cuts Timeline Signature Material Custom Names
PRINT RUNS B/WN 1-50 COPIES PER
NO PRICING ON QTY OF 5 OR LESS
PRIME PRINT RUN B/WN 1-5 COPIES PER
NO PRIME PRICING DUE TO SCARCITY
OVERALL AU-GU ODDS ONE PER PACK
T11 Cal Ripken B-H-J-P/50 125.00 200.00
T24 Willie Mays SFG B-B-J-J/50 125.00 200.00

2005 Prime Cuts Timeline Signature Material Custom Numbers
PRINT RUNS B/WN 1-50 COPIES PER
NO PRICING ON QTY OF 10 OR LESS
PRIME PRINT RUN B/WN 1-10 COPIES PER
NO PRIME PRICING DUE TO SCARCITY
OVERALL AU-GU ODDS ONE PER PACK
T24 Willie Mays SFG B-B-J-J/50 125.00 200.00
T46 Cal Ripken B-H-J-P/50 150.00 250.00
T47 Willie Mays NYM B-B-J-J/50 125.00 200.00

2008 Prime Cuts
COMMON CARD (1-100) .40 1.00
TWO BASE CARDS PER BOX
1-100 PRINT RUN 249 SER.#'d SETS
OVERALL AU/MEM ODDS 4 PER BOX
AUTO PRINT RUN 249 SER.#'d SETS
EXCHANGE DEADLINE 6/26/2010
1 Al Kaline 1.00 2.50
2 Alan Trammell .60 1.50
3 Andre Dawson .60 1.50
4 Barry Larkin .60 1.50
5 Billy Williams .60 1.50
6 Bo Jackson 1.00 2.50
7 Bob Feller .60 1.50
8 Bob Gibson .60 1.50
9 Bobby Doerr .60 1.50
10 Brooks Robinson .60 1.50
11 Bruce Sutter .60 1.50
12 Cal Ripken Jr. 3.00 8.00
13 Carl Erskine .40 1.00
14 Carl Yastrzemski 1.50 4.00
15 Carlton Fisk .60 1.50
16 Dale Murphy 1.00 2.50
17 Dave Winfield .60 1.50
18 Deion Sanders .60 1.50
19 Dennis Eckersley .60 1.50
20 Denny McLain .40 1.00
21 Dwight Gooden .40 1.00
22 Don Drysdale .60 1.50
23 Don Larsen .40 1.00
24 Don Mattingly 2.00 5.00
25 Don Sutton .60 1.50
26 Duke Snider .60 1.50
27 Eddie Mathews 1.00 2.50
28 Eddie Murray .60 1.50
29 Ernie Banks 1.00 2.50
30 Fergie Jenkins .60 1.50
31 Frank Howard .40 1.00
32 Frank Robinson .60 1.50
33 Fred Lynn .40 1.00
34 Gary Carter .60 1.50
35 Gaylord Perry .60 1.50
36 George Brett 2.00 5.00
37 George Kell .60 1.50
38 Gil Hodges .60 1.50
39 Hank Aaron 2.00 5.00
40 Harmon Killebrew 1.00 2.50
41 Jackie Robinson 1.00 2.50
42 Jim Palmer .60 1.50
43 Jim Rice .60 1.50
44 Jim Thorpe 1.00 2.50
45 Joe Cronin .40 1.00
46 Joe Jackson 1.25 3.00
47 Joe Medwick .40 1.00
48 Joe Morgan .60 1.50
49 Johnny Bench 1.00 2.50
50 Johnny Pesky .40 1.00
51 Juan Marichal .60 1.50
52 Arky Vaughan .40 1.00
53 Kirk Gibson .40 1.00
54 Larry Walker .60 1.50
55 Lou Boudreau .60 1.50
56 Lou Brock .60 1.50
57 Lou Gehrig 2.00 5.00
58 Luis Aparicio .60 1.50
59 Mark Fidrych .40 1.00
60 Marty Marion .40 1.00
61 Maury Wills .40 1.00
62 Mike Schmidt 1.50 4.00
63 Monte Irvin .60 1.50
64 Nellie Fox .60 1.50
65 Nolan Ryan 3.00 8.00
66 Orlando Cepeda .60 1.50
67 Ozzie Smith 1.25 3.00
68 Paul Molitor 1.00 2.50
69 Pete Rose 2.00 5.00
70 Phil Niekro .60 1.50
72 Randy Jones .40 1.00
73 Red Schoendienst .60 1.50
74 Reggie Jackson .60 1.50
75 Richie Ashburn .60 1.50
77 Roberto Clemente 2.50 6.00
78 Robin Roberts .60 1.50
79 Robin Yount 1.00 2.50
80 Rod Carew .60 1.50
81 Roger Maris 1.00 2.50
82 Ryne Sandberg 2.00 5.00
83 Satchel Paige 1.00 2.50
84 Sparky Anderson .60 1.50
85 Stan Musial 1.50 4.00
86 Steve Carlton .60 1.50
87 Steve Garvey .40 1.00
88 Ted Williams 2.00 5.00
89 Tim Raines .60 1.50
90 Tom Seaver .60 1.50
91 Tony Gwynn 1.00 2.50
92 Tony Perez .60 1.50
93 Wade Boggs .60 1.50
94 Warren Spahn .60 1.50
95 Whitey Ford .60 1.50
96 Will Clark .60 1.50
97 Willie Mays 2.00 5.00
98 Willie McCovey .60 1.50
99 Willie Stargell .60 1.50
100 Yogi Berra 1.00 2.50
101 Mike Stanton AU/249 75.00 200.00
102 L.Morrison AU/249 15.00 40.00
103 Daniel Cortes AU/249 3.00 8.00
104 Jhoulys Chacin AU/249 3.00 8.00
105 B.Crawford AU/249 6.00 15.00
106a Rick Porcello AU/249 8.00 20.00
106b R.Porcello Jsy AU/249 4.00 10.00
107 Neftali Feliz AU/249 6.00 15.00
108a Buster Posey AU/249 40.00 80.00
108b B.Posey Jsy AU/249 40.00 80.00
109a G.Beckham AU/249 6.00 15.00
109b G.Beckham Jsy AU/249 6.00 15.00
110a I.Davis AU/249 4.00 10.00
110b I.Davis Bat AU/249 4.00 10.00
111a A.Cashner AU/249 6.00 15.00
111b A.Cashner Jsy AU/249 8.00 20.00
112 Ryan Perry AU/249 4.00 10.00
113 Anthony Hewitt AU/249 4.00 10.00
114 Daniel Schlereth AU/249 4.00 10.00
115 Carlos Gutierrez AU/249 3.00 8.00
116 Shooter Hunt AU/249 6.00 15.00
117 Brad Holt AU/249 5.00 12.00
118 Zach Collier AU/249 5.00 12.00
119 Evan Frederickson AU/249 3.00 8.00
120 C.Friedrich AU/249 6.00 15.00
121 Cord Phelps AU/249 4.00 10.00
122 Danny Espinosa AU/249 12.50 30.00
124 Bryan Price AU/249 5.00 12.00
125 Juan Ramirez AU/249 3.00 8.00
126 Xavier Avery AU/249 5.00 12.00
127 Brad Hand AU/249 5.00 12.00
128 Jay Austin AU/249 3.00 8.00
129 Tyson Ross AU/249 3.00 8.00
130 Michael Taylor AU/249 12.50 30.00
131 Tyler Ladendorf AU/249 3.00 8.00
132 Rashun Dixon AU/249 12.50 30.00
133 Cody Adams AU/249 3.00 8.00
134 Michel Inoa AU/249 12.50 30.00
135 Wilin Rosario AU/249 6.00 15.00
136 Dennis Raben AU/249 5.00 12.00
137 Satterwhite Jsy AU/249 6.00 15.00
138 W.Flores AU/249 10.00 25.00
139 Z.Spruill AU/249 EXCH 5.00 12.00
140 Jason Knapp AU/249 5.00 12.00
141 C.Blackmon AU/249 15.00 40.00
142 Tyler Chatwood AU/187 5.00 12.00
143 Logan Schafer AU/249 4.00 10.00
144 Isaac Galloway AU/249 4.00 10.00
145 T.J. Steele AU/249 4.00 10.00
146 Chase D'Arnaud AU/249 3.00 8.00
147 Rolando Gomez AU/249 3.00 8.00
148 Anthony Gose AU/249 5.00 12.00
149 Adrian Nieto AU/249 3.00 8.00
150 Allan Dykstra AU/249 5.00 12.00

2008 Prime Cuts Auto Biography
OVERALL AU/MEM ODDS 4 PER BOX
PRINT RUNS B/WN 1-50 COPIES PER
NO PRICING ON SOME DUE TO SCARCITY
EXCHANGE DEADLINE 6/26/2010
9 Willie Mays/25 75.00 150.00
14 Cal Ripken Jr./25 30.00 80.00
15 Nolan Ryan/50 60.00 120.00
18 Mike Schmidt/50 20.00 50.00
19 Reggie Jackson/50 20.00 50.00
29 Willie Mays/25 75.00 150.00
35 Cal Ripken Jr./24 30.00 80.00

2008 Prime Cuts Bats
OVERALL AU/MEM ODDS 4 PER BOX
PRINT RUNS B/WN 1-99 COPIES PER
NO PRICING ON QTY 25 OR LESS
2 Alan Trammell/99 5.00 12.00
3 Andre Dawson/99 4.00 10.00
4 Barry Larkin/99 3.00 8.00
6 Bo Jackson/99 5.00 12.00
10 Brooks Robinson/99 4.00 10.00
12 Cal Ripken Jr./30 15.00 40.00
15 Carlton Fisk/27 4.00 10.00
16 Dale Murphy/99 6.00 15.00
18 Deion Sanders/49 6.00 15.00
21 Dwight Gooden/49 3.00 8.00
24 Don Mattingly/99 5.00 12.00
27 Eddie Mathews/99 6.00 15.00
28 Eddie Murray/99 4.00 10.00
34 Gary Carter/30 6.00 15.00
36 George Brett/30 10.00 25.00
40 Harmon Killebrew/31 6.00 15.00
48 Joe Morgan/99 3.00 8.00
49 Johnny Bench/35 4.00 10.00
52 Arky Vaughan/99 8.00 20.00
64 Nellie Fox/49 12.50 30.00
66 Orlando Cepeda/99 3.00 8.00
68 Paul Molitor/49 3.00 8.00
77 Roberto Clemente/50 20.00 50.00
79 Robin Yount/49 4.00 10.00
81 Roger Maris/99 12.50 30.00
86 Steve Carlton/29 4.00 10.00
91 Tony Gwynn/49 5.00 12.00
96 Will Clark/99 4.00 10.00
99 Willie Stargell/99 4.00 10.00

2008 Prime Cuts Biography
OVERALL INSERT ODDS 1 PER BOX
1 Lou Gehrig 4.00 10.00
2 Jackie Robinson 2.00 5.00
3 Ted Williams 4.00 10.00
4 Pete Rose 4.00 10.00
5 Jim Thorpe 2.00 5.00
6 Joe Jackson 2.50 6.00
7 Joe Medwick .75 2.00
8 Eddie Mathews 2.00 5.00
9 Willie Mays 4.00 10.00
10 Hank Aaron 4.00 10.00
11 Pete Rose 4.00 10.00
12 Gil Hodges 1.25 3.00
13 Roberto Clemente 5.00 12.00
14 Cal Ripken Jr. 6.00 15.00
15 Nolan Ryan 6.00 15.00
16 Satchel Paige 2.00 5.00
17 Roger Maris 2.00 5.00
18 Mike Schmidt 3.00 8.00
19 Reggie Jackson 1.25 3.00
20 George Brett 4.00 10.00
21 Pete Rose 4.00 10.00
22 Lou Gehrig 4.00 10.00
23 Jackie Robinson 2.00 5.00
24 Ted Williams 4.00 10.00
25 Jim Thorpe 2.00 5.00
26 Joe Jackson 2.50 6.00
27 Joe Medwick .75 2.00
28 Eddie Mathews 2.00 5.00
29 Willie Mays 4.00 10.00
30 Arky Vaughan .75 2.00
31 Gil Hodges 1.25 3.00
32 Roberto Clemente 5.00 12.00
33 Satchel Paige 2.00 5.00
34 Roger Maris 2.00 5.00
35 Cal Ripken Jr. 6.00 15.00

2008 Prime Cuts Biography Materials
OVERALL AU/MEM ODDS 4 PER BOX
PRINT RUNS B/WN 5-50 COPIES PER
NO PRICING ON MANY DUE TO SCARCITY
3 Ted Williams/25 50.00 100.00
6 Joe Jackson/25 125.00 250.00
7 Joe Medwick/50 20.00 50.00
8 Eddie Mathews/50 15.00 40.00
12 Gil Hodges/25 20.00 50.00
13 Roberto Clemente/50 30.00 60.00
14 Cal Ripken Jr./40 15.00 40.00
16 Satchel Paige/25 40.00 80.00
17 Roger Maris/50 20.00 50.00
20 George Brett/50 12.50 30.00
24 Ted Williams/25 50.00 100.00
26 Joe Jackson/25 125.00 250.00
27 Joe Medwick/50 10.00 25.00
28 Eddie Mathews/50 15.00 40.00
30 Arky Vaughan/50 20.00 50.00
31 Gil Hodges/25 20.00 50.00
32 Roberto Clemente/50 30.00 60.00

33 Satchel Paige/20 40.00 80.00
34 Roger Maris/50 20.00 50.00
35 Cal Ripken Jr./20 15.00 40.00

2008 Prime Cuts Colossal

OVERALL AU/MEM ODDS 4 PER BOX
PRINT RUNS B/WN 1-50 COPIES PER
NO PRICING ON MOST DUE TO SCARCITY
7 Nolan Ryan/30 20.00 50.00
21 Gil Hodges/50 10.00 25.00
23 Joe Medwick/49 12.50 30.00

2008 Prime Cuts Colossal Jersey Location

OVERALL AU/MEM ODDS 4 PER BOX
PRINT RUNS B/WN 1-99 COPIES PER
NO PRICING ON QTY 25 OR LESS
16 Tony Gwynn/99 8.00 20.00
21 Gil Hodges/50 15.00 40.00
23 Joe Medwick/49 12.00 30.00

2008 Prime Cuts Colossal Jersey Number

OVERALL AU/MEM ODDS 4 PER BOX
PRINT RUNS B/WN 1-50 COPIES PER
NO PRICING ON QTY 25 OR LESS
21 Gil Hodges/50 10.00 25.00
23 Joe Medwick/49 15.00 40.00

2008 Prime Cuts Colossal Jersey Position

OVERALL AU/MEM ODDS 4 PER BOX
PRINT RUNS B/WN 1-50 COPIES PER
NO PRICING ON QTY 25 OR LESS
16 Tony Gwynn/99 8.00 20.00
21 Gil Hodges/50 15.00 40.00
23 Joe Medwick/49 15.00 40.00

2008 Prime Cuts Colossal Jersey Position Prime

OVERALL AU/MEM ODDS 4 PER BOX
PRINT RUNS B/WN 1-25 COPIES PER
NO PRICING DUE TO SCARCITY

2008 Prime Cuts Dual Materials

OVERALL AU/MEM ODDS 4 PER BOX
PRINT RUNS B/WN 1-99 COPIES PER
NO PRICING ON QTY 25 OR LESS
2 Alan Trammell/60 10.00 25.00
16 Dale Murphy/50 12.50 30.00
21 Dwight Gooden/49 3.00 8.00
25 Don Sutton/99 3.00 8.00
34 Gary Carter/30 6.00 15.00
45 Joe Cronin/49 10.00 25.00
48 Joe Morgan/99 3.00 8.00
52 Arky Vaughan/99 20.00 50.00
68 Paul Molitor/49 4.00 10.00
73 Red Schoendienst/29 3.00 8.00
81 Roger Maris/49 20.00 50.00
86 Steve Carlton/29 4.00 10.00
91 Tony Gwynn/49 5.00 12.00
92 Tony Perez/49 5.00 12.00
93 Wade Boggs/26 10.00 25.00
99 Willie Stargell/99 4.00 10.00

2008 Prime Cuts Icons Silver

OVERALL INSERT ODDS 1 PER BOX
STATED PRINT RUN 10 SER.#'d SETS
NO PRICING DUE TO SCARCITY

2008 Prime Cuts Icons Bats

OVERALL AU/MEM ODDS 4 PER BOX
PRINT RUNS B/WN 1-99 COPIES PER
NO PRICING ON QTY 19 OR LESS
7 Brooks Robinson/60 5.00 12.00
17 Joe Morgan/50 4.00 10.00
21 Dale Murphy/99 6.00 15.00
22 Robin Yount/39 8.00 20.00
29 Barry Larkin/75 3.00 8.00
31 Roberto Clemente/50 20.00 50.00
32 Eddie Mathews/99 6.00 15.00
41 Roger Maris/99 12.50 30.00
45 Tony Gwynn/99 5.00 12.00
50 Will Clark/49 8.00 20.00

2008 Prime Cuts Icons Jersey Number

OVERALL AU/MEM ODDS 4 PER BOX
PRINT RUNS B/WN 1-99 COPIES PER
NO PRICING ON QTY 19 OR LESS
17 Joe Morgan/50 3.00 8.00
28 Dennis Eckersley/43 3.00 8.00
45 Tony Gwynn/99 4.00 10.00
49 Ozzie Smith/99 8.00 20.00

2008 Prime Cuts Icons Jersey Number Prime

OVERALL AU/MEM ODDS 4 PER BOX
PRINT RUNS B/WN 1-40 COPIES PER
NO PRICING ON QTY 25 OR LESS
23 Cal Ripken Jr./40 20.00 50.00

2008 Prime Cuts Icons Jersey Position

OVERALL AU/MEM ODDS 4 PER BOX
PRINT RUNS B/WN 1-99 COPIES PER
NO PRICING ON QTY 20 OR LESS
17 Joe Morgan/50 3.00 8.00
23 Cal Ripken Jr./35 15.00 40.00
45 Tony Gwynn/99 4.00 10.00
49 Ozzie Smith/90 8.00 20.00

2008 Prime Cuts Icons Materials Combos

OVERALL AU/MEM ODDS 4 PER BOX
PRINT RUNS B/WN 1-49 COPIES PER
NO PRICING ON QTY 20 OR LESS
17 Joe Morgan/49 6.00 15.00
21 Dale Murphy/49 10.00 25.00
30 Larry Walker/49 4.00 10.00
41 Roger Maris/49 20.00 50.00
45 Tony Gwynn/49 6.00 15.00

2008 Prime Cuts Icons Materials HOF

OVERALL AU/MEM ODDS 4 PER BOX
PRINT RUNS B/WN 1-99 COPIES PER
NO PRICING ON QTY 20 OR LESS
17 Joe Morgan/30 4.00 10.00
28 Dennis Eckersley/35 5.00 12.00
45 Tony Gwynn/99 5.00 12.00

2008 Prime Cuts Icons Materials Icon

OVERALL AU/MEM ODDS 4 PER BOX
PRINT RUNS B/WN 1-49 COPIES PER
NO PRICING ON QTY 20 OR LESS
28 Dennis Eckersley/35 3.00 8.00
29 Barry Larkin/30 10.00 25.00
45 Tony Gwynn/99 6.00 15.00

2008 Prime Cuts Icons Materials MVP

OVERALL AU/MEM ODDS 4 PER BOX
PRINT RUNS B/WN 1-50 COPIES PER
NO PRICING ON QTY 20 OR LESS
17 Joe Morgan/50 3.00 8.00

2008 Prime Cuts Icons Signature Materials MVP

OVERALL AU/MEM ODDS 4 PER BOX
PRINT RUNS B/WN 1-49 COPIES PER
NO PRICING ON MOST DUE TO SCARCITY
EXCHANGE DEADLINE 6/26/2010
17 Joe Morgan/49 15.00 40.00
28 Dennis Eckersley/30 8.00 20.00

2008 Prime Cuts Icons Signature Materials MVP Prime

OVERALL AU/MEM ODDS 4 PER BOX
PRINT RUNS B/WN 1-49 COPIES PER
NO PRICING ON MOST TO SCARCITY
EXCHANGE DEADLINE 6/26/2010
21 Dale Murphy/49 20.00 50.00

2008 Prime Cuts Jersey Number

OVERALL AU/MEM ODDS 4 PER BOX
PRINT RUNS B/WN 1-99 COPIES PER
NO PRICING ON QTY 25 OR LESS
2 Alan Trammell/75 6.00 15.00
3 Andre Dawson/50 4.00 10.00
5 Billy Williams/75 3.00 8.00
7 Bob Feller/49 6.00 15.00
9 Bobby Doerr/49 5.00 12.00
9 Bobby Doerr/49 5.00 12.00
10 Brooks Robinson/30 10.00 25.00
12 Cal Ripken Jr./30 12.00 30.00
16 Dale Murphy/75 10.00 25.00
17 Dave Winfield/31 4.00 10.00
18 Deion Sanders/75 5.00 12.00
21 Dwight Gooden/99 3.00 8.00
25 Don Sutton/99 3.00 8.00
28 Eddie Murray/33 6.00 15.00
35 Gaylord Perry/36 3.00 8.00
45 Joe Cronin/49 5.00 12.00
48 Joe Morgan/50 3.00 8.00
67 Ozzie Smith/75 6.00 15.00
68 Paul Molitor/49 4.00 10.00
70 Phil Niekro/49 3.00 8.00
86 Steve Carlton/49 3.00 8.00
91 Tony Gwynn/99 4.00 10.00
94 Warren Spahn/99 6.00 15.00
99 Willie Stargell/99 4.00 10.00

2008 Prime Cuts Jersey Position

OVERALL AU/MEM ODDS 4 PER BOX
PRINT RUNS B/WN 1-99 COPIES PER
NO PRICING ON QTY 25 OR LESS
2 Alan Trammell/75 6.00 15.00
3 Andre Dawson/99 3.00 8.00
5 Billy Williams/75 3.00 8.00
7 Bob Feller/49 6.00 15.00
9 Bobby Doerr/49 5.00 12.00
12 Cal Ripken Jr./30 20.00 50.00
16 Dale Murphy/49 10.00 25.00
18 Deion Sanders/99 5.00 12.00
21 Dwight Gooden/99 3.00 8.00
24 Don Mattingly/49 6.00 15.00
25 Don Sutton/99 3.00 8.00
45 Joe Cronin/49 5.00 12.00
48 Joe Morgan/50 3.00 8.00
67 Ozzie Smith/75 6.00 15.00
68 Paul Molitor/49 4.00 10.00
70 Phil Niekro/49 3.00 8.00
86 Steve Carlton/49 3.00 8.00
91 Tony Gwynn/99 4.00 10.00
92 Tony Perez/49 5.00 12.00
94 Warren Spahn/99 6.00 15.00
99 Willie Stargell/99 4.00 10.00

2008 Prime Cuts Leaf Limited Phenoms Autographs

OVERALL AU/MEM ODDS 4 PER BOX
EXCHANGE DEADLINE 6/26/2010
1 Rick Porcello 12.50 30.00
2 Buster Posey 25.00 60.00
3 Gordon Beckham 10.00 25.00
4 Ike Davis 10.00 25.00
5 Andrew Cashner 8.00 20.00
6 Jhoulys Chacin 8.00 20.00
7 Neftali Feliz 5.00 12.00
8 Ryan Perry 4.00 10.00
9 Anthony Hewitt 4.00 10.00
10 Daniel Schlereth 4.00 10.00
11 Michel Inoa 8.00 20.00
12 Logan Schafer 4.00 10.00
13 Rafael Rodriguez 10.00 25.00
14 Allan Dykstra 4.00 10.00
15 Neftali Soto 10.00 25.00
16 Wilson Ramos 8.00 20.00
17 Anthony Gose 4.00 10.00
18 Tyler Sample 4.00 10.00
19 Danny Espinosa 12.50 30.00
20 Rashun Dixon 6.00 15.00
21 Kyle Hudson 4.00 10.00
22 Tim Murphy 4.00 10.00
23 Jharmidy De Jesus 4.00 10.00
24 Will Smith 4.00 10.00
25 Derek Norris 8.00 20.00

2008 Prime Cuts Material Combos

OVERALL AU/MEM ODDS 4 PER BOX
PRINT RUNS B/WN 25-99 COPIES PER
NO PRICING ON QTY 25 OR LESS
5 Ted Williams 20.00 50.00
Lou Boudreau/99
9 Ted Williams 20.00 50.00
Tony Gwynn/99
10 Joe Medwick 10.00 25.00
Carl Yastrzemski/99

2008 Prime Cuts Material Triples

OVERALL AU/MEM ODDS 4 PER BOX
PRINT RUNS B/WN 5-50 COPIES PER
NO PRICING ON QTY 25 OR LESS
1 Rose/Rose/Rose/50 40.00 80.00

2008 Prime Cuts Material Quads

OVERALL AU/MEM ODDS 4 PER BOX
PRINT RUNS B/WN 5-99 COPIES PER
NO PRICING ON QTY 25 OR LESS
3 Bench/Schmidt/Mays/Molitor/99 20.00 50.00

2008 Prime Cuts Material Quads Prime

OVERALL AU/MEM ODDS 4 PER BOX
PRINT RUNS B/WN 1-5 COPIES PER
NO PRICING DUE TO SCARCITY

2008 Prime Cuts Playoff Contenders Autographs

OVERALL AU/MEM ODDS 4 PER BOX
EXCHANGE DEADLINE 6/26/2010
1 Rick Porcello 10.00 25.00
2 Buster Posey 40.00 80.00
3 Gordon Beckham 10.00 25.00
4 Ike Davis 10.00 25.00
5 Andrew Cashner 8.00 20.00
6 Jhoulys Chacin 6.00 15.00
7 Neftali Feliz 10.00 25.00
8 Ryan Perry 3.00 8.00
9 Anthony Hewitt 4.00 10.00
10 Daniel Schlereth 3.00 8.00
11 Michel Inoa 10.00 25.00
12 Logan Schafer 4.00 10.00
13 Rafael Rodriguez 10.00 25.00
14 Allan Dykstra 4.00 10.00
15 T.J. Steele 4.00 10.00
16 Aaron Shafer 3.00 8.00
17 Dennis Raben 4.00 10.00
18 Cody Satterwhite 8.00 20.00
19 James Darnell 4.00 10.00
20 Zeke Spruill EXCH 8.00 20.00
21 Jason Knapp 3.00 8.00
22 Charlie Blackmon 10.00 25.00
23 O.J. Mayo 30.00 60.00
24 Michael Beasley 15.00 40.00
25 Derrick Rose 150.00 300.00

2008 Prime Cuts Signature Century

OVERALL AU/MEM ODDS 4 PER BOX
PRINT RUNS B/WN 1-99 COPIES PER
NO PRICING ON QTY ON 25 OR LESS
EXCHANGE DEADLINE 6/26/2010
1 Al Kaline/28 20.00 50.00
10 Brooks Robinson/74 10.00 25.00
12 Cal Ripken Jr./29 30.00 80.00
25 Don Sutton/53 10.00 25.00
37 George Kell/99 10.00 25.00
51 Juan Marichal/43 10.00 25.00
60 Marty Marion/94 6.00 15.00
65 Nolan Ryan/32 40.00 80.00
85 Stan Musial/99 25.00 60.00
95 Whitey Ford/26 20.00 50.00

2008 Prime Cuts Souvenir Cuts

OVERALL AU/MEM ODDS 4 PER BOX
PRINT RUNS B/WN 1-250 COPIES PER
NO PRICING ON MOST DUE TO SCARCITY
EXCHANGE DEADLINE 6/26/2010
98 Joe DiMaggio/250 150.00 400.00

2008 Prime Cuts Stadium Souvenir Cuts

OVERALL AU/MEM ODDS 4 PER BOX
PRINT RUNS B/WN 1-250 COPIES PER
NO PRICING ON MOST DUE TO SCARCITY
EXCHANGE DEADLINE 6/26/2010
2 Joe DiMaggio/250 200.00 400.00

2008 Prime Cuts Timeline

OVERALL INSERT ODDS 1 PER BOX
STATED PRINT RUN 50 SER.#'d SETS
1 Stan Musial 5.00 12.00
2 Yogi Berra 3.00 8.00
3 Willie Mays 6.00 15.00
4 Hank Aaron 6.00 15.00
5 Ernie Banks 3.00 8.00
6 Frank Robinson 2.00 5.00
7 Brooks Robinson 2.00 5.00
8 Frank Robinson 2.00 5.00
9 Orlando Cepeda 2.00 5.00
10 Carl Yastrzemski 5.00 12.00
11 Bob Gibson 2.00 5.00
12 Willie McCovey 2.00 5.00
13 Harmon Killebrew 3.00 8.00
14 Johnny Bench 3.00 8.00
15 Pete Rose 6.00 15.00
16 Reggie Jackson 2.00 5.00
17 Joe Morgan 2.00 5.00
18 Rod Carew 2.00 5.00
19 Mike Schmidt 5.00 12.00
20 George Brett 6.00 15.00
21 Robin Yount 3.00 8.00
22 Cal Ripken Jr. 10.00 25.00
23 Ryne Sandberg 6.00 15.00
24 Don Mattingly 6.00 15.00
25 Roberto Clemente 8.00 20.00
26 Eddie Mathews 3.00 8.00
27 Gil Hodges 2.00 5.00
28 Jackie Robinson 3.00 8.00
29 Jim Thorpe 3.00 8.00
30 Joe Jackson 4.00 10.00
31 Joe Medwick 1.25 3.00
32 Lou Gehrig 6.00 15.00
33 Nellie Fox 2.00 5.00
34 Nolan Ryan 10.00 25.00
35 Roger Maris 3.00 8.00
36 Satchel Paige 3.00 8.00
37 Ted Williams 6.00 15.00
38 Tom Seaver 2.00 5.00
39 Tony Gwynn 3.00 8.00
40 Whitey Ford 2.00 5.00
41 Reggie Jackson 2.00 5.00
42 Casey Stengel 2.00 5.00
43 Early Wynn 2.00 5.00
44 Billy Martin 2.00 5.00
45 Don Drysdale 2.00 5.00
46 Lefty Grove 2.00 5.00
47 Enos Slaughter 2.00 5.00
48 Catfish Hunter 2.00 5.00
49 Carlton Fisk 2.00 5.00
50 Eddie Murray 2.00 5.00

2008 Prime Cuts Timeline Bats

OVERALL AU/MEM ODDS 4 PER BOX
PRINT RUNS B/WN 3-99 COPIES PER
NO PRICING ON QTY 25 OR LESS
7 Brooks Robinson/60 5.00 12.00
9 Orlando Cepeda/29 5.00 12.00
10 Carl Yastrzemski/67 5.00 12.00
17 Joe Morgan/50 4.00 10.00
24 Don Mattingly/60 5.00 12.00
25 Roberto Clemente/50 20.00 50.00
26 Eddie Mathews/99 6.00 15.00
35 Roger Maris/99 12.50 30.00
39 Tony Gwynn/49 5.00 12.00
50 Eddie Murray/99 4.00 10.00

2008 Prime Cuts Timeline Jersey Location

OVERALL AU/MEM ODDS 4 PER BOX
PRINT RUNS B/WN 1-99 COPIES PER
NO PRICING ON QTY 25 OR LESS
17 Joe Morgan/50 4.00 10.00
39 Tony Gwynn/99 5.00 12.00
49 Carlton Fisk/35 4.00 10.00

2008 Prime Cuts Timeline Jersey Number

OVERALL AU/MEM ODDS 4 PER BOX
PRINT RUNS B/WN 1-99 COPIES PER
NO PRICING ON QTY 25 OR LESS
17 Joe Morgan/50 4.00 10.00
22 Cal Ripken Jr./35 12.50 30.00
39 Tony Gwynn/99 5.00 12.00
49 Carlton Fisk/27 4.00 10.00

2008 Prime Cuts Timeline Jersey Position

OVERALL AU/MEM ODDS 4 PER BOX
PRINT RUNS B/WN 1-99 COPIES PER
NO PRICING ON QTY 25 OR LESS
17 Joe Morgan/99 4.00 10.00
22 Cal Ripken Jr./35 20.00 50.00
39 Tony Gwynn/99 5.00 12.00
49 Carlton Fisk/49 4.00 10.00

2008 Prime Cuts Timeline Materials Combos

OVERALL AU/MEM ODDS 4 PER BOX
PRINT RUNS B/WN 1-99 COPIES PER
NO PRICING ON QTY 25 OR LESS
17 Joe Morgan/50 4.00 10.00
39 Tony Gwynn/99 5.00 12.00
42 Casey Stengel/30 10.00 25.00

2008 Prime Cuts Timeline Materials Trios

OVERALL AU/MEM ODDS 4 PER BOX
PRINT RUNS B/WN 1-99 COPIES PER
NO PRICING ON QTY 25 OR LESS
17 Joe Morgan/40 4.00 10.00
39 Tony Gwynn/99 5.00 12.00
42 Casey Stengel/30 20.00 50.00

2008 Prime Cuts Timeline Materials Trios HOF

OVERALL AU/MEM ODDS 4 PER BOX
PRINT RUNS B/WN 1-99 COPIES PER
NO PRICING ON QTY 25 OR LESS
39 Tony Gwynn/99 5.00 12.00

2008 Prime Cuts Timeline Materials Trios Stats

OVERALL AU/MEM ODDS 4 PER BOX
PRINT RUNS B/WN 1-99 COPIES PER
NO PRICING ON QTY 25 OR LESS
39 Tony Gwynn/99 5.00 12.00

2008 Prime Cuts Timeline Materials Quads

OVERALL AU/MEM ODDS 4 PER BOX
PRINT RUNS B/WN 1-99 COPIES PER
NO PRICING ON QTY 25 OR LESS
39 Tony Gwynn/99 5.00 12.00

2008 Prime Cuts Timeline Materials Custom Nicknames

OVERALL AU/MEM ODDS 4 PER BOX
PRINT RUNS B/WN 1-99 COPIES PER
NO PRICING ON QTY 25 OR LESS
9 Orlando Cepeda/99 5.00 12.00
27 Gil Hodges/50 10.00 25.00
30 Joe Jackson/50 125.00 250.00
33 Nellie Fox/50 30.00 60.00
39 Tony Gwynn/99 5.00 12.00

2008 Prime Cuts Timeline Materials CY HR

OVERALL AU/MEM ODDS 4 PER BOX
PRINT RUNS B/WN 1-99 COPIES PER
NO PRICING ON QTY 25 OR LESS
17 Joe Morgan/50 4.00 10.00
30 Joe Jackson/50 100.00 200.00
39 Tony Gwynn/99 5.00 12.00

2008 Prime Cuts Timeline Signature Materials Quads Custom Numbers

OVERALL AU/MEM ODDS 4 PER BOX
PRINT RUNS B/W 1-49 COPIES PER
NO PRICING ON MOST DUE TO SCARCITY
EXCHANGE DEADLINE 6/26/2010
9 Orlando Cepeda/49 20.00 50.00

2008 Prime Cuts Timeline Signature Materials Quads Custom Numbers Prime

OVERALL AU/MEM ODDS 4 PER BOX
PRINT RUNS B/W 1-5 COPIES PER
NO PRICING DUE TO SCARCITY
EXCHANGE DEADLINE 6/26/2010

2011 Prime Cuts

COMMON CARD .60 1.50
STATED PRINT RUN 99 SER.#'d SETS
1 Adrian Gonzalez 1.25 3.00
2 Albert Pujols 2.00 5.00
3 Alex Rodriguez 2.00 5.00
4 Buster Posey 2.00 5.00
5 CC Sabathia 1.00 2.50
6 Carl Crawford 1.00 2.50
7 Chipper Jones 1.50 4.00
8 Clayton Kershaw 2.50 6.00
9 Cliff Lee 1.00 2.50
10 David Freese .60 1.50
11 David Ortiz 1.50 4.00
12 David Wright 1.25 3.00
13 Derek Jeter 4.00 10.00
14 Dustin Pedroia 1.50 4.00
15 Felix Hernandez 1.00 2.50
16 Hanley Ramirez 1.00 2.50
17 Hunter Pence 1.00 2.50
18 Ian Kinsler 1.00 2.50
19 Ichiro Suzuki 2.00 5.00
20 Jacoby Ellsbury 1.25 3.00
21 Joey Votto 1.50 4.00
22 Jose Bautista 1.00 2.50
23 Jose Reyes 1.00 2.50
24 Josh Hamilton 1.00 2.50
25 Justin Upton 1.00 2.50
26 Justin Verlander 1.50 4.00
27 Logan Morrison .60 1.50
28 Mariano Rivera 2.00 5.00
29 Mark Teixeira 1.00 2.50
30 Matt Kemp 1.25 3.00
31 Melky Cabrera .60 1.50
32 Michael Bourn .60 1.50
33 Michael Young .60 1.50
34 Miguel Cabrera 1.50 4.00
35 Mike Napoli .60 1.50
36 Giancarlo Stanton 1.50 4.00
37 Mike Trout RC 60.00 120.00
38 Nelson Cruz 1.50 4.00
39 Paul Konerko 1.00 2.50
40 Prince Fielder 1.00 2.50
41 Robinson Cano 1.00 2.50
42 Roy Halladay 1.00 2.50
43 Ryan Braun 1.00 2.50
44 Ryan Howard 1.25 3.00
45 Starlin Castro 1.00 2.50
46 Stephen Strasburg 1.50 4.00
47 Tim Lincecum 1.00 2.50
48 Todd Helton 1.00 2.50
49 Troy Tulowitzki 1.50 4.00
50 Yovani Gallardo .60 1.50

2011 Prime Cuts Auto Biography Materials

OVERALL AUTO ODDS 2 PER BOX
PRINT RUNS B/WN 10-49 COPIES PER
NO PRICING ON QTY 25 OR LESS
EXCHANGE DEADLINE 10/04/2013
5 Ralph Kiner/49 15.00 40.00
6 Red Schoendienst/49 15.00 40.00
9 Rod Carew/40 12.50 30.00
21 Tom Seaver/49 25.00 60.00

2011 Prime Cuts Biography Materials

OVERALL MEM ODDS 2 PER BOX
PRINT RUN B/WN 1-99 COPIES PER
NO PRICING ON QTY 25 OR LESS
1 Satchel Paige/49 20.00 50.00
6 Red Schoendienst/99 4.00 10.00
7 Reggie Jackson/99 5.00 12.00
9 Rod Carew/49 10.00 25.00
10 Ryne Sandberg/99 6.00 15.00
12 Curt Flood/99 8.00 20.00
13 Charlie Gehringer/99 10.00 25.00
14 Miller Huggins/99 15.00 40.00
15 Jim Bottomley/99 10.00 25.00
16 Deion Sanders/49 6.00 15.00
17 Bo Jackson/49 10.00 25.00
18 Lloyd Waner/99 10.00 25.00
19 Paul Waner/99 12.00 30.00
20 Arky Vaughan/99 10.00 25.00
21 Tom Seaver/99 10.00 25.00
22 Tony Gwynn/99 8.00 20.00
23 Wade Boggs/99 5.00 12.00
24 Josh Hamilton/99 4.00 10.00
25 Ken Griffey Jr./99 8.00 20.00

2011 Prime Cuts Colossal Materials

OVERALL MEM ODDS 2 PER BOX
PRINT RUNS B/WN 25-49 COPIES PER
NO PRICING ON QTY 25 OR LESS
1 Ken Griffey Jr./49 12.50 30.00
2 Josh Hamilton/49 5.00 12.00
3 Miguel Cabrera/49 6.00 15.00
4 Matt Kemp/49 8.00 20.00
5 CC Sabathia/49 4.00 10.00
7 Clayton Kershaw/49 5.00 12.00
10 Andre Dawson/49 4.00 10.00
11 Cal Ripken Jr./49 15.00 40.00
12 Dale Murphy/49 8.00 20.00
13 David Ortiz/49 4.00 10.00
14 Derek Jeter/49 12.50 30.00
15 Frank Robinson/49 4.00 10.00
17 Ichiro Suzuki/49 12.50 30.00
18 Nolan Ryan/49 12.50 30.00
19 Orlando Cepeda/49 10.00 25.00
22 Phil Niekro/49 10.00 25.00
23 Red Schoendienst/49 10.00 25.00
24 Tony Gwynn/49 12.50 30.00
25 Yogi Berra/49 10.00 25.00

2011 Prime Cuts Draft Pick Signatures

OVERALL AUTO ODDS 2 PER BOX
PRINT RUNS B/WN 248-249 COPIES PER
EXCHANGED DEADLINE 10/04/2013
AB Archie Bradley 8.00 20.00
AR Anthony Rendon 15.00 40.00
BG Brian Goodwin 4.00 10.00
BN Brandon Nimmo 6.00 15.00
BST Bubba Starling 4.00 10.00
BSW Blake Swihart 6.00 15.00
CS Cory Spangenberg 5.00 12.00
DBU Dylan Bundy 10.00 25.00
DH Danny Hultzen 6.00 15.00
FLI Francisco Lindor 30.00 80.00
GC Gerrit Cole 40.00 100.00
GS George Springer 8.00 20.00
HO Henry Owens 4.00 10.00
JAB Jackie Bradley Jr. 10.00 25.00
JB Javier Baez 10.00 25.00
JBE Josh Bell 12.00 30.00
KWO Kolten Wong/248 4.00 10.00
MM Mikie Mahtook 5.00 12.00
MP Matt Purke 4.00 10.00
SGR Sonny Gray 10.00 25.00
TB Trevor Bauer 20.00 50.00
TC Tyler Collins 4.00 10.00
TJ Taylor Jungmann 4.00 10.00
TJ Zach Cone 4.00 10.00
ZC Jed Bradley 4.00 10.00

2011 Prime Cuts Emblems of the Hall Materials

OVERALL MEM ODDS 2 PER BOX
PRINT RUNS B/WN 1-99 COPIES PER
NO PRICING ON QTY 25 OR LESS
EXCHANGE DEADLINE 10/04/2013
3 Roberto Alomar/99 4.00 10.00
9 Tony Gwynn/99 8.00 20.00
10 Cal Ripken Jr./99 8.00 20.00
12 Wade Boggs/99 5.00 12.00
13 Ryne Sandberg/99 8.00 20.00
14 Harmon Killebrew/49 8.00 20.00
15 Paul Molitor/99 4.00 10.00
17 Eddie Murray/99 6.00 15.00
18 Ozzie Smith/49 12.50 30.00
19 Dave Winfield/49 4.00 10.00
20 Sparky Anderson/99 6.00 15.00
21 Carlton Fisk/40 4.00 10.00
23 George Brett/99 8.00 20.00
24 Orlando Cepeda/99 4.00 10.00
25 Nolan Ryan/99 10.00 25.00

2011 Prime Cuts Emblems of the Hall Materials Signatures

OVERALL AUTO ODDS 2 PER BOX
PRINT RUNS B/WN 3-49 COPIES PER
NO PRICING ON QTY 25 OR LESS
EXCHANGE DEADLINE 10/04/2013
3 Roberto Alomar/49 10.00 25.00

2011 Prime Cuts Emblems of the Hall Signatures

OVERALL AUTO ODDS 2 PER PACK
PRINT RUNS B/WN 5-49 COPIES PER
NO PRICING ON QTY 25 OR LESS
EXCHANGE DEADLINE 10/04/2013
6 George Kell/49 10.00 25.00
12 Wade Boggs/49 12.50 30.00

2011 Prime Cuts Hats Off

OVERALL MEM ODDS 2 PER BOX
PRINT RUNS B/WN 1-49 COPIES PER
NO PRICING ON QTY 25 OR LESS
EXCHANGE DEADLINE 10/04/2013
8 Frank Robinson/49 5.00 12.00
11 Hanley Ramirez/49 4.00 10.00
19 Rickey Henderson/49 8.00 20.00
21 Rod Carew/49 5.00 12.00

2011 Prime Cuts Icons Bats

OVERALL MEM ODDS 2 PER BOX
PRINT RUNS B/WN 1-99 COPIES PER
NO PRICING ON QTY 25 OR LESS
3 Thurman Munson/49 6.00 15.00
8 Eddie Mathews/99 4.00 10.00
9 Dave Winfield/99 4.00 10.00
13 Willie Stargell/99 4.00 10.00
16 Wade Boggs/99 4.00 10.00
18 Derek Jeter/99 8.00 20.00
26 Josh Hamilton/99 6.00 15.00
29 Reggie Jackson/99 4.00 10.00
30 Alex Rodriguez/99 5.00 12.00

2011 Prime Cuts Icons Jersey Number

OVERALL MEM ODDS 2 PER BOX
PRINT RUNS B/WN 1-42 COPIES PER
NO PRICING ON QTY 25 OR LESS
1 Jackie Robinson/42 20.00 50.00
8 Eddie Mathews/41 6.00 15.00
9 Dave Winfield/31 4.00 10.00
11 Hoyt Wilhelm/31 5.00 12.00
19 Catfish Hunter/27 5.00 12.00
20 Juan Marichal/27 4.00 10.00
26 Josh Hamilton/32 5.00 12.00
28 Phil Niekro/35 4.00 10.00

2011 Prime Cuts Icons Materials

OVERALL MEM ODDS 2 PER BOX
PRINT RUNS B/WN 1-99 COPIES PER
NO PRICING ON QTY 25 OR LESS
3 Thurman Munson/49 10.00 25.00
5 Cal Ripken Jr./99 10.00 25.00
6 Duke Snider/99 5.00 12.00
8 Eddie Mathews/49 4.00 10.00
9 Dave Winfield/99 4.00 10.00
14 Yogi Berra/99 5.00 12.00
16 Wade Boggs/99 4.00 10.00
17 Johnny Mize/99 5.00 12.00
18 Derek Jeter/99 8.00 20.00
24 Albert Pujols/99 6.00 15.00
25 Todd Helton/99 4.00 10.00
26 Josh Hamilton/99 4.00 10.00
27 Chipper Jones/99 6.00 15.00
28 Phil Niekro/99 4.00 10.00

2011 Prime Cuts Icons Signatures

OVERALL AUTO ODDS 2 PER PACK
PRINT RUNS B/WN 5-49 COPIES PER
NO PRICING ON QTY 25 OR LESS
EXCHANGE DEADLINE 10/04/2013
9 Dave Winfield/49 15.00 40.00
15 Whitey Ford/49 20.00 50.00
16 Wade Boggs/49 10.00 40.00

2011 Prime Cuts Materials

OVERALL MEM ODDS 2 PER BOX
PRINT RUNS B/WN 49-199 COPIES PER
1 Adrian Gonzalez/199 3.00 8.00
2 Albert Pujols/199 5.00 12.00
3 Alex Rodriguez/199 5.00 12.00
4 Buster Posey/199 5.00 12.00
5 CC Sabathia/199 3.00 8.00
6 Carl Crawford/199 3.00 8.00
7 Chipper Jones/199 5.00 12.00
8 Clayton Kershaw/99 4.00 10.00
9 Cliff Lee/199 3.00 8.00
10 David Freese/199 5.00 12.00
11 David Ortiz/199 4.00 10.00
12 David Wright/199 3.00 8.00
13 Derek Jeter/199 6.00 15.00
14 Dustin Pedroia/199 3.00 8.00
15 Felix Hernandez/199 3.00 8.00
16 Hanley Ramirez/199 3.00 8.00
17 Hunter Pence/199 3.00 8.00
19 Ichiro Suzuki/199 6.00 15.00
20 Jacoby Ellsbury/199 3.00 8.00
21 Joey Votto/199 4.00 10.00
23 Jose Reyes/199 3.00 8.00
24 Josh Hamilton/199 6.00 15.00
25 Justin Upton/199 3.00 8.00
26 Justin Verlander/199 4.00 10.00
27 Logan Morrison/49 3.00 8.00
29 Mark Teixeira/99 3.00 8.00
30 Matt Kemp/199 4.00 10.00
31 Melky Cabrera/199 3.00 8.00
32 Michael Bourn/199 3.00 8.00
33 Michael Young/99 3.00 8.00
34 Miguel Cabrera/199 6.00 15.00
38 Nelson Cruz/199 3.00 8.00
39 Paul Konerko/199 3.00 8.00
40 Prince Fielder/199 3.00 8.00
41 Robinson Cano/199 4.00 10.00
42 Roy Halladay/199 3.00 8.00
43 Ryan Braun/199 4.00 10.00
44 Ryan Howard/199 3.00 8.00
45 Starlin Castro/199 4.00 10.00
48 Todd Helton/199 4.00 10.00
49 Troy Tulowitzki/199 3.00 8.00
50 Yovani Gallardo/199 3.00 8.00

2011 Prime Cuts Materials Century Silver

*SILVER p/r 49: .6X TO 1.5X BASIC p/r 199
*SILVER p/r 49: .6X TO 1.5X BASIC p/r 99
OVERALL MEM ODDS 2 PER BOX
PRINT RUNS B/WN 10-49 COPIES PER
NO PRICING ON QTY 25 OR LESS

2011 Prime Cuts Prospect Signatures

OVERALL AUTO ODDS 2 PER BOX
STATED PRINT RUN 299 SER.#'d SETS
EXCHANGE DEADLINE 10/04/2013
AC Adam Conley 4.00 10.00
AH Austin Hedges 3.00 8.00
AM Anthony Meo 4.00 10.00
AS Andrew Susac 4.00 10.00
BS Blake Snell 5.00 12.00
CC Chad Comer 3.00 8.00
CG Cameron Gallagher 4.00 10.00
CM Cory Mazzoni 3.00 8.00
CR Chris Reed 4.00 10.00
CT Carl Thomore 3.00 8.00
CT Charlie Tilson 4.00 10.00
DB Dante Bichette Jr. 6.00 15.00
DN Daniel Norris 3.00 8.00
DS Dwight Smith Jr. 4.00 10.00
DV Dan Vogelbach 6.00 15.00
EJ Erik Johnson 3.00 8.00
GG Grayson Garvin 3.00 8.00
GR Gabriel Rosa 3.00 8.00
HB Hudson Boyd 3.00 8.00
JA Jacob Anderson 5.00 12.00
JA Jeff Ames 3.00 8.00
JE Jason Esposito 3.00 8.00
JH Jake Hager 3.00 8.00
JM James McCann 8.00 20.00
JP Jace Peterson 5.00 12.00
JP Joe Panik 10.00 25.00
JR Joe Ross 3.00 8.00
KC Kyle Crick 3.00 8.00
KM Kevin Matthews 3.00 8.00
KW Keenyn Walker 3.00 8.00
LM Levi Michael 3.00 8.00
MB Matt Barnes 6.00 15.00
MF Michael Fulmer 12.00 30.00
MK Michael Kelly 3.00 8.00
RQ Roman Quinn 3.00 8.00
RS Robert Stephenson 6.00 15.00
SG Sean Gilmartin 4.00 10.00
TA Tyler Anderson 3.00 8.00
TG Taylor Guerrieri 3.00 8.00
TG Tyler Goeddel 3.00 8.00
TH Travis Harrison 3.00 8.00
TS Trevor Story 5.00 12.00
WJ Williams Jerez 3.00 8.00
WL Will Lamb 3.00 8.00
AHO Adrian Houser 4.00 10.00
BMI Brad Miller 4.00 10.00
BMI Brandon Martin 3.00 8.00
CCR C.J. Cron 4.00 10.00
GGO Granden Goetzman 3.00 8.00
JHA James Harris 3.00 8.00

2011 Prime Cuts Prospect Signatures Gold

*GOLD: .6X TO 1.5X BASIC
OVERALL AUTO ODDS 2 PER BOX
STATED PRINT RUN 49 SER.#'d SETS
EXCHANGE DEADLINE 10/04/2013

2011 Prime Cuts Prospect Signatures Silver

*SILVER: .4X TO 1X BASIC
OVERALL AUTO ODDS 2 PER BOX
STATED PRINT RUN 99 SER.#'d SETS
EXCHANGE DEADLINE 10/04/2013

2011 Prime Cuts Souvenir Cuts

OVERALL AUTO ODDS 2 PER BOX
PRINT RUNS B/WN 1-49 COPIES PER
NO PRICING ON QTY 25 OR LESS
EXCHANGE DEADLINE 10/04/2013
2 Edd Roush/49 12.50 30.00
3 Joe Sewell/49 12.50 30.00
5 Willie Kamm/49 12.50 30.00
6 Billy Herman/39 10.00 25.00
7 Bob Feller/35 12.50 30.00
8 Enos Slaughter/39 10.00 25.00
33 Joe Sewell/45 12.50 30.00
34 Edd Roush/39 12.50 30.00

2011 Prime Cuts Timeline Material Combos

OVERALL MEM ODDS 2 PER BOX
PRINT RUNS B/WN 5-99 COPIES PER
NO PRICING ON QTY 25 OR LESS
1 L.Waner/P.Waner/49 10.00 25.00
7 Chipper Jones 4.00 10.00
Michael Bourn/99
8 Todd Helton 5.00 12.00
Troy Tulowitzki/99
9 J.Verlander/M.Cabrera/99 12.50 30.00
10 C.Kershaw/M.Kemp/99 5.00 12.00
13 F.Hernandez/I.Suzuki/99 5.00 12.00
15 F.Hernandez/R.Halladay/99 8.00 20.00
16 C.Kershaw/J.Verlander/99 8.00 20.00
18 A.Pujols/J.Mauer/99 12.50 30.00
19 Joey Votto 6.00 15.00
Josh Hamilton/99

2011 Prime Cuts Timeline Material Quads

OVERALL MEM ODDS 2 PER BOX
PRINT RUNS B/WN 25-99 COPIES PER

NO PRICING ON QTY 25 OR LESS
2 Gonzalez/Ortiz/Pedroia/Ellsbury/99 12.50 30.00
3 ARod/Jeter/Teixeira/Cano/99 12.50 30.00
4 Pedroia/Mauer/Hamilton/Verlan/99 10.00 25.00

2011 Prime Cuts Timeline Material Triples

OVERALL MEM ODDS 2 PER BOX
PRINT RUNS B/WN 10-99 COPIES PER
NO PRICING ON QTY 10
1 Vaughan/Waner/Waner/99 30.00 60.00
2 Brooks/Brett/Boggs/99 12.50 30.00

2011 Prime Cuts Timeline Materials

OVERALL MEM ODDS 2 PER BOX
PRINT RUNS B/WN 1-49 COPIES PER
NO PRICING ON QTY 25 OR LESS
5 Mel Ott/49 10.00 25.00

2011 Prime Cuts Timeline Signatures

OVERALL AUTO ODDS 2 PER BOX
PRINT RUNS B/WN 5-49 COPIES PER
NO PRICING ON QTY 25 OR LESS
EXCHANGE DEADLINE 10/04/2013
17 Pete Rose/49 20.00 50.00

2011 Prime Cuts Timeline Trios Materials MVP

OVERALL MEM ODDS 2 PER BOX
PRINT RUNS B/WN 1-5 COPIES PER
NO PRICING DUE TO SCARCITY

2012 Prime Cuts

JSY PRINT RUN B/WN 40-99 COPIES PER
AU PRINT RUN B/WN 99-149 COPIES PER
EXCHANGE DEADLINE 5/28/2014
1 Adam Jones Jsy/99 4.00 10.00
2 Adrian Beltre Jsy/99 4.00 10.00
3 Albert Pujols Jsy/99 6.00 15.00
4 Alex Avila Jsy/99 5.00 12.00
5 Alex Rodriguez Jsy/99 6.00 15.00
7 Andrew McCutchen Jsy/99 5.00 12.00
8 Austin Jackson Pants/99 4.00 10.00
9 Brett Gardner Jsy/99 4.00 10.00
10 Bryce Harper Jsy/99 RC 10.00 25.00
11 Buster Posey Jsy/99 4.00 10.00
12 Carl Crawford Jsy/99 4.00 10.00
13 Chipper Jones Jsy/99 4.00 10.00
15 David Freese Jsy/99 4.00 10.00
16 David Ortiz Jsy/99 4.00 10.00
17 Derek Jeter Jsy/99 6.00 15.00
19 Evan Longoria Jsy/99 4.00 10.00
20 Hanley Ramirez Jsy/99 4.00 10.00
21 Hunter Pence Jsy/99 4.00 10.00
22 Ichiro Suzuki Bat/99 4.00 10.00
24 Joe Mauer Jsy/99 8.00 20.00
25 Joey Votto Jsy/99 4.00 10.00
26 Jose Bautista Jsy/99 4.00 10.00
27 Josh Hamilton Jsy/99 4.00 10.00
28 Justin Upton Jsy/99 4.00 10.00
29 Justin Verlander Jsy/99 4.00 10.00
31 Mark Teixeira Jsy/99 4.00 10.00
32 Matt Kemp Jsy/99 4.00 10.00
33 Michael Young Jsy/99 4.00 10.00
34 Miguel Cabrera Jsy/99 4.00 10.00
35 Mike Trout Jsy/99 30.00 80.00
37 Nelson Cruz Jsy/99 4.00 10.00
38 Nick Swisher Jsy/99 4.00 10.00
41 Robinson Cano Jsy/99 5.00 12.00
42 Roy Halladay Jsy/99 4.00 10.00
43 Ryan Braun Jsy/99 4.00 10.00
44 Ryan Howard Jsy/99 4.00 10.00
45 Starlin Castro Jsy/99 4.00 10.00
47 Tim Lincecum Jsy/99 5.00 12.00
48 Todd Helton Jsy/99 4.00 10.00
49 Troy Tulowitzki Jsy/99 4.00 10.00
50 Yu Darvish Jsy/99 RC 10.00 25.00
51 A.J. Pollock AU/149 RC 4.00 10.00
52 Addison Reed AU/149 RC 4.00 10.00
53 A.Simmons AU/199 RC 4.00 10.00
54 Anthony Gose AU/199 RC 4.00 10.00
56 Brett Lawrie AU/149 RC 8.00 20.00
57 Brett Jackson AU/199 RC 4.00 10.00
58 Casey Crosby AU/99 RC 4.00 10.00
59 Chris Archer AU/199 RC 4.00 10.00
60 David Phelps AU/149 RC 4.00 10.00
61 Dellin Betances AU/149 RC 10.00 25.00
62 Devin Mesoraco AU/149 RC 4.00 10.00
63 Drew Hutchison AU/149 RC 4.00 10.00
64 Drew Pomeranz AU/149 RC 4.00 10.00
65 Drew Smyly AU/149 RC 5.00 12.00
66 Dan Straily AU/199 RC 4.00 10.00
67 Derek Norris AU/199 RC EXCH 5.00 12.00
68 Garrett Richards AU/149 RC 5.00 12.00
69 Hector Sanchez AU/149 RC 4.00 10.00
70 Jarrod Parker AU/149 RC 4.00 10.00
71 Jemile Weeks AU/149 RC 4.00 10.00
72 Jesus Montero AU/149 RC 5.00 12.00
74 Jean Segura AU/199 RC 4.00 10.00
75 Leonys Martin AU/199 RC 4.00 10.00
76 Jordany Valdespin AU/149 RC 4.00 10.00
77 Martin Perez AU/99 RC 4.00 10.00
78 Matt Harvey AU/199 RC 25.00 60.00
79 Kelvin Herrera AU/149 RC 4.00 10.00
80 Kirk Nieuwenhuis AU/149 RC 4.00 10.00
81 Starling Marte AU/199 RC EXCH 4.00 10.00
82 Lucas Luetge AU/149 RC 4.00 10.00
83 Trevor Bauer AU/199 RC 12.00 30.00
85 Matt Moore AU/149 RC 4.00 10.00
86 Nick Hagadone AU/149 RC 4.00 10.00
87 Pat Corbin AU/149 RC 5.00 12.00
88 Robbie Ross AU/149 RC 4.00 10.00
89 Ryan Cook AU/149 RC 4.00 10.00
90 Steve Lombardozzi AU/149 RC 4.00 10.00
91 Tyler Thornburg AU/199 RC 4.00 10.00
92 Yasmani Grandal AU/99 RC 4.00 10.00
94 Tyler Moore AU/149 RC 4.00 10.00
95 Tyler Pastornicky AU/149 RC 4.00 10.00
96 Zach McAllister AU/99 RC 4.00 10.00
97 Wellington Castillo AU/149 4.00 10.00
98 Wilin Rosario AU/149 RC 4.00 10.00
99 Will Middlebrooks AU/149 RC 4.00 10.00
100 Y.Cespedes AU/199 RC 8.00 20.00

2012 Prime Cuts Century Silver

*SILVER: .4X TO 1X BASIC
PRINT RUNS B/WN 10-49 COPIE PER
NO PRICING ON QTY 25 OR LESS

2012 Prime Cuts Auto Biography

PRINT RUNS B/WN 8-49 COPIES PER
NO PRICING ON QTY 25 OR LESS
EXCHANGE DEADLINE 5/28/2014
1 Bernie Williams/49 20.00 50.00
4 Dale Murphy/49 12.50 30.00
8 Dwight Gooden/49 12.50 30.00
17 Minnie Minoso/49 12.00 30.00
19 Roberto Alomar/49 15.00 40.00

2012 Prime Cuts Biography Memorabilia

PRINT RUNS B/WN 25-99 COPIES PER
NO PRICING ON QTY 25 OR LESS
2 Cal Ripken Jr./99 10.00 25.00
9 Eddie Murray/99 8.00 20.00
13 Ken Griffey Jr./99 10.00 25.00
14 Lefty Williams/99 10.00 25.00
16 Miller Huggins/99 10.00 25.00
19 Roberto Alomar/49 20.00 50.00

2012 Prime Cuts Colossal Memorabilia

PRINT RUNS B/WN 10-49 COPIES PER
NO PRICING ON QTY 25 OR LESS
1 Adrian Gonzalez/49 4.00 10.00
2 Bernie Williams/49 6.00 15.00
3 Bert Blyleven/49 4.00 10.00
4 Billy Williams/49 4.00 10.00
5 Bo Jackson/49 10.00 25.00
6 Brooks Robinson/49 10.00 25.00
7 Cal Ripken Jr./49 20.00 50.00
10 Don Mattingly/49 15.00 40.00
12 John Smoltz/49 30.00 60.00
13 Justin Upton/49 4.00 10.00
15 Miguel Cabrera/49 4.00 10.00
16 Nolan Ryan/49 12.00 30.00
19 Pete Rose/49 10.00 25.00
20 Reggie Jackson/49 4.00 10.00
21 Rickey Henderson/49 20.00 50.00
23 Tony Gwynn/49 12.00 30.00
24 Tony Perez/49 10.00 25.00
25 Wade Boggs/49 12.00 30.00

2012 Prime Cuts Hats Off

STATED PRINT RUN 99 SER.#'d SETS
1 Cal Ripken Jr./99 10.00 25.00
2 Eddie Murray/99 6.00 15.00
3 Greg Maddux/99 10.00 25.00
5 Nolan Ryan/99 10.00 25.00
6 Ozzie Smith/99 10.00 25.00
7 Pete Rose/99 10.00 25.00
8 Robin Yount/99 4.00 10.00
9 Ron Santo/99 12.50 30.00
12 Tony Gwynn/99 12.50 30.00

2012 Prime Cuts Icons Bats

COMMON CARD 4.00 10.00
PRINT RUNS B/WN 1-99 COPIES PER
NO PRICING ON QTY 25 OR LESS
9 Duke Snider/99 6.00 15.00
10 Frank Robinson/99 4.00 10.00
18 Paul Molitor/99 4.00 10.00
20 Reggie Jackson/99 5.00 12.00
21 Rickey Henderson/99 6.00 15.00
22 Stan Musial/99 10.00 25.00
30 Joe Jackson/99 50.00 120.00
31 Arky Vaughan/99 10.00 25.00
33 Eddie Collins/99 12.00 30.00
34 George Kelly/99 12.00 30.00
35 Hack Wilson/99 4.00 10.00
36 Jim Bottomley/99 4.00 10.00
37 Lefty Williams/99 40.00 80.00
38 Lloyd Waner/99 10.00 25.00
39 Miller Huggins/99 8.00 20.00
40 Paul Waner/99 12.00 40.00

2012 Prime Cuts Icons Jersey Number

PRINT RUNS B/WN 1-54 COPIES PER
NO PRICING ON QTY 25 OR LESS
3 Bert Blyleven/28 6.00 15.00
11 Frank Thomas/35 15.00 40.00
12 Goose Gossage/54 4.00 10.00
17 Nolan Ryan/34 15.00 40.00

2012 Prime Cuts Icons Jersey Number Signatures

PRINT RUNS B/WN 1-54 COPIES PER
NO PRICING ON QTY 25 OR LESS
EXCHANGE DEADLINE 5/28/2014
15 Josh Hamilton/32 10.00 25.00
16 Mariano Rivera/42 100.00 200.00
17 Nolan Ryan/34 50.00 100.00
19 Randy Johnson/51 40.00 100.00

2012 Prime Cuts Icons Jerseys

PRINT RUNS B/WN 20-99 COPIES PER
NO PRICING ON QTY 25 OR LESS
1 Andre Dawson/99 5.00 12.00
2 Barry Larkin/49 5.00 12.00
3 Bert Blyleven/49 4.00 10.00
4 Bobby Doerr/49 5.00 12.00
5 Cal Ripken Jr./99 6.00 15.00
6 Carlton Fisk/99 4.00 10.00
7 Chipper Jones/99 6.00 15.00
9 Duke Snider/99 4.00 10.00
14 Jim Thorpe/25 40.00 100.00
16 Mariano Rivera/99 10.00 25.00
18 Paul Molitor/99 4.00 10.00
19 Randy Johnson/99 4.00 10.00
20 Reggie Jackson/99 5.00 12.00
21 Rickey Henderson/99 6.00 15.00
25 Tony Gwynn/99 4.00 10.00
26 Tony Perez/99 10.00 25.00
28 Yogi Berra/99 8.00 20.00

2012 Prime Cuts Legendary Bats

PRINT RUNS B/WN 10-99 COPIES PER
NO PRICING ON QTY 25 OR LESS
1 Albert Pujols/99 4.00 10.00
2 Alex Rodriguez/99 6.00 15.00
4 Billy Herman/99 4.00 10.00
6 Eddie Murray/99 4.00 10.00
8 George Brett/99 10.00 25.00
9 George Kelly/99 12.00 30.00
10 Hack Wilson/99 10.00 25.00
11 Ichiro Suzuki/99 5.00 12.00
12 Jim Bottomley/99 15.00 40.00
14 Joe Jackson/99 60.00 120.00
17 Lloyd Waner/99 10.00 25.00
20 Paul Molitor/99 4.00 10.00
21 Paul Waner/99 10.00 25.00
22 Pete Rose/99 12.00 30.00
23 Reggie Jackson/99 5.00 12.00
24 Stan Musial/99 6.00 15.00
25 Tony Gwynn/99 4.00 10.00

2012 Prime Cuts Legendary Bats Signatures

PRINT RUNS B/WN 5-49 COPIES PER
NO PRICING ON QTY 25 OR LESS
EXCHANGE DEADLINE 5/28/2014
6 Eddie Murray/49 12.00 30.00
8 George Brett/49 40.00 80.00
19 Mike Schmidt/49 20.00 50.00
22 Pete Rose/49 12.00 30.00
23 Reggie Jackson/49 15.00 40.00
24 Stan Musial/49 40.00 80.00
25 Tony Gwynn/49 20.00 50.00

2012 Prime Cuts Notable Nicknames

STATED PRINT RUN 49 SER.#'d SETS
EXCHANGE DEADLINE 5/28/2014
1 Bill Madlock/49 10.00 25.00
2 Billy Williams/49 12.00 30.00
3 Austin Jackson/49 6.00 15.00
4 Dave Parker/49 8.00 20.00
5 Dave Winfield/49 30.00 60.00
6 Don Sutton/49 10.00 25.00
7 Earl Weaver/49 12.00 30.00
8 Eddie Murray/49 50.00 100.00
9 Frank Howard/49 10.00 25.00
10 Frank Howard/49 25.00 50.00
11 Joe Morgan/49 20.00 50.00
12 Johnny Bench/49 25.00 60.00
13 Josh Hamilton/49 12.00 30.00
15 Larry Walker/49 EXCH 30.00 60.00
16 Lou Brock/49 30.00 60.00
17 Lou Piniella/49 6.00 15.00
18 Mariano Rivera/49 100.00 200.00
19 Mariano Rivera/49 100.00 200.00
20 Mike Schmidt/49 EXCH 25.00 60.00
21 Orel Hershiser/49 50.00 100.00
22 Pablo Sandoval/49 12.00 30.00
23 Paul Molitor/49 6.00 25.00
24 Paul O'Neill/49 6.00 15.00
25 Robin Yount/49 25.00 60.00
26 Rod Carew/49 8.00 20.00
27 Ron Cey/49 30.00 60.00
28 Ron Guidry/49 20.00 50.00
29 Ron Guidry/49 20.00 50.00
30 Steve Garvey/49 15.00 40.00
31 Tom Seaver/49 EXCH 40.00 100.00
32 Tom Seaver/49 EXCH 20.00 50.00
33 Wade Boggs/49 10.00 25.00
34 Whitey Ford/49 20.00 50.00
35 Willie Randolph/49 6.00 15.00

2012 Prime Cuts Retired Jersey Numbers

PRINT RUNS B/WN 1-44 COPIES PER
NO PRICING ON QTY 25 OR LESS
27 Greg Maddux/31 6.00 15.00
30 Phil Niekro/35 6.00 15.00
34 Willie McCovey/44 15.00 40.00
35 Reggie Jackson/44 8.00 20.00

2012 Prime Cuts Significant Signatures

PRINT RUNS B/WN 25-49 COPIES PER
NO PRICING ON QTY 25 OR LESS
EXCHANGE DEADLINE 5/28/2014
8 Fernando Valenzuela/49 10.00 25.00
54 Stan Musial/49 20.00 50.00
60 Vin Scully/49 150.00 300.00

2012 Prime Cuts Souvenir Cuts

PRINT RUNS B/WN 1-99 COPIES PER
NO PRICING ON QTY 25 OR LESS
EXCHANGE DEADLINE 5/28/2014
1 Al Barlick/49 20.00 50.00
3 Bob Feller/99 10.00 25.00
4 Bob Lemon/49 10.00 25.00
5 Bobby Thomson/99 10.00 25.00
9 Dick Williams/49 10.00 25.00
13 Enos Slaughter/99 15.00 40.00
15 George Kell/99 5.00 25.00
17 Harmon Killebrew/99 15.00 40.00
23 Lou Boudreau/99 12.50 30.00
27 Rick Ferrell/49 10.00 25.00
28 Robin Roberts/49 10.00 25.00
32 Tommy Henrich/49 10.00 25.00

2012 Prime Cuts Timeline Jersey Number

PRINT RUNS B/WN 1-53 COPIES PER
NO PRICING ON QTY 25 OR LESS
7 Buster Posey/28 8.00 20.00
11 Cliff Lee/33 4.00 10.00
18 Don Drysdale/53 12.50 30.00
23 Ichiro Suzuki/51 15.00 40.00
25 Jackie Robinson/42 20.00 50.00
30 Larry Walker/33 15.00 40.00
43 Roy Campanella/39 12.50 30.00

2012 Prime Cuts Timeline Memorabilia

PRINT RUNS B/WN 5-99 COPIES PER
NO PRICING ON QTY 25 OR LESS
3 Alex Rodriguez/99 5.00 12.00
9 Cal Ripken Jr./99 5.00 12.00
16 Derek Jeter/99 6.00 15.00
18 Don Drysdale/99 4.00 10.00
22 Greg Maddux/49 10.00 25.00
29 Ken Griffey Jr./99 12.50 30.00
31 Leo Durocher/99 6.00 15.00
38 Nolan Ryan/99 12.50 30.00
39 Pee Wee Reese/99 4.00 10.00
40 Pete Rose/99 10.00 25.00
43 Roy Campanella/99 8.00 20.00
49 Walter Alston/99 4.00 10.00

2012 Prime Cuts USA Baseball Collegiate National Team Game Jersey Signatures

STATED PRINT RUN 199 SER.#'d SETS
EXCHANGE DEADLINE 5/28/2014
2 Kris Bryant/199 40.00 100.00
4 Michael Conforto/199 10.00 25.00
5 Austin Cousino/199 4.00 10.00
6 Jonathon Crawford/199 4.00 10.00
7 Kyle Farmer/199 4.00 10.00
8 Johnny Field/199 4.00 10.00
9 Adam Frazier/199 4.00 10.00
10 Marco Gonzales/199 4.00 10.00
11 Brett Hambright/199 4.00 10.00
12 Jordan Hankins/199 4.00 10.00
13 Michael Lorenzen/199 4.00 10.00
14 D.J. Peterson/199 5.00 12.00
15 Colton Plaia/199 4.00 10.00
16 Adam Plutko/199 4.00 10.00
17 Jake Reed/199 4.00 10.00
18 Carlos Rodon/199 20.00 50.00
19 Ryne Stanek/199 4.00 10.00
20 Trea Turner/199 15.00 40.00
21 Bobby Wahl/199 4.00 10.00
22 Trevor Williams/199 4.00 10.00

2016 Prime Cuts

PRINT RUNS B/WN 5-149 COPIES PER
NO PRICING ON QTY 15 OR LESS
EXCHANGE DEADLINE 5/9/2018
2 A.Diaz AU/99 RC 10.00 25.00
3 D.Lee AU/99 RC 8.00 20.00
4 Ross Stripling AU/99 RC 4.00 10.00
5 S.Oh AU/99 RC 20.00 50.00
6 T.Naquin AU/99 RC 8.00 20.00
7 Raul A. Mondesi AU/99 RC 8.00 20.00
8 Tyler White AU/99 RC 4.00 10.00
9 Aaron Nola AU/99 RC 8.00 20.00
10 Rob Refsnyder AU/99 RC 5.00 12.00
11 Robert Stephenson AU/99 RC 4.00 10.00
12 Joey Rickard AU/99 RC 4.00 10.00
13 Mallex Smith AU/99 RC 4.00 10.00
14 Richie Shaffer AU/99 RC 4.00 10.00
15 Brandon Drury AU/99 RC 6.00 15.00
16 T.Story AU/99 RC 12.00 30.00
17 Luis Severino AU/99 RC 5.00 12.00
20 Ji-Man Choi AU/99 RC 5.00 12.00
21 Byung-ho Park JSY AU/99 RC 5.00 12.00
22 M.Sano JSY AU/99 RC 8.00 20.00
23 K.Schwarber JSY AU/99 RC 20.00 50.00
24 T.Thompson JSY AU/99 RC
25 N.Mazara JSY AU/99 RC 15.00 40.00
26 Peter O'Brien JSY AU/99 RC 4.00 10.00
27 Brian Johnson JSY AU/99 RC 4.00 10.00
28 Alex Dickerson JSY AU/99 RC 4.00 10.00
29 Dariel Alvarez JSY AU/99 RC 4.00 10.00
30 C.Seager JSY AU/99 RC 10.00 25.00
31 Jerad Eickhoff JSY AU/99 RC 6.00 15.00
32 Jonathan Gray JSY AU/99 RC 4.00 10.00
33 Jose Peraza JSY AU/99 RC 5.00 12.00
34 Michael Reed JSY AU/99 RC 4.00 10.00
36 S.Piscotty JSY AU/99 RC 6.00 15.00
37 Travis Jankowski JSY AU/99 RC 4.00 10.00
38 Zach Davies JSY AU/25 RC 6.00 15.00
39 Elias Diaz JSY AU/99 RC 4.00 10.00
40 John Lamb JSY AU/99 RC 4.00 10.00
41 Ketel Marte JSY AU/99 RC 8.00 20.00
42 Mac Williamson JSY AU/99 RC 4.00 10.00
44 Tom Murphy JSY AU/99 RC 4.00 10.00
45 T.Turner JSY AU/99 RC 12.00 30.00
46 Tyler Duffey JSY AU/99 RC 4.00 10.00
47 Edwards Jr. JSY AU/99 RC 5.00 12.00
48 A.Nola JSY AU/99 10.00 25.00
49 Alex Dickerson JSY AU/99 4.00 10.00
50 Brandon Drury JSY AU/99 6.00 15.00
51 Byung-ho Park JSY AU/99 5.00 12.00
52 Colin Rea JSY AU/99 RC 4.00 10.00
54 T.Story JSY AU/99 15.00 40.00
55 Jonathan Gray JSY AU/99 4.00 10.00
56 K.Schwarber JSY AU/99 20.00 50.00
57 Luis Severino JSY AU/99 5.00 12.00
58 M.Sano JSY AU/99 8.00 20.00
60 Travis Jankowski JSY AU/99 4.00 10.00
63 M.Trout JSY/149 8.00 20.00
65 N.Ryan JSY/149 6.00 15.00
67 S.Musial JSY/25 10.00 25.00
68 R.Clemente JSY/25 50.00 120.00
71 A.Rizzo JSY/149 5.00 12.00
72 Jose Fernandez JSY/149 4.00 10.00
73 Stephen Strasburg JSY/149 4.00 10.00
74 B.Harper JSY/149 6.00 15.00
75 Josh Donaldson JSY/149 3.00 8.00
76 Y.Molina JSY/149 5.00 12.00
77 B.Posey JSY/149 5.00 12.00
78 Masahiro Tanaka JSY/149 3.00 8.00
79 Jose Abreu JSY/149 4.00 10.00
80 Reggie Jackson JSY/149 4.00 10.00
81 Eddie Mathews BAT/149 4.00 10.00
82 Pee Wee Reese JSY/149 4.00 10.00
84 Gregory Polanco JSY/149 3.00 8.00
85 K.Griffey Jr. JSY/149 8.00 20.00
86 Jose Bautista JSY/149 3.00 8.00
87 Carlos Gonzalez JSY/99 3.00 8.00
88 Wil Myers JSY/149 3.00 8.00
89 M.Trout BAT/25 30.00 80.00
90 G.Brett BAT/149 8.00 20.00
91 R.Hornsby JSY/25 8.00 20.00
92 Edwin Encarnacion JSY/149 4.00 10.00
94 Brooks Robinson JSY/149 4.00 10.00
95 Ralph Kiner JSY/99 3.00 8.00
96 Albert Pujols BAT/99 5.00 12.00
97 Dustin Pedroia JSY/149 4.00 10.00
98 Reggie Jackson JSY/149 4.00 10.00
99 Lou Brock BAT/149 3.00 8.00
100 Ozzie Smith BAT/149 5.00 12.00
101 Roger Maris JSY/99 10.00 25.00
102 C.Kershaw JSY/149 5.00 12.00
103 Kris Bryant JSY/149 10.00 25.00
104 Nolan Arenado JSY/149 6.00 15.00
105 Xander Bogaerts JSY/149 4.00 10.00
106 Manny Machado JSY/149 4.00 10.00
107 Robinson Cano JSY/149 3.00 8.00
108 Max Scherzer JSY/149 4.00 10.00
109 Jose Altuve JSY/149 3.00 8.00
110 F.Lindor JSY/149 4.00 10.00
111 Paul Goldschmidt JSY/99 4.00 10.00
112 Lorenzo Cain JSY/149 2.50 6.00
113 A.J. Pollock JSY/149 2.50 6.00
114 Jake Arrieta JSY/149 3.00 8.00
115 Noah Syndergaard JSY/149 3.00 8.00
116 Yu Darvish JSY/149 4.00 10.00
117 Jackie Bradley Jr. JSY/149 4.00 10.00
118 Kirby Puckett JSY/149 10.00 25.00
119 F.Thomas JSY/149 5.00 12.00
120 Fergie Jenkins JSY/149 3.00 8.00
121 Jake Arrieta JSY/149 3.00 8.00
122 Todd Frazier JSY/149 2.50 6.00
123 Chris Davis JSY/149 2.50 6.00
124 Jacob deGrom JSY/149 8.00 20.00
125 Ryan Braun JSY/149 3.00 8.00
126 Phil Rizzuto JSY/149 5.00 12.00
127 Carlos Beltran JSY/149 3.00 8.00
128 Matt Carpenter JSY/149 4.00 10.00
129 Pedro Martinez JSY/149 3.00 8.00
130 Ozzie Smith JSY/149 5.00 12.00
131 Nolan Ryan JSY/149 6.00 15.00
132 Rickey Henderson JSY/149 4.00 10.00
133 M.Rivera JSY/149 6.00 15.00
134 Andres Galarraga JSY/149 3.00 8.00
135 Andres Galarraga JSY/149 3.00 8.00
136 Paul Molitor JSY/149 4.00 10.00
137 Eddie Murray JSY/149 5.00 12.00
138 Mike Piazza JSY/149 4.00 10.00
139 Giancarlo Stanton JSY/149 4.00 10.00
140 Pete Rose JSY/25
141 M.Cabrera JSY/149 4.00 10.00
142 Chris Sale JSY/149 4.00 10.00
143 Johnny Cueto JSY/149 3.00 8.00
144 David Ortiz JSY/149 6.00 15.00
145 Mookie Betts JSY/149 8.00 20.00
146 M.Bumgarner JSY/99 3.00 8.00
147 Adrian Beltre JSY/149 4.00 10.00
148 Victor Martinez JSY/149 3.00 8.00
149 Evan Longoria JSY/149 3.00 8.00
150 Cal Ripken JSY/149 10.00 25.00
151 K.Griffey Jr. JSY/149 8.00 20.00
153 Steve Carlton JSY/149 3.00 8.00
154 Felix Hernandez JSY/149 3.00 8.00
155 Jean Segura JSY/99 3.00 8.00
156 Tony Gwynn JSY/149 8.00 20.00
157 Dennis Eckersley JSY/149 3.00 8.00
158 Tom Seaver JSY/99 5.00 12.00
159 R.Clemens JSY/149 5.00 12.00
160 Bob Feller JSY/25 6.00 15.00
162 Steve Okert AU/99 4.00 10.00
163 Greg Mahle AU/99 4.00 10.00
164 A.Almora Jr. AU/49 8.00 20.00
165 J.Urias AU/99 RC 12.00 30.00
166 Alen Hanson AU/99 5.00 12.00
171 Jeff Bagwell AU/49 15.00 40.00
172 Vida Blue AU/99 6.00 15.00
177 R.A. Dickey AU/25 15.00 40.00
178 Mark Trumbo AU/99 6.00 15.00
179 J.J. Hardy AU/99 4.00 10.00
180 Jonathan Lucroy AU/99 5.00 12.00
181 Adam Eaton AU/99 5.00 12.00
187 Jean Segura AU/25 6.00 15.00
188 George Kell AU/25 8.00 20.00
191 Tino Martinez AU/25 8.00 20.00
192 Brandon Belt AU/99 5.00 12.00
197 C.Kershaw AU/25
202 S.Strasburg JSY AU/25
203 Brian McCann BAT AU/49 5.00 12.00
204 D.Strawberry BAT AU/49 4.00 10.00
206 A.Trammell JSY AU/49 15.00 40.00
207 Wil Myers BAT AU/99 5.00 12.00
209 Sonny Gray JSY AU/99 5.00 12.00
212 Schoendienst JSY AU/99 10.00 25.00
213 Joe Girardi JSY AU/99 5.00 12.00
214 Hisashi Iwakuma JSY AU/49 5.00 12.00
221 Tommy John JSY AU/25
222 Jose Berrios JSY AU/49 6.00 15.00
223 Anthony Rendon JSY AU/99 8.00 20.00
224 V.Guerrero BAT AU/25 15.00 40.00
226 G.Gossage JSY AU/25 12.00 30.00
228 Wade Boggs JSY AU/25 20.00 50.00
229 S.Perez JSY AU/25 12.00 30.00
230 P.Alvarez BAT AU/25
232 M.Scherzer JSY AU/25 15.00 40.00
234 Alex Gordon JSY AU/25 20.00 50.00
235 Ryan Braun JSY AU/25 12.00 30.00
236 J.Donaldson JSY AU/25 20.00 50.00
237 Brett Lawrie JSY AU/49 5.00 12.00
239 Jose Abreu JSY AU/25 8.00 20.00
240 M.Rivera JSY AU/20
241 Brian Ellington JSY AU/99 RC 4.00 10.00
242 Frankie Montas JSY AU/99 RC 5.00 12.00
243 G.Bird JSY AU/99 RC 5.00 12.00
244 Kaleb Cowart JSY AU/99 RC 4.00 10.00
245 Jorge Lopez JSY AU/99 RC 4.00 10.00
246 Kelby Tomlinson JSY AU/99 RC 4.00 10.00
247 Kyle Waldrop JSY AU/99 RC 5.00 12.00
248 Luke Jackson JSY AU/99 RC 4.00 10.00
249 Pedro Severino JSY AU/99 RC 4.00 10.00
250 Zack Godley JSY AU/99 RC 4.00 10.00
251 A.J. Reed JSY AU/99 RC 5.00 12.00
252 Lucas Giolito JSY AU/99 RC 6.00 15.00
253 B.Nimmo JSY AU/99 RC 8.00 20.00
254 W.Contreras JSY AU/99 RC 10.00 25.00
255 Tim Anderson JSY AU/99 RC 25.00 60.00
256 Jameson Taillon JSY AU/99 RC 5.00 12.00
257 M.Fulmer JSY AU/99 RC 6.00 15.00
258 Blake Snell JSY AU/99 RC 5.00 12.00
259 Aaron Blair JSY AU/99 RC 4.00 10.00
260 S.Manaea JSY AU/99 RC 4.00 10.00

2016 Prime Cuts Bronze

*BRNZE AU p/r 49: .4X TO 1X BASE
*BRNZE AU p/r 25: .5X TO 1.2X BASE
*BRNZE JSY p/r 49: .5X TO 1.2X BASE
*BRNZE JSY p/r 25: .6X TO 1.5X BASE
*BRNZE GU AU p/r 49: .4X TO 1X BASE
*BRNZE GU AU p/r 25: .5X TO 1.2X BASE
RANDOM INSERTS IN PACKS
PRINT RUNS B/WN 3-49 COPIES PER
NO PRICING ON QTY 15 OR LESS
EXCHANGE DEADLINE 5/9/2018
161 Ronald Torreyes AU/49 20.00 50.00

2016 Prime Cuts Holo Gold

*GOLD AU: .5X TO 1.2X BASE
*GOLD JSY: .75X TO 2X BASE
*GOLD GU AU: .5X TO 1.2X BASE
RANDOM INSERTS IN PACKS
PRINT RUNS B/WN 1-25 COPIES PER
NO PRICING ON QTY 15 OR LESS
EXCHANGE DEADLINE 5/9/2018

2016 Prime Cuts Auto Biography Materials

*GOLD/25: .5X TO 1.2X BASIC p/r 49-99
RANDOM INSERTS IN PACKS
PRINT RUNS B/WN 10-99 COPIES PER
NO PRICING ON QTY 15 OR LESS
EXCHANGE DEADLINE 5/9/2018
ABMAG Alex Gordon/25 20.00 50.00
ABMBW Bernie Williams/25 10.00 25.00
ABMCG Carlos Gonzalez/25
ABMDS Don Sutton/25
ABMDW David Wright/49 10.00 25.00
ABMDY Darryl Strawberry/49 12.00 30.00
ABMEH Eric Hosmer/25 10.00 25.00
ABMEL Evan Longoria/25 8.00 20.00
ABMGC Gerrit Cole/49 8.00 20.00
ABMJB Jeff Bagwell/49 25.00 60.00
ABMJG Joe Girardi/99 8.00 20.00
ABMJM Joe Mauer/25 8.00 20.00
ABMMC Matt Carpenter/99 8.00 20.00
ABMOC Orlando Cepeda/49 8.00 20.00
ABMPM Paul Molitor/25 15.00 40.00
ABMRB Ryan Braun/25 8.00 20.00
ABMRF Rollie Fingers/25 12.00 30.00

2016 Prime Cuts Auto Biography Materials Combos

*GOLD/25: .5X TO 1.2X BASIC p/r 99
RANDOM INSERTS IN PACKS
PRINT RUNS B/WN 5-99 COPIES PER
NO PRICING ON QTY 15 OR LESS
EXCHANGE DEADLINE 5/9/2018
ABMCBR Brooks Robinson/25 20.00 50.00
ABMCDP Dustin Pedroia/25
ABMCDP David Price/25 15.00 40.00
ABMCJA Jose Abreu/99 8.00 20.00
ABMCJC Jose Canseco/25 25.00 60.00
ABMCPM Paul Molitor/25 12.00 30.00
ABMCSS Steven Souza/99 6.00 15.00
ABMCVG Vladimir Guerrero/20 12.00 30.00
ABMCWB Wade Boggs/25 20.00 50.00

2016 Prime Cuts Auto Biography Materials Triples

*GOLD/25: .5X TO 1.2X BASIC p/r 49
RANDOM INSERTS IN PACKS
PRINT RUNS B/WN 5-49 COPIES PER
NO PRICING ON QTY 15 OR LESS
EXCHANGE DEADLINE 5/9/2018
ABMTAG Andres Galarraga/49 10.00 25.00
ABMTEM Edgar Martinez/49 12.00 30.00
ABMTFL Fred Lynn/25 10.00 25.00
ABMTOV Omar Vizquel/49 8.00 20.00
ABMTRG Ron Guidry/25 25.00 60.00
ABMTTJ Tommy John/49

2016 Prime Cuts Biography Materials

RANDOM INSERTS IN PACKS
PRINT RUNS B/WN 10-99 COPIES PER
NO PRICING ON QTY 15 OR LESS
*GOLD/25: .6X TO 1.5X BASIC
1 Cal Ripken/99 10.00 25.00
2 George Brett/99 12.00 30.00
4 Al Kaline/25 8.00 20.00
7 Dave Winfield/99 3.00 8.00
8 Ozzie Smith/99 5.00 12.00
9 Albert Pujols/49 5.00 12.00
10 Greg Maddux/99 5.00 12.00
11 Kenny Lofton/49 8.00 20.00
12 Jose Canseco/25 12.00 30.00
15 Mel Ott/99 6.00 15.00
16 Don Drysdale/99 5.00 12.00
17 Tony Gwynn/99 8.00 20.00
18 Ichiro Suzuki/25 8.00 20.00
19 Adrian Beltre/99 4.00 10.00
20 Roger Maris/99 12.00 30.00
21 Leo Durocher/99 2.50 6.00
22 Ralph Kiner/99 3.00 8.00
23 Ken Griffey Jr./99 8.00 20.00
24 Ken Boyer/25 10.00 25.00
25 Mariano Rivera/99 8.00 20.00
26 Gary Carter/99 5.00 12.00
27 Pee Wee Reese/99 4.00 10.00
29 Johnny Mize/99 3.00 8.00
33 Stan Musial/25 10.00 25.00
34 Wade Boggs/99 3.00 8.00
35 Rod Carew/49 3.00 8.00
36 Lou Brock/99 4.00 10.00
37 Joe Morgan/99 3.00 8.00
39 Tommy Lasorda/99 3.00 8.00
40 Phil Rizzuto/49 3.00 8.00
41 Darryl Strawberry/99 2.50 6.00
42 Nolan Ryan/99 8.00 20.00
43 Steve Carlton/99 3.00 8.00
44 Barry Bonds/99 6.00 15.00
45 Mark McGwire/49 6.00 15.00
48 Jeff Bagwell/99 4.00 10.00
49 Vladimir Guerrero/25 5.00 12.00
50 Orel Hershiser/99 2.50 6.00

2016 Prime Cuts Biography Materials Blue

*BLUE/49: .4X TO 1X BASIC
*BLUE/25: .6X TO 1.5X BASIC
RANDOM INSERTS IN PACKS
PRINT RUNS B/WN 5-49 COPIES PER
NO PRICING ON QTY 15 OR LESS
18 Ichiro Suzuki/49 5.00 12.00

2016 Prime Cuts Biography Materials Jumbo

RANDOM INSERTS IN PACKS
PRINT RUNS B/WN 15-99 COPIES PER
NO PRICING ON QTY 15
*BLUE/49: .4X TO 1X BASIC
*BLUE/25: .6X TO 1.5X BASIC
*GOLD/25: .6X TO 1.5X BASIC
2 Pete Rose/25 30.00 80.00
6 Jason Giambi/25 4.00 10.00
8 Ryne Sandberg/25 8.00 20.00
9 Robin Yount/25 6.00 15.00
10 Pedro Martinez/25 5.00 12.00
11 Barry Larkin/25 8.00 20.00
12 John Smoltz/49 4.00 10.00
13 Todd Helton/99 3.00 8.00

2016 Prime Cuts Combo Player Materials

RANDOM INSERTS IN PACKS
PRINT RUNS B/WN 5-99 COPIES PER
NO PRICING ON QTY 10 OR LESS
CPMAB J.Arrieta/K.Bryant/99 10.00 25.00
CPMBB J.Bradley Jr./M.Betts/99 6.00 15.00
CPMBD J.Bautista/J.Donaldson/99 6.00 15.00
CPMBO A.Beltre/R.Odor/99 4.00 10.00
CPMBR J.Bench/P.Rose/49 20.00 50.00
CPMDC A.Dawson/G.Carter/99 6.00 15.00
CPMDP A.Diaz/S.Piscotty/99 5.00 12.00
CPMFS T.Frazier/C.Sale/99 4.00 10.00
CPMGB N.Garciaparra/X.Bogaerts/99 4.00 10.00
CPMKD C.Kershaw/D.Drysdale/99 6.00 15.00
CPMKK A.Kaline/H.Kuenn/25 15.00 40.00
CPMKP H.Killebrew/K.Puckett/99 20.00 50.00
CPMMG E.Martinez/K.Griffey Jr./99 20.00 50.00
CPMMM J.Morgan/T.Munson/99 10.00 25.00
CPMMS N.Mazara/T.Story/99 12.00 30.00
CPMND H.Nomo/Y.Darvish/25 6.00 15.00
CPMPB B.Posey/M.Bumgarner/99 5.00 12.00
CPMRG A.Rizzo/P.Goldschmidt/99 5.00 12.00
CPMRM F.Robinson/R.Maris/49 15.00 40.00
CPMRR P.Reese/P.Reiser/49 12.00 30.00
CPMSA G.Springer/J.Altuve/99 3.00 8.00
CPMSC K.Schwarber/W.Contreras/99 8.00 20.00
CPMSP M.Sano/B.Park/99 4.00 10.00
CPMTM B.Thomson/J.Mize/25 5.00 12.00

2016 Prime Cuts Combo Player Materials Blue

*BLUE/49: .5X TO 1.2X BASIC p/r 99
*BLUE/25: .5X TO 1.2X BASIC p/r 49
*BLUE/25: .6X TO 1.5X BASIC p/r 99
RANDOM INSERTS IN PACKS
PRINT RUNS B/WN 5-49 COPIES PER
NO PRICING ON QTY 15 OR LESS
CPMMS Kenta Maeda 10.00 25.00
Corey Seager/49

2016 Prime Cuts Combo Player Materials Gold

*GOLD/25: .6X TO 1.5X BASIC p/r 99
RANDOM INSERTS IN PACKS
PRINT RUNS B/WN 1-25 COPIES PER
NO PRICING ON QTY 15 OR LESS
CPMMS Kenta Maeda 12.00 30.00
Corey Seager/25

2016 Prime Cuts Icons Bats

RANDOM INSERTS IN PACKS
PRINT RUNS B/WN 5-99 COPIES PER
NO PRICING ON QTY 15 OR LESS
*GOLD/25: .6X TO 1.5X BASIC
IBBL Barry Larkin/99 5.00 12.00
IBCB Craig Biggio/99 3.00 8.00
IBCJ Chipper Jones/99 4.00 10.00
IBDM Don Mattingly/99 8.00 20.00
IBEM Eddie Mathews/99 5.00 12.00
IBGA Gary Carter/99 3.00 8.00
IBGC George Case/49 6.00 15.00
IBJB Jeff Bagwell/49 4.00 10.00
IBJC Jose Canseco/25 12.00 30.00
IBKB Ken Boyer/25 10.00 25.00
IBKP Kirby Puckett/99 8.00 20.00
IBMO Mel Ott/99 6.00 15.00
IBMS Mike Schmidt/99 6.00 15.00
IBPM Paul Molitor/99 4.00 10.00
IBPR Pete Reiser/25 4.00 10.00
IBRH Rogers Hornsby/25 8.00 20.00
IBRM Roger Maris/25 10.00 25.00
IBRY Robin Yount/99 4.00 10.00
IBSM Stan Musial/25 10.00 25.00
IBWM Willie McCovey/99 3.00 8.00

2016 Prime Cuts Icons Jerseys

RANDOM INSERTS IN PACKS
PRINT RUNS B/WN 5-99 COPIES PER
NO PRICING ON QTY 10 OR LESS
*GOLD/25: .6X TO 1.5X BASIC
IJBB Barry Bonds/99 6.00 15.00
IJBF Bob Feller/99 5.00 12.00
IJBM Billy Martin/99 5.00 12.00
IJCR Cal Ripken/99 6.00 15.00
IJDM Dale Murphy/99 4.00 10.00
IJDS Duke Snider/99 3.00 8.00
IJEM Eddie Murray/99 5.00 12.00
IJFT Frank Thomas/99 4.00 10.00
IJGB George Brett/99 8.00 20.00
IJGG Goose Gossage/99 3.00 8.00
IJGM Greg Maddux/99 5.00 12.00
IJHP Herb Pennock/99 3.00 8.00
IJJP Jim Palmer/25 5.00 12.00
IJKG Ken Griffey Jr./99 8.00 20.00
IJMM Mark McGwire/99 6.00 15.00
IJMP Mike Piazza/99 4.00 10.00
IJMS Mike Schmidt/99 6.00 15.00
IJNR Nolan Ryan/99 5.00 12.00
IJOS Ozzie Smith/99 5.00 12.00
IJPM Pedro Martinez/99 3.00 8.00
IJPR Pee Wee Reese/99 4.00 10.00
IJRC Rod Carew/49 3.00 8.00
IJRJ Reggie Jackson/99 6.00 15.00
IJTG Tony Gwynn/99 8.00 20.00
IJTP Tony Perez/25 5.00 12.00
IJWB Wade Boggs/99 6.00 15.00
IJWC Will Clark/99 3.00 8.00
IJWF Whitey Ford/99 4.00 10.00

2016 Prime Cuts Icons Numbers Combos

RANDOM INSERTS IN PACKS
PRINT RUNS B/WN 15-99 COPIES PER
NO PRICING ON QTY 15
*GOLD/25: .6X TO 1.5X BASIC
INCAP Andy Pettitte/49 3.00 8.00
INCBG Bob Gibson/25 6.00 15.00
INCBS Bruce Sutter/49 3.00 8.00
INCCF Carlton Fisk/99 4.00 10.00
INCDW Dave Winfield/49 3.00 8.00
INCJW Jimmy Wynn/25 4.00 10.00
INCMR Mariano Rivera/49 8.00 20.00
INCNR Nolan Ryan/25 12.00 30.00
INCRA Roberto Alomar/99 5.00 12.00
INCRC Rod Carew/49 3.00 8.00
INCRF Rollie Fingers/99 4.00 10.00
INCTM Thurman Munson/25 12.00 30.00

2016 Prime Cuts Icons Numbers Quads

RANDOM INSERTS IN PACKS
PRINT RUNS B/WN 25-99 COPIES PER
*GOLD/25: .6X TO 1.5X BASIC
1 Cal Ripken/25 15.00 40.00
2 Nolan Ryan/25 12.00 30.00
3 Rickey Henderson/49 20.00 50.00
6 Barry Bonds/99 6.00 15.00
8 Craig Biggio/25 5.00 12.00
9 Pete Rose/25 30.00 80.00
10 Joe Morgan/49 3.00 8.00

2016 Prime Cuts Icons Numbers Trios

RANDOM INSERTS IN PACKS
PRINT RUNS B/WN 3-99 COPIES PER
NO PRICING ON QTY 3

*GOLD/25: .6X TO 1.5X BASIC
INTEM Edgar Martinez/25 5.00 12.00
INTFT Frank Thomas/25 6.00 15.00
INTGB George Brett/25 20.00 50.00
INTIS Ichiro Suzuki/25 8.00 20.00
INTKP Kirby Puckett/25 25.00 60.00
INTTG Tony Gwynn/25 12.00 30.00
INTTH Todd Helton/25 12.00 30.00
INTTW Ted Williams/25 20.00 50.00
INTWB Wade Boggs/99 6.00 15.00

2016 Prime Cuts Prime Signatures

*BRONZE/49: .4X TO 1X BASIC p/r 99
*BRONZE/25: .5X TO 1.2X BASIC p/r 49
*GOLD/25: .5X TO 1.2X BASIC p/r 99
RANDOM INSERTS IN PACKS
PRINT RUNS B/WN 25-99 COPIES PER
EXCHANGE DEADLINE 5/9/2018
PSAG Andres Galarraga/99 6.00 15.00
PSAR Anthony Rizzo/49 20.00 50.00
PSBB Barry Bonds/25 75.00 200.00
PSBJ Bo Jackson/25 30.00 80.00
PSCB Craig Biggio/49 10.00 25.00
PSCJ Chipper Jones/25 30.00 80.00
PSCR Cal Ripken/25
PSDM Don Mattingly/25 30.00 80.00
PSDW Dave Winfield/25 15.00 40.00
PSEM Edgar Martinez/99 6.00 15.00
PSFT Frank Thomas/25 30.00 80.00
PSGB George Brett/25 50.00 120.00
PSJA Jose Abreu/49 8.00 20.00
PSJC Jose Canseco/99 10.00 25.00
PSJD Josh Donaldson/49 8.00 20.00
PSJD Jacob deGrom/49 25.00 60.00
PSJH Jason Heyward/99 15.00 40.00
PSKG Ken Griffey Jr./25 60.00 150.00
PSMM Mark McGwire/25 40.00 100.00
PSMM Manny Machado/49 20.00 50.00
PSMP Mike Piazza/25
PSMS Mike Schmidt/25
PSNR Nolan Ryan/25
PSOV Omar Vizquel/99 6.00 15.00
PSPM Paul Molitor/99 8.00 20.00
PSPR Pete Rose/49 25.00 60.00
PSRA Roberto Alomar/49 8.00 20.00
PSRC Roger Clemens/25 20.00 50.00
PSRC Robinson Cano/25 10.00 25.00
PSRJ Reggie Jackson/25 20.00 50.00
PSRS Ryne Sandberg/25 20.00 50.00
PSSC Steve Carlton/25 10.00 25.00
PSTG Tom Glavine/49 6.00 15.00
PSTH Todd Helton/49 6.00 15.00
PSWB Wade Boggs/25 20.00 50.00
PSXB Xander Bogaerts/99 15.00 40.00
PSYC Yoenis Cespedes/49 8.00 20.00
PSYM Yadier Molina/49 25.00 60.00

2016 Prime Cuts Prime Six Signatures Booklets

RANDOM INSERTS IN PACKS
PRINT RUNS B/WN 5-25 COPIES PER
NO PRICING ON QTY 10 OR LESS
EXCHANGE DEADLINE 5/9/2018
1 Se/St/Di/Ma/Re/Tu/25

2016 Prime Cuts Rookie Autographs Jumbo Materials Booklets

RANDOM INSERTS IN PACKS
PRINT RUNS B/WN 25-99 COPIES PER
EXCHANGE DEADLINE 5/9/2018
RJSAD Aledmys Diaz/25 10.00 25.00
RJSBD Brandon Drury/25
RJSBP Byung-ho Park/25 8.00 20.00
RJSCS Corey Seager/25 50.00 120.00
RJSGB Greg Bird/99 6.00 15.00
RJSJB Jose Berrios/25 10.00 25.00
RJSKM Ketel Marte/99 10.00 25.00
RJSKS Kyle Schwarber/49 30.00 80.00
RJSLG Lucas Giolito/25 10.00 25.00
RJSLS Luis Severino/49 10.00 25.00
RJSMK Max Kepler/25
RJSMS Miguel Sano/25 12.00 30.00
RJSNM Nomar Mazara/25 20.00 50.00
RJSRR Rob Refsnyder/25 10.00 25.00
RJSSP Stephen Piscotty/25 15.00 40.00
RJSTN Tyler Naquin/49 12.00 30.00
RJSTS Trevor Story/49 20.00 50.00
RJSTT Trayce Thompson/25
RJSTT Trea Turner/25 25.00 60.00

2016 Prime Cuts Rookie Autographs Silhouette Combo Materials Booklets

RANDOM INSERTS IN PACKS
PRINT RUNS B/WN 25-99 COPIES PER
EXCHANGE DEADLINE 5/9/2018
1 C.Seager/T.Thompson/25 50.00 120.00
2 K.Schwarber/W.Contreras/49 40.00 100.00
3 B.Drury/P.O'Brien/25 12.00 30.00
4 J.Gray/T.Story/49 25.00 60.00
6 Refsnyder/Bird/99 8.00 20.00
7 T.Naquin/S.Piscotty/49 15.00 40.00
8 L.Giolito/T.Turner/25 30.00 80.00

2016 Prime Cuts Souvenir Cuts

RANDOM INSERTS IN PACKS
PRINT RUNS B/WN 1-99 COPIES PER
NO PRICING ON QTY 15 OR LESS
EXCHANGE DEADLINE 5/9/2018
SCAB Al Barlick/25 15.00 40.00
SCBL Bob Lemon/50 12.00 30.00
SCBT Bobby Thomson/99 12.00 30.00
SCBT Bill Terry/49 20.00 50.00
SCCH Catfish Hunter/25 15.00 40.00
SCDW Dick Williams/40
SCGC Gary Carter/99 12.00 30.00
SCGK George Kell/60 10.00 25.00
SCHK Harmon Killebrew/99 12.00 30.00
SCHN Hal Newhouser/25
SCJP Johnny Pesky/99 12.00 30.00
SCLB Lou Boudreau/99 12.00 30.00
SCPR Phil Rizzuto/20 20.00 50.00
SCRK Ralph Kiner/99 10.00 25.00
SCRR Robin Roberts/25 15.00 40.00
SCSM Stan Musial/99 15.00 40.00
SCTL Tommy Leach/20 75.00 200.00
SCWS Warren Spahn/99 12.00 30.00

2016 Prime Cuts Timeline Materials

RANDOM INSERTS IN PACKS
PRINT RUNS B/WN 3-99 COPIES PER
NO PRICING ON QTY 10 OR LESS
*GOLD/25: .6X TO 1.5X BASIC
TAV Arky Vaughan/49 6.00 15.00
TCB Craig Biggio/99 3.00 8.00
TCC Carlos Correa/99 4.00 10.00
TGB George Brett/99 12.00 30.00
TJA Jose Abreu/99 6.00 15.00
TJD Josh Donaldson/99 3.00 8.00
TKB Kris Bryant/99 5.00 12.00
TKG Ken Griffey Jr./99 8.00 20.00
TLB Lou Brock/99 4.00 10.00
TLW Lloyd Waner/25 5.00 12.00
TMB Madison Bumgarner/99 3.00 8.00
TMS Mike Schmidt/99 6.00 15.00
TMT Mike Trout/25 15.00 40.00
TNR Nolan Ryan/99 8.00 20.00
TPR Pete Rose/25 30.00 80.00
TSM Stan Musial/25 10.00 25.00
TTW Ted Williams/99 12.00 30.00

2016 Prime Cuts Timeline Materials Combos

RANDOM INSERTS IN PACKS
PRINT RUNS B/WN 5-99 COPIES PER
NO PRICING ON QTY 15 OR LESS
*GOLD/25: .6X TO 1.5X BASIC
TCAB Adrian Beltre/49 4.00 10.00
TCAP Albert Pujols/49 5.00 12.00
TCCK Clayton Kershaw/25 10.00 25.00
TCCR Cal Ripken/25 15.00 40.00
TCDO David Ortiz/49 12.00 30.00
TCDW David Wright/49 3.00 8.00
TCFR Frank Robinson/25 5.00 12.00
TCFT Frank Thomas/49 4.00 10.00
TCGH Gabby Hartnett/25 8.00 20.00
TCGS Giancarlo Stanton/49 4.00 10.00
TCJV Justin Verlander/99 4.00 10.00
TCKP Kirby Puckett/49 15.00 40.00
TCMH Miller Huggins/49 6.00 15.00
TCNA Nolan Arenado/49 6.00 15.00
TCRS Ryne Sandberg/25 8.00 20.00

2016 Prime Cuts Timeline Materials Quads

RANDOM INSERTS IN PACKS
PRINT RUNS B/WN 5-25 COPIES PER
NO PRICING ON QTY 10 OR LESS
TQAR Anthony Rizzo/25 8.00 20.00
TQBH Bryce Harper/25 10.00 25.00
TQCY Carl Yastrzemski/25 15.00 40.00
TQEM Eddie Murray/25 8.00 20.00
TQJB Jose Bautista/25 5.00 12.00
TQJB Johnny Bench/25 15.00 40.00
TQLA Luke Appling/25 6.00 15.00
TQMC Miguel Cabrera/25 6.00 15.00
TQMM Manny Machado/25 8.00 20.00
TQPR Pee Wee Reese/25 6.00 15.00
TQRC Rod Carew/25 5.00 12.00
TQRJ Reggie Jackson/25 10.00 25.00
TQTH Tommy Henrich/25 4.00 10.00

2016 Prime Cuts Timeline Materials Stats

RANDOM INSERTS IN PACKS
PRINT RUNS B/WN 5-99 COPIES PER
NO PRICING ON QTY 10 OR LESS
*GOLD/25: .6X TO 1.5X BASIC
5 Tony Gwynn/25 12.00 30.00
7 Stan Musial/25 10.00 25.00
9 Rickey Henderson/49 20.00 50.00
11 Pete Rose/49 20.00 50.00
12 Mark McGwire/49 6.00 15.00
13 Roger Maris/25 20.00 50.00

2016 Prime Cuts Timeline Materials Trios

RANDOM INSERTS IN PACKS
PRINT RUNS B/WN 5-99 COPIES PER
NO PRICING ON QTY 10 OR LESS
*GOLD/25: .6X TO 1.5X BASIC
TTBB Barry Bonds/25 10.00 25.00
TTCS Chris Sale/49 4.00 10.00
TTGG Goose Gossage/99 3.00 8.00
TTGM Gil McDougald/49 8.00 20.00
TTHP Herb Pennock/25 10.00 25.00
TTJD Jacob deGrom/25 12.00 30.00
TTMM Mark McGwire/25 10.00 25.00
TTOS Ozzie Smith/49 5.00 12.00
TTPG Paul Goldschmidt/49 4.00 10.00
TTSS Stephen Strasburg/25 6.00 15.00
TTWA Walter Alston/25 8.00 20.00
TTWB Wade Boggs/49 6.00 15.00
TTXB Xander Bogaerts/99 4.00 10.00
TTYM Yadier Molina/99 6.00 15.00

2005 Prime Patches

COMMON CARD (1-89) .75 2.00
1 Darin Erstad .75 2.00
2 Garret Anderson .75 2.00
3 Vladimir Guerrero 1.25 3.00
4 Luis Gonzalez .75 2.00
5 Shawn Green .75 2.00
6 Troy Glaus .75 2.00
7 Andruw Jones .75 2.00
8 Chipper Jones 2.00 5.00
9 John Smoltz 2.00 5.00
10 Tim Hudson 1.25 3.00
11 Brian Roberts .75 2.00
12 Melvin Mora .75 2.00
13 Miguel Tejada 1.25 3.00
14 Curt Schilling 1.25 3.00
15 David Ortiz 2.00 5.00
16 Johnny Damon 1.25 3.00
17 Manny Ramirez 2.00 5.00
18 Derrek Lee .75 2.00
19 Greg Maddux 2.50 6.00
20 Kerry Wood .75 2.00
21 Mark Prior 1.25 3.00
22 Mark Buehrle 1.25 3.00
23 Paul Konerko 1.25 3.00
24 Adam Dunn 1.25 3.00
25 Ken Griffey Jr. 4.00 10.00
26 Sean Casey .75 2.00
27 Travis Hafner .75 2.00
28 Victor Martinez 1.25 3.00
29 Todd Helton 1.25 3.00
30 Ivan Rodriguez 1.25 3.00
31 Carlos Delgado .75 2.00
32 Dontrelle Willis .75 2.00
33 Josh Beckett .75 2.00
34 Miguel Cabrera 2.00 5.00
35 Craig Biggio 1.25 3.00
36 Lance Berkman 1.25 3.00
37 Roger Clemens 2.50 6.00
38 Roy Oswalt 1.25 3.00
39 Mike Sweeney .75 2.00
40 Jeff Kent .75 2.00
41 Milton Bradley .75 2.00
42 Ben Sheets .75 2.00
43 Carlos Lee .75 2.00
44 Johan Santana 1.25 3.00
45 Justin Morneau 1.25 3.00
46 Torii Hunter .75 2.00
47 David Wright 1.50 4.00
48 Mike Piazza 2.00 5.00
49 Pedro Martinez 1.25 3.00
50 Alex Rodriguez 2.50 6.00
51 Derek Jeter 5.00 12.00
52 Gary Sheffield .75 2.00
53 Hideki Matsui 3.00 8.00
54 Randy Johnson 2.00 5.00
55 Barry Zito 1.25 3.00
56 Eric Chavez .75 2.00
57 Rich Harden .75 2.00
58 Bobby Abreu .75 2.00
59 Jim Thome 1.25 3.00
60 Pat Burrell .75 2.00
61 Jason Bay .75 2.00
62 Jake Peavy .75 2.00
63 Edgardo Alfonzo .75 2.00
64 Moises Alou .75 2.00
65 Adrian Beltre 2.00 5.00
66 Carlos Beltran 1.25 3.00
67 Ichiro Suzuki 2.50 6.00
68 Richie Sexson .75 2.00
69 Albert Pujols 2.50 6.00
70 Jim Edmonds 1.25 3.00
71 Mark Mulder .75 2.00
72 Scott Rolen 1.25 3.00
73 Aubrey Huff .75 2.00
74 Rocco Baldelli .75 2.00
75 Alfonso Soriano 1.25 3.00
76 Hank Blalock .75 2.00
77 Mark Teixeira 1.25 3.00
78 Michael Young .75 2.00
79 Roy Halladay 1.25 3.00
80 Vernon Wells .75 2.00
81 Jose Vidro .75 2.00
82 B.J. Upton 1.25 3.00
83 Ted Williams 4.00 10.00
84 Prince Fielder RC 4.00 10.00
85 Willie Mays 4.00 10.00
86 Stan Musial 3.00 8.00
87 Cal Ripken 6.00 15.00
88 George Brett 4.00 10.00
89 Nolan Ryan 6.00 15.00

2005 Prime Patches Materials Bat

*BAT p/r 81-150: .4X TO 1X JSY p/r 150
*BAT p/r 81-150: .3X TO .8X JSY p/r 50-69
*BAT p/r 81-150: .25X TO .6X JSY p/r 25
*BAT p/r 24-25: .4X TO 1X JSY p/r 25
TWO AUTOS OR GAME-USED PER PACK
PRINT RUNS B/WN 1-150 COPIES PER
NO PRICING ON QTY OF 5 OR LESS
1 Darin Erstad/150 2.50 6.00
3 Vladimir Guerrero/150 4.00 10.00
5 Shawn Green/150 2.50 6.00
6 Troy Glaus/150 2.50 6.00
7 Andruw Jones/150 3.00 8.00
8 Chipper Jones/150 4.00 10.00
10 Tim Hudson/100 2.50 6.00
15 David Ortiz/150 3.00 8.00
18 Derrek Lee/150 3.00 8.00
21 Mark Prior/150 3.00 8.00
24 Adam Dunn/150 2.50 6.00
30 Ivan Rodriguez/150 3.00 8.00
31 Carlos Delgado/150 2.50 6.00
32 Dontrelle Willis/150 2.50 6.00
33 Josh Beckett/150 2.50 6.00
36 Lance Berkman/150 2.50 6.00
39 Mike Sweeney/150 2.50 6.00
40 Jeff Kent/24 4.00 10.00
45 Justin Morneau/150 2.50 6.00
46 Torii Hunter/150 2.50 6.00
48 Mike Piazza/150 4.00 10.00
49 Pedro Martinez/150 3.00 8.00
54 Randy Johnson/45 5.00 12.00
59 Jim Thome/150 3.00 8.00
63 Edgardo Alfonzo/150 2.00 5.00
64 Moises Alou/150 2.50 6.00
68 Richie Sexson/150 2.50 6.00
69 Albert Pujols/150 8.00 20.00
77 Mark Teixeira/150 3.00 8.00
78 Michael Young/150 2.50 6.00
81 Jose Vidro/150 2.00 5.00
82 B.J. Upton/150 2.50 6.00

2005 Prime Patches Materials Jersey

TWO AUTOS OR GAME-USED PER PACK
PRINT RUNS B/WN 1-150 COPIES PER
NO PRICING ON QTY OF 10 OR LESS
9 John Smoltz/150 3.00 8.00
13 Miguel Tejada/25 4.00 10.00
14 Curt Schilling/150 3.00 8.00
17 Manny Ramirez/50 4.00 10.00
23 Paul Konerko/25 4.00 10.00
26 Sean Casey/150 2.50 6.00
27 Travis Hafner/150 2.50 6.00
29 Todd Helton/150 3.00 8.00
34 Miguel Cabrera/25 5.00 12.00
35 Craig Biggio/69 4.00 10.00
37 Roger Clemens/150 6.00 15.00
38 Roy Oswalt/150 2.50 6.00
58 Bobby Abreu/150 2.50 6.00
60 Pat Burrell/50 3.00 8.00
61 Jason Bay/50 3.00 8.00
65 Adrian Beltre/150 2.50 6.00
70 Jim Edmonds/150 2.50 6.00
72 Scott Rolen/150 3.00 8.00
74 Rocco Baldelli/150 2.50 6.00
75 Alfonso Soriano/150 2.50 6.00
83 Ted Williams/150 20.00 50.00
85 Willie Mays/25 10.00 25.00
86 Stan Musial/50 12.50 30.00
87 Cal Ripken/150 8.00 20.00

2005 Prime Patches Materials Name Plate Patch

*PATCH p/r 22-24: 1.25X TO 3X JSY p/r 150
TWO AUTOS OR GAME-USED PER PACK
PRINT RUNS B/WN 1-59 COPIES PER
NO PRICING ON QTY OF 13 OR LESS
3 Vladimir Guerrero/22 12.50 30.00
4 Luis Gonzalez/59 6.00 15.00
39 Mike Sweeney/24 8.00 20.00

2005 Prime Patches Materials Number Patch

*PATCH p/r 22-31: 1.25X TO 3X JSY p/r 150
TWO AUTOS OR GAME-USED PER PACK
PRINT RUNS B/WN 1-67 COPIES PER
NO PRICING ON QTY OF 10 OR LESS
4 Luis Gonzalez/40 6.00 15.00
7 Andruw Jones/22 10.00 25.00
19 Greg Maddux/24 15.00 40.00
31 Carlos Delgado/37 6.00 15.00
39 Mike Sweeney/67 5.00 12.00
59 Jim Thome/59 8.00 20.00

2005 Prime Patches Materials Sleeve Patch

TWO AUTOS OR GAME-USED PER PACK
PRINT RUNS B/WN 1-27 COPIES PER
NO PRICING ON QTY OF 9 OR LESS
39 Mike Sweeney/27 8.00 20.00

2005 Prime Patches Materials Team Logo Patch

*PATCH p/r 36-50: 1X TO 2.5X JSY p/r 150
*PATCH p/r 24-32: 1.25X TO 3X JSY p/r 150
TWO AUTOS OR GAME-USED PER PACK
PRINT RUNS B/WN 1-76 COPIES PER
NO PRICING ON QTY OF 15 OR LESS
4 Luis Gonzalez/70 5.00 12.00
8 Chipper Jones/50 12.50 30.00
39 Mike Sweeney/76 5.00 12.00
46 Torii Hunter/24 8.00 20.00
59 Jim Thome/32 10.00 25.00

2005 Prime Patches Autograph

TWO AUTOS OR GAME-USED PER PACK
TIER 1 QTY B/WN 1-50 COPIES PER
TIER 2 QTY B/WN 51-100 COPIES PER
TIER 3 QTY B/WN 101-250 COPIES PER
TIER 4 QTY B/WN 251-800 COPIES PER
TIER 5 QTY B/WN 801-1200 COPIES PER
CARDS ARE NOT SERIAL-NUMBERED
PRINT RUN INFO PROVIDED BY DONRUSS
2 Garret Anderson T2/100 * 8.00 20.00
10 Tim Hudson T1/50 * 10.00 25.00
11 Brian Roberts T4 6.00 15.00
12 Melvin Mora T2/67 * 5.00 12.00
15 David Ortiz T1/25 * 25.00 50.00
18 Derrek Lee T3 10.00 25.00
21 Mark Prior T1/25 * 10.00 25.00
22 Mark Buehrle T3 8.00 20.00
23 Paul Konerko T4 10.00 25.00
26 Sean Casey T2/100 * 8.00 20.00
27 Travis Hafner T4 6.00 15.00
28 Victor Martinez T2/100 * 5.00 12.00
29 Todd Helton T1/25 * 8.00 40.00
33 Josh Beckett T1/25 * 8.00 40.00
34 Miguel Cabrera T3 20.00 40.00
35 Craig Biggio T1/25 * 15.00 40.00
38 Roy Oswalt T3 6.00 15.00
41 Milton Bradley T3 4.00 10.00
42 Ben Sheets T1/25 * 10.00 25.00
43 Carlos Lee T5 6.00 15.00
44 Johan Santana T1/25 * 15.00 40.00
45 Justin Morneau T3 6.00 15.00
46 Torii Hunter T5 10.00 25.00
47 David Wright T1/43 * 20.00 50.00
52 Gary Sheffield T1/25 * 10.00 25.00
56 Eric Chavez T1/50 * 10.00 25.00
57 Rich Harden T5 6.00 15.00
61 Jason Bay T1/50 * 10.00 25.00
62 Jake Peavy T4 6.00 15.00
71 Mark Mulder T1/25 * 10.00 25.00
72 Scott Rolen T3 5.00 12.00
73 Aubrey Huff T4 4.00 10.00
75 Alfonso Soriano T1/25 * 10.00 25.00
77 Mark Teixeira T3 10.00 25.00
78 Michael Young T3 6.00 15.00
79 Roy Halladay T1/50 * 25.00 60.00
81 Jose Vidro T1/50 * 6.00 15.00
84 Prince Fielder T2/100 * 8.00 40.00
86 Stan Musial T2/100 * 20.00 50.00
88 George Brett T1/25 * 25.00 60.00
89 Nolan Ryan T2/100 * 30.00 80.00

2005 Prime Patches All-Star Materials Bat

*BAT p/r 100-150: .3X TO .8X JUM p/r 104-493
*BAT p/r 100-150: .25X TO .6X JUM p/r 40
*BAT p/r 100-150: .2X TO .5X JUM p/r 25
TWO AUTOS OR GAME-USED PER PACK
PRINT RUNS B/WN 4-150 COPIES PER
NO PRICING ON QTY OF 5 OR LESS
6 Mark Teixeira/150 3.00 8.00
13 Paul Lo Duca/150 2.50 6.00

2005 Prime Patches All-Star Materials Jersey

*JSY p/r 30: .5X TO 1.2X JUM p/r 104-493
TWO AUTOS OR GAME-USED PER PACK
PRINT RUNS B/WN 1-30 COPIES PER
NO PRICING ON QTY OF 1

2005 Prime Patches All-Star Materials Name Plate Patch

*PAT p/r 39-55: .75X TO 2X JUM p/r 107-493
*PAT p/r 39-55: .6X TO 1.5X JUM p/r 40
*PAT p/r 20-32: 1X TO 2.5X JUM p/r 107-493
TWO AUTOS OR GAME-USED PER PACK
PRINT RUNS B/WN 1-55 COPIES PER
NO PRICING ON QTY OF 15 OR LESS

2005 Prime Patches All-Star Materials Number Patch

*PAT p/r 72: .5X TO 1.2X JUM p/r 40
*PAT p/r 55-57 .75X TO 2X JUM p/r 107-493
*PAT p/r 20-35: 1X TO 2.5X JUM p/r 407-493
*PAT p/r 20-35: .6X TO 1.5X JUM p/r 25
TWO AUTOS OR GAME-USED PER PACK
PRINT RUNS B/WN 6-72 COPIES PER
NO PRICING ON QTY OF 17 OR LESS

2005 Prime Patches All-Star Materials Team Logo Patch

*PAT p/r 38-55: .75X TO 2X JUM p/r 407-493
*PAT p/r 20-35: 1X TO 2.5X JUM p/r 407-493
*PAT p/r 20-35: .75X TO 2X JUM p/r 40
*PAT p/r 20-35: .6X TO 1.5X JUM p/r 25
TWO AUTOS OR GAME-USED PER PACK
PRINT RUNS B/WN 1-55 COPIES PER
NO PRICING ON QTY OF 16 OR LESS

2005 Prime Patches All-Star Materials Jumbo Swatch

PRINT RUNS B/WN 1-493 COPIES PER
NO PRICING ON QTY OF 1
PRIME PRINT RUNS B/WN 1-20 COPIES
NO PRIME PRICING DUE TO SCARCITY
TWO AUTOS OR GAME-USED PER PACK
1 Johan Santana/277 5.00 12.00
3 Miguel Cabrera/145 4.00 10.00
4 Albert Pujols/493 10.00 25.00
7 Vernon Wells/297 3.00 8.00
8 Vladimir Guerrero/196 5.00 12.00
9 Jim Edmonds/359 3.00 8.00
10 Paul Konerko/25 5.00 12.00
11 Roy Oswalt/238 3.00 8.00
12 Johnny Damon/155 4.00 10.00
14 Miguel Tejada/228 3.00 8.00
15 Scott Rolen/324 4.00 10.00
16 Andruw Jones/40 5.00 12.00
17 Manny Ramirez/107 4.00 10.00
18 Derrek Lee/453 4.00 10.00

2005 Prime Patches All-Star Materials Double Patch

*DBL p/r 50: .75X TO 2X JUM p/r 104-493
TWO AUTOS OR GAME-USED PER PACK
PRINT RUNS B/WN 1-50 COPIES PER
NO PRICING ON QTY OF 10 OR LESS

2005 Prime Patches All-Star Materials Double Swatch

*DBL p/r 79-150: .4X TO 1X JUM p/r 104-493
*DBL p/r 79-150: .3X TO .8X JUM p/r 40
*DBL p/r 40-48: .5X TO 1.2X JUM p/r 104-493
TWO AUTOS OR GAME-USED PER PACK
PRINT RUNS B/WN 1-150 COPIES PER
NO PRICING ON QTY OF 15 OR LESS
5 Barry Zito Jsy-Jsy/48 4.00 10.00
13 P.LoDuca Chest Prot-Jsy/87 3.00 8.00

2005 Prime Patches All-Star Materials Double Swatch Prime

*DBL p/r 36-62: .6X TO 1.5X JUM p/r 104-493
*DBL p/r 36-62: .5X TO 1.2X JUM p/r 40
TWO AUTOS OR GAME-USED PER PACK
PRINT RUNS B/WN 1-62 COPIES PER
NO PRICING ON QTY OF 5 OR LESS
5 Barry Zito Jsy-Jsy/59 5.00 12.00

2005 Prime Patches All-Star Materials Triple Patch

*TRI p/r 25: 1.25X TO 3X JUM p/r 104-493
*TRI p/r 25: 1X TO 2.5X JUM p/r 40
TWO AUTOS OR GAME-USED PER PACK
PRINT RUNS B/WN 1-25 COPIES PER
NO PRICING ON QTY OF 10 OR LESS

2005 Prime Patches All-Star Materials Triple Swatch

*TRI p/r 75-150: .5X TO 1.2X JUM p/r 104-493
*TRI p/r 75-150: .3X TO .8X JUM p/r 25
*TRI p/r 47-55: .6X TO 1.5X JUM p/r 104-493
TWO AUTOS OR GAME-USED PER PACK
PRINT RUNS B/WN 1-150 COPIES PER
NO PRICING ON QTY OF 19 OR LESS
5 Barry Zito FG-H-J/32 6.00 15.00
6 Mark Teixeira B-H-SH/78 5.00 12.00
13 Paul Lo Duca B-J-SH/47 5.00 12.00

2005 Prime Patches All-Star Materials Triple Swatch Prime

*TRI p/r 103: .6X TO 1.5X JUM p/r 104-493
*TRI p/r 24-35: 1X TO 2.5X JUM p/r 104-493
*TRI p/r 24-35: .6X TO 1.5X JUM p/r 25
TWO AUTOS OR GAME-USED PER PACK
PRINT RUNS B/WN 1-103 COPIES PER
NO PRICING ON QTY OF 10 OR LESS
5 Barry Zito FG-J-SH/35 8.00 20.00

2005 Prime Patches All-Star Materials Autograph

TWO AUTOS OR GAME-USED PER PACK
TIER 1 QTY B/WN 1-50 COPIES PER
TIER 2 QTY B/WN 51-100 COPIES PER
TIER 4 QTY B/WN 251-800 COPIES PER
CARDS ARE NOT SERIAL-NUMBERED
PRINT RUN INFO PROVIDED BY DONRUSS
1 Johan Santana T1/50 * 15.00 40.00
2 Melvin Mora T1/50 * 6.00 15.00
3 Miguel Cabrera T1/50 * 20.00 50.00
6 Mark Teixeira T1/25 * 15.00 40.00
10 Paul Konerko T4 10.00 25.00
11 Roy Oswalt T1/25 * 10.00 25.00
15 Scott Rolen T1/25 * 15.00 40.00
18 Derrek Lee T2/75 * 15.00 40.00

2005 Prime Patches Hall of Fame Materials Bat

*BAT p/r 150: .3X TO .8X JUM p/r 105-230
TWO AUTOS OR GAME-USED PER PACK
PRINT RUNS B/WN 1-150 COPIES PER
NO PRICING ON QTY OF 12 OR LESS

2005 Prime Patches Hall of Fame Materials Jersey

*JSY p/r 138-150: .3X TO .8X JUM p/r 105-230
TWO AUTOS OR GAME-USED PER PACK
PRINT RUNS B/WN 1-150 COPIES PER
NO PRICING ON QTY OF 5 OR LESS
10 Reggie Jackson/24 5.00 12.00

2005 Prime Patches Hall of Fame Materials Name Plate Patch

*PAT p/r 39: .75X TO 2X JUM p/r 105-230
*PAT p/r 21-33: 1X TO 2.5X JUM p/r 105-230
TWO AUTOS OR GAME-USED PER PACK
PRINT RUNS B/WN 3-39 COPIES PER
NO PRICING ON QTY OF 17 OR LESS
4 Mike Schmidt/33 15.00 40.00

2005 Prime Patches Hall of Fame Materials Number Patch

*PAT p/r 75-86: .6X TO 1.5X JUM p/r 105-230
*PAT p/r 59: .75X TO 2X JUM p/r 105-230
*PAT p/r 21-35: 1X TO 2.5X JUM p/r 105-230
TWO AUTOS OR GAME-USED PER PACK
PRINT RUNS B/WN 19-86 COPIES PER
NO PRICING ON QTY OF 19 OR LESS
4 Mike Schmidt/77 10.00 25.00
5 George Brett/21 20.00 50.00
10 Reggie Jackson/86 6.00 15.00

2005 Prime Patches Hall of Fame Materials Team Logo Patch

*PAT p/r 56: .75X TO 2X JUM p/r 105-230
*PAT p/r 20-35: 1X TO 2.5X JUM p/r 105-230
TWO AUTOS OR GAME-USED PER PACK
PRINT RUNS B/WN 5-56 COPIES PER
NO PRICING ON QTY OF 19 OR LESS
4 Mike Schmidt/33 15.00 40.00

2005 Prime Patches Hall of Fame Materials Jumbo Swatch

PRINT RUNS B/WN 17-230 COPIES PER
NO PRICING ON QTY OF 17
PRIME PRINT RUNS B/WN 1-28 COPIES PER
NO PRIME PRICING DUE TO SCARCITY
TWO AUTOS OR GAME-USED PER PACK
1 Nolan Ryan/116 15.00 40.00
2 Eddie Murray/179 6.00 15.00
3 Paul Molitor/230 3.00 8.00
6 Dennis Eckersley/192 3.00 8.00
7 Dave Winfield/105 3.00 8.00
8 Rod Carew/107 4.00 10.00
9 Ozzie Smith/222 8.00 20.00

2005 Prime Patches Hall of Fame Materials Double Patch

*DBL p/r 25: 1X TO 2.5X JUM p/r 104-493
TWO AUTOS OR GAME-USED PER PACK
PRINT RUNS B/WN 1-25 COPIES PER
NO PRICING ON QTY OF 15 OR LESS

2005 Prime Patches Hall of Fame Materials Double Swatch

*DBL p/r 83-150: .4X TO 1X JUM p/r 105-230
*DBL p/r 55: .5X TO 1.2X JUM p/r 105-230
TWO AUTOS OR GAME-USED PER PACK
PRINT RUNS B/WN 1-150 COPIES PER
NO PRICING ON QTY OF 5 OR LESS
5 George Brett Hat-Hat/106 10.00 25.00
10 Reggie Jackson Jsy-Jsy/30 6.00 15.00

2005 Prime Patches Hall of Fame Materials Double Swatch Prime

*DBL p/r 100: .5X TO 1.2X JUM p/r 105-230
TWO AUTOS OR GAME-USED PER PACK
PRINT RUNS B/WN 1-100 COPIES PER
NO PRICING ON QTY OF 15 OR LESS
4 Mike Schmidt Jsy-Stirrup/64 12.50 30.00
5 George Brett Hat-Jsy/29 15.00 40.00

2005 Prime Patches Hall of Fame Materials Triple Swatch

*TRI p/r 150: .5X TO 1.2X JUM p/r 105-230
*TRI p/r 40-45: .6X TO 1.5X JUM p/r 105-230
TWO AUTOS OR GAME-USED PER PACK
PRINT RUNS B/WN 15-150 COPIES PER
NO PRICING ON QTY OF 15
4 Mike Schmidt H-H-ST/150 10.00 25.00
5 George Brett H-H-J/25 15.00 40.00
10 Reggie Jackson J-J-J/30 8.00 20.00

2005 Prime Patches Hall of Fame Materials Triple Swatch Prime

TWO AUTOS OR GAME-USED PER PACK
PRINT RUNS B/WN 1-40 COPIES PER
NO PRICING ON QTY OF 10 OR LESS
4 Mike Schmidt J-P-ST/40 15.00 40.00
5 George Brett B-H-J/22 20.00 50.00
10 Reggie Jackson J-J-J/25 10.00 25.00

2005 Prime Patches Hall of Fame Materials Quad Swatch

*QUADp/r101-150: .6XTO1.5X JUMp/r105-230
*QUAD p/r 52: .75X TO 2X JUM p/r 105-230
*QUAD p/r 2-30: 1X TO 2.5X JUM p/r 105-230
TWO AUTOS OR GAME-USED PER PACK
PRINT RUNS BAWN 1-150 COPIES PER
NO PRICING ON QTY OF 16 OR LESS
4 M.Schmidt BG-FG-H-JK/20 20.00 50.00
5 George Brett B-H-J-J/29 10.00 25.00
10 Reggie Jackson J-J-J-J/30 10.00 25.00

2005 Prime Patches Hall of Fame Materials Quad Swatch Prime

*QUADp/r44-60: 1X TO 2.5X JUMp/r105-230
TWO AUTOS OR GAME-USED PER PACK
PRINT RUNS B/WN 1-60 COPIES PER
NO PRICING ON QTY OF 17 OR LESS
4 M.Schmidt BL-J-J-ST/60 20.00 50.00
10 R.Jackson J-J-J-J/25 12.50 30.00

2005 Prime Patches Hall of Fame Materials Autograph

TWO AUTOS OR GAME-USED PER PACK
TIER 1 QTY B/WN 1-50 COPIES PER
CARDS ARE NOT SERIAL-NUMBERED
PRINT RUN INFO PROVIDED BY DONRUSS
NO PRICING ON QTY OF 5
1 Nolan Ryan T1/50 * 50.00 100.00
3 Paul Molitor T1/50 * 10.00 25.00
4 Mike Schmidt T1/50 * 15.00 40.00
5 George Brett T1/25 * 30.00 60.00
6 Dennis Eckersley T1/50 * 10.00 25.00
8 Rod Carew T1/25 * 15.00 40.00
9 Ozzie Smith T1/25 * 30.00 60.00

2005 Prime Patches Hall of Fame Materials Autograph Bat

*BAT p/r 50: .4X TO 1X AU T1
TWO AUTOS OR GAME-USED PER PACK
PRINT RUNS B/WN 5-50 COPIES PER
NO PRICING ON QTY OF 5

2005 Prime Patches Hall of Fame Materials Autograph Jersey

*JSY p/r 25-50: .4X TO 1X AU T1
TWO AUTOS OR GAME-USED PER PACK
PRINT RUNS B/WN 5-50 COPIES PER
NO PRICING ON QTY OF 5

2005 Prime Patches Hall of Fame Materials Autograph Number Patch

*PATCH p/r 25-30: .5X TO 1.2X AU T1
TWO AUTOS OR GAME-USED PER PACK
PRINT RUNS B/WN 1-30 COPIES PER
NO PRICING ON QTY OF 10 OR LESS

2005 Prime Patches Hall of Fame Materials Autograph Double Swatch

*DBL p/r 100: .3X TO .8X AU T1
*DBL p/r 25-50: .4X TO 1X AU T1
TWO AUTOS OR GAME-USED PER PACK
PRINT RUNS B/WN 1-100 COPIES PER
NO PRICING ON QTY OF 10 OR LESS

2005 Prime Patches Hall of Fame Materials Autograph Triple Swatch

*TRI p/r 25-50: .5X TO 1.2X AU T1
TWO AUTOS OR GAME-USED PER PACK
PRINT RUNS B/WN 1-50 COPIES PER
NO PRICING ON QTY OF 5 OR LESS

2005 Prime Patches Hall of Fame Materials Autograph Quad Swatch

*QUAD p/r 25: .6X TO 1.5X AU T1
TWO AUTOS OR GAME-USED PER PACK
PRINT RUNS B/WN 1-25 COPIES PER
NO PRICING ON QTY OF 10 OR LESS

2005 Prime Patches Major League Materials Bat

*BAT p/r 142-150: .3X TO .8X JUM p/r 70-532
*BAT p/r 142-150: .25X TO .6X JUM p/r 40-52
*BAT p/r 142-150: .2X TO .5X JUM p/r 23-34
TWO AUTOS OR GAME-USED PER PACK
PRINT RUNS B/WN 1-150 COPIES PER
NO PRICING ON QTY OF 2 OR LESS
2 Paul Konerko/150 2.50 6.00
9 Preston Wilson/42 2.50 6.00
17 Alfonso Soriano/150 2.50 6.00
22 B.J. Upton/150 2.50 6.00
25 Craig Wilson/150 2.00 5.00
33 Angel Berroa/150 2.00 5.00
38 Austin Kearns/150 2.00 5.00
39 Johnny Estrada/150 2.00 5.00
42 Orlando Hudson/150 2.00 5.00
52 Edgardo Alfonzo/150 -2.00 5.00
53 Jay Gibbons/142 2.00 5.00

2005 Prime Patches Major League Materials Jersey

*JSY p/r 150: .3X TO .8X JUM p/r 70-532
TWO AUTOS OR GAME-USED PER PACK
PRINT RUNS B/WN 1-150 COPIES PER
NO PRICING ON QTY OF 5 OR LESS
30 Nick Johnson/27 3.00 8.00

2005 Prime Patches Major League Materials Name Plate Patch

*PAT p/r 52-62: .75X TO 2X JUM p/r 70-532
*PAT p/r 20-34: 1X TO 2.5X JUM p/r 70-532
*PAT p/r 20-34: .75X TO 2X JUM p/r 40-52
TWO AUTOS OR GAME-USED PER PACK
PRINT RUNS B/WN 1-62 COPIES PER
NO PRICING ON QTY OF 18 OR LESS
11 David Dellucci/23 8.00 20.00
45 Juan Gonzalez/52 6.00 15.00

2005 Prime Patches Major League Materials Number Patch

*PAT p/r 69-111: .6X TO 1.5X JUM p/r 70-532
*PAT p/r 39-53: .75X TO 2X JUM p/r 70-532
*PAT p/r 25-30: 1X TO 2.5X JUM p/r 70-532
TWO AUTOS OR GAME-USED PER PACK
PRINT RUNS B/WN 1-111 COPIES PER
NO PRICING ON QTY OF 19 OR LESS
6 A.J. Pierzynski/69 5.00 12.00

2005 Prime Patches Major League Materials Sleeve Patch

*PAT p/r 20: 1X TO 2.5X JUM p/r 70-532
TWO AUTOS OR GAME-USED PER PACK
PRINT RUNS B/WN 1-20 COPIES PER
NO PRICING ON QTY OF 16 OR LESS

2005 Prime Patches Major League Materials Team Logo Patch

*PAT p/r 61-74: .6X TO 1.5X JUM p/r 70-532
*PAT p/r 42-46: .75X TO 2X JUM p/r 70-532
*PAT p/r 23-33: 1X TO 2.5X JUM p/r 70-532
TWO AUTOS OR GAME-USED PER PACK
PRINT RUNS B/WN 1-74 COPIES PER
NO PRICING ON QTY OF 15 OR LESS
6 A.J. Pierzynski/27 8.00 20.00
11 David Dellucci/28 8.00 20.00
22 B.J. Upton/23 8.00 20.00

2005 Prime Patches Major League Materials Jumbo Swatch

PRINT RUNS B/WN 1-532 COPIES PER
NO PRICING ON QTY OF 19 OR LESS
PRIME PRINT RUNS B/WN 1-10 COPIES PER
NO PRIME PRICING DUE TO SCARCITY
TWO AUTOS OR GAME-USED PER PACK
1 Roy Oswalt/23 5.00 12.00
3 Bill Hall/449 2.50 6.00
4 Jay Payton/500 2.50 6.00
10 Andy Pettitte/250 4.00 10.00
12 Craig Biggio/424 4.00 10.00
14 Steve Finley/261 3.00 8.00
15 Geoff Jenkins/375 2.50 6.00

20 Aaron Boone/245 3.00 8.00
21 Richie Sexson/532 3.00 8.00
24 Scott Podsednik/150 3.00 8.00
26 Al Leiter/34 5.00 12.00
27 Sean Casey/163 3.00 8.00
28 Jason Jennings/297 2.50 6.00
31 Lyle Overbay/40 3.00 8.00
32 Ben Grieve/96 2.50 6.00
35 Brian Giles/315 3.00 8.00
36 Cal Ripken/500 10.00 25.00
40 Rondell White/335 2.50 6.00
46 Gary Sheffield/346 3.00 8.00
47 Michael Cuddyer/52 3.00 8.00
48 Mike Cameron/222 2.50 6.00
49 Brad Radke/70 3.00 8.00
50 J.D. Drew/500 3.00 8.00
51 Curt Schilling/256 4.00 10.00

2005 Prime Patches Major League Materials Double Swatch
*DBL p/r 75-150: .4X TO 1X JUM p/r 70-532
*DBL p/r 22: .6X TO 1.5X JUM p/r 70-532
TWO AUTOS OR GAME-USED PER PACK
PRINT RUNS B/WN 1-150 COPIES PER
NO PRICING ON QTY OF 14 OR LESS
17 Alfonso Soriano Jsy-Jsy/107 3.00 8.00
30 N.Johnson Jsy-Jsy/150 2.50 6.00
41 Barry Zito Jsy-Jsy/75 3.00 8.00
52 E.Alfonzo Bat-Jsy/150 2.50 6.00

2005 Prime Patches Major League Materials Double Swatch Prime
*DBL p/r 96-143: .5X TO 1.2X JUM p/r 70-532
*DBL p/r 96-143: .3X TO .8X JUM p/r 23-34
*DBL p/r 41-63: .6X TO 1.5X JUM p/r 70-532
*DBL p/r 23-24: .75X TO 2X JUM p/r 70-532
TWO AUTOS OR GAME-USED PER PACK
PRINT RUNS B/WN 1-143 COPIES PER
NO PRICING ON QTY OF 13 OR LESS
17 Alfonso Soriano Jsy-Jsy/41 5.00 12.00

2005 Prime Patches Major League Materials Triple Swatch
*TRI p/r 81-150: .5X TO 1.2X JUM p/r 70-532
*TRI p/r 81-150: .4X TO 1X JUM p/r 40-52
*TRI p/r 36-65: .6X TO 1.5X JUM p/r 70-532
*TRI p/r 25: .5X TO 1.2X JUM p/r 23-34
TWO AUTOS OR GAME-USED PER PACK
PRINT RUNS B/WN 1-150 COPIES PER
NO PRICING ON QTY OF 18 OR LESS
29 Jody Gerut B-J-J/65 4.00 10.00
30 N.Johnson J-J-SH/50 4.00 10.00
39 J.Estrada B-B-SG/103 3.00 8.00
42 O.Hudson B-B-FG/150 3.00 8.00
52 E.Alfonzo B-J-J/115 3.00 8.00
53 Jay Gibbons B-B-SH/36 4.00 10.00

2005 Prime Patches Major League Materials Triple Swatch Prime
*TRI p/r 90: .6X TO 1.5X JUM p/r 70-532
*TRI p/r 60: .75X TO 2X JUM p/r 70-532
TWO AUTOS OR GAME-USED PER PACK
PRINT RUNS B/WN 1-90 COPIES PER
NO PRICING ON QTY OF 13 OR LESS

2005 Prime Patches Major League Materials Quad Swatch
*QUAD p/r 86-150: .6X TO 1.5X JUMp/r70-532
*QUAD p/r 86-150: .5X TO 1.2X JUM p/r 40-52
*QUAD p/r 86-150: .4X TO 1X JUM p/r 23-34
*QUAD p/r 52-59: .75X TO 2X JUM p/r 70-532
TWO AUTOS OR GAME-USED PER PACK
PRINT RUNS B/WN 1-150 COPIES PER
NO PRICING ON QTY OF 17 OR LESS
17 A.Soriano B-B-J-J/52 6.00 15.00
29 Jody Gerut B-J-J-J/100 4.00 10.00
30 N.Johnson J-J-J-SH/55 5.00 12.00
41 Barry Zito J-J-J-J/52 6.00 15.00
45 J.Gonzalez J-J-J-J/55 6.00 15.00

2005 Prime Patches Major League Materials Quad Swatch Prime
*QUAD p/r 73-120: .75X TO 2X JUMp/r70-532
*QUAD p/r 46-50: 1X TO 2.5X JUM p/r 70-532
*QUAD p/r 22-30: 1.25X TO 3X JUMp/r70-532
TWO AUTOS OR GAME-USED PER PACK
PRINT RUNS B/WN 1-120 COPIES PER
NO PRICING ON QTY OF 9 OR LESS
41 Barry Zito FG-J-J-J/22 10.00 25.00

2005 Prime Patches Major League Materials Autograph
TWO AUTOS OR GAME-USED PER PACK
TIER 1 QTY B/WN 1-50 COPIES PER
TIER 2 QTY B/WN 51-100 COPIES PER
TIER 3 QTY B/WN 101-250 COPIES PER
TIER 4 QTY B/WN 251-800 COPIES PER
TIER 5 QTY B/WN 801-1200 COPIES PER
CARDS ARE NOT SERIAL-NUMBERED
PRINT RUN INFO PROVIDED BY DONRUSS
NO PRICING ON QTY OF 16 OR LESS
1 Roy Oswalt T2/100 * 8.00 20.00
2 Paul Konerko T2/100 * 12.50 30.00
5 Danny Kolb T4 4.00 10.00
7 Wade Miller T5 4.00 10.00
8 Ben Sheets T1/25 * 4.00 10.00
9 Preston Wilson T4 4.00 10.00
11 David Dellucci T5 6.00 15.00
13 Edgar Renteria T4 6.00 15.00
14 Steve Finley T3 6.00 15.00
16 Livan Hernandez T5 6.00 15.00
17 Alfonso Soriano T1/25 * 10.00 25.00
18 Jamie Moyer T5 4.00 10.00
19 Brett Myers T5 4.00 10.00
22 B.J. Upton T4 8.00 20.00
23 Cliff Lee T4 6.00 15.00
25 Craig Wilson T4 4.00 10.00
27 Sean Casey T1/50 * 10.00 25.00
29 Jody Gerut T2/71 * 5.00 12.00
30 Nick Johnson T4 4.00 10.00
31 Lyle Overbay T4 4.00 10.00
33 Angel Berroa T1/37 * 6.00 15.00
34 Scott Rolen T1/25 * 15.00 40.00
37 Jermaine Dye T4 6.00 15.00
38 Austin Kearns T1/31 * 6.00 15.00
42 Orlando Hudson T5 4.00 10.00
43 Francisco Cordero T5 4.00 10.00
44 Bobby Crosby T4 6.00 15.00
45 Juan Gonzalez T5 6.00 15.00
46 Gary Sheffield T1/25 * 10.00 25.00
53 Jay Gibbons T2/87 * 5.00 12.00

2005 Prime Patches Major League Materials Autograph Bat
*BAT p/r 200-250: .4X TO 1X AU T3-T5
*BAT p/r 200-250: .3X TO .8X AU T2
*BAT p/r 200-250: .25X TO .6X AU T1
*BAT p/r 100: .5X TO 1.2X AU T3-T5
*BAT p/r 25-50: .6X TO 1.5X AU T3-T5
*BAT p/r 25-50: .5X TO 1.2X AU T2
*BAT p/r 25-50: .4X TO 1X AU T1
TWO AUTOS OR GAME-USED PER PACK
PRINT RUNS B/WN 1-250 COPIES PER
NO PRICING ON QTY OF 15 OR LESS
39 Johnny Estrada/250 4.00 10.00

2005 Prime Patches Major League Materials Autograph Jersey
*JSY p/r 119-250: .4X TO 1X AU T3-T5
*JSY p/r 81-100: .5X TO 1.2X AU T3-T5
*JSY p/r 25-50: .6X TO 1.5X AU T3-T5
*JSY p/r 25-50: .4X TO 1X AU T1
TWO AUTOS OR GAME-USED PER PACK
PRINT RUNS B/WN 1-250 COPIES PER
NO PRICING ON QTY OF 14 OR LESS
36 Cal Ripken/50 40.00 80.00

2005 Prime Patches Major League Materials Autograph Name Plate Patch
*PATCH p/r 20-50: .75X TO 2X AU T3-T5
TWO AUTOS OR GAME-USED PER PACK
PRINT RUNS B/WN 1-28 COPIES PER
NO PRICING ON QTY OF 18 OR LESS

2005 Prime Patches Major League Materials Autograph Number Patch
*PATCH p/r 20-33: .75X TO 2X AU T3-T5
*PATCH p/r 20-33: .6X TO 1.5X AU T2
*PATCH p/r 20-33: .5X TO 1.2X AU T1
TWO AUTOS OR GAME-USED PER PACK
PRINT RUNS B/WN 1-33 COPIES PER
NO PRICING ON QTY OF 8 OR LESS

2005 Prime Patches Major League Materials Autograph Team Logo Patch
*PATCH p/r 21-40: .75X TO 2X AU T3-T5
*PATCH p/r 21-40: .5X TO 1.2X AU T1
TWO AUTOS OR GAME-USED PER PACK
PRINT RUNS B/WN 1-40 COPIES PER
NO PRICING ON QTY OF 10 OR LESS

2005 Prime Patches Major League Materials Autograph Double Patch
TWO AUTOS OR GAME-USED PER PACK
PRINT RUNS B/WN 1-25 COPIES PER
NO PRICING ON QTY OF 5 OR LESS
4 Jay Payton/25 8.00 20.00

2005 Prime Patches Major League Materials Autograph Double Swatch
*DBL p/r 150-250: .4X TO 1X AU T3-T5
*DBL p/r 150-250: .25X TO .6X AU T1
*DBL p/r 75-100: .5X TO 1.2X AU T3-T5
*DBL p/r 75-100: .3X TO .8X AU T1
*DBL p/r 25-50: .6X TO 1.5X AU T3-T5
*DBL p/r 25-50: .5X TO 1.2X AU T2
*DBL p/r 25-50: .4X TO 1X AU T1
TWO AUTOS OR GAME-USED PER PACK
PRINT RUNS B/WN 1-250 COPIES PER
NO PRICING ON QTY OF 14 OR LESS
36 Cal Ripken Jkt-Jsy/50 75.00 150.00
41 Barry Zito Jsy-Jsy/75 8.00 20.00

2005 Prime Patches Major League Materials Autograph Double Swatch Prime
*DBL p/r 20: .4X TO 1X AU T1
TWO AUTOS OR GAME-USED PER PACK
PRINT RUNS B/WN 1-20 COPIES PER
NO PRICING ON QTY OF 15 OR LESS

2005 Prime Patches Major League Materials Autograph Triple Patch
TWO AUTOS OR GAME-USED PER PACK
PRINT RUNS B/WN 1-25 COPIES PER
NO PRICING ON QTY OF 5 OR LESS
4 Jay Payton/25 10.00 25.00

2005 Prime Patches Major League Materials Autograph Triple Swatch
*TRI p/r 105-250: .5X TO 1.2X AU T3-T5
*TRI p/r 105-250: .3X TO .8X AU T1
*TRI p/r 67-100: .6X TO 1.5X AU T3-T5
*TRI p/r 67-100: .5X TO 1.2X AU T2
*TRI p/r 67-100: .4X TO 1X AU T1
*TRI p/r 25-50: .75X TO 2X AU T3-T5
*TRI p/r 25-50: .6X TO 1.5X AU T2
*TRI p/r 25-50: .5X TO 1.2X AU T1
TWO AUTOS OR GAME-USED PER PACK
PRINT RUNS B/WN 1-250 COPIES PER
NO PRICING ON QTY OF 17 OR LESS
39 Johnny Estrada B-B-SG/25 8.00 20.00
41 Barry Zito J-J-J/40 12.50 30.00

2005 Prime Patches Major League Materials Autograph Triple Swatch Prime
*TRI p/r 25-42: 1X TO 2.5X AU T3-T5
TWO AUTOS OR GAME-USED PER PACK
PRINT RUNS B/WN 1-42 COPIES PER
NO PRICING ON QTY OF 10 OR LESS

2005 Prime Patches Major League Materials Autograph Quad Patch
TWO AUTOS OR GAME-USED PER PACK
PRINT RUNS B/WN 1-25 COPIES PER
NO PRICING ON QTY OF 5 OR LESS
4 Jay Payton/25 12.50 30.00

2005 Prime Patches Major League Materials Autograph Quad Swatch
*QUAD p/r 180-250: .6X TO 1.5X AU T3-T5
*QUAD p/r 68-100: .75X TO 2X AU T3-T5
*QUAD p/r 68-100: .5X TO 1.2X AU T1
*QUAD p/r 25-50: 1X TO 2.5X AU T3-T5
*QUAD p/r 25-50: .75X TO 2X AU T2
*QUAD p/r 25-50: .6X TO 1.5X AU T1
TWO AUTOS OR GAME-USED PER PACK
PRINT RUNS B/WN 1-250 COPIES PER
NO PRICING ON QTY OF 15 OR LESS
36 Cal Ripken JK-J-J-J/50 50.00 100.00
39 J.Estr B-B-SG-SG/100 8.00 20.00
41 Barry Zito J-J-J-J/25 15.00 40.00

2005 Prime Patches Major League Materials Autograph Quad Swatch Prime
*QUAD p/r 25: 1.25X TO 3X AU T3-T5
TWO AUTOS OR GAME-USED PER PACK
PRINT RUNS B/WN 1-25 COPIES PER
NO PRICING ON QTY OF 10 OR LESS

2005 Prime Patches Next Generation Bat
*BAT p/r 150: .3X TO .8X JUM p/r 96-399
*BAT p/r 28: .5X TO 1.2X JUM p/r 96-399
TWO AUTOS OR GAME-USED PER PACK
PRINT RUNS B/WN 1-150 COPIES PER
NO PRICING ON QTY OF 1
3 Johnny Estrada/150 2.00 5.00
4 Adam Dunn/150 2.50 6.00

2005 Prime Patches Next Generation Name Plate Patch
*PAT p/r 26-29: 1X TO 2.5X JUM p/r 96-399
TWO AUTOS OR GAME-USED PER PACK
PRINT RUNS B/WN 1-29 COPIES PER
NO PRICING ON QTY OF 18 OR LESS
4 Adam Dunn/29 8.00 20.00

2005 Prime Patches Next Generation Number Patch
TWO AUTOS OR GAME-USED PER PACK
PRINT RUNS B/WN 1-70 COPIES PER
NO PRICING ON QTY OF 19 OR LESS
4 Adam Dunn/70 5.00 12.00

2005 Prime Patches Next Generation Team Logo Patch
*PAT p/r 32: 1X TO 2.5X JUM p/r 96-399
TWO AUTOS OR GAME-USED PER PACK
PRINT RUNS B/WN 1-32 COPIES PER
NO PRICING ON QTY OF 15 OR LESS

2005 Prime Patches Next Generation Jumbo Swatch
PRINT RUNS B/WN 1-399 COPIES PER
NO PRICING ON QTY OF 12 OR LESS
PRIME PRINT RUNS B/WN 5-10 COPIES PER
NO PRIME PRICING DUE TO SCARCITY
TWO AUTOS OR GAME-USED PER PACK
2 Josh Beckett/391 3.00 8.00
5 Hank Blalock/229 3.00 8.00
6 David Wright/210 6.00 15.00
8 Carlos Zambrano/125 3.00 8.00
9 Cliff Lee/399 2.50 6.00
11 Justin Morneau/156 3.00 8.00
12 Dontrelle Willis/175 3.00 8.00
14 Edwin Jackson/96 2.50 6.00

2005 Prime Patches Next Generation Double Patch
*DBL p/r 113: .6X TO 1.5X JUM p/r 96-399
TWO AUTOS OR GAME-USED PER PACK
PRINT RUNS B/WN 1-113 COPIES PER
NO PRICING ON QTY OF 4 OR LESS
4 Adam Dunn/50 6.00 15.00
7 Ryan Wagner/35 6.00 15.00

2005 Prime Patches Next Generation Double Swatch
TWO AUTOS OR GAME-USED PER PACK
PRINT RUNS B/WN 1-20 COPIES PER
NO PRICING ON QTY OF 3 OR LESS
4 Adam Dunn Jsy-Jsy/20 5.00 12.00

2005 Prime Patches Next Generation Double Swatch Prime
TWO AUTOS OR GAME-USED PER PACK
PRINT RUNS B/WN 1-62 COPIES PER
NO PRICING ON QTY OF 15 OR LESS
4 Adam Dunn Jsy-Jsy/62 5.00 12.00

2005 Prime Patches Next Generation Triple Patch
*TRI p/r 43: 1X TO 2.5X JUM p/r 96-399
TWO AUTOS OR GAME-USED PER PACK
PRINT RUNS B/WN 1-43 COPIES PER
NO PRICING ON QTY OF 15 OR LESS

2005 Prime Patches Next Generation Triple Swatch
*TRI p/r 66-150: .5X TO 1.2X JUM p/r 96-399
TWO AUTOS OR GAME-USED PER PACK
PRINT RUNS B/WN 1-150 COPIES PER
NO PRICING ON QTY OF 15 OR LESS
4 Adam Dunn B-H-SH/62 5.00 12.00

2005 Prime Patches Next Generation Triple Swatch Prime
*TRI p/r 38: .75X TO 2X JUM p/r 96-399
*TRI p/r 30: 1X TO 2.5X JUM p/r 96-399
TWO AUTOS OR GAME-USED PER PACK
PRINT RUNS B/WN 5-84 COPIES PER
NO PRICING ON QTY OF 19 OR LESS
4 Adam Dunn B-B-J/84 5.00 12.00

2005 Prime Patches Next Generation Quad Swatch
*QUADp/r100-150:.6X TO 1.5X JUMp/r 96-399
*QUAD p/r 39-45: .75X TO 2X JUM p/r 96-399
TWO AUTOS OR GAME-USED PER PACK
PRINT RUNS B/WN 1-150 COPIES PER
NO PRICING ON QTY OF 7 OR LESS
4 Adam Dunn B-H-J-SH/101 5.00 12.00
7 Ryan Wagner J-J-J-J/150 4.00 10.00
10 Ken Harvey J-J-J-J/45 5.00 12.00
13 Carl Crawford J-J-J-J/150 5.00 12.00

2005 Prime Patches Next Generation Autograph
TWO AUTOS OR GAME-USED PER PACK
TIER 1 QTY B/WN 1-50 COPIES PER
TIER 3 QTY B/WN 101-250 COPIES PER
TIER 4 QTY B/WN 251-800 COPIES PER
CARDS ARE NOT SERIAL-NUMBERED
PRINT RUN INFO PROVIDED BY DONRUSS
NO PRICING ON QTY OF 10 OR LESS
1 Brian Roberts T4 6.00 15.00
3 Johnny Estrada T3 4.00 10.00
7 Ryan Wagner T4 4.00 10.00
8 Carlos Zambrano T1/33 * 10.00 25.00
9 Cliff Lee T4 6.00 15.00
10 Ken Harvey T4 4.00 10.00
14 Edwin Jackson T4 4.00 10.00

2005 Prime Patches Next Generation Autograph Bat
*BAT p/r 142-250: .4X TO 1X AU T3-T5
TWO AUTOS OR GAME-USED PER PACK
PRINT RUNS B/WN 25-250 COPIES PER
2 Josh Beckett/25 15.00 40.00
6 David Wright/150 6.00 15.00
11 Justin Morneau/150 6.00 15.00

2005 Prime Patches Next Generation Autograph Jersey
*JSY p/r 121-250: .4X TO 1X AU T3-T5
*JSY p/r 121-250: .25X TO .6X AU T1
*JSY p/r 79: .5X TO 1.2X AU T3-T5
*JSY p/r 25-41: .6X TO 1.5X AU T3-T5
TWO AUTOS OR GAME-USED PER PACK
PRINT RUNS B/WN 25-250 COPIES PER
6 David Wright/125 20.00 50.00
11 Justin Morneau/25 10.00 25.00

2005 Prime Patches Next Generation Autograph Name Plate Patch
*PATCH p/r 46: .5X TO 1.2X AU T1
TWO AUTOS OR GAME-USED PER PACK
PRINT RUNS B/WN 1-46 COPIES PER
NO PRICING ON QTY OF 15 OR LESS

2005 Prime Patches Next Generation Autograph Number Patch
*PATCH p/r 62-63: .75X TO 2X AU T3-T5
TWO AUTOS OR GAME-USED PER PACK
PRINT RUNS B/WN 7-63 COPIES PER
NO PRICING ON QTY OF 18 OR LESS

2005 Prime Patches Next Generation Autograph Team Logo Patch
*PATCH p/r 140: .5X TO 1.2X AU T3-T5
*PATCH p/r 31-41: .75X TO 2X AU T3-T5
*PATCH p/r 31-41: .5X TO 1.2X AU T1
TWO AUTOS OR GAME-USED PER PACK
PRINT RUNS B/WN 1-140 COPIES PER
NO PRICING ON QTY OF 1
9 Cliff Lee/140 10.00 25.00

2005 Prime Patches Next Generation Autograph Double Swatch
*DBL p/r 150: .4X TO 1X AU T3-T5
TWO AUTOS OR GAME-USED PER PACK
STATED PRINT RUN 150 SERIAL #'d SETS

2005 Prime Patches Next Generation Autograph Quad Patch
TWO AUTOS OR GAME-USED PER PACK
PRINT RUNS B/WN 1-10 COPIES PER
NO PRICING DUE TO SCARCITY

2005 Prime Patches Next Generation Autograph Quad Swatch
*QUAD p/r 150: .6X TO 1.5X AU T3-T5
*QUAD p/r 49: 1X TO 2.5X AU T3-T5
TWO AUTOS OR GAME-USED PER PACK
PRINT RUNS B/WN 1-150 COPIES PER
NO PRICING ON QTY OF 1

2005 Prime Patches Next Generation Autograph Quad Swatch Prime
TWO AUTOS OR GAME-USED PER PACK
STATED PRINT RUN 1 SERIAL #'d SET
NO PRICING DUE TO SCARCITY

2005 Prime Patches Past and Present Bat
*BAT p/r 118-150: .3X TO .8X JUM p/r 89-532
TWO AUTOS OR GAME-USED PER PACK
PRINT RUNS B/WN 1-150 COPIES PER
NO PRICING ON QTY OF 3 OR LESS
6 Rafael Palmeiro/50 4.00 10.00

2005 Prime Patches Past and Present Jersey
*JSY p/r 150: .3X TO .8X JUM p/r 89-532
TWO AUTOS OR GAME-USED PER PACK
PRINT RUNS B/WN 1-150 COPIES PER
NO PRICING ON QTY OF 13 OR LESS
6 Rafael Palmeiro/150 3.00 8.00

2005 Prime Patches Past and Present Jersey Combo
*COM p/r 150: .4X TO 1X JUM p/r 89-532
*COM p/r 55-56: .5X TO 1.2X JUM p/r 89-532
TWO AUTOS OR GAME-USED PER PACK
PRINT RUNS B/WN 1-150 COPIES PER
NO PRICING ON QTY OF 1
6 Rafael Palmeiro/55 5.00 12.00

2005 Prime Patches Past and Present Name Plate Patch
*PAT p/r 68-71: .6X TO 1.5X JUM p/r 89-532
*PAT p/r 38-51: .75X TO 2X JUM p/r 89-532
*PAT p/r 22-32: 1X TO 2.5X JUM p/r 89-532
TWO AUTOS OR GAME-USED PER PACK
PRINT RUNS B/WN 1-71 COPIES PER
NO PRICING ON QTY OF 18 OR LESS
12 Mark Mulder/22 8.00 20.00

2005 Prime Patches Past and Present Name Plate Patch Combo
*COM p/r 44-52: .75X TO 2X JUM p/r 89-532
*COM p/r 20-30: 1X TO 2.5X JUM p/r 89-532
TWO AUTOS OR GAME-USED PER PACK
PRINT RUNS B/WN 1-52 COPIES PER
NO PRICING ON QTY OF 13 OR LESS
6 Rafael Palmeiro/20 10.00 25.00

2005 Prime Patches Past and Present Number Patch
*PAT p/r 131: .6X TO 1.5X JUM p/r 89-532
*PAT p/r 84-125: .6X TO 1.5X JUM p/r 89-532
*PAT p/r 41-58: .75X TO 2X JUM p/r 89-532
*PAT p/r 22-33: 1X TO 2.5X JUM p/r 89-532
TWO AUTOS OR GAME-USED PER PACK
PRINT RUNS B/WN 1-131 COPIES PER
NO PRICING ON QTY OF 17 OR LESS
12 Mark Mulder/29 8.00 20.00

2005 Prime Patches Past and Present Number Patch Combo
*COM p/r 69: .6X TO 1.5X JUM p/r 89-532
*COM p/r 36-40: .75X TO 2X JUM p/r 89-532
*COM p/r 25-30: 1X TO 2.5X JUM p/r 89-532
TWO AUTOS OR GAME-USED PER PACK
PRINT RUNS B/WN 1-69 COPIES PER
NO PRICING ON QTY OF 13 OR LESS

2005 Prime Patches Past and Present Team Logo Patch
*PAT p/r 38-60: .75X TO 2X JUM p/r 89-532
*PAT p/r 23-35: 1X TO 2.5X JUM p/r 89-532
TWO AUTOS OR GAME-USED PER PACK
PRINT RUNS B/WN 1-60 COPIES PER
NO PRICING ON QTY OF 19 OR LESS
12 Mark Mulder/23 8.00 20.00

2005 Prime Patches Past and Present Team Logo Patch Combo
*COM p/r 40-43: .75X TO 2X JUM p/r 89-532
*COM p/r 21-35: 1X TO 2.5X JUM p/r 89-532
TWO AUTOS OR GAME-USED PER PACK
PRINT RUNS B/WN 1-43 COPIES PER
NO PRICING ON QTY OF 13 OR LESS

2005 Prime Patches Past and Present Jumbo Swatch
PRINT RUNS B/WN 89-532 COPIES PER
PRIME PRINT RUNS B/WN 1-52 COPIES PER
NO PRIME PRICING DUE TO SCARCITY
TWO AUTOS OR GAME-USED PER PACK
1 Greg Maddux/243 6.00 15.00
2 Ivan Rodriguez/500 4.00 10.00
3 Jim Edmonds/275 3.00 8.00
4 Carlos Delgado/198 3.00 8.00
5 Bret Boone/294 3.00 8.00
7 Carlos Lee/150 3.00 8.00
8 Adrian Beltre/494 3.00 8.00
9 Miguel Tejada/330 3.00 8.00
10 Junior Spivey/89 2.50 6.00
11 Aramis Ramirez/248 3.00 8.00
13 Derrek Lee/234 4.00 10.00
14 Vladimir Guerrero/163 5.00 12.00
15 Javy Lopez/384 3.00 8.00
16 Cliff Floyd/180 3.00 8.00
17 Shawn Green/532 3.00 8.00
18 Mike Mussina/134 4.00 10.00
19 Larry Walker/532 3.00 8.00
20 Mike Piazza/512 5.00 12.00

2005 Prime Patches Past and Present Double Patch Combo
*DBL p/r 25: 1.25X TO 3X JUM p/r 89-532
TWO AUTOS OR GAME-USED PER PACK
PRINT RUNS B/WN 1-25 COPIES PER
NO PRICING ON QTY OF 15 OR LESS

2005 Prime Patches Past and Present Double Swatch
*DBL p/r 99-150: .4X TO 1X JUM p/r 89-532
TWO AUTOS OR GAME-USED PER PACK
PRINT RUNS B/WN 1-150 COPIES PER
NO PRICING ON QTY OF 13 OR LESS
6 Rafael Palmeiro Jsy-Jsy/30 6.00 15.00

2005 Prime Patches Past and Present Double Swatch Prime
*DBL p/r 88-150: .5X TO 1.2X JUM p/r 89-532
*DBL p/r 38-59: .6X TO 1.5X JUM p/r 89-532
TWO AUTOS OR GAME-USED PER PACK
PRINT RUNS B/WN 1-150 COPIES PER
NO PRICING ON QTY OF 17 OR LESS

2005 Prime Patches Past and Present Double Swatch Combo
*DBL p/r 100-150: .6X TO 1.5X JUMp/r89-532
TWO AUTOS OR GAME-USED PER PACK
PRINT RUNS B/WN 1-150 COPIES PER
NO PRICING ON QTY OF 11 OR LESS
6 R.Palmeiro J-J-J-P/150 6.00 15.00

2005 Prime Patches Past and Present Double Swatch Combo Prime
*DBL p/r 69-128: .75X TO 2X JUM 89-532
*DBL p/r 50: 1X TO 2.5X JUM 89-532
*DBL p/r 20-31: 1.25X TO 3X JUM 89-532
TWO AUTOS OR GAME-USED PER PACK
PRINT RUNS B/WN 1-128 COPIES PER
NO PRICING ON QTY OF 15 OR LESS
12 M.Mulder J-J-J-J/100 6.00 15.00

2005 Prime Patches Past and Present Autograph
TWO AUTOS OR GAME-USED PER PACK
TIER 1 QTY B/WN 1-50 COPIES PER
TIER 2 QTY B/WN 51-100 COPIES PER
TIER 4 QTY B/WN 251-800 COPIES PER
TIER 5 QTY B/WN 801-1200 COPIES PER
CARDS ARE NOT SERIAL-NUMBERED
PRINT RUN INFO PROVIDED BY DONRUSS
NO PRICING ON QTY OF 5 OR LESS
6 Rafael Palmeiro T1/22 * 15.00 40.00
7 Carlos Lee T4 6.00 15.00
10 Junior Spivey T5 4.00 10.00
11 Aramis Ramirez T1/25 * 10.00 25.00
12 Mark Mulder T1/25 * 10.00 25.00
13 Derrek Lee T2/93 * 12.50 30.00

2005 Prime Patches Past and Present Autograph Bat
*BAT p/r 250: .4X TO 1X AU T3-T5
*BAT p/r 50: .5X TO 1.2X AU T2
TWO AUTOS OR GAME-USED PER PACK
PRINT RUNS B/WN 3-250 COPIES PER
NO PRICING ON QTY OF 5 OR LESS

2005 Prime Patches Past and Present Autograph Jersey
*JSY p/r 250: .4X TO 1X AU T3-T5
*JSY p/r 250: .3X TO .8X AU T2
*JSY p/r 20-25: .4X TO 1X AU T1
TWO AUTOS OR GAME-USED PER PACK
PRINT RUNS B/WN 5-250 COPIES PER
NO PRICING ON QTY OF 5
8 Adrian Beltre/20 10.00 25.00

2005 Prime Patches Past and Present Autograph Jersey Combo
*JSY p/r 125: .4X TO 1X AU T3-T5
*JSY p/r 20-50: .5X TO 1.2X AU T2
TWO AUTOS OR GAME-USED PER PACK
PRINT RUNS B/WN 5-125 COPIES PER
NO PRICING ON QTY OF 5
8 Adrian Beltre/20 10.00 25.00

2005 Prime Patches Past and Present Autograph Name Plate Patch
*PATCH p/r 25: .5X TO 1.2X AU T1
TWO AUTOS OR GAME-USED PER PACK
PRINT RUNS B/WN 1-25 COPIES PER
NO PRICING ON QTY OF 19 OR LESS

2005 Prime Patches Past and Present Autograph Number Patch
*PATCH p/r 98: .6X TO 1.5X AU T3-T5
*PATCH p/r 35-50: .75X TO 2X AU T3-T5
*PATCH p/r 35-50: .5X TO 1.2X AU T1
TWO AUTOS OR GAME-USED PER PACK
PRINT RUNS B/WN 1-98 COPIES PER
NO PRICING ON QTY OF 15 OR LESS

2005 Prime Patches Past and Present Autograph Number Patch Combo
*PATCH p/r 25: .75X TO 2X AU T3-T5
TWO AUTOS OR GAME-USED PER PACK
PRINT RUNS B/WN 1-25 COPIES PER
NO PRICING ON QTY OF 5 OR LESS

2005 Prime Patches Past and Present Autograph Sleeve Patch
*PATCH p/r 35: .75X TO 2X AU T3-T5
TWO AUTOS OR GAME-USED PER PACK
PRINT RUNS B/WN 1-35 COPIES PER
NO PRICING ON QTY OF 1

2005 Prime Patches Past and Present Autograph Team Logo Patch
*PATCH p/r 20-50: .75X TO 2X AU T3-T5
*PATCH p/r 20-50: .5X TO 1.2X AU T1
TWO AUTOS OR GAME-USED PER PACK
PRINT RUNS B/WN 1-50 COPIES PER
NO PRICING ON QTY OF 10 OR LESS

2005 Prime Patches Portraits Bat
*BAT p/r 100: .3X TO .8X JUM p/r 83-532
*BAT p/r 100: .25X TO .6X JUM p/r 37-64
*BAT p/r 100: .2X TO .5X JUM p/r 20-32
*BAT p/r 40-54 .4X TO 1X JUM p/r 83-532
*BAT p/r 25-31 .5X TO 1.2X JUM p/r 83-532
*BAT p/r 25-31 .3X TO .8X JUM p/r 20-32
TWO AUTOS OR GAME-USED PER PACK
PRINT RUNS B/WN 1-100 COPIES PER
NO PRICING ON QTY OF 10 OR LESS
11 Mark Teixeira/100 3.00 8.00
14 Rafael Palmeiro/50 4.00 10.00
17 Richie Sexson/100 2.50 6.00
18 Matt Williams/100 2.50 6.00
24 Paul Lo Duca/100 2.50 6.00
47 Jacque Jones/100 2.00 5.00
48 Magglio Ordonez/100 2.50 6.00
56 Dave Parker/100 2.50 6.00
57 Jose Vidro/100 2.00 5.00
64 Eric Hinske/100 2.00 5.00
70 Juan Gonzalez/40 3.00 8.00

2005 Prime Patches Portraits Jersey
*JSY p/r 108-150: .3X TO .8X JUM p/r 83-532
*JSY p/r 41-55: .4X TO 1X JUM p/r 83-532
*JSY p/r 25: .3X TO .8X JUM p/r 20-32
TWO AUTOS OR GAME-USED PER PACK
PRINT RUNS B/WN 1-150 COPIES PER
NO PRICING ON QTY OF 15 OR LESS

2005 Prime Patches Portraits Name Plate Patch
*PAT p/r 67-110: .6X TO 1.5X JUM p/r 83-532
*PAT p/r 36-63: .75X TO 2X JUM p/r 83-532
*PAT p/r 22-31: 1X TO 2.5X JUM p/r 83-532
*PAT p/r 22-31: .75X TO 2X JUM p/r 37-64
TWO AUTOS OR GAME-USED PER PACK
PRINT RUNS B/WN 1-110 COPIES PER
NO PRICING ON QTY OF 19 OR LESS
48 Magglio Ordonez/37 6.00 15.00
64 Eric Hinske/29 6.00 15.00
69 Carlos Beltran/54 6.00 15.00
82 Jose Canseco/52 10.00 25.00

2005 Prime Patches Portraits Number Patch
*PAT p/r 127-150: .6X TO 1.5X JUM p/r 83-532
*PAT p/r 74-113: .6X TO 1.5X JUM p/r 83-532
*PAT p/r 37-53: .75X TO 2X JUM p/r 83-532
*PAT p/r 20-35: 1X TO 2.5X JUM p/r 83-532
*PAT p/r 20-35: .75X TO 2X JUM p/r 37-64
TWO AUTOS OR GAME-USED PER PACK
PRINT RUNS B/WN 1-150 COPIES PER
NO PRICING ON QTY OF 18 OR LESS
17 Richie Sexson/20 8.00 20.00
64 Eric Hinske/37 5.00 12.00
69 Carlos Beltran/144 5.00 12.00
82 Jose Canseco/94 8.00 20.00

2005 Prime Patches Portraits Sleeve Patch
*PAT p/r 20-33: 1X TO 2.5X JUM p/r 83-532
TWO AUTOS OR GAME-USED PER PACK
PRINT RUNS B/WN 1-33 COPIES PER
NO PRICING ON QTY OF 17 OR LESS

2005 Prime Patches Portraits Team Logo Patch
*PAT p/r 126-150: .6X TO 1.5X JUM p/r 83-532
*PAT p/r 79-108: .6X TO 1.5X JUM p/r 83-532
*PAT p/r 79-108: .5X TO 1.2X JUM p/r 37-64
*PAT p/r 36-64: .75X TO 2X JUM p/r 83-532
*PAT p/r 21-34: 1X TO 2.5X JUM p/r 83-532
*PAT p/r 21-34: .75X TO 2X JUM p/r 37-64
TWO AUTOS OR GAME-USED PER PACK
PRINT RUNS B/WN 1-150 COPIES PER
NO PRICING ON QTY OF 19 OR LESS
64 Eric Hinske/31 6.00 15.00
69 Carlos Beltran/40 6.00 15.00
82 Jose Canseco/29 12.50 30.00

2005 Prime Patches Portraits Jumbo Swatch
PRINT RUNS B/WN 1-532 COPIES PER
NO PRICING ON QTY OF 17 OR LESS
PRIME PRINT RUNS B/WN 1-55 COPIES PER
NO PRIME PRICING DUE TO SCARCITY
TWO AUTOS OR GAME-USED PER PACK
1 Andruw Jones/107 4.00 10.00
2 Preston Wilson/88 2.50 6.00
3 Laynce Nix/40 3.00 8.00
4 Roberto Alomar/502 4.00 10.00
5 David Ortiz/237 5.00 12.00
6 Frank Thomas/150 5.00 12.00
7 Eric Chavez/48 4.00 10.00
9 Roy Oswalt/163 3.00 8.00
10 Jeff Bagwell/532 4.00 10.00
12 Ben Sheets/136 3.00 8.00
13 Shawn Green/490 3.00 8.00
15 Travis Hafner/501 3.00 8.00
16 Sammy Sosa/173 5.00 12.00
19 Lee Smith/144 3.00 8.00
20 Andy Pettitte/321 4.00 10.00
21 Michael Young/331 3.00 8.00
22 Curt Schilling/145 4.00 10.00
23 Will Clark/140 4.00 10.00
25 Tom Glavine/532 4.00 10.00
26 Dwight Gooden/424 2.50 6.00
27 Kerry Wood/115 3.00 8.00
29 Albert Pujols/150 10.00 25.00
30 Miguel Cabrera/55 5.00 12.00
31 Jim Thome/282 4.00 10.00
32 Aramis Ramirez/221 3.00 8.00
33 Rod Carew/163 4.00 10.00
34 Kazuo Matsui/99 3.00 8.00
35 Ivan Rodriguez/394 4.00 10.00
36 Rocco Baldelli/224 3.00 8.00
37 Kazuhisa Ishii/515 3.00 8.00
38 Edgar Martinez/269 4.00 10.00
41 John Olerud/136 3.00 8.00
42 Shea Hillenbrand/198 2.50 6.00
43 C.C. Sabathia/516 3.00 8.00
44 Matt Clement/214 3.00 8.00
45 Jim Edmonds/266 3.00 8.00
46 Moises Alou/270 3.00 8.00
49 Lance Berkman/150 3.00 8.00
50 Kirk Gibson/400 3.00 8.00
51 Pat Burrell/55 4.00 10.00
52 Jeromy Burnitz/327 3.00 8.00
53 Rich Aurilia/517 2.50 6.00
54 Jack Morris/218 3.00 8.00
55 Bo Jackson/489 10.00 25.00
58 Tino Martinez/177 4.00 10.00
59 Luis Gonzalez/340 3.00 8.00
60 Bobby Abreu/491 3.00 8.00
61 Milton Bradley/150 2.50 6.00
62 Edgardo Alfonzo/150 2.50 6.00
63 Shannon Stewart/219 2.50 6.00
65 Omar Vizquel/37 5.00 12.00
66 Chipper Jones/258 10.00 25.00
67 Mark Prior/59 5.00 12.00
68 Fred McGriff/222 4.00 10.00
72 Rickey Henderson/179 6.00 15.00
73 Hideo Nomo/353 6.00 15.00
74 Austin Kearns/60 3.00 8.00
75 Garret Anderson/20 5.00 12.00
76 Victor Martinez/64 4.00 10.00
77 Jason Bay/83 3.00 8.00
78 Willie Mays/30 20.00 50.00
79 Aubrey Huff/200 2.50 6.00
80 Rafael Palmeiro/304 4.00 10.00
81 Tony Gwynn/499 6.00 15.00
83 Pedro Martinez/32 6.00 15.00
84 Troy Glaus/154 3.00 8.00

2005 Prime Patches Portraits Double Patch
*DBL p/r 30: 1X TO 2.5X JUM p/r 83-532
TWO AUTOS OR GAME-USED PER PACK
PRINT RUNS B/WN 1-30 COPIES PER
NO PRICING ON QTY OF 13 OR LESS

2005 Prime Patches Portraits Double Swatch
*DBL p/r 73-150: .4X TO 1X JUM p/r 83-532
*DBL p/r 73-150: .3X TO .8X JUM p/r 37-64
*DBL p/r 73-150: .25X TO .6X JUM p/r 20-32
*DBL p/r 44-55: .5X TO 1.2X JUM p/r 83-532
*DBL p/r 20-30: .6X TO 1.5X JUM p/r 83-532
*DBL p/r 20-30: .4X TO 1X JUM p/r 20-32
TWO AUTOS OR GAME-USED PER PACK
PRINTS RUNS B/WN 1-150 COPIES PER
NO PRICING ON QTY OF 13 OR LESS
24 P.LoDuca Ch.Prot-Jsy/150 3.00 8.00
40 M.Buehrle Fld Glv-Hat/20 5.00 12.00
47 Jacque Jones Jsy-Jsy/55 3.00 8.00
48 M.Ordonez Jsy-Jsy/20 5.00 12.00
64 Eric Hinske Jsy-Jsy/24 4.00 10.00

2005 Prime Patches Portraits Double Swatch Prime
*DBL p/r 70-150: .5X TO 1.2X JUM p/r 83-532
*DBL p/r 37-59: .6X TO 1.5X JUM p/r 83-532
*DBL p/r 20-35: .75X TO 2X JUM p/r 83-532
*DBL p/r 20-35: .6X TO 1.5X JUM p/r 37-64
TWO AUTOS OR GAME-USED PER PACK
PRINT RUNS B/WN 1-150 COPIES PER
NO PRICING ON QTY OF 15 OR LESS
48 M.Ordonez Jsy-Jsy/35 6.00 15.00
56 Dave Parker Jsy-Jsy/20 5.00 12.00
69 Carlos Beltran Jsy-Jsy/86 4.00 10.00
82 Jose Canseco Jsy-Jsy/20 10.00 25.00

2005 Prime Patches Portraits Triple Patch
*TRI p/r 25: 1.25X TO 3X JUM p/r 83-532
TWO AUTOS OR GAME-USED PER PACK
PRINT RUNS B/WN 1-25 COPIES PER
NO PRICING ON QTY OF 11 OR LESS

2005 Prime Patches Portraits Triple Swatch
*TRI p/r 78-150: .5X TO 1.2X JUM p/r 83-532
*TRI p/r 78-150: .4X TO 1X JUM p/r 47-64
*TRI p/r 78-150: .3X TO .8X JUM p/r 20-32

*TRI p/r 42-65: .6X TO 1.5X JUM p/r 83-532
*TRI p/r 42-65: .5X TO 1.2X JUM p/r 37-64
*TRI p/r 25-33: .75X TO 2X JUM p/r 83-532
TWO AUTOS OR GAME-USED PER PACK
PRINT RUNS B/WN 1-150 COPIES PER
NO PRICING ON QTY OF 17 OR LESS
11 M.Teixeira B-FG-SH/150 5.00 12.00
14 R.Palmeiro B-J-SH/50 6.00 15.00
17 R.Sexson B-SH-SH/150 4.00 10.00
24 P.Lo Duca B-FG-H/150 4.00 10.00
47 Jacque Jones B-J-J/30 5.00 12.00
48 M.Ordonez B-J-SH/150 4.00 10.00
64 Eric Hinske FG-J-SH/126 3.00 8.00
82 Jose Canseco BG-H-J/33 10.00 25.00

2005 Prime Patches Portraits Triple Swatch Prime

*TRI p/r 68-150: .6X TO 1.5X JUM p/r 83-532
*TRI p/r 68-150: .5X TO 1.2X JUM p/r 37-64
*TRI p/r 39-64: .75X TO 2X JUM p/r 83-532
*TRI p/r 25-35: 1X TO 2.5X JUM p/r 83-532
*TRI p/r 25-35: .75X TO 2X JUM p/r 37-64
TWO AUTOS OR GAME-USED PER PACK
PRINT RUNS B/WN 1-150 COPIES PER
NO PRICING ON QTY OF 15 OR LESS
24 Paul Lo Duca B-CP-J/30 8.00 20.00
48 Magglio Ordonez J-J-J/25 8.00 20.00
56 Dave Parker J-J-J/31 8.00 20.00
69 Carlos Beltran H-J-SH/89 5.00 12.00

2005 Prime Patches Portraits Quad Patch

*QUAD p/r 30: 1.5X TO 4X JUM p/r 83-532
TWO AUTOS OR GAME-USED PER PACK
PRINT RUNS B/WN 1- COPIES PER
NO PRICING ON QTY OF OR LESS

2005 Prime Patches Portraits Quad Swatch

*QUAD p/r 66-150: .6X TO 1.5X JUMp/r83-532
*QUAD p/r 66-150: .5X TO 1.2X JUM p/r 47-64
*QUAD p/r 66-150: .4X TO 1X JUM p/r 20-32
*QUAD p/r 25-30: 1X TO 2.5X JUM p/r 83-532
*QUAD p/r 25-30: .75X TO 2X JUM p/r 37-64
TWO AUTOS OR GAME-USED PER PACK
PRINT RUNS B/WN 1-150 COPIES PER
NO PRICING ON QTY OF 10 OR LESS
8 D.Matt BG-H-J-SH/25 20.00 50.00
11 M.Teixeira FG-H-J-SH/50 8.00 20.00
14 R.Palm FG-J-SH-SH/50 8.00 20.00
17 R.Sexson B-BG-FG-SH/61 6.00 15.00
24 P.LoDuca FG-J-SG-SH/85 5.00 12.00
40 M.Buehrle BG-FG-H-SH/100 5.00 12.00
47 Jacque Jones B-B-J-J/82 4.00 10.00
48 M.Ordonez B-H-J-SH/150 5.00 12.00
56 Dave Parker J-J-J-J/85 5.00 12.00
64 E.Hinske BG-FG-J-SH/90 4.00 10.00
69 C.Beltran B-J-J-SH/75 5.00 12.00
82 J.Canseco BG-H-J-J/25 12.50 30.00

2005 Prime Patches Portraits Quad Swatch Prime

*QUAD p/r 75-150: .75X TO 2X JUMp/r83-532
*QUAD p/r 42-60: 1X TO 2.5X JUM p/r 83-532
*QUAD p/r 42-60: .75X TO 2X JUM p/r 37-64
*QUAD p/r 22-33: 1.25X TO 3X JUMp/r83-532
*QUAD p/r 22-33: .75X TO 2X JUM p/r 20-32
TWO AUTOS OR GAME-USED PER PACK
PRINT RUNS B/WN 1-150 COPIES PER
NO PRICING ON QTY OF 19 OR LESS
24 P.Lo Duca B-CP-H-J/43 8.00 20.00
48 M.Ord B-B-H-J/129 6.00 15.00
69 C.Beltran H-J-J-SH/28 10.00 25.00

2005 Prime Patches Portraits Autograph

TWO AUTOS OR GAME-USED PER PACK
TIER 1 QTY B/WN 1-50 COPIES PER
TIER 2 QTY B/WN 51-100 COPIES PER
TIER 3 QTY B/WN 101-250 COPIES PER
TIER 4 QTY B/WN 251-800 COPIES PER
TIER 5 QTY B/WN 801-1200 COPIES PER
CARDS ARE NOT SERIAL-NUMBERED
PRINT RUN INFO PROVIDED BY DONRUSS
NO PRICING ON QTY OF 24 OR LESS
2 Preston Wilson T4 4.00 10.00
3 Laynce Nix T5 4.00 10.00
4 Roberto Alomar T1/50 * 15.00 40.00
5 David Ortiz T1/25 * 20.00 50.00
8 Don Mattingly T1/25 * 40.00 80.00
9 Roy Oswalt T1/25 * 10.00 25.00
11 Mark Teixeira T1/25 * 15.00 40.00
12 Ben Sheets T1/25 * 10.00 25.00
14 Rafael Palmeiro T1/25 * 15.00 40.00
15 Travis Hafner T4 6.00 15.00
18 Matt Williams T2/90 * 8.00 20.00
21 Michael Young T3 6.00 15.00
23 Will Clark T1/25 * 15.00 40.00
26 Dwight Gooden T1/46 * 6.00 15.00
28 Orel Hershiser T1/25 * 10.00 25.00
30 Miguel Cabrera T1/50 * 20.00 50.00
33 Rod Carew T1/25 * 15.00 40.00
39 Jermaine Dye T4 6.00 15.00
40 Mark Buehrle T3 8.00 20.00
42 Shea Hillenbrand T1/50 * 6.00 15.00
47 Jacque Jones T2/100 * 5.00 12.00
48 Magglio Ordonez T1/25 * 10.00 25.00
50 Kirk Gibson T1/24 * 10.00 25.00
55 Bo Jackson T1/25 * 30.00 60.00
56 Dave Parker T3 6.00 15.00
57 Jose Vidro T3 4.00 10.00
61 Milton Bradley T4 4.00 10.00
65 Omar Vizquel T2/100 * 12.50 30.00
67 Mark Prior T1/25 * 10.00 25.00
70 Juan Gonzalez T2/100 * 8.00 20.00
71 Lew Ford T4 4.00 10.00
74 Austin Kearns T1/49 * 6.00 15.00
75 Garret Anderson T4 6.00 15.00
76 Victor Martinez T3 6.00 15.00
78 Willie Mays T2/100 * 60.00 120.00
79 Aubrey Huff T4 4.00 10.00
80 Rafael Palmeiro T1/25 * 15.00 40.00
81 Tony Gwynn T1/50 * 10.00 25.00

2005 Prime Patches Portraits Autograph Bat

*BAT p/r 150-250: .4X TO 1X AU T3-T5
*BAT p/r 150-250: .3X TO .8X AU T2
*BAT p/r 150-250: .25X TO .6X AU T1
*BAT p/r 100: .3X TO .8X AU T1
*BAT p/r 25-50: .6X TO 1.5X AU T3-T5
*BAT p/r 25-50: .5X TO 1.2X AU T2
*BAT p/r 25-50: .4X TO 1X AU T1
TWO AUTOS OR GAME-USED PER PACK
PRINT RUNS B/WN 1-150 COPIES PER
NO PRICING ON QTY OF 10 OR LESS
6 Frank Thomas/25 30.00 60.00
10 Jeff Bagwell/25 30.00 60.00
77 Jason Bay/150 6.00 15.00
82 Jose Canseco/25 20.00 50.00

2005 Prime Patches Portraits Autograph Jersey

*JSY p/r 125-250: .4X TO 1X AU T3-T5
*JSY p/r 125-250: .3X TO .8X AU T2
*JSY p/r 125-250: .25X TO .6X AU T1
*JSY p/r 20-50: .6X TO 1.5X AU T3-T5
*JSY p/r 20-50: .5X TO 1.2X AU T2
*JSY p/r 20-50: .4X TO 1X AU T1
TWO AUTOS OR GAME-USED PER PACK
PRINT RUNS B/WN 1-250 COPIES PER
NO PRICING ON QTY OF 13 OR LESS
6 Frank Thomas/150 25.00 60.00
7 Eric Chavez/100 8.00 20.00
10 Jeff Bagwell/25 30.00 60.00
19 Lee Smith/20 10.00 25.00
32 Aramis Ramirez/39 10.00 25.00
82 Jose Canseco/25 20.00 50.00

2005 Prime Patches Portraits Autograph Name Plate Patch

*PATCH p/r 22-36: .75X TO 2X AU T3-T5
*PATCH p/r 22-36: .5X TO 1.2X AU T1
TWO AUTOS OR GAME-USED PER PACK
PRINT RUNS B/WN 1-36 COPIES PER
NO PRICING ON QTY OF 15 OR LESS

2005 Prime Patches Portraits Autograph Number Patch

*PATCH p/r 132: .5X TO 1.2X AU T3-T5
*PATCH p/r 53-61: .6X TO 1.5X AU T3-T5
*PATCH p/r 25-50: .75X TO 2X AU T3-T5
*PATCH p/r 25-50: .5X TO 1.2X AU T1
TWO AUTOS OR GAME-USED PER PACK
PRINT RUNS B/WN 1-132 COPIES PER
NO PRICING ON QTY OF 16 OR LESS
82 Jose Canseco/25 25.00 60.00

2005 Prime Patches Portraits Autograph Team Logo Patch

*PATCH p/r 72: .6X TO 1.5X AU T3-T5
*PATCH p/r 25-50: .75X TO 2X AU T3-T5
*PATCH p/r 25-50: .6X TO 1.5X AU T2
TWO AUTOS OR GAME-USED PER PACK
PRINT RUNS B/WN 1-72 COPIES PER
NO PRICING ON QTY OF 15 OR LESS

2005 Prime Patches Portraits Autograph Double Patch

*PATCH p/r 25: .5X TO 1.2X AU T1
TWO AUTOS OR GAME-USED PER PACK
PRINT RUNS B/WN 1-25 COPIES PER
NO PRICING ON QTY OF 10 OR LESS
77 Jason Bay/25 12.50 30.00

2005 Prime Patches Portraits Autograph Double Swatch

*DBL p/r 113-150: .4X TO 1X AU T3-T5
*DBL p/r 113-150: .25X TO .6X AU T1
*DBL p/r 60-100: .4X TO 1X AU T2
*DBL p/r 20-50: .6X TO 1.5X AU T3-T5
*DBL p/r 20-50: .5X TO 1.2X AU T2
*DBL p/r 20-50: .4X TO 1X AU T1
TWO AUTOS OR GAME-USED PER PACK
PRINT RUNS B/WN 1-150 COPIES PER
NO PRICING ON QTY OF 18 OR LESS
7 Eric Chavez Jsy-Jsy/22 10.00 25.00
10 Jeff Bagwell Jsy-Jsy/25 30.00 60.00
32 Aramis Ramirez Jsy-Jsy/50 10.00 25.00
45 Jim Edmonds Jsy-Jsy/50 15.00 40.00
60 Bobby Abreu Jsy-Jsy/20 10.00 25.00
77 Jason Bay Jsy-Jsy/25 10.00 25.00

2005 Prime Patches Portraits Autograph Double Swatch Prime

*DBL p/r 25: .5X TO 1.2X AU T1
TWO AUTOS OR GAME-USED PER PACK
PRINT RUNS B/WN 1-25 COPIES PER
NO PRICING ON QTY OF 15 OR LESS
10 Jeff Bagwell Jsy-Jsy/25 25.00 60.00
45 Jim Edmonds Jsy-Jsy/25 20.00 50.00

2005 Prime Patches Portraits Autograph Triple Patch

*TRI p/r 25-50: 1X TO 2.5X AU T3-T5
*TRI p/r 25-50: .6X TO 1.5X AU T1
TWO AUTOS OR GAME-USED PER PACK
PRINT RUNS B/WN 1-50 COPIES PER
NO PRICING ON QTY OF 10 OR LESS

2005 Prime Patches Portraits Autograph Triple Swatch

*TRI p/r 133-250: .5X TO 1.2X AU T3-T5
*TRI p/r 133-250: .4X TO 1X AU T2
*TRI p/r 133-250: .3X TO .8X AU T1
*TRI p/r 60-70: .6X TO 1.5X AU T3-T5
*TRI p/r 60-70: .4X TO 1X AU T1
*TRI p/r 20-50: .75X TO 2X AU T3-T5
*TRI p/r 20-50: .6X TO 1.5X AU T2
*TRI p/r 20-50: .5X TO 1.2X AU T1
TWO AUTOS OR GAME-USED PER PACK
PRINT RUNS B/WN 1-250 COPIES PER
NO PRICING ON QTY OF 13 OR LESS
10 Jeff Bagwell H-J-P/25 25.00 60.00
32 Aramis Ramirez B-J-J/25 12.50 30.00
45 Jim Edmonds B-J-J/50 20.00 50.00
60 Bobby Abreu J-J-J/25 12.50 30.00
82 Jose Canseco BG-H-J/25 25.00 60.00

2005 Prime Patches Portraits Autograph Triple Swatch Prime

*TRI p/r 25: .6X TO 1.5X AU T1
TWO AUTOS OR GAME-USED PER PACK
PRINT RUNS B/WN 1-25 COPIES PER
NO PRICING ON QTY OF 15 OR LESS

2005 Prime Patches Portraits Autograph Quad Patch

*QUAD p/r 150: .75X TO 2X AU T3-T5
*QUAD p/r 25: .75X TO 2X AU T1
TWO AUTOS OR GAME-USED PER PACK
PRINT RUNS B/WN 1-150 COPIES PER
NO PRICING ON QTY OF 10 OR LESS

2005 Prime Patches Portraits Autograph Quad Swatch

*QUAD p/r 125-150: .6X TO 1.5X AU T3-T5
*QUAD p/r 125-150: .5X TO 1.2X AU T2
*QUAD p/r 125-150: .4X TO 1X AU T1
*QUAD p/r 68-100: .75X TO 2X AU T3-T5
*QUAD p/r 68-100: .6X TO 1.5X AU T2
*QUAD p/r 68-100: .5X TO 1.2X AU T1
*QUAD p/r 25-50: 1X TO 2.5X AU T3-T5
*QUAD p/r 25-50: .75X TO 2X AU T2
*QUAD p/r 25-50: .6X TO 1.5X AU T1
TWO AUTOS OR GAME-USED PER PACK
PRINT RUNS B/WN 1-150 COPIES PER
NO PRICING ON QTY OF 15 OR LESS
6 Frank Thomas B-J-J-P/95 25.00 60.00
7 Eric Chavez J-J-J-J/50 15.00 40.00
10 Jeff Bagwell B-H-J-J/25 30.00 80.00
45 J.Edmonds J-J-SH-SH/25 12.50 30.00
60 Bobby Abreu J-J-J-J/25 15.00 40.00
82 J.Canseco BG-H-J-J/25 30.00 80.00

2005 Prime Patches Portraits Autograph Quad Swatch Prime

*QUAD p/r 25: 1X TO 2.5X AU T2
TWO AUTOS OR GAME-USED PER PACK
PRINT RUNS B/WN 1-25 COPIES PER
NO PRICING ON QTY OF 10 OR LESS

2005 Prime Patches Team Materials Triple Name Plate Patch

*NAME p/r 67-74: .4X TO 1X NUM p/r 74-150
*NAME p/r 67-74: .25X TO .6X NUM p/r 20-35
*NAME p/r 39-55: .5X TO 1.2X NUMp/r74-150
*NAME p/r 39-55: .4X TO 1X NUM p/r 39-57
*NAME p/r 39-55: .3X TO .8X NUM p/r 20-35
*NAME p/r 20-34: .6X TO 1.5X NUMp/r74-150
*NAME p/r 20-34: .5X TO 1.2X NUM p/r 39-57
*NAME p/r 20-34: .4X TO 1X NUM p/r 20-35
TWO AUTOS OR GAME-USED PER PACK
PRINT RUNS B/WN 8 74 COPIES PER
NO PRICING ON QTY OF 15 OR LESS
6 Gooden/Carter/Cone/26 10.00 25.00
15 Davis/Deion/Boone/32 12.50 30.00

2005 Prime Patches Team Materials Triple Number Patch

TWO AUTOS OR GAME-USED PER PACK
PRINT RUNS B/WN 7-150 COPIES PER
NO PRICING ON QTY OF 15 OR LESS
1 Gibson/Trammell/Morris/30 10.00 25.00
2 Bedard/Gibbons/Matos/28 10.00 25.00
3 Thomas/Vent/Baines/35 15.00 40.00
4 Rickey/Sheff/Straw/107 10.00 25.00
5 Vidro/Vazquez/Armas/150 6.00 15.00
7 Smoltz/Glav/Maddux/107 40.00 80.00
8 Pedro/Vazquez/Randy/47 12.50 30.00
9 Braz/Backe/McGriff/39 8.00 20.00
10 Edgar/Moyer/Olerud/26 12.50 30.00
12 Nomo/Park/Ishii/50 12.50 30.00
13 Cruz/Sutton/Wagner/30 10.00 25.00
16 Glaus/Edmonds/Erstad/44 8.00 20.00
17 J.Gonz/Bo/Sweeney/107 10.00 25.00
18 Sheff/Jordan/Justice/55 10.00 25.00
20 Aurilia/Tucker/Snow/25 10.00 25.00
21 Branyan/Lee/Hafner/100 6.00 15.00
22 Giles/Kendall/Wilson/100 6.00 15.00
23 Finley/Kim/Womack/57 8.00 20.00
24 Cruz/Mondesi/Phelps/32 10.00 25.00
25 Burnitz/Pierre/Castilla/74 6.00 15.00
26 Mient/Romero/Mays/32 10.00 25.00
27 Long/Ludwick/Hudson/45 8.00 20.00
29 Jenkins/Hall/Pods/55 8.00 20.00
30 Ventura/Alfonzo/Leiter/45 8.00 20.00
31 Green/Cey/Brown/35 10.00 25.00
32 Drew/Edm/Taguchi/20 10.00 25.00

2005 Prime Patches Team Materials Triple Team Logo Patch

*LOGO p/r 67-93: .3X TO .8X NUM p/r 39-57
*LOGO p/r 67-93: .25X TO .6X NUM p/r 20-35
*LOGO p/r 37-63: .5X TO 1.2X NUM p/r 74-150
*LOGO p/r 37-63: .4X TO 1X NUM p/r 39-57
*LOGO p/r 37-63: .3X TO .8X NUM p/r 20-35
*LOGO p/r 28-35: .5X TO 1.2X NUM p/r 39-57
*LOGO p/r 28-35: .4X TO 1X NUM p/r 20-35
TWO AUTOS OR GAME-USED PER PACK
PRINT RUNS B/WN 1-93 COPIES PER
NO PRICING ON QTY OF 19 OR LESS
11 Haren/Drew/Renteria/51 8.00 20.00
14 Manny/Thome/Vizquel/35 12.50 30.00
19 Rolen/Burrell/Myers/29 12.50 30.00

1999 Private Stock

This 150-card set was distributed in six card packs with a suggested retail price of $4.49. The fronts feature color action player photos printed on super-thick 30 pt. card stock in holographic silver foil. The backs display selected box scores from the 1998 season.

COMPLETE SET (150) 12.50 30.00
1 Jeff Bagwell .30 .75
2 Roger Clemens 1.00 2.50
3 J.D. Drew .20 .50
4 Nomar Garciaparra .75 2.00
5 Juan Gonzalez .20 .50
6 Ken Griffey Jr. 1.00 2.50
7 Tony Gwynn .60 1.50
8 Derek Jeter 1.25 3.00
9 Chipper Jones .50 1.25
10 Travis Lee .10 .30
11 Greg Maddux .75 2.00
12 Mark McGwire 1.25 3.00
13 Mike Piazza .75 2.00
14 Manny Ramirez .30 .75
15 Cal Ripken 1.50 4.00
16 Alex Rodriguez .75 2.00
17 Ivan Rodriguez .30 .75
18 Sammy Sosa .50 1.25
19 Frank Thomas .50 1.25
20 Kerry Wood .20 .50
21 Roberto Alomar .30 .75
22 Moises Alou .20 .50
23 Albert Belle .20 .50
24 Craig Biggio .30 .75
25 Wade Boggs .30 .75
26 Barry Bonds 1.25 3.00
27 Jose Canseco .30 .75
28 Jim Edmonds .20 .50
29 Darin Erstad .20 .50
30 Andres Galarraga .20 .50
31 Tom Glavine .30 .75
32 Ben Grieve .10 .30
33 Vladimir Guerrero .50 1.25
34 Wilton Guerrero .10 .30
35 Todd Helton .30 .75
36 Andruw Jones .30 .75
37 Ryan Klesko .20 .50
38 Kenny Lofton .20 .50
39 Javy Lopez .20 .50
40 Pedro Martinez .30 .75
41 Paul Molitor .20 .50
42 Raul Mondesi .20 .50
43 Rafael Palmeiro .30 .75
44 Tim Salmon .30 .75
45 Jim Thome .30 .75
46 Mo Vaughn .20 .50
47 Larry Walker .20 .50
48 David Wells .20 .50
49 Bernie Williams .30 .75
50 Jaret Wright .10 .30
51 Bob Abreu .20 .50
52 Garret Anderson .20 .50
53 Rolando Arrojo .10 .30
54 Tony Batista .10 .30
55 Rod Beck .10 .30
56 Derek Bell .10 .30
57 Marvin Benard .10 .30
58 Dave Berg .10 .30
59 Dante Bichette .20 .50
60 Aaron Boone .20 .50
61 Bret Boone .20 .50
62 Scott Brosius .20 .50
63 Brant Brown .10 .30
64 Kevin Brown .30 .75
65 Jeromy Burnitz .20 .50
66 Ken Caminiti .20 .50
67 Mike Caruso .10 .30
68 Sean Casey .20 .50
69 Vinny Castilla .20 .50
70 Eric Chavez .20 .50
71 Ryan Christenson .10 .30
72 Jeff Cirillo .10 .30
73 Tony Clark .10 .30
74 Will Clark .30 .75
75 Edgard Clemente .10 .30
76 David Cone .20 .50
77 Marty Cordova .10 .30
78 Jose Cruz Jr. .10 .30
79 Eric Davis .20 .50
80 Carlos Delgado .20 .50
81 David Dellucci .10 .30
82 Delino DeShields .10 .30
83 Gary DiSarcina .10 .30
84 Damion Easley .10 .30
85 Dennis Eckersley .20 .50
86 Cliff Floyd .20 .50
87 Jason Giambi .20 .50
88 Doug Glanville .10 .30
89 Alex Gonzalez .10 .30
90 Mark Grace .30 .75
91 Rusty Greer .20 .50
92 Jose Guillen .20 .50
93 Carlos Guillen .20 .50
94 Jeffrey Hammonds .10 .30
95 Rick Helling .10 .30
96 Bob Henley .10 .30
97 Livan Hernandez .20 .50
98 Orlando Hernandez .20 .50
99 Bob Higginson .20 .50
100 Trevor Hoffman .20 .50
101 Randy Johnson .50 1.25
102 Brian Jordan .20 .50
103 Wally Joyner .20 .50
104 Eric Karros .20 .50
105 Jason Kendall .20 .50
106 Jeff Kent .20 .50
107 Jeff King .10 .30
108 Mark Kotsay .20 .50
109 Ray Lankford .20 .50
110 Barry Larkin .30 .75
111 Mark Loretta .10 .30
112 Edgar Martinez .30 .75
113 Tino Martinez .30 .75
114 Quinton McCracken .10 .30
115 Fred McGriff .30 .75
116 Ryan Minor .10 .30
117 Hal Morris .10 .30
118 Bill Mueller .20 .50
119 Mike Mussina .30 .75
120 Dave Nilsson .10 .30
121 Otis Nixon .10 .30
122 Hideo Nomo .50 1.25
123 Paul O'Neill .30 .75
124 Jose Offerman .10 .30
125 John Olerud .20 .50
126 Rey Ordonez .10 .30
127 David Ortiz .50 1.25
128 Dean Palmer .20 .50
129 Chan Ho Park .20 .50
130 Aramis Ramirez .20 .50
131 Edgar Renteria .20 .50
132 Armando Rios .10 .30
133 Henry Rodriguez .10 .30
134 Scott Rolen .30 .75
135 Curt Schilling .20 .50
136 David Segui .10 .30
137 Richie Sexson .20 .50
138 Gary Sheffield .20 .50
139 John Smoltz .30 .75
140 Matt Stairs .10 .30
141 Justin Thompson .10 .30
142 Greg Vaughn .10 .30
143 Omar Vizquel .30 .75
144 Tim Wakefield .30 .75
145 Todd Walker .10 .30
146 Devon White .10 .30
147 Rondell White .20 .50
148 Matt Williams .20 .50
149 Enrique Wilson .10 .30
150 Kevin Young .20 .50

1999 Private Stock Exclusive

COMPLETE SET (20) 250.00 500.00
*STARS: 3X TO 8X BASIC CARDS

1999 Private Stock Platinum

*STARS: 5X TO 12X BASIC CARDS

1999 Private Stock Home Run History

COMPLETE SET (22) 40.00 100.00
COMMON MCGWIRE 2.50 6.00
COMMON SOSA 1.25 3.00
STATED ODDS 2:25 HOB/1:17 RET
1 Mark McGwire 61 2.50 6.00
3 Mark McGwire 62 4.00 10.00
15 Mark McGwire 70 6.00 15.00
16 Sammy Sosa 66 4.00 10.00
17 M.McGwire w J.D.Drew 4.00 10.00
18 Sammy Sosa SPEC 1.25 3.00
19 S.Sosa M.McGwire 3.00 8.00
20 M.McGwire S.Sosa 3.00 8.00
21 M.McGwire Crown DC 6.00 15.00
22 Cal Ripken 8.00 20.00

1999 Private Stock Players Choice

These cards parallel the regular Private Stock set. They have a special "Players Choice" logo stamped on them and were given away at the Players Choice award ceremony in Las Vegas. Each card was printed in different quantities so we have put the quantity next to the players name. Due to market scarcity, no pricing is provided.

14 Manny Ramirez/25
18 Sammy Sosa/15

1999 Private Stock Preferred

*STARS: 2.5X TO 6X BASIC CARDS

1999 Private Stock PS-206

*PS-206: .75X TO 2X BASIC PRI.STOCK

1999 Private Stock PS-206 Red

*PS-206 RED: 5X TO 12X BASIC PRI.STOCK
STATED ODDS 1:25 HOB/1:33 RET

1999 Private Stock Vintage

*STARS: 8X TO 20X BASIC CARDS

2000 Private Stock

COMPLETE SET (150) 20.00 50.00
COMP.SET w/o SP's (125) 8.00 20.00
COMMON CARD (1-150) .20 .50
COMMON SP PROSPECT 1.00 2.50
SP PROSPECT ODDS 1:4 HOB, 1:6 RET
1 Darin Erstad .20 .50
2 Troy Glaus .20 .50
3 Tim Salmon .20 .50
4 Mo Vaughn .20 .50
5 Jay Bell .20 .50
6 Luis Gonzalez .20 .50
7 Randy Johnson .50 1.25
8 Matt Williams .20 .50
9 Andruw Jones .20 .50
10 Chipper Jones .50 1.25
11 Brian Jordan .20 .50
12 Greg Maddux .60 1.50
13 Kevin Millwood .20 .50
14 Albert Belle .20 .50
15 Mike Mussina .30 .75
16 Cal Ripken 1.50 4.00
17 B.J. Surhoff .20 .50
18 Nomar Garciaparra .30 .75
19 Butch Huskey .20 .50
20 Pedro Martinez .30 .75
21 Troy O'Leary .20 .50
22 Mark Grace .30 .75
23 Bo Porter SP 1.00 2.50
24 Henry Rodriguez .20 .50
25 Sammy Sosa .50 1.25
26 Kerry Wood .20 .50
27 Jason Dellaero SP 1.00 2.50
28 Ray Durham .20 .50
29 Paul Konerko .20 .50
30 Carlos Lee .20 .50
31 Magglio Ordonez .30 .75
32 Frank Thomas .50 1.25
33 Mike Cameron .20 .50
34 Sean Casey .20 .50
35 Barry Larkin .30 .75
36 Greg Vaughn .20 .50
37 Roberto Alomar .30 .75
38 Russell Branyan SP 1.00 2.50
39 Kenny Lofton .20 .50
40 Manny Ramirez .50 1.25
41 Richie Sexson .20 .50
42 Jim Thome .30 .75
43 Omar Vizquel .30 .75
44 Pedro Astacio .20 .50
45 Vinny Castilla .20 .50
46 Todd Helton .30 .75
47 Ben Petrick SP 1.00 2.50
48 Juan Sosa SP RC 1.00 2.50
49 Larry Walker .30 .75
50 Tony Clark .20 .50
51 Damion Easley .20 .50
52 Juan Encarnacion .20 .50
53 Robert Fick SP 1.00 2.50
54 Dean Palmer .20 .50
55 A.J. Burnett SP 1.00 2.50
56 Luis Castillo .20 .50
57 Alex Gonzalez .20 .50
58 Julio Ramirez SP 1.00 2.50
59 Preston Wilson .20 .50
60 Jeff Bagwell .30 .75
61 Craig Biggio .30 .75
62 Ken Caminiti .30 .75
63 Carl Everett .20 .50
64 Mike Hampton .20 .50
65 Billy Wagner .20 .50
66 Carlos Beltran .30 .75
67 Dermal Brown SP 1.00 2.50
68 Jermaine Dye .20 .50
69 Carlos Febles .20 .50
70 Mark Quinn SP 1.00 2.50
71 Mike Sweeney .20 .50
72 Kevin Brown .20 .50
73 Eric Gagne SP 1.00 2.50
74 Eric Karros .20 .50
75 Raul Mondesi .20 .50
76 Gary Sheffield .20 .50
77 Jeromy Burnitz .20 .50
78 Jeff Cirillo .20 .50
79 Geoff Jenkins .20 .50
80 David Nilsson .20 .50
81 Ron Coomer .20 .50
82 Jacque Jones .20 .50
83 Corey Koskie .20 .50
84 Brad Radke .20 .50
85 Tony Armas Jr. SP 1.00 2.50
86 Peter Bergeron SP 1.00 2.50
87 Vladimir Guerrero .30 .75
88 Jose Vidro .20 .50
89 Rondell White .20 .50
90 Edgardo Alfonzo .20 .50
91 Roger Cedeno .20 .50
92 Rickey Henderson .50 1.25
93 Jay Payton SP 1.00 2.50
94 Mike Piazza .50 1.25
95 Jorge Toca SP 1.00 2.50
96 Robin Ventura .20 .50
97 Roger Clemens .60 1.50
98 David Cone .20 .50
99 Derek Jeter 1.25 3.00
100 D'Angelo Jimenez SP 1.00 2.50
101 Tino Martinez .20 .50
102 Alfonso Soriano SP 2.50 6.00
103 Bernie Williams .30 .75
104 Jason Giambi .20 .50
105 Ben Grieve .20 .50
106 Tim Hudson .30 .75
107 Matt Stairs .20 .50
108 Bob Abreu .20 .50
109 Doug Glanville .20 .50
110 Scott Rolen .30 .75
111 Curt Schilling .30 .75
112 Brian Giles .20 .50
113 Chad Hermansen SP 1.00 2.50
114 Jason Kendall .20 .50
115 Warren Morris .20 .50
116 Rick Ankiel SP 1.50 4.00
117 J.D. Drew .20 .50
118 Adam Kennedy SP 1.00 2.50
119 Ray Lankford .20 .50
120 Mark McGwire .75 2.00
121 Fernando Tatis .20 .50
122 Mike Darr SP 1.00 2.50
123 Ben Davis .20 .50
124 Tony Gwynn .50 1.25
125 Trevor Hoffman .30 .75
126 Reggie Sanders .20 .50
127 Barry Bonds .75 2.00
128 Ellis Burks .20 .50
129 Jeff Kent .20 .50
130 J.T. Snow .20 .50
131 Freddy Garcia .20 .50
132 Ken Griffey Jr. 1.00 2.50
133 Carlos Guillen SP 1.00 2.50
134 Edgar Martinez .30 .75
135 Alex Rodriguez .60 1.50
136 Miguel Cairo .20 .50
137 Jose Canseco .30 .75
138 Steve Cox SP 1.00 2.50
139 Roberto Hernandez .20 .50
140 Fred McGriff .30 .75
141 Juan Gonzalez .20 .50
142 Rusty Greer .20 .50
143 Ruben Mateo SP 1.00 2.50
144 Rafael Palmeiro .30 .75
145 Ivan Rodriguez .30 .75
146 Carlos Delgado .20 .50
147 Tony Fernandez .20 .50
148 Shawn Green .20 .50
149 Shannon Stewart .20 .50
150 Vernon Wells SP 1.00 2.50

2000 Private Stock Gold Portraits

*STARS: 6X TO 15X BASIC CARDS
*PROSPECTS: 1.25X TO 3X BASIC CARDS

2000 Private Stock Premiere Date

*STARS: 10X TO 25X BASIC CARDS
*PROSPECTS: 2X TO 5X BASIC CARDS
STATED ODDS 1:24 HOBBY

2000 Private Stock Silver Portraits

*STARS: 4X TO 10X BASIC CARDS
*PROSPECTS: .75X TO 2X BASIC CARDS

2000 Private Stock Artist's Canvas

PROOFS PRINT RUN 1 SERIAL #'d SET
PROOFS NOT PRICED DUE TO SCARCITY
1 Chipper Jones 2.00 5.00
2 Greg Maddux 2.50 6.00
3 Cal Ripken 6.00 15.00
4 Nomar Garciaparra 1.25 3.00
5 Sammy Sosa 2.00 5.00
6 Frank Thomas 2.00 5.00
7 Manny Ramirez 2.00 5.00
8 Larry Walker 1.25 3.00
9 Jeff Bagwell 1.25 3.00
10 Vladimir Guerrero 1.25 3.00
11 Mike Piazza 2.00 5.00
12 Roger Clemens 2.50 6.00
13 Derek Jeter 5.00 12.00
14 Mark McGwire 3.00 8.00
15 Tony Gwynn 2.00 5.00
16 Barry Bonds 3.00 8.00
17 Ken Griffey Jr. 4.00 10.00
18 Alex Rodriguez 2.50 6.00
19 Juan Gonzalez .75 2.00
20 Ivan Rodriguez 1.25 3.00

2000 Private Stock Extreme Action

COMPLETE SET (20) 15.00 40.00
STATED ODDS 2:25
1 Andruw Jones .40 1.00
2 Chipper Jones 1.00 2.50
3 Cal Ripken 3.00 8.00
4 Nomar Garciaparra .60 1.50
5 Sammy Sosa 1.00 2.50
6 Frank Thomas 1.00 2.50
7 Roberto Alomar .60 1.50
8 Manny Ramirez 1.00 2.50
9 Larry Walker .60 1.50
10 Jeff Bagwell .60 1.50
11 Vladimir Guerrero .60 1.50
12 Mike Piazza 1.00 2.50
13 Derek Jeter 2.50 6.00
14 Bernie Williams .60 1.50
15 Scott Rolen .60 1.50
16 Mark McGwire 1.50 4.00
17 Tony Gwynn 1.00 2.50
18 Ken Griffey Jr. 2.00 5.00
19 Alex Rodriguez 1.25 3.00
20 Ivan Rodriguez .60 1.50

2000 Private Stock PS-2000 Action

COMPLETE SET (60) 15.00 40.00
1 Mo Vaughn .15 .40
2 Greg Maddux .50 1.25
3 Andruw Jones .15 .40
4 Chipper Jones .40 1.00
5 Cal Ripken 1.25 3.00
6 Nomar Garciaparra .25 .60
7 Pedro Martinez .25 .60
8 Sammy Sosa .40 1.00
9 Jason Dellaero .15 .40
10 Magglio Ordonez .25 .60
11 Frank Thomas .40 1.00
12 Sean Casey .15 .40
13 Russell Branyan .15 .40
14 Manny Ramirez .40 1.00
15 Richie Sexson .15 .40
16 Ben Petrick .15 .40
17 Juan Sosa .15 .40
18 Larry Walker .25 .60
19 Robert Fick .15 .40
20 Craig Biggio .25 .60
21 Jeff Bagwell .25 .60
22 Carlos Beltran .25 .60
23 Dermal Brown .15 .40
24 Mark Quinn .15 .40
25 Eric Gagne .15 .40
26 Jeromy Burnitz .15 .40
27 Tony Armas Jr. .15 .40
28 Peter Bergeron .15 .40
29 Vladimir Guerrero .25 .60
30 Edgardo Alfonzo .15 .40
31 Mike Piazza .40 1.00
32 Jorge Toca .15 .40
33 Roger Clemens .50 1.25
34 Alfonso Soriano .40 1.00
35 Bernie Williams .25 .60
36 Derek Jeter 1.00 2.50
37 Tim Hudson .25 .60
38 Bob Abreu .15 .40
39 Scott Rolen .25 .60
40 Brian Giles .15 .40
41 Chad Hermansen .15 .40
42 Warren Morris .15 .40
43 Rick Ankiel .25 .60
44 J.D. Drew .15 .40
45 Adam Kennedy .15 .40
46 Mark McGwire .60 1.50
47 Mike Darr .15 .40
48 Tony Gwynn .40 1.00
49 Barry Bonds .60 1.50
50 Ken Griffey Jr. .75 2.00
51 Carlos Guillen .15 .40
52 Alex Rodriguez .50 1.25
53 Juan Gonzalez .15 .40
54 Ruben Mateo .15 .40
55 Ivan Rodriguez .25 .60
56 Rafael Palmeiro .25 .60
57 Jose Canseco .25 .60
58 Steve Cox .15 .40
59 Shawn Green .15 .40
60 Vernon Wells .15 .40

2000 Private Stock PS-2000 New Wave

COMPLETE SET (20) 20.00 50.00
1 Andruw Jones .75 2.00
2 Chipper Jones 2.00 5.00
3 Nomar Garciaparra 1.25 3.00
4 Magglio Ordonez 1.25 3.00
5 Sean Casey .75 2.00
6 Manny Ramirez 2.00 5.00
7 Richie Sexson .75 2.00
8 Carlos Beltran 1.25 3.00
9 Jeromy Burnitz .75 2.00
10 Vladimir Guerrero 1.25 3.00
11 Edgardo Alfonzo .75 2.00
12 Derek Jeter 5.00 12.00
13 Tim Hudson 1.25 3.00
14 Bob Abreu .75 2.00
15 Scott Rolen 1.25 3.00
16 Brian Giles .75 2.00
17 Warren Morris .75 2.00
18 J.D. Drew .75 2.00
19 Alex Rodriguez 2.50 6.00
20 Shawn Green .75 2.00

2000 Private Stock PS-2000 Rookies

COMPLETE SET (20) 30.00 60.00
1 Jason Dellaero 1.50 4.00
2 Russell Branyan 1.50 4.00
3 Ben Petrick 1.50 4.00
4 Juan Sosa 1.50 4.00
5 Robert Fick 1.50 4.00
6 Dermal Brown 1.50 4.00
7 Mark Quinn 1.50 4.00
8 Eric Gagne 1.50 4.00
9 Tony Armas Jr. 1.50 4.00
10 Peter Bergeron 1.50 4.00
11 Jorge Toca 1.50 4.00
12 Alfonso Soriano 4.00 10.00
13 Chad Hermansen 1.50 4.00
14 Rick Ankiel 2.50 6.00
15 Adam Kennedy 1.50 4.00
16 Mike Darr 1.50 4.00
17 Carlos Guillen 1.50 4.00
18 Steve Cox 1.50 4.00
19 Ruben Mateo 1.50 4.00
20 Vernon Wells 1.50 4.00

2000 Private Stock PS-2000 Stars

COMPLETE SET (20) 60.00 120.00
1 Mo Vaughn 1.25 3.00
2 Greg Maddux 4.00 10.00
3 Cal Ripken 10.00 25.00
4 Pedro Martinez 2.00 5.00
5 Sammy Sosa 3.00 8.00
6 Frank Thomas 3.00 8.00
7 Larry Walker 2.00 5.00
8 Craig Biggio 2.00 5.00
9 Jeff Bagwell 2.00 5.00
10 Mike Piazza 3.00 8.00
11 Roger Clemens 4.00 10.00
12 Bernie Williams 2.00 5.00
13 Mark McGwire 5.00 12.00
14 Tony Gwynn 3.00 8.00
15 Barry Bonds 5.00 12.00
16 Ken Griffey Jr. 6.00 15.00
17 Juan Gonzalez 1.25 3.00
18 Ivan Rodriguez 2.00 5.00
19 Rafael Palmeiro 2.00 5.00
20 Jose Canseco 2.00 5.00

2000 Private Stock Reserve

COMPLETE SET (20) 75.00 150.00
1 Chipper Jones 3.00 8.00
2 Greg Maddux 4.00 10.00
3 Cal Ripken 10.00 25.00
4 Nomar Garciaparra 2.00 5.00
5 Sammy Sosa 3.00 8.00
6 Frank Thomas 3.00 8.00
7 Manny Ramirez 3.00 8.00
8 Larry Walker 2.00 5.00
9 Jeff Bagwell 2.00 5.00
10 Vladimir Guerrero 2.00 5.00
11 Mike Piazza 3.00 8.00
12 Roger Clemens 4.00 10.00
13 Derek Jeter 8.00 20.00
14 Mark McGwire 5.00 12.00
15 Tony Gwynn 3.00 8.00
16 Barry Bonds 5.00 12.00
17 Ken Griffey Jr. 6.00 15.00
18 Alex Rodriguez 4.00 10.00
19 Ivan Rodriguez 2.00 5.00
20 Shawn Green 1.25 3.00

2001 Private Stock

COMPLETE SET (150) 75.00 150.00
COMP.SET w/o SP's (125) 25.00 50.00
COMMON CARD (1-125) .20 .50
COMMON CARD (126-150) 2.00 5.00
1 Darin Erstad .20 .50
2 Troy Glaus .20 .50
3 Tim Salmon .30 .75
4 Mo Vaughn .20 .50
5 Steve Finley .20 .50
6 Luis Gonzalez .20 .50
7 Randy Johnson .50 1.25
8 Matt Williams .20 .50
9 Rafael Furcal .20 .50
10 Andres Galarraga .20 .50
11 Tom Glavine .30 .75
12 Andruw Jones .30 .75
13 Chipper Jones .50 1.25
14 Greg Maddux .75 2.00
15 B.J. Surhoff .20 .50
16 Brady Anderson .20 .50
17 Albert Belle .20 .50
18 Mike Mussina .30 .75
19 Cal Ripken 1.50 4.00
20 Carl Everett .20 .50
21 Nomar Garciaparra .75 2.00
22 Pedro Martinez .30 .75
23 Mark Grace .30 .75
24 Sammy Sosa .50 1.25
25 Kerry Wood .20 .50
26 Carlos Lee .20 .50
27 Magglio Ordonez .20 .50
28 Frank Thomas .50 1.25
29 Sean Casey .20 .50
30 Ken Griffey Jr. 1.00 2.50
31 Barry Larkin .30 .75
32 Pokey Reese .20 .50
33 Roberto Alomar .30 .75
34 Kenny Lofton .20 .50
35 Manny Ramirez .30 .75
36 Jim Thome .30 .75
37 Omar Vizquel .30 .75
38 Jeff Cirillo .20 .50
39 Jeffrey Hammonds .20 .50
40 Todd Helton .30 .75
41 Larry Walker .20 .50
42 Tony Clark .20 .50
43 Juan Encarnacion .20 .50
44 Juan Gonzalez .20 .50
45 Hideo Nomo .50 1.25
46 Cliff Floyd .20 .50
47 Derrek Lee .30 .75
48 Henry Rodriguez .20 .50
49 Preston Wilson .20 .50
50 Jeff Bagwell .30 .75
51 Craig Biggio .30 .75
52 Richard Hidalgo .20 .50
53 Moises Alou .20 .50
54 Carlos Beltran .20 .50
55 Johnny Damon .30 .75
56 Jermaine Dye .20 .50
57 Mac Suzuki .20 .50
58 Mike Sweeney .20 .50
59 Adrian Beltre .20 .50
60 Kevin Brown .20 .50
61 Shawn Green .20 .50
62 Eric Karros .20 .50
63 Chan Ho Park .20 .50
64 Gary Sheffield .20 .50
65 Jeromy Burnitz .20 .50
66 Geoff Jenkins .20 .50
67 Richie Sexson .20 .50
68 Jacque Jones .20 .50
69 Matt Lawton .20 .50
70 Eric Milton .20 .50
71 Vladimir Guerrero .50 1.25
72 Jose Vidro .20 .50
73 Edgardo Alfonzo .20 .50
74 Mike Hampton .20 .50
75 Mike Piazza .75 2.00
76 Robin Ventura .20 .50
77 Jose Canseco .30 .75
78 Roger Clemens 1.00 2.50
79 Derek Jeter 1.25 3.00
80 David Justice .20 .50
81 Jorge Posada .30 .75
82 Bernie Williams .30 .75
83 Jason Giambi .20 .50
84 Ben Grieve .20 .50
85 Tim Hudson .20 .50
86 Terrence Long .20 .50
87 Miguel Tejada .20 .50
88 Bob Abreu .20 .50
89 Pat Burrell .20 .50
90 Mike Lieberthal .20 .50
91 Scott Rolen .30 .75
92 Kris Benson .20 .50
93 Brian Giles .20 .50
94 Jason Kendall .20 .50
95 Aramis Ramirez .20 .50
96 Rick Ankiel .20 .50
97 Will Clark .30 .75
98 J.D. Drew .20 .50
99 Jim Edmonds .20 .50
100 Mark McGwire 1.25 3.00
101 Fernando Tatis .20 .50
102 Adam Eaton .20 .50
103 Tony Gwynn .60 1.50
104 Phil Nevin .20 .50
105 Eric Owens .20 .50
106 Barry Bonds 1.25 3.00
107 Jeff Kent .20 .50
108 J.T. Snow .20 .50
109 Rickey Henderson .50 1.25
110 Edgar Martinez .30 .75
111 John Olerud .20 .50
112 Alex Rodriguez .60 1.50
113 Kazuhiro Sasaki .20 .50
114 Vinny Castilla .20 .50
115 Fred McGriff .30 .75
116 Greg Vaughn .20 .50
117 Gabe Kapler .20 .50
118 Ruben Mateo .20 .50
119 Rafael Palmeiro .30 .75
120 Ivan Rodriguez .30 .75
121 Tony Batista .20 .50
122 Jose Cruz Jr. .20 .50
123 Carlos Delgado .20 .50
124 Shannon Stewart .20 .50
125 David Wells .20 .50
126 Shawn Wooten SP 2.00 5.00
127 George Lombard SP 2.00 5.00
128 Morgan Burkhart SP 2.00 5.00
129 Ross Gload SP 2.00 5.00
130 Corey Patterson SP 2.00 5.00
131 Julio Zuleta SP 2.00 5.00
132 Joe Crede SP 4.00 10.00
133 Matt Ginter SP 2.00 5.00
134 Travis Dawkins SP 2.00 5.00
135 Eric Munson SP 2.00 5.00
136 Dee Brown SP 2.00 5.00
137 Luke Prokopec SP 2.00 5.00
138 Timo Perez SP 2.00 5.00
139 Alfonso Soriano SP 3.00 8.00
140 Jake Westbrook SP 2.00 5.00
141 Eric Byrnes SP 2.00 5.00
142 Adam Hyzdu SP 2.00 5.00
143 Jimmy Rollins SP 3.00 8.00
144 Xavier Nady SP 2.00 5.00
145 Ryan Vogelsong SP 2.00 5.00
146 Joel Pineiro SP 3.00 8.00
147 Aubrey Huff SP 3.00 8.00
148 Kenny Kelly SP 2.00 5.00
149 Josh Phelps SP 2.00 5.00
150 Vernon Wells SP 2.00 5.00

2001 Private Stock Gold Portraits

*STARS 1-125: 8X TO 20X BASIC CARDS
*PROSPECTS 126-150: .75X TO 2X BASIC

2001 Private Stock Premiere Date

*STARS 1-125: 8X TO 20X BASIC CARDS
*PROSPECTS 126-150: .75X TO 2X BASIC

2001 Private Stock Silver

*STARS 1-125: .75X TO 2X BASIC CARDS
*PROSPECTS: 126-150: .4X TO 1X BASIC

2001 Private Stock Silver Portraits

*STARS 1-125: 3X TO 8X BASIC CARDS
*PROSPECTS 126-150: .5X TO 1.2X BASIC

2001 Private Stock Artist's Canvas

COMPLETE SET (20) 200.00 400.00
PROOFS PRINT RUN 1 SERIAL #'d SET
PROOFS NOT PRICED DUE TO SCARCITY
1 Randy Johnson 5.00 12.00
2 Chipper Jones 5.00 12.00
3 Greg Maddux 8.00 20.00
4 Cal Ripken 15.00 40.00
5 Nomar Garciaparra 8.00 20.00
6 Pedro Martinez 3.00 8.00
7 Sammy Sosa 5.00 12.00
8 Frank Thomas 5.00 12.00
9 Ken Griffey Jr. 10.00 25.00
10 Manny Ramirez 3.00 8.00
11 Vladimir Guerrero 5.00 12.00
12 Mike Piazza 8.00 20.00
13 Roger Clemens 10.00 25.00
14 Derek Jeter 12.50 30.00
15 Jason Giambi 3.00 8.00
16 Rick Ankiel 3.00 8.00
17 Mark McGwire 12.50 30.00
18 Barry Bonds 12.50 30.00
19 Alex Rodriguez 6.00 15.00
20 Ivan Rodriguez 3.00 8.00

2001 Private Stock Extreme Action

COMPLETE SET (20) 60.00 120.00
1 Darin Erstad .75 2.00
2 Troy Glaus .75 2.00
3 Rafael Furcal .75 2.00
4 Cal Ripken 6.00 15.00
5 Nomar Garciaparra 3.00 8.00
6 Sammy Sosa 2.00 5.00
7 Frank Thomas 2.00 5.00
8 Ken Griffey Jr. 4.00 10.00
9 Roberto Alomar 1.25 3.00
10 Vladimir Guerrero 2.00 5.00
11 Derek Jeter 5.00 12.00
12 Mike Piazza 3.00 8.00
13 Jason Giambi .75 2.00
14 Miguel Tejada .75 2.00
15 Jim Edmonds .75 2.00
16 Mark McGwire 5.00 12.00
17 Barry Bonds 5.00 12.00
18 Jeff Kent .75 2.00
19 Alex Rodriguez 2.50 6.00
20 Ivan Rodriguez 1.25 3.00

2001 Private Stock Game Gear

1 Garret Anderson Bat 4.00 10.00
2 Darin Erstad Jsy 4.00 10.00
3 Ron Gant Bat 4.00 10.00
4 Troy Glaus Jsy 4.00 10.00
5 Tim Salmon Bat 6.00 15.00
6 Mo Vaughn Jsy Grey 4.00 10.00
7 Mo Vaughn Jsy White 4.00 10.00
8 Mo Vaughn Bat 4.00 10.00
9 Jay Bell Jsy 4.00 10.00
10 Jay Bell Bat 4.00 10.00
11 Erubiel Durazo Jsy Black 4.00 10.00
12 Erubiel Durazo Jsy White 4.00 10.00
13 Erubiel Durazo Bat 4.00 10.00
14 Steve Finley Bat 4.00 10.00
15 Randy Johnson Jsy 6.00 15.00
16 Byung-Hyun Kim Jsy White 4.00 10.00
17 Byung-Hyun Kim Jsy Grey 4.00 10.00
18 Matt Williams Jsy Grey 4.00 10.00
19 Matt Williams Jsy White 4.00 10.00
20 Matt Williams Jsy Purple 4.00 10.00
21 Bobby Bonilla Jsy 4.00 10.00
22 Rafael Furcal Bat 4.00 10.00
23 Andruw Jones Bat 6.00 15.00
24 Chipper Jones Jsy 6.00 15.00
25 Chipper Jones Bat 6.00 15.00
26 Brian Jordan Jsy 4.00 10.00
27 Javier Lopez Bat 4.00 10.00
28 Greg Maddux Jsy 6.00 15.00
29 Greg Maddux Bat 6.00 15.00
30 Brady Anderson Bat 4.00 10.00
31 Albert Belle Bat 4.00 10.00
32 Nomar Garciaparra Bat 8.00 20.00
33 Pedro Martinez Bat 6.00 15.00
34 Jose Offerman Bat 4.00 10.00
35 Damon Buford Jsy 4.00 10.00
36 Jose Nieves Bat 4.00 10.00
38 Kerry Wood Bat 4.00 10.00
39 James Baldwin Jsy 4.00 10.00
40 Ray Durham Jsy 4.00 10.00
41 Ray Durham Bat 4.00 10.00
42 Carlos Lee Bat 4.00 10.00
43 Magglio Ordonez Jsy 4.00 10.00
44 Magglio Ordonez Bat 4.00 10.00
45 Chris Singleton Jsy 4.00 10.00
46 Aaron Boone Bat 4.00 10.00
47 Sean Casey Bat 4.00 10.00
48 Barry Larkin Jsy 6.00 15.00
49 Pokey Reese Jsy 4.00 10.00
50 Pokey Reese Bat 4.00 10.00
51 Dmitri Young Bat 4.00 10.00
52 Roberto Alomar Bat 6.00 15.00
53 Einar Diaz Bat 4.00 10.00
54 Kenny Lofton Jsy 4.00 10.00
55 David Segui Bat 4.00 10.00
56 Omar Vizquel Jsy 6.00 15.00
57 Luis Castillo Jsy 4.00 10.00
58 Jeff Cirillo Jsy 4.00 10.00
59 Jeff Frye Bat 4.00 10.00
60 Todd Helton Jsy 6.00 15.00
61 Todd Helton Bat 6.00 15.00
62 Neifi Perez Bat 4.00 10.00
63 Larry Walker Jsy 4.00 10.00
64 Larry Walker Bat 4.00 10.00
65 Masato Yoshii Jsy 4.00 10.00
66 Brad Ausmus Jsy 4.00 10.00
67 Rich Becker Bat 4.00 10.00
68 Tony Clark Bat 4.00 10.00
69 Deivi Cruz Bat 4.00 10.00
70 Juan Gonzalez Bat 4.00 10.00
71 Dean Palmer Bat 4.00 10.00
72 Cliff Floyd Jsy White 4.00 10.00
73 Cliff Floyd Jsy Teal 4.00 10.00
74 Cliff Floyd Bat 4.00 10.00
75 Alex Gonzalez Jsy 4.00 10.00
76 Alex Gonzalez Marlins Bat 4.00 10.00
77 Mark Kotsay Bat 4.00 10.00
78 Derrek Lee Bat 6.00 15.00
79 Pablo Ozuna Jsy 4.00 10.00
80 Craig Biggio Bat 6.00 15.00
81 Ken Caminiti Bat 4.00 10.00
82 Roger Cedeno Bat 4.00 10.00
83 Ricky Bottalico Bat 4.00 10.00
84 Dee Brown Bat 4.00 10.00
85 Jermaine Dye Bat 4.00 10.00
86 David McCarty Bat 4.00 10.00
87 Hector Ortiz Bat 4.00 10.00
88 Joe Randa Bat 4.00 10.00
89 Adrian Beltre Jsy 4.00 10.00
90 Kevin Brown Jsy 4.00 10.00
91 Alex Cora Bat 4.00 10.00
92 Darren Dreifort Bat 4.00 10.00
93 Shawn Green Jsy White 4.00 10.00
94 Shawn Green Jsy Grey 4.00 10.00
95 Shawn Green Bat 4.00 10.00
96 Todd Hundley Jsy 4.00 10.00
97 Eric Karros Bat 4.00 10.00
98 Chan Ho Park Jsy 4.00 10.00
99 Chan Ho Park Bat 4.00 10.00
101 Gary Sheffield Bat 4.00 10.00
102 Ismael Valdes Bat 4.00 10.00
103 Jeromy Burnitz Bat 4.00 10.00
104 Marquis Grissom Bat 4.00 10.00
105 Matt Lawton Bat 4.00 10.00
106 Fernando Seguignol Bat 4.00 10.00
107 E.Alfonzo Jsy White Swing 4.00 10.00
108 E.Alfonzo Jsy White Drop 4.00 10.00
109 Edgardo Alfonzo Jsy Black 4.00 10.00
110 Derek Bell Jsy White 4.00 10.00
111 Derek Bell Jsy Black 4.00 10.00
112 Armando Benitez Bat 4.00 10.00
113 Al Leiter Bat 4.00 10.00
114 Rey Ordonez Jsy Grey Field 4.00 10.00
115 Rey Ordonez Jsy White 4.00 10.00
116 Rey Ordonez Jsy Grey Bunt 4.00 10.00
117 Rey Ordonez Bat 4.00 10.00
118 Jay Payton Bat 4.00 10.00
119 Mike Piazza Jsy 8.00 20.00
120 Robin Ventura Jsy Black Hit 4.00 10.00
121 R.Ventura Jsy Black Field 4.00 10.00
122 Robin Ventura Jsy White 4.00 10.00
123 Luis Polonia Bat 4.00 10.00
124 Bernie Williams Bat 6.00 15.00
125 Eric Chavez Jsy 4.00 10.00
126 Jason Giambi Jsy 4.00 10.00
127 Jason Giambi Bat 4.00 10.00
128 Ben Grieve Jsy 4.00 10.00
129 Ben Grieve Bat 4.00 10.00
130 Ramon Hernandez Bat 4.00 10.00
131 Tim Hudson Jsy 4.00 10.00
132 Terrence Long Bat 4.00 10.00
133 Mark Mulder Jsy 4.00 10.00
134 Adam Piatt Jsy 4.00 10.00
135 Olmedo Saenz Bat 4.00 10.00
136 Matt Stairs Bat 4.00 10.00
137 Mike Stanley Bat 4.00 10.00
138 Miguel Tejada Bat 4.00 10.00
139 Travis Lee Bat 4.00 10.00
140 Brian Giles Bat 4.00 10.00
141 Jason Kendall Jsy 4.00 10.00
142 Will Clark Bat 6.00 15.00
143 J.D. Drew Bat 4.00 10.00
144 Jim Edmonds Bat 4.00 10.00
145 Mark McGwire Bat 12.50 30.00
146 Edgar Renteria Bat 4.00 10.00
147 Garrett Stephenson Jsy 4.00 10.00
148 Tony Gwynn Jsy 6.00 15.00
149 Ruben Rivera Bat 4.00 10.00
150 Barry Bonds Jsy 12.50 30.00
151 Barry Bonds Bat 12.50 30.00
152 Ellis Burks Jsy 4.00 10.00
153 J.T. Snow Bat 4.00 10.00
154 Jay Buhner Jsy 4.00 10.00
155 Jay Buhner Bat 4.00 10.00
156 Carlos Guillen Jsy 4.00 10.00
157 Carlos Guillen Bat 4.00 10.00
158 Rickey Henderson Bat 6.00 15.00
159 Edgar Martinez Bat 6.00 15.00
160 Gil Meche Jsy 4.00 10.00
161 John Olerud Bat 4.00 10.00
162 Joe Oliver Bat 4.00 10.00
163 Alex Rodriguez Jsy SP 50.00 100.00
164 Kazuhiro Sasaki Jsy 4.00 10.00
165 Dan Wilson Jsy 4.00 10.00
166 Dan Wilson Bat 4.00 10.00
167 Vinny Castilla Bat 4.00 10.00
168 Jose Guillen Bat 4.00 10.00
169 Fred McGriff Jsy 6.00 15.00
170 Rusty Greer Bat 4.00 10.00
171 Mike Lamb Bat 4.00 10.00
172 Ruben Mateo Jsy 4.00 10.00
173 Ruben Mateo Bat 4.00 10.00
174 Rafael Palmeiro Jsy 6.00 15.00
175 Rafael Palmeiro Bat 6.00 15.00
178 Tony Batista Bat 4.00 10.00
179 Marty Cordova Bat 4.00 10.00
180 Jose Cruz Jr. Bat 4.00 10.00
181 Alex Gonzalez Blue Jays Bat 4.00 10.00
182 Raul Mondesi Bat 4.00 10.00

2001 Private Stock Game Jersey Patch

2 Darin Erstad 10.00 25.00
4 Troy Glaus 10.00 25.00
6 Mo Vaughn Grey 10.00 25.00
7 Mo Vaughn White 10.00 25.00
9 Jay Bell 10.00 25.00
11 Erubiel Durazo Black 6.00 15.00
12 Erubiel Durazo White 6.00 15.00
15 Randy Johnson 30.00 60.00
16 Byung-Hyun Kim White 10.00 25.00
17 Byung-Hyun Kim Grey 10.00 25.00
18 Matt Williams Grey 10.00 25.00
19 Matt Williams White 10.00 25.00
20 Matt Williams Purple 10.00 25.00
21 Bobby Bonilla 10.00 25.00
24 Chipper Jones 30.00 60.00
26 Brian Jordan 10.00 25.00
28 Greg Maddux 60.00 120.00
35 Damon Buford 6.00 15.00
39 James Baldwin 6.00 15.00
40 Ray Durham 10.00 25.00
43 Magglio Ordonez 10.00 25.00
45 Chris Singleton 6.00 15.00
48 Barry Larkin 15.00 40.00
49 Pokey Reese 6.00 15.00
54 Kenny Lofton 15.00 40.00
56 Omar Vizquel 15.00 40.00
57 Luis Castillo 6.00 15.00
58 Jeff Cirillo 6.00 15.00
60 Todd Helton 15.00 40.00
63 Larry Walker 10.00 25.00
65 Masato Yoshii 6.00 15.00
66 Brad Ausmus 10.00 25.00
72 Cliff Floyd White 10.00 25.00
73 Cliff Floyd Teal 10.00 25.00
75 Alex Gonzalez 6.00 15.00
79 Pablo Ozuna 6.00 15.00
89 Adrian Beltre 10.00 25.00
90 Kevin Brown 10.00 25.00
93 Shawn Green White 10.00 25.00
94 Shawn Green Grey 10.00 25.00
96 Todd Hundley 6.00 15.00
98 Chan Ho Park 10.00 25.00
107 E.Alfonzo White Swing 6.00 15.00
108 E.Alfonzo White Drop 6.00 15.00
109 Edgardo Alfonzo Black 6.00 15.00
110 Derek Bell White 6.00 15.00
111 Derek Bell Black 6.00 15.00
114 Rey Ordonez Grey Field 6.00 15.00
115 Rey Ordonez White 6.00 15.00
116 Rey Ordonez Grey Bunt 6.00 15.00
119 Mike Piazza 60.00 120.00
120 Robin Ventura Black Hit 10.00 25.00
121 Robin Ventura Black Field 10.00 25.00
122 Robin Ventura White 10.00 25.00
125 Eric Chavez 10.00 25.00
126 Jason Giambi 10.00 25.00
128 Ben Grieve 6.00 15.00
131 Tim Hudson 10.00 25.00
133 Mark Mulder 10.00 25.00
134 Adam Piatt 6.00 15.00
141 Jason Kendall 10.00 25.00
147 Garrett Stephenson 6.00 15.00
148 Tony Gwynn 50.00 100.00
150 Barry Bonds 75.00 150.00
152 Ellis Burks 10.00 25.00
154 Jay Buhner 10.00 25.00
156 Carlos Guillen 10.00 25.00
160 Gil Meche 6.00 15.00
164 Kazuhiro Sasaki 10.00 25.00
165 Dan Wilson 6.00 15.00
169 Fred McGriff 15.00 40.00
172 Ruben Mateo 6.00 15.00
174 Rafael Palmeiro 15.00 40.00

2001 Private Stock PS-206 Action

COMPLETE SET (60) 10.00 25.00
1 Darin Erstad .15 .40
2 Troy Glaus .15 .40
3 Randy Johnson .40 1.00
4 Rafael Furcal .15 .40
5 Tom Glavine .25 .60
6 Andruw Jones .25 .60
7 Chipper Jones .40 1.00
8 Greg Maddux .60 1.50
9 Albert Belle .15 .40
10 Mike Mussina .25 .60
11 Cal Ripken 1.25 3.00
12 Nomar Garciaparra .60 1.50
13 Pedro Martinez .25 .60
14 Mark Grace .25 .60
15 Sammy Sosa .40 1.00
16 Kerry Wood .15 .40
17 Magglio Ordonez .15 .40
18 Frank Thomas .40 1.00
19 Ken Griffey Jr. .75 2.00
20 Barry Larkin .25 .60
21 Roberto Alomar .25 .60
22 Manny Ramirez .25 .60
23 Jim Thome .25 .60
24 Jeff Cirillo .15 .40
25 Todd Helton .25 .60
26 Larry Walker .15 .40
27 Juan Gonzalez .15 .40
28 Hideo Nomo .40 1.00
29 Preston Wilson .15 .40
30 Jeff Bagwell .25 .60
31 Craig Biggio .25 .60
32 Johnny Damon .25 .60
33 Jermaine Dye .15 .40
34 Shawn Green .15 .40
35 Gary Sheffield .15 .40
36 Vladimir Guerrero .40 1.00
37 Mike Piazza .60 1.50
38 Jose Canseco .25 .60
39 Roger Clemens .75 2.00
40 Derek Jeter 1.00 2.50
41 Bernie Williams .25 .60
42 Jason Giambi .15 .40
43 Ben Grieve .15 .40
44 Pat Burrell .15 .40
45 Scott Rolen .25 .60
46 Rick Ankiel .15 .40
47 J.D. Drew .15 .40
48 Jim Edmonds .15 .40
49 Mark McGwire 1.00 2.50
50 Tony Gwynn .50 1.25
51 Barry Bonds 1.00 2.50
52 Jeff Kent .15 .40
53 Edgar Martinez .25 .60
54 Alex Rodriguez .50 1.25
55 Kazuhiro Sasaki .15 .40
56 Fred McGriff .25 .60
57 Rafael Palmeiro .25 .60
58 Ivan Rodriguez .25 .60
59 Tony Batista .15 .40
60 Carlos Delgado .15 .40

2001 Private Stock PS-206 New Wave

COMPLETE SET (20) 60.00 120.00
1 Darin Erstad 2.00 5.00
2 Troy Glaus 2.00 5.00
3 Rafael Furcal 2.00 5.00
4 Andruw Jones 3.00 8.00
5 Magglio Ordonez 2.00 5.00
6 Carlos Lee 2.00 5.00
7 Todd Helton 3.00 8.00
8 Johnny Damon 3.00 8.00
9 Jermaine Dye 2.00 5.00
10 Vladimir Guerrero 5.00 12.00
11 Jason Giambi 2.00 5.00
12 Ben Grieve 2.00 5.00
13 Pat Burrell 2.00 5.00
14 Rick Ankiel 2.00 5.00
15 J.D. Drew 2.00 5.00
16 Adam Eaton 2.00 5.00
17 Kazuhiro Sasaki 2.00 5.00
18 Ruben Mateo 2.00 5.00
19 Tony Batista 2.00 5.00
20 Carlos Delgado 2.00 5.00

2001 Private Stock PS-206 Rookies

COMPLETE SET (20) 75.00 150.00
1 George Lombard 4.00 10.00
2 Morgan Burkhart 4.00 10.00
3 Corey Patterson 4.00 10.00
4 Julio Zuleta 4.00 10.00
5 Joe Crede 8.00 20.00
6 Matt Ginter 4.00 10.00
7 Aaron Myette 4.00 10.00
8 Travis Dawkins 4.00 10.00
9 Eric Munson 4.00 10.00
10 Dee Brown 4.00 10.00
11 Luke Prokopec 4.00 10.00
12 Jorge Toca 4.00 10.00
13 Alfonso Soriano 6.00 15.00
14 Eric Byrnes 4.00 10.00
15 Adam Hyzdu 4.00 10.00
16 Jimmy Rollins 4.00 10.00
17 Joel Pineiro 4.00 10.00
18 Aubrey Huff 4.00 10.00
19 Kenny Kelly 4.00 10.00
20 Vernon Wells 4.00 10.00

2001 Private Stock PS-206 Stars

COMPLETE SET (20) 125.00 250.00
1 Chipper Jones 4.00 10.00
2 Greg Maddux 6.00 15.00
3 Cal Ripken 12.50 30.00
4 Nomar Garciaparra 6.00 15.00
5 Pedro Martinez 3.00 8.00
6 Sammy Sosa 4.00 10.00
7 Frank Thomas 4.00 10.00
8 Ken Griffey Jr. 8.00 20.00
9 Manny Ramirez 3.00 8.00
10 Jeff Bagwell 3.00 8.00
11 Gary Sheffield 3.00 8.00
12 Mike Piazza 6.00 15.00
13 Roger Clemens 8.00 20.00
14 Derek Jeter 10.00 25.00
15 Rick Ankiel 3.00 8.00
16 Mark McGwire 10.00 25.00
17 Tony Gwynn 5.00 12.00
18 Barry Bonds 10.00 25.00
19 Alex Rodriguez 5.00 12.00
20 Ivan Rodriguez 3.00 8.00

2001 Private Stock Reserve

COMPLETE SET (20) 125.00 250.00
1 Randy Johnson 3.00 8.00
2 Chipper Jones 3.00 8.00
3 Greg Maddux 5.00 12.00
4 Cal Ripken 10.00 25.00
5 Nomar Garciaparra 5.00 12.00
6 Pedro Martinez 2.00 5.00
7 Sammy Sosa 3.00 8.00
8 Frank Thomas 3.00 8.00
9 Ken Griffey Jr. 6.00 15.00
10 Todd Helton 2.00 5.00
11 Vladimir Guerrero 3.00 8.00
12 Mike Piazza 5.00 12.00
13 Roger Clemens 6.00 15.00
14 Derek Jeter 8.00 20.00
15 Rick Ankiel 2.00 5.00
16 Mark McGwire 8.00 20.00
17 Tony Gwynn 4.00 10.00
18 Barry Bonds 8.00 20.00
19 Alex Rodriguez 4.00 10.00
20 Ivan Rodriguez 2.00 5.00

1994 Pro Mags Promo

These three cards were issued to introduce Pro Mags to the collectible market. They measure 2 1/8" by 3 3/8" and have blank backs. The cards are numbered with a "Promo Mag" logo near the bottom.

COMPLETE SET (3) 3.00 8.00
1 Ken Griffey 2.00 5.00
2 Greg Maddux 1.25 3.00
3 Frank Thomas 1.00 2.50

1994-95 Pro Mags

1994-95 Pro Mags were distributed in rack packs containing five random player magnets, one team magnet, and a checklist. Each player mag has rounded corners and measures 2 1/8" by 3 3/8" (team mags measure 2 1/8" by 3/4"). Fronts feature borderless color player action shots with name at the bottom and a team logo at upper left. The black magnetized backs are blank. The magnets are numbered on the front. Five hundred Joe Carter autograph magnets were randomly inserted into packs as well.

COMPLETE SET (140) 30.00 80.00
1 Terry Pendleton .08 .25
2 Ryan Klesko .20 .50
3 Fred McGriff .30 .75
4 David Justice .40 1.00
5 Greg Maddux 1.50 4.00
6 Brady Anderson .30 .75
7 Ben McDonald .08 .25
8 Cal Ripken 2.50 6.00
9 Mike Mussina .40 1.00
10 Jeffrey Hammonds .08 .25
11 Roger Clemens 1.25 3.00
12 Andre Dawson .30 .75
13 Mike Greenwell .08 .25
14 Mo Vaughn .20 .50
15 Otis Nixon .20 .50
16 Chad Curtis .08 .25
17 Mark Langston .08 .25
18 Tim Salmon .20 .50
19 Chuck Finley .08 .25
20 Eduardo Perez .08 .25
21 Steve Buechele .08 .25
22 Mark Grace .40 1.00
23 Sammy Sosa .75 2.00
24 Derrick May .08 .25
25 Shawon Dunston .08 .25
26 Jack McDowell .08 .25
27 Tim Raines .20 .50
28 Frank Thomas .60 1.50
29 Robin Ventura .30 .75
30 Julio Franco .20 .50
31 John Smiley .08 .25
32 Barry Larkin .40 1.00
33 Jose Rijo .08 .25
34 Reggie Sanders .20 .50
35 Kevin Mitchell .08 .25
36 Sandy Alomar .20 .50
37 Carlos Baerga .08 .25
38 Albert Belle .20 .50
39 Manny Ramirez .60 1.50
40 Eddie Murray .60 1.50
41 Dante Bichette .20 .50
42 Ellis Burks .20 .50
43 Andres Galarraga .40 1.00
44 Greg Harris .08 .25
45 David Nied .08 .25
46 Cecil Fielder .20 .50
47 Kirk Gibson .20 .50
48 Mickey Tettleton .08 .25
49 Lou Whitaker .20 .50
50 Travis Fryman .20 .50
51 Jeff Conine .20 .50
52 Charlie Hough .20 .50
53 Benito Santiago .20 .50
54 Gary Sheffield .60 1.50
55 Dave Magadan .08 .25
56 Jeff Bagwell .60 1.50
57 Luis Gonzalez .40 1.00
58 Andujar Cedeno .08 .25
59 Craig Biggio .30 .75
60 Doug Drabek .08 .25
61 Tom Gordon .08 .25
62 Brian McRae .08 .25
63 David Cone .30 .75
64 Wally Joyner .20 .50
65 Jeff Montgomery .08 .25
66 Eric Karros .30 .75
67 Tom Candiotti .08 .25
68 Delino DeShields .08 .25
69 Orel Hershiser .20 .50
70 Mike Piazza 1.50 4.00
71 Darryl Hamilton .08 .25
72 Kevin Seitzer .08 .25
73 B.J. Surhoff .20 .50
74 John Jaha .08 .25
75 Greg Vaughn .08 .25
76 Kent Hrbek .08 .25
77 Kirby Puckett .75 2.00
78 Kevin Tapani .08 .25
79 Dave Winfield .50 1.25
80 Chuck Knoblauch .20 .50
81 Moises Alou .20 .50
82 Wil Cordero .08 .25
83 Marquis Grissom .20 .50
84 Pedro Martinez .60 1.50
85 Larry Walker .40 1.00
86 Jim Abbott .08 .25
87 Wade Boggs .60 1.50
88 Don Mattingly 1.25 3.00
89 Luis Polonia .08 .25
90 Danny Tartabull .08 .25
91 Bobby Bonilla .08 .25
92 Todd Hundley .20 .50
93 Dwight Gooden .20 .50
94 Jeromy Burnitz .20 .50
95 Bret Saberhagen .08 .25
96 Dennis Eckersley .50 1.25
97 Mark McGwire 1.25 3.00
98 Ruben Sierra .20 .50
99 Terry Steinbach .08 .25
100 Rickey Henderson .75 2.00
101 Darren Daulton .20 .50
102 Lenny Dykstra .20 .50
103 Dave Hollins .08 .25
104 John Kruk .20 .50
105 Curt Schilling .75 2.00
106 Carlos Garcia .08 .25
107 Jay Bell .08 .25
108 Don Slaught .08 .25
109 Andy Van Slyke .08 .25
110 Orlando Merced .08 .25
111 Ray Lankford .20 .50
112 Mark Whiten .08 .25
113 Todd Zeile .08 .25
114 Ozzie Smith 1.00 2.50
115 Gregg Jefferies .20 .50
116 Derek Bell .08 .25
117 Andy Benes .08 .25
118 Phil Plantier .08 .25
119 Tony Gwynn 1.25 3.00
120 Bip Roberts .08 .25
121 Barry Bonds 1.25 3.00
122 John Burkett .08 .25
123 Robby Thompson .08 .25
124 Darren Lewis .08 .25
125 Willie McGee .08 .25
126 Jay Buhner .30 .75
127 Ken Griffey Jr. 1.50 4.00
128 Randy Johnson .60 1.50
129 Eric Anthony .08 .25
130 Edgar Martinez .30 .75
131 Kevin Brown .30 .75
132 Jose Canseco .60 1.50
133 Juan Gonzalez .40 1.00
134 Will Clark .40 1.00
135 Ivan Rodriguez .60 1.50
136 Roberto Alomar .40 1.00
137 Joe Carter .20 .50
138 Juan Guzman .08 .25
139 Paul Molitor .60 1.50
140 John Olerud .30 .75
AU137 Joe Carter AU 8.00 20.00

1996 Pro Mags All-Stars

These 24 magnet cards measure approximately 2" by 3 1/4". The set was distributed in 12-card packs for each league, including 10 players plus an All-Star Game logo and league logo card. The cards have rounded corners and the garish fronts feature the players portrait against either the National or American League background. There is also a league logo and a 1996 All-Star game logo on the front of the card. These cards are numbered in very small print in the lower left hand corner. The American League cards are 1-10, while the National League cards are #11-20.

COMPLETE SET (24) 20.00 50.00
1 Brady Anderson .40 1.00
2 Jose Canseco 1.00 2.50
3 Ken Griffey Jr. UER NNO 2.50 6.00
4 Kenny Lofton .60 1.50
5 Cal Ripken 4.00 10.00
6 Frank Thomas 1.00 2.50
7 Ivan Rodriguez 1.00 2.50
8 Mo Vaughn .40 1.00
9 Albert Belle .40 1.00
10 Alex Rodriguez 2.50 6.00
11 Hideo Nomo .75 2.00
12 Greg Maddux 2.50 6.00
13 Jeff Bagwell 1.00 2.50
14 Barry Bonds 1.50 4.00
15 Ryan Klesko .40 1.00
16 Mike Piazza 2.50 6.00
17 David Justice .75 2.00
18 Dante Bichette .20 .50
19 Barry Larkin .75 2.00
20 Tony Gwynn 2.00 5.00
NNO American League Logo .20 .50
NNO National League Logo .20 .50
NNO All-Star Game Logo .20 .50
NNO All-Star Game Logo .20 .50

1996 Pro Mags Die Cuts

This 25-card set was issued by Chris Martin Enterprises and features color action figures of some of the stars of Major League Baseball on a die-cut magnet.

COMPLETE SET (25) 25.00 60.00
1 David Justice .60 1.50
2 Ryan Klesko .60 1.50
3 Fred McGriff .75 2.00
4 Cal Ripken Jr. 4.00 10.00
5 Bobby Bonilla .40 1.00
6 Mo Vaughn .60 1.50
7 Tim Salmon 1.00 2.50
8 Frank Thomas 1.25 3.00
9 Barry Larkin 1.00 2.50
10 Albert Belle .60 1.50
11 Eddie Murray 1.25 3.00
12 Dante Bichette .40 1.00
13 Andres Galarraga 1.00 2.50

14 Cecil Fielder .60 1.50
15 Hideo Nomo 1.00 2.50
16 Mike Piazza 2.50 6.00
17 Kirby Puckett 1.50 4.00
18 Don Mattingly 2.00 5.00
19 Tony Gwynn 2.00 5.00
20 Barry Bonds 1.50 4.00
21 Ken Griffey Jr. 2.50 6.00
22 Randy Johnson 1.25 3.00
23 Will Clark 1.00 2.50
24 Juan Gonzalez 1.00 2.50
25 Joe Carter .60 1.50

1995 ProMint

This set of 15 diamond cards was produced by ProMint. The embossed gold-foil cards feature 22-karat gold on their fronts and a five-point diamond next to the player's name at the bottom. Each card is individually numbered and packaged in an acrylic holder.

COMPLETE SET (15) 200.00 400.00
1 Jeff Bagwell 10.00 25.00
2 Albert Belle 6.00 15.00
3 Barry Bonds 10.00 25.00
4 George Brett 10.00 25.00
5 Roger Clemens 10.00 25.00
6 Ken Griffey Jr. 12.50 30.00
7 Tony Gwynn 10.00 25.00
8 Greg Maddux 12.50 30.00
9 Don Mattingly 10.00 25.00
10 Mike Piazza 10.00 25.00
11 Kirby Puckett 8.00 20.00
12 Cal Ripken 15.00 40.00
13 Nolan Ryan 15.00 40.00
14 Ozzie Smith 10.00 25.00
15 Frank Thomas 10.00 25.00

1998 ProMint

These two cards honor the participants in the great home run chase of 1998.

COMPLETE SET 8.00 20.00
1 Mark McGwire/70 Homers 4.00 10.00
2 Sammy Sosa/66 Homers 4.00 10.00

1998 ProMint McGwire Fleer

Issued by ProMint and liscenced by Fleers, this 24K card commemorates Mark McGwire breaking the single season home run record

1 Mark McGwire 4.00 10.00
Smashing the Record

1993 ProMint 22K Gold

This 22 karat gold cards measure the standard size and features an embossed image of the player bordered by an embossed arrow design. The player's name, along with the ProMint logo, appear near the bottom. The horizontal back carries the player's name within a motion-streaked baseball icon at the upper left. Career highlights appear in the "outfield" of a baseball field design. The card carries its production number at the bottom right, but is otherwise unnumbered.

1 Barry Bonds 3.00 8.00
2 Nolan Ryan 3.00 8.00
5 George Brett

1991 Pro Set Pro Files

These cards measure the standard size. The fronts have full-bleed color photos, with facsimile autographs inscribed across the bottom of the pictures. Reportedly only 150 of each were produced and approximately 100 of each were handed out as part of a contest on the Pro Files TV show. Each week viewers were invited to send in their names and addresses to a Pro Set post office box. All subjects in the set made appearances on the TV show. The show was hosted by Craig James and Tim Brant and was aired on Saturday nights in Dallas and sponsored by Pro Set. The cards were subtitled "Signature Series". The cards are unnumbered and are listed in alphabetical order by subject in the checklist below. All of the cards were facsimile autographed except for Anne Smith who signed all of her cards personally.

COMPLETE SET (13) 120.00 300.00
5 Ferguson Jenkins 8.00 20.00
12 Vernon Wells 4.00 10.00

1967 Pro's Pizza

This set, which features members of both Chicago teams featrures a square design with the words "The Pro's Pizza" in a black box in the upper right. These photos are in black and white. Since these cards are unnumbered, we have sequenced them in alphabetical order. Ron Santo was involved in management of Pro's Pizza at the time this set was issued.

COMPLETE SET 1500.00 3000.00
1 Ted Abernathy 50.00 100.00
2 George Altman 50.00 100.00
3 Joe Amalfitano 50.00 100.00
4 Ernie Banks 400.00 800.00
5 Glenn Beckert 50.00 100.00
6 Ernie Broglio 50.00 100.00
7 Byron Browne 50.00 100.00
8 Don Buford 50.00 100.00
9 Billy Connors 50.00 100.00
10 Dick Ellsworth 50.00 100.00
11 Billy Hoeft 50.00 100.00
12 Ken Holtzman 100.00 200.00
13 Joel Horlen 50.00 100.00
14 Randy Hundley 50.00 100.00
15 Fergie Jenkins 250.00 500.00
16 Don Kessinger 50.00 100.00
17 Chris Krug 50.00 100.00
18 Gary Peters 50.00 100.00
19 Ron Santo 125.00 250.00
20 Carl Warwick 50.00 100.00
21 Billy Williams 250.00 500.00

1996 Pro Stamps

This 140-stamp set was issued by Chris Martin Enterprises and distributed on 3" by 7 1/2" sheets of six stamps, five players of the same team and team logo. The team logo stamps are unnumbered and not included in the checklist below. Each stamp measures approximately 1 1/2" by 1 15/16". A collector could receive more stamps and become an official Pro Stamps Club member by mailing in the form found on the back of the stamp sheets.

COMPLETE SET (140) 30.00 80.00
1 Gary Discarcina .08 .25
2 Tim Salmon .20 .50
3 J.T. Snow .20 .50
4 Brian Anderson .08 .25
5 Chili Davis .20 .50
6 Mark McGwire 1.00 2.50
7 Terry Steinbach .08 .25
8 Danny Tartabull .08 .25
9 Todd Stottlemyre .08 .25
10 Geronimo Berroa .08 .25
11 Derek Bell .08 .25
12 Craig Biggio .50 1.25
13 Jeff Bagwell .50 1.25
14 Doug Drabek .08 .25
15 Shane Reynolds .08 .25
16 Ed Sprague .08 .25
17 Pat Hentgen .08 .25
18 Joe Carter .20 .50
19 John Olerud .30 .75
20 Carlos Delgado .50 1.25
21 Fred McGriff .30 .75
22 Ryan Klesko .20 .50
23 David Justice .20 .50
24 Greg Maddux 1.25 3.00
25 Tom Glavine .40 1.00
26 Kevin Seitzer .08 .25
27 Greg Vaughn .08 .25
28 John Jaha .08 .25
29 Pat Listach .08 .25
30 Bill Wegman .08 .25
31 Brian Jordan .20 .50
32 Ray Lankford .20 .50
33 Tom Pagnozzi .08 .25
34 Bernard Gilkey .08 .25
35 Ozzie Smith .75 2.00
36 Mark Grace .40 1.00
37 Shawon Dunston .08 .25
38 Brian McRae .08 .25
39 Jaime Navarro .08 .25
40 Sammy Sosa .60 1.50
41 Mike Piazza 1.25 3.00
42 Eric Karros .20 .50
43 Raul Mondesi .40 1.00
44 Delino Deshields .08 .25
45 Hideo Nomo .50 1.25
46 Wilfredo Cordero .08 .25
47 Darrin Fletcher .08 .25
48 David Segui .08 .25
49 Pedro Martinez .50 1.25
50 Rondell White .20 .50
51 Matt Williams .30 .75
52 Barry Bonds .75 2.00
53 Deion Sanders .40 1.00
54 Mark Leiter .08 .25
55 Glenallen Hill .08 .25
56 Kenny Lofton .20 .50
57 Albert Belle .20 .50
58 Eddie Murray .50 1.25
59 Manny Ramirez .50 1.25
60 Charles Nagy .08 .25
61 Ken Griffey Jr. 1.25 3.00
62 Randy Johnson .50 1.25
63 Jay Buhner .20 .50
64 Edgar Martinez .30 .75
65 Alex Rodriguez 1.25 3.00
66 Gary Sheffield .50 1.25
67 Jeff Conine .20 .50
68 Terry Pendleton .08 .25
69 Chris Hammond .08 .25
70 Greg Colbrunn .08 .25
71 Todd Hundley .20 .50
72 Jose Vizcaino .08 .25
73 Jeff Kent .40 1.00
74 Rico Brogna .08 .25
75 Bobby Jones .08 .25
76 Cal Ripken 2.00 5.00
77 Bobby Bonilla .08 .25
78 Brady Anderson .20 .50
79 Mike Mussina .40 1.00
80 Rafael Palmeiro .40 1.00
81 Tony Gwynn .75 2.00
82 Ken Caminiti .40 1.00
83 Andujar Cedeno .08 .25
84 Andy Ashby .08 .25
85 Jody Reed .08 .25
86 Jim Eisenreich .08 .25
87 Gregg Jefferies .08 .25
88 Mickey Morandini .08 .25
89 Paul Quantrill .08 .25
90 Darren Daulton .20 .50
91 Orlando Merced .08 .25
92 Carlos Garcia .08 .25
93 Jay Bell .08 .25
94 Al Martin .08 .25
95 Denny Neagle .08 .25
96 Benji Gil .08 .25
97 Will Clark .40 1.00
98 Juan Gonzalez .50 1.25
99 Ivan Rodriguez .50 1.25
100 Dean Palmer .08 .25
101 Barry Larkin .40 1.00
102 Reggie Sanders .08 .25
103 Benito Santiago .20 .50
104 Jose Rijo .08 .25
105 Bret Boone .30 .75
106 Mo Vaughn .20 .50
107 Jose Canseco .50 1.25
108 Mike Greenwell .08 .25
109 John Valentin .08 .25
110 Roger Clemens 1.00 2.50
111 Dante Bichette .20 .50
112 Vinny Castilla .20 .50
113 Andres Galarraga .40 1.00
114 Larry Walker .20 .50
115 Walt Weiss .08 .25
116 Tom Goodwin .08 .25
117 Keith Lockhart .08 .25
118 Mark Gubicza .08 .25
119 Jon Nunnally .08 .25
120 Kevin Appier .20 .50
121 Chad Curtis .08 .25
122 Phil Nevin .08 .25
123 Travis Fryman .20 .50
124 Alan Trammell .30 .75
125 Cecil Fielder .20 .50
126 Chuck Knoblauch .40 1.00
127 Kirby Puckett 1.00 2.50
128 Marty Cordova .08 .25
129 Pedro Munoz .08 .25
130 Rich Aguilera .08 .25
131 Frank Thomas .60 1.50
132 Ozzie Guillen .30 .75
133 Robin Ventura .30 .75
134 Ron Karkovice .08 .25
135 Alex Fernandez .08 .25
136 Wade Boggs .50 1.25
137 Jimmy Key .20 .50
138 Paul O'Neill .20 .50
139 David Cone .30 .75
140 Bernie Williams .40 1.00

1972 Pro Stars Postcards

Printed in Canada by Pro Star Promotions, these 37 blank-backed postcards measure approximately 3 1/2" by 5 1/2" and feature white-bordered color player photos. The player's name appears within the lower white border and also as a facsimile autograph across the bottom of the photo. The postcards are unnumbered and checklisted below in alphabetical order within the Expos team (1-12), National League (13-24) and American League (25-36). In addition to the 36 players listed below, the checklist also carries a listing for 12 posters of major league players.

COMPLETE SET (37) 150.00 300.00
COMMON EXPOS (1-12) .60 1.50
COMMON ALL-STAR (13-36) .75 2.00
1 Bob Bailey .75 2.00
2 John Boccabella .75 2.00
3 Boots Day .60 1.50
4 Jim Fairey .60 1.50
5 Tim Foli .60 1.50
6 Ron Hunt .60 1.50
7 Mike Jorgensen .60 1.50
8 Ernie McAnally .60 1.50
9 Carl Morton .60 1.50
10 Steve Renko .60 1.50
11 Ken Singleton 1.25 3.00
12 Bill Stoneman .75 2.00
13 Hank Aaron 4.00 10.00
14 Johnny Bench 20.00 50.00
15 Roberto Clemente 50.00 100.00
16 Ferguson Jenkins 1.50 4.00
17 Juan Marichal 1.50 4.00
18 Willie Mays 50.00 100.00
19 Willie McCovey 2.50 6.00
20 Frank Robinson 2.50 6.00
21 Pete Rose 40.00 80.00
22 Tom Seaver 2.50 6.00
23 Willie Stargell 1.50 4.00
24 Joe Torre 1.25 3.00
25 Vida Blue 1.25 3.00
26 Reggie Jackson 2.50 6.00
27 Al Kaline 2.50 6.00
28 Harmon Killebrew 15.00 40.00
29 Mickey Lolich 1.25 3.00
30 Dave McNally 1.25 3.00
31 Bill Melton .75 2.00
32 Bobby Murcer 1.25 3.00
33 Fritz Peterson .75 2.00
34 Boog Powell 8.00 20.00
35 Merv Rettenmund .75 2.00
36 Brooks Robinson 12.50 30.00
37 Checklist Card .75 2.00

1991 Pro Stars Posters

These three posters were folded, cello wrapped, and inserted in Pro Stars cereal boxes. Through an offer on the side panel of the box, the collector could receive another poster by sending in three Pro Stars UPC symbols and 1.00 for postage and handling. In the cello packs, the posters measure approximately 4 1/2" by 4"; they unfold to a narrow poster that measures approximately 4 1/2" by 24". On a background of blue, purple, and bright yellow stars, a cartoon drawing portrays the athlete in an action pose. At the bottom of each poster appears a player profile in English and French. The backsides of all three posters combine to form a composite poster featuring all three players. The posters are unnumbered and listed below alphabetically.

COMPLETE SET (3) 4.00 10.00
1 Bo Jackson .60 1.50

1998-00 ProTalk Griffey

These four items, which feature a talking card and a displayable piece feature various highlights from the career of Ken Griffey Jr. Each card has about 45 seconds of actual game highlights which can be heard. These were originally available directly from ProTalk on their website for $4.99 each.

COMPLETE SET (4) 8.00 20.00
COMMON CARD (1-4) 2.00 5.00

1998-00 Protalk Talking Cards

Issued as a combination of talking card and displayable portrait, these items were available through stores as well as through the Fanaticsonline.com web site at a direct cost of $4.99 per. Each card features approximately 45 seconds of actual game highlights.

COMPLETE SET 30.00 80.00
1 Mark McGwire/500th career homer 3.00 8.00
2 Mark McGwire/70th homer 3.00 8.00
3 Sammy Sosa/300th career homer 2.50 6.00
4 Sammy Sosa/66th homer 2.50 6.00
5 Ken Griffey Jr. 2.50 6.00
Grand slam homer
6 Ken Griffey Jr. 2.50 6.00
Amazing Catch
7 New York Yankees 2.00 5.00
World Champions
8 Mike Piazza 2.50 6.00
Game Winning Homer
9 Chipper Jones 2.50 6.00
World Series Homer
10 Cal Ripken Jr./400th career homer 3.00 8.00
11 Derek Jeter 3.00 8.00
World Series Play
12 Derek Jeter 3.00 8.00
Spectacular Leaping Catch
13 Nomar Garciaparra/10 RBI Game 2.50 6.00
14 Ivan Rodriguez 2.00 5.00
Texas Ranger RBI Record
15 Alex Rodriguez 2.50 6.00
Joins the 40/40 Club

1990 Publications International Stickers

The 1990 Publications International baseball stickers set contains 648 unnumbered stickers bound in a book. Subsets of the 648-sticker set include All-Stars from each league, and young stars from each league. The stickers are put into the album over a question which pertains to each player pictured as a clue for where the sticker goes. Good stat information is available on this set in the album/book. The set numbering is ordered by teams. The album spaces are numbered and contain a trivia question answered by the players name. The set/book was licensed by Major League Baseball and MLBPA and was produced by Publications International. The only way to identify the stickers numbers is to have an album.

COMPLETE SET (648) 15.00 40.00
1 Dave Anderson .01 .05
2 Tim Belcher .01 .05
3 Mike Davis .01 .05
4 Rick Dempsey .02 .10
5 Kirk Gibson .05 .15
6 Alfredo Griffin .01 .05
7 Jeff Hamilton .01 .05
8 Mickey Hatcher .01 .05
9 Orel Hershiser .02 .10
10 Ricky Horton .01 .05
11 Jay Howell .01 .05
12 Tim Leary .01 .05
13 Mike Marshall .01 .05
14 Eddie Murray .30 .75
15 Alejandro Pena .01 .05
16 Willie Randolph .02 .10
17 Mike Scioscia .05 .15
18 John Shelby .01 .05
19 Franklin Stubbs .01 .05
20 John Tudor .01 .05
21 Fernando Valenzuela .02 .10
22 Todd Benzinger .01 .05
23 Tom Browning .01 .05
24 Norm Charlton .01 .05
25 Kal Daniels .01 .05
26 Eric Davis .02 .10
27 Bo Diaz .01 .05
28 Rob Dibble .01 .05
29 John Franco .02 .10
30 Ken Griffey .10 .30
31 Lenny Harris .01 .05
32 Danny Jackson .01 .05
33 Barry Larkin .08 .25
34 Rick Mahler .01 .05
35 Ron Oester .01 .05
36 Paul O'Neill .02 .10
37 Jeff Reed .01 .05
38 Jose Rijo .01 .05
39 Chris Sabo .01 .05
40 Kent Tekulve .02 .10
41 Manny Trillo .01 .05
42 Joel Youngblood .01 .05
43 Roberto Alomar .30 .75
44 Greg Booker .01 .05
45 Jack Clark .02 .10
46 Jerald Clark .01 .05
47 Mark Davis .01 .05
48 Tim Flannery .01 .05
49 Mark Grant .01 .05
50 Tony Gwynn .60 1.50
51 Bruce Hurst .01 .05
52 John Kruk .02 .10
53 Dave Leiper .01 .05
54 Carmelo Martinez .01 .05
55 Mark Parent .01 .05
56 Dennis Rasmussen .01 .05
57 Randy Ready .01 .05
58 Benito Santiago .02 .10
59 Eric Show .01 .05
60 Garry Templeton .01 .05
61 Walt Terrell .01 .05
62 Ed Whitson .01 .05
63 Marvell Wynne .01 .05
64 Brett Butler .02 .10
65 Will Clark .08 .25
66 Kelly Downs .01 .05
67 Scott Garrelts .01 .05
68 Rich(Goose) Gossage .02 .10
69 Atlee Hammaker .01 .05
70 Tracy Jones .01 .05
71 Terry Kennedy .01 .05
72 Mike Krukow .01 .05
73 Mike LaCoss .01 .05
74 Craig Lefferts .01 .05
75 Candy Maldonado .01 .05
76 Kirt Manwaring .01 .05
77 Kevin Mitchell .01 .05
78 Donell Nixon .01 .05
79 Rick Reuschel .02 .10
80 Ernest Riles .01 .05
81 Don Robinson .01 .05
82 Chris Speier .01 .05
83 Robby Thompson .01 .05
84 Jose Uribe .01 .05
85 Juan Agosto .01 .05
86 Larry Andersen .01 .05
87 Kevin Bass .01 .05
88 Craig Biggio .30 .75
89 Ken Caminiti .01 .05
90 Jim Clancy .01 .05
91 Danny Darwin .01 .05
92 Glenn Davis .01 .05
93 Jim Deshaies .01 .05
94 Bill Doran .01 .05
95 Bob Forsch .01 .05
96 Billy Hatcher .01 .05
97 Bob Knepper .01 .05
98 Terry Puhl .01 .05
99 Rafael Ramirez .01 .05
100 Craig Reynolds .01 .05
101 Rick Rhoden .01 .05
102 Mike Scott .01 .05
103 Dave Smith .01 .05
104 Alex Trevino .01 .05
105 Gerald Young .01 .05
106 Jose Alvarez .01 .05
107 Paul Assenmacher .01 .05
108 Bruce Benedict .01 .05
109 Jeff Blauser .01 .05
110 Joe Boever .01 .05
111 Jody Davis .01 .05
112 Darrell Evans .02 .10
113 Ron Gant .02 .10
114 Tommy Gregg .01 .05
115 Dion James .01 .05
116 Derek Lilliquist .01 .05
117 Dale Murphy .08 .25
118 Gerald Perry .01 .05
119 Charlie Puleo .01 .05
120 John Russell .01 .05
121 Lonnie Smith .01 .05
122 Pete Smith .01 .05
123 Zane Smith .01 .05
124 John Smoltz .08 .25
125 Bruce Sutter .25 .60
126 Andres Thomas .01 .05
127 Rick Aguilera .02 .10
128 Gary Carter .30 .75
129 David Cone .05 .15
130 Ron Darling .01 .05
131 Len Dykstra .02 .10
132 Kevin Elster .01 .05
133 Sid Fernandez .01 .05
134 Dwight Gooden .02 .10
135 Keith Hernandez .02 .10
136 Gregg Jefferies .01 .05
137 Howard Johnson .01 .05
138 Dave Magadan .01 .05
139 Lee Mazzilli .01 .05
140 Roger McDowell .01 .05
141 Kevin McReynolds .01 .05
142 Randy Myers .02 .10
143 Bob Ojeda .01 .05
144 Mackey Sasser .01 .05
145 Darryl Strawberry .02 .10
146 Tim Teufel .01 .05
147 Mookie Wilson .02 .10
148 Rafael Belliard .01 .05
149 Barry Bonds .60 1.50
150 Bobby Bonilla .02 .10
151 Sid Bream .01 .05
152 Benny Distefano .01 .05
153 Doug Drabek .01 .05
154 Brian Fisher .01 .05
155 Jim Gott .01 .05
156 Neal Heaton .01 .05
157 Bill Landrum .01 .05
158 Mike LaValliere .01 .05
159 Jose Lind .01 .05
160 Junior Ortiz .01 .05
161 Tom Prince .01 .05
162 Gary Redus .01 .05
163 R.J. Reynolds .01 .05
164 Jeff Robinson .01 .05
165 John Smiley .01 .05
166 Andy Van Slyke .02 .10
167 Bob Walk .01 .05
168 Glenn Wilson .01 .05
169 Hubie Brooks .01 .05
170 Tim Burke .01 .05
171 Mike Fitzgerald .01 .05
172 Tom Foley .01 .05
173 Andres Galarraga .08 .25
174 Kevin Gross .01 .05
175 Joe Hesketh .01 .05
176 Brian Holman .01 .05
177 Rex Hudler .02 .10
178 Wallace Johnson .01 .05
179 Mark Langston .01 .05
180 Dave Martinez .01 .05
181 Dennis Martinez .02 .10
182 Andy McGaffigan .01 .05
183 Otis Nixon .01 .05
184 Spike Owen .01 .05
185 Pascual Perez .01 .05
186 Tim Raines .02 .10
187 Nelson Santovenia .01 .05
188 Bryn Smith .01 .05
189 Tim Wallach .01 .05
190 Damon Berryhill .01 .05
191 Mike Bielecki .01 .05
192 Andre Dawson .08 .25
193 Shawon Dunston .01 .05
194 Mark Grace .20 .50
195 Darrin Jackson .01 .05
196 Paul Kilgus .01 .05
197 Vance Law .01 .05
198 Greg Maddux .60 1.50
199 Pat Perry .01 .05
200 Jeff Pico .01 .05
201 Ryne Sandberg .30 .75
202 Scott Sanderson .01 .05
203 Calvin Schiraldi .01 .05
204 Dwight Smith .01 .05
205 Rick Sutcliffe .02 .10
206 Gary Varsho .01 .05
207 Jerome Walton .01 .05
208 Mitch Webster .01 .05
209 Curtis Wilkerson .01 .05
210 Mitch Williams .01 .05
211 Tom Brunansky .01 .05
212 Cris Carpenter .01 .05
213 Vince Coleman .01 .05
214 John Costello .01 .05
215 Danny Cox .01 .05
216 Ken Dayley .01 .05
217 Jose DeLeon .01 .05
218 Frank DiPino .01 .05
219 Pedro Guerrero .02 .10
220 Joe Magrane .01 .05
221 Greg Mathews .01 .05
222 Willie McGee .02 .10
223 Jose Oquendo .01 .05
224 Tom Pagnozzi .01 .05
225 Tony Pena .01 .05
226 Terry Pendleton .02 .10
227 Dan Quisenberry .01 .05
228 Ozzie Smith .40 1.00
229 Scott Terry .01 .05
230 Milt Thompson .01 .05
231 Todd Worrell .01 .05
232 Steve Bedrosian .01 .05
233 Don Carman .01 .05
234 Darren Daulton .02 .10
235 Bob Dernier .01 .05
236 Marvin Freeman .01 .05
237 Greg Harris .01 .05
238 Von Hayes .01 .05
239 Tom Herr .01 .05
240 Ken Howell .01 .05
241 Chris James .01 .05
242 Steve Jeltz .01 .05
243 Ron Jones .01 .05
244 Ricky Jordan .01 .05
245 Steve Lake .01 .05
246 Mike Maddux .01 .05
247 Larry McWilliams .01 .05
248 Jeff Parrett .01 .05
249 Juan Samuel .01 .05
250 Mike Schmidt .30 .75
251 Dickie Thon .01 .05
252 Floyd Youmans .01 .05
253 Bobby Bonilla .02 .10
254 Will Clark .08 .25
255 Eric Davis .02 .10
256 Andre Dawson .08 .25
257 Bill Doran .01 .05
258 John Franco .02 .10
259 Kirk Gibson .02 .10
260 Dwight Gooden .02 .10
261 Tony Gwynn .60 1.50
262 Keith Hernandez .02 .10
263 Orel Hershiser .02 .10
264 Danny Jackson .01 .05
265 Howard Johnson .01 .05
266 Barry Larkin .08 .25
267 Joe Magrane .01 .05
268 Kevin McReynolds .01 .05
269 Tony Pena .01 .05
270 Ryne Sandberg .40 1.00
271 Benito Santiago .02 .10
272 Ozzie Smith .40 1.00
273 Darryl Strawberry .02 .10
274 Todd Worrell .01 .05
275 Harold Baines .02 .10
276 George Bell .01 .05
277 Wade Boggs .30 .75
278 Bob Boone .02 .10
279 Jose Canseco .20 .50
280 Joe Carter .02 .10
281 Roger Clemens .60 1.50
282 Dennis Eckersley .20 .50
283 Tony Fernandez .02 .10
284 Carlton Fisk .30 .75
285 Julio Franco .05 .15
286 Gary Gaetti .02 .10
287 Mike Greenwell .01 .05
288 Rickey Henderson .40 1.00
289 Ted Higuera .01 .05
290 Kent Hrbek .02 .10
291 Don Mattingly .60 1.50
292 Kirby Puckett .25 .60
293 Jeff Reardon .02 .10
294 Harold Reynolds .02 .10
295 Dave Stewart .02 .10
296 Alan Trammell .05 .15
297 Frank Viola .01 .05
298 Dave Winfield .30 .75
299 Todd Burns .01 .05
300 Greg Cadaret .01 .05
301 Jose Canseco .20 .50
302 Storm Davis .01 .05
303 Dennis Eckersley .20 .50
304 Mike Gallego .01 .05
305 Ron Hassey .01 .05
306 Dave Henderson .01 .05
307 Rick Honeycutt .01 .05
308 Stan Javier .01 .05
309 Carney Lansford .02 .10
310 Mark McGwire .50 1.25
311 Mike Moore .01 .05
312 Dave Parker .02 .10
313 Eric Plunk .01 .05
314 Luis Polonia .01 .05
315 Terry Steinbach .01 .05
316 Dave Stewart .02 .10
317 Walt Weiss .01 .05
318 Bob Welch .01 .05
319 Curt Young .01 .05
320 Allan Anderson .01 .05
321 Wally Backman .01 .05
322 Doug Baker .01 .05
323 Juan Berenguer .01 .05
324 Randy Bush .01 .05
325 Jim Dwyer .01 .05
326 Gary Gaetti .02 .10
327 Greg Gagne .01 .05
328 Dan Gladden .01 .05
329 Brian Harper .01 .05
330 Kent Hrbek .02 .10
331 Gene Larkin .01 .05
332 Tim Laudner .01 .05
333 John Moses .01 .05
334 Al Newman .01 .05
335 Kirby Puckett .25 .60
336 Shane Rawley .01 .05
337 Jeff Reardon .02 .10
338 Steve Shields .01 .05
339 Frank Viola .01 .05
340 Gary Wayne .01 .05
341 Luis Aquino .01 .05
342 Floyd Bannister .01 .05
343 Bob Boone .02 .10
344 George Brett .40 1.00
345 Bill Buckner .02 .10
346 Jim Eisenreich .01 .05
347 Steve Farr .01 .05
348 Tom Gordon .02 .10
349 Mark Gubicza .01 .05
350 Bo Jackson .08 .25
351 Charlie Leibrandt .01 .05
352 Mike Macfarlane .01 .05
353 Jeff Montgomery .02 .10
354 Bret Saberhagen .02 .10
355 Kevin Seitzer .01 .05
356 Kurt Stillwell .01 .05
357 Pat Tabler .01 .05
358 Danny Tartabull .01 .05
359 Gary Thurman .01 .05
360 Frank White .02 .10
361 Willie Wilson .01 .05
362 Jim Abbott .05 .15
363 Kent Anderson .01 .05
364 Tony Armas .01 .05
365 Dante Bichette .02 .10
366 Bert Blyleven .02 .10
367 Chili Davis .02 .10
368 Brian Downing .01 .05
369 Chuck Finley .02 .10
370 Willie Fraser .01 .05
371 Jack Howell .01 .05
372 Wally Joyner .02 .10
373 Kirk McCaskill .01 .05
374 Bob McClure .01 .05
375 Greg Minton .01 .05
376 Lance Parrish .01 .05
377 Dan Petry .01 .05
378 Johnny Ray .01 .05
379 Dick Schofield .01 .05
380 Claudell Washington .01 .05
381 Devon White .01 .05
382 Mike Witt .01 .05
383 Harold Baines .02 .10
384 Daryl Boston .01 .05
385 Ivan Calderon .01 .05
386 Carlton Fisk .30 .75
387 Dave Gallagher .01 .05
388 Ozzie Guillen .05 .15
389 Shawn Hillegas .01 .05
390 Barry Jones .01 .05
391 Ron Karkovice .01 .05
392 Eric King .01 .05
393 Ron Kittle .01 .05
394 Bill Long .01 .05
395 Steve Lyons .02 .10
396 Fred Manrique .01 .05
397 Donn Pall .01 .05
398 Dan Pasqua .01 .05
399 Melido Perez .01 .05
400 Jerry Reuss .01 .05
401 Bobby Thigpen .01 .05
402 Greg Walker .01 .05
403 Eddie Williams .01 .05
404 Buddy Bell .02 .10
405 Kevin Brown .08 .25
406 Steve Buechele .01 .05
407 Cecil Espy .01 .05
408 Scott Fletcher .01 .05
409 Julio Franco .05 .15
410 Cecilio Guante .01 .05
411 Jose Guzman .01 .05
412 Charlie Hough .02 .10
413 Pete Incaviglia .01 .05
414 Chad Kreuter .01 .05
415 Jeff Kunkel .01 .05
416 Rick Leach .01 .05
417 Jamie Moyer .05 .15
418 Rafael Palmeiro .20 .50
419 Geno Petralli .01 .05
420 Jeff Russell .01 .05
421 Nolan Ryan 1.00 2.50
422 Ruben Sierra .02 .10
423 Jim Sundberg .01 .05
424 Bobby Witt .01 .05
424 Steve Balboni .01 .05
426 Scott Bankhead .01 .05
427 Scott Bradley .01 .05
428 Mickey Brantley .01 .05
429 Darnell Coles .01 .05
430 Henry Cotto .01 .05
431 Alvin Davis .01 .05
432 Mario Diaz .01 .05
433 Ken Griffey Jr. .60 1.50
434 Erik Hanson .01 .05
435 Mike Jackson .02 .10
436 Jeffrey Leonard .01 .05
437 Edgar Martinez .05 .15
438 Tom Niedenfuer .01 .05
439 Jim Presley .01 .05
440 Jerry Reed .01 .05
441 Harold Reynolds .02 .10
442 Bill Swift .01 .05
443 Steve Trout .01 .05
444 David Valle .01 .05
445 Omar Vizquel .20 .50
446 Marty Barrett .01 .05
447 Mike Boddicker .01 .05
448 Wade Boggs .30 .75
449 Dennis(Oil Can) Boyd .01 .05
450 Ellis Burks .05 .15
451 Rick Cerone .01 .05
452 Roger Clemens .60 1.50
453 Nick Esasky .01 .05
454 Dwight Evans .02 .10
455 Wes Gardner .01 .05
456 Rich Gedman .01 .05
457 Mike Greenwell .01 .05
458 Sam Horn .01 .05
459 Randy Kutcher .01 .05
460 Dennis Lamp .01 .05
461 Rob Murphy .01 .05
462 Jody Reed .01 .05
463 Jim Rice .02 .10
464 Lee Smith .02 .10
465 Mike Smithson .01 .05
466 Bob Stanley .01 .05
467 Doyle Alexander .01 .05
468 Dave Bergman .01 .05
469 Chris Brown .01 .05
470 Paul Gibson .01 .05
471 Mike Heath .01 .05
472 Mike Henneman .01 .05
473 Guillermo Hernandez .01 .05
474 Charles Hudson .01 .05
475 Chet Lemon .01 .05
476 Fred Lynn .01 .05
477 Keith Moreland .01 .05
478 Jack Morris .02 .10
479 Matt Nokes .01 .05
480 Gary Pettis .01 .05
481 Jeff Robinson .01 .05
482 Pat Sheridan .01 .05
483 Frank Tanana .01 .05
484 Alan Trammell .05 .15
485 Lou Whitaker .02 .10
486 Frank Williams .01 .05
487 Kenny Williams .02 .10
488 Don August .01 .05
489 Mike Birkbeck .01 .05
490 Chris Bosio .01 .05

491 Glenn Braggs .01 .05
492 Greg Brock .01 .05
493 Chuck Crim .01 .05
494 Rob Deer .01 .05
495 Mike Felder .01 .05
496 Jim Gantner .01 .05
497 Ted Higuera .01 .05
498 Joey Meyer .01 .05
499 Paul Mirabella .01 .05
500 Paul Molitor .20 .50
501 Juan Nieves .01 .05
502 Charlie O'Brien .01 .05
503 Dan Plesac .01 .05
504 Gary Sheffield .40 1.00
505 B.J. Surhoff .02 .10
506 Dale Sveum .01 .05
507 Bill Wegman .01 .05
508 Robin Yount .30 .75
509 George Bell .01 .05
510 Pat Borders .01 .05
511 John Cerutti .01 .05
512 Rob Ducey .01 .05
513 Tony Fernandez .02 .10
514 Mike Flanagan .01 .05
515 Kelly Gruber .01 .05
516 Tom Henke .01 .05
517 Alexis Infante .01 .05
518 Jimmy Key .02 .10
519 Tom Lawless .01 .05
520 Manny Lee .01 .05
521 Al Leiter .08 .25
522 Nelson Liriano .01 .05
523 Fred McGriff .08 .25
524 Lloyd Moseby .01 .05
525 Rance Mulliniks .01 .05
526 Dave Stieb .02 .10
527 Todd Stottlemyre .01 .05
528 Duane Ward .01 .05
529 Ernie Whitt .01 .05
530 Jesse Barfield .01 .05
531 Bob Brower .01 .05
532 John Candelaria .01 .05
533 Richard Dotson .01 .05
534 Lee Guetterman .01 .05
535 Mel Hall .01 .05
536 Andy Hawkins .01 .05
537 Rickey Henderson .40 1.00
538 Roberto Kelly .01 .05
539 Dave LaPoint .01 .05
540 Don Mattingly .60 1.50
541 Lance McCullers .01 .05
542 Mike Pagliarulo .01 .05
543 Clay Parker .01 .05
544 Ken Phelps .01 .05
545 Dave Righetti .01 .05
546 Rafael Santana .01 .05
547 Steve Sax .01 .05
548 Don Slaught .01 .05
549 Wayne Tolleson .01 .05
550 Dave Winfield .30 .75
551 Andy Allanson .01 .05
552 Keith Atherton .01 .05
553 Scott Bailes .01 .05
554 Bud Black .01 .05
555 Jerry Browne .01 .05
556 Tom Candiotti .01 .05
557 Joe Carter .02 .10
558 David Clark .01 .05
559 John Farrell .01 .05
560 Felix Fermin .01 .05
561 Brook Jacoby .01 .05
562 Doug Jones .01 .05
563 Oddibe McDowell .01 .05
564 Luis Medina .01 .05
565 Pete O'Brien .01 .05
566 Jesse Orosco .02 .10
567 Joel Skinner .01 .05
568 Cory Snyder .01 .05
569 Greg Swindell .01 .05
570 Rich Yett .01 .05
571 Mike Young .01 .05
572 Brady Anderson .08 .25
573 Jeff Ballard .01 .05
574 Jose Bautista .01 .05
575 Phil Bradley .01 .05
576 Mike Devereaux .01 .05
577 Kevin Hickey .01 .05
578 Brian Holton .01 .05
579 Bob Melvin .02 .10
580 Bob Milacki .01 .05
581 Gregg Olson .01 .05
582 Joe Orsulak .01 .05
583 Bill Ripken .01 .05
584 Cal Ripken Jr. 1.00 2.50
585 Dave Schmidt .01 .05
586 Larry Sheets .01 .05
587 Mickey Tettleton .02 .10
588 Mark Thurmond .01 .05
589 Jay Tibbs .01 .05
590 Jim Traber .01 .05
591 Mark Williamson .01 .05
592 Craig Worthington .01 .05
593 Allan Anderson .01 .05
594 Ellis Burks .05 .15
595 Ken Griffey Jr. .75 2.00
596 Bo Jackson .08 .25
597 Roberto Kelly .01 .05
598 Kirk McCaskill .01 .05
599 Fred McGriff .08 .25
600 Mark McGwire .60 1.50
601 Bob Milacki .01 .05
602 Melido Perez .01 .05
603 Jeff Robinson .01 .05
604 Gary Sheffield .30 .75
605 Ruben Sierra .02 .10
606 Greg Swindell .01 .05
607 Roberto Alomar .40 1.00
608 Tim Belcher .01 .05
609 Vince Coleman .01 .05
610 Kal Daniels .01 .05
611 Andres Galarraga .08 .25
612 Ron Gant .02 .10
613 Mark Grace .08 .25
614 Gregg Jefferies .01 .05
615 Ricky Jordan .01 .05
616 Jose Lind .01 .05
617 Kevin Mitchell .01 .05
618 Gerald Young .01 .05
619 Base .01 .05
620 Batting helmets .01 .05
621 Bats .01 .05
622 Batting gloves .01 .05
623 Los Angeles Dodgers .01 .05
624 Cincinnati Reds .01 .05
625 San Diego Padres .01 .05
626 San Francisco Giants .01 .05
627 Houston Astros .01 .05
628 Atlanta Braves .01 .05
629 New York Mets .01 .05
630 Pittsburgh Pirates .01 .05
631 Montreal Expos .01 .05
632 Chicago Cubs .01 .05
633 St. Louis Cardinals .01 .05
634 Philadelphia Phillies .01 .05
635 Oakland Athletics .01 .05
636 Minnesota Twins .01 .05
637 Kansas City Royals .01 .05
638 California Angels .01 .05
639 Chicago White Sox .01 .05
640 Texas Rangers .01 .05
641 Seattle Mariners .01 .05
642 Boston Red Sox .01 .05
643 Detroit Tigers .01 .05
644 Milwaukee Brewers .01 .05
645 Toronto Blue Jays .01 .05
646 New York Yankees .01 .05
647 Cleveland Indians .01 .05
648 Baltimore Orioles .01 .05

1997 Puckett Glaucoma

This one card oversized set featured Kirby Puckett and information about Glaucoma. The front has an action shot of Kirby with the words "Don't Be Blindsided" on top and the sponsorship information on the bottom. The back has information about Glaucoma and information about two more sponsors: Allina Health System and Phillips Eye Institute.

1 Kirby Puckett 2.00 5.00

1997 Puckett Sight Night

This one-card set features a color action photo of Kirby Puckett in a red frame with a white border. The card was distributed at the April 30, 1997 Game between the Twins and the Orioles. The back displays sports eye safety tips and was sponsored by the Phillips Eye Institute.

1 Kirby Puckett 12.50 25.00

1954 Quaker Sports Oddities

This 27-card set features strange moments in sports and was issued as an insert inside Quaker Puffed Rice cereal boxes. Fronts of the cards are drawings depicting the person or the event. In a stripe at the top of the card face appear the words "Sports Oddities." Two colorful drawings fill the remaining space: the left half is a portrait, while the right half is action-oriented. A variety of sports are included. The cards measure approximately 2 1/4" by 3 1/2" and have rounded corners. The last line on the back of each card declares, "It's Odd but True." A person could also buy the complete set for fifteen cents and two box tops from Quaker Puffed Wheat or Quaker Rice. If a collector did send in their material to Quaker Oats the set came back in a specially marked box with the cards in cellophane wrapping. Sets in original wrapping are valued at 1.25x to 1.5X the high column listings in our checklist.

COMPLETE SET (27) 125.00 250.00
27 Yankee Stadium 7.50 15.00

1986 Quaker Granola

This set of 33 standard-size cards was available in packages of Quaker Oats Chewy Granola, three player cards plus a complete set offer card in each package. The set was also available through a mail-in offer where anyone sending in four UPC seals from Chewy Granola (before 12/31/86) would receive a complete set. The cards were produced by Topps for Quaker Oats. Card backs are printed in red and blue on gray card stock. The cards are numbered on the front and the back. Cards 1-17 feature National League players and cards 18-33 feature American League players. The first three cards in each sequence depict that league's MVP, Cy Young, and Rookie of the Year, respectively. The rest of the cards in each sequence are ordered alphabetically.

COMPLETE SET (33) 2.50 6.00
1 Willie McGee .07 .20
2 Dwight Gooden .10 .30
3 Vince Coleman .07 .20
4 Gary Carter .20 .50
5 Jack Clark .02 .10
6 Steve Garvey .10 .30
7 Tony Gwynn .40 1.00
8 Dale Murphy .15 .40
9 Dave Parker .07 .20
10 Tim Raines .07 .20
11 Pete Rose .20 .50
12 Nolan Ryan .75 2.00
13 Ryne Sandberg .15 .40
14 Mike Schmidt .20 .50
15 Ozzie Smith .20 .50
16 Darryl Strawberry .07 .20
17 Fernando Valenzuela .07 .20
18 Don Mattingly .40 1.00
19 Bret Saberhagen .07 .20
20 Ozzie Guillen .15 .40
21 Bert Blyleven .07 .20
22 Wade Boggs .20 .50
23 George Brett .40 1.00
24 Darrell Evans .02 .10
25 Rickey Henderson .25 .60
26 Reggie Jackson .20 .50
27 Eddie Murray .20 .50
28 Phil Niekro .20 .50
29 Dan Quisenberry .02 .10
30 Jim Rice .07 .20
31 Cal Ripken .75 2.00
32 Tom Seaver .20 .50
33 Dave Winfield .20 .50
NNO Offer Card for the complete set .02 .10

1997 R and N Ted Williams Porcelain

This 18-card limited edition set honors Ted Williams with previous card images of him printed on porcelain. Each card was hand numbered and came packaged in a plexi case with a display easel and a certificate of authenticity. The set was available in several versions besides just the white porcelain card version: white porcelain with a 23kt. gold trim, white porcelain with a .999 pure platinum trim, porcelain with gold covered surface (only 750 produced), porcelain with platinum covered surface (only 500 produced), and in a Collector Series Mug version. The cards are listed below according to the year they were produced by the card manufacturers also listed.

COMPLETE SET (18) 200.00 400.00
COMMON CARD (1-18) 10.00 25.00

1936 R311 Premiums

The 1936 R311 set of Portraits and Team Baseball Photos exist in two different forms, each measuring 6" by 8". Fifteen leather-like or uneven surface cards comprise the first type; these are indicated by the prefix L in the checklist below and are listed first. Twenty eight glossy surface, sepia or black and white cards comprise the second type. These glossy cards are indicated by the prefix G in the checklist below. The Boston Red Sox team exists with or without a sky above the building at the right of the card. Scarcities within the glossy subset include Pepper Martin, Mel Harder, Schoolboy Rowe, and the Dodgers, Pirates, Braves and Columbus team cards; these are asterisked in the checklist below.

COMPLETE SET (44) 1200.00 2400.00
COMMON GLOSSY (G1-G28) 10.00 20.00
COMMON LEATHER (L1-L15) 15.00 30.00
G1 Earl Averill 25.00 50.00
G2 Jim Bottomley 25.00 50.00
G3 Mickey Cochrane 30.00 60.00
G4 Joe Cronin 25.00 50.00
G5 Dizzy Dean 50.00 100.00
G6 Jimmy Dykes 12.50 25.00
G7 Jimmie Foxx 50.00 100.00
G8 Frankie Frisch 30.00 60.00
G9 Hank Greenberg 30.00 60.00
G10 Mel Harder 20.00 40.00
G11 Ken Keltner 15.00 30.00
G12 Pepper Martin 100.00 200.00
G13 Schoolboy Rowe 15.00 30.00
G14 Bill Terry 25.00 50.00
G15 Pie Traynor 25.00 50.00
G16 American League All Stars 1935 12.50 25.00
G17 Detroit Tigers 1934 25.00 50.00
G18 Boston Braves 1935 125.00 250.00
G19A Boston Red Sox with sky above building at right of the card 12.50 25.00
G19B Boston Red Sox without sky 50.00 100.00
G20 Brooklyn Dodgers1935 125.00 250.00
G21 Chicago White Sox/1935 12.50 25.00
G22 Columbus Red Birds 1934 Pennant Winners of Amer. Assoc. 12.50 25.00
G23 National League All Stars 1934 12.50 25.00
G24 National League Champions 1935 Chicago Cubs 12.50 25.00
G25 New York Yankees/1935 25.00 50.00
G26 Pittsburgh Pirates/1935 * 25.00 50.00
G27 St. Louis Browns/1935 12.50 25.00
G28 World Champions 1934 St. Louis Cardinals 12.50 25.00
L1 Paul Derringer 20.00 40.00
L2 Wes Ferrell 20.00 40.00
L3 Jimmie Foxx 60.00 120.00
L4 Charley Gehringer 40.00 80.00
L5 Mel Harder 20.00 40.00
L6 Gabby Hartnett 40.00 80.00
L7 Rogers Hornsby 60.00 120.00
L8 Connie Mack MG 50.00 100.00
L9 Van Mungo 20.00 40.00
L10 Steve O'Neill 20.00 40.00
L11 Red Ruffing 40.00 80.00
L12 Joe DiMaggio Frank Crosetti Tony Lazzeri 250.00 500.00
L13 Arky Vaughan Honus Wagner CO 60.00 120.00
L14 American League Pennant Winners 1935 Detroit Tigers 20.00 40.00
L15 National League Pennant Winners 1935 Chicago Cubs 20.00 40.00

1936 R312 Pastel Photos

The 1936 R312 Baseball Photos set contains 25 color tinted, single player cards, listed with the letter A in the checklist; 14 multiple player cards, listed with the letter B in the checklist; 6 action cards with handwritten signatures, listed with the letter C in the checklist; and 5 action cards with printed titles, listed with the letter D in the checklist. The pictures are reminiscent of a water-color type painting in soft pastels. The Allen card is reportedly more difficult to obtain than other cards in the set.

COMPLETE SET (50) 2500.00 5000.00
1 Johnny Allen 125.00 250.00
2 Cy Blanton 30.00 60.00
3 Mace Brown 30.00 60.00
4 Dolph Camilli 30.00 60.00
5 Mickey Cochrane 75.00 150.00
6 Rip Collins 30.00 60.00
7 KiKi Cuyler 60.00 120.00
8 Bill Dickey 75.00 150.00
9 Joe DiMaggio UER 600.00 1200.00
10 Chuck Dressen 40.00 80.00
11 Benny Frey 30.00 60.00
12 Hank Greenberg 75.00 150.00
13 Mel Harder 40.00 80.00
14 Rogers Hornsby 125.00 250.00
15 Ernie Lombardi 60.00 120.00
16 Pepper Martin 40.00 80.00
17 Johnny Mize 75.00 150.00
18 Van Lingle Mungo 30.00 60.00
19 Bud Parmalee 30.00 60.00
20 Red Ruffing 60.00 120.00
21 Eugene Schott 30.00 60.00
22 Casey Stengel 125.00 250.00
23 Billy Sullivan 30.00 60.00
24 Bill Swift 30.00 60.00
25 Ralph Winegarner 30.00 60.00
26 Ollie Bejma and Rollie Hemsley 30.00 60.00
27 Cliff Bolton and Earl Whitehill 30.00 60.00
28 Stan Bordagaray and George Earnshaw 30.00 60.00
29 Herman Cavarretta Hack 40.00 80.00
30 Fox White Goslin 40.00 80.00
31 Galan Herman Lindstrom Hartnett 40.00 80.00
32 Bucky Harris Joe Cronin 60.00 120.00
33 G. Hartnett L. Warneke 40.00 80.00
34 Myril Hoag Lefty Gomez 60.00 120.00
35 A. Sothoron R. Hornsby 60.00 120.00
36 Connie Mack Lefty Grove 100.00 200.00
37 Taylor Speaker Cuyler 60.00 120.00
38 Dixie Walker Mule Haas Mike Kreevich 30.00 60.00
39 P. Waner L.Waner Weaver 60.00 120.00
40 Nick Altrock Al Schacht 40.00 80.00
41 Bell (St. Louis) Out At First Zeke Bonura 30.00 60.00
42 Jim Collins (Safe) and Stan Hack 30.00 60.00
43 Jimmie Foxx Luke Sewell 60.00 120.00
44 Al Lopez Traps Two Cubs on Third Base 60.00 120.00
45 Pie Traynor Augie Galan 60.00 120.00
46 Alvin Crowder after victory in the World Series 30.00 60.00
48 Gabby Hartnett Crossing home plate after hitting homer 60.00 120.00
49 Schoolboy Rowe 30.00 60.00
50 Russ Van Atta/St. Louis pitcher out at plate/Rick Ferrell 30.00 60.00

1933 R337 Eclipse Import Series Of 24

The cards in this 24-card set measure 2 5/16" by 2 13/16". The "Series of 24" is similar to the MP and Co. issues in terms of style and quality. Produced in 1933, this set is numbered 401-424. The three missing numbers, 403, 413, and 414, probably correspond to the three known unnumbered players. Some dealers believe this is known as the "Eclipse Import" set.

COMPLETE SET (24) 1200.00 2400.00
401 Johnny Vergez 50.00 100.00
402 Babe Ruth 1000.00 2000.00
404 George Pipgras 50.00 100.00
405 Bill Terry 100.00 200.00
406 George Connally 50.00 100.00
407 Wilson Clark 50.00 100.00
408 Lefty Grove 150.00 300.00
409 Henry Johnson 50.00 100.00
410 Jimmy Dykes 50.00 100.00
411 Henry Hine Schuble 50.00 100.00
412 Washington Harris Makes Home Run 75.00 150.00
415 Al Simmons 100.00 200.00
416 Heinie Manush 75.00 150.00
417 Glen Myatt 50.00 100.00
418 Babe Herman 75.00 150.00
419 Frank Frisch# 100.00 200.00
420 A Safe Slide to the Home Plate 50.00 100.00
421 Paul Waner 75.00 150.00
422 Jimmy Wilson 50.00 100.00
423 Charles Grimm 75.00 150.00
424 Dick Bartell 50.00 100.00
NNO Jimmy Fox/(sic& Jimmie Foxx) Athletics/(unnumbe 150.00 300.00
NNO Roy Johnson unnumbered 50.00 100.00
NNO Traynor Pitss/(sic& Pittsburgh) is out/(unnumbe 100.00 200.00

1950 R423

Many numbers of these small and unattractive cards may be yet unknown for this issue of the early 1950s. The cards are printed on thin stock and measure 5/8" by 3/4"; sometimes they are found as a long horizontal strip of 13 cards connected by a perforation. Complete strips intact are worth 50 percent more than the sum of the individual players on the strip. The cards were available with a variety of back colors, red, green, blue, or purple, with the red and blue being the rarest of the varieties. The cards on the strip are in no apparent order, numerically or alphabetically. The producer's numbering of the cards in the set is very close to alphabetical order. Cards are so small they are sometimes lost. These strips were premiums or prizes in one-cent bubblegum machines; they were folded accordion style and held together by a small metal clip.

COMPLETE SET 600.00 1200.00
1 Grover C. Alexander 7.50 15.00
2 Richie Ashburn 7.50 15.00
3 Frank Baumholtz 2.50 5.00
4 Ralph Branca 3.00 6.00
5 Yogi Berra 20.00 40.00
6 Ewell Blackwell 3.00 6.00
7 Lou Boudreau 5.00 10.00
8 Harry Brecheen 2.50 5.00
9 Chico Carrasquel 2.50 5.00
10 Jerry Coleman 3.00 6.00
11 Walker Cooper 2.50 5.00
12 Roy Campanella 20.00 40.00
13 Phil Cavarretta 3.00 6.00
14A Ty Cobb Facsimile Auto 40.00 80.00
14B Ty Cobb No Auto 40.00 80.00
15 Mickey Cochrane 5.00 10.00
16 Eddie Collins 5.00 10.00
17 Frank Crosetti 3.00 6.00
18 Larry Doby 5.00 10.00
19 Walter Dropo 2.50 5.00
20 Alvin Dark 3.00 6.00
21 Dizzy Dean 15.00 30.00
22 Bill Dickey 5.00 10.00
23 Murray Dickson 2.50 5.00
24 Dom DiMaggio 5.00 10.00
25 Joe DiMaggio 40.00 80.00
26 Leo Durocher MG 5.00 10.00
27 Mel Parnell 3.00 6.00
28 Bob Elliott 3.00 6.00
29 Del Ennis 2.50 5.00
31 Bob Feller 15.00 30.00
32 Frank Frisch 5.00 10.00
33 Billy Goodman 2.50 5.00
34 Lefty Gomez
35 Lou Gehrig 40.00 80.00
36 Joe Gordon 3.00 6.00
38 Hank Greenberg 5.00 10.00
39 Lefty Grove 5.00 10.00
42 Ken Heintzelman 2.50 5.00
44 Jim Hearn 2.50 5.00
45 Gil Hodges 7.50 15.00
46 Harry Heilmann 5.00 10.00
47 Tommy Henrich 4.00 8.00
48 Roger Hornsby 12.50 25.00
49 Carl Hubbell 5.00 10.00
50 Eddie Joost 2.50 5.00
51 Nippy Jones 2.50 5.00
53 Nippy Jones 2.50 5.00
54 Walter Johnson 12.50 25.00
55 Ellis Kinder 2.50 5.00
56 Jim Konstanty 3.00 6.00
57 George Kell 5.00 10.00
58 Ralph Kiner 5.00 10.00
59 Bob Lemon 5.00 10.00
60 Whitey Lockman 3.00 6.00
61 Ed Lopat 3.00 6.00
62 Tony Lazzeri 5.00 10.00
63 Cass Michaels 2.50 5.00
64 Cliff Mapes 2.50 5.00
65 Willard Marshall 2.50 5.00
66 Clyde McCullough 2.50 5.00
67 Connie Mack 5.00 10.00
68 Christy Mathewson 12.50 25.00
69 Joe Medwick 5.00 10.00
70 Johnny Mize 5.00 10.00
71 Terry Moore 2.50 5.00
72 Stan Musial 25.00 50.00
73 Hal Newhouser 5.00 10.00
74 Don Newcombe 4.00 8.00
75 Lefty O'Doul 3.00 6.00
76 Mel Ott 5.00 10.00
77 Mel Parnell 2.50 5.00
79 Gerald Priddy 2.50 5.00
80 Dave Philley 2.50 5.00
81 Bob Porterfield 2.50 5.00
82 Andy Pafko 2.50 5.00
83 Howie Pollet 2.50 5.00
84 Herb Pennock 5.00 10.00
85 Al Rosen 3.00 6.00
86 Pee Wee Reese 5.00 10.00
87 Del Rice 2.50 5.00
88 Vic Raschi 3.00 6.00
89 Allie Reynolds 3.00 6.00
90 Phil Rizzuto 5.00 10.00
91 Jackie Robinson 40.00 80.00
92 Babe Ruth 50.00 100.00
93 Casey Stengel 5.00 10.00
94 Vern Stephens 3.00 6.00
95 Duke Snider 7.50 15.00
96 Enos Slaughter 5.00 10.00
97 Al Schoendienst 5.00 10.00
98 Gerald Staley 2.50 5.00
99 Clyde Shoun 2.50 5.00
102 Al Simmons 5.00 10.00
103 George Sisler 5.00 10.00
104 Tris Speaker 5.00 10.00
105 Ed Stanky 3.00 6.00
106 Virgil Trucks 2.50 5.00
107 Henry Thompson 2.50 5.00
109 Dazzy Vance 5.00 10.00
110 Lloyd Waner 5.00 10.00
111 Paul Waner 5.00 10.00
112 Gene Woodling 2.50 5.00
113 Ted Williams 40.00 80.00
114 Vic Wertz 2.50 5.00
115 Wes Westrum 2.50 5.00
116 Johnny Wyrostek 2.50 5.00
117 Eddie Yost 2.50 5.00
118 Al Zarilla 2.50 5.00
119 Gus Zernial 2.50 5.00
120 Sam Zoldak 2.50 5.00
XX Strip of 13 cards 10.00 20.00

1984 Ralston Purina

The cards in this 33-card set measure the standard size. In 1984 the Ralston Purina Company issued what it has entitled "The First Annual Collectors Edition of Baseball Cards." The cards feature portrait photos of the players rather than batting action shots. The Topps logo appears along with the Ralston logo on the front of the card. The backs are completely different from the Topps cards of this year; in fact, they contain neither a Topps logo nor a Topps copyright. Large quantities of these cards were obtained by card dealers for direct distribution into the organized hobby, hence the relatively low price of the set. These cards are very similar to the Topps Cereal issue of the same year -- note that the only difference is the Ralston Purina logo on the front.

COMPLETE SET (33) 2.00 5.00
1 Eddie Murray .15 .40
2 Ozzie Smith .30 .75
3 Ted Simmons .01 .05
4 Pete Rose .15 .40
5 Greg Luzinski .01 .05
6 Andre Dawson .10 .30
7 Dave Winfield .15 .40
8 Tom Seaver .15 .40
9 Jim Rice .02 .10
10 Fernando Valenzuela .02 .10
11 Wade Boggs .15 .40
12 Dale Murphy .10 .30
13 George Brett .30 .75
14 Nolan Ryan .60 1.50
15 Rickey Henderson .25 .60
16 Steve Carlton .15 .40
17 Rod Carew .15 .40
18 Steve Garvey .07 .20
19 Reggie Jackson .15 .40
20 Dave Concepcion .02 .10
21 Robin Yount .15 .40
22 Mike Schmidt .15 .40
23 Jim Palmer .15 .40
24 Bruce Sutter .01 .05
25 Dan Quisenberry .01 .05
26 Bill Madlock .02 .10
27 Cecil Cooper .02 .10
28 Gary Carter .15 .40
29 Fred Lynn .02 .10
30 Pedro Guerrero .01 .05
31 Ron Guidry .02 .10
32 Keith Hernandez .02 .10
33 Carlton Fisk .15 .40

1987 Ralston Purina

The Ralston Purina Company issued a set of 15 cards picturing players without their respective team logos. The cards measure approximately 2 1/2" by 3 3/8" and are in full-color on the front. The cards are numbered on the back in the lower right hand corner; the player's uniform number is prominently displayed on the front. The cards were distributed as inserts inside packages of certain flavors of Ralston Purina's breakfast cereals. Three cards and a contest card were packaged in cellophane and inserted within the cereal box. The set was also available as an uncut sheet through a mail-in offer. Since the uncut sheets are relatively common, the value of the sheet is essentially the same as the value of the sum of the individual cards. In fact there were two uncut sheets issued, one had "Honey Graham Chex" printed at the top and the other had "Cookie Crisp" printed at the top. Also cards were issued with (cards from cereal boxes) and without (cards cut from the uncut sheets) the words "1987 Collectors Edition" printed in blue on the front. Reportedly 100,000 of the uncut sheets were given away free via instant win certificates inserted in with the cereal or collectors could send in two non-winning contest cards plus 1.00 for each uncut sheet.

COMPLETE SET (15) 8.00 20.00
1 Nolan Ryan 2.00 5.00
2 Steve Garvey .30 .75
3 Wade Boggs .75 2.00
4 Dave Winfield .50 1.25
5 Don Mattingly 1.00 2.50
6 Don Sutton .50 1.25
7 Dave Parker .08 .25
8 Eddie Murray .50 1.25
9 Gary Carter .50 1.25
10 Roger Clemens 1.00 2.50
11 Fernando Valenzuela .20 .50
12 Cal Ripken 2.00 5.00
13 Ozzie Smith 1.00 2.50
14 Mike Schmidt .50 1.25
15 Ryne Sandberg 1.00 2.50

1909 Ramly T204

The cards in this 121-card set measure approximately 2" by 2 1/2". The Ramly baseball series, designated T204 in the catalog, contains unnumbered cards. This set is one of the most distinguished ever produced, containing ornate gold borders around a black and white portrait of each player. There are spelling errors, and two distinct backs, "Ramly" and "TTT", are known. There is a premium of up to 25 percent for the "TTT" back. Much of the obverse card detail is actually embossed. The players have been alphabetized and numbered for reference in the checklist below. A few players (so far only six are confirmed, and a seventh is rumored) are known with square frames with blank backs. It is possible that these are proofs. The confirmed square players are John Anderson, Frank Bancroft, Kitty Bransfield, Jesse Burkett, Bill Dineen and Pat Moran. Of note, pricing for raw cards is provided in VgEx condition due to the fact that most cards from this set are found in off-grade shape.

COMPLETE SET (121) 25000.00 50000.00
1 Whitey Alperman 250.00 500.00
2 John J. Anderson 150.00 300.00
3 Jimmy Archer 150.00 300.00
4 Frank Arrelanes 250.00 500.00
5 Jim Ball 150.00 300.00
6 Neal Ball 150.00 300.00
7 Frank Bancroft 150.00 300.00
8 Johnny Bates 150.00 300.00
9 Fred Beebe 150.00 300.00
10 George Bell 150.00 300.00
11 Chief Bender 600.00 1200.00
12 Walter Blair 150.00 300.00
13 Cliff Blankenship 150.00 300.00
14 Frank Bowerman 150.00 300.00
15 Kitty Bransfield 150.00 300.00
16 Roger Bresnahan 500.00 1000.00
17 Al Bridwell 150.00 300.00
18 Mordecai Brown 600.00 1200.00
19 Fred Burchell 150.00 300.00
20 Jesse Burkett 3000.00 6000.00
21 Bobby Byrne (Byrnes) 150.00 300.00
22 Bill Carrigan 150.00 300.00
23 Frank Chance 500.00 1000.00
24 Charles Chech 150.00 300.00
25 Eddie Cicolte 500.00 1000.00
26 Otis Clymer 150.00 300.00
27 Andrew Coakley 150.00 300.00
28 Eddie Collins 600.00 1200.00
29 Jimmy Collins 500.00 1000.00
30 Wid Conroy 150.00 300.00
31 Jack Coombs 250.00 500.00
32 Doc Crandall 150.00 300.00
33 Lou Criger 150.00 300.00
34 Harry Davis 150.00 300.00
35 Art Devlin 150.00 300.00
36 Bill Dineen 150.00 300.00
37 Pat Donahue 150.00 300.00
38 Mike Donlin 150.00 300.00
39 Bill Donovan 150.00 300.00
40 Gus Dorner 150.00 300.00
41 Joe Dunn 150.00 300.00
42 Kid Elberfield 150.00 300.00
43 Johnny Evers 600.00 1200.00
44 Bob Ewing 150.00 300.00
45 George Ferguson 150.00 300.00
46 Hobe Ferris 150.00 300.00
47 Jerry Freeman 150.00 300.00
48 Art Fromme 150.00 300.00
49 Bob Ganley 150.00 300.00
50 Doc Gessler 150.00 300.00
51 Peaches Graham 150.00 300.00
52 Clark Griffith 500.00 1000.00
53 Roy Hartzell 150.00 300.00
54 Charlie Hemphill 150.00 300.00
55 Dick Hoblitzell 150.00 300.00
56 George Howard 150.00 300.00
57 Harry Howell 150.00 300.00
58 Miller Huggins 500.00 1000.00
59 John Hummel 150.00 300.00
60 Walter Johnson 10000.00 20000.00
61 Tom Jones 150.00 300.00
62 Mike Kahoe 150.00 300.00
63 Ed Kargar 150.00 300.00
64 Willie Keeler 600.00 1200.00
65 Red Kleinon 150.00 300.00
66 John Knight 150.00 300.00
67 Ed Konetchey 150.00 300.00
68 Vive Lindaman 150.00 300.00
69 Hans Loebert 150.00 300.00
70 Harry Lord 150.00 300.00
71 Harry Lumley 150.00 300.00
72 Ernie Lush 150.00 300.00
73 Rube Manning 150.00 300.00
74 Jimmy McAleer 150.00 300.00
75 Amby McConnell 150.00 300.00
76 Moose McCormick 150.00 300.00
77 Matty McIntyre 150.00 300.00
78 Larry McLean 150.00 300.00
79 Fred Merkle 250.00 500.00
80 Clyde Milan 150.00 300.00
81 Mike Mitchell 150.00 300.00
82 Pat Moran 150.00 300.00
83 Harry Cy Morgan 150.00 300.00
84 Tim Murname 150.00 300.00
85 Danny Murphy 150.00 300.00
86 Red Murray 150.00 300.00
87 Doc Newton 150.00 300.00
88 Simon Nichols 150.00 300.00
89 Harry Niles 150.00 300.00
90 Bill O'Hare 150.00 300.00
91 Charley O'Leary 150.00 300.00
92 Dode Paskert 150.00 300.00
93 Barney Pelty 150.00 300.00
94 Jack Pfeister 150.00 300.00
95 Eddie Plank 1500.00 3000.00
96 Jack Powell 150.00 300.00
97 Bugs Raymond 150.00 300.00
98 Tom Reilly 150.00 300.00
99 Claude Ritchey 150.00 300.00
100 Nap Rucker 150.00 300.00
101 Ed Ruelbach 150.00 300.00
102 Slim Sallee 150.00 300.00
103 Germany Schaefer 150.00 300.00
104 Jimmy Schekard 150.00 300.00
105 Admiral Schlei 150.00 300.00
106 Wildfire Schulte 150.00 300.00
107 Jimmy Sebring 150.00 300.00
108 Bill Shipke 150.00 300.00
109 Charlie Smith 150.00 300.00
110 Tubby Spencer 150.00 300.00
111 Jake Stahl 250.00 500.00
112 Jim Stephens 150.00 300.00
113 Harry Stienfeldt (Steinfeldt) 250.00 500.00
114 Gabby Street 150.00 300.00
115 Bill Sweeney 150.00 300.00
116 Fred Tenney 150.00 300.00
117 Ira Thomas 150.00 300.00
118 Joe Tinker 700.00 1400.00
119 Bob Unglane 150.00 300.00
120 Heinie Wagner 150.00 300.00
121 Bobby Wallace 500.00 1000.00

1909 Ramly Square Frame T204

These few cards are known to exist with square picture frames. They can also be identified as the players full name is printed on the card. It is possible, although unlikely, that a few other players in this set may exist but no confirmation is known at this time.

COMPLETE SET 12500.00 25000.00
1 John Anderson 3000.00 6000.00
2 Frank Bancroft 3000.00 6000.00
3 Kitty Bransfield 3000.00 6000.00
4 Jesse Burkett 7500.00 15000.00
5 Bill Dineen 3000.00 6000.00
6 Pat Moran 5000.00 10000.00

1972 Rangers Team Issue

This 32-card set of the 1972 Texas Rangers measures approximately 3 1/2" by 5 3/4" and features black-and-white player portraits with white borders. A facsimile autograph is printed on the photo. Name, position, and Texas Rangers are printed across the bottom of the photo. The backs are blank. The cards are unnumbered and checklisted below in alphabetical order.

COMPLETE SET (32) 40.00 80.00
1 Larry Biittner .75 2.00
2 Dick Billings .75 2.00
3 Dick Bosman 1.25 3.00
4 Pete Broberg .75 2.00
5 Jeff Burroughs 2.00 5.00
6 Casey Cox .75 2.00
7 Jim Driscoll .75 2.00
8 Ted Ford .75 2.00
9 Bill Gogolewski .75 2.00
10 Tom Grieve 1.50 4.00
11 Rich Hand .75 2.00
12 Toby Harrah 2.00 5.00
13 Frank Howard 2.00 5.00
14 Sid Hudson CO .75 2.00

15 Dalton Jones .75 2.00
16 Hal King .75 2.00
17 Ted Kubiak .75 2.00
18 Paul Lindblad .75 2.00
19 Joe Lovitto .75 2.00
20 Elliott Maddox .75 2.00
21 Don Mincher .75 2.00
22 Dave Nelson .75 2.00
23 Jim Panther .75 2.00
24 Mike Paul .75 2.00
25 Horacio Pina .75 2.00
26 Lenny Randle .75 2.00
27 Jim Shellenback .75 2.00
28 Don Stanhouse 1.25 3.00
29 Ken Suarez .75 2.00
30 George Susce CO .75 2.00
31 Wayne Terwilliger CO .75 2.00
32 Ted Williams MG 6.00 15.00

1973 Rangers Team Issue

This set of the Texas Rangers measures approximately 3 1/2" by 5 3/4" and features black-and-white player portraits in a white border. The backs are blank. The cards are unnumbered and checklisted below in alphabetical order. Since the Rangers changed managers during the 1973 season, both Whitey Herzog and Billy Martin are listed as managers in our checklist.

COMPLETE SET 15.00 40.00
1 Lloyd Allen .40 1.00
2 Jim Bibby .75 2.00
3 Larry Biittner .40 1.00
4 Rich Billings .40 1.00
5 Pete Broberg .40 1.00
6 Jeff Burroughs 1.50 4.00
7 Rico Carty .75 2.00
8 David Clyde .75 2.00
9 Steve Dunning .40 1.00
10 Chuck Estrada CO .40 1.00
11 Steve Foucault .40 1.00
12 Bill Gogolewski .40 1.00
13 Rich Hand .40 1.00
14 Toby Harrah 1.25 3.00
15 Vic Harris .40 1.00
16 Whitey Herzog .75 2.00
17 Chuck Hiller CO .40 1.00
18 Charlie Hudson .40 1.00
19 Alex Johnson .75 2.00
20 Elliot Maddox .40 1.00
21 Billy Martin MG 2.00 5.00
22 Jim Mason .40 1.00
23 Jim Merritt .40 1.00
24 Dave Nelson .40 1.00
25 Mike Paul .40 1.00
26 Lenny Randle .40 1.00
27 Sonny Siebert .40 1.00
28 Don Stanhouse .40 1.00
29 Ken Suarez .40 1.00

1974 Rangers Team Issue

This set, which measured 3 1/2" by 5 3/4" featured members of the 1974 Texas Rangers. These black and white blank-backed cards feature the player's photo along with their name, position and Texas Rangers name on the bottom. Since these cards are unnumbered, we have sequenced them in alphabetical order. It is believed but not confirmed that cards were issued for Dick Billings and Don Stanhouse.

COMPLETE SET 12.50 30.00
1 Jim Bibby .40 1.00
2 Pete Broberg .40 1.00
3 Jackie Brown .40 1.00
4 Larry Brown .40 1.00
5 Jeff Burroughs .60 1.50
6 Leo Cardenas .40 1.00
7 David Clyde .40 1.00
8 Merrill Combs CO .40 1.00
9 Mike Cubbage .40 1.00
10 Don Durham .40 1.00
11 Steve Dunning .40 1.00
12 Chuck Estrada CO .40 1.00
13 Steve Foucault .40 1.00
14 Art Fowler CO .40 1.00
15 Jim Fregosi .40 1.00
16 Tom Grieve .60 1.50
17 Toby Harrah .40 1.00
18 Steve Hargan .40 1.00
19 Mike Hargrove 1.00 2.50
20 Fergie Jenkins 1.25 3.00
21 Alex Johnson .40 1.00
22 Joe Lovitto .40 1.00
23 Frank Lucchesi CO .40 1.00
24 Billy Martin MG 1.25 3.00
25 Jim Merritt .40 1.00
26 Jackie Moore .40 1.00
27 Dave Nelson .40 1.00
28 Lenny Randle .40 1.00
29 Jim Shellenback .40 1.00
30 Charlie Silvera CO .40 1.00
31 Jim Spencer .40 1.00
32 Jim Sundberg 1.00 2.50
33 Cesar Tovar .40 1.00

1975 Rangers Postcards

This 37-card set of the Texas Rangers features player photos on postcard-size cards. The cards are unnumbered and checklisted below in alphabetical order.

COMPLETE SET (37) 8.00 20.00
1 Mike Bacsik .20 .50
2 Jim Bibby .20 .50
3 Jackie Brown .20 .50
4 Jeff Burroughs .30 .75
5 Leo Cardenas .20 .50
6 Merrill Combs CO .20 .50
7 Mike Cubbage .20 .50
8 Bill Fahey .20 .50
9 Steve Foucault .20 .50
10 Art Fowler CO .20 .50
11 Jim Fregosi .30 .75
12 Tom Grieve .30 .75
13 Bill Hands .20 .50
14 Steve Hargan .20 .50
15 Mike Hargrove .60 1.50
16 Toby Harrah .30 .75
17 Roy Howell .20 .50
18 Fergie Jenkins .75 2.00
19 Joe Lovitto .20 .50
20 Frank Lucchesi CO .20 .50
21 Billy Martin MG .60 1.50
22 Jim Merritt .20 .50
23 Dave Moates .20 .50
24 Jackie Moore .20 .50
25 Tommy Joe Moore .20 .50
26 Dave Nelson .20 .50
27 Dave Nelson/(Autographed) .20 .50
28 Gaylord Perry .75 2.00
29 Lenny Randle .20 .50
30 Lenny Randle/(Autographed) .20 .50
31 Charlie Silvera CO .20 .50
32 Roy Smalley .30 .75
33 Jim Spencer .20 .50
34 Jim Sundberg .30 .75
35 Jim Sundberg/(Last year's picture) .30 .75
36 Stan Thomas .20 .50
37 Cesar Tovar .20 .50
38 Jim Umbarger .20 .50
39 Clyde Wright .20 .50

1976 Rangers Team Issue

This photo card set featured members of the 1976 Texas Rangers. The 3 1/2" by 5 3/4" blank-backed cards black and white cards feature player photos surrounded by a white border. The player's name is identified at the bottom of the card. Since the cards are unnumbered, we have sequenced them in alphabetical order.

COMPLETE SET 12.50 30.00
1 Steve Barr .40 1.00
2 Juan Beniquez .40 1.00
3 Bert Blyleven 1.00 2.50
4 Nelson Briles .40 1.00
5 Jeff Burroughs .40 1.00
6 Gene Clines .40 1.00
7 Pat Corrales CO .40 1.00
8 John Ellis .40 1.00
9 Bill Fahey .40 1.00
10 Steve Foucault .40 1.00
11 Jim Fregosi .40 1.00
12 Dick Gernert CO .40 1.00
13 Tom Grieve .60 1.50
14 Steve Hargan .40 1.00
15 Mike Hargrove .60 1.50
16 Toby Harrah .40 1.00
17 Joe Hoerner .40 1.00
18 Roy Lee Howell .40 1.00
19 Sid Hudson CO .40 1.00
20 Joe Lahoud .40 1.00
21 Dave Moates .40 1.00
22 Jackie Moore .40 1.00
23 Gaylord Perry 1.25 3.00
24 Lenny Randle .40 1.00
25 Jim Sundberg .60 1.50
26 Danny Thompson .40 1.00
27 Jim Umbarger .40 1.00
28 Bill Zeigler .40 1.00

1977 Rangers Team Issue

This set was issued to promote the members of the 1977 Texas Rangers. The black and white blank-backed cards measures approximately 3 1/2" by 5 3/4". The player's photo are surrounded by white borders. This checklist may be incomplete and any additions are appreciated. Since these cards are unnumbered, we have sequenced them in alphabetical order.

COMPLETE SET 10.00 25.00
1 Doyle Alexander .40 1.00
2 Bert Blyleven .75 2.00
3 Nelson Briles .40 1.00
4 Bert Campaneris .75 2.00
5 Adrian Devine .40 1.00
6 Dock Ellis .40 1.00
7 Bill Fahey .40 1.00
8 Tom Grieve .60 1.50
9 Mike Hargrove .60 1.50
10 Toby Harrah .40 1.00
11 Ken Henderson .40 1.00
12 Willie Horton .60 1.50
13 Billy Hunter MG .40 1.00
14 Darold Knowles .40 1.00
15 Paul Lindblad .40 1.00
16 Mike Marshall .40 1.00
17 Jim Mason .40 1.00
18 Dave May .40 1.00
19 Gaylord Perry 1.25 3.00
20 Jim Sundberg .60 1.50
21 Claudell Washington .40 1.00
22 Bump Wills .60 1.50

1978 Rangers Burger King

The cards in this 23-card set measure 2 1/2" by 3 1/2". This set of 22 numbered player cards (featuring the Texas Rangers) and one unnumbered checklist was issued regionally by Burger King in 1978. Asterisks denote poses different from those found in the regular Topps cards of this year.

COMPLETE SET (23) 6.00 15.00
1 Billy Hunter MG .20 .50
2 Jim Sundberg .40 1.00
3 John Ellis .20 .50
4 Doyle Alexander .30 .75
5 Jon Matlack * .30 .75
6 Dock Ellis .20 .50
7 Doc Medich .20 .50
8 Fergie Jenkins * 1.50 4.00
9 Len Barker .20 .50
10 Reggie Cleveland * .20 .50
11 Mike Hargrove .60 1.50
12 Bump Wills .20 .50
13 Toby Harrah .40 1.00
14 Bert Campaneris .30 .75
15 Sandy Alomar .30 .75
16 Kurt Bevacqua .20 .50
17 Al Oliver * .60 1.50
18 Juan Beniquez .20 .50
19 Claudell Washington .40 1.00
20 Richie Zisk .30 .75
21 John Lowenstein * .20 .50
22 Bobby Thompson * .20 .50
NNO Checklist Card TP .10 .25

1978-79 Rangers Team Issue

Issued over a period of years, these cards feature members of the late 1970's Texas Rangers. These black and white blank-backed cards measure 3 1/2" by 5 1/2". The player's photo is surrounded by white borders while his name is located at the bottom. Since the cards are unnumbered, we have sequenced this set in alphabetical order.

COMPLETE SET 12.50 30.00
1 Doyle Alexander .40 1.00
2 Sandy Alomar .40 1.00
3 Len Barker .60 1.50
4 Buddy Bell .60 1.50
5 Juan Beniquez .40 1.00
6 Kurt Bevacqua .40 1.00
7 Bobby Bonds 1.00 2.50
8 Bert Campaneris .60 1.50
9 Reggie Cleveland .40 1.00
10 Steve Comer .40 1.00
11 Pat Corrales CO .40 1.00
12 John Ellis .40 1.00
13 Bill Fahey .40 1.00
14 Mike Hargrove .60 1.50
15 Toby Harrah .40 1.00
16 Sid Hudson CO .40 1.00
17 Billy Hunter MG .40 1.00
18 Mike Jorgensen .40 1.00
19 Jim Kern .40 1.00
20 Fred Koenig CO .40 1.00
21 Paul Lindblad .40 1.00
22 John Lowenstein .40 1.00
23 Sparky Lyle .60 1.50
24 Jim Mason .40 1.00
25 Jon Matlack .40 1.00
26 George Doc Medich .40 1.00
27 Roger Moret .40 1.00
28 Al Oliver .75 2.00
29 Jim Sundberg .60 1.50
30 Jim Umbarger .40 1.00
31 Bump Wills .40 1.00
32 Richie Zisk .40 1.00

1980 Rangers Postcards

These postcards came in black and white with the player's name in a white border on the bottom. For some unexplained reason, both Billy Sample and Bump Wills have two poses. These cards are not numbered so we have sequenced them in alphabetical order.

COMPLETE SET 8.00 20.00
1 Buddy Bell .40 1.00
2 Steve Comer .20 .50
3 Pat Corrales MG .20 .50
4 Danny Darwin .20 .50
5 Adrian Devine .20 .50
6 Rich Donnelly CO .20 .50
7 John Ellis .20 .50
8 Pepe Frias .20 .50
9 John Grubb .20 .50
10 Bud Harrelson .20 .50
11 Fergie Jenkins .75 2.00
12 Jim Kern .20 .50
13 Fred Koenig CO .20 .50
14 Sparky Lyle .30 .75
15 Jon Matlack .20 .50
16 Doc Medich .20 .50
17 Jackie Moore CO .20 .50
18 Nelson Norman .20 .50
19 Jim Norris .20 .50
20 Al Oliver .40 1.00
21 Gaylord Perry .75 2.00
22 Pat Putnam .20 .50
23 Dave Rajsich .20 .50
24 Mickey Rivers .30 .75
25 Dave Roberts .20 .50
26 Billy Sample .20 .50
Patch on Uniform
27 Billy Sample .20 .50
No Patch
28 Rusty Staub .60 1.50
29 Jim Sundberg .20 .50
30 Jim Umbarger .20 .50
31 Bump Wills .20 .50
With facial hair
32 Bump Wills .20 .50
Clean shaven
33 Richie Zisk .30 .75

1983 Rangers Affiliated Food

The cards in this 28-card set measure 2 3/8" by 3 1/2". The Affiliated Food Stores chain of Arlington, Texas, produced this set of Texas Rangers late during the 1983 baseball season. Complete sets were given to children 13 and under at the September 3, 1983, Rangers game. The cards are numbered by uniform number and feature the player's name, card number, and the words "1983 Rangers" on the bottom front. The backs contain biographical data, career totals, a small black and white insert picture of the player, and the Affiliated Food Stores' logo. The coaches card is unnumbered.

COMPLETE SET (28) 2.00 5.00
1 Bill Stein .08 .25
2 Mike Richardt .08 .25
3 Wayne Tolleson .08 .25
5 Billy Sample .08 .25
6 Bobby Jones .08 .25
7 Bucky Dent .20 .50
8 Bobby Johnson .08 .25
9 Pete O'Brien .20 .50
10 Jim Sundberg .08 .25
11 Doug Rader MG .08 .25
12 Dave Hostetler .08 .25
14 Larry Biittner .08 .25
15 Larry Parrish .20 .50
17 Mickey Rivers .08 .25
21 Odell Jones .08 .25
24 Dave Schmidt .08 .25
25 Buddy Bell .40 1.00
26 George Wright .08 .25
28 Frank Tanana .30 .75
29 John Butcher .08 .25
32 Jon Matlack .08 .25
40 Rick Honeycutt .08 .25
41 Dave Tobik .08 .25
44 Danny Darwin .08 .25
46 Jim Anderson .08 .25
48 Mike Smithson .08 .25
49 Charlie Hough .30 .75
NNO Rangers Coaches .08 .25
Wayne Terwilliger
Merv Rettenmund

1984 Rangers Jarvis Press

The cards in this 30-card set measure 2 1/2" by 3 1/2". The Jarvis Press of Dallas issued this full-color regional set of Texas Rangers. Cards are numbered on the front by the players uniform number. The cards were issued on an uncut sheet. Twenty-seven player cards, a manager card, a trainer card (unnumbered) and a coaches card (unnumbered) comprise this set. The backs are black and white and contain biographical information, statistics, and an additional photo of the player.

COMPLETE SET (30) 2.00 5.00
1 Bill Stein .08 .25
2 Alan Bannister .08 .25
3 Wayne Tolleson .08 .25
5 Billy Sample .08 .25
6 Bobby Jones .08 .25
7 Ned Yost .20 .50
9 Pete O'Brien .20 .50
11 Doug Rader MG .08 .25
13 Tommy Dunbar .08 .25
14 Jim Anderson .08 .25
15 Larry Parrish .20 .50
16 Mike Mason .08 .25
17 Mickey Rivers .08 .25
19 Curtis Wilkerson .08 .25
20 Jeff Kunkel .08 .25
21 Odell Jones .08 .25
24 Dave Schmidt .08 .25
25 Buddy Bell .40 1.00
26 George Wright .08 .25
28 Frank Tanana .30 .75
30 Marv Foley .08 .25
31 Dave Stewart .40 1.00
32 Gary Ward .08 .25
36 Dickie Noles .08 .25
43 Donnie Scott .08 .25
44 Danny Darwin .20 .50
49 Charlie Hough .30 .75
53 Joey McLaughlin .08 .25
NNO Bill Zeigler TR .08 .25
NNO0 Rangers Coaches .08 .25
Merv Rettenmund
Rich Donnelly
G

1984 Rangers Team Issue 4 X 6

This 31-card set features members of the 1984 Texas Rangers. These black and white blank-backed cards measure approximately 4 1/8" by 6 1/2" and have the player's photo surrounded by a white border. The bottom is dedicated to the player's name as well as the Rangers logo. Since these cards are unnumbered, we have sequenced them in alphabetical order.

COMPLETE SET
1 Jim Anderson .20 .50
2 Alan Bannister .20 .50
3 Buddy Bell .30 .75
4 Danny Darwin .20 .50
5 Rich Donnelly .20 .50
6 Glenn Ezell .20 .50
7 Marv Foley .20 .50
8 Tom Henke .60 1.50
9 Charlie Hough .30 .75
10 Bobby Jones .20 .50
11 Odell Jones .20 .50
12 Mike Mason .20 .50
13 Pete O'Brien .20 .50
14 Larry Parrish .20 .50
15 Doug Rader MG .20 .50
16 Merv Rettenmund .20 .50
17 Mickey Rivers .30 .75
18 Billy Sample .20 .50
19 Dave Schmidt .20 .50
20 Donnie Scott .20 .50
21 Bill Stein .20 .50
22 Dave Stewart .20 .50
23 Dick Such CO .20 .50
24 Frank Tanana .30 .75
25 Wayne Terwilliger CO .20 .50
26 Dave Tobik .20 .50
27 Wayne Tolleson .20 .50
28 Gary Ward .20 .50
29 Curtis Wilkerson .20 .50
30 George Wright .20 .50
31 Ned Yost .20 .50

1984-85 Rangers Team Issue 3 X 5

These cards, issued over at least a two-year period, feature members of the mid-1980's Texas Rangers. These blank-back black and white cards measure approximately 3" by 5" and feature black and white photos surrounded by white borders. The bottom left has the player's name while the bottom right has the Rangers logo. Since these cards are unnumbered, we have checklisted them in alphabetical order.

COMPLETE SET 8.00 20.00
1 Jim Anderson .20 .50
2 Alan Bannister .20 .50
3 Buddy Bell .30 .75
4 Bobby Bragan .30 .75
5 Glenn Brummer .20 .50
6 Glen Cook .20 .50
7 Danny Darwin .20 .50
8 Rich Donnelly .20 .50
9 Tommy Dunbar .20 .50
10 Glenn Ezell .20 .50
11 Toby Harrah .20 .50
12 Greg Harris .20 .50
13 Burt Hooton .20 .50
14 Charlie Hough .30 .75
15 Tom House .20 .50
16 Art Howe .20 .50
17 Cliff Johnson .20 .50
18 Bobby Jones .20 .50
19 Mike Mason .20 .50
20 Oddibe McDowell .40 1.00
21 Dickie Noles .20 .50
22 Pete O'Brien .20 .50
23 Larry Parrish .20 .50
24 Luis Pujols .20 .50
25 Doug Rader MG .20 .50
26 Dave Rozema .20 .50
27 Billy Sample .20 .50
28 Dave Schmidt .20 .50
29 Don Slaught .20 .50
30 Bill Stein .20 .50
31 Dave Stewart .40 1.00
32 Frank Tanana .30 .75
33 Wayne Terwilliger CO .20 .50
34 Wayne Tolleson .20 .50
35 Gary Ward .20 .50
36 Chris Welsh .20 .50
37 Curtis Wilkerson .20 .50
38 Bobby Valentine MG .20 .50
39 George Wright .20 .50
40 Ned Yost .30 .75

1985 Rangers Performance

The cards in this 28-card set measure 2 3/8" by 3 1/2". Performance Printing sponsored this full-color regional set of Texas Rangers. Cards are numbered on the back by the players uniform number. The cards were also issued on an uncut sheet. Twenty-five player cards, a manager card, a trainer card (unnumbered) and a coaches card (unnumbered) comprise this set. The backs are black and white and contain biographical information, statistics, and an additional photo of the player.

COMPLETE SET (28) 2.00 5.00
0 Oddibe McDowell .30 .75
1 Bill Stein .08 .25
2 Bobby Valentine MG .20 .50
3 Wayne Tolleson .08 .25
4 Don Slaught .08 .25
5 Alan Bannister .08 .25
6 Bobby Jones .08 .25
7 Glenn Brummer .08 .25
8 Luis Pujols .08 .25
9 Pete O'Brien .20 .50
11 Toby Harrah .20 .50
13 Tommy Dunbar .08 .25
15 Larry Parrish .20 .50
16 Mike Mason .08 .25
19 Curtis Wilkerson .08 .25
24 Dave Schmidt .08 .25
25 Buddy Bell .40 1.00
27 Greg A. Harris .08 .25
30 Dave Rozema .08 .25
32 Gary Ward .08 .25
36 Dickie Noles .08 .25
41 Chris Welsh .08 .25
44 Cliff Johnson .20 .50
46 Burt Hooton .08 .25
48 Dave Stewart .40 1.00
49 Charlie Hough .30 .75
NNO Trainers:Bill Zeigler .08 .25
and Danny Wheat
NNO Rangers Coaches .08 .25
Art Howe
Rich Donnelly
Glenn Ez

1986 Rangers Greats TCMA

This 12-card standard-size set honors some of the leading Texas Rangers from their first 15 seasons. The player's photo, name and position are noted on the front. The backs have career information, vital statistics as well as a biography.

COMPLETE SET (12) 1.25 3.00
1 Gaylord Perry .40 1.00
2 Jon Matlack .08 .25
3 Jim Kern .08 .25
4 Billy Hunter MG .08 .25
5 Mike Hargrove .20 .50
6 Bump Wills .08 .25
7 Toby Harrah .20 .50
8 Lenny Randle .08 .25
9 Al Oliver .20 .50
10 Mickey Rivers .08 .25
11 Jeff Burroughs .08 .25
12 Dick Billings .08 .25

1986 Rangers Lite

This seven-card set of the Texas Rangers features color player portraits with white borders and measures approximately 4" by 6". The backs carry player biographical information and career statistics. The cards are unnumbered and checklisted below in alphabetical order. These cards are known with our without stats on the back, however all values are the same for cards no matter what the back.

COMPLETE SET 8.00 20.00
1 Bob Brower .20 .50
2 Steve Buechele .40 1.00
3 Edwin Correa .20 .50
4 Joe Ferguson .20 .50
5 Scott Fletcher .20 .50
6 Tim Foli CO .20 .50
7 Jose Guzman .30 .75
8 Toby Harrah .30 .75
9 Greg Harris .20 .50
10 Dwayne Henry .20 .50
11 Charlie Hough .40 1.00
12 Tom House CO .20 .50
13 Art Howe .20 .50
14 Pete Incaviglia .60 1.50
15 Mickey Mahler .20 .50
16 Mike Mason .20 .50
17 Oddibe McDowell .30 .75
18 Pete O'Brien .20 .50
19 Tom Paciorek .20 .50
20 Larry Parrish .30 .75
21 Geno Petralli .20 .50
22 Darrell Porter .30 .75
23 Tom Robson .20 .50
24 Don Slaught .20 .50
25 Bobby Valentine MG .30 .75
26 Gary Ward .20 .50
27 Curtis Wilkerson .20 .50
28 Mitch Williams .40 1.00
29 Bobby Witt .40 1.00
30 George Wright .20 .50
31 Ricky Wright .20 .50
32 Arlington Stadium .20 .50

1986 Rangers Performance

Performance Printing of Dallas produced a 28-card set of Texas Rangers which were given out at the stadium on August 23rd. Cards measure approximately 2 3/8" by 3 1/2" and are in full color. The cards are unnumbered except for uniform number which is given on the card back. Card backs feature black printing on white card stock with a small picture of the player's head in the upper left corner. The set seems to be more desirable than the previous Ranger sets due to the Rangers' 1986 success which was directly related to their outstanding rookie crop including Jose Guzman, Pete Incaviglia, Ruben Sierra, Mitch Williams, and Bobby Witt.

COMPLETE SET (28) 4.00 10.00
0 Oddibe McDowell .20 .50
1 Scott Fletcher .08 .25
2 Bobby Valentine MG .20 .50
3 Ruben Sierra .60 1.50
4 Don Slaught .08 .25
9 Pete O'Brien .20 .50
11 Toby Harrah .20 .50
12 Geno Petralli .08 .25
15 Larry Parrish .20 .50
16 Mike Mason .08 .25
17 Darrell Porter .20 .50
18 Edwin Correa .08 .25
19 Curtis Wilkerson .08 .25
22 Steve Buechele .20 .50
23 Jose Guzman .08 .25
24 Ricky Wright .08 .25
27 Greg A. Harris .08 .25
28 Mitch Williams .30 .75
29 Pete Incaviglia .30 .75
32 Gary Ward .08 .25
34 Dale Mohorcic .08 .25
40 Jeff Russell .08 .25
44 Tom Paciorek .08 .25
46 Mike Loynd .08 .25
48 Bobby Witt .40 1.00
49 Charlie Hough .40 1.00
NNO Coaching Staff .08 .25
Art Howe
Joe Ferguson
Tim Foli/
NNO Trainers:Bill Ziegler .08 .25
and Danny Wheat

1987 Rangers Mother's

This set consists of 28 full-color, rounded-corner cards each measuring 2 1/2" by 3 1/2". Starter sets (only 20 cards but also including a certificate for eight more cards) were given out at the ballpark and collectors were encouraged to trade to fill in the rest of their set. Cards were originally given out on July 17th during the game against the Yankees. Photos were taken by Barry Colla. The sets were reportedly given out free to the first 25,000 paid admissions at the game.

COMPLETE SET (28) 5.00 12.00
1 Bobby Valentine MG .20 .50
2 Pete Incaviglia .30 .75
3 Charlie Hough .30 .75
4 Oddibe McDowell .20 .50
5 Larry Parrish .20 .50
6 Scott Fletcher .08 .25
7 Steve Buechele .08 .25
8 Tom Paciorek .08 .25
9 Pete O'Brien .20 .50
10 Darrell Porter .20 .50
11 Greg A. Harris .08 .25
12 Don Slaught .08 .25
13 Ruben Sierra .60 1.50
14 Curtis Wilkerson .08 .25
15 Dale Mohorcic .08 .25
16 Ron Meridith .08 .25
17 Mitch Williams .40 1.00
18 Bob Brower .08 .25
19 Edwin Correa .08 .25
20 Geno Petralli .08 .25
21 Mike Loynd .08 .25
22 Jerry Browne .20 .50
23 Jose Guzman .08 .25
24 Jeff Kunkel .08 .25
25 Bobby Witt .40 1.00
26 Jeff Russell .20 .50
27 Rangers' Trainers .08 .25
Bill Ziegler
Danny Wheat
28 Checklist Card .08 .25
Tom Robson CO
Art Howe CO
Joe Fe

1987 Rangers Smokey

The U.S. Forestry Service (in conjunction with the Texas Rangers) produced this large, attractive 32-card set. The cards feature Smokey the Bear pictured in the upper-right corner of every player's card. The card backs give a cartoon fire safety tip. The cards measure approximately 4 1/4" by 6" and are subtitled "Wildfire Prevention" on the front. Card numbers 4 Mike Mason and 14 Tom Paciorek were withdrawn and were never formally released as part of the set and hence are quite scarce.

COMPLETE SET (32) 40.00 100.00
COMMON CARD (1-32) .10 .25
COMMON SP 40.00
1 Charlie Hough .40 1.00
2 Greg A. Harris .08 .25
3 Jose Guzman .08 .25
4 Mike Mason SP 15.00 40.00
5 Dale Mohorcic .08 .25
6 Bobby Witt .40 1.00
7 Mitch Williams .40 1.00
8 Geno Petralli .08 .25
9 Don Slaught .08 .25
10 Darrell Porter .08 .25
11 Steve Buechele .08 .25
12 Pete O'Brien .20 .50
13 Scott Fletcher .08 .25
14 Tom Paciorek SP 15.00 40.00
15 Pete Incaviglia .40 1.00
16 Oddibe McDowell .20 .50
17 Ruben Sierra .60 1.50
18 Larry Parrish .20 .50
19 Bobby Valentine MG .20 .50
20 Tom House CO .08 .25
21 Tom Robson CO .08 .25
22 Edwin Correa .08 .25
23 Mike Stanley .75 2.00
24 Joe Ferguson CO .08 .25
25 Art Howe CO .08 .25
26 Bob Brower .08 .25
27 Mike Loynd .08 .25
28 Curtis Wilkerson .08 .25
29 Tim Foli CO .08 .25
30 Dave Oliver CO .08 .25
31 Jerry Browne .08 .25
32 Jeff Russell .08 .25

1988 Rangers Mother's

This set consists of 28 full-color, rounded-corner cards each measuring 2 1/2" by 3 1/2". Starter sets (only 20 cards but also including a certificate for eight more cards) were given out at the ballpark and collectors were encouraged to trade to fill in the rest of their set. Cards were originally given out on August 7th. Photos were taken by Barry Colla. The sets were reportedly given out free to the first 25,000 paid admissions at the game.

COMPLETE SET (28) 3.00 8.00
1 Bobby Valentine MG .20 .50
2 Pete Incaviglia .20 .50
3 Charlie Hough .30 .75
4 Oddibe McDowell .20 .50
5 Larry Parrish .20 .50
6 Scott Fletcher .08 .25
7 Steve Buechele .08 .25
8 Steve Kemp .08 .25
9 Pete O'Brien .20 .50
10 Ruben Sierra .40 1.00
11 Mike Stanley .08 .25
12 Jose Cecena .08 .25
13 Cecil Espy .08 .25
14 Curtis Wilkerson .08 .25
15 Dale Mohorcic .08 .25
16 Ray Hayward .08 .25
17 Mitch Williams .30 .75
18 Bob Brower .08 .25
19 Paul Kilgus .08 .25
20 Geno Petralli .08 .25
21 James Steels .08 .25
22 Jerry Browne .08 .25
23 Jose Guzman .08 .25
24 DeWayne Vaughn .08 .25
25 Bobby Witt .08 .25
26 Jeff Russell .08 .25
27 Rangers' Coaches .08 .25
Richard Egan
Tom House
Art How
28 Checklist Card .08 .25
Danny Wheat TR
Bill Zeigler TR

1988 Rangers Smokey

The cards in this 21-card set measure approximately 3 1/2" by 5". This numbered, full color set features the Fire Prevention Bear, Smokey, and a Rangers player (or manager) on each card. The set was given out at Arlington Stadium to fans during the Smokey Bear Day game promotion on August 7th. The logos of the Texas Forest Service and the U.S. Forestry Service appear on the reverse in conjunction with a Smokey the Bear logo on the obverse. The backs contain short biographical data and a fire prevention hint from Smokey.

COMPLETE SET (21) 5.00 12.00
1 Tom O'Malley .20 .50
2 Pete O'Brien .30 .75
3 Geno Petralli .20 .50
4 Pete Incaviglia .30 .75
5 Oddibe McDowell .30 .75
6 Dale Mohorcic .20 .50
7 Bobby Witt .20 .50
8 Bobby Valentine MG .30 .75
9 Ruben Sierra .60 1.50
10 Scott Fletcher .20 .50
11 Mike Stanley .20 .50
12 Steve Buechele .20 .50
13 Charlie Hough .40 1.00
14 Larry Parrish .30 .75
15 Jerry Browne .20 .50
16 Bob Brower .20 .50
17 Jeff Russell .20 .50
18 Edwin Correa .20 .50
19 Mitch Williams .30 .75
20 Jose Guzman .30 .75
21 Curtis Wilkerson .20 .50

1989 Rangers Mother's

The 1989 Mother's Cookies Texas Rangers set contains 28 standard-size cards with rounded corners. The fronts have borderless color photos, and the horizontally oriented backs have biographical information. Starter sets containing 20 of these cards were given away at a Rangers home game during the 1989 season. Kenny Rogers appears in his Rookie Card season.

COMPLETE SET (28) 6.00 15.00
1 Bobby Valentine MG .20 .50
2 Nolan Ryan 3.00 8.00
3 Julio Franco .40 1.00
4 Charlie Hough .30 .75
5 Rafael Palmeiro 1.00 2.50
6 Jeff Russell .08 .25
7 Ruben Sierra .40 1.00
8 Steve Buechele .08 .25
9 Buddy Bell .30 .75
10 Pete Incaviglia .20 .50
11 Geno Petralli .08 .25
12 Cecil Espy .20 .50
13 Scott Fletcher .20 .50
14 Bobby Witt .08 .25
15 Brad Arnsberg .08 .25
16 Rick Leach .08 .25
17 Jamie Moyer .40 1.00
18 Kevin Brown .75 2.00
19 Jeff Kunkel .08 .25
20 Craig McMurtry .08 .25
21 Kenny Rogers .75 2.00
22 Mike Stanley .08 .25
23 Cecilio Guante .08 .25
24 Jim Sundberg .08 .25
25 Jose Guzman .20 .50
26 Jeff Stone .08 .25
27 Rangers' Coaches .08 .25

Dick Egan
Tom House
Toby Harra
28 Checklist Card .08 .25
Danny Wheat TR
Bill Ziegler TR

1989 Rangers Smokey

The 1989 Smokey Rangers set features 34 unnumbered cards measuring approximately 4 1/4" by 6". The fronts feature mugshot photos with white borders. The backs feature biographical information and fire prevention tips. The set was given away at a 1989 Rangers' home game.

COMPLETE SET (34) 10.00 25.00
1 Darrel Akerfelds .20 .50
2 Brad Arnsberg .20 .50
3 Buddy Bell .40 1.00
4 Kevin Brown 1.00 2.50
5 Steve Buechele .20 .50
6 Dick Egan CO .20 .50
7 Cecil Espy .20 .50
8 Scott Fletcher .20 .50
9 Julio Franco .40 1.00
10 Cecilio Guante .20 .50
11 Jose Guzman .20 .50
12 Drew Hall .20 .50
13 Toby Harrah CO .20 .50
14 Charlie Hough .40 1.00
15 Tom House CO .20 .50
16 Pete Incaviglia .30 .75
17 Chad Kreuter .20 .50
18 Jeff Kunkel .20 .50
19 Rick Leach .20 .50
20 Davey Lopes .30 .75
21 Craig McMurtry .20 .50
22 Jamie Moyer .60 1.50
23 Dave Oliver CO .20 .50
24 Rafael Palmeiro 2.00 5.00
25 Geno Petralli .20 .50
26 Tom Robson CO .20 .50
27 Kenny Rogers 1.25 3.00
28 Jeff Russell .20 .50
29 Nolan Ryan 5.00 12.00
30 Ruben Sierra .60 1.50
31 Mike Stanley .20 .50
32 Jim Sundberg .30 .75
33 Bobby Valentine MG .30 .75
34 Bobby Witt .20 .50

1990 Rangers Mother's

This 28-card, standard-size set features members of the 1990 Texas Rangers. The set has beautiful full-color photos on the front along with biographical information on the back. The set also features the now traditional Mother's Cookies rounded corners. The Rangers cards were distributed on July 22nd to the first 25,000 game attendees in Arlington. They were distributed in 20-card random packets at the game and eight more at the redemption booths. However, both groups of cards were random and there was no guarantee of getting a complete set in the cards. The promotional idea was that the only way one could finish the set was to trade for them. The redemption certificates (for eight more cards) were also able to be redeemed at the 17th Annual Dallas Card Convention on August 18-19, 1990.

COMPLETE SET (28) 6.00 15.00
1 Bobby Valentine MG .30 .75
2 Nolan Ryan 3.00 8.00
3 Ruben Sierra .40 1.00
4 Pete Incaviglia .20 .50
5 Charlie Hough .20 .50
6 Harold Baines .30 .75
7 Gino Petralli .08 .25
8 Jeff Russell .08 .25
9 Rafael Palmeiro .60 1.50
10 Julio Franco .40 1.00
11 Jack Daugherty .08 .25
12 Gary Pettis .08 .25
13 Brian Bohanon .10 .25
14 Steve Buechele .08 .25
15 Bobby Witt .08 .25
16 Thad Bosley .08 .25
17 Gary Mielke .08 .25
18 Jeff Kunkel .08 .25
19 Mike Jeffcoat .08 .25
20 Mike Stanley .08 .25
21 Kevin Brown 1.25 3.00
22 Kenny Rogers .40 1.00
23 Jeff Huson .08 .25
24 Jamie Moyer .40 1.00
25 Cecil Espy .08 .25
26 John Russell .08 .25
27 Coaches Card .08 .25
Dave Oliver
Davey Lopes
Tom Robson
28 Trainers Card .08 .25
Bill Zeigler TR
Joe Macko EQ.MG./

1990 Rangers Smokey

These oversize cards, which measure approximately 3 1/2" by 5" were given away at Rangers games in 1990. The cards were issued with the player photos in the middle, the Rangers logo on the upper left and the Smokey logo on the upper right. The backs have biographical information as well as a safety tip.

COMPLETE SET 8.00 20.00
1 Harold Baines .40 1.00
2 Brian Bohanon .20 .50
3 Thad Bosley .20 .50
4 Kevin Brown .60 1.50
5 Jack Daugherty .20 .50
6 Cecil Espy .20 .50
7 Julio Franco .60 1.50
8 Jeff Huson .20 .50
9 Pete Incaviglia .30 .75
10 Mike Jeffcoat .20 .50
11 Chad Kreuter .20 .50
12 Jeff Kunkel .20 .50
13 Gary Mielke .20 .50
14 Jamie Moyer .60 1.50
15 Rafael Palmeiro .75 2.00
16 Gary Pettis .20 .50
17 Kenny Rogers .60 1.50
18 Jeff Russell .20 .50
19 John Russell .20 .50
20 Nolan Ryan 2.00 5.00
21 Ruben Sierra .40 1.00
22 Bobby Valentine MG .30 .75
23 Bobby Witt .20 .50
24 Arlington Stadium .20 .50

1991 Rangers Mother's

The 1991 Mother's Cookies Texas Rangers set contains 28 cards with rounded corners measuring the standard size.

COMPLETE SET (28) 6.00 15.00
1 Bobby Valentine MG .30 .75
2 Nolan Ryan 3.00 8.00
3 Ruben Sierra .30 .75
4 Juan Gonzalez 2.50 6.00
5 Steve Buechele .08 .25
6 Bobby Witt .08 .25
7 Geno Petralli .08 .25
8 Jeff Russell .08 .25
9 Rafael Palmeiro .60 1.50
10 Julio Franco .30 .75
11 Jack Daugherty .08 .25
12 Gary Pettis .08 .25
13 John Barfield .08 .25
14 Scott Chiamparino .08 .25
15 Kevin Reimer .08 .25
16 Rich Gossage .40 1.00
17 Brian Downing .20 .50
18 Denny Walling .08 .25
19 Mike Jeffcoat .08 .25
20 Mike Stanley .08 .25
21 Kevin Brown .75 2.00
22 Kenny Rogers .30 .75
23 Jeff Huson .08 .25
24 Mario Diaz .08 .25
25 Brad Arnsberg .08 .25
26 John Russell .08 .25
27 Gerald Alexander .08 .25
28 Checklist Card .08 .25
Tom Robson CO
Toby Harrah CO
Orl

1992 Rangers Mother's

The 1992 Mother's Cookies Rangers set contains 28 cards with rounded corners measuring the standard size.

COMPLETE SET (28) 6.00 15.00
1 Bobby Valentine MG .30 .75
2 Nolan Ryan 2.00 5.00
3 Ruben Sierra .40 1.00
4 Juan Gonzalez 1.00 2.50
5 Ivan Rodriguez 2.00 5.00
6 Bobby Witt .08 .25
7 Geno Petralli .08 .25
8 Jeff Russell .08 .25
9 Rafael Palmeiro .60 1.50
10 Julio Franco .30 .75
11 Jack Daugherty .08 .25
12 Dickie Thon .08 .25
13 Floyd Bannister .08 .25
14 Scott Chiamparino .08 .25
15 Kevin Reimer .08 .25
16 Jeff M. Robinson .08 .25
17 Brian Downing .20 .50
18 Brian Bohanon .08 .25
19 Jose Guzman .08 .25
20 Terry Mathews .08 .25
21 Kevin Brown .60 1.50
22 Kenny Rogers .40 1.00
23 Jeff Huson .08 .25
24 Monty Fariss .08 .25
25 Al Newman .08 .25
26 Dean Palmer .40 1.00
27 John Cangelosi .08 .25
28 Coaches .08 .25
Checklist
Tom Robson
Ray Burris
Toby Ha

1992 Rangers Team Issue

This 27-card team photo set measures approximately 3" by 5". The fronts feature posed color player photos against a variegated gray studio background. The backs are blank. The cards are unnumbered and checklisted below in alphabetical order. Julio Franco, Brian Downing and Edwin Nunez all have a blue background.

COMPLETE SET (27) 4.00 10.00
1 Floyd Bannister .08 .25
2 Kevin Brown .50 1.25
3 John Cangelosi .08 .25
4 Scott Chiamparino .08 .25
5 Jack Daugherty .08 .25
6 Brian Downing .20 .50
7 Julio Franco .30 .75
8 Juan Gonzalez .50 1.25
9 Jose Guzman .08 .25
10 Jeff Huson .08 .25
11 Mike Jeffcoat .08 .25
12 Terry Mathews .08 .25
13 Al Newman .08 .25
14 Edwin Nunez .08 .25
15 Rafael Palmeiro .50 1.25
16 Dean Palmer .40 1.00
17 Geno Petralli .08 .25
18 Kevin Reimer .08 .25
19 Ivan Rodriguez 1.00 2.50
20 Kenny Rogers .40 1.00
21 Jeff Russell .08 .25
22 Nolan Ryan 1.25 3.00
23 Ruben Sierra .40 1.00
24 Dickie Thon .08 .25
25 Bobby Valentine MG .20 .50
26 Bobby Witt .08 .25
27 Model of New Ballpark .08 .25

1993 Rangers Dr. Pepper

The four cards comprising this set were issued with metal pins which came attached to cardboard tabs beneath the perforated card bottoms. The cards measure approximately 2 1/2" by 3 7/8" and feature white-bordered color photos on their fronts. Other than the card of Nolan Ryan; the other pin/card combinations feature a picture of Arlington Stadium and some highlights from the history there. The back of Nolan Ryan's card features his career statistics. The attached pin carries his name and uniform number and bids "Farewell to a Legend." The backs of the Arlington Stadium cards feature text that explains the history of the ballpark. The attached pins carry Rangers logos. Though the cards are unnumbered, the pins are numbered "X of 4" on the cardboard tabs and checklisted below accordingly.

COMPLETE SET (4) 6.00 15.00
COMMON PLAYER (1-4) .60 1.50
3 Nolan Ryan 5.00 12.00

1993 Rangers Decker

These blank-backed full-color cards were sponsored by Decker foods and featured members of the 1993 Texas Rangers. These cards measure approximately 3" by 5" and since the cards are not numbered, we have sequenced them in alphabetical order. Please note that this set was originally available from the Rangers for $6.50.

COMPLETE SET 10.00 25.00
1 Brian Bohanon .20 .50
2 Jeff Bronkey .20 .50
3 Kevin Brown .40 1.00
4 Todd Burns .20 .50
5 Jose Canseco .75 2.00
6 Doug Dascenzo .20 .50
7 Butch Davis .20 .50
8 Julio Franco .60 1.50
9 Jeff Frye .20 .50
10 Juan Gonzalez .60 1.50
11 Mickey Hatcher .20 .50
12 Tom Henke .30 .75
13 Perry Hill CO .20 .50
14 David Hulse .20 .50
15 Jeff Huson .20 .50
16 Kevin Kennedy MG .20 .50
17 Manuel Lee .20 .50
18 Craig Lefferts .20 .50
19 Charlie Leibrandt .20 .50
20 Jackie Moore CO .20 .50
21 Robb Nen .40 1.00
22 Dave Oliver CO .20 .50
23 Claude Osteen CO .20 .50
24 Rafael Palmeiro .75 2.00
25 Dean Palmer .40 1.00
26 Bob Patterson .20 .50
27 Roger Pavlik .20 .50
28 Geno Petralli .20 .50
29 Gary Redus .20 .50
30 Bill Ripken .20 .50
31 Ivan Rodriguez 1.00 2.50
32 Kenny Rogers .60 1.50
33 Nolan Ryan 1.25 3.00
34 Doug Strange .20 .50
35 Willie Upshaw .20 .50
36 Matt Whiteside .20 .50

1993 Rangers Keebler

The Keebler All-Time Texas Rangers Card Series was a 468-card set (446 player cards plus 22 stat cards that have SP prefixes) issued in eight series booklets of perforated card sheets that honored everyone who ever wore a Rangers uniform during its 22-year history. The set was sponsored by Keebler and Albertsons food stores. Booklets of perforated sheets were distributed free to 35,000 fans as an in-stadium promotion at specific games. The exception was on April 9, when 42,000 booklets were distributed. Series I highlights 1972 team members, while Series VIII features the 1993 team, with the balance of the Rangers appearing in alphabetical order in Series II-VII.

COMPLETE SET (468) 20.00 50.00
1 Ted Williams MG 1.50 4.00
2 Larry Biittner .20 .50
3 Rich Billings .20 .50
4 Dick Bosman .20 .50
5 Pete Broberg .20 .50
6 Jeff Burroughs .25 .60
7 Casey Cox .20 .50
8 Jim Driscoll .20 .50
9 Jan Dukes .20 .50
10 Bill Fahey .20 .50
11 Ted Ford .20 .50
12 Bill Gogolewski .20 .50
13 Tom Grieve .25 .60
14 Rich Hand .20 .50
15 Toby Harrah .25 .60
16 Vic Harris .20 .50
17 Rich Hinton .20 .50
18 Frank Howard .25 .60
19 Gerry Janeski .20 .50
20 Dalton Jones .20 .50
21 Hal King .20 .50
22 Ted Kubiak .20 .50
23 Steve Lawson .20 .50
24 Paul Lindblad .20 .50
25 Joe Lovitto .20 .50
26 Elliott Maddox .20 .50
27 Marty Martinez .20 .50
28 Jim Mason .20 .50
29 Don Mincher .20 .50
30 Dave Nelson .20 .50
31 Jim Panther .20 .50
32 Mike Paul .20 .50
33 Horacio Pina .20 .50
34 Tom Ragland .20 .50
35 Lenny Randle .20 .50
36 Jim Roland .20 .50
37 Jim Shellenback .20 .50
38 Don Stanhouse .20 .50
39 Ken Suarez .20 .50
40 Joe Camacho CO .20 .50
41 Nellie Fox CO .60 1.50
42 Sid Hudson CO .20 .50
43 George Susce CO .20 .50
44 Wayne Terwilliger CO .20 .50
45 Darrel Akerfelds .20 .50
46 Doyle Alexander .20 .50
47 Gerald Alexander .20 .50
48 Brian Allard .20 .50
49 Lloyd Allen .20 .50
50 Sandy Alomar .20 .50
51 Wilson Alvarez .20 .50
52 Jim Anderson .20 .50
53 Scott Anderson .20 .50
54 Brad Arnsberg .20 .50
55 Tucker Ashford .20 .50
56 Doug Ault .20 .50
57 Bob Babcock .20 .50
58 Mike Bacsik .20 .50
59 Harold Baines .25 .60
60 Alan Bannister .20 .50
61 Floyd Bannister .20 .50
62 John Barfield .20 .50
63 Len Barker .20 .50
64 Steve Barr .20 .50
65 Randy Bass .20 .50
66 Lew Beasley .20 .50
67 Kevin Belcher .20 .50
68 Buddy Bell .25 .60
69 Juan Beniquez .20 .50
70 Kurt Bevacqua .20 .50
71 Jim Bibby .20 .50
72 Joe Bitker .20 .50
73 Larvell Blanks .20 .50
74 Bert Blyleven .25 .60
75 Terry Bogener .20 .50
76 Tommy Boggs .20 .50
77 Dan Boitano .20 .50
78 Bobby Bonds .25 .60
79 Thad Bosley .20 .50
80 Dennis Boyd .20 .50
81 Nelson Briles .20 .50
82 Ed Brinkman .20 .50
83 Bob Brower .20 .50
84 Jackie Brown .20 .50
85 Larry Brown .20 .50
86 Jerry Browne .20 .50
87 Glenn Brummer .20 .50
88 Kevin Buckley .20 .50
89 Steve Buechele .20 .50
90 Ray Burris .20 .50
91 John Butcher .20 .50
92 Bert Campaneris .20 .50
93 Mike Campbell .20 .50
94 John Cangelosi .20 .50
95 Nick Capra .20 .50
96 Leo Cardenas .20 .50
97 Don Carman .20 .50
98 Rico Carty .20 .50
99 Don Castle .20 .50
100 Jose Cecena .20 .50
101 Dave Chalk .20 .50
102 Scott Chiamparino .20 .50
103 Ken Clay .20 .50
104 Reggie Cleveland .20 .50
105 Gene Clines .20 .50
106 David Clyde .20 .50
107 Cris Colon .20 .50
108 Merrill Combs CO .20 .50
109 Steve Comer .20 .50
110 Glen Cook .20 .50
111 Scott Coolbaugh .20 .50
112 Pat Corrales MG .20 .50
113 Edwin Correa .20 .50
114 Larry Cox .20 .50
115 Keith Creel .20 .50
116 Victor Cruz .20 .50
117 Mike Cubbage .20 .50
118 Bobby Cuellar .20 .50
119 Danny Darwin .20 .50
120 Jack Daugherty .20 .50
121 Doug Davis .20 .50
122 Odie Davis .20 .50
123 Willie Davis .20 .50
124 Bucky Dent .25 .60
125 Adrian Devine .20 .50
126 Mario Diaz .20 .50
127 Rich Donnelly CO .20 .50
128 Brian Downing .20 .50
129 Tommy Dunbar .20 .50
130 Steve Dunning .20 .50
131 Dan Duran .20 .50
132 Don Durham .20 .50
133 Dick Egan CO .20 .50
134 Dock Ellis .20 .50
135 John Ellis .20 .50
136 Mike Epstein .20 .50
137 Cecil Espy .20 .50
138 Chuck Estrada CO .20 .50
139 Glenn Ezell CO .20 .50
140 Hector Fajardo .20 .50
141 Monty Fariss .20 .50
142 Ed Farmer .20 .50
143 Jim Farr .20 .50
144 Joe Ferguson .20 .50
145 Ed Figueroa .20 .50
146 Steve Fireovid .20 .50
147 Scott Fletcher .20 .50
148 Doug Flynn .20 .50
149 Marv Foley .20 .50
150 Tim Foli .20 .50
151 Tony Fossas .20 .50
152 Steve Foucault .20 .50
153 Art Fowler CO .20 .50
154 Jim Fregosi .20 .50
155 Pepe Frias .20 .50
156 Oscar Gamble .20 .50
157 Barbaro Garbey .20 .50
158 Dick Gernert CO .20 .50
159 Jim Gideon .20 .50
160 Jerry Don Gleaton .20 .50
161 Orlando Gomez CO .20 .50
162 Rich Gossage .25 .60
163 Gary Gray .20 .50
164 Gary Green .20 .50
165 John Grubb .20 .50
166 Cecilio Guante .20 .50
167 Jose Guzman .20 .50
168 Drew Hall .20 .50
169 Bill Hands .20 .50
170 Steve Hargan .20 .50
171 Mike Hargrove .20 .50
172 Toby Harrah .25 .60
173 Bud Harrelson .20 .50
174 Donald Harris .20 .50
175 Greg A. Harris .20 .50
176 Mike Hart .20 .50
177 Bill Haselman .20 .50
178 Ray Hayward .20 .50
179 Tommy Helms .20 .50
180 Ken Henderson .20 .50
181 Rick Henninger .20 .50
182 Dwayne Henry .20 .50
183 Jose Hernandez .20 .50
184 Whitey Herzog MG .20 .50
185 Chuck Hiller CO .20 .50
186 Joe Hoerner .20 .50
187 Guy Hoffman .20 .50
188 Gary Holle .20 .50
189 Rick Honeycutt .20 .50
190 Burt Hooton .20 .50
191 John Hoover .20 .50
192 Willie Horton .20 .50
193 Dave Hostetler .20 .50
194 Charlie Hough .25 .60
195 Tom House .20 .50
196 Art Howe CO .20 .50
197 Steve Howe .20 .50
198 Roy Howell .20 .50
199 Charles Hudson .20 .50
200 Billy Hunter MG .20 .50
201 Pete Incaviglia .25 .60
202 Mike Jeffcoat .20 .50
203 Ferguson Jenkins .60 1.50
204 Alex Johnson .20 .50
205 Bobby Johnson .20 .50
206 Cliff Johnson .20 .50
207 Darrell Johnson MG .20 .50
208 John Henry Johnson .20 .50
209 Lamar Johnson .20 .50
210 Bobby Jones .20 .50
211 Odell Jones .20 .50
212 Mike Jorgensen .20 .50
213 Don Kainer .20 .50
214 Mike Kekich .20 .50
215 Steve Kemp .20 .50
216 Jim Kern .20 .50
217 Paul Kilgus .20 .50
218 Ed Kirkpatrick .20 .50
219 Darold Knowles .20 .50
220 Fred Koenig CO .20 .50
221 Jim Kremmel .20 .50
222 Chad Kreuter .20 .50
223 Jeff Kunkel .20 .50
224 Bob Lacey .20 .50
225 Al Lachowicz .20 .50
226 Joe Lahoud .20 .50
227 Rick Leach .20 .50
228 Danny Leon .20 .50
229 Dennis Lewallyn .20 .50
230 Rick Lisi .20 .50
231 Davey Lopes .20 .50
232 John Lowenstein .20 .50
233 Mike Loynd .20 .50
234 Frank Lucchesi MG .20 .50
235 Sparky Lyle .20 .50
236 Pete Mackanin .20 .50
237 Bill Madlock .20 .50
238 Greg Mahlberg .20 .50
239 Mickey Mahler .20 .50
240 Bob Malloy .20 .50
241 Ramon Manon .20 .50
242 Fred Manrique .20 .50
243 Barry Manuel .20 .50
244 Mike Marshall .20 .50
245 Billy Martin MG .25 .60
246 Mike Mason .20 .50
247 Terry Mathews .20 .50
248 Jon Matlack .20 .50
249 Rob Maurer .20 .50
250 Dave May .20 .50
251 Scott May .20 .50
252 Lee Mazzilli .20 .50
253 Larry McCall .20 .50
254 Lance McCullers .20 .50
255 Oddibe McDowell .20 .50
256 Russ McGinnis .20 .50
257 Joey McLaughlin .20 .50
258 Craig McMurtry .20 .50
259 Doc Medich .20 .50
260 Dave Meier .20 .50
261 Mario Mendoza .20 .50
262 Orlando Mercado .20 .50
263 Mark Mercer .20 .50
264 Ron Meridith .20 .50
265 Jim Merritt .20 .50
266 Gary Mielke .20 .50
267 Eddie Miller .20 .50
268 Paul Mirabella .20 .50
269 Dave Moates .20 .50
270 Dale Mohorcic .20 .50
271 Willie Montanez .20 .50
272 Tommy Moore .20 .50
273 Roger Moret .20 .50
274 Jamie Moyer .25 .60
275 Dale Murray .20 .50
276 Al Newman .20 .50
277 Dickie Noles .20 .50
278 Eric Nolte .20 .50
279 Nelson Norman .20 .50
280 Jim Norris .20 .50
281 Edwin Nunez .20 .50
282 Pete O'Brien .20 .50
283 Al Oliver .25 .60
284 Tom O'Malley .20 .50
285 Tom Paciorek .20 .50
286 Ken Pape .20 .50
287 Mark Parent .20 .50
288 Larry Parrish .20 .50
289 Gaylord Perry .60 1.50
290 Stan Perzanowski .20 .50
291 Fritz Peterson .20 .50
292 Mark Petkovsek .20 .50
293 Gary Pettis .20 .50
294 Jim Piersall CO .20 .50
295 John Poloni .20 .50
296 Jim Poole .20 .50
297 Tom Poquette .20 .50
298 Darrell Porter .20 .50
299 Ron Pruitt .20 .50
300 Greg Pryor .20 .50
301 Luis Pujols .20 .50
302 Pat Putnam .20 .50
303 Doug Rader MG .20 .50
304 Dave Rajsich .20 .50
305 Kevin Reimer .20 .50
306 Merv Rettenmund CO .20 .50
307 Mike Richardt .20 .50
308 Mickey Rivers .20 .50
309 Dave Roberts .20 .50
310 Leon Roberts .20 .50
311 Jeff M. Robinson .20 .50
312 Tom Robson .20 .50
313 Wayne Rosenthal .20 .50
314 Dave Rozema .20 .50
315 Jeff Russell .20 .50
316 Connie Ryan MG .20 .50
317 Billy Sample .20 .50
318 Jim Schaffer CO .20 .50
319 Calvin Schiraldi .20 .50
320 Dave Schmidt .20 .50
321 Donnie Scott .20 .50
322 Tony Scruggs .20 .50
323 Bob Sebra .20 .50
324 Larry See .20 .50
325 Sonny Siebert .20 .50
326 Ruben Sierra .60 1.50
327 Charlie Silvera CO .20 .50
328 Duke Sims .20 .50
329 Bill Singer .20 .50
330 Craig Skok .20 .50
331 Don Slaught .20 .50
332 Roy Smalley .20 .50
333 Dan Smith .20 .50
334 Keith Smith .20 .50
335 Mike Smithson .20 .50
336 Eric Soderholm .20 .50
337 Sammy Sosa 2.50 6.00
338 Jim Spencer .20 .50
339 Dick Such CO .20 .50
340 Eddie Stanky MG .20 .50
341 Mike Stanley .20 .50
342 Rusty Staub .25 .60
343 James Steels .20 .50
344 Bill Stein .20 .50
345 Rick Stelmaszek .20 .50
346 Ray Stephens .20 .50
347 Dave Stewart .20 .50
348 Jeff Stone .20 .50
349 Bill Sudakis .20 .50
350 Jim Sundberg .25 .60
351 Rich Surhoff .20 .50
352 Greg Tabor .20 .50
353 Frank Tanana .20 .50
354 Jeff Terpko .20 .50
355 Stan Thomas .20 .50
356 Bobby Thompson .20 .50
357 Danny Thompson .20 .50
358 Dickie Thon .20 .50
359 Dave Tobik .20 .50
360 Wayne Tolleson .20 .50
361 Cesar Tovar .20 .50
362 Jim Umbarger .20 .50
363 Bobby Valentine MG .20 .50
364 Ellis Valentine .20 .50
365 Ed Vande Berg .20 .50
366 DeWayne Vaughn .20 .50
367 Mark Wagner .20 .50
368 Rick Waits .20 .50
369 Duane Walker .20 .50
370 Mike Wallace .20 .50
371 Denny Walling .20 .50
372 Danny Walton .20 .50
373 Gary Ward .20 .50
374 Claudell Washington .20 .50
375 LaRue Washington UER
(Misspelled Wasington .20 .50
on ca
376 Chris Welsh .20 .50
377 Don Werner .20 .50
378 Len Whitehouse .20 .50
379 Del Wilber MG .20 .50
380 Curtis Wilkerson .20 .50
381 Matt Williams .20 .50
382 Mitch Williams .20 .50
383 Bump Wills .20 .50
384 Paul Wilmet .20 .50
385 Steve Wilson .20 .50
386 Bobby Witt .20 .50
387 Clyde Wright .20 .50
388 George Wright .20 .50
389 Ricky Wright .20 .50
390 Ned Yost .20 .50
391 Don Zimmer MG .25 .60
392 Richie Zisk .20 .50
393 Kevin Kennedy MG .20 .50
394 Steve Balboni .20 .50
395 Brian Bohanon .20 .50
396 Jeff Bronkey .20 .50
397 Kevin Brown .60 1.50
398 Todd Burns .20 .50
399 Jose Canseco 1.25 3.00
400 Cris Carpenter .20 .50
401 Doug Dascenzo .20 .50
402 Butch Davis .20 .50
403 Steve Dreyer .20 .50
404 Rob Ducey .20 .50
405 Julio Franco .25 .60
406 Jeff Frye .20 .50
407 Benji Gil .20 .50
408 Juan Gonzalez .75 2.00
409 Tom Henke .20 .50
410 David Hulse .20 .50
411 Jeff Huson .20 .50
412 Chris James .20 .50
413 Manuel Lee .20 .50
414 Craig Lefferts .20 .50
415 Charlie Leibrandt .20 .50
416 Gene Nelson .20 .50
417 Robb Nen .20 .50
418 Darren Oliver .20 .50
419 Rafael Palmeiro 1.25 3.00
420 Dean Palmer .20 .50
421 Bob Patterson .20 .50
422 Roger Pavlik .20 .50
423 Dan Peltier .20 .50
424 Geno Petralli .20 .50
425 Gary Redus .20 .50
426 Rick Reed .20 .50
427 Bill Ripken .20 .50
428 Ivan Rodriguez 2.50 6.00
429 Kenny Rogers .25 .60
430 John Russell .20 .50
431 Nolan Ryan 5.00 12.00
432 Mike Schooler .20 .50
433 Jon Shave .20 .50
434 Doug Strange .20 .50
435 Matt Whiteside .20 .50
436 Mickey Hatcher CO .20 .50
437 Perry Hill CO .20 .50
438 Jackie Moore CO .20 .50
439 Dave Oliver CO .20 .50
440 Claude Osteen CO .20 .50
441 Willie Upshaw CO .20 .50
442 Checklist 1-112 .20 .50
443 Checklist 113-224 .20 .50
444 Checklist 225-336 .20 .50
445 Checklist 337-446 .20 .50
446 Arlington Stadium .20 .50
SP1 1972 Team Photo .20 .50
SP2 Logo .20 .50
SP3 Logo .20 .50
SP4 Logo .20 .50
SP5 Logo .20 .50
SP6 Home Run Leaders .20 .50
SP7 RBI Leaders .20 .50
SP9 Win Leaders .20 .50
SP10 Save Leaders .20 .50
SP11 Hit Leaders .20 .50
SP12 Stolen Base Leaders .20 .50
SP13 Games Played Leaders .20 .50
SP14 Strikeout Leaders .20 .50
SP15 ERA Leaders .20 .50
SP16 Games Pitched .20 .50
Leaders
SP17 Innings Pitched .20 .50
Leaders
SP18 Attendance Records .20 .50
SP19 Top 20 Crowds .20 .50
SP20 Hitting Streaks .20 .50
SP21 All-Stars .20 .50
SP22 Top Draft Picks .20 .50

1993 Rangers Stadium Club

This 30-card standard-size set features the 1993 Texas Rangers. The set was issued in hobby (plastic box) and retail (blister) form.

COMP. FACT SET (30) 3.00 8.00
1 Nolan Ryan 1.50 4.00
2 Ritchie Moody .02 .10
3 Matt Whiteside .02 .10
4 David Hulse .02 .10
5 Roger Pavlik .02 .10
6 Dan Smith .02 .10
7 Donald Harris .02 .10
8 Butch Davis .02 .10
9 Benji Gil .02 .10
10 Ivan Rodriguez .75 2.00
11 Dean Palmer .30 .75
12 Jeff Huson .02 .10
13 Rob Maurer .02 .10
14 Gary Redus .02 .10
15 Doug Dascenzo .02 .10
16 Charlie Leibrandt .02 .10
17 Tom Henke .02 .10
18 Manuel Lee .02 .10
19 Kenny Rogers .30 .75
20 Kevin Brown .30 .75
21 Juan Gonzalez .50 1.25
22 Geno Petralli .02 .10
23 John Russell .02 .10
24 Robb Nen .30 .75
25 Julio Franco .30 .75
26 Rafael Palmeiro .50 1.25
27 Todd Burns .02 .10
28 Jose Canseco .50 1.25
29 Billy Ripken .02 .10
30 Dan Peltier .02 .10

1994 Rangers Magic Marker

This 40-card set was sponsored by Magic Marker and measures approximately 3" by 4 15/16". The fronts feature borderless color portraits of the 1994 Texas Rangers. The backs are blank. The cards are unnumbered and checklisted below in alphabetical order.

COMPLETE SET (40) 6.00 15.00
1 Jack Armstrong .08 .25
2 Esteban Beltre .08 .25
3 Kevin Brown .40 1.00
4 Jose Canseco .60 1.50
5 Cris Carpenter .08 .25
6 Will Clark .60 1.50
7 Steve Dreyer .08 .25
8 Rob Ducey .08 .25
9 Jeff Frye .08 .25
10 Juan Gonzalez .50 1.25
11 Mickey Hatcher CO .08 .25
12 Rick Helling .40 1.00
13 Tom Henke .20 .50
14 Perry Hill CO .08 .25
15 Rick Honeycutt .08 .25
16 Jay Howell .08 .25
17 David Hulse .08 .25
18 Bruce Hurst .08 .25
19 James Hurst .08 .25
20 Jeff Huson .08 .25
21 Chris James .08 .25
22 Kevin Kennedy MG .08 .25
23 Manuel Lee .08 .25
24 Oddibe McDowell .08 .25
25 Jackie Moore CO .08 .25
26 Darren Oliver .20 .50
27 Dave Oliver CO .08 .25
28 Junior Ortiz .08 .25
29 Claude Osteen CO .08 .25
30 Dean Palmer .40 1.00
31 Roger Pavlik .08 .25
32 Gary Redus .08 .25
33 Rick Reed .08 .25
34 Bill Ripken .08 .25
35 Ivan Rodriguez 1.00 2.50
36 Kenny Rogers .40 1.00
37 Doug Strange .08 .25
38 Willie Upshaw CO .08 .25
39 Matt Whiteside .08 .25
40 The Ballpark in Arlington .08 .25

1995 Rangers Crayola

This 36-card set measures approximately 3" by 5". The fronts feature full-bleed color posed player portraits with the team logo, sponsor name, player's name and position in a blue bar across the bottom. The backs are blank. The cards are unnumbered and checklisted below in alphabetical order. This set was originally available from the Ragers for $6.50.

COMPLETE SET (36) 4.00 10.00
1 The Ballpark in Arlington .08 .25
2 Jose Alberro .08 .25
3 Esteban Beltre .08 .25
4 Dick Bosman CO .08 .25
5 Terry Burrows .08 .25
6 Will Clark .60 1.50
7 Bucky Dent CO .20 .50
8 Hector Fajardo .08 .25

9 Jeff Frye .08 .25
10 Benji Gil .08 .25
11 Juan Gonzalez .50 1.25
12 Rusty Greer .60 1.50
13 Kevin Gross .08 .25
14 Larry Hardy CO .08 .25
15 Shawn Hare .08 .25
16 Rudy Jaramillo CO .08 .25
17 Roger McDowell .08 .25
18 Mark McLemore .08 .25
19 Ed Napoleon CO .08 .25
20 Jerry Narron CO .08 .25
21 Chris Nichting .08 .25
22 Otis Nixon .08 .25
23 Johnny Oates MG .08 .25
24 Darren Oliver .08 .25
25 Mike Pagliarulo .08 .25
26 Dean Palmer .40 1.00
27 Roger Pavlik .08 .25
28 Ivan Rodriguez .75 2.00
29 Kenny Rogers .40 1.00
30 Jeff Russell .08 .25
31 Mickey Tettleton .20 .50
32 Bob Tewksbury .08 .25
33 David Valle .08 .25
34 Jack Voigt .08 .25
35 Ed Vosberg .08 .25
36 Matt Whiteside .08 .25

1996 Rangers Dr Pepper

This 39-card set of the 1996 Texas Rangers was sponsored by the Dr. Pepper Bottling Co. of Texas and measures approximately 3" by 5". The fronts feature color player portraits on a blue background with the team logo, sponsor's name, player's name and position in a white box at the bottom. The backs are blank. The cards are unnumbered and checklisted below in alphabetical order. During the season, cards of Rene Gonzales, Rick Helling and Mike Stanton were pulled; however there is no real extra value for these cards.

COMPLETE SET (39) 5.00 12.00
1 Dick Bosman CO .08 .25
2 Mark Brandenburg .08 .25
3 Damon Buford .08 .25
4 Will Clark .40 1.00
5 Dennis Cook .08 .25
6 Bucky Dent CO .20 .50
7 Kevin Elster .08 .25
8 Lou Frazier .08 .25
9 Benji Gil .08 .25
10 Rene Gonzales .20 .50
11 Juan Gonzalez .40 1.00
12 Rusty Greer .40 1.00
13 Kevin Gross .08 .25
14 Darryl Hamilton .08 .25
15 Larry Hardy CO .08 .25
16 Rick Helling .20 .50
17 Gil Heredia .08 .25
18 Mike Henneman .08 .25
19 Ken Hill .08 .25
20 Rudy Jaramillo CO .08 .25
21 Mark McLemore .08 .25
22 Ed Napoleon CO .08 .25
23 Jerry Narron CO .08 .25
24 Warren Newson .08 .25
25 Johnny Oates MG .08 .25
26 Darren Oliver .08 .25
27 Dean Palmer .40 1.00
28 Roger Pavlik .08 .25
29 Ivan Rodriguez .60 1.50
30 Jeff Russell .08 .25
31 Mike Stanton .20 .50
32 Kurt Stillwell .08 .25
33 Mickey Tettleton .20 .50
34 David Valle .08 .25
35 Ed Vosberg .08 .25
36 Matt Whiteside .08 .25
37 Bobby Witt .08 .25
38 Craig Worthington .08 .25
39 The Ballpark in Arlington .08 .25

1996 Rangers Fleer

These 20 standard-size cards have the same design as the regular Fleer issue, except they are UV coated, use silver foil and are numbered "x of 20". The team set packs were available at retail locations and hobby shops in 10-card packs with an $1.99 SRP which came 36 packs to a box and 20 boxes to a case..

COMPLETE SET (20) 1.25 3.00
1 Mark Brandenburg .02 .10
2 Damon Buford .02 .10
3 Will Clark .15 .40
4 Kevin Elster .02 .10
5 Benji Gil .02 .10
6 Juan Gonzalez .15 .40
7 Rusty Greer .10 .30
8 Kevin Gross .02 .10
9 Darryl Hamilton .02 .10
10 Ken Hill .02 .10
11 Mark McLemore .02 .10
12 Dean Palmer .07 .20
13 Roger Pavlik .02 .10
14 Ivan Rodriguez .30 .75
15 Mickey Tettleton .07 .20
16 Dave Valle .02 .10
17 Ed Vosberg .02 .10
18 Matt Whiteside .02 .10
19 Logo card .02 .10
20 Checklist .02 .10

1996 Rangers Mother's

This 28-card set consists of borderless posed color player portraits in stadium settings. The player's and team's names appear in one of the top rounded corners. The backs carry biographical information and the sponsor's logo on a white background in red and purple print. A blank slot for the player's autograph rounds out the back.

COMPLETE SET (28) 4.00 10.00
1 Johnny Oates MG .08 .25
2 Will Clark .50 1.25
3 Juan Gonzalez .40 1.00
4 Ivan Rodriguez .60 1.50
5 Darryl Hamilton .08 .25
6 Dean Palmer .30 .75
7 Mickey Tettleton .20 .50
8 Craig Worthington .08 .25
9 Rusty Greer .40 1.00
10 Kevin Gross .08 .25
11 Rick Helling .08 .25
12 Kevin Elster .08 .25
13 Bobby Witt .08 .25
14 Mark McLemore .08 .25
15 Warren Newson .08 .25
16 Mike Henneman .08 .25
17 Ken Hill .08 .25
18 Gil Heredia .08 .25
19 Roger Pavlik .08 .25
20 David Valle .08 .25
21 Mark Brandenburg .08 .25
22 Kurt Stillwell .08 .25
23 Ed Vosberg .08 .25
24 Dennis Cook .08 .25
25 Damon Buford .08 .25
26 Benji Gil .08 .25
27 Darren Oliver .08 .25
28 Coaches Card CL .08 .25
Dick Bosman
Bucky Dent
Larry Ha

1997 Rangers Commemorative Sheet

This 11" by 8 1/2" card was given away at the April 21, 1997, game between the Texas Rangers and the Detroit Tigers and commemorates the 25th Anniversary of the Rangers' first game at Arlington Stadium. It also honors former Arlington Mayor, Judge Tom Vandergriff, who was instrumental in biringing Major League Baseball to the North Texas area. The front features art work by sports artist, Vernon Wells, and depicts various present and former Texas Rangers. The back displays information about the 25th anniversary and the artist. Only 50,000 of this card was produced and are sequentially numbered.

1 From the First Pitch 2.00 5.00

1997 Rangers Dr Pepper

This 34-card set sponsored by the Dr. Pepper Bottling Co. of Texas measures approximately 3" by 5" and features borderless color player portraits. The backs are blank. The cards are unnumbered and checklisted below in alphabetical order. During the season, the Dean Palmer card was pulled and was replaced by a card of Mark Sagmoen. This set was available from the Rangers for $5.

COMPLETE SET (34) 5.00 12.00
1 Dick Bosman CO .08 .25
2 Damon Buford .08 .25
3 John Burkett .08 .25
4 Domingo Cedeno .08 .25
5 Will Clark .40 1.00
6 Bucky Dent CO .08 .25
7 Mike Devereaux .08 .25
8 Benji Gil .08 .25
9 Juan Gonzalez .40 1.00
10 Rusty Greer .40 1.00
11 Eric Gunderson .08 .25
12 Xavier Hernandez .08 .25
13 Larry Hardy CO .08 .25
14 Ken Hill .08 .25
15 Rudy Jaramillo CO .08 .25
16 Mark McLemore .08 .25
17 Henry Mercedes .08 .25
18 Ed Napoleon CO .08 .25
19 Jerry Narron CO .08 .25
20 Warren Newson .08 .25
21 Johnny Oates MG .08 .25
22 Darren Oliver .08 .25
23 Dean Palmer .20 .50
24 Danny Patterson .08 .25
25 Roger Pavlik .08 .25
26 Bill Ripken .08 .25
27 Ivan Rodriguez .60 1.50
28 Marc Sagmoen .08 .25
29 Julio Santana .08 .25
30 Lee Stevens .08 .25
31 Mickey Tettleton .20 .50
32 Ed Vosberg .08 .25
33 John Wetteland .30 .75
34 Bobby Witt .08 .25
35 The Ballpark in Arlington .08 .25

1997 Rangers 1st Interleague Game

This one-card set and pin sponsored by Columbia Healthcare Systems was issued to commemorate the first regular season interleague game played in Major League Baseball on June 12, 1997. The American League Texas Rangers played the National League San Francisco Giants.

1 Mickey Tettleton 1.50 4.00
Will Clark
Barry Bonds
Dusty B

1997 Rangers Minyard Magnets

This six-card set sponsored by Minyard Food Stores and Powerade Thirst Quencher features action color player photos printed on die-cut magnets. The magnets are unnumbered and checklisted below in alphabetical order.

COMPLETE SET (6) 5.00 12.00
1 John Burkett .75 2.00
2 Will Clark 1.50 4.00
3 Rusty Greer 1.50 4.00
4 Ken Hill .75 2.00
5 Johnny Oates MG .75 2.00
6 Mickey Tettleton .75 2.00

1997 Rangers Mother's

This 28-card set of the Texas Rangers sponsored by Mother's Cookies consists of posed color player photos with rounded corners. The backs carry biographical information and the sponsor's logo on a white background in red and purple print. A blank slot for the player's autograph rounds out the back.

COMPLETE SET (28) 4.00 10.00
1 Johnny Oates MG .08 .25
2 Will Clark .40 1.00
3 Juan Gonzalez .40 1.00
4 Ivan Rodriguez .60 1.50
5 John Wetteland .30 .75
6 Mickey Tettleton .20 .50
7 Dean Palmer .20 .50
8 Rusty Greer .40 1.00
9 Ed Vosberg .08 .25
10 Lee Stevens .08 .25
11 Benji Gil .08 .25
12 Mike Devereaux .08 .25
13 Bobby Witt .08 .25
14 Mark McLemore .08 .25
15 Warren Newson .08 .25
16 Eric Gunderson .08 .25
17 Ken Hill .08 .25
18 Damon Buford .08 .25
19 Roger Pavlik .08 .25
20 Bill Ripken .08 .25
21 John Burkett .08 .25
22 Darren Oliver .08 .25
23 Mike Simms .08 .25
24 Julio Santana .08 .25
25 Henry Mercedes .08 .25
26 Xavier Hernandez .08 .25
27 Danny Patterson .08 .25
28 Coaches Card CL .08 .25
Dick Bosman
Bucky Dent
Larry Ha

1997 Rangers Score

This 15-card set of the Texas Rangers was issued in five-card packs with a suggested retail price of $1.30 each. The fronts feature color player photos with special team specific color foil stamping. The backs carry player information. Only 100 cases were made for each team. Platinum parallel cards were inserted at a rate of 1:6, Premier parallel cards at a rate of 1:31.

COMPLETE SET (15) 2.00 5.00
*PLATINUM: 5X BASIC CARDS
*PREMIER: 20X BASIC CARDS
1 Mickey Tettleton .20 .50
2 Will Clark .40 1.00
3 Ken Hill .08 .25
4 Rusty Greer .30 .75
5 Kevin Elster .08 .25
6 Darren Oliver .08 .25
7 Mark McLemore .08 .25
8 Roger Pavlik .08 .25
9 Dean Palmer .30 .75
10 Bobby Witt .08 .25
11 Juan Gonzalez .40 1.00
12 Ivan Rodriguez .60 1.50
13 Darryl Hamilton .08 .25
14 John Burkett .08 .25
15 Warren Newson .08 .25

1998 Rangers Dr. Pepper

This 34 card postcard set was issued by the Texas Rangers and was available to all fans through a mail in offer in the Rangers Program. The fronts feature posed shots against a blue background and blank banks. The backs are blank so we have sequenced them in alphabetical order. This set was available from the Rangers for a $5 cost.

COMPLETE SET (34) 5.00 12.00
1 Luis Alicea .08 .25
2 Scott Bailes .08 .25
3 Dick Bosman CO .08 .25
4 John Burkett .08 .25
5 Domingo Cedeno .08 .25
6 Will Clark .40 1.00
7 Tim Crabtree .08 .25
8 Bucky Dent CO .08 .25
9 Kevin Elster .08 .25
10 Juan Gonzalez .40 1.00
11 Tom Goodwin .08 .25
12 Rusty Greer .40 1.00
13 Eric Gunderson .08 .25
14 Larry Hardy CO .08 .25
15 Bill Haselman .08 .25
16 Rick Helling .08 .25
17 Xavier Hernandez .08 .25
18 Rudy Jarmaillo CO .08 .25
19 Roberto Kelly .08 .25
20 Mark McLemore .08 .25
21 Ed Napoleon CO .08 .25
22 Warren Newson .08 .25
23 Jerry Narron CO .08 .25
24 Johnny Oates MG .08 .25
25 Darren Oliver .08 .25
26 Danny Patterson .08 .25
27 Roger Pavlik .08 .25
28 Ivan Rodriguez .60 1.50
29 Aaron Sele .08 .25
30 Mike Simms .08 .25
31 Lee Stevens .08 .25
32 Fernando Tatis .08 .25
33 John Wetteland .30 .75
34 Bobby Witt .08 .25
35 Ballpark in Ariington .08 .25

1999 Rangers Postcards Dr Pepper

These postcards were available directly from the Texas Rangers and cost $7 when ordered from the program. The fronts are a player portrait against a solid blue background except for the Johnny Oates cards and the players name along with the Rangers logo and an ad for Dr. Pepper is on the bottom of the card. The cards are blank backed and we have sequenced them in alphabetical order.

COMPLETE SET 5.00 12.00
1 Luis Alicea .08 .25
2 Dick Bosman CO .08 .25
3 John Burkett .08 .25
4 Mark Clark .08 .25
5 Royce Clayton .08 .25
6 Tim Crabtree .08 .25
7 Bucky Dent CO .08 .25
8 Juan Gonzalez .40 1.00
9 Tom Goodwin .08 .25
10 Rusty Greer .30 .75
11 Ryan Glynn .08 .25
12 Eric Gunderson .08 .25
13 Larry Hardy CO .08 .25
14 Rick Helling .08 .25
15 Rudy Jaramillo CO .08 .25
16 Roberto Kelly .08 .25
17 Danny Kolb .08 .25
18 Esteban Loiaza .30 .75
19 Ruben Mateo .08 .25
20 Mark McLemore .08 .25
21 Mike Morgan .08 .25
22 Mike Munoz .08 .25
23 Ed Napoleon CO .08 .25
24 Jerry Narron CO .08 .25
25 Johnny Oates MG .08 .25
26 Rafael Palmeiro .50 1.25
27 Danny Patterson .08 .25
28 Ivan Rodriguez .60 1.50
29 Aaron Sele .08 .25
30 Jon Shave .08 .25
31 Mike Simms .08 .25
32 Lee Stevens .08 .25
33 Mike Venafro .08 .25
34 John Wetteland .30 .75
35 Gregg Zaun .08 .25
36 Todd Zeile .20 .50
37 Jeff Zimmerman .08 .25
38 The Ballpark in Arlington .08 .25

2000 Rangers Clayton Sickle-Cell

1 Royce Clayton .40 1.00

2000 Rangers Postcards Dr. Pepper

COMPLETE SET (37) 4.80 12.00
1 Luis Alicea .10 .25
2 Dick Bosman CO .10 .25
3 Frank Catalanotto .20 .50
4 Mark Clark .10 .25
5 Royce Clayton .10 .25
6 Francisco Cordero .10 .25
7 Tim Crabtree .10 .25
8 Chad Curtis .10 .25
9 Doug Davis .10 .25
10 Bucky Dent CO .10 .25
11 Tom Evans .10 .25
12 Ryan Glynn .10 .25
13 Rusty Greer .30 .75
14 Bill Haselman .10 .25
15 Rick Helling .10 .25
16 Rudy Jaramillo CO .10 .25
17 Bobby Jones CO .10 .25
18 Gabe Kapler .10 .25
19 Mike Lamb .20 .50
20 Esteban Loaiza .30 .75
21 Ruben Mateo .10 .25
22 Jason McDonald .10 .25
23 Mike Munoz .10 .25
24 Jerry Narron CO .10 .25
25 Johnny Oates MG .10 .25
Card does not have a Dr. Pepper l
26 Darren Oliver .10 .25
27 Rafael Palmeiro .50 1.25
28 Matt Perisho .10 .25
29 Ivan Rodriguez .60 1.50
30 Kenny Rogers .30 .75
31 David Segui .10 .25
32 Scott Sheldon .10 .25
33 Justin Thompson .10 .25
34 Mike Venafro .10 .25
35 John Wetteland .30 .75
36 Jeff Zimmerman .10 .25
37 The Ballpark in Arlington .10 .25

2000 Rangers Southwest Airline

COMPLETE SET (33) 4.00 10.00
1 Luis Alicea .10 .25
2 Frank Catalanotto .30 .75
3 Royce Clayton .10 .25
4 Francisco Cordero .40 1.00
5 Tim Crabtree .10 .25
6 Mark Clark .10 .25
7 Chad Curtis .10 .25
8 Tom Evans .10 .25
9 Scarborough Green .10 .25
10 Rusty Greer .30 .75
11 Bill Haselman .10 .25
12 Rick Helling .10 .25
13 Gabe Kapler .10 .25
14 Mike Lamb .10 .25
15 Esteban Loiaza .30 .75
16 Ruben Mateo .10 .25
17 Jason McDonald .10 .25
18 Mike Munoz .10 .25
19 Johnny Oates MG .10 .25
20 Darren Oliver .10 .25
21 Rafael Palmeiro .50 1.25
22 Matt Perisho .10 .25
23 Ivan Rodriguez .60 1.50
24 Kenny Rogers .40 1.00
25 David Segui .10 .25
26 Mike Simms .10 .25
27 Scott Sheldon .10 .25
28 Justin Thompson .10 .25
29 Mike Venafro .10 .25
30 John Wetteland .30 .75
31 Jeff Zimmerman .10 .25
32 Rudy Jaramillo CO .10 .25
Bucky Dent CO
Jerry Narron CO#
33 Southwest Airline .10 .25

2001 Rangers Mrs Baird

COMPLETE SET (10) 4.00 8.00
1 Ivan Rodriguez .60 1.50
2 Gabe Kapler .10 .25
3 Rusty Greer .30 .75
4 Rafael Palmeiro .50 1.25
5 Kenny Rogers .40 1.00
6 Alex Rodriguez 1.00 2.50
7 Ruben Mateo .10 .25
8 Rick Helling .10 .25
9 Ken Caminiti .30 .75
10 Andres Galarraga .40 1.00

2001 Rangers Postcards

COMPLETE SET 5.00 12.00
1 Jeff Brantley .20 .50
2 Ken Caminiti .30 .75
3 Frank Catalanotto .20 .50
4 Tim Crabtree .08 .25
5 Bobby Cuellar CO .08 .25
6 Chad Curtis .08 .25
7 Doug Davis .08 .25
8 Bucky Dent CO .08 .25
9 Andres Galarraga .20 .50
10 Ryan Glynn .08 .25
11 Rusty Greer .30 .75
12 Larry Hardy CO .08 .25
13 Bill Haselman .08 .25
14 Rick Helling .08 .25
15 Rudy Jaramillo CO .08 .25
16 Jonathan Johnson .08 .25
17 Bobby Jones CO .08 .25
18 Gabe Kapler .08 .25
19 Ricky Ledee .08 .25
20 Joe Macko TRIB .08 .25
21 Pat Mahomes .08 .25
22 Ruben Mateo .08 .25
23 Doug Mirabelli .08 .25
24 Jerry Narron CO .08 .25
25 Darren Oliver .08 .25
26 Rafael Palmeiro .50 1.25
27 Mark Petkovsek .08 .25
28 Bo Porter .08 .25
29 Alex Rodriguez .75 2.00
30 Ivan Rodriguez .50 1.25
31 Kenny Rogers .40 1.00
32 Scott Sheldon .08 .25
33 Justin Thompson .08 .25
34 Randy Velarde .08 .25
35 Mike Venafro .08 .25
36 Jeff Zimmerman .08 .25
37 The Ballpark in Arlington .08 .25

2001 Rangers Upper Deck Collectibles

COMPLETE SET 6.00 15.00
1 Alex Rodriguez .75 2.00
2 Rafael Palmeiro .50 1.25
3 Ivan Rodriguez .60 1.50
4 Andres Galarraga .40 1.00
5 Ken Caminiti .30 .75
6 Ruben Mateo .10 .25
7 Rusty Greer .30 .75
8 Rick Helling .10 .25
9 Gabe Kapler .10 .25
10 Kenny Rogers .40 1.00
11 Randy Velarde .10 .25
12 Doug Davis .10 .25
13 Bill Haselman .10 .25
14 Tim Crabtree .10 .25
15 Darren Oliver .10 .25
16 Jeff Zimmerman .10 .25
17 Ricky Ledee .10 .25
18 Mark Petkovsek .10 .25
19 Frank Catalanotto .10 .25
20 Nolan Ryan 2.00 5.00

2002 Rangers Postcards

COMPLETE SET 6.00 15.00
1 Oscar Acosta CO .08 .25
2 Hank Blalock 1.00 2.50
3 Dave Burba .08 .25
4 Frank Catalanotto .30 .75
5 Doug Davis .08 .25
6 Carl Everett .20 .50
7 Terry Francona CO .08 .25
8 Juan Gonzalez .40 1.00
9 Rusty Greer .30 .75
10 DeMarlo Hale CO .08 .25
11 Bill Haselman .08 .25
12 Hideki Irabu .08 .25
13 Gabe Kapler .08 .25
14 Rudy Jaramillo CO .08 .25
15 Mike Lamb .20 .50
16 Colby Lewis .08 .25
17 Kevin Mench .50 1.25
18 Chris Michalak .08 .25
19 Jerry Narron MG .08 .25
20 Rafael Palmeiro .50 1.25
21 Chan Ho Park .08 .25
22 Herbert Perry .08 .25
23 Jay Powell .08 .25
24 Jamie Quirk CO .08 .25
25 John Rocker .20 .50
26 Alex Rodriguez .75 2.00
27 Ivan Rodriguez .50 1.25
28 Rich Rodriguez .08 .25
29 Kenny Rogers .40 1.00
30 Rudy Seanez .08 .25
31 Steve Smith CO .08 .25
32 Ismael Valdes .08 .25
33 Todd Van Poppel .08 .25
34 Steve Woodard .08 .25
35 Michael Young .60 1.50
36 Jeff Zimmerman .08 .25
37 The Ballpark in Arlington .08 .25

2003 Rangers Dr. Pepper

COMPLETE SET 7.50 15.00
1 Joacquin Benoit .20 .50
2 Hank Blalock .75 2.00
3 Ryan Christenson .10 .25
4 Mark Connor CO .10 .25
5 Francisco Cordero .40 1.00
6 Einar Diaz .10 .25
7 R.A. Dickey .10 .25
8 Ryan Drese .10 .25
9 Carl Everett .20 .50
10 Aaron Fultz .10 .25
11 Rosman Garcia .10 .25
12 Doug Glanville .10 .25
13 Juan Gonzalez .40 1.00
14 Todd Greene .10 .25
15 Rusty Greer .30 .75
16 DeMarlo Hale CO .10 .25
17 Orel Hershiser CO .10 .25
18 Rudy Jaramillo CO .10 .25
19 Colby Lewis .10 .25
20 Kevin Mench .40 1.00
21 Chan Ho Park .10 .25
22 Rafael Palmeiro .50 1.25
23 Herbert Perry .10 .25
24 Jay Powell .10 .25
25 Alex Rodriguez 1.00 2.50
26 Buck Showalter MG .10 .25
27 Brian Shouse .10 .25
28 Ruben Sierra .20 .50
29 Steve Smith CO .10 .25
30 Mark Teixeira 1.25 3.00
31 John Thomson .10 .25
32 Ugueth Urbina .10 .25
33 Ismael Valdes .10 .25
34 Todd Van Poppel .10 .25
35 Don Wakamatsu CO .10 .25
36 Esteban Yan .10 .25
37 Michael Young .60 1.50
38 Jeff Zimmerman .10 .25

2004 Rangers Dr Pepper

COMPLETE SET
1 Carlos Almanzar .10 .25
2 Rod Barajas .20 .50
3 Joaquin Benoit .20 .50
4 Hank Blalock .75 2.00
5 Doug Brocail .10 .25
6 Mickey Callaway .10 .25
7 Mark Connor .10 .25
8 Jason Conti .10 .25
9 Francisco Cordero .40 1.00
10 David Dellucci .20 .50
11 R.A. Dickey .10 .25
12 Juan Dominguez .20 .50
13 Ryan Drese .10 .25
14 Frank Francisco .10 .25
15 Brad Fullmer .10 .25
16 Adrian Gonzalez .10 .25
17 Rusty Greer .40 1.00
18 DeMarlo Hale CO .10 .25
19 Orel Hersiser CO .20 .50
20 Ken Huckaby .10 .25
21 Rudy Jaramillo CO .10 .25
22 Brian Jordan .10 .25
23 Gerald Laird .10 .25
24 Colby Lewis .10 .25
25 Ron Mahay .10 .25
26 Gary Matthews Jr. .10 .25
27 Kevin Mench .40 1.00
28 Jeff Nelson .10 .25
28 Ramon Nivar .10 .25
30 Laynce Nix .30 .75
31 Chan Ho Park .10 .25
32 Herbert Perry .10 .25
33 Jay Powell .10 .25
34 Erasmo Ramirez .10 .25
35 Ricardo Rodriguez .10 .25
36 Kenny Rogers .40 1.00
37 Brian Shouse .10 .25
38 Buck Showalter MG .10 .25
39 Steve Smith CO .10 .25
40 Alfonso Soriano .40 1.00
41 Mark Teixeira 1.00 2.50
42 Don Wakamatsu CO .10 .25
43 John Wasdin .10 .25
44 John Wetteland CO .10 .25
45 Eric Young .10 .25
46 Michael Young .60 1.50
47 Jeff Zimmerman .10 .25
48 Ameriquest Field In Arlington .10 .25

2005 Rangers Uno

COMP.FACT SET (112)
COMPLETE SET
B1 Laynce Nix .20 .50
B2 Kenny Rogers .30 .75
B3 Michael Young .60 1.50
B4 Hank Blalock .75 2.00
B5 Ryan Drese .10 .25
B6 Alfonso Soriano .40 1.00
B7 Francisco Cordero .30 .75
B8 David Dellucci .20 .50
B9 Mark Teixeira 1.00 2.50
G1 Laynce Nix .20 .50
G2 Kenny Rogers .30 .75
G3 Michael Young .60 1.50
G4 Hank Blalock .75 2.00
G5 Ryan Drese .10 .25
G6 Alfonso Soriano .40 1.00
G7 Francisco Cordero .30 .75
G8 David Dellucci .20 .50
G9 Mark Teixeira 1.00 2.50
O1 Laynce Nix .10 .25
O2 Kenny Rogers .30 .75
O3 Michael Young .60 1.50
O4 Hank Blalock .75 2.00
O5 Ryan Drese .10 .25
O6 Alfonso Soriano .40 1.00
O7 Francisco Cordero .30 .75
O8 David Dellucci .20 .50
O9 Mark Teixeira 1.00 2.50
Y1 Laynce Nix .10 .25
Y2 Kenny Rogers .30 .75
Y3 Michael Young .60 1.50
Y4 Hank Blalock .75 2.00
Y5 Ryan Drese .10 .25
Y6 Alfonso Soriano .40 1.00
Y7 Francisco Cordero .30 .75
Y8 David Dellucci .20 .50
Y9 Mark Teixeira 1.00 2.50
BA Richard Hidalgo .10 .25
BD Michael Young .30 .75
Hank Blalock
BO Chan Ho Park .10 .25
BR David Dellucci .20 .50
BS Michael Young .60 1.50
GD Michael Young .30 .75
Hank Blalock
GO Chan Ho Park .10 .25
GR David Dellucci .20 .50
GS Michael Young .60 1.50
OD Michael Young .30 .75
Hank Blalock
OO Chan Ho Park .10 .25
OR David Dellucci .20 .50
OS Michael Young .60 1.50
YD Michael Young .30 .75
Hank Blalock
YO Chan Ho Park .10 .25
YR David Dellucci .20 .50
YS Michael Young .60 1.50
BLD Alfonso Soriano .30 .75
Mark Teixeira
BLW Francisco Cordero .30 .75

2006 Rangers Topps

COMPLETE SET (14) 3.00 8.00
TEX1 Hank Blalock .12 .30
TEX2 Mark Teixeira .20 .50
TEX3 Michael Young .12 .30
TEX4 Brad Wilkerson .12 .30
TEX5 David Dellucci .12 .30
TEX6 Adam Eaton .12 .30
TEX7 Laynce Nix .12 .30
TEX8 Phil Nevin .12 .30
TEX9 Kevin Mench .12 .30
TEX10 Rod Barajas .12 .30
TEX11 Francisco Cordero .12 .30
TEX12 Kevin Millwood .12 .30
TEX13 Edison Volquez .12 .30
TEX14 Vicente Padilla .12 .30

2007 Rangers Topps

COMPLETE SET (14) 3.00 8.00
TEX1 Michael Young .12 .30
TEX2 Brad Wilkerson .12 .30
TEX3 Frank Catalanotto .12 .30
TEX4 Ian Kinsler .20 .50
TEX5 Brandon McCarthy .12 .30
TEX6 Vicente Padilla .12 .30
TEX7 Eric Gagne .12 .30
TEX8 Mark Teixeira .20 .50
TEX9 Kenny Lofton .12 .30
TEX10 Kevin Millwood .12 .30
TEX11 Hank Blalock .12 .30
TEX12 Akinori Otsuka .12 .30
TEX13 Nelson Cruz .30 .75
TEX14 Gerald Laird .12 .30

2008 Rangers Topps

COMPLETE SET (14) 3.00 8.00
TEX1 Michael Young .12 .30
TEX2 Josh Hamilton .20 .50
TEX3 Frank Catalanotto .12 .30
TEX4 Ian Kinsler .20 .50
TEX5 Brandon McCarthy .12 .30
TEX6 Vicente Padilla .12 .30
TEX7 Jarrod Saltalamacchia .12 .30
TEX8 Marlon Byrd .12 .30
TEX9 Milton Bradley .12 .30
TEX10 Kevin Millwood .12 .30
TEX11 Hank Blalock .12 .30
TEX12 Ben Broussard .12 .30
TEX13 C.J. Wilson .12 .30
TEX14 Gerald Laird .12 .30

2009 Rangers Topps

TEX1 Josh Hamilton .25 .60
TEX2 Kevin Millwood .15 .40
TEX3 Michael Young .15 .40
TEX4 David Murphy .15 .40
TEX5 Nelson Cruz .40 1.00
TEX6 Vicente Padilla .15 .40
TEX7 Ian Kinsler .25 .60
TEX8 Matt Harrison .15 .40
TEX9 Jarrod Saltalamacchia .15 .40
TEX10 Hank Blalock .15 .40
TEX11 Taylor Teagarden .15 .40
TEX12 Frank Francisco .15 .40
TEX13 Chris Davis .25 .60
TEX14 Marlon Byrd .15 .40
TEX15 Rangers Captain .15 .40

2010 Rangers Topps

TEX1 Ian Kinsler .25 .60
TEX2 Elvis Andrus .25 .60
TEX3 Brandon McCarthy .15 .40
TEX4 Neftali Feliz .15 .40
TEX5 Chris Davis .25 .60
TEX6 Nelson Cruz .40 1.00
TEX7 Jarrod Saltalamacchia .15 .40
TEX8 Josh Hamilton .25 .60
TEX9 Rich Harden .15 .40
TEX10 Vladimir Guerrero .25 .60
TEX11 Frank Francisco .15 .40
TEX12 Derek Holland .15 .40
TEX13 Michael Young .15 .40
TEX14 Scott Feldman .15 .40
TEX15 Taylor Teagarden .15 .40
TEX16 David Murphy .15 .40
TEX17 Tommy Hunter .15 .40

2011 Rangers Topps

TEX1 Josh Hamilton .25 .60
TEX2 Julio Borbon .15 .40
TEX3 Ian Kinsler .25 .60
TEX4 Colby Lewis .15 .40
TEX5 Yorvit Torrealba .15 .40
TEX6 David Murphy .15 .40
TEX7 Mitch Moreland .15 .40
TEX8 C.J. Wilson .15 .40
TEX9 Michael Young .15 .40
TEX10 Tommy Hunter .15 .40
TEX11 Derek Holland .15 .40
TEX12 Nelson Cruz .40 1.00
TEX13 Brandon Webb .25 .60
TEX14 Adrian Beltre .40 1.00
TEX15 Elvis Andrus .25 .60
TEX16 Neftali Feliz .15 .40
TEX17 Rangers Ballpark in Arlington .15 .40

2012 Rangers Topps

TEX1 Josh Hamilton .30 .75
TEX2 Nelson Cruz .40 1.00
TEX3 Craig Gentry .25 .60
TEX4 Mitch Moreland .25 .60
TEX5 Michael Young .25 .60
TEX6 Joe Nathan .25 .60
TEX7 Mike Napoli .25 .60
TEX8 Adrian Beltre .40 1.00
TEX9 Ian Kinsler .30 .75
TEX10 Colby Lewis .25 .60
TEX11 Matt Harrison .25 .60
TEX12 David Murphy .25 .60
TEX13 Elvis Andrus .30 .75
TEX14 Derek Holland .25 .60
TEX15 Neftali Feliz .25 .60
TEX16 Alexi Ogando .25 .60
TEX17 Rangers Ballpark in Arlington .15 .40

2013 Rangers Topps

COMPLETE SET (17) 3.00 8.00
TEX1 Yu Darvish .25 .60
TEX2 Adrian Beltre .25 .60

TEX3 Elvis Andrus .20 .50
TEX4 Ian Kinsler .20 .50
TEX5 Matt Harrison .15 .40
TEX6 Lance Berkman .20 .50
TEX7 Alexi Ogando .25 .60
TEX8 Nelson Cruz .25 .60
TEX9 Derek Holland .15 .40
TEX10 Mike Olt .30 .75
TEX11 Jurickson Profar .30 .75
TEX12 David Murphy .25 .60
TEX13 Craig Gentry .15 .40
TEX14 Joe Nathan .25 .60
TEX15 A.J. Pierzynski .15 .40
TEX16 Mitch Moreland .25 .60
TEX17 Rangers Ballpark in Arlington .15 .40

2014 Rangers Topps

COMPLETE SET (17) 3.00 8.00
TEX1 Yu Darvish .25 .60
TEX2 Adrian Beltre .25 .60
TEX3 Elvis Andrus .20 .50
TEX4 Prince Fielder .20 .50
TEX5 Matt Harrison .15 .40
TEX6 Alex Rios .20 .50
TEX7 Alexi Ogando .15 .40
TEX8 Michael Choice .15 .40
TEX9 Derek Holland .15 .40
TEX10 Neftali Feliz .15 .40
TEX11 Jurickson Profar .20 .50
TEX12 Martin Perez .20 .50
TEX13 Shin-Soo Choo .20 .50
TEX14 Leonys Martin .15 .40
TEX15 Geovany Soto .20 .50
TEX16 Mitch Moreland .15 .40
TEX17 Rangers Ballpark In Arlington .15 .40

2015 Rangers Topps

COMPLETE SET (17) 3.00 8.00
TR1 Yu Darvish .25 .60
TR2 Adrian Beltre .25 .60
TR3 Michael Choice .15 .40
TR4 Shin-Soo Choo .20 .50
TR5 Elvis Andrus .20 .50
TR6 Prince Fielder .20 .50
TR7 Anthony Ranaudo .15 .40
TR8 Robinson Chirinos .15 .40
TR9 Rougned Odor .20 .50
TR10 Jurickson Profar .20 .50
TR11 Jake Smolinski .15 .40
TR12 Leonys Martin .15 .40
TR13 Mitch Moreland .15 .40
TR14 Neftali Feliz .15 .40
TR15 Yovani Gallardo .15 .40
TR16 Ross Detwiler .15 .40
TR17 Nick Martinez .15 .40

2016 Rangers Topps

COMPLETE SET (17) 3.00 8.00
TEX1 Elvis Andrus .20 .50
TEX2 Prince Fielder .20 .50
TEX3 Yu Darvish .25 .60
TEX4 Robinson Chirinos .15 .40
TEX5 Mitch Moreland .15 .40
TEX6 Rougned Odor .20 .50
TEX7 Adrian Beltre .25 .60
TEX8 Josh Hamilton .20 .50
TEX9 Delino DeShields Jr. .15 .40
TEX10 Shin-Soo Choo .20 .50
TEX11 Cole Hamels .20 .50
TEX12 Derek Holland .15 .40
TEX13 Martin Perez .20 .50
TEX14 Shawn Tolleson .15 .40
TEX15 Colby Lewis .15 .40
TEX16 Sam Dyson .15 .40
TEX17 Keone Kela .15 .40

2017 Rangers Topps

COMPLETE SET (17) 3.00 8.00
TEX1 Rougned Odor .20 .50
TEX2 Elvis Andrus .20 .50
TEX3 Matt Bush .20 .50
TEX4 Jurickson Profar .20 .50
TEX5 Andrew Cashner .15 .40
TEX6 Joey Gallo .20 .50
TEX7 Shin-Soo Choo .20 .50
TEX8 Yu Darvish .25 .60
TEX9 Keone Kela .15 .40
TEX10 Carlos Gomez .15 .40
TEX11 Sam Dyson .15 .40
TEX12 Martin Perez .20 .50
TEX13 Jonathan Lucroy .20 .50
TEX14 Ryan Rua .15 .40
TEX15 Adrian Beltre .25 .60
TEX16 Nomar Mazara .15 .40
TEX17 Cole Hamels .20 .50

2018 Rangers Topps

COMPLETE SET (17) 2.00 5.00
TR1 Joey Gallo .20 .50
TR2 Adrian Beltre .25 .60
TR3 Elvis Andrus .20 .50
TR4 Alex Claudio .15 .40
TR5 Shin-Soo Choo .20 .50
TR6 Rougned Odor .20 .50
TR7 Matt Bush .15 .40
TR8 Nomar Mazara .15 .40
TR9 Jake Diekman .15 .40
TR10 Doug Fister .15 .40
TR11 Cole Hamels .20 .50
TR12 Robinson Chirinos .15 .40
TR13 Mike Minor .15 .40
TR14 Tony Barnette .15 .40
TR15 Willie Calhoun .25 .60
TR16 Delino DeShields .15 .40
TR17 Martin Perez .20 .50

2019 Rangers Topps

COMPLETE SET (17) 2.00 5.00
TR1 Joey Gallo .20 .50
TR2 Rougned Odor .20 .50
TR3 Elvis Andrus .20 .50
TR4 Ronald Guzman .15 .40
TR5 Patrick Wisdom .15 .40
TR6 Isiah Kiner-Falefa .20 .50
TR7 Shin-Soo Choo .20 .50
TR8 Willie Calhoun .15 .40
TR9 Jose Leclerc .15 .40
TR10 Mike Minor .15 .40
TR11 Delino DeShields .15 .40
TR12 Nomar Mazara .15 .40
TR13 Ariel Jurado .15 .40
TR14 Drew Smyly .15 .40
TR15 Yohander Mendez .15 .40
TR16 Carlos Tocci .15 .40
TR17 Jeffrey Springs .15 .40

2020 Rangers Topps

TEX1 Mike Minor .15 .40
TEX2 Corey Kluber .20 .50
TEX3 Elvis Andrus .20 .50
TEX4 Rougned Odor .20 .50
TEX5 Lance Lynn .15 .40
TEX6 Kolby Allard .15 .40
TEX7 Jeff Mathis .20 .50
TEX8 Shin-Soo Choo .20 .50
TEX9 Willie Calhoun .15 .40
TEX10 Ariel Jurado
TEX11 Kyle Gibson .15 .40
TEX12 Danny Santana .15 .40
TEX13 Nick Solak .60 1.50
TEX14 Jose Trevino .15 .40
TEX15 Ronald Guzman .15 .40
TEX16 Isiah Kiner-Falefa .20 .50
TEX17 Brock Burke .15 .40

2017 Rangers Topps National Baseball Card Day

COMPLETE SET (10) 5.00 12.00
TEX1 Jonathan Lucroy .75 2.00
TEX2 Adrian Beltre 1.00 2.50
TEX3 Nomar Mazara .60 1.50
TEX4 Cole Hamels .75 2.00
TEX5 Yu Darvish 1.00 2.50
TEX6 Rougned Odor .75 2.00
TEX7 Carlos Gomez .60 1.50
TEX8 Elvis Andrus .75 2.00
TEX9 Shin-Soo Choo .75 2.00
TEX10 Ivan Rodriguez .75 2.00

1964-66 Rawlings Photos

These 8" by 9 1/2" photos parallel the glove box cut cards. These photos were given away with a purchase of a Rawlings Glove
COMPLETE SET
COMMON CARD

1955 Rawlings Musial

This six-card set was actually the side panels of the box containing a Rawlings baseball glove. Rawlings Sporting Goods was headquartered in St. Louis. The cards are numbered and come in two sizes. Cards 1-4 are larger, 2 5/8" by 3 3/4" whereas numbers 1A and 2A are smaller, 2 1/8" by 3 1/8". The cards are blank backed and have a black and white picture on a light blue background.
COMPLETE SET (6) 750.00 1500.00
1 Stan Musial/(portrait) 150.00 300.00
1A Stan Musial/(portrait with hand and bat visible) 100.00 200.00
2 Stan Musial/(kneeling) 150.00 300.00
2A Stan Musial/(portrait& same picture as number 1 100.00 200.00
3 Stan Musial/(swinging HOR) 150.00 300.00
4 Stan Musial/(batting stance) 150.00 300.00

1961 Rawlings

This set measures approximately 8 1/8" by 10 1/8" and features white-bordered, black-and-white player photos. A facsimile autograph and sponsor name is printed in a white box on one side of the picture. The backs are blank. The cards are unnumbered and checklisted below in alphabetical order. More photos, from more years, are believed to exist so any additions to this checklist are appreciated.
COMPLETE SET 300.00 600.00
1 Joe Adcock 8.00 20.00
2 Hank Aguirre 5.00 12.00
3 Bob Bailey 5.00 12.00
4 Ed Bailey 5.00 12.00
5 Dick Bertell 5.00 12.00
6 John Blanchard 5.00 12.00
7 Clete Boyer 8.00 20.00
8 Ken Boyer/2 different photos known 10.00 25.00
9 Lew Burdette 6.00 15.00
10 Bob Cerv 5.00 12.00
11 Gordon Coleman 5.00 12.00
12 Tony Conigliaro 5.00 12.00
13 Wes Covington 5.00 12.00
14 Joe Cunningham 5.00 12.00
15 Tommy Davis 6.00 15.00
16 Don Demeter 5.00 12.00
17 Jim Grant 5.00 12.00
18 Dick Groat 5.00 12.00
19 Harvey Haddix 5.00 12.00
20 Elston Howard 10.00 25.00
21 Larry Jackson 5.00 12.00
22 Tony Kubek 10.00 25.00
23 Vern Law 5.00 12.00
24 Sherm Lollar 5.00 12.00
25 Mickey Mantle 40.00 80.00
26 Eddie Mathews 12.50 30.00
27 Dal Maxvill 5.00 12.00
28 Wilmer Mizell 5.00 12.00
29 Wally Moon 6.00 15.00
30 Stan Musial 12.50 30.00
31 Charlie Neal 5.00 12.00
32 Rocky Nelson 5.00 12.00
33 Brooks Robinson 30.00 60.00
34 Herb Score 6.00 15.00
35 Roy Sievers 6.00 15.00
36 Bob Skinner 5.00 12.00
37 Duke Snider 40.00 80.00
38 Warren Spahn 40.00 80.00
39 Bob Turley 6.00 15.00
40 Billy Williams 6.00 15.00

1964-66 Rawlings

This set features borderless color player photos that measure 2 3/8" by 4" when properly cut off the glove boxes on which they were printed. The photos are of stars of the day posing with their Rawlings glove prominently displayed, and a facsimile autograph is printed across the bottom of the picture. The cards are unnumbered and checklisted below in alphabetical order. There was also a picture issue of 8" by 9 1/2" Advisory Staff photos given away upon purchase. The same players featured on the boxes were featured on these photos.
COMPLETE SET 100.00 200.00
1 Ken Boyer Cards 6.00 15.00
2 Ken Boyer Mets 6.00 15.00
3 Gordy Coleman 4.00 10.00
4 Tommy Davis 4.00 10.00
5 Willie Davis 5.00 12.00
6 Dick Groat 6.00 15.00
7 Mickey Mantle 20.00 50.00
8 Dal Maxvill 4.00 10.00
9 Brooks Robinson 10.00 25.00
10 Warren Spahn 8.00 20.00
11 Tom Tresh 5.00 12.00
12 Bill White Phillies 6.00 15.00
13 Billy Williams 8.00 20.00

1976 Rawlings

This card was distributed by Rawlings Sporting Goods Company honoring Cesar Cedeno on the winning of his 4th consecutive Golden Glove Award. It measures approximately 5" by 7" and features a color photo in a white border with a white facsimile autograph. The back displays player information and career statistics. This set may be incomplete.
1 Cesar Cedeno 1.25 3.00

1998 Rawlings

This 10 card standard-size set was issued by Rawlings to promote their line of gloves. Each card has the player's photo on the front surrounded by brown borders while the back has biographical information as well as career highlights. Since these cards are unnumbered, we have sequenced them in alphabetical order.
COMPLETE SET 6.00 15.00
1 Craig Biggio .30 .75
2 Ken Griffey Jr. .75 2.00
3 Tony Gwynn .75 2.00
4 Derek Jeter 1.50 4.00
5 Randy Johnson .50 1.25
6 Mark McGwire .60 1.50
7 Mike Piazza 1.00 2.50
8 Cal Ripken Jr. 1.50 4.00
9 Larry Walker .40 1.00
10 Bernie Williams .30 .75

2008 Rays Topps

COMPLETE SET (14) 3.00 8.00
TBR1 Carl Crawford .20 .50
TBR2 Matt Garza .12 .30
TBR3 Edwin Jackson .12 .30
TBR4 Al Reyes .12 .30
TBR5 Dioner Navarro .12 .30
TBR6 James Shields .12 .30
TBR7 Scott Kazmir .20 .50
TBR8 B.J. Upton .20 .50
TBR9 Carlos Pena .20 .50
TBR10 Cliff Floyd .12 .30
TBR11 Jason Bartlett .12 .30
TBR12 Jonny Gomes .12 .30
TBR13 Akinori Iwamura .12 .30
TBR14 Rocco Baldelli .12 .30

2009 Rays Topps

TBR1 Evan Longoria .25 .60
TBR2 Scott Kazmir .15 .40
TBR3 Carl Crawford .25 .60
TBR4 Matt Garza .15 .40
TBR5 Gabe Gross .15 .40
TBR6 James Shields .15 .40
TBR7 B.J. Upton .25 .60
TBR8 Pat Burrell .15 .40
TBR9 Carlos Pena .25 .60
TBR10 David Price .30 .75
TBR11 Willy Aybar .15 .40
TBR12 Akinori Iwamura .15 .40
TBR13 Jason Bartlett .15 .40
TBR14 Dioner Navarro .15 .40
TBR15 Raymond .15 .40

2010 Rays Topps

TBR1 Evan Longoria .25 .60
TBR2 Wade Davis .25 .60
TBR3 James Shields .15 .40
TBR4 Andy Sonnanstine .15 .40
TBR5 Ben Zobrist .25 .60
TBR6 Jeff Niemann .15 .40
TBR7 Jason Bartlett .15 .40
TBR8 David Price .30 .75
TBR9 Gabe Gross .15 .40
TBR10 J.P. Howell .15 .40
TBR11 Carl Crawford .25 .60
TBR12 Matt Garza .15 .40
TBR13 B.J. Upton .25 .60
TBR14 Dioner Navarro .15 .40
TBR15 Carlos Pena .25 .60
TBR16 Kelly Shoppach .15 .40
TBR17 Rafael Soriano .15 .40

2011 Rays Topps

TBR1 Evan Longoria .25 .60
TBR2 David Price .30 .75
TBR3 Sean Rodriguez .15 .40
TBR4 James Shields .15 .40
TBR5 Jeff Niemann .15 .40
TBR6 Desmond Jennings .25 .60
TBR7 John Jaso .15 .40
TBR8 Jeremy Hellickson .40 1.00
TBR9 J.P. Howell .15 .40
TBR10 Wade Davis .15 .40
TBR11 Ben Zobrist .25 .60
TBR12 Reid Brignac .15 .40
TBR13 Johnny Damon .25 .60
TBR14 Manny Ramirez .40 1.00
TBR15 B.J. Upton .25 .60
TBR16 Matt Joyce .15 .40
TBR17 Tropicana Field .15 .40

2012 Rays Topps

TB1 David Price .30 .75
TB2 Matt Joyce .25 .60
TB3 Desmond Jennings .30 .75
TB4 Wade Davis .30 .75
TB5 Sean Rodriguez .25 .60
TB6 Jeremy Hellickson .25 .60
TB7 B.J. Upton .30 .75
TB8 James Shields .25 .60
TB9 Kyle Farnsworth .30 .75
TB10 Evan Longoria .30 .75
TB11 Matt Moore .40 1.00
TB12 Ben Zobrist .30 .75
TB13 Reid Brignac .25 .60
TB14 Jeff Niemann .25 .60
TB15 Jose Molina .25 .60
TB16 Joe Maddon .15 .40
TB17 Tropicana Field .15 .40

2013 Rays Topps

COMPLETE SET (17) 3.00 8.00
TAM1 Evan Longoria .30 .75
TAM2 David Price .30 .75
TAM3 Ben Zobrist .20 .50
TAM4 Yunel Escobar .25 .60
TAM5 Fernando Rodney .25 .60
TAM6 Matt Joyce .15 .40
TAM7 Matt Moore .30 .75
TAM8 Jeremy Hellickson .15 .40
TAM9 Desmond Jennings .20 .50
TAM10 James Loney .20 .50
TAM11 Alex Cobb .15 .40
TAM12 Jose Molina .25 .60
TAM13 Sam Fuld .15 .40
TAM14 Kelly Johnson .25 .60
TAM15 Jake McGee .20 .50
TAM16 Jeff Niemann .25 .60
TAM17 Tropicana Field .15 .40

2014 Rays Topps

COMPLETE SET (17) 3.00 8.00
TAM1 Evan Longoria .20 .50
TAM2 David Price .20 .50
TAM3 Ben Zobrist .20 .50
TAM4 Yunel Escobar .15 .40
TAM5 Grant Balfour .15 .40
TAM6 Matt Joyce .15 .40
TAM7 Matt Moore .20 .50
TAM8 Jeremy Hellickson .15 .40
TAM9 Desmond Jennings .20 .50
TAM10 James Loney .15 .40
TAM11 Alex Cobb .15 .40
TAM12 Wil Myers .15 .40
TAM13 Chris Archer .15 .40
TAM14 David DeJesus .15 .40
TAM15 Ryan Hanigan .15 .40
TAM16 Heath Bell .15 .40
TAM17 Tropicana Field .15 .40

2015 Rays Topps

COMPLETE SET (17) 3.00 8.00
TBR1 Evan Longoria .20 .50
TBR2 Alex Cobb .15 .40
TBR3 David DeJesus .15 .40
TBR4 Nick Franklin .15 .40
TBR5 Asdrubal Cabrera .20 .50
TBR6 James Loney .15 .40
TBR7 Chris Archer .15 .40
TBR8 John Jaso .15 .40
TBR9 Desmond Jennings .20 .50
TBR10 Rene Rivera .15 .40
TBR11 Jake McGee .20 .50
TBR12 Drew Smyly .15 .40
TBR13 Steven Souza Jr. .20 .50
TBR14 Kevin Kiermaier .20 .50
TBR15 Brandon Guyer .15 .40
TBR16 Matt Moore .20 .50
TBR17 Kevin Cash .15 .40

2016 Rays Topps

COMPLETE SET (17) 3.00 8.00
TBR1 Kevin Kiermaier .20 .50
TBR2 Chris Archer .15 .40
TBR3 Jake McGee .15 .40
TBR4 Logan Forsythe .15 .40
TBR5 Brad Miller .20 .50
TBR6 Evan Longoria .20 .50
TBR7 Desmond Jennings .20 .50
TBR8 Steven Souza Jr. .20 .50
TBR9 Curt Casali .15 .40
TBR10 Jake Odorizzi .15 .40
TBR11 Brad Boxberger .15 .40
TBR12 Alex Cobb .15 .40
TBR13 Logan Morrison .15 .40
TBR14 Drew Smyly .15 .40
TBR15 Mikie Mahtook .15 .40
TBR16 Matt Moore .20 .50
TBR17 Brandon Guyer .15 .40

2017 Rays Topps

COMPLETE SET (17) 3.00 8.00
TB1 Kevin Kiermaier .20 .50
TB2 Alex Colome .15 .40
TB3 Chris Archer .15 .40
TB4 Brad Boxberger .15 .40
TB5 Tropicana Field .15 .40
TB6 Steven Souza Jr. .20 .50
TB7 Colby Rasmus .20 .50
TB8 Jake Odorizzi .15 .40
TB9 Evan Longoria .20 .50
TB10 Blake Snell .20 .50
TB11 Luke Maile .15 .40
TB12 Matt Duffy .15 .40
TB13 Alex Cobb .15 .40
TB14 Nick Franklin .15 .40
TB15 Corey Dickerson .15 .40
TB16 Brad Miller .20 .50
TB17 Mikie Mahtook .15 .40

2018 Rays Topps

COMPLETE SET (17) 2.00 5.00
TB1 Kevin Kiermaier .20 .50
TB2 Chris Archer .15 .40
TB3 Christian Arroyo .15 .40
TB4 Corey Dickerson .15 .40
TB5 Adeiny Hechavarria .15 .40
TB6 Chih-Wei Hu .15 .40
TB7 Mallex Smith .15 .40
TB8 Matt Duffy .15 .40
TB9 Alex Colome .15 .40
TB10 Jose de Leon .15 .40
TB11 Brad Miller .20 .50
TB12 Jesus Sucre .15 .40
TB13 Jacob Faria .15 .40
TB14 Wilson Ramos .15 .40
TB15 Blake Snell .20 .50
TB16 Steven Souza Jr. .20 .50
TB17 Dan Jennings .15 .40

2019 Rays Topps

COMPLETE SET (17) 2.00 5.00
TB1 Blake Snell .20 .50
TB2 Kevin Kiermaier .20 .50
TB3 Charlie Morton .25 .60
TB4 Joey Wendle .20 .50
TB5 Willy Adames .15 .40
TB6 Matt Duffy .15 .40
TB7 Tommy Pham .15 .40
TB8 Austin Meadows .25 .60
TB9 Mike Zunino .15 .40
TB10 Daniel Robertson .15 .40
TB11 Chaz Roe .15 .40
TB12 Wilmer Font .15 .40
TB13 Tyler Glasnow .25 .60
TB14 Ryan Yarbrough .15 .40
TB15 Jake Faria .15 .40
TB16 Nick Ciuffo .15 .40
TB17 Brandon Lowe .25 .60

2020 Rays Topps

TB1 Blake Snell .20 .50
TB2 Willy Adames .15 .40
TB3 Austin Meadows .25 .60
TB4 Kevin Kiermaier .20 .50
TB5 Charlie Morton .25 .60
TB6 Tyler Glasnow .25 .60
TB7 Hunter Renfroe .15 .40
TB8 Mike Zunino .15 .40
TB9 Yandy Diaz .20 .50
TB10 Joey Wendle .20 .50
TB11 Nate Lowe .40 1.00
TB12 Brandon Lowe .20 .50
TB13 Ji-Man Choi .15 .40
TB14 Yonny Chirinos .15 .40
TB15 Brendan McKay .25 .60
TB16 Ryan Yarbrough .15 .40
TB17 Emilio Pagan .15 .40

2017 Rays Topps National Baseball Card Day

COMPLETE SET (10) 5.00 12.00
TBR1 Steven Souza Jr. .75 2.00
TBR2 Kevin Kiermaier .75 2.00
TBR3 Blake Snell .75 2.00
TBR4 Chris Archer .60 1.50
TBR5 Evan Longoria .75 2.00
TBR6 Matt Duffy .60 1.50
TBR7 Brad Miller .75 2.00
TBR8 Jake Odorizzi .60 1.50
TBR9 Colby Rasmus .75 2.00
TBR10 Wade Boggs .75 2.00

1978 Reading Remembers

This 23-card set measures 3" by 4". The fronts feature brown and white tinted player action and posted photos. The backs carry the player's name, jersey number, position, biography, statistics, and other player facts. The cards are unnumbered and checklisted below in alphabetical order. This set was issued in three-card strips. This set was available upon release for $4 postpaid from the producers.
COMPLETE SET (23) 8.00 20.00
1 Tommy Brown .20 .50
2 Doug Clemens .20 .50
3 Dom Dallessandro .20 .50
4 George Eyrich .20 .50
5 Carl Furillo .60 1.50
6 Dick Gernert .20 .50
7 Randy Gumpert .20 .50
8 Bob Katz .20 .50
9 Betz Klopp .20 .50
10 Whitey Kurowski .30 .75
11 Lauer's Park .20 .50
12 Jesse Levan .20 .50
13 Carl Mathias .20 .50
14 Roger Maris 2.00 5.00
15 Lenny Moore 1.25 3.00
16 Robin Roberts 2.00 5.00
17 Harry Schaeffer .20 .50
18 Herb Score .60 1.50
19 Ty Stofflet .20 .50
20 John Updike .30 .75
21 Charlie Wagner .20 .50
22 Stan Wentzel .20 .50
23 Vic Wertz .20 .50

1995 Real Action Pop-Ups

COMPLETE SET (7) 2.50 6.00
1 Bert Blyleven .40 1.00
5 Mike Schmidt .50 1.25

1910-13 Red Cross T215

The cards in this set measure 1 1/2" by 2 5/8." There are actually three distinct groupings or types. Type 1 cards have brown captions. Type 2 cards have blue captions. Type 3 cards are distinguished by their "Pirate Cigarettes" backs printed in green ink. According to leading dealers and collectors, these cards were produced for Americans serving their country in the South Seas. The players have been alphabetized within Type and numbered for reference in the checklist below.
COMMON TYPE 1 (1-88) 75.00 150.00
COMMON TYPE 2 (89-167) 50.00 100.00
COMMON TYPE 3 (168-259)
1 Red Ames 200.00 400.00
2 Frank Baker 400.00 800.00
3 Neal Ball 200.00 400.00
4 Chief Bender (2) 400.00 800.00
5 Chief Bender (2) 400.00 800.00
6 Al Bridwell 200.00 400.00
7 Bobby Byrne 200.00 400.00
8 Howie Camnitz 200.00 400.00
9 Frank Chance 600.00 1200.00
10 Hal Chase 400.00 800.00
11 Ty Cobb 3000.00 6000.00
12 Eddie Collins 400.00 800.00
13 Wid Conroy 200.00 400.00
14 Doc Crandall 200.00 400.00
15 Sam Crawford 400.00 800.00
16 Birdie Cree 200.00 400.00
17 Harry Davis 200.00 400.00
18 Josh Devore 200.00 400.00
19 Mike Donlin 250.00 500.00
20 Mickey Doolan 200.00 400.00
21 Patsy Dougherty 200.00 400.00
22 Larry Doyle 250.00 500.00
23 Larry Doyle 250.00 500.00
24 Kid Elberfeld 200.00 400.00
25 Russ Ford 200.00 400.00
26 Art Fromme 200.00 400.00
27 Clark Griffith 400.00 800.00
28 Topsy Hartsel 200.00 400.00
29 Doc Hoblitzell 200.00 400.00
30 Danny Hofman 200.00 400.00
31 Del Howard 200.00 400.00
32 Miller Huggins 400.00 800.00
33 John Hummell 200.00 400.00
34 Hugh Jennings (2) 400.00 800.00
35 Hugh Jennings (2) 400.00 800.00
36 Walter Johnson 1000.00 2000.00
37 Ed Konetchy 200.00 400.00
38 Harry Krause 200.00 400.00
39 Nap Lajoie 750.00 1500.00
40 Bill Lange
41 Arlie Latham 200.00 400.00
42 Tommy Leach 200.00 400.00
43 Lefty Leifield 200.00 400.00
44 Harry Lord 200.00 400.00
45 Sherry Magee 300.00 600.00
46 Rube Marquard (2) 400.00 800.00
47 Rube Marquard (2) 400.00 800.00
48 Christy Mathewson 1000.00 2000.00
49 Christy Mathewson 1000.00 2000.00
50 Joe McGinnity 400.00 800.00
51 John McGraw (2) 600.00 1200.00
52 John McGraw (2) 600.00 1200.00
53 Matty McIntyre 200.00 400.00
54 Fred Merkle 300.00 600.00
55 Chief Meyers 250.00 500.00
56 Dots Miller 200.00 400.00
57 George Mullin 250.00 500.00
58 Danny Murphy 200.00 400.00
59 Red Murray 200.00 400.00
60 Rebel Oakes 200.00 400.00
61 Charley O'Leary 200.00 400.00
62 Dode Paskert 200.00 400.00
63 Barney Pelty 200.00 400.00
64 Jack Quinn 200.00 400.00
65 Ed Reulbach 250.00 500.00
66 Nap Rucker 250.00 500.00
67 Germany Schaefer 300.00 600.00
68 Frank Schulte 250.00 500.00
69 Jimmy Sheckard 200.00 400.00
70 Frank Smith 200.00 400.00
71 Smither 200.00 400.00
72 Tris Speaker 750.00 1500.00
73 Jake Stahl 250.00 500.00
74 Harry Steinfeldt 250.00 500.00
75 Gabby Street (2) 200.00 400.00
76 Gabby Street (2) 200.00 400.00
77 William Sweeney 200.00 400.00
78 Lee Tannehill 200.00 400.00
79 Joe Tinker (2) 400.00 800.00
80 Joe Tinker (2) 400.00 800.00
81 Honus Wagner 1000.00 2000.00
82 Jack Warhop 200.00 400.00
83 Zach Wheat 400.00 800.00
84 Doc White 200.00 400.00
85 Ed Willett 200.00 400.00
86 Owen Wilson 200.00 400.00
87 Hooks Wiltse (2) 200.00 400.00
88 Hooks Wiltse (2) 200.00 400.00
89 Cy Young 1250.00 2500.00
90 Red Ames 200.00 400.00
91 Chief Bender (2) 400.00 800.00
92 Chief Bender (2) 400.00 800.00
93 Roger Bresnahan 400.00 800.00
94 Mordecai Brown 400.00 800.00
95 Bobby Byrne 200.00 400.00
96 Howie Camnitz 200.00 400.00
97 Frank Chance 750.00 1500.00
98 Ty Cobb 4000.00 8000.00
99 Eddie Collins 400.00 800.00
100 Doc Crandall 200.00 400.00
101 Birdie Cree 200.00 400.00
102 Harry Davis 200.00 400.00
103 Josh Devore 200.00 400.00
104 Mike Donlin 250.00 500.00
105 Mickey Doolan (2) 200.00 400.00
106 Mickey Doolan (2) 200.00 400.00
107 Patsy Dougherty 200.00 400.00
108 Larry Doyle (2) 250.00 500.00
109 Larry Doyle (2) 250.00 500.00
110 Jean Dubuc 200.00 400.00
111 Kid Elberfeld 200.00 400.00
112 Johnny Evers 400.00 800.00
113 Russ Ford 200.00 400.00
114 Art Fromme 200.00 400.00
115 Clark Griffith 400.00 800.00
116 Bob Groom 200.00 400.00
117 Topsy Hartsel 200.00 400.00
118 Buck Herzog 200.00 400.00
119 Doc Hoblitzell 200.00 400.00
120 Solly Hofman 200.00 400.00
121 Miller Huggins (2) 750.00 1500.00
122 Miller Huggins (2) 750.00 1500.00
123 John Hummel 200.00 400.00
124 Hugh Jennings 400.00 800.00
125 Walter Johnson 1250.00 2500.00
126 Joe Kelley 400.00 800.00
127 Ed Konetchy 200.00 400.00
128 Harry Krause 200.00 400.00
129 Napolean Lajoie 1000.00 2000.00
130 Lake 200.00 400.00
131 Tommy Leach 200.00 400.00
132 Lefty Leifield 200.00 400.00
133 Harry Lord 200.00 400.00
134 Rube Marquard 400.00 800.00
135 Christy Mathewson 1250.00 2500.00
136 John McGraw (2) 600.00 1200.00
137 John McGraw (2) 600.00 1200.00
138 Larry McLean 200.00 400.00
139 Dots Miller 200.00 400.00
140 Michael Mitchell 200.00 400.00
141 Mike Mowrey 200.00 400.00
142 George Mullin 250.00 500.00
143 Danny Murphy 200.00 400.00
144 Red Murray 200.00 400.00
145 Rebel Oakes 200.00 400.00
146 Rube Oldring 200.00 400.00
147 Charley O'Leary 200.00 400.00
148 Dode Paskert 200.00 400.00
149 Barney Pelty 200.00 400.00
150 William Purtell 200.00 400.00
151 Ed Reulbach 250.00 500.00
152 Nap Rucker 250.00 500.00
153 Germany Schaefer (2) 250.00 500.00
154 Germany Schaefer (2) 250.00 500.00
155 Frank Schulte 250.00 500.00
156 Frank Smith (2) 200.00 400.00
157 Frank Smith (2) 200.00 400.00
158 Tris Speaker 1000.00 2000.00
159 Jake Stahl 200.00 400.00
160 Harry Steinfeldt 250.00 500.00
161 Ed Summers 200.00 400.00
162 William Sweeney 200.00 400.00
163 Joe Tinker 400.00 800.00
164 Honus Wagner 1250.00 2500.00
165 Jack Warhop 200.00 400.00
166 Doc White 200.00 400.00
167 Hooks Wiltse (2) 200.00 400.00
168 Hooks Wiltse (2) 200.00 400.00
169 Red Ames 500.00 1000.00
170 Frank Baker 1250.00 2500.00
171 Neal Ball 500.00 1000.00
172 Chief Bender 1250.00 2500.00
173 Al Bridwell 500.00 1000.00
174 Bobby Byrne 500.00 1000.00
175 Howie Camnitz 500.00 1000.00
176 Frank Chance 1500.00 3000.00
177 Hal Chase 1000.00 2000.00
178 Eddie Collins 2000.00 4000.00
179 Doc Crandall 500.00 1000.00
180 Sam Crawford 1500.00 3000.00
181 Birdie Cree 500.00 1000.00
182 Harry Davis 500.00 1000.00
183 Josh Devore 500.00 1000.00
184 Mike Donlin 600.00 1200.00
185 Mickey Doolan 500.00 1000.00
186 Mickey Doolan 500.00 1000.00
187 Patsy Dougherty 500.00 1000.00
188 Larry Doyle 600.00 1200.00
189 Larry Doyle 600.00 1200.00
190 Jean Dubuc 500.00 1000.00
191 Kid Eberfeld 500.00 1000.00
192 Steve Evans 500.00 1000.00
193 Johnny Evers 1500.00 3000.00
194 Russ Ford 500.00 1000.00
195 Art Fromme 500.00 1000.00
196 Clark Griffith 1500.00 3000.00
197 Bob Groom 500.00 1000.00
198 Topsy Hartsell 500.00 1000.00
199 Buck Herzog 1000.00 2000.00
200 Dick Hoblitzell 500.00 1000.00
201 Solly Hofman 500.00 1000.00
202 Del Howard 500.00 1000.00
203 Miller Huggins 1000.00 2000.00
204 Miller Huggins 1000.00 2000.00
205 John Hummel 500.00 1000.00
206 Hugh Jennings 1000.00 2000.00
207 Hugh Jennings 1000.00 2000.00
208 Walter Johnson 2500.00 5000.00
209 Joe Kelley 2500.00 5000.00
210 Ed Konetchy 500.00 1000.00
211 Harry Krause 500.00 1000.00
212 Nap Lajoie 1500.00 3000.00
213 Joe Lake 500.00 1000.00
214 Lefty Leifield 500.00 1000.00
215 Harry Lord 500.00 1000.00
216 Sherry Magee 600.00 1200.00
217 Rube Marquard 1000.00 2000.00
218 Rube Marquard 1000.00 2000.00
219 Joe McGinnity 1000.00 2000.00
220 John McGraw 1250.00 2500.00
221 John McGraw 1250.00 2500.00
222 Matty McIntyre Chicago Nat'l 500.00 1000.00
223 Matty McIntyre Bkln. and Chicago Nat'l 500.00 1000.00
224 Larry McLean 500.00 1000.00
225 Fred Merkle 600.00 1200.00
226 Chief Meyers 600.00 1200.00
227 Michael Mitchell 500.00 1000.00
228 Mike Mowrey 500.00 1000.00
229 George Mullin 600.00 1200.00
230 Danny Murphy 500.00 1000.00
231 Red Murray. 500.00 1000.00
232 Rebel Oakes 500.00 1000.00
233 Rube Oldring 500.00 1000.00
234 Charley O'Leary 500.00 1000.00
235 Dode Paskert 500.00 1000.00
236 Barney Pelty 500.00 1000.00
237 William Purtell 500.00 1000.00
238 Jack Quinn 600.00 1200.00
239 Ed Reulbach 750.00 1500.00
240 Nap Rucker 600.00 1200.00
241 Germany Schaefer 600.00 1200.00
242 Frank Schulte 600.00 1200.00
243 Jimmy Sheckard 600.00 1200.00
244 Frank Smith 500.00 1000.00
245 Tris Speaker 2000.00 4000.00
246 Jake Stahl 500.00 1000.00
247 Harry Steinfeldt 600.00 1200.00
248 Gabby Street 500.00 1000.00
249 Ed Summers 500.00 1000.00
250 William Sweeney 500.00 1000.00
251 Lee Tannehill 500.00 1000.00
252 Ira Thomas 500.00 1000.00
253 Joe Tinker 1500.00 3000.00
254 Heinie Wagner 500.00 1000.00
255 Jack Warhop 500.00 1000.00
256 Zack Wheat 1000.00 2000.00
257 Ed Willett 500.00 1000.00
258 Owen Wilson 600.00 1200.00
259 Hooks Wiltse 500.00 1000.00
260 Hooks Wiltse 500.00 1000.00

1954 Red Heart

The cards in this 33-card set measure approximately 2 5/8" by 3 3/4". The 1954 Red Heart baseball series was marketed by Red Heart dog food, which, incidentally, was a subsidiary of Morrell Meats. The set consists of three series of eleven unnumbered cards each of which could be ordered from the company via an offer (two can labels plus ten cents for each series) on the can label. Each series has a specific color background (red, green or blue) behind the color player photo. Cards with red backgrounds are considered scarcer and are marked with SP in the checklist (which has been alphabetized and numbered for reference). The catalog designation is F156. It is believed that some of the cards were available directly from Red Heart well into the 1970's.
COMPLETE SET (33) 2000.00 4000.00

COMMON CARD 25.00 50.00
COMMON CARD SP 30.00 60.00
1 Richie Ashburn SP 60.00 120.00
2 Frank Baumholtz SP 30.00 60.00
3 Gus Bell 25.00 50.00
4 Billy Cox 40.00 80.00
5 Alvin Dark 30.00 60.00
6 Carl Erskine SP 50.00 100.00
7 Ferris Fain 30.00 60.00
8 Dee Fondy 25.00 50.00
9 Nellie Fox 60.00 120.00
10 Jim Gilliam 40.00 80.00
11 Jim Hegan SP 50.00 100.00
12 George Kell 50.00 100.00
13 Ralph Kiner SP 60.00 120.00
14 Ted Kluszewski SP 60.00 120.00
15 Harvey Kuenn 40.00 80.00
16 Bob Lemon SP 50.00 100.00
17 Sherman Lollar 30.00 60.00
18 Mickey Mantle 500.00 1000.00
19 Billy Martin 50.00 100.00
20 Gil McDougald SP 40.00 80.00
21 Roy McMillan 30.00 60.00
22 Minnie Minoso 50.00 100.00
23 Stan Musial SP 200.00 400.00
24 Billy Pierce 30.00 60.00
25 Al Rosen SP 50.00 100.00
26 Hank Sauer 30.00 60.00
27 Red Schoendienst SP 60.00 120.00
28 Enos Slaughter 50.00 100.00
29 Duke Snider 50.00 100.00
30 Warren Spahn 60.00 120.00
31 Sammy White 25.00 50.00
32 Eddie Yost 25.00 50.00
33 Gus Zernial 30.00 60.00

1952 Red Man

The cards in this 52-card set measure approximately 3 1/2" by 4" (or 3 1/2" by 3 5/8" without the tab). This Red Man issue was the first nationally available tobacco issue since the T cards of the teens early in this century. This 52-card set contains 26 top players from each league. Cards that have the tab (coupon) attached are generally worth a multiplier of cards without tabs. Please refer to multiplier line below. The 1952 Red Man cards are considered to be the most difficult (of the Red Man sets) to find with tabs. Card numbers are located on the tabs. The prices listed below refer to cards without tabs. The numbering of the set is alphabetical by player within league with the exception of the managers who are listed first.

COMPLETE SET (52) 500.00 1000.00
*CARDS WITH TABS: 3X VALUES
AL1 Casey Stengel MG 15.00 30.00
AL2 Bobby Avila 5.00 10.00
AL3 Yogi Berra 25.00 50.00
AL4 Gil Coan 5.00 10.00
AL5 Dom DiMaggio 10.00 20.00
AL6 Larry Doby 12.50 25.00
AL7 Ferris Fain 5.00 10.00
AL8 Bob Feller 15.00 30.00
AL9 Nellie Fox 12.50 25.00
AL10 Johnny Groth 5.00 10.00
AL11 Jim Hegan 5.00 10.00
AL12 Eddie Joost 5.00 10.00
AL13 George Kell 12.50 25.00
AL14 Gil McDougald 7.50 15.00
AL15 Minnie Minoso 7.50 15.00
AL16 Billy Pierce 6.00 12.00
AL17 Bob Porterfield 5.00 10.00
AL18 Eddie Robinson 5.00 10.00
AL19 Saul Rogovin 5.00 10.00
AL20 Bobby Shantz 6.00 12.00
AL21 Vern Stephens 5.00 10.00
AL22 Vic Wertz 5.00 10.00
AL23 Ted Williams 500.00 1000.00
AL24 Early Wynn 12.50 25.00
AL25 Eddie Yost 5.00 10.00
AL26 Gus Zernial 6.00 12.00
NL1 Leo Durocher MG 10.00 20.00
NL2 Richie Ashburn 12.50 25.00
NL3 Ewell Blackwell 5.00 10.00
NL4 Cliff Chambers 5.00 10.00
NL5 Murry Dickson 5.00 10.00
NL6 Sid Gordon 5.00 10.00
NL7 Granny Hamner 5.00 10.00
NL8 Jim Hearn 5.00 10.00
NL9 Monte Irvin 12.50 25.00
NL10 Larry Jansen 5.00 10.00
NL11 Willie Jones 5.00 10.00
NL12 Ralph Kiner 12.50 25.00
NL13 Whitey Lockman 5.00 10.00
NL14 Sal Maglie 6.00 12.00
NL15 Willie Mays 250.00 500.00
NL16 Stan Musial 50.00 100.00
NL17 Pee Wee Reese 15.00 30.00
NL18 Robin Roberts 12.50 25.00
NL19 Red Schoendienst 12.50 25.00
NL20 Enos Slaughter 12.50 25.00
NL21 Duke Snider 30.00 60.00
NL22 Warren Spahn 15.00 30.00
NL23 Eddie Stanky 6.00 12.00
NL24 Bobby Thomson 7.50 15.00
NL25 Earl Torgeson 5.00 10.00
NL26 Wes Westrum 5.00 10.00

1953 Red Man

The cards in this 52-card set measure approximately 3 1/2" by 4" (or 3 1/2" by 3 5/8" without the tab). The 1953 Red Man set contains 26 National League stars and 26 American League stars. Card numbers are located both on the write-up of the player and on the tab. Cards that have the tab (coupon) attached are worth a multiplier of cards without tabs. Please refer to the multiplier line below. The prices listed below refer to cards without tabs.

COMPLETE SET (52) 400.00 800.00
*CARDS WITH TABS: 2.5X VALUES
AL1 Casey Stengel MG 15.00 30.00
AL2 Hank Bauer 5.00 10.00
AL3 Yogi Berra 25.00 50.00
AL4 Walt Dropo 4.00 8.00
AL5 Nellie Fox 12.50 25.00
AL6 Jackie Jensen 5.00 10.00
AL7 Eddie Joost 4.00 8.00
AL8 George Kell 10.00 20.00
AL9 Dale Mitchell 4.00 8.00
AL10 Phil Rizzuto 15.00 30.00
AL11 Eddie Robinson 4.00 8.00
AL12 Gene Woodling 6.00 12.00
AL13 Gus Zernial 6.00 12.00
AL14 Early Wynn 10.00 20.00
AL15 Joe Dobson 4.00 8.00
AL16 Billy Pierce 6.00 12.00
AL17 Bob Lemon 10.00 20.00
AL18 Johnny Mize 10.00 20.00
AL19 Bob Porterfield 4.00 8.00
AL20 Bobby Shantz 6.00 12.00
AL21 Mickey Vernon 6.00 12.00
AL22 Dom DiMaggio 7.50 15.00
AL23 Gil McDougald 5.00 10.00
AL24 Al Rosen 5.00 10.00
AL25 Mel Parnell 4.00 8.00
AL26 Bobby Avila 4.00 8.00
NL1 Charlie Dressen MG 4.00 8.00
NL2 Bobby Adams 4.00 8.00
NL3 Richie Ashburn 12.50 25.00
NL4 Joe Black 5.00 10.00
NL5 Roy Campanella 30.00 60.00
NL6 Ted Kluszewski 7.50 15.00
NL7 Whitey Lockman 4.00 8.00
NL8 Sal Maglie 5.00 10.00
NL9 Andy Pafko 4.00 8.00
NL10 Pee Wee Reese 15.00 30.00
NL11 Robin Roberts 10.00 20.00
NL12 Red Schoendienst 10.00 20.00
NL13 Enos Slaughter 10.00 20.00
NL14 Duke Snider 30.00 60.00
NL15 Ralph Kiner 10.00 20.00
NL16 Hank Sauer 5.00 10.00
NL17 Del Ennis 5.00 10.00
NL18 Granny Hamner 5.00 10.00
NL19 Warren Spahn 15.00 30.00
NL20 Wes Westrum 4.00 8.00
NL21 Hoyt Wilhelm 10.00 20.00
NL22 Murry Dickson 4.00 8.00
NL23 Warren Hacker 4.00 8.00
NL24 Gerry Staley 4.00 8.00
NL25 Bobby Thomson 7.50 15.00
NL26 Stan Musial 50.00 100.00

1954 Red Man

The cards in this 50-card set measure approximately 3 1/2" by 4" (or 3 1/2" by 3 5/8" without the tab). The 1954 Red Man set witnessed a reduction to 25 players from each league. George Kell, Sam Mele, and Dave Philley are known to exist with two different teams. Card number 19 of the National League exists as Enos Slaughter and as Gus Bell. Card numbers are on the write-ups of the players. Cards that have the tab (coupon) attached are worth a multiple of cards without tabs. Please refer to the values below for cards with tabs. The prices listed below refer to cards without tabs. The complete set price below refers to all 54 cards including the four variations.

COMPLETE SET (54) 500.00 800.00
*CARDS WITH TABS:2.5X VALUES
AL1 Bobby Avila 4.00 8.00
AL2 Jim Busby 4.00 8.00
AL3 Nellie Fox 12.00 20.00
AL4 George Kell/(Boston) 15.00 25.00
AL4 George Kell/(Chicago) 35.00 60.00
AL5 Sherman Lollar 4.00 8.00
AL6 Sam Mele/(Baltimore) 7.00 12.00
AL6 Sam Mele/(Chicago) 25.00 40.00
AL7 Minnie Minoso 6.00 10.00
AL8 Mel Parnell 4.00 8.00
AL9 Dave Philley/(Cleveland) 7.00 12.00
AL9 Dave Philley/(Philadelphia) 25.00 40.00
AL10 Billy Pierce 6.00 10.00
AL11 Jimmy Piersall 5.00 10.00
AL12 Al Rosen 6.00 10.00
AL13 Mickey Vernon 6.00 10.00
AL14 Sammy White 4.00 8.00
AL15 Gene Woodling 6.00 10.00
AL16 Whitey Ford 15.00 25.00
AL17 Phil Rizzuto 12.00 20.00
AL18 Bob Porterfield 4.00 8.00
AL19 Chico Carrasquel 4.00 8.00
AL20 Yogi Berra 25.00 40.00
AL21 Bob Lemon 9.00 15.00
AL22 Ferris Fain 4.00 8.00
AL23 Hank Bauer 6.00 10.00
AL24 Jim Delsing 4.00 8.00
AL25 Gil McDougald 6.00 10.00
NL1 Richie Ashburn 12.00 20.00
NL2 Billy Cox 6.00 10.00
NL3 Del Crandall 6.00 10.00
NL4 Carl Erskine 6.00 10.00
NL5 Monte Irvin 7.00 12.00
NL6 Ted Kluszewski 7.00 12.00
NL7 Don Mueller 4.00 8.00
NL8 Andy Pafko 4.00 8.00
NL9 Del Rice 4.00 8.00
NL10 Red Schoendienst 9.00 15.00
NL11 Warren Spahn 12.00 20.00
NL12 Curt Simmons 6.00 10.00
NL13 Roy Campanella 30.00 50.00
NL14 Jim Gilliam 6.00 10.00
NL15 Pee Wee Reese 15.00 25.00
NL16 Duke Snider 30.00 50.00
NL17 Rip Repulski 4.00 8.00
NL18 Robin Roberts 9.00 15.00
NL19 Enos Slaughter 35.00 60.00
NL19 Gus Bell 15.00 25.00
NL20 Johnny Logan 4.00 8.00
NL21 John Antonelli 4.00 8.00
NL22 Gil Hodges 12.00 20.00
NL23 Eddie Mathews 12.00 20.00
NL24 Lew Burdette 6.00 10.00
NL25 Willie Mays 50.00 80.00

1955 Red Man

The cards in this 50-card set measure approximately 3 1/2" by 4" (or 3 1/2" by 3 5/8" without the tab). The 1955 Red Man set contains 25 players from each league. Card numbers are on the write-ups of the players. Cards that have the tab (coupon) attached are generally worth a multiple of cards which have had their tabs removed. Please see multiplier values below. The prices listed below refer to cards without tabs.

COMPLETE SET (50) 300.00 600.00
*CARDS WITH TABS:2.5X VALUES
AL1 Ray Boone 4.00 8.00
AL2 Jim Busby 4.00 8.00
AL3 Whitey Ford 15.00 30.00
AL4 Nellie Fox 12.50 25.00
AL5 Bob Grim 4.00 8.00
AL6 Jack Harshman 4.00 8.00
AL7 Jim Hegan 4.00 8.00
AL8 Bob Lemon 10.00 20.00
AL9 Irv Noren 4.00 8.00
AL10 Bob Porterfield 4.00 8.00
AL11 Al Rosen 5.00 10.00
AL12 Mickey Vernon 6.00 12.00
AL13 Vic Wertz 4.00 8.00
AL14 Early Wynn 10.00 20.00
AL15 Bobby Avila 4.00 8.00
AL16 Yogi Berra 25.00 50.00
AL17 Joe Coleman 4.00 8.00
AL18 Larry Doby 10.00 20.00
AL19 Jackie Jensen 6.00 12.00
AL20 Pete Runnels 4.00 8.00
AL21 Jimmy Piersall 5.00 10.00
AL22 Hank Bauer 5.00 10.00
AL23 Chico Carrasquel 4.00 8.00
AL24 Minnie Minoso 6.00 12.00
AL25 Sandy Consuegra 4.00 8.00
NL1 Richie Ashburn 12.50 25.00
NL2 Del Crandall 4.00 8.00
NL3 Gil Hodges 12.50 25.00
NL4 Brooks Lawrence 4.00 8.00
NL5 Johnny Logan 4.00 8.00
NL6 Sal Maglie 5.00 10.00
NL7 Willie Mays 60.00 120.00
NL8 Don Mueller 4.00 8.00
NL9 Bill Sarni 4.00 8.00
NL10 Warren Spahn 12.50 25.00
NL11 Hank Thompson 4.00 8.00
NL12 Hoyt Wilhelm 10.00 20.00
NL13 John Antonelli 4.00 8.00
NL14 Carl Erskine 6.00 12.00
NL15 Granny Hamner 4.00 8.00
NL16 Ted Kluszewski 7.50 15.00
NL17 Pee Wee Reese 15.00 30.00
NL18 Red Schoendienst 10.00 20.00
NL19 Duke Snider 30.00 60.00
NL20 Frank Thomas 5.00 10.00
NL21 Ray Jablonski 4.00 8.00
NL22 Dusty Rhodes 5.00 10.00
NL23 Gus Bell 5.00 10.00
NL24 Curt Simmons 5.00 10.00
NL25 Marv Grissom 4.00 8.00

1912 Red Sox Boston American Series PC742-1

These cream-colored cards with sepia photo and printing were issued in 1912 by the Boston American newspaper. The set features players from the 1912 Red Sox, who won the World Series. It is reasonable to assume that additional cards will be found. All additions to this checklist are appreciated. Unlike the PC 742-2 Boston Daily American Souvenir set, this set features excellent quality photos. The two most commonly found postcards from this set are Tris Speaker and Joe Wood, the others are found only on rare occassions.

COMPLETE SET (6) 500.00 1000.00
1 Forest Cady 150.00 300.00
2 Hub Perdue 150.00 300.00
3 Tris Speaker 300.00 600.00
4 Jake Stahl 150.00 300.00
5 Heinie Wagner 150.00 300.00
6 Joe Wood 250.00 500.00

1912 Red Sox Boston Daily American Souvenir PC742-2

This black and white postcard set was issued in 1912 and features players from the World Champion Boston Red Sox of that year. The printing quality of the cards are rather poor. It is thought that this checklist may be incomplete, so any additions are appreciated.

COMPLETE SET (4) 300.00 600.00
1 Forest Cady 150.00 300.00
2 Ray Collins 150.00 300.00
3 Hub Perdue 150.00 300.00
4 Heinie Wagner 150.00 300.00

1940 Red Sox Team Issue

These 25 blank-backed cards, which measure 6 1/2" by 9" feature the players photo along with a facsimile autograph. The cards are unnumbered, so we have sequenced them in alphabetical order.

COMPLETE SET 150.00 300.00
1 Jim Bagby Jr 5.00 10.00
2 Bull Butland 5.00 10.00
3 Tom Carey 5.00 10.00
4 Doc Cramer 6.00 12.00
5 Joe Cronin 10.00 20.00
6 Gene Desautels 5.00 10.00
7 Emerson Dickman 5.00 10.00
8 Dom DiMaggio 12.50 25.00
9 Bobby Doerr 10.00 20.00
10 Lou Finney 5.00 10.00
11 Jimmie Foxx 20.00 40.00
12 Denny Galehouse 5.00 10.00
13 Joe Glenn 5.00 10.00
14 Lefty Grove 15.00 30.00
15 Mickey Harris 5.00 10.00
16 Herb Hash 5.00 10.00
17 Joe Hevering 5.00 10.00
18 Leo Nonnenkamp 5.00 10.00
19 Fritz Ostermueller 5.00 10.00
20 Marv Owen 5.00 10.00
21 John Peacock 5.00 10.00
22 Jim Tabor 5.00 10.00
23 Charlie Wagner 5.00 10.00
24 Ted Williams 30.00 60.00
25 Jack Wilson 5.00 10.00

1941 Red Sox Team Issue

These 25 blank-backed cards, which measure 6 1/2" by 9" feature the players photo along with a facsimile autograph. Since these cards are unnumbered, we have sequenced them in alphabetical order.

1 Tom Carey 5.00 10.00
2 Joe Cronin 10.00 20.00
3 Emerson Dickman 5.00 10.00
4 Dom DiMaggio 10.00 20.00
5 Joe Dobson 5.00 10.00
6 Bobby Doerr 10.00 20.00
7 Lou Finney 5.00 10.00
8 Bill Fleming 5.00 10.00
9 Pete Fox 5.00 10.00
10 Jimmie Foxx 15.00 30.00
11 Lefty Grove 12.50 25.00
12 Odell Hale 5.00 10.00
13 Mickey Harris 5.00 10.00
14 Earl Johnson 5.00 10.00
15 Lefty Judd 5.00 10.00
16 Skeeter Newsome 5.00 10.00
17 Dick Newsome 5.00 10.00
18 John Peacock 5.00 10.00
19 Frank Pytlak 5.00 10.00
20 Mike Ryba 5.00 10.00
21 Stan Spence 5.00 10.00
22 Jim Tabor 5.00 10.00
23 Charlie Wagner 5.00 10.00
24 Ted Williams 40.00 80.00
25 Jack Wilson 5.00 10.00

1942 Red Sox Team Issue

This set of the Boston Red Sox measures approximately 6 1/2" by 9". The black and white photos display fascimile autographs. The backs are blank. The cards are unnumbered and are checklisted below in alphabetical order.

COMPLETE SET (25) 150.00 300.00
1 Mace Brown 5.00 10.00
2 Bill Butland 5.00 10.00
3 Paul Campbell 5.00 10.00
4 Tom Carey 5.00 10.00
5 Ken Chase 5.00 10.00
6 Bill Conroy 5.00 10.00
7 Joe Cronin 10.00 20.00
8 Dominic DiMaggio 10.00 20.00
9 Joe Dobson 5.00 10.00
10 Bob Doerr 10.00 20.00
11 Lou Finney 5.00 10.00
12 Pete Fox 5.00 10.00
13 Jimmie Foxx 20.00 40.00
14 Tex Hughson 5.00 10.00
15 Oscar Judd 5.00 10.00
16 Tony Lupien 5.00 10.00
17 Dick Newsome 5.00 10.00
18 Skeeter Newsome 5.00 10.00
19 John Peacock 5.00 10.00
20 Johnny Pesky 7.50 15.00
21 Mike Ryba 5.00 10.00
22 Jim Tabor 5.00 10.00
23 Yank Terry 5.00 10.00
24 Charles Wagner 5.00 10.00
25 Ted Williams 40.00 80.00

1943 Red Sox Team Issue

This 24-card set of the Boston Red Sox measures approximately 6 1/2" by 9" and features black-and-white player portraits with a facsimile autograph. The cards are unnumbered and checklisted below in alphabetical order.

COMPLETE SET (24) 125.00 250.00
1 Mace Brown 5.00 10.00
2 Ken Chase 5.00 10.00
3 Bill Conroy 5.00 10.00
4 Joe Cronin 10.00 20.00
5 Joe Dobson 5.00 10.00
6 Bob Doerr 10.00 20.00
7 Pete Fox 5.00 10.00
8 Ford Garrison 5.00 10.00
9 Tex Hughson 5.00 10.00
10 Oscar Judd 5.00 10.00
11 Andy Karl 5.00 10.00
12 Eddie Lake 5.00 10.00
13 John Lazor 5.00 10.00
14 Lou Lucier 5.00 10.00
15 Tony Lupien 5.00 10.00
16 Dee Miles 5.00 10.00
17 Dick Newsome 5.00 10.00
18 Skeeter Newsome 5.00 10.00
19 Roy Partee 5.00 10.00
20 John Peacock 5.00 10.00
21 Mike Ryba 5.00 10.00
22 Al Simmons 25.00 50.00
23 Jim Tabor 5.00 10.00
24 Yank Terry 5.00 10.00

1946 Red Sox Team Issue

These 25 cards measure approximately 6 1/2" by 9". They feature members of the 1946 American League pennant winners Red Sox. The set can be dated by Ernie Andres whose only year in the majors was 1946.

COMPLETE SET (25) 150.00 300.00
1 Ernie Andres 4.00 8.00
2 Jim Bagby Jr 4.00 8.00
3 Mace Brown 4.00 8.00
4 Joe Cronin 12.50 25.00
5 Leon Culberson 4.00 8.00
6 Mel Deutsch 4.00 8.00
7 Dom DiMaggio 12.50 25.00
8 Joe Dobson 4.00 8.00
9 Bob Doerr 12.50 25.00
10 Dave Ferriss 4.00 8.00
11 Mickey Harris 4.00 8.00
12 Randy Heflin 4.00 8.00
13 Tex Hughson 4.00 8.00
14 Earl Johnson 4.00 8.00
15 Ed McGah 4.00 8.00
16 George Metkovich 4.00 8.00
17 Roy Partee 4.00 8.00
18 Eddie Pellagrini 4.00 8.00
19 Johnny Pesky 6.00 12.00
20 Rip Russell 4.00 8.00
21 Mike Ryba 4.00 8.00
22 Charlie Wagner 4.00 8.00
23 Hal Wagner 4.00 8.00
24 Ted Williams 40.00 80.00
25 Rudy York 6.00 12.00

1947 Red Sox Team Issue

This 25-card set of the Boston Red Sox team measures approximately 6 1/2" by 9" and features black-and-white player portraits. A facsimile autograph is printed on each photo. The backs are blank. The cards are unnumbered and checklisted below in alphabetical order.

COMPLETE SET (25) 150.00 300.00
1 Joe Cronin MG 7.50 15.00
2 Leon Culberson 4.00 8.00
3 Dom DiMaggio 7.50 15.00
4 Joseph Dobson 4.00 8.00
5 Bob Doerr 7.50 15.00
6 Harry Dorish 4.00 8.00
7 David Boo Ferriss 4.00 8.00
8 Tommy Fine 4.00 8.00
9 Don Gutteridge 4.00 8.00
10 Mickey Harris 4.00 8.00
11 Tex Hughson 4.00 8.00
12 Earl Johnson 4.00 8.00
13 Bob Klinger 4.00 8.00
14 Sam Mele 4.00 8.00
15 Wally Moses 5.00 10.00
16 Johnny Murphy 4.00 8.00
17 Mel Parnell 5.00 10.00
18 Roy Partee 4.00 8.00
19 Eddie Pellagrini 4.00 8.00
20 Johnny Pesky 6.00 12.00
21 Rip Russell 4.00 8.00
22 Birdie Tebbetts 5.00 10.00
23 Ted Williams 40.00 80.00
24 Rudy York 6.00 12.00
25 Bill Zuber 4.00 8.00

1948 Red Sox Team Issue

These 25 photos measure approximately 6 1/2" by 9". They feature members of the 1948 Boston Red Sox. The photos take up almost the entire surface and are surrounded by white borders. A fascimile autograph is also on each photo. The backs are blank and we have sequenced this set in alphabetical order.

COMPLETE SET (25) 150.00 300.00
1 Matt Batts 4.00 8.00
2 Dom DiMaggio 10.00 20.00
3 Joe Dobson 4.00 8.00
4 Bobby Doerr 10.00 20.00
5 Harry Dorish 4.00 8.00
6 Dave Boo Ferriss 4.00 8.00
7 Denny Galehouse 4.00 8.00
8 Bill Goodman 6.00 12.00
9 Mickey Harris 4.00 8.00
10 Billy Hitchcock 4.00 8.00
11 Earl Johnson 4.00 8.00
12 Jake Jones 4.00 8.00
13 Ellis Kinder 4.00 8.00
14 Jack Kramer 4.00 8.00
15 Joe McCarthy MG 10.00 20.00
16 Maurice McDermott 4.00 8.00
17 Sam Mele 4.00 8.00
18 Wally Moses 4.00 8.00
19 Mel Parnell 6.00 12.00
20 Johnny Pesky 6.00 12.00
21 Stan Spence 4.00 8.00
22 Vern Stephens 6.00 12.00
23 Chuck Stobbs 4.00 8.00
24 Birdie Tebbetts 4.00 8.00
25 Ted Williams 40.00 80.00

1949 Red Sox Team Issue

This 25-card set of the Boston Red Sox team measures approximately 6 1/2" by 9" and features black-and-white player portraits with white borders. A fascimile autograph is printed on each photo. The backs are blank. The cards are unnumbered and checklisted below in alphabetical order.

COMPLETE SET (25) 150.00 300.00
1 Matt Batts 4.00 8.00
2 Merrill Combs 4.00 8.00
3 Dom DiMaggio 7.50 15.00
4 Joe Dobson 4.00 8.00
5 Bob Doerr 7.50 15.00
6 David Boo Ferriss 4.00 8.00
7 Bill Goodman 6.00 12.00
8 Mickey Harris 4.00 8.00
9 Billy Hitchcock 4.00 8.00
10 Tex Hughson 4.00 8.00
11 Earl Johnson 4.00 8.00
12 Ellis Kinder 4.00 8.00
13 Jack Kramer 4.00 8.00
14 Joe McCarthy MG 7.50 15.00
15 Sam Mele 4.00 8.00
16 Tommy O'Brien 4.00 8.00
17 Mel Parnell 6.00 12.00
18 Johnny Pesky 6.00 12.00
19 Frank Quinn 4.00 8.00
20 Vern Stephens 6.00 12.00
21 Chuck Stobbs 4.00 8.00
22 Lou Stringer 4.00 8.00
23 Birdie Tebbetts 4.00 8.00
24 Ted Williams 40.00 80.00
25 Al Zarilla 4.00 8.00

1950 Red Sox Clark Locksmith

This four-card set features black-and-white photos of Boston Red Sox players and measures approximately 2 3/4" by 3 3/4".

COMPLETE SET (4) 25.00 50.00
1 Bobby Doerr 5.00 10.00
2 Ted Williams 12.50 25.00
3 Dom DiMaggio 7.50 15.00
4 Johnny Pesky 2.50 5.00

1950 Red Sox Team Issue

This 30-card set of the Boston Red Sox team measures approximately 6 1/2" by 9" and features black-and-white player portraits with white borders. A fascimile autograph is printed on each photo. The backs are blank. The cards are unnumbered and checklisted below in alphabetical order. Earl Johnson, Ken Keltner, Joe McCarthy, Al Papai and Charley Schanz were issued originally and were replaced in the second series with Dick Littlefield, Willard Nixon, Steve O'Neill, George Susce, and Clyde Vollmer. All of these 10 people are notated with SP's below.

COMPLETE SET (30) 125.00 250.00
COMMON CARD (1-30) 2.00 4.00
COMMON SP 5.00 10.00
1 Matt Batts 2.00 4.00
2 Earle Combs CO 4.00 8.00
3 Dom DiMaggio 4.00 8.00
4 Joe Dobson 2.00 4.00
5 Bob Doerr 4.00 8.00
6 Walter Dropo 2.50 5.00
7 Bill Goodman 2.00 4.00
8 Earl Johnson SP 5.00 10.00
9 Ken Keltner SP 6.00 12.00
10 Ellis Kinder 2.00 4.00
11 Dick Littlefield SP 5.00 10.00
12 Walter Masterson 2.00 4.00
13 Joe McCarthy MG SP 10.00 20.00
14 Maurice McDermott 2.00 4.00
15 Willard Nixon SP 5.00 10.00
16 Steve O'Neill MG SP 6.00 12.00
17 Al Papai SP 5.00 10.00
18 Mel Parnell 3.00 6.00
19 Johnny Pesky 3.00 6.00
20 Buddy Rosar 2.00 4.00
21 Charley Schanz SP 5.00 10.00
22 Vern Stephens 3.00 6.00
23 Chuck Stobbs 2.00 4.00
24 Lou Stringer 2.00 4.00
25 George Susce SP 5.00 10.00
26 Birdie Tebbetts 2.50 5.00
27 Clyde Vollmer SP 10.00 20.00
28 Ted Williams 20.00 40.00
29 Tom Wright 2.00 4.00
30 Al Zarilla 2.00 4.00

1953 Red Sox First National Super Market Stores

This four-card set features black-and-white player photos and measures approximately 3 3/4" by 5". The backs carry advertising for the stores. The cards are unnumbered and checklisted below in alphabetical order. A reprint of this set was made in the early 80's.

COMPLETE SET (4) 150.00 300.00
1 Bill Goodman 40.00 80.00
2 Ellis Kinder 40.00 80.00
3 Mel Parnell 50.00 100.00
4 Sammy White 40.00 80.00

1953 Red Sox Team Issue

This set of the Boston Red Sox measures approximately 6 1/2" by 9". The black-and-white player photos display fascimile autographs. The backs are blank. The cards are unnumbered and checklisted below in alphabetical order.

COMPLETE SET (30) 125.00 250.00
1 Milt Bolling 4.00 8.00
2 Lou Boudreau 7.50 15.00
3 Harold Brown 4.00 8.00
4 Bill Consolo 4.00 8.00
5 Dom DiMaggio 7.50 15.00
6 Hoot Evers 4.00 8.00
7 Ben Flowers 4.00 8.00
8 Hershell Freeman 4.00 8.00
9 Dick Gernert 4.00 8.00
10 Bill Goodman 6.00 12.00
11 Marv Grissom 4.00 8.00
12 Ken Holcombe 4.00 8.00
13 Sid Hudson 4.00 8.00
14 George Kell 7.50 15.00
15 Bill Kennedy 4.00 8.00
16 Ellis Kinder 6.00 12.00
17 Ted Lepcio 4.00 8.00
18 Johnny Lipon 4.00 8.00
19 Maurice McDermott 4.00 8.00
20 John Merson 4.00 8.00
21 Gus Niarhos 4.00 8.00
22 Willard Nixon 4.00 8.00
23 Mel Parnell 6.00 12.00
24 Jimmy Piersall 7.50 15.00
25 Gene Stephens 4.00 8.00
26 Tommy Umphlett 4.00 8.00
27 Bill Werle 4.00 8.00
28 Sam White 4.00 8.00
29 Del Wilber 4.00 8.00
30 Al Zarilla 4.00 8.00

1954 Red Sox Team Issue

These 30 blank-backed cards, which measure 6 1/2" by 9" feature members of the 1954 Boston Red Sox. The fronts feature the players photo along with a fascimile autograph. Since these cards are unnumbered, we have sequenced them in alphabetical order. One of the very few Harry Agganis cards printed during his short career is in this set.

COMPLETE SET 150.00 300.00
1 Harry Agganis 15.00 30.00
2 Milt Bolling 4.00 8.00
3 Lou Boudreau MG 7.50 15.00
4 Tom Brewer 4.00 8.00
5 Hal Brown 4.00 8.00
6 Tex Clevenger 4.00 8.00
7 Billy Consolo 4.00 8.00
8 Joe Dobson 4.00 8.00
9 Hoot Evers 4.00 8.00
10 Dick Gernert 4.00 8.00
11 Billy Goodman 5.00 10.00
12 Bill Henry 4.00 8.00
13 Tom Herrin 4.00 8.00
14 Sid Hudson 4.00 8.00
15 Jackie Jensen 6.00 12.00
16 George Kell 7.50 15.00
17 Leo Kiely 4.00 8.00
18 Ellis Kinder 4.00 8.00
19 Ted Lepcio 4.00 8.00
20 Charlie Maxwell 4.00 8.00
21 Willard Nixon 4.00 8.00
22 Karl Olson 4.00 8.00
23 Mickey Owen CO 4.00 8.00
24 Mel Parnell 5.00 10.00
25 Jimmy Piersall 6.00 12.00
26 Frank Sullivan 4.00 8.00
27 Bill Werle 4.00 8.00
28 Sammy White 4.00 8.00
29 Del Wilber 4.00 8.00
30 Ted Williams 40.00 80.00

1958 Red Sox Jay Publishing

This 12-card set of the Boston Red Sox measures approximately 5" by 7" and features black-and-white player photos in a white border. These cards were packaged 12 to a packet. The backs are blank. The cards are unnumbered and checklisted below in alphabetical order.

COMPLETE SET (12) 30.00 60.00
1 Tom Brewer 1.50 3.00
2 Don Buddin 1.50 3.00
3 Dick Gernert 1.50 3.00
4 Mike Higgins MG 1.50 3.00
5 Jack Jensen 2.50 5.00
6 Frank Malzone 2.50 5.00
7 Jim Piersall 2.50 5.00
8 Pete Runnels 2.00 4.00
9 Gene Stephens 1.50 3.00
10 Frank Sullivan 1.50 3.00
11 Sam White 1.50 3.00
12 Ted Williams 12.50 25.00

1959 Red Sox Jay Publishing

This 12-card set of the Boston Red Sox measures approximately 5" by 7" and features black-and-white player photos in a white border. These cards were packaged 12 to a packet and originally sold for 25 cents. The backs are blank. The cards are unnumbered and checklisted below in alphabetical order.

COMPLETE SET (12) 30.00 60.00
1 Tom Brewer 1.50 3.00
2 Dick Gernert 1.50 3.00
3 Mike Higgins 1.50 3.00
4 Jackie Jensen 2.50 5.00
5 Frank Malzone 2.50 5.00
6 Gene Mauch 1.50 3.00
7 Jimmy Piersall 2.50 5.00
8 Dave Sisler 1.50 3.00
9 Gene Stephens 1.50 3.00
10 Frank Sullivan 1.50 3.00
11 Sammy White 1.50 3.00
12 Ted Williams 12.50 25.00

1960 Red Sox Jay Publishing

This 12-card set of the Boston Red Sox measures approximately 5" by 7" and features black-and-white player photos in a white border. These cards were packaged 12 to a packet. The backs are blank. The cards are unnumbered and checklisted below in alphabetical order.

COMPLETE SET (12) 15.00 40.00
1 Tom Brewer .75 2.00
2 Don Buddin .75 2.00
3 Jerry Casale .75 2.00
4 Ike Delock .75 2.00
5 Jerry(Pumpsie) Green .75 2.00
6 Bill Jurges MG .75 2.00
7 Frank Malzone 1.25 3.00
8 Pete Runnels 1.00 2.50
9 Gene Stephens .75 2.00
10 Bobby Thomson 1.50 4.00
11 Vic Wertz .75 2.00
12 Ted Williams 10.00 25.00

1962 Red Sox Jay Publishing

Like other Jay Publishing issues these black-and-white, blank-backed, white-bordered, 5" X 7" photos. The player's name and team are printed in black within the lower margin. The photos are unnumbered and checklisted below in alphabetical order. This set has more than 12 cards since two different versions were issued during 1962.

COMPLETE SET 15.00 40.00
1 Ed Bressoud .75 2.00
2 Lou Clinton .75 2.00
3 Gene Conley 1.00 2.50
4 Gary Geiger .75 2.00
5 Carroll Hardy .75 2.00
6 Mike Higgins MG .75 2.00
7 Frank Malzone 1.25 3.00
8 Bill Monbouquette .75 2.00
9 Russ Nixon .75 2.00
10 Pete Runnels .75 2.00
11 Chuck Schilling .75 2.00
12 Don Schwall .75 2.00
13 Carl Yastrzemski UER 8.00 20.00
Misspelled Yastremski

1963 Red Sox Jay Publishing

This 12-card set of the Boston Red Sox measures approximately 5" by 7". The fronts feature black-and-white posed player photos with the player's and team name printed below in the white border. These cards were packaged 12 to a packet. The backs are blank. The cards are unnumbered and checklisted below in alphabetical order.

COMPLETE SET (12) 20.00 50.00
1 Ed Bressoud .75 2.00
2 Lou Clinton .75 2.00
3 Gary Geiger .75 2.00
4 Frank Malzone 1.25 3.00
5 Roman Mejias .75 2.00
6 Bill Monbouquette .75 2.00
7 Johnny Pesky MG 1.00 2.50
8 Dick Radatz 1.00 2.50
9 Chuck Schilling .75 2.00
10 Dick Stuart .75 2.00
11 Bob Tillman .75 2.00
12 Carl Yastrzemski 8.00 20.00

1964 Red Sox Jay Publishing

This 12-card set of the Boston Red Sox measures approximately 5" by 7". The fronts feature black-and-white posed player photos with the player's and team name printed below in the white border. These cards were packaged 12 to a packet. The backs are blank. The cards are unnumbered and checklisted below in alphabetical order.

COMPLETE SET (12) 20.00 50.00
1 Ed Bressoud .75 2.00
2 Lou Clinton .75 2.00
3 Gary Geiger .75 2.00
4 Frank Malzone 1.25 3.00
5 Felix Mantilla .75 2.00
6 Bill Monbouquette .75 2.00
7 Russ Nixon .75 2.00
8 Johnny Pesky MG 1.00 2.50
9 Dick Radatz 1.00 2.50
10 Chuck Schilling .75 2.00
11 Dick Stuart 1.00 2.50
12 Carl Yastrzemski 8.00 20.00

1964 Red Sox Team Issue

This eight-card set of the Boston Red Sox measures approximately 8" by 10" and features color portraits with a white border and a facsimile autograph. The backs are blank. The photos were packaged eight to a clear plastic packet and originally sold for 50 cents at the park or through the mail. They were also inserted one to each Red Sox year book. The cards are unnumbered and checklisted below in alphabetical order.

COMPLETE SET (8) 15.00 40.00
1 Ed Bressoud 1.50 4.00
2 Jack Lamabe 1.50 3.00
3 Frank Malzone 2.50 6.00
4 Bill Monbouquette 2.00 5.00
5 Johnny Pesky 2.00 5.00
6 Dick Radatz 2.00 5.00
7 Dick Stuart 2.00 5.00
8 Carl Yastrzemski 8.00 20.00

1965 Red Sox Jay Publishing

This 12-card set of the Boston Red Sox measures approximately 5" by 7". The fronts feature black-and-white posed player photos with the player's and team name printed below in the white border. These cards were packaged 12 to a packet. The backs are blank. The cards are unnumbered and checklisted below in alphabetical order.

COMPLETE SET (12)	15.00	40.00
1 Dennis Bennett	.75	2.00
2 Ed Bressoud	.75	2.00
3 Tony Conigliaro	2.00	5.00
4 Billy Herman MG	1.50	4.00
5 Frank Malzone	1.25	3.00
6 Felix Mantilla	.75	2.00
7 Bill Monbouquette	.75	2.00
8 Dick Radatz	1.00	2.50
9 Lee Thomas	.75	2.00
10 John Tillman	.75	2.00
11 Earl Wilson	.75	2.00
12 Carl Yastrzemski	8.00	20.00

1965 Red Sox Team Issue

This 18-card set of the 1965 Boston Red Sox features color player photos measuring approximately 7 7/8" by 9 7/8" with a white border. A facsimile autograph is printed across the bottom of the photo. The cards were packaged in a clear plastic packet and was originally sold for $1 at the park or through the mail. They were also inserted one to each Red Sox year book. The backs are blank. The cards are unnumbered and checklisted below in alphabetical order. Although the photos were sold 16 at a time, turnover within the team's roster made for an expanded set

COMPLETE SET	40.00	80.00
1 Dennis Bennett	1.50	4.00
2 Ed Bressoud	1.50	4.00
3 Tony Conigliaro	5.00	12.00
4 Bob Heffner	1.50	4.00
5 Billy Herman MG	3.00	8.00
6 Tony Horton		
7 Jack Lamabe	1.50	4.00
8 Frank Malzone	2.50	6.00
9 Felix Mantilla	1.50	4.00
10 Bill Monbouquette	1.50	4.00
11 Dave Morehead	1.50	4.00
12 Dick Radatz	2.00	5.00
13 Jerry Stephenson	1.50	4.00
14 Dick Stuart		
15 Lee Thomas	1.50	4.00
16 Bob Tillman	1.50	4.00
17 Earl Wilson	1.50	4.00
18 Carl Yastrzemski	12.50	30.00

1966 Red Sox Team Issue

This 16-card set of the 1966 Boston Red Sox features color player photos measuring approximately 7 3/4" by 9 7/8" with a white border. A facsimile autograph is printed at the bottom of the photo. The photos were packaged in a clear plastic packet and was originally sold for $1 at the park or through the mail. They were also inserted one to each Red Sox year book. The backs are blank. The cards are unnumbered and checklisted below in alphabetical order.

COMPLETE SET (16)	40.00	80.00
1 Dennis Bennett	1.50	4.00
2 Tony Conigliaro	3.00	8.00
3 Joe Foy	1.50	4.00
4 Jim Gosger	1.50	4.00
5 Tony Horton	2.00	5.00
6 Jim Lonborg	2.50	6.00
7 Dave Morehead	1.50	4.00
8 Dan Osinski	1.50	4.00
9 Rico Petrocelli	2.50	6.00
10 Dick Radatz	2.00	5.00
11 Mike Ryan	1.50	4.00
12 Bob Sadowski	1.50	4.00
13 George Smith	1.50	4.00
14 George Thomas	1.50	4.00
15 Earl Wilson	1.50	4.00
16 Carl Yastrzemski	10.00	25.00

1967 Red Sox Stickers Topps

This was a limited production "test" issue for Topps. It is very similar to the Pirates "test" issue preceding. The stickers are blank backed and measure 2 1/2" by 3 1/2". The stickers look like cards from the front and are somewhat attractive in spite of the "no neck" presentation of many of the players' photos. The cards are numbered on the front.

COMPLETE SET (33)	350.00	700.00
WRAPPER (5-CENT)	20.00	50.00
1 Dennis Bennett	10.00	25.00
2 Darrell Brandon	10.00	25.00
3 Tony Conigliaro	15.00	40.00
4 Don Demeter	10.00	25.00
5 Hank Fischer	10.00	25.00
6 Joe Foy	10.00	25.00
7 Mike Andrews	10.00	25.00
8 Dalton Jones	10.00	25.00
9 Jim Lonborg	12.50	30.00
10 Don McMahon	10.00	25.00
11 Dave Morehead	10.00	25.00
12 Reggie Smith	15.00	40.00
13 Rico Petrocelli	12.50	30.00
14 Mike Ryan	10.00	25.00
15 Jose Santiago	10.00	25.00
16 George Scott	12.50	30.00
17 Sal Maglie CO	12.50	30.00
18 George Smith	10.00	25.00
19 Lee Stange	10.00	25.00
20 Jerry Stephenson	10.00	25.00
21 Jose Tartabull	10.00	25.00
22 George Thomas	10.00	25.00
23 Bob Tillman	10.00	25.00
24 John Wyatt	10.00	25.00
25 Carl Yastrzemski	100.00	200.00
26 Dick Williams MG	15.00	40.00
27 I Love the Red Sox	10.00	25.00
28 Let's Go Red Sox	10.00	25.00
29 Carl Yastrzemski for Mayor	50.00	100.00
30 Tony Conigliaro is my Hero	20.00	50.00
31 Happiness is a Boston Win	10.00	25.00
32 Red Sox Logo	10.00	25.00
33 Red Sox Pennant	10.00	25.00

1967 Red Sox Team Issue

These 16 blank backed cards measure approximately 4" by 5 5/8" and have white borders. They were issued in two series and were available at the ball park or via the mail for 50 cents per pack. They were issued in two series and we have sequenced them alphabetically by series.

COMPLETE SET (16)	15.00	40.00
1 Tony Conigliaro A	1.50	4.00
2 Joe Foy A	.75	2.00
3 Jim Lonborg A	1.25	3.00
4 Don McMahon A	.75	2.00
5 Rico Petrocelli A	1.25	3.00
6 George Scott A	1.00	2.50
7 Lee Stange A	.75	2.00
8 Carl Yastrzemski A	4.00	10.00
9 Darrell Brandon B	.75	2.00
10 Russ Gibson B	.75	2.00
11 Bill Rohr B	.75	2.00
12 Mike Ryan B	.75	2.00
13 Reggie Smith B	2.50	6.00
14 Jose Tartabull B	.75	2.00
15 George Thomas B	.75	2.00
16 John Wyatt B	.75	2.00

1968 Red Sox Team Issue

This eight-card set of the 1968 Boston Red Sox measures approximately 5 1/2" by 7 1/2". The fronts feature black-and-white player portraits with facsimile autographs and white borders. The backs are blank. The cards are unnumbered and checklisted below in alphabetical order. The set may be incomplete and any confirmed additions would be appreciated.

COMPLETE SET (8)	10.00	25.00
1 Mike Andrews	.75	2.00
2 Darrell Brandon	.75	2.00
3 Bobby Doerr	2.00	5.00
4 Ken Harrelson	2.00	5.00
5 Jim Lonborg	1.50	4.00
6 Rico Petrocelli	2.00	5.00
7 Reggie Smith	2.00	5.00
8 Dick Williams MG	2.00	5.00

1969 Red Sox Arco Oil

Sponsored by Arco Oil, this 12-card set features photos of the 1969 Boston Red Sox. The cards are unnumbered and checklisted below in alphabetical order.

COMPLETE SET (12)	40.00	80.00
1 Mike Andrews	2.00	5.00
2 Tony Conigliaro	4.00	10.00
3 Ray Culp	2.00	5.00
4 Russ Gibson	2.00	5.00
5 Dalton Jones	2.00	5.00
6 Jim Lonborg	3.00	8.00
7 Sparky Lyle	4.00	10.00
8 Syd O'Brien	2.00	5.00
9 Rico Petrocelli	3.00	8.00
10 Geo. Scott	2.50	6.00
11 Reggie Smith	3.00	8.00
12 Carl Yastrzemski	8.00	20.00

1969 Red Sox Team Issue

This 12-card set of the Boston Red Sox measures approximately 4 1/4" by 7". The fronts display black-and-white player portraits bordered in white. The player's name and team are printed in the top margin. The backs are blank. The cards are unnumbered and checklisted below in alphabetical order.

COMPLETE SET (12)	12.50	30.00
1 Mike Andrews	.75	2.00
2 Tony Conigliaro	1.50	4.00
3 Russ Gibson	.75	2.00
4 Dalton Jones	.75	2.00
5 Bill Landis	.75	2.00
6 Jim Lonborg	1.25	3.00
7 Sparky Lyle	1.50	4.00
8 Rico Petrocelli	1.25	3.00
9 George Scott	1.00	2.50
10 Reggie Smith	1.00	2.50
11 Dick Williams MG	1.00	2.50
12 Carl Yastrzemski	3.00	8.00

1969 Red Sox Team Issue Color

This 10-card set features color portraits of the Boston Red Sox with white borders and measures approximately 7" by 8 3/4". The backs are blank. The cards are unnumbered and checklisted below in alphabetical order.

COMPLETE SET (10)	15.00	40.00
1 Mike Andrews	1.25	3.00
2 Tony Conigliaro	2.50	6.00
3 Ray Culp	1.25	3.00
4 Russ Gibson	1.25	3.00
5 James Lonborg	2.00	5.00
6 Rico Petrocelli	2.00	5.00
7 George Scott,	1.50	4.00
8 Reggie Smith	2.00	5.00
9 Dick Williams	1.50	4.00
10 Carl Yastrzemski	4.00	10.00

1970 Red Sox Color Photo Post Cards

This set features members of the 1970 Boston Red Sox. These color post cards are unnumbered and we have sequenced them in alphabetical order.

COMPLETE SET	12.50	30.00
1 Luis Alvarado	.40	1.00
2 Mike Andrews	.40	1.00
3 Ken Brett	.60	1.50
4 Bill Conigliaro	.60	1.50
5 Tony Conigliaro	1.00	2.50
6 Ray Culp	.40	1.00
7 Sparky Lyle	1.00	2.50
8 Gerry Moses	.40	1.00
9 Mike Nagy	.40	1.00
10 Gary Peters	.60	1.50
11 Rico Petrocelli	.75	2.00
12 George Scott	.60	1.50
13 Sonny Siebert	.40	1.00
14 Reggie Smith	.75	2.00
15 Lee Stange	.40	1.00
16 Carl Yastrzemski	3.00	8.00
17 Jim Lonborg (oversize)	.75	2.00

1971 Red Sox Arco Oil

Sponsored by Arco Oil, these 12 pictures of the 1971 Boston Red Sox measure approximately 8" by 10" and feature on their fronts white-bordered posed color player photos. The player's name is shown in black lettering within the white margin below the photo. His facsimile autograph appears across the picture. The white back carries the team's and player's names at the top, followed below by position, biography, career highlights, and statistics. An ad at the bottom for picture frames rounds out the back. The cards are unnumbered and checklisted below in alphabetical order.

COMPLETE SET (12)	30.00	60.00
1 Luis Aparicio	4.00	10.00
2 Ken Brett	2.00	5.00
3 Billy Conigliaro	2.50	6.00
4 Ray Culp	2.00	5.00
5 Doug Griffin	2.00	5.00
6 Bob Montgomery	2.00	5.00
7 Gary Peters	2.00	5.00
8 George Scott	2.50	6.00
9 Sonny Siebert	2.00	5.00
10 Reggie Smith	2.50	6.00
11 Ken Tatum	2.00	5.00
12 Carl Yastrzemski	5.00	12.00

1971 Red Sox Team Issue

These 12 photos measure approximately 4 1/4" by 7". The player's name and team are noted on the top with the rest of the front dedicated to a photo. The backs are blank. We have sequenced this set in alphabetical order. The set is dated 1971 as that was Luis Aparicio's first year with the Red Sox and Sparky Lyle's last season with the club.

COMPLETE SET (12)	10.00	25.00
1 Luis Aparicio	1.25	3.00
2 Billy Conigliaro	.75	2.00
3 Ray Culp	.60	1.50
4 Duane Josephson	.60	1.50
5 Jim Lonborg	1.00	2.50
6 Sparky Lyle	1.00	2.50
7 Gary Peters	.60	1.50
8 Rico Petrocelli	1.00	2.50
9 George Scott	.75	2.00
10 Sonny Siebert	.60	1.50
11 Reggie Smith	.75	2.00
12 Carl Yastrzemski	2.00	5.00

1972 Red Sox Team Issue

This 23-card set of the Boston Red Sox features borderless black-and-white player portraits with a facsimile autograph. The backs are blank. The cards are unnumbered and checklisted below in alphabetical order. Carlton Fisk has a card in his Rookie Card year.

COMPLETE SET (23)	8.00	20.00
1 Juan Beniquez	.20	.50
2 Bob Bolin	.20	.50
3 Danny Cater	.20	.50
4 John Curtis	.20	.50
5 Mike Fiore	.20	.50
6 Carlton Fisk	3.00	8.00
7 Phil Gagliano	.20	.50
8 Doug Griffin	.20	.50
9 Tommy Harper	.30	.75
10 John Kennedy	.20	.50
11 Lew Krausse	.20	.50
12 Joe Lahoud	.20	.50
13 Bill Lee	.40	1.00
14 Lynn McGlothlin	.20	.50
15 Rick Miller	.30	.75
16 Bob Montgomery	.20	.50
17 Roger Moret	.20	.50
18 Ben Oglivie	.30	.75
19 Marty Pattin	.20	.50
20 Don Pavletich	.20	.50
21 Ken Tatum	.20	.50
22 Luis Tiant	.40	1.00
23 Carl Yastrzemski	3.00	8.00

1975 Red Sox Herald

This 26 card set was issued as an insert in the two Boston Herald papers over a period of time and featured drawings by sports artist Phil Bissell.

COMPLETE SET	12.50	30.00
1 Carl Yastrzemski	2.00	5.00
2 Fred Lynn	2.00	5.00
3 Jim Rice	2.00	5.00
4 Carlton Fisk	2.00	5.00
5 Bill Lee	.40	1.00
6 Rick Wise	.20	.50
7 Rico Petrocelli	.40	1.00
8 Luis Tiant	.75	2.00
9 Bernie Carbo	.20	.50
10 Bob Heise	.20	.50
11 Juan Beniquez	.20	.50
12 Jim Willoughby	.20	.50
13 Jim Burton	.20	.50
14 Dick Pole	.20	.50
15 Reggie Cleveland	.20	.50
16 Tim Blackwell	.20	.50
17 Cecil Cooper	.40	1.00
18 Dick Drago	.20	.50
19 Dwight Evans	.75	2.00
20 Rick Burleson	.60	1.50
21 Doug Griffin	.20	.50
22 Rick Miller	.20	.50
23 Roger Moret	.20	.50
24 Diego Segui	.20	.50
25 Bob Montgomery	.20	.50
26 Denny Doyle	.20	.50

1975 Red Sox 1946 TCMA

This 43-card set of the 1946 Boston Red Sox team was printed in 1975 by TCMA and features white-and-blue tinted player photos with red lettering. The backs carry player information. The cards are unnumbered and checklisted below in alphabetical order. Card number 43 pictures five players and measures 3 1/2" by 5" instead of the standard size.

COMPLETE SET (43)	10.00	25.00
1 Jim Bagby	.20	.50
2 Floyd Baker	.20	.50
3 Mace Brown	.20	.50
4 Bill Butland	.20	.50
5 Paul Campbell	.20	.50
6 Tom Carey	.20	.50
7 Joe Cronin P MG	.75	2.00
8 Leon Culbertson	.20	.50
9 Tom Daly CO	.20	.50
10 Dom DiMaggio	.60	1.50
11 Joe Dobson	.20	.50
12 Bob Doerr	.75	2.00
13 Clem Dreisewerd	.20	.50
14 Boo Ferriss	.20	.50
15 Andy Gilbert	.20	.50
16 Don Gutteridge	.20	.50
17 Mickey Harris	.20	.50
18 Randy Heflin	.20	.50
19 Pinky Higgins	.20	.50
20 Tex Hughson	.20	.50
21 Earl Johnson	.20	.50
22 Bob Klinger	.20	.50
23 John Lazor	.20	.50
24 Thomas McBride	.20	.50
25 Ed McGah	.20	.50
26 Catfish Metkovich	.20	.50
27 Wally Moses	.40	1.00
28 Roy Partee	.20	.50
29 Eddie Pellargini	.20	.50
30 Johnny Pesky	.60	1.50
31 Frank Pytlak	.20	.50
32 Rip Russell	.20	.50
33 Mike Ryba	.20	.50
34 Ben Steiner	.20	.50
35 Charlie Wagner	.20	.50
36 Hal Wagner	.20	.50
37 Ted Williams	2.00	5.00
38 Larry Woodall CO	.20	.50
39 Larry Woodall CO Charlie Wagner Floyd Baker	.20	.50
40 Rudy York	.40	1.00
41 B. Zuber	.20	.50
42 Six player card	.40	1.00
43 Five player card	.40	1.00

1976 Red Sox Star Market

This 16-card set of the Boston Red Sox measures approximately 5 7/8" by 9". The white-bordered fronts feature color player head photos with a facsimile autograph. The backs are blank. The cards are unnumbered and checklisted below in alphabetical order.

COMPLETE SET (16)	15.00	40.00
1 Rick Burleson	.75	2.00
2 Reggie Cleveland	.40	1.00
3 Cecil Cooper	1.00	2.50
4 Denny Doyle	.40	1.00
5 Dwight Evans	1.50	4.00
6 Carlton Fisk	3.00	8.00
7 Tom House	.40	1.00
8 Fergie Jenkins	1.50	4.00
9 Bill Lee	.75	2.00
10 Fred Lynn	1.00	2.50
11 Rick Miller	.40	1.00
12 Rico Petrocelli	.75	2.00
13 Jim Rice	1.50	4.00
14 Luis Tiant	1.00	2.50
15 Rick Wise	.40	1.00
16 Carl Yastrzemski	3.00	8.00

1976-77 Red Sox

This nine-card set of the Boston Red Sox measures approximately 7" by 8 1/2". The fronts feature white-bordered color player action photos with the player's name printed in black in the bottom margin. The backs are blank. The cards are unnumbered and checklisted below in alphabetical order. These cards were issued over a two year period as eight card sets. They are listed together since there is no difference other than Rico Petrocelli retired after the 1976 season and was replaced by George Scott.

COMPLETE SET (9)	8.00	20.00
1 Rick Burleson	.75	2.00
2 Denny Doyle	.60	1.50
3 Dwight Evans	1.25	3.00
4 Carlton Fisk	2.00	5.00
5 Fred Lynn	1.25	3.00
6 Rico Petrocelli '76	1.00	2.50
7 Jim Rice	1.25	3.00
8 George Scott '77	1.00	2.50
9 Carl Yastrzemski	1.25	3.00

1979 Red Sox Early Favorites

This 25-card set measures 2 1/2" by 3 3/4". The set covers the early years of Tom Yawkey's ownership. The photos are all black and white.

COMPLETE SET (25)	8.00	20.00
1 New Fenway Park	.40	1.00
2 Mrs. Tom Yawkey Mrs. Eddie Collins	.30	.75
3 1932 Outfielders Tom Oliver Earl Webb Jack Roth	.30	.75
4 Ace Pitchers John Marcum Wes Ferrell Lefty Grov	.30	.75
5 John Gooch	.30	.75
6 Pitching recruits with (Joe Cronin Lee Rogers B	.40	1.00
7 Danny MacFayden	.30	.75
8 Dale Alexander	.30	.75
9 Robert Fothergill/(Fatsy)	.30	.75
10 Sunday Morning Workout	.30	.75
11 Jimmy Foxx (Jimmie) signs ball for Mrs. Tom Yawkey	.40	1.00
12 Lefty Grove receiving key for new car	.40	1.00
13 Lefty Grove Fireball	.40	1.00
14 Jack Rothrock Urbane Pickering	.30	.75
15 Tom Daly CO Al Schact CO Herb Pennock CO	.30	.75
16 Heinie Manush Eddie Collins	.40	1.00
17 Tris Speaker	.60	1.50
18 Jimmy Foxx (Jimmie)	.75	2.00
19 Smead Jolley	.30	.75
20 Hal Trosky James Foxx	.30	.75
21 Harold (Muddy) Ruel Wilcy (Fireman) Moore	.30	.75
22 Bob Quinn PR Shano Collins MG	.30	.75
23 Tom Oliver	.30	.75
24 Joe Cronin CO Herb Pennock CO Bud Buetter	.40	1.00
25 Jimmie Foxx	2.00	5.00

1979 Red Sox Vendor Cards

This standard-size set of the Boston Red Sox features black-and-white player portraits with biographical and statistical information on the backs except for one card which displays a picture of Garry Hancodk on one side and Stan Papi on the other. There are three other double player cards who need identifying. For now they are listed as two player cards. Any help on these three other cards is appreciated. According to the back, The Phantom Co. issued these cards. The cards came in a white packet with a picture of a Red Sox (apparently Yaz) rounding the bases.

COMPLETE SET	10.00	25.00
1 Gary Allenson	.20	.50
2 Jack Brohamer	.20	.50
3 Tom Burgmeier	.20	.50
4 Rick Burleson	.30	.75
5 Bill Campbell	.20	.50
6 Dick Drago	.20	.50
7 Dennis Eckersley	1.25	3.00
8 Dwight Evans	.60	1.50
9 Carlton Fisk	2.00	5.00
10 Andy Hassler	.20	.50
11 Butch Hobson	.20	.50
12 Fred Lynn	.60	1.50
13 Bob Montgomery	.20	.50
14 Mike O'Berry	.20	.50
15 Jerry Remy	.20	.50
16 Steve Renko	.20	.50
17 Jim Rice	.75	2.00
18 George Scott	.30	.75
19 Bob Stanley	.20	.50
20 Mike Torrez	.20	.50
21 Larry Wolfe	.20	.50
22 Jim Wright	.20	.50
23 Carl Yastrzemski	2.00	5.00
24 Garry Hancock Stan Papi	.20	.50
25 Two Player Card	.20	.50
26 Two Player Card	.20	.50
27 Two Player Card	.20	.50

1980 Red Sox Postcards

Issued by the team, these 19 cards are black and white and are postcard sized. Some of these cards were known to come with facsimile autographs. Since these cards are unnumbered we have sequenced them in alphabetical order.

COMPLETE SET	8.00	20.00
1 Gary Allenson	.20	.50
2 Jack Billingham	.20	.50
3 Jack Brohamer	.20	.50
4 Rick Burleson	.20	.50
5 Dick Drago	.20	.50
6 Dennis Eckersley	.75	2.00
7 Dwight Evans	.60	1.50
8 Carlton Fisk	1.25	3.00
9 Butch Hobson	.20	.50
10 Glenn Hoffman	.20	.50
11 Fred Lynn	.60	1.50
12 Tony Perez	.75	2.00
13 Chuck Rainey	.20	.50
14 Jerry Remy	.20	.50
15 Steve Renko	.20	.50
16 Jim Rice	.60	1.50
17 Bob Stanley	.20	.50
18 Mike Torrez	.20	.50
19 Carl Yastrzemski	2.00	5.00

1981 Red Sox Boston Globe

This standard size 128-card set consists of the Boston Globe's series featuring black-and-white photos surrounded by white borders of famous Boston Red Sox players. The set was issued in two series with cards 1-64 making up the first series and cards 65-128 being the second series. The horizontal backs have player information as well as career statistics. This set concentrates on players from the 60's. These photos were never intended to be issued as cards until a Globe employee got a hold of the printing plated and illegally produced this set in two series of 64 cards each. Series one featured players of the 50's while series two featured the 60's Red Sox players.

COMPLETE SET (128)	20.00	50.00
1 Harry Agganis	.40	1.00
2 Ken Aspromonte	.08	.25
3 Bobby Avila	.08	.25
4 Frank Baumann	.08	.25
5 Lou Berberet	.08	.25
6 Milt Bolling	.08	.25
7 Lou Boudreau	.40	1.00
8 Ted Bowsfield	.08	.25
9 Tom Brewer	.08	.25
10 Don Buddin	.08	.25
11 Jerry Casale	.08	.25
12 Billy Consolo UER (Harry Agganis pictured)	.30	.75
13 Pete Daley	.08	.25
14 Ike Delock	.08	.25
15 Dom DiMaggio	.40	1.00
16 Bobby Doerr	.40	1.00
17 Walt Dropo	.20	.50
18 Arnie Earley	.08	.25
19 Hoot Evers	.08	.25
20 Mike Fornieles	.08	.25
21 Gary Geiger	.08	.25
22 Don Gile	.08	.25
23 Joe Ginsburg	.08	.25
24 Billy Goodman	.08	.25
25 Pumpsie Green	.08	.25
26 Grady Hatton	.08	.25
27 Mike Higgins	.08	.25
28 Jackie Jensen	.30	.75
29 George Kell	.40	1.00
30 Marty Keough	.08	.25
31 Leo Kiely	.08	.25
32 Ellis Kinder	.08	.25
33 Billy Klaus	.08	.25
34 Don Lenhardt	.08	.25
35 Ted Lepcio	.08	.25
36 Frank Malzone	.30	.75
37 Gene Mauch	.08	.25
38 Maury McDermott	.08	.25
39 Bill Monboquette	.08	.25
40 Chet Nichols	.08	.25
41 Willard Nixon	.08	.25
42 Jim Pagliaroni	.08	.25
43 Mel Parnell	.30	.75
44 Johnny Pesky	.30	.75
45 Jimmy Piersall	.20	.50
46 Bob Porterfield	.08	.25
47 Pete Runnels	.08	.25
48 Dave Sisler	.08	.25
49 Riverboat Smith	.08	.25
50 Gene Stephens	.08	.25
51 Vern Stephens	.08	.25
52 Chuck Stobbs	.08	.25
53 Dean Stone	.08	.25
54 Frank Sullivan	.08	.25
55 Haywood Sullivan	.08	.25
56 Birdie Tebbetts	.08	.25
57 Mickey Vernon	.30	.75
58 Vic Wertz	.08	.25
59 Sammy White	.08	.25
60 Ted Williams	2.50	6.00
61 Ted Wills	.08	.25
62 Earl Wilson	.08	.25
63 Al Zarilla	.08	.25
64 Norm Zauchin	.08	.25
65 Ted Williams Carl Yastrzemski	1.25	3.00
66 Boston Globe Red Sox Dream Makers	.40	1.00
67 Tony Conigliaro Billy Conigliaro	.08	.25
68 Jerry Adair	.08	.25
69 Mike Andrews	.08	.25
70 Gary Bell	.08	.25
71 Dennis Bennett	.08	.25
72 Ed Bressoud	.08	.25
73 Ken Brett	.08	.25
74 Lu Clinton	.08	.25
75 Tony Conigliaro	.40	1.00
76 Billy Conigliaro	.08	.25
77 Gene Conley	.08	.25
78 Ray Culp	.08	.25
79 Dick Ellsworth	.08	.25
80 Joe Foy	.08	.25
81 Russ Gibson	.08	.25
82 Jim Gosger	.08	.25
83 Lennie Green	.08	.25
84 Ken Harrelson	.20	.50
85 Tony Horton	.08	.25
86 Elston Howard	.40	1.00
87 Dalton Jones	.08	.25
88 Eddie Kasko	.08	.25
89 Joe Lahoud	.08	.25
90 Jack Lamabe	.08	.25
91 Jim Lonborg	.30	.75
92 Sparky Lyle	.30	.75
93 Felix Mantilla	.08	.25
94 Roman Mejias	.08	.25
95 Don McMahon	.08	.25
96 Dave Morehead	.08	.25
97 Gerry Moses	.08	.25
98 Mike Nagy	.08	.25
99 Russ Nixon	.08	.25
100 Gene Oliver	.08	.25
101 Dan Osinski	.08	.25
102 Rico Petrocelli	.20	.50
103 Juan Pizarro	.08	.25
104 Dick Radatz	.20	.50
105 Vicente Romo	.08	.25
106 Mike Ryan	.08	.25
107 Jose Santiago	.08	.25
108 Chuck Schilling	.08	.25
109 Dick Schofield	.08	.25
110 Don Schwall	.08	.25
111 George Scott	.20	.50
112 Norm Siebern	.08	.25
113 Sonny Siebert	.08	.25
114 Reggie Smith	.20	.50
115 Bill Spanswick	.08	.25
116 Tracy Stallard	.08	.25
117 Lee Stange	.08	.25
118 Jerry Stephenson	.08	.25
119 Dick Stuart	.20	.50
120 Tom Sturdivant	.08	.25
121 Jose Tartabull	.08	.25
122 George Thomas	.08	.25
123 Lee Thomas	.08	.25
124 Bob Tillman	.08	.25
125 Gary Waslewski	.08	.25
126 Dick Williams	.20	.50
127 John Wyatt	.08	.25
128 Carl Yastrzemski	1.25	3.00

1982 Red Sox Coke

The cards in this 23-card set measure the standard size. This set of Boston Red Sox ballplayers was issued locally in the Boston area as a joint promotion by Brigham's Ice Cream Stores and Coca-Cola. The pictures are identical to those in the Topps regular 1982 issue, except that the colors are brighter and the Brigham and Coke logos appear inside the frame line. The reverses are done in red, black and gray, in contrast to the Topps set, and the number appears to the right of the position listing. The cards were initally distributed in three-card cello packs with an ice cream or Coca-Cola purchase but later became available as sets within the hobby. The unnumbered title or advertising card carries a premium offer on the reverse. The set numbering is in alphabetical order by player's name.

COMPLETE SET (23)	3.00	8.00
1 Gary Allenson	.08	.25
2 Tom Burgmeier	.08	.25
3 Mark Clear	.08	.25
4 Steve Crawford	.08	.25
5 Dennis Eckersley	.75	2.00
6 Dwight Evans	.40	1.00
7 Rich Gedman	.08	.25
8 Garry Hancock	.08	.25
9 Glenn Hoffman	.08	.25
10 Carney Lansford	.20	.50
11 Rick Miller	.08	.25
12 Reid Nichols	.08	.25
13 Bob Ojeda	.30	.75
14 Tony Perez	.75	2.00
15 Chuck Rainey	.08	.25
16 Jerry Remy	.08	.25
17 Jim Rice	.40	1.00
18 Bob Stanley	.20	.50
19 Dave Stapleton	.08	.25
20 Mike Torrez	.08	.25
21 John Tudor	.20	.50
22 Carl Yastrzemski	1.25	3.00
NNO Title Card	.05	.15

1982 Red Sox Herald Stamps

These stamps, which feature a mix of active and retired players for the Red Sox were issued by the Boston Herald. Stamps 1 through 26 feature players from the 1982 Red Sox, 39 through 42 feature prospect and the others feature all-time Red Sox greats.

COMPLETE SET	15.00	40.00
1 Jerry Remy	.08	.25
2 Glenn Hoffman	.08	.25
3 Luis Aponte	.08	.25
4 Jim Rice		1.25
5 Mark Clear	.08	.25
6 Reid Nichols	.08	.25
7 Wade Boggs	2.00	5.00
8 Dennis Eckersley	.60	1.50
9 Jeff Newman	.08	.25
10 Bob Ojeda	.08	.25
11 Ed Jurak	.08	.25
12 Rick Miller	.08	.25
13 Carl Yastrzemski	1.00	2.50
14 Mike Brown	.08	.25
15 Bob Stanley	.08	.25
16 John Tudor	.08	.25
17 Gary Allenson	.08	.25
18 Rich Gedman	.08	.25
19 Tony Armas	.20	.50
20 Doug Bird	.08	.25
21 Bruce Hurst	.08	.25
22 Dave Stapleton	.08	.25
23 Dwight Evans		1.00
24 Julio Valdez	.08	.25
25 John Henry Johnson	.08	.25
26 Ralph Houk MG	.08	.25
27 George Scott	.20	.50
28 Bobby Doerr		1.00
29 Frank Malzone	.20	.50
30 Rico Petrocelli	.20	.50
31 Carl Yastrzemski	.60	1.50
32 Ted Williams	2.00	5.00
33 Dwight Evans		1.25
34 Carlton Fisk	.75	2.00
35 Dick Radatz	.20	.50
36 Luis Tiant		1.00
37 Mel Parnell	.20	.50
38 Jim Rice		1.25
39 Dennis Boyd	.20	.50
40 Marty Barrett	.20	.50
41 Brian Denman	.08	.25
42 Steve Crawford	.08	.25
43 Cy Young		1.25
44 Jimmy Collins		1.25
45 Tris Speaker	.60	1.50
46 Harry Hooper		1.00
47 Lefty Grove	.75	2.00
48 Joe Cronin	.60	1.50
49 Jimmy Foxx (Jimmie)	.75	2.00
50 Ted Williams	2.00	5.00

1986 Red Sox Greats TCMA

This 12-card standard-size set features all-time leading Red Sox. The player's photo and his name are featured on the front. The back gives more information about that player.

COMPLETE SET (12)	3.00	8.00
1 Sammy White	.08	.25
2 Lefty Grove	.40	1.00
3 Cy Young	.40	1.00
4 Jimmie Foxx	.40	1.00
5 Bobby Doerr	.20	.50
6 Joe Cronin	.08	.25
7 Frank Malzone	.08	.25
8 Ted Williams	1.00	2.50
9 Carl Yastrzemski	.40	1.00
10 Tris Speaker	.30	.75
11 Dick Radatz	.08	.25
12 Dick Williams MG	.08	.25

1987 Red Sox 1946 TCMA

This nine-card standard-size set honors players on the 1946 Red Sox. This team would prove to be the only time Ted Williams would participate in post season play.

COMPLETE SET (9)	4.00	10.00
1 Joe Cronin MG	.20	.50
2 Rudy York	.08	.25
3 Bobby Doerr	.30	.75
4 Johnny Pesky	.20	.50
5 Dom DiMaggio	.30	.75
6 Ted Williams	1.00	2.50
7 Dave Boo Ferriss	.08	.25
8 Tex Hughson	.08	.25
9 Mickey Harris	.08	.25

1987 Red Sox Postcards

This 22-card set features photos of the 1987 Boston Red Sox printed on postcard-size cards. The cards are unnumbered and checklisted below in alphabetical order.

COMPLETE SET (22)	8.00	20.00
1 Marty Barrett	.20	.50
2 Don Baylor	.40	1.00
3 Wade Boggs	.75	2.00
4 Dennis Boyd	.20	.50
5 Ellis Burks	.75	2.00
6 Roger Clemens	1.50	4.00
7 Steve Crawford	.20	.50
8 Dwight Evans	.60	1.50
9 Wes Gardner	.20	.50
10 Rich Gedman	.20	.50
11 Mike Greenwell	.60	1.50
12 Dave Henderson	.20	.50
13 Bruce Hurst	.20	.50
14 Al Nipper	.20	.50

15 Spike Owen	.20	.50
16 Jim Rice	.40	1.00
17 Ed Romero	.20	.50
18 Joe Sambito	.20	.50
19 Calvin Schiraldi	.20	.50
20 Jeff Sellers	.20	.50
21 Bob Stanley	.20	.50
22 Marc Sullivan	.20	.50

1987 Red Sox Sports Action Postcards

These color postcards featured members of the 1987 Boston Red Sox. They were issued in sets of all ten players.

COMPLETE SET (10)	3.00	8.00
1 Marty Barrett	.20	.50
2 Don Baylor	.40	1.00
3 Wade Boggs	.75	2.00
4 Dennis Boyd	.20	.50
5 Bill Buckner	.30	.75
6 Roger Clemens	1.50	4.00
7 Dwight Evans	.60	1.50
8 Bruce Hurst	.20	.50
9 Spike Owen	.20	.50
10 Jim Rice	.40	1.00

1988 Red Sox Donruss Team Book

The 1988 Donruss Red Sox Team Book set features 27 cards (three pages with nine cards on each page) plus a large full-page puzzle of Stan Musial. Cards are in full color and are standard size. The set was distributed as a four-page book; although the puzzle page was perforated, the card pages were not. The cover of the "Team Collection" book is primarily bright red. Card fronts are very similar in design to the 1988 Donruss regular issue. The card numbers on the backs are the same for those players that are the same as in the regular Donruss set; the new players pictured are numbered on the back as "NEW." The book is usually sold intact. When cut from the book into individual cards, these cards are distinguishable from the regular 1988 Donruss cards since these have a 1988 copyright on the back whereas the regular issue has a 1987 copyright on the back.

COMPLETE SET (27)	1.50	4.00
41 Jody Reed RR	.08	.25
51 Roger Clemens	.75	2.00
92 Bob Stanley	.02	.10
129 Rich Gedman	.02	.10
153 Wade Boggs	.60	1.50
174 Ellis Burks	.30	1.00
216 Dwight Evans	.08	.25
252 Bruce Hurst	.02	.10
276 Marty Barrett	.02	.10
297 Todd Benzinger	.02	.10
339 Mike Greenwell	.02	.10
399 Jim Rice	.08	.25
421 John Marzano	.02	.10
462 Oil Can Boyd	.02	.10
498 Sam Horn	.02	.10
544 Spike Owen	.02	.10
585 Jeff Sellers	.02	.10
623 Ed Romero	.02	.10
634 Wes Gardner	.02	.10
NEW Brady Anderson	.50	1.00
NEW Rick Cerone	.02	.10
NEW Steve Ellsworth	.02	.10
NEW Dennis Lamp	.02	.10
NEW Kevin Romine	.02	.10
NEW Lee Smith	.08	.25
NEW Mike Smithson	.02	.10
NEW John Trautwein	.02	.10

1990 Red Sox Pepsi

The 1990 Pepsi Boston Red Sox set is a 20-card standard-size set, which is checklisted alphabetically below. This set was apparently prepared very early in the 1990 season as Bill Buckner and Lee Smith were still members of the Red Sox in this set. The cards were supposedly available as a store promotion with one card per specially marked 12-pack of Pepsi. The cards were difficult to remove from the boxes, thus making perfect mint cards worth an extra premium.

COMPLETE SET (20)	15.00	40.00
1 Marty Barrett	.40	1.00
2 Mike Boddicker	.40	1.00
3 Wade Boggs	4.00	10.00
4 Bill Buckner	.60	1.50
5 Ellis Burks	2.50	6.00
6 Roger Clemens	8.00	20.00
7 John Dopson	.40	1.00
8 Dwight Evans	1.00	2.50
9 Wes Gardner	.40	1.00
10 Rich Gedman	.40	1.00
11 Mike Greenwell	.75	2.00
12 Dennis Lamp	.40	1.00
13 Rob Murphy	.40	1.00
14 Tony Pena	.40	1.00
15 Carlos Quintana	.40	1.00
16 Jeff Reardon	.60	1.50
17 Jody Reed	.40	1.00
18 Luis Rivera	.40	1.00
19 Kevin Romine	.40	1.00
20 Lee Smith	1.00	2.50

1990 Red Sox Topps TV

This Red Sox team set contains 66 cards measuring the standard size. Cards numbered 1-33 were with the parent club, while cards 34-66 were in the farm system. The set features an early card of Mo Vaughn.

COMPLETE FACT. SET (66)	20.00	50.00
1 Joe Morgan MG	.10	.25
2 Dick Berardino CO	.08	.25
3 Al Bumbry CO	.08	.25
4 Bill Fischer CO	.08	.25
5 Richie Hebner CO	.08	.25
6 Rac Slider CO	.08	.25
7 Mike Boddicker	.08	.25
8 Roger Clemens	15.00	40.00
9 John Dopson	.08	.25
10 Wes Gardner	.08	.25
11 Greg A. Harris	.08	.25
12 Dana Kiecker	.08	.25
13 Dennis Lamp	.08	.25
14 Rob Murphy	.08	.25
15 Jeff Reardon	.20	.50
16 Mike Rochford	.08	.25
17 Lee Smith	.60	1.50
18 Rich Gedman	.08	.25
19 John Marzano	.08	.25
20 Tony Pena	.08	.25
21 Marty Barrett	.08	.25
22 Wade Boggs	8.00	20.00
23 Bill Buckner	.20	.50
24 Danny Heep	.08	.25
25 Jody Reed	.08	.25
26 Luis Rivera	.08	.25
27 Billy Joe Robidoux	.08	.25
28 Ellis Burks	1.25	3.00
29 Dwight Evans	.60	1.50
30 Mike Greenwell	.20	.50
31 Randy Kutcher	.08	.25
32 Carlos Quintana	.08	.25
33 Kevin Romine	.08	.25
34 Ed Nottle MG	.08	.25
35 Mark Meleski CO	.08	.25
36 Steve Bast	.08	.25
37 Greg Blosser	.08	.25
38 Tom Bolton	.08	.25
39 Scott Cooper	.08	.25
40 Zach Crouch	.08	.25
41 Steve Curry	.08	.25
42 Mike Dalton	.08	.25
43 John Flaherty	.08	.25
44 Angel Gonzalez	.08	.25
45 Eric Hetzel	.08	.25
46 Daryl Irvine	.08	.25
47 Joe Johnson	.08	.25
48 Rick Lancellotti	.08	.25
49 John Leister	.08	.25
50 Derek Livernois	.08	.25
51 Josias Manzanillo	.08	.25
52 Kevin Morton	.08	.25
53 Julius McDougal	.08	.25
54 Tim Naehring	.20	.50
55 Jim Pankovits	.08	.25
56 Mickey Pina	.08	.25
57 Phil Plantier	.20	.50
58 Jerry Reed	.08	.25
59 Larry Shikles	.08	.25
60 Tito Stewart	.08	.25
61 Jeff Stone	.08	.25
62 John Trautwein	.08	.25
63 Gary Tremblay	.08	.25
64 Mo Vaughn	4.00	10.00
65 Scott Wade	.08	.25
66 Eric Wedge	.75	2.00

1991 Red Sox Pepsi

This 20-card set was sponsored by Pepsi and officially licensed by Mike Schechter Associates on behalf of the MLBPA. The 1991 edition consists of 100,000 sets that were available from July 1 through August 10, 1991 in the New England area, with one card per specially marked pack of Pepsi and Diet Pepsi. The promotion also includes a sweepstakes offering a grand prize trip for four to Red Sox Spring training camp. The cards are unnumbered and checklisted below in alphabetical order.

COMPLETE SET (20)	8.00	20.00
1 Tom Bolton	.30	.75
2 Tom Brunansky	.30	.75
3 Ellis Burks	1.00	2.50
4 Jack Clark	.40	1.00
5 Roger Clemens	4.00	10.00
6 Danny Darwin	.30	.75
7 Jeff Gray	.30	.75
8 Mike Greenwell	.50	1.25
9 Greg A. Harris	.30	.75
10 Dana Kiecker	.30	.75
11 Dennis Lamp	.30	.75
12 John Marzano	.30	.75
13 Tim Naehring	.30	.75
14 Tony Pena	.40	1.00
15 Phil Plantier	.30	.75
16 Carlos Quintana	.30	.75
17 Jeff Reardon	.50	1.25
18 Jody Reed	.30	.75
19 Luis Rivera	.30	.75
20 Matt Young	.30	.75

1991 Red Sox Postcards

This 29-card set features photos of the 1991 Boston Red Sox printed on postcard-size cards. The cards are unnumbered and checklisted below in alphabetical order.

COMPLETE SET (29)	8.00	20.00
1 Wade Boggs	.75	2.00
2 Tom Bolton	.20	.50
3 Mike Brumley	.20	.50
4 Tom Brunansky	.30	.75
5 Ellis Burks	.60	1.50
6 Jack Clark	.30	.75
7 Roger Clemens	1.50	4.00
8 Danny Darwin	.20	.50
9 John Dopson	.20	.50
10 Tony Fossas	.20	.50
11 Mike Gardiner	.20	.50
12 Jeff Gray	.20	.50
13 Mike Greenwell	.30	.75
14 Greg Harris	.20	.50
15 Joe Hesketh	.20	.50
16 Dana Kiechker	.20	.50
17 Dennis Lamp	.20	.50
18 Steve Lyons	.30	.75
19 John Marzano	.20	.50
20 Kevin Morton	.20	.50
21 Tim Naehring	.20	.50
22 Carlos Quintana	.20	.50
23 Tony Pena	.20	.50
24 Jeff Reardon	.30	.75
25 Jody Reed	.20	.50
26 Luis Rivera	.20	.50
27 Kevin Romine	.20	.50
28 Mo Vaughn	1.00	2.50
29 Matt Young	.20	.50

1992 Red Sox Dunkin' Donuts

The 1992 Boston Red Sox Player Photo Collection was sponsored by Dunkin' Donuts and WVIT Channel 30 (Connecticut's NBC Station). It consists of three large sheets (each measuring approximately 9 3/8" by 10 3/4") joined together to form one continuous sheet. The first panel displays a color picture of Fenway Park and a WVIT Red Sox Schedule. The second and third panels, which are perforated, feature 15 player cards each. After perforation, the cards measure approximately 2 1/8" by 3 1/8". The set was also available sponsored by WJAR-10 TV in Providence, Rhode Island and by Rookie Red Sox Coke via a mail-in offer on 12-packs of Coke in the Boston area for 7.00.

COMPLETE SET (30)	5.00	12.00
1 Gary Allenson CO	.08	.25
2 Wade Boggs	.75	2.00
3 Tom Bolton	.08	.25
4 Tom Brunansky	.08	.25
5 Al Bumbry CO	.08	.25
6 Ellis Burks	.30	.75
7 Rick Burleson CO	.08	.25
8 Jack Clark	.20	.50
9 Roger Clemens	2.00	5.00
10 Danny Darwin	.08	.25
11 Tony Fossas	.08	.25
12 Rich Gale CO	.08	.25
13 Mike Gardiner	.08	.25
14 Mike Greenwell	.20	.50
15 Greg A. Harris	.08	.25
16 Joe Hesketh	.08	.25
17 Butch Hobson MG	.08	.25
18 John Marzano	.08	.25
19 Kevin Morton	.08	.25
20 Tim Naehring	.08	.25
21 Tony Pena	.08	.25
22 Phil Plantier	.08	.25
23 Carlos Quintana	.08	.25
24 Jeff Reardon	.20	.50
25 Jody Reed	.08	.25
26 Luis Rivera	.08	.25
27 Mo Vaughn	1.00	2.50
28 Frank Viola	.20	.50
29 Matt Young	.08	.25
30 Don Zimmer CO	.20	.50

1993 Red Sox Postcards

This 33-card set features photos of the 1993 Boston Red Sox printed on postcard-size cards. The cards are unnumbered and checklisted below in alphabetical order.

COMPLETE SET (33)	8.00	20.00
1 Gary Allenson CO	.20	.50
2 Scott Bankhead	.20	.50
3 Al Bumbry	.20	.50
4 Rick Burleson CO	.20	.50
5 Ivan Calderon	.20	.50
6 Roger Clemens	1.50	4.00
7 Scott Cooper	.20	.50
8 Danny Darwin	.20	.50
9 Andre Dawson	.60	1.50
10 John Dopson	.20	.50
11 Mike Easler CO	.20	.50
12 John Flaherty	.20	.50
13 Scott Fletcher	.20	.50
14 Tony Fossas	.20	.50
15 Rich Gale	.20	.50
16 Mike Greenwell	.30	.75
17 Greg Harris	.20	.50
18 Billy Hatcher	.20	.50
19 Joe Hesketh	.20	.50
20 Butch Hobson MG	.20	.50
21 Jose Melendez	.20	.50
22 Bob Melvin	.30	.75
23 Tim Naehring	.20	.50
24 Tony Pena	.20	.50
25 Paul Quantrill	.20	.50
26 Carlos Quintan	.20	.50
27 Ernest Riles	.20	.50
28 Luis Rivera	.20	.50
29 Jeff Russell	.20	.50
30 John Valentin	.20	.50
31 Mo Vaughn	.60	1.50
32 Frank Viola	.30	.75
33 Bob Zupcic	.20	.50

1993 Red Sox Winter Haven Police

This 28-card standard-size set features players who were invited to the 1993 Red Sox spring training camp. The fronts feature posed studio shots while the backs feature recent stats as well as listing the various sponsors. Many of the stats only go through the 1991 season.

COMPLETE SET (28)	4.00	10.00
1 Checklist	.08	.25
2 Scott Bankhead	.08	.25
3 Danny Darwin	.08	.25
4 Andre Dawson	.40	1.00
5 Scott Fletcher	.08	.25
6 Billy Hatcher	.08	.25
7 Jack Clark	.20	.50
8 Roger Clemens	1.25	3.00
9 Scott Cooper	.08	.25
10 John Dopson	.08	.25
11 Paul Quantrill	.08	.25
12 Mike Greenwell	.20	.50
13 Greg A. Harris	.08	.25
14 Joe Hesketh	.08	.25
15 Peter Hoy	.08	.25
16 Daryl Irvine	.08	.25
17 John Marzano	.08	.25
18 Jeff McNeely	.08	.25
19 Tim Naehring	.08	.25
20 Matt Young	.08	.25
21 Jeff Plympton	.08	.25
22 Bob Melvin	.20	.50
23 Tony Pena	.08	.25
24 Luis Rivera	.08	.25
25 Scott Taylor	.08	.25
26 John Valentin	.08	.25
27 Mo Vaughn	.50	1.25
28 Frank Viola	.20	.50

1996 Red Sox Fleer

These 20 standard-size cards feature the same design as the regular Fleer issue, except they are UV coated, use silver foil and are numbered "x of 20". The team set packs were available at retail locations and hobby shops in 10-card packs for a suggested retail price of $1.99.

COMPLETE SET (20)	1.50	4.00
1 Stan Belinda	.02	.10
2 Jose Canseco	.20	.50
3 Roger Clemens	.75	2.00
4 Wil Cordero	.02	.10
5 Vaughn Eshelman	.02	.10
6 Tom Gordon	.10	.30
7 Mike Greenwell	.02	.10
8 Dwayne Hosey	.02	.10
9 Kevin Mitchell	.02	.10
10 Tim Naehring	.02	.10
11 Troy O'Leary	.02	.10
12 Aaron Sele	.07	.20
13 Heathcliff Slocumb	.02	.10
14 Mike Stanley	.02	.10
15 Jeff Suppan	.07	.20
16 John Valentin	.02	.10
17 Mo Vaughn	.10	.30
18 Tim Wakefield	.15	.40
19 Logo card	.02	.10
20 Checklist	.02	.10

1997 Red Sox Score

This 15-card set of the Boston Red Sox was issued in five-card packs with a suggested retail price of $1.30 each. The fronts feature color player photos with special team specific color foil stamping. The backs carry player information. Only 100 cases were made for each team. Platinum parallel cards were inserted at a rate of 1:6, Premier parallel cards at a rate of 1:31.

COMPLETE SET (15)	2.00	5.00
*PLATINUM: 5X BASIC CARDS		
*PREMIER: 20X BASIC CARDS		
1 Wil Cordero	.08	.25
2 Mo Vaughn	.20	.50
3 John Valentin	.08	.25
4 Reggie Jefferson	.08	.25
5 Tom Gordon	.20	.50
6 Mike Stanley	.08	.25
7 Jose Canseco	.50	1.25
8 Roger Clemens	.75	2.00
9 Darren Bragg	.08	.25
10 Jeff Frye	.08	.25
11 Jeff Suppan	.20	.50
12 Mike Greenwell	.08	.25
13 Arquimedez Pozo	.08	.25
14 Tim Naehring	.08	.25
15 Troy O'Leary	.08	.25

1998 Red Sox Postcards

These 37 blank backed postcards measure 4" by 5 3/4". They are unnumbered so we have sequenced them in alphabetical order.

COMPLETE SET (37)	5.00	12.00
1 Steve Avery	.08	.25
2 Mike Benjamin	.08	.25
3 Darren Bragg	.08	.25
4 Damon Buford	.08	.25
5 Jin Ho Cho	.08	.25
6 Jim Corsi	.08	.25
7 Midre Cummings	.08	.25
8 Dennis Eckersley	.60	1.50
9 Nomar Garciaparra	1.25	3.00
10 Tom Gordon	.20	.50
11 Scott Hattenberg	.08	.25
12 Butch Henry	.08	.25
13 Joe Hudson	.08	.25
14 Dave Jauss CO	.08	.25
15 Reggie Jefferson	.08	.25
16 Wendell Kim CO	.08	.25
17 Joe Kerrigan CO	.08	.25
18 Mark Lemke	.08	.25
19 Darren Lewis	.08	.25
20 Grady Little CO	.08	.25
21 Derek Lowe	.30	.75
22 Ron Mahay	.08	.25
23 Pedro Martinez	.60	1.50
24 Lou Merloni	.08	.25
25 Tim Naehring	.08	.25
26 Troy O'Leary	.08	.25
27 Dick Pole CO	.08	.25
28 Jim Rice CO	.20	.50
29 Brian Rose	.08	.25
30 Bret Saberhagen	.20	.50
31 Donnie Sadler	.08	.25
32 John Valentin	.08	.25
33 Jason Varitek	.60	1.50
34 Mo Vaughn	.30	.75
35 Tim Wakefield	.40	1.00
36 John Wasdin	.08	.25
37 Jimy Williams MG	.08	.25

1998 Red Sox Score

This 15-card set was issued in special retail packs and features color photos of the Boston Red Sox team. The backs carry player information. A special platinum parallel set was also issued and randomly inserted in packs.

COMPLETE SET (15)	2.50	6.00
*PLATINUM: 5X BASIC CARDS		
1 Steve Avery	.08	.25
2 Aaron Sele	.08	.25
3 Tim Wakefield	.40	1.00
4 Darren Bragg	.08	.25
5 Scott Hatteberg	.08	.25
6 Jeff Suppan	.20	.50
7 Nomar Garciaparra	1.25	3.00
8 Tim Naehring	.08	.25
9 Reggie Jefferson	.08	.25
10 John Valentin	.08	.25
11 Jeff Frye	.08	.25
12 Wil Cordero	.08	.25
13 Troy O'Leary	.08	.25
14 Mo Vaughn	.20	.50
15 Shane Mack	.08	.25

2001 Red Sox Commemorative Set

COMPLETE SET (16)	4.80	12.00
1 Jimmy Collins	.10	.25
2 Cy Young	.40	1.00
3 Tris Speaker	.20	.50
4 Babe Ruth	1.20	3.00
5 Lefty Grove	.20	.50
6 Joe Cronin	.20	.50
7 Jimmie Foxx	.30	.75
8 Bobby Doerr	.20	.50
9 Ted Williams	1.00	2.50
10 Dom DiMaggio	.20	.50
11 Johnny Pesky	.10	.25
12 Carl Yastrzemski	.40	1.00
13 Carlton Fisk	.40	1.00
14 Jim Rice	.20	.50
15 Nomar Garciaparra	.60	1.50
16 Pedro Martinez	.50	1.25

2001 Red Sox Team Issue

COMPLETE SET (19)	4.00	10.00
1 Rolando Arrojo	.10	.25
2 Rod Beck	.10	.25
3 Dante Bichette	.10	.25
4 Frank Castillo	.10	.25
5 Paxton Crawford	.10	.25
6 Brian Daubach	.10	.25
7 Carl Everett	.30	.75
8 Shea Hillenbrand	.20	.50
9 Mike Lansing	.10	.25
10 Pedro Martinez	.80	2.00
11 Lou Merloni	.10	.25
12 Hideo Nomo	.60	1.50
13 Tomo Ohka	.10	.25
14 Manny Ramirez	.80	2.00
15 Pete Schourek	.10	.25
16 Chris Stynes	.10	.25
17 John Valentin	.10	.25
18 Tim Wakefield	.40	1.00
19 Wilton Veras	.10	.25

2002 Red Sox Polish Spring

COMPLETE SET	5.00	10.00
1 Rolando Arrojo	.08	.25
2 Carlos Baerga	.20	.50
3 John Burkett	.08	.25
4 Frank Castillo	.08	.25
5 Tony Clark	.08	.25
6 Johnny Damon	.60	1.50
7 Brian Daubach	.08	.25
8 Rich Garces	.08	.25
9 Nomar Garciaparra	.75	2.00
10 Rickey Henderson	.60	1.50
11 Shea Hillenbrand	.08	.25
12 Grady Little MG	.08	.25
13 Derek Lowe	.30	.75
14 Pedro Martinez	.60	1.50
15 Lou Merloni	.08	.25
16 Doug Mirabelli	.08	.25
17 Trot Nixon	.30	.75
18 Jose Offerman	.08	.25
19 Manny Ramirez	.60	1.50
20 Ugueth Urbina	.08	.25
21 Jason Varitek	.60	1.50
22 Tim Wakefield	.40	1.00
23 Wally Mascot	.08	.25

2003 Red Sox Team Issue

COMPLETE SET	5.00	10.00
1 John Burkett	.10	.25
2 Tony Cloninger CO	.10	.25
3 Mike Cubbage CO	.10	.25
4 Johnny Damon	.60	1.50
5 Alan Embree	.10	.25
6 Casey Fossum	.10	.25
7 Nomar Garciaparra	.75	2.00
8 Shea Hillenbrand	.20	.50
9 Damian Jackson	.10	.25
10 Ron Jackson CO	.10	.25
11 Byung-Hyun Kim	.20	.50
12 Grady Little MG	.10	.25
13 Brandon Lyon	.10	.25
14 Derek Lowe	.30	.75
15 Pedro Martinez	.60	1.50
16 Ramiro Mendoza	.10	.25
17 Lou Merloni	.10	.25
18 Kevin Millar	.30	.75
19 Doug Mirabelli	.10	.25
20 Bill Mueller	.30	.75
21 Jerry Narron CO	.10	.25
22 Trot Nixon	.40	1.00
23 David Ortiz	1.00	2.50
24 Robert Person	.10	.25
25 Euclidies Rojas	.10	.25
26 Manny Ramirez	.60	1.50
27 Freddy Sanchez	.10	.25
28 Mike Timlin	.10	.25
29 Tim Wakefield	.40	1.00
30 Todd Walker	.20	.50
31 Dallas Williams	.10	.25

2004 Red Sox Team Issue

COMPLETE SET (23)		
1 Bronson Arroyo	.30	.75
2 Mark Bellhorn	.30	.75
3 Cesar Crespo	.10	.25
4 Johnny Damon	.60	1.50
5 Lenny DiNardo	.20	.50
6 Alan Embree	.10	.25
7 Theo Epstein GM	.20	.50
8 Keith Foulke	.20	.50
9 Terry Francona MG	.20	.50
10 Gabe Kapler	.10	.25
11 Derek Lowe	.30	.75
12 David McCarty	.10	.25
13 Kevin Millar	.30	.75
14 Doug Mirabelli	.10	.25
15 Bill Mueller	.20	.50
16 Trot Nixon	.30	.75
17 David Ortiz	.75	2.00
18 Pokey Reese	.10	.25
19 Curt Schilling	.75	2.00
20 Jason Varitek	.60	1.50
21 Tim Wakefield	.40	1.00
22 Scott Williamson	.10	.25
23 Kevin Youkilis	.20	.50
24 Wally the Green Monster Mascot	.10	.25

2004 Red Sox Topps Chips

COMP. FACT SET (26)	8.00	20.00
1 Bronson Arroyo	.40	1.00
2 Mark Bellhorn	.40	1.00
3 Orlando Cabrera	.40	1.00
4 Johnny Damon	.60	1.50
5 Alan Embree	.40	1.00
6 Keith Foulke	.40	1.00
7 Terry Francona MG	.40	1.00
8 Gabe Kapler	.40	1.00
9 Curtis Leskanic	.40	1.00
10 Derek Lowe	.40	1.00
11 Pedro Martinez	.60	1.50
12 Ramiro Mendoza	.40	1.00
13 Doug Mientkiewicz	.40	1.00
14 Kevin Millar	.40	1.00
15 Doug Mirabelli	.40	1.00
16 Bill Mueller	.40	1.00
17 Mike Myers	.40	1.00
18 Trot Nixon	.40	1.00
19 David Ortiz	1.00	2.50
20 Manny Ramirez	1.00	2.50
21 Pokey Reese	.40	1.00
22 Dave Roberts	.60	1.50
23 Curt Schilling	.60	1.50
24 Mike Timlin	.40	1.00
25 Tim Wakefield	.60	1.50
26 Boston Red Sox World Series Chip	.40	1.00

2004 Red Sox Topps World Champions

COMP.FACT.SET (56)	12.00	20.00
ISSUED ONLY IN FACTORY SET FORM		
1 Bronson Arroyo	.10	.25
2 Alan Embree	.10	.25
3 Keith Foulke	.10	.25
4 Curtis Leskanic	.10	.25
5 Derek Lowe	.10	.25
6 Pedro Martinez	.15	.40
7 Ramiro Mendoza	.10	.25
8 Mike Myers	.10	.25
9 Curt Schilling	.15	.40
10 Mike Timlin	.10	.25
11 Tim Wakefield	.15	.40
12 Scott Williamson	.10	.25
13 Doug Mirabelli	.10	.25
14 Mark Bellhorn	.10	.25
15 Orlando Cabrera	.10	.25
16 Ricky Gutierrez	.10	.25
17 Doug Mientkiewicz	.10	.25
18 Kevin Millar	.10	.25
19 Bill Mueller	.10	.25
20 Pokey Reese	.10	.25
21 Kevin Youkilis	.10	.25
22 Johnny Damon	.15	.40
23 Gabe Kapler	.10	.25
24 David McCarty	.10	.25
25 Trot Nixon	.10	.25
26 Manny Ramirez	.25	.60
27 Dave Roberts	.15	.40
28 Ellis Burks	.10	.25
29 David Ortiz	.25	.60
30 Terry Francona MG	.10	.25
31 Boston Red Sox TC	.40	1.00
32 Curt Schilling SH	.15	.40
33 Kevin Millar SH	.10	.25
34 Manny Ramirez SH	.25	.60
35 Cabrera Mientkiewicz SH	.10	.25
36 Manny Ramirez SH	.25	.60
37 Schill Ortiz Manny SH	.25	.60
38 Pokey Reese SH	.10	.25
39 Bill Mueller SH	.10	.25
40 Curt Schilling ALDS1	.15	.40
41 Pedro Martinez ALDS2	.15	.40
42 David Ortiz ALDS3	.25	.60
43 Kevin Millar ALCS1	.10	.25
44 Johnny Damon ALCS2	.15	.40
45 Trot Nixon ALCS3	.10	.25
46 David Ortiz ALCS4	.25	.60
47 Keith Foulke ALCS5	.10	.25
48 Schilling Foulke ALCS6	.15	.40
49 Team Celebration ALCS7	.40	1.00
50 David Ortiz ALCS MVP	.25	.60
51 Mark Bellhorn WS1	.10	.25
52 Curt Schilling WS2	.15	.40
53 Pedro Martinez WS3	.15	.40
54 Team Celebration WS4	.40	1.00
55 Manny Ramirez WS MVP	.25	.60
NNO Boston Red Sox Jumbo TC	.40	1.00

2004 Red Sox Upper Deck

COMPLETE SET (20)	4.00	10.00
1 David Ortiz	.50	1.25
2 Mark Bellhorn	.20	.50
3 Orlando Cabrera	.20	.50
4 Bill Mueller	.20	.50
5 Manny Ramirez	.50	1.25
6 Johnny Damon	.30	.75
7 Trot Nixon	.20	.50
8 Jason Varitek	.50	1.25
9 Curt Schilling	.30	.75
10 Pedro Martinez	.30	.75
11 Bronson Arroyo	.20	.50
12 Tim Wakefield	.30	.75
13 Derek Lowe	.20	.50
14 Mike Timlin	.20	.50
15 Alan Embree	.20	.50
16 Keith Foulke	.20	.50
17 Johnny Damon MM	.30	.75
18 Curt Schilling MM	.30	.75
19 Team Card MM	.40	1.00
20 Manny Ramirez MVP	.50	1.25

2005 Red Sox McDonald's Upper Deck

COMPLETE SET (27)		
1 Manny Ramirez	.60	1.50
2 Curt Schilling	.50	1.25
3 Tim Wakefield	.40	1.00
4 Alan Embree	.10	.25
5 Mike Timlin	.10	.25
6 Kevin Youkilis	.20	.50
7 Bronson Arroyo	.30	.75
8 Bill Mueller	.20	.50
9 Boston Red Sox World Champions	.10	.25
10 Johnny Damon	.50	1.25
11 Jason Varitek	.50	1.25
12 Keith Foulke	.20	.50
13 Gabe Kapler	.10	.25
14 Doug Mientkiewicz	.10	.25
15 Orlando Cabrera	.10	.25
16 Pokey Reese	.10	.25
17 Curtis Leskanic	.10	.25
18 Wally the Green Monster	.10	.25
19 Doug Mirabelli	.10	.25
20 Trot Nixon	.30	.75
21 Mark Bellhorn	.20	.50
22 Derek Lowe	.30	.75
23 David Ortiz	.75	2.00
24 Mike Myers	.10	.25
25 Dave Roberts	.10	.25
26 Pedro Martinez	.50	1.25
27 Terry Francona MG	.10	.25

2006 Red Sox Topps

COMPLETE SET (14)	3.00	8.00
BOS1 David Ortiz	.30	.75
BOS2 Manny Ramirez	.30	.75
BOS3 Trot Nixon	.12	.30
BOS4 Mike Lowell	.12	.30
BOS5 Curt Schilling	.20	.50
BOS6 Mark Loretta	.12	.30
BOS7 Kevin Youkilis	.12	.30
BOS8 Tim Wakefield	.20	.50
BOS9 Bronson Arroyo	.12	.30
BOS10 David Wells	.12	.30
BOS11 Matt Clement	.12	.30
BOS12 Jon Papelbon	.60	1.50
BOS13 Keith Foulke	.12	.30
BOS14 Josh Beckett	.12	.30

2007 Red Sox Topps

COMPLETE SET (14)	3.00	8.00
BOS1 Daisuke Matsuzaka	.50	1.25
BOS2 Manny Ramirez	.30	.75
BOS3 Jason Varitek	.30	.75
BOS4 Julio Lugo	.12	.30
BOS5 Wily Mo Pena	.12	.30
BOS6 Curt Schilling	.20	.50
BOS7 Kevin Youkilis	.12	.30
BOS8 Jonathan Papelbon	.30	.75
BOS9 J.D. Drew	.12	.30
BOS10 Coco Crisp	.12	.30
BOS11 Mike Lowell	.12	.30
BOS12 Tim Wakefield	.20	.50
BOS13 Josh Beckett	.12	.30
BOS14 David Ortiz	.30	.75

2007 Red Sox Topps Gift Set

COMPLETE SET (55)	12.50	30.00
BOS1 Josh Beckett	.15	.40
BOS2 Brendan Donnelly	.15	.40
BOS3 Javier Lopez	.15	.40
BOS4 Daisuke Matsuzaka	.60	1.50
BOS5 Hideki Okajima	.75	2.00
BOS6 Jonathan Papelbon	.40	1.00
BOS7 Joel Pineiro	.15	.40
BOS8 J.C. Romero	.15	.40
BOS9 Curt Schilling	.25	.60
BOS10 Kyle Snyder	.15	.40
BOS11 Julian Tavarez	.15	.40
BOS12 Tim Wakefield	.25	.60
BOS13 Doug Mirabelli	.15	.40
BOS14 Jason Varitek	.40	1.00
BOS15 Alex Cora	.25	.60
BOS16 Eric Hinske	.15	.40
BOS17 Mike Lowell	.15	.40
BOS18 Julio Lugo	.15	.40
BOS19 Dustin Pedroia	.40	1.00
BOS20 Kevin Youkilis	.15	.40
BOS21 Coco Crisp	.15	.40
BOS22 J.D. Drew	.15	.40
BOS23 Wily Mo Pena	.15	.40
BOS24 Manny Ramirez	.40	1.00
BOS25 David Ortiz	.40	1.00
BOS26 Terry Francona MG	.25	.60
BOS27 Brad Mills CO	.15	.40
BOS28 Luis Alicea CO	.15	.40
BOS29 DeMarlo Hale CO	.15	.40
BOS30 John Farrell CO	.15	.40
BOS31 Dave Magadan CO	.15	.40
BOS32 Mike Lowell	.15	.40
BOS33 Manny Ramirez	.40	1.00
BOS34 David Ortiz	.40	1.00
BOS35 Mike Lowell	.15	.40
BOS36 David Ortiz	.40	1.00
BOS37 Curt Schilling	.25	.60
BOS38 Jonathan Papelbon	.40	1.00
BOS39 Josh Beckett	.15	.40
BOS40 Curt Schilling	.25	.60
BOS41 Ortiz/Ramirez/Lugo	.40	1.00
BOS42 A.Cora/J.Lugo	.25	.60
BOS43 J.Varitek/T.Wakefield	.40	1.00
BOS44 Manny Ramirez	.40	1.00
BOS45 Tim Wakefield	.25	.60
BOS46 Curt Schilling	.25	.60
BOS47 David Ortiz	.40	1.00
BOS48 J.D. Drew	.15	.40
BOS49 Jason Varitek	.40	1.00
BOS50 Kevin Youkilis	.15	.40
BOS51 Josh Beckett	.15	.40
BOS52 Dustin Pedroia	.40	1.00
BOS53 Hideki Okajima	.75	2.00
BOS54 Daisuke Matsuzaka	.60	1.50
BOS55 Wally the Green Monster	.15	.40

2007 Red Sox Upper Deck Boston Globe

COMPLETE SET (20)	4.00	10.00
1 Josh Beckett	.12	.30
2 Daisuke Matsuzaka	.50	1.25
3 Tim Wakefield	.20	.50
4 Jonathan Papelbon	.30	.75
5 Hideki Okajima	.60	1.50
6 Doug Mirabelli	.12	.30
7 Jacoby Ellsbury	.75	2.00
8 Mike Lowell	.12	.30
9 Julio Lugo	.12	.30
10 Julian Tavarez	.12	.30
11 Curt Schilling	.20	.50
12 Kevin Youkilis	.12	.30
13 Manny Ramirez	.30	.75
14 David Ortiz	.30	.75
15 Coco Crisp	.12	.30
16 J.D. Drew	.12	.30
17 Jason Varitek	.30	.75
18 Dustin Pedroia	.30	.75
19 Jon Lester	.20	.50
20 Alex Cora	.20	.50

2007 Red Sox Upper Deck World Series Champions

1 Josh Beckett	.20	.50
2 Alex Cora	.30	.75
3 Coco Crisp	.20	.50
4 Manny Delcarmen	.20	.50

5 J.D. Drew .20 .50
6 Jacoby Ellsbury 1.25 3.00
7 Eric Gagne .20 .50
8 Eric Hinske .20 .50
9 Bobby Kielty .20 .50
10 Jon Lester .30 .75
11 Javier Lopez .20 .50
12 Mike Lowell .20 .50
13 Julio Lugo .20 .50
14 Daisuke Matsuzaka .75 2.00
15 Doug Mirabelli .20 .50
16 Hideki Okajima 1.00 2.50
17 David Ortiz .50 1.25
18 Jonathan Papelbon .50 1.25
19 Dustin Pedroia .50 1.25
20 Manny Ramirez .50 1.25
21 Curt Schilling .30 .75
22 Kyle Snyder .20 .50
23 Mike Timlin .20 .50
24 Jason Varitek .50 1.25
25 Kevin Youkilis .20 .50

2007 Red Sox Upper Deck World Series Champions Memorable Moments

MM1 Manny Ramirez .50 1.25
MM2 Curt Schilling .30 .75
MM3 J.D. Drew .20 .50
MM4 Dustin Pedroia .50 1.25
MM5 Josh Beckett .20 .50
MM6 Daisuke Matsuzaka .75 2.00
MM7 Jacoby Ellsbury 1.25 3.00
MM8 Mike Lowell .20 .50
MM9 Jonathan Papelbon .50 1.25

2007 Red Sox Upper Deck World Series Champions MVP

MVP1 Mike Lowell .20 .50

2007 Red Sox Upper Deck World Series Champions Season Highlights

SH1 Daisuke Matsuzaka .75 2.00
SH2 Jonathan Papelbon .50 1.25
SH3 Jason Varitek .50 1.25
SH4 Hideki Okajima 1.00 2.50
SH5 Manny Ramirez .50 1.25
SH6 Julio Lugo .20 .50
SH7 Daisuke Matsuzaka .75 2.00
SH8 Kevin Youkilis .20 .50
SH9 Curt Schilling .30 .75
SH10 Manny Ramirez .50 1.25
SH11 David Ortiz .50 1.25
SH12 Tim Wakefield .30 .75
SH13 Clay Buchholz .60 1.50
SH14 Josh Beckett .20 .50
SH15 Josh Beckett .20 .50

2008 Red Sox Topps

COMPLETE SET (14) 3.00 8.00
BOS1 David Ortiz .30 .75
BOS2 Daisuke Matsuzaka .20 .50
BOS3 Manny Ramirez .30 .75
BOS4 Jason Varitek .30 .75
BOS5 Julio Lugo .12 .30
BOS6 Jacoby Ellsbury .25 .60
BOS7 Curt Schilling .20 .50
BOS8 Kevin Youkilis .12 .30
BOS9 Jonathan Papelbon .20 .50
BOS10 Dustin Pedroia .30 .75
BOS11 J.D. Drew .12 .30
BOS12 Mike Lowell .12 .30
BOS13 Hideki Okajima .20 .50
BOS14 Josh Beckett .12 .30

2009 Red Sox Topps

BOS1 Jacoby Ellsbury .30 .75
BOS2 Josh Beckett .15 .40
BOS3 Dustin Pedroia .40 1.00
BOS4 Jon Lester .25 .60
BOS5 David Ortiz .40 1.00
BOS6 Kevin Youkilis .15 .40
BOS7 Daisuke Matsuzaka .25 .60
BOS8 J.D. Drew .15 .40
BOS9 Jonathan Papelbon .25 .60
BOS10 Jed Lowrie .15 .40
BOS11 John Smoltz .40 1.00
BOS12 Brad Penny .15 .40
BOS13 Rocco Baldelli .15 .40
BOS14 Jason Bay .25 .60
BOS15 Wally The Green Monster .15 .40

2010 Red Sox Topps

BOS1 Dustin Pedroia .40 1.00
BOS2 Victor Martinez .25 .60
BOS3 Jonathan Papelbon .25 .60
BOS4 Kevin Youkilis .15 .40
BOS5 John Lackey .25 .60
BOS6 Clay Buchholz .15 .40
BOS7 Tim Wakefield .25 .60
BOS8 Adrian Beltre .40 1.00
BOS9 Jason Varitek .40 1.00
BOS10 Josh Beckett .15 .40
BOS11 J.D. Drew .15 .40
BOS12 David Ortiz .40 1.00
BOS13 Jacoby Ellsbury .30 .75
BOS14 Jon Lester .25 .60
BOS15 Daisuke Matsuzaka .25 .60
BOS16 Daniel Bard .15 .40
BOS17 Marco Scutaro .25 .60

2011 Red Sox Topps

BOS1 Carl Crawford .25 .60
BOS2 David Ortiz .40 1.00
BOS3 Jonathan Papelbon .25 .60
BOS4 Kevin Youkilis .15 .40
BOS5 Marco Scutaro .25 .60
BOS6 J.D. Drew .15 .40
BOS7 Jacoby Ellsbury .30 .75
BOS8 John Lackey .25 .60
BOS9 Jed Lowrie .15 .40
BOS10 Tim Wakefield .25 .60
BOS11 Jon Lester .25 .60
BOS12 Dustin Pedroia .40 1.00
BOS13 Jarrod Saltalamacchia .15 .40
BOS14 Adrian Gonzalez .30 .75
BOS15 Clay Buchholz .15 .40
BOS16 Josh Beckett .15 .40
BOS17 Fenway Park .15 .40

2012 Red Sox Topps

BOS1 Jacoby Ellsbury .30 .75
BOS2 Josh Beckett .25 .60
BOS3 Carl Crawford .30 .75
BOS4 Kevin Youkilis .40 1.00
BOS5 Adrian Gonzalez .30 .75
BOS6 Daniel Bard .25 .60
BOS7 Jon Lester .25 .60
BOS8 Dustin Pedroia .40 1.00
BOS9 David Ortiz .40 1.00
BOS10 Andrew Bailey .25 .60
BOS11 Clay Buchholz .25 .60
BOS12 Mike Aviles .25 .60
BOS13 Jarrod Saltalamacchia .25 .60
BOS14 Mark Melancon .25 .60
BOS15 Fenway Park 1912 .15 .40
BOS16 Fenway Park 1967 .15 .40
BOS17 Fenway Park Modern Day .15 .40

2013 Red Sox Topps

COMPLETE SET (17) 3.00 8.00
BOS1 David Ortiz .40 1.00
BOS2 Jacoby Ellsbury .30 .75
BOS3 Dustin Pedroia .25 .60
BOS4 Jon Lester .30 .75
BOS5 Will Middlebrooks .25 .60
BOS6 Clay Buchholz .15 .40
BOS7 Koji Uehara .25 .60
BOS8 Stephen Drew .25 .60
BOS9 Jarrod Saltalamacchia .25 .60
BOS10 Joel Hanrahan .25 .60
BOS11 Shane Victorino .30 .75
BOS12 Ryan Dempster .15 .40
BOS13 John Lackey .30 .75
BOS14 Felix Doubront .25 .60
BOS15 Jonny Gomes .25 .60
BOS16 Mike Napoli .15 .40
BOS17 Fenway Park .15 .40

2014 Red Sox Topps

COMPLETE SET (17) 3.00 8.00
BOS1 David Ortiz .25 .60
BOS2 Jake Peavy .15 .40
BOS3 Dustin Pedroia .25 .60
BOS4 Jon Lester .20 .50
BOS5 Will Middlebrooks .15 .40
BOS6 Clay Buchholz .15 .40
BOS7 Koji Uehara .15 .40
BOS8 Junichi Tazawa .15 .40
BOS9 Jackie Bradley Jr. .25 .60
BOS10 A.J. Pierzynski .15 .40
BOS11 Shane Victorino .20 .50
BOS12 Xander Bogaerts .50 1.25
BOS13 John Lackey .20 .50
BOS14 Felix Doubront .15 .40
BOS15 Jonny Gomes .15 .40
BOS16 Mike Napoli .15 .40
BOS17 Fenway Park .15 .40

2015 Red Sox Topps

COMPLETE SET (17) 3.00 8.00
BRS1 Pablo Sandoval .20 .50
BRS2 David Ortiz .25 .60
BRS3 Christian Vazquez .20 .50
BRS4 Mike Napoli .15 .40
BRS5 Dustin Pedroia .25 .60
BRS6 Xander Bogaerts .25 .60
BRS7 Hanley Ramirez .20 .50
BRS8 Rusney Castillo .20 .50
BRS9 Mookie Betts .50 1.25
BRS10 Wade Miley .15 .40
BRS11 Rick Porcello .20 .50
BRS12 Clay Buchholz .15 .40
BRS13 Joe Kelly .15 .40
BRS14 Justin Masterson .15 .40
BRS15 Koji Uehara .15 .40
BRS16 Junichi Tazawa .15 .40
BRS17 Matt Barnes .15 .40

2016 Red Sox Topps

COMPLETE SET (17) 3.00 8.00
BOS1 David Ortiz .25 .60
BOS2 Blake Swihart .20 .50
BOS3 Hanley Ramirez .20 .50
BOS4 Dustin Pedroia .25 .60
BOS5 Xander Bogaerts .25 .60
BOS6 Pablo Sandoval .20 .50
BOS7 Jackie Bradley Jr. .25 .60
BOS8 Mookie Betts .50 1.25
BOS9 Rusney Castillo .15 .40
BOS10 Clay Buchholz .15 .40
BOS11 Rick Porcello .20 .50
BOS12 Craig Kimbrel .20 .50
BOS13 Henry Owens .20 .50
BOS14 David Price .20 .50
BOS15 Brock Holt .15 .40
BOS16 Eduardo Rodriguez .15 .40
BOS17 Koji Uehara .15 .40

2017 Red Sox Topps

COMPLETE SET (17) 3.00 8.00
BOS1 Mookie Betts .50 1.25
BOS2 Eduardo Rodriguez .15 .40
BOS3 Pablo Sandoval .20 .50
BOS4 David Price .20 .50
BOS5 Andrew Benintendi .50 1.25
BOS6 Brock Holt .15 .40
BOS7 Hanley Ramirez .20 .50
BOS8 Mitch Moreland .15 .40
BOS9 Tyler Thornburg .15 .40
BOS10 Craig Kimbrel .20 .50
BOS11 Rick Porcello .20 .50
BOS12 Dustin Pedroia .25 .60
BOS13 Xander Bogaerts .25 .60
BOS14 Chris Young .15 .40
BOS15 Steven Wright .15 .40
BOS16 Jackie Bradley Jr. .25 .60
BOS17 Chris Sale .25 .60

2018 Red Sox Topps

COMPLETE SET (17) 2.50 6.00
RS1 Andrew Benintendi .25 .60
RS2 Mookie Betts .50 1.25
RS3 Rick Porcello .20 .50
RS4 Rafael Devers .50 1.25
RS5 Hanley Ramirez .20 .50
RS6 David Price .20 .50
RS7 Mitch Moreland .15 .40
RS8 Xander Bogaerts .25 .60
RS9 Drew Pomeranz .15 .40
RS10 Dustin Pedroia .25 .60
RS11 Eduardo Rodriguez .15 .40
RS12 Chris Sale .25 .60
RS13 Joe Kelly .15 .40
RS14 Tessie MASCOT .15 .40
RS15 Jackie Bradley Jr. .25 .60
RS16 Craig Kimbrel .20 .50
RS17 Christian Vazquez .20 .50

2019 Red Sox Topps

COMPLETE SET (17) 3.00 8.00
RS1 Mookie Betts .50 1.25
RS2 Chris Sale .25 .60
RS3 David Price .20 .50
RS4 Andrew Benintendi .25 .60
RS5 J.D. Martinez .25 .60
RS6 Dustin Pedroia .25 .60
RS7 Xander Bogaerts .25 .60
RS8 Rafael Devers .30 .75
RS9 Rick Porcello .20 .50
RS10 Steve Pearce .25 .60
RS11 Brock Holt .15 .40
RS12 Sandy Leon .15 .40
RS13 Mitch Moreland .15 .40
RS14 Matt Barnes .15 .40
RS15 Jackie Bradley Jr. .25 .60
RS16 Christian Vazquez .20 .50
RS17 Eduardo Rodriguez .15 .40

2020 Red Sox Topps

BOS1 Rafael Devers .30 .75
BOS2 Chris Sale .25 .60
BOS3 Andrew Benintendi .25 .60
BOS4 Dustin Pedroia .25 .60
BOS5 Jackie Bradley Jr .25 .60
BOS6 Nathan Eovaldi .20 .50
BOS7 Brandon Workman .15 .40
BOS8 Christian Vazquez .20 .50
BOS9 Matt Barnes .15 .40
BOS10 Xander Bogaerts .25 .60
BOS11 Darwinzon Hernandez .15 .40
BOS12 Boston Red Sox Team .15 .40
BOS13 Eduardo Rodriguez .15 .40
BOS14 Michael Chavis .20 .50
BOS15 J.D. Martinez .25 .60
BOS16 Wally The Green Monster .15 .40
BOS17 Tessie .15 .40

2017 Red Sox Topps National Baseball Card Day

COMPLETE SET (10) 8.00 20.00
BOS1 Xander Bogaerts 1.00 2.50
BOS2 Dustin Pedroia 1.00 2.50
BOS3 Mookie Betts 2.00 5.00
BOS4 Rick Porcello .75 2.00
BOS5 Jackie Bradley Jr. 1.00 2.50
BOS6 Andrew Benintendi 2.00 5.00
BOS7 Craig Kimbrel .75 2.00
BOS8 David Price .75 2.00
BOS9 Hanley Ramirez .75 2.00
BOS10 David Ortiz 1.00 2.50

2008 Red Sox Topps Gift Set

1 Terry Francona MG .25 .60
2 Clay Buchholz No-Hitter .25 .60
3 David Ortiz .40 1.00
4 David Ortiz/Mike Lowell/Manny Ramirez .40 1.00
5 Josh Beckett .15 .40
6 Jason Varitek .40 1.00
7 Daisuke Matsuzaka .25 .60
8 Manny Ramirez .40 1.00
9 Dustin Pedroia ROY .40 1.00
10 Josh Beckett/Curt Schilling
Daisuke Matsuzaka .25 .60
11 Jonathan Papelbon .25 .60
12 Mike Lowell .15 .40
13 J.D. Drew/Manny Ramirez/Mike Lowell .40 1.00
14 Tim Wakefield .25 .60
15 Brad Mills CO .15 .40
16 Josh Beckett ALCS MVP .15 .40
17 Dustin Pedroia .40 1.00
18 Hideki Okajima .15 .40
19 Daisuke Matsuzaka/Josh Beckett
Tim Wakefield .25 .60
20 Jacoby Ellsbury .30 .75
21 Mike Lowell/Julio Lugo .15 .40
22 Curt Schilling .25 .60
23 David Ortiz/Mike Lowell
Dustin Pedroia .40 1.00
24 David Ortiz/Manny Ramirez .40 1.00
25 Julio Lugo .15 .40
26 Luis Alicea CO .15 .40
27 Mike Timlin .15 .40
28 Mike Lowell WS MVP .15 .40
29 Kevin Youkilis .15 .40
30 Clay Buchholz .25 .60
31 Josh Beckett/Tim Wakefield
Daisuke Matsuzaka .25 .60
32 Kevin Cash .15 .40
33 Jon Lester .25 .60
34 DeMarlo Hale CO .15 .40
35 Daisuke Matsuzaka MLB Debut .25 .60
36 Coco Crisp .15 .40
37 Kyle Snyder .15 .40
38 Mike Lowell/David Ortiz
Dustin Pedroia .40 1.00
39 J.D. Drew .15 .40
40 Julian Tavarez .15 .40
41 John Farrell CO .15 .40
42 David Ortiz Silver Slugger .40 1.00
43 Alex Cora .25 .60
44 Javier Lopez .15 .40
45 Daisuke Matsuzaka/Josh Beckett
Tim Wakefield .25 .60
46 Curt Schilling One-Hitter .25 .60
47 Mike Lowell/David Ortiz
Manny Ramirez .40 1.00
48 Sean Casey .15 .40
49 Manny Ramirez/Kevin Youkilis .40 1.00
50 Manny Delcarmen .15 .40
51 Dave Magadan CO .15 .40
52 Mike Lowell/Manny Ramirez .40 1.00
53 Red Sox Win World Series .15 .40
54 Wally The Green Monster .15 .40
55 Fenway Park .15 .40

1869 Red Stockings Peck and Snyder

This card was issued by Peck and Snyder as an advertising trade piece. It comes in two versions (either with red or black borders). The black version is usually larger than the red version. Most of these cards are found trimmed to fit into CdV albums. The front features a photo of the 1869 Red Stockings while the back is an advertisment for Peck and Snyder.

1 Red Stockings Team 35000.00 70000.00

1891 Reds Cabinets Conly

These Cabinets feature members of the 1891 Cincinnati Reds. The players are all pictured in suit and tie. The back features an ad for Conly studios. This set is not numbered so we have sequenced them in alphabetical order.

COMPLETE SET 7500.00 15000.00
1 Tom Brown 1000.00 2000.00
2 Charlie Buffington 1000.00 2000.00
3 Bill Daley 1000.00 2000.00
4 Duke Farrell 1000.00 2000.00
5 Arthur Irwin 1000.00 2000.00
6 John Irwin 1000.00 2000.00
7 Morgan Murphy 1000.00 2000.00
8 Darby O'Brien 1000.00 2000.00
9 Paul Radford 1000.00 2000.00
10 Hardy Richardson 1000.00 2000.00
11 John Striker 1000.00 2000.00

1919-20 Reds World's Champions Postcards

This black and white set of Cincinnati players was issued in 1920 and appears with either of two captions in the border on the front of the card -- World Champions 1919 or National League Champions 1919. A glossy version of this set also exists.

COMPLETE SET 900.00 1800.00
1 Nick Allen 50.00 100.00
2 Rube Bressler 50.00 100.00
3 Jake Daubert 50.00 100.00
4 Pat Duncan 50.00 100.00
5 Hod Eller 50.00 100.00
6 Ray Fisher 50.00 100.00
7 Eddie Gerner 50.00 100.00
8 Heine Groh 75.00 150.00
9 Larry Kopf 50.00 100.00
10 Adolfo Luque 75.00 150.00
11 Sherwood Magee 60.00 120.00
12 Roy Mitchell 50.00 100.00
13 Pat Moran MG 50.00 100.00
14 Greasy Neale 75.00 150.00
15 Bill Rariden 50.00 100.00
16 Morris Rath 50.00 100.00
17 Jimmy Ring 50.00 100.00
18 Edd Roush 100.00 200.00
19 Walter Reuther 50.00 100.00
20 Harry Sallee 50.00 100.00
21 Hank Schreiber 50.00 100.00
22 Charles See 50.00 100.00
23 Jimmy Smith 50.00 100.00
24 Ivy Wingo 50.00 100.00
25 Team Card 300.00 600.00

1938-39 Reds Orange/Gray W711-1

The cards in this 32-card set measure approximately 2" by 3". The 1938-39 Cincinnati Reds Baseball player set was printed in orange and gray tones. Many back variations exist and there are two poses of Johnny VanderMeer, portrait (PORT) and an action (ACT) poses. The set was sold at the ballpark and was printed on thin cardboard stock. The cards are unnumbered but have been alphabetized and numbered in the checklist below.

COMPLETE SET (32) 600.00 1200.00
1 Wally Berger (2) 25.00 50.00
2 Nino Bongiovanni (39) 50.00 100.00
3 Stanley Bordagaray 50.00 100.00
Frenchy (39)
4 Joe Cascarella (38) 15.00 30.00
5 Allen Dusty Cooke (38) 15.00 30.00
6 Harry Craft 20.00 40.00
7 Ray(Peaches) Davis 15.00 30.00
8 Paul Derringer (2) 30.00 60.00
9 Linus Frey (2) 15.00 30.00
10 Lee Gamble (2) 15.00 30.00
11 Ival Goodman (2) 15.00 30.00
12 Hank Gowdy CO 20.00 40.00
13 Lee Grissom (2) 15.00 30.00
14 Willard Hershberger (2) 20.00 40.00
15 Eddie Joost (39) 20.00 40.00
16 Wes Livengood (39) 100.00 200.00
17 Ernie Lombardi (2) 60.00 120.00
18 Frank McCormick 25.00 50.00
19 Bill McKechnie (2) MG 30.00 60.00
20 Lloyd Whitey Moore (2) 15.00 30.00
21 Billy Myers (2) 15.00 30.00
22 Lew Riggs (2) 15.00 30.00
23 Eddie Roush CO (38) 50.00 100.00
24 Les Scarsella (39) 15.00 30.00
25 Gene Schott (38) 15.00 30.00
26 Eugene Thompson 15.00 30.00
27 Johnny VanderMeer 30.00 60.00
PORT
28 Johnny VanderMeer 30.00 60.00
ACT
29 Wm.(Bucky) Walters (2) 25.00 50.00
30 Jim Weaver 15.00 30.00
31 Bill Werber (39) 15.00 30.00
32 Jimmy Wilson (39) 15.00 30.00

1939 Reds Team Issue

This 25-card set of the Cincinnati Reds features player photos printed on cards with blank backs. The cards are unnumbered and checklisted below in alphabetical order. The cards measure approximaley 2" by 3", were printed in grey sepia and the players' name is printed in orange. It is believed that this set was issued by Kroger's. Although this set is similar to the W711-1 set, the difference in these cards is believed to be the distribution method

1 Wally Berger 15.00 30.00
2 Nino Bongiovanni 12.50 25.00
3 Frenchy Bordagaray 12.50 25.00
4 Joe Cascarella 12.50 25.00
5 Harry Craft 12.50 25.00
6 Paul Derringer 15.00 30.00
7 Linus Frey 12.50 25.00
8 Lee Gamble 12.50 25.00
9 Ival Goodman 12.50 25.00
10 Hank Gowdy CO 12.50 25.00
11 Willard Hershberger 20.00 40.00
12 Eddie Joost 15.00 30.00
13 Ernie Lombardi 25.00 50.00
14 Frank McCormick 15.00 30.00
15 Bill McKechnie MG 25.00 50.00
16 Whitey Moore 12.50 25.00
17 Billy Myers 12.50 25.00
18 Lew Riggs 12.50 25.00
19 Eddie Roush CO 25.00 50.00
20 Les Scarsella 12.50 25.00
21 Junior Thompson 12.50 25.00
22 Johnny VanderMeer 20.00 40.00
23 Jimmy Wilson CO 15.00 30.00
24 Bill Werber 15.00 30.00
25 Bucky Walters 20.00 40.00

1941 Reds Harry Hartman W711-2

The cards in this 34-card set measure approximately 2 1/8" by 2 5/8". The W711-2 Cincinnati Reds set contains unnumbered, black and white cards and was issued in boxes which had a reverse side resembling a mailing label. This issue is sometimes called the "Harry Hartman" set. The cards are numbered below in alphabetical order by player's name with non-player cards listed at the end. The set is worth about $100 more when it is in the original mailing box. The set originally cost 20 cents when ordered in 1940.

COMPLETE SET (34) 300.00 600.00
COMMON CARD (1-28) 7.50 15.00
COMMON CARD (29-34) 7.50 15.00
1 Morris Arnovich 12.50 25.00
2 William(Bill) Baker 12.50 25.00
3 Joseph Beggs 12.50 25.00
4 Harry Craft 15.00 30.00
5 Paul Derringer 25.00 50.00
6 Linus Frey 12.50 25.00
7 Ival Goodman 12.50 25.00
8 Hank Gowdy CO 15.00 30.00
9 Witt Guise 12.50 25.00
10 Willard Hershberger 15.00 30.00
11 John Hutchings 12.50 25.00
12 Edwin Joost 15.00 30.00
13 Ernie Lombardi 30.00 60.00
14 Frank McCormick 20.00 40.00
15 Myron McCormick 12.50 25.00
16 Bill McKechnie MG 25.00 50.00
17 Whitey Moore 12.50 25.00
18 William(Bill) Myers 12.50 25.00
19 Elmer Riddle 12.50 25.00
20 Lewis Riggs 12.50 25.00
21 James A. Ripple 12.50 25.00
22 Milburn Shoffner 12.50 25.00
23 Eugene Thompson 12.50 25.00
24 James Turner 15.00 30.00
25 John VanderMeer 25.00 50.00
26 Bucky Walters 20.00 40.00
27 Bill Werber 15.00 30.00
28 James Wilson 12.50 25.00
29 Results 1940 12.50 25.00
World Series
30 The Cincinnati Reds/(Title Card) 12.50 25.00
31 The Cincinnati Reds 12.50 25.00
World's Champions/(Title Car
32 Debt of Gratitude 12.50 25.00
to Wm. Koehl Co.
33 Tell the World 12.50 25.00
About Our Reds
34 Harry Hartman ANN 12.50 25.00

1954-55 Reds Postcards

These cards, which were issued over a two year period, have four distinct styles to them. They are: no name in the white 3/4" inch space at the bottom; no name in the box but a blue fascimile autograph; printed name and fascimile autograph in the bottom white box and printed name, Cincinnatie Redleg in white space plus the blue fascimile autograph. This set carries a catalog naming of PC746. These cards are unnumbered, so we have sequenced them in alphabetical order. At least 20 more players are considered to be possible additions to this set so any help is appreciated.

COMPLETE SET 250.00 500.00
1 Bobby Adams 3.00 6.00
Portrait
2 Bobby Adams 3.00 6.00
Fielding
3 Fred Baczewski 3.00 6.00
4 Ed Bailey 3.00 6.00
5 Dick Bartell CO 3.00 6.00
Neck Shows
6 Dick Bartell CO 3.00 6.00
No-Neck
7 Matt Batts 3.00 6.00
8 Gus Bell 4.00 8.00
Hitting
9 Gus Bell 4.00 8.00
Portrait
10 Joe Black 4.00 8.00
11 Bob Borkowski 3.00 6.00
12 Rocky Bridges 3.00 6.00
13 Smoky Burgess 3.00 6.00
14 Jackie Collum 3.00 6.00
Portrait
15 Jackie Collum 3.00 6.00
Pitching
16 Powell Crosley Jr. PRES 3.00 6.00
17 Jimmy Dykes MG 4.00 8.00
18 Nico Escalera 3.00 6.00
19 Tom Ferrick 3.00 6.00
20 Art Fowler 3.00 6.00
Portrait
21 Art Fowler 3.00 6.00
Pitching
22 Herschel Freeman 3.00 6.00
23 Jim Greengrass 3.00 6.00
24 Don Gross 3.00 6.00
25 Charley Harmon 3.00 6.00
26 Ray Jablonski 3.00 6.00
27 Howie Judson 3.00 6.00
28 Johnny Klippstein 3.00 6.00
29 Ted Kluszewski 10.00 20.00
Neck Shows, looking right
30 Ted Kluszewski 10.00 20.00
No-Beck, leaning right
31 Ted Kluszewski 10.00 20.00
Standing, holding 4 bats
32 Ted Kluszewski 10.00 20.00
Ready to hit; cut-out sleeves
33 Ted Kluszewski 10.00 20.00
Uniform number visible
34 Ted Kluszewski 10.00 20.00
Stretching at 1st
35 Ted Kluszewski 10.00 20.00
Ready to hit; hands at belt
36 Ted Kluszewski 10.00 20.00
Batting follow-through, lookin up
37 Ted Kluszewski 10.00 20.00
Batting follow-through; stands vis
38 Hobie Landrith 3.00 6.00
39 Bill McKechnie Jr. 3.00 6.00
40 Roy McMilian 4.00 8.00
Portrait
41 Roy McMilian 4.00 8.00
Batting
42 Lloyd Merriman 3.00 6.00
43 Rudy Minarcin 3.00 6.00
Neck shows
44 Rudy Minarcin 3.00 6.00
No-Neck
45 Joe Nuxhall 4.00 8.00
Portrait
46 Joe Nuxhall 4.00 8.00
Pitching
47 Stan Palys 3.00 6.00
48 Bud Podbielan 3.00 6.00
No Belt
49 Bud Podbielan 3.00 6.00
Belt
50 Wally Post 4.00 8.00
Ready to hit; only to hips
51 Wally Post 4.00 8.00
Ready to hit; belt shows
52 Wally Post 4.00 8.00
Follow-through; one pole
53 Wally Post 4.00 8.00
Follow-through; two posts
54 Wally Post 4.00 8.00
Portrait
56 Ken Raffensberger 3.00 6.00
57 Steve Ridzik 3.00 6.00
58 Connie Ryan 3.00 6.00
59 Andy Seminick 3.00 6.00
60 Al Silvera 3.00 6.00
61 Frank Smith 3.00 6.00
62 Milt Smith 3.00 6.00
63 Gerry Staley 3.00 6.00
64 Birdie Tebbetts 3.00 6.00
Neck
65 Birdie Tebbetts 3.00 6.00
No-Neck
66 Johnny Temple 3.00 6.00
Mouth closed
67 Johnny Temple 3.00 6.00
Mouth open
68 Corky Valentine 3.00 6.00
69 George Zuverink 3.00 6.00
70 Crosley Field 3.00 6.00

1956-65 Reds Burger Beer

This 23-card set features 8 1/2" by 11" black-and-white photos of various Cincinnati Reds from 1956 through 1965. Most of the backs are blank, but the 1959 photos have a Burger Beer ad on them. The cards are unnumbered and checklisted below in alphabetical order.

COMPLETE SET 250.00 500.00
COMMON BURGER BEER AD 15.00 40.00
1 Ed Bailey 60-61 6.00 12.00
2 Mel Bailey 57-58 7.50 15.00
3 Gus Bell 59-61 7.50 15.00
4 Smoky Burgess 56 12.50 25.00
5 Gordon Coleman 60-65 6.00 12.00
6 John Edwards 61-65 6.00 12.00
7 Gene Freese 61-63 6.00 12.00
8 Waite Hoyt ANN 60-65 7.50 15.00
Black Suit
9 Waite Hoyt ANN 60-65 7.50 15.00
Checkered Suit
10 Fred Hutchinson 1960-65 6.00 12.00
11 Joey Jay 60-65 6.00 12.00
12 Hal Jeffcoat 57-58 7.50 15.00
13 Eddie Kasko 60-63 6.00 12.00
14 Gene Kelly ANN 60-65 6.00 12.00
15 Jerry Lynch 59 7.50 15.00
16 Jim Maloney 60-65 6.00 12.00
17 Ray McMillan 56-58 10.00 20.00
18 Joe Nuxhall 60, 62-65 6.00 12.00
19 Jim O'Toole 60-65 6.00 12.00
Winding Up
20 Jim O'Toole 60-65 6.00 12.00
Follow Through
21 Vada Pinson 60-65 12.50 25.00
Hands on Knee
22 Vada Pinson 60-65 12.50 25.00
Catching Fly Ball
23 Vada Pinson 60-65 12.50 25.00
Batting
24 Wally Post 56 10.00 20.00
25 Bob Purkey 59-64 7.50 15.00
Portrait
26 Bob Purkey 59-64 7.50 15.00
Pitching
27 Frank Robinson 59-65 25.00 50.00
Portrait
28 Frank Robinson 59-65 25.00 50.00
Fielding
29 Pete Rose 63-65 30.00 60.00
30 Johnny Temple 58-59 6.00 12.00
31 Frank Thomas 58-59 7.50 15.00

1957 Reds Sohio

The 1957 Sohio Cincinnati Reds set consists of 18 perforated photos, approximately 5" by 7", in black and white with facsimile autographs on the front which were designed to be pasted into a special photo album issued by SOHIO (Standard Oil of Ohio). The set features an early Frank Robinson card. These unnumbered cards are listed below in alphabetical order for convenience.

COMPLETE SET (18) 125.00 250.00
1 Ed Bailey 4.00 10.00
2 Gus Bell 5.00 12.00
3 Rocky Bridges 4.00 10.00
4 Smoky Burgess 5.00 12.00
5 Hersh Freeman 4.00 10.00
6 Alex Grammas 4.00 10.00
7 Don Gross 4.00 10.00
8 Warren Hacker 4.00 10.00
9 Don Hoak 5.00 12.00
10 Hal Jeffcoat 4.00 10.00
11 Johnny Klippstein 4.00 10.00
12 Ted Kluszewski 20.00 40.00
13 Brooks Lawrence 4.00 10.00
14 Roy McMillan 4.00 10.00
15 Joe Nuxhall 5.00 12.00
16 Wally Post 5.00 12.00
17 Frank Robinson 40.00 80.00
18 John Temple 5.00 12.00

1957 Reds Team Issue

These 8" by 10" photos feature members of the 1957 Cincinnati Reds. The fronts have the players photo along with their name on the bottom. The backs are blank so we have sequenced these photos in alphabetical order. Some of these photos are also know with the Cincinnati Baseball Club stamp on the back.

COMPLETE SET 40.00 80.00
1 Tom Acker 2.00 4.00
2 Gus Bell 2.00 4.00
3 George Crowe 2.00 4.00
4 Jimmy Dykes CO 2.50 5.00
5 Tom Ferrick 2.00 4.00
6 Art Fowler 2.00 4.00
7 Hersh Freeman 2.00 4.00
8 Alex Grammas 2.00 4.00
9 Don Gross 2.00 4.00
10 Bobby Henrich 2.00 4.00
11 Don Hoak 2.00 4.00
12 Johnny Klippstein 2.00 4.00
13 Brooks Lawrence 2.00 4.00
14 Frank McCormick CO 2.00 4.00
15 Roy McMillan 2.00 4.00
16 Joe Nuxhall 2.50 5.00
17 Gabe Paul GM 2.00 4.00
18 Frank Robinson 7.50 15.00
19 Raul Sanchez 2.00 4.00
20 Birdie Tebbetts MG 2.00 4.00
21 Pete Whisenant 2.00 4.00

1958 Reds Enquirer

This set consists of Lou Smith's Redleg Scrapbook newspaper clippings from the Cincinnati Enquirer and features black-and-white photos of the members of the 1958 Cincinnati Reds team with information about the players. The clippings were designed to be placed in an album. They are unnumbered and checklisted below in alphabetical order.

COMPLETE SET (44) 40.00 80.00
1 Tom Acker .75 1.50
2 Chico Alvarez .75 1.50
3 Ed Bailey .75 1.50
4 Gus Bell .75 1.50
5 Steve Bilko .75 1.50
6 Smoky Burgess 1.00 2.00
7 Jerry Cade .75 1.50
8 George Crowe 1.00 2.00
9 Dutch Dotterer .75 1.50
10 Jimmy Dykes CO 1.25 2.50
11 Tom Ferrick CO .75 1.50
12 Dee Fondy .75 1.50
13 Hersh Freeman .75 1.50
14 Buddy Gilbert .75 1.50
15 Harvey Haddix 1.25 2.50
16 Bob Henrich .75 1.50
17 Don Hoak 1.00 2.00
18 Ken Hommel .75 1.50
19 Jay Hook .75 1.50
20 Hal Jeffcoat .75 1.50
21 Bob Kelly .75 1.50
22 John Klippstein .75 1.50
23 Marty Kutyna .75 1.50
24 Brooks Lawrence 1.00 2.00
25 Jerry Lynch .75 1.50
26 Roy McMillan .75 1.50
27 Joe Nuxhall 1.50 3.00
28 Jim O'Toole .75 1.50
29 Stan Palys .75 1.50
30 Bob Purkey .75 1.50
31 Charley Rabe .75 1.50
32 Johnny Riddle CO .75 1.50
33 Frank Robinson 5.00 10.00
34 Haven Schmidt .75 1.50
35 Willard Schmidt .75 1.50
36 Dave Skaugstad .75 1.50
37 John Smith .75 1.50
38 Birdie Tebbetts MG .75 1.50
39 John Temple .75 1.50
40 Bob Thurman .75 1.50
41 Pete Whisenant .75 1.50
42 Ted Wieand .75 1.50
43 Bill Wight .75 1.50
44 Album 7.50 15.00

1958 Reds Jay Publishing

This 12-card set of the Cincinnati Reds measures approximately 5" by 7" and features black-and-white player photos in a white border. These cards were packaged 12 to a packet. The backs are blank. The cards are unnumbered and checklisted below in alphabetical order.

COMPLETE SET (12) 20.00 40.00
1 Ed Bailey 1.50 3.00
2 Gus Bell 1.50 3.00
3 Steve Bilko 1.50 3.00
4 Smoky Burgess 2.00 4.00
5 George Crowe 2.00 4.00
6 Harvey Haddix 2.00 4.00
7 Don Hoak 1.50 3.00
8 Hal Jeffcoat 1.50 3.00
9 Roy McMillan 2.50 5.00
10 Bob Purkey 1.50 3.00
11 Frank Robinson 5.00 10.00
12 Birdie Tebbetts MG 2.00 4.00

1959 Reds Enquirer

This set consists of Lou Smith's Reds Scrapbook newspaper clippings from the Cincinnati Enquirer and features black-and-white photos of the members of the 1959 Cincinnati Reds team with information about the players. The clippings are unnumbered and checklisted below in alphabetical order.

COMPLETE SET (28) 40.00 80.00
1 Tom Acker 2.00 5.00
2 Ed Bailey 2.00 5.00
3 Chuck Coles 2.00 5.00
4 Dutch Dotterer 2.00 5.00
5 Walt Dropo 2.00 5.00
6 Del Ennis 2.50 6.00
7 Jim Fridley 2.00 5.00
8 Buddy Gilbert 2.00 5.00
9 Jesse Gonder 2.00 5.00
10 Bob Henrich 2.00 5.00
11 Hal Jeffcoat 2.00 5.00
12 Brooks Lawrence 2.00 5.00
13 Bobbie Mabe 2.00 5.00

14 Roy McMillan 2.00 5.00
15 Don Newcombe 4.00 10.00
16 Joe Nuxhall 3.00 8.00
17 Claude Osteen 3.00 8.00
18 Don Pavletich 2.00 5.00
19 Orlando Pena 2.00 5.00
20 Jim Pendleton 2.00 5.00
21 John Powers 2.00 5.00
22 Charley Rabe 2.00 5.00
23 Willard Schmidt 2.00 5.00
24 Mayo Smith MG 2.50 6.00
25 Johnny Temple 2.00 5.00
26 Frank Thomas 3.00 8.00
27 Bob Thurman 2.00 5.00
28 Ted Wieand 2.00 5.00

1959 Reds Jay Publishing

This 12-card set of the Cincinnati Reds measures approximately 5" by 7" and features black-and-white player photos in a white border. These cards were packaged 12 to a packet. The backs are blank. The cards are unnumbered and checklisted below in alphabetical order.

COMPLETE SET 15.00 40.00
1 Ed Bailey 1.50 3.00
2 Gus Bell 1.50 3.00
3 Brooks Lawrence 1.50 3.00
4 Jerry Lynch 1.50 3.00
5 Roy McMillan 2.00 4.00
6 Don Newcombe 2.00 4.00
7 Joe Nuxhall 2.00 4.00
8 Vada Pinson 3.00 6.00
9 Bob Purkey 1.50 3.00
10 Johnny Temple 1.50 3.00
11 Frank Robinson 6.00 12.00
12 Frank Thomas 1.50 3.00

1960 Reds Jay Publishing

This 12-card set of the Cincinnati Reds measures approximately 5" by 7". The fronts feature black-and-white posed player photos with the player's and team name printed below in the white border. These cards were packaged 12 in a packet and originally sold for 25 cents. The backs are blank. The cards are unnumbered and checklisted below in alphabetical order.

COMPLETE SET (12) 15.00 40.00
1 Gus Bell 1.25 3.00
2 Dutch Dotterer .75 2.00
3 Jay Hook .75 2.00
4 Fred Hutchinson MG 1.25 3.00
5 Roy McMillan 1.25 3.00
6 Don Newcombe 1.50 4.00
7 Joe Nuxhall 1.25 3.00
8 Jim O'Toole .75 2.00
9 Orlanda Pena .75 2.00
10 Vada Pinson 1.50 4.00
11 Bob Purkey .75 2.00
12 Frank Robinson 5.00 12.00

1961 Reds Jay Publishing

This 12-card set of the Cincinnati Reds measures approximately 5" by 7". The fronts feature black-and-white posed player photos with the player's and team name printed below in the white border. These cards were packaged 12 in a packet. The backs are blank. The cards are unnumbered and checklisted below in alphabetical order.

COMPLETE SET (12) 6.00 15.00
1 Ed Bailey .75 2.00
2 Jim Baumer .75 2.00
3 Gus Bell 1.25 3.00
4 Gordon Coleman .75 2.00
5 Fred Hutchinson MG 1.25 3.00
6 Joey Jay 1.00 2.50
7 Willie Jones .75 2.00
8 Eddie Kasko .75 2.00
9 Jerry Lynch .75 2.00
10 Claude Osteen 1.00 2.50
11 Vada Pinson 1.50 4.00
12 Frank Robinson 5.00 12.00

1961 Reds Postcards

These postcards feature members of the NL Champion Cincinnati Reds. Many of these cards have stamped blue signatures which appear to be the only year this approach was used. Since these cards are unnumbered, we have sequenced them in alphabetical order.

COMPLETE SET 75.00 150.00
1 Gus Bell 2.00 5.00
2 Don Blasingame 2.00 5.00
3 Marshall Bridges 2.00 5.00
4 Jim Brosnan 2.00 5.00
5 Leo Cardenas 2.00 5.00
6 Elio Chacon 2.00 5.00
7 Gordy Coleman 2.00 5.00
8 Otis Douglas 2.00 5.00
9 John Edwards 2.00 5.00
10 Gene Freese 2.00 5.00
11 Dick Gernert 2.00 5.00
12 Bill Henry 2.00 5.00
13 Ken Hunt 2.00 5.00
14 Fred Hutchinson MG 2.00 5.00
Black Background
15 Fred Hutchinson MG 2.00 5.00
Smiling
16 Joey Jay 2.00 5.00
17 Ken Johnson 2.00 5.00
18 Sherman Jones 2.00 5.00
19 Eddie Kasko 2.00 5.00
20 Jerry Lynch 2.00 5.00
Dark Background
21 Jerry Lynch 2.00 5.00
number 4 on back
22 Jim Maloney 3.00 8.00
23 Howie Nunn 2.00 5.00
24 Reggie Otero 2.00 5.00
25 Jim O'Toole 2.00 5.00
26 Vada Pinson 4.00 10.00
27 Wally Post 2.00 5.00
28 Bob Purkey 2.00 5.00
29 Frank Robinson 6.00 15.00
30 Dick Sisler 2.00 5.00
31 Bob Schmidt 2.00 5.00
32 Jim Turner CO 2.00 5.00
33 Pete Whisenant 2.00 5.00
34 Jerry Zimmerman 2.00 5.00

1962 Reds Enquirer

This set consists of newspaper clippings from the Cincinnati Enquirer and features black-and-white photos of the members of the 1962 Cincinnati Reds team with information about the players. They are unnumbered and checklisted below in alphabetical order.

COMPLETE SET (32) 50.00 100.00
1 Don Blasingame 1.25 3.00
2 Jim Brosnan 1.25 3.00
3 Leo Cardenas 1.50 4.00
4 Gordy Coleman 1.25 3.00
5 Cliff Cook 1.25 3.00
6 Myron Drabowsky 1.25 3.00
7 John Edwards 1.25 3.00
8 Gene Freese 1.25 3.00
9 Joe Gaines 1.25 3.00
10 Jesse Gonder 1.25 3.00
11 Tom Harper 1.50 4.00
12 Bill Henry 1.25 3.00
13 Dave Hillman 1.25 3.00
14 Ken Hunt 1.25 3.00
15 Fred Hutchinson MG 1.50 4.00
16 Joey Jay 1.25 3.00
17 Darrell Johnson 1.25 3.00
18 Eddie Kasko 1.25 3.00
19 Marty Keough 1.25 3.00
20 John Klippstein 1.25 3.00
21 Jerry Lynch 1.25 3.00
22 Jim Maloney 1.50 4.00
23 Bob Miller 1.25 3.00
24 Jim O'Toole 1.25 3.00
25 Don Pavletich 1.25 3.00
26 Vada Pinson 2.00 5.00
27 Wally Post 1.50 4.00
28 Bob Purkey 1.25 3.00
29 Frank Robinson 6.00 15.00
30 Octavio Rojas 2.00 5.00
31 Hiraldo Ruiz 1.25 3.00
32 Dave Sisler 1.25 3.00

1962 Reds Jay Publishing

This 12-card set features members of the Cincinnati Reds. Originally, this set came in a brown envelope that included a "picture pak order form". Printed on thin stock paper, the cards measure approximately 5" by 7". On a white background the fronts have a black-and-white posed player photo. The player's name and team appear in black letters under the photo. The backs are blank. The cards are unnumbered and checklisted below in alphabetical order.

COMPLETE SET (12) 15.00 40.00
1 Jim Brosnan .75 2.00
2 Leo Cardenas 1.00 2.50
3 Gordon Coleman .75 2.00
4 Jess Gonder .75 2.00
5 Fred Hutchinson MG 1.25 3.00
6 Joey Jay 1.25 3.00
7 Eddie Kasko .75 2.00
8 Jerry Lynch .75 2.00
9 Jim O'Toole 1.00 2.50
10 Vada Pinson 1.50 4.00
11 Wally Post 1.25 3.00
12 Frank Robinson 5.00 12.00

1962 Reds Postcards

These cards feature members of the 1962 Cincinnati Reds. For the first time, the stamped autographs are no longer on the card. Since these cards are unnumbered, we have sequenced them in alphabetical order.

COMPLETE SET 75.00 150.00
1 Don Blasingame 2.00 5.00
2 Jim Brosnan 2.00 5.00
3 Leo Cardenas 2.00 5.00
4 Gordy Coleman 2.00 5.00
5 Otis Douglas 2.00 5.00
6 Moe Drabowsky 2.00 5.00
7 John Edwards 2.00 5.00
8 Sammy Ellis 2.00 5.00
9 Hank Foiles 2.00 5.00
10 Gene Freese 2.00 5.00
11 Joe Gaines 2.00 5.00
12 Bill Henry 2.00 5.00
13 Fred Hutchinson MG 2.00 5.00
14 Joey Jay 2.00 5.00
15 Eddie Kasko 2.00 5.00
16 Marty Keough 2.00 5.00
17 Johnny Klippstein 2.00 5.00
18 Jerry Lynch 2.00 5.00
19 Howie Nunn 2.00 5.00
20 Reggie Otero CO 2.00 5.00
21 Jim O'Toole 2.00 5.00
22 Don Pavletich 2.00 5.00
23 Vada Pinson 4.00 10.00
24 Bob Purkey 2.00 5.00
25 Dr. Richard Rohde 2.00 5.00
26 Cookie Rojas 2.50 6.00
27 Ray Shore 2.00 5.00
28 Dave Sisler 2.00 5.00
29 Dick Sisler 2.00 5.00
30 Jim Turner CO 2.00 5.00
31 Pete Whisenant 2.00 5.00
32 Ted Wills 2.00 5.00
33 Don Zimmer 3.00 8.00

1963 Reds Enquirer

This set consists of newspaper clippings from the Reds' Scrapbook found in the Cincinnati Enquirer and features black-and-white photos of the members of the 1963 Cincinnati Reds team with information about the players. They are unnumbered and checklisted below in alphabetical order. Pete Rose appears in his rookie year.

COMPLETE SET (33) 100.00 200.00
1 Don Blasingame 1.25 3.00
2 Harry Bright 1.25 3.00
3 Jim Brosnan 1.25 3.00
4 Leo Cardenas 1.50 4.00
5 Gordy Coleman 1.25 3.00
6 John Edwards 1.25 3.00
7 Sam Ellis 1.25 3.00
8 Hank Foiles 1.25 3.00
9 Gene Freese 1.25 3.00
10 Jesse Gonder 1.25 3.00
11 Tom Harper 1.50 4.00
12 Bill Henry 1.25 3.00
13 Ken Hunt 1.25 3.00
14 Fred Hutchinson MG 2.00 2.50
15 Joey Jay 1.25 3.00
16 Eddie Kasko 1.25 3.00
17 Marty Keough 1.25 3.00
18 John Klippstein 1.25 3.00
19 Jerry Lynch 1.25 3.00
20 Jim Maloney 2.00 5.00
21 Joe Nuxall 2.00 5.00
22 Jim O'Toole 1.25 3.00
23 Jim Owens 1.25 3.00
24 Don Pavletich 1.25 3.00
25 Vada Pinson 2.50 6.00
26 Wally Post 1.50 4.00
27 Bob Purkey 1.25 3.00
28 Frank Robinson 8.00 20.00
29 Dave Sisler 1.25 3.00
30 John Tsitouris 1.25 3.00
31 Ken Walters 1.25 3.00
32 Pete Rose 20.00 50.00
33 Al Worthington 1.25 3.00

1963 Reds French Bauer Caps

These are a 32 "card" set of (cardboard) milk bottle caps featuring personnel of the Cincinnati Reds. These unattractive cardboard caps are blank-backed and unnumbered; they are numbered below for convenience in alphabetical order. The caps are approximately 1 1/4" in diameter. Blasingame was traded to the Senators early in the '63 season and Spencer was picked up from the Dodgers early in the '63 season; hence their caps are tougher to find than the others. Ken Walters and Don Pavletich also seem to be harder to find. We are listing those caps as SP's. Pete Rose has a cap in his rookie year.

COMPLETE SET (32) 250.00 500.00
COMMON PLAYER CAP 2.50 6.00
COMMON SP 6.00 15.00
1 Don Blasingame SP 6.00 15.00
2 Leo Cardenas 3.00 8.00
3 Gordon Coleman 2.50 6.00
4 Wm. O. DeWitt OWN 2.50 6.00
5 John Edwards 2.50 6.00
6 Jesse Gonder 2.50 6.00
7 Tommy Harper 3.00 8.00
8 Bill Henry 2.50 6.00
9 Fred Hutchinson MG 4.00 10.00
10 Joey Jay 3.00 8.00
11 Eddie Kasko 2.50 6.00
12 Marty Keough 2.50 6.00
13 Jim Maloney 4.00 10.00
14 Joe Nuxhall 4.00 10.00
15 Reggie Otero CO 2.50 6.00
16 Jim O'Toole 3.00 8.00
17 Jim Owens 2.50 6.00
18 Don Pavletich SP 6.00 15.00
19 Vada Pinson 5.00 12.00
20 Bob Purkey 2.50 6.00
21 Dr. Richard Rohde 2.50 6.00
22 Frank Robinson 30.00 60.00
23 Pete Rose 100.00 200.00
24 Ray Shore CO 2.50 6.00
25 Dick Sisler CO 2.50 6.00
26 Bob Skinner 2.50 6.00
27 Daryl Spencer SP 12.50 30.00
28 John Tsitouris 2.50 6.00
29 Jim Turner CO 3.00 8.00
30 Ken Walters SP 6.00 15.00
31 Al Worthington 2.50 6.00
32 Dom Zanni 2.50 6.00

1963 Reds Jay Publishing

This 12-card set features members of the Cincinnati Reds. Printed on thin stock paper, the cards measure approximately 5" by 7". On a white background the fronts have a black-and-white posed player photo. The player's name and team appear in black letters under the photo. The backs are blank. The cards are unnumbered and checklisted below in alphabetical order.

COMPLETE SET (12) 12.50 30.00
1 Jim Brosnan .75 2.00
2 Gordy Coleman .75 2.00
3 Fred Hutchinson MG 1.25 3.00
4 Joey Jay 1.00 2.50
5 Eddie Kasko .75 2.00
6 Marty Keough .75 2.00
7 Jerry Lynch .75 2.00
8 Jim O'Toole 1.00 2.50
9 Don Pavletich .75 2.00
10 Vada Pinson 1.50 4.00
11 Bob Purkey .75 2.00
12 Frank Robinson 5.00 12.00

1963 Reds Postcards

These cards feature members of the 1963 Cincinnati Reds. Since these cards are unnumbered, we have sequenced them in alphabetical order. A card of Pete Rose, issued during his rookie season, is included in this set.

COMPLETE SET 125.00 250.00
1 Jim Brosnan 2.00 5.00
2 Leo Cardenas 2.00 5.00
Hitting
3 Leo Cardenas 2.00 5.00
Fielding
4 Jim Coates 2.00 5.00
5 Gordy Coleman 2.00 5.00
6 John Edwards 2.00 5.00
7 Gene Freese 2.00 5.00
Fielding
8 Gene Freese 2.00 5.00
Hitting
9 Jesse Gonder 2.00 5.00
10 Gene Green 2.50 6.00
11 Tommy Harper 2.00 5.00
12 Bill Henry 2.00 5.00
13 Joey Jay 2.00 5.00
14 Eddie Kasko 2.00 5.00
15 Marty Keough 2.00 5.00
16 Jim Maloney 3.00 8.00
17 Charlie Neal 2.00 5.00
18 Jim O'Toole 2.00 5.00
19 Reggie Otero 2.00 5.00
20 Jim Owens 2.00 5.00
21 Don Pavletich 2.00 5.00
22 Vada Pinson 4.00 10.00
23 Bob Purkey 2.00 5.00
24 Frank Robinson 6.00 15.00
Batting
25 Frank Robinson 6.00 15.00
Portrait
26 Dr. Richard Rohde 2.00 5.00
27 Pete Rose 100.00 200.00
28 Ray Shore 2.00 5.00
29 Dick Sisler 2.00 5.00
30 Bob Skinner 2.00 5.00
31 Hal Smith 2.00 5.00
32 Daryl Spencer 2.00 5.00
33 Sammy Taylor 2.00 5.00
34 John Tsitouris 2.00 5.00
35 Ken Walters 2.00 5.00
36 Al Worthington 2.00 5.00
37 Dom Zanni 2.00 5.00

1964 Reds Enquirer Scrapbook

These newspaper "clippings" measure about 5" by 7" when cut from the Cincinnati Enquirer Newspaper. Each time, a different member of the 1964 Reds was featured with some biographical information, his statistics as well as a brief biography. Since these are unnumbered, we have sequenced them in alphabetical order.

COMPLETE SET 40.00 80.00
1 Steve Boros .75 2.00
2 Leo Cardenas .75 2.00
3 Gordy Coleman .75 2.00
4 Lincoln Curtis .75 2.00
5 Jim Dickson .75 2.00
6 John Edwards .75 2.00
7 Sam Ellis .75 2.00
8 Tommy Harper .75 2.00
9 Bill Henry .75 2.00
10 Fred Hutchinson MG .75 2.00
11 Joey Jay .75 2.00
12 Deron Johnson .75 2.00
13 Marty Keough .75 2.00
14 Jim Maloney 1.00 2.50
15 Billy McCool .75 2.00
16 Charley Neal .75 2.00
17 Chet Nichols .75 2.00
18 Joe Nuxhall 1.25 3.00
19 Vada Pinson 1.50 4.00
20 Bob Purkey .75 2.00
21 Mel Queen .75 2.00
22 Frank Robinson 3.00 8.00
23 Pete Rose 10.00 25.00
24 Chico Ruiz .75 2.00
25 Bob Skinner .75 2.00
26 Hal Smith .75 2.00
27 John Tsitouris .75 2.00
28 Al Worthington .75 2.00

1964 Reds Jay Publishing

This 12-card set of the Cincinnati Reds measures approximately 5" by 7". The fronts feature black-and-white posed player photos with the player's and team name printed below in the white border. These cards were packaged 12 in a packet. The backs are blank. The cards are unnumbered and checklisted below in alphabetical order.

COMPLETE SET (12) 30.00 60.00
1 Leo Cardenas .75 2.00
2 Gordy Coleman .75 2.00
3 Tommy Harper 1.00 2.50
4 Fred Hutchinson MG .75 2.00
5 Joey Jay 1.00 2.50
6 Jim Maloney 1.25 3.00
7 Joe Nuxhall 1.25 3.00
8 Jim O'Toole 1.00 2.50
9 Vada Pinson 1.50 4.00
10 Bob Purkey .75 2.00
11 Frank Robinson 5.00 12.00
12 Pete Rose 10.00 25.00

1964 Reds Postcards

This set features members of the 1964 Cincinnati Reds. These cards had no PC markings on the back. Since these cards were unnumbered, we have sequenced them in alphabetical order. A Pre-Rookie Card Tony Perez is in this set.

COMPLETE SET 125.00 250.00
1 Steve Boros 2.00 5.00
2 Leo Cardenas 2.00 5.00
3 Jim Coker 2.00 5.00
Arms Crossed
4 Jim Coker 2.00 5.00
Near the dugout
5 Gordy Coleman 2.00 5.00
6 Ryne Duren 2.00 5.00
7 John Edwards 2.00 5.00
8 Sam Ellis 2.00 5.00
9 Tommy Harper 2.00 5.00
10 Bill Henry 2.00 5.00
11 Fred Hutchinson MG 2.00 5.00
12 Joey Jay 2.00 5.00
13 Deron Johnson 2.00 5.00
14 Marty Keough 2.00 5.00
15 Bobby Klaus 2.00 5.00
16 Jim Maloney 2.50 6.00
17 Billy McCool 2.00 5.00
18 Tom Murphy TR 2.00 5.00
19 Joe Nuxhall 3.00 8.00
20 Reggie Otero CO 2.00 5.00
21 Jim O'Toole 2.00 5.00
22 Don Pavletich 2.00 5.00
23 Tony Perez 8.00 20.00
24 Vada Pinson 4.00 10.00
25 Bob Purkey 2.00 5.00
26 Mel Queen 2.00 5.00
27 Frank Robinson 6.00 15.00
28 Pete Rose 30.00 60.00
29 Chico Ruiz 2.00 5.00
30 Ray Shore 2.00 5.00
31 Dick Sisler CO 2.00 5.00
32 Johnny Temple 2.00 5.00
33 John Tsitouris 2.00 5.00
34 Jim Turner CO 2.00 5.00

1965 Reds Enquirer

This set consists of newspaper clippings from the Cincinnati Enquirer and features black-and-white photos of the members of the 1965 Cincinnati Reds team with information about the players. They are unnumbered and checklisted below in alphabetical order.

COMPLETE SET (29) 30.00 60.00
1 Gerry Arrigo .60 1.50
2 Steve Boros .60 1.50
3 Leo Cardenas .60 1.50
4 Jim Coker .60 1.50
5 Gordy Coleman .60 1.50
6 Roger Craig .75 2.00
7 Ryne Duren .75 2.00
8 John Edwards .60 1.50
9 Sammy Ellis .60 1.50
10 Tommy Harper .75 2.00
11 Tommy Helms .75 2.00
12 Bill Henry .60 1.50
13 Charley James .60 1.50
14 Joey Jay .60 1.50
15 Deron Johnson .60 1.50
16 Marty Keough .60 1.50
17 Jim Maloney 1.00 2.50
18 Bill McCool .60 1.50
19 Joe Nuxhall 1.00 2.50
20 Jim O'Toole .60 1.50
21 Don Pavletich .60 1.50
22 Tony Perez 3.00 8.00
23 Vada Pinson 1.25 3.00
24 Frank Robinson 4.00 10.00
25 Pete Rose 8.00 20.00
26 Hiraldo S.(Chico) Ruiz .60 1.50
27 Art Shamsky .60 1.50
28 Dick Sisler MG .60 1.50
29 John Tsitouris .60 1.50

1965 Reds Jay Publishing

This 12-card set of the Cincinnati Reds measures approximately 5" by 7". The fronts feature black-and-white posed player photos with the player's and team name printed below in the white border. These cards were packaged 12 to a packet. The backs are blank. The cards are unnumbered and checklisted below in alphabetical order.

COMPLETE SET (12) 20.00 50.00
1 Gerry Arrigo .75 2.00
2 Gordy Coleman .75 2.00
3 Sammy Ellis .75 2.00
4 Joey Jay 1.00 2.50
5 Marty Keough .75 2.00
6 Jim Maloney 1.25 3.00
7 Jim O'Toole 1.00 2.50
8 Vada Pinson 1.50 4.00
9 Mel Queen .75 2.00
10 Frank Robinson 5.00 12.00
11 Pete Rose 10.00 25.00
12 Dick Sisler MG .75 2.00

1965 Reds Postcards

Issued by the team, these postcards feature members of the 1965 Cincinnati Reds. Since these are unnumbered, we have sequenced them in alphabetical order. A Tony Perez card is in this series, which is also his Rookie Card year.

COMPLETE SET 100.00 200.00
1 Gerry Arrigo 2.00 5.00
2 Leo Cardenas 2.00 5.00
3 Jimmy Coker 2.00 5.00
4 Gordy Coleman 2.00 5.00
5 Roger Craig 2.00 5.00
6 Jim Duffalo 2.00 5.00
7 Johnny Edwards 2.00 5.00
8 Sammy Ellis 2.00 5.00
9 Tommy Harper 2.50 6.00
10 Charlie James 2.00 5.00
11 Joey Jay 2.00 5.00
12 Deron Johnson 2.00 5.00
13 Marty Keough 2.00 5.00
14 Jim Maloney 2.50 6.00
15 Billy McCool 2.00 5.00
16 Joe Nuxhall 3.00 8.00
17 Frank Oceak 2.00 5.00
18 Reggie Otero CO 2.00 5.00
19 Jim O'Toole 2.00 5.00
20 Don Pavletich 2.00 5.00
21 Tony Perez 40.00 80.00
22 Vada Pinson 4.00 10.00
23 Frank Robinson 8.00 20.00
24 Pete Rose 50.00 100.00
25 Chico Ruiz 2.00 5.00
26 Art Shamsky 2.00 5.00
27 Ray Shore 2.00 5.00
28 Dick Sisler MG 2.00 5.00
29 John Tsitouris 2.00 5.00
30 Jim Turner CO 2.00 5.00
Portrait to Belt
31 Jim Turner CO 2.00 5.00
Portrait shows entire right shoulde

1966 Reds Postcards

These 33 postcards were issued by the Cincinatti Reds and featured members of the 1966 Reds. Since they are unnumbered, we have sequenced them in alphabetical order. These cards can be identified as they were the last year the Reds printed cards on glossy stock.

COMPLETE SET 100.00 200.00
1 Jack Baldschun 2.00 5.00
2 Dave Bristol CO 2.00 5.00
3 Leo Cardenas 2.00 5.00
4 Jimmie Coker 2.00 5.00
5 Gordy Coleman 2.00 5.00
6 Ted Davidson 2.00 5.00
7 Johnny Edwards 2.00 5.00
8 Sammy Ellis 2.00 5.00
9 Bill Fischer 2.00 5.00
10 Mel Harder CO 2.00 5.00
11 Tommy Harper 2.50 6.00
12 Don Heffner MG 2.00 5.00
13 Tommy Helms 2.00 5.00
14 Joey Jay 2.00 5.00
15 Alex Johnson 2.00 5.00
16 Jim Maloney 2.50 6.00
17 Bill McCool 2.00 5.00
18 Don Nottebart 2.00 5.00
19 Joe Nuxhall 3.00 8.00
20 Darrell Osteen 2.00 5.00
21 Jim O'Toole 2.00 5.00
22 Milt Pappas 2.50 6.00
23 Don Pavletich 2.00 5.00
24 Tony Perez 6.00 15.00
25 Vada Pinson 4.00 10.00
26 Mel Queen 2.00 5.00
27 Pete Rose 15.00 40.00
28 Chico Ruiz 2.00 5.00
29 Art Shamsky 2.00 5.00
30 Ray Shore CO 2.00 5.00
31 Roy Sievers 2.50 6.00
32 Dick Simpson 2.00 5.00
33 Whitey Wietelmann 2.00 5.00

1966 Reds Team Issue

These 5" by 7" black and white glossy photos featured members of the 1966 Cincinnati Reds. Since they are unnumbered, we have sequenced them in alphabetical order. It is possible that there are more photos so any additions are greatly appreciated.

COMPLETE SET 40.00 80.00
1 Gerry Arrigo 1.50 4.00
2 Jack Baldschun 1.50 4.00
3 Leo Cardenas 1.50 4.00
4 Jim Coker 1.50 4.00
5 Gordy Coleman 1.50 4.00
6 Ted Davidson 1.50 4.00
7 Johnny Edwards 1.50 4.00
8 Sammy Ellis 1.50 4.00
9 Tommy Helms 1.50 4.00
10 Deron Johnson 1.50 4.00
11 Jim Maloney 2.00 5.00
12 Billy McCool 1.50 4.00
13 Don Nottebart 1.50 4.00
14 Milt Pappas 2.00 5.00
15 Vada Pinson 3.00 8.00
16 Pete Rose 8.00 20.00

1967 Reds Postcards

These 38 blank-backed black and white postcards measure 3 1/2" by 5 1/2" and feature members of the 1967 Reds. The fronts have a player photo, a blue fascimile autograph as well as the Cincinnati Reds in red lettering. Since the photos are unnumbered, we have sequenced them in alphabetical order. Darrell Osteen, who was pictured in the special folder made available to put these photos in, was not published as a postcard. A Johnny Bench postcard is known in this series which predates his Rookie Card.

COMPLETE SET (38) 75.00 150.00
1 Ted Abernathy 1.50 4.00
2 Gerry Arrigo 1.50 4.00
3 Jack Baldschun 1.50 4.00
4 Johnny Bench 12.50 30.00
5 Vern Benson CO 1.50 4.00
6 Jimmy Bragan CO 1.50 4.00
7 Dave Bristol MG 1.50 4.00
8 Leo Cardenas 1.50 4.00
9 Jim Coker 1.50 4.00
10 Ted Davidson 1.50 4.00
11 John Edwards 1.50 4.00
12 Sammy Ellis 1.50 4.00
13 Ray Evans CP 1.50 4.00
14 Mel Harder CO 2.00 5.00
15 Tommy Harper 1.50 4.00
16 Tommy Helms 1.50 4.00
17 Deron Johnson 1.50 4.00
18 Bob Lee 1.50 4.00
19 Jim Maloney 2.00 5.00
20 Lee May 2.00 5.00
21 Bill McCool 1.50 4.00
22 Tom Murphy CP 1.50 4.00
23 Gary Nolan 1.50 4.00
24 Don Nottebart 1.50 4.00
25 Don Pavletich 1.50 4.00
26 Milt Pappas 2.00 5.00
27 Tony Perez 4.00 10.00
28 Vada Pinson 3.00 8.00
29 Mel Queen 1.50 4.00
30 Floyd Robinson 1.50 4.00
31 Pete Rose 50.00 100.00
32 Chico Ruiz 1.50 4.00
33 Art Shamsky 1.50 4.00
34 Ray Shore CO 1.50 4.00
35 Dick Simpson 1.50 4.00
36 Jake Wood 1.50 4.00
37 Whitey Wietelmann CO 1.50 4.00
38 Al Wyider CP 1.50 4.00

1968 Reds Postcards

These 30 blank-backed black and white postcards features members of the 1968 Reds. The fronts have a player photo, a blue fascimile signature and "Cincinnati Reds" in red lettering. Since the cards are unnumbered, we have sequenced them in alphabetical order. John Bench is featured during his rookie season.

COMPLETE SET (30) 75.00 150.00
1 Ted Abernathy 1.50 4.00
2 Gerry Arrigo 1.50 4.00
3 Johnny Bench 40.00 80.00
4 Vern Benson CO 1.50 4.00
5 Jimmy Bragan CO 1.50 4.00
6 Dave Bristol MG 1.50 4.00
7 Leo Cardenas 1.50 4.00
8 Clay Carroll 1.50 4.00
9 Tony Cloninger 1.50 4.00
10 George Culver 1.50 4.00
11 Tommy Helms 1.50 4.00
12 Alex Johnson 1.50 4.00
13 Mack Jones 1.50 4.00
14 Bill Kelso 1.50 4.00
15 Bob Lee 1.50 4.00
16 Jim Maloney 2.00 5.00
17 Lee May 2.00 5.00
18 Bill McCool 1.50 4.00
19 Gary Nolan 1.50 4.00
20 Don Pavletich 1.50 4.00
21 Tony Perez 4.00 10.00
22 Vada Pinson 3.00 8.00
23 Mel Queen 1.50 4.00
24 Jay Ritchie 1.50 4.00
25 Pete Rose 8.00 20.00
26 Chico Ruiz 1.50 4.00
27 Jim Schaffer 1.50 4.00
28 Hal Smith CO 1.50 4.00
29 Fred Whitfield 1.50 4.00
30 Woody Woodward 1.50 4.00

1969 Reds Postcards

These 28 blank-backed black and white postcards feature members of the 1969 Cincinnati Reds. These postcards have a player photo, a black fascimile autograph and "Cincinnati Reds" in red lettering. Since these are unnumbered, we have sequenced them in alphabetical order.

COMPLETE SET (28) 50.00 100.00
1 Gerry Arrigo 1.25 3.00
2 Johnny Bench 6.00 15.00
3 Jim Beauchamp 1.25 3.00
4 Vern Benson CO 1.25 3.00
5 Jimmy Bragan CO 1.25 3.00
6 Dave Bristol MG 1.25 3.00
7 Clay Carroll 1.25 3.00
8 Darrel Chaney 1.25 3.00
9 Tony Cloninger 1.25 3.00
10 Pat Corrales 1.25 3.00
11 George Culver 1.25 3.00
12 Jack Fisher 1.25 3.00
13 Wayne Granger 1.25 3.00
14 Harvey Haddix CO 1.25 3.00
15 Tommy Helms 1.25 3.00
16 Alex Johnson 1.25 3.00
17 Jim Maloney 1.25 3.00
18 Lee May 1.50 4.00
19 Jim Merritt 1.25 3.00
20 Tony Perez 3.00 8.00
21 Pete Rose 6.00 15.00
22 Chico Ruiz 1.25 3.00
23 Ted Savage 1.25 3.00
24 Hal Smith CO 1.25 3.00
25 Jim Stewart 1.25 3.00
26 Bob Tolan 1.25 3.00
27 Fred Whitfield 1.25 3.00
28 Woody Woodward 1.25 3.00

1970 Reds Team Issue

These two 5" by 7" blank-backed cards feature members of the Cincinnati Reds circa 1970. It is probable that there are many more cards in this set and grouping so all additional information is appreciated. These cards are unnumbered so we have put them in alphabetical order. Interestingly enough, these are the same photos used in Partridge meats set around the same era.

COMPLETE SET 15.00 40.00
1 Johnny Bench 8.00 20.00
2 Pete Rose 8.00 20.00

1971 Reds Postcards

These 33 black and white blank-backed postcards feature members of the 1971 Cincinnati Reds. The fronts have a player photo, a black fascimile autograph and "Cincinnati Reds" in black lettering. Since these cards are unnumbered, we have sequenced them in alphabetical order.

COMPLETE SET 40.00 80.00
1 Sparky Anderson MG 2.00 5.00
2 Johnny Bench 4.00 10.00
3 Buddy Bradford .75 2.00
4 Bernie Carbo .75 2.00
5 Clay Carroll .75 2.00
6 Ty Cline .75 2.00
7 Tony Cloninger .75 2.00
8 Dave Concepcion 2.00 5.00
9 Pat Corrales .75 2.00
10 Al Ferrara .75 2.00
11 George Foster 2.50 6.00
12 Joe Gibbon .75 2.00
13 Alex Grammas CO .75 2.00
14 Wayne Granger .75 2.00
15 Ross Grimsley .75 2.00
16 Don Gullett 1.25 3.00
17 Tommy Helms .75 2.00
18 Ted Kluszewski 2.00 5.00
19 Lee May 1.25 3.00
20 Jim McGlothlin .75 2.00
21 Hal McRae .75 2.00
22 Jim Merritt .75 2.00
23 Gary Nolan .75 2.00
24 Tony Perez 2.50 6.00
25 Pete Rose 6.00 15.00
26 George Scherger CO .75 2.00
27 Larry Shepard .75 2.00
28 Willie Smith .75 2.00
29 Wayne Simpson .75 2.00
30 Jim Stewart .75 2.00
31 Bobby Tolan .75 2.00
32 Milt Wilcox .75 2.00
33 Woody Woodward .75 2.00

1973 Reds Postcards

These blank-backed cards feature members of the 1973 Cincinnati Reds. Each of the cards have the player's fascimile autograph in a white box with a Cincinnati Reds logo below the signature. It is believed that many of these cards were also issued during the 1974 season. Since these cards are unnumbered, we have sequenced them in alphabetical order.

COMPLETE SET 30.00 60.00
1 Sparky Anderson MG 1.00 2.50
2 Dick Baney .40 1.00
3 Bob Barton .40 1.00
4 Johnny Bench 2.00 5.00
5 Jack Billingham .40 1.00
6 Jack Billingham .40 1.00
Photo credit given
7 Pedro Borbon .40 1.00
8 Clay Carroll .40 1.00
9 Darrel Chaney .40 1.00
10 Dave Concepcion 1.00 2.50
11 Ed Crosby .40 1.00
12 Dan Driessen .40 1.00
13 Phil Gagliano .40 1.00
14 Cesar Geronimo .40 1.00
15 Alex Grammas CO .40 1.00

16 Ken Griffey 1.00 2.50
17 Ross Grimsley .40 1.00
18 Don Gullett .60 1.50
19 Joe Hague .40 1.00
20 Tom Hall .40 1.00
21 Hal King .40 1.00
22 Ted Kluszewski CO 1.00 2.50
23 Andy Kosco .40 1.00
24 Gene Locklear .40 1.00
25 Jim McGlothlin .40 1.00
26 Denis Menke .40 1.00
27 Joe Morgan 1.50 4.00
28 Roger Nelson .40 1.00
29 Gary Nolan .40 1.00
30 Fred Norman .40 1.00
31 Tony Perez 1.25 3.00
32 Bill Plummer .40 1.00
33 Pete Rose 3.00 8.00
34 Richie Scheinblum .40 1.00
35 George Scherger CO .40 1.00
36 Larry Shepard CO .40 1.00
37 Ed Sprague .40 1.00
38 Larry Stahl .40 1.00
39 Bobby Tolan .40 1.00
40 Dave Tomlin .40 1.00

1974 Reds 1939-40 Bra-Mac

This 48 card set, which measured 3 1/2" by 5" featured members of the NL Champions Cincinnati Reds and were issued by Bra-Mac using their extensive photo library. The 1939-40 Reds won consecutive NL pennants during that period.

COMPLETE SET 10.00 25.00
1 John Vander Meer .60 1.50
2 Jimmie Wilson .30 .75
3 Wally Berger .30 .75
4 Bucky Walters .60 1.50
5 Vince DiMaggio .30 .75
6 Johnny Rizzo .20 .50
7 Ival Goodman .20 .50
8 Junior Thompson .20 .50
9 Jim Turner .20 .50
10 Milt Shoffner .20 .50
11 Whitey Moore .20 .50
12 Moe Arnovich .20 .50
13 Ernie Lombardi .75 2.00
14 Mike Dejan .20 .50
15 Dick West .20 .50
16 Johnny Ripple .20 .50
17 Joe Beggs .20 .50
18 Harry Craft .20 .50
19 Lew Riggs .20 .50
20 Mike McCormick .20 .50
21 Red Barrett .20 .50
22 Paul Derringer .40 1.00
23 Johnny Riddle .20 .50
24 Witt Guise .20 .50
25 Billy Werber .30 .75
26 Johnny Hutchings .20 .50
27 Billy Myers .20 .50
28 Williard Hershberger .30 .75
29 Lonnie Frey .20 .50
30 Frank McCormick .30 .75
31 Bill Baker .20 .50
32 Lee Gamble .20 .50
33 Eddie Joost .30 .75
34 Nino Bongiovani .20 .50
35 French Bordagaray .20 .50
36 Peaches Davis .20 .50
37 Johnny Niggeling .20 .50
38 Les Scarsella .20 .50
39 Lee Grissom .20 .50
40 Wes Livengood .20 .50
41 Milt Galatzer .20 .50
42 Pete Noktenis .20 .50
43 Jim Weaver .20 .50
44 Art Jacobs .20 .50
45 Nolen Richardson .20 .50
46 Al Simmons .75 2.00
47 Hank Johnson .20 .50
48 Bill McKechnie MG .60 1.50

1976 Reds Icee Lids

This unnumbered and blank-backed set of "lids" is complete at 12. Cards are listed below in alphabetical order. They are circular cards with the bottom squared off. The circle is approximately 2" in diameter. The fronts contain the MLB logo as well as the player's name, position and team. The player photo is in black and white with the cap logo removed. If a collector acquired all 12 of these discs, they were then eligible to win free tickets to a Cincinnati Reds game. These discs were on the bottom of 12 ounce Icee drinks.

COMPLETE SET 40.00 80.00
1 Johnny Bench 8.00 20.00
2 Dave Concepcion 2.00 5.00
3 Rawley Eastwick .50 1.25
4 George Foster 1.50 4.00
5 Cesar Geronimo .50 1.25
6 Ken Griffey 1.50 4.00
7 Don Gullett .50 1.25
8 Will McEnaney .50 1.25
9 Joe Morgan 5.00 12.00
10 Gary Nolan .50 1.25
11 Tony Perez 4.00 10.00
12 Pete Rose 15.00 40.00

1976 Reds Kroger

This 16-card set of the Cincinnati Reds measures approximately 5 7/8" by 9". The white-bordered fronts feature color player head photos with a facsimile autograph below. The backs are blank. The cards are unnumbered and checklisted below in alphabetical order. They were printed on thin glossy paper.

COMPLETE SET (19) 10.00 25.00
1 Ed Armbrister .40 1.00
2 Bob Bailey .40 1.00
3 Johnny Bench 2.00 5.00
4 Jack Billingham .40 1.00
5 Dave Concepcion .75 2.00
6 Dan Driessen .40 1.00
7 Rawly Eastwick .40 1.00
8 George Foster .75 2.00
9 Cesar Geronimo .40 1.00
10 Ken Griffey 1.00 2.50
11 Don Gullett .40 1.00
12 Joe Morgan 1.50 4.00
13 Gary Nolan .40 1.00
14 Fred Norman .40 1.00
15 Tony Perez 1.00 2.50
16 Pete Rose 3.00 8.00

1976 Reds Parker Classic

These 24 cartoons honor various people who have been involved with the Reds as either a player or manager. These cartoons were drawn by noted sports artist Bob Parker.

COMPLETE SET (24) 50.00 100.00
1 Sparky Anderson MG 5.00 12.00
2 Wally Berger 1.50 4.00
3 Pedro Borbon 1.50 4.00
4 Rube Bressler 1.50 4.00
5 Gordy Coleman 1.50 4.00
6 Dave Concepcion 3.00 8.00
7 Harry Craft 1.50 4.00
8 Hugh Critz 1.50 4.00
9 Dan Driessen 1.50 4.00
10 Pat Duncan 1.50 4.00
11 Lonnie Frey 1.50 4.00
12 Ival Goodman 1.50 4.00
13 Heinie Groh 1.50 4.00
14 Noodles Hahn 2.50 6.00
15 Mike Lum 1.50 4.00
16 Bill McKechnie 5.00 12.00
17 Pat Moran 1.50 4.00
18 Billy Myers 1.50 4.00
19 Gary Nolan 1.50 4.00
20 Fred Norman 1.50 4.00
21 Jim O'Toole 1.50 4.00
22 Vada Pinson 3.00 8.00
23 Bucky Walters 3.00 8.00
24 Checklist 1.50 4.00

1977 Reds Cartoons Parker

This 24-card set features drawings of famous Cincinnati Reds players by cartoonist and photographer, Bob Parker. The set displays player head drawings along with cartoon illustrated player facts and could be obtained by mail for $3.50.

COMPLETE SET (24) 60.00 120.00
1 Ted Kluszewski 6.00 15.00
2 Johnny Bench 15.00 40.00
3 Jim Maloney .75 2.00
4 Bub Hargrave .75 2.00
5 Don Gullett .75 2.00
6 Joe Nuxhall .75 2.00
7 Eddie Roush 1.50 4.00
8 Wally Post 4.00 10.00
9 George Wright 2.50 6.00
10 George Foster 1.25 3.00
11 Pete Rose 20.00 50.00
12 Red Lucas .75 2.00
13 Joe Morgan 6.00 15.00
14 Eppa Rixey 1.50 4.00
15 Bill Werber .75 2.00
16 Frank Robinson 6.00 15.00
17 Dolf Luque .75 2.00
18 Frank McCormick .75 2.00
19 Paul Derringer .75 2.00
20 Ken Griffey 1.25 3.00
21 Jack Billingham .75 2.00
22 Larry Kopf .75 2.00
23 Ernie Lombardi 1.50 4.00
24 John Vandermeer 1.25 3.00

1977 Reds 1939-40 TCMA

This 45-card set features black-and-white player photos of the 1939-40 Cincinnati Reds in red borders. The backs carry 1939 and 1940 player statistics.

COMPLETE SET (45) 8.00 20.00
1 Vince DiMaggio .40 1.00
2 Wally Berger .40 1.00
3 Nolen Richardson .20 .50
4 Ernie Lombardi .75 2.00
5 Ival Goodman .20 .50
6 Jim Turner .40 1.00
7 Bucky Walters .60 1.50
8 Jimmy Ripple .20 .50
9 Hank Johnson .20 .50
10 Bill Baker .20 .50
11 Al Simmons .75 2.00
12 Johnny Hutchings .20 .50
13 Peaches Davis .20 .50
14 Willard Hershberger .40 1.00
15 Bill Werber .40 1.00
16 Harry Craft .20 .50
17 Milt Galatzer .20 .50
18 Dick West .20 .50
19 Art Jacobs .20 .50
20 Joe Beggs .20 .50
21 Frenchy Bordagary .20 .50
22 Lee Gamble .20 .50
23 Lee Grissom .20 .50
24 Eddie Joost .40 1.00
25 Milt Shofner .20 .50
26 Morrie Arnovich .20 .50
27 Pete Naktenis .20 .50
28 Jim Weaver .20 .50
29 Mike McCormick .20 .50
30 Johnny Niggeling .20 .50
31 Les Scarsella .20 .50
32 Lonny Frey .20 .50
33 Billy Myers .20 .50
34 Frank McCormick .40 1.00
35 Lew Riggs .20 .50
36 Nino Bongiovanni .20 .50
37 Johnny Rizzo .20 .50
38 Wes Livengood .20 .50
39 Junior Thompson .20 .50
40 Mike Dejan .20 .50
41 Jimmy Wilson .20 .50
42 Paul Derringer .40 1.00
43 Johnny VanderMeer .40 1.00
44 Whitey Moore .20 .50
45 Bill McKechnie MG .40 1.00

1980 Reds Enquirer

This set features members of the 1980 Cincinnati Reds. The cards are sequenced by uniform numbers of the organization. When cut out, these cards measure 3" by 4 7/16".

COMPLETE SET 5.00 12.00
2 Russ Nixon CO .08 .25
3 John McNamara MG .08 .25
4 Harry Dunlop CO .08 .25
5 Johnny Bench 1.50 4.00
6 Bill Fischer CO .08 .25
7 Hector Cruz .08 .25
9 Vic Correll .08 .25
11 Ron Plaza CO .08 .25
12 Harry Spilman .08 .25
13 Dave Concepcion .40 1.00
15 George Foster .40 1.00
16 Ron Oester .08 .25
19 Don Werner .08 .25
20 Cesar Geronimo .08 .25
22 Dan Driessen .08 .25
23 Rick Auerbach .08 .25
25 Ray Knight .20 .50
26 Junior Kennedy .08 .25
28 Sam Mejias .08 .25
29 Dave Collins .08 .25
30 Ken Griffey .40 1.00
31 Paul Moskau .08 .25
34 Sheldon Burnside .08 .25
35 Frank Pastore .08 .25
36 Mario Soto .20 .50
37 Dave Tomlin .08 .25
40 Doug Bair .08 .25
41 Tom Seaver 1.00 2.50
42 Bill Bonham .08 .25
44 Charlie Leibrandt .08 .25
47 Tom Hume .08 .25
51 Mike LaCoss .08 .25

1980 Reds 1961 TCMA

This 41-card set features photos of the 1961 Cincinnati Reds team with red lettering. The backs carry player information and statistics.

COMPLETE SET (41) 10.00 25.00
1 Eddie Kasko .08 .25
2 Wally Post .08 .25
3 Vada Pinson .30 .75
4 Frank Robinson .40 1.00
5 Pete Whisenant .08 .25
6 Reggie Otero CO .08 .25
7 Dick Sisler CO .08 .25
8 Jim Turner CO .20 .50
9 Fred Hutchinson MG .08 .25
10 Gene Freese .08 .25
11 Gordy Coleman .08 .25
12 Don Blasingame .08 .25
13 Gus Bell .08 .25
14 Leo Cardenas .08 .25
15 Elio Chacon .08 .25
16 Dick Gernert .08 .25
17 Jim Baumer .08 .25
18 Willie Jones .08 .25
19 Joe Gaines .08 .25
20 Cliff Cook .08 .25
21 Harry Anderson .08 .25
22 Jerry Zimmerman .08 .25
23 Johnny Edwards .08 .25
24 Bob Schmidt .08 .25
25 Darrell Johnson .08 .25
26 Ed Bailey .08 .25
27 Joey Jay .08 .25
28 Jim O'Toole .08 .25
29 Bob Purkey .08 .25
30 Jim Brosnan .08 .25
31 Ken Hunt .08 .25
32 Ken Johnson .08 .25
33 Jim Maloney .20 .50
34 Bill Henry .08 .25
35 Jerry Lynch .08 .25
36 Hal Bevan .08 .25
37 Howie Nunn .08 .25
38 Sherman Jones .08 .25
39 Jay Hook .08 .25
40 Claude Osteen .08 .25
41 Marshall Bridges .08 .25

1982 Reds Coke

The cards in this 23-card set measure the standard size. The 1982 Coca-Cola Cincinnati Reds set, issued in conjunction with Topps, contains 22 cards of current Reds players. Although the cards of 15 players feature the exact photo used in the Topps' regular issue, the Coke photos have better coloration and appear sharper than their Topps counterparts. Six players, Cedeno, Harris, Hurdle, Kern, Krenchicki, and Trevino are new to the Reds uniform via trades, while Paul Householder had formerly appeared on the Reds' 1982 Topps "Future Stars" card. The cards are numbered 1 to 22 on the red and gray reverse, and the Coke logo appears on both sides of the card. There is an unnumbered title card which contains a premium offer on the reverse. The set numbering is in alphabetical order by player's name.

COMPLETE SET (23) 3.00 8.00
1 Johnny Bench 1.25 3.00
2 Bruce Berenyi .08 .25
3 Larry Biittner .08 .25
4 Cesar Cedeno .20 .50
5 Dave Concepcion .30 .75
6 Dan Driessen .08 .25
7 Greg A. Harris .20 .50
8 Paul Householder .08 .25
9 Tom Hume .08 .25
10 Clint Hurdle .20 .50
11 Jim Kern .08 .25
12 Wayne Krenchicki .08 .25
13 Rafael Landestoy .08 .25
14 Charlie Leibrandt .08 .25
15 Mike O'Berry .08 .25
16 Ron Oester .08 .25
17 Frank Pastore .08 .25
18 Joe Price .08 .25
19 Tom Seaver 1.25 3.00
20 Mario Soto .20 .50
21 Alex Trevino .08 .25
22 Mike Vail .08 .25
NNO Title Card .05 .15

1983 Reds Yearbook

These perforated cards are found in the center of the 1983 Reds Yearbook; they are numbered by uniform number; cards are in full color; backs contain year by year statistical information. The yearbook itself originally sold (cover price) for $3.00. The cards are sequenced in uniform number order.

COMPLETE SET 2.00 5.00
2 Gary Redus .08 .25
5 Johnny Bench 1.00 2.50
7 Russ Nixon MG .08 .25
13 Dave Concepcion .30 .75
16 Ron Oester .08 .25
20 Eddie Milner .08 .25
21 Paul Householder .08 .25
22 Dan Driessen .08 .25
25 Charlie Puleo .08 .25
28 Cesar Cedeno .20 .50
29 Alex Trevino .08 .25
32 Rich Gale .08 .25
35 Frank Pastore .08 .25
36 Mario Soto .20 .50
38 Bruce Berenyi .08 .25
47 Tom Hume .08 .25
49 Joe Price .08 .25
xx Riverfront Stadium .08 .25

1984 Reds Borden's

This set of eight stickers featuring Eric Davis' first Cincinnati card, was produced as two sheets of four by Borden's Dairy. The sheets are perforated so that the individual stickers may be separated. The sheet of four stickers measures approximately 5 1/2" by 8" whereas the individual stickers measure 2 1/2" by 3 7/8". The backs of the stickers feature discount "cents off" coupons applicable to Borden's products. The fronts feature a full color photo of the player in a bold red border. The stickers are not numbered except that each player's uniform number is given prominently on the front. The sheets are arbitrarily numbered one and two and designated in the checklist below. We have noted either a 1 or a 2 after the player's name to notate which sheet their visage appeared on.

COMPLETE SET (8) 3.00 8.00
2 Gary Redus 2 .08 .25
16 Ron Oester 1 .08 .25
20 Eddie Milner 2 .08 .25
24 Tony Perez 2 1.00 2.50
36 Mario Soto 1 .08 .25
39 Dave Parker 1 .40 1.00
44 Eric Davis 1 1.50 4.00
46 Jeff Russell 2 .20 .50

1984 Reds Enquirer

This set consists of newspaper clippings from the Cincinnati Enquirer and features black-and-white head photos of the members of the 1984 Cincinnati Reds team with information about the players.

COMPLETE SET (32) 6.00 15.00
1 Tony Perez .40 1.00
2 Dan Driessen .08 .25
3 Ron Oester .08 .25
4 Tom Lawless .08 .25
5 Dave Concepcion .30 .75
6 Tom Foley .08 .25
7 Nick Esasky .08 .25
8 Wayne Krenchicki .08 .25
9 Gary Redus .08 .25
10 Duane Walker .08 .25
11 Eddie Milner .08 .25
12 Dave Parker .40 1.00
13 Cesar Cedeno .20 .50
14 Dann Bilardello .08 .25
15 Brad Gulden .08 .25
16 Jeff Russell .20 .50
17 Joe Price .08 .25
18 Bill Scherrer .08 .25
19 Tom Hume .08 .25
20 Bruce Berenyi .08 .25
21 Bob Owchinko .08 .25
22 Ted Power .08 .25
23 Frank Pastore .08 .25
24 John Franco .75 2.00
25 Mario Soto .20 .50
26 Eric Davis 2.00 5.00
27 Tommy Helms CO .08 .25
28 Bruce Kimm CO .08 .25
29 George Scherger CO .08 .25
30 Joe Sparks CO .08 .25
31 Stan Williams CO .08 .25
32 Vern Rapp MG .08 .25

1984 Reds Yearbook

These 18 standard-size cards were inserted into the 1984 Cincinnati Reds yearbook. The cards were issued in two nine-card sheets and could be perforated into standard-size cards. The player photo is surrounded by red trim with the player's name on top and the position on the bottom. The backs have biographical information and career statistics. Since the cards are unnumbered, we have sequenced them in alphabetical order.

COMPLETE SET (18) 4.00 10.00
1 Bruce Berenyi .20 .50
2 Dann Bilardello .20 .50
3 Dave Concepcion .75 2.00
4 Dan Driessen .20 .50
5 Nick Esasky .20 .50
6 Bob Howsam PRES .20 .50
7 Tom Hume .20 .50
8 Eddie Milner .20 .50
9 Ron Oester .20 .50
10 Dave Parker .75 2.00
11 Frank Pastore .20 .50
12 Tony Perez 1.25 3.00
13 Joe Price .20 .50
14 Vern Rapp MG .20 .50
15 Gary Redus .20 .50
16 Bill Scherrer .20 .50
17 Mario Soto .20 .50
18 Duane Walker .20 .50

1985 Reds Yearbook

When perforated, these 18 cards measure the standard size. These cards were included as an insert in the 1985 Cincinnati Reds Yearbook. The fronts feature photos, the player's name and his position. The horizontal backs feature vital statistics and career information. We have sequenced this set in alphabetical order.

COMPLETE SET (18) 3.00 8.00
1 Cesar Cedeno .20 .50
2 Dave Concepcion .30 .75
3 Eric Davis 1.00 2.50
4 Nick Esasky .08 .25
5 Tom Foley .08 .25
6 John Franco .60 1.50
7 Brad Gulden .08 .25
8 Wayne Krenchicki .08 .25
9 Eddie Milner .08 .25
10 Ron Oester .08 .25
11 Dave Parker .40 1.00
12 Ted Power .08 .25
13 Joe Price .08 .25
14 Pete Rose P .75 2.00
MG
15 Jeff Russell .08 .25
16 Mario Soto .08 .25
17 Jay Tibbs .08 .25
18 Duane Walker .08 .25

1986 Reds Greats TCMA

This 12-card standard-size set features some all-time leading Red players. The player's photo, name and position are on the front. The back contains more information about that player.

COMPLETE SET (12) 3.00 8.00
1 Clay Carroll .08 .25
2 Bill McKechnie MG .20 .50
3 Paul Derringer .20 .50
4 Eppa Rixey .30 .75
5 Frank Robinson .40 1.00
6 Vada Pinson .20 .50
7 Leo Cardenas .08 .25
8 Heinie Groh .08 .25
9 Ted Kluszewski .40 1.00
10 Joe Morgan .40 1.00
11 Edd Roush .30 .75
12 Johnny Bench .75 2.00

1986 Reds Texas Gold

Texas Gold Ice Cream is the sponsor of this 28-card set of Cincinnati Reds. The standard-size cards feature player photos in full color with a red and white border on the front of the card. The set was distributed to fans attending the Reds game at Riverfront Stadium on September 19th. The card backs contain the player's career statistics, uniform number, name, position, and the Texas Gold logo.

COMPLETE SET (28) 20.00 50.00
6 Bo Diaz .40 1.00
9 Max Venable .40 1.00
11 Kurt Stillwell .40 1.00
12 Nick Esasky .40 1.00
13 Dave Concepcion .75 2.00
14A Pete Rose INF 4.00 10.00
14B Pete Rose MG 4.00 10.00
14C Pete Rose(Commemorative) 4.00 10.00
16 Ron Oester .40 1.00
20 Eddie Milner .40 1.00
22 Sal Butera .40 1.00
24 Tony Perez 2.00 5.00
25 Buddy Bell .60 1.50
28 Kal Daniels .50 1.25
29 Tracy Jones .40 1.00
31 John Franco .75 2.00
32 Tom Browning .50 1.25
33 Ron Robinson .40 1.00
34 Bill Gullickson .40 1.00
36 Mario Soto .50 1.25
39 Dave Parker .75 2.00
40 John Denny .50 1.25
44 Eric Davis 1.50 4.00
45 Chris Welsh .40 1.00
48 Ted Power .40 1.00
49 Joe Price .40 1.00
NNO Reds Coaches .40 1.00
George Scherger
Bruce Kimm
Billy D
NNO Preferred Customer .40 1.00
Card (Discount Coupon)

1987 Reds Kahn's

This 28-card standard-size set was issued to the first 20,000 fans at the August 2nd game between the Reds and the San Francisco Giants at Riverfront Stadium by Kahn's Wieners. The cards are unnumbered except for uniform number and feature full-color photos bordered in red and white on the front. The Kahn's logo is printed in red in the corner of the reverse. The set features a card of Barry Larkin in his Rookie Card year.

COMPLETE SET (28) 10.00 25.00
6 Bo Diaz .20 .50
10 Terry Francona .30 .75
11 Kurt Stillwell .20 .50
12 Nick Esasky .20 .50
13 Dave Concepcion .50 1.25
15 Barry Larkin 4.00 10.00
16 Ron Oester .20 .50
21 Paul O'Neill 1.50 4.00
23 Lloyd McClendon .30 .75
25 Buddy Bell .40 1.00
28 Kal Daniels .30 .75
29 Tracy Jones .20 .50
30 Guy Hoffman .20 .50
31 John Franco .50 1.25
32 Tom Browning .30 .75
33 Ron Robinson .20 .50
34 Bill Gullickson .20 .50
35 Pat Pacillo .20 .50
39 Dave Parker .50 1.25
43 Bill Landrum .20 .50
44 Eric Davis 1.50 4.00
46 Rob Murphy .20 .50
47 Frank Williams .20 .50
48 Ted Power .20 .50
NNO Pete Rose MG 1.50 4.00
NNO Coaches Card .30 .75
Scott Breeden
Billy DeMars
Tommy H
NNO Ad Card .08 .25
Save 25 cents
on Corn Dogs
NNO Ad Card .08 .25
Save 30 cents
on Smokeys

1988 Reds Kahn's

These 26-card standard-size sets were issued to fans at the August 14th game between the Cincinnati Reds and the Atlanta Braves at Riverfront Stadium. The cards are unnumbered except for uniform number and feature full-color photos bordered in red and white on the front. The Kahn's logo is printed in red in the corner of the reverse. The cards are numbered below by uniform number which is listed parenthetically on the front of the cards.

COMPLETE SET (26) 6.00 15.00
6 Bo Diaz .08 .25
8 Terry McGriff .08 .25
9 Eddie Milner .08 .25
10 Leon Durham .08 .25
11 Barry Larkin 2.00 5.00
12 Nick Esasky .08 .25
13 Dave Concepcion .40 1.00
14 Pete Rose MG 1.00 2.50
15 Jeff Treadway .08 .25
17 Chris Sabo .40 1.00
20 Danny Jackson .08 .25
21 Paul O'Neill .50 1.25
22 Dave Collins .08 .25
27 Jose Rijo .08 .25
28 Kal Daniels .08 .25
29 Tracy Jones .08 .25
30 Lloyd McClendon .08 .25
31 John Franco .40 1.00
32 Tom Browning .20 .50
33 Ron Robinson .08 .25
40 Jack Armstrong .08 .25
44 Eric Davis .40 1.00
46 Rob Murphy .08 .25
47 Frank Williams .08 .25
48 Tim Birtsas .08 .25
NNO Reds Coaches .30 .75
Lee May
Tony Perez
Bruce Kimm
Tom

1989 Reds Kahn's

The 1989 Kahn's Reds set contains 28 standard-size cards; each card features a member of the Cincinnati Reds. The fronts have color photos with red borders. The horizontally oriented backs have career stats. The card numbering below is according to uniform number.

COMPLETE SET (28) 5.00 12.00
6 Bo Diaz .08 .25
7 Lenny Harris .20 .50
11 Barry Larkin 1.25 3.00
12 Joel Youngblood .08 .25
14 Pete Rose MG .75 2.00
16 Ron Oester .08 .25
17 Chris Sabo .20 .50
20 Danny Jackson .08 .25
21 Paul O'Neill .50 1.25
25 Todd Benzinger .08 .25
27 Jose Rijo .08 .25
28 Kal Daniels .08 .25
29 Herm Winningham .08 .25
30 Ken Griffey .30 .75
31 John Franco .40 1.00
32 Tom Browning .20 .50
33 Ron Robinson .08 .25
34 Jeff Reed .08 .25
36 Rolando Roomes .08 .25
37 Norm Charlton .20 .50
42 Rick Mahler .08 .25
43 Kent Tekulve .20 .50
44 Eric Davis .40 1.00
48 Tim Birtsas .08 .25
49 Rob Dibble .30 .75
XX Coaches Card .20 .50
Scott Breeden
Dave Bristol
Tommy H
xx Sponsor Coupon .05 .15
Kahn's Corndogs
xx Sponsor Coupon .05 .15
Kahn's Wieners

1990 Reds Kahn's

This 27-card, standard size set of Cincinnati Reds was issued by Kahn's Meats. This set which continued a more than 30-year tradition of Kahn's issuing Cincinnati Reds cards has the player's photos framed by red and white borders. The front have full-color photos while the back have a small black and white photo in the upper left hand corner and complete career statistics on the back of the card. The set is checklisted alphabetically since the cards are unnumbered.

COMPLETE SET (27) 4.00 10.00
1 Jack Armstrong .08 .25
2 Todd Benzinger .08 .25
3 Tim Birtsas .08 .25
4 Glenn Braggs .08 .25
5 Tom Browning .20 .50
6 Norm Charlton .08 .25
7 Eric Davis .50 1.25
8 Rob Dibble .20 .50
9 Mariano Duncan .08 .25
10 Ken Griffey .30 .75
11 Billy Hatcher .20 .50
12 Barry Larkin 1.00 2.50
13 Danny Jackson .08 .25
14 Tim Layana .08 .25
15 Rick Mahler .08 .25
16 Hal Morris .30 .75
17 Randy Myers .30 .75
18 Ron Oester .08 .25
19 Joe Oliver .08 .25
20 Paul O'Neill .40 1.00
21 Lou Piniella MG .30 .75
22 Luis Quinones .08 .25
23 Jeff Reed .08 .25
24 Jose Rijo .20 .50
25 Chris Sabo .08 .25
26 Herm Winningham .08 .25
27 Red Coaches .30 .75
Jackie Moore
Tony Perez
Sam Perlozz

1991 Reds Kahn's

The 1991 Kahn's Cincinnati Reds set contains 28 standard-size cards. The set is skip-numbered by uniform number and includes two Kahn's coupon cards.

COMPLETE SET (28) 3.00 8.00
NNO Schottzie .08 .25
Mascot
7 Mariano Duncan .08 .25
9 Joe Oliver .08 .25
10 Luis Quinones .08 .25
11 Barry Larkin 1.00 2.50
15 Glenn Braggs .08 .25
17 Chris Sabo .08 .25
19 Bill Doran .08 .25
21 Paul O'Neill .40 1.00
22 Billy Hatcher .08 .25
23 Hal Morris .08 .25
25 Todd Benzinger .08 .25
27 Jose Rijo .08 .25
28 Randy Myers .20 .50
29 Herm Winningham .08 .25
32 Tom Browning .20 .50
34 Jeff Reed .08 .25
36 Don Carman .08 .25
37 Norm Charlton .08 .25
40 Jack Armstrong .08 .25
41 Lou Piniella MG .30 .75
44 Eric Davis .40 1.00
45 Chris Hammond .20 .50
47 Scott Scudder .08 .25
48 Ted Power .08 .25
49 Rob Dibble .20 .50
57 Freddie Benavides .08 .25
NNO Coaches Card .20 .50
Jackie Moore
Tony Perez
Sam Perlozz

1991 Reds Pepsi

This 20-card standard-size set was produced by MSA (Michael Schechter Associates) for Pepsi-Cola of Ohio, and Pepsi logos adorn the upper corners of the card face. The cards were placed inside of 24-soda packs of Pepsi, Diet Pepsi, Caffeine-Free Pepsi, Caffeine Free Diet-Pepsi, Mountain Dew, and Diet Mountain Dew.

COMPLETE SET (20) 5.00 12.00
1 Jack Armstrong .20 .50
2 Todd Benzinger .20 .50
3 Glenn Braggs .20 .50
4 Tom Browning .30 .75
5 Norm Charlton .20 .50
6 Eric Davis .60 1.50
7 Rob Dibble .30 .75
8 Bill Doran .20 .50
9 Mariano Duncan .20 .50
10 Billy Hatcher .20 .50
11 Barry Larkin 1.00 2.50
12 Hal Morris .20 .50
13 Randy Myers .40 1.00
14 Joe Oliver .20 .50
15 Paul O'Neill .60 1.50
16 Lou Piniella MG .40 1.00
17 Jeff Reed .20 .50
18 Jose Rijo .20 .50
19 Chris Sabo .20 .50
20 Herm Winningham .20 .50

1992 Reds Kahn's

The 1992 Kahn's Cincinnati Reds set consists of 29 standard-size cards. The set included two manufacturer's coupons (one for 50 cents off Kahn's Wieners and another for the same amount off Kahn's Corn Dogs). The cards are skip-numbered by uniform number on both sides and checklisted below accordingly.

COMPLETE SET (29) 3.00 8.00
2 Schottzie(Mascot) .08 .25
9 Joe Oliver .08 .25
10 Bip Roberts .08 .25
11 Barry Larkin .75 2.00
12 Freddie Benavides .08 .25
15 Glenn Braggs .08 .25
16 Reggie Sanders .30 .75
17 Chris Sabo .08 .25
19 Bill Doran .08 .25
21 Paul O'Neill .40 1.00
23 Hal Morris .08 .25
25 Scott Bankhead .08 .25
26 Darnell Coles .08 .25
27 Jose Rijo .08 .25
28 Scott Ruskin .08 .25
29 Greg Swindell .08 .25
30 Dave Martinez .08 .25
31 Tim Belcher .08 .25
32 Tom Browning .08 .25
34 Jeff Reed .08 .25
37 Norm Charlton .08 .25
38 Troy Afenir .08 .25
41 Lou Piniella MG .30 .75
45 Chris Hammond .08 .25
48 Dwayne Henry .08 .25
49 Rob Dibble .20 .50
NNO Coaches Card .20 .50
Jackie Moore
John McLaren
Sam Perl
NNO Manufacturer's Coupon .05 .15
Kahn's Corn Dogs
NNO Manufacturer's Coupon .05 .15
Kahn's Beef Franks

1993 Reds Kahn's

This 27-card standard-size set was issued by Kahn's Meats. The cards are unnumbered and checklisted below in alphabetical order.

COMPLETE SET (30) 3.00 8.00
1 Bobby Ayala .08 .25
2 Tim Belcher .08 .25
3 Jeff Branson .08 .25
4 Marty Brennaman ANN .20 .50
Joe Nuxhall ANN
5 Tom Browning .20 .50
6 Jacob Brumfield .08 .25
7 Greg Cadaret .08 .25
8 Jose Cardenal CO .08 .25
Don Gullett CO
Ray Knight CO
D
9 Rob Dibble .20 .50
10 Davey Johnson MG .20 .50
11 Roberto Kelly .08 .25
12 Bill Landrum .08 .25
13 Barry Larkin .75 2.00
14 Randy Milligan .08 .25
15 Kevin Mitchell .20 .50
16 Hal Morris .08 .25

17 Joe Oliver .08 .25
18 Tim Pugh .08 .25
19 Jeff Reardon .20 .50
20 Jose Rijo .20 .50
21 Bip Roberts .08 .25
22 Chris Sabo .08 .25
23 Juan Samuel .08 .25
24 Reggie Sanders .30 .75
25 Schottzie (mascot) .08 .25
Marge Schott
26 John Smiley .08 .25
27 Gary Varsho .08 .25
28 Kevin Wickander .08 .25
NNO Manufacturer's Coupon (Kahn's hot dogs) .05 .15
NNO Manufacturer's Coupon (Kahn's corn dogs) .05 .15

1994 Reds Kahn's

These 33 standard-size cards were handed out at Riverfront Stadium to fans attending a Reds' home game on August 7. The cards are unnumbered and checklisted below in alphabetical order.

COMPLETE SET (35) 3.00 8.00
1 Bret Boone UER/(Misspelled Brett on front and ba .30 .75
2 Jeff Branson .08 .25
3 Jeff Brantley .20 .50
4 Tom Browning .20 .50
5 Jacob Brumfield .08 .25
6 Hector Carrasco .08 .25
7 Rob Dibble .08 .25
8 Brian Dorsett .08 .25
9 Tony Fernandez .20 .50
10 Tim Fortugno UER (Misspelled Fortungo on back) .08 .25
11 Steve Foster .08 .25
12 Ron Gant .20 .50
13 Erik Hanson .08 .25
14 Lenny Harris .08 .25
15 Thomas Howard .08 .25
16 Davey Johnson MG .20 .50
17 Barry Larkin .75 2.00
18 Chuck McElroy .08 .25
19 Kevin Mitchell .20 .50
20 Hal Morris .08 .25
21 Joe Oliver .08 .25
22 Tim Pugh .08 .25
23 Jose Rijo .08 .25
24 John Roper .08 .25
25 Johnny Ruffin .08 .25
26 Deion Sanders .40 1.00
27 Reggie Sanders .30 .75
28 Schottzie (Mascot) .08 .25
29 Pete Schourek .08 .25
30 John Smiley UER/(Front photo is Erik Hanson) .08 .25
31 Eddie Taubensee .08 .25
32 Jerome Walton .08 .25
33 Coaches .08 .25
Bob Boone
Don Gullett
Grant Jackson
Ra
NNO Manufacturer's Coupon Kahn's Wieners .05 .15
NNO Manufacturer's Coupon Kahn's Corn Dogs .05 .15

1995 Reds Kahn's

This 34-card standard-size set has white-bordered fronts feature color player action photos. The cards are unnumbered and checklisted below in alphabetical order.

COMPLETE SET (36) 2.50 6.00
1 Eric Anthony .02 .10
2 Damon Berryhill .02 .10
3 Bret Boone .30 .75
4 Jeff Branson .02 .10
5 Jeff Brantley .08 .25
6 Hector Carrasco .02 .10
7 Ron Gant .08 .25
8 Willie Greene .02 .10
9 Lenny Harris .02 .10
10 Xavier Hernandez .02 .10
11 Thomas Howard .02 .10
12 Brian Hunter .02 .10
13 Mike Jackson .02 .10
14 Kevin Jarvis .02 .10
15 Davey Johnson MG .08 .25
16 Barry Larkin .60 1.50
17 Mark Lewis .02 .10
18 Chuck McElroy .02 .10
19 Hal Morris .02 .10
20 C.J. Nitkowski .02 .10
21 Brad Pennington .02 .10
22 Tim Pugh .02 .10
23 Jose Rijo .02 .10
24 John Roper .02 .10
25 Johnny Ruffin .02 .10
26 Deion Sanders .30 .75
27 Reggie Sanders .20 .50
28 Benito Santiago .08 .25
29 Schottzie (Mascot) .02 .10
30 Pete Schourek .02 .10
31 John Smiley .02 .10
32 Eddie Taubensee .02 .10
33 Jerome Walton .02 .10
34 Coaches .02 .10
Ray Knight
Don Gullett
Grant Jackson
H
NNO Manufacturer's Coupon Kahn's Corn Dogs .01 .05
NNO Manufacturer's Coupon Kahn's Hot Dogs .01 .05

1996 Reds Kahn's

This 36 card standard-size set features members of the 1996 Cincinnati Reds. Since the cards are unnumbered, we have sequenced them in alphabetical order.

COMPLETE SET (36) 4.00 10.00
1 Eric Anthony .08 .25
2 Tim Belk .08 .25
3 Bret Boone .40 1.00
4 Jeff Branson .08 .25
5 Jeff Brantley .20 .50
6 Dave Burba .08 .25
7 Hector Carrasco .08 .25
8 Eric Davis .30 .75
9 Curtis Goodwin .08 .25
10 Willie Greene .08 .25
11 Lenny Harris .08 .25
12 Thomas Howard .08 .25
13 Kevin Jarvis .08 .25
14 Mike Kelly .08 .25
15 Ray Knight MG .08 .25
16 Barry Larkin .60 1.50
17 Hal Morris .08 .25
18 Joe Oliver .08 .25
19 Eric Owens .08 .25
20 Eduardo Perez .08 .25
21 Mark Portugal .08 .25
22 Jose Rijo .08 .25
23 Johnny Ruffin .08 .25
24 Chris Sabo .08 .25
25 Roger Salkeld .08 .25
26 Reggie Sanders .30 .75
27 Pete Schourek .08 .25
28 Scott Service .08 .25
29 Jeff Shaw .20 .50
30 John Smiley .08 .25
31 Bernie Stowe EQMG .08 .25
32 Eddie Taubensee .08 .25
33 Marc Bombard CO .08 .25
Don Gullett CO
Jim Lett CO
Hal
34 Schottzie 02 .08 .25
Mascot
35 Coupon .05 .15
36 Coupon .05 .15

1996 Reds '76 Klosterman

This 10-card set celebrates the 20th anniversary of the Cincinnati Reds 1976 World Championship team. Distributed by Klosterman Baking Co., one card was inserted in bags of Big White Bread product and released to participating Cincinnati-area grocery stores.

COMPLETE SET (10) 2.00 5.00
1 Sparky Anderson .20 .50
2 Johnny Bench .40 1.00
3 Big Four 1.00 2.50
Johnny Bench
Joe Morgan
Tony Perez
Pete Rose
4 Dave Concepcion .30 .75
5 George Foster .20 .50
6 Cesar Geronimo .08 .25
7 Ken Griffey .30 .75
8 Don Gullett .08 .25
9 Joe Morgan .40 1.00
10 Tony Perez .40 1.00

1997 Reds Kahn's

This 36 card standard-size set features members of the 1997 Cincinnati Reds. The players and uniform number are on the left of the card while the rest of the card is devoted to a borderless photo.

COMPLETE SET (36) 4.00 10.00
1 Stan Belinda .08 .25
2 Aaron Boone .08 .25
3 Bret Boone .20 .50
4 Jeff Branson .08 .25
5 Jeff Brantley .20 .50
6 Dave Burba .08 .25
7 Brook Fordyce .08 .25
8 Steve Gibralter .08 .25
9 Curtis Goodwin .08 .25
10 Willie Greene .08 .25
11 Lenny Harris .08 .25
12 Mike Kelly .08 .25
13 Ray Knight MG .08 .25
14 Barry Larkin .60 1.50
15 Kent Mercker .08 .25
16 Mike Morgan .08 .25
17 Hal Morris .08 .25
18 Joe Oliver .08 .25
19 Terry Pendleton .08 .25
20 Eduardo Perez .08 .25
21 Pokey Reese .08 .25
22 Mike Remlinger .08 .25
23 Jose Rijo .08 .25
24 Felix Rodriguez .08 .25
25 Deion Sanders .40 1.00
26 Reggie Sanders .30 .75
27 Pete Schourek .08 .25
28 Jeff Shaw .20 .50
29 John Smiley .08 .25
30 Scott Sullivan .08 .25
31 Eddie Taubensee .08 .25
32 Brett Tomko .08 .25
33 Ken Griffey Sr CO .08 .25
Don Gullett CO
Tom Hume CO
De
34 Schottzie 02 .08 .25
Mascot
35 Coupon .05 .15
36 Coupon .05 .15

1998 Reds Kahn's

This 36 card standard-size set features members of the 1998 Cincinnati Reds. Since the cards are unnumbered, we have sequenced them in alphabetical order.

COMPLETE SET (36) 5.00 12.00
1 Stan Belinda .08 .25
2 Aaron Boone .40 1.00
3 Bret Boone .40 1.00
4 Sean Casey .60 1.50
5 Steve Cooke .08 .25
6 Brook Fordyce .08 .25
7 Mike Frank .08 .25
8 Danny Graves .20 .50
9 Willie Greene .08 .25
10 Pete Harnisch .08 .25
11 John Hudek .08 .25
12 Damian Jackson .08 .25
13 Paul Konerko 1.00 2.50
14 Rick Krivda .08 .25
15 Barry Larkin .60 1.50
16 Jack McKeon MG .20 .50
17 Melvin Nieves .08 .25
18 Jon Nunnally .08 .25
19 Steve Parris .08 .25
20 Eduardo Perez .08 .25
21 Pokey Reese .08 .25
22 Mike Remlinger .08 .25
23 Reggie Sanders .30 .75
24 Chris Stynes .08 .25
25 Scott Sullivan .08 .25
26 Eddie Taubensee .08 .25
27 Brett Tomko .08 .25
28 Pat Watkins .08 .25
29 Gabe White .08 .25
30 Todd Williams .08 .25
31 Scott Winchester .08 .25
32 Dmitri Young .30 .75
33 Ken Griffey Sr. CO .08 .25
Tom Hume CO
Ron Oester CO
Do
34 Schottzie 02 .08 .25
Mascot
35 Coupon .05 .15
36 Coupon .05 .15

1999 Reds Kahns

This 34 card standard-size set features members of the 1999 Cincinnati Reds. The cards have the player's name and position running down the left side with the words, "1999 Cincinnati Reds" on the bottom. The rest of the borderless cards feature an action shot of the player. The back has biographical stats and complete career statistics. Other than the uniform numbers on the back, the cards are unnumbered, and therefore we have sequenced the cards in alphabetical order.

COMPLETE SET (34) 4.00 10.00
1 Steve Avery .08 .25
2 Stan Belinda .08 .25
3 Jason Bere .08 .25
4 Aaron Boone .20 .50
5 Mike Cameron .30 .75
6 Sean Casey .40 1.00
7 Danny Graves .20 .50
8 Jeffrey Hammonds .08 .25
9 Pete Harnisch .08 .25
10 Brian Johnson .08 .25
11 Barry Larkin .40 1.00
12 Jason LaRue .08 .25
13 Mark Lewis .08 .25
14 Jack McKeon MG .08 .25
15 Hal Morris .08 .25
16 Denny Neagle .08 .25
17 Steve Parris .08 .25
18 Pokey Reese .08 .25
19 Dennis Reyes .08 .25
20 Chris Stynes .08 .25
21 Scott Sullivan .08 .25
22 Eddie Taubensee .08 .25
23 Brett Tomko .08 .25
24 Michael Tucker .20 .50
25 Greg Vaughn .20 .50
26 Ron Villone .08 .25
27 Gabe White .08 .25
28 Scott Williamson .08 .25
29 Mark Wohlers .08 .25
30 Dmitri Young .30 .75
31 Schottzie .08 .25
Mascot
32 Marty Brennaman ANN .20 .50
Joe Nuxhall ANN
33 Ken Griffey Sr. CO .08 .25
Ron Oester CO
Denis Menke CO#
34 Don Gullett CO .08 .25
Tom Hume CO
Harry Dunlop INS
Mar
XX Kanh's Coupon .05 .15
Hot Dogs
XX Kahn's Coupon .05 .15
Corn Dogs

2000 Reds Kahn's

COMPLETE SET (34) 4.00 10.00
1 Manny Aybar .10 .25
2 Rob Bell .10 .25
3 Dante Bichette .20 .50
4 Aaron Boone .30 .75
5 Sean Casey .40 1.00
6 Juan Castro .10 .25
7 Elmer Dessens .10 .25
8 Osvaldo Fernandez .10 .25
9 Danny Graves .20 .50
10 Ken Griffey Jr. 1.20 3.00
11 Pete Harnisch .10 .25
12 Barry Larkin .60 1.50
13 Jack McKeon MG .10 .25
14 Hal Morris .10 .25
15 Denny Neagle .10 .25
16 Alex Ochoa .10 .25
17 Steve Parris .10 .25
18 Pokey Reese .10 .25
19 Dennys Reyes .10 .25
20 Benito Santiago .20 .50
21 Chris Stynes .10 .25
22 Scott Sullivan .10 .25
23 Eddie Taubensee .10 .25
24 Michael Tucker .20 .50
25 Ron Villone .10 .25
26 Scott Williamson .10 .25
27 Dmitri Young .30 .75
28 Ken Griffey Sr. CO .10 .25
Ron Oester CO
Denis Menke CO#
29 Don Gullett CO .10 .25
Tom Hume CO
Harry Dunlop CO
Mark
30 Marty Brennaman ANN .20 .50
Joe Nuxhall ANN
31 Red .10 .25
Mascot
32 Kahnlee .10 .25
Mascot-
33 Coupon .06 .15
34 Coupon .06 .15

2000 Reds Perez Sheet Pepsi

1 Tony Perez 1.20 3.00

2001 Reds Kahn

COMPLETE SET (33) 4.00 10.00
1 Juan Acevedo .10 .25
2 Aaron Boone .30 .75
3 Bob Boone MG .20 .50
4 Jim Brower .10 .25
5 Sean Casey .40 1.00
6 Juan Castro .10 .25
7 Brady Clark .10 .25
8 Lance Davis .10 .25
9 Elmer Dessens .10 .25
10 Adam Dunn .80 2.00
11 Osvaldo Fernandez .10 .25
12 Danny Graves .10 .25
13 Ken Griffey Jr 1.00 2.50
14 Pete Harnisch .10 .25
15 Barry Larkin .40 1.00
16 Jason Larue .20 .50
17 Hector Mercado .10 .25
18 Chris Nichting .10 .25
19 Pokey Reese .10 .25
20 Chris Reitsma .10 .25
21 Dennys Reyes .10 .25
22 John Riedling .10 .25
23 Ruben Rivera .10 .25
24 Bill Selby .10 .25
25 Kelly Stinnett .10 .25
26 Scott Sullivan .10 .25
27 Michael Tucker .10 .25
28 Scott Williamson .10 .25
29 Dmitri Young .30 .75
30 Marty Brennaman ANN .20 .50
Joe Nuxhall ANN
31 Mr. Red .10 .25
Mascot
32 Ken Griffey Sr. CO .10 .25
Ron Oester CO
Tim Foli CO
Bi
33 Don Gullett CO .10 .25
Tom Hume CO
Mark Berry CO
XX Manufacturer Coupon .04 .10
Hot Dogs
XX Manufacturer Coupon .04 .10
Corn Dogs

2002 Reds Kahn

COMPLETE SET 4.00 10.00
1 Aaron Boone .30 .75
2 Bob Boone MG .08 .25
3 Russell Branyan .20 .50
4 Sean Casey .40 1.00
5 Juan Castro .08 .25
6 Bruce Chen .20 .50
7 Ryan Dempster .20 .50
8 Elmer Dessens .08 .25
9 Adam Dunn .75 2.00
10 Jared Fernandez .08 .25
11 Danny Graves .20 .50
12 Ken Griffey Jr. 1.25 3.00
13 Joey Hamilton .08 .25
14 Jimmy Haynes .08 .25
15 Austin Kearns .50 1.25
16 Barry Larkin .50 1.25
17 Jason Larue .08 .25
18 Corky Miller .08 .25
19 Luis Pineda .08 .25
20 Chris Reitsma .08 .25
21 John Riedling .08 .25
22 Jose Rijo .08 .25
23 Jose Silva .08 .25
24 Kelly Stinnett .08 .25
25 Scott Sullivan .08 .25
26 Reggie Taylor .08 .25
27 Todd Walker .20 .50
28 Gabe White .08 .25
29 Scott Williamson .08 .25
30 Don Gullett CO .08 .25
Tom Hume CO
Mark Berry CO
31 Jim Lefebvre CO .08 .25
Tim Foli CO
Ray Knight CO
Jose
32 Joe Nuxhall ANN .20 .50
Marty Brennaman ANN
33 Cinergy Field .08 .25
XX Corn Dog Coupon .02 .10
XX Hot Dog Coupon .02 .10

2003 Reds Kahn's

COMPLETE SET 5.00 10.00
1 Aaron Boone .30 .75
2 Bob Boone MG .10 .25
3 Russell Branyan .20 .50
4 Sean Casey .40 1.00
5 Juan Castro .10 .25
6 Ryan Dempster .10 .25
7 Adam Dunn .60 1.50
8 Danny Graves .30 .75
9 Ken Griffey Jr. .75 2.00
10 Jose Guillen .50 1.25
11 Jimmy Haynes .10 .25
12 Felix Heredia .10 .25
13 Austin Kearns .40 1.00
14 Barry Larkin .50 1.25
15 Jason LaRue .10 .25
16 Kent Mercker .10 .25
17 Wily Mo Pena .40 1.00
18 Brian Reith .10 .25
19 Chris Reitsma .10 .25
20 John Riedling .10 .25
21 Kelly Stinnett .10 .25
22 Scott Sullivan .10 .25
23 Reggie Taylor .10 .25
24 Gabe White .10 .25
25 Scott Williamson .10 .25
26 Paul Wilson .10 .25
27 Tom Robson CO .10 .25
Tim Foli CO
Ray Knight CO
Jose Ca
28 Don Gullett CO .10 .25
Tom Hume CO
Mark Berry CO
29 Coupon Card (50 cents off) .10 .25
30 Coupon Card (75 cents off) .10 .25

2004 Reds Kahn's

COMPLETE SET (29) 4.00 10.00
1 Juan Acevedo .10 .25
2 Sean Casey .40 1.00
3 Juan Castro .10 .25
4 Brandon Claussen .10 .25
5 Jacob Cruz .10 .25
6 Adam Dunn .60 1.50
7 Ryan Freel .30 .75
8 Danny Graves .30 .75
9 Ken Griffey Jr. .75 2.00
10 Aaron Harang .10 .25
11 Tim Hummel .10 .25
12 D'Angelo Jimenez .20 .50
13 Austin Kearns .40 1.00
14 Barry Larkin .50 1.25
15 Brandon Larson .10 .25
16 Jason LaRue .10 .25
17 Cory Lidle .10 .25
18 Dave Miley MG .10 .25
19 Phil Norton .10 .25
20 Wily Mo Pena .40 1.00
21 John Riedling .10 .25
22 Javier Valentin .10 .25
23 John Vander Wal .10 .25
24 Todd Van Poppel .10 .25
25 Ryan Wagner .30 .75
26 Gabe White .10 .25
27 Paul Wilson .10 .25
28 Mark Berry CO .10 .25
Chris Chambliss CO
Don Gullett CO
Tom Hume CO
29 Jerry Narron CO .10 .25
Randy Whisler CO
Mike Stefanski BC
Mark Mann TR

2009 Reds Kahn's

COMPLETE SET (28) 4.00 10.00
CARDS LISTED ALPHABETICALLY
1 Bronson Arroyo .10 .25
2 Dusty Baker MG .10 .25
3 Jay Bruce .15 .40
4 Jared Burton .10 .25
5 Francisco Cordero .10 .25
6 Johnny Cueto .15 .40
7 Chris Dickerson .10 .25
8 Edwin Encarnacion .25 .60
9 Alex Gonzalez .10 .25
10 Jerry Hairston Jr .10 .25
11 Ryan Hanigan .10 .25
12 Aaron Harang .10 .25
13 Ramon Hernandez .10 .25
14 Daniel Ray Herrera .10 .25
15 Paul Janish .10 .25
16 Mike Lincoln .10 .25
17 Nick Masset .10 .25
18 Darnell McDonald .10 .25
19 Laynce Nix .10 .25
20 Micah Owings .10 .25
21 Brandon Phillips .10 .25
22 Arthur Rhodes .10 .25
23 Adam Rosales .10 .25
24 Willy Taveras .10 .25
25 Edinson Volquez .10 .25
26 Joey Votto .25 .60
27 David Weathers .10 .25

2006 Reds Topps

COMPLETE SET (14) 3.00 8.00
CIN1 Ryan Wagner .12 .30
CIN2 Adam Dunn .20 .50
CIN3 Austin Kearns .12 .30
CIN4 Wily Mo Pena .12 .30
CIN5 Jason LaRue .12 .30
CIN6 Felipe Lopez .12 .30
CIN7 Tony Womack .12 .30
CIN8 Ryan Freel .12 .30
CIN9 Eric Milton .12 .30
CIN10 Luke Hudson .12 .30
CIN11 Aaron Harang .12 .30
CIN12 Brandon Claussen .12 .30
CIN13 Edwin Encarnacion .30 .75
CIN14 Rich Aurilia .12 .30

2007 Reds Topps

COMPLETE SET (14) 3.00 8.00
CIN1 Ken Griffey Jr. .60 1.50
CIN2 Scott Hatteberg .12 .30
CIN3 David Ross .12 .30
CIN4 Jeff Conine .12 .30
CIN5 Bronson Arroyo .12 .30
CIN6 Edwin Encarnacion .30 .75
CIN7 Alex Gonzalez .12 .30
CIN8 Todd Coffey .12 .30
CIN9 Ryan Freel .12 .30
CIN10 Kyle Lohse .12 .30
CIN11 Eric Milton .12 .30
CIN12 Aaron Harang .12 .30
CIN13 Brandon Phillips .12 .30
CIN14 Adam Dunn .20 .50

2008 Reds Topps

COMPLETE SET (14) 3.00 8.00
CIN1 Brandon Phillips .12 .30
CIN2 Ken Griffey Jr. .60 1.50
CIN3 Scott Hatteberg .12 .30
CIN4 Homer Bailey .20 .50
CIN5 David Weathers .12 .30
CIN6 Bronson Arroyo .12 .30
CIN7 Edwin Encarnacion .30 .75
CIN8 Alex Gonzalez .12 .30
CIN9 Joey Votto 1.00 2.50
CIN10 Edinson Volquez .12 .30
CIN11 Norris Hopper .12 .30
CIN12 Francisco Cordero .12 .30
CIN13 Aaron Harang .12 .30
CIN14 Adam Dunn .20 .50

2009 Reds Topps

CIN1 Jay Bruce .25 .60
CIN2 Edinson Volquez .15 .40
CIN3 Joey Votto .40 1.00
CIN4 Bronson Arroyo .15 .40
CIN5 Brandon Phillips .15 .40
CIN6 Aaron Harang .15 .40
CIN7 Edwin Encarnacion .40 1.00
CIN8 Johnny Cueto .25 .60
CIN9 Chris Dickerson .15 .40
CIN10 Francisco Cordero .15 .40
CIN11 Willy Taveras .15 .40
CIN12 Ramon Hernandez .15 .40
CIN13 Jeff Keppinger .15 .40
CIN14 Micah Owings .15 .40
CIN15 Mr. Redlegs .15 .40

2010 Reds Topps

CIN1 Joey Votto .40 1.00
CIN2 Johnny Cueto .25 .60
CIN3 Brandon Phillips .15 .40
CIN4 Homer Bailey .15 .40
CIN5 Willy Taveras .15 .40
CIN6 Drew Stubbs .40 1.00
CIN7 Francisco Cordero .15 .40
CIN8 Micah Owings .15 .40
CIN9 Chris Dickerson .15 .40
CIN10 Scott Rolen .25 .60
CIN11 Edinson Volquez .15 .40
CIN12 Aaron Harang .15 .40
CIN13 Bronson Arroyo .15 .40
CIN14 Jay Bruce .25 .60
CIN15 Wladimir Balentien .15 .40
CIN16 Paul Janish .15 .40
CIN17 Ramon Hernandez .15 .40

2011 Reds Topps

CIN1 Joey Votto .40 1.00
CIN2 Jay Bruce .25 .60
CIN3 Edinson Volquez .15 .40
CIN4 Johnny Cueto .25 .60
CIN5 Bronson Arroyo .15 .40
CIN6 Scott Rolen .25 .60
CIN7 Francisco Cordero .15 .40
CIN8 Homer Bailey .15 .40
CIN9 Edgar Renteria .15 .40
CIN10 Aroldis Chapman .50 1.25
CIN11 Ramon Hernandez .15 .40
CIN12 Jonny Gomes .15 .40
CIN13 Mike Leake .25 .60
CIN14 Brandon Phillips .15 .40
CIN15 Drew Stubbs .15 .40
CIN16 Travis Wood .15 .40
CIN17 Home of the Reds .15 .40

2012 Reds Topps

CIN1 Joey Votto .40 1.00
CIN2 Jay Bruce .30 .75
CIN3 Mat Latos .30 .75
CIN4 Scott Rolen .30 .75
CIN5 Johnny Cueto .30 .75
CIN6 Homer Bailey .25 .60
CIN7 Drew Stubbs .25 .60
CIN8 Brandon Phillips .25 .60
CIN9 Ryan Hanigan .25 .60
CIN10 Bronson Arroyo .25 .60
CIN11 Mike Leake .25 .60
CIN12 Juan Francisco .30 .75
CIN13 Zack Cozart .25 .60
CIN14 Ryan Madson .25 .60
CIN15 Aroldis Chapman .40 1.00
CIN16 Chris Heisey .25 .60
CIN17 Great American Ball Park .15 .40

2013 Reds Topps

COMPLETE SET (17) 3.00 8.00
CIN1 Joey Votto .40 1.00
CIN2 Aroldis Chapman .25 .60
CIN3 Johnny Cueto .20 .50
CIN4 Brandon Phillips .15 .40
CIN5 Jay Bruce .20 .50
CIN6 Mat Latos .20 .50
CIN7 Jonathan Broxton .15 .40
CIN8 Chris Heisey .15 .40
CIN9 Ryan Ludwick .15 .40
CIN10 Shin-Soo Choo .20 .50
CIN11 Todd Frazier .15 .40
CIN12 Bronson Arroyo .15 .40
CIN13 Homer Bailey .15 .40
CIN14 Zack Cozart .15 .40
CIN15 Ryan Hanigan .25 .60
CIN16 Mike Leake .15 .40
CIN17 Great American Ball Park .15 .40

2014 Reds Topps

COMPLETE SET (17) 3.00 8.00
CIN1 Joey Votto .25 .60
CIN2 Aroldis Chapman .25 .60
CIN3 Johnny Cueto .20 .50
CIN4 Brandon Phillips .15 .40
CIN5 Jay Bruce .20 .50
CIN6 Mat Latos .20 .50
CIN7 Billy Hamilton .20 .50
CIN8 Tony Cingrani .20 .50
CIN9 Ryan Ludwick .15 .40
CIN10 Chris Heisey .15 .40
CIN11 Todd Frazier .15 .40
CIN12 Skip Schumaker .15 .40
CIN13 Homer Bailey .15 .40
CIN14 Zack Cozart .15 .40
CIN15 Devin Mesoraco .15 .40
CIN16 Mike Leake .15 .40
CIN17 Great American Ball Park .15 .40

2015 Reds Topps

COMPLETE SET (17) 3.00 8.00
CR1 Joey Votto .25 .60
CR2 Tony Cingrani .20 .50
CR3 Daniel Corcino .15 .40
CR4 Zack Cozart .15 .40
CR5 Todd Frazier .15 .40
CR6 Devin Mesoraco .15 .40
CR7 Manny Parra .15 .40
CR8 Brandon Phillips .15 .40
CR9 Aroldis Chapman .25 .60
CR10 Marlon Byrd .15 .40
CR11 Billy Hamilton .20 .50
CR12 Jay Bruce .20 .50
CR13 Johnny Cueto .20 .50
CR14 Homer Bailey .15 .40
CR15 Skip Schumaker .15 .40
CR16 Mike Leake .15 .40
CR17 Anthony DeSclafani .15 .40

2016 Reds Topps

COMPLETE SET (17) 3.00 8.00
CR1 Joey Votto .25 .60
CR2 Jose Peraza .20 .50
CR3 Devin Mesoraco .15 .40
CR4 Brandon Phillips .15 .40
CR5 Zack Cozart .15 .40
CR6 Adam Duvall .40 1.00
CR7 Billy Hamilton .20 .50
CR8 Jay Bruce .20 .50
CR9 Homer Bailey .15 .40
CR10 Anthony DeSclafani .15 .40
CR11 Raisel Iglesias .20 .50
CR12 J.J. Hoover .15 .40
CR13 Eugenio Suarez .20 .50
CR14 Tucker Barnhart .15 .40
CR15 Tony Cingrani .20 .50
CR16 Michael Lorenzen .15 .40
CR17 Jumbo Diaz .15 .40

2017 Reds Topps

COMPLETE SET (17) 3.00 8.00
CIN1 Joey Votto .25 .60
CIN2 Dilson Herrera .20 .50
CIN3 Drew Storen .15 .40
CIN4 Michael Lorenzen .15 .40
CIN5 Tucker Barnhart .15 .40
CIN6 Homer Bailey .15 .40
CIN7 Zack Cozart .15 .40
CIN8 Tony Cingrani .20 .50
CIN9 Eugenio Suarez .20 .50
CIN10 Brandon Phillips .15 .40
CIN11 Anthony DeSclafani .15 .40
CIN12 Raisel Iglesias .20 .50
CIN13 Billy Hamilton .20 .50
CIN14 Jose Peraza .20 .50
CIN15 Brandon Finnegan .15 .40
CIN16 Adam Duvall .20 .50
CIN17 Scott Schebler .20 .50

2018 Reds Topps

COMPLETE SET (17) 2.00 5.00
CR1 Joey Votto .25 .60
CR2 Homer Bailey .15 .40
CR3 Michael Lorenzen .15 .40
CR4 Luis Castillo .20 .50
CR5 Raisel Iglesias .20 .50
CR6 Robert Stephenson .15 .40
CR7 Eugenio Suarez .20 .50
CR8 Scooter Gennett .20 .50
CR9 Scott Schebler .20 .50
CR10 Wandy Peralta .15 .40
CR11 Jose Peraza .20 .50
CR12 Adam Duvall .20 .50
CR13 Anthony DeSclafani .15 .40
CR14 Tucker Barnhart .15 .40
CR15 Billy Hamilton .20 .50
CR16 Jesse Winker .25 .60
CR17 Brandon Finnegan .15 .40

2019 Reds Topps

COMPLETE SET (17) 2.00 5.00
CR1 Joey Votto .25 .60
CR2 Scooter Gennett .20 .50
CR3 Eugenio Suarez .20 .50
CR4 Yasiel Puig .25 .60
CR5 Jose Peraza .20 .50
CR6 Anthony DeSclafani .15 .40
CR7 Luis Castillo .20 .50
CR8 Scott Schebler .20 .50
CR9 Tucker Barnhart .15 .40
CR10 Phillip Ervin .15 .40
CR11 Raisel Iglesias .15 .40
CR12 Curt Casali .15 .40
CR13 Alex Wood .15 .40
CR14 Jesse Winker .25 .60
CR15 Matt Kemp .20 .50
CR16 Tanner Roark .15 .40
CR17 Sal Romano .15 .40

2020 Reds Topps

CIN1 Eugenio Suarez .20 .50
CIN2 Joey Votto .25 .60
CIN3 Luis Castillo .20 .50
CIN4 Nick Senzel .25 .60
CIN5 Jesse Winker .25 .60
CIN6 Freddy Galvis .15 .40
CIN7 Aristides Aquino .40 1.00
CIN8 Trevor Bauer .30 .75
CIN9 Phillip Ervin .15 .40
CIN10 Wade Miley .15 .40
CIN11 Sonny Gray .20 .50
CIN12 Raisel Iglesias .15 .40
CIN13 Michael Lorenzen .15 .40
CIN14 Tyler Mahle .15 .40
CIN15 Tucker Barnhart .15 .40
CIN16 Amir Garrett .15 .40
CIN17 Mike Moustakas .20 .50

2017 Reds Topps National Baseball Card Day

COMPLETE SET (10) 5.00 12.00
CIN1 Joey Votto 1.00 2.50
CIN2 Eugenio Suarez .75 2.00
CIN3 Billy Hamilton .75 2.00
CIN4 Anthony DeSclafani .60 1.50
CIN5 Adam Duvall .75 2.00
CIN6 Jose Peraza .75 2.00
CIN7 Raisel Iglesias .75 2.00
CIN8 Brandon Finnegan .60 1.50
CIN9 Homer Bailey .60 1.50
CIN10 Johnny Bench 1.00 2.50

2004 Reflections

COMP.SET w/o SP's (100) 15.00 40.00
COMP.UPDATE SET (50) 12.50 30.00
COMMON CARD (1-100) .30 .75
COMMON CARD (101-130) 1.00 2.50
101-130 STATED ODDS 1:8
101-130 PRINT RUN 1250 SERIAL #'d SETS
COMMON CARD (131-214) 2.50 6.00
COMMON SP (131-214) 3.00 8.00
SP CL: 132/142/144/146/153/156/159
SP CL: 161-162/164/178/184/186/188
SP CL: 190-191/197-198/201/207/214
SP INFO PROVIDED BY UPPER DECK
COMMON CARD (215-298) 3.00 8.00
131-298 OVERALL GU ODDS 1:2
215-298 PRINT RUN 100 SERIAL #'d SETS
COMMON CARD (299-340) 10.00 25.00
COMMON RETIRED 299-340 10.00 25.00

299-340 OVERALL AU ODDS 1:16
299-340 PRINT RUN 35 SERIAL #'d SETS
COMMON CARD (341-390) .40 1.00
ONE UPDATE SET PER 12 UD HOB.BOXES
1 Adam Dunn .50 1.25
2 Albert Pujols 1.00 2.50
3 Alex Rodriguez Yanks 1.00 2.50
4 Alfonso Soriano .50 1.25
5 Andruw Jones .30 .75
6 Austin Kearns .30 .75
7 Rafael Furcal .30 .75
8 Barry Zito .50 1.25
9 Bartolo Colon .30 .75
10 Ben Sheets .30 .75
11 Bernie Williams .50 1.25
12 Bobby Abreu .30 .75
13 Brandon Webb .30 .75
14 Bret Boone .30 .75
15 Brian Giles .30 .75
16 Carlos Beltran .50 1.25
17 Carlos Delgado .30 .75
18 Carlos Lee .30 .75
19 Chipper Jones .75 2.00
20 Corey Patterson .30 .75
21 Curt Schilling .50 1.25
22 Delmon Young .50 1.25
23 Derek Jeter 2.00 5.00
24 Dmitri Young .30 .75
25 Dontrelle Willis .30 .75
26 Edgar Martinez .50 1.25
27 Edgar Renteria .30 .75
28 Eric Chavez .30 .75
29 Eric Gagne .30 .75
30 Frank Thomas .75 2.00
31 Garrett Anderson .30 .75
32 Gary Sheffield .30 .75
33 Geoff Jenkins .30 .75
34 Greg Maddux 1.00 2.50
35 Hank Blalock .30 .75
36 Hideki Matsui 1.25 3.00
37 Hideo Nomo .75 2.00
38 Ichiro Suzuki 1.00 2.50
39 Ivan Rodriguez .50 1.25
40 Jacque Jones .30 .75
41 Jason Giambi .30 .75
42 Jason Schmidt .30 .75
43 Javy Lopez .30 .75
44 Jay Gibbons .30 .75
45 Jeff Bagwell .50 1.25
46 Jeff Kent .30 .75
47 Jeremy Bonderman .30 .75
48 Jim Edmonds .50 1.25
49 Jim Thome .50 1.25
50 Johnny Damon .50 1.25
51 Jorge Posada .50 1.25
52 Jose Contreras .30 .75
53 Jose Reyes .50 1.25
54 Jose Vidro .30 .75
55 Josh Beckett .30 .75
56 Juan Gonzalez .30 .75
57 Ken Griffey Jr. 1.50 4.00
58 Kerry Wood .30 .75
59 Kevin Brown .30 .75
60 Kevin Millwood .30 .75
61 Lance Berkman .50 1.25
62 Larry Walker .50 1.25
63 Luis Gonzalez .30 .75
64 Magglio Ordonez .50 1.25
65 Manny Ramirez .75 2.00
66 Mark Mulder .30 .75
67 Mark Prior .50 1.25
68 Mark Teixeira .50 1.25
69 Miguel Cabrera .75 2.00
70 Miguel Tejada .50 1.25
71 Mike Lowell .30 .75
72 Mike Mussina .50 1.25
73 Mike Piazza .75 2.00
74 Mike Sweeney .30 .75
75 Milton Bradley .30 .75
76 Nomar Garciaparra .50 1.25
77 Orlando Cabrera .30 .75
78 Pedro Martinez .50 1.25
79 Phil Nevin .30 .75
80 Preston Wilson .30 .75
81 Rafael Palmeiro .50 1.25
82 Randy Johnson .75 2.00
83 Rich Harden .30 .75
84 Richie Sexson .30 .75
85 Rickie Weeks .30 .75
86 Rocco Baldelli .30 .75
87 Roy Halladay .50 1.25
88 Roy Oswalt .50 1.25
89 Ryan Klesko .30 .75
90 Sammy Sosa .75 2.00
91 Scott Rolen .50 1.25
92 Shannon Stewart .30 .75
93 Shawn Green .30 .75
94 Tim Hudson .50 1.25
95 Todd Helton .50 1.25
96 Torii Hunter .30 .75
97 Trot Nixon .30 .75
98 Troy Glaus .30 .75
99 Vernon Wells .30 .75
100 Vladimir Guerrero .50 1.25
101 Brandon Medders RC 1.00 2.50
102 Colby Miller RC 1.00 2.50
103 Dave Crouthers RC 1.00 2.50
104 Dennis Sarfate RC 1.00 2.50
105 Donnie Kelly RC 1.50 4.00
106 Alec Zumwalt RC 1.00 2.50
107 Chris Aguila RC 1.00 2.50
108 Greg Dobbs RC 1.00 2.50
109 Ian Snell RC 1.00 2.50
110 Jake Woods RC 1.00 2.50
111 Jamie Brown RC 1.00 2.50
112 Jason Frasor RC 1.00 2.50
113 Jerome Gamble RC 1.00 2.50
114 Jesse Harper RC 1.00 2.50
115 Josh Labandeira RC 1.00 2.50
116 Justin Hampson RC 1.00 2.50
117 Justin Huisman RC 1.00 2.50
118 Justin Leone RC 1.00 2.50
119 Kazuo Matsui RC 1.50 4.00
120 Lincoln Holdzkom RC 1.00 2.50
121 Mike Bumatay RC 1.00 2.50
122 Mike Gosling RC 1.00 2.50
123 Mike Johnston RC 1.00 2.50
124 Mike Rouse RC 1.00 2.50
125 Nick Regilio RC 1.00 2.50
126 Ryan Meaux RC 1.00 2.50
127 Scott Dohmann RC 1.00 2.50
128 Sean Henn RC 1.00 2.50
129 Tim Bausher RC 1.00 2.50
130 Tim Bittner RC 1.00 2.50
131 Adam Dunn Jsy L1 2.50 6.00
132 Andruw Jones Jsy L1 SP 5.00 12.00
133 Austin Kearns Jsy L1 2.50 6.00
134 Bartolo Colon Jsy L1 2.50 6.00
135 Ben Sheets Jsy L1 2.50 6.00
136 Bernie Williams Jsy L1 4.00 10.00
137 Bobby Abreu Jsy L1 2.50 6.00
138 Brian Giles Jsy L1 2.50 6.00
139 Carlos Lee Jsy L1 2.50 6.00
140 Chipper Jones Jsy L1 4.00 10.00
141 Corey Patterson Jsy L1 2.50 6.00
142 Darin Erstad Jsy L1 SP 3.00 8.00
143 Edgar Martinez Jsy L1 4.00 10.00
144 Vladimir Guerrero Jsy L1 SP 5.00 12.00
145 Eric Gagne Jsy L1 2.50 6.00
146 Frank Thomas Jsy L1 SP 5.00 12.00
147 Garret Anderson Jsy L1 2.50 6.00
148 Roger Clemens Jsy L1 6.00 15.00
149 Greg Maddux Jsy L1 4.00 10.00
150 Jacque Jones Jsy L1 2.50 6.00
151 Randy Johnson Jsy L1 4.00 10.00
152 Javy Lopez Jsy L1 2.50 6.00
153 Mike Piazza Jsy L1 SP 6.00 15.00
154 Albert Pujols Jsy L1 6.00 15.00
155 Jim Edmonds Jsy L1 2.50 6.00
156 Eric Milton Jsy L1 SP 3.00 8.00
157 Jorge Posada Jsy L1 4.00 10.00
158 J.D. Drew Jsy L1 2.50 6.00
159 Jose Vidro Jsy L1 SP 3.00 8.00
160 Kevin Millwood Jsy L1 2.50 6.00
161 Larry Walker Jsy L1 SP 3.00 8.00
162 Luis Gonzalez Jsy L1 SP 3.00 8.00
163 Mike Sweeney Jsy L1 2.50 6.00
164 Kerry Wood Jsy L1 SP 3.00 8.00
165 Mike Cameron Jsy L1 2.50 6.00
166 Phil Nevin Jsy L1 2.50 6.00
167 Rocco Baldelli Jsy L1 2.50 6.00
168 Ryan Klesko Jsy L1 2.50 6.00
169 Shannon Stewart Jsy L1 2.50 6.00
170 Torii Hunter Jsy L1 2.50 6.00
171 Trot Nixon Jsy L1 2.50 6.00
172 Vernon Wells Jsy L1 2.50 6.00
173 Alfonso Soriano Jsy L2 2.50 6.00
174 Andruw Jones Jsy L2 4.00 10.00
175 Barry Zito Jsy L2 2.50 6.00
176 Brandon Webb Jsy L2 2.50 6.00
177 Bret Boone Jsy L2 2.50 6.00
178 Scott Rolen Jsy L2 SP 5.00 12.00
179 Carlos Delgado Jsy L2 2.50 6.00
180 Curt Schilling Jsy L2 4.00 10.00
181 Dontrelle Willis Jsy L2 4.00 10.00
182 Eric Chavez Jsy L2 2.50 6.00
183 Frank Thomas Jsy L2 4.00 10.00
184 Gary Sheffield Jsy L2 SP 3.00 8.00
185 Greg Maddux Jsy L2 4.00 10.00
186 Hank Blalock Jsy L2 SP 3.00 8.00
187 Hideki Matsui Jsy L2 10.00 25.00
188 Hideo Nomo Jsy L2 SP 5.00 12.00
189 Ichiro Suzuki Jsy L2 6.00 15.00
190 Ivan Rodriguez Jsy L2 SP 5.00 12.00
191 Jason Giambi Jsy L2 SP 3.00 8.00
192 Rafael Furcal Jsy L2 2.50 6.00
193 Jeff Bagwell Jsy L2 4.00 10.00
194 Jeff Kent Jsy L2 2.50 6.00
195 Jim Thome Jsy L2 4.00 10.00
196 Jose Reyes Jsy L2 2.50 6.00
197 Josh Beckett Jsy L2 SP 3.00 8.00
198 Juan Gonzalez Jsy L2 SP 3.00 8.00
199 Ken Griffey Jr. Jsy L2 6.00 15.00
200 Kevin Brown Jsy L2 2.50 6.00
201 Lance Berkman Jsy L2 SP 3.00 8.00
202 Magglio Ordonez Jsy L2 2.50 6.00
203 Mark Mulder Jsy L2 2.50 6.00
204 Mark Teixeira Jsy L2 4.00 10.00
205 Miguel Tejada Jsy L2 2.50 6.00
206 Mike Mussina Jsy L2 4.00 10.00
207 Preston Wilson Jsy L2 SP 3.00 8.00
208 Rafael Palmeiro Jsy L2 4.00 10.00
209 Alex Rodriguez Jsy L2 6.00 15.00
210 Richie Sexson Jsy L2 2.50 6.00
211 Roy Halladay Jsy L2 2.50 6.00
212 Roy Oswalt Jsy L2 2.50 6.00
213 Tim Hudson Jsy L2 2.50 6.00
214 Troy Glaus Jsy L2 SP 3.00 8.00
215 Adam Dunn Jsy L3 3.00 8.00
216 Austin Kearns Jsy L3 3.00 8.00
217 Bartolo Colon Jsy L3 3.00 8.00
218 Ben Sheets Jsy L3 3.00 8.00
219 Bernie Williams Jsy L3 5.00 12.00
220 Bobby Abreu Jsy L3 3.00 8.00
221 Bret Boone Jsy L3 3.00 8.00
222 Todd Helton Jsy L3 5.00 12.00
223 Chipper Jones Jsy L3 5.00 12.00
224 Corey Patterson Jsy L3 3.00 8.00
225 Darin Erstad Jsy L3 3.00 8.00
226 Dontrelle Willis Jsy L3 5.00 12.00
227 Edgar Martinez Jsy L3 5.00 12.00
228 Eric Gagne Jsy L3 3.00 8.00
229 Garret Anderson Jsy L3 3.00 8.00
230 Roger Clemens Jsy L3 8.00 20.00
231 Hank Blalock Jsy L3 3.00 8.00
232 Jacque Jones Jsy L3 3.00 8.00
233 Jeff Bagwell Jsy L3 5.00 12.00
234 Jeff Kent Jsy L3 3.00 8.00
235 Jeremy Bonderman Jsy L3 3.00 8.00
236 Jim Edmonds Jsy L3 3.00 8.00
237 Jorge Posada Jsy L3 5.00 12.00
238 J.D. Drew Jsy L3 3.00 8.00
239 Jose Reyes Jsy L3 3.00 8.00
240 Jose Vidro Jsy L3 3.00 8.00
241 Kevin Millwood Jsy L3 3.00 8.00
242 Luis Gonzalez Jsy L3 3.00 8.00
243 Mike Sweeney Jsy L3 3.00 8.00
244 Jason Giambi Jsy L3 3.00 8.00
245 Manny Ramirez Jsy L3 5.00 12.00
246 Phil Nevin Jsy L3 3.00 8.00
247 Preston Wilson Jsy L3 3.00 8.00
248 Alex Rodriguez Jsy L3 8.00 20.00
249 Richie Sexson Jsy L3 3.00 8.00
250 Rocco Baldelli Jsy L3 3.00 8.00
251 Ryan Klesko Jsy L3 3.00 8.00
252 Sammy Sosa Jsy L3 5.00 12.00
253 Torii Hunter Jsy L3 3.00 8.00
254 Mike Lowell Jsy L3 3.00 8.00
255 Troy Glaus Jsy L3 3.00 8.00
256 Vernon Wells Jsy L3 3.00 8.00
257 Albert Pujols Jsy L4 10.00 25.00
258 Alex Rodriguez Jsy L4 8.00 20.00
259 Alfonso Soriano Jsy L4 3.00 8.00
260 Roger Clemens Jsy L4 8.00 20.00
261 Barry Zito Jsy L4 3.00 8.00
262 Brandon Webb Jsy L4 3.00 8.00
263 Carlos Delgado Jsy L4 3.00 8.00
264 Curt Schilling Jsy L4 5.00 12.00
265 Derek Jeter Jsy L4 12.50 30.00
266 Eric Chavez Jsy L4 3.00 8.00
267 Gary Sheffield Jsy L4 3.00 8.00
268 Hideki Matsui Jsy L4 12.50 30.00
269 Hideo Nomo Jsy L4 5.00 12.00
270 Ichiro Suzuki Jsy L4 10.00 25.00
271 Ivan Rodriguez Jsy L4 5.00 12.00
272 Jason Giambi Jsy L4 3.00 8.00
273 Jim Thome Jsy L4 5.00 12.00
274 Josh Beckett Jsy L4 3.00 8.00
275 Juan Gonzalez Jsy L4 3.00 8.00
276 Ken Griffey Jr. Jsy L4 8.00 20.00
277 Kerry Wood Jsy L4 3.00 8.00
278 Kevin Brown Jsy L4 3.00 8.00
279 Lance Berkman Jsy L4 3.00 8.00
280 Magglio Ordonez Jsy L4 3.00 8.00
281 Manny Ramirez Jsy L4 5.00 12.00
282 Mark Mulder Jsy L4 3.00 8.00
283 Mark Prior Jsy L4 5.00 12.00
284 Mark Teixeira Jsy L4 5.00 12.00
285 Miguel Tejada Jsy L4 3.00 8.00
286 Mike Mussina Jsy L4 5.00 12.00
287 Mike Piazza Jsy L4 8.00 20.00
288 Pedro Martinez Jsy L4 5.00 12.00
289 Rafael Palmeiro Jsy L4 5.00 12.00
290 Randy Johnson Jsy L4 5.00 12.00
291 Roy Halladay Jsy L4 3.00 8.00
292 Roy Oswalt Jsy L4 3.00 8.00
293 Sammy Sosa Jsy L4 5.00 12.00
294 Scott Rolen Jsy L4 5.00 12.00
295 Shawn Green Jsy L4 3.00 8.00
296 Tim Hudson Jsy L4 3.00 8.00
297 Todd Helton Jsy L4 5.00 12.00
298 Vladimir Guerrero Jsy L4 5.00 12.00
299 Bret Boone AU 15.00 40.00
300 Alex Rodriguez AU 100.00 175.00
301 Dontrelle Willis AU 20.00 50.00
302 Barry Larkin AU 30.00 60.00
303 Barry Zito AU 20.00 50.00
304 Eric Chavez AU 10.00 25.00
305 Bernie Williams AU 60.00 120.00
306 Brandon Webb AU 10.00 25.00
307 Cal Ripken AU 125.00 200.00
308 Carl Yastrzemski AU 40.00 80.00
309 Carlos Delgado AU 15.00 40.00
310 Shawn Green AU 20.00 50.00
311 Eric Gagne AU 5.00 12.00
312 Frank Thomas AU 30.00 60.00
313 Carlos Lee AU 10.00 25.00
314 Garret Anderson AU 10.00 25.00
315 Hideki Matsui AU 200.00 350.00
316 Jim Edmonds AU 20.00 50.00
317 Jeff Bagwell AU 20.00 50.00
318 Luis Gonzalez AU 15.00 40.00
319 Mike Mussina AU 20.00 50.00
320 John Smoltz AU 50.00 100.00
321 Jose Reyes AU 15.00 40.00
322 Josh Beckett AU 20.00 50.00
323 Juan Gonzalez AU 15.00 40.00
324 Ken Griffey Jr. AU 75.00 150.00
325 Rich Harden AU 10.00 25.00
326 Pat Burrell AU 15.00 40.00
327 Mark Teixeira AU 20.00 50.00
328 Roy Oswalt AU 15.00 40.00
329 Miguel Tejada AU 20.00 50.00
330 Mike Hampton AU 15.00 40.00
331 Mike Piazza AU 50.00 100.00
332 Nolan Ryan AU 75.00 150.00
333 Orlando Hernandez AU 15.00 40.00
334 Paul Lo Duca AU 15.00 40.00
335 Roberto Alomar AU 20.00 50.00
336 Rocco Baldelli AU 15.00 40.00
337 Trevor Hoffman AU 20.00 50.00
338 Tom Glavine AU 20.00 50.00
339 Tom Seaver AU 30.00 80.00
340 Mark Prior AU 15.00 40.00
341 Shingo Takatsu RC .40 1.00
342 Franklyn Gracesqui RC .40 1.00
343 Angel Chavez RC .40 1.00
344 Jorge Sequea RC .40 1.00
345 David Aardsma RC .40 1.00
346 Ramon Ramirez RC .40 1.00
347 Lino Urdaneta RC .40 1.00
348 Orlando Rodriguez RC .40 1.00
349 Jason Szuminski RC .40 1.00
350 Luis A. Gonzalez RC .40 1.00
351 John Gall RC .40 1.00
352 Kevin Cave RC .40 1.00
353 Chris Oxspring RC .40 1.00
354 Freddy Guzman RC .40 1.00
355 Jeff Bennett RC .40 1.00
356 Jorge Vasquez RC .40 1.00
357 Merkin Valdez RC .40 1.00
358 Tim Hamulack RC .40 1.00
359 Hector Gimenez RC .40 1.00
360 Jerry Gil RC .40 1.00
361 Ryan Wing RC .40 1.00
362 Shawn Hill RC .40 1.00
363 Jason Bartlett RC 1.25 3.00
364 Renyel Pinto RC .40 1.00
365 Carlos Vasquez RC .40 1.00
366 Mike Vento RC .40 1.00
367 Casey Daigle RC .40 1.00
368 Chad Bentz RC .40 1.00
369 Chris Saenz RC .40 1.00
370 Shawn Camp RC .40 1.00
371 Carlos Hines RC .40 1.00
372 Edwin Moreno RC .40 1.00
373 Michael Wuertz RC .40 1.00
374 Aarom Baldiris RC .40 1.00
375 Ronny Cedeno RC .40 1.00
376 Akinori Otsuka RC .40 1.00
377 Jose Capellan RC .40 1.00
378 Justin Germano RC .40 1.00
379 Justin Knoedler RC .40 1.00
380 Mariano Gomez RC .40 1.00
381 Fernando Nieve RC .40 1.00
382 Scott Proctor RC .40 1.00
383 Roman Colon RC .40 1.00
384 Onil Joseph RC .40 1.00
385 Eddy Rodriguez RC .40 1.00
386 Enemencio Pacheco RC .40 1.00
387 William Bergolla RC .40 1.00
388 Ivan Ochoa RC .40 1.00
389 Rusty Tucker RC .40 1.00
390 Roberto Novoa RC .40 1.00
S38 Ichiro Suzuki Promo

2004 Reflections Black

1-100 OVERALL PARALLEL ODDS 1:4
101-130/299-340 OVERALL AU ODDS 1:16
173-214/257-298 OVERALL GU ODDS 1:2
1-100/173-340 PRINT RUN 1 SERIAL #'d SET
101-130 PRINT RUN 5 SERIAL #'d SETS
NO PRICING DUE TO SCARCITY

2004 Reflections Blue

*BLUE 1-100: 1.25X TO 3X BASIC
1-100 OVERALL PARALLEL ODDS 1:4
1-100 PRINT RUN 250 SERIAL #'d SETS
*BLUE JSY 215-256: 1.25X TO 3X BASIC
215-256 OVERALL GU ODDS 1:2
215-256 PRINT RUN 15 SERIAL #'d SETS

2004 Reflections Gold

*GOLD 1-100: 5X TO 12X BASIC
1-100 PRINT RUN 15 SERIAL #'d SETS
101-130 PRINT RUN 250 SERIAL #'d SETS
*GOLD JSY 131-172: 1.5X TO 4X BASIC
*GOLD JSY 131-172: 1.25X TO 3X BASIC SP
131-172 PRINT RUN 15 SERIAL #'d SETS
257-298 PRINT RUN 5 SERIAL #'d SETS
257-398 NO PRICING DUE TO SCARCITY
*GOLD AU JSY 299-340: .6X TO 1.2X BASIC
299-340 PRINT RUN 15 SERIAL #'d SETS
1-100 OVERALL PARALLEL ODDS 1:4
101-130/299-340 OVERALL AU ODDS 1:16
131-172/257-298 OVERALL GU ODDS 1:2
101 Brandon Medders AU 4.00 10.00
102 Colby Miller AU 4.00 10.00
103 Dave Crouthers AU 4.00 10.00
104 Dennis Sarfate AU 4.00 10.00
105 Donnie Kelly AU 4.00 10.00
106 Alec Zumwalt AU 4.00 10.00
107 Chris Aguila AU 4.00 10.00
108 Greg Dobbs AU 4.00 10.00
109 Ian Snell AU 8.00 20.00
110 Jake Woods AU 4.00 10.00
111 Jamie Brown AU 4.00 10.00
112 Jason Frasor AU 4.00 10.00
113 Jerome Gamble AU 4.00 10.00
114 Jesse Harper AU 4.00 10.00
115 Josh Labandeira AU 4.00 10.00
116 Justin Hampson AU 4.00 10.00
117 Justin Huisman AU 4.00 10.00
118 Justin Leone AU 6.00 15.00
120 Lincoln Holdzkom AU 4.00 10.00
121 Mike Bumatay AU 4.00 10.00
122 Mike Gosling AU 4.00 10.00
123 Mike Johnston AU 4.00 10.00
124 Mike Rouse AU 4.00 10.00
125 Nick Regilio AU 4.00 10.00
126 Ryan Meaux AU 4.00 10.00
127 Scott Dohmann AU 4.00 10.00
128 Sean Henn AU 4.00 10.00
129 Tim Bausher AU 4.00 10.00
130 Tim Bittner AU 4.00 10.00

2004 Reflections Gold Rookie Autograph 125

*GOLD AU 125: .4X TO 1X GOLD AU 250
OVERALL AU ODDS 1:16
STATED PRINT RUN 125 SERIAL #'d SETS

2004 Reflections Red

*RED 1-100: 2X TO 5X BASIC
1-100 OVERALL PARALLEL ODDS 1:4
*RED JSY 131-214: .6X TO 1.5X BASIC
*RED JSY 131-214: .5X TO 1.2X BASIC SP
*RED JSY 215-256: .5X TO 1.2X BASIC
131-256 OVERALL GU ODDS 1:2
STATED PRINT RUN 50 SERIAL #'d SETS

2005 Reflections

COMP.SET w/o SP's (100) 15.00 40.00
COMMON CARD (1-100) .30 .75
COMMON CARD (101-150) .50 1.25
COMMON CARD (151-200) .50 1.25
101-200 STATED ODDS 1:2
COMMON CARD (201-286) .30 .75
201-286 ONE PER '05 UD UPDATE PACK
1 Corey Patterson .30 .75
2 Curt Schilling .50 1.25
3 Todd Helton .50 1.25
4 Johnny Damon .50 1.25
5 Alex Rodriguez 1.00 2.50
6 Vladimir Guerrero .50 1.25
7 John Smoltz .75 2.00
8 Ivan Rodriguez .50 1.25
9 Roy Halladay .50 1.25
10 Carlos Beltran .50 1.25
11 Ichiro Suzuki 1.00 2.50
12 Jim Edmonds .50 1.25
13 Andruw Jones .30 .75
14 Scott Podsednik .30 .75
15 Troy Glaus .30 .75
16 Miguel Cabrera .75 2.00
17 Adrian Beltre .75 2.00
18 Ben Sheets .30 .75
19 Alfonso Soriano .50 1.25
20 Brian Giles .30 .75
21 Carl Crawford .50 1.25
22 Frank Thomas .75 2.00
23 Jeff Kent .30 .75
24 Eric Gagne .30 .75
25 Shawn Green .30 .75
26 Sammy Sosa .75 2.00
27 Carlos Lee .30 .75
28 Ken Griffey Jr. 1.50 4.00
29 Mike Lowell .30 .75
30 Magglio Ordonez .50 1.25
31 Aubrey Huff .30 .75
32 Travis Hafner .30 .75
33 Albert Pujols 1.00 2.50
34 Vernon Wells .30 .75
35 Roy Oswalt .50 1.25
36 Jose Guillen .30 .75
37 Jim Thome .50 1.25
38 Bobby Abreu .30 .75
39 Bret Boone .30 .75
40 Mark Teixeira .50 1.25
41 Garret Anderson .30 .75
42 Jose Reyes .50 1.25
43 Bernie Williams .50 1.25
44 Greg Maddux 1.00 2.50
45 Gary Sheffield .30 .75
46 Josh Beckett .30 .75
47 Chipper Jones .75 2.00
48 Hank Blalock .30 .75
49 C.C. Sabathia .50 1.25
50 Manny Ramirez .75 2.00
51 Pedro Martinez .50 1.25
52 Michael Young .30 .75
53 Jacque Jones .30 .75
54 Marcus Giles .30 .75
55 Steve Finley .30 .75
56 Miguel Tejada .50 1.25
57 Mike Sweeney .30 .75
58 Lance Berkman .50 1.25
59 J.D. Drew .30 .75
60 Jeromy Burnitz .30 .75
61 Johan Santana .50 1.25
62 Victor Martinez .50 1.25
63 Carl Pavano .30 .75
64 Roger Clemens 1.00 2.50
65 Richie Sexson .30 .75
66 Tim Hudson .50 1.25
67 Melvin Mora .30 .75
68 Angel Berroa .30 .75
69 Rafael Palmeiro .50 1.25
70 Randy Johnson .75 2.00
71 Torii Hunter .30 .75
72 Luis Gonzalez .30 .75
73 Kazuo Matsui .30 .75
74 Hideki Matsui 1.25 3.00
75 Mark Prior .50 1.25
76 Jeff Bagwell .50 1.25
77 Eric Chavez .30 .75
78 Mark Loretta .30 .75
79 Adam Dunn .50 1.25
80 Kerry Wood .30 .75
81 Jose Vidro .30 .75
82 Jason Schmidt .30 .75
83 Carlos Delgado .30 .75
84 Scott Rolen .50 1.25
85 David Ortiz .75 2.00
86 Edgar Renteria .30 .75
87 Nomar Garciaparra .50 1.25
88 Mike Piazza .75 2.00
89 Mark Mulder .30 .75
90 Tom Glavine .50 1.25
91 Paul Konerko .50 1.25
92 Larry Walker .50 1.25
93 Derek Jeter 2.00 5.00
94 Jake Peavy .30 .75
95 Carlos Zambrano .50 1.25
96 Russ Ortiz .30 .75
97 Barry Zito .50 1.25
98 Austin Kearns .30 .75
99 Pedro Feliz .30 .75
100 Rich Harden .30 .75
101 Adam LaRoche FUT .50 1.25
102 Brandon Claussen FUT .50 1.25
103 Gavin Floyd FUT .50 1.25
104 Daniel Cabrera FUT .50 1.25
105 Joe Mauer FUT 1.00 2.50
106 Khalil Greene FUT .50 1.25
107 David Wright FUT 1.00 2.50
108 Rickie Weeks FUT .50 1.25
109 Robb Quinlan FUT .50 1.25
110 Bucky Jacobsen FUT .50 1.25
111 Ryan Howard FUT 1.00 2.50
112 Jeff Francis FUT .50 1.25
113 Jason Lane FUT .50 1.25
114 Alexis Rios FUT .50 1.25
115 Bobby Madritsch FUT .50 1.25
116 Jesse Crain FUT .50 1.25
117 Oliver Perez FUT .50 1.25
118 Garrett Atkins FUT .50 1.25
119 Casey Kotchman FUT .50 1.25
120 B.J. Upton FUT .75 2.00
121 Laynce Nix FUT .50 1.25
122 Adrian Gonzalez FUT 1.00 2.50
123 Joe Blanton FUT .50 1.25
124 Gabe Gross FUT .50 1.25
125 Scott Kazmir FUT 1.25 3.00
126 Zack Greinke FUT 1.50 4.00
127 Edwin Jackson FUT .50 1.25
128 Jason Bay FUT .50 1.25
129 J.D. Closser FUT .50 1.25
130 Jason DuBois FUT .50 1.25
131 Dallas McPherson FUT .50 1.25
132 Chad Cordero FUT .50 1.25
133 Angel Guzman FUT .50 1.25
134 Jayson Werth FUT .75 2.00
135 Ryan Wagner FUT .50 1.25
136 Guillermo Quiroz FUT .50 1.25
137 Scott Proctor FUT .50 1.25
138 Chris Burke FUT .50 1.25
139 Nick Swisher FUT .75 2.00
140 David DeJesus FUT .50 1.25
141 Yhency Brazoban FUT .50 1.25
142 Bobby Crosby FUT .50 1.25
143 Chase Utley FUT .75 2.00
144 Wily Mo Pena FUT .50 1.25
145 Roman Colon FUT .50 1.25
146 Eddy Rodriguez FUT .50 1.25
147 Gerald Laird FUT .50 1.25
148 Jose Capellan FUT .50 1.25
149 Aaron Rowand FUT .50 1.25
150 Kevin Youkilis FUT .50 1.25
151 Bob Feller LGD .75 2.00
152 Robin Yount LGD 1.25 3.00
153 Willie Stargell LGD .75 2.00
154 Cal Ripken LGD 4.00 10.00
155 Monte Irvin LGD .75 2.00
156 Nolan Ryan LGD 4.00 10.00
157 Bob Lemon LGD .75 2.00
158 Richie Ashburn LGD .75 2.00
159 Billy Williams LGD .75 2.00
160 Luis Aparicio LGD .75 2.00
161 Phil Niekro LGD .75 2.00
162 Bobby Doerr LGD .75 2.00
163 Mike Schmidt LGD 2.00 5.00
164 Stan Musial LGD 2.00 5.00
165 George Kell LGD .75 2.00
166 Joe Morgan LGD .75 2.00
167 Whitey Ford LGD .75 2.00
168 Rick Ferrell LGD .50 1.25
169 Catfish Hunter LGD .75 2.00
170 Red Schoendienst LGD .75 2.00
171 Tom Seaver LGD .75 2.00
172 Pee Wee Reese LGD .75 2.00
173 Lou Boudreau LGD .75 2.00
174 Hal Newhouser LGD .75 2.00
175 Harmon Killebrew LGD 1.25 3.00
176 Jim Bunning LGD .75 2.00
177 Willie McCovey LGD .75 2.00
178 Bob Gibson LGD .75 2.00
179 Juan Marichal LGD .75 2.00
180 Robin Roberts LGD .75 2.00
181 Gaylord Perry LGD .75 2.00
182 Brooks Robinson LGD .75 2.00
183 Al Lopez LGD .50 1.25
184 Joe DiMaggio LGD 2.50 6.00
185 Al Kaline LGD 1.25 3.00
186 Rollie Fingers LGD .75 2.00
187 Mickey Mantle LGD 4.00 10.00
188 Enos Slaughter LGD .75 2.00
189 Ernie Banks LGD 1.25 3.00
190 Eddie Mathews LGD 1.25 3.00
191 Tommy Lasorda LGD .75 2.00
192 Fergie Jenkins LGD .75 2.00
193 Lou Brock LGD .75 2.00
194 Larry Doby LGD .75 2.00
195 Phil Rizzuto LGD .75 2.00
196 Warren Spahn LGD .75 2.00
197 Ralph Kiner LGD .75 2.00
198 Hoyt Wilhelm LGD .75 2.00
199 Early Wynn LGD .75 2.00
200 Yogi Berra LGD 1.25 3.00
201 Adam Shabala FR RC .30 .75
202 Ambiorix Burgos FR RC .30 .75
203 Ambiorix Concepcion FR RC .30 .75
204 Anibal Sanchez FR RC 1.25 3.00
205 Bill McCarthy FR RC .30 .75
206 Brandon McCarthy FR RC .50 1.25
207 Brian Burres FR RC .30 .75
208 Carlos Ruiz FR RC .50 1.25
209 Casey Rogowski FR RC .50 1.25
210 Chad Orvella FR RC .30 .75
211 Chris Resop FR RC .30 .75
212 Chris Roberson FR RC .30 .75
213 Chris Seddon FR RC .30 .75
214 Colter Bean FR RC .30 .75
215 Dae-Sung Koo FR RC .30 .75
216 Yuniesky Betancourt FR RC 1.25 3.00
217 Dave Gassner FR RC .30 .75
218 Brian Anderson FR RC .50 1.25
219 D.J. Houlton FR RC .30 .75
220 Derek Wathan FR RC .30 .75
221 Devon Lowery FR RC .30 .75
222 Enrique Gonzalez FR RC .30 .75
223 Ryan Zimmerman FR RC 1.50 4.00
224 Eude Brito FR RC .30 .75
225 Francisco Butto FR RC .30 .75
226 Franquelis Osoria FR RC .30 .75
227 Garrett Jones FR RC .50 1.25
228 Geovany Soto FR RC 1.50 4.00
229 Hayden Penn FR RC .30 .75
230 Ismael Ramirez FR RC .30 .75
231 Jared Gothreaux FR RC .30 .75
232 Jason Hammel FR RC .75 2.00
233 Chris Denorfia FR RC .30 .75
234 Jeff Miller FR RC .30 .75
235 Jeff Niemann FR RC .75 2.00
236 Dana Eveland FR RC .30 .75
237 Joel Peralta FR RC .30 .75
238 John Hattig FR RC .30 .75
239 Jorge Campillo FR RC .30 .75
240 Juan Morillo FR RC .30 .75
241 Justin Verlander FR RC 6.00 15.00
242 Ryan Garko FR RC .30 .75
243 Keiichi Yabu FR RC .30 .75
244 Kendry Morales FR RC .75 2.00
245 Luis Hernandez FR RC .30 .75
246 Jermaine Van Buren FR .30 .75
247 Luis Pena FR RC .30 .75
248 Luis O.Rodriguez FR RC .30 .75
249 Luke Scott FR RC .75 2.00
250 Marcos Carvajal FR RC .30 .75
251 Mark Woodyard FR RC .30 .75
252 Matt A.Smith FR RC .30 .75
253 Matthew Lindstrom FR RC .30 .75
254 Miguel Negron FR RC .50 1.25
255 Mike Morse FR RC 1.00 2.50
256 Nate McLouth FR RC .50 1.25
257 Nelson Cruz FR RC 4.00 10.00
258 Nick Masset FR RC .30 .75
259 Mark McLemore FR RC .30 .75
260 Oscar Robles FR RC .30 .75
261 Paulino Reynoso FR RC .30 .75
262 Pedro Lopez FR RC .30 .75
263 Pete Orr FR RC .50 1.25
264 Philip Humber FR RC .75 2.00
265 Prince Fielder FR RC 1.50 4.00
266 Randy Messenger FR RC .30 .75
267 Randy Williams FR RC .30 .75
268 Raul Tablado FR RC .30 .75
269 Ronny Paulino FR RC .50 1.25
270 Russ Rohlicek FR RC .30 .75
271 Russell Martin FR RC 1.00 2.50
272 Scott Baker FR RC .50 1.25
273 Scott Munter FR RC .30 .75
274 Sean Thompson FR RC .30 .75
275 Sean Tracey FR RC .30 .75
276 Shane Costa FR RC .30 .75
277 Stephen Drew FR RC 1.00 2.50
278 Steve Schmoll FR RC .30 .75
279 Ryan Spilborghs FR RC .75 2.00
280 Tadahito Iguchi FR RC .50 1.25
281 Tony Giarratano FR RC .30 .75
282 Tony Pena FR RC .30 .75
283 Travis Bowyer FR RC .30 .75
284 Ubaldo Jimenez FR RC .75 2.00
285 Wladimir Balentien FR RC .50 1.25
286 Yorman Bazardo FR RC .30 .75

2005 Reflections Blue

*BLUE 1-100: 1.5X TO 4X BASIC
*BLUE 101-150: 1X TO 2.5X BASIC
*BLUE 151-200: 1X TO 2.5X BASIC
1-200 OVERALL PARALLEL ODDS 1:6
*BLUE 201-286: 2.5X TO 6X BASIC
201-286 ISSUED IN '05 UD UPDATE PACKS
201-286 ONE #'d CARD OR AU PER PACK
STATED PRINT RUN 75 SERIAL #'d SETS

2005 Reflections Emerald

*EMERALD 1-100: 3X TO 8X BASIC
*EMERALD 101-150: 2X TO 5X BASIC
*EMERALD 151-200: 2X TO 5X BASIC
1-200 OVERALL PARALLEL ODDS 1:6
201-286 ISSUED IN '05 UD UPDATE PACKS
201-286 ONE #'d CARD OR AU PER PACK
STATED PRINT RUN 25 SERIAL #'d SETS
201-286 NO PRICING DUE TO SCARCITY

2005 Reflections Purple

*PURPLE 1-100: 1.5X TO 4X BASIC
*PURPLE 101-150: 1X TO 2.5X BASIC
*PURPLE 151-200: 1X TO 2.5X BASIC
1-200 OVERALL PARALLEL ODDS 1:6
*PURPLE 201-286: 2X TO 5X BASIC
201-286 ISSUED IN '05 UD UPDATE PACKS
201-286 ONE #'d CARD OR AU PER PACK
STATED PRINT RUN 99 SERIAL #'d SETS

2005 Reflections Red

*RED 1-100: 1.5X TO 4X BASIC
*RED 101-150: 1X TO 2.5X BASIC
*RED 151-200: 1X TO 2.5X BASIC
1-200 OVERALL PARALLEL ODDS 1:6
*RED 201-286: 2X TO 5X BASIC
201-286 ISSUED IN '05 UD UPDATE PACKS
201-286 ONE #'d CARD OR AU PER PACK
STATED PRINT RUN 99 SERIAL #'d SETS

2005 Reflections Turquoise

*TURQUOISE 1-100: 2X TO 5X BASIC
*TURQUOISE 101-150: 1.25X TO 3X BASIC
*TURQUOISE 151-200: 1.25X TO 3X BASIC
1-200 OVERALL PARALLEL ODDS 1:6
*TURQUOISE 201-286: 3X TO 8X BASIC
201-286 ISSUED IN '05 UD UPDATE PACKS
201-286 ONE #'d CARD OR AU PER PACK
STATED PRINT RUN 50 SERIAL #'d SETS

2005 Reflections Cut From the Same Cloth Dual Jersey

STATED PRINT RUN 225 SERIAL #'d SETS
*BLUE: .6X TO 1.5X BASIC
BLUE PRINT RUN 50 SERIAL #'d SETS
PLATINUM PRINT RUN 1 SERIAL #'d SET
NO PLATINUM PRICING DUE TO SCARCITY
*RED: .5X TO 1.2X BASIC
RED PRINT RUN 99 SERIAL #'d SETS
OVERALL DUAL GU ODDS 1:12
AA A.Beltre/A.Pujols 6.00 15.00
AB B.Abreu/C.Beltran 4.00 10.00
AG G.Anderson/V.Guerrero 5.00 12.00
AH A.Soriano/H.Blalock 4.00 10.00
AJ A.Pujols/J.Thome 6.00 15.00
AM A.Beltre/M.Cabrera 4.00 10.00
AT B.Abreu/J.Thome 4.00 10.00
AW A.Pujols/W.Clark 6.00 15.00
BB C.Biggio/J.Bagwell 5.00 12.00
BD1 C.Belt Mets/J.Damon Sox 4.00 10.00
BD2 C.Belt Ryl/J.Damon Ryl 4.00 10.00
BG C.Beltran/K.Griffey Jr. 6.00 15.00
BM G.Brett/P.Molitor 6.00 15.00
BO J.Beckett/R.Oswalt 4.00 10.00
BP J.Bench Pants/M.Piazza 6.00 15.00
BR A.Beltre/S.Rolen 4.00 10.00
BS G.Brett/M.Schmidt 10.00 25.00
BT H.Blalock/M.Teixeira 4.00 10.00
BW D.Wright/H.Blalock 6.00 15.00
CB B.Crosby/J.Bay 4.00 10.00
CC B.Crosby/E.Chavez 4.00 10.00
CG B.Crosby/K.Greene 4.00 10.00
CL M.Cabrera/M.Lowell 4.00 10.00
CP C.Crawford/S.Podsednik 4.00 10.00
CR E.Chavez/S.Rolen 4.00 10.00
CT B.Crosby/M.Tejada 4.00 10.00
DM D.Murphy Pants/M.Schmidt 10.00 25.00
DR J.Damon/M.Ramirez 4.00 10.00
GG1 K.Grif Jr./K.Grif Sr. Reds 8.00 20.00
GG2 K.Grif Jr./K.Grif Sr. M's 8.00 20.00
GI B.Giles/M.Giles 4.00 10.00
GS K.Griffey Jr./S.Sosa 6.00 15.00
GV J.Guillen/J.Vidro 4.00 10.00
HH R.Harden/T.Hudson 4.00 10.00
HK H.Killebrew/K.Hrbek 10.00 25.00
JD C.Jones/J.Drew 5.00 12.00
JH J.Jones/T.Hunter 4.00 10.00
JJ A.Jones/C.Jones 5.00 12.00
JM D.Jeter/D.Mattingly 15.00 40.00
JR N.Ryan/R.Johnson 10.00 25.00
JS J.Santana/S.Carlton 4.00 10.00
JT D.Jeter/M.Tejada 8.00 20.00
KH J.Kendall/T.Hudson 4.00 10.00
KM C.Kotchman/D.McPherson 4.00 10.00
MB D.Mattingly/W.Boggs Pants 10.00 25.00
MC D.Mattingly/W.Clark 10.00 25.00
MH M.Mulder/T.Hudson 4.00 10.00
MJ C.Jones/D.Murphy Pants 8.00 20.00
MK H.Killebrew/J.Morneau 8.00 20.00
MM H.Matsui/K.Matsui 15.00 40.00
MS J.Mauer/J.Santana 4.00 10.00
MW D.McPherson/D.Wright 6.00 15.00
MY P.Molitor/R.Yount 10.00 25.00
OD D.Ortiz/J.Damon 4.00 10.00
OT A.Otsuka/S.Takatsu 4.00 10.00
PB J.Bunning/J.Palmer 4.00 10.00
PC A.Pujols/M.Cabrera 8.00 20.00
PG A.Pujols/V.Guerrero 6.00 15.00
PP J.Posada/M.Piazza 5.00 12.00
PR A.Pujols/S.Rolen 6.00 15.00
PS M.Prior/T.Seaver 4.00 10.00
PT A.Pujols/M.Teixeira 6.00 15.00
RJ C.Ripken/D.Jeter 10.00 25.00
RM I.Rodriguez/V.Martinez 4.00 10.00
RO D.Ortiz/M.Ramirez 6.00 15.00

RP I.Rodriguez/M.Piazza 5.00 12.00
RR B.Robinson/C.Ripken 15.00 40.00
RT C.Ripken/M.Tejada 12.50 30.00
RW D.Wright/S.Rolen 6.00 15.00
SB R.Sandberg/W.Boggs 12.50 30.00
SM C.Schilling/P.Martinez 4.00 10.00
SO C.Schilling/D.Ortiz 4.00 10.00
SP B.Sheets/M.Prior 4.00 10.00
SR M.Schmidt/S.Rolen 6.00 15.00
ST A.Soriano/M.Teixeira 4.00 10.00
TC M.Teixeira/M.Cabrera 4.00 10.00
TH J.Thome/T.Helton 4.00 10.00
TP M.Tejada/R.Palmeiro 4.00 10.00
TR J.Thome/M.Ramirez 4.00 10.00
TS J.Thome/M.Schmidt 8.00 20.00
UJ B.Upton/D.Jeter 8.00 20.00
UK B.Upton/S.Kazmir 4.00 10.00
UW B.Upton/D.Wright 4.00 10.00
VJ J.Vidro/N.Johnson 4.00 10.00
WB B.Williams/C.Beltran 4.00 10.00
WJ B.Williams/D.Jeter 12.50 30.00
WM B.Williams/H.Matsui 12.50 30.00
WP K.Wood/M.Prior 6.00 15.00
WR K.Wood/N.Ryan 10.00 25.00
YR C.Yastrzemski/M.Ramirez 10.00 25.00
ZM B.Zito/M.Mulder 4.00 10.00

2005 Reflections Cut From the Same Cloth Dual Patch

*PATCH: 1X TO 2.5X BASIC
OVERALL PREMIUM AU-GU ODDS 1:24
STATED PRINT RUN 99 SERIAL #'d SETS
BS G.Brett/M.Schmidt 20.00 50.00
CP G.Carter/M.Piazza 12.50 30.00
GC K.Griffey Jr./M.Cabrera 20.00 50.00
JM D.Jeter/D.Mattingly 40.00 80.00
JR C.Ripken/D.Jeter 30.00 60.00
MP J.Mauer/M.Piazza 12.50 30.00
MY P.Molitor/R.Yount 10.00 25.00
OB D.Ortiz/W.Boggs 10.00 25.00
RJ N.Ryan/R.Johnson 20.00 50.00
RR B.Robinson/C.Ripken 30.00 60.00
RW K.Wood/N.Ryan 10.00 25.00
SB R.Sandberg/W.Boggs 15.00 40.00
TO M.Teixeira/D.Ortiz 10.00 25.00
YO C.Yastrzemski/D.Ortiz 20.00 50.00

2005 Reflections Dual Signatures

TIER 3 PRINT RUNS 275 OR MORE PER
TIER 2 PRINT RUNS B/WN 125-199 PER
TIER 1 PRINT RUNS 75 OR LESS PER
CARDS ARE NOT SERIAL-NUMBERED
PRINT RUN INFO PROVIDED BY UD
PLATINUM PRINT RUN 1 SERIAL #'d SET
NO PLATINUM PRICING DUE TO SCARCITY
OVERALL DUAL AUTO ODDS 1:12
EXCHANGE DEADLINE 06/07/08
ABDW A.Beltre/D.Wright T1 30.00 60.00
ABEC A.Beltre/E.Chavez T1 6.00 15.00
ABJL A.Beltre/J.Leone T1 10.00 25.00
AHBU A.Huff/B.Upton T1 12.00 30.00
AHCC A.Huff/C.Craw T1 6.00 15.00
AOST A.Otsuka/S.Takatsu T3 6.00 15.00
ARKG A.Rios/K.Griffey Jr. T1 40.00 80.00
ARTH A.Rosen/T.Hafner T2 10.00 25.00
BAKY B.Arroyo/K.Youkilis T1 10.00 25.00
BCDJ B.Crosby/D.Jeter T1 75.00 150.00
BCEC B.Crosby/E.Chav T1 EX 10.00 25.00
BGMG B.Giles/M.Giles T1 10.00 25.00
BPFH B.Powell/F.Howard T1 12.00 30.00
BRRS B.Robinson/R.Santo T1 30.00 60.00
BSJC B.Sheets/J.Capellan T2 8.00 20.00
BSRW B.Sheets/R.Weeks T1 10.00 25.00
BSSK B.Sheets/S.Kazmir T1 10.00 25.00
BUDJ B.Upton/D.Jeter T1 75.00 150.00
BURW B.Upton/R.Weeks T1 10.00 25.00
BUSK B.Upton/S.Kazmir T2 8.00 20.00
BWKG B.Will/K.Grif Jr. T1 50.00 100.00
CCNJ C.Cordero/N.Johnson T2 8.00 20.00
CKDM C.Kotch/D.McPh T3 EX 8.00 20.00
CKKH C.Kotch/K.Hernandez T3 8.00 20.00
CKMT C.Kotch/M.Teix T1 12.00 30.00
CTDM C.Thomas/D.Murphy T1 6.00 15.00
CTJC C.Thomas/J.Capellan T3 6.00 15.00
CTRH C.Thomas/R.Howard T3 6.00 15.00
DGDB D.Gooden/D.Brazelton T3 6.00 15.00
DGJB D.Gooden/J.Bouton T3 8.00 20.00
DJDM D.Jeter/D.Mattingly T1 150.00 250.00
DJKG D.Jeter/Khalil T1 EX * 75.00 150.00
DKFH D.Kingman/F.Howard T3 5.00 12.00
DMDW D.McPh/D.Wright T2 5.00 12.00
DMJB D.Murphy/J.Bay T1 10.00 25.00
DMJL D.McPh/J.Leone T3 EX 6.00 15.00
DMKY D.McPh/K.Youk T3 EX 6.00 15.00
DMMS D.McPh/M.Schm T1 12.00 30.00
DMRH D.McPh/R.How T3 6.00 15.00
DOKY D.Ortiz/K.Youkilis T1 30.00 60.00
DWJL D.Wright/J.Leone T3 12.00 30.00
DWKH D.Wright/K.Hern T1 20.00 50.00
DWKY D.Wright/K.Youkilis T3 8.00 20.00
DWMS D.Wright/M.Schmidt T1 50.00 100.00
DWSR D.Wright/S.Rolen T1 12.00 30.00
FHMT F.Howard/M.Teixeira T1 12.00 30.00
FHNJ F.Howard/N.Johnson T3 8.00 20.00
GPJP G.Perry/J.Peavy T1 10.00 25.00
ISJC I.Snell/J.Capellan T3 6.00 15.00
ISMV I.Snell/M.Valdez T3 6.00 15.00
ISSK I.Snell/S.Kazmir T3 6.00 15.00
JBIS J.Blanton/I.Snell T3 6.00 15.00
JBJP J.Bunning/J.Palmer T1 15.00 40.00
JBMV J.Blanton/M.Valdez T3 6.00 15.00
JBRH J.Blanton/R.Harden T3 8.00 20.00
JBSK J.Blanton/S.Kazmir T3 10.00 25.00
JCMV J.Capellan/M.Valdez T3 6.00 15.00
JLRH J.Leone/R.Howard T3 6.00 15.00
JPJB J.Blanton/J.Peavy T2 6.00 15.00
JPKG J.Peavy/K.Greene T1 8.00 20.00
JPRH J.Peavy/R.Harden T2 10.00 25.00
JPSK J.Peavy/S.Kazmir T1 10.00 25.00
JRDW J.Reyes/D.Wright T1 40.00 80.00
JSMP J.Sant/M.Prior T1 EX 40.00 80.00
JSSC J.Sant/S.Carlt T1 12.00 30.00
JVMG J.Vidro/M.Giles T1 6.00 15.00
KGKG K.Grif Sr./K.Grif Jr. T2 40.00 80.00
KGMC K.Grif Jr./M.Cabr T1 75.00 150.00
KYWB K.Youkilis/W.Boggs T1 10.00 25.00
MCRH M.Cabrera/R.Howard T1 40.00 80.00
MGRW M.Giles/R.Weeks T1 EX 10.00 25.00
MTHB M.Teix/H.Blalock T1 6.00 15.00
MTMC M.Teix/M.Cabrera T1 30.00 60.00
MTRH M.Teix/R.Howard T1 12.00 30.00
MVRH M.Valdez/R.Harden T3 8.00 20.00
PBKG P.Burr/K.Grif Jr. T1 Ex 40.00 80.00
PBMC P.Burr/M.Cabr T1 15.00 40.00
RHDO R.Howard/D.Ortiz T1 20.00 50.00
RHRO R.Harden/R.Oswalt T1 10.00 25.00
RHSK R.Harden/S.Kazmir T3 10.00 25.00
THVM T.Hafner/V.Martinez T1 12.00 30.00
TOKH T.Oliva/K.Hrbek T3 12.00 30.00
VMYM V.Martinez/Y.Molina T3 25.00 60.00

2005 Reflections Dual Signatures Blue

*BLUE: .6X TO 1.5X BASIC T3
*BLUE: .6X TO 1.5X BASIC T2
*BLUE: .5X TO 1.2X BASIC T1
OVERALL AUTO ODDS 1:12
STATED PRINT RUN 35 SERIAL #'d SETS
EXCHANGE DEADLINE 06/07/08
ABAR A.Beltre/A.Rosen 12.00 30.00
AKDM A.Kaline/D.Murphy 40.00 100.00
ARKG A.Rios/K.Griffey Jr. 50.00 100.00
BAKY B.Arroyo/K.Youkilis 10.00 25.00
BCCR B.Crosby/C.Rip 50.00 100.00
BCDJ B.Crosby/D.Jeter EX 90.00 150.00
BCKG B.Crosby/Khalil EX 15.00 40.00
BDWB B.Doerr/W.Boggs 30.00 60.00
BSSK B.Sheets/S.Kazmir 12.00 30.00
BUDJ B.Upton/D.Jeter 125.00 200.00
BWKG B.Williams/K.Griffey Jr. 60.00 120.00
CZLT C.Zambrano/L.Tiant 12.00 30.00
DJDM D.Jeter/D.Mattingly 175.00 300.00
DJKG D.Jeter/K.Greene 125.00 200.00
DMMS D.McPh/M.Schm 20.00 50.00
DMWC D.Mattingly/W.Clark 40.00 80.00
DWKH D.Wright/K.Hernandez 30.00 60.00
DWMS D.Wright/M.Schmidt 15.00 40.00
KGKG K.Griffey Sr./K.Griffey Jr. 50.00 100.00
MTHB M.Teixeira/H.Blalock 8.00 20.00
THVM T.Hafner/V.Martinez 15.00 40.00

2005 Reflections Dual Signatures Red

*RED: .5X TO 1.2X BASIC T3
*RED: .5X TO 1.2X BASIC T2
*RED: .4X TO 1X BASIC T1
OVERALL AUTO ODDS 1:12
STATED PRINT RUN 99 SERIAL #'d SETS
EXCHANGE DEADLINE 06/07/08
ABAR A.Beltre/A.Rosen 10.00 25.00
AKDM A.Kaline/D.Murphy 30.00 80.00
BAKY B.Arroyo/K.Youkilis 6.00 15.00
BDWB B.Doerr/W.Boggs 20.00 50.00
BSSK B.Sheets/S.Kazmir 10.00 25.00
BUDJ B.Upton/D.Jeter 100.00 200.00
BWKG B.Williams/K.Griffey Jr. 50.00 100.00
CZLT C.Zambrano/L.Tiant 10.00 25.00
DJDM D.Jeter/D.Mattingly 150.00 250.00
DJKG D.Jeter/K.Greene 75.00 150.00
DMWC D.Mattingly/W.Clark 50.00 100.00
DWKH D.Wright/K.Hernandez 40.00 80.00
DWMS D.Wright/M.Schmidt 30.00 60.00
DWSR D.Wright/S.Rolen 12.00 30.00
KGKG K.Griffey Sr./K.Griffey Jr. 30.00 60.00
MTHB M.Teixeira/H.Blalock 6.00 15.00
THVM T.Hafner/V.Martinez 10.00 25.00

2005 Reflections Fabric Jersey

STATED ODDS 1:12
SP INFO PROVIDED BY UPPER DECK
*PATCH/99: 1.2X TO 3X BASIC
AB Adrian Beltre 3.00 8.00
AP Albert Pujols 4.00 10.00
AS Alfonso Soriano 2.00 5.00
BW Bernie Williams 2.00 5.00
CB Carlos Beltran 2.00 5.00
CJ Chipper Jones 3.00 8.00
CR Cal Ripken SP 10.00 25.00
CS Curt Schilling 2.00 5.00
CY Carl Yastrzemski SP 6.00 15.00
DJ Derek Jeter SP 8.00 20.00
DM Don Mattingly SP 12.00 30.00
DO David Ortiz 3.00 8.00
DW David Wright 2.50 6.00
EC Eric Chavez 1.25 3.00
GB George Brett SP 6.00 15.00
GM Greg Maddux 4.00 10.00
HB Hank Blalock 1.25 3.00
HM Hideki Matsui 5.00 12.00
IR Ivan Rodriguez 2.00 5.00
JD Johnny Damon 2.00 5.00
JS Johan Santana 2.00 5.00
JT Jim Thome 2.00 5.00
KG Ken Griffey Jr. 6.00 15.00
KW Kerry Wood 1.25 3.00
MC Miguel Cabrera 3.00 8.00
MP Mark Prior 2.00 5.00
MR Manny Ramirez 3.00 8.00
MS Mike Schmidt SP 5.00 12.00
MT Mark Teixeira 2.00 5.00
NR Nolan Ryan SP 10.00 25.00
PI Mike Piazza 3.00 8.00
PM Paul Molitor SP 3.00 8.00
RJ Randy Johnson 3.00 8.00
RY Robin Yount SP 3.00 8.00
SR Scott Rolen 2.00 5.00
TE Miguel Tejada 2.00 5.00
TH Todd Helton 2.00 5.00
VG Vladimir Guerrero 2.00 5.00
WB Wade Boggs SP 2.00 5.00
WC Will Clark SP 2.00 5.00

2005 Reflections Fabric Patch Autograph

OVERALL PREMIUM AU-GU ODDS 1:24
STATED PRINT RUN 50 SERIAL #'d SETS
EXHANGE DEADLINE 06/07/08
AB Adrian Beltre 20.00 50.00
AJ Andruw Jones 6.00 15.00
AP Albert Pujols 175.00 300.00
BS Ben Sheets 15.00 40.00
BU B.J. Upton 15.00 40.00
CA Miguel Cabrera 50.00 100.00
CR Cal Ripken 150.00 250.00
CZ Carlos Zambrano 15.00 40.00
DG Dwight Gooden 20.00 50.00
DJ Derek Jeter 175.00 300.00
DM Dale Murphy 20.00 50.00
DO David Ortiz 40.00 100.00
DW David Wright 12.50 30.00
EC Eric Chavez 15.00 40.00
GP Gaylord Perry 15.00 40.00
GR Khalil Greene 20.00 50.00
HB Hank Blalock 6.00 15.00
JB Jason Bay 6.00 15.00
JP Jake Peavy 6.00 15.00
JS Johan Santana 6.00 15.00
KG Ken Griffey Jr. 75.00 150.00
MA Don Mattingly 40.00 80.00
MP Mark Prior 6.00 15.00
MS Mike Schmidt 60.00 120.00
MT Mark Teixeira 6.00 15.00
NR Nolan Ryan 75.00 150.00
PM Paul Molitor 15.00 40.00
RH Rich Harden 6.00 15.00
RJ Randy Johnson 60.00 120.00
RO Roy Oswalt 15.00 40.00
RY Robin Yount 40.00 80.00
SK Scott Kazmir 6.00 15.00
SR Scott Rolen 15.00 40.00
ST Shingo Takatsu 15.00 40.00
WB Wade Boggs 20.00 50.00

2005 Reflections Super Swatch

STATED PRINT RUN 50 SERIAL #'d SETS
BLUE PRINT RUN 10 SERIAL #'d SETS
NO BLUE PRICING DUE TO SCARCITY
RED PRINT RUN 25 SERIAL #'d SETS
NO RED PRICING DUE TO SCARCITY
OVERALL PREMIUM AU-GU ODDS 1:24
AB Adrian Beltre 6.00 15.00
AD Adam Dunn 6.00 15.00
AH Aubrey Huff 6.00 15.00
AJ Andruw Jones 6.00 15.00
AO Akinori Otsuka 10.00 25.00
AP Albert Pujols 15.00 40.00
AS Alfonso Soriano 6.00 15.00
BA Jeff Bagwell 6.00 15.00
BB Bret Boone 10.00 25.00
BC Bobby Crosby 6.00 15.00
BE Josh Beckett 6.00 15.00
BG Brian Giles 6.00 15.00
BI Craig Biggio 6.00 15.00
BO Bobby Abreu 6.00 15.00
BS Ben Sheets 6.00 15.00
BW Bernie Williams 6.00 15.00
BZ Barry Zito 6.00 15.00
CB Carlos Beltran 6.00 15.00
CC Carl Crawford 6.00 15.00
CD Carlos Delgado 6.00 15.00
CJ Chipper Jones 15.00 40.00
CP Corey Patterson 6.00 15.00
CS C.C. Sabathia 6.00 15.00
DA Johnny Damon 6.00 15.00
DJ Derek Jeter 20.00 50.00
DM Dallas McPherson 6.00 15.00
DO David Ortiz 6.00 15.00
DW David Wright 10.00 25.00
EC Eric Chavez 6.00 15.00
EG Eric Gagne 6.00 15.00
ER Edgar Renteria 6.00 15.00
GA Garret Anderson 6.00 15.00
GM Greg Maddux 15.00 40.00
GR Khalil Greene 6.00 15.00
GS Gary Sheffield 6.00 15.00
HA Roy Halladay 6.00 15.00
HB Hank Blalock 6.00 15.00
HE Todd Helton 6.00 15.00
HM Hideki Matsui 15.00 40.00
HN Hideo Nomo 15.00 40.00
HO Trevor Hoffman 6.00 15.00
HU Torii Hunter 6.00 15.00
IR Ivan Rodriguez 6.00 15.00
JB Jason Bay 6.00 15.00
JD J.D. Drew 6.00 15.00
JE Jim Edmonds 6.00 15.00
JG Jason Giambi 6.00 15.00
JJ Jacque Jones 6.00 15.00
JK Jason Kendall 6.00 15.00
JM Justin Morneau 6.00 15.00
JP Jorge Posada 6.00 15.00
JR Jose Reyes 6.00 15.00
JS Jason Schmidt 6.00 15.00
JT Jim Thome 6.00 15.00
JV Jose Vidro 6.00 15.00
KB Kevin Brown 6.00 15.00
KF Keith Foulke 6.00 15.00
KG Ken Griffey Jr. 15.00 40.00
KM Kazuo Matsui 6.00 15.00
KW Kerry Wood 6.00 15.00
LB Lance Berkman 6.00 15.00
LG Luis Gonzalez 6.00 15.00
MA Moises Alou 6.00 15.00
MC Miguel Cabrera 6.00 15.00
MG Marcus Giles 6.00 15.00
ML Mike Lowell 6.00 15.00
MM Mark Mulder 6.00 15.00
MO Magglio Ordonez 6.00 15.00
MP Mark Prior 6.00 15.00
MR Manny Ramirez 6.00 15.00
MS Mike Sweeney 6.00 15.00
MT Mark Teixeira 6.00 15.00
MU Mike Mussina 6.00 15.00
PI Mike Piazza 8.00 20.00
PM Pedro Martinez 6.00 15.00
RA Roberto Alomar 6.00 15.00
RB Rocco Baldelli 6.00 15.00
RH Rich Harden 6.00 15.00
RJ Randy Johnson 8.00 20.00
RO Roy Oswalt 6.00 15.00
RP Rafael Palmeiro 6.00 15.00
RS Richie Sexson 6.00 15.00
SA Johan Santana 8.00 20.00
SC Curt Schilling 6.00 15.00
SG Shawn Green 6.00 15.00
SK Scott Kazmir 6.00 15.00
SP Scott Podsednik 6.00 15.00
SR Scott Rolen 6.00 15.00
SS Sammy Sosa 8.00 20.00
ST Shingo Takatsu 6.00 15.00
TE Miguel Tejada 6.00 15.00
TG Tom Glavine 10.00 25.00
TH Tim Hudson 6.00 15.00
VG Vladimir Guerrero 8.00 20.00
VM Victor Martinez 6.00 15.00
VW Vernon Wells 6.00 15.00
WA Billy Wagner 6.00 15.00

1992 Rembrandt Ultra-Pro Promos

COMPLETE SET (19) 12.50 30.00
P1 Bobby Bonilla/(Holding both ends of bat across n .40 1.00
P2 Bobby Bonilla Front pose shot from waist up .40 1.00
P3 Bobby Bonilla Follow-through after golf swing .40 1.00
P4 Jose Canseco Posed in car 1.00 2.50
P5 Jose Canseco Batting stance 1.00 2.50
P6 Jose Canseco/(Front pose& bat resting on shoulde 1.00 2.50
P7 Hal Morris Front pose bat resting on shoulder .40 1.00
P8 Hal Morris Posed, tennis racket in hand .40 1.00
P9 Hal Morris Pose, shot from waist up .40 1.00
P10 Scott Erickson Posed, skis on shoulder .40 1.00
P11 Scott Erickson Front pose, shot from waist up .40 1.00
P12 Scott Erickson Batting stance .40 1.00
P13 Danny Tartabull Batting stance .40 1.00
P14 Danny Tartabull/(Front pose& bat resting on shou .40 1.00
P15 Danny Tartabull/(Posed with chrome dumbbell in l .40 1.00
P16 Danny Tartabull and Bobby Bonilla/(Posed in tuxe .40 1.00
P17 Bobby Bonilla Posed in tuxedo .40 1.00
P18 Danny Tartabull Bobby Bonilla Hologram 2.00 5.00
P19 Jose Canseco/(Holding Ultra-Pro sheet filled wit 1.00 2.50

1993 Rembrandt Ultra-Pro Karros

Eric Karros is the exclusive subject of this five-card, standard-size set that celebrates his National League Rookie of the Year award. The full-bleed action photos have a blue bar across the bottom with Karros' name and "Rookie of the Year" in white lettering. The borderless backs carry a head shot in the left with career highlights on the right. Below the picture, Karros' 1992 statistics are listed. The Rembrandt logo appears on a blue bar in the lower left.

COMPLETE SET (5) 1.50 4.00
COMMON PLAYER (1-5) .40 1.00

1994 Rembrandt Ultra-Pro Piazza Promos

Issued to promote Ultra-Pro's card storage products, these two standard-size cards feature on their borderless fronts color photos of Mike Piazza posed in front of a purple background and holding Ultra-Pro products. His name and the words "1993 Rookie of the Year" appear at the bottom. The pink back carries product information and a facsimile Mike Piazza autograph. The cards are unnumbered.

COMPLETE SET (2) .75 2.00
COMMON PLAYER (1-2) .40 1.00

1994 Rembrandt Ultra-Pro Piazza

These six standard-size cards feature on their borderless fronts color photos of Mike Piazza in various game and non-game situations. His name and "1993 Rookie of the Year" appear at the bottom. The pink back has a color head shot of Piazza, with career highlights and statistics below. One of these cards was inserted in each 200-count box of Ultra-Pro Mini Top Loaders. A black vinyl binder for displaying all six cards was also available. The cards are numbered on the back as "X of 6." There were refractors of these cards issued -- however they are thinly traded so no prices can be established at this time.

COMPLETE SET (6) 5.00 12.00
COMMON PLAYER (1-6) .80 2.00

1996 Rembrandt Ultra Pro Piazza

This nine-card set is actually a puzzle with each of the cards featuring a different portion of an action photo of Mike Piazza. The complete set could be mailed in for an uncut version of the photo. Gold and silver versions of the puzzle were also produced which, when completed, could be mailed in for monetary prizes. The gold version is distinguished by a gold foil emblem on each piece and could be exchanged for a prize of $250. The silver version displays a silver foil emblem and could be exchanged for $100. The mail-in prize offer expired April 1, 1997.

COMPLETE SET (9) 2.00 5.00
COMMON CARD (1-9) .30 .75

1985 Reuss Cystic Fibrosis

This one-card set measures approximately 3 1/2" by 5 1/2" and features a color photo of Jerry Reuss in a white border. The back displays information and a form for ordering the photo in a full color personally autographed 8" by 10" version which could be purchased by mail for $5 along with a 16" by 20" poster for $8. A portion of the proceeds was to be donated to the Cystic Fibrosis Foundation.

1 Jerry Reuss 2.00 5.00

1998 Revolution

The 1998 Revolution set (produced by Pacific) consists of 150 standard size cards. The three card packs retailed for a suggested price of $5.99. The fronts feature a color action photo atop a state-of-the-art silver foil sparkling background. The backs provide collectors with full year-by-year statistics of the featured player. The set release date was September, 1998. Rookie Cards inlcude Magglio Ordonez.

COMPLETE SET (150) 40.00 100.00
1 Garret Anderson .40 1.00
2 Jim Edmonds .40 1.00
3 Darin Erstad .40 1.00
4 Chuck Finley .40 1.00
5 Tim Salmon .60 1.50
6 Jay Bell .40 1.00
7 Travis Lee .25 .60
8 Devon White .40 1.00
9 Matt Williams .40 1.00
10 Andres Galarraga .40 1.00
11 Tom Glavine .60 1.50
12 Andruw Jones .60 1.50
13 Chipper Jones 1.00 2.50
14 Ryan Klesko .40 1.00
15 Javy Lopez .40 1.00
16 Greg Maddux 1.50 4.00
17 Walt Weiss .40 1.00
18 Roberto Alomar .60 1.50
19 Joe Carter .40 1.00
20 Mike Mussina .60 1.50
21 Rafael Palmeiro .60 1.50
22 Cal Ripken 3.00 8.00
23 B.J. Surhoff .40 1.00
24 Nomar Garciaparra 1.50 4.00
25 Reggie Jefferson .25 .60
26 Pedro Martinez .60 1.50
27 Troy O'Leary .25 .60
28 Mo Vaughn .40 1.00
29 Mark Grace .60 1.50
30 Mickey Morandini .25 .60
31 Henry Rodriguez .25 .60
32 Sammy Sosa 1.00 2.50
33 Kerry Wood .50 1.25
34 Albert Belle .40 1.00
35 Ray Durham .40 1.00
36 Magglio Ordonez RC 2.50 6.00
37 Frank Thomas 1.00 2.50
38 Robin Ventura .40 1.00
39 Bret Boone .40 1.00
40 Barry Larkin .60 1.50
41 Reggie Sanders .40 1.00
42 Brett Tomko .25 .60
43 Sandy Alomar Jr. .25 .60
44 David Justice .40 1.00
45 Kenny Lofton .40 1.00
46 Manny Ramirez .60 1.50
47 Jim Thome .60 1.50
48 Omar Vizquel .60 1.50
49 Jaret Wright .25 .60
50 Dante Bichette .40 1.00
51 Ellis Burks .40 1.00
52 Vinny Castilla .40 1.00
53 Todd Helton .60 1.50
54 Larry Walker .40 1.00
55 Tony Clark .25 .60
56 Deivi Cruz .25 .60
57 Damion Easley .25 .60
58 Bobby Higginson .40 1.00
59 Brian Hunter .25 .60
60 Cliff Floyd .40 1.00
61 Livan Hernandez .40 1.00
62 Derrek Lee .60 1.50
63 Edgar Renteria .40 1.00
64 Moises Alou .40 1.00
65 Jeff Bagwell .60 1.50
66 Derek Bell .25 .60
67 Craig Biggio .60 1.50
68 Richard Hidalgo .25 .60
69 Johnny Damon .60 1.50
70 Jeff King .25 .60
71 Hal Morris .25 .60
72 Dean Palmer .40 1.00
73 Bobby Bonilla .40 1.00
74 Charles Johnson .40 1.00
75 Eric Karros .40 1.00
76 Raul Mondesi .40 1.00
77 Gary Sheffield .40 1.00
78 Jeromy Burnitz .40 1.00
79 Marquis Grissom .40 1.00
80 Dave Nilsson .25 .60
81 Fernando Vina .25 .60
82 Marty Cordova .25 .60
83 Pat Meares .25 .60
84 Paul Molitor .40 1.00
85 Brad Radke .40 1.00
86 Terry Steinbach .25 .60
87 Todd Walker .25 .60
88 Brad Fullmer .25 .60
89 Vladimir Guerrero 1.00 2.50
90 Carl Pavano .40 1.00
91 Rondell White .40 1.00
92 Bernard Gilkey .25 .60
93 Hideo Nomo 1.00 2.50
94 John Olerud .40 1.00
95 Rey Ordonez .25 .60
96 Mike Piazza 1.50 4.00
97 Masato Yoshii RC .40 1.00
98 Hideki Irabu .25 .60
99 Derek Jeter 2.50 6.00
100 Chuck Knoblauch .40 1.00
101 Tino Martinez .60 1.50
102 Paul O'Neill .60 1.50
103 Darryl Strawberry .40 1.00
104 Bernie Williams .60 1.50
105 Jason Giambi .40 1.00
106 Ben Grieve .25 .60
107 Rickey Henderson 1.00 2.50
108 Matt Stairs .25 .60
109 Doug Glanville .25 .60
110 Desi Relaford .25 .60
111 Scott Rolen .60 1.50
112 Curt Schilling .40 1.00
113 Jason Kendall .40 1.00
114 Al Martin .25 .60
115 Jason Schmidt .40 1.00
116 Kevin Young .40 1.00
117 Delino DeShields .25 .60
118 Gary Gaetti .40 1.00
119 Brian Jordan .40 1.00
120 Ray Lankford .40 1.00
121 Mark McGwire 2.50 6.00
122 Kevin Brown .60 1.50
123 Steve Finley .40 1.00
124 Tony Gwynn 1.25 3.00
125 Wally Joyner .40 1.00
126 Greg Vaughn .25 .60
127 Barry Bonds 2.50 6.00
128 Orel Hershiser .40 1.00
129 Jeff Kent .40 1.00
130 Bill Mueller .40 1.00
131 Jay Buhner .40 1.00
132 Ken Griffey Jr. 2.00 5.00
133 Randy Johnson 1.00 2.50
134 Edgar Martinez .60 1.50
135 Alex Rodriguez 1.50 4.00
136 David Segui .25 .60
137 Rolando Arrojo RC .40 1.00
138 Wade Boggs .60 1.50
139 Quinton McCracken .25 .60
140 Fred McGriff .60 1.50
141 Will Clark .60 1.50
142 Juan Gonzalez .40 1.00
143 Tom Goodwin .25 .60
144 Ivan Rodriguez .60 1.50
145 Aaron Sele .25 .60
146 John Wetteland .40 1.00
147 Jose Canseco .60 1.50
148 Roger Clemens 2.00 5.00
149 Jose Cruz Jr. .25 .60
150 Carlos Delgado .40 1.00

1998 Revolution Shadow Series

*STARS: 4X TO 10X BASIC CARDS
*ROOKIES: 3X TO 8X BASIC CARDS
RANDOM INSERTS IN HOBBY PACKS
STATED PRINT RUN 99 SERIAL #'d SETS

1998 Revolution Foul Pole

COMPLETE SET (20) 50.00 120.00
STATED ODDS 1:49
1 Cal Ripken 12.00 30.00
2 Nomar Garciaparra 2.50 6.00
3 Mo Vaughn 1.50 4.00
4 Frank Thomas 4.00 10.00
5 Manny Ramirez 4.00 10.00
6 Bernie Williams 2.50 6.00
7 Ben Grieve 1.50 4.00
8 Ken Griffey Jr. 8.00 20.00
9 Alex Rodriguez 5.00 12.00
10 Juan Gonzalez 1.50 4.00
11 Ivan Rodriguez 2.50 6.00
12 Travis Lee 1.50 4.00
13 Chipper Jones 4.00 10.00
14 Sammy Sosa 4.00 10.00
15 Vinny Castilla 1.50 4.00
16 Moises Alou 1.50 4.00
17 Gary Sheffield 1.50 4.00
18 Mike Piazza 4.00 10.00
19 Mark McGwire 6.00 15.00
20 Barry Bonds 6.00 15.00

1998 Revolution Major League Icons

COMPLETE SET (10) 40.00 100.00
STATED ODDS 1:121
1 Cal Ripken 15.00 40.00
2 Nomar Garciaparra 8.00 20.00
3 Frank Thomas 5.00 12.00
4 Ken Griffey Jr. 10.00 25.00
5 Alex Rodriguez 8.00 20.00
6 Chipper Jones 5.00 12.00
7 Kerry Wood 2.50 6.00
8 Mike Piazza 8.00 20.00
9 Mark McGwire 12.50 30.00
10 Tony Gwynn 6.00 15.00

1998 Revolution Prime Time Performers

COMPLETE SET (20) 75.00 150.00
STATED ODDS 1:25
1 Cal Ripken 10.00 25.00
2 Nomar Garciaparra 5.00 12.00
3 Frank Thomas 3.00 8.00
4 Jim Thome 2.00 5.00
5 Hideki Irabu .75 2.00
6 Derek Jeter 8.00 20.00
7 Ben Grieve .75 2.00
8 Ken Griffey Jr. 6.00 15.00
9 Alex Rodriguez 5.00 12.00
10 Juan Gonzalez 1.25 3.00
11 Ivan Rodriguez 2.00 5.00
12 Travis Lee .75 2.00
13 Chipper Jones 3.00 8.00
14 Greg Maddux 5.00 12.00
15 Kerry Wood 1.50 4.00
16 Larry Walker 1.25 3.00
17 Jeff Bagwell 2.00 5.00
18 Mike Piazza 5.00 12.00
19 Mark McGwire 8.00 20.00
20 Tony Gwynn 4.00 10.00

1998 Revolution Rookies and Hardball Heroes

COMPLETE SET (30) 20.00 50.00
STATED ODDS 1:6 HOBBY
*GOLD 1-20: 6X TO 15X BASE CARD HI
GOLD 1-20 RANDOM INS.IN HOBBY PACKS
GOLD 1-20 PRINT RUN 50 SERIAL #'d SETS
1 Justin Baughman .40 1.00
2 Jarrod Washburn .40 1.00
3 Travis Lee .40 1.00
4 Kerry Wood .75 2.00
5 Magglio Ordonez 2.00 5.00
6 Todd Helton 1.00 2.50
7 Derrek Lee 1.00 2.50
8 Richard Hidalgo .40 1.00
9 Mike Caruso .40 1.00
10 David Ortiz .75 2.00
11 Brad Fullmer .40 1.00
12 Masato Yoshii .40 1.00
13 Orlando Hernandez 2.00 5.00
14 Ricky Ledee .60 1.50
15 Ben Grieve .40 1.00
16 Carlton Loewer .40 1.00
17 Desi Relaford .40 1.00
18 Ruben Rivera .60 1.50
19 Rolando Arrojo .40 1.00
20 Matt Perisho .40 1.00
21 Chipper Jones 1.50 4.00
22 Greg Maddux 2.50 6.00
23 Cal Ripken 5.00 12.00
24 Nomar Garciaparra 2.50 6.00
25 Frank Thomas 1.50 4.00
26 Mark McGwire 4.00 10.00
27 Tony Gwynn 2.00 5.00
28 Ken Griffey Jr. 3.00 8.00
29 Alex Rodriguez 2.50 6.00
30 Juan Gonzalez .60 1.50

1998 Revolution Showstoppers

COMPLETE SET (36) 100.00 200.00
STATED ODDS 2:25
1 Cal Ripken 8.00 20.00
2 Nomar Garciaparra 4.00 10.00
3 Pedro Martinez 1.50 4.00
4 Mo Vaughn 1.00 2.50
5 Frank Thomas 2.50 6.00
6 Manny Ramirez 1.50 4.00
7 Jim Thome 1.50 4.00
8 Jaret Wright .60 1.50
9 Paul Molitor 1.00 2.50
10 Orlando Hernandez 3.00 8.00
11 Derek Jeter 6.00 15.00
12 Bernie Williams 1.50 4.00
13 Ben Grieve .60 1.50
14 Ken Griffey Jr. 5.00 12.00
15 Alex Rodriguez 4.00 10.00
16 Wade Boggs 1.50 4.00
17 Juan Gonzalez 1.00 2.50
18 Ivan Rodriguez 1.50 4.00
19 Jose Canseco 1.50 4.00
20 Roger Clemens 5.00 12.00
21 Travis Lee .60 1.50
22 Andres Galarraga 1.00 2.50
23 Chipper Jones 2.50 6.00
24 Greg Maddux 4.00 10.00
25 Sammy Sosa 2.50 6.00
26 Kerry Wood 1.25 3.00
27 Vinny Castilla 1.00 2.50
28 Larry Walker 1.00 2.50
29 Moises Alou 1.00 2.50
30 Raul Mondesi 1.00 2.50
31 Gary Sheffield 1.00 2.50
32 Hideki Irabu .60 1.50
33 Mike Piazza 4.00 10.00
34 Mark McGwire 6.00 15.00
35 Tony Gwynn 3.00 8.00
36 Barry Bonds 6.00 15.00

1999 Revolution

The 1999 Revolution set (produced by Pacific) was issued in one series totalling 150 cards and distributed in three-card packs with a suggested retail price of $3.99. The set features color action player photos on dual-foiled, etched and embossed cards. The set contains a short-printed 25-card rookies subset inserted in packs at the rate of one in four. Rookie Cards include Freddy Garcia.

COMPLETE SET (150) 12.50 30.00
SP STATED ODDS 1:4
SP'S: 16/21/22/33/34/56/57/60/65/68/78/79
SP'S: 80/83/86/100/104/114/117/127/128/129
SP'S: 139/148/150
1 Jim Edmonds .40 1.00
2 Darin Erstad .25 .60
3 Troy Glaus .25 .60
4 Tim Salmon .25 .60
5 Mo Vaughn .25 .60
6 Steve Finley .25 .60
7 Luis Gonzalez .25 .60
8 Randy Johnson .60 1.50
9 Travis Lee .25 .60
10 Matt Williams .25 .60
11 Andruw Jones .25 .60
12 Chipper Jones .60 1.50
13 Brian Jordan .25 .60
14 Javy Lopez .25 .60
15 Greg Maddux .75 2.00
16 Kevin McGlinchy SP .40 1.00
17 John Smoltz .40 1.00
18 Brady Anderson .25 .60
19 Albert Belle .25 .60
20 Will Clark .40 1.00
21 Willis Otanez SP .40 1.00
22 Calvin Pickering SP .40 1.00
23 Cal Ripken 2.00 5.00
24 Nomar Garciaparra .40 1.00
25 Pedro Martinez .40 1.00
26 Troy O'Leary .25 .60
27 Jose Offerman .25 .60
28 Mark Grace .40 1.00
29 Mickey Morandini .25 .60
30 Henry Rodriguez .25 .60
31 Sammy Sosa .60 1.50
32 Ray Durham .25 .60
33 Carlos Lee SP .40 1.00
34 Jeff Liefer SP .40 1.00
35 Magglio Ordonez .40 1.00
36 Frank Thomas .60 1.50
37 Mike Cameron .25 .60
38 Sean Casey .25 .60
39 Barry Larkin .40 1.00
40 Greg Vaughn .25 .60
41 Roberto Alomar .40 1.00
42 Sandy Alomar Jr. .25 .60
43 David Justice .25 .60
44 Kenny Lofton .25 .60
45 Manny Ramirez .60 1.50
46 Richie Sexson .25 .60
47 Jim Thome .40 1.00
48 Dante Bichette .25 .60
49 Vinny Castilla .25 .60
50 Darryl Hamilton .25 .60
51 Todd Helton .40 1.00
52 Larry Walker .40 1.00
53 Tony Clark .25 .60
54 Damion Easley .25 .60
55 Bob Higginson .25 .60
56 Gabe Kapler SP .40 1.00
57 Alex Gonzalez SP .40 1.00
58 Mark Kotsay .25 .60
59 Kevin Orie .25 .60
60 Preston Wilson SP .40 1.00
61 Jeff Bagwell .40 1.00
62 Derek Bell .25 .60
63 Craig Biggio .40 1.00
64 Ken Caminiti .25 .60
65 Carlos Beltran SP .60 1.50

Card	Low	High
66 Johnny Damon	.40	1.00
67 Jermaine Dye	.25	.60
68 Carlos Febles SP	.40	1.00
69 Kevin Brown	.25	.60
70 Todd Hundley	.25	.60
71 Eric Karros	.25	.60
72 Raul Mondesi	.25	.60
73 Gary Sheffield	.25	.60
74 Jeromy Burnitz	.25	.60
75 Jeff Cirillo	.25	.60
76 Marquis Grissom	.25	.60
77 Fernando Vina	.25	.60
78 Chad Allen SP RC	.40	1.00
79 Corey Koskie SP	.40	1.00
80 Doug Mientkiewicz SP RC	.60	1.50
81 Brad Radke	.25	.60
82 Todd Walker	.25	.60
83 Michael Barrett SP	.40	1.00
84 Vladimir Guerrero	.40	1.00
85 Wilton Guerrero	.25	.60
86 Guillermo Mota SP RC	.40	1.00
87 Rondell White	.25	.60
88 Edgardo Alfonzo	.25	.60
89 Rickey Henderson	.60	1.50
90 John Olerud	.25	.60
91 Mike Piazza	.60	1.50
92 Robin Ventura	.25	.60
93 Roger Clemens	.75	2.00
94 Chili Davis	.25	.60
95 Derek Jeter	1.50	4.00
96 Chuck Knoblauch	.25	.60
97 Tino Martinez	.25	.60
98 Paul O'Neill	.40	1.00
99 Bernie Williams	.40	1.00
100 Eric Chavez SP	.40	1.00
101 Jason Giambi	.25	.60
102 Ben Grieve	.25	.60
103 John Jaha	.25	.60
104 Olmedo Saenz SP	.40	1.00
105 Bobby Abreu	.25	.60
106 Doug Glanville	.25	.60
107 Desi Relaford	.25	.60
108 Scott Rolen	.40	1.00
109 Curt Schilling	.25	.60
110 Brian Giles	.25	.60
111 Jason Kendall	.25	.60
112 Pat Meares	.25	.60
113 Kevin Young	.25	.60
114 J.D. Drew SP	.40	1.00
115 Ray Lankford	.25	.60
116 Eli Marrero	.25	.60
117 Joe McEwing SP RC	.40	1.00
118 Mark McGwire	1.00	2.50
119 Fernando Tatis	.25	.60
120 Tony Gwynn	.60	1.50
121 Trevor Hoffman	.40	1.00
122 Wally Joyner	.25	.60
123 Reggie Sanders	.25	.60
124 Barry Bonds	1.00	2.50
125 Ellis Burks	.25	.60
126 Jeff Kent	.25	.60
127 Ramon E.Martinez SP RC	.40	1.00
128 Joe Nathan SP RC	1.00	2.50
129 Freddy Garcia SP RC	1.00	2.50
130 Ken Griffey Jr.	1.25	3.00
131 Brian Hunter	.25	.60
132 Edgar Martinez	.40	1.00
133 Alex Rodriguez	.75	2.00
134 David Segui	.25	.60
135 Wade Boggs	.40	1.00
136 Jose Canseco	.40	1.00
137 Quinton McCracken	.25	.60
138 Fred McGriff	.40	1.00
139 Kelly Dransfeldt SP RC	.40	1.00
140 Juan Gonzalez	.25	.60
141 Rusty Greer	.25	.60
142 Rafael Palmeiro	.40	1.00
143 Ivan Rodriguez	.40	1.00
144 Lee Stevens	.25	.60
145 Jose Cruz Jr.	.25	.60
146 Carlos Delgado	.25	.60
147 Shawn Green	.25	.60
148 Roy Halladay SP	.60	1.50
149 Shannon Stewart	.25	.60
150 Kevin Witt SP	.40	1.00

1999 Revolution Premiere Date

*STARS: 5X TO 12X BASIC CARDS
*SP'S: 2X TO 5X BASIC SP'S
*SP RC'S: 2X TO 5X BASIC SP RC'S
STATED ODDS 1:25 HOBBY
STATED PRINT RUN 49 SERIAL #'d SETS

1999 Revolution Red

*STARS: 2X TO 5X BASIC CARDS
*SP'S: .1.2X TO 3X BASIC SP'S
RANDOM INSERTS IN RETAIL PACKS
STATED PRINT RUN 299 SERIAL #'d SETS

1999 Revolution Shadow Series

*STARS: 4X TO 10X BASIC CARDS
*SP'S: 2.5X TO 6X BASIC SP'S
RANDOM INSERTS IN HOBBY PACKS
STATED PRINT RUN 99 SERIAL #'d SETS

1999 Revolution Diamond Legacy

Card	Low	High
COMPLETE SET (36)	20.00	50.00
STATED ODDS 2:25		
1 Troy Glaus	.40	1.00
2 Mo Vaughn	.40	1.00
3 Matt Williams	.40	1.00
4 Chipper Jones	1.00	2.50
5 Andruw Jones	.40	1.00
6 Greg Maddux	1.25	3.00
7 Albert Belle	.40	1.00
8 Cal Ripken	3.00	8.00
9 Nomar Garciaparra	.60	1.50
10 Sammy Sosa	1.00	2.50
11 Frank Thomas	1.00	2.50
12 Manny Ramirez	1.00	2.50
13 Todd Helton	.60	1.50
14 Larry Walker	.60	1.50
15 Gabe Kapler	.40	1.00
16 Jeff Bagwell	.60	1.50
17 Craig Biggio	.60	1.50
18 Raul Mondesi	.40	1.00
19 Vladimir Guerrero	.60	1.50
20 Mike Piazza	1.00	2.50
21 Roger Clemens	1.25	3.00
22 Derek Jeter	2.50	6.00
23 Bernie Williams	.60	1.50
24 Ben Grieve	.40	1.00
25 Scott Rolen	.60	1.50
26 J.D. Drew	.40	1.00
27 Mark McGwire	1.50	4.00
28 Fernando Tatis	.40	1.00
29 Tony Gwynn	1.00	2.50
30 Barry Bonds	1.50	4.00
31 Ken Griffey Jr.	2.00	5.00
32 Alex Rodriguez	1.25	3.00
33 Jose Canseco	.60	1.50
34 Juan Gonzalez	.40	1.00
35 Ivan Rodriguez	.60	1.50
36 Shawn Green	.40	1.00

1999 Revolution Foul Pole

Card	Low	High
COMPLETE SET (20)	125.00	250.00
STATED ODDS 1:49		
1 Chipper Jones	2.50	6.00
2 Andruw Jones	1.00	2.50
3 Cal Ripken	8.00	20.00
4 Nomar Garciaparra	1.50	4.00
5 Sammy Sosa	2.50	6.00
6 Frank Thomas	2.50	6.00
7 Manny Ramirez	2.50	6.00
8 Jeff Bagwell	1.50	4.00
9 Raul Mondesi	1.00	2.50
10 Vladimir Guerrero	1.50	4.00
11 Mike Piazza	2.50	6.00
12 Derek Jeter	10.00	25.00
13 Bernie Williams	1.50	4.00
14 Scott Rolen	1.50	4.00
15 J.D. Drew	1.00	2.50
16 Mark McGwire	4.00	10.00
17 Tony Gwynn	2.50	6.00
18 Ken Griffey Jr.	5.00	12.00
19 Alex Rodriguez	3.00	8.00
20 Juan Gonzalez	1.00	2.50

1999 Revolution MLB Icons

Card	Low	High
STATED ODDS 1:121		
1 Cal Ripken	10.00	25.00
2 Nomar Garciaparra	2.00	5.00
3 Sammy Sosa	3.00	8.00
4 Frank Thomas	3.00	8.00
5 Mike Piazza	3.00	8.00
6 Derek Jeter	12.00	30.00
7 Mark McGwire	5.00	12.00
8 Tony Gwynn	3.00	8.00
9 Ken Griffey Jr.	6.00	15.00
10 Alex Rodriguez	4.00	10.00

1999 Revolution Thorn in the Side

Card	Low	High
COMPLETE SET (20)	40.00	100.00
STATED ODDS 1:25		
1 Mo Vaughn	1.00	2.50
2 Chipper Jones	2.50	6.00
3 Greg Maddux	3.00	8.00
4 Cal Ripken	8.00	20.00
5 Nomar Garciaparra	1.50	4.00
6 Sammy Sosa	2.50	6.00
7 Frank Thomas	2.50	6.00
8 Manny Ramirez	2.50	6.00
9 Jeff Bagwell	1.50	4.00
10 Mike Piazza	2.50	6.00
11 Derek Jeter	6.00	15.00
12 Bernie Williams	1.50	4.00
13 J.D. Drew	1.00	2.50
14 Mark McGwire	4.00	10.00
15 Tony Gwynn	2.50	6.00
16 Barry Bonds	4.00	10.00
17 Ken Griffey Jr.	5.00	12.00
18 Alex Rodriguez	3.00	8.00
19 Juan Gonzalez	1.00	2.50
20 Ivan Rodriguez	1.50	4.00

1999 Revolution Tripleheader

*TIER 1 (1-10): 3X TO 8X BASIC TRIPLE
TIER 1 PRINT RUN 99 SERIAL #'d SETS
*TIER 2 (11-20): 2X TO 5X BASIC TRIPLE
*TIER 2 DREW: 1X TO 2.5X BASE SP HI
TIER 2 PRINT RUN 199 SERIAL #'d SETS
*TIER 3 (21-30): 1.25X TO 3X BASIC TRIPLE
TIER 3 PRINT RUN 299 SERIAL #'d SETS
TIER CARDS RANDOM IN HOBBY PACKS

Card	Low	High
COMPLETE SET (30)	30.00	80.00
STATED ODDS 4:25 HOBBY		
1 Greg Maddux	2.00	5.00
2 Cal Ripken	4.00	10.00
3 Nomar Garciaparra	2.00	5.00
4 Sammy Sosa	1.25	3.00
5 Frank Thomas	1.25	3.00
6 Mike Piazza	2.00	5.00
7 Mark McGwire	3.00	8.00
8 Tony Gwynn	1.50	4.00
9 Ken Griffey Jr.	2.50	6.00
10 Alex Rodriguez	2.00	5.00
11 Mo Vaughn	.50	1.25
12 Chipper Jones	1.25	3.00
13 Manny Ramirez	.75	2.00
14 Larry Walker	.50	1.25
15 Jeff Bagwell	.75	2.00
16 Vladimir Guerrero	1.25	3.00
17 Derek Jeter	3.00	8.00
18 J.D. Drew	.40	1.00
19 Barry Bonds	3.00	8.00
20 Juan Gonzalez	.50	1.25
21 Troy Glaus	.75	2.00
22 Andruw Jones	.75	2.00
23 Matt Williams	.50	1.25
24 Craig Biggio	.75	2.00
25 Raul Mondesi	.50	1.25
26 Roger Clemens	2.50	6.00
27 Bernie Williams	.75	2.00
28 Scott Rolen	.75	2.00
29 Jose Canseco	.75	2.00
30 Ivan Rodriguez	.75	2.00

2000 Revolution

Card	Low	High
COMPLETE SET (150)	12.50	30.00
COMMON CARD (1-150)	.20	.50
COMMON SP	.40	1.00
SP STATED ODDS 1:4		
1 Darin Erstad	.20	.50
2 Troy Glaus	.20	.50
3 Adam Kennedy SP	.40	1.00
4 Mo Vaughn	.20	.50
5 Erubiel Durazo	.20	.50
6 Steve Finley	.20	.50
7 Luis Gonzalez	.20	.50
8 Randy Johnson	.50	1.25
9 Travis Lee	.20	.50
10 Vicente Padilla SP RC	1.00	2.50
11 Matt Williams	.20	.50
12 Rafael Furcal SP	.60	1.50
13 Andres Galarraga	.30	.75
14 Andruw Jones	.20	.50
15 Chipper Jones	.50	1.25
16 Greg Maddux	.60	1.50
17 Luis Rivera SP RC	.40	1.00
18 Albert Belle	.20	.50
19 Mike Bordick	.20	.50
20 Will Clark	.30	.75
21 Mike Mussina	.30	.75
22 Cal Ripken	1.50	4.00
23 B.J. Surhoff	.20	.50
24 Carl Everett	.20	.50
25 Nomar Garciaparra	.30	.75
26 Pedro Martinez	.30	.75
27 Jason Varitek	.50	1.25
28 Wilton Veras SP	.40	1.00
29 Shane Andrews	.20	.50
30 Scott Downs SP RC	.40	1.00
31 Mark Grace	.30	.75
32 Sammy Sosa	.50	1.25
33 Kerry Wood	.20	.50
34 Ray Durham	.20	.50
35 Paul Konerko	.20	.50
36 Carlos Lee	.20	.50
37 Magglio Ordonez	.30	.75
38 Frank Thomas	.50	1.25
39 Rob Bell SP	.40	1.00
40 Sean Casey	.20	.50
41 Ken Griffey Jr.	1.00	2.50
42 Barry Larkin	.30	.75
43 Pokey Reese	.20	.50
44 Roberto Alomar	.30	.75
45 David Justice	.20	.50
46 Kenny Lofton	.20	.50
47 Manny Ramirez	.50	1.25
48 Richie Sexson	.20	.50
49 Jim Thome	.30	.75
50 Jeff Cirillo	.20	.50
51 Jeffrey Hammonds	.20	.50
52 Todd Helton	.30	.75
53 Larry Walker	.30	.75
54 Tony Clark	.20	.50
55 Juan Gonzalez	.20	.50
56 Hideo Nomo	.50	1.25
57 Dean Palmer	.20	.50
58 Alex Gonzalez	.20	.50
59 Mike Lowell	.20	.50
60 Pablo Ozuna SP	.40	1.00
61 Brad Penny SP	.40	1.00
62 Preston Wilson	.20	.50
63 Moises Alou	.20	.50
64 Jeff Bagwell	.30	.75
65 Craig Biggio	.30	.75
66 Ken Caminiti	.20	.50
67 Julio Lugo SP	.40	1.00
68 Carlos Beltran	.30	.75
69 Johnny Damon UER	.30	.75
70 Jermaine Dye	.20	.50
71 Carlos Febles	.20	.50
72 Mark Quinn SP	.40	1.00
73 Kevin Brown	.20	.50
74 Shawn Green	.20	.50
75 Chan Ho Park	.30	.75
76 Gary Sheffield	.20	.50
77 Kevin Barker SP	.40	1.00
78 Ron Belliard	.20	.50
79 Jeromy Burnitz	.20	.50
80 Geoff Jenkins	.20	.50
81 Cristian Guzman	.20	.50
82 Jacque Jones	.20	.50
83 Corey Koskie	.20	.50
84 Matt Lawton	.20	.50
85 Peter Bergeron SP	.40	1.00
86 Vladimir Guerrero	.30	.75
87 Andy Tracy SP RC	.40	1.00
88 Jose Vidro	.20	.50
89 Rondell White	.20	.50
90 Edgardo Alfonzo	.20	.50
91 Derek Bell	.20	.50
92 Eric Cammack SP RC	.40	1.00
93 Mike Piazza	.50	1.25
94 Robin Ventura	.20	.50
95 Roger Clemens	.60	1.50
96 Orlando Hernandez	.20	.50
97 Derek Jeter	1.25	3.00
98 Tino Martinez	.20	.50
99 Alfonso Soriano SP	1.00	2.50
100 Bernie Williams	.30	.75
101 Eric Chavez	.20	.50
102 Jason Giambi	.20	.50
103 Ben Grieve	.20	.50
104 Terrence Long SP	.40	1.00
105 Mark Mulder SP	.40	1.00
106 Adam Piatt SP	.40	1.00
107 Bobby Abreu	.20	.50
108 Pat Burrell SP	.40	1.00
109 Rico Brogna	.20	.50
110 Doug Glanville	.20	.50
111 Mike Lieberthal	.20	.50
112 Scott Rolen	.30	.75
113 Brian Giles	.20	.50
114 Jason Kendall	.20	.50
115 Warren Morris	.20	.50
116 Rick Ankiel SP	.60	1.50
117 J.D. Drew	.20	.50
118 Jim Edmonds	.20	.50
119 Mark McGwire	.75	2.00
120 Fernando Tatis	.20	.50
121 Fernando Vina	.20	.50
122 Tony Gwynn	.50	1.25
123 Trevor Hoffman	.30	.75
124 Ryan Klesko	.20	.50
125 Eric Owens	.20	.50
126 Barry Bonds	.75	2.00
127 Ellis Burks	.20	.50
128 Bobby Estalella	.20	.50
129 Jeff Kent	.20	.50
130 Scott Linebrink SP RC	.40	1.00
131 Jay Buhner	.20	.50
132 Stan Javier	.20	.50
133 Edgar Martinez	.30	.75
134 John Olerud	.20	.50
135 Alex Rodriguez	.60	1.50
136 Kazuhiro Sasaki SP RC	1.00	2.50
137 Jose Canseco	.30	.75
138 Vinny Castilla	.20	.50
139 Fred McGriff	.30	.75
140 Greg Vaughn	.20	.50
141 Gabe Kapler	.20	.50
142 Mike Lamb SP RC	.40	1.00
143 Ruben Mateo SP	.40	1.00
144 Rafael Palmeiro	.30	.75
145 Ivan Rodriguez	.30	.75
146 Tony Batista	.20	.50
147 Jose Cruz Jr.	.20	.50
148 Carlos Delgado	.20	.50
149 Brad Fullmer	.20	.50
150 Raul Mondesi	.20	.50

2000 Revolution Premiere Date

*PREM.DATE: 3X TO 8X BASIC
*SP's: 1.5X TO 4X BASIC SP's
STATED ODDS 1:25 HOBBY
STATED PRINT RUN 99 SERIAL #'d SETS

2000 Revolution Red

*RED: 4X TO 10X BASIC
*SP's: 2X TO 5X BASIC SP's
STATED PRINT RUN 63 SERIAL #'d SETS

2000 Revolution Shadow Series

*SHADOW: 3X TO 8X BASIC
*SP's: 1.5X TO 4X BASIC SP's
STATED ODDS 1:25 HOBBY
STATED PRINT RUN 99 SERIAL #'d SETS

2000 Revolution Foul Pole

Card	Low	High
COMPLETE SET (20)	40.00	100.00
STATED ODDS 1:49		
1 Chipper Jones	2.00	5.00
2 Cal Ripken	6.00	15.00
3 Nomar Garciaparra	1.25	3.00
4 Pedro Martinez	1.25	3.00
5 Sammy Sosa	2.00	5.00
6 Frank Thomas	2.00	5.00
7 Ken Griffey Jr.	4.00	10.00
8 Manny Ramirez	2.00	5.00
9 Jeff Bagwell	1.25	3.00
10 Shawn Green	.75	2.00
11 Vladimir Guerrero	1.25	3.00
12 Mike Piazza	2.00	5.00
13 Derek Jeter	10.00	25.00
14 Pat Burrell	.75	2.00
15 Rick Ankiel	1.25	3.00
16 Mark McGwire	3.00	8.00
17 Tony Gwynn	2.00	5.00
18 Barry Bonds	3.00	8.00
19 Alex Rodriguez	2.50	6.00
20 Ivan Rodriguez	1.25	3.00

2000 Revolution MLB Game Ball Signatures

Card	Low	High
1 Randy Johnson	30.00	80.00
2 Greg Maddux	40.00	100.00
3 Rafael Furcal	6.00	15.00
4 Shane Andrews	4.00	10.00
5 Sean Casey	6.00	15.00
6 Travis Dawkins	4.00	10.00
7 Alex Gonzalez	4.00	10.00
8 Shane Reynolds	4.00	10.00
9 Eric Gagne	6.00	15.00
10 Kevin Barker	4.00	10.00
11 Eric Milton	4.00	10.00
12 Mark Quinn	4.00	10.00
13 Alfonso Soriano	6.00	15.00
14 Brian Giles	6.00	15.00
15 Mark Mulder	6.00	15.00
16 Adam Piatt	4.00	10.00
17 Warren Morris	4.00	10.00
18 Rick Ankiel	6.00	15.00
19 Adam Kennedy	6.00	15.00
20 Fernando Tatis	4.00	10.00
21 Barry Bonds	50.00	120.00
22 Alex Rodriguez	30.00	80.00
23 Ruben Mateo	4.00	10.00
24 Billy Koch	6.00	15.00
25 Brad Penny	6.00	15.00

2000 Revolution MLB Icons

Card	Low	High
STATED ODDS 1:121		
1 Randy Johnson	4.00	10.00
2 Chipper Jones	4.00	10.00
3 Greg Maddux	5.00	12.00
4 Cal Ripken	12.00	30.00
5 Nomar Garciaparra	2.50	6.00
6 Pedro Martinez	2.50	6.00
7 Sammy Sosa	4.00	10.00
8 Frank Thomas	4.00	10.00
9 Ken Griffey Jr.	8.00	20.00
10 Juan Gonzalez	1.50	4.00
11 Jeff Bagwell	2.50	6.00
12 Vladimir Guerrero	2.50	6.00
13 Mike Piazza	4.00	10.00
14 Roger Clemens	5.00	12.00
15 Derek Jeter	10.00	25.00
16 Mark McGwire	6.00	15.00
17 Tony Gwynn	4.00	10.00
18 Barry Bonds	6.00	15.00
19 Alex Rodriguez	5.00	12.00
20 Ivan Rodriguez	2.50	6.00

2000 Revolution On Deck

Card	Low	High
COMPLETE SET (20)	15.00	40.00
STATED ODDS 1:25		
1 Chipper Jones	1.00	2.50
2 Cal Ripken	3.00	8.00
3 Nomar Garciaparra	.60	1.50
4 Sammy Sosa	1.00	2.50
5 Frank Thomas	1.00	2.50
6 Ken Griffey Jr.	2.00	5.00
7 Manny Ramirez	1.00	2.50
8 Larry Walker	.60	1.50
9 Juan Gonzalez	.40	1.00
10 Jeff Bagwell	.60	1.50
11 Shawn Green	.40	1.00
12 Vladimir Guerrero	.60	1.50
13 Mike Piazza	1.00	2.50
14 Derek Jeter	2.50	6.00
15 Scott Rolen	.60	1.50
16 Mark McGwire	1.50	4.00
17 Tony Gwynn	1.00	2.50
18 Alex Rodriguez	1.25	3.00
19 Jose Canseco	.60	1.50
20 Ivan Rodriguez	.60	1.50

2000 Revolution Season Opener

Card	Low	High
COMPLETE SET (36)	20.00	50.00
STATED ODDS 2:25		
1 Erubiel Durazo	.40	1.00
2 Randy Johnson	1.00	2.50
3 Andruw Jones	.40	1.00
4 Chipper Jones	1.00	2.50
5 Greg Maddux	1.25	3.00
6 Cal Ripken	3.00	8.00
7 Nomar Garciaparra	.60	1.50
8 Pedro Martinez	.60	1.50
9 Sammy Sosa	1.00	2.50
10 Frank Thomas	1.00	2.50
11 Magglio Ordonez	.60	1.50
12 Ken Griffey Jr.	2.00	5.00
13 Barry Larkin	.60	1.50
14 Kenny Lofton	.40	1.00
15 Manny Ramirez	1.00	2.50
16 Jim Thome	.60	1.50
17 Larry Walker	.60	1.50
18 Juan Gonzalez	.40	1.00
19 Jeff Bagwell	.60	1.50
20 Craig Biggio	.60	1.50
21 Carlos Beltran	.60	1.50
22 Shawn Green	.40	1.00
23 Vladimir Guerrero	.60	1.50
24 Mike Piazza	1.00	2.50
25 Orlando Hernandez	.40	1.00
26 Derek Jeter	2.50	6.00
27 Bernie Williams	.60	1.50
28 Eric Chavez	.40	1.00
29 Scott Rolen	.60	1.50
30 Jim Edmonds	.40	1.00
31 Tony Gwynn	1.00	2.50
32 Barry Bonds	1.50	4.00
33 Alex Rodriguez	1.25	3.00
34 Jose Canseco	.60	1.50
35 Ivan Rodriguez	.60	1.50
36 Rafael Palmeiro	.60	1.50

2000 Revolution Triple Header

Card	Low	High
COMPLETE SET (30)	20.00	50.00
STATED ODDS 4:25		
1 Chipper Jones	1.00	2.50
2 Cal Ripken	3.00	8.00
3 Nomar Garciaparra	.60	1.50
4 Frank Thomas	1.00	2.50
5 Larry Walker	.60	1.50
6 Vladimir Guerrero	.60	1.50
7 Mike Piazza	1.00	2.50
8 Derek Jeter	2.50	6.00
9 Tony Gwynn	1.00	2.50
10 Ivan Rodriguez	.60	1.50
11 Sammy Sosa	1.00	2.50
12 Ken Griffey Jr.	2.00	5.00
13 Manny Ramirez	1.00	2.50
14 Jeff Bagwell	.60	1.50
15 Shawn Green	.40	1.00
16 Mark McGwire	1.50	4.00
17 Barry Bonds	1.50	4.00
18 Alex Rodriguez	1.25	3.00
19 Jose Canseco	.60	1.50
20 Rafael Palmeiro	.60	1.50
21 Randy Johnson	1.00	2.50
22 Tom Glavine	.60	1.50
23 Greg Maddux	1.25	3.00
24 Mike Mussina	.60	1.50
25 Pedro Martinez	.60	1.50
26 Kerry Wood	.40	1.00
27 Chuck Finley	.40	1.00
28 Kevin Brown	.40	1.00
29 Roger Clemens	1.25	3.00
30 Rick Ankiel	.60	1.50

2000 Revolution Triple Header Holographic Gold

*BTG.AVG. 1-10: 3X TO 8X BASIC TRIPLE HDR
1-10 PRINT RUN 99 SERIAL #'d SETS
*HR'S 11-20: 3X TO 8X BASIC TRIPLE HDR
11-20 PRINT RUN 99 SERIAL #'d SETS
*K'S 21-30: 1.25X TO 3X BASIC TRIPLE HDR
21-30 PRINT RUN 599 SERIAL #'d SETS

2000 Revolution Triple Header Holographic Silver

*K'S 21-30: 1.5X TO 4X BASIC TRIPLE HDR
STATED PRINT RUN 299 SERIAL #'d SETS

2000 Revolution Triple Header Platinum Blue

*BTG.AVG. 1-10: 1.5X TO 4X BASIC TRIPLE
1-10 PRINT RUN 359 SERIAL #'d SETS
*HR'S 11-20: 2.5X TO 6X BASIC TRIPLE HDR
11-20 PRINT RUN 199 SERIAL #'d SETS
*K'S 21-30: .75X TO 2X BASIC TRIPLE HDR
21-30 PRINT RUN 799 SERIAL #'d SETS

2000 Revolution Triple Header Silver

*BTG.AVG. 1-10: .75X TO 2X BASIC TRIPLE
BTG. 1-10 PRINT RUN 899 SERIAL #'d SETS
*HR'S 11-20: 1.5X TO 4X BASIC TRIPLE HDR
HR'S 11-20 PRINT RUN 399 SERIAL #'d SETS
*K'S 21-30: .75X TO 2X BASIC TRIPLE HDR
K'S 21-30 PRINT RUN 999 SERIAL #'d SETS

1992-93 Revolutionary Legends 1

Revolutionary Comics released this Series one card set and inserted three cards within each issue of Baseball Legends magazine. The individual cards measure approximately 2 1/2" by 3 5/8" but are combined on one strip and stapled to the center of the magazine. The strip measures 10 1/2" by 2 1/2". These are unauthorized cards according to Revolutionary Comics. The fronts display graphic illustrations by Scott Penzer on a red and black background within an irregular yellow and black border. The black and white backs carry biography, career highlights and career summary.

Card	Low	High
COMPLETE SET (15)	4.00	10.00
1 Willie Mays	.40	1.00
2 Willie Mays	.40	1.00
3 Willie Mays	.40	1.00
4 Honus Wagner	.30	.75
5 Honus Wagner	.30	.75
6 Honus Wagner	.30	.75
7 Roberto Clemente	.60	1.50
8 Roberto Clemente	.60	1.50
9 Roberto Clemente	.60	1.50
10 Yogi Berra	.30	.75
11 Yogi Berra	.30	.75
12 Yogi Berra	.30	.75
13 Billy Martin	.20	.50
14 Billy Martin	.20	.50
15 Billy Martin	.20	.50

1992-93 Revolutionary Superstars 1

1992-93 Baseball Superstars Series one was issued by Revolutionary Comics. The cards were inserted in the magazine Baseball Superstars. The cards measure approximately 2 1/2" by 3 5/8" individually and the strip of three measures 10 1/2" by 2 1/2". The graphic illustrations of these superstar players was by Scott Penzer. The fronts display a black background with black and white mottled corner design. The white backs have black print and include biography, career highlights and career summary.

Card	Low	High
COMPLETE SET (15)	5.00	12.00
1 Darryl Strawberry Rookie Year 1983	.20	.50
2 Darryl Strawberry	.20	.50
3 Darryl Strawberry Greatest Moment	.20	.50
4 Frank Thomas Rookie Year 1990	.75	2.00
5 Frank Thomas	.75	2.00
6 Frank Thomas Greatest Moment	.75	2.00
7 Ryne Sandberg Rookie Year 1981	.40	1.00
8 Ryne Sandberg	.40	1.00
9 Ryne Sandberg Greatest Moment	.40	1.00
10 Kirby Puckett Rookie Year 1984	.40	1.00
11 Kirby Puckett	.40	1.00
12 Kirby Puckett Greatest Moment	.40	1.00
13 Roberto Alomar Rookie Year 1988 Sandy Alomar Ro	.30	.75
14 Roberto Alomar Sandy Alomar	.30	.75
15 Roberto Alomar Sandy Alomar Greatest Moments	.30	.75

1993 Rice Council

Card	Low	High
COMPLETE SET (10)	4.00	10.00
1 Steve Sax BB	.20	.50
3 Roger Clemens BB	1.20	3.00
7 Steve Sax BB	.20	.50

1997 Bobby Richardson

This one card standard-size set was given out by Bobby Richardson, former star second baseman for the New York Yankees, as a promotional card he handed out to fans.

Card	Low	High
1 Bobby Richardson	.40	1.00

1989 Rini Postcards Gehrig

This set of 12 postcards measures 3 1/2" by 5 1/2" and honors Lou Gehrig. The fronts feature color drawings by Susan Rini. The cards are numbered on the back.

Card	Low	High
COMPLETE SET (10)	2.00	5.00
COMMON CARD (1-10)	.20	.50
4 Lou Gehrig/(Sitting with Babe Ruth)	.40	1.00

1989 Rini Postcards Mattingly 1

This set of 12 postcards measures 3 1/2" by 5 1/2" and honors Don Mattingly. The fronts feature color drawings by Susan Rini.

Card	Low	High
COMPLETE SET (12)	2.00	5.00
COMMON CARD (1-12)	.20	.50

1990 Rini Postcards Clemente

This 12-card set measures approximately 3 1/2" by 5 1/2" and honors Roberto Clemente. The fronts of the postcards feature the artwork of Susan Rini while the back notes that the set is limited to 5,000 copies of each postcard made.

Card	Low	High
COMPLETE SET (12)	2.00	5.00
COMMON PLAYER (1-12)	.20	.50

1990 Rini Postcards Munson

This set of 12 postcards measures 3 1/2" by 5 1/2" and honors Thurman Munson. The fronts feature color drawings by Susan Rini.

Card	Low	High
COMPLETE SET (12)	2.00	5.00
COMMON CARD (1-12)	.20	.50

1990 Rini Postcards Ryan 1

This set of 12 postcards measures 3 1/2" by 5 1/2" and honors Nolan Ryan. On a light blue background, the fronts feature color drawings by Susan Rini.

Card	Low	High
COMPLETE SET (12)	2.00	5.00
COMMON CARD (1-12)	.20	.50

1990 Rini Postcards Ryan 2

This set of 12 postcards measures 3 1/2" by 5 1/2" and honors Nolan Ryan. On a peach colored background, the fronts feature color drawings by Susan Rini.

Card	Low	High
COMPLETE SET (12)	2.00	5.00
COMMON CARD (1-12)	.20	.50

1991 Rini Postcards Mattingly 2

This set of 12 postcards measures approximately 3 1/2" by 5 1/2" and honors Don Mattingly. On a white background with blue stripes, the fronts feature color drawings by Susan Rini. The backs carry a postcard format.

Card	Low	High
COMPLETE SET (12)	2.00	5.00
COMMON CARD (1-12)	.20	.50

2001 Ripken Essay

Card	Low	High
1 Cal Ripken Jr	.80	2.00

1933 Rittenhouse Candy E285

These cards measure 2 1/4" by 1 7/16" and are found in four colors: red, green, orange or blue. The fronts feature a player photo in the middle surrounded by the suits symbol. The backs either feature one alphabetical character from the words "Rittnehouse Candy Co" or a description of the premium offers. We have sequenced the set in playing order by suit and numbers are assigned to Aces (1), Jacks (11A), Queens (12) and Kings (13). All colors are priced equally.

Card	Low	High
COMPLETE SET (52)	1875.00	3750.00
1C Doc Cramer	30.00	60.00
1D Babe Herman	50.00	100.00
1H Mule Haas	30.00	60.00
1S Babe Ruth	300.00	600.00
2C Bing Miller	30.00	60.00
2D Chick Hafey	60.00	120.00
2H Gus Mancuso	30.00	60.00
2S Billy Herman	60.00	120.00
3C Lefty O'Doul	60.00	120.00
3D Chuck Klein	60.00	120.00
3H George Earnshaw	40.00	80.00
3S Frankie Frisch	100.00	200.00
4C Mel Ott	100.00	200.00
4D Fred Brickell	30.00	60.00
4H Leroy Mahaffey	30.00	60.00
4S Dick Bartell	30.00	60.00
5C Kiki Cuyler	60.00	120.00
5D George Davis	30.00	60.00
5H Jimmy Dykes	40.00	80.00
5S Paul Waner	60.00	120.00
6C Hugh Critz	30.00	60.00
6D Paul Waner	60.00	120.00
6H Rogers Hornsby	125.00	250.00
6S Don Hurst	30.00	60.00
7C Walter Berger	40.00	80.00
7D Sugar Cain	30.00	60.00
7H Joe Cronin	60.00	120.00
7S Frankie Frisch	60.00	120.00
8C Dib Williams	30.00	60.00
8D Lefty Grove	100.00	200.00
8H Lou Finney	30.00	60.00
8S Ed. Cihocki	30.00	60.00
9C Hack Wilson	60.00	120.00
9D Al Simmons	60.00	120.00
9H Spud Davis	30.00	60.00
9S Hack Wilson	60.00	120.00
10C Pie Traynor	60.00	120.00
10D Bill Terry	60.00	120.00
10H Lloyd Waner	60.00	120.00
10S Jimmy Foxx (Jimmie)	100.00	200.00
11C Jumbo Elliott	30.00	60.00
11D Don Hurst	30.00	60.00
11H Pinky Higgins	30.00	60.00
11S Jim Bottomley	60.00	120.00
12C Pinky Whitney	30.00	60.00
12D Lloyd Waner	60.00	120.00
12H Eric McNair	30.00	60.00
12S Rube Walberg	30.00	60.00
13C Babe Ruth	300.00	600.00
13D Phil Collins	30.00	60.00
13H Gabby Hartnett	60.00	120.00
13S Max Bishop	30.00	60.00

1955 Robert Gould W605

The cards in this 28-card set measure 2 1/2" by 3 1/2". The 1955 Robert F. Gould set of black and white on green cards were toy store cardboard holders for small plastic statues. The statues were attached to the card by a rubber band through two holes on the side of the card. The catalog designation is W605. The cards are numbered in the bottom right corner of the obverse and are blank-backed.

Card	Low	High
COMPLETE SET (28)	5000.00	10000.00
1 Willie Mays	1250.00	2500.00
2 Gus Zernial	100.00	200.00
3 Red Schoendienst	200.00	400.00
4 Chico Carrasquel	100.00	200.00
5 Jim Hegan	100.00	200.00
6 Curt Simmons	125.00	250.00
7 Bob Porterfield	100.00	200.00
8 Jim Busby	100.00	200.00
9 Don Mueller	100.00	200.00
10 Ted Kluszewski	200.00	400.00
11 Ray Boone	100.00	200.00
12 Smoky Burgess	125.00	250.00
13 Bob Rush	100.00	200.00
14 Early Wynn	200.00	400.00
15 Bill Bruton	100.00	200.00
16 Gus Bell	100.00	200.00
17 Jim Finigan	100.00	200.00
18 Granny Hamner	100.00	200.00
19 Hank Thompson	100.00	200.00
20 Joe Coleman	100.00	200.00
21 Don Newcombe	150.00	300.00
22 Richie Ashburn	300.00	600.00
23 Bobby Thomson	150.00	300.00
24 Sid Gordon	100.00	200.00
25 Gerry Coleman	125.00	250.00
26 Ernie Banks	600.00	1200.00
27 Billy Pierce	125.00	250.00
28 Mel Parnell	125.00	250.00

1993 Brooks Robinson Country Time Legends

These eight cards measure approximately 2 1/2" by 3 5/8" and feature restored "colorized" black-and-white photos highlighting the 23-season career of HOFer Brooks Robinson. Each photo is overlaid upon a black diamond. The border around the photo is green, red, and black, and the set's logo rests at the lower right. The back carries career highlights within a white rectangle framed in yellow and bordered in gray, yellow and black. The cards are unnumbered and checklisted below chronologically and distinguished by pose descriptions.

Card	Low	High
COMPLETE SET	2.50	6.00
COMMON PLAYER (1-8)	.40	1.00

1947 Jackie Robinson Bond Bread

The 1947 Bond Bread Jackie Robinson set features 13 unnumbered cards of Jackie in different action or portrait poses; each card measures approximately 2 1/4" by 3 1/2". Card number 7, which is the only card in the set to contain a facsimile autograph, was apparently issued in greater quantity than other cards in the set and has been noted as a double print (DP) in the checklist below. Several of the cards have a horizontal format; these are marked in the checklist

below by HOR. The catalog designation for this set is D302.
COMPLETE SET (13) 4000.00 8000.00
COMMON DP
1 Jackie Robinson 400.00 800.00
Sliding into base
cap, ump in photo, HOR
2 Jackie Robinson 400.00 800.00
Running down 3rd base line
3 Jackie Robinson 400.00 800.00
Batting
bat behind head
facing camera
4 Jackie Robinson 400.00 800.00
Moving towards second
throw almost to glove
HOR
5 Jackie Robinson 400.00 800.00
Taking throw at first, HOR
6 Jackie Robinson 400.00 800.00
Jumping high in the air for ball
7 Jackie Robinson 250.00 500.00
Profile with glove in
front of head
facsimile autograph DP
8 Jackie Robinson 400.00 800.00
Leaping over second base
ready to throw
9 Jackie Robinson 400.00 800.00
Portrait
holding glove over head
10 Jackie Robinson 400.00 800.00
Portrait
holding bat perpendicular
to body
11 Jackie Robinson 400.00 800.00
Reaching for throw
glove near ankle
12 Jackie Robinson 400.00 800.00
Leaping for throw
no scoreboard
in background
13 Portrait, holding/bat parallel/to body 400.00800.00
XX Jackie Robinson/6 1/2 by 9
Premium Photo 750.00 1500.00

1993 Rockies Stadium Club

This 30-card standard-size set features the 1993 Colorado Rockies. The set was issued in hobby (plastic box) and retail (blister) form as well as being distributed in shrinkwrapped cardboard boxes with a manager card pictured on it.

COMP. FACT SET (30) 2.00 5.00
1 David Nied .02 .10
2 Quinton McCracken .02 .10
3 Charlie Hayes .02 .10
4 Bryn Smith .02 .10
5 Dante Bichette .30 .75
6 Alex Cole .02 .10
7 Scott Aldred .02 .10
8 Roberto Mejia .02 .10
9 Jeff Parrett .02 .10
10 Joe Girardi .08 .25
11 Andres Galarraga .60 1.50
12 Daryl Boston .02 .10
13 Jerald Clark .02 .10
14 Gerald Young .02 .10
15 Bruce Ruffin .02 .10
16 Rudy Seanez .02 .10
17 Darren Holmes .02 .10
18 Andy Ashby .02 .10
19 Chris Jones .02 .10
20 Mark Thompson .02 .10
21 Freddie Benavides .02 .10
22 Eric Wedge .08 .25
23 Vinny Castilla .30 .75
24 Butch Henry .02 .10
25 Jim Tatum .02 .10
26 Steve Reed .02 .10
27 Eric Young .20 .50
28 Danny Sheaffer .02 .10
29 Roger Bailey .02 .10
30 Brad Ausmus .08 .25

1993 Rockies U.S. Playing Cards

This 56-card standard-size set celebrates the 1993 Inaugural Year of the Colorado Rockies. Since this set is similar to a playing card set, the set is checklisted below as if it were a playing card deck. In the checklist C means Clubs, D means Diamonds, H means Hearts, S means Spades and JK means Joker. The cards are checklisted in playing order by suits and numbers are assigned to Aces, (1) Jacks, (11) Queens, (12) and Kings (13). Included in the set are a Rockies' opening day player roster card and a 1993 home schedule card. The jokers, home schedule card and the opening day player roster card are unnumbered and listed at the end of our checklist.

COMPLETE SET (56) 1.50 4.00
1C Jim Tatum .01 .05
1D Andres Galarraga .20 .50
1H Charlie Hayes .01 .05
1S David Nied .01 .05
2C Charlie Hayes .01 .05
2D David Nied .01 .05
2H Jim Tatum .01 .05
2S Andres Galarraga .20 .50
3C Dale Murphy .20 .50
3D Dante Bichette .08 .25
3H Andy Ashby .01 .05
3S Gary Wayne .01 .05
4C Scott Aldred .01 .05
4D Joe Girardi .02 .10
4H Vinny Castilla .08 .25
4S Freddie Benavides .01 .05
5C Braulio Castillo .01 .05
5D Bryn Smith .01 .05
5H Steve Reed .01 .05
5S Butch Henry .01 .05
6C Danny Sheaffer .01 .05
6D Darren Holmes .01 .05
6H Daryl Boston .01 .05
6S Gerald Young .01 .05
7C Jerald Clark .01 .05
7D Bruce Ruffin .01 .05
7H Alex Cole .01 .05
7S Jeff Parrett .01 .05
8C Willie Blair .01 .05
8D Eric Young .05 .15
8H Bryn Smith .01 .05
8S Braulio Castillo .01 .05
9C Daryl Boston .01 .05
9D Gerald Young .01 .05
9H Danny Sheaffer .01 .05
9S Darren Holmes .01 .05
10C Andy Ashby .01 .05
10D Gary Wayne .01 .05
10H Willie Blair .01 .05
10S Dale Murphy .20 .50
11C Butch Henry .01 .05
11D Steve Reed .01 .05
11H Dante Bichette .15 .40
11S Eric Young .05 .15
12C Alex Cole .01 .05
12D Jeff Parrett .01 .05
12H Jerald Clark .01 .05
12S Bruce Ruffin .01 .05
13C Vinny Castilla .08 .25
13D Freddie Benavides .01 .05
13H Scott Aldred .01 .05
13S Joe Girardi .02 .10
JKO National League Logo .01 .05
NNO 1993 Home Schedule .01 .05

1993 Rockies Upper Deck

This 27-card set of the Colorado Rockies features the same design as the players' 1993 regular Upper Deck cards. The difference is found in the gold foil stamping of the team's logo on the front. The cards are checklisted below according to their corresponding numbers in the regular Upper Deck set. These cards were issued in special "team sets" form.

COMPLETE SET 3.00 8.00
27 David Nied .02 .10
444 John Burke .02 .10
478 Dante Bichette .08 .25
David Nied
Andres Galarraga
521 Eric Young .08 .25
529 Jeff Parrett .02 .10
538 Alex Cole .02 .10
560 Vinny Castilla .15 .40
571 Joe Girardi .08 .25
593 Andres Galarraga .08 .25
647 Charlie Hayes .02 .10
653 Eric Wedge .08 .25
668 Darren Holmes .02 .10
670 Bruce Ruffin .02 .10
683 Dante Bichette .08 .25
706 Dale Murphy 2.50 6.00
720 Willie Blair .02 .10
723 Bryn Smith .02 .10
732 Freddie Benavides .02 .10
737 Daryl Boston .02 .10
740 Gerald Young .02 .10
752 Steve Reed .02 .10
761 Jim Tatum .02 .10
763 Andy Ashby .02 .10
770 Butch Henry .02 .10
793 Armando Reynoso .02 .10
797 Jerald Clark .02 .10
834 David Nied CL .02 .10

1994 Rockies Police

These 27 cards measure approximately 2 5/8" by 4" and feature color action and posed player photos on their yellow-bordered fronts. The cards are unnumbered and checklisted below in alphabetical order.

COMPLETE SET (27) 4.00 10.00
1 Don Baylor MG .30 .75
2 Dante Bichette .40 1.00
3 Willie Blair .08 .25
4 Kent Bottenfield .08 .25
5 Ellis Burks .40 1.00
6 Vinny Castilla .40 1.00
7 Marvin Freeman .08 .25
8 Andres Galarraga .75 2.00
9 Andres Galarraga/1993 Batting Champ.75 2.00
10 Joe Girardi .20 .50
11 Mike Harkey .08 .25
12 Greg W. Harris .08 .25
13 Charlie Hayes .08 .25
14 Darren Holmes .08 .25
15 Howard Johnson .08 .25
16 Nelson Liriano .08 .25
17 Roberto Mejia .08 .25
18 Mike Munoz .08 .25
19 David Nied .08 .25
20 Steve Reed .08 .25
21 Armando Reynoso .08 .25
22 Bruce Ruffin .08 .25
23 Danny Sheaffer .08 .25
24 Darrell Sherman .08 .25
25 Walt Weiss .08 .25
26 Eric Young .20 .50
27 Coaches Card .08 .25
Larry Bearnarth
Dwight Evans
Gene

1995 Rockies Police

This 12-card set of the Colorado Rockies measures 2 5/8" by 4" and was sponsored by the Kansas City Life Insurance Company. The cards are unnumbered and checklisted below in alphabetical order.

COMPLETE SET (12) 3.00 6.00
1 Jason Bates .08 .25
2 Don Baylor MG .20 .50
3 Dante Bichette .40 1.00
4 Ellis Burks .40 1.00
5 Vinny Castilla .40 1.00
6 Andres Galarraga .60 1.50
7 Joe Girardi .08 .25
8 Mike Kingery .08 .25
9 Bill Swift .08 .25
10 Larry Walker .60 1.50
11 Walt Weiss .08 .25
12 Eric Young .20 .50

1996 Rockies Fleer

These 20 standard-size cards are same as the regular Fleer issue, except they are UV coated, they use silver foil and they are numbered "x of 20". The team set packs were available at retail locations and hobby shops in 10-card packs for a suggested price of $1.99.

COMPLETE SET (20) .75 2.00
1 Jason Bates .02 .10
2 Dante Bichette .10 .30
3 Ellis Burks .10 .30
4 Vinny Castilla .10 .30
5 Andres Galarraga .15 .40
6 Darren Holmes .02 .10
7 Curt Leskanic .02 .10
8 Quinton McCracken .02 .10
9 Mike Munoz .04 .10
10 Jayhawk Owens .02 .10
11 Steve Reed .02 .10
12 Kevin Ritz .02 .10
13 Bret Saberhagen .07 .20
14 Bill Swift .02 .10
15 John Vander Wal .02 .10
16 Larry Walker .30 .75
17 Walt Weiss .02 .10
18 Eric Young .07 .20
19 Logo card .02 .10
20 Checklist .02 .10

1996 Rockies Police

This 27-card set measures approximately 2 5/8" by 4". This set features members of the 1996 Colorado Rockies. The cards are unnumbered and we have sequenced them in alphabetical order. The set was sponsored by Kansas City Life Insurance Company and the back features various safety tips.

COMPLETE SET (27) 3.00 8.00
1 Roger Bailey .08 .25
2 Jason Bates .08 .25
3 Don Baylor MG .20 .50
4 Dante Bichette .20 .50
5 Ellis Burks .40 1.00
6 Vinny Castilla .20 .50
7 Marvin Freeman .08 .25
8 Andres Galarraga .40 1.00
9 Darren Holmes .08 .25
10 Trenidad Hubbard .08 .25
11 Curt Leskanic .08 .25
12 Quinton McCracken .08 .25
13 Mike Munoz .08 .25
14 Jayhawk Owens .08 .25
15 Lance Painter .08 .25
16 Steve Reed .08 .25
17 Bryan Rekar .08 .25
18 Armando Reynoso .08 .25
19 Kevin Ritz .08 .25
20 Bruce Ruffin .08 .25
21 Bret Saberhagen .20 .50
22 Bill Swift .08 .25
23 Mark Thompson .08 .25
24 John Vander Wal .08 .25
25 Larry Walker .60 1.50
26 Walt Weiss .08 .25
27 Eric Young .20 .50

1997 Rockies Coke/7-11

This four-card set was produced by World Holographics and was available for purchase at participating 7-Eleven stores with the purchase of any Coca-Cola 12-pack. The set measures approximately 3" by 4" and features 3-D lenticular color action player photos. The cards are unnumbered and checklisted below alphabetically.

COMPLETE SET (4) 3.00 8.00
1 Dante Bichette/(Batting) .75 2.00
2 Dante Bichette/(Sliding) .75 2.00
3 Ellis Burks/(Batting) 1.00 2.50
4 Ellis Burks/(Sliding) 1.00 2.50

1997 Rockies Police

This 12-card set of the Colorado Rockies was sponsored by the Colorado Association of Chiefs of Police (CACP) and Decker. The fronts feature color action player photos in a thin white border. The backs carry player information and a safety message. The cards are unnumbered and checklisted below in alphabetical order.

COMPLETE SET (12) 4.00 10.00
1 Don Baylor MG .30 .75
2 Dante Bichette .40 1.00
3 Ellis Burks .60 1.50
4 Vinny Castilla .40 1.00
5 Dinger(Mascot) .20 .50
6 Andres Galarraga .75 2.00
7 Kirt Manwaring .20 .50
8 Quinton McCracken .20 .50
9 Bill Swift .20 .50
10 Larry Walker .75 2.00
11 Walt Weiss .20 .50
12 Eric Young .30 .75

1997 Rockies Score

This 15-card set of the Colorado Rockies was issued in five-card packs with a suggested retail price of $1.30 each. The fronts feature color player photos with special team specific color foil stamping. The backs carry player information. Only 100 cases were made for each team. Platinum parallel cards were inserted at a rate of 1:6, Premier parallel cards at a rate of 1:31.

COMPLETE SET (15) 2.00 5.00
*PLATINUM: 5X BASIC CARDS
*PREMIER: 20X BASIC CARDS
1 Dante Bichette .20 .50
2 Kevin Ritz .08 .25
3 Walt Weiss .08 .25
4 Ellis Burks .30 .75
5 Jamey Wright .08 .25
6 Andres Galarraga .40 1.00
7 Eric Young .20 .50
8 Larry Walker .60 1.50
9 Vinny Castilla .30 .75
10 Quinton McCracken .08 .25
11 Armando Reynoso .08 .25
12 Jayhawk Owens .08 .25
13 Mark Thompson .08 .25
14 Bruce Ruffin .08 .25
15 John Burke .08 .25

1998 Rockies Police

This 12 card standard-size set was issued by the Colorado Rockies and produced by Grandstand. The borderless cards feature a player portrait along with the player's name going down the side. The horizontal back has a player portrait, vital information and a safety tip. The cards were sponsored by "Decker", the hot dog manufacturer. The cards are unnumbered so we have sequenced them alphabetically.

COMPLETE SET 3.00 8.00
1 Pedro Astacio .20 .50
2 Don Baylor MG .20 .50
3 Dante Bichette .30 .75
4 Ellis Burks .40 1.00
5 Vinny Castilla .30 .75
6 Todd Helton 1.00 2.50
7 Darryl Kile .30 .75
8 Mike Lansing .20 .50
9 Kirt Manwaring .20 .50
10 Neifi Perez .20 .50
11 Larry Walker .75 2.00
12 Dinger .20 .50
Mascot

1999 Rockies Police

These 12 standard-size cards feature members of the 1999 Colorado Rockies. The borderless fronts have player photos with the player's name and position on the bottom and the words "Colorado Rockies" running along the side. The backs have a smaller player photo, biographical information and a safety tip. Since the cards are unnumbered, we have sequenced them in alphabetical order.

COMPLETE SET (12) 3.00 8.00
1 Dante Bichette .30 .75
2 Vinny Castilla .30 .75
3 Dinger .20 .50
Mascot
4 Jerry DiPoto .20 .50
5 Darryl Hamilton .20 .50
6 Todd Helton 1.00 2.50
7 Darryl Kile .30 .75
8 Mike Lansing .20 .50
9 Jim Leyland MG .20 .50
10 Kirt Manwaring .20 .50
11 Neifi Perez .20 .50
12 Larry Walker .75 2.00

2000 Rockies Police

COMPLETE SET (12) 3.20 8.00
1 Rolando Arrojo .20 .50
2 Buddy Bell MG .20 .50
3 Jeff Cirillo .20 .50
4 Tom Goodwin .20 .50
5 Jeffrey Hammonds .20 .50
6 Todd Helton 1.00 2.50
7 Mike Lansing .20 .50
8 Brent Mayne .20 .50
9 Neifi Perez .20 .50
10 Larry Walker .75 2.00
11 Dinger .20 .50
Mascot
12 Coors Field .20 .50

2002 Rockies Police

COMPLETE SET 2.50 6.00
1 Gary Bennett .08 .25
2 Mike Hampton .20 .50
3 Todd Helton .75 2.00
4 Todd Hollandsworth .08 .25
5 Clint Hurdle MG .08 .25
6 Denny Neagle .08 .25
7 Jose Ortiz .08 .25
8 Juan Pierre .60 1.50
9 Juan Uribe .08 .25
10 Larry Walker .60 1.50
11 Todd Zeile .20 .50
12 Dinger .08 .25
Mascot
XX Armour Coupon .08 .25

2004 Rockies Magnets

COMPLETE SET (6) 4.00 10.00
1 Vinny Castilla .60 1.50
2 Todd Helton 1.50 4.00
3 Javier A. Lopez .40 1.00
4 Larry Walker 1.25 3.00
5 Preston Wilson .60 1.50
6 Mascot Dinger .40 1.00

2006 Rockies Topps

COMPLETE SET (14) 3.00 8.00
COL1 Matt Holliday .30 .75
COL2 Todd Helton .20 .50
COL3 Garrett Atkins .12 .30
COL4 Clint Barmes .12 .30
COL5 Jeff Francis .12 .30
COL6 Brian Fuentes .12 .30
COL7 Yorvit Torrealba .12 .30
COL8 Brad Hawpe .12 .30
COL9 Ryan Shealy .12 .30
COL10 Aaron Cook .12 .30
COL11 Zach Day .12 .30
COL12 Jason Jennings .12 .30
COL13 Jose Mesa .12 .30
COL14 Luis Gonzalez .12 .30

2007 Rockies Topps

COMPLETE SET (14) 3.00 8.00
COL1 Todd Helton .20 .50
COL2 Jamey Carroll .12 .30
COL3 Ubaldo Jimenez .40 1.00
COL4 Chris Iannetta .12 .30
COL5 Troy Tulowitzki .40 1.00
COL6 Brad Hawpe .12 .30
COL7 Jeff Francis .12 .30
COL8 Willy Taveras .12 .30
COL9 Matt Holliday .30 .75
COL10 Cory Sullivan .12 .30
COL11 Garrett Atkins .12 .30
COL12 Aaron Cook .12 .30
COL13 Josh Fogg .12 .30
COL14 Brian Fuentes .12 .30

2008 Rockies Topps

COMPLETE SET (14) 3.00 8.00
COL1 Matt Holliday .30 .75
COL2 Ian Stewart .12 .30
COL3 Ubaldo Jimenez .12 .30
COL4 Chris Iannetta .12 .30
COL5 Troy Tulowitzki .30 .75
COL6 Brad Hawpe .12 .30
COL7 Jeff Francis .12 .30
COL8 Willy Taveras .12 .30
COL9 Todd Helton .20 .50
COL10 Ryan Spilborghs .12 .30
COL11 Garrett Atkins .12 .30
COL12 Aaron Cook .12 .30
COL13 Manny Corpas .12 .30
COL14 Yorvit Torrealba .12 .30

2009 Rockies Topps

COL1 Troy Tulowitzki .40 1.00
COL2 Ubaldo Jimenez .15 .40
COL3 Garrett Atkins .15 .40
COL4 Jeff Francis .15 .40
COL5 Clint Barmes .15 .40
COL6 Ryan Spilborghs .15 .40
COL7 Brad Hawpe .15 .40
COL8 Huston Street .15 .40
COL9 Todd Helton .25 .60
COL10 Dexter Fowler .25 .60
COL11 Chris Iannetta .15 .40
COL12 Aaron Cook .15 .40
COL13 Ian Stewart .15 .40
COL14 Jeff Baker .15 .40
COL15 Coors Field .15 .40

2010 Rockies Topps

COL1 Troy Tulowitzki .40 1.00
COL2 Eric Young Jr. .15 .40
COL3 Jhoulys Chacin .15 .40
COL4 Ian Stewart .15 .40
COL5 Dexter Fowler .25 .60
COL6 Chris Iannetta .15 .40
COL7 Huston Street .15 .40
COL8 Carlos Gonzalez .25 .60
COL9 Todd Helton .25 .60
COL10 Jorge De La Rosa .15 .40
COL11 Jason Hammel .25 .60
COL12 Brad Hawpe .15 .40
COL13 Ubaldo Jimenez .15 .40
COL14 Aaron Cook .15 .40
COL15 Jeff Francis .15 .40
COL16 Seth Smith .15 .40
COL17 Clint Barmes .15 .40

2011 Rockies Topps

COL1 Carlos Gonzalez .25 .60
COL2 Todd Helton .25 .60
COL3 Ian Stewart .15 .40
COL4 Seth Smith .15 .40
COL5 Ubaldo Jimenez .15 .40
COL6 Aaron Cook .15 .40
COL7 Jhoulys Chacin .15 .40
COL8 Eric Young Jr. .15 .40
COL9 Jorge De La Rosa .15 .40
COL10 Dexter Fowler .25 .60
COL11 Ty Wigginton .15 .40
COL12 Chris Iannetta .15 .40
COL13 Ryan Spilborghs .15 .40
COL14 Huston Street .15 .40
COL15 Troy Tulowitzki .40 1.00
COL16 Jason Hammel .25 .60
COL17 Coors Field .15 .40

2012 Rockies Topps

COL1 Troy Tulowitzki .40 1.00
COL2 Carlos Gonzalez .30 .75
COL3 Eric Young .25 .60
COL4 Jorge De La Rosa .25 .60
COL5 Todd Helton .30 .75
COL6 Drew Pomeranz .25 .60
COL7 Dexter Fowler .30 .75
COL8 Juan Nicasio .25 .60
COL9 Jason Giambi .25 .60
COL10 Jhoulys Chacin .25 .60
COL11 Ramon Hernandez .25 .60
COL12 Jordan Pacheco .25 .60
COL13 Jonathan Herrera .25 .60
COL14 Rafael Betancourt .25 .60
COL15 Michael Cuddyer .25 .60
COL16 Guillermo Moscoso .30 .75
COL17 Coors Field .15 .40

2013 Rockies Topps

COMPLETE SET (17) 3.00 8.00
COL1 Carlos Gonzalez .30 .75
COL2 Troy Tulowitzki .25 .60
COL3 Michael Cuddyer .15 .40
COL4 Todd Helton .30 .75
COL5 Jhoulys Chacin .15 .40
COL6 Chris Nelson .25 .60
COL7 Jordan Pacheco .25 .60
COL8 Juan Nicasio .15 .40
COL9 Josh Rutledge .15 .40
COL10 Jorge De La Rosa .15 .40
COL11 Rafael Betancourt .15 .40
COL12 Wilin Rosario .15 .40
COL13 Dexter Fowler .30 .75
COL14 Tyler Colvin .15 .40
COL15 Tyler Chatwood .15 .40
COL16 Drew Pomeranz .20 .50
COL17 Coors Field .15 .40

2014 Rockies Topps

COMPLETE SET (17) 3.00 8.00
COL1 Carlos Gonzalez .20 .50
COL2 Troy Tulowitzki .25 .60
COL3 Michael Cuddyer .15 .40
COL4 Nolan Arenado .40 1.00
COL5 Jhoulys Chacin .15 .40
COL6 Charlie Blackmon .25 .60
COL7 Drew Stubbs .15 .40
COL8 Juan Nicasio .15 .40
COL9 D.J. LeMahieu .25 .60
COL10 Jorge De La Rosa .15 .40
COL11 Rex Brothers .15 .40
COL12 Wilin Rosario .15 .40
COL13 Justin Morneau .20 .50
COL14 Jordan Pacheco .15 .40
COL15 Tyler Chatwood .15 .40
COL16 Brett Anderson .15 .40
COL17 Coors Field .15 .40

2015 Rockies Topps

COMPLETE SET (17) 3.00 8.00
COR1 Troy Tulowitzki .25 .60
COR2 Charlie Blackmon .25 .60
COR3 Rex Brothers .15 .40
COR4 Corey Dickerson .15 .40
COR5 Tommy Kahnle .15 .40
COR6 Jordan Lyles .15 .40
COR7 Wilin Rosario .15 .40
COR8 Nolan Arenado .40 1.00
COR9 Justin Morneau .20 .50
COR10 DJ LeMahieu .25 .60
COR11 Drew Stubbs .15 .40
COR12 Carlos Gonzalez .20 .50
COR13 Jorge De La Rosa .15 .40
COR14 Christian Bergman .15 .40
COR15 Tyler Matzek .15 .40
COR16 LaTroy Hawkins .15 .40
COR17 Jhoulys Chacin .15 .40

2016 Rockies Topps

COMPLETE SET (17) 3.00 8.00
COL1 Nolan Arenado .40 1.00
COL2 Carlos Gonzalez .20 .50
COL3 Nick Hundley .15 .40
COL4 Jordan Lyles .15 .40
COL5 DJ LeMahieu .25 .60
COL6 Jose Reyes .20 .50
COL7 Corey Dickerson .15 .40
COL8 Charlie Blackmon .25 .60
COL9 Jorge De La Rosa .15 .40
COL10 Mark Reynolds .15 .40
COL11 Tyler Chatwood .15 .40
COL12 Chad Bettis .15 .40
COL13 Ben Paulsen .15 .40
COL14 Brandon Barnes .15 .40
COL15 Chris Rusin .15 .40
COL16 Jon Gray
COL17 Tom Murphy .15 .40

2017 Rockies Topps

COMPLETE SET (17) 3.00 8.00
COL1 Nolan Arenado .40 1.00
COL2 Tyler Chatwood .15 .40
COL3 David Dahl .20 .50
COL4 Tony Wolters .15 .40
COL5 Ian Desmond .15 .40
COL6 Jon Gray .15 .40
COL7 Chad Bettis .15 .40
COL8 Charlie Blackmon .25 .60
COL9 Jason Motte .15 .40
COL10 Jake McGee .20 .50
COL11 Carlos Estevez .15 .40
COL12 Jeff Hoffman .15 .40
COL13 DJ LeMahieu .25 .60
COL14 Adam Ottavino .15 .40
COL15 Carlos Gonzalez .20 .50
COL16 Trevor Story .25 .60
COL17 Gerardo Parra .15 .40

2018 Rockies Topps

COMPLETE SET (17) 2.00 5.00
CO1 Nolan Arenado .40 1.00
CO2 Raimel Tapia .15 .40
CO3 Pat Valaika .15 .40
CO4 Jon Gray .15 .40
CO5 Mike Dunn .15 .40
CO6 Charlie Blackmon .25 .60
CO7 Kyle Freeland .20 .50
CO8 Chad Bettis .15 .40
CO9 Gerardo Parra .15 .40
CO10 Trevor Story .25 .60
CO11 Tony Wolters .15 .40
CO12 Tyler Anderson .15 .40
CO13 German Marquez .15 .40
CO14 Chris Rusin .15 .40
CO15 Ian Desmond .15 .40
CO16 DJ LeMahieu .25 .60
CO17 Adam Ottavino .15 .40

2019 Rockies Topps

COMPLETE SET (17) 2.00 5.00
CO1 Charlie Blackmon .25 .60
CO2 Nolan Arenado .40 1.00
CO3 Trevor Story .25 .60
CO4 David Dahl .15 .40
CO5 Ian Desmond .15 .40
CO6 Tyler Anderson .15 .40
CO7 Jon Gray .15 .40
CO8 Kyle Freeland .20 .50
CO9 Daniel Murphy .20 .50
CO10 Chris Iannetta .15 .40
CO11 Antonio Senzatela .15 .40
CO12 German Marquez .15 .40
CO13 Wade Davis .15 .40
CO14 Bryan Shaw .15 .40
CO15 Raimel Tapia .15 .40
CO16 Noel Cuevas .15 .40
CO17 Seung-hwan Oh .20 .50

2020 Rockies Topps

COL1 Charlie Blackmon .25 .60
COL2 Nolan Arenado .40 1.00
COL3 Trevor Story .25 .60
COL4 German Marquez .25 .60
COL5 Wade Davis .15 .40
COL6 Daniel Murphy .20 .50
COL7 Ryan McMahon .25 .60
COL8 Ian Desmond .15 .40
COL9 Raimel Tapia .15 .40
COL10 Garrett Hampson .15 .40
COL11 Tony Wolters .15 .40
COL12 Brendan Rodgers .25 .60
COL13 Kyle Freeland .20 .50
COL14 Scott Oberg .15 .40
COL15 Jon Gray .15 .40
COL16 Bryan Shaw
COL17 David Dahl .15 .40

2017 Rockies Topps National Baseball Card Day

COMPLETE SET (10) 5.00 12.00
COL1 Nolan Arenado 1.50 4.00
COL2 Chad Bettis .60 1.50
COL3 Charlie Blackmon 1.00 2.50
COL4 David Dahl .75 2.00
COL5 Ian Desmond .60 1.50
COL6 Carlos Gonzalez .75 2.00
COL7 Jon Gray .60 1.50
COL8 DJ LeMahieu 1.00 2.50
COL9 Trevor Story 1.00 2.50
COL10 Andres Galarraga .75 2.00

1999 Alex Rodriguez Bookmar

These five bookmarks feature star shortstop Alex Rodriguez and publicize his a-rod reading club program

COMPLETE SET 4.00 10.00
COMMON CARD .80 2.00

1998 Alex Rodriguez Taco Time Bookmarks

These four bookmarks feature Alex Rodriguez and promote the A-Rod reading club which encourage young kids to read at least five books. The fronts feature photos of Alex along with the message, "Hit the Books, not the streets". The backs have the Taco Time logo on the top and information on how to join the A-Rod reading club as well as information about his web site.

COMPLETE SET (4) 2.00 5.00
COMMON CARD (1-4) .60 1.50

2005 Alex Rodriguez Etopps Promos

AR1 Alex Rodriguez At Bat 2.00 5.00
AR2 Alex Rodriguez Fielding 2.00 5.00
AR3 Alex Rodriguez Swinging 2.00 5.00

1930 Rogers Peet

The Rogers Peet Department Store in New York released this set in early 1930. The cards were given out four at time to employees at the store for enrolling boys in Ropeco (the store's magazine club). Employees who completed the set, and pasted them in the album designed to house the cards, were eligible to win prizes. The blankbacked cards measure roughly 1 3/4" by 2 1/2" and feature a black and white photo of the famous athlete with his name and card number below the picture. Additions to this list are appreciated.

5 Dazzy Vance BB 60.00 100.00
13 Walter Johnson BB 200.00 400.00
16 Rogers Hornsby BB 100.00 200.00
18 Herb Pennock BB 60.00 100.00
28 Lou Gehrig BB 375.00 750.00
34 Ty Cobb BB 500.00 800.00
38 Tris Speaker BB 62.50 125.00
48 Babe Ruth BB 2500.00 4000.00

1964 Rollins Sheels Hardware

This blank-backed photograph, which measures approximately 7 1/2" by 9 1/2" features Twins star third baseman Rich Rollins. The front has a photo of Rollins along with a note at the bottom for Sheels Hardware which then had 3 locations in the Fargo-Moorehead, North Dakota area.

1 Rich Rollins 4.00 10.00

2018 Rookies and Stars

1 Shohei Ohtani RC 6.00 15.00
2 Buster Posey .30 .75
3 Ronald Acuna Jr. RC 8.00 20.00
4 Miguel Andujar RC 1.00 2.50
5 Rhys Hoskins RC 1.00 2.50
6 Chris Sale .25 .60
7 Austin Hays RC .40 1.00
8 Ozzie Albies RC .75 2.00
9 Bryce Harper .40 1.00
10 Joey Votto .25 .60
11 Cody Bellinger .50 1.25
12 Giancarlo Stanton .25 .60
13 Nolan Arenado .40 1.00
14 Kris Bryant .30 .75
15 Amed Rosario RC .30 .75
16 Gleyber Torres RC 2.50 6.00
17 Rafael Devers RC .75 2.00
18 Mike Trout 1.25 3.00
19 Clint Frazier RC .50 1.25
20 Marcell Ozuna .25 .60

2019 Rookies and Stars

RANDOM INSERTS IN PACKS
*GOLD/199: 1.2X TO 3X
*BLUE/99: 1.5X TO 4X
*RED/50: 2X TO 5X
*HOLO SLVR/25: 3X TO 8X
1 Pete Alonso RC 2.00 5.00
2 Eloy Jimenez RC .60 1.50
3 Fernando Tatis Jr. RC 2.00 5.00
4 Michael Kopech RC .50 1.25
5 Kyle Tucker RC .40 1.00
6 Yusei Kikuchi RC .25 .60
7 Chris Paddack RC .30 .75
8 Mike Trout 1.25 3.00
9 Bryce Harper .40 1.00
10 Aaron Judge .60 1.50
11 Kris Bryant .30 .75
12 Shohei Ohtani .40 1.00
13 Vladimir Guerrero Jr. RC 2.50 6.00
14 Nick Senzel RC .50 1.25
15 Carter Kieboom RC .25 .60
16 Xander Bogaerts .25 .60
17 Anthony Rendon .25 .60
18 Griffin Canning RC .25 .60
19 Cal Quantrill RC .15 .40
20 Nicky Lopez RC .25 .60

2020 Rookies and Stars

RANDOM INSERTS IN PACKS
1 Shogo Akiyama RC .40 1.00
2 Yordan Alvarez RC 2.50 6.00
3 Bo Bichette RC 3.00 8.00
4 Aristides Aquino RC .60 1.50
5 Gavin Lux RC 1.25 3.00
6 Yoshitomo Tsutsugo RC .60 1.50
7 Brendan McKay RC .40 1.00
8 Luis Robert RC 4.00 10.00
9 Sean Murphy RC .40 1.00
10 Yu Chang RC .40 1.00
11 Domingo Leyba RC .30 .75
12 Edwin Rios RC .60 1.50
13 Tony Gonsolin RC 1.00 2.50
14 Willi Castro RC .40 1.00
15 Tyrone Taylor RC .25 .60
16 Gleyber Torres .50 1.25
17 Stephen Strasburg .25 .60
18 Jose Altuve .20 .50
19 Ozzie Albies .25 .60
20 Shane Bieber .25 .60

2020 Rookies and Stars Signatures

RANDOM INSERTS IN PACKS

PRINT RUNS B/WN 10-99 COPIES PER
NO PRICING QTY 15 OR LESS
EXCHANGE DEADLINE 3/18/2022
1 Shogo Akiyama/49 6.00 15.00
2 Yordan Alvarez/50 40.00 100.00
3 Bo Bichette/30 30.00 80.00
4 Aristides Aquino/60 8.00 20.00
6 Yoshitomo Tsutsugo/99 8.00 20.00
8 Luis Robert EXCH/99 75.00 200.00
9 Sean Murphy/99 5.00 12.00
10 Yu Chang/99 5.00 12.00
11 Domingo Leyba/99 4.00 10.00
12 Edwin Rios/99 8.00 20.00
13 Tony Gonsolin/99 12.00 30.00
14 Willi Castro/99 5.00 12.00
16 Gleyber Torres EXCH/25 20.00 50.00

1908-09 Rose Company PC760

One of the most attractive postcards ever issued, The Rose Company postcards were issued during the end of the 20th century's first decade. The set features a black and white photo in a circle surrounded by a yellow and green baseball field, crossed bats and small figures. Imprints on the reverse contain the letters TRC, with the loop around the bottom of the C possibly accounting for a lower case "o," giving Co. The Rose Co. baseball series is listed in alphabetical order by teams in the checklist below-research indicates that each of the 16 major league teams is represented by 12 Rose postcards (to date not all have been found). And several minor league franchises are now believed to have 10 or more cards for them as well. The cards we currently list as 192 through 204 all feature members of the Springfield Mass baseball team. Although it is not confirmed that these are Rose postcards, the similarities are obvious enough that to add these to these listings makes sense.

COMPLETE SET 25000.00 50000.00
1 Ralph Glaze 300.00 600.00
2 Dad Hale 300.00 600.00
3 Frank LaPorte 300.00 600.00
4 Bris Lord 300.00 600.00
5 Tex Pruiett 300.00 600.00
6 Jack Thoney 300.00 600.00
7 Bob Unglaub 300.00 600.00
8 Heinie Wagner 300.00 600.00
9 George Winter 300.00 600.00
10 Cy Young 1500.00 3000.00
11 Nick Altrock 400.00 800.00
12 John Anderson 300.00 600.00
13 Jiggs Donohue 300.00 600.00
14 Fielder Jones 300.00 600.00
15 Freddy Parent 300.00 600.00
16 Frank Smith 300.00 600.00
17 Billy Sullivan 300.00 600.00
18 Lee Tannehill 300.00 600.00
19 Doc White 300.00 600.00
20 Harry Bemis 300.00 600.00
21 Joe Birmingham 300.00 600.00
22 Bill Bradley 300.00 600.00
23 Josh Clarke 300.00 600.00
24 Bill Hinchman 300.00 600.00
25 Addie Joss 1000.00 2000.00
26 Nap Lajoie 600.00 1200.00
27 Glen Liebhardt 300.00 600.00
28 Bob Rhoads 300.00 600.00
Spelled Rhoades on card
29 George Stovall 300.00 600.00
30 Terry Turner 300.00 600.00
31 Ty Cobb 3000.00 6000.00
32 Bill Coughlin 300.00 600.00
33 Sam Crawford 600.00 1200.00
34 Bill Donovan 400.00 800.00
35 Ed Killian 300.00 600.00
36 Matty McIntyre 300.00 600.00
37 George Mullin 400.00 800.00
38 Charley O'Leary 300.00 600.00
39 Claude Rossman 300.00 600.00
40 Germany Schaefer 400.00 800.00
41 Boss Schmidt 300.00 600.00
42 Ed Summers 300.00 600.00
43 Hal Chase 600.00 1200.00
44 Jack Chesbro 600.00 1200.00
45 Wid Conroy 300.00 600.00
46 Kid Elberfeld 300.00 600.00
47 Fred Glade 300.00 600.00
48 Charlie Hemphill 300.00 600.00
49 Willie Keeler 600.00 1200.00
50 Red Kleinow 300.00 600.00
51 Doc Newton 300.00 600.00
52 Harry Niles 300.00 600.00
53 Al Orth 300.00 600.00
54 Jake Stahl 300.00 600.00
55 Chief Bender 600.00 1200.00
56 Jimmy Collins 600.00 1200.00
57 Jack Coombs 300.00 600.00
58 Harry Davis 300.00 600.00
59 Jimmy Dygert 300.00 600.00
60 Topsy Hartsel 300.00 600.00
61 Danny Murphy 300.00 600.00
62 Simon Nicholls 300.00 600.00
63 Rube Oldring 300.00 600.00
64 Eddie Plank 600.00 1200.00
65 Ossee Schreck 300.00 600.00
66 Socks Seybold 300.00 600.00
67 Hobe Ferris 300.00 600.00
68 Danny Hoffman 300.00 600.00
69 Harry Howell 300.00 600.00
70 Tom Jones 300.00 600.00
71 Jack Powell 300.00 600.00
72 Tubby Spencer 300.00 600.00
73 George Stone 300.00 600.00
74 Rube Waddell 600.00 1200.00
75 Jimmy Williams 300.00 600.00
76 Otis Clymer 300.00 600.00
77 Frank Delahanty 300.00 600.00
78 Bob Ganley 300.00 600.00
79 Jerry Freeman 300.00 600.00
80 Tom Hughes 300.00 600.00
81 Walter Johnson 2000.00 4000.00
82 George McBride 300.00 600.00
83 Casey Patten 300.00 600.00
84 Clyde Milan 400.00 800.00
85 Bill Shipke 300.00 600.00
86 Charlie Smith 300.00 600.00
87 Jack Warner 300.00 600.00
88 Ginger Beaumont 300.00 600.00
89 Sam Brown 300.00 600.00
90 Bill Dahlen 300.00 600.00
91 George Ferguson 300.00 600.00
92 Vive Lindaman 300.00 600.00
93 Claude Ritchey 300.00 600.00
94 Whitey Alperman 300.00 600.00
95 John Hummel 300.00 600.00
96 Phil Lewis 300.00 600.00
97 Harry Lumley 300.00 600.00
98 Billy Maloney 300.00 600.00
99 Harry MacIntyre 300.00 600.00
100 Nap Rucker 300.00 600.00
101 Tommy Sheehan 300.00 600.00
102 Mordecai Brown 600.00 1200.00
103 Frank Chance 1000.00 2000.00
104 Johnny Evers 1000.00 2000.00
105 Solly Hofman 300.00 600.00
106 John Kling 300.00 600.00
107 Orvall Overall 300.00 600.00
108 Ed Reulbach 300.00 600.00
109 Frank Schulte 400.00 800.00
110 Jimmy Sheckard 300.00 600.00
111 Jimmy Slagle 300.00 600.00
112 Harry Steinfeldt 400.00 800.00
113 Joe Tinker 1000.00 2000.00
114 Billy Campbell 300.00 600.00
115 Andy Coakley 300.00 600.00
116 Bob Ewing 300.00 600.00
117 John Ganzel 300.00 600.00
118 Miller Huggins 600.00 1200.00
119 Rudy Hulswitt 300.00 600.00
120 Hans Lobert 300.00 600.00
121 Larry McLean 300.00 600.00
122 Mike Mitchell 300.00 600.00
123 Mike Mowery 300.00 600.00
124 Dode Paskert 300.00 600.00
125 Jake Weimer 300.00 600.00
126 Roger Bresnahan 600.00 1200.00
127 Al Bridwell 300.00 600.00
128 Art Devlin 300.00 600.00
129 Mike Donlin 400.00 800.00
130 Joe Doyle 400.00 800.00
131 Christy Mathewson 2000.00 4000.00
132 Joe McGinnity 600.00 1200.00
133 Cy Seymour 300.00 600.00
134 Spike Shannon 300.00 600.00
135 Dummy Taylor 400.00 800.00
136 Fred Tenney 300.00 600.00
137 Hooks Wiltse 300.00 600.00
138 Kitty Bransfield 300.00 600.00
139 Buster Brown 300.00 600.00
140 Frank Corridon 300.00 600.00
141 Red Dooin 300.00 600.00
142 Mickey Doolan 300.00 600.00
143 Eddie Grant 400.00 800.00
144 Otto Knabe 300.00 600.00
145 Sherry Magee 500.00 1000.00
146 George McQuillan 300.00 600.00
Spelled McQuillen on card
147 Fred Osborn 300.00 600.00
148 Tully Sparks 300.00 600.00
149 John Titus 300.00 600.00
150 Ed Abbaticchio 300.00 600.00
151 Bill Abstein 300.00 600.00
152 Howie Camnitz 300.00 600.00
153 Fred Clarke 600.00 1200.00
154 George Gibson 300.00 600.00
155 Jim Kane 300.00 600.00
156 Tommy Leach 300.00 600.00
157 Nick Maddox 300.00 600.00
158 Deacon Philippe 400.00 800.00
159 Roy Thomas 300.00 600.00
160 Honus Wagner 2000.00 4000.00
161 Owen Wilson 400.00 800.00
162 Irv Young 300.00 600.00
163 Shad Barry 300.00 600.00
164 Fred Beebe 300.00 600.00
165 Bobby Byrne 300.00 600.00
166 Joe Delahanty 300.00 600.00
167 Billy Gilbert 300.00 600.00
168 Art Hoelskoetter 300.00 600.00
169 Ed Karger 300.00 600.00
170 Ed Konetchy 300.00 600.00
171 Johnny Lush 300.00 600.00
172 Stoney McGlynn 300.00 600.00
173 Red Murray 300.00 600.00
174 Patsy O'Rourke 300.00 600.00
175 Beckendorf 300.00 600.00
Scranton
176 Bills 300.00 600.00
177 Graham 300.00 600.00
178 Groh 300.00 600.00
Scranton
179 Halligan 300.00 600.00
180 Houser 300.00 600.00
181 Isbel 300.00 600.00
182 Kellogg 300.00 600.00
Scranton
183 Kittredge 300.00 600.00
Scranton
184 Moran 300.00 600.00
185 Schultz 300.00 600.00
186 Steele 300.00 600.00
187 Andy Coakley 300.00 600.00
188 Knight 300.00 600.00
189 Schlei 300.00 600.00
190 Spade 300.00 600.00
191 Tris Speaker 600.00 1200.00
192 Thomas 300.00 600.00
193 Harl Maggert 300.00 600.00
194 Parker 300.00 600.00
195 James Burns 300.00 600.00
196 Edwin Warner 300.00 600.00
197 Rising 300.00 600.00
198 Connor 300.00 600.00
199 Wachob 300.00 600.00
200 McLean 300.00 600.00
201 Chet Waite 300.00 600.00
202 Luby 300.00 600.00
203 George Tacy 300.00 600.00
204 Collins 300.00 600.00
205 Louis Barbour 300.00 600.00
206 Big Jeff Pfeffer

2001 Rose Ballpark Café

1 Pete Rose 2.00 5.00

1992 Rose Dynasty

Produced by Dynasty Sports Cards, this 15-card, standard-size set is aptly titled "The Hit King" and showcases Pete Rose. The white-bordered color pictures on the fronts were painted by artist Tim Seeberger. A gold foil crown and a card subtitle are printed in the wider white border below the picture. On a white background in black print, backs carry the year in a diamond icon and running narrative summarizing Rose's illustrious career.

COMPLETE SET (15) 4.00 10.00
COMMON PLAYER (1-14) .30 .75

1968 Rose Jamesway Trucking

This one card set, which measures 4" by 5 1/4" featured a batting pose of Pete Rose and the "Jamesway Trucking Logo" on the bottom.

1 Pete Rose 200.00 400.00

1905 Rotograph Co. PC782

This rather distinguished looking set mesaures 3 1/4" by 5 3/8" and was printed by the Rotograph Company of New York in 1905. Some of the cards are numbered while others are not. The Clark Griffith card was initially issued with the name misspelled and was later corrected. The Rotograph identification is printed on the back of the card. Only New York teams are portrayed.

COMPLETE SET (9) 875.00 1750.00
1 Ambrose Puttman 100.00 200.00
2 Jack Chesbro (2) 200.00 400.00
3 George Brown 100.00 200.00
4 Bill Dahlen 100.00 200.00
5 John McGraw 300.00 600.00
6 Clark Griffill 200.00 400.00
Sic, Griffith
7 Clark Griffith 200.00 400.00
8 Joe McGinnity 200.00 400.00
Spelled Josep
9 Joe McGinnity 200.00 400.00
Spelled Joseph
10 Luther Taylor 100.00 200.00

1976 Rowe Exhibits

These collector issued exhibits feature the best major leaguers of the pre- World War 2 era. The cards are unnumbered and we have sequenced in alphabetical order by who appears in the upper left corner.

COMPLETE SET (16) 4.00 10.00
1 Luke Appling .15 .40
Ted Lyons
Red Ruffing
Red Faber
2 Jim Bottomley .20 .50
Earle Combs
George Sisler
Roger H
3 Dizzy Dean .30 .75
Stan Musial
Jesse Haines
Frank Frisc
4 Joe DiMaggio .40 1.00
Lou Gehrig
Lefty Gomez
Bill Dickey
5 Bob Feller .20 .50
Lou Boudreau
Earl Averill
Bob Lemon
6 Jimmie Foxx .15 .40
Grover C. Alexander
Robin Roberts
E
7 Hank Greenberg .40 1.00
Charlie Gehringer
Ty Cobb
Goose
8 Chick Hafey .15 .40
Edd Roush
Bill McKechnie
George Kel
9 Fred Lindstrom .15 .40
Billy Herman
Kiki Cuyler
Gabby H
10 Heinie Manush .20 .50
Walter Johnson
Bucky Harris
Sam R
11 Joe Medwick .15 .40
Max Carey
Dazzy Vance
Burleigh Grim
12 Mel Ott .20 .50
Carl Hubbell
Dave Bancroft
Bill Terry
13 Al Simmons .20 .50
Lefty Grove
Mickey Cochrane
Eddie Co
14 Warren Spahn .20 .50
Al Lopez
Casey Stengel
Rabbit Mara
15 Pie Traynor .20 .50
Lloyd Waner
Honus Wagner
Paul Waner
16 Ted Williams .40 1.00
Herb Pennock
Babe Ruth
Joe Cronin

1950-53 Royal Desserts

These cards were issued by Royal desserts over a period of years. These cards measure 2 1/2" by 3 1/2" and even though the same players are featured, variations exist when biographies were changed to keep the cards current. The backs are blank but the cards are numbered on the front. A set is considered complete with only one of each variation. These items were also made in blue. They have a value of 1X to2X the values listed below.

COMPLETE SET 1250.00 2500.00
COMMON PLAYER (1-24) 15.00 30.00
COMMON DP
1 Stan Musial DP 200.00 400.00
2 Pee Wee Reese DP 75.00 150.00
3 George Kell 60.00 120.00
4 Dom DiMaggio 40.00 80.00
5 Warren Spahn 75.00 150.00
6A Andy Pafko 20.00 40.00
Chicago Cubs
6B Andy Pafko 75.00 150.00
Brooklyn Dodgers
7A Andy Seminick 20.00 40.00
Philadelphia Phillies
7B Andy Seminick 20.00 40.00
Cincinnati Reds
8A Lou Brissie 20.00 40.00
Philadelphia A's
8B Lou Brissie 75.00 150.00
Cleveland Indians
9 Ewell Blackwell 20.00 40.00
10 Bobby Thomson 40.00 80.00
11 Phil Rizzuto DP 75.00 150.00
12 Tommy Henrich 40.00 80.00
13 Joe Gordon 40.00 80.00
14A Ray Scarborough 20.00 40.00
Washington Senators
14B Ray Scarborough 75.00 150.00
Chicago White Sox
14C Ray Scarborough 20.00 40.00
Boston Red Sox
15A Stan Rojek 20.00 40.00
Pittsburgh Pirates
15B Stan Rojek 75.00 150.00
St. Louis Browns
16 Luke Appling 60.00 120.00
17 Willard Marshall 20.00 40.00
18 Alvin Dark 40.00 80.00
19A Dick Sisler 20.00 40.00
Philadelphia Phillies
19B Dick Sisler 20.00 40.00
Cincinnati Reds
20 Johnny Ostrowski 20.00 40.00
21A Virgil Trucks 20.00 40.00
Detroit Tigers
21B Virgil Trucks 75.00 150.00
St. Louis Browns
22 Eddie Robinson 20.00 40.00
23 Nanny Fernandez 75.00 150.00
24 Ferris Fain 20.00 40.00

1952 Royal Premiums

These 16 photos measure approximately 5" by 7". These black and white photos are all facsimile signed with the expression "To a Royal Fan". The backs are blank and sequenced in alphabetical order.

COMPLETE SET (16) 400.00 800.00
1 Ewell Blackwell 15.00 30.00
2 Leland Brissie Jr. 15.00 30.00
3 Alvin Dark 20.00 40.00
4 Dom DiMaggio 30.00 60.00
5 Ferris Fain 15.00 30.00
6 George Kell 30.00 60.00
7 Stan Musial 100.00 200.00
8 Andy Pafko 15.00 30.00
9 Pee Wee Reese 50.00 100.00
10 Phil Rizzuto 50.00 100.00
11 Eddie Robinson 15.00 30.00
12 Ray Scarborough 15.00 30.00
13 Andy Seminick 15.00 30.00
14 Dick Sisler 15.00 30.00
15 Warren Spahn 50.00 100.00
16 Bobby Thomson 20.00 40.00

1969 Royals Solon

These 15 blank-backed cards measure approximately 2 1/8" by 3 3/8" and feature blue-screened posed player photos on their white-bordered fronts. The player's name and position, along with the Royals logo, appear in blue lettering in the lower white margin. The cards are unnumbered and checklisted below in alphabetical order. The set is given the appelation Solon because long-time hobbyist Bob Solon produced these cards.

COMPLETE SET (15) 6.00 15.00
1 Jerry Adair .40 1.00
2 Wally Bunker .40 1.00
3 Moe Drabowsky .40 1.00
4 Dick Drago .40 1.00
5 Joe Foy .40 1.00
6 Joe Gordon MG .60 1.50
7 Chuck Harrison .40 1.00
8 Mike Hedlund .40 1.00
9 Jack Hernandez .40 1.00
10 Pat Kelly .40 1.00
11 Roger Nelson .40 1.00
12 Bob Oliver .40 1.00
13 Lou Piniella 1.50 4.00
14 Ellie Rodriguez .40 1.00
15 Dave Wickersham .40 1.00

1969 Royals Team Issue

This 12-card set of the Kansas City Royals measures approximately 4 1/4" by 7". The fronts display black-and-white player portraits bordered in white. The player's name and team are printed in the top margin. The backs are blank. The cards are unnumbered and checklisted below in alphabetical order.

COMPLETE SET 6.00 15.00
1 Jerry Adair .60 1.50
2 Jimmy Campanis .60 1.50
3 Moe Drabowsky .60 1.50
4 Mike Fiore .60 1.50
5 Joe Foy .60 1.50
6 Joe Gordon MG 1.00 2.50
7 Pat Kelly .60 1.50
8 Joe Keough .60 1.50
9 Roger Nelson .60 1.50
10 Bob Oliver .60 1.50
11 Juan Rios .60 1.50
12 Dave Wickersham .60 1.50

1970 Royals Team Issue

This 38-card set measures approximately 3 3/8" by 5" and features black-and-white player portraits in a white border. A facsimile autograph across the bottom of the picture. The backs are blank. The cards are unnumbered and checklisted below in alphabetical order.

COMPLETE SET (38) 15.00 40.00
1 Ted Abernathy .40 1.00
2 Jerry Adair .40 1.00
3 Luis Alcaraz .40 1.00
4 Wally Bunker .40 1.00
5 Tom Burgmeier .40 1.00
6 Bill Butler .40 1.00
7 Jim Campanis .40 1.00
8 Dan Carnevale CO .40 1.00
9 Moe Drabowsky .40 1.00
10 Dick Drago .40 1.00
11 Harry Dunlop CO .40 1.00
12 Mike Fiore .40 1.00
13 Al Fitzmorris .40 1.00
14 Jack Hernandez .40 1.00
15 Bob Johnson .40 1.00
16 Pat Kelly .40 1.00
17 Joe Keough .40 1.00
18 Ed Kirkpatrick .40 1.00
19 Bob Lemon MG 1.00 2.50
20 Pat Locanto .40 1.00
21 Tommy Matchick .40 1.00
22 Charlie Metro CO .40 1.00
23 Aurelio Monteagudo .40 1.00
24 Dave Morehead .40 1.00
25 Bob Oliver .40 1.00
26 Amos Otis .60 1.50
27 Lou Piniella 1.00 2.50
28 Ellie Rodriguez .40 1.00
29 Cookie Rojas .60 1.50
30 Jim Rooker .40 1.00
31 Paul Schaal .40 1.00
32 Joe Schultz CO .60 1.50
33 Bill Sorrell .40 1.00
34 Rich Stevenson .40 1.00
35 George Strickland CO .40 1.00
36 Cedric Tallis GM .40 1.00
37 Bob Hawk Taylor .40 1.00
38 Ken Wright .40 1.00

1971 Royals Signature Series Team

These photos feature members of the 1971 Kansas City Royals. The photos are unnumbered and feature fascimile signatures on them and we have sequenced them in alphabetical order.

COMPLETE SET 12.50 30.00
1 Ted Abernathy .40 1.00
2 Wally Bunker .40 1.00
3 Galen Cisco .40 1.00
4 Bruce Dal Canton .40 1.00
5 Dick Drago .40 1.00
6 Harry Dunlop CO .40 1.00
7 Al Fitzmorris .60 1.50
8 Mike Hedlund .40 1.00
9 Chuck Harrison .40 1.00
10 Gail Hopkins .40 1.00
11 Pat Kelly .40 1.00
12 Ed Kirkpatrick .40 1.00
13 Bobby Knoop .40 1.00
14 Charley Lau CO .60 1.50
15 Bob Lemon MG 1.00 2.50
16 Jerry May .40 1.00
17 Dave Morehead .40 1.00
18 Roger Nelson .40 1.00
19 Bob Oliver .75 2.00
20 Amos Otis 1.00 2.50
21 Dennis Paepke .40 1.00
22 Fred Patek .75 2.00
23 Lou Piniella 1.00 2.50
24 Lou Piniella 1.00 2.50
25 Cookie Rojas .60 1.50
26 Ted Savage .40 1.00
27 Paul Splittorff .60 1.50
28 George Strickland CO .40 1.00
29 Cedric Talles GM .40 1.00
30 Carl Taylor .40 1.00
31 Ken Wright .40 1.00
32 Jim York .40 1.00

1972 Royals Team Issue

These photos feature members of the 1972 Kansas City Royals. They are unnumbered so we have sequenced them in alphabetical order.

COMPLETE SET 6.00 15.00
1 Ted Abernathy .20 .50
2 Tom Burgmeier .20 .50
3 Harry Dunlop GM .20 .50
4 Al Fitzmorris .20 .50
5 Bob Floyd .20 .50
6 Mike Hedlund .20 .50
7 Gail Hopkins .20 .50
8 Steve Hovley .20 .50
9 Joe Keough .20 .50
10 Ed Kirkpatrick .20 .50
11 Bobby Knoop .20 .50
12 Charley Lau CO .40 1.00
13 Bob Lemon MG .60 1.50
14 Jerry May .20 .50
15 John Mayberry .40 1.00
16 Roger Nelson .20 .50
17 Amos Otis .60 1.50
18 Fred Patek .40 1.00
19 Lou Pinella .60 1.50
20 Cookie Rojas .30 .75
21 Jim Rooker .20 .50
22 Paul Schaal .20 .50
23 Richie Scheinblum .20 .50
24 Paul Splittorff .30 .75
25 George Strickland CO .20 .50
26 Carl Taylor .20 .50
27 Ken Wright .20 .50

1974 Royals Postcards

This 29-card set of the Kansas City Royals features black-and-white player protraits measuring approximately 3 1/4" by 5" with a facsimile autograph. The set could originally be bought from the team for $2 or 10 cards for $1. The cards are unnumbered and checklisted below in alphabetical order. George Brett has a postcard in this set, a year before his Rookie Card.

COMPLETE SET (29) 15.00 40.00
1 Kurt Bevacqua .30 .75
2 Doug Bird .20 .50
3 George Brett 10.00 25.00
4 Nelson Briles .20 .50
5 Steve Busby .20 .50
6 Orlando Cepeda 2.00 5.00
7 Galen Cisco CO .20 .50
8 Al Cowens .30 .75
9 Bruce Dal Canton .20 .50
10 Harry Dunlop CO .20 .50
11 Al Fitzmorris .20 .50
12 Fran Healy .40 1.00
13 Joe Hoerner .20 .50
14 Charley Lau CO .30 .75
Card does not have a fascimile aut
15 Buck Martinez .30 .75
16 John Mayberry .40 1.00
17 Lindy McDaniel .20 .50
18 Jack McKeon MG .20 .50
19 Hal McRae .40 1.00
20 Steve Mingori .20 .50
21 Amos Otis .40 1.00
22 Fred Patek .30 .75
23 Marty Pattin .20 .50
24 Vada Pinson .60 1.50
25 Cookie Rojas .30 .75
26 Tony Solaita .20 .50
27 Paul Spittorff .20 .50
28 Frank White 1.25 3.00
29 Jim Wohlford .20 .50

1975 Royals Postcards

This 32-card set of the Kansas City Royals features player photos on postcard-size cards. The cards are unnumbered and checklisted below in alphabetical order.

COMPLETE SET (32) 10.00 25.00
1 Doug Bird .20 .50
2 George Brett 4.00 10.00
3 Steve Boros CO .20 .50
4 Nelson Briles .20 .50
5 Joe Burke GM .20 .50
6 Steve Busby .20 .50
7 Bruce Dal Canton .20 .50
8 Galen Cisco CO .20 .50
9 Al Cowens .20 .50
10 Harry Dunlop CO .20 .50
11 Al Fitzmorris .20 .50
12 Fran Healy .20 .50
13 Whitey Herzog MG .20 .50
14 Harmon Killebrew 1.25 3.00
15 Charlie Lau CO .20 .50
16 Dennis Leonard .20 .50
17 Burck Martinez .30 .75
18 John Mayberry .20 .50
19 Lindy McDaniel .30 .75
20 Jack McKeon FO .20 .50
21 Hal McRae .40 1.00
22 Steve Mingori .20 .50
23 Amos Otis .40 1.00
24 Fred Patek .30 .75
25 Marty Pattin .20 .50
26 Vada Pinson .60 1.50
27 Cookie Rojas .30 .75
28 Tony Solaita .20 .50
29 Paul Splittorff .20 .50
30 Bob Stinson .20 .50
31 Frank White .60 1.50
32 Jim Wohlford .20 .50

1976 Royals A and P

This 16-card set features color photos of the Kansas City Royals and is believed to measure approximately 5 7/8" by 9". The set was produced by the Atlantic and Pacific Tea Company and distributed in Missouri and surrounding areas. The cards are unnumbered and checklisted below in alphabetical order. These cards were issued over a four week period at a rate of four each week. The cards were available when a customer bought two specially priced items at the A and P.

COMPLETE SET (16) 8.00 20.00
1 Doug Bird .40 1.00
2 George Brett 3.00 8.00
3 Steve Busby .40 1.00
4 Al Cowens .40 1.00
5 Al Fitzmorris .40 1.00
6 Dennis Leonard .40 1.00
7 Buck Martinez .60 1.50
8 John Mayberry .40 1.00
9 Hal McRae .75 2.00
10 Amos Otis .75 2.00
11 Fred Patek .60 1.50
12 Tom Poquette .40 1.00
13 Cookie Rojas .60 1.50
14 Tony Solaita .40 1.00
15 Paul Splittorff .40 1.00
16 Jim Wohlford .40 1.00

1976 Royals Postcards

This 33-card set of the Kansas City Royals features player photos on postcard-size cards. The cards are unnumbered and checklisted below in alphabetical order.

COMPLETE SET (33) 8.00 20.00
1 Doug Bird .20 .50
2 Steve Boros CO .20 .50
3 George Brett 2.50 6.00
4 Joe Burke GM .20 .50
5 Steve Busby .20 .50
6 Galen Cisco CO .20 .50
7 Al Cowens .20 .50
8 Al Fitzsimmons .20 .50
9 Larry Gura .20 .50
10 Tom Hall .20 .50
11 Fran Healy .20 .50
12 Whitey Herzog MG .60 1.50
13 Chuck Hiller CO .20 .50
14 Charley Lau CO .20 .50
15 Dennis Leonard .20 .50
16 Mark Littell .20 .50
17 Buck Martinez .30 .75
18 John Mayberry .30 .75
19 Hal McRae .40 1.00
20 Steve Mingori .20 .50
21 Dave Nelson .20 .50
22 Amos Otis .40 1.00
23 Fred Patek .30 .75
24 Marty Pattin .20 .50
25 Tom Poquette .20 .50
26 Jamie Quirk .20 .50
27 Cookie Rojas .30 .75
28 Tony Solaita .20 .50
29 Paul Splittorff .20 .50
30 Bob Stinson .20 .50
31 John Wathan .30 .75
32 Frank White .40 1.00
33 Jim Wohlford .20 .50

1978 Royals

This 27-card set features the Kansas City Royals. The cards measure approximately 3 1/4" by 5". The fronts have black-and-white player portraits with a thin white border. The player's name, position, and team name are printed in a wider border beneath the picture. The backs are blank. The cards are unnumbered and checklisted below in alphabetical order.

COMPLETE SET (27) 10.00 25.00
1 Doug Bird .30 .75
2 Steve Braun .30 .75
3 George Brett 2.00 5.00
4 Al Cowens .30 .75
5 Rich Gale .30 .75
6 Larry Gura .30 .75
7 Whitey Herzog MG .60 1.50
8 Al Hrabosky .40 1.00
9 Clint Hurdle .60 1.50
10 Pete LaCock .30 .75
11 Dennis Leonard .30 .75
12 John Mayberry .40 1.00
13 Hal McRae .60 1.50
14 Steve Mingori .30 .75
15 Dave Nelson .30 .75
16 Amos Otis .60 1.50
17 Fred Patek .40 1.00
18 Marty Pattin .30 .75
19 Tom Poquette .30 .75
20 Darrell Porter .60 1.50
21 Paul Splittorff .30 .75
22 Jerry Terrell .30 .75
23 U.L. Washington .30 .75
24 John Wathan .30 .75
25 Frank White .60 1.50
26 Willie Wilson .75 2.00
27 Joe Zdeb .30 .75

1979-80 Royals Team Issue

These color photos feature members of the Kansas City Royals. The photos measure approximately 4" by 5 1/4" and have blank backs. A fascimile signature is on each photo and we have sequenced these photos in alphabetical order.

COMPLETE SET (13) 8.00 20.00
1 Willie Mays Aikens .30 .75
2 Steve Braun .20 .50
3 George Brett 2.00 5.00
4 Steve Busby .20 .50
5 Al Cowens .20 .50
6 Rich Gale .20 .50
7 Larry Gura .20 .50
8 Whitey Herzog MG .40 1.00
9 Al Hrabosky .20 .50
10 Clint Hurdle .40 1.00
11 Pete LaCock .20 .50
12 Dennis Leonard .30 .75
13 Renie Martin .20 .50
14 Hal McRae .40 1.00
15 Steve Mingori .20 .50
16 Amos Otis .40 1.00
17 Fred Patek .20 .50
18 Marty Pattin .20 .50
19 Tom Poquette .20 .50
20 Darrell Porter .30 .75
21 Jamie Quirk .20 .50
22 Dan Quisenberry .60 1.50
23 Ed Rodriguez .20 .50
24 Paul Splitorff .20 .50
25 Jerry Terrell .20 .50
26 U.L Washington .20 .50
27 John Wathan .20 .50
28 Frank White .40 1.00
29 Willie Wilson .40 1.00
30 Joe Zdeb .20 .50
31 Steve Boros CO .20 .50
Galen Cisco CO
32 John Sullivan CO .20 .50
Chuck Hiller CO

1981 Royals Police

The cards in this ten-card set measure approximately 2 1/2" by 4 1/8". The 1981 Police Kansas City Royals set features full color cards of Royals players. The fronts feature the player's name, position, height and weight, and the Royals' logo in addition to the photo and facsimile autograph of the player. The backs feature player statistics, Tips from the Royals, and identification of the sponsoring organizations. This set can be distinguished from the 1983 Police Royals set by the statistics on the backs of these 1981 cards, whereas the 1983 cards only show a biographical paragraph in the same space.

COMPLETE SET (10) 12.50 30.00
1 Willie Aikens .60 1.50
2 George Brett 6.00 15.00
3 Rich Gale .60 1.50
4 Clint Hurdle .75 2.00
5 Dennis Leonard .75 2.00
6 Hal McRae 1.00 2.50
7 Amos Otis 1.00 2.50
8 U.L. Washington .60 1.50
9 Frank White 1.25 3.00
10 Willie Wilson 1.25 3.00

1982 Royals

This set features members of the 1982 Kansas City Royals. Since the cards are unnumbered we have checklisted them below in alphabetical order.

COMPLETE SET (25) 10.00 25.00
1 Willie Aikens .08 .25
2 Mike Armstrong .08 .25
3 Vida Blue .20 .50
4 George Brett 12.50 30.00
5 Scott Brown .08 .25
6 Onix Concepcion .08 .25
7 Dave Frost .08 .25
8 Cesar Geronimo .08 .25
9 Larry Gura .08 .25
10 Dick Howser MG .08 .25
11 Dennis Leonard .08 .25
12 Jerry Martin .08 .25
13 Hal McRae .30 .75
14 Amos Otis .30 .75
15 Tom Poquette .08 .25
16 Greg Pryor .08 .25
17 Jamie Quirk .08 .25
18 Dan Quisenberry .30 .75
19 John Schuerholz GM .08 .25
20 Paul Splittorff .08 .25
21 U.L. Washington .08 .25

22 John Wathan .08 .25
23 Dennis Werth .08 .25
24 Frank White .30 .75
25 Willie Wilson .30 .75

1983 Royals Police

The cards in this ten-card set measure approximately 2 1/2" by 4 1/8". The 1983 Police Kansas City Royals set features full color cards of Royals players. The fronts feature the player's name, height and weight, and the Royals' logo in addition to the player's photo and a facsimile autograph. The backs feature Kids and Cops Facts about the players, Tips from the Royals, and identification of the sponsors of the set. The cards are unnumbered. This set can be distinguished from the 1981 Police Royals set by the absence of statistics on the backs of these 1983 cards, since these 1983 cards only show a brief biographical paragraph.

COMPLETE SET (10) 10.00 25.00
1 Willie Aikens .60 1.50
2 George Brett 5.00 12.00
3 Dennis Leonard .75 2.00
4 Hal McRae 1.00 2.50
5 Amos Otis 1.00 2.50
6 Dan Quisenberry 1.00 2.50
7 U.L. Washington .60 1.50
8 John Wathan .75 2.00
9 Frank White 1.25 3.00
10 Willie Wilson .75 2.00

1983 Royals Postcards

This 33-card set features photos of the 1983 Kansas City Royals printed on postcard-size cards. The cards are unnumbered and checklisted below in alphabetical order.

COMPLETE SET (33) 8.00 20.00
1 Willie Aikens .20 .50
2 Mike Armstrong .20 .50
3 Bud Black .20 .50
4 Vida Blue .30 .75
5 Cloyd Boyer CO .20 .50
6 George Brett 2.00 5.00
7 Bill Castro .20 .50
8 Rocky Colavito CO 1.00 2.50
9 Onix Concepcion .20 .50
10 Keith Creel .20 .50
11 Cesar Geronimo .20 .50
12 Larry Gura .20 .50
13 Don Hood .20 .50
14 Dick Howser MG .20 .50
15 Ron Johnson .20 .50
16 Dennis Leonard .20 .50
17 Jose Martinez CO .20 .50
18 Jerry Martin .20 .50
19 Hal McRae .30 .75
20 Joe Nossik CO .20 .50
21 Amos Otis .30 .75
22 Greg Pryor .20 .50
23 Dan Quisenberry .40 1.00
24 Steve Renko .20 .50
25 Leon Roberts .20 .50
26 Jim Schaffer CO .20 .50
27 John Scherholz GM .20 .50
28 Joe Simpson .20 .50
29 Don Slaught .20 .50
30 Paul Splittorff .20 .50
31 Bob Tufts .20 .50
32 U.L. Washington .20 .50
33 John Wathan .20 .50
34 Frank White .40 1.00
35 Willie Wilson .30 .75

1984 Royals Postcards

This 37-card set features black-and-white portraits of the 1984 Kansas City Royals in white borders printed on postcard-size cards. The backs are blank. The cards are unnumbered and checklisted below in alphabetical order.

COMPLETE SET (37) 6.00 15.00
1 Steve Balboni .08 .25
2 Howie Bedell CO .08 .25
3 Joe Beckwith .08 .25
4 Buddy Biancalana .08 .25
5 Bud Black .08 .25
6 Gary Blaylock CO .08 .25
7 George Brett 2.00 5.00
8 Onix Concepcion .08 .25
9 Butch Davis .08 .25
10 Mike Ferraro CO .08 .25
11 Mark Gubicza .40 1.00
12 Larry Gura .08 .25
13 Dick Howser MG .08 .25
14 Mark Huismann .08 .25
15 Dane Iorg .08 .25
16 Danny Jackson .08 .25
17 Lynn Jones .08 .25
18 Charlie Leibrandt .08 .25
19 Dennis Leonard .08 .25
20 Jose Martinez .08 .25
21 Lee May .20 .50
22 Hal McRae .30 .75
23 Darryl Motley .08 .25
24 Jorge Orta .08 .25
25 Greg Pryor .08 .25
26 Dan Quisenberry .30 .75
27 Leon Roberts .08 .25
28 Bret Saberhagen .75 2.00
29 Jim Schaffer CO .08 .25
30 John Schuerholz GM .08 .25
31 Pat Sheridan .08 .25
32 Don Slaught .08 .25
33 Paul Splittorff .08 .25
34 U.L. Washington .08 .25
35 John Wathan .08 .25
36 Frank White .30 .75
37 Willie Wilson .20 .50

1985 Royals Team Issue

This 33-card set features black-and-white photos of the Kansas City Royals measuring approximately 3 1/4" by 5". The cards are unnumbered and checklisted below in alphabetical order.

COMPLETE SET (33) 8.00 20.00
1 Steve Balboni .08 .25
2 Joe Beckwith .08 .25
3 Buddy Biancalana .08 .25
4 Bud Black .08 .25
5 Gary Blaylock CO .08 .25
6 George Brett 2.00 5.00
7 Onix Concepcion .08 .25
8 Mike Ferraro CO .08 .25
9 Mark Gubicza .20 .50
10 Larry Gura .08 .25
11 Dick Howser MG .08 .25
12 Dane Iorg .08 .25
13 Danny Jackson .08 .25
14 Lynn Jones .08 .25
15 Mike Jones .08 .25
16 Mike LaCoss .08 .25
17 Charlie Liebrandt .08 .25
18 Dennis Leonard .08 .25
19 Jose Martinez CO .08 .25
20 Lee May CO .08 .25
21 Hal McRae .30 .75
22 Darryl Motley .08 .25
23 Jorge Orta .08 .25
24 Dan Quisenberry .30 .75
25 Greg Pryor .08 .25
26 Bret Saberhagen .40 1.00
27 Jim Schaffer CO .08 .25
28 John Schuerholz GM .08 .25
29 Pat Sheridan .08 .25
30 Jim Sundberg .08 .25
31 John Wathan .08 .25
32 Frank White .30 .75
33 Willie Wilson .20 .50

1986 Royals Greats TCMA

This 12-card standard-size set features some of the best Kansas City Royals from their first two decades. The player's photo, name and position are noted on the front. There is more personal information about the player on the back.

COMPLETE SET (12) 1.25 3.00
1 John Mayberry .20 .50
2 Cookie Rojas .08 .25
3 Fred Patek .08 .25
4 Paul Schall .08 .25
5 Lou Piniella .30 .75
6 Amos Otis .20 .50
7 Tom Poquette .08 .25
8 Ed Kirkpatrick .08 .25
9 Steve Busby .08 .25
10 Paul Splittorff .08 .25
11 Mark Littell .08 .25
12 Jim Frey MG .08 .25

1986 Royals Kitty Clover Discs

This set of discs was distributed by Kitty Clover in 1986 to commemorate the Kansas City Royals' World Championship in 1985. Each disc measures 2 3/4" in diameter. Each disc has a white border on the front. Inside this white border is a full color photo of the player with his hat on. However the hat's team emblem has been deleted from the picture. The statistics on back of the disc give the player's 1985 pitching or hitting record as well as his vital statistics.

COMPLETE SET (20) 8.00 20.00
1 Lonnie Smith .20 .50
2 Buddy Biancalana .20 .50
3 Bret Saberhagen .60 1.50
4 Hal McRae .40 1.00
5 Onix Concepcion .20 .50
6 Jorge Orta .20 .50
7 Bud Black .20 .50
8 Dan Quisenberry .40 1.00
9 Dane Iorg .20 .50
10 Charlie Leibrandt .20 .50
11 Pat Sheridan .20 .50
12 John Wathan .20 .50
13 Frank White .40 1.00
14 Darryl Motley .20 .50
15 Willie Wilson .30 .75
16 Danny Jackson .20 .50
17 Steve Balboni .20 .50
18 Jim Sundberg .30 .75
19 Mark Gubicza .20 .50
20 George Brett 4.00 10.00

1986 Royals National Photo

The set contains 24 cards which are numbered only by uniform number except for the checklist card and discount card, which entitles the bearer to a 40 percent discount at National Photo. Cards measure approximately 2 7/8" by 4 1/4". Cards were distributed at the stadium on August 14th. The set was supposedly later available for 3.00 directly from the Royals.

COMPLETE SET (24) 5.00 12.00
1 Buddy Biancalana .08 .25
3 Jorge Orta .08 .25
4 Greg Pryor .08 .25
5 George Brett 2.50 6.00
6 Willie Wilson .40 1.00
8 Jim Sundberg .08 .25
10 Dick Howser MG .20 .50
11 Hal McRae .30 .75
20 Frank White .30 .75
21 Lonnie Smith .08 .25
22 Dennis Leonard .20 .50
23 Mark Gubicza .08 .25
24 Darryl Motley .08 .25
25 Danny Jackson .08 .25
26 Steve Farr .08 .25
29 Dan Quisenberry .30 .75
31 Bret Saberhagen .40 1.00
35 Lynn Jones .08 .25
37 Charlie Leibrandt .08 .25
38 Mark Huismann .08 .25
40 Bud Black .08 .25
45 Steve Balboni .08 .25
NNO Discount card .08 .25
NNO Checklist card .08 .25

1986 Royals Team Issue

This 27-card set of the Kansas City Royals measures approximately 3 1/4" by 5" and features black-and-white player portraits with white borders. The backs are blank. The cards are unnumbered and checklisted. David Cone has a postcard in this set which predates his Rookie Card.

COMPLETE SET (27) 4.00 10.00
1 Steve Balboni .08 .25
2 Scott Bankhead .08 .25
3 Buddy Biancalana .08 .25
4 Bud Black .08 .25
5 George Brett 1.00 2.50
6 David Cone 1.00 2.50
7 Steve Farr .08 .25
8 Mark Gubicza .08 .25
9 Dick Howser MG .08 .25
10 Danny Jackson .08 .25
11 Lynn Jones .08 .25
12 Mike Kingery .08 .25
13 Rudy Law .08 .25
14 Charlie Leibrandt .08 .25
15 Dennis Leonard .08 .25
16 Hal McRae .30 .75
17 Darryl Motley .08 .25
18 Jorge Orta .08 .25
19 Greg Pryor .08 .25
20 Jamie Quirk .08 .25
21 Dan Quisenberry .20 .50
22 Bret Saberhagen .30 .75
23 Angel Salazar .08 .25
24 Lonnie Smith .08 .25
25 Jim Sundberg .08 .25
26 Willie Wilson .20 .50
27 Frank White .30 .75

1988 Royals Smokey

This set of 28 cards features caricatures of the Kansas City Royals players. The cards are numbered on the back except for the unnumbered title/checklist card. The card set was distributed as a giveaway item at the stadium on August 14th to kids age 14 and under. The cards are approximately 3" by 5" and are in full color on the card fronts. The Smokey logo is in the upper right corner of every obverse.

COMPLETE SET (28) 5.00 12.00
1 John Wathan MG .08 .25
2 Royals Coaches .20 .50
3 Willie Wilson .20 .50
4 Danny Tartabull .20 .50
5 Bo Jackson .60 1.50
6 Gary Thurman .08 .25
7 Jerry Don Gleaton .08 .25
8 Floyd Bannister .08 .25
9 Bud Black .08 .25
10 Steve Farr .08 .25
11 Gene Garber .08 .25
12 Mark Gubicza .08 .25
13 Charlie Leibrandt .08 .25
14 Ted Power .08 .25
15 Dan Quisenberry .30 .75
16 Bret Saberhagen .40 1.00
17 Mike Macfarlane .20 .50
18 Scotti Madison .08 .25
19 Jamie Quirk .08 .25
20 George Brett 1.50 4.00
21 Kevin Seitzer .40 1.00
22 Bill Pecota .08 .25
23 Kurt Stillwell .08 .25
24 Brad Wellman .08 .25
25 Frank White .30 .75
26 Jim Eisenreich .20 .50
27 Smokey Bear .08 .25
NNO Checklist Card .08 .25

1988 Royals Team Issue

This 38-card set features black-and-white photos of the Kansas City Royals measuring approximately 3 1/4" by 5". The cards are unnumbered and checklisted below in alphabetical order.

COMPLETE SET (38) 5.00 12.00
1 Rick Anderson .08 .25
2 Steve Balboni .08 .25
3 Floyd Bannister .08 .25
4 Bud Black .08 .25
5 Thad Bosley .08 .25
6 George Brett 1.25 3.00
7 Bill Buckner .20 .50
8 Jim Eisenreich .20 .50
9 Steve Farr .08 .25
10 Frank Funk CO .08 .25
11 Gene Garber .20 .50
12 Adrian Garrett CO .08 .25
13 Jerry Don Gleaton .08 .25
14 Mark Gubicza .08 .25
15 Ed Hearn .08 .25
16 Bo Jackson .40 1.00
17 Charlie Liebrandt .08 .25
18 Mike Lum CO .08 .25
19 Mike Macfarlane .20 .50
20 Jeff Montgomery .40 1.00
21 Ed Napoleon CO .08 .25
22 Larry Owen .08 .25
23 Bill Pecota .08 .25
24 Ted Power .08 .25
25 Jamie Quirk .08 .25
26 Dan Quisenberry .30 .75
27 Bret Saberhagen .30 .75
28 Bob Schaefer CO .08 .25
29 Jim Schaffer CO .08 .25
30 Kevin Seitzer .08 .25
31 Kurt Stillwell .08 .25
32 Pat Tabler .08 .25
33 Danny Tartabull .08 .25
34 Gary Thurman .08 .25
35 John Wathan MG .08 .25
36 Brad Wellman .08 .25
37 Frank White .30 .75
38 Willie Wilson .20 .50

1989 Royals Taystee Discs

This set features members of the 1989 Kansas City Royals. These discs were issued by Tastee-Freez.

COMPLETE SET (12) 5.00 12.00
1 George Brett 3.00 8.00
2 Kevin Seitzer .30 .75
3 Pat Tabler .20 .50
4 Danny Tartabull .30 .75
5 Willie Wilson .30 .75
6 Bo Jackson .75 2.00
7 Frank White .40 1.00
8 Kurt Stillwell .20 .50
9 Mark Gubicza .20 .50
10 Charlie Leibrandt .20 .50
11 Bret Saberhagen .60 1.50
12 Steve Farr .20 .50

1990 Royals Postcards

This 29-card set features photos of the 1990 Kansas City Royals printed on postcard-size cards. The cards are unnumbered and checklisted below in alphabetical order.

COMPLETE SET (29) 4.00 10.00
1 Kevin Appier .40 1.00
2 Luis Aquino .08 .25
3 Bob Boone .30 .75
4 George Brett 1.25 3.00
5 Steve Crawford .08 .25
6 Mark Davis .08 .25
7 Jim Eisenreich .20 .50
8 Glenn Ezell CO .08 .25
9 Steve Farr .08 .25
10 Frank Funk CO .08 .25
11 Adrian Garrett CO .08 .25
12 Tom Gordon .40 1.00
13 Bo Jackson .60 1.50
14 Steve Jeltz .08 .25
15 Mike Macfarlane .08 .25
16 John Mayberry CO .08 .25
17 Jeff Montgomery .20 .50
18 Rey Palacios .08 .25
19 Bill Pecota .08 .25
20 Gerald Perry .08 .25
21 Bret Saberhagen .40 1.00
22 Kevin Seitzer .20 .50
23 Terry Shumpert .20 .50
24 Kurt Stillwell .08 .25
25 Pat Tabler .08 .25
26 Danny Tartabull .20 .50
27 John Wathan .08 .25
28 Frank White .30 .75
29 Willie Wilson .20 .50

1991 Royals Police

This 27-card set, measuring 2 5/"' by 4 1/8" was distributed by the Metropolitan Chiefs and Sheriffs Association. The cards are unnumbered and checklisted below in alphabetical order, with the coaches' cards listed at the end of our checklist. Supposedly many of the Bo Jackson cards were burned after Bo was released from the Royals.

COMPLETE SET (27) 8.00 20.00
COMMON SP 2.50 6.00
1 Kevin Appier .40 1.00
2 Luis Aquino .08 .25
3 Mike Boddicker .08 .25
4 George Brett 1.50 4.00
5 Steve Crawford .08 .25
6 Mark Davis .20 .50
7 Storm Davis .08 .25
8 Jim Eisenreich .20 .50
9 Kirk Gibson .30 .75
10 Tom Gordon .20 .50
11 Mark Gubicza .08 .25
12 Bo Jackson SP 2.50 6.00
13 Mike Macfarlane .08 .25
14 Andy McGaffigan .08 .25
15 Brian McRae .40 1.00
16 Jeff Montgomery .30 .75
17 Bill Pecota .08 .25
18 Bret Saberhagen .40 1.00
19 Kevin Seitzer .20 .50
20 Terry Shumpert .08 .25
21 Kurt Stillwell .08 .25
22 Danny Tartabull .20 .50
23 Gary Thurman .08 .25
24 John Wathan MG .08 .25
25 Coaches .08 .25
Pat Dobson
Adrian Garrett
26 Coaches .08 .25
Glenn Ezell
Lynn Jones
Bob Schaefer
27 Checklist Card .08 .25

1992 Royals Police

This 27-card set, given out as a promotion at the stadium, was sponsored by the Kansas City Life Insurance Company and distributed by the Metropolitan Chiefs and Sheriffs Association. It is rumored that two cards were pulled prior to release (the cards of Kevin Seitzer, who went to Milwaukee, and Kirk Gibson, who went to Pittsburgh). The cards are unnumbered and checklisted below in alphabetical order.

COMPLETE SET (27) 4.00 10.00
1 Kevin Appier .30 .75
2 Luis Aquino .08 .25
3 Mike Boddicker .08 .25
4 George Brett 1.25 3.00
5 Mark Davis .08 .25
6 Jim Eisenreich .20 .50
7 Kirk Gibson .30 .75
8 Tom Gordon .30 .75
9 Mark Gubicza .08 .25
10 Chris Gwynn .08 .25
11 David Howard .08 .25
12 Gregg Jefferies .08 .25
13 Joel Johnston .08 .25
14 Wally Joyner .20 .50
15 Mike Macfarlane .08 .25
16 Mike Magnante .08 .25
17 Brent Mayne .08 .25
18 Brian McRae .08 .25
19 Hal McRae MG .20 .50
20 Kevin McReynolds .08 .25
21 Bob Melvin CO .08 .25
22 Keith Miller .08 .25
23 Jeff Montgomery .30 .75
24 Kevin Seitzer .20 .50
25 Terry Shumpert .08 .25
26 Gary Thurman .08 .25
27 Coaches .08 .25
Glenn Ezell
Adrian Garrett
Guy Hansen/

1993 Royals Police

This 27-card set was given away to fans attending the Royals-Twins game of April 10. The set was sponsored by Kansas City Life Insurance and distributed by the Metropolitan Chiefs and Sheriffs Association. The cards are unnumbered and checklisted below in alphabetical order.

COMPLETE SET (27) 4.00 10.00
1 Hal McRae MG .20 .50
2 Kevin Appier .30 .75
3 Luis Aquino .08 .25
4 Mike Boddicker .08 .25
5 George Brett 1.25 3.00
6 David Cone .40 1.00
7 Greg Gagne .08 .25
8 Mark Gardner .08 .25
9 Tom Gordon .30 .75
10 Mark Gubicza .08 .25
11 Chris Gwynn .08 .25
12 Chris Haney .08 .25
13 Felix Jose .08 .25
14 Wally Joyner .20 .50
15 Kevin Koslofski .08 .25
16 Jose Lind .08 .25
17 Mike Macfarlane .08 .25
18 Brent Mayne .08 .25
19 Brian McRae .08 .25
20 Kevin McReynolds .08 .25
21 Rusty Meacham .08 .25
22 Keith Miller .08 .25
23 Jeff Montgomery .20 .50
24 Hipolito Pichardo .08 .25
25 Curtis Wilkerson .08 .25
26 Craig Wilson .08 .25
27 Royals Coaches .08 .25
Steve Boros
Glenn Ezell
Guy Hans

1993 Royals Stadium Club

This 30-card standard-size set features the 1993 Kansas City Royals. The set was issued in hobby (plastic box) and retail (blister) form.

COMP. FACT SET (30) 1.50 4.00
1 George Brett .75 2.00
2 Mike Macfarlane .02 .10
3 Tom Gordon .20 .50
4 Wally Joyner .08 .25
5 Kevin Appier .08 .25
6 Phil Hiatt .02 .10
7 Keith Miller .02 .10
8 Hipolito Pichardo .02 .10
9 Chris Gwynn .02 .10
10 Jose Lind .02 .10
11 Mark Gubicza .02 .10
12 Dennis Rasmussen .02 .10
13 Mike Magnante .02 .10
14 Joe Vitiello .02 .10
15 Kevin McReynolds .02 .10
16 Greg Gagne .02 .10
17 David Cone .30 .75
18 Brent Mayne .02 .10
19 Jeff Montgomery .08 .25
20 Joe Randa .40 1.00
21 Felix Jose .02 .10
22 Bill Sampen .02 .10
23 Curt Wilkerson .02 .10
24 Mark Gardner .02 .10
25 Brian McRae .02 .10
26 Hubie Brooks .02 .10
27 Chris Eddy .02 .10
28 Harvey Pulliam .02 .10
29 Rusty Meacham .02 .10
30 Danny Miceli .02 .10

1993 Royals Star 25th

Subtitled "Royals All-Time Team" this 16-card set celebrates the Royals' 25th Anniversary (1969-1993), features great Royals of the past, and was originally issued in a perforated sheet. The sheet measures approximately 10 3/8" by 14 3/8"; after perforation, each card would measure the standard size. The individual cards measure the standard size. The cards are unnumbered and checklisted below in alphabetical order.

COMPLETE SET (16) 8.00 20.00
1 George Brett 4.00 10.00
2 Steve Busby .40 1.00
3 Al Cowens .40 1.00
4 Dick Howser MG .60 1.50
5 Dennis Leonard .60 1.50
6 John Mayberry .60 1.50
7 Hal McRae .75 2.00
8 Amos Otis .75 2.00
9 Fred Patek .60 1.50
10 Darrell Porter .60 1.50
11 Dan Quisenberry .75 2.00
12 Bret Saberhagen .75 2.00
13 Paul Splittorff .40 1.00
14 Frank White .60 1.50
15 Willie Wilson .60 1.50
16 Title card .40 1.00

1995 Royals Postcards

These 5" by 7" blank-backed postcards feature members of the 1995 Kansas City Royals. The fronts have white borders, a color photo and the players name and team logo on the bottom. Since they are unnumbered we have sequenced them in alphabetical order.

COMPLETE SET (31) 3.00 8.00
1 Kevin Appier .20 .50
2 Bob Boone MG .20 .50
3 Pat Borders .08 .25
4 Billy Brewer .08 .25
5 Melvin Bunch .08 .25
6 Edgar Caceres .08 .25
7 Vince Coleman .20 .50
8 Gary Gaetti .20 .50
9 Greg Gagne .08 .25
10 Tom Goodwin .08 .25
11 Tom Gordon .30 .75
12 Jeff Grotewold .08 .25
13 Mark Gubicza .08 .25
14 Bob Hamelin .08 .25
15 Chris Haney .08 .25
16 Phil Hiatt .08 .25
17 David Howard .08 .25
18 Wally Joyner .20 .50
19 Keith Lockhart .08 .25
20 Brent Mayne .08 .25
21 Rusty Meacham .08 .25
22 Jeff Montgomery .20 .50
23 Les Norman .08 .25
24 Jon Nunnally .08 .25
25 Hipolito Pichardo .08 .25
26 Joe Randa .30 .75
27 Dennis Rasmussen .08 .25
28 Dilson Torres .08 .25
29 Michael Tucker .20 .50
30 Chris Stynes .08 .25
31 Joe Vitiello .08 .25

1996 Royals Police

This 26-card set of the Kansas City Royals measures 2 5/8" by 4" and was sponsored by the Kansas City Life Insurance Company. The fronts feature color action player photos in a thin white border. The backs carry player information, statistics, and a safety message. The cards are unnumbered and checklisted below in alphabetical order.

COMPLETE SET (26) 1.50 4.00
1 Kevin Appier .08 .25
2 Tim Belcher .02 .10
3 Bob Boone MG .08 .25
4 Melvin Bunch .02 .10
5 Terry Clark .02 .10
6 Jim Converse .02 .10
7 Johnny Damon 1.00 2.50
8 Tom Goodwin .02 .10
9 Mark Gubicza .02 .10
10 Bob Hamelin .02 .10
11 Chris Haney .02 .10
12 David Howard .02 .10
13 Rick Huisman .02 .10
14 Jason Jacome .02 .10
15 Keith Lockhart .02 .10
16 Mike Macfarlane .02 .10
17 Mike Magnante .20 .50
18 Rusty Meacham .02 .10
19 Jeff Montgomery .08 .25
20 Les Norman .02 .10
21 Jon Nunnally .02 .10
22 Jose Offerman .02 .10
23 Hipolito Pichardo .02 .10
24 Joe Randa .20 .50
25 Bip Roberts .02 .10
26 Michael Tucker .08 .25
27 Joe Vitiello .02 .10

1997 Royals Police

This 23-card set of the Kansas City Royals measures 2 5/8" by 4" and was sponsored by the Kansas City Life Insurance Company. The fronts feature color action player photos in a white border. The backs carry player information, statistics, and a safety message. The cards are unnumbered and checklisted below in alphabetical order.

COMPLETE SET (23) 3.00 8.00
1 Kevin Appier .20 .50
2 Tim Belcher .08 .25
3 Jay Bell .08 .25
4 Jaime Bluma .08 .25
5 Bob Boone MG .08 .25
6 Johnny Damon .75 2.00
7 Chili Davis .30 .75
8 Tom Goodwin .08 .25
9 Chris Haney .08 .25
10 David Howard .08 .25
11 Rick Huisman .08 .25
12 Jason Jacome .08 .25
13 Jeff King .08 .25
14 Mike Macfarlane .08 .25
15 Jeff Montgomery .20 .50
16 Jose Offerman .08 .25
17 Craig Paquette .08 .25
18 Hipolito Pichardo .08 .25
19 Bip Roberts .08 .25
20 Jose Rosado .08 .25
21 Mike Sweeney .60 1.50
22 Joe Vitiello .08 .25
23 Sluggerrr(Mascot) .08 .25

1999 Royals Postcards

These postcars measure 3" by 5" and feature members of the 1999 Kansas City Royals. The fronts have a player photo and identification and some cards were issued with the "Conoco" logo. No matter in what version these cards exist, the values are the same. Since the cards are not numbered we have sequenced them in alphabetical order.

COMPLETE SET 4.00 10.00
1 Kevin Appier .20 .50
2 Carlos Beltran .75 2.00
3 Tim Byrdak .08 .25
4 Johnny Damon .75 2.00
5 Jermaine Dye .20 .50
6 Carlos Febles .08 .25
7 Jeremy Giambi .08 .25
8 Jed Hansen .08 .25
9 Jeff King .08 .25
10 Chad Krueter .08 .25
11 Mendy Lopez .08 .25
12 Jeff Montgomery .20 .50
13 Alvin Morman .08 .25
14 Tony Muser MG .08 .25
15 Hipolito Pichardo .08 .25
16 Jim Pittsley .08 .25
17 Scott Pose .08 .25
18 Jamie Quirk .08 .25
19 Joe Randa .30 .75
20 Jose Rosado .08 .25
21 Glendon Rusch .08 .25
22 Rey Sanchez .08 .25
23 Scott Service .08 .25
24 Tim Spehr .08 .25
25 Jeff Suppan .08 .25
26 Larry Sutton .08 .25
27 Mac Suzuki .08 .25
28 Mike Sweeney .40 1.00
29 Matt Whisenant .08 .25
30 Frank White CO .20 .50
31 Jay Witasick .08 .25
32 Kauffman Stadium .08 .25

2000 Royals Safety

COMPLETE SET 6.00 15.00
1 Carlos Beltran 1.00 2.50
2 Ricky Bottalico .20 .50
3 Johnny Damon 1.00 2.50
4 Todd Dunwoody .20 .50
5 Chad Durbin .20 .50
6 Jermaine Dye .40 1.00
7 Carlos Febles .20 .50
8 Chris Fussell .20 .50
9 Ray Holbert .20 .50
10 Brian Johnson .20 .50
11 Tony Muser MG .20 .50
12 Scott Pose .20 .50
13 Mark Quinn .20 .50
14 Joe Randa .40 1.00
15 Jeff Reboulet .20 .50
16 Dan Reichert .20 .50
17 Jose Rosado .20 .50
18 Rey Sanchez .20 .50
19 Jose Santiago .20 .50
20 Jerry Spradlin .20 .50
21 Blake Stein .20 .50
22 Jeff Suppan .20 .50
23 Mike Sweeney .60 1.50
24 Jay Witasik .20 .50
25 Slugger .20 .50
Mascot

2001 Royals Police

COMPLETE SET 4.00 10.00
1 Carlos Beltran 1.00 2.50
2 Dee Brown .10 .25
3 Chad Durbin .10 .25
4 Jermaine Dye .30 .75
5 Carlos Febles .10 .25
6 Doug Henry .10 .25
7 Roberto Hernandez .20 .50
8 Dave McCarty .10 .25
9 Brian Meadows .10 .25
10 Scott Mullen .10 .25
11 Luis Ordaz .10 .25
12 Hector Ortiz .10 .25
13 Mark Quinn .10 .25
14 Joe Randa .30 .75
15 Dan Reichert .10 .25
16 Jose Rosado .10 .25
17 Rey Sanchez .10 .25
18 Jose Santiago .10 .25
19 Blake Stein .10 .25
20 Jeff Suppan .20 .50
21 Mac Suzuki .10 .25
22 Mike Sweeney .60 1.50
23 Kris Wilson .10 .25
24 Greg Zaun .10 .25

2002 Royals Police

COMPLETE SET 3.00 8.00
1 Luis Alicea .08 .25
2 Cory Bailey .08 .25
3 Carlos Beltran .75 2.00
4 Dee Brown .08 .25
5 Paul Byrd .20 .50
6 Chad Durbin .08 .25
7 Carlos Febles .08 .25
8 Jason Grimsley .08 .25
9 Roberto Hernandez .20 .50
10 A.J. Hinch .08 .25
11 Raul Ibanez .20 .50
12 Chuck Knoblauch .20 .50
13 Darrell May .08 .25
14 Brent Mayne .08 .25
15 Dave McCarty .08 .25
16 Tony Muser MG .08 .25
17 Neifi Perez .08 .25
18 Mark Quinn .08 .25
19 Joe Randa .30 .75
20 Dan Reichert .08 .25
21 Donnie Sadler .08 .25
22 Blake Stein .08 .25
23 Jeff Suppan .20 .50
24 Mike Sweeney .60 1.50
25 Michael Tucker .08 .25
26 Sluggerrr .08 .25
Mascot

2003 Royals Police

COMPLETE SET (27) 3.00 8.00
1 Jeremy Affeldt .30 .75
2 Miguel Asencio .10 .25
3 James Baldwin .10 .25
4 Carlos Beltran .75 2.00
5 Brandon Berger .10 .25
6 Angel Berroa .30 .75
7 Ryan Bukvich .10 .25
8 Mike DiFelice .10 .25
9 Carlos Febles .10 .25
10 Chris George .10 .25
11 Jason Grimsley .10 .25
12 Aaron Guiel .10 .25
13 Ken Harvey .10 .25
14 Runelvys Hernandez .10 .25
15 Raul Ibanez .20 .50
16 Albie Lopez .10 .25
17 Mike MacDougal .10 .25
18 Darrell May .10 .25
19 Brent Mayne .10 .25
20 Scott Mullen .10 .25
21 Tony Pena MG .10 .25
22 Joe Randa .30 .75
23 Desi Relaford .10 .25
24 Mike Sweeney .40 1.00
25 Michael Tucker .10 .25
26 Kris Wilson .10 .25
27 Sluggerrr .10 .25
Mascot

2003 Royals Team Issue

COMPLETE SET 4.00 10.00
1 Jeremy Affeldt .20 .50
2 Carlos Beltran 1.00 2.50
3 Angel Berroa .40 1.00
4 Dee Brown .20 .50
5 Mike DiFelice .20 .50
6 Jimmy Gobble .20 .50
7 Aaron Guiel .20 .50
8 Ken Harvey .20 .50
9 Raul Ibanez .30 .75
10 Mike MacDougal .20 .50
11 Darrell May .20 .50
12 Scott Mullen .20 .50
13 Tony Pena MG .20 .50
14 Desi Relaford .20 .50
15 Mike Sweeney .60 1.50
16 Michael Tucker .20 .50

2004 Royals Police

COMPLETE SET (27) 4.00 10.00
1 Jeremy Affeldt .30 .75
2 Brian Anderson .10 .25
3 Kevin Appier .20 .50
4 Carlos Beltran .75 2.00

5 Angel Berroa .20 .50
6 D.J. Carrasco .10 .25
7 Jaime Cerda .10 .25
8 David DeJesus .40 1.00
9 Jimmy Gobble .10 .25
10 Juan Gonzalez .40 1.00
11 Tony Graffanino .10 .25
12 Jason Grimsley .10 .25
13 Aaron Guiel .10 .25
14 Ken Harvey .10 .25
15 Curtis Leskanic .10 .25
16 Mike MacDougal .10 .25
17 Darrell May .10 .25
18 Tony Pena MG .10 .25
19 Joe Randa .30 .75
20 Desi Relaford .10 .25
21 Benito Santiago .10 .25
22 Matt Stairs .10 .25
23 Kelly Stinnett .10 .25
24 Scott Sullivan .10 .25
25 Mike Sweeney .40 1.00
26 Rich Thompson .10 .25
27 Mascot Sluggerrr .10 .25

2004 Royals Team Issue

COMPLETE SET
1 Jeremy Affeldt .20 .50
2 Brian Anderson .20 .50
3 Angel Berroa .30 .75
4 John Buck .20 .50
5 David DeJesus .50 1.25
6 Byron Gettis .20 .50
7 Jimmy Gobble .20 .50
8 Zack Greinke .20 .50
9 Jason Grimsley .20 .50
10 Ken Harvey .20 .50
11 Mike MacDougal .20 .50
12 Darrell May .20 .50
13 Tony Pena MG .20 .50
14 Joe Randa .40 1.00
15 Desi Relaford .20 .50
16 Benito Santiago .20 .50
17 Matt Stairs .20 .50
18 Mike Sweeney .50 1.25
19 Mike Wood .20 .50

2005 Royals Police

COMPLETE SET
1 Jeremy Affeldt .20 .50
2 Brian Anderson .20 .50
3 Denny Bautista .20 .50
4 Angel Berroa .30 .75
5 John Buck .20 .50
6 Shawn Camp .20 .50
7 Jaime Cerda .20 .50
8 David DeJesus .50 1.25
9 Nate Field .20 .50
10 Jimmy Gobble .20 .50
11 Ruben Gotay .20 .50
12 Tony Graffanino .20 .50
13 Zack Greinke .20 .50
14 Aaron Guiel .20 .50
15 Ken Harvey .20 .50
16 Runelvys Hernandez .20 .50
17 Jose Lima .20 .50
18 Terrence Long .30 .75
19 Mike MacDougal .30 .75
20 Eli Marrero .20 .50
21 Tony Pena MG .20 .50
22 Andy Sisco .30 .75
23 Matt Stairs .20 .50
24 Mike Sweeney .50 1.25
25 Mark Teahen .50 1.25
26 Mike Wood .20 .50
27 Sluggerrr .20 .50
Mascot

2006 Royals Topps

COMPLETE SET (14) 3.00 8.00
KCR1 Mike Sweeney .12 .30
KCR2 Angel Berroa .12 .30
KCR3 Mark Grudzielanek .12 .30
KCR4 Mark Teahen .12 .30
KCR5 Doug Mientkiewicz .12 .30
KCR6 David DeJesus .12 .30
KCR7 Joe Buck .12 .30
KCR8 Mike MacDougal .12 .30
KCR9 Andy Sisco .12 .30
KCR10 Reggie Sanders .12 .30
KCR11 Mark Redman .12 .30
KCR12 Zack Greinke .30 .75
KCR13 Runelvys Hernandez .12 .30
KCR14 Denny Bautista .12 .30

2007 Royals Topps

COMPLETE SET (14) 3.00 8.00
KCR1 Mark Teahen .12 .30
KCR2 Gil Meche .12 .30
KCR3 Ryan Shealy .12 .30
KCR4 Mark Grudzielanek .12 .30
KCR5 Octavio Dotel .12 .30
KCR6 Brian Bannister .12 .30
KCR7 Emil Brown .12 .30
KCR8 Jason LaRue .12 .30
KCR9 Joey Gathright .12 .30
KCR10 Angel Berroa .12 .30
KCR11 Reggie Sanders .12 .30
KCR12 Zack Greinke .30 .75
KCR13 David DeJesus .12 .30
KCR14 Mike Sweeney .12 .30

2008 Royals Topps

COMPLETE SET (14) 3.00 8.00
KCR1 Mark Teahen .12 .30
KCR2 Gil Meche .12 .30
KCR3 Alex Gordon .20 .50
KCR4 Mark Grudzielanek .12 .30
KCR5 Esteban German .12 .30
KCR6 Brian Bannister .12 .30
KCR7 Joakim Soria .12 .30
KCR8 John Buck .12 .30
KCR9 Joey Gathright .12 .30
KCR10 Billy Butler .12 .30
KCR11 Tony Pena .12 .30
KCR12 Zack Greinke .30 .75
KCR13 David DeJesus .12 .30
KCR14 Jose Guillen .12 .30

2009 Royals Topps

KCR1 Alex Gordon .25 .60
KCR2 Zack Greinke .40 1.00
KCR3 David DeJesus .15 .40
KCR4 Gil Meche .15 .40
KCR5 Mark Teahen .15 .40
KCR6 Brian Bannister .15 .40
KCR7 Billy Butler .15 .40
KCR8 Luke Hochevar .15 .40
KCR9 Coco Crisp .15 .40
KCR10 Kyle Davies .15 .40
KCR11 Miguel Olivo .15 .40
KCR12 Joakim Soria .15 .40
KCR13 Mike Jacobs .15 .40
KCR14 Mike Aviles .15 .40
KCR15 Kauffman Stadium .15 .40

2010 Royals Topps

KCR1 Zack Greinke .40 1.00
KCR2 Billy Butler .15 .40
KCR3 Chris Getz .15 .40
KCR4 Jose Guillen .15 .40
KCR5 David DeJesus .15 .40
KCR6 Alberto Callaspo .15 .40
KCR7 Gil Meche .15 .40
KCR8 Brian Bannister .15 .40
KCR9 Kyle Davies .15 .40
KCR10 Luke Hochevar .15 .40
KCR11 Joakim Soria .15 .40
KCR12 Scott Podsednik .15 .40
KCR13 Yuniesky Betancourt .15 .40
KCR14 Alex Gordon .25 .60
KCR15 Robinson Tejeda .15 .40
KCR16 Jason Kendall .15 .40
KCR17 Slugger .15 .40

2011 Royals Topps

KCR1 Billy Butler .15 .40
KCR2 Mike Aviles .15 .40
KCR3 Alcides Escobar .25 .60
KCR4 Chris Getz .15 .40
KCR5 Kyle Davies .15 .40
KCR6 Vin Mazzaro .15 .40
KCR7 Alex Gordon .25 .60
KCR8 Luke Hochevar .15 .40
KCR9 Kila Ka'aihue .15 .40
KCR10 Jason Kendall .15 .40
KCR11 Sean O'Sullivan .15 .40
KCR12 Joakim Soria .15 .40
KCR13 Wilson Betemit .15 .40
KCR14 Melky Cabrera .15 .40
KCR15 Jeremy Jeffress .15 .40
KCR16 Jeff Francoeur .25 .60
KCR17 Kauffman Stadium .15 .40

2012 Royals Topps

KAN1 Eric Hosmer .30 .75
KAN2 Jeff Francoeur .30 .75
KAN3 Alex Gordon .30 .75
KAN4 Salvador Perez .30 .75
KAN5 Johnny Giavotella .25 .60
KAN6 Yuniesky Betancourt .25 .60
KAN7 Bruce Chen .25 .60
KAN8 Alcides Escobar .30 .75
KAN9 Billy Butler .25 .60
KAN10 Lorenzo Cain .25 .60
KAN11 Danny Duffy .25 .60
KAN12 Mike Moustakas .30 .75
KAN13 Jonathan Sanchez .25 .60
KAN14 Luke Hochevar .25 .60
KAN15 Joakim Soria .25 .60
KAN16 Aaron Crow .25 .60
KAN17 Kauffman Stadium .15 .40

2013 Royals Topps

COMPLETE SET (17) 3.00 8.00
KCR1 Billy Butler .15 .40
KCR2 Alex Gordon .30 .75
KCR3 Mike Moustakas .30 .75
KCR4 Jeff Francoeur .20 .50
KCR5 Lorenzo Cain .15 .40
KCR6 Alcides Escobar .30 .75
KCR7 Johnny Giavotella .15 .40
KCR8 Eric Hosmer .20 .50
KCR9 James Shields .25 .60
KCR10 Bruce Chen .15 .40
KCR11 Ervin Santana .15 .40
KCR12 Jeremy Guthrie .15 .40
KCR13 Salvador Perez .20 .50
KCR14 Greg Holland .15 .40
KCR15 Aaron Crow .15 .40
KCR16 Wade Davis .15 .40
KCR17 Kauffman Stadium .15 .40

2014 Royals Topps

COMPLETE SET (17) 3.00 8.00
KCR1 Billy Butler .15 .40
KCR2 Alex Gordon .20 .50
KCR3 Mike Moustakas .20 .50
KCR4 Yordano Ventura .20 .50
KCR5 Lorenzo Cain .15 .40
KCR6 Alcides Escobar .20 .50
KCR7 Justin Maxwell .15 .40
KCR8 Eric Hosmer .20 .50
KCR9 James Shields .15 .40
KCR10 Danny Duffy .15 .40
KCR11 Omar Infante .15 .40
KCR12 Jeremy Guthrie .15 .40
KCR13 Salvador Perez .20 .50
KCR14 Greg Holland .15 .40
KCR15 Norichika Aoki .15 .40
KCR16 Jason Vargas .15 .40
KCR17 Kauffman Stadium .15 .40

2015 Royals Topps

COMPLETE SET (17) 3.00 8.00
KCR1 Eric Hosmer .20 .50
KCR2 Jeremy Guthrie .15 .40
KCR3 Greg Holland .15 .40
KCR4 Alcides Escobar .20 .50
KCR5 Salvador Perez .20 .50
KCR6 Jason Vargas .15 .40
KCR7 Yordano Ventura .20 .50
KCR8 Brandon Finnegan .15 .40
KCR9 Omar Infante .15 .40
KCR10 Mike Moustakas .20 .50
KCR11 Alex Gordon .20 .50
KCR12 Lorenzo Cain .15 .40
KCR13 Kris Medlen .20 .50
KCR14 Kendrys Morales .15 .40
KCR15 Luke Hochevar .15 .40
KCR16 Wade Davis .15 .40
KCR17 Alex Rios .20 .50

2016 Royals Topps

COMPLETE SET (17) 3.00 8.00
KCR1 Salvador Perez .20 .50
KCR2 Eric Hosmer .20 .50
KCR3 Danny Duffy .15 .40
KCR4 Alcides Escobar .20 .50
KCR5 Raul Mondesi .30 .75
KCR6 Mike Moustakas .20 .50
KCR7 Lorenzo Cain .15 .40
KCR8 Kendrys Morales .15 .40
KCR9 Chris Young .15 .40
KCR10 Yordano Ventura .20 .50
KCR11 Kris Medlen .20 .50
KCR12 Edinson Volquez .15 .40
KCR13 Wade Davis .15 .40
KCR14 Omar Infante .15 .40
KCR15 Jarrod Dyson .15 .40
KCR16 Alex Gordon .20 .50
KCR17 Christian Colon .15 .40

2017 Royals Topps

COMPLETE SET (17) 3.00 8.00
KC1 Salvador Perez .20 .50
KC2 Danny Duffy .15 .40
KC3 Hunter Dozier .15 .40
KC4 Kelvin Herrera .15 .40
KC5 Lorenzo Cain .15 .40
KC6 Cheslor Cuthbert .15 .40
KC7 Raul Mondesi Jr. .20 .50
KC8 Alcides Escobar .20 .50
KC9 Alex Gordon .20 .50
KC10 Joakim Soria .15 .40
KC11 Mike Moustakas .20 .50
KC12 Jorge Soler .25 .60
KC13 Matt Strahm .15 .40
KC14 Ian Kennedy .15 .40
KC15 Eric Hosmer .20 .50
KC16 Paulo Orlando .15 .40
KC17 Kauffman Stadium .15 .40

2018 Royals Topps

COMPLETE SET (17) 2.00 5.00
KR1 Salvador Perez .20 .50
KR2 Jorge Soler .25 .60
KR3 Raul Mondesi
KR4 Ian Kennedy .15 .40
KR5 Cheslor Cuthbert .15 .40
KR6 Danny Duffy .15 .40
KR7 Drew Butera .15 .40
KR8 Brandon Moss .15 .40
KR9 Alex Gordon .20 .50
KR10 Trevor Cahill .15 .40
KR11 Nathan Karns .15 .40
KR12 Jason Hammel .20 .50
KR13 Whit Merrifield .25 .60
KR14 Kelvin Herrera .15 .40
KR15 Mike Moustakas .20 .50
KR16 Jorge Bonifacio .15 .40
KR17 Eric Hosmer .20 .50

2019 Royals Topps

COMPLETE SET (17) 2.00 5.00
KR1 Whit Merrifield .25 .60
KR2 Salvador Perez .20 .50
KR3 Adalberto Mondesi .20 .50
KR4 Alex Gordon .20 .50
KR5 Brett Phillips .15 .40
KR6 Ryan O'Hearn .15 .40
KR7 Danny Duffy .15 .40
KR8 Brad Keller .15 .40
KR9 Jakob Junis .15 .40
KR10 Hunter Dozier .15 .40
KR11 Jorge Bonifacio .15 .40
KR12 Ian Kennedy .15 .40
KR13 Jorge Lopez .15 .40
KR14 Brian Goodwin .15 .40
KR15 Heath Fillmyer .15 .40
KR16 Chris Owings .15 .40
KR17 Billy Hamilton .20 .50

2020 Royals Topps

KC1 Whit Merrifield .25 .60
KC2 Salvador Perez .20 .50
KC3 Jorge Soler .25 .60
KC4 Ryan O'Hearn .15 .40
KC5 Cam Gallagher .15 .40
KC6 Bubba Starling .30 .75
KC7 Hunter Dozier .15 .40
KC8 Adalberto Mondesi .20 .50
KC9 Nicky Lopez .15 .40
KC10 Danny Duffy .15 .40
KC11 Brad Keller .15 .40
KC12 Ian Kennedy .15 .40
KC13 Meibrys Viloria .15 .40
KC14 Chance Adams .15 .40
KC15 Maikel Franco .20 .50
KC16 Jakob Junis .15 .40
KC17 Brett Phillips .15 .40

2017 Royals Topps National Baseball Card Day

COMPLETE SET (10) 5.00 12.00
KCR1 Ian Kennedy .60 1.50
KCR2 Raul Mondesi .75 2.00
KCR3 Paulo Orlando .60 1.50
KCR4 Joakim Soria .60 1.50
KCR5 Alex Gordon .75 2.00
KCR6 Jorge Soler 1.00 2.50
KCR7 Danny Duffy .60 1.50
KCR8 Salvador Perez .75 2.00
KCR9 Kelvin Herrera .60 1.50
KCR10 George Brett 2.00 5.00

1933 Blue Bird Soda

This card, which measures approximately 3 7/8" by 5 7/" features all-time slugger Babe Ruth. The photo shows the Babe in a batting pose, and the back has an advertisement for Blue Bird drink.

1 Babe Ruth Front View 500.00 1000.00
2 Babe Ruth Side View 500.00 1000.00

1996 Ruth Danbury Mint

This one card standard-size set features a card of Babe Ruth set against a gold relief border. The front has a photo of Ruth along with his name, team affiliation and position. The back has his vital stats along with his career stats. We suspect there might be more Danbury Mint cards so any further cards known would be appreciated.

1 Babe Ruth 4.00 10.00

1992 Delphi Bradford Exchange

These standard size cards were issued to promote the Legends of Baseball plates released by the Delphi company. With each plate in the series, collectors received a free old-fashioned Baseball Legends card depicting the player and recounting the milestones of his career. The cards are unnumbered. This checklist may be incomplete, so please contact us with any additions.

1 Grover Alexander .30 .75
2 Ty Cobb .75 2.00
3 Mickey Cochrane .30 .75
4 Jimmie Foxx .50 1.25
5 Lou Gehrig 1.00 2.50
6 Lefty Grove .30 .75
7 Rogers Hornsby .30 .75
8 Joe Jackson .60 1.50
9 Walter Johnson .50 1.25
10 Christy Mathewson .50 1.25
11 Mel Ott .50 1.25
12 Babe Ruth 1.25 3.00
13 Tris Speaker .30 .75
14 Honus Wagner .50 1.25
15 Cy Young .30 .75

1928 Ruth Fro Joy

The cards in this six-card set measure approximately 2 1/16" by 4". The Fro Joy set of 1928 was designed to exploit the advertising potential of the mighty Babe Ruth. Six black and white cards explained specific baseball techniques while the reverse advertising extolled the virtues of Fro Joy ice cream and ice cream cones. Unfortunately this small set has been illegally reprinted (several times) and many of these virtually worthless fakes have been introduced into the hobby. The easiest fakes to spot are those cards (or uncut sheets) that are slightly over-sized and blue tinted; however some of the other fakes are more cleverly faithful to the original. Be very careful before purchasing Fro-Joys; obtain a qualified opinion on authenticity from an experienced dealer (preferably one who is unrelated to the dealer trying to sell you his cards). You might also show the cards (before you commit to purchase them) to an experienced printer who can advise you on the true age of the paper stock. More than one dealer has been quoted as saying that 99 percent of the Fro Joys seen are fakes. In addition, a 8 1/2" by 12" premium photo was also issued as part of the release of this promotion.

COMPLETE SET (6) 300.00 600.00
1 Babe Ruth 150.00 300.00
George Herman Babe Ruth
2 Babe Ruth 100.00 200.00
Look Out Mr. Pitcher
3 Babe Ruth 100.00 200.00
Bang The Babe Lines one out
4 Babe Ruth/When the Babe Comes Out 100.00200.00
5 Babe Ruth 100.00 200.00
Babe Ruth's Grip
6 Babe Ruth 100.00 200.00
Ruth is a Crack Fielder
P1 Babe Ruth 150.00 300.00
Premium
NNO Uncut Sheet

1992 Ruth Gold Entertainment

Gold Entertainment produced this five-card holographic set celebrating the life and legend of Babe Ruth, along with Lou Gehrig and Roger Maris. The artwork for these cards was created by Hollywood artists Mike Butkus and Alan Hunter. This standard-size set was sold in box cases containing 20 five-card sets (16 in silver and four in gold) and four bonus holograms (of a surprise player). The gold sets are valued at one and a half times the (silver) values listed below. The production run is reported to be 12,500 boxes, with each box carrying a numbered holographic seal. Each set features two double-sided full-bleed holograms and three full-color backs presenting biography, statistics, and quotes. The cards are numbered on the front in a diamond in the upper left corner (the cards with the color backs also carry a number on the back).

COMPLETE SET (5) 4.00 10.00
2 Babe Ruth/(Two-sided hologram; 1.25 3.00
Ruth's stats on f
4 Babe Ruth/61 in 1961 - 60 in 1927/(Two-sided hol
1.25 3.00

1920 Ruth Heading Home

This six card blank-back set, which measure approximately 1 1/2" by 2 3/8", was issued to promote Babe Ruth in his first starring movie vehicle. That film was titled "Heading Home" and each card shows the Babe with a bat in his hand

COMPLETE SET (6) 4000.00
COMMON CARD 750.00

1928 Ruth Home Run Candy Membership

This one card set was issued to people who purchased a ruth's home run candy which cost a nickel and featured a photo of the Babe on the front and ten general rules for members on the back. Very few copies are known to exist of this card and any additional information is greatly appreciated. A few wrappers are also known to exist of this product.

1 Babe Ruth 1000.00 2000.00

1921 Ruth Pathe

This 7" by 9" card was issued as a premium card by the Pathe Freres Phonograph Company. This card is printed in green and gray tones and shows the Babe with his hands at the waist. The back describes his 1920 season when he set a then record with 54 homers in a season. This item was actually the sleeve of a 78 RPM record commemorating the great Babe.

1 Babe Ruth 1500.00 3000.00

1938 Ruth Quaker Oats

This 8" by 10" blank backed poster of Babe Ruth was produced in the 1930's by the Quaker Oats company.The poster features Ruth swinging and has a facsimile autograph with the words "To My Pal from "Babe" Ruth. The bottom of the poster has the words "Presented to Members of the the Babe Ruth Base Ball Clun by the Quaker Puffed Wheat and Puffed Rice." Like most promotional photos, it was sent in a mailing envelope to insure delivery in good condition

1 Babe Ruth 250.00 500.00

1995 Ruth Stamp Cards.

These 12 standard-size cards were issued by the Sport Stamps Collectors Association to honor the 100th anniversary of Babe ruth's birth. The fronts feature pictures of Babe Ruth surrounded by a frame. In the upper left corner is the word "Guyana" while on the right corner there is a $160 price tag. The backs describe various parts of Babe's life and also have a montage of some of the photos shown on the fronts. This set was issued in a special box and was a full reprint of the stamps issued in Guyana.

COMP.FACT SET 4.00 10.00
COMMON CARD .40 1.00
6 Babe Ruth .75 2.00
Lou Gehrig

1990 Ryan Arlington Yellow Pages

This card was distributed by the Greater Arlington/Mansfield Spotlight Yellow Pages and measures approximately 5 1/4" by 6 3/4". The front displays a color action picture of Nolan Ryan pitching, and his 17 Major League strike out records are printed on the back.

1 Nolan Ryan 2.00 5.00

1989 Ryan Best Western

This one-card standard-size set was sponsored by Best Western in conjunction with American Express to commemorate the 50th anniversary of Little League Baseball. The cards were distributed at a Texas Rangers home game in 1989. This card has a black and white photo of Nolan Ryan in his Little League uniform.

NNO Nolan Ryan 1.25 3.00
Little League photo

1994 Ryan Legends Postcard

This postcard features Texas Ranger great Nolan Ryan. This was issued after Ryan's career finished and is a tribute to his long and fabled career which included more than 300 wins and the shattering of the exsitng strikeout record.

1 Nolan Ryan .75 2.00

1994 Ryan SSCA

This 12-card set was distributed in sealed factory boxes and are actually official postage stamp cards issued by the Government of Guyana. The fronts feature color photos of Nolan Ryan with a gold foil simulated autograph. The backs carry information about Ryan's career. 1000 redemption cards were randomly seeded into sets which could be redeemed for a special card autographed by Nolan Ryan himself.

COMPLETE SET (12) 8.00 20.00
COMMON CARD (1-12) .80 2.00

1993 Ryan Texas Supermarket Stickers

These stickers featured reprints of Nolan Ryan Topps cards. They were regionally issued in various Texas Supermarkets: Minyards, Super S, Brookshire Borthers and Budget Chopper. over a period of ten weeks. Each sticker sheet contained three "reprint" cards. These stickers were issued by Big League Collectibles and measure 98 percent of the regular card size.

COMPLETE SET (30) 4.00 10.00
COMMON STICKER (1-30) .20 .50

1993 Ryan Whataburger

Subtitled "Recollections," these ten plastic-coated cards were produced by Triad and distributed by Whataburger. The standard-size fronts have a prismatic border and color action shots of Ryan, which lay under the diffraction grating plastic coating that gives a 3-D appearance. The cards are unnumbered.

COMPLETE SET (10) 4.00 10.00
COMMON CARD (1-10) .20 .50

1936 S and S (Green Backs) WG8

These cards were distributed as part of a baseball game produced in 1936. The cards each measure approximately 2 1/4" by 3 1/2" and have rounded corners. The card fronts are all oriented horizontally and show a small black and white photo of the player, his name, position, his team, vital statistics and the game outcome associated with that particular card. The card backs are evenly split between a plain green back with a thin white border or a plain back on a tannish paper stock. Since the cards are unnumbered, they are listed below in alphabetical order. Interestingly there are actually two box sizes. The box, which contained these fifty-two cards, and some other accoutrements to play the game, retailed for fifty cents when issued in 1936.

COMPLETE SET (52) 400.00 800.00
1 Luke Appling 15.00 30.00
2 Earl Averill 15.00 30.00
3 Zeke Bonura 7.50 15.00
4 Dolph Camilli 10.00 20.00
5 Ben Cantwell 7.50 15.00
6 Phil Cavarretta 12.50 25.00
7 Rip Collins 10.00 20.00
8 Joe Cronin 25.00 50.00
9 Frank Crosetti 12.50 25.00
10 Kiki Cuyler 15.00 30.00
11 Virgil Davis 7.50 15.00
12 Frank Demaree 10.00 20.00
13 Paul Derringer 15.00 30.00
14 Bill Dickey 30.00 60.00
15 Woody English 7.50 15.00
16 Fred Fitzsimmons 10.00 20.00
17 Rick Ferrell 15.00 30.00
18 Pete Fox 7.50 15.00
19 Jimmy Foxx 40.00 80.00
(Jimmie)
20 Larry French 7.50 15.00
21 Frank Frisch 25.00 50.00
22 August Galan 10.00 20.00
23 Charlie Gehringer 25.00 50.00
24 John Gill 7.50 15.00
25 Charles Grimm 12.50 25.00
26 Mule Haas 10.00 20.00
27 Stan Hack 12.50 25.00
28 Bill Hallahan 10.00 20.00
29 Mel Harder 12.50 25.00
30 Gabby Hartnett 15.00 30.00
31 Ray Hayworth 7.50 15.00
32 Ralston Hemsley 7.50 15.00
33 Billy Herman 15.00 30.00
34 Frank Higgins 7.50 15.00
35 Carl Hubbell 30.00 60.00
36 Bill Jurges 7.50 15.00
37 Vernon Kennedy 7.50 15.00
38 Chuck Klein 15.00 30.00
39 Mike Kreevich 7.50 15.00
40 Bill Lee 7.50 15.00
41 Joe Medwick 15.00 30.00
42 Van Mungo 10.00 20.00
43 James O'Dea 7.50 15.00
44 Mel Ott 30.00 60.00
45 Rip Radcliff 7.50 15.00
46 Pie Traynor 15.00 30.00
47 Arky Vaughan 15.00 30.00
48 Joe Vosmik 7.50 15.00
49 Lloyd Waner 15.00 30.00
50 Paul Waner 15.00 30.00
51 Lon Warneke 10.00 20.00
52 Floyd Young 7.50 15.00

1911 S74 Silks

Issued around 1911, these silk fabric collectibles have designs similar to the designs in the T205 Cigarette card set. The silk itself is 2" by 3" and the image is 1 1/4" by 2 3/8". The line work on the silks is in one color only, with colors of blue, red, brown and several variations between red and brown known to exist. The field or stock color is known in white and several pastel tints. The cards are unnumbered but have been numbered and listed by team alphabetical order and then player alphabetical order within the teams in the checklist below. Turkey Red and Old Mill Cigarettes are among the issuers of these silks. These silks were produced in more than one year and in fact may possibly be broken into two distinct sets. Silks with Helmar and Red Sun backs can also be found; although the Red Sun variations seem to be very scarce. White backgroung silks are valued 25% higher. Silks which still have the paper ad backing attached are worth double the prices listed below.

COMPLETE SET (122) 4000.00 8000.00
1 Bill Carrigan 50.00 100.00
2 Ed Cicotte 200.00 400.00
3 Tris Speaker 250.00 500.00
4 Jake Stahl 50.00 100.00
5 Hugh Duffy 150.00 300.00
6 Amby McConnell 50.00 100.00
7 Freddie Parent 50.00 100.00
8 Fred Payne 50.00 100.00
9 Lee Tannehill 50.00 100.00
10 Doc White 50.00 100.00
11 Terry Turner 50.00 100.00
12 Cy Young 250.00 500.00
13 Ty Cobb 1000.00 2000.00
14 Jim Delahanty 50.00 100.00
15 Davy Jones 50.00 100.00
16 George Moriarty 50.00 100.00
17 George Mullin 60.00 120.00
18 Ed Summers 50.00 100.00
19 Ed Willett 50.00 100.00
20 Hal Chase 100.00 200.00
21 Russ Ford 50.00 100.00
22 Charlie Hemphill 50.00 100.00
23 John Knight 50.00 100.00
24 John Quinn 60.00 120.00
25 Harry Wolter 50.00 100.00
26 Frank Baker 150.00 300.00
27 Jack Barry 50.00 100.00
28 Chief Bender 150.00 300.00
29 Eddie Collins 150.00 300.00
30 Jimmy Dygert 50.00 100.00
31 Topsy Hartsel 50.00 100.00
32 Harry Krause 50.00 100.00
33 Danny Murphy 50.00 100.00
34 Rube Oldring 50.00 100.00
35 Barney Pelty 50.00 100.00
36 George Stone 50.00 100.00
37 Bobby Wallace 150.00 300.00
38 Kid Elberfeld 50.00 100.00
39 Walter Johnson 500.00 1000.00
40 Germany Schaefer 60.00 120.00
41 Gabby Street 50.00 100.00
42 Fred Beck 50.00 100.00
43 Peaches Graham 50.00 100.00
44 Buck Herzog 50.00 100.00
45 Al Mattern 50.00 100.00
46 Dave Shean 50.00 100.00
47 Harry Steinfeldt 60.00 120.00
48 Cy Barger (2) 50.00 100.00
49 George Bell 50.00 100.00
50 Bill Bergen 50.00 100.00
51 Bill Dahlen 60.00 120.00
52 Jake Daubert 60.00 120.00
53 John Hummel 50.00 100.00
54 Nap Rucker 60.00 120.00
55 Doc Scanlan 50.00 100.00
56 Red Smith 50.00 100.00
57 Tony Smith 50.00 100.00
58 Zach Wheat 150.00 300.00
59 Mordecai Brown 150.00 300.00
60 Frank Chance 200.00 400.00
61 Johnny Evers 200.00 400.00
62 Bill Foxen 50.00 100.00
63 Peaches Graham 50.00 100.00
64 Johnny Kling 60.00 120.00
65 Harry McIntire 50.00 100.00
66 Tom Needham 50.00 100.00
67 Orval Overall 60.00 120.00
68 Ed Reulbach 60.00 120.00
69 Frank Schulte 60.00 120.00
70 Jimmy Sheckard 50.00 100.00
71 Harry Steinfeldt 60.00 120.00
72 Joe Tinker 200.00 400.00
73 Bob Bescher 50.00 100.00
74 Tom Downey 50.00 100.00
75 Art Fromme 50.00 100.00
76 Eddie Grant 50.00 100.00
77 Clark Griffith 150.00 300.00
78 Dick Hoblitzell 50.00 100.00
79 Mike Mitchell 50.00 100.00
80 Red Ames 50.00 100.00
81 Beals Becker 50.00 100.00
82 Al Bridwell 50.00 100.00
83 Doc Crandall 50.00 100.00
84 Art Devlin 50.00 100.00
85 Josh Devore 50.00 100.00
86 Larry Doyle 60.00 120.00
87 Art Fletcher 50.00 100.00
88 Rube Marquard 150.00 300.00
89 Christy Mathewson 500.00 1000.00
90 John McGraw MG 200.00 400.00
91 Fred Merkle 60.00 120.00
92 Chief Meyers 60.00 120.00
93 Red Murray 50.00 100.00
94 Bugs Raymond 50.00 100.00
95 Admiral Schlei 50.00 100.00
96 Fred Snodgrass 50.00 100.00
97 Hooks Wiltse (2) 50.00 100.00
98 Johnny Bates 50.00 100.00
99 Red Dooin 50.00 100.00
100 Mickey Doolan 50.00 100.00
101 Bob Ewing 50.00 100.00
102 Hans Lobert 50.00 100.00
103 Pat Moran 50.00 100.00
104 Dode Paskert 50.00 100.00
105 Jack Rowan 50.00 100.00
106 John Titus 50.00 100.00
107 Bobby Byrne 50.00 100.00
108 Howie Camnitz 50.00 100.00
109 Fred Clarke 150.00 300.00
110 John Flynn 50.00 100.00
111 George Gibson 50.00 100.00
112 Tommy Leach 50.00 100.00
113 Lefty Leifield 50.00 100.00
114 Dots Miller 50.00 100.00
115 Deacon Phillippe 60.00 120.00
116 Kirby White 50.00 100.00
117 Owen Wilson 50.00 100.00
118 Roger Bresnahan (2) 150.00 300.00
119 Steve Evans 50.00 100.00
120 Arnold Hauser 50.00 100.00
121 Miller Huggins 150.00 300.00
122 Ed Konetchy 50.00 100.00
123 Rebel Oakes 50.00 100.00

1911 S81 Large Silks

These large and attractive silks are found in two sizes, approximately 5" by 7" or 7" by 9". Unlike the smaller S74 Baseball Silks, these silks are numbered, beginning with number 86 and ending at number 110. The pose of the picture is the same as that of the T3 Turkey Red baseball cards. The silks were issued in 1911 and are frequently found grouped on pillow covers. For some reason the silk of Mathewson appears to be the most plentiful member of this admittedly scarce issue. Therefore no premium typically associated with a Hall of Famer exists for this card.

COMPLETE SET (25) 25000.00 35000.00
86 Rube Marquard 900.00 1500.00
87 Marty O'Toole 500.00 800.00
88 Rube Benton 500.00 800.00
89 Grover C. Alexander 900.00 1500.00
90 Russ Ford 500.00 800.00
91 John McGraw MG 900.00 1500.00
92 Nap Rucker 500.00 800.00
93 Mike Mitchell 500.00 800.00
94 Chief Bender 900.00 1500.00
95 Frank Baker 900.00 1500.00
96 Napoleon Lajoie 900.00 1500.00
97 Joe Tinker 900.00 1500.00
98 Sherry Magee 600.00 1000.00
99 Howie Camnitz 500.00 800.00
100 Eddie Collins 900.00 1500.00
101 Red Dooin 500.00 800.00
102 Ty Cobb 12500.00 25000.00
103 Hugh Jennings MG 900.00 1500.00
104 Roger Bresnahan 900.00 1500.00
105 Jake Stahl 500.00 800.00
106 Tris Speaker 900.00 1500.00
107 Ed Walsh 900.00 1500.00
108 Christy Mathewson 800.00 1200.00
109 Johnny Evers 900.00 1500.00
110 Walter Johnson 6000.00 12000.00

1889 S.F.Hess and Co. N338-2

In contrast to the color drawings in Hess' California League set N321, the players in this series of big league ballplayers are shown in sepia photographs. The cards are blank-backed and unnumbered; they have no printed detail except for the player's name and the advertisement for S.F. Hess and Co.'s Cigarettes found below the picture. Cards denoted by SPOT are "Spotted Ties".

COMPLETE SET 30000.00 60000.00
1 Bill Brown: New York 2500.00 5000.00
2 Roger Conner (sic) 10000.00 20000.00
New York
3 Ed Crane: New York 2500.00 5000.00
4 Buck Ewing: New York 10000.00 20000.00
SPOT
5 Elmer Foster: New York 2500.00 5000.00
6 William George: 2500.00 5000.00
New York
7 Joe Gerhardt: New York 2500.00 5000.00
SPOT
8 Charles Getzein: 2500.00 5000.00
Detroit
9 George Gore: New York 2500.00 5000.00
10 Gil Hatfield: New York 2500.00 5000.00
11 Arlie Latham: St.Louis 4000.00 8000.00
12 Pat Murphy: New York 2500.00 5000.00
13 Jim Mutrie: New York 4000.00 8000.00
14 Dave Orr: New York 2500.00 5000.00
SPOT
15 Danny Richardson: 2500.00 5000.00
New York
16 Mike Slattery: 2500.00 5000.00
New York
17 Lidell Titcomb: 2500.00 5000.00
New York
18 John M. Ward: New York 10000.00 20000.00
19 Curt Welch: St. Louis 3000.00 6000.00
20 Mickey Welch: 10000.00 20000.00
New York SPOT
21 Arthur Whitney: 2500.00 5000.00
New York

1948-1950 Safe-T-Card

Cards from this set were issued in the Washington D.C. area in the late 1940s and early 1950s. Each card was printed in either black or red and features an artist's rendering of a famous area athlete or personality from a variety of sports. The card backs feature an ad for Jim Gibbons Cartoon-A-Quiz television show along with an ad from a local business. The player's facsimile autograph and team or sport affiliation is included on the fronts.

11 Ossie Bluege Mgr BB 15.00 30.00
13 Gilbert Coan BB 15.00 30.00
19 Sam Dente BB 15.00 30.00
21 Jacob Early BB 20.00 40.00
23 Al Evans BB 15.00 30.00
29 Calvin Griffith BB 15.00 30.00
30 Clark Griffith BB 20.00 40.00
34 Bucky Harris BB 25.00 50.00
37 Sid Hudson BB 15.00 30.00
40 Joe Kuhel BB 15.00 30.00
41 Bob Lemon BB 25.00 50.00
45 Bill McGowan Ump BB 15.00 30.00
46 George McQuinn BB 15.00 30.00
48 Don Newcombe BB 25.00 50.00
50 Joe Ostrowski BB 15.00 30.00
52 Sam Rice BB 25.00 50.00
56 Ray Scarborough BB 15.00 30.00
57 Bert Shepard BB 15.00 30.00
62 Mickey Vernon BB 20.00 40.00
66 Early Wynn BB 25.00 50.00
67 Eddie Yost BB 20.00 40.00

1978 Saga Discs

This set is a parallel to the 1978 Tastee-Freez discs. They were issued through Saga and are significantly more difficult than the regular Tastee-Freez discs.

COMPLETE SET (26) 100.00 200.00
1 Buddy Bell 2.00 5.00
2 Jim Palmer 8.00 20.00
3 Steve Garvey 3.00 8.00
4 Jeff Burroughs 1.00 2.50
5 Greg Luzinski 2.00 5.00
6 Lou Brock 6.00 15.00
7 Thurman Munson 4.00 10.00
8 Rod Carew 6.00 15.00
9 George Brett 20.00 50.00
10 Tom Seaver 8.00 20.00
11 Willie Stargell 6.00 15.00
12 Jerry Koosman 1.00 2.50
13 Bill North 1.00 2.50
14 Richie Zisk 1.00 2.50
15 Bill Madlock 2.00 5.00
16 Carl Yastrzemski 6.00 15.00
17 Dave Cash 1.00 2.50
18 Bob Watson 2.00 5.00
19 Dave Kingman 4.00 10.00
20 Gene Tenace 1.00 2.50
21 Ralph Garr 1.00 2.50
22 Mark Fidrych 6.00 15.00
23 Frank Tanana 2.00 5.00
24 Larry Hisle 1.00 2.50
25 Bruce Bochte 1.00 2.50
26 Bob Bailor 1.00 2.50

1962 Sain Spinner Postcard

This one-card set features four small color photos of the New York Yankee's pitching coach, John Sain, demonstrating how to use the Spinner, a device to teach the mechanics of a Curveball, Fast Ball, Sinker, and Screwball. The back displays a postcard format with an ad for the Spinner and instructions on how to obtain it.

1 John Sain CO 8.00 20.00

1995 Tim Salmon

This one card standard-sized set features star outfielder Tim Salmon. Issued as a testimonial to his religious beliefs, the card has his player portrait surrounded by yellow borders. The back has some biographical information and also has further explanation of his religious beliefs. While the card shown is signed, not all of these cards come autographed.

1 Tim Salmon 2.00 5.00

1981 San Diego Sports Collectors

This 20-card standard-size rounded-corner set was presented by the San Diego Sports Collectors Association at the San Diego Show held August 22 and 23, 1981. The fronts feature borderless, glossy, black-and-white player photos. The backs are white and carry the player's name, advertisement information and an offer for 50 cents off admission to the show with the card.

COMPLETE SET (20) 8.00 20.00
1 Gary Butcher .08 .25
2 Hank Aaron .60 1.50
3 Duke Snider .40 1.00
4 Al Kaline .40 1.00
5 Vic Power .20 .50
6 Jackie Robinson .40 1.00
7 Carl Erskine .20 .50
8 Ted Williams/(Batting) .75 2.00
9 Ted Williams/(Portrait) .75 2.00
10 Mickey Mantle/(Portrait) 1.00 2.50
11 Mickey Mantle/(Holding bat) 1.00 2.50
12 Mickey Mantle .40 1.00
Willie Mays
13 Mickey Mantle .40 1.00
Stan Musial
14 Joe DiMaggio .75 2.00
15 Roger Maris/(Portrait) .40 1.00
16 Roger Maris/(Holding bat) .40 1.00
17 Lou Gehrig .75 2.00
18 Bill Dickey .40 1.00
Lou Gehrig
19 Lou Gehrig .30 .75
Joe Cronin
Bill Dickey
Joe DiMaggio
20 Gary Butcher .08 .25

1997 Sandberg Commemorative

This one-card set was given away by the Chicago Cubs on Ryne Sandberg day. The card measures approximately 6 1/4" by 9" and features color images of Ryne Sandberg on the front with a postcard format on the back and a message to group leaders about ticket discounts.

1 Ryne Sandberg Jumbo 4.00 10.00
2 Ryne Sandberg 2.00 5.00

2005 Sandberg Jersey Retirement Day

1 Ryne Sandberg 5.00 10.00

1932 Sanella Margarine

The cards in this set measure approximately 2 3/4" by 4 1/8" and feature color images of famous athletes printed on thin stock. The cards were created in Germany and originally designed to be pasted into an album called "Handbook of Sports." The Ruth, and possibly the other cards in the set, was created in four versions with slight differences being found on the cardbacks.

1 Japanese catcher 5.00 10.00
83A Babe Ruth Type 1 (Sanella Centered) 50.00100.00
83B Babe Ruth Type 2
(Sanella at Bottom) 50.00 100.00
83C Babe Ruth Type 3
(Sanella at Bottom with 83) 75.00 150.00
83D Babe Ruth Type 4
(Sanella Centered with 83) 100.00 200.00

1968 SCFS Old Timers

This 72-card set measures 3 1/2" X 4 1/4" and features black-and-white artistic renderings of old time baseball players. The player's name, position and years played are printed at the bottom. The first series backs are blank except for a small stamp at the bottom with the 1968 copyright date. The second series has more complete player information and have a 1969 copyright date. The cards are numbered on the front. The cards were produced by long time hobbyist Mike Aronstein. This set was available from the producer at time of issue for $6.50.

COMPLETE SET 125.00 250.00
1 Babe Ruth 20.00 50.00
2 Rube Marquard 3.00 8.00
3 Zack Wheat 3.00 8.00
4 John Clarkson 3.00 8.00
5 Honus Wagner 4.00 10.00
6 Crab Evers 3.00 8.00
7 Bill Dickey 3.00 8.00
8 Elmer Smith 1.00 2.50
9 Ty Cobb 10.00 25.00
10 Happy Jack Chesbro 3.00 8.00
11 Moon Gibson 1.00 2.50
12 Bullet Joe Bush 1.00 2.50
13 George Mullin 1.00 2.50
14 Buddy Myer 1.00 2.50
15 James Collins 3.00 8.00
16 William Wambsganss 1.00 2.50
17 Jack Barry 1.00 2.50
18 Dickie Kerr 1.00 2.50
19 Connie Mack 3.00 8.00
20 Rabbit Maranville 3.00 8.00
21 Roger Peckinpaugh 1.00 2.50
22 Mickey Cochrane 3.00 8.00
23 George Kelly 3.00 8.00
24 John Baker 1.00 2.50
25 Wally Schang 1.00 2.50
26 Eddie Plank 3.00 8.00
27 Bill Donovan 1.00 2.50
28 Red Faber 3.00 8.00
29 Hack Wilson 3.00 8.00
30 Three Fingered Brown 3.00 8.00
31 Frederick Merkle 1.00 2.50
32 Heinie Groh 1.00 2.50
33 Stuffy McInnis 1.00 2.50
34 Prince Hal Chase 3.00 8.00
35 Kenesaw Mountain 2.00 5.00
Landis COMM
36 Chief Bender 3.00 8.00
38 Tony Lazzeri
39 John McGraw
40 Mel Ott
41 Grover Cleveland Alexander
42 Rube Waddell
43 Wilbert Robinson
44 Cap Anson
45 Eddie Cicotte
46 Hank Gowdy
47 Frankie Frisch
48 Charles Comiskey
49 Clyde Milan
50 Jimmy Wilson 1.00 2.50
51 Christy Mathewson
52 Tim Keefe
53 Abner Doubleday
54 Ed Walsh
55 Jim Thorpe 10.00 25.00
56 Roger Bresnahan
57 Frank Chance
58 Heinie Manush
59 Max Carey
72 Bill Dineen
73 Kid Gleason

1921 Schapira Bros.

This seven card set, which measures approximately 1 3/4" by 2 1/2, were used as part of a contest by Schapira brothers for people to collect and turn in 250 of the portrait photos plus any one of the action photos for a signed Babe Ruth baseball. Since more portraits were needed for the contest than action shots, we are presuming that those cards were printed in greater supply and are more available then the action shots in this set.

COMPLETE SET (6) 2000.00 4000.00
1 Babe Ruth Portrait (without Arrows) 400.00 800.00
2 Babe Ruth Portrait (with Arrows) 400.00 800.00
3 Babe Ruth Clear the Bags 500.00 1000.00
4 Babe Ruth Home Run 500.00 1000.00
5 Babe Ruth Over the Fence 500.00 1000.00
6 Babe Ruth They Passed Him 500.00 1000.00
7 Babe Ruth Waiting for a High One 500.00 1000.00

1950 Schumacher Gas

Little is known about these two cards which measure approximately 2 1/2" by 3 1/2" and were cut fairly unevenly. The fronts feature a black and white picture of the player while the horizontal backs feature the then "Gulf" logo and just some basic details about Schumacher service station. Since these cards are unnumbered, we have sequenced them in alphabetical order. There may be more players in this set so any further checklisting help is appreciated.

COMPLETE SET 100.00 200.00
COMMON CARD 50.00 100.00
1 George Munger 50.00 100.00
2 Vern Stephens 60.00 120.00

1935 Schutter-Johnson R332

This set of 50 cards was issued by the Schutter-Johnson Candy Corporation around 1935. Each card measures 2 1/4" by 2 7/8". While each card in the series is numbered, the ones in the checklist below are the only ones known at the present time. These black line-drawing cards on a red field are entitled "Major League Secrets" and feature tips from major league players on the reverse.

COMPLETE SET (50) 2000.00 4000.00
1 Al Simmons 150.00 300.00
Swings 2 or 3 bats
2 Lloyd Waner's 150.00 300.00
Batting Stance
3 Kiki Cuyler's 150.00 300.00
Baserunning Tips
4 Frank Frisch 200.00 400.00
Chop Bunt
5 Chick Hafey 150.00 300.00
Get Jump On Fly Balls
6 Bill Klem UMP 200.00 400.00
Balk
7 How to Practice 300.00 600.00
Control (Rogers
Hornsby Pitch-/
8 Carl Mays 100.00 200.00
Underhand Ball
9 Umpire Charles Wrig- 100.00 200.00
ley (Pitcher's feet
with no
10 Christy Mathewson 400.00 800.00
Fade-Away Pitch
11 Bill Dickey 200.00 400.00
Waste Ball
12 Walter Berger 100.00 200.00
don't step in the bucket
13 George Earnshaw 100.00 200.00
Curve
14 Hack Wilson 200.00 400.00
grip bat at extreme end
15 Charley Grimm 100.00 200.00
testing pitcher at first
16 Waner Brothers 150.00 300.00
word signs in outfield
17 Chuck Klein 150.00 300.00
keep eye on ball
18 Woody English 100.00 200.00
bunt flat-footed
19 Grover Alexander 200.00 400.00
side arm fastball
20 Lou Gehrig 1000.00 2000.00
hit ball where pitched)
21 Wes Ferrell 100.00 200.00
Wind-up
22 Carl Hubbell 200.00 400.00
Wind-up Pitching Tips
23 Pie Traynor 150.00 300.00
Bunting Tips
24 Gus Mancuso 100.00 200.00
getting under foul ball
25 Ben Cantwell 100.00 200.00
curve ball grip
26 Babe Ruth 2000.00 4000.00
Advice
27 Goose Goslin 150.00 300.00
throw from outfield
28 Earle Combs 150.00 300.00
Hands Apart Grip
29 Kiki Cuyler 150.00 300.00
halfslide
30 Jimmy Wilson 100.00 200.00
delayed steal
31 Dizzy Dean 300.00 600.00
curveball
32 Mickey Cochrane 200.00 400.00
signs
33 Ted Lyons 200.00 400.00
Knuckle Ball
34 Si Johnson 100.00 200.00
Slow Ball
35 Dizzy Dean 300.00 600.00
Fork Ball
36 Pepper Martin 100.00 200.00
bunting
37 Joe Cronin 150.00 300.00
Battery Tips
38 Gabby Hartnett 150.00 300.00
Simple Batting Signs
39 Oscar Melillo (play 100.00 200.00
ball& don't let
ball play yo
40 Ben Chapman 100.00 200.00
hook slide)
41 John McGraw MG 200.00 400.00
Coaching Signs
42 Babe Ruth 2000.00 4000.00
choke grip
43 Red Lucas 100.00 200.00
illegal action
44 Charley Root 100.00 200.00
Holding Runners on First
45 Dazzy Vance 150.00 300.00
drop pitch
46 Hugh Critz 100.00 200.00
second baseman's throw
47 Firpo Marberry 100.00 200.00
Raise Ball
48 Grover Alexander 200.00 400.00
Full Windup
49 Lefty Grove 200.00 400.00
fast ball grip
50 Heine Meine 100.00 200.00
three types of curves

1996 Schwebels Discs

This 20-disc set measures approximately 2 3/4" in diameter. The fronts feature color player portraits in a blue-and-red border with fading stars. The player's name is printied in the top blue border with the year "1996" in the bottom red border. The backs carry the player's name, team, position, biographical information, season and career statistics.

COMPLETE SET (20) 8.00 20.00
1 Jim Thome .50 1.25
2 Orel Hershiser .20 .50
3 Greg Maddux 1.25 3.00
4 Charles Nagy .08 .25
5 Omar Vizquel .40 1.00
6 Manny Ramirez .50 1.25
7 Dennis Martinez .20 .50
8 Eddie Murray .50 1.25
9 Albert Belle .20 .50
10 Fred McGriff .30 .75
11 Jack McDowell .08 .25
12 Kenny Lofton .20 .50
13 Cal Ripken 2.00 5.00
14 Jose Mesa .20 .50
15 Randy Johnson .50 1.25
16 Ken Griffey Jr. 1.25 3.00
17 Carlos Baerga .08 .25
18 Frank Thomas .50 1.25
19 Sandy Alomar .08 .25
20 Barry Bonds .75 2.00

1954 Scoop

COMPLETE SET (156) 1500.00 3000.00
COMMON CARD (1-78) 3.00 8.00
COMMON CARD (79-156) 5.00 12.00
27 Bob Feller Strikeout King 30.00 60.00
41 Babe Ruth Sets Record 75.00 150.00
130 Braves Go to Milwaukee 20.00 40.00
154 26-Inning Tie 25.00 50.00

1988 Score Samples

COMPLETE SET (6) 15.00 40.00
30 Mark Langston 2.00 5.00
48 Tony Pena 2.00 5.00
71 Keith Moreland 2.00 5.00
72 Barry Larkin 8.00 20.00
121 Dennis Boyd 2.00 5.00
145 Denny Walling 2.00 5.00

1988 Score

This set consists of 660 standard-size cards. The set was distributed by Major League Marketing and features six distinctive border colors on the front. Subsets include Reggie Jackson Tribute (500-504), Highlights (652-660) and Rookie Prospects (623-647). Card number 501, showing Reggie as a member of the Baltimore Orioles, is one of the few opportunities collectors have to visually remember Reggie's one-year stay with the Orioles. The set is distinguished by the fact that each card back shows a full-color picture of the player. Rookie Cards in this set include Ellis Burks, Ken Caminiti, Tom Glavine and Matt Williams.

COMPLETE SET (660) 5.00 12.00
COMP.FACT.SET (660) 8.00 20.00
1 Don Mattingly .25 .60
2 Wade Boggs .05 .15
3 Tim Raines .02 .10
4 Andre Dawson .02 .10
5 Mark McGwire .60 1.50
6 Kevin Seitzer .01 .05
7 Wally Joyner .02 .10
8 Jesse Barfield .02 .10
9 Pedro Guerrero .02 .10
10 Eric Davis .02 .10
11 George Brett .20 .50
12 Ozzie Smith .10 .30
13 Rickey Henderson .07 .20
14 Jim Rice .02 .10
15 Matt Nokes RC .08 .25
16 Mike Schmidt .20 .50
17 Dave Parker .02 .10
18 Eddie Murray .07 .20
19 Andres Galarraga .02 .10
20 Tony Fernandez .01 .05
21 Kevin McReynolds .01 .05
22 B.J. Surhoff .02 .10
23 Pat Tabler .01 .05
24 Kirby Puckett .07 .20
25 Benny Santiago .02 .10
26 Ryne Sandberg .15 .40
27 Kelly Downs .01 .05
28 Jose Cruz .02 .10
29 Pete O'Brien .01 .05
30 Mark Langston .01 .05
31 Lee Smith .02 .10
32 Juan Samuel .01 .05
33 Kevin Bass .01 .05
34 R.J. Reynolds .01 .05
35 Steve Sax .01 .05
36 John Kruk .02 .10
37 Alan Trammell .02 .10
38 Chris Bosio .01 .05
39 Brook Jacoby .01 .05
40 Willie McGee UER .02 .10
Excited misspelled
as excitd
41 Dave Magadan .01 .05
42 Fred Lynn .02 .10
43 Kent Hrbek .02 .10
44 Brian Downing .02 .10
45 Jose Canseco .20 .50
46 Jim Presley .01 .05
47 Mike Stanley .01 .05
48 Tony Pena .01 .05
49 David Cone .02 .10
50 Rick Sutcliffe .02 .10
51 Doug Drabek .01 .05
52 Bill Doran .01 .05
53 Mike Scioscia .02 .10
54 Candy Maldonado .01 .05
55 Dave Winfield .02 .10
56 Lou Whitaker .02 .10
57 Tom Henke .01 .05
58 Ken Gerhart .01 .05
59 Glenn Braggs .01 .05
60 Julio Franco .02 .10
61 Charlie Leibrandt .01 .05
62 Gary Gaetti .02 .10
63 Bob Boone .02 .10
64 Luis Polonia RC .08 .25
65 Dwight Evans .05 .15
66 Phil Bradley .01 .05
67 Mike Boddicker .01 .05
68 Vince Coleman .01 .05
69 Howard Johnson .02 .10
70 Tim Wallach .01 .05
71 Keith Moreland .01 .05
72 Barry Larkin .05 .15
73 Alan Ashby .01 .05
74 Rick Rhoden .01 .05
75 Darrell Evans .02 .10
76 Dave Stieb .02 .10
77 Dan Plesac .01 .05
78 Will Clark UER .07 .20
Born 3/17/64
should be 3/13/64
79 Frank White .02 .10
80 Joe Carter .02 .10
81 Mike Witt .01 .05
82 Terry Steinbach .02 .10
83 Alvin Davis .01 .05
84 Tommy Herr .02 .10
85 Vance Law .01 .05
86 Kal Daniels .01 .05
87 Rick Honeycutt UER .01 .05
Wrong years for
stats on back
88 Alfredo Griffin .01 .05
89 Bret Saberhagen .02 .10
90 Bert Blyleven .02 .10
91 Jeff Reardon .02 .10
92 Cory Snyder .01 .05
93A Greg Walker ERR .75 2.00
93B Greg Walker COR .01 .05
93 of 660
94 Joe Magrane RC .08 .25
95 Rob Deer .01 .05
96 Ray Knight .02 .10
97 Casey Candaele .01 .05
98 John Cerutti .01 .05
99 Buddy Bell .02 .10
100 Jack Clark .02 .10
101 Eric Bell .01 .05
102 Willie Wilson .02 .10
103 Dave Schmidt .01 .05
104 Dennis Eckersley UER .05 .15
Complete games stats
are wrong
105 Don Sutton .02 .10
106 Danny Tartabull .01 .05
107 Fred McGriff .07 .20
108 Les Straker .01 .05
109 Lloyd Moseby .01 .05
110 Roger Clemens .40 1.00
111 Glenn Hubbard .01 .05
112 Ken Williams RC .01 .05
113 Ruben Sierra .02 .10
114 Stan Jefferson .01 .05
115 Milt Thompson .01 .05
116 Bobby Bonilla .02 .10
117 Wayne Tolleson .01 .05
118 Matt Williams RC .30 .75
119 Chet Lemon .02 .10
120 Dale Sveum .01 .05
121 Dennis Boyd .01 .05
122 Brett Butler .02 .10
123 Terry Kennedy .01 .05
124 Jack Howell .01 .05
125 Curt Young .01 .05
126A Dave Valle ERR .02 .10
Misspelled Dale
on card front
126B Dave Valle COR .01 .05
127 Curt Wilkerson .01 .05
128 Tim Teufel .01 .05
129 Ozzie Virgil .01 .05
130 Brian Fisher .01 .05
131 Lance Parrish .02 .10
132 Tom Browning .01 .05
133A Larry Andersen ERR .02 .10
Misspelled Anderson
on card front
133B Larry Andersen COR .01 .05
134A Bob Brenly ERR .02 .10
Misspelled Brenley
on card front
134B Bob Brenly COR .01 .05
135 Mike Marshall .01 .05
136 Gerald Perry .01 .05
137 Bobby Meacham .01 .05
138 Larry Herndon .01 .05
139 Fred Manrique .01 .05
140 Charlie Hough .02 .10
141 Ron Darling .02 .10
142 Herm Winningham .01 .05
143 Mike Diaz .01 .05
144 Mike Jackson RC .08 .25
145 Denny Walling .01 .05
146 Robby Thompson .01 .05
147 Franklin Stubbs .01 .05
148 Albert Hall .01 .05
149 Bobby Witt .01 .05
150 Lance McCullers .01 .05
151 Scott Bradley .01 .05
152 Mark McLemore .01 .05
153 Tim Laudner .01 .05
154 Greg Swindell .01 .05
155 Marty Barrett .01 .05
156 Mike Heath .01 .05
157 Gary Ward .01 .05
158A Lee Mazzilli ERR .02 .10
Misspelled Mazilli
on card front
158B Lee Mazzilli COR .02 .10
159 Tom Foley .01 .05
160 Robin Yount .10 .30
161 Steve Bedrosian .01 .05
162 Bob Walk .01 .05
163 Nick Esasky .01 .05
164 Ken Caminiti RC .75 2.00
165 Jose Uribe .01 .05
166 Dave Anderson .01 .05
167 Ed Whitson .01 .05
168 Ernie Whitt .01 .05
169 Cecil Cooper .02 .10
170 Mike Pagliarulo .01 .05
171 Pat Sheridan .01 .05
172 Chris Bando .01 .05
173 Lee Lacy .01 .05
174 Steve Lombardozzi .01 .05
175 Mike Greenwell .01 .05
176 Greg Minton .01 .05
177 Moose Haas .01 .05
178 Mike Kingery .01 .05
179 Greg A. Harris .01 .05
180 Bo Jackson .07 .20
181 Carmelo Martinez .01 .05
182 Alex Trevino .01 .05
183 Ron Oester .01 .05
184 Danny Darwin .01 .05
185 Mike Krukow .01 .05
186 Rafael Palmeiro .15 .40
187 Tim Burke .01 .05
188 Roger McDowell .01 .05
189 Garry Templeton .02 .10
190 Terry Pendleton .02 .10
191 Larry Parrish .01 .05
192 Rey Quinones .01 .05
193 Joaquin Andujar .02 .10
194 Tom Brunansky .01 .05
195 Donnie Moore .01 .05
196 Dan Pasqua .01 .05
197 Jim Gantner .01 .05
198 Mark Eichhorn .01 .05
199 John Grubb .01 .05
200 Bill Ripken RC .08 .25
201 Sam Horn RC .02 .10
202 Todd Worrell .01 .05
203 Terry Leach .01 .05
204 Garth Iorg .01 .05
205 Brian Dayett .01 .05
206 Bo Diaz .01 .05
207 Craig Reynolds .01 .05
208 Brian Holton .01 .05
209 Marvell Wynne UER .01 .05
Misspelled Marvelle
on card front
210 Dave Concepcion .02 .10
211 Mike Davis .01 .05
212 Devon White .02 .10
213 Mickey Brantley .01 .05
214 Greg Gagne .01 .05
215 Oddibe McDowell .01 .05
216 Jimmy Key .02 .10
217 Dave Bergman .01 .05
218 Calvin Schiraldi .01 .05
219 Larry Sheets .01 .05
220 Mike Easler .01 .05
221 Kurt Stillwell .01 .05
222 Chuck Jackson .01 .05
223 Dave Martinez .01 .05
224 Tim Leary .01 .05
225 Steve Garvey .02 .10
226 Greg Mathews .01 .05
227 Doug Sisk .01 .05
228 Dave Henderson .01 .05
Wearing Red Sox uniform;
Red Sox logo on back
229 Jimmy Dwyer .01 .05
230 Larry Owen .01 .05
231 Andre Thornton .01 .05
232 Mark Salas .01 .05
233 Tom Brookens .01 .05
234 Greg Brock .01 .05
235 Rance Mulliniks .01 .05
236 Bob Brower .01 .05
237 Joe Niekro .01 .05
238 Scott Bankhead .01 .05
239 Doug DeCinces .01 .05
240 Tommy John .02 .10
241 Rich Gedman .01 .05
242 Ted Power .01 .05
243 Dave Meads .01 .05
244 Jim Sundberg .02 .10
245 Ken Oberkfell .01 .05
246 Jimmy Jones .01 .05
247 Ken Landreaux .01 .05
248 Jose Oquendo .01 .05
249 John Mitchell RC .02 .10
250 Don Baylor .02 .10
251 Scott Fletcher .01 .05
252 Al Newman .01 .05
253 Carney Lansford .02 .10
254 Johnny Ray .01 .05
255 Gary Pettis .01 .05
256 Ken Phelps .01 .05
257 Rick Leach .01 .05
258 Tim Stoddard .01 .05
259 Ed Romero .01 .05
260 Sid Bream .01 .05
261A Tom Niedenfuer ERR .02 .10
Misspelled Neidenfuer
on card front
261B Tom Niedenfuer COR .01 .05
262 Rick Dempsey .01 .05
263 Lonnie Smith .01 .05
264 Bob Forsch .01 .05
265 Barry Bonds .75 2.00
266 Willie Randolph .02 .10
267 Mike Ramsey .01 .05
268 Don Slaught .01 .05
269 Mickey Tettleton .01 .05
270 Jerry Reuss .01 .05
271 Marc Sullivan .01 .05
272 Jim Morrison .01 .05
273 Steve Balboni .01 .05
274 Dick Schofield .01 .05
275 John Tudor .02 .10
276 Gene Larkin RC .08 .25
277 Harold Reynolds .02 .10
278 Jerry Browne .01 .05
279 Willie Upshaw .01 .05
280 Ted Higuera .01 .05
281 Terry McGriff .01 .05
282 Terry Puhl .01 .05
283 Mark Wasinger .01 .05
284 Luis Salazar .01 .05
285 Ted Simmons .02 .10
286 John Shelby .01 .05
287 John Smiley RC .08 .25
288 Curt Ford .01 .05
289 Steve Crawford .01 .05
290 Dan Quisenberry .01 .05
291 Alan Wiggins .01 .05
292 Randy Bush .01 .05
293 John Candelaria .01 .05
294 Tony Phillips .01 .05
295 Mike Morgan .01 .05
296 Bill Wegman .01 .05
297A Terry Francona ERR .02 .10
Misspelled Franconia
on card front
297B Terry Francona COR .02 .10
298 Mickey Hatcher .01 .05
299 Andres Thomas .01 .05
300 Bob Stanley .01 .05
301 Al Pedrique .01 .05
302 Jim Lindeman .01 .05
303 Wally Backman .01 .05
304 Paul O'Neill .05 .15
305 Hubie Brooks .01 .05
306 Steve Buechele .01 .05
307 Bobby Thigpen .01 .05
308 George Hendrick .02 .10
309 John Moses .01 .05
310 Ron Guidry .02 .10
311 Bill Schroeder .01 .05
312 Jose Nunez .01 .05
313 Bud Black .01 .05
314 Joe Sambito .01 .05
315 Scott McGregor .01 .05
316 Rafael Santana .01 .05
317 Frank Williams .01 .05
318 Mike Fitzgerald .01 .05
319 Rick Mahler .01 .05
320 Jim Gott .01 .05
321 Mariano Duncan .01 .05
322 Jose Guzman .01 .05
323 Lee Guetterman .01 .05
324 Dan Gladden .01 .05
325 Gary Carter .02 .10
326 Tracy Jones .01 .05
327 Floyd Youmans .01 .05
328 Bill Dawley .01 .05
329 Paul Noce .01 .05
330 Angel Salazar .01 .05
331 Goose Gossage .02 .10
332 George Frazier .01 .05
333 Ruppert Jones .01 .05
334 Billy Joe Robidoux .01 .05
335 Mike Scott .02 .10
336 Randy Myers .02 .10
337 Bob Sebra .01 .05
338 Eric Show .01 .05
339 Mitch Williams .01 .05
340 Paul Molitor .02 .10
341 Gus Polidor .01 .05
342 Steve Trout .01 .05
343 Jerry Don Gleaton .01 .05
344 Bob Knepper .01 .05
345 Mitch Webster .01 .05
346 John Morris .01 .05
347 Andy Hawkins .01 .05
348 Dave Leiper .01 .05
349 Ernest Riles .01 .05
350 Dwight Gooden .02 .10
351 Dave Righetti .02 .10
352 Pat Dodson .01 .05
353 John Habyan .01 .05
354 Jim Deshaies .01 .05
355 Butch Wynegar .01 .05
356 Bryn Smith .01 .05
357 Matt Young .01 .05
358 Tom Pagnozzi RC .02 .10
359 Floyd Rayford .01 .05
360 Darryl Strawberry .02 .10
361 Sal Butera .01 .05
362 Domingo Ramos .01 .05
363 Chris Brown .01 .05
364 Jose Gonzalez .01 .05
365 Dave Smith .01 .05
366 Andy McGaffigan .01 .05
367 Stan Javier .01 .05
368 Henry Cotto .01 .05
369 Mike Birkbeck .01 .05
370 Len Dykstra .02 .10
371 Dave Collins .01 .05
372 Spike Owen .01 .05
373 Geno Petralli .01 .05
374 Ron Karkovice .01 .05
375 Shane Rawley .01 .05
376 DeWayne Buice .01 .05
377 Bill Pecota RC .02 .10
378 Leon Durham .01 .05
379 Ed Olwine .01 .05
380 Bruce Hurst .01 .05
381 Bob McClure .01 .05
382 Mark Thurmond .01 .05
383 Buddy Biancalana .01 .05
384 Tim Conroy .01 .05
385 Tony Gwynn .10 .30
386 Greg Gross .01 .05
387 Barry Lyons .01 .05
388 Mike Felder .01 .05
389 Pat Clements .01 .05
390 Ken Griffey .02 .10
391 Mark Davis .01 .05
392 Jose Rijo .02 .10
393 Mike Young .01 .05
394 Willie Fraser .01 .05
395 Dion James .01 .05
396 Steve Shields .01 .05
397 Randy St.Claire .01 .05
398 Danny Jackson .01 .05
399 Cecil Fielder .02 .10
400 Keith Hernandez .02 .10
401 Don Carman .01 .05
402 Chuck Crim .01 .05
403 Rob Woodward .01 .05
404 Junior Ortiz .01 .05
405 Glenn Wilson .01 .05
406 Ken Howell .01 .05
407 Jeff Kunkel .01 .05
408 Jeff Reed .01 .05
409 Chris James .01 .05
410 Zane Smith .01 .05
411 Ken Dixon .01 .05
412 Ricky Horton .01 .05
413 Frank DiPino .01 .05
414 Shane Mack .01 .05
415 Danny Cox .01 .05
416 Andy Van Slyke .05 .15
417 Danny Heep .01 .05
418 John Cangelosi .01 .05
419A John Christensen ERR .02 .10
Christiansen

on card front
419B John Christensen COR .01 .05
420 Joey Cora RC .08 .25
421 Mike LaValliere .01 .05
422 Kelly Gruber .01 .05
423 Bruce Benedict .01 .05
424 Len Matuszek .01 .05
425 Kent Tekulve .01 .05
426 Rafael Ramirez .01 .05
427 Mike Flanagan .01 .05
428 Mike Gallego .01 .05
429 Juan Castillo .01 .05
430 Neal Heaton .01 .05
431 Phil Garner .02 .10
432 Mike Dunne .01 .05
433 Wallace Johnson .01 .05
434 Jack O'Connor .01 .05
435 Steve Jeltz .01 .05
436 Donell Nixon .01 .05
437 Jack Lazorko .01 .05
438 Keith Comstock .01 .05
439 Jeff D. Robinson .01 .05
440 Graig Nettles .02 .10
441 Mel Hall .01 .05
442 Gerald Young .01 .05
443 Gary Redus .01 .05
444 Charlie Moore .01 .05
445 Bill Madlock .02 .10
446 Mark Clear .01 .05
447 Greg Booker .01 .05
448 Rick Schu .01 .05
449 Ron Kittle .01 .05
450 Dale Murphy .05 .15
451 Bob Dernier .01 .05
452 Dale Mohorcic .01 .05
453 Rafael Belliard .01 .05
454 Charlie Puleo .01 .05
455 Dwayne Murphy .01 .05
456 Jim Eisenreich .01 .05
457 David Palmer .01 .05
458 Dave Stewart .02 .10
459 Pascual Perez .01 .05
460 Glenn Davis .01 .05
461 Dan Petry .01 .05
462 Jim Winn .01 .05
463 Darrell Miller .01 .05
464 Mike Moore .01 .05
465 Mike LaCoss .01 .05
466 Steve Farr .01 .05
467 Jerry Mumphrey .01 .05
468 Kevin Gross .01 .05
469 Bruce Bochy .01 .05
470 Orel Hershiser .02 .10
471 Eric King .01 .05
472 Ellis Burks RC .15 .40
473 Darren Daulton .02 .10
474 Mookie Wilson .02 .10
475 Frank Viola .02 .10
476 Ron Robinson .01 .05
477 Bob Melvin .01 .05
478 Jeff Musselman .01 .05
479 Charlie Kerfeld .01 .05
480 Richard Dotson .01 .05
481 Kevin Mitchell .02 .10
482 Gary Roenicke .01 .05
483 Tim Flannery .01 .05
484 Rich Yett .01 .05
485 Pete Incaviglia .01 .05
486 Rick Cerone .01 .05
487 Tony Armas .02 .10
488 Jerry Reed .01 .05
489 Dave Lopes .02 .10
490 Frank Tanana .02 .10
491 Mike Loynd .01 .05
492 Bruce Ruffin .01 .05
493 Chris Speier .01 .05
494 Tom Hume .01 .05
495 Jesse Orosco .01 .05
496 Robbie Wine UER .01 .05
Misspelled Robby
on card front
497 Jeff Montgomery RC .08 .25
498 Jeff Dedmon .01 .05
499 Luis Aguayo .01 .05
500 Reggie Jackson A's .05 .15
501 Reggie Jackson O's .05 .15
502 Reggie Jackson Yanks .05 .15
503 Reggie Jackson Angels .05 .15
504 Reggie Jackson A's .05 .15
505 Billy Hatcher .01 .05
506 Ed Lynch .01 .05
507 Willie Hernandez .01 .05
508 Jose DeLeon .01 .05
509 Joel Youngblood .01 .05
510 Bob Welch .02 .10
511 Steve Ontiveros .01 .05
512 Randy Ready .01 .05
513 Juan Nieves .01 .05
514 Jeff Russell .01 .05
515 Von Hayes .01 .05
516 Mark Gubicza .01 .05
517 Ken Dayley .01 .05
518 Don Aase .01 .05
519 Rick Reuschel .02 .10
520 Mike Henneman RC .08 .25
521 Rick Aguilera .02 .10
522 Jay Howell .01 .05
523 Ed Correa .01 .05
524 Manny Trillo .01 .05
525 Kirk Gibson .07 .20
526 Wally Ritchie .01 .05
527 Al Nipper .01 .05
528 Atlee Hammaker .01 .05
529 Shawon Dunston .01 .05
530 Jim Clancy .01 .05
531 Tom Paciorek .01 .05
532 Joel Skinner .01 .05
533 Scott Garrelts .01 .05
534 Tom O'Malley .01 .05
535 John Franco .02 .10
536 Paul Kilgus .01 .05
537 Darrell Porter .01 .05
538 Walt Terrell .01 .05
539 Bill Long .01 .05
540 George Bell .02 .10
541 Jeff Sellers .01 .05
542 Joe Boever .01 .05
543 Steve Howe .01 .05
544 Scott Sanderson .01 .05
545 Jack Morris .02 .10
546 Todd Benzinger RC .08 .25
547 Steve Henderson .01 .05
548 Eddie Milner .01 .05
549 Jeff M. Robinson .01 .05
550 Cal Ripken .30 .75
551 Jody Davis .01 .05
552 Kirk McCaskill .01 .05
553 Craig Lefferts .01 .05
554 Darnell Coles .01 .05
555 Phil Niekro .02 .10
556 Mike Aldrete .01 .05
557 Pat Perry .01 .05
558 Juan Agosto .01 .05
559 Rob Murphy .01 .05
560 Dennis Rasmussen .01 .05
561 Manny Lee .01 .05
562 Jeff Blauser RC .08 .25
563 Bob Ojeda .01 .05
564 Dave Dravecky .01 .05
565 Gene Garber .01 .05
566 Ron Roenicke .01 .05
567 Tommy Hinzo .01 .05
568 Eric Nolte .01 .05
569 Ed Hearn .01 .05
570 Mark Davidson .01 .05
571 Jim Walewander .01 .05
572 Donnie Hill UER .01 .05
84 Stolen Base
total listed as 7
573 Jamie Moyer .02 .10
574 Ken Schrom .01 .05
575 Nolan Ryan .40 1.00
576 Jim Acker .01 .05
577 Jamie Quirk .01 .05
578 Jay Aldrich .01 .05
579 Claudell Washington .01 .05
580 Jeff Leonard .01 .05
581 Carmen Castillo .01 .05
582 Daryl Boston .01 .05
583 Jeff DeWillis .01 .05
584 John Marzano .01 .05
585 Bill Gullickson .01 .05
586 Andy Allanson .01 .05
587 Lee Tunnell UER .01 .05
1987 stat line
reads .4.84 ERA
588 Gene Nelson .01 .05
589 Dave LaPoint .01 .05
590 Harold Baines .02 .10
591 Bill Buckner .02 .10
592 Carlton Fisk .05 .15
593 Rick Manning .01 .05
594 Doug Jones RC .08 .25
595 Tom Candiotti .01 .05
596 Steve Lake .01 .05
597 Jose Lind RC .08 .25
598 Ross Jones .01 .05
599 Gary Matthews .02 .10
600 Fernando Valenzuela .02 .10
601 Dennis Martinez .02 .10
602 Les Lancaster .01 .05
603 Ozzie Guillen .02 .10
604 Tony Bernazard .01 .05
605 Chili Davis .02 .10
606 Roy Smalley .01 .05
607 Ivan Calderon .01 .05
608 Jay Tibbs .01 .05
609 Guy Hoffman .01 .05
610 Doyle Alexander .01 .05
611 Mike Bielecki .01 .05
612 Shawn Hillegas RC .01 .05
613 Keith Atherton .01 .05
614 Eric Plunk .01 .05
615 Sid Fernandez .01 .05
616 Dennis Lamp .01 .05
617 Dave Engle .01 .05
618 Harry Spilman .01 .05
619 Don Robinson .01 .05
620 John Farrell RC .02 .10
621 Nelson Liriano RC .01 .05
622 Floyd Bannister .01 .05
623 Randy Milligan RC .02 .10
624 Kevin Elster .01 .05
625 Jody Reed RC .08 .25
626 Shawn Abner .01 .05
627 Kirt Manwaring RC .08 .25
628 Pete Stanicek RC .01 .05
629 Rob Ducey RC .01 .05
630 Steve Kiefer .01 .05
631 Gary Thurman RC .01 .05
632 Darrel Akerfelds RC .01 .05
633 Dave Clark .01 .05
634 Roberto Kelly RC .08 .25
635 Keith Hughes RC .01 .05
636 John Davis RC .01 .05
637 Mike Devereaux RC .08 .25
638 Tom Glavine RC UER 1.25 3.00
Struck out 34 in 32 innings, not 31
639 Keith A. Miller RC .08 .25
640 Chris Gwynn UER RC .08 .25
Wrong batting and
throwing on back
641 Tim Crews RC .08 .25
642 Mackey Sasser RC .08 .25
643 Vicente Palacios RC .01 .05
644 Kevin Romine RC .01 .05
645 Gregg Jefferies RC .08 .25
646 Jeff Treadway RC .08 .25
647 Ron Gant RC .15 .40
648 M.McGwire/M.Nokes .30 .75
649 Eric Davis .02 .10
Tim Raines
650 D.Mattingly/J.Clark .10 .30
651 Fernandez/Trammell/Ripken .08 .25
652 Vince Coleman HL .01 .05
653 Kirby Puckett HL .05 .15
654 Benito Santiago HL .01 .05
655 Juan Nieves HL .01 .05
656 Steve Bedrosian HL .01 .05
657 Mike Schmidt HL .07 .20
658 Don Mattingly HL .10 .30
659 Mark McGwire HL .30 .75
660 Paul Molitor HL .01 .05

1988 Score Glossy

COMP.FACT.SET (660) 60.00 120.00
*STARS: 5X TO 12X BASIC CARDS
*ROOKIES: 5X TO 12X BASIC CARDS
DISTRIBUTED ONLY IN FACTORY SET FORM

1988 Score Box Cards

COMPLETE SET (24) 4.00 10.00
1 Terry Kennedy .02 .10
2 Don Mattingly .60 1.50
3 Willie Randolph .07 .20
4 Wade Boggs .50 1.00
5 Cal Ripken 1.25 3.00
6 George Bell .02 .10
7 Rickey Henderson .50 1.25
8 Dave Winfield .30 .75
9 Bret Saberhagen .07 .20
10 Gary Carter .30 .75
11 Jack Clark .07 .20
12 Ryne Sandberg .60 1.50
13 Mike Schmidt .30 .75
14 Ozzie Smith .60 1.50
15 Eric Davis .07 .20
16 Andre Dawson .20 .50
17 Darryl Strawberry .07 .20
18 Mike Scott .02 .10
T1 Fenway Park '60 .75 2.00
Ted Williams Hits
To The End
T2 Comiskey Park '83 .07 .20
Grand Slam (Fred Lynn)
Breaks
T3 Anaheim Stadium '87 .75 2.00
Old Rookie Record
Falls (Mar
T4 Wrigley Field '38 .07 .20
Gabby (Hartnett) Gets
Pennant
T5 Comiskey Park '50 .07 .20
Red (Schoendienst)
Rips Winnin
T6 County Stadium '87 .20 .50
Rookie (John Farrell)
Stops H

1988 Score Rookie/Traded

This 110-card standard-size set was issued exclusively in a boxes factory-set form features traded players (1-65) and rookies (66-110) for the 1988 season. The cards are distinguishable from the regular Score set by the orange borders and by the fact that the numbering on the back has a T suffix. Apparently Score's first attempt at a Rookie/Traded set was produced very conservatively, resulting in a set which is now recognized as being much tougher to find than the other Rookie/Traded sets from the other major companies of that year. Extended Rookie Cards in this set include Roberto Alomar, Brady Anderson, Craig Biggio, Jay Buhner and Mark Grace.

COMP.FACT.SET (110) 15.00 40.00
1T Jack Clark .30 .75
2T Danny Jackson .08 .25
3T Brett Butler .30 .75
4T Kurt Stillwell .08 .25
5T Tom Brunansky .08 .25
6T Dennis Lamp .08 .25
7T Jose DeLeon .08 .25
8T Tom Herr .08 .25
9T Keith Moreland .08 .25
10T Kirk Gibson .75 2.00
11T Bud Black .08 .25
12T Rafael Ramirez .08 .25
13T Luis Salazar .08 .25
14T Goose Gossage .30 .75
15T Bob Welch .30 .75
16T Vance Law .08 .25
17T Ray Knight .30 .75
18T Dan Quisenberry .08 .25
19T Don Slaught .08 .25
20T Lee Smith .30 .75
21T Rick Cerone .08 .25
22T Pat Tabler .08 .25
23T Larry McWilliams .08 .25
24T Ricky Horton .08 .25
25T Graig Nettles .30 .75
26T Dan Petry .08 .25
27T Jose Rijo .30 .75
28T Chili Davis .30 .75
29T Dickie Thon .08 .25
30T Mackey Sasser .08 .25
31T Mickey Tettleton .08 .25
32T Rick Dempsey .08 .25
33T Ron Hassey .08 .25
34T Phil Bradley .08 .25
35T Jay Howell .08 .25
36T Bill Buckner .30 .75
37T Alfredo Griffin .08 .25
38T Gary Pettis .08 .25
39T Calvin Schiraldi .08 .25
40T John Candelaria .08 .25
41T Joe Orsulak .08 .25
42T Willie Upshaw .08 .25
43T Herm Winningham .08 .25
44T Ron Kittle .08 .25
45T Bob Dernier .08 .25
46T Steve Balboni .08 .25
47T Steve Shields .08 .25
48T Henry Cotto .08 .25
49T Dave Henderson .08 .25
50T Dave Parker .30 .75
51T Mike Young .08 .25
52T Mark Salas .08 .25
53T Mike Davis .08 .25
54T Rafael Santana .08 .25
55T Don Baylor .30 .75
56T Dan Pasqua .08 .25
57T Ernest Riles .08 .25
58T Glenn Hubbard .08 .25
59T Mike Smithson .08 .25
60T Richard Dotson .08 .25
61T Jerry Reuss .08 .25
62T Mike Jackson .30 .75
63T Floyd Bannister .08 .25
64T Jesse Orosco .08 .25
65T Larry Parrish .08 .25
66T Jeff Bittiger .08 .25
67T Ray Hayward .08 .25
68T Ricky Jordan XRC .30 .75
69T Tommy Gregg .08 .25
70T Brady Anderson XRC .50 1.25
71T Jeff Montgomery .30 .75
72T Darryl Hamilton XRC .30 .75
73T Cecil Espy XRC .08 .25
74T Greg Briley XRC .08 .25
75T Joey Meyer .08 .25
76T Mike Macfarlane XRC .30 .75
77T Oswald Peraza XRC .08 .25
78T Jack Armstrong XRC .08 .25
79T Don Heinkel .08 .25
80T Mark Grace XRC 3.00 8.00
81T Steve Curry .08 .25
82T Damon Berryhill XRC* .30 .75
83T Steve Ellsworth .08 .25
84T Pete Smith XRC* .08 .25
85T Jack McDowell XRC .50 1.25
86T Rob Dibble XRC .50 1.25
87T Bryan Harvey XRC .30 .75
88T John Dopson .08 .25
89T Dave Gallagher .08 .25
90T Todd Stottlemyre XRC .30 .75
91T Mike Schooler .08 .25
92T Don Gordon .08 .25
93T Sil Campusano .08 .25
94T Jeff Pico .08 .25
95T Jay Buhner XRC .75 2.00
96T Nelson Santovenia .08 .25
97T Al Leiter XRC 1.25 3.00
98T Luis Alicea XRC .30 .75
99T Pat Borders XRC .30 .75
100T Chris Sabo XRC .50 1.25
101T Tim Belcher .08 .25
102T Walt Weiss XRC* .50 1.25
103T Craig Biggio XRC 5.00 12.00
104T Don August .08 .25
105T Roberto Alomar XRC 4.00 10.00
106T Todd Burns .08 .25
107T John Costello XRC .08 .25
108T Melido Perez XRC* .30 .75
109T Darrin Jackson XRC* .08 .25
110T Orestes Destrade XRC .08 .25

1988 Score Rookie/Traded Glossy

COMP.FACT.SET (110) 75.00 150.00
*STARS: 1X TO 2.5X BASIC CARDS
*ROOKIES: 1X TO 2.5X BASIC CARDS
DISTRIBUTED ONLY IN FACTORY SET FORM

1988 Score Young Superstars I

COMPLETE SET (40) 3.00 8.00
1 Mark McGwire 1.00 2.50
2 Benito Santiago .02 .10
3 Sam Horn .01 .05
4 Chris Bosio .01 .05
5 Matt Nokes .01 .05
6 Ken Williams .05 .15
7 Dion James .01 .05
8 B.J. Surhoff .05 .15
9 Joe Magrane .01 .05
10 Kevin Seitzer .01 .05
11 Stanley Jefferson .01 .05
12 Devon White .02 .10
13 Nelson Liriano .01 .05
14 Chris James .01 .05
15 Mike Henneman .02 .10
16 Terry Steinbach .02 .10
17 John Kruk .02 .10
18 Matt Williams .40 1.00
19 Kelly Downs .01 .05
20 Bill Ripken .01 .05
21 Ozzie Guillen .05 .15
22 Luis Polonia .01 .05
23 Dave Magadan .01 .05
24 Mike Greenwell .01 .05
25 Will Clark .40 1.00
26 Mike Dunne .01 .05
27 Wally Joyner .02 .10
28 Robby Thompson .01 .05
29 Ken Caminiti .30 .75
30 Jose Canseco .40 1.00
31 Todd Benzinger .01 .05
32 Pete Incaviglia .01 .05
33 John Farrell .01 .05
34 Casey Candaele .01 .05
35 Mike Aldrete .01 .05
36 Ruben Sierra .05 .15
37 Ellis Burks .07 .20
38 Tracy Jones .01 .05
39 Kal Daniels .01 .05
40 Cory Snyder .01 .05

1988 Score Young Superstars II

COMP.FACT.SET (40) 2.00 5.00
1 Don Mattingly .40 1.00
2 Glenn Braggs .01 .05
3 Dwight Gooden .02 .10
4 Jose Lind .01 .05
5 Danny Tartabull .01 .05
6 Tony Fernandez .02 .10
7 Julio Franco .02 .10
8 Andres Galarraga .07 .20
9 Bobby Bonilla .02 .10
10 Eric Davis .02 .10
11 Gerald Young .01 .05
12 Barry Bonds .30 .75
13 Jerry Browne .01 .05
14 Jeff Blauser .02 .10
15 Mickey Brantley .01 .05
16 Floyd Youmans .01 .05
17 Bret Saberhagen .02 .10
18 Shawon Dunston .01 .05
19 Len Dykstra .02 .10
20 Darryl Strawberry .02 .10
21 Rick Aguilera .02 .10
22 Ivan Calderon .01 .05
23 Roger Clemens .40 1.00
24 Vince Coleman .01 .05
25 Gary Thurman .01 .05
26 Jeff Treadway .01 .05
27 Oddibe McDowell .01 .05
28 Fred McGriff .07 .20
29 Mark McLemore .01 .05
30 Jeff Musselman .01 .05
31 Mitch Williams .01 .05
32 Dan Plesac .01 .05
33 Juan Nieves .01 .05
34 Barry Larkin .07 .20
35 Greg Mathews .01 .05
36 Shane Mack .01 .05
37 Scott Bankhead .01 .05
38 Eric Bell .01 .05
39 Greg Swindell .01 .05
40 Kevin Elster .01 .05

1989 Score

This 660-card standard-size set was distributed by Major League Marketing. Cards were issued primarily in fin-wrapped plastic packs and factory sets. Cards feature six distinctive inner border (inside a white outer border) colors on the front. Subsets include Highlights (652-660) and Rookie Prospects (621-651). Rookie Cards in this set include Brady Anderson, Craig Biggio, Randy Johnson, Gary Sheffield, and John Smoltz.

COMPLETE SET (660) 6.00 15.00
COMP.FACT.SET (660) 6.00 15.00
1 Jose Canseco .08 .25
2 Andre Dawson .02 .10
3 Mark McGwire UER .40 1.00
4 Benito Santiago .02 .10
5 Rick Reuschel .01 .05
6 Fred McGriff .05 .15
7 Kal Daniels .01 .05
8 Gary Gaetti .01 .05
9 Ellis Burks .02 .10
10 Darryl Strawberry .02 .10
11 Julio Franco .02 .10
12 Lloyd Moseby .01 .05
13 Jeff Pico .01 .05
14 Johnny Ray .01 .05
15 Cal Ripken .30 .75
16 Dick Schofield .01 .05
17 Mel Hall .01 .05
18 Bill Ripken .01 .05
19 Brook Jacoby .01 .05
20 Kirby Puckett .08 .25
21 Bill Doran .01 .05
22 Pete O'Brien .01 .05
23 Matt Nokes .01 .05
24 Brian Fisher .01 .05
25 Jack Clark .02 .10
26 Gary Pettis .01 .05
27 Dave Valle .01 .05
28 Willie Wilson .02 .10
29 Curt Young .01 .05
30 Dale Murphy .05 .15
31 Barry Larkin .05 .15
32 Dave Stewart .02 .10
33 Mike LaValliere .01 .05
34 Glenn Hubbard .01 .05
35 Ryne Sandberg .15 .40
36 Tony Pena .01 .05
37 Greg Walker .01 .05
38 Von Hayes .01 .05
39 Kevin Mitchell .02 .10
40 Tim Raines .02 .10
41 Keith Hernandez .02 .10
42 Keith Moreland .01 .05
43 Ruben Sierra .02 .10
44 Chet Lemon .02 .10
45 Willie Randolph .02 .10
46 Andy Allanson .01 .05
47 Candy Maldonado .01 .05
48 Sid Bream .01 .05
49 Denny Walling .01 .05
50 Dave Winfield .02 .10
51 Alvin Davis .01 .05
52 Cory Snyder .01 .05
53 Hubie Brooks .01 .05
54 Chili Davis .02 .10
55 Kevin Seitzer .01 .05
56 Jose Uribe .01 .05
57 Tony Fernandez .01 .05
58 Tim Teufel .01 .05
59 Oddibe McDowell .01 .05
60 Les Lancaster .01 .05
61 Billy Hatcher .01 .05
62 Dan Gladden .01 .05
63 Marty Barrett .01 .05
64 Nick Esasky .01 .05
65 Wally Joyner .02 .10
66 Mike Greenwell .01 .05
67 Ken Williams .01 .05
68 Bob Horner .02 .10
69 Steve Sax .01 .05
70 Rickey Henderson .08 .25
71 Mitch Webster .01 .05
72 Rob Deer .01 .05
73 Jim Presley .01 .05
74 Albert Hall .01 .05
75 George Brett COR .25 .60
75A George Brett ERR .40 1.00
76 Brian Downing .02 .10
77 Dave Martinez .02 .10
78 Scott Fletcher .01 .05
79 Phil Bradley .01 .05
80 Ozzie Smith .15 .40
81 Larry Sheets .01 .05
82 Mike Aldrete .01 .05
83 Darnell Coles .01 .05
84 Len Dykstra .02 .10
85 Jim Rice .02 .10
86 Jeff Treadway .01 .05
87 Jose Lind .01 .05
88 Willie McGee .02 .10
89 Mickey Brantley .01 .05
90 Tony Gwynn .10 .30
91 R.J. Reynolds .01 .05
92 Milt Thompson .01 .05
93 Kevin McReynolds .01 .05
94 Eddie Murray UER .08 .25
'86 batting .205,
should be .305
95 Lance Parrish .02 .10
96 Ron Kittle .01 .05
97 Gerald Young .01 .05
98 Ernie Whitt .01 .05
99 Jeff Reed .01 .05
100 Don Mattingly .25 .60
101 Gerald Perry .01 .05
102 Vance Law .01 .05
103 John Shelby .01 .05
104 Chris Sabo RC .15 .40
105 Danny Tartabull .01 .05
106 Glenn Wilson .01 .05
107 Mark Davidson .01 .05
108 Dave Parker .02 .10
109 Eric Davis .02 .10
110 Alan Trammell .02 .10
111 Ozzie Virgil .01 .05
112 Frank Tanana .02 .10
113 Rafael Ramirez .01 .05
114 Dennis Martinez .02 .10
115 Jose DeLeon .01 .05
116 Bob Ojeda .01 .05
117 Doug Drabek .01 .05
118 Andy Hawkins .01 .05
119 Greg Maddux .20 .50
120 Cecil Fielder UER .02 .10
Reversed Photo on back
121 Mike Scioscia .02 .10
122 Dan Petry .01 .05
123 Terry Kennedy .01 .05
124 Kelly Downs .01 .05
125 Greg Gross UER .01 .05
Gregg on back
126 Fred Lynn .02 .10
127 Barry Bonds .60 1.50
128 Harold Baines .02 .10
129 Doyle Alexander .01 .05
130 Kevin Elster .01 .05
131 Mike Heath .01 .05
132 Teddy Higuera .01 .05
133 Charlie Leibrandt .01 .05
134 Tim Laudner .01 .05
135A Ray Knight ERR .02 .10
Reverse negative
135B Ray Knight COR .02 .10
136 Howard Johnson .02 .10
137 Terry Pendleton .02 .10
138 Andy McGaffigan .01 .05
139 Ken Oberkfell .01 .05
140 Butch Wynegar .01 .05
141 Rob Murphy .01 .05
142 Rich Renteria .01 .05
143 Jose Guzman .01 .05
144 Andres Galarraga .02 .10
145 Ricky Horton .01 .05
146 Frank DiPino .01 .05
147 Glenn Braggs .01 .05
148 John Kruk .02 .10
149 Mike Schmidt .20 .50
150 Lee Smith .02 .10
151 Robin Yount .15 .40
152 Mark Eichhorn .01 .05
153 DeWayne Buice .01 .05
154 B.J. Surhoff .02 .10
155 Vince Coleman .01 .05
156 Tony Phillips .01 .05
157 Willie Fraser .01 .05
158 Lance McCullers .01 .05
159 Greg Gagne .01 .05
160 Jesse Barfield .02 .10
161 Mark Langston .01 .05
162 Kurt Stillwell .01 .05
163 Dion James .01 .05
164 Glenn Davis .01 .05
165 Walt Weiss .01 .05
166 Dave Concepcion .02 .10
167 Alfredo Griffin .01 .05
168 Don Heinkel .01 .05
169 Luis Rivera .01 .05
170 Shane Rawley .01 .05
171 Darrell Evans .02 .10
172 Robby Thompson .01 .05
173 Jody Davis .01 .05
174 Andy Van Slyke .05 .15
175 Wade Boggs UER .05 .15
Bio says .364,
should be .356
176 Garry Templeton .02 .10
'85 stats
off-centered
177 Gary Redus .01 .05
178 Craig Lefferts .01 .05
179 Carney Lansford .02 .10
180 Ron Darling .02 .10
181 Kirk McCaskill .01 .05
182 Tony Armas .02 .10
183 Steve Farr .01 .05
184 Tom Brunansky .01 .05
185 Bryan Harvey RC UER .08 .25
'87 games 47,
should be 3
186 Mike Marshall .01 .05
187 Bo Diaz .01 .05
188 Willie Upshaw .01 .05
189 Mike Pagliarulo .01 .05
190 Mike Krukow .01 .05
191 Tommy Herr .01 .05
192 Jim Pankovits .01 .05
193 Dwight Evans .05 .15
194 Kelly Gruber .01 .05
195 Bobby Bonilla .02 .10
196 Wallace Johnson .01 .05
197 Dave Stieb .02 .10
198 Pat Borders RC .08 .25
199 Rafael Palmeiro .08 .25
200 Dwight Gooden .02 .10
201 Pete Incaviglia .01 .05
202 Chris James .01 .05
203 Marvell Wynne .01 .05
204 Pat Sheridan .01 .05
205 Don Baylor .02 .10
206 Paul O'Neill .05 .15
207 Pete Smith .01 .05
208 Mark McLemore .01 .05
209 Henry Cotto .01 .05
210 Kirk Gibson .02 .10
211 Claudell Washington .01 .05
212 Randy Bush .01 .05
213 Joe Carter .02 .10
214 Bill Buckner .02 .10
215 Bert Blyleven UER .02 .10
216 Brett Butler .02 .10
217 Lee Mazzilli .02 .10
218 Spike Owen .01 .05
219 Bill Swift .01 .05
220 Tim Wallach .01 .05
221 David Cone .02 .10
222 Don Carman .01 .05
223 Rich Gossage .02 .10
224 Bob Walk .01 .05
225 Dave Righetti .02 .10
226 Kevin Bass .01 .05
227 Kevin Gross .01 .05
228 Tim Burke .01 .05
229 Rick Mahler .01 .05
230 Lou Whitaker UER .02 .10
252 games in '85,
should be 152
231 Luis Alicea RC .08 .25
232 Roberto Alomar .08 .25
233 Bob Boone .02 .10
234 Dickie Thon .01 .05
235 Shawon Dunston .01 .05
236 Pete Stanicek .01 .05
237 Craig Biggio RC 1.50 4.00
238 Dennis Boyd .01 .05
239 Tom Candiotti .01 .05
240 Gary Carter .02 .10
241 Mike Stanley .01 .05
242 Ken Phelps .01 .05
243 Chris Bosio .01 .05
244 Les Straker .01 .05
245 Dave Smith .01 .05
246 John Candelaria .01 .05
247 Joe Orsulak .01 .05
248 Storm Davis .01 .05
249 Floyd Bannister UER .01 .05
ML Batting Record
250 Jack Morris .02 .10
251 Bret Saberhagen .02 .10
252 Tom Niedenfuer .01 .05
253 Neal Heaton .01 .05
254 Eric Show .01 .05
255 Juan Samuel .01 .05
256 Dale Sveum .01 .05
257 Jim Gott .01 .05
258 Scott Garrelts .01 .05
259 Larry McWilliams .01 .05
260 Steve Bedrosian .01 .05
261 Jack Howell .01 .05
262 Jay Tibbs .01 .05
263 Jamie Moyer .02 .10
264 Doug Sisk .01 .05
265 Todd Worrell .01 .05
266 John Farrell .01 .05
267 Dave Collins .01 .05
268 Sid Fernandez .01 .05
269 Tom Brookens .01 .05
270 Shane Mack .01 .05
271 Paul Kilgus .01 .05
272 Chuck Crim .01 .05
273 Bob Knepper .01 .05
274 Mike Moore .01 .05
275 Guillermo Hernandez .01 .05
276 Dennis Eckersley .05 .15
277 Graig Nettles .02 .10
278 Rich Dotson .01 .05
279 Larry Herndon .01 .05
280 Gene Larkin .01 .05
281 Roger McDowell .01 .05
282 Greg Swindell .01 .05
283 Juan Agosto .01 .05
284 Jeff M. Robinson .01 .05
285 Mike Dunne .01 .05
286 Greg Mathews .01 .05
287 Kent Tekulve .01 .05
288 Jerry Mumphrey .01 .05
289 Jack McDowell .02 .10
290 Frank Viola .02 .10
291 Mark Gubicza .01 .05
292 Dave Schmidt .01 .05
293 Mike Henneman .01 .05
294 Jimmy Jones .01 .05
295 Charlie Hough .02 .10
296 Rafael Santana .01 .05
297 Chris Speier .01 .05
298 Mike Witt .01 .05
299 Pascual Perez .01 .05
300 Nolan Ryan .40 1.00
301 Mitch Williams .01 .05
302 Mookie Wilson .02 .10
303 Mackey Sasser .01 .05
304 John Cerutti .01 .05
305 Jeff Reardon .02 .10
306 Randy Myers UER .02 .10
6 hits in '87,
should be 61
307 Greg Brock .01 .05
308 Bob Welch .02 .10
309 Jeff D. Robinson .01 .05
310 Harold Reynolds .02 .10
311 Jim Walewander .01 .05
312 Dave Magadan .01 .05
313 Jim Gantner .01 .05
314 Walt Terrell .01 .05
315 Wally Backman .01 .05
316 Luis Salazar .01 .05
317 Rick Rhoden .01 .05
318 Tom Henke .01 .05
319 Mike Macfarlane RC .08 .25
320 Dan Plesac .01 .05
321 Calvin Schiraldi .01 .05
322 Stan Javier .01 .05
323 Devon White .02 .10
324 Scott Bradley .01 .05
325 Bruce Hurst .01 .05
326 Manny Lee .01 .05
327 Rick Aguilera .02 .10
328 Bruce Ruffin .01 .05
329 Ed Whitson .01 .05
330 Bo Jackson .08 .25
331 Ivan Calderon .01 .05
332 Mickey Hatcher .01 .05
333 Barry Jones .01 .05
334 Ron Hassey .01 .05
335 Bill Wegman .01 .05
336 Damon Berryhill .01 .05
337 Steve Ontiveros .01 .05
338 Dan Pasqua .01 .05
339 Bill Pecota .01 .05
340 Greg Cadaret .01 .05

341 Scott Bankhead .01 .05
342 Ron Guidry .02 .10
343 Danny Heep .01 .05
344 Bob Brower .01 .05
345 Rich Gedman .01 .05
346 Nelson Santovenia .01 .05
347 George Bell .02 .10
348 Ted Power .01 .05
349 Mark Grant .01 .05
350 Roger Clemens COR .40 1.00
350A Roger Clemens ERR .75 2.00
351 Bill Long .01 .05
352 Jay Bell .02 .10
353 Steve Balboni .01 .05
354 Bob Kipper .01 .05
355 Steve Jeltz .01 .05
356 Jesse Orosco .01 .05
357 Bob Dernier .01 .05
358 Mickey Tettleton .01 .05
359 Duane Ward .01 .05
360 Darrin Jackson .02 .10
361 Rey Quinones .01 .05
362 Mark Grace .08 .25
363 Steve Lake .01 .05
364 Pat Perry .01 .05
365 Terry Steinbach .02 .10
366 Alan Ashby .01 .05
367 Jeff Montgomery .01 .05
368 Steve Buechele .01 .05
369 Chris Brown .01 .05
370 Orel Hershiser .02 .10
371 Todd Benzinger .01 .05
372 Ron Gant .02 .10
373 Paul Assenmacher .01 .05
374 Joey Meyer .01 .05
375 Neil Allen .01 .05
376 Mike Davis .01 .05
377 Jeff Parrett .01 .05
378 Jay Howell .01 .05
379 Rafael Belliard .01 .05
380 Luis Polonia UER .01 .05
2 triples in '87, should be 10
381 Keith Atherton .01 .05
382 Kent Hrbek .02 .10
383 Bob Stanley .01 .05
384 Dave LaPoint .01 .05
385 Rance Mulliniks .01 .05
386 Melido Perez .01 .05
387 Doug Jones .01 .05
388 Steve Lyons .01 .05
389 Alejandro Pena .01 .05
390 Frank White .02 .10
391 Pat Tabler .01 .05
392 Eric Plunk .01 .05
393 Mike Maddux .01 .05
394 Allan Anderson .01 .05
395 Bob Brenly .01 .05
396 Rick Cerone .01 .05
397 Scott Terry .01 .05
398 Mike Jackson .01 .05
399 Bobby Thigpen UER .01 .05
Bio says 37 saves in '88, should be 34
400 Don Sutton .02 .10
401 Cecil Espy .01 .05
402 Junior Ortiz .01 .05
403 Mike Smithson .01 .05
404 Bud Black .01 .05
405 Tom Foley .01 .05
406 Andres Thomas .01 .05
407 Rick Sutcliffe .02 .10
408 Brian Harper .01 .05
409 John Smiley .01 .05
410 Juan Nieves .01 .05
411 Shawn Abner .01 .05
412 Wes Gardner .01 .05
413 Darren Daulton .02 .10
414 Juan Berenguer .01 .05
415 Charles Hudson .01 .05
416 Rick Honeycutt .01 .05
417 Greg Booker .01 .05
418 Tim Belcher .01 .05
419 Don August .01 .05
420 Dale Mohorcic .01 .05
421 Steve Lombardozzi .01 .05
422 Atlee Hammaker .01 .05
423 Jerry Don Gleaton .01 .05
424 Scott Bailes .01 .05
425 Bruce Sutter .02 .10
426 Randy Ready .01 .05
427 Jerry Reed .01 .05
428 Bryn Smith .01 .05
429 Tim Leary .01 .05
430 Mark Clear .01 .05
431 Terry Leach .01 .05
432 John Moses .01 .05
433 Ozzie Guillen .02 .10
434 Gene Nelson .01 .05
435 Gary Ward .01 .05
436 Luis Aguayo .01 .05
437 Fernando Valenzuela .02 .10
438 Jeff Russell UER .01 .05
Saves total does not add up correctly
439 Cecilio Guante .01 .05
440 Don Robinson .01 .05
441 Rick Anderson .01 .05
442 Tom Glavine .08 .25
443 Daryl Boston .01 .05
444 Joe Price .01 .05
445 Stu Cliburn .01 .05
446 Manny Trillo .01 .05
447 Joel Skinner .01 .05
448 Charlie Puleo .01 .05
449 Carlton Fisk .05 .15
450 Will Clark .05 .15
451 Otis Nixon .01 .05
452 Rick Schu .01 .05
453 Todd Stottlemyre UER .01 .05
ML Batting Record
454 Tim Birtsas .01 .05
455 Dave Gallagher .01 .05
456 Barry Lyons .01 .05
457 Fred Manrique .01 .05
458 Ernest Riles .01 .05
459 Doug Jennings RC .01 .05
460 Joe Magrane .01 .05
461 Jamie Quirk .01 .05
462 Jack Armstrong RC .08 .25
463 Bobby Witt .01 .05
464 Keith A. Miller .01 .05
465 Todd Burns .01 .05
466 John Dopson .01 .05
467 Rich Yett .01 .05
468 Craig Reynolds .01 .05
469 Dave Bergman .01 .05
470 Rex Hudler .01 .05
471 Eric King .01 .05
472 Joaquin Andujar .02 .10
473 Sil Campusano .01 .05
474 Terry Mulholland .01 .05
475 Mike Flanagan .01 .05
476 Greg A. Harris .01 .05
477 Tommy John .02 .10
478 Dave Anderson .01 .05
479 Fred Toliver .01 .05
480 Jimmy Key .02 .10
481 Donell Nixon .01 .05
482 Mark Portugal .01 .05
483 Tom Pagnozzi .01 .05
484 Jeff Kunkel .01 .05
485 Frank Williams .01 .05
486 Jody Reed .01 .05
487 Roberto Kelly .01 .05
488 Shawn Hillegas UER .01 .05
165 innings in '87, should be 165.2
489 Jerry Reuss .01 .05
490 Mark Davis .01 .05
491 Jeff Sellers .01 .05
492 Zane Smith .01 .05
493 Al Newman .01 .05
494 Mike Young .01 .05
495 Larry Parrish .01 .05
496 Herm Winningham .01 .05
497 Carmen Castillo .01 .05
498 Joe Hesketh .01 .05
499 Darrell Miller .01 .05
500 Mike LaCoss .01 .05
501 Charlie Lea .01 .05
502 Bruce Benedict .01 .05
503 Chuck Finley .02 .10
504 Brad Wellman .01 .05
505 Tim Crews .01 .05
506 Ken Gerhart .01 .05
507A Brian Holton ERR .01 .05
Born 1/25/65 Denver, should be 11/29/59 in McKeesport
507B Brian Holton COR .75 2.00
508 Dennis Lamp .01 .05
509 Bobby Meacham UER .01 .05
'84 games 099
510 Tracy Jones .01 .05
511 Mike R. Fitzgerald .01 .05
512 Jeff Bittiger .01 .05
513 Tim Flannery .01 .05
514 Ray Hayward .01 .05
515 Dave Leiper .01 .05
516 Rod Scurry .01 .05
517 Carmelo Martinez .01 .05
518 Curtis Wilkerson .01 .05
519 Stan Jefferson .01 .05
520 Dan Quisenberry .01 .05
521 Lloyd McClendon .01 .05
522 Steve Trout .01 .05
523 Larry Andersen .01 .05
524 Don Aase .01 .05
525 Bob Forsch .01 .05
526 Geno Petralli .01 .05
527 Angel Salazar .01 .05
528 Mike Schooler .01 .05
529 Jose Oquendo .01 .05
530 Jay Buhner UER .02 .10
Wearing 43 on front, listed as 34 on back
531 Tom Bolton .01 .05
532 Al Nipper .01 .05
533 Dave Henderson .01 .05
534 John Costello RC .01 .05
535 Donnie Moore .01 .05
536 Mike Laga .01 .05
537 Mike Gallego .01 .05
538 Jim Clancy .01 .05
539 Joel Youngblood .01 .05
540 Rick Leach .01 .05
541 Kevin Romine .01 .05
542 Mark Salas .01 .05
543 Greg Minton .01 .05
544 Dave Palmer .01 .05
545 Dwayne Murphy UER .01 .05
Game-sinning
546 Jim Deshaies .01 .05
547 Don Gordon .01 .05
548 Ricky Jordan RC .08 .25
549 Mike Boddicker .01 .05
550 Mike Scott .02 .10
551 Jeff Ballard .01 .05
552A Jose Rijo ERR .02 .10
Uniform listed as 24 on back
552B Jose Rijo COR .02 .10
Uniform listed as 27 on back
553 Danny Darwin .01 .05
554 Tom Browning .01 .05
555 Danny Jackson .01 .05
556 Rick Dempsey .01 .05
557 Jeffrey Leonard .01 .05
558 Jeff Musselman .01 .05
559 Ron Robinson .01 .05
560 John Tudor .02 .10
561 Don Slaught UER .01 .05
237 games in 1987
562 Dennis Rasmussen .01 .05
563 Brady Anderson RC .15 .40
564 Pedro Guerrero .02 .10
565 Paul Molitor .02 .10
566 Terry Clark .01 .05
567 Terry Puhl .01 .05
568 Mike Campbell .01 .05
569 Paul Mirabella .01 .05
570 Jeff Hamilton .01 .05
571 Oswald Peraza RC .01 .05
572 Bob McClure .01 .05
573 Jose Bautista RC .02 .10
574 Alex Trevino .01 .05
575 John Franco .02 .10
576 Mark Parent RC .01 .05
577 Nelson Liriano .01 .05
578 Steve Shields .01 .05
579 Odell Jones .01 .05
580 Al Leiter .08 .25
581 Dave Stapleton .01 .05
582 Orel Hershiser .08 .25
Jose Canseco
Kirk Gibson
Dave Stewart WS
583 Donnie Hill .01 .05
584 Chuck Jackson .01 .05
585 Rene Gonzales .01 .05
586 Tracy Woodson .01 .05
587 Jim Adduci .01 .05
588 Mario Soto .02 .10
589 Jeff Blauser .01 .05
590 Jim Traber .01 .05
591 Jon Perlman .01 .05
592 Mark Williamson .01 .05
593 Dave Meads .01 .05
594 Jim Eisenreich .01 .05
595A Paul Gibson P1 .40 1.00
595B Paul Gibson P2 .01 .05
Airbrushed leg on player in background
596 Mike Birkbeck .01 .05
597 Terry Francona .02 .10
598 Paul Zuvella .01 .05
599 Franklin Stubbs .01 .05
600 Gregg Jefferies .01 .05
601 John Cangelosi .01 .05
602 Mike Sharperson .01 .05
603 Mike Diaz .01 .05
604 Gary Varsho .01 .05
605 Terry Blocker .01 .05
606 Charlie O'Brien .01 .05
607 Jim Eppard .01 .05
608 John Davis .01 .05
609 Ken Griffey Sr. .02 .10
610 Buddy Bell .02 .10
611 Ted Simmons UER .02 .10
'78 stats Cardinal
612 Matt Williams .08 .25
613 Danny Cox .01 .05
614 Al Pedrique .01 .05
615 Ron Oester .01 .05
616 John Smoltz RC .60 1.50
617 Bob Melvin .01 .05
618 Rob Dibble RC .15 .40
619 Kirt Manwaring .01 .05
620 Felix Fermin .01 .05
621 Doug Dascenzo .01 .05
622 Bill Brennan .01 .05
623 Carlos Quintana RC .02 .10
624 Mike Harkey RC UER .02 .10
13 and 31 walks in '88, should be 35 and 33
625 Gary Sheffield RC .60 1.50
626 Tom Prince .01 .05
627 Steve Searcy .01 .05
628 Charlie Hayes RC .08 .25
Listed as outfielder
629 Felix Jose RC UER .02 .10
Modesto misspelled as Modesta
630 Sandy Alomar Jr. RC .15 .40
Inconsistent design, portrait on front
631 Derek Lilliquist RC .02 .10
632 Geronimo Berroa .01 .05
633 Luis Medina .01 .05
634 Tom Gordon RC UER .20 .50
635 Ramon Martinez RC .08 .25
636 Craig Worthington .01 .05
637 Edgar Martinez .08 .25
638 Chad Kreuter RC .08 .25
639 Ron Jones .02 .10
640 Van Snider RC .02 .10
641 Lance Blankenship RC .02 .10
642 Dwight Smith RC UER .08 .25
10 HR's in '87, should be 18
643 Cameron Drew .01 .05
644 Jerald Clark RC .02 .10
645 Randy Johnson RC 1.25 3.00
646 Norm Charlton RC .08 .25
647 Todd Frohwirth UER .01 .05
Southpaw on back
648 Luis De Los Santos .01 .05
649 Tim Jones .01 .05
650 Dave West RC UER .02 .10
ML hits 3
should be 6
651 Bob Milacki .01 .05
652 Wrigley Field HL .02 .10
653 Orel Hershiser HL .01 .05
654A Wade Boggs HL ERR .05 .15
'seasno' on back
654B Wade Boggs HL COR .02 .10
655 Jose Canseco HL .08 .25
656 Doug Jones HL .01 .05
657 Rickey Henderson HL .05 .15
658 Tom Browning HL .01 .05
659 Mike Greenwell HL .01 .05
660 Boston Red Sox HL .01 .05

1989 Score Rookie/Traded

The 1989 Score Rookie and Traded set contains 110 standard-size cards. The set was issued exclusively in factory set form through hobby dealers. The set was distributed in a blue box with 10 Magic Motion trivia cards. The fronts have coral green borders with pink diamonds at the bottom. Cards 1-80 feature traded players; cards 81-110 feature 1989 rookies. Rookie Cards in this set include Jim Abbott, Joey (Albert) Belle, Ken Griffey Jr. and John Wetteland.

COMP.FACT.SET (110) 6.00 15.00
1T Rafael Palmeiro .08 .25
2T Nolan Ryan .60 1.50
3T Jack Clark .02 .10
4T Dave LaPoint .01 .05
5T Mike Moore .01 .05
6T Pete O'Brien .01 .05
7T Jeffrey Leonard .01 .05
8T Rob Murphy .01 .05
9T Tom Herr .01 .05
10T Claudell Washington .01 .05
11T Mike Pagliarulo .01 .05
12T Steve Lake .01 .05
13T Spike Owen .01 .05
14T Andy Hawkins .01 .05
15T Todd Benzinger .01 .05
16T Mookie Wilson .02 .10
17T Bert Blyleven .02 .10
18T Jeff Treadway .01 .05
19T Bruce Hurst .01 .05
20T Steve Sax .01 .05
21T Juan Samuel .01 .05
22T Jesse Barfield .02 .10
23T Carmen Castillo .01 .05
24T Terry Leach .01 .05
25T Mark Langston .01 .05
26T Eric King .01 .05
27T Steve Balboni .01 .05
28T Len Dykstra .02 .10
29T Keith Moreland .01 .05
30T Terry Kennedy .01 .05
31T Eddie Murray .08 .25
32T Mitch Williams .01 .05
33T Jeff Parrett .01 .05
34T Wally Backman .01 .05
35T Julio Franco .02 .10
36T Lance Parrish .02 .10
37T Nick Esasky .01 .05
38T Luis Polonia .01 .05
39T Kevin Gross .01 .05
40T John Dopson .01 .05
41T Willie Randolph .02 .10
42T Jim Clancy .01 .05
43T Tracy Jones .01 .05
44T Phil Bradley .01 .05
45T Milt Thompson .01 .05
46T Chris James .01 .05
47T Scott Fletcher .01 .05
48T Kal Daniels .01 .05
49T Steve Bedrosian .01 .05
50T Rickey Henderson .08 .25
51T Dion James .01 .05
52T Tim Leary .01 .05
53T Roger McDowell .01 .05
54T Mel Hall .01 .05
55T Dickie Thon .01 .05
56T Zane Smith .01 .05
57T Danny Heep .01 .05
58T Bob McClure .01 .05
59T Brian Holton .01 .05
60T Randy Ready .01 .05
61T Bob Melvin .01 .05
62T Harold Baines .02 .10
63T Lance McCullers .01 .05
64T Jody Davis .01 .05
65T Darrell Evans .02 .10
66T Joel Youngblood .01 .05
67T Frank Viola .02 .10
68T Mike Aldrete .01 .05
69T Greg Cadaret .01 .05
70T John Kruk .02 .10
71T Pat Sheridan .01 .05
72T Oddibe McDowell .01 .05
73T Tom Brookens .01 .05
74T Bob Boone .02 .10
75T Walt Terrell .01 .05
76T Joel Skinner .01 .05
77T Randy Johnson .75 2.00
78T Felix Fermin .01 .05
79T Rick Mahler .01 .05
80T Richard Dotson .01 .05
81T Cris Carpenter RC * .02 .10
82T Billy Spiers RC .08 .25
83T Junior Felix RC .02 .10
84T Joe Girardi RC .15 .40
85T Jerome Walton RC .08 .25
86T Greg Litton .01 .05
87T Greg W.Harris RC .02 .10
88T Jim Abbott RC .40 1.00
89T Kevin Brown .08 .25
90T John Wetteland RC .15 .40
91T Gary Wayne .01 .05
92T Rich Monteleone .01 .05
93T Bob Geren RC .01 .05
94T Clay Parker .01 .05
95T Steve Finley RC .30 .75
96T Gregg Olson RC .08 .25
97T Ken Patterson .01 .05
98T Ken Hill RC .08 .25
99T Scott Scudder RC .02 .10
100T Ken Griffey Jr. RC 3.00 8.00
101T Jeff Brantley RC .08 .25
102T Donn Pall .01 .05
103T Carlos Martinez RC .02 .10
104T Joe Oliver RC .08 .25
105T Omar Vizquel RC .40 1.00
106T Albert Belle RC .40 1.00
107T Kenny Rogers RC .75 2.00
108T Mark Carreon .01 .05
109T Rolando Roomes .01 .05
110T Pete Harnisch RC .08 .25

1989 Score Hottest 100 Rookies

This set was distributed by Publications International in January 1989 through many retail stores and chains; the card set was packaged along with a colorful 48-page book for a suggested retail price of 12.95. Supposedly 225,000 sets were produced. The cards measure the standard size and show full color on both sides of the card. The cards were produced by Score as indicated on the card backs. The set is subtitled "Rising Star" on the reverse. The first six cards (1-6) of a 12-card set of Score's trivia cards, subtitled "Rookies to Remember" is included along with each set. This set is distinguished by the sharp blue borders and the player's first initial inside a yellow triangle in the lower left corner of the obverse. The set features Dave Justice appearing one year before his Rookie Card year.

COMP.FACT.SET (100) 4.00 10.00
1 Gregg Jefferies .01 .05
2 Vicente Palacios .01 .05
3 Cameron Drew .01 .05
4 Doug Dascenzo .01 .05
5 Luis Medina .01 .05
6 Craig Worthington .01 .05
7 Rob Ducey .01 .05
8 Hal Morris .05 .15
9 Bill Brennan .01 .05
10 Gary Sheffield .40 1.00
11 Mike Devereaux .01 .05
12 Hensley Meulens .01 .05
13 Carlos Quintana .01 .05
14 Todd Frohwirth .01 .05
15 Scott Lusader .01 .05
16 Mark Carreon .01 .05
17 Torey Lovullo .01 .05
18 Randy Velarde .05 .15
19 Billy Bean .05 .15
20 Lance Blankenship .01 .05
21 Chris Gwynn .01 .05
22 Felix Jose .01 .05
23 Derek Lilliquist .01 .05
24 Gary Thurman .01 .05
25 Ron Jones .01 .05
26 Dave Justice .75 2.00
27 Johnny Paredes .01 .05
28 Tim Jones .01 .05
29 Jose Gonzalez .01 .05
30 Geronimo Berroa .01 .05
31 Trevor Wilson .01 .05
32 Morris Madden .01 .05
33 Lance Johnson .01 .05
34 Marvin Freeman .01 .05
35 Jose Cecena .01 .05
36 Jim Corsi .01 .05
37 Rolando Roomes .01 .05
38 Scott Medvin .01 .05
39 Charlie Hayes .01 .05
40 Edgar Martinez .20 .50
41 Van Snider .01 .05
42 John Fishel .01 .05
43 Bruce Fields .01 .05
44 Darryl Hamilton .01 .05
45 Tom Prince .01 .05
46 Kirt Manwaring .01 .05
47 Steve Searcy .01 .05
48 Mike Harkey .01 .05
49 German Gonzalez .01 .05
50 Tony Perezchica .01 .05
51 Chad Kreuter .01 .05
52 Luis DeLosSantos .01 .05
53 Steve Curry .01 .05
54 Greg Briley .01 .05
55 Ramon Martinez .08 .25
56 Ron Tingley .01 .05
57 Randy Kramer .01 .05
58 Alex Madrid .01 .05
59 Kevin Reimer .01 .05
60 Dave Otto .01 .05
61 Ken Patterson .01 .05
62 Keith Miller .01 .05
63 Randy Johnson 2.00 5.00
64 Dwight Smith .05 .15
65 Eric Yelding .01 .05
66 Bob Geren .01 .05
67 Shane Turner .01 .05
68 Tom Gordon .15 .40
69 Jeff Huson .01 .05
70 Marty Brown .01 .05
71 Nelson Santovenia .01 .05
72 Roberto Alomar .40 1.00
73 Mike Schooler .01 .05
74 Pete Smith .01 .05
75 John Costello .01 .05
76 Chris Sabo .01 .05
77 Damon Berryhill .01 .05
78 Mark Grace .75 2.00
79 Melido Perez .01 .05
80 Al Leiter .15 .40
81 Todd Stottlemyre .01 .05
82 Mackey Sasser .01 .05
83 Don August .01 .05
84 Jeff Treadway .01 .05
85 Jody Reed .01 .05
86 Mike Campbell .01 .05
87 Ron Gant .05 .15
88 Ricky Jordan .01 .05
89 Terry Clark .01 .05
90 Roberto Kelly .01 .05
91 Pat Borders .05 .15
92 Bryan Harvey .01 .05
93 Joey Meyer .01 .05
94 Tim Belcher .01 .05
95 Walt Weiss .01 .05
96 Dave Gallagher .01 .05
97 Mike Macfarlane .01 .05
98 Craig Biggio 1.00 2.50
99 Jack Armstrong .01 .05
100 Todd Burns .01 .05

1989 Score Hottest 100 Stars

This set was distributed by Publications International in January 1989 through many retail stores and chains; the card set was packaged along with a colorful 48-page book for a suggested retail price of 12.95. Supposedly 225,000 sets were produced. The cards measure the standard size and show full color on both sides of the card. The cards were produced by Score as indicated on the card backs. The set is subtitled "Superstar" on the reverse. The last six cards (7-12) of a 12-card set of Score's trivia cards, subtitled "Rookies to Remember" is included along with each set. This set is distinguished by the sharp red borders and the player's first initial inside a yellow triangle in the upper left corner of the obverse.

COMP. FACT.SET (100) 4.00 10.00
1 Jose Canseco .40 1.00
2 David Cone .20 .50
3 Dave Winfield .40 1.00
4 George Brett .75 2.00
5 Frank Viola .01 .05
6 Cory Snyder .01 .05
7 Alan Trammell .10 .30
8 Dwight Evans .05 .15
9 Tim Leary .01 .05
10 Don Mattingly .75 2.00
11 Kirby Puckett .40 1.00
12 Carney Lansford .05 .15
13 Dennis Martinez .05 .15
14 Kent Hrbek .05 .15
15 Dwight Gooden .05 .15
16 Dennis Eckersley .30 .75
17 Kevin Seitzer .05 .15
18 Lee Smith .05 .15
19 Danny Tartabull .01 .05
20 Gerald Perry .01 .05
21 Gary Gaetti .05 .15
22 Rick Reuschel .05 .15
23 Keith Hernandez .05 .15
24 Jeff Reardon .05 .15
25 Mark McGwire .60 1.50
26 Juan Samuel .01 .05
27 Jack Clark .01 .05
28 Robin Yount .40 1.00
29 Steve Bedrosian .01 .05
30 Kirk Gibson .05 .15
31 Barry Bonds .60 1.50
32 Dan Plesac .01 .05
33 Steve Sax .01 .05
34 Jeff M. Robinson .01 .05
35 Orel Hershiser .05 .15
36 Julio Franco .05 .15
37 Dave Righetti .01 .05
38 Bob Knepper .01 .05
39 Carlton Fisk .40 1.00
40 Tony Gwynn .75 2.00
41 Doug Jones .01 .05
42 Bobby Bonilla .05 .15
43 Ellis Burks .10 .30
44 Pedro Guerrero .01 .05
45 Rickey Henderson .60 1.50
46 Glenn Davis .01 .05
47 Benito Santiago .05 .15
48 Greg Maddux 1.00 2.50
49 Teddy Higuera .01 .05
50 Darryl Strawberry .05 .15
51 Ozzie Guillen .10 .30
52 Barry Larkin .20 .50
53 Tony Fernandez .05 .15
54 Ryne Sandberg .60 1.50
55 Joe Carter .10 .30
56 Rafael Palmeiro .30 .75
57 Paul Molitor .40 1.00
58 Eric Davis .05 .15
59 Mike Henneman .01 .05
60 Mike Scott .05 .15
61 Tom Browning .01 .05
62 Mark Davis .01 .05
63 Tom Henke .01 .05
64 Nolan Ryan 1.50 4.00
65 Fred McGriff .20 .50
66 Dale Murphy .20 .50
67 Mark Langston .01 .05
68 Bobby Thigpen .01 .05
69 Mark Gubicza .01 .05
70 Mike Greenwell .01 .05
71 Ron Darling .01 .05
72 Gerald Young .01 .05
73 Wally Joyner .05 .15
74 Andres Galarraga .20 .50
75 Danny Jackson .01 .05
76 Mike Schmidt .40 1.00
77 Cal Ripken 1.50 4.00
78 Alvin Davis .01 .05
79 Bruce Hurst .01 .05
80 Andre Dawson .20 .50
81 Bob Boone .05 .15
82 Harold Reynolds .05 .15
83 Eddie Murray .40 1.00
84 Robby Thompson .01 .05
85 Will Clark .20 .50
86 Vince Coleman .01 .05
87 Doug Drabek .01 .05
88 Ozzie Smith .60 1.50
89 Bob Welch .01 .05
90 Roger Clemens .75 2.00
91 George Bell .01 .05
92 Andy Van Slyke .05 .15
93 Willie McGee .05 .15
94 Todd Worrell .01 .05
95 Tim Raines .05 .15
96 Kevin McReynolds .01 .05
97 John Franco .05 .15
98 Jim Gott .01 .05
99 Johnny Ray .01 .05
100 Wade Boggs .40 1.00

1989 Scoremasters

COMP.FACT.SET (42) 4.00 10.00
DISTRIBUTED IN FACTORY SET FORM ONLY
1 Bo Jackson .08 .25
2 Jerome Walton .02 .10
3 Cal Ripken .30 .75
4 Mike Scott .01 .05
5 Nolan Ryan .40 1.00
6 Don Mattingly .25 .60
7 Tom Gordon .05 .15
8 Jack Morris .02 .10
9 Carlton Fisk .07 .20
10 Will Clark .05 .15
11 George Brett .25 .60
12 Kevin Mitchell .02 .10
13 Mark Langston .01 .05
14 Dave Stewart .02 .10
15 Dale Murphy .05 .15
16 Gary Gaetti .02 .10
17 Wade Boggs .05 .15
18 Eric Davis .02 .10
19 Kirby Puckett .08 .25
20 Roger Clemens .40 1.00
21 Orel Hershiser .02 .10
22 Mark Grace .08 .25
23 Ryne Sandberg .15 .40
24 Barry Larkin .05 .15
25 Ellis Burks .02 .10
26 Dwight Gooden .02 .10
27 Ozzie Smith .15 .40
28 Andre Dawson .02 .10
29 Julio Franco .02 .10
30 Ken Griffey Jr. 8.00 20.00
31 Ruben Sierra .02 .10
32 Mark McGwire .40 1.00
33 Andres Galarraga .02 .10
34 Joe Carter .02 .10
35 Vince Coleman .01 .05
36 Mike Greenwell .01 .05
37 Tony Gwynn .10 .30
38 Andy Van Slyke .05 .15
39 Gregg Jefferies .02 .10
40 Jose Canseco .08 .25
41 Dave Winfield .02 .10
42 Darryl Strawberry .02 .10
NNO Don Mattingly Promo 2.00 5.00
NNO Jose Canseco Sample

1989 Score Young Superstars I

COMPLETE SET (42) 3.00 8.00
ONE PER RACK PACK
1 Gregg Jefferies .15 .40
2 Jody Reed .08 .25
3 Mark Grace .40 1.00
4 Dave Gallagher .08 .25
5 Bo Jackson .40 1.00
6 Jay Buhner .15 .40
7 Melido Perez .08 .25
8 Bobby Witt .08 .25
9 David Cone .15 .40
10 Chris Sabo .08 .25
11 Pat Borders .08 .25
12 Mark Grant .08 .25
13 Mike Macfarlane .08 .25
14 Mike Jackson .08 .25
15 Ricky Jordan .08 .25
16 Ron Gant .15 .40
17 Al Leiter .40 1.00
18 Jeff Parrett .08 .25
19 Pete Smith .08 .25
20 Walt Weiss .15 .40
21 Doug Drabek .08 .25
22 Kirt Manwaring .08 .25
23 Keith Miller .08 .25
24 Damon Berryhill .08 .25
25 Gary Sheffield 2.00 5.00
26 Brady Anderson .25 .60
27 Mitch Williams .08 .25
28 Roberto Alomar .40 1.00
29 Bobby Thigpen .08 .25
30 Bryan Harvey UER .08 .25
31 Jose Rijo .08 .25
32 Dave West .08 .25
33 Joey Meyer .08 .25
34 Allan Anderson .08 .25
35 Rafael Palmeiro .40 1.00
36 Tim Belcher .08 .25
37 John Smiley .08 .25
38 Mackey Sasser .08 .25
39 Greg Maddux .75 2.00
40 Ramon Martinez .15 .40
41 Randy Myers .15 .40
42 Scott Bankhead .08 .25

1989 Score Young Superstars II

COMP.FACT.SET (42) 10.00 25.00
DISTRIBUTED IN FACTORY SET FORM ONLY
1 Sandy Alomar Jr. .25 .60
2 Tom Gordon .25 .60
3 Ron Jones .08 .25
4 Todd Burns .08 .25
5 Paul O'Neill .25 .60
6 Gene Larkin .08 .25
7 Eric King .08 .25
8 Jeff M. Robinson .08 .25
9 Bill Wegman .08 .25
10 Cecil Espy .08 .25
11 Jose Guzman .08 .25
12 Kelly Gruber .08 .25
13 Duane Ward .08 .25
14 Mark Gubicza .08 .25
15 Norm Charlton .15 .40
16 Jose Oquendo .08 .25
17 Geronimo Berroa .08 .25
18 Ken Griffey Jr. 8.00 20.00
19 Lance McCullers .08 .25
20 Todd Stottlemyre .25 .60
21 Craig Worthington .08 .25
22 Mike Devereaux .08 .25
23 Tom Glavine .40 1.00
24 Dale Sveum .08 .25
25 Roberto Kelly .15 .40
26 Luis Medina .08 .25
27 Steve Searcy .08 .25
28 Don August .08 .25
29 Shawn Hillegas .08 .25
30 Mike Campbell .08 .25
31 Mike Harkey .08 .25
32 Randy Johnson 4.00 10.00
33 Craig Biggio 2.00 5.00
34 Mike Schooler .08 .25
35 Andres Thomas .08 .25
36 Jerome Walton .15 .40
37 Cris Carpenter .08 .25
38 Kevin Mitchell .15 .40
39 Eddie Williams .08 .25
40 Chad Kreuter .08 .25
41 Danny Jackson .08 .25
42 Kurt Stillwell .08 .25

1990 Score Promos

*PROMOS: 10X TO 20X BASIC CARDS

1990 Score

The 1990 Score set contains 704 standard-size cards. Cards were distributed in plastic-wrap packs and factory sets. The front borders are red, blue, green or white. The vertically oriented backs are white with borders that match the fronts, and feature color mugshots. Subsets include Draft Picks (661-682) and Dream Team (683-695). A special black and white horizontal-designed card of Bo Jackson in football pads holding a bat above his shoulders was a big hit in 1990. That card traded for as much as $10 but has since cooled off. Nevertheless, it remains one of the most noteworthy cards issued in the early 1990's. Rookie Cards of note include Juan Gonzalez, Dave Justice, Chuck Knoblauch, Dean Palmer, Sammy Sosa, Frank Thomas, Mo Vaughn, Larry Walker and Bernie Williams. A ten-card set of Dream Team Rookies was inserted into each hobby factory set, but was not included in retail factory sets.

COMPLETE SET (704) 6.00 15.00
COMP.RETAIL SET (704) 6.00 15.00
COMP.HOBBY SET (714) 6.00 15.00
1 Don Mattingly .25 .60
2 Cal Ripken .30 .75

3 Dwight Evans .05 .15
4 Barry Bonds .40 1.00
5 Kevin McReynolds .01 .05
6 Ozzie Guillen .02 .10
7 Terry Kennedy .01 .05
8 Bryan Harvey .01 .05
9 Alan Trammell .02 .10
10 Cory Snyder .01 .05
11 Jody Reed .01 .05
12 Roberto Alomar .05 .15
13 Pedro Guerrero .01 .05
14 Gary Redus .01 .05
15 Marty Barrett .01 .05
16 Ricky Jordan .01 .05
17 Joe Magrane .01 .05
18 Sid Fernandez .01 .05
19 Richard Dotson .01 .05
20 Jack Clark .02 .10
21 Bob Walk .01 .05
22 Ron Karkovice .01 .05
23 Lenny Harris .01 .05
24 Phil Bradley .01 .05
25 Andres Galarraga .02 .10
26 Brian Downing .01 .05
27 Dave Martinez .01 .05
28 Eric King .01 .05
29 Barry Lyons .01 .05
30 Dave Schmidt .01 .05
31 Mike Boddicker .01 .05
32 Tom Foley .01 .05
33 Brady Anderson .02 .10
34 Jim Presley .01 .05
35 Lance Parrish .01 .05
36 Von Hayes .01 .05
37 Lee Smith .02 .10
38 Herm Winningham .01 .05
39 Alejandro Pena .01 .05
40 Mike Scott .01 .05
41 Joe Orsulak .01 .05
42 Rafael Ramirez .01 .05
43 Gerald Young .01 .05
44 Dick Schofield .01 .05
45 Dave Smith .01 .05
46 Dave Magadan .01 .05
47 Dennis Martinez .02 .10
48 Greg Minton .01 .05
49 Milt Thompson .01 .05
50 Orel Hershiser .02 .10
51 Bip Roberts .01 .05
52 Jerry Browne .01 .05
53 Bob Ojeda .01 .05
54 Fernando Valenzuela .02 .10
55 Matt Nokes .01 .05
56 Brook Jacoby .01 .05
57 Frank Tanana .01 .05
58 Scott Fletcher .01 .05
59 Ron Oester .01 .05
60 Bob Boone .02 .10
61 Dan Gladden .01 .05
62 Darnell Coles .01 .05
63 Gregg Olson .02 .10
64 Todd Burns .01 .05
65 Todd Benzinger .01 .05
66 Dale Murphy .05 .15
67 Mike Flanagan .01 .05
68 Jose Oquendo .01 .05
69 Cecil Espy .01 .05
70 Chris Sabo .01 .05
71 Shane Rawley .01 .05
72 Tom Brunansky .01 .05
73 Vance Law .01 .05
74 B.J. Surhoff .02 .10
75 Lou Whitaker .02 .10
76 Ken Caminiti UER .02 .10
Euclid and Ohio should be Hanford and California
77 Nelson Liriano .01 .05
78 Tommy Gregg .01 .05
79 Don Slaught .01 .05
80 Eddie Murray .08 .25
81 Joe Boever .01 .05
82 Charlie Leibrandt .01 .05
83 Jose Lind .01 .05
84 Tony Phillips .01 .05
85 Mitch Webster .01 .05
86 Dan Plesac .01 .05
87 Rick Mahler .01 .05
88 Steve Lyons .01 .05
89 Tony Fernandez .01 .05
90 Ryne Sandberg .15 .40
91 Nick Esasky .01 .05
92 Luis Salazar .01 .05
93 Pete Incaviglia .01 .05
94 Ivan Calderon .01 .05
95 Jeff Treadway .01 .05
96 Kurt Stillwell .01 .05
97 Gary Sheffield .08 .25
98 Jeffrey Leonard .01 .05
99 Andres Thomas .01 .05
100 Roberto Kelly .01 .05
101 Alvaro Espinoza .01 .05
102 Greg Gagne .01 .05
103 John Farrell .01 .05
104 Willie Wilson .01 .05
105 Glenn Braggs .01 .05
106 Chet Lemon .01 .05
107A Jamie Moyer ERR .02 .10
Scintilating
107B Jamie Moyer COR .20 .50
Scintillating
108 Chuck Crim .01 .05
109 Dave Valle .01 .05
110 Walt Weiss .01 .05
111 Larry Sheets .01 .05
112 Don Robinson .01 .05
113 Danny Heep .01 .05
114 Carmelo Martinez .01 .05
115 Dave Gallagher .01 .05
116 Mike LaValliere .01 .05
117 Bob McClure .01 .05
118 Rene Gonzales .01 .05
119 Mark Parent .01 .05
120 Wally Joyner .02 .10
121 Mark Gubicza .01 .05
122 Tony Pena .01 .05
123 Carmelo Castillo .01 .05
124 Howard Johnson .01 .05
125 Steve Sax .01 .05
126 Tim Belcher .01 .05
127 Tim Burke .01 .05
128 Al Newman .01 .05
129 Dennis Rasmussen .01 .05
130 Doug Jones .01 .05
131 Fred Lynn .01 .05
132 Jeff Hamilton .01 .05
133 German Gonzalez .01 .05
134 John Morris .01 .05
135 Dave Parker .02 .10
136 Gary Pettis .01 .05
137 Dennis Boyd .01 .05
138 Candy Maldonado .01 .05
139 Rick Cerone .01 .05
140 George Brett .25 .60
141 Dave Clark .01 .05
142 Dickie Thon .01 .05
143 Junior Ortiz .01 .05
144 Don August .01 .05
145 Gary Gaetti .02 .10
146 Kirt Manwaring .01 .05
147 Jeff Reed .01 .05
148 Jose Alvarez .01 .05
149 Mike Schooler .01 .05
150 Mark Grace .05 .15
151 Geronimo Berroa .01 .05
152 Barry Jones .01 .05
153 Geno Petralli .01 .05
154 Jim Deshaies .01 .05
155 Barry Larkin .05 .15
156 Alfredo Griffin .01 .05
157 Tom Henke .01 .05
158 Mike Jeffcoat .01 .05
159 Bob Welch .01 .05
160 Julio Franco .02 .10
161 Henry Cotto .01 .05
162 Terry Steinbach .01 .05
163 Damon Berryhill .01 .05
164 Tim Crews .01 .05
165 Tom Browning .01 .05
166 Fred Manrique .01 .05
167 Harold Reynolds .02 .10
168A Ron Hassey ERR .01 .05
27 on back
168B Ron Hassey COR .20 .50
24 on back
169 Shawon Dunston .01 .05
170 Bobby Bonilla .02 .10
171 Tommy Herr .01 .05
172 Mike Heath .01 .05
173 Rich Gedman .01 .05
174 Bill Ripken .01 .05
175 Pete O'Brien .01 .05
176A Lloyd McClendon ERR .01 .05
Uniform number on back listed as 1
176B Lloyd McClendon COR .20 .50
Uniform number on back listed as 10
177 Brian Holton .01 .05
178 Jeff Blauser .01 .05
179 Jim Eisenreich .01 .05
180 Bert Blyleven .02 .10
181 Rob Murphy .01 .05
182 Bill Doran .01 .05
183 Curt Ford .01 .05
184 Mike Henneman .01 .05
185 Eric Davis .02 .10
186 Lance McCullers .01 .05
187 Steve Davis RC .01 .05
188 Bill Wegman .01 .05
189 Brian Harper .01 .05
190 Mike Moore .01 .05
191 Dale Mohorcic .01 .05
192 Tim Wallach .01 .05
193 Keith Hernandez .02 .10
194 Dave Righetti .02 .10
195A Bret Saberhagen ERR .01 .05
Joke
195B Bret Saberhagen COR .20 .50
Joker
196 Paul Kilgus .01 .05
197 Bud Black .01 .05
198 Juan Samuel .01 .05
199 Kevin Seitzer .01 .05
200 Darryl Strawberry .02 .10
201 Dave Stieb .02 .10
202 Charlie Hough .02 .10
203 Jack Morris .02 .10
204 Rance Mulliniks .01 .05
205 Alvin Davis .01 .05
206 Jack Howell .01 .05
207 Ken Patterson .01 .05
208 Terry Pendleton .02 .10
209 Craig Lefferts .01 .05
210 Kevin Brown UER .02 .10
First mention of '89 Rangers should be '88
211 Dan Petry .01 .05
212 Dave Leiper .01 .05
213 Daryl Boston .01 .05
214 Kevin Hickey .01 .05
215 Mike Krukow .01 .05
216 Terry Francona .02 .10
217 Kirk McCaskill .01 .05
218 Scott Bailes .01 .05
219 Bob Forsch .01 .05
220A Mike Aldrete ERR .01 .05
25 on back
220B Mike Aldrete COR .20 .50
24 on back
221 Steve Buechele .01 .05
222 Jesse Barfield .01 .05
223 Juan Berenguer .01 .05
224 Andy McGaffigan .01 .05
225 Pete Smith .01 .05
226 Mike Witt .01 .05
227 Jay Howell .01 .05
228 Scott Bradley .01 .05
229 Jerome Walton .01 .05
230 Greg Swindell .01 .05
231 Atlee Hammaker .01 .05
232A Mike Devereaux ERR .01 .05
RF on front
232B Mike Devereaux COR .20 .50
CF on front
233 Ken Hill .02 .10
234 Craig Worthington .01 .05
235 Scott Terry .01 .05
236 Brett Butler .02 .10
237 Doyle Alexander .01 .05
238 Dave Anderson .01 .05
239 Bob Milacki .01 .05
240 Dwight Smith .01 .05
241 Otis Nixon .01 .05
242 Pat Tabler .01 .05
243 Derek Lilliquist .01 .05
244 Danny Tartabull .01 .05
245 Wade Boggs .05 .15
246 Scott Garrelts .01 .05
Should say Relief Pitcher on front
247 Spike Owen .01 .05
248 Norm Charlton .01 .05
249 Gerald Perry .01 .05
250 Nolan Ryan .40 1.00
251 Kevin Gross .01 .05
252 Randy Milligan .01 .05
253 Mike LaCoss .01 .05
254 Dave Bergman .01 .05
255 Tony Gwynn .10 .30
256 Felix Fermin .01 .05
257 Greg W. Harris .01 .05
258 Junior Felix .01 .05
259 Mark Davis .01 .05
260 Vince Coleman .01 .05
261 Paul Gibson .01 .05
262 Mitch Williams .01 .05
263 Jeff Russell .01 .05
264 Omar Vizquel .08 .25
265 Andre Dawson .02 .10
266 Storm Davis .01 .05
267 Guillermo Hernandez .01 .05
268 Mike Felder .01 .05
269 Tom Candiotti .01 .05
270 Bruce Hurst .01 .05
271 Fred McGriff .08 .25
272 Glenn Davis .01 .05
273 John Franco .02 .10
274 Rich Yett .01 .05
275 Craig Biggio .08 .25
276 Gene Larkin .01 .05
277 Rob Dibble .02 .10
278 Randy Bush .01 .05
279 Kevin Bass .01 .05
280A Bo Jackson ERR .08 .25
Watham
280B Bo Jackson COR .30 .75
Wathan
281 Wally Backman .01 .05
282 Larry Andersen .01 .05
283 Chris Bosio .01 .05
284 Juan Agosto .01 .05
285 Ozzie Smith .15 .40
286 George Bell .01 .05
287 Rex Hudler .01 .05
288 Pat Borders .01 .05
289 Danny Jackson .01 .05
290 Carlton Fisk .05 .15
291 Tracy Jones .01 .05
292 Allan Anderson .01 .05
293 Johnny Ray .01 .05
294 Lee Guetterman .01 .05
295 Paul O'Neill .05 .15
296 Carney Lansford .02 .10
297 Tom Brookens .01 .05
298 Claudell Washington .01 .05
299 Hubie Brooks .01 .05
300 Will Clark .05 .15
301 Kenny Rogers .02 .10
302 Darrell Evans .02 .10
303 Greg Briley .01 .05
304 Donn Pall .01 .05
305 Teddy Higuera .01 .05
306 Dan Pasqua .01 .05
307 Dave Winfield .02 .10
308 Dennis Powell .01 .05
309 Jose DeLeon .01 .05
310 Roger Clemens UER .40 1.00
311 Melido Perez .01 .05
312 Devon White .02 .10
313 Dwight Gooden .02 .10
314 Carlos Martinez .01 .05
315 Dennis Eckersley .02 .10
316 Clay Parker UER .01 .05
Height 6'11-inch
317 Rick Honeycutt .01 .05
318 Tim Laudner .01 .05
319 Joe Carter .02 .10
320 Robin Yount .15 .40
321 Felix Jose .01 .05
322 Mickey Tettleton .01 .05
323 Mike Gallego .01 .05
324 Edgar Martinez .05 .15
325 Dave Henderson .01 .05
326 Chili Davis .02 .10
327 Steve Balboni .01 .05
328 Jody Davis .01 .05
329 Shawn Hillegas .01 .05
330 Jim Abbott .05 .15
331 John Dopson .01 .05
332 Mark Williamson .01 .05
333 Jeff D. Robinson .01 .05
334 John Smiley .01 .05
335 Bobby Thigpen .01 .05
336 Garry Templeton .01 .05
337 Marvell Wynne .01 .05
338A Ken Griffey Sr. ERR .02 .10
Uniform number on back listed as 25
338B Ken Griffey Sr. COR .20 .50
Uniform number on back listed as 30
339 Steve Finley .02 .10
340 Ellis Burks .05 .15
341 Frank Williams .01 .05
342 Mike Morgan .01 .05
343 Kevin Mitchell .01 .05
344 Joel Youngblood .01 .05
345 Mike Greenwell .01 .05
346 Glenn Wilson .01 .05
347 John Costello .01 .05
348 Wes Gardner .01 .05
349 Jeff Ballard .01 .05
350 Mark Thurmond UER .01 .05
ERA is 192,
should be 1.92
351 Randy Myers .02 .10
352 Shawn Abner .01 .05
353 Jesse Orosco .01 .05
354 Greg Walker .01 .05
355 Pete Harnisch .01 .05
356 Steve Farr .01 .05
357 Dave LaPoint .01 .05
358 Willie Fraser .01 .05
359 Mickey Hatcher .01 .05
360 Rickey Henderson .08 .25
361 Mike Fitzgerald .01 .05
362 Bill Schroeder .01 .05
363 Mark Carreon .01 .05
364 Ron Jones .01 .05
365 Jeff Montgomery .02 .10
366 Bill Krueger .01 .05
367 John Cangelosi .01 .05
368 Jose Gonzalez .01 .05
369 Greg Hibbard RC .02 .10
370 John Smoltz .08 .25
371 Jeff Brantley .01 .05
372 Frank White .02 .10
373 Ed Whitson .01 .05
374 Willie McGee .02 .10
375 Jose Canseco .05 .15
376 Randy Ready .01 .05
377 Don Aase .01 .05
378 Tony Armas .01 .05
379 Steve Bedrosian .01 .05
380 Chuck Finley .02 .10
381 Kent Hrbek .02 .10
382 Jim Gantner .01 .05
383 Mel Hall .01 .05
384 Mike Marshall .01 .05
385 Mark McGwire .40 1.00
386 Wayne Tolleson .01 .05
387 Brian Holman .01 .05
388 John Wetteland .08 .25
389 Darren Daulton .02 .10
390 Rob Deer .01 .05
391 John Moses .01 .05
392 Todd Worrell .01 .05
393 Chuck Cary .01 .05
394 Stan Javier .01 .05
395 Willie Randolph .02 .10
396 Bill Buckner .01 .05
397 Robby Thompson .01 .05
398 Mike Scioscia .01 .05
399 Lonnie Smith .01 .05
400 Kirby Puckett .08 .25
401 Mark Langston .01 .05
402 Danny Darwin .01 .05
403 Greg Maddux .15 .40
404 Lloyd Moseby .01 .05
405 Rafael Palmeiro .05 .15
406 Chad Kreuter .01 .05
407 Jimmy Key .02 .10
408 Tim Birtsas .01 .05
409 Tim Raines .02 .10
410 Dave Stewart .02 .10
411 Eric Yelding RC .01 .05
412 Kent Anderson .01 .05
413 Les Lancaster .01 .05
414 Rick Dempsey .01 .05
415 Randy Johnson .20 .50
416 Gary Carter .02 .10
417 Rolando Roomes .01 .05
418 Dan Schatzeder .01 .05
419 Bryn Smith .01 .05
420 Ruben Sierra .02 .10
421 Steve Jeltz .01 .05
422 Ken Oberkfell .01 .05
423 Sid Bream .01 .05
424 Jim Clancy .01 .05
425 Kelly Gruber .01 .05
426 Rick Leach .01 .05
427 Len Dykstra .02 .10
428 Jeff Pico .01 .05
429 John Cerutti .01 .05
430 David Cone .02 .10
431 Jeff Kunkel .01 .05
432 Luis Aquino .01 .05
433 Ernie Whitt .01 .05
434 Bo Diaz .01 .05
435 Steve Lake .01 .05
436 Pat Perry .01 .05
437 Mike Davis .01 .05
438 Cecilio Guante .01 .05
439 Duane Ward .01 .05
440 Andy Van Slyke .05 .15
441 Gene Nelson .01 .05
442 Luis Polonia .01 .05
443 Kevin Elster .01 .05
444 Keith Moreland .01 .05
445 Roger McDowell .01 .05
446 Ron Darling .01 .05
447 Ernest Riles .01 .05
448 Mookie Wilson .02 .10
449A Billy Spiers ERR .01 .05
No birth year
449B Billy Spiers COR .20 .50
Born in 1966
450 Rick Sutcliffe .02 .10
451 Nelson Santovenia .01 .05
452 Andy Allanson .01 .05
453 Bob Melvin .01 .05
454 Benito Santiago .02 .10
455 Jose Uribe .01 .05
456 Bill Landrum .01 .05
457 Bobby Witt .01 .05
458 Kevin Romine .01 .05
459 Lee Mazzilli .01 .05
460 Paul Molitor .05 .15
461 Ramon Martinez .01 .05
462 Frank DiPino .01 .05
463 Walt Terrell .01 .05
464 Bob Geren .01 .05
465 Rick Reuschel .01 .05
466 Mark Grant .01 .05
467 John Kruk .02 .10
468 Gregg Jefferies .02 .10
469 R.J. Reynolds .01 .05
470 Harold Baines .02 .10
471 Dennis Lamp .01 .05
472 Tom Gordon .02 .10
473 Terry Puhl .01 .05
474 Curt Wilkerson .01 .05
475 Dan Quisenberry .01 .05
476 Oddibe McDowell .01 .05
477A Zane Smith ERR .01 .05
Career ERA .393
477B Zane Smith COR .20 .50
career ERA 3.93
478 Franklin Stubbs .01 .05
479 Wallace Johnson .01 .05
480 Jay Tibbs .01 .05
481 Tom Glavine .05 .15
482 Manny Lee .01 .05
483 Joe Hesketh UER .01 .05
Says Rookiess on back, should say Rookies
484 Mike Bielecki .01 .05
485 Greg Brock .01 .05
486 Pascual Perez .01 .05
487 Kirk Gibson .02 .10
488 Scott Sanderson .01 .05
489 Domingo Ramos .01 .05
490 Kal Daniels .01 .05
491A David Wells ERR .02 .10
Reverse negative photo on card back
491B David Wells COR .20 .50
492 Jerry Reed .01 .05
493 Eric Show .01 .05
494 Mike Pagliarulo .01 .05
495 Ron Robinson .01 .05
496 Brad Komminsk .01 .05
497 Greg Litton .01 .05
498 Chris James .01 .05
499 Luis Quinones .01 .05
500 Frank Viola .01 .05
501 Tim Teufel UER .01 .05
Twins '85, the s is lower case, should be upper case
502 Terry Leach .01 .05
503 Matt Williams UER .02 .10
Wearing 10 on front, listed as 9 on back
504 Tim Leary .01 .05
505 Doug Drabek .01 .05
506 Mariano Duncan .01 .05
507 Charlie Hayes .01 .05
508 Joey Belle .08 .25
509 Pat Sheridan .01 .05
510 Mackey Sasser .01 .05
511 Jose Rijo .01 .05
512 Mike Smithson .01 .05
513 Gary Ward .01 .05
514 Dion James .01 .05
515 Jim Gott .01 .05
516 Drew Hall .01 .05
517 Doug Bair .01 .05
518 Scott Scudder .01 .05
519 Rick Aguilera .02 .10
520 Rafael Belliard .01 .05
521 Jay Buhner .02 .10
522 Jeff Reardon .02 .10
523 Steve Rosenberg .01 .05
524 Randy Velarde .01 .05
525 Jeff Musselman .01 .05
526 Bill Long .01 .05
527 Gary Wayne .01 .05
528 Dave Wayne Johnson RC .01 .05
529 Ron Kittle .01 .05
530 Erik Hanson UER .01 .05
5th line on back says seson, should say season
531 Steve Wilson .01 .05
532 Joey Meyer .01 .05
533 Curt Young .01 .05
534 Kelly Downs .01 .05
535 Joe Girardi .05 .15
536 Lance Blankenship .01 .05
537 Greg Mathews .01 .05
538 Donell Nixon .01 .05
539 Mark Knudson .01 .05
540 Jeff Wetherby RC .01 .05
541 Darrin Jackson .01 .05
542 Terry Mulholland .01 .05
543 Eric Hetzel .01 .05
544 Rick Reed RC .08 .25
545 Dennis Cook .01 .05
546 Mike Jackson .01 .05
547 Brian Fisher .01 .05
548 Gene Harris .01 .05
549 Jeff King .01 .05
550 Dave Dravecky .08 .25
551 Randy Kutcher .01 .05
552 Mark Portugal .01 .05
553 Jim Corsi .01 .05
554 Todd Stottlemyre .02 .10
555 Scott Bankhead .01 .05
556 Ken Dayley .01 .05
557 Rick Wrona .01 .05
558 Sammy Sosa RC 1.00 2.50
559 Keith Miller .01 .05
560 Ken Griffey Jr. .40 1.00
561A R.Sandberg HL ERR 3.00 8.00
561B R.Sandberg HL COR .08 .25
562 Billy Hatcher .01 .05
563 Jay Bell .02 .10
564 Jack Daugherty RC .01 .05
565 Rich Monteleone .01 .05
566 Bo Jackson AS-MVP .02 .10
567 Tony Fossas RC .01 .05
568 Roy Smith .01 .05
569 Jaime Navarro .01 .05
570 Lance Johnson .01 .05
571 Mike Dyer RC .01 .05
572 Kevin Ritz RC .01 .05
573 Dave West .01 .05
574 Gary Mielke RC .01 .05
575 Scott Lusader .01 .05
576 Joe Oliver .01 .05
577 Sandy Alomar Jr. .02 .10
578 Andy Benes UER .02 .10
Extra comma between day and year
579 Tim Jones .01 .05
580 Randy McCament RC .01 .05
581 Curt Schilling .40 1.00
582 John Orton RC .02 .10
583A Milt Cuyler ERR RC .02 .10
583B Milt Cuyler COR .20 .50
584 Eric Anthony RC .02 .10
585 Greg Vaughn .01 .05
586 Deion Sanders .08 .25
587 Jose DeJesus .01 .05
588 Chip Hale RC .01 .05
589 John Olerud RC .20 .50
590 Steve Olin RC .08 .25
591 Marquis Grissom RC .15 .40
592 Moises Alou RC .30 .75
593 Mark Lemke .01 .05
594 Dean Palmer RC .08 .25
595 Robin Ventura .08 .25
596 Tino Martinez .20 .50
597 Mike Huff RC .01 .05
598 Scott Hemond RC .02 .10
599 Wally Whitehurst .01 .05
600 Todd Zeile .02 .10
601 Glenallen Hill .01 .05
602 Hal Morris .01 .05
603 Juan Bell .01 .05
604 Bobby Rose .01 .05
605 Matt Merullo .01 .05
606 Kevin Maas RC .08 .25
607 Randy Nosek RC .01 .05
608A Billy Bates RC .01 .05
608B Billy Bates .01 .05
Text has no mention of triples
609 Mike Stanton RC .08 .25
610 Mauro Gozzo RC .01 .05
611 Charles Nagy .01 .05
612 Scott Coolbaugh RC .01 .05
613 Jose Vizcaino RC .08 .25
614 Greg Smith RC .01 .05
615 Jeff Huson RC .02 .10
616 Mickey Weston RC .01 .05
617 John Pawlowski .01 .05
618A Joe Skalski ERR .01 .05
27 on back
618B Joe Skalski COR .20 .50
67 on back
619 Bernie Williams RC .60 1.50
620 Shawn Holman RC .01 .05
621 Gary Eave RC .01 .05
622 Darrin Fletcher UER RC .02 .10
623 Pat Combs .01 .05
624 Mike Blowers RC .02 .10
625 Kevin Appier .02 .10
626 Pat Austin .01 .05
627 Kelly Mann RC .01 .05
628 Matt Kinzer RC .01 .05
629 Chris Hammond RC .02 .10
630 Dean Wilkins RC .01 .05
631 Larry Walker RC .40 1.00
632 Blaine Beatty RC .01 .05
633A Tommy Barrett ERR .01 .05
633B Tommy Barrett COR .20 .50
14 on back
634 Stan Belinda RC .02 .10
635 Mike Texas Smith RC .01 .05
636 Hensley Meulens .01 .05
637 Juan Gonzalez RC .40 1.00
638 Lenny Webster RC .02 .10
639 Mark Gardner RC .02 .10
640 Tommy Greene RC .02 .10
641 Mike Hartley RC .01 .05
642 Phil Stephenson .01 .05
643 Kevin Mmahat RC .01 .05
644 Ed Whited RC .01 .05
645 Delino DeShields RC .08 .25
646 Kevin Blankenship .01 .05
647 Paul Sorrento RC .08 .25
648 Mike Roesler RC .01 .05
649 Jason Grimsley RC .02 .10
650 Dave Justice RC .20 .50
651 Scott Cooper RC .02 .10
652 Dave Eiland .01 .05
653 Mike Munoz RC .01 .05
654 Jeff Fischer RC .01 .05
655 Terry Jorgensen RC .01 .05
656 George Canale RC .01 .05
657 Brian DuBois UER RC .01 .05
658 Carlos Quintana .01 .05
659 Luis de los Santos .01 .05
660 Jerald Clark .01 .05
661 Donald Harris RC .01 .05
662 Paul Coleman RC .02 .10
663 Frank Thomas RC 1.00 2.50
664 Brent Mayne DC RC .08 .25
665 Eddie Zosky RC .02 .10
666 Steve Hosey RC .02 .10
667 Scott Bryant RC .02 .10
668 Tom Goodwin RC .08 .25
669 Cal Eldred RC .08 .25
670 Earl Cunningham RC .02 .10
671 Alan Zinter DC RC .02 .10
672 Chuck Knoblauch RC .15 .40
673 Kyle Abbott RC .01 .05
674 Roger Salkeld RC .02 .10
675 Mo Vaughn RC .20 .50
676 Keith Kiki Jones RC .01 .05
677 Tyler Houston RC .08 .25
678 Jeff Jackson RC .02 .10
679 Greg Gohr RC .02 .10
680 Ben McDonald DC RC .08 .25
681 Greg Blosser RC .02 .10
682 Willie Greene RC .08 .25
683A Wade Boggs DT ERR .02 .10
Text says 215 hits in '89, should be 205
683B Wade Boggs DT COR .20 .50
Text says 205 hits in '89
684 Will Clark DT .02 .10
685 Tony Gwynn DT UER .05 .15
Text reads battling instead of batting
686 Rickey Henderson DT .05 .15
687 Bo Jackson DT .02 .10
688 Mark Langston DT .01 .05
689 Barry Larkin DT .02 .10
690 Kirby Puckett DT .05 .15
691 Ryne Sandberg DT .08 .25
692 Mike Scott DT .01 .05
693A Terry Steinbach DT .01 .05
ERR catchers
693B Terry Steinbach DT .01 .05
COR catchers
694 Bobby Thigpen DT .01 .05
695 Mitch Williams DT .01 .05
696 Nolan Ryan HL .15 .40
697 Bo Jackson FB 2.00 5.00
BB
698 Rickey Henderson .05 .15
ALCS-MVP
699 Will Clark .02 .10
NLCS-MVP
700 Dave Stewart .02 .10
Mike Moore WS
701 Lights Out .08 .25
702 Carney Lansford .05 .15
Rickey Henderson
Jose Canseco
Dave Henderson WS
703 WS Game 4 .01 .05
Wrap-up
704 Wade Boggs HL .02 .10

1990 Score Magic Motion Trivia

COMPLETE SET (56) 1.00 2.50
COMMON CARD .02 .10

1990 Score Rookie Dream Team

COMPLETE SET (10) 1.50 4.00
ONE SET PER HOBBY FACTORY SET
B1 Bart Giamatti MEM .40 1.00
B2 Pat Combs .07 .20
B3 Todd Zeile .15 .40
B4 Luis de los Santos .07 .20
B5 Mark Lemke .07 .20
B6 Robin Ventura .40 1.00
B7 Jeff Huson .15 .40
B8 Greg Vaughn .07 .20
B9 Marquis Grissom .60 1.50
B10 Eric Anthony .15 .40

1990 Score Rookie/Traded

The standard-size 110-card 1990 Score Rookie and Traded set marked the third consecutive year Score had issued an end of the year set to note trades and give rookies early cards. The set was issued through hobby accounts and only in factory set form. The first 66 cards are traded players while the last 44 cards are rookie cards. Hockey star Eric Lindros is included in this set. Rookie Cards in the set include Derek Bell, Todd Hundley and Ray Lankford.

COMP.FACT.SET (110) 1.25 3.00
1T Dave Winfield .02 .10
2T Kevin Bass .01 .05
3T Nick Esasky .01 .05
4T Mitch Webster .01 .05
5T Pascual Perez .01 .05
6T Gary Pettis .01 .05
7T Tony Pena .01 .05
8T Candy Maldonado .01 .05
9T Cecil Fielder .02 .10
10T Carmelo Martinez .01 .05
11T Mark Langston .01 .05
12T Dave Parker .02 .10
13T Don Slaught .01 .05
14T Tony Phillips .01 .05
15T John Franco .02 .10
16T Randy Myers .02 .10
17T Jeff Reardon .02 .10
18T Sandy Alomar Jr. .02 .10
19T Joe Carter .02 .10
20T Fred Lynn .01 .05
21T Storm Davis .01 .05
22T Craig Lefferts .01 .05
23T Pete O'Brien .01 .05
24T Dennis Boyd .01 .05
25T Lloyd Moseby .01 .05
26T Mark Davis .01 .05
27T Tim Leary .01 .05
28T Gerald Perry .01 .05
29T Don Aase .01 .05
30T Ernie Whitt .01 .05
31T Dale Murphy .05 .15
32T Alejandro Pena .01 .05
33T Juan Samuel .01 .05
34T Hubie Brooks .01 .05
35T Gary Carter .02 .10
36T Jim Presley .01 .05
37T Wally Backman .01 .05
38T Matt Nokes .01 .05
39T Dan Petry .01 .05
40T Franklin Stubbs .01 .05
41T Jeff Huson .01 .05
42T Billy Hatcher .01 .05
43T Terry Leach .01 .05
44T Phil Bradley .01 .05
45T Claudell Washington .01 .05
46T Luis Polonia .01 .05
47T Daryl Boston .01 .05
48T Lee Smith .02 .10
49T Tom Brunansky .01 .05
50T Mike Witt .01 .05
51T Willie Randolph .02 .10
52T Stan Javier .01 .05
53T Brad Komminsk .01 .05
54T John Candelaria .01 .05
55T Bryn Smith .01 .05
56T Glenn Braggs .01 .05
57T Keith Hernandez .02 .10
58T Ken Oberkfell .01 .05
59T Steve Jeltz .01 .05
60T Chris James .01 .05
61T Scott Sanderson .01 .05
62T Bill Long .01 .05
63T Rick Cerone .01 .05
64T Scott Bailes .01 .05
65T Larry Sheets .01 .05
66T Junior Ortiz .01 .05
67T Francisco Cabrera .01 .05
68T Gary DiSarcina RC .08 .25

69T Greg Olson (C) RC .01 .05
70T Beau Allred RC .01 .05
71T Oscar Azocar .01 .05
72T Kent Mercker RC .08 .25
73T John Burkett .01 .05
74T Carlos Baerga RC .08 .25
75T Dave Hollins RC .08 .25
76T Todd Hundley RC .08 .25
77T Rick Parker RC .01 .05
78T Steve Cummings RC .01 .05
79T Bill Sampen RC .01 .05
80T Jerry Kutzler RC .01 .05
81T Derek Bell RC .08 .25
82T Kevin Tapani RC .08 .25
83T Jim Leyritz RC .08 .25
84T Ray Lankford RC .15 .40
85T Wayne Edwards RC .01 .05
86T Frank Thomas 1.00 2.50
87T Tim Naehring RC .02 .10
88T Willie Blair RC .02 .10
89T Alan Mills RC .02 .10
90T Scott Radinsky RC .02 .10
91T Howard Farmer RC .01 .05
92T Julio Machado RC .01 .05
93T Rafael Valdez RC .01 .05
94T Shawn Boskie RC .02 .10
95T David Segui RC .15 .40
96T Chris Hoiles RC .08 .25
97T D.J.Dozier RC .02 .10
98T Hector Villanueva RC .01 .05
99T Eric Gunderson RC .01 .05
100T Eric Lindros .40 1.00
101T Dave Otto .01 .05
102T Dana Kiecker RC .01 .05
103T Tim Drummond RC .01 .05
104T Mickey Pina RC .01 .05
105T Craig Grebeck RC .02 .10
106T Bernard Gilkey RC .08 .25
107T Tim Layana RC .01 .05
108T Scott Chiamparino RC .01 .05
109T Steve Avery .01 .05
110T Terry Shumpert RC .01 .05

1990 Score 100 Superstars

The 1990 Score Superstars set contains 100 standard size cards. The fronts are red, white, blue and purple. The vertically oriented backs feature a large color facial shot and career highlights. The cards were distributed as a set in a blister pack, which also included a full color booklet with more information about each player.

COMP.FACT.SET (100) 4.00 10.00
1 Kirby Puckett .30 .75
2 Steve Sax .01 .05
3 Tony Gwynn .60 1.50
4 Willie Randolph .02 .10
5 Jose Canseco .30 .75
6 Ozzie Smith .50 1.25
7 Rick Reuschel .01 .05
8 Bill Doran .01 .05
9 Mickey Tettleton .02 .10
10 Don Mattingly .50 1.25
11 Greg Swindell .01 .05
12 Bert Blyleven .02 .10
13 Dave Stewart .02 .10
14 Andres Galarraga .10 .30
15 Darryl Strawberry .02 .10
16 Ellis Burks .07 .20
17 Paul O'Neill .02 .10
18 Bruce Hurst .01 .05
19 Dave Smith .01 .05
20 Carney Lansford .02 .10
21 Robby Thompson .01 .05
22 Gary Gaetti .02 .10
23 Jeff Russell .01 .05
24 Chuck Finley .02 .10
25 Mark McGwire .50 1.25
26 Alvin Davis .01 .05
27 George Bell .01 .05
28 Cory Snyder .01 .05
29 Keith Hernandez .02 .10
30 Will Clark .10 .30
31 Steve Bedrosian .01 .05
32 Ryne Sandberg .40 1.00
33 Tom Browning .01 .05
34 Tim Burke .01 .05
35 John Smoltz .10 .30
36 Phil Bradley .01 .05
37 Bobby Bonilla .02 .10
38 Kirk McCaskill .01 .05
39 Dave Righetti .01 .05
40 Bo Jackson .20 .50
41 Alan Trammell .07 .20
42 Mike Moore UER/(Uniform number is 21& .01
.05
not 23 as
43 Harold Reynolds .02 .10
44 Nolan Ryan 1.25 3.00
45 Fred McGriff .07 .20
46 Brian Downing .01 .05
47 Brett Butler .02 .10
48 Mike Scioscia .02 .10
49 John Franco .02 .10
50 Kevin Mitchell .01 .05
51 Mark Davis .01 .05
52 Glenn Davis .01 .05
53 Barry Bonds .50 1.25
54 Dwight Evans .02 .10
55 Terry Steinbach .01 .05
56 Dave Gallagher .01 .05
57 Roberto Kelly .01 .05
58 Rafael Palmeiro .20 .50
59 Joe Carter .02 .10
60 Mark Grace .10 .30
61 Pedro Guerrero .01 .05
62 Von Hayes .01 .05
63 Benito Santiago .02 .10
64 Dale Murphy .10 .30
65 John Smiley .01 .05
66 Cal Ripken 1.25 3.00
67 Mike Greenwell .01 .05
68 Devon White .01 .05
69 Ed Whitson .01 .05
70 Carlton Fisk .20 .50
71 Lou Whitaker .02 .10
72 Danny Tartabull .01 .05
73 Vince Coleman .01 .05
74 Andre Dawson .20 .50
75 Tim Raines .02 .10
76 George Brett .40 1.00
77 Tom Herr .01 .05
78 Andy Van Slyke .02 .10
79 Roger Clemens .60 1.50
80 Wade Boggs .30 .75
81 Wally Joyner .02 .10
82 Lonnie Smith .01 .05
83 Howard Johnson .01 .05
84 Julio Franco .02 .10
85 Ruben Sierra .02 .10
86 Dan Plesac .01 .05
87 Bobby Thigpen .01 .05
88 Kevin Seitzer .01 .05
89 Dave Stieb .01 .05
90 Rickey Henderson .40 1.00
91 Jeffrey Leonard .01 .05
92 Robin Yount .20 .50
93 Mitch Williams .01 .05
94 Orel Hershiser .02 .10
95 Eric Davis .02 .10
96 Mark Langston .01 .05
97 Mike Scott .01 .05
98 Paul Molitor .30 .75
99 Dwight Gooden .02 .10
100 Kevin Bass .01 .05

1990 Score McDonald's

This 25-card standard-size set was produced by Score for McDonald's restaurants; included with the set were 15 World Series Trivia cards. The player cards were given away four to a pack and free with the purchase of fries and a drink, at only 11 McDonald's in the United States (in Idaho and Eastern Oregon) during a special promotion which lasted approximately three weeks. The front has color action player photos, with white and yellow borders on a purple card face that fades as one moves toward the middle of the card. The upper left corner of the picture is cut off to allow space for the McDonald's logo; the player's name and team logo at the bottom round out the card face. The backs have color mugshots, biography, statistics, and career summary.

COMPLETE SET (25) 400.00 800.00
1 Will Clark 12.50 30.00
2 Sandy Alomar Jr. 1.00 2.50
3 Julio Franco 3.00 8.00
4 Carlton Fisk 12.50 30.00
5 Rickey Henderson 15.00 40.00
6 Matt Williams 5.00 12.50
7 John Franco 3.00 8.00
8 Ryne Sandberg 15.00 40.00
9 Kelly Gruber 1.00 2.50
10 Andre Dawson 8.00 20.00
11 Barry Bonds 12.50 30.00
12 Gary Sheffield 12.50 30.00
13 Ramon Martinez 1.00 2.50
14 Len Dykstra 3.00 8.00
15 Benito Santiago 3.00 8.00
16 Cecil Fielder 3.00 8.00
17 John Olerud 5.00 12.50
18 Roger Clemens 20.00 50.00
19 George Brett 15.00 40.00
20 George Bell 1.00 2.50
21 Ozzie Guillen 5.00 12.50
22 Steve Sax 1.00 2.50
23 Dave Stewart 3.00 8.00
24 Ozzie Smith 15.00 40.00
25 Robin Yount 12.50 30.00

1990 Score Rising Stars

COMP.FACT.SET (100) 6.00 15.00
DISTRIBUTED IN FACTORY SET FORM ONLY
1 Tom Gordon .08 .25
2 Jerome Walton .02 .10
3 Ken Griffey Jr. 1.00 2.50
4 Dwight Smith .02 .10
5 Jim Abbott .15 .40
6 Todd Zeile .08 .25
7 Donn Pall .02 .10
8 Rick Reed .25 .60
9 Albert Belle .25 .60
10 Gregg Jefferies .08 .25
11 Kevin Ritz .02 .10
12 Charlie Hayes .02 .10
13 Kevin Appier .08 .25
14 Jeff Huson .02 .10
15 Gary Wayne .02 .10
16 Eric Yelding .02 .10
17 Clay Parker .02 .10
18 Junior Felix .02 .10
19 Derek Lilliquist .02 .10
20 Gary Sheffield .25 .60
21 Craig Worthington .02 .10
22 Jeff Brantley .02 .10
23 Eric Hetzel .02 .10
24 Greg W.Harris .02 .10
25 John Wetteland .25 .60
26 Joe Oliver .02 .10
27 Kevin Maas .08 .25
28 Kevin Brown .20 .50
29 Mike Stanton .02 .10
30 Greg Vaughn .02 .10
31 Ron Jones .02 .10
32 Gregg Olson .08 .25
33 Joe Girardi .15 .40
34 Ken Hill .08 .25
35 Sammy Sosa 1.25 3.00
36 Geronimo Berroa .02 .10
37 Omar Vizquel .25 .60
38 Dean Palmer .25 .60
39 John Olerud .40 1.00
40 Deion Sanders .25 .60
41 Randy Kramer .02 .10
42 Scott Lusader .02 .10
43 Dave Wayne Johnson .02 .10
44 Jeff Wetherby .02 .10
45 Eric Anthony .02 .10
46 Kenny Rogers .08 .25
47 Matt Winters .02 .10
48 Mauro Gozzo .02 .10
49 Carlos Quintana .02 .10
50 Bob Geren .02 .10
51 Chad Kreuter .02 .10
52 Randy Johnson .60 1.50
53 Hensley Meulens .02 .10
54 Gene Harris .02 .10
55 Bill Spiers .02 .10
56 Kelly Mann .02 .10
57 Tom McCarthy .02 .10
58 Steve Finley .08 .25
59 Ramon Martinez .02 .10
60 Greg Briley .02 .10
61 Jack Daugherty .02 .10
62 Tim Jones .02 .10
63 Doug Strange .02 .10
64 John Orton .02 .10
65 Scott Scudder .02 .10
66 Mark Gardner .02 .10
67 Mark Carreon .02 .10
68 Bob Milacki .02 .10
69 Andy Benes .08 .25
70 Carlos Martinez .02 .10
71 Jeff King .02 .10
72 Brad Arnsberg .02 .10
73 Rick Wrona .02 .10
74 Cris Carpenter .02 .10
75 Dennis Cook .02 .10
76 Pete Harnisch .02 .10
77 Greg Hibbard .02 .10
78 Ed Whited .02 .10
79 Scott Coolbaugh .02 .10
80 Billy Bates .02 .10
81 German Gonzalez .02 .10
82 Lance Blankenship .02 .10
83 Lenny Harris .02 .10
84 Milt Cuyler .02 .10
85 Erik Hanson .02 .10
86 Kent Anderson .02 .10
87 Hal Morris .02 .10
88 Mike Brumley .02 .10
89 Ken Patterson .02 .10
90 Mike Devereaux .02 .10
91 Greg Litton .02 .10
92 Rolando Roomes .02 .10
93 Ben McDonald .02 .10
94 Curt Schilling .75 2.00
95 Jose DeJesus .02 .10
96 Robin Ventura .25 .60
97 Steve Searcy .02 .10
98 Chip Hale .02 .10
99 Marquis Grissom .25 .60
100 Luis de los Santos .02 .10

1990 Score Sportflics Ryan

This standard-size card was issued by Optigraphics (producer of Score and Sportflics) to commemorate the 11th National Sports Card Collectors Convention held in Arlington, Texas in July of 1990. This card featured a Score front similar to the Ryan 1990 Score highlight card except for the 11th National Convention Logo on the bottom right of the card. On the other side a Ryan Sportflics card was printed that stated (reflected) either Sportflics or 1990 National Sports Collectors Convention on the bottom of the card. This issue was limited to a printing of 600 cards with Ryan himself destroying the printing plates.

NNO Nolan Ryan/(No number on back; 125.00 300.00
card back is actu

1990 Score Young Superstars I

COMPLETE SET (42) 4.00 10.00
ONE PER RACK PACK
1 Bo Jackson .50 1.25
2 Dwight Smith .08 .25
3 Albert Belle .50 1.25
4 Gregg Olson .08 .25
5 Jim Abbott .30 .75
6 Felix Fermin .08 .25
7 Brian Holman .08 .25
8 Clay Parker .08 .25
9 Junior Felix .08 .25
10 Joe Oliver .08 .25
11 Steve Finley .20 .50
12 Greg Briley .08 .25
13 Greg Vaughn .08 .25
14 Bill Spiers .08 .25
15 Eric Yelding .08 .25
16 Jose Gonzalez .08 .25
17 Mark Carreon .08 .25
18 Greg W. Harris .08 .25
19 Felix Jose .08 .25
20 Bob Milacki .08 .25
21 Kenny Rogers .20 .50
22 Rolando Roomes .08 .25
23 Bip Roberts .08 .25
24 Jeff Brantley .08 .25
25 Jeff Ballard .08 .25
26 John Dopson .08 .25
27 Ken Patterson .08 .25
28 Omar Vizquel .50 1.25
29 Kevin Brown .20 .50
30 Derek Lilliquist .08 .25
31 David Wells .20 .50
32 Ken Hill .20 .50
33 Greg Litton .08 .25
34 Rob Ducey .08 .25
35 Carlos Martinez .08 .25
36 John Smoltz .50 1.25
37 Lenny Harris .08 .25
38 Charlie Hayes .08 .25
39 Tommy Gregg .08 .25
40 John Wetteland .50 1.25
41 Jeff Huson .08 .25
42 Eric Anthony .08 .25

1990 Score Young Superstars II

COMP.FACT.SET (42) 10.00 25.00
DISTRIBUTED ONLY IN FACTORY SET FORM
1 Todd Zeile .20 .50
2 Ben McDonald .08 .25
3 Delino DeShields .60 1.50
4 Pat Combs .08 .25
5 John Olerud 1.25 3.00
6 Marquis Grissom .60 1.50
7 Mike Stanton .08 .25
8 Robin Ventura .60 1.50
9 Larry Walker 1.50 4.00
10 Dante Bichette .20 .50
11 Jack Armstrong .08 .25
12 Jay Bell .20 .50
13 Andy Benes .20 .50
14 Joey Cora .20 .50
15 Rob Dibble .20 .50
16 Jeff King .08 .25
17 Jeff Hamilton .08 .25
18 Erik Hanson .08 .25
19 Pete Harnisch .08 .25
20 Greg Hibbard .08 .25
21 Stan Javier .08 .25
22 Mark Lemke .08 .25
23 Steve Olin .20 .50
24 Tommy Greene .08 .25
25 Sammy Sosa 2.50 6.00
26 Gary Wayne .08 .25
27 Deion Sanders .60 1.50
28 Steve Wilson .08 .25
29 Joe Girardi .20 .50
30 John Orton .08 .25
31 Kevin Tapani .60 1.50
32 Carlos Baerga .20 .50
33 Glenallen Hill .08 .25
34 Mike Blowers .20 .50
35 Dave Hollins .20 .50
36 Lance Blankenship .08 .25
37 Hal Morris .08 .25
38 Lance Johnson .08 .25
39 Chris Gwynn .08 .25
40 Doug Dascenzo .08 .25
41 Jerald Clark .08 .25
42 Carlos Quintana .08 .25

1991 Score Promos

*PROMOS: 50X TO 100X BASIC CARDS

1991 Score

The 1991 Score set contains 893 standard-size cards issued in two separate series of 441 and 452 cards each. This set marks the fourth consecutive year that Score issued a major set but the first time Score issued the set in two series. Cards were distributed in plastic-wrap packs, blister packs and factory sets. The card fronts feature one of four different solid color borders (black, blue, teal and white) framing the full-color photo of the cards. Subsets include Rookie Prospects (331-379), First Draft Picks (380-391, 671-682), AL All-Stars (392-401), Master Blasters (402-406, 689-693), K-Men (407-411, 684-688), Rifleman (412-416, 694-698), NL All-Stars (661-670), No-Hitters (699-707), Franchise (849-874), Award Winners (875-881) and Dream Team (882-893). An American Flag card (737) was issued to honor the American soldiers involved in Desert Storm. Rookie Cards in the set include Carl Everett, Jeff Conine, Chipper Jones, Mike Mussina and Rondell White. There are a number of pitchers whose card backs show Innings Pitched totals which do not equal the added year-by-year total; the following card numbers were affected, 4, 24, 29, 30, 51, 81, 109, 111, 118, 141, 150, 156, 177, 204, 218, 232, 235, 255, 287, 289, 311, and 328.

COMPLETE SET (893) 8.00 20.00
COMP.FACT.SET (900) 10.00 25.00
SUBSET CARDS HALF VALUE OF BASE CARDS
1 Jose Canseco .05 .15
2 Ken Griffey Jr. .25 .60
3 Ryne Sandberg .15 .40
4 Nolan Ryan .40 1.00
5 Bo Jackson .08 .25
6 Bret Saberhagen UER .01 .05
In bio, missed
misspelled as mised
7 Will Clark .05 .15
8 Ellis Burks .02 .10
9 Joe Carter .02 .10
10 Rickey Henderson .08 .25
11 Ozzie Guillen .02 .10
12 Wade Boggs .05 .15
13 Jerome Walton .01 .05
14 John Franco .02 .10
15 Ricky Jordan UER .01 .05
League misspelled
as legue
16 Wally Backman .01 .05
17 Rob Dibble .02 .10
18 Glenn Braggs .01 .05
19 Cory Snyder .01 .05
20 Kal Daniels .01 .05
21 Mark Langston .01 .05
22 Kevin Gross .01 .05
23 Don Mattingly UER .25 .60
24 Dave Righetti .02 .10
25 Roberto Alomar .05 .15
26 Robby Thompson .01 .05
27 Jack McDowell .01 .05
28 Bip Roberts UER .01 .05
Bio reads playd
29 Jay Howell .01 .05
30 Dave Stieb UER .01 .05
17 wins in bio,
18 in stats
31 Johnny Ray .01 .05
32 Steve Sax .01 .05
33 Terry Mulholland .01 .05
34 Lee Guetterman .01 .05
35 Tim Raines .02 .10
36 Scott Fletcher .01 .05
37 Lance Parrish .02 .10
38 Tony Phillips UER .01 .05
Born 4/15(should be 4/25
39 Todd Stottlemyre .01 .05
40 Alan Trammell .02 .10
41 Todd Burns .01 .05
42 Mookie Wilson .02 .10
43 Chris Bosio .01 .05
44 Jeffrey Leonard .01 .05
45 Doug Jones .01 .05
46 Mike Scott UER .01 .05
In first line,
dominate should
read dominating
47 Andy Hawkins .01 .05
48 Harold Reynolds .02 .10
49 Paul Molitor .02 .10
50 John Farrell .01 .05
51 Danny Darwin .01 .05
52 Jeff Blauser .01 .05
53 John Tudor UER .01 .05
41 wins in '81
54 Milt Thompson .01 .05
55 Dave Justice .02 .10
56 Greg Olson .01 .05
57 Willie Blair .01 .05
58 Rick Parker .01 .05
59 Shawn Boskie .01 .05
60 Kevin Tapani .01 .05
61 Dave Hollins .01 .05
62 Scott Radinsky .01 .05
63 Francisco Cabrera .01 .05
64 Tim Layana .01 .05
65 Jim Leyritz .01 .05
66 Wayne Edwards .01 .05
67 Lee Stevens .01 .05
68 Bill Sampen UER .01 .05
Fourth line, long is spelled along
69 Craig Grebeck UER .01 .05
Born in Cerritos, not Johnstown
70 John Burkett .01 .05
71 Hector Villanueva .01 .05
72 Oscar Azocar .01 .05
73 Alan Mills .01 .05
74 Carlos Baerga .01 .05
75 Charles Nagy .01 .05
76 Tim Drummond .01 .05
77 Dana Kiecker .01 .05
78 Tom Edens RC .01 .05
79 Kent Mercker .01 .05
80 Steve Avery .01 .05
81 Lee Smith .02 .10
82 Dave Martinez .01 .05
83 Dave Winfield .02 .10
84 Bill Spiers .01 .05
85 Dan Pasqua .01 .05
86 Randy Milligan .01 .05
87 Tracy Jones .01 .05
88 Greg Myers .01 .05
89 Keith Hernandez .02 .10
90 Todd Benzinger .01 .05
91 Mike Jackson .01 .05
92 Mike Stanley .01 .05
93 Candy Maldonado .01 .05
94 John Kruk UER .02 .10
No decimal point
before 1990 BA
95 Cal Ripken UER .30 .75
96 Willie Fraser .01 .05
97 Mike Felder .01 .05
98 Bill Landrum .01 .05
99 Chuck Crim .01 .05
100 Chuck Finley .02 .10
101 Kirt Manwaring .01 .05
102 Jaime Navarro .01 .05
103 Dickie Thon .01 .05
104 Brian Downing .01 .05
105 Jim Abbott .05 .15
106 Tom Brookens .01 .05
107 Darryl Hamilton UER .01 .05
Bio info is for
Jeff Hamilton
108 Bryan Harvey .01 .05
109 Greg A. Harris UER .01 .05
Shown pitching lefty, bio says righty
110 Greg Swindell .01 .05
111 Juan Berenguer .01 .05
112 Mike Heath .01 .05
113 Scott Bradley .01 .05
114 Jack Morris .02 .10
115 Barry Jones .01 .05
116 Kevin Romine .01 .05
117 Garry Templeton .01 .05
118 Scott Sanderson .01 .05
119 Roberto Kelly .01 .05
120 George Brett .25 .60
121 Oddibe McDowell .01 .05
122 Jim Acker .01 .05
123 Bill Swift UER .01 .05
Born 12/27/61,
should be 10/27
124 Eric King .01 .05
125 Jay Buhner .02 .10
126 Matt Young .01 .05
127 Alvaro Espinoza .01 .05
128 Greg Hibbard .01 .05
129 Jeff M. Robinson .01 .05
130 Mike Greenwell .01 .05
131 Dion James .01 .05
132 Donn Pall UER .01 .05
1988 ERA in stats 0.00
133 Lloyd Moseby .01 .05
134 Randy Velarde .01 .05
135 Allan Anderson .01 .05
136 Mark Davis .01 .05
137 Eric Davis .02 .10
138 Phil Stephenson .01 .05
139 Felix Fermin .01 .05
140 Pedro Guerrero .02 .10
141 Charlie Hough .02 .10
142 Mike Henneman .01 .05
143 Jeff Montgomery .01 .05
144 Lenny Harris .01 .05
145 Bruce Hurst .01 .05
146 Eric Anthony .01 .05
147 Paul Assenmacher .01 .05
148 Jesse Barfield .01 .05
149 Carlos Quintana .01 .05
150 Dave Stewart .02 .10
151 Roy Smith .01 .05
152 Paul Gibson .01 .05
153 Mickey Hatcher .01 .05
154 Jim Eisenreich .01 .05
155 Kenny Rogers .02 .10
156 Dave Schmidt .01 .05
157 Lance Johnson .01 .05
158 Dave West .01 .05
159 Steve Balboni .01 .05
160 Jeff Brantley .01 .05
161 Craig Biggio .05 .15
162 Brook Jacoby .01 .05
163 Dan Gladden .01 .05
164 Jeff Reardon UER .02 .10
Total IP shown as
943.2, should be 943.1
165 Mark Carreon .01 .05
166 Mel Hall .01 .05
167 Gary Mielke .01 .05
168 Cecil Fielder .02 .10
169 Darrin Jackson .01 .05
170 Rick Aguilera .02 .10
171 Walt Weiss .01 .05
172 Steve Farr .01 .05
173 Jody Reed .01 .05
174 Mike Jeffcoat .01 .05
175 Mark Grace .05 .15
176 Larry Sheets .01 .05
177 Bill Gullickson .01 .05
178 Chris Gwynn .01 .05
179 Melido Perez .01 .05
180 Sid Fernandez UER .01 .05
779 runs in 1990
181 Tim Burke .01 .05
182 Gary Pettis .01 .05
183 Rob Murphy .01 .05
184 Craig Lefferts .01 .05
185 Howard Johnson .01 .05
186 Ken Caminiti .02 .10
187 Tim Belcher .01 .05
188 Greg Cadaret .01 .05
189 Matt Williams .02 .10
190 Dave Magadan .01 .05
191 Geno Petralli .01 .05
192 Jeff D. Robinson .01 .05
193 Jim Deshaies .01 .05
194 Willie Randolph .02 .10
195 George Bell .01 .05
196 Hubie Brooks .01 .05
197 Tom Gordon .01 .05
198 Mike Fitzgerald .01 .05
199 Mike Pagliarulo .01 .05
200 Kirby Puckett .08 .25
201 Shawon Dunston .01 .05
202 Dennis Boyd .01 .05
203 Junior Felix UER .01 .05
Text has him in NL
204 Alejandro Pena .01 .05
205 Pete Smith .01 .05
206 Tom Glavine UER .05 .15
Lefty spelled leftie
207 Luis Salazar .01 .05
208 John Smoltz .05 .15
209 Doug Dascenzo .01 .05
210 Tim Wallach .01 .05
211 Greg Gagne .01 .05
212 Mark Gubicza .01 .05
213 Mark Parent .01 .05
214 Ken Oberkfell .01 .05
215 Gary Carter .02 .10
216 Rafael Palmeiro .05 .15
217 Tom Niedenfuer .01 .05
218 Dave LaPoint .01 .05
219 Jeff Treadway .01 .05
220 Mitch Williams UER .01 .05
'89 ERA shown as 2.76,
should be 2.64
221 Jose DeLeon .01 .05
222 Mike LaValliere .01 .05
223 Darrel Akerfelds .01 .05
224A Kent Anderson ERR .02 .10
First line& flachy
should read flashy
224B Kent Anderson COR .02 .10
Corrected in
factory sets
225 Dwight Evans .05 .15
226 Gary Redus .01 .05
227 Paul O'Neill .05 .15
228 Marty Barrett .01 .05
229 Tom Browning .01 .05
230 Terry Pendleton .02 .10
231 Jack Armstrong .01 .05
232 Mike Boddicker .01 .05
233 Neal Heaton .01 .05
234 Marquis Grissom .02 .10
235 Bert Blyleven .02 .10
236 Curt Young .01 .05
237 Don Carman .01 .05
238 Charlie Hayes .01 .05
239 Mark Knudson .01 .05
240 Todd Zeile .01 .05
241 Larry Walker UER .08 .25
Maple River, should
be Maple Ridge
242 Jerald Clark .01 .05
243 Jeff Ballard .01 .05
244 Jeff King .01 .05
245 Tom Brunansky .01 .05
246 Darren Daulton .02 .10
247 Scott Terry .01 .05
248 Rob Deer .01 .05
249 Brady Anderson UER .02 .10
1990 Hagerstown 1 hit,
should say 13 hits
250 Len Dykstra .02 .10
251 Greg W. Harris .01 .05
252 Mike Hartley .01 .05
253 Joey Cora .01 .05
254 Ivan Calderon .01 .05
255 Ted Power .01 .05
256 Sammy Sosa .08 .25
257 Steve Buechele .01 .05
258 Mike Devereaux UER .01 .05
No comma between
city and state
259 Brad Komminsk UER .01 .05
Last text line,
Ba should be BA
260 Ted Higuera .01 .05
261 Shawn Abner .01 .05
262 Dave Valle .01 .05
263 Jeff Huson .01 .05
264 Edgar Martinez .05 .15
265 Carlton Fisk .05 .15
266 Steve Finley .02 .10
267 John Wetteland .02 .10
268 Kevin Appier .02 .10
269 Steve Lyons .01 .05
270 Mickey Tettleton .01 .05
271 Luis Rivera .01 .05
272 Steve Jeltz .01 .05
273 R.J. Reynolds .01 .05
274 Carlos Martinez .01 .05
275 Dan Plesac .01 .05
276 Mike Morgan UER .01 .05
Total IP shown as
1149.1, should be 1149
277 Jeff Russell .01 .05
278 Pete Incaviglia .01 .05
279 Kevin Seitzer UER .01 .05
Bio has 200 hits twice
and .300 four times,
should be once and
three times
280 Bobby Thigpen .01 .05
281 Stan Javier UER .01 .05
Born 1/9,
should say 9/1
282 Henry Cotto .01 .05
283 Gary Wayne .01 .05
284 Shane Mack .01 .05
285 Brian Holman .01 .05
286 Gerald Perry .01 .05
287 Steve Crawford .01 .05
288 Nelson Liriano .01 .05
289 Don Aase .01 .05
290 Randy Johnson .10 .30
291 Harold Baines .02 .10
292 Kent Hrbek .02 .10
293A Les Lancaster ERR .01 .05
No comma between
Dallas and Texas
293B Les Lancaster COR .01 .05
Corrected in
factory sets
294 Jeff Musselman .01 .05
295 Kurt Stillwell .01 .05
296 Stan Belinda .01 .05
297 Lou Whitaker .02 .10
298 Glenn Wilson .01 .05
299 Omar Vizquel UER .05 .15
Born 5/15, should be
4/24, there is a decimal
before GP total for '90
300 Ramon Martinez .01 .05
301 Dwight Smith .01 .05
302 Tim Crews .01 .05
303 Lance Blankenship .01 .05
304 Sid Bream .01 .05
305 Rafael Ramirez .01 .05
306 Steve Wilson .01 .05
307 Mackey Sasser .01 .05
308 Franklin Stubbs .01 .05
309 Jack Daugherty UER .01 .05
Born 6/3/60,
should say July
310 Eddie Murray .08 .25
311 Bob Welch .01 .05
312 Brian Harper .01 .05
313 Lance McCullers .01 .05
314 Dave Smith .01 .05
315 Bobby Bonilla .02 .10
316 Jerry Don Gleaton .01 .05
317 Greg Maddux .15 .40
318 Keith Miller .01 .05
319 Mark Portugal .01 .05
320 Robin Ventura .02 .10
321 Bob Ojeda .01 .05
322 Mike Harkey .01 .05
323 Jay Bell .02 .10
324 Mark McGwire .30 .75
325 Gary Gaetti .02 .10
326 Jeff Pico .01 .05
327 Kevin McReynolds .01 .05
328 Frank Tanana .01 .05
329 Eric Yelding UER .01 .05
Listed as 6'3
should be 5'11
330 Barry Bonds .40 1.00
331 Brian McRae RC .08 .25
332 Pedro Munoz RC .02 .10
333 Daryl Irvine RC .01 .05
334 Chris Hoiles .01 .05
335 Thomas Howard .01 .05
336 Jeff Schulz RC .01 .05
337 Jeff Manto .01 .05
338 Beau Allred .01 .05
339 Mike Bordick RC .15 .40
340 Todd Hundley .01 .05
341 Jim Vatcher UER RC .01 .05
342 Luis Sojo .01 .05
343 Jose Offerman UER .01 .05
Born 1969, should
say 1968
344 Pete Coachman RC .01 .05
345 Mike Benjamin .01 .05
346 Ozzie Canseco .01 .05
347 Tim McIntosh .01 .05
348 Phil Plantier RC .02 .10
349 Terry Shumpert .01 .05
350 Darren Lewis .01 .05
351 David Walsh RC .01 .05
352A Scott Chiamparino .02 .10
ERR
Bats left, should be right
352B Scott Chiamparino .02 .10
COR
corrected in factory sets
353 Julio Valera .01 .05
UER Progressed mis-
spelled as progessed
354 Anthony Telford RC .01 .05
355 Kevin Wickander .01 .05
356 Tim Naehring .01 .05
357 Jim Poole .01 .05
358 Mark Whiten UER .01 .05
Shown hitting lefty, bio says righty
359 Terry Wells RC .01 .05
360 Rafael Valdez .01 .05
361 Mel Stottlemyre Jr. .01 .05
362 David Segui .01 .05
363 Paul Abbott RC .01 .05
364 Steve Howard .01 .05
365 Karl Rhodes .01 .05
366 Rafael Novoa RC .01 .05
367 Joe Grahe RC .01 .05
368 Darren Reed .01 .05
369 Jeff McKnight .01 .05
370 Scott Leius .01 .05
371 Mark Dewey RC .01 .05
372 Mark Lee UER RC .02 .10
373 Rosario Rodriguez UER RC .01 .05
374 Chuck McElroy .01 .05
375 Mike Bell RC .01 .05
376 Mickey Morandini .01 .05
377 Bill Haselman RC .01 .05

378 Dave Pavlas RC .01 .05
379 Derrick May .01 .05
380 Jeromy Burnitz RC .15 .40
381 Donald Peters RC .01 .05
382 Alex Fernandez FDP .01 .05
383 Mike Mussina RC 1.00 2.50
384 Dan Smith RC .02 .10
385 Lance Dickson RC .02 .10
386 Carl Everett RC .20 .50
387 Tom Nevers RC .02 .10
388 Adam Hyzdu RC .08 .25
389 Todd Van Poppel RC .08 .25
390 Rondell White RC .15 .40
391 Marc Newfield RC .02 .10
392 Julio Franco AS .01 .05
393 Wade Boggs AS .02 .10
394 Ozzie Guillen AS .01 .05
395 Cecil Fielder AS .01 .05
396 Ken Griffey Jr. AS .10 .30
397 Rickey Henderson AS .05 .15
398 Jose Canseco AS .02 .10
399 Roger Clemens AS .15 .40
400 Sandy Alomar Jr. AS .01 .05
401 Bobby Thigpen AS .01 .05
402 Bobby Bonilla MB .01 .05
403 Eric Davis MB .01 .05
404 Fred McGriff MB .02 .10
405 Glenn Davis MB .01 .05
406 Kevin Mitchell MB .01 .05
407 Rob Dibble KM .01 .05
408 Ramon Martinez KM .01 .05
409 David Cone KM .01 .05
410 Bobby Witt KM .01 .05
411 Mark Langston KM .01 .05
412 Bo Jackson RIF .02 .10
413 Shawon Dunston RIF .01 .05
UER
In the baseball, should say in baseball
414 Jesse Barfield RIF .01 .05
415 Ken Caminiti RIF .01 .05
416 Benito Santiago RIF .01 .05
417 Nolan Ryan HL .20 .50
418 Bobby Thigpen HL UER .01 .05
Back refers to Hal
McRae Jr., should
say Brian McRae
419 Ramon Martinez HL .01 .05
420 Bo Jackson HL .02 .10
421 Carlton Fisk HL .02 .10
422 Jimmy Key .01 .05
423 Junior Noboa .01 .05
424 Al Newman .01 .05
425 Pat Borders .01 .05
426 Von Hayes .01 .05
427 Tim Teufel .01 .05
428 Eric Plunk UER .01 .05
Text says Eric's had, no apostrophe needed
429 John Moses .01 .05
430 Mike Witt .01 .05
431 Otis Nixon .01 .05
432 Tony Fernandez .01 .05
433 Rance Mulliniks .01 .05
434 Dan Petry .01 .05
435 Bob Geren .01 .05
436 Steve Frey .01 .05
437 Jamie Moyer .02 .10
438 Junior Ortiz .01 .05
439 Tom O'Malley .01 .05
440 Pat Combs .01 .05
441 Jose Canseco DT .05 .15
442 Alfredo Griffin .01 .05
443 Andres Galarraga .02 .10
444 Bryn Smith .01 .05
445 Andre Dawson .02 .10
446 Juan Samuel .01 .05
447 Mike Aldrete .01 .05
448 Ron Gant .02 .10
449 Fernando Valenzuela .02 .10
450 Vince Coleman UER .01 .05
Should say topped
majors in steals four
times, not three times
451 Kevin Mitchell .01 .05
452 Spike Owen .01 .05
453 Mike Bielecki .01 .05
454 Dennis Martinez .02 .10
455 Brett Butler .02 .10
456 Ron Darling .01 .05
457 Dennis Rasmussen .01 .05
458 Ken Howell .01 .05
459 Steve Bedrosian .01 .05
460 Frank Viola .02 .10
461 Jose Lind .01 .05
462 Chris Sabo .01 .05
463 Dante Bichette .02 .10
464 Rick Mahler .01 .05
465 John Smiley .01 .05
466 Devon White .02 .10
467 John Orton .01 .05
468 Mike Stanton .01 .05
469 Billy Hatcher .01 .05
470 Wally Joyner .02 .10
471 Gene Larkin .01 .05
472 Doug Drabek .01 .05
473 Gary Sheffield .02 .10
474 David Wells .02 .10
475 Andy Van Slyke .05 .15
476 Mike Gallego .01 .05
477 B.J. Surhoff .02 .10
478 Gene Nelson .01 .05
479 Mariano Duncan .01 .05
480 Fred McGriff .05 .15
481 Jerry Browne .01 .05
482 Alvin Davis .01 .05
483 Bill Wegman .01 .05
484 Dave Parker .02 .10
485 Dennis Eckersley .02 .10
486 Erik Hanson UER .01 .05
Basketball misspelled
as basketball
487 Bill Ripken .01 .05
488 Tom Candiotti .01 .05
489 Mike Schooler .01 .05
490 Gregg Olson .01 .05
491 Chris James .01 .05
492 Pete Harnisch .01 .05
493 Julio Franco .02 .10
494 Greg Briley .01 .05
495 Ruben Sierra .02 .10
496 Steve Olin .01 .05
497 Mike Fetters .01 .05
498 Mark Williamson .01 .05
499 Bob Tewksbury .01 .05
500 Tony Gwynn .10 .30
501 Randy Myers .01 .05
502 Keith Comstock .01 .05
503 Craig Worthington UER .01 .05
DeCinces misspelled
DiCinces on back
504 Mark Eichhorn UER .01 .05
Stats incomplete,
doesn't have '89 Braves stint
505 Barry Larkin .05 .15
506 Dave Johnson .01 .05
507 Bobby Witt .01 .05
508 Joe Orsulak .01 .05
509 Pete O'Brien .01 .05
510 Brad Arnsberg .01 .05
511 Storm Davis .01 .05
512 Bob Milacki .01 .05
513 Bill Pecota .01 .05
514 Glenallen Hill .01 .05
515 Danny Tartabull .01 .05
516 Mike Moore .01 .05
517 Ron Robinson UER .01 .05
577 K's in 1990
518 Mark Gardner .01 .05
519 Rick Wrona .01 .05
520 Mike Scioscia .01 .05
521 Frank Wills .01 .05
522 Greg Brock .01 .05
523 Jack Clark .02 .10
524 Bruce Ruffin .01 .05
525 Robin Yount .15 .40
526 Tom Foley .01 .05
527 Pat Perry .01 .05
528 Greg Vaughn .01 .05
529 Wally Whitehurst .01 .05
530 Norm Charlton .01 .05
531 Marvell Wynne .01 .05
532 Jim Gantner .01 .05
533 Greg Litton .01 .05
534 Manny Lee .01 .05
535 Scott Bailes .01 .05
536 Charlie Leibrandt .01 .05
537 Roger McDowell .01 .05
538 Andy Benes .01 .05
539 Rick Honeycutt .01 .05
540 Dwight Gooden .02 .10
541 Scott Garrelts .01 .05
542 Dave Clark .01 .05
543 Lonnie Smith .01 .05
544 Rick Reuschel .01 .05
545 Delino DeShields UER .02 .10
Rockford misspelled
as Rock Ford in '88
546 Mike Sharperson .01 .05
547 Mike Kingery .01 .05
548 Terry Kennedy .01 .05
549 David Cone .02 .10
550 Orel Hershiser .02 .10
551 Matt Nokes .01 .05
552 Eddie Williams .01 .05
553 Frank DiPino .01 .05
554 Fred Lynn .01 .05
555 Alex Cole .01 .05
556 Terry Leach .01 .05
557 Chet Lemon .01 .05
558 Paul Mirabella .01 .05
559 Bill Long .01 .05
560 Phil Bradley .01 .05
561 Duane Ward .01 .05
562 Dave Bergman .01 .05
563 Eric Show .01 .05
564 Xavier Hernandez .01 .05
565 Jeff Parrett .01 .05
566 Chuck Cary .01 .05
567 Ken Hill .01 .05
568 Bob Welch Hand .01 .05
Complement should be
compliment UER
569 John Mitchell .01 .05
570 Travis Fryman .02 .10
571 Derek Lilliquist .01 .05
572 Steve Lake .01 .05
573 John Barfield .01 .05
574 Randy Bush .01 .05
575 Joe Magrane .01 .05
576 Eddie Diaz .01 .05
577 Casey Candaele .01 .05
578 Jesse Orosco .01 .05
579 Tom Henke .01 .05
580 Rick Cerone UER .01 .05
Actually his third
go-round with Yankees
581 Drew Hall .01 .05
582 Tony Castillo .01 .05
583 Jimmy Jones .01 .05
584 Rick Reed .01 .05
585 Joe Girardi .01 .05
586 Jeff Gray RC .01 .05
587 Luis Polonia .01 .05
588 Joe Klink .01 .05
589 Rex Hudler .01 .05
590 Kirk McCaskill .01 .05
591 Juan Agosto .01 .05
592 Wes Gardner .01 .05
593 Rich Rodriguez RC .01 .05
594 Mitch Webster .01 .05
595 Kelly Gruber .01 .05
596 Dale Mohorcic .01 .05
597 Willie McGee .02 .10
598 Bill Krueger .01 .05
599 Bob Walk UER .01 .05
Cards says he's 33,
but actually he's 34
600 Kevin Maas .01 .05
601 Danny Jackson .01 .05
602 Craig McMurtry UER .01 .05
Anonymously misspelled
anonimously
603 Curtis Wilkerson .01 .05
604 Adam Peterson .01 .05
605 Sam Horn .01 .05
606 Tommy Gregg .01 .05
607 Ken Dayley .01 .05
608 Carmelo Castillo .01 .05
609 John Shelby .01 .05
610 Don Slaught .01 .05
611 Calvin Schiraldi .01 .05
612 Dennis Lamp .01 .05
613 Andres Thomas .01 .05
614 Jose Gonzalez .01 .05
615 Randy Ready .01 .05
616 Kevin Bass .01 .05
617 Mike Marshall .01 .05
618 Daryl Boston .01 .05
619 Andy McGaffigan .01 .05
620 Joe Oliver .01 .05
621 Jim Gott .01 .05
622 Jose Oquendo .01 .05
623 Jose DeJesus .01 .05
624 Mike Brumley .01 .05
625 John Olerud .02 .10
626 Ernest Riles .01 .05
627 Gene Harris .01 .05
628 Jose Uribe .01 .05
629 Darnell Coles .01 .05
630 Carney Lansford .02 .10
631 Tim Leary .01 .05
632 Tim Hulett .01 .05
633 Kevin Elster .01 .05
634 Tony Fossas .01 .05
635 Francisco Oliveras .01 .05
636 Bob Patterson .01 .05
637 Gary Ward .01 .05
638 Rene Gonzales .01 .05
639 Don Robinson .01 .05
640 Darryl Strawberry .02 .10
641 Dave Anderson .01 .05
642 Scott Scudder .01 .05
643 Reggie Harris UER .01 .05
Hepatitis misspelled
as hepititis
644 Dave Henderson .01 .05
645 Ben McDonald .01 .05
646 Bob Kipper .01 .05
647 Hal Morris UER .01 .05
It's should be its
648 Tim Birtsas .01 .05
649 Steve Searcy .01 .05
650 Dale Murphy .05 .15
651 Ron Oester .01 .05
652 Mike LaCoss .01 .05
653 Ron Jones .01 .05
654 Kelly Downs .01 .05
655 Roger Clemens .30 .75
656 Herm Winningham .01 .05
657 Trevor Wilson .01 .05
658 Jose Rijo .01 .05
659 Dann Bilardello UER .01 .05
Bio has 13 games, 1 hit,
and 32 AB, stats show 19, 2, and 37
660 Gregg Jefferies .01 .05
661 Doug Drabek AS UER .01 .05
Through is mis-
spelled though
662 Randy Myers AS .01 .05
663 Benny Santiago AS .01 .05
664 Will Clark AS .02 .10
665 Ryne Sandberg AS .08 .25
666 Barry Larkin AS UER .02 .10
Line 13, coolly misspelled cooly
667 Matt Williams AS .01 .05
668 Barry Bonds AS .20 .50
669 Eric Davis AS .01 .05
670 Bobby Bonilla AS .01 .05
671 Chipper Jones RC 2.00 5.00
672 Eric Christopherson RC .02 .10
673 Robbie Beckett RC .02 .10
674 Shane Andrews RC .08 .25
675 Steve Karsay RC .08 .25
676 Aaron Holbert RC .02 .10
677 Donovan Osborne RC .02 .10
678 Todd Ritchie RC .08 .25
679 Ronnie Walden RC .02 .10
680 Tim Costo RC .02 .10
681 Dan Wilson RC .08 .25
682 Kurt Miller RC .02 .10
683 Mike Lieberthal RC .15 .40
684 Roger Clemens KM .15 .40
685 Dwight Gooden KM .01 .05
686 Nolan Ryan KM .20 .50
687 Frank Viola KM .01 .05
688 Erik Hanson KM .01 .05
689 Matt Williams MB .01 .05
690 Jose Canseco MB UER .02 .10
Mammoth misspelled
as monmouth
691 Darryl Strawberry MB .01 .05
692 Bo Jackson MB .02 .10
693 Cecil Fielder MB .01 .05
694 Sandy Alomar Jr. RF .01 .05
695 Cory Snyder RF .01 .05
696 Eric Davis RF .01 .05
697 Ken Griffey Jr. RF .10 .30
698 Andy Van Slyke RF UER .02 .10
Line 2, outfielders
does not need
699 Mark Langston NH .01 .05
Mike Witt
700 Randy Johnson NH .05 .15
701 Nolan Ryan NH .20 .50
702 Dave Stewart NH .01 .05
703 Fernando Valenzuela NH .01 .05
704 Andy Hawkins NH .01 .05
705 Melido Perez NH .01 .05
706 Terry Mulholland NH .01 .05
707 Dave Stieb NH .01 .05
708 Brian Barnes RC .01 .05
709 Bernard Gilkey .01 .05
710 Steve Decker RC .01 .05
711 Paul Faries RC .01 .05
712 Paul Marak RC .01 .05
713 Wes Chamberlain RC .02 .10
714 Kevin Belcher RC .02 .10
715 Dan Boone UER .01 .05
IP adds up to 101,
but card has 101.2
716 Steve Adkins RC .01 .05
717 Geronimo Pena .01 .05
718 Howard Farmer .01 .05
719 Mark Leonard RC .01 .05
720 Tom Lampkin .01 .05
721 Mike Gardiner RC .01 .05
722 Jeff Conine RC .15 .40
723 Efrain Valdez RC .01 .05
724 Chuck Malone .01 .05
725 Leo Gomez .01 .05
726 Paul McClellan RC .01 .05
727 Mark Leiter RC .02 .10
728 Rich DeLucia UER RC .01 .05
729 Mel Rojas .01 .05
730 Hector Wagner RC .01 .05
731 Ray Lankford .02 .10
732 Turner Ward RC .02 .10
733 Gerald Alexander RC .01 .05
734 Scott Anderson RC .01 .05
735 Tony Perezchica .01 .05
736 Jimmy Kremers .01 .05
737 American Flag .08 .25
Pray for Peace
738 Mike York RC .01 .05
739 Mike Rochford .01 .05
740 Scott Aldred .01 .05
741 Rico Brogna .01 .05
742 Dave Burba RC .08 .25
743 Ray Stephens RC .01 .05
744 Eric Gunderson .01 .05
745 Troy Afenir RC .01 .05
746 Jeff Shaw .01 .05
747 Orlando Merced RC .02 .10
748 Omar Olivares UER RC .02 .10
749 Jerry Kutzler .01 .05
750 Mo Vaughn UER .02 .10
44 SB's in 1990
751 Matt Stark RC .01 .05
752 Randy Hennis RC .01 .05
753 Andujar Cedeno .01 .05
754 Kelvin Torve .01 .05
755 Joe Kraemer .01 .05
756 Phil Clark RC .02 .10
757 Ed Vosberg RC .01 .05
758 Mike Perez RC .02 .10
759 Scott Lewis RC .01 .05
760 Steve Chitren RC .01 .05
761 Ray Young RC .01 .05
762 Andres Santana .01 .05
763 Rodney McCray RC .01 .05
764 Sean Berry UER RC .02 .10
765 Brent Mayne .01 .05
766 Mike Simms RC .01 .05
767 Glenn Sutko RC .01 .05
768 Gary DiSarcina .01 .05
769 George Brett HL .08 .25
770 Cecil Fielder HL .01 .05
771 Jim Presley .01 .05
772 John Dopson .01 .05
773 Bo Jackson Breaker .02 .10
774 Brent Knackert UER .01 .05
Born in 1954,
shown throwing righty,
but bio says lefty
775 Bill Doran UER .01 .05
Reds in NL East
776 Dick Schofield .01 .05
777 Nelson Santovenia .01 .05
778 Mark Guthrie .01 .05
779 Mark Lemke .01 .05
780 Terry Steinbach .01 .05
781 Tom Bolton .01 .05
782 Randy Tomlin RC .02 .10
783 Jeff Kunkel .01 .05
784 Felix Jose .01 .05
785 Rick Sutcliffe .02 .10
786 John Cerutti .01 .05
787 Jose Vizcaino UER .01 .05
Offerman, not Opperman
788 Curt Schilling .08 .25
789 Ed Whitson .01 .05
790 Tony Pena .01 .05
791 John Candelaria .01 .05
792 Carmelo Martinez .01 .05
793 Sandy Alomar Jr. UER .01 .05
Indian's should
say Indians'
794 Jim Neidlinger RC .01 .05
795 Barry Larkin WS .02 .10
and Chris Sabo
796 Paul Sorrento .01 .05
797 Tom Pagnozzi .01 .05
798 Tino Martinez .08 .25
799 Scott Ruskin UER .01 .05
Text says first three
seasons but lists
averages for four
800 Kirk Gibson .02 .10
801 Walt Terrell .01 .05
802 John Russell .01 .05
803 Chili Davis .02 .10
804 Chris Nabholz .01 .05
805 Juan Gonzalez .08 .25
806 Ron Hassey .01 .05
807 Todd Worrell .01 .05
808 Tommy Greene .01 .05
809 Joel Skinner UER .01 .05
Joel, not Bob, was drafted in 1979
810 Benito Santiago .02 .10
811 Pat Tabler UER .01 .05
Line 3, always misspelled always
812 Scott Erickson UER RC .01 .05
813 Moises Alou .02 .10
814 Dale Sveum .01 .05
815 Ryne Sandberg MANYR .08 .25
816 Rick Dempsey .01 .05
817 Scott Bankhead .01 .05
818 Jason Grimsley .01 .05
819 Doug Jennings .01 .05
820 Tom Herr .01 .05
821 Rob Ducey .01 .05
822 Luis Quinones .01 .05
823 Greg Minton .01 .05
824 Mark Grant .01 .05
825 Ozzie Smith UER .15 .40
826 Dave Eiland .01 .05
827 Danny Heep .01 .05
828 Hensley Meulens .01 .05
829 Charlie O'Brien .01 .05
830 Glenn Davis .01 .05
831 John Marzano UER .01 .05
International mis-
spelled Internaional
832 Steve Ontiveros .01 .05
833 Ron Karkovice .01 .05
834 Jerry Goff .01 .05
835 Ken Griffey Sr. .02 .10
836 Kevin Reimer .01 .05
837 Randy Kutcher UER .01 .05
Infectious mis-
spelled infectous
838 Mike Blowers .01 .05
839 Mike Macfarlane .01 .05
840 Frank Thomas UER .08 .25
1989 Sarasota stats,
15 games but 188 AB
841 K.Griffey Jr./K.Griffey Sr. .20 .50
842 Jack Howell .01 .05
843 Goose Gozzo .01 .05
844 Gerald Young .01 .05
845 Zane Smith .01 .05
846 Kevin Brown .02 .10
847 Sil Campusano .01 .05
848 Larry Andersen .01 .05
849 Cal Ripken FRAN .15 .40
850 Roger Clemens FRAN .15 .40
851 Sandy Alomar Jr. FRAN .01 .05
852 Alan Trammell FRAN .02 .10
853 George Brett FRAN .08 .25
854 Robin Yount FRAN .08 .25
855 Kirby Puckett FRAN .05 .15
856 Don Mattingly FRAN .10 .30
857 Rickey Henderson FRAN .05 .15
858 Ken Griffey Jr. FRAN .15 .40
859 Ruben Sierra FRAN .01 .05
860 John Olerud FRAN .01 .05
861 Dave Justice FRAN .01 .05
862 Ryne Sandberg FRAN .08 .25
863 Eric Davis FRAN .01 .05
864 Darryl Strawberry FRAN .01 .05
865 Tim Wallach FRAN .01 .05
866 Dwight Gooden FRAN .01 .05
867 Len Dykstra FRAN .01 .05
868 Barry Bonds FRAN .20 .50
869 Todd Zeile FRAN UER .01 .05
Powerful misspelled
as poweful
870 Benito Santiago FRAN .01 .05
871 Will Clark FRAN .02 .10
872 Craig Biggio FRAN .02 .10
873 Wally Joyner FRAN .01 .05
874 Frank Thomas FRAN .05 .15
875 Rickey Henderson MVP .05 .15
876 Barry Bonds MVP .20 .50
877 Bob Welch CY .01 .05
878 Doug Drabek CY .01 .05
879 Sandy Alomar Jr. ROY .01 .05
880 Dave Justice ROY .01 .05
881 Damon Berryhill .01 .05
882 Frank Viola DT .01 .05
883 Dave Stewart DT .01 .05
884 Doug Jones DT .01 .05
885 Randy Myers DT .01 .05
886 Will Clark DT .02 .10
887 Roberto Alomar DT .02 .10
888 Barry Larkin DT .02 .10
889 Wade Boggs DT .05 .15
890 Rickey Henderson DT .08 .25
891 Kirby Puckett DT .05 .15
892 Ken Griffey Jr DT .25 .60
893 Benny Santiago DT .02 .10

1991 Score Cooperstown

COMPLETE SET (7) 2.50 6.00
ONE SET PER FACTORY SET
B1 Wade Boggs .25 .60
B2 Barry Larkin .25 .60
B3 Ken Griffey Jr. 1.00 2.50
B4 Rickey Henderson .40 1.00
B5 George Brett 1.00 2.50
B6 Will Clark .25 .60
B7 Nolan Ryan 1.50 4.00

1991 Score Hot Rookies

COMPLETE SET (10) 3.00 8.00
ONE PER BLISTER PACK
1 David Justice .40 1.00
2 Kevin Maas .20 .50
3 Hal Morris .20 .50
4 Frank Thomas .75 2.00
5 Jeff Conine .20 .50
6 Sandy Alomar Jr. .20 .50
7 Ray Lankford .40 1.00
8 Steve Decker .20 .50
9 Juan Gonzalez .75 2.00
10 Jose Offerman .20 .50

1991 Score Mantle

COMPLETE SET (7) 20.00 50.00
COMMON MANTLE (1-7) 6.00 15.00
RANDOM INSERTS IN SER.2 PACKS
ONE PROMO SET SENT TO EACH DEALER
DEALER PROMOS NUMBERED OUT OF 5000
AU Mickey Mantle AU/2500 250.00 500.00

1991 Score Mantle Promos

COMPLETE SET (7) 20.00 50.00
COMMON MANTLE 4.00 10.00

1991 Score Rookie/Traded

The 1991 Score Rookie and Traded contains 110 standard-size player cards and was issued exclusively in factory set form along with 10 "World Series II" magic motion trivia cards through hobby dealers. The front design is identical to the regular issue 1991 Score set except for the distinctive mauve borders and T-suffixed numbering. Cards 1T-80T feature traded players, while cards 81T-110T focus on rookies. Rookie Cards in the set include Jeff Bagwell and Ivan Rodriguez.

COMP.FACT.SET (110) 2.00 5.00
1T Bo Jackson .20 .50
2T Mike Flanagan .02 .10
3T Pete Incaviglia .02 .10
4T Jack Clark .08 .25
5T Hubie Brooks .02 .10
6T Ivan Calderon .02 .10
7T Glenn Davis .02 .10
8T Wally Backman .02 .10
9T Dave Smith .02 .10
10T Tim Raines .08 .25
11T Joe Carter .08 .25
12T Sid Bream .02 .10
13T George Bell .02 .10
14T Steve Bedrosian .02 .10
15T Willie Wilson .02 .10
16T Darryl Strawberry .08 .25
17T Danny Jackson .02 .10
18T Kirk Gibson .08 .25
19T Willie McGee .08 .25
20T Junior Felix .02 .10
21T Steve Farr .02 .10
22T Pat Tabler .02 .10
23T Brett Butler .08 .25
24T Danny Darwin .02 .10
25T Mickey Tettleton .02 .10
26T Gary Carter .08 .25
27T Mitch Williams .02 .10
28T Candy Maldonado .02 .10
29T Otis Nixon .02 .10
30T Brian Downing .02 .10
31T Tom Candiotti .02 .10
32T John Candelaria .02 .10
33T Rob Murphy .02 .10
34T Deion Sanders .15 .40
35T Willie Randolph .08 .25
36T Pete Harnisch .02 .10
37T Dante Bichette .08 .25
38T Garry Templeton .02 .10
39T Gary Gaetti .08 .25
40T John Cerutti .02 .10
41T Rick Cerone .02 .10
42T Mike Pagliarulo .02 .10
43T Ron Hassey .02 .10
44T Roberto Alomar .15 .40
45T Mike Boddicker .02 .10
46T Bud Black .02 .10
47T Rob Deer .02 .10
48T Devon White .08 .25
49T Luis Sojo .02 .10
50T Terry Pendleton .08 .25
51T Kevin Gross .02 .10
52T Mike Huff .02 .10
53T Dave Righetti .08 .25
54T Matt Young .02 .10
55T Ernest Riles .02 .10
56T Bill Gullickson .02 .10
57T Vince Coleman .02 .10
58T Fred McGriff .15 .40
59T Franklin Stubbs .02 .10
60T Eric King .02 .10
61T Cory Snyder .02 .10
62T Dwight Evans .15 .40
63T Gerald Perry .02 .10
64T Eric Show .02 .10
65T Shawn Hillegas .02 .10
66T Tony Fernandez .02 .10
67T Tim Teufel .02 .10
68T Mitch Webster .02 .10
69T Mike Heath .02 .10
70T Chili Davis .08 .25
71T Larry Andersen .02 .10
72T Gary Varsho .02 .10
73T Juan Berenguer .02 .10
74T Jack Morris .08 .25
75T Barry Jones .02 .10
76T Rafael Belliard .02 .10
77T Steve Buechele .02 .10
78T Scott Sanderson .02 .10
79T Bob Ojeda .02 .10
80T Curt Schilling .20 .50
81T Brian Drahman RC .02 .10
82T Ivan Rodriguez RC .75 2.00
83T David Howard RC .02 .10
84T Heathcliff Slocumb RC .08 .25
85T Mike Timlin RC .08 .25
86T Darryl Kile .08 .25
87T Pete Schourek RC .08 .25
88T Bruce Walton RC .02 .10
89T Al Osuna RC .02 .10
90T Gary Scott RC .02 .10
91T Doug Simons RC .02 .10
92T Chris Jones RC .02 .10
93T Chuck Knoblauch .08 .25
94T Dana Allison RC .02 .10
95T Erik Pappas RC .02 .10
96T Jeff Bagwell RC .60 1.50
97T Kirk Dressendorfer RC .02 .10
98T Freddie Benavides RC .02 .10
99T Luis Gonzalez RC .20 .50
100T Wade Taylor RC .02 .10
101T Ed Sprague .02 .10
102T Bob Scanlan RC .02 .10
103T Rick Wilkins RC .02 .10
104T Chris Donnels RC .02 .10
105T Joe Slusarski RC .02 .10
106T Mark Lewis .02 .10
107T Pat Kelly RC .02 .10
108T John Briscoe RC .02 .10
109T Luis Lopez RC .02 .10
110T Jeff Johnson RC .02 .10

1991 Score All-Star Fanfest

This 11-card standard-size set was issued with a 3-D 1946 World Series trivia card. The cards feature on the fronts color action player photos, with red borders above and below the pictures. The card face is lime green with miniature yellow baseballs and blue player icons, and it can be seen at the top and bottom of the card front. The backs have a similar pattern on a white background and present biographical information as well as career highlights. The set features young players, who were apparently projected by Score to be future All-Stars. The cards are numbered on the back as "X of 10."

COMPLETE SET (10) 2.00 5.00
1 Ray Lankford .60 1.50
2 Steve Decker .08 .25
3 Gary Scott .08 .25
4 Hensley Meulens .08 .25
5 Tim Naehring .08 .25
6 Mark Whiten .08 .25
7 Ed Sprague .08 .25
8 Charles Nagy .08 .25
9 Terry Shumpert .08 .25
10 Chuck Knoblauch 1.00 2.50
NNO Title Card .08 .25

1991 Score 100 Rising Stars

The 1991 Score 100 Rising Stars sets were issued by Score with or without special books which goes with the cards. The standard-size cards feature 100 of the most popular rising stars. The sets (with the special book with brief biography on the players) are marketed for retail purposes at a suggested price of 12.95.

COMP. FACT SET (100) 3.00 8.00
1 Sandy Alomar Jr. .01 .05
2 Tom Edens .01 .05
3 Terry Shumpert .01 .05
4 Shawn Boskie .01 .05
5 Steve Avery .01 .05
6 Deion Sanders .08 .25
7 John Burkett .01 .05
8 Stan Belinda .01 .05
9 Thomas Howard .01 .05
10 Wayne Edwards .01 .05
11 Rick Parker .01 .05
12 Randy Veres .01 .05
13 Alex Cole .01 .05
14 Scott Chiamparino .01 .05
15 Greg Olson .01 .05
16 Jose DeJesus .01 .05
17 Mike Blowers .01 .05
18 Jeff Huson .01 .05
19 Willie Blair .01 .05
20 Howard Farmer .01 .05
21 Larry Walker .20 .50
22 Scott Hemond .01 .05
23 Mel Stottlemyre Jr. .01 .05
24 Mark Whiten .01 .05
25 Jeff Schulz .01 .05
26 Gary DiSarcina .01 .05
27 George Canale .01 .05
28 Dean Palmer .07 .20
29 Jim Leyritz .01 .05
30 Carlos Baerga .01 .05
31 Rafael Valdez .01 .05
32 Derek Bell .01 .05
33 Francisco Cabrera .01 .05
34 Chris Hoiles .01 .05
35 Craig Grebeck .01 .05
36 Scott Coolbaugh .01 .05
37 Kevin Wickander .01 .05
38 Marquis Grissom .07 .20
39 Chip Hale .01 .05
40 Kevin Maas .01 .05
41 Juan Gonzalez .25 .60
42 Eric Anthony .01 .05
43 Luis Sojo .01 .05
44 Paul Sorrento .01 .05
45 Dave Justice .07 .20
46 Oscar Azocar .01 .05
47 Charles Nagy .01 .05
48 Robin Ventura .07 .20
49 Reggie Harris .01 .05
50 Ben McDonald .01 .05
51 Hector Villanueva .01 .05
52 Kevin Tapani .01 .05
53 Brian Bohanon .01 .05
54 Tim Layana .01 .05
55 Delino DeShields .02 .10
56 Beau Allred .01 .05
57 Eric Gunderson .01 .05
58 Kent Mercker .01 .05
59 Juan Bell .01 .05
60 Glenallen Hill .01 .05
61 David Segui .01 .05
62 Alan Mills .01 .05
63 Mike Harkey .01 .05
64 Bill Sampen .01 .05
65 Greg Vaughn .07 .20
66 Alex Fernandez .07 .20
67 Mike Hartley .01 .05
68 Travis Fryman .07 .20
69 Dave Rohde .01 .05
70 Tom Lampkin .01 .05
71 Mark Gardner .01 .05
72 Pat Combs .01 .05
73 Kevin Appier .07 .20
74 Mike Fetters .01 .05
75 Greg Myers .01 .05
76 Steve Searcy .01 .05
77 Tim Naehring .01 .05
78 Frank Thomas .40 1.00
79 Todd Hundley .07 .20
80 Ed Vosberg .01 .05
81 Todd Zeile .02 .10
82 Lee Stevens .01 .05
83 Scott Radinsky .01 .05
84 Hensley Meulens .01 .05
85 Brian DuBois .01 .05
86 Steve Olin .01 .05
87 Julio Machado .01 .05
88 Jose Vizcaino .01 .05
89 Mark Lemke .01 .05
90 Felix Jose .01 .05
91 Wally Whitehurst .01 .05
92 Dana Kiecker .01 .05
93 Mike Munoz .01 .05
94 Adam Peterson .01 .05
95 Tim Drummond .01 .05
96 Dave Hollins .01 .05
97 Craig Wilson .01 .05
98 Hal Morris .01 .05
99 Jose Offerman .01 .05
100 John Olerud .01 .05

1991 Score 100 Superstars

The 1991 Score 100 Superstars sets were issued by Score with or without special books which came with the cards. The standard-size cards feature 100 of the most popular superstars. The sets (with the special book with brief biography on the players) are marketed for retail purposes at a suggested price of 12.95.

COMP. FACT SET (100) 3.00 8.00
1 Jose Canseco .20 .50
2 Bo Jackson .15 .40
3 Wade Boggs .20 .50
4 Will Clark .07 .20

5 Ken Griffey Jr. .60 1.50
6 Doug Drabek .01 .05
7 Kirby Puckett .25 .60
8 Joe Orsulak .01 .05
9 Eric Davis .02 .10
10 Rickey Henderson .30 .75
11 Len Dykstra .02 .10
12 Ruben Sierra .02 .10
13 Paul Molitor .20 .50
14 Ron Gant .02 .10
15 Ozzie Guillen .05 .15
16 Ramon Martinez .01 .05
17 Edgar Martinez .05 .15
18 Ozzie Smith .30 .75
19 Charlie Hayes .01 .05
20 Barry Larkin .07 .20
21 Cal Ripken .75 2.00
22 Andy Van Slyke .02 .10
23 Don Mattingly .40 1.00
24 Dave Stewart .02 .10
25 Nolan Ryan .75 2.00
26 Barry Bonds .30 .75
27 Gregg Olson .01 .05
28 Chris Sabo .01 .05
29 John Franco .02 .10
30 Gary Sheffield .20 .50
31 Jeff Treadway .01 .05
32 Tom Browning .01 .05
33 Jose Lind .01 .05
34 Dave Magadan .01 .05
35 Dale Murphy .07 .20
36 Tom Candiotti .01 .05
37 Willie McGee .02 .10
38 Robin Yount .20 .50
39 Mark McGwire .40 1.00
40 George Bell .02 .10
41 Carlton Fisk .20 .50
42 Bobby Bonilla .02 .10
43 Randy Milligan .01 .05
44 Dave Parker .02 .10
45 Shawon Dunston .01 .05
46 Brian Harper .01 .05
47 John Tudor .01 .05
48 Ellis Burks .02 .10
49 Bob Welch .01 .05
50 Roger Clemens .40 1.00
51 Mike Henneman .01 .05
52 Eddie Murray .15 .40
53 Kal Daniels .01 .05
54 Doug Jones .01 .05
55 Craig Biggio .05 .15
56 Rafael Palmeiro .15 .40
57 Wally Joyner .02 .10
58 Tim Wallach .01 .05
59 Bret Saberhagen .02 .10
60 Ryne Sandberg .30 .75
61 Benito Santiago .02 .10
62 Darryl Strawberry .02 .10
63 Alan Trammell .05 .15
64 Kelly Gruber .01 .05
65 Dwight Gooden .02 .10
66 Dave Winfield .20 .50
67 Rick Aguilera .02 .10
68 Dave Righetti .01 .05
69 Jim Abbott .02 .10
70 Frank Viola .01 .05
71 Fred McGriff .05 .15
72 Steve Sax .01 .05
73 Dennis Eckersley .15 .40
74 Cory Snyder .01 .05
75 Mackey Sasser .01 .05
76 Candy Maldonado .01 .05
77 Matt Williams .05 .15
78 Kent Hrbek .02 .10
79 Randy Myers .02 .10
80 Gregg Jefferies .01 .05
81 Joe Carter .02 .10
82 Mike Greenwell .01 .05
83 Jack Armstrong .01 .05
84 Julio Franco .02 .10
85 George Brett .30 .75
86 Howard Johnson .01 .05
87 Andre Dawson .07 .20
88 Cecil Fielder .02 .10
89 Tim Raines .02 .10
90 Chuck Finley .02 .10
91 Mark Grace .07 .20
92 Brook Jacoby .01 .05
93 Dave Stieb .01 .05
94 Tony Gwynn .40 1.00
95 Bobby Thigpen .01 .05
96 Roberto Kelly .01 .05
97 Kevin Seitzer .01 .05
98 Kevin Mitchell .01 .05
99 Dwight Evans .02 .10
100 Roberto Alomar .07 .20

1991 Score Rookies

This 40-card standard-sized set was distributed with five magic motion trivia cards. The fronts feature high glossy color action player photos, on a blue card face with meandering green lines.

COMP.FACT.SET (40) 1.50 4.00
1 Mel Rojas .01 .05
2 Ray Lankford .10 .30
3 Scott Aldred .01 .05
4 Turner Ward .01 .05
5 Omar Olivares .01 .05
6 Mo Vaughn .60 1.50
7 Phil Clark .01 .05
8 Brent Mayne .01 .05
9 Scott Lewis .01 .05
10 Brian Barnes .01 .05
11 Bernard Gilkey .01 .05
12 Steve Decker .01 .05
13 Paul Marak .01 .05
14 Wes Chamberlain .01 .05
15 Kevin Belcher .01 .05
16 Steve Adkins .01 .05
17 Geronimo Pena .01 .05
18 Mark Leonard .01 .05
19 Jeff Conine .02 .10
20 Leo Gomez .01 .05
21 Chuck Malone .01 .05
22 Beau Allred .01 .05
23 Todd Hundley .10 .30
24 Lance Dickson .01 .05
25 Mike Benjamin .01 .05
26 Jose Offerman .01 .05
27 Terry Shumpert .01 .05
28 Darren Lewis .01 .05
29 Scott Chiamparino .01 .05
30 Tim Naehring .01 .05
31 David Segui .02 .10
32 Karl Rhodes .01 .05
33 Mickey Morandini .01 .05
34 Chuck McElroy .01 .05
35 Tim McIntosh .01 .05
36 Derrick May .01 .05
37 Rich DeLucia .01 .05
38 Tino Martinez .40 1.00
39 Hensley Meulens .01 .05
40 Andujar Cedeno .01 .05

1991 Score Ryan Life and Times

This four-card standard-size set was manufactured by Score to commemorate four significant milestones in Nolan Ryan's illustrious career beginning with his years growing up in Alvin, Texas, his years with the Mets and Angels, with the Astros and Rangers, and his career statistics. Each card commemorates a career milestone (all occur with the Rangers) and features Ryan's color photo on the front. They are part of "The Life and Times of Nolan Ryan," by Tarrant Printing, a special collector set that consists of four volumes (8 1/2" by 11" booklets) along with the cards packaged in a folder.

COMPLETE SET (4) 8.00 20.00
COMMON CARD (1-4) 2.00 5.00

1992 Score Samples

COMPLETE SET (6) 8.00 20.00
COMMON PLAYER (1-6) .20 .50
COMMON SP .50 1.00
1 Ken Griffey Jr. 4.00 10.00
2 Dave Justice .75 2.00
3 Robin Ventura .75 2.00
4 Steve Avery .20 .50
5 Ryne Sandberg SP 3.00 8.00
6 Shane Mack SP .40 1.00

1992 Score

The 1992 Score set marked the second year that Score released their set in two different series. The first series contains 442 cards while the second series contains 451 cards. Cards were distributed in plastic wrapped packs, blister packs, jumbo packs and factory sets. Each pack included a special "World Series II" trivia card. Topical subsets include Rookie Prospects (395-424/736-772/814-877), No-Hit Club (425-428/784-787), Highlights (429-430), AL All-Stars (431-440; with color montages displaying Chris Greco's player caricatures), Dream Team (441-442/883-893), NL All-Stars (773-782), Highlights (783, 795-797), Draft Picks (799-810), and Memorabilia (878-882). The memorabilia cards all feature items from the famed Barry Halper collection. Halper was a part-owner of Score at the time. All of the Rookie Prospects (736-772) can be found with or without the Rookie Prospect stripe. Rookie Cards in the set include Vinny Castilla and Manny Ramirez. Chuck Knoblauch, 1991 American League Rookie of the Year, autographed 3,000 of his own 1990 Score Draft Pick cards (card number 672) in gold ink, 2,989 were randomly inserted in Series two poly packs, while the other 11 were given away in a sweepstakes. The backs of these Knoblauch autograph cards have special holograms to differentiate them.

COMPLETE SET (893) 6.00 15.00
COMP.FACT.SET (910) 8.00 20.00
COMPLETE SERIES 1 (442) 3.00 8.00
COMPLETE SERIES 2 (451) 3.00 8.00
SUBSET CARDS HALF VALUE OF BASE CARDS
1 Ken Griffey Jr. .20 .50
2 Nolan Ryan .40 1.00
3 Will Clark .05 .15
4 Dave Justice .02 .10
5 Dave Henderson .01 .05
6 Bret Saberhagen .02 .10
7 Fred McGriff .05 .15
8 Erik Hanson .01 .05
9 Darryl Strawberry .02 .10
10 Dwight Gooden .02 .10
11 Juan Gonzalez .05 .15
12 Mark Langston .01 .05
13 Lonnie Smith .01 .05
14 Jeff Montgomery .01 .05
15 Roberto Alomar .05 .15
16 Delino DeShields .01 .05
17 Steve Bedrosian .01 .05
18 Terry Pendleton .02 .10
19 Mark Carreon .01 .05
20 Mark McGwire .25 .60
21 Roger Clemens .20 .50
22 Chuck Crim .01 .05
23 Don Mattingly .25 .60
24 Dickie Thon .01 .05
25 Ron Gant .02 .10
26 Milt Cuyler .01 .05
27 Mike Macfarlane .01 .05
28 Dan Gladden .01 .05
29 Melido Perez .01 .05
30 Willie Randolph .02 .10
31 Albert Belle .02 .10
32 Dave Winfield .02 .10
33 Jimmy Jones .01 .05
34 Kevin Gross .01 .05
35 Andres Galarraga .02 .10
36 Mike Devereaux .01 .05
37 Chris Bosio .01 .05
38 Mike LaValliere .01 .05
39 Gary Gaetti .02 .10
40 Felix Jose .01 .05
41 Alvaro Espinoza .01 .05
42 Rick Aguilera .02 .10
43 Mike Gallego .01 .05
44 Eric Davis .02 .10
45 George Bell .01 .05
46 Tom Brunansky .01 .05
47 Steve Farr .01 .05
48 Duane Ward .01 .05
49 David Wells .02 .10
50 Cecil Fielder .02 .10
51 Walt Weiss .01 .05
52 Todd Zeile .01 .05
53 Doug Jones .01 .05
54 Bob Walk .01 .05
55 Rafael Palmeiro .05 .15
56 Rob Deer .01 .05
57 Paul O'Neill .05 .15
58 Jeff Reardon .02 .10
59 Randy Ready .01 .05
60 Scott Erickson .01 .05
61 Paul Molitor .02 .10
62 Jack McDowell .01 .05
63 Jim Acker .01 .05
64 Jay Buhner .02 .10
65 Travis Fryman .02 .10
66 Marquis Grissom .02 .10
67 Mike Harkey .01 .05
68 Luis Polonia .01 .05
69 Ken Caminiti .02 .10
70 Chris Sabo .01 .05
71 Gregg Olson .01 .05
72 Carlton Fisk .05 .15
73 Juan Samuel .01 .05
74 Todd Stottlemyre .01 .05
75 Andre Dawson .02 .10
76 Alvin Davis .01 .05
77 Bill Doran .01 .05
78 B.J. Surhoff .02 .10
79 Kirk McCaskill .01 .05
80 Dale Murphy .05 .15
81 Jose DeLeon .01 .05
82 Alex Fernandez .01 .05
83 Ivan Calderon .01 .05
84 Brent Mayne .01 .05
85 Jody Reed .01 .05
86 Randy Tomlin .01 .05
87 Randy Milligan .01 .05
88 Pascual Perez .01 .05
89 Hensley Meulens .01 .05
90 Joe Carter .02 .10
91 Mike Moore .01 .05
92 Ozzie Guillen .02 .10
93 Shawn Hillegas .01 .05
94 Chili Davis .02 .10
95 Vince Coleman .01 .05
96 Jimmy Key .02 .10
97 Billy Ripken .01 .05
98 Dave Smith .01 .05
99 Tom Bolton .01 .05
100 Barry Larkin .05 .15
101 Kenny Rogers .02 .10
102 Mike Boddicker .01 .05
103 Kevin Elster .01 .05
104 Ken Hill .01 .05
105 Charlie Leibrandt .01 .05
106 Pat Combs .01 .05
107 Hubie Brooks .01 .05
108 Julio Franco .02 .10
109 Vicente Palacios .01 .05
110 Kal Daniels .01 .05
111 Bruce Hurst .01 .05
112 Willie McGee .02 .10
113 Ted Power .01 .05
114 Milt Thompson .01 .05
115 Doug Drabek .01 .05
116 Rafael Belliard .01 .05
117 Scott Garrelts .01 .05
118 Terry Mulholland .01 .05
119 Jay Howell .01 .05
120 Danny Jackson .01 .05
121 Scott Ruskin .01 .05
122 Robin Ventura .02 .10
123 Bip Roberts .01 .05
124 Jeff Russell .01 .05
125 Hal Morris .01 .05
126 Teddy Higuera .01 .05
127 Luis Sojo .01 .05
128 Carlos Baerga .01 .05
129 Jeff Ballard .01 .05
130 Tom Gordon .01 .05
131 Sid Bream .01 .05
132 Rance Mulliniks .01 .05
133 Andy Benes .01 .05
134 Mickey Tettleton .01 .05
135 Rich DeLucia .01 .05
136 Tom Pagnozzi .01 .05
137 Harold Baines .02 .10
138 Danny Darwin .01 .05
139 Kevin Bass .01 .05
140 Chris Nabholz .01 .05
141 Pete O'Brien .01 .05
142 Jeff Treadway .01 .05
143 Mickey Morandini .01 .05
144 Eric King .01 .05
145 Danny Tartabull .01 .05
146 Lance Johnson .01 .05
147 Casey Candaele .01 .05
148 Felix Fermin .01 .05
149 Rich Rodriguez .01 .05
150 Dwight Evans .05 .15
151 Joe Klink .01 .05
152 Kevin Reimer .01 .05
153 Orlando Merced .01 .05
154 Mel Hall .01 .05
155 Randy Myers .01 .05
156 Greg A. Harris .01 .05
157 Jeff Brantley .01 .05
158 Jim Eisenreich .01 .05
159 Luis Rivera .01 .05
160 Cris Carpenter .01 .05
161 Bruce Ruffin .01 .05
162 Omar Vizquel .05 .15
163 Gerald Alexander .01 .05
164 Mark Guthrie .01 .05
165 Scott Lewis .01 .05
166 Bill Sampen .01 .05
167 Dave Anderson .01 .05
168 Kevin McReynolds .01 .05
169 Jose Vizcaino .01 .05
170 Bob Geren .01 .05
171 Mike Morgan .01 .05
172 Jim Gott .01 .05
173 Mike Pagliarulo .01 .05
174 Mike Jeffcoat .01 .05
175 Craig Lefferts .01 .05
176 Steve Finley .02 .10
177 Wally Backman .01 .05
178 Kent Mercker .01 .05
179 John Cerutti .01 .05
180 Jay Bell .02 .10
181 Dale Sveum .01 .05
182 Greg Gagne .01 .05
183 Donnie Hill .01 .05
184 Rex Hudler .01 .05
185 Pat Kelly .01 .05
186 Jeff D. Robinson .01 .05
187 Jeff Gray .01 .05
188 Jerry Willard .01 .05
189 Carlos Quintana .01 .05
190 Dennis Eckersley .02 .10
191 Kelly Downs .01 .05
192 Gregg Jefferies .01 .05
193 Darrin Fletcher .01 .05
194 Mike Jackson .01 .05
195 Eddie Murray .08 .25
196 Bill Landrum .01 .05
197 Eric Yelding .01 .05
198 Devon White .02 .10
199 Larry Walker .05 .15
200 Ryne Sandberg .15 .40
201 Dave Magadan .01 .05
202 Steve Chitren .01 .05
203 Scott Fletcher .01 .05
204 Dwayne Henry .01 .05
205 Scott Coolbaugh .01 .05
206 Tracy Jones .01 .05
207 Von Hayes .01 .05
208 Bob Melvin .01 .05
209 Scott Scudder .01 .05
210 Luis Gonzalez .02 .10
211 Scott Sanderson .01 .05
212 Chris Donnels .01 .05
213 Heathcliff Slocumb .01 .05
214 Mike Timlin .01 .05
215 Brian Harper .01 .05
216 Juan Berenguer UER .01 .05
Decimal point missing
in IP total
217 Mike Henneman .01 .05
218 Bill Spiers .01 .05
219 Scott Terry .01 .05
220 Frank Viola .02 .10
221 Mark Eichhorn .01 .05
222 Ernest Riles .01 .05
223 Ray Lankford .02 .10
224 Pete Harnisch .01 .05
225 Bobby Bonilla .02 .10
226 Mike Scioscia .01 .05
227 Joel Skinner .01 .05
228 Brian Holman .01 .05
229 Gilberto Reyes .01 .05
230 Matt Williams .02 .10
231 Jaime Navarro .01 .05
232 Jose Rijo .01 .05
233 Atlee Hammaker .01 .05
234 Tim Teufel .01 .05
235 John Kruk .02 .10
236 Kurt Stillwell .01 .05
237 Dan Pasqua .01 .05
238 Tim Crews .01 .05
239 Dave Gallagher .01 .05
240 Leo Gomez .01 .05
241 Steve Avery .01 .05
242 Bill Gullickson .01 .05
243 Mark Portugal .01 .05
244 Lee Guetterman .01 .05
245 Benito Santiago .02 .10
246 Jim Gantner .01 .05
247 Robby Thompson .01 .05
248 Terry Shumpert .01 .05
249 Mike Bell .01 .05
250 Harold Reynolds .02 .10
251 Mike Felder .01 .05
252 Bill Pecota .01 .05
253 Bill Krueger .01 .05
254 Alfredo Griffin .01 .05
255 Lou Whitaker .02 .10
256 Roy Smith .01 .05
257 Jerald Clark .01 .05
258 Sammy Sosa .08 .25
259 Tim Naehring .01 .05
260 Dave Righetti .02 .10
261 Paul Gibson .01 .05
262 Chris James .01 .05
263 Larry Andersen .01 .05
264 Storm Davis .01 .05
265 Jose Lind .01 .05
266 Greg Hibbard .01 .05
267 Norm Charlton .01 .05
268 Paul Kilgus .01 .05
269 Greg Maddux .15 .40
270 Ellis Burks .02 .10
271 Frank Tanana .01 .05
272 Gene Larkin .01 .05
273 Ron Hassey .01 .05
274 Jeff M. Robinson .01 .05
275 Steve Howe .01 .05
276 Daryl Boston .01 .05
277 Mark Lee .01 .05
278 Jose Segura .01 .05
279 Lance Blankenship .01 .05
280 Don Slaught .01 .05
281 Russ Swan .01 .05
282 Bob Tewksbury .01 .05
283 Geno Petralli .01 .05
284 Shane Mack .01 .05
285 Bob Scanlan .01 .05
286 Tim Leary .01 .05
287 John Smoltz .05 .15
288 Pat Borders .01 .05
289 Mark Davidson .01 .05
290 Sam Horn .01 .05
291 Lenny Harris .01 .05
292 Franklin Stubbs .01 .05
293 Thomas Howard .01 .05
294 Steve Lyons .01 .05
295 Francisco Oliveras .01 .05
296 Terry Leach .01 .05
297 Barry Jones .01 .05
298 Lance Parrish .02 .10
299 Wally Whitehurst .01 .05
300 Bob Welch .01 .05
301 Charlie Hayes .01 .05
302 Charlie Hough .02 .10
303 Gary Redus .01 .05
304 Scott Bradley .01 .05
305 Jose Oquendo .01 .05
306 Pete Incaviglia .01 .05
307 Marvin Freeman .01 .05
308 Gary Pettis .01 .05
309 Joe Slusarski .01 .05
310 Kevin Seitzer .01 .05
311 Jeff Reed .01 .05
312 Pat Tabler .01 .05
313 Mike Maddux .01 .05
314 Bob Milacki .01 .05
315 Eric Anthony .01 .05
316 Dante Bichette .02 .10
317 Steve Decker .01 .05
318 Jack Clark .02 .10
319 Doug Dascenzo .01 .05
320 Scott Leius .01 .05
321 Jim Lindeman .01 .05
322 Bryan Harvey .01 .05
323 Spike Owen .01 .05
324 Roberto Kelly .01 .05
325 Stan Belinda .01 .05
326 Joey Cora .01 .05
327 Jeff Innis .01 .05
328 Willie Wilson .01 .05
329 Juan Agosto .01 .05
330 Charles Nagy .01 .05
331 Scott Bailes .01 .05
332 Pete Schourek .01 .05
333 Mike Flanagan .01 .05
334 Omar Olivares .01 .05
335 Dennis Lamp .01 .05
336 Tommy Greene .01 .05
337 Randy Velarde .01 .05
338 Tom Lampkin .01 .05
339 John Russell .01 .05
340 Bob Kipper .01 .05
341 Todd Burns .01 .05
342 Ron Jones .01 .05
343 Dave Valle .01 .05
344 Mike Heath .01 .05
345 John Olerud .02 .10
346 Gerald Young .01 .05
347 Ken Patterson .01 .05
348 Les Lancaster .01 .05
349 Steve Crawford .01 .05
350 John Candelaria .01 .05
351 Mike Aldrete .01 .05
352 Mariano Duncan .01 .05
353 Julio Machado .01 .05
354 Ken Williams .01 .05
355 Walt Terrell .01 .05
356 Mitch Williams .01 .05
357 Al Newman .01 .05
358 Bud Black .01 .05
359 Joe Hesketh .01 .05
360 Paul Assenmacher .01 .05
361 Bo Jackson .08 .25
362 Jeff Blauser .01 .05
363 Mike Brumley .01 .05
364 Jim Deshaies .01 .05
365 Brady Anderson .02 .10
366 Chuck McElroy .01 .05
367 Matt Merullo .01 .05
368 Tim Belcher .01 .05
369 Luis Aquino .01 .05
370 Joe Oliver .01 .05
371 Greg Swindell .01 .05
372 Lee Stevens .01 .05
373 Mark Knudson .01 .05
374 Bill Wegman .01 .05
375 Jerry Don Gleaton .01 .05
376 Pedro Guerrero .02 .10
377 Randy Bush .01 .05
378 Greg W. Harris .01 .05
379 Eric Plunk .01 .05
380 Jose DeJesus .01 .05
381 Bobby Witt .01 .05
382 Curtis Wilkerson .01 .05
383 Gene Nelson .01 .05
384 Wes Chamberlain .01 .05
385 Tom Henke .01 .05
386 Mark Lemke .01 .05
387 Greg Briley .01 .05
388 Rafael Ramirez .01 .05
389 Tony Fossas .01 .05
390 Henry Cotto .01 .05
391 Tim Hulett .01 .05
392 Dean Palmer .02 .10
393 Glenn Braggs .01 .05
394 Mark Salas .01 .05
395 Rusty Meacham .01 .05
396 Andy Ashby .01 .05
397 Jose Melendez .01 .05
398 Warren Newson .01 .05
399 Frank Castillo .01 .05
400 Chito Martinez .01 .05
401 Bernie Williams .05 .15
402 Derek Bell .02 .10
403 Javier Ortiz .01 .05
404 Tim Sherrill .01 .05
405 Rob MacDonald .01 .05
406 Phil Plantier .01 .05
407 Troy Afenir .01 .05
408 Gino Minutelli .01 .05
409 Reggie Jefferson .01 .05
410 Mike Remlinger .01 .05
411 Carlos Rodriguez .01 .05
412 Joe Redfield .01 .05
413 Alonzo Powell .01 .05
414 Scott Livingstone UER .01 .05
Travis Fryman,
not Woodie, should be
referenced on back
415 Scott Kamieniecki .01 .05
416 Tim Spehr .01 .05
417 Brian Hunter .01 .05
418 Ced Landrum .01 .05
419 Bret Barberie .01 .05
420 Kevin Morton .01 .05
421 Doug Henry RC .02 .10
422 Doug Piatt .01 .05
423 Pat Rice .01 .05
424 Juan Guzman .01 .05
425 Nolan Ryan NH .20 .50
426 Tommy Greene NH .01 .05
427 Bob Milacki and .01 .05
Mike Flanagan NH
Mark Williamson
and Gregg Olson
428 Wilson Alvarez NH .01 .05
429 Otis Nixon HL .01 .05
430 Rickey Henderson HL .05 .15
431 Cecil Fielder AS .01 .05
432 Julio Franco AS .01 .05
433 Cal Ripken AS .15 .40
434 Wade Boggs AS .02 .10
435 Joe Carter AS .01 .05
436 Ken Griffey Jr. AS .10 .30
437 Ruben Sierra AS .01 .05
438 Scott Erickson AS .01 .05
439 Tom Henke AS .01 .05
440 Terry Steinbach AS .01 .05
441 Rickey Henderson DT .08 .25
442 Ryne Sandberg DT .15 .40
443 Otis Nixon .01 .05
444 Scott Radinsky UER .01 .05
Photo on front is Tom Drees
445 Mark Grace .05 .15
446 Tony Pena .01 .05
447 Billy Hatcher .01 .05
448 Glenallen Hill .01 .05
449 Chris Gwynn .01 .05
450 Tom Glavine .05 .15
451 John Habyan .01 .05
452 Al Osuna .01 .05
453 Tony Phillips .01 .05
454 Greg Cadaret .01 .05
455 Rob Dibble .02 .10
456 Rick Honeycutt .01 .05
457 Jerome Walton .01 .05
458 Mookie Wilson .02 .10
459 Mark Gubicza .01 .05
460 Craig Biggio .05 .15
461 Dave Cochrane .01 .05
462 Keith Miller .01 .05
463 Alex Cole .01 .05
464 Pete Smith .01 .05
465 Brett Butler .02 .10
466 Jeff Huson .01 .05
467 Steve Lake .01 .05
468 Lloyd Moseby .01 .05
469 Tim McIntosh .01 .05
470 Dennis Martinez .02 .10
471 Greg Myers .01 .05
472 Mackey Sasser .01 .05
473 Junior Ortiz .01 .05
474 Greg Olson .01 .05
475 Steve Sax .01 .05
476 Ricky Jordan .01 .05
477 Max Venable .01 .05
478 Brian McRae .01 .05
479 Doug Simons .01 .05
480 Rickey Henderson .08 .25
481 Gary Varsho .01 .05
482 Carl Willis .01 .05
483 Rick Wilkins .01 .05
484 Donn Pall .01 .05
485 Edgar Martinez .05 .15
486 Tom Foley .01 .05
487 Mark Williamson .01 .05
488 Jack Armstrong .01 .05
489 Gary Carter .02 .10
490 Ruben Sierra .02 .10
491 Gerald Perry .01 .05
492 Rob Murphy .01 .05
493 Zane Smith .01 .05
494 Darryl Kile .02 .10
495 Kelly Gruber .01 .05
496 Jerry Browne .01 .05
497 Darryl Hamilton .01 .05
498 Mike Stanton .01 .05
499 Mark Leonard .01 .05
500 Jose Canseco .05 .15
501 Dave Martinez .01 .05
502 Jose Guzman .01 .05
503 Terry Kennedy .01 .05
504 Ed Sprague .01 .05
505 Frank Thomas UER .08 .25
His Gulf Coast League
stats are wrong
506 Darren Daulton .02 .10
507 Kevin Tapani .01 .05
508 Luis Salazar .01 .05
509 Paul Faries .01 .05
510 Sandy Alomar Jr. .01 .05
511 Jeff King .01 .05
512 Gary Thurman .01 .05
513 Chris Hammond .01 .05
514 Pedro Munoz .01 .05
515 Alan Trammell .02 .10
516 Geronimo Pena .01 .05
517 Rodney McCray UER .01 .05
Stole 6 bases in 1990, not 5;
career totals are correct at 7
518 Manny Lee .01 .05
519 Junior Felix .01 .05
520 Kirk Gibson .02 .10
521 Darrin Jackson .01 .05
522 John Burkett .01 .05
523 Jeff Johnson .01 .05
524 Jim Corsi .01 .05
525 Robin Yount .15 .40
526 Jamie Quirk .01 .05
527 Bob Ojeda .01 .05
528 Mark Lewis .01 .05
529 Bryn Smith .01 .05
530 Kent Hrbek .02 .10
531 Dennis Boyd .01 .05
532 Ron Karkovice .01 .05
533 Don August .01 .05
534 Todd Frohwirth .01 .05
535 Wally Joyner .02 .10
536 Dennis Rasmussen .01 .05
537 Andy Allanson .01 .05
538 Rich Gossage .02 .10
539 John Marzano .01 .05
540 Cal Ripken .30 .75
541 Bill Swift UER .01 .05
Brewers logo on front
542 Kevin Appier .02 .10
543 Dave Bergman .01 .05
544 Bernard Gilkey .01 .05
545 Mike Greenwell .01 .05
546 Jose Uribe .01 .05
547 Jesse Orosco .01 .05
548 Bob Patterson .01 .05
549 Mike Stanley .01 .05
550 Howard Johnson .01 .05
551 Joe Orsulak .01 .05
552 Dick Schofield .01 .05
553 Dave Hollins .01 .05
554 David Segui .01 .05
555 Barry Bonds .40 1.00
556 Mo Vaughn .02 .10
557 Craig Wilson .01 .05
558 Bobby Rose .01 .05
559 Rod Nichols .01 .05
560 Len Dykstra .02 .10
561 Craig Grebeck .01 .05
562 Darren Lewis .01 .05
563 Todd Benzinger .01 .05
564 Ed Whitson .01 .05
565 Jesse Barfield .01 .05
566 Lloyd McClendon .01 .05
567 Dan Plesac .01 .05
568 Danny Cox .01 .05
569 Skeeter Barnes .01 .05
570 Bobby Thigpen .01 .05
571 Deion Sanders .05 .15
572 Chuck Knoblauch .02 .10
573 Matt Nokes .01 .05
574 Herm Winningham .01 .05
575 Tom Candiotti .01 .05
576 Jeff Bagwell .08 .25
577 Brook Jacoby .01 .05
578 Chico Walker .01 .05
579 Brian Downing .01 .05
580 Dave Stewart .02 .10
581 Francisco Cabrera .01 .05
582 Rene Gonzales .01 .05
583 Stan Javier .01 .05
584 Randy Johnson .08 .25
585 Chuck Finley .02 .10
586 Mark Gardner .01 .05
587 Mark Whiten .01 .05
588 Garry Templeton .01 .05
589 Gary Sheffield .02 .10
590 Ozzie Smith .15 .40
591 Candy Maldonado .01 .05
592 Mike Sharperson .01 .05
593 Carlos Martinez .01 .05
594 Scott Bankhead .01 .05
595 Tim Wallach .01 .05
596 Tino Martinez .05 .15
597 Roger McDowell .01 .05
598 Cory Snyder .01 .05
599 Andujar Cedeno .01 .05
600 Kirby Puckett .08 .25
601 Rick Parker .01 .05
602 Todd Hundley .01 .05
603 Greg Litton .01 .05
604 Dave Johnson .01 .05
605 John Franco .02 .10
606 Mike Fetters .01 .05
607 Luis Alicea .01 .05
608 Trevor Wilson .01 .05
609 Rob Ducey .01 .05
610 Ramon Martinez .01 .05
611 Dave Burba .01 .05
612 Dwight Smith .01 .05
613 Kevin Maas .01 .05
614 John Costello .01 .05
615 Glenn Davis .01 .05
616 Shawn Abner .01 .05
617 Scott Hemond .01 .05
618 Tom Prince .01 .05
619 Wally Ritchie .01 .05
620 Jim Abbott .05 .15
621 Charlie O'Brien .01 .05
622 Jack Daugherty .01 .05
623 Tommy Gregg .01 .05
624 Jeff Shaw .01 .05
625 Tony Gwynn .10 .30
626 Mark Leiter .01 .05
627 Jim Clancy .01 .05
628 Tim Layana .01 .05
629 Jeff Schaefer .01 .05
630 Lee Smith .02 .10
631 Wade Taylor .01 .05
632 Mike Simms .01 .05
633 Terry Steinbach .01 .05
634 Shawon Dunston .01 .05
635 Tim Raines .02 .10
636 Kirt Manwaring .01 .05
637 Warren Cromartie .01 .05
638 Luis Quinones .01 .05
639 Greg Vaughn .01 .05
640 Kevin Mitchell .01 .05
641 Chris Hoiles .01 .05
642 Tom Browning .01 .05
643 Mitch Webster .01 .05
644 Steve Olin .01 .05
645 Tony Fernandez .01 .05
646 Juan Bell .01 .05
647 Joe Boever .01 .05
648 Carney Lansford .02 .10
649 Mike Benjamin .01 .05
650 George Brett .25 .60
651 Tim Burke .01 .05
652 Jack Morris .02 .10
653 Orel Hershiser .02 .10
654 Mike Schooler .01 .05
655 Andy Van Slyke .05 .15
656 Dave Stieb .01 .05
657 Dave Clark .01 .05
658 Ben McDonald .01 .05
659 John Smiley .01 .05
660 Wade Boggs .05 .15
661 Eric Bullock .01 .05
662 Eric Show .01 .05
663 Lenny Webster .01 .05
664 Mike Huff .01 .05
665 Rick Sutcliffe .02 .10
666 Jeff Manto .01 .05
667 Mike Fitzgerald .01 .05
668 Matt Young .01 .05
669 Dave West .01 .05
670 Mike Hartley .01 .05
671 Curt Schilling .05 .15
672 Brian Bohanon .01 .05
673 Cecil Espy .01 .05
674 Joe Grahe .01 .05
675 Sid Fernandez .01 .05
676 Edwin Nunez .01 .05
677 Hector Villanueva .01 .05
678 Sean Berry .01 .05
679 Dave Eiland .01 .05
680 David Cone .02 .10
681 Mike Bordick .01 .05
682 Tony Castillo .01 .05

683 John Barfield .01 .05
684 Jeff Hamilton .01 .05
685 Ken Dayley .01 .05
686 Carmelo Martinez .01 .05
687 Mike Capel .01 .05
688 Scott Chiamparino .01 .05
689 Rich Gedman .01 .05
690 Rich Monteleone .01 .05
691 Alejandro Pena .01 .05
692 Oscar Azocar .01 .05
693 Jim Poole .01 .05
694 Mike Gardiner .01 .05
695 Steve Buechele .01 .05
696 Rudy Seanez .01 .05
697 Paul Abbott .01 .05
698 Steve Searcy .01 .05
699 Jose Offerman .01 .05
700 Ivan Rodriguez .08 .25
701 Joe Girardi .01 .05
702 Tony Perezchica .01 .05
703 Paul McClellan .01 .05
704 David Howard .01 .05
705 Dan Petry .01 .05
706 Jack Howell .01 .05
707 Jose Mesa .01 .05
708 Randy St. Claire .01 .05
709 Kevin Brown .02 .10
710 Ron Darling .01 .05
711 Jason Grimsley .01 .05
712 John Orton .01 .05
713 Shawn Boskie .01 .05
714 Pat Clements .01 .05
715 Brian Barnes .01 .05
716 Luis Lopez .01 .05
717 Bob McClure .01 .05
718 Mark Davis .01 .05
719 Dann Bilardello .01 .05
720 Tom Edens .01 .05
721 Willie Fraser .01 .05
722 Curt Young .01 .05
723 Neal Heaton .01 .05
724 Craig Worthington .01 .05
725 Mel Rojas .01 .05
726 Daryl Irvine .01 .05
727 Roger Mason .01 .05
728 Kirk Dressendorfer .01 .05
729 Scott Aldred .01 .05
730 Willie Blair .01 .05
731 Allan Anderson .01 .05
732 Dana Kiecker .01 .05
733 Jose Gonzalez .01 .05
734 Brian Drahman .01 .05
735 Brad Komminsk .01 .05
736 Arthur Rhodes .01 .05
737 Terry Mathews .01 .05
738 Jeff Fassero .01 .05
739 Mike Magnante RC .02 .10
740 Kip Gross .01 .05
741 Jim Hunter .01 .05
742 Jose Mota .01 .05
743 Joe Bitker .01 .05
744 Tim Mauser .01 .05
745 Ramon Garcia .01 .05
746 Rod Beck RC .08 .25
747 Jim Austin RC .01 .05
748 Keith Mitchell .01 .05
749 Wayne Rosenthal .01 .05
750 Bryan Hickerson RC .02 .10
751 Bruce Egloff .01 .05
752 John Wehner .01 .05
753 Darren Holmes .01 .05
754 Dave Hansen .01 .05
755 Mike Mussina .08 .25
756 Anthony Young .01 .05
757 Ron Tingley .01 .05
758 Ricky Bones .01 .05
759 Mark Wohlers .01 .05
760 Wilson Alvarez .01 .05
761 Harvey Pulliam .01 .05
762 Ryan Bowen .01 .05
763 Terry Bross .01 .05
764 Joel Johnston .01 .05
765 Terry McDaniel .01 .05
766 Esteban Beltre .01 .05
767 Rob Maurer RC .01 .05
768 Ted Wood .01 .05
769 Mo Sanford .01 .05
770 Jeff Carter .01 .05
771 Gil Heredia RC .08 .25
772 Monty Fariss .01 .05
773 Will Clark AS .02 .10
774 Ryne Sandberg AS .08 .25
775 Barry Larkin AS .02 .10
776 Howard Johnson AS .01 .05
777 Barry Bonds AS .20 .50
778 Brett Butler AS .01 .05
779 Tony Gwynn AS .05 .15
780 Ramon Martinez AS .01 .05
781 Lee Smith AS .01 .05
782 Mike Scioscia AS .01 .05
783 Dennis Martinez HL UER .01 .05
Card has both 13th
and 15th perfect game
in Major League history
784 Dennis Martinez NH .01 .05
785 Mark Gardner NH .01 .05
786 Bret Saberhagen NH .01 .05
787 Kent Mercker NH .01 .05
Mark Wohlers
Alejandro Pena
788 Cal Ripken MVP .15 .40
789 Terry Pendleton MVP .01 .05
790 Roger Clemens CY .08 .25
791 Tom Glavine CY .02 .10
792 Chuck Knoblauch ROY .01 .05
793 Jeff Bagwell ROY .05 .15
794 Cal Ripken MANYR .15 .40
795 David Cone HL .01 .05
796 Kirby Puckett HL .05 .15
797 Steve Avery HL .01 .05
798 Jack Morris HL .01 .05
799 Allen Watson RC .02 .10
800 Manny Ramirez RC 1.50 4.00
801 Cliff Floyd RC .30 .75
802 Al Shirley RC .02 .10
803 Brian Barber RC .02 .10
804 Jon Farrell RC .02 .10
805 Brent Gates RC .02 .10
806 Scott Ruffcorn RC .02 .10
807 Tyrone Hill RC .02 .10
808 Benji Gil RC .08 .25
809 Aaron Sele RC .08 .25
810 Tyler Green RC .02 .10
811 Chris Jones .01 .05
812 Steve Wilson .01 .05
813 Freddie Benavides .01 .05
814 Don Wakamatsu RC .01 .05
815 Mike Humphreys .01 .05
816 Scott Servais .01 .05
817 Rico Rossy .01 .05
818 John Ramos .01 .05
819 Rob Mallicoat .01 .05
820 Milt Hill .01 .05
821 Carlos Garcia .01 .05
822 Stan Royer .01 .05
823 Jeff Plympton .01 .05
824 Braulio Castillo .01 .05
825 David Haas .01 .05
826 Luis Mercedes .01 .05
827 Eric Karros .02 .10
828 Shawn Hare RC .02 .10
829 Reggie Sanders .02 .10
830 Tom Goodwin .01 .05
831 Dan Gakeler .01 .05
832 Stacy Jones .01 .05
833 Kim Batiste .01 .05
834 Cal Eldred .01 .05
835 Chris George .01 .05
836 Wayne Housie .01 .05
837 Mike Ignasiak .01 .05
838 Josias Manzanillo RC .02 .10
839 Jim Olander .01 .05
840 Gary Cooper .01 .05
841 Royce Clayton .01 .05
842 Hector Fajardo RC .02 .10
843 Blaine Beatty .01 .05
844 Jorge Pedre .01 .05
845 Kenny Lofton .05 .15
846 Scott Brosius RC .20 .50
847 Chris Cron .01 .05
848 Denis Boucher .01 .05
849 Kyle Abbott .01 .05
850 Bob Zupcic RC .02 .10
851 Rheal Cormier .01 .05
852 Jimmy Lewis RC .01 .05
853 Anthony Telford .01 .05
854 Cliff Brantley .01 .05
855 Kevin Campbell .01 .05
856 Craig Shipley .01 .05
857 Chuck Carr .01 .05
858 Tony Eusebio .02 .10
859 Jim Thome .08 .25
860 Vinny Castilla RC .40 1.00
861 Dann Howitt .01 .05
862 Kevin Ward .01 .05
863 Steve Wapnick .01 .05
864 Rod Brewer RC .02 .10
865 Todd Van Poppel .01 .05
866 Jose Hernandez RC .08 .25
867 Amalio Carreno .01 .05
868 Calvin Jones .01 .05
869 Jeff Gardner .01 .05
870 Jarvis Brown .01 .05
871 Eddie Taubensee RC .08 .25
872 Andy Mota .01 .05
873 Chris Haney .01 .05
874 Roberto Hernandez .01 .05
875 Laddie Renfroe .01 .05
876 Scott Cooper .01 .05
877 Armando Reynoso RC .08 .25
878 Ty Cobb MEMO .08 .25
879 Babe Ruth MEMO .20 .50
880 Honus Wagner MEMO .08 .25
881 Lou Gehrig MEMO .15 .40
882 Satchel Paige MEMO .08 .25
883 Will Clark DT .02 .10
884 Cal Ripken DT .75 2.00
885 Wade Boggs DT .02 .10
886 Kirby Puckett DT .05 .15
887 Tony Gwynn DT .05 .15
888 Craig Biggio DT .02 .10
889 Scott Erickson DT .01 .05
890 Tom Glavine DT .02 .10
891 Rob Dibble DT .02 .10
892 Mitch Williams DT .01 .05
893 Frank Thomas DT .05 .15
X672 Knoblauch 90 Score AU/3000 12.50 30.00

1992 Score DiMaggio

COMPLETE SET (5) 25.00 60.00
COMMON DIMAGGIO (1-5) 6.00 15.00
RANDOM INSERTS IN SER.1 PACKS
AU Joe DiMaggio AU/2500 200.00 400.00

1992 Score Factory Inserts

COMPLETE SET (17) 3.00 8.00
ONE SET PER FACTORY SET
B1 Greg Gagne WS .15 .40
B2 Scott Leius WS .15 .40
B3 Mark Lemke WS .15 .40
David Justice
B4 Lonnie Smith WS .15 .40
Brian Harper
B5 David Justice WS .30 .75
B6 Kirby Puckett WS .75 2.00
B7 Gene Larkin WS .15 .40
B8 Carlton Fisk COOP .50 1.25
B9 Ozzie Smith COOP 1.25 3.00
B10 Dave Winfield COOP .30 .75
B11 Robin Yount COOP 1.25 3.00
B12 Joe DiMaggio .40 1.00
B13 Joe DiMaggio .40 1.00
B14 Joe DiMaggio .40 1.00
B15 Carl Yastrzemski .20 .50
B16 Carl Yastrzemski .20 .50
B17 Carl Yastrzemski .20 .50

1992 Score Franchise

COMPLETE SET (4) 12.50 30.00
RANDOM INSERTS IN SER.2 PACKS
STATED PRINT RUN 150,000 SETS
1 Stan Musial 2.00 5.00
2 Mickey Mantle 4.00 10.00
3 Carl Yastrzemski 2.00 5.00
4 Musial 4.00 10.00
Mantle
Yaz

1992 Score Franchise Autographs

RANDOM INSERTS IN SER.2 PACKS
1-3 PRINT RUN 2000 SERIAL #'d SETS
COMBO CARD PRINT RUN 500 #'d COPIES
AU1 Stan Musial 60.00 120.00
AU2 Mickey Mantle 250.00 500.00
AU3 Carl Yastrzemski 50.00 100.00
AU4 Musial/Mantle/Yaz 450.00 900.00

1992 Score Hot Rookies

COMPLETE SET (10) 3.00 8.00
ONE PER BLISTER PACK
1 Cal Eldred .20 .50
2 Royce Clayton .20 .50
3 Kenny Lofton .75 2.00
4 Todd Van Poppel .20 .50
5 Scott Cooper .20 .50
6 Todd Hundley .20 .50
7 Tino Martinez .75 2.00
8 Anthony Telford .20 .50
9 Derek Bell .20 .50
10 Reggie Jefferson .20 .50

1992 Score Impact Players

COMPLETE SET (90) 8.00 20.00
COMPLETE SERIES 1 (45) 5.00 12.00
COMPLETE SERIES 2 (45) 2.50 6.00
FIVE PER JUMBO PACK
1 Chuck Knoblauch .10 .30
2 Jeff Bagwell .30 .75
3 Juan Guzman .05 .15
4 Milt Cuyler .05 .15
5 Ivan Rodriguez .30 .75
6 Rich DeLucia .05 .15
7 Orlando Merced .05 .15
8 Ray Lankford .10 .30
9 Brian Hunter .05 .15
10 Roberto Alomar .20 .50
11 Wes Chamberlain .05 .15
12 Steve Avery .05 .15
13 Scott Erickson .05 .15
14 Jim Abbott .20 .50
15 Mark Whiten .05 .15
16 Leo Gomez .05 .15
17 Doug Henry .10 .30
18 Brent Mayne .05 .15
19 Charles Nagy .05 .15
20 Phil Plantier .05 .15
21 Mo Vaughn .10 .30
22 Craig Biggio .20 .50
23 Derek Bell .10 .30
24 Royce Clayton .05 .15
25 Gary Cooper .05 .15
26 Scott Cooper .05 .15
27 Juan Gonzalez .20 .50
28 Ken Griffey Jr. .60 1.50
29 Larry Walker .20 .50
30 John Smoltz .20 .50
31 Todd Hundley .05 .15
32 Kenny Lofton .20 .50
33 Andy Mota .05 .15
34 Todd Zeile .05 .15
35 Arthur Rhodes .05 .15
36 Jim Thome .30 .75
37 Todd Van Poppel .05 .15
38 Mark Wohlers .05 .15
39 Anthony Young .05 .15
40 Sandy Alomar Jr. .05 .15
41 John Olerud .10 .30
42 Robin Ventura .10 .30
43 Frank Thomas .30 .75
44 David Justice .10 .30
45 Hal Morris .05 .15
46 Ruben Sierra .10 .30
47 Travis Fryman .10 .30
48 Mike Mussina .30 .75
49 Tom Glavine .20 .50
50 Barry Larkin .20 .50
51 Will Clark .20 .50
52 Jose Canseco .20 .50
53 Bo Jackson .30 .75
54 Dwight Gooden .10 .30
55 Barry Bonds 1.25 3.00
56 Fred McGriff .20 .50
57 Roger Clemens .60 1.50
58 Benito Santiago .10 .30
59 Darryl Strawberry .10 .30
60 Cecil Fielder .10 .30
61 John Franco .10 .30
62 Matt Williams .10 .30
63 Marquis Grissom .10 .30
64 Danny Tartabull .05 .15
65 Ron Gant .10 .30
66 Paul O'Neill .20 .50
67 Devon White .10 .30
68 Rafael Palmeiro .20 .50
69 Tom Gordon .05 .15
70 Shawon Dunston .05 .15
71 Rob Dibble .10 .30
72 Eddie Zosky .05 .15
73 Jack McDowell .05 .15
74 Len Dykstra .10 .30
75 Ramon Martinez .05 .15
76 Reggie Sanders .10 .30
77 Greg Maddux .50 1.25
78 Ellis Burks .10 .30
79 John Smiley .05 .15
80 Roberto Kelly .05 .15
81 Ben McDonald .05 .15
82 Mark Lewis .05 .15
83 Jose Rijo .05 .15
84 Ozzie Guillen .10 .30
85 Lance Dickson .05 .15
86 Kim Batiste .05 .15
87 Gregg Olson .05 .15
88 Andy Benes .05 .15
89 Cal Eldred .05 .15
90 David Cone .10 .30

1992 Score Rookie/Traded

The 1992 Score Rookie and Traded set contains 110 standard-size cards featuring traded veterans and rookies. This set was issued in complete set form and was released through hobby dealers. The set is arranged numerically such that cards 1T-79T are traded players and cards 80T-110T feature rookies. Notable Rookie Cards in this set include Brian Jordan and Jeff Kent.

COMP.FACT.SET (110) 3.00 8.00
1T Gary Sheffield .10 .30
2T Kevin Seitzer .07 .20
3T Danny Tartabull .07 .20
4T Steve Sax .07 .20
5T Bobby Bonilla .10 .30
6T Frank Viola .10 .30
7T Dave Winfield .10 .30
8T Rick Sutcliffe .10 .30
9T Jose Canseco .20 .50
10T Greg Swindell .07 .20
11T Eddie Murray .30 .75
12T Randy Myers .07 .20
13T Wally Joyner .10 .30
14T Kenny Lofton .20 .50
15T Jack Morris .10 .30
16T Charlie Hayes .07 .20
17T Pete Incaviglia .07 .20
18T Kevin Mitchell .07 .20
19T Kurt Stillwell .07 .20
20T Bret Saberhagen .10 .30
21T Steve Buechele .07 .20
22T John Smiley .07 .20
23T Sammy Sosa Cubs .30 .75
24T George Bell .07 .20
25T Curt Schilling .20 .50
26T Dick Schofield .07 .20
27T David Cone .10 .30
28T Dan Gladden .07 .20
29T Kirk McCaskill .07 .20
30T Mike Gallego .07 .20
31T Kevin McReynolds .07 .20
32T Bill Swift .07 .20
33T Dave Martinez .07 .20
34T Storm Davis .07 .20
35T Willie Randolph .10 .30
36T Melido Perez .07 .20
37T Mark Carreon .07 .20
38T Doug Jones .07 .20
39T Gregg Jefferies .07 .20
40T Mike Jackson .07 .20
41T Dickie Thon .07 .20
42T Eric King .07 .20
43T Herm Winningham .07 .20
44T Derek Lilliquist .07 .20
45T Dave Anderson .07 .20
46T Jeff Reardon .10 .30
47T Scott Bankhead .07 .20
48T Cory Snyder .07 .20
49T Al Newman .07 .20
50T Keith Miller .07 .20
51T Dave Burba .07 .20
52T Bill Pecota .07 .20
53T Chuck Crim .07 .20
54T Mariano Duncan .07 .20
55T Dave Gallagher .07 .20
56T Chris Gwynn .07 .20
57T Scott Ruskin .07 .20
58T Jack Armstrong .07 .20
59T Gary Carter .10 .30
60T Andres Galarraga .10 .30
61T Ken Hill .07 .20
62T Eric Davis .10 .30
63T Ruben Sierra .10 .30
64T Darrin Fletcher .07 .20
65T Tim Belcher .07 .20
66T Mike Morgan .07 .20
67T Scott Scudder .07 .20
68T Tom Candiotti .07 .20
69T Hubie Brooks .07 .20
70T Kal Daniels .07 .20
71T Bruce Ruffin .07 .20
72T Billy Hatcher .07 .20
73T Bob Melvin .07 .20
74T Lee Guetterman .07 .20
75T Rene Gonzales .07 .20
76T Kevin Bass .07 .20
77T Tom Bolton .07 .20
78T John Wetteland .10 .30
79T Bip Roberts .07 .20
80T Pat Listach RC .15 .40
81T John Doherty RC .07 .20
82T Sam Militello .07 .20
83T Brian Jordan RC .25 .60
84T Jeff Kent RC 1.25 3.00
85T Dave Fleming .07 .20
86T Jeff Tackett .07 .20
87T Chad Curtis RC .15 .40
88T Eric Fox RC .07 .20
89T Denny Neagle .10 .30
90T Donovan Osborne .07 .20
91T Carlos Hernandez .07 .20
92T Tim Wakefield RC 1.25 3.00
93T Tim Salmon .20 .50
94T Dave Nilsson .07 .20
95T Mike Perez .07 .20
96T Pat Hentgen .07 .20
97T Frank Seminara RC .07 .20
98T Ruben Amaro .07 .20
99T Archi Cianfrocco RC .07 .20
100T Andy Stankiewicz .07 .20
101T Jim Bullinger .07 .20
102T Pat Mahomes RC .15 .40
103T Hipolito Pichardo RC .07 .20
104T Bret Boone .20 .50
105T John Vander Wal .07 .20
106T Vince Horsman .07 .20
107T Jim Austin .07 .20
108T Brian Williams RC .07 .20
109T Dan Walters .07 .20
110T Wil Cordero .07 .20

1992 Score 100 Rising Stars

The 1992 Score Rising Stars set contains 100 standard size player cards and six "Magic Motion" trivia cards.

COMPLETE SET (100) 3.00 8.00
1 Milt Cuyler .01 .05
2 David Howard .01 .05
3 Brian R. Hunter .01 .05
4 Darryl Kile .02 .10
5 Pat Kelly .01 .05
6 Luis Gonzalez .08 .25
7 Mike Benjamin .01 .05
8 Eric Anthony .01 .05
9 Moises Alou .05 .15
10 Darren Lewis .01 .05
11 Chuck Knoblauch .08 .25
12 Geronimo Pena .01 .05
13 Jeff Plympton .01 .05
14 Bret Barberie .01 .05
15 Chris Haney .01 .05
16 Rick Wilkins .01 .05
17 Julio Valera .01 .05
18 Joe Slusarski .01 .05
19 Jose Melendez .01 .05
20 Pete Schourek .01 .05
21 Jeff Conine .02 .10
22 Paul Faries .01 .05
23 Scott Kamieniecki .01 .05
24 Bernard Gilkey .01 .05
25 Wes Chamberlain .01 .05
26 Charles Nagy .01 .05
27 Juan Guzman .01 .05
28 Heath Slocumb .01 .05
29 Eddie Taubensee .02 .10
30 Cedric Landrum .01 .05
31 Jose Offerman .01 .05
32 Andres Santana .01 .05
33 David Segui .02 .10
34 Bernie Williams .50 1.25
35 Jeff Bagwell 1.00 2.50
36 Kevin Morton .01 .05
37 Kirk Dressendorfer .01 .05
38 Mike Fetters .01 .05
39 Darren Holmes .01 .05
40 Jeff Johnson .01 .05
41 Scott Aldred .01 .05
42 Kevin Ward .01 .05
43 Ray Lankford .08 .25
44 Terry Shumpert .01 .05
45 Wade Taylor .01 .05
46 Rob MacDonald .01 .05
47 Jose Mota .01 .05
48 Reggie Harris .01 .05
49 Mike Remlinger .01 .05
50 Mark Lewis .01 .05
51 Tino Martinez .08 .25
52 Ed Sprague .01 .05
53 Freddie Benavides .01 .05
54 Rich DeLucia .01 .05
55 Brian Drahman .01 .05
56 Steve Decker .01 .05
57 Scott Livingstone .01 .05
58 Mike Timlin .01 .05
59 Bob Scanlan .01 .05
60 Dean Palmer .05 .15
61 Frank Castillo .01 .05
62 Mark Leonard .01 .05
63 Chuck McElroy .01 .05
64 Derek Bell .01 .05
65 Andujar Cedeno .01 .05
66 Leo Gomez .01 .05
67 Rusty Meacham .01 .05
68 Dann Howitt .01 .05
69 Chris Jones .01 .05
70 Dave Cochrane .01 .05
71 Carlos Martinez .01 .05
72 Hensley Meulens .01 .05
73 Rich Reed .01 .05
74 Pedro Munoz .01 .05
75 Orlando Merced .01 .05
76 Chito Martinez .01 .05
77 Ivan Rodriguez 1.00 2.50
78 Brian Barnes .01 .05
79 Chris Donnels .01 .05
80 Todd Hundley .02 .10
81 Gary Scott .01 .05
82 John Wehner .01 .05
83 Al Osuna .01 .05
84 Luis Lopez .01 .05
85 Brent Mayne .01 .05
86 Phil Plantier .01 .05
87 Joe Bitker .01 .05
88 Scott Cooper .01 .05
89 Chris Hammond .02 .10
90 Tim Sherrill .01 .05
91 Doug Simons .01 .05
92 Kip Gross .01 .05
93 Tim McIntosh .01 .05
94 Larry Casian .01 .05
95 Mike Dalton .01 .05
96 Lance Dickson .01 .05
97 Joe Grahe .01 .05
98 Glenn Sutko .01 .05
99 Gerald Alexander .01 .05
100 Mo Vaughn .08 .25

1992 Score 100 Superstars

The 1992 Score Superstars set contains 100 standard-size player cards and six "Magic Motion" trivia cards.

COMPLETE SET (100) 5.00 12.00
1 Ken Griffey Jr. .75 2.00
2 Scott Erickson .01 .05
3 John Smiley .01 .05
4 Rick Aguilera .02 .10
5 Jeff Reardon .02 .10
6 Chuck Finley .02 .10
7 Kirby Puckett .25 .60
8 Paul Molitor .15 .40
9 Dave Winfield .15 .40
10 Mike Greenwell .01 .05
11 Bret Saberhagen .02 .10
12 Pete Harnisch .01 .05
13 Ozzie Guillen .05 .15
14 Hal Morris .01 .05
15 Tom Glavine .15 .40
16 David Cone .05 .15
17 Edgar Martinez .05 .15
18 Willie McGee .02 .10
19 Jim Abbott .02 .10
20 Mark Grace .05 .15
21 George Brett .50 1.25
22 Jack McDowell .01 .05
23 Don Mattingly .60 1.50
24 Will Clark .08 .25
25 Dwight Gooden .02 .10
26 Barry Bonds .50 1.25
27 Rafael Palmeiro .15 .40
28 Lee Smith .02 .10
29 Wally Joyner .02 .10
30 Wade Boggs .30 .75
31 Tom Henke .01 .05
32 Mark Langston .01 .05
33 Robin Ventura .08 .25
34 Steve Avery .01 .05
35 Joe Carter .02 .10
36 Benito Santiago .02 .10
37 Dave Stieb .01 .05
38 Julio Franco .02 .10
39 Albert Belle .02 .10
40 Dale Murphy .08 .25
41 Rob Dibble .01 .05
42 Dave Justice .08 .25
43 Jose Rijo .01 .05
44 Eric Davis .02 .10
45 Terry Pendleton .01 .05
46 Kevin Maas .01 .05
47 Ozzie Smith .40 1.00
48 Andre Dawson .05 .15
49 Sandy Alomar Jr. .02 .10
50 Nolan Ryan 1.25 3.00
51 Frank Thomas .30 .75
52 Craig Biggio .05 .15
53 Doug Drabek .01 .05
54 Bobby Thigpen .01 .05
55 Darryl Strawberry .02 .10
56 Dennis Eckersley .15 .40
57 John Franco .02 .10
58 Paul O'Neill .05 .15
59 Scott Sanderson .01 .05
60 Dave Stewart .02 .10
61 Ivan Calderon .01 .05
62 Frank Viola .01 .05
63 Mark McGwire .60 1.50
64 Kelly Gruber .01 .05
65 Fred McGriff .05 .15
66 Cecil Fielder .02 .10
67 Jose Canseco .15 .40
68 Howard Johnson .01 .05
69 Juan Gonzalez .25 .60
70 Tim Wallach .01 .05
71 John Olerud .08 .25
72 Carlton Fisk .15 .40
73 Otis Nixon .01 .05
74 Roger Clemens .60 1.50
75 Ramon Martinez .02 .10
76 Ron Gant .02 .10
77 Barry Larkin .08 .25
78 Eddie Murray .15 .40
79 Vince Coleman .01 .05
80 Bobby Bonilla .01 .05
81 Tony Gwynn .50 1.25
82 Roberto Alomar .08 .25
83 Ellis Burks .02 .10
84 Robin Yount .20 .50
85 Ryne Sandberg .20 .50
86 Len Dykstra .02 .10
87 Ruben Sierra .02 .10
88 George Bell .01 .05
89 Cal Ripken 1.25 3.00
90 Danny Tartabull .01 .05
91 Gregg Olson .01 .05
92 Dave Henderson .01 .05
93 Kevin Mitchell .01 .05
94 Ben McDonald .01 .05
95 Matt Williams .05 .15
96 Roberto Kelly .01 .05
97 Dennis Martinez .02 .10
98 Kent Hrbek .02 .10
99 Felix Jose .01 .05
100 Rickey Henderson .30 .75

1992 Score/Pinnacle Promo Panels

COMPLETE SET (25) 20.00 50.00
1 Nolan Ryan 4.00 10.00
Terry Pendleton
Willie McGee
Lonnie
2 Will Clark .75 2.00
Mark Langston
Paul Molitor
Devon Whi
3 Frank Thomas 3.00 8.00
David Justice
Mark Carreon
Dave He
4 Kirby Puckett 2.50 6.00
Ryne Sandberg
Roberto Alomar
Davi
5 Ozzie Smith 1.50 4.00
Darryl Strawberry
Kevin Seitzer
Jef
6 Robin Yount .75 2.00
Jay Buhner
Chuck Crim
Jimmy Jones
7 Don Mattingly 1.50 4.00
Matt Williams
Dave Winfield
Georg
8 Orel Hershisher .40 1.00
Wes Chamberlain
Gary Gaetti
Dic
9 Ron Gant .75 2.00
Andres Galarraga
Bruce Hurst
Alex Fern
10 Albert Belle .60 1.50
Ellis Burks
Melido Perez
Kevin Gro
11 Ivan Calderon .40 1.00
Bill Doran
Rick Aguilera
Doug Jon
12 Todd Zeile .40 1.00
Mike Gallego
Lenny Harris
Jack Clark
13 Harold Baines .40 1.00
Walt Weiss
Eric Davis
Randy Ready
14 N.Ryan 6.00 15.00
G.Brett
G.Bell
R.Palmeiro
15 Chili Davis .40 1.00
Phil Plantier
David Wells
Bob Walk
16 John Olerud .40 1.00
Dave Hollins
Jack McDowell
Juan Sam
17 Carlton Fisk .60 1.50
Kent Hrbek
Denny Martinez
Jim Acke
18 Jay Buhner .60 1.50
Gregg Olson
Terry Steinbach
Kirk McC
19 Jeff Bagwell 1.50 4.00
Darryl Strawberry
Travis Fryman
An
20 Alex Cole .60 1.50
Jim Gantner
Ken Caminiti
Todd Stottle
21 Alex Fernandez .40 1.00
Bill Gullickson
Jose Guzman
Shaw
22 Bernard Gilkey .40 1.00
Omar Vizquel
Ivan Calderon
Ozzie
23 Gary Gaetti .40 1.00
Doug Drabek
Brent Mayne
Tom Bolton
24 David Justice .75 2.00
Kevin Maas
Jody Reed
Vince Colema
25 Chili Davis .40 1.00
Hensley Meulens
David Howard
Mark L

1992 Score Proctor and Gamble

This 18-card standard-size set was produced by Score for Proctor and Gamble as a mail-in premium and contains 18 players from the 1992 All-Star Game line-up. The production run comprised 2,000,000 sets and 25 uncut sheets. A three-card sample set was also produced for sales representatives with a print run of 5,000,000 sets and 25 uncut sheets. The three sample cards, featuring Griffey, Sandberg, and Henderson, are stamped "sample" on the back. Collectors could obtain the set by sending in a required certificate, 99 cents, three UPC symbols from three different Proctor and Gamble products, and 50 cents for postage and handling. The certificate was published in a flyer inserted in Sunday, August 16 newspapers. The card fronts feature color action player cutouts superimposed on a diagonally striped background showing a large star behind the player. Card numbers 1-9 have a blue star on a graded magenta background, while card numbers 10-18 show a red star on blue-green. The backs display a close-up photo, biographical and statistical information, and career summary on a graded yellow-orange background. The cards are numbered "X/18" at the lower right corner.

COMPLETE SET (18) 2.00 5.00
1 Sandy Alomar Jr. .05 .15
2 Mark McGwire .40 1.00
3 Roberto Alomar .08 .25
4 Wade Boggs .15 .40
5 Cal Ripken .75 2.00
6 Kirby Puckett .20 .50
7 Ken Griffey Jr. .60 1.50
8 Jose Canseco .15 .40
9 Kevin Brown .07 .20
10 Benito Santiago .05 .15
11 Fred McGriff .07 .20
12 Ryne Sandberg .30 .75
13 Terry Pendleton .02 .10
14 Ozzie Smith .30 .75
15 Barry Bonds .30 .75
16 Tony Gwynn .40 1.00
17 Andy Van Slyke .02 .10
18 Tom Glavine .08 .25

1992 Score Rookies

This 40-card boxed set measures the standard size and features glossy color action player photos on a kelly green face with meandering purple stripes.

COMP.FACT SET (40) 1.50 4.00
1 Todd Van Poppel .01 .05
2 Kyle Abbott .01 .05
3 Derek Bell .01 .05
4 Jim Thome .60 1.50
5 Mark Wohlers .01 .05
6 Todd Hundley .08 .25
7 Arthur Lee Rhodes .01 .05
8 John Ramos .01 .05
9 Chris George .01 .05
10 Kenny Lofton .40 1.00
11 Ted Wood .01 .05
12 Royce Clayton .01 .05
13 Scott Cooper .01 .05
14 Anthony Young .01 .05
15 Joel Johnston .01 .05
16 Andy Mota .01 .05

17 Lenny Webster .01 .05
18 Andy Ashby .01 .05
19 Jose Mota .01 .05
20 Tim McIntosh .01 .05
21 Terry Bross .01 .05
22 Harvey Pulliam .01 .05
23 Hector Fajardo .01 .05
24 Esteban Beltre .01 .05
25 Gary DiSarcina .01 .05
26 Mike Humphreys .01 .05
27 Jarvis Brown .01 .05
28 Gary Cooper .01 .05
29 Chris Donnels .01 .05
30 Monty Fariss .01 .05
31 Eric Karros .30 .75
32 Braulio Castillo .01 .05
33 Cal Eldred .01 .05
34 Tom Goodwin .01 .05
35 Reggie Sanders .20 .50
36 Scott Servais .01 .05
37 Kim Batiste .01 .05
38 Eric Wedge .08 .25
39 Willie Banks .01 .05
40 Mo Sanford .01 .05

1993 Score

The 1993 Score baseball set consists of 660 standard-size cards issued in one single series. The cards were distributed in 16-card poly packs and 35-card jumbo superpacks. Topical subsets featured are Award Winners (481-486), Draft Picks (487-501), All-Star Caricature (502-512 [AL], 522-531 [NL]), Highlights (513-519), World Series Highlights (520-521), Dream Team (532-542) and Rookies (sprinkled throughout the set). Rookie Cards in this set include Derek Jeter, Jason Kendall and Shannon Stewart.

COMPLETE SET (660) 15.00 40.00
SUBSET CARDS HALF VALUE OF BASE CARDS
1 Ken Griffey Jr. .40 1.00
2 Gary Sheffield .07 .20
3 Frank Thomas .20 .50
4 Ryne Sandberg .30 .75
5 Larry Walker .07 .20
6 Cal Ripken .60 1.50
7 Roger Clemens .40 1.00
8 Bobby Bonilla .07 .20
9 Carlos Baerga .02 .10
10 Darren Daulton .07 .20
11 Travis Fryman .07 .20
12 Andy Van Slyke .10 .30
13 Jose Canseco .10 .30
14 Roberto Alomar .10 .30
15 Tom Glavine .10 .30
16 Barry Larkin .10 .30
17 Gregg Jefferies .02 .10
18 Craig Biggio .10 .30
19 Shane Mack .02 .10
20 Brett Butler .07 .20
21 Dennis Eckersley .07 .20
22 Will Clark .10 .30
23 Don Mattingly .50 1.25
24 Tony Gwynn .25 .60
25 Ivan Rodriguez .10 .30
26 Shawon Dunston .02 .10
27 Mike Mussina .10 .30
28 Marquis Grissom .07 .20
29 Charles Nagy .02 .10
30 Len Dykstra .07 .20
31 Cecil Fielder .07 .20
32 Jay Bell .07 .20
33 B.J. Surhoff .07 .20
34 Bob Tewksbury .02 .10
35 Danny Tartabull .02 .10
36 Terry Pendleton .07 .20
37 Jack Morris .07 .20
38 Hal Morris .02 .10
39 Luis Polonia .02 .10
40 Ken Caminiti .07 .20
41 Robin Ventura .07 .20
42 Darryl Strawberry .07 .20
43 Wally Joyner .07 .20
44 Fred McGriff .10 .30
45 Kevin Tapani .02 .10
46 Matt Williams .07 .20
47 Robin Yount .30 .75
48 Ken Hill .02 .10
49 Edgar Martinez .10 .30
50 Mark Grace .10 .30
51 Juan Gonzalez .07 .20
52 Curt Schilling .07 .20
53 Dwight Gooden .07 .20
54 Chris Hoiles .02 .10
55 Frank Viola .07 .20
56 Ray Lankford .07 .20
57 George Brett .50 1.25
58 Kenny Lofton .07 .20
59 Nolan Ryan .75 2.00
60 Mickey Tettleton .02 .10
61 John Smoltz .10 .30
62 Howard Johnson .02 .10
63 Eric Karros .07 .20
64 Rick Aguilera .02 .10
65 Steve Finley .07 .20
66 Mark Langston .02 .10
67 Bill Swift .02 .10
68 John Olerud .07 .20
69 Kevin McReynolds .02 .10
70 Jack McDowell .02 .10
71 Rickey Henderson .20 .50
72 Brian Harper .02 .10
73 Mike Morgan .02 .10
74 Rafael Palmeiro .10 .30
75 Dennis Martinez .07 .20
76 Tino Martinez .10 .30
77 Eddie Murray .20 .50
78 Ellis Burks .07 .20
79 John Kruk .07 .20
80 Gregg Olson .02 .10
81 Bernard Gilkey .02 .10
82 Milt Cuyler .02 .10
83 Mike LaValliere .02 .10
84 Albert Belle .07 .20
85 Bip Roberts .02 .10
86 Melido Perez .02 .10
87 Otis Nixon .02 .10
88 Bill Spiers .02 .10
89 Jeff Bagwell .10 .30
90 Orel Hershiser .07 .20
91 Andy Benes .02 .10
92 Devon White .07 .20
93 Willie McGee .07 .20
94 Ozzie Guillen .07 .20
95 Ivan Calderon .02 .10
96 Keith Miller .02 .10
97 Steve Buechele .02 .10
98 Kent Hrbek .07 .20
99 Dave Hollins .02 .10
100 Mike Bordick .02 .10
101 Randy Tomlin .02 .10
102 Omar Vizquel .10 .30
103 Lee Smith .07 .20
104 Leo Gomez .02 .10
105 Jose Rijo .02 .10
106 Mark Whiten .02 .10
107 David Justice .07 .20
108 Eddie Taubensee .02 .10
109 Lance Johnson .02 .10
110 Felix Jose .02 .10
111 Mike Harkey .02 .10
112 Randy Milligan .02 .10
113 Anthony Young .02 .10
114 Rico Brogna .02 .10
115 Bret Saberhagen .07 .20
116 Sandy Alomar Jr. .02 .10
117 Terry Mulholland .02 .10
118 Darryl Hamilton .02 .10
119 Todd Zeile .02 .10
120 Bernie Williams .10 .30
121 Zane Smith .02 .10
122 Derek Bell .02 .10
123 Deion Sanders .10 .30
124 Luis Sojo .02 .10
125 Joe Oliver .02 .10
126 Craig Grebeck .02 .10
127 Andujar Cedeno .02 .10
128 Brian McRae .02 .10
129 Jose Offerman .02 .10
130 Pedro Munoz .02 .10
131 Bud Black .02 .10
132 Mo Vaughn .07 .20
133 Bruce Hurst .02 .10
134 Dave Henderson .02 .10
135 Tom Pagnozzi .02 .10
136 Erik Hanson .02 .10
137 Orlando Merced .02 .10
138 Dean Palmer .07 .20
139 John Franco .07 .20
140 Brady Anderson .07 .20
141 Ricky Jordan .02 .10
142 Jeff Blauser .02 .10
143 Sammy Sosa .20 .50
144 Bob Walk .02 .10
145 Delino DeShields .02 .10
146 Kevin Brown .07 .20
147 Mark Lemke .02 .10
148 Chuck Knoblauch .07 .20
149 Chris Sabo .02 .10
150 Bobby Witt .02 .10
151 Luis Gonzalez .07 .20
152 Ron Karkovice .02 .10
153 Jeff Brantley .02 .10
154 Kevin Appier .07 .20
155 Darrin Jackson .02 .10
156 Kelly Gruber .02 .10
157 Royce Clayton .02 .10
158 Chuck Finley .07 .20
159 Jeff King .02 .10
160 Greg Vaughn .02 .10
161 Geronimo Pena .02 .10
162 Steve Farr .02 .10
163 Jose Oquendo .02 .10
164 Mark Lewis .02 .10
165 John Wetteland .07 .20
166 Mike Henneman .02 .10
167 Todd Hundley .02 .10
168 Wes Chamberlain .02 .10
169 Steve Avery .02 .10
170 Mike Devereaux .02 .10
171 Reggie Sanders .07 .20
172 Jay Buhner .07 .20
173 Eric Anthony .02 .10
174 John Burkett .02 .10
175 Tom Candiotti .02 .10
176 Phil Plantier .02 .10
177 Doug Henry .02 .10
178 Scott Leius .02 .10
179 Kirt Manwaring .02 .10
180 Jeff Parrett .02 .10
181 Don Slaught .02 .10
182 Scott Radinsky .02 .10
183 Luis Alicea .02 .10
184 Tom Gordon .02 .10
185 Rick Wilkins .02 .10
186 Todd Stottlemyre .02 .10
187 Moises Alou .07 .20
188 Joe Grahe .02 .10
189 Jeff Kent .20 .50
190 Bill Wegman .02 .10
191 Kim Batiste .02 .10
192 Matt Nokes .02 .10
193 Mark Wohlers .02 .10
194 Paul Sorrento .02 .10
195 Chris Hammond .02 .10
196 Scott Livingstone .02 .10
197 Doug Jones .02 .10
198 Scott Cooper .02 .10
199 Ramon Martinez .02 .10
200 Dave Valle .02 .10
201 Mariano Duncan .02 .10
202 Ben McDonald .02 .10
203 Darren Lewis .02 .10
204 Kenny Rogers .07 .20
205 Manuel Lee .02 .10
206 Scott Erickson .02 .10
207 Dan Gladden .02 .10
208 Bob Welch .02 .10
209 Greg Olson .02 .10
210 Dan Pasqua .02 .10
211 Tim Wallach .02 .10
212 Jeff Montgomery .02 .10
213 Derrick May .02 .10
214 Ed Sprague .02 .10
215 David Haas .02 .10
216 Darrin Fletcher .02 .10
217 Brian Jordan .07 .20
218 Jaime Navarro .02 .10
219 Randy Velarde .02 .10
220 Ron Gant .07 .20
221 Paul Quantrill .02 .10
222 Damion Easley .02 .10
223 Charlie Hough .07 .20
224 Brad Brink .02 .10
225 Barry Manuel .02 .10
226 Kevin Koslofski .02 .10
227 Ryan Thompson .02 .10
228 Mike Munoz .02 .10
229 Dan Wilson .07 .20
230 Peter Hoy .02 .10
231 Pedro Astacio .02 .10
232 Matt Stairs .02 .10
233 Jeff Reboulet .02 .10
234 Manny Alexander .02 .10
235 Willie Banks .02 .10
236 John Jaha .02 .10
237 Scooter Tucker .02 .10
238 Russ Springer .02 .10
239 Paul Miller .02 .10
240 Dan Peltier .02 .10
241 Ozzie Canseco .02 .10
242 Ben Rivera .02 .10
243 John Valentin .02 .10
244 Henry Rodriguez .02 .10
245 Derek Parks .02 .10
246 Carlos Garcia .02 .10
247 Tim Pugh RC .02 .10
248 Melvin Nieves .02 .10
249 Rich Amaral .02 .10
250 Willie Greene .02 .10
251 Tim Scott .02 .10
252 Dave Silvestri .02 .10
253 Rob Mallicoat .02 .10
254 Donald Harris .02 .10
255 Craig Colbert .02 .10
256 Jose Guzman .02 .10
257 Domingo Martinez RC .02 .10
258 William Suero .02 .10
259 Juan Guerrero .02 .10
260 J.T.Snow RC .20 .50
261 Tony Pena .02 .10
262 Tim Fortugno .02 .10
263 Tom Marsh .02 .10
264 Kurt Knudsen .02 .10
265 Tim Costo .02 .10
266 Steve Shifflett .02 .10
267 Billy Ashley .02 .10
268 Jerry Nielsen .02 .10
269 Pete Young .02 .10
270 Johnny Guzman .02 .10
271 Greg Colbrunn .02 .10
272 Jeff Nelson .02 .10
273 Kevin Young .07 .20
274 Jeff Frye .02 .10
275 J.T. Bruett .02 .10
276 Todd Pratt RC .08 .25
277 Mike Butcher .02 .10
278 John Flaherty .02 .10
279 John Patterson .02 .10
280 Eric Hillman .02 .10
281 Bien Figueroa .02 .10
282 Shane Reynolds .02 .10
283 Rich Rowland .02 .10
284 Steve Foster .02 .10
285 Dave Mlicki .02 .10
286 Mike Piazza 1.25 3.00
287 Mike Trombley .02 .10
288 Jim Pena .02 .10
289 Bob Ayrault .02 .10
290 Henry Mercedes .02 .10
291 Bob Wickman .02 .10
292 Jacob Brumfield .02 .10
293 David Hulse RC .02 .10
294 Ryan Klesko .07 .20
295 Doug Linton .02 .10
296 Steve Cooke .02 .10
297 Eddie Zosky .02 .10
298 Gerald Williams .02 .10
299 Jonathan Hurst .02 .10
300 Larry Carter RC .02 .10
301 William Pennyfeather .02 .10
302 Cesar Hernandez .02 .10
303 Steve Hosey .02 .10
304 Blas Minor .02 .10
305 Jeff Grotewald .02 .10
306 Bernardo Brito .02 .10
307 Rafael Bournigal .02 .10
308 Jeff Branson .02 .10
309 Tom Quinlan RC .02 .10
310 Pat Gomez RC .02 .10
311 Sterling Hitchcock RC .08 .25
312 Kent Bottenfield .02 .10
313 Alan Trammell .07 .20
314 Cris Colon .02 .10
315 Paul Wagner .02 .10
316 Matt Maysey .02 .10
317 Mike Stanton .02 .10
318 Rick Trlicek .02 .10
319 Kevin Rogers .02 .10
320 Mark Clark .02 .10
321 Pedro Martinez .40 1.00
322 Al Martin .02 .10
323 Mike Macfarlane .02 .10
324 Rey Sanchez .02 .10
325 Roger Pavlik .02 .10
326 Troy Neel .02 .10
327 Kerry Woodson .02 .10
328 Wayne Kirby .02 .10
329 Ken Ryan RC .08 .25
330 Jesse Levis .02 .10
331 Jim Austin .02 .10
332 Dan Walters .02 .10
333 Brian Williams .02 .10
334 Wil Cordero .02 .10
335 Bret Boone .07 .20
336 Hipolito Pichardo .02 .10
337 Pat Mahomes .02 .10
338 Andy Stankiewicz .02 .10
339 Jim Bullinger .02 .10
340 Archi Cianfrocco .02 .10
341 Ruben Amaro .02 .10
342 Frank Seminara .02 .10
343 Pat Hentgen .02 .10
344 Dave Nilsson .02 .10
345 Mike Perez .02 .10
346 Tim Salmon .10 .30
347 Tim Wakefield .20 .50
348 Carlos Hernandez .02 .10
349 Donovan Osborne .02 .10
350 Denny Neagle .07 .20
351 Sam Militello .02 .10
352 Eric Fox .02 .10
353 John Doherty .02 .10
354 Chad Curtis .02 .10
355 Jeff Tackett .02 .10
356 Dave Fleming .02 .10
357 Pat Listach .02 .10
358 Kevin Wickander .02 .10
359 John Vander Wal .02 .10
360 Arthur Rhodes .02 .10
361 Bob Scanlan .02 .10
362 Bob Zupcic .02 .10
363 Mel Rojas .02 .10
364 Jim Thome .10 .30
365 Bill Pecota .02 .10
366 Mark Carreon .02 .10
367 Mitch Williams .02 .10
368 Cal Eldred .02 .10
369 Stan Belinda .02 .10
370 Pat Kelly .02 .10
371 Rheal Cormier .02 .10
372 Juan Guzman .02 .10
373 Damon Berryhill .02 .10
374 Gary DiSarcina .02 .10
375 Norm Charlton .02 .10
376 Roberto Hernandez .02 .10
377 Scott Kamieniecki .02 .10
378 Rusty Meacham .02 .10
379 Kurt Stillwell .02 .10
380 Lloyd McClendon .02 .10
381 Mark Leonard .02 .10
382 Jerry Browne .02 .10
383 Glenn Davis .02 .10
384 Randy Johnson .20 .50
385 Mike Greenwell .02 .10
386 Scott Chiamparino .02 .10
387 George Bell .02 .10
388 Steve Olin .02 .10
389 Chuck McElroy .02 .10
390 Mark Gardner .02 .10
391 Rod Beck .02 .10
392 Dennis Rasmussen .02 .10
393 Charlie Leibrandt .02 .10
394 Julio Franco .07 .20
395 Pete Harnisch .02 .10
396 Sid Bream .02 .10
397 Milt Thompson .02 .10
398 Glenallen Hill .02 .10
399 Chico Walker .02 .10
400 Alex Cole .02 .10
401 Trevor Wilson .02 .10
402 Jeff Conine .07 .20
403 Kyle Abbott .02 .10
404 Tom Browning .02 .10
405 Jerald Clark .02 .10
406 Vince Horsman .02 .10
407 Kevin Mitchell .02 .10
408 Pete Smith .02 .10
409 Jeff Innis .02 .10
410 Mike Timlin .02 .10
411 Charlie Hayes .02 .10
412 Alex Fernandez .02 .10
413 Jeff Russell .02 .10
414 Jody Reed .02 .10
415 Mickey Morandini .02 .10
416 Darnell Coles .02 .10
417 Xavier Hernandez .02 .10
418 Steve Sax .02 .10
419 Joe Girardi .02 .10
420 Mike Fetters .02 .10
421 Danny Jackson .02 .10
422 Jim Gott .02 .10
423 Tim Belcher .02 .10
424 Jose Mesa .02 .10
425 Junior Felix .02 .10
426 Thomas Howard .02 .10
427 Julio Valera .02 .10
428 Dante Bichette .07 .20
429 Mike Sharperson .02 .10
430 Darryl Kile .07 .20
431 Lonnie Smith .02 .10
432 Monty Fariss .02 .10
433 Reggie Jefferson .02 .10
434 Bob McClure .02 .10
435 Craig Lefferts .02 .10
436 Duane Ward .02 .10
437 Shawn Abner .02 .10
438 Roberto Kelly .02 .10
439 Paul O'Neill .10 .30
440 Alan Mills .02 .10
441 Roger Mason .02 .10
442 Gary Pettis .02 .10
443 Steve Lake .02 .10
444 Gene Larkin .02 .10
445 Larry Andersen .02 .10
446 Doug Dascenzo .02 .10
447 Daryl Boston .02 .10
448 John Candelaria .02 .10
449 Storm Davis .02 .10
450 Tom Edens .02 .10
451 Mike Maddux .02 .10
452 Tim Naehring .02 .10
453 John Orton .02 .10
454 Joey Cora .02 .10
455 Chuck Crim .02 .10
456 Dan Plesac .02 .10
457 Mike Bielecki .02 .10
458 Terry Jorgensen .02 .10
459 John Habyan .02 .10
460 Pete O'Brien .02 .10
461 Jeff Treadway .02 .10
462 Frank Castillo .02 .10
463 Jimmy Jones .02 .10
464 Tommy Greene .02 .10
465 Tracy Woodson .02 .10
466 Rich Rodriguez .02 .10
467 Joe Hesketh .02 .10
468 Greg Myers .02 .10
469 Kirk McCaskill .02 .10
470 Ricky Bones .02 .10
471 Lenny Webster .02 .10
472 Francisco Cabrera .02 .10
473 Turner Ward .02 .10
474 Dwayne Henry .02 .10
475 Al Osuna .02 .10
476 Craig Wilson .02 .10
477 Chris Nabholz .02 .10
478 Rafael Belliard .02 .10
479 Terry Leach .02 .10
480 Tim Teufel .02 .10
481 Dennis Eckersley AW .07 .20
482 Barry Bonds MVP .30 .75
483 Dennis Eckersley AW .07 .20
484 Greg Maddux CY .20 .50
485 Pat Listach AW .02 .10
486 Eric Karros AW .02 .10
487 Jamie Arnold RC .02 .10
488 B.J.Wallace .02 .10
489 Derek Jeter RC 12.00 30.00
490 Jason Kendall RC .40 1.00
491 Rick Helling .02 .10
492 Derek Wallace RC .02 .10
493 Sean Lowe RC .02 .10
494 Shannon Stewart RC .30 .75
495 Benji Grigsby RC .02 .10
496 Todd Steverson RC .02 .10
497 Dan Serafini RC .02 .10
498 Michael Tucker .02 .10
499 Chris Roberts .02 .10
500 Pete Janicki RC .02 .10
501 Jeff Schmidt RC .02 .10
502 Edgar Martinez AS .07 .20
503 Omar Vizquel AS .07 .20
504 Ken Griffey Jr. AS .25 .60
505 Kirby Puckett AS .10 .30
506 Joe Carter AS .02 .10
507 Ivan Rodriguez AS .07 .20
508 Jack Morris AS .02 .10
509 Dennis Eckersley AS .07 .20
510 Frank Thomas AS .10 .30
511 Roberto Alomar AS .07 .20
512 Mickey Morandini AS .02 .10
513 Dennis Eckersley HL .07 .20
514 Jeff Reardon HL .02 .10
515 Danny Tartabull HL .02 .10
516 Bip Roberts HL .02 .10
517 George Brett HL .25 .60
518 Robin Yount HL .20 .50
519 Kevin Gross HL .02 .10
520 Ed Sprague WS .02 .10
521 Dave Winfield WS .02 .10
522 Ozzie Smith AS .20 .50
523 Barry Bonds AS .30 .75
524 Andy Van Slyke AS .07 .20
525 Tony Gwynn AS .10 .30
526 Darren Daulton AS .02 .10
527 Greg Maddux AS .20 .50
528 Fred McGriff AS .10 .30
529 Lee Smith AS .02 .10
530 Ryne Sandberg AS .20 .50
531 Gary Sheffield AS .02 .10
532 Ozzie Smith DT .20 .50
533 Kirby Puckett DT .10 .30
534 Gary Sheffield DT .02 .10
535 Andy Van Slyke DT .07 .20
536 Ken Griffey Jr. DT .25 .60
537 Ivan Rodriguez DT .07 .20
538 Charles Nagy DT .02 .10
539 Tom Glavine DT .07 .20
540 Dennis Eckersley DT .07 .20
541 Frank Thomas DT .10 .30
542 Roberto Alomar DT .07 .20
543 Sean Berry .02 .10
544 Mike Schooler .02 .10
545 Chuck Carr .02 .10
546 Lenny Harris .02 .10
547 Gary Scott .02 .10
548 Derek Lilliquist .02 .10
549 Brian Hunter .02 .10
550 Kirby Puckett MOY .10 .30
551 Jim Eisenreich .02 .10
552 Andre Dawson .07 .20
553 David Nied .02 .10
554 Spike Owen .02 .10
555 Greg Gagne .02 .10
556 Sid Fernandez .02 .10
557 Mark McGwire .50 1.25
558 Bryan Harvey .02 .10
559 Harold Reynolds .07 .20
560 Barry Bonds .60 1.50
561 Eric Wedge RC .08 .25
562 Ozzie Smith .30 .75
563 Rick Sutcliffe .07 .20
564 Jeff Reardon .07 .20
565 Alex Arias .02 .10
566 Greg Swindell .02 .10
567 Brook Jacoby .02 .10
568 Pete Incaviglia .02 .10
569 Butch Henry .02 .10
570 Eric Davis .07 .20
571 Kevin Seitzer .02 .10
572 Tony Fernandez .02 .10
573 Steve Reed RC .02 .10
574 Cory Snyder .02 .10
575 Joe Carter .07 .20
576 Greg Maddux .30 .75
577 Bert Blyleven UER .07 .20
578 Kevin Bass .02 .10
579 Carlton Fisk .10 .30
580 Doug Drabek .02 .10
581 Mark Gubicza .02 .10
582 Bobby Thigpen .02 .10
583 Chili Davis .07 .20
584 Scott Bankhead .02 .10
585 Harold Baines .07 .20
586 Eric Young .02 .10
587 Lance Parrish .07 .20
588 Juan Bell .02 .10
589 Bob Ojeda .02 .10
590 Joe Orsulak .02 .10
591 Benito Santiago .07 .20
592 Wade Boggs .10 .30
593 Robby Thompson .02 .10
594 Eric Plunk .02 .10
595 Hensley Meulens .02 .10
596 Lou Whitaker .07 .20
597 Dale Murphy .10 .30
598 Paul Molitor .07 .20
599 Greg W. Harris .02 .10
600 Darren Holmes .02 .10
601 Dave Martinez .02 .10
602 Tom Henke .02 .10
603 Mike Benjamin .02 .10
604 Rene Gonzales .02 .10
605 Roger McDowell .02 .10
606 Kirby Puckett .20 .50
607 Randy Myers .02 .10
608 Ruben Sierra .07 .20
609 Wilson Alvarez .02 .10
610 David Segui .02 .10
611 Juan Samuel .02 .10
612 Tom Brunansky .02 .10
613 Willie Randolph .07 .20
614 Tony Phillips .02 .10
615 Candy Maldonado .02 .10
616 Chris Bosio .02 .10
617 Bret Barberie .02 .10
618 Scott Sanderson .02 .10
619 Ron Darling .02 .10
620 Dave Winfield .07 .20
621 Mike Felder .02 .10
622 Greg Hibbard .02 .10
623 Mike Scioscia .02 .10
624 John Smiley .02 .10
625 Alejandro Pena .02 .10
626 Terry Steinbach .02 .10
627 Freddie Benavides .02 .10
628 Kevin Reimer .02 .10
629 Braulio Castillo .02 .10
630 Dave Stieb .02 .10
631 Dave Magadan .02 .10
632 Scott Fletcher .02 .10
633 Cris Carpenter .02 .10
634 Kevin Maas .02 .10
635 Todd Worrell .02 .10
636 Rob Deer .02 .10
637 Dwight Smith .02 .10
638 Chito Martinez .02 .10
639 Jimmy Key .07 .20
640 Greg A. Harris .02 .10
641 Mike Moore .02 .10
642 Pat Borders .02 .10
643 Bill Gullickson .02 .10
644 Gary Gaetti .07 .20
645 David Howard .02 .10
646 Jim Abbott .10 .30
647 Willie Wilson .02 .10
648 David Wells .07 .20
649 Andres Galarraga .07 .20
650 Vince Coleman .02 .10
651 Rob Dibble .07 .20
652 Frank Tanana .02 .10
653 Steve Decker .02 .10
654 David Cone .07 .20
655 Jack Armstrong .02 .10
656 Dave Stewart .07 .20
657 Billy Hatcher .02 .10
658 Tim Raines .07 .20
659 Walt Weiss .02 .10
660 Jose Lind .02 .10

1993 Score Boys of Summer

COMPLETE SET (30) 20.00 50.00
RANDOM INSERTS IN JUMBO PACKS
1 Billy Ashley .60 1.50
2 Tim Salmon 1.25 3.00
3 Pedro Martinez 4.00 10.00
4 Luis Mercedes .60 1.50
5 Mike Piazza 4.00 10.00
6 Troy Neel .60 1.50
7 Melvin Nieves .60 1.50
8 Ryan Klesko .75 2.00
9 Ryan Thompson .60 1.50
10 Kevin Young .75 2.00
11 Gerald Williams .60 1.50
12 Willie Greene .60 1.50
13 John Patterson .60 1.50
14 Carlos Garcia .60 1.50
15 Ed Zosky .60 1.50
16 Sean Berry .60 1.50
17 Rico Brogna .60 1.50
18 Larry Carter .60 1.50
19 Bobby Ayala .60 1.50
20 Alan Embree .60 1.50
21 Donald Harris .60 1.50
22 Sterling Hitchcock .75 2.00
23 David Nied .60 1.50
24 Henry Mercedes .60 1.50
25 Ozzie Canseco .60 1.50
26 David Hulse .60 1.50
27 Al Martin .60 1.50
28 Dan Wilson .60 1.50
29 Paul Miller .60 1.50
30 Rich Rowland .60 1.50

1993 Score Franchise

COMPLETE SET (28) 60.00 120.00
STATED ODDS 1:24
1 Cal Ripken 10.00 25.00
2 Roger Clemens 6.00 15.00
3 Mark Langston .60 1.50
4 Frank Thomas 3.00 8.00
5 Carlos Baerga .60 1.50
6 Cecil Fielder 1.25 3.00
7 Gregg Jefferies .60 1.50
8 Robin Yount 5.00 12.00
9 Kirby Puckett 3.00 8.00
10 Don Mattingly 8.00 20.00
11 Dennis Eckersley 1.25 3.00
12 Ken Griffey Jr. 6.00 15.00
13 Juan Gonzalez 1.25 3.00
14 Roberto Alomar 2.00 5.00
15 Terry Pendleton 1.25 3.00
16 Ryne Sandberg 5.00 12.00
17 Barry Larkin 2.00 5.00
18 Jeff Bagwell 2.00 5.00
19 Brett Butler 1.25 3.00
20 Larry Walker 1.25 3.00
21 Bobby Bonilla 1.25 3.00
22 Darren Daulton 1.25 3.00
23 Andy Van Slyke 2.00 5.00
24 Ray Lankford 1.25 3.00
25 Gary Sheffield 1.25 3.00
26 Will Clark 2.00 5.00
27 Bryan Harvey .60 1.50
28 David Nied .60 1.50

1993 Score Gold Dream Team

COMPLETE SET (12) 2.00 5.00
SETS DISTRIBUTED VIA MAIL-IN OFFER
1 Ozzie Smith .30 .75
2 Kirby Puckett .20 .50
3 Gary Sheffield .07 .20
4 Andy Van Slyke .10 .30
5 Ken Griffey Jr. .40 1.00
6 Ivan Rodriguez .10 .30
7 Charles Nagy .02 .10
8 Tom Glavine .10 .30
9 Dennis Eckersley .07 .20
10 Frank Thomas .20 .50
11 Roberto Alomar .10 .30
NNO Header Card .02 .10

1993 Score Proctor and Gamble

This ten-card standard-size set was produced by Score as a promotion for Proctor and Gamble. The set was advertised through store displays; the set could be acquired by sending in three UPC symbols and money to cover postage and handling.

COMPLETE SET (10) 2.50 6.00
1 Wil Cordero .08 .25
2 Pedro Martinez 1.50 4.00
3 Bret Boone .75 2.00
4 Melvin Nieves .08 .25
5 Ryan Klesko .40 1.00
6 Ryan Thompson .08 .25
7 Kevin Young .08 .25
8 Willie Greene .08 .25
9 Eric Wedge .20 .50
10 David Nied .08 .25

1994 Score Samples

COMPLETE SET (19) 15.00 40.00
1 Barry Bonds .75 2.00
1GR Barry Bonds 1.25 3.00
2 John Olerud .20 .50
2GR John Olerud .60 1.50
3 Ken Griffey Jr. 1.25 3.00
3GR Ken Griffey Jr. 4.00 10.00
4 Jeff Bagwell .50 1.25
4GR Jeff Bagwell 2.00 5.00
5 John Burkett .08 .25
5GR John Burkett .40 1.00
6 Jack McDowell .08 .25
6GR Jack McDowell .40 1.00
7 Albert Belle .20 .50
7GR Albert Belle .60 1.50
8 Andres Galarraga .40 1.00
8GR Andres Galarraga 1.00 2.50
DT5 Barry Larkin 1.50 4.00
NNO Hobby Ad Card .08 .25
NNO Retail Ad Card .08 .25

1994 Score

The 1994 Score set of 660 standard-size cards was issued in two series of 330. Cards were distributed in 14-card hobby and retail packs. Each pack contained 13 basic cards plus one Gold Rush parallel card. Cards were also distributed in retail Jumbo packs. 4,875 cases of 1994 Score baseball were printed for the hobby. This figure does not take into account additional product printed for retail outlets. Among the subsets are American League stadiums (317-330) and National League stadiums (647-660). Rookie Cards include Trot Nixon and Billy Wagner.

COMPLETE SET (660) 10.00 25.00
COMPLETE SERIES 1 (330) 5.00 12.00
COMPLETE SERIES 2 (330) 5.00 12.00
SUBSET CARDS HALF VALUE OF BASE CARDS
1 Barry Bonds .60 1.50
2 John Olerud .07 .20
3 Ken Griffey Jr. .40 1.00
4 Jeff Bagwell .10 .30
5 John Burkett .02 .10
6 Jack McDowell .02 .10
7 Albert Belle .07 .20
8 Andres Galarraga .07 .20
9 Mike Mussina .10 .30
10 Will Clark .10 .30
11 Travis Fryman .07 .20
12 Tony Gwynn .25 .60
13 Robin Yount .30 .75
14 Dave Magadan .02 .10
15 Paul O'Neill .10 .30
16 Ray Lankford .07 .20
17 Damion Easley .02 .10
18 Andy Van Slyke .10 .30
19 Brian McRae .02 .10
20 Ryne Sandberg .30 .75
21 Kirby Puckett .20 .50
22 Dwight Gooden .07 .20
23 Don Mattingly .50 1.25
24 Kevin Mitchell .02 .10
25 Roger Clemens .40 1.00
26 Eric Karros .07 .20
27 Juan Gonzalez .07 .20
28 John Kruk .07 .20
29 Gregg Jefferies .02 .10
30 Tom Glavine .10 .30
31 Ivan Rodriguez .10 .30
32 Jay Bell .07 .20
33 Randy Johnson .20 .50
34 Darren Daulton .07 .20
35 Rickey Henderson .20 .50
36 Eddie Murray .20 .50
37 Brian Harper .02 .10
38 Delino DeShields .02 .10
39 Jose Lind .02 .10
40 Benito Santiago .07 .20
41 Frank Thomas .20 .50
42 Mark Grace .10 .30
43 Roberto Alomar .10 .30
44 Andy Benes .02 .10
45 Luis Polonia .02 .10
46 Brett Butler .07 .20
47 Terry Steinbach .02 .10
48 Craig Biggio .10 .30
49 Greg Vaughn .02 .10
50 Charlie Hayes .02 .10
51 Mickey Tettleton .02 .10

Card	Low	High
52 Jose Rijo	.02	.10
53 Carlos Baerga	.02	.10
54 Jeff Blauser	.02	.10
55 Leo Gomez	.02	.10
56 Bob Tewksbury	.02	.10
57 Mo Vaughn	.07	.20
58 Orlando Merced	.02	.10
59 Tino Martinez	.10	.30
60 Lenny Dykstra	.07	.20
61 Jose Canseco	.10	.30
62 Tony Fernandez	.02	.10
63 Donovan Osborne	.02	.10
64 Ken Hill	.02	.10
65 Kent Hrbek	.07	.20
66 Bryan Harvey	.02	.10
67 Wally Joyner	.07	.20
68 Derrick May	.02	.10
69 Lance Johnson	.02	.10
70 Willie McGee	.07	.20
71 Mark Langston	.02	.10
72 Terry Pendleton	.07	.20
73 Joe Carter	.07	.20
74 Barry Larkin	.10	.30
75 Jimmy Key	.07	.20
76 Joe Girardi	.02	.10
77 B.J. Surhoff	.07	.20
78 Pete Harnisch	.02	.10
79 Lou Whitaker UER	.07	.20
80 Cory Snyder	.02	.10
81 Kenny Lofton	.07	.20
82 Fred McGriff	.10	.30
83 Mike Greenwell	.02	.10
84 Mike Perez	.02	.10
85 Cal Ripken	.60	1.50
86 Don Slaught	.02	.10
87 Omar Vizquel	.10	.30
88 Curt Schilling	.07	.20
89 Chuck Knoblauch	.07	.20
90 Moises Alou	.07	.20
91 Greg Gagne	.02	.10
92 Bret Saberhagen	.07	.20
93 Ozzie Guillen	.07	.20
94 Matt Williams	.07	.20
95 Chad Curtis	.02	.10
96 Mike Harkey	.02	.10
97 Devon White	.07	.20
98 Walt Weiss	.02	.10
99 Kevin Brown	.07	.20
100 Gary Sheffield	.07	.20
101 Wade Boggs	.10	.30
102 Orel Hershiser	.07	.20
103 Tony Phillips	.02	.10
104 Andujar Cedeno	.02	.10
105 Bill Spiers	.02	.10
106 Otis Nixon	.02	.10
107 Felix Fermin	.02	.10
108 Bip Roberts	.02	.10
109 Dennis Eckersley	.07	.20
110 Dante Bichette	.07	.20
111 Ben McDonald	.02	.10
112 Jim Poole	.02	.10
113 John Dopson	.02	.10
114 Rob Dibble	.07	.20
115 Jeff Treadway	.02	.10
116 Ricky Jordan	.02	.10
117 Mike Henneman	.02	.10
118 Willie Blair	.02	.10
119 Doug Henry	.02	.10
120 Gerald Perry	.02	.10
121 Greg Myers	.02	.10
122 John Franco	.07	.20
123 Roger Mason	.02	.10
124 Chris Hammond	.02	.10
125 Hubie Brooks	.02	.10
126 Kent Mercker	.02	.10
127 Jim Abbott	.10	.30
128 Kevin Bass	.02	.10
129 Rick Aguilera	.02	.10
130 Mitch Webster	.02	.10
131 Eric Plunk	.02	.10
132 Mark Carreon	.02	.10
133 Dave Stewart	.07	.20
134 Willie Wilson	.02	.10
135 Dave Fleming	.02	.10
136 Jeff Tackett	.02	.10
137 Geno Petralli	.02	.10
138 Gene Harris	.02	.10
139 Scott Bankhead	.02	.10
140 Trevor Wilson	.02	.10
141 Alvaro Espinoza	.02	.10
142 Ryan Bowen	.02	.10
143 Mike Moore	.02	.10
144 Bill Pecota	.02	.10
145 Jaime Navarro	.02	.10
146 Jack Daugherty	.02	.10
147 Bob Wickman	.02	.10
148 Chris Jones	.02	.10
149 Todd Stottlemyre	.02	.10
150 Brian Williams	.02	.10
151 Chuck Finley	.07	.20
152 Lenny Harris	.02	.10
153 Alex Fernandez	.02	.10
154 Candy Maldonado	.02	.10
155 Jeff Montgomery	.02	.10
156 David West	.02	.10
157 Mark Williamson	.02	.10
158 Milt Thompson	.02	.10
159 Ron Darling	.02	.10
160 Stan Belinda	.02	.10
161 Henry Cotto	.02	.10
162 Mel Rojas	.02	.10
163 Doug Strange	.02	.10
164 Rene Arocha	.02	.10
165 Tim Hulett	.02	.10
166 Steve Avery	.02	.10
167 Jim Thome	.10	.30
168 Tom Browning	.02	.10
169 Mario Diaz	.02	.10
170 Steve Reed	.02	.10
171 Scott Livingstone	.02	.10
172 Chris Donnels	.02	.10
173 John Jaha	.02	.10
174 Carlos Hernandez	.02	.10
175 Dion James	.02	.10
176 Bud Black	.02	.10
177 Tony Castillo	.02	.10
178 Jose Guzman	.02	.10
179 Torey Lovullo	.02	.10
180 John Vander Wal	.02	.10
181 Mike LaValliere	.02	.10
182 Sid Fernandez	.02	.10
183 Brent Mayne	.02	.10
184 Terry Mulholland	.02	.10
185 Willie Banks	.02	.10
186 Steve Cooke	.02	.10
187 Brent Gates	.02	.10
188 Erik Pappas	.02	.10
189 Bill Haselman	.02	.10
190 Fernando Valenzuela	.07	.20
191 Gary Redus	.02	.10
192 Danny Darwin	.02	.10
193 Mark Portugal	.02	.10
194 Derek Lilliquist	.02	.10
195 Charlie O'Brien	.02	.10
196 Matt Nokes	.02	.10
197 Danny Sheaffer	.02	.10
198 Bill Gullickson	.02	.10
199 Alex Arias	.02	.10
200 Mike Fetters	.02	.10
201 Brian Jordan	.07	.20
202 Joe Grahe	.02	.10
203 Tom Candiotti	.02	.10
204 Jeremy Hernandez	.02	.10
205 Mike Stanton	.02	.10
206 David Howard	.02	.10
207 Darren Holmes	.02	.10
208 Rick Honeycutt	.02	.10
209 Danny Jackson	.02	.10
210 Rich Amaral	.02	.10
211 Blas Minor	.02	.10
212 Kenny Rogers	.07	.20
213 Jim Leyritz	.02	.10
214 Mike Morgan	.02	.10
215 Dan Gladden	.02	.10
216 Randy Velarde	.02	.10
217 Mitch Williams	.02	.10
218 Hipolito Pichardo	.02	.10
219 Dave Burba	.02	.10
220 Wilson Alvarez	.02	.10
221 Bob Zupcic	.02	.10
222 Francisco Cabrera	.02	.10
223 Julio Valera	.02	.10
224 Paul Assenmacher	.02	.10
225 Jeff Branson	.02	.10
226 Todd Frohwirth	.02	.10
227 Armando Reynoso	.02	.10
228 Rich Rowland	.02	.10
229 Freddie Benavides	.02	.10
230 Wayne Kirby	.02	.10
231 Darryl Kile	.07	.20
232 Skeeter Barnes	.02	.10
233 Ramon Martinez	.02	.10
234 Tom Gordon	.02	.10
235 Dave Gallagher	.02	.10
236 Ricky Bones	.02	.10
237 Larry Andersen	.02	.10
238 Pat Meares	.02	.10
239 Zane Smith	.02	.10
240 Tim Leary	.02	.10
241 Phil Clark	.02	.10
242 Danny Cox	.02	.10
243 Mike Jackson	.02	.10
244 Mike Gallego	.02	.10
245 Lee Smith	.07	.20
246 Todd Jones	.02	.10
247 Steve Bedrosian	.02	.10
248 Troy Neel	.02	.10
249 Jose Bautista	.02	.10
250 Steve Frey	.02	.10
251 Jeff Reardon	.07	.20
252 Stan Javier	.02	.10
253 Mo Sanford	.02	.10
254 Steve Sax	.02	.10
255 Luis Aquino	.02	.10
256 Domingo Jean	.02	.10
257 Scott Servais	.02	.10
258 Brad Pennington	.02	.10
259 Dave Hansen	.02	.10
260 Rich Gossage	.07	.20
261 Jeff Fassero	.02	.10
262 Junior Ortiz	.02	.10
263 Anthony Young	.02	.10
264 Chris Bosio	.02	.10
265 Ruben Amaro	.02	.10
266 Mark Eichhorn	.02	.10
267 Dave Clark	.02	.10
268 Gary Thurman	.02	.10
269 Les Lancaster	.02	.10
270 Jamie Moyer	.07	.20
271 Ricky Gutierrez	.02	.10
272 Greg A. Harris	.02	.10
273 Mike Benjamin	.02	.10
274 Gene Nelson	.02	.10
275 Damon Berryhill	.02	.10
276 Scott Radinsky	.02	.10
277 Mike Aldrete	.02	.10
278 Jerry DiPoto	.02	.10
279 Chris Haney	.02	.10
280 Richie Lewis	.02	.10
281 Jarvis Brown	.02	.10
282 Juan Bell	.02	.10
283 Joe Klink	.02	.10
284 Graeme Lloyd	.02	.10
285 Casey Candaele	.02	.10
286 Bob MacDonald	.02	.10
287 Mike Sharperson	.02	.10
288 Gene Larkin	.02	.10
289 Brian Barnes	.02	.10
290 David McCarty	.02	.10
291 Jeff Innis	.02	.10
292 Bob Patterson	.02	.10
293 Ben Rivera	.02	.10
294 John Habyan	.02	.10
295 Rich Rodriguez	.02	.10
296 Edwin Nunez	.02	.10
297 Rod Brewer	.02	.10
298 Mike Timlin	.02	.10
299 Jesse Orosco	.02	.10
300 Gary Gaetti	.07	.20
301 Todd Benzinger	.02	.10
302 Jeff Nelson	.02	.10
303 Rafael Belliard	.02	.10
304 Matt Whiteside	.02	.10
305 Vinny Castilla	.07	.20
306 Matt Turner	.02	.10
307 Eduardo Perez	.02	.10
308 Joel Johnston	.02	.10
309 Chris Gomez	.02	.10
310 Pat Rapp	.02	.10
311 Jim Tatum	.02	.10
312 Kirk Rueter	.02	.10
313 John Flaherty	.02	.10
314 Tom Kramer	.02	.10
315 Mark Whiten	.02	.10
316 Chris Bosio	.02	.10
317 Baltimore Orioles CL	.02	.10
318 Boston Red Sox CL UER (Viola listed as 316; shoul	.02	.10
319 California Angels CL	.02	.10
320 Chicago White Sox CL	.02	.10
321 Cleveland Indians CL	.02	.10
322 Detroit Tigers CL	.02	.10
323 Kansas City Royals CL	.02	.10
324 Milwaukee Brewers CL	.02	.10
325 Minnesota Twins CL	.02	.10
326 New York Yankees CL	.02	.10
327 Oakland Athletics CL	.02	.10
328 Seattle Mariners CL	.02	.10
329 Texas Rangers CL	.02	.10
330 Toronto Blue Jays CL	.02	.10
331 Frank Viola	.07	.20
332 Ron Gant	.07	.20
333 Charles Nagy	.02	.10
334 Roberto Kelly	.02	.10
335 Brady Anderson	.07	.20
336 Alex Cole	.02	.10
337 Alan Trammell	.07	.20
338 Derek Bell	.02	.10
339 Bernie Williams	.10	.30
340 Jose Offerman	.02	.10
341 Bill Wegman	.02	.10
342 Ken Caminiti	.07	.20
343 Pat Borders	.02	.10
344 Kirt Manwaring	.02	.10
345 Chili Davis	.07	.20
346 Steve Buechele	.02	.10
347 Robin Ventura	.07	.20
348 Teddy Higuera	.02	.10
349 Jerry Browne	.02	.10
350 Scott Kamieniecki	.02	.10
351 Kevin Tapani	.02	.10
352 Marquis Grissom	.07	.20
353 Jay Buhner	.07	.20
354 Dave Hollins	.02	.10
355 Dan Wilson	.02	.10
356 Bob Walk	.02	.10
357 Chris Hoiles	.02	.10
358 Todd Zeile	.02	.10
359 Kevin Appier	.07	.20
360 Chris Sabo	.02	.10
361 David Segui	.02	.10
362 Jerald Clark	.02	.10
363 Tony Pena	.02	.10
364 Steve Finley	.07	.20
365 Roger Pavlik	.02	.10
366 John Smoltz	.10	.30
367 Scott Fletcher	.02	.10
368 Jody Reed	.02	.10
369 David Wells	.07	.20
370 Jose Vizcaino	.02	.10
371 Pat Listach	.02	.10
372 Orestes Destrade	.02	.10
373 Danny Tartabull	.02	.10
374 Greg W. Harris	.02	.10
375 Juan Guzman	.02	.10
376 Larry Walker	.07	.20
377 Gary DiSarcina	.02	.10
378 Bobby Bonilla	.07	.20
379 Tim Raines	.07	.20
380 Tommy Greene	.02	.10
381 Chris Gwynn	.02	.10
382 Jeff King	.02	.10
383 Shane Mack	.02	.10
384 Ozzie Smith	.30	.75
385 Eddie Zambrano RC	.02	.10
386 Mike Devereaux	.02	.10
387 Erik Hanson	.02	.10
388 Scott Cooper	.02	.10
389 Dean Palmer	.07	.20
390 John Wetteland	.07	.20
391 Reggie Jefferson	.02	.10
392 Mark Lemke	.02	.10
393 Cecil Fielder	.07	.20
394 Reggie Sanders	.07	.20
395 Darryl Hamilton	.02	.10
396 Daryl Boston	.02	.10
397 Pat Kelly	.02	.10
398 Joe Orsulak	.02	.10
399 Ed Sprague	.02	.10
400 Eric Anthony	.02	.10
401 Scott Sanderson	.02	.10
402 Jim Gott	.02	.10
403 Ron Karkovice	.02	.10
404 Phil Plantier	.02	.10
405 David Cone	.07	.20
406 Robby Thompson	.02	.10
407 Dave Winfield	.07	.20
408 Dwight Smith	.02	.10
409 Ruben Sierra	.07	.20
410 Jack Armstrong	.02	.10
411 Mike Felder	.02	.10
412 Wil Cordero	.02	.10
413 Julio Franco	.07	.20
414 Howard Johnson	.02	.10
415 Mark McLemore	.02	.10
416 Pete Incaviglia	.02	.10
417 John Valentin	.02	.10
418 Tim Wakefield	.10	.30
419 Jose Mesa	.02	.10
420 Bernard Gilkey	.02	.10
421 Kirk Gibson	.07	.20
422 David Justice	.07	.20
423 Tom Brunansky	.02	.10
424 John Smiley	.02	.10
425 Kevin Maas	.02	.10
426 Doug Drabek	.02	.10
427 Paul Molitor	.07	.20
428 Darryl Strawberry	.07	.20
429 Tim Naehring	.02	.10
430 Bill Swift	.02	.10
431 Ellis Burks	.07	.20
432 Greg Hibbard	.02	.10
433 Felix Jose	.02	.10
434 Bret Barberie	.02	.10
435 Pedro Munoz	.02	.10
436 Darrin Fletcher	.02	.10
437 Bobby Witt	.02	.10
438 Wes Chamberlain	.02	.10
439 Mackey Sasser	.02	.10
440 Mark Whiten	.02	.10
441 Harold Reynolds	.07	.20
442 Greg Olson	.02	.10
443 Billy Hatcher	.02	.10
444 Joe Oliver	.02	.10
445 Sandy Alomar Jr.	.02	.10
446 Tim Wallach	.02	.10
447 Karl Rhodes	.02	.10
448 Royce Clayton	.02	.10
449 Cal Eldred	.02	.10
450 Rick Wilkins	.02	.10
451 Mike Stanley	.02	.10
452 Charlie Hough	.07	.20
453 Jack Morris	.07	.20
454 Jon Ratliff RC	.02	.10
455 Rene Gonzales	.02	.10
456 Eddie Taubensee	.02	.10
457 Roberto Hernandez	.02	.10
458 Todd Hundley	.02	.10
459 Mike Macfarlane	.02	.10
460 Mickey Morandini	.02	.10
461 Scott Erickson	.02	.10
462 Lonnie Smith	.02	.10
463 Dave Henderson	.02	.10
464 Ryan Klesko	.07	.20
465 Edgar Martinez	.10	.30
466 Tom Pagnozzi	.02	.10
467 Charlie Leibrandt	.02	.10
468 Brian Anderson RC	.08	.25
469 Harold Baines	.07	.20
470 Tim Belcher	.02	.10
471 Andre Dawson	.07	.20
472 Eric Young	.02	.10
473 Paul Sorrento	.02	.10
474 Luis Gonzalez	.07	.20
475 Rob Deer	.02	.10
476 Mike Piazza	.40	1.00
477 Kevin Reimer	.02	.10
478 Jeff Gardner	.02	.10
479 Melido Perez	.02	.10
480 Darren Lewis	.02	.10
481 Duane Ward	.02	.10
482 Rey Sanchez	.02	.10
483 Mark Lewis	.02	.10
484 Jeff Conine	.07	.20
485 Joey Cora	.02	.10
486 Trot Nixon RC	.40	1.00
487 Kevin McReynolds	.02	.10
488 Mike Lansing	.02	.10
489 Mike Pagliarulo	.02	.10
490 Mariano Duncan	.02	.10
491 Mike Bordick	.02	.10
492 Kevin Young	.02	.10
493 Dave Valle	.02	.10
494 Wayne Gomes RC	.02	.10
495 Rafael Palmeiro	.10	.30
496 Deion Sanders	.10	.30
497 Rick Sutcliffe	.07	.20
498 Randy Milligan	.02	.10
499 Carlos Quintana	.02	.10
500 Chris Turner	.02	.10
501 Thomas Howard	.02	.10
502 Greg Swindell	.02	.10
503 Chad Kreuter	.02	.10
504 Eric Davis	.07	.20
505 Dickie Thon	.02	.10
506 Matt Drews RC	.02	.10
507 Spike Owen	.02	.10
508 Rod Beck	.02	.10
509 Pat Hentgen	.02	.10
510 Sammy Sosa	.20	.50
511 J.T. Snow	.07	.20
512 Chuck Carr	.02	.10
513 Bo Jackson	.20	.50
514 Dennis Martinez	.07	.20
515 Phil Hiatt	.02	.10
516 Jeff Kent	.10	.30
517 Brooks Kieschnick RC	.02	.10
518 Kirk Presley RC	.02	.10
519 Kevin Seitzer	.02	.10
520 Carlos Garcia	.02	.10
521 Mike Blowers	.02	.10
522 Luis Alicea	.02	.10
523 David Hulse	.02	.10
524 Greg Maddux	.30	.75
525 Gregg Olson	.02	.10
526 Hal Morris	.02	.10
527 Daron Kirkreit	.02	.10
528 David Nied	.02	.10
529 Jeff Russell	.02	.10
530 Kevin Gross	.02	.10
531 John Doherty	.02	.10
532 Matt Brunson RC	.02	.10
533 Dave Nilsson	.02	.10
534 Randy Myers	.02	.10
535 Steve Farr	.02	.10
536 Billy Wagner RC	.50	1.25
537 Darnell Coles	.02	.10
538 Frank Tanana	.02	.10
539 Tim Salmon	.10	.30
540 Kim Batiste	.02	.10
541 George Bell	.02	.10
542 Tom Henke	.02	.10
543 Sam Horn	.02	.10
544 Doug Jones	.02	.10
545 Scott Leius	.02	.10
546 Al Martin	.02	.10
547 Bob Welch	.02	.10
548 Scott Christman RC	.02	.10
549 Norm Charlton	.02	.10
550 Mark McGwire	.50	1.25
551 Greg McMichael	.02	.10
552 Tim Costo	.02	.10
553 Rodney Bolton	.02	.10
554 Pedro Martinez	.20	.50
555 Marc Valdes	.02	.10
556 Darrell Whitmore	.02	.10
557 Tim Bogar	.02	.10
558 Steve Karsay	.02	.10
559 Danny Bautista	.02	.10
560 Jeffrey Hammonds	.02	.10
561 Aaron Sele	.02	.10
562 Russ Springer	.02	.10
563 Jason Bere	.02	.10
564 Billy Brewer	.02	.10
565 Sterling Hitchcock	.02	.10
566 Bobby Munoz	.02	.10
567 Craig Paquette	.02	.10
568 Bret Boone	.07	.20
569 Dan Peltier	.02	.10
570 Jeromy Burnitz	.07	.20
571 John Wasdin RC	.02	.10
572 Chipper Jones	.20	.50
573 Jamey Wright RC	.02	.10
574 Jeff Granger	.02	.10
575 Jay Powell RC	.02	.10
576 Ryan Thompson	.02	.10
577 Lou Frazier	.02	.10
578 Paul Wagner	.02	.10
579 Brad Ausmus	.10	.30
580 Jack Voigt	.02	.10
581 Kevin Rogers	.02	.10
582 Damon Buford	.02	.10
583 Paul Quantrill	.02	.10
584 Marc Newfield	.02	.10
585 Derrek Lee RC	.60	1.50
586 Shane Reynolds	.02	.10
587 Cliff Floyd	.07	.20
588 Jeff Schwarz	.02	.10
589 Ross Powell RC	.02	.10
590 Gerald Williams	.02	.10
591 Mike Trombley	.02	.10
592 Ken Ryan	.02	.10
593 John O'Donoghue	.02	.10
594 Rod Correia	.02	.10
595 Darrell Sherman	.02	.10
596 Steve Scarsone	.02	.10
597 Sherman Obando	.02	.10
598 Kurt Abbott RC	.02	.10
599 Dave Telgheder	.02	.10
600 Rick Trlicek	.02	.10
601 Carl Everett	.07	.20
602 Luis Ortiz	.02	.10
603 Larry Luebbers	.02	.10
604 Kevin Roberson	.02	.10
605 Butch Huskey	.02	.10
606 Benji Gil	.02	.10
607 Todd Van Poppel	.02	.10
608 Mark Hutton	.02	.10
609 Chip Hale	.02	.10
610 Matt Maysey	.02	.10
611 Scott Ruffcorn	.02	.10
612 Hilly Hathaway	.02	.10
613 Allen Watson	.02	.10
614 Carlos Delgado	.10	.30
615 Roberto Mejia	.02	.10
616 Turk Wendell	.02	.10
617 Tony Tarasco	.02	.10
618 Raul Mondesi	.07	.20
619 Kevin Stocker	.02	.10
620 Javier Lopez	.07	.20
621 Keith Kessinger	.02	.10
622 Bob Hamelin	.02	.10
623 John Roper	.02	.10
624 Lenny Dykstra WS	.02	.10
625 Joe Carter WS	.02	.10
626 Jim Abbott HL	.07	.20
627 Lee Smith HL	.02	.10
628 Ken Griffey Jr. HL	.25	.60
629 Dave Winfield HL	.02	.10
630 Darryl Kile HL	.02	.10
631 Frank Thomas MVP	.10	.30
632 Barry Bonds MVP	.30	.75
633 Jack McDowell AL CY	.02	.10
634 Greg Maddux CY	.20	.50
635 Tim Salmon ROY	.07	.20
636 Mike Piazza ROY	.20	.50
637 Brian Turang RC	.02	.10
638 Rondell White	.07	.20
639 Nigel Wilson	.02	.10
640 Torii Hunter RC	.40	1.00
641 Salomon Torres	.02	.10
642 Kevin Higgins	.02	.10
643 Eric Wedge	.02	.10
644 Roger Salkeld	.02	.10
645 Manny Ramirez	.20	.50
646 Jeff McNeely	.02	.10
647 Checklist Atlanta Braves	.02	.10
648 Checklist Chicago Cubs	.02	.10
649 Checklist Cincinnati Reds	.02	.10
650 Checklist Colorado Rockies	.02	.10
651 Checklist Florida Marlins	.02	.10
652 Checklist Houston Astros	.02	.10
653 Checklist Los Angeles Dodgers	.02	.10
654 Checklist Montreal Expos	.02	.10
655 Checklist New York Mets	.02	.10
656 Checklist Philadelphia Phillies	.02	.10
657 Checklist Pittsburgh Pirates	.02	.10
658 Checklist St. Louis Cardinals	.02	.10
659 Checklist San Diego Padres	.02	.10
660 Checklist San Francisco Giants	.02	.10

1994 Score Gold Rush

COMPLETE SET (660)	20.00	50.00
COMPLETE SERIES 1 (330)	10.00	25.00
COMPLETE SERIES 2 (330)	10.00	25.00

*STARS: 1.5X TO 4X BASIC CARDS
*ROOKIES: 1.25X TO 3X BASIC
ONE PER PACK
TWO PER JUMBO

1994 Score Boys of Summer

COMPLETE SET (60)	25.00	60.00
COMPLETE SERIES 1 (30)	10.00	25.00
COMPLETE SERIES 2 (30)	15.00	35.00
STATED ODDS 1:4 SUPER PACKS		
1 Jeff Conine	.75	2.00
2 Aaron Sele	.40	1.00
3 Kevin Stocker	.40	1.00
4 Pat Meares	.40	1.00
5 Jeromy Burnitz	.75	2.00
6 Mike Piazza	3.00	8.00
7 Allen Watson	.40	1.00
8 Jeffrey Hammonds	.40	1.00
9 Kevin Roberson	.40	1.00
10 Hilly Hathaway	.40	1.00
11 Kirk Rueter	.40	1.00
12 Eduardo Perez	.40	1.00
13 Ricky Gutierrez	.40	1.00
14 Domingo Jean	.40	1.00
15 David Nied	.40	1.00
16 Wayne Kirby	.40	1.00
17 Mike Lansing	.40	1.00
18 Jason Bere	.40	1.00
19 Brent Gates	.40	1.00
20 Javier Lopez	.75	2.00
21 Greg McMichael	.40	1.00
22 David Hulse	.40	1.00
23 Roberto Mejia	.40	1.00
24 Tim Salmon	1.25	3.00
25 Rene Arocha	.40	1.00
26 Bret Boone	.75	2.00
27 David McCarty	.40	1.00
28 Todd Van Poppel	.40	1.00
29 Lance Painter	.40	1.00
30 Erik Pappas	.40	1.00
31 Chuck Carr	.40	1.00
32 Mark Hutton	.40	1.00
33 Jeff McNeely	.40	1.00
34 Willie Greene	.40	1.00
35 Nigel Wilson	.40	1.00
36 Rondell White	.75	2.00
37 Brian Turang	.40	1.00
38 Manny Ramirez	2.00	5.00
39 Salomon Torres	.40	1.00
40 Melvin Nieves	.40	1.00
41 Ryan Klesko	.75	2.00
42 Keith Kessinger	.40	1.00
43 Brad Ausmus	1.25	3.00
44 Bob Hamelin	.40	1.00
45 Carlos Delgado	1.25	3.00
46 Marc Newfield	.40	1.00
47 Raul Mondesi	.75	2.00
48 Tim Costo	.40	1.00
49 Pedro Martinez	2.00	5.00
50 Steve Karsay	.40	1.00
51 Danny Bautista	.40	1.00
52 Butch Huskey	.40	1.00
53 Kurt Abbott	.40	1.00
54 Darrell Sherman	.40	1.00
55 Damon Buford	.40	1.00
56 Ross Powell	.40	1.00
57 Darrell Whitmore	.40	1.00
58 Chipper Jones	2.00	5.00
59 Jeff Granger	.40	1.00
60 Cliff Floyd	.75	2.00

1994 Score Cycle

COMPLETE SET (20)	20.00	50.00
SER.2 STATED ODDS 1:72, 1:36 JUM		
TC1 Brett Butler	1.25	3.00
TC2 Kenny Lofton	1.25	3.00
TC3 Paul Molitor	3.00	8.00
TC4 Carlos Baerga	1.25	3.00
TC5 G.Jefferies T.Phillips	1.25	3.00
TC6 John Olerud	1.25	3.00
TC7 Charlie Hayes	1.25	3.00
TC8 Lenny Dykstra	1.25	3.00
TC9 Dante Bichette	1.25	3.00
TC10 Devon White	1.25	3.00
TC11 Lance Johnson	1.25	3.00
TC12 J.Cora S.Finley	1.25	3.00
TC13 Tony Fernandez	1.25	3.00
TC14 D.Hulse B.Butler	1.25	3.00
TC15 Bell McRae Morandini	1.25	3.00
TC16 J.Gonzalez B.Bonds	6.00	15.00
TC17 Ken Griffey Jr.	6.00	15.00
TC18 Frank Thomas	3.00	8.00
TC19 David Justice	1.25	3.00
TC20 M.Williams A.Belle	1.25	3.00

1994 Score Dream Team

COMPLETE SET (10)	25.00	60.00
SER.1 STATED ODDS 1:72, 1:36 JUM		
1 Mike Mussina	3.00	8.00
2 Tom Glavine	3.00	8.00
3 Don Mattingly	12.50	30.00
4 Carlos Baerga	1.00	2.50
5 Barry Larkin	3.00	8.00
6 Matt Williams	2.00	5.00
7 Juan Gonzalez	2.00	5.00
8 Andy Van Slyke	3.00	8.00
9 Larry Walker	2.00	5.00
10 Mike Stanley	1.00	2.50
S5 Barry Larkin Sample	.40	1.00

1994 Score Gold Stars

COMPLETE SET (60)	50.00	120.00
COMPLETE NL SERIES (30)	25.00	60.00
COMPLETE AL SERIES (30)	25.00	60.00
STATED ODDS 1:18 HOBBY		
1 Barry Bonds	3.00	8.00
2 Orlando Merced	.60	1.50
3 Mark Grace	1.00	2.50
4 Darren Daulton	.60	1.50
5 Jeff Blauser	.60	1.50
6 Deion Sanders	1.00	2.50
7 John Kruk	.60	1.50
8 Jeff Bagwell	1.00	2.50
9 Gregg Jefferies	.60	1.50
10 Matt Williams	.60	1.50
11 Andres Galarraga	1.00	2.50
12 Jay Bell	.60	1.50
13 Mike Piazza	1.50	4.00
14 Ron Gant	.60	1.50
15 Barry Larkin	1.00	2.50
16 Tom Glavine	1.00	2.50
17 Len Dykstra	.60	1.50
18 Fred McGriff	1.00	2.50
19 Andy Van Slyke	.60	1.50
20 Gary Sheffield	.60	1.50
21 John Burkett	.60	1.50
22 Dante Bichette	.60	1.50
23 Tony Gwynn	1.50	4.00
24 David Justice	.60	1.50
25 Marquis Grissom	.60	1.50
26 Bobby Bonilla	.60	1.50
27 Larry Walker	1.00	2.50
28 Brett Butler	.60	1.50
29 Robby Thompson	.60	1.50
30 Jeff Conine	.60	1.50
31 Joe Carter	1.00	2.50
32 Ken Griffey Jr.	3.00	8.00
33 Juan Gonzalez	1.00	2.50
34 Rickey Henderson	1.50	4.00
35 Bo Jackson	1.50	4.00
36 Cal Ripken	5.00	12.00
37 John Olerud	.60	1.50
38 Carlos Baerga	.60	1.50
39 Jack McDowell	.60	1.50
40 Cecil Fielder	.60	1.50
41 Kenny Lofton	.60	1.50
42 Roberto Alomar	1.00	2.50
43 Randy Johnson	1.50	4.00
44 Tim Salmon	.60	1.50
45 Frank Thomas	1.50	4.00
46 Albert Belle	.60	1.50
47 Greg Vaughn		
48 Travis Fryman	.60	1.50
49 Don Mattingly	3.00	8.00
50 Wade Boggs	1.00	2.50
51 Mo Vaughn	.60	1.50
52 Kirby Puckett	1.50	4.00
53 Devon White	.60	1.50
54 Tony Phillips	.60	1.50
55 Brian Harper	.60	1.50
56 Chad Curtis	.60	1.50
57 Paul Molitor	1.50	4.00
58 Ivan Rodriguez	1.00	2.50
59 Rafael Palmeiro	1.00	2.50
60 Brian McRae	.60	1.50

1994 Score Rookie/Traded Samples

COMPLETE SET (11)	5.00	12.00
CP2 Rafael Palmeiro	1.00	2.50
RT1 Will Clark	.75	2.00
RT2 Lee Smith	.30	.75
RT3 Bo Jackson	.75	2.00
RT4 Ellis Burks	.30	.75
RT5 Eddie Murray	1.00	2.50
RT6 Delino DeShields	.20	.50
RT102 Carlos Delgado	1.00	2.50
SU2 Manny Ramirez	1.00	2.50
NNO Title Card	.20	.50
NNO September Call-Up Redemption Sample	.20	.50

1994 Score Rookie/Traded

The 1994 Score Rookie and Traded set consists of 165 standard-size cards featuring rookie standouts, traded players, and new young prospects. The set is delineated by traded players (RT1-RT70) and rookies/young prospects (RT71-RT163). The set closes with checklists (RT164-RT165). Each foil pack contained one Gold Rush card. The cards are numbered on the back with an "RT" prefix. Several leading dealers are under the belief that Jose Lima's card (number RT158) was short-printed. Conversely, extra cards of John Mabry are typically found in place of the short Lima's. A special unnumbered September Call-Up Redemption card could be exchanged for an Alex Rodriguez card. The expiration date was January 31st, 1995. Odds of finding a redemption card were approximately one in 240 retail and hobby packs. Rookie Cards include Jose Lima and Chan Ho Park.

COMPLETE SET (165)	6.00	15.00
A.ROD CALL UP EXCH.STATED ODDS 1:240		
A.ROD CALL-UP VIA MAIL PER EXCH.CARD		
ACTUAL CARD REDEEMED IN 1995		
RT1 Will Clark	.20	.50
RT2 Lee Smith	.10	.30
RT3 Bo Jackson	.30	.75
RT4 Ellis Burks	.10	.30
RT5 Eddie Murray	.30	.75
RT6 Delino DeShields	.05	.15
RT7 Erik Hanson	.05	.15
RT8 Rafael Palmeiro	.20	.50
RT9 Luis Polonia	.05	.15
RT10 Omar Vizquel	.20	.50
RT11 Kurt Abbott	.05	.15
RT12 Vince Coleman	.05	.15
RT13 Rickey Henderson	.30	.75
RT14 Terry Mulholland	.05	.15
RT15 Greg Hibbard	.05	.15
RT16 Walt Weiss	.05	.15
RT17 Chris Sabo	.05	.15
RT18 Dave Henderson	.05	.15
RT19 Rick Sutcliffe	.10	.30
RT20 Harold Reynolds	.10	.30
RT21 Jack Morris	.10	.30
RT22 Dan Wilson	.05	.15
RT23 Dave Magadan	.05	.15
RT24 Dennis Martinez	.10	.30
RT25 Wes Chamberlain	.05	.15
RT26 Otis Nixon	.05	.15
RT27 Eric Anthony	.05	.15
RT28 Randy Milligan	.05	.15
RT29 Julio Franco	.10	.30
RT30 Kevin McReynolds	.05	.15
RT31 Anthony Young	.05	.15
RT32 Brian Harper	.05	.15
RT33 Gene Harris	.05	.15
RT34 Eddie Taubensee	.05	.15
RT35 David Segui	.05	.15
RT36 Stan Javier	.05	.15
RT37-Felix Fermin	.05	.15
RT38 Darrin Jackson	.05	.15

RT39 Tony Fernandez .05 .15
RT40 Jose Vizcaino .05 .15
RT41 Willie Banks .05 .15
RT42 Brian Hunter .05 .15
RT43 Reggie Jefferson .05 .15
RT44 Junior Felix .05 .15
RT45 Jack Armstrong .05 .15
RT46 Bip Roberts .05 .15
RT47 Jerry Browne .05 .15
RT48 Marvin Freeman .05 .15
RT49 Jody Reed .05 .15
RT50 Alex Cole .05 .15
RT51 Sid Fernandez .05 .15
RT52 Pete Smith .05 .15
RT53 Xavier Hernandez .05 .15
RT54 Scott Sanderson .05 .15
RT55 Turner Ward .05 .15
RT56 Rex Hudler .05 .15
RT57 Deion Sanders .20 .50
RT58 Sid Bream .05 .15
RT59 Tony Pena .05 .15
RT60 Bret Boone .10 .30
RT61 Bobby Ayala .05 .15
RT62 Pedro Martinez .30 .75
RT63 Howard Johnson .05 .15
RT64 Mark Portugal .05 .15
RT65 Roberto Kelly .05 .15
RT66 Spike Owen .05 .15
RT67 Jeff Treadway .05 .15
RT68 Mike Harkey .05 .15
RT69 Doug Jones .05 .15
RT70 Steve Farr .05 .15
RT71 Billy Taylor RC .05 .15
RT72 Manny Ramirez .30 .75
RT73 Bob Hamelin .05 .15
RT74 Steve Karsay .05 .15
RT75 Ryan Klesko .10 .30
RT76 Cliff Floyd .10 .30
RT77 Jeffrey Hammonds .05 .15
RT78 Javier Lopez .10 .30
RT79 Roger Salkeld .05 .15
RT80 Hector Carrasco .05 .15
RT81 Gerald Williams .05 .15
RT82 Raul Mondesi .10 .30
RT83 Sterling Hitchcock .05 .15
RT84 Danny Bautista .05 .15
RT85 Chris Turner .05 .15
RT86 Shane Reynolds .05 .15
RT87 Rondell White .10 .30
RT88 Salomon Torres .05 .15
RT89 Turk Wendell .05 .15
RT90 Tony Tarasco .05 .15
RT91 Shawn Green .30 .75
RT92 Greg Colbrunn .05 .15
RT93 Eddie Zambrano .05 .15
RT94 Rich Becker .05 .15
RT95 Chris Gomez .05 .15
RT96 John Patterson .05 .15
RT97 Derek Parks .05 .15
RT98 Rich Rowland .05 .15
RT99 James Mouton .05 .15
RT100 Tim Hyers RC .05 .15
RT101 Jose Valentin .05 .15
RT102 Carlos Delgado .20 .50
RT103 Robert Eenhoorn .05 .15
RT104 John Hudek RC .05 .15
RT105 Domingo Cedeno .05 .15
RT106 Denny Hocking .05 .15
RT107 Greg Pirkl .05 .15
RT108 Mark Smith .05 .15
RT109 Paul Shuey .05 .15
RT110 Jorge Fabregas .05 .15
RT111 Rikkert Faneyte RC .05 .15
RT112 Rob Butler .05 .15
RT113 Darren Oliver RC .10 .30
RT114 Troy O'Leary .05 .15
RT115 Scott Brow .05 .15
RT116 Tony Eusebio .05 .15
RT117 Carlos Reyes .05 .15
RT118 J.R. Phillips .05 .15
RT119 Alex Diaz .05 .15
RT120 Charles Johnson .10 .30
RT121 Nate Minchey .05 .15
RT122 Scott Sanders .05 .15
RT123 Daryl Boston .05 .15
RT124 Joey Hamilton .05 .15
RT125 Brian Anderson .10 .30
RT126 Dan Miceli .05 .15
RT127 Tom Brunansky .05 .15
RT128 Dave Staton .05 .15
RT129 Mike Oquist .05 .15
RT130 John Mabry RC .10 .30
RT131 Norberto Martin .05 .15
RT132 Hector Fajardo .05 .15
RT133 Mark Hutton .05 .15
RT134 Fernando Vina .05 .15
RT135 Lee Tinsley .05 .15
RT136 Chan Ho Park RC .20 .50
RT137 Paul Spoljaric .05 .15
RT138 Matias Carrillo .05 .15
RT139 Mark Kiefer .05 .15
RT140 Stan Royer .05 .15
RT141 Bryan Eversgerd .05 .15
RT142 Brian L. Hunter .05 .15
RT143 Joe Hall .05 .15
RT144 Johnny Ruffin .05 .15
RT145 Alex Gonzalez .05 .15
RT146 Keith Lockhart RC .10 .30
RT147 Tom Marsh .05 .15
RT148 Tony Longmire .05 .15
RT149 Keith Mitchell .05 .15
RT150 Melvin Nieves .05 .15
RT151 Kelly Stinnett RC .05 .15
RT152 Miguel Jimenez .05 .15
RT153 Jeff Juden .05 .15
RT154 Matt Walbeck .05 .15
RT155 Marc Newfield .05 .15
RT156 Matt Mieske .05 .15
RT157 Marcus Moore .05 .15
RT158 Jose Lima SP RC 2.00 5.00
RT159 Mike Kelly .05 .15
RT160 Jim Edmonds .30 .75
RT161 Steve Trachsel .05 .15
RT162 Greg Blosser .05 .15
RT163 Mark Acre RC .05 .15
RT164 AL Checklist .05 .15
RT165 NL Checklist .05 .15
HC1 Alex Rodriguez CU 60.00 150.00
NNO September Call-Up Trade EXP .75 2.00

1994 Score Rookie/Traded Gold Rush

COMPLETE SET (165) 20.00 50.00
*STARS: 1X TO 2.5X BASIC CARDS
*ROOKIES: 1X TO 2.5X BASIC CARDS
ONE GOLD RUSH PER PACK

1994 Score Rookie/Traded Changing Places

COMPLETE SET (10) 12.50 30.00
STATED ODDS 1:36 HOB/RET
CP1 Will Clark 2.50 6.00
CP2 Rafael Palmeiro 2.50 6.00
CP3 Roberto Kelly .75 2.00
CP4 Bo Jackson 4.00 10.00
CP5 Otis Nixon .75 2.00
CP6 Rickey Henderson 4.00 10.00
CP7 Ellis Burks 1.50 4.00
CP8 Lee Smith 1.50 4.00
CP9 Delino DeShields .75 2.00
CP10 Deion Sanders 2.50 6.00

1994 Score Rookie/Traded Super Rookies

COMPLETE SET (18) 10.00 25.00
STATED ODDS 1:36 HOBBY
SU1 Carlos Delgado 1.50 4.00
SU2 Manny Ramirez 2.00 5.00
SU3 Ryan Klesko 1.00 2.50
SU4 Raul Mondesi 1.00 2.50
SU5 Bob Hamelin .75 2.00
SU6 Steve Karsay .75 2.00
SU7 Jeffrey Hammonds .75 2.00
SU8 Cliff Floyd 1.00 2.50
SU9 Kurt Abbott .75 2.00
SU10 Marc Newfield .75 2.00
SU11 Javier Lopez 1.00 2.50
SU12 Rich Becker .75 2.00
SU13 Greg Pirkl .75 2.00
SU14 Rondell White 1.00 2.50
SU15 James Mouton .75 2.00
SU16 Tony Tarasco .75 2.00
SU17 Brian Anderson 1.00 2.50
SU18 Jim Edmonds 2.00 5.00

1995 Score Samples

COMPLETE SET (10) 4.00 10.00
2 Roberto Alomar .40 1.00
4 Jose Canseco .50 1.25
5 Matt Williams .30 .75
221 Jeff Bagwell .60 1.50
223 Albert Belle .20 .50
224 Chuck Carr .08 .25
288 Jorge Fabregas .08 .25
DP8 McKay Christensen .08 .25
HG5 Cal Ripken 2.00 5.00
NNO Title Card .08 .25

1995 Score

The 1995 Score set consists of 605 standard-size cards issued in hobby, retail and jumbo packs. Hobby packs featured a special signed Ryan Klesko (RG1)card. Retail packs also had a Klesko card (SG1) but these were not signed.

COMPLETE SET (605) 10.00 25.00
COMPLETE SERIES 1 (330) 5.00 12.00
COMPLETE SERIES 2 (275) 5.00 12.00
SUBSET CARDS HALF VALUE OF BASE CARDS
KLESKO RG1 SER.1 ODDS 1:720 RET
KLESKO SG1 SER.1 ODDS 1:720 HOB
1 Frank Thomas .20 .50
2 Roberto Alomar .10 .30
3 Cal Ripken .60 1.50
4 Jose Canseco .10 .30
5 Matt Williams .07 .20
6 Esteban Beltre .02 .10
7 Domingo Cedeno .02 .10
8 John Valentin .02 .10
9 Glenallen Hill .02 .10
10 Rafael Belliard .02 .10
11 Randy Myers .02 .10
12 Mo Vaughn .07 .20
13 Hector Carrasco .02 .10
14 Chili Davis .07 .20
15 Dante Bichette .07 .20
16 Darrin Jackson .02 .10
17 Mike Piazza .30 .75
18 Junior Felix .02 .10
19 Moises Alou .07 .20
20 Mark Gubicza .02 .10
21 Bret Saberhagen .07 .20
22 Lenny Dykstra .07 .20
23 Steve Howe .02 .10
24 Mark Dewey .02 .10
25 Brian Harper .02 .10
26 Ozzie Smith .30 .75
27 Scott Erickson .02 .10
28 Tony Gwynn .25 .60
29 Bob Welch .02 .10
30 Barry Bonds .60 1.50
31 Leo Gomez .02 .10
32 Greg Maddux .30 .75
33 Mike Greenwell .02 .10
34 Sammy Sosa .20 .50
35 Darnell Coles .02 .10
36 Tommy Greene .02 .10
37 Will Clark .10 .30
38 Steve Ontiveros .02 .10
39 Stan Javier .02 .10
40 Bip Roberts .02 .10
41 Paul O'Neill .10 .30
42 Bill Haselman .02 .10
43 Shane Mack .02 .10
44 Orlando Merced .02 .10
45 Kevin Seitzer .02 .10
46 Trevor Hoffman .07 .20
47 Greg Gagne .02 .10
48 Jeff Kent .07 .20
49 Tony Phillips .02 .10
50 Ken Hill .02 .10
51 Carlos Baerga .02 .10
52 Henry Rodriguez .02 .10
53 Scott Sanderson .02 .10
54 Jeff Conine .07 .20
55 Chris Turner .02 .10
56 Ken Caminiti .07 .20
57 Harold Baines .07 .20
58 Charlie Hayes .02 .10
59 Roberto Kelly .02 .10
60 John Olerud .07 .20
61 Tim Davis .02 .10
62 Rich Rowland .02 .10
63 Rey Sanchez .02 .10
64 Junior Ortiz .02 .10
65 Ricky Gutierrez .02 .10
66 Rex Hudler .02 .10
67 Johnny Ruffin .02 .10
68 Jay Buhner .07 .20
69 Tom Pagnozzi .02 .10
70 Julio Franco .07 .20
71 Eric Young .02 .10
72 Mike Bordick .02 .10
73 Don Slaught .02 .10
74 Goose Gossage .07 .20
75 Lonnie Smith .02 .10
76 Jimmy Key .07 .20
77 Dave Hollins .02 .10
78 Mickey Tettleton .02 .10
79 Luis Gonzalez .07 .20
80 Dave Winfield .07 .20
81 Ryan Thompson .02 .10
82 Felix Jose .02 .10
83 Rusty Meacham .02 .10
84 Darryl Hamilton .02 .10
85 John Wetteland .07 .20
86 Tom Brunansky .02 .10
87 Mark Lemke .02 .10
88 Spike Owen .02 .10
89 Shawon Dunston .02 .10
90 Wilson Alvarez .02 .10
91 Lee Smith .07 .20
92 Scott Kamieniecki .02 .10
93 Jacob Brumfield .02 .10
94 Kirk Gibson .07 .20
95 Joe Girardi .02 .10
96 Mike Macfarlane .02 .10
97 Greg Colbrunn .02 .10
98 Ricky Bones .02 .10
99 Delino DeShields .02 .10
100 Pat Meares .02 .10
101 Jeff Fassero .02 .10
102 Jim Leyritz .02 .10
103 Gary Redus .02 .10
104 Terry Steinbach .02 .10
105 Kevin McReynolds .02 .10
106 Felix Fermin .02 .10
107 Danny Jackson .02 .10
108 Chris James .02 .10
109 Jeff King .02 .10
110 Pat Hentgen .02 .10
111 Gerald Perry .02 .10
112 Tim Raines .07 .20
113 Eddie Williams .02 .10
114 Jamie Moyer .07 .20
115 Bud Black .02 .10
116 Chris Gomez .02 .10
117 Luis Lopez .02 .10
118 Roger Clemens .40 1.00
119 Javier Lopez .07 .20
120 Dave Nilsson .02 .10
121 Karl Rhodes .02 .10
122 Rick Aguilera .02 .10
123 Tony Fernandez .02 .10
124 Bernie Williams .10 .30
125 James Mouton .02 .10
126 Mark Langston .02 .10
127 Mike Lansing .02 .10
128 Tino Martinez .10 .30
129 Joe Orsulak .02 .10
130 David Hulse .02 .10
131 Pete Incaviglia .02 .10
132 Mark Clark .02 .10
133 Tony Eusebio .02 .10
134 Chuck Finley .07 .20
135 Lou Frazier .02 .10
136 Craig Grebeck .02 .10
137 Kelly Stinnett .02 .10
138 Paul Shuey .02 .10
139 David Nied .02 .10
140 Billy Brewer .02 .10
141 Dave Weathers .02 .10
142 Scott Leius .02 .10
143 Brian Jordan .07 .20
144 Melido Perez .02 .10
145 Tony Tarasco .02 .10
146 Dan Wilson .02 .10
147 Rondell White .07 .20
148 Mike Henneman .02 .10
149 Brian Johnson .02 .10
150 Tom Henke .02 .10
151 John Patterson .02 .10
152 Bobby Witt .02 .10
153 Eddie Taubensee .02 .10
154 Pat Borders .02 .10
155 Ramon Martinez .02 .10
156 Mike Kingery .02 .10
157 Zane Smith .02 .10
158 Benito Santiago .07 .20
159 Matias Carrillo .02 .10
160 Scott Brosius .07 .20
161 Dave Clark .02 .10
162 Mark McLemore .02 .10
163 Curt Schilling .07 .20
164 J.T. Snow .07 .20
165 Rod Beck .02 .10
166 Scott Fletcher .02 .10
167 Bob Tewksbury .02 .10
168 Mike LaValliere .02 .10
169 Dave Hansen .02 .10
170 Pedro Martinez .10 .30
171 Kirk Rueter .02 .10
172 Jose Lind .02 .10
173 Luis Alicea .02 .10
174 Mike Moore .02 .10
175 Andy Ashby .02 .10
176 Jody Reed .02 .10
177 Darryl Kile .07 .20
178 Carl Willis .02 .10
179 Jeromy Burnitz .07 .20
180 Mike Gallego .02 .10
181 Bill VanLandingham .02 .10
182 Sid Fernandez .02 .10
183 Kim Batiste .02 .10
184 Greg Myers .02 .10
185 Steve Avery .02 .10
186 Steve Farr .02 .10
187 Robb Nen .07 .20
188 Dan Pasqua .02 .10
189 Bruce Ruffin .02 .10
190 Jose Valentin .02 .10
191 Willie Banks .02 .10
192 Mike Aldrete .02 .10
193 Randy Milligan .02 .10
194 Steve Karsay .02 .10
195 Mike Stanley .02 .10
196 Jose Mesa .02 .10
197 Tom Browning .02 .10
198 John Vander Wal .02 .10
199 Kevin Brown .07 .20
200 Mike Oquist .02 .10
201 Greg Swindell .02 .10
202 Eddie Zambrano .02 .10
203 Joe Boever .02 .10
204 Gary Varsho .02 .10
205 Chris Gwynn .02 .10
206 David Howard .02 .10
207 Jerome Walton .02 .10
208 Danny Darwin .02 .10
209 Darryl Strawberry .07 .20
210 Todd Van Poppel .02 .10
211 Scott Livingstone .02 .10
212 Dave Fleming .02 .10
213 Todd Worrell .02 .10
214 Carlos Delgado .07 .20
215 Bill Pecota .02 .10
216 Jim Lindeman .02 .10
217 Rick White .02 .10
218 Jose Oquendo .02 .10
219 Tony Castillo .02 .10
220 Fernando Vina .02 .10
221 Jeff Bagwell .10 .30
222 Randy Johnson .20 .50
223 Albert Belle .07 .20
224 Chuck Carr .02 .10
225 Mark Leiter .02 .10
226 Hal Morris .02 .10
227 Robin Ventura .07 .20
228 Mike Munoz .02 .10
229 Jim Thome .10 .30
230 Mario Diaz .02 .10
231 John Doherty .02 .10
232 Bobby Jones .02 .10
233 Raul Mondesi .07 .20
234 Ricky Jordan .02 .10
235 John Jaha .02 .10
236 Carlos Garcia .02 .10
237 Kirby Puckett .20 .50
238 Orel Hershiser .07 .20
239 Don Mattingly .50 1.25
240 Sid Bream .02 .10
241 Brent Gates .02 .10
242 Tony Longmire .02 .10
243 Robby Thompson .02 .10
244 Rick Sutcliffe .07 .20
245 Dean Palmer .07 .20
246 Marquis Grissom .07 .20
247 Paul Molitor .07 .20
248 Mark Carreon .02 .10
249 Jack Voigt .02 .10
250 Greg McMichael UER .02 .10
251 Damon Berryhill .02 .10
252 Brian Dorsett .02 .10
253 Jim Edmonds .10 .30
254 Barry Larkin .10 .30
255 Jack McDowell .02 .10
256 Wally Joyner .07 .20
257 Eddie Murray .20 .50
258 Lenny Webster .02 .10
259 Milt Cuyler .02 .10
260 Todd Benzinger .02 .10
261 Vince Coleman .02 .10
262 Todd Stottlemyre .02 .10
263 Turner Ward .02 .10
264 Ray Lankford .07 .20
265 Matt Walbeck .02 .10
266 Deion Sanders .10 .30
267 Gerald Williams .02 .10
268 Jim Gott .02 .10
269 Jeff Frye .02 .10
270 Jose Rijo .02 .10
271 David Justice .07 .20
272 Ismael Valdes .02 .10
273 Ben McDonald .02 .10
274 Darren Lewis .02 .10
275 Graeme Lloyd .02 .10
276 Luis Ortiz .02 .10
277 Julian Tavarez .02 .10
278 Mark Dalesandro .02 .10
279 Brett Merriman .02 .10
280 Ricky Bottalico .02 .10
281 Robert Eenhoorn .02 .10
282 Rikkert Faneyte .02 .10
283 Mike Kelly .02 .10
284 Mark Smith .02 .10
285 Turk Wendell .02 .10
286 Greg Blosser .02 .10
287 Garey Ingram .02 .10
288 Jorge Fabregas .02 .10
289 Blaise Ilsley .02 .10
290 Joe Hall .02 .10
291 Orlando Miller .02 .10
292 Jose Lima .02 .10
293 Greg O'Halloran RC .02 .10
294 Mark Kiefer .02 .10
295 Jose Oliva .02 .10
296 Rich Becker .02 .10
297 Brian L.Hunter .02 .10
298 Dave Silvestri .02 .10
299 Armando Benitez .02 .10
300 Darren Dreifort .02 .10
301 John Mabry .02 .10
302 Greg Pirkl .02 .10
303 J.R. Phillips .02 .10
304 Shawn Green .07 .20
305 Roberto Petagine .02 .10
306 Keith Lockhart .02 .10
307 Jonathan Hurst .02 .10
308 Paul Spoljaric .02 .10
309 Mike Lieberthal .07 .20
310 Garret Anderson .07 .20
311 John Johnstone .02 .10
312 Alex Rodriguez .50 1.25
313 Kent Mercker .02 .10
314 John Valentin .02 .10
315 Kenny Rogers .07 .20
316 Fred McGriff AS MVP .07 .20
317 Braves .02 .10
Orioles CL
318 Cubs .02 .10
Red Sox CL
319 Reds .02 .10
Angels CL
320 Rockies .02 .10
White Sox CL
321 Marlins .02 .10
Indians CL
322 Astros .02 .10
Tigers CL
323 Dodgers .02 .10
Royals CL
324 Expos .02 .10
Brewers CL
325 Mets .02 .10
Twins CL
326 Phillies .02 .10
Yankees CL
327 Pirates .02 .10
Athletics CL
328 Padres .02 .10
Mariners CL
329 Giants .02 .10
Rangers CL
330 Cardinals .02 .10
Blue Jays CL
331 Pedro Munoz .02 .10
332 Ryan Klesko .07 .20
333 Andre Dawson .07 .20
334 Derrick May .02 .10
335 Aaron Sele .02 .10
336 Kevin Mitchell .02 .10
337 Steve Trachsel .02 .10
338 Andres Galarraga .07 .20
339 Terry Pendleton .07 .20
340 Gary Sheffield .07 .20
341 Travis Fryman .07 .20
342 Bo Jackson .20 .50
343 Gary Gaetti .07 .20
344 Brett Butler .07 .20
345 B.J. Surhoff .07 .20
346 Larry Walker .07 .20
347 Kevin Tapani .02 .10
348 Rick Wilkins .02 .10
349 Wade Boggs .10 .30
350 Mariano Duncan .02 .10
351 Ruben Sierra .07 .20
352 Andy Van Slyke .10 .30
353 Reggie Jefferson .02 .10
354 Gregg Jefferies .02 .10
355 Tim Naehring .02 .10
356 John Roper .02 .10
357 Joe Carter .07 .20
358 Kurt Abbott .02 .10
359 Lenny Harris .02 .10
360 Lance Johnson .02 .10
361 Brian Anderson .02 .10
362 Jim Eisenreich .02 .10
363 Jerry Browne .02 .10
364 Mark Grace .10 .30
365 Devon White .07 .20
366 Reggie Sanders .07 .20
367 Ivan Rodriguez .10 .30
368 Kirt Manwaring .02 .10
369 Pat Kelly .02 .10
370 Ellis Burks .07 .20
371 Charles Nagy .02 .10
372 Kevin Bass .02 .10
373 Lou Whitaker .07 .20
374 Rene Arocha .02 .10
375 Derek Parks .02 .10
376 Mark Whiten .02 .10
377 Mark McGwire .50 1.25
378 Doug Drabek .02 .10
379 Greg Vaughn .02 .10
380 Al Martin .02 .10
381 Ron Darling .02 .10
382 Tim Wallach .02 .10
383 Alan Trammell .07 .20
384 Randy Velarde .02 .10
385 Chris Sabo .02 .10
386 Wil Cordero .02 .10
387 Darrin Fletcher .02 .10
388 David Segui .02 .10
389 Steve Buechele .02 .10
390 Dave Gallagher .02 .10
391 Thomas Howard .02 .10
392 Chad Curtis .02 .10
393 Cal Eldred .02 .10
394 Jason Bere .02 .10
395 Bret Barberie .02 .10
396 Paul Sorrento .02 .10
397 Steve Finley .07 .20
398 Cecil Fielder .07 .20
399 Eric Karros .07 .20
400 Jeff Montgomery .02 .10
401 Cliff Floyd .07 .20
402 Matt Mieske .02 .10
403 Brian Hunter .02 .10
404 Alex Cole .02 .10
405 Kevin Stocker .02 .10
406 Eric Davis .07 .20
407 Marvin Freeman .02 .10
408 Dennis Eckersley .07 .20
409 Todd Zeile .02 .10
410 Keith Mitchell .02 .10
411 Andy Benes .02 .10
412 Juan Bell .02 .10
413 Royce Clayton .02 .10
414 Ed Sprague .02 .10
415 Mike Mussina .10 .30
416 Todd Hundley .02 .10
417 Pat Listach .02 .10
418 Joe Oliver .02 .10
419 Rafael Palmeiro .10 .30
420 Tim Salmon .10 .30
421 Brady Anderson .07 .20
422 Kenny Lofton .07 .20
423 Craig Biggio .10 .30
424 Bobby Bonilla .07 .20
425 Kenny Rogers .07 .20
426 Derek Bell .02 .10
427 Scott Cooper .02 .10
428 Ozzie Guillen .07 .20
429 Omar Vizquel .10 .30
430 Phil Plantier .02 .10
431 Chuck Knoblauch .07 .20
432 Darren Daulton .07 .20
433 Bob Hamelin .02 .10
434 Tom Glavine .10 .30
435 Walt Weiss .02 .10
436 Jose Vizcaino .02 .10
437 Ken Griffey Jr. .40 1.00
438 Jay Bell .07 .20
439 Juan Gonzalez .07 .20
440 Jeff Blauser .02 .10
441 Rickey Henderson .20 .50
442 Bobby Ayala .02 .10
443 David Cone .07 .20
444 Pedro Martinez .10 .30
445 Manny Ramirez .10 .30
446 Mark Portugal .02 .10
447 Damion Easley .02 .10
448 Gary DiSarcina .02 .10
449 Roberto Hernandez .02 .10
450 Jeffrey Hammonds .02 .10
451 Jeff Treadway .02 .10
452 Jim Abbott .10 .30
453 Carlos Rodriguez .02 .10
454 Joey Cora .02 .10
455 Bret Boone .07 .20
456 Danny Tartabull .02 .10
457 John Franco .07 .20
458 Roger Salkeld .02 .10
459 Fred McGriff .10 .30
460 Pedro Astacio .02 .10
461 Jon Lieber .02 .10
462 Luis Polonia .02 .10
463 Geronimo Pena .02 .10
464 Tom Gordon .02 .10
465 Brad Ausmus .07 .20
466 Willie McGee .07 .20
467 Doug Jones .02 .10
468 John Smoltz .10 .30
469 Troy Neel .02 .10
470 Luis Sojo .02 .10
471 John Smiley .02 .10
472 Rafael Bournigal .02 .10
473 Bill Taylor .02 .10
474 Juan Guzman .02 .10
475 Dave Magadan .02 .10
476 Mike Devereaux .02 .10
477 Andujar Cedeno .02 .10
478 Edgar Martinez .10 .30
479 Milt Thompson .02 .10
480 Allen Watson .02 .10
481 Ron Karkovice .02 .10
482 Joey Hamilton .02 .10
483 Vinny Castilla .07 .20
484 Tim Belcher .02 .10
485 Bernard Gilkey .02 .10
486 Scott Servais .02 .10
487 Cory Snyder .02 .10
488 Mel Rojas .02 .10
489 Carlos Reyes .02 .10
490 Chip Hale .02 .10
491 Bill Swift .02 .10
492 Pat Rapp .02 .10
493 Brian McRae .02 .10
494 Mickey Morandini .02 .10
495 Tony Pena .02 .10
496 Danny Bautista .02 .10
497 Armando Reynoso .02 .10
498 Ken Ryan .02 .10
499 Billy Ripken .02 .10
500 Pat Mahomes .02 .10
501 Mark Acre .02 .10
502 Geronimo Berroa .02 .10
503 Norberto Martin .02 .10
504 Chad Kreuter .02 .10
505 Howard Johnson .02 .10
506 Eric Anthony .02 .10
507 Mark Wohlers .02 .10
508 Scott Sanders .02 .10
509 Pete Harnisch .02 .10
510 Wes Chamberlain .02 .10
511 Tom Candiotti .02 .10
512 Albie Lopez .02 .10
513 Denny Neagle .07 .20
514 Sean Berry .02 .10
515 Billy Hatcher .02 .10
516 Todd Jones .02 .10
517 Wayne Kirby .02 .10
518 Butch Henry .02 .10
519 Sandy Alomar Jr. .02 .10
520 Kevin Appier .07 .20
521 Roberto Mejia .02 .10
522 Steve Cooke .02 .10
523 Terry Shumpert .02 .10
524 Mike Jackson .02 .10
525 Kent Mercker .02 .10
526 David Wells .07 .20
527 Juan Samuel .02 .10
528 Salomon Torres .02 .10
529 Duane Ward .02 .10
530 Rob Dibble .07 .20
531 Mike Blowers .02 .10
532 Mark Eichhorn .02 .10
533 Alex Diaz .02 .10
534 Dan Miceli .02 .10
535 Jeff Branson .02 .10
536 Dave Stevens .02 .10
537 Charlie O'Brien .02 .10
538 Shane Reynolds .02 .10
539 Rich Amaral .02 .10
540 Rusty Greer .07 .20
541 Alex Arias .02 .10
542 Eric Plunk .02 .10
543 John Hudek .02 .10
544 Kirk McCaskill .02 .10
545 Jeff Reboulet .02 .10
546 Sterling Hitchcock .02 .10
547 Warren Newson .02 .10
548 Bryan Harvey .02 .10
549 Mike Huff .02 .10
550 Lance Parrish .07 .20
551 Ken Griffey Jr. HIT .25 .60
552 Matt Williams HIT .02 .10
553 Roberto Alomar HIT .07 .20
554 Jeff Bagwell HIT .07 .20
555 David Justice HIT .02 .10
556 Cal Ripken HIT .30 .75
557 Albert Belle HIT .02 .10
558 Mike Piazza HIT .15 .40
559 Kirby Puckett HIT .10 .30
560 Wade Boggs HIT .07 .20
561 Tony Gwynn HIT .10 .30
562 Barry Bonds HIT .30 .75
563 Mo Vaughn HIT .02 .10
564 Don Mattingly HIT .25 .60
565 Carlos Baerga HIT .02 .10
566 Paul Molitor HIT .02 .10
567 Raul Mondesi HIT .02 .10
568 Manny Ramirez HIT .07 .20
569 Alex Rodriguez HIT .20 .50
570 Will Clark HIT .07 .20
571 Frank Thomas HIT .10 .30
572 Moises Alou HIT .02 .10
573 Jeff Conine HIT .02 .10
574 Joe Ausanio .02 .10
575 Charles Johnson .07 .20
576 Ernie Young .02 .10
577 Jeff Granger .02 .10
578 Robert Perez .02 .10
579 Melvin Nieves .02 .10
580 Gar Finnvold .02 .10
581 Duane Singleton .02 .10
582 Chan Ho Park .07 .20
583 Fausto Cruz .02 .10
584 Dave Staton .02 .10
585 Denny Hocking .02 .10
586 Nate Minchey .02 .10
587 Marc Newfield .02 .10
588 Jayhawk Owens .02 .10
589 Darren Bragg .02 .10
590 Kevin King .02 .10
591 Kurt Miller .02 .10
592 Aaron Small .02 .10
593 Troy O'Leary .02 .10
594 Phil Stidham .02 .10
595 Steve Dunn .02 .10
596 Cory Bailey .02 .10
597 Alex Gonzalez .02 .10
598 Jim Bowie RC .02 .10
599 Jeff Cirillo .02 .10
600 Mark Hutton .02 .10
601 Russ Davis .02 .10
602 Checklist .02 .10
603 Checklist .02 .10
604 Checklist .02 .10
605 Checklist .02 .10
RG1 R.Klesko Rook.Great. .40 1.00
SG1 Ryan Klesko AU/6100 4.00 10.00

1995 Score Gold Rush

COMPLETE SET (605) 20.00 50.00
COMPLETE SERIES 1 (330) 10.00 25.00
COMPLETE SERIES 2 (275) 10.00 25.00
*STARS: 2X TO 5X BASIC CARDS
ONE PER PACK

1995 Score Platinum Team Sets

*STARS: 5X TO 12X BASIC CARDS
ONE PLAT.TEAM VIA MAIL PER G.RUSH TEAM

1995 Score You Trade Em

COMPLETE SET (11) .60 1.50
ONE SET VIA MAIL PER REDEMPTION CARD
333T Andre Dawson .15 .40
339T Terry Pendleton .15 .40
344T Brett Butler .15 .40
346T Larry Walker .15 .40
352T Andy Van Slyke .25 .60
392T Chad Curtis .07 .20
427T Scott Cooper .07 .20
443T David Cone .15 .40
452T Jim Abbott .25 .60
493T Brian McRae .07 .20
530T Rob Dibble .15 .40
NNO Expired Trade Card .20 .50

1995 Score Airmail

COMPLETE SET (18) 20.00 50.00
SER.2 STATED ODDS 1:24 JUMBO
AM1 Bob Hamelin .60 1.50
AM2 John Mabry .60 1.50
AM3 Marc Newfield .60 1.50
AM4 Jose Oliva .60 1.50
AM5 Charles Johnson 1.00 2.50
AM6 Russ Davis .60 1.50
AM7 Ernie Young .60 1.50
AM8 Billy Ashley .60 1.50
AM9 Ryan Klesko 1.00 2.50
AM10 J.R. Phillips .60 1.50
AM11 Cliff Floyd 1.00 2.50
AM12 Carlos Delgado 1.00 2.50
AM13 Melvin Nieves .60 1.50
AM14 Raul Mondesi 1.00 2.50
AM15 Manny Ramirez 1.50 4.00
AM16 Mike Kelly .60 1.50
AM17 Alex Rodriguez 6.00 15.00
AM18 Rusty Greer 1.00 2.50

1995 Score Contest Redemption

COMPLETE SET 3.00 8.00
AD1 Alex Rodriguez 2.50 6.00
AD2 Ivan Rodriguez 1.25 3.00

1995 Score Double Gold Champs

COMPLETE SET (12) 30.00 80.00
SER.2 STATED ODDS 1:36 HOBBY
GC1 Frank Thomas 2.00 5.00
GC2 Ken Griffey Jr. 4.00 10.00
GC3 Barry Bonds 6.00 15.00
GC4 Tony Gwynn 2.50 6.00
GC5 Don Mattingly 5.00 12.00
GC6 Greg Maddux 3.00 8.00
GC7 Roger Clemens 4.00 10.00
GC8 Kenny Lofton .75 2.00
GC9 Jeff Bagwell 1.25 3.00
GC10 Matt Williams .75 2.00
GC11 Kirby Puckett 2.00 5.00
GC12 Cal Ripken 6.00 15.00

1995 Score Draft Picks

COMPLETE SET (18) 10.00 25.00
SER.1 STATED ODDS 1:36 HOBBY
DP1 McKay Christensen .40 1.00
DP2 Bret Wagner .40 1.00
DP3 Paul Wilson .40 1.00
DP4 C.J. Nitkowski .40 1.00
DP5 Josh Booty .40 1.00
DP6 Antone Williamson .40 1.00
DP7 Paul Konerko 2.00 5.00
DP8 Scott Elarton .60 1.50
DP9 Jacob Shumate .40 1.00

DP10 Terrence Long .40 1.00
DP11 Mark Johnson .60 1.50
DP12 Ben Grieve .40 1.00
DP13 Doug Million .40 1.00
DP14 Jayson Peterson .40 1.00
DP15 Dustin Hermanson .40 1.00
DP16 Matt Smith .40 1.00
DP17 Kevin Witt .40 1.00
DP18 Brian Buchanan .40 1.00

1995 Score Dream Team

COMPLETE SET (12) 10.00 25.00
SER.1 STATED ODDS 1:72
DG1 Frank Thomas 1.50 4.00
DG2 Roberto Alomar 1.00 2.50
DG3 Cal Ripken 5.00 12.00
DG4 Matt Williams .60 1.50
DG5 Mike Piazza 1.50 4.00
DG6 Albert Belle .60 1.50
DG7 Ken Griffey Jr. 3.00 8.00
DG8 Tony Gwynn 1.50 4.00
DG9 Paul Molitor 1.50 4.00
DG10 Jimmy Key .60 1.50
DG11 Greg Maddux 2.50 6.00
DG12 Lee Smith .60 1.50

1995 Score Hall of Gold

COMPLETE SET (110) 12.50 30.00
COMPLETE SERIES 1 (55) 8.00 20.00
COMPLETE SERIES 2 (55) 5.00 12.00
STATED ODDS 1:6H/R, 1:4J, 1:3ANCO
*YTE CARDS: .4X TO 1X BASIC HALL
ONE YTE SET VIA MAIL PER YTE TRADE CARD
HG1 Ken Griffey Jr. 2.50 6.00
HG2 Matt Williams .50 1.25
HG3 Roberto Alomar .75 2.00
HG4 Jeff Bagwell .75 2.00
HG5 David Justice .50 1.25
HG6 Cal Ripken 4.00 10.00
HG7 Randy Johnson 1.25 3.00
HG8 Barry Larkin .75 2.00
HG9 Albert Belle .50 1.25
HG10 Mike Piazza 2.00 5.00
HG11 Kirby Puckett 1.25 3.00
HG12 Moises Alou .50 1.25
HG13 Jose Canseco .75 2.00
HG14 Tony Gwynn 1.50 4.00
HG15 Roger Clemens 2.50 6.00
HG16 Barry Bonds 4.00 10.00
HG17 Mo Vaughn .50 1.25
HG18 Greg Maddux 2.00 5.00
HG19 Dante Bichette .50 1.25
HG20 Will Clark .75 2.00
HG21 Lenny Dykstra .50 1.25
HG22 Don Mattingly 3.00 8.00
HG23 Carlos Baerga .25 .60
HG24 Ozzie Smith 2.00 5.00
HG25 Paul Molitor .50 1.25
HG26 Paul O'Neill .75 2.00
HG27 Deion Sanders .75 2.00
HG28 Jeff Conine .50 1.25
HG29 John Olerud .50 1.25
HG30 Jose Rijo .25 .60
HG31 Sammy Sosa 1.25 3.00
HG32 Robin Ventura .50 1.25
HG33 Raul Mondesi .50 1.25
HG34 Eddie Murray 1.25 3.00
HG35 Marquis Grissom .50 1.25
HG36 Darryl Strawberry .50 1.25
HG37 Dave Nilsson .25 .60
HG38 Manny Ramirez .75 2.00
HG39 Delino DeShields .25 .60
HG40 Lee Smith .50 1.25
HG41 Alex Rodriguez 3.00 8.00
HG42 Julio Franco .50 1.25
HG43 Bret Saberhagen .50 1.25
HG44 Ken Hill .25 .60
HG45 Roberto Kelly .25 .60
HG46 Hal Morris .25 .60
HG47 Jimmy Key .50 1.25
HG48 Terry Steinbach .25 .60
HG49 Mickey Tettleton .25 .60
HG50 Tony Phillips .25 .60
HG51 Carlos Garcia .25 .60
HG52 Jim Edmonds .75 2.00
HG53 Rod Beck .25 .60
HG54 Shane Mack .25 .60
HG55 Ken Caminiti .50 1.25
HG56 Frank Thomas 1.25 3.00
HG57 Kenny Lofton .50 1.25
HG58 Juan Gonzalez .50 1.25
HG59 Jason Bere .25 .60
HG60 Joe Carter .50 1.25
HG61 Gary Sheffield .50 1.25
HG62 Andres Galarraga .50 1.25
HG63 Ellis Burks .50 1.25
HG64 Bobby Bonilla .50 1.25
HG65 Tom Glavine .75 2.00
HG66 John Smoltz .75 2.00
HG67 Fred McGriff .75 2.00
HG68 Craig Biggio .75 2.00
HG69 Reggie Sanders .50 1.25
HG70 Kevin Mitchell .25 .60
HG71 Larry Walker .50 1.25
HG72 Carlos Delgado .50 1.25
HG73 Alex Gonzalez .25 .60
HG74 Ivan Rodriguez .75 2.00
HG75 Ryan Klesko .50 1.25
HG76 John Kruk .25 .60
HG77 Brian McRae .25 .60
HG78 Tim Salmon .75 2.00
HG79 Travis Fryman .50 1.25
HG80 Chuck Knoblauch .50 1.25
HG81 Jay Bell .50 1.25
HG82 Cecil Fielder .50 1.25
HG83 Cliff Floyd .50 1.25
HG84 Ruben Sierra .50 1.25
HG85 Mike Mussina .75 2.00
HG86 Mark Grace .75 2.00
HG87 Dennis Eckersley .50 1.25
HG88 Dennis Martinez .25 .60
HG89 Rafael Palmeiro .75 2.00
HG90 Ben McDonald .25 .60
HG91 Dave Hollins .25 .60
HG92 Steve Avery .25 .60
HG93 David Cone .50 1.25
HG94 Darren Daulton .50 1.25
HG95 Bret Boone .50 1.25
HG96 Wade Boggs .75 2.00
HG97 Doug Drabek .25 .60
HG98 Andy Benes .25 .60
HG99 Jim Thome .75 2.00
HG100 Chili Davis .50 1.25
HG101 Jeffrey Hammonds .25 .60
HG102 Rickey Henderson 1.25 3.00
HG103 Brett Butler .50 1.25
HG104 Tim Wallach .25 .60
HG105 Wil Cordero .25 .60
HG106 Mark Whiten .25 .60
HG107 Bob Hamelin .25 .60
HG108 Rondell White .50 1.25
HG109 Devon White .50 1.25
HG110 Tony Tarasco .25 .60

1995 Score Hall of Gold You Trade Em

COMPLETE SET (5) 1.25 3.00
ONE SET VIA MAIL PER GOLD TRADE CARD
HG71T Larry Walker .50 1.25
HG76T John Kruk .25 .60
HG77T Brian McRae .25 .60
HG93T David Cone .50 1.25
HG110T Tony Tarasco .25 .60
NNO Exp. Hall of Gold Trade Card .20 .50

1995 Score Rookie Dream Team

COMPLETE SET (12) 25.00 60.00
SER.2 STAT.ODDS 1:72 HOB/RET, 1:43 ANCO
RDT PREFIX ON CARD NUMBERS
RDT1 J.R. Phillips 1.00 2.50
RDT2 Alex Gonzalez 1.00 2.50
RDT3 Alex Rodriguez 8.00 20.00
RDT4 Jose Oliva 1.00 2.50
RDT5 Charles Johnson 2.00 5.00
RDT6 Shawn Green 2.00 5.00
RDT7 Brian L.Hunter 1.00 2.50
RDT8 Garret Anderson 2.00 5.00
RDT9 Julian Tavarez 1.00 2.50
RDT10 Jose Lima 1.00 2.50
RDT11 Armando Benitez 1.00 2.50
RDT12 Ricky Bottalico 1.00 2.50

1995 Score Rules

COMPLETE SET (30) 60.00 120.00
SER.1 STATED ODDS 1:8 JUMBO
*JUMBO'S: .5X TO 1.2X
JUMBOS ISSUED ONE PER COLLECTOR KIT
SR1 Ken Griffey Jr. 4.00 10.00
SR2 Frank Thomas 2.00 5.00
SR3 Mike Piazza 3.00 8.00
SR4 Jeff Bagwell 1.25 3.00
SR5 Alex Rodriguez 5.00 12.00
SR6 Albert Belle .75 2.00
SR7 Matt Williams .75 2.00
SR8 Roberto Alomar 1.25 3.00
SR9 Barry Bonds 6.00 15.00
SR10 Raul Mondesi .75 2.00
SR11 Jose Canseco 1.25 3.00
SR12 Kirby Puckett 2.00 5.00
SR13 Fred McGriff 1.25 3.00
SR14 Kenny Lofton .75 2.00
SR15 Greg Maddux 3.00 8.00
SR16 Juan Gonzalez .75 2.00
SR17 Cliff Floyd .75 2.00
SR18 Cal Ripken 6.00 15.00
SR19 Will Clark 1.25 3.00
SR20 Tim Salmon 1.25 3.00
SR21 Paul O'Neill 1.25 3.00
SR22 Jason Bere .40 1.00
SR23 Tony Gwynn 2.50 6.00
SR24 Manny Ramirez 1.25 3.00
SR25 Don Mattingly 5.00 12.00
SR26 David Justice .75 2.00
SR27 Javier Lopez .75 2.00
SR28 Ryan Klesko .75 2.00
SR29 Carlos Delgado .75 2.00
SR30 Mike Mussina 1.25 3.00

1995 Score Rules Jumbos

STATED PRINT RUN 3000 SER.#'d SETS
SR1 Ken Griffey Jr. 15.00 40.00
SR2 Frank Thomas 15.00 40.00
SR3 Mike Piazza 12.50 30.00
SR4 Jeff Bagwell 6.00 15.00
SR5 Alex Rodriguez 5.00 12.00
SR6 Albert Belle 6.00 15.00
SR7 Matt Williams 2.00 5.00
SR8 Roberto Alomar 4.00 10.00
SR9 Barry Bonds 3.00 8.00
SR10 Raul Mondesi 2.50 6.00
SR11 Jose Canseco 1.50 4.00
SR12 Kirby Puckett 40.00 80.00
SR13 Fred McGriff 1.50 4.00
SR14 Kenny Lofton 4.00 10.00
SR15 Greg Maddux 12.50 30.00
SR16 Juan Gonzalez 3.00 8.00
SR17 Cliff Floyd .60 1.50
SR18 Cal Ripken 20.00 50.00
SR19 Will Clark 20.00 50.00
SR20 Tim Salmon 2.50 6.00
SR21 Paul O'Neill 1.25 3.00
SR22 Jason Bere .60 1.50
SR23 Tony Gwynn 10.00 25.00
SR24 Manny Ramirez 5.00 12.00
SR25 Don Mattingly 6.00 15.00
SR26 David Justice 1.25 3.00
SR27 Javier Lopez 1.50 4.00
SR28 Ryan Klesko 3.00 8.00
SR29 Carlos Delgado 1.25 3.00
SR30 Mike Mussina 2.50 6.00

1996 Score Samples

COMPLETE SET (8) 3.00 8.00
3 Ryan Klesko .20 .50
4 Jim Edmonds .40 1.00
5 Barry Larkin .40 1.00
6 Jim Thome .50 1.25
7 Raul Mondesi .30 .75
110 Derek Bell .08 .25
240 Derek Jeter 2.00 5.00
241 Michael Tucker .20 .50

1996 Score

This set consists of 517 standard-size cards. These cards were issued in packs of 10 that retailed for 99 cents per pack. The fronts feature an action photo surrounded by white borders. The "Score 96" logo is in the upper left, while the player is identified on the bottom. The backs have season and career stats as well as a player photo and some text. A Cal Ripken tribute card was issued at a rate of 1 every 300 packs.

COMPLETE SET (517) 12.50 30.00
COMPLETE SERIES 1 (275) 6.00 15.00
COMPLETE SERIES 2 (242) 6.00 15.00
RIPKEN 2131 ODDS 1:300 H/R, 1:150 JUM
1 Will Clark .10 .30
2 Rich Becker .07 .20
3 Ryan Klesko .07 .20
4 Jim Edmonds .07 .20
5 Barry Larkin .10 .30
6 Jim Thome .10 .30
7 Raul Mondesi .07 .20
8 Don Mattingly .50 1.25
9 Jeff Conine .07 .20
10 Rickey Henderson .20 .50
11 Chad Curtis .07 .20
12 Darren Daulton .07 .20
13 Larry Walker .07 .20
14 Carlos Garcia .07 .20
15 Carlos Baerga .07 .20
16 Tony Gwynn .25 .60
17 Jon Nunnally .07 .20
18 Deion Sanders .10 .30
19 Mark Grace .10 .30
20 Alex Rodriguez .40 1.00
21 Frank Thomas .20 .50
22 Brian Jordan .07 .20
23 J.T. Snow .07 .20
24 Shawn Green .07 .20
25 Tim Wakefield .07 .20
26 Curtis Goodwin .07 .20
27 John Smoltz .10 .30
28 Devon White .07 .20
29 Brian L. Hunter .07 .20
30 Rusty Greer .07 .20
31 Rafael Palmeiro .10 .30
32 Bernard Gilkey .07 .20
33 John Valentin .07 .20
34 Randy Johnson .20 .50
35 Garret Anderson .07 .20
36 Rikkert Faneyte .07 .20
37 Ray Durham .07 .20
38 Bip Roberts .07 .20
39 Jaime Navarro .07 .20
40 Mark Johnson .07 .20
41 Darren Lewis .07 .20
42 Tyler Green .07 .20
43 Bill Pulsipher .07 .20
44 Jason Giambi .07 .20
45 Kevin Ritz .07 .20
46 Jack McDowell .07 .20
47 Felipe Lira .07 .20
48 Rico Brogna .07 .20
49 Terry Pendleton .07 .20
50 Rondell White .07 .20
51 Andre Dawson .07 .20
52 Kirby Puckett .20 .50
53 Wally Joyner .07 .20
54 B.J. Surhoff .07 .20
55 Randy Velarde .07 .20
56 Greg Vaughn .07 .20
57 Roberto Alomar .10 .30
58 David Justice .07 .20
59 Kevin Seitzer .07 .20
60 Cal Ripken .60 1.50
61 Ozzie Smith .30 .75
62 Mo Vaughn .07 .20
63 Ricky Bones .07 .20
64 Gary DiSarcina .07 .20
65 Matt Williams .07 .20
66 Wilson Alvarez .07 .20
67 Lenny Dykstra .07 .20
68 Brian McRae .07 .20
69 Todd Stottlemyre .07 .20
70 Bret Boone .07 .20
71 Sterling Hitchcock .07 .20
72 Albert Belle .07 .20
73 Todd Hundley .07 .20
74 Vinny Castilla .07 .20
75 Moises Alou .07 .20
76 Cecil Fielder .07 .20
77 Brad Radke .07 .20
78 Quilvio Veras .07 .20
79 Eddie Murray .20 .50
80 James Mouton .07 .20
81 Pat Listach .07 .20
82 Mark Gubicza .07 .20
83 Dave Winfield .07 .20
84 Fred McGriff .10 .30
85 Darryl Hamilton .07 .20
86 Jeffrey Hammonds .07 .20
87 Pedro Munoz .07 .20
88 Craig Biggio .10 .30
89 Cliff Floyd .07 .20
90 Tim Naehring .07 .20
91 Brett Butler .07 .20
92 Kevin Foster .07 .20
93 Pat Kelly .07 .20
94 John Smiley .07 .20
95 Terry Steinbach .07 .20
96 Orel Hershiser .07 .20
97 Darrin Fletcher .07 .20
98 Walt Weiss .07 .20
99 John Wetteland .07 .20
100 Alan Trammell .07 .20
101 Steve Avery .07 .20
102 Tony Eusebio .07 .20
103 Sandy Alomar Jr. .07 .20
104 Joe Girardi .07 .20
105 Rick Aguilera .07 .20
106 Tony Tarasco .07 .20
107 Chris Hammond .07 .20
108 Mike Macfarlane .07 .20
109 Doug Drabek .07 .20
110 Derek Bell .07 .20
111 Ed Sprague .07 .20
112 Todd Hollandsworth .07 .20
113 Otis Nixon .07 .20
114 Keith Lockhart .07 .20
115 Donovan Osborne .07 .20
116 Dave Magadan .07 .20
117 Edgar Martinez .10 .30
118 Chuck Carr .07 .20
119 J.R. Phillips .07 .20
120 Sean Bergman .07 .20
121 Andujar Cedeno .07 .20
122 Eric Young .07 .20
123 Al Martin .07 .20
124 Mark Lemke .07 .20
125 Jim Eisenreich .07 .20
126 Benito Santiago .07 .20
127 Ariel Prieto .07 .20
128 Jim Bullinger .07 .20
129 Russ Davis .07 .20
130 Jim Abbott .10 .30
131 Jason Isringhausen .07 .20
132 Carlos Perez .07 .20
133 David Segui .07 .20
134 Troy O'Leary .07 .20
135 Pat Meares .07 .20
136 Chris Hoiles .07 .20
137 Ismael Valdes .07 .20
138 Jose Oliva .07 .20
139 Carlos Delgado .07 .20
140 Tom Goodwin .07 .20
141 Bob Tewksbury .07 .20
142 Chris Gomez .07 .20
143 Jose Oquendo .07 .20
144 Mark Lewis .07 .20
145 Salomon Torres .07 .20
146 Luis Gonzalez .07 .20
147 Mark Carreon .07 .20
148 Lance Johnson .07 .20
149 Melvin Nieves .07 .20
150 Lee Smith .07 .20
151 Jacob Brumfield .07 .20
152 Armando Benitez .07 .20
153 Curt Schilling .07 .20
154 Javier Lopez .07 .20
155 Frank Rodriguez .07 .20
156 Alex Gonzalez .07 .20
157 Todd Worrell .07 .20
158 Benji Gil .07 .20
159 Greg Gagne .07 .20
160 Tom Henke .07 .20
161 Randy Myers .07 .20
162 Joey Cora .07 .20
163 Scott Ruffcorn .07 .20
164 W. VanLandingham .07 .20
165 Tony Phillips .07 .20
166 Eddie Williams .07 .20
167 Bobby Bonilla .07 .20
168 Denny Neagle .07 .20
169 Troy Percival .07 .20
170 Billy Ashley .07 .20
171 Andy Van Slyke .10 .30
172 Jose Offerman .07 .20
173 Mark Parent .07 .20
174 Edgardo Alfonzo .07 .20
175 Trevor Hoffman .07 .20
176 David Cone .07 .20
177 Dan Wilson .07 .20
178 Steve Ontiveros .07 .20
179 Dean Palmer .07 .20
180 Mike Kelly .07 .20
181 Jim Leyritz .07 .20
182 Ron Karkovice .07 .20
183 Kevin Brown .07 .20
184 Jose Valentin .07 .20
185 Jorge Fabregas .07 .20
186 Jose Mesa .07 .20
187 Brent Mayne .07 .20
188 Carl Everett .07 .20
189 Paul Sorrento .07 .20
190 Pete Schourek .07 .20
191 Scott Kamieniecki .07 .20
192 Roberto Hernandez .07 .20
193 Randy Johnson RR .10 .30
194 Greg Maddux RR .20 .50
195 Hideo Nomo RR .10 .30
196 David Cone RR .07 .20
197 Mike Mussina RR .07 .20
198 Andy Benes RR .07 .20
199 Kevin Appier RR .07 .20
200 John Smoltz RR .07 .20
201 John Wetteland RR .07 .20
202 Mark Wohlers RR .07 .20
203 Stan Belinda .07 .20
204 Brian Anderson .07 .20
205 Mike Devereaux .07 .20
206 Mark Wohlers .07 .20
207 Omar Vizquel .10 .30
208 Jose Rijo .07 .20
209 Willie Blair .07 .20
210 Jamie Moyer .07 .20
211 Craig Shipley .07 .20
212 Shane Reynolds .07 .20
213 Chad Fonville .07 .20
214 Jose Vizcaino .07 .20
215 Sid Fernandez .07 .20
216 Andy Ashby .07 .20
217 Frank Castillo .07 .20
218 Kevin Tapani .07 .20
219 Kent Mercker .07 .20
220 Karim Garcia .07 .20
221 Antonio Osuna .07 .20
222 Tim Unroe .07 .20
223 Johnny Damon .10 .30
224 LaTroy Hawkins .07 .20
225 Mariano Rivera 4.00 10.00
226 Jose Alberro .07 .20
227 Angel Martinez .07 .20
228 Jason Schmidt .10 .30
229 Tony Clark .07 .20
230 Kevin Jordan .07 .20
231 Mark Thompson .07 .20
232 Jim Dougherty .07 .20
233 Roger Cedeno .07 .20
234 Ugueth Urbina .07 .20
235 Ricky Otero .07 .20
236 Mark Smith .07 .20
237 Brian Barber .07 .20
238 Kevin Flora .07 .20
239 Joe Rosselli .07 .20
240 Derek Jeter .50 1.25
241 Michael Tucker .07 .20
242 Ben Blomdahl .07 .20
243 Joe Vitiello .07 .20
244 Todd Steverson .07 .20
245 James Baldwin .07 .20
246 Alan Embree .07 .20
247 Shannon Penn .07 .20
248 Chris Stynes .07 .20
249 Oscar Munoz .07 .20
250 Jose Herrera .07 .20
251 Scott Sullivan .07 .20
252 Reggie Williams .07 .20
253 Mark Grudzielanek .07 .20
254 Steve Rodriguez .07 .20
255 Terry Bradshaw .07 .20
256 F.P. Santangelo .07 .20
257 Lyle Mouton .07 .20
258 George Williams .07 .20
259 Larry Thomas .07 .20
260 Rudy Pemberton .07 .20
261 Jim Pittsley .07 .20
262 Les Norman .07 .20
263 Ruben Rivera .07 .20
264 Cesar Devarez .07 .20
265 Greg Zaun .07 .20
266 Dustin Hermanson .07 .20
267 John Frascatore .07 .20
268 Joe Randa .07 .20
269 Jeff Bagwell CL .07 .20
270 Mike Piazza CL .20 .50
271 Dante Bichette CL .07 .20
272 Frank Thomas CL .10 .30
273 Ken Griffey Jr. CL .25 .60
274 Cal Ripken CL .30 .75
275 G.Maddux .07 .20
A.Belle CL
276 Greg Maddux .30 .75
277 Pedro Martinez .10 .30
278 Bobby Higginson .07 .20
279 Ray Lankford .07 .20
280 Shawon Dunston .07 .20
281 Gary Sheffield .07 .20
282 Ken Griffey Jr. .40 1.00
283 Paul Molitor .07 .20
284 Kevin Appier .07 .20
285 Chuck Knoblauch .07 .20
286 Alex Fernandez .07 .20
287 Steve Finley .07 .20
288 Jeff Blauser .07 .20
289 Charles Johnson .07 .20
290 John Franco .07 .20
291 Mark Langston .07 .20
292 Bret Saberhagen .07 .20
293 John Mabry .07 .20
294 Ramon Martinez .07 .20
295 Mike Blowers .07 .20
296 Paul O'Neill .10 .30
297 Dave Nilsson .07 .20
298 Dante Bichette .07 .20
299 Marty Cordova .07 .20
300 Jay Bell .07 .20
301 Mike Mussina .10 .30
302 Ivan Rodriguez .10 .30
303 Jose Canseco .10 .30
304 Jeff Bagwell .10 .30
305 Manny Ramirez .10 .30
306 Dennis Martinez .07 .20
307 Charlie Hayes .07 .20
308 Joe Carter .07 .20
309 Travis Fryman .07 .20
310 Mark McGwire .50 1.25
311 Reggie Sanders .07 .20
312 Julian Tavarez .07 .20
313 Jeff Montgomery .07 .20
314 Andy Benes .07 .20
315 John Jaha .07 .20
316 Jeff Kent .07 .20
317 Mike Piazza .30 .75
318 Erik Hanson .07 .20
319 Kenny Rogers .07 .20
320 Hideo Nomo .20 .50
321 Gregg Jefferies .07 .20
322 Chipper Jones .20 .50
323 Jay Buhner .07 .20
324 Dennis Eckersley .07 .20
325 Kenny Lofton .07 .20
326 Robin Ventura .07 .20
327 Tom Glavine .10 .30
328 Tim Salmon .10 .30
329 Andres Galarraga .07 .20
330 Hal Morris .07 .20
331 Brady Anderson .07 .20
332 Chili Davis .07 .20
333 Roger Clemens .40 1.00
334 Marquis Grissom .07 .20
335 Mike Greenwell UER front
reads Jeff Greenwell .07 .20
336 Sammy Sosa .20 .50
337 Ron Gant .07 .20
338 Ken Caminiti .07 .20
339 Danny Tartabull .07 .20
340 Barry Bonds .60 1.50
341 Ben McDonald .07 .20
342 Ruben Sierra .07 .20
343 Bernie Williams .10 .30
344 Wil Cordero .07 .20
345 Wade Boggs .10 .30
346 Gary Gaetti .07 .20
347 Greg Colbrunn .07 .20
348 Juan Gonzalez .07 .20
349 Marc Newfield .07 .20
350 Charles Nagy .07 .20
351 Robby Thompson .07 .20
352 Roberto Petagine .07 .20
353 Darryl Strawberry .07 .20
354 Tino Martinez .10 .30
355 Eric Karros .07 .20
356 Cal Ripken SS .30 .75
357 Cecil Fielder SS .07 .20
358 Kirby Puckett SS .10 .30
359 Jim Edmonds SS .07 .20
360 Matt Williams SS .07 .20
361 Alex Rodriguez SS .20 .50
362 Barry Larkin SS .07 .20
363 Rafael Palmeiro SS .07 .20
364 David Cone SS .07 .20
365 Roberto Alomar SS .07 .20
366 Eddie Murray SS .10 .30
367 Randy Johnson SS .10 .30
368 Ryan Klesko SS .07 .20
369 Raul Mondesi SS .07 .20
370 Mo Vaughn SS .07 .20
371 Will Clark SS .07 .20
372 Carlos Baerga SS .07 .20
373 Frank Thomas SS .10 .30
374 Larry Walker SS .07 .20
375 Garret Anderson SS .07 .20
376 Edgar Martinez SS .07 .20
377 Don Mattingly SS .25 .60
378 Tony Gwynn SS .10 .30
379 Albert Belle SS .07 .20
380 Jason Isringhausen SS .07 .20
381 Ruben Rivera SS .07 .20
382 Johnny Damon SS .07 .20
383 Karim Garcia SS .07 .20
384 Derek Jeter SS .25 .60
385 David Justice SS .07 .20
386 Royce Clayton .07 .20
387 Mark Whiten .07 .20
388 Mickey Tettleton .07 .20
389 Steve Trachsel .07 .20
390 Danny Bautista .07 .20
391 Midre Cummings .07 .20
392 Scott Leius .07 .20
393 Manny Alexander .07 .20
394 Brent Gates .07 .20
395 Rey Sanchez .07 .20
396 Andy Pettitte .10 .30
397 Jeff Cirillo .07 .20
398 Kurt Abbott .07 .20
399 Lee Tinsley .07 .20
400 Paul Assenmacher .07 .20
401 Scott Erickson .07 .20
402 Todd Zeile .07 .20
403 Tom Pagnozzi .07 .20
404 Ozzie Guillen .07 .20
405 Jeff Frye .07 .20
406 Kirt Manwaring .07 .20
407 Chad Ogea .07 .20
408 Harold Baines .07 .20
409 Jason Bere .07 .20
410 Chuck Finley .07 .20
411 Jeff Fassero .07 .20
412 Joey Hamilton .07 .20
413 John Olerud .07 .20
414 Kevin Stocker .07 .20
415 Eric Anthony .07 .20
416 Aaron Sele .07 .20
417 Chris Bosio .07 .20
418 Michael Mimbs .07 .20
419 Orlando Miller .07 .20
420 Stan Javier .07 .20
421 Matt Mieske .07 .20
422 Jason Bates .07 .20
423 Orlando Merced .07 .20
424 John Flaherty .07 .20
425 Reggie Jefferson .07 .20
426 Scott Stahoviak .07 .20
427 John Burkett .07 .20
428 Rod Beck .07 .20
429 Bill Swift .07 .20
430 Scott Cooper .07 .20
431 Mel Rojas .07 .20
432 Todd Van Poppel .07 .20
433 Bobby Jones .07 .20
434 Mike Harkey .07 .20
435 Sean Berry .07 .20
436 Glenallen Hill .07 .20
437 Ryan Thompson .07 .20
438 Luis Alicea .07 .20
439 Esteban Loaiza .07 .20
440 Jeff Reboulet .07 .20
441 Vince Coleman .07 .20
442 Ellis Burks .07 .20
443 Allen Battle .07 .20
444 Jimmy Key .07 .20
445 Ricky Bottalico .07 .20
446 Delino DeShields .07 .20
447 Albie Lopez .07 .20
448 Mark Petkovsek .07 .20
449 Tim Raines .07 .20
450 Bryan Harvey .07 .20
451 Pat Hentgen .07 .20
452 Tim Laker .07 .20
453 Tom Gordon .07 .20
454 Phil Plantier .07 .20
455 Ernie Young .07 .20
456 Pete Harnisch .07 .20
457 Roberto Kelly .07 .20
458 Mark Portugal .07 .20
459 Mark Leiter .07 .20
460 Tony Pena .07 .20
461 Roger Pavlik .07 .20
462 Jeff King .07 .20
463 Bryan Rekar .07 .20
464 Al Leiter .07 .20
465 Phil Nevin .07 .20
466 Jose Lima .07 .20
467 Mike Stanley .07 .20
468 David McCarty .07 .20
469 Herb Perry .07 .20
470 Geronimo Berroa .07 .20
471 David Wells .07 .20
472 Vaughn Eshelman .07 .20
473 Greg Swindell .07 .20
474 Steve Sparks .07 .20
475 Luis Sojo .07 .20
476 Derrick May .07 .20
477 Joe Oliver .07 .20
478 Alex Arias .07 .20
479 Brad Ausmus .07 .20
480 Gabe White .07 .20
481 Pat Rapp .07 .20
482 Damon Buford .07 .20
483 Turk Wendell .07 .20
484 Jeff Brantley .07 .20
485 Curtis Leskanic .07 .20
486 Robb Nen .07 .20
487 Lou Whitaker .07 .20
488 Melido Perez .07 .20
489 Luis Polonia .07 .20
490 Scott Brosius .07 .20
491 Robert Perez .07 .20
492 Mike Sweeney RC .30 .75
493 Mark Loretta .07 .20
494 Alex Ochoa .07 .20
495 Matt Lawton RC .07 .20
496 Shawn Estes .07 .20
497 John Wasdin .07 .20
498 Marc Kroon .07 .20
499 Chris Snopek .07 .20
500 Jeff Suppan .07 .20
501 Terrell Wade .07 .20
502 Marvin Benard RC .07 .20
503 Chris Widger .07 .20
504 Quinton McCracken .07 .20
505 Bob Wolcott .07 .20
506 C.J. Nitkowski .07 .20
507 Aaron Ledesma .07 .20
508 Scott Hatteberg .07 .20
509 Jimmy Haynes .07 .20
510 Howard Battle .07 .20
511 Marty Cordova CL .07 .20
512 Randy Johnson CL .10 .30
513 Mo Vaughn CL .07 .20
514 Hideo Nomo CL .07 .20
515 Greg Maddux CL .20 .50
516 Barry Larkin CL .07 .20
517 Tom Glavine CL .07 .20
2131 Cal Ripken 2131 8.00 20.00

1996 Score All-Stars

COMPLETE SET (20) 25.00 60.00
SER.2 STATED ODDS 1:9 JUMBO
1 Frank Thomas 1.25 3.00
2 Albert Belle .50 1.25
3 Ken Griffey Jr. 2.50 6.00
4 Cal Ripken 4.00 10.00
5 Mo Vaughn .50 1.25
6 Matt Williams .50 1.25
7 Barry Bonds 4.00 10.00
8 Dante Bichette .50 1.25
9 Tony Gwynn 1.50 4.00
10 Greg Maddux 2.00 5.00
11 Randy Johnson 1.25 3.00
12 Hideo Nomo 1.25 3.00
13 Tim Salmon .75 2.00
14 Jeff Bagwell .75 2.00
15 Edgar Martinez .75 2.00
16 Reggie Sanders .50 1.25
17 Larry Walker .50 1.25
18 Chipper Jones 1.25 3.00
19 Manny Ramirez .75 2.00
20 Eddie Murray 1.25 3.00

1996 Score Big Bats

COMPLETE SET (20) 10.00 25.00
SER.1 STATED ODDS 1:31 RETAIL
1 Cal Ripken 3.00 8.00
2 Ken Griffey Jr. 2.00 5.00
3 Frank Thomas 1.00 2.50
4 Jeff Bagwell .60 1.50
5 Mike Piazza 1.00 2.50
6 Barry Bonds 1.50 4.00
7 Matt Williams .40 1.00
8 Raul Mondesi .40 1.00
9 Tony Gwynn 1.00 2.50
10 Albert Belle .40 1.00
11 Manny Ramirez .60 1.50
12 Carlos Baerga .40 1.00
13 Mo Vaughn .40 1.00
14 Derek Bell .40 1.00
15 Larry Walker .60 1.50
16 Kenny Lofton .40 1.00
17 Edgar Martinez .60 1.50
18 Reggie Sanders .40 1.00
19 Eddie Murray .60 1.50
20 Chipper Jones 1.00 2.50

1996 Score Diamond Aces

COMPLETE SET (30) 60.00 120.00
SER.1 STATED ODDS 1:8 JUMBO
1 Hideo Nomo 2.00 5.00
2 Brian L.Hunter .75 2.00
3 Ray Durham .75 2.00
4 Frank Thomas 2.00 5.00
5 Cal Ripken 3.00 8.00
6 Barry Bonds 6.00 15.00
7 Greg Maddux 3.00 8.00
8 Chipper Jones 2.00 5.00
9 Raul Mondesi .75 2.00
10 Mike Piazza 3.00 8.00
11 Derek Jeter 5.00 12.00
12 Bill Pulsipher .75 2.00
13 Larry Walker .75 2.00
14 Ken Griffey Jr. 4.00 10.00
15 Alex Rodriguez 4.00 10.00
16 Manny Ramirez 1.25 3.00
17 Mo Vaughn .75 2.00
18 Reggie Sanders .75 2.00
19 Derek Bell .75 2.00
20 Jim Edmonds .75 2.00
21 Albert Belle .75 2.00
22 Eddie Murray 2.00 5.00
23 Tony Gwynn 2.50 6.00
24 Jeff Bagwell 1.25 3.00
25 Carlos Baerga .75 2.00
26 Matt Williams .75 2.00
27 Garret Anderson .75 2.00
28 Todd Hollandsworth .75 2.00
29 Johnny Damon .75 2.00
30 Tim Salmon 1.25 3.00

1996 Score Dream Team

COMPLETE SET (9) 25.00 60.00
SER.1 STATED ODDS 1:72 HOB/RET
1 Cal Ripken 6.00 15.00
2 Frank Thomas 2.00 5.00
3 Carlos Baerga .75 2.00
4 Matt Williams .75 2.00
5 Mike Piazza 3.00 8.00
6 Barry Bonds 6.00 15.00
7 Ken Griffey Jr. 4.00 10.00

8 Manny Ramirez 1.25 3.00
9 Greg Maddux 3.00 8.00

1996 Score Dugout Collection

COMPLETE SERIES 1 (110) 20.00 50.00
COMPLETE SERIES 2 (110) 20.00 50.00
*DUGOUT: 1.5X TO 4X BASIC
STATED ODDS 1:3 HOB/RET
SUBSET CARDS HALF VALUE OF BASE CARDS
*AP DUGOUT: 10X TO 25X BASIC
AP STATED ODDS 1:36 HOB/RET

1996 Score Dugout Collection Artist's Proofs

*STARS: 2.5X TO 6X BASIC DUGOUT
STATED ODDS 1:36

1996 Score Future Franchise

COMPLETE SET (16) 40.00 100.00
SER.2 STATED ODDS 1:72 HOB/RET
1 Jason Isringhausen 1.50 4.00
2 Chipper Jones 4.00 10.00
3 Derek Jeter 10.00 25.00
4 Alex Rodriguez 8.00 20.00
5 Alex Ochoa 1.50 4.00
6 Manny Ramirez 2.50 6.00
7 Johnny Damon 1.50 4.00
8 Ruben Rivera 1.50 4.00
9 Karim Garcia 1.50 4.00
10 Garret Anderson 1.50 4.00
11 Marty Cordova 1.50 4.00
12 Bill Pulsipher 1.50 4.00
13 Hideo Nomo 4.00 10.00
14 Marc Newfield 1.50 4.00
15 Charles Johnson 1.50 4.00
16 Raul Mondesi 1.50 4.00

1996 Score Gold Stars

COMPLETE SET (30) 20.00 50.00
SER.2 STATED ODDS 1:15 HOB/RET
1 Ken Griffey Jr. 2.00 5.00
2 Frank Thomas 1.00 2.50
3 Reggie Sanders .40 1.00
4 Tim Salmon .60 1.50
5 Mike Piazza 1.50 4.00
6 Tony Gwynn 1.25 3.00
7 Gary Sheffield .40 1.00
8 Matt Williams .40 1.00
9 Bernie Williams .60 1.50
10 Jason Isringhausen .40 1.00
11 Albert Belle .40 1.00
12 Chipper Jones 1.00 2.50
13 Edgar Martinez .60 1.50
14 Barry Larkin .60 1.50
15 Barry Bonds 3.00 8.00
16 Jeff Bagwell .60 1.50
17 Greg Maddux 1.50 4.00
18 Mo Vaughn .40 1.00
19 Ryan Klesko .40 1.00
20 Sammy Sosa 1.00 2.50
21 Darren Daulton .40 1.00
22 Ivan Rodriguez .60 1.50
23 Dante Bichette .40 1.00
24 Hideo Nomo 1.00 2.50
25 Cal Ripken 3.00 8.00
26 Rafael Palmeiro .60 1.50
27 Larry Walker .40 1.00
28 Carlos Baerga .40 1.00
29 Randy Johnson 1.00 2.50
30 Manny Ramirez .60 1.50

1996 Score Numbers Game

COMPLETE SET (30) 25.00 60.00
SER.1 STATED ODDS 1:15 HOB/RET
1 Cal Ripken 3.00 8.00
2 Frank Thomas 1.00 2.50
3 Ken Griffey Jr. 2.00 5.00
4 Mike Piazza 1.00 2.50
5 Barry Bonds 1.50 4.00
6 Greg Maddux 1.50 4.00
7 Jeff Bagwell .60 1.50
8 Derek Bell .40 1.00
9 Tony Gwynn 1.00 2.50
10 Hideo Nomo 1.00 2.50
11 Raul Mondesi .40 1.00
12 Manny Ramirez .60 1.50
13 Albert Belle .40 1.00
14 Matt Williams .40 1.00
15 Jim Edmonds .40 1.00
16 Edgar Martinez .60 1.50
17 Mo Vaughn .40 1.00
18 Reggie Sanders .40 1.00
19 Chipper Jones 1.00 2.50
20 Larry Walker .60 1.50
21 Juan Gonzalez .40 1.00
22 Kenny Lofton .40 1.00
23 Don Mattingly 2.00 5.00
24 Ivan Rodriguez .60 1.50
25 Randy Johnson 1.00 2.50
26 Derek Jeter 2.50 6.00
27 J.T. Snow .40 1.00
28 Will Clark .60 1.50
29 Rafael Palmeiro .60 1.50
30 Alex Rodriguez 1.25 3.00

1996 Score Power Pace

COMPLETE SET (18) 25.00 60.00
SER.2 STATED ODDS 1:31 RETAIL
1 Mark McGwire 4.00 10.00
2 Albert Belle .60 1.50
3 Jay Buhner .60 1.50
4 Frank Thomas 1.50 4.00
5 Matt Williams .60 1.50
6 Gary Sheffield .60 1.50
7 Mike Piazza 2.50 6.00
8 Larry Walker .60 1.50
9 Mo Vaughn .60 1.50
10 Rafael Palmeiro 1.00 2.50
11 Dante Bichette .60 1.50
12 Ken Griffey Jr. 3.00 8.00
13 Barry Bonds 5.00 12.00
14 Manny Ramirez 1.00 2.50
15 Sammy Sosa 1.50 4.00
16 Tim Salmon 1.00 2.50
17 Dave Justice .60 1.50
18 Eric Karros .60 1.50

1996 Score Reflextions

COMPLETE SET (20) 40.00 100.00
SER.1 STATED ODDS 1:15 HOBBY
1 C.Ripken 6.00 15.00
C.Jones
2 K.Griffey Jr. 4.00 10.00
A.Rodriguez
3 F.Thomas 2.00 5.00
M.Vaughn
4 K.Lofton .75 2.00
B.L.Hunter
5 D.Mattingly 5.00 12.00
J.T.Snow
6 M.Ramirez 1.25 3.00
R.Mondesi
7 T.Gwynn 2.50 6.00
G.Anderson
8 R.Alomar 1.25 3.00
C.Baerga
9 A.Dawson .75 2.00
L.Walker
10 D.Jeter 5.00 12.00
B.Larkin
11 B.Bonds 6.00 15.00
R.Sanders
12 M.Piazza 3.00 8.00
A.Belle
13 W.Boggs 1.25 3.00
E.Martinez
14 D.Cone .75 2.00
J.Smoltz
15 J.Bagwell 1.25 3.00
W.Clark
16 M.McGwire 5.00 12.00
C.Fielder
17 G.Maddux 3.00 8.00
M.Mussina
18 H.Nomo 2.00 5.00
R.Johnson
19 J.Thome 1.25 3.00
D.Palmer
20 C.Knoblauch 1.25 3.00
C.Biggio

1996 Score Titanic Taters

COMPLETE SET (18) 30.00 80.00
SER.2 STATED ODDS 1:31 HOBBY
1 Albert Belle .75 2.00
2 Frank Thomas 2.00 5.00
3 Mo Vaughn .75 2.00
4 Ken Griffey Jr. 4.00 10.00
5 Matt Williams .75 2.00
6 Mark McGwire 5.00 12.00
7 Dante Bichette .75 2.00
8 Tim Salmon 1.25 3.00
9 Jeff Bagwell 1.25 3.00
10 Rafael Palmeiro 1.25 3.00
11 Mike Piazza 3.00 8.00
12 Cecil Fielder .75 2.00
13 Larry Walker .75 2.00
14 Sammy Sosa 2.00 5.00
15 Manny Ramirez 1.25 3.00
16 Gary Sheffield .75 2.00
17 Barry Bonds 6.00 15.00
18 Jay Buhner .75 2.00

1997 Score

The 1997 Score set has a total of 550 cards. With cards 1-330 distributed in series one packs and cards 331-550 in series two packs. The 10-card Series one packs and the 12-card Series two packs carried a suggested retail price of $.99 each and were distributed exclusively to retail outlets. The fronts feature color player action photos in a white border. The backs carry player information and career statistics. The Hideki Irabu card (551A and B) is shortprinted (about twice as tough to pull as a basic card). One final note on the Irabu card, in the retail packs and factory sets, the card text is in English. In the Hobby Reserve packs, text is in Japanese. Notable Rookie Cards include Brian Giles.

COMPLETE SET (551) 15.00 40.00
COMP.FACT.SET (551) 15.00 40.00
COMPLETE SERIES 1 (330) 6.00 15.00
COMPLETE SERIES 2 (221) 10.00 25.00
IRABU ENGLISH IN FACT.SET/RETAIL PACKS
1 Jeff Bagwell .12 .30
2 Mickey Tettleton .07 .20
3 Johnny Damon .12 .30
4 Jeff Conine .07 .20
5 Bernie Williams .12 .30
6 Will Clark .12 .30
7 Ryan Klesko .07 .20
8 Cecil Fielder .07 .20
9 Paul Wilson .07 .20
10 Gregg Jefferies .07 .20
11 Chili Davis .07 .20
12 Albert Belle .07 .20
13 Ken Hill .07 .20
14 Cliff Floyd .07 .20
15 Jaime Navarro .07 .20
16 Ismael Valdes .07 .20
17 Jeff King .07 .20
18 Chris Bosio .07 .20
19 Reggie Sanders .07 .20
20 Darren Daulton .07 .20
21 Ken Caminiti .07 .20
22 Mike Piazza .20 .50
23 Chad Mottola .07 .20
24 Darin Erstad .07 .20
25 Dante Bichette .07 .20
26 Frank Thomas .20 .50
27 Ben McDonald .07 .20
28 Raul Casanova .07 .20
29 Kevin Ritz .07 .20
30 Garret Anderson .07 .20
31 Jason Kendall .07 .20
32 Billy Wagner .07 .20
33 Dave Justice .07 .20
34 Marty Cordova .07 .20
35 Derek Jeter .50 1.25
36 Trevor Hoffman .07 .20
37 Geronimo Berroa .07 .20
38 Walt Weiss .07 .20
39 Kirt Manwaring .07 .20
40 Alex Gonzalez .07 .20
41 Sean Berry .07 .20
42 Kevin Appier .07 .20
43 Rusty Greer .07 .20
44 Pete Incaviglia .07 .20
45 Rafael Palmeiro .07 .20
46 Eddie Murray .12 .30
47 Moises Alou .07 .20
48 Mark Lewis .07 .20
49 Hal Morris .07 .20
50 Edgar Renteria .07 .20
51 Rickey Henderson .20 .50
52 Pat Listach .07 .20
53 John Wasdin .07 .20
54 James Baldwin .07 .20
55 Brian Jordan .07 .20
56 Edgar Martinez .12 .30
57 Wil Cordero .07 .20
58 Danny Tartabull .07 .20
59 Keith Lockhart .07 .20
60 Rico Brogna .07 .20
61 Ricky Bottalico .07 .20
62 Terry Pendleton .07 .20
63 Bret Boone .07 .20
64 Charlie Hayes .07 .20
65 Marc Newfield .07 .20
66 Sterling Hitchcock .07 .20
67 Roberto Alomar .12 .30
68 John Jaha .07 .20
69 Greg Colbrunn .07 .20
70 Sal Fasano .07 .20
71 Brooks Kieschnick .07 .20
72 Pedro Martinez .12 .30
73 Kevin Elster .07 .20
74 Ellis Burks .07 .20
75 Chuck Finley .07 .20
76 John Olerud .07 .20
77 Jay Bell .07 .20
78 Allen Watson .07 .20
79 Darryl Strawberry .07 .20
80 Orlando Miller .07 .20
81 Jose Herrera .07 .20
82 Andy Pettitte .12 .30
83 Juan Guzman .07 .20
84 Alan Benes .07 .20
85 Jack McDowell .07 .20
86 Ugueth Urbina .07 .20
87 Rocky Coppinger .07 .20
88 Jeff Cirillo .07 .20
89 Tom Glavine .12 .30
90 Robby Thompson .07 .20
91 Barry Bonds .30 .75
92 Carlos Delgado .07 .20
93 Mo Vaughn .07 .20
94 Ryne Sandberg .30 .75
95 Alex Rodriguez .25 .60
96 Brady Anderson .07 .20
97 Scott Brosius .07 .20
98 Dennis Eckersley .12 .30
99 Brian McRae .07 .20
100 Rey Ordonez .07 .20
101 John Valentin .07 .20
102 Brett Butler .07 .20
103 Eric Karros .07 .20
104 Harold Baines .12 .30
105 Javier Lopez .07 .20
106 Alan Trammell .12 .30
107 Jim Thome .12 .30
108 Frank Rodriguez .07 .20
109 Bernard Gilkey .07 .20
110 Reggie Jefferson .07 .20
111 Scott Stahoviak .07 .20
112 Steve Gibralter .07 .20
113 Todd Hollandsworth .07 .20
114 Ruben Rivera .07 .20
115 Dennis Martinez .07 .20
116 Mariano Rivera .25 .60
117 John Smoltz .12 .30
118 John Mabry .07 .20
119 Tom Gordon .07 .20
120 Alex Ochoa .07 .20
121 Jamey Wright .07 .20
122 Dave Nilsson .07 .20
123 Bobby Bonilla .07 .20
124 Al Leiter .07 .20
125 Rick Aguilera .07 .20
126 Jeff Brantley .07 .20
127 Kevin Brown .07 .20
128 George Arias .07 .20
129 Darren Oliver .07 .20
130 Bill Pulsipher .07 .20
131 Roberto Hernandez .07 .20
132 Delino DeShields .07 .20
133 Mark Grudzielanek .07 .20
134 John Wetteland .07 .20
135 Carlos Baerga .07 .20
136 Paul Sorrento .07 .20
137 Leo Gomez .07 .20
138 Andy Ashby .07 .20
139 Julio Franco .07 .20
140 Brian Hunter .07 .20
141 Jermaine Dye .07 .20
142 Tony Clark .07 .20
143 Ruben Sierra .07 .20
144 Donovan Osborne .07 .20
145 Mark McLemore .07 .20
146 Terry Steinbach .07 .20
147 Bob Wells .07 .20
148 Chan Ho Park .07 .20
149 Tim Salmon .07 .20
150 Paul O'Neill .12 .30
151 Cal Ripken .60 1.50
152 Wally Joyner .07 .20
153 Omar Vizquel .12 .30
154 Mike Mussina .12 .30
155 Andres Galarraga .12 .30
156 Ken Griffey Jr. .40 1.00
157 Kenny Lofton .07 .20
158 Ray Durham .07 .20
159 Hideo Nomo .12 .30
160 Ozzie Guillen .07 .20
161 Roger Pavlik .07 .20
162 Manny Ramirez .12 .30
163 Mark Lemke .07 .20
164 Mike Stanley .07 .20
165 Chuck Knoblauch .07 .20
166 Kimera Bartee .07 .20
167 Wade Boggs .12 .30
168 Jay Buhner .07 .20
169 Eric Young .07 .20
170 Jose Canseco .12 .30
171 Dwight Gooden .07 .20
172 Fred McGriff .12 .30
173 Sandy Alomar Jr. .07 .20
174 Andy Benes .07 .20
175 Dean Palmer .07 .20
176 Larry Walker .12 .30
177 Charles Nagy .07 .20
178 David Cone .07 .20
179 Mark Grace .12 .30
180 Robin Ventura .07 .20
181 Roger Clemens .25 .60
182 Bobby Witt .07 .20
183 Vinny Castilla .07 .20
184 Gary Sheffield .07 .20
185 Dan Wilson .07 .20
186 Roger Cedeno .07 .20
187 Mark McGwire .30 .75
188 Darren Bragg .07 .20
189 Quinton McCracken .07 .20
190 Randy Myers .07 .20
191 Jeromy Burnitz .07 .20
192 Randy Johnson .20 .50
193 Chipper Jones .20 .50
194 Greg Vaughn .07 .20
195 Travis Fryman .07 .20
196 Tim Naehring .07 .20
197 B.J. Surhoff .07 .20
198 Juan Gonzalez .07 .20
199 Terrell Wade .07 .20
200 Jeff Frye .07 .20
201 Joey Cora .07 .20
202 Raul Mondesi .07 .20
203 Ivan Rodriguez .12 .30
204 Armando Reynoso .07 .20
205 Jeffrey Hammonds .07 .20
206 Darren Dreifort .07 .20
207 Kevin Seitzer .07 .20
208 Tino Martinez .12 .30
209 Jim Bruske SP .07 .20
210 Jeff Suppan .07 .20
211 Mark Carreon .07 .20
212 Wilson Alvarez .07 .20
213 John Burkett .07 .20
214 Tony Phillips .07 .20
215 Greg Maddux .30 .75
216 Mark Whiten .07 .20
217 Curtis Pride .07 .20
218 Lyle Mouton .07 .20
219 Todd Hundley .07 .20
220 Greg Gagne .07 .20
221 Rich Amaral .07 .20
222 Tom Goodwin .07 .20
223 Chris Hoiles .07 .20
224 Jayhawk Owens .07 .20
225 Kenny Rogers .07 .20
226 Mike Greenwell .07 .20
227 Mark Wohlers .07 .20
228 Henry Rodriguez .07 .20
229 Robert Perez .07 .20
230 Jeff Kent .07 .20
231 Darryl Hamilton .07 .20
232 Alex Fernandez .07 .20
233 Ron Karkovice .07 .20
234 Jimmy Haynes .07 .20
235 Craig Biggio .12 .30
236 Ray Lankford .07 .20
237 Lance Johnson .07 .20
238 Matt Williams .07 .20
239 Chad Curtis .07 .20
240 Mark Thompson .07 .20
241 Jason Giambi .07 .20
242 Barry Larkin .12 .30
243 Paul Molitor .20 .50
244 Sammy Sosa .12 .30
245 Kevin Tapani .07 .20
246 Marquis Grissom .07 .20
247 Joe Carter .07 .20
248 Ramon Martinez .07 .20
249 Tony Gwynn .20 .50
250 Andy Fox .07 .20
251 Troy O'Leary .07 .20
252 Warren Newson .07 .20
253 Troy Percival .07 .20
254 Jamie Moyer .07 .20
255 Danny Graves .07 .20
256 David Wells .07 .20
257 Todd Zeile .07 .20
258 Raul Ibanez .12 .30
259 Tyler Houston .07 .20
260 LaTroy Hawkins .07 .20
261 Joey Hamilton .07 .20
262 Mike Sweeney .07 .20
263 Brant Brown .07 .20
264 Pat Hentgen .07 .20
265 Mark Johnson .07 .20
266 Robb Nen .07 .20
267 Justin Thompson .07 .20
268 Ron Gant .07 .20
269 Jeff D'Amico .07 .20
270 Shawn Estes .07 .20
271 Derek Bell .07 .20
272 Fernando Valenzuela .07 .20
273 Tom Pagnozzi .07 .20
274 John Burke .07 .20
275 Ed Sprague .07 .20
276 F.P. Santangelo .07 .20
277 Todd Greene .07 .20
278 Butch Huskey .07 .20
279 Steve Finley .07 .20
280 Eric Davis .07 .20
281 Shawn Green .07 .20
282 Al Martin .07 .20
283 Michael Tucker .07 .20
284 Shane Reynolds .07 .20
285 Matt Mieske .07 .20
286 Jose Rosado .07 .20
287 Mark Langston .07 .20
288 Ralph Milliard .07 .20
289 Mike Lansing .07 .20
290 Scott Servais .07 .20
291 Royce Clayton .07 .20
292 Mike Grace .07 .20
293 James Mouton .07 .20
294 Charles Johnson .07 .20
295 Gary Gaetti .07 .20
296 Kevin Mitchell .07 .20
297 Carlos Garcia .07 .20
298 Desi Relaford .07 .20
299 Jason Thompson .07 .20
300 Osvaldo Fernandez .07 .20
301 Fernando Vina .07 .20
302 Jose Offerman .07 .20
303 Yamil Benitez .07 .20
304 J.T. Snow .07 .20
305 Rafael Bournigal .07 .20
306 Jason Isringhausen .07 .20
307 Bobby Higginson .07 .20
308 Nerio Rodriguez RC .07 .20
309 Brian Giles RC .40 1.00
310 Andruw Jones .07 .20
311 Tony Graffanino .07 .20
312 Arquimedez Pozo .07 .20
313 Jermaine Allensworth .07 .20
314 Jeff Darwin .07 .20
315 George Williams .07 .20
316 Karim Garcia .07 .20
317 Trey Beamon .07 .20
318 Mac Suzuki .07 .20
319 Robin Jennings .07 .20
320 Danny Patterson .07 .20
321 Damon Mashore .07 .20
322 Wendell Magee .07 .20
323 Dax Jones .07 .20
324 Todd Walker .07 .20
325 Marvin Benard .07 .20
326 Mike Cameron .07 .20
327 Marcus Jensen .07 .20
328 Eddie Murray CL .12 .30
329 Paul Molitor CL .20 .50
330 Todd Hundley CL .07 .20
331 Norm Charlton .07 .20
332 Bruce Ruffin .07 .20
333 John Wetteland .07 .20
334 Marquis Grissom .07 .20
335 Sterling Hitchcock .07 .20
336 John Olerud .07 .20
337 David Wells .07 .20
338 Chili Davis .07 .20
339 Mark Lewis .07 .20
340 Kenny Lofton .07 .20
341 Alex Fernandez .07 .20
342 Ruben Sierra .07 .20
343 Delino DeShields .07 .20
344 John Wasdin .07 .20
345 Dennis Martinez .07 .20
346 Kevin Elster .07 .20
347 Bobby Bonilla .07 .20
348 Jaime Navarro .07 .20
349 Chad Curtis .07 .20
350 Terry Steinbach .07 .20
351 Ariel Prieto .07 .20
352 Jeff Kent .07 .20
353 Carlos Garcia .07 .20
354 Mark Whiten .07 .20
355 Todd Zeile .07 .20
356 Eric Davis .07 .20
357 Greg Colbrunn .07 .20
358 Moises Alou .07 .20
359 Allen Watson .07 .20
360 Jose Canseco .12 .30
361 Matt Williams .07 .20
362 Jeff King .07 .20
363 Darryl Hamilton .07 .20
364 Mark Clark .07 .20
365 J.T. Snow .07 .20
366 Kevin Mitchell .07 .20
367 Orlando Miller .07 .20
368 Rico Brogna .07 .20
369 Mike James .07 .20
370 Brad Ausmus .07 .20
371 Darryl Kile .07 .20
372 Edgardo Alfonzo .07 .20
373 Julian Tavarez .07 .20
374 Darren Lewis .07 .20
375 Steve Karsay .07 .20
376 Lee Stevens .07 .20
377 Albie Lopez .07 .20
378 Orel Hershiser .07 .20
379 Lee Smith .07 .20
380 Rick Helling .07 .20
381 Carlos Perez .07 .20
382 Tony Tarasco .07 .20
383 Melvin Nieves .07 .20
384 Benji Gil .07 .20
385 Devon White .07 .20
386 Armando Benitez .07 .20
387 Bill Swift .07 .20
388 John Smiley .07 .20
389 Midre Cummings .07 .20
390 Tim Belcher .07 .20
391 Tim Raines .12 .30
392 Todd Worrell .07 .20
393 Quilvio Veras .07 .20
394 Matt Lawton .07 .20
395 Aaron Sele .07 .20
396 Bip Roberts .07 .20
397 Denny Neagle .07 .20
398 Tyler Green .07 .20
399 Hipolito Pichardo .07 .20
400 Scott Erickson .07 .20
401 Bobby Jones .07 .20
402 Jim Edmonds .07 .20
403 Chad Ogea .07 .20
404 Cal Eldred .07 .20
405 Pat Listach .07 .20
406 Todd Stottlemyre .07 .20
407 Phil Nevin .07 .20
408 Otis Nixon .07 .20
409 Billy Ashley .07 .20
410 Jimmy Key .07 .20
411 Mike Timlin .07 .20
412 Joe Vitiello .07 .20
413 Rondell White .07 .20
414 Jeff Fassero .07 .20
415 Rex Hudler .07 .20
416 Curt Schilling .07 .20
417 Rich Becker .07 .20
418 William Van Landingham .07 .20
419 Chris Snopek .07 .20
420 David Segui .07 .20
421 Eddie Murray .12 .30
422 Shane Andrews .07 .20
423 Gary DiSarcina .07 .20
424 Brian Hunter .07 .20
425 Willie Greene .07 .20
426 Felipe Crespo .07 .20
427 Jason Bates .07 .20
428 Albert Belle .07 .20
429 Rey Sanchez .07 .20
430 Roger Clemens .25 .60
431 Deion Sanders .12 .30
432 Ernie Young .07 .20
433 Jay Bell .07 .20
434 Jeff Blauser .07 .20
435 Lenny Dykstra .07 .20
436 Chuck Carr .07 .20
437 Russ Davis .07 .20
438 Carl Everett .07 .20
439 Damion Easley .07 .20
440 Pat Kelly .07 .20
441 Pat Rapp .07 .20
442 Dave Justice .07 .20
443 Graeme Lloyd .07 .20
444 Damon Buford .07 .20
445 Jose Valentin .07 .20
446 Jason Schmidt .07 .20
447 Dave Martinez .07 .20
448 Danny Tartabull .07 .20
449 Jose Vizcaino .07 .20
450 Steve Avery .07 .20
451 Mike Devereaux .07 .20
452 Jim Eisenreich .07 .20
453 Mark Leiter .07 .20
454 Roberto Kelly .07 .20
455 Benito Santiago .07 .20
456 Steve Trachsel .07 .20
457 Gerald Williams .07 .20
458 Pete Schourek .07 .20
459 Esteban Loaiza .07 .20
460 Mel Rojas .07 .20
461 Tim Wakefield .12 .30
462 Tony Fernandez .07 .20
463 Doug Drabek .07 .20
464 Joe Girardi .07 .20
465 Mike Bordick .07 .20
466 Jim Leyritz .07 .20
467 Erik Hanson .07 .20
468 Michael Tucker .07 .20
469 Tony Womack RC .07 .20
470 Doug Glanville .07 .20
471 Rudy Pemberton .07 .20
472 Keith Lockhart .07 .20
473 Nomar Garciaparra .12 .30
474 Scott Rolen .12 .30
475 Jason Dickson .07 .20
476 Glendon Rusch .07 .20
477 Todd Walker .07 .20
478 Dmitri Young .07 .20
479 Rod Myers .07 .20
480 Wilton Guerrero .07 .20
481 Jorge Posada .12 .30
482 Brant Brown .07 .20
483 Bubba Trammell RC .07 .20
484 Jose Guillen .07 .20
485 Scott Spiezio .07 .20
486 Bob Abreu .12 .30
487 Chris Holt .07 .20
488 Deivi Cruz RC .07 .20
489 Vladimir Guerrero .12 .30
490 Julio Santana .07 .20
491 Ray Montgomery RC .07 .20
492 Kevin Orie .07 .20
493 Todd Hundley GY .07 .20
494 Tim Salmon GY .07 .20
495 Albert Belle GY .07 .20
496 Manny Ramirez GY .12 .30
497 Rafael Palmeiro GY .07 .20
498 Juan Gonzalez GY .07 .20
499 Ken Griffey Jr. GY .40 1.00
500 Andruw Jones GY .07 .20
501 Mike Piazza GY .20 .50
502 Jeff Bagwell GY .12 .30
503 Bernie Williams GY .12 .30
504 Barry Bonds GY .30 .75
505 Ken Caminiti GY .07 .20
506 Darin Erstad GY .07 .20
507 Alex Rodriguez GY .25 .60
508 Frank Thomas GY .20 .50
509 Chipper Jones GY .20 .50
510 Mo Vaughn GY .07 .20
511 Mark McGwire GY .30 .75
512 Fred McGriff GY .12 .30
513 Jay Buhner GY .07 .20
515A Gary Sheffield GY .07 .20
515B Jim Thome GY .12 .30
516 Dean Palmer GY .07 .20
517 Henry Rodriguez GY .07 .20
518 Andy Pettitte RF .12 .30
519 Mike Mussina RF .12 .30
520 Greg Maddux RF .30 .75
521 John Smoltz RF .12 .30
522 Hideo Nomo RF .12 .30
523 Troy Percival RF .07 .20
524 John Wetteland RF .07 .20
525 Roger Clemens RF .25 .60
526 Charles Nagy RF .07 .20
527 Mariano Rivera RF .25 .60
528 Tom Glavine RF .12 .30
529 Randy Johnson RF .20 .50
530 Jason Isringhausen RF .07 .20
531 Alex Fernandez RF .07 .20
532 Kevin Brown RF .07 .20
533 Chuck Knoblauch TG .07 .20
534 Rusty Greer TG .07 .20
535 Tony Gwynn TG .20 .50
536 Ryan Klesko TG .07 .20
537 Ryne Sandberg TG .30 .75
538 Barry Larkin TG .12 .30
539 Will Clark TG .12 .30
540 Kenny Lofton TG .07 .20
541 Paul Molitor TG .20 .50
542 Roberto Alomar TG .12 .30
543 Rey Ordonez TG .07 .20
544 Jason Giambi TG .07 .20
545 Derek Jeter TG .50 1.25
546 Cal Ripken TG .60 1.50
547 Ivan Rodriguez TG .12 .30
548 Ken Griffey Jr. CL .40 1.00
549 Frank Thomas CL .20 .50
550 Mike Piazza CL .20 .50
551A Hideki Irabu English SP 1.00 2.50
551B Hideki Irabu Japanese SP 1.00 2.50

1997 Score Artist's Proofs White Border

*STARS: 12.5X TO 30X BASIC CARDS
*ROOKIES: 4X TO 10X BASIC CARDS
RANDOM INSERTS IN RETAIL PACKS

1997 Score Hobby Reserve

*HOBBY RESERVE: .6X TO 1.5X
HR331 Norm Charlton 1.25 3.00
HR332 Bruce Ruffin 1.25 3.00
HR333 John Wetteland 1.25 3.00
HR334 Marquis Grissom 1.25 3.00
HR335 Sterling Hitchcock 1.25 3.00
HR336 John Olerud 1.25 3.00
HR337 David Wells 1.25 3.00
HR338 Chili Davis 1.25 3.00
HR339 Mark Lewis 1.25 3.00
HR340 Kenny Lofton 1.25 3.00
HR341 Alex Fernandez 1.25 3.00
HR342 Ruben Sierra 1.25 3.00
HR343 Delino DeShields 1.25 3.00
HR344 John Wasdin 1.25 3.00
HR345 Dennis Martinez 1.25 3.00
HR346 Kevin Elster 1.25 3.00
HR347 Bobby Bonilla 1.25 3.00
HR348 Jaime Navarro 1.25 3.00
HR349 Chad Curtis 1.25 3.00
HR350 Terry Steinbach 1.25 3.00
HR351 Ariel Prieto 1.25 3.00
HR352 Jeff Kent 1.25 3.00
HR353 Carlos Garcia 1.25 3.00
HR354 Mark Whiten 1.25 3.00
HR355 Todd Zeile 1.25 3.00
HR356 Eric Davis 1.25 3.00
HR357 Greg Colbrunn 1.25 3.00
HR358 Moises Alou 1.25 3.00
HR359 Allen Watson 1.25 3.00
HR360 Jose Canseco 2.00 5.00
HR361 Matt Williams 1.25 3.00
HR362 Jeff King 1.25 3.00
HR363 Darryl Hamilton 1.25 3.00
HR364 Mark Clark 1.25 3.00
HR365 J.T. Snow 1.25 3.00
HR366 Kevin Mitchell 1.25 3.00
HR367 Orlando Miller 1.25 3.00
HR368 Rico Brogna 1.25 3.00
HR369 Mike James 1.25 3.00
HR370 Brad Ausmus 1.25 3.00
HR371 Darryl Kile 1.25 3.00
HR372 Edgardo Alfonzo 1.25 3.00
HR373 Julian Tavarez 1.25 3.00
HR374 Darren Lewis 1.25 3.00
HR375 Steve Karsay 1.25 3.00
HR376 Lee Stevens 1.25 3.00
HR377 Albie Lopez 1.25 3.00
HR378 Orel Hershiser 1.25 3.00
HR379 Lee Smith 1.25 3.00
HR380 Rick Helling 1.25 3.00
HR381 Carlos Perez 1.25 3.00
HR382 Tony Tarasco 1.25 3.00
HR383 Melvin Nieves 1.25 3.00
HR384 Benji Gil 1.25 3.00
HR385 Devon White 1.25 3.00
HR386 Armando Benitez 1.25 3.00
HR387 Bill Swift 1.25 3.00
HR388 John Smiley 1.25 3.00
HR389 Midre Cummings 1.25 3.00
HR390 Tim Belcher 1.25 3.00
HR391 Tim Raines 2.00 5.00
HR392 Todd Worrell 1.25 3.00
HR393 Quilvio Veras 1.25 3.00
HR394 Matt Lawton 1.25 3.00
HR395 Aaron Sele 1.25 3.00
HR396 Bip Roberts 1.25 3.00
HR397 Denny Neagle 1.25 3.00
HR398 Tyler Green 1.25 3.00
HR399 Hipolito Pichardo 1.25 3.00
HR400 Scott Erickson 1.25 3.00
HR401 Bobby Jones 1.25 3.00
HR402 Jim Edmonds 1.25 3.00
HR403 Chad Ogea 1.25 3.00
HR404 Cal Eldred 1.25 3.00
HR405 Pat Listach 1.25 3.00
HR406 Todd Stottlemyre 1.25 3.00
HR407 Phil Nevin 1.25 3.00
HR408 Otis Nixon 1.25 3.00
HR409 Billy Ashley 1.25 3.00
HR410 Jimmy Key 1.25 3.00
HR411 Mike Timlin 1.25 3.00
HR412 Joe Vitiello 1.25 3.00
HR413 Rondell White 1.25 3.00
HR414 Jeff Fassero 1.25 3.00
HR415 Rex Hudler 1.25 3.00
HR416 Curt Schilling 1.25 3.00
HR417 Rich Becker 1.25 3.00
HR418 William Van Landingham 1.25 3.00
HR419 Chris Snopek 1.25 3.00
HR420 David Segui 1.25 3.00
HR421 Eddie Murray 2.00 5.00
HR422 Shane Andrews 1.25 3.00
HR423 Gary DiSarcina 1.25 3.00
HR424 Brian Hunter 1.25 3.00
HR425 Willie Greene 1.25 3.00
HR426 Felipe Crespo 1.25 3.00
HR427 Jason Bates 1.25 3.00
HR428 Albert Belle 1.25 3.00
HR429 Rey Sanchez 1.25 3.00
HR430 Roger Clemens 4.00 10.00
HR431 Deion Sanders 2.00 5.00
HR432 Ernie Young
HR433 Jay Bell 1.25 3.00
HR434 Jeff Blauser 1.25 3.00
HR435 Lenny Dykstra 1.25 3.00
HR436 Chuck Carr 1.25 3.00
HR437 Russ Davis 1.25 3.00
HR438 Carl Everett 1.25 3.00
HR439 Damion Easley 1.25 3.00
HR440 Pat Kelly 1.25 3.00
HR441 Pat Rapp 1.25 3.00
HR442 Dave Justice 1.25 3.00
HR443 Graeme Lloyd 1.25 3.00
HR444 Damon Buford 1.25 3.00
HR445 Jose Valentin 1.25 3.00
HR446 Jason Schmidt 1.25 3.00
HR447 Dave Martinez 1.25 3.00
HR448 Danny Tartabull 1.25 3.00
HR449 Jose Vizcaino 1.25 3.00
HR450 Steve Avery 1.25 3.00
HR451 Mike Devereaux 1.25 3.00
HR452 Jim Eisenreich 1.25 3.00
HR453 Mark Leiter 1.25 3.00
HR454 Roberto Kelly 1.25 3.00
HR455 Benito Santiago 1.25 3.00
HR456 Steve Trachsel 1.25 3.00
HR457 Gerald Williams 1.25 3.00
HR458 Pete Schourek 1.25 3.00
HR459 Esteban Loaiza 1.25 3.00

HR460 Mel Rojas 1.25 3.00
HR461 Tim Wakefield 2.00 5.00
HR462 Tony Fernandez 1.25 3.00
HR463 Doug Drabek 1.25 3.00
HR464 Joe Girardi 1.25 3.00
HR465 Mike Bordick 1.25 3.00
HR466 Jim Leyritz 1.25 3.00
HR467 Erik Hanson 1.25 3.00
HR468 Michael Tucker 1.25 3.00
HR469 Tony Womack 1.25 3.00
HR470 Doug Glanville 1.25 3.00
HR471 Rudy Pemberton 1.25 3.00
HR472 Keith Lockhart 1.25 3.00
HR473 Nomar Garciaparra 2.00 5.00
HR474 Scott Rolen 2.00 5.00
HR475 Jason Dickson 1.25 3.00
HR476 Glendon Rusch 1.25 3.00
HR477 Todd Walker 1.25 3.00
HR478 Dmitri Young 1.25 3.00
HR479 Rod Myers 1.25 3.00
HR480 Wilton Guerrero 1.25 3.00
HR481 Jorge Posada 2.00 5.00
HR482 Brant Brown 1.25 3.00
HR483 Bubba Trammell 1.25 3.00
HR484 Jose Guillen 1.25 3.00
HR485 Scott Spiezio 1.25 3.00
HR486 Bob Abreu 2.00 5.00
HR487 Chris Holt 1.25 3.00
HR488 Deivi Cruz 1.25 3.00
HR489 Vladimir Guerrero 2.00 5.00
HR490 Julio Santana 1.25 3.00
HR491 Ray Montgomery 1.25 3.00
HR492 Kevin Orie 1.25 3.00
HR493 Todd Hundley GY 1.25 3.00
HR494 Tim Salmon GY 1.25 3.00
HR495 Albert Belle GY 1.25 3.00
HR496 Manny Ramirez GY 2.00 5.00
HR497 Rafael Palmeiro GY 1.25 3.00
HR498 Juan Gonzalez GY 1.25 3.00
HR499 Ken Griffey Jr. GY 6.00 15.00
HR500 Andruw Jones GY 1.25 3.00
HR501 Mike Piazza GY 3.00 8.00
HR502 Jeff Bagwell GY 2.00 5.00
HR503 Bernie Williams GY 2.00 5.00
HR504 Barry Bonds GY 5.00 12.00
HR505 Ken Caminiti GY 1.25 3.00
HR506 Darin Erstad GY 1.25 3.00
HR507 Alex Rodriguez GY 4.00 10.00
HR508 Frank Thomas GY 3.00 8.00
HR509 Chipper Jones GY 3.00 8.00
HR510 Mo Vaughn GY 1.25 3.00
HR511 Mark McGwire GY 5.00 12.00
HR512 Fred McGriff GY 2.00 5.00
HR513 Jay Buhner GY 1.25 3.00
HR514 Jim Thome GY 2.00 5.00
HR515 Gary Sheffield GY 1.25 3.00
HR516 Dean Palmer GY 1.25 3.00
HR517 Henry Rodriguez GY 1.25 3.00
HR518 Andy Pettitte RF 2.00 5.00
HR519 Mike Mussina RF 2.00 5.00
HR520 Greg Maddux RF 5.00 12.00
HR521 John Smoltz RF 2.00 5.00
HR522 Hideo Nomo RF 2.00 5.00
HR523 Troy Percival RF 1.25 3.00
HR524 John Wetteland RF 1.25 3.00
HR525 Roger Clemens RF 4.00 10.00
HR526 Charles Nagy RF 1.25 3.00
HR527 Mariano Rivera RF 4.00 10.00
HR528 Tom Glavine RF 2.00 5.00
HR529 Randy Johnson RF 3.00 8.00
HR530 Jason Isringhausen RF 1.25 3.00
HR531 Alex Fernandez RF 1.25 3.00
HR532 Kevin Brown RF 1.25 3.00
HR533 Chuck Knoblauch TG 1.25 3.00
HR534 Rusty Greer TG 1.25 3.00
HR535 Tony Gwynn TG 3.00 8.00
HR536 Ryan Klesko TG 1.25 3.00
HR537 Ryne Sandberg TG 5.00 12.00
HR538 Barry Larkin TG 2.00 5.00
HR539 Will Clark TG 2.00 5.00
HR540 Kenny Lofton TG 1.25 3.00
HR541 Paul Molitor TG 3.00 8.00
HR542 Roberto Alomar TG 2.00 5.00
HR543 Rey Ordonez TG 1.25 3.00
HR544 Jason Giambi TG 1.25 3.00
HR545 Derek Jeter TG 8.00 20.00
HR546 Cal Ripken TG 10.00 25.00
HR547 Ivan Rodriguez TG 2.00 5.00
HR548 Ken Griffey Jr. CL 6.00 15.00
HR549 Frank Thomas CL 3.00 8.00
HR550 Mike Piazza CL 3.00 8.00

1997 Score Premium Stock

COMPLETE SET (330) 30.00 80.00
COMPLETE SERIES 1 (330) 15.00 40.00
*STARS: .75X TO 2X BASIC CARDS
*ROOKIES: .6X TO 1.5X BASIC CARDS
*IRABU: .4X TO 1X BASIC IRABU
PRM.STOCK DIST.ONLY IN HOBBY BOXES
IRABU JAPANESE IN HOBBY RESERVE PACKS

1997 Score Reserve Collection

*STARS: 5X TO 12X BASIC CARDS
*ROOKIES: 2.5X TO 6X BASIC CARDS
*IRABU: 1.5X TO 3X BASIC IRABU
SER.2 ODDS 1:11 HOBBY

1997 Score Showcase Series

*STARS: 3X TO 8X BASIC CARDS
*ROOKIES: 1.5X TO 4X BASIC CARDS
*IRABU: .5X TO 1.2X BASIC IRABU
SER.1 ODDS 1:7 H/R, 1:2 JUM, 1:4 MAG
SER.2 ODDS 1:5 HOBBY, 1:7 RETAIL

1997 Score Showcase Series Artist's Proofs

*STARS: 10X TO 25X BASIC CARDS
*ROOKIES: 4X TO 10X BASIC CARDS
*IRABU: 2X TO 5X BASIC IRABU
SER.1 ODDS 1:35 H/R, 1:7 JUM, 1:17 MAG
SER.2 ODDS 1:23 HOBBY, 1:35 RETAIL

1997 Score All-Star Fanfest

COMPLETE SET (20) 30.00 80.00
1 Frank Thomas 1.50 4.00
2 Jeff Bagwell 2.00 5.00
3 Chuck Knoblauch .75 2.00
4 Ryne Sandberg 2.00 5.00
5 Alex Rodriguez 4.00 10.00
6 Chipper Jones 3.00 8.00
7 Jim Thome 1.25 3.00
8 Ken Caminiti .60 1.50
9 Albert Belle .60 1.50
10 Tony Gwynn 3.00 8.00
11 Ken Griffey Jr. 5.00 12.00
12 Andruw Jones 2.50 6.00
13 Juan Gonzalez 1.25 3.00
14 Brian Jordan .60 1.50
15 Ivan Rodriguez 2.00 5.00
16 Mike Piazza 4.00 10.00
17 Andy Pettitte .75 2.00
18 John Smoltz 1.25 3.00
19 John Wetteland .60 1.50
20 Mark Wohlers .40 1.00

1997 Score Blast Masters

COMPLETE SET (18) 40.00 100.00
SER.2 ODDS 1:35 RETAIL, 1:23 HOBBY
1 Mo Vaughn .75 2.00
2 Mark McGwire 5.00 12.00
3 Juan Gonzalez .75 2.00
4 Albert Belle .75 2.00
5 Barry Bonds 6.00 15.00
6 Ken Griffey Jr. 4.00 10.00
7 Andruw Jones 1.25 3.00
8 Chipper Jones 2.00 5.00
9 Mike Piazza 3.00 8.00
10 Jeff Bagwell 1.25 3.00
11 Dante Bichette .75 2.00
12 Alex Rodriguez 3.00 8.00
13 Gary Sheffield .75 2.00
14 Ken Caminiti .75 2.00
15 Sammy Sosa 2.00 5.00
16 Vladimir Guerrero 2.00 5.00
17 Brian Jordan .75 2.00
18 Tim Salmon 1.25 3.00

1997 Score Franchise

COMPLETE SET (9) 8.00 20.00
SER.1 ODDS 1:72 H/R, 1:17 JUM, 1:35 MAG
*GLOWING: .6X TO 1.5X BASIC
GLOW.SER.1 ODDS 1:240H/R, 1:79J, 1:120M
1 Ken Griffey Jr. 2.00 5.00
2 John Smoltz .60 1.50
3 Cal Ripken 3.00 8.00
4 Chipper Jones 1.00 2.50
5 Mike Piazza 1.00 2.50
6 Albert Belle .40 1.00
7 Frank Thomas 1.00 2.50
8 Sammy Sosa .60 1.50
9 Roberto Alomar .60 1.50

1997 Score Heart of the Order

COMPLETE SET (36) 40.00 100.00
STATED ODDS 1:23 RETAIL, 1:15 HOBBY
1 Will Clark 1.00 2.50
2 Ivan Rodriguez 1.00 2.50
3 Juan Gonzalez .60 1.50
4 Frank Thomas 1.50 4.00
5 Albert Belle .60 1.50
6 Robin Ventura .60 1.50
7 Alex Rodriguez 2.50 6.00
8 Jay Buhner .60 1.50
9 Ken Griffey Jr. 3.00 8.00
10 Rafael Palmeiro 1.00 2.50
11 Roberto Alomar 1.00 2.50
12 Cal Ripken 5.00 12.00
13 Manny Ramirez 1.00 2.50
14 Matt Williams .60 1.50
15 Jim Thome 1.00 2.50
16 Derek Jeter 4.00 10.00
17 Wade Boggs 1.00 2.50
18 Bernie Williams 1.00 2.50
19 Chipper Jones 1.50 4.00
20 Andruw Jones 1.00 2.50
21 Ryan Klesko .60 1.50
22 Mike Piazza 2.50 6.00
23 Wilton Guerrero .60 1.50
24 Raul Mondesi .60 1.50
25 Tony Gwynn 2.00 5.00
26 Greg Vaughn .60 1.50
27 Ken Caminiti .60 1.50
28 Brian Jordan .60 1.50
29 Ron Gant .60 1.50
30 Dmitri Young .60 1.50
31 Darin Erstad .60 1.50
32 Tim Salmon 1.00 2.50
33 Jim Edmonds .60 1.50
34 Chuck Knoblauch .60 1.50
35 Paul Molitor .60 1.50
36 Todd Walker .60 1.50

1997 Score Highlight Zone

COMPLETE SET (18) 75.00 150.00
SER.1 ODDS 1:35 HOBBY, 1:9 JUMBO PS
1 Frank Thomas 2.50 6.00
2 Ken Griffey Jr. 5.00 12.00
3 Mo Vaughn 1.00 2.50
4 Albert Belle 1.00 2.50
5 Mike Piazza 4.00 10.00
6 Barry Bonds 8.00 20.00
7 Greg Maddux 4.00 10.00
8 Sammy Sosa 2.50 6.00
9 Jeff Bagwell 1.50 4.00
10 Alex Rodriguez 4.00 10.00
11 Chipper Jones 2.50 6.00
12 Brady Anderson 1.00 2.50
13 Ozzie Smith 1.00 2.50
14 Edgar Martinez 1.50 4.00
15 Cal Ripken 8.00 20.00
16 Ryan Klesko 1.00 2.50
17 Randy Johnson 2.50 6.00
18 Eddie Murray 2.50 6.00

1997 Score Pitcher Perfect

COMPLETE SET (15) 2.00 5.00
SER.1 ODDS 1:23 H/R,1:11 MAG,1:15 JUM PS
1 Cal Ripken .60 1.50
2 Alex Rodriguez .30 .75
3 A.Rodriguez 1.25 3.00
C.Ripken
4 Edgar Martinez .10 .30
5 Ivan Rodriguez .10 .30
6 Mark McGwire .50 1.25
7 Tim Salmon .10 .30
8 Chili Davis .07 .20
9 Joe Carter .07 .20
10 Frank Thomas .20 .50
11 Will Clark .10 .30
12 Mo Vaughn .07 .20
13 Wade Boggs .10 .30
14 Ken Griffey Jr. .40 1.00
15 Randy Johnson .20 .50

1997 Score Stand and Deliver

COMPLETE SET (24) 125.00 250.00
SER.2 ODDS 1:41 HOBBY, 1:71 RETAIL
1 Andruw Jones 2.50 6.00
2 Greg Maddux 6.00 15.00
3 Chipper Jones 4.00 10.00
4 John Smoltz 2.50 6.00
5 Ken Griffey Jr. 8.00 20.00
6 Alex Rodriguez 6.00 15.00
7 Jay Buhner 1.50 4.00
8 Randy Johnson 4.00 10.00
9 Derek Jeter 10.00 25.00
10 Andy Pettitte 2.50 6.00
11 Bernie Williams 2.50 6.00
12 Mariano Rivera 4.00 10.00
13 Mike Piazza 6.00 15.00
14 Hideo Nomo 4.00 10.00
15 Raul Mondesi 1.50 4.00
16 Todd Hollandsworth 1.50 4.00
17 Manny Ramirez 2.50 6.00
18 Jim Thome 2.50 6.00
19 Dave Justice 1.50 4.00
20 Matt Williams 1.50 4.00
21 Juan Gonzalez W 1.50 4.00
22 Jeff Bagwell W 2.50 6.00
23 Cal Ripken W 12.50 30.00
24 Frank Thomas W 4.00 10.00

1997 Score Stellar Season

COMPLETE SET (18) 25.00 60.00
SER.1 STATED ODDS 1:35 MAGAZINE
1 Juan Gonzalez .60 1.50
2 Chuck Knoblauch .60 1.50
3 Jeff Bagwell 1.00 2.50
4 John Smoltz 1.00 2.50
5 Mark McGwire 4.00 10.00
6 Ken Griffey Jr. 3.00 8.00
7 Frank Thomas 1.50 4.00
8 Alex Rodriguez 2.50 6.00
9 Mike Piazza 2.50 6.00
10 Albert Belle .60 1.50
11 Roberto Alomar 1.00 2.50
12 Sammy Sosa 1.50 4.00
13 Mo Vaughn .60 1.50
14 Brady Anderson .60 1.50
15 Henry Rodriguez .60 1.50
16 Eric Young .60 1.50
17 Gary Sheffield .60 1.50
18 Ryan Klesko .60 1.50

1997 Score Titanic Taters

COMPLETE SET (18) 60.00 120.00
SER.1 STATED ODDS 1:35 RETAIL
1 Mark McGwire 6.00 15.00
2 Mike Piazza 4.00 10.00
3 Ken Griffey Jr. 5.00 12.00
4 Juan Gonzalez 1.00 2.50
5 Frank Thomas 2.50 6.00
6 Albert Belle 1.00 2.50
7 Sammy Sosa 2.50 6.00
8 Jeff Bagwell 1.50 4.00
9 Todd Hundley 1.00 2.50
10 Ryan Klesko 1.00 2.50
11 Brady Anderson 1.00 2.50
12 Mo Vaughn 1.00 2.50
13 Jay Buhner 1.00 2.50
14 Chipper Jones 2.50 6.00
15 Barry Bonds 8.00 20.00
16 Gary Sheffield 1.00 2.50
17 Alex Rodriguez 4.00 10.00
18 Cecil Fielder 1.00 2.50

1997 Score Andruw Jones Blister Pack Special

1 Andruw Jones .75 2.00

1997 Score Jumbos

1 Frank Thomas 2.50 6.00
2 Ken Griffey Jr. 5.00 12.00
3 Cal Ripken 8.00 20.00
4 Chipper Jones 2.50 6.00
5 Mike Piazza 2.50 6.00
6 Juan Gonzalez 1.00 2.50
7 Derek Jeter 6.00 15.00
8 Andruw Jones 1.00 2.50
9 Alex Rodriguez 3.00 8.00

1998 Score Samples

COMPLETE SET (6) 5.00 12.00
10 Alex Rodriguez .75 2.00
24 Mike Piazza 1.00 2.50
34 Ken Griffey Jr. 1.25 3.00
43 Cal Ripken 1.50 4.00
51 Chipper Jones .75 2.00
60 Carlos Delgado .40 1.00

1998 Score

This 270-card set was distributed in 10-card packs exclusively to retail outlets with a suggested retail price of $.99. The fronts feature color player photos in a thin white border. The backs carry player information and statistics. In addition, two unnumbered checklist cards were created. The first card was available only in regular issue packs and provided listings for the standard 270-card set. A blank-backed checklist card was randomly seeded exclusively into All-Star Edition packs (released about three months after the regular packs went live). This checklist card provided listings only for the three insert sets exclusively distributed in All-Star Edition packs (First Pitch, Loaded Lineup and New Season).

COMPLETE SET (270) 15.00 40.00
1 Andruw Jones .10 .30
2 Dan Wilson .07 .20
3 Hideo Nomo .20 .50
4 Chuck Carr .07 .20
5 Barry Bonds .60 1.50
6 Jack McDowell .07 .20
7 Albert Belle .07 .20
8 Francisco Cordova .07 .20
9 Greg Maddux .30 .75
10 Alex Rodriguez .30 .75
11 Steve Avery .07 .20
12 Chuck McElroy .07 .20
13 Larry Walker .07 .20
14 Hideki Irabu .07 .20
15 Roberto Alomar .10 .30
16 Neifi Perez .07 .20
17 Jim Thome .10 .30
18 Rickey Henderson .20 .50
19 Andres Galarraga .07 .20
20 Jeff Fassero .07 .20
21 Kevin Young .07 .20
22 Derek Jeter .50 1.25
23 Andy Benes .07 .20
24 Mike Piazza .30 .75
25 Todd Stottlemyre .07 .20
26 Michael Tucker .07 .20
27 Denny Neagle .07 .20
28 Javier Lopez .07 .20
29 Aaron Sele .07 .20
30 Ryan Klesko .07 .20
31 Dennis Eckersley .07 .20
32 Quinton McCracken .07 .20
33 Brian Anderson .07 .20
34 Ken Griffey Jr. .40 1.00
35 Shawn Estes .07 .20
36 Tim Wakefield .07 .20
37 Jimmy Key .07 .20
38 Jeff Bagwell .10 .30
39 Edgardo Alfonzo .07 .20
40 Mike Cameron .07 .20
41 Mark McGwire .50 1.25
42 Tino Martinez .10 .30
43 Cal Ripken .60 1.50
44 Curtis Goodwin .07 .20
45 Bobby Ayala .07 .20
46 Sandy Alomar Jr. .07 .20
47 Bobby Jones .07 .20
48 Omar Vizquel .10 .30
49 Roger Clemens .40 1.00
50 Tony Gwynn .25 .60
51 Chipper Jones .20 .50
52 Ron Coomer .07 .20
53 Dmitri Young .07 .20
54 Brian Giles .07 .20
55 Steve Finley .07 .20
56 David Cone .07 .20
57 Andy Pettitte .10 .30
58 Wilton Guerrero .07 .20
59 Deion Sanders .10 .30
60 Carlos Delgado .07 .20
61 Jason Giambi .07 .20
62 Ozzie Guillen .07 .20
63 Jay Bell .07 .20
64 Barry Larkin .10 .30
65 Sammy Sosa .20 .50
66 Bernie Williams .10 .30
67 Terry Steinbach .07 .20
68 Scott Rolen .10 .30
69 Melvin Nieves .07 .20
70 Craig Biggio .10 .30
71 Todd Greene .07 .20
72 Greg Gagne .07 .20
73 Shigetoshi Hasegawa .07 .20
74 Mark McLemore .07 .20
75 Darren Bragg .07 .20
76 Brett Butler .07 .20
77 Ron Gant .07 .20
78 Mike Difelice RC .07 .20
79 Charles Nagy .07 .20
80 Scott Hatteberg .07 .20
81 Brady Anderson .07 .20
82 Jay Buhner .07 .20
83 Todd Hollandsworth .07 .20
84 Geronimo Berroa .07 .20
85 Jeff Suppan .07 .20
86 Pedro Martinez .10 .30
87 Roger Cedeno .07 .20
88 Ivan Rodriguez .10 .30
89 Jaime Navarro .07 .20
90 Chris Hoiles .07 .20
91 Nomar Garciaparra .30 .75
92 Rafael Palmeiro .10 .30
93 Darin Erstad .07 .20
94 Kenny Lofton .07 .20
95 Mike Timlin .07 .20
96 Chris Clemons .07 .20
97 Vinny Castilla .07 .20
98 Charlie Hayes .07 .20
99 Lyle Mouton .07 .20
100 Jason Dickson .07 .20
101 Justin Thompson .07 .20
102 Pat Kelly .07 .20
103 Chan Ho Park .07 .20
104 Ray Lankford .07 .20
105 Frank Thomas .20 .50
106 Jermaine Allensworth .07 .20
107 Doug Drabek .07 .20
108 Todd Hundley .07 .20
109 Carl Everett .07 .20
110 Edgar Martinez .10 .30
111 Robin Ventura .07 .20
112 John Wetteland .07 .20
113 Mariano Rivera .20 .50
114 Jose Rosado .07 .20
115 Ken Caminiti .07 .20
116 Paul O'Neill .10 .30
117 Tim Salmon .10 .30
118 Eduardo Perez .07 .20
119 Mike Jackson .07 .20
120 John Smoltz .10 .30
121 Brant Brown .07 .20
122 John Mabry .07 .20
123 Chuck Knoblauch .07 .20
124 Reggie Sanders .07 .20
125 Ken Hill .07 .20
126 Mike Mussina .10 .30
127 Chad Curtis .07 .20
128 Todd Worrell .07 .20
129 Chris Widger .07 .20
130 Damon Mashore .07 .20
131 Kevin Brown .10 .30
132 Bip Roberts .07 .20
133 Tim Naehring .07 .20
134 Dave Martinez .07 .20
135 Jeff Blauser .07 .20
136 David Justice .07 .20
137 Dave Hollins .07 .20
138 Pat Hentgen .07 .20
139 Darren Daulton .07 .20
140 Ramon Martinez .07 .20
141 Raul Casanova .07 .20
142 Tom Glavine .10 .30
143 J.T. Snow .07 .20
144 Tony Graffanino .07 .20
145 Randy Johnson .20 .50
146 Orlando Merced .07 .20
147 Jeff Juden .07 .20
148 Darryl Kile .07 .20
149 Ray Durham .07 .20
150 Alex Fernandez .07 .20
151 Joey Cora .07 .20
152 Royce Clayton .07 .20
153 Randy Myers .07 .20
154 Charles Johnson .07 .20
155 Alan Benes .07 .20
156 Mike Bordick .07 .20
157 Heathcliff Slocumb .07 .20
158 Roger Bailey .07 .20
159 Reggie Jefferson .07 .20
160 Ricky Bottalico .07 .20
161 Scott Erickson .07 .20
162 Matt Williams .07 .20
163 Robb Nen .07 .20
164 Matt Stairs .07 .20
165 Ismael Valdes .07 .20
166 Lee Stevens .07 .20
167 Gary DiSarcina .07 .20
168 Brad Radke .07 .20
169 Mike Lansing .07 .20
170 Armando Benitez .07 .20
171 Mike James .07 .20
172 Russ Davis .07 .20
173 Lance Johnson .07 .20
174 Joey Hamilton .07 .20
175 John Valentin .07 .20
176 David Segui .07 .20
177 David Wells .07 .20
178 Delino DeShields .07 .20
179 Eric Karros .07 .20
180 Jim Leyritz .07 .20
181 Raul Mondesi .07 .20
182 Travis Fryman .07 .20
183 Todd Zeile .07 .20
184 Brian Jordan .07 .20
185 Rey Ordonez .07 .20
186 Jim Edmonds .07 .20
187 Terrell Wade .07 .20
188 Marquis Grissom .07 .20
189 Chris Snopek .07 .20
190 Shane Reynolds .07 .20
191 Jeff Frye .07 .20
192 Paul Sorrento .07 .20
193 James Baldwin .07 .20
194 Brian McRae .07 .20
195 Fred McGriff .10 .30
196 Troy Percival .07 .20
197 Rich Amaral .07 .20
198 Juan Guzman .07 .20
199 Cecil Fielder .07 .20
200 Willie Blair .07 .20
201 Chili Davis .07 .20
202 Gary Gaetti .07 .20
203 B.J. Surhoff .07 .20
204 Steve Cooke .07 .20
205 Chuck Finley .07 .20
206 Jeff Kent .07 .20
207 Ben McDonald .07 .20
208 Jeffrey Hammonds .07 .20
209 Tom Goodwin .07 .20
210 Billy Ashley .07 .20
211 Wil Cordero .07 .20
212 Shawon Dunston .07 .20
213 Tony Phillips .07 .20
214 Jamie Moyer .07 .20
215 John Jaha .07 .20
216 Troy O'Leary .07 .20
217 Brad Ausmus .07 .20
218 Garret Anderson .07 .20
219 Wilson Alvarez .07 .20
220 Kent Mercker .07 .20
221 Wade Boggs .10 .30
222 Mark Wohlers .07 .20
223 Kevin Appier .07 .20
224 Tony Fernandez .07 .20
225 Ugueth Urbina .07 .20
226 Gregg Jefferies .07 .20
227 Mo Vaughn .07 .20
228 Arthur Rhodes .07 .20
229 Jorge Fabregas .07 .20
230 Mark Gardner .07 .20
231 Shane Mack .07 .20
232 Jorge Posada .10 .30
233 Jose Cruz Jr. .07 .20
234 Paul Konerko .07 .20
235 Derrek Lee .10 .30
236 Steve Woodard .07 .20
237 Todd Dunwoody .07 .20
238 Fernando Tatis .07 .20
239 Jacob Cruz .07 .20
240 Pokey Reese .07 .20
241 Mark Kotsay .07 .20
242 Matt Morris .07 .20
243 Antone Williamson .07 .20
244 Ben Grieve .07 .20
245 Ryan McGuire .07 .20
246 Lou Collier .07 .20
247 Shannon Stewart .07 .20
248 Brett Tomko .07 .20
249 Bobby Estalella .07 .20
250 Livan Hernandez .07 .20
251 Todd Helton .10 .30
252 Jaret Wright .07 .20
253 Darryl Hamilton IM .07 .20
254 Stan Javier IM .07 .20
255 Glenallen Hill IM .07 .20
256 Mark Gardner IM .07 .20
257 Cal Ripken IM .30 .75
258 Mike Mussina IM .07 .20
259 Mike Piazza IM .20 .50
260 Sammy Sosa IM .10 .30
261 Todd Hundley IM .07 .20
262 Eric Karros IM .07 .20
263 Denny Neagle IM .07 .20
264 Jeromy Burnitz IM .07 .20
265 Greg Maddux IM .20 .50
266 Tony Clark IM .07 .20
267 Vladimir Guerrero IM .10 .30
268 Cal Ripken CL UER .30 .75
269 Ken Griffey Jr. CL .25 .60
270 Mark McGwire CL .25 .60
NNO Checklist Regular Issue .07 .20
NNO Checklist All-Star Edition .10 .30

1998 Score Showcase Series

*SHOWCASE: 2X TO 5X BASIC CARDS
STATED ODDS 1:7

1998 Score Showcase Series Artist's Proofs

*SHOWCASE AP: 8X TO 20X BASIC CARDS
STATED ODDS 1:35

1998 Score All Score Team

COMPLETE SET (20) 12.00 30.00
STATED ODDS 1:35
1 Mike Piazza 1.00 2.50
2 Ivan Rodriguez .60 1.50
3 Frank Thomas 1.00 2.50
4 Mark McGwire 1.50 4.00
5 Ryne Sandberg 1.50 4.00
6 Roberto Alomar .60 1.50
7 Cal Ripken 3.00 8.00
8 Barry Larkin .60 1.50
9 Paul Molitor 1.00 2.50
10 Travis Fryman .40 1.00
11 Kirby Puckett 1.00 2.50
12 Tony Gwynn 1.00 2.50
13 Ken Griffey Jr. 2.00 5.00
14 Juan Gonzalez .40 1.00
15 Barry Bonds 1.50 4.00
16 Andruw Jones .40 1.00
17 Roger Clemens 1.25 3.00
18 Randy Johnson 1.00 2.50
19 Greg Maddux 1.25 3.00
20 Dennis Eckersley .60 1.50

1998 Score All-Score Team Gold Jones Autograph

1 Andruw Jones Gold AU 10.00 25.00

1998 Score Complete Players

COMPLETE SET (30) 75.00 150.00
STATED ODDS 1:23
THREE CARDS PER PLAYER
ALL 3 VARIETIES SAME PRICE
*GOLD: .4X TO 1X BASIC COMP.PLAY.
GOLD: RANDOM IN SCORE TEAM SETS
1A Ken Griffey Jr. 3.00 8.00
2A Mark McGwire 4.00 10.00
3A Derek Jeter 4.00 10.00
4A Cal Ripken 5.00 12.00
5A Mike Piazza 2.50 6.00
6A Darin Erstad .60 1.50
7A Frank Thomas 1.50 4.00
8A Andruw Jones 1.00 2.50
9A Nomar Garciaparra 2.50 6.00
10A Manny Ramirez 1.50 4.00

1998 Score First Pitch

COMPLETE SET (20) 25.00 60.00
STATED ODDS 1:11 AS EDIT.
1 Ken Griffey Jr. 2.00 5.00
2 Frank Thomas 1.00 2.50
3 Alex Rodriguez 1.50 4.00
4 Cal Ripken 3.00 8.00
5 Chipper Jones 1.00 2.50
6 Juan Gonzalez 1.00 2.50
7 Derek Jeter 2.50 6.00
8 Mike Piazza 1.50 4.00
9 Andruw Jones .60 1.50
10 Nomar Garciaparra 1.50 4.00
11 Barry Bonds 3.00 8.00
12 Jeff Bagwell .60 1.50
13 Scott Rolen .60 1.50
14 Hideo Nomo 1.00 2.50
15 Roger Clemens 2.00 5.00
16 Mark McGwire 2.50 6.00
17 Greg Maddux 1.50 4.00
18 Albert Belle .40 1.00
19 Ivan Rodriguez .60 1.50
20 Mo Vaughn .40 1.00

1998 Score Andruw Jones Icon Order Card

1 Andruw Jones .40 1.00

1998 Score Loaded Lineup

COMPLETE SET (10) 25.00 60.00
STATED ODDS 1:45 AS EDIT.
LL1 Chuck Knoblauch .75 2.00
LL2 Tony Gwynn 2.50 6.00
LL3 Frank Thomas 2.00 5.00
LL4 Ken Griffey Jr. 4.00 10.00
LL5 Mike Piazza 3.00 8.00
LL6 Barry Bonds 6.00 15.00
LL7 Cal Ripken 6.00 15.00
LL8 Paul Molitor 2.00 5.00
LL9 Nomar Garciaparra 3.00 8.00
LL10 Greg Maddux 3.00 8.00

1998 Score New Season

COMPLETE SET (15) 20.00 50.00
STATED ODDS 1:23 AS EDIT.
NS1 Kenny Lofton .75 2.00
NS2 Nomar Garciaparra 2.50 6.00
NS3 Todd Helton 1.00 2.50
NS4 Miguel Tejada 1.25 3.00
NS5 Jaret Wright .60 1.50
NS6 Alex Rodriguez 2.50 6.00
NS7 Vladimir Guerrero 1.25 3.00
NS8 Ken Griffey Jr. 4.00 10.00
NS9 Ben Grieve .60 1.50
NS10 Travis Lee .60 1.50
NS11 Jose Cruz Jr. .60 1.50
NS12 Paul Konerko .75 2.00
NS13 Frank Thomas 1.25 3.00
NS14 Chipper Jones 1.25 3.00
NS15 Cal Ripken 5.00 12.00

1998 Score Rookie Traded

The 1998 Score Rookie and Traded set was issued in one series totalling 270 cards. The 10-card packs retail for $.99 each. The set contains the subset: Spring Training (253-267). Cards numbered one through 50 were inserted one per pack making them short prints compared to the other cards in the set. Paul Konerko signed 500 cards which were also randomly seeded into packs. Notable Rookie Cards include Magglio Ordonez.

COMPLETE SET (270) 15.00 40.00
COMMON SP (1-50) .10 .30
COMMON CARD (51-270) .07 .20
COMMON RC (51-270) .07 .20
KONERKO AU RANDOM INSERT IN PACKS
1 Tony Clark .10 .30
2 Juan Gonzalez .10 .30
3 Frank Thomas .30 .75
4 Greg Maddux .50 1.25
5 Barry Larkin .20 .50
6 Derek Jeter .75 2.00
7 Randy Johnson .30 .75
8 Roger Clemens .60 1.50
9 Tony Gwynn .40 1.00
10 Barry Bonds .75 2.00
11 Jim Edmonds .10 .30
12 Bernie Williams .20 .50
13 Ken Griffey Jr. .60 1.50
14 Tim Salmon .20 .50
15 Mo Vaughn .10 .30
16 David Justice .10 .30
17 Jose Cruz Jr. .10 .30
18 Andruw Jones .20 .50
19 Sammy Sosa .30 .75
20 Jeff Bagwell .20 .50
21 Scott Rolen .20 .50
22 Darin Erstad .10 .30
23 Andy Pettitte .20 .50
24 Mike Mussina .20 .50
25 Mark McGwire .75 2.00
26 Hideo Nomo .30 .75
27 Chipper Jones .30 .75
28 Cal Ripken 1.00 2.50
29 Chuck Knoblauch .10 .30
30 Alex Rodriguez .50 1.25
31 Jim Thome .20 .50
32 Mike Piazza .50 1.25
33 Ivan Rodriguez .20 .50
34 Roberto Alomar .20 .50
35 Nomar Garciaparra .50 1.25
36 Albert Belle .10 .30
37 Vladimir Guerrero .30 .75
38 Raul Mondesi .10 .30
39 Larry Walker .10 .30
40 Manny Ramirez .20 .50
41 Tino Martinez .20 .50
42 Craig Biggio .20 .50
43 Jay Buhner .10 .30
44 Kenny Lofton .10 .30
45 Pedro Martinez .20 .50
46 Edgar Martinez .20 .50
47 Gary Sheffield .10 .30
48 Jose Guillen .10 .30
49 Ken Caminiti .10 .30
50 Bobby Higginson .10 .30
51 Alan Benes .07 .20
52 Shawn Green .07 .20
53 Ron Coomer .07 .20
54 Charles Nagy .07 .20
55 Steve Karsay .07 .20
56 Matt Morris .07 .20
57 Bobby Jones .07 .20
58 Jason Kendall .07 .20
59 Jeff Conine .07 .20
60 Joe Girardi .07 .20
61 Mark Kotsay .07 .20
62 Eric Karros .07 .20
63 Bartolo Colon .07 .20
64 Mariano Rivera .20 .50
65 Alex Gonzalez .07 .20
66 Scott Spiezio .07 .20
67 Luis Castillo .07 .20
68 Joey Cora .07 .20
69 Mark McLemore .07 .20
70 Reggie Jefferson .07 .20
71 Lance Johnson .07 .20
72 Damian Jackson .07 .20
73 Jeff D'Amico .07 .20
74 David Ortiz .30 .75
75 J.T. Snow .07 .20
76 Todd Hundley .07 .20
77 Billy Wagner .07 .20
78 Vinny Castilla .07 .20
79 Ismael Valdes .07 .20
80 Neifi Perez .07 .20
81 Derek Bell .07 .20
82 Ryan Klesko .07 .20
83 Rey Ordonez .07 .20
84 Carlos Garcia .07 .20
85 Curt Schilling .07 .20
86 Robin Ventura .07 .20
87 Pat Hentgen .07 .20
88 Glendon Rusch .07 .20
89 Hideki Irabu .07 .20
90 Antone Williamson .07 .20
91 Denny Neagle .07 .20
92 Kevin Orie .07 .20
93 Reggie Sanders .07 .20
94 Brady Anderson .07 .20
95 Andy Benes .07 .20
96 John Valentin .07 .20
97 Bobby Bonilla .07 .20
98 Walt Weiss .07 .20

99 Robin Jennings .07 .20
100 Marty Cordova .07 .20
101 Brad Ausmus .07 .20
102 Brian Rose .07 .20
103 Calvin Maduro .07 .20
104 Raul Casanova .07 .20
105 Jeff King .07 .20
106 Sandy Alomar Jr. .07 .20
107 Tim Naehring .07 .20
108 Mike Cameron .07 .20
109 Omar Vizquel .10 .30
110 Brad Radke .07 .20
111 Jeff Fassero .07 .20
112 Deivi Cruz .07 .20
113 Dave Hollins .07 .20
114 Dean Palmer .07 .20
115 Esteban Loaiza .07 .20
116 Brian Giles .07 .20
117 Steve Finley .07 .20
118 Jose Canseco .10 .30
119 Al Martin .07 .20
120 Eric Young .07 .20
121 Curtis Goodwin .07 .20
122 Ellis Burks .07 .20
123 Mike Hampton .07 .20
124 Lou Collier .07 .20
125 John Olerud .07 .20
126 Ramon Martinez .07 .20
127 Todd Dunwoody .07 .20
128 Jermaine Allensworth .07 .20
129 Eduardo Perez .07 .20
130 Dante Bichette .07 .20
131 Edgar Renteria .07 .20
132 Bob Abreu .07 .20
133 Rondell White .07 .20
134 Michael Coleman .07 .20
135 Jason Giambi .07 .20
136 Brant Brown .07 .20
137 Michael Tucker .07 .20
138 Dave Nilsson .07 .20
139 Benito Santiago .07 .20
140 Ray Durham .07 .20
141 Jeff Kent .07 .20
142 Matt Stairs .07 .20
143 Kevin Young .07 .20
144 Eric Davis .07 .20
145 John Wetteland .07 .20
146 Esteban Yan RC .10 .30
147 Wilton Guerrero .07 .20
148 Moises Alou .07 .20
149 Edgardo Alfonzo .07 .20
150 Andy Ashby .07 .20
151 Todd Walker .07 .20
152 Jermaine Dye .07 .20
153 Brian Hunter .07 .20
154 Shawn Estes .07 .20
155 Bernard Gilkey .07 .20
156 Tony Womack .07 .20
157 John Smoltz .10 .30
158 Delino DeShields .07 .20
159 Jacob Cruz .07 .20
160 Javier Valentin .07 .20
161 Chris Hoiles .07 .20
162 Garret Anderson .07 .20
163 Dan Wilson .07 .20
164 Paul O'Neill .10 .30
165 Matt Williams .07 .20
166 Travis Fryman .07 .20
167 Javier Lopez .07 .20
168 Ray Lankford .07 .20
169 Bobby Estalella .07 .20
170 Henry Rodriguez .07 .20
171 Quinton McCracken .07 .20
172 Jaret Wright .07 .20
173 Darryl Kile .07 .20
174 Wade Boggs .10 .30
175 Orel Hershiser .07 .20
176 B.J. Surhoff .07 .20
177 Fernando Tatis .07 .20
178 Carlos Delgado .07 .20
179 Jorge Fabregas .07 .20
180 Tony Saunders .07 .20
181 Devon White .07 .20
182 Dmitri Young .07 .20
183 Ryan McGuire .07 .20
184 Mark Bellhorn .07 .20
185 Joe Carter .07 .20
186 Kevin Stocker .07 .20
187 Mike Lansing .07 .20
188 Jason Dickson .07 .20
189 Charles Johnson .07 .20
190 Will Clark .10 .30
191 Shannon Stewart .07 .20
192 Johnny Damon .10 .30
193 Todd Greene .07 .20
194 Carlos Baerga .07 .20
195 David Cone .07 .20
196 Pokey Reese .07 .20
197 Livan Hernandez .07 .20
198 Tom Glavine .10 .30
199 Geronimo Berroa .07 .20
200 Darryl Hamilton .07 .20
201 Terry Steinbach .07 .20
202 Robb Nen .07 .20
203 Ron Gant .07 .20
204 Rafael Palmeiro .10 .30
205 Rickey Henderson .20 .50
206 Justin Thompson .07 .20
207 Jeff Suppan .07 .20
208 Kevin Brown .10 .30
209 Jimmy Key .07 .20
210 Brian Jordan .07 .20
211 Aaron Sele .07 .20
212 Fred McGriff .10 .30
213 Jay Bell .07 .20
214 Andres Galarraga .07 .20
215 Mark Grace .10 .30
216 Brett Tomko .07 .20
217 Francisco Cordova .07 .20
218 Rusty Greer .07 .20
219 Bubba Trammell .07 .20
220 Derrek Lee .10 .30
221 Brian Anderson .07 .20
222 Mark Grudzielanek .07 .20
223 Marquis Grissom .07 .20
224 Gary DiSarcina .07 .20
225 Jim Leyritz .07 .20
226 Jeffrey Hammonds .07 .20
227 Karim Garcia .07 .20
228 Chan Ho Park .07 .20
229 Brooks Kieschnick .07 .20
230 Trey Beamon .07 .20
231 Kevin Appier .07 .20
232 Wally Joyner .07 .20
233 Richie Sexson .07 .20
234 Frank Catalanotto RC .20 .50
235 Rafael Medina .07 .20
236 Travis Lee .07 .20
237 Eli Marrero .07 .20
238 Carl Pavano .07 .20
239 Enrique Wilson .07 .20
240 Richard Hidalgo .07 .20
241 Todd Helton .10 .30
242 Ben Grieve .07 .20
243 Mario Valdez .07 .20
244 Magglio Ordonez RC .60 1.50
245 Juan Encarnacion .07 .20
246 Russell Branyan .07 .20
247 Sean Casey .07 .20
248 Abraham Nunez .07 .20
249 Brad Fullmer .07 .20
250 Paul Konerko .07 .20
251 Miguel Tejada .20 .50
252 Mike Lowell RC .40 1.00
253 Ken Griffey Jr. ST .25 .60
254 Frank Thomas ST .10 .30
255 Alex Rodriguez ST .20 .50
256 Jose Cruz Jr. ST .07 .20
257 Jeff Bagwell ST .07 .20
258 Chipper Jones ST .10 .30
259 Mo Vaughn ST .07 .20
260 Nomar Garciaparra ST .20 .50
261 Jim Thome ST .07 .20
262 Derek Jeter ST .25 .60
263 Mike Piazza ST .20 .50
264 Tony Gwynn ST .10 .30
265 Scott Rolen ST .10 .30
266 Andruw Jones ST .10 .30
267 Cal Ripken ST .30 .75
268 Checklist 1 .07 .20
269 Checklist 2 .07 .20
270 Checklist 3 .07 .20
S250 Paul Konerko AU/500 6.00 15.00

1998 Score Rookie Traded Showcase Series

*SHOWCASE 1-50: 1.25X TO 3X BASIC
*SHOWCASE 51-270: 2X TO 5X BASIC
*SHOWCASE RC'S 51-270: 1.5X TO 4X BASIC
STATED ODDS 1:7

1998 Score Rookie Traded Showcase Series Artist's Proofs

*SHOWCASE AP 1-50: 5X TO 12X BASIC
*SHOWCASE AP 51-270: 8X TO 20X BASIC
*SHOWCASE AP RC'S 51-270: 3X TO 8X BASIC
STATED ODDS 1:35

1998 Score Rookie Traded Showcase Series Artist's Proofs 1 of 1's

RANDOM INSERTS IN HOBBY PACKS
STATED PRINT RUN 1 SET
NO PRICING DUE TO SCARCITY

1998 Score Rookie Traded Complete Players Samples

COMPLETE SET (30) 20.00 50.00
THREE CARDS PER PLAYER
1A Ken Griffey Jr. 2.00 5.00
2A Larry Walker .40 1.00
3A Alex Rodriguez 1.00 2.50
4A Jose Cruz Jr. .20 .50
5A Jeff Bagwell .50 1.25
6A Greg Maddux 1.25 3.00
7A Ivan Rodriguez .50 1.25
8A Roger Clemens 1.00 2.50
9A Chipper Jones 1.00 2.50
10A Hideo Nomo .40 1.00

1998 Score Rookie Traded Complete Players

COMPLETE SET (30) 20.00 50.00
STATED ODDS 1:11
THREE CARDS PER PLAYER
ALL 3 VERSIONS SAME PRICE
1A Ken Griffey Jr. 1.50 4.00
2A Larry Walker .30 .75
3A Alex Rodriguez 1.25 3.00
4A Jose Cruz Jr. .30 .75
5A Jeff Bagwell .50 1.25
6A Greg Maddux 1.25 3.00
7A Ivan Rodriguez .50 1.25
8A Roger Clemens 1.50 4.00
9A Chipper Jones .75 2.00
10A Hideo Nomo .75 2.00

1998 Score Rookie Traded Star Gazing

COMPLETE SET (20) 10.00 25.00
STATED ODDS 1:35
1 Ken Griffey Jr. 1.25 3.00
2 Frank Thomas .60 1.50
3 Chipper Jones .60 1.50
4 Mark McGwire 1.50 4.00
5 Cal Ripken 2.00 5.00
6 Mike Piazza 1.00 2.50
7 Nomar Garciaparra 1.00 2.50
8 Derek Jeter 1.50 4.00
9 Juan Gonzalez .25 .60
10 Vladimir Guerrero .60 1.50
11 Alex Rodriguez 1.00 2.50
12 Tony Gwynn .75 2.00
13 Andruw Jones .40 1.00
14 Scott Rolen .40 1.00
15 Jose Cruz Jr. .25 .60
16 Mo Vaughn .25 .60
17 Bernie Williams .40 1.00
18 Greg Maddux 1.00 2.50
19 Tony Clark .25 .60
20 Ben Grieve .15 .40

2012 Score Hot Rookies Toronto Fall Expo

CRACKED ICE/25: 1.5X TO 4X BASE HI
13 Mike Trout 10.00 25.00
14 Brett Lawrie 2.00 5.00
15 Bryce Harper 5.00 12.00
16 Yu Darvish 4.00 10.00
17 Yoenis Cespedes 3.00 8.00
18 Drew Pomeranz .75 2.00

2018 Score

1 Mike Trout 1.25 3.00
2 Austin Hays RC .40 1.00
3 Amed Rosario RC .30 .75
4 Kris Bryant .30 .75
5 Aaron Judge .60 1.50
6 Bryce Harper .40 1.00
7 Yadier Molina .30 .75
8 Ozzie Albies RC .75 2.00
9 Chance Sisco RC .30 .75
10 Ronald Acuna Jr. RC 8.00 20.00
11 Shohei Ohtani RC 6.00 15.00
12 Rafael Devers RC .75 2.00
13 Nolan Arenado .40 1.00
14 Manny Machado .25 .60
15 J.P. Crawford RC .25 .60
16 Shohei Ohtani RC 6.00 15.00
17 Max Scherzer .25 .60
18 Cody Bellinger .50 1.25
19 Alex Verdugo RC .40 1.00
20 Nick Williams RC .30 .75
21 Jose Altuve .20 .50
22 Giancarlo Stanton .20 .50
23 Rhys Hoskins RC 1.00 2.50
24 Clint Frazier RC .50 1.25
25 Ryan McMahon RC .60 1.50
26 Victor Robles RC .60 1.50
27 Gleyber Torres RC 2.50 6.00
28 Dominic Smith RC .30 .75
29 Walker Buehler RC 1.25 3.00
30 Miguel Andujar RC 1.00 2.50

2019 Score

RANDOM INSERTS IN PACKS
*RED/99: 1.5X TO 4X
*BLUE/50: 2X TO 5X
*PINK/25: 3X TO 8X
1 Kyle Tucker .40 1.00
2 Max Scherzer .25 .60
3 Aaron Judge .60 1.50
4 Pete Alonso RC 3.00 8.00
5 Michael Kopech RC .50 1.25
6 Yusei Kikuchi RC .25 .60
7 Jacob deGrom .50 1.25
8 Mookie Betts .50 1.25
9 Vladimir Guerrero Jr. RC 2.50 6.00
10 Christian Yelich .30 .75
11 Jose Altuve .20 .50
12 Kris Bryant .30 .75
13 Mike Trout 1.25 3.00
14 Bryce Harper .40 1.00
15 Eloy Jimenez RC .60 1.50
16 Fernando Tatis Jr. RC 4.00 10.00
17 Chris Paddack RC .30 .75
18 Cody Bellinger .50 1.25
19 Khris Davis .25 .60
20 Shohei Ohtani .40 1.00

2020 Score

RANDOM INSERTS IN PACKS
1 Yordan Alvarez RC 2.50 6.00
2 Bo Bichette RC 3.00 8.00
3 Aristides Aquino RC .60 1.50
4 Gavin Lux RC 1.25 3.00
5 Luis Robert RC 4.00 10.00
6 Brendan McKay RC .40 1.00
7 Shogo Akiyama RC .40 1.00
8 Yoshitomo Tsutsugo RC .60 1.50
9 Logan Webb RC .40 1.00
10 Deivy Grullon RC .25 .60
11 Ronald Bolanos RC .25 .60
12 Danny Mendick RC .30 .75
13 Kwang-Hyun Kim RC .50 1.25
14 Shun Yamaguchi RC .30 .75
15 Lewis Thorpe RC .25 .60
16 Luis Castillo .20 .50
17 Charlie Morton .25 .60
18 Manny Machado .25 .60
19 Chris Paddack .25 .60
20 Gary Sanchez .25 .60
21 Mike Trout 2.00 5.00
22 Nolan Arenado .40 1.00
23 Ronald Acuna Jr. 1.50 4.00
24 Gerrit Cole .40 1.00
25 Walker Buehler .30 .75
26 Anthony Rendon .25 .60
27 Javier Baez .30 .75
28 Pete Alonso .60 1.50
29 Vladimir Guerrero Jr. .40 1.00
30 Ken Griffey Jr. .50 1.25

2020 Score Signatures

RANDOM INSERTS IN PACKS
PRINT RUNS B/WN 5-99 COPIES PER
NO PRICING QTY 15 OR LESS
EXCHANGE DEADLINE 3/18/2022
1 Yordan Alvarez/50 40.00 100.00
2 Bo Bichette/30 30.00 80.00
3 Aristides Aquino/60 8.00 20.00
5 Luis Robert EXCH/99 75.00 200.00
7 Shogo Akiyama/49 6.00 15.00
8 Yoshitomo Tsutsugo/99 8.00 20.00
9 Logan Webb/96 5.00 12.00
10 Deivy Grullon/99 3.00 8.00
13 Kwang-Hyun Kim/99 6.00 15.00
14 Shun Yamaguchi/99 4.00 10.00
18 Manny Machado/25

1994 Score Board National Promos

COMPLETE SET (20) 20.00 40.00
11 Nolan Ryan 1.50 4.00
20D Nolan Ryan CL 1.25 3.00

1997 Scoreboard Mantle

This 75-card set features color and blue-and-white photos of Baseball great Mickey Mantle and some special events that occurred in his life. Cards numbers 1, 6, 7, 70, and 74 are die cut with special gold foil enhancements. Cards numbers 51-69 are replicas of his 1951-1969 trading cards.

COMPLETE SET (75) 20.00 50.00
COMMON CARD (1-50) .20 .50
COMMON REPLICA CARD .40 1.00
COMMON DIE CUT 1.50 4.00
1 Mickey Mantle Summary of the Legend 1.50 4.00
2 Mickey Mantle Triple Crown 1956 .20 .50
3 Mickey Mantle MVP 1956 .20 .50
4 Mickey Mantle MVP 1957 .20 .50
5 Mickey Mantle MVP 1962 .20 .50
6 Mickey Mantle Uniform #6 1.50 4.00
7 Mickey Mantle Uniform #7 1.50 4.00
8 Mickey Mantle Sparkling Defense .20 .50
9 Mickey Mantle/20-Time All-Star .20 .50
10 Mickey Mantle/4-Time HR Champion .20 .50
11 Mickey Mantle World Series Records .20 .50
12 Mickey Mantle Dirty Dozen .20 .50
13 Mickey Mantle World Champion 1951 .20 .50
14 Mickey Mantle World Champion 1952 .20 .50
15 Mickey Mantle World Champion 1953 .20 .50
16 Mickey Mantle World Champion 1956 .20 .50
17 Mickey Mantle World Champion 1958 .20 .50
18 Mickey Mantle World Champion 1961 .20 .50
19 Mickey Mantle World Champion 1962 .20 .50
20 Mickey Mantle Replacing A Legend .20 .50
21 Mickey Mantle Casey On Mantle .20 .50
22 Mickey Mantle Mickey and the Media .20 .50
23 Mickey Mantle Family Man .20 .50
24 Mickey Mantle Fan Favorite .20 .50
25 Mickey Mantle Playing Injured .20 .50
26 Mickey Mantle Clubhouse Leader .20 .50
27 Mickey Mantle Team Leader .20 .50
28 Mickey Mantle Cleanup Hitter Roger Maris .60 1.50
29 Mickey Mantle Legendary Friendships .20 .50
30 Mickey Mantle Time Out .20 .50
31 Mickey Mantle Mantle Is Born .20 .50
32 Mickey Mantle Mutt Mantle .20 .50
33 Mickey Mantle Growing Up .20 .50
34 Mickey Mantle/5-Tool Player-Arm .20 .50
35 Mickey Mantle/5-Tool Player-Defense .20 .50
36 Mickey Mantle/5-Tool Player-Average .20 .50
37 Mickey Mantle/5-Tool Player-Speed .20 .50
38 Mickey Mantle/5-Tool Player-Power .20 .50
39 Mickey Mantle First Home Run .20 .50
40 Mickey Mantle/100th Home Run .20 .50
41 Mickey Mantle/200th Home Run .20 .50
42 Mickey Mantle/300th Home Run .20 .50
43 Mickey Mantle/400th Home Run .20 .50
44 Mickey Mantle/500th Home Run .20 .50
45 Mickey Mantle/536 Career Home Runs .20 .50
46 Mickey Mantle Yankee Stadium Blasts .20 .50
47 Mickey Mantle Switch-Hit Home Runs .20 .50
48 Mickey Mantle/565-ft. Home Run .20 .50
49 Mickey Mantle Signs 1st Pro Contract .20 .50
50 Mickey Mantle Mickey in the Minors .20 .50
51 Mickey Mantle/1951 Trading Card .40 1.00
52 Mickey Mantle/1952 Trading Card .40 1.00
53 Mickey Mantle/1953 Trading Card .40 1.00
54 Mickey Mantle/1954 Trading Card .40 1.00
55 Mickey Mantle/1955 Trading Card .40 1.00
56A Mickey Mantle/1956 Trading Card Batting left .40 1.00
56B Mickey Mantle/1956 Trading Card/(Batting right) .40 1.00
57 Mickey Mantle/1957 Trading Card .40 1.00
58 Mickey Mantle/1958 Trading Card .40 1.00
59 Mickey Mantle/1959 Trading Card .40 1.00
60 Mickey Mantle/1960 Trading Card .40 1.00
61 Mickey Mantle/1961 Trading Card .40 1.00
62 Mickey Mantle/1962 Trading Card .40 1.00
63 Mickey Mantle/1963 Trading Card .40 1.00
64 Mickey Mantle/1964 Trading Card .40 1.00
65 Mickey Mantle/1965 Trading Card .40 1.00
66 Mickey Mantle/1966 Trading Card .40 1.00
67 Mickey Mantle/1967 Trading Card .40 1.00
68 Mickey Mantle/1968 Trading Card .40 1.00
69 Mickey Mantle/1969 Trading Card .40 1.00
70 Mickey Mantle/#7 Retired by Yankees 1.50 4.00
71 Mickey Mantle Mickey Mantle Day 1965 Bobby Kenne .20 .50
72 Mickey Mantle Mickey Mantle Day 1969 .20 .50
73 Mickey Mantle Life After Baseball .20 .50
74 Mickey Mantle Hall of Fame Induction 1.50 4.00
P1 Mickey Mantle Summary of the Legend .60 1.50
P7 Mickey Mantle Uniform #7 .60 1.50

1997 Scoreboard Mantle 7

The first six cards of this seven-card set were randomly inserted in packs of Mickey Mantle Shoe Box Collection cards at the rate of one in 16 with card number 7 having an insertion rate of one in 320. The complete set could be mailed in for a chance to win a $7,000 Mickey Mantle prepaid phone card or a $700 one. The fronts feature color photos of Mickey Mantle. The backs display the game rules.

COMPLETE SET (7) 30.00 80.00
COMMON CARD (1-7) 3.20 8.00
5 Mickey Mantle/(Head and shoulder view while batti 4.00 10.00
7 Mickey Mantle/(Hand on hip) 20.00 50.00

1998 Scoreboard 23K Collection

These cards, issued in the style of the Bleachers cards, were produced by Scoreboard in their final days as a company in 1998. These cards are produced in 23K and feature photos on the front along with player information on the back. These cards are all credited to the Score Board Inc. but as Scoreboard in the process of declaring bankruptcy during this period, any further information would be greatly appreciated.

1 Reggie Jackson/500 Home Run Club 6.00 15.00
2 Mark McGwire Numbered to 6262 8.00 20.00
3 Mark McGwire Chasing Sixty-One, Numbered to 9861 6.00 15.00
4 Mark McGwire History Breaking in Red, Numbered to 8.00 20.00
5 Mark McGwire History Breaking in Black, Individua 12.50 30.00

1888 Scrapps Die Cuts

These cards are unnumbered; they are ordered below alphabetically within team. The first nine players (1-9) are St. Louis and the second nine (10-18) are Detroit players.

COMPLETE SET (18) 7500.00 15000.00
1 Doc Bushong 500.00 1000.00
2 Bob Caruthers 500.00 1000.00
3 Charles Comiskey 1500.00 3000.00
4 Dave. Foutz 500.00 1000.00
5 Bill Gleason 750.00 1500.00
6 Arlie Latham 600.00 1200.00
7 Tip O'Neill 500.00 1000.00
8 Yank Robinson 500.00 1000.00
9 Curt Welch 600.00 1200.00
10 C.W. Bennett 500.00 1000.00
11 Dan Brouthers 2000.00 4000.00
12 Fred Dunlap 500.00 1000.00
13 Charlie Getzen (sic) 500.00 1000.00
14 Ned Hanlon 1000.00 2000.00
15 Hardie Richardson 500.00 1000.00
16 Jack Rowe 500.00 1000.00
17 Sam Thompson 1500.00 3000.00
18 Deacon White 500.00 1000.00

1946 Sears-East St. Louis PC783

This black and white blank-backed set measures 3 1/2" by 5 3/8" and was issued in 1946 and given away by Sears at their East St. Louis location. The set features players from St. Louis teams. Two poses of John Miller exist. The cards are unnumbered so we have listed them alphabetically. Famed broadcaster Joe Garagiola has an early card in this set.

COMPLETE SET 3000.00 6000.00
1 Buster Adams 40.00 80.00
2 Red Barrett 40.00 80.00
3 Johnny Beazley 40.00 80.00
4 Johnny Berardino 60.00 120.00
5 Frank Biscan 40.00 80.00
6 Al Brazle 40.00 80.00
7 Harry Breechen 50.00 100.00
8 Ken Burkhardt 40.00 80.00
9 Jerry Burmeister 40.00 80.00
10 Mark Christman 40.00 80.00
11 Joffre Cross 40.00 80.00
12 Babe Dahlgren 50.00 100.00
13 Murray Dickson 40.00 80.00
14 Bob Dillinger 50.00 100.00
15 George Duckins 40.00 80.00
16 Blix Donnelly 40.00 80.00
17 Erv Dusak 40.00 80.00
18 Eddie Dyer MG 40.00 80.00
19 Bill Endicott 40.00 80.00
20 Stanley Ferens 40.00 80.00
21 Denny Galehouse 40.00 80.00
22 Joe Garagiola 100.00 200.00
23 Mike Gonzales CO 40.00 80.00
24 Joe Grace 40.00 80.00
25 Jeff Heath 40.00 80.00
26 Henry Helf 40.00 80.00
27 Fred Hoffman 40.00 80.00
28 Walt Judnich 40.00 80.00
29 Ellis Kinder 40.00 80.00
30 Lou Klein 40.00 80.00
31 Clyde Kluttz 40.00 80.00
32 Jack Kramer 40.00 80.00
33 Howard Krist 40.00 80.00
34 Whitey Kurowski 50.00 100.00
35 Chet Laabs 40.00 80.00
36 Al LaMacchia 40.00 80.00
37 John Lucadello 40.00 80.00
38 Frank Mancuso 40.00 80.00
39 Marty Marion 60.00 120.00
40 Fred Martin 40.00 80.00
41 George McQuillen 40.00 80.00
42 John Miller (2) 40.00 80.00
43 Al Milnar 40.00 80.00
44 Terry Moore 60.00 120.00
45 Bob Muncrief 40.00 80.00
46 Stan Musial 1000.00 2000.00
47 Ken O'Dea 40.00 80.00
48 Howie Pollet 40.00 80.00
49 Nelson Potter 40.00 80.00
50 Del Rice 40.00 80.00
51 Len Schulte 40.00 80.00
52 Red Schoendienst 75.00 150.00
53 Ken Sears 40.00 80.00
54 Walt Sessi 40.00 80.00
55 Luke Sewell MG 50.00 100.00
56 Joe Schultz 40.00 80.00
57 Tex Shirley 40.00 80.00
58 Dick Sisler 40.00 80.00
59 Enos Slaughter 75.00 150.00
60 Vern Stephens 60.00 120.00
61 Chuck Stevens 40.00 80.00
62 Max Surkont 40.00 80.00
63 Zack Taylor MG 40.00 80.00
64 Harry Walker 50.00 100.00
65 Buzzy Wares 40.00 80.00
66 Ernie White 40.00 80.00
67 Ted Wilks 40.00 80.00
68 Al Zarilla 40.00 80.00
69 Sam Zoldak 40.00 80.00

1993 Seaver Chemical Bank

This one card standard-size set was issued by Chemical Bank and featured their spokesman Tom Seaver. Seaver is natily attired in a business suit holding a baseball on the front while the back has complete career statistics.

1 Tom Seaver 2.00 5.00

1993 Select Samples

COMPLETE SET (8) 10.00 25.00
22 Robin Yount 2.50 6.00
24 Don Mattingly 4.00 10.00
26 Sandy Alomar Jr. .75 2.00
41 Gary Sheffield 2.50 6.00
56 Brady Anderson .75 2.00
65 Rob Dibble .75 2.00
75 John Smiley .40 1.00
79 Mitch Williams .40 1.00

1993 Select

Seeking a niche in the premium, mid-price market, Score produced a new 405-card standard-size set entitled Select in 1993. The set includes regular players, rookies, and draft picks, and was sold in 15-card hobby and retail packs and 28-card super packs. Subset cards include Draft Picks and Rookies, both sprinkled throughout the latter part of the set. Rookie Cards in this set include Derek Jeter, Jason Kendall and Shannon Stewart.

COMPLETE SET (405) 12.50 30.00
1 Barry Bonds .60 1.50
2 Ken Griffey Jr. .40 1.00
3 Will Clark .10 .30
4 Kirby Puckett .20 .50
5 Tony Gwynn .25 .60
6 Frank Thomas .20 .50
7 Tom Glavine .10 .30
8 Roberto Alomar .10 .30
9 Andre Dawson .07 .20
10 Ron Darling .05 .15
11 Bobby Bonilla .07 .20
12 Danny Tartabull .05 .15
13 Darren Daulton .07 .20
14 Roger Clemens .40 1.00
15 Ozzie Smith .30 .75
16 Mark McGwire .50 1.25
17 Terry Pendleton .07 .20
18 Cal Ripken .60 1.50
19 Fred McGriff .10 .30
20 Cecil Fielder .07 .20
21 Darryl Strawberry .07 .20
22 Robin Yount .30 .75
23 Barry Larkin .10 .30
24 Don Mattingly .50 1.25
25 Craig Biggio .10 .30
26 Sandy Alomar Jr. .05 .15
27 Larry Walker .07 .20
28 Junior Felix .05 .15
29 Eddie Murray .20 .50
30 Robin Ventura .07 .20
31 Greg Maddux .30 .75
32 Dave Winfield .07 .20
33 John Kruk .07 .20
34 Wally Joyner .07 .20
35 Andy Van Slyke .10 .30
36 Chuck Knoblauch .07 .20
37 Tom Pagnozzi .05 .15
38 Dennis Eckersley .07 .20
39 David Justice .07 .20
40 Juan Gonzalez .07 .20
41 Gary Sheffield .07 .20
42 Paul Molitor .07 .20
43 Delino DeShields .05 .15
44 Travis Fryman .07 .20
45 Hal Morris .05 .15
46 Greg Olson .05 .15
47 Ken Caminiti .07 .20
48 Wade Boggs .10 .30
49 Orel Hershiser .07 .20
50 Albert Belle .07 .20
51 Bill Swift .05 .15
52 Mark Langston .05 .15
53 Joe Girardi .05 .15
54 Keith Miller .05 .15
55 Gary Carter .07 .20
56 Brady Anderson .07 .20
57 Dwight Gooden .07 .20
58 Julio Franco .07 .20
59 Lenny Dykstra .07 .20
60 Mickey Tettleton .05 .15
61 Randy Tomlin .05 .15
62 B.J. Surhoff .07 .20
63 Todd Zeile .05 .15
64 Roberto Kelly .05 .15
65 Rob Dibble .07 .20
66 Leo Gomez .05 .15
67 Doug Jones .05 .15
68 Ellis Burks .07 .20
69 Mike Scioscia .05 .15
70 Charles Nagy .05 .15
71 Cory Snyder .05 .15
72 Devon White .07 .20
73 Mark Grace .10 .30
74 Luis Polonia .05 .15
75 John Smiley 2X .05 .15
76 Carlton Fisk .10 .30
77 Luis Sojo .05 .15
78 George Brett .50 1.25
79 Mitch Williams .05 .15
80 Kent Hrbek .07 .20
81 Jay Bell .07 .20
82 Edgar Martinez .10 .30
83 Lee Smith .07 .20
84 Deion Sanders .10 .30
85 Bill Gullickson .05 .15
86 Paul O'Neill .10 .30
87 Kevin Seitzer .05 .15
88 Steve Finley .07 .20
89 Mel Hall .05 .15
90 Nolan Ryan .75 2.00
91 Eric Davis .07 .20
92 Mike Mussina .10 .30
93 Tony Fernandez .05 .15
94 Frank Viola .07 .20
95 Matt Williams .07 .20
96 Joe Carter .07 .20
97 Ryne Sandberg .30 .75
98 Jim Abbott .10 .30
99 Marquis Grissom .07 .20
100 George Bell .05 .15
101 Howard Johnson .05 .15
102 Kevin Appier .07 .20
103 Dale Murphy .10 .30
104 Shane Mack .05 .15
105 Jose Lind .05 .15
106 Rickey Henderson .20 .50
107 Bob Tewksbury .05 .15
108 Kevin Mitchell .05 .15
109 Steve Avery .05 .15
110 Candy Maldonado .05 .15
111 Bip Roberts .05 .15
112 Lou Whitaker .07 .20
113 Jeff Bagwell .10 .30
114 Dante Bichette .07 .20
115 Brett Butler .07 .20
116 Melido Perez .05 .15
117 Andy Benes .05 .15
118 Randy Johnson .20 .50
119 Willie McGee .07 .20
120 Jody Reed .05 .15
121 Shawon Dunston .05 .15
122 Carlos Baerga .05 .15
123 Bret Saberhagen .07 .20
124 John Olerud .07 .20
125 Ivan Calderon .05 .15
126 Bryan Harvey .05 .15
127 Terry Mulholland .05 .15
128 Ozzie Guillen .07 .20
129 Steve Buechele .05 .15
130 Kevin Tapani .05 .15
131 Felix Jose .05 .15
132 Terry Steinbach .05 .15
133 Ron Gant .07 .20
134 Harold Reynolds .07 .20
135 Chris Sabo .05 .15
136 Ivan Rodriguez .10 .30
137 Eric Anthony .05 .15
138 Mike Henneman .05 .15
139 Robby Thompson .05 .15
140 Scott Fletcher .05 .15
141 Bruce Hurst .05 .15
142 Kevin Maas .05 .15
143 Tom Candiotti .05 .15
144 Chris Hoiles .05 .15
145 Mike Morgan .05 .15
146 Mark Whiten .05 .15
147 Dennis Martinez .07 .20
148 Tony Pena .05 .15
149 Dave Magadan .05 .15
150 Mark Lewis .05 .15
151 Mariano Duncan .05 .15
152 Gregg Jefferies .05 .15
153 Doug Drabek .05 .15
154 Brian Harper .05 .15
155 Ray Lankford .07 .20
156 Carney Lansford .07 .20
157 Mike Sharperson .05 .15
158 Jack Morris .07 .20
159 Otis Nixon .05 .15
160 Steve Sax .05 .15
161 Mark Lemke .05 .15
162 Rafael Palmeiro .10 .30
163 Jose Rijo .05 .15
164 Omar Vizquel .10 .30
165 Sammy Sosa .20 .50
166 Milt Cuyler .05 .15
167 John Franco .07 .20
168 Darryl Hamilton .05 .15
169 Ken Hill .05 .15
170 Mike Devereaux .05 .15
171 Don Slaught .05 .15
172 Steve Farr .05 .15
173 Bernard Gilkey .05 .15
174 Mike Fetters .05 .15
175 Vince Coleman .05 .15
176 Kevin McReynolds .05 .15
177 John Smoltz .10 .30
178 Greg Gagne .05 .15
179 Greg Swindell .05 .15
180 Juan Guzman .05 .15
181 Kal Daniels .05 .15
182 Rick Sutcliffe .07 .20
183 Orlando Merced .05 .15
184 Bill Wegman .05 .15
185 Mark Gardner .05 .15
186 Rob Deer .05 .15
187 Dave Hollins .05 .15
188 Jack Clark .07 .20
189 Brian Hunter .05 .15
190 Tim Wallach .05 .15
191 Tim Belcher .05 .15
192 Walt Weiss .05 .15
193 Kurt Stillwell .05 .15
194 Charlie Hayes .05 .15
195 Willie Randolph .07 .20
196 Jack McDowell .05 .15
197 Jose Offerman .05 .15
198 Chuck Finley .07 .20
199 Darrin Jackson .05 .15
200 Kelly Gruber .05 .15
201 John Wetteland .07 .20
202 Jay Buhner .07 .20
203 Mike LaValliere .05 .15
204 Kevin Brown .07 .20
205 Luis Gonzalez .07 .20
206 Rick Aguilera .05 .15
207 Norm Charlton .05 .15
208 Mike Bordick .05 .15
209 Charlie Leibrandt .05 .15
210 Tom Brunansky .05 .15
211 Tom Henke .05 .15
212 Randy Milligan .05 .15
213 Ramon Martinez .05 .15
214 Mo Vaughn .07 .20

215 Randy Myers .05 .15
216 Greg Hibbard .05 .15
217 Wes Chamberlain .05 .15
218 Tony Phillips .05 .15
219 Pete Harnisch .05 .15
220 Mike Gallego .05 .15
221 Bud Black .05 .15
222 Greg Vaughn .05 .15
223 Milt Thompson .05 .15
224 Ben McDonald .05 .15
225 Billy Hatcher .05 .15
226 Paul Sorrento .05 .15
227 Mark Gubicza .05 .15
228 Mike Greenwell .05 .15
229 Curt Schilling .07 .20
230 Alan Trammell .07 .20
231 Zane Smith .05 .15
232 Bobby Thigpen .05 .15
233 Greg Olson .05 .15
234 Joe Orsulak .05 .15
235 Joe Oliver .05 .15
236 Tim Raines .07 .20
237 Juan Samuel .05 .15
238 Chili Davis .07 .20
239 Spike Owen .05 .15
240 Dave Stewart .07 .20
241 Jim Eisenreich .05 .15
242 Phil Plantier .05 .15
243 Sid Fernandez .05 .15
244 Dan Gladden .05 .15
245 Mickey Morandini .05 .15
246 Tino Martinez .10 .30
247 Kirt Manwaring .05 .15
248 Dean Palmer .07 .20
249 Tom Browning .05 .15
250 Brian McRae .05 .15
251 Scott Leius .05 .15
252 Bert Blyleven .07 .20
253 Scott Erickson .05 .15
254 Bob Welch .05 .15
255 Pat Kelly .05 .15
256 Felix Fermin .05 .15
257 Harold Baines .07 .20
258 Duane Ward .05 .15
259 Bill Spiers .05 .15
260 Jaime Navarro .05 .15
261 Scott Sanderson .05 .15
262 Gary Gaetti .07 .20
263 Bob Ojeda .05 .15
264 Jeff Montgomery .05 .15
265 Scott Bankhead .05 .15
266 Lance Johnson .05 .15
267 Rafael Belliard .05 .15
268 Kevin Reimer .05 .15
269 Benito Santiago .07 .20
270 Mike Moore .05 .15
271 Dave Fleming .05 .15
272 Moises Alou .07 .20
273 Pat Listach .05 .15
274 Reggie Sanders .07 .20
275 Kenny Lofton .07 .20
276 Donovan Osborne .05 .15
277 Rusty Meacham .05 .15
278 Eric Karros .07 .20
279 Andy Stankiewicz .05 .15
280 Brian Jordan .07 .20
281 Gary DiSarcina .05 .15
282 Mark Wohlers .05 .15
283 Dave Nilsson .05 .15
284 Anthony Young .05 .15
285 Jim Bullinger .05 .15
286 Derek Bell .05 .15
287 Brian Williams .05 .15
288 Julio Valera .05 .15
289 Dan Walters .05 .15
290 Chad Curtis .05 .15
291 Michael Tucker .05 .15
292 Bob Zupcic .05 .15
293 Todd Hundley .05 .15
294 Jeff Tackett .05 .15
295 Greg Colbrunn .05 .15
296 Cal Eldred .05 .15
297 Chris Roberts .05 .15
298 John Doherty .05 .15
299 Denny Neagle .07 .20
300 Arthur Rhodes .05 .15
301 Mark Clark .05 .15
302 Scott Cooper .05 .15
303 Jamie Arnold RC .05 .15
304 Jim Thome .10 .30
305 Frank Seminara .05 .15
306 Kurt Knudsen .05 .15
307 Tim Wakefield .20 .50
308 John Jaha .05 .15
309 Pat Hentgen .05 .15
310 B.J.Wallace .05 .15
311 Roberto Hernandez .05 .15
312 Hipolito Pichardo .05 .15
313 Eric Fox .05 .15
314 Willie Banks .05 .15
315 Sam Militello .05 .15
316 Vince Horsman .05 .15
317 Carlos Hernandez .05 .15
318 Jeff Kent .20 .50
319 Mike Perez .05 .15
320 Scott Livingstone .05 .15
321 Jeff Conine .07 .20
322 Jim Austin .05 .15
323 John Vander Wal .05 .15
324 Pat Mahomes .05 .15
325 Pedro Astacio .05 .15
326 Bret Boone UER .07 .20
327 Matt Stairs .05 .15
328 Damion Easley .05 .15
329 Ben Rivera .05 .15
330 Reggie Jefferson .05 .15
331 Luis Mercedes .05 .15
332 Kyle Abbott .05 .15
333 Eddie Taubensee .05 .15
334 Tim McIntosh .05 .15
335 Phil Clark .05 .15
336 Wil Cordero .05 .15
337 Russ Springer .05 .15
338 Craig Colbert .05 .15
339 Tim Salmon .10 .30
340 Braulio Castillo .05 .15
341 Donald Harris .05 .15
342 Eric Young .05 .15
343 Bob Wickman .05 .15
344 John Valentin .05 .15
345 Dan Wilson .07 .20
346 Steve Hosey .05 .15
347 Mike Piazza 1.25 3.00
348 Willie Greene .05 .15
349 Tom Goodwin .05 .15
350 Eric Hillman .05 .15
351 Steve Reed RC .05 .15
352 Dan Serafini RC .05 .15
353 Todd Steverson RC .05 .15
354 Benji Grigsby RC .05 .15
355 Shannon Stewart RC .30 .75
356 Sean Lowe RC .05 .15
357 Derek Wallace RC .05 .15
358 Rick Helling .05 .15
359 Jason Kendall RC .40 1.00
360 Derek Jeter RC 8.00 20.00
361 David Cone .07 .20
362 Jeff Reardon .07 .20
363 Bobby Witt .05 .15
364 Jose Canseco .10 .30
365 Jeff Russell .05 .15
366 Ruben Sierra .07 .20
367 Alan Mills .05 .15
368 Matt Nokes .05 .15
369 Pat Borders .05 .15
370 Pedro Munoz .05 .15
371 Danny Jackson .05 .15
372 Geronimo Pena .05 .15
373 Craig Lefferts .05 .15
374 Joe Grahe .05 .15
375 Roger McDowell .05 .15
376 Jimmy Key .07 .20
377 Steve Olin .05 .15
378 Glenn Davis .05 .15
379 Rene Gonzales .05 .15
380 Manuel Lee .05 .15
381 Ron Karkovice .05 .15
382 Sid Bream .05 .15
383 Gerald Williams .05 .15
384 Lenny Harris .05 .15
385 J.T.Snow RC .20 .50
386 Dave Stieb .05 .15
387 Kirk McCaskill .05 .15
388 Lance Parrish .07 .20
389 Craig Grebeck .05 .15
390 Rick Wilkins .05 .15
391 Manny Alexander .05 .15
392 Mike Schooler .05 .15
393 Bernie Williams .10 .30
394 Kevin Koslofski .05 .15
395 Willie Wilson .05 .15
396 Jeff Parrett .05 .15
397 Mike Harkey .05 .15
398 Frank Tanana .05 .15
399 Doug Henry .05 .15
400 Royce Clayton .05 .15
401 Eric Wedge RC .08 .25
402 Derrick May .05 .15
403 Carlos Garcia .05 .15
404 Henry Rodriguez .05 .15
405 Ryan Klesko .07 .20

1993 Select Aces

COMPLETE SET (24) 12.00 30.00
STATED ODDS 1:4 JUMBO
1 Roger Clemens 3.00 8.00
2 Tom Glavine 1.00 2.50
3 Jack McDowell .50 1.25
4 Greg Maddux 2.50 6.00
5 Jack Morris .60 1.50
6 Dennis Martinez .60 1.50
7 Kevin Brown .60 1.50
8 Dwight Gooden .60 1.50
9 Kevin Appier .60 1.50
10 Mike Morgan .50 1.25
11 Juan Guzman .50 1.25
12 Charles Nagy .50 1.25
13 John Smiley .50 1.25
14 Ken Hill .50 1.25
15 Bob Tewksbury .50 1.25
16 Doug Drabek .50 1.25
17 John Smoltz 1.00 2.50
18 Greg Swindell .50 1.25
19 Bruce Hurst .50 1.25
20 Mike Mussina 1.00 2.50
21 Cal Eldred .50 1.25
22 Melido Perez .50 1.25
23 Dave Fleming .50 1.25
24 Kevin Tapani .50 1.25

1993 Select Chase Rookies

COMPLETE SET (21) 20.00 50.00
STATED ODDS 1:18 HOBBY
1 Pat Listach 1.00 2.50
2 Moises Alou 2.00 5.00
3 Reggie Sanders 2.00 5.00
4 Kenny Lofton 2.00 5.00
5 Eric Karros 2.00 5.00
6 Brian Williams 1.00 2.50
7 Donovan Osborne 1.00 2.50
8 Sam Militello 1.00 2.50
9 Chad Curtis 1.00 2.50
10 Bob Zupcic 1.00 2.50
11 Tim Salmon 3.00 8.00
12 Jeff Conine 2.00 5.00
13 Pedro Astacio 1.00 2.50
14 Arthur Rhodes 1.00 2.50
15 Cal Eldred 1.00 2.50
16 Tim Wakefield 4.00 10.00
17 Andy Stankiewicz 1.00 2.50
18 Wil Cordero 1.00 2.50
19 Todd Hundley 1.00 2.50
20 Dave Fleming 1.00 2.50
21 Bret Boone 2.00 5.00

1993 Select Chase Stars

COMPLETE SET (24) 40.00 100.00
STATED ODDS 1:18 RETAIL
1 Fred McGriff 1.50 4.00
2 Ryne Sandberg 4.00 10.00
3 Ozzie Smith 4.00 10.00
4 Gary Sheffield 1.00 2.50
5 Darren Daulton 1.00 2.50
6 Andy Van Slyke 1.50 4.00
7 Barry Bonds 8.00 20.00
8 Tony Gwynn 3.00 8.00
9 Greg Maddux 4.00 10.00
10 Tom Glavine 1.50 4.00
11 John Franco 1.00 2.50
12 Lee Smith 1.00 2.50
13 Cecil Fielder 1.00 2.50
14 Roberto Alomar 1.50 4.00
15 Cal Ripken 8.00 20.00
16 Edgar Martinez 1.50 4.00
17 Ivan Rodriguez 1.50 4.00
18 Kirby Puckett 2.50 6.00
19 Ken Griffey Jr. 5.00 12.00
20 Joe Carter 1.00 2.50
21 Roger Clemens 5.00 12.00
22 Dave Fleming .75 2.00
23 Paul Molitor 1.00 2.50
24 Dennis Eckersley 1.00 2.50

1993 Select Stat Leaders

COMPLETE SET (90) 3.00 8.00
ONE PER SCORE PACK
1 Edgar Martinez .07 .20
2 Kirby Puckett .10 .30
3 Frank Thomas .10 .30
4 Gary Sheffield .02 .10
5 Andy Van Slyke .07 .20
6 John Kruk .02 .10
7 Kirby Puckett .10 .30
8 Carlos Baerga .02 .10
9 Paul Molitor .02 .10
10 T.Pendleton .02 .10
A.Van Slyke
11 Ryne Sandberg .20 .50
12 Mark Grace .07 .20
13 F.Thomas .10 .30
E.Martinez
14 D.Mattingly .30 .75
Yount
15 Ken Griffey Jr. .25 .60
16 Andy Van Slyke .07 .20
17 Duncan .02 .10
Clark
Lankford
18 M.Grissom .02 .10
T.Pendleton
19 Lance Johnson .02 .10
20 Mike Devereaux .02 .10
21 Brady Anderson .02 .10
22 Deion Sanders .07 .20
23 Steve Finley .02 .10
24 Andy Van Slyke .07 .20
25 Juan Gonzalez .02 .10
26 Mark McGwire .30 .75
27 Cecil Fielder .02 .10
28 Fred McGriff .07 .20
29 Barry Bonds .40 1.00
30 Gary Sheffield .02 .10
31 Cecil Fielder .02 .10
32 Joe Carter .02 .10
33 Frank Thomas .10 .30
34 Darren Daulton .02 .10
35 Terry Pendleton .02 .10
36 Fred McGriff .07 .20
37 Tony Phillips .02 .10
38 Frank Thomas .10 .30
39 Roberto Alomar .07 .20
40 Barry Bonds .40 1.00
41 Dave Hollins .02 .10
42 Andy Van Slyke .07 .20
43 Mark McGwire .30 .75
44 Edgar Martinez .07 .20
45 Frank Thomas .10 .30
46 Barry Bonds .40 1.00
47 Gary Sheffield .02 .10
48 Fred McGriff .07 .20
49 Frank Thomas .10 .30
50 Danny Tartabull .02 .10
51 Roberto Alomar .07 .20
52 Barry Bonds .40 1.00
53 John Kruk .02 .10
54 Brett Butler .02 .10
55 Kenny Lofton .02 .10
56 Pat Listach .02 .10
57 Brady Anderson .02 .10
58 Marquis Grissom .02 .10
59 Delino DeShields .02 .10
60 B.Roberts .02 .10
S.Finley
61 Jack McDowell .02 .10
62 K.Brown .25 .60
R.Clemens
63 C.Nagy .02 .10
M.Perez
64 Terry Mulholland .02 .10
65 C.Schilling .02 .10
D.Drabek
66 G.Maddux .20 .50
J.Smoltz
67 Dennis Eckersley .02 .10
68 Rick Aguilera .02 .10
69 Jeff Montgomery .02 .10
70 Lee Smith .02 .10
71 Randy Myers .02 .10
72 John Wetteland .02 .10
73 Randy Johnson .10 .30
74 Melido Perez .02 .10
75 Roger Clemens .25 .60
76 John Smoltz .07 .20
77 David Cone .02 .10
78 Greg Maddux .20 .50
79 Roger Clemens .25 .60
80 Kevin Appier .02 .10
81 Mike Mussina .07 .20
82 Bill Swift .02 .10
83 Bob Tewksbury .02 .10
84 Greg Maddux .20 .50
85 J.Morris .02 .10
K.Brown
86 Jack McDowell .02 .10
87 R.Clemens .25 .60
M.Mussina
88 T.Glavine .20 .50
G.Maddux
89 K.Hill .02 .10
B.Tewksbury
90 M.Morgan .02 .10
D.Martinez

1993 Select Triple Crow

COMPLETE SET (3) 20.00 50.00
RANDOM INSERTS IN HOBBY PACKS
1 Mickey Mantle 15.00 40.00
2 Frank Robinson 4.00 10.00
3 Carl Yastrzemski 4.00 10.00

1993 Select Rookie/Traded

These 150 standard-size cards feature rookies and traded veteran players. The production run comprised 1,950 individually numbered cases. Cards were distributed in foil packs. Card design is similar to the regular 1993 Select cards excpt for the dramatic royal blue borders (instead of emerald green for the regular cards) and T-suffixed numbering. There are no key Rookie Cards in this set. Two Rookie of the Year insert cards and a Nolan Ryan Tribute card were randomly inserted in the foil packs. The chances of finding a Nolan Ryan card was listed at not less than one per 288 packs. The two ROY cards, featuring American League Rookie of the Year, Tim Salmon and National League Rookie of the Year, Mike Piazza were randomly inserted into one in every 576 packs.

COMPLETE SET (150) 6.00 15.00
COMMON CARD (1T-150T) .15 .40
COMMON RC .15 .40
RYAN TRIBUTE STATED ODDS 1:288
ROY STATED ODDS 1:576
1T Rickey Henderson .60 1.50
2T Rob Deer .15 .40
3T Tim Belcher .15 .40
4T Gary Sheffield .25 .60
5T Fred McGriff .40 1.00
6T Mark Whiten .15 .40
7T Jeff Russell .15 .40
8T Harold Baines .25 .60
9T Dave Winfield .25 .60
10T Ellis Burks .25 .60
11T Andre Dawson .25 .60
12T Gregg Jefferies .15 .40
13T Jimmy Key .25 .60
14T Harold Reynolds .25 .60
15T Tom Henke .15 .40
16T Paul Molitor .25 .60
17T Wade Boggs .40 1.00
18T David Cone .25 .60
19T Tony Fernandez .15 .40
20T Roberto Kelly .15 .40
21T Paul O'Neill .40 1.00
22T Jose Lind .15 .40
23T Barry Bonds 1.50 4.00
24T Dave Stewart .25 .60
25T Randy Myers .15 .40
26T Benito Santiago .25 .60
27T Tim Wallach .15 .40
28T Greg Gagne .15 .40
29T Kevin Mitchell .15 .40
30T Jim Abbott .40 1.00
31T Lee Smith .25 .60
32T Bobby Munoz .15 .40
33T Mo Sanford .15 .40
34T John Roper .15 .40
35T David Hulse RC .15 .40
36T Pedro Martinez 1.25 3.00
37T Chuck Carr .15 .40
38T Armando Reynoso .15 .40
39T Ryan Thompson .15 .40
40T Carlos Garcia .15 .40
41T Matt Whiteside RC .15 .40
42T Benji Gil .15 .40
43T Rodney Bolton .15 .40
44T J.T.Snow .40 1.00
45T David McCarty .15 .40
46T Paul Quantrill .15 .40
47T Al Martin .15 .40
48T Lance Painter RC .15 .40
49T Lou Frazier RC .15 .40
50T Eduardo Perez .15 .40
51T Kevin Young .25 .60
52T Mike Trombley .15 .40
53T Sterling Hitchcock RC .25 .60
54T Tim Bogar RC .15 .40
55T Hilly Hathaway RC .15 .40
56T Wayne Kirby .15 .40
57T Craig Paquette .15 .40
58T Bret Boone .25 .60
59T Greg McMichael RC .15 .40
60T Mike Lansing RC .25 .60
61T Brent Gates .15 .40
62T Rene Arocha RC .25 .60
63T Ricky Gutierrez .15 .40
64T Kevin Rogers .15 .40
65T Ken Ryan RC .15 .40
66T Phil Hiatt .15 .40
67T Pat Meares RC .25 .60
68T Troy Neel .15 .40
69T Steve Cooke .15 .40
70T Sherman Obando RC .15 .40
71T Blas Minor .15 .40
72T Angel Miranda .15 .40
73T Tom Kramer RC .15 .40
74T Chip Hale .15 .40
75T Brad Pennington .15 .40
76T Graeme Lloyd RC .25 .60
77T Darrell Whitmore RC .15 .40
78T David Nied .15 .40
79T Todd Van Poppel .15 .40
80T Chris Gomez RC .25 .60
81T Jason Bere .15 .40
82T Jeffrey Hammonds .15 .40
83T Brad Ausmus .60 1.50
84T Kevin Stocker .15 .40
85T Jeromy Burnitz .25 .60
86T Aaron Sele .15 .40
87T Roberto Mejia RC .15 .40
88T Kirk Rueter RC .25 .60
89T Kevin Roberson RC .15 .40
90T Allen Watson .15 .40
91T Charlie Leibrandt .15 .40
92T Eric Davis .25 .60
93T Jody Reed .15 .40
94T Danny Jackson .15 .40
95T Gary Gaetti .25 .60
96T Norm Charlton .15 .40
97T Doug Drabek .15 .40
98T Scott Fletcher .15 .40
99T Greg Swindell .15 .40
100T John Smiley .15 .40
101T Kevin Reimer .15 .40
102T Andres Galarraga .25 .60
103T Greg Hibbard .15 .40
104T Chris Hammond .15 .40
105T Darnell Coles .15 .40
106T Mike Felder .15 .40
107T Jose Guzman .15 .40
108T Chris Bosio .15 .40
109T Spike Owen .15 .40
110T Felix Jose .15 .40
111T Cory Snyder .15 .40
112T Craig Lefferts .15 .40
113T David Wells .25 .60
114T Pete Incaviglia .15 .40
115T Mike Pagliarulo .15 .40
116T Dave Magadan .15 .40
117T Charlie Hough .25 .60
118T Ivan Calderon .15 .40
119T Manuel Lee .15 .40
120T Bob Patterson .15 .40
121T Bob Ojeda .15 .40
122T Scott Bankhead .15 .40
123T Greg Maddux 1.00 2.50
124T Chili Davis .25 .60
125T Milt Thompson .15 .40
126T Dave Martinez .15 .40
127T Frank Tanana .15 .40
128T Phil Plantier .15 .40
129T Juan Samuel .15 .40
130T Eric Young .15 .40
131T Joe Orsulak .15 .40
132T Derek Bell .15 .40
133T Darrin Jackson .15 .40
134T Tom Brunansky .15 .40
135T Jeff Reardon .25 .60
136T Kevin Higgins .15 .40
137T Joel Johnston .15 .40
138T Rick Trlicek .15 .40
139T Richie Lewis RC .15 .40
140T Jeff Gardner .15 .40
141T Jack Voigt RC .15 .40
142T Rod Correja RC .15 .40
143T Billy Brewer .15 .40
144T Terry Jorgensen .15 .40
145T Rich Amaral .15 .40
146T Sean Berry .15 .40
147T Dan Peltier .15 .40
148T Paul Wagner .15 .40
149T Damon Buford .15 .40
150T Wil Cordero .15 .40
NR1 Nolan Ryan Tribute 10.00 25.00
ROY1 Tim Salmon AL ROY 2.00 5.00
ROY2 Mike Piazza NL ROY 15.00 40.00

1993 Select Rookie/Traded All-Star Rookies

COMPLETE SET (10) 40.00 100.00
STATED ODDS 1:58
1 Jeff Conine 4.00 10.00
2 Brent Gates 2.00 5.00
3 Mike Lansing 4.00 10.00
4 Kevin Stocker 2.00 5.00
5 Mike Piazza 15.00 40.00
6 Jeffrey Hammonds 2.00 5.00
7 David Hulse 2.00 5.00
8 Tim Salmon 4.00 10.00
9 Rene Arocha 4.00 10.00
10 Greg McMichael 2.00 5.00

1994 Select Samples

COMPLETE SET (9) 3.00 8.00
3 Paul Molitor .75 2.00
17 Kirby Puckett .75 2.00
19 Randy Johnson .75 2.00
24 John Kruk .20 .50
51 Jose Lind .08 .25
197 Ryan Klesko/94 Rookie Prospect .20 .50
CC1 Lenny Dykstra .60 1.50
Crown Contenders
RS1 Cliff Floyd .60 1.50
Rookie Surge '94
NNO Title Card .08 .25

1994 Select

Measuring the standard size, the 1994 Select set consists of 420 cards that were issued in two series of 210. The horizontal fronts feature a color player action photo and a duo-tone player shot. The backs are vertical and contain a photo, 1993 and career statistics and highlights. Special Dave Winfield and Cal Ripken cards were inserted in first series packs. A Paul Molitor MVP card and a Carlos Delgado Rookie of the Year card were inserted in second series packs. The insertion rate for each card was one in 360 packs. Rookie Cards include Chan Ho Park.

COMPLETE SET (420) 10.00 25.00
COMPLETE SERIES 1 (210) 6.00 15.00
COMPLETE SERIES 2 (210) 4.00 10.00
SER.1 SALUTE STATED ODDS 1:360
SER.2 MVP/ROY STATED ODDS 1:360
1 Ken Griffey Jr. .60 1.50
2 Greg Maddux .50 1.25
3 Paul Molitor .10 .30
4 Mike Piazza .60 1.50
5 Jay Bell .10 .30
6 Frank Thomas .30 .75
7 Barry Larkin .20 .50
8 Paul O'Neill .20 .50
9 Darren Daulton .10 .30
10 Mike Greenwell .05 .15
11 Chuck Carr .05 .15
12 Joe Carter .10 .30
13 Lance Johnson .05 .15
14 Jeff Blauser .05 .15
15 Chris Hoiles .05 .15
16 Rick Wilkins .05 .15
17 Kirby Puckett .30 .75
18 Larry Walker .10 .30
19 Randy Johnson .30 .75
20 Bernard Gilkey .05 .15
21 Devon White .10 .30
22 Randy Myers .05 .15
23 Don Mattingly .75 2.00
24 John Kruk .10 .30
25 Ozzie Guillen .10 .30
26 Jeff Conine .10 .30
27 Mike Macfarlane .05 .15
28 Dave Hollins .05 .15
29 Chuck Knoblauch .10 .30
30 Ozzie Smith .50 1.25
31 Harold Baines .10 .30
32 Ryne Sandberg .50 1.25
33 Ron Karkovice .05 .15
34 Terry Pendleton .10 .30
35 Wally Joyner .10 .30
36 Mike Mussina .20 .50
37 Felix Jose .05 .15
38 Derrick May .05 .15
39 Scott Cooper .05 .15
40 Jose Rijo .05 .15
41 Robin Ventura .10 .30
42 Charlie Hayes .05 .15
43 Jimmy Key .10 .30
44 Eric Karros .10 .30
45 Ruben Sierra .10 .30
46 Ryan Thompson .05 .15
47 Brian McRae .05 .15
48 Pat Hentgen .05 .15
49 John Valentin .05 .15
50 Al Martin .05 .15
51 Jose Lind .05 .15
52 Kevin Stocker .05 .15
53 Mike Gallego .05 .15
54 Dwight Gooden .10 .30
55 Brady Anderson .10 .30
56 Jeff King .05 .15
57 Mark McGwire .75 2.00
58 Sammy Sosa .30 .75
59 Ryan Bowen .05 .15
60 Mark Lemke .05 .15
61 Roger Clemens .60 1.50
62 Brian Jordan .10 .30
63 Andres Galarraga .10 .30
64 Kevin Appier .10 .30
65 Don Slaught .05 .15
66 Mike Blowers .05 .15
67 Wes Chamberlain .05 .15
68 Troy Neel .05 .15
69 John Wetteland .10 .30
70 Joe Girardi .05 .15
71 Reggie Sanders .10 .30
72 Edgar Martinez .20 .50
73 Todd Hundley .05 .15
74 Pat Borders .05 .15
75 Roberto Mejia .05 .15
76 David Cone .10 .30
77 Tony Gwynn .40 1.00
78 Jim Abbott .20 .50
79 Jay Buhner .10 .30
80 Mark McLemore .05 .15
81 Wil Cordero .05 .15
82 Pedro Astacio .05 .15
83 Bob Tewksbury .05 .15
84 Dave Winfield .10 .30
85 Jeff Kent .20 .50
86 Todd Van Poppel .05 .15
87 Steve Avery .05 .15
88 Mike Lansing .05 .15
89 Lenny Dykstra .10 .30
90 Jose Guzman .05 .15
91 Brian R. Hunter .05 .15
92 Tim Raines .10 .30
93 Andre Dawson .10 .30
94 Joe Orsulak .05 .15
95 Ricky Jordan .05 .15
96 Billy Hatcher .05 .15
97 Jack McDowell .05 .15
98 Tom Pagnozzi .05 .15
99 Darryl Strawberry .10 .30
100 Mike Stanley .05 .15
101 Bret Saberhagen .10 .30
102 Willie Greene .05 .15
103 Bryan Harvey .05 .15
104 Tim Bogar .05 .15
105 Jack Voigt .05 .15
106 Brad Ausmus .20 .50
107 Ramon Martinez .05 .15
108 Mike Perez .05 .15
109 Jeff Montgomery .05 .15
110 Danny Darwin .05 .15
111 Wilson Alvarez .05 .15
112 Kevin Mitchell .05 .15
113 David Nied .05 .15
114 Rich Amaral .05 .15
115 Stan Javier .05 .15
116 Mo Vaughn .10 .30
117 Ben McDonald .05 .15
118 Tom Gordon .05 .15
119 Carlos Garcia .05 .15
120 Phil Plantier .05 .15
121 Mike Morgan .05 .15
122 Pat Meares .05 .15
123 Kevin Young .05 .15
124 Jeff Fassero .05 .15
125 Gene Harris .05 .15
126 Bob Welch .05 .15
127 Walt Weiss .05 .15
128 Bobby Witt .05 .15
129 Andy Van Slyke .20 .50
130 Steve Cooke .05 .15
131 Mike Devereaux .05 .15
132 Joey Cora .05 .15
133 Bret Barberie .05 .15
134 Orel Hershiser .10 .30
135 Ed Sprague .05 .15
136 Shawon Dunston .05 .15
137 Alex Arias .05 .15
138 Archi Cianfrocco .05 .15
139 Tim Wallach .05 .15
140 Bernie Williams .20 .50
141 Karl Rhodes .05 .15
142 Pat Kelly .05 .15
143 Dave Magadan .05 .15
144 Kevin Tapani .05 .15
145 Eric Young .05 .15
146 Derek Bell .05 .15
147 Dante Bichette .10 .30
148 Geronimo Pena .05 .15
149 Joe Oliver .05 .15
150 Orestes Destrade .05 .15
151 Tim Naehring .05 .15
152 Ray Lankford .10 .30
153 Phil Clark .05 .15
154 David McCarty .05 .15
155 Tommy Greene .05 .15
156 Wade Boggs .20 .50
157 Kevin Gross .05 .15
158 Hal Morris .05 .15
159 Moises Alou .10 .30
160 Rick Aguilera .05 .15
161 Curt Schilling .10 .30
162 Chip Hale .05 .15
163 Tino Martinez .20 .50
164 Mark Whiten .05 .15
165 Dave Stewart .10 .30
166 Steve Buechele .05 .15
167 Bobby Jones .05 .15
168 Darrin Fletcher .05 .15
169 John Smiley .05 .15
170 Cory Snyder .05 .15
171 Scott Erickson .05 .15
172 Kirk Rueter .05 .15
173 Dave Fleming .05 .15
174 John Smoltz .20 .50
175 Ricky Gutierrez .05 .15
176 Mike Bordick .05 .15
177 Chan Ho Park RC .20 .50
178 Alex Gonzalez .05 .15
179 Steve Karsay .05 .15
180 Jeffrey Hammonds .05 .15
181 Manny Ramirez .30 .75
182 Salomon Torres .05 .15
183 Raul Mondesi .10 .30
184 James Mouton .05 .15
185 Cliff Floyd .10 .30
186 Danny Bautista .05 .15
187 Kurt Abbott RC .05 .15
188 Javier Lopez .10 .30
189 John Patterson .05 .15
190 Greg Blosser .05 .15
191 Bob Hamelin .05 .15
192 Tony Eusebio .05 .15
193 Carlos Delgado .20 .50
194 Chris Gomez .05 .15
195 Kelly Stinnett RC .10 .30
196 Shane Reynolds .05 .15
197 Ryan Klesko .10 .30
198 Jim Edmonds .30 .75
199 James Hurst RC .05 .15
200 Dave Staton .05 .15
201 Rondell White .10 .30
202 Keith Mitchell .05 .15
203 Matt Walbeck .05 .15
204 Mike Matheny RC .25 .60
205 Chris Turner .05 .15
206 Matt Mieske .05 .15
207 NL Team Checklist .05 .15
208 NL Team Checklist .05 .15
209 AL Team Checklist .05 .15
210 AL Team Checklist .05 .15
211 Barry Bonds .75 2.00
212 Juan Gonzalez .10 .30
213 Jim Eisenreich .05 .15
214 Ivan Rodriguez .20 .50
215 Tony Phillips .05 .15
216 John Jaha .05 .15
217 Lee Smith .10 .30
218 Bip Roberts .05 .15
219 Dave Hansen .05 .15
220 Pat Listach .05 .15
221 Willie McGee .10 .30
222 Damion Easley .05 .15
223 Dean Palmer .10 .30
224 Mike Moore .05 .15
225 Brian Harper .05 .15
226 Gary DiSarcina .05 .15
227 Delino DeShields .05 .15
228 Otis Nixon .05 .15
229 Roberto Alomar .20 .50
230 Mark Grace .20 .50
231 Kenny Lofton .10 .30
232 Gregg Jefferies .05 .15
233 Cecil Fielder .10 .30
234 Jeff Bagwell .20 .50
235 Albert Belle .10 .30
236 David Justice .10 .30
237 Tom Henke .05 .15
238 Bobby Bonilla .10 .30
239 John Olerud .10 .30
240 Robby Thompson .05 .15
241 Dave Valle .05 .15
242 Marquis Grissom .10 .30
243 Greg Swindell .05 .15
244 Todd Zeile .05 .15
245 Dennis Eckersley .10 .30
246 Jose Offerman .05 .15
247 Greg McMichael .05 .15
248 Tim Belcher .05 .15
249 Cal Ripken 1.00 2.50
250 Tom Glavine .20 .50
251 Luis Polonia .05 .15
252 Bill Swift .05 .15
253 Juan Guzman .05 .15
254 Rickey Henderson .30 .75
255 Terry Mulholland .05 .15
256 Gary Sheffield .10 .30
257 Terry Steinbach .05 .15
258 Brett Butler .10 .30
259 Jason Bere .05 .15
260 Doug Strange .05 .15
261 Kent Hrbek .10 .30
262 Graeme Lloyd .05 .15
263 Lou Frazier .05 .15
264 Charles Nagy .05 .15
265 Bret Boone .10 .30
266 Kirk Gibson .10 .30
267 Kevin Brown .10 .30
268 Fred McGriff .20 .50
269 Matt Williams .10 .30
270 Greg Gagne .05 .15
271 Mariano Duncan .05 .15
272 Jeff Russell .05 .15
273 Eric Davis .10 .30
274 Shane Mack .05 .15
275 Jose Vizcaino .05 .15
276 Jose Canseco .20 .50
277 Roberto Hernandez .05 .15
278 Royce Clayton .05 .15

279 Carlos Baerga .05 .15
280 Pete Incaviglia .05 .15
281 Brent Gates .05 .15
282 Jeromy Burnitz .10 .30
283 Chili Davis .10 .30
284 Pete Harnisch .05 .15
285 Alan Trammell .10 .30
286 Eric Anthony .05 .15
287 Ellis Burks .10 .30
288 Julio Franco .10 .30
289 Jack Morris .10 .30
290 Erik Hanson .05 .15
291 Chuck Finley .10 .30
292 Reggie Jefferson .05 .15
293 Kevin McReynolds .05 .15
294 Greg Hibbard .05 .15
295 Travis Fryman .10 .30
296 Craig Biggio .20 .50
297 Kenny Rogers .10 .30
298 Dave Henderson .05 .15
299 Jim Thome .20 .50
300 Rene Arocha .05 .15
301 Pedro Munoz .05 .15
302 David Hulse .05 .15
303 Greg Vaughn .05 .15
304 Darren Lewis .05 .15
305 Deion Sanders .20 .50
306 Danny Tartabull .05 .15
307 Darryl Hamilton .05 .15
308 Andujar Cedeno .05 .15
309 Tim Salmon .20 .50
310 Tony Fernandez .05 .15
311 Alex Fernandez .05 .15
312 Roberto Kelly .05 .15
313 Harold Reynolds .10 .30
314 Chris Sabo .05 .15
315 Howard Johnson .05 .15
316 Mark Portugal .05 .15
317 Rafael Palmeiro .20 .50
318 Pete Smith .05 .15
319 Will Clark .20 .50
320 Henry Rodriguez .05 .15
321 Omar Vizquel .20 .50
322 David Segui .05 .15
323 Lou Whitaker .10 .30
324 Felix Fermin .05 .15
325 Spike Owen .05 .15
326 Darryl Kile .10 .30
327 Chad Kreuter .05 .15
328 Rod Beck .05 .15
329 Eddie Murray .30 .75
330 B.J. Surhoff .10 .30
331 Mickey Tettleton .05 .15
332 Pedro Martinez .30 .75
333 Roger Pavlik .05 .15
334 Eddie Taubensee .05 .15
335 John Doherty .05 .15
336 Jody Reed .05 .15
337 Aaron Sele .05 .15
338 Leo Gomez .05 .15
339 Dave Nilsson .05 .15
340 Rob Dibble .10 .30
341 John Burkett .05 .15
342 Wayne Kirby .05 .15
343 Dan Wilson .05 .15
344 Armando Reynoso .05 .15
345 Chad Curtis .05 .15
346 Dennis Martinez .10 .30
347 Cal Eldred .05 .15
348 Luis Gonzalez .10 .30
349 Doug Drabek .05 .15
350 Jim Leyritz .05 .15
351 Mark Langston .05 .15
352 Darrin Jackson .05 .15
353 Sid Fernandez .05 .15
354 Benito Santiago .10 .30
355 Kevin Seitzer .05 .15
356 Bo Jackson .30 .75
357 David Wells .10 .30
358 Paul Sorrento .05 .15
359 Ken Caminiti .10 .30
360 Eduardo Perez .05 .15
361 Orlando Merced .05 .15
362 Steve Finley .10 .30
363 Andy Benes .05 .15
364 Manuel Lee .05 .15
365 Todd Benzinger .05 .15
366 Sandy Alomar Jr. .05 .15
367 Rex Hudler .05 .15
368 Mike Henneman .05 .15
369 Vince Coleman .05 .15
370 Kirt Manwaring .05 .15
371 Ken Hill .05 .15
372 Glenallen Hill .05 .15
373 Sean Berry .05 .15
374 Geronimo Berroa .05 .15
375 Duane Ward .05 .15
376 Allen Watson .05 .15
377 Marc Newfield .05 .15
378 Dan Miceli .05 .15
379 Denny Hocking .05 .15
380 Mark Kiefer .05 .15
381 Tony Tarasco .05 .15
382 Tony Longmire .05 .15
383 Brian Anderson RC .10 .30
384 Fernando Vina .05 .15
385 Hector Carrasco .05 .15
386 Mike Kelly .05 .15
387 Greg Colbrunn .05 .15
388 Roger Salkeld .05 .15
389 Steve Trachsel .05 .15
390 Rich Becker .05 .15
391 Bill Taylor RC .10 .30
392 Rich Rowland .05 .15
393 Carl Everett .10 .30
394 Johnny Ruffin .05 .15
395 Keith Lockhart RC .10 .30
396 J.R. Phillips .05 .15
397 Sterling Hitchcock .05 .15
398 Jorge Fabregas .05 .15
399 Jeff Granger .05 .15
400 Eddie Zambrano RC .05 .15
401 Rikkert Faneyte RC .05 .15
402 Gerald Williams .05 .15
403 Joey Hamilton .05 .15
404 Joe Hall RC .05 .15
405 John Hudek RC .05 .15
406 Roberto Petagine .05 .15
407 Charles Johnson .10 .30
408 Mark Smith .05 .15
409 Jeff Juden .05 .15
410 Carlos Pulido RC .05 .15
411 Paul Shuey .05 .15
412 Rob Butler .05 .15
413 Mark Acre RC .05 .15
414 Greg Pirkl .05 .15
415 Melvin Nieves .05 .15
416 Tim Hyers RC .05 .15
417 NL Checklist .05 .15
418 NL Checklist .05 .15
419 AL Checklist .05 .15
420 AL Checklist .05 .15
RY1 Carlos Delgado ROY 2.00 5.00
SS1 Cal Ripken Salute 8.00 20.00
SS2 Dave Winfield Salute 1.50 4.00
MVP1 Paul Molitor MVP 2.00 5.00

1994 Select Crown Contenders

COMPLETE SET (10) 25.00 60.00
SER.1 STATED ODDS 1:24
CC1 Lenny Dykstra .75 2.00
CC2 Greg Maddux 3.00 8.00
CC3 Roger Clemens 4.00 10.00
CC4 Randy Johnson 2.00 5.00
CC5 Frank Thomas 2.00 5.00
CC6 Barry Bonds 5.00 12.00
CC7 Juan Gonzalez .75 2.00
CC8 John Olerud .75 2.00
CC9 Mike Piazza 4.00 10.00
CC10 Ken Griffey Jr. 4.00 10.00

1994 Select Rookie Surge

COMPLETE SET (18) 12.50 30.00
COMPLETE SERIES 1 (9) 5.00 12.00
COMPLETE SERIES 2 (9) 6.00 15.00
STATED ODDS 1:48
RS1 Cliff Floyd 1.25 3.00
RS2 Bob Hamelin .75 2.00
RS3 Ryan Klesko 1.25 3.00
RS4 Carlos Delgado 2.00 5.00
RS5 Jeffrey Hammonds .75 2.00
RS6 Rondell White 1.25 3.00
RS7 Salomon Torres .75 2.00
RS8 Steve Karsay .75 2.00
RS9 Javier Lopez 1.25 3.00
RS10 Manny Ramirez 3.00 8.00
RS11 Tony Tarasco .75 2.00
RS12 Kurt Abbott .75 2.00
RS13 Chan Ho Park 2.00 5.00
RS14 Rich Becker .75 2.00
RS15 James Mouton .75 2.00
RS16 Alex Gonzalez .75 2.00
RS17 Raul Mondesi 1.25 3.00
RS18 Steve Trachsel .75 2.00

1994 Select Skills

COMPLETE SET (10) 10.00 25.00
SER.2 STATED ODDS 1:24
SK1 Randy Johnson 2.50 6.00
SK2 Barry Larkin 1.50 4.00
SK3 Lenny Dykstra 1.00 2.50
SK4 Kenny Lofton 1.00 2.50
SK5 Juan Gonzalez 1.50 4.00
SK6 Barry Bonds 5.00 12.00
SK7 Marquis Grissom 1.00 2.50
SK8 Ivan Rodriguez 1.50 4.00
SK9 Larry Walker 1.50 4.00
SK10 Travis Fryman 1.00 2.50

1995 Select Samples

COMPLETE SET (4) 5.00 12.00
34 Roberto Alomar .75 2.00
37 Jeff Bagwell 1.25 3.00
241 Alex Rodriguez 3.00 8.00
NNO Title Card .20 .50

1995 Select

This 250-card set was issued in 12-card packs with 24 packs per box and 24 boxes per case. There was an announced production run of 4,950 cases. A special card of Hideo Nomo (number 251) was issued to hobby dealers who had bought cases of the Select product.

COMPLETE SET (250) 6.00 15.00
SUBSET CARDS HALF VALUE OF BASE CARDS
NOMO CARD ISSUED DIRECT TO DEALERS
1 Cal Ripken .60 1.50
2 Robin Ventura .07 .20
3 Al Martin .02 .10
4 Jeff Frye .02 .10
5 Darryl Strawberry .07 .20
6 Chan Ho Park .07 .20
7 Steve Avery .02 .10
8 Bret Boone .07 .20
9 Danny Tartabull .02 .10
10 Dante Bichette .07 .20
11 Rondell White .07 .20
12 Dave McCarty .02 .10
13 Bernard Gilkey .02 .10
14 Mark McGwire .50 1.25
15 Ruben Sierra .07 .20
16 Wade Boggs .10 .30
17 Mike Piazza .30 .75
18 Jeffrey Hammonds .02 .10
19 Mike Mussina .10 .30
20 Darryl Kile .07 .20
21 Greg Maddux .30 .75
22 Frank Thomas .20 .50
23 Kevin Appier .07 .20
24 Jay Bell .07 .20
25 Kirk Gibson .07 .20
26 Pat Hentgen .02 .10
27 Joey Hamilton .02 .10
28 Bernie Williams .10 .30
29 Aaron Sele .02 .10
30 Delino DeShields .02 .10
31 Danny Bautista .02 .10
32 Jim Thome .10 .30
33 Rikkert Faneyte .02 .10
34 Roberto Alomar .10 .30
35 Paul Molitor .07 .20
36 Allen Watson .02 .10
37 Jeff Bagwell .10 .30
38 Jay Buhner .07 .20
39 Marquis Grissom .07 .20
40 Jim Edmonds .10 .30
41 Ryan Klesko .07 .20
42 Fred McGriff .10 .30
43 Tony Tarasco .02 .10
44 Darren Daulton .07 .20
45 Marc Newfield .02 .10
46 Barry Bonds .60 1.50
47 Bobby Bonilla .07 .20
48 Greg Pirkl .02 .10
49 Steve Karsay .02 .10
50 Bob Hamelin .02 .10
51 Javier Lopez .07 .20
52 Barry Larkin .10 .30
53 Kevin Young .02 .10
54 Sterling Hitchcock .02 .10
55 Tom Glavine .10 .30
56 Carlos Delgado .07 .20
57 Darren Oliver .02 .10
58 Cliff Floyd .07 .20
59 Tim Salmon .10 .30
60 Albert Belle .07 .20
61 Salomon Torres .02 .10
62 Gary Sheffield .07 .20
63 Ivan Rodriguez .10 .30
64 Charles Nagy .02 .10
65 Eduardo Perez .02 .10
66 Terry Steinbach .02 .10
67 David Justice .07 .20
68 Jason Bere .02 .10
69 Dave Nilsson .02 .10
70 Brian Anderson .02 .10
71 Billy Ashley .02 .10
72 Roger Clemens .40 1.00
73 Jimmy Key .07 .20
74 Wally Joyner .07 .20
75 Andy Benes .02 .10
76 Ray Lankford .07 .20
77 Jeff Kent .07 .20
78 Moises Alou .07 .20
79 Kirby Puckett .20 .50
80 Joe Carter .07 .20
81 Manny Ramirez .10 .30
82 J.R. Phillips .02 .10
83 Matt Mieske .02 .10
84 John Olerud .07 .20
85 Andres Galarraga .07 .20
86 Juan Gonzalez .07 .20
87 Pedro Martinez .10 .30
88 Dean Palmer .07 .20
89 Ken Griffey Jr. .40 1.00
90 Brian Jordan .07 .20
91 Hal Morris .02 .10
92 Lenny Dykstra .07 .20
93 Wil Cordero .02 .10
94 Tony Gwynn .25 .60
95 Alex Gonzalez .02 .10
96 Cecil Fielder .07 .20
97 Mo Vaughn .07 .20
98 John Valentin .02 .10
99 Will Clark .10 .30
100 Geronimo Pena .02 .10
101 Don Mattingly .50 1.25
102 Charles Johnson .07 .20
103 Raul Mondesi .07 .20
104 Reggie Sanders .07 .20
105 Royce Clayton .02 .10
106 Reggie Jefferson .02 .10
107 Craig Biggio .10 .30
108 Jack McDowell .02 .10
109 James Mouton .02 .10
110 Mike Greenwell .02 .10
111 David Cone .07 .20
112 Matt Williams .07 .20
113 Garret Anderson .07 .20
114 Carlos Garcia .02 .10
115 Alex Fernandez .02 .10
116 Deion Sanders .10 .30
117 Chili Davis .07 .20
118 Mike Kelly .02 .10
119 Jeff Conine .07 .20
120 Kenny Lofton .07 .20
121 Rafael Palmeiro .10 .30
122 Chuck Knoblauch .07 .20
123 Ozzie Smith .30 .75
124 Carlos Baerga .02 .10
125 Brett Butler .07 .20
126 Sammy Sosa .20 .50
127 Ellis Burks .07 .20
128 Bret Saberhagen .07 .20
129 Doug Drabek .02 .10
130 Dennis Martinez .07 .20
131 Paul O'Neill .10 .30
132 Travis Fryman .07 .20
133 Brent Gates .02 .10
134 Rickey Henderson .20 .50
135 Randy Johnson .20 .50
136 Mark Langston .02 .10
137 Greg Colbrunn .02 .10
138 Jose Rijo .02 .10
139 Bryan Harvey .02 .10
140 Dennis Eckersley .07 .20
141 Ron Gant .07 .20
142 Carl Everett .07 .20
143 Jeff Granger .02 .10
144 Ben McDonald .02 .10
145 Kurt Abbott .02 .10
146 Jim Abbott .10 .30
147 Jason Jacome .02 .10
148 Rico Brogna .02 .10
149 Cal Eldred .02 .10
150 Rich Becker .02 .10
151 Pete Harnisch .02 .10
152 Roberto Petagine .02 .10
153 Jacob Brumfield .02 .10
154 Todd Hundley .02 .10
155 Roger Cedeno .02 .10
156 Harold Baines .07 .20
157 Steve Dunn .02 .10
158 Tim Belk .02 .10
159 Marty Cordova .02 .10
160 Russ Davis .02 .10
161 Jose Malave .02 .10
162 Brian L.Hunter .02 .10
163 Andy Pettitte .10 .30
164 Brooks Kieschnick .02 .10
165 Midre Cummings .02 .10
166 Frank Rodriguez .02 .10
167 Chad Mottola .02 .10
168 Brian Barber .02 .10
169 Tim Unroe RC .02 .10
170 Shane Andrews .02 .10
171 Kevin Flora .02 .10
172 Ray Durham .07 .20
173 Chipper Jones .20 .50
174 Butch Huskey .02 .10
175 Ray McDavid .02 .10
176 Jeff Cirillo .02 .10
177 Terry Pendleton .07 .20
178 Scott Ruffcorn .02 .10
179 Ray Holbert .02 .10
180 Joe Randa .07 .20
181 Jose Oliva .02 .10
182 Andy Van Slyke .10 .30
183 Albie Lopez .02 .10
184 Chad Curtis .02 .10
185 Ozzie Guillen .07 .20
186 Chad Ogea .02 .10
187 Dan Wilson .02 .10
188 Tony Fernandez .02 .10
189 John Smoltz .10 .30
190 Willie Greene .02 .10
191 Darren Lewis .02 .10
192 Orlando Miller .02 .10
193 Kurt Miller .02 .10
194 Andrew Lorraine .02 .10
195 Ernie Young .02 .10
196 Jimmy Haynes .02 .10
197 Raul Casanova RC .08 .25
198 Joe Vitiello .02 .10
199 Brad Woodall RC .02 .10
200 Juan Acevedo RC .02 .10
201 Michael Tucker .02 .10
202 Shawn Green .07 .20
203 Alex Rodriguez .50 1.25
204 Julian Tavarez .02 .10
205 Jose Lima .02 .10
206 Wilson Alvarez .02 .10
207 Rich Aude .02 .10
208 Armando Benitez .02 .10
209 Dwayne Hosey .02 .10
210 Gabe White .02 .10
211 Joey Eischen .02 .10
212 Bill Pulsipher .02 .10
213 Robby Thompson .02 .10
214 Toby Borland .02 .10
215 Rusty Greer .07 .20
216 Fausto Cruz .02 .10
217 Luis Ortiz .02 .10
218 Duane Singleton .02 .10
219 Troy Percival .07 .20
220 Gregg Jefferies .02 .10
221 Mark Grace .10 .30
222 Mickey Tettleton .02 .10
223 Phil Plantier .02 .10
224 Larry Walker .07 .20
225 Ken Caminiti .07 .20
226 Dave Winfield .07 .20
227 Brady Anderson .07 .20
228 Kevin Brown .07 .20
229 Andujar Cedeno .02 .10
230 Roberto Kelly .02 .10
231 Jose Canseco .10 .30
232 Scott Ruffcorn ST .02 .10
233 Billy Ashley ST .02 .10
234 J.R. Phillips ST .02 .10
235 Chipper Jones ST .10 .30
236 Charles Johnson ST .02 .10
237 Midre Cummings ST .02 .10
238 Brian L.Hunter ST .02 .10
239 Garret Anderson ST .02 .10
240 Shawn Green ST .02 .10
241 Alex Rodriguez ST .20 .50
242 Frank Thomas CL .10 .30
243 Ken Griffey Jr. CL .25 .60
244 Albert Belle CL .02 .10
245 Cal Ripken CL .30 .75
246 Barry Bonds CL .30 .75
247 Raul Mondesi CL .02 .10
248 Mike Piazza CL .20 .50
249 Jeff Bagwell CL .07 .20
250 Bag .25 .60
Thom
Grif
Piaz CL
251S Hideo Nomo .40 1.00

1995 Select Artist's Proofs

*STARS: 12.5X TO 30X BASIC CARDS
STATED ODDS 1:24
NOMO CARD ISSUED DIRECT TO DEALERS

1995 Select Big Sticks

COMPLETE SET (12) 15.00 40.00
STATED ODDS 1:48
BS1 Frank Thomas 1.50 4.00
BS2 Ken Griffey Jr. 3.00 8.00
BS3 Cal Ripken 5.00 12.00
BS4 Mike Piazza 1.50 4.00
BS5 Don Mattingly 3.00 8.00
BS6 Will Clark .60 1.50
BS7 Tony Gwynn 1.50 4.00
BS8 Jeff Bagwell 1.00 2.50
BS9 Barry Bonds 2.50 6.00
BS10 Paul Molitor 1.50 4.00
BS11 Matt Williams .60 1.50
BS12 Albert Belle .60 1.50

1995 Select Can't Miss

COMPLETE SET (12) 20.00 50.00
STATED ODDS 1:24
CM1 Cliff Floyd 1.00 2.50
CM2 Ryan Klesko 1.00 2.50
CM3 Charles Johnson 1.00 2.50
CM4 Raul Mondesi 1.00 2.50
CM5 Manny Ramirez 1.25 3.00
CM6 Billy Ashley .60 1.50
CM7 Alex Gonzalez .60 1.50
CM8 Carlos Delgado 1.00 2.50
CM9 Garret Anderson 1.00 2.50
CM10 Alex Rodriguez 5.00 12.00
CM11 Chipper Jones 2.00 5.00
CM12 Shawn Green 1.00 2.50

1995 Select Sure Shots

COMPLETE SET (10) 12.50 30.00
STATED ODDS 1:90
SS1 Ben Grieve 1.25 3.00
SS2 Kevin Witt 1.25 3.00
SS3 Mark Farris 1.25 3.00
SS4 Paul Konerko 4.00 10.00
SS5 Dustin Hermanson 1.25 3.00
SS6 Ramon Castro 1.25 3.00
SS7 McKay Christensen 1.25 3.00
SS8 Brian Buchanan 1.25 3.00
SS9 Paul Wilson 1.25 3.00
SS10 Terrence Long 1.25 3.00

1996 Select

The 1996 Select set was issued in one series totalling 200 cards. The 10-card packs retailed for $1.99 each. The fronts feature a color action player photo over most of the card with a small player photo framed and name in gold foil printing. The backs carry another player photo, player information and statistics. The set contains the topical subsets: Lineup Leaders (151-160) and Rookies (161-195).

COMPLETE SET (200) 6.00 15.00
SUBSET CARDS HALF VALUE OF BASE CARDS
1 Wade Boggs .10 .30
2 Shawn Green .07 .20
3 Andres Galarraga .07 .20
4 Bill Pulsipher .07 .20
5 Chuck Knoblauch .07 .20
6 Ken Griffey Jr. .40 1.00
7 Greg Maddux .30 .75
8 Manny Ramirez .10 .30
9 Ivan Rodriguez .10 .30
10 Tim Salmon .10 .30
11 Frank Thomas .20 .50
12 Jeff Bagwell .10 .30
13 Travis Fryman .07 .20
14 Kenny Lofton .07 .20
15 Matt Williams .07 .20
16 Jay Bell .07 .20
17 Ken Caminiti .07 .20
18 Ray Lankford .07 .20
19 Cal Ripken .60 1.50
20 Roger Clemens .40 1.00
21 Carlos Baerga .07 .20
22 Mike Piazza .30 .75
23 Gregg Jefferies .07 .20
24 Reggie Sanders .07 .20
25 Rondell White .07 .20
26 Sammy Sosa .20 .50
27 Kevin Appier .07 .20
28 Kevin Seitzer .07 .20
29 Gary Sheffield .07 .20
30 Mike Mussina .10 .30
31 Mark McGwire .50 1.25
32 Barry Larkin .10 .30
33 Marc Newfield .07 .20
34 Ismael Valdes .07 .20
35 Marty Cordova .07 .20
36 Albert Belle .07 .20
37 Johnny Damon .10 .30
38 Garret Anderson .07 .20
39 Cecil Fielder .07 .20
40 John Mabry .07 .20
41 Chipper Jones .20 .50
42 Omar Vizquel .10 .30
43 Jose Rijo .07 .20
44 Charles Johnson .07 .20
45 Alex Rodriguez .40 1.00
46 Rico Brogna .07 .20
47 Joe Carter .07 .20
48 Mo Vaughn .07 .20
49 Moises Alou .07 .20
50 Raul Mondesi .07 .20
51 Robin Ventura .07 .20
52 Jim Thome .10 .30
53 David Justice .07 .20
54 Jeff King .07 .20
55 Brian L.Hunter .07 .20
56 Juan Gonzalez .07 .20
57 John Olerud .07 .20
58 Rafael Palmeiro .10 .30
59 Tony Gwynn .25 .60
60 Eddie Murray .20 .50
61 Jason Isringhausen .07 .20
62 Dante Bichette .07 .20
63 Randy Johnson .20 .50
64 Kirby Puckett .20 .50
65 Jim Edmonds .07 .20
66 David Cone .07 .20
67 Ozzie Smith .30 .75
68 Fred McGriff .10 .30
69 Darren Daulton .07 .20
70 Edgar Martinez .10 .30
71 J.T. Snow .07 .20
72 Butch Huskey .07 .20
73 Hideo Nomo .20 .50
74 Pedro Martinez .10 .30
75 Bobby Bonilla .07 .20
76 Jeff Conine .07 .20
77 Ryan Klesko .07 .20
78 Bernie Williams .10 .30
79 Andre Dawson .07 .20
80 Trevor Hoffman .07 .20
81 Mark Grace .10 .30
82 Benji Gil .07 .20
83 Eric Karros .07 .20
84 Pete Schourek .07 .20
85 Edgardo Alfonzo .07 .20
86 Jay Buhner .07 .20
87 Vinny Castilla .07 .20
88 Bret Boone .07 .20
89 Ray Durham .07 .20
90 Brian Jordan .07 .20
91 Jose Canseco .10 .30
92 Paul O'Neill .10 .30
93 Chili Davis .07 .20
94 Tom Glavine .10 .30
95 Julian Tavarez .07 .20
96 Derek Bell .07 .20
97 Will Clark .10 .30
98 Larry Walker .07 .20
99 Denny Neagle .07 .20
100 Alex Fernandez .07 .20
101 Barry Bonds .60 1.50
102 Ben McDonald .07 .20
103 Andy Pettitte .10 .30
104 Tino Martinez .10 .30
105 Sterling Hitchcock .07 .20
106 Royce Clayton .07 .20
107 Jim Abbott .10 .30
108 Rickey Henderson .20 .50
109 Ramon Martinez .07 .20
110 Paul Molitor .07 .20
111 Dennis Eckersley .07 .20
112 Alex Gonzalez .07 .20
113 Marquis Grissom .07 .20
114 Greg Vaughn .07 .20
115 Lance Johnson .07 .20
116 Todd Stottlemyre .07 .20
117 Jack McDowell .07 .20
118 Ruben Sierra .07 .20
119 Brady Anderson .07 .20
120 Julio Franco .07 .20
121 Brooks Kieschnick .07 .20
122 Roberto Alomar .10 .30
123 Greg Gagne .07 .20
124 Wally Joyner .07 .20
125 John Smoltz .10 .30
126 John Valentin .07 .20
127 Russ Davis .07 .20
128 Joe Vitiello .07 .20
129 Shawon Dunston .07 .20
130 Frank Rodriguez .07 .20
131 Charlie Hayes .07 .20
132 Andy Benes .07 .20
133 B.J. Surhoff .07 .20
134 Dave Nilsson .07 .20
135 Carlos Delgado .07 .20
136 Walt Weiss .07 .20
137 Mike Stanley .07 .20
138 Greg Colbrunn .07 .20
139 Mike Kelly .07 .20
140 Ryne Sandberg .30 .75
141 Lee Smith .07 .20
142 Dennis Martinez .07 .20
143 Bernard Gilkey .07 .20
144 Lenny Dykstra .07 .20
145 Danny Tartabull .07 .20
146 Dean Palmer .07 .20
147 Craig Biggio .10 .30
148 Juan Acevedo .07 .20
149 Michael Tucker .07 .20
150 Bobby Higginson .07 .20
151 Ken Griffey Jr. LUL .25 .60
152 Frank Thomas LUL .10 .30
153 Cal Ripken LUL .30 .75
154 Albert Belle LUL .07 .20
155 Mike Piazza LUL .20 .50
156 Barry Bonds LUL .30 .75
157 Sammy Sosa LUL .10 .30
158 Mo Vaughn LUL .07 .20
159 Greg Maddux LUL .20 .50
160 Jeff Bagwell LUL .07 .20
161 Derek Jeter .50 1.25
162 Paul Wilson .07 .20
163 Chris Snopek .07 .20
164 Jason Schmidt .10 .30
165 Jimmy Haynes .07 .20
166 George Arias .07 .20
167 Steve Gibralter .07 .20
168 Bob Wolcott .07 .20
169 Jason Kendall .07 .20
170 Greg Zaun .07 .20
171 Quinton McCracken .07 .20
172 Alan Benes .07 .20
173 Rey Ordonez .07 .20
174 Livan Hernandez RC .40 1.00
175 Osvaldo Fernandez .07 .20
176 Marc Barcelo .07 .20
177 Sal Fasano .07 .20
178 Mike Grace .07 .20
179 Chan Ho Park .07 .20
180 Robert Perez .07 .20
181 Todd Hollandsworth .07 .20
182 Wilton Guerrero RC .08 .25
183 John Wasdin .07 .20
184 Jim Pittsley .07 .20
185 LaTroy Hawkins .07 .20
186 Jay Powell .07 .20
187 Felipe Crespo .07 .20
188 Jermaine Dye .07 .20
189 Bob Abreu .20 .50
190 Matt Luke .07 .20
191 Richard Hidalgo .07 .20
192 Karim Garcia .07 .20
193 Marvin Benard RC .07 .20
194 Andy Fox .07 .20
195 Terrell Wade .07 .20
196 Frank Thomas CL .10 .30
197 Ken Griffey Jr. CL .25 .60
198 Greg Maddux CL .20 .50
199 Mike Piazza CL .20 .50
200 Cal Ripken CL .30 .75

1996 Select Artist's Proofs

COMPLETE SET (200) 750.00 1500.00
*STARS: 12.5X TO 30X BASIC CARDS
*ROOKIES: 8X TO 20X BASIC CARDS
STATED ODDS 1:35

1996 Select Claim To Fame

COMPLETE SET (20) 125.00 250.00
STATED ODDS 1:72
1 Cal Ripken 12.50 30.00
2 Greg Maddux 6.00 15.00
3 Ken Griffey Jr. 8.00 20.00
4 Frank Thomas 4.00 10.00
5 Mo Vaughn 1.50 4.00
6 Albert Belle 1.50 4.00
7 Jeff Bagwell 2.50 6.00
8 Sammy Sosa 4.00 10.00
9 Reggie Sanders 1.50 4.00
10 Hideo Nomo 4.00 10.00
11 Chipper Jones 4.00 10.00
12 Mike Piazza 6.00 15.00
13 Matt Williams 1.50 4.00
14 Tony Gwynn 5.00 12.00
15 Johnny Damon 2.50 6.00
16 Dante Bichette 1.50 4.00
17 Kirby Puckett 4.00 10.00
18 Barry Bonds 12.50 30.00
19 Randy Johnson 4.00 10.00
20 Eddie Murray 4.00 10.00
S8 Sammy Sosa Sample .75 2.00

1996 Select En Fuego

COMPLETE SET (25) 40.00 100.00
STATED ODDS 1:48
1 Ken Griffey Jr. 5.00 12.00
2 Frank Thomas 2.50 6.00
3 Cal Ripken 8.00 20.00
4 Greg Maddux 4.00 10.00
5 Jeff Bagwell 1.50 4.00
6 Barry Bonds 4.00 10.00
7 Mo Vaughn 1.00 2.50
8 Albert Belle 1.00 2.50
9 Sammy Sosa 2.50 6.00
10 Reggie Sanders 1.00 2.50
11 Mike Piazza 2.50 6.00
12 Chipper Jones 2.50 6.00
13 Tony Gwynn 2.50 6.00
14 Kirby Puckett 2.50 6.00
15 Wade Boggs 1.50 4.00
16 Dan Patrick 1.00 2.50
17 Gary Sheffield 1.00 2.50
18 Dante Bichette 1.00 2.50
19 Randy Johnson 2.50 6.00
20 Matt Williams 1.00 2.50
21 Alex Rodriguez 3.00 8.00
22 Tim Salmon 1.00 2.50
23 Johnny Damon 1.50 4.00
24 Manny Ramirez 1.50 4.00
25 Hideo Nomo 2.50 6.00

1996 Select Team Nucleus

COMPLETE SET (28) 15.00 40.00
STATED ODDS 1:18
1 Ramirez .60 1.50
Belle
Baerga
2 Lankford 1.25 3.00
Jordan
Smith
3 J.Bell .40 1.00
J.King
D.Neagle
4 Bichette .60 1.50
Galarraga
Walker
5 McGwire 1.50 4.00
Bordick
Steinbach
6 Boggs .60 1.50
B.Williams
Cone
7 S.Green .40 1.00
Carter
Gonzalez
8 Clemens 1.25 3.00
Vaughn
Canseco
9 Griffey 2.00 5.00
Martinez
Johnson
10 Jefferies .40 1.00
Daulton
Dykstra
11 Piazza 1.00 2.50
Nomo
Mondesi
12 Maddux 1.50 4.00
Jones
Klesko
13 Fielder .40 1.00
Fryman
Nevin
14 Gonzalez .60 1.50
Rodriguez
Clark
15 Sosa 1.50 4.00
Sandberg
Grace
16 Sheffield .40 1.00
Johnson
Dawson
17 Damon .60 1.50
Tucker
Appier
18 Bonds 1.50 4.00
Williams
Beck
19 Puckett 1.00 2.50
Knobl
Cordova
20 Ripken 3.00 8.00
Bonilla
Mussina
21 Isring .40 1.00
Puls
Brogna
22 Gwynn 1.00 2.50
Caminiti
Newfield
23 Salmon .40 1.00
Anders
Edmonds
24 M.Alou .40 1.00
R.White
C.Floyd
25 Larkin .60 1.50
Sanders
Boone
26 Bagwell .60 1.50
Biggio
Bell
27 Thomas 1.00 2.50
Ventura
Fernandez
28 Jaha .40 1.00
Vaughn
Seitzer

1997 Select

The 1997 Select set was issued in two series totalling 200 cards and was distributed in hobby only six-card packs with a suggested retail price of $2.99. The 150-card first series set contains 100 common "Red" cards and 50 short-printed Blue cards. Each card features a distinctive silver-foil treatment with either a red or blue foil accent. The red cards are twice as easy to find than the blue cards. The fronts display a color action player photo over most of the card with a small player photo

at the bottom. The backs carry another player photo, player information and statistics.
COMPLETE SET (200) 25.00 60.00
COMPLETE SERIES 1 (150) 15.00 40.00
COMPLETE HI SERIES (50) 10.00 25.00
COMMON RED (1-150) .10 .30
COMMON BLUE (1-150) .25 .60
BLUE CARDS 2X TOUGHER THAN RED
COMMON CARD (151-200) .25 .60
SUBSET CARDS HALF VALUE OF BASE CARDS
ALL HI SERIES FRONTS ERRONEOUSLY
HAVE "SELECT COMPANY" TEXT ON THEM
1 Juan Gonzalez B .25 .60
2 Mo Vaughn B .25 .60
3 Tony Gwynn R .40 1.00
4 Manny Ramirez B .40 1.00
5 Jose Canseco R .20 .50
6 David Cone R .10 .30
7 Chan Ho Park R .10 .30
8 Frank Thomas B .60 1.50
9 Todd Hollandsworth R .10 .30
10 Marty Cordova R .10 .30
11 Gary Sheffield B .25 .60
12 John Smoltz B .40 1.00
13 Mark Grudzielanek R .10 .30
14 Sammy Sosa B .60 1.50
15 Paul Molitor R .10 .30
16 Kevin Brown R .10 .30
17 Albert Belle B .25 .60
18 Eric Young R .10 .30
19 John Wetteland R .10 .30
20 Ryan Klesko B .25 .60
21 Joe Carter R .10 .30
22 Alex Ochoa R .10 .30
23 Greg Maddux B 1.00 2.50
24 Roger Clemens B 1.25 3.00
25 Ivan Rodriguez B .40 1.00
26 Barry Bonds B 1.50 4.00
27 Kenny Lofton B .25 .60
28 Javy Lopez R .10 .30
29 Hideo Nomo B .60 1.50
30 Rusty Greer R .10 .30
31 Rafael Palmeiro R .20 .50
32 Mike Piazza B 1.00 2.50
33 Ryne Sandberg R .50 1.25
34 Wade Boggs R .20 .50
35 Jim Thome B .40 1.00
36 Ken Caminiti B .25 .60
37 Mark Grace R .20 .50
38 Brian Jordan B .25 .60
39 Craig Biggio R .20 .50
40 Henry Rodriguez R .10 .30
41 Dean Palmer R .10 .30
42 Jason Kendall R .10 .30
43 Bill Pulsipher R .10 .30
44 Tim Salmon B .40 1.00
45 Marc Newfield R .10 .30
46 Pat Hentgen R .10 .30
47 Ken Griffey Jr. B 1.25 3.00
48 Paul Wilson R .10 .30
49 Jay Buhner B .25 .60
50 Rickey Henderson R .30 .75
51 Jeff Bagwell B .40 1.00
52 Cecil Fielder R .10 .30
53 Alex Rodriguez B .75 2.00
54 John Jaha R .10 .30
55 Brady Anderson B .25 .60
56 Andres Galarraga R .10 .30
57 Raul Mondesi R .10 .30
58 Andy Pettitte R .20 .50
59 Roberto Alomar B .40 1.00
60 Derek Jeter B 1.50 4.00
61 Charles Johnson R .10 .30
62 Travis Fryman R .10 .30
63 Chipper Jones B .60 1.50
64 Edgar Martinez R .20 .50
65 Bobby Bonilla R .10 .30
66 Greg Vaughn R .10 .30
67 Bobby Higginson R .10 .30
68 Garret Anderson R .10 .30
69 Chuck Knoblauch B .25 .60
70 Jermaine Dye R .10 .30
71 Cal Ripken B 2.00 5.00
72 Jason Giambi R .10 .30
73 Trey Beamon R .10 .30
74 Shawn Green R .10 .30
75 Mark McGwire B 1.50 4.00
76 Carlos Delgado R .10 .30
77 Jason Isringhausen R .10 .30
78 Randy Johnson B .60 1.50
79 Troy Percival B .25 .60
80 Ron Gant R .10 .30
81 Ellis Burks R .10 .30
82 Mike Mussina B .40 1.00
83 Todd Hundley R .10 .30
84 Jim Edmonds R .10 .30
85 Charles Nagy R .10 .30
86 Dante Bichette B .25 .60
87 Mariano Rivera R .30 .75
88 Matt Williams B .25 .60
89 Rondell White R .10 .30
90 Steve Finley R .10 .30
91 Alex Fernandez R .10 .30
92 Barry Larkin R .20 .50
93 Tom Goodwin R .10 .30
94 Will Clark R .20 .50
95 Michael Tucker R .10 .30
96 Derek Bell R .10 .30
97 Larry Walker R .10 .30
98 Alan Benes R .10 .30
99 Tom Glavine R .20 .50
100 Darin Erstad B .25 .60
101 Andruw Jones B .40 1.00
102 Scott Rolen R .10 .30
103 Todd Walker B .25 .60
104 Dmitri Young R .10 .30
105 Vladimir Guerrero B .60 1.50
106 Nomar Garciaparra R .50 1.25
107 Danny Patterson R .10 .30
108 Karim Garcia R .10 .30
109 Todd Greene R .10 .30
110 Ruben Rivera R .10 .30
111 Raul Casanova R .10 .30
112 Mike Cameron R .10 .30
113 Bartolo Colon R .10 .30
114 Rod Myers R .10 .30
115 Todd Dunn R .10 .30
116 Torii Hunter R .10 .30
117 Jason Dickson R .10 .30
118 Eugene Kingsale R .10 .30
119 Rafael Medina R .10 .30
120 Raul Ibanez R .10 .30
121 Bobby Henley R RC .10 .30
122 Scott Spiezio R .10 .30
123 Bobby Smith R .10 .30
124 J.J. Johnson R .10 .30
125 Bubba Trammell R RC .20 .50
126 Jeff Abbott R .10 .30
127 Neifi Perez R .10 .30
128 Derrek Lee R .20 .50
129 Kevin Brown C R .10 .30
130 Mendy Lopez R .10 .30
131 Kevin Orie R .10 .30
132 Ryan Jones R .10 .30
133 Juan Encarnacion R .10 .30
134 Jose Guillen B .10 .30
135 Greg Norton R .10 .30
136 Richie Sexson R .10 .30
137 Jay Payton R .10 .30
138 Bob Abreu R .20 .50
139 Ron Belliard R RC .30 .75
140 Wilton Guerrero B .25 .60
141 Alex Rodriguez SS B .50 1.25
142 Juan Gonzalez SS B .25 .60
143 Ken Caminiti SS B .25 .60
144 Frank Thomas SS B .60 1.50
145 Ken Griffey Jr. SS B .75 2.00
146 John Smoltz SS B .40 1.00
147 Mike Piazza SS B .30 .75
148 Derek Jeter SS B .75 2.00
149 Frank Thomas CL R .20 .50
150 Ken Griffey Jr. CL R .40 1.00
151 Jose Cruz Jr. RC .40 1.00
152 Moises Alou .25 .60
153 Hideki Irabu RC .40 1.00
154 Glendon Rusch .25 .60
155 Ron Coomer .25 .60
156 Jeremi Gonzalez RC .25 .60
157 Fernando Tatis RC .25 .60
158 John Olerud .25 .60
159 Rickey Henderson .30 .75
160 Shannon Stewart .25 .60
161 Kevin Polcovich RC .25 .60
162 Jose Rosado .25 .60
163 Ray Lankford .25 .60
164 David Justice .25 .60
165 Mark Kotsay RC 1.00 2.50
166 Deivi Cruz RC .40 1.00
167 Billy Wagner .25 .60
168 Jacob Cruz .25 .60
169 Matt Morris .10 .30
170 Brian Banks .25 .60
171 Brett Tomko .25 .60
172 Todd Helton .60 1.50
173 Eric Young .25 .60
174 Bernie Williams .40 1.00
175 Jeff Fassero .25 .60
176 Ryan McGuire .25 .60
177 Darryl Kile .25 .60
178 Kelvim Escobar RC .60 1.50
179 Dave Nilsson .25 .60
180 Geronimo Berroa .25 .60
181 Livan Hernandez .25 .60
182 Tony Womack RC .40 1.00
183 Deion Sanders .40 1.00
184 Jeff Kent .25 .60
185 Brian Hunter .25 .60
186 Jose Malave .25 .60
187 Steve Woodard RC .25 .60
188 Brad Radke .25 .60
189 Todd Dunwoody .25 .60
190 Joey Hamilton .25 .60
191 Denny Neagle .25 .60
192 Bobby Jones .25 .60
193 Tony Clark .25 .60
194 Jaret Wright RC .40 1.00
195 Matt Stairs .25 .60
196 Francisco Cordova .25 .60
197 Justin Thompson .25 .60
198 Pokey Reese .25 .60
199 Garrett Stephenson .25 .60
200 Carl Everett .25 .60

1997 Select Artist's Proofs
*STARS: 5X TO 12X BASIC CARDS
STATED ODDS 1:71 RED, 1:355 BLUE

1997 Select Company
*BLUE 1-150: .4X TO 1X BASIC
*RED 1-150: .75X TO 2X BASIC
*HI SERIES 151-200: .4X TO 1X BASIC
COMPANY FRONTS HAVE COARSE FINISH
P121 Bobby Henley PROMO .20 .50

1997 Select Registered Gold
*STARS: 1.25X TO 3X BASIC CARDS
STATED ODDS 1:11 RED, 1:47 BLUE

1997 Select Rookie Autographs
COMPLETE SET (4) 20.00 50.00
RANDOM INSERTS IN PACKS
PRINT RUNS B/WN 2500-3000 PER
1 Jose Guillen/3000 6.00 15.00
2 Wilton Guerrero/3000 3.00 8.00
3 Andruw Jones/2500 6.00 15.00
4 Todd Walker/3000 6.00 15.00

1997 Select Rookie Revolution
COMPLETE SET (20) 40.00 100.00
STATED ODDS 1:56
1 Andruw Jones 2.00 5.00
2 Derek Jeter 6.00 15.00
3 Todd Hollandsworth .75 2.00
4 Edgar Renteria 1.25 3.00
5 Jason Kendall 1.25 3.00
6 Rey Ordonez .75 2.00
7 F.P. Santangelo .75 2.00
8 Jermaine Dye 1.25 3.00
9 Alex Ochoa .75 2.00
10 Vladimir Guerrero 2.50 6.00
11 Dmitri Young 1.25 3.00
12 Todd Walker .75 2.00
13 Scott Rolen 2.00 5.00
14 Nomar Garciaparra 4.00 10.00
15 Ruben Rivera .75 2.00
16 Darin Erstad 1.25 3.00
17 Todd Greene .75 2.00
18 Mariano Rivera 2.50 6.00
19 Trey Beamon .75 2.00
20 Karim Garcia .75 2.00

1997 Select Tools of the Trade
COMPLETE SET (25) 60.00 120.00
STATED ODDS 1:9
*MIRROR BLUE: 2X TO 5X BASIC MIRROR
MIRROR BLUE STATED ODDS 1:240
1 K.Griffey Jr. 3.00 8.00
A.Jones
2 G.Maddux 2.50 6.00
A.Pettitte
3 C.Ripken 3.00 8.00
C.Jones
4 M.Piazza 2.50 6.00
J.Kendall
5 A.Belle .50 1.25
K.Garcia
6 M.Vaughn .50 1.25
D.Young
7 J.Gonzalez 1.25 3.00
V.Guerrero
8 T.Gwynn 2.00 5.00
J.Dye
9 B.Bonds 4.00 10.00
A.Ochoa
10 J.Bagwell .75 2.00
J.Giambi
11 D.Erstad .50 1.25
K.Lofton
12 M.Ramirez .75 2.00
G.Sheffield
13 T.Salmon .75 2.00
T.Hollandsworth
14 S.Sosa 1.25 3.00
R.Rivera
15 P.Molitor .50 1.25
G.Arias
16 J.Thome .75 2.00
T.Walker
17 W.Boggs .75 2.00
S.Rolen
18 R.Sandberg 2.50 6.00
C.Knoblauch
19 M.McGwire 3.00 8.00
F.Thomas
20 I.Rodriguez .75 2.00
C.Johnson
21 B.Jordan .50 1.25
R.Greer
22 R.Clemens 3.00 8.00
T.Percival
23 J.Smoltz .75 2.00
M.Mussina
24 A.Rodriguez 2.50 6.00
R.Ordonez
25 D.Jeter 3.00 8.00
N.Garciaparra

2002 Select Rookies and Prospects
COMPLETE SET 200.00 500.00
1 Abraham Nunez 2.00 5.00
2 Adam Bernero 2.00 5.00
3 Adam Pettyjohn 2.00 5.00
Black Autograph
4 Alex Escobar 2.00 5.00
5 Allan Simpson 2.00 5.00
6 Andres Torres 2.00 5.00
7 Andy Pratt 2.00 5.00
8 Bert Snow 2.00 5.00
Black Autograph
8A Bert Snow 2.00 5.00
Blue Autograph
9 Bill Ortega 2.00 5.00
10 Billy Sylvester 2.00 5.00
11 Brad Voyles 2.00 5.00
12 Brandon Backe 4.00 10.00
13 Brent Abernathy 2.00 5.00
14 Brian Mallette 2.00 5.00
15 Brian Rogers 2.00 5.00
16 Cam Esslinger 2.00 5.00
17 Carlos Garcia 2.00 5.00
18 Carlos Valderrama 2.00 5.00
19 Cesar Izturis 6.00 15.00
Black Autograph
20 Chad Durbin 2.00 5.00
21 Chris Baker 2.00 5.00
22 Claudio Vargas 2.00 5.00
23 Cory Aldridge 2.00 5.00
24 Craig Monroe 6.00 15.00
25 David Elder 2.00 5.00
26 David Brous 2.00 5.00
27 David Espinosa 2.00 5.00
28 Derrick Lewis 2.00 5.00
29 Elio Serrano 2.00 5.00
30 Elpidio Guzman 2.00 5.00
31 Eric Cyr 2.00 5.00
32 Eric Valent 2.00 5.00
33 Erik Bedard 3.00 8.00
34 Esix Snead 2.00 5.00
35 Francis Beltran 2.00 5.00
36 George Perez 2.00 5.00
37 Gene Altman 2.00 5.00
38 Greg Miller 2.00 5.00
39 Horacio Ramirez 2.00 5.00
40 Jason Hart 2.00 5.00
41 Jason Karnuth 2.00 5.00
42 Jason Romano 2.00 5.00
43 Jeff Deardorff 2.00 5.00
44 Jeremy Affeldt 3.00 8.00
45 Jeremy Lambert 2.00 5.00
46 John Ennis 2.00 5.00
47 John Grabow 2.00 5.00
48 Jose Cueto 2.00 5.00
49 Jose Mieses 2.00 5.00
Black Autograph
50 Jose Ortiz 2.00 5.00
51 Josh Pearce 2.00 5.00
52 Josue Perez 2.00 5.00
53 Juan Diaz 2.00 5.00
54 Juan Pena 2.00 5.00
55 Keith Ginter 2.50 6.00
Black Autograph
56 Kevin Frederick 2.00 5.00
57 Kevin Joseph 2.00 5.00
58 Kevin Olsen 2.00 5.00
60 Kris Keller 2.00 5.00
61 Larry Bigbie 3.00 8.00
62 Les Walrond 2.00 5.00
63 Luis Pineda 2.00 5.00
64 Luis Rivas 2.00 5.00
65 Luis Rivera 2.00 5.00
66 Luke Hudson 2.00 5.00
67 Marcus Giles 6.00 15.00
68 Mark Ellis 2.00 5.00
69 Martin Vargas 2.00 5.00
70 Matt Childers 2.00 5.00
71 Matt Guerrier 2.00 5.00
72 Matt Thornton 2.00 5.00
73 Matt White 2.00 5.00
74 Mike Penney 2.00 5.00
75 Nate Teut 2.00 5.00
76 Nick Maness 2.00 5.00
77 Orlando Woodards 2.00 5.00
78 Paul Phillips 2.00 5.00
79 Pedro Feliz 4.00 10.00
80 Ramon Vazquez 2.00 5.00
81 Raul Chavez 2.00 5.00
82 Reed Johnson 2.50 6.00
83 Ryan Freel 6.00 15.00
84 Ryan Jamison 2.00 5.00
85 Ryan Ludwick 2.00 5.00
86 Saul Rivera 2.00 5.00
87 Steve Bechler 4.00 10.00
88 Steve Green 2.00 5.00
89 Steve Smyth 2.00 5.00
90 Tike Redman 2.50 6.00
91 Tom Shearn 2.00 5.00
92 Tomas De La Rosa 2.00 5.00
93 Tony Cogan 2.00 5.00
94 Travis Hafner 8.00 20.00
95 Travis Hughes 2.50 6.00
96 Wilkin Ruan 2.00 5.00
97 Will Ohman 2.00 5.00
98 Wilmy Caceras 2.00 5.00
99 Wilson Guzman 2.00 5.00
100 Winston Abreu 2.00 5.00

1995 Select Certified Samples
COMPLETE SET (8) 8.00 20.00
2 Reggie Sanders .20 .50
3 Cal Ripken 4.00 10.00
Gold Team
10 Mo Vaughn .20 .50
39 Mike Piazza 2.50 6.00
50 Mark McGwire 2.50 6.00
75 Roberto Alomar .30 .75
89 Larry Walker .50 1.25
110 Ray Durham .30 .75

1995 Select Certified
This 135-card standard-size set was issued through hobby outlets only. This product was issued in six-card packs. The cards are made with 24-point stock and are all metallic and double laminated. Rookie Cards in this set include Bobby Higginson and Hideo Nomo. Card number 18 was never printed; Cal Ripken is featured on a special card numbered 2131, which is included in the complete set of 135.
COMPLETE SET (135) 15.00 40.00
SET INCLUDES CARD 2131
CARD NUMBER 18 DOES NOT EXIST
1 Barry Bonds 1.25 3.00
2 Reggie Sanders .20 .50
3 Terry Steinbach .08 .25
4 Eduardo Perez .08 .25
5 Frank Thomas .50 1.25
6 Wil Cordero .08 .25
7 John Olerud .20 .50
8 Deion Sanders .30 .75
9 Mike Mussina .30 .75
10 Mo Vaughn .20 .50
11 Will Clark .30 .75
12 Chili Davis .20 .50
13 Jimmy Key .20 .50
14 Eddie Murray .50 1.25
15 Bernard Gilkey .08 .25
16 David Cone .20 .50
17 Tim Salmon .30 .75
19 Steve Ontiveros .08 .25
20 Andres Galarraga .20 .50
21 Don Mattingly 1.25 3.00
22 Kevin Appier .20 .50
23 Paul Molitor .20 .50
24 Edgar Martinez .30 .75
25 Andy Benes .08 .25
26 Rafael Palmeiro .30 .75
27 Barry Larkin .30 .75
28 Gary Sheffield .20 .50
29 Wally Joyner .20 .50
30 Wade Boggs .30 .75
31 Rico Brogna .08 .25
32 Eddie Murray 3000th Hit .30 .75
33 Kirby Puckett .50 1.25
34 Bobby Bonilla .20 .50
35 Hal Morris .08 .25
36 Moises Alou .20 .50
37 Javier Lopez .20 .50
38 Chuck Knoblauch .20 .50
39 Mike Piazza .75 2.00
40 Travis Fryman .20 .50
41 Rickey Henderson .50 1.25
42 Jim Thome .30 .75
43 Carlos Baerga .08 .25
44 Dean Palmer .20 .50
45 Kirk Gibson .20 .50
46 Bret Saberhagen .20 .50
47 Cecil Fielder .20 .50
48 Manny Ramirez .30 .75
49 Derek Bell .08 .25
50 Mark McGwire 1.25 3.00
51 Jim Edmonds .30 .75
52 Robin Ventura .20 .50
53 Ryan Klesko .20 .50
54 Jeff Bagwell .30 .75
55 Ozzie Smith .75 2.00
56 Albert Belle .20 .50
57 Darren Daulton .20 .50
58 Jeff Conine .20 .50
59 Greg Maddux .75 2.00
60 Lenny Dykstra .20 .50
61 Randy Johnson .50 1.25
62 Fred McGriff .30 .75
63 Ray Lankford .20 .50
64 David Justice .20 .50
65 Paul O'Neill .30 .75
66 Tony Gwynn .60 1.50
67 Matt Williams .20 .50
68 Dante Bichette .20 .50
69 Craig Biggio .30 .75
70 Ken Griffey Jr. 1.00 2.50
71 J.T. Snow .20 .50
72 Cal Ripken 1.50 4.00
73 Jay Bell .20 .50
74 Joe Carter .20 .50
75 Roberto Alomar .30 .75
76 Benji Gil .08 .25
77 Ivan Rodriguez .30 .75
78 Raul Mondesi .20 .50
79 Cliff Floyd .20 .50
80 Karros .50 1.25
Piazza
Mondesi
81 Royce Clayton .08 .25
82 Billy Ashley .08 .25
83 Joey Hamilton .08 .25
84 Sammy Sosa .50 1.25
85 Jason Bere .08 .25
86 Dennis Martinez .20 .50
87 Greg Vaughn .08 .25
88 Roger Clemens 1.00 2.50
89 Larry Walker .20 .50
90 Mark Grace .30 .75
91 Kenny Lofton .20 .50
92 Carlos Perez RC .20 .50
93 Roger Cedeno .08 .25
94 Scott Ruffcorn .08 .25
95 Jim Pittsley .08 .25
96 Andy Pettitte .30 .75
97 James Baldwin .08 .25
98 Hideo Nomo RC 1.50 4.00
99 Ismael Valdes .08 .25
100 Armando Benitez .08 .25
101 Jose Malave .08 .25
102 Bob Higginson RC .40 1.00
103 LaTroy Hawkins .08 .25
104 Russ Davis .08 .25
105 Shawn Green .08 .25
106 Joe Vitiello .08 .25
107 Chipper Jones .50 1.25
108 Shane Andrews .08 .25
109 Jose Oliva .08 .25
110 Ray Durham .08 .25
111 Jon Nunnally .08 .25
112 Alex Gonzalez .08 .25
113 Vaughn Eshelman .08 .25
114 Marty Cordova .08 .25
115 Mark Grudzielanek RC .40 1.00
116 Brian L.Hunter .08 .25
117 Charles Johnson .20 .50
118 Alex Rodriguez 1.25 3.00
119 David Bell .08 .25
120 Todd Hollandsworth .08 .25
121 Joe Randa .20 .50
122 Derek Jeter 1.25 3.00
123 Frank Rodriguez .08 .25
124 Curtis Goodwin .08 .25
125 Bill Pulsipher .08 .25
126 John Mabry .08 .25
127 Julian Tavarez .08 .25
128 Edgardo Alfonzo .08 .25
129 Orlando Miller .08 .25
130 Juan Acevedo RC .08 .25
131 Jeff Cirillo .08 .25
132 Roberto Petagine .08 .25
133 Antonio Osuna .08 .25
134 Michael Tucker .08 .25
135 Garret Anderson .20 .50
2131 Cal Ripken TRIB 1.50 4.00

1995 Select Certified Mirror Gold
*STARS: 4X TO 10X BASIC CARDS
*ROOKIES: 5X TO 12X BASIC
STATED ODDS 1:5
122 Derek Jeter 30.00 60.00

1995 Select Certified Checklists
COMPLETE SET (7) 1.25 3.00
ONE PER PACK
1 Ken Griffey Jr. .25 .60
2 Frank Thomas .10 .30
3 Cal Ripken .40 1.00
4 Jeff Bagwell .07 .20
5 Mike Piazza .20 .50
6 Barry Bonds .30 .75
7 M.Ramirez .07 .20
R.Mondesi

1995 Select Certified Future
COMPLETE SET (10) 5.00 12.00
STATED ODDS 1:19
1 Chipper Jones 1.00 2.50
2 Curtis Goodwin .40 1.00
3 Hideo Nomo 1.00 2.50
4 Shawn Green .40 1.00
5 Ray Durham .40 1.00
6 Todd Hollandsworth .40 1.00
7 Brian L.Hunter .40 1.00
8 Carlos Delgado .40 1.00
9 Michael Tucker UER .40 1.00
10 Alex Rodriguez 2.50 6.00

1995 Select Certified Gold Team
COMPLETE SET (12) 40.00 80.00
STATED ODDS 1:41
1 Ken Griffey Jr. 10.00 25.00
2 Frank Thomas 3.00 8.00
3 Cal Ripken 10.00 25.00
4 Jeff Bagwell 2.00 5.00
5 Mike Piazza 5.00 12.00
6 Barry Bonds 8.00 20.00
7 Matt Williams 1.25 3.00
8 Don Mattingly 8.00 20.00
9 Will Clark 2.00 5.00
10 Tony Gwynn 4.00 10.00
11 Kirby Puckett 3.00 8.00
12 Jose Canseco 3.00 8.00

1995 Select Certified Potential Unlimited 1975
COMPLETE SET (20) 60.00 120.00
STATED ODDS 1:32
STATED PRINT RUN 1975 SETS
*903 CARDS: .6X TO 1.5X 1975 CARDS
ONE 903 CARD PER SEALED BOX
STATED PRINT RUN 903 SETS
1975 CARDS PRICED BELOW
1 Cliff Floyd 1.50 4.00
2 Manny Ramirez 2.50 6.00
3 Raul Mondesi 1.50 4.00
4 Scott Ruffcorn 1.50 4.00
5 Billy Ashley 1.50 4.00
6 Alex Gonzalez 1.50 4.00
7 Midre Cummings 1.50 4.00
8 Charles Johnson 1.50 4.00
9 Garret Anderson 1.50 4.00
10 Hideo Nomo 6.00 15.00
11 Chipper Jones 4.00 10.00
12 Curtis Goodwin 1.50 4.00
13 Frank Rodriguez 1.50 4.00
14 Shawn Green 1.50 4.00
15 Ray Durham 1.50 4.00
16 Todd Hollandsworth 1.50 4.00
17 Brian L.Hunter 1.50 4.00
18 Carlos Delgado 1.50 4.00
19 Michael Tucker 1.50 4.00
20 Alex Rodriguez 12.50 30.00

1996 Select Certified
The 1996 Select Certified hobby only set was issued in one series totalling 144 cards. Each six-card pack carried a suggested retail price of $4.99. Printed on special 24-point silver mirror mylar card stock, the fronts feature a color player photo on a gray and black background. The backs carry another color player photo with information about his playing abilities.
COMPLETE SET (144) 15.00 40.00
1 Frank Thomas .40 1.00
2 Tino Martinez .25 .60
3 Gary Sheffield .15 .40
4 Kenny Lofton .15 .40
5 Joe Carter .15 .40
6 Alex Rodriguez .75 2.00
7 Chipper Jones .40 1.00
8 Roger Clemens .75 2.00
9 Jay Bell .15 .40
10 Eddie Murray .40 1.00
11 Will Clark .25 .60
12 Mike Mussina .25 .60
13 Hideo Nomo .75 2.00
14 Andres Galarraga .15 .40
15 Marc Newfield .15 .40
16 Jason Isringhausen .15 .40
17 Randy Johnson .40 1.00
18 Chuck Knoblauch .15 .40
19 J.T. Snow .15 .40
20 Mark McGwire 1.00 2.50
21 Tony Gwynn .50 1.25
22 Albert Belle .15 .40
23 Gregg Jefferies .15 .40
24 Reggie Sanders .15 .40
25 Bernie Williams .25 .60
26 Ray Lankford .15 .40
27 Johnny Damon .25 .60
28 Ryne Sandberg .60 1.50
29 Rondell White .15 .40
30 Mike Piazza .60 1.50
31 Barry Bonds 1.00 2.50
32 Greg Maddux .60 1.50
33 Craig Biggio .25 .60
34 John Valentin .15 .40
35 Ivan Rodriguez .25 .60
36 Rico Brogna .15 .40
37 Tim Salmon .25 .60
38 Sterling Hitchcock .15 .40
39 Charles Johnson .15 .40
40 Travis Fryman .15 .40
41 Barry Larkin .25 .60
42 Tom Glavine .25 .60
43 Marty Cordova .15 .40
44 Shawn Green .15 .40
45 Ben McDonald .15 .40
46 Robin Ventura .15 .40
47 Ken Griffey Jr. .75 2.00
48 Orlando Merced .15 .40
49 Paul O'Neill .25 .60
50 Ozzie Smith .60 1.50
51 Manny Ramirez .25 .60
52 Ismael Valdes .15 .40
53 Cal Ripken 1.25 3.00
54 Jeff Bagwell .25 .60
55 Greg Vaughn .15 .40
56 Juan Gonzalez .15 .40
57 Raul Mondesi .15 .40
58 Carlos Baerga .15 .40
59 Sammy Sosa .40 1.00
60 Mike Kelly .15 .40
61 Edgar Martinez .25 .60
62 Kirby Puckett .40 1.00
63 Cecil Fielder .15 .40
64 David Cone .15 .40
65 Moises Alou .15 .40
66 Fred McGriff .25 .60
67 Mo Vaughn .15 .40
68 Edgardo Alfonzo .15 .40
69 Jim Thome .25 .60
70 Rickey Henderson .40 1.00
71 Dante Bichette .15 .40
72 Lenny Dykstra .15 .40
73 Benji Gil .15 .40
74 Wade Boggs .25 .60
75 Jim Edmonds .15 .40
76 Michael Tucker .15 .40
77 Carlos Delgado .15 .40
78 Butch Huskey .15 .40
79 Billy Ashley .15 .40
80 Dean Palmer .15 .40
81 Paul Molitor .15 .40
82 Ryan Klesko .15 .40
83 Brian L.Hunter .15 .40
84 Jay Buhner .15 .40
85 Larry Walker .15 .40
86 Mike Bordick .15 .40
87 Matt Williams .15 .40
88 Jack McDowell .15 .40
89 Hal Morris .15 .40
90 Brian Jordan .15 .40
91 Andy Pettitte .25 .60
92 Melvin Nieves .15 .40
93 Pedro Martinez .25 .60
94 Mark Grace .25 .60
95 Garret Anderson .15 .40
96 Andre Dawson .15 .40
97 Ray Durham .15 .40
98 Jose Canseco .25 .60
99 Roberto Alomar .25 .60
100 Derek Jeter 1.00 2.50
101 Alan Benes .15 .40
102 Karim Garcia .15 .40
103 Robin Jennings .15 .40
104 Bob Abreu .15 .40
105 Sal Fasano UER .15 .40
105A Sal Fasano
Correct Name on Front of Card
106 Steve Gibralter .15 .40
107 Jermaine Dye .15 .40
108 Jason Kendall .15 .40
109 Mike Grace RC .15 .40
110 Jason Schmidt .25 .60
111 Paul Wilson .15 .40
112 Rey Ordonez .15 .40
113 Wilton Guerrero RC .15 .40
114 Brooks Kieschnick .15 .40
115 George Arias .15 .40
116 Osvaldo Fernandez RC .15 .40
117 Todd Hollandsworth .15 .40
118 John Wasdin .15 .40
119 Eric Owens .15 .40
120 Chan Ho Park .15 .40
121 Mark Loretta .15 .40
122 Richard Hidalgo .15 .40
123 Jeff Suppan .15 .40
124 Jim Pittsley .15 .40
125 LaTroy Hawkins .15 .40
126 Chris Snopek .15 .40
127 Justin Thompson .15 .40
128 Jay Powell .15 .40
129 Alex Ochoa .15 .40
130 Felipe Crespo .15 .40
131 Matt Lawton RC .15 .40
132 Jimmy Haynes .15 .40
133 Terrell Wade .15 .40
134 Ruben Rivera .15 .40
135 Frank Thomas PP .25 .60
136 Ken Griffey Jr. PP .50 1.25
137 Greg Maddux PP .40 1.00
138 Mike Piazza PP .40 1.00
139 Cal Ripken PP .60 1.50
140 Albert Belle PP .15 .40
141 Mo Vaughn PP .15 .40
142 Chipper Jones PP .25 .60
143 Hideo Nomo PP .25 .60
144 Ryan Klesko PP .15 .40

1996 Select Certified Artist's Proofs
*STARS: 2.5X TO 6X BASIC CARDS
STATED ODDS 1:18
100 Derek Jeter 60.00 150.00

1996 Select Certified Certified Blue
*STARS: 5X TO 12X BASIC CARDS
*ROOKIES: 2.5X TO 6X BASIC CARDS
STATED ODDS 1:50
ANNCD PRINT RUN OF 180
100 Derek Jeter 300.00 600.00

1996 Select Certified Certified Red
COMPLETE SET (144) 250.00 500.00
*STARS: 1X TO 2.5X BASIC CARDS
STATED ODDS 1:5
100 Derek Jeter 40.00 100.00

1996 Select Certified Mirror Blue
*STARS: 40X TO 100X BASIC
*PP STARS 135-144: 30X TO 80X BASIC
*ROOKIES: 20X TO 50X BASIC
STATED ODDS 1:200
STATED PRINT RUN 45 SETS
100 Derek Jeter 4000.00 8000.00

1996 Select Certified Mirror Gold
*GOLD 1-134: 50X TO 120X BASIC
*PP 135-144: 50X TO 120X BASIC
*ROOKIES: 30X TO 80X BASIC
STATED ODDS 1:300
STATED PRINT RUN 30 SETS
53 Cal Ripken 1200.00 1500.00
100 Derek Jeter 5000.00 10000.00
139 Cal Ripken PP 1200.00 1500.00

1996 Select Certified Mirror Red
*STARS: 25X TO 60X BASIC CARDS
*ROOKIES: 10X TO 25X BASIC CARDS
STATED ODDS 1:100
STATED PRINT RUN 90 SETS
100 Derek Jeter 3000.00 6000.00

1996 Select Certified Interleague Preview
COMPLETE SET (25) 100.00 200.00
STATED ODDS 1:42
1 K.Griffey Jr. 4.00 10.00
H.Nomo
2 G.Maddux 3.00 8.00
M.Vaughn
3 S.Sosa 2.00 5.00
F.Thomas
4 M.Piazza 3.00 8.00
J.Edmonds
5 R.Clemens 4.00 10.00
R.Klesko
6 D.Jeter 20.00 50.00
R.Ordonez
7 J.Damon 1.25 3.00
R.Lankford
8 M.Ramirez 1.25 3.00
R.Sanders

9 B.Bonds 5.00 12.00
J.Buhner
10 J.Isringhausen 1.25 3.00
W.Boggs
11 C.Jones 2.00 5.00
D.Cone
12 J.Bagwell 1.25 3.00
W.Clark
13 T.Gwynn 2.50 6.00
R.Johnson
14 C.Ripken 6.00 15.00
T.Glavine
15 K.Puckett 2.00 5.00
A.Benes
16 G.Sheffield 1.25 3.00
M.Mussina
17 R.Mondesi 1.25 3.00
T.Salmon
18 R.White .75 2.00
C.Delgado
19 R.Sandberg 3.00 8.00
C.Fielder
20 K.Lofton .75 2.00
B.Hunter
21 P.Wilson 1.25 3.00
P.O'Neill
22 I.Valdes 1.25 3.00
E.Martinez
23 M.McGwire 5.00 12.00
M.Williams
24 A.Belle 1.25 3.00
B.Larkin
25 B.Anderson .75 2.00
M.Grissom
S6 D.Jeter
R.Ordonez SAMPLE
S7 J.Damon
R.Lankford SAMPLE
S8 M.Ramirez
R.Sanders SAMPLE
S24 A.Belle
B.Larkin SAMPLE

1996 Select Certified Select Few

COMPLETE SET (18) 100.00 200.00
STATED ODDS 1:60
1 Sammy Sosa 5.00 12.00
2 Derek Jeter 12.00 30.00
3 Ken Griffey Jr. 10.00 25.00
4 Albert Belle 2.00 5.00
5 Cal Ripken 15.00 40.00
6 Greg Maddux 8.00 20.00
7 Frank Thomas 5.00 12.00
8 Mo Vaughn 2.00 5.00
9 Chipper Jones 5.00 12.00
10 Mike Piazza 5.00 12.00
11 Ryan Klesko 2.00 5.00
12 Hideo Nomo 5.00 12.00
13 Alan Benes 2.00 5.00
14 Manny Ramirez 3.00 8.00
15 Gary Sheffield 2.00 5.00
16 Barry Bonds 8.00 20.00
17 Matt Williams 2.00 5.00
18 Johnny Damon 3.00 8.00

2013 Select

AU RC PRINT RUNS B/WN 500-750 COPIES PER
EXCHANGE DEADLINE 6/25/2015
1 Torii Hunter .25 .60
2 Prince Fielder .30 .75
3 Giancarlo Stanton .40 1.00
4 Jacoby Ellsbury .30 .75
5 Derek Jeter 1.50 4.00
6 Chris Sale .40 1.00
7 Matt Cain .30 .75
8 Elvis Andrus .30 .75
9 Andrew McCutchen .40 1.00
10 Todd Helton .30 .75
11 Yadier Molina .50 1.25
12 J.J. Hardy .25 .60
13 Jordan Zimmermann .30 .75
14 Mat Latos .30 .75
15 Ichiro Suzuki .50 1.25
16 Edwin Encarnacion .40 1.00
17 Gerardo Parra .25 .60
18 Ryan Howard .30 .75
19 Joey Votto .40 1.00
20 Carlos Beltran .30 .75
21 Freddie Freeman .50 1.25
22 Mike Trout 5.00 12.00
23 David Price .30 .75
24 Hisashi Iwakuma .30 .75
25 CC Sabathia .30 .75
26 Alex Gordon .30 .75
27 Jason Kipnis .30 .75
28 Tim Lincecum .30 .75
29 Justin Morneau .30 .75
30 Pablo Sandoval .30 .75
31 Adam Jones .30 .75
32 Nick Swisher .30 .75
33 Buster Posey .50 1.25
34 Matt Kemp .30 .75
35 Justin Verlander .40 1.00
36 Dustin Pedroia .40 1.00
37 Stephen Strasburg .40 1.00
38 Chase Headley .25 .60
39 Carlos Gonzalez .30 .75
40 Robinson Cano .30 .75
41 Roy Halladay .30 .75
42 Ryan Zimmerman .30 .75
43 Felix Hernandez .30 .75
44 Marco Scutaro .30 .75
45 Michael Bourn .25 .60
46 Josh Hamilton .30 .75
47 B.J. Upton .30 .75
48 Adam Wainwright .30 .75
49 Adrian Gonzalez .30 .75
50 Brian Wilson .40 1.00
51 Domonic Brown .30 .75
52 David Ortiz .40 1.00
53 Chase Utley .30 .75
54 Chris Johnson .25 .60
55 Troy Tulowitzki .40 1.00
56 Mike Napoli .25 .60
57 David Wright .30 .75
58 Matt Moore .30 .75
59 Mark Trumbo .25 .60
60 Alfonso Soriano .30 .75
61 Paul Goldschmidt .40 1.00
62 Ian Kinsler .30 .75
63 Norichika Aoki .25 .60
64 Raul Ibanez .30 .75
65 Jose Reyes .30 .75
66 Starling Marte .30 .75
67 Craig Kimbrel .30 .75
68 Alex Rios .30 .75
69 Bartolo Colon .25 .60
70 Hunter Pence .30 .75
71 Miguel Cabrera .40 1.00
72 Mariano Rivera .50 1.25
73 Anthony Rizzo .50 1.25
74 Matt Harvey .30 .75
75 Justin Upton .30 .75
76 Curtis Granderson .30 .75
77 Yoenis Cespedes .40 1.00
78 Clay Buchholz .25 .60
79 Jered Weaver .30 .75
80 Brandon Phillips .25 .60
81 Joe Mauer .30 .75
82 Allen Craig .30 .75
83 Wei-Yin Chen .25 .60
84 Jose Altuve .30 .75
85 Clayton Kershaw .60 1.50
86 Jose Bautista .30 .75
87 Starlin Castro .25 .60
88 Adrian Beltre .40 1.00
89 R.A. Dickey .30 .75
90 Evan Longoria .30 .75
91 Shin-Soo Choo .30 .75
92 James Shields .25 .60
93 Jason Heyward .30 .75
94 Albert Pujols .50 1.25
95 Chris Davis .30 .75
96 Jean Segura .30 .75
97 Max Scherzer .40 1.00
98 Bryce Harper .60 1.50
99 Pat Corbin .30 .75
100 Yu Darvish .40 1.00
101 Rickey Henderson 1.25 3.00
102 Ken Griffey Jr. 8.00 20.00
103 Mike Schmidt 2.00 5.00
104 Ken Griffey Jr. 8.00 20.00
105 Bob Gibson 1.00 2.50
106 Roger Clemens 1.50 4.00
107 Dwight Gooden .75 2.00
108 Nolan Ryan 4.00 10.00
109 Nomar Garciaparra 1.00 2.50
110 Frank Thomas 1.25 3.00
111 Ernie Banks 1.25 3.00
112 Pete Rose 2.50 6.00
113 Bo Jackson 1.25 3.00
114 George Brett 2.50 6.00
115 Craig Biggio 1.00 2.50
116 Nolan Ryan 4.00 10.00
117 Don Mattingly 2.50 6.00
118 Ryne Sandberg 2.50 6.00
119 Ozzie Smith 1.50 4.00
120 Darryl Strawberry .75 2.00
121 Will Clark 1.00 2.50
122 Randy Johnson 1.25 3.00
123 Chipper Jones 1.25 3.00
124 Mike Piazza 1.25 3.00
125 Cal Ripken Jr. 4.00 10.00
126 Yasiel Puig RC 10.00 25.00
127 Cody Asche RC 1.25 3.00
128 Josh Phegley RC .75 2.00
129 Kyuji Fujikawa RC 1.25 3.00
130 Alberto Cabrera RC .75 2.00
131 Nolan Arenado RC 20.00 50.00
132 Oswaldo Arcia RC .75 2.00
133 Marcell Ozuna RC 2.00 5.00
134 Carlos Martinez RC 1.25 3.00
135 Carlos Triunfel RC 1.00 2.50
136 Neftali Soto RC 1.00 2.50
137 Kyle Gibson RC 1.25 3.00
138 Yan Gomes RC 1.00 2.50
139 Justin Grimm RC .75 2.00
140 Christian Garcia RC .75 2.00
141 Jean Machi RC .75 2.00
142 A.J. Ramos RC 1.00 2.50
143 Paul Clemens RC .75 2.00
144 Alfredo Marte RC .75 2.00
145 Robbie Grossman RC .75 2.00
146 Matt Magill RC .75 2.00
147 Scott Rice RC 1.25 3.00
148 Nate Freiman RC .75 2.00
149 Ryan Pressly RC 1.00 2.50
150 T.J. McFarland RC .75 2.00
151 Yoervis Medina RC .75 2.00
152 Hiram Burgos RC .75 2.00
153 Seth Maness RC .75 2.00
154 Tyler Lyons RC .75 2.00
155 Munenori Kawasaki RC 1.25 3.00
156 Robert Carson RC .75 2.00
157 Jordy Mercer RC .75 2.00
158 Jose Ortega RC .75 2.00
159 Hector Rondon RC 1.00 2.50
160 Nick Noonan RC 1.00 2.50
161 Leury Garcia RC .75 2.00
162 Luis D. Jimenez RC .75 2.00
163 Juan Lagares RC 1.00 2.50
164 Jose Cisnero RC .75 2.00
165 Vidal Nuno RC .75 2.00
166 Zach Lutz RC .75 2.00
167 David Adams RC 1.00 2.50
168 Donovan Hand RC .75 2.00
169 Cesar Hernandez RC .75 2.00
170 Alex Wood RC 1.00 2.50
171 Todd Redmond RC .75 2.00
172 Deunte Heath RC .75 2.00
173 Pedro Villarreal RC .75 2.00
174 Nathan Karns RC .75 2.00
175 Ryan Reid RC .75 2.00
176 Nick Tepesch AU/750 RC 3.00 8.00
177 Aaron Hicks AU/750 RC 4.00 10.00
178 Aaron Loup AU/750 RC 2.50 6.00
179 Adam Warren AU/750 RC 2.50 6.00
180 Jackie Bradley Jr. AU/750 RC 12.00 30.00
181 Alex Wilson AU/750 RC EXCH 2.50 6.00
182 Jonathan Pettibone AU/500 RC 4.00 10.00
183 Allen Webster AU/500 RC EXCH 3.00 8.00
184 Tony Cingrani AU/500 RC 5.00 12.00
185 Andrew Taylor AU/750 RC 2.50 6.00
186 Andrew Werner AU/750 RC 2.50 6.00
187 Bobby LaFromboise AU/750 RC 2.50 6.00
188 Brandon Barnes AU/750 RC 2.50 6.00
189 Brandon Maurer AU/750 RC 3.00 8.00
190 Christian Yelich AU/500 RC 40.00 100.00
191 Brooks Raley AU/750 RC 2.50 6.00
192 Bruce Rondon AU/750 RC 2.50 6.00
193 Bryan Morris AU/750 RC 2.50 6.00
194 Carlos Martinez AU/750 RC 4.00 10.00
195 Preston Claiborne AU/500 RC 2.50 6.00
196 Carter Capps AU/750 RC 2.50 6.00
197 Jedd Gyorko AU/500 RC 3.00 8.00
198 Chad Jenkins AU/750 RC 2.50 6.00
199 Chris Herrmann AU/750 RC 2.50 6.00
200 Tyler Cloyd AU/500 RC 3.00 8.00
201 Chris Rusin AU/750 RC 2.50 6.00
202 Justin Wilson AU/500 RC EXCH 2.50 6.00
203 Corey Kluber AU/750 RC 8.00 20.00
204 Cory Burns AU/750 RC 2.50 6.00
205 Chris Leroux AU/750 RC 2.50 6.00
206 Derek Dietrich AU/750 RC 3.00 8.00
207 Derrick Robinson AU/750 RC 2.50 6.00
208 Didi Gregorius AU/750 RC 10.00 25.00
209 Evan Gattis AU/750 RC 5.00 12.00
210 Tyler Skaggs AU/500 RC 4.00 10.00
211 Kevin Gausman AU/750 RC 8.00 20.00
212 Jose Dominguez AU/750 RC 2.50 6.00
213 Wil Myers AU/500 RC 8.00 20.00
214 Nick Maronde AU/750 RC 3.00 8.00
215 Steven Lerud AU/750 (RC) 2.50 6.00
216 Junior Lake AU/750 RC 2.50 6.00
217 Tom Koehler AU/750 RC 2.50 6.00
218 Tyson Brummett AU/750 RC 2.50 6.00
219 Zack Wheeler AU/750 RC 5.00 12.00
220 Adam Eaton AU/500 RC 4.00 10.00
221 Zoilo Almonte AU/500 RC 3.00 8.00
222 Avisail Garcia AU/500 RC 3.00 8.00
223 Brock Holt AU/500 RC 3.00 8.00
224 Casey Kelly AU/500 RC 3.00 8.00
225 Collin McHugh AU/500 RC 2.50 6.00
226 Darin Ruf AU/750 RC 5.00 12.00
227 David Lough AU/500 RC 2.50 6.00
228 Dylan Bundy AU/500 RC 6.00 15.00
229 Eury Perez AU/500 RC 3.00 8.00
230 M.Machado AU/500 RC 15.00 40.00
231 Jake Odorizzi AU/500 RC 3.00 8.00
232 Jaye Chapman AU/500 RC 2.50 6.00
233 Jeurys Familia AU/500 RC 4.00 10.00
234 Jurickson Profar AU/500 RC 3.00 8.00
235 L.J. Hoes AU/500 RC 3.00 8.00
236 Michael Wacha AU/500 RC 3.00 8.00
237 Melky Mesa AU/500 RC EXCH 3.00 8.00
238 Mike Olt AU/500 RC 3.00 8.00
239 Mike Zunino AU/500 RC 4.00 10.00
240 Paco Rodriguez AU/500 RC 4.00 10.00
241 Rob Brantly AU/500 RC 2.50 6.00
242 Rob Scahill AU/500 RC 2.50 6.00
243 Shawn Tolleson AU/750 RC 2.50 6.00
244 Shelby Miller AU/500 RC 6.00 15.00
245 Sonny Gray AU/750 RC 4.00 10.00
246 J.Fernandez AU/750 RC 6.00 15.00
247 Gerrit Cole AU/500 RC 60.00 150.00
248 Nick Franklin AU/750 RC 3.00 8.00
249 Anthony Rendon AU/500 RC 15.00 40.00
250 H.Jin Ryu AU/750 RC EXCH 6.00 15.00

2013 Select Prizm

*PRIZM VET: 1X TO 2.5X BASIC
*PRIZM RET: .6X TO 1.5X BASIC
*PRIZM RC: 1X TO 2.5X BASIC
PRIZM RC PRINT RUN 99 SER.#'d SETS
*PRIZM AU RC: .5X TO 1.2X BASIC
PRIZM AU PRINT RUN 99 SER.#'d SETS
EXCHANGE DEADLINE 6/25/2015
22 Mike Trout 25.00 60.00
126 Yasiel Puig 12.00 30.00
247 Gerrit Cole AU 75.00 200.00

2013 Select En Fuego

1 Bryce Harper 3.00 8.00
2 Mike Trout 15.00 40.00
3 Derek Jeter 5.00 12.00
4 Albert Pujols 2.50 6.00
5 Buster Posey 2.50 6.00
6 Miguel Cabrera 2.00 5.00
7 Andrew McCutchen 2.00 5.00
8 Matt Harvey 1.50 4.00
9 Paul Goldschmidt 2.00 5.00
10 Justin Verlander 2.00 5.00
11 Joey Votto 2.00 5.00
12 Troy Tulowitzki 2.00 5.00
13 Evan Longoria 1.50 4.00
14 Joe Mauer 1.50 4.00
15 Felix Hernandez 1.50 4.00
16 Adam Jones 1.50 4.00
17 Clayton Kershaw 5.00 12.00
18 Yu Darvish 2.00 5.00
19 Ken Griffey Jr. 4.00 10.00
20 Justin Upton 1.50 4.00
21 Cal Ripken Jr. 6.00 15.00
22 Robinson Cano 1.50 4.00
23 David Wright 1.50 4.00
24 Jean Segura 1.50 4.00
25 Dustin Pedroia 2.00 5.00
26 Brandon Phillips 1.00 2.50
27 Matt Kemp 1.50 4.00
28 Chase Utley 1.50 4.00
29 Jose Bautista 1.50 4.00
30 Yasiel Puig 5.00 12.00

2013 Select En Fuego Prizm

*PRIZM: .5X TO 1.2X BASIC

2013 Select Select Future

1 Mark Appel 2.00 5.00
2 Kris Bryant 8.00 20.00
3 Jonathan Gray 1.50 4.00
4 Kohl Stewart 1.50 4.00
5 Clint Frazier 6.00 15.00
6 Colin Moran 1.50 4.00
7 Trey Ball 2.00 5.00
8 Hunter Dozier 1.25 3.00
9 Austin Meadows 3.00 8.00
10 Dominic Smith 2.00 5.00
11 D.J. Peterson 1.25 3.00
12 Hunter Renfroe 2.00 5.00
13 Reese McGuire 1.50 4.00
14 Braden Shipley 1.25 3.00
15 J.P. Crawford 2.00 5.00

2013 Select Select Future Prizm

*PRIZM: .5X TO 1.2X BASIC

2013 Select Select Team

1 Carlos Gonzalez 1.50 4.00
2 Clayton Kershaw 3.00 8.00
3 Mike Trout 15.00 40.00
4 Buster Posey 2.50 6.00
5 Nick Swisher 1.50 4.00
6 Anthony Rizzo 2.50 6.00
7 Andrew McCutchen 2.00 5.00
8 Elvis Andrus 1.50 4.00
9 Matt Kemp 1.50 4.00
10 Felix Hernandez 1.50 4.00

2013 Select Select Team Prizm

*PRIZM: .5X TO 1.2X BASIC

2013 Select Signatures

EXCHANGE DEADLINE 6/25/2015
MOST NOT PRICED DUE TO LACK OF INFO
2 Adam LaRoche 5.00 12.00
4 Alex Gordon 4.00 10.00
6 Aramis Ramirez 4.00 10.00
7 Asdrubal Cabrera 4.00 10.00
8 Zach McAllister 4.00 10.00
9 Brandon Phillips 10.00 25.00
10 Brett Gardner 15.00 40.00
11 Brett Jackson 4.00 10.00
16 Chris Perez 4.00 10.00
17 Chris Sale 4.00 10.00
21 Cory Luebke 4.00 10.00
23 Yoenis Cespedes 12.50 30.00
24 Curt Schilling 12.50 30.00
25 Darryl Strawberry 12.50 30.00
26 Darwin Barney 4.00 10.00
27 Dave Kingman 6.00 15.00
28 David Freese 5.00 12.00
29 David Ortiz 20.00 50.00
30 Wilin Rosario 4.00 10.00
33 Drew Stubbs 4.00 10.00
38 Glen Perkins 4.00 10.00
39 Harold Reynolds 10.00 25.00
41 Tim Wakefield EXCH 20.00 50.00
42 James Shields 5.00 12.00
43 Jarrod Parker 4.00 10.00
44 Jason Grilli 4.00 10.00
45 Jason Kipnis 5.00 12.00
46 Jason Motte 4.00 10.00
47 Jay Bruce 8.00 20.00
48 Vinnie Pestano 5.00 12.00
54 Josh Johnson 5.00 12.00
55 Josh Reddick 4.00 10.00
58 Kirk Nieuwenhuis 4.00 10.00
60 Lance Lynn 5.00 12.00
62 Logan Morrison 6.00 15.00
63 Lucas Duda 4.00 10.00
64 Mark Trumbo 4.00 10.00
65 Martin Prado 4.00 10.00
66 Matt Adams 6.00 15.00
67 Tyler Flowers 4.00 10.00
69 Mike Mussina EXCH 8.00 20.00
71 Troy Tulowitzki 5.00 12.00
72 Mitchell Boggs 4.00 10.00
73 Nelson Cruz 4.00 10.00
76 Pablo Sandoval 4.00 10.00
80 Troy Glaus EXCH 6.00 15.00
82 Thomas Neal 4.00 10.00
85 Skip Schumaker 4.00 10.00
86 Starlin Castro 4.00 10.00
87 Stephen Strasburg 30.00 60.00
89 Todd Frazier 4.00 10.00
90 Robinson Cano EXCH 6.00 15.00
MM Mitch Moreland 4.00 10.00
92 Michael Morse 4.00 10.00
95 Jean Segura EXCH 3.00 8.00
96 Scott Van Slyke 4.00 10.00
97 Alex Wood 6.00 15.00
98 Chris Davis EXCH 10.00 25.00
99 Bobby Parnell 4.00 10.00
OT Oscar Taveras 12.00 30.00

2013 Select Skills

1 Miguel Cabrera 2.00 5.00
2 Mike Trout 15.00 40.00
3 Derek Jeter 5.00 12.00
4 Andrew McCutchen 2.00 5.00
5 Bryce Harper 3.00 8.00
6 Buster Posey 2.50 6.00
7 Joe Mauer 1.50 4.00
8 Robinson Cano 1.50 4.00
9 Joey Votto 2.00 5.00
10 Evan Longoria 1.50 4.00
11 Troy Tulowitzki 2.00 5.00
12 Josh Hamilton 1.50 4.00
13 Elvis Andrus 1.50 4.00
14 Michael Bourn 1.25 3.00
15 Adrian Beltre 2.00 5.00
16 Mark Teixeira 1.50 4.00
17 Brandon Phillips 1.25 3.00
18 David Wright 1.50 4.00
19 Austin Jackson 1.25 3.00
20 Alex Gordon 1.50 4.00
21 Aramis Ramirez 1.25 3.00
22 Albert Pujols 2.50 6.00
23 Jose Reyes 1.50 4.00
24 Adam Dunn 1.50 4.00
25 Edwin Encarnacion 2.00 5.00
26 Justin Verlander 2.00 5.00
27 Yu Darvish 2.00 5.00
28 Clayton Kershaw 3.00 8.00
29 Mariano Rivera 2.50 6.00
30 Matt Harvey 1.50 4.00
31 Craig Kimbrel 1.50 4.00
32 Jim Johnson 1.25 3.00
33 Ichiro Suzuki 2.50 6.00
34 Yadier Molina 2.50 6.00
35 Wade Boggs 1.50 4.00
36 Cal Ripken Jr. 6.00 15.00
37 Ken Griffey Jr. 4.00 10.00
38 George Brett 4.00 10.00
39 Ozzie Smith 2.50 6.00
40 Nolan Ryan 6.00 15.00
41 Roger Clemens 2.50 6.00
42 Randy Johnson 2.00 5.00
43 Bo Jackson 2.00 5.00
44 Greg Maddux 2.50 6.00
45 Tony Gwynn 2.00 5.00

2013 Select Skills Prizm

*PRIZM: .5X TO 1.2X BASIC

2013 Select Statisticians

1 Buster Posey 2.50 6.00
2 Miguel Cabrera 2.00 5.00
3 Mike Trout 15.00 40.00
4 Derek Jeter 5.00 12.00
5 Albert Pujols 2.50 6.00
6 Giancarlo Stanton 2.00 5.00
7 Andrew McCutchen 2.00 5.00
8 Justin Verlander 2.00 5.00
9 David Price 1.50 4.00
10 Gio Gonzalez 1.50 4.00
11 R.A. Dickey 1.50 4.00
12 Clayton Kershaw 3.00 8.00
13 Jered Weaver 1.50 4.00
14 George Brett 4.00 10.00
15 Ken Griffey Jr. 4.00 10.00

2013 Select Statisticians Prizm

*PRIZM: .5X TO 1.2X BASIC

2013 Select Thunder Alley

1 Miguel Cabrera 2.00 5.00
2 Jose Bautista 1.50 4.00
3 Josh Hamilton 1.50 4.00
4 Bryce Harper 3.00 8.00
5 Paul Goldschmidt 2.00 5.00
6 Adam Dunn 1.50 4.00
7 Justin Upton 1.50 4.00
8 Chris Davis 1.50 4.00
9 Carlos Gonzalez 1.50 4.00
10 Adrian Beltre 2.00 5.00
11 Prince Fielder 1.50 4.00
12 Anthony Rizzo 2.50 6.00
13 Mark Trumbo 1.25 3.00
14 Albert Pujols 2.50 6.00
15 Matt Kemp 1.50 4.00
16 Robinson Cano 1.50 4.00
17 Edwin Encarnacion 2.00 5.00
18 David Ortiz 2.00 5.00
19 Carlos Beltran 1.50 4.00
20 Mike Trout 15.00 40.00
21 Yoenis Cespedes 2.00 5.00
22 Yasiel Puig 5.00 12.00
23 Curtis Granderson 1.50 4.00
24 Adam Jones 1.50 4.00
25 Andrew McCutchen 2.00 5.00

2013 Select Thunder Alley Prizm

*PRIZM: .5X TO 1.2X BASIC

2013 Select Youngbloods

*PRIZM: .5X TO 1.2X BASIC
1 Bryce Harper 2.00 5.00
2 Mike Trout 10.00 25.00
3 Yu Darvish 1.25 3.00
4 Buster Posey 1.50 4.00
5 Matt Harvey 1.00 2.50
6 Giancarlo Stanton 1.25 3.00
7 Yasiel Puig 3.00 8.00
8 Matt Moore 1.00 2.50
9 Stephen Strasburg 1.25 3.00
10 Jean Segura 1.00 2.50

2018 Select

INSERTED IN '18 CHRONICLES PACKS
1 Dominic Smith RC .50 1.25
2 Ronald Acuna Jr. RC 10.00 25.00
3 Shohei Ohtani RC 10.00 25.00
4 Aaron Judge 1.00 2.50
5 Kris Bryant .50 1.25
6 Rhys Hoskins RC 1.50 4.00
7 Bryce Harper .60 1.50
8 Cody Bellinger .75 2.00
9 Victor Robles RC 1.00 2.50
10 Clint Frazier RC .50 1.25
11 Miguel Andujar RC 1.50 4.00
12 Manny Machado .40 1.00
13 Amed Rosario RC .50 1.25
14 Mookie Betts .75 2.00
15 Juan Soto RC 30.00 80.00
16 Jose Altuve .30 .75
17 Austin Hays RC .60 1.50
18 Mike Trout 2.00 5.00
19 Yadier Molina .50 1.25
20 Gleyber Torres RC 4.00 10.00
21 Ozzie Albies RC 1.25 3.00
22 Nolan Arenado .60 1.50
23 Rafael Devers RC 1.25 3.00
24 Willy Adames RC .50 1.25
25 Ryan McMahon RC 1.00 2.50

2018 Select Aqua

*AQUA: .75X TO 2X BASIC
*AQUA RC: .5X TO 1.2X BASIC
INSERTED IN '18 CHRONICLES PACKS
STATED PRINT RUN 299 SER.#'d SETS

2018 Select Black

*BLACK: 2.5X TO 6X BASIC
*BLACK RC:1.5X TO 4X BASIC
INSERTED IN '18 CHRONICLES PACKS
STATED PRINT RUN 25 SER.#'d SETS

2018 Select Blue

*BLUE: 1X TO 2.5X BASIC
*BLUE RC: .6X TO 1.5X BASIC
INSERTED IN '18 CHRONICLES PACKS
STATED PRINT RUN 149 SER.#'d SETS

2018 Select Carolina Blue

*CAR.BLUE: 1.5X TO 4X BASIC
*CAR.BLUE RC: 1X TO 2.5X BASIC
INSERTED IN '18 CHRONICLES PACKS
STATED PRINT RUN 50 SER.#'d SETS

2018 Select Orange

*ORANGE: 1X TO 2.5X BASIC
*ORANGE RC: .6X TO 1.5X BASIC
INSERTED IN '18 CHRONICLES PACKS
STATED PRINT RUN 199 SER.#'d SETS

2018 Select Prizm

*PRIZM: .75X TO 2X BASIC
*PRIZM RC: .5X TO 1.2X BASIC
INSERTED IN '18 CHRONICLES PACKS

2018 Select Red

*RED: 1.2X TO 3X BASIC
*RED RC: .75X TO 2X BASIC
INSERTED IN '18 CHRONICLES PACKS
STATED PRINT RUN 99 SER.#'d SETS

2018 Select Signatures

RANDOM INSERTS IN PACKS
1 Christian Villanueva 2.50 6.00
4 Luiz Gohara 2.50 6.00
5 Austin Hays 4.00 10.00
8 Lucas Sims 2.50 6.00
9 Anthony Santander 2.50 6.00
10 Cameron Gallagher 2.50 6.00
11 Nicky Delmonico 2.50 6.00
15 Dan Vogelbach 2.50 6.00
16 Daniel Norris 4.00 10.00
19 Tucker Barnhart 4.00 10.00
20 Jose Osuna 2.50 6.00

2020 Select

RANDOM INSERTS IN PACKS
1 Joe Palumbo RC .50 1.25
2 Brad Keller .25 .60
3 Yasmani Grandal .25 .60
4 Starling Marte .30 .75
5 Pete Alonso 1.00 2.50
6 Abraham Toro RC .60 1.50
7 Bo Bichette RC 5.00 12.00
8 Jake Fraley RC .60 1.50
9 Cody Bellinger .75 2.00
10 Michael Chavis .30 .75
11 Anthony Rendon .40 1.00
12 Shogo Akiyama RC .75 2.00
13 Andres Munoz RC .75 2.00
14 Sean Manaea .25 .60
15 Ramon Laureano .30 .75
16 Kyle Lewis RC 4.00 10.00
17 Eddie Rosario .30 .75
18 Cole Hamels .30 .75
19 DJ LeMahieu .40 1.00
20 Tyrone Taylor RC .50 1.25
21 Jose Abreu .40 1.00
22 Josh Bell .30 .75
23 Liam Hendriks .25 .60
24 Justin Dunn RC .60 1.50
25 Mike Moustakas .30 .75
26 Kyle Hendricks .40 1.00
27 Nico Hoerner RC 2.00 5.00
28 Adalberto Mondesi .30 .75
29 Sheldon Neuse RC .60 1.50
30 Josh Rojas RC .50 1.25
31 Bryce Harper .60 1.50
32 Kris Bryant .50 1.25
33 Kolten Wong .30 .75
34 Evan Longoria .30 .75
35 Juan Soto 1.25 3.00
36 Clayton Kershaw .60 1.50
37 Dallas Keuchel .30 .75
38 Lorenzo Cain .25 .60
39 Patrick Sandoval RC .75 2.00
40 Jonathan Hernandez RC .50 1.25
41 Deivy Grullon RC .50 1.25
42 Michael King RC .75 2.00
43 Marcell Ozuna .40 1.00
44 Kyle Seager .25 .60
45 Bobby Bradley RC .50 1.25
46 Julio Teheran .30 .75
47 Kirby Yates .25 .60
48 Marco Gonzales .25 .60
49 Stephen Strasburg .40 1.00
50 Hyun-Jin Ryu .30 .75
51 Joey Votto .40 1.00
52 Ken Giles .25 .60
53 John Means .40 1.00
54 Zac Gallen RC 1.25 3.00
55 Spencer Turnbull .25 .60
56 Logan Allen RC .50 1.25
57 Tony Gonsolin RC 2.00 5.00
58 Michael Brantley .30 .75
59 Randy Arozarena RC 4.00 10.00
60 Lourdes Gurriel .30 .75
61 Howie Kendrick .25 .60
62 Tommy Pham .25 .60
63 George Springer .30 .75
64 Bryan Abreu RC .50 1.25
65 Buster Posey .50 1.25
66 Brusdar Graterol RC .75 2.00
67 Yonathan Daza RC .60 1.50
68 Jake Odorizzi .25 .60
69 Justin Turner .40 1.00
70 Austin Meadows .40 1.00
71 Charlie Blackmon .40 1.00
72 James Paxton .30 .75
73 Jorge Soler .40 1.00
74 T.J. Zeuch RC .50 1.25
75 Gleyber Torres .75 2.00
76 Isan Diaz RC .75 2.00
77 Marcus Stroman .30 .75
78 Jack Flaherty .40 1.00
79 Michel Baez RC .50 1.25
80 Brandon Lowe .30 .75
81 Luis Castillo .30 .75
82 David Fletcher .40 1.00
83 Willy Adames .25 .60
84 Matt Thaiss RC .60 1.50
85 Niko Goodrum .30 .75
86 Domingo Leyba RC .60 1.50
87 Trent Grisham RC 2.00 5.00
88 Aaron Nola .30 .75
89 Brandon Woodruff .40 1.00
90 Shin-Soo Choo .30 .75
91 Lucas Giolito .30 .75
92 Jacob deGrom .75 2.00
93 Gary Sanchez .40 1.00
94 Aaron Judge 1.00 2.50
95 Manny Machado .40 1.00
96 Eduardo Rodriguez .25 .60
97 Shane Bieber .40 1.00
98 Jonathan Gray .25 .60
99 Keston Hiura .50 1.25
100 Gio Urshela .40 1.00
101 Xander Bogaerts PRM .60 1.50
102 Jeff McNeil PRM .50 1.25
103 Corey Kluber PRM .50 1.25
104 Justin Verlander PRM .60 1.50
105 Omar Narvaez PRM .40 1.00
106 Ronald Acuna Jr. PRM 2.50 6.00
107 Miguel Cabrera PRM .60 1.50
108 Eloy Jimenez PRM 1.25 3.00
109 Javier Baez PRM .75 2.00
110 Josh Hader PRM .50 1.25
111 Sonny Gray PRM .50 1.25
112 Shohei Ohtani PRM 1.00 2.50
113 J.T. Realmuto PRM .60 1.50
114 A.J. Puk PRM RC 1.25 3.00
115 Carlos Santana PRM .50 1.25
116 Danny Mendick PRM RC 1.00 2.50
117 Mike Soroka PRM .60 1.50
118 Mookie Betts PRM 1.25 3.00
119 Max Fried PRM .60 1.50
120 Lance Lynn PRM .40 1.00
121 Vladimir Guerrero Jr. PRM 1.00 2.50
122 Noah Syndergaard PRM .50 1.25
123 Rafael Devers PRM .75 2.00
124 Masahiro Tanaka PRM .60 1.50
125 Logan Webb PRM RC 1.25 3.00
126 Mike Trout PRM 4.00 10.00
127 Yu Darvish PRM .60 1.50
128 Adrian Morejon PRM RC .75 2.00
129 Fernando Tatis Jr. PRM 2.50 6.00
130 Miguel Sano PRM .50 1.25
131 Matt Carpenter PRM .60 1.50
132 Jesus Luzardo PRM RC 1.50 4.00
133 Hanser Alberto PRM .40 1.00
134 Brendan McKay PRM RC 1.25 3.00
135 Sandy Alcantara PRM .40 1.00
136 Cavan Biggio PRM .75 2.00
137 Yusei Kikuchi PRM .50 1.25
138 Dustin May PRM RC 2.50 6.00
139 Adbert Alzolay PRM RC 1.00 2.50
140 Ketel Marte PRM .50 1.25
141 Luis Robert PRM RC 10.00 25.00
142 Hunter Dozier PRM .40 1.00
143 Gerrit Cole PRM 1.00 2.50
144 Dakota Hudson PRM .50 1.25
145 Trent Thornton PRM .40 1.00
146 Walker Buehler PRM .75 2.00
147 Kevin Newman PRM .60 1.50
148 Yu Chang PRM RC 1.25 3.00
149 Jordan Yamamoto PRM RC .75 2.00
150 Dylan Cease PRM RC 1.25 3.00
151 Max Scherzer PRM .60 1.50
152 Matt Olson PRM .60 1.50
153 Shun Yamaguchi PRM RC 1.00 2.50
154 Yordan Alvarez PRM RC 8.00 20.00
155 Max Kepler PRM .50 1.25
156 Jake Rogers PRM RC .75 2.00
157 Michael Conforto PRM .50 1.25
158 Brock Burke PRM RC .75 2.00
159 Aristides Aquino PRM RC 2.00 5.00
160 Travis Demeritte PRM RC 1.25 3.00
161 Mitch Garver PRM .40 1.00
162 Chris Sale PRM .60 1.50
163 Chris Paddack PRM .60 1.50
164 Ronald Bolanos PRM RC .75 2.00
165 Rico Garcia PRM RC 1.25 3.00
166 Paul Goldschmidt PRM .60 1.50
167 Jorge Polanco PRM .50 1.25
168 Nick Ahmed PRM .40 1.00
169 German Marquez PRM .60 1.50
170 Gavin Lux PRM RC 4.00 10.00
171 Marcus Semien PRM .60 1.50
172 Victor Robles PRM .75 2.00
173 Trea Turner PRM .50 1.25
174 Matt Chapman PRM .60 1.50
175 Yoshitomo Tsutsugo PRM RC 2.00 5.00
176 Bryan Reynolds PRM .50 1.25
177 Jaylin Davis PRM RC 1.25 3.00
178 Trevor Bauer PRM .75 2.00
179 Freddie Freeman PRM .75 2.00
180 Alex Bregman PRM .60 1.50
181 Christian Yelich PRM .75 2.00
182 Patrick Corbin PRM .50 1.25
183 Tyler Glasnow PRM .60 1.50
184 Tim Anderson PRM .60 1.50
185 Nelson Cruz PRM .60 1.50
186 Eduardo Escobar PRM .40 1.00
187 Mauricio Dubon PRM RC 1.00 2.50
188 Willi Castro PRM RC 1.25 3.00
189 Francisco Lindor PRM .60 1.50
190 Max Muncy PRM .50 1.25
191 Scott Kingery PRM .50 1.25
192 David Dahl PRM .40 1.00
193 Yadier Molina PRM .75 2.00
194 Eugenio Suarez PRM .50 1.25
195 Jose Berrios PRM .50 1.25
196 Matt Boyd PRM .40 1.00
197 Giancarlo Stanton PRM .60 1.50
198 Sean Murphy PRM RC 1.25 3.00
199 Danny Duffy PRM .40 1.00
200 Mike Clevinger PRM .50 1.25
201 Robbie Ray DMD .50 1.25
202 Tres Barrera DMD RC 2.00 5.00
203 Carlos Correa DMD .75 2.00
204 Albert Pujols DMD 1.00 2.50
205 Aaron Civale DMD RC 2.00 5.00
206 Kwang-Hyun Kim DMD RC 2.00 5.00
207 Caleb Smith DMD .50 1.25
208 Zack Greinke DMD .75 2.00
209 J.D. Martinez DMD .75 2.00
210 Trey Mancini DMD .75 2.00
211 Anthony Kay DMD RC 1.00 2.50
212 Willson Contreras DMD .75 2.00
213 Blake Snell DMD .60 1.50
214 Yoan Moncada DMD .75 2.00
215 Mike Minor DMD .50 1.25
216 Whit Merrifield DMD .75 2.00
217 Lewis Thorpe DMD RC 1.00 2.50
218 Danny Santana DMD .50 1.25
219 Nolan Arenado DMD 1.25 3.00
220 Christian Vazquez DMD .60 1.50
221 Mike Yastrzemski DMD 1.25 3.00
222 Jonathan Villar DMD .50 1.25
223 James McCann DMD .60 1.50
224 Rhys Hoskins DMD 1.00 2.50
225 J.D. Davis DMD .50 1.25
226 Ozzie Albies DMD .75 2.00
227 Nicholas Castellanos DMD .75 2.00
228 Edwin Rios DMD RC 2.50 6.00
229 Joey Gallo DMD .75 2.00
230 Brian Anderson DMD .50 1.25
231 Josh Donaldson DMD .60 1.50
232 Jose Altuve DMD .60 1.50
233 Donnie Walton DMD RC 2.50 6.00
234 Trevor Story DMD .75 2.00
235 Tommy Edman DMD .75 2.00
236 Anthony Rizzo DMD 1.00 2.50
237 Zack Collins DMD RC 1.25 3.00
238 Sam Hilliard DMD RC 1.50 4.00
239 Zack Wheeler DMD .60 1.50
240 Will Smith DMD .75 2.00
241 Kyle Schwarber DMD .75 2.00
242 Corey Seager DMD .75 2.00
243 Mitch Haniger DMD .60 1.50
244 Jose Ramirez DMD .60 1.50
245 Dan Vogelbach DMD .50 1.25
246 Madison Bumgarner DMD .60 1.50
247 Paul DeJong DMD .75 2.00

248 Nick Solak DMD RC 4.00 10.00
249 Charlie Morton DMD .75 2.00
250 Merrill Kelly DMD .50 1.25

2020 Select Prizms Blue

*BLUE 1-100: 1.5X TO 4X BASIC
*BLUE 1-100 RC: .8X TO 2X BASIC RC
*BLUE 101-200: 1X TO 2.5X BASIC
*BLUE 101-200 RC: .5X TO 1.2X BASIC
RANDOM INSERTS IN PACKS
STATED PRINT RUN 149 COPIES PER
7 Bo Bichette 15.00 40.00
9 Cody Bellinger 5.00 12.00
10 Michael Chavis 3.00 8.00
12 Shogo Akiyama 10.00 25.00
16 Kyle Lewis 5.00 12.00
75 Gleyber Torres 10.00 25.00
94 Aaron Judge 10.00 25.00
106 Ronald Acuna Jr. PRM 12.00 30.00
121 Vladimir Guerrero Jr. PRM 6.00 15.00
126 Mike Trout PRM 25.00 60.00
129 Fernando Tatis Jr. PRM 8.00 20.00
141 Luis Robert PRM 30.00 80.00
154 Yordan Alvarez PRM 15.00 40.00
155 Max Kepler PRM 8.00 20.00
159 Aristides Aquino PRM 12.00 30.00
170 Gavin Lux PRM 12.00 30.00
181 Christian Yelich PRM 10.00 25.00
189 Francisco Lindor PRM 4.00 10.00
193 Yadier Molina PRM 4.00 10.00

2020 Select Prizms Carolina Blue

RANDOM INSERTS IN PACKS
STATED PRINT RUN 35 COPIES PER
5 Pete Alonso 12.00 30.00
7 Bo Bichette 50.00 120.00
9 Cody Bellinger 10.00 25.00
10 Michael Chavis 5.00 12.00
12 Shogo Akiyama 15.00 40.00
16 Kyle Lewis 12.00 30.00
27 Nico Hoerner 15.00 40.00
75 Gleyber Torres 12.00 30.00
94 Aaron Judge 15.00 40.00
106 Ronald Acuna Jr. PRM 20.00 50.00
118 Mookie Betts PRM 8.00 20.00
121 Vladimir Guerrero Jr. PRM 12.00 30.00
126 Mike Trout PRM 50.00 120.00
129 Fernando Tatis Jr. PRM 12.00 30.00
132 Jesus Luzardo PRM 12.00 30.00
141 Luis Robert PRM 50.00 120.00
149 Jordan Yamamoto PRM 12.00 30.00
154 Yordan Alvarez PRM 25.00 60.00
155 Max Kepler PRM 12.00 30.00
156 Jake Rogers PRM 25.00 60.00
159 Aristides Aquino PRM 25.00 60.00
170 Gavin Lux PRM 30.00 80.00
181 Christian Yelich PRM 15.00 40.00
189 Francisco Lindor PRM 6.00 15.00
193 Yadier Molina PRM 10.00 25.00

2020 Select Prizms Cracked Ice

*CRKD ICE 1-100: 3X TO 8X BASIC
*CRKD ICE 1-100 RC: 1.5X TO 4X BASIC RC
*CRKD ICE 101-200: 2X TO 5X BASIC
*CRKD ICE 101-200 RC: 1X TO 2.5X BASIC
RANDOM INSERTS IN PACKS
STATED PRINT RUN 25 COPIES PER
5 Pete Alonso 15.00 40.00
7 Bo Bichette 60.00 150.00
9 Cody Bellinger 20.00 50.00
10 Michael Chavis 8.00 20.00
12 Shogo Akiyama 20.00 50.00
16 Kyle Lewis 15.00 40.00
27 Nico Hoerner 20.00 50.00
75 Gleyber Torres 25.00 60.00
94 Aaron Judge 20.00 50.00
106 Ronald Acuna Jr. PRM 25.00 60.00
118 Mookie Betts PRM 10.00 25.00
121 Vladimir Guerrero Jr. PRM 15.00 40.00
126 Mike Trout PRM 75.00 200.00
129 Fernando Tatis Jr. PRM 40.00 100.00
132 Jesus Luzardo PRM 20.00 50.00
141 Luis Robert PRM 60.00 150.00
149 Jordan Yamamoto PRM 15.00 40.00
154 Yordan Alvarez PRM 30.00 80.00
155 Max Kepler PRM 15.00 40.00
156 Jake Rogers PRM 30.00 80.00
159 Aristides Aquino PRM 30.00 80.00
170 Gavin Lux PRM 40.00 100.00
181 Christian Yelich PRM 20.00 50.00
189 Francisco Lindor PRM 8.00 20.00
193 Yadier Molina PRM 12.00 30.00

2020 Select Prizms Holo

RANDOM INSERTS IN PACKS
7 Bo Bichette 15.00 40.00
9 Cody Bellinger 5.00 12.00
10 Michael Chavis 3.00 8.00
12 Shogo Akiyama 10.00 25.00
16 Kyle Lewis 5.00 12.00
75 Gleyber Torres 10.00 25.00
94 Aaron Judge 10.00 25.00
106 Ronald Acuna Jr. PRM 15.00 40.00
121 Vladimir Guerrero Jr. PRM 10.00 25.00
126 Mike Trout PRM 30.00 80.00
129 Fernando Tatis Jr. PRM 10.00 25.00
132 Jesus Luzardo PRM 8.00 20.00
141 Luis Robert PRM 40.00 100.00
149 Jordan Yamamoto PRM 10.00 25.00
154 Yordan Alvarez PRM 20.00 50.00
155 Max Kepler PRM 10.00 25.00
159 Aristides Aquino PRM 20.00 50.00
170 Gavin Lux PRM 25.00 60.00
181 Christian Yelich PRM 12.00 30.00
189 Francisco Lindor PRM 5.00 12.00
193 Yadier Molina PRM 5.00 12.00

2020 Select Prizms Neon Green

*NEON GRN 1-100: 2X TO 5X BASIC
*NEON GRN 1-100 RC: 1X TO 2.5X BASIC RC
*NEON GRN 101-200: 1.2X TO 3X BASIC
*NEON GRN 101-200 RC: .6X TO 1.5X BASIC
RANDOM INSERTS IN PACKS
STATED PRINT RUN 99 COPIES PER
5 Pete Alonso 10.00 25.00
7 Bo Bichette 20.00 50.00
9 Cody Bellinger 8.00 20.00
10 Michael Chavis 4.00 10.00
12 Shogo Akiyama 12.00 30.00
16 Kyle Lewis 6.00 15.00
27 Nico Hoerner 12.00 30.00
75 Gleyber Torres 12.00 30.00
94 Aaron Judge 12.00 30.00
106 Ronald Acuna Jr. PRM 15.00 40.00
121 Vladimir Guerrero Jr. PRM 10.00 25.00
126 Mike Trout PRM 40.00 100.00
129 Fernando Tatis Jr. PRM 10.00 25.00
132 Jesus Luzardo PRM 8.00 20.00
141 Luis Robert PRM 40.00 100.00
149 Jordan Yamamoto PRM 10.00 25.00
154 Yordan Alvarez PRM 20.00 50.00
155 Max Kepler PRM 10.00 25.00
159 Aristides Aquino PRM 15.00 40.00
170 Gavin Lux PRM 25.00 60.00
181 Christian Yelich PRM 12.00 30.00
189 Francisco Lindor PRM 5.00 12.00
193 Yadier Molina PRM 5.00 12.00

2020 Select Prizms Red

*RED 1-100: 1.5X TO 4X BASIC
*RED 1-100 RC: .8X TO 2X BASIC RC
*RED 101-200: 1X TO 2.5X BASIC
*RED 101-200 RC: .5X TO 1.2X BASIC
RANDOM INSERTS IN PACKS
STATED PRINT RUN 199 COPIES PER
7 Bo Bichette 15.00 40.00
10 Michael Chavis 3.00 8.00
12 Shogo Akiyama 10.00 25.00
75 Gleyber Torres 10.00 25.00
94 Aaron Judge 10.00 25.00
106 Ronald Acuna Jr. PRM 12.00 30.00
121 Vladimir Guerrero Jr. PRM 6.00 15.00
126 Mike Trout PRM 25.00 60.00
129 Fernando Tatis Jr. PRM 8.00 20.00
141 Luis Robert PRM 30.00 80.00
154 Yordan Alvarez PRM 15.00 40.00
155 Max Kepler PRM 8.00 20.00
159 Aristides Aquino PRM 12.00 30.00
170 Gavin Lux PRM 12.00 30.00
181 Christian Yelich PRM 10.00 25.00
189 Francisco Lindor PRM 4.00 10.00

2020 Select Prizms Tie Dye

RANDOM INSERTS IN PACKS
STATED PRINT RUN 20 COPIES PER
5 Pete Alonso 40.00 100.00
7 Bo Bichette 60.00 150.00
9 Cody Bellinger 20.00 50.00
10 Michael Chavis 8.00 20.00
12 Shogo Akiyama 20.00 50.00
16 Kyle Lewis 15.00 40.00
27 Nico Hoerner 20.00 50.00
34 Evan Longoria 15.00 40.00
75 Gleyber Torres 25.00 60.00
94 Aaron Judge 20.00 50.00
104 Justin Verlander PRM 15.00 40.00
106 Ronald Acuna Jr. PRM 25.00 60.00
118 Mookie Betts PRM 10.00 25.00
121 Vladimir Guerrero Jr. PRM 15.00 40.00
126 Mike Trout PRM 150.00 400.00
129 Fernando Tatis Jr. PRM 40.00 100.00
132 Jesus Luzardo PRM 30.00 80.00
138 Dustin May PRM 10.00 25.00
141 Luis Robert PRM 60.00 150.00
149 Jordan Yamamoto PRM 15.00 40.00
154 Yordan Alvarez PRM 30.00 80.00
155 Max Kepler PRM 15.00 40.00
156 Jake Rogers PRM 30.00 80.00
159 Aristides Aquino PRM 30.00 80.00
170 Gavin Lux PRM 40.00 100.00
181 Christian Yelich PRM 20.00 50.00
189 Francisco Lindor PRM 8.00 20.00
193 Yadier Molina PRM 12.00 30.00

2020 Select Prizms Tri-Color

*TRI CLR 1-100: 1.2X TO 3X BASIC
*TRI CLR 1-100 RC: .6X TO 1.5X BASIC RC
*TRI CLR 101-200: .8X TO 2X BASIC
*TRI CLR 101-200 RC: .4X TO 1X BASIC
RANDOM INSERTS IN PACKS
7 Bo Bichette 12.00 30.00
12 Shogo Akiyama 5.00 12.00
75 Gleyber Torres 8.00 20.00
94 Aaron Judge 8.00 20.00
106 Ronald Acuna Jr. PRM 10.00 25.00
121 Vladimir Guerrero Jr. PRM 5.00 12.00
126 Mike Trout PRM 20.00 50.00
129 Fernando Tatis Jr. PRM 8.00 20.00
141 Luis Robert PRM 25.00 60.00
155 Max Kepler PRM 6.00 15.00
170 Gavin Lux PRM 12.00 30.00
181 Christian Yelich PRM 2.50 6.00

2020 Select Prizms White

*WHITE 1-100: 2X TO 5X BASIC
*WHITE 1-100 RC: 1X TO 2.5X BASIC RC
*WHITE 101-200: 1.2X TO 3X BASIC
*WHITE 101-200 RC: .6X TO 1.5X BASIC
RANDOM INSERTS IN PACKS
STATED PRINT RUN 50 COPIES PER
5 Pete Alonso 10.00 25.00
7 Bo Bichette 40.00 100.00
9 Cody Bellinger 8.00 20.00
10 Michael Chavis 4.00 10.00
12 Shogo Akiyama 12.00 30.00
16 Kyle Lewis 6.00 15.00
27 Nico Hoerner 12.00 30.00
75 Gleyber Torres 12.00 30.00
94 Aaron Judge 12.00 30.00
106 Ronald Acuna Jr. PRM 15.00 40.00
121 Vladimir Guerrero Jr. PRM 10.00 25.00
126 Mike Trout PRM 40.00 100.00
129 Fernando Tatis Jr. PRM 10.00 25.00
132 Jesus Luzardo PRM 8.00 20.00
141 Luis Robert PRM 40.00 100.00
149 Jordan Yamamoto PRM 10.00 25.00
154 Yordan Alvarez PRM 20.00 50.00
155 Max Kepler PRM 10.00 25.00
159 Aristides Aquino PRM 20.00 50.00
170 Gavin Lux PRM 25.00 60.00
181 Christian Yelich PRM 12.00 30.00
189 Francisco Lindor PRM 5.00 12.00
193 Yadier Molina PRM 5.00 12.00

2020 Select Artistic Impressions

1 Yordan Alvarez 30.00 80.00
2 Bo Bichette 20.00 50.00
3 Shohei Ohtani 10.00 25.00
4 Aaron Judge 20.00 50.00
5 Alex Bregman 12.00 30.00
6 Mookie Betts 15.00 40.00
7 Mike Trout 30.00 80.00
8 Juan Soto 25.00 60.00
9 Bryce Harper 12.00 30.00
10 Ronald Acuna Jr. 15.00 40.00

2020 Select '93 Retro Select Materials

RANDOM INSERTS IN PACKS
1 Cal Ripken 6.00 15.00
2 Ozzie Smith 6.00 15.00
3 Tony Gwynn 4.00 87.00
4 Roberto Alomar 4.00 10.00
5 Tom Glavine 2.50 6.00
6 Ivan Rodriguez 5.00 12.00
7 Greg Maddux 4.00 10.00
8 Paul Molitor 3.00 8.00
9 Roger Clemens 4.00 10.00
10 Dennis Eckersley 5.00 12.00
11 Ryne Sandberg 6.00 15.00
12 Barry Larkin 6.00 15.00
13 Mike Piazza 3.00 8.00
14 Wade Boggs 4.00 10.00
15 Randy Johnson 5.00 12.00
16 Frank Thomas 3.00 8.00
17 Juan Gonzalez 2.00 5.00
18 Kenny Lofton 10.00 25.00
19 Craig Biggio 2.50 6.00
20 Larry Walker 2.50 6.00

2020 Select '93 Retro Select Materials Prizms Holo

*HOLO: .5X TO 1.2X BASIC
RANDOM INSERTS IN PACKS
STATED PRINT RUN 75 COPIES PER
3 Tony Gwynn 6.00 15.00
14 Wade Boggs 8.00 20.00
19 Craig Biggio 5.00 12.00

2020 Select '93 Retro Select Materials Prizms Tri-Color

*TRI CLR: .5X TO 1.2X BASIC
RANDOM INSERTS IN PACKS
STATED PRINT RUN 49 COPIES PER
3 Tony Gwynn 6.00 15.00
14 Wade Boggs 8.00 20.00
19 Craig Biggio 5.00 12.00

2020 Select 25-Man

RANDOM INSERTS IN PACKS
1 J.T. Realmuto .75 2.00
2 Pete Alonso 2.00 5.00
3 DJ LeMahieu .75 2.00
4 Alex Bregman .75 2.00
5 Xander Bogaerts .75 2.00
6 Juan Soto 2.50 6.00
7 Mike Trout 4.00 10.00
8 Christian Yelich 1.00 2.50
9 Cody Bellinger 1.50 4.00
10 Justin Verlander .75 2.00
11 Jacob deGrom 1.50 4.00
12 Gerrit Cole 1.25 3.00
13 Max Scherzer .75 2.00
14 Stephen Strasburg .75 2.00
15 Liam Hendriks .50 1.25
16 Brandon Workman .50 1.25
17 Josh Hader .60 1.50
18 Ken Giles .50 1.25
19 Will Harris .75 2.00
20 Zack Britton .50 1.25
21 Kirby Yates .50 1.25
22 Mookie Betts 1.50 4.00
23 Jose Altuve .60 1.50
24 Anthony Rendon .75 2.00
25 Ronald Acuna Jr. 3.00 8.00

2020 Select 25-Man Prizms Holo

*HOLO: .6X TO 1.5X BASIC
RANDOM INSERTS IN PACKS
7 Mike Trout 8.00 20.00

2020 Select Hot Rookies

RANDOM INSERTS IN PACKS
*HOLO: .6X TO 1.5X BASIC
1 A.J. Puk .75 2.00
2 Bo Bichette 4.00 10.00
3 Brusdar Graterol .75 2.00
4 Gavin Lux 2.50 6.00
5 Yoshitomo Tsutsugo 1.25 3.00
6 Nick Solak 2.00 5.00
7 Sean Murphy .75 2.00
8 Yordan Alvarez 5.00 12.00
9 Zack Collins .60 1.50
10 Zac Gallen 1.25 3.00
11 Trent Grisham 2.00 5.00
12 Luis Robert 8.00 20.00
13 Mauricio Dubon .60 1.50
14 Jesus Luzardo 1.00 2.50
15 Dylan Cease .75 2.00
16 Brendan McKay .75 2.00
17 Aristides Aquino 1.25 3.00
18 Shun Yamaguchi .60 1.50
19 Kwang-Hyun Kim 1.00 2.50
20 Dustin May 1.50 4.00
21 Isan Diaz .75 2.00
22 Kyle Lewis 4.00 10.00
23 Nico Hoerner 2.00 5.00
24 Tony Gonsolin 2.00 5.00
25 Shogo Akiyama .75 2.00

2020 Select Launch Angle Autographs

6 Aristides Aquino 20.00 50.00
10 Yordan Alvarez 20.00 50.00

2020 Select Moon Shots

RANDOM INSERTS IN PACKS
1 Nomar Mazara .50 1.25
2 Ronald Acuna Jr. 3.00 8.00
3 Christian Yelich 1.00 2.50
4 Cody Bellinger 1.50 4.00
5 Josh Bell .60 1.50
6 Yordan Alvarez 5.00 12.00
7 Eugenio Suarez .60 1.50
8 Pete Alonso 2.00 5.00
9 Kyle Schwarber .75 2.00
10 Mike Trout 4.00 10.00
11 Nelson Cruz .75 2.00
12 Freddie Freeman 1.00 2.50
13 Aaron Judge 2.00 5.00
14 Shohei Ohtani 1.25 3.00
15 George Springer .60 1.50
16 Bryce Harper 1.25 3.00
17 Jorge Soler .75 2.00
18 Kris Bryant 1.00 2.50
19 Alex Bregman .75 2.00
20 Rhys Hoskins 1.00 2.50

2020 Select Moon Shots Prizms Holo

RANDOM INSERTS IN PACKS
4 Cody Bellinger 8.00 20.00
10 Mike Trout 8.00 20.00
14 Shohei Ohtani 6.00 15.00

2020 Select Phenomenon

RANDOM INSERTS IN PACKS
1 Rafael Devers 1.00 2.50
2 Juan Soto 2.50 6.00
3 Ronald Acuna Jr. 3.00 8.00
4 Vladimir Guerrero Jr. 1.25 3.00
5 Fernando Tatis Jr. 4.00 10.00
6 Eloy Jimenez 1.50 4.00
7 Gavin Lux 4.00 10.00
8 Jack Flaherty .75 2.00
9 Ozzie Albies .75 2.00
10 Yordan Alvarez 5.00 12.00
11 Bo Bichette 6.00 15.00
12 Luis Robert 4.00 10.00
13 Jo Adell 2.00 5.00
14 Wander Franco 5.00 12.00
15 Gleyber Torres 1.50 4.00

2020 Select Phenomenon Prizms Holo

RANDOM INSERTS IN PACKS
4 Vladimir Guerrero Jr. 10.00 25.00
7 Gavin Lux 10.00 25.00

2020 Select Phenoms

RANDOM INSERTS IN PACKS
*HOLO: .6X TO 1.5X BASIC
1 Wander Franco 5.00 12.00
2 Luis Robert 4.00 10.00
3 Jo Adell 2.00 5.00
4 Adley Rutschman 6.00 15.00
5 Casey Mize 1.50 4.00
6 Bobby Witt Jr. 5.00 12.00
7 Royce Lewis 1.25 3.00
8 Nate Pearson 1.50 4.00
9 Cristian Pache 1.50 4.00
10 Alex Kirilloff 1.00 2.50
11 Forrest Whitley .75 2.00
12 Jasson Dominguez 20.00 50.00
13 Joey Bart 1.50 4.00
14 Andrew Vaughn 2.00 5.00
15 Sixto Sanchez 1.50 4.00
16 Dylan Carlson 2.00 5.00
17 Julio Rodriguez 3.00 8.00
18 JJ Bleday 1.50 4.00
19 Ian Anderson 1.50 4.00
20 Alec Bohm 3.00 8.00
21 Keibert Ruiz 2.50 6.00
22 Nick Madrigal 2.00 5.00
23 CJ Abrams 1.50 4.00
24 Oneil Cruz .60 1.50
25 Tarik Skubal 2.50 6.00

2020 Select Rookie Jersey Autographs

RANDOM INSERTS IN PACKS
STATED PRINT RUN BTW 199-209 SER.#'d SET
EXCHANGE DEADLINE 10/15/2021
1 Randy Arozarena/209 25.00 60.00
2 Jordan Yamamoto /209 8.00 20.00
3 Adrian Morejon/209 3.00 8.00
4 Gavin Lux/209 20.00 50.00
5 Joe Palumbo/209 3.00 8.00
6 Isan Diaz/209 8.00 20.00
7 Adbert Alzolay/209 4.00 10.00
8 Mauricio Dubon/209 4.00 10.00
9 Jake Fraley/209 4.00 10.00
10 Matt Thaiss/209 4.00 10.00
11 Rico Garcia/209 5.00 12.00
12 Patrick Sandoval/209 5.00 12.00
13 T.J. Zeuch/209 3.00 8.00
14 Yu Chang/209 6.00 15.00
15 Sam Hilliard/209 5.00 12.00
16 Zack Collins/209 4.00 10.00
17 Ronald Bolanos/209 3.00 8.00
18 Danny Mendick/209 4.00 10.00
19 Aristides Aquino/209 15.00 40.00
20 Brock Burke/209 3.00 8.00
21 A.J. Puk/209 5.00 12.00
22 Tres Barrera/209 6.00 15.00
23 Kyle Lewis/209 25.00 60.00
24 Jaylin Davis/209 5.00 12.00
25 Logan Allen/209 3.00 8.00
26 Anthony Kay/209 3.00 8.00
27 Brendan McKay/209 8.00 20.00
28 Trent Grisham/209 12.00 30.00
29 Michel Baez/209 3.00 8.00
30 Bryan Abreu/209 3.00 8.00
31 Jonathan Hernandez/209 3.00 8.00
32 Domingo Leyba/209 4.00 10.00
33 Yordan Alvarez/209 30.00 80.00
34 Josh Rojas/209 3.00 8.00
35 Travis Demeritte/209 5.00 12.00
36 Bobby Bradley/209 3.00 8.00
37 Logan Webb/209 5.00 12.00
38 Andres Munoz/209 5.00 12.00
39 Justin Dunn/209 4.00 10.00
40 Yonathan Daza/209 4.00 10.00
41 Michael King/209 5.00 12.00
42 Jesus Luzardo/209 12.00 30.00
43 Nick Solak/209 6.00 15.00
44 Abraham Toro/209 8.00 20.00
45 Dustin May/199 20.00 50.00
46 Tony Gonsolin/209 4.00 10.00
47 Jake Rogers/209 3.00 8.00
48 Sean Murphy/209 5.00 12.00
49 Lewis Thorpe/209 3.00 8.00
50 Sheldon Neuse/209 4.00 10.00
51 Aaron Civale/209 8.00 20.00
52 Dylan Cease/209 5.00 12.00
53 Edwin Rios/209 4.00 10.00
54 Deivy Grullon/209 3.00 8.00
55 Donnie Walton/209 8.00 20.00
56 Zac Gallen/209 6.00 15.00
57 Bo Bichette/209 25.00 60.00
58 Nico Hoerner/209 12.00 30.00
59 Willi Castro/209 10.00 25.00
60 Brusdar Graterol/209 5.00 12.00
61 Tyrone Taylor/209 3.00 8.00
62 Luis Robert/199 EXCH 60.00 150.00

2020 Select Rookie Jersey Autographs Prizms Cracked Ice

*CRKD ICE: .6X TO 1.5X BASIC
RANDOM INSERTS IN PACKS
STATED PRINT RUN 25 SER.#'d SETS
NO PRICING DUE TO SCARCITY
EXCHANGE DEADLINE 10/15/2021
2 Jordan Yamamoto 15.00 40.00
6 Isan Diaz 20.00 50.00
8 Mauricio Dubon 15.00 40.00
9 Jake Fraley 20.00 50.00
10 Matt Thaiss 15.00 40.00
19 Aristides Aquino 125.00 300.00
23 Kyle Lewis 25.00 60.00
24 Jaylin Davis 40.00 100.00
31 Jonathan Hernandez 10.00 25.00
38 Andres Munoz 12.00 30.00
43 Nick Solak 8.00 20.00
50 Sheldon Neuse 15.00 40.00
56 Zac Gallen 30.00 80.00
57 Bo Bichette 75.00 200.00
60 Brusdar Graterol 15.00 40.00

2020 Select Rookie Jersey Autographs Prizms Holo

*HOLO: .5X TO 1.2X BASIC
RANDOM INSERTS IN PACKS
STATED PRINT RUN 99 SER.#'d SETS
EXCHANGE DEADLINE 10/15/2021
19 Aristides Aquino 50.00 120.00
23 Kyle Lewis 20.00 50.00
57 Bo Bichette 60.00 150.00

2020 Select Rookie Jersey Autographs Prizms Orange Pulsar

*ORNG PLSR/20: .6X TO 1.5X BASIC
RANDOM INSERTS IN PACKS
STATED PRINT RUN BTW 5-20 SER.#'d SET
NO PRICING QTY 15 OR LESS
EXCHANGE DEADLINE 10/15/2021
19 Aristides Aquino/20 125.00 300.00
33 Yordan Alvarez/20 125.00 300.00
57 Bo Bichette/20 75.00 200.00
62 Luis Robert/20 150.00 400.00

2020 Select Rookie Jersey Autographs Prizms Tri-Color

*TRI CLR: .5X TO 1.2X BASIC
RANDOM INSERTS IN PACKS
STATED PRINT RUN 49 SER.#'d SETS
EXCHANGE DEADLINE 10/15/2021
2 Jordan Yamamoto 12.00 30.00
6 Isan Diaz 15.00 40.00
8 Mauricio Dubon 12.00 30.00
10 Matt Thaiss 12.00 30.00
19 Aristides Aquino 100.00 250.00
23 Kyle Lewis 20.00 50.00
24 Jaylin Davis 30.00 80.00
31 Jonathan Hernandez 8.00 20.00
38 Andres Munoz 10.00 25.00
57 Bo Bichette 60.00 150.00

2020 Select Rookie Jumbo Swatch

RANDOM INSERTS IN PACKS
*HOLO: .4X TO 1X BASIC
1 Jordan Yamamoto 2.00 5.00
2 Adrian Morejon 2.00 5.00
3 Gavin Lux 6.00 15.00
4 Isan Diaz 3.00 8.00
5 Adbert Alzolay 2.50 6.00
6 Mauricio Dubon 2.50 6.00
7 Jake Fraley 2.50 6.00
8 Matt Thaiss 2.50 6.00
9 Patrick Sandoval 3.00 8.00
11 Yu Chang 4.00 10.00
12 Sam Hilliard 3.00 8.00
13 Zack Collins 2.50 6.00
15 Aristides Aquino 5.00 12.00
16 A.J. Puk 3.00 8.00
17 Kyle Lewis 15.00 40.00
18 Jaylin Davis 3.00 8.00
19 Luis Robert 10.00 25.00
20 Anthony Kay 2.00 5.00
21 Brendan McKay 3.00 8.00
22 Trent Grisham 8.00 20.00
23 Michel Baez 2.00 5.00
24 Domingo Leyba 2.50 6.00
25 Yordan Alvarez 8.00 20.00
26 Travis Demeritte 3.00 8.00
27 Bobby Bradley 2.00 5.00
28 Logan Webb 3.00 8.00
29 Justin Dunn 2.50 6.00
30 Yonathan Daza 2.50 6.00
31 Jesus Luzardo 3.00 8.00
32 Nick Solak 8.00 20.00
33 Abraham Toro 2.50 6.00
34 Dustin May 6.00 15.00
35 Tony Gonsolin 8.00 20.00
36 Jake Rogers 2.00 5.00
37 Sean Murphy 3.00 8.00
38 Lewis Thorpe 2.00 5.00
39 Sheldon Neuse 4.00 10.00
40 Aaron Civale 4.00 10.00
41 Dylan Cease 3.00 8.00
42 Edwin Rios 5.00 12.00
43 Deivy Grullon 2.00 5.00
44 Donnie Walton 5.00 12.00
45 Zac Gallen 5.00 12.00
46 Bo Bichette 8.00 20.00
47 Nico Hoerner 5.00 12.00
48 Willi Castro 3.00 8.00
49 Brusdar Graterol 3.00 8.00
50 Tyrone Taylor 2.00 5.00

2020 Select Rookie Jumbo Swatch Prizms Cracked Ice

*CRKD ICE/25: .6X TO 1.5X BASIC
RANDOM INSERTS IN PACKS
STATED PRINT RUN 25 COPIES PER
3 Gavin Lux 30.00 80.00
9 Patrick Sandoval 10.00 25.00
15 Aristides Aquino 25.00 60.00
19 Luis Robert 20.00 50.00
25 Yordan Alvarez 30.00 80.00
46 Bo Bichette 40.00 100.00

2020 Select Rookie Jumbo Swatch Prizms Tri-Color

*TRI CLR: .5X TO 1.2X BASIC
RANDOM INSERTS IN PACKS
STATED PRINT RUN 99 COPIES PER
25 Yordan Alvarez 12.00 30.00

2020 Select Rookie Signatures

RANDOM INSERTS IN PACKS
STATED PRINT RUN 199 COPIES PER
EXCHANGE DEADLINE 10/15/2021
*HOLO: .5X TO 1.2X BASIC
*TRI CLR: .5X TO 1.2X BASIC
1 Nico Hoerner 10.00 25.00
2 Gavin Lux 15.00 40.00
3 Dylan Cease 4.00 10.00
4 Isan Diaz 8.00 20.00
RSBB Bo Bichette 40.00 100.00
6 Jesus Luzardo 5.00 12.00
7 Luis Robert 75.00 200.00
8 Brendan McKay 10.00 25.00
10 Sean Murphy 4.00 10.00

2020 Select Rookie Signatures Prizms Cracked Ice

*CRKD ICE: .6X TO 1.5X BASIC
RANDOM INSERTS IN PACKS
STATED PRINT RUN 25 SER.#'d SETS
NO PRICING DUE TO SCARCITY
EXCHANGE DEADLINE 10/15/2021
1 Nico Hoerner 25.00 60.00
10 Sean Murphy 12.00 30.00

2020 Select Select Stars

RANDOM INSERTS IN PACKS
1 Vladimir Guerrero Jr. 1.25 3.00
2 Anthony Rendon .75 2.00
3 Albert Pujols 1.00 2.50
4 Mike Trout 4.00 10.00
5 Yoan Moncada .75 2.00
6 Christian Yelich 1.00 2.50
7 Bryce Harper 1.25 3.00
8 Manny Machado .75 2.00
9 Justin Verlander .75 2.00
10 Jacob deGrom 1.50 4.00
11 Clayton Kershaw 1.25 3.00
12 Matt Chapman .75 2.00
13 Buster Posey 1.00 2.50
14 Anthony Rizzo 1.00 2.50
15 Max Scherzer .75 2.00

2020 Select Select Stars Prizms Holo

*HOLO: .6X TO 1.5X BASIC
RANDOM INSERTS IN PACKS
1 Vladimir Guerrero Jr. 10.00 25.00
4 Mike Trout 8.00 20.00
6 Christian Yelich 5.00 12.00

2020 Select Select Swatches

RANDOM INSERTS IN PACKS
1 Mike Trout 10.00 25.00
2 Aaron Judge 6.00 15.00
3 Pete Alonso 8.00 20.00
4 Rafael Devers 4.00 10.00
5 Cody Bellinger 6.00 15.00
6 Ronald Acuna Jr. 6.00 15.00
7 Freddie Freeman 4.00 10.00
8 Mookie Betts 6.00 15.00
9 Jose Altuve 2.50 6.00
10 Juan Soto 10.00 25.00
11 Ozzie Albies 3.00 8.00
12 Alex Bregman 3.00 8.00
13 Jose Abreu 3.00 8.00
14 Fernando Tatis Jr. 5.00 12.00
15 Justin Verlander 3.00 8.00
16 Shohei Ohtani 5.00 12.00
17 Anthony Rizzo 4.00 10.00
18 Javier Baez 4.00 10.00
19 Clayton Kershaw 5.00 12.00
20 Kris Bryant 4.00 10.00

2020 Select Select Swatches Prizms Cracked Ice

*CRKD ICE/24-25: .6X TO 1.5X BASIC
RANDOM INSERTS IN PACKS
PRINT RUN BTW 24-25 SER.#'d SETS
4 Rafael Devers/24 10.00 25.00
6 Ronald Acuna Jr./25 40.00 100.00
7 Freddie Freeman/25 10.00 25.00
13 Jose Abreu/25 10.00 25.00
14 Fernando Tatis Jr./25 20.00 50.00
19 Clayton Kershaw/25 10.00 25.00

2020 Select Select Swatches Prizms Holo

*HOLO: .4X TO 1X BASIC
RANDOM INSERTS IN PACKS
PRINT RUN BTW 149- 250 SER.#'d SETS
6 Ronald Acuna Jr./250 10.00 25.00
7 Freddie Freeman/149 5.00 12.00
13 Jose Abreu/250 6.00 15.00
19 Clayton Kershaw/149 6.00 15.00

2020 Select Select Swatches Prizms Tri-Color

*TRI CLR: .5X TO 1.2X BASIC
RANDOM INSERTS IN PACKS
STATED PRINT RUN 75 COPIES PER
4 Rafael Devers 8.00 20.00
6 Ronald Acuna Jr. 12.00 30.00
7 Freddie Freeman 6.00 15.00
13 Jose Abreu 8.00 20.00
19 Clayton Kershaw 8.00 20.00

2020 Select Sensations

RANDOM INSERTS IN PACKS
1 Aaron Judge 2.00 5.00
2 Javier Baez 1.00 2.50
3 Cody Bellinger 1.50 4.00
4 Gerrit Cole 1.25 3.00
5 Trevor Story .75 2.00
6 Jose Altuve .60 1.50
7 Christian Yelich 1.00 2.50
8 Mike Trout 4.00 10.00
9 Tim Anderson .75 2.00
10 Trea Turner .60 1.50
11 Francisco Lindor .75 2.00
12 Juan Soto 2.50 6.00
13 Adalberto Mondesi .60 1.50
14 Mookie Betts 1.50 4.00
15 Shohei Ohtani 1.25 3.00

2020 Select Sensations Prizms Holo

*HOLO: .6X TO 1.5X BASIC
RANDOM INSERTS IN PACKS
8 Mike Trout 8.00 20.00

2020 Select Signature Materials

RANDOM INSERTS IN PACKS
STATED PRINT RUN BTW 48-99 SER.#'d SET
EXCHANGE DEADLINE 10/15/2021
1 Brandon Woodruff/99 6.00 15.00
2 Carlos Correa/48 6.00 15.00
3 Paul Goldschmidt/49 12.00 30.00
4 Xander Bogaerts/99 25.00 60.00
10 Jorge Polanco/75 5.00 12.00
12 Anthony Rizzo/49 20.00 50.00
14 Curt Schilling/49 25.00 60.00
16 Rickey Henderson/75 40.00 100.00
18 Frank Thomas/75 30.00 80.00

2020 Select Signature Materials Prizms Holo

5 Jose Abreu/79 10.00 25.00
8 Manny Machado/75 25.00 60.00
9 Corey Seager/49 15.00 40.00
13 Ken Griffey Jr./25 150.00 400.00
15 John Smoltz/49 10.00 25.00
19 Mark McGwire/49 50.00 120.00

2020 Select Signature Materials Prizms Tri-Color

*TRI CLR/29-49: .5X TO 1.2X BASIC
*TRI CLR/25: .6X TO 1.5X BASIC
RANDOM INSERTS IN PACKS
STATED PRINT RUN BTW 10-49 SER.#'d SET
NO PRICING QTY 15 OR LESS
EXCHANGE DEADLINE 10/15/2021
5 Jose Abreu/35 10.00 25.00
6 Josh Bell/49 12.00 30.00
8 Manny Machado/49 25.00 60.00
9 Corey Seager/35 15.00 40.00
15 John Smoltz/29 10.00 25.00

2020 Select Signatures

RANDOM INSERTS IN PACKS
STATED PRINT RUN BTW 75-199 SER.#'d SET
EXCHANGE DEADLINE 10/15/2021
2 Josh Rojas/199 2.50 6.00
4 Michel Baez/199 2.50 6.00
6 Rico Garcia/199 4.00 10.00
7 Donnie Walton/199 6.00 15.00
8 Jake Fraley/199 8.00 20.00
9 Joe Palumbo/199 2.50 6.00
10 T.J. Zeuch/199 2.50 6.00
11 Jose Abreu/79 12.00 30.00
12 Ronald Bolanos/199 2.50 6.00
15 Fernando Tatis Jr./75 60.00 150.00
16 Vladimir Guerrero Jr./99 30.00 80.00
17 Kenny Lofton/99 12.00 30.00
18 Ben Zobrist/99 10.00 25.00
19 Jasson Dominguez/149 EXCH 200.00 500.00
22 Adalberto Mondesi/99 4.00 10.00
26 Michael Chavis/199 8.00 20.00
27 Jo Adell/199 EXCH 25.00 60.00
28 Nomar Mazara/99 6.00 15.00
29 Nick Senzel/199 8.00 20.00
30 Eloy Jimenez/99 15.00 40.00

2020 Select Signatures Prizms Cracked Ice

*CRKD ICE/25: .6X TO 1.5X BASIC p/r 149-199
*CRKD ICE/25: .5X TO 1.2X BASIC p/r 75-99
RANDOM INSERTS IN PACKS
STATED PRINT RUN BTW 15-25 SER.#'d SET
NO PRICING QTY 15 OR LESS
EXCHANGE DEADLINE 10/15/2021
1 Freddie Freeman/25 30.00 80.00
3 Ronald Acuna Jr./15
5 Josh Bell/25 15.00 40.00
10 T.J. Zeuch/25 6.00 15.00
13 Xander Bogaerts/25 50.00 120.00
14 Juan Soto/25 100.00 250.00
19 Jasson Dominguez/25 EXCH 400.00 800.00
21 Corey Seager/25 20.00 50.00
25 Shohei Ohtani/15
29 Nick Senzel/25 20.00 50.00

2020 Select Signatures Prizms Holo

*HOLO/35-99: .4X TO 1X BASIC p/r 75-99
*HOLO/35-99: .5X TO 1.2X BASIC p/r 149-199
RANDOM INSERTS IN PACKS
STATED PRINT RUN BTW 35-99 SER.#'d SET
EXCHANGE DEADLINE 10/15/2021
3 Ronald Acuna Jr./49 50.00 120.00
5 Josh Bell/49 12.00 30.00
24 Omar Vizquel/35 4.00 10.00
25 Shohei Ohtani/49 60.00 150.00

2020 Select Signatures Prizms Tri-Color

*TRI CLR/49: .5X TO 1.2X BASIC p/r 149-199
*TRI CLR/49: .4X TO 1X BASIC p/r 75-99
*TRI CLR/25: .6X TO 1.5X BASIC p/r 149-199
*TRI CLR/25: .5X TO 1.2X BASIC p/r 75-99
RANDOM INSERTS IN PACKS
STATED PRINT RUN BTW 25-49 SER.#'d SET
EXCHANGE DEADLINE 10/15/2021
1 Freddie Freeman/49 25.00 60.00
3 Ronald Acuna Jr./25 60.00 150.00
13 Xander Bogaerts/49 40.00 100.00
19 Jasson Dominguez/49 EXCH 300.00 600.00
21 Corey Seager/49 15.00 40.00
24 Omar Vizquel/25 5.00 12.00
25 Shohei Ohtani/25 75.00 200.00

2020 Select Sparks

RANDOM INSERTS IN PACKS
1 Mookie Betts 1.50 4.00
2 Francisco Lindor .75 2.00
3 Pete Alonso 2.00 5.00
4 Gleyber Torres 1.50 4.00
5 Mike Trout 4.00 10.00
6 Javier Baez 1.00 2.50
7 Fernando Tatis Jr. 3.00 8.00
8 Ketel Marte .60 1.50
9 Whit Merrifield .75 2.00
10 Jeff McNeil .60 1.50

2020 Select Sparks Prizms Holo

RANDOM INSERTS IN PACKS
5 Mike Trout 8.00 20.00

2020 Select Sparks Signatures

RANDOM INSERTS IN PACKS
STATED PRINT RUN 199 COPIES PER
EXCHANGE DEADLINE 10/15/2021
1 Zac Gallen 6.00 15.00
2 Zack Collins 3.00 8.00
3 Tony Gonsolin 10.00 25.00
4 Travis Demeritte 3.00 8.00
5 Bryan Abreu 2.50 6.00
6 Yu Chang 5.00 12.00
7 Brusdar Graterol 6.00 15.00
8 Trent Grisham 10.00 25.00
9 Logan Webb 4.00 10.00
10 Randy Arozarena 25.00 60.00
11 Anthony Kay 2.50 6.00
12 Jaylin Davis 4.00 10.00
13 Adbert Alzolay 3.00 8.00
14 Aaron Civale 6.00 15.00
15 Yonathan Daza 3.00 8.00
16 Patrick Sandoval 4.00 10.00
17 Tyrone Taylor 2.50 6.00
18 Andres Munoz 4.00 10.00
19 Jonathan Hernandez 2.50 6.00
20 Deivy Grullon 2.50 6.00
21 Tres Barrera 8.00 20.00
22 Michael King 4.00 10.00
23 Sheldon Neuse 3.00 8.00
24 Lewis Thorpe 2.50 6.00
25 Abraham Toro 3.00 8.00
26 Jake Rogers 8.00 20.00
27 Logan Allen 2.50 6.00
28 Danny Mendick 3.00 8.00
29 Domingo Leyba 3.00 8.00
30 Brock Burke 2.50 6.00
31 Justin Dunn 3.00 8.00
32 Mauricio Dubon 3.00 8.00
33 Adrian Morejon 2.50 6.00
34 Willi Castro 4.00 10.00
35 Jordan Yamamoto 2.50 6.00
36 Edwin Rios 8.00 20.00
37 A.J. Puk 4.00 10.00
38 Sam Hilliard 4.00 10.00
39 Bobby Bradley 2.50 6.00
40 Matt Thaiss 3.00 8.00

2020 Select Sparks Signatures Prizms Cracked Ice

*CRKD ICE: .6X TO 1.5X BASIC
RANDOM INSERTS IN PACKS
STATED PRINT RUN 25 SER.#'d SETS
EXCHANGE DEADLINE 10/15/2021
12 Jaylin Davis 20.00 50.00
27 Logan Allen 6.00 15.00
35 Jordan Yamamoto 20.00 50.00
37 A.J. Puk 15.00 40.00

2020 Select Sparks Signatures Prizms Holo

*HOLO: .5X TO 1.2X BASIC
RANDOM INSERTS IN PACKS
STATED PRINT RUN 99 SER.#'d SETS
EXCHANGE DEADLINE 10/15/2021
37 A.J. Puk 12.00 30.00

2020 Select Sparks Signatures Prizms Tri-Color

*TRI CLR: .5X TO 1.2X BASIC
RANDOM INSERTS IN PACKS
STATED PRINT RUN 49 SER.#'d SETS
EXCHANGE DEADLINE 10/15/2021
37 A.J. Puk 12.00 30.00

2020 Select X-Factor Material Signatures

RANDOM INSERTS IN PACKS
STATED PRINT RUN BTW 49-149 SER.#'d SET
EXCHANGE DEADLINE 10/15/2021
2 Byron Buxton/99 6.00 15.00
3 Fernando Tatis Jr./49 75.00 200.00
4 Gary Sanchez/149 12.00 30.00
6 Marcell Ozuna/99 6.00 15.00
12 Yoan Moncada/75 12.00 30.00
14 Ketel Marte/49 5.00 12.00
17 Jorge Polanco/75 5.00 12.00
20 Gleyber Torres/99 40.00 100.00

2020 Select X-Factor Material Signatures Prizms Cracked Ice

*CRKD ICE/25: .6X TO 1.5X BASIC p/r 149
*CRKD ICE/25: .5X TO 1.2X BASIC pr 49-99
RANDOM INSERTS IN PACKS
STATED PRINT RUN BTW 15-25 SER.#'d SET
NO PRICING QTY 15 OR LESS
EXCHANGE DEADLINE 10/15/2021
5 Gerrit Cole/20
10 Eloy Jimenez/25 EXCH 20.00 50.00
11 Juan Soto/25 50.00 120.00
15 Rafael Devers/15

2020 Select X-Factor Material Signatures Prizms Holo

RANDOM INSERTS IN PACKS
STATED PRINT RUN BTW 35-99 SER.#'d SET
EXCHANGE DEADLINE 10/15/2021
8 Ronald Acuna Jr./49 60.00 150.00
10 Eloy Jimenez/99 EXCH 15.00 40.00
15 Rafael Devers/75 10.00 25.00
18 Pete Alonso/75 50.00 120.00

2020 Select X-Factor Material Signatures Prizms Tri-Color

*TRI CLR/49: .5X TO 1.2X BASIC p/r 149
*TRI CLR/49: .4X TO 1X BASIC p/r 49-99
*TRI CLR/25: .5X TO 1.2X BASIC 49-99
RANDOM INSERTS IN PACKS
STATED PRINT RUN BTW 25-49 SER.#'d SET
EXCHANGE DEADLINE 10/15/2021
13 Stephen Strasburg/49
15 Rafael Devers/49 25.00 60.00
16 Whit Merrifield/49 12.00 30.00
18 Pete Alonso/49 50.00 120.00

1894 Senators Cabinets Bell

These cabinets feature members of the 19th century Washington Senators and were produced at the Bell Studio on Pennsylvania Avenue. These cabinets feature mainly players in uniform but a couple of players are posed in suit and tie. Since these cabinets are unnumbered, we have sequenced them in alphabetical order.

COMPLETE SET 6000.00 12000.00
1 Charles Abbey 750.00 1500.00
2 Ed Cartwright 750.00 1500.00
3 Dan Dugdale 750.00 1500.00
4 Jim McGuire 750.00 1500.00
5 Tim O'Rourke 750.00 1500.00
6 Al Selbach 750.00 1500.00
7 Otis Stocksdale 750.00 1500.00
8 Mike Sullivan 750.00 1500.00
9 George Tebeau 750.00 1500.00
10 Frank Ward 750.00 1500.00

1909 Senators Barr-Farnham Postcards

This extremely rare set of real photo postcards was produced by Barr-Farnham Picture Postcards Co. located in Washington, DC in 1909. Ten cards have been positively identified but there are undoubtedly others, probably every member of the team. There is a strong possibility there is a team postcard as well. All additions to this checklist are greatly appreciated. All views show a full body close up of the player taken on the outfield grass with the ball park in the background.

COMPLETE SET (10) 1250.00 2500.00
11 Bob Unglaub 100.00 200.00
1 Otis Clymer 100.00 200.00
2 Wid Conroy 100.00 200.00
3 Bob Ganley 100.00 200.00
4 Dolly Gray 100.00 200.00
5 Bob Groom 100.00 200.00
6 Tom Hughes 100.00 200.00
7 Walter Johnson 400.00 800.00
8 George McBride 100.00 200.00
9 Charlie Smith 100.00 200.00
10 Jesse Tannehill 100.00 200.00

1912 Senators National Photo Company

The National Photo Company located in Washington, DC published a rare set of real photo postcards. The Postcards were also titled "The Climbers" and was probably produced in 1912 when the Senators climbed to second place from a seventh place finish the season before. The two known players are all time great pitcher Walter Johnson and fleet outfielder Clyde Milan. Both players had superb seasons in 1912. There might be other players in this set so additions to the checklist are appreciated.

COMPLETE SET (2) 350.00 700.00
1 Walter Johnson 300.00 600.00
2 Clyde Milan 100.00 200.00

1925 Senators Holland Creameries

These 18 cards, which feature members of the Washington Senators, were issued in Canada by an ice cream company. These cards, which measure approximately 1 1/2" by 3", feature the players photo and his position on the front and the back describes the prize is all 18 cards are returned. Roger Peckinpaugh, number 16, is believed to have been deliberately short printed to make winning the prize extremely hard.

COMPLETE SET (18) 1500.00 3000.00
COMMON CARD (1-18) 60.00 120.00
COMMON SP
1 Ralph Miller 300.00 600.00
2 Earl McNeely 300.00 600.00
3 Allan Russell 300.00 600.00
4 Ernest Shirley 300.00 600.00
5 Sam Rice 600.00 1200.00
6 Muddy Ruel 300.00 600.00
7 Ossie Bluege 400.00 800.00
8 Nemo Leibold 300.00 600.00
9 Paul Zahniser 300.00 600.00
10 Firpo Marberry 400.00 800.00
11 Warren Ogden 300.00 600.00
12 George Mogridge 300.00 600.00
13 Tom Zachary 300.00 600.00
14 Goose Goslin 600.00 1200.00
15 Joe Judge 400.00 800.00
16 Roger Peckinpaugh SP 1000.00 2000.00
17 Bucky Harris 600.00 1200.00
18 Walter Johnson 2500.00 5000.00

1925 Senators Oakland Tribune

This one-card set measures approximately 3" by 4 3/4" and was issued to commemorate the Washington Senators 1924 Series victory. The card features a blue tinted photo of Walter Johnson who was close to purchasing the Oakland minor league team at the time.

1 Walter Johnson 2500.00 5000.00

1931 Senators Team Issue Photos W-UNC

This 30-card team set of the Washington Senators measures approximately 6 1/8" by 9 3/8" and features sepia-toned player photos printed on thin paper stock. The backs are blank. The cards are unnumbered and checklisted below in alphabetical order.

COMPLETE SET (30) 125.00 250.00
1 Nick Altrock CO 6.00 12.00
2 Oswald Bluege 7.50 15.00
3 Cliff Bolton 5.00 10.00
4 Lloyd Brown 5.00 10.00
5 Robert Burke 5.00 10.00
6 Joe Cronin 20.00 40.00
7 Alvin Crowder 5.00 10.00
8 E.B. Eynon Jr. 5.00 10.00
9 Charles Fischer 5.00 10.00
10 Edward Gharrity 5.00 10.00
11 Clark Griffith OWN 20.00 40.00
12 Irving Hadley 5.00 10.00
13 William Hargrave 5.00 10.00
14 David Harris 5.00 10.00
15 Jack Hayes 5.00 10.00
16 Walter Johnson MG 75.00 150.00
17 Sam Jones 6.00 12.00
18 Baxter Jordan 5.00 10.00
19 Joe Judge 5.00 10.00
20 Joe Kuhel 5.00 10.00
21 Henry Manush 10.00 20.00
22 Fred Marberry 6.00 12.00
23 Mike Martin 5.00 10.00
24 Walter Masters 5.00 10.00
25 Charles Myer 6.00 12.00
26 Harry Rice 5.00 10.00
27 Sam Rice 20.00 40.00
28 Al Schacht CO 10.00 20.00
29 Ray Spencer 5.00 10.00
30 Sam West 5.00 10.00

1947 Senators Gunther Beer PC

These postcards usually featuring two players on the front were issued around 1947-48 based on the players in the set. The cards feature the players photos on the front along with their names in big bold black letters on the bottom. The backs have room for messages to be sent, usually from the Senators announcer at the time, Arch MacDonald. This listing may be incomplete so additions are welcome.

COMMON PLAYER 500.00 1000.00
1 Joe Kuhel 50.00 100.00
2 Al Evans 50.00 100.00
  Scott Cary
3 Tom Ferrick 50.00 100.00
  Harold Keller
4 Mickey Haefner 50.00 100.00
  Forrest Thompson
5 Sid Hudson 50.00 100.00
  Al Kozar
6 Walter Masterson 60.00 120.00
  Rick Ferrell
7 Tom McBride 50.00 100.00
  Milo Candini
8 Marino Pieretti 50.00 100.00
  Leon Culberson
9 Sherrard Robertson 50.00 100.00
  Eddie Lyons
10 Ray Scarborough 50.00 100.00
  Kenneth McCreight
11 Mickey Vernon 60.00 120.00
  Gil Coan

1958 Senators Jay Publishing

This 12-card set of the Washington Senators measures approximately 5" by 7" and features black-and-white player photos in a white border. These cards were packaged 12 to a packet. The backs are blank. The cards are unnumbered and checklisted below in alphabetical order.

COMPLETE SET (12) 20.00 40.00
1 Rocky Bridges 2.00 4.00
2 Truman Clevenger 1.50 3.00
3 Clint Courtney 1.50 3.00
4 Dick Hyde 1.50 3.00
5 Cookie Lavagetto MG 2.00 4.00
6 Jim Lemon 1.50 3.00
7 Camilo Pascual 2.50 5.00
8 Albie Pearson 2.00 4.00
9 Herb Plews 1.50 3.00
10 Pedro Ramos 1.50 3.00
11 Roy Sievers 2.00 4.00
12 Eddie Yost 2.00 4.00

1958 Senators Team Issue

This 29-card set of the Washington Senators measures approximately 4" by 5" and features black-and-white player photos in a white border with a facsimile autograph printed on the front. These cards were originally sold through the mail by the club for 10 cents each. The cards are unnumbered and checklisted below in alphabetical order.

COMPLETE SET (29) 75.00 150.00
1 Ozzie Alvarez 2.50 5.00
2 Ken Aspromonte 2.50 5.00
3 Boom-Boom Beck CO 2.50 5.00
4 Julio Becquer 2.50 5.00
5 Rocky Bridges 3.00 6.00
6 Neil Chrisley 2.50 5.00
7 Ellis Clary CO 2.50 5.00
8 Truman Clevenger 2.50 5.00
9 Clint Courtney 2.50 5.00
10 Ed Fitzgerald 2.50 5.00
11 Hal Griggs 2.50 5.00
12 Dick Hyde 2.50 5.00
13 Walter Johnson 5.00 10.00
14 Bill Jurges CO 2.50 5.00
15 Russ Kemmerer 2.50 5.00
16 Steve Korcheck 2.50 5.00
17 Cookie Lavagetto MG 3.00 6.00
18 Jim Lemon 2.50 5.00
19 Bob Malkmus 2.50 5.00
20 Camilio Pascual 4.00 8.00
21 Albie Pearson 3.00 6.00
22 Herb Plews 2.50 5.00
23 Pedro Ramos 2.50 5.00
24 Roy Sievers 4.00 8.00
25 Faye Throneberry 2.50 5.00
26 Vito Valentinetti 2.50 5.00
27 Eddie Yost 3.00 6.00
28 Norm Zauchin 2.50 5.00
29 Team Picture 10.00 20.00

1959 Senators Team Issue

This Washington Senators team set features black-and-white player photos in a white border and measures approximately 4" by 5". The cards are unnumbered and checklisted below in alphabetical order. This checklist may be incomplete and any known additions are welcomed.

COMPLETE SET 40.00 80.00
1 Ken Aspromonte 2.50 5.00
2 Julio Becquer 2.50 5.00
3 Reno Bertoia 2.50 5.00
4 Tex Clevenger 2.50 5.00
5 Billy Consolo 2.50 5.00
6 Clint Courtney 2.50 5.00
7 Bill Fischer 2.50 5.00
8 Hal Griggs 2.50 5.00
9 Russ Kemmerer 2.50 5.00
10 Ralph Lumenti 2.50 5.00
11 Hal Naragon 2.50 5.00
12 Camilo Pascual 4.00 8.00
13 J.W. Porter 2.50 5.00
14 Pedro Ramos 2.50 5.00
15 John Romonosky 2.50 5.00
16 Ron Samford 2.50 5.00
17 Jose Valdivielso 2.50 5.00
18 Hal Woodeshick 2.50 5.00

1959 Senators Team Issue 5 by 7

Measuring 5" by 7", these photos were issued by the Senators in 1959. Since these photos are unnumbered, we have sequenced them in alphabetical order.

COMPLETE SET 10.00 25.00
1 Reno Bertoia 1.50 3.00
2 Clint Courtney 1.50 3.00
3 Ed Fitzgerald 1.50 3.00
4 Dick Hyde 1.50 3.00
5 Cookie Lavagetto MG 1.50 3.00
6 Jim Lemon 1.50 3.00
7 Camilio Pascual 2.00 4.00
8 Albie Pearson 1.50 3.00
9 Herb Plews 1.50 3.00
10 Pedro Ramos 1.50 3.00
11 Roy Sievers 2.00 4.00
12 Norm Zauchin 1.50 3.00

1960 Senators Universal Match Corp.

This 20-cover set produced by the Universal Match Corp. of Washington, D.C. titled "Famous Senators" features a facial cut-out of a player on a cream. The "Mr. Senator" logo is printed in red, blue and black. The set was sponsored by 1st Federal Savings and Loan Associatiion. Complete matchbooks carry a fifty percent premium.

COMPLETE SET (20) 60.00 120.00
1 Nick Altrock 2.50 6.00
2 Ossie Bluege 2.50 6.00
3 Joe Cronin 5.00 12.00
4 Alvin Crowder 2.50 6.00
5 Goose Goslin 5.00 12.00
6 Clark Griffith 5.00 12.00
7 Bucky Harris 5.00 12.00
8 Walter Johnson 6.00 15.00
9 Joe Judge 2.50 6.00
10 Harmon Killebrew 6.00 15.00
11 Joe Kuhel 2.50 6.00
12 Buddy Lewis 2.50 6.00
13 Clyde Milan 2.50 6.00
14 Buddy Myer 2.50 6.00
15 Roger Peckinpaugh 2.50 6.00
16 Sam Rice 5.00 12.00
17 Roy Sievers 3.00 8.00
18 Stan Spence 2.50 6.00
19 Mickey Vernon 3.00 8.00
20 Sam West 2.50 6.00

1960 Senators Jay Publishing

This 12-card set of the Washington Senators measures approximately 5" by 7" and features black-and-white player photos in a white border. These cards were packaged 12 to a packet. The backs are blank. The cards are unnumbered and checklisted below in alphabetical order.

COMPLETE SET (12) 12.50 30.00
1 Bob Allison 1.25 3.00
2 Julio Becquer .75 2.00
3 Truman Clevenger .75 2.00
4 Billy Consolo .75 2.00
5 Dan Dobbek .75 2.00
6 William(Billy) Gardner .75 2.00
7 Harmon Killebrew 4.00 10.00
8 Steve Korchek .75 2.00
9 Cookie Lavagetto MG 1.00 2.50
10 Jim Lemon .75 2.00
11 Camilo Pascual 1.25 3.00
12 Pedro Ramos .75 2.00

1961 Senators Jay Publishing

This 12-card set of the first year expansion Washington Senators measures approximately 5" by 7". The fronts feature black-and-white posed player photos with the player's and team name printed below in the white border. These cards were packaged 12 in a packet. The backs are blank. The cards are unnumbered and checklisted below in alphabetical order.

COMPLETE SET (12) 8.00 20.00
1 Harry Bright .75 2.00
2 Pete Daley .75 2.00
3 Bennie Daniels .75 2.00
4 Dick Donovan .75 2.00
5 Bob Johnson .75 2.00
6 Marty Keough .75 2.00
7 R.C. Stevens .75 2.00
8 Willie Tasby .75 2.00
9 Coot Veal .75 2.00
10 Mickey Vernon MG 1.00 2.50
11 Gene Woodling 1.00 2.50
12 Bud Zipfel .75 2.00

1962 Senators Jay Publishing

Produced by Jay Publishing, this 12-card set features members of the Washington Senators. Originally, this set came in a plastic sack that included a "picture pak order form" and sold for 25 cents. Printed on thin stock paper, the cards measure approximately 5" by 7". On a white background the fronts have a black-and-white posed player photo. The player's name and team appear in black letters under the photo. The backs are blank. The cards are unnumbered and checklisted below in alphabetical order.

COMPLETE SET (12) 15.00 40.00
1 Pete Burnside 1.50 4.00
2 Chuck Cottier 1.50 4.00
3 Bernie Daniels 1.50 4.00
4 Bob Johnson 1.50 4.00
5 Marty Kutyna 1.50 4.00
6 Joe McClain 1.50 4.00
7 Danny O'Connell 1.50 4.00
8 Ken Retzer 1.50 4.00
9 Willie Tasby 1.50 4.00
10 Mickey Vernon MG 2.50 6.00
11 Gene Wooding 2.00 5.00
12 Bud Zipfel 1.50 4.00

1962 Senators Newberrys Little Pro

This one-card set was a promotional card for a batting practice device. The card measures approximately 4" by 5" and features a photo of Jimmy Piersall. The back displays a statement by Roger Maris as to the effectiveness of the device as a batting aid and a list of six reasons as to why it is a good batting tool.

1 Jimmy Piersall 6.00 15.00

1963 Senators Jay Publishing

This 12-card set of the Washington Senators measures approximately 5" by 7". The fronts feature black-and-white posed player photos with the player's and team name printed below in the white border. These cards were packaged 12 to a packet. The backs are blank. The cards are unnumbered and checklisted below in alphabetical order.

COMPLETE SET (12) 15.00 40.00
1 Tom Cheney 1.50 4.00
2 Bennie Daniels 1.50 4.00
3 Ken Hamlin 1.50 4.00
4 Chuck Hinton 1.50 4.00
5 Don Lock 1.50 4.00
6 Claude Osteen 2.50 6.00
7 Jim Piersall 3.00 8.00
8 Ken Retzer 1.50 4.00
9 Don Rudolph 1.50 4.00
10 Bob Schmidt 1.50 4.00
11 Dave Stenhouse 1.50 4.00
12 Mickey Vernon MG 2.00 5.00

1964 Senators Jay Publishing

This 12-card set of the Washington Senators measures approximately 5" by 7". The fronts feature black-and-white posed player photos with the player's and team name printed below in the white border. These cards were packaged 12 to a packet. The backs are blank. The cards are unnumbered and checklisted below in alphabetical order.

COMPLETE SET (12) 20.00 50.00
1 Don Blasingame 1.50 4.00
2 Tom Cheney 1.50 4.00
3 Chuck Cottier 1.50 4.00
4 Chuck Hinton 1.50 4.00
5 Gil Hodges MG 4.00 10.00
6 Jim King 1.50 4.00
7 Ron Kline 1.50 4.00
8 Don Leppert 1.50 4.00
9 Don Lock 1.50 4.00
10 Claude Osteen 2.50 6.00
11 Ed Roebuck 1.50 4.00
12 Don Rudolph 1.50 4.00

1965 Senators Jay Publishing

This 12-card set of the Washington Senators measures approximately 5" by 7". The fronts feature black-and-white posed player photos with the player's and team name printed below in the white border. These cards were packaged 12 to a packet. The backs are blank. The cards are unnumbered and checklisted below in alphabetical order.

COMPLETE SET (12) 8.00 20.00
1 Don Blasingame .75 2.00
2 Ed Brinkman .75 2.00
3 Mike Brumley .75 2.00
4 Woodie Held .75 2.00
5 Gil Hodges MG 2.00 5.00
6 Frank Howard 1.50 4.00
7 Jim King .75 2.00
8 Don Lock .75 2.00
9 Ken McMullen .75 2.00
10 Buster Narum .75 2.00
11 Phil Ortega .75 2.00
12 Pete Richert .75 2.00

1966 Senators Team Issue

This 12-card set of the Washington Senators measures approximately 5" by 7" and is printed on textured paper stock. The fronts feature black-and-white posed player photos with the player's and team name printed below in the white border. These cards were packaged 12 to a packet and could be obtained from the team through a mail-in offer. The twelfth player in the pack is unknown. The backs are blank. The cards are unnumbered and checklisted below in alphabetical order.

COMPLETE SET (12) 12.50 30.00
1 Don Blasingame 1.00 2.50
2 Ed Brinkman/(Without hat) 1.00 2.50
3 Mike Brumley 1.00 2.50
4 Bob Chance 1.00 2.50
5 Bennie Daniels 1.00 2.50
6 Woodie Held 1.00 2.50
7 Gil Hodges 2.50 6.00
8 Frank Howard 2.00 5.00
9 Don Lock 1.00 2.50
10 Phil Ortega 1.00 2.50
11 Pete Richert/(With plain cap) 1.00 2.50
12 Unknown player

1967 Senators Postcards

This 22-card set of the Washington Senators features borderless black-and-white player photos with a facsimile autograph in a white bar at the bottom. The cards measure approximately 3 1/2" by 5 13/16". The backs are blank. The cards are unnumbered and checklisted below in alphabetical order.

COMPLETE SET (22) 8.00 20.00
1 Bernie Allen .40 1.00
2 Hank Allen .40 1.00
3 Dave Baldwin .40 1.00
4 Frank Bertaina .40 1.00
5 Ed Brinkman .40 1.00
6 Doug Camilli .40 1.00
7 Paul Casanova .40 1.00
8 Joe Coleman .40 1.00
9 Tim Cullen .40 1.00
10 Mike Esptein .40 1.00
11 Frank Howard 2.00 5.00
12 Bob Humphreys .40 1.00
13 Darold Knowles .40 1.00
14 Dick Lines .40 1.00
15 Ken McMullen .40 1.00
16 Dick Nen .40 1.00
17 Phil Ortega .40 1.00
18 Camilo Pascual .60 1.50
19 Cap Peterson .40 1.00
20 Bob Priddy .40 1.00
21 Bob Saverine .40 1.00
22 Fred Valentine .40 1.00

1967 Senators Team Issue

This 12-card set of the Washington Senators measures approximately 5" by 7" and is printed on textured paper stock. The fronts feature black-and-white posed player photos with the player's and team name printed below in the white border. These cards were packaged 12 to a packet and could be obtained from the team through a mail-in offer. The backs are blank. The cards are unnumbered and checklisted below in alphabetical order.

COMPLETE SET (12) 10.00 25.00
1 Bernie Allen .75 2.00
2 Ed Brinkman/(With hat) .75 2.00
3 Paul Casanova .75 2.00
4 Ken Harrelson 1.50 4.00
5 Gil Hodges 2.50 6.00
6 Frank Howard 2.00 5.00
7 Jim Lemon .75 2.00
8 Ken McMullen .75 2.00
9 Phil Ortega .75 2.00
10 Camilo Pascual 1.25 3.00
11 Pete Richert/(With Senators cap) .75 2.00
12 Fred Valentine .75 2.00

1968 Senators Team Issue

This 12-card set of the Washington Senators measures approximately 5" by 7" and is printed on textured paper stock. The fronts feature black-and-white posed player photos with the player's and team name printed below in the white border. These cards were packaged 12 to a packet and could be obtained from the team through a mail-in offer. The backs are blank. The cards are unnumbered and checklisted below in alphabetical order.

COMPLETE SET (12) 10.00 25.00
1 Frank Bertaina 1.00 2.50
2 Paul Casanova 1.00 2.50
3 Frank Coggins 1.00 2.50
4 Mike Epstein 1.00 2.50
5 Ron Hansen 1.00 2.50
6 Frank Howard 2.00 5.00
7 Jim Lemon 1.00 2.50
8 Ken McMullen 1.00 2.50
9 Phil Ortega 1.00 2.50
10 Camilo Pascual 1.25 3.00
11 Cap Peterson 1.00 2.50
12 Fred Valentine 1.00 2.50

1968 Senators Team Issue 8 1/2x 11

This set features black-and-white player photos in white borders and measures 8 1/2" by 11". The backs are blank. The cards are unnumbered and checklisted below in alphabetical order. The checklist is incomplete and any known additions are welcomed.

COMPLETE SET 8.00 20.00
1 Ed Brinkman 4.00 10.00
2 Sid Hudson CO 4.00 10.00

1969-70 Senators Team Issue

This 16-card set of the Washington Senators measures approximately 4 1/4" by 7". The fronts display black-and-white player portraits bordered in white and printed on a grainy, textured card stock. The player's name and team are printed in the top margin. The backs are blank. The cards are unnumbered and checklisted below in alphabetical order.

COMPLETE SET (16) 15.00 40.00
1 Hank Allen .75 2.00
2 Dick Bosman .75 2.00
3 Ed Brinkman .75 2.00
4 George Brunet .75 2.00
5 Paul Casanova .75 2.00
6 Joe Coleman 1.00 2.50
7 Mike Epstein .75 2.00
8 Jim Hannan .75 2.00
9 Frank Howard 1.50 4.00
10 Lee Maye .75 2.00
11 Ken McMullen .75 2.00
12 Camilo Pascual 1.25 3.00
13 Aurelio Rodriguez .75 2.00
14 Ed Stroud .75 2.00
15 Del Unser .75 2.00
16 Ted Williams 6.00 15.00

1969 Senators Team Issue 8x10

This 20-card set features black-and-white player photos in white borders and measuring 8" by 10". The backs are blank. The cards are unnumbered and checklisted below in alphabetical order.

COMPLETE SET (20) 40.00 80.00
1 Bernie Allen 1.25 3.00
2 Hank Allen 1.25 3.00
3 Dave Baldwin 1.25 3.00
4 Dick Bosman 1.25 3.00
5 Ed Brinkman/(Batting) 1.25 3.00
6 Ed Brinkman/(Throwing) 1.25 3.00
7 Doug Camilli 1.25 3.00
8 Joe Coleman 1.50 4.00
9 Casey Cox 1.25 3.00
10 Mike Epstein 1.25 3.00
11 Nellie Fox CO 4.00 10.00
12 Frank Howard 2.50 6.00
13 Darold Knowles 1.25 3.00
14 Ken McMullen 1.25 3.00
15 Phil Ortega 1.25 3.00
16 Camilo Pascual 2.00 5.00
17 Cap Peterson 1.25 3.00
18 Del Unser 1.25 3.00
19 Fred Valentine 1.25 3.00
20 Ted Williams MG 8.00 20.00

1970 Senators Police Yellow

The 1970 Washington Senators Police set was issued on a thin unperforated cardboard sheet measuring approximately 12 1/2" by 8". The sheet is divided into ten cards by thin black lines. When the players are cut into individual cards, they measure approximately 2 1/2" by 4". The color of the sheet is yellow, and consequently the black and white borderless player photos have a similar cast. The player's name, position, and team name appear below the pictures. The backs have different safety messages sponsored by the Office of Traffic Safety, D.C. Department of Motor Vehicles. The cards are unnumbered and checklisted below in alphabetical order.

COMPLETE SET (10) 12.50 30.00
1 Dick Bosman 1.25 3.00
2 Eddie Brinkman 1.00 2.50
3 Paul Casanova 1.00 2.50
4 Mike Epstein 1.25 3.00
5 Frank Howard 3.00 8.00
6 Darold Knowles 1.00 2.50
7 Lee Maye 1.00 2.50
8 Aurelio Rodriguez 1.25 3.00
9 John Roseboro 1.25 3.00
10 Ed Stroud 1.00 2.50

1971 Senators Police Pink

The 1971 Washington Senators Police set was issued on a thin unperforated cardboard sheet measuring approximately 12 1/2" by 8". In contrast to the previous year's issue, the sheet is not divided up into separate cards by thin black lines. If the sheet were cut into individual player cards, each player's card would measure approximately 2 1/2" by 4". The color of the sheet ranges from pink to peach, and consequently the black and white borderless player photos have a similar cast. The player's name, position, and team name appear below the pictures. The backs have different safety messages sponsored by the Office of Traffic Safety, D.C. Department of Motor Vehicles. The cards are unnumbered and checklisted below in alphabetical order. The set is dated by the fact that it is Denny McLain's only year on the Senators.

COMPLETE SET (10) 12.50 30.00
1 Dick Bosman 1.25 3.00
2 Paul Casanova 1.00 2.50
3 Tim Cullen 1.00 2.50
4 Joe Foy 1.00 2.50
5 Toby Harrah 2.00 5.00
6 Frank Howard 3.00 8.00
7 Elliott Maddox 1.25 3.00
8 Tom McCraw 1.00 2.50
9 Denny McLain 2.00 5.00
10 Don Wert 1.00 2.50

1971 Senators Team Issue W-UNC

This 24-card set of the Washington Senators features black-and-white player photos with a facsimile autograph in the bottom margin. The cards measure approximately 3 1/2" by 5 3/4" and have blank backs. The cards are unnumbered and checklisted below in alphabetical order.

COMPLETE SET (24) 40.00 80.00
1 Bernie Allen 1.25 3.00
2 Larry Biitner 1.25 3.00
3 Dick Billings 1.25 3.00
4 Dick Bosman 1.50 4.00
5 Pete Broberg 1.25 3.00
6 Jackie Brown 1.25 3.00
7 Paul Casanova 1.25 3.00
8 Casey Cox 1.25 3.00
9 Tim Cullen 1.25 3.00
10 Bill Gogolewski 1.25 3.00
11 Joe Grzenda 1.25 3.00
12 Toby Harrah 2.50 6.00
13 Frank Howard 2.50 6.00
14 Paul Lindblad 1.25 3.00
15 Elliott Maddox 1.25 3.00
16 Denny McLain 2.50 6.00
17 Don Mincher 1.25 3.00
18 Dave Nelson 1.25 3.00
19 Horacio Pina 1.25 3.00
20 Lenny Randle 1.25 3.00
21 Denny Riddleberger 1.25 3.00
22 Jim Shellenback 1.25 3.00
23 Mike Thompson 1.25 3.00
24 Del Unser 1.25 3.00

1975 Senators 1924-25 TCMA

This 40-card set features black-and-white photos of the 1924-25 Washington Senators in white borders. The cards measure approximately 2 3/8" by 3 3/8". The backs carry player information and statistics. The cards are unnumbered and checklisted below in alphabetical order except for cards 38-40 which are jumbo cards.

COMPLETE SET (41) 10.00 25.00
1 Spencer Adams .20 .50
2 Nick Altrock .75 2.00
3 Ossie Bluege .40 1.00
4 Stan Coveleski .75 2.00
5 Alex Ferguson .20 .50
6 Showboat Fischer .20 .50
7 Goose Goslin .75 2.00
8 Bert Griffith .20 .50
9 Pinky Hargrave .20 .50
10 Bucky Harris P MG .75 2.00
11 Joe Harris .20 .50
12 Tex Jeans .20 .50
13 Walter Johnson 1.50 4.00
14 Joe Judge .60 1.50
15 Wade Lefler .20 .50
16 Nemo Leibold .20 .50
17 Fripo Marberry .20 .50
18 Joe Martina .20 .50
19 Wid Matthews .20 .50
20 Mike McNally .20 .50
21 Ralph Miller .20 .50
22 George Mogridge .20 .50
23 Buddy Myer .20 .50
24 Curly Ogden .20 .50
25 Roger Peckinpaugh .40 1.00
26 Sam Rice .20 .50
27 Muddy Ruel .20 .50
28 Dutch Ruether .20 .50
29 Allen Russell .20 .50
30 Hank Severeid .20 .50
31 Everett Scott .20 .50
32 Mule Shirley .20 .50
33 By Speece .20 .50
34 Bennie Tate .20 .50
35 Bobby Veach .20 .50
36 Tom Zachary .20 .50
37 Paul Zahniser .20 .50
38 Bucky Harris .40 1.00
  Bill McKechnie
39 Ossie Bluege .40 1.00
  Roger Peckinpaugh
  Harris
  Joe Judge
40 Tom Zachary .75 2.00
  Firpo Marberry
  Alex Ferguson
  Walter
41 Earl McNeely .40 1.00

1981 Senators 1924-25 TCMA

This set almost exactly mirrors the 1975 Senators 1924-25 TCMA issue wth several minor changes. Ralph Miller replaced Tommy Taylor and different photos were used for both By Speece and Hank Severeid.

COMPLETE SET (41) 10.00 25.00
1 Spencer Adams .20 .50
2 Nick Altrock .75 2.00
3 Ossie Bluege .30 .75
4 Stan Coveleski .75 2.00
5 Alex Ferguson .20 .50
6 Showboat Fischer .20 .50

7 Goose Goslin .75 2.00
8 Bert Griffith .20 .50
9 Pinky Hargrave .20 .50
10 Bucky Harris P .75 2.00
MG
11 Joe Harris .20 .50
12 Tex Jeans .20 .50
13 Walter Johnson 1.50 4.00
14 Joe Judge .50 1.25
15 Wade Lefler .20 .50
16 Nemo Leibold .20 .50
17 Fripo Marberry .20 .50
18 Joe Martina .20 .50
19 Wid Matthews .20 5.00
20 Mike McNally .20 .50
21 Tommy Taylor .20 .50
22 Beorge Mogridge .20 .50
23 Buddy Myer .20 .50
24 Curly Ogden .20 .50
25 Roger Peckinpaugh .30 .75
26 Sam Rice .20 .50
27 Muddy Ruel .20 .50
28 Dutch Ruether .20 .50
29 Allen Russell .20 .50
30 Hank Severeid .20 .50
31 Everett Scott .20 .50
32 Mule Shirley .20 .50
33 By Speece .20 .50
34 Bennie Tate .20 .50
35 Bobby Veach .20 .50
36 Tom Zachary .20 .50
37 Paul Zahniser .20 .50
38 Bucky Harris .30 .75
Bill McKechnie
39 Ossie Bluege .30 .75
Roger Peckinpaugh
Harris
Joe Judge
40 Tom Zachary .75 2.00
Firpo Marberry
Alex Ferguson
Walter
41 Earl McNeely .30 .75

1999 Senators 69 Reunion

These 28 cards feature members of the 1969 Washington Senators and was issued by the Washington Senators Historical Society. These cards measure 2" by 2 1/2" and feature commentary on each player as if it were written at the end of the 1969 season.

COMPLETE SET (28) 4.00 10.00
1 Bernie Allen .08 .25
2 Hank Allen .08 .25
3 Frank Bertania .08 .25
4 Dick Billings .08 .25
5 Dick Bosman .08 .25
6 Ed Brinkman .08 .25
7 Johnny Holliday ANN .08 .25
8 Joe Camacho CO .08 .25
9 Casey Cox .08 .25
10 Tim Cullen .08 .25
11 Mike Epstein .08 .25
12 Jim French .08 .25
13 Jim Hannan .08 .25
14 Ron Menchine ANN .08 .25
15 Denny Higgins .08 .25
16 Frank Howard .40 1.00
17 Sid Hudson CO .20 .50
18 Bob Humphreys .08 .25
19 Frank Kruetzer .08 .25
20 Lee Maye .08 .25
21 Shelby Whitfield ANN .08 .25
22 Ken McMullen .08 .25
23 Ed Stroud .08 .25
24 Wayne Terwillger CO. .08 .25
25 Del Unser .08 .25
26 Fred Valentine .08 .25
27 Ted Williams MG 2.00 5.00
28 Checklist Card .20 .50
All Players printed in front

1910 Sepia Anon PC796

This sepia with white border set measures 3 1/2" by 5 1/2", was issued circa 1910 and features 25 cards of popular players of the era. No markings are found either on the front or on the backs to indicate a manufacturer or issuer. The Cobb and Wagner card spells Honus' name as Honas. The same checklist is also used for the PC Novelty Cultery Co set. The pictures in that set have been reduced and enclosed in an ornate frame border. Postcards by either issuer are valued the same.

COMPLETE SET (25) 3750.00 7500.00
1 Roger Bresnahan 500.00 1000.00
Full catching pose
2 Al Bridwell 250.00 500.00
Stooped fielding
3 Mordecai Brown 400.00 800.00
Pitching - left leg up
4 Ty Cobb Batting to Hips 2000.00 4000.00
5 T.Cobb/H.Wagner Shaking Hands 1250.00 2500.00
6 Frank Chance MG 500.00 1000.00
Throwing
7 Hal Chase 400.00 800.00
Fielding at first
8 Eddie Collins 400.00 800.00
Batting
9 Sam Crawford 400.00 800.00
Batting
10 Johnny Evers 500.00 1000.00
Germany Schaefer
Standing
11 Art Devlin 250.00 500.00
Glove outstretched
12 Red Dooin 250.00 500.00
Arms High
Ball in one hand; Glove the
13 Sam Frock 250.00 500.00
Portrait
14 George Gibson 250.00 500.00
Full catching position
15 Artie Hoffman 250.00 500.00
Fielding for high one
16 Walter Johnson 1000.00 2000.00
Pitching
17 Nap Lajoie 500.00 1000.00
Full batting pose
18 Harry Lord 250.00 500.00
Throwing
19 Christy Mathewson 1000.00 2000.00
Pitching -- right leg up
20 Orvall Overall 250.00 500.00
Pitching -- left leg up
21 Eddie Plank 400.00 800.00
Portrait -- hand over head
22 Tris Speaker 500.00 1000.00
Batting pose
23 Charley Street 250.00 500.00
Full catching about to throw
24 Honus Wagner 1000.00 2000.00
Full batting pose
25 Ed Walsh 400.00 800.00
Full bunting pose

1977 Sertoma Stars

1 Hank Aaron 6.00 15.00
2 Bob Allison 2.50 6.00
3 Clete Boyer 2.50 6.00
4 Don Buford 2.50 6.00
5 Rod Carew 3.00 8.00
6 Rico Carty 2.50 6.00
7 Roberto Clemente 10.00 25.00
8 Jim Ray Hart 2.50 6.00
9 Dave Johnson 2.50 6.00
10 Harmon Killebrew 4.00 10.00
11 Mickey Mantle 12.50 30.00
12 Juan Marichal 3.00 8.00
13 Bill Mazeroski 3.00 8.00
14 Joe Morgan 3.00 8.00
15 Phil Niekro 3.00 8.00
16 Tony Oliva 3.00 8.00
17 Gaylord Perry 3.00 8.00
18 Boog Powell 2.50 6.00
19 Brooks Robinson 3.00 8.00
20 Frank Robinson 3.00 8.00
21 John Roseboro 2.50 6.00
22 Rusty Staub 2.50 6.00
23 Joe Torre 3.00 8.00
24 Jim Wynn 2.50 6.00

1977 Sertoma Stars Puzzle Backs

This 25-card set, measures approximately 2 3/4" by 4 1/4". The fronts feature a black-and-white player portrait in a black-framed circle on a yellor background. The player's name, position, sponsor logo, and card name are printed in black and red between a top and bottom row of black stars which border the card. The backs carry a puzzle piece which, when placed in the right position, form a picture of the 1913 Pittsburgh Nationals. The cards are unnumbered and checklisted below in alphabetical order. Although a 1978 set was planned and a checklist was distributed into the hobby; those cards were never produced.

COMPLETE SET (25) 30.00 60.00
1 Bernie Allen .20 .50
2 Frank(Home Run) Baker .75 2.00
3 Ted Beard .20 .50
4 Don Buford .20 .50
5 Eddie Cicotte .75 2.00
6 Roberto Clemente 2.50 6.00
7 Dom Dallessandro .20 .50
8 Carl Erskine .40 1.00
9 Nellie Fox .75 2.00
10 Lou Gehrig 2.50 6:00
11 Joe Jackson 2.50 6.00
12 Len Johnston .20 .50
13 Benny Kauff .20 .50
14 Dick Kenworthy .20 .50
15 Harmon Killebrew .75 2.00
16 Bob(Lefty) Logan .20 .50
17 Willie Mays 2.50 6.00
18 Satchell Paige 2.50 6.00
19 Edd Roush .75 2.00
20 Chico Ruiz .20 .50
21 Babe Ruth 4.00 10.00
22 Herb Score .40 1.00
23 George Sisler .75 2.00
24 George(Buck) Weaver .75 2.00
25 Early Wynn .75 2.00

1961 Seven-Eleven

The 1961 7-Eleven set consists of 30 cards, each measuring approximately 2 7/16" by 3 3/8". The checklist card states that this is the first series, and that a new series was to be released every two weeks (though apparently no other series were issued). The cards are printed on pink cardboard stock and the backs are blank and were available as seven cards for five cents. The fronts have a black and white headshot in the upper left portion and brief biographical information to the right of the picture. The player's name appears across the top of each front. The remainder of the front carries "1960 Hi Lites," which consist of a list of dates and the player's achievements on those dates. The team name across the bottom of the card rounds out the front. The cards are numbered on the front in the lower right corner.

COMPLETE SET (30) 1100.00 2200.00
1 Dave Sisler 100.00 200.00
2 Don Mossi 30.00 60.00
3 Joey Jay 20.00 50.00
4 Bob Purkey 20.00 50.00
5 Jack Fisher 20.00 50.00
6 John Romano 20.00 50.00
7 Russ Snyder 20.00 50.00
8 Johnny Temple 20.00 50.00
9 Roy Sievers 30.00 60.00
10 Ron Hansen 20.00 50.00
11 Pete Runnels 30.00 60.00
12 Gene Woodling 30.00 60.00
13 Clint Courtney 20.00 50.00
14 Whitey Herzog 40.00 80.00
15 Warren Spahn 75.00 150.00
16 Stan Musial 150.00 300.00
17 Willie Mays 150.00 300.00
18 Ken Boyer 40.00 80.00
19 Joe Cunningham 30.00 60.00
20 Orlando Cepeda 50.00 100.00
21 Gil Hodges 50.00 100.00
22 Yogi Berra 100.00 200.00
23 Ernie Banks 200.00 400.00
24 Lou Burdette 40.00 80.00
25 Roger Maris 200.00 400.00
26 Charlie Smith 20.00 50.00
27 Jimmie Foxx 50.00 100.00
28 Mel Ott 50.00 100.00
29 Don Nottebart 20.00 50.00
NNO Checklist Card 150.00 300.00

1981 7-Up Jumbos

These thin-stock cards, measuring approximately 5 1/4" x 8 1/2", were given away at 7-Up point-of-purchase displays. With the slogan "Feelin' 7-Up", the cards were produced highlighting the cola's different sports spokesmen of that time. The fronts contain a full-bleed color posed player photograph and a facsimile autograph. The backs have a green border, and some highlights of the player inside a white box. The cards were first available during the 1980-81 basketball season, and therefore Magic Johnson's card is one of his earliest professional pieces. Ann Meyers, another basketball great in her own right, is also represented in the set. Any other additions to this checklist would be greatly appreciated. The cards are unnumbered and checklisted below in alphabetical order.

COMPLETE SET (7) 30.00 75.00
2 George Brett BB 8.00 20.00
6 Dave Parker BB 4.00 10.00
7 Mike Schmidt BB 8.00 20.00

1975 Shakey's Pizza

This 18-card set measures 2 3/4" by 3 1/2" and features black-and-white players photos on a white card face. The red Shakey's Pizza logo overlaps the lower left corner of the picture. The phrase "West Coast Greats" cuts diagonally across the upper left corner of the picture. The player's name is printed below the photo in red. Red and brown stars accent the margins. The backs carry a Shakey's Pizza advertisement encouraging consumers to visit Shakey's Pizza parlors in Bellevue, Lake City, Aurora and West Seattle. The DiMaggio back has an offer for $1.00 off on a family-size pizza and were given away to the 1st 1,000 attendees at a Seattle card convention. The cards are numbered on the front below the picture.

COMPLETE SET (18) 40.00 80.00
1 Joe DiMaggio 6.00 15.00
2 Paul Waner 1.50 4.00
3 Lefty Gomez 1.50 4.00
4 Earl Averill 1.50 4.00
5 Ernie Lombardi 1.50 4.00
6 Joe Cronin 1.50 4.00
7 George Burns 1.25 3.00
8 Casey Stengel 2.50 6.00
9 Sam Crawford 1.50 4.00
10 Ted Williams 6.00 15.00
11 Fred Hutchinson 1.25 3.00
12 Duke Snider 2.50 6.00
13 Hal Chase 1.25 3.00
14 Bobby Doerr 1.50 4.00
15 Arky Vaughan 1.50 4.00
16 Tony Lazzeri 1.50 4.00
17 Lefty O'Doul 1.25 3.00
18 Stan Hack 1.25 3.00

1976 Shakey's Pizza

The 1976 Shakey's Pizza set contains 159 standard-size cards. The cards were part of a promotion at five Seattle-area Shakey's restaurants, and the "A" card could be exchanged for $1.00 off on any family-size pizza. The set is arranged according to year of induction into the Baseball Hall of Fame. The fronts feature vintage black and white player photos framed by red and white border stripes against a blue card face. The player's name appears in a baseball icon at the bottom of the picture. The backs have biography, career summary and player statistics.

COMPLETE SET (159) 50.00 100.00
1 Ty Cobb 2.50 6.00
2 Babe Ruth 4.00 10.00
3 Walter Johnson .75 2.00
4 Christy Mathewson .75 2.00
5 Honus Wagner 1.00 2.50
6 Nap Lajoie .75 2.00
7 Tris Speaker .60 1.50
8 Cy Young .75 2.00
9 Morgan G. Bulkeley .10 .25
10 Ban Johnson PRES .10 .25
11 John McGraw .60 1.50
12 Connie Mack .60 1.50
13 George Wright .20 .50
14 Grover Cleveland .40 1.00
Alexander
15 Alexander Cartwright .10 .25
16 Henry Chadwick .10 .25
17 Eddie Collins .60 1.50
18 Lou Gehrig 2.50 6.00
19 Willie Keeler .20 .50
20 George Sisler .60 1.50
21 Cap Anson .60 1.50
22 Charles Comiskey .20 .50
23 Candy Cummings .20 .50
24 Buck Ewing .20 .50
25 Old Hoss Radbourne .20 .50
26 Al Spalding .20 .50
27 Rogers Hornsby .60 1.50
28 Kenesaw Landis COMM .10 .25
29 Roger Bresnahan .20 .50
30 Dan Brouthers .20 .50
31 Fred Clarke .20 .50
32 Jimmy Collins .20 .50
33 Ed Delahanty .20 .50
34 Hugh Duffy .20 .50
35 Hugh Jennings .20 .50
36 Mike King Kelly .20 .50
37 Jim O'Rourke .20 .50
38 Wilbert Robinson .20 .50
39 Jesse Burkett .20 .50
40 Frank Chance .60 1.50
41 Jack Chesbro .20 .50
42 Johnny Evers .60 1.50
43 Clark Griffith .20 .50
44 Tommy McCarthy .20 .50
45 Joe McGinnity .20 .50
46 Eddie Plank .20 .50
47 Joe Tinker .60 1.50
48 Rube Waddell .20 .50
49 Ed Walsh .20 .50
50 Mickey Cochrane .60 1.50
51 Frankie Frisch .20 .50
52 Lefty Grove .60 1.50
53 Carl Hubbell .20 .50
54 Herb Pennock .20 .50
55 Pie Traynor .60 1.50
56 Charley Gehringer .20 .50
57 Mordecai Brown .20 .50
58 Kid Nichols .20 .50
59 Jimmie Foxx .75 2.00
60 Mel Ott .60 1.50
61 Harry Heilmann .20 .50
62 Paul Waner .20 .50
63 Dizzy Dean .75 2.00
64 Al Simmons .20 .50
65 Ed Barrow .10 .25
66 Chief Bender .20 .50
67 Tommy Connolly .10 .25
68 Bill Klem .10 .25
69 Bobby Wallace .20 .50
70 Harry Wright .20 .50
71 Bill Dickey .60 1.50
72 Rabbit Maranville .20 .50
73 Bill Terry .20 .50
74 Joe DiMaggio 2.50 6.00
75 Gabby Hartnett .20 .50
76 Ted Lyons .20 .50
77 Dazzy Vance .20 .50
78 Home Run Baker .20 .50
79 Ray Schalk .20 .50
80 Joe Cronin .20 .50
81 Hank Greenberg .60 1.50
82 Sam Crawford .20 .50
83 Joe McCarthy MG .10 .25
84 Zack Wheat .20 .50
85 Max Carey .20 .50
86 Billy Hamilton .20 .50
87 Bob Feller .75 2.00
88 Jackie Robinson 2.50 6.00
89 Bill McKechnie .10 .25
90 Edd Roush .20 .50
91 John Clarkson .20 .50
92 Elmer Flick .20 .50
93 Sam Rice .20 .50
94 Eppa Rixey .20 .50
95 Luke Appling .20 .50
96 Red Faber .20 .50
97 Burleigh Grimes .20 .50
98 Miller Huggins .20 .50
99 Tim Keefe .20 .50
100 Heinie Manush .20 .50
101 Monte Ward .20 .50
102 Pud Galvin .20 .50
103 Ted Williams 2.50 6.00
104 Casey Stengel .60 1.50
105 Red Ruffing .20 .50
106 Branch Rickey .10 .25
107 Lloyd Waner .20 .50
108 Joe Medwick .20 .50
109 Kiki Cuyler .20 .50
110 Goose Goslin .20 .50
111 Roy Campanella .75 2.00
112 Stan Musial 1.00 2.50
113 Stan Coveleski .20 .50
114 Waite Hoyt .20 .50
115 Lou Boudreau .20 .50
116 Earle Combs .20 .50
117 Ford Frick COMM .10 .25
118 Jesse Haines .20 .50
119 Dave Bancroft .20 .50
120 Jake Beckley .20 .50
121 Chick Hafey .20 .50
122 Harry Hooper .20 .50
123 Joe Kelley .20 .50
124 Rube Marquard .20 .50
125 Satchel Paige 1.00 2.50
126 George Weiss GM .10 .25
127 Yogi Berra .60 1.50
128 Josh Gibson 1.00 2.50
129 Lefty Gomez .20 .50
130 Will Harridge PRES .10 .25
131 Sandy Koufax .60 1.50
132 Buck Leonard .20 .50
133 Early Wynn .20 .50
134 Ross Youngs .20 .50
135 Roberto Clemente 2.50 6.00
136 Billy Evans .10 .25
137 Monte Irvin .20 .50
138 George Kelly .20 .50
139 Warren Spahn .20 .50
140 Mickey Welch .10 .25
141 Cool Papa Bell .10 .25
142 Jim Bottomley .10 .25
143 Jocko Conlan .10 .25
144 Whitey Ford .10 .25
145 Mickey Mantle 4.00 10.00
146 Sam Thompson .20 .50
147 Earl Averill .20 .50
148 Bucky Harris .20 .50
149 Billy Herman .20 .50
150 Judy Johnson .20 .50
151 Ralph Kiner .40 1.00
152 Oscar Charleston .20 .50
153 Roger Connor .20 .50
154 Cal Hubbard .20 .50
155 Bob Lemon .20 .50
156 Fred Lindstrom .20 .50
157 Robin Roberts .40 1.00
158 Robin Roberts .40 1.00
Same picture and text
as previous
A Earl Averill .10 .25

1977 Shakey's Pizza

In this 28-card commemorative set, cards A-C were issued in honor of baseball's "1977 WASSCA Convention Superstars." Cards 1-25 honor "All-Time Superstars." They were available at five Seattle area Shakey's: Bellevue, Lake City, Aurora, West Seattle and at Elliott and Broad. The cards measure 2 1/4" by 3" and feature posed and action black-and-white player photos with faded maroon borders. A blue facsimile autograph runs across the bottom of each picture. The backs carry the player's name, career highlights and statistics in the form of "Seasonal Bests."

COMPLETE SET (28) 20.00 50.00
1 Connie Mack .60 1.50
2 John McGraw .40 1.00
3 Cy Young .60 1.50
4 Walter Johnson .60 1.50
5 Grover C. Alexander .60 1.50
6 Christy Mathewson .60 1.50
7 Lefty Grove .60 1.50
8 Mickey Cochrane .40 1.00
9 Bill Dickey .40 1.00
10 Lou Gehrig 2.50 6.00
11 George Sisler .40 1.00
12 Cap Anson .40 1.00
13 Jimmie Foxx .60 1.50
14 Rogers Hornsby 1.00 2.50
15 Nap Lajoie .60 1.50
16 Eddie Collins .40 1.00
17 Pie Traynor .40 1.00
18 Honus Wagner .60 1.50
19 Ty Cobb 2.50 6.00
20 Babe Ruth 3.00 8.00
21 Joe Jackson 2.00 5.00
22 Tris Speaker .60 1.50
23 Ted Williams 2.00 5.00
24 Joe DiMaggio 2.00 5.00
25 Stan Musial 1.00 2.50
A Earl Averill .30 .75
B Johnny Mize .30 .75
C Bob Johnson .20 .50

1990 Mike Shannon Restaurant

This 5" by 7" blank-backed card features three photos of Mike Shannon (two from his playing career and one as an announcer) and has some information about his restaurant (location, hours and specialities).

1 Mike Shannon 1.25 3.00

1998 Monty Sheldon Promos Tri-Fold

Monty Sheldon, a sports artist, draws elaborate hand-painted baseballs. These 12 cards, issued in the stule of the T202 Hassan Triple Folder set, were produced to show what these baseballs look like upon completion. Since these cards are unnumbered, we have sequenced them in alphabetical order.

COMPLETE SET (12) 25.00 60.00
1 Ty Cobb 2.50 6.00
2 Joe DiMaggio 3.00 8.00
3 Joe Jackson 3.00 8.00
4 Walter Johnson 2.00 5.00
5 Sadaharu Oh 1.50 4.00
6 Satchel Paige 1.50 4.00
7 Cal Ripken 3.00 8.00
8 Babe Ruth 4.00 10.00
9 Rube Waddell 1.50 4.00
10 Honus Wagner 2.00 5.00
11 Ted Williams 3.00 8.00
12 Artie Wilson .40 1.00

1998-99 Monty Sheldon Promos

These small sized cards, which measure approximately 2" by 2" feature the artwork of Monty Sheldon who creates special art baseballs featuring requested players. Since these cards are unnumbered, we have sequenced them in alphabetical order.

COMPLETE SET 75.00 150.00
1 Hank Aaron 2.50 6.00
2 Grover C. Alexander 1.50 4.00
3 Roger Clemens 2.00 5.00
5 Ty Cobb 2.50 6.00
6 Eddie Collins 1.50 4.00
7 Joe DiMaggio 3.00 8.00
8 Whitey Ford 2.00 5.00
9 Eddie Gaedel .75 2.00
10 Lou Gehrig 3.00 8.00
11 Josh Gibson 3.00 8.00
12 Ken Griffey Jr 2.50 6.00
13 Tony Gwynn 2.00 5.00
14 Joe Jackson 2.50 6.00
15 Walter Johnson 2.50 6.00
16 Michael Jordan 4.00 10.00
17 Sandy Koufax 2.50 6.00
18 Mickey Mantle 4.00 10.00
19 Christy Mathewson 2.00 5.00
20 Willie Mays 3.00 8.00
21 Mark McGwire 2.00 5.00
22 Stan Musial 2.50 6.00
23 Bill Raimondi .40 1.00
24 Cal Ripken Jr 3.00 8.00
25 Alex Rodriguez 3.00 8.00
26 Pete Rose 2.00 5.00
27 Babe Ruth 4.00 10.00
28 Duke Snider 2.00 5.00
29 Sammy Sosa 2.00 5.00
30 Warren Spahn 1.50 4.00
31 Rube Waddell 1.50 4.00
32 Honus Wagner 2.00 5.00
33 Ted Williams 3.00 8.00
34 Artie Wilson .40 1.00
35 Carl Yastrzemski 1.50 4.00

1991 Sierra United Way

This one-card standard-size set features star outfielder Ruben Sierra. An United Way logo is in the upper left corner. There is also a photo and the player and his team is identified on the bottom. The back has vital statistics and career information about Sierra. This card was issued with six different sponsors; Etheridge Printing Company, National Semi-Conductor Corporation and Pier 1 Imports, Electro-Com Automation and General Dynamics; Stripling and Cox and the Tandy Corporation; John Deere Company and NCNB, and County Seat Stores, Inc. and Dallas Times-Herald. Each card has two different sponsors except for the ones with Etheridge.

1 Ruben Sierra .40 1.00

1991 SilverStar Holograms

These hologram cards measure the standard size and were issued to commemorate outstanding achievements of the players. The backs of the hologram cards are brightly colored and have statistics as well as a player profile. Each card also comes with a 2 1/16" by 5 3/8" blank-backed ticket. The tickets have a color player photo, serial number, and a description of the achievement honored. The Henderson hologram honors him as the all-time stolen base leader; the Ryan hologram celebrates his 7th no-hitter; and the Justice hologram commemorates his two-run homer against the Reds on October 1 that led to a 7-6 Braves' victory during the NL West pennant race. The cards are unnumbered and checklisted below chronologically by release dates. Cards numbered 5 though 8 were released later and are unnumbered. These cards are sequenced in alphabetical order.

COMPLETE SET (8) 4.00 10.00
1 Rickey Henderson .50 1.25
2 Nolan Ryan 1.25 3.00
3 Dave Justice .30 .75
4 Cal Ripken 1.25 3.00
5 Will Clark .40 1.00
6 Roger Clemens .60 1.50
7 Rawlings Gold Glove .08 .25
8 Darryl Strawberry .20 .50

1992 Silverstar Holograms

NNO Roger Clemens
NNO Roger Clemens
TICKET
NNO Dodger Stadium/30th Anniversary 2.00 5.00
NNO Roger Clemens 2.00 5.00
PROMO

1991 Simon and Schuster More Little Big Leaguers

This 96-page album was published by Simon and Schuster and includes boyhood stories of today's pro baseball players. Moreover, five 8 1/2" by 11" sheets of cards (9 cards per sheet) are inserted at the end of the album; after perforation, the cards measure the standard size. The fronts feature black and white photos of these players as kids. The pictures are bordered in green on a white card face. The backs have the same design, only with biography and career summary in place of the picture. The cards are unnumbered and checklisted below in alphabetical order.

COMPLETE SET (45) 3.00 8.00
1 Jim Abbott .07 .20
2 Jesse Barfield .02 .10
3 Kevin Bass .02 .10
4 Craig Biggio .15 .40
5 Phil Bradley .02 .10
6 Jeff Brantley .07 .20
7 Tom Brunansky .02 .10
8 Ken Caminiti .20 .50
9 Will Clark .15 .40
10 Vince Coleman .02 .10
11 David Cone .07 .20
12 Alvin Davis .02 .10
13 Andre Dawson .15 .40
14 Bill Doran .02 .10
15 Nick Esasky .02 .10
16 Dwight Gooden .07 .20
17 Tom Gordon .07 .20
18 Ken Griffey Jr. .50 1.25
19 Kevin Gross .02 .10
20 Kelly Gruber .02 .10
21 Lee Guetterman .02 .10
22 Terry Kennedy .02 .10
23 John Kruk .07 .20
24 Bill Landrum .02 .10
25 Mark Langston .02 .10
26 Barry Larkin .10 .30
27 Dave Magadan .02 .10
28 Don Mattingly .40 1.00
29 Mark McGwire .40 1.00
30 Kevin Mitchell .02 .10
31 Bob Ojeda .02 .10
32 Gregg Olson .02 .10
33 Terry Pendleton .02 .10
34 Ted Power .02 .10
35 Kirby Puckett .25 .60
36 Terry Puhl .02 .10
37 Bret Saberhagen .02 .10
38 Chris Sabo .02 .10
39 Kevin Seitzer .02 .10
40 Don Slaught .02 .10
41 Lonnie Smith .02 .10
42 Darryl Strawberry .07 .20
43 Mickey Tettleton .02 .10
44 Bobby Thigpen .02 .10
45 Frank White .07 .20

1995 Skin Bracer

Sponsored by Colgate-Palmolive Co., this three-card standard-size set was included in specially marked Skin Bracer toiletries bags and five-ounce Skin Bracer gift cartons. Also autographed 8" by 10" photos commemorating the same players and events were available for $7.99 with a proof-of-purchase from Skin Bracer, Afta skin conditioner or Colgate shave cream. The autographed photo offer was available via in-store tear pads and on-pack. The cards are unnumbered and checklisted below in alphabetical order.

COMPLETE SET (3) 6.00 15.00
1 Don Larsen 2.00 5.00
WS Perfect Game
2 Bill Mazeroski 2.00 5.00
WS-ending Home Run
3 Bobby Thomson 2.00 5.00
Shot Heard 'Round the World

2001 Skippy Derek Jeter

COMPLETE SET (4) 3.00 8.00
1 Derek Jeter 1.25 3.00
2 Derek Jeter 1.25 3.00
3 Derek Jeter 1.25 3.00
4 Derek Jeter 1.25 3.00

2000 SkyBox

COMP.MASTER SET (300) 50.00 100.00
COMP.SET w/o SP's (250) 12.50 30.00
COMMON CARD (1-250) .12 .30
COMMON ROOKIE (201-250) .20 .50
COMMON SP (201S-240S) .60 1.50
SP 201-240 STATED ODDS 1:8
DUAL SP STATED ODDS 1:12
SP CARDS 201S-250S ARE HORIZONTAL
BASIC CARDS 201-250 ARE VERTICAL
1 Cal Ripken 1.00 2.50
2 Ivan Rodriguez .20 .50
3 Chipper Jones .30 .75
4 Dean Palmer .12 .30
5 Devon White .12 .30
6 Ugueth Urbina .12 .30
7 Doug Glanville .12 .30
8 Damian Jackson .12 .30
9 Jose Canseco .20 .50
10 Billy Koch .12 .30
11 Brady Anderson .12 .30
12 Vladimir Guerrero .20 .50
13 Dan Wilson .12 .30
14 Kevin Brown .12 .30
15 Eddie Taubensee .12 .30
16 Jose Lima .12 .30
17 Greg Maddux .40 1.00
18 Manny Ramirez .30 .75
19 Brad Fullmer .12 .30
20 Ron Gant .12 .30
21 Edgar Martinez .20 .50
22 Pokey Reese .12 .30
23 Jason Varitek .30 .75
24 Neifi Perez .12 .30
25 Shane Reynolds .12 .30
26 Robin Ventura .12 .30
27 Scott Rolen .20 .50
28 Trevor Hoffman .20 .50
29 John Valentin .12 .30
30 Shannon Stewart .12 .30
31 Troy Glaus .12 .30
32 Kerry Wood .12 .30
33 Jim Thome .20 .50
34 Rafael Roque .12 .30
35 Tino Martinez .12 .30
36 Jeffrey Hammonds .12 .30
37 Orlando Hernandez .12 .30
38 Kris Benson .12 .30
39 Fred McGriff .20 .50
40 Brian Jordan .12 .30
41 Trot Nixon .12 .30
42 Matt Clement .12 .30
43 Ray Durham .12 .30
44 Johnny Damon .20 .50
45 Todd Hollandsworth .12 .30
46 Edgardo Alfonzo .12 .30
47 Tim Hudson .20 .50
48 Tony Gwynn .30 .75
49 Barry Bonds .50 1.25
50 Andruw Jones .12 .30
51 Pedro Martinez .20 .50
52 Mike Hampton .12 .30
53 Miguel Tejada .20 .50
54 Kevin Young .12 .30
55 J.T. Snow .12 .30
56 Carlos Delgado .12 .30
57 Bobby Howry .12 .30
58 Andres Galarraga .20 .50
59 Paul Konerko .12 .30
60 Mike Cameron .12 .30
61 Jeremy Giambi .12 .30
62 Todd Hundley .12 .30
63 Al Leiter .12 .30
64 Matt Stairs .12 .30
65 Edgar Renteria .12 .30
66 Jeff Kent .12 .30
67 John Wetteland .12 .30
68 Nomar Garciaparra .20 .50
69 Jeff Weaver .12 .30
70 Matt Williams .12 .30
71 Kyle Farnsworth .12 .30
72 Brad Radke .12 .30
73 Eric Chavez .12 .30
74 J.D. Drew .12 .30
75 Steve Finley .12 .30
76 Pete Harnisch .12 .30
77 Chad Kreuter .12 .30
78 Todd Pratt .12 .30
79 John Jaha .12 .30
80 Armando Rios .12 .30
81 Luis Gonzalez .12 .30
82 Ryan Minor .12 .30
83 Juan Gonzalez .12 .30
84 Rickey Henderson .30 .75
85 Jason Giambi .12 .30
86 Shawn Estes .12 .30
87 Chad Curtis .12 .30
88 Jeff Cirillo .12 .30
89 Juan Encarnacion .12 .30
90 Tony Womack .12 .30
91 Mike Mussina .20 .50
92 Jeff Bagwell .20 .50
93 Rey Ordonez .12 .30
94 Joe McEwing .12 .30
95 Robb Nen .12 .30
96 Will Clark .20 .50
97 Chris Singleton .12 .30
98 Jason Kendall .12 .30
99 Ken Griffey Jr. .60 1.50
100 Rusty Greer .12 .30
101 Charles Johnson .12 .30
102 Carlos Lee .12 .30
103 Brad Ausmus .12 .30
104 Preston Wilson .12 .30
105 Ronnie Belliard .12 .30
106 Mike Lieberthal .12 .30
107 Alex Rodriguez .40 1.00
108 Jay Bell .12 .30
109 Frank Thomas .30 .75
110 Adrian Beltre .30 .75
111 Ron Coomer .12 .30
112 Ben Grieve .12 .30
113 Darryl Kile .12 .30
114 Erubiel Durazo .12 .30
115 Maggio Ordonez .20 .50
116 Gary Sheffield .12 .30
117 Joe Mays .12 .30
118 Fernando Tatis .12 .30
119 David Wells .12 .30
120 Tim Salmon .12 .30
121 Troy O'Leary .12 .30
122 Roberto Alomar .20 .50
123 Damion Easley .12 .30
124 Brant Brown .12 .30
125 Carlos Beltran .20 .50
126 Eric Karros .12 .30
127 Geoff Jenkins .12 .30
128 Roger Clemens .40 1.00
129 Warren Morris .12 .30
130 Eric Owens .12 .30
131 Jose Cruz Jr. .12 .30
132 Mo Vaughn .12 .30
133 Eric Young .12 .30
134 Kenny Lofton .12 .30
135 Marquis Grissom .12 .30
136 A.J. Burnett .12 .30
137 Bernie Williams .20 .50
138 Javy Lopez .12 .30
139 Jose Offerman .12 .30
140 Sean Casey .12 .30
141 Alex Gonzalez .12 .30
142 Carlos Febles .12 .30
143 Mike Piazza .30 .75
144 Curt Schilling .20 .50
145 Ben Davis .12 .30
146 Rafael Palmeiro .20 .50
147 Scott Williamson .12 .30
148 Darin Erstad .12 .30
149 Joe Girardi .20 .50
150 Gerald Williams .12 .30
151 Richie Sexson .12 .30

152 Corey Koskie .12 .30
153 Paul O'Neill .20 .50
154 Chad Hermansen .12 .30
155 Randy Johnson .30 .75
156 Henry Rodriguez .12 .30
157 Bartolo Colon .12 .30
158 Tony Clark .12 .30
159 Mike Lowell .12 .30
160 Moises Alou .12 .30
161 Todd Walker .12 .30
162 Mariano Rivera .40 1.00
163 Mark McGwire .50 1.25
164 Roberto Hernandez .12 .30
165 Larry Walker .20 .50
166 Albert Belle .12 .30
167 Barry Larkin .20 .50
168 Rolando Arrojo .12 .30
169 Mark Kotsay .12 .30
170 Ken Caminiti .12 .30
171 Dermal Brown .12 .30
172 Michael Barrett .12 .30
173 Jay Buhner .12 .30
174 Ruben Mateo .12 .30
175 Jim Edmonds .12 .30
176 Sammy Sosa .30 .75
177 Omar Vizquel .20 .50
178 Todd Helton .20 .50
179 Kevin Barker .12 .30
180 Derek Jeter .75 2.00
181 Brian Giles .12 .30
182 Greg Vaughn .12 .30
183 Roy Halladay .20 .50
184 Tom Glavine .20 .50
185 Craig Biggio .20 .50
186 Jose Vidro .12 .30
187 Andy Ashby .12 .30
188 Freddy Garcia .12 .30
189 Garret Anderson .12 .30
190 Mark Grace .20 .50
191 Travis Fryman .12 .30
192 Jeromy Burnitz .12 .30
193 Jacque Jones .12 .30
194 David Cone .12 .30
195 Ryan Rupe .12 .30
196 John Smoltz .30 .75
197 Daryle Ward .12 .30
198 Rondell White .12 .30
199 Bobby Abreu .12 .30
200 Justin Thompson .12 .30
201 Norm Hutchins .12 .30
201S Norm Hutchins SP .60 1.50
202 Ramon Ortiz .12 .30
202S Ramon Ortiz SP .60 1.50
203 Dan Wheeler .12 .30
203S Dan Wheeler SP .60 1.50
204 Matt Riley .12 .30
204S Matt Riley SP .60 1.50
205 Steve Lomasney .12 .30
205S Steve Lomasney SP .60 1.50
206 Chad Meyers .12 .30
206S Chad Meyers SP .60 1.50
207 Gary Glover RC .20 .50
207S Gary Glover SP .60 1.50
208 Joe Crede .12 .30
208S Joe Crede SP .60 1.50
209 Kip Wells .12 .30
209S Kip Wells SP .60 1.50
210 Travis Dawkins .12 .30
210S Travis Dawkins SP .60 1.50
211 Denny Stark RC .20 .50
211S Denny Stark SP .60 1.50
212 Ben Petrick .12 .30
212S Ben Petrick SP .60 1.50
213 Eric Munson .12 .30
213S Eric Munson SP .60 1.50
214 Josh Beckett .25 .60
214S Josh Beckett SP 1.25 3.00
215 Pablo Ozuna .12 .30
215S Pablo Ozuna SP .60 1.50
216 Brad Penny .12 .30
216S Brad Penny SP .60 1.50
217 Julio Ramirez .12 .30
217S Julio Ramirez SP .60 1.50
218 Danny Peoples .12 .30
218S Danny Peoples SP .60 1.50
219 Wilfredo Rodriguez RC .20 .50
219S Wilfredo Rodriguez SP .60 1.50
220 Julio Lugo .12 .30
220S Julio Lugo SP .60 1.50
221 Mark Quinn .12 .30
221S Mark Quinn SP .60 1.50
222 Eric Gagne .12 .30
222S Eric Gagne SP .60 1.50
223 Chad Green .12 .30
223S Chad Green SP .60 1.50
224 Tony Armas Jr. .12 .30
224S Tony Armas Jr. SP .60 1.50
225 Milton Bradley .12 .30
225S Milton Bradley SP .60 1.50
226 Rob Bell .12 .30
226S Rob Bell SP .60 1.50
227 Alfonso Soriano .30 .75
227S Alfonso Soriano SP 1.50 4.00
228 Wily Pena .12 .30
228S Wily Pena SP .60 1.50
229 Nick Johnson .12 .30
229S Nick Johnson SP .60 1.50
230 Ed Yarnall .12 .30
230S Ed Yarnall SP .60 1.50
231 Ryan Bradley .12 .30
231S Ryan Bradley SP .60 1.50
232 Adam Piatt .12 .30
232S Adam Piatt SP .60 1.50
233 Chad Harville .12 .30
233S Chad Harville SP .60 1.50
234 Alex Sanchez .12 .30
234S Alex Sanchez SP .60 1.50
235 Michael Coleman .12 .30
235S Michael Coleman SP .60 1.50
236 Pat Burrell .12 .30
236S Pat Burrell SP .60 1.50
237 Wascar Serrano RC .20 .50
237S Wascar Serrano SP .60 1.50
238 Rick Ankiel .20 .50
238S Rick Ankiel SP 1.00 2.50
239 Mike Lamb RC .20 .50
239S Mike Lamb SP .60 1.50
240 Vernon Wells .12 .30
240S Vernon Wells SP .60 1.50
241 J.Toca .12 .30
G.Tomlinson
241S J.Toca .60 1.50
G.Tomlinson SP
242 J.Phelps RC .20 .50
S.Hillenbrand
242S J.Phelps .60 1.50
S.Hillenbrand SP
243 A.Myette .12 .30
D.Davis
243S A.Myette .60 1.50
D.Davis SP
244 B.Laxton .12 .30
R.Ramsay
244S B.Laxton .60 1.50
R.Ramsay SP
245 B.J.Ryan .12 .30
C.Lee
245S B.J.Ryan .60 1.50
C.Lee SP
246 C.Haas .12 .30
W.Veras
246S C.Haas .60 1.50
W.Veras SP
247 J.Anderson .12 .30
K.Peterson
247S J.Anderson .60 1.50
K.Peterson SP
248 J.Dewey .12 .30
G.Chiaramonte
248S J.Dewey .60 1.50
G.Chiaramonte SP
249 G.Mota .12 .30
O.Moreno
249S G.Mota .60 1.50
O.Moreno SP
250 J.Zuleta RC .20 .50
S.Cox
250S J.Zuleta .60 1.50
S.Cox SP

2000 SkyBox Star Rubies

*RUBIES: 4X TO 10X BASIC CARDS
*ROOKIES: 2.5X TO 6X BASIC VERTICAL
STATED ODDS 1:12
DUAL VERSIONS DO NOT EXIST FOR 201-250

2000 SkyBox Star Rubies Extreme

*RUBIES EXTREME: 15X TO 40X BASIC
*ROOKIES: 6X TO 15X BASIC CARDS
STATED PRINT RUN 50 SERIAL #'d SETS
DUAL VERSIONS DO NOT EXIST FOR 201-250

2000 SkyBox Autographics

DOMINION STATED ODDS 1:144
E-X STATED ODDS 1:24
IMPACT STATED ODDS 1:216
METAL STATED ODDS 1:96
SKYBOX STATED ODDS 1:72
DM SUFFIX ON DOMINION DISTRIBUTION
EX SUFFIX ON E-X DISTRIBUTION
IM SUFFIX ON IMPACT DISTRIBUTION
MT SUFFIX ON METAL DISTRIBUTION
SB SUFFIX ON SKYBOX DISTRIBUTION
*PURPLE FOIL: 1X TO 2.5X BASIC
PURPLE RANDOM IN SKYBOX PRODUCTS
PURPLE STATED PRINT RUN 50 #'d SETS
1 Bobby Abreu 10.00 25.00
2 Chad Allen 4.00 10.00
3 Moises Alou 6.00 15.00
4 Marlon Anderson 4.00 10.00
5 Rick Ankiel 6.00 15.00
6 Glen Barker 4.00 10.00
7 Michael Barrett 4.00 10.00
8 Josh Beckett 8.00 20.00
9 Rob Bell 4.00 10.00
10 Mark Bellhorn 20.00 50.00
11 Carlos Beltran 8.00 20.00
12 Adrian Beltre 25.00 60.00
13 Peter Bergeron 4.00 10.00
14 Lance Berkman 6.00 15.00
15 Wade Boggs 10.00 25.00
16 Barry Bonds 50.00 100.00
17 Kent Bottenfield 4.00 10.00
18 Milton Bradley 6.00 15.00
19 Rico Brogna 4.00 10.00
20 Pat Burrell 6.00 15.00
21 Orlando Cabrera 6.00 15.00
22 Miguel Cairo 4.00 10.00
23 Mike Cameron 6.00 15.00
24 Chris Carpenter 10.00 25.00
25 Sean Casey 6.00 15.00
26 Roger Cedeno 4.00 10.00
27 Eric Chavez 6.00 15.00
28 Bruce Chen 4.00 10.00
29 Will Clark 12.50 30.00
30 Johnny Damon 10.00 25.00
31 Mike Darr 6.00 15.00
32 Ben Davis 4.00 10.00
33 Russ Davis 4.00 10.00
34 Carlos Delgado 10.00 25.00
35 Jason Dewey 4.00 10.00
36 Einar Diaz 4.00 10.00
37 Octavio Dotel 4.00 10.00
38 J.D. Drew 6.00 15.00
39 Erubiel Durazo 4.00 10.00
40 Ray Durham 6.00 15.00
41 Damion Easley 4.00 10.00
42 Scott Elarton 4.00 10.00
43 Kelvim Escobar 4.00 10.00
44 Carlos Febles 4.00 10.00
45 Freddy Garcia 6.00 15.00
46 Jason Giambi 5.00 12.00
47 Jeremy Giambi 4.00 10.00
48 Doug Glanville 6.00 15.00
49 Troy Glaus 6.00 15.00
50 Alex Gonzalez 4.00 10.00
51 Shawn Green 10.00 25.00
52 Todd Greene 4.00 10.00
53 Jason Grilli 4.00 10.00
54 Vladimir Guerrero 12.00 30.00
55 Tony Gwynn 20.00 50.00
56 Jerry Hairston Jr. 4.00 10.00
57 Mike Hampton 6.00 15.00
58 Todd Helton 4.00 10.00
59 Trevor Hoffman 10.00 25.00
60 Bobby Howry 4.00 10.00
61 Tim Hudson 8.00 20.00
62 Norm Hutchins 4.00 10.00
63 John Jaha 4.00 10.00
64 Derek Jeter 200.00 400.00
65 D'Angelo Jimenez 4.00 10.00
66 Nick Johnson 6.00 15.00
67 Randy Johnson 40.00 80.00
68 Andruw Jones 10.00 25.00
69 Jacque Jones 6.00 15.00
70 Gabe Kapler 6.00 15.00
71 Jason Kendall 6.00 15.00
72 Adam Kennedy 4.00 10.00
73 Cesar King 4.00 10.00
74 Paul Konerko 8.00 20.00
75 Mark Kotsay 6.00 15.00
76 Ray Lankford 6.00 15.00
77 Jason LaRue 4.00 10.00
78 Matt Lawton 4.00 10.00
79 Carlos Lee 6.00 15.00
80 Mike Lieberthal 6.00 15.00
81 Cole Liniak 4.00 10.00
82 Steve Lomasney 4.00 10.00
83 Jose Macias 4.00 10.00
84 Greg Maddux 50.00 120.00
85 Edgar Martinez 6.00 15.00
86 Pedro Martinez 100.00 200.00
87 Ruben Mateo 4.00 10.00
88 Gary Matthews Jr. 4.00 10.00
89 Aaron McNeal 4.00 10.00
90 Kevin Millwood 6.00 15.00
91 Raul Mondesi 6.00 15.00
92 Orber Moreno 4.00 10.00
93 Warren Morris 5.00 12.00
94 Eric Munson 4.00 10.00
95 Heath Murray 4.00 10.00
96 Mike Mussina 10.00 25.00
97 Joe Nathan 5.00 12.00
98 Magglio Ordonez 10.00 25.00
99 Eric Owens 4.00 10.00
100 Rafael Palmeiro 12.00 30.00
101 Jim Parque 4.00 10.00
102 Angel Pena 4.00 10.00
103 Adam Piatt 3.00 8.00
104 Wily Pena 12.00 30.00
105 Pokey Reese 6.00 15.00
106 Matt Riley 4.00 10.00
107 Cal Ripken 50.00 100.00
108 Alex Rodriguez 20.00 50.00
109 Scott Rolen 4.00 10.00
110 Jimmy Rollins 20.00 50.00
111 Ryan Rupe 4.00 10.00
112 B.J. Ryan 6.00 15.00
113 Tim Salmon 10.00 25.00
114 Randall Simon 4.00 10.00
115 Chris Singleton 4.00 10.00
116 J.T. Snow 6.00 15.00
117 Alfonso Soriano 5.00 12.00
118 Shannon Stewart 6.00 15.00
119 Mike Sweeney 6.00 15.00
120 Miguel Tejada 10.00 25.00
121 Frank Thomas 30.00 80.00
122 Wilton Veras 4.00 10.00
123 Jose Vidro 4.00 10.00
124 Billy Wagner 10.00 25.00
125 Jeff Weaver 6.00 15.00
126 Rondell White 6.00 15.00
127 Scott Williamson 4.00 10.00
128 Randy Wolf 6.00 15.00
129 Tony Womack 6.00 15.00
130 Jaret Wright 4.00 10.00
131 Ed Yarnall 4.00 10.00
132 Kevin Young 4.00 10.00

2000 SkyBox E-Ticket

COMPLETE SET (15) 6.00 15.00
STATED ODDS 1:4
*STAR RUBY: 8X TO 20X BASIC E-TICKET
STAR RUBIES PR.RUN 100 SERIAL #'d SETS
ET1 Alex Rodriguez .60 1.50
ET2 Derek Jeter 1.25 3.00
ET3 Nomar Garciaparra .30 .75
ET4 Cal Ripken 1.50 4.00
ET5 Sean Casey .20 .50
ET6 Mark McGwire .75 2.00
ET7 Sammy Sosa .50 1.25
ET8 Ken Griffey Jr. 1.00 2.50
ET9 Tony Gwynn .50 1.25
ET10 Pedro Martinez .30 .75
ET11 Chipper Jones .50 1.25
ET12 Vladimir Guerrero .30 .75
ET13 Roger Clemens .60 1.50
ET14 Mike Piazza .50 1.25
ET15 Randy Johnson .50 1.25

2000 SkyBox Genuine Coverage

HR STATED ODDS 1:399 HOBBY/RETAIL
H STATED ODDS 1:144 HOBBY
AU PRINT RUN 20 SERIAL #'d SETS
NO AU PRICING DUE TO SCARCITY
1 Jose Canseco H 6.00 15.00
2 J.D. Drew H 4.00 10.00
3 Troy Glaus HR 4.00 10.00
4 Manny Ramirez H 6.00 15.00
5 Cal Ripken HR 15.00 40.00
6 Alex Rodriguez HR 10.00 25.00
7 Ivan Rodriguez H 6.00 15.00
8 Frank Thomas H 6.00 15.00
9 Robin Ventura HR 4.00 10.00
10 Matt Williams HR 4.00 10.00

2000 SkyBox Higher Level

COMPLETE SET (10) 10.00 25.00
STATED ODDS 1:24
*STAR RUBIES: 5X TO 12X BASIC HIGH.LEVEL
STAR RUBIES PRINT RUN 50 SERIAL #'d SETS
1 Cal Ripken 3.00 8.00
2 Derek Jeter 2.50 6.00
3 Nomar Garciaparra .60 1.50
4 Chipper Jones 1.00 2.50
5 Mike Piazza 1.00 2.50
6 Ivan Rodriguez .60 1.50
7 Ken Griffey Jr. 2.00 5.00
8 Sammy Sosa 1.00 2.50
9 Alex Rodriguez 1.25 3.00
10 Mark McGwire 1.50 4.00

2000 SkyBox Preeminence

COMPLETE SET (10) 8.00 20.00
STATED ODDS 1:24
*STAR RUBIES: 5X TO 12X BASIC PRE-EM
STAR RUBIES PRINT RUN 50 SERIAL #'d SETS
1 Pedro Martinez .60 1.50
2 Derek Jeter 2.50 6.00
3 Nomar Garciaparra .60 1.50
4 Alex Rodriguez 1.25 3.00
5 Mark McGwire 1.50 4.00
6 Sammy Sosa 1.00 2.50
7 Sean Casey .40 1.00
8 Mike Piazza 1.00 2.50
9 Chipper Jones 1.00 2.50
10 Ivan Rodriguez .60 1.50

2000 SkyBox Skylines

COMPLETE SET (10) 6.00 15.00
STATED ODDS 1:11
*STAR RUBIES: 10X TO 25X BASIC SKYLINE
STAR RUBIES PRINT RUN 50 SERIAL #'d SETS
1 Cal Ripken 2.00 5.00
2 Mark McGwire 1.00 2.50
3 Alex Rodriguez .75 2.00
4 Sammy Sosa .60 1.50
5 Derek Jeter 1.50 4.00
6 Mike Piazza .60 1.50
7 Nomar Garciaparra .40 1.00
8 Chipper Jones .60 1.50
9 Ken Griffey Jr. 1.25 3.00
10 Manny Ramirez .60 1.50

2000 SkyBox Speed Merchants

COMPLETE SET (10) 5.00 12.00
STATED ODDS 1:8
*STAR RUBIES: 6X TO 15X BASIC MERCHANT
STAR RUBIES PRINT RUN 100 SERIAL #'d SETS
1 Derek Jeter 1.25 3.00
2 Sammy Sosa .50 1.25
3 Nomar Garciaparra .30 .75
4 Alex Rodriguez .60 1.50
5 Randy Johnson .50 1.25
6 Ken Griffey Jr. 1.00 2.50
7 Pedro Martinez .30 .75
8 Pat Burrell .20 .50
9 Barry Bonds .75 2.00
10 Mark McGwire .75 2.00

2000 SkyBox Technique

COMPLETE SET (15) 10.00 25.00
STATED ODDS 1:11
*STAR RUBIES: 8X TO 20X BASIC TECHNIQUE
STAR RUBIES PRINT RUN 50 SERIAL #'d SETS
1 Alex Rodriguez 1.00 2.50
2 Tony Gwynn .75 2.00
3 Sean Casey .30 .75
4 Mark McGwire 1.25 3.00
5 Sammy Sosa .75 2.00
6 Ken Griffey Jr. 1.50 4.00
7 Mike Piazza .75 2.00
8 Nomar Garciaparra .50 1.25
9 Derek Jeter 2.00 5.00
10 Vladimir Guerrero .50 1.25
11 Cal Ripken 2.50 6.00
12 Chipper Jones .75 2.00
13 Frank Thomas .75 2.00
14 Manny Ramirez .75 2.00
15 Jeff Bagwell .50 1.25

2000 SkyBox Hobby Bullpen

COMPLETE SET (15) 8.00 20.00
1 Cal Ripken 2.00 5.00
2 Ivan Rodriguez .40 1.00
3 Chipper Jones .60 1.50
12 Vladimir Guerrero .40 1.00
17 Greg Maddux .75 2.00
18 Manny Ramirez .60 1.50
48 Tony Gwynn .60 1.50
49 Barry Bonds 1.00 2.50
51 Pedro Martinez .40 1.00
68 Nomar Garciaparra .40 1.00
98 Jason Kendall .25 .60
99 Ken Griffey Jr. 1.25 3.00
163 Mark McGwire 1.00 2.50
176 Sammy Sosa .60 1.50
180 Derek Jeter 1.50 4.00

2000 SkyBox National

COMPLETE SET (6) 4.00 10.00
1 Cal Ripken 2.00 5.00
2 Ken Griffey Jr. 1.25 3.00
3 Derek Jeter 1.50 4.00
4 Alex Rodriguez .75 2.00
5 Mark McGwire 1.00 2.50
6 Mike Piazza .60 1.50

2004 SkyBox Autographics

COMP.SET w/o SP's (65) 15.00 40.00
COMMON CARD (1-65) .30 .75
COMMON CARD (66-100) .75 2.00
66-100 ODDS 1:1 HOBBY, 1:72 RETAIL
66-100 PRINT RUN 1500 SERIAL #'d SETS
1 Albert Pujols 1.00 2.50
2 Richie Sexson .30 .75
3 Scott Rolen .50 1.25
4 Rafael Palmeiro .50 1.25
5 Ichiro Suzuki 1.00 2.50
6 Craig Biggio .50 1.25
7 Todd Helton .50 1.25
8 Miguel Cabrera .75 2.00
9 Ken Griffey Jr. 1.50 4.00
10 Pat Burrell .30 .75
11 Jose Reyes .50 1.25
12 Hideki Matsui 1.25 3.00
13 Geoff Jenkins .30 .75
14 Mark Prior .50 1.25
15 Gary Sheffield .30 .75
16 Nomar Garciaparra .50 1.25
17 Luis Gonzalez .30 .75
18 Troy Glaus .30 .75
19 Rocco Baldelli .30 .75
20 Hank Blalock .30 .75
21 Bret Boone .30 .75
22 Mike Sweeney .30 .75
23 Dmitri Young .30 .75
24 Dontrelle Willis .30 .75
25 Austin Kearns .30 .75
26 Jason Kendall .30 .75
27 Derek Jeter 2.00 5.00
28 Miguel Tejada .50 1.25
29 Torii Hunter .30 .75
30 Sammy Sosa .75 2.00
31 Chipper Jones .75 2.00
32 Pedro Martinez .50 1.25
33 Curt Schilling .50 1.25
34 Roy Halladay .50 1.25
35 Jim Edmonds .50 1.25
36 Alex Rodriguez Yanks 1.00 2.50
37 Jason Schmidt .30 .75
38 Jeff Bagwell .50 1.25
39 Omar Vizquel .50 1.25
40 Ivan Rodriguez .50 1.25
41 Magglio Ordonez .50 1.25
42 Jim Thome .50 1.25
43 Mike Piazza .75 2.00
44 Alfonso Soriano .50 1.25
45 Hideo Nomo .75 2.00
46 Kerry Wood .30 .75
47 Greg Maddux 1.00 2.50
48 Tony Batista .30 .75
49 Randy Johnson .75 2.00
50 Garret Anderson .30 .75
51 Mark Teixeira .50 1.25
52 Carlos Delgado .30 .75
53 Darin Erstad .30 .75
54 Shawn Green .30 .75
55 Josh Beckett .30 .75
56 Lance Berkman .50 1.25
57 Adam Dunn .50 1.25
58 Brian Giles .30 .75
59 Jason Giambi .30 .75
60 Barry Zito .50 1.25
61 Vladimir Guerrero .50 1.25
62 Frank Thomas .75 2.00
63 Jay Gibbons .30 .75
64 Manny Ramirez .75 2.00
65 Andruw Jones .30 .75
66 Rickie Weeks PR .75 2.00
67 Chad Bentz PR RC .75 2.00
68 Bobby Crosby PR .75 2.00
69 Greg Dobbs PR RC .75 2.00
70 John Gall PR RC .75 2.00
71 Kaz Matsui PR RC 1.25 3.00
72 Dallas McPherson PR .75 2.00
73 Brandon Watson PR .75 2.00
74 Jerry Gil PR RC .75 2.00
75 Garrett Atkins PR .75 2.00
76 Cory Sullivan PR RC .75 2.00
77 Khalil Greene PR 1.25 3.00
78 Shawn Hill PR RC .75 2.00
79 Graham Koonce PR .75 2.00
80 Chien-Ming Wang PR 3.00 8.00
81 John Labandeira PR RC .75 2.00
82 Jonny Gomes PR .75 2.00
83 Edwin Jackson PR .75 2.00
84 Alfredo Simon PR RC 1.25 3.00
85 Delmon Young PR 1.25 3.00
86 Jason Bartlett PR RC 2.50 6.00
87 Angel Chavez PR RC .75 2.00
88 Angel Guzman PR .75 2.00
89 Ryan Howard PR 1.50 4.00
90 Scott Hairston PR .75 2.00
91 Ronny Cedeno PR RC .75 2.00
92 Don Kelly PR RC 1.25 3.00
93 Ivan Ochoa PR RC .75 2.00
94 Edwin Encarnarcion PR 2.00 5.00
95 Byron Gettis PR .75 2.00
96 Kevin Youkilis PR .75 2.00
97 Grady Sizemore PR 1.25 3.00
98 Mariano Gomez PR RC .75 2.00
99 Hector Gimenez PR RC .75 2.00
100 Ruddy Yan PR .75 2.00

2004 SkyBox Autographics Insignia

*INSIGNIA 1-65: 1.25X TO 3X BASIC
*INSIGNIA 66-100: .6X TO 1.5X BASIC
OVERALL PARALLEL ODDS 1:4 H, 1:192 R
STATED PRINT RUN 150 SERIAL #'d SETS
INSIGNIA IS SILVER BACKGROUND

2004 SkyBox Autographics Royal Insignia

*ROYAL INS. 1-65: 3X TO 8X BASIC
*ROYAL INS. 66-100: 1X TO 2.5X BASIC
OVERALL PARALLEL ODDS 1:4 H, 1:192 R
STATED PRINT RUN 25 SERIAL #'d SETS
ROYAL INSIGNIA IS PURPLE BACKGROUND

2004 SkyBox Autographics Autoclassics

STATED ODDS 1:12 HOBBY/RETAIL
1 Johnny Bench 1.00 2.50
2 Steve Carlton .60 1.50
3 Carlton Fisk .60 1.50
4 Bill Mazeroski .60 1.50
5 Jim Palmer .60 1.50
6 Warren Spahn .60 1.50
7 Duke Snider .60 1.50
8 Wade Boggs .60 1.50
9 Nolan Ryan 3.00 8.00
10 Mike Schmidt 1.50 4.00
11 Albert Chandler .40 1.00
12 Ty Cobb 1.50 4.00
13 Sal Maglie .40 1.00
14 George Kelly .40 1.00
15 Joe Sewell .60 1.50

2004 SkyBox Autographics Autoclassics Memorabilia

OVERALL AU-GU ODDS 1:1 HOB, 1:24 RET
STATED PRINT RUN 350 SERIAL #'d SETS
BM Bill Mazeroski Bat 6.00 15.00
CF Carlton Fisk Jsy 6.00 15.00
DS Duke Snider Jsy 6.00 15.00
JB Johnny Bench Jsy 6.00 15.00
JP Jim Palmer Jsy 4.00 10.00
MS Mike Schmidt Bat 6.00 15.00
NR Nolan Ryan Jsy 10.00 25.00
SC Steve Carlton Jsy 4.00 10.00
WB Wade Boggs Jsy 6.00 15.00
WS Warren Spahn Jsy 6.00 15.00

2004 SkyBox Autographics Autoclassics Signature

OVERALL AU-GU ODDS 1:1 HOB, 1:24 RET
PRINT RUNS B/WN 3-50 COPIES PER
NO PRICING ON QTY OF 3 OR LESS
AC Albert Chandler/25 75.00 150.00
BM Bill Mazeroski/50 10.00 25.00
CF Carlton Fisk/50 15.00 40.00
DS Duke Snider/50 15.00 40.00
GK George Kelly/25 100.00 175.00
JB Johnny Bench/50 20.00 50.00
JP Jim Palmer/50 10.00 25.00
JS Joe Sewell/25 50.00 100.00
NR Nolan Ryan/38 75.00 150.00
SC Steve Carlton/50 10.00 25.00
SM Mike Schmidt/25 60.00 120.00
SM Sal Maglie/25 100.00 175.00
WB Wade Boggs/50 15.00 40.00
WS Warren Spahn/50 20.00 50.00

2004 SkyBox Autographics Jerseygraphics Blue

STATED PRINT RUN 250 SERIAL #'d SETS
*GOLD: 1X TO 2.5X BLUE
GOLD PRINT RUN 25 SERIAL #'d SETS
PURPLE PRINT RUN 1 SERIAL #'d SET
NO PURPLE PRICING DUE TO SCARCITY
*SILVER: .5X TO 1.2X BLUE
SILVER PRINT RUN 100 SERIAL #'d SETS
OVERALL AU-GU ODDS 1:1 HOB, 1:24 RET
AD Adam Dunn 3.00 8.00
AJ Andruw Jones 4.00 10.00
AK Austin Kearns 3.00 8.00
AP Albert Pujols 6.00 15.00
AR Alex Rodriguez 5.00 12.00
AS Alfonso Soriano 3.00 8.00
BA Bobby Abreu 3.00 8.00
BZ Barry Zito 3.00 8.00
CB Craig Biggio 4.00 10.00
CD Carlos Delgado 3.00 8.00
CJ Chipper Jones 4.00 10.00
CS Curt Schilling 3.00 8.00
DE Darin Erstad 3.00 8.00
DJ Derek Jeter 8.00 20.00
DO David Ortiz 4.00 10.00
DW Dontrelle Willis 4.00 10.00
FT Frank Thomas 4.00 10.00
GM Greg Maddux 5.00 12.00
HB Hank Blalock 3.00 8.00
HN Hideo Nomo 4.00 10.00
IR Ivan Rodriguez 4.00 10.00
JB Josh Beckett 3.00 8.00
JE Jim Edmonds 3.00 8.00
JG1 Jason Giambi 3.00 8.00
JG2 Jay Gibbons 3.00 8.00
JR Jose Reyes 3.00 8.00
JT Jim Thome 4.00 10.00
KM Kevin Millwood 3.00 8.00
KW Kerry Wood 3.00 8.00
LB Lance Berkman 3.00 8.00
MC Miguel Cabrera 4.00 10.00
MO Magglio Ordonez 3.00 8.00
MP1 Mike Piazza 5.00 12.00
MP2 Mark Prior 4.00 10.00
MR Manny Ramirez 4.00 10.00
MT1 Mark Teixeira 4.00 10.00
MT2 Miguel Tejada 3.00 8.00
NG Nomar Garciaparra 5.00 12.00
PB Pat Burrell 3.00 8.00
PM Pedro Martinez 4.00 10.00
RB Rocco Baldelli 3.00 8.00
RH Roy Halladay 3.00 8.00
RP Rafael Palmeiro 4.00 10.00
SG Shawn Green 3.00 8.00
SR Scott Rolen 4.00 10.00
SS Sammy Sosa 4.00 10.00
TG Troy Glaus 3.00 8.00
TH1 Todd Helton 4.00 10.00
TH2 Torii Hunter 3.00 8.00
VG Vladimir Guerrero 4.00 10.00

2004 SkyBox Autographics Prospects Endorsed

STATED ODDS 1:4 HOBBY, 1:8 RETAIL
1 A.Pujols 1.25 3.00
D.Young
2 E.Gagne .40 1.00
B.Jenks
3 B.Larkin .60 1.50
E.Encarnacion
4 A.Jones .40 1.00
J.Gomes
5 H.Nomo 1.50 4.00
C.Wang
6 G.Sheffield .40 1.00
C.Sullivan
7 B.Wagner .75 2.00
R.Howard
8 J.Posada .60 1.50
K.Hill
9 C.Schilling .60 1.50
R.Wagner
10 J.Reyes .60 1.50
R.Weeks
11 A.Soriano .60 1.50
M.Kata
12 B.Zito .60 1.50
R.Harden
13 R.Johnson 1.00 2.50
B.Webb
14 A.Rodriguez 1.25 3.00
A.Berroa
15 D.Willis .40 1.00
E.Jackson

2004 SkyBox Autographics Prospects Endorsed Dual Autograph

OVERALL AU-GU ODDS 1:1 HOB, 1:24 RET
STATED PRINT RUN 50 SERIAL #'d SETS
AJJG A.Jones/J.Gomes 15.00 40.00
APDY A.Pujols/D.Young 175.00 300.00
BLEE B.Larkin/E.Encarnacion 30.00 60.00
BWRH B.Wagner/R.Howard 50.00 100.00
EGBJ E.Gagne/B.Jenks 15.00 40.00
GSCS G.Sheffield/C.Sullivan 10.00 25.00
JRRW J.Reyes/R.Weeks 15.00 40.00

2004 SkyBox Autographics Prospects Endorsed Dual Jersey

STATED PRINT RUN 500 SERIAL #'d SETS
*PATCH: 1.25X TO 3X BASIC
PATCH PRINT RUN 50 SERIAL #'d SETS
OVERALL AU-GU ODDS 1:1 HOB, 1:24 RET
APDY A.Pujols 6.00 15.00
D.Young
ARAB A.Rodriguez/A.Berroa 4.00 10.00
ASMK A.Soriano/M.Kata 3.00 8.00
BLKM B.Larkin/K.Matsui Bat 4.00 10.00
BZRH B.Zito/R.Harden 3.00 8.00
CSRW C.Schilling/R.Wagner 4.00 10.00
DWEJ D.Willis/E.Jackson 4.00 10.00
HNCW H.Nomo/C.Wang 30.00 60.00
JRRW J.Reyes/R.Weeks 3.00 8.00
RJBW R.Johnson/B.Webb 4.00 10.00

2004 SkyBox Autographics Signatures Blue

PRINT RUNS B/WN 100-485 COPIES PER
*GOLD: 1X TO 2X BLUE p/r 200-485
*GOLD: 1X TO 2X BLUE p/r 100-197
GOLD PRINT RUN 25 SERIAL #'d SETS
*ON LOCATION: .4X TO 1X BLUE p/r 200-485
*ON LOCATION: .4X TO 1X BLUE p/r 100-197
ON LOCATION PRINT 99 SERIAL #'d SETS
PURPLE PRINT RUN 1 SERIAL #'d SET
NO PURPLE PRICING DUE TO SCARCITY
*SILVER: .4X TO 1X BLUE p/r 200-485
*SILVER: .4X TO 1X BLUE p/r 100-197
SILVER PRINT RUN 100 SERIAL #'d SETS
OVERALL AU-GU ODDS 1:1 HOB, 1:24 RET
AB1 Angel Berroa/182 4.00 10.00
AB2 A.J. Burnett/485 6.00 15.00
AH Aubrey Huff/296 6.00 15.00
AK Austin Kearns/275 4.00 10.00
AM Aaron Miles/140 4.00 10.00
AP Albert Pujols/103 40.00 100.00
BJ Bobby Jenks/307 6.00 15.00
BL Barry Larkin/195 15.00 40.00
BW1 Billy Wagner/180 10.00 25.00
BW2 Brandon Webb/310 4.00 10.00
CP Corey Patterson/220 4.00 10.00
CS1 Chris Snelling/200 4.00 10.00
CS2 Cory Sullivan/170 4.00 10.00
CW Chien-Ming Wang/195 12.00 30.00
DH Dan Haren/176 4.00 10.00
DM Dallas McPherson/179 6.00 15.00
DW Dontrelle Willis/225 10.00 25.00
DY Delmon Young/205 10.00 25.00
EE Edwin Encarnarcion/188 15.00 40.00
EG Eric Gagne/225 10.00 25.00
EJ Edwin Jackson/224 4.00 10.00
GA Garrett Atkins/175 4.00 10.00
GK Graham Koonce/190 4.00 10.00
GS Gary Sheffield/210 4.00 10.00
HB Hank Blalock/205 6.00 15.00
JB Josh Beckett/100 6.00 15.00
JG Jonny Gomes/265 6.00 15.00
JP Juan Pierre/220 6.00 15.00
JR1 Jose Reyes/195 6.00 15.00
JR2 Juan Richardson/345 4.00 10.00
JV Javier Vazquez/210 6.00 15.00
KG Khalil Greene/190 10.00 25.00
KH Koyie Hill/240 4.00 10.00
KW Kerry Wood/191 10.00 25.00
LN Laynce Nix/185 4.00 10.00
MB Marlon Byrd/240 4.00 10.00
MK Matt Kata/197 4.00 10.00
MM Mark Mulder/186 6.00 15.00
RB Rocco Baldelli/255 6.00 15.00
RH1 Rich Harden/185 6.00 15.00
RH2 Ryan Howard/170 10.00 25.00
RW Rickie Weeks/187 6.00 15.00
SH Shea Hillenbrand/213 6.00 15.00
SP Scott Podsednik/210 4.00 10.00
SS Shannon Stewart/340 6.00 15.00
TH1 Tim Hudson/169 10.00 25.00
TH2 Torii Hunter/215 6.00 15.00
TN Trot Nixon/210 6.00 15.00

2004 SkyBox Autographics Signatures Game Jersey

STATED PRINT RUN 125 SERIAL #'d SETS
*PATCH: 1X TO 2X BASIC
PATCH PRINT RUN 25 SERIAL #'d SETS
OVERALL AU-GU ODDS 1:1 HOB, 1:24 RET
AP Albert Pujols 75.00 150.00
BW1 Billy Wagner 6.00 15.00
BW2 Brandon Webb 6.00 15.00
CP Corey Patterson 6.00 15.00
DW Dontrelle Willis 15.00 40.00
HB Hank Blalock 10.00 25.00
JB Josh Beckett 8.00 20.00
RB Rocco Baldelli 10.00 25.00
TH2 Torii Hunter 10.00 25.00

2005 SkyBox Autographics

COMP.SET w/o SP's (60) 15.00 40.00
COMMON CARD (1-60) .30 .75
1-60 GOLD FOIL FACSIMILE SIGS ON ALL
COMMON CARD (61-90) 1.00 2.50
61-90 STATED ODDS 1:6 H
61-90 PRINT RUN 750 SERIAL #'d SETS
61-90 BLACK FOIL FACSIMILE SIGS ON ALL
COMMON CARD (91-115) .50 1.25
91-115 STATED ODDS 1:6
91-115 PRINT RUN 750 SERIAL #'d SETS
SUBSETS 61-115/PARALLEL ODDS 1:6 R
1 Vladimir Guerrero .50 1.25
2 Garret Anderson .30 .75
3 Troy Glaus .30 .75
4 Shawn Green .30 .75
5 Chipper Jones .75 2.00
6 Andruw Jones .30 .75
7 Miguel Tejada .50 1.25
8 Melvin Mora .30 .75
9 Manny Ramirez .75 2.00
10 Curt Schilling .50 1.25
11 Nomar Garciaparra .50 1.25
12 Mark Prior .50 1.25
13 Sammy Sosa .75 2.00
14 Frank Thomas .75 2.00
15 Paul Konerko .50 1.25
16 Adam Dunn .50 1.25
17 Ken Griffey Jr. 1.50 4.00
18 Victor Martinez .50 1.25
19 Travis Hafner .30 .75
20 Todd Helton .50 1.25
21 Ivan Rodriguez .50 1.25
22 Carlos Guillen .30 .75
23 Miguel Cabrera .75 2.00
24 Juan Pierre .30 .75

25 Roger Clemens 1.00 2.50
26 Jeff Bagwell .50 1.25
27 Lance Berkman .50 1.25
28 Mike Sweeney .30 .75
29 Eric Gagne .30 .75
30 J.D. Drew .30 .75
31 Ben Sheets .30 .75
32 Lyle Overbay .30 .75
33 Johan Santana .50 1.25
34 Torii Hunter .30 .75
35 Mike Piazza .75 2.00
36 Pedro Martinez .50 1.25
37 Carlos Beltran .50 1.25
38 Derek Jeter 2.00 5.00
39 Alex Rodriguez 1.00 2.50
40 Hideki Matsui 1.25 3.00
41 Randy Johnson .75 2.00
42 Eric Chavez .30 .75
43 Jim Thome .50 1.25
44 Craig Wilson .30 .75
45 Khalil Greene .30 .75
46 Jake Peavy .30 .75
47 Jason Schmidt .30 .75
48 Ichiro Suzuki 1.00 2.50
49 Adrian Beltre .75 2.00
50 Albert Pujols 1.00 2.50
51 Scott Rolen .50 1.25
52 Carl Crawford .50 1.25
53 Rocco Baldelli .30 .75
54 Alfonso Soriano .50 1.25
55 Hank Blalock .30 .75
56 Vernon Wells .30 .75
57 Jose Vidro .30 .75
58 David Ortiz .75 2.00
59 Bobby Abreu .30 .75
60 Gary Sheffield .30 .75
61 Nolan Ryan GT 8.00 20.00
62 Mike Schmidt GT 4.00 10.00
63 Johnny Bench GT 2.50 6.00
64 Lou Brock GT 1.50 4.00
65 Dennis Eckersley GT 1.50 4.00
66 Carlton Fisk GT 1.50 4.00
67 Bob Gibson GT 1.50 4.00
68 Reggie Jackson GT 1.50 4.00
69 Al Kaline GT 2.50 6.00
70 Bill Mazeroski GT 1.50 4.00
71 Willie McCovey GT 1.50 4.00
72 Jim Palmer GT 1.50 4.00
73 Phil Rizzuto GT 1.50 4.00
74 Warren Spahn GT 1.50 4.00
75 Brooks Robinson GT 1.50 4.00
76 Willie Stargell GT 1.50 4.00
77 Catfish Hunter GT 1.50 4.00
78 Tony Perez GT 1.50 4.00
79 George Kell GT 1.50 4.00
80 Robin Yount GT 2.50 6.00
81 Fergie Jenkins GT 1.50 4.00
82 Tom Seaver GT 1.50 4.00
83 Eddie Mathews GT 2.50 6.00
84 Enos Slaughter GT 1.50 4.00
85 Pee Wee Reese GT 1.50 4.00
86 Harmon Killebrew GT 2.50 6.00
87 Eddie Murray GT 1.50 4.00
88 Orlando Cepeda GT 1.50 4.00
89 Billy Williams GT 1.50 4.00
90 Ralph Kiner GT 1.50 4.00
91 Ryan Raburn ROO .50 1.25
92 Justin Morneau ROO .75 2.00
93 Zack Greinke ROO 1.50 4.00
94 David Aardsma ROO .50 1.25
95 B.J. Upton ROO .75 2.00
96 Gavin Floyd ROO .50 1.25
97 David Wright ROO 1.00 2.50
98 Russ Adams ROO .50 1.25
99 Jose Lopez ROO .50 1.25
100 Scott Kazmir ROO 1.25 3.00
101 Mike Gosling ROO .50 1.25
102 Jeff Keppinger ROO .50 1.25
103 Dave Krynzel ROO .50 1.25
104 Jeff Niemann ROO RC 1.25 3.00
105 Ruben Gotay ROO .50 1.25
106 Dioner Navarro ROO .50 1.25
107 Nick Swisher ROO .75 2.00
108 Yadier Molina ROO 5.00 12.00
109 Joey Gathright ROO .50 1.25
110 Jon Knott ROO .50 1.25
111 J.D. Durbin ROO .50 1.25
112 Andres Blanco ROO .50 1.25
113 Charlton Jimerson ROO .50 1.25
114 Sean Burnett ROO .50 1.25
115 Justin Verlander ROO RC 10.00 25.00

2005 SkyBox Autographics Insignia

*1-60: 1.25X TO 3X BASIC
*61-90: .6X TO 1.5X BASIC
*91-115: 1.2X TO 3X BASIC
OVERALL PARALLEL ODDS 1:6 H
SUBSETS 61-115/PARALLEL ODDS 1:6 R
STATED PRINT RUN 150 SERIAL #'d SETS
GOLD FOIL FACSIMILE SIGS ON ALL

2005 SkyBox Autographics Royal Insignia

*1-60: 3X TO 8X BASIC
*61-90: 1X TO 2.5X BASIC
*91-115: 2X TO 5X BASIC
OVERALL PARALLEL ODDS 1:6 H
SUBSETS 61-115/PARALLEL ODDS 1:6 R
STATED PRINT RUN 25 SERIAL #'d SETS
NO PRICING AVAIL.ON CARDS 104 AND 115
PURPLE FOIL FACSIMILE SIGS ON ALL

2005 SkyBox Autographics Future Signs

STATED ODDS 1:6 H, 1:12 R
1 Bobby Crosby .40 1.00
2 David Aardsma .40 1.00
3 Russ Adams .40 1.00
4 J.D. Durbin .40 1.00
5 Johnny Estrada .40 1.00
6 Chone Figgins .40 1.00
7 Jason Bay .40 1.00
8 Gavin Floyd .40 1.00
9 Lew Ford .40 1.00
10 Victor Martinez .60 1.50
11 Joe Mauer .75 2.00
12 Justin Morneau .60 1.50
13 Laynce Nix .40 1.00
14 Sean Burnett .40 1.00
15 B.J. Upton .60 1.50
16 Justin Verlander 8.00 20.00
17 David Wright .75 2.00
18 Delmon Young 1.00 2.50
19 Michael Young .40 1.00
20 Zack Greinke 1.25 3.00

2005 SkyBox Autographics Future Signs Autograph Blue

STATED ODDS 1:25 HOBBY
PRINT RUNS B/WN 8-639 COPIES PER
CARDS ARE NOT SERIAL-NUMBERED
PRINT RUN INFO PROVIDED BY UD
NO PRICING ON QTY OF 8
AO Akinori Otsuka/639 * 6.00 15.00
JB Jason Bay/264 * 6.00 15.00
JM Justin Morneau/224 * 5.00 12.00
JV Justin Verlander/505 * 20.00 50.00
VM Victor Martinez/500 * 6.00 15.00
ZG Zack Greinke/264 * 8.00 20.00

2005 SkyBox Autographics Future Signs Autograph Gold

*GOLD: .5X TO 1.2X BLUE
OVERALL AU ODDS 1:4 H, AU-GU 1:24 R
STATED PRINT RUN 65 SERIAL #'d SETS
AS Alfredo Simon/30 UER 5.00 12.00
BU B.J. Upton 8.00 20.00
DW David Wright 8.00 20.00
EE Edwin Encarnacion 15.00 40.00
JD J.D. Durbin 5.00 12.00
RW Rickie Weeks 8.00 20.00
SB Sean Burnett 5.00 12.00
SH Scott Hairston/31 UER 5.00 12.00
VMJ Val Majewski 5.00 12.00

2005 SkyBox Autographics Future Signs Autograph Gold Embossed

*GOLD EMB: .5X TO 1.2X BLUE
OVERALL AU ODDS 1:4 H, AU-GU 1:24 R
STATED PRINT RUN 45 SERIAL #'d SETS
AS Alfredo Simon/30 UER 5.00 12.00
BU B.J. Upton 8.00 20.00
DW David Wright 8.00 20.00
DY Delmon Young 12.00 30.00
EE Edwin Encarnacion 15.00 40.00
JD J.D. Durbin 5.00 12.00
RW Rickie Weeks 8.00 20.00
SB Sean Burnett 5.00 12.00
SH Scott Hairston/28 UER 5.00 12.00
VMJ Val Majewski 5.00 12.00

2005 SkyBox Autographics Future Signs Autograph Platinum

*PLAT: .6X TO 1.5X BLUE
STATED PRINT RUN 25 SERIAL #'d SETS
NO PRICING AVAIL ON CARDS JN AND JV
EMBOSSED PLAT.PRINT RUN 5 #'d SETS
NO EMB.PLAT.PRICING DUE TO SCARCITY
OVERALL AU ODDS 1:4 H, AU-GU 1:24 R
AS Alfredo Simon 6.00 15.00
BU B.J. Upton 10.00 25.00
DW David Wright 10.00 25.00
DY Delmon Young 15.00 40.00
EE Edwin Encarnacion 20.00 50.00
JD J.D. Durbin 6.00 15.00
RW Rickie Weeks 10.00 25.00
SB Sean Burnett 6.00 15.00
SH Scott Hairston 6.00 15.00
VMJ Val Majewski 6.00 15.00

2005 SkyBox Autographics Future Signs Autograph Silver

*SILVER: .4X TO 1X BLUE
OVERALL AU ODDS 1:4 H, AU-GU 1:24 R
STATED PRINT RUN 100 SERIAL #'d SETS
AS Alfredo Simon/54 UER 4.00 10.00
BU B.J. Upton/34 UER 6.00 15.00
DW David Wright 6.00 15.00
EE Edwin Encarnacion/95 UER 12.00 30.00
JD J.D. Durbin/53 UER 4.00 10.00
RW Rickie Weeks/36 UER 6.00 15.00
SB Sean Burnett/51 UER 4.00 10.00
VMJ Val Majewski/55 UER 4.00 10.00

2005 SkyBox Autographics Future Signs Autograph Silver Embossed

*SILVER EMB: .4X TO 1X BLUE
OVERALL AU ODDS 1:4 H, AU-GU 1:24 R
STATED PRINT RUN 85 SERIAL #'d SETS
AS Alfredo Simon/40 UER 4.00 10.00
BU B.J. Upton 6.00 15.00
DW David Wright 6.00 15.00
DY Delmon Young/29 UER 10.00 25.00
EE Edwin Encarnacion 12.00 30.00
JD J.D. Durbin/70 UER 4.00 10.00
RW Rickie Weeks 6.00 15.00
SB Sean Burnett/60 UER 4.00 10.00
SH Scott Hairston/40 UER 4.00 10.00
VMJ Val Majewski 4.00 10.00

2005 SkyBox Autographics Jerseygraphics Blue

STATED ODDS 1:40 RETAIL
*GOLD: .75X TO 2X BLUE
GOLD STATED ODDS 1:240 RETAIL
*SILVER: .5X TO 1.2X BLUE
SILVER STATED ODDS 1:80 RETAIL
AB Adrian Beltre 2.00 5.00
AD Adam Dunn 2.00 5.00
AK Austin Kearns 2.00 5.00
BG Brian Giles 2.00 5.00
BS Ben Sheets 2.00 5.00
CD Carlos Delgado 2.00 5.00
EG Eric Gagne 2.00 5.00
GA Garret Anderson 2.00 5.00
HB Hank Blalock 2.00 5.00
JB Jeff Bagwell 3.00 8.00
JBE Josh Beckett 2.00 5.00
JR Jose Reyes 2.00 5.00
MB Marlon Byrd 2.00 5.00
MC Miguel Cabrera 3.00 8.00
MO Magglio Ordonez 2.00 5.00
MT Mark Teixeira 3.00 8.00
RB Rocco Baldelli 2.00 5.00
TG Troy Glaus 2.00 5.00
TGL Tom Glavine 2.00 5.00
TH Torii Hunter 2.00 5.00

2005 SkyBox Autographics Jerseygraphics Silver

STATED ODDS 1:80 RETAIL
AB Adrian Beltre 2.50 6.00

2005 SkyBox Autographics Signature Moments

STATED ODDS 1:12 H, 1:24 R
1 Manny Ramirez 2.00 5.00
2 Derek Jeter 4.00 10.00
3 Ichiro Suzuki 3.00 8.00
4 Roger Clemens 3.00 8.00
5 Albert Pujols 4.00 10.00
6 Nolan Ryan 4.00 10.00
7 Reggie Jackson 2.00 5.00
8 Carlton Fisk 2.00 5.00
9 Mike Schmidt 4.00 10.00
10 Johnny Bench 2.00 5.00

2005 SkyBox Autographics Signatures Blue

STATED ODDS 1:19 H
PRINT RUNS B/WN 137-590 COPIES PER
CARDS ARE NOT SERIAL-NUMBERED
PRINT RUN INFO PROVIDED BY UD
AE Adam Everett/590 * 4.00 10.00
BL Brad Lidge/164 * 10.00 25.00
CC Carl Crawford/150 * 6.00 15.00
CK Casey Kotchman/227 * 6.00 15.00
CP Corey Patterson/329 * 4.00 10.00
DE David Eckstein/546 * 4.00 10.00
EP Eduardo Perez/584 * 4.00 10.00
JB Jeremy Bonderman/369 * 6.00 15.00
JK Jason Kubel/137 * 4.00 10.00
JO John Olerud/446 * 6.00 15.00
JS Johan Santana/200 * 12.00 30.00
LG Luis Gonzalez/187 * 6.00 15.00
MC Miguel Cabrera/250 * 20.00 50.00
MCA Mike Cameron/200 * 4.00 10.00
OH Orlando Hudson/231 * 4.00 10.00
SK Scott Kazmir/231 * 8.00 20.00
TH Trevor Hoffman/590 * 15.00 30.00
THA Travis Hafner/246 * 6.00 15.00

2005 SkyBox Autographics Signatures Game Jersey Gold

*JSY GOLD: .6X TO 1.5X BLUE
OVERALL AU ODDS 1:4 H, AU-GU 1:24 R
STATED PRINT RUN 45 SERIAL #'d SETS
MG Marcus Giles 10.00 25.00
MT Mark Teixeira 15.00 40.00
RB Rocco Baldelli/40 UER 10.00 25.00
RH Roy Halladay 10.00 25.00
SS Shannon Stewart 6.00 15.00

2005 SkyBox Autographics Signatures Game Jersey Gold Embossed

*JSY GOLD EMB: .75X TO 2X BLUE
OVERALL AU ODDS 1:4 H, AU-GU 1:24 R
STATED PRINT RUN 30 SERIAL #'d SETS
MG Marcus Giles 12.50 30.00
MT Mark Teixeira 20.00 50.00
RB Rocco Baldelli 12.50 30.00
SS Shannon Stewart 12.50 30.00

2005 SkyBox Autographics Signatures Game Jersey Silver

*JSY SILVER: .5X TO 1.2X BLUE
OVERALL AU ODDS 1:4 H, AU-GU 1:24 R
STATED PRINT RUN 100 SERIAL #'d SETS
MT Mark Teixeira/70 UER 12.50 30.00
RB Rocco Baldelli/58 UER 8.00 20.00
SS Shannon Stewart 5.00 12.00

2005 SkyBox Autographics Signatures Game Jersey Silver Embossed

*JSY SILVER EMB: .5X TO 1.2X BLUE
OVERALL AU ODDS 1:4 H, AU-GU 1:24 R
STATED PRINT RUN 75 SERIAL #'d SETS
MG Marcus Giles 8.00 20.00
MT Mark Teixeira 12.50 30.00
RB Rocco Baldelli/50 UER 8.00 20.00
SS Shannon Stewart 5.00 12.00

2005 SkyBox Autographics Signatures Game Patch Silver

*PATCH SILVER: 1X TO 2.5X BLUE
OVERALL AUTO ODDS 1:4 H
STATED PRINT RUN 25 SERIAL #'d SETS
NO GILES PRICING DUE TO SCARCITY
MT Mark Teixeira 25.00 60.00
RB Rocco Baldelli 15.00 40.00
SS Shannon Stewart 15.00 40.00

2000 SkyBox Dominion

COMPLETE SET (300) 15.00 40.00
COMMON CARD (1-250) .07 .20
COMMON PROS (251-300) .15 .40
1 M.McGwire .40 1.00
K.Griffey Jr. LL
2 M.McGwire .30 .75
M.Ramirez LL
3 L.Walker .12 .30
N.Garciaparra LL
4 T.Womack .07 .20
B.Hunter LL
5 M.Hampton .12 .30
P.Martinez LL
6 R.Johnson .20 .50
P.Martinez LL
7 R.Johnson .20 .50
P.Martinez LL
8 U.Urbina .25 .60
M.Rivera LL
9 Vinny Castilla HL .07 .20
10 Orioles .07 .20
Cuban Nat'l HL
11 Jose Canseco HL .12 .30
12 Fernando Tatis HL .07 .20
13 Robin Ventura HL .07 .20
14 Roger Clemens HL .25 .60
15 Jose Jimenez HL .07 .20
16 David Cone HL .07 .20
17 Mark McGwire HL .30 .75
18 Cal Ripken HL .60 1.50
19 Tony Gwynn HL .20 .50
20 Wade Boggs HL .12 .30
21 Ivan Rodriguez HL .12 .30
22 Chuck Finley HL UER .07 .20
23 Eric Milton HL .07 .20
24 Adrian Beltre .20 .50
25 Brad Radke .07 .20
26 Derek Bell .07 .20
27 Garret Anderson .07 .20
28 Ivan Rodriguez .12 .30
29 Jeff Kent .07 .20
30 Jeremy Giambi .07 .20
31 John Franco .07 .20
32 Jose Hernandez .07 .20
33 Jose Offerman .07 .20
34 Jose Rosado .07 .20
35 Kevin Appier .07 .20
36 Kris Benson .07 .20
37 Mark McGwire .30 .75
38 Matt Williams .07 .20
39 Paul O'Neill .12 .30
40 Rickey Henderson .20 .50
41 Todd Greene .07 .20
42 Russ Ortiz .07 .20
43 Sean Casey .07 .20
44 Tony Womack .07 .20
45 Troy O'Leary .07 .20
46 Ugueth Urbina .07 .20
47 Tom Glavine .12 .30
48 Mike Mussina .12 .30
49 Carlos Febles .07 .20
50 Jon Lieber .07 .20
51 Juan Gonzalez .07 .20
52 Matt Clement .07 .20
53 Moises Alou .07 .20
54 Ray Durham .07 .20
55 Robb Nen .07 .20
56 Tino Martinez .07 .20
57 Troy Glaus .07 .20
58 Curt Schilling .12 .30
59 Mike Sweeney .07 .20
60 Steve Finley .07 .20
61 Roger Cedeno .07 .20
62 Bobby Jones .07 .20
63 John Smoltz .20 .50
64 Darin Erstad .07 .20
65 Carlos Delgado .07 .20
66 Ray Lankford .07 .20
67 Todd Stottlemyre .07 .20
68 Andy Ashby .07 .20
69 Bob Abreu .07 .20
70 Chuck Finley .07 .20
71 Damion Easley .07 .20
72 Dustin Hermanson .07 .20
73 Frank Thomas .20 .50
74 Kevin Brown .07 .20
75 Kevin Millwood .07 .20
76 Mark Grace .12 .30
77 Matt Stairs .07 .20
78 Mike Hampton .07 .20
79 Omar Vizquel .12 .30
80 Preston Wilson .07 .20
81 Robin Ventura .07 .20
82 Todd Helton .12 .30
83 Tony Clark .07 .20
84 Al Leiter .07 .20
85 Alex Fernandez .07 .20
86 Bernie Williams .12 .30
87 Edgar Martinez .12 .30
88 Edgar Renteria .07 .20
89 Fred McGriff .12 .30
90 Jermaine Dye .07 .20
91 Joe McEwing .07 .20
92 John Halama .07 .20
93 Lee Stevens .07 .20
94 Matt Lawton .07 .20
95 Mike Piazza .20 .50
96 Pete Harnisch .07 .20
97 Scott Karl .07 .20
98 Tony Fernandez .07 .20
99 Sammy Sosa .20 .50
100 Bobby Higginson .07 .20
101 Tony Gwynn .20 .50
102 J.D. Drew .07 .20
103 Roberto Hernandez .07 .20
104 Rondell White .07 .20
105 David Nilsson .07 .20
106 Shane Reynolds .07 .20
107 Jaret Wright .07 .20
108 Jeff Bagwell .12 .30
109 Jay Bell .07 .20
110 Kevin Tapani .07 .20
111 Michael Barrett .07 .20
112 Neifi Perez .07 .20
113 Pat Hengen .07 .20
114 Roger Clemens .25 .60
115 Travis Fryman .07 .20
116 Aaron Sele .07 .20
117 Eric Davis .07 .20
118 Trevor Hoffman .12 .30
119 Chris Singleton .07 .20
120 Ryan Klesko .07 .20
121 Scott Rolen .12 .30
122 Jorge Posada .12 .30
123 Abraham Nunez .07 .20
124 Alex Gonzalez .07 .20
125 B.J. Surhoff .07 .20
126 Barry Bonds .30 .75
127 Billy Koch .07 .20
128 Billy Wagner .07 .20
129 Brad Ausmus .07 .20
130 Bret Boone .07 .20
131 Cal Ripken .60 1.50
132 Chad Allen .07 .20
133 Chris Carpenter .12 .30
134 Craig Biggio .12 .30
135 Dante Bichette .07 .20
136 Dean Palmer .07 .20
137 Derek Jeter .50 1.25
138 Ellis Burks .07 .20
139 Freddy Garcia .07 .20
140 Gabe Kapler .07 .20
141 Greg Maddux .25 .60
142 Greg Vaughn .07 .20
143 Jason Kendall .07 .20
144 Jim Parque .07 .20
145 John Valentin .07 .20
146 Jose Vidro .07 .20
147 Ken Griffey Jr. .40 1.00
148 Kenny Lofton .07 .20
149 Kenny Rogers .07 .20
150 Kent Bottenfield .07 .20
151 Chuck Knoblauch .07 .20
152 Larry Walker .12 .30
153 Manny Ramirez .20 .50
154 Mickey Morandini .07 .20
155 Mike Cameron .07 .20
156 Mike Lieberthal .07 .20
157 Mo Vaughn .07 .20
158 Randy Johnson .20 .50
159 Rey Ordonez .07 .20
160 Roberto Alomar .12 .30
161 Scott Williamson .07 .20
162 Shawn Estes .07 .20
163 Tim Wakefield .12 .30
164 Tony Batista .07 .20
165 Will Clark .12 .30
166 Wade Boggs .12 .30
167 David Cone .07 .20
168 Doug Glanville .07 .20
169 Jeff Cirillo .07 .20
170 John Jaha .07 .20
171 Mariano Rivera .25 .60
172 Tom Gordon .07 .20
173 Wally Joyner .07 .20
174 Alex Gonzalez .07 .20
175 Andruw Jones .07 .20
176 Barry Larkin .12 .30
177 Bartolo Colon .07 .20
178 Brian Giles .07 .20
179 Carlos Lee .07 .20
180 Darren Dreifort .07 .20
181 Eric Chavez .07 .20
182 Henry Rodriguez .07 .20
183 Ismael Valdes .07 .20
184 Jason Giambi .07 .20
185 John Wetteland .07 .20
186 Juan Encarnacion .07 .20
187 Luis Gonzalez .07 .20
188 Reggie Sanders .07 .20
189 Richard Hidalgo .07 .20
190 Ryan Rupe .07 .20
191 Sean Berry .07 .20
192 Rick Helling .07 .20
193 Randy Wolf .07 .20
194 Cliff Floyd .07 .20
195 Jose Lima .07 .20
196 Chipper Jones .20 .50
197 Charles Johnson .07 .20
198 Nomar Garciaparra .12 .30
199 Magglio Ordonez .12 .30
200 Shawn Green .07 .20
201 Travis Lee .07 .20
202 Jose Canseco .12 .30
203 Fernando Tatis .07 .20
204 Bruce Aven .07 .20
205 Johnny Damon .12 .30
206 Gary Sheffield .07 .20
207 Ken Caminiti .07 .20
208 Ben Grieve .07 .20
209 Sidney Ponson .07 .20
210 Vinny Castilla .07 .20
211 Alex Rodriguez .25 .60
212 Chris Widger .07 .20
213 Carl Pavano .07 .20
214 J.T. Snow .07 .20
215 Jim Thome .12 .30
216 Kevin Young .07 .20
217 Mike Sirotka .07 .20
218 Rafael Palmeiro .12 .30
219 Rico Brogna .07 .20
220 Todd Walker .07 .20
221 Todd Zeile .07 .20
222 Brian Rose .07 .20
223 Chris Fussell .07 .20
224 Corey Koskie .07 .20
225 Rich Aurilia .07 .20
226 Geoff Jenkins .07 .20
227 Pedro Martinez .12 .30
228 Todd Hundley .07 .20
229 Brian Jordan .07 .20
230 Cristian Guzman .07 .20
231 Raul Mondesi .07 .20
232 Tim Hudson .12 .30
233 Albert Belle .07 .20
234 Andy Pettitte .12 .30
235 Brady Anderson .07 .20
236 Brian Bohanon .07 .20
237 Carlos Beltran .12 .30
238 Doug Mientkiewicz .07 .20
239 Jason Schmidt .07 .20
240 Jeff Zimmerman .07 .20
241 John Olerud .07 .20
242 Paul Byrd .07 .20
243 Vladimir Guerrero .12 .30
244 Warren Morris .07 .20
245 Eric Karros .07 .20
246 Jeff Weaver .07 .20
247 Jeromy Burnitz .07 .20
248 David Bell .07 .20
249 Rusty Greer .07 .20
250 Kevin Stocker .07 .20
251 Shea Hillenbrand PROS .15 .40
252 Alfonso Soriano PROS .40 1.00
253 Micah Bowie PROS .15 .40
254 Gary Matthews Jr. PROS .15 .40
255 Lance Berkman PROS .25 .60
256 Pat Burrell PROS .15 .40
257 Ruben Mateo PROS .15 .40
258 Kip Wells PROS .15 .40
259 Wilton Veras PROS .15 .40
260 Ben Davis PROS .15 .40
261 Eric Munson PROS .15 .40
262 Ramon Hernandez PROS .15 .40
263 Tony Armas Jr. PROS .15 .40
264 Erubiel Durazo PROS .15 .40
265 Chad Meyers PROS .15 .40
266 Rick Ankiel PROS .25 .60
267 Ramon Ortiz PROS .15 .40
268 Adam Kennedy PROS .15 .40
269 Vernon Wells PROS .15 .40
270 Chad Hermansen PROS .15 .40
271 N.Hutchins .15 .40
T.Durrington
272 G.Molina .15 .40
B.J. Ryan
273 J.Pena .15 .40
T.Ohka RC
274 P.Daneker .15 .40
A.Myette
275 J.Rakers .15 .40
R.Branyan
276 B.Graterol .15 .40
D.Borkowski
277 M.Quinn .15 .40
D.Reichert
278 M.Redman .15 .40
J.Jones
279 W.Pena .15 .40
E.Yarnall
280 C.Harville .15 .40
B.Laxton
281 A.Scheffer .15 .40
G.Meche
282 J.Morris .40 1.00
D.Wheeler
283 D.Kolb .15 .40
K.Dransfeldt
284 P.Munro .15 .40
C.Blake
285 R.Ryan .15 .40
B.Kim
286 D.Ebert .15 .40
P.Matos
287 R.Barker .15 .40
K.Farnsworth
288 J.LaRue .15 .40
T.Dawkins
289 C.Sexton .15 .40
E.Clemente
290 A.Garcia .15 .40
A.Burnett
291 C.Hernandez .15 .40
D.Ward
292 Eric Gagne .15 .40
293 K.Peterson .15 .40
K.Barker
294 F.Seguignol .15 .40
G.Mota
295 M.Mora .15 .40
O.Dotel
296 A.Shumaker .15 .40
C.Politte
297 Y.Haad .15 .40
J.Anderson
298 R.Heiserman .15 .40
C.Hutchinson
299 M.Darr .15 .40
W.Gonzalez
300 J.Nathan .15 .40
C.Murray
P211 Alex Rodriguez Promo .60 1.50

2000 SkyBox Dominion Double Play

COMPLETE SET (10) 10.00 25.00
STATED ODDS 1:9
*PLUS: 1.5X TO 4X BASIC DOUBLE PLAY
PLUS STATED ODDS 1:90
*WARP TEK: 12X TO 30X BASIC DOUBLE PLAY
WARP TEK STATED ODDS 1:900
1 N.Garciaparra .60 1.50
A.Rodriguez
2 P.Martinez .50 1.25
R.Johnson
3 C.Jones .50 1.25
S.Rolen
4 M.McGwire 1.00 2.50
K.Griffey Jr.
5 C.Ripken 1.50 4.00
D.Jeter
6 R.Clemens .60 1.50
G.Maddux
7 J.Gonzalez .50 1.25
M.Ramirez
8 T.Gwynn .50 1.25
S.Green
9 S.Sosa .50 1.25
F.Thomas
10 M.Piazza .50 1.25
I.Rodriguez

2000 SkyBox Dominion Eye on October

COMPLETE SET (15) 12.50 30.00
STATED ODDS 1:24
*PLUS: 2X TO 5X BASIC OCTOBER
PLUS STATED ODDS 1:240
1 Ken Griffey Jr. 2.00 5.00
2 Mark McGwire 1.50 4.00
3 Derek Jeter 2.50 6.00
4 Juan Gonzalez .40 1.00
5 Chipper Jones 1.00 2.50
6 Sammy Sosa 1.00 2.50
7 Greg Maddux 1.25 3.00
8 Frank Thomas 1.00 2.50
9 Nomar Garciaparra .60 1.50
10 Shawn Green .40 1.00
11 Cal Ripken 3.00 8.00
12 Manny Ramirez 1.00 2.50
13 Scott Rolen .60 1.50
14 Mike Piazza 1.00 2.50
15 Alex Rodriguez 1.25 3.00

2000 SkyBox Dominion Hats Off

STATED ODDS 1:468 HOBBY
1 Wade Boggs 10.00 25.00
2 Barry Bonds 10.00 25.00
3 J.D. Drew 6.00 15.00
4 Shawn Green 6.00 15.00
5 Vladimir Guerrero 10.00 25.00
6 Randy Johnson 10.00 25.00
7 Andruw Jones 10.00 25.00
8 Greg Maddux 12.00 30.00
9 Pedro Martinez 10.00 25.00
10 Mike Mussina 10.00 25.00
11 Rafael Palmeiro 10.00 25.00
12 Alex Rodriguez 10.00 25.00
13 Scott Rolen 10.00 25.00
14 Tim Salmon 10.00 25.00
15 Robin Ventura 6.00 15.00

2000 SkyBox Dominion Milestones

COMPLETE SET (6) 50.00 100.00
STATED ODDS 1:1999
1 Mark McGwire 10.00 25.00
2 Roger Clemens 8.00 20.00
3 Tony Gwynn 6.00 15.00
4 Wade Boggs 4.00 10.00
5 Cal Ripken 20.00 50.00
6 Jose Canseco 4.00 10.00

2000 SkyBox Dominion New Era

COMPLETE SET (20) 4.00 10.00
STATED ODDS 1:3
*PLUS: 1.5X TO 4X BASIC NEW ERA
PLUS STATED ODDS 1:30
*WARP TEK: 5X TO 12X BASIC NEW ERA
WARP TEK STATED ODDS 1:300
1 Pat Burrell .40 1.00
2 Ruben Mateo .40 1.00
3 Wilton Veras .40 1.00
4 Eric Munson .40 1.00
5 Jeff Weaver .40 1.00
6 Tim Hudson .60 1.50
7 Carlos Beltran .60 1.50
8 Chris Singleton .40 1.00
9 Lance Berkman .60 1.50
10 Freddy Garcia .40 1.00
11 Erubiel Durazo .40 1.00
12 Randy Wolf .40 1.00
13 Shea Hillenbrand .40 1.00
14 Kip Wells .40 1.00
15 Alfonso Soriano 1.00 2.50
16 Rick Ankiel .60 1.50
17 Ramon Ortiz .40 1.00
18 Adam Kennedy .40 1.00
19 Vernon Wells .40 1.00
20 Chad Hermansen .40 1.00

1998 SkyBox Dugout Axcess

The 1998 SkyBox Dugout Axcess set was issued in one series totalling 150 cards. The 12-card packs retailed for $1.59 each. The set contains the topical subsets: The Insiders (1-90), Little Dawgs (91-120), 7th Inning Sketch (121-132), Name Plates (133-140), and Trivia Cards (141-150). Notable Rookie Cards include Magglio Ordonez. In addition, an Alex Rodriguez sample card was distributed to dealers and hobby media a few months prior to the release of the product. The card is identical to the standard 1998 SkyBox Axcess Alex Rodriguez except for the text 'PROMOTIONAL SAMPLE" diagonally written across the front and back. Also, Todd Helton signed 800 copies of his Little Dawgs subset card (number 120) for the 1999 Fleer Baseball Card Flipping Challenge. A total of 380 hobby shops participated in the program and each shop received two cards. One copy was intended to be given to the winner of each shop's card flipping tournament and the other one was to be kept by the shop owner as a gift for participating. Though the cards lack any serial numbering, they do feature an embossed SkyBox seal of authenticity and the print run was publicly released by the manufacturer. The additional 40 cards not used in the Flipping Challenge were mostly used as grab bag prizes at the 1999 MLB All-Star Fanfest in Boston.

COMPLETE SET (150) 6.00 15.00
COMMON RC YR .07 .20
1 Travis Lee .07 .20
2 Matt Williams .07 .20
3 Andy Benes .07 .20
4 Chipper Jones .20 .50
5 Ryan Klesko .07 .20
6 Greg Maddux .30 .75
7 Sammy Sosa .20 .50
8 Henry Rodriguez .07 .20
9 Mark Grace .10 .30
10 Barry Larkin .07 .20
11 Bret Boone .07 .20
12 Reggie Sanders .07 .20
13 Vinny Castilla .07 .20
14 Larry Walker .07 .20
15 Darryl Kile .07 .20
16 Charles Johnson .07 .20
17 Edgar Renteria .07 .20
18 Gary Sheffield .07 .20
19 Jeff Bagwell .10 .30
20 Craig Biggio .10 .30
21 Moises Alou .10 .30
22 Mike Piazza .30 .75
23 Hideo Nomo .20 .50
24 Raul Mondesi .07 .20
25 John Jaha .07 .20
26 Jeff Cirillo .07 .20
27 Jeromy Burnitz .07 .20
28 Mark Grudzielanek .07 .20
29 Vladimir Guerrero .20 .50
30 Rondell White .07 .20
31 Edgardo Alfonzo .07 .20
32 Rey Ordonez .07 .20
33 Bernard Gilkey .07 .20
34 Scott Rolen .10 .30
35 Curt Schilling .07 .20
36 Ricky Bottalico .07 .20
37 Tony Womack .07 .20
38 Al Martin .07 .20
39 Jason Kendall .07 .20
40 Ron Gant .07 .20
41 Mark McGwire .50 1.25
42 Ray Lankford .07 .20
43 Tony Gwynn .25 .60
44 Ken Caminiti .07 .20
45 Kevin Brown .10 .30
46 Barry Bonds .60 1.50
47 J.T. Snow .07 .20
48 Shawn Estes .07 .20
49 Jim Edmonds .07 .20
50 Tim Salmon .10 .30

51 Jason Dickson .07 .20
52 Cal Ripken .60 1.50
53 Mike Mussina .10 .30
54 Roberto Alomar .10 .30
55 Mo Vaughn .07 .20
56 Pedro Martinez .10 .30
57 Nomar Garciaparra .30 .75
58 Albert Belle .07 .20
59 Frank Thomas .20 .50
60 Robin Ventura .07 .20
61 Jim Thome .10 .30
62 Sandy Alomar Jr. .07 .20
63 Jaret Wright .07 .20
64 Bobby Higginson .10 .30
65 Tony Clark .07 .20
66 Justin Thompson .07 .20
67 Dean Palmer .07 .20
68 Kevin Appier .07 .20
69 Johnny Damon .10 .30
70 Paul Molitor .07 .20
71 Marty Cordova .07 .20
72 Brad Radke .07 .20
73 Derek Jeter .50 1.25
74 Bernie Williams .10 .30
75 Andy Pettitte .10 .30
76 Matt Stairs .07 .20
77 Ben Grieve .20 .50
78 Jason Giambi .07 .20
79 Randy Johnson .20 .50
80 Ken Griffey Jr. .40 1.00
81 Alex Rodriguez .30 .75
82 Fred McGriff .10 .30
83 Wade Boggs .10 .30
84 Wilson Alvarez .07 .20
85 Juan Gonzalez .07 .20
86 Ivan Rodriguez .10 .30
87 Fernando Tatis .07 .20
88 Roger Clemens .40 1.00
89 Jose Cruz Jr. .07 .20
90 Shawn Green .07 .20
91 Jeff Suppan .07 .20
92 Eli Marrero .07 .20
93 Mike Lowell RC .50 1.25
94 Ben Grieve .20 .50
95 Cliff Politte .07 .20
96 Rolando Arrojo RC .10 .30
97 Mike Caruso .07 .20
98 Miguel Tejada .20 .50
99 Rod Myers .07 .20
100 Juan Encarnacion .07 .20
101 Enrique Wilson .07 .20
102 Brian Giles .07 .20
103 Magglio Ordonez RC .60 1.50
104 Brian Rose .07 .20
105 Ryan Jackson RC .07 .20
106 Mark Kotsay .07 .20
107 Desi Relaford .07 .20
108 A.J. Hinch .07 .20
109 Eric Milton .07 .20
110 Ricky Ledee .07 .20
111 Karim Garcia .07 .20
112 Derrek Lee .10 .30
113 Brad Fullmer .07 .20
114 Travis Lee .20 .50
115 Greg Norton .07 .20
116 Rich Butler RC .07 .20
117 Masato Yoshii RC .10 .30
118 Paul Konerko .07 .20
119 Richard Hidalgo .07 .20
120 Todd Helton .10 .30
121 Nomar Garciaparra 7TH .20 .50
122 Scott Rolen 7TH .07 .20
123 Cal Ripken 7TH .30 .75
124 Derek Jeter 7TH .25 .60
125 Mike Piazza 7TH .20 .50
126 Tony Gwynn 7TH .10 .30
127 Mark McGwire 7TH .25 .60
128 Kenny Lofton 7TH .07 .20
129 Greg Maddux 7TH .20 .50
130 Jeff Bagwell 7TH .07 .20
131 Randy Johnson 7TH .10 .30
132 Alex Rodriguez 7TH .20 .50
133 Mo Vaughn NAME .07 .20
134 Chipper Jones NAME .10 .30
135 Juan Gonzalez NAME .07 .20
136 Tony Clark NAME .07 .20
137 Fred McGriff NAME .07 .20
138 Roger Clemens NAME .20 .50
139 Ken Griffey Jr. NAME .25 .60
140 Ivan Rodriguez NAME .07 .20
141 Vinny Castilla TRIV .07 .20
142 Livan Hernandez TRIV .07 .20
143 Jose Cruz Jr. TRIV .07 .20
144 Andruw Jones TRIV .07 .20
145 Rafael Palmeiro TRIV .07 .20
146 Chuck Knoblauch TRIV .07 .20
147 Jay Buhner TRIV .07 .20
148 Andres Galarraga TRIV .07 .20
149 Frank Thomas TRIV .10 .30
150 Todd Hundley TRIV .07 .20
S120 Todd Helton AU/800 15.00 30.00
NNO Alex Rodriguez Sample .75 2.00

1998 SkyBox Dugout Axcess Inside Axcess

*STARS: 10X TO 25X BASIC CARDS
*ROOKIES: 10X TO 25X BASIC
RANDOM INSERTS IN ALL PACKS
STATED PRINT RUN 50 SERIAL #'d SETS

1998 SkyBox Dugout Axcess Autograph Redemptions

STATED ODDS 1:96 HOBBY
GLOVE EXCH.CARDS TOO SCARCE TO PRICE
EXPIRATION DATE 3/31/99
1 Jay Buhner Ball .40 1.00
2 Roger Clemens Ball .40 1.00
3 Jose Cruz Jr. Ball .40 1.00
4 Darin Erstad Glove .40 1.00
5 Nomar Garciaparra Ball .40 1.00
6 Tony Gwynn Ball .40 1.00
7 Roberto Hernandez Ball .40 1.00
8 Todd Hollandsworth Glove .40 1.00
9 Greg Maddux Ball .40 1.00
10 Alex Ochoa Glove .40 1.00
11 Alex Rodriguez Ball .40 1.00
12 Scott Rolen Ball .40 1.00
13 Scott Rolen Glove .40 1.00
14 Todd Walker Glove .40 1.00
15 Tony Womack Ball .40 1.00

1998 SkyBox Dugout Axcess Dishwashers

COMPLETE SET (10) 4.00 10.00
STATED ODDS 1:8
D1 Greg Maddux .75 2.00
D2 Kevin Brown .30 .75
D3 Pedro Martinez .30 .75
D4 Randy Johnson .50 1.25
D5 Curt Schilling .20 .50
D6 John Smoltz .20 .50
D7 Darryl Kile .20 .50
D8 Roger Clemens 1.00 2.50
D9 Andy Pettitte .30 .75
D10 Mike Mussina .30 .75

1998 SkyBox Dugout Axcess Double Header

COMPLETE SET (20) 2.00 5.00
DH1 Jeff Bagwell .05 .15
DH2 Albert Belle .02 .10
DH3 Barry Bonds .30 .75
DH4 Derek Jeter .25 .60
DH5 Tony Clark .02 .10
DH6 Nomar Garciaparra .15 .40
DH7 Juan Gonzalez .02 .10
DH8 Ken Griffey Jr. .20 .50
DH9 Chipper Jones .08 .25
DH10 Kenny Lofton .02 .10
DH11 Mark McGwire .25 .60
DH12 Mo Vaughn .02 .10
DH13 Mike Piazza .15 .40
DH14 Cal Ripken .30 .75
DH15 Ivan Rodriguez .05 .15
DH16 Scott Rolen .05 .15
DH17 Frank Thomas .08 .25
DH18 Tony Gwynn .10 .30
DH19 Travis Lee .02 .10
DH20 Jose Cruz Jr. .02 .10

1998 SkyBox Dugout Axcess Frequent Flyers

COMPLETE SET (10) 1.00 2.50
STATED ODDS 1:4
FF1 Brian Hunter .07 .20
FF2 Kenny Lofton .07 .20
FF3 Chuck Knoblauch .07 .20
FF4 Tony Womack .07 .20
FF5 Marquis Grissom .07 .20
FF6 Craig Biggio .15 .40
FF7 Barry Bonds .40 1.00
FF8 Tom Goodwin .07 .20
FF9 Delino DeShields .07 .20
FF10 Eric Young .07 .20

1998 SkyBox Dugout Axcess Gronks

COMPLETE SET (10) 25.00 60.00
STATED ODDS 1:72 HOBBY
G1 Jeff Bagwell 2.00 5.00
G2 Albert Belle 1.25 3.00
G3 Juan Gonzalez 1.25 3.00
G4 Ken Griffey Jr. 6.00 15.00
G5 Mark McGwire 8.00 20.00
G6 Mike Piazza 5.00 12.00
G7 Frank Thomas 3.00 8.00
G8 Mo Vaughn 1.25 3.00
G9 Ken Caminiti 1.25 3.00
G10 Tony Clark 1.25 3.00

1998 SkyBox Dugout Axcess SuperHeroes

COMPLETE SET (10) 12.50 30.00
STATED ODDS 1:20
SH1 Barry Bonds 4.00 10.00
SH2 Andres Galarraga .50 1.25
SH3 Ken Griffey Jr. 2.50 6.00
SH4 Chipper Jones 1.25 3.00
SH5 Andruw Jones .50 1.25
SH6 Hideo Nomo 1.25 3.00
SH7 Cal Ripken 4.00 10.00
SH8 Alex Rodriguez 2.00 5.00
SH9 Frank Thomas 1.25 3.00
SH10 Mo Vaughn .50 1.25

2004 SkyBox LE

COMP.SET w/o SP'S (110) 15.00 40.00
COMMON CARD (1-110) .25 .60
1-110 HOBBY CARDS ARE ALL DIE-CUT
COMMON CARD p/r 299 5.00
COMMON CARD p/r 99 4.00 10.00
111-160 ODDS 1:18 HOBBY, 1:144 RETAIL
111-160 PRINTS B/WN 99-299 COPIES PER
1 Juan Pierre .25 .60
2 Derek Jeter 1.50 4.00
3 Brandon Webb .25 .60
4 Jeff Bagwell .40 1.00
5 Jason Schmidt .25 .60
6 Marlon Byrd .25 .60
7 Garret Anderson .25 .60
8 Miguel Cabrera .60 1.50
9 Jose Reyes .40 1.00
10 Rocco Baldelli .25 .60
11 Tony Batista .25 .60
12 Carlos Beltran .40 1.00
13 Nomar Garciaparra .40 1.00
14 Shawn Green .25 .60
15 Albert Pujols .75 2.00
16 Magglio Ordonez .40 1.00
17 Kip Wells .25 .60
18 Andruw Jones .25 .60
19 Ryan Wagner .25 .60
20 Alex Rodriguez .75 2.00
21 Vernon Wells .25 .60
22 Todd Helton .40 1.00
23 David Ortiz .60 1.50
24 Troy Glaus .25 .60
25 Jim Thome .40 1.00
26 Greg Maddux .75 2.00
27 Roberto Alomar .40 1.00
28 Edgardo Alfonzo .25 .60
29 Hee Seop Choi .25 .60
30 Ken Griffey Jr. 1.25 3.00
31 Tim Hudson .40 1.00
32 Shannon Stewart .25 .60
33 Ichiro Suzuki .75 2.00
34 Luis Gonzalez .25 .60
35 Darin Erstad .25 .60
36 Dmitri Young .25 .60
37 Ivan Rodriguez .40 1.00
38 Scott Podsednik .25 .60
39 Jose Vidro .25 .60
40 Mark Prior .40 1.00
41 Mike Mussina .40 1.00
42 Gary Sheffield .25 .60
43 Manny Ramirez .60 1.50
44 C.C. Sabathia .40 1.00
45 Curt Schilling .40 1.00
46 Scott Rolen .40 1.00
47 Hideo Nomo .60 1.50
48 Torii Hunter .25 .60
49 Aubrey Huff .25 .60
50 Javy Lopez .25 .60
51 Austin Kearns .25 .60
52 Mike Piazza .60 1.50
53 Sean Burroughs .25 .60
54 Kerry Wood .25 .60
55 Marquis Grissom .25 .60
56 Preston Wilson .25 .60
57 Angel Berroa .25 .60
58 Jason Kendall .25 .60
59 Rafael Palmeiro .40 1.00
60 Mike Lowell .25 .60
61 Eric Chavez .25 .60
62 Bartolo Colon .25 .60
63 Adam Dunn .40 1.00
64 Pedro Martinez .40 1.00
65 Lance Berkman .40 1.00
66 Bret Boone .25 .60
67 Eric Gagne .25 .60
68 Vladimir Guerrero .40 1.00
69 Jay Gibbons .25 .60
70 Larry Walker .40 1.00
71 Orlando Cabrera .25 .60
72 Jorge Posada .40 1.00
73 Jamie Moyer .25 .60
74 Carl Crawford .40 1.00
75 Hank Blalock .25 .60
76 Josh Beckett .25 .60
77 Jody Gerut .25 .60
78 Kevin Brown .25 .60
79 Sammy Sosa .60 1.50
80 Chipper Jones .60 1.50
81 Tom Glavine .40 1.00
82 Barry Zito .40 1.00
83 Edgar Renteria .25 .60
84 Esteban Loaiza .25 .60
85 Jason Giambi .25 .60
86 Miguel Tejada .40 1.00
87 Randy Johnson .60 1.50
88 A.J. Burnett .25 .60
89 Richie Sexson .25 .60
90 Reggie Sanders .25 .60
91 Carlos Delgado .25 .60
92 Pat Burrell .25 .60
93 Jacque Jones .25 .60
94 Roy Oswalt .40 1.00
95 Frank Thomas .60 1.50
96 Melvin Mora .25 .60
97 Jeremy Bonderman .25 .60
98 Mike Sweeney .25 .60
99 Brian Giles .25 .60
100 Edgar Martinez .40 1.00
101 Mark Teixeira .40 1.00
102 Sean Casey .25 .60
103 Javier Vazquez .25 .60
104 Hideki Matsui 1.00 2.50
105 Jim Edmonds .40 1.00
106 Roy Halladay .40 1.00
107 Craig Biggio .40 1.00
108 Geoff Jenkins .25 .60
109 Alfonso Soriano .40 1.00
110 Barry Larkin .40 1.00
111 Chris Bootcheck PR/299 .75 2.00
112 Dallas McPherson PR/99 2.00 5.00
113 Matt Kata PR/99 2.00 5.00
114 Scott Hairston PR/299 .75 2.00
115 Bobby Crosby PR/299 .75 2.00
116 Adam Wainright PR/99 3.00 8.00
117 Daniel Cabrera PR/299 .75 2.00
118 Kevin Youkilis PR/299 .75 2.00
119 Ronny Cedeno PR/299 RC .75 2.00
120 Ruddy Yan PR/299 .75 2.00
121 Ryan Wing PR/299 RC .75 2.00
122 William Bergolla PR/299 RC .75 2.00
123 Edwin Encarnacion PR/299 2.00 5.00
124 Jonny Gomes PR/299 .75 2.00
125 Garrett Atkins PR/299 .75 2.00
126 Clint Barmes PR/299 1.25 3.00
127 Wilfredo Ledezma PR/299 .75 2.00
128 Cody Ross PR/299 2.00 5.00
129 Josh Willingham PR/99 3.00 8.00
130 Chin-Hui Tsao PR/299 .75 2.00
131 Hector Gimenez PR/299 RC .75 2.00
132 David DeJesus PR/299 .75 2.00
133 Jimmy Gobble PR/299 .75 2.00
134 Edwin Jackson PR/99 2.00 5.00
135 Koyie Hill PR/299 .75 2.00
136 Rickie Weeks PR/99 2.00 5.00
137 Graham Koonce PR/299 .75 2.00
138 Rob Bowen PR/299 .75 2.00
139 Shawn Hill PR/299 RC .75 2.00
140 Craig Brazell PR/299 .75 2.00
141 Mike Hessman PR/299 .75 2.00
142 Jorge De Paula PR/299 .75 2.00
143 Chien-Ming Wang PR/99 8.00 20.00
144 Rich Harden PR/299 .75 2.00
145 Ryan Howard PR/99 4.00 10.00
146 Alfredo Simon PR/299 RC 1.25 3.00
147 Ian Snell PR RC/299 RC .75 2.00
148 Ryan Doumit PR/299 .75 2.00
149 Khalil Greene PR/99 3.00 8.00
150 Angel Chavez PR/299 RC .75 2.00
151 Dan Haren PR/299 .75 2.00
152 Chris Snelling PR/299 .75 2.00
153 Aaron Miles PR/299 .75 2.00
154 John Gall PR/299 RC .75 2.00
155 Chris Narveson PR/299 .75 2.00
156 Delmon Young PR/99 3.00 8.00
157 Chad Gaudin PR/299 .75 2.00
158 Gerald Laird PR/299 .75 2.00
159 Alexis Rios PR/299 .75 2.00
160 Jason Arnold PR/299 .75 2.00

2004 SkyBox LE Artist Proof

*AP 1-110: 3X TO 8X BASIC
*AP 111-160: 1X TO 2.5X BASIC p/r 299
*AP 111-160: .4X TO 1X BASIC p/r 99
OVERALL PARALLEL ODDS 1:6 H, 1:48 R
STATED PRINT RUN 50 SERIAL #'d SETS

2004 SkyBox LE Gold Proof

*GOLD 1-110: 1.5X TO 4X BASIC
*GOLD 111-160: .5X TO 1.2X BASIC p/r 299
*GOLD 111-160: .2X TO .5X BASIC p/r 99
OVERALL PARALLEL ODDS 1:6 H, 1:48 R
STATED PRINT RUN 150 SERIAL #'d SETS

2004 SkyBox LE Photographer Proof

*PHOTO 1-110: 5X TO 12X BASIC
*PHOTO 111-160: 1.5X TO 4X BASIC p/r 299
*PHOTO 111-160: .6X TO 1.5X BASIC p/r 99
OVERALL PARALLEL ODDS 1:6 H, 1:48 R
STATED PRINT RUN 25 SERIAL #'d SETS

2004 SkyBox LE Retail

*RETAIL 1-110: .15X TO .4X BASIC
ISSUED ONLY IN RETAIL PACKS
RETAIL CARDS ARE NOT DIE CUT

2004 SkyBox LE Jersey Proof

STATED PRINT RUN 299 SERIAL #'d SETS
GOLD PRINT RUN 10 SERIAL #'d SETS
NO GOLD PRICING DUE TO SCARCITY
*SILVER: .6X TO 1.5X BASIC
SILVER PRINT RUN 50 SERIAL #'d SETS
OVERALL GU ODDS 1:9 H, 1:48 R
1 Troy Glaus 3.00 8.00
2 Curt Schilling 3.00 8.00
3 Randy Johnson 4.00 10.00
4 Brandon Webb 3.00 8.00
5 Gary Sheffield 3.00 8.00
6 Greg Maddux 6.00 15.00
7 Chipper Jones 4.00 10.00
8 David Ortiz 4.00 10.00
9 Nomar Garciaparra 6.00 15.00
10 Pedro Martinez 4.00 10.00
11 Manny Ramirez 4.00 10.00
12 Kerry Wood 3.00 8.00
13 Mark Prior 4.00 10.00
14 Sammy Sosa 4.00 10.00
15 Frank Thomas 4.00 10.00
17 Todd Helton 4.00 10.00
18 Preston Wilson 3.00 8.00
19 Juan Pierre 3.00 8.00
20 Josh Beckett 3.00 8.00
21 Ivan Rodriguez 4.00 10.00
22 Miguel Cabrera 4.00 10.00
23 Mike Lowell 3.00 8.00
24 Lance Berkman 3.00 8.00
25 Jeff Bagwell 4.00 10.00
26 Angel Berroa 3.00 8.00
27 Hideo Nomo 6.00 15.00
28 Eric Gagne 3.00 8.00
29 Scott Podsednik 3.00 8.00
30 Richie Sexson 3.00 8.00
31 Torii Hunter 3.00 8.00
32 Mike Piazza 6.00 15.00
33 Jose Reyes 3.00 8.00
34 Tom Glavine 4.00 10.00
35 Derek Jeter 12.50 30.00
36 Jorge Posada 4.00 10.00
37 Jason Giambi 3.00 8.00
38 Alfonso Soriano 3.00 8.00
39 Eric Chavez 3.00 8.00
40 Miguel Tejada 3.00 8.00
41 Jim Thome 4.00 10.00
42 Albert Pujols 8.00 20.00
43 Scott Rolen 4.00 10.00
44 Rocco Baldelli 3.00 8.00
45 Alex Rodriguez 5.00 12.00
46 Hank Blalock 3.00 8.00
47 Mark Teixeira 4.00 10.00
48 Rafael Palmeiro 4.00 10.00
49 Carlos Delgado 3.00 8.00
50 Roy Halladay 3.00 8.00

2004 SkyBox LE History Draft 90's Autograph Black

STATED PRINT RUN 199 SERIAL #'d SETS
*COPPER: .4X TO 1X BASIC
COPPER PRINTS B/WN 93-99 COPIES PER
GOLD PRINT RUN 10 SERIAL #'d SETS
NO GOLD PRICING DUE TO SCARCITY
*SILVER: .5X TO 1.2X BASIC
SILVER PRINT RUN 50 SERIAL #'d SETS
OVERALL AUTO ODDS 1:18 HOBBY
AH Aubrey Huff 6.00 15.00
AK Austin Kearns 4.00 10.00
AP Albert Pujols 125.00 200.00
CP Corey Patterson 4.00 10.00
HB Hank Blalock 6.00 15.00
JP Juan Pierre 6.00 15.00
MB Marlon Byrd 4.00 10.00
ML Mike Lowell 6.00 15.00
RH Roy Halladay 40.00 80.00
SP Scott Podsednik 10.00 25.00
SR Scott Rolen 10.00 25.00
TH Torii Hunter 6.00 15.00
VW Vernon Wells 6.00 15.00

2004 SkyBox LE History Draft 90's Jersey

PRINT RUNS B/WN 90-99 COPIES PER
GOLD PRINT RUN 10 SERIAL #'d SETS
NO GOLD PRICING DUE TO SCARCITY
*SILVER: .5X TO 1.2X BASIC
SILVER PRINT RUN 50 SERIAL #'d SETS
OVERALL GU ODDS 1:9 H, 1:48 R
AB A.J. Burnett/95 4.00 10.00
AD Adam Dunn/98 4.00 10.00
AH Aubrey Huff/98 4.00 10.00
AK Austin Kearns/98 4.00 10.00
AP Albert Pujols/99 10.00 25.00
AR Alex Rodriguez/93 6.00 15.00
BB Bret Boone/90 4.00 10.00
BZ Barry Zito/99 4.00 10.00
CB Carlos Beltran/95 4.00 10.00
CJ Chipper Jones/90 5.00 12.00
CP Corey Patterson/98 4.00 10.00
DE Darin Erstad/95 4.00 10.00
DJ Derek Jeter/92 12.00 30.00
EC Eric Chavez/96 4.00 10.00
GA Garret Anderson/90 4.00 10.00
HB Hank Blalock/99 4.00 10.00
JB Josh Beckett/99 4.00 10.00
JG Jason Giambi/92 4.00 10.00
JPI Juan Pierre/98 4.00 10.00
JPO Jorge Posada/90 5.00 12.00
JS Jason Schmidt/91 4.00 10.00
JV Javier Vazquez/94 4.00 10.00
KW Kerry Wood/95 4.00 10.00
LB Lance Berkman/97 4.00 10.00
MB Marlon Byrd/99 4.00 10.00
ML Mike Lowell/95 4.00 10.00
MM Mike Mussina/90 5.00 12.00
MR Manny Ramirez/91 5.00 12.00
NG Nomar Garciaparra/94 8.00 20.00
PB Pat Burrell/98 4.00 10.00
RH Roy Halladay/95 4.00 10.00
RS Richie Sexson/93 4.00 10.00
SG Shawn Green/91 4.00 10.00
SP Scott Podsednik/94 4.00 10.00
SR Scott Rolen/93 5.00 12.00
SS Shannon Stewart/92 4.00 10.00
THE Todd Helton/95 5.00 12.00
THN Torii Hunter/93 4.00 10.00
THU Tim Hudson/97 4.00 10.00
VW Vernon Wells/97 4.00 10.00

2004 SkyBox LE League Leaders

STATED ODDS 1:18 HOBBY, 1:12 RETAIL
EXECUTIVE RANDOM INSERTS IN PACKS
EXECUTIVE PRINT RUN 1 SERIAL #'d SET
NO EXECUTIVE PRICING DUE TO SCARCITY
1 Alex Rodriguez 1.25 3.00
2 Jim Thome .60 1.50
3 Albert Pujols 1.25 3.00
4 Pedro Martinez .60 1.50
5 Roy Halladay .60 1.50
6 Jason Schmidt .40 1.00
7 Kerry Wood .40 1.00
8 Juan Pierre .40 1.00
9 Preston Wilson .40 1.00
10 Carlos Delgado .40 1.00

2004 SkyBox LE League Leaders Jersey

STATED PRINT RUN 75 SERIAL #'d SETS
GOLD PRINT RUN 10 SERIAL #'d SETS
NO GOLD PRICING DUE TO SCARCITY
*SILVER: .5X TO 1.2X BASIC
SILVER PRINT RUN 50 SERIAL #'d SETS
OVERALL GU ODDS 1:9 H, 1:48 R
AP Albert Pujols 10.00 25.00
AR Alex Rodriguez 6.00 15.00
CD Carlos Delgado 4.00 10.00
JP Juan Pierre 4.00 10.00
JS Jason Schmidt 4.00 10.00
JT Jim Thome 5.00 12.00
KW Kerry Wood 4.00 10.00
PM Pedro Martinez 5.00 12.00
PW Preston Wilson 4.00 10.00
RH Roy Halladay 4.00 10.00

2004 SkyBox LE Rare Form

STATED ODDS 1:288 HOBBY, 1:576 RETAIL
NO MORE THAN 130 SETS PRODUCED
PRINT RUN INFO PROVIDED BY FLEER
EXECUTIVE RANDOM INSERTS IN PACKS
EXECUTIVE PRINT RUN 1 SERIAL #'d SET
NO EXECUTIVE PRICING DUE TO SCARCITY
1 Albert Pujols 8.00 20.00
2 Miguel Cabrera 6.00 15.00
3 Jim Thome 4.00 10.00
4 Derek Jeter 15.00 40.00
5 Nomar Garciaparra 4.00 10.00
6 Mike Piazza 6.00 15.00
7 Alex Rodriguez 8.00 20.00
8 Delmon Young 4.00 10.00
9 Chipper Jones 6.00 15.00
10 Rickie Weeks 2.50 6.00

2004 SkyBox LE Rare Form Autograph Black

STATED PRINT RUN 299 SERIAL #'d SETS
*COPPER: .5X TO 1.2X BASIC
COPPER PRINT RUN 99 SERIAL #'d SETS
GOLD PRINT RUN 10 SERIAL #'d SETS
NO GOLD PRICING DUE TO SCARCITY
*SILVER: .6X TO 1.5X BASIC
SILVER PRINT RUN 50 SERIAL #'d SETS
OVERALL AUTO ODDS 1:18 HOBBY
1 Dallas McPherson 6.00 15.00
2 Delmon Young 10.00 25.00
3 Rickie Weeks 6.00 15.00
4 Brandon Webb 4.00 10.00
5 Matt Kata 4.00 10.00
6 Edwin Jackson 4.00 10.00
7 Rocco Baldelli 6.00 15.00
8 Angel Berroa 4.00 10.00
9 Rich Harden 6.00 15.00

2004 SkyBox LE Rare Form Game Used Silver

STATED PRINT RUN 50 SERIAL #'d SETS
GOLD PRINT RUN 10 SERIAL #'d SETS
NO GOLD PRICING DUE TO SCARCITY
*NUMBER p/r 31: .5X TO 1.2X BASIC
*NUMBER p/r 20-25: .6X TO 1.5X BASIC
NUMBER PRINTS B/WN 2-31 COPIES PER
NO NUMBER PRICING ON 25 OR LESS
OVERALL GU ODDS 1:9 H, 1:48 R
AP Albert Pujols Jsy 12.50 30.00
AR Alex Rodriguez Jsy 8.00 20.00
CJ Chipper Jones Jsy 6.00 15.00
DJ Derek Jeter Jsy 20.00 50.00
JT Jim Thome Jsy 6.00 15.00
MC Miguel Cabrera Jsy 6.00 15.00
MP Mike Piazza Jsy 10.00 25.00
NG Nomar Garciaparra Jsy 10.00 25.00
RB Rocco Baldelli Jsy 5.00 12.00
RW Rickie Weeks Bat 5.00 12.00

2004 SkyBox LE Sky's the Limit

STATED ODDS 1:6 HOBBY, 1:8 RETAIL
EXECUTIVE RANDOM INSERTS IN PACKS
EXECUTIVE PRINT RUN 1 SERIAL #'d SET
NO EXECUTIVE PRICING DUE TO SCARCITY
1 Dontrelle Willis .40 1.00
2 Rocco Baldelli .40 1.00
3 Miguel Cabrera 1.00 2.50
4 Mark Prior .60 1.50
5 Hideki Matsui 1.50 4.00
6 Kerry Wood .40 1.00
7 Alfonso Soriano .60 1.50
8 Ichiro Suzuki 1.25 3.00
9 Brandon Webb .40 1.00
10 Alex Rodriguez 1.25 3.00
11 Barry Zito .60 1.50
12 Hank Blalock .40 1.00
13 Jose Reyes .60 1.50
14 Torii Hunter .40 1.00
15 Josh Beckett .40 1.00
16 Manny Ramirez 1.00 2.50
17 Andruw Jones .40 1.00
18 Vladimir Guerrero .60 1.50
19 Miguel Tejada .60 1.50
20 Carlos Delgado .40 1.00

2004 SkyBox LE Sky's the Limit Jersey

STATED PRINT RUN 99 SERIAL #'d SETS
GOLD PRINT RUN 10 SERIAL #'d SETS
NO GOLD PRICING DUE TO SCARCITY
*SILVER: .5X TO 1.2X BASIC
SILVER PRINT RUN 50 SERIAL #'d SETS
OVERALL GU ODDS 1:9 H, 1:48 R
AJ Andruw Jones 5.00 12.00
AR Alex Rodriguez 6.00 15.00
AS Alfonso Soriano 4.00 10.00
BW Brandon Webb 4.00 10.00
BZ Barry Zito 4.00 10.00
CD Carlos Delgado 4.00 10.00
DW Dontrelle Willis 5.00 12.00
HB Hank Blalock 4.00 10.00
JB Josh Beckett 4.00 10.00
JR Jose Reyes 4.00 10.00
KW Kerry Wood 4.00 10.00
MC Miguel Cabrera 5.00 12.00
MP Mark Prior 5.00 12.00
MR Manny Ramirez 5.00 12.00
MT Miguel Tejada 4.00 10.00
RB Rocco Baldelli 4.00 10.00
TH Torii Hunter 4.00 10.00
VG Vladimir Guerrero 5.00 12.00

1999 SkyBox Molten Metal

The 1999 SkyBox Molten Metal set was issued in one series and distributed in six-card packs with a suggested retail price of $4.99. The set features 100 of the game's top veterans in the Metal Smiths (cards 1-100) subset with an insertion rate of 4:1 pack; 30 of today's power hitters in the Heavy Metal subset (101-130) inserted one per pack; and 20 of 1999's hottest rookies in the Supernatural subset(131-150) with an insertion rate of 1:2 packs. The cards are silver-foil on 24-point stock and enhanced with additional holofoil and wet laminate. Rookie Cards inlcude Pat Burrell and Freddy Garcia. Finally, special National Edition boxes were printed and distributed exclusively at the National Sportscard Collectors Convention in Atlanta in July 1999.

COMPLETE SET (150) 15.00 40.00
COMMON CARD (1-100) .15 .40
METALSMITHS 1-100 ODDS 4:1
COMMON CARD (101-130) .15 .40
HEAVY METAL 101-130 ODDS 1:1
COMMON CARD (131-150) .30 .75
SUPERNATURAL 131-150 ODDS 1:2
1 Larry Walker MS .15 .40
2 Jose Canseco MS .25 .60
3 Brian Jordan MS .15 .40
4 Rafael Palmeiro MS .25 .60
5 Edgar Renteria MS .15 .40
6 Dante Bichette MS .15 .40
7 Mark Kotsay MS .15 .40
8 Denny Neagle MS .15 .40
9 Ellis Burks MS .15 .40
10 Paul O'Neill MS .25 .60
11 Miguel Tejada MS .15 .40
12 Ken Caminiti MS .15 .40
13 David Cone MS .15 .40
14 Jason Kendall MS .15 .40
15 Ruben Rivera MS .15 .40
16 Todd Walker MS .15 .40
17 Bobby Higginson MS .15 .40
18 Derrek Lee MS .25 .60
19 Rondell White MS .15 .40
20 Pedro Martinez MS .25 .60
21 Jeff Kent MS .15 .40
22 Randy Johnson MS .40 1.00
23 Matt Williams MS .15 .40
24 Sean Casey MS .15 .40
25 Eric Davis MS .15 .40
26 Ryan Klesko MS .15 .40
27 Curt Schilling MS .15 .40
28 Geoff Jenkins MS .15 .40
29 Bob Abreu MS .15 .40
30 Vinny Castilla MS .15 .40
31 Will Clark MS .25 .60
32 Ray Durham MS .15 .40
33 Ray Lankford MS .15 .40
34 Richie Sexson MS .15 .40
35 Derrick Gibson MS .15 .40
36 Mark Grace MS .25 .60
37 Greg Vaughn MS .15 .40
38 Bartolo Colon MS .15 .40
39 Steve Finley MS .15 .40
40 Chuck Knoblauch MS .15 .40
41 Ricky Ledee MS .15 .40
42 John Smoltz MS .25 .60
43 Moises Alou MS .15 .40
44 Jim Edmonds MS .15 .40
45 Cliff Floyd MS .15 .40
46 Javy Lopez MS .15 .40
47 Jim Thome MS .25 .60
48 J.T. Snow MS .15 .40
49 Sandy Alomar Jr. MS .15 .40
50 Andy Pettitte MS .25 .60
51 Juan Encarnacion MS .15 .40
52 Travis Fryman MS .15 .40
53 Eli Marrero MS .15 .40
54 Jeff Cirillo MS .15 .40
55 Brady Anderson MS .15 .40
56 Jose Cruz Jr. MS .15 .40
57 Edgar Martinez MS .25 .60
58 Garret Anderson MS .15 .40
59 Paul Konerko MS .15 .40
60 Eric Milton MS .15 .40
61 Jason Giambi MS .15 .40
62 Tom Glavine MS .25 .60
63 Justin Thompson MS .15 .40
64 Brad Fullmer MS .15 .40
65 Marquis Grissom MS .15 .40
66 Fernando Tatis MS .15 .40
67 Carlos Beltran MS .25 .60
68 Charles Johnson MS .15 .40
69 Raul Mondesi MS .15 .40
70 Richard Hildago MS .15 .40
71 Barry Larkin MS .25 .60
72 David Wells MS .15 .40
73 Jay Buhner MS .15 .40
74 Matt Clement MS .15 .40
75 Eric Karros MS .15 .40
76 Carl Pavano MS .15 .40
77 Mariano Rivera MS .40 1.00
78 Livan Hernandez MS .15 .40
79 A.J. Hinch MS .15 .40
80 Tino Martinez MS .25 .60
81 Rusty Greer MS .15 .40
82 Jose Guillen MS .15 .40
83 Robin Ventura MS .15 .40
84 Kevin Brown MS .25 .60
85 Chan Ho Park MS .15 .40
86 John Olerud MS .15 .40
87 Johnny Damon MS .25 .60
88 Todd Hundley MS .15 .40
89 Fred McGriff MS .25 .60
90 Wade Boggs MS .25 .60
91 Mike Cameron MS .15 .40
92 Gary Sheffield MS .15 .40
93 Rickey Henderson MS .40 1.00
94 Pat Hentgen MS .15 .40
95 Omar Vizquel MS .25 .60
96 Craig Biggio MS .25 .60
97 Mike Caruso MS .15 .40
98 Neifi Perez MS .15 .40
99 Mike Mussina MS .25 .60
100 Carlos Delgado MS .15 .40
101 Andruw Jones HM .25 .60
102 Pat Burrell HM RC .75 2.00
103 Orlando Hernandez HM .15 .40
104 Darin Erstad HM .15 .40
105 Roberto Alomar HM .25 .60
106 Tim Salmon HM .25 .60
107 Albert Belle HM .15 .40
108 Chad Allen HM RC .15 .40
109 Travis Lee HM .15 .40
110 Jesse Garcia HM RC .15 .40
111 Tony Clark HM .15 .40
112 Ivan Rodriguez HM .25 .60
113 Troy Glaus HM .25 .60
114 A.J. Burnett HM RC .40 1.00
115 David Justice HM .15 .40
116 Adrian Beltre HM .15 .40
117 Eric Chavez HM .15 .40
118 Kenny Lofton HM .15 .40
119 Michael Barrett HM .15 .40
120 Jeff Weaver HM RC .25 .60
121 Manny Ramirez HM .25 .60
122 Barry Bonds HM 1.25 3.00
123 Bernie Williams HM .25 .60
124 Freddy Garcia HM RC .40 1.00
125 Scott Hunter HM RC .15 .40
126 Jeremy Giambi HM .15 .40
127 Masao Kida HM RC .15 .40
128 Todd Helton HM .25 .60
129 Mike Figga HM .15 .40
130 Mo Vaughn HM .15 .40
131 J.D. Drew SN .30 .75
132 Cal Ripken SN 2.00 5.00
133 Ken Griffey Jr. SN 1.25 3.00
134 Mark McGwire SN 1.50 4.00
135 Nomar Garciaparra SN 1.00 2.50
136 Greg Maddux SN 1.00 2.50
137 Mike Piazza SN 1.00 2.50
138 Alex Rodriguez SN 1.00 2.50
139 Frank Thomas SN .60 1.50
140 Juan Gonzalez SN .30 .75
141 Tony Gwynn SN .75 2.00
142 Derek Jeter SN 1.50 4.00
143 Chipper Jones SN .60 1.50
144 Scott Rolen SN .40 1.00
145 Sammy Sosa SN .60 1.50
146 Kerry Wood SN .30 .75
147 Roger Clemens SN 1.25 3.00
148 Jeff Bagwell SN .40 1.00
149 Vladimir Guerrero SN .60 1.50
150 Ben Grieve SN .30 .75

1999 SkyBox Molten Metal Xplosion

COMPLETE SET (150) 300.00 600.00
*METALSMITHS 1-100: 2.5X TO 6X BASIC
*HEAVY METAL 101-130: 2X TO 5X BASIC
*HVY.MTL RC'S 101-130: 1.25X TO 3X BASIC
*S'NATURAL 131-150: 1.5X TO 4X BASIC
XPLOSION STATED ODDS 1:2
NNO Kerry Wood Sample .40 1.00

1999 SkyBox Molten Metal Fusion

COMPLETE SET (50) 200.00 400.00
COMMON CARD (1-30) .75 2.00
HEAVY METAL 1-30 ODDS 1:12
COMMON CARD (31-50) 2.00 5.00
SUPERNATURAL 31-50 ODDS 1:24
1 Andruw Jones HM .75 2.00
2 Pat Burrell HM 2.50 6.00
3 Orlando Hernandez HM .75 2.00
4 Darin Erstad HM .75 2.00
5 Roberto Alomar HM .75 2.00
6 Tim Salmon HM .75 2.00
7 Albert Belle HM .75 2.00
8 Chad Allen HM .75 2.00
9 Travis Lee HM .75 2.00
10 Jesse Garcia HM .75 2.00
11 Tony Clark HM .75 2.00
12 Ivan Rodriguez HM .75 2.00
13 Troy Glaus HM .75 2.00
14 A.J. Burnett HM 1.25 3.00
15 David Justice HM .75 2.00
16 Adrian Beltre HM .75 2.00
17 Eric Chavez HM .75 2.00

18 Kenny Lofton HM .75 2.00
19 Michael Barrett HM .75 2.00
20 Jeff Weaver HM .75 2.00
21 Manny Ramirez HM .75 2.00
22 Barry Bonds HM 6.00 15.00
23 Bernie Williams HM .75 2.00
24 Freddy Garcia HM 1.25 3.00
25 Scott Hunter HM .75 2.00
26 Jeremy Giambi HM .75 2.00
27 Masao Kida HM .75 2.00
28 Todd Helton HM .75 2.00
29 Mike Figga HM .75 2.00
30 Mo Vaughn HM .75 2.00
31 J.D. Drew SN 2.00 5.00
32 Cal Ripken SN 10.00 25.00
33 Ken Griffey Jr. SN 6.00 15.00
34 Mark McGwire SN 8.00 20.00
35 Nomar Garciaparra SN 5.00 12.00
36 Greg Maddux SN 5.00 12.00
37 Mike Piazza SN 5.00 12.00
38 Alex Rodriguez SN 8.00 20.00
39 Frank Thomas SN 2.00 5.00
40 Juan Gonzalez SN 2.00 5.00
41 Tony Gwynn SN 4.00 10.00
42 Derek Jeter SN 8.00 20.00
43 Chipper Jones SN 2.00 5.00
44 Scott Rolen SN 2.00 5.00
45 Sammy Sosa SN 2.00 5.00
46 Kerry Wood SN 2.00 5.00
47 Roger Clemens SN 6.00 15.00
48 Jeff Bagwell SN 2.00 5.00
49 Vladimir Guerrero SN 2.00 5.00
50 Ben Grieve SN 2.00 5.00

1999 SkyBox Molten Metal Oh Atlanta

COMPLETE SET (30) 40.00 100.00
ONE PER NATIONAL EDITION PACK
1 Kenny Lofton 1.25 3.00
2 Kevin Millwood 1.25 3.00
3 Bret Boone 1.25 3.00
4 Otis Nixon .75 2.00
5 Vinny Castilla 1.25 3.00
6 Brian Jordan 1.25 3.00
7 Chipper Jones 3.00 8.00
8 David Justice 1.25 3.00
9 Micah Bowie .75 2.00
10 Fred McGriff 2.00 5.00
11 Ron Gant 1.25 3.00
12 Andruw Jones 2.00 5.00
13 Kent Mercker .75 2.00
14 Greg McMichael .75 2.00
15 Steve Avery .75 2.00
16 Marquis Grissom 1.25 3.00
17 Jason Schmidt 1.25 3.00
18 Ryan Klesko 1.25 3.00
19 Charlie O'Brien .75 2.00
20 Terry Pendleton 1.25 3.00
21 Denny Neagle .75 2.00
22 Greg Maddux 6.00 15.00
23 Tom Glavine 2.00 5.00
24 Javy Lopez 1.25 3.00
25 John Rocker 1.25 3.00
26 Walt Weiss .75 2.00
27 John Smoltz 2.00 5.00
28 Michael Tucker .75 2.00
29 Odalis Perez .75 2.00
30 Andres Galarraga 1.25 3.00

1999 SkyBox Premium

The 1999 SkyBox Premium set was issued in one series for a total of 350 cards and distributed in eight-card packs with a suggested retail price of $2.69. The set features color action player photos with a team colored action-trail and gold-foil stamping. The set contains the following subsets: Spring Fling (273-297) and two versions of the 50 Rookies. In an effoty to satisfy fans of both complete sets and short-printed Rookie Cards, dual version rookie and prospect cards were created. The commonly available versions feature close-up shots of the players and these are considered the true Rookie Card. The short-printed versions feature full-body action shots and are seeded at a rate of one in eight packs. Both versions of these cards are numbered but we've added an "S" suffix on the short-prints for checklisting purposes. Notable Rookie Cards include Pat Burrell and Freddy Garcia.

COMP.MASTER SET (350) 100.00 200.00
COMP.SET w/o SP's (300) 10.00 25.00
COMMON (1-222/273-300) .07 .20
COMMON CARD (223-272) .10 .30
COMMON SP (223-272) .75 2.00
SP STATED ODDS 1:8
223-272: TWO VERSIONS OF EACH EXIST
SP CARDS FEATURE FULL BODY SHOTS
BASIC CARDS FEATURE CLOSE UP SHOTS
1 Alex Rodriguez .50 1.25
2 Sidney Ponson .07 .20
3 Shawn Green .10 .30
4 Dan Wilson .07 .20
5 Rolando Arrojo .07 .20
6 Roberto Alomar .20 .50
7 Matt Anderson .07 .20
8 David Segui .07 .20
9 Alex Gonzalez .07 .20
10 Edgar Renteria .10 .30
11 Benito Santiago .10 .30
12 Todd Stottlemyre .07 .20
13 Rico Brogna .07 .20
14 Troy Glaus .20 .50
15 Al Leiter .10 .30
16 Pedro Martinez .20 .50
17 Paul O'Neill .20 .50
18 Manny Ramirez .20 .50
19 Scott Rolen .20 .50
20 Curt Schilling .10 .30
21 Bob Abreu .10 .30
22 Robb Nen .10 .30
23 Andy Pettitte .20 .50
24 John Wetteland .10 .30
25 Bobby Bonilla .10 .30
26 Darin Erstad .10 .30
27 Shawn Estes .07 .20
28 John Franco .10 .30
29 Nomar Garciaparra .50 1.25
30 Rick Helling .07 .20
31 David Justice .10 .30
32 Chuck Knoblauch .10 .30
33 Quinton McCracken .07 .20
34 Kenny Rogers .10 .30
35 Brian Giles .10 .30
36 Armando Benitez .07 .20
37 Trevor Hoffman .10 .30
38 Charles Johnson .10 .30
39 Travis Lee .07 .20
40 Tom Glavine .20 .50
41 Rondell White .10 .30
42 Orlando Hernandez .10 .30
43 Mickey Morandini .07 .20
44 Darryl Kile .10 .30
45 Greg Vaughn .07 .20
46 Gregg Jefferies .07 .20
47 Mark McGwire .75 2.00
48 Kerry Wood .10 .30
49 Jeromy Burnitz .10 .30
50 Ron Gant .10 .30
51 Vinny Castilla .10 .30
52 Doug Glanville .07 .20
53 Juan Guzman .07 .20
54 Dustin Hermanson .07 .20
55 Jose Hernandez .07 .20
56 Bobby Higginson .10 .30
57 A.J. Hinch .07 .20
58 Randy Johnson .30 .75
59 Eli Marrero .07 .20
60 Rafael Palmeiro .20 .50
61 Carl Pavano .10 .30
62 Brett Tomko .07 .20
63 Jose Guillen .10 .30
64 Mike Lieberthal .10 .30
65 Jim Abbott .20 .50
66 Dante Bichette .10 .30
67 Jeff Cirillo .07 .20
68 Eric Davis .10 .30
69 Delino DeShields .07 .20
70 Steve Finley .10 .30
71 Mark Grace .20 .50
72 Jason Kendall .10 .30
73 Jeff Kent .10 .30
74 Desi Relaford .07 .20
75 Ivan Rodriguez .20 .50
76 Shannon Stewart .10 .30
77 Geoff Jenkins .07 .20
78 Ben Grieve .07 .20
79 Cliff Floyd .10 .30
80 Jason Giambi .10 .30
81 Rod Beck .07 .20
82 Derek Bell .07 .20
83 Will Clark .20 .50
84 David Dellucci .07 .20
85 Joey Hamilton .07 .20
86 Livan Hernandez .10 .30
87 Barry Larkin .20 .50
88 Matt Mantei .07 .20
89 Dean Palmer .10 .30
90 Chan Ho Park .10 .30
91 Jim Thome .20 .50
92 Miguel Tejada .10 .30
93 Justin Thompson .07 .20
94 David Wells .10 .30
95 Bernie Williams .20 .50
96 Jeff Bagwell .20 .50
97 Derrek Lee .20 .50
98 Devon White .10 .30
99 Jeff Shaw .07 .20
100 Brad Radke .10 .30
101 Mark Grudzielanek .07 .20
102 Javy Lopez .10 .30
103 Mike Sirotka .07 .20
104 Robin Ventura .10 .30
105 Andy Ashby .07 .20
106 Juan Gonzalez .10 .30
107 Albert Belle .10 .30
108 Andy Benes .07 .20
109 Jay Buhner .10 .30
110 Ken Caminiti .10 .30
111 Roger Clemens .60 1.50
112 Mike Hampton .10 .30
113 Pete Harnisch .07 .20
114 Mike Piazza .50 1.25
115 J.T. Snow .10 .30
116 John Olerud .10 .30
117 Tony Womack .07 .20
118 Todd Zeile .10 .30
119 Tony Gwynn .40 1.00
120 Brady Anderson .10 .30
121 Sean Casey .10 .30
122 Jose Cruz Jr. .07 .20
123 Carlos Delgado .10 .30
124 Edgar Martinez .20 .50
125 Jose Mesa .07 .20
126 Shane Reynolds .07 .20
127 John Valentin .07 .20
128 Mo Vaughn .10 .30
129 Kevin Young .10 .30
130 Jay Bell .10 .30
131 Aaron Boone .10 .30
132 John Smoltz .20 .50
133 Mike Stanley .07 .20
134 Bret Saberhagen .10 .30
135 Tim Salmon .20 .50
136 Mariano Rivera .30 .75
137 Ken Griffey Jr. .60 1.50
138 Jose Offerman .07 .20
139 Troy Percival .10 .30
140 Greg Maddux .50 1.25
141 Frank Thomas .30 .75
142 Steve Avery .07 .20
143 Kevin Millwood .10 .30
144 Sammy Sosa .30 .75
145 Larry Walker .10 .30
146 Matt Williams .10 .30
147 Mike Caruso .07 .20
148 Todd Helton .20 .50
149 Andruw Jones .20 .50
150 Ray Lankford .10 .30
151 Craig Biggio .20 .50
152 Ugueth Urbina .07 .20
153 Wade Boggs .20 .50
154 Derek Jeter .75 2.00
155 Wally Joyner .10 .30
156 Mike Mussina .20 .50
157 Gregg Olson .07 .20
158 Henry Rodriguez .07 .20
159 Reggie Sanders .10 .30
160 Fernando Tatis .07 .20
161 Dmitri Young .10 .30
162 Rick Aguilera .07 .20
163 Marty Cordova .07 .20
164 Johnny Damon .20 .50
165 Ray Durham .10 .30
166 Brad Fullmer .07 .20
167 Chipper Jones .30 .75
168 Bobby Smith .07 .20
169 Omar Vizquel .20 .50
170 Todd Hundley .07 .20
171 David Cone .10 .30
172 Royce Clayton .07 .20
173 Ryan Klesko .10 .30
174 Jeff Montgomery .07 .20
175 Magglio Ordonez .10 .30
176 Billy Wagner .10 .30
177 Masato Yoshii .07 .20
178 Jason Christiansen .07 .20
179 Chuck Finley .10 .30
180 Tom Gordon .07 .20
181 Wilton Guerrero .07 .20
182 Rickey Henderson .30 .75
183 Sterling Hitchcock .07 .20
184 Kenny Lofton .10 .30
185 Tino Martinez .20 .50
186 Fred McGriff .20 .50
187 Matt Stairs .07 .20
188 Neifi Perez .07 .20
189 Bob Wickman .07 .20
190 Barry Bonds .75 2.00
191 Jose Canseco .20 .50
192 Damion Easley .07 .20
193 Jim Edmonds .10 .30
194 Juan Encarnacion .07 .20
195 Travis Fryman .10 .30
196 Tom Goodwin .07 .20
197 Rusty Greer .10 .30
198 Roberto Hernandez .07 .20
199 B.J. Surhoff .10 .30
200 Scott Brosius .10 .30
201 Brian Jordan .10 .30
202 Paul Konerko .10 .30
203 Ismael Valdes .07 .20
204 Eric Milton .07 .20
205 Adrian Beltre .10 .30
206 Tony Clark .07 .20
207 Bartolo Colon .10 .30
208 Cal Ripken 1.00 2.50
209 Moises Alou .10 .30
210 Wilson Alvarez .07 .20
211 Kevin Brown .20 .50
212 Orlando Cabrera .10 .30
213 Vladimir Guerrero .30 .75
214 Jose Rosado .07 .20
215 Raul Mondesi .10 .30
216 David Nilsson .07 .20
217 Carlos Perez .07 .20
218 Jason Schmidt .10 .30
219 Richie Sexson .10 .30
220 Gary Sheffield .10 .30
221 Fernando Vina .07 .20
222 Todd Walker .07 .20
223 Scott Sauerbeck RC .10 .30
223S Scott Sauerbeck SP .75 2.00
224 Pascual Matos RC .10 .30
224S Pascual Matos SP .75 2.00
225 Kyle Farnsworth RC .10 .30
225S Kyle Farnsworth SP .75 2.00
226 Freddy Garcia RC .30 .75
226S Freddy Garcia SP 1.25 3.00
227 David Lundquist RC .10 .30
227S David Lundquist SP .75 2.00
228 Jolbert Cabrera RC .10 .30
228S Jolbert Cabrera SP .75 2.00
229 Dan Perkins RC .10 .30
229S Dan Perkins SP .75 2.00
230 Warren Morris .10 .30
230S Warren Morris SP .75 2.00
231 Carlos Febles .10 .30
231S Carlos Febles SP .75 2.00
232 Brett Hinchliffe RC .10 .30
232S Brett Hinchliffe SP .75 2.00
233 Jason Phillips RC .10 .30
233S Jason Phillips SP .75 2.00
234 Glen Barker RC .10 .30
234S Glen Barker SP .75 2.00
235 Jose Macias RC .10 .30
235S Jose Macias SP .75 2.00
236 Joe Mays RC .10 .30
236S Joe Mays SP .75 2.00
237 Chad Allen RC .10 .30
237S Chad Allen SP .75 2.00
238 Miguel Del Toro RC .10 .30
238S Miguel Del Toro SP .75 2.00
239 Chris Singleton .10 .30
239S Chris Singleton SP .75 2.00
240 Jesse Garcia RC .10 .30
240S Jesse Garcia SP .75 2.00
241 Kris Benson .10 .30
241S Kris Benson SP .75 2.00
242 Clay Bellinger RC .10 .30
242S Clay Bellinger SP .75 2.00
243 Scott Williamson .10 .30
243S Scott Williamson SP .75 2.00
244 Masao Kida RC .10 .30
244S Masao Kida SP .75 2.00
245 Guillermo Garcia RC .10 .30
245S Guillermo Garcia SP .75 2.00
246 A.J. Burnett RC .30 .75
246S A.J. Burnett SP 1.25 3.00
247 Bo Porter RC .10 .30
247S Bo Porter SP .75 2.00
248 Pat Burrell RC .60 1.50
248S Pat Burrell SP 2.50 6.00
249 Carlos Lee .10 .30
249S Carlos Lee SP .75 2.00
250 Jeff Weaver RC .20 .50
250S Jeff Weaver SP .75 2.00
251 Ruben Mateo .10 .30
251S Ruben Mateo SP .75 2.00
252 J.D. Drew .10 .30
252S J.D. Drew SP .75 2.00
253 Jeremy Giambi .10 .30
253S Jeremy Giambi SP .75 2.00
254 Gary Bennett RC .10 .30
254S Gary Bennett SP .75 2.00
255 Edwards Guzman RC .10 .30
255S Edwards Guzman SP .75 2.00
256 Ramon E.Martinez RC .10 .30
256S Ramon E.Martinez SP .75 2.00
257 Giomar Guevara RC .10 .30
257S Giomar Guevara SP .75 2.00
258 Joe McEwing RC .10 .30
258S Joe McEwing SP .75 2.00
259 Tom Davey RC .10 .30
259S Tom Davey SP .75 2.00
260 Gabe Kapler .10 .30
260S Gabe Kapler SP .75 2.00
261 Ryan Rupe RC .10 .30
261S Ryan Rupe SP .75 2.00
262 Kelly Dransfeldt RC .10 .30
262S Kelly Dransfeldt SP .75 2.00
263 Michael Barrett .10 .30
263S Michael Barrett SP .75 2.00
264 Eric Chavez .10 .30
264S Eric Chavez SP .75 2.00
265 Orber Moreno RC .10 .30
265S Orber Moreno SP .75 2.00
266 Marlon Anderson .10 .30
266S Marlon Anderson SP .75 2.00
267 Carlos Beltran .20 .50
267S Carlos Beltran SP .75 2.00
268 Doug Mientkiewicz RC .20 .50
268S Doug Mientkiewicz SP .75 2.00
269 Roy Halladay .30 .75
269S Roy Halladay SP 2.00 5.00
270 Torii Hunter .10 .30
270S Torii Hunter SP .75 2.00
271 Stan Spencer .10 .30
271S Stan Spencer SP .75 2.00
272 Alex Gonzalez .10 .30
272S Alex Gonzalez SP .75 2.00
273 Mark McGwire SF .40 1.00
274 Scott Rolen SF .10 .30
275 Jeff Bagwell SF .10 .30
276 Derek Jeter SF .40 1.00
277 Tony Gwynn SF .20 .50
278 Frank Thomas SF .20 .50
279 Sammy Sosa SF .20 .50
280 Nomar Garciaparra SF .30 .75
281 Cal Ripken SF .50 1.25
282 Albert Belle SF .07 .20
283 Kerry Wood SF .10 .30
284 Greg Maddux SF .30 .75
285 Barry Bonds SF .40 1.00
286 Juan Gonzalez SF .07 .20
287 Ken Griffey Jr. SF .40 1.00
288 Alex Rodriguez SF .30 .75
289 Ben Grieve SF .07 .20
290 Travis Lee SF .07 .20
291 Mo Vaughn SF .07 .20
292 Mike Piazza SF .30 .75
293 Roger Clemens SF .30 .75
294 J.D. Drew SF .07 .20
295 Randy Johnson SF .20 .50
296 Chipper Jones SF .20 .50
297 Vladimir Guerrero SF .20 .50
298 Nomar Garciaparra CL .30 .75
299 Ken Griffey Jr. CL .40 1.00
300 Mark McGwire CL .40 1.00
S83 Ben Grieve Sample .40 1.00

1999 SkyBox Premium Star Rubies

*STARS: 40X TO 100X BASIC CARDS
*PROSPECTS 223-272: 40X TO 100X BASIC
*ROOKIES 223-272: 25X TO 60X BASIC RC'S
STATED PRINT RUN 50 SERIAL #'d SETS
SP PRINT RUN 15 SERIAL #'d SETS
RANDOM INSERTS IN PACKS
NO SP PRICING DUE TO SCARCITY

1999 SkyBox Premium Autographics

STATED ODDS 1:68
UNNUMBERED CARDS LISTED IN ALPH.ORDER
1 Roberto Alomar 12.50 30.00
2 Paul Bako 4.00 10.00
3 Michael Barrett 4.00 10.00
4 Kris Benson 6.00 15.00
5 Micah Bowie 4.00 10.00
6 Roosevelt Brown 4.00 10.00
7 A.J. Burnett 4.00 10.00
8 Pat Burrell 10.00 25.00
9 Ken Caminiti 15.00 40.00
10 Royce Clayton 4.00 10.00
11 Edgard Clemente 4.00 10.00
12 Bartolo Colon 6.00 15.00
13 J.D. Drew 6.00 15.00
14 Damion Easley 4.00 10.00
15 Derrin Ebert 4.00 10.00
16 Mario Encarnacion 4.00 10.00
17 Juan Encarnacion 6.00 15.00
18 Troy Glaus 15.00 40.00
19 Tom Glavine 20.00 50.00
20 Juan Gonzalez SP 60.00 120.00
21 Shawn Green 10.00 25.00
22 Wilton Guerrero 4.00 10.00
23 Jose Guillen 6.00 15.00
24 Tony Gwynn 15.00 40.00
25 Mark Harriger 4.00 10.00
26 Todd Hollandsworth 4.00 10.00
27 Scott Hunter 4.00 10.00
28 Gabe Kapler 6.00 15.00
29 Scott Karl 4.00 10.00
30 Mike Kinkade 4.00 10.00
31 Ray Lankford 6.00 15.00
32 Barry Larkin 20.00 50.00
33 Matt Lawton 4.00 10.00
34 Ricky Ledee 4.00 10.00
35 Travis Lee 4.00 10.00
36 Eli Marrero 4.00 10.00
37 Ruben Mateo 4.00 10.00
38 Joe McEwing 4.00 10.00
39 Doug Mientkiewicz 6.00 15.00
40 Russ Ortiz 4.00 10.00
41 Jim Parque 4.00 10.00
42 Robert Person 4.00 10.00
43 Alex Rodriguez 60.00 120.00
44 Scott Rolen 6.00 15.00
45 Benj Sampson 4.00 10.00
46 Luis Saturria 4.00 10.00
47 Curt Schilling 12.00 30.00
48 David Segui 6.00 15.00
49 Fernando Tatis 4.00 10.00
50 Peter Tucci 4.00 10.00
51 Javier Vazquez 6.00 15.00
52 Robin Ventura 6.00 15.00

1999 SkyBox Premium Autographics Blue Ink

*BLUE INK STARS: 1X TO 2.5X BASIC AU'S
*BLUE INK RC's: .75X TO 2X BASIC AU'S
RANDOM INSERTS IN PACKS
BLUE INK PRINT RUN 50 SERIAL #'d SETS
NNO CARDS LISTED IN ALPH.ORDER

1999 SkyBox Premium Diamond Debuts

COMPLETE SET (15) 30.00 80.00
STATED ODDS 1:49
1 Eric Chavez 3.00 8.00
2 Kyle Farnsworth 3.00 8.00
3 Ryan Rupe 3.00 8.00
4 Jeremy Giambi 3.00 8.00
5 Marlon Anderson 3.00 8.00
6 J.D. Drew 3.00 8.00
7 Carlos Febles 3.00 8.00
8 Joe McEwing 3.00 8.00
9 Jeff Weaver 5.00 12.00
10 Alex Gonzalez 2.00 5.00
11 Chad Allen 3.00 8.00
12 Michael Barrett 3.00 8.00
13 Gabe Kapler 3.00 8.00
14 Carlos Lee 3.00 8.00
15 Edwards Guzman 3.00 8.00

1999 SkyBox Premium Intimidation Nation

STATED PRINT RUN 99 SERIAL #'d SETS
1 Cal Ripken 60.00 150.00
2 Tony Gwynn 20.00 50.00
3 Nomar Garciaparra 12.00 30.00
4 Frank Thomas 20.00 50.00
5 Mike Piazza 20.00 50.00
6 Mark McGwire 30.00 80.00
7 Scott Rolen 12.00 30.00
8 Chipper Jones 20.00 50.00
9 Greg Maddux 25.00 60.00
10 Ken Griffey Jr. 40.00 100.00
11 Juan Gonzalez 8.00 20.00
12 Derek Jeter 50.00 125.00
13 J.D. Drew 8.00 20.00
14 Roger Clemens 25.00 60.00
15 Alex Rodriguez 25.00 60.00

1999 SkyBox Premium Live Bats

COMPLETE SET (15) 10.00 25.00
STATED ODDS 1:7
1 Juan Gonzalez .20 .50
2 Mark McGwire 1.25 3.00
3 Jeff Bagwell .30 .75
4 Frank Thomas .50 1.25
5 Mike Piazza .75 2.00
6 Nomar Garciaparra .75 2.00
7 Alex Rodriguez .75 2.00
8 Scott Rolen .30 .75
9 Travis Lee .10 .30
10 Tony Gwynn .60 1.50
11 Derek Jeter 1.25 3.00
12 Ben Grieve .10 .30
13 Chipper Jones .50 1.25
14 Ken Griffey Jr. 1.00 2.50
15 Cal Ripken 1.50 4.00

1999 SkyBox Premium Show Business

COMPLETE SET (15) 12.00 30.00
STATED ODDS 1:70
1 Mark McGwire 2.00 5.00
2 Tony Gwynn 1.25 3.00
3 Nomar Garciaparra .75 2.00
4 Juan Gonzalez .50 1.25
5 Roger Clemens 1.50 4.00
6 Chipper Jones 1.25 3.00
7 Cal Ripken 4.00 10.00
8 Alex Rodriguez 1.50 4.00
9 Orlando Hernandez .50 1.25
10 Greg Maddux 1.50 4.00
11 Mike Piazza 1.25 3.00
12 Frank Thomas 1.25 3.00
13 Ken Griffey Jr. 2.50 6.00
14 Scott Rolen .75 2.00
15 Derek Jeter 3.00 8.00

1999 SkyBox Premium Soul of the Game

COMPLETE SET (15) 25.00 60.00
STATED ODDS 1:14
1 Alex Rodriguez 1.50 4.00
2 Vladimir Guerrero 1.00 2.50
3 Chipper Jones 1.00 2.50
4 Derek Jeter 2.50 6.00
5 Tony Gwynn 1.25 3.00
6 Scott Rolen .60 1.50
7 Juan Gonzalez .40 1.00
8 Mark McGwire 2.50 6.00
9 Ken Griffey Jr. 2.00 5.00
10 Jeff Bagwell .60 1.50
11 Cal Ripken 3.00 8.00
12 Frank Thomas 1.00 2.50
13 Mike Piazza 1.50 4.00
14 Nomar Garciaparra 1.50 4.00
15 Sammy Sosa 1.00 2.50

1999 SkyBox Thunder

The 1999 SkyBox Thunder set was issued in one series totalling 300 cards. The set was distributed in eight-card packs with a suggested retail price of $1.59. The fronts feature color action player photos with computer-enhanced graphics. The backs carry player information. The regular player cards (1-140) have an insertion rate of four or five per pack. Veteran stars (141-240) come two per pack. Superstars (241-300) are seeded 1:1. A sample card featuring Ben Grieve was distributed to dealers and hobby media several weeks prior to the product shipping. The card can be easily distinguished by the text "Promotional Sample" running diagonally across the front and back.

COMPLETE SET (300) 15.00 40.00
COMMON CARD (1-140) .07 .20
1-140 FOUR TO FIVE PER PACK
COMMON CARD (141-240) .10 .30
141-240 TWO PER PACK
COMMON CARD (241-300) .15 .40
241-300 ONE PER PACK
1 John Smoltz .10 .30
2 Garret Anderson .07 .20
3 Matt Williams .07 .20
4 Daryle Ward .07 .20
5 Andy Ashby .07 .20
6 Miguel Tejada .07 .20
7 Dmitri Young .07 .20
8 Roberto Alomar .10 .30
9 Kevin Brown .10 .30
10 Eric Young .07 .20
11 Odalis Perez .07 .20
12 Preston Wilson .07 .20
13 Jeff Abbott .07 .20
14 Bret Boone .07 .20
15 Mendy Lopez .07 .20
16 B.J. Surhoff .07 .20
17 Steve Woodard .07 .20
18 Ron Coomer .07 .20
19 Rondell White .07 .20
20 Edgardo Alfonzo .07 .20
21 Kevin Millwood .07 .20
22 Jose Canseco .10 .30
23 Blake Stein .07 .20
24 Quilvio Veras .07 .20
25 Chuck Knoblauch .07 .20
26 David Segui .07 .20
27 Eric Davis .07 .20
28 Francisco Cordova .07 .20
29 Randy Winn .07 .20
30 Will Clark .10 .30
31 Billy Wagner .07 .20
32 Kevin Witt .07 .20
33 Jim Edmonds .07 .20
34 Todd Stottlemyre .07 .20
35 Shane Andrews .07 .20
36 Michael Tucker .07 .20
37 Sandy Alomar Jr. .07 .20
38 Neifi Perez .07 .20
39 Jaret Wright .07 .20
40 Devon White .07 .20
41 Edgar Renteria .07 .20
42 Shane Reynolds .07 .20
43 Jeff King .07 .20
44 Darren Dreifort .07 .20
45 Fernando Vina .07 .20
46 Marty Cordova .07 .20
47 Ugueth Urbina .07 .20
48 Bobby Bonilla .07 .20
49 Omar Vizquel .10 .30
50 Tom Gordon .07 .20
51 Ryan Christenson .07 .20
52 Aaron Boone .07 .20
53 Jamie Moyer .07 .20
54 Brian Giles .07 .20
55 Kevin Tapani .07 .20
56 Scott Brosius .07 .20
57 Ellis Burks .07 .20
58 Al Leiter .07 .20
59 Royce Clayton .07 .20
60 Chris Carpenter .07 .20
61 Bubba Trammell .07 .20
62 Tom Glavine .10 .30
63 Shannon Stewart .07 .20
64 Todd Zeile .07 .20
65 J.T. Snow .07 .20
66 Matt Clement .07 .20
67 Matt Stairs .07 .20
68 Ismael Valdes .07 .20
69 Todd Walker .07 .20
70 Jose Lima .07 .20
71 Mike Caruso .07 .20
72 Brett Tomko .07 .20
73 Mike Lansing .07 .20
74 Justin Thompson .07 .20
75 Damion Easley .07 .20
76 Derrek Lee .10 .30
77 Derek Bell .07 .20
78 Brady Anderson .07 .20
79 Charles Johnson .07 .20
80 Rafael Roque RC .07 .20
81 Corey Koskie .07 .20
82 Fernando Seguignol .07 .20
83 Jay Tessmer .07 .20
84 Jason Giambi .07 .20
85 Mike Lieberthal .07 .20
86 Jose Guillen .07 .20
87 Jim Leyritz .07 .20
88 Shawn Estes .07 .20
89 Ray Lankford .07 .20
90 Paul Sorrento .07 .20
91 Javy Lopez .07 .20
92 John Wetteland .07 .20
93 Sean Casey .07 .20
94 Chuck Finley .07 .20
95 Trot Nixon .07 .20
96 Ray Durham .07 .20
97 Reggie Sanders .07 .20
98 Bartolo Colon .07 .20
99 Henry Rodriguez .07 .20
100 Rolando Arrojo .07 .20
101 Geoff Jenkins .07 .20
102 Darryl Kile .07 .20
103 Mark Kotsay .07 .20
104 Craig Biggio .10 .30
105 Omar Daal .07 .20
106 Carlos Febles .07 .20
107 Eric Karros .07 .20
108 Matt Lawton .07 .20
109 Carl Pavano .07 .20
110 Brian McRae .07 .20
111 Mariano Rivera .20 .50
112 Jay Buhner .07 .20
113 Doug Glanville .07 .20
114 Jason Kendall .07 .20
115 Wally Joyner .07 .20
116 Jeff Kent .07 .20
117 Shane Monahan .07 .20
118 Eli Marrero .07 .20
119 Bobby Smith .07 .20
120 Shawn Green .07 .20
121 Kirk Rueter .07 .20
122 Tom Goodwin .07 .20
123 Andy Benes .07 .20
124 Ed Sprague .07 .20
125 Mike Mussina .10 .30
126 Jose Offerman .07 .20
127 Mickey Morandini .07 .20
128 Paul Konerko .07 .20
129 Denny Neagle .07 .20
130 Travis Fryman .07 .20
131 John Rocker .07 .20
132 Robert Fick .07 .20
133 Livan Hernandez .07 .20
134 Ken Caminiti .07 .20
135 Johnny Damon .10 .30
136 Jeff Kubenka .07 .20
137 Marquis Grissom .07 .20
138 Doug Mientkiewicz RC .10 .30
139 Dustin Hermanson .07 .20
140 Carl Everett .07 .20
141 Hideo Nomo .30 .75
142 Jorge Posada .20 .50
143 Rickey Henderson .30 .75
144 Robb Nen .10 .30
145 Ron Gant .10 .30
146 Aramis Ramirez .10 .30
147 Trevor Hoffman .10 .30
148 Bill Mueller .10 .30
149 Edgar Martinez .20 .50
150 Fred McGriff .20 .50
151 Rusty Greer .10 .30
152 Tom Evans .10 .30
153 Todd Greene .10 .30
154 Jay Bell .10 .30
155 Mike Lowell .10 .30
156 Orlando Cabrera .10 .30
157 Troy O'Leary .10 .30
158 Jose Hernandez .10 .30
159 Magglio Ordonez .10 .30
160 Barry Larkin .20 .50
161 David Justice .10 .30
162 Derrick Gibson .10 .30
163 Luis Gonzalez .10 .30
164 Alex Gonzalez .10 .30
165 Scott Elarton .10 .30
166 Dermal Brown .10 .30
167 Eric Milton .10 .30
168 Raul Mondesi .10 .30
169 Jeff Cirillo .10 .30
170 Benj Sampson .10 .30
171 John Olerud .10 .30
172 Andy Pettitte .20 .50
173 A.J. Hinch .10 .30
174 Rico Brogna .10 .30
175 Jason Schmidt .10 .30
176 Dean Palmer .10 .30
177 Matt Morris .10 .30
178 Quinton McCracken .10 .30
179 Rick Helling .10 .30
180 Walt Weiss .10 .30
181 Troy Percival .10 .30
182 Tony Batista .10 .30
183 Brian Jordan .10 .30
184 Jerry Hairston Jr. .10 .30
185 Bret Saberhagen .10 .30
186 Mark Grace .20 .50
187 Brian Simmons .10 .30
188 Pete Harnisch .10 .30
189 Kenny Lofton .10 .30
190 Vinny Castilla .10 .30
191 Bobby Higginson .10 .30
192 Joey Hamilton .10 .30
193 Cliff Floyd .10 .30
194 Andres Galarraga .10 .30
195 Chan Ho Park .10 .30
196 Jeromy Burnitz .10 .30
197 David Ortiz .40 1.00
198 Wilton Guerrero .10 .30
199 Rey Ordonez .10 .30
200 Paul O'Neill .20 .50
201 Kenny Rogers .10 .30
202 Marlon Anderson .10 .30
203 Tony Womack .10 .30
204 Robin Ventura .10 .30
205 Russ Ortiz .10 .30
206 Mike Frank .10 .30
207 Fernando Tatis .10 .30
208 Miguel Cairo .10 .30
209 Ivan Rodriguez .20 .50
210 Carlos Delgado .10 .30
211 Tim Salmon .20 .50
212 Brian Anderson .10 .30
213 Ryan Klesko .10 .30
214 Scott Erickson .10 .30
215 Mike Stanley .10 .30
216 Brant Brown .10 .30
217 Rod Beck .10 .30
218 Guillermo Garcia RC .10 .30
219 David Wells .10 .30
220 Dante Bichette .10 .30
221 Armando Benitez .10 .30
222 Todd Dunwoody .10 .30
223 Kelvim Escobar .10 .30
224 Richard Hidalgo .10 .30
225 Angel Pena .10 .30
226 Ronnie Belliard .10 .30
227 Brad Radke .10 .30
228 Brad Fullmer .10 .30
229 Jay Payton .10 .30
230 Tino Martinez .20 .50
231 Scott Spiezio .10 .30
232 Bob Abreu .10 .30
233 John Valentin .10 .30
234 Kevin Young .10 .30
235 Steve Finley .10 .30
236 David Cone .10 .30
237 Armando Rios .10 .30
238 Russ Davis .10 .30
239 Wade Boggs .20 .50
240 Aaron Sele .10 .30
241 Jose Cruz Jr. .15 .40
242 George Lombard .15 .40
243 Todd Helton .25 .60
244 Andruw Jones .25 .60
245 Troy Glaus .25 .60
246 Manny Ramirez .25 .60
247 Ben Grieve .15 .40

248 Richie Sexson	.15	.40
249 Juan Encarnacion	.15	.40
250 Randy Johnson	.40	1.00
251 Gary Sheffield	.15	.40
252 Rafael Palmeiro	.25	.60
253 Roy Halladay	.40	1.00
254 Mike Piazza	.60	1.50
255 Tony Gwynn	.50	1.25
256 Juan Gonzalez	.15	.40
257 Jeremy Giambi	.15	.40
258 Ben Davis	.15	.40
259 Russ Branyan	.15	.40
260 Pedro Martinez	.25	.60
261 Frank Thomas	.40	1.00
262 Calvin Pickering	.15	.40
263 Chipper Jones	.40	1.00
264 Ryan Minor	.15	.40
265 Roger Clemens	.75	2.00
266 Sammy Sosa	.40	1.00
267 Mo Vaughn	.15	.40
268 Carlos Beltran	.25	.60
269 Jim Thome	.25	.60
270 Mark McGwire	1.00	2.50
271 Travis Lee	.15	.40
272 Darin Erstad	.15	.40
273 Derek Jeter	1.00	2.50
274 Greg Maddux	.60	1.50
275 Ricky Ledee	.15	.40
276 Alex Rodriguez	.60	1.50
277 Vladimir Guerrero	.40	1.00
278 Greg Vaughn	.15	.40
279 Scott Rolen	.25	.60
280 Carlos Guillen	.15	.40
281 Jeff Bagwell	.25	.60
282 Bruce Chen	.15	.40
283 Tony Clark	.15	.40
284 Albert Belle	.15	.40
285 Cal Ripken	1.25	3.00
286 Barry Bonds	1.00	2.50
287 Curt Schilling	.15	.40
288 Eric Chavez	.15	.40
289 Larry Walker	.15	.40
290 Orlando Hernandez	.15	.40
291 Moises Alou	.15	.40
292 Ken Griffey Jr.	.75	2.00
293 Kerry Wood	.15	.40
294 Nomar Garciaparra	.60	1.50
295 Gabe Kapler	.15	.40
296 Bernie Williams	.25	.60
297 Matt Anderson	.15	.40
298 Adrian Beltre	.15	.40
299 J.D. Drew	.15	.40
300 Ryan Bradley	.15	.40
S247 Ben Grieve Sample	.40	1.00

1999 SkyBox Thunder Rant

*RANT 1-140: 4X TO 10X BASIC 1-140
*RANT 141-240: 2.5X TO 6X BASIC 141-240
*RANT 241-300: 2X TO 5X BASIC 241-300
STATED ODDS 1:2 RETAIL

1999 SkyBox Thunder Rave

*RAVE 1-140: 15X TO 40X BASIC 1-140
*RAVE 141-240: 10X TO 25X BASIC 141-240
*RAVE 241-300: 8X TO 20X BASIC 241-300
RANDOM INSERTS IN HOBBY PACKS
STATED PRINT RUN 150 SERIAL #'d SETS

273 Derek Jeter	75.00	150.00

1999 SkyBox Thunder Super Rave

*S.RAVE 1-140: 30X TO 80X BASIC
*S.RAVE 141-240: 20X TO 50X BASIC
*S.RAVE 241-300: 15X TO 40X BASIC
RANDOM INSERTS IN HOBBY PACKS
STATED PRINT RUN 25 SERIAL #'d SETS
NO RC PRICING DUE TO SCARCITY

1999 SkyBox Thunder Dial 1

COMPLETE SET (10)	100.00	200.00
STATED ODDS 1:300		
D1 Nomar Garciaparra	10.00	25.00
D2 Juan Gonzalez	2.50	6.00
D3 Ken Griffey Jr.	12.50	30.00
D4 Chipper Jones	6.00	15.00
D5 Mark McGwire	15.00	40.00
D6 Mike Piazza	10.00	25.00
D7 Manny Ramirez	4.00	10.00
D8 Alex Rodriguez	10.00	25.00
D9 Sammy Sosa	6.00	15.00
D10 Mo Vaughn	2.50	6.00

1999 SkyBox Thunder Hip-No-Tized

COMPLETE SET (15)	40.00	100.00
STATED ODDS 1:36		
H1 J.D. Drew	.60	1.50
H2 Nomar Garciaparra	2.50	6.00
H3 Juan Gonzalez	.60	1.50
H4 Ken Griffey Jr.	3.00	8.00
H5 Derek Jeter	4.00	10.00
H6 Randy Johnson	1.50	4.00
H7 Chipper Jones	1.50	4.00
H8 Mark McGwire	4.00	10.00
H9 Mike Piazza	2.50	6.00
H10 Cal Ripken	5.00	12.00
H11 Alex Rodriguez	2.50	6.00
H12 Sammy Sosa	1.50	4.00
H13 Frank Thomas	1.50	4.00
H14 Jim Thome	1.00	2.50
H15 Kerry Wood	.60	1.50

1999 SkyBox Thunder In Depth

COMPLETE SET (10)	12.50	30.00
STATED ODDS 1:24		
ID1 Albert Belle	.40	1.00
ID2 Barry Bonds	2.50	6.00
ID3 Roger Clemens	2.00	5.00
ID4 Juan Gonzalez	.40	1.00
ID5 Ken Griffey Jr.	2.00	5.00
ID6 Mark McGwire	2.50	6.00
ID7 Mike Piazza	1.50	4.00
ID8 Sammy Sosa	1.00	2.50
ID9 Mo Vaughn	.40	1.00
ID10 Kerry Wood	.40	1.00

1999 SkyBox Thunder Turbo-Charged

COMPLETE SET (10)	25.00	60.00
STATED ODDS 1:72		
TC1 Jose Canseco	.60	1.50
TC2 Juan Gonzalez	.75	2.00
TC3 Ken Griffey Jr.	4.00	10.00
TC4 Vladimir Guerrero	2.00	5.00
TC5 Mark McGwire	5.00	12.00
TC6 Mike Piazza	3.00	8.00
TC7 Manny Ramirez	1.25	3.00
TC8 Alex Rodriguez	3.00	8.00
TC9 Sammy Sosa	2.00	5.00
TC10 Mo Vaughn	.75	2.00

1999 SkyBox Thunder Unleashed

COMPLETE SET (15)	6.00	15.00
STATED ODDS 1:6		
U1 Carlos Beltran	.60	1.50
U2 Adrian Beltre	.40	1.00
U3 Eric Chavez	.40	1.00
U4 J.D. Drew	.40	1.00
U5 Juan Encarnacion	.40	1.00
U6 Jeremy Giambi	.40	1.00
U7 Troy Glaus	.60	1.50
U8 Ben Grieve	.40	1.00
U9 Todd Helton	.60	1.50
U10 Orlando Hernandez	.40	1.00
U11 Gabe Kapler	.40	1.00
U12 Travis Lee	.40	1.00
U13 Calvin Pickering	.40	1.00
U14 Richie Sexson	.40	1.00
U15 Kerry Wood	.40	1.00

1999 SkyBox Thunder www.batterz.com

COMPLETE SET (10)	12.50	30.00
STATED ODDS 1:18		
WB1 J.D. Drew	.30	.75
WB2 Nomar Garciaparra	1.25	3.00
WB3 Ken Griffey Jr.	1.50	4.00
WB4 Tony Gwynn	1.00	2.50
WB5 Derek Jeter	2.00	5.00
WB6 Mark McGwire	2.00	5.00
WB7 Alex Rodriguez	1.25	3.00
WB8 Scott Rolen	.50	1.25
WB9 Sammy Sosa	.75	2.00
WB10 Bernie Williams	.50	1.25

1988 SLU Baseball

This 124-piece set was issued by Cincinnati-based Kenner Toy Company. The statues feature top Major League Baseball stars in action poses and are accompanied by a standard-size card of each player. The card front has either a posed or action color shot. The back has biographical and statistical information along with a facsimile signature. This was the first set produced under the Starting Lineup brand. The four modes of distribution for the '88 Baseball set were regionally issued team cases (24 pieces), nationally distributed All-Star cases (24 pieces), via a 1-800 number that offered team sets and complete sets, and through the J.C. Penney and Sears catalogs. The retail catalogs offered 72 of the figures in 36 different 2-player combinations. Each player was teamed with another player from their respective team. The Montreal Expos and Toronto Blue Jays were the only teams not to offer 2 player hook-ups due to Tim Raines and George Bell being each of the Canadian teams sole representative in the set. There were two Nationally distributed All-Star cases, an American League and a National League. The American League case consisted of the following 11 players: George Bell, Wade Boggs, George Brett, Roger Clemens, Rickey Henderson, Wally Joyner, Don Mattingly, Eddie Murray, Kirby Puckett, Alan Trammell and Dave Winfield. The 13 players featured in the National League case were Gary Carter, Eric Davis, Andre Dawson, Dwight Gooden, Pedro Guerrero, Tony Gwynn, Dale Murphy, Tim Raines, Mike Schmidt, Mike Scott, Ozzie Smith, Darryl Strawberry and Fernando Valenzuela. Each package that the figure came in also was issued in two variations, one with and one without the All-Star baseball offer. This offer was part of the front of the packaging. This ad wasn't a sticker; it was a part of the cardboard. The offer that appeared in a yellow starburst type ad right where the cardboard turns into the blue area was for a facsimile autographed baseball of all 24 of the nationally issued All-Star players. The baseball has a current retail value of $15-$35 but was available in 1988 for only five proofs of purchase and $3.99. Some of the key figures in the set include Barry Bonds, Cal Ripken and Nolan Ryan. The values listed below refer to unopened packages. The figures are unnumbered and checklisted below in alphabetical order.

BLUE SHOWCASE	25.00	45.00
BLUE DISP.STAND	40.00	70.00
SEND-OFF AU.BB	25.00	40.00
1988-90 PRICES NM IN PACKAGE		
1 Alan Ashby	8.00	20.00
2 Harold Baines	6.00	15.00
3 Kevin Bass	6.00	15.00
4 Steve Bedrosian	6.00	15.00
5 Buddy Bell	8.00	20.00
6 George Bell	6.00	15.00
7 Mike Boddicker	15.00	25.00
8 Wade Boggs	8.00	20.00
9 Barry Bonds	40.00	100.00
10 Bobby Bonilla	6.00	15.00
11 Sid Bream	6.00	15.00
12 George Brett	15.00	40.00
13 Chris Brown	6.00	15.00
14 Tom Brunansky	10.00	25.00
15 Ellis Burks	8.00	20.00
16 Jose Canseco	12.00	30.00
17 Gary Carter	8.00	20.00
18 Joe Carter	10.00	25.00
19 Jack Clark	8.00	20.00
20 Will Clark	8.00	20.00
21 Roger Clemens	15.00	40.00
22 Vince Coleman	6.00	15.00
23 Kal Daniels	6.00	15.00
24 Alvin Davis	6.00	15.00
25 Eric Davis	6.00	15.00
26 Glenn Davis	6.00	15.00
27 Jody Davis	10.00	25.00
28 Andre Dawson	8.00	20.00
29 Rob Deer	6.00	15.00
30 Brian Downing	8.00	20.00
31 Mike Dunne	6.00	15.00
32 Shawon Dunston	8.00	20.00
33 Leon Durham	6.00	15.00
34 Lenny Dykstra	8.00	20.00
35 Dwight Evans	8.00	20.00
36 Carlton Fisk	15.00	40.00
37 John Franco	6.00	15.00
38 Julio Franco	6.00	15.00
39 Gary Gaetti	10.00	20.00
40 Dwight Gooden	8.00	20.00
41 Ken Griffey Sr.	12.00	30.00
42 Pedro Guerrero	6.00	15.00
43 Ozzie Guillen	6.00	15.00
44 Tony Gwynn	30.00	80.00
45 Mel Hall	6.00	15.00
46 Billy Hatcher	12.00	30.00
47 Von Hayes	8.00	20.00
48 Rickey Henderson	12.00	30.00
49 Keith Hernandez	6.00	15.00
50 Willie Hernandez	6.00	15.00
51 Tom Herr	6.00	15.00
52 Ted Higuera	6.00	15.00
53 Charlie Hough	6.00	15.00
54 Kent Hrbek	8.00	20.00
55 Pete Incaviglia	6.00	15.00
56 Howard Johnson	8.00	20.00
57 Wally Joyner	6.00	15.00
58 Terry Kennedy	6.00	15.00
59 John Kruk	10.00	25.00
60 Mark Langston	10.00	25.00
61 Carney Lansford	8.00	20.00
62 Jeffrey Leonard	6.00	15.00
63 Fred Lynn	12.00	30.00
64 Candy Maldonado	6.00	15.00
65 Mike Marshall	6.00	15.00
66 Don Mattingly	10.00	25.00
67 Willie McGee	8.00	20.00
68 Mark McGwire	30.00	80.00
69 Kevin McReynolds	8.00	20.00
70 Paul Molitor	20.00	50.00
71 Donnie Moore	10.00	25.00
72 Jack Morris	8.00	20.00
73 Dale Murphy	10.00	25.00
74 Eddie Murray	25.00	60.00
75 Matt Nokes	6.00	15.00
76 Pete O'Brien	6.00	15.00
77 Ken Oberkfell	6.00	15.00
78 Dave Parker	10.00	25.00
79 Larry Parrish	6.00	15.00
80 Ken Phelps	6.00	15.00
81 Jim Presley	6.00	15.00
82 Kirby Puckett	15.00	40.00
83 Dan Quisenberry	8.00	20.00
84 Tim Raines	6.00	15.00
85 Willie Randolph	8.00	20.00
86 Shane Rawley	6.00	15.00
87 Jeff Reardon	10.00	25.00
88 Gary Redus	6.00	15.00
89 Rick Reuschel	6.00	15.00
90 Jim Rice	8.00	20.00
91 Dave Righetti	10.00	25.00
92 Cal Ripken	40.00	100.00
93 Pete Rose	10.00	25.00
94 Nolan Ryan	40.00	100.00
95 Bret Saberhagen	6.00	15.00
96 Juan Samuel	6.00	15.00
97 Ryne Sandberg	20.00	50.00
98 Benito Santiago	6.00	15.00
99 Steve Sax	6.00	15.00
100 Mike Schmidt	20.00	50.00
101 Mike Scott	6.00	15.00
102 Kevin Seitzer	6.00	15.00
103 Ruben Sierra	6.00	15.00
104 Ozzie Smith	15.00	40.00
105 Zane Smith	6.00	15.00
106 Cory Snyder	6.00	15.00
107 Darryl Strawberry	8.00	20.00
108 Franklin Stubbs	6.00	15.00
109 B.J. Surhoff	10.00	25.00
110 Rick Sutcliffe	8.00	20.00
111 Pat Tabler	6.00	15.00
112 Danny Tartabull	6.00	15.00
113 Alan Trammell	8.00	20.00
114 Fernando Valenzuela	6.00	15.00
115 Andy Van Slyke	10.00	25.00
116 Frank Viola	8.00	20.00
117 Ozzie Virgil	6.00	15.00
118 Greg Walker	6.00	15.00
119 Lou Whitaker	10.00	25.00
120 Devon White	10.00	25.00
121 Dave Winfield	12.00	30.00
122 Mike Witt	6.00	15.00
123 Todd Worrell	6.00	15.00
124 Robin Yount	15.00	40.00

1989 SLU Baseball

This 168-piece set was issued by Cincinnati-based Kenner Toy Company. The statues feature top Major League Baseball stars in action poses and are accompanied by a standard-size card of each player. The front of each card has either a posed or action color shot. The back has biographical and statistical information and a facsimile signature. At 168 pieces, this is the largest set issued under the Starting Lineup brand. The three modes of distribution for these figures were regionally issued team cases (24 pieces), nationally distributed All-Star cases (24 pieces) and a 1-800 number. The 1-800 number was through a fulfillment house in conjunction with Kenner and offered team sets and complete sets. The regionally issued team cases were 24 count but each player in the team case was not equally distributed. This caused some figures to be shorter than others. The 24 count All-Star cases were divided into American League and National League. The 14 American League players in the 24-piece AL cases were George Bell, Wade Boggs, Jose Canseco, Roger Clemens, Mike Greenwell, Rickey Henderson, Wally Joyner, Don Mattingly, Mark McGwire, Paul Molitor, Kirby Puckett, Alan Trammell, Frank Viola and Dave Winfield. The 13 National League players that were featured in the 24-piece NL cases were Bobby Bonilla, Will Clark, Vince Coleman, Eric Davis, Andre Dawson, Kirk Gibson, Dwight Gooden, Dale Murphy, Tim Raines, Ryne Sandberg, Mike Scott, Ozzie Smith and Darryl Strawberry. The key first appearances include Roberto Alomar, Ron Gant, and Greg Maddux. The figures of the California Angels team, except for Wally Joyner, are the toughest pieces to find. The values listed below refer to unopened packages. The figures are unnumbered and checklisted below in alphabetical order.

DISPLAY w/14 FIG.	160.00	275.00
1 Roberto Alomar FP	75.00	200.00
2 Brady Anderson FP	50.00	120.00
3 Harold Baines	12.00	30.00
4 Marty Barrett FP	6.00	15.00
5 Kevin Bass	6.00	15.00
6 Steve Bedrosian	6.00	15.00
7 George Bell	6.00	15.00
8 Damon Berryhill FP	6.00	15.00
9 Wade Boggs	6.00	15.00
10 Barry Bonds	30.00	80.00
11 Bobby Bonilla	6.00	15.00
12 Phil Bradley FP	8.00	20.00
13 Glenn Braggs FP	8.00	20.00
14 Mickey Brantley FP	10.00	25.00
15 George Brett	15.00	40.00
16 Tom Brookens FP	10.00	25.00
17 Tom Brunansky	6.00	15.00
18 Steve Buechele FP	10.00	25.00
19 Ellis Burks	6.00	15.00
20 Brett Butler FP	8.00	20.00
21 Ivan Calderon FP	6.00	15.00
22 Jose Canseco	10.00	25.00
23 Gary Carter	8.00	20.00
24 Joe Carter	6.00	15.00
25 Will Clark	8.00	20.00
26 Roger Clemens	10.00	25.00
27 Vince Coleman	6.00	15.00
28 David Cone FP	15.00	40.00
29 Kal Daniels	6.00	15.00
30 Alvin Davis	6.00	15.00
31 Chili Davis FP	40.00	100.00
32 Eric Davis	6.00	15.00
33 Glenn Davis	6.00	15.00
34 Mark Davis FP	12.00	30.00
35 Andre Dawson	10.00	25.00
36 Rob Deer	8.00	20.00
37 Bo Diaz FP	12.00	30.00
38 Bill Doran FP	8.00	20.00
39 Doug Drabek FP	10.00	25.00
40 Shawon Dunston	10.00	25.00
41 Lenny Dykstra	10.00	25.00
42 Dennis Eckersley FP	25.00	60.00
43 Kevin Elster FP	6.00	15.00
44 Scott Fletcher FP	30.00	80.00
45 John Franco	10.00	25.00
46 Gary Gaetti	8.00	20.00
47 Ron Gant FP	60.00	150.00
48 Kirk Gibson FP	10.00	25.00
49 Dan Gladden FP	8.00	20.00
50 Dwight Gooden	6.00	15.00
51 Mark Grace FP	10.00	25.00
52 Mike Greenwell FP	6.00	15.00
53 Mark Gubicza FP	6.00	15.00
54 Pedro Guerrero	6.00	15.00
55 Ozzie Guillen	10.00	25.00
56 Tony Gwynn	125.00	300.00
57 Albert Hall FP	8.00	20.00
58 Mel Hall	6.00	15.00
59 Billy Hatcher	8.00	20.00
60 Von Hayes	6.00	15.00
61 Rickey Henderson	8.00	20.00
62 Mike Henneman FP	6.00	15.00
63 Keith Hernandez	6.00	15.00
64 Orel Hershiser FP	12.00	30.00
65 Ted Higuera	15.00	40.00
66 Jack Howell FP	30.00	80.00
67 Kent Hrbek	10.00	25.00
68 Pete Incaviglia	6.00	15.00
69 Bo Jackson FP	10.00	25.00
70 Danny Jackson FP	10.00	25.00
71 Brook Jacoby FP	8.00	20.00
72 Chris James FP	6.00	15.00
73 Dion James FP	10.00	25.00
74 Gregg Jefferies FP	10.00	25.00
75 Doug Jones FP	6.00	15.00
76 Wally Joyner	6.00	15.00
77 John Kruk	12.00	30.00
78 Mark Langston	8.00	20.00
79 Carney Lansford	8.00	20.00
80 Barry Larkin FP	15.00	40.00
81 Tim Laudner FP	12.00	30.00
82 Mike LaValliere FP	10.00	25.00
83 Al Leiter FP	10.00	25.00
84 Chet Lemon FP	6.00	15.00
85 Jose Lind FP	8.00	20.00
86 Greg Maddux FP	60.00	150.00
87 Candy Maldonado	6.00	15.00
88 Mike Marshall	10.00	25.00
89 Don Mattingly	10.00	25.00
90 Willie McGee	10.00	25.00
91 Mark McGwire	30.00	80.00
92 Kevin McReynolds	6.00	15.00
93 Kevin Mitchell FP	6.00	15.00
94 Paul Molitor	15.00	40.00
95 Jack Morris	10.00	25.00
96 Dale Murphy	10.00	25.00
97 Randy Myers FP	6.00	15.00
98 Matt Nokes	6.00	15.00
99 Mike Pagliarulo FP	6.00	15.00
100 Dave Parker	8.00	20.00
101 Dan Pasqua FP	6.00	15.00
102 Tony Pena FP	10.00	25.00
103 Terry Pendleton FP	8.00	20.00
104 Melido Perez FP	12.00	30.00
105 Gerald Perry FP	10.00	25.00
106 Dan Plesac FP	8.00	20.00
107 Kirby Puckett	12.00	30.00
108 Rey Quinones FP	12.00	30.00
109 Tim Raines	6.00	15.00
110 Johnny Ray FP	40.00	100.00
111 Jeff Reardon	12.00	30.00
112 Harold Reynolds FP	12.00	30.00
113 Jim Rice	8.00	20.00
114 Dave Righetti	8.00	20.00
115 Cal Ripken	75.00	200.00
116 Jeff Russell FP	12.00	30.00
117 Bret Saberhagen	8.00	20.00
118 Chris Sabo FP	8.00	20.00
119 Luis Salazar FP	6.00	15.00
120 Juan Samuel	6.00	15.00
121 Ryne Sandberg	15.00	40.00
122 Benito Santiago	8.00	20.00
123 Mike Schmidt	12.00	30.00
124 Dick Schofield FP	40.00	100.00
125 Mike Scioscia FP	50.00	120.00
126 Mike Scott	6.00	15.00
127 Kevin Seitzer	6.00	15.00
128 Larry Sheets FP	10.00	25.00
129 John Shelby FP	12.00	30.00
130 Ruben Sierra	10.00	25.00
131 Don Slaught FP	8.00	20.00
132 Dave Smith FP	8.00	20.00
133 Lee Smith FP	20.00	50.00
134 Ozzie Smith	15.00	40.00
135 Zane Smith	8.00	20.00
136 Cory Snyder	8.00	20.00
137 Pete Stanicek FP	10.00	25.00
138 Terry Steinbach FP	10.00	25.00
139 Dave Stewart FP	10.00	25.00
140 Kurt Stillwell FP	6.00	15.00
141 Darryl Strawberry	6.00	15.00
142 B.J. Surhoff	15.00	40.00
143 Rick Sutcliffe	8.00	20.00
144 Bruce Sutter FP	15.00	40.00
145 Greg Swindell FP	6.00	15.00
146 Pat Tabler	6.00	15.00
147 Danny Tartabull	6.00	15.00
148 Bobby Thigpen FP	12.00	30.00
149 Milt Thompson FP	12.00	30.00
150 Robby Thompson FP	8.00	20.00
151 Alan Trammell	6.00	15.00
152 Jeff Treadway FP	12.00	30.00
153 Jose Uribe FP	6.00	15.00
154 Fernando Valenzuela	8.00	20.00
155 Andy Van Slyke	6.00	15.00
156 Frank Viola	6.00	15.00
157 Bob Walk FP	12.00	30.00
158 Greg Walker	10.00	25.00
159 Walt Weiss FP	10.00	25.00
160 Bob Welch FP	12.00	30.00
161 Lou Whitaker	12.00	30.00
162 Devon White	40.00	100.00
163 Dave Winfield	12.00	30.00
164 Mike Witt	30.00	80.00
165 Todd Worrell	6.00	15.00
166 Marvell Wynne FP	12.00	30.00
167 Gerald Young FP	10.00	25.00
168 Robin Yount	25.00	60.00

1989 SLU Baseball Greats

This 10-piece set was issued by Cincinnati-based Kenner Toy Company. There are two legendary Major League Baseball players per package along with a collectors card for each player. The fronts of the cards feature an action or posed shot. The backs of the carfeature biographical and statistical information. The packages usually feature two of the greatest players from a particular organization. The only piece that doesn't is the Hank Aaron and Carl Yastrzemski package. There are also three variations of the Babe Ruth/Lou Gehrig piece. The common version has Ruth in a gray uniform and Gehrig in a white uniform. The second version has the uniform colors reversed and the third version has both wearing a white uniform. The third version is the scarest. The complete set price only reflects the common version. The pieces came in 2 different 12-piece case assortments. The values listed below refer to unopened packages. The cards and figures are unnumbered and checklisted below.

SET ONLY INC.RUTH/GEHRIG G/W VER.		
1 J.Bench/P.Rose	10.00	25.00
2 Drysdale/R.Jackson	10.00	25.00
3 M.Mantle/DiMaggio	15.00	40.00
4 E.Mathews/H.Aaron	10.00	25.00
5 W.Mays/W.McCovey	10.00	25.00
6 S.Musial/B.Gibson	15.00	40.00
7A Ruth/Gehrig G/W	15.00	40.00
7B Ruth/Gehrig W/G	20.00	50.00
7C Ruth/Gehrig W/W	20.00	50.00
8 Stargell/R.Clemente	12.00	30.00
9 B.Williams/E.Banks	10.00	25.00
10 C.Yaz/H.Aaron	15.00	40.00

1990 SLU Baseball

This 85-piece set was issued by Cincinnati-based Kenner Toy Company. The statues feature top Major League Baseball stars in action poses and are accompanied by two cards. There is a regular card which features a posed or action color shot on front. The back has biographical and statistical information along with a facsimile signature. The second card is titled a "Rookie" card. The front has an action or posed shot along with a banner in the upper part that has the "Rookie Year" for that particular player. The back features biographical information. Figures were distributed through regionally issued team cases (16 pieces), nationally issued All-Star cases (24 pieces), via a 1-800 number and through extended series cases (24 pieces). This was the last year that the baseball series had the distribution through the regional team cases. The All-Star cases were divided into American and National League. The 15 players included in the American League All-Star cases were Wade Boggs, Jose Canseco, Roger Clemens, Mike Greenwell, Ken Griffey Jr. (Sliding), Rickey Henderson, Bo Jackson, Don Mattingly (Bat in Hand), Fred McGriff, Mark McGwire, Paul Molitor, Kirby Puckett, Cal Ripken, Nolan Ryan and Steve Sax. The 16 players included in the National League cases were Will Clark (Batting), Vince Coleman, Eric Davis, Andre Dawson, Andres Galarraga, Kirk Gibson, Dwight Gooden, Mark Grace (Batting), Orel Hershiser, Gregg Jefferies, Kevin Mitchell, Chris Sabo, Ryne Sandberg, Mike Scott, Ozzie Smith and Darryl Strawberry (Batting). This was also the first year of the Extend series release. The key first pieces are both of the Ken Griffey Jr. poses, one of which appears in the extended series. The most valuable, Greg Maddux was available only in Chicago regional cases and is tougher to find than his 1989 figure. The values listed below refer to unopened packages. The figures are unnumbered and checklisted below in alphabetical order.

3 Allan Anderson FP	6.00	15.00
4 Wally Backman FP	6.00	15.00
5 Jeff Ballard FP	6.00	15.00
6 Jesse Barfield FP	6.00	15.00
7 Steve Bedrosian	6.00	15.00
8 Todd Benzinger FP	6.00	15.00
9 Damon Berryhill	6.00	15.00
10 Wade Boggs	8.00	20.00
11 Barry Bonds	25.00	60.00
12 Bobby Bonilla	6.00	15.00
13 Chris Bosio FP	8.00	20.00
14 Ellis Burks	6.00	15.00
15 Jose Canseco	6.00	15.00
17 Will Clark Batting	6.00	15.00
18 Will Clark Power	6.00	15.00
19 Roger Clemens	8.00	20.00
20 Vince Coleman	6.00	15.00
21 Ron Darling FP	8.00	20.00
22 Eric Davis	6.00	15.00
23 Andre Dawson	8.00	20.00
24 Rob Dibble FP	10.00	25.00
25 Lenny Dykstra	8.00	20.00
26 Dennis Eckersley	15.00	40.00
27 Nick Esasky FP	10.00	25.00
28 Gary Gaetti	6.00	15.00
29 Andres Galarraga FP	10.00	25.00
30 Kirk Gibson	6.00	15.00
31 Dwight Gooden	6.00	15.00
32 Mark Grace Batting	8.00	20.00
33 Mark Grace Power	8.00	20.00
34 Mike Greenwell	6.00	15.00
35 Ken Griffey Jr. Slide FP	30.00	80.00
37 Pedro Guerrero	6.00	15.00
38 Von Hayes FP	6.00	15.00
39 Dave Henderson FP	6.00	15.00
40 Rickey Henderson	6.00	15.00
41 Tom Herr	6.00	15.00
42 Orel Hershiser	8.00	20.00
43 Kent Hrbek	6.00	15.00
45 Gregg Jefferies	6.00	15.00
46 Howard Johnson	6.00	15.00
47 Ricky Jordan FP	6.00	15.00
48 Roberto Kelly FP	6.00	15.00
49 Barry Larkin	10.00	25.00
50 Greg Maddux	100.00	250.00
51 Joe Magrane FP	6.00	15.00
52 Don Mattingly Batting	8.00	20.00
53 Don Mattingly Power	8.00	20.00
55 Fred McGriff FP	15.00	40.00
56 Mark McGwire	20.00	50.00
57 Kevin McReynolds	6.00	15.00
58 Kevin Mitchell	6.00	15.00
59 Paul Molitor	12.00	30.00
60 Eddie Murray	30.00	80.00
61 Matt Nokes	6.00	15.00
62 Paul O'Neill FP	20.00	50.00
63 Jose Oquendo FP	8.00	20.00
64 Gary Pettis FP	12.00	30.00
65 Kirby Puckett	10.00	25.00
66 Willie Randolph	6.00	15.00
67 Jody Reed FP	6.00	15.00
68 Rick Reuschel	6.00	15.00
69 Dave Righetti	6.00	15.00
70 Cal Ripken	30.00	80.00
71 Nolan Ryan	15.00	40.00
72 Chris Sabo	6.00	15.00
73 Juan Samuel	6.00	15.00
74 Ryne Sandberg	10.00	25.00
75 Steve Sax	6.00	15.00
76 Mike Scott	6.00	15.00
77 Gary Sheffield FP	12.00	30.00
78 John Smiley FP	6.00	15.00
79 Ozzie Smith	10.00	25.00
80 Dave Stewart	6.00	15.00
81 Darryl Strawberry Batting	6.00	15.00
82 Darryl Strawberry Field	6.00	15.00
83 Rick Sutcliffe	6.00	15.00
84 Mickey Tettleton FP	8.00	20.00
85 Alan Trammell	6.00	15.00
86 Andy Van Slyke	6.00	15.00
87 Frank Viola	6.00	15.00
89 Lou Whitaker	6.00	15.00
90 Mitch Williams FP	6.00	15.00
91 Dave Winfield	15.00	40.00
92 Robin Yount	15.00	40.00

1990 SLU Baseball Extended

This 7-piece set was issued by Cincinnati-based Kenner Toy Company. The statues feature top Major League Baseball stars in action poses and are accompanied by two cards. There is a regular card which features a posed or action color shot on front. The back has biographical and statistical information along with a facsimile signature. The second card is titled a "Rookie" card. The front has an action or posed shot along with a banner in the upper part that has the "Rookie Year" for that particular player. The back features biographical information. The extended case had five new figures and four previously released figures. The breakdown for the extended case is Sandy Alomar (2), Jim Abbott (3), Jose Canseco (4), Joe Carter, Ken Griffey Jr. Jumping (4), Bo Jackson (4), Ben McDonald (2), Nolan Ryan (2) and Jerome Walton (2). The key first piece is of Ken Griffey Jr, while the first piece of catcher Sandy Alomar Jr. apprears here as well. The values listed below refer to unopened packages. The figures are unnumbered and checklisted below in alphabetical order.

1 Jim Abbott FP	6.00	15.00
2 Sandy Alomar Jr. FP	6.00	15.00
16 Joe Carter	6.00	15.00
36 Ken Griffey Jr. FP	40.00	100.00
44 Bo Jackson	6.00	15.00
54 Ben McDonald FP	6.00	15.00
88 Jerome Walton FP	6.00	15.00

1991 SLU Baseball

This 46-piece set was issued by Cincinnati-based Kenner Toy Company. The statues feature top Major League Baseball stars in action poses and are accompanied by a standard-size card and a collector coin of each player. The card front has either a posed or action color shot. The back has biographical and statistical information and a facsimile signature. The coin features a embossed player portrait and came in two different variations, steel and aluminum. This was the first year for distribution to be only through American League and National League case assortments. There were at least two 16-piece case assortments for each league that made up the distribution for the 46 original pieces. Later in the year a nine-piece extended series was released. Nolan Ryan was the only figure that was previously released. The only difference in the two Ryans is that the UPC number on the back was different on the second version. Collectors have deemed the difference too insignificant to make any difference in price. The key first piece is Matt Williams. The values listed below refer to unopened packages. The figures are unnumbered and checklisted below in alphabetical order.

SENDOFF POSTER	7.50	15.00
1 Jim Abbott	4.00	10.00
2 Sandy Alomar Jr.	4.00	10.00
3 Jack Armstrong FP	5.00	12.00
5 Barry Bonds	15.00	40.00
6 Bobby Bonilla	4.00	10.00
7 Tom Browning FP	4.00	10.00
8 Jose Canseco	6.00	15.00
9 Will Clark	6.00	15.00
11 Eric Davis	4.00	10.00
13 Andre Dawson	6.00	15.00
14 Delino DeShields FP	5.00	12.00
15 Doug Drabek	4.00	10.00
16 Shawon Dunston	4.00	10.00
17 Lenny Dykstra	5.00	12.00
18 Cecil Fielder FP	6.00	15.00
19 John Franco	6.00	15.00
20 Dwight Gooden	4.00	10.00
21 Mark Grace	6.00	15.00
22 Ken Griffey Jr. Batting	12.50	30.00
25 Kelly Gruber FP	4.00	10.00
26 Ozzie Guillen	4.00	10.00
27 Rickey Henderson	6.00	15.00
28 Bo Jackson Royals	4.00	10.00
30 Gregg Jefferies	4.00	10.00
31 Howard Johnson	4.00	10.00
33 Roberto Kelly	4.00	10.00
34 Barry Larkin	4.00	10.00
35 Kevin Maas FP	4.00	10.00
36 Dave Magadan FP	4.00	10.00
37 Ramon Martinez FP	4.00	10.00
38 Don Mattingly	6.00	15.00
39 Ben McDonald	4.00	10.00
40 Mark McGwire	12.00	30.00
41 Kevin Mitchell	4.00	10.00
42 Kirby Puckett	8.00	20.00
44 Nolan Ryan	12.00	30.00
45 Chris Sabo	4.00	10.00
46 Ryne Sandberg	8.00	20.00
47 Benito Santiago	4.00	10.00
48 Steve Sax	4.00	10.00
49 Dave Stewart	4.00	10.00
50 Darryl Strawberry Mets	4.00	10.00
52 Alan Trammell	4.00	10.00
53 Frank Viola	4.00	10.00
54 Matt Williams FP	10.00	25.00
55 Todd Zeile FP	6.00	15.00

1991 SLU Baseball Extended

This nine-piece set was issued by Cincinnati-based Kenner Toy Company. The statues feature top Major League Baseball stars in action poses and are accompanied by a standard-size card and a collector coin of each player. The card front has either a posed or action color shot. The back has biographical and statistical information and a facsimile signature. The coin features a embossed player portrait and came in two different variations, steel and aluminum. The 16-piece case assortment that the extended series came in had 10 different players. The key first issued piece in the set is Dave Justice. Other pieces in the set showcase players in their new uniforms such as Bo Jackson in the White Sox and Darryl Strawberry in the Dodgers uniform. The values listed below refer to unopened packages. The figures are unnumbered and checklisted below in alphabetical order.

4 George Bell	4.00	10.00
10 Vince Coleman	5.00	12.00
12 Glenn Davis	4.00	10.00
23 Ken Griffey Jr. Run	15.00	40.00
24 Ken Griffey Sr.	10.00	25.00
29 Bo Jackson -Sox	6.00	15.00
32 Dave Justice FP	10.00	25.00
43 Tim Raines	4.00	10.00
51 Darryl Strawberry -LA	4.00	10.00

1992 SLU Baseball

This 37-piece set was issued by Cincinnati-based Kenner Toy Company. The statues feature top Major League Baseball stars in action poses and are accompanied by a standard-size card and a poster of each player. The card front has either a posed or action color shot. The back has biographical and statistical information and a facsimile signature. The poster folds out to be a 11" X 14" shot of the player. The figures came in 16-piece cases and each case was either American League or National League player specific. A nine-piece extended series was released later in the year. Some of the key first pieces include Craig Biggio, Albert Belle, Tom Glavine, Juan Gonzalez and Frank Thomas. The values listed below refer to unopened packages. The figures are unnumbered and checklisted below in alphabetical order.

GIVE AWAY CARD POSTER	7.50	15.00
1 Roberto Alomar	8.00	20.00
3 George Bell	3.00	8.00
4 Albert Belle FP	6.00	15.00
5 Craig Biggio FP	8.00	20.00
6 Barry Bonds	12.00	30.00
8 Ivan Calderon	3.00	8.00
9 Jose Canseco	6.00	15.00
10 Will Clark	4.00	10.00
11 Roger Clemens	6.00	15.00
13 Rob Dibble	3.00	8.00
14 Scott Erickson FP	4.00	10.00
15 Cecil Fielder	3.00	8.00
16 Chuck Finley FP	5.00	12.00
17 Tom Glavine FP	10.00	25.00
18 Juan Gonzalez FP	10.00	25.00
19 Ken Griffey Jr. Regular	10.00	25.00
20 Ken Griffey Jr. Spring	12.50	30.00
21 Tony Gwynn	10.00	25.00
22 Dave Henderson	4.00	10.00
23 Rickey Henderson	4.00	10.00
24 Bo Jackson Regular	4.00	10.00
25 Bo Jackson Spring	4.00	10.00
26 Howard Johnson	3.00	8.00
27 Felix Jose FP	3.00	8.00
28 Dave Justice	8.00	20.00
29 Kevin Maas	3.00	8.00
30 Ramon Martinez	4.00	10.00

31 Fred McGriff 6.00 15.00
32 Brian McRae FP 3.00 8.00
34 Cal Ripken 15.00 40.00
35 Nolan Ryan 12.00 30.00
37 Chris Sabo 3.00 8.00
38 Ryne Sandberg 6.00 15.00
40 Ruben Sierra 4.00 10.00
41 Darryl Strawberry 4.00 10.00
43 Frank Thomas Field FP 10.00 25.00
46 Matt Williams 6.00 15.00

1992 SLU Baseball Extended

This 9-piece set was issued by Cincinnati-based Kenner Toy Company. The statues feature top Major League Baseball stars in action poses and are accompanied by a standard-size card and a poster of each player. The card front has either a posed or action color shot. The back has biographical and statistical information and a facsimile signature. The poster folds out to be a 11" X 14" shot of the player. The 16-piece case assortment that the extended series came in had nine different players. Bret Saberhagen and Danny Tartabull were the only players in the extended case that came one per case while the other seven players were two per case. Some of the key first pieces include Tom Seaver and Frank Thomas. The values listed below refer to unopened packages. The figures are unnumbered and checklisted below in alphabetical order.

2 Steve Avery FP 4.00 10.00
7 Bobby Bonilla 4.00 10.00
12 Eric Davis 4.00 10.00
33 Kirby Puckett 10.00 25.00
36 Bret Saberhagen 4.00 10.00
39 Tom Seaver FP 10.00 25.00
42 Danny Tartabull 5.00 12.00
44 Frank Thomas - Batting FP 12.00 30.00
45 Todd Van Poppel FP 4.00 10.00

1992 SLU Baseball Headline Collection

This seven-piece set was the first of the Headline Collection brand issued by Cincinnati-based Kenner Toy Company. The pieces feature Top Major League Baseball players in action poses. The figures are accompanied by an authentic newspaper article and a high gloss, black base used to insert the article and display the figure. The article is framed and describes a memorable moment from the previous season. The pieces came in 12-count case assortments. The values listed below refer to unopened packages. The figures are unnumbered and listed below in alphabetical order.

1 George Brett 10.00 25.00
2 Cecil Fielder 4.00 10.00
3 Ken Griffey Jr. 15.00 40.00
4 Rickey Henderson 6.00 15.00
5 Bo Jackson 6.00 15.00
6 Nolan Ryan 12.00 30.00
7 Ryne Sandberg 12.00 30.00

1993 SLU Baseball

This 40-piece set was issued by Cincinnati-based Kenner Toy Company. The statues feature top Major League Baseball stars in action poses and are accompanied by two cards of each player. The regular card front has either a posed or action color shot. The back has biographical and statistical information and a facsimile signature. The second card is one of a titled subset. The front feature either a posed or action color shot. The back features a paragraph about the accomplishments of that player. The figures came in 16-piece case. Ken Griffey Jr. and Frank Thomas were the widest distributed figures even being included in cases that primarily contained National League players. A seven-piece extended series was released later in the year. Key first pieces include Jeff Bagwell, John Smoltz, Larry Walker, and Mike Mussina. The values listed below refer to unopened packages. The figures are unnumbered and checklisted below in alphabetical order. The set price does not include the two without eyeblack variations on Ken Griffey and Cal Ripken.

1 Roberto Alomar 4.00 10.00
2 Carlos Baerga FP 4.00 10.00
3 Jeff Bagwell FP 12.00 30.00
4 Barry Bonds Pirates 8.00 20.00
6 Kevin Brown FP 4.00 10.00
7 Jose Canseco 4.00 10.00
8 Will Clark 4.00 10.00
9 Roger Clemens 5.00 12.00
10 David Cone 5.00 12.00
12 Travis Fryman FP 4.00 10.00
13 Tom Glavine 8.00 20.00
14 Juan Gonzalez 8.00 20.00
15 Ken Griffey Jr. 12.50 30.00
15B Ken Griffey Jr. w o Eyeblack 12.50 30.00
16 Marquis Grissom FP 4.00 10.00
17 Juan Guzman FP 4.00 10.00
19 Eric Karros FP 6.00 15.00
20 Roberto Kelly 4.00 10.00
21 John Kruk 4.00 10.00
22 Ray Lankford FP 4.00 10.00
23 Barry Larkin 5.00 12.00
24 Shane Mack FP 5.00 12.00
26 Jack McDowell FP 4.00 10.00
27 Fred McGriff 4.00 10.00
28 Mark McGwire 15.00 40.00
29 Mike Mussina FP 8.00 20.00
31 Dean Palmer FP 4.00 10.00
32 Terry Pendleton 4.00 10.00
33 Kirby Puckett 6.00 15.00
34 Cal Ripken 12.00 30.00
34B Cal Ripken w o Eyeblack 15.00 35.00
35 Bip Roberts FP 4.00 10.00
36 Nolan Ryan 10.00 25.00
38 Ryne Sandberg 6.00 15.00
40 Gary Sheffield 4.00 10.00
41 John Smoltz FP 8.00 20.00
42 Frank Thomas 6.00 15.00
43 Andy Van Slyke 5.00 12.00
44 Robin Ventura FP 6.00 15.00
45 Larry Walker FP 6.00 15.00

1993 SLU Baseball Extended

This 7-piece set was issued by Cincinnati-based Kenner Toy Company. The statues feature top Major League Baseball stars in action poses and are accompanied by two cards of each player. The regular card front has either a posed or action color shot. The back has biographical and statistical information and a facsimile signature. The second card is one of a titled subset. The front feature either a posed or action color shot. The back features a paragraph about the accomplishments of that player. Nolan Ryan Retirement figure was the only piece to appear more than twice in the extended cases, showing up four per case. The David Neid and Benito Santiago extend series pieces were the first Starting Lineup figures to feature a player in the Colorado Rockies and Florida Marlin uniform respectively.

5 Barry Bonds Giants 10.00 25.00
11 Carlton Fisk 8.00 20.00
18 Bo Jackson 4.00 10.00
25 Greg Maddux 20.00 50.00
30 David Nied FP 4.00 10.00
37 Nolan Ryan Retirement 25.00 60.00
39 Benito Santiago 4.00 10.00

1993 SLU Baseball Headline Collection

This eight-piece set was the last in the Headline Collection series to be issued by Cincinnati-based Kenner Toy Company. The pieces feature top Major League Baseball players in action poses. The figures are accompanied by an authentic newspaper article and a high gloss, black base used to insert the article and display the figure. The article is framed and describes a memorable moment from the previous season. The pieces came in 12 count case assortments. The values listed below refer to unopened packages. The figures are unnumbered and listed below in alphabetical order.

1 Jim Abbott 6.00 15.00
2 Roberto Alomar 6.00 15.00
3 Tom Glavine 6.00 15.00
4 Mark McGwire 15.00 40.00
5 Cal Ripken 15.00 40.00
6 Nolan Ryan 15.00 40.00
7 Deion Sanders 8.00 20.00
8 Frank Thomas 10.00 25.00

1993 SLU Baseball Stadium Stars

This six-piece set was issued by the Cincinnati-based Kenner Toy Company. This was the first release of the Stadium Star brand. The figures are 25% larger than the typical Starting Lineup pieces. Each player is featured on top of a replica of their respective home stadium. The figures are also packaged in a window style display box. There were at least two different case assortments and eight figures in each case. A special case that featured only Nolan Ryan was issued late in the production release cycle. These cases were mainly distributed in the Southwest region of the U.S. The values listed below refer to unopened packages. The pieces are unnumbered and checklisted below in alphabetical order.

1 Roger Clemens 10.00 25.00
2 Cecil Fielder 6.00 15.00
3 Ken Griffey Jr. 15.00 40.00
4 Nolan Ryan 15.00 40.00
5 Ryne Sandberg 10.00 25.00
6 Frank Thomas 12.00 30.00

1994 SLU Baseball

This 57-piece set was issued by Cincinnati-based Kenner Toy Company. The statues feature top Major League Baseball stars in action poses and are accompanied by a standard-size card of each player. The card front has either a posed or action color shot. The back has biographical and statistical information. The figures came in 16-piece cases and each case was either American League or National League. An eight-piece extended series was released later in the year. Key first pieces include Randy Johnson, Ivan "Pudge" Rogriguez, Mo Vaughn, Tim Salmon, and catcher Mike Piazza. The values listed below refer to unopened packages. The figures are unnumbered and checklisted below in alphabetical order.

1 Kevin Appier FP 4.00 10.00
2 Steve Avery 4.00 10.00
3 Carlos Baerga 4.00 10.00
4 Jeff Bagwell 8.00 20.00
5 Derek Bell FP 4.00 10.00
6 Jay Bell FP 4.00 10.00
7 Albert Belle 4.00 10.00
8 Wade Boggs 5.00 12.00
9 Barry Bonds 8.00 20.00
10 John Burkett FP 4.00 10.00
12 Joe Carter 4.00 10.00
14 Roger Clemens 5.00 12.00
15 David Cone 4.00 10.00
16 Chad Curtis FP 4.00 10.00
17 Darren Daulton FP 6.00 15.00
18 Delino DeShields 4.00 10.00
20 Alex Fernandez FP 5.00 12.00
21 Cecil Fielder 4.00 10.00
22 Andres Galarraga 5.00 12.00
24 Tommy Greene FP 4.00 10.00
25 Ken Griffey Jr. 10.00 25.00
26 Mark Grace 4.00 10.00
27 Brian Harper FP 4.00 10.00
28 Bryan Harvey FP 4.00 10.00
29 Charlie Hayes FP 4.00 10.00
30 Chris Hoiles FP 4.00 10.00
31 Dave Hollins FP 4.00 10.00
32 Gregg Jefferies 4.00 10.00
33 Randy Johnson FP 12.00 30.00
34 Dave Justice 4.00 10.00
35 Eric Karros 4.00 10.00
36 Jimmy Key FP 6.00 15.00
37 Darryl Kile FP 6.00 15.00
38 Chuck Knoblauch FP 8.00 20.00
39 Mark Langston 4.00 10.00
41 Don Mattingly 6.00 15.00
43 Orlando Merced FP 4.00 10.00
44 Paul Molitor 5.00 12.00
45 Mike Mussina 4.00 10.00
46 John Olerud FP 6.00 15.00
48 Tony Phillips FP 4.00 10.00
49 Mike Piazza FP 12.00 30.00
50 Jose Rijo FP 4.00 10.00
51 Cal Ripken 10.00 25.00
52 Ivan Rodriguez FP 10.00 25.00
53 Tim Salmon FP 5.00 12.00
54 Ryne Sandberg 10.00 25.00
55 Curt Schilling FP 8.00 20.00
56 Gary Sheffield 4.00 10.00
58 J.T. Snow FP 6.00 15.00
59 Frank Thomas 6.00 15.00
60 Robby Thompson 4.00 10.00
61 Greg Vaughn FP 5.00 12.00
62 Mo Vaughn FP 6.00 15.00
63 Robin Ventura 4.00 10.00
64 Matt Williams 5.00 12.00
65 Dave Winfield 6.00 15.00

1994 SLU Baseball Extended

This 8-piece extended set was issued by Cincinnati-based Kenner Toy Company. The statues feature top Major League Baseball stars in action poses and are accompanied by a standard-size card of each player. The card front has either a posed or action color shot. The back has biographical and statistical information. The extended figures came in a 16-piece case assortment. The key first pieces in this set include the Rafeal Palmerio and Kenny Lofton.

11 Steve Carlton FP 8.00 20.00
13 Will Clark 5.00 12.00
19 Lenny Dykstra 5.00 12.00
23 Juan Gonzalez 8.00 20.00
40 Kenny Lofton FP 8.00 20.00
42 Fred McGriff 6.00 15.00
47 Rafeal Palmerio FP 8.00 20.00
57 Gary Sheffield 5.00 12.00

1994 SLU Baseball Stadium Stars

This eight-piece set was issued by the Cincinnati-based Kenner Toy Company. The figures are 25% larger than the typical Starting Lineup pieces. Each player is featured on top of a replica of their respective home stadium. The figures are also packaged in a window style display box. The figures came in at least three different eight count case assortments. The Bo Jackson figure is the shortest piece in the series. The values listed below refer to unopened packages. The pieces are unnumbered and checklisted below in alphabetical order.

1 Barry Bonds 10.00 25.00
2 Will Clark 10.00 25.00
3 Dennis Eckersley 8.00 20.00
4 Tom Glavine 10.00 25.00
5 Juan Gonzalez 10.00 25.00
6 Bo Jackson 10.00 25.00
7 Kirby Puckett 10.00 25.00
8 Deion Sanders 10.00 25.00

1994 SLU Cooperstown Collection

This eight-piece set is the first in the Cooperstown Collection line to be released by Cincinnati-based Kenner Toy Company. Each figure is a Hall of Fame player in an action pose and is accompanied by a standard size card. Each card features a posed or an action shot on the front. The back has biographical and statistical information. The figures came in 16 count case assortments with Babe Ruth being the most prolific figure at three per case. One of the most valuable Starting Lineup figures is the #44 jersey variation of the Jackie Robinson figure. The values listed below refer to unopened packages. The figures are unnumbered and checklisted below in alphabetical order.

5B NOT INCLUDED IN SET PRICE

1 Ty Cobb 6.00 15.00
2 Lou Gehrig 6.00 15.00
3 Reggie Jackson 10.00 25.00
4 Willie Mays 6.00 15.00
5A Jackie Robinson (42) 6.00 15.00
5B Jackie Robinson (44) 300.00 550.00
6 Babe Ruth 6.00 15.00
7 Honus Wagner 10.00 25.00
8 Cy Young 6.00 15.00

1995 SLU Baseball

This 58-piece set was issued by Cincinnati-based Kenner Toy Company. The statues feature top Major League Baseball stars in action poses and are accompanied by a standard-size card of each player. The card front has either a posed or action color shot. The back has biographical and statistical information. The figures came in 16-piece cases and each case was either American League or National League. A nine-piece extended series was released later in the year. The key first piece in the set is of homerun slugger Sammy Sosa. Other key first pieces include Dante Bichette, Ryan Klesko, Javier Lopez, Raul Mondesi, Moises Alou, and Calos Delgado. The values listed below refer to unopened packages. The figures are unnumbered and checklisted below in alphabetical order.

1 Jim Abbott 6.00 15.00
2 Moises Alou FP 5.00 12.00
3 Carlos Baerga 4.00 10.00
4 Jeff Bagwell 8.00 20.00
5 Albert Belle 4.00 10.00
6 Geronimo Berroa FP 4.00 10.00
7 Dante Bichette FP 6.00 15.00
8 Barry Bonds 6.00 15.00
9 Jay Buhner FP 6.00 15.00
10 Jose Canseco 5.00 12.00
12 Chuck Carr FP 4.00 10.00
13 Joe Carter 4.00 10.00
14 Andujar Cedeno FP 4.00 10.00
15 Will Clark 5.00 12.00
16 Roger Clemens 5.00 12.00
17 Jeff Conine FP 4.00 10.00
18 Scott Cooper FP 4.00 10.00
19 Darren Daulton 4.00 10.00
20 Carlos Delgado FP 8.00 20.00
21 Cecil Fielder 4.00 10.00
22 Cliff Floyd FP 5.00 12.00
23 Julio Franco 4.00 10.00
24 Juan Gonzalez 5.00 12.00
26 Ken Griffey Jr. 8.00 20.00
27 Tony Gwynn 6.00 15.00
28 Bob Hamelin FP 4.00 10.00
29 Jeffery Hammonds FP 4.00 10.00
30 Randy Johnson 6.00 15.00
31 Jeff Kent FP 6.00 15.00
32 Jeff King FP 4.00 10.00
33 Ryan Klesko FP 5.00 12.00
34 Chuck Knoblauch 5.00 12.00
35 John Kruk 4.00 10.00
36 Ray Lankford 4.00 10.00
37 Barry Larkin 4.00 10.00
39 Javier Lopez FP 8.00 20.00
40 Al Martin FP 4.00 10.00
41 Brian McRae 4.00 10.00
42 Paul Molitor 5.00 12.00
43 Raul Mondesi FP 8.00 20.00
44 Mike Mussina 4.00 10.00
45 Troy Neel FP 4.00 10.00
46 Dave Nilsson FP 5.00 12.00
47 John Olerud 4.00 10.00
48 Paul O'Neill 5.00 12.00
50 Mike Piazza 10.00 25.00
52 Kirby Puckett 6.00 15.00
54 Cal Ripken 12.00 30.00
57 Tim Salmon 4.00 10.00
58 Deion Sanders 8.00 20.00
59 Reggie Sanders FP 4.00 10.00
61 Sammy Sosa FP 20.00 50.00
62 Mickey Tettleton 4.00 10.00
63 Frank Thomas 6.00 15.00
64 Andy Van Slyke 4.00 10.00
65 Mo Vaughn 5.00 12.00
66 Rick Wilkins FP 4.00 10.00
67 Matt Williams 4.00 10.00

1995 SLU Baseball Extended

This 9-piece extended set was issued by Cincinnati-based Kenner Toy Company. The statues feature top Major League Baseball stars in action poses and are accompanied by a standard-size card of each player. The card front has either a posed or action color shot. The back has biographical and statistical information. The extended figures came in a 16-piece case assortment. The extended series was highlighted by the Cal Ripken figure that features him in a 1982 Orioles uniform and has a sticker on the packaging that pays tribute to his breaking Lou Gehrig's streak. The key first pieces in this set include the short-printed Manny Ramirez and Alex Rodriguez.

11 Jose Canseco 4.00 10.00
25 Rusty Greer FP 5.00 12.00
38 Kenny Lofton 10.00 25.00
49 Tom Pagnozzi FP 4.00 10.00
51 Mike Piazza 6.00 15.00
53 Manny Ramirez FP 15.00 40.00
55 Cal Ripken '82 Ori. 15.00 40.00
56 Alex Rodriguez FP 20.00 50.00
60 Mike Schmidt 5.00 12.00

1995 SLU Baseball Stadium Stars

This nine-piece set was issued by the Cincinnati-based Kenner Toy Company. The figures are 25% larger than the typical Starting Lineup pieces. Each player is featured on top of a replica of their respective home stadium. The figures are also packaged in a window style display box. The figures came in at least three different eight count case assortments. Darren Daulton, Randy Johnson and Mark McGwire appear to be the shortest pieces in the series. The values listed below refer to unopened packages. The pieces are unnumbered and checklisted below in alphabetical order.

1 Darren Daulton 10.00 25.00
2 Lenny Dykstra 10.00 25.00
3 Ken Griffey Jr. 15.00 40.00
4 Randy Johnson 12.00 30.00
5 Dave Justice 8.00 20.00
6 Greg Maddux 12.00 30.00
7 Mark McGwire 20.00 50.00
8 Frank Thomas 10.00 25.00
9 Mo Vaughn 8.00 20.00

1995 SLU Cooperstown Collection

This 10-piece set was issued by Cincinnati-based Kenner Toy Company. Each figure is a Hall of Fame player in an action pose and is accompanied by a standard size card. Each card features a posed or an action shot on the front. The back has biographical and statistical information. The figures came in 16-count case assortments with Babe Ruth being available at a rate of three per case. Harmon Killebrew and Eddie Mathews are the toughest, being inserted only one per case respectively. The values listed below refer to unopened packages. Since the cards are unnumbered, we have listed this set in alphabetical order.

1 Rod Carew 3.00 8.00
2 Dizzy Dean 4.00 10.00
3 Don Drysdale 3.00 8.00
4 Bob Feller 3.00 8.00
5 Whitey Ford 3.00 8.00
6 Bob Gibson 3.00 8.00
7 Harmon Killebrew 4.00 10.00
8 Eddie Mathews 6.00 15.00
9 Satchel Paige 4.00 10.00
10 Babe Ruth 6.00 15.00

1996 SLU Baseball

This 51-piece set was issued by Cincinnati-based Kenner Toy Company. The statues feature top Major League Baseball stars in action poses and are accompanied by a standard-size card of each player. The card front has either a posed or action color shot. The back has biographical and statistical information. The figures came in 16-piece cases and each case was either American League or National League. Cal Ripken and Hideo Nomo appear in two different poses in the set. Key first pieces are Derek Jeter, Chipper Jones and both Hideo Nomos. Other popular first pieces include Ken Caminiti and Jim Thome. The values listed below refer to unopened packages. The figures are unnumbered and checklisted below in alphabetical order.

1 Roberto Alomar 5.00 12.00
5A Jeff Bagwell (Blk Tan) 5.00 12.00
5B Jeff Bagwell Tan Bat 5.00 12.00
6 Albert Belle 4.00 10.00
8 Craig Biggio 5.00 12.00
9 Barry Bonds 5.00 12.00
10 Ricky Bones FP 4.00 10.00
11 Rico Brogna FP 4.00 10.00
12 Ken Caminiti FP 6.00 15.00
14 Vinny Castilla FP 5.00 12.00
15 Will Clark 4.00 10.00
16 David Cone 4.00 10.00
18 Wil Cordero FP 4.00 10.00
19 Marty Cordova FP 4.00 10.00
21 Shawon Dunston 4.00 10.00
22 Lenny Dykstra 4.00 10.00
23 Jim Edmonds FP 6.00 15.00
24 Jim Eisenreich FP 4.00 10.00
25 Gary Gaetti 4.00 10.00
26 Ron Gant 4.00 10.00
28 Ken Griffey Jr. 8.00 20.00
30 Marquis Grissom 4.00 10.00
31 Ozzie Guillen 4.00 10.00
32 Brian L. Hunter FP 4.00 10.00
33 Derek Jeter FP 15.00 40.00
34 Charles Johnson FP 5.00 12.00
35 Chipper Jones FP 20.00 50.00
39 Greg Maddux 10.00 25.00
40 Jeff Manto FP 4.00 10.00
41 Edgar Martinez FP 6.00 15.00
43 Fred McGriff 4.00 10.00
44 Mark McGwire 12.00 30.00
45 Raul Mondesi 4.00 10.00
47 Eddie Murray 5.00 12.00
49 Hideo Nomo White FP 6.00 15.00
50 Hideo Nomo Gray FP 6.00 15.00
51 Paul O'Neill 5.00 12.00
53 Mike Piazza 6.00 15.00
54 Kirby Puckett 5.00 12.00
55 Cal Ripken Field 8.00 20.00
56 Cal Ripken Slide 8.00 20.00
57 Ivan Rodriguez 5.00 12.00
58 Deion Sanders 4.00 10.00
59 Ozzie Smith 6.00 15.00
60 Sammy Sosa 12.00 30.00
61 Terry Steinbach 4.00 10.00
62 Frank Thomas 6.00 15.00
63 Jim Thome FP 8.00 20.00
64 Ryan Thompson FP 4.00 10.00
65 John Valentin FP 4.00 10.00
66 Mo Vaughn 5.00 12.00
67 Larry Walker 5.00 12.00
68 Rondell White FP 4.00 10.00
69 Matt Williams 4.00 10.00

1996 SLU Baseball Extended

This 16-piece extended set was issued by Cincinnati-based Kenner Toy Company. The statues feature top Major League Baseball stars in action poses and are accompanied by a standard-size card of each player. The values listed below refer to unopened packages. The figures are unnumbered and checklisted below in alphabetical order. Some of the more popular pieces from this set include Ken Griffey Jr. and Don Mattingly's last regular issued piece.

2 Moises Alou 5.00 12.00
3 Garret Anderson FP 5.00 12.00
4 Carlos Baerga 4.00 10.00
7 Dante Bichette 4.00 10.00
13 Joe Carter 4.00 10.00
17 Jeff Conine 4.00 10.00
20 Chad Curtis 4.00 10.00
27 Juan Gonzalez 6.00 15.00
29 Ken Griffey Jr. 15.00 40.00
36 David Justice 5.00 12.00
37 Eric Karros 4.00 10.00
38 Barry Larkin 5.00 12.00
42 Don Mattingly 8.00 20.00
46 Hal Morris 4.00 10.00
48 Denny Neagle FP 6.00 15.00
52 Rafael Palmeiro 6.00 15.00

1996 SLU Baseball Stadium Stars

This 11-piece set was issued by the Cincinnati-based Kenner Toy Company. The figures are 25% larger than the typical Starting Lineup pieces. Most players are featured on top of a replica of their respective home stadium. Due to contractual problems, Albert Belle, Mike Piazza, and Cal Ripken appear on top of Veteran Stadium. Veteran Stadium was chosen as a replacement since that was were the 1996 All-Star game was held. The figures are also packaged in a window style display box. The figures came in at least two different eight count case assortments. The values listed below refer to unopened packages. The pieces are unnumbered and checklisted below in alphabetical order.

1 Albert Belle 8.00 20.00
2 Jay Buhner 8.00 20.00
3 Jose Canseco 8.00 20.00
4 Darren Daulton 8.00 20.00
5 Mark Grace 8.00 20.00
6 Chuck Knoblauch 8.00 20.00
7 Javier Lopez 12.00 30.00
8 Mike Piazza 12.00 30.00
9 Cal Ripken 15.00 40.00
10 Robin Ventura 8.00 20.00
11 Matt Williams 8.00 20.00

1996 SLU Cooperstown Collection

This 10-piece set was issued by Cincinnati-based Kenner Toy Company. Each figure is a Hall of Fame player in an action pose and is accompanied by a standard size card. Each card features a posed or an action shot on the front. The back has biographical and statistical information. The figures came in two 16-count case assortments. There are two special figures that were produced in the Cooperstown Collection packaging but are not part of the 10-piece set. Those two figures are Richie Ashburn and Rod Carew. The Richie Ashburn figure was available through a Clover stores, a retail chain. The second figure, Rod Carew, was available for $10 to attendees of the 1996 National Sports Collectors Convention in Anaheim. These two piece are not valued in the complete set price. The values listed below refer to unopened packages. Since the figures are unnumbered, we have listed this set in alphabetical order.

ASHBURN NOT INCLUDED IN SET PRICE

1 Hank Aaron 6.00 15.00
2 Richie Ashburn Spec. 8.00 20.00
3 Rod Carew 5.00 12.00
4 Grover Cleveland Alexander 5.00 12.00
5 Roberto Clemente 6.00 15.00
6 Jimmie Foxx 5.00 12.00
7 Hank Greenberg 5.00 12.00
8 Rogers Hornsby 5.00 12.00
9 Joe Morgan 5.00 12.00
10 Mel Ott 5.00 12.00
11 Robin Roberts 5.00 12.00
12 Jackie Robinson 6.00 15.00

1996 SLU Cooperstown Collection 12-inch Figures

This series of six figures was Kenner's first entry into the 12" figure market. The figures featued Hall of Fame players from the early part of the 20th century. Each figure was done with actual cloth uniforms and simiulated wood bats and gloves. Two of the pieces were exclusive to mass market retailers. The Babe Ruth Red Sox piece was only available at Kay Bee Toys and the Honus Wagner was only available at Toys-R-Us. These pieces carried an original retail price between $24.95 and $29.95.

1 Ty Cobb 12.00 30.00
2 Lou Gehrig 15.00 40.00
3 Babe Ruth Red Sox (KB) 15.00 40.00
4 Babe Ruth Yankees 15.00 40.00
5 Honus Wagner (Toys-R-Us) 12.00 30.00
6 Cy Young 12.00 30.00

1997 SLU Baseball

This 48-piece set was issued by Cincinnati-based Kenner Toy Company. The statues feature top Major League Baseball stars in action poses and are accompanied by a standard-size card of each player. The card front has either a posed or action color shot. The back has biographical and statistical information. The figures came in 16-piece cases and each case was either American League or National League. Tino Martinez and Bernie Williams both of the Yankees were amoung the key First Pieces. Brady Anderson first piece since 1989, the second Chipper Jones piece, and the second Alex Rodriguez piece are some of the most desirable in the set. The values listed below refer to unopened packages. The figures are unnumbered and checklisted below in alphabetical order.

1 Roberto Alomar 5.00 12.00
2 Brady Anderson 5.00 12.00
3 Jeff Bagwell 5.00 12.00
4 Derek Bell 4.00 10.00
5 Albert Belle 3.00 8.00
7 Dante Bichette 5.00 12.00
8 Barry Bonds 6.00 15.00
10 Scott Brosius FP 5.00 12.00
11 Ellis Burks 5.00 12.00
14 Roger Clemens 5.00 12.00
16 Johnny Damon FP 4.00 10.00
18 Steve Finley FP 6.00 15.00
19 Tom Glavine 6.00 15.00
20 Rusty Greer 4.00 10.00
21 Ken Griffey Jr. 10.00 25.00
22 Todd Hundley FP 5.00 12.00
23 Jason Isringhausen FP 4.00 10.00
24 John Jaha FP 4.00 10.00
26 Randy Johnson 6.00 15.00
28 Chipper Jones 10.00 25.00
29 Brian Jordan 4.00 10.00
30 Wally Joyner 4.00 10.00
31 Jason Kendall FP 6.00 15.00
32 Ryan Klesko 4.00 10.00
33 Javier Lopez 4.00 10.00
34 Tino Martinez FP 10.00 25.00
36 Brian McRae 3.00 8.00
37 Jose Mesa FP 3.00 8.00
38 Paul Molitor 5.00 12.00
39 Raul Mondesi 4.00 10.00
41 Hideo Nomo 5.00 12.00
42 Rey Ordonez FP 6.00 15.00
43 Chan Ho Park FP 6.00 15.00
45 Mike Piazza 5.00 12.00
46 Manny Ramirez 6.00 15.00
47 Cal Ripken 8.00 20.00
48 Alex Rodriguez 6.00 15.00
50 Henry Rodriguez FP 5.00 12.00
51 Ivan Rodriguez 5.00 12.00
52 Ryne Sandberg 6.00 15.00
54 Reggie Sanders 3.00 8.00
55 John Smoltz 8.00 20.00
56 J.T. Snow 4.00 10.00
57 Frank Thomas 6.00 15.00
58 Ismael Valdes FP 5.00 12.00
59 Devon White 4.00 10.00
60 Bernie Williams FP 8.00 20.00
61 Matt Williams 4.00 10.00

1997 SLU Baseball Extended

This 14-piece extended set was issued by Cincinnati-based Kenner Toy Company. The statues feature top Major League Baseball stars in action poses and are accompanied by a standard-size card of each player. The values listed below refer to unopened packages. The figures are unnumbered and checklisted below in alphabetical order. The Mark McGwire is a retro figure using the 1989 same style as in 1989. The key first piece from this set is Braves outfielder Andruw Jones.

6 Albert Belle 4.00 10.00
9 Ricky Bottalico FP 5.00 12.00
12 Ken Caminiti 5.00 12.00
13 Tony Clark FP 6.00 15.00
15 Roger Clemens Jays 5.00 12.00
17 Dennis Eckersley 5.00 12.00
25 Derek Jeter 10.00 25.00
27 Andruw Jones FP 10.00 25.00
35 Mark McGwire '89 12.00 30.00
40 Mike Mussina 5.00 12.00
44 Andy Pettitte FP 10.00 25.00
49 Alex Rodriguez 8.00 20.00
53 Deion Sanders 4.00 10.00
62 Matt Williams Ind. 6.00 15.00

1998 SLU Baseball

This 53-piece set was issued by Cincinnati-based Kenner Toy Company. The statues feature top Major League Baseball stars in action poses and are accompanied by a standard-size card of each player. The card front has either a posed or action color shot. The back has biographical and statistical information. The figures came in three different assortments. The set does not include either special Mark Grace or Sammy Sosa pieces that were issued at Wrigly Field. The extended set was released with 14 pieces. Key first pieces include Darin Erstad, Nomar Garciaparra, Hideki Irabu, Mariano Rivera and Scott Rolen. The values listed below refer to unopened packages. The figures are unnumbered and checklisted below in alphabetical order.

4 Albert Belle 3.00 8.00
5 Craig Biggio 3.00 8.00
6 Barry Bonds 7.50 15.00
7 Kevin Brown 3.00 8.00
8 Jose Canseco 5.00 12.00
9 Will Clark 5.00 12.00
11 Darin Erstad FP 7.50 15.00
12 Andres Galarraga 3.00 8.00
13 Nomar Garciaparra FP 10.00 25.00
14 Tom Glavine 3.00 8.00
15 Juan Gonzalez 4.00 10.00
16 Mark Grace 4.00 10.00
16A Mark Grace Wrigley 15.00 40.00
17 Ken Griffey Jr. 8.00 20.00
19 Mark Grudzielanek FP 4.00 10.00
20 Tony Gwynn 4.00 10.00
21 Bobby Higginson FP 5.00 12.00
22 Glenallen Hill FP 4.00 10.00
24 Derek Jeter 7.50 15.00
25 Chipper Jones 6.00 12.00
26 Dave Justice 3.00 8.00
27 Chuck Knoblauch 3.00 8.00
28 Ray Lankford 3.00 8.00
29 Barry Larkin 4.00 10.00
32A Mark McGwire HR Hero 10.00 20.00
33 Mickey Morandini FP 4.00 10.00
34 Marc Newfield FP 3.00 8.00
35 Hideo Nomo 5.00 12.00
36 Rafael Palmeiro 3.00 8.00
38 Mike Piazza 4.00 10.00
39 Cal Ripken 8.00 20.00
40 Mariano Rivera FP 10.00 20.00
41 Alex Rodriguez 6.00 12.00
43 Deion Sanders 4.00 10.00
44 Gary Sheffield 3.00 8.00
45A Sammy Sosa HR Hero 8.00 20.00
46 Sammy Sosa Wrigley 25.00 60.00
47 Ed Sprague FP 4.00 10.00
48 Frank Thomas 4.00 10.00
49 Jim Thome 4.00 10.00
50 Mo Vaughn 3.00 8.00
51 Larry Walker 4.00 10.00
53 Bernie Williams 3.00 8.00

1998 SLU Baseball 12-inch Figures

Released for the second year by Kenner, this four-piece set features MLB figures 12 inches tall. Prices below refer to in-package pieces.

1 Derek Jeter 20.00 50.00
2 Chipper Jones 10.00 25.00
3 Hideo Nomo 10.00 25.00
4 Alex Rodriguez 10.00 25.00

1998 SLU Baseball Classic Doubles

This is the second consecutive year that Kenner has released their Classic Double line. This 10-piece set contains five pieces that feature current players and five legends. The pieces are not numbered and listed below in alphabetical order.

1 A.Belle/F.Thomas 10.00 25.00
2 J.Bench/J.Morgan 10.00 25.00
3 Y.Berra/T.Munson 10.00 25.00
4 J.Cnsco/M.McGwire 20.00 50.00
5 R.Jackson/C.Hunter 10.00 25.00
6 D.Jeter/R.Ordonez 12.00 30.00
6A McGwire/Sosa HR.Hero 30.00 60.00
7 M.Piazza/I.Rodriguez 10.00 25.00
8 A.Rod/K.Griffey Jr. 15.00 40.00
9 N.Ryan/W.Johnson 10.00 25.00
10 B.Ruth/R.Maris 10.00 25.00

1998 SLU Baseball Extended

This 14-piece extended set was issued by Cincinnati-based Kenner Toy Company. The statues feature top Major League Baseball stars in action poses and are accompanied by a standard-size card of each player. The values listed below refer to unopened packages. The figures are unnumbered and checklisted below in alphabetical order. The key figure in the set is of Mark McGwire featured on his first St. Louis Cardinals figure. Some of the more popular first pieces from this set include Scott Rolen and Hideki Irabu.

1 Sandy Alomar 5.00 12.00
2 Moises Alou 4.00 10.00
3 Jay Bell 3.00 8.00
10 Jim Edmonds 5.00 12.00
18 Ken Griffey Jr. 8.00 20.00
23 Hideki Irabu FP 5.00 12.00
30 Greg Maddux 5.00 12.00
31 Fred McGriff 4.00 10.00
32 Mark McGwire 10.00 25.00
37 Dean Palmer 3.00 8.00
42 Scott Rolen FP 8.00 20.00
45 Sammy Sosa 10.00 25.00
52 Larry Walker 7.50 15.00
54 Tony Womack FP 5.00 12.00

1998 SLU Baseball Freeze Frames

Sold exclusively through Toys R Us, this 6-piece set is the second year Kenner has release the Freeze Frame series. The pieces came in two different assortments with a retail issue price of $25. The pieces are not numbered and listed below in alphabetical order.

1 Jeff Bagwell 12.50 25.00
2 Barry Bonds 12.50 25.00
3 Derek Jeter 20.00 35.00
4 Greg Maddux 10.00 20.00
5 Cal Ripken 15.00 40.00
6 Alex Rodriguez 20.00 35.00

1998 SLU Baseball Stadium Stars

This 7-piece set was issued by the Cincinnati-based Kenner Toy Company. The figures are 25% larger than the typical Starting Lineup pieces. Most players are featured on top of a replica of their respective home stadium. The figures are packaged in a window style display box. The figures came in two different assortments. The values listed below refer to unopened packages. The pieces are unnumbered and checklisted below in alphabetical order.

1 Albert Belle 5.00 10.00
2 Ken Griffey Jr. 12.50 30.00
3 Mike Piazza 10.00 20.00
4 Cal Ripken 12.50 25.00
5 Ivan Rodriguez 8.00 20.00
6 John Smoltz 7.50 15.00
7 Bernie Williams 10.00 20.00

1998 SLU Cooperstown Collection

This version of the Cooperstown Collection was released in two assortments. It was the fifth consecutive year for the line. The pieces are not numbered and listed below in alphabetical order.

1 Yogi Berra 4.00 8.00

2 Lou Brock	4.00	8.00
3 Roy Campanella	4.00	8.00
4 Roberto Clemente	5.00	10.00
5 Buck Leonard	4.00	8.00
6 Phil Niekro	4.00	8.00
7 Jim Palmer	4.00	8.00
8 Frank Robinson	4.00	8.00
9 Tom Seaver	4.00	8.00
10 Warren Spahn	4.00	8.00
11 Tris Speaker	4.00	8.00

1999 SLU Baseball

This 38-piece regular set was issued by Cincinnati-based Kenner Toy Company. The statues feature top Major League Baseball stars in action poses and are accompanied by a standard-size card of each player. The values listed below refer to unopened packages. The figures are unnumbered and checklisted below in alphabetical order. Some of the more popular first pieces from this set include Vladimir Guerrero and Pedro Martinez.

1 Wilson Alvarez	5.00	12.00
2 Edgardo Alfonzo FP	12.00	30.00
3 Jeff Bagwell	6.00	15.00
6 Vinny Castilla	5.00	12.00
7 Tony Clark	5.00	12.00
8 Roger Clemens	5.00	12.00
9 David Cone	5.00	12.00
10 Jose Cruz, Jr. FP	8.00	20.00
12 Darin Erstad	5.00	12.00
13 Nomar Garciaparra	6.00	15.00
15 Juan Gonzalez	5.00	12.00
17 Ken Griffey. Jr.	8.00	20.00
18 Vladimir Guerrero FP	20.00	40.00
19 Jose Guillen FP	5.00	12.00
20 Tony Gwynn	6.00	15.00
21 Livan Hernandez FP	5.00	12.00
22 Derek Jeter	6.00	15.00
23 Randy Johnson	5.00	12.00
24 Chipper Jones	5.00	12.00
25 Travis Lee FP	5.00	12.00
26 Kenny Lofton	6.00	15.00
28 Pedro Martinez FP	10.00	25.00
29 Tino Martinez	5.00	12.00
30 Mark McGwire	10.00	25.00
31 Denny Neagle	5.00	12.00
32 Chan Ho Park	5.00	12.00
33 Mike Piazza	6.00	15.00
34 Brad Radke FP	5.00	12.00
35 Manny Ramirez	8.00	20.00
36 Edgar Renteria FP	5.00	12.00
37 Cal Ripken, Jr.	5.00	12.00
38 Scott Rolen	5.00	12.00
39 Alex Rodriguez	5.00	12.00
40 Ivan Rodriguez	6.00	15.00
41 Sammy Sosa	6.00	15.00
43 Omar Vizquel FP	12.00	30.00
44 Larry Walker	5.00	12.00
47 Kerry Wood FP	6.00	15.00

1999 SLU Baseball Classic Doubles

A twist on the Classic Doubles theme, this set actually featured two poses of the same player: one minor league uniform and one major league jersey.

1 Sandy Alomar	6.00	15.00
2 Darin Erstad	6.00	15.00
3 Nomar Garciaparra	8.00	20.00
4 Ken Griffey, Jr.	15.00	40.00
5 Derek Jeter	10.00	25.00
6 Javy Lopez	8.00	20.00
7 Greg Maddux	6.00	15.00
8 Mark McGwire	10.00	25.00
9 Raul Mondesi	8.00	20.00
10 Alex Rodriguez	10.00	25.00

1999 SLU Baseball Extended

This 10-piece extended set was issued by Cincinnati-based Kenner Toy Company. The statues feature top Major League Baseball stars in action poses and are accompanied by a standard-size card of each player. The values listed below refer to unopened packages. The figures are unnumbered and checklisted below in alphabetical order. Some of the more popular first pieces from this set include short-printed Sean Casey, J.D.Drew, and Ben Grieve.

4 Kevin Brown	4.00	10.00
5 Sean Casey FP	10.00	25.00
11 J.D. Drew FP	6.00	15.00
14 Nomar Garciaparra	4.00	10.00
16 Ben Grieve FP	4.00	10.00
27 Greg Maddux	4.00	10.00
42 Mo Vaughn	4.00	10.00
45 David Wells FP	5.00	12.00
46 Bernie Williams	4.00	10.00
48 Jaret Wright FP	4.00	10.00

1999 SLU Baseball One On One

Another series in the popular One On One two-figure packaging schemes, this set included five pairs of players.

1 S.Alomar/K.Griffey Jr.	12.50	30.00
2 Garciaparra/Edmonds	6.00	15.00
3 C.Jones/L.Walker	6.00	15.00
4 J.Kendall/R.Ordonez	6.00	15.00
5 C.Ripken/K.Lofton	8.00	20.00

1999 SLU Baseball Stadium Stars

These seven figures are displayed amidst their home stadium scenery. The set features Mark McGwire, Alex Rodriguez and Derek Jeter.

1 Roger Clemens	8.00	20.00
2 Nomar Garciaparra	8.00	20.00
3 Derek Jeter	10.00	25.00
4 Chipper Jones	8.00	20.00
5 Kenny Lofton	8.00	20.00
6 Mark McGwire	8.00	20.00
7 Alex Rodriguez	8.00	20.00

1999 SLU Baseball Wal-Mart Exclusives

Banking on the phenomenal home run record chase, this Walmart exclusive set offered numerous poses of Sammy Sosa and Mark McGwire.

1 Mark McGwire Reg.	6.00	15.00
1A Mark McGwire Reg.Blue VAR	12.00	30.00
2 Sammy Sosa Reg.	6.00	15.00
3 Mark McGwire Stad. Star	12.00	30.00
4 Sammy Sosa Stad. Star	12.00	30.00
5 Mark McGwire Sports Star	8.00	20.00
6 Sammy Sosa Sports Star	8.00	20.00
7 Mark McGwire	10.00	25.00
Roger Maris CD		
8 Sammy Sosa	10.00	25.00
Roger Maris CD		

1999 SLU Cooperstown Collection

Seven retro-themed Hall-of-Famers make up this SLU set, including Nolan Ryan, George Brett, and Ted Williams.

1 George Brett	6.00	15.00
2 Pepper Davis	4.00	10.00
3 Bob Gibson	4.00	10.00
4 Juan Marichal	4.00	10.00
5 Nolan Ryan	6.00	15.00
6 Earl Weaver	5.00	12.00
7 Ted Williams	10.00	25.00

2000 SLU Baseball

SET DOESN'T INC.McGWIRE 500 HR WALMART
SET COMPLETE WITH ONE McGWIRE FIGURE

1 Roberto Alomar	5.00	12.00
3 Barry Bonds	5.00	12.00
4 Bret Boone FP	4.00	10.00
5 Jose Canseco	6.00	15.00
6 Roger Clemens	4.00	10.00
7 J.D. Drew	4.00	10.00
8 Nomar Garciaparra	5.00	12.00
9 Troy Glaus FP	8.00	20.00
10 Ken Griffey Jr.	6.00	15.00
11 Shawn Green FP	6.00	15.00
12 Vladimir Guerrero	8.00	20.00
13 Todd Helton FP	10.00	25.00
14 Orlando Hernandez FP	6.00	15.00
15 Trevor Hoffman FP	5.00	12.00
16 Derek Jeter	6.00	15.00
17 Randy Johnson	5.00	12.00
18 Barry Larkin	5.00	12.00
19 Greg Maddux	4.00	10.00
20 Pedro Martinez	4.00	10.00
21A Mark McGwire	6.00	15.00
21B Mark McGwire w/SG	6.00	15.00
21C Mark McGwire 500 HR Wal.	8.00	20.00
21D Mark McGwire Salute Wal.	6.00	15.00
22 Mike Piazza	4.00	10.00
23 Shane Reynolds FP	4.00	10.00
24 Cal Ripken Jr.	8.00	20.00
25 Aaron Sele FP	5.00	12.00
26 Curt Schilling	4.00	10.00
27 Sammy Sosa	4.00	10.00
28 Matt Stairs FP	5.00	12.00
29 Robin Ventura	8.00	20.00
30 Bernie Williams	4.00	10.00

2000 SLU Baseball Classic Doubles

10 D.Jeter/M.Piazza	8.00	20.00
20 R.Clemens/C.Schilling	6.00	15.00
30 J.Thome/S.Casey	6.00	15.00
40 P.Martinez/J.Smoltz	6.00	15.00
50 C.Ripken/C.Jones	8.00	20.00

2000 SLU Baseball Elite

10 Ken Griffey Jr.	10.00	25.00
20 Derek Jeter	10.00	25.00
30 Greg Maddux	8.00	20.00
40 Mark McGwire	8.00	20.00
50 Mike Piazza	10.00	25.00
60 Sammy Sosa	8.00	20.00

2000 SLU Baseball Extended

10 Roger Cedeno FP	4.00	10.00
20 Ken Griffey Jr. Reds	8.00	20.00
30 Tony Gwynn 3000 Hits	6.00	15.00
40 Mike Hampton FP	4.00	10.00
50 Chipper Jones	5.00	12.00
60 Kevin Millwood FP	5.00	12.00
70 Cal Ripken Jr. 3000 Hits	8.00	20.00
80 Alex Rodriguez	5.00	12.00
90 Scott Williamson FP	5.00	12.00

2001 SLU Baseball

20 Rick Ankiel FP	8.00	20.00
30 Barry Bonds	10.00	25.00
40 Pat Burrell FP	8.00	20.00
50 Rafael Furcal FP	8.00	20.00
60 Nomar Garciaparra	6.00	15.00
70 Jason Giambi FP	10.00	25.00
80 Shawn Green	8.00	20.00
90 Ken Griffey Jr.	8.00	20.00
100 Vladimir Guerrero	6.00	15.00
110 Todd Helton	6.00	15.00
120 Derek Jeter Fielding	8.00	20.00
130 Randy Johnson	6.00	15.00
140 Chipper Jones	6.00	15.00
150 Dave Justice Toys 'R Us	12.00	30.00
160 Pedro Martinez White	6.00	15.00
170 Mark McGwire	6.00	15.00
180 Magglio Ordonez FP	8.00	20.00
190 Mike Piazza	6.00	15.00
200 Pokey Reese FP	6.00	15.00
210 Cal Ripken Jr.	8.00	20.00
220 Ivan Rodriguez	6.00	15.00
230 Sammy Sosa	6.00	15.00
240 Jim Thome Toys 'R Us	10.00	25.00

2001 SLU Baseball Classic Doubles

40 K.Griffey Jr./A.Jones	10.00	25.00
50 T.Hudson/G.Maddux	12.00	30.00
60 D.Jeter/O.Vizquel	12.00	30.00
70 M.McGwire/T.Helton	8.00	20.00
80 S.Sosa/V.Guerrero	8.00	20.00

2001 SLU Baseball Extended

20 Jeff Bagwell	5.00	12.00
30 Jim Edmonds	5.00	12.00
40 Tom Glavine	5.00	12.00
60 Jorge Posada FP	8.00	20.00
70 Alex Rodriguez	6.00	15.00
80 Frank Thomas	5.00	12.00

2001 SLU Baseball Inserts

10 Bobby Abreu	12.00	30.00
20 Brian Giles	12.00	30.00
30 Andruw Jones	12.00	30.00
40 Preston Wilson	12.00	30.00

2001 SLU Baseball Wal-Mart Exclusives

20 Jermaine Dye	6.00	15.00
30 Andres Galarraga	6.00	15.00
50 Derek Jeter Batting	10.00	25.00
60 Pedro Martinez Grey	8.00	20.00
80 Gary Sheffield	6.00	15.00

2001 SLU Cooperstown Collection

20 Reggie Jackson	5.00	12.00
30 Willie McCovey	5.00	12.00
40 Brooks Robinson	5.00	12.00
50 Nolan Ryan	6.00	15.00
60 Tom Seaver	5.00	12.00
70 Willie Stargell	6.00	15.00
80 Robin Yount	8.00	20.00

1949 R447 Smack-A-Roo

1 Pop Fly	10.00	25.00
2 Ball Hits Home Plate	10.00	25.00
3 Ball Hits Batter	10.00	25.00
4 Hit by Pitcher	10.00	25.00
5 Scoring Descision	10.00	25.00
6 Pitcher Drops Ball	10.00	25.00
7 Fan Reaches Over Fence	10.00	25.00
8 Municipal Stadium	10.00	25.00
9 Longest Distances	10.00	25.00
10 Longest Game in History	10.00	25.00
11 Double Play	10.00	25.00
12 Babe Ruth	12.50	30.00
13 New York Giants	10.00	25.00
14 Base Measurements	10.00	25.00
15 Fielder Throws Glove	10.00	25.00
16 Bunted Ball	10.00	25.00

1987 Smokey American League

The U.S. Forestry Service (in conjunction with Major League Baseball) produced this large, attractive 14-player card set to commemorate the 43rd birthday of Smokey. The cards feature Smokey the Bear pictured on every card with the player. The card backs give a fire safety tip. The cards measure approximately 4" by 6" and are subtitled "National Smokey Bear Day 1987" on the front. The cards were printed on an uncut (but perforated) sheet that measured 18" by 24".

COMPLETE SET (16)	3.00	8.00
1 Jose Canseco	.75	2.00
2 Dennis Oil Can Boyd	.08	.25
3 John Candelaria	.08	.25
4 Harold Baines	.20	.50
5 Joe Carter	.30	.75
6 Jack Morris	.20	.50
7 Buddy Biancalana	.08	.25
8 Kirby Puckett	1.00	2.50
9 Mike Pagliarulo	.08	.25
10 Larry Sheets	.08	.25
11 Mike Moore	.08	.25
12 Charlie Hough	.08	.25
13 National Smokey	.08	.25
Bear Day 1987		
14 Tom Henke	.20	.50
15 Jim Gantner	.08	.25
16 American League	.08	.25
Smokey Bear Day 1987		

1987 Smokey National League

The U.S. Forestry Service (in conjunction with Major League Baseball) produced this large, attractive 14 player card set to commemorate the 43rd birthday of Smokey. The cards feature Smokey the Bear pictured on every card with the player. The card backs give a fire safety tip. The cards measure approximately 4" by 6" and are subtitled "National Smokey Bear Day 1987" on the front. The set price below does not include the more difficult variation cards.

COMPLETE SET (15)	3.00	8.00
1 Steve Sax	.08	.25
2A Dale Murphy	1.25	3.00
Holding bat		
2B Dale Murphy	5.00	12.00
No bat		
arm around Smokey		
3A Jody Davis	.20	.50
Kneeling with Smokey		
3B Jody Davis	3.00	8.00
Standing, shaking Smokey's hand		
4 Bill Gullickson	.08	.25
5 Mike Scott	.08	.25
6 Roger McDowell	.08	.25
7 Steve Bedrosian	.08	.25
8 Johnny Ray	.08	.25
9 Ozzie Smith	1.00	2.50
10 Steve Garvey	.30	.75
11 National Smokey	.08	.25
Bear Day		
12 Mike Krukow	.08	.25
13 Smokey the Bear	.08	.25
14 Mike Fitzgerald	.08	.25
15 National League Logo	.08	.25

1995 Sonic/Pepsi Greats

This 12-card standard-size set was released at Sonic restaurants which served Pepsi products. Some players apparently signed cards for this set. The cards were issued in three-card cello packs. The fronts display color player photos inside red borders. Team logos have been airbrushed off hats and jerseys. In blue print on a white background, the backs present career summary, honors received, player profile, and career statistics. The cards are unnumbered and checklisted below in alphabetical order.

COMPLETE SET (12)	3.00	8.00
1 Bert Campaneris	.30	.75
2 George Foster	.30	.75
3 Steve Garvey	.40	1.00
4 Ferguson Jenkins	.60	1.50
5 Tommy John	.30	.75
6 Harmon Killebrew	.60	1.50
7 Sparky Lyle	.30	.75
8 Fred Lynn	.30	.75
9 Joe Morgan	.60	1.50
10 Graig Nettles	.30	.75
11 Warren Spahn	.60	1.50
12 Maury Wills	.40	1.00

1999 Sotheby's Halper Auction

This 15-card standard-size set was issued to preview the auction of Barry Halper's collection through the Sotheby's auction house. This set features some of the most important moments or people in baseball history and what lots in the auction feature items apropos to that event. The fronts feature black and white photos with white borders with the words, "The Barry Halper Collection of Baseball Memorabilia" on the front. At the bottom is a description of the moment or person pictured. The back, styled similarly to the 1953 Topps set, features more information about the items. These sets were first displayed at the Atlanta National in 1999.

COMPLETE SET (15)	8.00	20.00
1 Babe Ruth	2.00	5.00
Auction Catalogue Information		
2 Babe Ruth	2.00	5.00
Last Bat		
3 Lou Gehrig	1.25	3.00
Day		
4 Joe DiMaggio	1.25	3.00
PCL Rookie		
5 Joe Jackson	1.25	3.00
Black Sox Scandal		
6 Mookie Wilson	.20	.50
Bill Buckner/1986 World Series		
7 Bobby Thomson	.20	.50
Ralph Branca		
Shot Heard Round the		
8 1888 World Tour	.08	.25
9 Henry Chadwick	.08	.25
Father of Baseball		
10 Ty Cobb	1.25	3.00
Famous Slide into 3rd		
11 George Brett	.40	1.00
Don Slaught		
Pine Tar Outburst		
12 Mickey Mantle	2.00	5.00
Roger Maris		
The M and M Boys		
13 Willie Mays	1.25	3.00
The Catch		
14 Autographed Baseball	.08	.25
Babe Ruth Ball against a com		
XX Header Card	.08	.25

1999 Sotheby's Halper Auction Amazon

This 16 card set was one of the two sets issued to preview the sale of the Barry Halper collection. This set was issued in conjunction with Amazon.com and is slightly different from the set issued directly from Sotheby's.

COMPLETE SET (16)	10.00	25.00
1 Header	.08	.25
Card is numbered		
2 Babe Ruth	2.00	5.00
Last Bat		
3 Lou Gehrig	1.25	3.00
Day		
4 Joe DiMaggio	1.25	3.00
Rookie Year		
5 Joe Jackson/1919 World Series	1.25	3.00
6 Roger Maris	1.25	3.00
Mickey Mantle/1961 Yankees		
7 Willie Mays/1954 World Series Catch	1.25	3.00
8 Bobby Thomson	.20	.50
Ralph Branca/1951 Playoff Game		
9 Ty Cobb	1.25	3.00
Famous Slide into 3rd		
10 George Brett	.40	1.00
Pine Tar Game		
11 Babe Ruth Ball	.08	.25
Shown against computer screen		
12 Pete Rose/4,000 Hit	.75	2.00
13 Babe Ruth	2.00	5.00
Shows kids how to play		
14 Babe Ruth	2.00	5.00
Newspaperman		
15 Bob Feller#[Satchel Paige	.40	1.00
Barnstormers		
16 Jackie Robinson	1.25	3.00
Keeps his promise		

1993 SP

This 290-card standard-size set, produced by Upper Deck, features fronts with action color player photos. Special subsets include All Star players (1-18) and Foil Prospects (271-290). Cards 19-270 are in alphabetical order by team nickname. Notable Rookie Cards include Johnny Damon and Derek Jeter.

COMPLETE SET (290)	150.00	400.00
COMMON CARD (1-270)	.20	.50
FOIL PROSPECTS (271-290)	.40	1.00
FOIL CARDS ARE CONDITION SENSITIVE		
1 Roberto Alomar AS	.50	1.25
2 Wade Boggs AS	.50	1.25
3 Joe Carter AS	.20	.50
4 Ken Griffey Jr. AS	1.50	4.00
5 Mark Langston AS	.20	.50
6 John Olerud AS	.30	.75
7 Kirby Puckett AS	.75	2.00
8 Cal Ripken AS	2.50	6.00
9 Ivan Rodriguez AS	.50	1.25
10 Barry Bonds AS	2.00	5.00
11 Darren Daulton AS	.30	.75
12 Marquis Grissom AS	.30	.75
13 David Justice AS	.30	.75
14 John Kruk AS	.30	.75
15 Barry Larkin AS	.50	1.25
16 Terry Mulholland AS	.20	.50
17 Ryne Sandberg AS	1.25	3.00
18 Gary Sheffield AS	.30	.75
19 Chad Curtis	.20	.50
20 Chili Davis	.30	.75
21 Gary DiSarcina	.20	.50
22 Damion Easley	.20	.50
23 Chuck Finley	.30	.75
24 Luis Polonia	.20	.50
25 Tim Salmon	.50	1.25
26 J.T.Snow RC	.50	1.25
27 Russ Springer	.20	.50
28 Jeff Bagwell	.50	1.25
29 Craig Biggio	.50	1.25
30 Ken Caminiti	.30	.75
31 Andujar Cedeno	.20	.50
32 Doug Drabek	.20	.50
33 Steve Finley	.30	.75
34 Luis Gonzalez	.30	.75
35 Pete Harnisch	.20	.50
36 Darryl Kile	.30	.75
37 Mike Bordick	.20	.50
38 Dennis Eckersley	.30	.75
39 Brent Gates	.20	.50
40 Rickey Henderson	.75	2.00
41 Mark McGwire	2.00	5.00
42 Craig Paquette	.20	.50
43 Ruben Sierra	.30	.75
44 Terry Steinbach	.20	.50
45 Todd Van Poppel	.20	.50
46 Pat Borders	.20	.50
47 Tony Fernandez	.20	.50
48 Juan Guzman	.20	.50
49 Pat Hentgen	.20	.50
50 Paul Molitor	.30	.75
51 Jack Morris	.30	.75
52 Ed Sprague	.20	.50
53 Duane Ward	.20	.50
54 Devon White	.30	.75
55 Steve Avery	.20	.50
56 Jeff Blauser	.20	.50
57 Ron Gant	.30	.75
58 Tom Glavine	.50	1.25
59 Greg Maddux	1.25	3.00
60 Fred McGriff	.50	1.25
61 Terry Pendleton	.30	.75
62 Deion Sanders	.50	1.25
63 John Smoltz	.50	1.25
64 Cal Eldred	.20	.50
65 Darryl Hamilton	.20	.50
66 John Jaha	.20	.50
67 Pat Listach	.20	.50
68 Jaime Navarro	.20	.50
69 Kevin Reimer	.20	.50
70 B.J. Surhoff	.30	.75
71 Greg Vaughn	.20	.50
72 Robin Yount	1.25	3.00
73 Rene Arocha RC	.30	.75
74 Bernard Gilkey	.20	.50
75 Gregg Jefferies	.20	.50
76 Ray Lankford	.30	.75
77 Tom Pagnozzi	.20	.50
78 Lee Smith	.30	.75
79 Ozzie Smith	1.25	3.00
80 Bob Tewksbury	.20	.50
81 Mark Whiten	.20	.50
82 Steve Buechele	.20	.50
83 Mark Grace	.50	1.25
84 Jose Guzman	.20	.50
85 Derrick May	.20	.50
86 Mike Morgan	.20	.50
87 Randy Myers	.20	.50
88 Kevin Roberson RC	.20	.50
89 Sammy Sosa	.75	2.00
90 Rick Wilkins	.20	.50
91 Brett Butler	.30	.75
92 Eric Davis	.30	.75
93 Orel Hershiser	.30	.75
94 Eric Karros	.30	.75
95 Ramon Martinez	.20	.50
96 Raul Mondesi	.30	.75
97 Jose Offerman	.20	.50
98 Mike Piazza	2.00	5.00
99 Darryl Strawberry	.30	.75
100 Moises Alou	.30	.75
101 Wil Cordero	.20	.50
102 Delino DeShields	.20	.50
103 Darrin Fletcher	.20	.50
104 Ken Hill	.20	.50
105 Mike Lansing RC	.30	.75
106 Dennis Martinez	.30	.75
107 Larry Walker	.30	.75
108 John Wetteland	.30	.75
109 Rod Beck	.20	.50
110 John Burkett	.20	.50
111 Will Clark	.50	1.25
112 Royce Clayton	.20	.50
113 Darren Lewis	.20	.50
114 Willie McGee	.30	.75
115 Bill Swift	.20	.50
116 Robby Thompson	.20	.50
117 Matt Williams	.30	.75
118 Sandy Alomar Jr.	.20	.50
119 Carlos Baerga	.20	.50
120 Albert Belle	.30	.75
121 Reggie Jefferson	.20	.50
122 Wayne Kirby	.20	.50
123 Kenny Lofton	.30	.75
124 Carlos Martinez	.20	.50
125 Charles Nagy	.20	.50
126 Paul Sorrento	.20	.50
127 Rich Amaral	.20	.50
128 Jay Buhner	.30	.75
129 Norm Charlton	.20	.50
130 Dave Fleming	.20	.50
131 Erik Hanson	.20	.50
132 Randy Johnson	.75	2.00
133 Edgar Martinez	.50	1.25
134 Tino Martinez	.50	1.25
135 Omar Vizquel	.50	1.25
136 Bret Barberie	.20	.50
137 Chuck Carr	.20	.50
138 Jeff Conine	.30	.75
139 Orestes Destrade	.20	.50
140 Chris Hammond	.20	.50
141 Bryan Harvey	.20	.50
142 Benito Santiago	.30	.75
143 Walt Weiss	.20	.50
144 Darrell Whitmore RC	.20	.50
145 Tim Bogar RC	.20	.50
146 Bobby Bonilla	.30	.75
147 Jeromy Burnitz	.30	.75
148 Vince Coleman	.20	.50
149 Dwight Gooden	.30	.75
150 Todd Hundley	.20	.50
151 Howard Johnson	.20	.50
152 Eddie Murray	.75	2.00
153 Bret Saberhagen	.30	.75
154 Brady Anderson	.30	.75
155 Mike Devereaux	.20	.50
156 Jeffrey Hammonds	.20	.50
157 Chris Hoiles	.20	.50
158 Ben McDonald	.20	.50
159 Mark McLemore	.20	.50
160 Mike Mussina	.50	1.25
161 Gregg Olson	.20	.50
162 David Segui	.20	.50
163 Derek Bell	.20	.50
164 Andy Benes	.20	.50
165 Archi Cianfrocco	.20	.50
166 Ricky Gutierrez	.20	.50
167 Tony Gwynn	1.00	2.50
168 Gene Harris	.20	.50
169 Trevor Hoffman	.75	2.00
170 Ray McDavid RC	.20	.50
171 Phil Plantier	.20	.50
172 Mariano Duncan	.20	.50
173 Len Dykstra	.30	.75
174 Tommy Greene	.20	.50
175 Dave Hollins	.20	.50
176 Pete Incaviglia	.20	.50
177 Mickey Morandini	.20	.50
178 Curt Schilling	.30	.75
179 Kevin Stocker	.20	.50
180 Mitch Williams	.20	.50
181 Stan Belinda	.20	.50
182 Jay Bell	.30	.75
183 Steve Cooke	.20	.50
184 Carlos Garcia	.20	.50
185 Jeff King	.20	.50
186 Orlando Merced	.20	.50
187 Don Slaught	.20	.50
188 Andy Van Slyke	.50	1.25
189 Kevin Young	.30	.75
190 Kevin Brown	.30	.75
191 Jose Canseco	.50	1.25
192 Julio Franco	.30	.75
193 Benji Gil	.20	.50
194 Juan Gonzalez	.30	.75
195 Tom Henke	.20	.50
196 Rafael Palmeiro	.50	1.25
197 Dean Palmer	.30	.75
198 Nolan Ryan	3.00	8.00
199 Roger Clemens	1.50	4.00
200 Scott Cooper	.20	.50
201 Andre Dawson	.30	.75
202 Mike Greenwell	.20	.50
203 Carlos Quintana	.20	.50
204 Jeff Russell	.20	.50
205 Aaron Sele	.20	.50
206 Mo Vaughn	.30	.75
207 Frank Viola	.30	.75
208 Rob Dibble	.30	.75
209 Roberto Kelly	.20	.50
210 Kevin Mitchell	.20	.50
211 Hal Morris	.20	.50
212 Joe Oliver	.20	.50
213 Jose Rijo	.20	.50
214 Bip Roberts	.20	.50
215 Chris Sabo	.20	.50
216 Reggie Sanders	.30	.75
217 Dante Bichette	.30	.75
218 Jerald Clark	.20	.50
219 Alex Cole	.20	.50
220 Andres Galarraga	.30	.75
221 Joe Girardi	.20	.50
222 Charlie Hayes	.20	.50
223 Roberto Mejia RC	.20	.50
224 Armando Reynoso	.20	.50
225 Eric Young	.20	.50
226 Kevin Appier	.30	.75
227 George Brett	2.00	5.00
228 David Cone	.30	.75
229 Phil Hiatt	.20	.50
230 Felix Jose	.20	.50
231 Wally Joyner	.30	.75
232 Mike Macfarlane	.20	.50
233 Brian McRae	.20	.50
234 Jeff Montgomery	.20	.50
235 Rob Deer	.20	.50
236 Cecil Fielder	.30	.75
237 Travis Fryman	.30	.75
238 Mike Henneman	.20	.50
239 Tony Phillips	.20	.50
240 Mickey Tettleton	.20	.50
241 Alan Trammell	.30	.75
242 David Wells	.30	.75
243 Lou Whitaker	.30	.75
244 Rick Aguilera	.20	.50
245 Scott Erickson	.20	.50
246 Brian Harper	.20	.50
247 Kent Hrbek	.30	.75
248 Chuck Knoblauch	.30	.75
249 Shane Mack	.20	.50
250 David McCarty	.20	.50
251 Pedro Munoz	.20	.50
252 Dave Winfield	.30	.75
253 Alex Fernandez	.20	.50
254 Ozzie Guillen	.30	.75
255 Bo Jackson	.75	2.00
256 Lance Johnson	.20	.50
257 Ron Karkovice	.20	.50
258 Jack McDowell	.20	.50
259 Tim Raines	.30	.75
260 Frank Thomas	.75	2.00
261 Robin Ventura	.30	.75
262 Jim Abbott	.50	1.25
263 Steve Farr	.20	.50
264 Jimmy Key	.30	.75
265 Don Mattingly	2.00	5.00
266 Paul O'Neill	.50	1.25
267 Mike Stanley	.20	.50
268 Danny Tartabull	.20	.50
269 Bob Wickman	.20	.50
270 Bernie Williams	.50	1.25
271 Jason Bere FOIL	.40	1.00
272 Roger Cedeno FOIL RC	.60	1.50
273 Johnny Damon FOIL RC	3.00	8.00
274 Russ Davis FOIL RC	.60	1.50
275 Carlos Delgado FOIL	1.50	4.00
276 Carl Everett FOIL	.60	1.50
277 Cliff Floyd FOIL	.30	.75
278 Alex Gonzalez FOIL	.40	1.00
279 Derek Jeter FOIL RC !	300.00	800.00
280 Chipper Jones FOIL	1.50	4.00
281 Javier Lopez FOIL	.50	1.25
282 Chad Mottola FOIL RC	.40	1.00
283 Marc Newfield FOIL	.40	1.00
284 Eduardo Perez FOIL	.40	1.00
285 Manny Ramirez FOIL	2.00	5.00
286 Todd Steverson FOIL RC	.40	1.00
287 Michael Tucker FOIL	.40	1.00
288 Allen Watson FOIL	.40	1.00
289 Rondell White FOIL	.60	1.50
290 Dmitri Young FOIL	.60	1.50

1993 SP Platinum Power

COMPLETE SET (20)	10.00	25.00
STATED ODDS 1:9		
PP1 Albert Belle	.75	2.00
PP2 Barry Bonds	5.00	12.00
PP3 Joe Carter	.50	1.25
PP4 Will Clark	1.25	3.00
PP5 Darren Daulton	.75	2.00
PP6 Cecil Fielder	.75	2.00
PP7 Ron Gant	.75	2.00
PP8 Juan Gonzalez	.75	2.00
PP9 Ken Griffey Jr.	4.00	10.00
PP10 Dave Hollins	.50	1.25
PP11 David Justice	.75	2.00
PP12 Fred McGriff	1.25	3.00
PP13 Mark McGwire	5.00	12.00
PP14 Dean Palmer	.75	2.00
PP15 Mike Piazza	5.00	12.00
PP16 Tim Salmon	1.25	3.00
PP17 Ryne Sandberg	3.00	8.00
PP18 Gary Sheffield	.75	2.00
PP19 Frank Thomas	2.00	5.00
PP20 Matt Williams	.75	2.00

1994 SP Previews

COMPLETE SET (15)	75.00	150.00
COMPLETE CENTRAL (5)	25.00	60.00
COMPLETE EAST (5)	15.00	40.00
COMPLETE WEST (5)	25.00	60.00
STATED ODDS 1:35 REG'L SER.2 UD HOBBY		
CR1 Jeff Bagwell	2.00	5.00
CR2 Michael Jordan	8.00	20.00
CR3 Kirby Puckett	3.00	8.00
CR4 Manny Ramirez	3.00	8.00
CR5 Frank Thomas	3.00	8.00
ER1 Roberto Alomar	2.00	5.00
ER2 Cliff Floyd	1.25	3.00
ER3 Javier Lopez	1.25	3.00
ER4 Don Mattingly	8.00	20.00
ER5 Cal Ripken	10.00	25.00
WR1 Barry Bonds	8.00	20.00
WR2 Juan Gonzalez	1.25	3.00
WR3 Ken Griffey Jr.	6.00	15.00
WR4 Mike Piazza	6.00	15.00
WR5 Tim Salmon	2.00	5.00

1994 SP

This 200-card standard-size set distributed in foil packs contains the game's top players and prospects. The first 20 cards in the set are Foil Prospects which are brighter and more metallic than the rest of the set. These cards therefore are highly condition sensitive. Cards 21-200 are in alphabetical order by team nickname. Rookie Cards include Brad Fullmer, Derrek Lee, Chan Ho Park and Alex Rodriguez.

COMPLETE SET (200)	50.00	100.00
COMMON CARD (21-200)	.07	.20
COMMON FOIL (1-20)	.20	.50
REGULAR CARDS HAVE GOLD HOLOGRAMS		
FOIL CARDS CONDITION SENSITIVE		
1 Mike Bell FOIL RC	.20	.50
2 D.J. Boston FOIL RC	.20	.50
3 Johnny Damon FOIL	.75	2.00
4 Brad Fullmer FOIL RC	.40	1.00
5 Joey Hamilton FOIL	.20	.50
6 Todd Hollandsworth FOIL	.20	.50
7 Brian L.Hunter FOIL	.20	.50
8 LaTroy Hawkins FOIL RC	.40	1.00
9 Brooks Kieschnick FOIL RC	.20	.50
10 Derrek Lee FOIL RC	5.00	12.00
11 Trot Nixon FOIL RC	1.50	4.00
12 Alex Ochoa FOIL	.20	.50
13 Chan Ho Park FOIL RC	.75	2.00
14 Kirk Presley FOIL RC	.20	.50
15 Alex Rodriguez FOIL RC	30.00	80.00
16 Jose Silva FOIL RC	.20	.50
17 Terrell Wade FOIL RC	.20	.50
18 Billy Wagner FOIL RC	1.50	4.00
19 Glenn Williams FOIL RC	.20	.50
20 Preston Wilson FOIL	.40	1.00
21 Brian Anderson RC	.15	.40
22 Chad Curtis	.07	.20
23 Chili Davis	.15	.40
24 Bo Jackson	.40	1.00
25 Mark Langston	.07	.20
26 Tim Salmon	.25	.60
27 Jeff Bagwell	.25	.60
28 Craig Biggio	.25	.60
29 Ken Caminiti	.15	.40
30 Doug Drabek	.07	.20
31 John Hudek RC	.07	.20
32 Greg Swindell	.07	.20
33 Brent Gates	.07	.20
34 Rickey Henderson	.40	1.00
35 Steve Karsay	.07	.20
36 Mark McGwire	1.00	2.50
37 Ruben Sierra	.15	.40
38 Terry Steinbach	.07	.20
39 Roberto Alomar	.25	.60
40 Joe Carter	.15	.40
41 Carlos Delgado	.25	.60
42 Alex Gonzalez	.07	.20
43 Juan Guzman	.07	.20
44 Paul Molitor	.15	.40
45 John Olerud	.15	.40
46 Devon White	.15	.40
47 Steve Avery	.07	.20
48 Jeff Blauser	.07	.20
49 Tom Glavine	.25	.60
50 David Justice	.15	.40
51 Roberto Kelly	.07	.20
52 Ryan Klesko	.15	.40
53 Javier Lopez	.15	.40
54 Greg Maddux	.60	1.50
55 Fred McGriff	.25	.60
56 Ricky Bones	.07	.20
57 Cal Eldred	.07	.20
58 Brian Harper	.07	.20
59 Pat Listach	.07	.20
60 B.J. Surhoff	.15	.40
61 Greg Vaughn	.07	.20
62 Bernard Gilkey	.07	.20
63 Gregg Jefferies	.07	.20
64 Ray Lankford	.15	.40
65 Ozzie Smith	.60	1.50
66 Bob Tewksbury	.07	.20

67 Mark Whiten .07 .20
68 Todd Zeile .07 .20
69 Mark Grace .25 .60
70 Randy Myers .07 .20
71 Ryne Sandberg .60 1.50
72 Sammy Sosa .40 1.00
73 Steve Trachsel .07 .20
74 Rick Wilkins .07 .20
75 Brett Butler .15 .40
76 Delino DeShields .07 .20
77 Orel Hershiser .15 .40
78 Eric Karros .15 .40
79 Raul Mondesi .15 .40
80 Mike Piazza .75 2.00
81 Tim Wallach .07 .20
82 Moises Alou .15 .40
83 Cliff Floyd .15 .40
84 Marquis Grissom .15 .40
85 Pedro Martinez .40 1.00
86 Larry Walker .15 .40
87 John Wetteland .15 .40
88 Rondell White .15 .40
89 Rod Beck .07 .20
90 Barry Bonds 1.00 2.50
91 John Burkett .07 .20
92 Royce Clayton .07 .20
93 Billy Swift .07 .20
94 Robby Thompson .07 .20
95 Matt Williams .15 .40
96 Carlos Baerga .07 .20
97 Albert Belle .15 .40
98 Kenny Lofton .15 .40
99 Dennis Martinez .15 .40
100 Eddie Murray .40 1.00
101 Manny Ramirez .40 1.00
102 Eric Anthony .07 .20
103 Chris Bosio .07 .20
104 Jay Buhner .15 .40
105 Ken Griffey Jr. .75 2.00
106 Randy Johnson .40 1.00
107 Edgar Martinez .25 .60
108 Chuck Carr .07 .20
109 Jeff Conine .15 .40
110 Carl Everett .15 .40
111 Chris Hammond .07 .20
112 Bryan Harvey .07 .20
113 Charles Johnson .15 .40
114 Gary Sheffield .15 .40
115 Bobby Bonilla .15 .40
116 Dwight Gooden .15 .40
117 Todd Hundley .07 .20
118 Bobby Jones .07 .20
119 Jeff Kent .25 .60
120 Bret Saberhagen .15 .40
121 Jeffrey Hammonds .07 .20
122 Chris Hoiles .07 .20
123 Ben McDonald .07 .20
124 Mike Mussina .25 .60
125 Rafael Palmeiro .25 .60
126 Cal Ripken 1.25 3.00
127 Lee Smith .15 .40
128 Derek Bell .07 .20
129 Andy Benes .07 .20
130 Tony Gwynn .50 1.25
131 Trevor Hoffman .25 .60
132 Phil Plantier .07 .20
133 Bip Roberts .07 .20
134 Darren Daulton .15 .40
135 Lenny Dykstra .15 .40
136 Dave Hollins .07 .20
137 Danny Jackson .07 .20
138 John Kruk .15 .40
139 Kevin Stocker .07 .20
140 Jay Bell .15 .40
141 Carlos Garcia .07 .20
142 Jeff King .07 .20
143 Orlando Merced .07 .20
144 Andy Van Slyke .25 .60
145 Paul Wagner .07 .20
146 Jose Canseco .25 .60
147 Will Clark .25 .60
148 Juan Gonzalez .15 .40
149 Tom Henke .07 .20
150 Dean Palmer .15 .40
151 Ivan Rodriguez .25 .60
152 Roger Clemens .75 2.00
153 Scott Cooper .07 .20
154 Andre Dawson .15 .40
155 Mike Greenwell .07 .20
156 Aaron Sele .07 .20
157 Mo Vaughn .15 .40
158 Bret Boone .15 .40
159 Barry Larkin .25 .60
160 Kevin Mitchell .07 .20
161 Jose Rijo .07 .20
162 Deion Sanders .25 .60
163 Reggie Sanders .15 .40
164 Dante Bichette .15 .40
165 Ellis Burks .15 .40
166 Andres Galarraga .15 .40
167 Charlie Hayes .07 .20
168 David Nied .07 .20
169 Walt Weiss .07 .20
170 Kevin Appier .15 .40
171 David Cone .15 .40
172 Jeff Granger .07 .20
173 Felix Jose .07 .20
174 Wally Joyner .15 .40
175 Brian McRae .07 .20
176 Cecil Fielder .15 .40
177 Travis Fryman .15 .40
178 Mike Henneman .07 .20
179 Tony Phillips .07 .20
180 Mickey Tettleton .07 .20
181 Alan Trammell .15 .40
182 Rick Aguilera .07 .20
183 Rich Becker .07 .20
184 Scott Erickson .07 .20
185 Chuck Knoblauch .15 .40
186 Kirby Puckett .40 1.00
187 Dave Winfield .15 .40
188 Wilson Alvarez .07 .20
189 Jason Bere .07 .20
190 Alex Fernandez .07 .20
191 Julio Franco .15 .40
192 Jack McDowell .07 .20
193 Frank Thomas .40 1.00
194 Robin Ventura .15 .40
195 Jim Abbott .25 .60
196 Wade Boggs .25 .60
197 Jimmy Key .15 .40
198 Don Mattingly 1.00 2.50
199 Paul O'Neill .25 .60
200 Danny Tartabull .07 .20
P24 Ken Griffey Jr. Promo 1.00 2.50

1994 SP Die Cuts

COMPLETE SET (200) 75.00 150.00
*STARS: .75X TO 2X BASIC CARDS
*ROOKIES: .6X TO 1.5X BASIC CARDS
ONE DIE CUT PER PACK
DIE CUTS HAVE SILVER HOLOGRAMS
10 Derrek Lee FOIL 6.00 15.00
15 Alex Rodriguez FOIL 30.00 80.00

1994 SP Holoviews

STATED ODDS 1:5
1 Roberto Alomar 1.25 3.00
2 Kevin Appier .75 2.00
3 Jeff Bagwell 1.25 3.00
4 Jose Canseco 1.25 3.00
5 Roger Clemens 4.00 10.00
6 Carlos Delgado 1.25 3.00
7 Cecil Fielder .75 2.00
8 Cliff Floyd .75 2.00
9 Travis Fryman .75 2.00
10 Andres Galarraga .75 2.00
11 Juan Gonzalez .75 2.00
12 Ken Griffey Jr. 4.00 10.00
13 Tony Gwynn 2.50 6.00
14 Jeffrey Hammonds .60 1.50
15 Bo Jackson 2.00 5.00
16 Michael Jordan 6.00 15.00
17 David Justice .75 2.00
18 Steve Karsay .60 1.50
19 Jeff Kent 1.25 3.00
20 Brooks Kieschnick .60 1.50
21 Ryan Klesko .75 2.00
22 John Kruk .75 2.00
23 Barry Larkin 1.25 3.00
24 Pat Listach .60 1.50
25 Don Mattingly 5.00 12.00
26 Mark McGwire 5.00 12.00
27 Raul Mondesi .75 2.00
28 Trot Nixon 2.50 6.00
29 Mike Piazza 3.00 8.00
30 Kirby Puckett 2.00 5.00
31 Manny Ramirez 2.00 5.00
32 Cal Ripken 6.00 15.00
33 Alex Rodriguez 12.00 30.00
34 Tim Salmon 1.25 3.00
35 Gary Sheffield .75 2.00
36 Ozzie Smith 3.00 8.00
37 Sammy Sosa 2.00 5.00
38 Andy Van Slyke 1.25 3.00

1994 SP Holoviews Die Cuts

*DIE CUTS: 2.5X TO 6X BASIC HOLO
*DIE CUTS: 1.5X TO 4X BASIC HOLO RC YR
STATED ODDS 1:75
12 Ken Griffey Jr. 30.00 80.00
16 Michael Jordan 75.00 150.00
33 Alex Rodriguez 150.00 400.00

1995 SP

This set consists of 207 cards being sold in eight-card, hobby-only packs with a suggested retail price of $3.99. Subsets featured are Salute (1-4) and Premier Prospects (5-24). The only notable Rookie Card in this set is Hideo Nomo. Dealers who ordered a certain quantity of Upper Deck baseball cases received as a bonus, a certified autographed SP card of Ken Griffey Jr.

COMPLETE SET (207) 15.00 40.00
COMMON CARD (1-207) .07 .20
COMMON FOIL (5-24) .20 .50
GRIFFEY AU SENT TO DEALERS AS BONUS
1 Cal Ripken Salute 1.25 3.00
2 Nolan Ryan Salute 1.50 4.00
3 George Brett Salute 1.00 2.50
4 Mike Schmidt Salute .60 1.50
5 Dustin Hermanson FOIL .20 .50
6 Antonio Osuna FOIL .20 .50
7 Mark Grudzielanek FOIL RC .50 1.25
8 Ray Durham FOIL .30 .75
9 Ugueth Urbina FOIL .20 .50
10 Ruben Rivera FOIL .20 .50
11 Curtis Goodwin FOIL .20 .50
12 Jimmy Hurst FOIL .20 .50
13 Jose Malave FOIL .20 .50
14 Hideo Nomo FOIL RC 1.50 4.00
15 Juan Acevedo RC FOIL .20 .50
16 Tony Clark FOIL .20 .50
17 Jim Pittsley FOIL .20 .50
18 Freddy Adrian Garcia RC FOIL .20 .50
19 Carlos Perez RC FOIL .30 .75
20 Raul Casanova FOIL RC .20 .50
21 Quilvio Veras FOIL .20 .50
22 Edgardo Alfonzo FOIL .20 .50
23 Marty Cordova FOIL .20 .50
24 C.J. Nitkowski FOIL .20 .50
25 Wade Boggs CL .15 .40
26 Dave Winfield CL .07 .20
27 Eddie Murray CL .25 .60
28 David Justice .15 .40
29 Marquis Grissom .15 .40
30 Fred McGriff .25 .60
31 Greg Maddux .60 1.50
32 Tom Glavine .25 .60
33 Steve Avery .07 .20
34 Chipper Jones .40 1.00
35 Sammy Sosa .40 1.00
36 Jaime Navarro .07 .20
37 Randy Myers .07 .20
38 Mark Grace .25 .60
39 Todd Zeile .07 .20
40 Brian McRae .07 .20
41 Reggie Sanders .15 .40
42 Ron Gant .15 .40
43 Deion Sanders .25 .60
44 Bret Boone .15 .40
45 Barry Larkin .25 .60
46 Jose Rijo .07 .20
47 Jason Bates .07 .20
48 Andres Galarraga .15 .40
49 Bill Swift .07 .20
50 Larry Walker .15 .40
51 Vinny Castilla .15 .40
52 Dante Bichette .15 .40
53 Jeff Conine .15 .40
54 John Burkett .07 .20
55 Gary Sheffield .15 .40
56 Andre Dawson .15 .40
57 Terry Pendleton .15 .40
58 Charles Johnson .15 .40
59 Brian L.Hunter .07 .20
60 Jeff Bagwell .25 .60
61 Craig Biggio .25 .60
62 Phil Nevin .15 .40
63 Doug Drabek .07 .20
64 Derek Bell .07 .20
65 Raul Mondesi .15 .40
66 Eric Karros .15 .40
67 Roger Cedeno .07 .20
68 Delino DeShields .07 .20
69 Ramon Martinez .07 .20
70 Mike Piazza .60 1.50
71 Billy Ashley .07 .20
72 Jeff Fassero .07 .20
73 Shane Andrews .07 .20
74 Wil Cordero .07 .20
75 Tony Tarasco .07 .20
76 Rondell White .15 .40
77 Pedro Martinez .25 .60
78 Moises Alou .15 .40
79 Rico Brogna .07 .20
80 Bobby Bonilla .15 .40
81 Jeff Kent .15 .40
82 Brett Butler .15 .40
83 Bobby Jones .07 .20
84 Bill Pulsipher .07 .20
85 Bret Saberhagen .15 .40
86 Gregg Jefferies .07 .20
87 Lenny Dykstra .15 .40
88 Dave Hollins .07 .20
89 Charlie Hayes .07 .20
90 Darren Daulton .15 .40
91 Curt Schilling .15 .40
92 Heathcliff Slocumb .07 .20
93 Carlos Garcia .07 .20
94 Denny Neagle .15 .40
95 Jay Bell .15 .40
96 Orlando Merced .07 .20
97 Dave Clark .07 .20
98 Bernard Gilkey .07 .20
99 Scott Cooper .07 .20
100 Ozzie Smith .60 1.50
101 Tom Henke .07 .20
102 Ken Hill .07 .20
103 Brian Jordan .15 .40
104 Ray Lankford .15 .40
105 Tony Gwynn .50 1.25
106 Andy Benes .07 .20
107 Ken Caminiti .15 .40
108 Steve Finley .15 .40
109 Joey Hamilton .07 .20
110 Bip Roberts .07 .20
111 Eddie Williams .07 .20
112 Rod Beck .07 .20
113 Matt Williams .15 .40
114 Glenallen Hill .07 .20
115 Barry Bonds 1.00 2.50
116 Robby Thompson .07 .20
117 Mark Portugal .07 .20
118 Brady Anderson .15 .40
119 Mike Mussina .25 .60
120 Rafael Palmeiro .25 .60
121 Chris Hoiles .07 .20
122 Harold Baines .15 .40
123 Jeffrey Hammonds .07 .20
124 Tim Naehring .07 .20
125 Mo Vaughn .15 .40
126 Mike Macfarlane .07 .20
127 Roger Clemens .75 2.00
128 John Valentin .07 .20
129 Aaron Sele .07 .20
130 Jose Canseco .25 .60
131 J.T. Snow .15 .40
132 Mark Langston .07 .20
133 Chili Davis .15 .40
134 Chuck Finley .15 .40
135 Tim Salmon .25 .60
136 Tony Phillips .07 .20
137 Jason Bere .07 .20
138 Robin Ventura .15 .40
139 Tim Raines .15 .40
140 Frank Thomas .40 1.00
140A Frank Thomas ERR .40 1.00
141 Alex Fernandez .07 .20
142 Jim Abbott .25 .60
143 Wilson Alvarez .07 .20
144 Carlos Baerga .07 .20
145 Albert Belle .15 .40
146 Jim Thome .25 .60
147 Dennis Martinez .15 .40
148 Eddie Murray .40 1.00
149 Dave Winfield .15 .40
150 Kenny Lofton .15 .40
151 Manny Ramirez .25 .60
152 Chad Curtis .07 .20
153 Lou Whitaker .15 .40
154 Alan Trammell .15 .40
155 Cecil Fielder .15 .40
156 Kirk Gibson .15 .40
157 Michael Tucker .07 .20
158 Jon Nunnally .07 .20
159 Wally Joyner .15 .40
160 Kevin Appier .15 .40
161 Jeff Montgomery .07 .20
162 Greg Gagne .07 .20
163 Ricky Bones .07 .20
164 Cal Eldred .07 .20
165 Greg Vaughn .07 .20
166 Kevin Seitzer .07 .20
167 Jose Valentin .07 .20
168 Joe Oliver .07 .20
169 Rick Aguilera .07 .20
170 Kirby Puckett .40 1.00
171 Scott Stahoviak .07 .20
172 Kevin Tapani .07 .20
173 Chuck Knoblauch .15 .40
174 Rich Becker .07 .20
175 Don Mattingly 1.00 2.50
176 Jack McDowell .07 .20
177 Jimmy Key .15 .40
178 Paul O'Neill .25 .60
179 John Wetteland .15 .40
180 Wade Boggs .25 .60
181 Derek Jeter 1.00 2.50
182 Rickey Henderson .40 1.00
183 Terry Steinbach .07 .20
184 Ruben Sierra .15 .40
185 Mark McGwire 1.00 2.50
186 Todd Stottlemyre .07 .20
187 Dennis Eckersley .15 .40
188 Alex Rodriguez 1.00 2.50
189 Randy Johnson .40 1.00
190 Ken Griffey Jr. .75 2.00
191 Tino Martinez .25 .60
192 Jay Buhner .15 .40
193 Edgar Martinez .25 .60
194 Mickey Tettleton .07 .20
195 Juan Gonzalez .15 .40
196 Benji Gil .07 .20
197 Dean Palmer .15 .40
198 Ivan Rodriguez .25 .60
199 Kenny Rogers .15 .40
200 Will Clark .25 .60
201 Roberto Alomar .25 .60
202 David Cone .15 .40
203 Paul Molitor .15 .40
204 Shawn Green .15 .40
205 Joe Carter .15 .40
206 Alex Gonzalez .07 .20
207 Pat Hentgen .07 .20
P100 Ken Griffey Jr. Promo 1.00 2.50
AU100 Ken Griffey Jr. AU 30.00 60.00

1995 SP Silver

COMPLETE SET (207) 40.00 100.00
*STARS: 1X TO 2.5X BASIC CARDS
*ROOKIES: .75X TO 2X BASIC CARDS
ONE PER PACK

1995 SP Platinum Power

COMPLETE SET (20) 8.00 20.00
STATED ODDS 1:5
PP1 Jeff Bagwell .30 .75
PP2 Barry Bonds 1.25 3.00
PP3 Ron Gant .20 .50
PP4 Fred McGriff .30 .75
PP5 Raul Mondesi .20 .50
PP6 Mike Piazza .75 2.00
PP7 Larry Walker .20 .50
PP8 Matt Williams .20 .50
PP9 Albert Belle .20 .50
PP10 Cecil Fielder .20 .50
PP11 Juan Gonzalez .20 .50
PP12 Ken Griffey Jr. 1.00 2.50
PP13 Mark McGwire 1.25 3.00
PP14 Eddie Murray .50 1.25
PP15 Manny Ramirez .30 .75
PP16 Cal Ripken 1.50 4.00
PP17 Tim Salmon .30 .75
PP18 Frank Thomas .50 1.25
PP19 Jim Thome .30 .75
PP20 Mo Vaughn .20 .50

1995 SP Special FX

COMPLETE SET (48) 50.00 120.00
STATED ODDS 1:75
1 Jose Canseco 1.00 2.50
2 Roger Clemens 3.00 8.00
3 Mo Vaughn .75 2.00
4 Tim Salmon .75 2.00
5 Chuck Finley .75 2.00
6 Robin Ventura .75 2.00
7 Jason Bere .75 2.00
8 Carlos Baerga .75 2.00
9 Albert Belle .75 2.00
10 Kenny Lofton .75 2.00
11 Manny Ramirez 1.25 3.00
12 Jeff Montgomery .75 2.00
13 Kirby Puckett 2.00 5.00
14 Wade Boggs 1.25 3.00
15 Don Mattingly 4.00 10.00
16 Cal Ripken 6.00 15.00
17 Ruben Sierra .75 2.00
18 Ken Griffey Jr. 10.00 25.00
19 Randy Johnson 2.00 5.00
20 Alex Rodriguez 6.00 15.00
21 Will Clark .75 2.00
22 Juan Gonzalez 1.25 3.00
23 Roberto Alomar 1.25 3.00
24 Joe Carter .75 2.00
25 Alex Gonzalez .75 2.00
26 Paul Molitor 2.00 5.00
27 Ryan Klesko .75 2.00
28 Fred McGriff 1.25 3.00
29 Greg Maddux 6.00 15.00
30 Sammy Sosa 2.00 5.00
31 Bret Boone .75 2.00
32 Barry Larkin 1.25 3.00
33 Reggie Sanders .75 2.00
34 Dante Bichette .75 2.00
35 Andres Galarraga 1.25 3.00
36 Charles Johnson .75 2.00
37 Gary Sheffield .75 2.00
38 Jeff Bagwell 1.25 3.00
39 Craig Biggio 1.25 3.00
40 Eric Karros .75 2.00
41 Billy Ashley .75 2.00
42 Raul Mondesi .75 2.00
43 Mike Piazza 2.00 5.00
44 Rondell White .75 2.00
45 Bret Saberhagen .75 2.00
46 Tony Gwynn 2.00 5.00
47 Melvin Nieves .75 2.00
48 Matt Williams .75 2.00

1996 SP Previews FanFest

These eight standard-size cards were issued to promote the 1996 Upper Deck SP Issue. The fronts feature a color action photo as well as a small inset player shot. The 1996 All-Star game logo as well as the SP logo are on the bottom left corner. The backs have another photo as well as some biographical information.

COMPLETE SET (8) 15.00 40.00
1 Ken Griffey Jr. 4.00 10.00
2 Frank Thomas 1.50 4.00
3 Albert Belle .60 1.50
4 Mo Vaughn .60 1.50
5 Barry Bonds 2.50 6.00
6 Mike Piazza 4.00 10.00
7 Matt Williams .75 2.00
8 Sammy Sosa 2.00 5.00

1996 SP

The 1996 SP set was issued in one series totalling 188 cards. The eight-card packs retailed for $4.19 each. Cards number 1-20 feature color action player photos with "Premier Prospects" printed in silver foil across the top and the player's name and team at the bottom in the border. The backs carry player information and statistics. Cards number 21-185 display unique player photos with an outer wood-grain border and inner thin platinum foil border as well as a small inset player shot. The only notable Rookie Card in this set is Darin Erstad.

COMPLETE SET (188) 12.00 30.00
SUBSET CARDS HALF VALUE OF BASE CARDS
1 Rey Ordonez FOIL .15 .40
2 George Arias FOIL .15 .40
3 Osvaldo Fernandez FOIL .15 .40
4 Darin Erstad FOIL RC 2.00 5.00
5 Paul Wilson FOIL .15 .40
6 Richard Hidalgo FOIL .15 .40
7 Justin Thompson FOIL .15 .40
8 Jimmy Haynes FOIL .15 .40
9 Edgar Renteria FOIL .15 .40
10 Ruben Rivera FOIL .15 .40
11 Chris Snopek FOIL .15 .40
12 Billy Wagner FOIL .15 .40
13 Mike Grace FOIL RC .15 .40
14 Todd Greene FOIL .15 .40
15 Karim Garcia FOIL .15 .40
16 John Wasdin FOIL .15 .40
17 Jason Kendall FOIL .15 .40
18 Bob Abreu FOIL .40 1.00
19 Jermaine Dye FOIL .15 .40
20 Jason Schmidt FOIL .25 .60
21 Javy Lopez .15 .40
22 Ryan Klesko .15 .40
23 Tom Glavine .25 .60
24 John Smoltz .25 .60
25 Greg Maddux .60 1.50
26 Chipper Jones .40 1.00
27 Fred McGriff .25 .60
28 David Justice .15 .40
29 Roberto Alomar .25 .60
30 Cal Ripken 1.25 3.00
31 B.J. Surhoff .15 .40
32 Bobby Bonilla .15 .40
33 Mike Mussina .25 .60
34 Randy Myers .15 .40
35 Rafael Palmeiro .25 .60
36 Brady Anderson .15 .40
37 Tim Naehring .15 .40
38 Jose Canseco .25 .60
39 Roger Clemens .75 2.00
40 Mo Vaughn .15 .40
41 John Valentin .15 .40
42 Kevin Mitchell .15 .40
43 Chili Davis .15 .40
44 Garret Anderson .15 .40
45 Tim Salmon .25 .60
46 Chuck Finley .15 .40
47 Troy Percival .15 .40
48 Jim Abbott .25 .60
49 J.T. Snow .15 .40
50 Jim Edmonds .15 .40
51 Sammy Sosa .40 1.00
52 Brian McRae .15 .40
53 Ryne Sandberg .60 1.50
54 Jaime Navarro .15 .40
55 Mark Grace .25 .60
56 Harold Baines .15 .40
57 Robin Ventura .15 .40
58 Tony Phillips .15 .40
59 Alex Fernandez .15 .40
60 Frank Thomas .40 1.00
61 Ray Durham .15 .40
62 Bret Boone .15 .40
63 Reggie Sanders .15 .40
64 Pete Schourek .15 .40
65 Barry Larkin .25 .60
66 John Smiley .15 .40
67 Carlos Baerga .15 .40
68 Jim Thome .25 .60
69 Eddie Murray .40 1.00
70 Albert Belle .15 .40
71 Dennis Martinez .15 .40
72 Jack McDowell .15 .40
73 Kenny Lofton .15 .40
74 Manny Ramirez .25 .60
75 Dante Bichette .15 .40
76 Vinny Castilla .15 .40
77 Andres Galarraga .15 .40
78 Walt Weiss .15 .40
79 Ellis Burks .15 .40
80 Larry Walker .15 .40
81 Cecil Fielder .15 .40
82 Melvin Nieves .15 .40
83 Travis Fryman .15 .40
84 Chad Curtis .15 .40
85 Alan Trammell .15 .40
86 Gary Sheffield .15 .40
87 Charles Johnson .15 .40
88 Andre Dawson .15 .40
89 Jeff Conine .15 .40
90 Greg Colbrunn .15 .40
91 Derek Bell .15 .40
92 Brian L.Hunter .15 .40
93 Doug Drabek .15 .40
94 Craig Biggio .25 .60
95 Jeff Bagwell .25 .60
96 Kevin Appier .15 .40
97 Jeff Montgomery .15 .40
98 Michael Tucker .15 .40
99 Bip Roberts .15 .40
100 Johnny Damon .25 .60
101 Eric Karros .15 .40
102 Raul Mondesi .15 .40
103 Ramon Martinez .15 .40
104 Ismael Valdes .15 .40
105 Mike Piazza .60 1.50
106 Hideo Nomo .40 1.00
107 Chan Ho Park .15 .40
108 Ben McDonald .15 .40
109 Kevin Seitzer .15 .40
110 Greg Vaughn .15 .40
111 Jose Valentin .15 .40
112 Rick Aguilera .15 .40
113 Marty Cordova .15 .40
114 Brad Radke .15 .40
115 Kirby Puckett .40 1.00
116 Chuck Knoblauch .15 .40
117 Paul Molitor .15 .40
118 Pedro Martinez .25 .60
119 Mike Lansing .15 .40
120 Rondell White .15 .40
121 Moises Alou .15 .40
122 Mark Grudzielanek .15 .40
123 Jeff Fassero .15 .40
124 Rico Brogna .15 .40
125 Jason Isringhausen .15 .40
126 Jeff Kent .15 .40
127 Bernard Gilkey .15 .40
128 Todd Hundley .15 .40
129 David Cone .15 .40
130 Andy Pettitte .25 .60
131 Wade Boggs .25 .60
132 Paul O'Neill .25 .60
133 Ruben Sierra .15 .40
134 John Wetteland .15 .40
135 Derek Jeter 1.00 2.50
136 Geronimo Berroa .15 .40
137 Terry Steinbach .15 .40
138 Ariel Prieto .15 .40
139 Scott Brosius .15 .40
140 Mark McGwire 1.00 2.50
141 Lenny Dykstra .15 .40
142 Todd Zeile .15 .40
143 Benito Santiago .15 .40
144 Mickey Morandini .15 .40
145 Gregg Jefferies .15 .40
146 Denny Neagle .15 .40
147 Orlando Merced .15 .40
148 Charlie Hayes .15 .40
149 Carlos Garcia .15 .40
150 Jay Bell .15 .40
151 Ray Lankford .15 .40
152 Alan Benes .15 .40
Andy Benes
153 Dennis Eckersley .15 .40
154 Gary Gaetti .15 .40
155 Ozzie Smith .60 1.50
156 Ron Gant .15 .40
157 Brian Jordan .15 .40
158 Ken Caminiti .15 .40
159 Rickey Henderson .40 1.00
160 Tony Gwynn .50 1.25
161 Wally Joyner .15 .40
162 Andy Ashby .15 .40
163 Steve Finley .15 .40
164 Glenallen Hill .15 .40
165 Matt Williams .15 .40
166 Barry Bonds 1.00 2.50
167 William Vanlandingham .15 .40
168 Rod Beck .15 .40
169 Randy Johnson .40 1.00
170 Ken Griffey Jr. .75 2.00
171 Alex Rodriguez .75 2.00
172 Edgar Martinez .25 .60
173 Jay Buhner .15 .40
174 Russ Davis .15 .40
175 Juan Gonzalez .15 .40
176 Mickey Tettleton .15 .40
177 Will Clark .25 .60
178 Ken Hill .15 .40
179 Dean Palmer .15 .40
180 Ivan Rodriguez .25 .60
181 Carlos Delgado .15 .40
182 Alex Gonzalez .15 .40
183 Shawn Green .15 .40
184 Juan Guzman .15 .40
185 Joe Carter .15 .40
186 Hideo Nomo CL .25 .60
187 Cal Ripken CL .60 1.50
188 Ken Griffey Jr. CL .50 1.25

1996 SP Baseball Heroes

COMPLETE SET (10) 30.00 80.00
STATED ODDS 1:96
CONDITION SENSITIVE SET
82 Frank Thomas 4.00 10.00
83 Albert Belle 1.50 4.00
84 Barry Bonds 6.00 15.00
85 Chipper Jones 4.00 10.00
86 Hideo Nomo 4.00 10.00
87 Mike Piazza 4.00 10.00
88 Manny Ramirez 2.50 6.00
89 Greg Maddux 6.00 15.00
90 Ken Griffey Jr. 8.00 20.00
NNO Ken Griffey Jr. HDR 8.00 20.00

1996 SP Marquee Matchups

COMPLETE SET (20) 15.00 40.00
STATED ODDS 1:5
*DIE CUTS: 1.2X TO 3X BASIC MARQUEE
DC STATED ODDS 1:61
MM1 Ken Griffey Jr. 2.00 5.00
MM2 Hideo Nomo 1.00 2.50
MM3 Derek Jeter 2.50 6.00
MM4 Rey Ordonez .40 1.00
MM5 Tim Salmon .40 1.00
MM6 Mike Piazza 1.00 2.50
MM7 Mark McGwire 1.50 4.00
MM8 Barry Bonds 1.50 4.00
MM9 Cal Ripken 3.00 8.00
MM10 Greg Maddux 1.50 4.00
MM11 Albert Belle .40 1.00
MM12 Barry Larkin .60 1.50
MM13 Jeff Bagwell .60 1.50
MM14 Juan Gonzalez .40 1.00
MM15 Frank Thomas 1.00 2.50
MM16 Sammy Sosa 1.00 2.50
MM17 Mike Mussina .60 1.50
MM18 Chipper Jones 1.00 2.50
MM19 Roger Clemens 1.25 3.00
MM20 Fred McGriff .60 1.50

1996 SP Special FX

COMPLETE SET (48) 50.00 100.00
STATED ODDS 1:5
*DIE CUTS: 1X TO 2.5X BASIC SPECIAL FX
DIE CUTS STATED ODDS 1:75
1 Greg Maddux 3.00 8.00
2 Eric Karros .75 2.00
3 Mike Piazza 3.00 8.00
4 Raul Mondesi .75 2.00
5 Hideo Nomo 2.00 5.00
6 Jim Edmonds .75 2.00
7 Jason Isringhausen .75 2.00
8 Jay Buhner .75 2.00
9 Barry Larkin 1.25 3.00
10 Ken Griffey Jr. 4.00 10.00
11 Gary Sheffield .75 2.00
12 Craig Biggio 1.25 3.00
13 Paul Wilson .75 2.00
14 Rondell White .75 2.00
15 Chipper Jones 2.00 5.00
16 Kirby Puckett 2.00 5.00
17 Ron Gant .75 2.00
18 Wade Boggs 1.25 3.00
19 Fred McGriff 1.25 3.00
20 Cal Ripken 6.00 15.00
21 Jason Kendall .75 2.00
22 Johnny Damon 1.25 3.00
23 Kenny Lofton .75 2.00
24 Roberto Alomar 1.25 3.00
25 Barry Bonds 5.00 12.00
26 Dante Bichette .75 2.00
27 Mark McGwire 5.00 12.00
28 Rafael Palmeiro 1.25 3.00
29 Juan Gonzalez .75 2.00
30 Albert Belle .75 2.00
31 Randy Johnson 2.00 5.00
32 Jose Canseco 1.25 3.00
33 Sammy Sosa 2.00 5.00
34 Eddie Murray 2.00 5.00
35 Frank Thomas 2.00 5.00
36 Tom Glavine 1.25 3.00
37 Matt Williams .75 2.00
38 Roger Clemens 4.00 10.00
39 Paul Molitor .75 2.00
40 Tony Gwynn 2.50 6.00
41 Mo Vaughn .75 2.00
42 Tim Salmon 1.25 3.00
43 Manny Ramirez 1.25 3.00
44 Jeff Bagwell 1.25 3.00
45 Edgar Martinez 1.25 3.00
46 Rey Ordonez .75 2.00
47 Osvaldo Fernandez .75 2.00
48 Derek Jeter 5.00 12.00

1997 SP

The 1997 SP set was issued in one series totalling 183 cards and was distributed in eight-card packs with a suggested retail of $4.39. Athough unconfirmed by the manufacturer, it is perceived in some circles that cards numbered between 160 and 180 are in slightly shorter supply. Notable Rookie Cards include Jose Cruz Jr. and Hideki Irabu.

COMPLETE SET (184) 15.00 40.00
1 Andruw Jones FOIL .40 1.00
2 Kevin Orie FOIL .20 .50
3 Nomar Garciaparra FOIL 1.00 2.50
4 Jose Guillen FOIL .30 .75
5 Todd Walker FOIL .20 .50
6 Derrick Gibson FOIL .20 .50
7 Aaron Boone FOIL .30 .75
8 Bartolo Colon FOIL .30 .75
9 Derrek Lee FOIL .40 1.00
10 Vladimir Guerrero FOIL .60 1.50
11 Wilton Guerrero FOIL .20 .50
12 Luis Castillo FOIL .20 .50
13 Jason Dickson FOIL .20 .50
14 Bubba Trammell FOIL RC .30 .75
15 Jose Cruz Jr. FOIL RC .30 .75
16 Eddie Murray .40 1.00
17 Darin Erstad .15 .40
18 Garret Anderson .15 .40
19 Jim Edmonds .15 .40
20 Tim Salmon .25 .60
21 Chuck Finley .15 .40
22 John Smoltz .25 .60
23 Greg Maddux .60 1.50
24 Kenny Lofton .15 .40
25 Chipper Jones .40 1.00
26 Ryan Klesko .15 .40
27 Javy Lopez .15 .40
28 Fred McGriff .25 .60
29 Roberto Alomar .25 .60
30 Rafael Palmeiro .25 .60
31 Mike Mussina .25 .60
32 Brady Anderson .15 .40
33 Rocky Coppinger .15 .40
34 Cal Ripken 1.25 3.00
35 Mo Vaughn .15 .40
36 Steve Avery .15 .40
37 Tom Gordon .15 .40
38 Tim Naehring .15 .40
39 Troy O'Leary .15 .40
40 Sammy Sosa .40 1.00
41 Brian McRae .15 .40
42 Mel Rojas .15 .40
43 Ryne Sandberg .60 1.50
44 Mark Grace .25 .60
45 Albert Belle .15 .40
46 Robin Ventura .15 .40
47 Roberto Hernandez .15 .40
48 Ray Durham .15 .40
49 Harold Baines .15 .40
50 Frank Thomas .40 1.00
51 Bret Boone .15 .40
52 Reggie Sanders .15 .40
53 Deion Sanders .25 .60
54 Hal Morris .15 .40
55 Barry Larkin .25 .60
56 Jim Thome .25 .60
57 Marquis Grissom .15 .40
58 David Justice .15 .40
59 Charles Nagy .15 .40
60 Manny Ramirez .25 .60
61 Matt Williams .15 .40
62 Jack McDowell .15 .40
63 Vinny Castilla .15 .40

64 Dante Bichette .15 .40
65 Andres Galarraga .15 .40
66 Ellis Burks .15 .40
67 Larry Walker .15 .40
68 Eric Young .15 .40
69 Brian L. Hunter .15 .40
70 Travis Fryman .15 .40
71 Tony Clark .15 .40
72 Bobby Higginson .15 .40
73 Melvin Nieves .15 .40
74 Jeff Conine .15 .40
75 Gary Sheffield .15 .40
76 Moises Alou .15 .40
77 Edgar Renteria .15 .40
78 Alex Fernandez .15 .40
79 Charles Johnson .15 .40
80 Bobby Bonilla .15 .40
81 Darryl Kile .15 .40
82 Derek Bell .15 .40
83 Shane Reynolds .15 .40
84 Craig Biggio .25 .60
85 Jeff Bagwell .25 .60
86 Billy Wagner .15 .40
87 Chili Davis .15 .40
88 Kevin Appier .15 .40
89 Jay Bell .15 .40
90 Johnny Damon .25 .60
91 Jeff King .15 .40
92 Hideo Nomo .40 1.00
93 Todd Hollandsworth .15 .40
94 Eric Karros .15 .40
95 Mike Piazza .60 1.50
96 Ramon Martinez .15 .40
97 Todd Worrell .15 .40
98 Raul Mondesi .15 .40
99 Dave Nilsson .15 .40
100 John Jaha .15 .40
101 Jose Valentin .15 .40
102 Jeff Cirillo .15 .40
103 Jeff D'Amico .15 .40
104 Ben McDonald .15 .40
105 Paul Molitor .15 .40
106 Rich Becker .15 .40
107 Frank Rodriguez .15 .40
108 Marty Cordova .15 .40
109 Terry Steinbach .15 .40
110 Chuck Knoblauch .15 .40
111 Mark Grudzielanek .15 .40
112 Mike Lansing .15 .40
113 Pedro Martinez .25 .60
114 Henry Rodriguez .15 .40
115 Rondell White .15 .40
116 Rey Ordonez .15 .40
117 Carlos Baerga .15 .40
118 Lance Johnson .15 .40
119 Bernard Gilkey .15 .40
120 Todd Hundley .15 .40
121 John Franco .15 .40
122 Bernie Williams .25 .60
123 David Cone .15 .40
124 Cecil Fielder .15 .40
125 Derek Jeter 1.00 2.50
126 Tino Martinez .25 .60
127 Mariano Rivera .40 1.00
128 Andy Pettitte .25 .60
129 Wade Boggs .25 .60
130 Mark McGwire 1.00 2.50
131 Jose Canseco .25 .60
132 Geronimo Berroa .15 .40
133 Jason Giambi .15 .40
134 Ernie Young .15 .40
135 Scott Rolen .25 .60
136 Ricky Bottalico .15 .40
137 Curt Schilling .15 .40
138 Gregg Jefferies .15 .40
139 Mickey Morandini .15 .40
140 Jason Kendall .15 .40
141 Kevin Elster .15 .40
142 Al Martin .15 .40
143 Joe Randa .15 .40
144 Jason Schmidt .15 .40
145 Ray Lankford .15 .40
146 Brian Jordan .15 .40
147 Andy Benes .15 .40
148 Alan Benes .15 .40
149 Gary Gaetti .15 .40
150 Ron Gant .15 .40
151 Dennis Eckersley .15 .40
152 Rickey Henderson .40 1.00
153 Joey Hamilton .15 .40
154 Ken Caminiti .15 .40
155 Tony Gwynn .50 1.25
156 Steve Finley .15 .40
157 Trevor Hoffman .15 .40
158 Greg Vaughn .15 .40
159 J.T. Snow .15 .40
160 Barry Bonds 1.00 2.50
161 Glenallen Hill .15 .40
162 Bill Van Landingham .15 .40
163 Jeff Kent .15 .40
164 Jay Buhner .15 .40
165 Ken Griffey Jr. .75 2.00
166 Alex Rodriguez .60 1.50
167 Randy Johnson .40 1.00
168 Edgar Martinez .25 .60
169 Dan Wilson .15 .40
170 Ivan Rodriguez .25 .60
171 Roger Pavlik .15 .40
172 Will Clark .25 .60
173 Dean Palmer .15 .40
174 Rusty Greer .15 .40
175 Juan Gonzalez .15 .40
176 John Wetteland .15 .40
177 Joe Carter .15 .40
178 Ed Sprague .15 .40
179 Carlos Delgado .15 .40
180 Roger Clemens .75 2.00
181 Juan Guzman .15 .40
182 Pat Hentgen .15 .40
183 Ken Griffey Jr. CL .50 1.25
184 Hideki Irabu RC .15 .40

1997 SP Game Film

COMPLETE SET (10) 125.00 250.00
RANDOM INSERTS IN PACKS
STATED PRINT RUN 500 SERIAL #'d SETS
GF1 Alex Rodriguez 12.00 30.00
GF2 Frank Thomas 10.00 25.00
GF3 Andruw Jones 4.00 10.00
GF4 Cal Ripken 30.00 80.00
GF5 Mike Piazza 10.00 25.00
GF6 Derek Jeter 25.00 60.00
GF7 Mark McGwire 15.00 40.00
GF8 Chipper Jones 10.00 25.00
GF9 Barry Bonds 15.00 40.00
GF10 Ken Griffey Jr. 20.00 50.00

1997 SP Griffey Heroes

COMPLETE SET (10) 20.00 50.00
COMMON CARD (91-100) 3.00 8.00

1997 SP Inside Info

COMPLETE SET (25) 75.00 150.00
ONE PER SEALED BOX
CONDITION SENSITIVE SET
1 Ken Griffey Jr. 5.00 12.00
2 Mark McGwire 6.00 15.00
3 Kenny Lofton 1.00 2.50
4 Paul Molitor 1.00 2.50
5 Frank Thomas 2.50 6.00
6 Greg Maddux 4.00 10.00
7 Mo Vaughn 1.00 2.50
8 Cal Ripken 8.00 20.00
9 Jeff Bagwell 1.50 4.00
10 Alex Rodriguez 4.00 10.00
11 John Smoltz 1.50 4.00
12 Manny Ramirez 1.50 4.00
13 Sammy Sosa 2.50 6.00
14 Vladimir Guerrero 4.00 10.00
15 Albert Belle 1.00 2.50
16 Mike Piazza 4.00 10.00
17 Derek Jeter 6.00 15.00
18 Scott Rolen 1.50 4.00
19 Tony Gwynn 3.00 8.00
20 Barry Bonds 6.00 15.00
21 Ken Caminiti 1.00 2.50
22 Chipper Jones 2.50 6.00
23 Juan Gonzalez 1.00 2.50
24 Roger Clemens 5.00 12.00
25 Andruw Jones 2.50 6.00

1997 SP Marquee Matchups

COMPLETE SET (20) 20.00 50.00
STATED ODDS 1:5
MM1 Ken Griffey Jr. 1.50 4.00
MM2 Andres Galarraga .30 .75
MM3 Barry Bonds 2.00 5.00
MM4 Mark McGwire 2.00 5.00
MM5 Mike Piazza 1.25 3.00
MM6 Tim Salmon .50 1.25
MM7 Tony Gwynn 1.00 2.50
MM8 Alex Rodriguez 1.25 3.00
MM9 Chipper Jones .75 2.00
MM10 Derek Jeter 2.00 5.00
MM11 Manny Ramirez .50 1.25
MM12 Jeff Bagwell .50 1.25
MM13 Greg Maddux 1.25 3.00
MM14 Cal Ripken 2.50 6.00
MM15 Mo Vaughn .30 .75
MM16 Gary Sheffield .30 .75
MM17 Jim Thome .50 1.25
MM18 Barry Larkin .50 1.25
MM19 Frank Thomas .75 2.00
MM20 Sammy Sosa .75 2.00

1997 SP Special FX

COMPLETE SET (48) 100.00 200.00
STATED ODDS 1:9
1 Ken Griffey Jr. 4.00 10.00
2 Frank Thomas 2.00 5.00
3 Barry Bonds 5.00 12.00
4 Albert Belle .75 2.00
5 Mike Piazza 3.00 8.00
6 Greg Maddux 3.00 8.00
7 Chipper Jones 2.00 5.00
8 Cal Ripken 6.00 15.00
9 Jeff Bagwell 1.25 3.00
10 Alex Rodriguez 3.00 8.00
11 Mark McGwire 5.00 12.00
12 Kenny Lofton .75 2.00
13 Juan Gonzalez .75 2.00
14 Mo Vaughn .75 2.00
15 John Smoltz 1.25 3.00
16 Derek Jeter 5.00 12.00
17 Tony Gwynn 2.50 6.00
18 Ivan Rodriguez 1.25 3.00
19 Barry Larkin 1.25 3.00
20 Sammy Sosa 2.00 5.00
21 Mike Mussina 1.25 3.00
22 Gary Sheffield .75 2.00
23 Brady Anderson .75 2.00
24 Roger Clemens 4.00 10.00
25 Ken Caminiti .75 2.00
26 Roberto Alomar 1.25 3.00
27 Hideo Nomo 2.00 5.00
28 Bernie Williams 1.25 3.00
29 Todd Hundley .75 2.00
30 Manny Ramirez 1.25 3.00
31 Eric Karros .75 2.00
32 Tim Salmon 1.25 3.00
33 Jay Buhner .75 2.00
34 Andy Pettitte 1.25 3.00
35 Jim Thome 1.25 3.00
36 Ryne Sandberg 3.00 8.00
37 Matt Williams .75 2.00
38 Ryan Klesko .75 2.00
39 Jose Canseco 1.25 3.00
40 Paul Molitor .75 2.00
41 Eddie Murray 2.00 5.00
42 Darin Erstad .75 2.00
43 Todd Walker 1.00 2.50
44 Wade Boggs 1.25 3.00
45 Andruw Jones 2.00 5.00
46 Scott Rolen 1.25 3.00
47 Vladimir Guerrero 3.00 8.00
49 Alex Rodriguez '96 4.00 10.00

1997 SP SPx Force

COMPLETE SET (10) 100.00 200.00
RANDOM INSERTS IN PACKS
STATED PRINT RUN 500 SERIAL #'d SETS
1 Griffey 12.50 30.00
Buhn
Gala
Bich
2 McGwire 15.00 40.00
Belle
B.And
Fielder
3 F.Thom 6.00 15.00
Mo
Bagw
Camin
4 Sosa 6.00 15.00
Bonds
Cans
Sheff
5 Madd 10.00 25.00
Clem
Smoltz
R.John
6 A.Rod 15.00 40.00
Jeter
Chipper
Ordon
7 Piazza 10.00 25.00
Nomo
Mond
T.Holl
8 J.Gonz 4.00 10.00
M.Ram
Alom
I.Rod
9 Gwynn 8.00 20.00
Boggs
Murray
Molit
10 Vlad 10.00 25.00
Rolen
Andruw
T.Walk

1997 SP SPx Force Autographs

STATED PRINT RUN 100 SERIAL #'d SETS
1 Ken Griffey Jr. 150.00 250.00
2 Albert Belle 15.00 40.00
3 Mo Vaughn 15.00 40.00
4 Gary Sheffield 20.00 50.00
5 Greg Maddux 75.00 150.00
6 Alex Rodriguez 100.00 175.00
7 Todd Hollandsworth 10.00 25.00
8 Roberto Alomar 20.00 50.00
9 Tony Gwynn 40.00 80.00
10 Andruw Jones 6.00 15.00

1997 SP Vintage Autographs

RANDOM INSERTS IN PACKS
PRINT RUNS B/WN 4-367 COPIES PER
NO PRICING ON QTY OF 25 OR LESS
1 Jeff Bagwell 93/7
2 Jeff Bagwell 95/173 30.00 60.00
3 Jeff Bagwell 96/292 12.00 30.00
4 Jeff Bagwell 96 MM/23
5 Jay Buhner 95/57 6.00 15.00
6 Jay Buhner 96/79 6.00 15.00
7 Jay Buhner 96 FX/27 6.00 15.00
8 Ken Griffey Jr. 93/16
9 Ken Griffey Jr. 93 PP/5
10 Ken Griffey Jr. 94/103 50.00 100.00
11 Ken Griffey Jr. 95/38 75.00 150.00
12 Ken Griffey Jr. 96/312 40.00 80.00
13 Tony Gwynn 93/17
14 Tony Gwynn 94/367 15.00 40.00
15 Tony Gwynn 94 HV/31 60.00 120.00
16 Tony Gwynn 95/64 30.00 60.00
17 Tony Gwynn 96/20
18 Todd Hollandsworth 94/167 6.00 15.00
19 Chipper Jones 93/34 50.00 100.00
20 Chipper Jones 95/60 40.00 80.00
21 Chipper Jones 96/102 30.00 60.00
22 Rey Ordonez 96/111 6.00 15.00
23 Rey Ordonez 96 MM/40 10.00 25.00
24 Alex Rodriguez 94/94 1000.00 1600.00
25 Alex Rodriguez 95/63 60.00 120.00
26 Alex Rodriguez 96/73 60.00 120.00
27 Gary Sheffield 94/130 15.00 40.00
28 Gary Sheffield 94 HVDC/4
29 Gary Sheffield 95/221 10.00 25.00
30 Gary Sheffield 96/58 30.00 60.00
31 Mo Vaughn 95/75 6.00 15.00
32 Mo Vaughn 97/293 6.00 15.00

1998 SP Authentic

The 1998 SP Authentic set was issued in one series totalling 198 cards. The five-card packs retailed for $4.99 each. The set contains the topical subset: Future Watch (1-30). Rookie Cards include Magglio Ordonez. A sample card featuring Ken Griffey Jr. was issued prior to the product's release and distributed along with dealer order forms. The card is identical to the basic issue Griffey Jr. card (number 123) except for the term "SAMPLE" in red print running diagonally against the card back.

COMPLETE SET (198) 15.00 40.00
1 Travis Lee FOIL .15 .40
2 Mike Caruso FOIL .15 .40
3 Kerry Wood FOIL .20 .50
4 Mark Kotsay FOIL .15 .40
5 Magglio Ordonez FOIL RC 5.00 12.00
6 Scott Elarton FOIL .15 .40
7 Carl Pavano FOIL .15 .40
8 A.J. Hinch FOIL .15 .40
9 Rolando Arrojo FOIL RC .15 .40
10 Ben Grieve FOIL .15 .40
11 Gabe Alvarez FOIL .15 .40
12 Mike Kinkade FOIL RC .15 .40
13 Bruce Chen FOIL .15 .40
14 Juan Encarnacion FOIL .15 .40
15 Todd Helton FOIL .25 .60
16 Aaron Boone FOIL .15 .40
17 Sean Casey FOIL .15 .40
18 Ramon Hernandez FOIL .15 .40
19 Daryle Ward FOIL .15 .40
20 Paul Konerko FOIL .15 .40
21 David Ortiz FOIL .50 1.25
22 Derrek Lee FOIL .25 .60
23 Brad Fullmer FOIL .15 .40
24 Javier Vazquez FOIL .15 .40
25 Miguel Tejada FOIL .40 1.00
26 Dave Dellucci FOIL RC .25 .60
27 Alex Gonzalez FOIL .15 .40
28 Matt Clement FOIL .15 .40
29 Masato Yoshii FOIL RC .15 .40
30 Russell Branyan FOIL .15 .40
31 Chuck Finley .15 .40
32 Jim Edmonds .15 .40
33 Darin Erstad .15 .40
34 Jason Dickson .15 .40
35 Tim Salmon .25 .60
36 Cecil Fielder .15 .40
37 Todd Greene .15 .40
38 Andy Benes .15 .40
39 Jay Bell .15 .40
40 Matt Williams .15 .40
41 Brian Anderson .15 .40
42 Karim Garcia .15 .40
43 Javy Lopez .15 .40
44 Tom Glavine .25 .60
45 Greg Maddux .60 1.50
46 Andruw Jones .25 .60
47 Chipper Jones .40 1.00
48 Ryan Klesko .15 .40
49 John Smoltz .25 .60
50 Andres Galarraga .15 .40
51 Rafael Palmeiro .25 .60
52 Mike Mussina .25 .60
53 Roberto Alomar .25 .60
54 Joe Carter .15 .40
55 Cal Ripken 1.25 3.00
56 Brady Anderson .15 .40
57 Mo Vaughn .15 .40
58 John Valentin .15 .40
59 Dennis Eckersley .15 .40
60 Nomar Garciaparra .60 1.50
61 Pedro Martinez .25 .60
62 Jeff Blauser .15 .40
63 Kevin Orie .15 .40
64 Henry Rodriguez .15 .40
65 Mark Grace .25 .60
66 Albert Belle .15 .40
67 Mike Cameron .15 .40
68 Robin Ventura .15 .40
69 Frank Thomas .40 1.00
70 Barry Larkin .25 .60
71 Brett Tomko .15 .40
72 Willie Greene .15 .40
73 Reggie Sanders .15 .40
74 Sandy Alomar Jr. .15 .40
75 Kenny Lofton .15 .40
76 Jaret Wright .15 .40
77 David Justice .15 .40
78 Omar Vizquel .25 .60
79 Manny Ramirez .25 .60
80 Jim Thome .25 .60
81 Travis Fryman .15 .40
82 Neifi Perez .15 .40
83 Mike Lansing .15 .40
84 Vinny Castilla .15 .40
85 Larry Walker .15 .40
86 Dante Bichette .15 .40
87 Darryl Kile .15 .40
88 Justin Thompson .15 .40
89 Damion Easley .15 .40
90 Tony Clark .15 .40
91 Bobby Higginson .15 .40
92 Brian Hunter .15 .40
93 Edgar Renteria .15 .40
94 Craig Counsell .15 .40
95 Mike Piazza .60 1.50
96 Livan Hernandez .15 .40
97 Todd Zeile .15 .40
98 Richard Hidalgo .15 .40
99 Moises Alou .15 .40
100 Jeff Bagwell .25 .60
101 Mike Hampton .15 .40
102 Craig Biggio .25 .60
103 Dean Palmer .15 .40
104 Tim Belcher .15 .40
105 Jeff King .15 .40
106 Jeff Conine .15 .40
107 Johnny Damon .25 .60
108 Hideo Nomo .40 1.00
109 Raul Mondesi .15 .40
110 Gary Sheffield .15 .40
111 Ramon Martinez .15 .40
112 Chan Ho Park .15 .40
113 Eric Young .15 .40
114 Charles Johnson .15 .40
115 Eric Karros .15 .40
116 Bobby Bonilla .15 .40
117 Jeromy Burnitz .15 .40
118 Cal Eldred .15 .40
119 Jeff D'Amico .15 .40
120 Marquis Grissom .15 .40
121 Dave Nilsson .15 .40
122 Brad Radke .15 .40
123 Marty Cordova .15 .40
124 Ron Coomer .15 .40
125 Paul Molitor .15 .40
126 Todd Walker .15 .40
127 Rondell White .15 .40
128 Mark Grudzielanek .15 .40
129 Carlos Perez .15 .40
130 Vladimir Guerrero .40 1.00
131 Dustin Hermanson .15 .40
132 Butch Huskey .15 .40
133 John Franco .15 .40
134 Rey Ordonez .15 .40
135 Todd Hundley .15 .40
136 Edgardo Alfonzo .15 .40
137 Bobby Jones .15 .40
138 John Olerud .15 .40
139 Chili Davis .15 .40
140 Tino Martinez .25 .60
141 Andy Pettitte .25 .60
142 Chuck Knoblauch .15 .40
143 Bernie Williams .25 .60
144 David Cone .15 .40
145 Derek Jeter 1.00 2.50
146 Paul O'Neill .25 .60
147 Rickey Henderson .40 1.00
148 Jason Giambi .15 .40
149 Kenny Rogers .15 .40
150 Scott Rolen .25 .60
151 Curt Schilling .15 .40
152 Ricky Bottalico .15 .40
153 Mike Lieberthal .15 .40
154 Francisco Cordova .15 .40
155 Jose Guillen .15 .40
156 Jason Schmidt .15 .40
157 Jason Kendall .15 .40
158 Kevin Young .15 .40
159 Delino DeShields .15 .40
160 Mark McGwire 1.00 2.50
161 Ray Lankford .15 .40
162 Brian Jordan .15 .40
163 Ron Gant .15 .40
164 Todd Stottlemyre .15 .40
165 Ken Caminiti .15 .40
166 Kevin Brown .25 .60
167 Trevor Hoffman .15 .40
168 Steve Finley .15 .40
169 Wally Joyner .15 .40
170 Tony Gwynn .50 1.25
171 Shawn Estes .15 .40
172 J.T. Snow .15 .40
173 Jeff Kent .15 .40
174 Robb Nen .15 .40
175 Barry Bonds 1.00 2.50
176 Randy Johnson .40 1.00
177 Edgar Martinez .25 .60
178 Jay Buhner .15 .40
179 Alex Rodriguez .60 1.50
180 Ken Griffey Jr. .75 2.00
181 Ken Cloude .15 .40
182 Wade Boggs .25 .60
183 Tony Saunders .15 .40
184 Wilson Alvarez .15 .40
185 Fred McGriff .25 .60
186 Roberto Hernandez .15 .40
187 Kevin Stocker .15 .40
188 Fernando Tatis .15 .40
189 Will Clark .25 .60
190 Juan Gonzalez .15 .40
191 Rusty Greer .15 .40
192 Ivan Rodriguez .25 .60
193 Jose Canseco .25 .60
194 Carlos Delgado .15 .40
195 Roger Clemens .75 2.00
196 Pat Hentgen .15 .40
197 Randy Myers .15 .40
198 Ken Griffey Jr. CL .50 1.25
S123 Ken Griffey Jr. Sample 1.00 2.50

1998 SP Authentic Chirography

STATED ODDS 1:25
1000 OR MORE OF EACH UNLESS STATED
SP PRINT RUNS STATED BELOW
GRIFFEY EXCH.DEADLINE 07/27/99
AJ Andruw Jones 6.00 15.00
AR Alex Rodriguez SP/800 40.00 100.00
BG Ben Grieve 6.00 15.00
CJ Charles Johnson 6.00 15.00
CP Chipper Jones SP/800 40.00 100.00
DE Darin Erstad 6.00 15.00
GS Gary Sheffield 10.00 25.00
IR Ivan Rodriguez 8.00 20.00
JC Jose Cruz Jr. 6.00 15.00
JW Jaret Wright 6.00 15.00
KG Ken Griffey Jr. SP/400 100.00 200.00
KGEX Ken Griffey Jr. EXCH 6.00 15.00
LH Livan Hernandez 6.00 15.00
MK Mark Kotsay 6.00 15.00
MM Mike Mussina 20.00 50.00
MT Miguel Tejada 6.00 15.00
MV Mo Vaughn SP/800 6.00 15.00
NG Nomar Garciaparra SP/400 20.00 50.00
PK Paul Konerko 6.00 15.00
PM Paul Molitor SP/800 12.00 30.00
RA Roberto Alomar SP/800 15.00 40.00
RB Russell Branyan 6.00 15.00
RC Roger Clemens SP/400 30.00 80.00
RL Ray Lankford 6.00 15.00
SC Sean Casey 6.00 15.00
SR Scott Rolen 10.00 25.00
TC Tony Clark 6.00 15.00
TG Tony Gwynn SP/850 20.00 50.00
TH Todd Helton 10.00 25.00
TL Travis Lee 6.00 15.00
VG Vladimir Guerrero 12.00 30.00

1998 SP Authentic Griffey 300th HR Redemption

300 Ken Griffey Jr. 15.00 40.00

1998 SP Authentic Game Jersey 5 x 7

ONE PER JERSEY TRADE CARD VIA MAIL
PRINT RUNS B/WN 125-415 COPIES PER
EXCH.DEADLINE WAS 8/1/99
1 Ken Griffey Jr./125 40.00 80.00
2 Gary Sheffield/125 10.00 25.00
3 Greg Maddux/125 40.00 80.00
4 Alex Rodriguez/125 40.00 80.00
5 Tony Gwynn/415 20.00 50.00
6 Jay Buhner/125 10.00 25.00

1998 SP Authentic Sheer Dominance

COMPLETE SET (42) 40.00 100.00
STATED ODDS 1:3
*GOLD: 1.25X TO 3X BASIC DOMINANCE
GOLD: RANDOM INSERTS IN PACKS
GOLD PRINT RUN 2000 SERIAL #'d SETS
*TITANIUM: 3X TO 8X BASIC DOMINANCE
TITANIUM: RANDOM INSERTS IN PACKS
TITANIUM PRINT RUN 100 SERIAL #'d SETS
SD1 Ken Griffey Jr. 2.00 5.00
SD2 Rickey Henderson 1.00 2.50
SD3 Jaret Wright .40 1.00
SD4 Craig Biggio .60 1.50
SD5 Travis Lee .40 1.00
SD6 Kenny Lofton .40 1.00
SD7 Raul Mondesi .40 1.00
SD8 Cal Ripken 3.00 8.00
SD9 Matt Williams .40 1.00
SD10 Mark McGwire 2.50 6.00
SD11 Alex Rodriguez 1.50 4.00
SD12 Fred McGriff .60 1.50
SD13 Scott Rolen .60 1.50
SD14 Paul Molitor .40 1.00
SD15 Nomar Garciaparra 1.50 4.00
SD16 Vladimir Guerrero 1.00 2.50
SD17 Andruw Jones .60 1.50
SD18 Manny Ramirez .60 1.50
SD19 Tony Gwynn 1.25 3.00
SD20 Barry Bonds 2.50 6.00
SD21 Ben Grieve .40 1.00
SD22 Ivan Rodriguez .60 1.50
SD23 Jose Cruz Jr. 1.00 2.50
SD24 Pedro Martinez .60 1.50
SD25 Chipper Jones 1.00 2.50
SD26 Albert Belle .40 1.00
SD27 Todd Helton .60 1.50
SD28 Paul Konerko .40 1.00
SD29 Sammy Sosa 1.00 2.50
SD30 Frank Thomas 1.00 2.50
SD31 Greg Maddux 1.50 4.00
SD32 Randy Johnson 1.00 2.50
SD33 Larry Walker .40 1.00
SD34 Roberto Alomar .60 1.50
SD35 Roger Clemens 2.00 5.00
SD36 Mo Vaughn .40 1.00
SD37 Jim Thome .60 1.50
SD38 Jeff Bagwell .60 1.50
SD39 Tino Martinez .60 1.50
SD40 Mike Piazza 1.50 4.00
SD41 Derek Jeter 2.50 6.00
SD42 Juan Gonzalez .40 1.00

1998 SP Authentic Trade Cards

COMMON CARD (B1-B5) 6.00 15.00
COMMON CARD (J1-J6) 6.00 15.00
COMMON CARD (KG1-KG4) 6.00 15.00
STATED ODDS 1:291
PRINT RUNS LISTED BELOW
EXCHANGE DEADLINE WAS 8/1/99
GRIFFEY GLOVE/JERS.TOO SCARCE TO PRICE
B1 R.Alomar Ball/100 10.00 25.00
B2 A.Belle Ball/100 6.00 15.00
B3 B.Jordan Ball/50 6.00 15.00
B4 R.Mondesi Ball/100 6.00 15.00
B5 R.Ventura Ball/50 10.00 25.00
J1 J.Buhner Jsy Card/125 6.00 15.00
J2 K.Griffey Jr. Jsy Card/125 30.00 80.00
J3 T.Gwynn Jsy Card/415 10.00 25.00
J4 G.Maddux Jsy Card/125 25.00 60.00
J5 A.Rodriguez Jsy Card/125 20.00 50.00
J6 G.Sheffield Jsy Card/125 6.00 15.00
KG1 K.Griffey Jr.300 Card/1000 8.00 20.00
KG2 K.Griffey Jr.AU Glove/30
KG3 K.Griffey Jr.AU Jersey/30
KG4 K.Griffey Jr.Standee/200 12.50 30.00

1999 SP Authentic

The 1999 SP Authentic set was issued in one series totalling 135 cards and distributed in five-card packs with a suggested retail price of $4.99. The fronts feature color action player photos with player information printed on the backs. The set features the following limited edition subsets: Future Watch (91-120) serially numbered to 2700 and Season to Remember (121-135) numbered to 2700 also. 350 Ernie Banks A Piece of History 500 Club bat cards were randomly seeded into packs. Also, Banks signed and numbered twenty additional copies. Pricing for these bat cards can be referenced under 1999 Upper Deck A Piece of History 500 Club.

COMP.SET w/o SP's (90) 10.00 25.00
COMMON CARD (1-90) .15 .40
COMMON FW (91-120) 4.00 10.00
FW PRINT RUN 2700 SERIAL #'d SUBSETS
COMMON STR (121-135) 1.25 3.00
STR PRINT RUN 2700 SERIAL #'d SUBSETS
91-135 RANDOM IN PACKS
E.BANKS BAT LISTED W/UD APH 500 CLUB
1 Mo Vaughn .15 .40
2 Jim Edmonds .15 .40
3 Darin Erstad .15 .40
4 Travis Lee .15 .40
5 Matt Williams .15 .40
6 Randy Johnson .40 1.00
7 Chipper Jones .40 1.00
8 Greg Maddux .60 1.50
9 Andruw Jones .25 .60
10 Andres Galarraga .15 .40
11 Tom Glavine .25 .60
12 Cal Ripken 1.25 3.00
13 Brady Anderson .15 .40
14 Albert Belle .15 .40
15 Nomar Garciaparra .60 1.50
16 Donnie Sadler .15 .40
17 Pedro Martinez .25 .60
18 Sammy Sosa .40 1.00
19 Kerry Wood .15 .40
20 Mark Grace .25 .60
21 Mike Caruso .15 .40
22 Frank Thomas .40 1.00
23 Paul Konerko .15 .40
24 Sean Casey .15 .40
25 Barry Larkin .25 .60
26 Kenny Lofton .15 .40
27 Manny Ramirez .25 .60
28 Jim Thome .25 .60
29 Bartolo Colon .15 .40
30 Jaret Wright .15 .40
31 Larry Walker .15 .40
32 Todd Helton .25 .60
33 Tony Clark .15 .40
34 Dean Palmer .15 .40
35 Mark Kotsay .15 .40
36 Cliff Floyd .15 .40
37 Ken Caminiti .15 .40
38 Craig Biggio .25 .60
39 Jeff Bagwell .25 .60
40 Moises Alou .15 .40
41 Johnny Damon .25 .60
42 Larry Sutton .15 .40
43 Kevin Brown .25 .60
44 Gary Sheffield .15 .40
45 Raul Mondesi .15 .40
46 Jeromy Burnitz .15 .40
47 Jeff Cirillo .15 .40
48 Todd Walker .15 .40
49 David Ortiz .40 1.00
50 Brad Radke .15 .40
51 Vladimir Guerrero .40 1.00
52 Rondell White .15 .40
53 Brad Fullmer .15 .40
54 Mike Piazza .60 1.50
55 Robin Ventura .15 .40
56 John Olerud .15 .40
57 Derek Jeter 1.00 2.50
58 Tino Martinez .25 .60
59 Bernie Williams .25 .60
60 Roger Clemens .75 2.00
61 Ben Grieve .15 .40
62 Miguel Tejada .15 .40
63 A.J. Hinch .15 .40
64 Scott Rolen .25 .60
65 Curt Schilling .15 .40
66 Doug Glanville .15 .40
67 Aramis Ramirez .15 .40
68 Tony Womack .15 .40
69 Jason Kendall .15 .40
70 Tony Gwynn .50 1.25
71 Wally Joyner .15 .40
72 Greg Vaughn .15 .40
73 Barry Bonds 1.00 2.50
74 Ellis Burks .15 .40
75 Jeff Kent .15 .40
76 Ken Griffey Jr. .75 2.00
77 Alex Rodriguez .60 1.50
78 Edgar Martinez .25 .60
79 Mark McGwire 1.00 2.50
80 Eli Marrero .15 .40
81 Matt Morris .15 .40
82 Rolando Arrojo .15 .40
83 Quinton McCracken .15 .40
84 Jose Canseco .25 .60
85 Ivan Rodriguez .25 .60
86 Juan Gonzalez .15 .40
87 Royce Clayton .15 .40
88 Shawn Green .15 .40
89 Jose Cruz Jr. .15 .40
90 Carlos Delgado .15 .40
91 Troy Glaus FW 5.00 12.00
92 George Lombard FW 4.00 10.00
93 Ryan Minor FW 4.00 10.00
94 Calvin Pickering FW 4.00 10.00
95 Jin Ho Cho FW 4.00 10.00
96 Russ Branyan FW 4.00 10.00
97 Derrick Gibson FW 4.00 10.00
98 Gabe Kapler FW 4.00 10.00
99 Matt Anderson FW 4.00 10.00
100 Preston Wilson FW 4.00 10.00
101 Alex Gonzalez FW 4.00 10.00
102 Carlos Beltran FW 4.00 10.00
103 Dee Brown FW 4.00 10.00
104 Jeremy Giambi FW 4.00 10.00
105 Angel Pena FW 4.00 10.00
106 Geoff Jenkins FW 4.00 10.00
107 Corey Koskie FW 4.00 10.00
108 A.J. Pierzynski FW 4.00 10.00
109 Michael Barrett FW 4.00 10.00
110 Fernando Seguignol FW 4.00 10.00
111 Mike Kinkade FW 4.00 10.00
112 Ricky Ledee FW 4.00 10.00
113 Mike Lowell FW 4.00 10.00
114 Eric Chavez FW 4.00 10.00
115 Matt Clement FW 4.00 10.00
116 Shane Monahan FW 4.00 10.00
117 J.D. Drew FW 4.00 10.00
118 Bubba Trammell FW 4.00 10.00
119 Kevin Witt FW 4.00 10.00
120 Roy Halladay FW 10.00 25.00
121 Mark McGwire STR 5.00 12.00
122 M.McGwire 4.00 10.00
S.Sosa STR
123 Sammy Sosa STR 2.00 5.00
124 Ken Griffey Jr. STR 4.00 10.00
125 Cal Ripken STR 6.00 15.00
126 Juan Gonzalez STR 1.25 3.00
127 Kerry Wood STR 1.25 3.00
128 Trevor Hoffman STR 1.25 3.00
129 Barry Bonds STR 5.00 12.00
130 Alex Rodriguez STR 3.00 8.00
131 Ben Grieve STR 1.25 3.00
132 Tom Glavine STR 1.25 3.00
133 David Wells STR 1.25 3.00
134 Mike Piazza STR 3.00 8.00
135 Scott Brosius STR 1.25 3.00

1999 SP Authentic Chirography

STATED ODDS 1:24
EXCH.DEADLINE 02/24/00
AG Alex Gonzalez 3.00 8.00
BC Bruce Chen 3.00 8.00
BF Brad Fullmer 3.00 8.00
BG Ben Grieve 3.00 8.00
CB Carlos Beltran 10.00 25.00
CJ Chipper Jones 30.00 80.00
CK Corey Koskie 4.00 10.00
CP Calvin Pickering 3.00 8.00
CR Cal Ripken 60.00 120.00
EC Eric Chavez 4.00 10.00
GK Gabe Kapler 4.00 10.00
GL George Lombard 3.00 8.00
GM Greg Maddux 50.00 120.00
GMJ Gary Matthews Jr. 3.00 8.00
GV Greg Vaughn 3.00 8.00
IR Ivan Rodriguez 15.00 40.00
JD J.D. Drew 4.00 10.00
JG Jeremy Giambi 3.00 8.00
JR Ken Griffey Jr. 60.00 150.00
JT Jim Thome 25.00 60.00
KW Kevin Witt 3.00 8.00
KW Kerry Wood 10.00 25.00
MA Matt Anderson 3.00 8.00
MK Mike Kinkade 3.00 8.00
ML Mike Lowell 5.00 12.00
NG Nomar Garciaparra 20.00 50.00
RB Russell Branyan 3.00 8.00
RH Richard Hidalgo 3.00 8.00
RL Ricky Ledee 3.00 8.00
RM Ryan Minor 3.00 8.00
RR Ruben Rivera 3.00 8.00
SM Shane Monahan 3.00 8.00
SR Scott Rolen 6.00 15.00
TG Tony Gwynn 10.00 25.00
TGL Troy Glaus 5.00 12.00
TH Todd Helton 8.00 20.00
TL Travis Lee 3.00 8.00
TW Todd Walker 4.00 10.00
VG Vladimir Guerrero 8.00 20.00
CRX Cal Ripken EXCH 4.00 10.00
JRX Ken Griffey Jr. EXCH 5.00 12.00
RRX Ruben Rivera EXCH .40 1.00
SRX Scott Rolen EXCH 1.00 2.50

1999 SP Authentic Chirography Gold

RANDOM INSERTS IN PACKS
CARDS SERIAL #'d TO PLAYER'S JERSEY

NO PRICING ON QTY OF 25 OR LESS
EXCHANGE DEADLINE 02/24/00
AG Alex Gonzalez/22
BC Bruce Chen/48 10.00 25.00
BF Brad Fullmer/20
BG Ben Grieve/14
CB Carlos Beltran/36 40.00 100.00
CJ Chipper Jones/10
CK Corey Koskie/47 15.00 40.00
CP Calvin Pickering/6
CR Cal Ripken/8
EC Eric Chavez/30 15.00 40.00
GK Gabe Kapler/51 15.00 40.00
GL George Lombard/26 10.00 25.00
GM Greg Maddux/31 125.00 250.00
GMJ Gary Matthews Jr./68 10.00 25.00
GV Greg Vaughn/23
IR Ivan Rodriguez/7
JD J.D. Drew/8
JG Jeremy Giambi/15
JR Ken Griffey Jr./24
JT Jim Thome/25
KW Kevin Witt/6
KW Kerry Wood/34 30.00 60.00
MA Matt Anderson/14
MK Mike Kinkade/33 10.00 25.00
ML Mike Lowell/60 20.00 50.00
NG Nomar Garciaparra/5
RB Russ Branyan/66 10.00 25.00
RH Richard Hidalgo/15
RL Ricky Ledee/38 10.00 25.00
RM Ryan Minor/10
RR Ruben Rivera/28 10.00 25.00
SM Shane Monahan/12
SR Scott Rolen/17
TG Tony Gwynn/19
TGL Troy Glaus/14
TH Todd Helton/17
TL Travis Lee/16
TW Todd Walker/12
VG Vladimir Guerrero/27 60.00 120.00
CRX Cal Ripken EXCH
JRX Ken Griffey Jr. EXCH
RRX Ruben Rivera EXCH
SRX Scott Rolen EXCH

1999 SP Authentic Epic Figures

COMPLETE SET (30) 40.00 100.00
STATED ODDS 1:7
E1 Mo Vaughn .60 1.50
E2 Travis Lee .60 1.50
E3 Andres Galarraga .60 1.50
E4 Andruw Jones 1.00 2.50
E5 Chipper Jones 1.50 4.00
E6 Greg Maddux 2.50 6.00
E7 Cal Ripken 5.00 12.00
E8 Nomar Garciaparra 2.50 6.00
E9 Sammy Sosa 1.50 4.00
E10 Frank Thomas 1.50 4.00
E11 Kerry Wood .60 1.50
E12 Kenny Lofton .60 1.50
E13 Manny Ramirez 1.00 2.50
E14 Larry Walker .60 1.50
E15 Jeff Bagwell 1.00 2.50
E16 Paul Molitor 1.50 4.00
E17 Vladimir Guerrero 1.50 4.00
E18 Derek Jeter 4.00 10.00
E19 Tino Martinez 1.00 2.50
E20 Mike Piazza 2.50 6.00
E21 Ben Grieve .60 1.50
E22 Scott Rolen 1.00 2.50
E23 Mark McGwire 4.00 10.00
E24 Tony Gwynn 2.00 5.00
E25 Barry Bonds 4.00 10.00
E26 Ken Griffey Jr. 3.00 8.00
E27 Alex Rodriguez 2.50 6.00
E28 J.D. Drew .60 1.50
E29 Juan Gonzalez .60 1.50
E30 Kevin Brown 1.00 2.50

1999 SP Authentic Home Run Chronicles

COMPLETE SET (70) 25.00 60.00
*DIE CUTS: 5X TO 12X BASIC HR CHRON.
DIE CUTS RANDOM INSERTS IN PACKS
DIE CUT PRINT RUN 70 SERIAL #'d SETS
HR1 Mark McGwire 1.50 4.00
HR2 Sammy Sosa .40 1.00
HR3 Ken Griffey Jr. .75 2.00
HR4 Mark McGwire 1.00 2.50
HR5 Mark McGwire 1.00 2.50
HR6 Albert Belle .15 .40
HR7 Jose Canseco .25 .60
HR8 Juan Gonzalez .15 .40
HR9 Manny Ramirez .25 .60
HR10 Rafael Palmeiro .40 1.00
HR11 Mo Vaughn .15 .40
HR12 Carlos Delgado .15 .40
HR13 Nomar Garciaparra .60 1.50
HR14 Barry Bonds 1.00 2.50
HR15 Alex Rodriguez .60 1.50
HR16 Tony Clark .15 .40
HR17 Jim Thome .25 .60
HR18 Edgar Martinez .25 .60
HR19 Frank Thomas .40 1.00
HR20 Greg Vaughn .15 .40
HR21 Vinny Castilla .15 .40
HR22 Andres Galarraga .15 .40
HR23 Moises Alou .15 .40
HR24 Jeromy Burnitz .15 .40
HR25 Vladimir Guerrero .40 1.00
HR26 Jeff Bagwell .25 .60
HR27 Chipper Jones .40 1.00
HR28 Javier Lopez .15 .40
HR29 Mike Piazza .60 1.50
HR30 Andruw Jones .25 .60
HR31 Henry Rodriguez .15 .40
HR32 Jeff Kent .15 .40
HR33 Ray Lankford .15 .40
HR34 Scott Rolen .25 .60
HR35 Raul Mondesi .15 .40
HR36 Ken Caminiti .15 .40
HR37 J.D. Drew .15 .40
HR38 Troy Glaus .25 .60
HR39 Gabe Kapler .15 .40
HR40 Alex Rodriguez .60 1.50
HR41 Ken Griffey Jr. .75 2.00
HR42 Sammy Sosa .40 1.00
HR43 Mark McGwire 1.00 2.50
HR44 Sammy Sosa .40 1.00
HR45 Mark McGwire 1.00 2.50
HR46 Vinny Castilla .15 .40
HR47 Sammy Sosa .40 1.00
HR48 Mark McGwire 1.00 2.50
HR49 Sammy Sosa .40 1.00
HR50 Greg Vaughn .15 .40
HR51 Sammy Sosa .40 1.00
HR52 Mark McGwire 1.00 2.50
HR53 Sammy Sosa .40 1.00
HR54 Mark McGwire 1.00 2.50
HR55 Sammy Sosa .40 1.00
HR56 Ken Griffey Jr. .75 2.00
HR57 Sammy Sosa .40 1.00
HR58 Mark McGwire 1.00 2.50
HR59 Sammy Sosa .40 1.00
HR60 Mark McGwire 1.00 2.50
HR61 Mark McGwire 1.50 4.00
HR62 Mark McGwire 2.00 5.00
HR63 Mark McGwire 1.00 2.50
HR64 Mark McGwire 1.00 2.50
HR65 Mark McGwire 1.00 2.50
HR66 Sammy Sosa 2.00 5.00
HR67 Mark McGwire 1.00 2.50
HR68 Mark McGwire 1.00 2.50
HR69 Mark McGwire 1.00 2.50
HR70 Mark McGwire 4.00 10.00

1999 SP Authentic Redemption Cards

STATED ODDS 1:864
EXPIRATION DATE: 03/01/00
PRICES BELOW REFER TO TRADE CARDS
1 K.Griffey Jr. AU Jersey/25
2 K.Griffey Jr. AU Baseball/75
3 K.Griffey Jr. AU SI Cover/75
4 K.Griffey Jr. AU Mini Helmet/75
5 M.McGwire AU 62 Ticket/1
6 M.McGwire AU 70 Ticket/3
7 K.Griffey Jr. Standee/300 6.00 15.00
8 K.Griffey Jr. Glove Card/200 20.00 50.00
9 K.Griffey Jr. HR Cel Card/346 12.50 30.00
10 K.Griffey Jr. SI Cover/200 10.00 25.00

1999 SP Authentic Reflections

COMPLETE SET (30) 30.00 80.00
STATED ODDS 1:23
R1 Mo Vaughn .60 1.50
R2 Travis Lee .60 1.50
R3 Andres Galarraga 1.00 2.50
R4 Andruw Jones .60 1.50
R5 Chipper Jones 1.50 4.00
R6 Greg Maddux 2.00 5.00
R7 Cal Ripken 5.00 12.00
R8 Nomar Garciaparra 1.00 2.50
R9 Sammy Sosa 1.50 4.00
R10 Frank Thomas 1.50 4.00
R11 Kerry Wood .60 1.50
R12 Kenny Lofton .60 1.50
R13 Manny Ramirez 1.50 4.00
R14 Larry Walker 1.00 2.50
R15 Jeff Bagwell 1.00 2.50
R16 Paul Molitor 1.50 4.00
R17 Vladimir Guerrero 1.00 2.50
R18 Derek Jeter 4.00 10.00
R19 Tino Martinez .60 1.50
R20 Mike Piazza 1.50 4.00
R21 Ben Grieve .60 1.50
R22 Scott Rolen 1.00 2.50
R23 Mark McGwire 2.50 6.00
R24 Tony Gwynn 1.50 4.00
R25 Barry Bonds 2.50 6.00
R26 Ken Griffey Jr 3.00 8.00
R27 Alex Rodriguez 2.00 5.00
R28 J.D. Drew .60 1.50
R29 Juan Gonzalez .60 1.50
R30 Roger Clemens 2.00 5.00

2000 SP Authentic

COMP.BASIC w/o SP's (90) 10.00 25.00
COMP.UPDATE w/o SP'S (30) 4.00 10.00
COMMON CARD (1-90) .15 .40
COMMON SUP (91-105) .40 1.00
91-105 PRINT RUN 2500 SERIAL #'d SETS
COMMON FW (106-135) .60 1.50
FW 106-135 PR.RUN 2500 SERIAL #'d SETS
COMMON FW (136-164) .75 2.00
FW 136-164 PRINT RUN 1700 #'d SETS
COMMON CARD (166-195) .25 .60
136-195 DISTRIBUTED IN ROOKIE.UPD.PACKS
CARD NUMBER 165 DOES NOT EXIST
WANER/SPEAKER 3K LIST.W/UD 3000 CLUB
1 Mo Vaughn .15 .40
2 Troy Glaus .15 .40
3 Jason Giambi .15 .40
4 Tim Hudson .25 .60
5 Eric Chavez .15 .40
6 Shannon Stewart .15 .40
7 Raul Mondesi .15 .40
8 Carlos Delgado .15 .40
9 Jose Canseco .25 .60
10 Vinny Castilla .15 .40
11 Greg Vaughn .15 .40
12 Manny Ramirez .40 1.00
13 Roberto Alomar .25 .60
14 Jim Thome .25 .60
15 Richie Sexson .15 .40
16 Alex Rodriguez .50 1.25
17 Freddy Garcia .15 .40
18 John Olerud .15 .40
19 Albert Belle .15 .40
20 Cal Ripken 1.25 3.00
21 Mike Mussina .25 .60
22 Ivan Rodriguez .25 .60
23 Gabe Kapler .15 .40
24 Rafael Palmeiro .25 .60
25 Nomar Garciaparra .25 .60
26 Pedro Martinez .25 .60
27 Carl Everett .15 .40
28 Carlos Beltran .25 .60
29 Jermaine Dye .15 .40
30 Juan Gonzalez .15 .40
31 Dean Palmer .15 .40
32 Corey Koskie .15 .40
33 Jacque Jones .15 .40
34 Frank Thomas .40 1.00
35 Paul Konerko .15 .40
36 Magglio Ordonez .25 .60
37 Bernie Williams .25 .60
38 Derek Jeter 1.00 2.50
39 Roger Clemens .50 1.25
40 Mariano Rivera .50 1.25
41 Jeff Bagwell .25 .60
42 Craig Biggio .25 .60
43 Jose Lima .15 .40
44 Moises Alou .15 .40
45 Chipper Jones .40 1.00
46 Greg Maddux .50 1.25
47 Andruw Jones .15 .40
48 Andres Galarraga .25 .60
49 Jeromy Burnitz .15 .40
50 Geoff Jenkins .15 .40
51 Mark McGwire .60 1.50
52 Fernando Tatis .15 .40
53 J.D. Drew .15 .40
54 Sammy Sosa .40 1.00
55 Kerry Wood .15 .40
56 Mark Grace .25 .60
57 Matt Williams .15 .40
58 Randy Johnson .40 1.00
59 Erubiel Durazo .15 .40
60 Gary Sheffield .15 .40
61 Kevin Brown .15 .40
62 Shawn Green .15 .40
63 Vladimir Guerrero .25 .60
64 Michael Barrett .15 .40
65 Barry Bonds .60 1.50
66 Jeff Kent .15 .40
67 Russ Ortiz .15 .40
68 Preston Wilson .15 .40
69 Mike Lowell .15 .40
70 Mike Piazza .40 1.00
71 Mike Hampton .15 .40
72 Robin Ventura .15 .40
73 Edgardo Alfonzo .15 .40
74 Tony Gwynn .40 1.00
75 Ryan Klesko .15 .40
76 Trevor Hoffman .25 .60
77 Scott Rolen .25 .60
78 Bob Abreu .15 .40
79 Mike Lieberthal .15 .40
80 Curt Schilling .25 .60
81 Jason Kendall .15 .40
82 Brian Giles .15 .40
83 Kris Benson .15 .40
84 Ken Griffey Jr. .75 2.00
85 Sean Casey .15 .40
86 Pokey Reese .15 .40
87 Barry Larkin .25 .60
88 Larry Walker .25 .60
89 Todd Helton .25 .60
90 Jeff Cirillo .15 .40
91 Ken Griffey Jr. SUP 2.00 5.00
92 Mark McGwire SUP 1.50 4.00
93 Chipper Jones SUP 1.00 2.50
94 Derek Jeter SUP 2.50 6.00
95 Shawn Green SUP .40 1.00
96 Pedro Martinez SUP .60 1.50
97 Mike Piazza SUP 1.00 2.50
98 Alex Rodriguez SUP 1.25 3.00
99 Jeff Bagwell SUP .60 1.50
100 Cal Ripken SUP 3.00 8.00
101 Sammy Sosa SUP 1.00 2.50
102 Barry Bonds SUP 1.50 4.00
103 Jose Canseco SUP .60 1.50
104 Nomar Garciaparra SUP .60 1.50
105 Ivan Rodriguez SUP .60 1.50
106 Rick Ankiel FW 1.00 2.50
107 Pat Burrell FW .60 1.50
108 Vernon Wells FW .60 1.50
109 Nick Johnson FW .60 1.50
110 Kip Wells FW .60 1.50
111 Matt Riley FW .60 1.50
112 Alfonso Soriano FW 1.50 4.00
113 Josh Beckett FW 1.25 3.00
114 Danys Baez FW RC .60 1.50
115 Travis Dawkins FW .60 1.50
116 Eric Gagne FW .60 1.50
117 Mike Lamb FW RC .60 1.50
118 Eric Munson FW .60 1.50
119 Wilfredo Rodriguez FW RC .60 1.50
120 Kazuhiro Sasaki FW RC 1.50 4.00
121 Chad Hutchinson FW .60 1.50
122 Peter Bergeron FW .60 1.50
123 Wascar Serrano FW RC .60 1.50
124 Tony Armas Jr. FW .60 1.50
125 Ramon Ortiz FW .60 1.50
126 Adam Kennedy FW .60 1.50
127 Joe Crede FW .60 1.50
128 Roosevelt Brown FW .60 1.50
129 Mark Mulder FW .60 1.50
130 Brad Penny FW .60 1.50
131 Terrence Long FW .60 1.50
132 Ruben Mateo FW .60 1.50
133 Wily Mo Pena FW .60 1.50
134 Rafael Furcal FW 1.00 2.50
135 Mario Encarnacion FW .60 1.50
136 Barry Zito FW RC 6.00 15.00
137 Aaron McNeal FW RC .75 2.00
138 Timo Perez FW RC 1.25 3.00
139 Sun Woo Kim FW RC .75 2.00
140 Xavier Nady FW RC 2.00 5.00
141 Matt Wheatland FW RC .75 2.00
142 Brent Abernathy FW RC .75 2.00
143 Cory Vance FW RC .75 2.00
144 Scott Heard FW RC .75 2.00
145 Mike Meyers FW RC 1.25 3.00
146 Ben Diggins FW RC .75 2.00
147 Luis Matos FW RC .75 2.00
148 Ben Sheets FW RC 2.00 5.00
149 Kurt Ainsworth FW RC .75 2.00
150 Dave Krynzel FW RC .75 2.00
151 Alex Cabrera FW RC .75 2.00
152 Mike Tonis FW RC .75 2.00
153 Dane Sardinha FW RC .75 2.00
154 Keith Ginter FW RC .75 2.00
155 David Espinosa FW RC .75 2.00
156 Joe Torres FW RC .75 2.00
157 Daylan Holt FW RC .75 2.00
158 Koyie Hill FW RC .75 2.00
159 Brad Wilkerson FW RC 2.00 5.00
160 Juan Pierre FW RC 4.00 10.00
161 Matt Ginter FW RC .75 2.00
162 Dane Artman FW RC .75 2.00
163 Jon Rauch FW RC .75 2.00
164 Sean Burnett FW RC .75 2.00
166 Darin Erstad .25 .60
167 Ben Grieve .25 .60
168 David Wells .25 .60
169 Fred McGriff .40 1.00
170 Bob Wickman .25 .60
171 Al Martin .25 .60
172 Melvin Mora .25 .60
173 Ricky Ledee .25 .60
174 Dante Bichette .25 .60
175 Mike Sweeney .25 .60
176 Bobby Higginson .25 .60
177 Matt Lawton .25 .60
178 Charles Johnson .25 .60
179 David Justice .25 .60
180 Richard Hidalgo .25 .60
181 B.J. Surhoff .25 .60
182 Richie Sexson .25 .60
183 Jim Edmonds .25 .60
184 Rondell White .25 .60
185 Curt Schilling .40 1.00
186 Tom Goodwin .25 .60
187 Jose Vidro .25 .60
188 Ellis Burks .25 .60
189 Henry Rodriguez .25 .60
190 Mike Bordick .25 .60
191 Eric Owens .25 .60
192 Travis Lee .25 .60
193 Kevin Young .25 .60
194 Aaron Boone .25 .60
195 Todd Hollandsworth .25 .60
SPA Ken Griffey Jr. Sample 1.00 2.50

2000 SP Authentic Limited

*LIMITED 1-90: 8X TO 20X BASIC
*LTD 91-105: 3X TO 8X BASIC
*LTD 106-135: 2X TO 5X BASIC
*LTD 106-135 RC: 1.5X TO 4X BASIC
STATED PRINT RUN 100 SERIAL #'d SETS

2000 SP Authentic Buybacks

STATED ODDS 1:95
PRINT RUNS B/WN 1-539 COPIES PER
NO PRICING ON QTY OF 25 OR LESS
1 Jeff Bagwell 93/58 12.50 30.00
2 Jeff Bagwell 94/46 12.50 30.00
3 Jeff Bagwell 95/60 12.50 30.00
4 Jeff Bagwell 96/74 12.50 30.00
5 Jeff Bagwell 97/53 12.50 30.00
6 Jeff Bagwell 98/38 12.50 30.00
7 Jeff Bagwell 99/539 10.00 25.00
9 Craig Biggio 93/59 15.00 40.00
10 Craig Biggio 94/69 15.00 40.00
11 Craig Biggio 95/171 10.00 25.00
12 Craig Biggio 96/71 15.00 40.00
13 Craig Biggio 97/46 15.00 40.00
14 Craig Biggio 98/40 15.00 40.00
15 Craig Biggio 99/125 10.00 25.00
22 Barry Bonds 99/520 30.00 60.00
23 Jose Canseco 93/29 20.00 50.00
29 Jose Canseco 99/502 15.00 40.00
31 Sean Casey 99/139 6.00 15.00
32 Roger Clemens 93/68 15.00 40.00
33 Roger Clemens 94/60 15.00 40.00
34 Roger Clemens 95/68 15.00 40.00
35 Roger Clemens 96/68 15.00 40.00
38 Roger Clemens 99/134 15.00 40.00
39 Jason Giambi 97/34 20.00 50.00
41 Tom Glavine 93/99 15.00 40.00
42 Tom Glavine 94/107 15.00 40.00
43 Tom Glavine 95/97 15.00 40.00
44 Tom Glavine 96/42 10.00 25.00
45 Tom Glavine 98/40 20.00 50.00
46 Tom Glavine 99/138 15.00 40.00
47 Shawn Green 96/55 15.00 40.00
48 Shawn Green 99/530 10.00 25.00
55 Ken Griffey Jr. 99/403 40.00 80.00
63 Tony Gwynn 99/129 25.00 60.00
64 Tony Gwynn 99/369 20.00 50.00
70 Derek Jeter 99/119 100.00 200.00
71 Randy Johnson 93/60 20.00 50.00
72 Randy Johnson 94/45 20.00 50.00
73 Randy Johnson 95/70 20.00 50.00
74 Randy Johnson 96/60 20.00 50.00
77 Randy Johnson 99/113 40.00 80.00
78 Andruw Jones 97/70 10.00 25.00
79 Andruw Jones 98/56 15.00 40.00
80 Andruw Jones 99/531 6.00 15.00
85 Chipper Jones 97/63 50.00 120.00
87 Chipper Jones 99/541 30.00 80.00
89 Kenny Lofton 94/100 8.00 20.00
90 Kenny Lofton 95/84 8.00 20.00
91 Kenny Lofton 96/34 20.00 50.00
92 Kenny Lofton 97/82 12.50 30.00
94 Kenny Lofton 99/99 12.50 30.00
95 Javy Lopez 93/106 6.00 15.00
96 Javy Lopez 94/160 6.00 15.00
97 Javy Lopez 96/99 6.00 15.00
98 Javy Lopez 97/61 10.00 25.00
99 Javy Lopez 98/26 12.50 30.00
106 Greg Maddux 99/504 40.00 80.00
107 Paul O'Neill 93/110 8.00 20.00
108 Paul O'Neill 94/97 12.00 30.00
109 Paul O'Neill 95/142 8.00 20.00
110 Paul O'Neill 96/70 8.00 20.00
116 Manny Ramirez 97/42 20.00 50.00
117 Manny Ramirez 98/36 20.00 50.00
118 Manny Ramirez 99/532 12.50 30.00
126 Cal Ripken 99/510 20.00 50.00
128 Alex Rodriguez 95/57 40.00 80.00
129 Alex Rodriguez 96/37 40.00 80.00
132 Alex Rodriguez 99/408 30.00 60.00
134 Ivan Rodriguez 93/29 30.00 60.00
139 Ivan Rodriguez 98/27 30.00 60.00
142 Scott Rolen 98/31 20.00 50.00
148 Frank Thomas 98/29 30.00 60.00
149 Frank Thomas 99/100 15.00 40.00
150 Greg Vaughn 93/79 4.00 10.00
151 Greg Vaughn 94/75 4.00 10.00
152 Greg Vaughn 95/155 4.00 10.00
153 Greg Vaughn 96/113 4.00 10.00
154 Greg Vaughn 97/29 8.00 20.00
155 Greg Vaughn 99/527 4.00 10.00
156 Mo Vaughn 93/119 6.00 15.00
157 Mo Vaughn 94/96 6.00 15.00
158 Mo Vaughn 95/121 6.00 15.00
159 Mo Vaughn 96/114 6.00 15.00
160 Mo Vaughn 97/61 10.00 25.00
161 Mo Vaughn 98/29 12.50 30.00
162 Mo Vaughn 99/537 4.00 10.00
163 Robin Ventura 93/59 10.00 25.00
164 Robin Ventura 94/49 10.00 25.00
165 Robin Ventura '95/125 6.00 15.00
166 Robin Ventura 96/55 10.00 25.00
167 Robin Ventura 97/44 10.00 25.00
168 Robin Ventura 98/28 12.50 30.00
169 Robin Ventura 99/370 6.00 15.00
170 Matt Williams 93/55 15.00 40.00
171 Matt Williams 94/50 15.00 40.00
172 Matt Williams 95/137 10.00 25.00
173 Matt Williams 96/77 10.00 25.00
174 Matt Williams 97/54 15.00 40.00
175 Matt Williams 98/29 20.00 50.00
176 Matt Williams 99/529 10.00 25.00
177 Preston Wilson '94/249 6.00 15.00
178 Preston Wilson '99/195 6.00 15.00
179 Authentication Card .20 .50

2000 SP Authentic Chirography

STATED ODDS 1:23
EXCHANGE DEADLINE 03/30/01
AJ Andruw Jones 6.00 15.00
AR Alex Rodriguez 30.00 60.00
AS Alfonso Soriano 4.00 10.00
BB Barry Bonds 50.00 120.00
BP Ben Petrick 4.00 10.00
CBE Carlos Beltran 10.00 25.00
CJ Chipper Jones 30.00 80.00
CR Cal Ripken 30.00 80.00
DJ Derek Jeter 125.00 300.00
EC Eric Chavez 6.00 15.00
ED Erubiel Durazo 4.00 10.00
EM Eric Munson 4.00 10.00
EY Ed Yarnall 4.00 10.00
IR Ivan Rodriguez 12.00 30.00
JB Jeff Bagwell 10.00 25.00
JC Jose Canseco 6.00 15.00
JD J.D. Drew 6.00 15.00
JG Jason Giambi 6.00 15.00
JK Josh Kalinowski 4.00 10.00
JL Jose Lima 4.00 10.00
JMA Joe Mays 4.00 10.00
JMO Jim Morris 10.00 25.00
JOB John Bale 4.00 10.00
KL Kenny Lofton 8.00 20.00
MQ Mark Quinn 4.00 10.00
MR Manny Ramirez 10.00 25.00
MRI Matt Riley 4.00 10.00
MV Mo Vaughn 6.00 15.00
NJ Nick Johnson 6.00 15.00
PB Pat Burrell 4.00 10.00
RA Rick Ankiel 6.00 15.00
RC Roger Clemens 30.00 60.00
RF Rafael Furcal 6.00 15.00
RP Robert Person 4.00 10.00
SC Sean Casey 4.00 10.00
SK Sandy Koufax 75.00 200.00
SR Scott Rolen 4.00 10.00
TG Tony Gwynn 20.00 50.00
TGL Troy Glaus 4.00 10.00
VG Vladimir Guerrero 10.00 25.00
VW Vernon Wells 4.00 10.00
WG Wilton Guerrero 4.00 10.00

2000 SP Authentic Chirography Gold

STATED PRINT RUNS LISTED BELOW
NO PRICING ON QTY OF 25 OR LESS
EXCHANGE DEADLINE 03/30/01
GAS Alfonso Soriano/53 8.00 20.00
GED Erubiel Durazo/44 6.00 15.00
GEY Ed Yarnall/41 6.00 15.00
GJC Jose Canseco/33 50.00 120.00
GJK Josh Kalinowski/62 6.00 15.00
GJL Jose Lima/42 6.00 15.00
GJMA Joe Mays/53 6.00 15.00
GJMO Jim Morris/63 40.00 100.00
GJOB John Bale/49 6.00 15.00
GMV Mo Vaughn/42 12.00 30.00
GNJ Nick Johnson/63 10.00 25.00
GPB Pat Burrell/33 15.00 40.00
GRA Rick Ankiel/66 10.00 25.00
GRP Robert Person/31 6.00 15.00
GVG Vladimir Guerrero/27 50.00 100.00

2000 SP Authentic Cornerstones

COMPLETE SET (7) 8.00 20.00
STATED ODDS 1:23
C1 Ken Griffey Jr 2.00 5.00
C2 Cal Ripken 3.00 8.00
C3 Mike Piazza 1.00 2.50
C4 Derek Jeter 2.50 6.00
C5 Mark McGwire 1.50 4.00
C6 Nomar Garciaparra .60 1.50
C7 Sammy Sosa 1.00 2.50

2000 SP Authentic DiMaggio Memorabilia

STATED PRINT RUNS LISTED BELOW
1 J.DiMaggio Jsy/500 30.00 60.00
2 J.DiMaggio Jsy Gold/56 100.00 200.00

2000 SP Authentic Midsummer Classics

COMPLETE SET (10) 8.00 20.00
STATED ODDS 1:12
MC1 Cal Ripken 3.00 8.00
MC2 Roger Clemens 1.25 3.00
MC3 Jeff Bagwell .60 1.50
MC4 Barry Bonds 1.50 4.00
MC5 Jose Canseco .60 1.50
MC6 Frank Thomas 1.00 2.50
MC7 Mike Piazza 1.00 2.50
MC8 Tony Gwynn 1.00 2.50
MC9 Juan Gonzalez .40 1.00
MC10 Greg Maddux 1.25 3.00

2000 SP Authentic Premier Performers

COMPLETE SET (10) 10.00 25.00
STATED ODDS 1:12
PP1 Mark McGwire 1.50 4.00
PP2 Alex Rodriguez 1.25 3.00
PP3 Cal Ripken 3.00 8.00
PP4 Nomar Garciaparra .60 1.50
PP5 Ken Griffey Jr. 2.00 5.00
PP6 Chipper Jones 1.00 2.50
PP7 Derek Jeter 2.50 6.00
PP8 Ivan Rodriguez .60 1.50
PP9 Vladimir Guerrero .60 1.50
PP10 Sammy Sosa 1.00 2.50

2000 SP Authentic Supremacy

COMPLETE SET (7) 4.00 10.00
STATED ODDS 1:23
S1 Alex Rodriguez 1.25 3.00
S2 Shawn Green .40 1.00
S3 Pedro Martinez .60 1.50
S4 Chipper Jones 1.00 2.50
S5 Tony Gwynn 1.00 2.50
S6 Ivan Rodriguez .60 1.50
S7 Jeff Bagwell .60 1.50

2000 SP Authentic United Nations

COMPLETE SET (10) 5.00 12.00
STATED ODDS 1:4
UN1 Sammy Sosa 1.00 2.50
UN2 Ken Griffey Jr. 2.00 5.00
UN3 Orlando Hernandez .40 1.00
UN4 Andres Galarraga .60 1.50
UN5 Kazuhiro Sasaki 1.00 2.50
UN6 Larry Walker .60 1.50
UN7 Vinny Castilla .40 1.00
UN8 Andruw Jones .40 1.00
UN9 Ivan Rodriguez .60 1.50
UN10 Chan Ho Park .60 1.50

2001 SP Authentic

COMP.BASIC w/o SP's (90) 10.00 25.00
COMP.UPDATE w/o SP's (30) 4.00 10.00
COMMON CARD (1-90) .15 .40
COMMON FW (91-135) 3.00 8.00
FW 91-135 RANDOM INSERTS IN PACKS
FW 91-135 PRINT RUN 1250 SERIAL #'d SETS
COMMON SS (136-180) 2.00 5.00
SS 136-180 RANDOM INSERTS IN PACKS
SS 136-180 PRINT RUN 1250 SERIAL #'d SETS
COMMON CARD (181-210) .25 .60
COMMON CARD (211-240) 2.50 6.00
211-240 RANDOM IN ROOKIE UPD.PACKS
211-240 PRINT RUN 1500 SERIAL #'d SETS
181-240 DISTRIBUTED IN ROOKIE UPD.PACKS
1 Troy Glaus .15 .40
2 Darin Erstad .15 .40
3 Jason Giambi .15 .40
4 Tim Hudson .15 .40
5 Eric Chavez .15 .40
6 Miguel Tejada .15 .40
7 Jose Ortiz .15 .40
8 Carlos Delgado .15 .40
9 Tony Batista .15 .40
10 Raul Mondesi .15 .40
11 Aubrey Huff .15 .40
12 Greg Vaughn .15 .40
13 Roberto Alomar .25 .60
14 Juan Gonzalez .15 .40
15 Jim Thome .25 .60
16 Omar Vizquel .25 .60
17 Edgar Martinez .25 .60
18 Freddy Garcia .15 .40
19 Cal Ripken 1.25 3.00
20 Ivan Rodriguez .25 .60
21 Rafael Palmeiro .25 .60
22 Alex Rodriguez .50 1.25
23 Manny Ramirez Sox .25 .60
24 Pedro Martinez .25 .60
25 Nomar Garciaparra .60 1.50
26 Mike Sweeney .15 .40
27 Jermaine Dye .15 .40
28 Bobby Higginson .15 .40
29 Dean Palmer .15 .40
30 Matt Lawton .15 .40
31 Eric Milton .15 .40
32 Frank Thomas .40 1.00
33 Magglio Ordonez .15 .40
34 David Wells .15 .40
35 Paul Konerko .15 .40
36 Derek Jeter 1.00 2.50
37 Bernie Williams .25 .60
38 Roger Clemens .75 2.00
39 Mike Mussina .25 .60
40 Jorge Posada .25 .60
41 Jeff Bagwell .25 .60
42 Richard Hidalgo .15 .40
43 Craig Biggio .25 .60
44 Greg Maddux .60 1.50
45 Chipper Jones .40 1.00
46 Andruw Jones .25 .60
47 Rafael Furcal .15 .40
48 Tom Glavine .25 .60
49 Jeromy Burnitz .15 .40
50 Jeffrey Hammonds .15 .40
51 Mark McGwire 1.00 2.50
52 Jim Edmonds .15 .40
53 Rick Ankiel .15 .40
54 J.D. Drew .15 .40
55 Sammy Sosa .40 1.00
56 Corey Patterson .15 .40
57 Kerry Wood .15 .40
58 Randy Johnson .40 1.00
59 Luis Gonzalez .15 .40
60 Curt Schilling .15 .40
61 Gary Sheffield .15 .40
62 Shawn Green .15 .40
63 Kevin Brown .15 .40
64 Vladimir Guerrero .40 1.00
65 Jose Vidro .15 .40
66 Barry Bonds 1.00 2.50
67 Jeff Kent .15 .40
68 Livan Hernandez .15 .40
69 Preston Wilson .15 .40
70 Charles Johnson .15 .40
71 Ryan Dempster .15 .40
72 Mike Piazza .60 1.50
73 Al Leiter .15 .40
74 Edgardo Alfonzo .15 .40
75 Robin Ventura .15 .40
76 Tony Gwynn .50 1.25
77 Phil Nevin .15 .40
78 Trevor Hoffman .15 .40
79 Scott Rolen .25 .60
80 Pat Burrell .15 .40
81 Bob Abreu .15 .40
82 Jason Kendall .15 .40
83 Brian Giles .15 .40
84 Kris Benson .15 .40
85 Ken Griffey Jr. .75 2.00
86 Barry Larkin .25 .60
87 Sean Casey .15 .40
88 Todd Helton .25 .60
89 Mike Hampton .15 .40
90 Larry Walker .15 .40
91 Ichiro Suzuki FW RC 300.00 800.00
92 Wilson Betemit FW RC 6.00 15.00
93 Adrian Hernandez FW RC 3.00 8.00
94 Juan Uribe FW RC 4.00 10.00
95 Travis Hafner FW RC 20.00 50.00
96 Morgan Ensberg FW RC 6.00 15.00
97 Sean Douglass FW RC 3.00 8.00
98 Juan Diaz FW RC 3.00 8.00
99 Erick Almonte FW RC 3.00 8.00
100 Ryan Freel FW RC 3.00 8.00
101 Elpidio Guzman FW RC 3.00 8.00
102 Christian Parker FW RC 3.00 8.00
103 Josh Fogg FW RC 3.00 8.00
104 Bert Snow FW RC 3.00 8.00
105 Horacio Ramirez FW RC 4.00 10.00
106 Ricardo Rodriguez FW RC 3.00 8.00
107 Tyler Walker FW RC 3.00 8.00
108 Jose Mieses FW RC 3.00 8.00
109 Billy Sylvester FW RC 3.00 8.00
110 Martin Vargas FW RC 3.00 8.00
111 Andres Torres FW RC 3.00 8.00
112 Greg Miller FW RC 3.00 8.00
113 Alexis Gomez FW RC 3.00 8.00
114 Grant Balfour FW RC 3.00 8.00
115 Henry Mateo FW RC 3.00 8.00
116 Esix Snead FW RC 3.00 8.00
117 Jackson Melian FW RC 3.00 8.00
118 Nate Teut FW RC 3.00 8.00
119 Tsuyoshi Shinjo FW RC 4.00 10.00
120 Carlos Valderrama FW RC 3.00 8.00
121 Johnny Estrada FW RC 4.00 10.00
122 Jason Michaels FW RC 3.00 8.00
123 William Ortega FW RC 3.00 8.00
124 Jason Smith FW RC 3.00 8.00
125 Brian Lawrence FW RC 3.00 8.00
126 Albert Pujols FW RC 125.00 300.00
127 Wilkin Ruan FW RC 3.00 8.00
128 Josh Towers FW RC 4.00 10.00
129 Kris Keller FW RC 3.00 8.00
130 Nick Maness FW RC 3.00 8.00
131 Jack Wilson FW RC 4.00 10.00
132 Brandon Duckworth FW RC 3.00 8.00
133 Mike Penney FW RC 3.00 8.00
134 Jay Gibbons FW RC 4.00 10.00
135 Cesar Crespo FW RC 3.00 8.00
136 Ken Griffey Jr. SS 5.00 12.00
137 Mark McGwire SS 6.00 15.00
138 Derek Jeter SS 6.00 15.00
139 Alex Rodriguez SS 3.00 8.00
140 Sammy Sosa SS 2.50 6.00
141 Carlos Delgado SS 2.00 5.00
142 Cal Ripken SS 8.00 20.00
143 Pedro Martinez SS 2.00 5.00
144 Frank Thomas SS 2.50 6.00
145 Juan Gonzalez SS 2.00 5.00
146 Troy Glaus SS 2.00 5.00
147 Jason Giambi SS 2.00 5.00
148 Ivan Rodriguez SS 2.00 5.00
149 Chipper Jones SS 2.50 6.00
150 Vladimir Guerrero SS 2.50 6.00
151 Mike Piazza SS 4.00 10.00
152 Jeff Bagwell SS 2.00 5.00
153 Randy Johnson SS 2.50 6.00
154 Todd Helton SS 2.00 5.00
155 Gary Sheffield SS 2.00 5.00
156 Tony Gwynn SS 3.00 8.00
157 Barry Bonds SS 6.00 15.00
158 Nomar Garciaparra SS 4.00 10.00
159 Bernie Williams SS 2.00 5.00
160 Greg Vaughn SS 2.00 5.00
161 David Wells SS 2.00 5.00
162 Roberto Alomar SS 2.00 5.00
163 Jermaine Dye SS 2.00 5.00
164 Rafael Palmeiro SS 2.00 5.00
165 Andruw Jones SS 2.00 5.00
166 Preston Wilson SS 2.00 5.00
167 Edgardo Alfonzo SS 2.00 5.00
168 Pat Burrell SS 2.00 5.00
169 Jim Edmonds SS 2.00 5.00
170 Mike Hampton SS 2.00 5.00
171 Jeff Kent SS 2.00 5.00
172 Kevin Brown SS 2.00 5.00
173 Manny Ramirez Sox SS 2.00 5.00
174 Magglio Ordonez SS 2.00 5.00
175 Roger Clemens SS 5.00 12.00
176 Jim Thome SS 2.00 5.00
177 Barry Zito SS 2.00 5.00
178 Brian Giles SS 2.00 5.00
179 Rick Ankiel SS 2.00 5.00
180 Corey Patterson SS 2.00 5.00
181 Garret Anderson .25 .60
182 Jermaine Dye .25 .60
183 Shannon Stewart .25 .60
184 Ben Grieve .25 .60
185 Ellis Burks .25 .60
186 John Olerud .25 .60
187 Tony Batista .25 .60
188 Ruben Sierra .25 .60
189 Carl Everett .25 .60
190 Neifi Perez .25 .60
191 Tony Clark .25 .60
192 Doug Mientkiewicz .25 .60
193 Carlos Lee .25 .60
194 Jorge Posada .40 1.00
195 Lance Berkman 2.00 5.00
196 Ken Caminiti .25 .60
197 Ben Sheets .40 1.00
198 Matt Morris .25 .60
199 Fred McGriff .40 1.00
200 Mark Grace .40 1.00
201 Paul LoDuca .25 .60
202 Tony Armas Jr. .25 .60
203 Andres Galarraga .25 .60
204 Cliff Floyd .25 .60
205 Matt Lawton .25 .60
206 Ryan Klesko .25 .60

207 Jimmy Rollins .25 .60
208 Aramis Ramirez .25 .60
209 Aaron Boone .25 .60
210 Jose Ortiz .25 .60
211 Mark Prior FW RC 6.00 15.00
212 Mark Teixeira FW RC 10.00 25.00
213 Bud Smith FW RC 2.50 6.00
214 Wilmy Caceres FW RC 2.50 6.00
215 Dave Williams FW RC 2.50 6.00
216 Delvin James FW RC 2.50 6.00
217 Endy Chavez FW RC 2.50 6.00
218 Doug Nickle FW RC 2.50 6.00
219 Bret Prinz FW RC 2.50 6.00
220 Troy Mattes FW RC 2.50 6.00
221 Duaner Sanchez FW RC 2.50 6.00
222 Dewon Brazelton FW RC 2.50 6.00
223 Brian Bowles FW RC 2.50 6.00
224 Donaldo Mendez FW RC 2.50 6.00
225 Jorge Julio FW RC 2.50 6.00
226 Matt White FW RC 2.50 6.00
227 Casey Fossum FW RC 2.50 6.00
228 Mike Rivera FW RC 2.50 6.00
229 Joe Kennedy FW RC 3.00 8.00
230 Kyle Lohse FW RC 5.00 12.00
231 Juan Cruz FW RC 2.50 6.00
232 Jeremy Affeldt FW RC 2.50 6.00
233 Brandon Lyon FW RC 2.50 6.00
234 Brian Roberts FW RC 8.00 20.00
235 Willie Harris FW RC 2.50 6.00
236 Pedro Santana FW RC 2.50 6.00
237 Rafael Soriano FW RC 2.50 6.00
238 Steve Green FW RC 2.50 6.00
239 Junior Spivey FW RC 3.00 8.00
240 Rob Mackowiak FW RC 3.00 8.00
NNO Ken Griffey Jr. Promo 1.00 2.50

2001 SP Authentic Limited

*STARS 1-90: 10X TO 25X BASIC 1-90
*FW 91-135: 1X TO 2.5X BASIC 91-135
*SS 136-180: 1.5X TO 4X BASIC 136-180
STATED PRINT RUN 50 SERIAL #'d SETS
91 Ichiro Suzuki FW 750.00 2000.00
126 Albert Pujols FW 250.00 600.00

2001 SP Authentic BuyBacks

STATED ODDS 1:144
STATED PRINT RUNS LISTED BELOW
NO PRICING ON QTY OF 25 OR LESS
1 Edgardo Alfonzo 95/77 10.00 25.00
3 Edgardo Alfonzo 00/280 10.00 25.00
4 Barry Bonds 93/75 40.00 80.00
5 Barry Bonds 94/103 40.00 80.00
6 Barry Bonds 95/31 40.00 80.00
8 Barry Bonds 96/49 40.00 80.00
11 Barry Bonds 00/146 40.00 80.00
12 Roger Clemens 00/145 20.00 50.00
13 Roger Clemens 99/150 20.00 50.00
16 Carlos Delgado 94/272 6.00 15.00
18 Carlos Delgado 96/81 10.00 25.00
19 Carlos Delgado 98/29 20.00 50.00
20 Carlos Delgado 00/169 6.00 15.00
21 Jim Edmonds 96/72 15.00 40.00
22 Jim Edmonds 97/38 30.00 60.00
26 Jason Giambi 00/290 6.00 15.00
27 Troy Glaus 00/340 6.00 15.00
28 Shawn Green 00/340 10.00 25.00
29 Ken Griffey Jr. 93/34 125.00 300.00
30 Ken Griffey Jr. 94/182 40.00 100.00
31 Ken Griffey Jr. 95/116 40.00 100.00
33 Ken Griffey Jr. 96/53 60.00 150.00
36 Ken Griffey Jr. 00/333 40.00 100.00
37 Tony Gwynn 93/101 20.00 50.00
38 Tony Gwynn 94/88 20.00 50.00
39 Tony Gwynn 95/179 20.00 50.00
40 Tony Gwynn 96/92 20.00 50.00
43 Tony Gwynn 00/95 20.00 50.00
44 Todd Helton 00/194 10.00 25.00
45 Tim Hudson 00/291 10.00 25.00
46 Randy Johnson 93/97 30.00 60.00
47 Randy Johnson 94/146 30.00 60.00
48 Randy Johnson 95/121 30.00 60.00
50 Randy Johnson 96/78 50.00 100.00
53 Randy Johnson 00/213 30.00 60.00
56 Andruw Jones 00/336 30.00 60.00
58 Chipper Jones 95/118 30.00 80.00
59 Chipper Jones 96/72 40.00 100.00
62 Chipper Jones 00/303 30.00 80.00
64 Cal Ripken 94/99 40.00 100.00
65 Cal Ripken 95/37 75.00 150.00
70 Cal Ripken 00/266 60.00 120.00
72 Alex Rodriguez 95/117 50.00 100.00
74 Alex Rodriguez 96/72 50.00 100.00
77 Alex Rodriguez 00/332 20.00 50.00
78 Ivan Rodriguez 93/89 10.00 25.00
81 Ivan Rodriguez 96/64 10.00 25.00
84 Ivan Rodriguez 00/163 10.00 25.00
85 Gary Sheffield 93/82 8.00 20.00
87 Gary Sheffield 95/70 8.00 20.00
88 Gary Sheffield 96/67 8.00 20.00
89 Gary Sheffield 97/43 12.50 30.00
90 Gary Sheffield 98/27 15.00 40.00
91 Gary Sheffield 00/146 5.00 12.00
92 Sammy Sosa 93/73 50.00 100.00
94 Sammy Sosa 95/30 50.00 100.00
97 Fernando Tatis 00/267 4.00 10.00
98 Frank Thomas 93/79 30.00 60.00
99 Frank Thomas 94/165 30.00 60.00
101 Frank Thomas 97/34 50.00 100.00
103 Frank Thomas 00/302 20.00 50.00
105 Mo Vaughn 93/94 10.00 25.00
106 Mo Vaughn 94/102 10.00 25.00
107 Mo Vaughn 95/129 6.00 15.00
109 Mo Vaughn 96/81 10.00 25.00
110 Mo Vaughn 97/36 15.00 40.00
112 Mo Vaughn 00/309 6.00 15.00
113 Robin Ventura 00/340 6.00 15.00
114 Matt Williams 00/340 10.00 25.00

2001 SP Authentic Chirography

STATED ODDS 1:72
SP PRINT RUNS LISTED BELOW
SP'S ARE NOT SERIAL NUMBERED
SP PRINT RUNS PROVIDED BY UPPER DECK
AB Albert Belle 6.00 15.00
AJ Andruw Jones 6.00 15.00
AP Albert Pujols 200.00 500.00
AR Alex Rodriguez SP/229 * 40.00 100.00
BS Ben Sheets 4.00 10.00
CB Carlos Beltran 6.00 15.00
CD Carlos Delgado 4.00 10.00
CF Cliff Floyd 6.00 15.00
CJ Chipper Jones SP/184 * 30.00 60.00
CR Cal Ripken SP/109 * 50.00 100.00
DD Darren Dreifort SP/206 * 4.00 10.00
DER Darin Erstad 4.00 10.00
DES David Espinosa 4.00 10.00
DJ David Justice 8.00 20.00
DS Dane Sardinha 4.00 10.00
DW David Wells 15.00 40.00
EA Edgardo Alfonzo 6.00 15.00
JC Jose Canseco 10.00 25.00
JD J.D. Drew 8.00 20.00
JE Jim Edmonds 8.00 20.00
JG Jason Giambi 6.00 15.00
KG Ken Griffey Jr. SP/126 * 50.00 100.00
LG Luis Gonzalez SP/271 * 10.00 25.00
MB Milton Bradley 6.00 15.00
MK Mark Kotsay SP/228 * 6.00 15.00
MS Mike Sweeney 6.00 15.00
MV Mo Vaughn SP/103 * 6.00 15.00
MW Matt Williams 10.00 25.00
PB Pat Burrell 6.00 15.00
RF Rafael Furcal SP/222 * 6.00 15.00
RH Rick Helling SP/211 * 4.00 10.00
RJ Randy Johnson SP/143 * 40.00 100.00
RW Rondell White 6.00 15.00
SG Shawn Green SP/82 * 6.00 15.00
SS Sammy Sosa SP/76 * 50.00 100.00
TH Tim Hudson 4.00 10.00
TL Travis Lee SP/226 * 4.00 10.00
TOG Tony Gwynn SP/76 * 20.00 50.00
TOH Todd Helton SP/152 * 10.00 25.00
TRG Troy Glaus 10.00 25.00

2001 SP Authentic Chirography Gold

STATED PRINT RUNS LISTED BELOW
NO PRICING ON QTY OF 25 OR LESS
GAB Albert Belle/88 20.00 50.00
GDD Darren Dreifort/37 10.00 25.00
GDES David Espinosa/79 10.00 25.00
GDJ David Justice/28 25.00 60.00
GDS Dane Sardinha/50 10.00 25.00
GDW David Wells/33 10.00 25.00
GKG Ken Griffey Jr./30 75.00 150.00
GMS Mike Sweeney/29 20.00 50.00
GMV Mo Vaughn/42 20.00 50.00
GRH Rick Helling/32 10.00 25.00
GRJ Randy Johnson/51 50.00 120.00

2001 SP Authentic Chirography Update

STATED PRINT RUN 250 SERIAL #'d SETS
SPCR Cal Ripken 40.00 80.00
SPDM Doug Mientkiewicz 6.00 15.00
SPIS Ichiro Suzuki 400.00 1000.00
SPJP Jorge Posada 40.00 80.00
SPKG Ken Griffey Jr. 40.00 80.00
SPLB Lance Berkman 6.00 15.00
SPMS Mike Sweeney 6.00 15.00
SPTG Tony Gwynn 10.00 25.00

2001 SP Authentic Chirography Update Silver

STATED PRINT RUN 100 SERIAL #'d SETS
SPCR Cal Ripken 75.00 150.00
SPDM Doug Mientkiewicz 10.00 25.00
SPJP Jorge Posada 50.00 100.00
SPKG Ken Griffey Jr. 50.00 100.00
SPLB Lance Berkman 15.00 40.00
SPMS Mike Sweeney 10.00 25.00
SPTG Tony Gwynn 15.00 40.00

2001 SP Authentic Cooperstown Calling Game Jersey

OVERALL JERSEY ODDS 1:24
SP PRINT RUNS PROVIDED BY UD
CCAD Andre Dawson 3.00 8.00
CCBM Bill Mazeroski 10.00 25.00
CCCR Cal Ripken 8.00 20.00
CCDM Don Mattingly 10.00 25.00
CCDW Dave Winfield 3.00 8.00
CCEM Eddie Murray 3.00 8.00
CCGC Gary Carter 3.00 8.00
CCGG Goose Gossage 3.00 8.00
CCIS Ichiro Suzuki SP 750.00 2000.00
CCJB Jeff Bagwell 3.00 8.00
CCKP Kirby Puckett 5.00 12.00
CCKS Kazuhiro Sasaki 2.00 5.00
CCMP Mike Piazza SP 10.00 25.00
CCMR Manny Ramirez Sox SP 5.00 12.00
CCOS Ozzie Smith 6.00 15.00
CCPM Pedro Martinez SP 3.00 8.00
CCPM Paul Molitor 5.00 12.00
CCRC Roger Clemens 8.00 20.00
CCRM Roger Maris SP/243 * 12.00 30.00
CCRS Ryne Sandberg 10.00 25.00
CCSG Steve Garvey 2.00 5.00
CCTG Tony Gwynn 5.00 12.00
CCWB Wade Boggs 3.00 8.00

2001 SP Authentic Stars of Japan

COMPLETE SET (30) 20.00 50.00
ONE 3-CARD PACK PER SPA HOBBY BOX
RS1 I.Suzuki 4.00 10.00
T.Shinjo
RS2 S.Hasegawa .75 2.00
H.Irabu
RS3 T.Ohka .75 2.00
M.Suzuki
RS4 T.Shinjo .75 2.00
H.Irabu
RS5 I.Suzuki 5.00 12.00
H.Nomo
RS6 T.Shinjo .75 2.00
M.Suzuki
RS7 T.Shinjo .75 2.00
K.Sasaki
RS8 H.Nomo .75 2.00
T.Ohka
RS9 I.Suzuki 4.00 10.00
M.Suzuki
RS10 H.Nomo .75 2.00
S.Hasegawa
RS11 H.Nomo .75 2.00
M.Yoshii
RS12 H.Nomo .75 2.00
H.Irabu
RS13 S.Hasegawa .75 2.00
K.Sasaki
RS14 S.Hasegawa .75 2.00
M.Suzuki
RS15 T.Shinjo .75 2.00
H.Nomo
RS16 T.Shinjo .75 2.00
T.Ohka
RS17 I.Suzuki 5.00 12.00
K.Sasaki
RS18 M.Yoshii .75 2.00
H.Irabu
RS19 I.Suzuki 4.00 10.00
T.Ohka
RS20 H.Irabu .75 2.00
K.Sasaki
RS21 T.Shinjo .75 2.00
M.Yoshii
RS22 I.Suzuki 4.00 10.00
S.Hasegawa
RS23 M.Suzuki .75 2.00
K.Sasaki
RS24 I.Suzuki 4.00 10.00
H.Irabu
RS25 T.Ohka .75 2.00
K.Sasaki
RS26 T.Shinjo .75 2.00
S.Hasegawa
RS27 M.Yoshii .75 2.00
K.Sasaki
RS28 H.Nomo .75 2.00
K.Sasaki
RS29 I.Suzuki 4.00 10.00
M.Yoshii
RS30 H.Nomo .75 2.00
M.Suzuki

2001 SP Authentic Stars of Japan Game Ball

OVERALL MEMORABILIA ODDS 1:12 SOJ
SP PRINT RUNS PROVIDED BY UD
NO PRICING ON QTY OF 40 OR LESS
GOLD RANDOM INSERTS IN PACKS
GOLD PRINT RUN 25 SERIAL #'d SETS
GOLD NO PRICING DUE TO SCARCITY
BBHI Hideki Irabu 4.00 10.00
BBIS Ichiro Suzuki 40.00 100.00
BBKS Kazuhiro Sasaki 6.00 15.00
BBMY Masato Yoshii 4.00 10.00
BBTS Tsuyoshi Shinjo SP/50 * 6.00 15.00

2001 SP Authentic Stars of Japan Game Ball-Base Combos

OVERALL SOJ COMBO ODDS 1:576 BASIC
SP PRINT RUNS PROVIDED BY UD
NO PRICING ON QTY OF 40 OR LESS
GOLD RANDOM INSERTS IN PACKS
GOLD PRINT RUN 25 SERIAL #'d SETS
GOLD NO PRICING DUE TO SCARCITY
HNKS Nomo/Sasaki SP/50 * 40.00 80.00
HNSH Nomo/Hasegawa 10.00 25.00
ISMY Ichiro/Yoshii 40.00 100.00
ISSH Ichiro/Hasegawa SP/72 * 60.00 150.00
TOKS Ohka/Sasaki 4.00 10.00

2001 SP Authentic Stars of Japan Game Bat

OVERALL MEMORABILIA ODDS 1:12 SOJ
SP PRINT RUNS PROVIDED BY UD
NO PRICING ON QTY OF 40 OR LESS
GOLD RANDOM INSERTS IN PACKS
GOLD PRINT RUN 25 SERIAL #'d SETS
GOLD NO PRICING DUE TO SCARCITY
BMY Masato Yoshii 4.00 10.00

2001 SP Authentic Stars of Japan Game Bat-Jersey Combos

OVERALL SOJ COMBO ODDS 1:576 BASIC
SASAKI-HASEGAWA IS DUAL JERSEY
HASEGAWA SHINJO IS DUAL BAT
GOLD RANDOM INSERTS IN PACKS
GOLD PRINT RUN 25 SERIAL #'d SETS
GOLD NO PRICING DUE TO SCARCITY
BBHS Hasegawa/Shinjo 10.00 25.00
JBNN Nomo/Nomo 30.00 60.00
JBSN Sasaki/Nomo 10.00 25.00
JJSH Sasaki/Hasegawa 6.00 15.00

2001 SP Authentic Stars of Japan Game Jersey

OVERALL MEMORABILIA ODDS 1:12 SOJ
SP PRINT RUNS PROVIDED BY UD
GOLD RANDOM INSERTS IN PACKS
GOLD PRINT RUN 25 SERIAL #'d SETS
NO GOLD PRICING DUE TO SCARCITY
JHN Hideo Nomo 6.00 15.00
JIS Ichiro Suzuki SP/260 * 25.00 60.00
JKS Kazuhiro Sasaki 4.00 10.00
JMY Masato Yoshii 4.00 10.00
JSH Shigetoshi Hasegawa 4.00 10.00
JTS Tsuyoshi Shinjo 6.00 15.00

2001 SP Authentic Sultan of Swatch Memorabilia

PRINT RUNS B/WN 14-94 COPIES PER
NO PRICING ON QTY OF 24 OR LESS
SOS2 B.Ruth 29.2 Inn/29 250.00 500.00
SOS3 B.Ruth 94 Wins/94 250.00 500.00
SOS4 B.Ruth 54 HRs/54 250.00 500.00
SOS5 B.Ruth 59 HRs/59 250.00 500.00
SOS6 B.Ruth 3 HRs WS/26 250.00 500.00
SOS7 B.Ruth 60 HRs/27 250.00 500.00
SOS8 B.Ruth Called Shot/32 250.00 500.00
SOS13 B.Ruth 40 HRs/26 250.00 500.00
SOS14 B.Ruth HR Title/27 250.00 500.00
SOS15 B.Ruth 50 HRs/28 250.00 500.00
SOS16 B.Ruth Leads Way/29 250.00 500.00
SOS17 B.Ruth 49 HRs/30 250.00 500.00
SOS18 B.Ruth Last Title/31 250.00 500.00
SOS19 B.Ruth 1st AS/33 250.00 500.00
SOS20 B.Ruth 1st HOF/36 250.00 500.00
SOS21 B.Ruth House/48 250.00 500.00

2001 SP Authentic UD Exclusives Game Jersey

OVERALL JERSEY ODDS 1:24
SP PRINT RUNS PROVIDED BY UD
AR Alex Rodriguez 6.00 15.00
GG Gary Sheffield 4.00 10.00
JD Joe DiMaggio SP/243 * 30.00 60.00
KG Ken Griffey Jr. 6.00 15.00
MM Mickey Mantle SP/243 * 75.00 150.00
SS Sammy Sosa 6.00 15.00

2001 SP Authentic UD Exclusives Game Jersey Combos

OVERALL JERSEY ODDS 1:24
SP PRINT RUNS PROVIDED BY UD
GD Griffey/DiMag SP/98 * 60.00 120.00
MD Mantle/DiMag SP/98 * 75.00 150.00
MG Mantle/Griffey Jr. SP/98 * 75.00 150.00
RS A.Rodriguez/O.Smith 10.00 25.00
SD Sosa/Dawson 10.00 25.00
SW Sheffield/Winfield 10.00 25.00

2002 SP Authentic

COMP.LOW w/o SP's (90) 6.00 15.00
COMP.UPDATE w/o SP's (30) 4.00 10.00
COMMON CARD (1-90) .15 .40
COMMON (91-135/201-230) 2.00 5.00
91-135/201-230 PRINT 1999 SERIAL #'d SETS
COMMON CARD (136-170) 4.00 10.00
136-170 PRINT RUN 999 SERIAL #'d SETS
146/152/157 PRINT 249 SERIAL #'d SETS
91-170/201-230 RANDOM IN PACKS
COMMON CARD (171-200) .25 .60
DIMAG POSTER EXCH RANDOM IN PACKS
DIMAGGIO EXCH.DEADLINE 08/08/05
1 Troy Glaus .15 .40
2 Darin Erstad .15 .40
3 Barry Zito .15 .40
4 Eric Chavez .15 .40
5 Tim Hudson .15 .40
6 Miguel Tejada .15 .40
7 Carlos Delgado .15 .40
8 Shannon Stewart .15 .40
9 Ben Grieve .15 .40
10 Jim Thome .25 .60
11 C.C. Sabathia .15 .40
12 Ichiro Suzuki .75 2.00
13 Freddy Garcia .15 .40
14 Edgar Martinez .25 .60
15 Bret Boone .15 .40
16 Jeff Conine .15 .40
17 Alex Rodriguez .50 1.50
18 Juan Gonzalez .15 .40
19 Ivan Rodriguez .25 .60
20 Rafael Palmeiro .25 .60
21 Hank Blalock .25 .60
22 Pedro Martinez .25 .60
23 Manny Ramirez .25 .60
24 Nomar Garciaparra .60 1.50
25 Carlos Beltran .15 .40
26 Mike Sweeney .15 .40
27 Randall Simon .15 .40
28 Dmitri Young .15 .40
29 Bobby Higginson .15 .40
30 Corey Koskie .15 .40
31 Eric Milton .15 .40
32 Torii Hunter .15 .40
33 Joe Mays .15 .40
34 Frank Thomas .40 1.00
35 Mark Buehrle .15 .40
36 Magglio Ordonez .15 .40
37 Kenny Lofton .15 .40
38 Roger Clemens .75 2.00
39 Derek Jeter 1.00 2.50
40 Jason Giambi .15 .40
41 Bernie Williams .25 .60
42 Alfonso Soriano .15 .40
43 Lance Berkman .15 .40
44 Roy Oswalt .15 .40
45 Jeff Bagwell .25 .60
46 Craig Biggio .25 .60
47 Chipper Jones .40 1.00
48 Greg Maddux .60 1.50
49 Gary Sheffield .15 .40
50 Andruw Jones .25 .60
51 Ben Sheets .15 .40
52 Richie Sexson .15 .40
53 Albert Pujols .75 2.00
54 Matt Morris .15 .40
55 J.D. Drew .15 .40
56 Sammy Sosa .40 1.00
57 Kerry Wood .15 .40
58 Corey Patterson .15 .40
59 Mark Prior .25 .60
60 Randy Johnson .40 1.00
61 Luis Gonzalez .15 .40
62 Curt Schilling .15 .40
63 Shawn Green .15 .40
64 Kevin Brown .15 .40
65 Hideo Nomo .40 1.00
66 Vladimir Guerrero .40 1.00
67 Jose Vidro .15 .40
68 Barry Bonds 1.00 2.50
69 Jeff Kent .15 .40
70 Rich Aurilia .15 .40
71 Preston Wilson .15 .40
72 Josh Beckett .15 .40
73 Mike Lowell .15 .40
74 Roberto Alomar .25 .60
75 Mo Vaughn .15 .40
76 Jeromy Burnitz .15 .40
77 Mike Piazza .60 1.50
78 Sean Burroughs .15 .40
79 Phil Nevin .15 .40
80 Bobby Abreu .15 .40
81 Pat Burrell .15 .40
82 Scott Rolen .25 .60
83 Jason Kendall .15 .40
84 Brian Giles .15 .40
85 Ken Griffey Jr. .75 2.00
86 Adam Dunn .15 .40
87 Sean Casey .15 .40
88 Todd Helton .25 .60
89 Larry Walker .15 .40
90 Mike Hampton .15 .40
91 Brandon Puffer FW RC 2.00 5.00
92 Tom Shearn FW RC 2.00 5.00
93 Chris Baker FW RC 2.00 5.00
94 Gustavo Chacin FW RC 3.00 8.00
95 Joe Orloski FW RC 2.00 5.00
96 Mike Smith FW RC 2.00 5.00
97 John Ennis FW RC 2.00 5.00
98 John Foster FW RC 2.00 5.00
99 Kevin Gryboski FW RC 2.00 5.00
100 Brian Mallette FW RC 2.00 5.00
101 Takahito Nomura FW RC 2.00 5.00
102 So Taguchi FW RC 3.00 8.00
103 Jeremy Lambert FW RC 2.00 5.00
104 Jason Simontacchi FW RC 2.00 5.00
105 Jorge Sosa FW RC 3.00 8.00
106 Brandon Backe FW RC 3.00 8.00
107 P.J. Bevis FW RC 2.00 5.00
108 Jeremy Ward FW RC 2.00 5.00
109 Doug Devore FW RC 2.00 5.00
110 Ron Chiavacci FW 2.00 5.00
111 Ron Calloway FW RC 2.00 5.00
112 Nelson Castro FW RC 2.00 5.00
113 Deivis Santos FW 2.00 5.00
114 Earl Snyder FW RC 2.00 5.00
115 Julio Mateo FW RC 2.00 5.00
116 J.J. Putz FW RC 2.00 5.00
117 Allan Simpson FW RC 2.00 5.00
118 Satoru Komiyama FW RC 2.00 5.00
119 Adam Walker FW RC 2.00 5.00
120 Oliver Perez FW RC 3.00 8.00
121 Cliff Bartosh FW RC 2.00 5.00
122 Todd Donovan FW RC 2.00 5.00
123 Elio Serrano FW RC 2.00 5.00
124 Pete Zamora FW RC 2.00 5.00
125 Mike Gonzalez FW RC 2.00 5.00
126 Travis Hughes FW RC 2.00 5.00
127 Jorge De La Rosa FW RC 2.00 5.00
128 Anastacio Martinez FW RC 2.00 5.00
129 Colin Young FW RC 2.00 5.00
130 Nate Field FW RC 2.00 5.00
131 Tim Kalita FW RC 2.00 5.00
132 Julius Matos FW RC 2.00 5.00
133 Terry Pearson FW RC 2.00 5.00
134 Kyle Kane FW RC 2.00 5.00
135 Mitch Wylie FW RC 2.00 5.00
136 Rodrigo Rosario AU RC 4.00 10.00
137 Franklyn German AU RC 4.00 10.00
138 Reed Johnson AU RC 8.00 20.00
139 Luis Martinez AU RC 4.00 10.00
140 Michael Crudale AU RC 4.00 10.00
141 Francis Beltran AU RC 4.00 10.00
142 Steve Kent AU RC 4.00 10.00
143 Felix Escalona AU RC 4.00 10.00
144 Jose Valverde AU RC 6.00 15.00
145 Victor Alvarez AU RC 4.00 10.00
146 Kazuhisa Ishii AU/249 RC 8.00 20.00
147 Jorge Nunez AU RC 4.00 10.00
148 Eric Good AU RC 4.00 10.00
149 Luis Ugueto AU RC 4.00 10.00
150 Matt Thornton AU RC 4.00 10.00
151 Wilson Valdez AU RC 4.00 10.00
152 Hansel Izquierdo AU/249 RC 15.00 40.00
153 Jaime Cerda AU RC 4.00 10.00
154 Mark Corey AU RC 4.00 10.00
155 Tyler Yates AU RC 4.00 10.00
156 Steve Bechler AU RC 4.00 10.00
157 Ben Howard AU/249 RC 15.00 40.00
158 Anderson Machado AU RC 4.00 10.00
159 Jorge Padilla AU RC 4.00 10.00
160 Eric Junge AU RC 4.00 10.00
161 Adrian Burnside AU RC 4.00 10.00
162 Josh Hancock AU RC 8.00 20.00
163 Chris Booker AU RC 4.00 10.00
164 Cam Esslinger AU RC 4.00 10.00
165 Rene Reyes AU RC 4.00 10.00
166 Aaron Cook AU RC 6.00 15.00
167 Juan Brito AU RC 4.00 10.00
168 Miguel Ascencio AU RC 4.00 10.00
169 Kevin Frederick AU RC 4.00 10.00
170 Edwin Almonte AU RC 4.00 10.00
171 Erubiel Durazo .25 .60
172 Junior Spivey .25 .60
173 Geronimo Gil .25 .60
174 Cliff Floyd .25 .60
175 Brandon Larson .25 .60
176 Aaron Boone .25 .60
177 Shawn Estes .25 .60
178 Austin Kearns .25 .60
179 Joe Borchard .25 .60
180 Russell Branyan .25 .60
181 Jay Payton .25 .60
182 Andres Torres .25 .60
183 Andy Van Hekken .25 .60
184 Alex Sanchez .25 .60
185 Endy Chavez .25 .60
186 Bartolo Colon .25 .60
187 Raul Mondesi .25 .60
188 Robin Ventura .25 .60
189 Mike Mussina .40 1.00
190 Jorge Posada .40 1.00
191 Ted Lilly .25 .60
192 Ray Durham .25 .60
193 Brett Myers .25 .60
194 Marlon Byrd .25 .60
195 Vicente Padilla .25 .60
196 Josh Fogg .25 .60
197 Kenny Lofton .25 .60
198 Scott Rolen .40 1.00
199 Jason Lane .25 .60
200 Josh Phelps .25 .60
201 Travis Driskill FW RC 2.00 5.00
202 Howie Clark FW RC 2.00 5.00
203 Mike Mahoney FW 2.00 5.00
204 Brian Tallet FW RC 2.00 5.00
205 Kirk Saarloos FW RC 2.00 5.00
206 Barry Wesson FW RC 2.00 5.00
207 Aaron Guiel FW RC 2.00 5.00
208 Shawn Sedlacek FW RC 2.00 5.00
209 Jose Diaz FW RC 2.00 5.00
210 Jorge Nunez FW 2.00 5.00
211 Danny Mota FW RC 2.00 5.00
212 David Ross FW RC 3.00 8.00
213 Jayson Durocher FW RC 2.00 5.00
214 Shane Nance FW RC 2.00 5.00
215 Wil Nieves FW RC 2.00 5.00
216 Freddy Sanchez FW RC 4.00 10.00
217 Alex Pelaez FW RC 2.00 5.00
218 Jamey Carroll FW RC 3.00 8.00
219 J.J. Trujillo FW RC 2.00 5.00
220 Kevin Pickford FW RC 2.00 5.00
221 Clay Condrey FW RC 2.00 5.00
222 Chris Snelling FW RC 2.50 6.00
223 Cliff Lee FW RC 4.00 10.00
224 Jeremy Hill FW RC 2.00 5.00
225 Jose Rodriguez FW RC 2.00 5.00
226 Lance Carter FW RC 2.00 5.00
227 Ken Huckaby FW RC 2.00 5.00
228 Scott Wiggins FW RC 2.00 5.00
229 Corey Thurman FW RC 2.00 5.00
230 Kevin Cash FW RC 2.00 5.00
RJD Joe DiMaggio AU Poster 125.00 200.00

2002 SP Authentic Limited

*LTD 1-90: 5X TO 12X BASIC
*LTD 91-135: .6X TO 1.5X BASIC
*LTD 136-170: .4X TO 1X BASIC
*LTD 146/152/157: .3X TO .8X BASIC
STATED PRINT RUN 125 SERIAL #'d SETS

2002 SP Authentic Limited Gold

*GOLD 1-90: 10X TO 25X BASIC
*GOLD 91-135: 1X TO 2.5X BASIC
*GOLD 136-170: .6X TO 1.5X BASIC
*GOLD 146/152/157: .5X TO 1.2X BASIC
STATED PRINT RUN 50 SERIAL #'d SETS
146 Kazuhisa Ishii FW AU 30.00 60.00

2002 SP Authentic Chirography

STATED ODDS 1:72
STATED PRINT RUNS LISTED BELOW
EXCHANGE DEADLINE 9/10/05
AD Adam Dunn/348 10.00 25.00
AG Alex Graman/418 4.00 10.00
AR Alex Rodriguez/391 20.00 50.00
BB Barry Bonds/112 20.00 50.00
BBo Bret Boone/500 6.00 15.00
BZ Barry Zito/419 6.00 15.00
CF Cliff Floyd/313 6.00 15.00
CS C.C. Sabathia/442 10.00 25.00
DE Darin Erstad/80 6.00 15.00
DM Doug Mientkiewicz/478 6.00 15.00
FG Freddy Garcia/456 6.00 15.00
HB Hank Blalock/282 6.00 15.00
IS Ichiro Suzuki/78 300.00 500.00
JB John Buck/427 6.00 15.00
JG Jason Giambi/244 6.00 15.00
JL Jon Lieber/462 6.00 15.00
JM Joe Mays/469 4.00 10.00
KG Ken Griffey Jr./238 40.00 80.00
MBr Milton Bradley/470 6.00 15.00
MBu Mark Buehrle/438 12.50 30.00
MM Mark McGwire/50 150.00 300.00
MS Mike Sweeney/265 6.00 15.00
RS Richie Sexson/483 6.00 15.00
SB Sean Burroughs/275 4.00 10.00
SS Sammy Sosa/247 25.00 60.00
TG Tom Glavine/376 15.00 40.00
TGw Tony Gwynn/75 10.00 25.00

2002 SP Authentic Chirography Gold

SEE BECKETT.COM FOR PRINT RUNS
NO PRICING ON QTY OF 25 OR LESS
AD Adam Dunn/44 20.00 50.00
AG Alex Graman/76 6.00 15.00
BZ Barry Zito/75 10.00 25.00
CF Cliff Floyd/30 15.00 40.00
CS C.C. Sabathia/52 20.00 50.00
FG Freddy Garcia/34 15.00 40.00
IS Ichiro Suzuki/51 600.00 1200.00
JL Jon Lieber/32 15.00 40.00
KG Ken Griffey Jr./30 75.00 150.00
MBu Mark Buehrle/56 30.00 60.00
MS Mike Sweeney/29 15.00 40.00
TG Tom Glavine/47 15.00 40.00

2002 SP Authentic Game Jersey

STATED ODDS 1:24
SP INFO PROVIDED BY UPPER DECK
SP'S ARE NOT SERIAL-NUMBERED
JAJ Andruw Jones 6.00 15.00
JAP Andy Pettitte 6.00 15.00
JAR Alex Rodriguez 8.00 20.00
JBW Bernie Williams 6.00 15.00
JBZ Barry Zito 4.00 10.00
JCC C.C. Sabathia 4.00 10.00
JCD Carlos Delgado 4.00 10.00
JCJ Chipper Jones 6.00 15.00
JCS Curt Schilling 4.00 10.00
JDE Darin Erstad 4.00 10.00
JGM Greg Maddux 6.00 15.00
JGS Gary Sheffield 4.00 10.00
JIR Ivan Rodriguez 6.00 15.00
JIS Ichiro Suzuki SP 10.00 25.00
JJBA Jeff Bagwell 6.00 15.00
JJBU Jeromy Burnitz SP 6.00 15.00
JJE Jim Edmonds 4.00 10.00
JJGO Juan Gonzalez 4.00 10.00
JJGR Jason Giambi 4.00 10.00
JJK Jason Kendall 4.00 10.00
JJT Jim Thome 6.00 15.00
JKG Ken Griffey Jr. SP/95 * 8.00 20.00
JKI Kazuhisa Ishii 6.00 15.00
JMM Mark McGwire SP 75.00 150.00
JMO Magglio Ordonez 4.00 10.00
JMP Mike Piazza 6.00 15.00
JMR Manny Ramirez 6.00 15.00
JOV Omar Vizquel 6.00 15.00
JPW Preston Wilson 4.00 10.00
JRA Roberto Alomar 6.00 15.00
JRC Roger Clemens 8.00 20.00
JRJ Randy Johnson 6.00 15.00
JRV Robin Ventura 4.00 10.00
JSG Shawn Green 4.00 10.00
JSR Scott Rolen 6.00 15.00
JSS Sammy Sosa 6.00 15.00
JTH Todd Helton 6.00 15.00
JTS Tsuyoshi Shinjo 6.00 15.00

2002 SP Authentic Game Jersey Gold

STATED PRINT RUNS LISTED BELOW
NO PRICING ON QTY OF 25 OR LESS
JAP Andy Pettitte/46 12.50 30.00
JBW Bernie Williams/51 12.50 30.00
JBZ Barry Zito/75 8.00 20.00
JCC C.C. Sabathia/52 8.00 20.00
JCS Curt Schilling/38 10.00 25.00
JGM Greg Maddux/31 40.00 80.00
JIS Ichiro Suzuki/51 60.00 120.00
JKG Ken Griffey Jr./30 15.00 40.00
JMO Magglio Ordonez/30 10.00 25.00
JMP Mike Piazza/31 40.00 80.00
JPW Preston Wilson/44 8.00 20.00
JRJ Randy Johnson/51 15.00 40.00

2002 SP Authentic Prospects Signatures

STATED ODDS 1:36
PAG Alex Graman 3.00 8.00
PBH Bill Hall 4.00 10.00
PDM Dustan Mohr 3.00 8.00
PDW Danny Wright 3.00 8.00
PJC Jose Cueto 3.00 8.00
PJDE Jeff Deardorff 3.00 8.00
PJDI Jose Diaz 3.00 8.00
PKH Ken Huckaby 3.00 8.00
PMG Matt Guerrier 3.00 8.00
PMS Marcos Scutaro 6.00 15.00
PST Steve Torrealba 3.00 8.00
PXN Xavier Nady 3.00 8.00

2002 SP Authentic Signed Big Mac

RANDOM INSERTS IN PACKS
SEE BECKETT.COM FOR PRINT RUNS
NO PRICING ON QTY OF 25 OR LESS
MM6 Mark McGwire/70 75.00 200.00

2002 SP Authentic USA Future Watch

RANDOM INSERTS IN PACKS
STATED PRINT RUN 1999 SERIAL #'d SETS
USA1 Chad Cordero 4.00 10.00
USA2 Philip Humber 5.00 12.00
USA3 Grant Johnson 2.00 5.00
USA4 Wes Littleton 2.00 5.00
USA5 Kyle Sleeth 2.00 5.00
USA6 Huston Street 4.00 10.00
USA7 Brad Sullivan 2.00 5.00
USA8 Bob Zimmermann 2.00 5.00
USA9 Abe Alvarez 2.00 5.00
USA10 Kyle Bakker 2.00 5.00
USA11 Landon Powell 2.00 5.00
USA12 Clint Sammons 2.00 5.00
USA13 Michael Aubrey 3.00 8.00
USA14 Aaron Hill 4.00 10.00
USA15 Conor Jackson 6.00 15.00
USA16 Eric Patterson 3.00 8.00
USA17 Dustin Pedroia 10.00 25.00
USA18 Rickie Weeks 10.00 25.00
USA19 Shane Costa 2.00 5.00
USA20 Mark Jurich 2.00 5.00
USA21 Sam Fuld 6.00 15.00
USA22 Carlos Quentin 3.00 8.00

2002 SP Authentic Hawaii Sign of the Times Duke Snider

DS Duke Snider/500 12.50 30.00

2003 SP Authentic

91-123 PRINT RUN 2500 SERIAL #'d SETS
124-150 PRINT RUN 1993 SERIAL #'d SETS
151-180 PRINT RUN 2003 SERIAL #'d SETS
181-189 PRINT RUN 500 SERIAL #'d SETS
91-189 RANDOM INSERTS IN PACKS
190-239 RANDOM IN 03 UD FINITE PACKS
190-239 PRINT RUN 699 SERIAL #'d SETS
J.CONTRERAS IS PART LIVE/PART EXCH
J.CONTRERAS EXCH DEADLINE 05/21/06
1 Darin Erstad .15 .40
2 Garret Anderson .15 .40
3 Troy Glaus .15 .40
4 Eric Chavez .15 .40
5 Barry Zito .25 .60
6 Miguel Tejada .25 .60
7 Eric Hinske .15 .40
8 Carlos Delgado .15 .40
9 Josh Phelps .15 .40
10 Ben Grieve .15 .40
11 Carl Crawford .25 .60
12 Omar Vizquel .25 .60
13 Matt Lawton .15 .40
14 C.C. Sabathia .25 .60
15 Ichiro Suzuki .50 1.25
16 John Olerud .15 .40
17 Freddy Garcia .15 .40
18 Jay Gibbons .15 .40
19 Tony Batista .15 .40
20 Melvin Mora .15 .40
21 Alex Rodriguez .50 1.25
22 Rafael Palmeiro .25 .60
23 Hank Blalock .15 .40
24 Nomar Garciaparra .25 .60
25 Pedro Martinez .25 .60
26 Johnny Damon .25 .60
27 Mike Sweeney .15 .40
28 Carlos Febles .15 .40
29 Carlos Beltran .25 .60
30 Carlos Pena .25 .60
31 Eric Munson .15 .40
32 Bobby Higginson .15 .40
33 Torii Hunter .15 .40
34 Doug Mientkiewicz .15 .40
35 Jacque Jones .15 .40
36 Paul Konerko .25 .60
37 Bartolo Colon .15 .40
38 Magglio Ordonez .25 .60
39 Derek Jeter 1.00 2.50
40 Bernie Williams .25 .60
41 Jason Giambi .15 .40
42 Alfonso Soriano .25 .60
43 Roger Clemens .50 1.25
44 Jeff Bagwell .25 .60
45 Jeff Kent .15 .40
46 Lance Berkman .15 .40
47 Chipper Jones .40 1.00
48 Andruw Jones .15 .40
49 Gary Sheffield .15 .40
50 Ben Sheets .15 .40
51 Richie Sexson .15 .40
52 Geoff Jenkins .15 .40
53 Jim Edmonds .25 .60
54 Albert Pujols .50 1.25
55 Scott Rolen .25 .60
56 Sammy Sosa .40 1.00
57 Kerry Wood .15 .40
58 Eric Karros .15 .40
59 Luis Gonzalez .15 .40
60 Randy Johnson .40 1.00
61 Curt Schilling .25 .60

62 Fred McGriff .25 .60
63 Shawn Green .15 .40
64 Paul Lo Duca .15 .40
65 Vladimir Guerrero .25 .60
66 Jose Vidro .15 .40
67 Barry Bonds .60 1.50
68 Rich Aurilia .15 .40
69 Edgardo Alfonzo .15 .40
70 Ivan Rodriguez .25 .60
71 Mike Lowell .15 .40
72 Derrek Lee .15 .40
73 Tom Glavine .25 .60
74 Mike Piazza .40 1.00
75 Roberto Alomar .25 .60
76 Ryan Klesko .15 .40
77 Phil Nevin .15 .40
78 Mark Kotsay .15 .40
79 Jim Thome .25 .60
80 Pat Burrell .15 .40
81 Bobby Abreu .15 .40
82 Jason Kendall .15 .40
83 Brian Giles .15 .40
84 Aramis Ramirez .15 .40
85 Austin Kearns .15 .40
86 Ken Griffey Jr. .75 2.00
87 Adam Dunn .25 .60
88 Larry Walker .25 .60
89 Todd Helton .25 .60
90 Preston Wilson .15 .40
91 Derek Jeter RA 2.50 6.00
92 Johnny Damon RA .60 1.50
93 Chipper Jones RA 1.00 2.50
94 Manny Ramirez RA 1.00 2.50
95 Trot Nixon RA .40 1.00
96 Alex Rodriguez RA 1.25 3.00
97 Chan Ho Park RA .60 1.50
98 Brad Fullmer RA .40 1.00
99 Billy Wagner RA .40 1.00
100 Hideo Nomo RA 1.00 2.50
101 Freddy Garcia RA .40 1.00
102 Darin Erstad RA .40 1.00
103 Jose Cruz Jr. RA .40 1.00
104 Nomar Garciaparra RA .60 1.50
105 Magglio Ordonez RA .60 1.50
106 Kerry Wood RA .40 1.00
107 Troy Glaus RA .40 1.00
108 J.D. Drew RA .40 1.00
109 Alfonso Soriano RA .60 1.50
110 Danys Baez RA .40 1.00
111 Kazuhiro Sasaki RA .40 1.00
112 Barry Zito RA .60 1.50
113 Brent Abernathy RA .40 1.00
114 Ben Diggins RA .40 1.00
115 Ben Sheets RA .40 1.00
116 Brad Wilkerson RA .40 1.00
117 Juan Pierre RA .40 1.00
118 Jon Rauch RA .40 1.00
119 Ichiro Suzuki RA 1.25 3.00
120 Albert Pujols RA 1.25 3.00
121 Mark Prior RA .60 1.50
122 Mark Teixeira RA .60 1.50
123 Kazuhisa Ishii RA .40 1.00
124 Troy Glaus B93 .40 1.00
125 Randy Johnson B93 1.00 2.50
126 Curt Schilling B93 .60 1.50
127 Chipper Jones B93 1.00 2.50
128 Greg Maddux B93 1.25 3.00
129 Nomar Garciaparra B93 .60 1.50
130 Pedro Martinez B93 .60 1.50
131 Sammy Sosa B93 1.00 2.50
132 Mark Prior B93 .60 1.50
133 Ken Griffey Jr. B93 2.00 5.00
134 Adam Dunn B93 .60 1.50
135 Jeff Bagwell B93 .60 1.50
136 Vladimir Guerrero B93 .60 1.50
137 Mike Piazza B93 1.00 2.50
138 Tom Glavine B93 .60 1.50
139 Derek Jeter B93 2.50 6.00
140 Roger Clemens B93 1.25 3.00
141 Jason Giambi B93 .40 1.00
142 Alfonso Soriano B93 .60 1.50
143 Miguel Tejada B93 .60 1.50
144 Barry Zito B93 .60 1.50
145 Jim Thome B93 .60 1.50
146 Barry Bonds B93 1.50 4.00
147 Ichiro Suzuki B93 1.25 3.00
148 Albert Pujols B93 1.25 3.00
149 Alex Rodriguez B93 1.25 3.00
150 Carlos Delgado B93 .40 1.00
151 Rich Fischer FW RC 1.25 3.00
152 Brandon Webb FW RC 4.00 10.00
153 Rob Hammock FW RC 1.25 3.00
154 Matt Kata FW RC 1.25 3.00
155 Tim Olson FW RC 1.25 3.00
156 Oscar Villarreal FW RC 1.25 3.00
157 Michael Hessman FW RC 1.25 3.00
158 Daniel Cabrera FW RC 2.00 5.00
159 Jon Leicester FW RC 1.25 3.00
160 Todd Wellemeyer FW RC 1.25 3.00
161 Felix Sanchez FW RC 1.25 3.00
162 David Sanders FW RC 1.25 3.00
163 Josh Stewart FW RC 1.25 3.00
164 Arnie Munoz FW RC 1.25 3.00
165 Ryan Cameron FW RC 1.25 3.00
166 Clint Barmes FW RC 3.00 8.00
167 Josh Willingham FW RC 4.00 10.00
169 Willie Eyre FW RC 1.25 3.00
170 Brent Hoard FW RC 1.25 3.00
171 Termel Sledge FW RC 1.25 3.00
172 Phil Seibel FW RC 1.25 3.00
173 Craig Brazell FW RC 1.25 3.00
174 Jeff Duncan FW RC 1.25 3.00
176 Bernie Castro FW RC 1.25 3.00
177 Mike Nicolas FW RC 1.25 3.00
178 Rett Johnson FW RC 1.25 3.00
179 Bobby Madritsch FW RC 1.25 3.00
180 Chris Capuano FW RC 1.25 3.00
181 Hid Matsui FW AU RC 200.00 400.00
182 Jose Contreras FW AU RC 12.50 30.00
183 Lew Ford FW AU RC 10.00 25.00
184 Jeremy Griffiths FW AU RC 6.00 15.00
185 G.Quiroz FW AU RC 6.00 15.00
186 Alej.Machado FW AU RC 6.00 15.00
187 Fran Cruceta FW AU RC 6.00 15.00
188 Prentice Redman FW AU RC 6.00 15.00
189 Shane Bazzell FW AU RC 6.00 15.00
190 Aaron Looper FW RC 1.25 3.00
191 Alex Prieto FW RC 1.25 3.00
192 Alfredo Gonzalez FW RC 1.25 3.00
193 Andrew Brown FW RC 1.25 3.00
194 Anthony Ferrari FW RC 1.25 3.00
195 Aquilino Lopez FW RC 1.25 3.00
196 Beau Kemp FW RC 1.25 3.00
197 Bo Hart FW RC 1.25 3.00
198 Chad Gaudin FW RC 1.25 3.00
199 Colin Porter FW RC 1.25 3.00
200 D.J. Carrasco FW RC 1.25 3.00
201 Dan Haren FW RC 6.00 15.00
202 Danny Garcia FW RC 1.25 3.00
203 Jon Switzer FW 1.25 3.00
204 Edwin Jackson FW RC 2.00 5.00
205 Fernando Cabrera FW RC 1.25 3.00
206 Garrett Atkins FW 1.25 3.00
207 Gerald Laird FW 1.25 3.00
208 Greg Jones FW RC 1.25 3.00
209 Ian Ferguson FW RC 1.25 3.00
210 Jason Roach FW RC 1.25 3.00
211 Jason Shiell FW RC 1.25 3.00
212 Jeremy Bonderman FW RC 5.00 12.00
213 Jeremy Wedel FW RC 1.25 3.00
214 Jhonny Peralta FW 1.25 3.00
215 Delmon Young FW RC 8.00 20.00
216 Jorge DePaula FW 1.25 3.00
217 Josh Hall FW RC 1.25 3.00
218 Julio Manon FW RC 1.25 3.00
219 Kevin Correia FW RC 1.25 3.00
220 Kevin Ohme FW RC 1.25 3.00
221 Kevin Tolar FW RC 1.25 3.00
222 Luis Ayala FW RC 1.25 3.00
223 Luis De Los Santos FW 1.25 3.00
224 Chad Cordero FW RC 1.25 3.00
225 Mark Malaska FW RC 1.25 3.00
226 Khalil Greene FW 2.00 5.00
227 Michael Nakamura FW RC 1.25 3.00
228 Michel Hernandez FW RC 1.25 3.00
229 Miguel Ojeda FW RC 1.25 3.00
230 Mike Neu FW RC 1.25 3.00
231 Nate Bland FW RC 1.25 3.00
232 Pete LaForest FW RC 1.25 3.00
233 Rickie Weeks FW RC 4.00 10.00
234 Rosman Garcia FW RC 1.25 3.00
235 Ryan Wagner FW RC 1.25 3.00
236 Lance Niekro FW 1.25 3.00
237 Tom Gregorio FW RC 1.25 3.00
238 Tommy Phelps FW 1.25 3.00
239 Wilfredo Ledezma FW RC 1.25 3.00

2003 SP Authentic Matsui Future Watch Autograph Parallel

RANDOM INSERTS IN PACKS
PRINT RUNS B/WN 10-75 COPIES PER
NO PRICING ON QTY OF 25 OR LESS
181A H.Matsui Bronze/75 175.00 300.00

2003 SP Authentic 500 HR Club

RANDOM INSERTS IN PACKS
GOLD PRINT RUN 25 SERIAL #'d CARDS
NO GOLD PRICING DUE TO SCARCITY
500 Sos/Ted/Mick/Mac/Bond 75.00 200.00

2003 SP Authentic Chirography

PRINT RUNS B/WN 50-350 COPIES PER
NO BRONZE PRICING ON 25 OR LESS
SILVER PRINT B/WN 15-50 COPIES PER
NO SILVER PRICING ON 25 OR LESS
GOLD PRINT RUN 10 SERIAL #'d SETS
NO GOLD PRICING DUE TO SCARCITY
EXCHANGE DEADLINE 05/21/06
AD Adam Dunn/170 6.00 15.00
BA Jeff Bagwell/175 30.00 60.00
CR Cal Ripken/250 30.00 80.00
FC Rafael Furcal/150 6.00 15.00
FG Freddy Garcia/345 6.00 15.00
FL Cliff Floyd/125 4.00 10.00
GA1 Garret Anderson/350 6.00 15.00
GI Jason Giambi/250 6.00 15.00
GJ Ken Griffey Jr./350 40.00 80.00
GL Brian Giles/225 6.00 15.00
IC Ichiro Suzuki/85 400.00 600.00
IS Ichiro Suzuki/75 400.00 600.00
JD Johnny Damon/245 6.00 15.00
JE2 Jim Edmonds/350 10.00 25.00
JM Joe Mays/245 4.00 10.00
JR Ken Griffey Jr./350 40.00 80.00
JT1 Jim Thome/250 15.00 40.00
KE Jason Kendall/145 6.00 15.00
LG1 Luis Gonzalez/195 6.00 15.00
MM Mark McGwire/50 175.00 300.00
RO Scott Rolen/50 6.00 15.00
RS Richie Sexson/245 6.00 15.00
SA Sammy Sosa/335 40.00 80.00
SO Sammy Sosa/335 20.00 50.00
SW Mike Sweeney/125 6.00 15.00
TO Torii Hunter/245 6.00 15.00
TS Tim Salmon/350 6.00 15.00

2003 SP Authentic Chirography Bronze

RANDOM INSERTS IN PACKS
PRINT RUNS B/WN 25-100 COPIES PER
NO PRICING ON QTY OF 25 OR LESS
EXCHANGE DEADLINE 05/21/06
A FEW CARDS FEATURE INSCRIPTIONS
AD Adam Dunn/50 15.00 40.00
BA Jeff Bagwell/50 40.00 100.00
CR Cal Ripken/75 40.00 100.00
FC Rafael Furcal/50 10.00 25.00
FG Freddy Garcia/100 10.00 25.00
FL Cliff Floyd/50 6.00 15.00
GI Jason Giambi/50 10.00 25.00
GJ Ken Griffey Jr./100 50.00 100.00
GL Brian Giles/50 10.00 25.00
IC Ichiro Suzuki ROY/50 1000.00 2000.00
IS Ichiro Suzuki MVP/50 1000.00 2000.00
JD Johnny Damon/100 10.00 25.00
JM Joe Mays/100 6.00 15.00
JR Ken Griffey Jr./100 50.00 100.00
KE Jason Kendall/50 10.00 25.00
RO Scott Rolen/100 25.00 60.00
RS Richie Sexson/100 10.00 25.00
SA Sammy Sosa/100 50.00 100.00
SO Sammy Sosa/100 30.00 60.00
SW Mike Sweeney/75 10.00 25.00
TO Torii Hunter/100 6.00 15.00

2003 SP Authentic Chirography Silver

RANDOM INSERTS IN PACKS
PRINT RUNS B/WN 15-50 COPIES PER
NO PRICING ON QTY OF 25 OR LESS
EXCHANGE DEADLINE 05/21/06
A FEW CARDS FEATURE INSCRIPTIONS
FG Freddy Garcia/50 15.00 40.00
JD Johnny Damon/50 15.00 40.00
JM Joe Mays/50 10.00 25.00
RO Scott Rolen/50 40.00 100.00
RS Richie Sexson/50 15.00 40.00
SA Sammy Sosa/50 50.00 100.00
SO Sammy Sosa/50 30.00 60.00
TO Torii Hunter/50 10.00 25.00

2003 SP Authentic Chirography Dodgers Stars

PRINT RUNS B/WN 170-345 COPIES PER
SILVER PRINT RUN 50 SERIAL #'d SETS
GOLD PRINT RUN 10 SERIAL #'d SETS
NO GOLD PRICING DUE TO SCARCITY
BB Bill Buckner/245 8.00 20.00
BI Bill Russell/245 6.00 15.00
CE Ron Cey/345 6.00 15.00
DL Davey Lopes/245 6.00 15.00
DN Don Newcombe/345 8.00 20.00
DS Duke Snider/345 10.00 25.00
JN Tommy John/170 6.00 15.00
MW Maury Wills/320 6.00 15.00
SG Steve Garvey/320 6.00 15.00
SU Don Sutton/245 6.00 15.00
SY Steve Yeager/345 6.00 15.00

2003 SP Authentic Chirography Dodgers Stars Bronze

*BRONZE: .6X TO 1.5X BASIC DODGER
RANDOM INSERTS IN PACKS
STATED PRINT RUN 100 SERIAL #'d SETS
T.JOHN PRINT RUN 75 SERIAL #'d CARDS
ALL HAVE DODGERS INSCRIPTION

2003 SP Authentic Chirography Dodgers Stars Silver

*SILVER: .75X TO 2X BASIC DODGER
RANDOM INSERTS IN PACKS
STATED PRINT RUN 50 SERIAL #'d SETS
MOST HAVE 81 WS CHAMPS INSCRIPTION

2003 SP Authentic Chirography Doubles

PRINT RUNS B/WN 10-150 COPIES PER
NO PRICING ON QTY OF 25 OR LESS
EXCHANGE DEADLINE 05/21/06
FB W.Ford/Y.Berra/75 75.00 200.00
FE C.Fisk/D.Evans/75 40.00 80.00
FM C.Fisk/B.Mazeroski/75 30.00 60.00
GG K.Griffey/J.Giambi/75 60.00 120.00
GR S.Garvey/R.Cey/75 30.00 60.00
JI K.Griffey/I.Suzuki/125 400.00 600.00
KR T.Kubek/B.Richardson/75 50.00 100.00
KT J.Koosman/T.Seaver/75 40.00 100.00
SJ S.Sosa/J.Giambi/75 30.00 60.00
WB M.Wilson/B.Buckner/150 25.00 60.00

2003 SP Authentic Chirography Flashback

PRINT RUNS B/WN 55-350 COPIES PER
NO BRONZE PRICING ON QTY OF 25 OR LESS
SILVER PRINT B/WN 15-50 COPIES PER
NO SILVER PRICING ON QTY OF 25 OR LESS
GOLD PRINT RUN 10 SERIAL #'d SETS
NO GOLD PRICING DUE TO SCARCITY
EXCHANGE DEADLINE 05/21/06
BN Brian Giles/245 6.00 15.00
CF1 Cliff Floyd/350 6.00 15.00
GM Ken Griffey Jr./350 60.00 150.00
JA Jason Giambi/350 6.00 15.00
JE1 Jim Edmonds/350 10.00 25.00
LA Luis Gonzalez/200 8.00 20.00
MA Mark McGwire/55 150.00 300.00
SR Sammy Sosa/245 20.00 50.00

2003 SP Authentic Chirography Flashback Bronze

RANDOM INSERTS IN PACKS
PRINT RUNS B/WN 25-100 COPIES PER
NO PRICING ON QTY OF 25 OR LESS
EXCHANGE DEADLINE 05/21/06
MOST CARDS FEATURE INSCRIPTIONS
BN Brian Giles/50 10.00 25.00
GM Ken Griffey Jr./100 75.00 200.00
JA Jason Giambi/100 10.00 25.00
LA Luis Gonzalez/75 12.50 30.00
SR Sammy Sosa/100 20.00 50.00

2003 SP Authentic Chirography Flashback Silver

RANDOM INSERTS IN PACKS
PRINT RUNS B/WN 15-50 COPIES PER
NO PRICING ON QTY OF 25 OR LESS
EXCHANGE DEADLINE 05/21/06
MOST CARDS HAVE TEAM INSCRIPTION
JA0 Jason Giambi/50 12.50 30.00
SR Sammy Sosa/50 30.00 60.00

2003 SP Authentic Chirography Hall of Famers

PRINT RUNS B/WN 150-350 COPIES PER
SILVER PRINT B/WN 25-50 COPIES PER
NO SILVER PRICING ON QTY OF 25 OR LESS
GOLD PRINT RUN 10 SERIAL #'d SETS
NO GOLD PRICING DUE TO SCARCITY
BG Bob Gibson/245 12.50 30.00
CF Carlton Fisk/240 15.00 40.00
DS Duke Snider/250 10.00 25.00
DW2 Dave Winfield/350 10.00 25.00
GC1 Gary Carter/350 12.00 30.00
JB1 Johnny Bench/350 30.00 60.00
NR Nolan Ryan/170 50.00 120.00
OC Orlando Cepeda/245 10.00 25.00
RF Rollie Fingers/170 6.00 15.00
RR Robin Roberts/170 10.00 25.00
RY Robin Yount/350 20.00 50.00
TP Tony Perez/320 6.00 15.00
TS Tom Seaver/170 25.00 60.00
WF Whitey Ford/150 20.00 50.00

2003 SP Authentic Chirography Hall of Famers Bronze

RANDOM INSERTS IN PACKS
PRINT RUNS B/WN 50-100 COPIES PER
ALL HAVE HOF INSCRIPTION
BG Bob Gibson/100 20.00 50.00
CF Carlton Fisk/100 25.00 60.00
DS Duke Snider/100 15.00 40.00
NR Nolan Ryan/100 60.00 150.00
OC Orlando Cepeda/100 15.00 40.00
RF Rollie Fingers/50 10.00 25.00
RR Robin Roberts/50 15.00 40.00
TP Tony Perez/100 10.00 25.00
TS Tom Seaver/75 40.00 100.00
WF Whitey Ford/75 25.00 60.00

2003 SP Authentic Chirography Hall of Famers Silver

RANDOM INSERTS IN PACKS
PRINT RUNS B/WN 25-50 COPIES PER
NO PRICING ON QTY OF 25 OR LESS
ALL HAVE HOF YEAR INSCRIPTION
BG Bob Gibson/50 30.00 80.00
CF Carlton Fisk/50 30.00 80.00
DS Duke Snider/50 20.00 50.00
OC Orlando Cepeda/50 20.00 50.00
TP Tony Perez/50 12.50 30.00
TS Tom Seaver/50 50.00 120.00

2003 SP Authentic Chirography Triples

RANDOM INSERTS IN PACKS
PRINT RUN B/WN 10-75 COPIES PER CARD
NO PRICING ON QTY OF 10 OR LESS
EXCHANGE DEADLINE 05/21/06
BKR Berra/Kubek/Richardson 75.00 200.00
FCG Fisk/Carter/Gibson EXCH 40.00 100.00
GIS Griffey/Suzuki/Sosa EXCH 400.00 600.00
GLC Garvey/Lopes/Cey 50.00 100.00
GRC Garvey/Russell/Cey 50.00 100.00
GSG Griffey/Sosa/Giambi EXCH 150.00 250.00
GSJ Giambi/Sosa/Griffey 75.00 150.00
ISG Suzuki/Sosa/Giambi 250.00 500.00
SEA Salmon/Erstad/Anderson 30.00 60.00
SKM Seaver/Koosman/McGraw 60.00 150.00

2003 SP Authentic Chirography World Series Heroes

PRINT RUNS B/WN 145-350 COPIES PER
SILVER PRINT B/WN 25-50 COPIES PER
NO SILVER PRICING ON QTY OF 25 OR LESS
GOLD PRINT RUN 10 SERIAL #'d SETS
NO GOLD PRICING DUE TO SCARCITY
EXCHANGE DEADLINE 05/21/06
AJ1 Andruw Jones/350 8.00 20.00
BM Bill Mazeroski/245 8.00 20.00
CF Carlton Fisk/200 15.00 40.00
CR Cal Ripken/295 25.00 60.00
CS Curt Schilling/345 10.00 25.00
DE Darin Erstad/245 8.00 20.00
DJ David Justice/170 10.00 25.00
ER Edgar Renteria/220 8.00 20.00
GA Garret Anderson/245 8.00 20.00
GC Gary Carter/345 12.00 30.00
GO Luis Gonzalez/225 8.00 20.00
GS Ken Griffey Sr./295 8.00 20.00
JK Jerry Koosman/170 10.00 25.00
JP Jorge Posada/350 20.00 50.00
KG Kirk Gibson/145 10.00 25.00
TI Tim Salmon/245 10.00 25.00
TM Tug McGraw/170 20.00 50.00

2003 SP Authentic Chirography World Series Heroes Bronze

RANDOM INSERTS IN PACKS
PRINT RUNS B/WN 50-100 COPIES PER
EXCHANGE DEADLINE 05/21/06
ALL HAVE WS YEAR INSCRIPTION
BM Bill Mazeroski/100 12.00 30.00
CF Carlton Fisk/75 25.00 60.00
CS Curt Schilling/100 15.00 40.00
DE Darin Erstad/100 12.50 30.00
DJ David Justice/75 15.00 40.00
ER Edgar Renteria/75 12.50 30.00
GA Garret Anderson/100 12.50 30.00
GC Gary Carter/100 20.00 50.00
GO Luis Gonzalez/100 12.50 30.00
GS Ken Griffey Sr./100 12.50 30.00
JK Jerry Koosman/75 15.00 40.00
KG Kirk Gibson/50 15.00 40.00
TI Tim Salmon/100 15.00 40.00
TM Tug McGraw/100 30.00 80.00

2003 SP Authentic Chirography World Series Heroes Silver

RANDOM INSERTS IN PACKS
PRINT RUNS B/WN 25-50 COPIES PER
NO PRICING ON QTY OF 25 OR LESS
MOST FEATURE WS EVENT INSCRIPTIONS
BM Bill Mazeroski/50 15.00 40.00
CS Curt Schilling/50 20.00 50.00
DE Darin Erstad/50 15.00 40.00
DJ David Justice/50 20.00 50.00
GA Garret Anderson/50 20.00 50.00
GC Gary Carter/50 20.00 50.00
GO Luis Gonzalez/50 15.00 40.00
GS Ken Griffey Sr./50 15.00 40.00
JK Jerry Koosman/50 20.00 50.00
TI Tim Salmon/50 20.00 50.00
TM Tug McGraw Believe/50 50.00 100.00

2003 SP Authentic Chirography Yankees Stars

RANDOM INSERTS IN PACKS
PRINT RUNS B/WN 210-350 COPIES PER
SILVER PRINT B/WN 25-75 COPIES PER
NO SILVER PRICING ON QTY OF 25 OR LESS
GOLD PRINT RUN 25 SERIAL #'d SETS
NO GOLD PRICING DUE TO SCARCITY
BR Bobby Richardson/320 10.00 25.00
DM Don Mattingly/295 20.00 50.00
DW1 Dave Winfield/350 12.00 30.00
HK Ralph Houk/245 6.00 15.00
JB Jim Bouton/345 6.00 15.00
JG Jason Giambi/275 6.00 15.00
KS Ken Griffey Sr./350 6.00 15.00
RC Roger Clemens/210 30.00 60.00
SL Sparky Lyle/345 6.00 15.00
ST Mel Stottlemyre/345 6.00 15.00
TH Tommy Henrich/345 8.00 20.00
TJ Tommy John/245 6.00 15.00
TK Tony Kubek/345 12.50 30.00
YB Yogi Berra/270 30.00 80.00

2003 SP Authentic Chirography Yankees Stars Bronze

RANDOM INSERTS IN PACKS
PRINT RUNS B/WN 60-100 COPIES PER
MOST HAVE YANKEES INSCRIPTION
BR Bobby Richardson/100 15.00 40.00
DM Don Mattingly/100 30.00 80.00
HK Ralph Houk/100 10.00 25.00
JB Jim Bouton/100 10.00 25.00
JG Jason Giambi/60 10.00 25.00
KS Ken Griffey Sr./100 10.00 25.00
RC Roger Clemens/75 30.00 60.00
SL Sparky Lyle/100 10.00 25.00
ST Mel Stottlemyre/100 10.00 25.00
TH Tommy Henrich/100 12.50 30.00
TJ Tommy John/100 10.00 25.00
TK Tony Kubek/100 20.00 50.00
YB Yogi Berra/100 50.00 120.00

2003 SP Authentic Chirography Yankees Stars Silver

RANDOM INSERTS IN PACKS
PRINT RUNS B/WN 25-75 COPIES PER
NO PRICING ON QTY OF 25 OR LESS
MOST HAVE NEW YORK INSCRIPTION
BR Bobby Richardson/50 20.00 50.00
DM Don Mattingly/50 40.00 80.00
HK Ralph Houk/50 12.50 30.00
JB Jim Bouton/50 12.50 30.00
RC Roger Clemens/50 30.00 60.00
SL Sparky Lyle/50 12.50 30.00
ST Mel Stottlemyre/50 12.50 30.00
TH Tommy Henrich/50 15.00 40.00
TJ Tommy John/50 12.50 30.00
TK Tony Kubek/50 30.00 60.00
YB Yogi Berra/75 60.00 150.00

2003 SP Authentic Chirography Young Stars

RANDOM INSERTS IN PACKS
PRINT RUNS B/WN 150-350 COPIES PER
BRONZE PRINT RUN 100 SERIAL #'d SETS
SILVER PRINT RUN 50 SERIAL #'d SETS
SILVER PRIOR PRINT RUN 25 #'d CARDS
NO SILVER PRIOR PRICING AVAILABLE
GOLD PRINT RUN 10 SERIAL #'d SETS
NO GOLD PRICING DUE TO SCARCITY
EXCHANGE DEADLINE 05/21/06
AP A.J. Pierzynski/245 6.00 15.00
BO Joe Borchard/245 4.00 10.00
BP1 Brandon Phillips/350 4.00 10.00
BZ Barry Zito/350 10.00 25.00
CP Corey Patterson/245 4.00 10.00
DH Drew Henson/245 4.00 10.00
DI1 Ben Diggins/350 4.00 10.00
EH Eric Hinske/245 4.00 10.00
FS Freddy Sanchez/350 6.00 15.00
HB Hank Blalock/245 6.00 15.00
JJ Jacque Jones/245 6.00 15.00
JJ1 Jimmy Journell/350 4.00 10.00
JL Jason Lane/245 6.00 15.00
JP Josh Phelps/245 4.00 10.00
JS Jayson Werth/350 6.00 15.00
MB Marlon Byrd/245 4.00 10.00
MI Doug Mientkiewicz/245 6.00 15.00
MP Mark Prior/150 10.00 25.00
MY Brett Myers/245 6.00 15.00
OH Orlando Hudson/245 4.00 10.00
OP Oliver Perez/245 6.00 15.00
PE Carlos Pena/245 4.00 10.00
SB Sean Burroughs/245 4.00 10.00
TX Mark Teixeira/245 4.00 10.00

2003 SP Authentic Chirography Young Stars Bronze

*BRONZE: .6X TO 1.5X BASIC YS
*BRONZE PRIOR: .75X TO 2X BASIC YS
RANDOM INSERTS IN PACKS
STATED PRINT RUN 100 SERIAL #'d SETS
PRIOR PRINT RUN 50 SERIAL #'d CARDS
MOST FEATURE CITY INSCRIPTION
EXCHANGE DEADLINE 05/21/06

2003 SP Authentic Chirography Young Stars Silver

*SILVER: .75X TO 2X BASIC YS
RANDOM INSERTS IN PACKS
STATED PRINT RUN 50 SERIAL #'d SETS
PRIOR PRINT RUN 25 SERIAL #'d CARDS
NO PRIOR PRICING DUE TO SCARCITY
EXCHANGE DEADLINE 05/21/06
MOST FEATURE TEAM INSCRIPTION

2003 SP Authentic Simply Splendid

COMMON CARD (TW1-TW30) 3.00 8.00
RANDOM INSERTS IN PACKS
STATED PRINT RUN 406 SERIAL #'d SETS

2003 SP Authentic Splendid Jerseys

RANDOM INSERTS IN PACKS
STATED PRINT RUN 406 SERIAL #'d SETS
SJTW Ted Williams 25.00 60.00

2003 SP Authentic Splendid Signatures

RANDOM INSERTS IN PACKS
STATED PRINT RUNS LISTED BELOW
NO T.WILLIAMS PRICING DUE TO SCARCITY
GA Nomar Garciaparra/406 10.00 25.00

2003 SP Authentic Splendid Swatches Pairs

RANDOM INSERTS IN PACKS
STATED PRINT RUN 406 SERIAL #'d SETS
EXCHANGE DEADLINE 05/21/06
IS T.Williams/I.Suzuki 20.00 50.00
JG T.Williams/J.Giambi 15.00 40.00
KG T.Williams/K.Griffey Jr. 20.00 50.00
MM T.Williams/M.McGwire 12.00 30.00
NM1 T.Williams/Nomar 10.00 25.00
NM2 T.Williams/Nomar 10.00 25.00
SS T.Williams/S.Sosa 10.00 25.00
TW T.Williams/M.Mantle 60.00 120.00

2003 SP Authentic Spotlight Godzilla

COMMON MATSUI (HM1-HM15) 3.00 8.00
STATED PRINT RUN 500 SERIAL #'d SETS
*RED: 1X TO 2.5X BASIC GODZILLA
RED PRINT RUN 55 SERIAL #'d SETS

2003 SP Authentic Superstar Flashback

RANDOM INSERTS IN PACKS
STATED PRINT RUN 2003 SERIAL #'d SETS
SF1 Tim Salmon .60 1.50
SF2 Darin Erstad .60 1.50
SF3 Troy Glaus .60 1.50
SF4 Randy Johnson 1.50 4.00
SF5 Curt Schilling 1.00 2.50
SF6 Steve Finley .60 1.50
SF7 Greg Maddux 2.00 5.00
SF8 Chipper Jones 1.50 4.00
SF9 Andruw Jones .60 1.50
SF10 Gary Sheffield .60 1.50
SF11 Manny Ramirez 1.50 4.00
SF12 Pedro Martinez 1.00 2.50
SF13 Nomar Garciaparra 1.00 2.50
SF14 Sammy Sosa 1.50 4.00
SF15 Frank Thomas 1.50 4.00
SF16 Kerry Wood .60 1.50
SF17 Paul Konerko 1.00 2.50
SF18 Corey Patterson .60 1.50
SF19 Mark Prior 1.00 2.50
SF20 Ken Griffey Jr. 3.00 8.00
SF21 Adam Dunn 1.00 2.50
SF22 Larry Walker 1.00 2.50
SF23 Preston Wilson .60 1.50
SF24 Todd Helton 1.00 2.50
SF25 Ivan Rodriguez 1.00 2.50
SF26 Josh Beckett .60 1.50
SF27 Jeff Bagwell 1.00 2.50
SF28 Jeff Kent .60 1.50
SF29 Lance Berkman 1.00 2.50
SF30 Carlos Beltran 1.00 2.50
SF31 Shawn Green .60 1.50
SF32 Richie Sexson .60 1.50
SF33 Vladimir Guerrero 1.00 2.50
SF34 Mike Piazza 1.50 4.00
SF35 Roberto Alomar 1.00 2.50
SF36 Roger Clemens 2.00 5.00
SF37 Derek Jeter 4.00 10.00
SF38 Jason Giambi .60 1.50
SF39 Bernie Williams 1.00 2.50
SF40 Nick Johnson .60 1.50
SF41 Alfonso Soriano 1.00 2.50
SF42 Miguel Tejada 1.00 2.50
SF43 Eric Chavez .60 1.50
SF44 Barry Zito 1.00 2.50
SF45 Jim Thome 1.00 2.50
SF46 Pat Burrell .60 1.50
SF47 Marlon Byrd .60 1.50
SF48 Jason Kendall .60 1.50
SF49 Aramis Ramirez .60 1.50
SF50 Brian Giles .60 1.50
SF51 Phil Nevin .60 1.50
SF52 Barry Bonds 2.50 6.00
SF53 Ichiro Suzuki 2.00 5.00
SF54 Scott Rolen 1.00 2.50
SF55 J.D. Drew .60 1.50
SF56 Albert Pujols 2.00 5.00
SF57 Mark Teixeira 1.00 2.50
SF58 Hank Blalock .60 1.50
SF59 Carlos Delgado .60 1.50
SF60 Roy Halladay 1.00 2.50

2004 SP Authentic

COMP.SET w/o SP's (90) 6.00 15.00
COMMON CARD (1-90) .15 .40
COMMON (91-132/178-191) 1.25 3.00
91-132/178-191 OVERALL FW ODDS 1:24
91-132/178-179/181-191 PRINT 704 #'d SETS
91-132/178-179/181-191 #'d FROM 296-999
CARD 180 PRINT RUN 999 #'d COPIES
CARD 180 #'d FROM 1-999
COMMON CARD (133-177) .40 1.00
133-177 STATED ODDS 1:24
133-177 PRINT RUN 999 SERIAL #'d SETS
1 Bret Boone .15 .40
2 Gary Sheffield .15 .40
3 Rafael Palmeiro .25 .60
4 Jorge Posada .25 .60
5 Derek Jeter 1.00 2.50
6 Garret Anderson .15 .40
7 Bartolo Colon .15 .40
8 Kevin Brown .15 .40
9 Shea Hillenbrand .15 .40
10 Ryan Klesko .15 .40
11 Bobby Abreu .15 .40
12 Scott Rolen .25 .60
13 Alfonso Soriano .25 .60
14 Jason Giambi .15 .40
15 Tom Glavine .25 .60
16 Hideo Nomo .40 1.00
17 Johan Santana .25 .60
18 Sammy Sosa .40 1.00
19 Rickie Weeks .15 .40
20 Barry Zito .25 .60
21 Kerry Wood .15 .40
22 Austin Kearns .15 .40
23 Shawn Green .15 .40
24 Miguel Cabrera .40 1.00
25 Richard Hidalgo .15 .40
26 Andruw Jones .15 .40
27 Randy Wolf .15 .40
28 David Ortiz .40 1.00
29 Roy Oswalt .25 .60
30 Vernon Wells .15 .40
31 Ben Sheets .15 .40
32 Mike Lowell .15 .40
33 Todd Helton .25 .60
34 Jacque Jones .15 .40
35 Mike Sweeney .15 .40
36 Hank Blalock .15 .40
37 Jason Schmidt .15 .40
38 Jeff Kent .15 .40
39 Josh Beckett .15 .40
40 Manny Ramirez .40 1.00
41 Torii Hunter .15 .40
42 Brian Giles .15 .40
43 Javier Vazquez .15 .40
44 Jim Edmonds .25 .60
45 Dmitri Young .15 .40
46 Preston Wilson .15 .40
47 Jeff Bagwell .25 .60
48 Pedro Martinez .25 .60
49 Eric Chavez .15 .40
50 Ken Griffey Jr. .75 2.00
51 Shannon Stewart .15 .40
52 Rafael Furcal .15 .40
53 Brandon Webb .15 .40
54 Juan Pierre .15 .40
55 Roger Clemens .50 1.25
56 Geoff Jenkins .15 .40
57 Lance Berkman .25 .60
58 Albert Pujols .50 1.25
59 Frank Thomas .40 1.00
60 Edgar Martinez .25 .60
61 Tim Hudson .25 .60
62 Eric Gagne .15 .40
63 Richie Sexson .15 .40
64 Corey Patterson .15 .40
65 Nomar Garciaparra .25 .60
66 Hideki Matsui .60 1.50
67 Mark Teixeira .25 .60
68 Troy Glaus .15 .40
69 Carlos Lee .15 .40
70 Mike Mussina .25 .60
71 Magglio Ordonez .25 .60
72 Roy Halladay .25 .60
73 Ichiro Suzuki .50 1.25
74 Randy Johnson .40 1.00
75 Luis Gonzalez .15 .40
76 Mark Prior .25 .60
77 Carlos Beltran .25 .60
78 Ivan Rodriguez .25 .60
79 Alex Rodriguez .50 1.25
80 Dontrelle Willis .15 .40
81 Mike Piazza .40 1.00
82 Curt Schilling .25 .60
83 Vladimir Guerrero .25 .60
84 Greg Maddux .50 1.25
85 Jim Thome .25 .60
86 Miguel Tejada .25 .60
87 Carlos Delgado .15 .40
88 Jose Reyes .25 .60
89 Matt Morris .15 .40
90 Mark Mulder .15 .40
91 Angel Chavez FW RC 1.25 3.00
92 Brandon Medders FW RC 1.25 3.00
93 Carlos Vasquez FW RC 1.25 3.00
94 Chris Aguila FW RC 1.25 3.00
95 Colby Miller FW RC 1.25 3.00
96 Dave Crouthers FW RC 1.25 3.00
97 Dennis Sarfate FW RC 1.25 3.00
98 Donnie Kelly FW RC 2.00 5.00
99 Merkin Valdez FW RC 1.25 3.00
100 Eddy Rodriguez FW RC 1.25 3.00
101 Edwin Moreno FW RC 1.25 3.00
102 Enemencio Pacheco FW RC 1.25 3.00
103 Roberto Novoa FW RC 1.25 3.00
104 Greg Dobbs FW RC 1.25 3.00
105 Hector Gimenez FW RC 1.25 3.00
106 Ian Snell FW RC 1.25 3.00
107 Jake Woods FW RC 1.25 3.00
108 Jamie Brown FW RC 1.25 3.00
109 Jason Frasor FW RC 1.25 3.00
110 Jerome Gamble FW RC 1.25 3.00
111 Jerry Gil FW RC 1.25 3.00
112 Jesse Harper FW RC 1.25 3.00
113 Jorge Vasquez FW RC 1.25 3.00
114 Jose Capellan FW RC 1.25 3.00
115 Josh Labandeira FW RC 1.25 3.00
116 Justin Hampson FW RC 1.25 3.00
117 Justin Huisman FW RC 1.25 3.00
118 Justin Leone FW RC 1.25 3.00
119 Lincoln Holdzkom FW RC 1.25 3.00
120 Lino Urdaneta FW RC 1.25 3.00
121 Mike Gosling FW RC 1.25 3.00
122 Mike Johnston FW RC 1.25 3.00
123 Mike Rouse FW RC 1.25 3.00
124 Scott Proctor FW RC 1.25 3.00
125 Roman Colon FW RC 1.25 3.00
126 Ronny Cedeno FW RC 1.25 3.00
127 Ryan Meaux FW RC 1.25 3.00
128 Scott Dohmann FW RC 1.25 3.00
129 Sean Henn FW RC 1.25 3.00
130 Tim Bausher FW RC 1.25 3.00
131 Tim Bittner FW RC 1.25 3.00
132 William Bergolla FW RC 1.25 3.00
133 Rick Ferrell ASM .40 1.00
134 Joe DiMaggio ASM 2.00 5.00
135 Bob Feller ASM .60 1.50
136 Ted Williams ASM 2.00 5.00
137 Stan Musial ASM 1.50 4.00
138 Larry Doby ASM .60 1.50
139 Red Schoendienst ASM .60 1.50
140 Enos Slaughter ASM .60 1.50
141 Stan Musial ASM 1.50 4.00
142 Mickey Mantle ASM 3.00 8.00
143 Ted Williams ASM 2.00 5.00
144 Mickey Mantle ASM 3.00 8.00
145 Stan Musial ASM 1.50 4.00
146 Tom Seaver ASM .60 1.50
147 Willie McCovey ASM .60 1.50
148 Bob Gibson ASM .60 1.50
149 Frank Robinson ASM .60 1.50
150 Joe Morgan ASM .60 1.50
151 Billy Williams ASM .60 1.50
152 Catfish Hunter ASM .60 1.50
153 Joe Morgan ASM .60 1.50
154 Joe Morgan ASM .60 1.50
155 Mike Schmidt ASM 1.50 4.00
156 Tommy Lasorda ASM .60 1.50
157 Robin Yount ASM 1.00 2.50
158 Nolan Ryan ASM 3.00 8.00
159 John Franco ASM .40 1.00
160 Nolan Ryan ASM 3.00 8.00
161 Ken Griffey Jr. ASM 2.00 5.00
162 Cal Ripken ASM 3.00 8.00
163 Ken Griffey Jr. ASM 2.00 5.00
164 Gary Sheffield ASM .40 1.00
165 Fred McGriff ASM .40 1.00
166 Hideo Nomo ASM 1.00 2.50
167 Mike Piazza ASM 1.00 2.50
168 Sandy Alomar Jr. ASM .40 1.00
169 Roberto Alomar ASM .60 1.50
170 Ted Williams ASM 2.00 5.00
171 Pedro Martinez ASM .60 1.50
172 Derek Jeter ASM 2.50 6.00
173 Cal Ripken ASM 3.00 8.00

174 Torii Hunter ASM .40 1.00
175 Alfonso Soriano ASM .60 1.50
176 Hank Blalock ASM .40 1.00
177 Ichiro Suzuki ASM 1.25 3.00
178 Orlando Rodriguez FW RC 1.25 3.00
179 Ramon Ramirez FW RC 1.25 3.00
180 Kazuo Matsui FW RC 2.00 5.00
181 Kevin Cave FW RC 1.25 3.00
182 John Gall FW RC 1.25 3.00
183 Freddy Guzman FW RC 1.25 3.00
184 Chris Oxspring FW RC 1.25 3.00
185 Rusty Tucker FW RC 1.25 3.00
186 Jorge Sequea FW RC 1.25 3.00
187 Carlos Hines FW RC 1.25 3.00
188 Michael Vento FW RC 1.25 3.00
189 Ryan Wing FW RC 1.25 3.00
190 Jeff Bennett FW RC 1.25 3.00
191 Luis A. Gonzalez FW RC 1.25 3.00

2004 SP Authentic 199/99

*199/99 1-90: 3X TO 8X BASIC
*199/99 91-132/178-191: 1X TO 2.5X BASIC
1-132/178-191 PRINT RUN SER. 99 #'d SETS
*199/99 133-177: .75X TO 2X BASIC
133-177 PRINT RUN 199 SERIAL #'d SETS
OVERALL PARALLEL ODDS 1:8

2004 SP Authentic 499/249

*499/249 1-90: 1.5X TO 4X BASIC
*499/249 133-177: .6X TO 1.5X BASIC
1-90/133-177 PRINT RUN 499 #'d SETS
*499/249 91-132/178-191: .75X TO 2X BASIC
91-132/178-191 PRINT RUN 249 #'d SETS
OVERALL PARALLEL ODDS 1:8

2004 SP Authentic Future Watch Autograph

STATED PRINT RUN 295 SERIAL #'d SETS
*AUTO 195: .5X TO 1.2X BASIC
AUTO 195 PRINT RUN 195 SERIAL #'d SETS
OVERALL FUTURE WATCH ODDS 1:24
91 Angel Chavez FW 4.00 10.00
92 Brandon Medders FW 4.00 10.00
93 Carlos Vasquez FW 6.00 15.00
94 Chris Aguila FW 4.00 10.00
95 Colby Miller FW 4.00 10.00
96 Dave Crouthers FW 4.00 10.00
97 Dennis Sarfate FW 4.00 10.00
98 Donnie Kelly FW 4.00 10.00
99 Merkin Valdez FW 4.00 10.00
100 Eddy Rodriguez FW 6.00 15.00
101 Edwin Moreno FW 4.00 10.00
102 Enemencio Pacheco FW 4.00 10.00
103 Roberto Novoa FW 4.00 10.00
104 Greg Dobbs FW 4.00 10.00
105 Hector Gimenez FW 4.00 10.00
106 Ian Snell FW 10.00 25.00
107 Jake Woods FW 4.00 10.00
108 Jamie Brown FW 4.00 10.00
109 Jason Frasor FW 4.00 10.00
110 Jerome Gamble FW 4.00 10.00
111 Jerry Gil FW 4.00 10.00
112 Jesse Harper FW 4.00 10.00
113 Jorge Vasquez FW 4.00 10.00
114 Jose Capellan FW 4.00 10.00
115 Josh Labandeira FW 4.00 10.00
116 Justin Hampson FW 4.00 10.00
117 Justin Huisman FW 4.00 10.00
118 Justin Leone FW 6.00 15.00
119 Lincoln Holdzkom FW 4.00 10.00
120 Lino Urdaneta FW 4.00 10.00
121 Mike Gosling FW 4.00 10.00
122 Mike Johnston FW 4.00 10.00
123 Mike Rouse FW 4.00 10.00
124 Scott Proctor FW 6.00 15.00
125 Roman Colon FW 4.00 10.00
126 Ronny Cedeno FW 6.00 15.00
127 Ryan Meaux FW 4.00 10.00
128 Scott Dohmann FW 4.00 10.00
129 Sean Henn FW 4.00 10.00
130 Tim Bausher FW 4.00 10.00
131 Tim Bittner FW 4.00 10.00
132 William Bergolla FW 4.00 10.00
178 Orlando Rodriguez FW 4.00 10.00
179 Ramon Ramirez FW 4.00 10.00
181 Kevin Cave FW 4.00 10.00
182 John Gall FW 6.00 15.00
183 Freddy Guzman FW 4.00 10.00
184 Chris Oxspring FW 4.00 10.00
185 Rusty Tucker FW 6.00 15.00
186 Jorge Sequea FW 4.00 10.00
187 Carlos Hines FW 4.00 10.00
188 Michael Vento FW 6.00 15.00
189 Ryan Wing FW 4.00 10.00
190 Jeff Bennett FW 4.00 10.00
191 Luis A. Gonzalez FW 6.00 15.00

2004 SP Authentic Buybacks

OVERALL AUTO INSERT ODDS 1:12
PRINT RUNS B/WN 1-105 COPIES PER
NO PRICING ON QTY OF 14 OR LESS
EXCHANGE DEADLINE 06/04/07
AB1 Angel Berroa 04 VIN/70 4.00 10.00
AD1 Andre Dawson 04 SSC/50 6.00 15.00
AK1 Al Kaline 03 SP LC/20 30.00 80.00
AK2 Al Kaline 04 SSC/70 25.00 50.00
AL1 Al Leiter 04 FP/80 6.00 15.00
AL2 Al Leiter 04 UD/60 6.00 15.00
BA1 Bobby Abreu 03 CP/63 6.00 15.00
BA3 Bobby Abreu 03 SPx/63 6.00 15.00
BA4 Bobby Abreu 03 SS/64 6.00 15.00
BA5 Bobby Abreu 03 UDA/63 6.00 15.00
BA6 Bobby Abreu 04 DAS/53 6.00 15.00
BA7 Bobby Abreu 04 FP/53 6.00 15.00
BA8 Bobby Abreu 04 UD/65 6.00 15.00
BA9 Bobby Abreu 04 VIN/53 6.00 15.00
BB1 Bret Boone 03 CP/66 15.00 40.00
BB2 Bret Boone 03 PC/15 30.00 60.00
BB3 Bret Boone 03 SPx/29 20.00 50.00
BB4 Bret Boone 03 SS/44 15.00 40.00
BB5 Bret Boone 03 UDA/63 15.00 40.00
BB6 Bret Boone 04 DAS/57 15.00 40.00
BB7 Bret Boone 04 VIN/53 15.00 40.00
BD1 Bobby Doerr 03 SP LCB/50 6.00 15.00
BD2 Bobby Doerr 04 SSC/73 6.00 15.00
BG1 Bob Gibson 04 SSC/23 15.00 40.00
BHI1 Bobby Hill 03 40M/40 4.00 10.00
BHI2 Bobby Hill 03 UDA/17 8.00 20.00
BHI3 Bobby Hill 04 FP/17 8.00 20.00
BHI4 Bobby Hill 04 UD/17 8.00 20.00
BHI5 Bobby Hill 04 VIN/34 6.00 15.00
BH1 Bo Hart 03 SPx/50 4.00 10.00
BH2 Bo Hart 04 VIN/45 4.00 10.00
BR1 B.Robinson 03 SP LC/50 10.00 25.00
BR2 B.Robinson 04 SSC/70 10.00 25.00
BS1 Ben Sheets 03 40M/25 10.00 25.00
BS2 Ben Sheets 03 CP/15 12.50 30.00
BS3 Ben Sheets 03 PC/15 12.50 30.00
BS4 Ben Sheets 03 SPx/15 12.50 30.00
BS5 Ben Sheets 04 DAS/15 12.50 30.00
BS7 Ben Sheets 04 UD/25 10.00 25.00
BS8 Ben Sheets 04 VIN/15 12.50 30.00
BW1 Brandon Webb 03 SPx/20 6.00 15.00
BW2 Brandon Webb 03 UD/65 4.00 10.00
BW4 Brandon Webb 04 DAS/50 4.00 10.00
BW5 Brandon Webb 04 FP/30 10.00 25.00
BW6 Brandon Webb 04 VIN/85 4.00 10.00
BZ1 Barry Zito 03 40M/30 15.00 40.00
BZ2 Barry Zito 03 CP/41 10.00 25.00
BZ3 Barry Zito 03 HR/60 10.00 25.00
BZ4 Barry Zito 03 PC/15 20.00 50.00
BZ5 Barry Zito 03 SPx/46 10.00 25.00
BZ6 Barry Zito 03 SS/63 10.00 25.00
BZ7 Barry Zito 03 UDA/40 10.00 25.00
BZ8 Barry Zito 04 FP/69 10.00 25.00
BZ9 Barry Zito 04 UD/61 10.00 25.00
BZ10 Barry Zito 04 VIN/50 10.00 25.00
CB2 Carlos Beltran 03 CP/15 12.50 30.00
CB3 Carlos Beltran 03 PC/15 12.50 30.00
CB5 Carlos Beltran 03 SS/15 12.50 30.00
CB6 Carlos Beltran 04 DAS/15 12.50 30.00
CB7 Carlos Beltran 04 VIN/15 12.50 30.00
CD5 C.Delgado 03 UDA/43 6.00 15.00
CF1 C.Fisk 03 SP LC/38 15.00 40.00
CF2 C.Fisk 03 SP LCB/55 15.00 40.00
CLL1 Cliff Lee 04 FP/40 30.00 60.00
CLL2 Cliff Lee 04 UD/50 30.00 60.00
CL1 Carlos Lee 04 FP/70 6.00 15.00
CL2 Carlos Lee 04 UD/70 6.00 15.00
CL3 Carlos Lee 04 VIN/70 6.00 15.00
CPO1 Colin Porter 03 CP/60 4.00 10.00
CPO3 Colin Porter 04 FP/70 4.00 10.00
CP1 C.Patterson 03 40M/20 6.00 15.00
CP2 C.Patterson 03 PC/20 6.00 15.00
CP3 C.Patterson 03 SPx/20 6.00 15.00
CP4 C.Patterson 03 SS/20 6.00 15.00
CP5 C.Patterson 04 FP/20 6.00 15.00
CP6 C.Patterson 04 UD/20 6.00 15.00
CP7 C.Patterson 04 VIN/20 6.00 15.00
CR1 Cal Ripken 04 SSC/45 75.00 150.00
CW1 C.Wang 04 FP/26 75.00 150.00
CY1 C.Yastrzemski 04 SSC/22 40.00 80.00
CZ1 C.Zambrano 04 VIN/70 10.00 25.00
DJ1 Derek Jeter 03 40M/30 90.00 180.00
DJ3 Derek Jeter 03 HR/25 100.00 200.00
DJ4 Derek Jeter 03 PC/25 100.00 200.00
DJ6 Derek Jeter 03 SS/30 125.00 250.00
DJ10 Derek Jeter 04 UD/25 100.00 200.00
DJ11 Derek Jeter 04 VIN/25 100.00 200.00
DS1 Duke Snider 04 SSC/23 20.00 50.00
DW1 D.Willis 04 DAS/70 10.00 25.00
DW2 D.Willis 04 FP/80 10.00 25.00
DW3 D.Willis 04 UD SR/45 10.00 25.00
DW4 D.Willis 04 VIN/105 10.00 25.00
DY3 Delmon Young 04 VIN/35 15.00 40.00
EC1 Eric Chavêz 03 40M/30 6.00 15.00
EC5 Eric Chavez 03 SS/25 6.00 15.00
EG1 Eric Gagne 03 40M/38 10.00 25.00
EG2 Eric Gagne 04 FP/26 15.00 40.00
EG3 Eric Gagne 04 UD/38 10.00 25.00
EG4 Eric Gagne 04 VIN/38 10.00 25.00
EM1 E.Martinez 04 DAS/70 15.00 40.00
GA1 G.Anderson 03 40M/30 10.00 25.00
GA4 G.Anderson 03 SS/20 10.00 25.00
GA5 G.Anderson 04 DAS/16 12.50 30.00
GA6 G.Anderson 04 VIN/16 12.50 30.00
HB1 Hank Blalock 03 40M/20 10.00 25.00
HB5 Hank Blalock 03 SS/15 12.50 30.00
HK1 H.Killebrew 03 SP LC/20 40.00 80.00
HR1 H.Ramirez 03 40M/25 6.00 15.00
HR3 Horacio Ramirez 04 UD/15 8.00 20.00
JB1 Josh Beckett 03 40M/21 15.00 40.00
JB3 Josh Beckett 03 HR/21 15.00 40.00
JB6 Josh Beckett 03 SS/21 15.00 40.00
JE1 Jim Edmonds 03 CP/25 15.00 40.00
JE2 Jim Edmonds 03 HR/15 20.00 50.00
JE3 Jim Edmonds 03 SPx/25 15.00 40.00
JE4 Jim Edmonds 03 SS/45 10.00 25.00
JE5 Jim Edmonds 03 UDA/25 15.00 40.00
JE6 Jim Edmonds 04 DAS/15 20.00 50.00
JE7 Jim Edmonds 04 FP/15 20.00 50.00
JE8 Jim Edmonds 04 UD/25 15.00 40.00
JE9 Jim Edmonds 04 VIN/15 20.00 50.00
JGE1 Jody Gerut 04 DAS/70 4.00 10.00
JGE2 Jody Gerut 04 VIN/70 4.00 10.00
JG1 Juan Gonzalez 03 40M/19 12.50 30.00
JG3 Juan Gonzalez 03 PC/19 12.50 30.00
JG4 Juan Gonzalez 03 SS/19 12.50 30.00
JG6 Juan Gonzalez 04 UD/19 12.50 30.00
JG7 Juan Gonzalez 04 VIN/20 10.00 25.00
JJ1 Jacque Jones 03 40M/40 6.00 15.00
JJ3 Jacque Jones 03 SPx/35 10.00 25.00
JJ4 Jacque Jones 03 SS/35 10.00 25.00
JL1 Javy Lopez 03 40M/30 10.00 25.00
JL2 Javy Lopez 04 FP/18 12.50 30.00
JL3 Javy Lopez 04 UD/29 10.00 25.00
JL4 Javy Lopez 04 VIN/18 12.50 30.00
JO1 John Olerud 03 CP/50 10.00 25.00
JO2 John Olerud 03 SS/45 10.00 25.00
JO3 John Olerud 04 VIN/70 10.00 25.00
JS1 John Smoltz 04 FP/67 30.00 60.00
JS2 John Smoltz 04 UD/67 30.00 60.00
JS3 John Smoltz 04 VIN/70 30.00 60.00
JT1 Joe Torre 04 SSC/70 10.00 25.00
JV1 Javier Vazquez 04 DAS/70 6.00 15.00
JV2 Javier Vazquez 04 VIN/70 6.00 15.00
JWS3 Jae Seo 04 UD/15 12.50 30.00
JWS4 Jae Seo 04 VIN/15 12.50 30.00
JW1 Jer.Williams 04 UD/70 4.00 10.00
JW2 Jer.Williams 04 VIN/60 4.00 10.00
KG1 K.Grif 02 SUP Silv/45 50.00 100.00
KG3 K.Grif 02 SUP SK Blue/19 75.00 150.00
KG4 K.Grif 03 40M Blue/20 60.00 120.00
KG6 K.Grif 03 40M 92 AS/18 75.00 150.00
KG7 K.Grif 03 40M 97 AL/18 75.00 150.00
KG8 K.Grif 03 40MHR94 Blk/31 60.00 120.00
KG9 K.Grif 03 40MHR94 Blu/27 60.00 120.00
KG10 K.Grif 03 40MHR98 Sil/28 60.00 120.00
KG13 K.Grif 03 40M HR99 Sil/48 50.00 100.00
KG14 K.Grif 03 40M T40 Blu/35 60.00 120.00
KG15 K.Grif 03 40M T40 AL/29 50.00 100.00
KG16 K.Grif 03 GF Black/40 50.00 100.00
KG17 K.Grif 03 GF Blue/23 60.00 120.00
KG19 K.Grif 03 GF 92AS/19 75.00 150.00
KG20 K.Grif 03 HR 92AS/15 75.00 150.00
KG21 K.Grif 03 HR 97AL/37 60.00 120.00
KG23 K.Grif 03 MVP Blk/56 50.00 100.00
KG25 K.Grif 03 MVP GG/15 75.00 150.00
KG27 K.Grif 03 PC Black/27 60.00 120.00
KG30 K.Grif 03 PB Black/15 75.00 150.00
KG32 K.Grif 03 PB 56 HR/15 75.00 150.00
KG34 K.Grif 03 SPA 56 HR/15 75.00 150.00
KG35 K.Grif 03 SPA 92 AS/20 60.00 120.00
KG36 K.Grif 03 SPA B93/20 60.00 120.00
KG39 K.Grif 03 SPx 97 AL/26 60.00 120.00
KG40 K.Grif 03 SS 97 AL/32 50.00 120.00
KG42 K.Grif 03 VIC Blk/57 50.00 100.00
KG43 K.Grif 03 VIC 92 AS/18 75.00 150.00
KW1 Kerry Wood 03 40M/34 15.00 40.00
KW6 Kerry Wood 03 SS/34 15.00 40.00
LA1 L.Aparicio 03 SP LC/20 10.00 25.00
LG1 L.Gonzalez 03 40M HR/25 10.00 25.00
LG2 Luis Gonzalez 03 CP/20 10.00 25.00
LG3 Luis Gonzalez 03 HR/20 10.00 25.00
LG5 Luis Gonzalez 03 SS/40 6.00 15.00
LG9 Luis Gonzalez 04 VIN/20 10.00 25.00
MB1 Marlon Byrd 04 VIN/70 4.00 10.00
MC1 M.Cabrera 03 SPx/25 20.00 50.00
MC2 M.Cabrera 04 DAS/20 20.00 50.00
MC3 M.Cabrera 04 FP/20 20.00 50.00
MC4 M.Cabrera 04 VIN/20 20.00 50.00
ME1 M.Ensberg 04 FP/70 6.00 15.00
ME2 M.Ensberg 04 UD/70 6.00 15.00
ME3 M.Ensberg 04 VIN/70 6.00 15.00
MG1 Marcus Giles 04 VIN/70 6.00 15.00
MH1 Mike Hampton 03 UDA/60 4.00 10.00
MH2 Mike Hampton 04 FP/34 6.00 15.00
MH3 Mike Hampton 04 UD/47 4.00 10.00
MI1 Monte Irvin 03 SP LC/20 10.00 25.00
ML1 Mike Lowell 03 40M/19 8.00 20.00
ML2 Mike Lowell 04 DAS/19 8.00 20.00
ML3 Mike Lowell 04 FP/19 8.00 20.00
ML4 Mike Lowell 04 UD/19 8.00 20.00
ML5 Mike Lowell 04 VIN/19 8.00 20.00
MM2 Mike Mussina 03 HR/20 15.00 40.00
MM3 Mike Mussina 03 HR/25 15.00 40.00
MM5 Mike Mussina 03 SS/60 10.00 25.00
MM6 Mike Mussina 03 UDA/45 10.00 25.00
MM7 Mike Mussina 04 FP/58 10.00 25.00
MM8 Mike Mussina 04 UD/45 10.00 25.00
MM9 Mike Mussina 04 VIN/45 10.00 25.00
MP1 Mark Prior 03 40M/22 12.50 30.00
MP4 Mark Prior 03 HR/22 12.50 30.00
MP5 Mark Prior 03 PC/22 12.50 30.00
MP6 Mark Prior 03 SPx/22 12.50 30.00
MP7 Mark Prior 03 SS/22 12.50 30.00
MP10 Mark Prior 04 FP/22 12.50 30.00
MP11 Mark Prior 04 UD/22 12.50 30.00
MP12 Mark Prior 04 VIN/22 12.50 30.00
MS1 M.Schmidt 03 SP LC/20 20.00 50.00
MTE1 Miguel Tejada 03 CP/38 6.00 15.00
MTE2 Miguel Tejada 03 HR/36 10.00 25.00
MTE3 M.Tejada 03 SPx/30 15.00 40.00
MTE4 M.Tejada 03 UDA/58 10.00 25.00
MTE5 Miguel Tejada 04 DAS/37 10.00 25.00
MTE6 Miguel Tejada 04 VIN/70 6.00 15.00
MT1 M.Teix 03 40M RWB/45 10.00 25.00
MT4 Mark Teixeira 03 SPx/40 10.00 25.00
MT5 Mark Teixeira 03 SS/23 15.00 40.00
MT6 Mark Teixeira 03 SS/25 15.00 40.00
MT7 Mark Teixeira 03 UDA/21 15.00 40.00
MT10 Mark Teixeira 04 UD/23 15.00 40.00
MW1 Maury Wills 04 SSC/70 6.00 15.00
NR1 Nolan Ryan 03 UDA/20 60.00 120.00
OD1 Octavio Dotel 04 FP/70 4.00 10.00
OD2 Octavio Dotel 04 UD/70 4.00 10.00
OD3 Octavio Dotel 04 VIN/70 4.00 10.00
PB1 Pat Burrell 03 CP/50 6.00 15.00
PB2 Pat Burrell 03 HR/25 10.00 25.00
PB3 Pat Burrell 03 SS/50 6.00 15.00
PB4 Pat Burrell 03 UDA/50 6.00 15.00
PB5 Pat Burrell 04 VIN/68 6.00 15.00
PL1 P.LoDuca 03 40M RWB/60 6.00 15.00
PL2 Paul Lo Duca 04 VIN/60 6.00 15.00
PL3 P.Lo Duca 04 VIN BW/20 10.00 25.00
PR1 Phil Rizzuto 03 SP LC/21 15.00 40.00
RB3 Rocco Baldelli 03 SPx/15 12.50 30.00
RB7 R.Baldelli 04 PB Red/25 10.00 25.00
RB8 R.Baldelli 04 PB Blue/25 10.00 25.00
RHL1 Roy Halladay 03 40M/32 20.00 50.00
RHL5 Roy Halladay 04 UD/32 20.00 50.00
RHM1 R.Hammock 03 40M/35 6.00 15.00
RHM2 R.Hammock 03 PC/15 8.00 20.00
RHM4 R.Hammock 04 UD/30 6.00 15.00
RHR1 R.Hernandez 03 40M/55 4.00 10.00
RHR2 R.Hernandez 03 UDA/40 4.00 10.00
RI1 Raul Ibanez 04 FP/70 8.00 20.00
RI2 Raul Ibanez 04 UD/65 8.00 20.00
RI3 Raul Ibanez 04 VIN/70 8.00 20.00
RK1 Ralph Kiner 03 SP LC/20 15.00 40.00
RO1 Roy Oswalt 03 40M/44 6.00 15.00
RO2 Roy Oswalt 03 HR/55 6.00 15.00
RO3 Roy Oswalt 03 SS/20 10.00 25.00
RO4 Roy Oswalt 04 UD/52 6.00 15.00
RR1 R.Roberts 03 SP LC/15 12.50 30.00
RW1 Rickie Weeks 03 UD/30 15.00 40.00
RW2 Rickie Weeks 04 FP/15 12.50 30.00
RW3 Rickie Weeks 04 VIN/50 6.00 15.00
RY1 Robin Yount 03 SP LC/20 50.00 100.00
SG3 Shawn Green 03 SS/15 20.00 50.00
SG6 Shawn Green 04 FP/15 20.00 50.00
SG8 Shawn Green 04 VIN/15 20.00 50.00
SM1 S.Musial 03 SP LC/16 50.00 100.00
THO1 T.Hoffman 04 FP/67 10.00 25.00
THO2 T.Hoffman 04 UD/51 10.00 25.00
TH1 Travis Hafner 03 40M/32 6.00 15.00
TH4 Travis Hafner 03 SS/32 6.00 15.00
TS1 Tom Seaver 03 SP LC/15 30.00 80.00
VG1 Vlad Guerrero 03 CP/20 12.00 30.00
VG3 Vlad Guerrero 03 SPx/34 12.00 30.00
VG4 Vlad Guerrero 03 SS/27 12.00 30.00
VG5 Vlad Guerrero 03 UDA/54 10.00 25.00
VG6 Vlad Guerrero 04 DAS/27 12.00 30.00
VG7 Vlad Guerrero 04 FP/28 12.00 30.00
VG9 Vlad Guerrero 04 VIN/27 12.00 30.00
VW1 Vernon Wells 03 40M/15 12.50 30.00
WE1 Willie Eyre 03 40M/45 4.00 10.00
WE2 W.Eyre 03 40M RWB/45 4.00 10.00
YB1 Yogi Berra 03 SP LC/23 30.00 80.00

2004 SP Authentic Chirography

STATED PRINT RUN 75 SERIAL #'d SETS
BASIC CHIRO. HAVE RED BACKGROUNDS
*DT w/NOTE: .5X TO 1.2X BASIC
*DT w/o NOTE: .4X TO 1X BASIC
DUO TONE PRINT RUN 75 SERIAL #'d SETS
MOST DT FEATURE UNIFORM # NOTATION
*BRONZE: .4X TO 1X BASIC
BRONZE PRINT RUN 65 SERIAL #'d SETS
*BRONZE DT w/NOTE: .5X TO 1.2X BASIC
*BRONZE DT w/o NOTE: .4X TO 1X BASIC
BRONZE DUO TONE PRINT RUN 60 #'d SETS
MOST BRONZE DT FEATURE TEAM NAMES
*SILVER: .4X TO 1X BASIC
SILVER PRINT RUN 60 SERIAL #'d SETS
*SILVER DT w/NOTE: .6X TO 1.5X BASIC
*SILVER DT w/o NOTE: .5X TO 1.2X BASIC
SILVER DT PRINT RUN 30 SERIAL #'d SETS
MOST SILVER DT HAVE KEY ACHIEVEMENT
OVERALL AUTO INSERT ODDS 1:12
EXCHANGE DEADLINE 06/04/07
AK Austin Kearns 5.00 12.00
BA Bobby Abreu 8.00 20.00
BB Bret Boone 12.50 30.00
BH Bo Hart 5.00 12.00
BS Ben Sheets 8.00 20.00
BW Brandon Webb 6.00 15.00
BZ Barry Zito 8.00 20.00
CB Carlos Beltran 8.00 20.00
CL Cliff Lee 15.00 40.00
CP Colin Porter 5.00 12.00
CR Cal Ripken 40.00 80.00
CW Chien-Ming Wang 75.00 150.00
DE Dennis Eckersley 12.50 30.00
DJ Derek Jeter 100.00 200.00
DW Dontrelle Willis 12.50 30.00
DY Delmon Young 6.00 15.00
EC Eric Chavez 8.00 20.00
EG Eric Gagne 12.50 30.00
GA Garret Anderson 8.00 20.00
HA Robby Hammock 5.00 12.00
HB Hank Blalock 8.00 20.00
HE Runelvys Hernandez 5.00 12.00
HI Bobby Hill 5.00 12.00
HR Horacio Ramirez 5.00 12.00
HY Roy Halladay 12.50 30.00
JB Josh Beckett 8.00 20.00
JG Juan Gonzalez 10.00 25.00
JJ Jacque Jones 11 8.00 20.00
JL Javy Lopez 5.00 12.00
JR Jose Reyes 10.00 25.00
JS Jae Weong Seo 5.00 12.00
JV Javier Vazquez 5.00 12.00
JW Jerome Williams 5.00 12.00
KW Kerry Wood 6.00 15.00
MC Miguel Cabrera 20.00 50.00
ML Mike Lowell 8.00 20.00
MP Mark Prior 5.00 12.00
MT Mark Teixeira 12.50 30.00
PA Corey Patterson 5.00 12.00
PI Mike Piazza 25.00 60.00
PL Paul Lo Duca 8.00 20.00
RB Rocco Baldelli 8.00 20.00
RO Roy Oswalt 5.00 12.00
RW Rickie Weeks 8.00 20.00
TH Travis Hafner 5.00 12.00
VW Vernon Wells 8.00 20.00
WE Willie Eyre 5.00 12.00

2004 SP Authentic Chirography Gold

*GOLD p/r 40: .5X TO 1.2X BASIC
STATED PRINT RUN 40 SERIAL #'d SETS
EDGAR/LEITER/SMOLTZ 75 #'d COPIES PER
*GLD DT p/r 20 w/NOTE: .6X TO 1.5X p/r 40
*GLD DT p/r20 w/o NOTE:.5X TO 1.2X p/r 40
*GOLD DT p/r 75: .4X TO 1X GOLD p/r 75
GOLD DT PRINT RUN 20 SERIAL #'d SETS
MOST GOLD DT HAVE KEY ACHIEVEMENT
OVERALL AUTO INSERT ODDS 1:12
EXCHANGE DEADLINE 06/04/07
AL Al Leiter/75 10.00 25.00
AR Alex Rodriguez 100.00 175.00
EM Edgar Martinez/75 10.00 25.00
SM John Smoltz/75 20.00 50.00

2004 SP Authentic Chirography Dual

OVERALL AUTO INSERT ODDS 1:12
STATED PRINT RUN 50 SERIAL #'d SETS
EXCHANGE DEADLINE 06/04/07
BC B.Boone/E.Chavez 10.00 25.00
BL J.Beckett/M.Lowell 10.00 25.00
BP C.Beltran/C.Patterson 10.00 25.00
BT H.Blalock/M.Teixeira 6.00 15.00
EG D.Eckersley/E.Gagne 30.00 60.00
HW R.Halladay/V.Wells 30.00 60.00
JM J.Bench/M.Piazza 175.00 300.00
KG A.Kearns/K.Griffey Jr. 40.00 80.00
PB J.Posada/Y.Berra 50.00 100.00
RR A.Rodriguez/C.Ripken 250.00 500.00
SG I.Suzuki/K.Griffey Jr. 400.00 600.00
SM O.Smith/S.Musial 125.00 200.00
WC D.Willis/M.Cabrera 15.00 40.00
WJ C.Wang/D.Jeter 300.00 500.00
WR K.Wood/N.Ryan 175.00 300.00
WW B.Webb/D.Willis 30.00 60.00
ZC B.Zito/E.Chavez 30.00 60.00

2004 SP Authentic Chirography Hall of Famers

STATED PRINT RUN 40 SERIAL #'d SETS
*DUO TONE: .5X TO 1.2X BASIC
DUO TONE PRINT RUN 25 SERIAL #'d SETS
SOME DT FEATURE HOF NOTATION
OVERALL AUTO INSERT ODDS 1:12
AK Al Kaline 30.00 80.00
BD Bobby Doerr 10.00 25.00
BG Bob Gibson 15.00 40.00
BR B.Robinson UER B/W 15.00 40.00
CF Carlton Fisk 15.00 40.00
CY Carl Yastrzemski HOF 89 50.00 100.00
DE Dennis Eckersley 15.00 40.00
DS Duke Snider 15.00 40.00
HK Harmon Killebrew 20.00 50.00
JB Johnny Bench 30.00 60.00
KP Kirby Puckett 50.00 100.00
LA Luis Aparicio Hall of Famer 10.00 25.00
MI Monte Irvin 10.00 25.00
MS Mike Schmidt 30.00 80.00
NR Nolan Ryan 75.00 150.00
OS Ozzie Smith 50.00 100.00
PM Paul Molitor 10.00 25.00
PR Phil Rizzuto Hall of Famer 15.00 40.00
RK Ralph Kiner HOF 1975 10.00 25.00
RR Robin Roberts Hall of Famer 15.00 40.00
RY Robin Yount 50.00 100.00
SM Stan Musial 60.00 120.00
TP Tony Perez Hall of Famer 10.00 25.00
TS Tom Seaver 20.00 50.00
YB Yogi Berra 30.00 80.00

2004 SP Authentic Chirography Triple

OVERALL AUTO INSERT ODDS 1:12
STATED PRINT RUN 25 SERIAL #'d SETS
EXCHANGE DEADLINE 06/04/07
BWR Beck/Wood/Ryan 60.00 150.00
FBB Fisk/Bench/Berra 200.00 400.00
GSM Gibson/Ozzie/Musial 150.00 300.00
JVB Jeter/Vazquez/Berra 75.00 200.00
PRC Porter/Reyes/Cabrera 25.00 60.00
RBT A.Rod/Blalock/Teixeira 125.00 300.00
RRR A.Rod/Ripken/Rizz 75.00 200.00
SJB Ichiro/Jacque/Baldelli 250.00 500.00
WLE Wang/C.Lee/Eyre 60.00 150.00
WPB Webb/Prior/Beckett 60.00 150.00
YYM Yaz/Yount/Musial 200.00 400.00
ZHO Zito/Halladay/Oswalt 50.00 120.00

2004 SP Authentic USA Signatures 445

STATED PRINT RUN 445 SERIAL #'d SETS
*USA SIG 50: .6X TO 1.5X BASIC
USA SIG 50 PRINT RUN 50 #'d SETS
OVERALL AUTO INSERT ODDS 1:12
1 Ernie Young 4.00 10.00
2 Chris Burke 6.00 15.00
3 Jesse Crain 6.00 15.00
4 Justin Duchscherer 6.00 15.00
5 J.D. Durbin 4.00 10.00
6 Gerald Laird 6.00 15.00
7 John Grabow 4.00 10.00
8 Gabe Gross 6.00 15.00
9 J.J. Hardy 15.00 40.00
10 Jeremy Reed 6.00 15.00
11 Graham Koonce 4.00 10.00
12 Mike Lamb 4.00 10.00
13 Justin Leone 6.00 15.00
14 Ryan Madson 8.00 20.00
15 Joe Mauer 10.00 25.00
16 Todd Williams 4.00 10.00
17 Horacio Ramirez 4.00 10.00
18 Mike Rouse 4.00 10.00
19 Jason Stanford 4.00 10.00
20 John Van Benschoten 4.00 10.00
21 Grady Sizemore 12.50 30.00

2004 SP Authentic USA Signatures 50

OVERALL AUTO INSERT ODDS 1:12
STATED PRINT RUN 50 SERIAL #'d SETS
9 J.J. Hardy 40.00 80.00

2005 SP Authentic

COMP.BASIC SET (100) 10.00 25.00
COMMON CARD (1-100) .15 .40
COMMON RETIRED 1-100 .15 .40
1-100 ISSUED IN 05 SP COLLECTION PACKS
COMMON AUTO (101-186) 4.00 10.00
101-186 ODDS APPX 1:8 '05 UD UPDATE
101-186 PRINT RUN 185 SERIAL #'d SETS
105, 115, 118-119, 142, 154 DO NOT EXIST
161, 180, 183, 186 DO NOT EXIST
1 A.J. Burnett .15 .40
2 Aaron Rowand .15 .40
3 Adam Dunn .25 .60
4 Adrian Beltre .40 1.00
5 Adrian Gonzalez .30 .75
6 Akinori Otsuka .15 .40
7 Albert Pujols .50 1.25
8 Andre Dawson .25 .60
9 Andruw Jones .15 .40
10 Aramis Ramirez .15 .40
11 Barry Larkin .25 .60
12 Ben Sheets .15 .40
13 Bo Jackson .40 1.00
14 Bobby Abreu .15 .40
15 Bobby Crosby .15 .40
16 Bronson Arroyo .15 .40
17 Cal Ripken 1.25 3.00
18 Carl Crawford .25 .60
19 Carlos Zambrano .25 .60
20 Casey Kotchman .15 .40
21 Cesar Izturis .15 .40
22 Chone Figgins .15 .40
23 Corey Patterson .15 .40
24 Craig Biggio .25 .60
25 Dale Murphy .40 1.00
26 Dallas McPherson .15 .40
27 Danny Haren .15 .40
28 Darryl Strawberry .15 .40
29 David Ortiz .40 1.00
30 David Wright .30 .75
31 Derek Jeter 1.00 2.50
32 Derrek Lee .15 .40
33 Don Mattingly .75 2.00
34 Dwight Gooden .15 .40
35 Edgar Renteria .15 .40
36 Eric Chavez .15 .40
37 Eric Gagne .15 .40
38 Gary Sheffield .15 .40
39 Gavin Floyd .15 .40
40 Pedro Martinez .25 .60
41 Greg Maddux .50 1.25
42 Hank Blalock .15 .40
43 Huston Street .15 .40
44 J.D. Drew .15 .40
45 Jake Peavy .15 .40
46 Jake Westbrook .15 .40
47 Jason Bay .15 .40
48 Austin Kearns .15 .40
49 Jeremy Reed .15 .40
50 Jim Rice .25 .60
51 Jimmy Rollins .25 .60
52 Joe Blanton .15 .40
53 Joe Mauer .30 .75
54 Johan Santana .25 .60
55 John Smoltz .40 1.00
56 Johnny Estrada .15 .40
57 Jose Reyes .25 .60
58 Ken Griffey Jr. .75 2.00
59 Kerry Wood .15 .40
60 Khalil Greene .15 .40
61 Marcus Giles .15 .40
62 Melvin Mora .15 .40
63 Mark Grace .25 .60
64 Mark Mulder .15 .40
65 Mark Prior .25 .60
66 Mark Teixeria .25 .60
67 Matt Clement .15 .40
68 Michael Young .15 .40
69 Miguel Cabrera .40 1.00
70 Miguel Tejada .25 .60
71 Mike Piazza .40 1.00
72 Mike Schmidt .60 1.50
73 Nolan Ryan 1.25 3.00
74 Oliver Perez .15 .40
75 Nick Johnson .15 .40
76 Paul Molitor .40 1.00
77 Rafael Palmeiro .25 .60
78 Randy Johnson .40 1.00
79 Reggie Jackson .25 .60
80 Rich Harden .15 .40
81 Rickie Weeks .15 .40
82 Robin Yount .40 1.00
83 Roger Clemens .50 1.25
84 Roy Oswalt .25 .60
85 Ryan Howard .30 .75
86 Ryne Sandberg .75 2.00
87 Scott Kazmir .40 1.00
88 Scott Rolen .25 .60
89 Sean Burroughs .15 .40
90 Sean Casey .15 .40
91 Shingo Takatsu .15 .40
92 Tim Hudson .25 .60
93 Tony Gwynn .50 1.25
94 Torii Hunter .15 .40
95 Travis Hafner .15 .40
96 Victor Martinez .25 .60
97 Vladimir Guerrero .25 .60
98 Wade Boggs .25 .60
99 Will Clark .25 .60
100 Yadier Molina 1.50 4.00
101 Adam Shabala AU RC 4.00 10.00
102 Ambiorix Burgos AU RC 4.00 10.00
103 Ambiorix Concepcion AU RC 4.00 10.00
104 Anibal Sanchez AU RC 6.00 15.00
106 Brandon McCarthy AU RC 8.00 20.00
107 Brian Burres AU RC 4.00 10.00
108 Carlos Ruiz AU RC 8.00 20.00
109 Casey Rogowski AU RC 4.00 10.00
110 Chad Orvella AU RC 4.00 10.00
111 Chris Resop AU RC 6.00 15.00
112 Chris Roberson AU RC 4.00 10.00
113 Chris Seddon AU RC 4.00 10.00
114 Colter Bean AU RC 6.00 15.00
116 Dave Gassner AU RC 4.00 10.00
117 Brian Anderson AU RC 6.00 15.00
120 Devon Lowery AU RC 4.00 10.00
121 Enrique Gonzalez AU RC 6.00 15.00
122 Eude Brito AU RC 4.00 10.00
123 Francisco Butto AU RC 4.00 10.00
124 Franquelis Osoria AU RC 4.00 10.00
125 Garrett Jones AU RC 10.00 25.00
126 Geovany Soto AU RC 4.00 10.00
127 Hayden Penn AU RC 6.00 15.00
128 Ismael Ramirez AU RC 4.00 10.00
129 Jared Gothreaux AU RC 4.00 10.00
130 Jason Hammel AU RC 4.00 10.00
131 Jeff Miller AU RC 4.00 10.00
132 Jeff Niemann AU RC 12.50 30.00
133 Joel Peralta AU RC 4.00 10.00
134 John Hattig AU RC 4.00 10.00
135 Jorge Campillo AU RC 4.00 10.00
136 Juan Morillo AU RC 4.00 10.00
137 Justin Verlander AU RC 75.00 200.00
138 Ryan Garko AU RC 4.00 10.00
139 Keiichi Yabu AU RC 6.00 15.00
140 Kendry Morales AU RC 10.00 25.00
141 Luis Hernandez AU RC 4.00 10.00
143 Luis O.Rodriguez AU RC 4.00 10.00
144 Luke Scott AU RC 10.00 25.00
145 Marcos Carvajal AU RC 4.00 10.00
146 Mark Woodyard AU RC 4.00 10.00
147 Matt A.Smith AU RC 4.00 10.00
148 Matthew Lindstrom AU RC 4.00 10.00
149 Miguel Negron AU RC 6.00 15.00
150 Mike Morse AU RC 10.00 25.00
151 Nate McLouth AU RC 6.00 15.00
152 Nelson Cruz AU RC 60.00 150.00
153 Nick Masset AU RC 4.00 10.00
155 Paulino Reynoso AU RC 4.00 10.00
156 Pedro Lopez AU RC 4.00 10.00
157 Pete Orr AU RC 4.00 10.00
158 Philip Humber AU RC 6.00 15.00
159 Prince Fielder AU RC 15.00 40.00
160 Randy Messenger AU RC 4.00 10.00
162 Raul Tablado AU RC 4.00 10.00
163 Ronny Paulino AU RC 6.00 15.00
164 Russ Rohlicek AU RC 4.00 10.00
165 Russell Martin AU RC 10.00 25.00
166 Scott Baker AU RC 6.00 15.00
167 Scott Munter AU RC 4.00 10.00
168 Sean Thompson AU RC 4.00 10.00
169 Sean Tracey AU RC 4.00 10.00
170 Shane Costa AU RC 4.00 10.00
171 Stephen Drew AU RC 12.50 30.00
172 Steve Schmoll AU RC 4.00 10.00
173 Tadahito Iguchi AU RC 15.00 40.00
174 Tony Giarratano AU RC 4.00 10.00
175 Tony Pena AU RC 4.00 10.00
176 Travis Bowyer AU RC 4.00 10.00
177 Ubaldo Jimenez AU RC 10.00 25.00
178 Wladimir Balentien AU RC 8.00 20.00
179 Yorman Bazardo AU RC 4.00 10.00
181 Ryan Zimmerman AU RC 40.00 100.00
182 Chris Denorfia AU RC 6.00 15.00
184 Jermaine Van Buren AU 4.00 10.00
185 Mark McLemore AU RC 4.00 10.00

2005 SP Authentic Jersey

STATED PRINT RUN 199 SERIAL #'d SETS
*GOLD: .5X TO 1.2X BASIC
GOLD PRINT RUN 99 SERIAL #'d SETS
ISSUED IN 05 SP COLLECTION PACKS
OVERALL GAME-USED ODDS 1:10
1 A.J. Burnett 2.00 5.00
2 Aaron Rowand 2.00 5.00
3 Adam Dunn 2.00 5.00
4 Adrian Beltre 2.00 5.00
5 Adrian Gonzalez 2.00 5.00
6 Akinori Otsuka 2.00 5.00
7 Albert Pujols 6.00 15.00
8 Andre Dawson 3.00 8.00
9 Andruw Jones 3.00 8.00
10 Aramis Ramirez 2.00 5.00
11 Barry Larkin 3.00 8.00
12 Ben Sheets 2.00 5.00
13 Bo Jackson 4.00 10.00
14 Bobby Abreu 2.00 5.00
15 Bobby Crosby 2.00 5.00
16 Bronson Arroyo 2.00 5.00
17 Cal Ripken Pants 8.00 20.00
18 Carl Crawford 2.00 5.00
19 Carlos Zambrano 2.00 5.00
20 Casey Kotchman 2.00 5.00
21 Cesar Izturis 2.00 5.00
22 Chone Figgins 2.00 5.00
23 Corey Patterson 2.00 5.00
24 Craig Biggio 3.00 8.00
25 Dale Murphy 4.00 10.00
26 Dallas McPherson 2.00 5.00
27 Danny Haren 2.00 5.00
28 Darryl Strawberry 3.00 8.00
29 David Ortiz 3.00 8.00
30 David Wright 4.00 10.00
31 Derek Jeter Pants 8.00 20.00
32 Derrek Lee 3.00 8.00
33 Don Mattingly 6.00 15.00
34 Dwight Gooden 3.00 8.00
35 Edgar Renteria 2.00 5.00
36 Eric Chavez 2.00 5.00
37 Eric Gagne 2.00 5.00
38 Gary Sheffield 2.00 5.00
39 Gavin Floyd 2.00 5.00
40 Pedro Martinez 3.00 8.00
41 Greg Maddux 4.00 10.00
42 Hank Blalock 2.00 5.00
43 Huston Street 3.00 8.00
44 J.D. Drew 2.00 5.00
45 Jake Peavy 2.00 5.00
46 Jake Westbrook 2.00 5.00
47 Jason Bay 2.00 5.00
48 Austin Kearns 2.00 5.00
49 Jeremy Reed 2.00 5.00
50 Jim Rice 3.00 8.00
51 Jimmy Rollins 2.00 5.00
52 Joe Blanton 2.00 5.00
53 Joe Mauer 4.00 10.00
54 Johan Santana 4.00 10.00
55 John Smoltz 3.00 8.00
56 Johnny Estrada 2.00 5.00
57 Jose Reyes 2.00 5.00
58 Ken Griffey Jr. 6.00 15.00
59 Kerry Wood 2.00 5.00
60 Khalil Greene 3.00 8.00
61 Marcus Giles 2.00 5.00
62 Melvin Mora 2.00 5.00
63 Mark Grace 4.00 10.00
64 Mark Mulder 2.00 5.00
65 Mark Prior 3.00 8.00
66 Mark Teixeria 3.00 8.00
67 Matt Clement 2.00 5.00
68 Michael Young 2.00 5.00
69 Miguel Cabrera 3.00 8.00
70 Miguel Tejada 2.00 5.00
71 Mike Piazza 4.00 10.00
72 Mike Schmidt 6.00 15.00
73 Nolan Ryan Pants 8.00 20.00
74 Oliver Perez 2.00 5.00
75 Nick Johnson 2.00 5.00
76 Paul Molitor 3.00 8.00
77 Rafael Palmeiro 4.00 10.00
78 Randy Johnson 4.00 10.00
79 Reggie Jackson 4.00 10.00
80 Rich Harden 2.00 5.00
81 Rickie Weeks 2.00 5.00
82 Robin Yount 4.00 10.00
83 Roger Clemens Pants 4.00 10.00
84 Roy Oswalt 2.00 5.00
85 Ryan Howard 10.00 25.00
86 Ryne Sandberg 6.00 15.00
87 Scott Kazmir 2.00 5.00
88 Scott Rolen 3.00 8.00
89 Sean Burroughs 2.00 5.00
90 Sean Casey 2.00 5.00
91 Shingo Takatsu 2.00 5.00
92 Tim Hudson 2.00 5.00
93 Tony Gwynn 4.00 10.00
94 Torii Hunter 2.00 5.00
95 Travis Hafner 2.00 5.00
96 Victor Martinez 2.00 5.00
97 Vladimir Guerrero 4.00 10.00
98 Wade Boggs 4.00 10.00
99 Will Clark 4.00 10.00
100 Yadier Molina 5.00 12.00

2005 SP Authentic Signature

PRINT RUNS B/WN 25-550 COPIES PER
GOLD PRINT RUN 10 SERIAL #'d SETS
NO GOLD PRICING DUE TO SCARCITY
ISSUED IN 05 SP COLLECTION PACKS
OVERALL AUTO ODDS 1:10
2 Aaron Rowand/550 10.00 25.00
3 Adam Dunn/25 10.00 25.00
4 Adrian Beltre/125 6.00 15.00
5 Adrian Gonzalez/550 6.00 15.00
6 Akinori Otsuka/475 6.00 15.00
7 Albert Pujols/25 150.00 250.00
8 Andre Dawson/125 6.00 15.00

9 Andruw Jones/25 20.00 50.00
10 Aramis Ramirez/475 6.00 15.00
11 Barry Larkin/125 20.00 50.00
12 Ben Sheets/350 6.00 15.00
13 Bo Jackson/25 40.00 80.00
15 Bobby Crosby/350 6.00 15.00
16 Bronson Arroyo/550 8.00 20.00
18 Carl Crawford/475 6.00 15.00
20 Casey Kotchman/550 6.00 15.00
21 Cesar Izturis/550 4.00 10.00
22 Chone Figgins/550 6.00 15.00
23 Corey Patterson/350 4.00 10.00
24 Craig Biggio/125 15.00 40.00
25 Dale Murphy/350 12.00 30.00
26 Dallas McPherson/550 4.00 10.00
27 Danny Haren/550 4.00 10.00
28 Darryl Strawberry/125 6.00 15.00
30 David Wright/350 12.50 30.00
31 Derek Jeter/150 125.00 300.00
32 Derrek Lee/350 10.00 25.00
33 Don Mattingly/25 40.00 80.00
34 Dwight Gooden/475 6.00 15.00
36 Eric Chavez/75 8.00 20.00
38 Gary Sheffield/25 15.00 40.00
39 Gavin Floyd/550 4.00 10.00
42 Hank Blalock/25 10.00 25.00
43 Huston Street/550 10.00 25.00
45 Jake Peavy/475 6.00 15.00
46 Jake Westbrook/550 4.00 10.00
47 Jason Bay/475 6.00 15.00
48 Austin Kearns/75 5.00 12.00
49 Jeremy Reed/550 4.00 10.00
50 Jim Rice/350 6.00 15.00
52 Joe Blanton/550 4.00 10.00
53 Joe Mauer/350 12.50 30.00
55 John Smoltz/25 20.00 50.00
57 Jose Reyes/475 6.00 15.00
59 Kerry Wood/25 10.00 25.00
60 Khalil Greene/350 10.00 25.00
62 Melvin Mora/475 6.00 15.00
63 Mark Grace/25 15.00 40.00
64 Mark Mulder/350 6.00 15.00
65 Mark Prior/25 10.00 25.00
66 Mark Teixeria/125 10.00 25.00
67 Matt Clement/350 6.00 15.00
68 Michael Young/475 6.00 15.00
69 Miguel Cabrera/125 12.50 30.00
70 Miguel Tejada/25 10.00 25.00
71 Mike Piazza/25 50.00 120.00
72 Mike Schmidt/25 40.00 80.00
73 Nolan Ryan/25 50.00 100.00
74 Oliver Perez/475 4.00 10.00
75 Nick Johnson/550 6.00 15.00
76 Paul Molitor/25 10.00 25.00
77 Rafael Palmeiro/25 15.00 40.00
78 Randy Johnson/25 50.00 100.00
79 Reggie Jackson/25 25.00 60.00
83 Roger Clemens/25 125.00 200.00
84 Roy Oswalt/125 6.00 15.00
85 Ryan Howard/550 10.00 25.00
86 Ryne Sandberg/25 40.00 80.00
87 Scott Kazmir/475 10.00 25.00
89 Sean Burroughs/475 4.00 10.00
91 Shingo Takatsu/550 6.00 15.00
92 Tim Hudson/25 10.00 25.00
93 Tony Gwynn/25 30.00 60.00
94 Torii Hunter/125 6.00 15.00
97 Vladimir Guerrero/25 15.00 40.00
98 Wade Boggs/25 15.00 40.00
99 Will Clark/25 20.00 50.00

2005 SP Authentic Honors

ISSUED IN 05 SP COLLECTION PACKS
OVERALL INSERT ODDS 1:10
STATED PRINT RUN 299 SERIAL #'d SETS
AB Adrian Beltre 1.50 4.00
AP Albert Pujols 2.00 5.00
AR Aramis Ramirez .60 1.50
BC Bobby Crosby .60 1.50
BJ Bo Jackson 1.50 4.00
BL Barry Larkin 1.00 2.50
BO Jeremy Bonderman .60 1.50
BS Ben Sheets .60 1.50
BU B.J. Upton 1.00 2.50
CA Miguel Cabrera 1.50 4.00
CC Carl Crawford 1.00 2.50
CP Corey Patterson .60 1.50
CR Cal Ripken 5.00 12.00
CZ Carlos Zambrano 1.00 2.50
DG Dwight Gooden .60 1.50
DJ Derek Jeter 4.00 10.00
DM Dale Murphy 1.50 4.00
DO David Ortiz 1.50 4.00
DW David Wright 1.25 3.00
GR Khalil Greene .60 1.50
JB Jason Bay .60 1.50
JM Joe Mauer 1.25 3.00
JP Jake Peavy .60 1.50
JR Jimmy Rollins 1.00 2.50
JS Johan Santana 1.00 2.50
JW Jake Westbrook .60 1.50
KG Ken Griffey Jr. 3.00 8.00
MC Dallas McPherson .60 1.50
MG Marcus Giles .60 1.50
MO Justin Morneau 1.00 2.50
MS Mike Schmidt 2.50 6.00
MT Mark Teixeria 1.00 2.50
MY Michael Young .60 1.50
NR Nolan Ryan 5.00 12.00
OP Oliver Perez .60 1.50
PM Paul Molitor 1.50 4.00
RC Roger Clemens 2.00 5.00
RE Jose Reyes 1.00 2.50
RH Rich Harden .60 1.50
RS Ryne Sandberg 3.00 8.00
SK Scott Kazmir 1.50 4.00
SM John Smoltz 1.50 4.00
ST Shingo Takatsu .60 1.50
TE Miguel Tejada 1.00 2.50
TG Tony Gwynn 2.00 5.00
TH Travis Hafner .60 1.50
VM Victor Martinez 1.00 2.50
WB Wade Boggs 1.00 2.50
WC Will Clark 1.00 2.50
ZG Zack Greinke 2.00 5.00

2005 SP Authentic Honors Jersey

ISSUED IN 05 SP COLLECTION PACKS
OVERALL PREMIUM AU-GU ODDS 1:20
STATED PRINT RUN 130 SERIAL #'d SETS
AB Adrian Beltre 2.00 5.00
AP Albert Pujols 6.00 15.00
AR Aramis Ramirez 2.00 5.00
BC Bobby Crosby 2.00 5.00
BJ Bo Jackson 4.00 10.00
BL Barry Larkin 3.00 8.00
BO Jeremy Bonderman 2.00 5.00
BS Ben Sheets 2.00 5.00
BU B.J. Upton 2.00 5.00
CA Miguel Cabrera 3.00 8.00
CC Carl Crawford 2.00 5.00
CP Corey Patterson 2.00 5.00
CR Cal Ripken Pants 8.00 20.00
CZ Carlos Zambrano 2.00 5.00
DG Dwight Gooden 3.00 8.00
DJ Derek Jeter Pants 8.00 20.00
DM Dale Murphy 4.00 10.00
DO David Ortiz 3.00 8.00
DW David Wright 4.00 10.00
GR Khalil Greene 3.00 8.00
JB Jason Bay 2.00 5.00
JM Joe Mauer 4.00 10.00
JP Jake Peavy 2.00 5.00
JR Jimmy Rollins 2.00 5.00
JS Johan Santana 4.00 10.00
JW Jake Westbrook 2.00 5.00
KG Ken Griffey Jr. 6.00 15.00
MC Dallas McPherson 2.00 5.00
MG Marcus Giles 2.00 5.00
MO Justin Morneau 2.00 5.00
MS Mike Schmidt 6.00 15.00
MT Mark Teixeria 3.00 8.00
MY Michael Young 2.00 5.00
NR Nolan Ryan Pants 8.00 20.00
OP Oliver Perez 2.00 5.00
PM Paul Molitor 3.00 8.00
RC Roger Clemens Pants 4.00 10.00
RE Jose Reyes 2.00 5.00
RH Rich Harden 2.00 5.00
RS Ryne Sandberg 6.00 15.00
SK Scott Kazmir 2.00 5.00
SM John Smoltz 3.00 8.00
ST Shingo Takatsu 2.00 5.00
TE Miguel Tejada 2.00 5.00
TG Tony Gwynn 4.00 10.00
TH Travis Hafner 2.00 5.00
VM Victor Martinez 2.00 5.00
WB Wade Boggs 4.00 10.00
WC Will Clark 4.00 10.00
ZG Zack Greinke 2.00 5.00

2006 SP Authentic

COMP.SET w/o SP's (100) 6.00 15.00
101-200 STATED ODDS 1:8
101-200 PRINT RUN 899 #'d SETS
201-300 AU STATED ODDS 1:16
201-300 AU PRINTS B/WN 125-899 PER
EXCH: 214/235/242/247/249/253/277
EXCH: 279/280/291
EXCHANGE DEADLINE 12/05/09
1 Erik Bedard .15 .40
2 Corey Patterson .15 .40
3 Ramon Hernandez .15 .40
4 Kris Benson .15 .40
5 Miguel Batista .15 .40
6 Orlando Hudson .15 .40
7 Shawn Green .15 .40
8 Jeff Francoeur .40 1.00
9 Marcus Giles .15 .40
10 Edgar Renteria .15 .40
11 Tim Hudson .25 .60
12 Tim Wakefield .25 .60
13 Mark Loretta .15 .40
14 Kevin Youkilis .15 .40
15 Mike Lowell .15 .40
16 Coco Crisp .15 .40
17 Tadahito Iguchi .15 .40
18 Scott Podsednik .15 .40
19 Jermaine Dye .15 .40
20 Jose Contreras .15 .40
21 Carlos Zambrano .25 .60
22 Aramis Ramirez .15 .40
23 Jacque Jones .15 .40
24 Austin Kearns .15 .40
25 Felipe Lopez .15 .40
26 Brandon Phillips .15 .40
27 Aaron Harang .15 .40
28 Cliff Lee .25 .60
29 Jhonny Peralta .15 .40
30 Jason Michaels .15 .40
31 Clint Barmes .15 .40
32 Brad Hawpe .15 .40
33 Aaron Cook .15 .40
34 Kenny Rogers .15 .40
35 Carlos Guillen .15 .40
36 Brian Moehler .15 .40
37 Andy Pettitte .25 .60
38 Wandy Rodriguez .15 .40
39 Morgan Ensberg .15 .40
40 Preston Wilson .15 .40
41 Mark Grudzielanek .15 .40
42 Angel Berroa .15 .40
43 Jeremy Affeldt .15 .40
44 Zack Greinke .40 1.00
45 Orlando Cabrera .15 .40
46 Garret Anderson .15 .40
47 Ervin Santana .15 .40
48 Derek Lowe .15 .40
49 Nomar Garciaparra .25 .60
50 J.D. Drew .15 .40
51 Rafael Furcal .15 .40
52 Rickie Weeks .15 .40
53 Geoff Jenkins .15 .40
54 Bill Hall .15 .40
55 Chris Capuano .15 .40
56 Derrick Turnbow .15 .40
57 Justin Morneau .25 .60
58 Michael Cuddyer .15 .40
59 Luis Castillo .15 .40
60 Hideki Matsui .40 1.00
61 Jason Giambi .15 .40
62 Jorge Posada .25 .60
63 Mariano Rivera .50 1.25
64 Billy Wagner .15 .40
65 Carlos Delgado .15 .40
66 Jose Reyes .25 .60
67 Nick Swisher .25 .60
68 Bobby Crosby .15 .40
69 Frank Thomas .40 1.00
70 Ryan Howard .30 .75
71 Pat Burrell .15 .40
72 Jimmy Rollins .25 .60
73 Craig Wilson .15 .40
74 Freddy Sanchez .15 .40
75 Sean Casey .15 .40
76 Mike Piazza .40 1.00
77 Dave Roberts .25 .60
78 Chris Young .15 .40
79 Noah Lowry .15 .40
80 Armando Benitez .15 .40
81 Pedro Feliz .15 .40
82 Jose Lopez .15 .40
83 Adrian Beltre .40 1.00
84 Jamie Moyer .15 .40
85 Jason Isringhausen .15 .40
86 Jason Marquis .15 .40
87 David Eckstein .15 .40
88 Juan Encarnacion .15 .40
89 Julio Lugo .15 .40
90 Ty Wigginton .15 .40
91 Jorge Cantu .15 .40
92 Akinori Otsuka .15 .40
93 Hank Blalock .15 .40
94 Kevin Mench .15 .40
95 Lyle Overbay .15 .40
96 Shea Hillenbrand .15 .40
97 B.J. Ryan .15 .40
98 Tony Armas .15 .40
99 Chad Cordero .15 .40
100 Jose Guillen .15 .40
101 Miguel Tejada 1.00 2.50
102 Brian Roberts .60 1.50
103 Melvin Mora .60 1.50
104 Brandon Webb 1.00 2.50
105 Chad Tracy .60 1.50
106 Luis Gonzalez .60 1.50
107 Andruw Jones .60 1.50
108 Chipper Jones 1.50 4.00
109 John Smoltz 1.50 4.00
110 Curt Schilling 1.00 2.50
111 Josh Beckett .60 1.50
112 David Ortiz 1.50 4.00
113 Manny Ramirez 1.50 4.00
114 Jason Varitek 1.50 4.00
115 Jim Thome 1.00 2.50
116 Paul Konerko 1.00 2.50
117 Javier Vazquez .60 1.50
118 Mark Prior 1.00 2.50
119 Derrek Lee .60 1.50
120 Greg Maddux 2.00 5.00
121 Ken Griffey Jr. 3.00 8.00
122 Adam Dunn 1.00 2.50
123 Bronson Arroyo .60 1.50
124 Travis Hafner .60 1.50
125 Victor Martinez 1.00 2.50
126 Grady Sizemore 1.00 2.50
127 C.C. Sabathia 1.00 2.50
128 Todd Helton 1.00 2.50
129 Matt Holliday 1.50 4.00
130 Garrett Atkins .60 1.50
131 Jeff Francis .60 1.50
132 Jeremy Bonderman .60 1.50
133 Ivan Rodriguez 1.00 2.50
134 Chris Shelton .60 1.50
135 Magglio Ordonez 1.00 2.50
136 Dontrelle Willis .60 1.50
137 Miguel Cabrera 1.50 4.00
138 Roger Clemens 2.00 5.00
139 Roy Oswalt 1.00 2.50
140 Lance Berkman 1.00 2.50
141 Reggie Sanders .60 1.50
142 Vladimir Guerrero 1.00 2.50
143 Bartolo Colon .60 1.50
144 Chone Figgins .60 1.50
145 Francisco Rodriguez 1.00 2.50
146 Brad Penny .60 1.50
147 Jeff Kent .60 1.50
148 Eric Gagne .60 1.50
149 Carlos Lee .60 1.50
150 Ben Sheets .60 1.50
151 Johan Santana 1.00 2.50
152 Torii Hunter .60 1.50
153 Joe Nathan .60 1.50
154 Alex Rodriguez 2.00 5.00
155 Derek Jeter 4.00 10.00
156 Randy Johnson 1.50 4.00
157 Johnny Damon 1.00 2.50
158 Mike Mussina 1.00 2.50
159 Pedro Martinez 1.00 2.50
160 Tom Glavine 1.00 2.50
161 David Wright 1.25 3.00
162 Carlos Beltran 1.00 2.50
163 Rich Harden .60 1.50
164 Barry Zito 1.00 2.50
165 Eric Chavez .60 1.50
166 Huston Street .60 1.50
167 Bobby Abreu .60 1.50
168 Chase Utley 1.00 2.50
169 Brett Myers .60 1.50
170 Jason Bay .60 1.50
171 Zach Duke .60 1.50
172 Jake Peavy .60 1.50
173 Brian Giles .60 1.50
174 Khalil Greene .60 1.50
175 Trevor Hoffman 1.00 2.50
176 Jason Schmidt .60 1.50
177 Randy Winn .60 1.50
178 Omar Vizquel 1.00 2.50
179 Kenji Johjima 1.50 4.00
180 Ichiro Suzuki 2.00 5.00
181 Richie Sexson .60 1.50
182 Felix Hernandez 1.00 2.50
183 Albert Pujols 2.00 5.00
184 Chris Carpenter 1.00 2.50
185 Jim Edmonds 1.00 2.50
186 Scott Rolen 1.00 2.50
187 Carl Crawford 1.00 2.50
188 Scott Kazmir 1.00 2.50
189 Jonny Gomes .60 1.50
190 Mark Teixeira 1.00 2.50
191 Michael Young .60 1.50
192 Kevin Millwood .60 1.50
193 Vernon Wells .60 1.50
194 Troy Glaus .60 1.50
195 Roy Halladay 1.00 2.50
196 Alex Rios .60 1.50
197 Nick Johnson .60 1.50
198 Livan Hernandez .60 1.50
199 Alfonso Soriano 1.00 2.50
200 Jose Vidro .60 1.50
201 A.Rakers AU/399 (RC) 3.00 8.00
202 A.Pagan AU/399 (RC) 4.00 10.00
203 B.Hendrick AU/399 (RC) 3.00 8.00
204 B.Livingston AU/399 (RC) 3.00 8.00
205 D.Rasner AU/399 (RC) 3.00 8.00
206 B.Bannister AU/399 (RC) 4.00 10.00
207 B.Wilson AU/899 RC 10.00 25.00
208 B.Keppel AU/199 (RC) 6.00 15.00
209 C.Freeman AU/399 (RC) 3.00 8.00
210 C.Booker AU/899 (RC) 3.00 8.00
211 C.Britton AU/399 (RC) 4.00 10.00
212 C.Demaria AU/329 RC 4.00 10.00
213 C.Resop AU/899 (RC) 3.00 8.00
214 T.Gwynn Jr. AU/399 (RC) 4.00 10.00
215 E.Reed AU/399 (RC) 3.00 8.00
216 F.Castro AU/399 RC 8.00 20.00
217 F.Nieve AU/299 (RC) 4.00 10.00
218 F.Bynum AU/899 (RC) 3.00 8.00
219 G.Quiroz AU/399 (RC) 3.00 8.00
220 H.Kuo AU/899 (RC) 6.00 15.00
221 R.Theriot AU/399 RC 3.00 8.00
222 J.Taschner AU/899 (RC) 3.00 8.00
223 J.Bergmann AU/899 (RC) 3.00 8.00
224 J.Hammel AU/899 (RC) 5.00 12.00
225 J.Harris AU/399 RC 3.00 8.00
226 J.Accardo AU/399 RC 4.00 10.00
227 T.Taubenheim AU/399 RC 12.50 30.00
228 J.Zumaya AU/399 (RC) 6.00 15.00
229 J.Koronka AU/399 (RC) 3.00 8.00
230 E.Aybar AU/399 (RC) 3.00 8.00
231 J.Tata AU/399 RC 6.00 15.00
232 R.Martin AU/399 (RC) 5.00 12.00
233 J.Rupe AU/399 (RC) 3.00 8.00
234 K.Frandsen AU/399 (RC) 6.00 15.00
235 M.Prado AU/399 (RC) 6.00 15.00
236 M.Capps AU/399 (RC) 3.00 8.00
237 A.Montero AU/199 (RC) 4.00 10.00
238 M.Thompson AU/399 RC 3.00 8.00
239 N.McLouth AU/399 (RC) 4.00 10.00
240 P.Moylan AU/399 RC 3.00 8.00
241 R.Abercrom AU/399 (RC) 3.00 8.00
242 C.Quentin AU/399 (RC) 8.00 20.00
243 R.Flores AU/399 RC 3.00 8.00
244 R.Shealy AU/399 (RC) 8.00 20.00
245 M.Rouse AU/399 (RC) 3.00 8.00
246 S.Ramirez AU/399 (RC) 3.00 8.00
247 C.Hensley AU/899 (RC) 3.00 8.00
248 S.Schumaker AU/399 (RC) 6.00 15.00
249 E.Alfonzo AU/899 RC 3.00 8.00
250 S.Stemle AU/399 RC 3.00 8.00
251 T.Hamulack AU/399 (RC) 3.00 8.00
252 T.Pena Jr. AU/299 (RC) 4.00 10.00
253 E.Fruto AU/899 RC 3.00 8.00
254 W.Nieves AU/399 (RC) 4.00 10.00
255 J.Devine AU/399 RC 4.00 10.00
256 A.Wainwright AU/399 (RC) 12.50 30.00
257 A.Ethier AU/399 (RC) 6.00 15.00
258 B.Johnson AU/399 (RC) 3.00 8.00
259 B.Logan AU/399 RC 6.00 15.00
260 C.Denorfia AU/899 (RC) 4.00 10.00
261 A.Soler AU/299 RC 6.00 15.00
262 C.Ross AU/899 (RC) 6.00 15.00
263 D.Gassner AU/399 (RC) 3.00 8.00
264 F.Carmona AU/399 (RC) 10.00 25.00
265 J.Sowers AU/299 (RC) 10.00 25.00
266 J.Kubel AU/399 (RC) 4.00 10.00
267 J.VanBenSch AU/399 (RC) 3.00 8.00
268 J.Capellan AU/399 (RC) 3.00 8.00
269 J.Wilson AU/399 (RC) 3.00 8.00
270 K.Shoppach AU/399 (RC) 3.00 8.00
271 M.McBride AU/399 (RC) 4.00 10.00
272 M.Cain AU/399 (RC) 10.00 25.00
273 M.Jacobs AU/399 (RC) 6.00 15.00
274 P.Maholm AU/399 (RC) 4.00 10.00
275 C.Billingsley AU/399 (RC) 3.00 8.00
276 R.Lugo AU/399 (RC) 3.00 8.00
277 J.Lester AU/399 RC 15.00 40.00
278 S.Marshall AU/383 (RC) 6.00 15.00
279 Me.Cabrera AU/399 (RC) 15.00 40.00
280 Y.Petit AU/399 (RC) 3.00 8.00
281 A.Hernandez AU/299 (RC) 4.00 10.00
282 B.Anderson AU/699 (RC) 4.00 10.00
283 C.Hamels AU/299 (RC) 8.00 20.00
284 B.Bonser AU/299 (RC) 6.00 15.00
285 D.Uggla AU/199 (RC) 10.00 25.00
286 F.Liriano AU/299 (RC) 5.00 12.00
287 H.Ramirez AU/199 (RC) 12.50 30.00
288 I.Kinsler AU/299 (RC) 8.00 20.00
289 J.Hermida AU/299 (RC) 6.00 15.00
290 J.Papelbon AU/199 (RC) 20.00 50.00
291 J.Weaver AU/199 (RC) 12.50 30.00
292 J.Johnson AU/299 (RC) 6.00 15.00
293 J.Willingham AU/199 (RC) 6.00 15.00
294 J.Verlander AU/199 (RC) 20.00 50.00
295 S.Drew AU/299 (RC) 6.00 15.00
296 P.Fielder AU/125 (RC) 6.00 15.00
297 R.Zimmer AU/199 (RC) 10.00 25.00
298 T.Saito AU/283 RC 10.00 25.00
299 T.Buchholz AU/299 (RC) 4.00 10.00
300 Co.Jackson AU/299 (RC) 6.00 15.00

2006 SP Authentic Baseball Heroes

COMPLETE SET (70) 50.00 100.00
STATED ODDS 1:4
1 Albert Pujols 1.25 3.00
2 Andruw Jones .40 1.00
3 Aramis Ramirez .40 1.00
4 Brian Roberts .40 1.00
5 Carl Crawford .60 1.50
6 Carlos Lee .40 1.00
7 Vladimir Guerrero .60 1.50
8 Chris Carpenter .60 1.50
9 Craig Biggio .60 1.50
10 David Ortiz 1.00 2.50
11 David Wright .75 2.00
12 Derrek Lee .40 1.00
13 Dontrelle Willis .40 1.00
14 Felix Hernandez .60 1.50
15 Garrett Atkins .40 1.00
16 Grady Sizemore .60 1.50
17 Huston Street .40 1.00
18 Jake Peavy .40 1.00
19 Jason Bay .40 1.00
20 Joe Mauer .60 1.50
21 John Smoltz 1.00 2.50
22 Jonny Gomes .40 1.00
23 Jorge Cantu .40 1.00
24 Ken Griffey Jr. 2.00 5.00
25 Marcus Giles .40 1.00
26 Mark Teixeira .60 1.50
27 Matt Cain 2.50 6.00
28 Michael Young .40 1.00
29 Miguel Cabrera 1.00 2.50
30 Johan Santana .60 1.50
31 Nick Swisher .60 1.50
32 Prince Fielder 2.00 5.00
33 Joe Blanton .40 1.00
34 Roy Oswalt .60 1.50
35 Ryan Howard .75 2.00
36 Scott Kazmir .60 1.50
37 Tadahito Iguchi .40 1.00
38 Travis Hafner .40 1.00
39 Victor Martinez .60 1.50
40 Jose Reyes .60 1.50
41 C.Carpenter/A.Pujols 1.25 3.00
42 A.Pujols/M.Cabrera 1.25 3.00
43 K.Griffey Jr./A.Jones 2.00 5.00
44 D.Lee/A.Ramirez .40 1.00
45 R.Howard/P.Fielder 2.00 5.00
46 R.Oswalt/J.Peavy .60 1.50
47 C.Biggio/M.Ensberg .60 1.50
48 T.Hafner/D.Ortiz 1.00 2.50
49 D.Jeter/D.Wright 2.50 6.00
50 K.Griffey Jr./D.Jeter 2.50 6.00
51 D.Jeter/M.Young 2.50 6.00
52 S.Kazmir/D.Willis .60 1.50
53 G.Sizemore/J.Bay .60 1.50
54 M.Young/M.Teixeira .60 1.50
55 B.Roberts/T.Iguchi .40 1.00
56 Wang/Cain/Felix 2.50 6.00
57 D.Lee/Pujols/Teixeira 1.25 3.00
58 Griffey/Pujols/Cabrera 2.00 5.00
59 Andruw/Smoltz/M.Giles 1.00 2.50
60 Wood/D.Lee/Aramis .40 1.00
61 Aramis/Ensberg/Wright .75 2.00
62 Crawford/Cantu/Gomes .60 1.50
63 Smoltz/Carpenter/Peavy 1.00 2.50
64 Hafner/V.Mart/Sizemore .60 1.50
65 Ortiz/Howard/Fielder 2.00 5.00
66 Smoltz/Carp/Peavy/Willis 1.00 2.50
67 Griffey/Jeter/Ortiz/Pujols 2.50 6.00
68 Andruw/D.Lee/Ortiz/Teix 1.00 2.50
69 Biggio/B.Rob/Giles/Iguchi .60 1.50
70 Wright/Teix/M.Cab/Bay 1.00 2.50

2006 SP Authentic By the Letter

STATED ODDS 1:24
PRINT RUNS B/WN 4-400 COPIES PER
EXCH: AJ, AR, CS, CZ, FH, FH2, GM, HO
EXCH: HU, JM, JR, JV, JW, KG, KG2, KG3
EXCH: KG4, KM, KW, MT, SM, TE
EXCHANGE DEADLINE 12/05/09
ABB A.J. Burnett B/50 6.00 15.00
ABE A.J. Burnett E/50 6.00 15.00
ABN A.J. Burnett N/50 6.00 15.00
ABR A.J. Burnett R/50 6.00 15.00
ABT A.J. Burnett T/100 6.00 15.00
ABU A.J. Burnett U/50 6.00 15.00
ADD Adam Dunn D/50 10.00 25.00
ADN Adam Dunn N/100 10.00 25.00
ADU Adam Dunn U/50 10.00 25.00
AGG Tony Gwynn Jr. G/150 8.00 20.00
AGN Tony Gwynn Jr. N/300 8.00 20.00
AGW Tony Gwynn Jr. W/150 8.00 20.00
AGY Tony Gwynn Jr. Y/150 8.00 20.00
AJE Andruw Jones E/20 60.00 120.00
AJJ Andruw Jones J/20 60.00 120.00
AJN Andruw Jones N/20 60.00 120.00
AJO Andruw Jones O/20 60.00 120.00
AJS Andruw Jones S/20 60.00 120.00
APJ Albert Pujols J/5 200.00 400.00
APL Albert Pujols L/5 200.00 400.00
APO Albert Pujols O/5 200.00 400.00
APP Albert Pujols P/5 200.00 400.00
APS Albert Pujols S/5 200.00 400.00
APU Albert Pujols U/5 200.00 400.00
AP2M Albert Pujols MVP M/10 200.00 400.00
AP2P Albert Pujols MVP P/10 200.00 400.00
AP2V Albert Pujols MVP V/10 200.00 400.00
ARI Alex Rios I/100 20.00 40.00
ARO Alex Rios O/100 20.00 40.00
ARR Alex Rios R/100 20.00 40.00
ARS Alex Rios S/100 20.00 40.00
BAA Bronson Arroyo A/80 6.00 15.00
BAO Bronson Arroyo O/160 6.00 15.00
BAR Bronson Arroyo R/160 6.00 15.00
BAY Bronson Arroyo Y/80 6.00 15.00
BIB Chad Billingsley B/75 6.00 15.00
BIE Chad Billingsley E/75 6.00 15.00
BIG Chad Billingsley G/75 6.00 15.00
BII Chad Billingsley I/150 6.00 15.00
BIL Chad Billingsley L/225 6.00 15.00
BIN Chad Billingsley N/75 6.00 15.00
BIS Chad Billingsley S/75 6.00 15.00
BIY Chad Billingsley Y/75 6.00 15.00
BRB Brian Roberts B/14 40.00 80.00
BRE Brian Roberts E/14 40.00 80.00
BRO Brian Roberts O/14 40.00 80.00
BRR Brian Roberts R/28 40.00 80.00
BRS Brian Roberts S/14 40.00 80.00
BRT Brian Roberts T/14 40.00 80.00
BSE Ben Sheets E/250 6.00 15.00
BSH Ben Sheets H/125 6.00 15.00
BSS Ben Sheets S/250 6.00 15.00
BST Ben Sheets T/125 6.00 15.00
BUN B.J. Upton N/20 25.00 50.00
BUO B.J. Upton O/20 25.00 50.00
BUP B.J. Upton P/20 25.00 50.00
BUT B.J. Upton T/20 25.00 50.00
BUU B.J. Upton U/20 25.00 50.00
CBB Craig Biggio B/55 30.00 60.00
CBG Craig Biggio G/110 30.00 60.00
CBI Craig Biggio I/110 30.00 60.00
CBO Craig Biggio O/55 30.00 60.00
CCA Chris Carpenter A/4 40.00 80.00
CCC Chris Carpenter C/4 40.00 80.00
CCE Chris Carpenter E/8 40.00 80.00
CCN Chris Carpenter N/4 40.00 80.00
CCP Chris Carpenter P/4 40.00 80.00
CCR Chris Carpenter R/8 40.00 80.00
CCT Chris Carpenter T/4 40.00 80.00
CC2C Chris Carpenter CY C/8 40.00 80.00
CC2G Chris Carpenter CY G/8 40.00 80.00
CC2N Chris Carpenter CY N/8 40.00 80.00
CC2O Chris Carpenter CY O/8 40.00 80.00
CC2U Chris Carpenter CY U/8 40.00 80.00
CC2Y Chris Carpenter CY Y/16 40.00 80.00
CHA Craig Hansen A/30 6.00 15.00
CHE Craig Hansen E/30 6.00 15.00
CHH Craig Hansen H/30 6.00 15.00
CHN Craig Hansen N/60 6.00 15.00
CHS Craig Hansen S/30 6.00 15.00
COA Cole Hamels A/120 10.00 25.00
COE Cole Hamels E/120 10.00 25.00
COH Cole Hamels H/120 10.00 25.00
COL Cole Hamels L/120 10.00 25.00
COM Cole Hamels M/120 10.00 25.00
COS Cole Hamels S/120 10.00 25.00
CSA C.C. Sabathia A/120 20.00 40.00
CSB C.C. Sabathia B/40 20.00 40.00
CSH C.C. Sabathia H/40 20.00 40.00
CSI C.C. Sabathia I/40 20.00 40.00
CSS C.C. Sabathia S/40 20.00 40.00
CST C.C. Sabathia T/40 20.00 40.00
CUE Chase Utley E/25 30.00 60.00
CUL Chase Utley L/25 30.00 60.00
CUT Chase Utley T/25 30.00 60.00
CUU Chase Utley U/25 30.00 60.00
CUY Chase Utley Y/25 30.00 60.00
CZA Carlos Zambrano A/34 50.00 100.00
CZB Carlos Zambrano B/17 50.00 100.00
CZM Carlos Zambrano M/17 50.00 100.00
CZN Carlos Zambrano N/17 50.00 100.00
CZO Carlos Zambrano O/17 50.00 100.00
CZR Carlos Zambrano R/17 50.00 100.00
CZZ Carlos Zambrano Z/17 50.00 100.00
DHA Danny Haren A/180 8.00 20.00
DHE Danny Haren E/180 8.00 20.00
DHH Danny Haren H/180 8.00 20.00
DHN Danny Haren N/180 8.00 20.00
DHR Danny Haren R/180 8.00 20.00
DJE Derek Jeter E/12 175.00 350.00
DJJ Derek Jeter J/6 175.00 350.00
DJR Derek Jeter R/6 175.00 350.00
DJT Derek Jeter T/6 175.00 350.00
DJ2A Derek Jeter Captain A/10 175.00 350.00
DJ2C Derek Jeter Captain C/5 175.00 350.00
DJ2I Derek Jeter Captain I/5 175.00 350.00
DJ2N Derek Jeter Captain N/5 175.00 350.00
DJ2P Derek Jeter Captain P/5 175.00 350.00
DJ2T Derek Jeter Captain T/5 175.00 350.00
DLE Derrek Lee E/400 6.00 15.00
DLL Derrek Lee L/200 6.00 15.00
DUA Dan Uggla A/100 10.00 25.00
DUG Dan Uggla G/200 10.00 25.00
DUL Dan Uggla L/100 10.00 25.00
DUU Dan Uggla U/100 10.00 25.00
DWI Dontrelle Willis I/300 6.00 15.00
DWL Dontrelle Willis L/300 6.00 15.00
DWS Dontrelle Willis S/150 6.00 15.00
DWW Dontrelle Willis W/150 6.00 15.00
ECA Eric Chavez A/75 20.00 40.00
ECC Eric Chavez C/75 20.00 40.00
ECE Eric Chavez E/75 20.00 40.00
ECH Eric Chavez H/75 20.00 40.00
ECV Eric Chavez V/75 20.00 40.00
ECZ Eric Chavez Z/75 20.00 40.00
FHA Felix Hernandez A/40 20.00 50.00
FHD Felix Hernandez D/40 20.00 50.00
FHE Felix Hernandez E/80 20.00 50.00
FHH Felix Hernandez H/40 20.00 50.00
FHN Felix Hernandez N/80 20.00 50.00
FHR Felix Hernandez R/40 20.00 50.00
FHZ Felix Hernandez Z/40 20.00 50.00
FH2G Felix Hernandez King G/75 20.00 50.00
FH2I Felix Hernandez King I/75 20.00 50.00
FH2K Felix Hernandez King K/75 20.00 50.00
FH2N Felix Hernandez King N/75 20.00 50.00
FLA Francisco Liriano A/100 8.00 20.00
FLI Francisco Liriano I/200 8.00 20.00
FLL Francisco Liriano L/100 8.00 20.00
FLN Francisco Liriano N/100 8.00 20.00
FLO Francisco Liriano O/100 8.00 20.00
FLR Francisco Liriano R/100 8.00 20.00
GMA Greg Maddux A/25 75.00 150.00
GMD Greg Maddux D/50 75.00 150.00
GMM Greg Maddux M/25 75.00 150.00
GMU Greg Maddux U/25 75.00 150.00
GMX Greg Maddux X/25 75.00 150.00
HBA Hank Blalock A/50 6.00 15.00
HBB Hank Blalock B/50 6.00 15.00
HBC Hank Blalock C/50 6.00 15.00
HBK Hank Blalock K/50 6.00 15.00
HBL Hank Blalock L/100 6.00 15.00
HBO Hank Blalock O/50 6.00 15.00
HKC Howie Kendrick C/75 6.00 15.00
HKD Howie Kendrick D/75 6.00 15.00
HKE Howie Kendrick E/75 6.00 15.00
HKI Howie Kendrick I/75 6.00 15.00
HKK Howie Kendrick K/150 6.00 15.00
HKN Howie Kendrick N/75 6.00 15.00
HKR Howie Kendrick R/75 6.00 15.00
HOA Trevor Hoffman A/8 10.00 25.00
HOF Trevor Hoffman F/16 10.00 25.00
HOH Trevor Hoffman H/8 10.00 25.00
HOM Trevor Hoffman M/8 10.00 25.00
HON Trevor Hoffman N/8 10.00 25.00
HOO Trevor Hoffman O/8 10.00 25.00
HRA Hanley Ramirez A/125 10.00 25.00
HRE Hanley Ramirez E/125 10.00 25.00
HRI Hanley Ramirez I/125 10.00 25.00
HRM Hanley Ramirez M/125 10.00 25.00
HRR Hanley Ramirez R/250 10.00 25.00
HRZ Hanley Ramirez Z/125 10.00 25.00
HSE Huston Street E/150 6.00 15.00
HSR Huston Street R/75 6.00 15.00
HSS Huston Street S/75 6.00 15.00
HST Huston Street T/150 6.00 15.00
HUD Tim Hudson D/50 20.00 40.00
HUH Tim Hudson H/50 20.00 40.00
HUN Tim Hudson N/50 20.00 40.00
HUO Tim Hudson O/50 20.00 40.00
HUS Tim Hudson S/50 20.00 40.00
HUU Tim Hudson U/50 20.00 40.00
IKE Ian Kinsler E/125 8.00 20.00
IKI Ian Kinsler I/125 8.00 20.00
IKK Ian Kinsler K/125 8.00 20.00
IKL Ian Kinsler L/125 8.00 20.00
IKN Ian Kinsler N/125 8.00 20.00
IKR Ian Kinsler R/125 8.00 20.00
IKS Ian Kinsler S/125 8.00 20.00
JBA Jason Bay A/110 6.00 15.00
JBB Jason Bay B/110 6.00 15.00
JBY Jason Bay Y/110 6.00 15.00
JB2O Jason Bay ROY O/50 6.00 15.00
JB2R Jason Bay ROY R/50 6.00 15.00
JB2Y Jason Bay ROY Y/50 6.00 15.00
JGE Jonny Gomes E/175 6.00 15.00
JGG Jonny Gomes G/175 6.00 15.00
JGM Jonny Gomes M/175 6.00 15.00
JGO Jonny Gomes O/175 6.00 15.00
JGS Jonny Gomes S/175 6.00 15.00
JHA Jeremy Hermida A/125 15.00 30.00
JHD Jeremy Hermida D/125 15.00 30.00
JHE Jeremy Hermida E/125 15.00 30.00
JHH Jeremy Hermida H/125 15.00 30.00
JHI Jeremy Hermida I/125 15.00 30.00
JHM Jeremy Hermida M/125 15.00 30.00
JHR Jeremy Hermida R/125 15.00 30.00
JMA Joe Mauer A/25 40.00 80.00
JME Joe Mauer E/25 40.00 80.00
JMM Joe Mauer M/25 40.00 80.00
JMR Joe Mauer R/25 40.00 80.00
JMU Joe Mauer U/25 40.00 80.00
JNA Joe Nathan A/200 6.00 15.00
JNH Joe Nathan H/100 6.00 15.00
JNN Joe Nathan N/200 6.00 15.00
JNT Joe Nathan T/100 6.00 15.00
JPA Jonathan Papelbon A/100 8.00 20.00
JPB Jonathan Papelbon B/100 8.00 20.00
JPE Jonathan Papelbon E/100 8.00 20.00
JPL Jonathan Papelbon L/100 8.00 20.00
JPN Jonathan Papelbon N/100 8.00 20.00
JPO Jonathan Papelbon O/100 8.00 20.00
JPP Jonathan Papelbon P/200 8.00 20.00
JRE Jose Reyes E/150 40.00 80.00
JRR Jose Reyes R/75 40.00 80.00
JRS Jose Reyes S/75 40.00 80.00
JRY Jose Reyes Y/75 40.00 80.00
JSE Jeremy Sowers E/50 25.00 50.00
JSO Jeremy Sowers O/50 25.00 50.00
JSR Jeremy Sowers R/50 25.00 50.00
JSS Jeremy Sowers S/100 25.00 50.00
JSW Jeremy Sowers W/50 25.00 50.00
JTE Jim Thome E/30 30.00 60.00
JTH Jim Thome H/30 30.00 60.00
JTM Jim Thome M/30 30.00 60.00
JTO Jim Thome O/30 30.00 60.00
JTT Jim Thome T/30 30.00 60.00
JVA Justin Verlander A/20 40.00 80.00
JVD Justin Verlander D/20 40.00 80.00
JVE Justin Verlander E/40 40.00 80.00
JVL Justin Verlander L/20 40.00 80.00
JVN Justin Verlander N/20 40.00 80.00
JVR Justin Verlander R/40 40.00 80.00
JVV Justin Verlander V/20 40.00 80.00
JWA Jered Weaver A/40 12.50 30.00
JWE Jered Weaver E/80 12.50 30.00
JWR Jered Weaver R/40 12.50 30.00
JWV Jered Weaver V/40 12.50 30.00
JWW Jered Weaver W/40 12.50 30.00
JZA Joel Zumaya A/250 6.00 15.00
JZM Joel Zumaya M/125 6.00 15.00
JZU Joel Zumaya U/125 6.00 15.00
JZY Joel Zumaya Y/125 6.00 15.00
JZZ Joel Zumaya Z/125 6.00 15.00
KGE Ken Griffey Jr. Reds E/25 75.00 150.00
KGF Ken Griffey Jr. Reds F/50 75.00 150.00
KGG Ken Griffey Jr. Reds G/25 75.00 150.00
KGI Ken Griffey Jr. Reds I/25 75.00 150.00
KGR Ken Griffey Jr. Reds R/25 75.00 150.00
KGY Ken Griffey Jr. Reds Y/25 75.00 150.00
KG2I Ken Griffey Jr. Junior I/25 75.00 150.00
KG2J Ken Griffey Jr. Junior J/25 75.00 150.00
KG2N Ken Griffey Jr. Junior N/25 75.00 150.00
KG2O Ken Griffey Jr. Junior O/25 75.00 150.00
KG2R Ken Griffey Jr. Junior R/25 75.00 150.00
KG2U Ken Griffey Jr. Junior U/25 75.00 150.00
KG3E Ken Griffey Jr. M's E/25 75.00 150.00
KG3F Ken Griffey Jr. M's F/50 75.00 150.00
KG3G Ken Griffey Jr. M's G/25 75.00 150.00
KG3I Ken Griffey Jr. M's I/25 75.00 150.00
KG3R Ken Griffey Jr. M's R/25 75.00 150.00
KG3Y Ken Griffey Jr. M's Y/25 75.00 150.00
KG4D Ken Griffey Jr. The Kid D/25 75.00 150.00
KG4E Ken Griffey Jr. The Kid E/25 75.00 150.00
KG4H Ken Griffey Jr. The Kid H/25 75.00 150.00
KG4I Ken Griffey Jr. The Kid I/25 75.00 150.00
KG4K Ken Griffey Jr. The Kid K/25 75.00 150.00
KG4T Ken Griffey Jr. The Kid T/25 75.00 150.00
KHE Khalil Greene E/225 6.00 15.00
KHG Khalil Greene G/75 6.00 15.00
KHN Khalil Greene N/75 6.00 15.00
KHR Khalil Greene R/75 6.00 15.00
KMA Kendry Morales A/20 10.00 25.00
KME Kendry Morales E/20 10.00 25.00
KML Kendry Morales L/20 10.00 25.00
KMM Kendry Morales M/20 10.00 25.00
KMO Kendry Morales O/20 10.00 25.00
KMR Kendry Morales R/20 10.00 25.00
KMS Kendry Morales S/20 10.00 25.00
KWD Kerry Wood D/10 40.00 80.00
KWO Kerry Wood O/20 40.00 80.00
KWW Kerry Wood W/10 40.00 80.00
LEE Carlos Lee E/50 20.00 40.00
LEL Carlos Lee L/25 20.00 40.00
MCA Miguel Cabrera A/70 40.00 80.00
MCB Miguel Cabrera B/35 40.00 80.00
MCC Miguel Cabrera C/35 40.00 80.00
MCE Miguel Cabrera E/35 40.00 80.00
MCR Miguel Cabrera R/70 40.00 80.00
MGE Marcus Giles E/136 6.00 15.00
MGG Marcus Giles G/136 6.00 15.00
MGI Marcus Giles I/136 6.00 15.00
MGL Marcus Giles L/136 6.00 15.00

MGS Marcus Giles S/136 6.00 15.00
MHA Matt Holliday A/37 15.00 40.00
MHD Matt Holliday D/37 15.00 40.00
MHH Matt Holliday H/37 15.00 40.00
MHI Matt Holliday I/37 15.00 40.00
MHL Matt Holliday L/74 15.00 40.00
MHO Matt Holliday O/37 15.00 40.00
MHY Matt Holliday Y/37 15.00 40.00
MMD Mark Mulder D/50 6.00 15.00
MME Mark Mulder E/50 6.00 15.00
MML Mark Mulder L/50 6.00 15.00
MMM Mark Mulder M/50 6.00 15.00
MMR Mark Mulder R/50 6.00 15.00
MMU Mark Mulder U/50 6.00 15.00
MOA Justin Morneau A/75 12.50 30.00
MOE Justin Morneau E/75 12.50 30.00
MOM Justin Morneau M/75 12.50 30.00
MON Justin Morneau N/75 12.50 30.00
MOO Justin Morneau O/75 12.50 30.00
MOR Justin Morneau R/75 12.50 30.00
MOU Justin Morneau U/75 12.50 30.00
MTA Mark Teixeira A/5 30.00 60.00
MTE Mark Teixeira E/10 30.00 60.00
MTI Mark Teixeira I/10 30.00 60.00
MTR Mark Teixeira R/5 30.00 60.00
MTT Mark Teixeira T/5 30.00 60.00
MTX Mark Teixeira X/5 30.00 60.00
MYG Michael Young G/50 12.50 30.00
MYN Michael Young N/50 12.50 30.00
MYO Michael Young O/50 12.50 30.00
MYU Michael Young U/50 12.50 30.00
MYY Michael Young Y/50 12.50 30.00
NSE Nick Swisher E/170 8.00 20.00
NSH Nick Swisher H/170 8.00 20.00
NSI Nick Swisher I/170 8.00 20.00
NSR Nick Swisher R/170 8.00 20.00
NSS Nick Swisher S/340 8.00 20.00
NSW Nick Swisher W/170 8.00 20.00
PEA Jake Peavy A/20 15.00 40.00
PEE Jake Peavy E/20 15.00 40.00
PEP Jake Peavy P/20 15.00 40.00
PEV Jake Peavy V/20 15.00 40.00
PEY Jake Peavy Y/20 15.00 40.00
RCC Roger Clemens C/15 30.00 60.00
RCE Roger Clemens E/30 30.00 60.00
RCL Roger Clemens L/15 30.00 60.00
RCM Roger Clemens M/15 30.00 60.00
RCN Roger Clemens N/15 30.00 60.00
RCS Roger Clemens S/15 30.00 60.00
RC2C Roger Clemens The Rocket C/15 30.00 60.00
RC2E Roger Clemens The Rocket E/30 30.00 60.00
RC2H Roger Clemens The Rocket H/15 30.00 60.00
RC2K Roger Clemens The Rocket K/15 30.00 60.00
RC2O Roger Clemens The Rocket O/15 30.00 60.00
RC2R Roger Clemens The Rocket R/15 30.00 60.00
RC2T Roger Clemens The Rocket T/30 30.00 60.00
ROA Roy Oswalt A/50 10.00 25.00
ROL Roy Oswalt L/50 10.00 25.00
ROO Roy Oswalt O/50 10.00 25.00
ROS Roy Oswalt S/50 10.00 25.00
ROT Roy Oswalt T/50 10.00 25.00
ROW Roy Oswalt W/50 10.00 25.00
RWE Rickie Weeks E/200 10.00 25.00
RWK Rickie Weeks K/100 10.00 25.00
RWS Rickie Weeks S/100 10.00 25.00
RWW Rickie Weeks W/100 10.00 25.00
RZA Ryan Zimmerman A/17 30.00 60.00
RZE Ryan Zimmerman E/17 30.00 60.00
RZI Ryan Zimmerman I/17 30.00 60.00
RZM Ryan Zimmerman M/51 30.00 60.00
RZN Ryan Zimmerman N/17 30.00 60.00
RZR Ryan Zimmerman R/17 30.00 60.00
RZZ Ryan Zimmerman Z/17 30.00 60.00
SKA Scott Kazmir A/6 50.00 100.00
SKI Scott Kazmir I/6 50.00 100.00
SKK Scott Kazmir K/6 50.00 100.00
SKM Scott Kazmir M/6 50.00 100.00
SKR Scott Kazmir R/6 50.00 100.00
SKZ Scott Kazmir Z/6 50.00 100.00
SML John Smoltz L/75 20.00 50.00
SMM John Smoltz M/75 20.00 50.00
SMO John Smoltz O/75 20.00 50.00
SMS John Smoltz S/75 20.00 50.00
SMT John Smoltz T/75 20.00 50.00
SMZ John Smoltz Z/75 20.00 50.00
TEA Miguel Tejada A/50 8.00 20.00
TED Miguel Tejada D/25 8.00 20.00
TEE Miguel Tejada E/25 8.00 20.00
TEJ Miguel Tejada J/25 8.00 20.00
TET Miguel Tejada T/25 8.00 20.00
THA Travis Hafner A/10 50.00 100.00
THE Travis Hafner E/10 50.00 100.00
THF Travis Hafner F/10 50.00 100.00
THH Travis Hafner H/10 50.00 100.00
THN Travis Hafner N/10 50.00 100.00
THR Travis Hafner R/10 50.00 100.00
TH2K Travis Hafner Pronk K/8 10.00 25.00
TH2N Travis Hafner Pronk N/8 10.00 25.00
TH2O Travis Hafner Pronk O/8 10.00 25.00
TH2P Travis Hafner Pronk P/8 10.00 25.00
TH2R Travis Hafner Pronk R/8 10.00 25.00
TIC Tadahito Iguchi C/20 20.00 50.00
TIG Tadahito Iguchi G/20 20.00 50.00
TIH Tadahito Iguchi H/20 20.00 50.00
TII Tadahito Iguchi I/40 20.00 50.00
TIU Tadahito Iguchi U/20 20.00 50.00
VGE Vladimir Guerrero E/50 20.00 50.00
VGG Vladimir Guerrero G/25 20.00 50.00
VGO Vladimir Guerrero O/25 20.00 50.00
VGR Vladimir Guerrero R/75 20.00 50.00
VGU Vladimir Guerrero U/25 20.00 50.00
VMA Victor Martinez A/75 6.00 15.00
VME Victor Martinez E/75 6.00 15.00
VMI Victor Martinez I/75 6.00 15.00
VMM Victor Martinez M/75 6.00 15.00
VMN Victor Martinez N/75 6.00 15.00
VMR Victor Martinez R/75 6.00 15.00
VMT Victor Martinez T/75 6.00 15.00
VMZ Victor Martinez Z/75 6.00 15.00
WIA Josh Willingham A/75 6.00 15.00
WIG Josh Willingham G/75 6.00 15.00
WIH Josh Willingham H/75 6.00 15.00
WII Josh Willingham I/150 6.00 15.00
WIL Josh Willingham L/150 6.00 15.00
WIM Josh Willingham M/75 6.00 15.00
WIN Josh Willingham N/75 6.00 15.00
WIW Josh Willingham W/75 6.00 15.00

2006 SP Authentic Chirography

STATED ODDS 1:96
PRINT RUNS B/WN 25-75 COPIES PER
NO PRICING ON QTY OF 25
EXCHANGE DEADLINE 12/05/09
AE Andre Ethier/75 12.50 30.00
AG Tony Gwynn Jr./75 6.00 15.00
AH Anderson Hernandez/75 4.00 10.00
AN Brian Anderson/75 4.00 10.00
AS Alfonso Soriano/75 12.50 30.00
AW Adam Wainwright/75 20.00 50.00
BA Brian Bannister/75 6.00 15.00
BB Brandon Backe/75 4.00 10.00
BC Bobby Crosby/75 6.00 15.00
BI Chad Billingsley/75 10.00 25.00
BL Boone Logan/75 4.00 10.00
BO Boof Bonser/75 6.00 15.00
BS Ben Sheets/75 10.00 25.00
CB Craig Biggio/75 15.00 40.00
CD Chris Denorfia/75 4.00 10.00
CF Choo Freeman/75 4.00 10.00
CG Carlos Guillen/75 10.00 25.00
CH Cole Hamels/75 10.00 25.00
CJ Conor Jackson/75 6.00 15.00
CK Casey Kotchman/75 4.00 10.00
CL Cliff Lee/75 15.00 40.00
CP Corey Patterson/75 6.00 15.00
CR Cody Ross/75 10.00 25.00
CS C.C. Sabathia/75 8.00 20.00
DB Denny Bautista/75 4.00 10.00
DD David DeJesus/75 6.00 15.00
DG David Gassner/75 4.00 10.00
DJ Derek Jeter/75 150.00 400.00
DU Dan Uggla/75 4.00 10.00
DW Dontrelle Willis/75 10.00 25.00
FC Fausto Carmona/75 4.00 10.00
FL Felipe Lopez/75 4.00 10.00
FT Frank Thomas/75 40.00 80.00
GA Garret Anderson/75 6.00 15.00
GR Ken Griffey Jr./75 60.00 120.00
HA Jeff Harris/75 4.00 10.00
HB Hank Blalock/75 6.00 15.00
HK Hong-Chih Kuo/75 50.00 100.00
HR Hanley Ramirez/75 6.00 15.00
IK Ian Kinsler/75 6.00 15.00
IR Ivan Rodriguez/75 20.00 50.00
JB Joe Blanton/75 6.00 15.00
JC Jose Capellan/75 4.00 10.00
JD Joey Devine/75 4.00 10.00
JE Johnny Estrada/75 4.00 10.00
JF Jeff Francis/75 10.00 25.00
JH Jeremy Hermida/75 6.00 15.00
JJ Josh Johnson/75 10.00 25.00
JK Jason Kubel/75 4.00 10.00
JL Jon Lester/75 15.00 40.00
JN Joe Nathan/75 6.00 15.00
JP Jonathan Papelbon/75 6.00 15.00
JR Josh Rupe/75 4.00 10.00
JS Jeremy Sowers/75 6.00 15.00
JW Josh Willingham/75 4.00 10.00
KF Keith Foulke/75 8.00 20.00
KG Khalil Greene/75 10.00 25.00
KM Kevin Mench/75 6.00 15.00
KS Kelly Shoppach/75 4.00 10.00
KY Kevin Youkilis/75 6.00 15.00
LI Francisco Liriano/75 4.00 10.00
LO Lyle Overbay/40 6.00 15.00
MC Matt Cain/75 40.00 80.00
MM Macay McBride/75 4.00 10.00
NS Nick Swisher/75 6.00 15.00
OP Oliver Perez/75 6.00 15.00
PM Paul Maholm/75 4.00 10.00
RE Eric Reed/75 4.00 10.00
RH Rich Harden/75 6.00 15.00
RZ Ryan Zimmerman/75 10.00 25.00
SC Sean Casey/75 10.00 25.00
SD Stephen Drew/75 6.00 15.00
SH Chris Shelton/75 4.00 10.00
SM Sean Marshall/75 12.50 30.00
SO Alay Soler/75 6.00 15.00
TB Taylor Buchholz/75 4.00 10.00
TH Travis Hafner/75 10.00 25.00
TP Tony Pena Jr./75 4.00 10.00
TS Takashi Saito/75 20.00 50.00
VA John Van Benschoten/75 4.00 10.00
VE Justin Verlander/75 50.00 100.00
VM Victor Martinez/75 10.00 25.00
WE Jered Weaver/75 4.00 10.00
WI Josh Wilson/75 4.00 10.00
WM Wily Mo Pena/75 6.00 15.00

2006 SP Authentic Sign of the Times

STATED ODDS 1:96
PRINT RUNS B/WN 25-75 COPIES PER
NO PRICING ON QTY OF 25
EXCHANGE DEADLINE 12/05/09
AB Adrian Beltre/75 10.00 25.00
AE Andre Ethier/75 12.50 30.00
AH Anderson Hernandez/75 4.00 10.00
AJ Andruw Jones/75 6.00 15.00
AN Brian Anderson/75 4.00 10.00
AR Aramis Ramirez/75 6.00 15.00
AS Alay Soler/75 6.00 15.00
AW Adam Wainwright/75 10.00 25.00
BA Bobby Abreu/75 30.00 60.00
BB Boof Bonser/75 6.00 15.00
BI Chad Billingsley/75 10.00 25.00
BJ Ben Johnson/75 4.00 10.00
BL Boone Logan/75 4.00 10.00
BR Brian Bannister/75 6.00 15.00
CA Matt Cain/75 10.00 25.00
CB Chris Booker/75 4.00 10.00
CC Carl Crawford/75 6.00 15.00
CD Chris Demaria/75 4.00 10.00
CH Cole Hamels/75 20.00 50.00
CR Cody Ross/75 10.00 25.00
CS Curt Schilling/75 25.00 60.00
CY Clay Hensley/75 4.00 10.00
DE Chris Denorfia/75 4.00 10.00
DG David Gassner/75 4.00 10.00
DJ Derek Jeter/75 100.00 175.00
DL Derrek Lee/75 6.00 15.00
DU Dan Uggla/75 12.50 30.00
EG Eric Gagne/75 10.00 25.00
ER Eric Reed/75 4.00 10.00
FC Fausto Carmona/75 10.00 25.00
FL Francisco Liriano/75 15.00 40.00
FR Ron Flores/75 4.00 10.00
GM Greg Maddux/75 60.00 120.00
HA Tim Hamulack/75 4.00 10.00
HE Jeremy Hermida/75 6.00 15.00
HR Hanley Ramirez/75 8.00 20.00
IK Ian Kinsler/75 6.00 15.00
JA Conor Jackson/75 6.00 15.00
JC Jose Capellan/75 4.00 10.00
JD J.D. Drew/75 10.00 25.00
JE Jered Weaver/75 20.00 50.00
JG Jose Guillen/75 4.00 10.00
JH Jason Hammel/75 4.00 10.00
JJ Josh Johnson/75 10.00 25.00
JK Jason Kendall/75 10.00 25.00
JM Joe Mauer/75 20.00 50.00
JP Jake Peavy/75 6.00 15.00
JS John Smoltz/75 10.00 25.00
JV John Van Benschoten/75 4.00 10.00
JW Josh Willingham/75 4.00 10.00
JY Jeremy Sowers/75 6.00 15.00
KG Ken Griffey Jr./75 60.00 120.00
KU Jason Kubel/75 4.00 10.00
MA Macay McBride/75 4.00 10.00
MC Miguel Cabrera/75 20.00 50.00
MI Mike Thompson/75 4.00 10.00
MJ Mike Jacobs/75 6.00 15.00
MK Mark Kotsay/75 6.00 15.00
MM Mark Mulder/75 6.00 15.00
MO Justin Morneau/75 6.00 15.00
MT Mark Teixeira/75 10.00 25.00
PA Jonathan Papelbon/75 10.00 25.00
PE Joel Peralta/75 4.00 10.00
PM Paul Maholm/75 4.00 10.00
RA Reggie Abercrombie/75 4.00 10.00
RF Rafael Furcal/75 6.00 15.00
RH Ramon Hernandez/75 10.00 25.00
RJ Randy Johnson/75 50.00 100.00
RM Russell Martin/75 4.00 10.00
RS Ryan Shealy/75 6.00 15.00
RW Rickie Weeks/75 10.00 25.00
RZ Ryan Zimmerman/75 20.00 50.00
SA Santiago Ramirez/75 4.00 10.00
SD Stephen Drew/75 20.00 50.00
SM Sean Marshall/75 10.00 25.00
SP Scott Podsednik/75 6.00 15.00
SS Skip Schumaker/75 4.00 10.00
ST Steve Stemle/75 4.00 10.00
TB Taylor Buchholz/75 4.00 10.00
TE Miguel Tejada/75 10.00 25.00
TH Tim Hudson/75 10.00 25.00
TP Tony Pena Jr./75 4.00 10.00
TS Takashi Saito/75 20.00 50.00
VE Justin Verlander/75 40.00 80.00
VG Vladimir Guerrero/75 15.00 40.00
VW Vernon Wells/75 6.00 15.00
WI Josh Wilson/75 4.00 10.00
YB Yuniesky Betancourt/75 6.00 15.00
ZG Zack Greinke/75 10.00 25.00

2006 SP Authentic WBC Future Watch

STATED ODDS 1:7
STATED PRINT RUN 999 SERIAL #'d SETS
1 Adrian Burnside 1.00 2.50
2 Gavin Fingleson 1.00 2.50
3 Bradley Harman 1.50 4.00
4 Brendan Kingman 1.00 2.50
5 Brett Roneberg 1.00 2.50
6 Paul Rutgers 1.00 2.50
7 Phil Stockman 1.00 2.50
8 Stubby Clapp 1.00 2.50
9 Steve Green 1.00 2.50
10 Pete LaForest 1.00 2.50
11 Adam Loewen 1.00 2.50
12 Ryan Radmanovich 1.00 2.50
13 Chenhao Li 1.00 2.50
14 Guangbiao Liu 1.00 2.50
15 Guogan Yang 1.00 2.50
16 Jingchao Wang 1.00 2.50
17 Lei Li 1.00 2.50
18 Lingfeng Sun 1.00 2.50
19 Nan Wang 1.00 2.50
20 Shuo Yang 1.00 2.50
21 Tao Bu 1.00 2.50
22 Wei Wang 1.00 2.50
23 Yi Feng 1.00 2.50
24 Chien-Ming Chiang 2.50 6.00
25 Yung-Chi Chen 1.50 4.00
26 Chia-Hsien Hseih 2.50 6.00
27 Chin-Lung Hu 1.00 2.50
28 En-Yu Lin 2.50 6.00
29 Wei-Lun Pan 2.50 6.00
30 Ariel Borrero 1.00 2.50
31 Yadel Marti 1.00 2.50
32 Yulieski Gourriel 3.00 8.00
33 Frederich Cepeda 1.00 2.50
34 Yadiel Pedroso 1.00 2.50
35 Pedro Luis Lazo 1.50 4.00
36 Elier Sanchez 1.00 2.50
37 Norberto Gonzalez 1.00 2.50
38 Carlos Tabares 1.00 2.50
39 Eduardo Paret 1.00 2.50
40 Osmany Urrutia 1.00 2.50
41 Alexi Ramirez 6.00 15.00
42 Yoandy Garlobo 1.00 2.50
43 Vicyohandry Odelin 1.00 2.50
44 Michel Enriquez 1.00 2.50
45 Ormari Romero 1.00 2.50
46 Ariel Pestano 1.00 2.50
47 Francisco Liriano 2.50 6.00
48 Dustin Delucchi 1.00 2.50
49 Tony Giarratano 1.00 2.50
50 Tom Gregorio 1.00 2.50
51 Mark Saccomanno 1.00 2.50
52 Takahiro Arai 1.50 4.00
53 Akinori Iwamura 3.00 8.00
54 Munenori Kawasaki 5.00 12.00
55 Nobuhiko Matsunaka 1.50 4.00
56 Daisuke Matsuzaka 3.00 8.00
57 Shinya Miyamoto 1.50 4.00
58 Tsuyoshi Nishioka 6.00 15.00
59 Tomoya Satozaki 1.50 4.00
60 Koji Uehara 3.00 8.00
61 Shunsuke Watanabe 1.50 4.00
62 Sadaharu Oh 6.00 15.00
63 Byung Kyu Lee 1.00 2.50
64 Ji Man Song 1.00 2.50
65 Jin Man Park 1.00 2.50
66 Jong Beom Lee 1.00 2.50
67 Jong Kook Kim 1.00 2.50
68 Min Han Son 1.00 2.50
69 Min Jae Kim 1.00 2.50
70 Seung Yeop Lee 1.50 4.00
71 Luis A. Garcia 1.00 2.50
72 Mario Valenzuela 1.00 2.50
73 Sharnol Adriana 1.00 2.50
74 Rob Cordemans 1.00 2.50
75 Michael Duursma 1.00 2.50
76 Percy Isenia 1.00 2.50
77 Sidney de Jong 1.00 2.50
78 Dirk Klooster 1.00 2.50
79 Raylinoe Legito 1.00 2.50
80 Shairon Martis 1.00 2.50
81 Harvey Monte 1.00 2.50
82 Hainley Statia 1.00 2.50
83 Roger Deago 1.00 2.50
84 Audes De Leon 1.00 2.50
85 Freddy Herrera 1.00 2.50
86 Yoni Lasso 1.00 2.50
87 Orlando Miller 1.00 2.50
88 Len Pecota 1.00 2.50
89 Federico Baez 1.00 2.50
90 Dicky Gonzalez 1.00 2.50
91 Josue Matos 1.00 2.50
92 Orlando Roman 1.00 2.50
93 Paul Bell 1.00 2.50
94 Kyle Botha 1.00 2.50
95 Jason Cook 1.00 2.50
96 Nicholas Dempsey 1.00 2.50
97 Victor Moreno 1.00 2.50
98 Ricardo Palma 1.00 2.50
99 Huston Street 1.00 2.50
100 Chase Utley 1.50 4.00

2007 SP Authentic

COMP.SET w/o RCs (100) 6.00 15.00
COMMON CARD (1-100) .15 .40
COMMON AU RC (101-158) 5.00 12.00
OVERALL BY THE LETTER AUTOS 1:12
AU RC PRINT RUN B/WN 20-120 COPIES PER
EXCHANGE DEADLINE 11/08/2008
1 Chipper Jones .40 1.00
2 Andruw Jones .15 .40
3 John Smoltz .40 1.00
4 Carlos Quentin .15 .40
5 Randy Johnson .40 1.00
6 Brandon Webb .25 .60
7 Alfonso Soriano .25 .60
8 Derrek Lee .15 .40
9 Aramis Ramirez .15 .40
10 Carlos Zambrano .25 .60
11 Ken Griffey Jr. .75 2.00
12 Adam Dunn .25 .60
13 Josh Hamilton .50 1.25
14 Todd Helton .25 .60
15 Jeff Francis .15 .40
16 Matt Holliday .40 1.00
17 Hanley Ramirez .25 .60
18 Dontrelle Willis .15 .40
19 Miguel Cabrera .40 1.00
20 Lance Berkman .25 .60
21 Roy Oswalt .25 .60
22 Carlos Lee .15 .40
23 Nomar Garciaparra .25 .60
24 Derek Lowe .15 .40
25 Juan Pierre .15 .40
26 Rafael Furcal .15 .40
27 Rickie Weeks .15 .40
28 Prince Fielder .25 .60
29 Ben Sheets .15 .40
30 David Wright .30 .75
31 Jose Reyes .25 .60
32 Tom Glavine .25 .60
33 Carlos Beltran .25 .60
34 Cole Hamels .30 .75
35 Jimmy Rollins .25 .60
36 Ryan Howard .30 .75
37 Jason Bay .25 .60
38 Freddy Sanchez .15 .40
39 Ian Snell .15 .40
40 Jake Peavy .15 .40
41 Greg Maddux .50 1.25
42 Trevor Hoffman .25 .60
43 Matt Cain .25 .60
44 Barry Zito .25 .60
45 Ray Durham .15 .40
46 Albert Pujols .50 1.25
47 Chris Carpenter .25 .60
48 Jim Edmonds .25 .60
49 Scott Rolen .25 .60
50 Ryan Zimmerman .25 .60
51 Felipe Lopez .15 .40
52 Austin Kearns .15 .40
53 Miguel Tejada .25 .60
54 Erik Bedard .15 .40
55 Daniel Cabrera .15 .40
56 David Ortiz .40 1.00
57 Curt Schilling .25 .60
58 Manny Ramirez .40 1.00
59 Jonathan Papelbon .40 1.00
60 Jim Thome .25 .60
61 Paul Konerko .25 .60
62 Bobby Jenks .15 .40
63 Grady Sizemore .25 .60
64 Victor Martinez .25 .60
65 Travis Hafner .15 .40
66 Ivan Rodriguez .25 .60
67 Justin Verlander .40 1.00
68 Joel Zumaya .15 .40
69 Jeremy Bonderman .15 .40
70 Gil Meche .15 .40
71 Mike Sweeney .15 .40
72 Mark Teahen .15 .40
73 Vladimir Guerrero .25 .60
74 Howie Kendrick .15 .40
75 Francisco Rodriguez .25 .60
76 Johan Santana .25 .60
77 Justin Morneau .25 .60
78 Joe Mauer .30 .75
79 Joe Nathan .15 .40
80a Alex Rodriguez .50 1.25
80b A.Rodriguez Angels 10.00 25.00
80c A.Rodriguez Cubs 12.00 30.00
80d A.Rodriguez Dodgers 12.00 30.00
80e A.Rodriguez Mets 12.00 30.00
80f A.Rodriguez Red Sox 12.00 30.00
81 Derek Jeter 1.00 2.50
82 Johnny Damon .25 .60
83 Chien-Ming Wang .25 .60
84 Rich Harden .15 .40
85 Mike Piazza .40 1.00
86 Dan Haren .15 .40
87 Ichiro Suzuki .50 1.25
88 Felix Hernandez .25 .60
89 Kenji Johjima .40 1.00
90 Adrian Beltre .40 1.00
91 Carl Crawford .25 .60
92 Scott Kazmir .25 .60
93 Delmon Young .25 .60
94 Michael Young .15 .40
95 Mark Teixeira .25 .60
96 Eric Gagne .15 .40
97 Hank Blalock .15 .40
98 Vernon Wells .15 .40
99 Roy Halladay .25 .60
100 Frank Thomas .40 1.00
101 Joaquin Arias AU/75 (RC) 5.00 12.00
102 Jeff Baker AU (RC) 5.00 12.00
103 M.Bourn AU/75 (RC) 6.00 15.00
104 Brian Burres AU/75 (RC) 6.00 15.00
105 Jared Burton AU/75 RC 6.00 15.00
106 Ryan Braun AU/50 (RC) 10.00 25.00
107a Y.Gallardo AU/75 (RC) 8.00 20.00
107b Yovani Gallardo AU/35 10.00 25.00
108a H.Gimenez AU/75 (RC) 6.00 15.00
108b Hector Gimenez AU/50 6.00 15.00
109 Alex Gordon AU/50 RC 10.00 25.00
110a J.Hamilton AU/50 (RC) 15.00 40.00
110b J.Hamilton AU/35 20.00 50.00
111a Justin Hampson AU/75 (RC) 5.00 12.00
111b Justin Hampson AU/50 5.00 12.00
112 Sean Henn AU/75 (RC) 10.00 25.00
113 P.Hughes AU (RC) 40.00 80.00
114 Kei Igawa AU/25 RC 8.00 20.00
115 A.Iwamura AU/20 RC 10.00 25.00
116a M.Reynolds AU/75 RC 5.00 12.00
116b Mark Reynolds AU/35 6.00 15.00
117a Homer Bailey AU/75 (RC) 4.00 10.00
117b Homer Bailey AU/50 (RC) 4.00 10.00
118a K.Kouzmanoff AU/75 (RC) 5.00 12.00
118b Kevin Kouzmanoff AU/40 5.00 12.00
119 Adam Lind AU/75 (RC) 6.00 15.00
120a Carlos Gomez AU/75 RC 8.00 20.00
120b Carlos Gomez AU/50 8.00 20.00
121a Glen Perkins AU/75 (RC) 5.00 12.00
121b Glen Perkins AU/50 5.00 12.00
122a R.Vanden Hurk AU/75 RC 5.00 12.00
122b Rick Vanden Hurk AU/35 5.00 12.00
123 Brad Salmon AU/75 RC 5.00 12.00
124a Zack Segovia AU/75 (RC) 5.00 12.00
124b Zack Segovia AU/50 5.00 12.00
125a Kurt Suzuki AU/75 (RC) 6.00 15.00
125b Kurt Suzuki AU/50 6.00 15.00
126a Chris Stewart AU/75 RC 5.00 12.00
126b Chris Stewart AU/50 5.00 12.00
127 Cesar Jimenez AU RC 5.00 12.00
128a Ryan Sweeney AU/50 (RC) 5.00 12.00
128b Ryan Sweeney AU/40 5.00 12.00
129a T.Tulowit AU/20 (RC) 15.00 40.00
129b T.Tulowit AU/10 15.00 40.00
130 Chase Wright AU/75 RC 6.00 15.00
131 Delmon Young AU/20 (RC) 5.00 12.00
132a Tony Abreu AU/75 RC 10.00 25.00
132h Tony Abreu AU/57 10.00 25.00
132c Tony Abreu AU/50 10.00 25.00
133 Brian Barden AU/75 RC 5.00 12.00
134a C.Thigpen AU/75 (RC) 4.00 10.00
134b Curtis Thigpen AU/40 4.00 10.00
135a Jon Coutlangus AU/75 (RC) 5.00 12.00
135b Jon Coutlangus AU/55 5.00 12.00
136a Kevin Cameron AU/75 RC 5.00 12.00
136b Kevin Cameron AU/50 5.00 12.00
137 Billy Butler AU/75 (RC) 6.00 15.00
138a A.Casilla AU/75 RC 5.00 12.00
138b Alexi Casilla AU/50 5.00 12.00
139 Kory Casto AU/75 (RC) 5.00 12.00
140 Matt Chico AU/75 (RC) 6.00 15.00
141 John Danks AU/75 RC 6.00 15.00
142 Andrew Miller AU/50 RC 8.00 20.00
143a B.Francisco AU/75 (RC) 6.00 15.00
143b Ben Francisco AU/40 6.00 15.00
144a Andy Gonzalez AU/75 RC 5.00 12.00
144b Andy Gonzalez AU/50 5.00 12.00
145 D.Hansack AU RC 6.00 15.00
146 Mike Rabelo AU/75 RC 6.00 15.00
147a Tim Lincecum AU/50 RC 20.00 50.00
147b Tim Lincecum AU/25 25.00 60.00
148a M.Lindstrom AU/75 (RC) 6.00 15.00
148b Matt Lindstrom AU/40 6.00 15.00
149a Jay Marshall AU/75 RC 5.00 12.00
149b Jay Marshall AU/50 5.00 12.00
150a D.Matsuzaka AU/20 RC 20.00 50.00
151a M.Montero AU/75 (RC) 5.00 12.00
151b Miguel Montero AU/60 5.00 12.00
152 Micah Owings AU/75 (RC) 6.00 15.00
153 Hunter Pence AU/75 (RC) 10.00 25.00
154a Brandon Wood AU/75 (RC) 6.00 15.00
155a Felix Pie AU/75 (RC) 6.00 15.00
155b Felix Pie AU/70 6.00 15.00
156 Danny Putnam AU/75 (RC) 6.00 15.00
157a Andy LaRoche AU/50 (RC) 5.00 12.00
157b Andy LaRoche AU/40 5.00 12.00
158a J.Saltalamac AU/75 (RC) 5.00 12.00
158b Jarrod Saltalamacchia AU/25 6.00 15.00
159 Doug Slaten AU/75 RC 6.00 15.00
160 Joe Smith AU/75 RC 8.00 20.00
161 Justin Upton AU/120 RC 10.00 25.00
162 J.Chamberlain AU/60 RC 8.00 20.00

2007 SP Authentic By the Letter Signatures

OVERALL BY THE LETTER AUTOS 1:12
PRINT RUNS B/WN 5-199 COPIES PER
NO PRICING ON SOME DUE TO SCARCITY
EXCHANGE DEADLINE 11/08/2008
1 Derek Jeter 150.00 300.00
2a Ken Griffey Jr./25 100.00 250.00
2b Ken Griffey Jr./20 100.00 250.00
4a Justin Verlander/25 25.00 60.00
4b Justin Verlander/15 30.00 80.00
5a Adrian Gonzalez/60 6.00 15.00
5b Adrian Gonzalez/50 6.00 15.00
8 Josh Beckett/15 10.00 25.00
9a Carlos Quentin/75 6.00 15.00
9b Carlos Quentin/50 6.00 15.00
10 Aramis Ramirez/25 6.00 15.00
11 Austin Kearns/50 6.00 15.00
12a B.J. Upton/25 8.00 20.00
12b B.J. Upton/15 8.00 20.00
13a Boof Bonser/75 6.00 15.00
13b Boof Bonser/50 6.00 15.00
14a Bronson Arroyo/75 6.00 15.00
14b Bronson Arroyo/10 10.00 25.00
15a Troy Tulowitzki 15.00 40.00
15b Troy Tulowitzki 15.00 40.00
16 Felix Pie/75 12.50 30.00
17 Alex Gordon/25 6.00 15.00
18a Chris Duffy/75 6.00 15.00
18b Chris Duffy 6.00 15.00
19a Chris Young/75 6.00 15.00
19b Chris Young/50 6.00 15.00
20a Cliff Lee/75 6.00 15.00
20b Cliff Lee/50 6.00 15.00
21a Cole Hamels/25 10.00 25.00
21b Cole Hamels/15 10.00 25.00
22 Adam Lind/75 8.00 20.00
23a Akinori Iwamura/25 6.00 15.00
23b Akinori Iwamura/15 6.00 15.00
24a Dan Uggla/25 8.00 20.00
24b Dan Uggla/21 8.00 20.00
25 Dan Haren/25 6.00 15.00
26 David Ortiz/10 40.00 80.00
27 Felix Hernandez/10 30.00 60.00
28a Tony Gwynn Jr. 6.00 15.00
28b Tony Gwynn Jr. 6.00 15.00
29a Josh Hamilton/75 10.00 30.00
29b Josh Hamilton/50 10.00 30.00
29c Josh Hamilton/10 15.00 40.00
30a Phil Hughes 6.00 15.00
30b Phil Hughes 8.00 20.00
31 Khalil Greene/25 12.50 30.00
32a Dontrelle Willis/25 6.00 15.00
32b Dontrelle Willis/20 6.00 15.00
33a Hanley Ramirez/50 10.00 25.00
33b Hanley Ramirez/25 12.00 30.00
34a Howie Kendrick/60 6.00 15.00
34b Howie Kendrick/50 6.00 15.00
35a Huston Street/50 6.00 15.00
35b Huston Street/25 8.00 20.00
37a Jason Bay/50 6.00 15.00
37b Jason Bay/25 10.00 25.00
40a Joe Mauer/25 50.00 100.00
40b Joe Mauer/15 50.00 100.00
41 Jonathan Papelbon/40 8.00 20.00
42a Tim Lincecum/50 15.00 40.00
42b Tim Lincecum/40 15.00 40.00
43a Matt Cain/75 8.00 20.00
43b Matt Cain/40 8.00 20.00
44 Victor Martinez/25 12.00 30.00
45 Roger Clemens/5 50.00 100.00
46 Ryan Zimmerman/25 12.00 30.00
47a Stephen Drew/25 6.00 15.00
47b Stephen Drew/10 6.00 15.00
48 Travis Hafner/25 6.00 15.00
49a Josh Willingham 6.00 15.00
49b Josh Willingham/50 6.00 15.00
50a Torii Hunter/25 8.00 20.00
51 Billy Butler/50 6.00 15.00
52a Justin Morneau/25 10.00 25.00
52b Justin Morneau/15 10.00 25.00
53a Andy LaRoche/75 6.00 15.00
53b Andy LaRoche/60 6.00 15.00
53c Andy LaRoche/50 6.00 15.00
54a Brandon Wood/75 6.00 15.00
54b Brandon Wood/50 6.00 15.00
55 Hunter Pence/50 12.00 30.00
56a Devern Hansack/199 6.00 15.00
56b Devern Hansack/75 6.00 15.00
56c Devern Hansack/50 10.00 25.00
58a Derrek Lee/25 8.00 50.00
58b Derrek Lee/10 8.00 20.00
59a Prince Fielder/25 8.00 20.00
59b Prince Fielder/10 10.00 25.00
60a Kevin Kouzmanoff/50 8.00 20.00

2007 SP Authentic Authentic Power

COMPLETE SET (50) 8.00 20.00
STATED ODDS 1:2
AP1 Adam Dunn .30 .75
AP2 Albert Pujols .60 1.50
AP3 Alex Rodriguez .60 1.50
AP4 Alfonso Soriano .30 .75
AP5 Andruw Jones .20 .50
AP6 Aramis Ramirez .20 .50
AP7 Bill Hall .20 .50
AP8 Carlos Beltran .30 .75
AP9 Carlos Delgado .20 .50
AP10 Carlos Lee .20 .50
AP11 Chase Utley .30 .75
AP12 Chipper Jones .50 1.25
AP13 Dan Uggla .20 .50
AP14 David Ortiz .50 1.25
AP15 David Wright .40 1.00
AP16 Derrek Lee .20 .50
AP17 Eric Chavez .20 .50
AP18 Frank Thomas .50 1.25
AP19 Garrett Atkins .20 .50
AP20 Gary Sheffield .20 .50
AP21 Hideki Matsui .50 1.25
AP22 J.D. Drew .20 .50
AP23 Jason Bay .30 .75
AP24 Jason Giambi .20 .50
AP25 Jeff Francoeur .50 1.25
AP26 Jermaine Dye .20 .50
AP27 Jim Thome .30 .75
AP28 Justin Morneau .30 .75
AP29 Ken Griffey Jr. 1.00 2.50
AP30 Lance Berkman .30 .75
AP31 Magglio Ordonez .30 .75
AP32 Manny Ramirez .50 1.25
AP33 Mark Teixeira .30 .75
AP34 Matt Holliday .50 1.25
AP35 Miguel Cabrera .50 1.25
AP36 Miguel Tejada .30 .75
AP37 Mike Piazza .50 1.25
AP38 Nick Swisher .30 .75
AP39 Pat Burrell .20 .50
AP40 Paul Konerko .30 .75
AP41 Prince Fielder .30 .75
AP42 Richie Sexson .20 .50
AP43 Ryan Howard .40 1.00
AP44 Sammy Sosa .50 1.25
AP45 Todd Helton .30 .75
AP46 Travis Hafner .20 .50
AP47 Troy Glaus .20 .50
AP48 Vernon Wells .20 .50
AP49 Victor Martinez .30 .75
AP50 Vladimir Guerrero .30 .75

2007 SP Authentic Authentic Speed

COMPLETE SET (50) 8.00 20.00
STATED ODDS 1:2
AS1 Alex Rios .20 .50
AS2 Alex Rodriguez .60 1.50
AS3 Alfonso Soriano .30 .75
AS4 B.J. Upton .20 .50
AS5 Bobby Abreu .20 .50
AS6 Brandon Phillips .20 .50
AS7 Brian Roberts .20 .50
AS8 Carl Crawford .30 .75
AS9 Carlos Beltran .30 .75
AS10 Chase Utley .30 .75
AS11 Chone Figgins .20 .50
AS12 Chris Burke .20 .50
AS13 Chris Duffy .20 .50
AS14 Coco Crisp .20 .50
AS15 Corey Patterson .20 .50
AS16 Dave Roberts .30 .75
AS17 David Wright .40 1.00
AS18 Derek Jeter 1.25 3.00
AS19 Edgar Renteria .20 .50
AS20 Eric Byrnes .20 .50
AS21 Felipe Lopez .20 .50
AS22 Gary Matthews .20 .50
AS23 Grady Sizemore .30 .75
AS24 Hanley Ramirez .30 .75
AS25 Ian Kinsler .30 .75
AS26 Ichiro Suzuki .60 1.50
AS27 Jacque Jones .20 .50
AS28 Jimmy Rollins .30 .75
AS29 Johnny Damon .30 .75
AS30 Jose Reyes .30 .75
AS31 Juan Pierre .20 .50
AS32 Julio Lugo .20 .50
AS33 Kenny Lofton .20 .50
AS34 Luis Castillo .20 .50
AS35 Marcus Giles .20 .50
AS36 Melky Cabrera .20 .50
AS37 Mike Cameron .20 .50
AS38 Orlando Cabrera .20 .50
AS39 Rafael Furcal .20 .50
AS40 Randy Winn .20 .50
AS41 Rickie Weeks .20 .50
AS42 Rocco Baldelli .20 .50
AS43 Ryan Freel .20 .50
AS44 Ryan Theriot .20 .50
AS45 Scott Podsednik .20 .50
AS46 Shane Victorino .20 .50
AS47 Tadahito Iguchi .20 .50
AS48 Torii Hunter .20 .50
AS49 Vernon Wells .20 .50
AS50 Willy Taveras .20 .50

2007 SP Authentic Chirography Dual

RANDOM INSERTS IN PACKS
PRINT RUNS B/WN 75-175 COPIES PER
EXCHANGE DEADLINE 11/05/2008
CG Chavez/Gordon/75 EXCH 8.00 20.00
CL Lincecum/Cain/175 40.00 80.00
HD Dunn/Hafner/75 8.00 20.00
HW Haren/Jer.Weaver/175 10.00 25.00
MI Matsuzaka/Iwamura/75 100.00 200.00
ML A.Miller/Lincecum/175 15.00 40.00
MZ Markakis/Zimmerman/75 10.00 25.00
RJ Ripken Jr./Jeter/75 EXCH 200.00 300.00
VH Hernandez/Verland/175 EXCH 50.00 100.00

2007 SP Authentic Sign of the Times Dual

RANDOM INSERTS IN PACKS
PRINT RUNS B/WN 75-175 COPIES PER
EXCHANGE DEADLINE 11/05/2008
BP Beckett/Papelbon/75 10.00 25.00
CJ Clemens/Jeter/75 150.00 400.00
CL Cain/Lincecum/175 75.00 150.00
CW Willis/Cabrera/75 20.00 50.00
FL Furcal/LaRoche/175 6.00 15.00
TK Teixeira/Kinsler/75 12.00 30.00
VM Verlander/Miller/75 12.00 30.00

2008 SP Authentic

COMP.SET w/o RCs (100) 8.00 20.00
COMMON CARD .15 .40
COMMON AU RC (101-191) 3.00 8.00
AU PRINT RUNS 149-999 PER
OVERALL AU ODDS 1:8 HOBBY
COMMON JSY AU RC (101-191) 4.00 10.00
JSY AU PRINT RUN 299-999 PER
OVERALL AU ODDS 1:8 HOBBY
EXCH DEADLINE 9/18/2010
1 Ken Griffey Jr. .75 2.00
2 Derek Jeter 1.00 2.50
3 Albert Pujols .50 1.25
4 Ichiro Suzuki .50 1.25
5 Daisuke Matsuzaka .25 .60
6 Vladimir Guerrero .25 .60
7 Magglio Ordonez .25 .60
8 Eric Chavez .15 .40
9 Randy Johnson .40 1.00
10 Ryan Braun .25 .60
11 Phil Hughes .15 .40
12 Joba Chamberlain .15 .40
13 B.J. Upton .25 .60
14 Frank Thomas .40 1.00
15 Greg Maddux .50 1.25
16 Delmon Young .25 .60
17 Carlos Beltran .25 .60
18 Derrek Lee .15 .40
19 Aramis Ramirez .15 .40
20 Miguel Tejada .25 .60
21 Manny Ramirez .40 1.00

22 Justin Upton .25 .60
23 Miguel Cabrera .40 1.00
24 Prince Fielder .25 .60
25 Adam Dunn .25 .60
26 Jose Reyes .25 .60
27 Chase Utley .25 .60
28 Jimmy Rollins .25 .60
29 Joe Blanton .15 .40
30 Mark Teixeira .25 .60
31 Brian McCann .25 .60
32 Russell Martin .15 .40
33 Ian Kinsler .25 .60
34 Travis Hafner .15 .40
35 Victor Martinez .25 .60
36 Grady Sizemore .25 .60
37 Alex Rodriguez .50 1.25
38 David Wright .25 .60
39 Ryan Howard .25 .60
40 Carlos Lee .15 .40
41 Lance Berkman .25 .60
42 Hunter Pence .25 .60
43 John Lackey .25 .60
44 C.C. Sabathia .25 .60
45 Michael Young .15 .40
46 Carl Crawford .25 .60
47 Carlos Pena .25 .60
48 Justin Verlander .40 1.00
49 Cole Hamels .30 .75
50 Carlos Zambrano .25 .60
51 Jake Peavy .15 .40
52 Khalil Greene .15 .40
53 Chris Young .15 .40
54 Vernon Wells .15 .40
55 Alex Rios .15 .40
56 Roy Halladay .25 .60
57 Roy Oswalt .25 .60
58 Ben Sheets .15 .40
59 J.J. Hardy .15 .40
60 Pedro Martinez .25 .60
61 Nick Swisher .25 .60
62 Curtis Granderson .25 .60
63 Johnny Damon .25 .60
64 Mariano Rivera .50 1.25
65 Josh Beckett .15 .40
66 Erik Bedard .15 .40
67 Johan Santana .25 .60
68 Joe Mauer .30 .75
69 Justin Morneau .25 .60
70 Torii Hunter .15 .40
71 Alex Gordon .25 .60
72 Jose Guillen .15 .40
73 Jim Thome .25 .60
74 Paul Konerko .25 .60
75 Josh Hamilton .25 .60
76 Hanley Ramirez .25 .60
77 Dontrelle Willis .15 .40
78 Dan Uggla .15 .40
79 Brandon Phillips .15 .40
80 Rick Ankiel .15 .40
81 Nick Markakis .30 .75
82 Ryan Zimmerman .25 .60
83 Brian Roberts .15 .40
84 Lastings Milledge .15 .40
85 Freddy Sanchez .15 .40
86 Barry Zito .25 .60
87 Matt Cain .25 .60
88 Andruw Jones .15 .40
89 Dan Haren .15 .40
90 Chien-Ming Wang .25 .60
91 Jonathan Papelbon .25 .60
92 Felix Hernandez .25 .60
93 David Ortiz .40 1.00
94 Jason Bay .25 .60
95 Matt Holliday .40 1.00
96 Troy Tulowitzki .40 1.00
97 Hideki Matsui .40 1.00
98 Jeff Francoeur .25 .60
99 Alfonso Soriano .25 .60
100 Curt Schilling .25 .60
101 Alex Romero Jsy AU/799 (RC) 4.00 10.00
102 Matt Tolbert Jsy/699 RC 5.00 12.00
103 Bobby Wilson AU/699 RC 6.00 15.00
104 B.Lillibridge AU/599 (RC) 5.00 12.00
105 Brian Barton AU/698 RC 6.00 15.00
106 B.Bass Jsy AU/799 (RC) 4.00 10.00
107 Brian Bixler AU/698 (RC) 3.00 8.00
108 Brian Bocock Jsy AU/599 RC 4.00 10.00
109 B.Badenhop AU/797 RC 3.00 8.00
110 C.Hu Jsy AU/999 (RC) 4.00 10.00
111 Chris Perez AU/699 RC 3.00 8.00
112 Buchholz Jsy AU/999 (RC) 5.00 12.00
114 Colt Morton Jsy AU/574 RC 4.00 10.00
115 Daric Barton Jsy AU/799 (RC) 4.00 10.00
116 Darren O'Day AU/798 RC 3.00 8.00
117 David Purcey AU/599 (RC) 3.00 8.00
118 D.Span Jsy AU/299 (RC) EXCH 8.00 20.00
119 E.Johnson AU/798 (RC) 3.00 8.00
120 E.Burriss AU/299 RC EXCH 4.00 10.00
121 E.Longoria Jsy AU/499 RC 15.00 40.00
122 Evan Meek Jsy AU/649 RC 5.00 12.00
123 Felipe Paulino Jsy AU/799 RC 4.00 10.00
125 German Duran AU/699 RC 3.00 8.00
126 Greg Reynolds AU/149 RC 3.00 8.00
127 Greg Smith Jsy AU/799 RC 5.00 12.00
128 Harvey Garcia Jsy AU/799 (RC) 4.00 10.00
129 Hernan Iribarren Jsy AU/799 (RC) 4.00 10.00
130 I.Kennedy Jsy AU/699 RC 6.00 15.00
131 J.R. Towles Jsy AU/499 RC 4.00 10.00
132 Jay Bruce Jsy AU/549 (RC) 4.00 10.00
133 Jayson Nix Jsy AU/299 (RC) EXCH 4.00 10.00
134 Jed Lowrie AU/499 (RC) 10.00 25.00
135 Jeff Clement AU/399 (RC) 4.00 10.00
136 Jonathan Herrera AU/699 RC 3.00 8.00
137 Joey Votto Jsy AU/999 (RC) 40.00 100.00
138 J.Cueto Jsy AU/999 RC 4.00 10.00
139 Jonathan Albaladejo Jsy AU/799 RC 4.00 10.00
140 J.Masterson AU/699 RC 6.00 15.00
141 J.Ruggiano AU/149 RC 3.00 8.00
142 Kevin Hart Jsy AU/749 (RC) 4.00 10.00
143 K.Fukudome Jsy/799 RC 6.00 15.00
144 Luis Mendoza Jsy AU/299 (RC) 4.00 10.00
145 Luke Carlin AU/699 RC 6.00 15.00
146 L.Hochevar AU/798 RC 4.00 10.00
148 M.Hoffpauir AU/699 RC 8.00 20.00
149 Mike Parisi AU/699 RC 8.00 20.00
150 N.Adenhart AU/599 (RC) 10.00 25.00
151 Blackburn Jsy AU/799 RC 8.00 20.00
152 Nyjer Morgan Jsy AU/999 (RC) 4.00 10.00
153 Troncoso Jsy AU/399 RC 5.00 12.00
154 Randor Bierd Jsy AU/799 RC 4.00 10.00
155 R.Thompson AU/398 RC 5.00 12.00
156 Washington Jsy AU/799 (RC) 4.00 10.00
157 Ross Ohlendorf Jsy AU/999 RC 4.00 10.00
158 Steve Holm Jsy AU/999 RC 4.00 10.00
159 Wesley Wright Jsy AU/849 RC 4.00 10.00
160 Wladimir Balentien AU/599 (RC) 3.00 8.00
161 Alex Hinshaw AU/699 RC EXCH 5.00 12.00
162 Bobby Korecky AU/999 RC 3.00 8.00
163 Brad Harman AU/999 RC 5.00 12.00
164 Brandon Boggs AU/999 (RC) 3.00 8.00
165 Callix Crabbe AU/325 (RC) 3.00 8.00
166 Clay Timpner AU/849 (RC) 3.00 8.00
167 Clete Thomas AU/850 RC 3.00 8.00
168 Cory Wade AU/999 (RC) 3.00 8.00
169 Doug Mathis AU/999 RC 3.00 8.00
170 Eider Torres AU/999 (RC) 5.00 12.00
171 Gregorio Petit AU/999 RC 4.00 10.00
172 M.Aubrey AU/699 RC EXCH 4.00 10.00
173 Jesse Carlson AU/999 RC 8.00 20.00
174 Billy Buckner AU/999 (RC) 3.00 8.00
175 Josh Newman AU/699 RC 3.00 8.00
176 Matt Tupman AU/999 RC 5.00 12.00
177 Matt Joyce AU/999 RC 6.00 15.00
178 Paul Janish AU/999 (RC) 5.00 12.00
179 Robinzon Diaz AU/999 (RC) 3.00 8.00
180 Fernando Hernandez AU/999 RC 3.00 8.00
181 Brandon Jones AU/999 RC 3.00 8.00
182 Eddie Bonine AU/899 RC 3.00 8.00
183 Chris Smith AU/384 (RC) 6.00 15.00
184 J.Van Every AU/999 RC 4.00 10.00
185 Marino Salas AU/999 RC 4.00 10.00
186 Mike Aviles AU/899 RC 6.00 15.00
187 M.Boggs AU/699 (RC) EXCH 6.00 15.00
188 C.Carter AU/699 (RC) EXCH 5.00 12.00
189 Travis Denker AU/699 RC EXCH 3.00 8.00
190 Carlos Rosa AU/699 RC 5.00 12.00
191 E.Longoria AU/350 (RC) 6.00 15.00

2008 SP Authentic Gold

*GOLD 1-100: 5X TO 12X BASIC
*GLD AU RC: .75X TO 2X BASIC
*GLD JSY AU RC: .75X TO 2X BASIC
RANDOM INSERTS IN PACKS
PRINT RUN B/WN 10-50 SER.#'d SETS
NO VOTTO PRICING AVAILABLE
EXCH DEADLINE 9/18/2010
4 Ichiro Suzuki 20.00 50.00
121 Evan Longoria Jsy AU/50 40.00 100.00
191 Evan Longoria AU/50 75.00 150.00

2008 SP Authentic Authentic Achievements

STATED ODDS 1:2 HOBBY
AA1 Derek Jeter 2.00 5.00
AA2 Ken Griffey Jr. 1.50 4.00
AA3 Randy Johnson .75 2.00
AA4 Frank Thomas .75 2.00
AA5 Tom Glavine .50 1.25
AA6 Matt Holliday .75 2.00
AA7 Justin Verlander .75 2.00
AA8 Manny Ramirez .75 2.00
AA9 Scott Rolen .50 1.25
AA10 Brandon Webb .50 1.25
AA11 Erik Bedard .30 .75
AA12 Daisuke Matsuzaka .50 1.25
AA13 Johan Santana .50 1.25
AA14 Carlos Lee .30 .75
AA15 Alfonso Soriano .50 1.25
AA16 Grady Sizemore .50 1.25
AA17 Jose Reyes .50 1.25
AA18 Chase Utley .50 1.25
AA19 Roy Oswalt .50 1.25
AA20 David Ortiz .75 2.00
AA21 Jake Peavy .30 .75
AA22 Hanley Ramirez .50 1.25
AA23 Alex Rodriguez 1.00 2.50
AA24 Ryan Howard .50 1.25
AA25 David Wright .50 1.25
AA26 Trevor Hoffman .50 1.25
AA27 Prince Fielder .50 1.25
AA28 Ichiro Suzuki 1.00 2.50
AA29 Jimmy Rollins .50 1.25
AA30 Mariano Rivera 1.00 2.50
AA31 Pedro Martinez .50 1.25
AA32 Torii Hunter .30 .75
AA33 Ivan Rodriguez .50 1.25
AA34 Jim Thome .50 1.25
AA35 Chipper Jones .75 2.00
AA36 John Smoltz .75 2.00
AA37 Jeff Kent .30 .75
AA38 Albert Pujols 1.00 2.50
AA39 Lance Berkman .50 1.25
AA40 Justin Morneau .50 1.25
AA41 Andruw Jones .30 .75
AA42 Adam Dunn .50 1.25
AA43 Greg Maddux 1.00 2.50
AA44 Billy Wagner .30 .75
AA45 Vladimir Guerrero .50 1.25
AA46 C.C. Sabathia .50 1.25
AA47 Mark Teixeira .50 1.25
AA48 Mark Buehrle .50 1.25
AA49 Miguel Cabrera .75 2.00
AA50 Josh Beckett .30 .75

2008 SP Authentic By The Letter Autographs

OVERALL AU ODDS 1:8 HOBBY
ANNCD PRINT RUNS LISTED
SER.# ON CARDS ARE DIFFERENT
EXCH DEADLINE 9/18/2010
AD Adam Dunn/140 * 10.00 25.00
AG Adrian Gonzalez/110 * 4.00 10.00
BH Bill Hall/1570 * 8.00 20.00
BP Brandon Phillips/1259 * 8.00 20.00
BW Billy Wagner/125 * 20.00 50.00
CB Chad Billingsley/1306 * 5.00 12.00
CJ Chipper Jones/100 * 50.00 100.00
CL Carlos Lee/160 * 10.00 25.00
CW Chien-Ming Wang/80 * 40.00 80.00
DA David Murphy/1837 * 10.00 25.00
DJ Derek Jeter/240 * EXCH 125.00 250.00
DM Daisuke Matsuzaka/125 * 30.00 60.00
EE Edwin Encarnacion/1570 * 5.00 12.00
FC Fausto Carmona/844 * 8.00 20.00
GA Garrett Atkins/588 * 8.00 20.00
GJ Geoff Jenkins/1200 * 5.00 12.00
GS Grady Sizemore/240 * 12.00 30.00
JB Joe Blanton/580 * 6.00 15.00
JE Jeff Francoeur/275 * 12.00 30.00
JF Jeff Francis/335 * 12.00 30.00
JG Jeremy Guthrie/985 * 6.00 15.00
JH Jeremy Hermida/505 * 5.00 12.00
JL James Loney/1275 * EXCH 6.00 15.00
JN Joe Nathan/365 * 5.00 12.00
JO John Lackey/187 * 12.00 30.00
JP Jonathan Papelbon/550 * 4.00 10.00
JS Jon Lester/235 * 40.00 80.00
KE Kevin Youkilis/365 * 15.00 40.00
KG Ken Griffey Jr./275 * EXCH 100.00 175.00
KJ Kelly Johnson/1399 * 5.00 12.00
LB Lance Berkman/165 * 15.00 40.00
ME Mark Ellis/995 * 5.00 12.00
MG Matt Garza/235 * 8.00 20.00
MK Matt Kemp/1369 * 12.00 30.00
MM Melvin Mora/490 * EXCH 8.00 20.00
NL Noah Lowry/1440 * 5.00 12.00
NS Nick Swisher/1150 * 6.00 15.00
PF Prince Fielder/245 * 6.00 15.00
PH Phil Hughes/385 * 8.00 20.00
PK Paul Konerko/175 * 15.00 40.00
RH Rich Hill/220 * 6.00 15.00
RM Russell Martin/265 * 8.00 20.00
RO Roy Halladay/160 * 30.00 60.00
SB Scott Baker/1248 * 6.00 15.00
TG Tom Gorzelanny/1082 * 5.00 12.00
TT Troy Tulowitzki/252 * 10.00 25.00

2008 SP Authentic Chirography Signatures Dual

OVERALL AU ODDS 1:8 HOBBY
PRINT RUNS B/WN 10-99 COPIES PER
NO PRICING ON MOST CARDS
EXCH DEADLINE 9/18/2010
GB T.Gorzelanny/C.Billingsley/96 12.50 30.00
HK P.Hughes/I.Kennedy/99 EXCH 10.00 25.00
MH D.Murphy/J.Hamilton/99 6.00 15.00
MK Nick Markakis 25.00 60.00
Matt Kemp/99
PE B.Phillips/E.Encarnacion/99 5.00 12.00

2008 SP Authentic Marquee Matchups

STATED ODDS 1:2 HOBBY
MM1 D.Jeter/C.Schilling 2.00 5.00
MM2 J.Beckett/D.Jeter 2.00 5.00
MM3 A.Pujols/B.Lidge 1.00 2.50
MM4 D.Matsuzaka/A.Rodriguez 1.00 2.50
MM5 K.Griffey Jr./J.Smoltz 1.50 4.00
MM6 J.Smoltz/D.Wright .75 2.00
MM7 Jonathan Papelbon/Gary Sheffield .50 1.25
MM8 R.Braun/R.Oswalt .50 1.25
MM9 Mariano Rivera/David Ortiz 1.00 2.50
MM10 C.Zambrano/A.Pujols 1.00 2.50
MM11 Dontrelle Willis/Travis Hafner .30 .75
MM12 Felix Hernandez/Victor Martinez .50 1.25
MM13 Carlos Zambrano/Carlos Lee .50 1.25
MM14 C.Wang/M.Ramirez .75 2.00
MM15 Felix Hernandez/Justin Morneau .50 1.25
MM16 I.Suzuki/F.Rodriguez 1.00 2.50
MM17 Grady Sizemore/Erik Bedard .50 1.25
MM18 V.Guerrero/J.Verlander .75 2.00
MM19 D.Matsuzaka/I.Suzuki 1.00 2.50
MM20 Alfonso Soriano/Chris Carpenter .50 1.25
MM21 Hanley Ramirez/Pedro Martinez .50 1.25
MM22 Chase Utley/Randy Johnson .75 2.00
MM23 K.Griffey Jr./R.Oswalt 1.50 4.00
MM24 R.Johnson/K.Griffey Jr. 1.50 4.00
MM25 Jimmy Rollins/Johan Santana .50 1.25
MM26 Matt Cain/Andruw Jones .50 1.25
MM27 P.Martinez/R.Howard .50 1.25
MM28 C.Hamels/D.Wright .60 1.50
MM29 C.Jones/J.Santana .75 2.00
MM30 Billy Wagner/Mark Teixeira .50 1.25
MM31 C.C. Sabathia/Magglio Ordonez .50 1.25
MM32 Jose Reyes/Tom Glavine .50 1.25
MM33 D.Jeter/J.Papelbon 2.00 5.00
MM34 J.Santana/A.Rodriguez 1.00 2.50
MM35 Alfonso Soriano/Jake Peavy .50 1.25
MM36 J.Santana/R.Howard .50 1.25
MM37 Jake Peavy/Russell Martin .30 .75
MM38 Carlos Zambrano/Prince Fielder .50 1.25
MM39 Cole Hamels/Carlos Beltran .60 1.50
MM40 J.Beckett/A.Rodriguez 1.00 2.50
MM41 R.Halladay/D.Jeter 2.00 5.00
MM42 H.Matsui/D.Matsuzaka .75 2.00
MM43 C.C. Sabathia/Joe Mauer .60 1.50
MM44 Francisco Rodriguez
Manny Ramirez .75 2.00
MM45 J.Weaver/M.Cabrera .75 2.00
MM46 D.Wright/J.Peavy .50 1.25
MM47 G.Maddux/K.Griffey Jr. 1.50 4.00
MM48 John Smoltz/Hanley Ramirez .75 2.00
MM49 P.Martinez/A.Rodriguez 1.00 2.50
MM50 Trevor Hoffman/Matt Holliday .75 2.00

2008 SP Authentic Rookie Exclusives

RANDOM INSERTS IN PACKS
AH Alex Hinshaw 1.25 3.00
AR Alex Romero 1.25 3.00
BA Brian Barton 1.25 3.00
BB Brandon Boggs 1.25 3.00
BH Brad Harman 1.25 3.00
BI Brian Bixler .75 2.00
BK Bobby Korecky .75 2.00
BO Brian Bocock .75 2.00
BR Brian Bass .75 2.00
BU Burke Badenhop 1.25 3.00
BW Bobby Wilson .75 2.00
CB Clay Buchholz 1.25 3.00
CC Callix Crabbe .75 2.00
CM Colt Morton 1.25 3.00
CT Clay Timpner .75 2.00
CU Johnny Cueto 2.00 5.00
CW Cory Wade .75 2.00
DB Daric Barton .75 2.00
DM Doug Mathis .75 2.00
DS Denard Span 1.25 3.00
EB Emmanuel Burriss 1.25 3.00
EJ Elliot Johnson .75 2.00
EM Evan Meek .75 2.00
ET Eider Torres 1.25 3.00
FH Fernando Hernandez .75 2.00
FP Felipe Paulino 1.25 3.00
GD German Duran 1.25 3.00
GP Gregorio Petit 1.25 3.00
GS Greg Smith .75 2.00
HI Hernan Iribarren 1.25 3.00
IK Ian Kennedy 2.00 5.00
JA Jonathan Albaladejo 1.25 3.00
JB Jay Bruce 2.50 6.00
JC Jesse Carlson 1.25 3.00
JH Jonathan Herrera 1.25 3.00
JL Jed Lowrie .75 2.00
JN Jayson Nix .75 2.00
JT J.R. Towles 1.25 3.00
KH Kevin Hart .75 2.00
LC Luke Carlin .75 2.00
LM Luis Mendoza .75 2.00
MA Matt Tolbert 1.25 3.00
MH Micah Hoffpauir 2.50 6.00
MJ Matt Joyce 2.00 5.00
MP Mike Parisi 1.25 3.00
MT Matt Tupman .75 2.00
NA Nick Adenhart .75 2.00
NB Nick Blackburn 1.25 3.00
NE Josh Newman 1.25 3.00
NM Nyjer Morgan .75 2.00
RA Alexei Ramirez 2.50 6.00
RB Randor Bierd .75 2.00
RD Robinzon Diaz .75 2.00
RI Rich Thompson 1.25 3.00
RO Ross Ohlendorf 1.25 3.00
RT Ramon Troncoso .75 2.00
RW Rico Washington .75 2.00
SH Steve Holm .75 2.00
TH Clete Thomas 1.25 3.00
WB Wladimir Balentien .75 2.00
WW Wesley Wright .75 2.00

2008 SP Authentic Sign of the Times Dual

OVERALL AU ODDS 1:8 HOBBY
PRINT RUNS B/WN 10-99 COPIES PER
MOST CARDS NOT PRICED
EXCH DEADLINE 9/18/2010
NW J.Nathan/B.Wagner/74 10.00 25.00
PW F.Pie/J.Willingham/99 6.00 15.00

2008 SP Authentic Sign of the Times Triple

OVERALL AU ODDS 1:8 HOBBY
PRINT RUNS B/WN 10-50 COPIES PER
NO PRICING ON QTY 14 OR LESS
EXCH DEADLINE 9/18/2010
HGK Jeremy Hermida/Carlos Gomez/Matt Kemp/50
10.00 25.00

2008 SP Authentic USA Junior National Team Jersey Autographs

OVERALL AU ODDS 1:8 HOBBY
STATED PRINT RUN 120 SER.#'d SETS
AA Andrew Aplin 10.00 25.00
AM Austin Maddox 5.00 12.00
CC Colton Cain 5.00 12.00
CG Cameron Garfield 12.50 30.00
CT Cecil Tanner 4.00 10.00
DN David Nick 4.00 10.00
DT Donovan Tate 10.00 25.00
FR Nick Franklin 5.00 12.00
HM Harold Martinez 10.00 25.00
JB Jake Barrett 6.00 15.00
MA Jeff Malm 6.00 15.00
ME Jonathan Meyer 8.00 20.00
MP Matthew Purke 8.00 20.00
MS Max Stassi 4.00 10.00
NF Nolan Fontana 5.00 12.00
TU Jacob Turner 6.00 15.00
WH Wes Hatton 10.00 25.00

2008 SP Authentic USA Junior National Team Patch Autographs

OVERALL AU ODDS 1:8 HOBBY
STATED PRINT RUN 50 SER.#'d SETS
AA Andrew Aplin 10.00 25.00
CC Colton Cain 10.00 25.00
DN David Nick 6.00 15.00
JB Jake Barrett 6.00 15.00
MS Max Stassi 10.00 25.00
NF Nolan Fontana 12.50 30.00
RW Ryan Weber 12.50 30.00
TU Jacob Turner 25.00 60.00
WH Wes Hatton 15.00 40.00

2008 SP Authentic USA National Team By the Letter Autographs

OVERALL AU ODDS 1:8 HOBBY
PRINT RUNS BW/N 50-181 PER
AG A.J. Griffin/105 4.00 10.00
AO Andrew Oliver/105 4.00 10.00
BS Blake Smith/105 4.00 10.00
CC Christian Colon/105 4.00 10.00
CH Chris Hernandez/180 4.00 10.00
DD Derek Dietrich/105 10.00 25.00
HM Hunter Morris/106 12.00 30.00
KD Kentrail Davis/103 12.00 30.00
KG Kyle Gibson/181 30.00 60.00
KR Kevin Rhoderick/172 4.00 10.00
KV Kendal Volz/105 4.00 10.00
MD Matt den Dekker/105 4.00 10.00
MG Micah Gibbs/180 4.00 10.00
ML Mike Leake/180 4.00 10.00
MM Mike Minor/105 4.00 10.00
RJ Ryan Jackson/104 4.00 10.00
SS Stephen Strasburg/105 25.00 60.00
TL Tyler Lyons/104 4.00 10.00

2009 SP Authentic

COMP.SET w/o AU's (200) 50.00 100.00
COMP.SET w/o SPs (100) 12.50 30.00
COMMON CARD (1-128) .15 .40
COMMON RC (129-170) 1.00 2.50
COMMON SP (171-200) .50 1.25
171-200 APPX.ODDS 1:8 HOBBY
COMMON SP (201-225) .60 1.50
201-225 RANDOMLY INSERTED
201-225 PRINT RUN 495 SER.#'d SETS
COMMON AUTO (226-250) 3.00 8.00
OVERALL AUTO ODDS 1:8 HOBBY
AUTO PRINT RUN B/WN 100-500 PER
1 Kosuke Fukudome .25 .60
2 Derek Jeter 1.00 2.50
3 Evan Longoria .25 .60
4 Yadier Molina .50 1.25
5 Albert Pujols .50 1.25
6 Ryan Howard .30 .75
7 Joe Mauer .30 .75
8 Ryan Braun .25 .60
9 Hunter Pence .25 .60
10 Gary Sheffield .15 .40
11 Ryan Zimmerman .25 .60
12 Alfonso Soriano .25 .60
13 Alex Rodriguez .50 1.25
14 Paul Konerko .25 .60
15 Dustin Pedroia .40 1.00
16 Brian McCann .25 .60
17 Lance Berkman .25 .60
18 Daisuke Matsuzaka .25 .60
19 Josh Beckett .15 .40
20 Carlos Quentin .15 .40
21 Carlos Delgado .15 .40
22 Clayton Kershaw .60 1.50
23 Zack Greinke .40 1.00
24 Ken Griffey Jr. .75 2.00
25 Mark Teixeira .25 .60
26 Chase Utley .25 .60
27 Vladimir Guerrero .25 .60
28 Prince Fielder .25 .60
29 Adrian Beltre .40 1.00
30 Magglio Ordonez .25 .60
31 Jon Lester .25 .60
32 Josh Hamilton .25 .60
33 Justin Morneau .25 .60
34 Felix Hernandez .25 .60
35 Cole Hamels .30 .75
36 Edinson Volquez .15 .40
37 Hideki Okajima .15 .40
38 Carlos Zambrano .25 .60
39 Aaron Harang .15 .40
40 Chien-Ming Wang .25 .60
41 Shin-Soo Choo .25 .60
42 Mariano Rivera .50 1.25
43 Josh Johnson .25 .60
44 Roy Oswalt .25 .60
45 Carlos Lee .15 .40
46 Ryan Dempster .15 .40
47 Ryan Ludwick .25 .60
48 Joakim Soria .15 .40
49 Jair Jurrjens .15 .40
50 John Danks .15 .40
51 Ichiro Suzuki .50 1.25
52 CC Sabathia .25 .60
53 Yovani Gallardo .15 .40
54 Ervin Santana .15 .40
55 Tim Lincecum .25 .60
56 Mark Buehrle .25 .60
57 Johan Santana .25 .60
58 Chad Billingsley .25 .60
59 Francisco Liriano .15 .40
60 Joey Votto .40 1.00
61 Matt Kemp .30 .75
62 Joba Chamberlain .15 .40
63 Hiroki Kuroda .15 .40
64 Brian Roberts .15 .40
65 Randy Johnson .40 1.00
66 Jay Bruce .25 .60
67 Curtis Granderson .30 .75
68 Hideki Matsui .40 1.00
69 Todd Helton .25 .60
70 Nick Markakis .30 .75
71 Andy Pettitte .25 .60
72 Ian Kinsler .25 .60
73 Brandon Inge .15 .40
74 Adrian Gonzalez .30 .75
75 Francisco Rodriguez .25 .60
76 Derek Lowe .15 .40
77 Carlos Beltran .25 .60
78 Matt Holliday .40 1.00
79 Jake Peavy .15 .40
80 Scott Kazmir .15 .40
81 David Ortiz .40 1.00
82 Dan Haren .15 .40
83 Hanley Ramirez .25 .60
84 Jim Thome .25 .60
85 Brad Hawpe .15 .40
86 Vernon Wells .15 .40
87 B.J. Upton .25 .60
88 James Shields .15 .40
89 Jason Giambi .15 .40
90 Adam Dunn .25 .60
91 Brandon Webb .25 .60
92 Roy Halladay .25 .60
93 Miguel Cabrera .40 1.00
94 Jose Reyes .25 .60
95 Chipper Jones .40 1.00
96 Grady Sizemore .25 .60
97 Jason Varitek .40 1.00
98 David Wright .30 .75
99 Manny Ramirez .40 1.00
100 Kevin Youkilis .15 .40
101 Bengie Molina .15 .40
102 Ivan Rodriguez .25 .60
103 Andruw Jones .15 .40
104 Jorge Cantu .15 .40
105 Corey Hart .15 .40
106 Adam Wainwright .25 .60
107 Raul Ibanez .25 .60
108 Jason Bay .25 .60
109 Chris Volstad .15 .40
110 Jermaine Dye .15 .40
111 Torii Hunter .15 .40
112 Brad Ziegler .15 .40
113 Carl Crawford .25 .60
114 Troy Tulowitzki .40 1.00
115 Aramis Ramirez .15 .40
116 Nomar Garciaparra .25 .60
117 Pedro Martinez .25 .60
118 Ryan Theriot .15 .40
119 Matt Cain .25 .60
120 Carlos Pena .25 .60
121 Nick Swisher .25 .60
122 Javier Vazquez .15 .40
123 John Lackey .25 .60
124 Jack Cust .15 .40
125 Justin Upton .25 .60
126 Michael Young .15 .40
127 Jeff Samardzija .25 .60
128 John Smoltz .40 1.00
129 Josh Reddick RC 1.50 4.00
130 Chris Tillman RC 1.50 4.00
131 Aaron Cunningham RC 1.00 2.50
132 Andrew McCutchen (RC) 5.00 12.00
133 Anthony Ortega RC 1.00 2.50
134 Anthony Swarzak (RC) 1.00 2.50
135 Antonio Bastardo RC 1.00 2.50
136 Brad Bergesen (RC) 1.00 2.50
137 Brett Cecil RC 1.00 2.50
138 Neftali Feliz RC 1.50 4.00
139 Chris Coghlan RC 2.50 6.00
140 Daniel Bard RC 1.00 2.50
141 Daniel Schlereth RC 1.00 2.50
142 Donald Veal RC 1.50 4.00
143 Brad Mills RC 1.00 2.50
144 David Huff RC 1.00 2.50
145 Elvis Andrus RC 2.50 6.00
146 Everth Cabrera RC 1.50 4.00
147 Mat Latos RC 3.00 8.00
148 Shairon Martis RC 1.50 4.00
149 Jess Todd RC 1.00 2.50
150 Jonathon Niese RC 1.50 4.00
151 Jose Mijares RC 2.50 6.00
152 Jhoulys Chacin RC 1.50 4.00
153 Kyle Blanks RC 1.50 4.00
154 Kris Medlen RC 2.50 6.00
155 Fu-Te Ni RC 1.50 4.00
156 Bud Norris RC 1.00 2.50
157 Julio Borbon RC 1.00 2.50
158 Mat Gamel RC 2.50 6.00
159 Matt LaPorta RC 1.50 4.00
160 Michael Bowden (RC) 1.00 2.50
161 Michael Saunders RC 2.50 6.00
162 Ricky Romero (RC) 1.50 4.00
163 Marc Rzepczynski RC 1.50 4.00
164 Ryan Perry RC 2.50 6.00
165 Sean O'Sullivan RC 1.00 2.50
166 Sean West (RC) 1.50 4.00
167 Trevor Cahill RC 2.50 6.00
168 Mike Carp (RC) 1.50 4.00
169 Vin Mazzaro RC 1.00 2.50
170 Wilkin Ramirez RC 1.00 2.50
171 Albert Pujols FG SP 1.50 4.00
172 Alfonso Soriano FG SP .75 2.00
173 Brandon Webb FG SP .75 2.00
174 Carlos Quentin FG SP .50 1.25
175 Carlos Zambrano FG SP .75 2.00
176 CC Sabathia FG SP .75 2.00
177 Chase Utley FG SP .75 2.00
178 Chipper Jones FG SP 1.25 3.00
179 Cole Hamels FG SP 1.00 2.50
180 Daisuke Matsuzaka FG SP .75 2.00
181 David Wright FG SP 1.00 2.50
182 Derek Jeter FG SP 3.00 8.00
183 Derek Lowe FG SP .50 1.25
184 Dustin Pedroia FG SP 1.25 3.00
185 Felix Hernandez FG SP .75 2.00
186 Grady Sizemore FG SP .75 2.00
187 Jason Giambi FG SP .50 1.25
188 Joba Chamberlain FG SP .50 1.25
189 Joe Mauer FG SP 1.00 2.50
190 Johan Santana FG SP .75 2.00
191 Jose Reyes FG SP .75 2.00
192 Josh Beckett FG SP .50 1.25
193 Josh Hamilton FG SP .75 2.00
194 Ken Griffey Jr. FG SP 2.50 6.00
195 Manny Ramirez FG SP 1.25 3.00
196 Prince Fielder FG SP .75 2.00
197 Randy Johnson FG SP 1.25 3.00
198 Ryan Braun FG SP .75 2.00
199 Ryan Howard FG SP 1.00 2.50
200 Tim Lincecum FG SP .75 2.00
201 A.J. Burnett FW FB .60 1.50
202 Adam Dunn FW FB 1.00 2.50
203 Alex Rodriguez FW FB 2.00 5.00
204 Alfonso Soriano FW FB 1.00 2.50
205 Andy Pettitte FW FB 1.00 2.50
206 Bobby Abreu FW FB .60 1.50
207 Carlos Beltran FW FB 1.00 2.50
208 Chipper Jones FW FB 1.50 4.00
209 Dan Haren FW FB .60 1.50
210 Derek Jeter FW FB 4.00 10.00
211 Derek Lowe FW FB .60 1.50
212 Gary Sheffield FW FB .60 1.50
213 Ivan Rodriguez FW FB 1.00 2.50
214 Jamie Moyer FW FB .60 1.50
215 Jason Giambi FW FB .60 1.50
216 Jim Thome FW FB 1.00 2.50
217 Johan Santana FW FB 1.00 2.50
218 John Smoltz FW FB 1.50 4.00
219 Johnny Damon FW FB 1.00 2.50
220 Josh Beckett FW FB .60 1.50
221 Ken Griffey Jr. FW FB 3.00 8.00
222 Manny Ramirez FW FB 1.50 4.00
223 Mark Teixeira FW FB 1.00 2.50
224 Randy Johnson FW FB 1.50 4.00
225 Tim Wakefield FW FB 1.00 2.50
226 Aaron Poreda AU/300 RC 3.00 8.00
227 B.Anderson AU/371 RC 5.00 12.00
228 M.LaPorta AU/225 5.00 12.00
229 C.Rasmus AU/300 (RC) 5.00 12.00
230 D.Price AU/222 RC 6.00 15.00
231 D.Holland AU/195 RC 5.00 12.00
232 D.Fowler AU/490 (RC) 5.00 12.00
233 F.Martinez AU/243 RC 8.00 20.00
234 G.Parra AU/299 RC 5.00 12.00
235 G.Beckham AU/136 RC 5.00 12.00
236 James McDonald AU/500 RC 8.00 20.00
237 James Parr AU/500 (RC) 3.00 8.00
238 J.Motte AU/415 (RC) 5.00 12.00
239 J.Schafer AU/475 (RC) 5.00 12.00
240 J.Zimmermann AU/417 RC 8.00 20.00
241 K.Kawakami AU/425 RC 5.00 12.00
242 K.Uehara AU/200 RC 8.00 20.00
243 Luis Perdomo AU/275 RC 3.00 8.00
244 Tuiasosopo AU/500 (RC) 3.00 8.00
245 M.Wieters AU/200 RC 10.00 25.00
246 N.Reimold AU/135 (RC) 3.00 8.00
247 P.Sandoval AU/230 (RC) 6.00 15.00
248 R.Porcello AU/225 RC 10.00 25.00
249 T.Hanson AU/198 RC 8.00 20.00
250 T.Snider AU/100 RC 5.00 12.00

2009 SP Authentic Copper

*1-128 COPPER: 2X TO 5X BASIC
1-128 PRINT RUN 99 SER.#'d SETS
*129-170 COPPER: ..6X TO 1.5X BASIC
129-170 PRINT RUN 99 SER.#'d SETS
*171-200 COPPER: .6X TO 1.5X BASIC
171-200 PRINT RUN 99 SER.#'d SETS
*201-225 COPPER: 1.2X TO 3X BASIC
1-225 RANDOMLY INSERTED IN PACKS
201-225 PRINT RUN 29 SER.#'d SETS
OVERALL AUTO ODDS 1:8 HOBBY
AU PRINT RUNS B/WN 10-50 COPIES
NO PRICING ON QTY 25 OR LESS
226 Aaron Poreda AU/50 4.00 10.00
227 Brett Anderson AU/50 6.00 15.00
228 Matt LaPorta AU/50 6.00 15.00
229 Colby Rasmus AU/50 6.00 15.00
230 David Price AU/50 8.00 20.00
231 Derek Holland AU/35 6.00 15.00
232 Dexter Fowler AU/50 6.00 15.00
233 Fernando Martinez AU/50 10.00 25.00
234 Gerardo Parra AU/50 6.00 15.00
235 Gordon Beckham AU/40 6.00 15.00
236 James McDonald AU/50 10.00 25.00
237 James Parr AU/50 4.00 10.00
238 Jason Motte AU/50 6.00 15.00
239 Jordan Schafer AU/50 6.00 15.00
240 Jordan Zimmermann AU/50 10.00 25.00
241 Kenshin Kawakami AU/50 6.00 15.00
243 Luis Perdomo AU/50 4.00 10.00
244 Matt Tuiasosopo AU/50 4.00 10.00
247 Pablo Sandoval AU/50 8.00 20.00
249 Tommy Hanson AU/35 10.00 25.00

2009 SP Authentic Gold

*1-128 GOLD: 1.5X TO 4X BASIC
1-128 PRINT RUN 299 SER.#'d SETS
*129-170 GOLD: .6X TO 1.5X BASIC
129-170 PRINT RUN 299 SER.#'d SETS
*171-200 GOLD: .5X TO 1.2X BASIC
171-200 PRINT RUN 299 SER.#'d SETS
*201-225 GOLD: .5X TO 1.2X BASIC
1-225 RANDOMLY INSERTED IN PACKS
201-225 PRINT RUN 99 SER.#'d SETS
OVERALL AUTO ODDS 1:8 HOBBY
AU PRINT RUNS B/WN 25-125 COPIES
NO PRICING ON QTY 25 OR LESS
226 Aaron Poreda AU/124 3.00 8.00
227 Brett Anderson AU/125 5.00 12.00
228 Matt LaPorta AU/125 5.00 12.00
229 Colby Rasmus AU/100 5.00 12.00
230 David Price AU/125 6.00 15.00
231 Derek Holland AU/90 6.00 15.00
232 Dexter Fowler AU/125 5.00 12.00
233 Fernando Martinez AU/125 8.00 20.00
234 Gerardo Parra AU/125 5.00 12.00
235 Gordon Beckham AU/85 6.00 15.00
236 James McDonald AU/125 8.00 20.00
237 James Parr AU/125 3.00 8.00
238 Jason Motte AU/125 5.00 12.00
239 Jordan Schafer AU/125 5.00 12.00
240 Jordan Zimmermann AU/125 8.00 20.00
241 Kenshin Kawakami AU/125 5.00 12.00
243 Luis Perdomo AU/125 3.00 8.00
244 Matt Tuiasosopo AU/125 3.00 8.00
245 Matt Wieters AU/50 12.00 30.00
246 Nolan Reimold AU/65 4.00 10.00
247 Pablo Sandoval AU/75 8.00 20.00
248 Rick Porcello AU/75 12.00 30.00
249 Tommy Hanson AU/65 10.00 25.00
250 Travis Snider AU/50 6.00 15.00

2009 SP Authentic Silver

*1-128 SILVER: 2.5X TO 6X BASIC
1-128 PRINT RUN 59 SER.#'d SETS
*129-170 SILVER: .75X TO 2X BASIC
129-170 PRINT RUN 59 SER.#'d SETS
*171-200 SILVER: 2.5X TO 6X BASIC
1-200 RANDOMLY INSERTED IN PACKS
171-200 PRINT RUN 59 SER.#'d SETS
OVERALL AUTO ODDS 1:8 HOBBY
226-250 AU PR B/WN 4-25 SER.#'d SETS
NO 201-250 PRICING DUE TO SCARCITY

2009 SP Authentic By The Letter Rookie Signatures

OVERALL LETTER AU ODDS 1:12
SER.#'d B/WN 11-100 COPIES PER
TOTAL PRINT RUNS LISTED BELOW
EXCHANGE DEADLINE 9/18/2011
BA B.Anderson/599 * 6.00 15.00
CR Colby Rasmus/450 * 6.00 15.00
DF David Freese/450 * 12.00 30.00
DH Derek Holland/270 * 6.00 15.00
DP David Patton/600 * 6.00 15.00
DV Donald Veal/715 * 6.00 15.00
EA Elvis Andrus/660 * 10.00 25.00
EC Everth Cabrera/715 * 6.00 15.00
FO Dexter Fowler/715 * 6.00 15.00
GK George Kottaras/715 * 4.00 10.00
JM James McDonald/715 * 10.00 25.00
JS Jordan Schafer/510 * 6.00 15.00
JZ J.Zimmermann/297 * 10.00 25.00
KJ Kevin Jepsen/600 * 4.00 10.00
KK K.Kawakami/600 * 6.00 15.00
KU Koji Uehara/400 * 10.00 25.00
MO Jason Motte/600 * 6.00 15.00
MW Matt Wieters/165 * 12.00 30.00
PC Phil Coke/709 * 6.00 15.00
PD David Price/168 * 8.00 20.00
PE Ryan Perry/300 * 10.00 25.00
PR David Price/140 * 8.00 20.00
PS P.Sandoval/308 * 8.00 20.00
RP Rick Porcello/510 * 12.00 30.00
RR R.Romero/715 * 6.00 15.00
SM Shairon Martis/715 * 6.00 15.00
TC Trevor Cahill/510 * 10.00 25.00
TR Trevor Crowe/715 * 4.00 10.00
TS Travis Snider/540 * 6.00 15.00
UE Koji Uehara/190 * 10.00 25.00

2009 SP Authentic By The Letter Signatures

OVERALL LETTER AU ODDS 1:12
SER.#'d B/WN 2-60 COPIES PER
TOTAL PRINT RUNS LISTED BELOW
EXCHANGE DEADLINE 9/18/2011
AH Alex Hinshaw/473* 6.00 15.00
AR Alex Romero/400* 5.00 12.00
BJ B.Jones/360* 8.00 20.00

BM B.McCann/220* 12.00 30.00
BR Jay Bruce/350* 5.00 12.00
BU B.J. Upton/26* 8.00 20.00
CG C.Gonzalez/495* 6.00 15.00
CH C.Hu/120* 6.00 15.00
CJ Chipper Jones/24* 60.00 150.00
CK C.Kershaw/140* 100.00 250.00
CV Chris Volstad/300* 5.00 12.00
CW C.Wang/60* 40.00 80.00
DJ Derek Jeter/200* 150.00 250.00
DM D.Murphy/360* 5.00 12.00
DP David Purcey/341* 5.00 12.00
DU D.Pedroia/390* 20.00 50.00
EB Emmanuel Burriss/375* 5.00 12.00
EC Eric Chavez/54* 8.00 20.00
EL E.Longoria/60* 75.00 150.00
FH F.Hernandez/80* EXCH 20.00 50.00
GA Garrett Atkins/65* 8.00 20.00
GF Gavin Floyd/400* 6.00 15.00
GP Glen Perkins/385* 5.00 12.00
GS Geovany Soto/40* 20.00 50.00
HA Cole Hamels/100* 12.00 30.00
HP Hunter Pence/48* 8.00 20.00
HR H.Ramirez/52* 10.00 25.00
HU C.Hu/270* 10.00 25.00
JB Jay Bruce/494* 10.00 30.00
JC J.Chamberlain/150* 30.00 60.00
JJ J.Johnson/297* 6.00 15.00
JN Joe Nathan/324* 5.00 12.00
JT J.R. Towles/400* 5.00 12.00
KG K.Griffey Jr./144* 75.00 150.00
KM Kyle McClellan/390* 6.00 15.00
KS Kelly Shoppach/494* 5.00 12.00
KY K.Youkilis/260* 6.00 15.00
LE Jon Lester/270* 10.00 25.00
LJ Jed Lowrie/297* 10.00 25.00
MA Mike Aviles/500* 10.00 25.00
MC Matt Cain/400* 10.00 25.00
MD D.Murphy/385* 6.00 15.00
MG Matt Garza/450* 3.00 8.00
MN N.Markakis/315* 6.00 15.00
MO N.Morgan/385* 8.00 20.00
MR N.Markakis/360* 6.00 15.00
NA Joe Nathan/350* 5.00 12.00
NM N.McLouth/495* 3.00 8.00
PE D.Pedroia/408* 20.00 50.00
RB Ryan Braun/90* 40.00 80.00
RH R.Halladay/110* 40.00 80.00
RJ R.Johnson/21* 50.00 120.00
TT T.Tulowitzki/420* 12.00 30.00
UB B.J. Upton/210* 8.00 20.00
WA Cory Wade/400* 6.00 15.00

2009 SP Authentic Derek Jeter 1993 SP Buyback Autograph

RANDOMLY INSERTED IN PACKS
STATED PRINT RUN 93 SER.#'d SETS
279 Derek Jeter/93 2000.00 3000.00

2009 SP Authentic Pennant Run Heroes

STATED ODDS 1:20 HOBBY
PR1 Alfonso Soriano .60 1.50
PR2 B.J. Upton .60 1.50
PR3 Brad Lidge .40 1.00
PR4 Brandon Webb .60 1.50
PR5 Carlos Quentin .40 1.00
PR6 Chad Billingsley .60 1.50
PR7 Chase Utley .60 1.50
PR8 Chris B. Young .40 1.00
PR9 Clayton Kershaw 1.50 4.00
PR10 Cole Hamels .75 2.00
PR11 David Ortiz 1.00 2.50
PR12 David Price .75 2.00
PR13 Derek Jeter 2.50 6.00
PR14 Evan Longoria .60 1.50
PR15 John Lackey .60 1.50
PR16 Jonathan Papelbon .60 1.50
PR17 Kevin Youkilis .40 1.00
PR18 Lance Berkman .60 1.50
PR19 Magglio Ordonez .60 1.50
PR20 Mariano Rivera 1.25 3.00

2009 SP Authentic Platinum Power

STATED ODDS 1:10 HOBBY
PP1 A.J. Burnett .40 1.00
PP2 Adam Dunn .60 1.50
PP3 Adrian Gonzalez .75 2.00
PP4 Albert Pujols 1.25 3.00
PP5 Alex Rodriguez 1.25 3.00
PP6 Alfonso Soriano .60 1.50
PP7 Brandon Webb .60 1.50
PP8 Bronson Arroyo .40 1.00
PP9 Carlos Delgado .40 1.00
PP10 Carlos Lee .40 1.00
PP11 Carlos Pena .60 1.50
PP12 Carlos Quentin .40 1.00
PP13 CC Sabathia .60 1.50
PP14 Chad Billingsley .60 1.50
PP15 Chase Utley .60 1.50
PP16 Cole Hamels .75 2.00
PP17 Dan Haren .40 1.00
PP18 David Wright .75 2.00
PP19 Edinson Volquez .40 1.00
PP20 Evan Longoria .60 1.50
PP21 Felix Hernandez .60 1.50
PP22 Grady Sizemore .60 1.50
PP23 Ian Kinsler .60 1.50
PP24 Jack Cust .40 1.00
PP25 Jake Peavy .40 1.00
PP26 James Shields .40 1.00
PP27 Jason Bay .60 1.50
PP28 Jason Giambi .40 1.00
PP29 Javier Vazquez .40 1.00
PP30 Jermaine Dye .40 1.00
PP31 Jim Thome .60 1.50
PP32 Joey Votto 1.00 2.50
PP33 Johan Santana .60 1.50
PP34 Josh Beckett .40 1.00
PP35 Josh Hamilton .60 1.50
PP36 Josh Johnson .60 1.50
PP37 Justin Verlander 1.00 2.50
PP38 Lance Berkman .60 1.50
PP39 Manny Ramirez 1.00 2.50
PP40 Mark Teixeira .60 1.50
PP41 Matt Cain .60 1.50
PP42 Miguel Cabrera 1.00 2.50
PP43 Mike Jacobs .40 1.00
PP44 Nick Markakis .75 2.00
PP45 Prince Fielder .60 1.50
PP46 Randy Johnson 1.00 2.50
PP47 Ricky Nolasco .40 1.00
PP48 Roy Halladay .60 1.50
PP49 Roy Oswalt .60 1.50
PP50 Ryan Braun .60 1.50
PP51 Ryan Dempster .40 1.00
PP52 Ryan Howard .75 2.00
PP53 Ryan Ludwick .60 1.50
PP54 Scott Kazmir .40 1.00
PP55 Tim Lincecum .60 1.50
PP56 Ubaldo Jimenez .40 1.00
PP57 Vladimir Guerrero .60 1.50
PP58 Wandy Rodriguez .40 1.00
PP59 Yovani Gallardo .40 1.00
PP60 Zack Greinke 1.00 2.50

2009 SP Authentic Signatures

OVERALL AUTO ODDS 1:8 HOBBY
SP INFO PROVIDED BY UD
SAN Andy LaRoche SP 8.00 20.00
SAR Aaron Rowand SP 6.00 15.00
SAS Anibal Sanchez SP 3.00 8.00
SCB Chad Billingsley SP 5.00 12.00
SCH Chase Headley SP 4.00 10.00
SCW Cory Wade SP 5.00 12.00
SDB Daric Barton SP 5.00 12.00
SDE David Eckstein SP 8.00 20.00
SDJ Derek Jeter SP 150.00 250.00
SDL Derek Lowe SP 3.00 8.00
SDU Dan Uggla SP 4.00 10.00
SEB Emilio Bonifacio 3.00 8.00
SEJ Edwin Jackson SP 5.00 12.00
SFC Fausto Carmona SP 3.00 8.00
SFJ Jeff Francoeur SP 3.00 8.00
SFL Felipe Lopez SP 3.00 8.00
SGG Greg Golson SP 3.00 8.00
SGP Glen Perkins SP 3.00 8.00
SHE Jeremy Hermida SP 4.00 10.00
SHJ Josh Hamilton SP 12.50 30.00
SJD John Danks SP 4.00 10.00
SJH J.A. Happ 12.50 30.00
SJL John Lackey SP 20.00 50.00
SJM J.Masterson SP 8.00 20.00
SJS Joe Smith 3.00 8.00
SJS James Shields SP 5.00 12.00
SKG Ken Griffey Jr. SP 75.00 150.00
SKS Kurt Suzuki SP 4.00 10.00
SKY Kevin Youkilis SP 8.00 20.00
SLA Adam Lind SP 4.00 10.00
SMA D.Matsuzaka SP 40.00 80.00
SME Mark Ellis SP 3.00 8.00
SMG Matt Garza SP 4.00 10.00
SMU David Murphy SP 3.00 8.00
SNM Nick Markakis SP 15.00 40.00
SNS Nick Swisher SP 12.50 30.00
SRC Ryan Church SP 3.00 8.00
SRM Russell Martin SP 6.00 15.00
SRT Ryan Theriot 5.00 12.00
SSA Jarrod Saltalamacchia SP 3.00 8.00
SSM Sean Marshall 3.00 8.00
SSO Joakim Soria SP 3.00 8.00
STS Takashi Saito SP 20.00 50.00
SVM Victor Martinez SP 6.00 15.00

1995 SP Championship

This set contains 200 cards that were sold in six-card retail packs for a suggested price of $2.99. The fronts have a full-bleed action photo with the words "SP Championship Series" in gold-foil in the bottom left-hand corner. In the bottom right-hand corner is the team's name in blue (National League) and red (American League) foil. The backs have a small head shot and player information. Statistics and team name are also on the back in blue or red just like on the front. Subsets featured are Diamonds in the Rough (1-20), October Legends (100-114) and Major League Profiles. Rookie Cards in this set include Bobby Higginson and Hideo Nomo. In addition, two special "one-shot" Cal Ripken cards (a basic design and a scarcer parallel die cut version) were randomly seeded into packs to commemorate his consecutive games streak record.

COMPLETE SET (200) 15.00 40.00
CR1 RIPKEN CARDS RANDOM IN PACKS
1 Hideo Nomo RC 1.00 2.50
2 Roger Cedeno .07 .20
3 Curtis Goodwin .07 .20
4 Jon Nunnally .07 .20
5 Bill Pulsipher .07 .20
6 Garret Anderson .15 .40
7 Dustin Hermanson .07 .20
8 Marty Cordova .07 .20
9 Ruben Rivera .07 .20
10 Ariel Prieto RC .07 .20
11 Edgardo Alfonzo .07 .20
12 Ray Durham .15 .40
13 Quilvio Veras .07 .20
14 Ugueth Urbina .07 .20
15 Carlos Perez RC .15 .40
16 Glenn Dishman RC .07 .20
17 Jeff Suppan .15 .40
18 Jason Bates .07 .20
19 Jason Isringhausen .15 .40
20 Derek Jeter 1.00 2.50
21 Fred McGriff MLP .15 .40
22 Marquis Grissom .15 .40
23 Fred McGriff .25 .60
24 Tom Glavine .25 .60
25 Greg Maddux .60 1.50
26 Chipper Jones .40 1.00
27 Sammy Sosa MLP .25 .60
28 Randy Myers .07 .20
29 Mark Grace .25 .60
30 Sammy Sosa .40 1.00
31 Todd Zeile .07 .20
32 Brian McRae .07 .20
33 Ron Gant MLP .07 .20
34 Reggie Sanders .15 .40
35 Ron Gant .15 .40
36 Barry Larkin .25 .60
37 Bret Boone .15 .40
38 John Smiley .07 .20
39 Larry Walker MLP .07 .20
40 Andres Galarraga .15 .40
41 Bill Swift .07 .20
42 Larry Walker .15 .40
43 Vinny Castilla .15 .40
44 Dante Bichette .15 .40
45 Jeff Conine MLP .07 .20
46 Charles Johnson .15 .40
47 Gary Sheffield .15 .40
48 Andre Dawson .15 .40
49 Jeff Conine .15 .40
50 Jeff Bagwell MLP .15 .40
51 Phil Nevin .15 .40
52 Craig Biggio .25 .60
53 Brian L.Hunter .07 .20
54 Doug Drabek .07 .20
55 Jeff Bagwell .25 .60
56 Derek Bell .07 .20
57 Mike Piazza MLP .40 1.00
58 Raul Mondesi .15 .40
59 Eric Karros .15 .40
60 Mike Piazza .60 1.50
61 Ramon Martinez .07 .20
62 Billy Ashley .07 .20
63 Rondell White MLP .07 .20
64 Jeff Fassero .07 .20
65 Moises Alou .15 .40
66 Tony Tarasco .07 .20
67 Rondell White .15 .40
68 Pedro Martinez .25 .60
69 Bobby Jones MLP .07 .20
70 Bobby Bonilla .15 .40
71 Bobby Jones .07 .20
72 Bret Saberhagen .15 .40
73 Darren Daulton MLP .07 .20
74 Darren Daulton .15 .40
75 Gregg Jefferies .07 .20
76 Tyler Green .07 .20
77 Heathcliff Slocumb .07 .20
78 Lenny Dykstra .15 .40
79 Jay Bell MLP .07 .20
80 Denny Neagle .15 .40
81 Orlando Merced .07 .20
82 Jay Bell .15 .40
83 Ozzie Smith MLP .40 1.00
84 Ken Hill .07 .20
85 Ozzie Smith .60 1.50
86 Bernard Gilkey .07 .20
87 Ray Lankford .15 .40
88 Tony Gwynn MLP .25 .60
89 Ken Caminiti .15 .40
90 Tony Gwynn .50 1.25
91 Joey Hamilton .07 .20
92 Bip Roberts .07 .20
93 Deion Sanders MLP .15 .40
94 Glenallen Hill .07 .20
95 Matt Williams .15 .40
96 Barry Bonds 1.00 2.50
97 Rod Beck .07 .20
98 Eddie Murray CL .25 .60
99 Cal Ripken CL .60 1.50
100 Roberto Alomar OL .15 .40
101 George Brett OL 1.00 2.50
102 Joe Carter OL .07 .20
103 Will Clark OL .15 .40
104 Dennis Eckersley OL .15 .40
105 Whitey Ford OL .25 .60
106 Steve Garvey OL .07 .20
107 Kirk Gibson OL .15 .40
108 Orel Hershiser OL .07 .20
109 Reggie Jackson OL .25 .60
110 Paul Molitor OL .07 .20
111 Kirby Puckett OL .25 .60
112 Mike Schmidt OL .60 1.50
113 Dave Stewart OL .07 .20
114 Alan Trammell OL .15 .40
115 Cal Ripken MLP .60 1.50
116 Brady Anderson .15 .40
117 Mike Mussina .25 .60
118 Rafael Palmeiro .25 .60
119 Chris Hoiles .07 .20
120 Cal Ripken 1.25 3.00
121 Mo Vaughn MLP .07 .20
122 Roger Clemens .75 2.00
123 Tim Naehring .07 .20
124 John Valentin .07 .20
125 Mo Vaughn .15 .40
126 Tim Wakefield .15 .40
127 Jose Canseco .25 .60
128 Rick Aguilera .07 .20
129 Chili Davis MLP .07 .20
130 Lee Smith .15 .40
131 Jim Edmonds .25 .60
132 Chuck Finley .15 .40
133 Chili Davis .15 .40
134 J.T. Snow .15 .40
135 Tim Salmon .25 .60
136 Frank Thomas MLP .25 .60
137 Jason Bere .07 .20
138 Robin Ventura .15 .40
139 Tim Raines .15 .40
140 Frank Thomas .40 1.00
141 Alex Fernandez .07 .20
142 Eddie Murray MLP .25 .60
143 Carlos Baerga .07 .20
144 Eddie Murray .40 1.00
145 Albert Belle .15 .40
146 Jim Thome .25 .60
147 Dennis Martinez .15 .40
148 Dave Winfield .15 .40
149 Kenny Lofton .15 .40
150 Manny Ramirez .25 .60
151 Cecil Fielder MLP .07 .20
152 Lou Whitaker .15 .40
153 Alan Trammell .15 .40
154 Kirk Gibson .15 .40
155 Cecil Fielder .15 .40
156 Bob Higginson RC .25 .60
157 Kevin Appier MLP .07 .20
158 Wally Joyner .15 .40
159 Jeff Montgomery .07 .20
160 Kevin Appier .15 .40
161 Gary Gaetti .15 .40
162 Greg Gagne .07 .20
163 Ricky Bones MLP .07 .20
164 Greg Vaughn .07 .20
165 Kevin Seitzer .07 .20
166 Ricky Bones .07 .20
167 Kirby Puckett MLP .25 .60
168 Pedro Munoz .07 .20
169 Chuck Knoblauch .15 .40
170 Kirby Puckett .40 1.00
171 Don Mattingly MLP .50 1.25
172 Wade Boggs .25 .60
173 Paul O'Neill .25 .60
174 John Wetteland .15 .40
175 Don Mattingly 1.00 2.50
176 Jack McDowell .07 .20
177 Mark McGwire MLP .50 1.25
178 Rickey Henderson .40 1.00
179 Terry Steinbach .07 .20
180 Ruben Sierra .15 .40
181 Mark McGwire 1.00 2.50
182 Dennis Eckersley .15 .40
183 Ken Griffey Jr. MLP .50 1.25
184 Alex Rodriguez 1.00 2.50
185 Ken Griffey Jr. .75 2.00
186 Randy Johnson .40 1.00
187 Jay Buhner .15 .40
188 Edgar Martinez .25 .60
189 Will Clark MLP .15 .40
190 Juan Gonzalez .15 .40
191 Benji Gil .07 .20
192 Ivan Rodriguez .25 .60
193 Kenny Rogers .15 .40
194 Will Clark .25 .60
195 Paul Molitor MLP .07 .20
196 Roberto Alomar .25 .60
197 David Cone .15 .40
198 Paul Molitor .15 .40
199 Shawn Green .15 .40
200 Joe Carter .15 .40
CR1 Cal Ripken 2131 4.00 10.00
CR1 Cal Ripken 2131 DC 15.00 40.00

1995 SP Championship Die Cuts

COMPLETE SET (200) 60.00 120.00
*STARS: 1X TO 2.5X BASIC CARDS
*ROOKIES: .75X TO 2X BASIC CARDS
ONE PER PACK

1995 SP Championship Classic Performances

COMPLETE SET (10) 6.00 15.00
STATED ODDS 1:15
*DIE CUTS: 1.2X TO 3X BASIC CLASSIC PERF.
DC STATED ODDS 1:75
CP1 Reggie Jackson .60 1.50
CP2 Nolan Ryan 3.00 8.00
CP3 Kirk Gibson .40 1.00
CP4 Joe Carter .40 1.00
CP5 George Brett 2.00 5.00
CP6 Roberto Alomar .60 1.50
CP7 Ozzie Smith 1.25 3.00
CP8 Kirby Puckett 1.00 2.50
CP9 Bret Saberhagen .40 1.00
CP10 Steve Garvey .40 1.00

1995 SP Championship Fall Classic

COMPLETE SET (9) 12.00 30.00
STATED ODDS 1:40
*DIE CUTS: .6X TO 1.5X BASIC FALL CLASSIC
DC STATED ODDS 1:75
1 Ken Griffey Jr. 6.00 15.00
2 Frank Thomas 3.00 8.00
3 Albert Belle 1.25 3.00
4 Mike Piazza 3.00 8.00
5 Don Mattingly 6.00 15.00
6 Hideo Nomo 3.00 8.00
7 Greg Maddux 5.00 12.00
8 Fred McGriff 2.00 5.00
9 Barry Bonds 5.00 12.00

2005 SP Collection of Stars

ISSUED IN 05 SP COLLECTION PACKS
OVERALL INSERT ODDS 1:10
STATED PRINT RUN 299 SERIAL #'d SETS
AB A.J. Burnett .60 1.50
AG Adrian Gonzalez 1.25 3.00
AM Andy Marte .60 1.50
AP Albert Pujols 2.00 5.00
AR Aaron Rowand .60 1.50
BA Clint Barmes .60 1.50
BE Adrian Beltre 1.50 4.00
BH Bill Hall .60 1.50
BI Brandon Inge .60 1.50
BL Joe Blanton .60 1.50
BM Brett Myers .60 1.50
BO Jeremy Bonderman .60 1.50
BR Bronson Arroyo .60 1.50
BU B.J. Upton 1.00 2.50
CA Jorge Cantu .60 1.50
CB Chris Burke .60 1.50
CC Carl Crawford 1.00 2.50
CD Chris Duffy .60 1.50
CF Chone Figgins .60 1.50
CG Carlos Guillen .60 1.50
CH Chad Cordero .60 1.50
CI Cesar Izturis .60 1.50
CK Casey Kotchman .60 1.50
CL Cliff Lee 1.00 2.50
CO Coco Crisp .60 1.50
CP Corey Patterson .60 1.50
CR Cal Ripken 5.00 12.00
CS Chris Shelton .60 1.50
CT Chad Tracy .60 1.50
CZ Carlos Zambrano 1.00 2.50
DB Dave Bush .60 1.50
DC Daniel Cabrera .60 1.50
DD David DeJesus .60 1.50
DH Danny Haren .60 1.50
DJ Derek Jeter 4.00 10.00
DM Dallas McPherson .60 1.50
DO David Ortiz 1.50 4.00
DU Jason DuBois .60 1.50
DW David Wright 1.25 3.00
EJ Edwin Jackson .60 1.50
GA Garrett Atkins .60 1.50
GC Gustavo Chacin .60 1.50
GF Gavin Floyd .60 1.50
GM Greg Maddux 2.00 5.00
GO Jonny Gomes .60 1.50
GR Khalil Greene .60 1.50
GS Grady Sizemore 1.00 2.50
HO Ryan Howard 1.25 3.00
HS Huston Street .60 1.50
JA Jason Bay .60 1.50
JB Jason Bartlett .60 1.50
JC Jesse Crain .60 1.50
JD J.D. Closser .60 1.50
JE Jeff Baker .60 1.50
JF Jeff Francis .60 1.50
JG Joey Gathright .60 1.50
JL Jason Lane .60 1.50
JM Joe Mauer 1.25 3.00
JP Jake Peavy .60 1.50
JR Jeremy Reed .60 1.50
JS Johan Santana 1.00 2.50
JW Jake Westbrook .60 1.50
KG Ken Griffey Jr. 3.00 8.00
KY Kevin Youkilis .60 1.50
LE Brandon League .60 1.50
LS Luke Scott 1.50 4.00
MC Miguel Cabrera 1.50 4.00
MH Matt Holliday 1.50 4.00
MI Miguel Tejada 1.00 2.50
MM Melvin Mora .60 1.50
MO Guillermo Mota .60 1.50
MP Mark Prior 1.00 2.50
MS Mike Schmidt 2.50 6.00
MT Mark Teahen .60 1.50
MY Michael Young .60 1.50
NJ Nick Johnson .60 1.50
NS Nick Swisher 1.00 2.50
OP Oliver Perez .60 1.50
PI Joel Pineiro .60 1.50
RA Aramis Ramirez .60 1.50
RC Roger Clemens 2.00 5.00
RE Jose Reyes 1.00 2.50
RF Ryan Freel .60 1.50
RH Rich Harden .60 1.50
RI Alex Rios .60 1.50
RJ Reed Johnson .60 1.50
RO Jimmy Rollins 1.00 2.50
RQ Robb Quinlan .60 1.50
SK Scott Kazmir 1.50 4.00
SM John Smoltz 1.50 4.00
ST Shingo Takatsu .60 1.50
TE Mark Teixeria 1.00 2.50
TH Charles Thomas .60 1.50
TR Travis Hafner .60 1.50
WE Jayson Werth 1.00 2.50
WM Wily Mo Pena .60 1.50
WT Willy Taveras .60 1.50
YB Yhency Brazoban .60 1.50
YM Yadier Molina 6.00 15.00
ZG Zack Greinke 2.00 5.00

2005 SP Collection of Stars Jersey

ISSUED IN 05 SP COLLECTION PACKS
OVERALL PREMIUM AU-GU ODDS 1:20
STATED PRINT RUN 130 SERIAL #'d SETS
AB A.J. Burnett 2.00 5.00
AG Adrian Gonzalez 2.00 5.00
AM Andy Marte 2.00 5.00
AP Albert Pujols 6.00 15.00
AR Aaron Rowand 2.00 5.00
BA Clint Barmes 2.00 5.00
BE Adrian Beltre 2.00 5.00
BH Bill Hall 2.00 5.00
BI Brandon Inge 2.00 5.00
BL Joe Blanton 2.00 5.00
BM Brett Myers 2.00 5.00
BO Jeremy Bonderman 2.00 5.00
BR Bronson Arroyo 2.00 5.00
BU B.J. Upton 2.00 5.00
CA Jorge Cantu 2.00 5.00
CB Chris Burke 2.00 5.00
CC Carl Crawford 2.00 5.00
CD Chris Duffy 2.00 5.00
CF Chone Figgins 2.00 5.00
CG Carlos Guillen 2.00 5.00
CH Chad Cordero 2.00 5.00
CI Cesar Izturis 2.00 5.00
CK Casey Kotchman 2.00 5.00
CL Cliff Lee 2.00 5.00
CO Coco Crisp 2.00 5.00
CP Corey Patterson 2.00 5.00
CR Cal Ripken Pants 8.00 20.00
CS Chris Shelton 3.00 8.00
CT Chad Tracy 2.00 5.00
CZ Carlos Zambrano 2.00 5.00
DB Dave Bush 2.00 5.00
DC Daniel Cabrera 2.00 5.00
DD David DeJesus 2.00 5.00
DH Danny Haren 2.00 5.00
DJ Derek Jeter Pants 8.00 20.00
DM Dallas McPherson 2.00 5.00
DO David Ortiz 3.00 8.00
DU Jason DuBois 2.00 5.00
DW David Wright 4.00 10.00
EJ Edwin Jackson 2.00 5.00
GA Garrett Atkins 2.00 5.00
GC Gustavo Chacin 2.00 5.00
GF Gavin Floyd 2.00 5.00
GM Greg Maddux 4.00 10.00
GO Jonny Gomes 2.00 5.00
GR Khalil Greene 3.00 8.00
GS Grady Sizemore 3.00 8.00
HO Ryan Howard 10.00 25.00
HS Huston Street 3.00 8.00
JA Jason Bay 2.00 5.00
JB Jason Bartlett 2.00 5.00
JC Jesse Crain 2.00 5.00
JD J.D. Closser 2.00 5.00
JE Jeff Baker 2.00 5.00
JF Jeff Francis 2.00 5.00
JG Joey Gathright 2.00 5.00
JL Jason Lane 2.00 5.00
JM Joe Mauer 4.00 10.00
JP Jake Peavy 2.00 5.00
JR Jeremy Reed 2.00 5.00
JS Johan Santana 4.00 10.00
JW Jake Westbrook 2.00 5.00
KG Ken Griffey Jr. 6.00 15.00
KY Kevin Youkilis 2.00 5.00
LE Brandon League 2.00 5.00
LS Luke Scott 4.00 10.00
MC Miguel Cabrera 3.00 8.00
MH Matt Holliday 2.50 6.00
MI Miguel Tejada 2.00 5.00
MM Melvin Mora 2.00 5.00
MO Guillermo Mota 2.00 5.00
MP Mark Prior 3.00 8.00
MS Mike Schmidt 6.00 15.00
MT Mark Teahen 2.00 5.00
MY Michael Young 2.00 5.00
NJ Nick Johnson 2.00 5.00
NS Nick Swisher 2.00 5.00
OP Oliver Perez 2.00 5.00
PI Joel Pineiro 2.00 5.00
RA Aramis Ramirez 2.00 5.00
RC Roger Clemens Pants 4.00 10.00
RE Jose Reyes 2.00 5.00
RF Ryan Freel 2.00 5.00
RH Rich Harden 2.00 5.00
RI Alex Rios 2.00 5.00
RJ Reed Johnson 2.00 5.00
RO Jimmy Rollins 2.00 5.00
RQ Robb Quinlan 2.00 5.00
SK Scott Kazmir 2.00 5.00
SM John Smoltz 3.00 8.00
ST Shingo Takatsu 2.00 5.00
TE Mark Teixeria 3.00 8.00
TH Charles Thomas 2.00 5.00
TR Travis Hafner 2.00 5.00
WE Jayson Werth 2.00 5.00
WM Wily Mo Pena 2.00 5.00
WT Willy Taveras 2.00 5.00
YB Yhency Brazoban 2.00 5.00
YM Yadier Molina 2.00 5.00
ZG Zack Greinke 2.00 5.00

2001 SP Game Bat Edition

COMPLETE SET (90) 20.00 50.00
1 Troy Glaus .40 1.00
2 Darin Erstad .40 1.00
3 Mo Vaughn .40 1.00
4 Jason Giambi .40 1.00
5 Ben Grieve .40 1.00
6 Eric Chavez .40 1.00
7 Carlos Delgado .40 1.00
8 Tony Batista .40 1.00
9 Shannon Stewart .40 1.00
10 Jose Cruz Jr. .40 1.00
11 Fred McGriff .60 1.50
12 Greg Vaughn .40 1.00
13 Roberto Alomar .60 1.50
14 Manny Ramirez .60 1.50
15 Jim Thome .60 1.50
16 Russell Branyan .40 1.00
17 Alex Rodriguez 1.25 3.00
18 John Olerud .40 1.00
19 Edgar Martinez .60 1.50
20 Cal Ripken 3.00 8.00
21 Albert Belle .40 1.00
22 Ivan Rodriguez .60 1.50
23 Rafael Palmeiro .60 1.50
24 Nomar Garciaparra 1.50 4.00
25 Carl Everett .40 1.00
26 Dante Bichette .40 1.00
27 Mike Sweeney .40 1.00
28 Jermaine Dye .40 1.00
29 Carlos Beltran .40 1.00
30 Juan Gonzalez .40 1.00
31 Dean Palmer .40 1.00
32 Bobby Higginson .40 1.00
33 Matt Lawton .40 1.00
34 Jacque Jones .40 1.00
35 Frank Thomas 1.00 2.50
36 Magglio Ordonez .40 1.00
37 Paul Konerko .40 1.00
38 Carlos Lee .40 1.00
39 Bernie Williams .60 1.50
40 Derek Jeter 2.50 6.00
41 Paul O'Neill .60 1.50
42 Jose Canseco .60 1.50
43 Ken Caminiti .40 1.00
44 Jeff Bagwell .60 1.50
45 Craig Biggio .60 1.50
46 Richard Hidalgo .40 1.00
47 Andruw Jones .60 1.50
48 Chipper Jones 1.00 2.50
49 Andres Galarraga .40 1.00
50 B.J. Surhoff .40 1.00
51 Jeromy Burnitz .40 1.00
52 Geoff Jenkins .40 1.00
53 Richie Sexson .40 1.00
54 Mark McGwire 2.50 6.00
55 Jim Edmonds .40 1.00
56 J.D. Drew .40 1.00
57 Fernando Tatis .40 1.00
58 Sammy Sosa 1.00 2.50
59 Mark Grace .60 1.50
60 Eric Young .40 1.00
61 Matt Williams .40 1.00
62 Luis Gonzalez .40 1.00
63 Steve Finley .40 1.00
64 Shawn Green .40 1.00
65 Gary Sheffield .40 1.00
66 Eric Karros .40 1.00
67 Vladimir Guerrero 1.00 2.50
68 Jose Vidro .40 1.00
69 Barry Bonds 2.50 6.00
70 Jeff Kent .40 1.00
71 Preston Wilson .40 1.00
72 Mike Lowell .40 1.00
73 Luis Castillo .40 1.00
74 Mike Piazza 1.50 4.00
75 Robin Ventura .40 1.00
76 Edgardo Alfonzo .40 1.00
77 Tony Gwynn 1.25 3.00
78 Eric Owens .40 1.00
79 Ryan Klesko .40 1.00
80 Scott Rolen .60 1.50
81 Bobby Abreu .40 1.00
82 Pat Burrell .40 1.00
83 Brian Giles .40 1.00
84 Jason Kendall .40 1.00
85 Aaron Boone .40 1.00
86 Ken Griffey Jr. 2.00 5.00
87 Barry Larkin .60 1.50
88 Todd Helton .60 1.50
89 Larry Walker .40 1.00
90 Jeffrey Hammonds .40 1.00

2001 SP Game Bat Edition Big League Hit Parade

COMPLETE SET (6) 12.50 30.00
STATED ODDS 1:15
HP1 Nomar Garciaparra 2.00 5.00
HP2 Ken Griffey Jr. 2.50 6.00
HP3 Sammy Sosa 1.25 3.00
HP4 Alex Rodriguez 1.50 4.00
HP5 Mark McGwire 3.00 8.00
HP6 Ivan Rodriguez 1.25 3.00

2001 SP Game Bat Edition In the Swing

COMPLETE SET (15) 20.00 50.00
STATED ODDS 1:7
IS1 Ken Griffey Jr. 2.50 6.00
IS2 Jim Edmonds .50 1.25
IS3 Carlos Delgado .50 1.25
IS4 Frank Thomas 1.25 3.00
IS5 Barry Bonds 3.00 8.00
IS6 Nomar Garciaparra 2.00 5.00
IS7 Gary Sheffield .50 1.25
IS8 Vladimir Guerrero 1.25 3.00
IS9 Alex Rodriguez 1.50 4.00
IS10 Todd Helton .75 2.00
IS11 Darin Erstad .50 1.25
IS12 Derek Jeter 3.00 8.00
IS13 Sammy Sosa 1.25 3.00
IS14 Mark McGwire 3.00 8.00
IS15 Jason Giambi .50 1.25

2001 SP Game Bat Edition Line Up Time

COMPLETE SET (11) 20.00 50.00
STATED ODDS 1:8
LT1 Mark McGwire 3.00 8.00
LT2 Roberto Alomar 1.25 3.00
LT3 Alex Rodriguez 1.50 4.00
LT4 Chipper Jones 1.25 3.00
LT5 Ivan Rodriguez 1.25 3.00
LT6 Ken Griffey Jr. 2.50 6.00
LT7 Sammy Sosa 1.25 3.00
LT8 Barry Bonds 3.00 8.00
LT9 Frank Thomas 1.25 3.00
LT10 Pedro Martinez 1.25 3.00
LT11 Derek Jeter 3.00 8.00

2001 SP Game Bat Edition Lumber Yard

COMPLETE SET (10) 15.00 40.00
STATED ODDS 1:10
Y1 Jason Giambi .50 1.25
Y2 Chipper Jones 1.25 3.00
Y3 Carl Everett .50 1.25
Y4 Alex Rodriguez 1.50 4.00
Y5 Frank Thomas 1.25 3.00
Y6 Barry Bonds 3.00 8.00
Y7 Jeff Bagwell .75 2.00
Y8 Sammy Sosa 1.25 3.00
Y9 Carlos Delgado .50 1.25
Y10 Mike Piazza 2.00 5.00

2001 SP Game Bat Edition Piece of the Game

STATED ODDS 1:1
SP PRINT RUN 1500 OR FEWER OF EACH
SP INFO PROVIDED BY UPPER DECK
GOLD RANDOM INSERTS IN PACKS
GOLD PRINT RUN 25 SERIAL #'d SETS
NO GOLD PRICING DUE TO SCARCITY
AJ Andruw Jones 3.00 8.00
AR Alex Rodriguez 6.00 15.00
BB Barry Bonds 6.00 15.00
BG Bob Gibson SP 6.00 15.00
BW Bernie Williams 3.00 8.00
CB Carlos Beltran 2.00 5.00
CD Carlos Delgado 2.00 5.00
CJ Chipper Jones 5.00 12.00
CR Cal Ripken SP 12.00 30.00
DE Darin Erstad SP 4.00 10.00
DJ David Justice 2.00 5.00
EA Edgardo Alfonzo SP 4.00 10.00
EM Edgar Martinez 3.00 8.00
FM Fred McGriff SP 6.00 15.00
FT Frank Thomas 5.00 12.00
GM Greg Maddux 6.00 15.00
GS Gary Sheffield 2.00 5.00
GV Greg Vaughn 2.00 5.00
IR Ivan Rodriguez 3.00 8.00
JB Jeff Bagwell SP 6.00 15.00
JB Johnny Bench SP 10.00 25.00
JC Jose Canseco 3.00 8.00
JD J.D. Drew 2.00 5.00
JE Jim Edmonds 3.00 8.00
JO John Olerud 2.00 5.00
JOD Joe DiMaggio SP 60.00 120.00
KB Kevin Brown SP 4.00 10.00
KG Ken Griffey Jr. 6.00 15.00
KL Kenny Lofton 2.00 5.00
MG Mark Grace 3.00 8.00
MO Magglio Ordonez 2.00 5.00
MQ Mark Quinn SP 4.00 10.00
MR Manny Ramirez 5.00 12.00
MV Mo Vaughn 2.00 5.00
MW Matt Williams 2.00 5.00
NR Nolan Ryan SP 12.00 30.00
PB Pat Burrell 2.00 5.00
PN Phil Nevin SP 4.00 10.00
PO Paul O'Neill 3.00 8.00
PW Preston Wilson 2.00 5.00
RA Rick Ankiel 2.00 5.00
RA Roberto Alomar 3.00 8.00
REJ Reggie Jackson SP 8.00 20.00
RF Rafael Furcal 2.00 5.00
RJ Randy Johnson 5.00 12.00
RV Robin Ventura 2.00 5.00
SA Sandy Alomar Jr. 2.00 5.00
SAS Sammy Sosa SP 6.00 15.00
SG Shawn Green 2.00 5.00
SR Scott Rolen 3.00 8.00
SS Shannon Stewart 2.00 5.00
TGL Tom Glavine SP 6.00 15.00
TGW Tony Gwynn 5.00 12.00
TH Todd Helton 3.00 8.00
THU Todd Hundley SP 4.00 10.00
TM Tino Martinez 3.00 8.00
TS Tim Salmon SP 6.00 15.00
WC Will Clark 3.00 8.00

2001 SP Game Bat Edition Piece of the Game Autograph

STATED ODDS 1:96
GOLD RANDOM INSERTS IN PACKS
GOLD PRINT RUN 25 SERIAL #'d SETS
NO GOLD PRICING DUE TO SCARCITY
SAJ Andruw Jones 8.00 20.00
SAR Alex Rodriguez 50.00 100.00
SBB Barry Bonds 100.00 175.00
SFT Frank Thomas 40.00 80.00
SJC Jose Canseco 20.00 50.00
SKG Ken Griffey Jr. 60.00 120.00
SNR Nolan Ryan 60.00 120.00
SSS Sammy Sosa 50.00 100.00
STGW Tony Gwynn 40.00 80.00

2001 SP Game Bat Milestone

COMP.SET w/o SP's (90) 30.00 80.00
COMMON CARD (1-90) .40 1.00
COMMON BAT (91-96) 4.00 10.00
BAT 91-96 RANDOM INSERTS IN PACKS
BAT 91-96 PRINT RUN 500 SERIAL #'d SETS
1 Troy Glaus .40 1.00
2 Darin Erstad .40 1.00
3 Jason Giambi .40 1.00
4 Jermaine Dye .40 1.00
5 Eric Chavez .40 1.00
6 Carlos Delgado .40 1.00
7 Raul Mondesi .40 1.00
8 Shannon Stewart .40 1.00
9 Greg Vaughn .40 1.00
10 Aubrey Huff .40 1.00
11 Juan Gonzalez .40 1.00
12 Roberto Alomar .60 1.50
13 Jim Thome .60 1.50
14 Omar Vizquel .60 1.50
15 Mike Cameron .40 1.00
16 Edgar Martinez .60 1.50
17 John Olerud .40 1.00
18 Bret Boone .40 1.00
19 Cal Ripken 3.00 8.00
20 Tony Batista .40 1.00
21 Alex Rodriguez 1.25 3.00
22 Ivan Rodriguez .60 1.50
23 Rafael Palmeiro .60 1.50
24 Manny Ramirez Sox .60 1.50
25 Pedro Martinez .60 1.50
26 Nomar Garciaparra 1.50 4.00
27 Carl Everett .40 1.00
28 Mike Sweeney .40 1.00
29 Neifi Perez .40 1.00
30 Mark Quinn .40 1.00
31 Bobby Higginson .40 1.00
32 Tony Clark .40 1.00
33 Doug Mientkiewicz .40 1.00
34 Cristian Guzman .40 1.00
35 Joe Mays .40 1.00
36 David Ortiz 1.00 2.50
37 Frank Thomas 1.00 2.50
38 Magglio Ordonez .40 1.00
39 Carlos Lee .40 1.00
40 Alfonso Soriano .60 1.50
41 Bernie Williams .60 1.50
42 Derek Jeter 2.50 6.00
43 Roger Clemens 2.00 5.00
44 Jeff Bagwell .60 1.50
45 Richard Hidalgo .40 1.00
46 Moises Alou .40 1.00
47 Chipper Jones 1.00 2.50
48 Greg Maddux 1.50 4.00
49 Rafael Furcal .40 1.00
50 Andruw Jones .60 1.50
51 Jeromy Burnitz .40 1.00
52 Geoff Jenkins .40 1.00
53 Richie Sexson .40 1.00
54 Edgar Renteria .40 1.00
55 Mark McGwire 2.50 6.00
56 Jim Edmonds .40 1.00
57 J.D. Drew .40 1.00
58 Sammy Sosa 1.00 2.50
59 Fred McGriff .60 1.50
60 Luis Gonzalez .40 1.00
61 Randy Johnson 1.00 2.50
62 Gary Sheffield .40 1.00
63 Shawn Green .40 1.00
64 Kevin Brown .40 1.00
65 Vladimir Guerrero 1.00 2.50
66 Jose Vidro .40 1.00
67 Fernando Tatis .40 1.00
68 Barry Bonds 2.50 6.00
69 Jeff Kent .40 1.00
70 Rich Aurilia .40 1.00
71 Preston Wilson .40 1.00
72 Charles Johnson .40 1.00
73 Cliff Floyd .40 1.00
74 Mike Piazza 1.50 4.00
75 Matt Lawton .40 1.00
76 Edgardo Alfonzo .40 1.00
77 Tony Gwynn 1.25 3.00
78 Phil Nevin .40 1.00
79 Scott Rolen .60 1.50
80 Pat Burrell .40 1.00
81 Bobby Abreu .40 1.00
82 Brian Giles .40 1.00
83 Jason Kendall .40 1.00
84 Aramis Ramirez .40 1.00
85 Sean Casey .40 1.00
86 Ken Griffey Jr. 2.00 5.00
87 Barry Larkin .60 1.50
88 Todd Helton .60 1.50
89 Mike Hampton .40 1.00
90 Larry Walker .40 1.00
91 Ichiro Suzuki BAT RC 30.00 80.00
92 Albert Pujols BAT RC 25.00 60.00
93 Tsuyoshi Shinjo BAT RC 6.00 15.00
94 Jack Wilson BAT RC 6.00 15.00
95 Donaldo Mendez BAT RC 4.00 10.00
96 Junior Spivey BAT RC 6.00 15.00

2001 SP Game Bat Milestone Art of Hitting

COMPLETE SET (12) 20.00 50.00
STATED ODDS 1:5
AH1 Tony Gwynn 1.50 4.00
AH2 Manny Ramirez Sox .75 2.00
AH3 Todd Helton .75 2.00
AH4 Nomar Garciaparra 2.00 5.00
AH5 Vladimir Guerrero 1.25 3.00
AH6 Ichiro Suzuki 10.00 25.00
AH7 Darin Erstad .75 2.00
AH8 Alex Rodriguez 1.50 4.00
AH9 Carlos Delgado .75 2.00
AH10 Edgar Martinez .75 2.00
AH11 Luis Gonzalez .75 2.00
AH12 Barry Bonds 3.00 8.00

2001 SP Game Bat Milestone Piece of Action Autographs

STATED ODDS 1:100
SAR Alex Rodriguez SP/97 60.00 120.00
SCD Carlos Delgado SP/97 10.00 25.00
SGS Gary Sheffield SP/194 10.00 25.00
SIS Ichiro Suzuki SP/53 600.00 1500.00
SJD J.D. Drew 10.00 25.00
SJD Jermaine Dye 10.00 25.00
SJK Jason Kendall 10.00 25.00
SJK Jeff Kent SP/194 40.00 80.00
SJV Jose Vidro 10.00 25.00
SLG Luis Gonzalez 10.00 25.00
SMT Miguel Tejada 10.00 25.00
SPW Preston Wilson 10.00 25.00
SRB Russell Branyan 10.00 25.00

2001 SP Game Bat Milestone Piece of Action Bound for the Hall

ONE GAME BAT PER PACK
ASTERISKS PERCEIVED GREATER SUPPLY
BAR Alex Rodriguez Rangers 6.00 15.00
BBB Barry Bonds 10.00 25.00
BCD Carlos Delgado 4.00 10.00
BCR Cal Ripken 15.00 40.00
BEM Edgar Martinez 6.00 15.00
BFM Fred McGriff 6.00 15.00
BGM Greg Maddux 6.00 15.00
BIR Ivan Rodriguez 6.00 15.00
BJG Jason Giambi 4.00 10.00
BMP Mike Piazza 4.00 10.00
BRC Roger Clemens SP/203 15.00 40.00
BRP Rafael Palmeiro 6.00 15.00
BSS Sammy Sosa 6.00 15.00
BTG Tony Gwynn 6.00 15.00
BKGM Ken Griffey Jr. M's * 8.00 20.00
BKGR Ken Griffey Jr. Reds 8.00 20.00

2001 SP Game Bat Milestone Piece of Action Bound for the Hall Gold

STATED PRINT RUN 35 SERIAL #'d SETS
BAR Alex Rodriguez 20.00 50.00
BBB Barry Bonds 20.00 50.00
BCD Carlos Delgado 10.00 25.00
BCR Cal Ripken 30.00 80.00
BEM Edgar Martinez 15.00 40.00
BFM Fred McGriff 15.00 40.00
BGM Greg Maddux 20.00 50.00
BIR Ivan Rodriguez 15.00 40.00
BJG Jason Giambi 10.00 25.00
BMP Mike Piazza 12.50 30.00
BRC Roger Clemens 20.00 50.00
BRP Rafael Palmeiro 15.00 40.00
BSS Sammy Sosa 15.00 40.00
BTG Tony Gwynn 20.00 50.00
BKGM K.Griffey Jr. Mariners 20.00 50.00
BKGR Ken Griffey Jr. Reds 20.00 50.00

2001 SP Game Bat Milestone Piece of Action International

ONE GAME BAT PER PACK
ASTERISKS PERCEIVED GREATER SUPPLY
IAB Adrian Beltre 4.00 10.00
IAJ Andruw Jones 6.00 15.00
IAP Albert Pujols 15.00 40.00
ICP Chan Ho Park 4.00 10.00
IHN Hideo Nomo SP/275 6.00 15.00
IIS Ichiro Suzuki SP/203 25.00 60.00
IJG Juan Gonzalez 4.00 10.00
IJP Jorge Posada 6.00 15.00
IMO Magglio Ordonez 4.00 10.00
IMR Manny Ramirez Sox 6.00 15.00
IMT Miguel Tejada 4.00 10.00
IOV Omar Vizquel * 6.00 15.00
IPM Pedro Martinez 6.00 15.00
IRA Roberto Alomar 6.00 15.00
IRF Rafael Furcal 4.00 10.00
ITS Tsuyoshi Shinjo 6.00 15.00

2001 SP Game Bat Milestone Piece of Action International Gold

STATED PRINT RUN 35 SERIAL #'d SETS
IAB Adrian Beltre 10.00 25.00
IAJ Andruw Jones 15.00 40.00
IAP Albert Pujols 100.00 250.00
ICP Chan Ho Park 10.00 25.00
IHN Hideo Nomo 15.00 40.00
IIS Ichiro Suzuki 60.00 150.00
IJG Juan Gonzalez 10.00 25.00
IJP Jorge Posada 15.00 40.00
IMO Magglio Ordonez 10.00 25.00
IMR Manny Ramirez Sox 15.00 40.00
IMT Miguel Tejada 10.00 25.00
IOV Omar Vizquel 15.00 40.00
IPM Pedro Martinez 15.00 40.00
IRA Roberto Alomar 15.00 40.00
IRF Rafael Furcal 10.00 25.00
ITS Tsuyoshi Shinjo 15.00 40.00

2001 SP Game Bat Milestone Piece of Action Milestone

ONE GAME BAT PER PACK
ASTERISKS PERCEIVED GREATER SUPPLY
AR Alex Rodriguez Mariners 6.00 15.00
BB Barry Bonds 10.00 25.00
CHJ Chipper Jones 6.00 15.00
CR Cal Ripken 15.00 40.00
DE Darin Erstad 4.00 10.00
FT Frank Thomas * 6.00 15.00
GS Gary Sheffield 4.00 10.00
IS Ichiro Suzuki SP/203 40.00 100.00
JB Jeff Bagwell 6.00 15.00
JBU Jeromy Burnitz 4.00 10.00
JT Jim Thome 6.00 15.00
KG Ken Griffey Jr. 8.00 20.00
LG Luis Gonzalez * 4.00 10.00
MP Mike Piazza 6.00 15.00
RB Russell Branyan 4.00 10.00
RC Roger Clemens 8.00 20.00
SS Sammy Sosa * 6.00 15.00
TH Todd Helton 6.00 15.00

2001 SP Game Bat Milestone Piece of Action Milestone Gold

STATED PRINT RUN 35 SERIAL #'d SETS
AR Alex Rodriguez 25.00 60.00
BB Barry Bonds 30.00 80.00
CHJ Chipper Jones 15.00 40.00
CR Cal Ripken 40.00 100.00
DE Darin Erstad 10.00 25.00
FT Frank Thomas 15.00 40.00
GS Gary Sheffield 10.00 25.00
IS Ichiro Suzuki 60.00 150.00
JB Jeff Bagwell 15.00 40.00
JBU Jeromy Burnitz 10.00 25.00
JT Jim Thome 15.00 40.00
KG Ken Griffey Jr. 25.00 60.00
LG Luis Gonzalez 10.00 25.00
MP Mike Piazza 30.00 80.00
RB Russell Branyan 10.00 25.00
RC Roger Clemens 30.00 80.00
SS Sammy Sosa 15.00 40.00
TH Todd Helton 15.00 40.00

2001 SP Game Bat Milestone Piece of Action Quads

STATED ODDS 1:50
GDBS Griffey/Drew/Burn/Sosa 20.00 50.00
GGRR Griffey/Griffey/Arod/Arod 40.00 80.00
GHSK Gonz/Helt/Sheff/Kent 15.00 40.00
GRBM Gwynn/Ripken/Bonds/McG 15.00 40.00
GRSB Griffey/Arod/Sosa/Bonds 20.00 50.00
JJFM Chip/Jones/Furc/Maddux 15.00 40.00
JVBW Chipper/Vent/Burr/Wilson 15.00 40.00
OJCP O'Neill/Just/Clemens/Posada 10.00 25.00
ONRD O'Neill/Nomo/Ripken/Delg 12.50 30.00
PWSG Puck/Winf/Smith/Garv 15.00 40.00
RGGM Arod/Glaus/Palm/Martinez 20.00 50.00
RRPM Arod/Irod/Palm/Mateo 10.00 25.00
SGBP Gary Sheffield 10.00 25.00
Shawn Green
Adrian Beltre
Chan Ho Park
TDTA Thom/Dye/Thome/Alomar 15.00 40.00
TVAL Thome/Vizq/Alomar/Lofton 15.00 40.00

2001 SP Game Bat Milestone Piece of Action Trios

STATED ODDS 1:50
CMG Clemens/Maddux/Glavine 20.00 50.00
GBM Griffey/Bonds/McGriff 15.00 40.00
GRB Gwynn/Ripken/Bonds 15.00 40.00
GRS Griffey/A.Rod/Sosa 10.00 25.00
JJF C.Jones/A.Jones/Furcal 15.00 40.00
KGR Kendall/B.Giles/A.Ramirez 10.00 25.00
OJC O'Neill/Justice/Clemens 20.00 50.00
OTA Ordonez/Thomas/S.Alomar 15.00 40.00
PWS Puckett/Winfield/O.Smith 15.00 40.00
RRP A.Rod/I.Rod/Palmeiro 10.00 25.00
SFR A.Soriano/Furcal/A.Ramirez 15.00 40.00
SGB Sheffield/Green/Beltre 10.00 25.00
TVA Thome/Vizquel/R.Alomar 15.00 40.00
VSA Ventura/Shinjo/Alfonzo 15.00 40.00

2001 SP Game Bat Milestone Slugging Sensations

COMPLETE SET (12) 15.00 40.00
STATED ODDS 1:5
SS1 Troy Glaus .50 1.25
SS2 Mark McGwire 3.00 8.00
SS3 Sammy Sosa 1.25 3.00
SS4 Juan Gonzalez .50 1.25
SS5 Barry Bonds 3.00 8.00
SS6 Jeff Bagwell .75 2.00
SS7 Jason Giambi .50 1.25
SS8 Ivan Rodriguez .75 2.00
SS9 Mike Piazza 2.00 5.00
SS10 Chipper Jones 1.25 3.00
SS11 Ken Griffey Jr. 2.50 6.00
SS12 Gary Sheffield .50 1.25

2001 SP Game Bat Milestone Trophy Room

COMPLETE SET (6) 12.50 30.00
STATED ODDS 1:10
TR1 Sammy Sosa 1.25 3.00
TR2 Jason Giambi 1.25 3.00
TR3 Todd Helton 1.25 3.00
TR4 Alex Rodriguez 1.50 4.00
TR5 Mark McGwire 3.00 8.00
TR6 Ken Griffey Jr. 2.50 6.00

2001 SP Game Used Edition

COMP.SET w/o SP's (60) 30.00 80.00
COMMON CARD (1-60) .50 1.25
COMMON CARD (61-90) 3.00 8.00
61-90 RANDOM INSERTS IN PACKS
61-90 PRINT RUN 500 SERIAL #'d SETS
1 Garret Anderson .50 1.25
2 Troy Glaus .50 1.25
3 Darin Erstad .50 1.25
4 Jason Giambi .50 1.25
5 Tim Hudson .50 1.25
6 Johnny Damon .75 2.00
7 Carlos Delgado .50 1.25
8 Greg Vaughn .50 1.25
9 Juan Gonzalez .50 1.25
10 Roberto Alomar .75 2.00
11 Jim Thome .75 2.00
12 Edgar Martinez .75 2.00
13 Cal Ripken 4.00 10.00
14 Andres Galarraga .50 1.25
15 Alex Rodriguez 1.50 4.00
16 Rafael Palmeiro .75 2.00
17 Ivan Rodriguez .75 2.00
18 Manny Ramirez Sox .75 2.00
19 Nomar Garciaparra 2.00 5.00
20 Pedro Martinez .75 2.00
21 Jermaine Dye .50 1.25
22 Dean Palmer .50 1.25
23 Matt Lawton .50 1.25
24 Frank Thomas 1.25 3.00
25 David Wells .50 1.25
26 Magglio Ordonez .50 1.25
27 Derek Jeter 3.00 8.00
28 Bernie Williams .75 2.00
29 Roger Clemens 2.50 6.00
30 Jeff Bagwell .75 2.00
31 Richard Hidalgo .50 1.25
32 Chipper Jones 1.25 3.00
33 Andruw Jones .75 2.00
34 Greg Maddux 2.00 5.00
35 Jeffrey Hammonds .50 1.25
36 Mark McGwire 3.00 8.00
37 Jim Edmonds .50 1.25
38 Sammy Sosa 1.25 3.00
39 Corey Patterson .50 1.25
40 Randy Johnson 1.25 3.00
41 Luis Gonzalez .50 1.25
42 Gary Sheffield .50 1.25
43 Shawn Green .50 1.25
44 Kevin Brown .50 1.25
45 Vladimir Guerrero 1.25 3.00
46 Barry Bonds 3.00 8.00
47 Jeff Kent .50 1.25
48 Preston Wilson .50 1.25
49 Charles Johnson .50 1.25
50 Mike Piazza 2.00 5.00
51 Edgardo Alfonzo .50 1.25
52 Tony Gwynn 1.50 4.00
53 Scott Rolen .75 2.00
54 Pat Burrell .50 1.25
55 Brian Giles .50 1.25
56 Jason Kendall .50 1.25
57 Ken Griffey Jr. 2.50 6.00
58 Mike Hampton .50 1.25
59 Todd Helton .75 2.00
60 Larry Walker .50 1.25
61 Wilson Betemit RC 6.00 15.00
62 Travis Hafner RC 12.50 30.00
63 Ichiro Suzuki RC 50.00 120.00
64 Juan Diaz RC 3.00 8.00
65 Morgan Ensberg RC 6.00 15.00
66 Horacio Ramirez RC 4.00 10.00
67 Ricardo Rodriguez RC 3.00 8.00
68 Sean Douglass RC 3.00 8.00
69 Brandon Duckworth RC 3.00 8.00
70 Jackson Melian RC 3.00 8.00
71 Adrian Hernandez RC 3.00 8.00
72 Kyle Kessel RC 3.00 8.00
73 Jason Michaels RC 3.00 8.00
74 Esix Snead RC 3.00 8.00
75 Jason Smith RC 3.00 8.00
76 Tyler Walker RC 3.00 8.00
77 Juan Uribe RC 4.00 10.00
78 Adam Pettyjohn RC 3.00 8.00
79 Tsuyoshi Shinjo RC 4.00 10.00
80 Mike Penney RC 3.00 8.00
81 Josh Towers RC 4.00 10.00
82 Erick Almonte RC 3.00 8.00
83 Ryan Freel RC 4.00 10.00
84 Juan Pena 3.00 8.00
85 Albert Pujols RC 75.00 200.00
86 Henry Mateo RC 3.00 8.00
87 Greg Miller RC 3.00 8.00
88 Jose Mieses RC 3.00 8.00
89 Jack Wilson RC 4.00 10.00
90 Carlos Valderrama RC 3.00 8.00

2001 SP Game Used Edition Authentic Fabric

STATED ODDS 1:1
PRINT RUNS LISTED BELOW AS AVAILABLE
DP'S PERCEIVED AS LARGER SUPPLY
AH Aubrey Huff 1.25 3.00
AJ Andruw Jones 2.00 5.00
AL Al Leiter 1.25 3.00
AP Adam Piatt 1.25 3.00
ARH Alex Rodriguez Rangers 4.00 10.00
ARM Alex Rodriguez Mariners DP 4.00 10.00
BB Barry Bonds 5.00 12.00
BG Brian Giles SP 2.50 6.00
BL Barry Larkin 2.00 5.00
CD Carlos Delgado SP 2.50 6.00
CJ Chipper Jones 3.00 8.00
CJO Charles Johnson 1.25 3.00
CR Cal Ripken 6.00 15.00
DE Darin Erstad 1.25 3.00
DW David Wells SP 2.50 6.00
DY Dmitri Young 1.25 3.00
EA Edgardo Alfonzo 1.25 3.00
EC Eric Chavez 1.25 3.00
EM Edgar Martinez DP 2.00 5.00
FM Fred McGriff 2.00 5.00
FTA Fernando Tatis 1.25 3.00
FTH Frank Thomas 3.00 8.00
GM Greg Maddux DP 5.00 12.00
GS Gary Sheffield 1.25 3.00
GV Greg Vaughn 1.25 3.00
IR Ivan Rodriguez 2.00 5.00
JB Jeromy Burnitz 1.25 3.00
JCH Jose Canseco 2.00 5.00
JCI Jeff Cirillo 1.25 3.00
JDI Joe DiMaggio SP/50 * 125.00 250.00
JDR J.D. Drew DP 1.25 3.00
JDY Jermaine Dye SP 2.50 6.00
JE Jim Edmonds DP 2.00 5.00
JG Jason Giambi 1.25 3.00
JI Jason Isringhausen SP 2.50 6.00
JK Jason Kendall 1.25 3.00
JK Jeff Kent 1.25 3.00
JO John Olerud 1.25 3.00
JT Jim Thome 2.00 5.00
JV Jose Vidro 1.25 3.00
KB Kevin Brown 2.00 5.00
KGH Ken Griffey Jr. Reds 6.00 15.00
KGM Ken Griffey Jr. Mariners DP 6.00 15.00
KL Kenny Lofton 1.25 3.00
KM Kevin Millwood 1.25 3.00
LG Luis Gonzalez 1.25 3.00
MG Mark Grace 2.00 5.00
MH Mike Hampton 1.25 3.00
MM Mickey Mantle SP/50 * 125.00 250.00
MO Magglio Ordonez 1.25 3.00
MR Mariano Rivera 3.00 8.00
MT Miguel Tejada 1.25 3.00
MW Matt Williams 1.25 3.00
NR Nolan Ryan Rangers SP/50 * 20.00 50.00
NRA Nolan Ryan Astros SP/50 * 20.00 50.00
PB Pat Burrell 1.25 3.00
PN Phil Nevin 1.25 3.00
PW Preston Wilson 1.25 3.00
RA Rick Ankiel DP 1.25 3.00
RAL Roberto Alomar 2.00 5.00
RC Roger Clemens 6.00 15.00
RJ Randy Johnson 3.00 8.00
RM Roger Maris SP 15.00 40.00
RV Robin Ventura 1.25 3.00
SG Shawn Green 1.25 3.00
SR Scott Rolen 2.00 5.00
SSH Sammy Sosa Home 2.00 5.00
SSR Sammy Sosa Road 2.00 5.00
TB Tony Batista SP 2.50 6.00
TGL Troy Glaus 1.25 3.00
TGW Tony Gwynn DP 3.00 8.00
TH Tim Hudson 1.25 3.00
THE Todd Helton 2.00 5.00
TL Terrence Long 1.25 3.00
TM Tino Martinez 3.00 8.00
TOG Tom Glavine 2.00 5.00
TRH Trevor Hoffman 2.00 5.00
TS Tom Seaver Mets SP/50 * 15.00 40.00
TSR Tom Seaver Reds SP/50 * 15.00 40.00
TZ Todd Zeile 1.25 3.00

2001 SP Game Used Edition Authentic Fabric Autographs

STATED PRINT RUN 50 SERIAL #'d SETS
EXCHANGE DEADLINE TBD
SAJ Andruw Jones 20.00 50.00
SAR Alex Rodriguez 100.00 175.00
SBB Barry Bonds 125.00 200.00
SCD Carlos Delgado 20.00 50.00
SCJ Chipper Jones 60.00 120.00
SCR Cal Ripken 125.00 200.00
SDW David Wells 20.00 50.00
SEA Edgardo Alfonzo 20.00 50.00
SFTH Frank Thomas 60.00 120.00
SIR Ivan Rodriguez 60.00 120.00
SJC Jose Canseco 40.00 80.00
SJDR J.D. Drew 20.00 50.00
SJG Jason Giambi 20.00 50.00
SKG Ken Griffey Jr. 75.00 150.00
SNR Nolan Ryan 125.00 200.00
SRA Rick Ankiel 30.00 60.00
SRJ Randy Johnson 60.00 120.00
SSS Sammy Sosa 50.00 100.00
STGL Troy Glaus 40.00 80.00
STH Tim Hudson 40.00 80.00

2001 SP Game Used Edition Authentic Fabric Duos

STATED PRINT RUN 50 SERIAL #'d SETS
BC B.Bonds/J.Canseco 40.00 80.00
CW R.Clemens/B.Williams 20.00 50.00
GR K.Griffey Jr./A.Rodriguez 30.00 60.00
GS K.Griffey Jr./S.Sosa 30.00 60.00
HG T.Hudson/J.Giambi 15.00 40.00
JJ C.Jones/A.Jones 20.00 50.00
JR R.Johnson/N.Ryan 50.00 100.00
MD M.Mantle/J.DiMaggio 250.00 400.00
MM M.Mantle/R.Maris 250.00 400.00
RR A.Rodriguez/I.Rodriguez 30.00 60.00
RS N.Ryan/T.Seaver 60.00 120.00
SG G.Sheffield/S.Green 15.00 40.00
SR S.Sosa/A.Rodriguez 30.00 60.00
ST S.Sosa/F.Thomas 20.00 50.00

2004 SP Game Used Patch

COMP.UPDATE SET (50) 40.00 100.00
COMMON CARD 1-60 .60 1.50
COMMON (61-90) p/r 400-684 .75 2.00
COMMON 61-90 p/r 262-384 .75 2.00
COMMON 61-90 p/r 165-236 .75 2.00
COMMON 61-90 p/r 86 .75 2.00
61-90 PRINT RUN B/WN 86-684 COPIES PER
COMMON CARD (91-119) 2.50 6.00
91-119 PRINT RUN 375 SERIAL #'d SETS
61-119 RANDOM INSERTS IN PACKS
COMMON CARD (121-135) .60 1.50
COMMON CARD (136-170) .75 2.00
ONE UPDATE SET PER 48 UD2 HOB.BOXES
1 Miguel Cabrera 1.50 4.00
2 Alex Rodriguez Yanks 2.00 5.00
3 Edgar Renteria .60 1.50
4 Juan Gonzalez .60 1.50
5 Mike Lowell .60 1.50
6 Andruw Jones .60 1.50
7 Eric Chavez .60 1.50
8 Jim Edmonds 1.00 2.50
9 Mike Piazza 1.50 4.00
10 Angel Berroa .60 1.50
11 Eric Gagne .60 1.50
12 Jody Gerut .60 1.50
13 Orlando Cabrera .60 1.50
14 Austin Kearns .60 1.50
15 Frank Thomas 1.50 4.00
16 Johan Santana 1.00 2.50
17 Randy Johnson 1.50 4.00
18 Preston Wilson .60 1.50
19 Garret Anderson .60 1.50
20 Jorge Posada 1.00 2.50
21 Rich Harden .60 1.50
22 Barry Zito 1.00 2.50
23 Gary Sheffield .60 1.50
24 Jose Reyes 1.00 2.50
25 Roy Halladay 1.00 2.50
26 Ben Sheets .60 1.50
27 Geoff Jenkins .60 1.50
28 Josh Beckett .60 1.50
29 Roy Oswalt 1.00 2.50
30 Bobby Abreu .60 1.50
31 Hank Blalock .60 1.50
32 Kerry Wood .60 1.50
33 Ryan Klesko .60 1.50
34 Rafael Furcal .60 1.50
35 Tom Glavine 1.00 2.50
36 Kevin Brown .60 1.50
37 Scott Rolen 1.00 2.50
38 Bret Boone .60 1.50
39 Ichiro Suzuki 2.00 5.00
40 Lance Berkman 1.00 2.50
41 Tim Hudson 1.00 2.50
42 Carlos Delgado .60 1.50
43 Ivan Rodriguez 1.00 2.50
44 Luis Gonzalez .60 1.50
45 Torii Hunter .60 1.50
46 Carlos Lee .60 1.50
47 Jacque Jones .60 1.50
48 Manny Ramirez 1.50 4.00
49 Troy Glaus .60 1.50
50 Corey Patterson .60 1.50
51 Jason Schmidt .60 1.50
52 Mark Mulder .60 1.50
53 Vernon Wells .60 1.50
54 Curt Schilling 1.00 2.50
55 Javy Lopez .60 1.50
56 Mark Prior 1.00 2.50
57 Dontrelle Willis .60 1.50
58 Derek Jeter 4.00 10.00
59 Jeff Bagwell 1.00 2.50
60 Marlon Byrd .60 1.50
61 Rafael Palmeiro SN/500 1.25 3.00
62 Kevin Millwood SN/165 .75 2.00
63 Greg Maddux SN/273 2.50 6.00
64 Adam Dunn SN/400 1.25 3.00
65 Richie Sexson SN/469 .75 2.00
66 Magglio Ordonez SN/567 1.25 3.00
67 Hideo Nomo SN/236 2.00 5.00
68 Albert Pujols SN/194 2.50 6.00
69 Rocco Baldelli SN/368 .75 2.00
70 Mark Teixeira SN/86 1.25 3.00
71 Jason Giambi SN/660 .75 2.00
72 Alfonso Soriano SN/230 1.25 3.00
73 Roger Clemens SN/300 2.50 6.00
74 Miguel Tejada SN/359 1.25 3.00
75 Jeff Kent SN/684 .75 2.00
76 Bernie Williams SN/342 1.25 3.00
77 Sammy Sosa SN/470 2.00 5.00
78 Mike Mussina SN/641 1.25 3.00
79 Jim Thome SN/334 1.25 3.00
80 Brian Giles SN/506 .75 2.00
81 Shawn Green SN/234 .75 2.00
82 Mike Sweeney SN/340 .75 2.00
83 John Smoltz SN/262 2.00 5.00
84 Carlos Beltran SN/319 1.25 3.00
85 Todd Helton SN/384 1.25 3.00
86 Nomar Garciaparra SN/372 1.25 3.00
87 Ken Griffey Jr. SN/481 4.00 10.00
88 Chipper Jones SN/633 2.00 5.00
89 Vladimir Guerrero SN/226 1.25 3.00
90 Pedro Martinez SN/313 1.25 3.00
91 Brandon Medders RD RC 2.50 6.00
92 Colby Miller RD RC 2.50 6.00
93 Dave Crouthers RD RC 2.50 6.00
94 Dennis Sarfate RD RC 2.50 6.00
95 Donald Kelly RD RC 4.00 10.00
96 Alec Zumwalt RD RC 2.50 6.00
97 Chris Aguila RD RC 2.50 6.00
98 Greg Dobbs RD RC 2.50 6.00
99 Ian Snell RD RC 2.50 6.00
100 Jake Woods RD RC 2.50 6.00
101 Jamie Brown RD RC 2.50 6.00
102 Jason Frasor RD RC 2.50 6.00
103 Jerome Gamble RD RC 2.50 6.00
104 Jesse Harper RD RC 2.50 6.00
105 Josh Labandeira RD RC 2.50 6.00
106 Justin Hampson RD RC 2.50 6.00
107 Justin Huisman RD RC 2.50 6.00
108 Justin Leone RD RC 2.50 6.00
109 Lincoln Holdzkom RD RC 2.50 6.00
110 Mike Bumatay RD RC 2.50 6.00
111 Mike Gosling RD RC 2.50 6.00
112 Mike Johnston RD RC 2.50 6.00
113 Mike Rouse RD RC 2.50 6.00
114 Nick Regilio RD RC 2.50 6.00
115 Ryan Meaux RD RC 2.50 6.00
116 Scott Dohmann RD RC 2.50 6.00
117 Sean Henn RD RC 2.50 6.00
118 Tim Bausher RD RC 2.50 6.00
119 Tim Bittner RD RC 2.50 6.00
121 Richie Sexson .60 1.50
122 Javier Vazquez .60 1.50
123 Alex Rodriguez Yanks 2.00 5.00
124 Javy Lopez .60 1.50
125 Miguel Tejada 1.00 2.50
126 Bartolo Colon .60 1.50
127 Ivan Rodriguez 1.00 2.50
128 Rafael Palmeiro 1.00 2.50
129 Kevin Brown .60 1.50
130 Gary Sheffield .60 1.50
131 Greg Maddux 2.00 5.00
132 Curt Schilling 1.00 2.50
133 Roger Clemens 2.00 5.00
134 Alfonso Soriano 1.00 2.50
135 Vladimir Guerrero 1.00 2.50
136 Carlos Vasquez RC .75 2.00
137 Roman Colon RC .75 2.00
138 William Bergolla RC .75 2.00
139 Jason Bartlett RC 2.50 6.00
140 Casey Daigle RC .75 2.00
141 Ryan Wing RC .75 2.00
142 Chris Saenz RC .75 2.00
143 Edwin Moreno RC .75 2.00
144 Shawn Hill RC .75 2.00
145 Eddy Rodriguez RC .75 2.00
146 Justin Knoedler RC .75 2.00
147 Renyel Pinto RC .75 2.00
148 Kevin Cave RC .75 2.00
149 Carlos Hines RC .75 2.00
150 Merkin Valdez RC .75 2.00
151 Tim Hamulack RC .75 2.00
152 Hector Gimenez RC .75 2.00
153 Mike Vento RC .75 2.00
154 Scott Proctor RC .75 2.00
155 Rusty Tucker RC .75 2.00
156 Akinori Otsuka RC .75 2.00
157 Ronny Cedeno RC .75 2.00
158 Jose Capellan RC .75 2.00
159 Justin Germano RC .75 2.00
160 Shingo Takatsu RC .75 2.00
161 Fernando Nieve RC .75 2.00
162 Michael Wuertz RC .75 2.00
163 Jerry Gil RC .75 2.00
164 Jorge Vasquez RC .75 2.00
165 Chad Bentz RC .75 2.00
166 Luis A. Gonzalez RC .75 2.00
167 Ivan Ochoa RC .75 2.00
168 Onil Joseph RC .75 2.00
169 Enemencio Pacheco RC .75 2.00
170 Kazuo Matsui RC 1.25 3.00

2004 SP Game Used Patch All-Star

RANDOM INSERTS IN PACKS
STATED PRINT RUN 50 SERIAL #'d SETS
AP Albert Pujols 40.00 80.00
AR Alex Rodriguez 30.00 60.00
AS Alfonso Soriano 10.00 25.00
BZ Barry Zito 10.00 25.00
CD Carlos Delgado 10.00 25.00
CJ Chipper Jones 15.00 40.00
CS Curt Schilling 15.00 40.00
DJ Derek Jeter 50.00 100.00
EC Eric Chavez 10.00 25.00
FT Frank Thomas 15.00 40.00
GS Gary Sheffield 10.00 25.00
HE Todd Helton 15.00 40.00
HN Hideo Nomo 40.00 80.00
IS Ichiro Suzuki 50.00 100.00
JG Juan Gonzalez 10.00 25.00
JT Jim Thome 15.00 40.00
KG Ken Griffey Jr. 30.00 60.00
MP Mark Prior 15.00 40.00
SS Sammy Sosa 15.00 40.00
TH Tim Hudson 10.00 25.00
VW Vernon Wells 10.00 25.00

2004 SP Game Used Patch All-Star Number

RANDOM INSERTS IN PACKS
PRINT RUNS B/WN 3-50 COPIES PER
NO PRICING ON QTY OF 12 OR LESS
AJ Andruw Jones/25 20.00 50.00
AP Andy Pettitte/42 15.00 40.00
BZ Barry Zito/50 10.00 25.00
CD Carlos Delgado/25 15.00 40.00
CD1 Carlos Delgado/25 15.00 40.00
CS Curt Schilling Sox/38 15.00 40.00
CS1 Curt Schilling D'backs/38 10.00 25.00
FT Frank Thomas/35 15.00 40.00
GA Garret Anderson/16 15.00 40.00
GM Greg Maddux Braves/31 30.00 60.00
GM1 Greg Maddux Cubs/31 30.00 60.00
HE Todd Helton/17 20.00 50.00
IS Ichiro Suzuki/50 50.00 100.00
JG Juan Gonzalez/19 15.00 40.00
JP Jorge Posada/20 20.00 50.00
JT Jim Thome/25 20.00 50.00
KG Ken Griffey Jr./30 40.00 80.00
MM Mike Mussina/35 15.00 40.00
MO Magglio Ordonez/30 10.00 25.00
PM Pedro Martinez/45 15.00 40.00
RC Roger Clemens/22 40.00 80.00
RH Roy Halladay/32 10.00 25.00
RP Rafael Palmeiro/25 20.00 50.00
SG Shawn Green/15 15.00 40.00
SR Scott Rolen/27 15.00 40.00
SS Sammy Sosa Cubs/21 20.00 50.00
SS1 Sammy Sosa Sox/21 20.00 50.00
TH Tim Hudson/15 15.00 40.00
TH1 Tim Hudson/15 15.00 40.00

2004 SP Game Used Patch Famous Nicknames

RANDOM INSERTS IN PACKS
PRINT RUNS B/WN 1-27 COPIES PER
NO PRICING ON QTY OF 14 OR LESS
BR Brooks Robinson/23 20.00 50.00
CR Cal Ripken Glove Down/21 60.00 120.00
CR1 Cal Ripken Glove Up/21 60.00 120.00
CY Carl Yastrzemski/23 40.00 80.00
DS Darryl Strawberry/17 15.00 40.00
ES Duke Snider/18 20.00 50.00
GA Sparky Anderson/27 10.00 25.00
GC Gary Carter/19 20.00 50.00
HK Harmon Killebrew/22 50.00 100.00
JF Nellie Fox/19 100.00 200.00
JG Juan Gonzalez/15 15.00 40.00
JH Catfish Hunter/15 20.00 50.00
KG Ken Griffey Jr./15 60.00 120.00
LB Yogi Berra/19 30.00 60.00
NR Nolan Ryan Astros/27 30.00 80.00
NR1 Nolan Ryan Rgr/27 30.00 80.00
OC Orlando Cepeda/17 15.00 40.00
OS Ozzie Smith/19 40.00 80.00
PN Phil Niekro/24 15.00 40.00
RC Roger Clemens/20 40.00 80.00
RJ Randy Johnson/16 20.00 50.00
RY Robin Yount/20 20.00 50.00
SM Stan Musial/22 75.00 150.00
SS Sammy Sosa Cubs/15 20.00 50.00
SS1 Sammy Sosa Sox/15 20.00 50.00
TS Tom Seaver/20 20.00 50.00
WS Willie Stargell/21 20.00 50.00

2004 SP Game Used Patch Famous Nicknames Autograph

RANDOM INSERTS IN PACKS
STATED PRINT RUN 50 SERIAL #'d SETS
AD Andre Dawson 30.00 60.00
AR Alex Rodriguez Rgr 100.00 200.00
AR1 Alex Rodriguez M's 100.00 200.00
BM Bill Mazeroski 40.00 80.00
BR Brooks Robinson 30.00 80.00
DM Don Mattingly 60.00 150.00
FT Frank Thomas 50.00 100.00
HK Harmon Killebrew 60.00 120.00
HM Hideki Matsui 125.00 300.00
JB Jeff Bagwell 60.00 120.00
JG Juan Gonzalez 30.00 60.00
KG Ken Griffey Jr. 100.00 200.00
LJ Chipper Jones Hand Up 60.00 120.00
MM Mike Mussina 40.00 80.00
NR Nolan Ryan 40.00 80.00
OS Ozzie Smith 40.00 100.00
PN Phil Niekro 30.00 60.00
RC Roger Clemens 100.00 250.00
RY Robin Yount 60.00 120.00
TS Tom Seaver 50.00 120.00
WI Dontrelle Willis 40.00 80.00

2004 SP Game Used Patch HOF Numbers

RANDOM INSERTS IN PACKS
PRINT RUNS B/WN 1-50 COPIES PER
NO PRICING ON QTY OF 11 OR LESS
AJ Andruw Jones/25 20.00 50.00
BG Bob Gibson/45 15.00 40.00
BW Billy Williams/26 15.00 40.00
CD Carlos Delgado/25 15.00 40.00
CH Catfish Hunter/27 15.00 40.00
CL Roger Clemens/22 40.00 80.00
CS Curt Schilling/38 15.00 40.00
DD Don Drysdale/50 30.00 60.00
DS Don Sutton/20 15.00 40.00
EG Eric Gagne/38 10.00 25.00

EM Eddie Mathews/41 40.00 80.00
FR Frank Robinson/20 15.00 40.00
FT Frank Thomas/35 40.00 80.00
GL Tom Glavine/47 15.00 40.00
GM Greg Maddux/31 30.00 60.00
GO Juan Gonzalez Royals/19 15.00 40.00
GO1 Juan Gonzalez Rgr/19 15.00 40.00
GP Gaylord Perry/36 10.00 25.00
HE Todd Helton/17 20.00 50.00
IS Ichiro Suzuki/50 50.00 100.00
JC Jose Canseco/33 15.00 40.00
JG Jason Giambi/25 15.00 40.00
JI Jim Thome/25 20.00 50.00
JP Jim Palmer/22 15.00 40.00
KG Ken Griffey Jr./30 30.00 60.00
MA Juan Marichal/27 15.00 40.00
MP Mike Piazza/31 30.00 60.00
MR Manny Ramirez/24 20.00 50.00
MS Mike Schmidt/20 40.00 80.00
MZ Pedro Martinez/45 15.00 40.00
NR Nolan Ryan/34 40.00 80.00
OC Orlando Cepeda/30 10.00 25.00
PI Mark Prior Look Right/22 15.00 40.00
PI1 Mark Prior Look Left/22 15.00 40.00
RC Roberto Clemente/21 200.00 350.00
RF Rollie Fingers/34 10.00 25.00
RH Rickey Henderson/25 20.00 50.00
RP Rafael Palmeiro O's/25 20.00 50.00
RP1 Rafael Palmeiro Rgr/25 20.00 50.00
RY Robin Yount/19 20.00 50.00
SC Steve Carlton/32 10.00 25.00
SG Shawn Green/15 15.00 40.00
SR Scott Rolen/27 15.00 40.00
SS Sammy Sosa Cubs/21 20.00 50.00
SS1 Sammy Sosa Sox/21 20.00 50.00
TH Tim Hudson/15 15.00 40.00
TS Tom Seaver/41 15.00 40.00
WB Wade Boggs/26 15.00 40.00
WS Warren Spahn/21 20.00 50.00

2004 SP Game Used Patch Legendary Fabrics

RANDOM INSERTS IN PACKS
PRINT RUNS B/WN 6-50 COPIES PER
NO PRICING ON QTY OF 10 OR LESS
BE Johnny Bench w Mask/50 15.00 40.00
BE1 Johnny Bench Hitting/50 15.00 40.00
BG Bob Gibson/50 15.00 40.00
BW Billy Williams/50 10.00 25.00
CH Catfish Hunter/50 15.00 40.00
CR Cal Ripken Fielding/50 50.00 100.00
CR1 Cal Ripken Running/50 50.00 100.00
CY Carl Yastrzemski/31 30.00 60.00
EM Eddie Mathews/50 40.00 80.00
FR Frank Robinson O's/50 15.00 40.00
FR1 Frank Robinson Reds/50 15.00 40.00
GP Gaylord Perry/50 10.00 25.00
HK Harmon Killebrew Twins/50 40.00 80.00
HK1 H.Killebrew Senators/50 40.00 80.00
JC Jose Canseco/50 15.00 40.00
JM Joe Morgan Reds/50 10.00 25.00
JM1 Joe Morgan Giants/50 10.00 25.00
JT Joe Torre/50 10.00 25.00
LA Luis Aparicio/50 10.00 25.00
LD Leo Durocher/50 15.00 40.00
MS Mike Schmidt Bat Hand/50 30.00 60.00
MS1 Mike Schmidt Swing/50 30.00 60.00
NR Nolan Ryan Astros/50 30.00 60.00
NR1 Nolan Ryan Rgr/50 30.00 60.00
OC Orlando Cepeda/50 10.00 25.00
OS Ozzie Smith/50 20.00 50.00
PO Paul O'Neill/50 15.00 40.00
RF Rollie Fingers/50 10.00 25.00
RY Robin Yount Bat Up/50 15.00 40.00
RY1 Robin Yount Bat Down/50 15.00 40.00
SC Steve Carlton/50 10.00 25.00
TS Tom Seaver Mets/50 15.00 40.00
TS1 Tom Seaver Reds/50 15.00 40.00
WS W.Spahn Arms Down/50 20.00 50.00
WS1 W.Spahn Arms Up/50 20.00 50.00

2004 SP Game Used Patch Legendary Fabrics Autograph Dual

RANDOM INSERTS IN PACKS
PRINT RUNS B/WN 10-25 COPIES PER
NO PRICING ON QTY OF 13 OR LESS
AD Andre Dawson/25 12.00 30.00
BE Johnny Bench/25 75.00 150.00
BR Brooks Robinson/25 60.00 120.00
BW Billy Williams/25 12.00 30.00
CR Cal Ripken/25 75.00 200.00
CY Carl Yastrzemski/17 75.00 200.00
DE Dwight Evans/25 60.00 120.00
DM Don Mattingly/25 60.00 150.00
DS Don Sutton/25 40.00 100.00
FL Fred Lynn/25 15.00 40.00
FR Frank Robinson/25 60.00 120.00
GP Gaylord Perry/25 25.00 60.00
HK Harmon Killebrew/25 75.00 200.00
JC Jose Canseco/25 60.00 120.00
JM Joe Morgan/25 30.00 80.00
JP Jim Palmer/25 50.00 100.00
JT Joe Torre Cards/25 50.00 100.00
JT1 Joe Torre Braves/25 50.00 100.00
KP Kirby Puckett/25 150.00 300.00
LA Luis Aparicio/25 40.00 80.00
NR Nolan Ryan Astros/25 75.00 150.00
NR1 Nolan Ryan Rgr/25 75.00 150.00
OC Orlando Cepeda/25 40.00 80.00
OS Ozzie Smith/25 60.00 120.00
PM Paul Molitor/25 50.00 100.00
PO Paul O'Neill/25 25.00 60.00
RC Roger Clemens/25 150.00 250.00
RF Rollie Fingers/25 10.00 25.00
RY Robin Yount Look Ahead/25 100.00 175.00
SG Steve Garvey/25 50.00 100.00
ST Darryl Strawberry/25 12.00 30.00
TG Tony Gwynn Look Left/25 75.00 150.00
TG1 Tony Gwynn Look Right/25 75.00 150.00
TS Tom Seaver Mets/25 60.00 150.00
TS1 Tom Seaver Reds/25 60.00 150.00
WB Wade Boggs Yanks/25 50.00 120.00
WB1 Wade Boggs Sox/25 50.00 210.00
WI Maury Wills/25 40.00 80.00
YO Robin Yount Look Right/25 100.00 175.00

2004 SP Game Used Patch MLB Masters

RANDOM INSERTS IN PACKS
PRINT RUNS B/WN 3-50 COPIES PER
NO PRICING ON QTY OF 12 OR LESS
AJ Andruw Jones/25 20.00 50.00
BE Josh Beckett/25 15.00 40.00
CD Carlos Delgado/25 15.00 40.00
CS Curt Schilling/38 15.00 40.00
FT Frank Thomas/35 15.00 40.00
GM Greg Maddux Braves/31 15.00 40.00
GM1 Greg Maddux Cubs/31 15.00 40.00
GO Juan Gonzalez/19 15.00 40.00
HE Todd Helton/17 20.00 50.00
IS Ichiro Suzuki/50 50.00 100.00
JG Jason Giambi/25 15.00 40.00
JP Jorge Posada/20 20.00 50.00
JT Jim Thome Phils/25 20.00 50.00
JT1 Jim Thome Indians/25 20.00 50.00
KG Ken Griffey Jr./30 40.00 80.00
MO Magglio Ordonez/30 10.00 25.00
MP Mark Prior/22 20.00 50.00
MR Manny Ramirez/24 20.00 50.00
PI Mike Piazza/31 15.00 40.00
PM Pedro Martinez/45 15.00 40.00
RC Roger Clemens/22 40.00 80.00
RH Roy Halladay/32 10.00 25.00
SG Shawn Green/15 15.00 40.00
SR Scott Rolen/27 15.00 40.00
SS Sammy Sosa/21 20.00 50.00
TH Tim Hudson Glove Up/15 15.00 40.00
TH1 Tim Hudson Glove Down/15 15.00 40.00

2004 SP Game Used Patch MVP

RANDOM INSERTS IN PACKS
STATED PRINT RUN 25 SERIAL #'d SETS
AR Alex Rodriguez 30.00 60.00
BR Brooks Robinson 20.00 50.00
BW Bernie Williams 20.00 50.00
CJ Chipper Jones 20.00 50.00
CR Cal Ripken 75.00 150.00
CS Curt Schilling 20.00 50.00
DJ Derek Jeter 60.00 120.00
FT Frank Thomas 20.00 50.00
GA Garret Anderson 15.00 40.00
IS Ichiro Suzuki 60.00 120.00
IV Ivan Rodriguez 20.00 50.00
JB Josh Beckett 15.00 40.00
JG Jason Giambi 15.00 40.00
KG Ken Griffey Jr. 40.00 80.00
MP Mike Piazza 30.00 60.00
MT Miguel Tejada 15.00 40.00
PM Pedro Martinez 20.00 50.00
RC Roger Clemens 40.00 80.00
RJ Randy Johnson 20.00 50.00
SS Sammy Sosa 20.00 50.00
TG Troy Glaus 15.00 40.00

2004 SP Game Used Patch Premium

RANDOM INSERTS IN PACKS
STATED PRINT RUN 50 SERIAL #'d SETS
GARCIAPARRA PRINT RUN 11 #'d CARDS
MATSUI PRINT RUN 17 #'d CARDS
SORIANO PRINT RUN 34 #'d CARDS
NO PRICING ON QTY OF 11 OR LESS
AD Adam Dunn 10.00 25.00
AP Albert Pujols 40.00 80.00
AR Alex Rodriguez Rgr 30.00 60.00
AR1 A.Rodriguez Yanks Cap 40.00 80.00
AR2 A.Rodriguez Yanks Helmet 40.00 80.00
AS Alfonso Soriano/34 10.00 25.00
BE Josh Beckett 10.00 25.00
BW Bernie Williams 15.00 40.00
BZ Barry Zito 10.00 25.00
CD Carlos Delgado 10.00 25.00
CJ Chipper Jones 15.00 40.00
CS Curt Schilling Glove Up 15.00 40.00
CS1 Curt Schilling Hand in Air 15.00 40.00
DJ Derek Jeter 40.00 100.00
DW Dontrelle Willis 15.00 40.00
EC Eric Chavez 10.00 25.00
FT Frank Thomas 15.00 40.00
GM Greg Maddux Braves 20.00 50.00
GM1 Greg Maddux Cubs 20.00 50.00
GO Juan Gonzalez 10.00 25.00
HM Hideki Matsui/17 125.00 200.00
IR Ivan Rodriguez 15.00 40.00
IS Ichiro Suzuki Profile 30.00 60.00
IS1 Ichiro Suzuki Arm Out 30.00 60.00
JB Jeff Bagwell 15.00 40.00
JG Jason Giambi 10.00 25.00
JP Jorge Posada 15.00 40.00
JT Jim Thome 15.00 40.00
KB Kevin Brown 10.00 25.00
KG Ken Griffey Jr. Arm Out 30.00 60.00
KG1 K.Griffey Jr. Red Helmet 30.00 60.00
MO Magglio Ordonez 10.00 25.00
MP Mark Prior 15.00 40.00
MR Manny Ramirez 15.00 40.00
MT Miguel Tejada 10.00 25.00
NR Nolan Ryan 30.00 60.00
PI Mike Piazza 10.00 25.00
PM Pedro Martinez 15.00 40.00
RC Roger Clemens 20.00 50.00
RH Roy Halladay 10.00 25.00
RI Mariano Rivera 15.00 40.00
RJ Randy Johnson 15.00 40.00
RP Rafael Palmeiro 15.00 40.00
SG Shawn Green 10.00 25.00
SR Scott Rolen 15.00 40.00
SS Sammy Sosa Swing 15.00 40.00
SS1 Sammy Sosa Bat Down 15.00 40.00
TE Mark Teixeira 15.00 40.00
TG Tom Glavine 15.00 40.00
TH Tim Hudson 10.00 25.00

2004 SP Game Used Patch Premium Update

ONE PER SPGU UPDATE FACTORY SET
ONE UPDATE SET PER 48 UD2 HOB.BOXES
STATED PRINT RUN 20 SERIAL #'d SETS
V.WELLS PRINT RUN 21 SERIAL #'d CARDS
AK Austin Kearns 15.00 40.00
BA Bobby Abreu 15.00 40.00
BB Bret Boone 15.00 40.00
BC Bartolo Colon 15.00 40.00
BW Brandon Webb 15.00 40.00
CP Corey Patterson 15.00 40.00
EG Eric Gagne 15.00 40.00
EM Edgar Martinez 30.00 60.00
GA Garret Anderson 15.00 40.00
HB Hank Blalock 15.00 40.00
HN Hideo Nomo 40.00 80.00
JE Jim Edmonds 15.00 40.00
JJ Jacque Jones 15.00 40.00
JK Jeff Kent 15.00 40.00
JR Jose Reyes 15.00 40.00
KM Kevin Millwood 15.00 40.00
KW Kerry Wood 15.00 40.00
LB Lance Berkman 15.00 40.00
MM Mark Mulder 15.00 40.00
MS Mike Sweeney 15.00 40.00
RB Rocco Baldelli 15.00 40.00
RK Ryan Klesko 15.00 40.00
RO Roy Oswalt 15.00 40.00
RS Richie Sexson 15.00 40.00
TG Troy Glaus 15.00 40.00
TH Torii Hunter 15.00 40.00
VG Vladimir Guerrero 40.00 80.00
VW Vernon Wells /21 15.00 40.00

2004 SP Game Used Patch Premium Autograph

RANDOM INSERTS IN PACKS
STATED PRINT RUN 50 SERIAL #'d SETS
GARCIAPARRA PRINT 33 SERIAL #'d CARDS
AK Austin Kearns 10.00 25.00
AR Alex Rodriguez 100.00 175.00
BZ Barry Zito 10.00 25.00
CD Carlos Delgado 30.00 60.00
DW Dontrelle Willis 40.00 80.00
EC Eric Chavez 30.00 60.00
EG Eric Gagne 10.00 25.00
HM Hideki Matsui 250.00 400.00
IR Ivan Rodriguez 50.00 100.00
IS Ichiro Suzuki 1000.00 2000.00
KB Kevin Brown 30.00 60.00
KG Ken Griffey Jr. Reds 100.00 200.00
KG1 Ken Griffey Jr. M's 175.00 350.00
MP Mark Prior 30.00 60.00
MT Miguel Tejada 10.00 25.00
NG Nomar Garciaparra/33 75.00 150.00
RC Roger Clemens 90.00 150.00
SG Shawn Green 10.00 25.00
TG Troy Glaus 40.00 80.00
TH Tim Hudson 12.00 30.00
VG Vladimir Guerrero 50.00 100.00

2004 SP Game Used Patch Significant Numbers

RANDOM INSERTS IN PACKS
PRINT RUNS B/WN 1-27 COPIES PER
NO PRICING ON QTY OF 14 OR LESS
CR Cal Ripken/21 100.00 200.00
CS Curt Schilling/16 20.00 50.00
CY Carl Yastrzemski/23 40.00 80.00
DS Darryl Strawberry/17 15.00 40.00
EM Eddie Mathews/17 60.00 120.00
GM Greg Maddux/18 40.00 80.00
GO Juan Gonzalez/15 15.00 40.00
GS Gary Sheffield/16 15.00 40.00
KG Ken Griffey Jr./15 60.00 120.00
NR Nolan Ryan/27 30.00 60.00
PO Paul O'Neill/17 20.00 50.00
RC Roger Clemens/20 40.00 80.00
RF Rollie Fingers/17 15.00 40.00
RJ Randy Johnson/16 20.00 50.00
RP Rafael Palmeiro/18 20.00 50.00
SN Duke Snider/18 20.00 50.00
SS Sammy Sosa/15 20.00 50.00
TG Tom Glavine/17 20.00 50.00
TS Tom Seaver/20 20.00 50.00

2004 SP Game Used Patch Significant Numbers Autograph

RANDOM INSERTS IN PACKS
STATED PRINT RUN 50 SERIAL #'d SETS
BROCK PRINT RUN 16 SERIAL #'d CARDS
PUCKETT PRINT RUN 3 SERIAL #'d CARDS
NO PUCKETT PRICING DUE TO SCARCITY
AR Alex Rodriguez Rgr 100.00 200.00
AR1 Alex Rodriguez M's 100.00 200.00
BA Bobby Abreu 30.00 60.00
BG Brian Giles 30.00 60.00
BW Bernie Williams 60.00 120.00
BZ Barry Zito 10.00 25.00
CD Carlos Delgado 30.00 60.00
CJ Chipper Jones 90.00 150.00
EC Eric Chavez 30.00 60.00
EG Eric Gagne 40.00 80.00
GM Greg Maddux 75.00 150.00
HE Todd Helton 40.00 80.00
HM Hideki Matsui 250.00 400.00
JG Juan Gonzalez Royals 30.00 60.00
JG1 Juan Gonzalez Rgr 30.00 60.00
KB Kevin Brown 30.00 60.00
KG Ken Griffey Jr. Reds 100.00 200.00
KG1 Ken Griffey Jr. M's 100.00 200.00
LB Lou Brock/16 20.00 50.00
LG Luis Gonzalez 30.00 60.00
MM Mike Mussina Yanks 40.00 80.00
MM1 Mike Mussina O's 20.00 50.00
MP Mike Piazza 150.00 250.00
MS Mike Schmidt 40.00 80.00
MT Miguel Tejada O's 15.00 40.00
MT1 Miguel Tejada A's 15.00 40.00
NR Nolan Ryan 40.00 80.00
PB Pat Burrell 30.00 60.00
PO Paul O'Neill 20.00 50.00
PR Mark Prior 15.00 40.00
RA Roberto Alomar 20.00 50.00
RB Rocco Baldelli 15.00 40.00
RF Rollie Fingers 30.00 60.00
RO Roy Oswalt Arm Up 15.00 40.00
RO1 Roy Oswalt Elbow Out 15.00 40.00
RP Rafael Palmeiro 20.00 50.00
RS Ryne Sandberg 20.00 50.00
SG Shawn Green 40.00 80.00
TG Tom Glavine 40.00 80.00
TH Tim Hudson 40.00 80.00
VG Vladimir Guerrero 50.00 100.00

2004 SP Game Used Patch Significant Numbers Autograph Dual

RANDOM INSERTS IN PACKS
STATED PRINT RUN 25 SERIAL #'d SETS
BROCK PRINT RUN 14 SERIAL #'d CARDS
NO BROCK PRICING DUE TO SCARCITY
AR Alex Rodriguez Rgr 125.00 250.00
BA Bobby Abreu 50.00 100.00
BG Brian Giles 40.00 80.00
BW Bernie Williams 125.00 200.00
BZ Barry Zito 20.00 50.00
CD Carlos Delgado 50.00 100.00
CJ Chipper Jones 125.00 250.00
DW Dontrelle Willis 20.00 50.00
EC Eric Chavez 20.00 50.00
EG Eric Gagne 60.00 120.00
GI Bob Gibson 60.00 120.00
GM Greg Maddux 125.00 200.00
HE Todd Helton 40.00 80.00
HM Hideki Matsui 400.00 600.00
JG Juan Gonzalez Royals 50.00 100.00
JG1 Juan Gonzalez Rgr 50.00 100.00
KB Kevin Brown 50.00 100.00
KG Ken Griffey Jr. Reds 125.00 250.00
KP Kirby Puckett 75.00 150.00
LG Luis Gonzalez 40.00 80.00
MM Mike Mussina Yanks 30.00 60.00
MM1 Mike Mussina O's 30.00 60.00
MP Mike Piazza 200.00 350.00
MR Troy Glaus 60.00 120.00
MS Mike Schmidt 75.00 150.00
MT Miguel Tejada O's 20.00 50.00
MT1 Miguel Tejada A's 20.00 50.00
NR Nolan Ryan 90.00 150.00
PB Pat Burrell 50.00 100.00
PO Paul O'Neill 60.00 120.00
RA Roberto Alomar 60.00 120.00
RF Rollie Fingers 20.00 50.00
RP Rafael Palmeiro 50.00 100.00
RS Ryne Sandberg 150.00 250.00
SG Shawn Green Dodgers 12.00 30.00
SG1 Shawn Green Jays 12.00 30.00
TG Tom Glavine 60.00 120.00
TH Tim Hudson 60.00 120.00
TO Tony Gwynn 75.00 150.00
TS Tom Seaver 30.00 80.00
VG Vladimir Guerrero 75.00 150.00

2004 SP Game Used Patch Star Potential

PRINT RUNS B/WN 3-50 COPIES PER
NO PRICING ON QTY OF 12 OR LESS
BW Brandon Webb/50 10.00 25.00
CP Corey Patterson/20 15.00 40.00
DWO D.Willis Arm Up/35 15.00 40.00
DW1 D.Willis Arm Down/35 15.00 40.00
HA Roy Halladay/32 10.00 25.00
IS Ichiro Suzuki/50 50.00 100.00
JB Josh Beckett/21 15.00 40.00
LB Lance Berkman/17 15.00 40.00
MM Mark Mulder/20 15.00 40.00
MPO M.Prior Hand in Glove/22 20.00 50.00
MP1 Mark Prior Throwing/22 20.00 50.00
MT M.Teixeira Hands Back/23 20.00 50.00
MT1 M.Teixeira Hands Fwd/23 20.00 50.00
RH Rich Harden/40 10.00 25.00
RO Roy Oswalt/44 10.00 25.00
RW Rickie Weeks/23 15.00 40.00
TG Troy Glaus/25 15.00 40.00
TH Tim Hudson/15 15.00 40.00

2004 SP Game Used Patch Stellar Combos Dual

RANDOM INSERTS IN PACKS
PRINT RUNS B/WN 1-25 COPIES PER
NO PRICING ON QTY OF 8 OR LESS
AD A.Soriano/D.Jeter/8 60.00 120.00
AJ A.Rodriguez/J.Gonzalez/25 40.00 80.00
AT B.Abreu/J.Thome/25 15.00 40.00
BK J.Bagwell/J.Kent/25 15.00 40.00
BT H.Blalock/M.Teixeira/25 15.00 40.00
CA J.Carter/R.Alomar/25 15.00 40.00
CO R.Clemens/R.Oswalt/25 40.00 80.00
CR C.Schilling/R.Johnson/25 15.00 40.00
DG C.Delgado/J.Giambi/25 15.00 40.00
DK A.Dunn/A.Kearns/25 15.00 40.00
GH E.Gagne/T.Hoffman/25 15.00 40.00
GT G.Maddux/T.Glavine/25 50.00 100.00
JJ A.Jones/C.Jones/25 15.00 40.00
KR J.Koosman/N.Ryan/25 100.00 200.00
LP A.Leiter/M.Piazza/25 40.00 80.00
LS F.Lynn/I.Suzuki/25 60.00 120.00
MG D.Mattingly/J.Giambi/25 15.00 40.00
MT E.Martinez/F.Thomas/25 15.00 40.00
MY P.Molitor/R.Yount/25 15.00 40.00
NB H.Nomo/K.Brown/25 15.00 40.00
NY A.Soriano/J.Reyes/25 15.00 40.00
PC M.Prior/R.Clemens/25 50.00 100.00
PE A.Pujols/J.Edmonds/25 60.00 120.00
PM A.Pettitte/M.Mussina/25 15.00 40.00
PP J.Posada/M.Piazza/25 40.00 80.00
PS R.Palmeiro/S.Sosa/25 15.00 40.00
RB I.Rodriguez/J.Beckett/25 15.00 40.00
RG2 C.Ripken/L.Gehrig/25 300.00 500.00
RJ1 A.Rod Rgr/D.Jeter/25 75.00 150.00
RJ2 A.Rod Yanks/D.Jeter/25 100.00 200.00
RR A.Rodriguez/C.Ripken/25 150.00 250.00
RS B.Robinson/M.Schmidt/25 40.00 80.00
SC I.Suzuki/T.Cobb Pants/25 150.00 250.00
SG D.Snider/S.Green/25 15.00 40.00
SJ G.Sheffield/R.Johnson/25 15.00 40.00
SM C.Schilling/P.Martinez/25 15.00 40.00
SR C.Schilling/N.Ryan/25 30.00 60.00
TO F.Thomas/M.Ordonez/25 15.00 40.00
WC D.Wells/R.Clemens/25 40.00 80.00
WH L.Walker/T.Helton/25 15.00 40.00
WS B.Williams/S.Sosa/25 15.00 40.00
ZH B.Zito/T.Hudson/25 15.00 40.00

2004 SP Game Used Patch World Series

RANDOM INSERTS IN PACKS
PRINT RUNS B/WN 15-50 COPIES PER
AJ Andruw Jones/50 15.00 40.00
AP Andy Pettitte/15 20.00 50.00
AS0 A.Soriano Hands on Bat/15 15.00 40.00
AS1 A.Soriano Hands Apart/15 15.00 40.00
BL Barry Larkin/50 15.00 40.00
BW Bernie Williams/50 15.00 40.00
CA Jose Canseco/50 15.00 40.00
CJ Chipper Jones/50 15.00 40.00
CS Curt Schilling D'backs/50 10.00 25.00
CS1 Curt Schilling Sox/50 15.00 40.00
CY Carl Yastrzemski/31 30.00 60.00
DW Dontrelle Willis/50 15.00 40.00
GA Garret Anderson/50 10.00 25.00
GL Troy Glaus Run/50 10.00 25.00
GL1 Troy Glaus Walk/50 10.00 25.00
GM Greg Maddux Arm Up/50 10.00 25.00
GM1 Greg Maddux Cubs/50 10.00 25.00
GM2 G.Maddux Glove Out/50 12.50 30.00
HM Hideki Matsui/17 125.00 200.00
IR Ivan Rodriguez/50 15.00 40.00
JB Josh Beckett Leaning/50 10.00 25.00
JB1 Josh Beckett Leg Kick/50 10.00 25.00
JE Derek Jeter Gray/50 40.00 100.00
JE1 Derek Jeter Stripes/50 75.00 150.00
JM Joe Morgan/50 10.00 25.00
JP Jorge Posada/50 15.00 40.00
JT Jim Thome Indians/50 15.00 40.00
JT1 Jim Thome Phils/50 15.00 40.00
KB Kevin Brown/50 10.00 25.00
MM Mike Mussina Yanks/50 10.00 25.00
MM1 Mike Mussina O's/43 6.00 15.00
MP Mike Piazza Mets/50 20.00 50.00
MP1 Mike Piazza Dodgers/50 20.00 50.00
MR Mariano Rivera/50 50.00 100.00
MS Mike Schmidt/50 15.00 40.00
PM Paul Molitor/50 10.00 25.00
PO Paul O'Neill/50 15.00 40.00
RC Roger Clemens/50 20.00 50.00
RF Rollie Fingers/50 15.00 40.00
RJ Randy Johnson/50 15.00 40.00
TG Tom Glavine/50 15.00 40.00

2001 SP Legendary Cuts

COMPLETE SET (90) 12.50 30.00
1 Al Simmons .10 .30
2 Jimmie Foxx .30 .75
3 Mickey Cochrane .20 .50
4 Phil Niekro .10 .30
5 Eddie Mathews .30 .75
6 Gary Matthews .10 .30
7 Hank Aaron .60 1.50
8 Joe Adcock .10 .30
9 Warren Spahn .20 .50
10 George Sisler .10 .30
11 Stan Musial .50 1.25
12 Dizzy Dean .30 .75
13 Frankie Frisch .10 .30
14 Harvey Haddix .10 .30
15 Johnny Mize .20 .50
16 Ken Boyer .10 .30
17 Rogers Hornsby .30 .75
18 Cap Anson .30 .75
19 Andre Dawson .10 .30
20 Billy Williams .10 .30
21 Billy Herman .10 .30
22 Hack Wilson .20 .50
23 Ron Santo .20 .50
24 Ryne Sandberg .50 1.25
25 Ernie Banks .30 .75
26 Burleigh Grimes .10 .30
27 Don Drysdale .20 .50
28 Gil Hodges .30 .75
29 Jackie Robinson .30 .75
30 Tommy Lasorda .10 .30
31 Pee Wee Reese .30 .75
32 Roy Campanella .30 .75
33 Tommy Davis .10 .30
34 Branch Rickey .10 .30
35 Leo Durocher .20 .50
36 Walt Alston .10 .30
37 Bill Terry .10 .30
38 Carl Hubbell .20 .50
39 Eddie Stanky .10 .30
40 George Kelly .10 .30
41 Mel Ott .30 .75
42 Juan Marichal .10 .30
43 Rube Marquard .10 .30
44 Travis Jackson .10 .30
45 Bob Feller .10 .30
46 Earl Averill .10 .30
47 Elmer Flick .10 .30
48 Ken Keltner .10 .30
49 Lou Boudreau .20 .50
50 Early Wynn .20 .50
51 Satchel Paige .30 .75
52 Ron Hunt .10 .30
53 Tom Seaver .20 .50
54 Richie Ashburn .20 .50
55 Mike Schmidt .60 1.50
56 Honus Wagner .40 1.00
57 Lloyd Waner .20 .50
58 Max Carey .10 .30
59 Paul Waner .20 .50
60 Roberto Clemente .75 2.00
61 Nolan Ryan .75 2.00
62 Bobby Doerr .20 .50
63 Carlton Fisk .20 .50
64 Joe Cronin .10 .30
65 Joe Wood .20 .50
66 Tony Conigliaro .20 .50
67 Edd Roush .10 .30
68 Johnny VanderMeer .10 .30
69 Walter Johnson .30 .75
70 Charlie Gehringer .10 .30
71 Al Kaline .30 .75
72 Ty Cobb .50 1.25
73 Tony Oliva .10 .30
74 Luke Appling .10 .30
75 Minnie Minoso .10 .30
76 Nellie Fox .20 .50
77 Joe Jackson .60 1.50
78 Babe Ruth 1.00 2.50
79 Bill Dickey .20 .50
80 Elston Howard .20 .50
81 Joe DiMaggio .60 1.50
82 Lefty Gomez .30 .75
83 Lou Gehrig .60 1.50
84 Mickey Mantle 1.25 3.00
85 Reggie Jackson .20 .50
86 Roger Maris .30 .75
87 Whitey Ford .20 .50
88 Waite Hoyt .10 .30
89 Yogi Berra .30 .75
90 Casey Stengel .30 .75

2001 SP Legendary Cuts Autographs

STATED ODDS 1:252
PRINT RUNS BETWEEN 1-275 COPIES PER
NO PRICING ON QTY OF 25 OR LESS
CBD Bill Dickey/28 250.00 400.00
CBHE Billy Herman/88 75.00 150.00
CBS Bob Shawkey/39 75.00 200.00
CBT Bill Terry/184 60.00 120.00
CCH Carl Hubbell/30 250.00 400.00
CDDE Dizzy Dean/56 400.00 800.00
CEA Earl Averill/189 40.00 80.00
CER Edd Roush/83 60.00 120.00
CGH Gabby Hartnett/32 175.00 300.00
CGK George Kelly/52 125.00 200.00
CHM Heinie Manush/50 175.00 300.00
CJC Jocko Conlan/26 250.00 400.00
CJD2 Joe DiMaggio/50 300.00 800.00
CJD3 Joe DiMaggio/150 250.00 600.00
CJD4 Joe DiMaggio/275 250.00 600.00
CJMC Joe McCarthy/40 175.00 350.00
CJMI Johnny Mize/84 100.00 200.00
CJR Jackie Robinson/147 1500.00 2000.00
CJS Joe Sewell/55 150.00 250.00
CJW Joe Wood/43 300.00 500.00
CLA Luke Appling/45 125.00 200.00
CLD Leo Durocher/45 175.00 300.00
CLG Lefty Grove/34 300.00 500.00
CLGO Lefty Gomez/85 100.00 250.00
CLW Lloyd Waner/217 60.00 120.00
CMC Max Carey/73 150.00 250.00
CMK Mark Koenig/30 250.00 400.00
CROM Roger Maris/73 600.00 1200.00
CRP Roger Peckinpaugh/45 150.00 250.00
CRS Rip Sewell/39 150.00 250.00
CSC Stanley Coveleski/42 125.00 200.00
CSP Satchel Paige/36 1200.00 1700.00
CTJ Travis Jackson/35 100.00 250.00
CTL2 Ted Lyons/59 100.00 200.00
CVM Johnny VanderMeer/65 75.00 150.00
CVR Vic Raschi/26 175.00 300.00
CWA Walt Alston/34 250.00 400.00
CWH Waite Hoyt/38 100.00 200.00
CWJ Walter Johnson/113 1500.00 2500.00

2001 SP Legendary Cuts Debut Game Bat

STATED ODDS 1:18
ASTERISKS PERCEIVED AS LARGER SUPPLY
BAT Alan Trammell * 4.00 10.00
BBB Bobby Bonds 4.00 10.00
BBF Bill Freehan 4.00 10.00
BGL Greg Luzinski 4.00 10.00
BLW Lou Whitaker 4.00 10.00
BSS Steve Sax * 4.00 10.00
BSY Steve Yeager 4.00 10.00
BWH Willie Horton 4.00 10.00
BWP Wes Parker * 4.00 10.00
DBB Bill Buckner * 4.00 10.00
DBD Bobby Doerr SP 10.00 25.00
DBF Bob Feller SP 10.00 25.00
DBH Billy Herman SP 10.00 25.00
DBM Bill Mazeroski 6.00 15.00
DBR Bobby Richardson SP 12.00 30.00
DCG Charlie Gehringer 15.00 40.00
DEH Elston Howard SP 10.00 25.00
DES Eddie Stanky 4.00 10.00
DFF Frankie Frisch SP 10.00 25.00
DGM Gary Matthews 4.00 10.00
DGS George Sisler 10.00 25.00
DHW Hack Wilson SP 20.00 50.00
DJA Joe Adcock SP 20.00 50.00
DJC Joe Cronin 6.00 15.00
DJJ Joe Jackson 75.00 150.00
DKB Ken Boyer SP 10.00 25.00
DLA Luke Appling SP 12.00 30.00
DLB Lou Boudreau 4.00 10.00
DMC Mickey Cochrane 25.00 60.00
DMM Minnie Minoso SP 12.50 30.00
DPW Paul Waner SP 10.00 25.00
DRA Richie Ashburn SP 15.00 40.00
DRH Ron Hunt 4.00 10.00
DTC Tony Conigliaro SP 15.00 40.00
DTO Tony Oliva 4.00 10.00

2001 SP Legendary Cuts Game Bat

STATED ODDS 1:18
ASTERISKS PERCEIVED AS LARGER SUPPLY
BAD Andre Dawson * 4.00 10.00
BAS Al Simmons SP 20.00 50.00
BBR Babe Ruth SP 125.00 200.00
BBT Bill Terry SP 30.00 60.00
BCF Carlton Fisk 6.00 15.00
BDD Don Drysdale SP 15.00 40.00
BDJ Davey Johnson 4.00 10.00
BEM Eddie Mathews 6.00 15.00
BGB George Brett * 6.00 15.00
BGH Gil Hodges SP 12.50 30.00
BHA Hank Aaron SP 10.00 25.00
BJD Joe DiMaggio SP 20.00 50.00
BJF Jimmie Foxx 10.00 25.00
BJR Jackie Robinson SP 15.00 40.00
BKC Kiki Cuyler 12.50 30.00
BMM Mickey Mantle SP 60.00 150.00
BMM Manny Mota 4.00 10.00
RMO Mel Ott SP 20.00 50.00
BMW Maury Wills * 4.00 10.00
BNF Nellie Fox 6.00 15.00
BNR Nolan Ryan SP 8.00 20.00
BPM Paul Molitor 4.00 10.00
BRC Rico Carty 4.00 10.00
BRCA Roy Campanella SP 12.50 30.00
BRCL Roberto Clemente 30.00 80.00
BRJ Reggie Jackson * 6.00 15.00
BRM Roger Maris SP 25.00 60.00
BRS Ryne Sandberg * 10.00 25.00
BRY Robin Yount * 6.00 15.00
BTC Ty Cobb SP 40.00 80.00
BTD Tommy Davis SP 40.00 80.00
BTHO Tommy Holmes 4.00 10.00
BVP Vada Pinson 10.00 25.00
BWB Wade Boggs * 4.00 10.00
BWMC Willie McCovey * 4.00 10.00
BYB Yogi Berra 6.00 15.00

2001 SP Legendary Cuts Game Jersey

STATED ODDS 1:18
ASTERISKS PERCEIVED AS LARGER SUPPLY
MOST SP'S NOT PRICED DUE TO SCARCITY
JBD Bill Dickey Uni 5.00 12.00
JBL Bob Lemon Uni 6.00 15.00
JBR Bobby Richardson Uni 6.00 15.00
JBR Babe Ruth Uni SP 600.00 900.00
JBRO Brooks Robinson Uni 6.00 15.00
JBT Bobby Thomson Uni 6.00 15.00
JBW Billy Williams Jsy 4.00 10.00
JCS Casey Stengel Uni 4.00 10.00
JGH Gil Hodges Jsy 6.00 15.00
JGP Gaylord Perry Jsy 4.00 10.00
JHW Honus Wagner Uni SP 300.00 600.00
JJF Jim Fregosi Jsy 4.00 10.00
JJM Juan Marichal Jsy * 4.00 10.00
JJN Joe Nuxhall Jsy 10.00 25.00
JLD Leo Durocher Jsy 4.00 10.00
JMM Mickey Mantle Uni SP 150.00 300.00
JMW Maury Wills Jsy 4.00 10.00
JNF Nellie Fox Uni 6.00 15.00
JNR Nolan Ryan Jsy 6.00 15.00
JRC Roberto Clemente Jsy 30.00 80.00
JRJ Reggie Jackson Jsy 6.00 15.00
JRY Robin Yount Jsy 6.00 15.00
JTC Tony Conigliaro Jsy 10.00 25.00
JTC Ty Cobb Uni SP 300.00 600.00
JTHO Tommy Holmes Uni * 4.00 10.00
JTK Ted Kluszewski Jsy 8.00 20.00
JVL Vic Lombardi Jsy 4.00 10.00
JWB Wade Boggs Jsy 6.00 15.00
JWF Whitey Ford Uni 10.00 25.00
JWM Willie McCovey Uni * 4.00 10.00
JYB Yogi Berra Uni 6.00 15.00

2002 SP Legendary Cuts

COMPLETE SET (90) 12.50 30.00
MCGWIRE EXCH DEADLINE 09/12/03
1 Al Kaline .60 1.50
2 Alvin Dark .25 .60
3 Andre Dawson .25 .60
4 Babe Ruth 2.00 5.00
5 Ernie Banks .60 1.50
6 Bob Lemon .40 1.00
7 Bobby Bonds .25 .60
8 Carl Erskine .25 .60
9 Carl Hubbell .40 1.00
10 Casey Stengel .60 1.50
11 Charlie Gehringer .40 1.00
12 Christy Mathewson .60 1.50
13 Dale Murphy .40 1.00
14 Dave Concepcion .25 .60
15 Dave Parker .25 .60
16 Dazzy Vance .25 .60
17 Dizzy Dean .40 1.00
18 Don Baylor .25 .60
19 Don Drysdale .40 1.00
20 Duke Snider .40 1.00
21 Earl Averill .25 .60
22 Early Wynn .25 .60
23 Edd Roush .25 .60
24 Elston Howard .25 .60
25 Ferguson Jenkins .25 .60
26 Frank Crosetti .25 .60
27 Frankie Frisch .25 .60
28 Gaylord Perry .25 .60
29 George Foster .25 .60
30 George Kell .25 .60
31 Gil Hodges .40 1.00
32 Hank Greenberg .60 1.50
33 Phil Niekro .25 .60
34 Harvey Haddix .25 .60
35 Harvey Kuenn .25 .60
36 Honus Wagner 1.00 2.50
37 Jackie Robinson .60 1.50
38 Orlando Cepeda .25 .60
39 Joe Adcock .25 .60
40 Joe Cronin .25 .60
41 Joe DiMaggio 1.00 2.50
42 Joe Morgan .25 .60
43 Johnny Mize .25 .60
44 Lefty Gomez .40 1.00
45 Lefty Grove .40 1.00
46 Jim Palmer .25 .60
47 Lou Boudreau .25 .60
48 Lou Gehrig 1.00 2.50
49 Luke Appling .25 .60
50 Mark McGwire 2.00 5.00
51 Mel Ott .60 1.50
52 Mickey Cochrane .40 1.00
53 Mickey Mantle 2.00 5.00
54 Minnie Minoso .25 .60
55 Brooks Robinson .40 1.00
56 Nellie Fox .40 1.00
57 Nolan Ryan 1.50 4.00
58 Rollie Fingers .25 .60
59 Pee Wee Reese .40 1.00
60 Phil Rizzuto .40 1.00
61 Ralph Kiner .25 .60
62 Ray Dandridge .25 .60
63 Richie Ashburn .40 1.00
64 Robin Yount .60 1.50
65 Rocky Colavito .40 1.00
66 Roger Maris .60 1.50
67 Rogers Hornsby .60 1.50
68 Ron Santo .25 .60
69 Ryne Sandberg 1.25 3.00
70 Stan Musial 1.00 2.50
71 Sam McDowell .25 .60
72 Satchel Paige .60 1.50
73 Willie McCovey .25 .60
74 Steve Garvey .25 .60
75 Ted Kluszewski .40 1.00
76 Catfish Hunter .40 1.00
77 Terry Moore .15 .40
78 Thurman Munson .60 1.50
79 Tom Seaver .40 1.00
80 Tommy John .25 .60
81 Tony Gwynn .75 2.00
82 Tony Kubek .40 1.00
83 Tony Lazzeri .25 .60
84 Ty Cobb 1.00 2.50
85 Wade Boggs .40 1.00
86 Waite Hoyt .25 .60
87 Walter Johnson .60 1.50
88 Willie Stargell .40 1.00
89 Yogi Berra .60 1.50
90 Zack Wheat .25 .60

2002 SP Legendary Cuts Autographs

STATED ODDS 1:128
STATED PRINT RUNS LISTED BELOW
NO PRICING ON QTY OF 25 OR LESS
BDA Babe Dahlgren/51 30.00 60.00
BFA Bibb Falk/44 30.00 60.00
BGO Bill Goodman/53 75.00 150.00

BHA Buddy Hassett/56 30.00 80.00
BIL Bill Lee/40 75.00 150.00
BKA Bob Kahle/53 60.00 120.00
BOL Bob Lemon/91 30.00 60.00
BSH Bob Shawkey/118 30.00 80.00
BWA Bucky Walters/31 30.00 80.00
CHM Chet Morgan/27 125.00 200.00
CKE Charlie Keller/29 150.00 250.00
EJO Earl Johnson/31 125.00 200.00
ELO Ed Lopat/58 30.00 80.00
ERO Edd Roush/101 30.00 60.00
ERO2 Edd Roush/155 30.00 80.00
FFR Frankie Frisch/35 250.00 400.00
GBU Guy Bush/38 75.00 150.00
GCA George Case/35 125.00 200.00
GPI George Pipgras/34 125.00 200.00
HCH Happy Chandler/96 30.00 60.00
HGR Hank Greenberg/94 200.00 400.00
HHA Harvey Haddix/37 40.00 100.00
HNE Hal Newhouser/81 60.00 120.00
JAD Joe Adcock/48 30.00 60.00
JCO Johnny Cooney/64 30.00 60.00
JCR Joe Cronin/185 40.00 100.00
JDI Joe DiMaggio/103 350.00 500.00
JDU Joe Dugan/39 125.00 200.00
JJO Judy Johnson/86 40.00 100.00
JSE Joe Sewell/136 25.00 60.00
LAP Luke Appling/53 25.00 60.00
LBO Lou Boudreau/85 30.00 60.00
LGR Lefty Grove/194 100.00 250.00
LJA Larry Jackson/37 30.00 60.00
NJA Bucky Jacobs/44 125.00 200.00
PRE Pete Reiser/73 25.00 60.00
RDA Ray Dandridge/179 25.00 60.00
SCO Stan Coveleski/85 25.00 60.00
SHA Stan Hack/36 60.00 120.00
SMA Sal Maglie/29 125.00 200.00
TDO Taylor Douthit/60 30.00 80.00
TMO Terry Moore/86 25.00 60.00
VRA Vic Raschi/98 30.00 80.00
WHO Waite Hoyt/61 30.00 80.00
WKA Willie Kamm/57 25.00 60.00
WST Willie Stargell/153 30.00 80.00
ZWH Zack Wheat/127 200.00 300.00

2002 SP Legendary Cuts Game Bat

STATED ODDS 1:8
SP INFO PROVIDED BY UPPER DECK
DP PERCEIVED AS LARGER SUPPLY
BADA Alvin Dark DP 4.00 10.00
BAND Andre Dawson DP 3.00 8.00
BBBO Bobby Bonds DP 3.00 8.00
BBRU Babe Ruth SP 60.00 150.00
BCRI Cal Ripken 6.00 15.00
BDBA Don Baylor DP 3.00 8.00
BDMU Dale Murphy DP 4.00 10.00
BDPA Dave Parker DP 3.00 8.00
BDSN Duke Snider 6.00 15.00
BEHO Elston Howard SP * 6.00 15.00
BEWY Early Wynn 4.00 10.00
BGFO George Foster DP 3.00 8.00
BGKE George Kell 4.00 10.00
BGPE Gaylord Perry 3.00 8.00
BHGR Hank Greenberg SP 8.00 20.00
BJAR Jackie Robinson SP * 25.00 60.00
BJMI Johnny Mize SP * 8.00 20.00
BLGR Lefty Grove 8.00 20.00
BMMA Mickey Mantle SP 50.00 100.00
BMMC Mark McGwire DP 6.00 15.00
BNFO Nellie Fox 6.00 15.00
BNRY Nolan Ryan 15.00 40.00
BPWE Pee Wee Reese DP 6.00 15.00
BRCO Rocky Colavito DP 8.00 20.00
BRKI Ralph Kiner 4.00 10.00
BRMA Roger Maris SP * 10.00 25.00
BRSA Ryne Sandberg DP 6.00 15.00
BRYO Robin Yount DP 3.00 8.00
BSGA Steve Garvey 3.00 8.00
BTGW Tony Gwynn SP * 8.00 20.00
BTKU Tony Kubek 3.00 8.00
BTLA Tony Lazzeri 6.00 15.00
BTMU Thurman Munson 10.00 25.00
BTSE Tom Seaver SP 8.00 20.00
BWST Willie Stargell 4.00 10.00
BYBE Yogi Berra SP 10.00 25.00

2002 SP Legendary Cuts Game Jersey

STATED ODDS 1:24
DP PERCEIVED AS LARGER SUPPLY
JAND Andre Dawson 4.00 10.00
JBBO Bobby Bonds Pants 2.50 6.00
JDBA Don Baylor 2.50 6.00
JDPA Dave Parker Pants DP 2.50 6.00
JFCR Frank Crosetti 2.50 6.00
JGFO George Foster 2.50 6.00
JJRO J.Robinson Pants SP * 25.00 60.00
JMMA M.Mantle Pants SP * 25.00 60.00
JNRY Nolan Ryan Pants 15.00 40.00
JPWE Pee Wee Reese 4.00 10.00
JRMA Roger Maris Pants 12.00 30.00
JRSA Ryne Sandberg SP * 8.00 20.00
JSGA Steve Garvey 2.50 6.00
JTSE Tom Seaver 4.00 10.00
JYBE Yogi Berra Pants DP 10.00 25.00

2002 SP Legendary Cuts Game Swatches

STATED ODDS 1:24
SCER Carl Erskine Pants 4.00 10.00
SCRJ Cal Ripken 10.00 25.00
SDBA Don Baylor 3.00 8.00
SDDR Don Drysdale Pants 10.00 25.00
SDPA Dave Parker 3.00 8.00
SFCR Frank Crosetti 4.00 10.00
SFJE Ferguson Jenkins Pants 3.00 8.00
SJMO Joe Morgan 3.00 8.00
SMMI Minnie Minoso 4.00 10.00
SMOT Mel Ott Pants 12.00 30.00
SRSA Ron Santo 6.00 15.00
SSMC Sam McDowell 3.00 8.00
STGW Tony Gwynn 6.00 15.00
STJO Tommy John 3.00 8.00
SWBO Wade Boggs 4.00 10.00

2003 SP Legendary Cuts

COMP.SET w/o SP's (100) 15.00 40.00
COMMON CARD .15 .40
COMMON SP 3.00 8.00
SP STATED ODDS 1:12
SP PRINT RUN 1299 SERIAL #'d SETS
1 Luis Aparicio .25 .60
2 Al Barlick .15 .40
3 Al Lopez .25 .60
4 Ernie Banks .60 1.50
5 Alexander Cartwright .25 .60
6 Lou Brock .40 1.00
7 Babe Ruth/1299 6.00 15.00
8 Bill Dickey .40 1.00
9 Bill Mazeroski .40 1.00
10 Bob Feller .25 .60
11 Billy Herman .25 .60
12 Billy Williams .25 .60
13 Bob Gibson/1299 4.00 10.00
14 Bob Lemon .25 .60
15 Bobby Doerr .25 .60
16 Branch Rickey .25 .60
17 Gary Carter .25 .60
18 Burleigh Grimes .25 .60
19 Cap Anson .40 1.00
20 Carl Hubbell .40 1.00
21 Carlton Fisk .40 1.00
22 Casey Stengel .40 1.00
23 Charlie Gehringer .25 .60
24 Chief Bender .25 .60
25 Christy Mathewson/1299 4.00 10.00
26 Cy Young .60 1.50
27 Dave Winfield .25 .60
28 Dazzy Vance .25 .60
29 Dizzy Dean/1299 4.00 10.00
30 Don Drysdale/1299 4.00 10.00
31 Duke Snider/1299 4.00 10.00
32 Earl Averill .25 .60
33 Earle Combs .25 .60
34 Edd Roush .25 .60
35 Earl Weaver .25 .60
36 Eddie Collins .25 .60
37 Eddie Plank .25 .60
38 Elmer Flick .25 .60
39 Enos Slaughter .25 .60
40 Ernie Lombardi .25 .60
41 Ford Frick .15 .40
42 Jim Hunter .40 1.00
43 Frankie Frisch .25 .60
44 Gabby Hartnett .25 .60
45 George Kell .25 .60
46 Early Wynn .25 .60
47 Ferguson Jenkins .25 .60
48 Al Kaline .60 1.50
49 Harmon Killebrew .60 1.50
50 Hal Newhouser .25 .60
51 Hank Greenberg/1299 4.00 10.00
52 Harry Caray .40 1.00
53 Tommy Lasorda .25 .60
54 Honus Wagner/1299 4.00 10.00
55 Hoyt Wilhelm/1299 3.00 8.00
56 Jackie Robinson/1299 4.00 10.00
57 Jim Bottomley .25 .60
58 Jim Bunning/1299 4.00 10.00
59 Jimmie Foxx/1299 4.00 10.00
60 Eddie Mathews .60 1.50
61 Joe Cronin .25 .60
62 Joe DiMaggio/1299 4.00 10.00
63 Joe McCarthy/1299 3.00 8.00
64 Joe Morgan/1299 3.00 8.00
65 Willie McCovey .25 .60
66 Joe Tinker .25 .60
67 Johnny Bench/1299 4.00 10.00
68 Johnny Evers/1299 3.00 8.00
69 Johnny Mize/1299 3.00 8.00
70 Josh Gibson/1299 4.00 10.00
71 Juan Marichal .25 .60
72 Judy Johnson .25 .60
73 Stan Musial 1.00 2.50
74 Kiki Cuyler .25 .60
75 Larry Doby .25 .60
76 Nap Lajoie .40 1.00
77 Larry MacPhail .15 .40
78 Phil Niekro .25 .60
79 Lefty Gomez/1299 4.00 10.00
80 Lefty Grove/1299 4.00 10.00
81 Leo Durocher/1299 3.00 8.00
82 Leon Day .25 .60
83 Gaylord Perry/1299 3.00 8.00
84 Lou Boudreau .25 .60
85 Lou Gehrig 1.00 2.50
86 Luke Appling .25 .60
87 Max Carey .25 .60
88 Mel Allen/1299 3.00 8.00
89 Mel Ott/1299 4.00 10.00
90 Mickey Cochrane .25 .60
91 Mickey Mantle 2.00 5.00
92 Brooks Robinson .40 1.00
93 Monte Irvin .25 .60
94 Nellie Fox .40 1.00
95 Nolan Ryan/1299 5.00 12.00
96 Ozzie Smith/1299 4.00 10.00
97 Mike Schmidt 1.25 3.00
98 Pee Wee Reese/1299 4.00 10.00
99 Phil Rizzuto .40 1.00
100 Ralph Kiner .25 .60
101 Ray Dandridge .25 .60
102 Richie Ashburn .40 1.00
103 Rick Ferrell .25 .60
104 Roberto Clemente 1.50 4.00
105 Robin Roberts .25 .60
106 Robin Yount .60 1.50
107 Rogers Hornsby .60 1.50
108 Rollie Fingers .25 .60
109 Roy Campanella .60 1.50
110 Rube Marquard .25 .60
111 Sam Crawford .25 .60
112 Steve Carlton .25 .60
113 Satchel Paige/1299 4.00 10.00
114 Sparky Anderson .25 .60
115 Stan Coveleski .25 .60
116 Red Schoendienst .40 1.00
117 Ted Williams 1.25 3.00
118 Tom Seaver .40 1.00
119 Tom Yawkey .15 .40
120 Tony Lazzeri .25 .60
121 Tony Perez .25 .60
122 Tris Speaker .60 1.50
123 Ty Cobb 1.00 2.50
124 Waite Hoyt/1299 3.00 8.00
125 Walter Alston .25 .60
126 Walter Johnson .60 1.50
127 Warren Spahn .40 1.00
128 Whitey Ford .40 1.00
129 Willie Stargell .40 1.00
130 Yogi Berra .60 1.50

2003 SP Legendary Cuts Blue

*BLUE POST-WAR: 2X TO 5X BASIC
*BLUE PRE-WAR: 1.5X TO 4X BASIC
*BLUE POST-WAR: .6X TO 1.5X BASIC SP
*BLUE PRE-WAR: .5X TO 1.2X BASIC SP
RANDOM INSERTS IN PACKS
STATED PRINT RUN 275 SERIAL #'d SETS

2003 SP Legendary Cuts Autographs

OVERALL CUT SIG ODDS 1:196
PRINT RUNS B/WN 1-96 COPIES PER
NO PRICING ON QTY OF 25 OR LESS
BG Burleigh Grimes/34 175.00 300.00
BI Billy Herman/30 75.00 150.00
BL Bob Lemon/34 75.00 150.00
BL1 Bob Lemon/41 75.00 150.00
CH Carl Hubbell/47 50.00 100.00
CH1 Carl Hubbell/63 30.00 80.00
EA Earl Averill/96 30.00 60.00
EC Earle Combs/45 75.00 200.00
ES Enos Slaughter/30 100.00 200.00
HC Harry Caray/29 175.00 300.00
HC1 Harry Caray/35 175.00 300.00
HG Hank Greenberg/30 250.00 400.00
JD Joe DiMaggio/50 300.00 500.00
JD1 Joe DiMaggio/28 350.00 550.00
LB Lou Boudreau/82 30.00 60.00
LB1 Lou Boudreau/49 40.00 80.00
LU Luke Appling/52 40.00 80.00
RM Rube Marquard/40 150.00 250.00
WA Walter Alston/30 100.00 200.00

2003 SP Legendary Cuts Autographs Blue

OVERALL CUT SIG ODDS 1:196
PRINT RUNS B/WN 1-50 COPIES PER
NO PRICING ON QTY OF 25 OR LESS
EA Earl Averill/50 75.00 150.00
HC1 Harry Caray/35 175.00 300.00
HN1 Hal Newhouser B2B/29 75.00 150.00
JD1 Joe DiMaggio/40 300.00 500.00

2003 SP Legendary Cuts Etched in Time 400

STATED PRINT RUN 400 SERIAL #'d SETS
*ETCHED 300: .4X TO 1X BASIC 400
ETCHED 300 PRINT RUN 300 #'d SETS
*ETCHED 175: .5X TO 1.2X BASIC 400
ETCHED 175 PRINT RUN 175 #'d SETS
OVERALL ETCHED ODDS 1:12
AB Al Barlick 2.00 5.00
AC Alexander Cartwright 2.00 5.00
BR Babe Ruth 6.00 15.00
CG Charlie Gehringer 2.00 5.00
CH Carl Hubbell 3.00 8.00
CM Christy Mathewson 3.00 8.00
CS Casey Stengel 3.00 8.00
CY Cy Young 3.00 8.00
DD Dizzy Dean 3.00 8.00
DO Don Drysdale 3.00 8.00
EC Eddie Collins 2.00 5.00
EL Ernie Lombardi 2.00 5.00
GH Gabby Hartnett 2.00 5.00
HC Harry Caray 3.00 8.00
HG Hank Greenberg 3.00 8.00
HW Honus Wagner 3.00 8.00
JD Joe DiMaggio 4.00 10.00
JF Jimmie Foxx 3.00 8.00
JG Josh Gibson 3.00 8.00
JM Joe McCarthy 2.00 5.00
JO Johnny Mize 2.00 5.00
JR Jackie Robinson 3.00 8.00
LB Lou Boudreau 2.00 5.00
LD Leo Durocher 2.00 5.00
LE Lefty Grove 3.00 8.00
LG Lefty Gomez 3.00 8.00
LO Lou Gehrig 5.00 12.00
ME Mel Allen 2.00 5.00
MM Mickey Mantle 10.00 25.00
MO Mel Ott 3.00 8.00
PR Pee Wee Reese 3.00 8.00
RA Richie Ashburn 3.00 8.00
RC Roberto Clemente 6.00 15.00
RH Rogers Hornsby 3.00 8.00
RO Roy Campanella 3.00 8.00
SP Satchel Paige 3.00 8.00
TC Ty Cobb 4.00 10.00
TL Tony Lazzeri 2.00 5.00
TS Tris Speaker 3.00 8.00
TW Ted Williams 4.00 10.00

2003 SP Legendary Cuts Hall Marks Autographs

OVERALL HALL MARKS ODDS 1:196
BLACK INK PRINTS B/WN 10-99 COPIES PER
BLUE INK PRINTS B/WN 10-15 COPIES PER
RED INK PRINT RUN 5 #'d COPIES PER
NO PRICING ON QTY OF 15 OR LESS
BD1 Bobby Doerr Black/50 10.00 40.00
BM1 Bill Mazeroski Black/50 10.00 25.00
CF1 Carlton Fisk Black/50 20.00 50.00
CY1 Carl Yastrzemski Black/45 40.00 80.00
DS1 Duke Snider Black/50 12.50 30.00
GC1 Gary Carter Black/50 10.00 25.00
GK1 George Kell Black/50 10.00 25.00
JM1 Juan Marichal Black/50 15.00 40.00
JO1 Joe Morgan Black/75 15.00 40.00
LA1 Luis Aparicio Black/45 10.00 25.00
MI1 Monte Irvin Black/85 10.00 25.00
OS1 Ozzie Smith Black/45 25.00 60.00
PR1 Phil Rizzuto Black/50 30.00 60.00
RF1 Rollie Fingers Black/99 10.00 25.00
RK1 Ralph Kiner Black/50 10.00 25.00
RR1 Robin Roberts Black/65 30.00 60.00
RY1 Robin Yount Black/45 40.00 80.00
SA1 Sparky Anderson Black/30 15.00 40.00
TP1 Tony Perez Black/50 15.00 40.00
WS1 Warren Spahn Black/35 40.00 80.00
YB1 Yogi Berra Black/50 40.00 100.00

2003 SP Legendary Cuts Historic Lumber

OVERALL GAME USED ODDS 1:12
PRINT RUNS B/WN 50-350 COPIES PER
BR Babe Ruth Away/150 75.00 150.00
BR1 Babe Ruth Home/150 50.00 100.00
CF Carlton Fisk R.Sox/50 10.00 25.00
CF1 Carlton Fisk W.Sox/50 10.00 25.00
CY C.Yastrzemski w/Bat/300 12.50 30.00
CY1 C.Yastrzemski w/Cap/350 12.50 30.00
CY2 C.Yaz w Helmet/350 12.50 30.00
DW Dave Winfield Padres/350 4.00 10.00
DW1 Dave Winfield Yanks/350 4.00 10.00
FR Frank Robinson O's/300 6.00 15.00
FR1 Frank Robinson Reds/350 6.00 15.00
FR2 Frank Robinson Angels/350 6.00 15.00
GC Gary Carter Mets/300 4.00 10.00
GC1 G.Carter Helmet Expos/100 4.00 10.00
GC2 G.Carter Cap Expos/100 4.00 10.00
HK Harmon Killebrew/350 6.00 15.00
JB Johnny Bench w/Bat/350 6.00 15.00
JB1 Johnny Bench Swing/350 6.00 15.00
JM Joe Morgan Reds/350 4.00 10.00
JM1 Joe Morgan Astros/350 4.00 10.00
MM Mickey Mantle/300 30.00 60.00
NR Nolan Ryan Rgr/225 12.50 30.00
OS Ozzie Smith Cards/300 10.00 25.00
OS1 Ozzie Smith Padres/350 10.00 25.00
RS R.Schoen Look Right/165 6.00 15.00
RS1 R.Schoen Look Left/165 6.00 15.00
SC Steve Carlton/350 4.00 10.00
TP Tony Perez Swing/350 4.00 10.00
TP1 Tony Perez Portrait/350 4.00 10.00
TS Tom Seaver/100 6.00 15.00
TW Ted Williams w/3 Bats/150 20.00 50.00
TW1 Ted Williams Portrait/150 20.00 50.00
WS W.Stargell Arms Down/150 6.00 15.00
WS1 W.Stargell Arms Up/150 6.00 15.00
YB Yogi Berra Shout/350 6.00 15.00
YB1 Yogi Berra w/Bat/350 6.00 15.00

2003 SP Legendary Cuts Historic Lumber Green

OVERALL GAME USED ODDS 1:12
PRINT RUNS BETWEEN 50-125 COPIES PER
BR Babe Ruth Away/75 100.00 200.00
BR1 Babe Ruth Home/75 100.00 200.00
CY C.Yastrzemski w Bat/125 15.00 40.00
CY1 C.Yastrzemski w Cap/125 10.00 25.00
CY2 C.Yaz w Helmet/125 10.00 25.00
DW Dave Winfield Padres/125 4.00 10.00
DW1 Dave Winfield Yanks/125 4.00 10.00
FR Frank Robinson O's/125 6.00 15.00
FR1 Frank Robinson Reds/125 6.00 15.00
FR2 Frank Robinson Angels/125 6.00 15.00
GC Gary Carter Mets/125 4.00 10.00
GC1 G.Carter Helmet Expos/125 4.00 10.00
GC2 G.Carter Cap Expos/125 4.00 10.00
HK Harmon Killebrew/125 6.00 15.00
JB Johnny Bench w Bat/125 6.00 15.00
JB1 Johnny Bench Swing/125 6.00 15.00
JM Joe Morgan Reds/125 4.00 10.00
JM1 Joe Morgan Astros/125 4.00 10.00
MM Mickey Mantle/75 40.00 80.00
NR Nolan Ryan Astros/50 10.00 25.00
OS Ozzie Smith Cards/125 12.50 30.00
OS1 Ozzie Smith Padres/125 12.50 30.00
RS R.Schoen Look Right/125 6.00 15.00
RS1 R.Schoen Look Left/125 6.00 15.00
SC Steve Carlton/125 4.00 10.00
TP Tony Perez Swing/125 4.00 10.00
TP1 Tony Perez Portrait/125 4.00 10.00
TS Tom Seaver/50 10.00 25.00
TW Ted Williams w/3 Bats/75 40.00 80.00
TW1 Ted Williams Portrait/75 40.00 80.00
WS W.Stargell Arms Down/125 6.00 15.00
WS1 W.Stargell Arms Up/125 6.00 15.00
YB Yogi Berra Shout/125 6.00 15.00
YB1 Yogi Berra w Bat/125 6.00 15.00

2003 SP Legendary Cuts Historic Swatches

OVERALL GAME USED ODDS 1:12
PRINT RUNS B/WN 48-350 COPIES PER
BG Bob Gibson CO Jsy/350 6.00 15.00
BM Bill Mazeroski Pants/50 10.00 25.00
BW Billy Williams Jsy/190 4.00 10.00
CF Carlton Fisk Pants/350 6.00 15.00
CM C.Mathewson Pants/300 125.00 300.00
CS Casey Stengel Jsy/275 12.50 30.00
CY Carl Yastrzemski Jsy/350 10.00 25.00
CY1 Carl Yastrzemski Pants/350 10.00 25.00
DS Duke Snider Jsy/350 6.00 15.00
DW1 D.Winfield Twins Jsy/300 4.00 10.00
FR F.Robinson O's Jsy/350 6.00 15.00
FR1 F.Robinson Angels Jsy/350 6.00 15.00
GC G.Carter Mets Jsy/350 4.00 10.00
GC1 G.Carter Expos Jsy/350 4.00 10.00
HW Honus Wagner Pants/275 40.00 80.00
JB Johnny Bench Jsy/150 6.00 15.00
JM Joe Morgan Jsy/350 4.00 10.00
JN Juan Marichal Pants/225 4.00 10.00
JN1 Juan Marichal Jsy/48 6.00 15.00
LA Luis Aparicio Jsy/230 4.00 10.00
LB Lou Boudreau Jsy/265 4.00 10.00
MM Mickey Mantle Pants/350 30.00 60.00
NR N.Ryan Rgr Pants/350 12.50 30.00
NR1 N.Ryan Astros Pants/350 12.50 30.00
OS Ozzie Smith Jsy/85 15.00 40.00
RF Rollie Fingers Jsy/105 4.00 10.00
RY R.Yount Portrait Jsy/350 6.00 15.00
RY1 R.Yount Swing Jsy/350 6.00 15.00
SA Sparky Anderson Jsy/350 4.00 10.00
SC Steve Carlton Jsy/350 6.00 15.00
SM Stan Musial Jsy/350 10.00 25.00
TC Ty Cobb Pants/300 50.00 100.00
TP Tony Perez Jsy/350 4.00 10.00
TS Tom Seaver Jsy/350 6.00 15.00
TS1 Tom Seaver Pants/350 6.00 15.00
TW Ted Williams Jsy/250 15.00 40.00
WA W.Alston Look Left Jsy/350 4.00 10.00
WA1 W.Alston Ahead Jsy/350 4.00 10.00
WI Willie Stargell Jsy/55 10.00 25.00
WS Warren Spahn CO Jsy/350 6.00 15.00
YB Yogi Berra Jsy/300 8.00 20.00

2003 SP Legendary Cuts Historic Swatches Blue

*BLUE: .6X TO 1.5X BASIC p/r 225-350
*BLUE: .6X TO 1.5X BASIC p/r 150-190
OVERALL GAME USED ODDS 1:12
STATED PRINT RUN 50 SERIAL #'d SETS

2003 SP Legendary Cuts Historic Swatches Green

*GREEN: .5X TO 1.2X BASIC SWATCH
OVERALL GAME USED ODDS 1:12
PRINT RUNS B/WN 160-250 COPIES PER
DW D.Winfield Yanks Jsy/160 4.00 10.00

2003 SP Legendary Cuts Historic Swatches Purple

*PURPLE p/r 150: .5X TO 1.2X BASIC
*PURPLE p/r 75-100: .6X TO 1.5X BASIC
OVERALL GAME USED ODDS 1:12
PRINT RUNS B/WN 75-150 COPIES PER

2003 SP Legendary Cuts Historical Impressions

STATED PRINT RUN 350 SERIAL #'d SETS
*GOLD 200: .6X TO 1.5X BASIC
GOLD 200 PRINT RUN 200 SERIAL #'d SETS
*GOLD 75: 1.25X TO 3X BASIC
GOLD 75 PRINT RUN 75 SERIAL #'d SETS
*SILVER: .75X TO 2X BASIC
SILVER PRINT RUN 250 SERIAL #'d SETS
OVERALL HIST.IMP.ODDS 1:12
AC Alexander Cartwright 3.00 8.00
BR Babe Ruth 8.00 20.00
CG Charlie Gehringer 3.00 8.00
CH Carl Hubbell 4.00 10.00
CM Christy Mathewson 4.00 10.00
CS Casey Stengel 4.00 10.00
CY Cy Young 4.00 10.00
DD Dizzy Dean 4.00 10.00
DO Don Drysdale 4.00 10.00
EC Eddie Collins 3.00 8.00
ES Enos Slaughter 3.00 8.00
GH Gabby Hartnett 3.00 8.00
HC Harry Caray 4.00 10.00
HG Hank Greenberg 4.00 10.00
HO Hoyt Wilhelm 3.00 8.00
HW Honus Wagner 4.00 10.00
JD Joe DiMaggio 5.00 12.00
JF Jimmie Foxx 4.00 10.00
JM Johnny Mize 3.00 8.00
JO Joe McCarthy 3.00 8.00
JR Jackie Robinson 4.00 10.00
LB Lou Boudreau 3.00 8.00
LD Leo Durocher 3.00 8.00
LE Lefty Grove 4.00 10.00
LG Lefty Gomez 4.00 10.00
LO Lou Gehrig 5.00 12.00
MA Mel Allen 3.00 8.00
MC Mickey Cochrane 3.00 8.00
MM Mickey Mantle 12.50 30.00
MO Mel Ott 4.00 10.00
PR Pee Wee Reese 4.00 10.00
RA Richie Ashburn 4.00 10.00
RC Roberto Clemente 8.00 20.00
RH Rogers Hornsby 4.00 10.00
RO Roy Campanella 4.00 10.00
SP Satchel Paige 4.00 10.00
TL Tony Lazzeri 3.00 8.00
TS Tris Speaker 4.00 10.00
TW Ted Williams 5.00 12.00
TY Ty Cobb 5.00 12.00

2004 SP Legendary Cuts

COMPLETE SET (126) 15.00 40.00
COMMON CARD (1-126) .20 .50
1 Al Kaline .50 1.25
2 Al Lopez .20 .50
3 Alan Trammell .30 .75
4 Andre Dawson .30 .75
5 Babe Ruth 1.25 3.00
6 Bert Campaneris .20 .50
7 Bill Mazeroski .30 .75
8 Bill Russell .20 .50
9 Billy Williams .30 .75
10 Bob Feller .30 .75
11 Bob Gibson .30 .75
12 Bob Lemon .30 .75
13 Bobby Doerr .30 .75
14 Brooks Robinson .30 .75
15 Cal Ripken 1.50 4.00
16 Carl Yastrzemski .50 1.25
17 Carlton Fisk .30 .75
18 Catfish Hunter .30 .75
19 Dale Murphy .50 1.25
20 Darryl Strawberry .20 .50
21 Dave Concepcion .20 .50
22 Dave Winfield .30 .75
23 Dennis Eckersley .30 .75
24 Denny McLain .20 .50
25 Don Drysdale .30 .75
26 Don Larsen .20 .50
27 Don Mattingly 1.00 2.50
28 Don Sutton .30 .75
29 Duke Snider .30 .75
30 Dusty Baker .20 .50
31 Dwight Gooden .20 .50
32 Earl Weaver .30 .75
33 Early Wynn .30 .75
34 Eddie Mathews .50 1.25
35 Eddie Murray .30 .75
36 Enos Slaughter .30 .75
37 Ernie Banks .50 1.25
38 Fergie Jenkins .30 .75
39 Frank Robinson .30 .75
40 Fred Lynn .20 .50
41 Gary Carter .30 .75
42 Gaylord Perry .30 .75
43 George Brett 1.00 2.50
44 George Foster .20 .50
45 George Kell .30 .75
46 Greg Luzinski .20 .50
47 Hal Newhouser .30 .75
48 Hank Greenberg .50 1.25
49 Harmon Killebrew .50 1.25
50 Honus Wagner .50 1.25
51 Hoyt Wilhelm .30 .75
52 Jackie Robinson .50 1.25
53 Jim Bunning .30 .75
54 Jim Palmer .30 .75
55 Jimmie Foxx .50 1.25
56 Joe Carter .20 .50
57 Joe DiMaggio 1.00 2.50
58 Joe Morgan .30 .75
59 Joe Torre .30 .75
60 Johnny Bench .50 1.25
61 Johnny Podres .20 .50
62 Johnny Roseboro .20 .50
63 Johnny Sain .20 .50
64 Juan Marichal .30 .75
65 Keith Hernandez .20 .50
66 Kirby Puckett .50 1.25
67 Kirk Gibson .20 .50
68 Will Clark .30 .75
69 Jim Rice .30 .75
70 Larry Doby .30 .75
71 Lou Boudreau .30 .75
72 Lou Brock .30 .75
73 Lou Gehrig 1.00 2.50
74 Lou Piniella .20 .50
75 Luis Aparicio .30 .75
76 Mark Grace .30 .75
77 Mel Ott .50 1.25
78 Mickey Lolich .20 .50
79 Mickey Mantle 1.50 4.00
80 Mike Greenwell .20 .50
81 Mike Schmidt .75 2.00
82 Monte Irvin .30 .75
83 Nellie Fox .30 .75
84 Nolan Ryan 1.50 4.00
85 Orlando Cepeda .30 .75
86 Ozzie Smith .60 1.50
87 Paul Molitor .50 1.25
88 Pee Wee Reese .30 .75
89 Phil Niekro .30 .75
90 Phil Rizzuto .30 .75
91 Ralph Kiner .30 .75
92 Red Rolfe .20 .50
93 Red Schoendienst .30 .75
94 Reggie Smith .20 .50
95 Rich Gossage .30 .75
96 Richie Ashburn .30 .75
97 Rick Ferrell .20 .50
98 Elston Howard .20 .50
99 Roberto Clemente 1.25 3.00
100 Robin Roberts .30 .75
101 Robin Yount .50 1.25
102 Roger Maris .50 1.25
103 Rollie Fingers .30 .75
104 Ron Santo .30 .75
105 Roy Campanella .50 1.25
106 Ryne Sandberg 1.00 2.50
107 Sparky Anderson .30 .75
108 Sparky Lyle .20 .50
109 Stan Musial .75 2.00
110 Steve Carlton .30 .75
111 Steve Garvey .20 .50
112 Ted Williams 1.00 2.50
113 Thurman Munson .50 1.25
114 Tom Seaver .30 .75
115 Tommy Henrich .20 .50
116 Tommy Lasorda .30 .75
117 Tony Gwynn .50 1.25
118 Tony Perez .30 .75
119 Ty Cobb .75 2.00
120 Wade Boggs .30 .75
121 Warren Spahn .30 .75
122 Whitey Ford .30 .75
123 Willie McCovey .30 .75
124 Willie Randolph .20 .50
125 Willie Stargell .30 .75
126 Yogi Berra .50 1.25

2004 SP Legendary Cuts Significant Fact Memorabilia

COMMON CARD p/r 50-61 15.00 40.00
MINOR STARS p/r 50-61 15.00 40.00
SEMISTARS p/r 50-61 20.00 50.00
UNLISTED STARS p/r 50-61 30.00 60.00
STATED ODDS 1:96
B/WN 5-99 VARIATIONS PER CARD EXIST
VARIATION PRINT RUNS PROVIDED BY UD
DIFT.FACTS FEATURED ON EACH CARD
EACH VARIATION SERIAL #'d AS 1 OF 1
NO PRICING ON QTY OF 10 OR LESS
SEE BECKETT.COM FOR ALL PRINT RUNS
1 Al Kaline Bat/50 * 30.00 60.00
3 Alan Trammell Jsy/25 * 20.00 50.00
4 Andre Dawson Jsy/25 * 20.00 50.00
7 Bill Mazeroski Bat/50 * 60.00 120.00
8 Bill Russell Pants/25 * 20.00 50.00
9 Billy Williams Jsy/99 * 10.00 25.00
11 Bob Gibson Jsy/99 * 15.00 40.00
13 Bobby Doerr Pants/99 * 15.00 40.00
14 Brooks Robinson Bat/99 * 15.00 40.00
15 Cal Ripken Jsy/99 * 50.00 100.00
16 Carl Yastrzemski Pants/99 * 30.00 60.00
17 Carlton Fisk Bat/99 * 15.00 40.00
18 Catfish Hunter Jsy/99 * 15.00 40.00
19 Dale Murphy Jsy/99 * 15.00 40.00
20 Darryl Strawberry Jsy/25 * 20.00 50.00
21 Dave Concepcion Jsy/99 * 10.00 25.00
22 Dave Winfield Jsy/99 * 10.00 25.00
23 Dennis Eckersley Jsy/25 * 20.00 50.00
25 Don Drysdale Jsy/99 * 20.00 50.00
26 Don Larsen Pants/50 * 20.00 50.00
27 Don Mattingly Jsy/99 * 75.00 150.00
28 Don Sutton Jsy/99 * 10.00 25.00
29 Duke Snider Jsy/99 * 15.00 40.00
30 Dusty Baker Jsy/50 * 10.00 25.00
31 Dwight Gooden Jsy/25 * 20.00 50.00
32 Earl Weaver Jsy/25 * 20.00 50.00
34 Eddie Mathews Jsy/99 * 20.00 50.00
35 Eddie Murray Jsy/99 * 75.00 150.00
37 Ernie Banks Jsy/99 * 20.00 50.00
38 Fergie Jenkins Pants/99 * 10.00 25.00
39 Frank Robinson Jsy/99 * 10.00 25.00
40 Fred Lynn Jsy/25 * 20.00 50.00
41 Gary Carter Jsy/99 * 10.00 25.00
42 Gaylord Perry Jsy/99 * 10.00 25.00
43 George Brett Jsy/99 * 60.00 120.00
49 Harmon Killebrew Jsy/99 * 20.00 50.00
51 Hoyt Wilhelm Pants/99 * 15.00 40.00
52 Jackie Robinson Jsy/99 * 75.00 150.00
53 Jim Bunning Pants/25 * 20.00 50.00
54 Jim Palmer Jsy/25 * 10.00 25.00
56 Joe Carter Jsy/99 * 50.00 100.00
58 Joe Morgan Bat/50 * 15.00 40.00
59 Joe Torre Jsy/25 * 30.00 60.00
60 Johnny Bench Jsy/99 * 20.00 50.00
61 Johnny Podres Jsy/99 * 10.00 25.00
62 Johnny Roseboro Bat/50 * 15.00 40.00
63 Johnny Sain Jsy/25 * 20.00 50.00
64 Juan Marichal Jsy/99 * 10.00 25.00
66 Kirby Puckett Bat/50 * 50.00 100.00
69 Jim Rice Jsy/99 * 10.00 25.00
71 Lou Boudreau Bat/25 * 30.00 60.00
72 Lou Brock Bat/99 * 15.00 40.00
74 Lou Piniella Jsy/25 * 20.00 50.00
75 Luis Aparicio Jsy/25 * 20.00 50.00
76 Mark Grace Jsy/25 * 30.00 60.00
78 Mickey Lolich Jsy/25 * 20.00 50.00
79 Mickey Mantle Bat/25 * 200.00 350.00
81 Mike Schmidt Jsy/99 * 75.00 150.00
83 Nellie Fox Jsy/99 * 60.00 120.00
84 Nolan Ryan Pants/99 * 75.00 150.00
85 Orlando Cepeda Pants/99 * 10.00 25.00
86 Ozzie Smith Bat/99 * 40.00 80.00
87 Paul Molitor Pants/99 * 10.00 25.00
88 Pee Wee Reese Jsy/99 * 15.00 40.00
89 Phil Niekro Jsy/99 * 10.00 25.00
90 Phil Rizzuto Jsy/99 * 15.00 40.00
92 Red Rolfe Bat/25 * 20.00 50.00
95 Rich Gossage Jsy/50 * 15.00 40.00
98 Elston Howard Jsy/99 * 15.00 40.00
101 Robin Yount Jsy/99 * 10.00 25.00
102 Roger Maris Pants/50 * 75.00 150.00
103 Rollie Fingers Jsy/99 * 10.00 25.00
105 Roy Campanella Pants/50 * 20.00 50.00
106 Ryne Sandberg Jsy/50 * 40.00 80.00
107 Sparky Anderson Jsy/50 * 15.00 40.00
108 Sparky Lyle Jsy/50 * 15.00 40.00
109 Stan Musial Pants/99 * 50.00 100.00
110 Steve Carlton Bat/99 * 10.00 25.00
111 Steve Garvey Jsy/99 * 10.00 25.00
113 Thurman Munson Jsy/99 * 20.00 50.00
114 Tom Seaver Jsy/61 * 20.00 50.00
116 Tommy Lasorda Jsy/25 * 20.00 50.00
117 Tony Gwynn Jsy/99 * 30.00 60.00
118 Tony Perez Jsy/99 * 10.00 25.00
120 Wade Boggs Jsy/99 * 15.00 40.00
121 Warren Spahn Jsy/99 * 20.00 50.00
123 Willie McCovey Pants/99 * 15.00 40.00
124 Willie Randolph Jsy/25 * 20.00 50.00
125 Willie Stargell Jsy/99 * 15.00 40.00
126 Yogi Berra Jsy/99 * 20.00 50.00

2004 SP Legendary Cuts All-Time Autos

OVERALL AU ODDS 1:64
STATED PRINT RUN 50 SERIAL #'d SETS
EXCHANGE DEADLINE 11/19/07
AK Al Kaline 25.00 50.00
BD Bobby Doerr 10.00 25.00
BM Bill Mazeroski 15.00 40.00
CF Carlton Fisk 20.00 50.00
CR Cal Ripken 40.00 100.00
DE Dennis Eckersley 30.00 60.00
DM Dale Murphy 15.00 40.00
DN Don Newcombe 10.00 25.00
DS Don Sutton 10.00 25.00
FJ Fergie Jenkins 10.00 25.00
FL Fred Lynn 6.00 15.00
GC Gary Carter 20.00 50.00
GK George Kell 20.00 50.00
GP Gaylord Perry 10.00 25.00
HK Harmon Killebrew 30.00 60.00
JC Joe Carter 10.00 25.00
JP Johnny Podres 6.00 15.00
LA Luis Aparicio 12.00 30.00
MA Don Mattingly 40.00 100.00
MC Denny McLain 10.00 25.00
MI Monte Irvin 15.00 40.00
MW Maury Wills 10.00 25.00
NR Nolan Ryan 60.00 120.00
OC Orlando Cepeda 10.00 25.00
PN Phil Niekro 10.00 25.00
RF Rollie Fingers 10.00 25.00
RR Robin Roberts 20.00 50.00
RS Red Schoendienst 10.00 25.00
RY Robin Yount 30.00 60.00
SA Ryne Sandberg 40.00 100.00
SM Stan Musial 40.00 80.00
TG Tony Gwynn 20.00 50.00
TP Tony Perez 15.00 40.00
TS Tom Seaver 30.00 80.00
WB Wade Boggs 20.00 50.00
WC Will Clark 15.00 40.00
WF Whitey Ford 20.00 50.00
WM Willie McCovey 15.00 40.00
YB Yogi Berra 25.00 60.00

2004 SP Legendary Cuts Autographs

OVERALL CUT AU ODDS 1:128
PRINT RUNS B/WN 1-199 COPIES PER
NO PRICING ON QTY OF 19 OR LESS
EXCHANGE DEADLINE 11/19/07
AR Allie Reynolds/25 100.00 200.00
BD Bill Dickey/82 50.00 100.00
BH Billy Herman/134 20.00 50.00
BJ Bob Johnson/32 150.00 250.00
BL Bob Lemon/199 20.00 50.00
BU Burleigh Grimes/83 75.00 150.00
CA Max Carey/72 40.00 80.00
CG Charlie Gehringer/171 20.00 50.00
CH Carl Hubbell/199 30.00 60.00
CR Joe Cronin/84 20.00 50.00
CS Casey Stengel/38 300.00 500.00
DD Dizzy Dean/33 500.00 800.00
DR Don Drysdale/66 50.00 120.00
EC Earle Combs/27 175.00 300.00
EL Ernie Lombardi/39 50.00 100.00
EM Eddie Mathews/27 175.00 300.00
ER Edd Roush/129 40.00 80.00
ES Enos Slaughter/147 20.00 50.00
EW Early Wynn/54 40.00 80.00
FF Frankie Frisch/57 200.00 350.00
GP George Pipgras/46 100.00 200.00
GR Lefty Grove/75 200.00 400.00
GS George Sisler/32 300.00 600.00

HG Hank Greenberg/37 250.00 400.00
HK Harvey Kuenn/49 60.00 120.00
HN Hal Newhouser/51 75.00 150.00
JD Joe DiMaggio/111 200.00 400.00
JH Jim Hunter/25 150.00 250.00
JM Joe Medwick/32 250.00 400.00
JS Joe Sewell/199 20.00 50.00
LB Lou Boudreau/199 20.00 50.00
LD Leo Durocher/75 150.00 300.00
LG Lefty Gomez/98 50.00 100.00
LU Luke Appling/108 40.00 100.00
MI Johnny Mize/118 40.00 80.00
PB James Cool Papa Bell/47 350.00 500.00
PR Pee Wee Reese/35 175.00 300.00
RA Richie Ashburn/31 175.00 300.00
RD Ray Dandridge/199 30.00 60.00
RF Rick Ferrell/43 50.00 100.00
RR Red Ruffing/30 175.00 300.00
RU Rube Marquard/59 150.00 250.00
SP Satchel Paige/28 500.00 800.00
SR Sam Rice/28 175.00 300.00
ST Stan Coveleski/102 75.00 150.00
SW Joe Wood/79 150.00 300.00
TL Ted Lyons/199 20.00 50.00
TW Ted Williams/28 1000.00 1200.00
WA Walter Alston/74 50.00 100.00
WF Wes Ferrell/36 150.00 250.00
WH Waite Hoyt/106 40.00 100.00
WM Hoyt Wilhelm/115 20.00 50.00
WS Willie Stargell/39 75.00 150.00

2004 SP Legendary Cuts Game Graphs Memorabilia 25

OVERALL AU ODDS 1:64
STATED PRINT RUN 25 SERIAL #'d SETS
GRAPH 10 PRINT RUN 10 SERIAL #'d SETS
NO GRAPH 10 PRICING DUE TO SCARCITY
EXCHANGE DEADLINE 11/19/07
AK Al Kaline Bat 40.00 100.00
BG Bob Gibson Jsy 20.00 50.00
BM Bill Mazeroski Bat 20.00 50.00
BR Brooks Robinson Bat 20.00 50.00
CF Carlton Fisk Jsy 20.00 50.00
CR Cal Ripken Jsy 50.00 120.00
CY Carl Yastrzemski Jsy 50.00 100.00
DM Dale Murphy Jsy 20.00 50.00
DS Don Sutton Jsy 12.50 30.00
DW Dave Winfield Pants 20.00 50.00
EB Ernie Banks Jsy 40.00 80.00
EM Eddie Murray Jsy 50.00 100.00
FR Frank Robinson Jsy 20.00 50.00
GB George Brett Jsy 60.00 120.00
GC Gary Carter Jsy 15.00 40.00
HK Harmon Killebrew Jsy 50.00 100.00
JB Johnny Bench Jsy 50.00 100.00
JC Joe Carter Jsy 15.00 40.00
JM Juan Marichal Jsy 15.00 40.00
KP Kirby Puckett Bat 50.00 100.00
LA Luis Aparicio Jsy 15.00 40.00
LB Lou Brock Jsy 20.00 50.00
MA Don Mattingly Jsy 60.00 120.00
MO Joe Morgan Bat 15.00 40.00
MS Mike Schmidt Jsy 50.00 100.00
NR Nolan Ryan Jsy 75.00 150.00
OS Ozzie Smith Jsy 40.00 80.00
PM Paul Molitor Jsy 15.00 40.00
PN Phil Niekro Jsy 15.00 40.00
PR Phil Rizzuto Jsy 20.00 50.00
RF Rollie Fingers Jsy 12.50 30.00
RS Ryne Sandberg Jsy 60.00 120.00
RY Robin Yount Jsy 40.00 80.00
SM Stan Musial Jsy 50.00 100.00
SN Duke Snider Jsy 20.00 50.00
TG Tony Gwynn Jsy 40.00 80.00
WB Wade Boggs Jsy 40.00 80.00
WM Willie McCovey Pants 25.00 60.00
YB Yogi Berra Jsy 40.00 100.00

2004 SP Legendary Cuts Historic Patches

OVERALL GU ODDS 1:4
STATED PRINT RUN 25 SERIAL #'d SETS
BG Bob Gibson 15.00 40.00
CR Cal Ripken 60.00 120.00
CY Carl Yastrzemski 30.00 60.00
DD Don Drysdale 15.00 40.00
DS Duke Snider 15.00 40.00
EB Ernie Banks 30.00 60.00
EM Eddie Mathews 40.00 80.00
GB George Brett 20.00 50.00
JB Johnny Bench 15.00 40.00
MS Mike Schmidt 20.00 50.00
NR Nolan Ryan 40.00 80.00
RY Robin Yount 15.00 40.00
SM Stan Musial 40.00 80.00
TG Tony Gwynn 15.00 40.00
TS Tom Seaver 15.00 40.00

2004 SP Legendary Cuts Historic Swatches

OVERALL GU ODDS 1:4
SP INFO PROVIDED BY UPPER DECK
AN Sparky Anderson Jsy 3.00 8.00
BR Brooks Robinson Bat 4.00 10.00
CF Carlton Fisk Pants 4.00 10.00
CH Catfish Hunter Pants 4.00 10.00
CR Cal Ripken Jsy 8.00 20.00
DC Dave Concepcion Jsy 3.00 8.00
DD Don Drysdale Pants 4.00 10.00
DL Don Larsen Pants SP 10.00 25.00
DM Don Mattingly Jsy 6.00 15.00
DS Don Sutton Jsy 3.00 8.00
DW Dave Winfield Pants 3.00 8.00
EM Eddie Murray Jsy SP 6.00 15.00
FJ Fergie Jenkins Pants 3.00 8.00
GB George Brett Jsy 6.00 15.00
GC Gary Carter Pants 3.00 8.00
GF George Foster Bat 3.00 8.00
GP Gaylord Perry Jsy 3.00 8.00
HK Harmon Killebrew Jsy 4.00 10.00
HW Hoyt Wilhelm Pants 3.00 8.00
JB Johnny Bench Pants SP 6.00 15.00
JC Joe Carter Jsy 3.00 8.00
JM Joe Morgan Bat 3.00 8.00
JP Johnny Podres Jsy 3.00 8.00
JR Jim Rice Jsy 3.00 8.00
KP Kirby Puckett Bat 4.00 10.00
LB Lou Brock Jsy 4.00 10.00
MA Eddie Mathews Jsy 4.00 10.00
ML Mickey Lolich Jsy 3.00 8.00
MU Dale Murphy Jsy 4.00 10.00
NR Nolan Ryan Jsy 8.00 20.00
OS Ozzie Smith Jsy 6.00 15.00
PM Paul Molitor Jsy 3.00 8.00
PN Phil Niekro Jsy 3.00 8.00
RF Rollie Fingers Pants 10.00 25.00
RY Robin Yount Pants 4.00 10.00
SG Steve Garvey Jsy 3.00 8.00
SL Sparky Lyle Jsy 3.00 8.00
SM Stan Musial Pants 10.00 25.00
TM Thurman Munson Jsy 4.00 10.00
TS Tom Seaver Pants 4.00 10.00

2004 SP Legendary Cuts Historic Swatches 25

*SWATCH 25: .75X TO 2X BASIC
*SWATCH 25: .75X TO 2X BASIC SP
OVERALL GU ODDS 1:4
STATED PRINT RUN 25 SERIAL #'d SETS
CR Cal Ripken Jsy 30.00 60.00
PR Phil Rizzuto Jsy 8.00 20.00

2004 SP Legendary Cuts Legendary Duels Memorabilia

OVERALL GU ODDS 1:4
STATED PRINT RUN 25 SERIAL #'d SETS
BG Brett Jsy/Gossage Jsy 30.00 60.00
DW DiMaggio Jsy/T.Will Jsy 75.00 150.00
EG Eckersley Jsy/K.Gibs Bat 15.00 40.00
FM Fisk Pants/Morgan Bat 15.00 40.00
GL B.Gibson Jsy/Lolich Jsy 15.00 40.00
MW Mantle Pants/T.Will Jsy 150.00 250.00
PL Podres Jsy/Larsen Jsy 15.00 40.00
RM Roseboro Bat/Marichal Pants 10.00 25.00
RR Reese Jsy/Rizzuto Pants 15.00 40.00
SM Snider Jsy/Mantle Pants 100.00 200.00
SS Ozzie Jsy/Sandberg Jsy 40.00 80.00
WB H.Wagner Pants/Banks Jsy 75.00 150.00

2004 SP Legendary Cuts Legendary Duos Memorabilia

OVERALL GU ODDS 1:4
STATED PRINT RUN 25 SERIAL #'d SETS
CM Concepcion Jsy/Morgan Bat 10.00 25.00
DM DiMaggio Jsy 100.00 200.00
Mantle Pants
LB Larsen Jsy 40.00 80.00
Berra Jsy
MB Mantle Pants 75.00 150.00
Berra Jsy
MM Mantle Pants 175.00 300.00
Maris Jsy
MY Molitor Jsy 20.00 50.00
Yount Jsy
PJ Reese Jsy 40.00 80.00
Jackie Jsy
RR Brooks Bat 40.00 80.00
Ripken Jsy
RS Ryan Jsy 75.00 150.00
Seaver Jsy
SC Snider Jsy 30.00 60.00
Campy Pants
SS Sain Jsy 12.00 30.00
Spahn Jsy
WB B.Will Jsy 20.00 50.00
Banks Jsy

2004 SP Legendary Cuts Legendary Sigs

OVERALL AU ODDS 1:64
STATED PRINT RUN 50 SERIAL #'d SETS
AK Al Kaline 25.00 50.00
BD Bobby Doerr 10.00 25.00
BF Bob Feller 10.00 25.00
BG Bob Gibson 15.00 40.00
BR Brooks Robinson 15.00 40.00
CR Cal Ripken 50.00 120.00
CY Carl Yastrzemski 30.00 60.00
DE Dennis Eckersley 15.00 40.00
DM Dale Murphy 15.00 40.00
DN Don Newcombe 10.00 25.00
DS Don Sutton 10.00 25.00
EB Ernie Banks 30.00 60.00
EM Eddie Murray 30.00 80.00
FL Fred Lynn 6.00 15.00
GC Gary Carter 20.00 50.00
GK George Kell 10.00 25.00
GP Gaylord Perry 10.00 25.00
HK Harmon Killebrew UER 30.00 60.00
JB Johnny Bench 30.00 60.00
JC Joe Carter 10.00 25.00
JM Juan Marichal 10.00 25.00
JP Johnny Podres 6.00 15.00
LA Luis Aparicio 10.00 25.00
MA Don Mattingly 25.00 60.00
MC Denny McLain 10.00 25.00
MI Monte Irvin 15.00 40.00
MS Mike Schmidt 40.00 80.00
MW Maury Wills 10.00 25.00
OS Ozzie Smith 30.00 60.00
PA Jim Palmer 10.00 25.00
PR Phil Rizzuto 15.00 40.00
RF Rollie Fingers 10.00 25.00
RK Ralph Kiner 15.00 40.00
RR Robin Roberts 20.00 50.00
RS Red Schoendienst 10.00 25.00
SA Ryne Sandberg 40.00 80.00
SN Duke Snider 15.00 40.00
TG Tony Gwynn 20.00 50.00
WB Wade Boggs 15.00 40.00
WC Will Clark 15.00 40.00
WM Willie McCovey 15.00 40.00

2004 SP Legendary Cuts Legendary Swatches

SP INFO PROVIDED BY UPPER DECK
SWATCH 15 PRINT RUN 15 #'d SETS
NO SWATCH 15 PRICING DUE TO SCARCITY
OVERALL GU ODDS 1:4
AK Al Kaline Bat 4.00 10.00
BD Bobby Doerr Pants 3.00 8.00
BG Bob Gibson Jsy 6.00 15.00
BW Billy Williams Jsy 3.00 8.00
CF Carlton Fisk Pants 4.00 10.00
CH Catfish Hunter Jsy 4.00 10.00
CR Cal Ripken Jsy 10.00 25.00
CY Carl Yastrzemski Jsy 6.00 15.00
DD Don Drysdale Pants 4.00 10.00
DM Don Mattingly Jsy 6.00 15.00
DS Duke Snider Pants 4.00 10.00
DW Dave Winfield Jsy 3.00 8.00
EB Ernie Banks Jsy SP 6.00 15.00
EH Elston Howard Jsy 4.00 10.00
EM Eddie Mathews Jsy 4.00 10.00
FR Frank Robinson Pants 3.00 8.00
GB George Brett Jsy 6.00 15.00
HK Harmon Killebrew Jsy 4.00 10.00
JB Johnny Bench Jsy 4.00 10.00
JR Jim Rice Jsy 3.00 8.00
MA Juan Marichal Pants 3.00 8.00
MS Mike Schmidt Jsy 6.00 15.00
NF Nellie Fox Jsy 4.00 10.00
NR Nolan Ryan Jsy 10.00 25.00
OC Orlando Cepeda Pants 3.00 8.00
PO Johnny Podres Jsy 3.00 8.00
PR Pee Wee Reese Jsy 4.00 10.00
RC Roy Campanella Pants 4.00 10.00
RI Phil Rizzuto Pants 12.50 30.00
RY Robin Yount Pants 4.00 10.00
SC Steve Carlton Bat 3.00 8.00
SM Stan Musial Jsy 8.00 20.00
ST Willie Stargell Jsy 4.00 10.00
TG Tony Gwynn Pants 4.00 10.00
TM Thurman Munson Jsy 8.00 20.00
TP Tony Perez Jsy 3.00 8.00
TS Tom Seaver Jsy 4.00 10.00
WB Wade Boggs Pants 4.00 10.00
WM Willie McCovey Pants 4.00 10.00
WS Warren Spahn Jsy 4.00 10.00
YB Yogi Berra Pants 4.00 10.00

2004 SP Legendary Cuts Marked for the Hall Autos

OVERALL AU ODDS 1:64
STATED PRINT RUN 50 SERIAL #'d SETS
EXCHANGE DEADLINE 11/19/07
AK Al Kaline 25.00 50.00
BD Bobby Doerr 10.00 25.00
BF Bob Feller 15.00 40.00
BG Bob Gibson 15.00 40.00
BM Bill Mazeroski 15.00 40.00
BR Brooks Robinson 15.00 40.00
CF Carlton Fisk 15.00 40.00
CY Carl Yastrzemski 30.00 80.00
DS Duke Snider 15.00 40.00
DW Dave Winfield 20.00 50.00
EB Ernie Banks 30.00 80.00
EM Eddie Murray 30.00 100.00
FR Frank Robinson 30.00 80.00
GB George Brett 50.00 120.00
GC Gary Carter 20.00 50.00
GP Gaylord Perry 10.00 25.00
HK Harmon Killebrew 40.00 100.00
JB Johnny Bench 40.00 100.00
JM Joe Morgan 10.00 25.00
JP Jim Palmer 10.00 25.00
KP Kirby Puckett 150.00 300.00
LA Luis Aparicio 10.00 25.00
LB Lou Brock 15.00 40.00
MA Juan Marichal 10.00 25.00
MS Mike Schmidt 40.00 80.00
NR Nolan Ryan 50.00 120.00
OC Orlando Cepeda 10.00 25.00
OS Ozzie Smith 25.00 60.00
PM Paul Molitor 10.00 25.00
PN Phil Niekro 15.00 40.00
PR Phil Rizzuto 15.00 40.00
RK Ralph Kiner 15.00 40.00
RR Robin Roberts 20.00 50.00
RY Robin Yount 30.00 80.00
SC Steve Carlton 12.00 30.00
SM Stan Musial 50.00 100.00
TP Tony Perez 15.00 40.00
TS Tom Seaver 25.00 60.00
WF Whitey Ford 15.00 40.00
WM Willie McCovey 25.00 60.00
YB Yogi Berra 30.00 80.00

2004 SP Legendary Cuts Marks of Greatness Autos

OVERALL AU ODDS 1:64
STATED PRINT RUN 50 SERIAL #'d SETS
EXCHANGE DEADLINE 11/19/07
AK Al Kaline 25.00 50.00
BG Bob Gibson 15.00 40.00
BR Brooks Robinson 20.00 50.00
BW Billy Williams 12.50 30.00
CF Carlton Fisk 15.00 40.00
CR Cal Ripken 75.00 150.00
DM Dale Murphy 20.00 50.00
DN Don Newcombe 10.00 25.00
DS Duke Snider 15.00 40.00
DW Dave Winfield 15.00 40.00
EB Ernie Banks 30.00 60.00
FJ Fergie Jenkins 10.00 25.00
FL Fred Lynn 6.00 15.00
FR Frank Robinson 15.00 40.00
GB George Brett 40.00 80.00
HK Harmon Killebrew 30.00 60.00
JB Johnny Bench 30.00 60.00
JC Joe Carter 10.00 25.00
JM Joe Morgan 10.00 25.00
JP Jim Palmer 10.00 25.00
KP Kirby Puckett 150.00 300.00
LB Lou Brock 15.00 40.00
MA Don Mattingly 15.00 40.00
MC Denny McLain 10.00 25.00
MS Mike Schmidt 40.00 80.00
NR Nolan Ryan 60.00 120.00
OC Orlando Cepeda 10.00 25.00
OZ Ozzie Smith 40.00 80.00
PM Paul Molitor 10.00 25.00
PN Phil Niekro 10.00 25.00
RF Rollie Fingers 10.00 25.00
RS Ryne Sandberg 20.00 50.00
RY Robin Yount 30.00 60.00
SM Stan Musial 40.00 80.00
TG Tony Gwynn 20.00 50.00
TP Tony Perez 15.00 40.00
TS Tom Seaver 25.00 60.00
WB Wade Boggs 15.00 40.00
WC Will Clark 15.00 40.00
WF Whitey Ford 15.00 40.00
YB Yogi Berra 40.00 100.00

2004 SP Legendary Cuts Significant Swatches

OVERALL GU ODDS 1:4
SP INFO PROVIDED BY UPPER DECK
BD Bobby Doerr Pants 3.00 8.00
BM Bill Mazeroski Bat 4.00 10.00
CF Carlton Fisk Pants 4.00 10.00
CH Catfish Hunter Pants 4.00 10.00
CR Cal Ripken Jsy 5.00 12.00
CY Carl Yastrzemski Jsy 6.00 15.00
DC Dave Concepcion Jsy 3.00 8.00
DD Don Drysdale Jsy 5.00 12.00
DM Dale Murphy Bat 4.00 10.00
DS Don Sutton Jsy 3.00 8.00
DW Dave Winfield Pants 3.00 8.00
EB Ernie Banks Pants SP 6.00 15.00
ED Eddie Mathews Jsy 5.00 12.00
EM Eddie Murray Jsy SP 6.00 15.00
FJ Fergie Jenkins Pants 3.00 8.00
FR Frank Robinson Jsy 3.00 8.00
GC Gary Carter Jsy 3.00 8.00
GF George Foster Bat 5.00 12.00
GP Gaylord Perry Jsy 3.00 8.00
HW Hoyt Wilhelm Pants 3.00 8.00
JC Joe Carter Jsy 3.00 8.00
JP Johnny Podres Jsy 3.00 8.00
LB Lou Brock Jsy SP 6.00 15.00
MA Don Mattingly Jsy 6.00 15.00
MS Mike Schmidt Pants 6.00 15.00
NR Nolan Ryan Jsy 10.00 25.00
OC Orlando Cepeda Pants 3.00 8.00
PM Paul Molitor Bat 3.00 8.00
PN Phil Niekro Jsy SP 4.00 10.00
RF Rollie Fingers Pants 3.00 8.00
RM Roger Maris Pants 12.50 30.00
RY Robin Yount Bat 4.00 10.00
SA Sparky Anderson Jsy 3.00 8.00
SG Steve Garvey Jsy 3.00 8.00
SL Sparky Lyle Jsy 3.00 8.00
SN Duke Snider Pants 3.00 8.00
ST Willie Stargell Jsy SP 6.00 15.00
TM Thurman Munson Pants 8.00 20.00
TP Tony Perez Jsy 3.00 8.00
TS Tom Seaver Pants 4.00 10.00
WM Willie McCovey Pants 4.00 10.00
WS Warren Spahn Jsy 5.00 12.00

2004 SP Legendary Cuts Significant Swatches 25

*SWATCH 25: .75X TO 2X BASIC
*SWATCH 25: .75X TO 2X BASIC SP
OVERALL GU ODDS 1:4
STATED PRINT RUN 25 SERIAL #'d SETS
CR Cal Ripken Jsy 20.00 50.00

2004 SP Legendary Cuts Ultimate Autos

OVERALL AU ODDS 1:64
STATED PRINT RUN 25 SERIAL #'d SETS
EXCHANGE DEADLINE 11/19/07
AK Al Kaline 30.00 80.00
BF Bob Feller 12.50 30.00
BG Bob Gibson 15.00 40.00
BM Bill Mazeroski 15.00 40.00
BR Brooks Robinson 30.00 80.00
CY Carl Yastrzemski 40.00 100.00
DE Dennis Eckersley 15.00 40.00
DM Don Mattingly 50.00 120.00
DS Don Sutton 10.00 25.00
DW Dave Winfield 15.00 40.00
EB Ernie Banks 30.00 80.00
EM Eddie Murray 40.00 100.00
FJ Fergie Jenkins 12.50 30.00
FR Frank Robinson 25.00 60.00
GB George Brett 50.00 120.00
GK George Kell 30.00 80.00
HK Harmon Killebrew 40.00 100.00
JB Johnny Bench 30.00 80.00
JM Joe Morgan 12.00 30.00
JP Johnny Podres 10.00 25.00
KP Kirby Puckett 125.00 250.00
LB Lou Brock 40.00 100.00
MA Juan Marichal 25.00 60.00
MI Monte Irvin 15.00 40.00
MS Mike Schmidt 40.00 100.00
MW Maury Wills 12.00 30.00
NR Nolan Ryan 60.00 120.00
OS Ozzie Smith 30.00 80.00
PA Jim Palmer 12.00 30.00
PM Paul Molitor 12.00 30.00
PR Phil Rizzuto 15.00 40.00
RK Ralph Kiner 15.00 40.00
RS Red Schoendienst 12.00 30.00
RY Robin Yount 30.00 80.00
SA Ryne Sandberg 50.00 120.00
SM Stan Musial 60.00 120.00
SN Duke Snider 20.00 50.00
TS Tom Seaver 40.00 100.00
WF Whitey Ford 15.00 40.00
YB Yogi Berra 40.00 100.00

2004 SP Legendary Cuts Ultimate Swatches

SP INFO PROVIDED BY UPPER DECK
SWATCH 10 PRINT RUN 10 #'d SETS
NO SWATCH 10 PRICING DUE TO SCARCITY
OVERALL GU ODDS 1:4
BG Bob Gibson Jsy 4.00 10.00
BR Brooks Robinson Bat 4.00 10.00
BW Billy Williams Jsy 3.00 8.00
CH Catfish Hunter Jsy 4.00 10.00
CR Cal Ripken Jsy 10.00 25.00
CY Carl Yastrzemski Jsy 6.00 15.00
DD Don Drysdale Jsy 4.00 10.00
DM Don Mattingly Jsy 6.00 15.00
DS Duke Snider Jsy SP 6.00 15.00
DW Dave Winfield Jsy 3.00 8.00
EB Ernie Banks Jsy 6.00 15.00
EM Eddie Mathews Jsy 4.00 10.00
FR Frank Robinson Pants 3.00 8.00
GB George Brett Jsy 6.00 15.00
HG Hank Greenberg Bat 6.00 15.00
HK Harmon Killebrew Jsy 4.00 10.00
HW Honus Wagner Pants SP 40.00 100.00
JB Johnny Bench Jsy 4.00 10.00
JD Joe DiMaggio Jsy SP 20.00 50.00
JR Jackie Robinson Jsy 15.00 40.00
KP Kirby Puckett Bat 4.00 10.00
MA Juan Marichal Jsy 3.00 8.00
MM Mickey Mantle Pants SP 25.00 60.00
MS Mike Schmidt Jsy 6.00 15.00
NF Nellie Fox Jsy 4.00 10.00
NR Nolan Ryan Jsy 8.00 20.00
OS Ozzie Smith Jsy 6.00 15.00
PR Pee Wee Reese Jsy 6.00 15.00
RC Roy Campanella Pants 4.00 10.00
RM Roger Maris Jsy 12.00 30.00
RY Robin Yount Jsy 4.00 10.00
SC Steve Carlton Bat 3.00 8.00
SM Stan Musial Jsy 8.00 20.00
TG Tony Gwynn Jsy 4.00 10.00
TM Thurman Munson Jsy 5.00 12.00
TS Tom Seaver Jsy SP 6.00 15.00
TW Ted Williams Pants SP 12.00 30.00
WB Wade Boggs Jsy 4.00 10.00
WM Willie McCovey Pants 4.00 10.00
WS Warren Spahn Jsy 5.00 12.00
YB Yogi Berra Pants 4.00 10.00

2005 SP Legendary Cuts

COMPLETE SET (90) 10.00 25.00
COMMON CARD (1-90) .25 .60
1 Al Kaline .60 1.50
2 Babe Ruth 1.50 4.00
3 Bill Mazeroski .40 1.00
4 Billy Williams .40 1.00
5 Bob Feller .40 1.00
6 Bob Gibson .40 1.00
7 Bob Lemon .40 1.00
8 Bobby Doerr .40 1.00
9 Brooks Robinson .40 1.00
10 Carl Yastrzemski .75 2.00
11 Carlton Fisk .40 1.00
12 Casey Stengel .40 1.00
13 Catfish Hunter .40 1.00
14 Christy Mathewson .60 1.50
15 Cy Young .60 1.50
16 Dennis Eckersley .40 1.00
17 Dizzy Dean .40 1.00
18 Don Drysdale .40 1.00
19 Don Sutton .40 1.00
20 Duke Snider .40 1.00
21 Early Wynn .40 1.00
22 Eddie Mathews .60 1.50
23 Eddie Murray .40 1.00
24 Enos Slaughter .40 1.00
25 Ernie Banks .60 1.50
26 Fergie Jenkins .40 1.00
27 Frank Robinson .40 1.00
28 Gary Carter .40 1.00
29 Gaylord Perry .40 1.00
30 Reggie Jackson .40 1.00
31 George Kell .40 1.00
32 George Sisler .40 1.00
33 Hal Newhouser .40 1.00
34 Harmon Killebrew .60 1.50
35 Honus Wagner .40 1.00
36 Jackie Robinson .40 1.00
37 Jim Bunning .40 1.00
38 Jim Palmer .40 1.00
39 Jimmie Foxx .40 1.00
40 Joe DiMaggio 1.25 3.00
41 Joe Morgan .40 1.00
42 Johnny Bench .60 1.50
43 Johnny Mize .40 1.00
44 Juan Marichal .40 1.00
45 Kirby Puckett .60 1.50
46 Larry Doby .40 1.00
47 Lefty Grove .40 1.00
48 Lou Boudreau .40 1.00
49 Lou Brock .40 1.00
50 Lou Gehrig 1.25 3.00
51 Luis Aparicio .40 1.00
52 Mel Ott .60 1.50
53 Mickey Cochrane .40 1.00
54 Mickey Mantle 2.00 5.00
55 Mike Schmidt 1.00 2.50
56 Monte Irvin .40 1.00
57 Nolan Ryan 2.00 5.00
58 Orlando Cepeda .40 1.00
59 Ozzie Smith .75 2.00
60 Paul Molitor .60 1.50
61 Pee Wee Reese .40 1.00
62 Phil Niekro .40 1.00
63 Phil Rizzuto .40 1.00
64 Ralph Kiner .40 1.00
65 Red Schoendienst .40 1.00
66 Richie Ashburn .40 1.00
67 Rick Ferrell .25 .60
68 Robin Roberts .40 1.00
69 Robin Yount .60 1.50
70 Rod Carew .40 1.00
71 Rogers Hornsby .25 .60
72 Rollie Fingers .40 1.00
73 Roy Campanella .40 1.00
74 Ryne Sandberg 1.25 3.00
75 Satchel Paige .60 1.50
76 Stan Musial 1.00 2.50
77 Steve Carlton .40 1.00
78 Ted Williams 1.25 3.00
79 Thurman Munson .40 1.00
80 Tom Seaver .40 1.00
81 Tony Gwynn .75 2.00
82 Tony Perez .40 1.00
83 Ty Cobb 1.00 2.50
84 Wade Boggs .40 1.00
85 Walter Johnson .40 1.00
86 Warren Spahn .40 1.00
87 Whitey Ford .40 1.00
88 Willie McCovey .40 1.00
89 Willie Stargell .40 1.00
90 Yogi Berra .60 1.50

2005 SP Legendary Cuts HoloFoil

*HOLOFOIL: 2X TO 5X BASIC
RANDOM INSERTS IN PACKS
STATED PRINT RUN 50 SERIAL #'d SETS
54 Mickey Mantle 10.00 25.00

2005 SP Legendary Cuts Autograph Cuts

OVERALL CUT AU ODDS 1:196
PRINT RUNS B/WN 1-108 COPIES PER
NO PRICING ON QTY OF 19 OR LESS
BD Bill Dickey/95 75.00 150.00
BH Billy Herman/99 20.00 50.00
BL Bob Lemon/108 20.00 50.00
BU Burleigh Grimes/99 75.00 150.00
BW Bucky Walters/34 75.00 150.00
CF Carl Furillo/25 50.00 100.00
CG Charlie Gehringer/97 40.00 80.00
CH Carl Hubbell/99 40.00 100.00
CK Charlie Keller/98 75.00 150.00
CR Joe Cronin/76 75.00 150.00
CS Casey Stengel/61 175.00 350.00
DD Don Drysdale/50 100.00 175.00
DE Dizzy Dean/21 450.00 600.00
DU Leo Durocher/57 75.00 150.00
EA Earl Averill/91 50.00 100.00
EM Eddie Mathews/80 30.00 80.00
ER Edd Roush/99 20.00 50.00
ES Enos Slaughter/99 30.00 80.00
EW Early Wynn/89 30.00 60.00
FE Rick Ferrell/80 20.00 50.00
GH Gabby Hartnett/50 125.00 200.00
GO Lefty Gomez/68 50.00 100.00
GR Lefty Grove/41 150.00 250.00
HA Chick Hafey/52 100.00 175.00
HC Happy Chandler/39 60.00 120.00
HG Hank Greenberg/44 150.00 300.00
HK Harvey Kuenn/33 50.00 100.00
HM Heinie Manush/25 125.00 250.00
HN Hal Newhouser/96 50.00 100.00
HU Catfish Hunter/65 60.00 120.00
JB Cool Papa Bell/78 100.00 250.00
JC Jocko Conlan/40 40.00 80.00
JD Joe DiMaggio/56 350.00 500.00
JH Jesse Haines/90 75.00 150.00
JJ Jackie Jensen/48 100.00 200.00
JO Judy Johnson/39 100.00 175.00
JS Joe Sewell/76 20.00 50.00
JW Hoyt Wilhelm/48 20.00 50.00
LA Luke Appling/85 60.00 120.00
LB Lou Boudreau/99 40.00 80.00
LD Larry Doby/32 50.00 100.00
LE Buck Leonard/71 40.00 80.00
LO Ernie Lombardi/29 100.00 200.00
MC Max Carey/84 40.00 100.00
MI Johnny Mize/90 60.00 120.00
PR Pee Wee Reese/69 100.00 175.00
RD1 Ray Dandridge/23 75.00 150.00
RD2 Ray Dandridge/76 60.00 120.00
RE Red Ruffing/22 100.00 200.00
RI Richie Ashburn/83 125.00 200.00
RO Roy McMillan/23 75.00 150.00
RU Rube Marquard/60 60.00 120.00
SI George Sisler/21 450.00 600.00
SR Sam Rice/41 125.00 200.00
ST Stan Coveleski/71 30.00 80.00
TK Ted Kluszewski/50 40.00 80.00
VR Vic Raschi/21 75.00 150.00
WA Warren Spahn/92 30.00 60.00
WH Waite Hoyt/99 30.00 60.00
WS Willie Stargell/63 50.00 100.00

2005 SP Legendary Cuts Battery Cuts

OVERALL CUT AU ODDS 1:196
PRINT RUNS B/WN 6-99 COPIES PER
NO PRICING ON QTY OF 9 OR LESS
BD Bill Dickey/22 75.00 200.00
CH Carl Hubbell/99 40.00 80.00
DD Don Drysdale/31 125.00 200.00
EW Early Wynn/32 75.00 150.00
HN Hal Newhouser/32 75.00 150.00
JH Jesse Haines/28 75.00 150.00
LG Lefty Gomez/77 75.00 150.00
SC Stan Coveleski/25 100.00 175.00
WH Waite Hoyt/58 60.00 120.00
WS Warren Spahn/43 40.00 80.00

2005 SP Legendary Cuts Classic Careers

STATED PRINT RUN 399 SERIAL #'d SETS
*GOLD: .6X TO 1.5X BASIC
GOLD PRINT RUN 75 SERIAL #'d SETS
PLATINUM PRINT RUN 1 SERIAL #'d SET
NO PLATINUM PRICING DUE TO SCARCITY
OVERALL INSERT ODDS 1:6
AD Andre Dawson 1.00 2.50
AR Al Rosen .60 1.50
AV Andy Van Slyke .60 1.50
BD Bobby Doerr 1.00 2.50
BF Bill Freehan .60 1.50
BH Bob Horner .60 1.50
BL Barry Larkin 1.00 2.50
BM Bill Madlock .60 1.50
CA Jose Canseco 1.00 2.50
CE Carl Erskine .60 1.50
CF Carlton Fisk 1.00 2.50
CR Cal Ripken 5.00 12.00
CY Carl Yastrzemski 2.00 5.00
DC David Cone .60 1.50
DE Dennis Martinez .60 1.50
DG Dwight Gooden .60 1.50
DM Dale Murphy 1.50 4.00
DO Don Sutton 1.00 2.50
DS Darryl Strawberry .60 1.50
FJ Fergie Jenkins 1.00 2.50
GC Gary Carter 1.00 2.50
GF George Foster .60 1.50
GG Goose Gossage .60 1.50
GM Gary Matthews .60 1.50
GN Graig Nettles .60 1.50
GP Gaylord Perry 1.00 2.50
GU Don Gullett .60 1.50
HB Harold Baines 1.00 2.50
JB Jay Buhner .60 1.50
JC Jack Clark .60 1.50
JM Jack Morris 1.00 2.50
JP Johnny Podres .60 1.50
JR Jim Rice 1.00 2.50
KH Keith Hernandez .60 1.50
LA Luis Aparicio 1.00 2.50
LD Lenny Dykstra .60 1.50
LT Luis Tiant .60 1.50
MA Don Mattingly 3.00 8.00
MG Mark Grace 1.00 2.50
MU Bobby Murcer .60 1.50
OC Orlando Cepeda 1.00 2.50
PN Phil Niekro 1.00 2.50
RG Ron Guidry .60 1.50
SF Sid Fernandez .60 1.50
SL Sparky Lyle .60 1.50
ST Dave Stewart .60 1.50
SU Bruce Sutter 1.00 2.50
TO Tony Oliva .60 1.50
TR Tim Raines 1.00 2.50
WC Will Clark 1.00 2.50

2005 SP Legendary Cuts Classic Careers Material

OVERALL GAME-USED ODDS 1:6
*GOLD: .5X TO 1.2X BASIC
GOLD PRINT RUN 75 SERIAL #'d SETS
PLATINUM PRINT RUN 1 SERIAL #'d SET
NO PLATINUM PRICING DUE TO SCARCITY
OVERALL #'d GAME-USED ODDS 1:40
AD Andre Dawson Jsy 2.00 5.00
AR Al Rosen Pants 3.00 8.00
AV Andy Van Slyke Jsy 3.00 8.00
BD Bobby Doerr Jsy 2.00 5.00
BF Bill Freehan Jsy 2.00 5.00
BH Bob Horner Jsy 2.00 5.00
BL Barry Larkin Jsy 3.00 8.00
BM Bill Madlock Jsy 2.00 5.00
CA Jose Canseco Jsy 3.00 8.00
CE Carl Erskine Pants 3.00 8.00
CF Carlton Fisk Jsy 3.00 8.00
CR Cal Ripken Jsy 8.00 20.00
CY Carl Yastrzemski Jsy 4.00 10.00
DC David Cone Jsy 2.00 5.00
DE Dennis Martinez Jsy 2.00 5.00
DG Dwight Gooden Jsy 2.00 5.00
DM Dale Murphy Jsy 3.00 8.00
DO Don Sutton Jsy 2.00 5.00
DS Darryl Strawberry Jsy 2.00 5.00
FJ Fergie Jenkins Jsy 2.00 5.00
GC Gary Carter Jsy 2.00 5.00
GF George Foster Jsy 2.00 5.00
GG Goose Gossage Jsy 2.00 5.00
GM Gary Matthews Jsy 2.00 5.00
GN Graig Nettles Jsy 2.00 5.00
GP Gaylord Perry Jsy 2.00 5.00
GU Don Gullett Jsy 2.00 5.00
HB Harold Baines Jsy 2.00 5.00
JB Jay Buhner Jsy 3.00 8.00
JC Jack Clark Jsy 2.00 5.00
JM Jack Morris Jsy 2.00 5.00
JP Johnny Podres Jsy 3.00 8.00
JR Jim Rice Jsy 2.00 5.00
KH Keith Hernandez Jsy 2.00 5.00
LA Luis Aparicio Jsy 2.00 5.00
LD Lenny Dykstra Jsy 2.00 5.00
LT Luis Tiant Jsy 2.00 5.00
MA Don Mattingly Jsy 5.00 12.00
MG Mark Grace Jsy 3.00 8.00
MU Bobby Murcer Pants 3.00 8.00
OC Orlando Cepeda Jsy 2.00 5.00
PN Phil Niekro Jsy 2.00 5.00
RG Ron Guidry Pants 3.00 8.00
SF Sid Fernandez Jsy 2.00 5.00
SL Sparky Lyle Pants 2.00 5.00
ST Dave Stewart Jsy 2.00 5.00
SU Bruce Sutter Jsy 2.00 5.00
TO Tony Oliva Jsy 2.00 5.00
TR Tim Raines Jsy 2.00 5.00
WC Will Clark Jsy 3.00 8.00

2005 SP Legendary Cuts Classic Careers Patch

*PATCH p/r 50: 1X TO 2.5X MATERIAL
*PATCH p/r 20: 1.25X TO 3X MATERIAL
STATED PRINT RUN 50 SERIAL #'d SETS
J.BUHNER PRINT RUN 14 CARDS
D.MARTINEZ PRINT RUN 20 CARDS
NO BUHNER PRICING AVAILABLE
GOLD PRINT RUN 10 SERIAL #'d SETS
NO GOLD PRICING DUE TO SCARCITY
PLATINUM PRINT RUN 1 SERIAL #'d SET
NO PLATINUM PRICING DUE TO SCARCITY
OVERALL PATCH ODDS 1:96

2005 SP Legendary Cuts Classic Careers Autograph

STATED PRINT RUN 25 SERIAL #'d SETS
GOLD PRINT RUN 10 SERIAL #'d SETS
NO GOLD PRICING DUE TO SCARCITY
PLATINUM PRINT RUN 1 SERIAL #'d SET
NO PLATINUM PRICING DUE TO SCARCITY
OVERALL AUTO ODDS 1:96
EXCHANGE DEADLINE 11/10/08
AD Andre Dawson 6.00 15.00
AR Al Rosen 6.00 15.00
AV Andy Van Slyke 10.00 25.00
BD Bobby Doerr 4.00 10.00
BF Bill Freehan 6.00 15.00
BH Bob Horner 4.00 10.00
BL Barry Larkin 12.50 30.00
BM Bill Madlock 6.00 15.00
CA Jose Canseco 12.50 30.00
CE Carl Erskine 6.00 15.00
CF Carlton Fisk 10.00 25.00
CY Carl Yastrzemski 12.50 30.00
DC David Cone 4.00 10.00
DE Dennis Martinez 4.00 10.00
DG Dwight Gooden 4.00 10.00
DM Dale Murphy 10.00 25.00
DO Don Sutton 6.00 15.00
DS Darryl Strawberry 6.00 15.00
FJ Fergie Jenkins 6.00 15.00
GC Gary Carter 6.00 15.00
GF George Foster 4.00 10.00
GG Goose Gossage 6.00 15.00
GM Gary Matthews 4.00 10.00
GN Graig Nettles 6.00 15.00
GP Gaylord Perry 6.00 15.00
GU Don Gullett 4.00 10.00
HB Harold Baines 6.00 15.00
JB Jay Buhner 10.00 25.00
JC Jack Clark 6.00 15.00
JM Jack Morris 4.00 10.00
JP Johnny Podres 6.00 15.00
JR Jim Rice 10.00 25.00
KH Keith Hernandez 4.00 10.00
LA Luis Aparicio 6.00 15.00
LD Lenny Dykstra 4.00 10.00
LT Luis Tiant 4.00 10.00
MA Don Mattingly 15.00 40.00
MG Mark Grace 12.00 30.00
OC Orlando Cepeda 6.00 15.00
PN Phil Niekro 8.00 20.00
RG Ron Guidry 10.00 25.00
SF Sid Fernandez 4.00 10.00
SL Sparky Lyle 4.00 10.00
ST Dave Stewart 6.00 15.00
SU Bruce Sutter 10.00 25.00
TO Tony Oliva 6.00 15.00
TR Tim Raines 6.00 15.00
WC Will Clark 10.00 25.00

2005 SP Legendary Cuts Classic Careers Autograph Material

*AUTO MAT: .4X TO 1X AUTO
STATED PRINT RUN 25 SERIAL #'d SETS

GOLD PRINT RUN 10 SERIAL #'d SETS
NO GOLD PRICING DUE TO SCARCITY
PLATINUM PRINT RUN 1 SERIAL #'d SET
NO PLATINUM PRICING DUE TO SCARCITY
OVERALL AU-GU ODDS 1:96
EXCHANGE DEADLINE 11/10/08

2005 SP Legendary Cuts Classic Careers Autograph Patch
*AUTO PATCH: .6X TO 1.5X AUTO
STATED PRINT RUN 25 SERIAL #'d SETS
GOLD PRINT RUN 5 SERIAL #'d SETS
NO GOLD PRICING DUE TO SCARCITY
PLATINUM PRINT RUN 1 SERIAL #'d SET
NO PLATINUM PRICING DUE TO SCARCITY
OVERALL AU-PATCH ODDS 1:196
EXCHANGE DEADLINE 11/10/08

2005 SP Legendary Cuts Cornerstone Cuts
OVERALL CUT AU ODDS 1:196
PRINT RUNS B/WN 1-79 COPIES PER
NO PRICING ON QTY OF 16 OR LESS
DC Dolph Camilli/79 40.00 80.00
EM Eddie Mathews/50 20.00 50.00
JM Johnny Mize/44 75.00 150.00
RD Ray Dandridge/27 75.00 150.00
WS Willie Stargell/36 20.00 50.00

2005 SP Legendary Cuts Glory Days
STATED PRINT RUN 399 SERIAL #'d SETS
*GOLD: .6X TO 1.5X BASIC
GOLD PRINT RUN 75 SERIAL #'d SETS
PLATINUM PRINT RUN 1 SERIAL #'d SET
NO PLATINUM PRICING DUE TO SCARCITY
OVERALL INSERT ODDS 1:6
AD Andre Dawson 1.00 2.50
AR Al Rosen .60 1.50
AV Andy Van Slyke .60 1.50
BD Bobby Doerr 1.00 2.50
BF Bill Freehan .60 1.50
BH Bob Horner .60 1.50
BL Barry Larkin 1.00 2.50
BM Bill Madlock .60 1.50
BS Bruce Sutter 1.00 2.50
CA Jose Canseco 1.00 2.50
CR Cal Ripken 5.00 12.00
DC David Cone .60 1.50
DE Dennis Martinez .60 1.50
DG Dwight Gooden .60 1.50
DM Dale Murphy 1.50 4.00
DS Darryl Strawberry .60 1.50
FJ Fergie Jenkins 1.00 2.50
FL Fred Lynn .60 1.50
GF George Foster .60 1.50
GM Gary Matthews .60 1.50
GN Graig Nettles .60 1.50
GU Don Gullett .60 1.50
HB Harold Baines 1.00 2.50
JB Jay Buhner .60 1.50
JC Jack Clark .60 1.50
JM Jack Morris 1.00 2.50
JP Jim Palmer 1.00 2.50
JR Jim Rice 1.00 2.50
KG Kirk Gibson .60 1.50
KH Keith Hernandez .60 1.50
LB Lou Brock 1.00 2.50
LD Lenny Dykstra .60 1.50
LT Luis Tiant .60 1.50
MA Juan Marichal 1.00 2.50
MU Bobby Murcer .60 1.50
NR Nolan Ryan 5.00 12.00
PM Paul Molitor 1.50 4.00
RG Ron Guidry .60 1.50
RS Red Schoendienst 1.00 2.50
RY Robin Yount 1.50 4.00
SF Sid Fernandez .60 1.50
SL Sparky Lyle .60 1.50
SN Duke Snider 1.00 2.50
ST Dave Stewart .60 1.50
TG Tony Gwynn 2.00 5.00
TO Tony Oliva .60 1.50
TR Tim Raines 1.00 2.50
WC Will Clark 1.00 2.50
WF Whitey Ford 1.00 2.50
YB Yogi Berra 1.50 4.00

2005 SP Legendary Cuts Glory Days Material
OVERALL GAME-USED ODDS 1:6
*GOLD: .5X TO 1.2X BASIC
GOLD PRINT RUN 75 SERIAL #'d SETS
PLATINUM PRINT RUN 1 SERIAL #'d SET
NO PLATINUM PRICING DUE TO SCARCITY
OVERALL #'d GAME-USED ODDS 1:40
AD Andre Dawson Jsy 2.00 5.00
AR Al Rosen Pants 3.00 8.00
AV Andy Van Slyke Jsy 3.00 8.00
BD Bobby Doerr Jsy 2.00 5.00
BF Bill Freehan Jsy 2.00 5.00
BH Bob Horner Jsy 2.00 5.00
BL Barry Larkin Jsy 3.00 8.00
BM Bill Madlock Jsy 2.00 5.00
BS Bruce Sutter Jsy 2.00 5.00
CA Jose Canseco Jsy 3.00 8.00
CR Cal Ripken Jsy 8.00 20.00
DC David Cone Jsy 2.00 5.00
DE Dennis Martinez Jsy 2.00 5.00
DG Dwight Gooden Jsy 2.00 5.00
DM Dale Murphy Jsy 3.00 8.00
DS Darryl Strawberry Jsy 2.00 5.00
FJ Fergie Jenkins Jsy 2.00 5.00
FL Fred Lynn Bat 2.00 5.00
GF George Foster Jsy 2.00 5.00
GM Gary Matthews Jsy 2.00 5.00
GN Graig Nettles Jsy 2.00 5.00
GU Don Gullett Jsy 2.00 5.00
HB Harold Baines Jsy 2.00 5.00
JB Jay Buhner Jsy 3.00 8.00
JC Jack Clark Jsy 2.00 5.00
JM Jack Morris Jsy 2.00 5.00
JP Jim Palmer Jsy 2.00 5.00
JR Jim Rice Jsy 2.00 5.00
KG Kirk Gibson Jsy 2.00 5.00
KH Keith Hernandez Jsy 2.00 5.00
LB Lou Brock Jsy * 3.00 8.00
LD Lenny Dykstra Jsy 2.00 5.00
LT Luis Tiant Jsy 2.00 5.00
MA Juan Marichal Jsy 3.00 8.00
MU Bobby Murcer Pants 3.00 8.00
NR Nolan Ryan Jsy 6.00 15.00
PM Paul Molitor Bat 2.00 5.00
RG Ron Guidry Pants 3.00 8.00
RS Red Schoendienst Jsy 3.00 8.00
RY Robin Yount Jsy 4.00 10.00
SF Sid Fernandez Jsy 2.00 5.00
SL Sparky Lyle Pants 2.00 5.00
SN Duke Snider Pants 4.00 10.00
ST Dave Stewart Jsy 2.00 5.00
TG Tony Gwynn Jsy 4.00 10.00
TO Tony Oliva Jsy 2.00 5.00
TR Tim Raines Jsy 2.00 5.00
WC Will Clark Jsy 3.00 8.00
WF Whitey Ford Jsy 5.00 12.00
YB Yogi Berra Pants 5.00 12.00

2005 SP Legendary Cuts Glory Days Patch
*PATCH: 1X TO 2.5X MATERIAL
STATED PRINT RUN 50 SERIAL #'d SETS
K.HERNANDEZ PRINT RUN 37 CARDS
L.TIANT PRINT RUN 40 CARDS
GOLD PRINT RUN 10 SERIAL #'d SETS
NO GOLD PRICING DUE TO SCARCITY
PLATINUM PRINT RUN 1 SERIAL #'d SET
NO PLATINUM PRICING DUE TO SCARCITY
OVERALL PATCH ODDS 1:96

2005 SP Legendary Cuts Glory Days Autograph
STATED PRINT RUN 25 SERIAL #'d SETS
GOLD PRINT RUN 10 SERIAL #'d SETS
NO GOLD PRICING DUE TO SCARCITY
PLATINUM PRINT RUN 1 SERIAL #'d SET
NO PLATINUM PRICING DUE TO SCARCITY
OVERALL AUTO ODDS 1:96
EXCHANGE DEADLINE 11/10/08
AD Andre Dawson 10.00 25.00
AR Al Rosen 10.00 25.00
AV Andy Van Slyke 15.00 40.00
BD Bobby Doerr 6.00 15.00
BF Bill Freehan 10.00 25.00
BH Bob Horner 6.00 15.00
BL Barry Larkin 20.00 50.00
BM Bill Madlock 10.00 25.00
BS Bruce Sutter 15.00 40.00
CA Jose Canseco 20.00 50.00
DC David Cone 6.00 15.00
DE Dennis Martinez 6.00 15.00
DG Dwight Gooden 6.00 15.00
DM Dale Murphy 15.00 40.00
DS Darryl Strawberry 10.00 25.00
FJ Fergie Jenkins 10.00 25.00
FL Fred Lynn 10.00 25.00
GF George Foster 10.00 25.00
GM Gary Matthews 6.00 15.00
GN Graig Nettles 10.00 25.00
GU Don Gullett 6.00 15.00
HB Harold Baines 10.00 25.00
JB Jay Buhner 15.00 40.00
JC Jack Clark 10.00 25.00
JM Jack Morris 6.00 15.00
JP Jim Palmer 10.00 25.00
JR Jim Rice 10.00 25.00
KG Kirk Gibson 10.00 25.00
KH Keith Hernandez 6.00 15.00
LB Lou Brock 15.00 40.00
LD Lenny Dykstra 6.00 15.00
LT Luis Tiant 6.00 15.00
MA Juan Marichal 10.00 25.00
NR Nolan Ryan 50.00 100.00
PM Paul Molitor 10.00 25.00
RG Ron Guidry 15.00 40.00
RS Red Schoendienst 10.00 25.00
RY Robin Yount 20.00 50.00
SF Sid Fernandez 6.00 15.00
SL Sparky Lyle 6.00 15.00
SN Duke Snider 10.00 25.00
ST Dave Stewart 10.00 25.00
TG Tony Gwynn 20.00 50.00
TO Tony Oliva 10.00 25.00
TR Tim Raines 10.00 25.00
WC Will Clark 15.00 40.00
WF Whitey Ford 15.00 40.00
YB Yogi Berra 30.00 80.00

2005 SP Legendary Cuts Glory Days Autograph Material
*AUTO MAT: .4X TO 1X AUTO
STATED PRINT RUN 25 SERIAL #'d SETS
GOLD PRINT RUN 10 SERIAL #'d SETS
NO GOLD PRICING DUE TO SCARCITY
PLATINUM PRINT RUN 1 SERIAL #'d SET
NO PLATINUM PRICING DUE TO SCARCITY
OVERALL AU-GU ODDS 1:96
EXCHANGE DEADLINE 11/10/08

2005 SP Legendary Cuts Glory Days Autograph Patch
*AUTO PATCH: .6X TO 1.5X AUTO
STATED PRINT RUN 25 SERIAL #'d SETS
D.GULLETT PRINT RUN 7 CARDS
NO D.GULLETT PRICING DUE TO SCARCITY
GOLD PRINT RUN 5 SERIAL #'d SETS
NO GOLD PRICING DUE TO SCARCITY
PLATINUM PRINT RUN 1 SERIAL #'d SET
NO PLATINUM PRICING DUE TO SCARCITY
OVERALL AU-PATCH ODDS 1:196

2005 SP Legendary Cuts Glovemen Cuts
OVERALL CUT AU ODDS 1:196
PRINT RUNS B/WN 1-75 COPIES PER
NO PRICING ON QTY OF 19 OR LESS
CP Cool Papa Bell/29 300.00 400.00
EA Earl Averill/39 60.00 120.00
ES Enos Slaughter/65 30.00 60.00
JD Joe DiMaggio/75 250.00 400.00
MC Max Carey/50 30.00 60.00
RA Richie Ashburn/20 150.00 250.00

2005 SP Legendary Cuts Lasting Legends
STATED PRINT RUN 399 SERIAL #'d SETS
*GOLD: .6X TO 1.5X BASIC
GOLD PRINT RUN 75 SERIAL #'d SETS
PLATINUM PRINT RUN 1 SERIAL #'d SET
NO PLATINUM PRICING DUE TO SCARCITY
OVERALL INSERT ODDS 1:6
AK Al Kaline 1.50 4.00
BD Bobby Doerr 1.00 2.50
BE Johnny Bench 1.50 4.00
BG Bob Gibson 1.00 2.50
BL Barry Larkin 1.00 2.50
BM Bill Mazeroski 1.00 2.50
BR Brooks Robinson 1.00 2.50
BS Bruce Sutter 1.00 2.50
CF Carlton Fisk 1.00 2.50
CR Cal Ripken 5.00 12.00
CY Carl Yastrzemski 2.00 5.00
DE Dennis Eckersley 1.00 2.50
DG Dwight Gooden .60 1.50
DM Don Mattingly 3.00 8.00
DS Don Sutton 1.00 2.50
EB Ernie Banks 1.50 4.00
EM Eddie Murray 1.00 2.50
FJ Fergie Jenkins 1.00 2.50
FR Frank Robinson 1.00 2.50
GC Gary Carter 1.00 2.50
GN Graig Nettles .60 1.50
GP Gaylord Perry 1.00 2.50
JM Joe Morgan 1.00 2.50
JP Jim Palmer 1.00 2.50
JR Jim Rice 1.00 2.50
KH Keith Hernandez .60 1.50
KP Kirby Puckett 1.50 4.00
LA Luis Aparicio 1.00 2.50
LB Lou Brock 1.00 2.50
MA Juan Marichal 1.00 2.50
MS Mike Schmidt 2.50 6.00
MU Dale Murphy 1.50 4.00
NR Nolan Ryan 5.00 12.00
OC Orlando Cepeda 1.00 2.50
OS Ozzie Smith 2.00 5.00
PM Paul Molitor 1.50 4.00
PN Phil Niekro 1.00 2.50
RC Rod Carew 1.00 2.50
RF Rollie Fingers 1.00 2.50
RS Red Schoendienst 1.00 2.50
RY Robin Yount 1.50 4.00
SA Ryne Sandberg 3.00 8.00
SC Steve Carlton 1.00 2.50
SM Stan Musial 2.50 6.00
SN Duke Snider 1.50 4.00
TG Tony Gwynn 2.00 5.00
TP Tony Perez 1.00 2.50
WB Wade Boggs 1.00 2.50
WF Whitey Ford 1.00 2.50
YB Yogi Berra 1.50 4.00

2005 SP Legendary Cuts Lasting Legends Material
OVERALL GAME-USED ODDS 1:6
*GOLD: .5X TO 1.2X BASIC
GOLD PRINT RUN 75 SERIAL #'d SETS
PLATINUM PRINT RUN 1 SERIAL #'d SET
NO PLATINUM PRICING DUE TO SCARCITY
OVERALL #'d GAME-USED ODDS 1:40
AK Al Kaline Bat 4.00 10.00
BD Bobby Doerr Pants 2.00 5.00
BE Johnny Bench Jsy 4.00 10.00
BG Bob Gibson Jsy 3.00 8.00
BL Barry Larkin Jsy 3.00 8.00
BM Bill Mazeroski Jsy 3.00 8.00
BR Brooks Robinson Jsy 3.00 8.00
BS Bruce Sutter Jsy 2.00 5.00
CF Carlton Fisk Jsy 3.00 8.00
CR Cal Ripken Jsy 8.00 20.00
CY Carl Yastrzemski Jsy 4.00 10.00
DE Dennis Eckersley Jsy 2.00 5.00
DG Dwight Gooden Jsy 2.00 5.00
DM Don Mattingly Jsy 5.00 12.00
DS Don Sutton Jsy 2.00 5.00
EB Ernie Banks Pants 4.00 10.00
EM Eddie Murray Jsy 4.00 10.00
FJ Fergie Jenkins Jsy 2.00 5.00
FR Frank Robinson Jsy 3.00 8.00
GC Gary Carter Jsy 2.00 5.00
GN Graig Nettles Jsy 2.00 5.00
GP Gaylord Perry Jsy 2.00 5.00
JM Joe Morgan Jsy 2.00 5.00
JP Jim Palmer Jsy 2.00 5.00
JR Jim Rice Jsy 2.00 5.00
KH Keith Hernandez Jsy 2.00 5.00
KP Kirby Puckett Jsy 4.00 10.00
LA Luis Aparicio Jsy 2.00 5.00
LB Lou Brock Jsy * 3.00 8.00
MA Juan Marichal Jsy 3.00 8.00
MS Mike Schmidt Jsy 5.00 12.00
MU Dale Murphy Jsy 3.00 8.00
NR Nolan Ryan Jsy 6.00 15.00
OC Orlando Cepeda Jsy 2.00 5.00
OS Ozzie Smith Jsy 4.00 10.00
PM Paul Molitor Bat 2.00 5.00
PN Phil Niekro Jsy 2.00 5.00
RC Rod Carew Jsy 3.00 8.00
RF Rollie Fingers Jsy 2.00 5.00
RS Red Schoendienst Jsy 3.00 8.00
RY Robin Yount Jsy 4.00 10.00
SA Ryne Sandberg Jsy 5.00 12.00
SC Steve Carlton Jsy 2.00 5.00
SM Stan Musial Jsy 6.00 15.00
SN Duke Snider Pants 4.00 10.00
TG Tony Gwynn Jsy 4.00 10.00
TP Tony Perez Jsy 2.00 5.00
WB Wade Boggs Jsy 3.00 8.00
WF Whitey Ford Jsy 5.00 12.00
YB Yogi Berra Pants 8.00 20.00

2005 SP Legendary Cuts Lasting Legends Patch
*PATCH: 1X TO 2.5X MATERIAL
STATED PRINT RUN 50 SERIAL #'d SETS
P.MOLITOR PRINT RUN 2 CARDS
B.ROBINSON PRINT RUN 43 CARDS
N.RYAN PRINT RUN 11 CARDS
NO MOLITOR/RYAN PRICING AVAILABLE
GOLD PRINT RUN 10 SERIAL #'d SETS
NO GOLD PRICING DUE TO SCARCITY
PLATINUM PRINT RUN 1 SERIAL #'d SET
NO PLATINUM PRICING DUE TO SCARCITY
OVERALL PATCH ODDS 1:96

2005 SP Legendary Cuts Lasting Legends Autograph
STATED PRINT RUN 25 SERIAL #'d SETS
GOLD PRINT RUN 10 SERIAL #'d SETS
NO GOLD PRICING DUE TO SCARCITY
PLATINUM PRINT RUN 1 SERIAL #'d SET
NO PLATINUM PRICING DUE TO SCARCITY
OVERALL AUTO ODDS 1:96
EXCHANGE DEADLINE 11/10/08
AK Al Kaline 25.00 50.00
BD Bobby Doerr 6.00 15.00
BE Johnny Bench 20.00 50.00
BG Bob Gibson 15.00 40.00
BL Barry Larkin 20.00 50.00
BM Bill Mazeroski 15.00 40.00
BR Brooks Robinson 20.00 50.00
BS Bruce Sutter 15.00 40.00
CF Carlton Fisk 15.00 40.00
CY Carl Yastrzemski 30.00 60.00
DE Dennis Eckersley 10.00 25.00
DG Dwight Gooden 6.00 15.00
DM Don Mattingly 30.00 60.00
DS Don Sutton 10.00 25.00
EB Ernie Banks 30.00 60.00
FJ Fergie Jenkins 10.00 25.00
FR Frank Robinson 10.00 25.00
GC Gary Carter 12.00 30.00
GN Graig Nettles 10.00 25.00
GP Gaylord Perry 10.00 25.00
JM Joe Morgan 10.00 25.00
JP Jim Palmer 10.00 25.00
JR Jim Rice 10.00 25.00
KH Keith Hernandez 6.00 15.00
KP Kirby Puckett 50.00 100.00
LA Luis Aparicio 10.00 25.00
LB Lou Brock 15.00 40.00
MA Juan Marichal 10.00 25.00
MS Mike Schmidt 30.00 60.00
MU Dale Murphy 15.00 40.00
NR Nolan Ryan 50.00 100.00
OC Orlando Cepeda 10.00 25.00
OS Ozzie Smith 20.00 50.00
PM Paul Molitor 10.00 25.00
PN Phil Niekro 10.00 25.00
RC Rod Carew 15.00 40.00
RF Rollie Fingers 10.00 25.00
RS Red Schoendienst 10.00 25.00
RY Robin Yount 20.00 50.00
SA Ryne Sandberg 30.00 60.00
SC Steve Carlton 10.00 25.00
SM Stan Musial 40.00 80.00
SN Duke Snider 20.00 50.00
TG Tony Gwynn 20.00 50.00
TP Tony Perez 10.00 25.00
WB Wade Boggs 15.00 40.00
WF Whitey Ford 15.00 40.00
YB Yogi Berra 30.00 80.00

2005 SP Legendary Cuts Lasting Legends Autograph Material
*AUTO MAT: .4X TO 1X AUTO
STATED PRINT RUN 25 SERIAL #'d SETS
C.FISK PRINT RUN 21 CARDS
GOLD PRINT RUN 10 SERIAL #'d SETS
NO GOLD PRICING DUE TO SCARCITY
PLATINUM PRINT RUN 1 SERIAL #'d SET
NO PLATINUM PRICING DUE TO SCARCITY
OVERALL AU-GU ODDS 1:96
EXCHANGE DEADLINE 11/10/08

2005 SP Legendary Cuts Lasting Legends Autograph Patch
*AUTO PATCH: .6X TO 1.5X AUTO
STATED PRINT RUN 25 SERIAL #'d SETS
L.BROCK PRINT RUN 6 CARDS
K.PUCKETT PRINT RUN 6 CARDS
NO BROCK/PUCKETT PRICING AVAILABLE
GOLD PRINT RUN 5 SERIAL #'d SETS
NO GOLD PRICING DUE TO SCARCITY
PLATINUM PRINT RUN 1 SERIAL #'d SET
NO PLATINUM PRICING DUE TO SCARCITY
OVERALL AU-PATCH ODDS 1:196

2005 SP Legendary Cuts Legendary Duels Material
OVERALL #'d GAME-USED ODDS 1:40
STATED PRINT RUN 25 SERIAL #'d SETS
OVERALL PATCH ODDS 1:96
PATCH PRINT RUN 10 SERIAL #'d SETS
NO PATCH PRICING DUE TO SCARCITY
BM E.Banks Pants/S.Musial Jsy 30.00 60.00
CC J.Canseco Jsy/W.Clark Jsy 15.00 40.00
DM L.Dykstra Jsy/P.Molitor Jsy 6.00 15.00
EG D.Eck Jsy/K.Gibson Jsy 10.00 25.00
FB C.Fisk Jsy/J.Bench Jsy 15.00 40.00
FR G.Foster Jsy/J.Rice Jsy 6.00 15.00
JY R.Jackson Jsy/C.Yaz Jsy 15.00 40.00
MC P.Moli Pants/R.Carew Jsy 10.00 25.00
MH D.Matt Jsy/K.Hern Jsy 15.00 40.00
SF D.Snider Pants/W.Ford Jsy 15.00 40.00
SG D.Sutt Jsy/R.Guid Pants 10.00 25.00
SS O.Smith Jsy/R.Sand Jsy 30.00 60.00
YS R.Yount Jsy/M.Schmidt Jsy 15.00 40.00

2005 SP Legendary Cuts Legendary Duos Material
OVERALL #'d GAME-USED ODDS 1:40
STATED PRINT RUN 25 SERIAL #'d SETS
OVERALL PATCH ODDS 1:96
PATCH PRINT RUN 10 SERIAL #'d SETS
NO PATCH PRICING DUE TO SCARCITY
CO R.Carew Jsy 10.00 25.00
T.Oliva Jsy
ES C.Erskine Jsy/D.Snider Jsy 10.00 25.00
FB W.Ford Jsy/Y.Berra Pants 15.00 40.00
GS M.Grace Jsy/R.Sand Jsy 20.00 50.00
JG R.Jack Jsy/R.Guidry Pants 10.00 25.00
MB J.Morgan Jsy/J.Bench Jsy 15.00 40.00
MY P.Molitor Pants/R.Yount Jsy 15.00 40.00
RB J.Rice Jsy/W.Boggs Jsy 10.00 25.00
RC C.Ripken Jsy/W.Clark Jsy 20.00 50.00
RM C.Ripken Jsy/E.Murray Jsy 30.00 60.00
RR B.Rob Jsy/F.Rob Jsy 10.00 25.00
SC M.Schmidt Jsy/S.Carlt Jsy 15.00 40.00
SG D.Straw Jsy/D.Gooden Jsy 6.00 15.00

2005 SP Legendary Cuts Legendary Lineage
STATED PRINT RUN 399 SERIAL #'d SETS
*GOLD: .6X TO 1.5X BASIC
GOLD PRINT RUN 75 SERIAL #'d SETS
PLATINUM PRINT RUN 1 SERIAL #'d SET
NO PLATINUM PRICING DUE TO SCARCITY
OVERALL INSERT ODDS 1:6
AD Andre Dawson 1.00 2.50
AR Al Rosen .60 1.50
AV Andy Van Slyke .60 1.50
BD Bobby Doerr 1.00 2.50
BF Bill Freehan .60 1.50
BH Bob Horner .60 1.50
BL Barry Larkin 1.00 2.50
BM Bill Madlock .60 1.50
BR Brooks Robinson 1.00 2.50
CA Jose Canseco 1.00 2.50
CR Cal Ripken 5.00 12.00
DC David Cone .60 1.50
DE Dennis Martinez .60 1.50
DG Dwight Gooden .60 1.50
DM Dale Murphy 1.50 4.00
DS Dave Stewart .60 1.50
EC Dennis Eckersley 1.00 2.50
FJ Fergie Jenkins 1.00 2.50
GG Goose Gossage 1.00 2.50
GM Gary Matthews .60 1.50
GN Graig Nettles .60 1.50
GU Don Gullett .60 1.50
HB Harold Baines 1.00 2.50
JB Jay Buhner .60 1.50
JC Jack Clark .60 1.50
JM Jack Morris 1.00 2.50
JP Jim Palmer 1.00 2.50
JR Jim Rice 1.00 2.50
KH Keith Hernandez .60 1.50
KP Kirby Puckett 1.50 4.00
LD Lenny Dykstra .60 1.50
LT Luis Tiant .60 1.50
MA Don Mattingly 3.00 8.00
MG Mark Grace 1.00 2.50
MS Mike Schmidt 2.50 6.00
MU Bobby Murcer .60 1.50
OS Ozzie Smith 2.00 5.00
PM Paul Molitor 1.50 4.00
RG Ron Guidry .60 1.50
RJ Reggie Jackson 1.00 2.50
SC Steve Carlton 1.00 2.50
SF Sid Fernandez .60 1.50
SL Sparky Lyle .60 1.50
SN Duke Snider 1.00 2.50
ST Darryl Strawberry .60 1.50
SU Bruce Sutter 1.00 2.50
TG Tony Gwynn 2.00 5.00
TO Tony Oliva .60 1.50
TR Tim Raines 1.00 2.50
WC Will Clark 1.00 2.50

2005 SP Legendary Cuts Legendary Lineage Material
OVERALL GAME-USED ODDS 1:6
*GOLD: .5X TO 1.2X BASIC
GOLD PRINT RUN 75 SERIAL #'d SETS
PLATINUM PRINT RUN 1 SERIAL #'d SET
NO PLATINUM PRICING DUE TO SCARCITY
OVERALL #'d GAME-USED ODDS 1:40
AD Andre Dawson Jsy 2.00 5.00
AR Al Rosen Pants 3.00 8.00
AV Andy Van Slyke Jsy 3.00 8.00
BD Bobby Doerr Jsy 2.00 5.00
BF Bill Freehan Jsy 2.00 5.00
BH Bob Horner Jsy 2.00 5.00
BL Barry Larkin Jsy 3.00 8.00
BM Bill Madlock Jsy 2.00 5.00
BR Brooks Robinson Jsy 3.00 8.00
CA Jose Canseco Jsy 3.00 8.00
CR Cal Ripken Jsy 8.00 20.00
DC David Cone Jsy 2.00 5.00
DE Dennis Martinez Jsy 2.00 5.00
DG Dwight Gooden Jsy 2.00 5.00
DM Dale Murphy Jsy 3.00 8.00
DS Dave Stewart Jsy 2.00 5.00
EC Dennis Eckersley Jsy 2.00 5.00
FJ Fergie Jenkins Jsy 2.00 5.00
GG Goose Gossage Jsy 2.00 5.00
GM Gary Matthews Jsy 2.00 5.00
GN Graig Nettles Jsy 2.00 5.00
GU Don Gullett Jsy 2.00 5.00
HB Harold Baines Jsy 2.00 5.00
JB Jay Buhner Jsy 3.00 8.00
JC Jack Clark Jsy 2.00 5.00
JM Jack Morris Jsy 2.00 5.00
JP Jim Palmer Jsy 2.00 5.00
JR Jim Rice Jsy 2.00 5.00
KH Keith Hernandez Jsy 2.00 5.00
KP Kirby Puckett Jsy 4.00 10.00
LD Lenny Dykstra Jsy 2.00 5.00
LT Luis Tiant Jsy 2.00 5.00
MA Don Mattingly Jsy 5.00 12.00
MG Mark Grace Jsy 3.00 8.00
MS Mike Schmidt Jsy 5.00 12.00
MU Bobby Murcer Pants 3.00 8.00
OS Ozzie Smith Jsy 4.00 10.00
PM Paul Molitor Bat 2.00 5.00
RG Ron Guidry Pants 3.00 8.00
RJ Reggie Jackson Jsy 3.00 8.00
SC Steve Carlton Jsy 2.00 5.00
SF Sid Fernandez Jsy 2.00 5.00
SL Sparky Lyle Pants 2.00 5.00
SN Duke Snider Pants 4.00 10.00
ST Darryl Strawberry Jsy 2.00 5.00
SU Bruce Sutter Jsy 2.00 5.00
TG Tony Gwynn Jsy 4.00 10.00
TO Tony Oliva Jsy 2.00 5.00
TR Tim Raines Jsy 2.00 5.00
WC Will Clark Jsy 3.00 8.00

2005 SP Legendary Cuts Legendary Lineage Patch
*PATCH: 1X TO 2.5X MATERIAL
STATED PRINT RUN 50 SERIAL #'d SETS
K.HERNANDEZ PRINT RUN 39 CARDS
B.MADLOCK PRINT RUN 43 CARDS
P.MOLITOR PRINT RUN 5 CARDS
J.RICE PRINT RUN 12 CARDS
NO MOLITOR/RICE PRICING AVAILABLE
GOLD PRINT RUN 10 SERIAL #'d SETS
NO GOLD PRICING DUE TO SCARCITY
PLATINUM PRINT RUN 1 SERIAL #'d SET
NO PLATINUM PRICING DUE TO SCARCITY
OVERALL PATCH ODDS 1:96

2005 SP Legendary Cuts Legendary Lineage Autograph
STATED PRINT RUN 25 SERIAL #'d SETS
GOLD PRINT RUN 10 SERIAL #'d SETS
NO GOLD PRICING DUE TO SCARCITY
PLATINUM PRINT RUN 1 SERIAL #'d SET
NO PLATINUM PRICING DUE TO SCARCITY
OVERALL AUTO ODDS 1:96
EXCHANGE DEADLINE 11/10/08
AD Andre Dawson 10.00 25.00
AR Al Rosen 10.00 25.00
AV Andy Van Slyke 15.00 40.00
BD Bobby Doerr 6.00 15.00
BF Bill Freehan 10.00 25.00
BH Bob Horner 6.00 15.00
BL Barry Larkin 20.00 50.00
BM Bill Madlock 10.00 25.00
BR Brooks Robinson 15.00 40.00
CA Jose Canseco 20.00 50.00
DC David Cone 6.00 15.00
DE Dennis Martinez 6.00 15.00
DG Dwight Gooden 6.00 15.00
DM Dale Murphy 15.00 40.00
DS Dave Stewart 6.00 15.00
EC Dennis Eckersley 10.00 25.00
FJ Fergie Jenkins 10.00 25.00
GG Goose Gossage 10.00 25.00
GM Gary Matthews 6.00 15.00
GN Graig Nettles 10.00 25.00
GU Don Gullett 6.00 15.00
HB Harold Baines 10.00 25.00
JB Jay Buhner 15.00 40.00
JC Jack Clark 10.00 25.00
JM Jack Morris 6.00 15.00
JP Jim Palmer 10.00 25.00
JR Jim Rice 10.00 25.00
KH Keith Hernandez 6.00 15.00
KP Kirby Puckett 150.00 250.00
LD Lenny Dykstra 6.00 15.00
LT Luis Tiant 6.00 15.00
MA Don Mattingly 30.00 60.00
MG Mark Grace 15.00 40.00
MS Mike Schmidt 30.00 60.00
OS Ozzie Smith 20.00 50.00
PM Paul Molitor 10.00 25.00
RG Ron Guidry 15.00 40.00
RJ Reggie Jackson 30.00 60.00
SC Steve Carlton 10.00 25.00
SF Sid Fernandez 6.00 15.00
SL Sparky Lyle 6.00 15.00
SN Duke Snider 20.00 50.00
ST Darryl Strawberry 10.00 25.00
SU Bruce Sutter 15.00 40.00
TG Tony Gwynn 20.00 50.00
TO Tony Oliva 10.00 25.00
TR Tim Raines 10.00 25.00
WC Will Clark 15.00 40.00

2005 SP Legendary Cuts Legendary Lineage Autograph Material
*AUTO MAT: .4X TO 1X AUTO
STATED PRINT RUN 25 SERIAL #'d SETS
GOLD PRINT RUN 10 SERIAL #'d SETS
NO GOLD PRICING DUE TO SCARCITY
PLATINUM PRINT RUN 1 SERIAL #'d SET
NO PLATINUM PRICING DUE TO SCARCITY
OVERALL AU-GU ODDS 1:96
EXCHANGE DEADLINE 11/10/08

2005 SP Legendary Cuts Legendary Lineage Autograph Patch
*AUTO PATCH: .6X TO 1.5X AUTO
STATED PRINT RUN 25 SERIAL #'d SETS
T.OLIVA PRINT RUN 16 CARDS
NO T.OLIVA PRICING DUE TO SCARCITY
GOLD PRINT RUN 5 SERIAL #'d SETS
NO GOLD PRICING DUE TO SCARCITY
PLATINUM PRINT RUN 1 SERIAL #'d SET
NO PLATINUM PRICING DUE TO SCARCITY
OVERALL AU-PATCH ODDS 1:196
EXCHANGE DEADLINE 11/10/08

2005 SP Legendary Cuts Material
STATED PRINT RUN 75 SERIAL #'d SETS
H.WAGNER PRINT RUN 22 CARDS
GOLD PRINT RUN 15 SERIAL #'d SETS
GOLD H.WAGNER PRINT RUN 5 CARDS
NO GOLD PRICING DUE TO SCARCITY
OVERALL MATERIAL ODDS 1:196
BD Bill Dickey Jsy 15.00 40.00
BL Bob Lemon Jsy 10.00 25.00
BR Babe Ruth Bat 150.00 250.00
CA Roy Campanella Pants 15.00 40.00
CM Christy Mathewson Pants 100.00 200.00
CO Mickey Cochrane Bat 15.00 40.00
CR Joe Cronin Bat 10.00 25.00
CS Casey Stengel Jsy 15.00 40.00
DD Don Drysdale Pants 10.00 25.00
DE Dizzy Dean Jsy 40.00 80.00
EM Eddie Mathews Jsy 12.50 30.00
ES Enos Slaughter Bat 10.00 25.00
EW Early Wynn Pants 6.00 15.00
HG Hank Greenberg Bat 20.00 50.00
HO Gil Hodges Bat 20.00 50.00
HU Catfish Hunter Jsy 6.00 15.00
HW Honus Wagner Pants/22 90.00 150.00
JD Joe DiMaggio Jsy 30.00 60.00
JF Jimmie Foxx Bat 30.00 60.00
JR Jackie Robinson Pants 20.00 50.00
JW Hoyt Wilhelm Jsy 10.00 25.00
LG Lou Gehrig Pants 125.00 200.00
MI Johnny Mize Pants 10.00 25.00
MM Mickey Mantle Pants 60.00 120.00
MO Mel Ott Jsy 15.00 40.00
PR Pee Wee Reese Jsy 10.00 25.00
RC Roberto Clemente Pants 25.00 60.00
RH Rogers Hornsby Jkt 40.00 80.00
RM Roger Maris Pants 20.00 50.00
SI George Sisler Bat 15.00 40.00
SP Satchel Paige Pants 30.00 60.00
TC Ty Cobb Bat 50.00 100.00
TK Ted Kluszewski Jsy 10.00 25.00
TL Tony Lazzeri Bat 15.00 40.00
TM Thurman Munson Pants 15.00 40.00
TW Ted Williams Pants 15.00 40.00
WS Warren Spahn Jsy 12.00 30.00

2005 SP Legendary Cuts Middlemen Cuts
OVERALL CUT AU ODDS 1:196
PRINT RUNS B/WN 2-99 COPIES PER
NO PRICING ON QTY OF 18 OR LESS
BH Billy Herman/90 30.00 60.00
CG Charlie Gehringer/95 40.00 80.00
FF Frankie Frisch/23 125.00 200.00
JC Joe Cronin/30 100.00 200.00
JS Joe Sewell/76 50.00 100.00
LA Luke Appling/32 30.00 60.00
LB Lou Boudreau/99 50.00 100.00
PW Pee Wee Reese/39 125.00 200.00

2006 SP Legendary Cuts
COMP.SET w/o SP's (100) 10.00 25.00
COMMON CARD (1-100) .25 .60
COMMON CARD (101-200) 2.00 5.00
101-200: ONE BASIC OR BRONZE PER BOX
101-200 PRINT RUN 550 SERIAL #'d SETS
EXQUISITE EXCH ODDS 1:60
EXQUISITE EXCH DEADLINE 07/27/07
1 Juan Marichal .40 1.00
2 Monte Irvin .25 .60
3 Will Clark .40 1.00
4 Willie McCovey .40 1.00
5 Eddie Gaedel .25 .60
6 Ken Williams .25 .60
7 Earl Battey .25 .60
8 Rick Ferrell .25 .60
9 Bob Gibson .40 1.00
10 Elmer Flick .40 1.00
11 Joe Medwick .25 .60
12 Lou Brock .40 1.00
13 Ozzie Smith .75 2.00
14 Red Schoendienst .40 1.00
15 Stan Musial 1.00 2.50
16 Tony Oliva .25 .60
17 Phil Niekro .40 1.00
18 Boog Powell .25 .60
19 Brooks Robinson .40 1.00
20 Cal Ripken 2.00 5.00
21 Eddie Murray .40 1.00
22 Frank Robinson .40 1.00
23 Jim Palmer .40 1.00
24 Jocko Conlon .25 .60
25 Carlton Fisk .40 1.00
26 Dwight Evans .25 .60
27 Fred Lynn .25 .60
28 Jim Rice .40 1.00
29 Ted Williams 1.25 3.00
30 Wade Boggs .40 1.00
31 Hugh Duffy .40 1.00
32 Kid Nichols .25 .60
33 Johnny Vander Meer .25 .60
34 Dolph Camilli .25 .60
35 Carl Yastrzemski 1.00 2.50
36 Chick Hafey .25 .60
37 Kirby Higbe .25 .60
38 Pee Wee Reese .40 1.00
39 Pete Reiser .25 .60
40 Don Sutton .25 .60
41 Rod Carew .40 1.00
42 Andre Dawson .40 1.00
43 Billy Herman .25 .60
44 Billy Williams .40 1.00
45 Charley Root .25 .60
46 Hack Wilson .40 1.00
47 Ernie Banks .60 1.50
48 Fergie Jenkins .40 1.00
49 Gabby Hartnett .40 1.00
50 Ken Hubbs .25 .60
51 Kiki Cuyler .40 1.00
52 Mark Grace .40 1.00
53 Ryne Sandberg 1.25 3.00
54 Harold Newhouser .25 .60
55 Charlie Robertson .25 .60
56 Harold Baines .40 1.00
57 Luis Aparicio .40 1.00
58 Luke Appling .40 1.00
59 Nellie Fox .40 1.00
60 Ray Schalk .25 .60
61 Red Faber .25 .60
62 Sloppy Thurston .25 .60
63 Freddie Lindstrom .25 .60
64 Vern Kennedy .25 .60
65 Barry Larkin .40 1.00
66 Bucky Walters .25 .60
67 Dolf Luque .25 .60
68 Al Campanis .25 .60
69 Ernie Lombardi .25 .60
70 George Foster .25 .60
71 Joe Morgan .40 1.00
72 Johnny Bench .60 1.50
73 Ken Griffey Sr. .25 .60
74 Ted Kluszewski .40 1.00
75 Tony Perez .40 1.00
76 Wally Post .25 .60
77 Bob Feller .40 1.00
78 Bob Lemon .40 1.00
79 Earl Averill .25 .60
80 Joe Sewell .25 .60
81 Johnny Hodapp .25 .60
82 Larry Doby .25 .60
83 Lou Boudreau .40 1.00
84 Rocky Colavito .40 1.00
85 Stan Coveleski .40 1.00
86 Nap Lajoie .60 1.50
87 Al Kaline .60 1.50
88 Alan Trammell .40 1.00
89 Charlie Gehringer .25 .60
90 Denny McLain .25 .60
91 Hank Greenberg .60 1.50
92 Jack Morris .40 1.00
93 Mark Fidrych .25 .60
94 Ray Boone .25 .60
95 Rudy York .25 .60
96 Buck Leonard .25 .60
97 Bo Jackson .60 1.50
98 Zoilo Versalles .25 .60
99 John Kruk .25 .60
100 Don Drysdale .40 1.00
101 Cecil Cooper 2.00 5.00
102 Vic Wertz 2.00 5.00
103 Kirk Gibson 2.00 5.00
104 Maury Wills 2.00 5.00
105 Steve Garvey 2.00 5.00
106 Warren Spahn 3.00 8.00
107 Paul Molitor 5.00 12.00
108 Robin Yount 3.00 8.00
109 Rollie Fingers 3.00 8.00
110 Bob Allison 2.00 5.00
111 Kirby Puckett 3.00 8.00
112 Tim Raines 3.00 8.00
113 George Pipgras 2.00 5.00
114 Eddie Grant 2.00 5.00
115 Hoyt Wilhelm 3.00 8.00
116 Sal Maglie 2.00 5.00

117 Ron Santo 3.00 8.00
118 Wally Joyner 2.00 5.00
119 Tom Seaver 3.00 8.00
120 Tommie Agee 2.00 5.00
121 Harmon Killebrew 3.00 8.00
122 Bill Dickey 2.00 5.00
123 Early Wynn 3.00 8.00
124 Bobby Murcer 2.00 5.00
125 Bucky Dent 2.00 5.00
126 Dave Winfield 3.00 8.00
127 Don Larsen 2.00 5.00
128 Don Mattingly 5.00 12.00
129 Earle Combs 2.00 5.00
130 Ed Lopat 2.00 5.00
131 Elston Howard 2.00 5.00
132 Everett Scott 2.00 5.00
133 Goose Gossage 3.00 8.00
134 Graig Nettles 2.00 5.00
135 Joe DiMaggio 5.00 12.00
136 Lou Piniella 2.00 5.00
137 Bill Skowron 2.00 5.00
138 Phil Rizzuto 3.00 8.00
139 Red Ruffing 2.00 5.00
140 Reggie Jackson 3.00 8.00
141 Roger Maris 3.00 8.00
142 Ron Guidry 2.00 5.00
143 Tiny Bonham 2.00 5.00
144 Bruce Sutter 3.00 8.00
145 Tony Lazzeri 3.00 8.00
146 Waite Hoyt 2.00 5.00
147 Whitey Ford 3.00 8.00
148 Steve Sax 2.00 5.00
149 Yogi Berra 3.00 8.00
150 Enos Slaughter 3.00 8.00
151 Catfish Hunter 3.00 8.00
152 Dennis Eckersley 3.00 8.00
153 Jose Canseco 3.00 8.00
154 Al Rosen 2.00 5.00
155 Al Simmons 3.00 8.00
156 Chief Bender 3.00 8.00
157 Cy Williams 2.00 5.00
158 Mike Schmidt 4.00 10.00
159 Richie Ashburn 3.00 8.00
160 Robin Roberts 3.00 8.00
161 Steve Carlton 3.00 8.00
162 Judy Johnson 2.00 5.00
163 Al Oliver 2.00 5.00
164 Bill Mazeroski 3.00 8.00
165 Dave Parker 2.00 5.00
166 Max Carey 2.00 5.00
167 Pie Traynor 3.00 8.00
168 Ralph Kiner 3.00 8.00
169 Roberto Clemente 6.00 15.00
170 Willie Stargell 3.00 8.00
171 Gaylord Perry 3.00 8.00
172 Tony Gwynn 3.00 8.00
173 Nolan Ryan 8.00 20.00
174 Joe Carter 2.00 5.00
175 Frank Howard 2.00 5.00
176 George Kell 3.00 8.00
177 Heinie Manush 2.00 5.00
178 Sam Rice 3.00 8.00
179 Babe Ruth 6.00 15.00
180 Casey Stengel 3.00 8.00
181 Christy Mathewson 3.00 8.00
182 Cy Young 3.00 8.00
183 Dizzy Dean 3.00 8.00
184 Eddie Mathews 3.00 8.00
185 George Sisler 3.00 8.00
186 Honus Wagner 3.00 8.00
187 Jackie Robinson 3.00 8.00
188 Jimmie Foxx 3.00 8.00
189 Johnny Mize 3.00 8.00
190 Lefty Gomez 2.00 5.00
191 Lou Gehrig 5.00 12.00
192 Mel Ott 2.00 5.00
193 Mickey Cochrane 3.00 8.00
194 Rogers Hornsby 3.00 8.00
195 Roy Campanella 3.00 8.00
196 Satchel Paige 3.00 8.00
197 Thurman Munson 3.00 8.00
198 Ty Cobb 4.00 10.00
199 Walter Johnson 3.00 8.00
200 Lefty Grove 3.00 8.00

2006 SP Legendary Cuts Bronze

*101-200 BRONZE: .6X TO 1.5X BASIC
101-200: ONE BASIC OR BRONZE PER BOX
STATED PRINT RUN 99 SERIAL #'d SETS

2006 SP Legendary Cuts A Place in History Cuts

OVERALL CUT AU ODDS 1:96
PRINT RUNS B/WN 1-98 COPIES PER
NO PRICING ON QTY OF 25 OR LESS
BA Bob Allison/94 30.00 60.00
BD Bill Dickey/29 75.00 200.00
BG Burleigh Grimes/43 75.00 150.00
BL Bob Lemon/47 20.00 50.00
CG Charlie Gehringer/57 30.00 60.00
CH Carl Hubbell/32 125.00 200.00
CW Cy Williams/29 150.00 250.00
DH Dick Howser/28 75.00 150.00
DL Leo Durocher/42 30.00 60.00
EA Earl Averill/75 20.00 50.00
EM Eddie Mathews/34 60.00 120.00
ER Edd Roush/98 50.00 100.00
EW Early Wynn/36 40.00 80.00
FF Ford Frick/30 100.00 175.00
GS George Sisler/42 300.00 500.00
HC Happy Chandler/61 50.00 100.00
HG Hank Greenberg/31 125.00 250.00
HI Kirby Higbe/59 20.00 50.00
JC Joe Cronin/30 30.00 60.00
JH Johnny Hodapp/26 30.00 60.00
JM Joe McCarthy/58 50.00 100.00
JS Joe Sewell/87 20.00 50.00
LA Luke Appling/94 60.00 120.00
LB Lou Boudreau/88 30.00 60.00
LG Lefty Gomez/30 100.00 175.00
ME Joe Medwick/60 75.00 150.00
PR Pee Wee Reese/57 100.00 200.00
RD Ray Dandridge/43 30.00 60.00
RE Pete Reiser/75 30.00 60.00
RO Charlie Robertson/42 75.00 150.00
RS Ray Schalk Best/37 200.00 400.00
RS2 Ray Schalk/75 175.00 300.00
SM Sal Maglie/73 50.00 100.00
VK Vern Kennedy/61 30.00 60.00
WG Warren Giles/45 75.00 150.00
WI Hoyt Wilhelm/65 20.00 50.00
WS Warren Spahn/41 75.00 150.00

2006 SP Legendary Cuts Baseball Chronology Gold

STATED PRINT RUN 550 SERIAL #'d SETS
*PLATINUM: .6X TO 1.5X BASIC
PLATINUM PRINT RUN 99 SERIAL #'d SETS
OVERALL CHRONOLOGY ODDS 1:12
AD Andre Dawson .75 2.00
AK Al Kaline 1.25 3.00
AT Alan Trammell .75 2.00
BD Bucky Dent .50 1.25
BF Bob Feller .75 2.00
BG Bob Gibson .75 2.00
BL Bob Lemon .75 2.00
BM Bill Mazeroski .75 2.00
BO Bo Jackson 1.25 3.00
BR Babe Ruth 3.00 8.00
BR2 Babe Ruth 3.00 8.00
BR3 Babe Ruth 3.00 8.00
BW Billy Williams .75 2.00
CA Rod Carew .75 2.00
CF Carlton Fisk .75 2.00
CH Catfish Hunter .75 2.00
CL Roberto Clemente 3.00 8.00
CM Christy Mathewson 1.25 3.00
CN Joe Cronin .50 1.25
CR Cal Ripken 4.00 10.00
CS Casey Stengel Yanks .75 2.00
CS2 Casey Stengel Mets .75 2.00
CY Cy Young 1.25 3.00
DD Don Drysdale .75 2.00
DE Dennis Eckersley .75 2.00
DL Don Larsen .50 1.25
DM Don Mattingly 2.50 6.00
DS Don Sutton .50 1.25
DZ Dizzy Dean .75 2.00
EB Ernie Banks 1.25 3.00
EB2 Ernie Banks 1.25 3.00
EM Eddie Murray .75 2.00
ES Enos Slaughter .75 2.00
FL Fred Lynn .50 1.25
FR Frank Robinson .75 2.00
GH Gil Hodges .75 2.00
GP Gaylord Perry .75 2.00
GS George Sisler .75 2.00
HG Hank Greenberg 1.25 3.00
HW Honus Wagner 1.25 3.00
HY Hoyt Wilhelm .75 2.00
JB Johnny Bench 1.25 3.00
JC Joe Carter .50 1.25
JD Joe DiMaggio 2.50 6.00
JF Jimmie Foxx A's 1.25 3.00
JF2 Jimmie Foxx Sox 1.25 3.00
JM Johnny Mize .75 2.00
JO Joe Morgan .75 2.00
JR Jackie Robinson 1.25 3.00
KG Kirk Gibson .50 1.25
KP Kirby Puckett 1.25 3.00
LB Lou Boudreau .75 2.00
LG Lou Gehrig 2.50 6.00
LG2 Lou Gehrig 2.50 6.00
LO Lou Brock .75 2.00
MC Mickey Cochrane .75 2.00
MF Mark Fidrych .50 1.25
MO Mel Ott .50 1.25
MS Mike Schmidt 2.00 5.00
MW Maury Wills .50 1.25
NL Nap Lajoie 1.25 3.00
NR Nolan Ryan Angels 4.00 10.00
NR2 Nolan Ryan Rgr 4.00 10.00
NR3 Nolan Ryan Rgr 4.00 10.00
OS Ozzie Smith 1.50 4.00
PM Paul Molitor 1.25 3.00
PN Phil Niekro .75 2.00
PW Pee Wee Reese .75 2.00
RC Roy Campanella 1.25 3.00
RF Rollie Fingers .75 2.00
RH Rogers Hornsby .75 2.00
RI Jim Rice .75 2.00
RJ Reggie Jackson .75 2.00
RK Ralph Kiner .75 2.00
RM Roger Maris 1.25 3.00
RO Brooks Robinson .75 2.00
RS Ryne Sandberg 2.50 6.00
RY Robin Yount 1.25 3.00
SC Steve Carlton Cards .75 2.00
SC2 Steve Carlton Phils .75 2.00
SG Steve Garvey .50 1.25
SM Stan Musial 2.00 5.00
SP Satchel Paige 1.25 3.00
ST Willie Stargell .75 2.00
TC Ty Cobb Tigers 2.00 5.00
TC2 Ty Cobb A's 2.00 5.00
TG Tony Gwynn 1.25 3.00
TM Thurman Munson 1.25 3.00
TS Tom Seaver .75 2.00
TW Ted Williams 2.50 6.00
TW2 Ted Williams 2.50 6.00
WB Wade Boggs Sox .75 2.00
WB2 Wade Boggs Rays .75 2.00
WC Will Clark .75 2.00
WF Whitey Ford .75 2.00
WJ Walter Johnson 1.25 3.00
WM Willie McCovey .75 2.00
WS Warren Spahn .75 2.00
YB Yogi Berra 1.25 3.00
YZ Carl Yastrzemski 2.00 5.00

2006 SP Legendary Cuts Baseball Chronology Materials

STATED ODDS 1:12
SP PRINT RUNS PROVIDED BY UD
NO PRICING ON QTY OF 25 OR LESS
AD Andre Dawson Pants 3.00 8.00
AK Al Kaline Bat 4.00 10.00
AT Alan Trammell Bat 3.00 8.00
BD Bucky Dent Jsy 3.00 8.00
BF Bob Feller Pants 4.00 10.00
BG Bob Gibson Jsy 3.00 8.00
BL Bob Lemon Jsy 3.00 8.00
BM B.Mazeroski Bat SP/59 * 12.50 30.00
BO Bo Jackson Jsy 4.00 10.00
BW Billy Williams Bat 3.00 8.00
CA Rod Carew Bat 3.00 8.00
CF Carlton Fisk Bat 3.00 8.00
CH Catfish Hunter Jsy 3.00 8.00
CL R.Clemente Pants SP/100 * 25.00 60.00
CM C.Mathew Pants SP/49 * 60.00 120.00
CN Joe Cronin Bat 4.00 10.00
CR Cal Ripken Pants 6.00 15.00
CS C.Stengel Yanks Jsy SP/199 * 10.00 25.00
CS2 C.Stengel Mets Jsy SP/100 * 10.00 25.00
DD Don Drysdale Jsy SP/94 * 10.00 25.00
DE Dennis Eckersley Jsy 3.00 8.00
DL Don Larsen Pants 3.00 8.00
DM Don Mattingly Pants 4.00 10.00
DS Don Sutton Jsy 3.00 8.00
DZ Dizzy Dean Jsy SP/100 * 30.00 60.00
EB Ernie Banks MVP Jsy 6.00 15.00
EB2 E.Banks 500 Jsy SP/100 * 6.00 15.00
EM Eddie Murray Jsy 3.00 8.00
ES E.Slaughter Bat SP/100 * 6.00 15.00
FL Fred Lynn Bat 3.00 8.00
FR Frank Robinson Jsy 3.00 8.00
GH Gil Hodges Bat SP/50 * 10.00 25.00
GP Gaylord Perry Jsy 3.00 8.00
GS George Sisler Bat SP/100 * 8.00 20.00
HG H.Greenberg Bat SP/198 * 10.00 25.00
HY Hoyt Wilhelm Jsy SP/46 * 4.00 10.00
JB Johnny Bench Jsy 4.00 10.00
JC Joe Carter Jsy 3.00 8.00
JD J.DiMaggio Jsy SP/100 * 40.00 80.00
JF J.Foxx A's Bat SP/50 * 12.50 30.00
JF2 J.Foxx Sox Bat SP/100 * 12.50 30.00
JM Johnny Mize Pants 4.00 10.00
JO Joe Morgan Jsy 3.00 8.00
KG Kirk Gibson Jsy 3.00 8.00
KP Kirby Puckett Bat 4.00 10.00
LB Lou Boudreau Jsy 4.00 10.00
LO Lou Brock Jsy 3.00 8.00
MF Mark Fidrych Jsy 6.00 15.00
MO Mel Ott Jsy SP/100 * 15.00 40.00
MS Mike Schmidt Bat 4.00 10.00
MW Maury Wills Bat 3.00 8.00
NR N.Ryan Angels Jsy SP/109 * 10.00 25.00
NR2 Nolan Ryan 5000 Jsy 10.00 25.00
NR3 Nolan Ryan 7th NH Jsy 10.00 25.00
OS Ozzie Smith Jkt-Jsy 4.00 10.00
PM Paul Molitor Bat 3.00 8.00
PN Phil Niekro Jsy 3.00 8.00
PW Pee Wee Reese Bat 4.00 10.00
RC R.Campy Pants SP/154 * 6.00 15.00
RF Rollie Fingers Jsy 3.00 8.00
RI Jim Rice Bat 3.00 8.00
RJ Reggie Jackson Jsy 4.00 10.00
RK Ralph Kiner Bat SP/154 * 4.00 10.00
RM Roger Maris Jsy 12.50 30.00
RO Brooks Robinson Bat 4.00 10.00
RS Ryne Sandberg Jsy 4.00 10.00
RY Robin Yount Pants 3.00 8.00
SC Steve Carlton Cards Bat 3.00 8.00
SC2 Steve Carlton Phils Bat 3.00 8.00
SG Steve Garvey Jsy 3.00 8.00
SM Stan Musial Bat 10.00 25.00
SP S.Paige Pants SP/50 * 30.00 60.00
ST Willie Stargell Bat 4.00 10.00
TG Tony Gwynn Jsy 6.00 15.00
TM Thurman Munson Jsy 8.00 20.00
TS Tom Seaver Jsy 3.00 8.00
TW T.Williams Pants SP/198 * 20.00 50.00
TW2 Ted Williams Bat 12.00 30.00
WB Wade Boggs Jsy 3.00 8.00
WB2 Wade Boggs Bat 3.00 8.00
WC Will Clark Jsy 3.00 8.00
WM Willie McCovey Jsy 3.00 8.00
WS Warren Spahn Jsy 6.00 15.00
YB Yogi Berra Jsy 6.00 15.00
YZ Carl Yastrzemski Jsy 4.00 10.00

2006 SP Legendary Cuts Legendary Materials Gold

PRINT RUNS B/WN 99-225 COPIES PER
*BRONZE: .5X TO 1.2X GOLD
BRONZE PRINT RUNS B/WN 25-99 PER
NO BRONZE PRICING ON QTY OF 25
PLATINUM PRINT RUNS B/WN 5-15 PER
NO PLATINUM PRICING DUE TO SCARCITY
*SILVER: .4X TO 1X GOLD
SILVER PRINT RUNS B/WN 50-199 PER
OVERALL #'d GU ODDS 1:12
AD Andre Dawson Pants/225 3.00 8.00
AK Al Kaline Bat/225 4.00 10.00
AO Al Oliver Bat/225 3.00 8.00
AR Al Rosen Bat/225 3.00 8.00
BD Bucky Dent Jsy/225 3.00 8.00
BF Bob Feller Pants/225 4.00 10.00
BG Bob Gibson Jsy/225 3.00 8.00
BL Barry Larkin Bat/225 3.00 8.00
BM Bill Mazeroski Bat/225 4.00 10.00
BO Bo Jackson Bat/225 4.00 10.00
BP Boog Powell Bat/225 3.00 8.00
BR Babe Ruth Pants/99 150.00 250.00
BS Bruce Sutter Pants/225 3.00 8.00
BW Billy Williams Bat/225 3.00 8.00
CC Cecil Cooper Pants/225 3.00 8.00
CF Carlton Fisk Pants/225 3.00 8.00
CR Cal Ripken Pants/225 6.00 15.00
CW Rod Carew Pants/225 3.00 8.00
CY Carl Yastrzemski Pants/225 4.00 10.00
DC Dave Concepcion Bat/225 3.00 8.00
DE Dennis Eckersley Jsy/225 3.00 8.00
DE2 Dennis Eckersley Jsy/225 3.00 8.00
DL Don Larsen Pants/225 3.00 8.00
DP Dave Parker Jsy/225 3.00 8.00
DW Dave Winfield Bat/225 3.00 8.00
EB Ernie Banks Jsy/225 4.00 10.00
EM Eddie Murray Jsy/225 3.00 8.00
EV Dwight Evans Jsy/225 3.00 8.00
FH Frank Howard Bat/225 3.00 8.00
FJ Fergie Jenkins Jsy/225 3.00 8.00
FL Fred Lynn Pants/225 3.00 8.00
FR Frank Robinson Pants/225 3.00 8.00
FR2 Frank Robinson Bat/225 3.00 8.00
GF George Foster Bat/225 3.00 8.00
GG Goose Gossage Jsy/225 3.00 8.00
GN Graig Nettles Jsy/225 3.00 8.00
GP Gaylord Perry Jsy/225 3.00 8.00
GP2 Gaylord Perry Jsy/225 3.00 8.00
GU Ron Guidry Pants/225 3.00 8.00
HB Harold Baines Bat/225 3.00 8.00
JB Johnny Bench Jsy/225 4.00 10.00
JC Jose Canseco Jsy/225 4.00 10.00
JD Joe DiMaggio Jsy/99 20.00 50.00
JK John Kruk Bat/225 3.00 8.00
JM Jack Morris Jsy/225 3.00 8.00
JO Joe Morgan Jsy/225 3.00 8.00
JP Jim Palmer Jsy/225 3.00 8.00
JP2 Jim Palmer Jsy/225 3.00 8.00
JR Jim Rice Pants/225 3.00 8.00
JT Joe Torre Bat/225 4.00 10.00
JU Juan Marichal Jsy/225 3.00 8.00
KG Ken Griffey Sr. Pants/225 3.00 8.00
KI Kirk Gibson Jsy/225 3.00 8.00
KP Kirby Puckett Jsy/225 4.00 10.00
LB Lou Brock Jsy/225 3.00 8.00
LB2 Lou Brock Jsy/225 3.00 8.00
LP Lou Piniella Jsy/225 3.00 8.00
MA Don Mattingly Pants/225 4.00 10.00
MG Mark Grace Bat/225 3.00 8.00
MS Mike Schmidt Jsy/225 4.00 10.00
MU Bobby Murcer Bat/225 3.00 8.00
MW Maury Wills Bat/225 3.00 8.00
NR Nolan Ryan Jkt/225 6.00 15.00
OS Ozzie Smith Jsy/225 4.00 10.00
PM Paul Molitor Bat/225 3.00 8.00
PN Phil Niekro Jsy/225 3.00 8.00
PN2 Phil Niekro Jsy/225 3.00 8.00
PR Phil Rizzuto Jsy/99 5.00 12.00
RC Rocky Colavito Bat/225 6.00 15.00
RE Red Schoendienst Jsy/99 5.00 12.00
RF Rollie Fingers Jsy/225 3.00 8.00
RJ Reggie Jackson Bat/225 4.00 10.00
RK Ralph Kiner Bat/225 4.00 10.00
RN Ron Santo Jsy/125 4.00 10.00
RN2 Ron Santo Jsy/125 4.00 10.00
RO Brooks Robinson Jsy/175 4.00 10.00
RR Robin Roberts Pants/225 4.00 10.00
RS Ryne Sandberg Jsy/225 4.00 10.00
RY Robin Yount Jsy/225 3.00 8.00
SC Steve Carlton Bat/225 3.00 8.00
SC2 Steve Carlton Bat/225 3.00 8.00
SG Steve Garvey Jsy/225 3.00 8.00
SK Bill Skowron Bat/225 3.00 8.00
SM Stan Musial Bat/225 6.00 15.00
SS Steve Sax Jsy/225 3.00 8.00
SU Don Sutton Jsy/225 3.00 8.00
TG Tony Gwynn Jsy/225 3.00 8.00
TO Tony Oliva Bat/225 3.00 8.00
TP Tony Perez Pants/225 3.00 8.00
TS Tom Seaver Jsy/225 3.00 8.00
WB Wade Boggs Jsy/225 3.00 8.00
WC Will Clark Jsy/225 3.00 8.00
WC2 Will Clark Jsy/99 3.00 8.00
WJ Wally Joyner Jsy/225 3.00 8.00
WM Willie McCovey Jsy/225 3.00 8.00
YB Yogi Berra Bat/225 6.00 15.00

2006 SP Legendary Cuts Legendary Signature Cuts

OVERALL CUT AU ODDS 1:96
PRINT RUNS B/WN 1-90 COPIES PER
NO PRICING ON QTY OF 25 OR LESS
BD Bill Dickey/34 125.00 250.00
BG Burleigh Grimes/33 75.00 150.00
BL Bob Lemon/77 20.00 50.00
BW Bucky Walters/52 30.00 60.00
CG Charlie Gehringer/76 20.00 50.00
CS Casey Stengel/35 200.00 400.00
DC Dolph Camilli/58 20.00 50.00
DR Don Drysdale/45 75.00 150.00
EA Earl Averill/50 60.00 120.00
EB Ed Barrow/35 150.00 250.00
EC Earle Combs/65 150.00 250.00
EL Ed Lopat/32 100.00 175.00
EM Eddie Mathews/59 30.00 60.00
ER Edd Roush/90 30.00 60.00
HE Billy Herman/87 20.00 50.00
HG Hank Greenberg/60 175.00 300.00
HK Harvey Kuehn/89 60.00 120.00
JA Joe Adcock/47 75.00 150.00
JC Jocko Conlon/76 50.00 100.00
JJ Judy Johnson/40 40.00 100.00
JM Joe McCarthy/67 75.00 200.00
JO Joe Cronin/30 50.00 100.00
JS Joe Sewell/83 30.00 80.00
LA Luke Appling/84 20.00 50.00
LB Lou Boudreau/86 20.00 50.00
LG Lefty Gomez/44 40.00 100.00
MA Mel Allen/67 75.00 150.00
MC Max Carey/79 30.00 60.00
ME Joe Medwick/82 100.00 175.00
MI Johnny Mize/90 60.00 120.00
PR Pee Wee Reese/47 60.00 120.00
PT Pie Traynor/26 400.00 600.00
RB Ray Boone/51 60.00 120.00
RD Ray Dandridge/35 30.00 60.00
RR Red Ruffing/72 125.00 200.00
SR Sam Rice/31 75.00 200.00
ST Stan Coveleski/81 20.00 50.00
WA Walter Alston/27 50.00 100.00
WH Waite Hoyt/49 75.00 150.00
WI Hoyt Wilhelm/47 50.00 100.00
WP Wally Post/66 25.00 60.00
WS Warren Spahn/52 75.00 150.00

2006 SP Legendary Cuts Memorable Moments Autographs

OVERALL AU STATED ODDS 1:192
PRINT RUNS B/WN 1-99 COPIES PER
NO PRICING ON QTY OF 25 OR LESS
AD Andre Dawson/99 6.00 15.00
BL Barry Larkin/50 30.00 60.00
CC Cesar Cedeno/99 6.00 15.00
CE Cecil Cooper/99 5.00 12.00
DC David Cone/99 6.00 15.00
DM Don Mattingly/50 60.00 120.00
GP Gaylord Perry/99 6.00 15.00
JK John Kruk/99 6.00 15.00
PR Phil Rizzuto/99 15.00 40.00
RF Rollie Fingers/47 8.00 20.00
TR Tim Raines/50 20.00 50.00
TS Tom Seaver/44 30.00 80.00

2006 SP Legendary Cuts Memorable Moments Materials

OVERALL #'d GU ODDS 1:12
PRINT RUNS B/WN 223-225 COPIES PER
AD Andre Dawson Pants/225 3.00 8.00
BF Bob Feller Pants/225 4.00 10.00
BJ Bo Jackson Bat/225 4.00 10.00
BL Barry Larkin Pants/225 4.00 10.00
BM Bobby Murcer Pants/225 3.00 8.00
BS Bruce Sutter Pants/225 3.00 8.00
CC Cesar Cedeno Pants/225 3.00 8.00
CE Cecil Cooper Jsy/225 3.00 8.00
CF Carlton Fisk Pants/225 3.00 8.00
DC David Cone Jsy/225 3.00 8.00
DE Dwight Evans Jsy/225 3.00 8.00
DM Don Mattingly Pants/225 4.00 10.00
DP Dave Parker Jsy/225 3.00 8.00
DS Don Sutton Jsy/225 3.00 8.00
EM Eddie Mathews Pants/225 6.00 15.00
GF George Foster Bat/225 3.00 8.00
GG Goose Gossage Jsy/225 3.00 8.00
GP Gaylord Perry Bat/225 3.00 8.00
JB Johnny Bench Jsy/225 4.00 10.00
JK John Kruk Bat/225 3.00 8.00
JM Johnny Mize Pants/225 4.00 10.00
KG Kirk Gibson Jsy/225 3.00 8.00
MA Juan Marichal Jsy/225 3.00 8.00
MO Joe Morgan Jsy/225 3.00 8.00
MS Mike Schmidt Jsy/225 4.00 10.00
MU Eddie Murray Jsy/225 3.00 8.00
OS Ozzie Smith Jsy/225 4.00 10.00
PO Paul O'Neill Jsy/225 3.00 8.00
PR Phil Rizzuto Jsy/225 4.00 10.00
RC Rocky Colavito Bat/225 6.00 15.00
RF Rollie Fingers Jsy/225 3.00 8.00
RG Ron Guidry Jsy/223 3.00 8.00
RJ Reggie Jackson Jsy/225 4.00 10.00
RS Ron Santo Bat/225 4.00 10.00
RY Robin Yount Jsy/225 3.00 8.00
SG Steve Garvey Jsy/225 3.00 8.00
SM Stan Musial Bat/225 6.00 15.00
SS Steve Sax Jsy/223 3.00 8.00
TG Tony Gwynn Pants/225 3.00 8.00
TR Tim Raines Jsy/225 3.00 8.00
TS Tom Seaver Jsy/225 3.00 8.00

2006 SP Legendary Cuts Place in History Autographs

OVERALL AU STATED ODDS 1:192
PRINT RUNS B/WN 6-99 COPIES PER
NO PRICING ON QTY OF 25 OR LESS
AD Andre Dawson/99 6.00 15.00
AR Al Rosen/99 10.00 25.00
BD Bucky Dent/99 6.00 15.00
BF Bob Feller/35 15.00 40.00
BL Barry Larkin/49 30.00 60.00
BM Bill Mazeroski/99 10.00 25.00
BO Bo Jackson/99 20.00 50.00
BP Boog Powell/99 6.00 15.00
BR Brooks Robinson/35 15.00 40.00
BR2 Brooks Robinson/35 15.00 40.00
BS Bruce Sutter/99 10.00 25.00
BW Billy Williams/99 6.00 15.00
CC Cecil Cooper/99 5.00 12.00
CF Carlton Fisk/99 15.00 40.00
CR Cal Ripken/35 40.00 80.00
CY Carl Yastrzemski/45 20.00 50.00
DE Dennis Eckersley/99 6.00 15.00
DE2 Dennis Eckersley/99 6.00 15.00
EV Dwight Evans/99 10.00 25.00
FH Frank Howard/99 10.00 25.00
FJ Fergie Jenkins/99 6.00 15.00
FL Fred Lynn/99 6.00 15.00
FR Frank Robinson Reds/45 15.00 40.00
FR2 Frank Robinson O's/45 15.00 40.00
GF George Foster/56 6.00 15.00
GN Graig Nettles/99 6.00 15.00
GP Gaylord Perry Rgr/99 6.00 15.00
GP2 Gaylord Perry Giants/99 6.00 15.00
HB Harold Baines/45 8.00 20.00
JB Johnny Bench/42 30.00 60.00
JC Jose Canseco/99 25.00 60.00
JM Jack Morris/82 6.00 15.00
JO Joe Morgan/50 12.50 30.00
JP Jim Palmer/99 10.00 25.00
JR Jim Rice/75 10.00 25.00
JT Joe Torre/99 15.00 40.00
JU Juan Marichal/29 12.50 30.00
JY Johnny Podres/38 12.50 30.00
KG Ken Griffey Sr./99 6.00 15.00
KP Kirby Puckett/99 75.00 150.00
LA Luis Aparicio/99 20.00 50.00
LA2 Luis Aparicio/99 20.00 50.00
LB Lou Brock/99 10.00 25.00
LB2 Lou Brock/99 10.00 25.00
LP Lou Piniella/99 10.00 25.00
MA Don Mattingly/50 25.00 60.00
MC Denny McLain/31 6.00 15.00
MG Mark Grace/99 10.00 25.00
MW Maury Wills/96 6.00 15.00
OS Ozzie Smith/99 30.00 60.00
PM Paul Molitor/99 10.00 25.00
PN Phil Niekro/52 8.00 20.00
PN2 Phil Niekro/52 8.00 20.00
PR Phil Rizzuto/99 15.00 40.00
RD Red Schoendienst/99 15.00 40.00
RK Ralph Kiner/99 10.00 25.00
RO Ron Santo/99 15.00 40.00
RO2 Ron Santo/99 15.00 40.00
RR Robin Roberts/55 8.00 20.00
RY Robin Yount/99 15.00 40.00
SC Steve Carlton/99 10.00 25.00
SC2 Steve Carlton/99 10.00 25.00
SG Steve Garvey/99 10.00 25.00
SM Stan Musial/45 30.00 60.00
SS Steve Sax/99 5.00 12.00
TG Tony Gwynn/26 40.00 80.00
TO Tony Oliva/99 12.50 30.00
TO2 Tony Oliva/99 12.50 30.00
TR Tim Raines/97 6.00 15.00
TS Tom Seaver/55 30.00 80.00
WB Wade Boggs/50 20.00 50.00
WC Will Clark/92 10.00 25.00
WC2 Will Clark/92 10.00 25.00
WF Whitey Ford/35 30.00 60.00
WJ Wally Joyner/99 10.00 25.00

2006 SP Legendary Cuts When It Was A Game Silver

STATED PRINT RUN 550 SERIAL #'d SETS
*GOLD: .6X TO 1.5X BASIC
GOLD PRINT RUN 99 SERIAL #'d SETS
OVERALL WIWAG ODDS 1:12
AD Andre Dawson .75 2.00
AK Al Kaline 1.25 3.00
AR Al Rosen .50 1.25
BF Bob Feller .75 2.00
BG Bob Gibson .75 2.00
BM Bill Mazeroski .75 2.00
BR Babe Ruth 3.00 8.00
BS Bruce Sutter .75 2.00
BW Billy Williams .75 2.00
CA Rod Carew .75 2.00
CF Carlton Fisk .75 2.00
CO Rocky Colavito .75 2.00
CR Cal Ripken 4.00 10.00
CY Cy Young 1.25 3.00
DD Don Drysdale .75 2.00
DE Dennis Eckersley .75 2.00
DL Don Larsen .50 1.25
DP Dave Parker .50 1.25
DY Denny McLain .50 1.25
EB Ernie Banks 1.25 3.00
ED Eddie Murray .75 2.00
EM Eddie Mathews 1.25 3.00
EV Dwight Evans .50 1.25
FH Frank Howard .50 1.25
FJ Fergie Jenkins .75 2.00
FL Fred Lynn .50 1.25
FR Frank Robinson Reds .75 2.00
FR2 Frank Robinson O's .75 2.00
GG Goose Gossage .75 2.00
GN Graig Nettles .50 1.25
GP Gaylord Perry .75 2.00
GS George Sisler .75 2.00
GU Ron Guidry .50 1.25
HB Harold Baines .75 2.00
HG Hank Greenberg 1.25 3.00
HO Rogers Hornsby .75 2.00
HW Honus Wagner 1.25 3.00
JB Johnny Bench 1.25 3.00
JD Joe DiMaggio 2.50 6.00
JF Jimmie Foxx 1.25 3.00
JK John Kruk .50 1.25
JM Jack Morris .75 2.00
JO Joe Morgan .75 2.00
JP Jim Palmer .75 2.00
JR Jackie Robinson 1.25 3.00
JT Joe Torre .75 2.00
JU Juan Marichal .75 2.00
KG Ken Griffey Sr. .50 1.25
KI Kirk Gibson .50 1.25
KP Kirby Puckett 1.25 3.00
LA Luis Aparicio .75 2.00
LB Lou Brock .75 2.00
LG Lou Gehrig 2.50 6.00
LP Lou Piniella .50 1.25
MA Don Mattingly 2.50 6.00
MC Mickey Cochrane .75 2.00
MO Mel Ott .50 1.25
MS Mike Schmidt 2.00 5.00
MU Bobby Murcer .50 1.25
MW Maury Wills .50 1.25
MZ Johnny Mize .75 2.00
NR Nolan Ryan 4.00 10.00
OS Ozzie Smith 1.50 4.00
PM Paul Molitor 1.25 3.00
PN Phil Niekro .75 2.00
PR Phil Rizzuto .75 2.00
PS Johnny Podres .50 1.25
RC Roberto Clemente 3.00 8.00
RF Rollie Fingers .75 2.00
RI Jim Rice .75 2.00
RJ Reggie Jackson .75 2.00
RK Ralph Kiner .75 2.00
RN Ron Santo .75 2.00
RO Brooks Robinson .75 2.00
RO2 Brooks Robinson .75 2.00
RR Robin Roberts .75 2.00
RS Red Schoendienst .75 2.00
RY Robin Yount 1.25 3.00
SA Ryne Sandberg 2.50 6.00
SC Steve Carlton .75 2.00
SC2 Steve Carlton .75 2.00
SG Steve Garvey .50 1.25
SK Bill Skowron .50 1.25
SM Stan Musial 2.00 5.00
SP Satchel Paige 1.25 3.00
SU Don Sutton .50 1.25
TG Tony Gwynn 1.25 3.00
TM Thurman Munson 1.25 3.00
TO Tony Oliva .50 1.25
TO2 Tony Oliva .50 1.25
TP Tony Perez .75 2.00
TR Tim Raines .75 2.00
TS Tom Seaver .75 2.00
WB Wade Boggs .75 2.00
WC Will Clark .75 2.00
WF Whitey Ford .75 2.00
WJ Wally Joyner .50 1.25
WM Willie McCovey .75 2.00
YB Yogi Berra 1.25 3.00
YZ Carl Yastrzemski 2.00 5.00

2006 SP Legendary Cuts When It Was A Game Materials

OVERALL #'d GU ODDS 1:12
PRINT RUNS B/WN 5-75 COPIES PER
NO PRICING ON QTY OF 25 OR LESS
AD Andre Dawson Pants/75 4.00 10.00
AR Al Rosen Pants/75 4.00 10.00
BF Bob Feller Pants/75 5.00 12.00
BG Bob Gibson Jsy/75 4.00 10.00
BM Bill Mazeroski Jsy/75 5.00 12.00
BS Bruce Sutter Pants/75 4.00 10.00
BW Billy Williams Jsy/75 4.00 10.00
CA Rod Carew Jsy/75 4.00 10.00
CF Carlton Fisk Pants/75 4.00 10.00
CO Rocky Colavito Jsy/75 8.00 20.00
CR Cal Ripken Pants/75 8.00 20.00
DD Don Drysdale Pants/75 10.00 25.00
DE Dennis Eckersley Jsy/75 4.00 10.00
DL Don Larsen Pants/75 4.00 10.00
DP Dave Parker Jsy/75 4.00 10.00
EB Ernie Banks Jsy/75 5.00 12.00
ED Eddie Murray Jsy/75 4.00 10.00
EM Eddie Mathews Pants/75 8.00 20.00
FJ Fergie Jenkins Jsy/75 4.00 10.00
FL Fred Lynn Jsy/75 5.00 12.00
FR Frank Robinson Reds Bat/75 4.00 10.00
FR2 Frank Robinson O's Bat/75 10.00 25.00
GN Graig Nettles Jsy/75 4.00 10.00
GP Gaylord Perry Bat/75 4.00 10.00
GS George Sisler Bat/75 10.00 25.00
GU Ron Guidry Jsy/75 4.00 10.00
HG Hank Greenberg Bat/75 15.00 40.00
HO Rogers Hornsby Bat/75 15.00 40.00
JB Johnny Bench Jsy/75 5.00 12.00
JD Joe DiMaggio Jsy/75 40.00 80.00
JF Jimmie Foxx Bat/75 15.00 40.00
JK John Kruk Bat/75 4.00 10.00
JO Joe Morgan Jsy/75 4.00 10.00
JP Jim Palmer Jsy/75 4.00 10.00
JR Jackie Robinson Jsy/75 20.00 50.00
JT Joe Torre Bat/75 5.00 12.00
JU Juan Marichal Jsy/75 5.00 12.00
KG Ken Griffey Sr. Jsy/75 4.00 10.00
KI Kirk Gibson Jsy/75 4.00 10.00
KP Kirby Puckett Jsy/75 20.00 50.00
LG Lou Gehrig Bat/75 50.00 100.00
LP Lou Piniella Jsy 4.00 10.00
MA Don Mattingly Pants/75 5.00 12.00
MO Mel Ott Jsy/75 15.00 40.00
MS Mike Schmidt Jsy/75 8.00 20.00
MU Bobby Murcer Pants/75 4.00 10.00
MW Maury Wills Jsy/75 4.00 10.00
MZ Johnny Mize Pants/75 5.00 12.00
OS Ozzie Smith Jkt-Jsy/75 5.00 12.00
PM Paul Molitor Bat/75 4.00 10.00
PN Phil Niekro Jsy/75 4.00 10.00
RC Roberto Clemente Jsy/75 40.00 80.00
RF Rollie Fingers Pants/75 4.00 10.00
RI Jim Rice Jsy-Pants/75 4.00 10.00
RK Ralph Kiner Bat/75 5.00 12.00
RN Ron Santo Jsy/75 5.00 12.00
RR Robin Roberts Pants/75 5.00 12.00
RS Red Schoendienst Jsy/75 5.00 12.00
RY Robin Yount Jsy/75 4.00 10.00
SC Steve Carlton Pants/75 4.00 10.00
SC2 Steve Carlton Pants/75 4.00 10.00
SG Steve Garvey Jsy/75 4.00 10.00
SK Bill Skowron Bat/75 4.00 10.00
SM Stan Musial Bat/75 8.00 20.00
SU Don Sutton Jsy/75 4.00 10.00
TG Tony Gwynn Jsy/75 4.00 10.00
TM T.Munson Pants/75 10.00 25.00
TO Tony Oliva Jsy/75 4.00 10.00
TO2 Tony Oliva Jsy/75 4.00 10.00
TP Tony Perez Pants/75 4.00 10.00
TR Tim Raines Jsy/75 4.00 10.00
TS Tom Seaver Jsy/75 4.00 10.00
WB Wade Boggs Jsy/75 4.00 10.00
WC Will Clark Jsy/75 4.00 10.00
WJ Wally Joyner Jsy/75 4.00 10.00
WM Willie McCovey Jsy/75 4.00 10.00
YB Yogi Berra Pants/75 8.00 20.00
YZ C.Yaz Jsy-Pants/75 5.00 12.00

2006 SP Legendary Cuts When It Was A Game Cuts

OVERALL CUT AU ODDS 1:96
PRINT RUNS B/WN 2-99 COPIES PER
NO PRICING ON QTY OF 25 OR LESS
AC Al Campanis/30 30.00 60.00
BG Burleigh Grimes/56 50.00 100.00
BL Bob Lemon/79 30.00 60.00
CG Charlie Gehringer/64 30.00 60.00
CH Carl Hubbell/80 75.00 150.00
CR Joe Cronin/34 75.00 150.00
EA Earl Averill/67 30.00 60.00
EM Eddie Mathews/33 100.00 175.00
ER Edd Roush/98 30.00 60.00
EW Early Wynn/40 60.00 120.00
FF Ford Frick/30 75.00 150.00
GS George Sisler/37 300.00 500.00
HC Happy Chandler/64 30.00 60.00
HE Billy Herman/99 30.00 60.00
HM Heinie Manush/29 100.00 250.00
HU Catfish Hunter/34 40.00 80.00
HW Hoyt Wilhelm/56 10.00 25.00
JC Jocko Conlon/73 50.00 100.00
JD Joe Dugan/30 50.00 100.00
JM Joe McCarthy/51 75.00 150.00
JS Joe Sewell/78 30.00 60.00
JV Johnny Vander Meer/45 40.00 80.00
LA Luke Appling/83 30.00 60.00
LB Lou Boudreau/50 30.00 60.00
LG Lefty Gomez/36 40.00 80.00
LO Ed Lopat/28 40.00 80.00
MC Max Carey/71 20.00 50.00
ME Joe Medwick/57 60.00 120.00
MI Johnny Mize/70 25.00 60.00
PR Pee Wee Reese/52 125.00 200.00
RB Ray Boone/68 30.00 60.00
RD Ray Dandridge/75 20.00 50.00
RR Red Ruffing/44 100.00 200.00
SC Stan Coveleski/91 30.00 60.00
SE George Selkirk/30 30.00 60.00
SM Sal Maglie/68 40.00 80.00
SR Sam Rice/33 60.00 150.00
ST Willie Stargell/27 100.00 200.00
TK Ted Kluszewski/50 40.00 80.00
VK Vern Kennedy/58 40.00 80.00
VW Vic Wertz/30 20.00 50.00
WH Waite Hoyt/70 30.00 60.00
WP Wally Post/66 30.00 60.00
WS Warren Spahn/78 30.00 60.00

2007 SP Legendary Cuts

COMP.SET w/o SP's (100) 10.00 25.00
COMMON CARD (1-100) .25 .60
COMMON CARD (101-200) 2.00 5.00
101-200 RANDOMLY INSERTED
101-200 PRINT RUN 550 SERIAL #'d SETS
1 Phil Niekro .40 1.00
2 Brooks Robinson .40 1.00
3 Frank Robinson .40 1.00
4 Jim Palmer .40 1.00
5 Cal Ripken Jr. 2.00 5.00
6 Warren Spahn .40 1.00
7 Cy Young .60 1.50
8 Carl Yastrzemski 1.00 2.50
9 Wade Boggs .40 1.00
10 Carlton Fisk .40 1.00
11 Joe Cronin .25 .60
12 Bobby Doerr .40 1.00
13 Roy Campanella .60 1.50
14 Pee Wee Reese .40 1.00
15 Rod Carew .40 1.00
16 Ernie Banks .60 1.50
17 Fergie Jenkins .40 1.00
18 Billy Williams .40 1.00
19 Gabby Hartnett .25 .60
20 Luis Aparicio .40 1.00
21 Nellie Fox .40 1.00
22 Luke Appling .40 1.00
23 Joe Morgan .40 1.00
24 Johnny Bench .60 1.50

25 Tony Perez .40 1.00
26 George Foster .25 .60
27 Johnny Vander Meer .25 .60
28 Bob Feller .40 1.00
29 Bob Lemon .40 1.00
30 Lou Boudreau .40 1.00
31 Early Wynn .40 1.00
32 Charlie Gehringer .25 .60
33 George Kell .40 1.00
34 Hal Newhouser .40 1.00
35 Al Kaline .60 1.50
36 Ted Kluszewski .40 1.00
37 Harvey Kuenn .25 .60
38 Maury Wills .25 .60
39 Don Drysdale .40 1.00
40 Don Sutton .40 1.00
41 Eddie Mathews .60 1.50
42 Joe Adcock .25 .60
43 Paul Molitor .60 1.50
44 Kirby Puckett .60 1.50
45 Harmon Killebrew .60 1.50
46 Monte Irvin .40 1.00
47 Ralph Kiner .40 1.00
48 Christy Mathewson .60 1.50
49 Hoyt Wilhelm .40 1.00
50 Tom Seaver .40 1.00
51 Allie Reynolds .25 .60
52 Joe DiMaggio 1.25 3.00
53 Lou Gehrig 1.25 3.00
54 Babe Ruth 1.50 4.00
55 Casey Stengel .40 1.00
56 Phil Rizzuto .40 1.00
57 Thurman Munson .60 1.50
58 Johnny Mize .25 .60
59 Yogi Berra .60 1.50
60 Rube Marquard .40 1.00
61 Don Mattingly 1.25 3.00
62 Ray Dandridge .25 .60
63 Rollie Fingers .40 1.00
64 Roberto Clemente 1.50 4.00
65 Reggie Jackson .40 1.00
66 Dennis Eckersley .40 1.00
67 Robin Yount .60 1.50
68 Jimmie Foxx .60 1.50
69 Lefty Grove .40 1.00
70 Richie Ashburn .40 1.00
71 Jim Bunning .40 1.00
72 Steve Carlton .40 1.00
73 Robin Roberts .40 1.00
74 Mike Schmidt 1.00 2.50
75 Willie Stargell .40 1.00
76 Ozzie Smith .75 2.00
77 Bill Mazeroski .40 1.00
78 Honus Wagner .60 1.50
79 Pie Traynor .40 1.00
80 Tony Gwynn .60 1.50
81 Willie McCovey .40 1.00
82 Gaylord Perry .40 1.00
83 Juan Marichal .40 1.00
84 Orlando Cepeda .40 1.00
85 Satchel Paige .60 1.50
86 George Sisler .40 1.00
87 Ken Boyer .25 .60
88 Joe Medwick .25 .60
89 Travis Jackson .25 .60
90 Stan Musial 1.00 2.50
91 Dizzy Dean .40 1.00
92 Bob Gibson .40 1.00
93 Red Schoendienst .40 1.00
94 Lou Brock .40 1.00
95 Enos Slaughter .25 .60
96 Nolan Ryan 2.00 5.00
97 Smokey Burgess .25 .60
98 Mickey Vernon .25 .60
99 Vern Stephens .25 .60
100 Rick Ferrell .25 .60
101 Phil Niekro LL 2.00 5.00
102 Brooks Robinson LL 3.00 8.00
103 Frank Robinson LL 2.00 5.00
104 Jim Palmer LL 2.00 5.00
105 Cal Ripken Jr. LL 5.00 12.00
106 Warren Spahn LL 3.00 8.00
107 Cy Young LL 3.00 8.00
108 Nellie Fox LL 3.00 8.00
109 Carl Yastrzemski LL 3.00 8.00
110 Joe Sewell LL 2.00 5.00
111 Wade Boggs LL 3.00 8.00
112 Carlton Fisk LL 3.00 8.00
113 Jackie Robinson LL 3.00 8.00
114 Roy Campanella LL 3.00 8.00
115 Pee Wee Reese LL 3.00 8.00
116 Earl Averill LL 2.00 5.00
117 Rod Carew LL 3.00 8.00
118 Ernie Banks LL 3.00 8.00
119 Fergie Jenkins LL 2.00 5.00
120 Billy Williams LL 2.00 5.00
121 Al Lopez LL 2.00 5.00
122 Luis Aparicio LL 2.00 5.00
123 Luke Appling LL 2.00 5.00
124 Joe Morgan LL 2.00 5.00
125 Johnny Bench LL 3.00 8.00
126 Tony Perez LL 2.00 5.00
127 George Foster LL 2.00 5.00
128 Bob Feller LL 2.00 5.00
129 Bob Lemon LL 2.00 5.00
130 Larry Doby LL 2.00 5.00
131 Lou Boudreau LL 2.00 5.00
132 George Kell LL 2.00 5.00
133 Hal Newhouser LL 2.00 5.00
134 Al Kaline LL 3.00 8.00
135 Ty Cobb LL 4.00 10.00
136 Charlie Keller LL 2.00 5.00
137 Buck Leonard LL 2.00 5.00
138 Maury Wills LL 2.00 5.00
139 Don Drysdale LL 3.00 8.00
140 Don Sutton LL 2.00 5.00
141 Eddie Mathews LL 3.00 8.00
142 Paul Molitor LL 2.00 5.00
143 Kirby Puckett LL 4.00 10.00
144 Harmon Killebrew LL 3.00 8.00
145 Monte Irvin LL 2.00 5.00
146 Mel Ott LL 2.00 5.00
147 Charlie Gehringer LL 2.00 5.00
148 Hoyt Wilhelm LL 2.00 5.00
149 Tom Seaver LL 3.00 8.00
150 Ted Kluszewski LL 3.00 8.00
151 Joe DiMaggio LL 4.00 10.00
152 Lou Gehrig LL 4.00 10.00
153 Babe Ruth LL 5.00 12.00
154 Casey Stengel LL 2.00 5.00
155 Phil Rizzuto LL 3.00 8.00
156 Thurman Munson LL 3.00 8.00
157 Johnny Mize LL 2.00 5.00
158 Yogi Berra LL 3.00 8.00
159 Roger Maris LL 3.00 8.00
160 Early Wynn LL 2.00 5.00
161 Bobby Doerr LL 2.00 5.00
162 Joe Cronin LL 2.00 5.00
163 Don Mattingly LL 4.00 10.00
164 Ray Dandridge LL 2.00 5.00
165 Rollie Fingers LL 2.00 5.00
166 Christy Mathewson LL 3.00 8.00
167 Reggie Jackson LL 3.00 8.00
168 Dennis Eckersley LL 2.00 5.00
169 Mickey Cochrane LL 2.00 5.00
170 Jimmie Foxx LL 3.00 8.00
171 Lefty Gomez LL 2.00 5.00
172 Jim Bunning LL 2.00 5.00
173 Steve Carlton LL 2.00 5.00
174 Robin Roberts LL 2.00 5.00
175 Richie Ashburn LL 3.00 8.00
176 Mike Schmidt LL 3.00 8.00
177 Ralph Kiner LL 3.00 8.00
178 Willie Stargell LL 3.00 8.00
179 Roberto Clemente LL 6.00 15.00
180 Bill Mazeroski LL 3.00 8.00
181 Honus Wagner LL 3.00 8.00
182 Pie Traynor LL 2.00 5.00
183 Tony Gwynn LL 3.00 8.00
184 Willie McCovey LL 3.00 8.00
185 Gaylord Perry LL 2.00 5.00
186 Juan Marichal LL 2.00 5.00
187 Orlando Cepeda LL 2.00 5.00
188 Satchel Paige LL 3.00 8.00
189 George Sisler LL 2.00 5.00
190 Rogers Hornsby LL 3.00 8.00
191 Stan Musial LL 3.00 8.00
192 Dizzy Dean LL 3.00 8.00
193 Bob Gibson LL 3.00 8.00
194 Red Schoendienst LL 2.00 5.00
195 Lou Brock LL 3.00 8.00
196 Enos Slaughter LL 2.00 5.00
197 Nolan Ryan LL 5.00 12.00
198 Mickey Vernon LL 2.00 5.00
199 Walter Johnson LL 3.00 8.00
200 Rick Ferrell LL 2.00 5.00

2007 SP Legendary Cuts Retail

*RETAIL: .4X TO 1X BASIC
INSERTED IN RETAIL PACKS

2007 SP Legendary Cuts A Stitch in Time Memorabilia

OVERALL AU-GU ODDS 1:12
BG Bob Gibson 3.00 8.00
BR Brooks Robinson 4.00 10.00
BW Billy Williams 3.00 8.00
CR Cal Ripken Jr. 6.00 15.00
DE Dwight Evans 3.00 8.00
DM Don Mattingly 4.00 10.00
EM Eddie Murray 3.00 8.00
GP Gaylord Perry 3.00 8.00
HK Harmon Killebrew 4.00 10.00
JB Johnny Bench 4.00 10.00
JR Jim Rice 3.00 8.00
KP Kirby Puckett 6.00 15.00
MS Mike Schmidt 5.00 12.00
PM Paul Molitor 3.00 8.00
RC Rod Carew 3.00 8.00
RJ Reggie Jackson 4.00 10.00
TG Tony Gwynn 4.00 10.00

2007 SP Legendary Cuts Enshrinement Cuts

OVERALL CUT ODDS 1:96
PRINT RUNS B/WN 1-86 COPIES PER
NO PRICING ON QTY 25 OR LESS
AB Al Barlick/44 30.00 60.00
BL Bob Lemon/53 20.00 50.00
CG Charlie Gehringer/65 20.00 50.00
CH Carl Hubbell/31 100.00 200.00
EC Earle Combs/27 100.00 250.00
ER Edd Roush/65 20.00 50.00
GH Gabby Hartnett/31 90.00 150.00
HN Hal Newhouser/40 30.00 60.00
JC Joe Cronin/86 40.00 80.00
LA Luke Appling/45 30.00 60.00
LB Lou Boudreau/30 30.00 60.00
WH Waite Hoyt/33 50.00 100.00
WS Warren Spahn/35 60.00 120.00

2007 SP Legendary Cuts Inside the Numbers Cuts

OVERALL CUT ODDS 1:96
PRINT RUNS B/WN 4-119 COPIES PER
NO PRICING ON QTY 25 OR LESS
BD Bill Dickey/28 60.00 120.00
BH Babe Herman/99 30.00 60.00
BL Bob Lemon/75 30.00 60.00
CG Charlie Gehringer/60 40.00 80.00
CH Carl Hubbell/70 30.00 60.00
CK Charlie Keller/38 50.00 100.00
EA Earl Averill/57 30.00 60.00
EL Ernie Lombardi/38 75.00 150.00
EM Eddie Mathews/70 30.00 60.00
ES Enos Slaughter/69 30.00 60.00
EW Early Wynn/34 40.00 80.00
FS Fred Snodgrass/75 75.00 150.00
GR Lefty Grove/73 150.00 200.00
JC Joe Cronin/29 60.00 120.00
JM Joe Medwick/119 60.00 120.00
JV Johnny Vander Meer/39 30.00 60.00
LG Lefty Gomez/75 50.00 100.00
RM Rube Marquard/33 75.00 150.00
SC Stan Coveleski/72 50.00 100.00
VK Vern Kennedy/45 30.00 60.00
WH Waite Hoyt/65 40.00 80.00
WI Hoyt Wilhelm/55 40.00 80.00
WS Warren Spahn/55 50.00 100.00

2007 SP Legendary Cuts Legendary Americana

RANDOM INSERTS IN PACKS
STATED PRINT RUN 550 SER.#'d SETS
1 George Washington Carver 1.25 3.00
2 George Custer 1.25 3.00
3 Frederick Douglass 1.25 3.00
4 Crazy Horse UER 1.25 3.00
5 William Cody 1.25 3.00
6 Abraham Lincoln 2.00 5.00
7 Thomas Edison 1.25 3.00
8 Andrew Carnegie 1.25 3.00
9 Eli Whitney 1.25 3.00
10 Harriet Tubman 1.25 3.00
11 Davy Crockett 1.25 3.00
12 Robert E. Lee 2.00 5.00
13 John D. Rockefeller 1.25 3.00
14 Billy the Kid 1.25 3.00
15 Ulysses S. Grant 2.00 5.00
16 Doc Holliday 1.25 3.00
17 Annie Oakley 1.25 3.00
18 Kit Carson 1.25 3.00
19 Francis Scott Key 1.25 3.00
20 Franklin Delano Roosevelt 1.25 3.00
21 Mark Twain 1.25 3.00
22 Thomas Paine 1.25 3.00
23 Walt Whitman 1.25 3.00
24 Alexander Graham Bell 1.25 3.00
25 Susan B. Anthony 1.25 3.00
26 Harriet Beecher Stowe 1.25 3.00
27 Eleanor Roosevelt 1.25 3.00
28 John F. Kennedy 2.00 5.00
29 P.T. Barnum 1.25 3.00
30 Frank Lloyd Wright 1.25 3.00
31 Wilbur Wright 1.25 3.00
32 Casey Jones 1.25 3.00
33 Theodore Roosevelt 1.25 3.00
34 Henry Ford 1.25 3.00
35 Dwight D. Eisenhower 1.25 3.00
36 Daniel Boone 1.25 3.00
37 Florence Nightingale 1.25 3.00
38 William Randolph Hearst 1.25 3.00
39 Charles Lindbergh 1.25 3.00
40 Wild Bill Hickok 1.25 3.00
41 William T. Sherman 2.00 5.00
42 Wyatt Earp 2.00 5.00
43 Jesse James 1.25 3.00
44 Boss Tweed 1.25 3.00
45 Daniel Webster 1.25 3.00
46 Joseph Pulitzer 1.25 3.00
47 Abner Doubleday 1.25 3.00
48 Harry Truman 1.25 3.00
49 Amelia Earhart 1.25 3.00
50 Eugene V. Debs 1.25 3.00
51 Bat Masterson 1.25 3.00
52 Will Rogers 1.25 3.00
53 Orville Wright 1.25 3.00
54 Johnny Appleseed 1.25 3.00
55 Jack London 1.25 3.00
56 Washington Irving 1.25 3.00
57 F. Scott Fitzgerald 1.25 3.00
58 Geronimo 4.00 10.00
59 Andrew Jackson 1.25 3.00
60 Zachary Taylor 1.25 3.00
61 George Eastman 1.25 3.00
62 Jefferson Davis 2.00 5.00
63 Sitting Bull 4.00 10.00
64 Clara Barton 1.25 3.00
65 Dorothea Dix 1.25 3.00
66 Booker T. Washington 1.25 3.00
67 Al Capone 4.00 10.00
68 Samuel F.B. Morse 1.25 3.00
69 Alexander Cartwright 1.25 3.00
70 John Marshall 1.25 3.00
71 William Seward 1.25 3.00
72 Andrew Johnson 1.25 3.00
73 Rutherford B. Hayes 1.25 3.00
74 James A. Garfield 1.25 3.00
75 Chester Arthur 1.25 3.00
76 Grover Cleveland 1.25 3.00
77 Benjamin Harrison 1.25 3.00
78 William McKinley 1.25 3.00
79 William H. Taft 1.25 3.00
80 Woodrow Wilson 1.25 3.00
81 Warren G. Harding 1.25 3.00
82 Calvin Coolidge 1.25 3.00
83 Herbert Hoover 1.25 3.00
84 Lyndon B. Johnson 1.25 3.00
85 Richard M. Nixon 1.25 3.00
86 Gerald Ford 1.25 3.00
87 Robert Johnson 1.25 3.00
88 Ronald Reagan 1.25 3.00
89 Chief Joseph 3.00 8.00
90 Butch Cassidy 2.00 5.00
91 Sundance Kid 2.00 5.00
92 Babe Ruth 5.00 12.00
93 Jackie Robinson 3.00 8.00
94 Frederick Winslow Taylor 1.25 3.00
95 Sojourner Truth 1.25 3.00
96 William Lloyd Garrison 1.25 3.00
97 Ira Hayes 1.25 3.00
98 Calamity Jane 1.25 3.00
99 Stonewall Jackson 2.00 5.00
100 Mary Harris Jones 1.25 3.00

2007 SP Legendary Cuts Legendary Cut Signatures

OVERALL CUT ODDS 1:96
PRINT RUNS B/WN 4-119 COPIES PER
NO PRICING ON QTY 25 OR LESS
AB Al Barlick/49 20.00 50.00
AH Happy Chandler/44 20.00 50.00
AR Allie Reynolds/40 60.00 120.00
BA Bob Allison/31 50.00 100.00
BD Bill Dickey/50 50.00 100.00
BG Burleigh Grimes/52 50.00 100.00
BH Babe Herman/99 20.00 50.00
BU Lew Burdette/50 30.00 60.00
BV Bill Veeck/47 200.00 300.00
CA Max Carey/40 50.00 100.00
CG Charlie Gehringer/50 40.00 80.00
CH Carl Hubbell/54 40.00 80.00
CR Joe Cronin/28 30.00 60.00
DI Joe DiMaggio/52 200.00 400.00
DU Leo Durocher/84 60.00 120.00
EA Earl Averill/62 40.00 80.00
EB Ewell Blackwell/50 20.00 50.00
EL Ed Lopat/66 20.00 50.00
EM Eddie Mathews/69 20.00 50.00
ER Edd Roush/50 30.00 60.00
ES Enos Slaughter/47 20.00 50.00
EW Early Wynn/40 20.00 50.00
FF Ford Frick/88 20.00 50.00
FL Freddy Lindstrom/45 100.00 250.00
GH Gabby Hartnett/50 60.00 150.00
GK George Kelly/95 40.00 80.00
GP George Pipgras/70 40.00 80.00
GR Lefty Grove/66 75.00 150.00
HG Hank Greenberg/59 75.00 200.00
HH Harvey Haddix/44 60.00 150.00
HU Catfish Hunter/26 40.00 80.00
JA Joe Adcock/49 40.00 80.00
JC Jocko Conlan/54 30.00 60.00
JD Joe Dugan/46 30.00 60.00
JO Judy Johnson/54 30.00 60.00
JS Joe Sewell/100 40.00 80.00
JV Johnny Vander Meer/49 40.00 80.00
LA Luke Appling/92 20.00 50.00
LD Larry Doby/50 50.00 100.00
MI Johnny Mize/133 30.00 60.00
PR Pee Wee Reese/39 75.00 150.00
RA Richie Ashburn/50 75.00 150.00
RD Ray Dandridge/50 40.00 80.00
RM Rube Marquard/52 50.00 100.00
RS Ray Schalk/44 125.00 250.00
SC Stan Coveleski/84 50.00 100.00
SW Warren Spahn/95 30.00 60.00
TJ Travis Jackson/88 40.00 80.00
VD Vince DiMaggio/34 100.00 175.00
WA Walter Alston/48 40.00 80.00
WH Waite Hoyt/79 20.00 50.00
WI Hoyt Wilhelm/60 20.00 50.00
WS Willie Stargell/71 40.00 80.00

2007 SP Legendary Cuts Legendary Materials

OVERALL AU-GU ODDS 1:12
PRINT RUN B/WN 189-199 COPIES PER
AD1 Andre Dawson/199 3.00 8.00
AD2 Andre Dawson/199 3.00 8.00
AK1 Al Kaline/189 4.00 10.00
AK2 Al Kaline/199 4.00 10.00
AO Al Oliver/199 3.00 8.00
BJ Bo Jackson/199 4.00 10.00
BL Barry Larkin/199 4.00 10.00
BR1 Brooks Robinson/199 4.00 10.00
BR2 Brooks Robinson/199 4.00 10.00
BS Bruce Sutter/199 3.00 8.00
BW Billy Williams/199 3.00 8.00
CA Roy Campanella/199 4.00 10.00
CF1 Carlton Fisk/199 3.00 8.00
CF2 Carlton Fisk/199 3.00 8.00
CR1 Cal Ripken Jr./199 8.00 20.00
CR2 Cal Ripken Jr./199 8.00 20.00
CY1 Carl Yastrzemski/199 4.00 10.00
CY2 Carl Yastrzemski/199 4.00 10.00
DD Don Drysdale/199 4.00 10.00
DE Dwight Evans/199 3.00 8.00
DM1 Don Mattingly/199 4.00 10.00
DM2 Don Mattingly/199 4.00 10.00
DP Dave Parker/199 3.00 8.00
DS Don Sutton/199 3.00 8.00
DW1 Dave Winfield/199 3.00 8.00
DW2 Dave Winfield/199 3.00 8.00
EC Dennis Eckersley/199 3.00 8.00
EM1 Eddie Murray/199 3.00 8.00
EM2 Eddie Murray/199 3.00 8.00
FJ Fergie Jenkins/199 3.00 8.00
FL1 Fred Lynn/199 3.00 8.00
FL2 Fred Lynn/199 3.00 8.00
FR Frank Robinson/199 3.00 8.00
GF George Foster/199 3.00 8.00
GG Goose Gossage/199 3.00 8.00
GP1 Gaylord Perry/199 3.00 8.00
GP2 Gaylord Perry/199 3.00 8.00
HB Harold Baines/199 3.00 8.00
HK1 Harmon Killebrew/199 4.00 10.00
HK2 Harmon Killebrew/199 4.00 10.00
HU Catfish Hunter/199 3.00 8.00
JB1 Johnny Bench/199 4.00 10.00
JB2 Johnny Bench/199 4.00 10.00
JM1 Jack Morris/199 3.00 8.00
JM2 Jack Morris/199 3.00 8.00
JP Jim Palmer/199 3.00 8.00
JR1 Jim Rice/199 3.00 8.00
JR2 Jim Rice/199 3.00 8.00
JT Joe Torre/199 4.00 10.00
KG Ken Griffey Sr./199 3.00 8.00
KG1 Kirk Gibson/199 3.00 8.00
KG2 Kirk Gibson/199 3.00 8.00
KP1 Kirby Puckett/199 10.00 25.00
KP2 Kirby Puckett/199 10.00 25.00
LA Luis Aparicio/199 3.00 8.00
LB1 Lou Brock/199 3.00 8.00
LB2 Lou Brock/199 3.00 8.00
MA Bill Madlock/199 3.00 8.00
MG Mark Grace/199 3.00 8.00
MS1 Mike Schmidt/199 5.00 12.00
MS2 Mike Schmidt/199 5.00 12.00
NR1 Nolan Ryan/199 8.00 20.00
NR2 Nolan Ryan/199 8.00 20.00
OS1 Ozzie Smith/199 5.00 12.00
OS2 Ozzie Smith/199 5.00 12.00
PM1 Paul Molitor/199 3.00 8.00
PM2 Paul Molitor/199 3.00 8.00
PN Phil Niekro/199 3.00 8.00
PO Paul O'Neill/199 3.00 8.00
PW Pee Wee Reese/199 5.00 12.00
RA Roberto Alomar/199 3.00 8.00
RC Roberto Clemente/199 20.00 50.00
RC1 Rod Carew/199 3.00 8.00
RC2 Rod Carew/199 3.00 8.00
RF Rollie Fingers/199 3.00 8.00
RG Ron Guidry/199 3.00 8.00
RJ1 Reggie Jackson/199 3.00 8.00
RJ2 Reggie Jackson/199 3.00 8.00
RM Roger Maris/199 10.00 25.00
RS Ryne Sandberg/199 5.00 12.00
RY1 Robin Yount/199 5.00 12.00
RY2 Robin Yount/199 5.00 12.00
SC Red Schoendienst/199 4.00 10.00
SC1 Steve Carlton/199 3.00 8.00
SC2 Steve Carlton/199 3.00 8.00
SG1 Steve Garvey/199 3.00 8.00
SG2 Steve Garvey/199 3.00 8.00
TG1 Tony Gwynn/199 4.00 10.00
TG2 Tony Gwynn/199 4.00 10.00
TO Tony Oliva/199 3.00 8.00
TP Tony Perez/199 3.00 8.00
WB1 Wade Boggs/199 3.00 8.00
WB2 Wade Boggs/199 3.00 8.00
WC1 Will Clark/199 3.00 8.00
WC2 Will Clark/199 3.00 8.00

2007 SP Legendary Cuts Legendary Materials Dual

*DUAL: .5X TO 1.2X BASIC
OVERALL AU-GU ODDS 1:12
PRINT RUN B/WN 63-125 COPIES PER
AK1 Al Kaline/125 8.00 20.00
AK2 Al Kaline/125 8.00 20.00
BJ Bo Jackson/125 8.00 20.00
CR1 Cal Ripken Jr./125 8.00 20.00
CR2 Cal Ripken Jr./125 8.00 20.00
EM Eddie Mathews/125 8.00 20.00
HK2 Harmon Killebrew/63 6.00 15.00
KP1 Kirby Puckett/125 10.00 25.00
KP2 Kirby Puckett/125 10.00 25.00

2007 SP Legendary Cuts Legendary Materials Triple

*TRIPLE: .6X TO 1.5X BASIC
OVERALL AU-GU ODDS 1:12
PRINT RUN B/WN 9-99 COPIES PER
NO PRICING ON QTY 25 OR LESS
AK1 Al Kaline/32 10.00 25.00
BJ Bo Jackson/99 10.00 25.00
CR1 Cal Ripken Jr./99 10.00 25.00
CR2 Cal Ripken Jr./99 10.00 25.00
KP1 Kirby Puckett/99 12.50 30.00
KP2 Kirby Puckett/99 12.50 30.00
RC Roberto Clemente/99 30.00 60.00

2007 SP Legendary Cuts Legendary Signatures

OVERALL AU-GU ODDS 1:12
PRINT RUN B/WN 15-199 COPIES PER
NO PRICING ON QTY 25 OR LESS
ASTERISK EQUALS PARTIAL EXCH
EXCH DEADLINE 8/22/2010
AD1 Andre Dawson/199 6.00 15.00
AD2 Andre Dawson/199 6.00 15.00
AK1 Al Kaline/199 12.00 30.00
AK2 Al Kaline/199 12.00 30.00
BF1 Bob Feller/199 12.50 30.00
BF2 Bob Feller/199 12.50 30.00
BF3 Bob Feller/189 12.50 30.00
BG1 Bob Gibson/50 10.00 25.00
BG2 Bob Gibson/50 10.00 25.00
BG3 Bob Gibson/40 10.00 25.00
BJ1 Bo Jackson/100 20.00 50.00
BJ2 Bo Jackson/100 20.00 50.00
BM1 Bill Mazeroski/189 10.00 25.00
BM2 Bill Mazeroski/199 10.00 25.00
BR1 Brooks Robinson/150 10.00 25.00
BR2 Brooks Robinson/140 10.00 25.00
BW1 Billy Williams/199 8.00 20.00
BW2 Billy Williams/189 8.00 20.00
CF1 Carlton Fisk/75 15.00 40.00
CF2 Carlton Fisk/75 15.00 40.00
CF3 Carlton Fisk/65 15.00 40.00
CR1 Cal Ripken Jr./99 30.00 60.00
CR2 Cal Ripken Jr./50 30.00 60.00
FJ1 Fergie Jenkins/125 5.00 12.00
FJ2 Fergie Jenkins/125 5.00 12.00
FJ3 Fergie Jenkins/125 5.00 12.00
FR1 Frank Robinson/50 12.50 30.00
FR2 Frank Robinson/50 12.50 30.00
FR3 Frank Robinson/40 12.50 30.00
GP1 Gaylord Perry/199 6.00 15.00
GP2 Gaylord Perry/199 6.00 15.00
HK1 Harmon Killebrew/100 15.00 40.00
HK2 Harmon Killebrew/90 15.00 40.00
JM1 Juan Marichal/199 8.00 20.00
JM2 Juan Marichal/199 8.00 20.00
JM3 Juan Marichal/189 8.00 20.00
JP1 Jim Palmer/199 8.00 20.00
JP2 Jim Palmer/199 8.00 20.00
JP3 Jim Palmer/199 8.00 20.00
JT Joe Torre/99 20.00 50.00
KG Kirk Gibson/199 8.00 20.00
LA1 Luis Aparicio/199 8.00 20.00
LA2 Luis Aparicio/186 8.00 20.00
MS1 Mike Schmidt/35 20.00 50.00
MS2 Mike Schmidt/35 20.00 50.00
OS1 Ozzie Smith/100 15.00 40.00
OS2 Ozzie Smith/100 15.00 40.00
OS3 Ozzie Smith/100 15.00 40.00
PM1 Paul Molitor/100 10.00 25.00
PM2 Paul Molitor/90 10.00 25.00
RC1 Rod Carew/35 20.00 50.00
RC2 Rod Carew/35 20.00 50.00
RY1 Robin Yount/35 30.00 60.00
RY2 Robin Yount/35 30.00 60.00
SC1 Steve Carlton/199 10.00 25.00
SC2 Steve Carlton/199 10.00 25.00
SC3 Steve Carlton/189 10.00 25.00
TP1 Tony Perez/199 6.00 15.00
TP2 Tony Perez/199 6.00 15.00
WB1 Wade Boggs/35 15.00 40.00
WB2 Wade Boggs/35 15.00 40.00
WB3 Wade Boggs/35 15.00 40.00
WC1 Will Clark/199 8.00 20.00
WC2 Will Clark/199 8.00 20.00

2007 SP Legendary Cuts Masterful Materials

OVERALL AU-GU ODDS 1:12
AD Andre Dawson 3.00 8.00
BJ Bo Jackson 4.00 10.00
BL Barry Larkin 3.00 8.00
BM Bill Madlock 3.00 8.00
BR Brooks Robinson 4.00 10.00
BS Bruce Sutter 3.00 8.00
CF Carlton Fisk 3.00 8.00
CR Cal Ripken Jr. 6.00 15.00
CY Carl Yastrzemski 4.00 10.00
DE Dwight Evans 3.00 8.00
DM Don Mattingly 4.00 10.00
DP Dave Parker 3.00 8.00
DS Don Sutton 3.00 8.00
DW Dave Winfield 3.00 8.00
EM Eddie Mathews 4.00 10.00
FL Fred Lynn 3.00 8.00
FR Frank Robinson 3.00 8.00
GP Gaylord Perry 3.00 8.00
JB Johnny Bench 4.00 10.00
JR Jim Rice 3.00 8.00
KG Ken Griffey Sr. 3.00 8.00
KP Kirby Puckett 6.00 15.00
MS Mike Schmidt 5.00 12.00
MU Eddie Murray 3.00 8.00
NR Nolan Ryan 6.00 15.00
PM Paul Molitor 3.00 8.00
RJ Reggie Jackson 4.00 10.00
RS Ryne Sandberg 4.00 10.00
RY Robin Yount 4.00 10.00
SC Steve Carlton 3.00 8.00
SG Steve Garvey 3.00 8.00
TG Tony Gwynn 4.00 10.00
WB Wade Boggs 3.00 8.00
WC Will Clark 3.00 8.00
WM Willie McCovey 4.00 10.00
YB Yogi Berra 6.00 15.00

2007 SP Legendary Cuts Quotation Cuts

OVERALL CUT ODDS 1:96
PRINT RUNS B/WN 1-109 COPIES PER
NO PRICING ON QTY 25 OR LESS
BL Bob Lemon/80 30.00 60.00
CH Carl Hubbell/65 30.00 60.00
CK Charlie Keller/45 50.00 100.00
CS Casey Stengel/36 200.00 300.00
HC Happy Chandler/44 30.00 60.00
HH Harvey Haddix/30 30.00 60.00
JM Joe McCarthy/109 50.00 100.00
LB Lou Boudreau/28 30.00 60.00
MI Johnny Mize/45 40.00 80.00
RA Richie Ashburn/48 75.00 150.00
RD Ray Dandridge/72 40.00 80.00
RM Rube Marquard/35 50.00 100.00
SC Stan Coveleski/71 30.00 60.00
WA Walter Alston/31 40.00 80.00
WI Hoyt Wilhelm/37 50.00 100.00
WS Warren Spahn/60 40.00 80.00

2007 SP Legendary Cuts Reel History Film Frame

STATED ODDS 1:576
ANNOUNCED PRINT RUNS LISTED
CARDS SERIAL #'d TO ONE
PRINT RUNS PROVIDED BY UD
BR Babe Ruth/785 * 40.00 100.00
LG Lou Gehrig/473 * 30.00 60.00

2007 SP Legendary Cuts When it Was a Game Memorabilia

OVERALL AU-GU ODDS 1:12
AT Alan Trammell 3.00 8.00
BF Bob Feller 3.00 8.00
BG Bob Gibson 3.00 8.00
BM Bill Mazeroski 4.00 10.00
BW Billy Williams 3.00 8.00
CF Carlton Fisk 3.00 8.00
CY Carl Yastrzemski 4.00 10.00
DE Dennis Eckersley 3.00 8.00
DM Don Mattingly 4.00 10.00
DW Dave Winfield 3.00 8.00
EM Eddie Murray 3.00 8.00
FJ Fergie Jenkins 3.00 8.00
FL Fred Lynn 3.00 8.00
FR Frank Robinson 3.00 8.00
GP Gaylord Perry 3.00 8.00
HK Harmon Killebrew 4.00 10.00
JP Jim Palmer 3.00 8.00
JR Jim Rice 3.00 8.00
KG Kirk Gibson 3.00 8.00
KP Kirby Puckett 6.00 15.00
LB Lou Brock 4.00 10.00
MS Mike Schmidt 5.00 12.00
NR Nolan Ryan 8.00 20.00
PM Paul Molitor 3.00 8.00
PW Pee Wee Reese 4.00 10.00
RF Rollie Fingers 3.00 8.00
RJ Reggie Jackson 4.00 10.00
RM Roger Maris 10.00 25.00
RS Red Schoendienst 3.00 8.00
TG Tony Gwynn 4.00 10.00

2008 SP Legendary Cuts

COMP.SET w/o SP's (100) 8.00 20.00
COMMON CARD (1-100) .20 .50
COMMON CARD (101-146) 2.00 5.00
COMMON CARD (147-200) 2.00 5.00
101-200 RANDOMLY INSERTED
101-200 PRINT RUN 550 SERIAL #'d SETS
1 Ken Griffey Jr. 1.00 2.50
2 Derek Jeter 1.25 3.00
3 Albert Pujols .60 1.50
4 Ichiro Suzuki .60 1.50
5 Ryan Braun .30 .75
6 Manny Ramirez .50 1.25
7 David Ortiz .50 1.25
8 Greg Maddux .60 1.50
9 Roger Clemens .60 1.50
10 Chase Utley .30 .75
11 Vladimir Guerrero .30 .75
12 Johan Santana .30 .75
13 Chipper Jones .50 1.25
14 Tom Glavine .30 .75
15 Ryan Howard .30 .75
16 Hunter Pence .30 .75
17 Prince Fielder .30 .75
18 Jeff Francoeur .30 .75
19 David Wright .30 .75
20 Carlos Beltran .30 .75
21 Carlos Lee .20 .50
22 Cole Hamels .40 1.00
23 Jered Weaver .30 .75
24 B.J. Upton .30 .75
25 Akinori Iwamura .20 .50
26 Daisuke Matsuzaka .30 .75
27 Curt Schilling .30 .75
28 Adam Dunn .30 .75
29 Jose Reyes .30 .75
30 Nomar Garciaparra .30 .75
31 Hideki Matsui .50 1.25
32 Matt Holliday .50 1.25
33 Jason Bay .30 .75
34 Grady Sizemore .30 .75
35 Travis Hafner .20 .50
36 Victor Martinez .30 .75
37 C.C. Sabathia .30 .75
38 Justin Morneau .30 .75
39 Torii Hunter .20 .50
40 Joe Mauer .40 1.00
41 Russell Martin .20 .50
42 Frank Thomas .50 1.25
43 Miguel Tejada .30 .75
44 Brian Roberts .20 .50
45 Justin Verlander .50 1.25
46 Gary Sheffield .20 .50
47 Magglio Ordonez .30 .75
48 Alex Rodriguez .60 1.50
49 Bobby Abreu .20 .50
50 Mark Teixeira .30 .75
51 Andruw Jones .20 .50
52 Derrek Lee .20 .50
53 Aramis Ramirez .20 .50
54 Carlos Zambrano .30 .75
55 Alfonso Soriano .30 .75
56 Omar Vizquel .30 .75
57 Lance Berkman .30 .75
58 Roy Oswalt .30 .75
59 Jake Peavy .20 .50
60 Chris R. Young .20 .50
61 Khalil Greene .20 .50
62 Troy Tulowitzki .50 1.25
63 Todd Helton .30 .75
64 Josh Beckett .20 .50
65 Miguel Cabrera .50 1.25
66 Hanley Ramirez .30 .75
67 Dan Uggla .20 .50
68 Scott Kazmir .30 .75
69 Delmon Young .30 .75
70 Erik Bedard .20 .50
71 Alex Gordon .30 .75
72 Felix Hernandez .30 .75
73 Kenji Johjima .20 .50
74 John Lackey .30 .75
75 Ryan Zimmerman .30 .75
76 Jeremy Bonderman .20 .50
77 Chien-Ming Wang .30 .75
78 Jim Thome .30 .75
79 Jimmy Rollins .30 .75
80 Mariano Rivera .60 1.50
81 Curtis Granderson .30 .75
82 Nick Markakis .40 1.00
83 Trevor Hoffman .30 .75
84 Barry Zito .30 .75
85 Yovani Gallardo .20 .50
86 Dan Haren .20 .50
87 Vernon Wells .20 .50
88 Ian Kennedy RC .50 1.25
89 Phil Hughes .20 .50
90 Brian McCann .30 .75
91 J.J. Hardy .20 .50
92 Roy Halladay .30 .75
93 Mike Piazza .50 1.25
94 Ivan Rodriguez .30 .75
95 Dontrelle Willis .20 .50
96 Brandon Webb .30 .75
97 Carl Crawford .30 .75
98 Tim Lincecum .30 .75
99 Jason Varitek .50 1.25
100 Freddy Sanchez .20 .50
101 Abraham Lincoln 4.00 10.00
102 Ulysses S. Grant 3.00 8.00
103 Andrew Johnson 2.00 5.00
104 George Washington 3.00 8.00
105 Thomas Jefferson 2.00 5.00
106 Andrew Jackson 3.00 8.00
107 James Madison 2.00 5.00
108 James Monroe 2.00 5.00
109 Benjamin Franklin 2.50 6.00
110 Alexander Graham Bell 2.00 5.00
111 Thomas Edison 2.00 5.00
112 Red Baron 2.00 5.00
113 Robert E. Lee 3.00 8.00
114 Mark Twain 2.00 5.00
115 Arthur Conan Doyle 2.00 5.00
116 Bram Stoker 2.00 5.00
117 Jules Verne 2.00 5.00
118 Billy the Kid 2.50 6.00
119 Harriet Beecher Stowe 2.00 5.00
120 Andrew Carnegie 2.00 5.00
121 Lewis Carroll 2.00 5.00
122 Cornelius Vanderbilt 2.00 5.00
123 Brigham Young 2.00 5.00
124 Charles Dickens 2.00 5.00
125 Vincent Van Gogh 2.00 5.00
126 Claude Monet 2.00 5.00
127 Jesse James 2.50 6.00
128 John D. Rockefeller 2.00 5.00
129 Harry Longabaugh 2.00 5.00
130 John F. Kennedy 4.00 10.00
131 Richard Nixon 2.50 6.00
132 Lyndon B. Johnson 2.50 6.00
133 Dwight D. Eisenhower 2.00 5.00
134 Franklin D. Roosevelt 2.00 5.00
135 Harry Truman 2.00 5.00
136 Ronald Reagan 4.00 10.00
137 Bill Clinton 2.50 6.00
138 George H.W. Bush 2.50 6.00
139 Jimmy Carter 2.50 6.00
140 Gerald Ford 2.50 6.00
141 Herbert Hoover 2.00 5.00
142 Calvin Coolidge 2.00 5.00
143 Warren G. Harding 2.00 5.00
144 Woodrow Wilson 2.00 5.00
145 William Taft 2.00 5.00
146 Theodore Roosevelt 2.50 6.00
147 Phil Niekro 3.00 8.00
148 Brooks Robinson 3.00 8.00
149 Cal Ripken Jr. 6.00 15.00
150 Eddie Murray 3.00 8.00
151 Jim Palmer 3.00 8.00
152 Abner Doubleday 2.00 5.00
153 Wade Boggs 3.00 8.00
154 Carl Yastrzemski 5.00 12.00
155 Bobby Doerr 3.00 8.00
156 Carlton Fisk 3.00 8.00
157 Pee Wee Reese 3.00 8.00
158 Ernie Banks 3.00 8.00
159 Fergie Jenkins 3.00 8.00
160 Billy Williams 3.00 8.00
161 Ryne Sandberg 4.00 10.00
162 Luis Aparicio 3.00 8.00
163 Joe Morgan 3.00 8.00
164 Johnny Bench 3.00 8.00
165 Tony Perez 3.00 8.00
166 Bob Feller 3.00 8.00
167 Larry Doby 3.00 8.00
168 Bob Lemon 3.00 8.00
169 Al Kaline 3.00 8.00
170 Warren Spahn 3.00 8.00
171 Robin Yount 3.00 8.00
172 Rollie Fingers 3.00 8.00
173 Harmon Killebrew 3.00 8.00
174 Rod Carew 3.00 8.00
175 Babe Ruth 5.00 12.00
176 Monte Irvin 3.00 8.00
177 Tom Seaver 3.00 8.00
178 Phil Rizzuto 3.00 8.00

179 Jack Chesbro 2.00 5.00
180 Catfish Hunter 3.00 8.00
181 Babe Ruth 5.00 12.00
182 Reggie Jackson 3.00 8.00
183 Dennis Eckersley 3.00 8.00
184 Steve Carlton 3.00 8.00
185 Ed Delahanty 2.00 5.00
186 Mike Schmidt 4.00 10.00
187 Jim Bunning 3.00 8.00
188 Robin Roberts 3.00 8.00
189 Willie Stargell 3.00 8.00
190 Bill Mazeroski 3.00 8.00
191 Ralph Kiner 3.00 8.00
192 Tony Gwynn 5.00 12.00
193 Juan Marichal 3.00 8.00
194 Willie McCovey 3.00 8.00
195 Orlando Cepeda 3.00 8.00
196 Stan Musial 4.00 10.00
197 Ozzie Smith 4.00 10.00
198 Bob Gibson 3.00 8.00
199 Bruce Sutter 3.00 8.00
200 Nolan Ryan 5.00 12.00

2008 SP Legendary Cuts Destination Stardom Memorabilia

RANDOM INSERTS IN PACKS
AG Alex Gordon 4.00 10.00
AI Akinori Iwamura 3.00 8.00
AM Andrew Miller 3.00 8.00
AR Alex Rios 3.00 8.00
BB Billy Butler 3.00 8.00
BM Brian McCann 3.00 8.00
BU B.J. Upton 3.00 8.00
CB Chad Billingsley 3.00 8.00
CD Chris Duncan 3.00 8.00
CG Curtis Granderson 3.00 8.00
CH Cole Hamels 3.00 8.00
DH Dan Haren 3.00 8.00
DM Daisuke Matsuzaka 5.00 12.00
DU Dan Uggla 3.00 8.00
DY Delmon Young 3.00 8.00
FH Felix Hernandez 3.00 8.00
FI Josh Fields 3.00 8.00
GA Garrett Atkins 3.00 8.00
GS Grady Sizemore 3.00 8.00
HA Corey Hart 3.00 8.00
HK Howie Kendrick 3.00 8.00
HP Hunter Pence 3.00 8.00
HR Hanley Ramirez 4.00 10.00
JF Jeff Francoeur 3.00 8.00
JH J.J. Hardy 3.00 8.00
JL James Loney 3.00 8.00
JM John Maine 3.00 8.00
JO Josh Hamilton 10.00 25.00
JP Jon Papelbon 4.00 10.00
JV Justin Verlander 3.00 8.00
JW Jered Weaver 3.00 8.00
KG Khalil Greene 3.00 8.00
LE Jon Lester 3.00 8.00
MH Matt Holliday 3.00 8.00
NM Nick Markakis 3.00 8.00
PF Prince Fielder 4.00 10.00
PH Phil Hughes 4.00 10.00
RB Ryan Braun 4.00 10.00
RG Ryan Garko 3.00 8.00
RH Rich Hill 3.00 8.00
RM Russell Martin 3.00 8.00
RZ Ryan Zimmerman 3.00 8.00
SD Stephen Drew 3.00 8.00
TB Travis Buck 3.00 8.00
TL Tim Lincecum 5.00 12.00
TT Troy Tulowitzki 3.00 8.00
YG Yovani Gallardo 3.00 8.00

2008 SP Legendary Cuts Destined for History Memorabilia

RANDOM INSERTS IN PACKS
AD Adam Dunn 3.00 8.00
AJ Andruw Jones 3.00 8.00
AP Albert Pujols 6.00 15.00
AP Andy Petitte 3.00 8.00
AR Alex Rodriguez 6.00 15.00
AS Alfonso Soriano 3.00 8.00
BW Brandon Webb 3.00 8.00
CB Carlos Beltran 3.00 8.00
CD Carlos Delgado 3.00 8.00
CJ Chipper Jones 4.00 10.00
CL Carlos Lee 3.00 8.00
CM Chien-Ming Wang 5.00 12.00
CS Curt Schilling 3.00 8.00
CZ Carlos Zambrano 3.00 8.00
DJ Derek Jeter 8.00 20.00
DL Derrek Lee 3.00 8.00
DO David Ortiz 4.00 10.00
DW Dontrelle Willis 3.00 8.00
FT Frank Thomas 4.00 10.00
GM Greg Maddux 4.00 10.00
GS Gary Sheffield 3.00 8.00
HA Travis Hafner 3.00 8.00
IR Ivan Rodriguez 3.00 8.00
JM Justin Morneau 3.00 8.00
JR Jimmy Rollins 3.00 8.00
JS John Smoltz 3.00 8.00
JT Jim Thome 3.00 8.00
MC Miguel Cabrera 3.00 8.00
MO Magglio Ordonez 3.00 8.00
MP Mike Piazza 4.00 10.00
MR Manny Ramirez 4.00 10.00
MT Mark Teixeira 3.00 8.00
MY Michael Young 3.00 8.00
OV Omar Vizquel 3.00 8.00
PM Pedro Martinez 3.00 8.00
RA Aramis Ramirez 3.00 8.00
RC Roger Clemens 4.00 10.00
RE Jose Reyes 3.00 8.00
RH Roy Halladay 3.00 8.00
RJ Randy Johnson 4.00 10.00
RO Roy Oswalt 3.00 8.00
SA Johan Santana 3.00 8.00
SS Sammy Sosa 3.00 8.00
TE Miguel Tejada 3.00 8.00
TG Tom Glavine 3.00 8.00
TH Todd Helton 3.00 8.00
TH Trevor Hoffman 3.00 8.00
VG Vladimir Guerrero 3.00 8.00

2008 SP Legendary Cuts Future Legends Signatures

RANDOM INSERTS IN PACKS
STATED PRINT RUN 99 SER.#'d SETS
BM Brian McCann 5.00 12.00
BU B.J. Upton 5.00 12.00
BW Brandon Wood 5.00 12.00
CB Clay Buchholz 10.00 25.00
CB Chad Billingsley 6.00 15.00
CD Chris Duncan 6.00 15.00
CH Chin-Lung Hu 15.00 40.00
CH Cole Hamels 8.00 20.00
CH Corey Hart 4.00 10.00
DB Daric Barton 5.00 12.00
DM Daisuke Matsuzaka 25.00 60.00
DU Dan Uggla 6.00 15.00
FC Fausto Carmona 5.00 12.00
FH Felix Hernandez 12.50 30.00
GA Garrett Atkins 5.00 12.00
HK Hong-Chih Kuo 6.00 15.00
HR Hanley Ramirez 10.00 25.00
IK Ian Kennedy 10.00 25.00
IK2 Ian Kinsler 6.00 15.00
JF Jeff Francis 5.00 12.00
JH Josh Hamilton 12.50 30.00
JL Jon Lester 12.00 30.00
JM John Maine 6.00 15.00
JP Jonathan Papelbon 10.00 25.00
KG Ken Griffey Jr. 40.00 80.00
KY Kevin Youkilis 10.00 25.00
LH Luke Hochevar 6.00 15.00
MC Matt Cain 20.00 50.00
MG Matt Garza 5.00 12.00
NM Nick Markakis 8.00 20.00
PH Phil Hughes 5.00 12.00
RH Rich Hill 5.00 12.00
TH Travis Hafner 6.00 15.00
YG Yovani Gallardo 6.00 15.00

2008 SP Legendary Cuts Generations Dual Autographs

RANDOM INSERTS IN PACKS
ASTERISK EQUALS PARTIAL EXCHANGE
NO PRICING ON SOME DUE TO SCARCITY
EXCHANGE DEADLINE 5/22/2010
AR Aparico/Hanley 20.00 50.00
BM Bench/Martin 20.00 50.00
CH S.Carlton/C,Hamels 60.00 120.00
GG Gwynn Sr./Gwynn Jr. 30.00 60.00
GM K.Griffey Jr./S.Musial 150.00 250.00
JJ Jeter/Reggie 150.00 400.00
MB W.McCovey/L.Berkman 12.00 30.00
MH P.Molitor/T.Hafner 8.00 20.00
PC Gaylord Perry/Fausto Carmona 12.00 30.00
PK Jim Palmer/Ian Kennedy 12.00 30.00
RC Brooks Robinson/Eric Chavez 12.00 30.00
YH Yount/Hart EXCH * 20.00 50.00

2008 SP Legendary Cuts Generations Dual Memorabilia

RANDOM INSERTS IN PACKS
AR Luis Aparicio / Hanley Ramirez 5.00 12.00
BC Lou Brock / Carl Crawford 4.00 10.00
BL E.Banks/D.Lee 8.00 20.00
BM Johnny Bench / Victor Martinez 5.00 12.00
BM Johnny Bench / Joe Mauer 6.00 15.00
BP Lance Berkman / Hunter Pence 4.00 10.00
BY Wade Boggs / Kevin Youkilis 5.00 12.00
CD C.Ripken/D.Jeter 15.00 40.00
CG R.Clemente/V.Guerrero 12.00 30.00
CH Roger Clemens / Philip Hughes 4.00 10.00
CK Rod Carew / Howie Kendrick 4.00 10.00
CM Will Clark / Justin Morneau 4.00 10.00
CP Orlando Cepeda / Albert Pujols 5.00 12.00
CS Steve Carlton / Johan Santana 4.00 10.00
DC Don Sutton / Chad Billingsley 4.00 10.00
DD D.Mattingly/D.Jeter 12.50 30.00
DJ J.DiMaggio/D.Jeter 50.00 100.00
DP B.Dickey/J.Posada 10.00 25.00
DS Andre Dawson / Alfonso Soriano 6.00 15.00
DT Don Mattingly / Todd Helton 4.00 10.00
EA E.Slaughter/A.Pujols 8.00 20.00
EC Eddie Murray / Chipper Jones 4.00 10.00
FF Frank Robinson / Frank Thomas 5.00 12.00
FP Carlton Fisk / Mike Piazza 4.00 10.00
FS Rollie Fingers / Huston Street 4.00 10.00
FV Carlton Fisk / Jason Varitek 4.00 10.00
GC B.Gibson/C.Carpenter 6.00 15.00
GF Tony Gwynn / Prince Fielder 5.00 12.00
GG Gaylord Perry / Greg Maddux 4.00 10.00
GH K.Griffey Jr./J.Hamilton 20.00 50.00
GL Tom Glavine/Jon Lester 4.00 10.00
GP Goose Gossage/Jon Papelbon 4.00 10.00
GR G.Gossage/M.Rivera 10.00 25.00
HH Catfish Hunter/Philip Hughes 5.00 12.00
HU R.Hornsby/C.Utley 12.00 30.00
JD Jim Rice/David Ortiz 5.00 12.00
JG F.Robinson/K.Griffey Jr. 8.00 20.00
JG R.Jackson/K.Griffey Jr. 20.00 50.00
JH Reggie Jackson/Travis Hafner 4.00 10.00
JJ R.Jackson/D.Jeter 10.00 25.00
KB R.Kiner/J.Bay 10.00 25.00
KD Ted Kluszewski/Adam Dunn 5.00 12.00
KH Harmon Killebrew/Travis Hafner 4.00 10.00
KK K.Griffey Sr./K.Griffey Jr. 12.50 30.00
KT Harmon Killebrew/Frank Thomas 5.00 12.00
LM Fred Lynn/Nick Markakis 4.00 10.00
MA Mike Schmidt/Albert Pujols 8.00 20.00
MB P.Molitor/R.Braun 8.00 20.00
MJ R.Maris/D.Jeter 15.00 40.00
MM Juan Marichal/Pedro Martinez 4.00 10.00
MS Mazeroski/Sandberg 8.00 20.00
NW Phil Niekro/Tim Wakefield 4.00 10.00
OJ Ozzie Smith/Jose Reyes 5.00 12.00
PB Jim Palmer/Erik Bedard 4.00 10.00
PH Gaylord Perry/Roy Halladay 4.00 10.00
PL Gaylord Perry/Tim Lincecum 5.00 12.00
PM Mike Piazza/Russell Martin 4.00 10.00
PO Dave Parker/David Ortiz 5.00 12.00
PY Gaylord Perry/Chris Young 4.00 10.00
RC Nolan Ryan/Roger Clemens 8.00 20.00
RD Ryne Sandberg/Dan Uggla 4.00 10.00
RJ P.Rizzuto/D.Jeter 12.50 30.00
RM C.Ripken/N.Markakis 8.00 20.00
RM B.Ruth/R.Maris 100.00 200.00
RO Nolan Ryan/Roy Oswalt 8.00 20.00
RR Randy Johnson/Rich Hill 4.00 10.00
RT Cal Ripken/Troy Tulowitzki 6.00 15.00
RV N.Ryan/J.Verlander 12.00 30.00
RW Nolan Ryan/Jered Weaver 5.00 12.00
SA S.Musial/A.Pujols 15.00 40.00
SB M.Schmidt/R.Braun 8.00 20.00
SC Steve Carlton/Cole Hamels 5.00 12.00
SG Ben Sheets/Yovani Gallardo 4.00 10.00
SJ Mike Schmidt/Chipper Jones 5.00 12.00
SL John Smoltz/Tim Lincecum 5.00 12.00
SM Tom Seaver/John Maine 5.00 12.00
SP Tom Seaver/Jake Peavy 4.00 10.00
SR Ron Santo/Aramis Ramirez 6.00 15.00
SU Ryne Sandberg/Chase Utley 6.00 15.00
SY Gary Sheffield/Delmon Young 4.00 10.00
SZ Mike Schmidt/Ryan Zimmerman 5.00 12.00
TM Todd Helton/Matt Holliday 5.00 12.00
TR Cal Ripken/Miguel Tejada 5.00 12.00
YH Robin Yount/J.J. Hardy 5.00 12.00
YJ R.Yount/D.Jeter 8.00 20.00
YO Carl Yastrzemski/David Ortiz 6.00 15.00

2008 SP Legendary Cuts Headliners and Heroes Cut Signatures

RANDOM INSERTS IN PACKS
NO PRICING ON MOST DUE TO SCARCITY
AB Al Barlick/32 20.00 50.00
AL Al Lopez/45 20.00 50.00
BC Ben Chapman/28 100.00 200.00
BH Babe Herman/44 20.00 50.00
BH Billy Herman/76 20.00 50.00
BL1 Buck Leonard/68 20.00 50.00
BL2 Buck Leonard/58 20.00 50.00
BL3 Bob Lemon/39 20.00 50.00
BT Bill Terry/94 20.00 50.00
CG Charlie Gehringer/40 20.00 50.00
EL Ed Lopat/46 20.00 50.00
ER Edd Roush/122 20.00 50.00
ES Enos Slaughter/36 20.00 50.00
EW Eugene Woodling/72 20.00 50.00
GK George Kelly/77 30.00 60.00
HC Happy Chandler/75 20.00 50.00
HH Harry Hooper/34 75.00 150.00
JH Jesse Haines/37 50.00 100.00
JJ Judy Johnson/38 40.00 80.00
JM Johnny Mize/41 20.00 50.00
JS Joe Sewell/59 20.00 50.00
JS Johnny Sain/50 20.00 50.00
LA Luke Appling/45 30.00 60.00
LB Lou Boudreau/52 30.00 60.00
MC Max Carey/31 50.00 100.00
PR Pee Wee Reese/52 50.00 100.00
RC Roy Campanella/37 300.00 600.00
RD Ray Dandridge/38 20.00 50.00
SH Stan Hack/10 60.00 120.00
TJ Travis Jackson/39 20.00 50.00
TL Ted Lyons/34 20.00 50.00

2008 SP Legendary Cuts Legendary Cut Signatures

RANDOM INSERTS IN PACKS
NO PRICING ON MOST DUE TO SCARCITY
AB Al Barlick/52 30.00 60.00
BH Babe Herman/30 40.00 80.00
BH Billy Herman/79 20.00 50.00
BL Buck Leonard/62 30.00 60.00
BL Bob Lemon/40 20.00 50.00
CF Curt Flood/26 175.00 300.00
CG Charlie Gehringer/45 20.00 50.00
CH Carl Hubbell/31 40.00 80.00
CK Charlie Keller/34 30.00 60.00
EA Earl Averill/44 30.00 60.00
HC Happy Chandler/55 20.00 50.00
HC Happy Chandler/60 20.00 50.00
HN Hal Newhouser/52 20.00 50.00
HU Catfish Hunter/37 20.00 50.00
HW Hoyt Wilhelm/32 20.00 50.00
JC Jocko Conlan/40 20.00 50.00
JH Jesse Haines/40 40.00 80.00
JJ Judy Johnson/29 20.00 50.00
JM Johnny Mize/41 20.00 50.00
JM Joe McCarthy/27 40.00 80.00
JS Joe Sewell/46 20.00 50.00
LA Luke Appling/32 20.00 50.00
LB Lou Boudreau/54 20.00 50.00
LB Lou Boudreau/50 20.00 50.00
LW Lloyd Waner/60 20.00 50.00
RC Roy Campanella/26 200.00 400.00
RF Rick Ferrell/108 20.00 50.00
SB Smoky Burgess/28 30.00 60.00
SC Stan Coveleski/45 30.00 60.00
TL Ted Lyons/32 40.00 80.00
WS Warren Spahn/39 40.00 80.00

2008 SP Legendary Cuts Legendary Memorabilia 99

RANDOM INSERTS IN PACKS
STATED PRINT RUN 99 SER.#'d SETS
AD Andre Dawson 4.00 10.00
BF Bob Feller 6.00 15.00
BR Brooks Robinson 4.00 10.00
BS Bruce Sutter 3.00 8.00
BW Billy Williams 4.00 10.00
CA Rod Carew 3.00 8.00
CF2 Carlton Fisk 4.00 10.00
CR Cal Ripken Jr. 8.00 20.00
CY Carl Yastrzemski 6.00 15.00
DM Don Mattingly 5.00 12.00
DP2 Dave Parker 3.00 8.00
DP2 Dave Parker 3.00 8.00
DS Don Sutton 3.00 8.00
DW Dave Winfield 3.00 8.00
EB Ernie Banks 5.00 12.00
EH Elston Howard 3.00 8.00
EM Eddie Murray 3.00 8.00
EW Early Wynn 3.00 8.00
FJ Fergie Jenkins 3.00 8.00
FL Fred Lynn 3.00 8.00
FR Frank Robinson 3.00 8.00
GG Goose Gossage 3.00 8.00
GP Gaylord Perry 3.00 8.00
HK Harmon Killebrew 10.00 25.00
JB Johnny Bench 3.00 8.00
JB2 Jim Bunning 3.00 8.00
JC Joe Carter 4.00 10.00
JM Juan Marichal 3.00 8.00
JM Joe Morgan 3.00 8.00
JT Joe Torre 4.00 10.00
LA Luis Aparicio 3.00 8.00
LE Bob Lemon 3.00 8.00
MA Edgar Martinez 4.00 10.00
MG Mark Grace 3.00 8.00
MS Mike Schmidt 4.00 10.00
NR Nolan Ryan 6.00 15.00
OS Ozzie Smith 4.00 10.00
OS2 Ozzie Smith 4.00 10.00
PM2 Paul Molitor 4.00 10.00
PN Phil Niekro 3.00 8.00
PO Paul O'Neill 3.00 8.00
RC Roberto Clemente 25.00 60.00
RF Rollie Fingers 3.00 8.00
RG Ron Guidry 4.00 10.00
RI Jim Rice 3.00 8.00
RJ Reggie Jackson 5.00 12.00
RM Roger Maris 12.50 30.00
RS Red Schoendienst 3.00 8.00
RS Ryne Sandberg 5.00 12.00
RY Robin Yount 4.00 10.00
SA Ron Santo 5.00 12.00
SM Stan Musial 6.00 15.00
ST Steve Carlton 3.00 8.00
TG2 Tony Gwynn 4.00 10.00
TP Tony Perez 3.00 8.00
TR Tim Raines 3.00 8.00
TS Tom Seaver 3.00 8.00
WB Wade Boggs 3.00 8.00
WB2 Wade Boggs 3.00 8.00
WC Will Clark 4.00 10.00
WF Whitey Ford 5.00 12.00

2008 SP Legendary Cuts Legendary Memorabilia 75

*MEM 75: .4X TO 1X MEM 99
RANDOM INSERTS IN PACKS
STATED PRINT RUN 75 SER.#'d SETS
BJ Bo Jackson 4.00 10.00
OC Orlando Cepeda 3.00 8.00

2008 SP Legendary Cuts Legendary Memorabilia 50

*MEM 50: .4X TO 1X MEM 99
RANDOM INSERTS IN PACKS
STATED PRINT RUN 50 SER.#'d SETS
BD Bill Dickey 5.00 12.00
BJ Bo Jackson 6.00 15.00
BM Bill Mazeroski 5.00 12.00
FM Fred McGriff 4.00 10.00
JD Joe DiMaggio 20.00 50.00
OC Orlando Cepeda 3.00 8.00

2008 SP Legendary Cuts Legendary Memorabilia 35

*MEM 35: .6X TO 1.5X MEM 99
RANDOM INSERTS IN PACKS
STATED PRINT RUN 35 SER.#'d SETS

2008 SP Legendary Cuts Mystery Cut Signatures

EXCHANGE DEADLINE 12/31/2010
AC Art Carney/27 20.00 50.00
CH Charlton Heston/31 75.00 150.00
EA2 Eddie Arcaro/136 20.00 50.00
EH J.Edgar Hoover/36 125.00 250.00
GF1 Gerald Ford/35 100.00 200.00
JG2 Sir John Gielgud/55 20.00 50.00
JH Jack Haley/34 50.00 100.00
KH Kim Hunter/31 20.00 40.00
LB1 Lucille Ball/51 125.00 250.00
MS1 Max Schmelling/30 60.00 120.00
VP Vincent Price/37 50.00 100.00
NNO Mystery EXCH 250.00 350.00

2009 SP Legendary Cuts

COMP.SET w/o SP's (100) 10.00 25.00
COMMON CARD (1-100) .15 .40
COMMON CARD (101-147) 2.00 5.00
COMMON CARD (148-200) 2.00 5.00
101-200 APPX.ODDS ONE PER BOX
101-200 PRINT RUN 550 SERIAL #'d SETS
1 Brian Roberts .15 .40
2 Derek Jeter 1.00 2.50
3 Evan Longoria .25 .60
4 Brandon Phillips .15 .40
5 David Wright .30 .75
6 Ryan Howard .30 .75
7 Jose Reyes .25 .60
8 Ryan Braun .25 .60
9 Jim Thome .25 .60
10 Chipper Jones .40 1.00
11 Jimmy Rollins .25 .60
12 Alfonso Soriano .25 .60
13 Alex Rodriguez .50 1.25
14 David Price RC .60 1.50
15 Carlos Beltran .25 .60
16 Aramis Ramirez .15 .40
17 Ken Griffey Jr. .75 2.00
18 Daisuke Matsuzaka .25 .60
19 Josh Beckett .15 .40
20 Kevin Youkilis .15 .40
21 Carlos Delgado .15 .40
22 Clayton Kershaw .60 1.50
23 Adrian Gonzalez .30 .75
24 Grady Sizemore .25 .60
25 Mark Teixeira .25 .60
26 Chase Utley .25 .60
27 Vladimir Guerrero .25 .60
28 Prince Fielder .25 .60
29 Jeff Samardzija .25 .60
30 Magglio Ordonez .25 .60
31 Cliff Lee .25 .60
32 Josh Hamilton .25 .60
33 Justin Morneau .25 .60
34 David Ortiz .40 1.00
35 Cole Hamels .30 .75
36 Edinson Volquez .15 .40
37 Nick Markakis .30 .75
38 Carlos Zambrano .25 .60
39 Max Scherzer .40 1.00
40 Rich Harden .15 .40
41 Ryan Doumit .15 .40
42 Mariano Rivera .50 1.25
43 Alexei Ramirez .25 .60
44 Jake Peavy .15 .40
45 Trevor Hoffman .25 .60
46 Ryan Dempster .15 .40
47 Francisco Liriano .15 .40
48 Travis Hafner .15 .40
49 Joakim Soria .15 .40
50 Albert Pujols .50 1.25
51 Ichiro Suzuki .50 1.25
52 CC Sabathia .25 .60
53 Ryan Ludwick .25 .60
54 Mike Lowell .15 .40
55 Tim Lincecum .25 .60
56 Francisco Rodriguez .25 .60
57 Johan Santana .25 .60
58 Jonathan Papelbon .25 .60
59 Geovany Soto .25 .60
60 Jacoby Ellsbury .30 .75
61 Jon Lester .25 .60
62 Joba Chamberlain .15 .40
63 Rick Ankiel .15 .40
64 Chad Billingsley .25 .60
65 Chien-Ming Wang .25 .60
66 Stephen Drew .15 .40
67 Roy Halladay .25 .60
68 Ian Kinsler .25 .60
69 Scott Kazmir .15 .40
70 Miguel Tejada .25 .60
71 Carlos Lee .15 .40
72 Hanley Ramirez .25 .60
73 Carlos Pena .25 .60
74 Alex Gordon .25 .60
75 Pat Burrell .15 .40
76 Dan Uggla .15 .40
77 Joe Mauer .30 .75
78 Felix Hernandez .25 .60
79 Jermaine Dye .15 .40
80 Carlos Quentin .15 .40
81 Lance Berkman .25 .60
82 Randy Johnson .40 1.00
83 Matt Holliday .40 1.00
84 Curtis Granderson .30 .75
85 Miguel Cabrera .40 1.00
86 Matt Cain .25 .60
87 Troy Tulowitzki .40 1.00
88 Brian McCann .25 .60
89 Adam Dunn .25 .60
90 Matt Kemp .30 .75
91 B.J. Upton .25 .60
92 A.J. Burnett .15 .40
93 Carl Crawford .25 .60
94 Nate McLouth .15 .40
95 Derrek Lee .15 .40
96 Dustin Pedroia .40 1.00
97 Russell Martin .15 .40
98 John Lackey .25 .60
99 Manny Ramirez .40 1.00
100 Jay Bruce .25 .60
101 Ozzie Smith 4.00 10.00
102 Luis Aparicio 3.00 8.00
103 Johnny Bench 3.00 8.00
104 Yogi Berra 3.00 8.00
105 Lou Brock 2.50 6.00
106 Rod Carew 2.50 6.00
107 Whitey Ford 2.50 6.00
108 Dennis Eckersley 3.00 8.00
109 Bob Feller 3.00 8.00
110 Rollie Fingers 3.00 8.00
111 Carlton Fisk 2.50 6.00
112 Bob Gibson 2.50 6.00
113 Catfish Hunter 2.00 5.00
114 Reggie Jackson 2.50 6.00
115 Fergie Jenkins 3.00 8.00
116 Al Kaline 3.00 8.00
117 Harmon Killebrew 3.00 8.00
118 Ralph Kiner 2.50 6.00
119 Juan Marichal 3.00 8.00
120 Vince Coleman 2.00 5.00
121 Bill Mazeroski 2.50 6.00
122 Don Newcombe 2.00 5.00
123 Joe Morgan 3.00 8.00
124 Eddie Murray 3.00 8.00
125 Phil Niekro 3.00 8.00
126 Mike Schmidt 4.00 10.00
127 John Kruk 2.00 5.00
128 Steve Carlton 3.00 8.00
129 Brooks Robinson 2.50 6.00
130 Nolan Ryan 6.00 15.00
131 Dave Winfield 3.00 8.00
132 Bo Jackson 3.00 8.00
133 Paul Molitor 3.00 8.00
134 Billy Williams 3.00 8.00
135 Robin Yount 3.00 8.00
136 Don Mattingly 5.00 12.00
137 Cal Ripken Jr. 6.00 15.00
138 Bobby Doerr 3.00 8.00
139 Goose Gossage 3.00 8.00
140 Wade Boggs 2.50 6.00
141 Jim Palmer 3.00 8.00
142 Carl Yastrzemski 4.00 10.00
143 Frank Robinson 2.50 6.00
144 Joe Carter 2.00 5.00
145 Oil Can Boyd 2.00 5.00
146 Tony Perez 3.00 8.00
147 Gaylord Perry 3.00 8.00
148 Jules Verne 2.00 5.00
149 James K. Polk 2.00 5.00
150 William Henry Harrison 2.00 5.00
151 Manfred von Richthofen 2.00 5.00
152 William Jennings Bryan 2.00 5.00
153 Susan B. Anthony 2.00 5.00
154 Gentleman Jim Corbett 3.00 8.00
155 Cornelius Vanderbilt 2.00 5.00
156 John L. Sullivan 3.00 8.00
157 Daniel Boone 2.00 5.00
158 Davy Crockett 3.00 8.00
159 Edgar Allen Poe 2.00 5.00
160 George Custer 2.00 5.00
161 Harriet Tubman 2.00 5.00
162 Adolphus Busch 2.00 5.00
163 Bonnie Parker 2.00 5.00
164 Clyde Barrow 2.00 5.00
165 Winston Churchill 2.00 5.00
166 Sir Isaac Newton 2.00 5.00
167 Christopher Columbus 2.00 5.00
168 Doc Holliday 2.00 5.00
169 Wyatt Earp 2.00 5.00
170 Sam Houston 2.00 5.00
171 Francis Scott Key 2.00 5.00
172 Betsy Ross 2.00 5.00
173 John Hancock 2.00 5.00
174 Vincent Van Gogh 2.00 5.00
175 Charles Dickens 2.00 5.00
176 Pope John Paul II 3.00 8.00
177 Woodrow Wilson 2.00 5.00
178 James A. Garfield 2.00 5.00
179 Robert E. Lee 3.00 8.00
180 Julius Caesar 2.00 5.00
181 Napoleon Bonaparte 2.00 5.00
182 Alexander Hamilton 2.00 5.00
183 Frederick Douglass 2.00 5.00
184 Booker T. Washington 2.00 5.00
185 Paul Revere 2.00 5.00
186 Grover Cleveland 2.00 5.00
187 Andrew Johnson 2.00 5.00
188 Billy the Kid 2.00 5.00
189 Samuel Adams 2.00 5.00
190 Dwight D. Eisenhower 2.00 5.00
191 Theodore Roosevelt 2.00 5.00
192 Ulysses S. Grant 2.00 5.00
193 George Washington 4.00 10.00
194 John D. Rockefeller 2.00 5.00
195 Martin Van Buren 2.00 5.00
196 John Adams 2.00 5.00
197 Andrew Jackson 2.00 5.00
198 Jesse James 3.00 8.00
199 Thomas Jefferson 2.00 5.00
200 Abraham Lincoln 4.00 10.00

2009 SP Legendary Cuts Destination Stardom Memorabilia

OVERALL MEM ODDS 1:3
BP Brandon Phillips 3.00 8.00
BS Ben Sheets 3.00 8.00
BU B.J. Upton 3.00 8.00
BW Brandon Webb 4.00 10.00
CB Carlos Beltran 3.00 8.00
CU Chase Utley 4.00 10.00
CZ Carlos Zambrano 3.00 8.00
DL Derrek Lee 3.00 8.00
DS Denard Span 3.00 8.00
EV Edinson Volquez 3.00 8.00
FH Felix Hernandez 3.00 8.00
FL Francisco Liriano 3.00 8.00
GS Grady Sizemore 3.00 8.00
JB Josh Beckett 4.00 10.00
JC Joba Chamberlain 4.00 10.00
JE Jacoby Ellsbury 5.00 12.00
JH Josh Hamilton 5.00 12.00
JM Joe Mauer 4.00 10.00
JP Jonathan Papelbon 3.00 8.00
JV Justin Verlander 3.00 8.00
MH Matt Holliday 3.00 8.00
MO Justin Morneau 3.00 8.00
MT Mark Teixeira 3.00 8.00
PE Jake Peavy 3.00 8.00
PF Prince Fielder 3.00 8.00
RC Robinson Cano 3.00 8.00
RM Russell Martin 3.00 8.00
SK Scott Kazmir 3.00 8.00

2009 SP Legendary Cuts Destined for History Memorabilia

OVERALL MEM ODDS 1:3
AP Albert Pujols 6.00 15.00
AR Aramis Ramirez 3.00 8.00
AS Alfonso Soriano 3.00 8.00
CD Carlos Delgado 3.00 8.00
CH Cole Hamels 4.00 10.00
CJ Chipper Jones 4.00 10.00
CS Curt Schilling 3.00 8.00
DJ Derek Jeter 10.00 25.00
DO David Ortiz 4.00 10.00
FT Frank Thomas 5.00 12.00
GS Gary Sheffield 3.00 8.00
HE Todd Helton 3.00 8.00
JG Jason Giambi 3.00 8.00
JP Jorge Posada 3.00 8.00
JS John Smoltz 3.00 8.00
JT Jim Thome 3.00 8.00
JV Jason Varitek 3.00 8.00
KG Ken Griffey Jr. 6.00 15.00
LB Lance Berkman 3.00 8.00
MO Magglio Ordonez 3.00 8.00
MR Mariano Rivera 6.00 15.00
PE Andy Pettitte 3.00 8.00
PM Pedro Martinez 3.00 8.00
RA Manny Ramirez 3.00 8.00
RH Roy Halladay 4.00 10.00
RJ Randy Johnson 4.00 10.00
RO Roy Oswalt 3.00 8.00
TG Tom Glavine 3.00 8.00
TH Trevor Hoffman 3.00 8.00
VG Vladimir Guerrero 3.00 8.00

2009 SP Legendary Cuts Future Legends Signatures

RANDOM INSERTS IN PACKS
PRINT RUNS B/WN 10-125 COPIES PER
NO PRICING ON QTY 25 OR LESS
AG Adrian Gonzalez/125 6.00 15.00
BM Brian McCann/125 10.00 25.00
BP Brandon Phillips/125 10.00 25.00
BU B.J. Upton/125 6.00 15.00
BZ Clay Buchholz/125 8.00 20.00
CG Carlos Gonzalez/125 12.00 30.00
CL Carlos Lee/125 4.00 10.00
CY Chris B. Young/34 4.00 10.00
DJ Derek Jeter/45 150.00 250.00
DP Dustin Pedroia/125 10.00 25.00
EE Edwin Encarnacion/125 4.00 10.00
FH Felix Hernandez/125 15.00 40.00
IK Ian Kennedy/125 4.00 10.00
JC Johnny Cueto/125 6.00 15.00
JF Jeff Francoeur/125 6.00 15.00
JL John Lackey/125 6.00 15.00
JN Joe Nathan/125 4.00 10.00
JP Jonathan Papelbon/125 10.00 25.00
JW Josh Willingham/125 6.00 15.00
KG Ken Griffey Jr./125 40.00 80.00
MK Matt Kemp/125 15.00 40.00
MU David Murphy/125 4.00 10.00
RZ Ryan Zimmerman/125 6.00 15.00
TT Troy Tulowitzki/125 12.00 30.00
VM Victor Martinez/125 10.00 25.00
YG Yovani Gallardo/125 8.00 20.00

2009 SP Legendary Cuts Generations Dual Memorabilia

OVERALL MEM ODDS 1:3
GM1B J.Giambi/D.Mattingly 6.00 15.00
GMAV Jason Varitek/Luis Aparicio 4.00 10.00
GMBC C.Beltran/R.Clemente 15.00 40.00
GMBJ D.Jeter/E.Banks 8.00 20.00
GMBL E.Longoria/W.Boggs 6.00 15.00
GMBO David Ortiz/Wade Boggs 8.00 20.00
GMBP P.Martinez/B.Gibson 6.00 15.00
GMBR E.Banks/H.Ramirez 6.00 15.00
GMBS Brooks Robinson/Scott Rolen 4.00 10.00
GMBY R.Braun/R.Yount 8.00 20.00
GMCG R.Clemente/V.Guerrero 10.00 25.00
GMCH Cole Hamels/Steve Carlton 5.00 12.00
GMCM C.Ripken/M.Tejada 10.00 25.00
GMCP Steve Carlton/Andy Pettitte 4.00 10.00
GMDB J.DiMaggio/C.Beltran 20.00 50.00
GMDD D.Matsuzaka/D.Sutton 8.00 20.00
GMDJ D.Jeter/B.Dent 12.50 30.00
GMDM Eddie Murray/Carlos Delgado 4.00 10.00
GMDS J.DiMaggio/G.Sizemore 20.00 50.00
GMEA Ernie Banks/Aramis Ramirez 5.00 12.00
GMED Derrek Lee/Ernie Banks 4.00 10.00
GMEH Trevor Hoffman/Dennis Eckersley 4.00 10.00
GMEJ Edgar Martinez/Jason Bay 4.00 10.00
GMEP Jonathan Papelbon / Dennis Eckersley 4.00 10.00
GMES Dennis Eckersley/Huston Street 4.00 10.00
GMFM Carlton Fisk/Joe Mauer 4.00 10.00
GMFP Jorge Posada/Carlton Fisk 4.00 10.00
GMFV Carlton Fisk/Jason Varitek 4.00 10.00
GMGG Tony Gwynn/Brian Giles 4.00 10.00
GMGJ Goose Gossage / Jonathan Papelbon 4.00 10.00
GMGM Jason Giambi/Tino Martinez 4.00 10.00
GMGP J.Peavy/B.Gibson 6.00 15.00
GMGR Mariano Rivera/Goose Gossage 5.00 12.00
GMGY Yastrzemski/K.Griffey Jr. 10.00 25.00
GMHG Todd Helton/Mark Grace 5.00 12.00
GMHJ Josh Hamilton/Reggie Jackson 5.00 12.00
GMHY Robin Yount/J.J. Hardy 5.00 12.00
GMJB Brian McCann/Johnny Bench 4.00 10.00
GMJH J.Hamilton/B.Jackson 6.00 15.00
GMJJ R.Jackson/D.Jeter 10.00 25.00
GMJO David Ortiz/Reggie Jackson 5.00 12.00
GMJP B.Jackson/A.Pujols 8.00 20.00
GMJR N.Ryan/R.Johnson 12.50 30.00
GMJS Mike Schmidt/Chipper Jones 5.00 12.00
GMJV Johnny Bench/Victor Martinez 4.00 10.00
GMLA Don Sutton/Chad Billingsley 4.00 10.00
GMLG Mark Grace/Derrek Lee 5.00 12.00
GMLH Phil Hughes/Sparky Lyle 4.00 10.00
GMLR Sparky Lyle/Mariano Rivera 4.00 10.00
GMMB Paul Molitor/Ryan Braun 5.00 12.00
GMMH Matt Holliday/Edgar Martinez 4.00 10.00
GMMJ D.Mattingly/D.Jeter 12.50 30.00
GMMK Joe Morgan/Ian Kinsler 4.00 10.00
GMMM Justin Morneau/Paul Molitor 4.00 10.00
GMMP Jake Peavy/Jack Morris 4.00 10.00
GMMR B.Robinson/M.Mora 8.00 20.00
GMMT Eddie Murray/Mark Teixeira 5.00 12.00
GMMU Chase Utley/Joe Morgan 4.00 10.00
GMMV Jack Morris/Justin Verlander 4.00 10.00
GMNC Graig Nettles/Robinson Cano 4.00 10.00
GMNY J.DiMaggio/D.Jeter 40.00 80.00
GMPB Josh Beckett/Jake Peavy 5.00 12.00
GMPF Dave Parker/Prince Fielder 4.00 10.00
GMPG K.Puckett/K.Griffey Jr. 12.00 30.00
GMPL Gaylord Perry/John Lackey 4.00 10.00
GMPM Tino Martinez/Jorge Posada 10.00 25.00
GMPP Gaylord Perry/Jake Peavy 4.00 10.00
GMPV Jason Varitek/Tony Perez 4.00 10.00
GMRA A.Ramirez/R.Santo 10.00 25.00
GMRB Ivan Rodriguez/Johnny Bench 4.00 10.00
GMRK N.Ryan/S.Kazmir 8.00 20.00
GMRL E.Longoria/B.Robinson 10.00 25.00
GMRN Graig Nettles/Aramis Ramirez 4.00 10.00
GMRO R.Oswalt/N.Ryan 8.00 20.00
GMRR C.Ripken/Hanley 6.00 15.00
GMRT C.Ripken/Troy Tulo 1.00 25.00
GMSA A.Pujols/S.Musial 12.50 30.00
GMSB P.Burrell/M.Schmidt 6.00 15.00
GMSD Jake Peavy/Tony Gwynn 4.00 10.00
GMSG K.Greene/O.Smith 8.00 20.00
GMSJ O.Smith/D.Jeter 8.00 20.00
GMSL M.Schmidt/E.Longoria 10.00 25.00
GMSP O.Smith/A.Pujols 12.50 30.00
GMSR Mike Schmidt/Aramis Ramirez 5.00 12.00
GMSS D.Jeter/C.Ripken 15.00 40.00
GMST Tom Glavine/Steve Carlton 4.00 10.00
GMSW D.Sutton/B.Webb 4.00 10.00
GMTA Adrian Gonzalez/Tino Martinez 4.00 10.00
GMTB Tom Glavine/Chad Billingsley 4.00 10.00
GMTC Carlos Beltran/Tony Perez 4.00 10.00
GMTJ Jose Reyes/Tim Raines 4.00 10.00
GMTX N.Ryan/J.Beckett 10.00 25.00
GMWK Wade Boggs/Kevin Youkilis 5.00 12.00
GMWM Wade Boggs/Mike Lowell 4.00 10.00
GMYE Yaz/J.Ellsbury 6.00 15.00
GMYO Yaz/D.Ortiz 8.00 20.00

2009 SP Legendary Cuts Legendary Cut Signatures

OVERALL CUT SIG ODDS TWO PER CASE
PRINT RUNS B/WN 5-55 COPIES PER

NO PRICING ON QTY 25 OR LESS
LC6 Wally Berger/50 20.00 50.00
LC107 Bob O'Farrell/26 20.00 50.00
LC109 Bill Stafford/26 15.00 40.00
LC201 Al Barlick/50 15.00 40.00
LC202 Luke Appling/33 30.00 60.00
LC203 Allie Reynolds/39 50.00 100.00
LC204 Aurelio Rodriguez/50 20.00 50.00
LC205 Bibb Falk/36 15.00 40.00
LC206 Bob Grim/37 15.00 40.00
LC208 Billy Herman/50 30.00 60.00
LC210 Bob Lemon/50 30.00 60.00
LC211 Barney McCosky/43 20.00 50.00
LC213 Bob Buhl/44 20.00 50.00
LC214 Bucky Walters/42 40.00 80.00
LC215 Clete Boyer/42 20.00 50.00
LC216 Charlie Gehringer/36 20.00 50.00
LC218 Del Ennis/27 40.00 80.00
LC220 Dick Donovan/31 30.00 60.00
LC221 Doc Cramer/39 15.00 40.00
LC223 Dick Sisler/27 30.00 60.00
LC229 Frank McCormick/50 15.00 40.00
LC230 Charlie Grimm/50 30.00 60.00
LC231 George Kelly/26 30.00 60.00
LC232 Gus Suhr/55 30.00 60.00
LC233 Gene Woodling/47 20.00 50.00
LC234 Hank Borowy/33 40.00 80.00
LC235 Happy Chandler/28 30.00 60.00
LC237 Harvey Kuenn/32 20.00 50.00
LC238 Hank Sauer/33 15.00 40.00
LC239 Hal Trosky/34 50.00 100.00
LC240 Joe Adcock/30 50.00 100.00
LC244 Joe Niekro/28 30.00 60.00
LC245 Joe Sewell/50 15.00 40.00
LC246 Jim Turner/32 30.00 60.00
LC247 Johnny Vander Meer/42 20.00 50.00
LC249 Clem Labine/26 20.00 50.00
LC250 Lew Fonseca/29 20.00 50.00
LC252 Lloyd Waner/50 75.00 150.00
LC254 Mel Harder/41 15.00 40.00
LC257 Pete Runnels/28 30.00 60.00
LC259 Ray Boone/37 30.00 60.00
LC260 Ray Dandridge/31 30.00 60.00
LC262 Roger Peckinpaugh/41 20.00 50.00
LC263 Rip Repulski/48 15.00 40.00
LC265 Stan Coveleski/42 20.00 50.00
LC266 Riggs Stephenson/39 30.00 60.00
LC269 Vic Wertz/43 15.00 40.00
LC270 Walker Cooper/44 20.00 50.00
LC275 Walter O'Malley/50 200.00 400.00
LC276 Buck Leonard/52 40.00 80.00
LC277 Cool Papa Bell/30 100.00 175.00
LC278 Catfish Hunter/40 30.00 60.00
LC280 Dutch Leonard/27 40.00 80.00
LC281 Ewell Blackwell/48 20.00 50.00
LC283 Hank Bauer/33 50.00 100.00
LC284 Hoyt Wilhelm/35 20.00 50.00
LC285 Harry Walker/45 20.00 50.00
LC287 Johnny Callison/26 40.00 80.00
LC289 Lou Boudreau/50 15.00 40.00
LC290 Larry French/45 20.00 50.00
LC291 Phil Rizzuto/50 40.00 80.00
LC296 Tony Cuccinello/37 40.00 80.00
LC297 Tommy Holmes/41 40.00 80.00
LC298 Terry Moore/50 20.00 50.00
LC299 Sammy White/28 30.00 60.00
LC300 Warren Spahn/39 30.00 60.00
LC309 Edd Roush/31 20.00 50.00
LC311 Enos Slaughter/43 20.00 50.00

2009 SP Legendary Cuts Legendary Memorabilia

OVERALL MEM ODDS 1:3
PRINT RUNS B/WN 40-125 COPIES PER
BD Bucky Dent/125 3.00 8.00
BG Bob Gibson/40 5.00 12.00
BO Bo Jackson/125 10.00 25.00
BR Brooks Robinson/125 5.00 12.00
BW Billy Williams/125 3.00 8.00
CA Rod Carew/125 3.00 8.00
CF Carlton Fisk/125 4.00 10.00
CR Cal Ripken Jr./125 12.50 30.00
CY Carl Yastrzemski/125 6.00 15.00
DE Dennis Eckersley/125 3.00 8.00
DM Don Mattingly/125 6.00 15.00
DS Don Sutton/125 3.00 8.00
DW Dave Winfield/125 3.00 8.00
EB Ernie Banks/125 5.00 12.00
EM Edgar Martinez/125 4.00 10.00
FR Frank Robinson/125 3.00 8.00
GG Goose Gossage/125 3.00 8.00
GK Kirk Gibson/125 5.00 12.00
GP Gaylord Perry/125 3.00 8.00
JB Johnny Bench/125 4.00 10.00
JC Joe Carter/125 3.00 8.00
JM Joe Morgan/125 3.00 8.00
JP Jim Palmer/125 4.00 10.00
JR Jim Rice/125 3.00 8.00
KG Ken Griffey Sr./125 3.00 8.00
LA Luis Aparicio/125 4.00 10.00
LB Lou Brock/125 5.00 12.00
MG Mark Grace/125 4.00 10.00
MO Jack Morris/125 4.00 10.00
MS Mike Schmidt/125 6.00 15.00
NR Nolan Ryan/125 8.00 20.00
OS Ozzie Smith/125 8.00 20.00
PM Paul Molitor/125 4.00 10.00
RJ Reggie Jackson/125 3.00 8.00
RS Ryne Sandberg/125 6.00 15.00
RY Robin Yount/125 4.00 10.00
SA Ron Santo/125 8.00 20.00
SC Steve Carlton/125 3.00 8.00
SL Sparky Lyle/125 3.00 8.00
SM Stan Musial/100 10.00 25.00
TG Tony Gwynn/125 5.00 12.00
TM Tino Martinez/125 4.00 10.00
TP Tony Perez/125 3.00 8.00
TR Tim Raines/125 4.00 10.00
TW Ted Williams/50 30.00 60.00
WB Wade Boggs/125 5.00 12.00
BG2 Bob Gibson/40 5.00 12.00
BO2 Bo Jackson/125 6.00 15.00
BR2 Brooks Robinson/125 5.00 12.00
BW2 Billy Williams/125 3.00 8.00
BW3 Billy Williams/125 3.00 8.00
CA2 Rod Carew/125 3.00 8.00
CA3 Rod Carew/125 3.00 8.00
CF2 Carlton Fisk/125 4.00 10.00
CF3 Carlton Fisk/125 4.00 10.00
CR2 Cal Ripken Jr./125 12.50 30.00
CR3 Cal Ripken Jr./125 12.50 30.00
CY2 Carl Yastrzemski/125 6.00 15.00
DE2 Dennis Eckersley/125 3.00 8.00
DM2 Don Mattingly/125 6.00 15.00
DM3 Don Mattingly/125 6.00 15.00
DS2 Don Sutton/125 3.00 8.00
EB2 Ernie Banks/125 5.00 12.00
GG2 Goose Gossage/125 3.00 8.00
GK2 Kirk Gibson/125 5.00 12.00
GP2 Gaylord Perry/125 3.00 8.00
GP3 Gaylord Perry/125 3.00 8.00
GP4 Gaylord Perry/125 3.00 8.00
JB2 Johnny Bench/125 4.00 10.00
JC2 Joe Carter/125 3.00 8.00
JM2 Joe Morgan/125 3.00 8.00
JP2 Jim Palmer/125 4.00 10.00
JR2 Jim Rice/125 3.00 8.00
LB2 Lou Brock/125 5.00 12.00
MG2 Mark Grace/125 4.00 10.00
MO2 Jack Morris/125 4.00 10.00
MS2 Mike Schmidt/125 6.00 15.00
NR2 Nolan Ryan/125 8.00 20.00
OS2 Ozzie Smith/125 8.00 20.00
OS3 Ozzie Smith/125 8.00 20.00
PM2 Paul Molitor/125 4.00 10.00
RJ2 Reggie Jackson/125 3.00 8.00
RS2 Ryne Sandberg/125 5.00 12.00
RY2 Robin Yount/125 4.00 10.00
SA2 Ron Santo/125 8.00 20.00
SC2 Steve Carlton/125 3.00 8.00
SL2 Sparky Lyle/125 3.00 8.00
SM2 Stan Musial/100 10.00 25.00
SM3 Stan Musial/100 10.00 25.00
TG2 Tony Gwynn/125 5.00 12.00
TM2 Tino Martinez/125 4.00 10.00
TP2 Tony Perez/125 3.00 8.00
TR2 Tim Raines/125 4.00 10.00
TW2 Ted Williams/50 15.00 40.00
WB2 Wade Boggs/125 5.00 12.00

2009 SP Legendary Cuts Legendary Memorabilia Blue

OVERALL MEM ODDS 1:3
PRINT RUNS B/WN 30-100 COPIES PER
BD Bucky Dent/100 3.00 8.00
BG Bob Gibson/30 5.00 12.00
BO Bo Jackson/100 6.00 15.00
BR Brooks Robinson/100 5.00 12.00
BW Billy Williams/100 3.00 8.00
CA Rod Carew/100 3.00 8.00
CF Carlton Fisk/100 4.00 10.00
CR Cal Ripken Jr./100 12.50 30.00
CY Carl Yastrzemski/100 6.00 15.00
DE Dennis Eckersley/100 3.00 8.00
DM Don Mattingly/100 6.00 15.00
DS Don Sutton/100 3.00 8.00
DW Dave Winfield/75 4.00 10.00
DW2 Dave Winfield/100 3.00 8.00
EB Ernie Banks/100 5.00 12.00
EM Edgar Martinez/100 4.00 10.00
FR Frank Robinson/100 3.00 8.00
GG Goose Gossage/100 3.00 8.00
GK Kirk Gibson/100 5.00 12.00
GP Gaylord Perry/100 3.00 8.00
JB Johnny Bench/100 4.00 10.00
JC Joe Carter/100 3.00 8.00
JM Joe Morgan/100 3.00 8.00
JR Jim Rice/100 3.00 8.00
KG Ken Griffey Sr./100 3.00 8.00
LA Luis Aparicio/100 4.00 10.00
LB Lou Brock/100 5.00 12.00
MG Mark Grace/100 4.00 10.00
MO Jack Morris/100 4.00 10.00
MS Mike Schmidt/100 6.00 15.00
OS Ozzie Smith/100 6.00 15.00
PM Paul Molitor/100 4.00 10.00
RJ Reggie Jackson/100 3.00 8.00
RS Ryne Sandberg/100 6.00 15.00
RY Robin Yount/100 4.00 10.00
SA Ron Santo/100 8.00 20.00
SC Steve Carlton/100 3.00 8.00
SL Sparky Lyle/100 3.00 8.00
SM Stan Musial/75 12.50 30.00
TG Tony Gwynn/100 5.00 12.00
TM Tino Martinez/100 4.00 10.00
TP Tony Perez/100 3.00 8.00
TR Tim Raines/100 4.00 10.00
TW Ted Williams/40 40.00 80.00
WB Wade Boggs/100 5.00 12.00
BG2 Bob Gibson/30 5.00 12.00
BO2 Bo Jackson/100 6.00 15.00
BR2 Brooks Robinson/100 5.00 12.00
BW2 Billy Williams/100 3.00 8.00
BW3 Billy Williams/100 3.00 8.00
CA2 Rod Carew/100 3.00 8.00
CA3 Rod Carew/100 3.00 8.00
CF2 Carlton Fisk/100 4.00 10.00
CF3 Carlton Fisk/100 4.00 10.00
CR2 Cal Ripken Jr./100 12.50 30.00
CR3 Cal Ripken Jr./100 12.50 30.00
CY2 Carl Yastrzemski/100 6.00 15.00
DE2 Dennis Eckersley/100 3.00 8.00
DM2 Don Mattingly/100 6.00 15.00
DM3 Don Mattingly/100 6.00 15.00
DS2 Don Sutton/100 3.00 8.00
EB2 Ernie Banks/100 5.00 12.00
GG2 Goose Gossage/100 3.00 8.00
GK2 Kirk Gibson/100 5.00 12.00
GP2 Gaylord Perry/100 3.00 8.00
GP3 Gaylord Perry/100 3.00 8.00
GP4 Gaylord Perry/100 3.00 8.00
JB2 Johnny Bench/100 4.00 10.00
JC2 Joe Carter/100 3.00 8.00
JM2 Joe Morgan/100 3.00 8.00
JP2 Jim Palmer/100 4.00 10.00
JR2 Jim Rice/100 3.00 8.00
LB2 Lou Brock/100 5.00 12.00
MG2 Mark Grace/100 4.00 10.00
MO2 Jack Morris/100 4.00 10.00
MS2 Mike Schmidt/100 6.00 15.00
OS2 Ozzie Smith/100 6.00 15.00
OS3 Ozzie Smith/100 6.00 15.00
PM2 Paul Molitor/100 4.00 10.00
RJ2 Reggie Jackson/100 3.00 8.00
RS2 Ryne Sandberg/100 5.00 12.00
RY2 Robin Yount/100 4.00 10.00
SA2 Ron Santo/100 8.00 20.00
SC2 Steve Carlton/100 3.00 8.00
SL2 Sparky Lyle/100 3.00 8.00
SM2 Stan Musial/75 12.50 30.00
SM3 Stan Musial/75 12.50 30.00
TG2 Tony Gwynn/100 5.00 12.00
TM2 Tino Martinez/100 4.00 10.00
TP2 Tony Perez/100 3.00 8.00
TR2 Tim Raines/100 4.00 10.00
TW2 Ted Williams/40 15.00 40.00
WB2 Wade Boggs/100 5.00 12.00

2009 SP Legendary Cuts Legendary Memorabilia Brown

OVERALL MEM ODDS 1:3
PRINT RUNS B/WN 20-50 COPIES PER
BD Bucky Dent 4.00 10.00
BG Bob Gibson/20 6.00 15.00
BO Bo Jackson 8.00 20.00
BR Brooks Robinson 6.00 15.00
BW Billy Williams 4.00 10.00
CA Rod Carew 4.00 10.00
CF Carlton Fisk 5.00 12.00
CR Cal Ripken Jr. 15.00 40.00
CY Carl Yastrzemski 8.00 20.00
DE Dennis Eckersley 4.00 10.00
DM Don Mattingly 8.00 20.00
DS Don Sutton 4.00 10.00
DW Dave Winfield 4.00 10.00
EB Ernie Banks 6.00 15.00
EM Edgar Martinez 5.00 12.00
FR Frank Robinson 4.00 10.00
GG Goose Gossage 4.00 10.00
GK Kirk Gibson 6.00 15.00
GP Gaylord Perry 4.00 10.00
JB Johnny Bench 5.00 12.00
JC Joe Carter 4.00 10.00
JM Joe Morgan 4.00 10.00
JP Jim Palmer 5.00 12.00
JR Jim Rice 4.00 10.00
KG Ken Griffey Sr. 4.00 10.00
LA Luis Aparicio 5.00 12.00
LB Lou Brock 6.00 15.00
MG Mark Grace 5.00 12.00
MO Jack Morris 5.00 12.00
MS Mike Schmidt 8.00 20.00
NR Nolan Ryan 10.00 25.00
OS Ozzie Smith 8.00 20.00
PM Paul Molitor 5.00 12.00
RC Roger Clemens 4.00 10.00
RC2 Roger Clemens 4.00 10.00
RJ Reggie Jackson 4.00 10.00
RS Ryne Sandberg 8.00 20.00
RY Robin Yount 5.00 12.00
SA Ron Santo 6.00 15.00
SC Steve Carlton 4.00 10.00
SL Sparky Lyle 4.00 10.00
SM Stan Musial 12.50 30.00
TG Tony Gwynn 6.00 15.00
TM Tino Martinez 5.00 12.00
TP Tony Perez 4.00 10.00
TR Tim Raines 5.00 12.00
TW Ted Williams 30.00 60.00
WB Wade Boggs 6.00 15.00
BG2 Bob Gibson/20 6.00 15.00
BO2 Bo Jackson 8.00 20.00
BR2 Brooks Robinson 6.00 15.00
BW2 Billy Williams 4.00 10.00
BW3 Billy Williams 4.00 10.00
CA2 Rod Carew 4.00 10.00
CA3 Rod Carew 4.00 10.00
CF2 Carlton Fisk 5.00 12.00
CF3 Carlton Fisk 5.00 12.00
CR2 Cal Ripken Jr. 15.00 40.00
CR3 Cal Ripken Jr. 15.00 40.00
CY2 Carl Yastrzemski 8.00 20.00
DE2 Dennis Eckersley 4.00 10.00
DM2 Don Mattingly 8.00 20.00
DM3 Don Mattingly 8.00 20.00
DS2 Don Sutton 4.00 10.00
EB2 Ernie Banks 6.00 15.00
GG2 Goose Gossage 4.00 10.00
GK2 Kirk Gibson 6.00 15.00
GP2 Gaylord Perry 4.00 10.00
GP3 Gaylord Perry 4.00 10.00
GP4 Gaylord Perry 4.00 10.00
JB2 Johnny Bench 5.00 12.00
JC2 Joe Carter 4.00 10.00
JM2 Joe Morgan 4.00 10.00
JP2 Jim Palmer 5.00 12.00
JR2 Jim Rice 4.00 10.00
LB2 Lou Brock 6.00 15.00
MG2 Mark Grace 5.00 12.00
MO2 Jack Morris 5.00 12.00
MS2 Mike Schmidt 8.00 20.00
NR2 Nolan Ryan 10.00 25.00
OS2 Ozzie Smith 8.00 20.00
OS3 Ozzie Smith 8.00 20.00
PM2 Paul Molitor 5.00 12.00
RJ2 Reggie Jackson 4.00 10.00
RS2 Ryne Sandberg 6.00 15.00
RY2 Robin Yount 5.00 12.00
SA2 Ron Santo 6.00 15.00
SC2 Steve Carlton 4.00 10.00
SL2 Sparky Lyle 4.00 10.00
SM2 Stan Musial 12.50 30.00
SM3 Stan Musial 12.50 30.00
TG2 Tony Gwynn 6.00 15.00
TM2 Tino Martinez 5.00 12.00
TP2 Tony Perez 4.00 10.00
TR2 Tim Raines 5.00 12.00
TW2 Ted Williams 15.00 40.00
WB2 Wade Boggs 6.00 15.00

2009 SP Legendary Cuts Legendary Memorabilia Red

OVERALL MEM ODDS 1:3
PRINT RUNS B/WN 25-75 COPIES PER
BD Bucky Dent 4.00 10.00
BG Bob Gibson/25 6.00 15.00
BO Bo Jackson 8.00 20.00
BR Brooks Robinson 6.00 15.00
BW Billy Williams 4.00 10.00
CA Rod Carew 4.00 10.00
CF Carlton Fisk 5.00 12.00
CR Cal Ripken Jr. 15.00 40.00
CY Carl Yastrzemski 8.00 20.00
DE Dennis Eckersley 4.00 10.00
DM Don Mattingly 8.00 20.00
DS Don Sutton 4.00 10.00
DW Dave Winfield 4.00 10.00
EB Ernie Banks 6.00 15.00
EM Edgar Martinez 5.00 12.00
FR Frank Robinson 4.00 10.00
GG Goose Gossage 4.00 10.00
GK Kirk Gibson 6.00 15.00
GP Gaylord Perry 4.00 10.00
JB Johnny Bench 5.00 12.00
JC Joe Carter 4.00 10.00
JM Joe Morgan 4.00 10.00
JP Jim Palmer 5.00 12.00
JR Jim Rice 4.00 10.00
KG Ken Griffey Sr. 4.00 10.00
LA Luis Aparicio 5.00 12.00
LB Lou Brock 6.00 15.00
MG Mark Grace 5.00 12.00
MO Jack Morris 5.00 12.00
MS Mike Schmidt 8.00 20.00
NR Nolan Ryan 10.00 25.00
OS Ozzie Smith 8.00 20.00
PM Paul Molitor 5.00 12.00
RJ Reggie Jackson 4.00 10.00
RS Ryne Sandberg 8.00 20.00
RY Robin Yount 5.00 12.00
SA Ron Santo 6.00 15.00
SC Steve Carlton 4.00 10.00
SL Sparky Lyle 4.00 10.00
SM Stan Musial 12.50 30.00
TG Tony Gwynn 6.00 15.00
TM Tino Martinez 5.00 12.00
TP Tony Perez 4.00 10.00
TR Tim Raines 5.00 12.00
TW Ted Williams 30.00 60.00
WB Wade Boggs 6.00 15.00
BG2 Bob Gibson/25 6.00 15.00
BO2 Bo Jackson 8.00 20.00
BR2 Brooks Robinson 6.00 15.00
BW2 Billy Williams 4.00 10.00
BW3 Billy Williams 4.00 10.00
CA2 Rod Carew 4.00 10.00
CA3 Rod Carew 4.00 10.00
CF2 Carlton Fisk 5.00 12.00
CF3 Carlton Fisk 5.00 12.00
CR2 Cal Ripken Jr. 15.00 40.00
CR3 Cal Ripken Jr. 15.00 40.00
CY2 Carl Yastrzemski 8.00 20.00
DE2 Dennis Eckersley 4.00 10.00
DM2 Don Mattingly 8.00 20.00
DM3 Don Mattingly 8.00 20.00
DS2 Don Sutton 4.00 10.00
EB2 Ernie Banks 6.00 15.00
GG2 Goose Gossage 4.00 10.00
GK2 Kirk Gibson 6.00 15.00
GP2 Gaylord Perry 4.00 10.00
GP3 Gaylord Perry 4.00 10.00
GP4 Gaylord Perry 4.00 10.00
JB2 Johnny Bench 5.00 12.00
JC2 Joe Carter 4.00 10.00
JM2 Joe Morgan 4.00 10.00
JP2 Jim Palmer 5.00 12.00
JR2 Jim Rice 4.00 10.00
LB2 Lou Brock 6.00 15.00
MG2 Mark Grace 5.00 12.00
MO2 Jack Morris 5.00 12.00
MS2 Mike Schmidt 8.00 20.00
NR2 Nolan Ryan 10.00 25.00
OS2 Ozzie Smith 8.00 20.00
OS3 Ozzie Smith 8.00 20.00
PM2 Paul Molitor 5.00 12.00
RJ2 Reggie Jackson 4.00 10.00
RS2 Ryne Sandberg 6.00 15.00
RY2 Robin Yount 5.00 12.00
SA2 Ron Santo 6.00 15.00
SC2 Steve Carlton 4.00 10.00
SL2 Sparky Lyle 4.00 10.00
SM2 Stan Musial 12.50 30.00
SM3 Stan Musial 12.50 30.00
TG2 Tony Gwynn 6.00 15.00
TM2 Tino Martinez 5.00 12.00
TP2 Tony Perez 4.00 10.00
TR2 Tim Raines 5.00 12.00
TW2 Ted Williams 15.00 40.00
WB2 Wade Boggs 6.00 15.00

2009 SP Legendary Cuts Legendary Memorabilia Violet

OVERALL MEM ODDS 1:3
STATED PRINT RUN 25 SER.#'d SETS
BD Bucky Dent 5.00 12.00
BG Bob Gibson 6.00 15.00
BO Bo Jackson 10.00 25.00
BR Brooks Robinson 8.00 20.00
BW Billy Williams 5.00 12.00
CA Rod Carew 5.00 12.00
CF Carlton Fisk 6.00 15.00
CR Cal Ripken Jr. 20.00 50.00
CY Carl Yastrzemski 10.00 25.00
DE Dennis Eckersley 5.00 12.00
DM Don Mattingly 10.00 25.00
DS Don Sutton 5.00 12.00
DW Dave Winfield 5.00 12.00
EB Ernie Banks 8.00 20.00
EM Edgar Martinez 6.00 15.00
FR Frank Robinson 5.00 12.00
GG Goose Gossage 5.00 12.00
GK Kirk Gibson 8.00 20.00
GP Gaylord Perry 5.00 12.00
JB Johnny Bench 6.00 15.00
JC Joe Carter 5.00 12.00
JM Joe Morgan 5.00 12.00
JP Jim Palmer 6.00 15.00
JR Jim Rice 5.00 12.00
KG Ken Griffey Sr. 5.00 12.00
LA Luis Aparicio 6.00 15.00
LB Lou Brock 8.00 20.00
MG Mark Grace 6.00 15.00
MO Jack Morris 6.00 15.00
MS Mike Schmidt 10.00 25.00
NR Nolan Ryan 12.50 30.00
OS Ozzie Smith 10.00 25.00
PM Paul Molitor 6.00 15.00
RC Roger Clemens 5.00 12.00
RJ Reggie Jackson 5.00 12.00
RS Ryne Sandberg 10.00 25.00
RY Robin Yount 6.00 15.00
SA Ron Santo 8.00 20.00
SC Steve Carlton 5.00 12.00
SL Sparky Lyle 5.00 12.00
SM Stan Musial 15.00 40.00
TG Tony Gwynn 8.00 20.00
TM Tino Martinez 6.00 15.00
TP Tony Perez 5.00 12.00
TR Tim Raines 6.00 15.00
TW Ted Williams 40.00 80.00
WB Wade Boggs 8.00 20.00
BG2 Bob Gibson 6.00 15.00
BO2 Bo Jackson 10.00 25.00
BR2 Brooks Robinson 8.00 20.00
BW2 Billy Williams 5.00 12.00
BW3 Billy Williams 5.00 12.00
CA2 Rod Carew 5.00 12.00
CA3 Rod Carew 5.00 12.00
CF2 Carlton Fisk 6.00 15.00
CF3 Carlton Fisk 6.00 15.00
CR2 Cal Ripken Jr. 20.00 50.00
CR3 Cal Ripken Jr. 20.00 50.00
CY2 Carl Yastrzemski 10.00 25.00
DE2 Dennis Eckersley 5.00 12.00
DM2 Don Mattingly 10.00 25.00
DM3 Don Mattingly 10.00 25.00
DS2 Don Sutton 5.00 12.00
EB2 Ernie Banks 8.00 20.00
GG2 Goose Gossage 5.00 12.00
GK2 Kirk Gibson 8.00 20.00
GP2 Gaylord Perry 5.00 12.00
GP3 Gaylord Perry 5.00 12.00
GP4 Gaylord Perry 5.00 12.00
JB2 Johnny Bench 6.00 15.00
JC2 Joe Carter 5.00 12.00
JM2 Joe Morgan 5.00 12.00
JP2 Jim Palmer 6.00 15.00
JR2 Jim Rice 5.00 12.00
LB2 Lou Brock 8.00 20.00
MG2 Mark Grace 6.00 15.00
MO2 Jack Morris 6.00 15.00
MS2 Mike Schmidt 10.00 25.00
NR2 Nolan Ryan 12.50 30.00
OS2 Ozzie Smith 10.00 25.00
OS3 Ozzie Smith 10.00 25.00
PM2 Paul Molitor 6.00 15.00
RJ2 Reggie Jackson 5.00 12.00
RS2 Ryne Sandberg 8.00 20.00
RY2 Robin Yount 6.00 15.00
SA2 Ron Santo 8.00 20.00
SC2 Steve Carlton 5.00 12.00
SL2 Sparky Lyle 5.00 12.00
SM2 Stan Musial 15.00 40.00
SM3 Stan Musial 15.00 40.00
TG2 Tony Gwynn 8.00 20.00
TM2 Tino Martinez 6.00 15.00
TP2 Tony Perez 5.00 12.00
TR2 Tim Raines 6.00 15.00
TW2 Ted Williams 20.00 50.00
WB2 Wade Boggs 8.00 20.00

2009 SP Legendary Cuts Mystery Cuts

STATED ODDS ONE PER CASE
EA Eddy Arnold/26 60.00 120.00
GD Glenn Davis/37 10.00 25.00
GM George McAfee/34 12.50 30.00
HL Harry Litwack/49 10.00 25.00
LB Lucille Ball/92 100.00 200.00
RA Red Auerbach/35 50.00 100.00
SD Sammy Davis Jr./91 100.00 200.00
TC Tom Cheney/74 12.50 30.00
NNO Exchange Card 175.00 350.00

2011 SP Legendary Cuts Legendary Signatures

OVERALL AUTO ODDS 1:1
PRINT RUNS B/WN 5-36 COPIES PER
NO PRICING ON MOST QTY 25 OR LESS
1 Al Barlick/35 40.00 80.00
2 Al Lopez/35 12.50 30.00
9 Bill Dickey/35 50.00 100.00
11 Bill Terry/25 30.00 60.00
14 Billy Herman/35 15.00 40.00
16 Bob Lemon/34 10.00 25.00
22 Buck Leonard/35 20.00 50.00
23 Buck O'Neil/10 50.00 100.00
31 Carl Hubbell/35 40.00 80.00
33 Catfish Hunter/34 20.00 50.00
34 Charlie Gehringer/35 40.00 80.00
35 Charlie Grimm/15 30.00 60.00
40 Cool Papa Bell/24 90.00 150.00
42 Cy Williams/10 60.00 120.00
51 Duffy Lewis/13 75.00 150.00
52 Earl Averill/35 15.00 40.00
54 Earle Combs/12 60.00 150.00
55 Early Wynn/32 30.00 60.00
56 Ed Lopat/16 20.00 50.00
57 Edd Roush/35 20.00 50.00
58 Eddie Mathews/35 40.00 80.00
61 Enos Slaughter/35 12.00 30.00
63 Ernie Lombardi/10 90.00 150.00
66 Frank McCormick/15 20.00 50.00
68 Frankie Frisch/10 125.00 250.00
71 Freddie Lindstrom/15 60.00 120.00
74 Gene Benson/10 20.00 50.00
77 George Kell/35 10.00 25.00
78 George Kelly/33 10.00 25.00
82 George Uhle/15 15.00 40.00
84 Glenn Wright/17 12.50 30.00
85 Hal Newhouser/35 12.50 30.00
88 Happy Chandler/35 15.00 40.00
99 Jesse Haines/19 25.00 60.00
103 Jocko Conlan/34 20.00 50.00
105 Joe Cronin/15 20.00 50.00
106 Joe DiMaggio/35 200.00 400.00
113 Joe Sewell/35 20.00 50.00
115 Johnny Mize/33 40.00 80.00
116 Johnny Murphy/7 50.00 100.00
127 Lefty O'Doul/13 75.00 150.00
131 Lloyd Waner/36 50.00 100.00
133 Lou Boudreau/35 15.00 40.00
134 Luke Appling/35 20.00 50.00
138 Max Carey/35 20.00 50.00
139 Mel Allen/7 40.00 80.00
146 Pete Reiser/10 40.00 80.00
147 Phil Rizzuto/30 50.00 100.00
149 Ray Dandridge/25 15.00 40.00
150 Ray Schalk/10 200.00 400.00
153 Red Rolfe/12 90.00 150.00
156 Rick Ferrell/33 20.00 50.00
165 Rube Marquard/35 50.00 100.00
166 Rube Walberg/10 30.00 60.00
172 Spud Davis/13 30.00 60.00
173 Stan Coveleski/35 15.00 40.00
175 Ted Kluszewski/14 30.00 60.00
176 Ted Lyons/35 15.00 40.00
177 Ted Williams/23 300.00 600.00
180 Tommy Leach/10 30.00 60.00
182 Travis Jackson/25 30.00 60.00
187 Vern Stephens/10 50.00 100.00
191 Waite Hoyt/35 30.00 60.00
195 Warren Spahn/33 20.00 50.00

2011 SP Legendary Cuts Legendary Black Signatures

OVERALL AUTO ODDS 1:1
PRINT RUNS B/WN 1-40 COPIES PER
NO PRICING ON MOST QTY 25 OR LESS
NYBD Babe Dahlgren/33 20.00 50.00
NYBG Bob Grim/17 30.00 60.00
NYBJ Billy Johnson/37 10.00 25.00
NYCH Catfish Hunter/14 30.00 60.00
NYEL Ed Lopat/32 20.00 50.00
NYFC Frankie Crosetti/34 20.00 50.00
NYGW Gene Woodling/29 10.00 25.00
NYHB Hank Bauer/35 10.00 25.00
NYHR Hal Reniff/35 12.50 30.00
NYJD Joe DiMaggio/30 200.00 400.00
NYJL Johnny Lindell/18 15.00 40.00
NYMR Marius Russo/35 10.00 25.00
NYNE Nick Etten/28 10.00 25.00
NYOH Oral Hildebrand/11 30.00 60.00
NYPR Phil Rizzuto/17 40.00 80.00
NYSS Spec Shea/33 10.00 25.00
NYTB Tommy Byrne/14 30.00 60.00
NYTT Tom Tresh/40 15.00 40.00
BALMB Mark Belanger/13 20.00 50.00
BOSBW Bill Werber/38 15.00 40.00
BOSDC Doc Cramer/29 10.00 25.00
BOSPR Pete Runnels/35 10.00 25.00
CINER Edd Roush/17 20.00 50.00
CINJV Johnny Vander Meer/20 30.00 60.00
CLEES Elmer Smith/15 15.00 40.00
CLEJS Joe Sewell/20 20.00 40.00
DETBH Billy Hoeft/15 20.00 50.00
DETBM Barney McCoskey/25 20.00 50.00
DETHE Hoot Evers/25 10.00 25.00
DETHK Harvey Kuenn/27 40.00 80.00
DETJB Johnny Bassler/10 20.00 50.00
NLGBO Buck O'Neil/35 40.00 80.00
NLGLD Leon Day/15 50.00 100.00
NYBDI Bill Dickey/21 25.00 60.00
PHIEA Ethan Allen/26 12.50 30.00
PITGS Gus Suhr/10 30.00 60.00
PITVD Vince DiMaggio/10 40.00 80.00
STLAH Andy High/15 20.00 50.00
STLBO Bob O'Farrell/36 15.00 40.00
STLHB Harry Brecheen/35 15.00 40.00
STLHH Harvey Haddix/35 20.00 50.00
STLHW Harry Walker/33 10.00 25.00
STLJH Johnny Hopp/35 10.00 25.00
STLJR Jack Rothrock/16 20.00 50.00
STLSD Spud Davis/29 15.00 40.00
STLSJ Syl Johnson/36 15.00 40.00
STLTM Terry Moore/35 20.00 50.00
STLWC Walker Cooper/15 20.00 50.00
STLWK Whitey Kurowski/34 15.00 40.00
WASCT Cecil Travis/35 20.00 50.00
WASDL Dutch Leonard/26 20.00 50.00
WASOB Ossie Bluege/35 20.00 50.00
WASTC Tom Cheney/40 10.00 25.00
BOMIWB Wally Berger/35 20.00 50.00
BRLABH Babe Herman/35 10.00 25.00
BRLABP Babe Phelps/36 10.00 25.00
BRLADC Dolph Camilli/16 15.00 40.00
BRLAFB Frenchy Bordagaray/35 10.00 25.00
BRLAGC George Cutshaw/14 20.00 50.00
BRLAMO Mickey Owen/35 12.50 30.00
BRLATC Tony Cuccinello/32 10.00 25.00
BRLAWW Whit Wyatt/35 15.00 40.00
CHINAG Augie Galan/35 10.00 25.00
CHINBN Bill Nicholson/35 10.00 25.00
CHINHS Hank Sauer/35 20.00 50.00
CHINWE Woody English/32 20.00 50.00
CHISBF Bibb Falk/17 30.00 60.00
CHISRR Reb Russell/11 30.00 60.00
NYSFBJ Billy Jurges/40 20.00 50.00
NYSFBR Bill Rigney/30 10.00 25.00
NYSFCH Carl Hubbell/15 40.00 80.00
NYSFDB Dick Bartell/27 10.00 25.00
NYSFFF Freddie Fitzsimmons/35 20.00 50.00
NYSFGM Gus Mancuso/35 10.00 25.00
NYSFHC Hughie Critz/25 10.00 25.00
NYSFHD Harry Danning/25 20.00 40.00
NYSFJS Jack Sanford/27 20.00 50.00
NYSFSG Sid Gordon/15 40.00 80.00
NYSFWM Willard Marshall/29 15.00 40.00
NYSFWW Wes Westrum/30 12.50 30.00
PHKCPL Paddy Livingston/15 20.00 50.00
PHKCSC Sam Chapman/35 10.00 25.00
BRLACLV Cookie Lavagetto/37 20.00 50.00
BRLAJPO Johnny Podres/35 20.00 50.00
BRLAPRO Preacher Roe/35 20.00 50.00

2011 SP Legendary Cuts Legendary Dual Signatures

OVERALL AUTO ODDS 1:1
PRINT RUNS B/WN 1-25 COPIES PER
NO PRICING ON MOST DUE TO SCARCITY
FTWW D.Walker/H.Walker/10 75.00 150.00
CHIAL L.Appling/T.Lyons/15 40.00 80.00
NLGDJ R.Dandridge/J.Johnson/15 60.00 120.00
UMPBC A.Barlick/J.Conlan/15 30.00 60.00
1948LS B.Lemon/J.Sain/10 30.00 60.00
BR41CH D.Camilli/B.Herman/10 30.00 60.00
CL48DL L.Doby/B.Lemon/10 50.00 100.00
DASHSW E.Slaughter/H.Walker/15 30.00 60.00
NY37DG B.Dickey/L.Gomez/10 100.00 175.00
NY39KS C.Keller/G.Selkirk/15 60.00 120.00
SPITCG S.Coveleski/B.Grimes/15 60.00 120.00
NYK20KT G.Kelly/B.Terry/10 50.00 100.00
NYK20LT F.Lindstrom/B.Terry/15 75.00 150.00
NYK33HT C.Hubbell/B.Terry/15 75.00 150.00

2004 SP Prospects

COMP.ROOKIES SET (198) 20.00 50.00
COMMON CARD (1-90) .30 .75
1-90 APPX. 2X TOUGHER THAN 91-290
COMMON CARD (91-190 .40 1.00
91-190 ODDS TWO PER PACK
COMMON CARD (191-290) .40 1.00
191-290 APPX.TWO PER PACK
COM.AU (291-447) p/r 500-600 2.50 6.00
COM.AU (291-447) p/r 325-499 2.50 6.00
OVERALL AU ODDS 1:5
AU PRINT RUNS B/WN 400-600 PER
233/237/345/438-443/445 DO NOT EXIST
1 Roger Clemens 1.00 2.50
2 Melvin Mora .30 .75
3 Dontrelle Willis .30 .75
4 Jose Vidro .30 .75
5 Oliver Perez .30 .75
6 Carlos Zambrano .50 1.25
7 Chipper Jones .75 2.00
8-Greg Maddux 1.00 2.50
9 Curt Schilling .50 1.25
10 Jose Reyes .50 1.25
11 David Ortiz .75 2.00
12 Mike Piazza .75 2.00
13 Jason Schmidt .30 .75
14 Randy Johnson .75 2.00
15 Magglio Ordonez .50 1.25
16 Mike Mussina .50 1.25
17 Jake Peavy .30 .75
18 Jim Edmonds .50 1.25
19 Ken Griffey Jr. 1.50 4.00
20 Jason Giambi .30 .75
21 Mike Sweeney .30 .75
22 Carlos Lee .30 .75
23 Craig Wilson .30 .75
24 Pedro Martinez .50 1.25
25 Bobby Abreu .30 .75
26 Mike Lowell .30 .75
27 Miguel Cabrera .75 2.00
28 Hank Blalock .30 .75
29 Frank Thomas .75 2.00
30 Manny Ramirez .75 2.00
31 Mark Mulder .30 .75
32 Scott Podsednik .30 .75
33 Albert Pujols 1.00 2.50
34 Preston Wilson .30 .75
35 Todd Helton .50 1.25
36 Victor Martinez .50 1.25
37 Kerry Wood .30 .75
38 Carlos Beltran .50 1.25
39 Vernon Wells .30 .75
40 Sammy Sosa .75 2.00
41 Pat Burrell .30 .75
42 Tim Hudson .50 1.25
43 Eric Gagne .30 .75
44 Jim Thome .50 1.25
45 Vladimir Guerrero .50 1.25
46 Travis Hafner .30 .75
47 Rickie Weeks .30 .75
48 Miguel Tejada .50 1.25
49 Ivan Rodriguez .50 1.25
50 J.D. Drew .30 .75
51 Ben Sheets .30 .75
52 Garret Anderson .30 .75
53 Aubrey Huff .30 .75
54 Nomar Garciaparra .50 1.25
55 Luis Gonzalez .30 .75
56 Lance Berkman .50 1.25
57 Ichiro Suzuki 1.00 2.50
58 Torii Hunter .30 .75
59 Adam Dunn .50 1.25
60 Mark Teixeira .50 1.25
61 Bret Boone .30 .75
62 Roy Oswalt .50 1.25
63 Joe Mauer .60 1.50
64 Scott Rolen .50 1.25
65 Hideki Matsui 1.25 3.00
66 Richie Sexson .30 .75
67 Jeff Kent .30 .75
68 Barry Zito .50 1.25
69 C.C. Sabathia .50 1.25
70 Carlos Delgado .30 .75
71 Gary Sheffield .30 .75
72 Shawn Green .30 .75
73 Jason Bay .50 1.25
74 Andruw Jones .30 .75
75 Jeff Bagwell .50 1.25
76 Rafael Palmeiro .50 1.25
77 Alex Rodriguez 1.00 2.50
78 Adrian Beltre .75 2.00
79 Troy Glaus .30 .75
80 Tom Glavine .50 1.25
81 Paul Konerko .50 1.25
82 Alfonso Soriano .50 1.25
83 Roy Halladay .50 1.25
84 Derek Jeter 2.00 5.00
85 Josh Beckett .30 .75
86 Delmon Young .50 1.25
87 Brian Giles .30 .75
88 Eric Chavez .30 .75
89 Lyle Overbay .30 .75
90 Mark Prior .50 1.25
91 Shawn Camp RC .40 1.00
92 Travis Smith .40 1.00
93 Juan Padilla RC .40 1.00
94 Brad Halsey RC .40 1.00
95 Scott Kazmir RC 2.00 5.00
96 Sam Narron RC .40 1.00
97 Frank Francisco RC .40 1.00
98 Mike Johnston RC .40 1.00
99 Sam McConnell RC .40 1.00
100 Josh Labandeira RC .40 1.00
101 Kazuhito Tadano RC .40 1.00
102 Hector Gimenez RC .40 1.00
103 David Aardsma RC .40 1.00
104 Charles Thomas RC .40 1.00
105 Ian Snell RC .40 1.00
106 Jeff Keppinger RC .60 1.50
107 Michael Vento RC .40 1.00
108 Jerry Gil RC .40 1.00
109 Marty McLeary RC .40 1.00
110 Donnie Kelly RC .60 1.50
111 Roman Colon RC .40 1.00
112 Travis Blackley RC .40 1.00
113 Edwardo Sierra RC .40 1.00
114 Chris Shelton RC .40 1.00
115 Bartolome Fortunato RC .40 1.00
116 Brandon Medders RC .40 1.00
117 Merkin Valdez RC .40 1.00
118 Carlos Vasquez RC .40 1.00
119 Shingo Takatsu RC .40 1.00
120 Aarom Baldiris RC .40 1.00
121 Chris Aguila RC .40 1.00
122 Jimmy Serrano RC .40 1.00
123 Mike Gosling RC .40 1.00
124 Brian Dallimore RC .40 1.00
125 Ronald Belisario RC .40 1.00

126 George Sherrill RC .40 1.00
127 Fernando Nieve RC .40 1.00
128 Abe Alvarez RC .40 1.00
129 Jeff Bennett RC .40 1.00
130 Ryan Meaux RC .40 1.00
131 Edwin Moreno RC .40 1.00
132 Jesse Crain RC .60 1.50
133 Scott Dohmann RC .40 1.00
134 Ronny Cedeno RC .40 1.00
135 Orlando Rodriguez RC .40 1.00
136 Michael Wuertz RC .40 1.00
137 Justin Hampson RC .40 1.00
138 Matt Treanor RC .40 1.00
139 Andy Green RC .40 1.00
140 Yadier Molina RC 20.00 50.00
141 Joe Nelson RC .40 1.00
142 Justin Lehr RC .40 1.00
143 Ryan Wing RC .40 1.00
144 Kevin Cave RC .40 1.00
145 Evan Rust RC .40 1.00
146 Mike Rouse RC .40 1.00
147 Lance Cormier RC .40 1.00
148 Eduardo Villacis RC .40 1.00
149 Justin Knoedler RC .40 1.00
150 Freddy Guzman RC .40 1.00
151 Casey Daigle RC .40 1.00
152 Joey Gathright RC .40 1.00
153 Tim Bittner RC .40 1.00
154 Scott Atchison RC .40 1.00
155 Ivan Ochoa RC .40 1.00
156 Lincoln Holdzkom RC .40 1.00
157 Onil Joseph RC .40 1.00
158 Jason Bartlett RC 1.25 3.00
159 Jon Knott RC .40 1.00
160 Jake Woods RC .40 1.00
161 Jerome Gamble RC .40 1.00
162 Sean Henn RC .40 1.00
163 Kazuo Matsui RC .60 1.50
164 Roberto Novoa RC .40 1.00
165 Eddy Rodriguez RC .40 1.00
166 Ramon Ramirez RC .40 1.00
167 Enemencio Pacheco RC .40 1.00
168 Chad Bentz RC .40 1.00
169 Chris Oxspring RC .40 1.00
170 Justin Leone RC .40 1.00
171 Joe Horgan RC .40 1.00
172 Jose Capellan RC .40 1.00
173 Greg Dobbs RC .40 1.00
174 Jason Frasor RC .40 1.00
175 Shawn Hill RC .40 1.00
176 Carlos Hines RC .40 1.00
177 John Gall RC .40 1.00
178 Steve Andrade RC .40 1.00
179 Scott Proctor RC .40 1.00
180 Rusty Tucker RC .40 1.00
181 Dave Crouthers RC .40 1.00
182 Franklyn Gracesqui RC .40 1.00
183 Justin Germano RC .40 1.00
184 Alfredo Simon RC .60 1.50
185 Jorge Sequea RC .40 1.00
186 Nick Regilio RC .40 1.00
187 Justin Huisman RC .40 1.00
188 Akinori Otsuka RC .40 1.00
189 Luis Gonzalez RC .40 1.00
190 Renyel Pinto RC .40 1.00
191 Joshua Leblanc RC .40 1.00
192 Devin Ivany RC .40 1.00
193 Chad Blackwell RC .40 1.00
194 Brandon Burgess RC .40 1.00
195 Cory Patton RC .40 1.00
196 Daniel Batz RC .40 1.00
197 Adam Russell RC .40 1.00
198 Jarrett Hoffpauir RC .40 1.00
199 Patrick Bryant RC .40 1.00
200 Sean Gamble RC .40 1.00
201 Jermaine Brock RC .40 1.00
202 Ben Zobrist RC 2.00 5.00
203 Clay Meredith RC .40 1.00
204 Derek Tharpe RC .40 1.00
205 Bradley McCann RC .40 1.00
206 Justin Hedrick RC .40 1.00
207 Clint Sammons RC .40 1.00
208 Richard Steik RC .40 1.00
209 Fernando Perez RC .40 1.00
210 Mark Jecmen RC .40 1.00
211 Benjamin Harrison RC .40 1.00
212 Jason Quarles RC .40 1.00
213 William Layman RC .40 1.00
214 Koley Kolberg RC .40 1.00
215 Randy Dicken RC .40 1.00
216 Barry Richmond RC .40 1.00
217 Timothy Murphey RC .40 1.00
218 John Hardy RC .40 1.00
219 Sebastien Boucher RC .40 1.00
220 Andrew Alvarado RC .40 1.00
221 Patrick Perry RC .40 1.00
222 Jarod McAuliff RC .40 1.00
223 Jared Gaston RC .40 1.00
224 William Thompson RC .40 1.00
225 Lucas French RC .40 1.00
226 Brandon Parillo RC .40 1.00
227 Gregory Goetz RC .40 1.00
228 David Haehnel RC .40 1.00
229 James Miller RC .40 1.00
230 Mark Roberts RC .40 1.00
231 Eric Ridener RC .40 1.00
232 Freddy Sandoval RC .40 1.00
234 Carlos Medero-Stullz RC .40 1.00
235 Matthew Shepherd RC .40 1.00
236 Thomas Hubbard RC .40 1.00
238 Kyle Bono RC .40 1.00
239 Craig Moldrem RC .40 1.00
240 Brandon Timm RC .40 1.00
241 Mike Carp RC 1.25 3.00
242 Joseph Muro RC .40 1.00
243 Derek Decarlo RC .40 1.00
244 Christopher Niesel RC .40 1.00
245 Trevor Lawhorn RC .40 1.00
246 Joey Howell RC .40 1.00
247 Dustin Hahn RC .40 1.00
248 James Fasano RC .40 1.00
249 Hainley Statia RC .40 1.00
250 Brandon Conway RC .40 1.00
251 Christopher McConnell RC .40 1.00
252 Austin Shappi RC .40 1.00
253 Joseph Metropoulos RC .40 1.00
254 David Nicholson RC .40 1.00
255 Ryan McCarthy RC .40 1.00
256 Michael Parisi RC .40 1.00
257 Andrew Macfarlane RC .40 1.00
258 Jeffrey Dominguez RC .40 1.00
259 Troy Patton RC .40 1.00
260 Ryan Norwood RC .40 1.00
261 Chad Boyd RC .40 1.00
262 Grant Plumley RC .40 1.00
263 Jeffrey Katz RC .40 1.00
264 Cory Middleton RC .40 1.00
265 Andrew Moffitt RC .40 1.00
266 Jarrett Grube RC .40 1.00
267 Derek Hankins RC .40 1.00
268 Douglas Reinhardt RC .40 1.00
269 Duron Legrande RC .40 1.00
270 Steven Jackson RC .40 1.00
271 Brian Hall RC .40 1.00
272 Cory Wade RC .40 1.00
273 John Grogan RC .40 1.00
274 Robert Asanovich RC .40 1.00
275 Kevin Hart RC .40 1.00
276 Matthew Guillory RC .40 1.00
277 Clifton Remole RC .40 1.00
278 David Trahan RC .40 1.00
279 Kristian Bell RC .40 1.00
280 Christopher Westervelt RC .40 1.00
281 Garry Bakker RC .40 1.00
282 Jonathan Ash RC .40 1.00
283 Ryan Phillips RC .40 1.00
284 Wesley Letson RC .40 1.00
285 Jeffrey Landing RC .40 1.00
286 Mark Worrell RC .40 1.00
287 Sean Gallagher RC .40 1.00
288 Nicholas Blasi RC .40 1.00
289 Kevin Frandsen RC .40 1.00
290 Richard Mercado RC .40 1.00
291 Matt Bush AU/400 RC 4.00 10.00
292 Mark Rogers AU/400 RC 4.00 10.00
293 Homer Bailey AU/400 RC 4.00 10.00
294 Chris Nelson AU/400 RC 2.50 6.00
295 Thomas Diamond AU/400 RC 2.50 6.00
296 Neil Walker AU/400 RC 8.00 20.00
297 Bill Bray AU/400 RC 2.50 6.00
298 David Purcey AU/400 RC 4.00 10.00
299 Scott Elbert AU/400 RC 2.50 6.00
300 Josh Fields AU/400 RC 4.00 10.00
301 Chris Lambert AU/400 RC 2.50 6.00
302 Trevor Plouffe AU/400 RC 6.00 15.00
303 Greg Golson AU/400 RC 2.50 6.00
304 Philip Hughes AU/400 RC 6.00 15.00
305 Kyle Waldrop AU/400 RC 2.50 6.00
306 Richie Robnett AU/350 RC 2.50 6.00
307 T.Tankersley AU/400 RC 2.50 6.00
308 Blake Dewitt AU/400 RC 4.00 10.00
309 Eric Hurley AU/400 RC 2.50 6.00
310 J.Howell AU/400 RC EX * 2.50 6.00
311 Zachary Jackson AU/400 RC 2.50 6.00
312 Justin Orenduff AU/400 RC 4.00 10.00
313 Tyler Lumsden AU/400 RC 2.50 6.00
314 Matthew Fox AU/600 RC 2.50 6.00
315 Danny Putnam AU/450 RC 2.50 6.00
316 Jon Poterson AU/400 RC 2.50 6.00
317 Gio Gonzalez AU/400 RC 4.00 10.00
318 Jay Rainville AU 475 RC 2.50 6.00
319 Huston Street AU/400 RC 4.00 10.00
320 Jeff Marquez AU/400 RC 2.50 6.00
321 Eric Beattie AU/500 RC 2.50 6.00
322 Reid Brignac AU/325 RC 6.00 15.00
323 Y.Gallardo AU/400 RC 6.00 15.00
324 Justin Hoyman AU/400 RC 2.50 6.00
325 B.J. Szymanski AU/400 RC 2.50 6.00
326 Seth Smith AU/600 RC 4.00 10.00
327 Karl Herren AU/600 RC 2.50 6.00
328 Brian Bixler AU/600 RC 2.50 6.00
329 Wesley Whisler AU/600 RC 2.50 6.00
330 E.San Pedro AU/400 RC 2.50 6.00
331 Billy Buckner AU/400 RC 2.50 6.00
332 Jon Zeringue AU/400 RC 2.50 6.00
333 Curtis Thigpen AU/400 RC 2.50 6.00
334 Blake Johnson AU/400 RC 2.50 6.00
335 Donald Lucy AU/400 RC 2.50 6.00
336 Michael Ferris AU/600 RC 2.50 6.00
337 A.Swarzak AU/600 RC 4.00 10.00
338 Jason Jaramillo AU/400 RC 2.50 6.00
339 Hunter Pence AU/600 RC 10.00 25.00
340 Dustin Pedroia AU/400 RC 30.00 80.00
341 Grant Johnson AU/400 RC 2.50 6.00
342 Kurt Suzuki AU/400 RC 4.00 10.00
343 Jason Vargas AU/600 RC 4.00 10.00
344 Raymond Liotta AU/400 RC 2.50 6.00
346 Eric Campbell AU/400 RC 2.50 6.00
347 Jeffrey Frazier AU/400 RC 2.50 6.00
348 G.Hernandez AU/400 RC 4.00 10.00
349 Wade Davis AU/600 RC 6.00 15.00
350 J.Wahpepah AU/400 RC 2.50 6.00
351 Scott Lewis AU/400 RC 2.50 6.00
352 Jeff Fiorentino AU/400 RC 2.50 6.00
353 S.Register AU/600 RC 2.50 6.00
354 Michael Schlact AU/400 RC 2.50 6.00
355 Eddie Prasch AU/400 RC 2.50 6.00
356 Adam Lind AU/400 RC 4.00 10.00
357 Ian Desmond AU/400 RC 4.00 10.00
358 Josh Johnson AU/575 RC 2.50 6.00
359 Garrett Mock AU/600 RC 2.50 6.00
360 Danny Hill AU/600 RC 2.50 6.00
361 Cory Dunlap AU/600 RC 2.50 6.00
362 Grant Hansen AU/600 RC 2.50 6.00
363 Eric Haberer AU/400 RC 2.50 6.00
364 E.Morlan AU/400 RC 4.00 10.00
365 James Happ AU/600 RC 6.00 15.00
366 M.Tuiasosopo AU/600 RC 6.00 15.00
367 Jordan Parraz AU/400 RC 4.00 10.00
368 Andrew Dobies AU/400 RC 2.50 6.00
369 Mark Reed AU/400 RC 2.50 6.00
370 Jason Windsor AU/400 RC 2.50 6.00
371 Gregory Burns AU/600 RC 2.50 6.00
372 Christian Garcia AU/600 RC 4.00 10.00
373 John Bowker AU/575 RC 2.50 6.00
374 J.C. Holt AU/550 RC 2.50 6.00
375 Daryl Jones AU/400 RC 2.50 6.00
376 Collin Mahoney AU/400 RC 2.50 6.00
377 A.Hathaway AU/400 RC 2.50 6.00
378 Matthew Spring AU/400 RC 2.50 6.00
379 Joshua Baker AU/400 RC 2.50 6.00
380 Charles Lofgren AU/400 RC 2.50 6.00
381 Raf Gonzalez AU/400 RC 2.50 6.00
382 Brad Bergesen AU/575 RC 2.50 6.00
383 Brandon Boggs AU/400 RC 2.50 6.00
384 J.Bauserman AU/400 RC 2.50 6.00
385 Collin Balester AU/500 RC 2.50 6.00
386 James Moore AU/400 RC 2.50 6.00
387 Robert Janssen AU/400 RC 2.50 6.00
388 Luis Guerra AU/400 RC 6.00 15.00
389 Lucas Harrell AU/550 RC 2.50 6.00
390 Donnie Smith AU/500 RC 2.50 6.00
391 Mark Robinson AU/525 RC 2.50 6.00
392 Louis Marson AU/550 RC 4.00 10.00
393 Rob Johnson AU/600 RC 2.50 6.00
394 L.Santangelo AU/600 RC 2.50 6.00
395 T.Hottovy AU/400 RC 2.50 6.00
396 Ryan Webb AU/400 RC 2.50 6.00
397 Jamar Walton AU/400 RC 2.50 6.00
398 Jason Jones AU/400 RC 2.50 6.00
399 Clay Timpner AU/600 RC 2.50 6.00
400 James Parr AU/400 RC 2.50 6.00
401 Sean Kazmar AU/400 RC 2.50 6.00
402 Andrew Kown AU/400 RC 2.50 6.00
403 Jacob McGee AU/600 RC 6.00 15.00
404 Michael Butia AU/600 RC 2.50 6.00
405 Paul Janish AU/500 RC 4.00 10.00
406 Matthew Macri AU/400 RC 4.00 10.00
407 Mike Nickeas AU/500 RC 2.50 6.00
408 Kyle Bloom AU/550 RC 2.50 6.00
409 Luis Rivera AU/500 RC 2.50 6.00
410 William Bunn AU/600 RC 2.50 6.00
411 Enrique Barrera AU/400 RC 2.50 6.00
412 R.Klosterman AU/400 RC 2.50 6.00
413 John Raglani AU/515 RC 2.50 6.00
414 Brandon Allen AU/500 RC 2.50 6.00
415 A.Baldwin AU/600 RC 2.50 6.00
416 Mark Lowe AU/400 RC 4.00 10.00
417 Mitch Einertson AU/400 RC 2.50 6.00
418 Ryan Schroyer AU/600 RC 2.50 6.00
419 Bradley Davis AU/400 RC 2.50 6.00
420 Jesse Hoover AU/500 RC 2.50 6.00
421 G.Broshuis AU/400 RC 2.50 6.00
422 Peter Pope AU/400 RC 2.50 6.00
423 Brent Dlugach AU/400 RC 2.50 6.00
424 Ryan Coultas AU/400 RC 2.50 6.00
425 Ryan Royster AU/400 RC 2.50 6.00
426 S.Chapman AU/400 RC 2.50 6.00
427 B.Chamberlin AU/400 RC 2.50 6.00
428 J.Koshansky AU/550 RC 2.50 6.00
429 William Susdorf AU/400 RC 2.50 6.00
430 A.J. Johnson AU/400 RC 2.50 6.00
431 Jeremy Sowers AU/400 RC 2.50 6.00
432 Justin Pekarek AU/400 RC 2.50 6.00
433 Brett Smith AU/400 RC 2.50 6.00
434 Matt Durkin AU/400 RC 2.50 6.00
435 Daniel Barone AU/400 RC 2.50 6.00
436 Scott Hyde AU/400 RC 2.50 6.00
437 T.Everidge AU/400 RC 2.50 6.00
444 Mark Trumbo AU/400 RC 6.00 15.00
446 Eric Patterson AU/400 RC 2.50 6.00
447 Michael Rozier AU/400 RC 2.50 6.00

2004 SP Prospects Autograph Bonus

OVERALL AU ODDS 1:5
PRINT RUNS B/WN 325-600 COPIES PER
AA Andrew Alvarado/400 3.00 8.00
AM Andrew Moffitt/400 3.00 8.00
AR Adam Russell/550 3.00 8.00
AS Austin Shappi/475 6.00 15.00
BB Brandon Burgess/400 6.00 15.00
BC Brandon Conway/400 3.00 8.00
BE Benjamin Harrison/387 3.00 8.00
BH Brian Hall/400 6.00 15.00
BL Chad Blackwell/400 3.00 8.00
BM Bradley McCann/400 10.00 25.00
BO Kyle Bono/400 3.00 8.00
BP Brandon Parillo/475 6.00 15.00
BR Barry Richmond/400 3.00 8.00
BT Brandon Timm/475 3.00 8.00
BZ Ben Zobrist/600 20.00 50.00
CA Mike Carp/400 3.00 8.00
CB Chad Boyd/475 3.00 8.00
CH Christopher McConnell/400 3.00 8.00
CL Clay Meredith/400 3.00 8.00
CM Cory Middleton/400 3.00 8.00
CN Christopher Niesel/475 6.00 15.00
CP Cory Patton/400 3.00 8.00
CR Clifton Remole/400 3.00 8.00
CS Clint Sammons/400 3.00 8.00
CW Cory Wade/400 6.00 15.00
DA David Haehnel/475 6.00 15.00
DB Daniel Batz/400 3.00 8.00
DD Derek Decarlo/400 3.00 8.00
DH Derek Hankins/400 3.00 8.00
DI Devin Ivany/550 3.00 8.00
DL Duron Legrande/400 3.00 8.00
DN David Nicholson/475 3.00 8.00
DR Douglas Reinhardt/400 3.00 8.00
DT Derek Tharpe/400 3.00 8.00
ER Eric Ridener/475 3.00 8.00
FP Fernando Perez/400 20.00 50.00
FS Freddy Sandoval/400 6.00 15.00
GA Jared Gaston/400 3.00 8.00
GB Garry Bakker/400 3.00 8.00
GG Gregory Goetz/400 3.00 8.00
GP Grant Plumley/475 3.00 8.00
GR John Grogan/400 3.00 8.00
HA Dustin Hahn/400 3.00 8.00
HE Justin Hedrick/400 3.00 8.00
HO Joey Howell/400 3.00 8.00
HS Hainley Statia/400 5.00 12.00
JA Jonathan Ash/400 8.00 20.00
JB Jermaine Brock/400 6.00 15.00
JD Jeffrey Dominguez/400 3.00 8.00
JF James Fasano/400 3.00 8.00
JG Jarrett Grube/400 3.00 8.00
JH Jarrett Hoffpauir/400 6.00 15.00
JK Jeffrey Katz/400 3.00 8.00
JL Joshua Leblanc/400 3.00 8.00
JM Joseph Metropoulos/400 6.00 15.00
JO John Hardy/475 3.00 8.00
JQ Jason Quarles/400 3.00 8.00
KB Kristian Bell/400 3.00 8.00
KF Kevin Frandsen/400 10.00 25.00
KH Kevin Hart/400 5.00 12.00
KK Koley Kolberg/400 3.00 8.00
LA Jeffrey Landing/400 3.00 8.00
LE Wesley Letson/400 3.00 8.00
LF Lucas French/400 3.00 8.00
MA Andrew Macfarlane/400 3.00 8.00
MC Jarod McAuliff/400 3.00 8.00
ME Carlos Medero-Stullz/400 3.00 8.00
MG Matthew Guillory/400 3.00 8.00
MI James Miller/475 3.00 8.00
MJ Mark Jecmen/600 3.00 8.00
MO Craig Moldrem/400 3.00 8.00
MP Michael Parisi/475 3.00 8.00
MR Mark Roberts/400 3.00 8.00
MS Matthew Shepherd/400 3.00 8.00
MU Joseph Muro/400 3.00 8.00
MW Mark Worrell/400 6.00 15.00
NB Nicholas Blasi/400 3.00 8.00
PB Patrick Bryant/400 3.00 8.00
PP Patrick Perry/475 6.00 15.00
RA Robert Asanovich/400 6.00 15.00
RD Randy Dicken/475 3.00 8.00
RI Richard Mercado/400 3.00 8.00
RM Ryan McCarthy/400 8.00 20.00
RN Ryan Norwood/400 10.00 25.00
RP Ryan Phillips/400 3.00 8.00
RS Richard Steik/400 3.00 8.00
SB Sebastien Boucher/325 6.00 15.00
SE Sean Gallagher/400 30.00 60.00
SG Sean Gamble/400 3.00 8.00
SJ Steven Jackson/475 3.00 8.00
TH Thomas Hubbard/400 3.00 8.00
TL Trevor Lawhorn/475 6.00 15.00
TM Timothy Murphey/400 3.00 8.00
TP Troy Patton/400 3.00 8.00
TR David Trahan/400 3.00 8.00
WE Christopher Westervelt/400 3.00 8.00
WL William Layman/400 3.00 8.00
WT William Thompson/475 3.00 8.00

2004 SP Prospects Draft Duos Dual Autographs

OVERALL AU ODDS 1:5
STATED PRINT RUN 175 SERIAL #'d SETS
BB B.Bray/C.Balester 10.00 25.00
BG H.Bailey/R.Gonzalez 15.00 40.00
BH M.Bush/P.Hughes 6.00 15.00
BI B.Bray/I.Desmond 6.00 15.00
BJ M.Bush/D.Jones 4.00 10.00
BK M.Bush/S.Kazmar 4.00 10.00
BM B.Buckner/J.Moore 5.00 12.00
BN M.Bush/C.Nelson 8.00 20.00
BP M.Bush/T.Plouffe 6.00 15.00
BR R.Brignac/R.Royster 5.00 12.00
BS H.Bailey/B.Szymanski 4.00 10.00
BT T.Diamond/B.Boggs 4.00 10.00
CF B.Chamberlin/J.Fiorentino 10.00 25.00
CH R.Coultas/A.Hathaway 5.00 12.00
CL J.Hoyman/J.Sowers 12.50 30.00
CO S.Register/S.Smith 10.00 25.00
DB B.Dewitt/D.Batz 4.00 10.00
DG C.Dunlap/L.Guerra 5.00 12.00
DH T.Diamond/E.Hurley 10.00 25.00
DR B.Dewitt/J.Raglani 5.00 12.00
DZ D.Purcey/Z.Jackson 4.00 10.00
EA E.Beattie/A.Kown 5.00 12.00
EC E.Beattie/C.Mahoney 5.00 12.00
ED S.Elbert/B.Dewitt 10.00 25.00
EJ E.Campbell/J.Holt 4.00 10.00
EM E.Hurley/M.Nickeas 10.00 25.00
ER S.Elbert/J.Raglani 5.00 12.00
FB J.Fiorentino/B.Bergesen 10.00 25.00
FH J.Fields/L.Harrell 15.00 40.00
FM J.Frazier/C.Mahoney 5.00 12.00
FW J.Fields/W.Whisler 4.00 10.00
GB H.Bailey/G.Goetz 8.00 20.00
GG G.Golson/S.Gamble 10.00 25.00
GH G.Golson/J.Happ 15.00 40.00
GM G.Gonzalez/T.Murphey 8.00 20.00
GW Y.Gallardo/J.Wahpepah 6.00 15.00
HB J.Howell/C.Blackwell 4.00 10.00
HG P.Hughes/C.Garcia 20.00 50.00
HH G.Hernandez/A.Hathaway 12.50 30.00
HJ H.Pence/J.Parraz 6.00 15.00
HM J.Marquez/P.Hughes 20.00 50.00
HP P.Hughes/J.Poterson 20.00 50.00
HS K.Herren/M.Schlact 5.00 12.00
JB B.Buckner/J.Johnson 4.00 10.00
JE J.Frazier/E.Beattie 5.00 12.00
JH J.Howell/J.Johnson 5.00 12.00
JJ J.Poterson/J.Jones 5.00 12.00
JK Z.Jackson/R.Klosterman 4.00 10.00
JM J.Jaramillo/L.Marson 5.00 12.00
JP J.Rainville/P.Bryant 10.00 25.00
JR G.Johnson/M.Reed 4.00 10.00
JS J.Sowers/S.Lewis 5.00 12.00
KB K.Waldrop/P.Bryant 5.00 12.00
KH M.Durkin/A.Hathaway 4.00 10.00
LA R.Liotta/B.Allen 5.00 12.00
LF C.Lambert/M.Ferris 5.00 12.00
LG T.Lumsden/G.Gonzalez 4.00 10.00
LH D.Lucy/G.Hansen 4.00 10.00
LK A.Lind/R.Klosterman 5.00 12.00
LR T.Lumsden/A.Russell 5.00 12.00
LS C.Lambert/D.Smith 4.00 10.00
MH J.Marquez/J.Hoover 5.00 12.00
MR E.Morlan/M.Robinson 5.00 12.00
MS J.Marquez/B.Smith 5.00 12.00
NB N.Walker/B.Bixler 10.00 25.00
NK N.Walker/K.Bloom 6.00 15.00
NM C.Nelson/M.Macri 12.00 30.00
NS C.Nelson/S.Smith 4.00 10.00
OG J.Orenduff/L.Guerra 5.00 12.00
OJ J.Orenduff/B.Johnson 5.00 12.00
PB E.Prasch/J.Bauserman 5.00 12.00
PD D.Pedroia/A.Dobies 15.00 40.00
PI E.San Pedro/D.Ivany 5.00 12.00
PJ D.Purcey/R.Janssen 4.00 10.00
PR T.Plouffe/M.Robinson 4.00 10.00
PT D.Putnam/D.Tharpe 5.00 12.00
PW T.Plouffe/K.Waldrop 4.00 10.00
PZ J.Parraz/B.Zobrist 10.00 25.00
RB M.Rogers/J.Baker 4.00 10.00
RD C.Dunlap/J.Raglani 5.00 12.00
RG M.Rogers/Y.Gallardo 8.00 20.00
RH R.Robnett/H.Street 4.00 10.00
RL L.Rivera/W.Layman 5.00 12.00
RP R.Robnett/D.Putnam 5.00 12.00
RS J.Rainville/A.Swarzak 4.00 10.00
RW R.Robnett/J.Windsor 5.00 12.00
SB J.Sowers/H.Bailey 6.00 15.00
SH B.Smith/P.Hughes 6.00 15.00
SJ B.Szymanski/P.Janish 5.00 12.00
SK S.Smith/J.Koshansky 4.00 10.00
SL J.Sowers/C.Lofgren 6.00 15.00
SR R.Robnett/K.Suzuki 4.00 10.00
SS H.Street/K.Suzuki 12.50 30.00
SW H.Street/R.Webb 4.00 10.00
TD T.Tankersley/B.Davis 4.00 10.00
TH C.Thigpen/D.Hill 5.00 12.00
TV T.Tankersley/J.Vargas 4.00 10.00
WB J.Wahpepah/J.Baker 4.00 10.00
WE B.Buckner/E.Barrera 4.00 10.00
WF K.Waldrop/M.Fox 5.00 12.00
WJ B.Buckner/J.Howell 4.00 10.00
WR R.Brignac/W.Davis 4.00 10.00
ZM J.Zeringue/G.Mock 10.00 25.00
ZP H.Pence/B.Zobrist 10.00 25.00

2004 SP Prospects Link to the Future Dual Autographs

OVERALL AU ODDS 1:5
STATED PRINT RUN 100 SERIAL #'d SETS
BD Adrian Beltre 15.00 40.00
Blake Dewitt
BG Carlos Beltran 10.00 25.00
Greg Golson
BH Angel Berroa 10.00 25.00
James Howell
CD Roger Clemens 20.00 50.00
Thomas Diamond
CF Matt Clement 6.00 15.00
Matthew Fox
EJ Eric Chavez 6.00 15.00
Josh Fields
GB Nomar Garciaparra 6.00 15.00
Matt Bush
GP Brian Giles 10.00 25.00
Danny Putnam
GS Ken Griffey Jr. 30.00 60.00
B.J. Szymanski
GZ Luis Gonzalez 10.00 25.00
Jonathan Zeringue
HS Todd Helton 15.00 40.00
Seth Smith
HW Rich Harden 10.00 25.00
Kyle Waldrop
JB Jason Kendall 6.00 15.00
Brian Bixler
JJ Edwin Jackson 6.00 15.00
Blake Johnson
JR Andruw Jones 8.00 20.00
Richie Robnett
KB Scott Kazmir 10.00 25.00
Reid Brignac
KW Jason Kendall 10.00 25.00
Neil Walker
LS Paul LoDuca 10.00 25.00
Erick San Pedro
MB Mark Mulder 10.00 25.00
Bill Bray
MH Mike Mussina 30.00 60.00
Philip Hughes
MP Joe Mauer 20.00 50.00
Trevor Plouffe
MS Mike Mussina 6.00 15.00
Brett Smith
OH Magglio Ordonez 10.00 25.00
Karl Herren
PE Odalis Perez 10.00 25.00
Scott Elbert
PJ Mark Prior 15.00 40.00
Grant Johnson
QT Guillermo Quiroz 6.00 15.00
Curtis Thigpen
RE Roy Oswalt 10.00 25.00
Eric Hurley
RF Scott Rolen 15.00 40.00
Michael Ferris
RL Scott Rolen 6.00 15.00
Chris Lambert
RP Alexis Rios 10.00 25.00
David Purcey
SJ Johan Santana 8.00 20.00
Jay Rainville
SR Ben Sheets 20.00 40.00
Mark Rogers
SW Johan Santana 6.00 15.00
Kyle Waldrop
TJ Tom Glavine 15.00 40.00
Jeremy Sowers
TN Miguel Tejada 6.00 15.00
Chris Nelson
TS Tim Hudson 15.00 40.00
Huston Street
VD Victor Martinez 10.00 25.00
Donald Lucy
VM Javier Vazquez 10.00 25.00
Jeff Marquez
VP Javier Vazquez 6.00 15.00
Jonathan Poterson
WB Kerry Wood 8.00 20.00
Homer Bailey
WT Dontrelle Willis 10.00 25.00
Taylor Tankersley

2004 SP Prospects Link to the Future Triple Autographs

OVERALL AU ODDS 1:5
STATED PRINT RUN 50 SERIAL #'d SETS
PRICING UNAVAILABLE AT THIS TIME
GBG Ken Griffey Jr. 20.00 50.00
Homer Bailey
Rafael Gonzalez
JJB Edwin Jackson 10.00 25.00
Blake Johnson
Daniel Batz

2004 SP Prospects Link to the Past Dual Autographs

OVERALL AU ODDS 1:5
STATED PRINT RUN 50 SERIAL #'d SETS
NO PRICING DUE TO LOW VOLUME
AB A.Dawson/B.Bray 10.00 25.00
AF L.Aparicio/J.Fields 15.00 40.00
AS Bi.Williams/R.Robnett 10.00 25.00
BH G.Brett/J.Howell 30.00 60.00
BJ G.Brett/J.Johnson 20.00 50.00
BP Y.Berra/J.Poterson 15.00 40.00
BR B.Blyleven/J.Rainville 8.00 20.00
BW J.Bench/N.Walker 25.00 60.00
CH D.Cone/J.Howell 8.00 20.00
CP J.Carter/D.Purcey 10.00 25.00
CR J.Canseco/R.Robnett 20.00 50.00
DB D.Snider/B.Dewitt 10.00 25.00
DE D.McLain/E.Beattie 10.00 25.00
DT A.Dawson/T.Tankersley 10.00 25.00
FG C.Fisk/G.Gonzalez 10.00 25.00
FH B.Feller/J.Hoyman 8.00 20.00
FL C.Fisk/T.Lumsden 10.00 25.00
FS B.Feller/J.Sowers 15.00 40.00
GL B.Gibson/C.Lambert 12.00 30.00
GM R.Guidry/J.Marquez 10.00 25.00
JD J.Canseco/D.Putnam 20.00 50.00
JE F.Jenkins/E.Hurley 6.00 15.00
KP H.Killebrew/T.Plouffe 12.50 30.00
KW J.Kaat/K.Waldrop 10.00 25.00
MB B.Mazeroski/B.Bixler 10.00 25.00
MN D.Murphy/C.Nelson 20.00 50.00
NO D.Newcombe/J.Orenduff 10.00 25.00
PD G.Perry/T.Diamond 8.00 20.00
PE J.Podres/S.Elbert 8.00 20.00
PP K.Puckett/T.Plouffe 30.00 80.00
PS T.Perez/B.Szymanski 12.00 30.00
RB N.Ryan/H.Bailey 50.00 100.00
RH R.Fingers/H.Street 8.00 20.00
RY R.Fingers/Y.Gallardo 20.00 50.00
SB O.Smith/M.Bush 20.00 50.00
SD T.Seaver/M.Durkin 15.00 40.00
SG M.Schmidt/G.Golson 15.00 40.00
TF L.Tiant/M.Fox 6.00 15.00
WB W.Ford/B.Smith 12.50 30.00
WJ D.Winfield/Z.Jackson 8.00 20.00
WP W.Ford/P.Hughes 20.00 50.00
WR W.Boggs/R.Brignac 6.00 15.00
YR R.Yount/M.Rogers 15.00 40.00

2004 SP Prospects National Honors USA Jersey

STATED ODDS 1:12
AG Alex Gordon 4.00 10.00
BC J. Brent Cox 3.00 8.00
BH Brett Hayes 3.00 8.00
CR Cesar Ramos 3.00 8.00
CV Chris Valaika 3.00 8.00
DB Daniel Bard 3.00 8.00
DS Drew Stubbs 3.00 8.00
IK Ian Kennedy 4.00 10.00
JC Jeff Clement 3.00 8.00
JD Joey Devine 3.00 8.00
JL Jed Lowrie 3.00 8.00
JM John Mayberry Jr. 3.00 8.00
LH Luke Hochevar 3.00 8.00
MP Mike Pelfrey 4.00 10.00
MR Mark Romanczuk 3.00 8.00
RR Ricky Romero 3.00 8.00
RZ Ryan Zimmerman 5.00 12.00
SK Stephen Kahn 3.00 8.00
TB Travis Buck 3.00 8.00
TC Trevor Crowe 3.00 8.00
TE Taylor Teagarden 3.00 8.00
TT Troy Tulowitzki 5.00 12.00

1999 SP Signature

The 1999 SP Signature set was issued in one series totalling 180 cards and distributed in three card packs with a suggested retail price of $19.99. The expensive SRP was due to the fact that there is one autograph card per pack. The set features color action player photos with player information on the cardback. Rookie Cards include A.J. Burnett and Pat Burrell. 350 Mel Ott A Piece of History 500 Club bat cards were randomly seeded into packs. Pricing for these bat cards can be referenced under 1999 Upper Deck A Piece of History 500 Club.

COMPLETE SET (180) 75.00 150.00
1 Nomar Garciaparra 1.50 4.00
2 Ken Griffey Jr. 2.00 5.00
3 J.D. Drew .40 1.00
4 Alex Rodriguez 1.50 4.00
5 Juan Gonzalez .40 1.00
6 Mo Vaughn .40 1.00
7 Greg Maddux 1.50 4.00
8 Chipper Jones 1.00 2.50
9 Frank Thomas 1.00 2.50
10 Vladimir Guerrero 1.00 2.50
11 Mike Piazza 1.50 4.00
12 Eric Chavez .40 1.00
13 Tony Gwynn 1.25 3.00
14 Orlando Hernandez .40 1.00
15 Pat Burrell RC 3.00 8.00
16 Darin Erstad .40 1.00
17 Greg Vaughn .30 .75
18 Russ Branyan .30 .75
19 Gabe Kapler .40 1.00
20 Craig Biggio .60 1.50
21 Troy Glaus .60 1.50
22 Pedro Martinez .60 1.50
23 Carlos Beltran .60 1.50
24 Derrek Lee .60 1.50
25 Manny Ramirez .60 1.50
26 Shea Hillenbrand RC 1.50 4.00
27 Carlos Lee .40 1.00
28 Angel Pena .30 .75
29 Rafael Roque RC .40 1.00
30 Octavio Dotel .30 .75
31 Jeromy Burnitz .40 1.00
32 Jeremy Giambi .30 .75
33 Andruw Jones .60 1.50
34 Todd Helton .60 1.50
35 Scott Rolen .60 1.50
36 Jason Kendall .40 1.00
37 Trevor Hoffman .40 1.00
38 Barry Bonds 2.50 6.00
39 Ivan Rodriguez .60 1.50
40 Roy Halladay 1.00 2.50
41 Rickey Henderson 1.00 2.50
42 Ryan Minor .30 .75
43 Brian Jordan .40 1.00
44 Alex Gonzalez .30 .75
45 Raul Mondesi .40 1.00
46 Corey Koskie .30 .75
47 Paul O'Neill .60 1.50
48 Todd Walker .30 .75
49 Carlos Febles .30 .75
50 Travis Fryman .40 1.00
51 Albert Belle .40 1.00
52 Travis Lee .30 .75
53 Bruce Chen .30 .75
54 Reggie Taylor .30 .75
55 Jerry Hairston Jr. .30 .75
56 Carlos Guillen .40 1.00
57 Michael Barrett .30 .75
58 Jason Conti .30 .75
59 Joe Lawrence .30 .75
60 Jeff Cirillo .30 .75
61 Juan Melo .30 .75
62 Chad Hermansen .30 .75
63 Ruben Mateo .30 .75
64 Ben Davis .30 .75
65 Mike Caruso .30 .75
66 Jason Giambi .40 1.00
67 Jose Canseco .60 1.50
68 Chad Hutchinson RC .60 1.50
69 Mitch Meluskey .30 .75
70 Adrian Beltre .40 1.00
71 Mark Kotsay .40 1.00
72 Juan Encarnacion .30 .75
73 Dermal Brown .30 .75
74 Kevin Witt .30 .75
75 Vinny Castilla .40 1.00
76 Aramis Ramirez .40 1.00
77 Marlon Anderson .30 .75
78 Mike Kinkade .30 .75
79 Kevin Barker .30 .75
80 Ron Belliard .30 .75
81 Chris Haas .30 .75
82 Bob Henley .30 .75
83 Fernando Seguignol .30 .75
84 Damon Minor .30 .75
85 A.J. Burnett RC 1.50 4.00
86 Calvin Pickering .30 .75
87 Mike Darr .30 .75
88 Cesar King .30 .75
89 Rob Bell .30 .75
90 Derrick Gibson .30 .75
91 Orber Moreno RC .40 1.00
92 Robert Fick .30 .75
93 Doug Mientkiewicz RC 1.00 2.50
94 A.J. Pierzynski .40 1.00
95 Orlando Palmeiro .30 .75
96 Sidney Ponson .30 .75
97 Ivanon Coffie RC .40 1.00
98 Juan Pena RC .40 1.00
99 Matt Karchner .30 .75
100 Carlos Castillo .30 .75
101 Bryan Ward RC .40 1.00
102 Mario Valdez .30 .75
103 Billy Wagner .40 1.00
104 Miguel Tejada .40 1.00
105 Jose Cruz Jr. .30 .75
106 George Lombard .30 .75
107 Geoff Jenkins .30 .75
108 Ray Lankford .40 1.00
109 Todd Stottlemyre .30 .75
110 Mike Lowell .40 1.00
111 Matt Clement .40 1.00
112 Scott Brosius .40 1.00
113 Preston Wilson .40 1.00
114 Bartolo Colon .40 1.00
115 Rolando Arrojo .30 .75
116 Jose Guillen .40 1.00
117 Ron Gant .40 1.00
118 Ricky Ledee .30 .75
119 Carlos Delgado .40 1.00
120 Abraham Nunez .30 .75
121 John Olerud .40 1.00
122 Chan Ho Park .40 1.00
123 Brad Radke .40 1.00
124 Al Leiter .40 1.00
125 Gary Matthews Jr. .30 .75
126 F.P. Santangelo .30 .75
127 Brad Fullmer .30 .75
128 Matt Anderson .30 .75
129 A.J. Hinch .30 .75
130 Sterling Hitchcock .30 .75
131 Edgar Martinez .60 1.50
132 Fernando Tatis .30 .75
133 Bobby Smith .30 .75
134 Paul Konerko .40 1.00
135 Sean Casey .40 1.00
136 Donnie Sadler .30 .75
137 Denny Neagle .30 .75
138 Sandy Alomar Jr. .30 .75
139 Mariano Rivera 1.00 2.50
140 Emil Brown .30 .75
141 J.T. Snow .40 1.00
142 Eli Marrero .30 .75
143 Rusty Greer .40 1.00
144 Johnny Damon .60 1.50
145 Damion Easley .30 .75
146 Eric Milton .30 .75
147 Rico Brogna .30 .75
148 Ray Durham .40 1.00
149 Wally Joyner .40 1.00
150 Royce Clayton .30 .75
151 David Ortiz 1.00 2.50
152 Wade Boggs .60 1.50
153 Ugueth Urbina .30 .75
154 Richard Hidalgo .30 .75
155 Bob Abreu .40 1.00
156 Robb Nen .40 1.00
157 David Segui .30 .75
158 Sean Berry .30 .75
159 Kevin Tapani .30 .75
160 Jason Varitek 1.00 2.50
161 Fernando Vina .30 .75
162 Jim Leyritz .30 .75
163 Enrique Wilson .30 .75
164 Jim Parque .30 .75
165 Doug Glanville .30 .75
166 Jesus Sanchez .30 .75
167 Nolan Ryan 2.50 6.00
168 Robin Yount 1.50 4.00
169 Stan Musial 1.50 4.00
170 Tom Seaver .60 1.50
171 Mike Schmidt 2.00 5.00
172 Willie Stargell .60 1.50
173 Rollie Fingers .40 1.00
174 Willie McCovey .40 1.00
175 Harmon Killebrew 1.00 2.50
176 Eddie Mathews 1.00 2.50

177 Reggie Jackson .60 1.50
178 Frank Robinson .60 1.50
179 Ken Griffey Sr. .40 1.00
180 Eddie Murray 1.00 2.50
S1 Ken Griffey Jr. Sample 1.00 2.50

1999 SP Signature Autographs

ONE PER PACK
EXCHANGE DEADLINE 5/12/00
AB Albert Belle 6.00 15.00
ABE Adrian Beltre 10.00 25.00
AG Alex Gonzalez 3.00 8.00
AJ Andruw Jones 12.00 30.00
AJB A.J. Burnett 4.00 10.00
AJP A.J. Pierzynski 6.00 15.00
AL Al Leiter 3.00 8.00
AN Abraham Nunez 3.00 8.00
AP Angel Pena 6.00 15.00
AR Alex Rodriguez 40.00 80.00
ARA Aramis Ramirez 3.00 8.00
BA Bob Abreu 6.00 15.00
BB Barry Bonds 50.00 100.00
BC Bruce Chen 3.00 8.00
BCO Bartolo Colon 10.00 25.00
BD Ben Davis 3.00 8.00
BF Brad Fullmer 3.00 8.00
BH Bob Henley 3.00 8.00
BR Brad Radke 6.00 15.00
BS Bobby Smith 3.00 8.00
BW Bryan Ward 3.00 8.00
BWA Billy Wagner 10.00 25.00
CBE Carlos Beltran 12.00 30.00
CC Carlos Castillo 3.00 8.00
CD Carlos Delgado 6.00 15.00
CF Carlos Febles 3.00 8.00
CH Chad Hermansen 3.00 8.00
CHA Chris Haas 3.00 8.00
CHU Chad Hutchinson 3.00 8.00
CJ Chipper Jones 75.00 200.00
CK Corey Koskie 3.00 8.00
CKI Cesar King 3.00 8.00
CL Carlos Lee 3.00 8.00
CP Calvin Pickering 3.00 8.00
DAM Damon Minor 3.00 8.00
DB Dermal Brown 3.00 8.00
DE Darin Erstad 3.00 8.00
DEA Damion Easley 3.00 8.00
DG Derrick Gibson 3.00 8.00
DGL Doug Glanville 3.00 8.00
DL Derrek Lee 6.00 15.00
DO David Ortiz 30.00 80.00
DOM Doug Mientkiewicz 3.00 8.00
DS Donnie Sadler 3.00 8.00
DSE David Segui 3.00 8.00
EB Emil Brown 3.00 8.00
EC Eric Chavez 3.00 8.00
ED Orlando Hernandez SP 15.00 40.00
ELI Eli Marrero 3.00 8.00
EM Edgar Martinez 15.00 40.00
EMA Eddie Mathews 25.00 60.00
EMI Eric Milton 3.00 8.00
EW Enrique Wilson 3.00 8.00
FR Frank Robinson 30.00 80.00
FS Fernando Seguignol 3.00 8.00
FT Frank Thomas 50.00 100.00
FTA Fernando Tatis 3.00 8.00
FV Fernando Vina 3.00 8.00
GJ Geoff Jenkins 3.00 8.00
GK Gabe Kapler 6.00 15.00
GM Greg Maddux 50.00 120.00
GMJ Gary Matthews Jr. 3.00 8.00
GV Greg Vaughn 3.00 8.00
HK Harmon Killebrew 25.00 60.00
IC Ivanon Coffie 3.00 8.00
JAG Jason Giambi 3.00 8.00
JC Jason Conti 3.00 8.00
JCI Jeff Cirillo 6.00 15.00
JD J.D. Drew 6.00 15.00
JDA Johnny Damon 6.00 15.00
JE Juan Encarnacion 3.00 8.00
JEG Jeremy Giambi 3.00 8.00
JG Jose Guillen 3.00 8.00
JHJ Jerry Hairston Jr. 3.00 8.00
JK Jason Kendall 3.00 8.00
JLA Joe Lawrence 3.00 8.00
JLE Jim Leyritz 3.00 8.00
JM Juan Melo 3.00 8.00
JO John Olerud 8.00 20.00
JOC Jose Canseco 15.00 40.00
JP Jim Parque 3.00 8.00
JR Ken Griffey Jr. 75.00 150.00
JS Jesus Sanchez 3.00 8.00
JT J.T. Snow 3.00 8.00
JV Jason Varitek 20.00 50.00
KB Kevin Barker 3.00 8.00
KW Kevin Witt 3.00 8.00
MA Marlon Anderson 3.00 8.00
MB Michael Barrett 3.00 8.00
MC Mike Caruso 3.00 8.00
MCL Matt Clement 6.00 15.00
MK Mark Kotsay 6.00 15.00
MKA Matt Karchner 3.00 8.00
MKI Mike Kinkade 3.00 8.00
MME Mitch Meluskey 3.00 8.00
MO Mo Vaughn 6.00 15.00
MP Mike Piazza 60.00 150.00
MR Manny Ramirez 15.00 40.00
MRI Mariano Rivera 125.00 300.00
MS Mike Schmidt 25.00 60.00
MT Miguel Tejada 3.00 8.00
MV Mario Valdez 3.00 8.00
NG Nomar Garciaparra 15.00 40.00
NR Nolan Ryan 60.00 150.00
OD Octavio Dotel 3.00 8.00
OP Orlando Palmeiro 3.00 8.00
PB Pat Burrell 3.00 8.00
PG Ivan Rodriguez 15.00 40.00
PK Paul Konerko 6.00 15.00
PM Pedro Martinez 20.00 50.00
PO Paul O'Neill 10.00 25.00
POP Willie Stargell 20.00 50.00
RB Russ Branyan 3.00 8.00
RBE Ron Belliard 3.00 8.00
RC Royce Clayton 3.00 8.00
RD Ray Durham 6.00 15.00
RGA Ron Gant SP 3.00 8.00
RGR Rusty Greer 6.00 15.00
RH Roy Halladay 75.00 200.00
RJ Reggie Jackson SP 40.00 100.00
RL Ray Lankford 6.00 15.00
RM Ryan Minor 3.00 8.00
RMA Ruben Mateo 3.00 8.00
RN Robb Nen 6.00 15.00
ROB Rob Bell 3.00 8.00
ROB Robert Fick 3.00 8.00
ROL Rollie Fingers 8.00 20.00
RR Rafael Roque 3.00 8.00
RT Reggie Taylor 3.00 8.00
RY Robin Yount 25.00 60.00
SA Sandy Alomar Jr. 6.00 15.00
SB Scott Brosius SP 12.00 30.00
SC Sean Casey 5.00 12.00
SHH Shea Hillenbrand 3.00 8.00
SM Stan Musial 40.00 100.00
SP Sidney Ponson 3.00 8.00
SR Ken Griffey Sr. 6.00 15.00
SR Scott Rolen 4.00 10.00
STH Sterling Hitchcock 3.00 8.00
TG Tony Gwynn 30.00 60.00
TGL Troy Glaus 5.00 12.00
THE Todd Helton 10.00 25.00
THO Trevor Hoffman 12.00 30.00
TSE Tom Seaver 50.00 120.00
TST Todd Stottlemyre 3.00 8.00
TW Todd Walker 6.00 15.00
VC Vinny Castilla 3.00 8.00
VG Vladimir Guerrero 15.00 40.00
WJ Wally Joyner 6.00 15.00
WMC Willie McCovey 15.00 40.00

1999 SP Signature Autographs Gold

RANDOM INSERTS IN PACKS
STATED PRINT RUN 50 SERIAL #'d SETS
11 PLAYERS DID NOT SIGN THEIR CARDS
UNSIGNED CARDS MARKED AS NO AU
EXCHANGE DEADLINE 5/12/00
AB Albert Belle 8.00 20.00
ABE Adrian Beltre 12.00 30.00
AG Alex Gonzalez 6.00 15.00
AJ Andruw Jones 30.00 80.00
AJB A.J. Burnett SP/20
AP Angel Pena 12.50 30.00
AR Alex Rodriguez 50.00 100.00
ARA Aramis Ramirez 4.00 10.00
BB Barry Bonds 150.00 300.00
BC Bruce Chen 6.00 15.00
BD Ben Davis 6.00 15.00
BH Bob Henley 6.00 15.00
BJ Brian Jordan NO AU 2.50 6.00
CB Craig Biggio NO AU 2.50 6.00
CBE Carlos Beltran 25.00 60.00
CF Carlos Febles 6.00 15.00
CG Carlos Guillen NO AU 2.50 6.00
CH Chad Hermansen 6.00 15.00
CHA Chris Haas 6.00 15.00
CHU Chad Hutchinson 6.00 15.00
CJ Chipper Jones 125.00 300.00
CK Corey Koskie 8.00 20.00
CKI Cesar King 6.00 15.00
CL Carlos Lee 4.00 10.00
CP Calvin Pickering 6.00 15.00
DAM Damon Minor 6.00 15.00
DB Dermal Brown 6.00 15.00
DE Darin Erstad 8.00 20.00
DG Derrick Gibson 6.00 15.00
DL Derrek Lee 6.00 15.00
EC Eric Chavez 8.00 20.00
ED Orlando Hernandez 125.00 200.00
FS Fernando Seguignol 6.00 15.00
FT Frank Thomas 125.00 200.00
GK Gabe Kapler 8.00 20.00
GM Greg Maddux 100.00 250.00
GV Greg Vaughn 3.00 8.00
JAG Jason Giambi 6.00 15.00
JB Jeromy Burnitz NO AU 2.50 6.00
JC Jason Conti 6.00 15.00
JCI Jeff Cirillo 6.00 15.00
JD J.D. Drew 8.00 20.00
JE Juan Encarnacion 4.00 10.00
JEG Jeremy Giambi NO AU 2.50 6.00
JHJ Jerry Hairston Jr. 6.00 15.00
JK Jason Kendall 4.00 10.00
JLA Joe Lawrence 6.00 15.00
JM Juan Melo 6.00 15.00
JOC Jose Canseco 50.00 100.00
JR Ken Griffey Jr. 150.00 250.00
JUG Juan Gonzalez NO AU 2.50 6.00
KB Kevin Barker 6.00 15.00
KW Kevin Witt 6.00 15.00
MA Marlon Anderson 6.00 15.00
MB Michael Barrett 6.00 15.00
MC Mike Caruso 6.00 15.00
MD Mike Darr NO AU 2.50 6.00
MK Mark Kotsay 6.00 15.00
MKI Mike Kinkade 6.00 15.00
MME Mitch Meluskey 6.00 15.00
MO Mo Vaughn 8.00 20.00
MP Mike Piazza 125.00 300.00
MR Manny Ramirez 75.00 150.00
NG Nomar Garciaparra 75.00 150.00
OD Octavio Dotel 6.00 15.00
PB Pat Burrell 6.00 15.00
PG Ivan Rodriguez 60.00 150.00
PM Pedro Martinez 100.00 200.00
PO Paul O'Neill 50.00 100.00
RB Russ Branyan 6.00 15.00
RBE Ron Belliard 6.00 15.00
RH Roy Halladay 150.00 400.00
RHE Rickey Henderson NO AU 2.50 6.00
RM Ryan Minor 6.00 15.00
RMA Ruben Mateo 6.00 15.00
RMO Raul Mondesi NO AU 2.50 6.00
ROB Rob Bell 6.00 15.00
RR Rafael Roque 6.00 15.00
RT Reggie Taylor 6.00 15.00
SHH Shea Hillenbrand 4.00 10.00
SR Scott Rolen 50.00 100.00
TF Travis Fryman NO AU 2.50 6.00
TG Tony Gwynn 40.00 100.00
TGL Troy Glaus 10.00 25.00
THE Todd Helton 15.00 40.00
THO Trevor Hoffman 20.00 50.00
TL Travis Lee NO AU 2.50 6.00
TW Todd Walker 8.00 20.00
VC Vinny Castilla 6.00 15.00
VG Vladimir Guerrero 60.00 150.00

2012 SP Signature

GROUP A ODDS 1:39 HOBBY
GROUP B ODDS 1:14 HOBBY
GROUP C ODDS 1:3.5 HOBBY
GROUP D ODDS 1:2.5 HOBBY
GROUP E ODDS 1:1.5 HOBBY
GROUP F ODDS 1:1 HOBBY
20121 Karsten Whitson A 6.00 15.00
20122 Nolan Fontana F 3.00 8.00
ATL1 Phil Niekro B 8.00 20.00
ATL2 Tom Glavine B 8.00 20.00
ATL3 Chipper Jones D 25.00 60.00
ATL4 Tommy Hanson B 10.00 25.00
ATL6 Tyler Stovall F 3.00 8.00
ATL7 Ryan Weber F 3.00 8.00
AZ1 Stephen Drew E 3.00 8.00
AZ3 Chris B. Young D 3.00 8.00
AZ4 Justin Upton C 4.00 10.00
AZ5 Zach Duke E 4.00 10.00
AZ6 Melvin Mora D 3.00 8.00
AZ7 Dan Hudson E 3.00 8.00
AZ8 Ian Kennedy F 3.00 8.00
AZ9 Wade Miley F 6.00 15.00
AZ10 Trevor Bauer A 12.00 30.00
BAL1 Frank Robinson B 10.00 25.00
BAL2 Cal Ripken Jr. E 30.00 60.00
BAL3 Nick Markakis D 8.00 20.00
BAL4 Adam Jones E 8.00 20.00
BAL5 Vladimir Guerrero A 20.00 50.00
BAL6 Mark Reynolds E 4.00 10.00
BAL7 Brian Matusz F 4.00 10.00
BAL8 Matt Wieters E 6.00 15.00
BAL9 Chris Tillman D 3.00 8.00
BAL10 Tommy Hunter D 3.00 8.00
BAL11 Ryan Flaherty F 3.00 8.00
BAL12 Xavier Avery C 6.00 15.00
BOS1 Bobby Doerr C 3.00 8.00
BOS2 Johnny Pesky E 8.00 20.00
BOS3 Carl Yastrzemski A 20.00 50.00
BOS4 Carlton Fisk A 10.00 25.00
BOS5 Luis Tiant C 6.00 15.00
BOS6 Jim Rice C 10.00 25.00
BOS7 Fred Lynn B 5.00 12.00
BOS8 Wade Boggs A 12.00 30.00
BOS9 Oil Can Boyd B 5.00 12.00
BOS10 Roger Clemens A 20.00 50.00
BOS12 Jason Varitek D 6.00 15.00
BOS13 Kevin Youkilis B 12.00 30.00
BOS14 Josh Beckett D 6.00 15.00
BOS15 Jon Lester B 12.00 30.00
BOS16 Dustin Pedroia B 10.00 25.00
BOS17 Clay Buchholz F 5.00 12.00
BOS18 J.D. Drew E 4.00 10.00
BOS19 Adrian Gonzalez B 12.00 30.00
BOS20 Josh Reddick E 4.00 10.00
BOS21 Junichi Tazawa E 4.00 10.00
BOS22 Jarrod Saltalamacchia B 6.00 15.00
BOS23 Garin Cecchini C 5.00 12.00
BOS24 Che-Hsuan Lin F 4.00 10.00
BOS25 Pete Hissey F 3.00 8.00
BOS26 Derrik Gibson C 3.00 8.00
BOS27 Stephen Fife F 4.00 10.00
BOS28 Ryan Westmoreland C 3.00 8.00
BOS29 Hunter Cervenka E 3.00 8.00
BOS30 Bryce Brentz C 4.00 10.00
CHC1 Ernie Banks C 15.00 40.00
CHC2 Billy Williams B 8.00 20.00
CHC3 Ron Santo C 8.00 20.00
CHC4 Ferguson Jenkins A 6.00 15.00
CHC5 Ryne Sandberg C 12.00 30.00
CHC6 Andre Dawson C 8.00 20.00
CHC7 Mark Grace B 4.00 10.00
CHC9 Matt Garza F 3.00 8.00
CHC10 Nelson Perez C 4.00 10.00
CHC11 Kevin Rhoderick F 3.00 8.00
CHC12 Junior Lake D 3.00 8.00
CHW2 Frank Thomas E 20.00 50.00
CHW3 John Danks F 3.00 8.00
CHW4 Alexei Ramirez F 5.00 12.00
CHW5 Adam Dunn C 6.00 15.00
CHW6 Gordon Beckham B 6.00 15.00
CHW7 Brent Lillibridge E 4.00 10.00
CHW8 Tyler Flowers C 4.00 10.00
CHW9 Jordan Danks E 4.00 10.00
CIN2 Ken Griffey Sr. E 5.00 12.00
CIN3 Brandon Phillips F 3.00 8.00
CIN4 Drew Stubbs F 4.00 10.00
CIN5 Paul Janish E 3.00 8.00
CIN6 Juan Francisco E 3.00 8.00
CIN8 Juan Duran E 3.00 8.00
CIN9 Yorman Rodriguez C 3.00 8.00
CLV1 Bob Feller B 12.50 30.00
CLV3 Rocky Colavito C 12.00 30.00
CLV4 Travis Hafner E 4.00 10.00
CLV5 Grady Sizemore C 10.00 25.00
CLV6 Fausto Carmona F 3.00 8.00
CLV7 Derek Lowe C 4.00 10.00
CLV8 Carlos Carrasco E 3.00 8.00
CLV9 Matt LaPorta B 4.00 10.00
CLV10 Michael Brantley F 3.00 8.00
CLV11 Chen-Chang Lee E 8.00 20.00
COL1 Dexter Fowler F 3.00 8.00
COL2 Carlos Gonzalez D 6.00 15.00
COL3 John Maine E 4.00 10.00
COL4 Jhoulys Chacin D 3.00 8.00
COL5 Tyler Colvin E 6.00 15.00
COL6 Peter Tago E 3.00 8.00
COL7 Drew Pomeranz B 8.00 20.00
DET1 Al Kaline B 15.00 40.00
DET2 Jack Morris D 6.00 15.00
DET3 Brandon Inge E 3.00 8.00
DET4 Justin Verlander C 15.00 40.00
DET5 Miguel Cabrera A 30.00 60.00
DET6 Fu-Te Ni F 4.00 10.00
DET7 Victor Martinez E 6.00 15.00
DET8 Prince Fielder E 4.00 10.00
DET9 Alex Avila D 6.00 15.00
DET10 Nick Castellanos A 12.00 30.00
DET11 Jacob Turner C 6.00 15.00
HOU2 Jeff Bagwell A 15.00 40.00
HOU3 Carlos Lee E 3.00 8.00
HOU4 J.A. Happ F 3.00 8.00
HOU5 Jed Lowrie F 3.00 8.00
HOU6 Jordan Lyles C 3.00 8.00
HOU7 Jay Austin C 3.00 8.00
HOU8 Ross Seaton C 3.00 8.00
HOU9 Jonathan Meyer F 3.00 8.00
HOU10 Jason Castro F 3.00 8.00
KC1 Bret Saberhagen E 6.00 15.00
KC3 Billy Butler C 8.00 20.00
KC4 Jeff Francis B 4.00 10.00
KC5 Jeff Francoeur E 4.00 10.00
KC6 Luke Hochevar D 3.00 8.00
KC7 Sean O'Sullivan E 3.00 8.00
KC8 Alcides Escobar F 3.00 8.00
KC9 Kendal Volz D 3.00 8.00
KC10 Aaron Crow C 6.00 15.00
KC11 Eric Hosmer D 6.00 15.00
KC12 Tim Melville C 3.00 8.00
KC13 Christian Colon B 6.00 15.00
LA1 Duke Snider E 10.00 25.00
LA2 Carl Erskine D 8.00 20.00
LA5 Frank Howard C 5.00 12.00
LA6 Steve Garvey C 10.00 25.00
LA7 Ron Cey D 5.00 12.00
LA8 Davey Lopes A 4.00 10.00
LA9 Dusty Baker D 6.00 15.00
LA10 Chad Billingsley E 3.00 8.00
LA11 Matt Kemp E 6.00 15.00
LA12 Andre Ethier D 3.00 8.00
LA13 Clayton Kershaw B 10.00 25.00
LA14 Ethan Martin D 3.00 8.00
LAA1 Wally Joyner D 6.00 15.00
LAA2 David Eckstein E 3.00 8.00
LAA3 Albert Pujols B 100.00 200.00
LAA4 Michael Kohn E 3.00 8.00
LAA5 Wes Hatton F 3.00 8.00
MIA1 Josh Johnson E 3.00 8.00
MIA2 Hanley Ramirez C 3.00 8.00
MIA3 Gaby Sanchez E 3.00 8.00
MIA4 Emilio Bonifacio C 4.00 10.00
MIA5 Mike Dunn D 3.00 8.00
MIA6 Kyle Skipworth F 3.00 8.00
MIA7 Marcell Ozuna C 5.00 12.00
MIL1 Cecil Cooper D 3.00 8.00
MIL2 Paul Molitor C 5.00 12.00
MIL4 Rickie Weeks E 4.00 10.00
MIL5 Corey Hart F 4.00 10.00
MIL6 Yovani Gallardo F 4.00 10.00
MIL7 Nyjer Morgan D 4.00 10.00
MIL8 Cameron Garfield E 3.00 8.00
MIL9 Seth Lintz F 3.00 8.00
MIL10 Jose Garcia E 3.00 8.00
MIL12 Kentrail Davis B 4.00 10.00
MIN1 Tony Oliva C 8.00 20.00
MIN2 Rod Carew C 10.00 25.00
MIN3 Kent Hrbek A 8.00 20.00
MIN4 Joe Mauer C 10.00 25.00
MIN5 Nick Blackburn E 3.00 8.00
MIN6 Denard Span E 4.00 10.00
MIN7 Josh Willingham F 3.00 8.00
MIN8 Francisco Liriano A 5.00 12.00
MIN9 Glen Perkins F 3.00 8.00
MIN10 Bobby Lanigan E 3.00 8.00
MIN11 Aaron Hicks C 5.00 12.00
MIN12 Kyle Gibson C 4.00 10.00
NYM1 Lee Mazzilli E 3.00 8.00
NYM2 Darryl Strawberry E 6.00 15.00
NYM3 Sid Fernandez C 4.00 10.00
NYM5 Gary Carter C 8.00 20.00
NYM7 Mike Pelfrey E 4.00 10.00
NYM8 Jason Bay E 3.00 8.00
NYM9 Tobi Stoner E 4.00 10.00
NYM10 Josh Thole E 3.00 8.00
NYM11 Chin-Lung Hu E 3.00 8.00
NYM12 Reese Havens C 3.00 8.00
NYY1 Whitey Ford C 8.00 20.00
NYY2 Don Larsen B 6.00 15.00
NYY3 Bobby Murcer C 8.00 20.00
NYY4 Chris Chambliss C 5.00 12.00
NYY5 Ron Guidry D 8.00 20.00
NYY6 Reggie Jackson C 20.00 50.00
NYY7 Bucky Dent C 10.00 25.00
NYY8 Don Mattingly D 15.00 40.00
NYY9 Tino Martinez A 6.00 15.00
NYY10 Tim Raines C 6.00 15.00
NYY11 Mike Mussina C 8.00 20.00
NYY13 Nick Swisher C 8.00 20.00
NYY14 Russell Martin D 3.00 8.00
NYY16 Garrison Lassiter E 4.00 10.00
NYY17 Jeremy Bleich E 3.00 8.00
NYY18 Brett Marshall F 5.00 12.00
NYY19 Andrew Aplin E 3.00 8.00
NYY20 David Adams E 4.00 10.00
NYY21 D.J. Mitchell C 4.00 10.00
OAK1 Jose Canseco C 12.00 30.00
OAK2 Dennis Eckersley A 6.00 15.00
OAK3 Eric Chavez D 3.00 8.00
OAK4 Mark Mulder B 3.00 8.00
OAK5 Rich Harden D 3.00 8.00
OAK6 Kurt Suzuki E 5.00 12.00
OAK7 Brandon Allen E 3.00 8.00
OAK8 Collin Cowgill C 3.00 8.00
OAK10 Jemile Weeks C 3.00 8.00
OAK11 Cecil Tanner E 3.00 8.00
OAK12 Max Stassi E 3.00 8.00
OAK13 Michael Choice D 4.00 10.00
OAK14 Kila Kaaihue E 3.00 8.00
PHI1 Greg Luzinski C 5.00 12.00
PHI2 Steve Carlton C 8.00 20.00
PHI3 Mike Schmidt A 12.00 30.00
PHI4 John Kruk E 5.00 12.00
PHI5 Jim Thome D 15.00 40.00
PHI6 Cole Hamels B 8.00 20.00
PHI7 Joe Blanton F 3.00 8.00
PHI8 Roy Halladay C 10.00 25.00
PHI9 Hunter Pence B 6.00 15.00
PHI10 Jonathan Papelbon C 5.00 12.00
PHI11 Dontrelle Willis C 3.00 8.00
PHI12 Harold Martinez E 3.00 8.00
PHI13 Aaron Altherr B 5.00 12.00
PIT1 Frank J. Thomas E 10.00 25.00
PIT2 Bill Madlock A 4.00 10.00
PIT4 Casey McGehee F 3.00 8.00
PIT5 Garrett Jones D 4.00 10.00
PIT6 Dinesh Kumar Patel C 3.00 8.00
PIT8 Pedro Alvarez C 5.00 12.00
PIT9 Colton Cain E 3.00 8.00
PIT10 Gerrit Cole B 15.00 40.00
PIT11 Jameson Taillon A 10.00 25.00
SD1 Tony Gwynn C 20.00 50.00
SD3 Huston Street B 6.00 15.00
SD4 Edinson Volquez F 3.00 8.00
SD5 Micah Owings F 3.00 8.00
SD6 Kyle Blanks F 3.00 8.00
SD7 Casey Kelly C 3.00 8.00
SD9 Donavan Tate E 3.00 8.00
SD10 Yasmani Grandal C 3.00 8.00
SEA1 Edgar Martinez B 8.00 20.00
SEA2 Randy Johnson A 20.00 50.00
SEA3 Ken Griffey Jr. C 40.00 80.00
SEA4 Felix Hernandez E 4.00 10.00
SEA5 Chone Figgins E 4.00 10.00
SEA6 Brandon League E 4.00 10.00
SEA7 Michael Saunders D 4.00 10.00
SEA8 Adam Moore F 3.00 8.00
SEA9 Justin Smoak C 3.00 8.00
SEA10 Casper Wells C 4.00 10.00
SEA11 Nick Franklin C 6.00 15.00
SEA12 Marcus Littlewood E 4.00 10.00
SF2 Orlando Cepeda C 6.00 15.00
SF3 Willie McCovey C 12.00 30.00
SF4 Juan Marichal C 8.00 20.00
SF5 Gaylord Perry B 5.00 12.00
SF6 Dave Kingman A 10.00 25.00
SF7 Jack Clark E 4.00 10.00
SF8 Will Clark C 8.00 20.00
SF9 Kevin Mitchell A 4.00 10.00
SF10 Miguel Tejada B 5.00 12.00
STL1 Bob Gibson B 8.00 20.00
STL2 Lou Brock A 20.00 50.00
STL3 Joe Torre A 12.00 30.00
STL4 Keith Hernandez E 6.00 15.00
STL5 Albert Pujols A 60.00 120.00
STL7 Matt Holliday B 10.00 25.00
STL8 Lance Berkman C 8.00 20.00
STL9 Kyle McClellan F 3.00 8.00
STL10 Kolten Wong B 4.00 10.00
TB1 Ben Zobrist F 5.00 12.00
TB2 James Shields E 4.00 10.00
TB3 Jeff Niemann F 3.00 8.00
TB4 Casey Kotchman D 3.00 8.00
TB5 Luke Scott D 3.00 8.00
TB6 Carlos Pena E 3.00 8.00
TB7 David Price B 6.00 15.00
TB8 Reid Brignac C 4.00 10.00
TB9 Matt Joyce D 8.00 20.00
TB10 Wade Davis D 3.00 8.00
TB11 Jeff Malm F 3.00 8.00
TB12 Austin Maddox F 4.00 10.00
TB13 Kyle Lobstein F 3.00 8.00
TEX1 Nolan Ryan A 60.00 120.00
TEX2 Ian Kinsler C 5.00 12.00
TEX3 David Murphy F 3.00 8.00
TEX4 Josh Hamilton E 8.00 20.00
TEX5 Joe Nathan F 5.00 12.00
TEX6 Neftali Feliz E 3.00 8.00
TEX7 Robbie Ross F 6.00 15.00
TEX8 Tommy Mendonca F 3.00 8.00
TEX9 Phillip Pfeifer D 3.00 8.00
TOR1 John Olerud D 5.00 12.00
TOR2 Joe Carter B 10.00 25.00
TOR3 Adam Lind C 6.00 15.00
TOR4 Kelly Johnson F 3.00 8.00
TOR5 Travis Snider D 10.00 25.00
TOR6 Colby Rasmus D 5.00 12.00
TOR7 Brett Lawrie C 6.00 15.00
TOR8 David Cooper C 5.00 12.00
TOR9 Jake Barrett E 3.00 8.00
TOR10 Asher Wojciechowski B 3.00 8.00
TOR11 Andrew Liebel E 3.00 8.00
WAS1 Ryan Zimmerman E 6.00 15.00
WAS2 Mike Morse F 3.00 8.00
WAS4 Shairon Martis E 3.00 8.00
WAS5 Stephen Strasburg A 50.00 100.00
WAS7 Destin Hood E 4.00 10.00
WAS9 Bryce Harper A 60.00 120.00
WAS10 Matthew Purke C 3.00 8.00

2012 SP Signature Compatriots Signatures Dual

OVERALL AUTO ODDS 3:1
PRINT RUNS B/WN 10-50 COPIES PER
NO PRICING ON QTY 25 OR LESS
JPN J.Tazawa/K.Uehara/50 25.00 60.00
TWN C.Hu/C.Lin/50 10.00 25.00

2012 SP Signature Compatriots Signatures Triple

OVERALL AUTO ODDS 3:1
PRINT RUNS B/WN 3-50 COPIES PER
NO PRICING ON QTY 25 OR LESS
USA1 Hosmer/Matusz/Skipworth/50 10.00 25.00
USA4 Alvarez/Castro/Smoak/50 10.00 25.00

2012 SP Signature Dual Signatures

GROUP A ODDS 1:39 HOBBY
GROUP B ODDS 1:14 HOBBY
GROUP C ODDS 1:3.5 HOBBY
GROUP D ODDS 1:2.5 HOBBY
GROUP E ODDS 1:1.5 HOBBY
GROUP F ODDS 1:1 HOBBY
2012DRAFT N.Fontana/K.Whitson B 5.00 12.00
ATL8 Tyler Stovall/Ryan Weber F 4.00 10.00
AZST1 Andrew Aplin/Jake Barrett F 4.00 10.00
BAL13 B.Matusz/M.Wieters F 6.00 15.00
BAL14 Brian Matusz/Chris Tillman E 8.00 20.00
BAL15 Xavier Avery/Ryan Flaherty F 4.00 10.00
BOS31 Che-Hsuan Lin/Josh Reddick F 4.00 10.00
BOS32 D.Gibson/P.Hissey F 5.00 12.00
BOS33 Stephen Fife
Ryan Westmoreland F 4.00 10.00
BOS34 C.Lin/J.Tazawa E 6.00 15.00
CAN1 B.Lawrie/M.Saunders E 6.00 15.00
CHW10 J.Danks/T.Flowers E 4.00 10.00
CHC13 J.Lake/N.Perez C 10.00 25.00
CIN10 M.Latos/Y.Rodriguez E 6.00 15.00
CLV12 M.Brantley/M.LaPorta C 6.00 15.00
COL8 Jhoulys Chacin/Peter Tago D 4.00 10.00
DET12 D.Schlereth/J.Turner C 8.00 20.00
HOU11 Jason Castro/Jordan Lyles E 4.00 10.00
HOU12 Jed Lowrie/Ross Seaton E 4.00 10.00
HOU13 Jordan Lyles/Ross Seaton F 4.00 10.00
KC14 A.Escobar/E.Hosmer E 10.00 25.00
KC15 A.Crow/E.Hosmer F 6.00 15.00
KC16 Aaron Crow/Tim Melville F 4.00 10.00
LA15 Chad Billingsley/Ethan Martin E 4.00 10.00
MIA8 Gaby Sanchez/Kyle Skipworth F 4.00 10.00
MIA9 Mike Dunn/Kyle Skipworth F 4.00 10.00
MIA10 Mike Dunn/Gaby Sanchez F 4.00 10.00
MIL13 Yovani Gallardo/Seth Lintz E 4.00 10.00
MIL14 Cutter Dykstra/Yovani Gallardo E 4.00 10.00
MIN13 K.Gibson/A.Hicks F 6.00 15.00
NYM13 Reese Havens/Josh Thole F 4.00 10.00
NYY22 Jeremy Bleich/D.J. Mitchell F 4.00 10.00
NYY23 Garrison Lassiter/D.J. Mitchell F 4.00 10.00
NYY24 Garrison Lassiter/Brett Marshall F 4.00 10.00
OAK15 Collin Cowgill/Jemile Weeks E 4.00 10.00
OAK16 Max Stassi/Jemile Weeks E 4.00 10.00
OAK17 Brandon Allen/Collin Cowgill E 4.00 10.00
PIT12 P.Alvarez/C.Cain F 6.00 15.00
PIT13 P.Alvarez/G.Cole C 6.00 15.00
SD11 C.Kelly/D.Tate F 5.00 12.00
SEA13 N.Franklin/J.Smoak F 5.00 12.00
TB14 Reid Brignac/Kyle Lobstein E 4.00 10.00
TB15 Wade Davis/Jeff Malm F 4.00 10.00
TB16 W.Davis/D.Price C 8.00 20.00
TEX11 N.Feliz/R.Ross E 5.00 12.00
TOR12 David Cooper/Andrew Liebel E 4.00 10.00
TOR13 D.Cooper/B.Lawrie B 6.00 15.00
WAS11 Bryce Harper
Stephen Strasburg A 100.00 200.00
WAS12 Destin Hood/Matthew Purke F 4.00 10.00

2012 SP Signature Enshrinement Signatures

OVERALL AUTO ODDS 3:1
PRINT RUNS B/WN 2-100 COPIES PER
NO PRICING ON QTY 25 OR LESS
AD Andre Dawson/50 8.00 20.00
AK Al Kaline/60 20.00 50.00
BG Bob Gibson/50 10.00 25.00
CR Cal Ripken Jr./100 25.00 60.00
DS Duke Snider/100 10.00 25.00
EB Ernie Banks/50 25.00 60.00
JR Jim Rice/50 12.50 30.00
MS Mike Schmidt/25 15.00 40.00
OS Ozzie Smith/34 30.00 60.00

2012 SP Signature Enshrinement Signatures Dual

OVERALL AUTO ODDS 3:1
PRINT RUNS B/WN 5-75 COPIES PER
NO PRICING ON QTY 25 OR LESS
5 W.Boggs/R.Sandberg/48 20.00 50.00
7 T.Gwynn/C.Ripken Jr./75 60.00 120.00
80 A.Kaline/D.Snider/60 30.00 80.00

2012 SP Signature Franchise Focus Signatures Dual

OVERALL AUTO ODDS 3:1
PRINT RUNS B/WN 5-75 COPIES PER
NO PRICING ON QTY 25 OR LESS
CHC A.Soriano/B.Williams/35 10.00 25.00
NYM G.Carter/J.Thole/50 10.00 25.00
SEA1 K.Griffey Jr./E.Martinez/30 60.00 120.00
SEA2 M.Saunders/J.Smoak/75 6.00 15.00

2012 SP Signature Franchise Focus Signatures Triple

OVERALL AUTO ODDS 3:1
PRINT RUNS B/WN 1-50 COPIES PER
NO PRICING ON QTY 25 OR LESS
CHC Lake/Perez/Rhod/50 6.00 15.00
CIN Juan Duran/Juan Francisco
Yorman Rodriguez/50 6.00 15.00
HOU Jay Austin/Jordan
Lyles/Ross Seaton/50 6.00 15.00
SEA1 Franklin/Littlewood/Smoak/50 10.00 25.00

2012 SP Signature Pride of a Nation Signatures

OVERALL AUTO ODDS 3:1
PRINT RUNS B/WN 15-99 COPIES PER
NO PRICING ON QTY 25 OR LESS
CB Craig Biggio/99 20.00 50.00
CZ Carlos Zambrano/99 4.00 10.00
DE Dennis Eckersley/99 6.00 15.00
DN Don Newcombe/99 10.00 25.00
JO John Olerud/99 8.00 20.00
LT Luis Tiant/99 10.00 25.00
MI Monte Irvin/99 8.00 20.00
MP Mike Piazza/99 30.00 80.00
MW Maury Wills/99 6.00 15.00
RK Ralph Kiner/99 12.00 30.00
RO Roy Oswalt/99 3.00 8.00
SR Ken Griffey Sr./99 6.00 15.00
WF Whitey Ford/99 12.00 30.00

2012 SP Signature Quad Signatures

GROUP A ODDS 1:39 HOBBY
GROUP B ODDS 1:14 HOBBY
GROUP C ODDS 1:3.5 HOBBY
GROUP D ODDS 1:2.5 HOBBY
GROUP E ODDS 1:1.5 HOBBY
GROUP F ODDS 1:1 HOBBY
BAL17 Avery/Mat/Till/Wiet C 10.00 25.00
BOS37 Stephen Fife/Derrik Gibson/Pete Hissey/Che-Hsuan Lin D 8.00 20.00
BOS38 Che-Hsuan Lin/Josh Reddick/Junichi Tazawa/Ryan Westmoreland D 8.00 20.00
CHW12 Beck/Danks/Flowers/Lill C 8.00 20.00
CIN11 Cueto/Duran/Latos/Rodri A 10.00 25.00
CIN12 Juan Duran/Juan Francisco/Paul Janish/Yorman Rodriguez C 8.00 20.00
CLV14 Brant/Carras/LaPort/Lee C 15.00 40.00
HOU15 Aust/Low/Lyles/Seaton D 8.00 20.00
KC18 Colon/Escob/Hos/O'Sul C 10.00 25.00
KC19 Colon/Crow/Hos/Melvil B 10.00 25.00
MIA11 Mike Dunn/Marcell Ozuna/Gaby Sanchez/Kyle Skipworth C 8.00 20.00
MIL16 Cutter Dykstra/Jose Garcia/Cameron Garfield/Seth Lintz D 8.00 20.00
MIN15 Danny Espinosa/Kyle Gibson/Aaron Hicks/Bobby Lanigan C 8.00 20.00
NYM15 Hav/Hu/Stoner/Thole D 8.00 20.00
NYY26 Aplin/Lass/Marsh/Mitch C 8.00 20.00
OAK20 Brandon Allen/Collin Cowgill/Brett Hunter/Cecil Tanner C 8.00 20.00
OAK21 Brett Hunter/Max Stassi/Cecil Tanner/Jemile Weeks D 8.00 20.00
PIT15 Pedro Alvarez/Casey McGehee/Dinesh Kumar Patel/Rinku Singh D 8.00 20.00
SD13 Bank/Kell/Owing/Tate C 10.00 25.00
SEA15 Frank/Moore/Saun/Smoak D 10.00 25.00
SEA16 Frank/Moore/Smoak/Wells D 10.00 25.00
TB19 Brig/Davis/Lobs/Malm D 8.00 20.00
TEX13 Feliz/Mend/Pfeil/Ross C 10.00 25.00
TOR15 Coop/Law/Liebel/Woj B 6.00 15.00

2012 SP Signature Signature Season Signatures Dual

OVERALL AUTO ODDS 3:1
PRINT RUNS B/WN 2-50 COPIES PER
NO PRICING ON QTY 25 OR LESS
02WS D.Eckstein/J.Lackey/48 8.00 20.00
06WS2 C.Duncan/D.Eckstein/50 8.00 20.00
07WS1 D.Pedroia/K.Youkilis/50 15.00 40.00
08WS J.Blanton/C.Hamels/50 10.00 25.00
08WS1 S.Victorino/J.Werth/50 12.00 30.00
10WS Fontenot/Sandoval/32 8.00 20.00
81WS D.Baker/R.Cey/50 8.00 20.00
86WS1 Fernandez/Strawberry/50 10.00 25.00
86WS2 G.Carter/D.Strawberry/35 30.00 60.00
93WS J.Carter/P.Molitor/50 15.00 40.00
95WS T.Glavine/C.Jones/30 60.00 120.00

2012 SP Signature Superstars Signatures Dual

OVERALL AUTO ODDS 3:1
PRINT RUNS B/WN 9-50 COPIES PER
NO PRICING ON QTY 25 OR LESS
KL J.Kruk/G.Luzinski/50 6.00 15.00
MEDIA1 D.Patrick/S.Scott/50 30.00 80.00
MEDIA2 L.Cohn/K.Mayne/50 8.00 20.00
SH E.Hosmer/J.Smoak/50 8.00 20.00

2012 SP Signature Superstars Signatures Triple

OVERALL AUTO ODDS 3:1
PRINT RUNS B/WN 5-50 COPIES PER
NO PRICING ON QTY 25 OR LESS
08DRAFT Alv/Hos/Mat/50 10.00 25.00
09DRAFT Crow/Frank/Tur/50 12.50 30.00

2012 SP Signature Triple Signatures

GROUP A ODDS 1:39 HOBBY
GROUP B ODDS 1:14 HOBBY
GROUP C ODDS 1:3.5 HOBBY
GROUP D ODDS 1:2.5 HOBBY
GROUP E ODDS 1:1.5 HOBBY
GROUP F ODDS 1:1 HOBBY
AZ11 Hudson/Miley/Owings E 6.00 15.00
BAL16 Avery/Flaherty/Matusz E 8.00 20.00
BOS35 Stephen Fife/Derrik
Gibson/Che-Hsuan Lin E 5.00 12.00
BOS36 Hunter Cervenka/Pete Hissey/Ryan Westmoreland E 5.00 12.00
CHC15 Lake/Perez/Rhod C 15.00 40.00
CHW11 Danks/Flowers/Lillibridge E 5.00 12.00
CLV13 Brantley/Carrasco/Lee E 5.00 12.00
DET13 Avila/Castel/Turner A 6.00 15.00
HOU14 Jason Castro/Jordan
Lyles/Ross Seaton E 5.00 12.00
KC17 Crow/Hosmer/Melville E 8.00 20.00
MIL15 Kentrail Davis
Cameron Garfield/Seth Lintz C 5.00 12.00
MIN14 Kyle Gibson/Aaron
Hicks/Bobby Lanigan E 5.00 12.00
NYM14 Havens/Hu/Stoner E 6.00 15.00
NYY25 Jeremy Bleich/Garrison
Lassiter/D.J. Mitchell E 5.00 12.00
OAK18 Brett Hunter
Max Stassi/Jemile Weeks E 5.00 12.00
OAK19 Brett Hunter/Ceci
l Tanner/Jemile Weeks E 5.00 12.00
PIT14 Alvarez/Cole/Taillon A 6.00 15.00
SD12 Blanks/Kelly/Tate C 8.00 20.00
SEA14 Franklin/Saunders/Smoak E 8.00 20.00
TAI1 Hu/Lee/Lin E 5.00 12.00
TB17 Brignac/Davis/Lobstein E 6.00 15.00
TB18 Brignac/Davis/Joyce E 8.00 20.00
TEX12 Mendonca/Pfeifer/Ross E 6.00 15.00
TOR14 Cooper/Lawrie/Liebel E 6.00 15.00
WAS13 Destin Hood/Shairon
Martis/Matthew Purke E 5.00 12.00

1993 Spectrum Gold Signature Griffey Jr.

This standard-size card features Ken Griffey Jr. Each of the 4,000 gold signature cards comes with a certificate of authenticity.

1 Ken Griffey Jr. 4.00 10.00

1993 Spectrum Gold Signature Herman

This card honors Hall of Fame second baseman Billy Herman. Each of the 4,000 gold signature cards comes with a certificate of authenticity.

1 Billy Herman .75 2.00

1993 Spectrum Gold Signature Seaver

This card honors Tom Seaver, whose career 311 wins and 3,640 strikeouts earned him a first year induction into the Hall of Fame. Each of the 5,000 gold signature cards comes with a certificate of authenticity.

1 Tom Seaver 1.50 4.00

1993 Spectrum HOF I

This five-card standard-size set features on its fronts borderless black-and-white vintage player photos that are trimmed in gold foil. The set includes an official certificate of authenticity giving the set serial number and the production run figures (5,000). The cards are numbered on the back. There was also a Gold Signature version (5,000 sets produced) of the cards which are similar to the regular 1993 Spectrum HOF set, except for the addition of embossed facsimile 24-karat gold signatures across their fronts. The regular cards may also be distinguished from the "Gold Signature" series by different vintage player photos. Each of the Signature cards comes with its own 1/2" Lucite card holder and carries a serial number out of a 5,000-card production run. The Gold Signature cards are valued at two to three times the prices listed below.

COMPLETE SET (5) 2.50 6.00
1 Babe Ruth .60 1.50
2 Ty Cobb .60 1.50
3 Satchel Paige .50 1.25
4 Rogers Hornsby .40 1.00
5 Dizzy Dean .40 1.00

1993 Spectrum HOF II

This five-card standard-size set features on its fronts borderless black-and-white vintage player photos that are trimmed in gold foil. "Spectrum" is printed diagonally in gold foil across the upper left corner. Cards are distinguishable from the "Gold Signature" series not only by the absence of embossed signatures but also by different vintage player photos. The set includes an official certificate of authenticity giving the set serial number and the production run figures (5,000). There was also a Gold Signature version (5,000 sets produced) of the cards which are similar to the regular 1993 Spectrum HOF set, except for the addition of embossed facsimile 24-karat gold signatures across their fronts. The regular cards may also be distinguished from the "Gold Signature" series by different vintage player photos. Each of the Signature cards comes with its own 1/2" Lucite card holder and carries a serial number out of a 5,000-card production run. The Gold Signature cards are valued at two to three times the prices listed below. The Grover Alexander card was also issued as a promo, with the disclaimer "For Promotional Use Only" in an oval on the back.

COMPLETE SET (5) 2.50 6.00
1 Lou Gehrig .60 1.50
2 Grover Alexander .40 1.00
3 Honus Wagner .50 1.25
4 Cy Young .50 1.25
5 Casey Stengel .40 1.00
P2 Grover Alexander

1993 Spectrum Ryan 10

This ten-card set was produced by Spectrum Holdings Group, Inc. to commemorate Nolan Ryan's career. A card certifying authenticity is included in the set which indicates that 5,000 sets were produced. There is a Gold Signature version (5,000 sets produced) of the cards which are identical to the regular 1993 Spectrum Nolan Ryan set, except for the addition of embossed facsimile gold signatures across their fronts. The Gold Signature cards are valued at double the prices listed below.

COMPLETE SET (10) 6.00 15.00
COMMON PLAYER (1-10) .60 1.50

1993 Spectrum Ryan 23K

Produced by Spectrum Holdings Group, Inc., this three-card set was accompanied by a certificate of authenticity carrying the set serial number and the production figures (10,000).

COMPLETE SET (3) 8.00 20.00
COMMON PLAYER (1-3) 2.40 6.00

1993 Spectrum Ryan 5

This five-card standard-size set was produced by Spectrum Holdings Group, Inc. to celebrate Nolan Ryan's career. The set included a certificate of authenticity carrying the set serial number and the production run figures (5,000). Only the first card carries an embossed facsimile gold signature across it.

COMPLETE SET (5) 3.00 8.00
COMMON PLAYER (1-5) .80 2.00

1993 Spectrum Ryan Tribute Sheet

This blank-backed borderless color sheet measures 8 1/2" by 11" and pays tribute to Nolan Ryan for his record-breaking 27 major league seasons. It features two color action shots of Ryan that are obliquely superimposed upon a background consisting of artificial turf, home plate, a ball and glove and Ryan's jersey. His gold signature appears in the lower left, below the Spectrum gold seal containing the production number out of a total of 5,000.

1 Nolan Ryan Sheet 2.00 5.00

1926 Sport Company of America

This 151-card set encompasses athletes from a multitude of different sports. There are 49-cards representing baseball and 14-cards for football. Each includes a black-and-white player photo within a fancy frame border. The player's name and sport are printed at the bottom. The backs carry a short player biography and statistics. The cards originally came in a small glassine envelope along with a coupon that could be redeemed for sporting equipment and are often still found in this form. The cards are unnumbered and have been checklisted below in alphabetical order within sport. We've assigned prefixes to the card numbers which serves to group the cards by sport (BB-baseball, FB- football).

BB1 Babe Adams 40.00 80.00
BB2 Grover Alexander 75.00 150.00
BB3 Nick Altrock 25.00 50.00
BB4 Dave Bancroft 75.00 150.00
BB5 Jesse Barnes 25.00 50.00
BB6 Ossie Bluege 25.00 50.00
BB7 Jim Bottomley 50.00 100.00
BB8 Max Carey 50.00 100.00
BB9 Ty Cobb 500.00 800.00
BB10 Mickey Cochrane 75.00 150.00
BB11 Eddie Collins 75.00 150.00
BB12 Stan Coveleski 50.00 100.00
BB13 Kiki Cuyler 50.00 100.00
BB14 Hank DeBerry 25.00 50.00
BB15 Jack Fournier 25.00 50.00
BB16 Goose Goslin 50.00 100.00
BB17 Charley Grimm 40.00 80.00
BB18 Bucky Harris 50.00 100.00
BB19 Gabby Hartnett 50.00 100.00
BB20 Fred Hofmann 25.00 50.00
BB21 Rogers Hornsby 100.00 200.00
BB22 Waite Hoyt 50.00 100.00
BB23 Walter Johnson 200.00 400.00
BB24 Joe Judge 25.00 50.00
BB25 Willie Kamm 25.00 50.00
BB26 Tony Lazzeri 50.00 100.00
BB27 Rabbit Maranville 50.00 100.00
BB28 Firpo Marberry 25.00 50.00
BB29 Rube Marquard 50.00 100.00
BB30 Stuffy McInnis 25.00 50.00
BB31 Babe Pinelli 25.00 50.00
BB32 Wally Pipp 25.00 50.00
BB33 Sam Rice 50.00 100.00
BB34 Emory Rigney 25.00 50.00
BB35 Dutch Ruether 25.00 50.00
BB36 Babe Ruth 600.00 1000.00
BB37 Ray Schalk 50.00 100.00
BB38 Joe Sewell 50.00 100.00
BB39 Urban Shocker 40.00 80.00
BB40 Al Simmons 50.00 100.00
BB41 George Sisler 75.00 150.00
BB42 Tris Speaker 100.00 200.00
BB43 Pie Traynor 75.00 150.00
BB44 George Uhle 25.00 50.00
BB45 Paul Waner 75.00 150.00
BB46 Aaron Ward 25.00 50.00
BB47 Ken Williams 40.00 80.00
BB48 Glenn Wright 25.00 50.00
BB49 Emil Yde 25.00 50.00

1967-71 Sport Hobbyist Famous Cards

This 48-card set was issued in two series. The first two series (1-30), measuring approximately 2 1/4" by 3 3/4", features black-and-white player photos. The card numbered 2 is unknown. The second series (31-51), measuring approximately 2" by 3", features black-and-white player photos with red borders. There are no cards numbered 42, 44, nor 46. Each of the first two series cost $1 from the producer of these cards.

COMPLETE SET (48) 30.00 60.00
1 Honus Wagner 4.00 10.00
T206
2 Unknown
3 Simmons .40 1.00
C46
4 Christy Mathewson 1.00 2.50
M116
5 Jack Barry .40 1.00
M101-5
6 Mordecai Brown 1.00 2.50
T204
7 Webb .40 1.00
D322 Tip Top Bread
8 Lou Criger .40 1.00
S74
9 Kiki Cuyler .75 2.00
R333
10 Nap Lajoie 1.00 2.50
R319
11 John McGraw 1.00 2.50
T205
12 Addie Joss .75 2.00
E107
13 George Sisler .75 2.00
W502
14 Buck Ewing .60 1.50
Allen & Ginter #29
15 Chief Bender .60 1.50
E90
16 George Mullin .40 1.00
E104
17 Fred Merkle .40 1.00
E95
18 Walter Schang .40 1.00
E121
19 Tim Keefe .40 1.00
Allen & Ginter #28
20 Harold Muddy Ruel .40 1.00
E120
21 Irving Jack Burns .40 1.00
D382
22 George Connally .40 1.00
D382
23 Myril Hoag .40 1.00
D382
24 Willie Kamm .40 1.00
D382
25 Dutch Leonard .40 1.00
D382
26 Clyde Manion .40 1.00
D382
27 Johnny Vergez .40 1.00
D382
28 Tom Zachary .40 1.00
D382
29 Ty Cobb E145 .40 1.00
30 Richardson .40 1.00
Playing Card
31 Ed Abbaticchio .40 1.00
T206
32 Barbeau .40 1.00
T206
33 Burch .40 1.00
T206
34 Mordecai Brown 1.00 2.50
T206
35 Hal Chase .75 2.00
T206
36 Ball .40 1.00
T206
37 Abstein .40 1.00
T206
38 Bowerman .40 1.00
T206
39 Hal Chase .75 2.00
T206
40 Criss .40 1.00
T206
41 Beck .40 1.00
T206
43 Bradley .40 1.00
T206
45 Kitty Bransfield .40 1.00
T206
47 Bell .40 1.00
T206
48 Bergen .40 1.00
T206
49 Chief Bender .75 2.00
T206
50 Bush .40 1.00
T206
51 Jack Chesbro .60 1.50
T206

1985-86 Sportflics Prototypes

COMPLETE SET (5) 75.00 150.00
1 Joe DiMaggio 40.00 80.00
Small size
2 Mike Schmidt 12.50 30.00
Biographical back
3 Mike Schmidt 20.00 50.00
Stats on back
4 Bruce Sutter 3.00 8.00
Stats on back
5 Dave Winfield 6.00 15.00
Biographical back
6 Dave Winfield 10.00 25.00
Stats on back

1985-86 Sportflics Samples

COMPLETE SET (3) 20.00 50.00
1 RBI Sluggers 6.00 15.00
Mike Schmidt
Dale Murphy
Jim Rice
43 Pete Rose/(Pictured with batting helmet; Pete# 8.00 20.00
45 Tom Seaver/(Tom is number 25 in regular 1986 set 8.00 20.00

1986 Sportflics

This 200-card standard-size set was marketed with 133 small trivia cards. This inaugural set for Sportflics was initially fairly well received by collectors. Sportflics was distributed by Major League Marketing; the company also maintained distribution agreements with Wrigley and Amurol. The set features 139 single player "magic motion" cards (which can be tilted to show three different pictures of the same player), 50 "Tri-Stars" (which show three different players), 10 "Big Six" cards (which show six players who share similar achievements), and one World Champs card featuring 12 members of the victorious Kansas City Royals. Some of the cards also have (limited production and rarely seen) proof versions with some player selection differences; a proof version of number 178 includes Jim Wilson instead of Mark Funderburk. Also a proof of number 179 with Karl Best, Mark Funderburk, Andres Galarraga, Dwayne Henry, Pete Incaviglia, and Todd Worrell was produced. The following sequences can be found to be in alphabetical order, 26-49, 76-99, 101-124, 151-174, and 187-199. Cards 1-24 seem to be Sportflics' selection of top players and cards 25, 50, 100, 125, and 175 all set milestones or records during the 1985 season. The Robin Yount Yankee error (#42A) is not considered part of the complete set.

COMP.FACT.SET (200) 10.00 25.00
1 George Brett .60 1.50
2 Don Mattingly .75 2.00
3 Wade Boggs .15 .40
4 Eddie Murray .25 .60
5 Dale Murphy .15 .40
6 Rickey Henderson .25 .60
7 Harold Baines .08 .25
8 Cal Ripken 1.00 2.50
9 Orel Hershiser .25 .60
10 Bret Saberhagen .08 .25
11 Tim Raines .08 .25
12 Fernando Valenzuela .08 .25
13 Tony Gwynn .40 1.00
14 Pedro Guerrero .08 .25
15 Keith Hernandez .08 .25
16 Earnie Riles .05 .15
17 Jim Rice .08 .25
18 Ron Guidry .08 .25
19 Willie McGee .08 .25
20 Ryne Sandberg .50 1.25
21 Kirk Gibson .08 .25
22 Ozzie Guillen .75 2.00
23 Dave Parker .08 .25
24 Vince Coleman .15 .40
25 Tom Seaver .15 .40
26 Brett Butler .08 .25
27 Steve Carlton .08 .25
28 Gary Carter .08 .25
29 Cecil Cooper .08 .25
30 Jose Cruz .08 .25
31 Alvin Davis .05 .15
32 Dwight Evans .15 .40
33 Julio Franco .08 .25
34 Damaso Garcia .05 .15
35 Steve Garvey .08 .25
36 Kent Hrbek .08 .25
37 Reggie Jackson .15 .40
38 Fred Lynn .08 .25
39 Paul Molitor .08 .25
40 Jim Presley .05 .15
41 Dave Righetti .08 .25
42A R.Yount ERR Yankees Logo 20.00 50.00
42B R.Yount COR Brewers Logo .40 1.00
43 Nolan Ryan 1.00 2.50
44 Mike Schmidt .60 1.50
45 Lee Smith .08 .25
46 Rick Sutcliffe .08 .25
47 Bruce Sutter .08 .25
48 Lou Whitaker .08 .25
49 Dave Winfield .08 .25
50 Pete Rose .60 1.50
51 NL MVP's Sandberg .25 .60
Rose
52 Slugging Stars George Brett .25 .60
53 No-Hitters .05 .15
54 Big Hitters Matt .50 1.25
Ripken
Yount
55 Bullpen Aces .05 .15
56 ROY Pete Rose .25 .60
57 AL MVP's Ripken .25 .60
Reggie
58 Batting Champs Pete Rose .25 .60
59 Cy Young Winners .05 .15
60 DAW Valen .08 .25
Sutcliffe
Seaver
61 HR Champs Reggie Jackson .08 .25
62 NL MVP's Mike Schmidt .25 .60
63 AL MVP's Yount .25 .60
Brett
64 Comeback Players .05 .15
65 Cy Young Relievers .05 .15
66 ROY Andre Dawson .05 .15
67 ROY Fisk .08 .25
Seaver
68 HR Champs Mike Schmidt .25 .60
69 DAW Ripken .15 .40
Carew
Rose
70 Cy Young Winners Carlton .08 .25
Seaver
71 Top Sluggers Jackson .25 .60
Yount
72 ROY Righetti .05 .15
Fernando
73 ROY Murray .25 .60
Ripken
74 ROY Rod Carew .08 .25
75 Btg Champs Mattingly .40 1.00
Boggs
76 Jesse Barfield .08 .25
77 Phil Bradley .05 .15
78 Chris Brown
79 Tom Browning .05 .15
80 Tom Brunansky .05 .15
81 Bill Buckner .08 .25
82 Chili Davis .08 .25
83 Mike Davis .05 .15
84 Rich Gedman .05 .15
85 Willie Hernandez .05 .15
86 Ron Kittle .05 .15
87 Lee Lacy .05 .15
88 Bill Madlock .08 .25
89 Mike Marshall .05 .15
90 Keith Moreland .05 .15
91 Graig Nettles .08 .25
92 Lance Parrish .08 .25
93 Kirby Puckett .40 1.00
94 Juan Samuel .05 .15
95 Steve Sax .05 .15
96 Dave Stieb .08 .25
97 Darryl Strawberry .15 .40
98 Willie Upshaw .05 .15
99 Frank Viola .08 .25
100 Dwight Gooden .25 .60
101 Joaquin Andujar .08 .25
102 George Bell .08 .25
103 Bert Blyleven .08 .25
104 Mike Boddicker .05 .15
105 Britt Burns .05 .15
106 Rod Carew .15 .40
107 Jack Clark .08 .25
108 Danny Cox .05 .15
109 Ron Darling .08 .25
110 Andre Dawson .08 .25
111 Leon Durham .05 .15
112 Tony Fernandez .05 .15
113 Tommy Herr .05 .15
114 Teddy Higuera .08 .25
115 Bob Horner .08 .25
116 Dave Kingman .08 .25
117 Jack Morris .08 .25
118 Dan Quisenberry .05 .15
119 Jeff Reardon .08 .25
120 Bryn Smith .05 .15
121 Ozzie Smith .40 1.00
122 John Tudor .08 .25
123 Tim Wallach .05 .15
124 Willie Wilson .08 .25
125 Carlton Fisk .15 .40
126 RBI Sluggers .05 .15
127 Run Scorers Ryne Sandberg .25 .60
128 Run Scorers Cal Ripken .25 .60
129 No-Hitters .08 .25
130 WS MVP's Pete Rose .25 .60
131 All-Star Game MVP's .08 .25
132 Cy Young Winners .05 .15
133 Comeback Players .05 .15
134 Big Winners .08 .25
135 Veteran Pitchers Tom Seaver .08 .25
136 ROY Dwight Gooden .08 .25
137 All-Star Game MVP's .08 .25
138 Veteran Hitters Pete Rose .25 .60
139 Power Hitters Mike Schmidt .25 .60
140 Btg Champs Tony Gwynn .15 .40
141 No-Hitters Nolan Ryan .40 1.00
142 No-Hitters Tom Seaver .08 .25
143 Strikeout Kings Nolan Ryan .40 1.00
144 Base Stealers .08 .25
145 RBI Sluggers Eddie Murray .15 .40
146 AL MVP's Rod Carew .08 .25
147 WS MVP's Reggie Jackson .08 .25
148 WS MVP's Mike Schmidt .25 .60
149 ERA Leaders .05 .15
150 Comeback Players Reggie .08 .25
151 Buddy Bell .08 .25
152 Dennis Boyd .05 .15
153 Dave Concepcion .08 .25
154 Brian Downing .08 .25
155 Shawon Dunston .05 .15
156 John Franco .08 .25
157 Scott Garrelts .05 .15
158 Bob James .05 .15
159 Charlie Leibrandt .05 .15
160 Oddibe McDowell .05 .15
161 Roger McDowell .05 .15
162 Mike Moore .05 .15
163 Phil Niekro .08 .25
164 Al Oliver .08 .25
165 Tony Pena .05 .15
166 Ted Power .05 .15
167 Mike Scioscia .08 .25
168 Mario Soto .08 .25
169 Bob Stanley .05 .15
170 Garry Templeton .08 .25
171 Andre Thornton .05 .15
172 Alan Trammell .08 .25
173 Doug DeCinces .05 .15
174 Greg Walker .05 .15
175 Don Sutton .08 .25
176 1985 AW O.Guillen .25 .60
Saber
177 1985 Hot Rookies .05 .15
178 Jose Canseco 2.50 6.00
179 1985 Gold Glove .60 1.50
180 Active Lifetime .300 .60 1.50
181 Active Lifetime .300 Pete Rose .25 .60
182 1985 Milestones .15 .40
183 1985 Triple Crown .40 1.00
184 1985 Highlights .15 .40
185 1985 20 Game Winners .15 .40
186 World Series Champs .15 .40
187 Hubie Brooks .05 .15
188 Glenn Davis .05 .15
189 Darrell Evans .08 .25
190 Rich Gossage .08 .25
191 Andy Hawkins .05 .15
192 Jay Howell .05 .15
193 LaMarr Hoyt .05 .15
194 Davey Lopes .08 .25
195 Mike Scott .08 .25
196 Ted Simmons .08 .25
197 Gary Ward .05 .15
198 Bob Welch .08 .25
199 Mike Young .05 .15
200 Buddy Biancalana .05 .15

1986 Sportflics Rookies

This set of 50 three-phase "animated" standard-size cards features top rookies of 1986 as well as a few outstanding rookies from the past. These "Magic Motion" cards feature a distinctive light blue border on the front of the card. Cards were distributed in a light blue box, which also contained 34 trivia cards, each measuring 1 3/4" by 2". There are 47 single player cards along with two Tri-Stars and one Big Six. The statistics on the card backs are inclusive up through the just-completed 1986 season. An very early card of Barry Bonds is the key to this set.

COMP.FACT.SET (50) 6.00 15.00
1 John Kruk .60 1.50
2 Edwin Correa .02 .10
3 Pete Incaviglia .08 .25
4 Dale Sveum .02 .10
5 Juan Nieves .02 .10
6 Will Clark .60 1.50
7 Wally Joyner .15 .40
8 Lance McCullers .02 .10
9 Scott Bailes .02 .10
10 Dan Plesac .08 .25
11 Jose Canseco 1.25 3.00
12 Bobby Witt .08 .25
13 Barry Bonds 6.00 15.00
14 Andres Thomas .02 .10
15 Jim Deshaies .02 .10
16 Ruben Sierra .30 .75
17 Steve Lombardozzi .02 .10
18 Cory Snyder .02 .10
19 Reggie Williams .02 .10
20 Mitch Williams .08 .25
21 Glenn Braggs .02 .10
22 Danny Tartabull .08 .25
23 Charlie Kerfeld .02 .10
24 Paul Assenmacher .08 .25
25 Robby Thompson .08 .25
26 Bobby Bonilla .15 .40
27 Andres Galarraga .30 .75
28 Billy Joe Robidoux .02 .10
29 Bruce Ruffin .02 .10
30 Greg Swindell .08 .25
31 John Cangelosi .02 .10
32 Jim Traber .02 .10
33 Russ Morman .02 .10
34 Barry Larkin 2.00 5.00
35 Todd Worrell .08 .25
36 John Cerutti .02 .10
37 Mike Kingery .02 .10
38 Mark Eichhorn .02 .10
39 Scott Bankhead .02 .10
40 Bo Jackson 2.50 6.00
41 Greg Mathews .02 .10
42 Eric King .02 .10
43 Kal Daniels .08 .25
44 Calvin Schiraldi .02 .10
45 Mickey Brantley .02 .10
46 Willie Mays .30 .75
Pete Rose
Fred Lynn
47 Tri-Stars Tom Seaver .08 .25
48 Big Six Cal Ripken .30 .75
49 Kevin Mitchell .15 .40
50 Mike Diaz .02 .10

1986 Sportflics Decade Greats Samples

COMPLETE SET (2) 3.00 8.00
1 Dwight Gooden 1.25 3.00
2 Mel Ott 2.00 5.00

1986 Sportflics Decade Greats

This set of 75 three-phase "animated" standard-size cards was produced by Sportflics and manufactured by Opti-Graphics of Arlington, Texas. The cards feature both sepia (players of the '30s and '40s) and full color cards. The concept of the set was that the best players at each position for each decade (from the '30s to the '80s) were chosen. The bios were written by Les Woodcock. Also included with the set in the specially designed collector box are 51 trivia cards with historical questions about the six decades of All-Star games.

COMPLETE FACT.SET (75) 8.00 20.00
1 Babe Ruth 1.50 4.00
2 Jimmie Foxx .15 .40
3 Lefty Grove .15 .40
4 Hank Greenberg .15 .40
5 Al Simmons .07 .20
6 Carl Hubbell .10 .30
7 Joe Cronin .07 .20
8 Mel Ott .15 .40
9 Lefty Gomez .15 .40
10 Lou Gehrig 1.25 3.00
11 Pie Traynor .10 .30
12 Charlie Gehringer .10 .30
13 Best '30s Catchers .07 .20
Bill Dickey
Mickey Cochrane/
14 Best '30s Pitchers .10 .30
Dizzy Dean
Red Ruffing
Paul
15 Best '30s Outfielders .07 .20
Paul Waner
Joe Medwick
Ea
16 Bob Feller .30 .75
17 Lou Boudreau .10 .30
18 Enos Slaughter .10 .30
19 Hal Newhouser .10 .30
20 Joe DiMaggio 1.25 3.00
21 Pee Wee Reese .15 .40
22 Phil Rizzuto .15 .40
23 Ernie Lombardi .07 .20
24 Best '40s Infielders .10 .30
Johnny Mize
Joe Gordon
Geo
25 Ted Williams 1.25 3.00
26 Mickey Mantle 1.50 4.00
27 Warren Spahn .15 .40
28 Jackie Robinson .60 1.50
29 Ernie Banks .15 .40
30 Stan Musial .40 1.00
31 Yogi Berra .15 .40
32 Duke Snider .15 .40
33 Roy Campanella .40 1.00
34 Eddie Mathews .15 .40
35 Ralph Kiner .10 .30
36 Early Wynn .10 .30
37 Nellie Fox .15 .40
Luis Aparicio
38 Best '50s First Base .02 .10
Gil Hodges
Ted Kluszewski/
39 Best '50s Pitchers .07 .20
Bob Lemon
Don Newcombe
Robin
40 Henry Aaron .60 1.50
41 Frank Robinson .10 .30
42 Bob Gibson .10 .30
43 Roberto Clemente .75 2.00
44 Whitey Ford .15 .40
45 Brooks Robinson .15 .40
46 Juan Marichal .10 .30
47 Carl Yastrzemski .15 .40
48 Best '60s First Base .10 .30
Willie McCovey
Harmon Kille
49 Best '60s Catchers .02 .10
Joe Torre
Elston Howard
Bill
50 Willie Mays .60 1.50
51 Best '60s Outfielders .10 .30
Al Kaline
Tony Oliva
Bill
52 Tom Seaver .15 .40
53 Reggie Jackson .15 .40
54 Steve Carlton .15 .40
55 Mike Schmidt .60 1.50
56 Joe Morgan .15 .40
57 Jim Rice .07 .20
58 Jim Palmer .15 .40
59 Lou Brock .10 .30
60 Pete Rose .60 1.50
61 Steve Garvey .10 .30
62 Best '70s Catchers .15 .40
Thurman Munson
Carlton Fisk/
63 Best '70s Pitchers .60 1.50
Vida Blue
Catfish Hunter
Nol
64 George Brett .75 2.00
65 Don Mattingly .75 2.00
66 Fernando Valenzuela .02 .10
67 Dale Murphy .15 .40
68 Wade Boggs .15 .40
69 Rickey Henderson .40 1.00
70 Eddie Murray .15 .40
71 Ron Guidry .02 .10
72 Best '80s Catchers .07 .20
Gary Carter
Lance Parrish
To
73 Best '80s Infielders .75 2.00
Cal Ripken
Lou Whitaker
Ro
74 Best '80s Outfielders .10 .30
Pedro Guerrero
Tim Raines#
75 Dwight Gooden .15 .40
XX Mel Ott 1.25 3.00
Sample, Blank Back
XX Dwight Gooden 2.00 5.00
Sample, Blank Back

1987 Sportflics

This 200-card standard-size color set was produced by Sportflics and again features three sequence action pictures on each card. Also included with the cards were 136 small team logo and trivia cards. There are 165 individual players, 20 Tri-Stars (the top three players in each league at each position), and 15 other miscellaneous multi-player cards. The cards feature a red border on the front. The cards in the factory-collated sets are copyrighted 1986, while the cards in the wax packs are copyrighted 1987 or show no copyright year on the back. Cards from wax packs with 1987 copyright are 1-35, 41-75, 81-115, 121-155, and 161-195; the rest of the numbers (when taken from wax packs) are found without a copyright year.

COMPLETE SET (200) 8.00 20.00
COMP.FACT.SET (200) 8.00 20.00
1 Don Mattingly .75 2.00
2 Wade Boggs .15 .40
3 Dale Murphy .15 .40
4 Rickey Henderson .25 .60
5 George Brett .60 1.50
6 Eddie Murray .25 .60
7 Kirby Puckett .40 1.00
8 Ryne Sandberg .50 1.25
9 Cal Ripken 1.00 2.50
10 Roger Clemens 1.25 3.00
11 Ted Higuera .05 .15
12 Steve Sax .05 .15
13 Chris Brown .05 .15
14 Jesse Barfield .08 .25
15 Kent Hrbek .08 .25
16 Robin Yount .40 1.00
17 Glenn Davis .05 .15
18 Hubie Brooks .05 .15
19 Mike Scott .08 .25
20 Darryl Strawberry .08 .25
21 Alvin Davis .05 .15
22 Eric Davis .15 .40
23 Danny Tartabull .05 .15
24A Cory Snyder ERR '86 .05 .15
24B Cory Snyder ERR '87 .05 .15
24C Cory Snyder COR '86 .05 .15
25 Pete Rose .60 1.50
26 Wally Joyner .15 .40
27 Pedro Guerrero .08 .25
28 Tom Seaver .15 .40
29 Bob Knepper .05 .15
30 Mike Schmidt .60 1.50
31 Tony Gwynn .40 1.00
32 Don Slaught .05 .15
33 Todd Worrell .05 .15
34 Tim Raines .08 .25
35 Dave Parker .08 .25
36 Bob Ojeda .05 .15
37 Pete Incaviglia .08 .25
38 Bruce Hurst .05 .15
39 Bobby Witt .08 .25
40 Steve Garvey .08 .25
41 Dave Winfield .08 .25
42 Jose Cruz .08 .25
43 Orel Hershiser .15 .40
44 Reggie Jackson .15 .40
45 Chili Davis .08 .25
46 Robby Thompson .08 .25
47 Dennis Boyd .05 .15
48 Kirk Gibson .08 .25
49 Fred Lynn .08 .25
50 Gary Carter .08 .25
51 George Bell .08 .25
52 Pete O'Brien .05 .15
53 Ron Darling .08 .25
54 Paul Molitor .08 .25
55 Mike Pagliarulo .05 .15
56 Mike Boddicker .05 .15
57 Dave Righetti .08 .25
58 Len Dykstra .08 .25
59 Mike Witt .05 .15
60 Tony Bernazard .05 .15
61 John Kruk .40 1.00
62 Mike Krukow .05 .15
63 Sid Fernandez .05 .15
64 Gary Gaetti .08 .25
65 Vince Coleman .05 .15
66 Pat Tabler .05 .15
67 Mike Scioscia .08 .25
68 Scott Garrelts .05 .15
69 Brett Butler .08 .25
70 Bill Buckner .08 .25
71A Dennis Rasmussen ERR '86 .25 .60
71B Dennis Rasmussen COR '87 .08 .25
72 Tim Wallach .05 .15
73 Bob Horner .08 .25
74 Willie McGee .08 .25
75 Tri-Stars Don Mattingly .40 1.00
76A Jesse Orosco COR/'86 copyright .05 .15
76B Jesse Orosco ERR/'87 copyright
(Number on back i .05 .15
77 Tri-Stars Worrell .05 .15
Reardon
Smith
78 Candy Maldonado .05 .15
79 Tri-Stars Ozzie Smith .25 .60
80 Tri-Stars Jose Canseco .25 .60
81 Bert Blyleven .08 .25
82 Mike Marshall .05 .15
83 Ron Guidry .08 .25
84 Julio Franco .08 .25
85 Willie Wilson .08 .25
86 Lee Lacy .05 .15
87 Jack Morris .08 .25
88 Ray Knight .08 .25
89 Phil Bradley .05 .15
90 Jose Canseco .40 1.00
91 Gary Ward .05 .15
92 Mike Easler .05 .15
93 Tony Pena .05 .15
94 Dave Smith .05 .15
95 Will Clark .75 2.00
96 Lloyd Moseby/(See also 76B) .05 .15
97 Jim Rice .08 .25
98 Shawon Dunston .05 .15
99 Don Sutton .08 .25
100 Dwight Gooden .15 .40
101 Lance Parrish .08 .25
102 Mark Langston .05 .15
103 Floyd Youmans .05 .15
104 Lee Smith .08 .25
105 Willie Hernandez .05 .15
106 Doug DeCinces .05 .15
107 Ken Schrom .05 .15
108 Don Carman .05 .15
109 Brook Jacoby .05 .15
110 Steve Bedrosian .05 .15
111 Tri-Stars Roger Clemens .25 .60
112 Tri-Stars Lou Whitaker .05 .15
113 Tri-Stars Cal Ripken .25 .60
114 Tri-Stars Boggs .25 .60
Brett
115 Tri-Stars Mike Schmidt .25 .60
116 Tri-Stars Ryne Sandberg .25 .60
117 Tri-Stars Tony Gwynn .15 .40
118 T.Steinbach .08 .25
B.Santiago
119 Hi-Lite Tri-Stars .05 .15
120 Tri-Stars Fernando .08 .25
Gooden
121 Johnny Ray .05 .15
122 Keith Moreland .05 .15
123 Juan Samuel .05 .15
124 Wally Backman .05 .15
125 Nolan Ryan 1.00 2.50
126 Greg A. Harris .05 .15
127 Kirk McCaskill .05 .15
128 Dwight Evans .15 .40
129 Rick Rhoden .05 .15
130 Bill Madlock .08 .25
131 Oddibe McDowell .05 .15
132 Darrell Evans .08 .25
133 Keith Hernandez .08 .25
134 Tom Brunansky .05 .15
135 Kevin McReynolds .05 .15
136 Scott Fletcher .05 .15
137 Lou Whitaker .08 .25
138 Carney Lansford .08 .25
139 Andre Dawson .08 .25
140 Carlton Fisk .15 .40
141 Buddy Bell .08 .25
142 Ozzie Smith .40 1.00
143 Dan Pasqua .05 .15
144 Kevin Mitchell .15 .40
145 Bret Saberhagen .08 .25
146 Charlie Kerfeld .05 .15
147 Phil Niekro .08 .25
148 John Candelaria .05 .15
149 Rich Gedman .05 .15
150 Fernando Valenzuela .08 .25
151 Tri-Stars Gary Carter .05 .15
152 Tri-Stars Raines .05 .15
Cruz
Coleman

153 Tri-Stars Dave Winfield .05 .15
154 Tri-Stars Parrish .05 .15
Slaught
Gedman
155 Tri-Stars Dale Murphy .15 .40
156 Hi-Lite Tri-Stars Mike Schmidt .25 .60
157 Speedburners R.Henderson .15 .40
158 Rafael Palmeiro 2.00 5.00
159 Big Six Mattingly .40 1.00
Clemens
160 Roger McDowell .05 .15
161 Brian Downing .08 .25
162 Bill Doran .05 .15
163 Don Baylor .08 .25
164A Alfredo Griffin ERR# .08 .25
164B Alfredo Griffin COR .05 .15
165 Don Aase .05 .15
166 Glenn Wilson .05 .15
167 Dan Quisenberry .05 .15
168 Frank White .08 .25
169 Cecil Cooper .08 .25
170 Jody Davis .05 .15
171 Harold Baines .08 .25
172 Rob Deer .05 .15
173 John Tudor .08 .25
174 Larry Parrish .05 .15
175 Kevin Bass .05 .15
176 Joe Carter .08 .25
177 Mitch Webster .05 .15
178 Dave Kingman .08 .25
179 Jim Presley .05 .15
180 Mel Hall .05 .15
181 Shane Rawley .05 .15
182 Marty Barrett .05 .15
183 Damaso Garcia .05 .15
184 Bobby Grich .08 .25
185 Leon Durham .05 .15
186 Ozzie Guillen .15 .40
187 Tony Fernandez .05 .15
188 Alan Trammell .08 .25
189 Jim Clancy .05 .15
190 Bo Jackson 2.50 6.00
191 Bob Forsch .05 .15
192 John Franco .08 .25
193 Von Hayes .05 .15
194 Tri-Stars Aase .05 .15
Righetti
Eichhorn
195 Tri-Stars Will Clark .25 .60
196 Hi-Lite Tri-Stars R.Clemens .25 .60
197 Big Six Brett .25 .60
Gwynn
Ryno
198 Tri-Stars Puckett .25 .60
Henderson
199 Speedburners Raines .08 .25
Cole
Davis
200 Steve Carlton .08 .25

1987 Sportflics Dealer Panels

These "Magic Motion" card panels of four were issued only to dealers who were ordering other Sportflics product in quantity. If cut into individual cards, the interior white borders will be slightly narrower than the regular issue Sportflics since the panels of four measure a shade under 4 7/8" by 6 7/8". The cards have a 1986 copyright on the back same as the factory collated sets. Other than the slight difference in size, these cards are essentially styled the same as the regular issue of 1987 Sportflics. This set of sixteen top players was accompanied by the inclusion of four smaller panels of four team logo/team fact cards. The 16 small team cards correspond directly to the 16 players in the sets. The checklist below prices the panels and gives the card number for each player, which is the same as the player's card number in the Sportflics regular set.

COMPLETE SET (4) 20.00 50.00
Don Mattingly 1 8.00 20.00
Roger Clemens 10
Mike Schmidt 30
Wade Boggs 2 2.00 5.00
Eddie Murray 6
Wally Joyner 26
Fer
Dale Murphy 3 5.00 12.00
Tony Gwynn 31
Jim Rice 97
Keith H
Rickey Henderson 4 8.00 20.00
George Brett 5
Cal Ripken 9/

1987 Sportflics Rookies I

These "Magic Motion" cards were issued as a series of 25 standard-size cards packaged in its own complete set box, along with 17 trivia cards. The cards in the set are numbered essentially in alphabetical order by player's name.

COMPLETE FACT.SET (25) 2.00 5.00
Eric Bell .02 .10
Chris Bosio .07 .20
Bob Brower .02 .10
Jerry Browne .02 .10
Ellis Burks .40 1.00
Casey Candaele .02 .10
Ken Gerhart .02 .10
Mike Greenwell .20 .50
Stan Jefferson .02 .10
Dave Magadan .07 .20
Joe Magrane .07 .20
Fred McGriff .60 1.50
Mark McGwire 1.00 2.50
Mark McLemore .07 .20
Jeff Musselman .02 .10
Matt Nokes .02 .10
Paul O'Neill .20 .50
Luis Polonia .07 .20
Benito Santiago .07 .20
Kevin Seitzer .20 .50
John Smiley .07 .20
Terry Steinbach .20 .50
B.J. Surhoff .20 .50
Devon White .20 .50
Matt Williams .60 1.50

1987 Sportflics Rookies II

These "Magic Motion" cards were issued as a series of 25 cards packaged in its own complete set box along with 17 trivia cards. Cards are standard sized. In this second set the card numbering begins with number 26. The three front photos show the player in two action poses and one portrait pose. The card backs also provide a full-color photo (approximately 1 3/8" by 2 1/4") of the player as well as the usual statistics and biographical notes.

COMPLETE FACT.SET (25) 3.00 8.00
26 DeWayne Buice .02 .10
27 Willie Fraser .02 .10
28 Billy Ripken .02 .10
29 Mike Henneman .10 .30
30 Shawn Hillegas .02 .10
31 Shane Mack .07 .20
32 Rafael Palmeiro 1.00 2.50
33 Mike Jackson .15 .40
34 Gene Larkin .07 .20
35 Jimmy Jones .02 .10
36 Gerald Young .02 .10
37 Ken Caminiti .75 2.00
38 Sam Horn .02 .10
39 David Cone 1.25 3.00
40 Mike Dunne .02 .10
41 Ken Williams .10 .30
42 John Morris .02 .10
43 Jim Lindeman .02 .10
44 Mike Stanley .10 .30
45 Les Straker .02 .10
46 Jeff M. Robinson .02 .10
47 Todd Benzinger .02 .10
48 Jeff Blauser .10 .30
49 John Marzano .02 .10
50 Keith Miller .02 .10

1987 Sportflics Rookie Discs

These seven oversize discs feature some of the leading rookies of the 1987 season. The discs feature the traditional sportflic magic motion three photos on the disc. The backs have career stats through 1986 as well as a biography of the playe.

COMPLETE SET (7) 8.00 20.00
1 Casey Candaele .40 1.00
2 Mark McGwire 5.00 12.00
3 Kevin Seitzer .75 2.00
4 Joe Magrane .40 1.00
5 Benito Santiago .60 1.50
6 Dave Magadan .60 1.50
7 Devon White .60 1.50

1987 Sportflics Rookie Packs

This two pack-set consists of ten "rookie" players and two trivia cards. Each of the two different packs had half the set and the outside of the wrapper told which cards were inside. Each card below has the pack number indicated by P1 or P2. The cards measure the standard size. Dealers received one rookie pack with every Team Preview set they ordered. The card backs also feature a full-color small photo of the player.

COMPLETE SET (10) 3.00 8.00
1 Terry Steinbach P2 .40 1.00
2 Rafael Palmeiro P1 1.25 3.00
3 Dave Magadan P2 .20 .50
4 Marvin Freeman P2 .08 .25
5 Brick Smith P2 .08 .25
6 B.J. Surhoff P1 .40 1.00
7 John Smiley P1 .20 .50
8 Alonzo Powell P2 .08 .25
9 Benito Santiago P1 .20 .50
10 Devon White P1 .40 1.00

1987 Sportflics Superstar Discs

These 18 discs, measuring approximately 4 5/8" in diameter, featured leading players. The player's photo was surrounded by a red border. Player information is located on the back.

COMPLETE SET (18) 15.00 40.00
1 Joe Carter 1.00 2.50
2 Mike Scott .40 1.00
3 Ryne Sandberg 2.00 5.00
4 Mike Schmidt 1.00 2.50
5 Dale Murphy 1.00 2.50
6 Fernando Valenzuela .60 1.50
7 Tony Gwynn 2.50 6.00
8 Cal Ripken Jr. 5.00 12.00
9 Gary Carter 1.25 3.00
10 Cory Snyder .40 1.00
11 Kirby Puckett 1.50 4.00
12 George Brett 2.00 5.00
13 Keith Hernandez .60 1.50
14 Rickey Henderson 1.25 3.00
15 Tim Raines .60 1.50
16 Bo Jackson 1.25 3.00
17 Pete Rose 2.00 5.00
18 Eric Davis .75 2.00

1987 Sportflics Team Preview

This 26-card standard-size set features a card for each Major League team. Each card shows 12 different players on that team via four "Magic Motion" trios. The narrative on the back gives Outlook, Newcomers to Watch, and Summary for each team. The list of players appearing on the front is given at the bottom of the reverse of each card. The was distributed as a complete set in its own box along with 26 team logo trivia cards measuring approximately 1 3/4" by 2". Tom Glavine has his only 1987 Major League card in this set.

COMPLETE SET (26) 10.00 25.00
1 Texas Rangers .75 2.00
Pete Incaviglia
Mitch Williams
Bo
2 New York Mets .40 1.00
Bob Ojeda
Lenny Dykstra
Darryl St
3 Cleveland Indians .20 .50
Joe Carter
Mel Hall
Cory Snyd
4 Cincinnati Reds .75 2.00
Eric Davis
Dave Parker
Bill Gul
5 Toronto Blue Jays .20 .50
Willie Upshaw
Tony Fernandez/
6 Philadelphia Phillies .40 1.00
Von Hayes
Steve Bedrosian#
7 New York Yankees 1.25 3.00
Bob Tewksbury
Dave Righetti
Da
8 Houston Astros 1.50 4.00
Glenn Davis
Bob Knepper
Kevin Ba
9 Boston Red Sox 1.25 3.00
Wade Boggs
Roger Clemens
Dennis
10 San Francisco Giants .40 1.00
Chris Brown
Mike Krukow
Wi
11 California Angels .20 .50
Don Sutton
Mike Witt
Donnie M
12 St. Louis Cardinals .60 1.50
Terry Pendleton
Tom Herr
To
13 Kansas City Royals 1.00 2.50
Bo Jackson
Danny Tartabull
G
14 Los Angeles Dodgers .20 .50
Mike Scioscia
Steve Fax
Fer
15 Detroit Tigers .60 1.50
Lou Whitaker
Dan Petry
Alan Tram
16 San Diego Padres .75 2.00
Tony Gwynn
John Kruk
Kevin Mit
17 Minnesota Twins .60 1.50
Gary Gaetti
Roy Smalley
Kirby P
18 Pittsburgh Pirates 4.00 10.00
John Smiley
Sid Bream
Mike D
19 Milwaukee Brewers .40 1.00
Ernest Riles
Rob Deer
Billy J
20 Montreal Expos .20 .50
Floyd Youmans
Tim Burke
Casey Ca
21 Baltimore Orioles 2.00 5.00
Don Aase
Mike Boddicker
Eric
22 Chicago Cubs 2.00 5.00
Maddux
Palmeiro
23 Oakland Athletics 1.50 4.00
Terry Steinbach
Mike Davis
Ca
24 Atlanta Braves 2.00 5.00
Rick Mahler
Ken Oberkfell
Gene G
25 Seattle Mariners .20 .50
Dave Valle
Donell Nixon
Scott
26 Chicago White Sox .40 1.00
Carlton Fisk
Harold Baines
Jo

1988 Sportflics

This 225-card standard-size full-color set was produced by Sportflics and again features three sequence action pictures on each card. There are 219 individual players, three Highlights trios, and three Rookie Prospect trio cards. The cards feature a red border on the front. A full-color action picture of the player is printed on the back of the card.

COMPLETE FACT.SET (225) 10.00 25.00
1 Don Mattingly .75 2.00
2 Tim Raines .08 .25
3 Andre Dawson .08 .25
4 George Bell .08 .25
5 Joe Carter .08 .25
6 Matt Nokes .15 .40
7 Dave Winfield .08 .25
8 Kirby Puckett .25 .60
9 Will Clark .25 .60
10 Eric Davis .08 .25
11 Rickey Henderson .25 .60
12 Ryne Sandberg .50 1.25
13 Jesse Barfield UER/(Misspelled Jessie .08 .25
on card ba
14 Ozzie Guillen .08 .25
15 Bret Saberhagen .08 .25
16 Tony Gwynn .40 1.00
17 Kevin Seitzer .05 .15
18 Jack Clark .05 .15
19 Danny Tartabull .05 .15
20 Ted Higuera .05 .15
21 Charlie Leibrandt UER .05 .15
22 Benito Santiago .08 .25
23 Fred Lynn .08 .25
24 Robby Thompson .05 .15
25 Alan Trammell .08 .25
26 Tony Fernandez .05 .15
27 Rick Sutcliffe .08 .25
28 Gary Carter .08 .25
29 Cory Snyder .05 .15
30 Lou Whitaker .08 .25
31 Keith Hernandez .08 .25
32 Mike Witt .05 .15
33 Harold Baines .08 .25
34 Robin Yount .40 1.00
35 Mike Schmidt .60 1.50
36 Dion James .05 .15
37 Tom Candiotti .05 .15
38 Tracy Jones .05 .15
39 Nolan Ryan 1.00 2.50
40 Fernando Valenzuela .08 .25
41 Vance Law .05 .15
42 Roger McDowell .05 .15
43 Carlton Fisk .15 .40
44 Scott Garrelts .05 .15
45 Lee Guetterman .05 .15
46 Mark Langston .05 .15
47 Willie Randolph .08 .25
48 Bill Doran .05 .15
49 Larry Parrish .05 .15
50 Wade Boggs .15 .40
51 Shane Rawley .05 .15
52 Alvin Davis .05 .15
53 Jeff Reardon .08 .25
54 Jim Presley .05 .15
55 Kevin Bass .05 .15
56 Kevin McReynolds .05 .15
57 B.J. Surhoff .08 .25
58 Julio Franco .08 .25
59 Eddie Murray .25 .60
60 Jody Davis .05 .15
61 Todd Worrell .05 .15
62 Von Hayes .05 .15
63 Billy Hatcher .05 .15
64 John Kruk .08 .25
65 Tom Henke .05 .15
66 Mike Scott .08 .25
67 Vince Coleman .05 .15
68 Ozzie Smith .40 1.00
69 Ken Williams .05 .15
70 Steve Bedrosian .05 .15
71 Luis Polonia .05 .15
72 Brook Jacoby .05 .15
73 Ron Darling .08 .25
74 Lloyd Moseby .05 .15
75 Wally Joyner .08 .25
76 Dan Quisenberry .05 .15
77 Scott Fletcher .05 .15
78 Kirk McCaskill .05 .15
79 Paul Molitor .08 .25
80 Mike Aldrete .05 .15
81 Neal Heaton .05 .15
82 Jeffrey Leonard .05 .15
83 Dave Magadan .05 .15
84 Danny Cox .05 .15
85 Lance McCullers .05 .15
86 Jay Howell .05 .15
87 Charlie Hough .08 .25
88 Gene Garber .05 .15
89 Jesse Orosco .05 .15
90 Don Robinson .05 .15
91 Willie McGee .08 .25
92 Bert Blyleven .08 .25
93 Phil Bradley .05 .15
94 Terry Kennedy .05 .15
95 Kent Hrbek .08 .25
96 Juan Samuel .05 .15
97 Pedro Guerrero .08 .25
98 Sid Bream .05 .15
99 Devon White .08 .25
100 Mark McGwire 1.25 3.00
101 Dave Parker .08 .25
102 Glenn Davis .05 .15
103 Greg Walker .05 .15
104 Rick Rhoden .05 .15
105 Mitch Webster .05 .15
106 Len Dykstra .08 .25
107 Gene Larkin .05 .15
108 Floyd Youmans .05 .15
109 Andy Van Slyke .15 .40
110 Mike Scioscia .08 .25
111 Kirk Gibson .25 .60
112 Kal Daniels .05 .15
113 Ruben Sierra .08 .25
114 Sam Horn .05 .15
115 Ray Knight .08 .25
116 Jimmy Key .08 .25
117 Bo Diaz .05 .15
118 Mike Greenwell .05 .15
119 Barry Bonds 1.25 3.00
120 Reggie Jackson UER .15 .40
121 Mike Pagliarulo .05 .15
122 Tommy John .08 .25
123 Bill Madlock .08 .25
124 Ken Caminiti .75 2.00
125 Gary Ward .05 .15
126 Candy Maldonado .05 .15
127 Harold Reynolds .08 .25
128 Joe Magrane .08 .25
129 Mike Henneman .08 .25
130 Jim Gantner .05 .15
131 Bobby Bonilla .08 .25
132 John Farrell .05 .15
133 Frank Tanana .05 .15
134 Zane Smith .05 .15
135 Dave Righetti .08 .25
136 Rick Reuschel .08 .25
137 Dwight Evans .15 .40
138 Howard Johnson .08 .25
139 Terry Leach .05 .15
140 Casey Candaele .05 .15
141 Tom Herr .05 .15
142 Tony Pena .05 .15
143 Lance Parrish .08 .25
144 Ellis Burks .40 1.00
145 Pete O'Brien .05 .15
146 Mike Boddicker .05 .15
147 Buddy Bell .08 .25
148 Bo Jackson .25 .60
149 Frank White .08 .25
150 George Brett .60 1.50
151 Tim Wallach .05 .15
152 Cal Ripken 1.00 2.50
153 Brett Butler .08 .25
154 Gary Gaetti .08 .25
155 Darryl Strawberry .08 .25
156 Alfredo Griffin .05 .15
157 Marty Barrett .05 .15
158 Jim Rice .08 .25
159 Terry Pendleton .08 .25
160 Orel Hershiser .08 .25
161 Larry Sheets .05 .15
162 Dave Stewart UER .08 .25
163 Shawon Dunston .05 .15
164 Keith Moreland .05 .15
165 Ken Oberkfell .05 .15
166 Ivan Calderon .05 .15
167 Bob Welch .08 .25
168 Fred McGriff .25 .60
169 Pete Incaviglia .05 .15
170 Dale Murphy .15 .40
171 Mike Dunne .05 .15
172 Chili Davis .08 .25
173 Milt Thompson .05 .15
174 Terry Steinbach .08 .25
175 Oddibe McDowell .05 .15
176 Jack Morris .08 .25
177 Sid Fernandez .05 .15
178 Ken Griffey Sr. .08 .25
179 Lee Smith .08 .25
180 HL 1987 Puckett .25 .60
Schmidt
181 Brian Downing .08 .25
182 Andres Galarraga .08 .25
183 Rob Deer .05 .15
184 Greg Brock .05 .15
185 Doug DeCinces .05 .15
186 Johnny Ray .05 .15
187 Hubie Brooks .05 .15
188 Darrell Evans .08 .25
189 Mel Hall .05 .15
190 Jim Deshaies .05 .15
191 Dan Plesac .05 .15
192 Willie Wilson .08 .25
193 Mike LaValliere .05 .15
194 Tom Brunansky .05 .15
195 John Franco .08 .25
196 Frank Viola .08 .25
197 Bruce Hurst .05 .15
198 John Tudor .08 .25
199 Bob Forsch .05 .15
200 Dwight Gooden .08 .25
201 Jose Canseco .40 1.00
202 Carney Lansford .08 .25
203 Kelly Downs .05 .15
204 Glenn Wilson .05 .15
205 Pat Tabler .05 .15
206 Mike Davis .05 .15
207 Roger Clemens .75 2.00
208 Dave Smith .05 .15
209 Curt Young .05 .15
210 Mark Eichhorn .05 .15
211 Juan Nieves .05 .15
212 Bob Boone .08 .25
213 Don Sutton .08 .25
214 Willie Upshaw .05 .15
215 Jim Clancy .05 .15
216 Bill Ripken .05 .15
217 Ozzie Virgil .05 .15
218 Dave Concepcion .08 .25
219 Alan Ashby .05 .15
220 Mike Marshall .05 .15
221 HL 1987 Mark McGwire .50 1.25
222 HL 1987 Don Mattingly .40 1.00
223 Jay Buhner .30 .75
224 Crews .08 .25
Palacios
Davis
225 Reed .15 .40
Treadway
Miller

1988 Sportflics Gamewinners

This 25-card set of "Gamewinners" was distributed in a green and yellow box along with 17 trivia cards by Weiser Card Company of New Jersey. The 25 players selected for the set show a strong New York preference. The set was ostensibly produced for use as a youth organizational fund raiser. The cards are the standard size and are done in the typical Sportflics' Magic Motion (three picture) style.

COMPLETE FACT.SET (25) 4.00 10.00
1 Don Mattingly 1.00 2.50
2 Mark McGwire 1.00 2.50
3 Wade Boggs .40 1.25
4 Will Clark .15 .40
5 Eric Davis .07 .20
6 Willie Randolph .07 .20
7 Dave Winfield .40 1.25
8 Rickey Henderson .60 1.50
9 Dwight Gooden .07 .20
10 Benito Santiago .07 .20
11 Keith Hernandez .07 .20
12 Juan Samuel .02 .10
13 Kevin Seitzer .02 .10
14 Gary Carter .12 1.25
15 Darryl Strawberry .07 .20
16 Rick Rhoden .02 .10
17 Howard Johnson .02 .10
18 Matt Nokes .02 .10
19 Dave Righetti .02 .10
20 Roger Clemens 1.00 2.50
21 Mike Schmidt .40 1.00
22 Kevin McReynolds .02 .10
23 Mike Pagliarulo .02 .10
24 Kevin Elster .02 .10
25 Jack Clark .07 .20

1989 Sportflics

This 225-card standard-size full-color set was produced by Sportflics (distributed by Major League Marketing) and again features three sequence action pictures on each card. There are 220 individual players, two Highlights trios, and three Rookie Prospect trio cards. The cards feature a white border on the front with red and blue inner trim colors. A full-color action picture of the player is printed on the back of the card.

COMPLETE SET (225) 10.00 25.00
COMPLETE FACT.SET (225) 10.00 25.00
1 Jose Canseco .30 .75
2 Wally Joyner .08 .25
3 Roger Clemens 1.00 2.50
4 Greg Swindell .05 .15
5 Jack Morris .08 .25
6 Mickey Brantley .05 .15
7 Jim Presley .05 .15
8 Pete O'Brien .05 .15
9 Jesse Barfield .08 .25
10 Frank Viola .08 .25
11 Kevin Bass .05 .15
12 Glenn Wilson .05 .15
13 Chris Sabo .20 .50
14 Fred McGriff .20 .50
15 Mark Grace .30 .75
16 Devon White .08 .25
17 Juan Samuel .05 .15
18 Lou Whitaker UER .08 .25
19 Greg Walker .05 .15
20 Roberto Alomar .30 .75
21 Mike Schmidt .60 1.50
22 Benito Santiago .08 .25
23 Dave Stewart .08 .25
24 Dave Winfield .08 .25
25 George Bell .08 .25
26 Jack Clark .08 .25
27 Doug Drabek .05 .15
28 Ron Gant .08 .25
29 Glenn Braggs .05 .15
30 Rafael Palmeiro .30 .75
31 Brett Butler .08 .25
32 Ron Darling .08 .25
33 Alvin Davis .05 .15
34 Bob Walk .05 .15
35 Dave Stieb .08 .25
36 Orel Hershiser .08 .25
37 John Farrell .05 .15
38 Doug Jones .05 .15
39 Kelly Downs .05 .15
40 Bob Boone .08 .25
41 Gary Sheffield UER 1.25 3.00
42 Doug Dascenzo .05 .15
43 Chad Kreuter .05 .15
44 Ricky Jordan .08 .25
45 Dave West .05 .15
46 Danny Tartabull .05 .15
47 Teddy Higuera .05 .15
48 Gary Gaetti .08 .25
49 Dave Parker .08 .25
50 Don Mattingly .75 2.00
51 David Cone .08 .25
52 Kal Daniels .08 .25
53 Carney Lansford .08 .25
54 Mike Marshall .05 .15
55 Kevin Seitzer .05 .15
56 Mike Henneman .05 .15
57 Bill Doran .05 .15
58 Steve Sax .05 .15
59 Lance Parrish .08 .25
60 Keith Hernandez .08 .25
61 Jose Uribe .05 .15
62 Jose Lind .05 .15
63 Steve Bedrosian .05 .15
64 George Brett UER .75 2.00
65 Kirk Gibson .08 .25
66 Cal Ripken 1.00 2.50
67 Mitch Webster .05 .15
68 Fred Lynn .05 .15
69 Eric Davis .08 .25
70 Bo Jackson .30 .75
71 Kevin Elster .05 .15
72 Rick Reuschel .08 .25
73 Tim Burke .05 .15
74 Mark Davis .05 .15
75 Claudell Washington .05 .15
76 Lance McCullers .05 .15
77 Mike Moore .05 .15
78 Robby Thompson .05 .15
79 Roger McDowell .05 .15
80 Danny Jackson .05 .15
81 Tim Leary .05 .15
82 Bobby Witt .05 .15
83 Jim Gott .05 .15
84 Andy Hawkins .05 .15
85 Ozzie Guillen .08 .25
86 John Tudor .08 .25
87 Todd Burns .05 .15
88 Dave Gallagher .05 .15
89 Jay Buhner .08 .25
90 Gregg Jefferies .05 .15
91 Bob Welch .08 .25
92 Charlie Hough .08 .25
93 Tony Fernandez .05 .15
94 Ozzie Virgil .05 .15
95 Andre Dawson .08 .25
96 Hubie Brooks .05 .15
97 Kevin McReynolds .05 .15
98 Mike LaValliere .05 .15
99 Terry Pendleton .08 .25
100 Wade Boggs .20 .50
101 Dennis Eckersley .20 .50
102 Mark Gubicza .05 .15
103 Frank Tanana .05 .15
104 Joe Carter .08 .25
105 Ozzie Smith .50 1.25
106 Dennis Martinez .08 .25
107 Jeff Treadway .05 .15
108 Greg Maddux .50 1.25
109 Bret Saberhagen .08 .25
110 Dale Murphy .20 .50
111 Rob Deer .05 .15
112 Pete Incaviglia .05 .15
113 Vince Coleman .05 .15
114 Tim Wallach .05 .15
115 Nolan Ryan 1.00 2.50
116 Walt Weiss .05 .15
117 Brian Downing .08 .25
118 Melido Perez .05 .15
119 Terry Steinbach .08 .25
120 Mike Scott .08 .25
121 Tim Belcher .05 .15
122 Mike Boddicker .05 .15
123 Len Dykstra .08 .25
124 Fernando Valenzuela .08 .25
125 Gerald Young .05 .15
126 Tom Henke .05 .15
127 Dave Henderson .05 .15
128 Dan Plesac .05 .15
129 Chili Davis .08 .25
130 Bryan Harvey .05 .15
131 Don August .05 .15
132 Mike Harkey
133 Luis Polonia .05 .15
134 Craig Worthington .05 .15
135 Joey Meyer .05 .15
136 Barry Larkin .20 .50
137 Glenn Davis .05 .15
138 Mike Scioscia .08 .25
139 Andres Galarraga .08 .25
140 Dwight Gooden .08 .25
141 Keith Moreland .05 .15
142 Kevin Mitchell .08 .25
143 Mike Greenwell .05 .15
144 Mel Hall .05 .15
145 Rickey Henderson .30 .75
146 Barry Bonds 1.00 2.50
147 Eddie Murray .30 .75
148 Lee Smith .08 .25
149 Julio Franco .08 .25
150 Tim Raines .08 .25
151 Mitch Williams .05 .15
152 Tim Laudner .05 .15
153 Mike Pagliarulo .05 .15
154 Floyd Bannister .05 .15
155 Gary Carter .08 .25
156 Kirby Puckett .30 .75
157 Harold Baines .08 .25
158 Dave Righetti .08 .25
159 Mark Langston .05 .15
160 Tony Gwynn .40 1.00
161 Tom Brunansky .05 .15
162 Vance Law .05 .15
163 Kelly Gruber .05 .15
164 Gerald Perry .05 .15
165 Harold Reynolds .08 .25
166 Andy Van Slyke .20 .50
167 Jimmy Key .08 .25
168 Jeff Reardon .08 .25
169 Milt Thompson .05 .15
170 Will Clark .20 .50
171 Chet Lemon .08 .25
172 Pat Tabler .05 .15
173 Jim Rice .08 .25
174 Billy Hatcher .05 .15
175 Bruce Hurst .05 .15
176 John Franco .08 .25
177 Van Snider .05 .15
178 Ron Jones .05 .15
179 Jerald Clark .05 .15
180 Tom Browning .08 .25
181 Von Hayes .05 .15
182 Bobby Bonilla .08 .25
183 Todd Worrell .05 .15
184 John Kruk .08 .25
185 Scott Fletcher .05 .15
186 Willie Wilson .08 .25
187 Jody Davis .05 .15
188 Kent Hrbek .08 .25
189 Ruben Sierra .08 .25
190 Shawon Dunston .05 .15
191 Ellis Burks .08 .25
192 Brook Jacoby .05 .15
193 Jeff M. Robinson .05 .15
194 Rich Dotson .05 .15
195 Johnny Ray .05 .15
196 Cory Snyder .05 .15
197 Mike Witt .05 .15
198 Marty Barrett .05 .15
199 Robin Yount .50 1.25
200 Mark McGwire 1.00 2.50
201 Ryne Sandberg .50 1.25
202 John Candelaria .05 .15
203 Matt Nokes .05 .15
204 Dwight Evans .20 .50
205 Darryl Strawberry .08 .25
206 Willie McGee .08 .25
207 Bobby Thigpen .05 .15
208 B.J. Surhoff .08 .25
209 Paul Molitor .08 .25
210 Jody Reed .05 .15
211 Doyle Alexander .05 .15
212 Dennis Rasmussen .05 .15
213 Kevin Gross .05 .15
214 Kirk McCaskill .05 .15
215 Alan Trammell .08 .25
216 Damon Berryhill .05 .15
217 Rick Sutcliffe .08 .25
218 Don Slaught .05 .15
219 Carlton Fisk .20 .50
220 Allan Anderson .05 .15
221 Canseco .20 .50
Boggs
Greenwell
222 Orel Hershiser .08 .25
Dennis Eckersley
Tom Browning
223 Sheffield .60 1.50
Jefferies
S.Alomar Jr.
224 Randy Johnson 3.00 8.00
Ramon Martinez
Bob Milacki
225 C.Drew .05 .15
G.Berroa
R.Jones

1990 Sportflics

The 1990 Sportflics set contains 225 standard-size cards. On the fronts, the black, white, orange, and yellow borders surround two photos, which can each be seen depending on the angle. The set is considered an improvement over the previous years' versions by many collectors due to the increased clarity of the fronts, caused by having two images rather than three. The backs are dominated by large color photos.

COMPLETE SET (225) 12.50 30.00
COMPLETE FACT.SET (225) 12.50 30.00
1 Kevin Mitchell .07 .20
2 Wade Boggs .20 .50
3 Cory Snyder .07 .20
4 Paul O'Neill .20 .50
5 Will Clark .20 .50
6 Tony Fernandez .07 .20
7 Ken Griffey Jr. 1.00 2.50
8 Nolan Ryan 1.00 2.50
9 Rafael Palmeiro .20 .50
10 Jesse Barfield .07 .20
11 Kirby Puckett .30 .75
12 Steve Sax .07 .20
13 Fred McGriff .20 .50

14 Gregg Jefferies .07 .20
15 Mark Grace .20 .50
16 Ozzie Smith .50 1.25
17 George Bell .07 .20
18 Robin Yount .50 1.25
19 Glenn Davis .07 .20
20 Jeffrey Leonard .07 .20
21 Chili Davis .10 .30
22 Craig Biggio .30 .75
23 Jose Canseco .20 .50
24 Derek Lilliquist .07 .20
25 Chris Bosio .07 .20
26 Dave Stieb .10 .30
27 Bobby Thigpen .07 .20
28 Jack Clark .10 .30
29 Kevin Ritz .07 .20
30 Tom Gordon .10 .30
31 Bryan Harvey .07 .20
32 Jim Deshaies .07 .20
33 Terry Steinbach .07 .20
34 Tom Glavine .20 .50
35 Bob Welch .10 .30
36 Charlie Hayes .07 .20
37 Jeff Reardon .10 .30
38 Joe Orsulak .07 .20
39 Scott Garrelts .07 .20
40 Bob Boone .10 .30
41 Scott Bankhead .07 .20
42 Tom Henke .07 .20
43 Greg Briley .07 .20
44 Teddy Higuera .07 .20
45 Pat Borders .07 .20
46 Kevin Seitzer .07 .20
47 Bruce Hurst .07 .20
48 Ozzie Guillen .10 .30
49 Wally Joyner .10 .30
50 Mike Greenwell .07 .20
51 Gary Gaetti .10 .30
52 Gary Sheffield UER .30 .75
53 Dennis Martinez .10 .30
54 Ryne Sandberg .50 1.25
55 Mike Scott .07 .20
56 Todd Benzinger .07 .20
57 Kelly Gruber .07 .20
58 Jose Lind .07 .20
59 Allan Anderson .07 .20
60 Robby Thompson .07 .20
61 John Smoltz .30 .75
62 Mark Davis .07 .20
63 Tom Herr .07 .20
64 Randy Johnson .50 1.25
65 Lonnie Smith .07 .20
66 Pedro Guerrero .10 .30
67 Jerome Walton .07 .20
68 Ramon Martinez .07 .20
69 Tim Raines .10 .30
70 Matt Williams .10 .30
71 Joe Oliver .07 .20
72 Nick Esasky .07 .20
73 Kevin Brown .10 .30
74 Walt Weiss .07 .20
75 Roger McDowell .07 .20
76 Jose DeLeon .07 .20
77 Brian Downing .10 .30
78 Jay Howell .07 .20
79 Jose Uribe .07 .20
80 Ellis Burks .10 .30
81 Sammy Sosa 2.50 6.00
82 Johnny Ray .07 .20
83 Danny Darwin .07 .20
84 Carney Lansford .10 .30
85 Jose Oquendo .07 .20
86 John Cerutti .07 .20
87 Dave Winfield .10 .30
88 Dave Righetti .10 .30
89 Danny Jackson .07 .20
90 Andy Benes .10 .30
91 Tom Browning .07 .20
92 Pete O'Brien .07 .20
93 Roberto Alomar .20 .50
94 Bret Saberhagen .10 .30
95 Phil Bradley .07 .20
96 Doug Jones .07 .20
97 Eric Davis .10 .30
98 Tony Gwynn .40 1.00
99 Jim Abbott .20 .50
100 Cal Ripken 1.00 2.50
101 Andy Van Slyke .20 .50
102 Dan Plesac .07 .20
103 Lou Whitaker .10 .30
104 Steve Bedrosian .07 .20
105 Dave Gallagher .07 .20
106 Keith Hernandez .10 .30
107 Duane Ward .07 .20
108 Andre Dawson .10 .30
109 Howard Johnson .07 .20
110 Mark Langston .07 .20
111 Jerry Browne .07 .20
112 Alvin Davis .07 .20
113 Sid Fernandez .07 .20
114 Mike Devereaux .07 .20
115 Benito Santiago .10 .30
116 Bip Roberts .07 .20
117 Craig Worthington .07 .20
118 Kevin Elster .07 .20
119 Harold Reynolds .10 .30
120 Joe Carter .10 .30
121 Brian Harper .07 .20
122 Frank Viola .10 .30
123 Jeff Ballard .07 .20
124 John Kruk .10 .30
125 Harold Baines .10 .30
126 Tom Candiotti .07 .20
127 Kevin McReynolds .07 .20
128 Mookie Wilson .10 .30
129 Danny Tartabull .07 .20
130 Craig Lefferts .07 .20
131 Jose DeJesus .07 .20
132 John Orton .07 .20
133 Curt Schilling .60 1.50
134 Marquis Grissom .30 .75
135 Greg Vaughn .07 .20
136 Brett Butler .10 .30
137 Rob Deer .07 .20
138 John Franco .10 .30
139 Keith Moreland .07 .20
140 Dave Smith .07 .20
141 Mark McGwire 1.00 2.50
142 Vince Coleman .07 .20
143 Barry Bonds .75 2.00
144 Mike Henneman .07 .20
145 Dwight Gooden .10 .30
146 Darryl Strawberry .10 .30
147 Von Hayes .07 .20
148 Andres Galarraga .10 .30
149 Roger Clemens 1.00 2.50
150 Don Mattingly .75 2.00
151 Joe Magrane .07 .20
152 Dwight Smith .07 .20
153 Ricky Jordan .07 .20
154 Alan Trammell .10 .30
155 Brook Jacoby .07 .20
156 Len Dykstra .10 .30
157 Mike LaValliere .07 .20
158 Julio Franco .10 .30
159 Joey Belle .30 .75
160 Barry Larkin .20 .50
161 Rick Reuschel .07 .20
162 Nelson Santovenia .07 .20
163 Mike Scioscia .07 .20
164 Damon Berryhill .07 .20
165 Todd Worrell .07 .20
166 Jim Eisenreich .07 .20
167 Ivan Calderon .07 .20
168 Mauro Gozzo .07 .20
169 Kirk McCaskill .07 .20
170 Dennis Eckersley .10 .30
171 Mickey Tettleton .07 .20
172 Chuck Finley .10 .30
173 Dave Magadan .07 .20
174 Terry Pendleton .10 .30
175 Willie Randolph .10 .30
176 Jeff Huson .07 .20
177 Todd Zeile .10 .30
178 Steve Olin .07 .20
179 Eric Anthony .07 .20
180 Scott Coolbaugh .07 .20
181 Rick Sutcliffe .10 .30
182 Tim Wallach .07 .20
183 Paul Molitor .10 .30
184 Roberto Kelly .07 .20
185 Mike Moore .07 .20
186 Junior Felix .07 .20
187 Mike Schooler .07 .20
188 Ruben Sierra .07 .20
189 Dale Murphy .20 .50
190 Dan Gladden .07 .20
191 John Smiley .07 .20
192 Jeff Russell .07 .20
193 Bert Blyleven .10 .30
194 Dave Stewart .10 .30
195 Bobby Bonilla .10 .30
196 Mitch Williams .07 .20
197 Orel Hershiser .10 .30
198 Kevin Bass .07 .20
199 Tim Burke .07 .20
200 Bo Jackson .30 .75
201 David Cone .10 .30
202 Gary Pettis .07 .20
203 Kent Hrbek .10 .30
204 Carlton Fisk .20 .50
205 Bob Geren .07 .20
206 Bill Spiers .07 .20
207 Oddibe McDowell .07 .20
208 Rickey Henderson .30 .75
209 Ken Caminiti .10 .30
210 Devon White .10 .30
211 Greg Maddux .50 1.25
212 Ed Whitson .07 .20
213 Carlos Martinez .07 .20
214 George Brett .75 2.00
215 Gregg Olson .07 .20
216 Kenny Rogers .10 .30
217 Dwight Evans .20 .50
218 Pat Tabler .07 .20
219 Jeff Treadway .07 .20
220 Scott Fletcher .07 .20
221 Deion Sanders .30 .75
222 Robin Ventura .30 .75
223 Chip Hale .07 .20
224 Tommy Greene .07 .20
225 Dean Palmer .30 .75

1994 Sportflics Samples

COMPLETE SET (4) 2.50 6.00
1 Len Dykstra .30 .75
7 Javier Lopez .60 1.50
193 Greg Maddux 2.00 5.00
NNO Sportflics 2000/94
Hobby Baseball/(Ad card) .20 .50

1994 Sportflics

After a three-year hiatus, Pinnacle resumed producing these lenticular "three-dimensional" cards, issued in hobby and retail packs. Each of the 193 "Magic Motion" cards features two images, which alternate when the card is viewed from different angles and creates the illusion of movement. Cards 176-193 are Starflics featuring top stars. The two commemorative cards, featuring Cliff Floyd and Paul Molitor, were inserted at a rate of one in every 360 packs.

COMPLETE SET (193) 10.00 25.00
SPECIAL CARDS STATED ODDS 1:360
1 Lenny Dykstra .10 .30
2 Mike Stanley .05 .15
3 Alex Fernandez .05 .15
4 Mark McGwire .75 2.00
5 Eric Karros .10 .30
6 David Justice .10 .30
7 Jeff Bagwell .20 .50
8 Darren Lewis .05 .15
9 David McCarty .05 .15
10 Albert Belle .10 .30
11 Ben McDonald .05 .15
12 Joe Carter .10 .30
13 Benito Santiago .10 .30
14 Rob Dibble .10 .30
15 Roger Clemens .60 1.50
16 Travis Fryman .10 .30
17 Doug Drabek .05 .15
18 Jay Buhner .10 .30
19 Orlando Merced .05 .15
20 Ryan Klesko .10 .30
21 Chuck Finley .10 .30
22 Dante Bichette .10 .30
23 Wally Joyner .10 .30
24 Robin Yount .50 1.25
25 Tony Gwynn .40 1.00
26 Allen Watson .05 .15
27 Rick Wilkins .05 .15
28 Gary Sheffield .10 .30
29 John Burkett .05 .15
30 Randy Johnson .30 .75
31 Roberto Alomar .20 .50
32 Fred McGriff .20 .50
33 Ozzie Guillen .10 .30
34 Jimmy Key .10 .30
35 Juan Gonzalez .10 .30
36 Wil Cordero .05 .15
37 Aaron Sele .05 .15
38 Mark Langston .05 .15
39 David Cone .10 .30
40 John Jaha .05 .15
41 Ozzie Smith .50 1.25
42 Kirby Puckett .30 .75
43 Kenny Lofton .10 .30
44 Mike Mussina .20 .50
45 Ryne Sandberg .50 1.25
46 Robby Thompson .05 .15
47 Bryan Harvey .05 .15
48 Marquis Grissom .10 .30
49 Bobby Bonilla .10 .30
50 Dennis Eckersley .10 .30
51 Curt Schilling .10 .30
52 Andy Benes .05 .15
53 Greg Maddux .50 1.25
54 Bill Swift .05 .15
55 Andres Galarraga .10 .30
56 Tony Phillips .05 .15
57 Darryl Hamilton .05 .15
58 Duane Ward .05 .15
59 Bernie Williams .20 .50
60 Steve Avery .05 .15
61 Eduardo Perez .05 .15
62 Jeff Conine .10 .30
63 Dave Winfield .10 .30
64 Phil Plantier .05 .15
65 Ray Lankford .10 .30
66 Robin Ventura .10 .30
67 Mike Piazza .60 1.50
68 Jason Bere .05 .15
69 Cal Ripken 1.00 2.50
70 Frank Thomas .30 .75
71 Carlos Baerga .05 .15
72 Darryl Kile .10 .30
73 Ruben Sierra .10 .30
74 Gregg Jefferies .05 .15
75 John Olerud .10 .30
76 Andy Van Slyke .10 .30
77 Larry Walker .10 .30
78 Cecil Fielder .10 .30
79 Andre Dawson .10 .30
80 Tom Glavine .20 .50
81 Sammy Sosa .30 .75
82 Charlie Hayes .05 .15
83 Chuck Knoblauch .10 .30
84 Kevin Appier .10 .30
85 Dean Palmer .10 .30
86 Royce Clayton .05 .15
87 Moises Alou .10 .30
88 Ivan Rodriguez .20 .50
89 Tim Salmon .20 .50
90 Ron Gant .10 .30
91 Barry Bonds .75 2.00
92 Jack McDowell .05 .15
93 Alan Trammell .10 .30
94 Dwight Gooden .10 .30
95 Jay Bell .10 .30
96 Devon White .10 .30
97 Wilson Alvarez .05 .15
98 Jim Thome .20 .50
99 Ramon Martinez .05 .15
100 Kent Hrbek .10 .30
101 John Kruk .10 .30
102 Wade Boggs .20 .50
103 Greg Vaughn .05 .15
104 Tom Henke .05 .15
105 Brian Jordan .10 .30
106 Paul Molitor .10 .30
107 Cal Eldred .05 .15
108 Deion Sanders .20 .50
109 Barry Larkin .20 .50
110 Mike Greenwell .05 .15
111 Jeff Blauser .05 .15
112 Jose Rijo .05 .15
113 Pete Harnisch .05 .15
114 Chris Hoiles .05 .15
115 Edgar Martinez .20 .50
116 Juan Guzman .05 .15
117 Todd Zeile .05 .15
118 Danny Tartabull .05 .15
119 Chad Curtis .05 .15
120 Mark Grace .20 .50
121 J.T. Snow .10 .30
122 Mo Vaughn .10 .30
123 Lance Johnson .05 .15
124 Eric Davis .10 .30
125 Orel Hershiser .10 .30
126 Kevin Mitchell .05 .15
127 Don Mattingly .75 2.00
128 Darren Daulton .10 .30
129 Rod Beck .05 .15
130 Charles Nagy .05 .15
131 Mickey Tettleton .05 .15
132 Kevin Brown .10 .30
133 Pat Hentgen .05 .15
134 Terry Mulholland .05 .15
135 Steve Finley .10 .30
136 John Smoltz .20 .50
137 Frank Viola .10 .30
138 Jim Abbott .20 .50
139 Matt Williams .10 .30
140 Bernard Gilkey .05 .15
141 Jose Canseco .20 .50
142 Mark Whiten .05 .15
143 Ken Griffey Jr. .60 1.50
144 Rafael Palmeiro .20 .50
145 Dave Hollins .05 .15
146 Will Clark .20 .50
147 Paul O'Neill .20 .50
148 Bobby Jones .05 .15
149 Butch Huskey .05 .15
150 Jeffrey Hammonds .05 .15
151 Manny Ramirez .30 .75
152 Bob Hamelin .05 .15
153 Kurt Abbott RC .05 .15
154 Scott Stahoviak .05 .15
155 Steve Hosey .05 .15
156 Salomon Torres .05 .15
157 Sterling Hitchcock .05 .15
158 Nigel Wilson .05 .15
159 Luis Lopez .05 .15
160 Chipper Jones .30 .75
161 Norberto Martin .05 .15
162 Raul Mondesi .10 .30
163 Steve Karsay .05 .15
164 J.R. Phillips .05 .15
165 Marc Newfield .05 .15
166 Mark Hutton .05 .15
167 Curtis Pride RC .10 .30
168 Carl Everett .10 .30
169 Scott Ruffcorn .05 .15
170 Turk Wendell .05 .15
171 Jeff McNeely .05 .15
172 Javier Lopez .10 .30
173 Cliff Floyd .10 .30
174 Rondell White .10 .30
175 Scott Lydy .05 .15
176 Frank Thomas SF .20 .50
177 Roberto Alomar SF .10 .30
178 Travis Fryman AS .05 .15
179 Cal Ripken SF .50 1.25
180 Chris Hoiles AS .05 .15
181 Ken Griffey Jr. SF .40 1.00
182 Juan Gonzalez SF .05 .15
183 Joe Carter SF .05 .15
184 Jack McDowell AS .05 .15
185 Fred McGriff SF .10 .30
186 Robby Thompson AS .05 .15
187 Matt Williams SF .05 .15
188 Jay Bell AS .05 .15
189 Mike Piazza SF .30 .75
190 Barry Bonds SF .40 1.00
191 Lenny Dykstra AS .05 .15
192 David Justice SF .05 .15
193 Greg Maddux SF .30 .75
NNO Cliff Floyd SPEC 1.25 3.00
NNO Paul Molitor SPEC 3.00 8.00

1994 Sportflics Movers

COMPLETE SET (12) 20.00 50.00
STATED ODDS 1:24 RETAIL
MM1 Gregg Jefferies .50 1.25
MM2 Ryne Sandberg 4.00 10.00
MM3 Cecil Fielder 1.00 2.50
MM4 Kirby Puckett 2.50 6.00
MM5 Tony Gwynn 3.00 8.00
MM6 Andres Galarraga 1.00 2.50
MM7 Sammy Sosa 2.50 6.00
MM8 Rickey Henderson 2.00 5.00
MM9 Don Mattingly 6.00 15.00
MM10 Joe Carter 1.00 2.50
MM11 Carlos Baerga .50 1.25
MM12 Lenny Dykstra 1.00 2.50

1994 Sportflics Shakers

COMPLETE SET (12) 25.00 60.00
STATED ODDS 1:24 HOBBY
SH1 Kenny Lofton 1.25 3.00
SH2 Tim Salmon 2.00 5.00
SH3 Jeff Bagwell 2.00 5.00
SH4 Jason Bere .60 1.50
SH5 Salomon Torres .60 1.50
SH6 Rondell White 1.25 3.00
SH7 Javier Lopez 1.25 3.00
SH8 Dean Palmer 1.25 3.00
SH9 Jim Thome 2.00 5.00
SH10 J.T. Snow 1.25 3.00
SH11 Mike Piazza 6.00 15.00
SH12 Manny Ramirez 3.00 8.00

1994 Sportflics Rookie/Traded Samples

COMPLETE SET (9) 3.00 8.00
1 Will Clark 1.00 2.50
14 Bret Boone .40 1.00
20 Ellis Burks .40 1.00
25 Deion Sanders .40 1.00
65 Chris Turner .20 .50
82 Tony Tarasco .20 .50
102 Rich Becker .20 .50
GG1 Gary Sheffield
(Going& Going& Gone) 1.25 3.00
NNO Title Card .20 .50

1994 Sportflics Rookie/Traded

This set of 150 standard-size cards was distributed in five-card retail packs at a suggested price of $1.89. The set features top rookies and traded players. This set was released only through retail (non-hobby) outlets. The fronts feature the "Magic Motion" printing with two action views of the player which change with the tilting of the card. The player's name is printed in red and expands and contracts with the tilting of the card. Numbered backs include a player biography and career stats and the 1994 performance of the rookie or how the player was acquired in a trade. A full-color photo of the player is framed at an angle with a red and black background. Rookie Cards in this set include Chan Ho Park and Alex Rodriguez.

COMPLETE SET (150) 15.00 40.00
ROY STATED ODDS 1:360
1 Will Clark .30 .75
2 Sid Fernandez .08 .25
3 Joe Magrane .08 .25
4 Pete Smith .08 .25
5 Roberto Kelly .08 .25
6 Delino DeShields .08 .25
7 Brian Harper .08 .25
8 Darrin Jackson .08 .25
9 Omar Vizquel .30 .75
10 Luis Polonia .08 .25
11 Reggie Jefferson .08 .25
12 Geronimo Berroa .08 .25
13 Mike Harkey .08 .25
14 Bret Boone .20 .50
15 Dave Henderson .08 .25
16 Pedro Martinez .50 1.25
17 Jose Vizcaino .08 .25
18 Xavier Hernandez .08 .25
19 Eddie Taubensee .08 .25
20 Ellis Burks .20 .50
21 Turner Ward .08 .25
22 Terry Mulholland .08 .25
23 Howard Johnson .08 .25
24 Vince Coleman .08 .25
25 Deion Sanders .30 .75
26 Rafael Palmeiro .30 .75
27 Dave Weathers .08 .25
28 Kent Mercker .08 .25
29 Gregg Olson .08 .25
30 Cory Bailey RC .08 .25
31 Brian L. Hunter .08 .25
32 Garey Ingram RC .08 .25
33 Daniel Smith .08 .25
34 Denny Hocking .08 .25
35 Charles Johnson .20 .50
36 Otis Nixon .08 .25
37 Hector Fajardo .08 .25
38 Lee Smith .20 .50
39 Phil Stidham .08 .25
40 Melvin Nieves .08 .25
41 Julio Franco .20 .50
42 Greg Gohr .08 .25
43 Steve Dunn .08 .25
44 Tony Fernandez .08 .25
45 Toby Borland RC .08 .25
46 Paul Shuey .08 .25
47 Shawn Hare .08 .25
48 Shawn Green .50 1.25
49 Julian Tavarez RC .20 .50
50 Ernie Young RC .20 .50
51 Chris Sabo .08 .25
52 Greg O'Halloran .08 .25
53 Donnie Elliott .08 .25
54 Jim Converse .08 .25
55 Ray Holbert .08 .25
56 Keith Lockhart RC .20 .50
57 Tony Longmire .08 .25
58 Jorge Fabregas .08 .25
59 Ravelo Manzanillo .08 .25
60 Marcus Moore .08 .25
61 Carlos Rodriguez .08 .25
62 Mark Portugal .08 .25
63 Yorkis Perez .08 .25
64 Dan Miceli .08 .25
65 Chris Turner .08 .25
66 Mike Oquist .08 .25
67 Tom Quinlan .08 .25
68 Matt Walbeck .08 .25
69 Dave Staton .08 .25
70 W.VanLandingham RC .08 .25
71 Dave Stevens .08 .25
72 Domingo Cedeno .08 .25
73 Alex Diaz .08 .25
74 Darren Bragg RC .08 .25
75 James Hurst .08 .25
76 Alex Gonzalez .08 .25
77 Steve Dreyer .08 .25
78 Robert Eenhoorn .08 .25
79 Derek Parks .08 .25
80 Jose Valentin .08 .25
81 Wes Chamberlain .08 .25
82 Tony Tarasco .08 .25
83 Steve Traschel .08 .25
84 Willie Banks .08 .25
85 Rob Butler .08 .25
86 Miguel Jimenez .08 .25
87 Gerald Williams .08 .25
88 Aaron Small .20 .50
89 Matt Mieske .08 .25
90 Tim Hyers RC .08 .25
91 Eddie Murray .50 1.25
92 Dennis Martinez .20 .50
93 Tony Eusebio .08 .25
94 Brian Anderson RC .20 .50
95 Blaise Ilsley .08 .25
96 Johnny Ruffin .08 .25
97 Carlos Reyes .08 .25
98 Greg Pirkl .08 .25
99 Jack Morris .20 .50
100 John Mabry RC .20 .50
101 Mike Kelly .08 .25
102 Rich Becker .08 .25
103 Chris Gomez .08 .25
104 Jim Edmonds .50 1.25
105 Rich Rowland .08 .25
106 Damon Buford .08 .25
107 Mark Kiefer .08 .25
108 Matias Carrillo .08 .25
109 James Mouton .08 .25
110 Kelly Stinnett RC .08 .25
111 Billy Ashley .08 .25
112 Fausto Cruz RC .08 .25
113 Roberto Petagine .08 .25
114 Joe Hall .08 .25
115 Brian Johnson RC .08 .25
116 Kevin Jarvis .08 .25
117 Tim Davis .08 .25
118 John Patterson .08 .25
119 Stan Royer .08 .25
120 Jeff Juden .08 .25
121 Bryan Eversgerd .08 .25
122 Chan Ho Park RC .30 .75
123 Shane Reynolds .08 .25
124 Danny Bautista .08 .25
125 Rikkert Faneyte RC .08 .25
126 Carlos Pulido .08 .25
127 Mike Matheny RC .30 .75
128 Hector Carrasco .08 .25
129 Eddie Zambrano .08 .25
130 Lee Tinsley .08 .25
131 Roger Salkeld .08 .25
132 Carlos Delgado .30 .75
133 Troy O'Leary .08 .25
134 Keith Mitchell .08 .25
135 Lance Painter .08 .25
136 Nate Minchey .08 .25
137 Eric Anthony .08 .25
138 Rafael Bournigal .08 .25
139 Joey Hamilton .08 .25
140 Bobby Munoz .08 .25
141 Rex Hudler .08 .25
142 Alex Cole .08 .25
143 Stan Javier .08 .25
144 Jose Oliva .08 .25
145 Tom Brunansky .08 .25
146 Greg Colbrunn .08 .25
147 Luis Lopez .08 .25
148 Alex Rodriguez RC 8.00 20.00
149 Darryl Strawberry .20 .50
150 Bo Jackson .50 1.25
RO1 R.Klesko 1.50 4.00
M.Ramirez ROY

1994 Sportflics Rookie/Traded Artist's Proofs

*STARS: 10X TO 25X HI COLUMN
*ROOKIES: 10X TO 25X HI
STATED ODDS 1:24

1994 Sportflics Rookie/Traded Going Going Gone

COMPLETE SET (12) 25.00 60.00
STATED ODDS 1:18
GG1 Gary Sheffield 1.00 2.50
GG2 Matt Williams 1.00 2.50
GG3 Juan Gonzalez 1.00 2.50
GG4 Ken Griffey Jr. 5.00 12.00
GG5 Mike Piazza 5.00 12.00
GG6 Frank Thomas 2.50 6.00
GG7 Tim Salmon 1.50 4.00
GG8 Barry Bonds 6.00 15.00
GG9 Fred McGriff 1.50 4.00
GG10 Cecil Fielder 1.00 2.50
GG11 Albert Belle 1.00 2.50
GG12 Joe Carter 1.00 2.50

1994 Sportflics Rookie/Traded Rookie Starflics

COMPLETE SET (18) 75.00 150.00
STATED ODDS 1:36
TR1 John Hudek 2.00 5.00
TR2 Manny Ramirez 6.00 15.00
TR3 Jeffrey Hammonds 2.00 5.00
TR4 Carlos Delgado 4.00 10.00
TR5 Javier Lopez 3.00 8.00
TR6 Alex Gonzalez 2.00 5.00
TR7 Raul Mondesi 3.00 8.00
TR8 Bob Hamelin 2.00 5.00
TR9 Ryan Klesko 3.00 8.00
TR10 Brian Anderson 3.00 8.00
TR11 Alex Rodriguez 25.00 60.00
TR12 Cliff Floyd 3.00 8.00
TR13 Chan Ho Park 4.00 10.00
TR14 Steve Karsay 2.00 5.00
TR15 Rondell White 3.00 8.00
TR16 Shawn Green 6.00 15.00
TR17 Rich Becker 2.00 5.00
TR18 Charles Johnson 3.00 8.00

1994 Sportflics FanFest All-Stars

At Fanfest, collectors received redemption coupons at various locations. These redemption coupons could be turned in at certain distribution centers for the Sportflics cards. It is noted on the backs that 10,000 sets were produced. The cards measure the standard size. The borderless fronts carry two-dimensional color action photos featuring an American League player and a National League player. The player's names appear in the upper left and bottom right corners. The backs carry headshots and statistics for each player. According to reports, between 10-20 percent of the mintage of this set was destroyed at the end of fanfest.

COMPLETE SET (9) 40.00 100.00
AS1 Fred McGriff 4.00 10.00
Frank Thomas
AS2 Ryne Sandberg 3.00 8.00
Roberto Alomar
AS3 Matt Williams 1.50 4.00
Travis Fryman
AS4 Ozzie Smith 10.00 25.00
Cal Ripken Jr.
AS5 Mike Piazza 6.00 15.00
Ivan Rodriguez
AS6 Barry Bonds 4.00 10.00
Juan Gonzalez
AS7 Lenny Dykstra 10.00 25.00
Ken Griffey Jr.
AS8 Gary Sheffield 4.00 10.00
Kirby Puckett
AS9 Greg Maddux 5.00 12.00
Mike Mussina

1995 Sportflix Samples

COMPLETE SET (9) 100.00 200.00
3 Fred McGriff 5.00 12.00
20 Frank Thomas 8.00 20.00
105 Manny Ramirez 8.00 20.00
122 Cal Ripken 15.00 40.00
128 Roberto Alomar 6.00 15.00
152 Russ Davis 3.00 8.00
162 Chipper Jones 15.00 40.00
DE2 Matt Williams (Detonator) 5.00 12.00
NNO Title card 3.00 8.00

1995 Sportflix

This 170 card standard-size set was released by Pinnacle brands. The set was issued in five card packs that had a suggested retail price of $1.89 per pack. Thirty-six of these packs are contained in a full box. Jumbo packs were also issued: these packs contained eight cards per pack and had 36 packs in a box. Card fronts feature Pinnacle's "Magic Motion" printing which shows the player in two different action shots when the card is tilted. The player's position is printed diagonally on the top right with the team logo underneath. Horizontal backs feature a full-color player photo on the right. Subsets include a rookies section (141-165) and a checklist grouping (166-170).

COMPLETE SET (170) 8.00 20.00
1 Ken Griffey Jr. .60 1.50
2 Jeffrey Hammonds .05 .15
3 Fred McGriff .20 .50
4 Rickey Henderson .30 .75
5 Derrick May .05 .15
6 Robin Ventura .10 .30
7 Royce Clayton .05 .15
8 Paul Molitor .10 .30
9 Charlie Hayes .05 .15
10 David Nied .05 .15
11 Ellis Burks .10 .30
12 Bernard Gilkey .05 .15
13 Don Mattingly .75 2.00
14 Albert Belle .10 .30
15 Doug Drabek .05 .15
16 Tony Gwynn .40 1.00
17 Delino DeShields .05 .15
18 Bobby Bonilla .10 .30
19 Cliff Floyd .10 .30
20 Frank Thomas .30 .75
21 Raul Mondesi .10 .30
22 Dave Nilsson .05 .15
23 Todd Zeile .05 .15
24 Bernie Williams .20 .50
25 Kirby Puckett .30 .75
26 David Cone .10 .30
27 Darren Daulton .10 .30
28 Marquis Grissom .10 .30
29 Randy Johnson .30 .75
30 Jeff Kent .10 .30
31 Orlando Merced .05 .15
32 David Justice .10 .30
33 Ivan Rodriguez .20 .50
34 Kirk Gibson .10 .30
35 Alex Fernandez .05 .15
36 Rick Wilkins .05 .15
37 Andy Benes .05 .15
38 Bret Saberhagen .10 .30
39 Billy Ashley .05 .15
40 Jose Rijo .05 .15
41 Matt Williams .10 .30
42 Lenny Dykstra .10 .30
43 Jay Bell .10 .30
44 Reggie Jefferson .05 .15
45 Greg Maddux .50 1.25
46 Gary Sheffield .10 .30
47 Bret Boone .10 .30
48 Jeff Bagwell .20 .50
49 Ben McDonald .05 .15
50 Eric Karros .10 .30
51 Roger Clemens .60 1.50
52 Sammy Sosa .30 .75
53 Barry Bonds .75 2.00
54 Joey Hamilton .05 .15
55 Brian Jordan .10 .30
56 Wil Cordero .05 .15
57 Aaron Sele .05 .15
58 Paul O'Neill .20 .50
59 Carlos Garcia .05 .15
60 Mike Mussina .20 .50
61 John Olerud .10 .30
62 Kevin Appier .10 .30
63 Matt Mieske .05 .15
64 Carlos Baerga .05 .15
65 Ryan Klesko .10 .30
66 Jimmy Key .10 .30
67 James Mouton .05 .15
68 Tim Salmon .20 .50
69 Hal Morris .05 .15
70 Albie Lopez .05 .15
71 Dave Hollins .05 .15
72 Greg Colbrunn .05 .15
73 Juan Gonzalez .10 .30
74 Wally Joyner .10 .30
75 Bob Hamelin .05 .15
76 Brady Anderson .10 .30
77 Deion Sanders .20 .50
78 Javier Lopez .10 .30
79 Brian McRae .05 .15
80 Craig Biggio .20 .50
81 Kenny Lofton .10 .30
82 Cecil Fielder .10 .30
83 Mike Piazza .50 1.25
84 Rafael Palmeiro .20 .50
85 Jim Thome .20 .50
86 Ruben Sierra .10 .30
87 Mark Langston .05 .15
88 John Valentin .05 .15
89 Shawon Dunston .05 .15
90 Travis Fryman .10 .30
91 Chuck Knoblauch .10 .30
92 Dean Palmer .10 .30
93 Robby Thompson .05 .15
94 Barry Larkin .20 .50
95 Darren Lewis .05 .15
96 Andres Galarraga .10 .30
97 Tony Phillips .05 .15
98 Mo Vaughn .10 .30
99 Pedro Martinez .20 .50
100 Chad Curtis .05 .15
101 Brent Gates .05 .15
102 Pat Hentgen .05 .15
103 Rico Brogna .05 .15
104 Carlos Delgado .10 .30
105 Manny Ramirez .20 .50
106 Mike Greenwell .05 .15
107 Wade Boggs .20 .50
108 Ozzie Smith .50 1.25
109 Rusty Greer .10 .30
110 Willie Greene .05 .15
111 Chili Davis .10 .30
112 Reggie Sanders .10 .30
113 Roberto Kelly .05 .15
114 Tom Glavine .20 .50
115 Moises Alou .10 .30
116 Dennis Eckersley .10 .30
117 Danny Tartabull .05 .15
118 Jeff Conine .10 .30
119 Will Clark .20 .50
120 Joe Carter .10 .30
121 Mark McGwire .75 2.00
122 Cal Ripken 1.00 2.50
123 Danny Jackson .05 .15
124 Phil Plantier .05 .15
125 Dante Bichette .10 .30
126 Jack McDowell .05 .15
127 Jose Canseco .20 .50
128 Roberto Alomar .20 .50
129 Rondell White .10 .30
130 Ray Lankford .10 .30
131 Ryan Thompson .05 .15
132 Ken Caminiti .10 .30
133 Gregg Jefferies .05 .15
134 Omar Vizquel .20 .50
135 Mark Grace .20 .50
136 Derek Bell .05 .15
137 Mickey Tettleton .05 .15
138 Wilson Alvarez .05 .15

139 Larry Walker	.10	.30
140 Bo Jackson	.30	.75
141 Alex Rodriguez	.75	2.00
142 Orlando Miller	.05	.15
143 Shawn Green	.10	.30
144 Steve Dunn	.05	.15
145 Midre Cummings	.05	.15
146 Chan Ho Park	.10	.30
147 Jose Oliva	.05	.15
148 Armando Benitez	.05	.15
149 J.R. Phillips	.05	.15
150 Charles Johnson	.10	.30
151 Garret Anderson	.10	.30
152 Russ Davis	.05	.15
153 Brian L.Hunter	.05	.15
154 Ernie Young	.05	.15
155 Marc Newfield	.05	.15
156 Greg Pirkl	.05	.15
157 Scott Ruffcorn	.05	.15
158 Rikkert Faneyte	.05	.15
159 Duane Singleton	.05	.15
160 Gabe White	.05	.15
161 Alex Gonzalez	.05	.15
162 Chipper Jones	.30	.75
163 Mike Kelly	.05	.15
164 Kurt Miller	.05	.15
165 Roberto Petagine	.05	.15
166 Jeff Bagwell CL	.10	.30
167 Mike Piazza CL	.30	.75
168 Ken Griffey Jr. CL	.40	1.00
169 Frank Thomas CL	.20	.50
170 C.Ripken	1.00	2.50
B.Bonds CL		

1995 Sportflix Artist's Proofs

*STARS: 6X TO 15X BASIC CARDS
STATED ODDS 1:36
STATED PRINT RUN 700 SETS

1995 Sportflix Detonators

COMPLETE SET (9)	8.00	20.00
STATED ODDS 1:16		
DE1 Jeff Bagwell	.60	1.50
DE2 Matt Williams	.40	1.00
DE3 Ken Griffey Jr.	2.00	5.00
DE4 Frank Thomas	1.00	2.50
DE5 Mike Piazza	1.50	4.00
DE6 Barry Bonds	2.50	6.00
DE7 Albert Belle	.40	1.00
DE8 Cliff Floyd	.40	1.00
DE9 Juan Gonzalez	.40	1.00

1995 Sportflix Double Take

COMPLETE SET (12)	40.00	100.00
STATED ODDS 1:48		
1 F.Thomas	2.50	6.00
J.Bagwell		
2 W.Clark	1.50	4.00
F.McGriff		
3 R.Alomar	1.50	4.00
J.Kent		
4 M.Williams	1.50	4.00
W.Boggs		
5 C.Ripken	8.00	20.00
O.Smith		
6 A.Rodriguez	6.00	15.00
W.Cordero		
7 M.Piazza	4.00	10.00
C.Delgado		
8 K.Lofton	1.00	2.50
D.Justice		
9 K.Griffey Jr.	5.00	12.00
B.Bonds		
10 A.Belle	1.00	2.50
R.Mondesi		
11 T.Gwynn	2.50	6.00
K.Puckett		
12 G.Maddux	4.00	10.00
J.Key		

1995 Sportflix Hammer Team

COMPLETE SET (18)	10.00	25.00
STATED ODDS 1:4		
HT1 Ken Griffey Jr.	1.00	2.50
HT2 Frank Thomas	.50	1.25
HT3 Jeff Bagwell	.30	.75
HT4 Mike Piazza	.75	2.00
HT5 Cal Ripken	1.50	4.00
HT6 Albert Belle	.20	.50
HT7 Barry Bonds	1.25	3.00
HT8 Don Mattingly	1.25	3.00
HT9 Will Clark	.30	.75
HT10 Tony Gwynn	.60	1.50
HT11 Matt Williams	.20	.50
HT12 Kirby Puckett	.50	1.25
HT13 Manny Ramirez	.30	.75
HT14 Fred McGriff	.30	.75
HT15 Juan Gonzalez	.20	.50
HT16 Kenny Lofton	.20	.50
HT17 Raul Mondesi	.20	.50
HT18 Tim Salmon	.30	.75

1995 Sportflix ProMotion

COMPLETE SET (12)	40.00	100.00
STATED ODDS 1:18 JUMBO		
PM1 Ken Griffey Jr.	5.00	12.00
PM2 Frank Thomas	2.50	6.00
PM3 Cal Ripken	8.00	20.00
PM4 Jeff Bagwell	1.50	4.00
PM5 Mike Piazza	4.00	10.00
PM6 Matt Williams	1.00	2.50
PM7 Albert Belle	1.00	2.50
PM8 Jose Canseco	1.50	4.00
PM9 Don Mattingly	6.00	15.00
PM10 Barry Bonds	6.00	15.00
PM11 Will Clark	1.50	4.00
PM12 Kirby Puckett	2.50	6.00

1996 Sportflix

With retail only distribution, this 144 card set comes in five card packs that retail for $1.99. Regular cards picture two different pieces of photography. The set contains the UC3 Subset (97-120), Rookies Subset (121-141), and Checklists (142-144). The UC3 Subset features veteran superstars in 3-D animation. The 21-card Rookie subset carries color player photos on a background of part of a baseball that changes into a wooden baseball bat section when moved.

COMPLETE SET (144)	10.00	25.00
1 Wade Boggs	.20	.50
2 Tim Salmon	.20	.50
3 Will Clark	.20	.50
4 Dante Bichette	.10	.30
5 Barry Bonds	.75	2.00
6 Kirby Puckett	.30	.75
7 Albert Belle	.10	.30
8 Greg Maddux	.50	1.25
9 Tony Gwynn	.40	1.00
10 Mike Piazza	.50	1.25
11 Ivan Rodriguez	.20	.50
12 Marty Cordova	.10	.30
13 Frank Thomas	.30	.75
14 Raul Mondesi	.10	.30
15 Johnny Damon	.20	.50
16 Mark McGwire	.75	2.00
17 Len Dykstra	.10	.30
18 Ken Griffey Jr.	.60	1.50
19 Chipper Jones	.30	.75
20 Alex Rodriguez	.60	1.50
21 Jeff Bagwell	.20	.50
22 Jim Edmonds	.10	.30
23 Edgar Martinez	.20	.50
24 David Cone	.10	.30
25 Tom Glavine	.20	.50
26 Eddie Murray	.30	.75
27 Paul Molitor	.10	.30
28 Ryan Klesko	.10	.30
29 Rafael Palmeiro	.20	.50
30 Manny Ramirez	.20	.50
31 Mo Vaughn	.10	.30
32 Rico Brogna	.10	.30
33 Marc Newfield	.10	.30
34 J.T. Snow	.10	.30
35 Reggie Sanders	.10	.30
36 Fred McGriff	.20	.50
37 Craig Biggio	.20	.50
38 Jeff King	.10	.30
39 Kenny Lofton	.10	.30
40 Gary Gaetti	.10	.30
41 Eric Karros	.10	.30
42 Jason Isringhausen	.10	.30
43 B.J. Surhoff	.10	.30
44 Michael Tucker	.10	.30
45 Gary Sheffield	.10	.30
46 Chili Davis	.10	.30
47 Bobby Bonilla	.10	.30
48 Hideo Nomo	.30	.75
49 Ray Durham	.10	.30
50 Phil Nevin	.10	.30
51 Randy Johnson	.30	.75
52 Bill Pulsipher	.10	.30
53 Ozzie Smith	.50	1.25
54 Cal Ripken	1.00	2.50
55 Cecil Fielder	.10	.30
56 Matt Williams	.10	.30
57 Sammy Sosa	.30	.75
58 Roger Clemens	.60	1.50
59 Brian L.Hunter	.10	.30
60 Barry Larkin	.20	.50
61 Charles Johnson	.10	.30
62 David Justice	.10	.30
63 Garret Anderson	.10	.30
64 Rondell White	.10	.30
65 Derek Bell	.10	.30
66 Andres Galarraga	.10	.30
67 Moises Alou	.10	.30
68 Travis Fryman	.10	.30
69 Pedro Martinez	.20	.50
70 Carlos Baerga	.10	.30
71 John Valentin	.10	.30
72 Larry Walker	.10	.30
73 Roberto Alomar	.20	.50
74 Mike Mussina	.20	.50
75 Kevin Appier	.10	.30
76 Bernie Williams	.20	.50
77 Ray Lankford	.10	.30
78 Gregg Jefferies	.10	.30
79 Robin Ventura	.10	.30
80 Kenny Rogers	.10	.30
81 Paul O'Neill	.20	.50
82 Mark Grace	.20	.50
83 Deion Sanders	.20	.50
84 Tino Martinez	.20	.50
85 Joe Carter	.10	.30
86 Pete Schourek	.10	.30
87 Jack McDowell	.10	.30
88 John Mabry	.10	.30
89 Darren Daulton	.10	.30
90 Jim Thome	.20	.50
91 Jay Buhner	.10	.30
92 Jay Bell	.10	.30
93 Kevin Seitzer	.10	.30
94 Jose Canseco	.20	.50
95 Juan Gonzalez	.10	.30
96 Jeff Conine	.10	.30
97 Chipper Jones UC3	.20	.50
98 Ken Griffey Jr. UC3	.40	1.00
99 Frank Thomas UC3	.20	.50
100 Cal Ripken UC3	.50	1.25
101 Albert Belle UC3	.10	.30
102 Mike Piazza UC3	.30	.75
103 Dante Bichette UC3	.10	.30
104 Sammy Sosa UC3	.20	.50
105 Mo Vaughn UC3	.10	.30
106 Tim Salmon UC3	.10	.30
107 Reggie Sanders UC3	.10	.30
108 Gary Sheffield UC3	.10	.30
109 Ruben Rivera UC3	.10	.30
110 Rafael Palmeiro UC3	.10	.30
111 Edgar Martinez UC3	.10	.30
112 Barry Bonds UC3	.40	1.00
113 Manny Ramirez UC3	.10	.30
114 Larry Walker UC3	.10	.30
115 Jeff Bagwell UC3	.10	.30
116 Matt Williams UC3	.10	.30
117 Mark McGwire UC3	.40	1.00
118 Johnny Damon UC3	.10	.30
119 Eddie Murray UC3	.20	.50
120 Jay Buhner UC3	.10	.30
121 Tim Unroe	.10	.30
122 Todd Hollandsworth	.10	.30
123 Tony Clark	.10	.30
124 Roger Cedeno	.10	.30
125 Jim Pittsley	.10	.30
126 Ruben Rivera	.10	.30
127 Bob Wolcott	.10	.30
128 Chan Ho Park	.10	.30
129 Chris Snopek	.10	.30
130 Alex Ochoa	.10	.30
131 Yamil Benitez	.10	.30
132 Jimmy Haynes	.10	.30
133 Dustin Hermanson	.10	.30
134 Shawn Estes	.10	.30
135 Howard Battle	.10	.30
136 Matt Lawton RC	.10	.30
137 Terrell Wade	.10	.30
138 Jason Schmidt	.20	.50
139 Derek Jeter	.75	2.00
140 Shannon Stewart	.10	.30
141 Chris Stynes	.10	.30
142 Ken Griffey Jr. CL	.40	1.00
143 Greg Maddux CL	.30	.75
144 Cal Ripken CL	.50	1.25

1996 Sportflix Artist's Proofs

*STARS: 10X TO 25X BASIC CARDS
*ROOKIES: 6X TO 15X BASIC CARDS
STATED ODDS 1:48

1996 Sportflix Double Take

COMPLETE SET (12)	25.00	60.00
STATED ODDS 1:22 JUMBO		
1 C.Ripken	5.00	12.00
B.Larkin		
2 R.Alomar	1.00	2.50
C.Biggio		
3 C.Jones	1.50	4.00
M.Williams		
4 K.Griffey	3.00	8.00
R.Rivera		
5 G.Maddux	2.50	6.00
H.Nomo		
6 F.Thomas	1.50	4.00
M.Vaughn		
7 M.Piazza	2.50	6.00
I.Rodriguez		
8 B.Bonds	4.00	10.00
A.Belle		
9 A.Rodriguez	10.00	25.00
D.Jeter		
10 T.Gwynn	2.00	5.00
K.Puckett		
11 S.Sosa	1.50	4.00
M.Ramirez		
12 J.Bagwell	1.00	2.50
R.Brogna		

1996 Sportflix Hit Parade

COMPLETE SET (16)	12.50	30.00
STATED ODDS 1:35		
1 Ken Griffey Jr.	2.00	5.00
2 Cal Ripken	3.00	8.00
3 Frank Thomas	1.00	2.50
4 Mike Piazza	1.00	2.50
5 Mo Vaughn	.40	1.00
6 Albert Belle	.40	1.00
7 Jeff Bagwell	.60	1.50
8 Matt Williams	.40	1.00
9 Sammy Sosa	1.00	2.50
10 Kirby Puckett	1.00	2.50
11 Dante Bichette	.40	1.00
12 Gary Sheffield	.40	1.00
13 Tony Gwynn	1.00	2.50
14 Wade Boggs	.60	1.50
15 Chipper Jones	1.00	2.50
16 Barry Bonds	1.50	4.00

1996 Sportflix Power Surge

COMPLETE SET (24)	60.00	120.00
STATED ODDS 1:35 RETAIL		
1 Chipper Jones	2.50	6.00
2 Ken Griffey Jr.	5.00	12.00
3 Frank Thomas	2.50	6.00
4 Cal Ripken	8.00	20.00
5 Albert Belle	1.00	2.50
6 Mike Piazza	4.00	10.00
7 Dante Bichette	1.00	2.50
8 Sammy Sosa	2.50	6.00
9 Mo Vaughn	1.00	2.50
10 Tim Salmon	1.50	4.00
11 Reggie Sanders	1.00	2.50
12 Gary Sheffield	1.00	2.50
13 Ruben Rivera	1.00	2.50
14 Rafael Palmeiro	1.50	4.00
15 Edgar Martinez	1.50	4.00
16 Barry Bonds	6.00	15.00
17 Manny Ramirez	1.50	4.00
18 Larry Walker	1.00	2.50
19 Jeff Bagwell	1.50	4.00
20 Matt Williams	1.00	2.50
21 Mark McGwire	6.00	15.00
22 Johnny Damon	1.50	4.00
23 Eddie Murray	2.50	6.00
24 Jay Buhner	1.00	2.50

1996 Sportflix ProMotion

COMPLETE SET (20)	20.00	50.00
STATED ODDS 1:17		
1 Cal Ripken	3.00	8.00
2 Greg Maddux	1.50	4.00
3 Mo Vaughn	.40	1.00
4 Albert Belle	.40	1.00
5 Mike Piazza	1.50	4.00
6 Ken Griffey Jr.	2.00	5.00
7 Frank Thomas	1.00	2.50
8 Jeff Bagwell	.60	1.50
9 Hideo Nomo	1.00	2.50
10 Chipper Jones	1.00	2.50
11 Tony Gwynn	1.25	3.00
12 Don Mattingly	2.00	5.00
13 Dante Bichette	.40	1.00
14 Matt Williams	.40	1.00
15 Manny Ramirez	.60	1.50
16 Barry Bonds	2.50	6.00
17 Reggie Sanders	.40	1.00
18 Tim Salmon	.60	1.50
19 Ruben Rivera	.40	1.00
20 Garret Anderson	.40	1.00

1996 Sportflix Rookie Jumbos

COMPLETE SET	12.50	30.00
1 Jason Schmidt	3.00	8.00
2 Chris Snopek	.75	2.00
3 Tony Clark	.75	2.00
4 Todd Hollandsworth	.75	2.00
5 Alex Ochoa	.75	2.00
6 Derek Jeter	40.00	80.00
7 Howard Battle	.75	2.00
8 Bob Wolcott	.75	2.00

1910-11 Sporting Life M116

The cards in this 288-card set (326 with all variations) measure approximately 1 1/2" by 2 5/8". The Sporting Life set was offered as a premium to the publication's subscribers in 1910 and 1911. Each of the 24 series of 12 cards, which cost four cents for each series, came in an envelope printed with a list of the players within. Cards marked with S1 or S2 followed by an asterisk can be found with both a blue background and a more common pastel background. Cards marked with S3 followed with an asterisk are found with either a blue or black printed Sporting Life advertisement on the reverse. McConnell appears with both Boston AL (common) and Chicago White Sox (scarce). Pricing is unavailable on the McConnell White Sox card, but a copy was sold at auction in 2007 graded EX+ by SGC for $31,024. McQuillan appears with Phillies (common) and Cincinnati (scarce). A card featuring Johnny Bates as a member of the Cincinnati Reds was recently discovered, and the first known copy sold for slightly more than $20,000 early in 2006.

COMPLETE SET (290)	20000.00	40000.00
COMMON MAJOR (1-280)	40.00	80.00
COMMON MINOR (280-288)	40.00	80.00
COMMON S19-S24	50.00	120.00
1 Ed Abbaticchio	70.00	120.00
2A Babe Adams Black Back	70.00	120.00
2B Babe Adams Blue Back	70.00	120.00
3 Red Ames	70.00	120.00
4 Jimmy Archer	70.00	120.00
5 Frank Arellanes	70.00	120.00
6 Tommy Atkins	70.00	120.00
7 Jimmy Austin	70.00	120.00
8 Les Bachman	70.00	120.00
9 Bill Bailey	70.00	120.00
10A Frank Baker Black Back	250.00	400.00
10B Frank Baker Blue Back	250.00	400.00
11 Cy Barger	70.00	120.00
12 Jack Barry	70.00	120.00
13A Johnny Bates Phil	70.00	120.00
13B Johnny Bates Cinc		
14 Ginger Beaumont	70.00	120.00
15 Fred Beck	70.00	120.00
16 Heine Beckendorf	70.00	120.00
17 Fred Beebe	70.00	120.00
18 George Bell	70.00	120.00
19 Harry Bemis	70.00	120.00
20A Chief Bender Blue	300.00	500.00
20B Chief Bender Pastel	250.00	400.00
21 Bill Bergen	70.00	120.00
22 Charles Berger	70.00	120.00
23 Bob Bescher	70.00	120.00
24 Joseph Dirmingham	70.00	120.00
25 Lena Blackburn	70.00	120.00
26 Jack Bliss	70.00	120.00
27 James J. Block	70.00	120.00
28 Hugh Bradley	70.00	120.00
29 Kitty Bransfield	70.00	120.00
30A Roger Bresnahan Blue	300.00	500.00
30B Roger Bresnahan Pastel	250.00	400.00
31 Al Bridwell	70.00	120.00
32 Buster Brown	70.00	120.00
33A Mordecai Brown Blue	300.00	500.00
33B Mordecai Brown Pastel	250.00	400.00
34 Al Burch	70.00	120.00
35 Donie Bush	70.00	120.00
36 Bobby Byrne	70.00	120.00
37 Howie Camnitz	70.00	120.00
38 Vin Campbell	70.00	120.00
39 Bill Carrigan	70.00	120.00
40A Frank Chance Blue	300.00	500.00
40B Frank Chance Pastel	250.00	400.00
41 Chappy Charles	70.00	120.00
42A Hal Chase Blue	250.00	400.00
42B Hal Chase Pastel	175.00	300.00
43 Ed Cicotte	250.00	400.00
44A Fred Clarke Black Back	250.00	400.00
44B Fred Clarke Blue Back	250.00	400.00
45 Nig Clarke	70.00	120.00
46 Tommy Clarke	70.00	120.00
47A Ty Cobb Blue	2500.00	4000.00
47B Ty Cobb Pastel	1800.00	3000.00
48A Eddie Collins Blue	350.00	600.00
48B Eddie Collins Pastel	300.00	500.00
49 Ray Collins	70.00	120.00
50 Wid Conroy	70.00	120.00
51 Jack Coombs	70.00	120.00
52 Frank Corridon	70.00	120.00
53 Harry Coveleski	90.00	150.00
54 Doc Crandall	70.00	120.00
55A Sam Crawford Blue	300.00	500.00
55B Sam Crawford Pastel	250.00	400.00
56 Birdie Cree	70.00	120.00
57 Lou Criger	70.00	120.00
58 Dode Criss	70.00	120.00
59 Cliff Curtis	70.00	120.00
60 Bill Dahlen MG	70.00	120.00
61 William Davidson	70.00	120.00
62A Harry Davis Blue	90.00	150.00
62B Harry Davis Pastel	70.00	120.00
63 Jim Delehanty	70.00	120.00
64 Ray Demmitt	70.00	120.00
65 Frank Dessau	70.00	120.00
66A Art Devlin Black Back	70.00	120.00
66B Art Devlin Blue Back	70.00	120.00
67 Josh Devore	70.00	120.00
68 Pat Donahue	70.00	120.00
69 Patsy Donovan MG	70.00	120.00
70A Bill Donovan Blue	70.00	120.00
70B Bill Donovan Pastel	70.00	120.00
71A Red Dooin Blue	90.00	150.00
71B Red Dooin Pastel	70.00	120.00
72 Mickey Doolan	70.00	120.00
73 Patsy Dougherty	70.00	120.00
74 Tom Downey	70.00	120.00
75 Jim Doyle	70.00	120.00
76A Larry Doyle Blue	90.00	150.00
76B Larry Doyle Pastel	70.00	120.00
77 Hugh Duffy MG	250.00	400.00
78 Jimmy Dygert	70.00	120.00
79 Dick Eagan	70.00	120.00
80 Kid Elberfeld	70.00	120.00
81 Rube Ellis	70.00	120.00
82 Arthur Engle	70.00	120.00
83 Tex Erwin	70.00	120.00
84 Steve Evans	70.00	120.00
85A Johnny Evers Black Back	300.00	500.00
85B Johnny Evers Blue Back	300.00	500.00
86 Bob Ewing	70.00	120.00
87 Cy Falkenberg	70.00	120.00
88 George Ferguson	70.00	120.00
89 Art Fletcher	70.00	120.00
90 Elmer Flick	250.00	400.00
91 John Flynn	70.00	120.00
92 Russ Ford	70.00	120.00
93 Ed Foster	70.00	120.00
94 Bill Foxen	70.00	120.00
95 John Frill	70.00	120.00
96 Samuel Frock	70.00	120.00
97 Art Fromme	70.00	120.00
98 Earle Gardner New York	70.00	120.00
99 Larry Gardner Boston	70.00	120.00
100 Harry Gaspar	70.00	120.00
101 Doc Gessler	70.00	120.00
102A George Gibson Blue	90.00	150.00
102B George Gibson Pastel	70.00	120.00
103 Bert Graham	70.00	120.00
104 Peaches Graham	70.00	120.00
105 Eddie Grant	70.00	120.00
106 Clark Griffith MG	250.00	400.00
107 Ed Hahn	70.00	120.00
108 Charles Hall	70.00	120.00
109 Bob Harmon	70.00	120.00
110 Topsy Hartsel	70.00	120.00
111 Roy Hartzell	70.00	120.00
112 Heinie Heitmuller	70.00	120.00
113 Buck Herzog	70.00	120.00
114 Doc Hoblitzel	70.00	120.00
115 Danny Hoffman	70.00	120.00
116 Solly Hofman	70.00	120.00
117 Harry Hooper	250.00	400.00
118 Harry Howell	70.00	120.00
119 Miller Huggins	250.00	400.00
120 Tom Hughes ML	70.00	120.00
121 Rudy Hulswitt	70.00	120.00
122 John Hummel	70.00	120.00
123 George Hunter	70.00	120.00
124 Ham Hyatt	70.00	120.00
125 Fred Jacklitsch	70.00	120.00
126A Hugh Jennings MG Blue	300.00	500.00
126B Hugh Jennings MG Pastel	250.00	400.00
127 Walter Johnson	900.00	1500.00
128A Davy Jones Blue	70.00	120.00
128B Davy Jones Pastel	70.00	120.00
129 Tom Jones	70.00	120.00
130A Tim Jordan Blue	90.00	150.00
130B Tim Jordan Pastel	70.00	120.00
131 Addie Joss	250.00	400.00
132 John Kane	70.00	120.00
133 Edwin Karge	70.00	120.00
134 Red Killifer	70.00	120.00
135 Johnny Kling	70.00	120.00
136 Otto Knabe	70.00	120.00
137 John Knight	70.00	120.00
138 Ed Konetchy	70.00	120.00
139 Harry Krause	70.00	120.00
140 Rube Kroh	70.00	120.00
141 Otto Krueger ML	70.00	120.00
142A Napoleon Lajoie Blue	600.00	1000.00
142B Napoleon Lajoie Pastel	500.00	800.00
143 Joe Lake	70.00	120.00
144 Fred Lake MG	70.00	120.00
145 Frank LaPorte	70.00	120.00
146 Jack Lapp	70.00	120.00
147 Chick Lathers	70.00	120.00
148A Tommy Leach Blue	90.00	150.00
148B Tommy Leach Pastel	70.00	120.00
149 Sam Leever	70.00	120.00
150 Lefty Leifield	70.00	120.00
151 Ed Lennox	70.00	120.00
152 Frederick Link	70.00	120.00
153 Paddy Livingstone	70.00	120.00
154 Hans Lobert	70.00	120.00
155 Bris Lord	70.00	120.00
156A Harry Lord Blue	90.00	150.00
156B Harry Lord Pastel	70.00	120.00
157 Johnny Lush	70.00	120.00
158 Connie Mack MG	350.00	600.00
159 Thomas Madden	70.00	120.00
160 Nick Maddox	70.00	120.00
161 Sherry Magee	70.00	120.00
162A Christy Mathewson Blue	900.00	1500.00
162B Christy Mathewson Pastel	900.00	1500.00
163 Al Mattern	70.00	120.00
164 Jimmy McAleer MG	70.00	120.00
165 George McBride	70.00	120.00
166A Amby McConnell Bos	70.00	120.00
166B Amby McConnell Chi		
167 Pryor McElveen	70.00	120.00
168 John McGraw MG	300.00	500.00
169 Deacon McGuire MG	70.00	120.00
170 Stuffy McInnis	70.00	120.00
171 Harry McIntire	70.00	120.00
172 Matty McIntyre	70.00	120.00
173 Larry McLean	70.00	120.00
174 Tommy McMillan	70.00	120.00
175A G.McQuillan Cinc	3500.00	6000.00
175B G.McQuillan Phil Blue	90.00	150.00
175C G.McQuillan Phil Pastel	70.00	120.00
176 Paul Meloan	70.00	120.00
177 Fred Merkle	70.00	120.00
178 Chief Meyers	70.00	120.00
179 Clyde Milan	70.00	120.00
180 Dots Miller	70.00	120.00
181 Warren Miller	70.00	120.00
182 Fred Mitchell ML	70.00	120.00
183 Mike Mitchell	70.00	120.00
184 Earl Moore	70.00	120.00
185 Pat Moran	70.00	120.00
186A Lew Moren Black Back	70.00	120.00
186B Lew Moren Blue Back	90.00	150.00
187 Cy Morgan	70.00	120.00
188 George Moriarty	70.00	120.00
189 Mike Mowery	70.00	120.00
190A George Mullin Black Back	70.00	120.00
190B George Mullin Blue Back	90.00	150.00
191 Danny Murphy	70.00	120.00
192 Red Murray	70.00	120.00
193 Tom Needham	70.00	120.00
194 Harry Niles	70.00	120.00
195 Rebel Oakes	70.00	120.00
196 Jack O'Conner	70.00	120.00
197 Paddy O'Connor	70.00	120.00
198 Bill O'Hara ML	70.00	120.00
199 Rube Oldring	70.00	120.00
200 Charley O'Leary	70.00	120.00
201 Orvie Overall	70.00	120.00
202 Fred Parent	70.00	120.00
203 Dode Paskert	70.00	120.00
204 Frederick Payne	70.00	120.00
205 Barney Pelty	70.00	120.00
206 Hub Pernoll	70.00	120.00
207 George Perring ML	70.00	120.00
208 Big Jeff Pfeffer	70.00	120.00
209 Jack Pfiester	70.00	120.00
210 Art Phelan	70.00	120.00
211 Ed Phelps	70.00	120.00
212 Deacon Phillipe	70.00	120.00
213 Eddie Plank	700.00	1200.00
214 Jack Powell	70.00	120.00
215 Billy (William) Purtell	70.00	120.00
216 Farmer Ray ML	70.00	120.00
217 Bugs Raymond	70.00	120.00
218 Doc Reisling	70.00	120.00
219 Ed Reulbach	70.00	120.00
220 Lew Richie	70.00	120.00
221 Jack Rowan	70.00	120.00
222A Nap Rucker Black Back	70.00	120.00
222B Nap Rucker Blue Back	70.00	120.00
223 Slim Sallee	70.00	120.00
224 Doc Scanlon	70.00	120.00
225 Germany Schaefer	70.00	120.00
226 Lou Schettler	70.00	120.00
227 Admiral Schlei	70.00	120.00
228 Boss Schmidt	70.00	120.00
229 Frank Schulte	70.00	120.00
230 Al Schweitzer	70.00	120.00
231 James Scott	70.00	120.00
232 James Seymour	70.00	120.00
233 Tillie Shafer	70.00	120.00
234 David Shean	70.00	120.00
235 Bayard Sharpe	70.00	120.00
236 Jimmy Sheckard	70.00	120.00
237 Mike Simon	70.00	120.00
238 Charlie Smith	70.00	120.00
239 Frank Smith	70.00	120.00
240 Harry Smith	70.00	120.00
241 Fred Snodgrass	70.00	120.00
242 Bob Spade UER	70.00	120.00
243 Tully Sparks	70.00	120.00
244 Tris Speaker	1200.00	2000.00
245 Jake Stahl	70.00	120.00
246 George Stallings MG	70.00	120.00
247 Oscar Stanage	70.00	120.00
248 Harry Steinfeldt	70.00	120.00
249 Jim Stephens	70.00	120.00
250 George Stone	70.00	120.00
251 George Stovall	70.00	120.00
252 Gabby Street	70.00	120.00
253 Sailor Stroud	70.00	120.00
254 Amos Strunk	70.00	120.00
255 George Suggs	70.00	120.00
256 Billy Sullivan	70.00	120.00
257A Ed Summers Black Back	70.00	120.00
257B Ed Summers Blue Back	70.00	120.00
258 Bill Sweeney	70.00	120.00
259 Jeff Sweeney	70.00	120.00
260 Lee Tannehill	70.00	120.00
261A Fred Tenney Blue	90.00	150.00
262B Fred Tenney Pastel	70.00	120.00
262A Ira Thomas Blue	90.00	150.00
262B Ira Thomas Pastel	70.00	120.00
263 John Thoney	70.00	120.00
264A Joe Tinker Black Back	250.00	400.00
264B Joe Tinker Blue Back	250.00	400.00
265 John Titus	70.00	120.00
266 Terry Turner	70.00	120.00
267 Bob Unglaub	70.00	120.00
268A Rube Waddell Black Back	250.00	400.00
268B Rube Waddell Blue Back	250.00	400.00
269A Hans Wagner Blue	5000.00	8000.00
269B Hans Wagner Pastel	3000.00	5000.00
270 Heinie Wagner	70.00	120.00
271 Bobby Wallace	175.00	300.00
272 Ed Walsh	250.00	400.00
273 Jimmy Walsh Gray	175.00	300.00
274 Jimmy Walsh White	175.00	300.00
275 Doc White	70.00	120.00
276 Kaiser Wilhelm	70.00	120.00
277 Ed Willett	70.00	120.00
278 Vic Willis	250.00	400.00
279 Art Wilson	70.00	120.00
280 Chief Wilson	70.00	120.00
281 Hooks Wiltse	70.00	120.00
282 Harry Wolter	70.00	120.00
283 Joe Wood	1200.00	2000.00
284 Ralph Works	70.00	120.00
285A Cy Young Black Back	900.00	1500.00
285B Cy Young Blue Back	900.00	1500.00
286 Irv Young	70.00	120.00
287 Heinie Zimmerman	70.00	120.00
288 Dutch Zwilling	70.00	120.00

1910-11 Sporting Life M116 Blank Backs

20A Chief Bender Blue
40A Frank Chance Blue
42A Hal Chase Blue
47A Ty Cobb Blue
48A Eddie Collins Blue
62A Harry Davis Blue
71A Red Dooin Blue
76A Larry Doyle Blue
126A Hugh Jennings Blue MG
162A Christy Mathewson Blue
175B George McQuillan Philadelphia Blue
269A Hans Wagner Blue

1911 Sporting Life Cabinets M110

This six-card set which measures approximately 5 5/8" by 7 1/2" was issued as a premium offer to the Sporting Life card set. These cards have a player photo surrounded by green borders with the players name on the bottom. The backs contain an advertisement for the Sporting Life newspaper. Since the cards are unnumbered, we have put them in alphabetical order.

COMPLETE SET (6)	20000.00	40000.00
1 Frank Chance	3000.00	6000.00
2 Hal Chase	2500.00	5000.00
3 Ty Cobb	6000.00	12000.00
4 Larry Lajoie	4000.00	8000.00
5 Christy Mathewson	5000.00	10000.00
6 Honus Wagner	5000.00	10000.00

1902-11 Sporting Life Cabinets W600

These large and attractive cabinet-type cards were issued by the Sporting Life Publishing Company over a period of years between 1902 and 1911. The exact number of cards in the set is not known but is estimated to be about 450. The cards are not numbered and might appear to have a slight reddish or sepia tinit. Many are found still in the glassine envelope in which they were issued. The backs are blank.

COMPLETE SET	75000.00	150000.00
1 Bill Abstein	600.00	1200.00
2 Babe Adams	600.00	1200.00
3 Whitey Alperman	600.00	1200.00
4 Nick Altrock	750.00	1500.00
5 Red Ames	600.00	1200.00
6 Frank Arelanes	600.00	1200.00
7 Charlie Armbruster	600.00	1200.00
8 Bill Armour MG	600.00	1200.00
9 Harry Arndt	600.00	1200.00
10 Harry Aubrey	600.00	1200.00
11 Jimmy Austin	750.00	1500.00
12 Charlie Babb	600.00	1200.00
13 Frank Baker	2000.00	4000.00
14 Jap Barbeau	600.00	1200.00
15 George Barclay	600.00	1200.00
16 Cy Barger	600.00	1200.00
17 Jimmy Barrett	600.00	1200.00
18 Shad Barry	600.00	1200.00
19 Jack Barry	600.00	1200.00
20 Harry Barton	600.00	1200.00
21 Emil Batch	600.00	1200.00
22 Johnny Bates	600.00	1200.00
23 Harry Bay	600.00	1200.00
24 Ginger Beaumont	600.00	1200.00
25 Fred Beck	600.00	1200.00
26 Henie Beckendorf	600.00	1200.00
26a Jake Beckley		
27 Fred Beebe	600.00	1200.00
28 George Bell	600.00	1200.00
29 Harry Bemis	600.00	1200.00
30 Chief Bender	1250.00	2500.00
31 Pug Bennett	600.00	1200.00
32 Bill Bergen	600.00	1200.00
33 C. Berger	600.00	1200.00
34 Bill Bernhard	600.00	1200.00
35 Bob Bescher	600.00	1200.00
36 W. Beville	600.00	1200.00
37 Lena Blackburne	600.00	1200.00
38 Elmer Bliss	600.00	1200.00
39 Frank Bowerman	600.00	1200.00
40 Bill Bradley	600.00	1200.00
41 W. Bradley	600.00	1200.00
42 Dave Brain	600.00	1200.00
43 Kitty Bransfield	600.00	1200.00
44 Roger Bresnahan	1250.00	2500.00
45 Al Bridwell	600.00	1200.00
46 Buster Brown	600.00	1200.00
47 Mordecai Brown	1250.00	2500.00
48 Sam Brown	600.00	1200.00
49 George Browne	600.00	1200.00
50 Jimmy Burke	600.00	1200.00
51 Jesse Burkett	1250.00	2500.00
52 Nixey Callahan	600.00	1200.00
53 Howie Camnitz	600.00	1200.00
54 Rip Cannell	600.00	1200.00
55 Joe Cantillon MG	600.00	1200.00
56 Pat Carney	600.00	1200.00
57 Charlie Carr	600.00	1200.00
58 Bill Carrigan	600.00	1200.00
59 Doc Casey	600.00	1200.00
60 Louis Castro		
61 Frank Chance	3000.00	6000.00
62 Hal Chase	1000.00	2000.00
63 Jack Chesbro	1250.00	2500.00
64 Eddie Cicotte	1250.00	2500.00
65 Fred Clarke	1250.00	2500.00
66 Nig Clarke	600.00	1200.00
67 T. Clarke	600.00	1200.00
68 Walter Clarkson	600.00	1200.00
69 Otis Clymer	600.00	1200.00
70 Andy Coakley	600.00	1200.00
71 Ty Cobb	10000.00	20000.00
72 Eddie Collins	1250.00	2500.00
73 Jimmy Collins	2000.00	4000.00
74 Bunk Congalton	600.00	1200.00
75 Wid Conroy	600.00	1200.00
76 Duff Cooley	600.00	1200.00
77 Jack Coombs	750.00	1500.00
78 Frank Corridon	600.00	1200.00
79 Bill Coughlin	600.00	1200.00
80 Ernie Courtney	600.00	1200.00
81 Doc Crandall	600.00	1200.00
82 Sam Crawford	1250.00	2500.00
83 Lou Criger	600.00	1200.00
84 Dode Criss	600.00	1200.00
85 John Cronin	750.00	1500.00
86 Lave Cross	600.00	1200.00
87 Monte Cross	600.00	1200.00
88 Clarence Currie	600.00	1200.00
89 Bill Dahlen	750.00	1500.00
90 George Davis	2000.00	4000.00
91 Harry Davis	600.00	1200.00

92 Jim Delehanty 750.00 1500.00
93 Art Devlin 750.00 1500.00
94 Pop Dillon 600.00 1200.00
95 Bill Dineen 600.00 1200.00
96 John Dobbs 600.00 1200.00
97 Ed Doheny 600.00 1200.00
98 Cozy Dolan 600.00 1200.00
99 Jiggs Donahue 600.00 1200.00
100 Mike Donlin 1000.00 2000.00
101 Patsy Donovan 600.00 1200.00
102 Bill Donovan 600.00 1200.00
103 Red Dooin 600.00 1200.00
104 Mickey Doolan 600.00 1200.00
105 Tom Doran 600.00 1200.00
106 Gus Dorner 600.00 1200.00
107 Patsy Dougherty 600.00 1200.00
108 Tom Downey 600.00 1200.00
109 Red Downs 600.00 1200.00
110 Jim Doyle 600.00 1200.00
111 Joe Doyle 600.00 1200.00
112 Larry Doyle 750.00 1500.00
113 Hugh Duffy 1250.00 2500.00
114 Bill Duggleby 600.00 1200.00
115 Gus Dundon 600.00 1200.00
116 Jack Dunleavy 600.00 1200.00
117 Jack Dunn 750.00 1500.00
118 Jimmy Dygert 600.00 1200.00
119 Dick Egan 600.00 1200.00
120 Kid Elberfeld 750.00 1500.00
121 Claude Elliott 600.00 1200.00
122 Rube Ellis 600.00 1200.00
123 Johnny Evers 2000.00 4000.00
124 Bob Ewing 600.00 1200.00
125 Cy Falkenberg 600.00 1200.00
126 John Farrell 600.00 1200.00
127 George Ferguson 600.00 1200.00
128 Hobe Ferris 600.00 1200.00
129 Tom Fisher 600.00 1200.00
130 Patsy Flaherty 600.00 1200.00
131 Elmer Flick 1250.00 2500.00
132 John Flynn 600.00 1200.00
133 Bill Foxen 600.00 1200.00
134 Chick Fraser 600.00 1200.00
135 Bill Friel 600.00 1200.00
136 Art Fromme 600.00 1200.00
137 Dave Fultz 600.00 1200.00
138 Bob Ganley 600.00 1200.00
139 John Ganzel 600.00 1200.00
140 Ned Garvin 600.00 1200.00
141 Harry Gasper 600.00 1200.00
142 Phil Geier 600.00 1200.00
143 Doc Gessler 600.00 1200.00
144 George Gibson 600.00 1200.00
145 Norwood Gibson 600.00 1200.00
146 Billy Gilbert 600.00 1200.00
147 Fred Glade 600.00 1200.00
148 Harry Gleason 750.00 1500.00
149 Eddie Grant 750.00 1500.00
150 Danny Green 600.00 1200.00
151 Ed Gremminger 600.00 1200.00
152 Clark Griffith 1250.00 2500.00
153 Moose Grimshaw 600.00 1200.00
154 H. Hackett 600.00 1200.00
155 Ed Hahn 600.00 1200.00
156 Noodles Hahn 750.00 1500.00
157 Charley Hall 600.00 1200.00
158 Bill Hallman 600.00 1200.00
159 Ned Hanlon MG 1250.00 2500.00
160 Bob Harmon 600.00 1200.00
161 Jack Harper 600.00 1200.00
162 Hub Hart 600.00 1200.00
163 Topsy Hartsel 600.00 1200.00
164 Roy Hartzell 600.00 1200.00
165 Charlie Hemphill 600.00 1200.00
166 Weldon Henley 600.00 1200.00
167 Otto Hess 600.00 1200.00
168 Mike Heydon 600.00 1200.00
169 Piano Legs Hickman 600.00 1200.00
170 Hunter Hill 600.00 1200.00
171 Homer Hillebrand 600.00 1200.00
172 Harry Hinchman 600.00 1200.00
173 Bill Hinchman 600.00 1200.00
174 Dick Hoblitzel 600.00 1200.00
175 Danny Hoffman 600.00 1200.00
176 Solly Hofman 600.00 1200.00
177 Bill Hogg 600.00 1200.00
178 A. Holesketter 600.00 1200.00
179 Ducky Holmes 600.00 1200.00
180 Del Howard 600.00 1200.00
181 Harry Howell 600.00 1200.00
182 J. Huelsman 600.00 1200.00
183 Miller Huggins 1250.00 2500.00
184 Jim Hughes 600.00 1200.00
185 Tom Hughes 600.00 1200.00
186 Rudy Hulswitt 600.00 1200.00
187 John Hummell 600.00 1200.00
189 Ham Hyatt 600.00 1200.00
188 Berthold Hustings
190 Frank Isbell 600.00 1200.00
191 Fred Jacklitsch 600.00 1200.00
192 Joe Jackson 6000.00 12000.00
193 H. Jacobson 600.00 1200.00
194 Hugh Jennings MG 1250.00 2500.00
195 Charlie Jones 600.00 1200.00
196 Davy Jones 600.00 1200.00
197 Oscar Jones 600.00 1200.00
198 Tom Jones 600.00 1200.00
199 Dutch Jordan 600.00 1200.00
200 Addie Joss 1250.00 2500.00
201 Mike Kahoe 600.00 1200.00
202 Ed Karger 600.00 1200.00
203 Bob Keefe 600.00 1200.00
204 Willie Keeler 2500.00 5000.00
205 Bill Keister 600.00 1200.00
206 Joe Kelley 1250.00 2500.00
207 Brickyard Kennedy 600.00 1200.00
208 Ed Killian 600.00 1200.00
209 J. Kissinger 600.00 1200.00
210 Frank Kitson 600.00 1200.00
211 Mal Kittridge 600.00 1200.00
212 Red Kleinrow 600.00 1200.00
213 Johnny Kling 750.00 1500.00
214 Ben Koehler 600.00 1200.00
215 Ed Konetchy 600.00 1200.00
216 Harry Krause 600.00 1200.00
217 Otto Krueger 600.00 1200.00
218 Candy LaChance 600.00 1200.00
219 Nap Lajoie 3000.00 6000.00
220 Joe Lake 600.00 1200.00
221 Frank Laporte 600.00 1200.00
222 L. Laroy 600.00 1200.00
223 Tommy Leach 750.00 1500.00
224 Watty Lee 600.00 1200.00
225 Sam Leever 600.00 1200.00
226 Phil Lewis 600.00 1200.00
227 Vive Lindaman 600.00 1200.00
228 Paddy Livingstone 600.00 1200.00
229 Hans Lobert 750.00 1500.00
230 Herman Long 600.00 1200.00
231 Bris Lord 600.00 1200.00
232 Harry Lord 750.00 1500.00
233 Harry Lumley 600.00 1200.00
234 Carl Lundgren 600.00 1200.00
235 Johnny Lush 600.00 1200.00
236 Connie Mack MG 2500.00 5000.00
237 Nick Maddox 600.00 1200.00
238 Sherry Magee 1000.00 2000.00
239 George Magoon 600.00 1200.00
240 John Malarkey 600.00 1200.00
241 Billy Maloney 600.00 1200.00
242 Doc Marshall 600.00 1200.00
243 Christy Mathewson 5000.00 10000.00
244 Jimmy McAleer 600.00 1200.00
245 Sport McAlister 600.00 1200.00
246 Jack McCarthy 600.00 1200.00
247 John McCloskey 600.00 1200.00
248 Amby McConnell 600.00 1200.00
249 Moose McCormick 600.00 1200.00
250 Chappie McFarland 600.00 1200.00
251 Herm McFarland 600.00 1200.00
252 Dan McGann 600.00 1200.00
253 Joe McGinnity 1250.00 2500.00
254 John McGraw MG 2500.00 5000.00
255 Deacon McGuire 750.00 1500.00
256 Harry McIntyre 600.00 1200.00
257 Matty McIntyre 600.00 1200.00
258 Larry McLean 600.00 1200.00
259 Fred Merkle 1000.00 2000.00
260 Sam Mertes 600.00 1200.00
261 Clyde Milan 750.00 1500.00
262 Dots Miller 600.00 1200.00
263 Billy Milligan 600.00 1200.00
264 Fred Mitchell 600.00 1200.00
265 Mike Mitchell 600.00 1200.00
266 Earl Moore 600.00 1200.00
267 Pat Moran 750.00 1500.00
268 Lew Moren 600.00 1200.00
269 Cy Morgan 600.00 1200.00
270 E. Moriarty 600.00 1200.00
271 Jack Morrissey 600.00 1200.00
272 Mike Mowery 600.00 1200.00
273 George Mullin 750.00 1500.00
274 Danny Murphy 600.00 1200.00
275 Red Murray 600.00 1200.00
276 W. Murray 600.00 1200.00
277 Jim Nealon 600.00 1200.00
278 D. Needham 600.00 1200.00
279 Doc Newton 600.00 1200.00
280 Harry Niles 600.00 1200.00
281 Rabbit Nill 600.00 1200.00
282 Pete Noonan 600.00 1200.00
283 Jack O'Brien 600.00 1200.00
284 Pete O'Brien 600.00 1200.00
285 Rube Oldring 600.00 1200.00
286 Charley O'Leary 600.00 1200.00
287 Jack O'Neil 600.00 1200.00
288 Mike O'Neil 600.00 1200.00
289 Al Orth 600.00 1200.00
290 Orvie Overall 600.00 1200.00
291 Frank Owens 600.00 1200.00
292 Freddie Parent 600.00 1200.00
293 Dode Paskert 600.00 1200.00
294 Jim Pastorious 600.00 1200.00
295 Roy Paterson 600.00 1200.00
296 Fred Payne 600.00 1200.00
297 Barney Pelty 600.00 1200.00
298 Blg Jeff Pfeiffer 600.00 1200.00
299 Jack Pfiester 600.00 1200.00
300 Ed Phelps 600.00 1200.00
301 Deacon Phillippe 750.00 1500.00
302 Bill Phillips 600.00 1200.00
303 Ollie Pickering 600.00 1200.00
304 Eddie Plank 2500.00 5000.00
305 Ed Poole 600.00 1200.00
306 Jack Powell 600.00 1200.00
307 Maurice Powers
308 Billy Purtell 600.00 1200.00
309 Ambrose Puttman 600.00 1200.00
310 Tommy Raub 600.00 1200.00
311 Fred Raymer 600.00 1200.00
312 Bill Reidy 600.00 1200.00
313 Ed Reulbach 1000.00 2000.00
314 Bob Rhoads 600.00 1200.00
315 D. Richie 600.00 1200.00
316 Claude Ritchey 600.00 1200.00
317 Lew Ritter 600.00 1200.00
318 C. Robinson 600.00 1200.00
319 George Rohe 600.00 1200.00
320 Claude Rossman 600.00 1200.00
321 Frank Roth 600.00 1200.00
322 Jack Rowan 600.00 1200.00
323 Slim Sallee 600.00 1200.00
324 Germany Schaefer 750.00 1500.00
325 Admiral Schiel 600.00 1200.00
326 Boss Schmidt 600.00 1200.00
327 Harry Schmidt
328 Ossie Schreckengost
329 Frank Schulte 600.00 1200.00
330 T. Sebring 600.00 1200.00
331 Al Schweitzer 600.00 1200.00
332 Kip Selbach 600.00 1200.00
333 Cy Seymour 600.00 1200.00
334 Spike Shannon 600.00 1200.00
335 Danny Shay 600.00 1200.00
336 Ralph Seybold
337 Dave Shean 600.00 1200.00
338 Jimmy Sheckard 600.00 1200.00
339 Ed Siever 600.00 1200.00
340 Jimmy Slagle 600.00 1200.00
341 Jack Slattery 600.00 1200.00
342 Charlie Smith 600.00 1200.00
343 E. Smith 600.00 1200.00
344 Frank Smith 600.00 1200.00
345 Harry Smith 600.00 1200.00
346 Homer Smoot 600.00 1200.00
347 Tully Sparks 600.00 1200.00
348 Chick Stahl 750.00 1500.00
349 Jake Stahl 750.00 1500.00
350 Joe Stanley 600.00 1200.00
351 Harry Steinfeldt 750.00 1500.00
352 George Stone 600.00 1200.00
353 George Stovall 600.00 1200.00
354 Jesss Stovall 600.00 1200.00
355 Sammy Strang 600.00 1200.00
356 Elmer Stricklett 600.00 1200.00
357 Willie Sudhoff 600.00 1200.00
358 Joe Sugden 600.00 1200.00
359 Billy Sullivan 600.00 1200.00
360 Ed Summers 600.00 1200.00
361 Bill Sweeney 600.00 1200.00
362 Lee Tannehill 600.00 1200.00
363 Jack Taylor 600.00 1200.00
364 Dummy Taylor 600.00 1200.00
365 Fred Tenney 600.00 1200.00
366 Ira Thomas 600.00 1200.00
367 Jack Thoney 600.00 1200.00
368 Joe Tinker 1250.00 2500.00
369 Terry Turner 600.00 1200.00
370 Bob Unglaub 600.00 1200.00
371 George Van Haltren 600.00 1200.00
372 Bucky Veil 600.00 1200.00
373 Rube Waddell 2000.00 4000.00
374 Heinie Wagner 600.00 1200.00
375 Honus Wagner 4000.00 8000.00
376 Bobby Wallace 1250.00 2500.00
377 Ed Walsh 2000.00 4000.00
378 Jack Warner 600.00 1200.00
379 Art Weaver 600.00 1200.00
380 Jake Weimer 600.00 1200.00
381 Kirby White 600.00 1200.00
382 Bob Wicker 600.00 1200.00
383 F. Wilhelm 600.00 1200.00
384 Ed Willett 600.00 1200.00
385 Jimmy Williams 600.00 1200.00
386 Otto Williams 600.00 1200.00
387 Hooks Wiltse 750.00 1500.00
388 George Winter 600.00 1200.00
389 Bill Wolfe 600.00 1200.00
390 Harry Wolverton 600.00 1200.00
391 Howard Wilson
392 Joe Yeager 600.00 1200.00
393 Cy Young 4000.00 8000.00
394 Irv Young 600.00 1200.00
395 Chief Zimmer 600.00 1200.00
396 Henie Zimmerman 600.00 1200.00

1899-00 Sporting News Supplements M101-1

Measuring approximately 9" by 11", these photos were issued as supplements in the Sporting News. This list is far from complete, so any additions are appreciated.

COMPLETE SET 7500.00 15000.00
1 Ted Breitenstein 250.00 500.00
2 Frank Chance 400.00 800.00
3 Jack Chesbro 300.00 600.00
4 Tom Corcoran 200.00 400.00
5 Bill Dahlen 250.00 500.00
6 Lou Criger 150.00 300.00
7 Lave Cross 150.00 300.00
8 George Davis 400.00 800.00
9 Ed Delahanty 300.00 600.00
10 Hugh Duffy 400.00 800.00
11 Frank Donahue 150.00 300.00
12 Patsy Donovan 200.00 400.00
13 Bill Dineen 200.00 400.00
14 Buck Freeman 200.00 400.00
15 Noodles Hahn 200.00 400.00
16 Ned Hanlon MG 300.00 600.00
18 Cowboy Jones 150.00 300.00
17 Hugh Jennings 400.00 800.00
19 Sam Leever 150.00 300.00
20 Herman Long 200.00 400.00
21 John McGraw 500.00 1000.00
22 Heinie Peitz 150.00 300.00
23 Deacon Phillippe 250.00 500.00
24 Wilbert Robinson 400.00 800.00
25 Ed Scott 150.00 300.00
26 Chick Stahl 200.00 400.00
27 Jesse Tannehill 200.00 400.00
28 Roy Thomas 200.00 400.00
29 Honus Wagner 1000.00 2000.00
30 James Williams 150.00 300.00
31 Vic Willis 400.00 800.00
32 Cy Young 750.00 1500.00
33 George Yeager 200.00 400.00

1909-13 Sporting News Supplements M101-2

These 100 8" x 10" sepia supplements were inserted in various issues of the Sporting News. We have identified the player and then given the date of the issue in which this supplement appears. The set is sequenced in order of appearence. No photos were issued between 4/14 and 8/25 in 1910. No photos were issued between 3/30 and 10/19 in 1911. No photos were issued between 1/18 and 10/03 in 1912.

COMPLETE SET (101) 6000.00 12000.00
1 Roger Bresnahan 75.00 150.00
St. Louis NL/7/22/09
2 Denton T. Young 100.00 200.00
Cleveland AL
and Louis Criger#
3 Christopher Mathewson 200.00 400.00
New York-N/8/5/09
4 Nap Lajoie 125.00 250.00
Cleve/8/10/09
5 Tyrus R. Cobb 8/12/09 300.00 600.00
6 Nap Lajoie 125.00 250.00
Cleveland/8/19/09
7 Sherwood N. Magee 30.00 60.00
Philadelphia-N/8/26/09
8 Frank L. Chance 125.00 250.00
Chicago-N/9/02/09
9 Edward Walsh 50.00 100.00
Chicago-A/9/9/09
10 Nap Rucker 25.00 50.00
Brooklyn/9/16/09
11 Honus Wagner 200.00 400.00
Pittsburgh/9/23/09
12 Hugh Jennings MG 50.00 100.00
Detroit/9/30/09
13 Fred C. Clarke 100.00 200.00
Pittsburgh/10/07/09
14 Ban Johnson AL PRES/10/14/09 100.00 200.00
15 Charles Comiskey OWN 75.00 150.00
Chicago White Sox/10/21/09
16 Eddie Collins 75.00 150.00
Philadelphia-A/10/28/09
17 James A. McAleer 25.00 50.00
Washington/11/04/09
18 Pittsburgh Pirates/11/11/09 50.00 100.00
19 Detroit Team/11/18/09 50.00 100.00
20 George Bell 25.00 50.00
Brooklyn/11/25/09
21 Tris Speaker 150.00 300.00
Boston-A/12/02/09
22 Mordecai Brown 100.00 200.00
Chicago-N/12/09/09
23 Hal Chase 50.00 100.00
New York-A/12/16/09
24 Thomas W. Leach 30.00 60.00
Pittsburgh/12/23/09
25 Owen Bush 25.00 50.00
Detroit/12/30/09
26 John J. Evers 75.00 150.00
Chicago-N/1/6/10
27 Harry Krause 25.00 50.00
Philadelphia-A/1/13/10
28 Babe Adams 30.00 60.00
Pittsburgh/1/20/10
29 Addie Joss 125.00 250.00
Cleveland/1/27/10
30 Orval Overall 25.00 50.00
Chicago-N/2/3/10
31 Samuel E. Crawford 100.00 200.00
Detroit/2/10/10
32 Fred Merkle 30.00 60.00
New York-N/2/17/10
33 George Mullin 30.00 60.00
Detroit/2/24/10
34 Edward Konetchy 25.00 50.00
St. Louis-N/3/3/10
35 George Gibson 25.00 50.00
Pitt.
Bugs Raymond
NY NL/3/10/10
36 T.Cobb/H.Wagner 3/17/10 250.00 500.00
37 Connie Mack MG 150.00 300.00
Phila.-AL/3/24/10
38 Bill Evans UMP 25.00 50.00
Silk O'Loughlin UMP
Bill Klem UMP
39 Edward Plank 75.00 150.00
Philadelphia-AL/4/7/10
40 Walter Johnson 150.00 300.00
Gabby Street
Wash./9/1/10
41 John C. Kling 25.00 50.00
Chicago-N/9/8/10
42 Frank Baker 75.00 150.00
Philadelphia-A/9/15/10
43 Charles S. Dooin 25.00 50.00
Philadelphia-A/9/22/10
44 Wm. F. Carrigan 25.00 50.00
Boston-A/9/29/10
45 John B. McLean 25.00 50.00
Cincinnati/10/06/10
46 John W. Coombs 30.00 60.00
Philadelphia-A/10/13/10
47 Jos. B. Tinker 100.00 200.00
Chicago-N/10/20/10
48 John I. Taylor OWN 25.00 50.00
Boston-A/10/27/10
49 Russell Ford 25.00 50.00
New York-A/11/03/10
50 Leonard L. Cole 25.00 50.00
Chicago-N/11/10/10
51 Harry Lord 25.00 50.00
Chicago-A/11/17/10
52 Philadelphia-A Team/11/24/10 50.00 100.00
53 Chicago-N Team/12/1/10 50.00 100.00
54 Charles A. Bender 50.00 100.00
Philadelphia-A/12/08/10
55 Arthur Hofman 25.00 50.00
Chicago-N/12/15/10
56 Bobby Wallace 50.00 100.00
St. Louis-A/12/21/10
57 John J. McGraw MG 150.00 300.00
New York-N/12/28/10
58 Harry H. Davis/1/5/11 25.00 50.00
Philadelphia-A
59 James P. Archer 25.00 50.00
Chicago-N/1/12/11
60 Ira Thomas 25.00 50.00
Philadelphia-A/1/19/11
61 Robert Byrnes 25.00 50.00
Pittsbutrgh/1/26/11
62 Clyde Milan 30.00 60.00
Washington/2/2/11
63 John T. Meyer 30.00 60.00
New York-N/2/9/11
64 Robert Bescher 25.00 50.00
Cincinnati/2/16/11
65 John J. Barry 25.00 50.00
Philadelphia-A/2/23/11
66 Frank Schulte 30.00 60.00
Chicago-N/3/2/11
67 C. Harris White 25.00 50.00
Chicago-A/3/9/11
68 Lawrence Doyle 30.00 60.00
New York-N/3/16/11
69 Joe Jackson 400.00 800.00
Cleveland/3/23/11
70 Martin O'Toole 25.00 50.00
William Kelly
Pittsburgh/10/26/1
71 Vean Gregg 25.00 50.00
Cleveland/11/2/11
72 Richard W. Marquard 75.00 150.00
New York-N/11/9/11
73 John E. McInnis 30.00 60.00
Philadelphia-N/11/16/11
74 Grover C. Alexander 125.00 250.00
Philadelphia-N/11/23/11
75 Del Gainor 25.00 50.00
Detroit/11/30/11
76 Fred Snodgrass 30.00 60.00
New York-N/12/7/11
77 James J. Callahan 30.00 60.00
Chicago-A/12/14/11
78 Robert Harmon 25.00 50.00
St. Louis-N/12/21/11
79 George Stovall 25.00 50.00
Cleveland/12/28/11
80 Zack D. Wheat 75.00 150.00
Brooklyn/1/4/12
81 Frank 'Ping' Bodie 25.00 50.00
Chicago-A/1/11/12
82 Boston-A Team/10/10/1912 50.00 100.00
83 New York-NTeam/10/17/1912 50.00 100.00
84 Jake Stahl MG 30.00 60.00
Boston-A/10/24/12
85 Joe Wood 40.00 80.00
Boston-A/10/31/12
86 Charles Wagner 25.00 50.00
Boston-A/11/07/12
87 Lew Ritchie 25.00 50.00
Chicago-N/11/14/12
88 Clark Griffith MG 50.00 100.00
Washington/11/21/12
89 Arnold Houser 25.00 50.00
St. Louis-N/11/28/12
90 Charles Herzog 25.00 50.00
New York-N/12/05/12
91 James Lavender 25.00 50.00
Chicago-N/12/12/12
92 Jeff Tesreau 25.00 50.00
New York-N/12/19/12
93 August Herrrman OWN 30.00 60.00
Cincinnati
94 Jake Daubert 30.00 60.00
Brooklyn/10/23/13
95 Heinie Zimmerman 25.00 50.00
Chicago-N/10/30/13
96 Ray Schalk 75.00 150.00
Chicago-A/11/07/13
97 Hans Lobert 25.00 50.00
Philadelphia-N/11/13/13
98 Albert W. Demaree 25.00 50.00
New York-N/11/20/13
99 Arthur Fletcher 25.00 50.00
New York-N/11/27/13
100 Charles A. Somers OWN 25.00 50.00
Cleveland/12/04/13
101 Joe Birmingham MG 25.00 50.00
Cleveland/12/11/13

1911 Sporting News

Little is know about this set. The front featured an posed action photo of the featured player along with his name, position and year and team on the bottom. The back is stamped "a picture given with every 5 cents in trade at". Any more information on this set is very appreciated.

COMPLETE SET
1 Solly Hofman

1916 M101-5 Blank Back

The cards in this set measure approximately 1 5/8" by 3". Issued in 1916 as a premium offer, the M101-5 set features black and white photos of current ballplayers. Each card is numbered on the front and the backs carry either a blank back or a sponsoring company's information. The fronts are the same as D329, H801-9 and the unclassified Famous and Barr set. Most of the players in this set also appear in the M101-4 set but the majority feature a different card number in both sets. Those cards which are asterisked in the checklist below are those cards which appeared in both the M101-5 and M101-4 sets identically and those have only been cataloged once in their respective M101-5 versions. The M101-5 cards are known to exist in these back variations but not every card has been confirmed to exist in every version: blank back, Block and Kuhl, Famous and Barr, Gimbels (large block letters), Gimbels (small block letters), Herpolsheimer, Holmes to Holmes, Morehouse Baking, Standard Biscuit, and Successful Farming. It is thought that the blank backs, Famous and Barr and Standard Biscuit versions are the most common with Holmes to Homes being the most difficult to find.

COMPLETE SET (200) 12500.00 25000.00
1 Babe Adams * 60.00 120.00
2 Sam Agnew Browns 50.00 100.00
3 Eddie Ainsmith * 50.00 100.00
4 Grover Alexander * 250.00 500.00
5 Leon Ames * 50.00 100.00
6 Jimmy Archer * 50.00 100.00
7 Jimmy Austin * 50.00 100.00
8 Frank Baker 100.00 200.00
9 Dave Bancroft 100.00 200.00
10 Jack Barry 60.00 120.00
11 Zinn Beck 50.00 100.00
12A Beals Becker SP
12B Lute Boone * 60.00 120.00
13 Joe Benz 50.00 100.00
14 Bob Bescher 50.00 100.00
15 Al Betzel 3rd B. 50.00 100.00
16 Roger Bresnahan 100.00 200.00
17 Eddie Burns 50.00 100.00
18 Geo. J. Burns 50.00 100.00
19 Joe Bush 60.00 120.00
20 Owen J. Bush 60.00 120.00
21 Art Butler 50.00 100.00
22 Bobby Byrne 50.00 100.00
23A Mordecai Brown 100.00 200.00
23B Forrest Cady SP
24 Jimmy Callahan 50.00 100.00
25 Ray Caldwell 50.00 100.00
26 Max Carey 100.00 200.00
27 George Chalmers 50.00 100.00
28 Frank Chance 150.00 300.00
29 Ray Chapman 60.00 120.00
30 Larry Cheney 50.00 100.00
31 Eddie Cicotte 150.00 300.00
32 Tom Clarke 50.00 100.00
33 Eddie Collins 100.00 200.00
34 Shauno Collins 50.00 100.00
35 Charles Comiskey UER 100.00 200.00
(Misspelled Comisky)
36 Joe Connolly 50.00 100.00
37 Luther Cook 60.00 120.00
38 Jack Coombs 100.00 200.00
39 Dan Costello 60.00 120.00
40 Harry Coveleski UER 60.00 120.00
(misspelled Coveleskie)
41 Gavvy Cravath 60.00 120.00
42 Sam Crawford 100.00 200.00
43 Jean Dale 50.00 100.00
44 Jake Daubert 60.00 120.00
45 George Davis Jr. 60.00 120.00
46 Charles Deal 50.00 100.00
47 Al Demaree 50.00 100.00
48 William Doak 50.00 100.00
49 Bill Donovan 50.00 100.00
50 Charles Dooin 50.00 100.00
51 Mike Doolan 50.00 100.00
52 Larry Doyle 60.00 120.00
53 Jean Dubuc 50.00 100.00
54 Oscar Dugey 50.00 100.00
55 Johnny Evers 150.00 300.00
56 Urban Faber 100.00 200.00
57 Hap Felsch R.F. 150.00 300.00
58 Bill Fischer 50.00 100.00
59 Ray Fisher Hands Over Head 50.00 100.00
60 Max Flack 50.00 100.00
61 Art Fletcher 50.00 100.00
62 Eddie Foster 50.00 100.00
63 Jacques Fournier 50.00 100.00
64 Del Gainer UER 50.00 100.00
(misspelled Gainor)
65 Larry Gardner * 50.00 100.00
66 Joe Gedeon * 50.00 100.00
67 Gus Getz * 50.00 100.00
68 Geo. Gibson (eo Not Missing) 50.00 100.00
69 Wilbur Good * 50.00 100.00
70 Hank Gowdy * 60.00 120.00
71 Jack Graney * 60.00 120.00
72 Tom Griffith 50.00 100.00
73 Heinie Groh 60.00 120.00
74 Earl Hamilton 50.00 100.00
75 Bob Harmon 50.00 100.00
76 Roy Hartzell Am. 50.00 100.00
77 Claude Hendrix 50.00 100.00
78 Olaf Henriksen 50.00 100.00
79 John Henry 50.00 100.00
80 Buck Herzog 50.00 100.00
81 Hugh High 50.00 100.00
82 Dick Hoblitzell 50.00 100.00
83 Harry Hooper 100.00 200.00
84 Ivan Howard 1st B. 50.00 100.00
85 Miller Huggins 100.00 200.00
86 Joe Jackson 4000.00 8000.00
87 William James 50.00 100.00
88 Harold Janvrin 50.00 100.00
89 Hughie Jennings 100.00 200.00
90 Walter Johnson 600.00 1200.00
91 Fielder Jones 50.00 100.00
92 Benny Kauff 50.00 100.00
93 Bill Killefer Jr. 50.00 100.00
94 Ed Konetchy 50.00 100.00
95 Napoleon Lajoie 300.00 600.00
96 Jack Lapp 50.00 100.00
97 John Lavan 50.00 100.00
98 Jimmy Lavender 50.00 100.00
99 Nemo Leibold 50.00 100.00
100 Hubert Leonard 60.00 120.00
101 Duffy Lewis 60.00 120.00
102 Hans Lobert 50.00 100.00
103 Tom Long 50.00 100.00
104 Fred Luderus 50.00 100.00
105 Connie Mack 200.00 400.00
106 Lee Magee 2nd B. 50.00 100.00
107 Albert Mamaux 50.00 100.00
108 Leslie Mann C.F. 50.00 100.00
109 Rabbit Maranville 100.00 200.00
110 Rube Marquard 100.00 200.00
111 Armando Marsans 60.00 120.00
112 J. Erskine Mayer 50.00 100.00
113 George McBride 50.00 100.00
114 John J. McGraw 150.00 300.00
115 Jack McInnis 60.00 120.00
116 Fred Merkle 60.00 120.00
117 Chief Meyers 50.00 100.00
118 Clyde Milan 60.00 120.00
119 Otto Miller 50.00 100.00
120 Willie Mitchell UER 50.00 100.00
(misspelled Mitchel)
121 Fred Mollwitz 50.00 100.00
122 J. Herbert Moran 60.00 120.00
123 Pat Moran 50.00 100.00
124 Ray Morgan 50.00 100.00
125 George Moriarty 50.00 100.00
126 Guy Morton 50.00 100.00
127 Ed. Murphy UER Photo 50.00 100.00
128 John Murray 60.00 120.00
129 Hy Myers 50.00 100.00
130 J. A. Niehoff 50.00 100.00
131 Leslie Nunamaker 60.00 120.00
132 Rube Oldring 50.00 100.00
133 Oliver O'Mara 50.00 100.00
134 Steve O'Neill 60.00 120.00
135 Dode Paskert C. 50.00 100.00
136 Roger Peckinpaugh UER Photo 60.00 120.00
137 E. J. Pfeffer 60.00 120.00
138 George Pierce UER 60.00 120.00
(misspelled Pearce)
139 Wally Pipp 60.00 120.00
140 Derrill Pratt UER 50.00 100.00
(misspelled Derril)
141 Bill Rariden * 50.00 100.00
142 Eppa Rixey * 100.00 200.00
143 Davey Robertson * 50.00 100.00
144 Wilbert Robinson * 150.00 300.00
145 Bob Roth C.F. 50.00 100.00
146 Edd Roush C.F. 100.00 200.00
147 Clarence Rowland * 50.00 100.00
148 Nap Rucker * 60.00 120.00
149 Dick Rudolph * 50.00 100.00
150 Reb Russell * 50.00 100.00
151 Babe Ruth * 50000.00 80000.00
152 Vic Saier * 50.00 100.00
153 Slim Sallee * 50.00 100.00
154 Germany Schaefer 60.00 120.00
155 Ray Schalk 100.00 200.00
156 Walter Schang 60.00 120.00
157 Charles Schmidt 60.00 120.00
158 Frank Schulte 50.00 100.00
159 Jim Scott 50.00 100.00
160 Everett Scott 60.00 120.00
161 Tom Seaton 50.00 100.00
162 Howard Shanks 50.00 100.00
163 Bob Shawkey UER Photo 60.00 120.00
164 Ernie Shore 60.00 120.00
165 Burt Shotton 50.00 100.00
166 George Sisler P 150.00 300.00
167 J. Carlisle Smith 50.00 100.00
168 Fred Snodgrass 60.00 120.00
169 George Stallings 50.00 100.00
170 Oscar Stanage UER Photo 50.00 100.00
171 Casey Stengel 600.00 1200.00
172 Milton Stock 50.00 100.00
173 Amos Strunk UER Photo 50.00 100.00
174 Billy Sullivan 60.00 120.00
175 Jeff Tesreau 50.00 100.00
176 Jim Thorpe 4000.00 8000.00
177 Joe Tinker 150.00 300.00
178 Fred Toney 50.00 100.00
179 Terry Turner 3rd B. 50.00 100.00
180 Jim Vaughn 50.00 100.00
181 Bob Veach 50.00 100.00
182 James Viox 2nd B. 50.00 100.00
183 Oscar Vitt 50.00 100.00
184 Honus Wagner 1000.00 2000.00
185 Clarence Walker Browns UER Photo 50.00 100.00
186A Zach Wheat 100.00 200.00
186B Bobby Wallace SP
187 Ed Walsh 100.00 200.00
188 Buck Weaver S.S. 200.00 400.00
189 Carl Weilman 50.00 100.00
190 George Whitted Nat'ls 50.00 100.00
191 Fred Williams 50.00 100.00
192 Art Wilson 50.00 100.00
193 J. Owen Wilson 50.00 100.00
194 Ivy Wingo 50.00 100.00
195 Mel Wolfgang 50.00 100.00
196 Joe Wood 100.00 200.00
197 Steve Yerkes 50.00 100.00
198 Rollie Zeider * 50.00 100.00
199 Heiny Zimmerman * 50.00 100.00
200 Edward Zwilling * 50.00 100.00

1916 M101-5 Block and Kuhl

BLOCK AND KUHL TOO SCARCE TO PRICE

1916 M101-5 Famous and Barr

*FAMOUS AND BARR: .4X TO 1X BLANK BACK

1916 M101-5 Gimbels (Large Block)

GIMBELS (LARGE) TOO SCARCE TO PRICE

1916 M101-5 Gimbels (Small Block)

GIMBELS (SMALL) TOO SCARCE TO PRICE

1916 M101-5 Herpolsheimer

HERPOLSHEIMER TOO SCARCE TO PRICE

1916 M101-5 Holmes to Homes

HOLMES TO HOMES TOO SCARCE TO PRICE

1916 M101-5 Morehouse Baking

MOREHOUSE BAKING TOO SCARCE TO PRICE

1916 M101-5 Standard Biscuit

*STANDARD BISCUIT: .4X TO 1X BLANK BACK

1916 M101-5 Successful Farming

SUCCESSFUL FARMING TOO SCARCE TO PRICE

1915 Sporting News Postcards M101-3

These 3 1/2" by 5 1/2" borderless postcards feature color, a rare commodity in early baseball postcards. The inscription "published by the Sporting News" appears on the front of the card along with the player's name and team. The postcards are believed to have been issued as premiums and mailed in an envelope, and the set is believed to be complete at six cards.

COMPLETE SET (6) 750.00 1500.00
1 Roger Bresnahan 100.00 200.00
2 Ty Cobb 400.00 800.00
3 Eddie Collins 100.00 200.00
4 Vean Gregg 50.00 100.00
5 Walter Johnson 150.00 300.00
Gabby Street
6 Rube Marquard 100.00 200.00

1916 M101-4 Blank Back

The cards in this set measure approximately 1 5/8" by 3". Issued in 1916 as a premium offer, the M101-4 set features black and white photos of current ballplayers with each card numbered on the front and the backs carry either a blank back, a Sporting News advertisement, or another company's sponsoring information. The fronts are the same as D329, H801-9 and the Famous and Barr set. Most of the players in this also appear in the M101-5 set, issued earlier that same year, but the majority feature a different card number in both sets. Block and Kuhl, Famous and Barr, Herpolsheimer, Morehouse Baking and Standard Baking sets identically are checklisted only in the M101-5 set and not listed below since there is no distinction between the two (cards: 1/3/4/5/6/7/65/66/67/69/70/71/141/142/143/144/147/148/149/150/151/152/153/198/199/200). At present, 17 different backs are known for M101-4: Altoona Tribune, blank back, Block and Kuhl, Burgess-Nash, Everybody's, Famous and Barr, Gimbels (Italic lettering), Globe, Green-Joyce, Herposheimer, Indianapolis Brewing Co, Mall Theatre, Morehouse Baking, Sporting News, Standard Biscuit, Ware's Basement, and Weil Baking. It is thought that the blank backs, Sporting News, Famous and Barr and Standard Biscuit versions are the most common with Everyboby's, Green-Joyce, and Mall Theatre being the most difficult to find.

COMPLETE SET (200) 10000.00 20000.00
2 Sam Agnew Red Sox 50.00 100.00
4 Grover Alexander 250.00 500.00
8 H. D. Baird C.F. 50.00 100.00
9 Frank Baker 75.00 150.00
10 Dave Bancroft 60.00 120.00
11 Jack Barry 50.00 100.00
12 Zinn Beck 40.00 80.00
13 Chief Bender 75.00 150.00
14 Joe Benz 40.00 80.00
15 Bob Bescher 40.00 80.00
16 Al Betzel 2nd B. 40.00 80.00
17 Mordecai Brown 60.00 120.00
18 Eddie Burns 40.00 80.00
19 George Burns 50.00 100.00
20 Geo. J. Burns 40.00 80.00
21 Joe Bush 50.00 100.00

22 Donie Bush 50.00 100.00
23 Art Butler 40.00 80.00
24 Bobbie Byrne 40.00 80.00
25 Forrest Cady 50.00 100.00
26 Jimmy Callahan 40.00 80.00
27 Ray Caldwell 40.00 80.00
28 Max Carey 60.00 120.00
29 George Chalmers 40.00 80.00
30 Ray Chapman 50.00 100.00
31 Larry Cheney 40.00 80.00
32 Eddie Cicotte 150.00 300.00
33 Tom Clarke 40.00 80.00
34 Eddie Collins 75.00 150.00
35 Shauno Collins 40.00 80.00
36 Charles Comiskey 75.00 150.00
37 Joe Connolly 40.00 80.00
38 Ty Cobb 2000.00 4000.00
39 Harry Coveleski UER 40.00 80.00
(misspelled Coveleskie)
40 Gavvy Cravath 50.00 100.00
41 Sam Crawford 60.00 120.00
42 Jean Dale 40.00 80.00
43 Jake Daubert 50.00 100.00
44 Charles Deal 40.00 80.00
45 Al Demaree 40.00 80.00
46 Josh Devore 50.00 100.00
47 William Doak 40.00 80.00
48 Bill Donovan 40.00 80.00
49 Charles Dooin 40.00 80.00
50 Mike Doolan 50.00 100.00
51 Larry Doyle 50.00 100.00
52 Jean Dubuc 40.00 80.00
53 Oscar Dugey 40.00 80.00
54 Johnny Evers 75.00 150.00
55 Urban Faber 60.00 120.00
56 Hap Felsch C.F. 150.00 300.00
57 Bill Fischer 40.00 80.00
58 Ray Fisher Pitching 40.00 80.00
59 Max Flack 40.00 80.00
60 Art Fletcher 40.00 80.00
61 Eddie Foster 40.00 80.00
62 Jacques Fournier 40.00 80.00
63 Del Gainer UER 40.00 80.00
(misspelled Gainor)
64 Chic Gandil 100.00 200.00
68 Geo. Gibson (eo Missing) 50.00 100.00
72 Clark Griffith 75.00 150.00
73 Tom Griffith 40.00 80.00
74 Heinie Groh 50.00 100.00
75 Earl Hamilton 40.00 80.00
76 Bob Harmon 40.00 80.00
77 Roy Hartzell Americans 40.00 80.00
78 Claude Hendrix 40.00 80.00
79 Olaf Henriksen 40.00 80.00
80 John Henry 40.00 80.00
81 Buck Herzog 40.00 80.00
82 Hugh High 40.00 80.00
83 Dick Hoblitzell 40.00 80.00
84 Harry Hooper 60.00 120.00
85 Ivan Howard 3rd B. 40.00 80.00
86 Miller Huggins 60.00 120.00
87 Joe Jackson 5000.00 10000.00
88 William James 40.00 80.00
89 Harold Janvrin 40.00 80.00
90 Hughie Jennings 60.00 120.00
91 Walter Johnson 300.00 600.00
92 Fielder Jones 40.00 80.00
93 Joe Judge 50.00 100.00
94 Benny Kauff 40.00 80.00
95 Bill Killefer Jr. 40.00 80.00
96 Ed Konetchy 40.00 80.00
97 Napoleon Lajoie 250.00 500.00
98 Jack Lapp 40.00 80.00
99 John Lavan 40.00 80.00
100 Jimmy Lavender 40.00 80.00
101 Nemo Leibold 40.00 80.00
102 Hubert Leonard 50.00 100.00
103 Duffy Lewis 50.00 100.00
104 Hans Lobert 40.00 80.00
105 Tom Long 40.00 80.00
106 Fred Luderus 40.00 80.00
107 Connie Mack 200.00 400.00
108 Lee Magee L.F. 40.00 80.00
109 Sherwood Magee 50.00 100.00
110 Al Mamaux 40.00 80.00
111 Leslie Mann L.F. 40.00 80.00
112 Rabbit Maranville 60.00 120.00
113 Rube Marquard 60.00 120.00
114 J. Erskine Mayer 40.00 80.00
115 George McBride 40.00 80.00
116 John J. McGraw 150.00 300.00
117 Jack McInnis 50.00 100.00
118 Fred Merkle 50.00 100.00
119 Chief Meyers 50.00 100.00
120 Clyde Milan 40.00 80.00
121 John Miller 50.00 100.00
122 Otto Miller 40.00 80.00
123 Willie Mitchell 40.00 80.00
124 Fred Mollwitz 40.00 80.00
125 Pat Moran 40.00 80.00
126 Ray Morgan 40.00 80.00
127 George Moriarty 40.00 80.00
128 Guy Morton 40.00 80.00
129 Mike Mowrey 50.00 100.00
130 Edward Murphy 40.00 80.00
131 Hy Myers 40.00 80.00
132 J. A. Niehoff 40.00 80.00
133 Rube Oldring 40.00 80.00
134 Oliver O'Mara 40.00 80.00
135 Steve O'Neill 50.00 100.00
136 Dode Paskert C.F. 40.00 80.00
137 Roger Peckinpaugh 50.00 100.00
138 Wally Pipp 50.00 100.00
139 Derrill Pratt UER 40.00 80.00
(misspelled Derril)
140 Pat Ragan 50.00 100.00
142 Eppa Rixey 100.00 200.00
144 Wilbert Robinson 150.00 300.00
145 Bob Roth R.F. 40.00 80.00
146 Edd Roush R.F. UER 75.00 150.00
(misspelled Rousch)
151 Babe Ruth 50000.00 80000.00
154 Ray Schalk 60.00 120.00
155 Walter Schang 50.00 100.00
156 Frank Schulte 40.00 80.00
157 Everett Scott 50.00 100.00
158 Jim Scott 40.00 80.00
159 Tom Seaton 40.00 80.00
160 Howard Shanks 40.00 80.00
161 Bob Shawkey 50.00 100.00
162 Ernie Shore 50.00 100.00
163 Burt Shotton 40.00 80.00
164 George Sisler 1st B. 150.00 300.00
165 J. Carlisle Smith 40.00 80.00
166 Fred Snodgrass 50.00 100.00
167 George Stallings 40.00 80.00
168A Oscar Stanage Portrait SP
168B Oscar Stanage Catching 40.00 80.00
169 Casey Stengel 600.00 1200.00
170 Milton Stock 40.00 80.00
171 Amos Strunk 40.00 80.00
172 Billy Sullivan 50.00 100.00
173 Jeff Tesreau 40.00 80.00
174 Joe Tinker 75.00 150.00
175 Fred Toney 40.00 80.00
176 Terry Turner 2nd B. 40.00 80.00
177 George Tyler 50.00 100.00
178 Jim Vaughn 40.00 80.00
179 Bob Veach 40.00 80.00
180 James Viox 3rd B. 40.00 80.00
181 Oscar Vitt 40.00 80.00
182 Honus Wagner 600.00 1200.00
183 Clarence Walker Red Sox 40.00 80.00
184 Ed Walsh 60.00 120.00
185 W. Wambsganss UER Photo 50.00 100.00
186 Buck Weaver 3rd B. 200.00 400.00
187 Carl Weilman 40.00 80.00
188 Zach Wheat 60.00 120.00
189 George Whitted Nationals 40.00 80.00
190 Fred Williams 40.00 80.00
191 Art Wilson 40.00 80.00
192 J. Owen Wilson 40.00 80.00
193 Ivy Wingo 40.00 80.00
194 Mel Wolfgang 40.00 80.00
195 Joe Wood 60.00 120.00
196 Steve Yerkes 40.00 80.00
197 Pep Young 50.00 100.00

1916 M101-4 Altoona Tribune
ALTOONA TRIBUNE TOO SCARCE TO PRICE

1916 M101-4 Block and Kuhl
BLOCK AND KUHL TOO SCARCE TO PRICE

1916 M101-4 Burgess-Nash
BURGESS-NASH TOO SCARCE TO PRICE

1916 M101-4 Everybody's
EVERYBODY'S TOO SCARCE TO PRICE

1916 M101-4 Famous and Barr
*FAMOUS AND BARR: .4X TO 1X BLANK BACK

1916 M101-4 Gimbels Italic
GIMBLES ITALIC TOO SCARCE TO PRICE

1916 M101-4 Globe
GLOBE TOO SCARCE TO PRICE

1916 M101-4 Green-Joyce
GREEN-JOYCE TOO SCARCE TO PRICE

1916 M101-4 Herpolsheimer
HERPOLSHEIMER TOO SCARCE TO PRICE

1916 M101-4 Indianapolis Brewing
INDY BREWING TOO SCARCE TO PRICE

1916 M101-4 Mall Theatre
MALL THEATRE TOO SCARCE TO PRICE

1916 M101-4 Morehouse Baking
MOREHOUSE BAKING TOO SCARCE TO PRICE

1916 M101-4 Sporting News
*SPORTING NEWS: .4X TO 1X BLANK BACK
1 Babe Adams 50.00 100.00
3 Eddie Ainsmith 40.00 80.00
4 Grover Alexander 250.00 500.00
5 Leon Ames 50.00 100.00
6 Jimmy Archer 50.00 100.00
7 Jimmy Austin 50.00 100.00
65 Larry Gardner 50.00 100.00
66 Joe Gedeon 50.00 100.00
67 Gus Getz 50.00 100.00
69 Wilbur Good 40.00 80.00
70 Hank Gowdy 50.00 100.00
71 John Graney 50.00 100.00
141 Bill Rariden 40.00 80.00
142 Eppa Rixey 60.00 120.00
143 Davey Robertson 40.00 80.00
147 Clarence Rowland 40.00 80.00
148 Nap Rucker 50.00 100.00
149 Dick Rudolph 50.00 100.00
150 Reb Russell 40.00 80.00
151 Babe Ruth 50000.00 80000.00
152 Vic Saier 40.00 80.00
153 Slim Sallee 50.00 100.00
168A Stanage Port SP
198 Rollie Zeider 50.00 100.00
199 Heiny Zimmerman 50.00 100.00
200 Edward Zwilling 50.00 100.00

1916 M101-4 Ware's Basement
WARE'S BASEMENT TOO SCARCE TO PRICE

1916 M101-4 Weil Baking
WEIL BAKING TOO SCARCE TO PRICE

1926-27 Sporting News Supplements M101-7
These 11 cards were included as inserts of the "Sporting News" publication. They are known to come in two sizes, 7" by 10" and 10" by 14 1/2". We have basically sequenced this set in alphabetical order.
COMPLETE SET (11) 600.00 1200.00
1 Kiki Cuyler 60.00 120.00
16-Dec
2 Babe Ruth 250.00 500.00
30-Dec
3 Rogers Hornsby 125.00 250.00
2-Dec
4 Tony Lazzeri 60.00 120.00
5 Heinie Manush 60.00 120.00
11-Nov
6 John Mostil 40.00 80.00
7 Harry Rice 60.00 120.00
January 13,1927
8 Al Simmons 75.00 150.00
23-Dec
9 Pie Traynor 75.00 150.00
26-Nov
10 George Uhle 40.00 80.00
11 Glenn Wright 40.00 80.00
4-Nov
12 New York Yankees
13 St. Louis Cardinals

1932 Sporting News Supplement M101-8
These four supplements were issued in 1932 as an supplement to the popular Baseball weekly, the Sporting News. Unlike most of the other supplements, these photos have biographical information and stats on the back. Since these are unnumbered, we have sequenced them in alphabetical order.
COMPLETE SET (4) 250.00 500.00
1 Kiki Cuyler 150.00 300.00
2 Dizzy Dean 200.00 400.00
3 Charlie Grimm 100.00 200.00
4 Lon Warneke 75.00 150.00

1939 Sporting News Premiums
All of these premiums are blank-backed. The players premiums measure approximately 8" by 10" while the team premiums measure approximately 11" by 16". The catalog number on this set is M101-9.
1 New York Yankees 100.00 200.00
Double Size
October 19
2 Joe DiMaggio 150.00 300.00
26-Oct-39
3 Bob Feller 125.00 250.00
9-Nov-39
4 Cincinnati Reds 50.00 100.00
November 2, 1939
Double Size
5 St. Louis Cardinals 50.00 100.00
November 16,1939

1888-89 Sporting Times M117
These 27 cards which measure 7 1/2" by 4 1/2" were included as premiums in the Sporting Times weekly newspaper. The cards are sequenced in alphabetical order and some of the other photos (most noticably) the Anson were used in other sets.
COMPLETE SET (27) 100000.00 200000.00
1 Cap Anson 12500.00 25000.00
2 Jersey Bakely 3000.00 6000.00
3 Dan Brouthers 6000.00 12000.00
4 Doc Bushong 3000.00 6000.00
5 Jack Clements 3000.00 6000.00
6 Charles Comiskey 6000.00 12000.00
7 Hank O'Day 3000.00 6000.00
8 Jerry Denny 3000.00 6000.00
9 Buck Ewing 5000.00 12000.00
10 Dude Esterbrook 3000.00 6000.00
11 Jay Faatz 3000.00 6000.00
12 Pud Galvin 6000.00 12000.00
13 Jack Glasscock 4000.00 8000.00
14 Tim Keefe 6000.00 12000.00
15 King Kelly 6000.00 12000.00
16 Matt Kilroy 3000.00 6000.00
17 Arlie Latham 4000.00 8000.00
18 Doggie Miller 3000.00 6000.00
19 Fred Pfeffer 3000.00 6000.00
20 Henry Porter 3000.00 6000.00
21 Toad Ramsey 3000.00 6000.00
22 John Reilly 3000.00 6000.00
23 Elmer Smith 3000.00 6000.00
24 Harry Stovey 4000.00 8000.00
25 Sam Thompson 6000.00 12000.00
26 John Montgomery Ward 6000.00 12000.00
27 Curt Welch 4000.00 8000.00

1933 Sport Kings
The cards in this 48-card set measure 2 3/8" by 2 7/8". The 1933 Sport Kings set, issued by the Goudey Gum Company, contains cards for the most famous athletic heroes of the times. No less than 18 different sports are represented in the set. The baseball cards of Cobb, Hubbell, and Ruth, and the football cards of Rockne, Grange and Thorpe command premium prices. The cards were issued in one-card penny packs which came 100 packs to a box along with a piece of gum. The catalog designation for this set is R338.
COMPLETE SET 10000.00 16000.00
1 Ty Cobb BB 2000.00 4000.00
2 Babe Ruth BB 5000.00 10000.00
42 Carl Hubbell BB 300.00 600.00

2007 Sportkings
6 Roger Clemens 5.00 12.00
7 Roberto Clemente 15.00 30.00
24 Don Mattingly 6.00 15.00
25 Stan Musial 10.00 25.00
27 Jackie Robinson 10.00 25.00
28 Pete Rose 20.00 40.00
31 Nolan Ryan 10.00 25.00
34 Tom Seaver 4.00 10.00
45 Ted Williams 8.00 20.00
47 Carl Yastrzemski 6.00 15.00

2007 Sportkings Mini
*MINIS: 1X TO 2X BASIC
ONE PER PACK
ANNOUNCED PRINT RUN 93 SETS

2007 Sportkings Autograph Gold
*GOLD: 1.2X TO 2X BASIC
RANDOM INSERTS IN PACKS
ANNOUNCED PRINT RUN 10 SETS
ANR Nolan Ryan 90.00 150.00
APRO Pete Rose 300.00 600.00

2007 Sportkings Autograph Silver
RANDOM INSERTS IN PACKS
ANNOUNCED PRINT RUN B/WN 95-99 PER
ACY Carl Yastrzemski 25.00 50.00
ADM Don Mattingly 25.00 50.00
ANR Nolan Ryan 60.00 100.00
APRO Pete Rose 150.00 300.00
ARC Roger Clemens 50.00 80.00
ASM Stan Musial 30.00 60.00
ATS Tom Seaver 20.00 50.00

2007 Sportkings Autograph Memorabilia Gold
*GOLD/10: 1.2X TO 2X SILVER/40
ANNOUNCED PRINT RUN 10 SETS
AMNR Nolan Ryan Jsy 125.00 200.00

2007 Sportkings Autograph Memorabilia Silver
RANDOM INSERTS IN PACKS
ANNOUNCED PRINT RUN 40 SETS
AMCY Carl Yastrzemski Jsy 30.00 60.00
AMDM Don Mattingly Jsy 30.00 60.00
AMNR Nolan Ryan Jsy 70.00 120.00
AMPRO Pete Rose Jsy 300.00 500.00
AMRC Roger Clemens Jsy 60.00 100.00
AMSM Stan Musial Jsy 50.00 80.00
AMTS Tom Seaver Jsy 25.00 60.00

2007 Sportkings Cityscapes Silver
ANNOUNCED PRINT RUN 20 SETS
*GOLD: .5X TO 1.2X BASIC
GOLD ANNOUNCED PRINT RUN 10 SETS
RANDOM INSERTS IN PACKS
CS02 P.Rose/P.Roy 100.00 175.00
CS03 R.Clemens/M.Schmidt 20.00 40.00
CS04 C.Yastrzemski/L.Bird 20.00 40.00
CS05 D.Mattingly/R.Clemens 25.00 50.00
CS06 T.Williams/L.Bird 40.00 80.00
CS07 R.Clemente/M.Lemieux 40.00 80.00

2007 Sportkings Decades Silver
ANNOUNCED PRINT RUN 20 SETS
*GOLD: .5X TO 1.2X BASIC
GOLD ANNOUNCED PRINT RUN 10 SETS
RANDOM INSERTS IN PACKS
D01 Williams/Richard/Musial 40.00 80.00
D02 Sawchuk/Shoe/Schmidt 40.00 80.00
D03 Yaz/Andretti/Clemente 50.00 100.00
D04 Rose/Holmes/Knievel 90.00 150.00
D05 Hogan/Mattingly/Magic 50.00 100.00
D06 Aikman/Roy/Clemens 40.00 80.00

2007 Sportkings Double Memorabilia Gold
*GOLD: .6X TO 1.5X BASIC
RANDOM INSERTS IN PACKS
ANNOUNCED PRINT RUN 10 SETS
DM15, DM16 ANNOUNCED PRINT RUN 1 PER
NO DM15, DM16 PRICING DUE TO SCARCITY
DM8 Pete Rose Jsy-Jsy 125.00 200.00

2007 Sportkings Double Memorabilia Silver
RANDOM INSERTS IN PACKS
ANNOUNCED PRINT RUN 4-40 SETS
DM15, DM16 ANNOUNCED PRINT RUN 4 PER
NO DM15, DM16 PRICING DUE TO SCARCITY
DM1 Don Mattingly 15.00 40.00
DM6 Nolan Ryan 20.00 50.00
DM8 Pete Rose 75.00 150.00
DM11 Roberto Clemente 40.00 80.00
DM12 Roger Clemens 12.50 30.00
DM13 Stan Musial 20.00 50.00

2007 Sportkings Hats Off Silver
ANNOUNCED PRINT RUN 20 SETS
*GOLD: .5X TO 1.2X BASIC
GOLD ANNOUNCED PRINT RUN 10 SETS
RANDOM INSERTS IN PACKS
HO1 Nolan Ryan Houston 25.00 50.00
HO2 Nolan Ryan Texas 25.00 50.00
HO3 Carl Yastrzemski 20.00 40.00
HO4 Roberto Clemente 50.00 80.00
HO5 Tom Seaver 15.00 30.00
HO6 Pete Rose Philadelphia 50.00 80.00
HO7 Pete Rose Cincinnati 60.00 100.00
HO8 Pete Rose Triple 125.00 200.00

2007 Sportkings Lumber Gold
*GOLD: .75X TO 1.5 BASIC
RANDOM INSERTS IN PACKS
ANNOUNCED PRINT RUN 10 SETS
WORDED SWATCHES COMMAND PREMIUMS
L8 Pete Rose Barrel 175.00 300.00

2007 Sportkings Lumber Silver
RANDOM INSERTS IN PACKS
ANNOUNCED PRINT RUN 30 SETS
WORDED SWATCHES COMMAND PREMIUMS
L6 Stan Musial Bat 40.00 80.00
L7 Don Mattingly Bat 40.00 80.00
L8 Pete Rose Bat 150.00 250.00

2007 Sportkings Patch Silver
ANNOUNCED PRINT RUN 20 SETS
P28-P30 ANNOUNCED PRINT RUN 4 PER
NO P28-P30 PRICING DUE TO SCARCITY
*GOLD: .6X TO 1.2X BASIC
GOLD ANNOUNCED PRINT RUN 10 SETS
GOLD P28-P30 ANCD. PRINT RUN 1 PER
GOLD P28-P30 NO PRICING AVAILABLE
RANDOM INSERTS IN PACKS
P1 Carl Yastrzemski Jsy 20.00 50.00
P3 Don Mattingly Jsy 15.00 40.00
P15 Nolan Ryan Texas Jsy 30.00 60.00
P16 Nolan Ryan Houston Jsy 30.00 60.00
P18 Pete Rose Cincinnati Jsy 100.00 175.00
P19 Pete Rose Montreal Jsy 125.00 200.00
P22 Roger Clemens Jsy 15.00 40.00
P23 Stan Musial Jsy 30.00 60.00
P26 Tom Seaver Jsy 15.00 40.00

2007 Sportkings Single Memorabilia Silver
RANDOM INSERTS IN PACKS
ANNOUNCED PRINT RUN 90 SETS
SM3, SM13 ANNOUNCED PRINT RUN 4 PER
NO SM3, SM13 PRICING DUE TO SCARCITY
SM02 Carl Yastrzemski Jsy 8.00 20.00
SM04 Don Mattingly Jsy 8.00 20.00
SM17 Pete Rose Cincinnati Jsy 40.00 80.00
SM22 Roberto Clemente Jsy 15.00 40.00
SM25 Stan Musial Jsy 10.00 25.00
SM27 Ted Williams Jsy 20.00 50.00
SM32 Roger Clemens Bos Jsy 6.00 15.00
SM33 Roger Clemens NY Jsy 6.00 15.00
SM41 Nolan Ryan Houston Jsy 10.00 25.00
SM44 Pete Rose Montreal Jsy 25.00 50.00
SM45 Tom Seaver Jsy 6.00 15.00
SM47 Nolan Ryan Texas Jsy 10.00 25.00

2007 Sportkings Triple Memorabilia Silver
ANNOUNCED PRINT RUN 10 SETS
TM7, TM8 ANNOUNCED PRINT RUN 4 PER
NO TM7, TM8 PRICING DUE TO SCARCITY
GOLD ANNOUNCED PRINT RUN 1 SET
NO GOLD PRICING DUE TO SCARCITY
RANDOM INSERTS IN PACKS
TM02 Nolan Ryan 50.00 100.00
TM03 Pete Rose 175.00 300.00

2008 Sportkings
FIVE CARDS PER BOX
54 Lou Brock 5.00 10.00
68 Bob Gibson 5.00 10.00
72 Johnny Bench 6.00 12.00
76 Tony Perez 4.00 8.00
79 Andre Dawson 4.00 8.00
98 Ernie Banks 6.00 12.00
99 Gary Carter 4.00 8.00
100 Ozzie Smith 6.00 12.00
102 Juan Marichal 4.00 8.00

2008 Sportkings Mini
*MINI: 1X TO 2X BASIC
ONE PER BOX

2008 Sportkings Autograph Silver
ANNOUNCED PRINT RUN B/WN 20-90 PER
RANDOM INSERTS IN PACKS
AD Andre Dawson/80 * 15.00 30.00
BG Bob Gibson/70 * 20.00 40.00
EB Ernie Banks/40 * 30.00 60.00
GC Gary Carter/50 * 15.00 30.00
JM Juan Marichal/80 * 15.00 30.00
EB2 Ernie Banks/40 * 30.00 60.00
GC2 Gary Carter/50 * 10.00 25.00
LBR Lou Brock/80 * 15.00 30.00
OS1 Ozzie Smith/40 * 20.00 40.00
OS2 Ozzie Smith/40 * 20.00 40.00
PRO Pete Rose/95
TP1 Tony Perez/30 * 20.00 40.00
TP2 Tony Perez/30 * 20.00 40.00
JBEN1 Johnny Bench/25 * 25.00 50.00
JBEN2 Johnny Bench/25 * 25.00 50.00

2008 Sportkings Autograph Memorabilia Silver
ANNOUNCED PRINT RUN B/WN 15-50 PER
NO GOLD PRICING DUE TO SCARCITY
RANDOM INSERTS IN PACKS
AD Andre Dawson/40 * 20.00 40.00
BG Bob Gibson/40 * 25.00 50.00
EB Ernie Banks/40 * 40.00 80.00
GC Gary Carter/20 * 20.00 40.00
JB Jason Bay/40 * 15.00 30.00
JBEN1 Johnny Bench/25 * 40.00 80.00
JBEN2 Johnny Bench/25 * 40.00 80.00
JM Juan Marichal/40 * 25.00 50.00
JMO Justin Morneau/40 * 15.00 30.00
LBR Lou Brock/40 * 25.00 50.00
OS Ozzie Smith/40 * 25.00 50.00
TP1 Tony Perez/20 * 25.00 50.00
TP2 Tony Perez/20 * 25.00 50.00

2008 Sportkings Cityscapes Double Silver
RANDOM INSERTS IN PACKS
3 G.Carter/J.Beliveau 15.00 40.00
5 E.Banks/B.Hull 20.00 50.00
6 B.Gibson/B.Hull 15.00 40.00
9 J.Montana/J.Marichal 20.00 50.00

2008 Sportkings Cityscapes Triple Silver
RANDOM INSERTS IN PACKS
1 Bird/Clemens/Parish 30.00 60.00
3 Rose/Bench/Perez 50.00 100.00
4 Montana/Young/Marichal 40.00 80.00
5 Carter/Rose/Beliveau 30.00 60.00
6 Messier/Mattingly/Pele 75.00 125.00
7 Brock/Smith/Hull 20.00 50.00

2008 Sportkings Decades Silver
RANDOM INSERTS IN PACKS
1 Banks/Beliveau/Hogan 40.00 80.00
2 Brown/Plante/Marichal 20.00 50.00

2008 Sportkings Double Memorabilia Silver
RANDOM INSERTS IN PACKS
2 O.Smith/L.Brock 15.00 40.00
13 Bo Jackson BB-FB 20.00 50.00
14 Deion Sanders BB-FB 15.00 40.00

2008 Sportkings Future Sportkings Autograph Silver
RANDOM INSERTS IN PACKS
JB1 Jason Bay/40 * 10.00 25.00
JB2 Jason Bay/40 * 10.00 25.00
JM1 Justin Morneau/40 * 10.00 25.00
JM2 Justin Morneau/40 * 10.00 25.00

2008 Sportkings Passing the Torch Silver
RANDOM INSERTS IN PACKS
1 E.Banks/P.Rose 50.00 100.00
9 B.Gibson/N.Ryan 15.00 40.00

2008 Sportkings Patch Silver
RANDOM INSERTS IN PACKS
1 Andre Dawson 10.00 25.00
3 Bo Jackson 20.00 50.00
4 Bob Gibson 12.50 30.00
8 Gary Carter 10.00 25.00
11 Jason Bay 10.00 25.00
15 Justin Morneau 10.00 25.00
16 Lou Brock 10.00 25.00
21 Ozzie Smith 15.00 40.00
24 Tony Perez 12.50 30.00

2008 Sportkings Single Memorabilia Silver
RANDOM INSERTS IN PACKS
1 Andre Dawson 6.00 15.00
8 Bob Gibson 8.00 20.00
13 Ernie Banks 10.00 25.00
14 Gary Carter 6.00 15.00
18 Jason Bay 6.00 15.00
25 Juan Marichal 6.00 15.00
26 Justin Morneau 6.00 15.00
27 Lou Brock 6.00 15.00
31 Ozzie Smith 10.00 25.00
40 Tony Perez 6.00 15.00

2008 Sportkings Triple Memorabilia Silver
RANDOM INSERTS IN PACKS
3 Rose/Clemente/Banks 90.00 150.00

2008 Sportkings National Convention VIP Promo
9 Pete Rose 3.00 8.00
Carl Hubbell

2009 Sportkings
COMPLETE SET (52) 250.00 450.00
COMMON CARD (109-160) 5.00 12.00
SEMISTARS 6.00 15.00
UNLISTED STARS 8.00 20.00
110 Reggie Jackson 6.00 15.00
111 Orlando Cepeda 6.00 15.00
138 Satchel Paige 8.00 20.00
152 Tony Oliva 6.00 15.00
153 Mike Schmidt 12.00 30.00

2009 Sportkings Mini
*MINI: .6X TO 1.5X BASIC CARDS
STATED ODDS ONE PER BOX
UNPRICED SILVER PRINT RUN 7 SETS
UNPRICED GOLD PRINT RUN 3 SETS

2009 Sportkings Autograph Silver
ANNOUNCED PRINT RUN B/WN 15-70 PER
UNPRICED GOLD PRINT RUN 10
OC1 Orlando Cepeda/40* 20.00 40.00
OC2 Orlando Cepeda/40* 20.00 40.00
RJ1 Reggie Jackson/25* 50.00 100.00
RJ2 Reggie Jackson/25* 50.00 100.00
TO1 Tony Oliva/40* 20.00 40.00
TO2 Tony Oliva/40* 20.00 40.00
MSC1 Mike Schmidt/35* 50.00 100.00
MSC2 Mike Schmidt/35* 50.00 100.00

2009 Sportkings Autograph Memorabilia Silver
ANNOUNCED PRINT RUN B/WN 15-40 PER
UNPRICED GOLD PRINT RUN 10
RANDOM INSERTS IN PACKS
OC1 Orlando Cepeda Jsy/40* 15.00 30.00
OC2 Orlando Cepeda Jsy/40* 15.00 30.00
TO1 Tony Oliva Jsy/40* 20.00 40.00
TO2 Tony Oliva Jsy/40* 20.00 40.00
MSC1 Mike Schmidt Jsy/35* 60.00 120.00
MSC2 Mike Schmidt Jsy/35* 60.00 120.00
RJA1 Reggie Jackson Jsy/25* 40.00 80.00
RJA2 Reggie Jackson Jsy/25* 40.00 80.00

2009 Sportkings Cityscapes Double Silver
ANNOUNCED PRINT RUN 19 SETS
UNPRICED GOLD PRINT RUN 1
RANDOM INSERTS IN PACKS
1 R.Jackson Jsy/J.Namath Jsy 25.00 50.00
4 M.Schmidt Jsy/B.Parent Jsy 25.00 50.00

2009 Sportkings Cityscapes Triple Silver
ANNOUNCED PRINT RUN 19 SETS
UNPRICED GOLD PRINT RUN 1
RANDOM INSERTS IN PACKS
1 Reggie/Namath/Pele 50.00 100.00
2 Rice/Montana/Cepeda 60.00 120.00
3 Taylor/Reggie/P.Esposito 25.00 50.00

2009 Sportkings Decades Silver
ANNOUNCED PRINT RUN 19 SETS
UNPRICED GOLD PRINT RUN 1
RANDOM INSERTS IN PACKS
1 Pele/Namath/Cepeda 50.00 100.00
2 Tretiak/Reggie/Karolyi 50.00 100.00
3 Taylor/Wallace/Schmidt 40.00 80.00

2009 Sportkings Double Memorabilia Silver
ANNOUNCED PRINT RUN B/WN 1-19
UNPRICED GOLD PRINT RUN 1
RANDOM INSERTS IN PACKS
3 Reggie Jackson/19* 20.00 40.00
9 M.Schmidt/T.Oliva/19* 30.00 60.00
10 Jackson/Schmidt/19* 30.00 60.00

2009 Sportkings Patch Silver
ANNOUNCED PRINT RUN B/WN 4-19
UNPRICED GOLD PRINT RUN 1 SET
RANDOM INSERTS IN PACKS
3 Reggie Jackson/19*
4 Reggie Jackson/19* 20.00 40.00
5 Reggie Jackson/19* 20.00 40.00
13 Mike Schmidt/19* 20.00 40.00

2009 Sportkings Single Memorabilia Silver
ANNOUNCED PRINT RUN B/WN 4-29
UNPRICED GOLD PRINT RUN B/WN 1-4
RANDOM INSERTS IN PACKS
11 Orlando Cepeda Jsy/29* 6.00 15.00
13 Reggie Jackson Jsy/29* 12.00 30.00
17 Mike Schmidt Jsy/29* 30.00 60.00
21 Tony Oliva Jsy/29* 12.00 30.00

2009 Sportkings Triple Memorabilia Silver
ANNOUNCED PRINT RUN B/WN 3-19
UNPRICED GOLD PRINT RUN 1 SET
RANDOM INSERTS IN PACKS
5 Cepeda/Jackson/Oliva/19* 30.00 60.00
8 Schmidt/Oliva/Cepeda/19* 20.00 40.00

2010 Sportkings
COMPLETE SET (48) 150.00 300.00
COMP.SET w/o ALI SP (47) 100.00 200.00
162 Duke Snider 5.00 12.00
180 Tony Gwynn 5.00 12.00
186 Mark McGwire 6.00 15.00
194 Steve Carlton 5.00 12.00

2010 Sportkings Mini
COMPLETE SET (48) 175.00 350.00
*MINI: .5X TO 1.2X BASIC CARDS
STATED ODDS 1:2

2010 Sportkings Autograph Silver
ANNOUNCED PRINT RUN 10-50
UNPRICED GOLD PRINT RUN 5-10
ASC1 Steve Carlton/25* 20.00 40.00
ASC2 Steve Carlton/25* 20.00 40.00
ATG1 Tony Gwynn/20* 30.00 60.00
ATG2 Tony Gwynn/20* 30.00 60.00
ATG3 Tony Gwynn/20* 30.00 60.00
ADSN1 Duke Snider/25* 20.00 40.00
ADSN2 Duke Snider/25* 20.00 40.00
AMMC1 Mark McGwire/25* 125.00 225.00
AMMC2 Mark McGwire/25* 125.00 225.00

2010 Sportkings Autograph Memorabilia Silver
ANNOUNCED PRINT RUN 10-40
UNPRICED GOLD PRINT RUN 5-10
AMSC1 Steve Carlton Jsy/25* 20.00 40.00
AMSC2 Steve Carlton Jsy/25* 20.00 40.00
AMTG1 Tony Gwynn Jsy/15* 35.00 70.00
AMTG2 Tony Gwynn Jsy/15* 35.00 70.00
AMTG3 Tony Gwynn Jsy/15* 35.00 70.00
AMDSN1 Duke Snider Jsy/25* 20.00 40.00
AMDSN2 Duke Snider Jsy/25* 20.00 40.00
AMMMC1 Mark McGwire Jsy/25* 150.00 250.00
AMMMC2 Mark McGwire Jsy/25* 150.00 250.00

2010 Sportkings Patch Silver
STATED PRINT RUN 20
UNPRICED GOLD PRINT RUN 10
P3 Mark McGwire 25.00 60.00
P5 Steve Carlton 10.00 25.00
P9 Mark McGwire 25.00 60.00
P10 Tony Gwynn 20.00 50.00

2010 Sportkings Single Memorabilia Silver
STATED PRINT RUN 26 UNLESS NOTED
SM9 Duke Snider 10.00 20.00
SM15 Mark McGwire 25.00 50.00
SM16 Mark McGwire 25.00 50.00
SM27 Steve Carlton 12.00 25.00
SM28 Tony Gwynn 12.00 25.00

2010 Sportkings Triple Memorabilia Silver
SILVER PRINT RUN 4-20
UNPRICED GOLD PRINT RUN 1-10
TM6 McGwire/Snider/Gwynn 25.00 50.00

2012 Sportkings
209 Cal Ripken Jr. 8.00 20.00
210 Ryne Sandberg 6.00 15.00
211 Ken Griffey Jr. 6.00 15.00
212 Roberto Alomar 4.00 10.00
213 Rickey Henderson 5.00 12.00
214 Paul Molitor 4.00 10.00
215 Eddie Murray 5.00 12.00
216 Rod Carew 4.00 10.00
217 Dave Winfield 4.00 10.00

2012 Sportkings Autograph Memorabilia Silver
ANNOUNCED PRINT RUN 15-50
AMCRJ1 Cal Ripken Jr. 60.00 120.00
AMCRJ2 Cal Ripken Jr. 60.00 120.00
AMCRJ3 Cal Ripken Jr. 60.00 120.00
AMDWI1 Dave Winfield 20.00 40.00
AMDWI2 Dave Winfield 20.00 40.00
AMEM Eddie Murray 25.00 50.00
AMEM2 Eddie Murray 25.00 50.00
AMKGRJ1 Ken Griffey Jr. 100.00 200.00
AMKGRJ2 Ken Griffey Jr. 100.00 200.00
AMPM1 Paul Molitor 15.00 30.00
AMPM2 Paul Molitor 15.00 30.00
AMPM3 Paul Molitor 15.00 30.00
AMRA1 Roberto Alomar 25.00 50.00
AMRA2 Roberto Alomar 25.00 50.00
AMRCA1 Rod Carew 15.00 30.00
AMRCA2 Rod Carew 15.00 30.00
AMRH1 Rickey Henderson 40.00 80.00
AMRH2 Rickey Henderson 40.00 80.00
AMRH3 Rickey Henderson 40.00 80.00
AMRS1 Ryne Sandberg 35.00 70.00
AMRS2 Ryne Sandberg 35.00 70.00

2012 Sportkings Autographs Silver
ANNOUNCED PRINT RUN 15-130
ACRJ1 Cal Ripken Jr. 50.00 100.00
ACRJ2 Cal Ripken Jr. 50.00 100.00
ACRJ3 Cal Ripken Jr. 50.00 100.00
ADWI1 Dave Winfield 15.00 30.00
ADWI2 Dave Winfield 15.00 30.00
AEM Eddie Murray 25.00 50.00
AEM2 Eddie Murray 25.00 50.00
AKGJR1 Ken Griffey Jr. 75.00 150.00
AKGJR2 Ken Griffey Jr. 75.00 150.00
AKGJR3 Ken Griffey Jr. 75.00 150.00
APM1 Paul Molitor 15.00 30.00
APM2 Paul Molitor 15.00 30.00
ARA Roberto Alomar 15.00 30.00
ARA2 Roberto Alomar 15.00 30.00
ARCA1 Rod Carew 12.00 25.00
ARCA2 Rod Carew 12.00 25.00
ARH1 Rickey Henderson 30.00 60.00
ARH2 Rickey Henderson 30.00 60.00
ARS1 Ryne Sandberg 30.00 60.00
ARS2 Ryne Sandberg 30.00 60.00

2012 Sportkings Cityscapes Double Silver
ANNOUNCED PRINT RUN 30
CS1 R.Alomar/P.Molitor 15.00 30.00
CS2 R.Carew/P.Molitor 15.00 30.00
CS3 D.Winfield/R.Henderson 25.00 50.00
CS4 F.Harris/D.Parker 10.00 25.00
CS6 E.Murray/C.Ripken Jr. 25.00 50.00
CS7 D.Mattingly/D.Winfield 20.00 40.00
CS9 R.Jackson/R.Henderson 25.00 50.00
CS10 S.Pippen/F.Thomas 25.00 50.00
CS11 T.Raines/P.Roy 10.00 25.00
CS12 G.Sayers/R.Sandberg 20.00 40.00

2012 Sportkings Double Memorabilia Silver
ANNOUNCED PRINT RUN 60
DM1 R.Alomar/P.Molitor 10.00 25.00
DM2 D.Winfield/R.Henderson 12.50 30.00
DM3 R.Carew/P.Molitor 10.00 25.00
DM4 C.Ripken Jr./E.Murray 15.00 30.00

2012 Sportkings Greatest Moments Silver
ANNOUNCED PRINT RUN 40
GM1 Roberto Alomar 10.00 20.00
GM5 Cal Ripken Jr. 25.00 50.00

2012 Sportkings Mini
*MINI: .5X TO 1.2X BASIC CARDS
RANDOM INSERT IN PACKS

2012 Sportkings Premium Back
*SINGLES: .5X TO 1.2X BASIC CARDS
STATED ODDS ONE PER PACK

2012 Sportkings Quad Memorabilia Silver
ANNOUNCED PRINT RUN 30
QM1 Moltr/Hndrsn/Alomr/Winfld 30.00 60.00
QM2 Ripk/Reggie/Thoms/Ryne 30.00 60.00

2012 Sportkings Single Memorabilia Silver
ANNOUNCED PRINT RUN 90
SM1 Roberto Alomar 15.00 30.00
SM2 Rod Carew 7.50 15.00
SM3 Ken Griffey Jr. 15.00 30.00
SM4 Rickey Henderson 15.00 30.00
SM6 Paul Molitor 7.50 15.00
SM7 Eddie Murray 10.00 20.00
SM8 Cal Ripken, Jr. 10.00 25.00
SM13 Dave Winfield 7.50 15.00

2012 Sportkings Triple Memorabilia Silver
ANNOUNCED PRINT RUN 30
TM1 Alomar/Winfield/Molitor 10.00 25.00
TM2 Ripken/Alomar/Henderson 35.00 70.00
TM3 Murray/Griffey/Carew 15.00 40.00

2013 Sportkings
COMPLETE SET (48) 60.00 120.00
273 Josh Gibson 3.00 8.00
284 Pedro Martinez 3.00 8.00
288 David Ortiz 3.00 8.00
293 Mariano Rivera 4.00 10.00
294 Brooks Robinson 4.00 10.00
300 Frank Thomas 4.00 10.00
301 Fernando Valenzuela 3.00 8.00

2013 Sportkings Autograph Memorabilia Silver
PRINT RUN 20-50
AMBRO1 Brooks Robinson/40* 12.00 30.00
AMBRO2 Brooks Robinson/40* 12.00 30.00
AMFT1 Frank Thomas/30* 20.00 50.00
AMFT2 Frank Thomas/30* 20.00 50.00
AMFT3 Frank Thomas/30* 20.00 50.00
AMFV1 Fernando Valenzuela/30* 20.00 50.00
AMFV2 Fernando Valenzuela/30* 20.00 50.00
AMFV3 Fernando Valenzuela/30* 20.00 50.00
AMMR1 Mariano Rivera/30* 100.00 175.00
AMMR2 Mariano Rivera/30* 100.00 175.00
AMMR3 Mariano Rivera/20* 100.00 175.00

2013 Sportkings Autographs Silver
PRINT RUN 15-60
ABRO1 Brooks Robinson/40* 10.00 25.00
ABRO2 Brooks Robinson/40* 10.00 25.00
AFT1 Frank Thomas/30* 20.00 50.00
AFT2 Frank Thomas/30* 20.00 50.00
AFT3 Frank Thomas/30* 20.00 50.00
AFV1 Fernando Valenzuela/30* 15.00 40.00
AFV2 Fernando Valenzuela/30* 15.00 40.00
AFV3 Fernando Valenzuela/30* 15.00 40.00
AMR1 Mariano Rivera/20* 100.00 175.00
AMR2 Mariano Rivera/20* 100.00 175.00
AMR3 Mariano Rivera/20* 100.00 175.00

2013 Sportkings Cityscapes Double Silver
ANNOUNCED PRINT RUN 40
CSD2 D.Ortiz/P.Martinez 5.00 12.00
CSD3 M.Rivera/W.Boggs 10.00 25.00
CSD4 F.Valenzuela/S.O'Neal 6.00 15.00
CSD6 M.Rivera/R.Alomar 8.00 20.00

2013 Sportkings Cityscapes Triple Silver
ANNOUNCED PRINT RUN 30
CST1 Rivera/Boggs/Winfield 10.00 25.00
CST2 Thomas/Pippen/Hull 10.00 25.00
CST3 O'Neal/Valenzuela/Sawchuk

2013 Sportkings Decades Silver
ANNOUNCED PRINT RUN 40
D1 Orti/Rive/Shaq/Ortiz 8.00 20.00
D2 Thom/Pipp/Strg/Yzer 10.00 25.00
D3 Vale/Drex/Bogg/Chav 12.00 30.00
D4 Howe/Hays/Robi/Jack 12.00 30.00

2013 Sportkings Double Memorabilia Silver
ANNOUNCED PRINT RUN 60
DM3 F.Thomas/D.Ortiz 6.00 15.00
DM5 P.Martinez/M.Rivera 6.00 15.00

2013 Sportkings Four Sport Silver
ANNOUNCED PRINT RUN 19
FSQM1 Thom/Shaq/Cohn/Will 8.00 20.00
FSQM2 Vale/Pipp/Hays/Ortiz 10.00 25.00
FSQM3 Rive/Drex/Howe/Strug 12.00 30.00
FSQM4 Ortiz/Robi/Chav/Yama 12.00 30.00

2013 Sportkings Mini
*MINI: .5X TO 1.2X BASIC CARDS
STATED ODDS 1:2

2013 Sportkings Premium Back
*PREM.BACK: .5X TO 1.2X BASIC CARDS
ONE PREMIUM BACK PER BOX
288 David Ortiz SP 30.00 60.00

2013 Sportkings Quad Memorabilia Silver
ANNOUNCED PRINT RUN 40
QM1 Rive/Thom/Bogg/Ortiz 12.00 30.00

2013 Sportkings Single Memorabilia Silver
ANNOUNCED PRINT RUN 90
SM3 Brooks Robinson 6.00 15.00
SM5 David Ortiz 5.00 12.00
SM6 David Ortiz/19* 8.00 20.00
SM7 Fernando Valenzuela 5.00 12.00
SM8 Frank Thomas 6.00 15.00
SM13 Mariano Rivera 6.00 15.00
SM14 Pedro Martinez 5.00 12.00
SM21 Wade Boggs 5.00 12.00

2013 Sportkings Triple Memorabilia Silver
ANNOUNCED PRINT RUN 40
TM2 Pedro/Rivera/Valenzuela 8.00 20.00
TM4 Ortiz/Robinson/Thomas 10.00 25.00

2009 Sportkings National Convention VIP Promo
COMPLETE SET (7)
2 Leslie/Namath/Flutie/Tretiak/Oliva/Taro 5.00 12.00
3 Cepeda/Negreanu/Walcott
Slater/Piper/Schmidt 4.00 10.00
5 Lewis/Jackson/Thorpe/Warner
Seabiscuit/Joyner-Kersee 5.00 12.00

2010 Sportkings National Convention VIP Promo
2 Duke Snider 1.25 3.00
16 Mark McGwire 6.00 15.00

1953 Sport Magazine Premiums
This 10-card set features 5 1/2" by 7" color portraits and was issued as a subscription premium by Sport Magazine. These photos were taken by noted sports photographer Ozzie Sweet. Each features a top player from a number of different sports. The photo backs are blank and unnumbered. We've checklisted the set below in alphabetical order.
COMPLETE SET (10) 30.00 60.00
1 Joe Black BB 5.00 10.00
6 Stan Musial BB 7.50 15.00
8 Allie Reynolds BB 5.00 10.00
9 Robin Roberts BB 6.00 12.00
10 Bobby Shantz BB 4.00 8.00

1968-73 Sport Pix
These 8" by 10" blank-backed photos feature black and white photos with the players name and the words "Sport Pix" on the bottom. The address for Sport Pix is also on the bottom. Since the cards are not numbered, we have sequenced them in alphabetical order.
COMPLETE SET (22) 150.00 300.00
12 Willie Mays 12.50 25.00
15 Casey Stengel 7.50 15.00
22 Ted Williams 12.50 25.00

1981 Sportrait Hall of Fame
This 25-card set measures approximately 3 5/8" by 5" and features a Hall of Fame player's sketch by Stan Sypulski inside a thin color frame on a white background. The player's name and card number are printed at the bottom in the frame color. The backs are blank.
COMPLETE SET (25) 8.00 20.00
1 Honus Wagner .40 1.00
2 Miller Huggins .20 .50
3 Babe Ruth 1.50 4.00
4 Connie Mack .20 .50
5 Ty Cobb 1.25 3.00
6 Lou Gehrig 1.25 3.00
7 Eddie Collins .30 .75
8 Chuck Klein .20 .50
9 Ted Williams 1.25 3.00
10 Jimmy Foxx .40 1.00
(Jimmie)
11 Frank Baker .20 .50
12 Nap Lajoie .30 .75
13 Casey Stengel .30 .75
14 Joe Dimaggio 1.25 3.00
15 Mickey Mantle 1.50 4.00
16 Frank Frisch .20 .50
17 Bill Terry .20 .50
18 Jackie Robinson 1.00 2.50
19 Sam Rice .20 .50
20 Mickey Cochrane .20 .50
21 George Sisler .30 .75
22 Bob Feller .40 1.00
23 Walter Johnson .40 1.00
24 Tris Speaker .40 1.00
NNO Checklist .08 .25

1970 Sports Cards for Collectors Old-Timer Postcards
This 32-card set was issued by Sports Cards for Collectors of New York and features black-and-white portraits and action photos of some of baseball's old-timer great players in white borders. Some of the cards display facsimile player autographs. The backs carry a postcard format.
COMPLETE SET (32) 20.00 50.00
1 Title Card 1.50 4.00
Babe Ruth
Lou Gehrig
2 Larry Doby .40 1.00
3 Mike Garcia .20 .50
4 Bob Feller .60 1.50
5 Early Wynn .40 1.00
6 Burleigh Grimes .40 1.00
7 Rabbit Maranville .40 1.00
8 Babe Ruth 2.00 5.00
Batting
9 Lou Gehrig 1.50 4.00
10 Joe Dimaggio 1.50 4.00
11 Ty Cobb 1.50 4.00
12 Lou Boudreau .40 1.00
13 Jimmy Foxx 1.25 3.00
(Jimmie)
14 Casey Stengle .60 1.50
15 Kenesaw Landis .40 1.00
16 Max Carey .40 1.00
17 Wilbert Robinson .40 1.00
18 Paul Richards .20 .50
19 Zack Wheat .40 1.00
20 Rube Marquard .40 1.00
21 Dave Bancroft .20 .50
22 Bobby Thomson .20 .50
23 Melvin Ott .60 1.50
24 Bobo Newsom .20 .50
25 John Mize .40 1.00
26 Walker Cooper .20 .50
27 Dixie Walker .20 .50
28 Augie Galan .20 .50
29 George Stirnweiss .20 .50
30 Floyd Herman .20 .50
31 Babe Ruth 2.00 5.00
Glove on knee
32 Babe Ruth 2.00 5.00
Waist up

1977-79 Sportscaster Series 1
COMPLETE SET (24) 17.50 35.00
121 Tom Seaver 2.00 4.00

1977-79 Sportscaster Series 2
COMPLETE SET (24) 30.00 60.00
208 Joe DiMaggio 5.00 10.00
216 1969 Mets 5.00 10.00

1977-79 Sportscaster Series 3
COMPLETE SET (24) 15.00 30.00
316 Henry Aaron 2.50 5.00

1977-79 Sportscaster Series 4
COMPLETE SET (24) 15.00 30.00
422 Johnny Bench 2.00 4.00

1977-79 Sportscaster Series 5
COMPLETE SET (24) 12.50 25.00
511 Babe Ruth 4.00 8.00
514 Bobby Thomson .75 1.50
522 The 1927 Yankees 1.00 2.00

1977-79 Sportscaster Series 6
COMPLETE SET (24) 12.50 25.00
624 Johnny Vander Meer .75 1.50

1977-79 Sportscaster Series 7
COMPLETE SET (24) 15.00 30.00
716 Roger Maris 5.00 10.00

1977-79 Sportscaster Series 8
COMPLETE SET (24) 12.50 25.00
804 Pete Rose 2.50 5.00

1977-79 Sportscaster Series 9
COMPLETE SET (24) 15.00 30.00
923 Jackie Robinson 7.50 15.00

1977-79 Sportscaster Series 10
COMPLETE SET (24) 17.50 35.00
1006 The Hall of Fame .75 1.50
1007 Rod Carew 1.25 2.50

1977-79 Sportscaster Series 11
COMPLETE SET (25) 20.00 40.00
1106 Willie Mays 2.50 5.00
1109 The Rules 1.50 3.00
Hank Aaron

1977-79 Sportscaster Series 12
COMPLETE SET (24) 12.50 25.00
1207 Ernie Banks 1.50 3.00

1977-79 Sportscaster Series 13
COMPLETE SET (24) 12.50 25.00
1303 Ted Williams 4.00 8.00
1305 Glenn Davis .75 1.50

1977-79 Sportscaster Series 14
COMPLETE SET (24) 17.50 35.00
1410 Jim Hunter 1.25 2.50
1411 Maury Wills .75 1.50

1977-79 Sportscaster Series 15
COMPLETE SET (24) 12.50 25.00
1509 A Century and a Half of History 1.00 2.00
Johnny Bench

1977-79 Sportscaster Series 16
COMPLETE SET (24) 15.00 30.00
1607 Brooks Robinson 1.25 2.50

1977-79 Sportscaster Series 17
COMPLETE SET (24) 10.00 20.00
1704 Randy Jones .50 1.00

1977-79 Sportscaster Series 18
COMPLETE SET (24) 12.50 25.00
1805 Joe Morgan 1.25 2.50
1811 Mark Fidrych 1.50 3.00
1816 Lingo II .75 1.50

1977-79 Sportscaster Series 19
COMPLETE SET (24) 25.00 50.00
1920 Gaylord Perry .75 1.50

1977-79 Sportscaster Series 20
COMPLETE SET (24) 7.50 15.00
2002 The Astrodome .25 .50
2005 Thurman Munson 1.50 3.00

1977-79 Sportscaster Series 21
COMPLETE SET (24) 15.00 30.00
2104 Lingo I .50 1.00
2105 Joe Rudi .50 1.00
2109 Vada Pinson .50 1.00
2116 Stan Musial 2.00 4.00

1977-79 Sportscaster Series 23
COMPLETE SET (24) 20.00 40.00
2304 Nolan Ryan 15.00 30.00
2323 Warren Spahn 1.50 3.00

1977-79 Sportscaster Series 24
COMPLETE SET (24) 10.00 20.00
2416 Lou Brock 1.25 2.50

1977-79 Sportscaster Series 25
COMPLETE SET (24) 10.00 20.00
2518 Frank Tanana .75 1.50

1977-79 Sportscaster Series 26
COMPLETE SET (24) 15.00 30.00
2615 Jim Palmer 1.50 3.00

1977-79 Sportscaster Series 27
COMPLETE SET (24) 12.50 25.00
2702 Steve Carlton 1.50 3.00
2721 Dave Kingman .75 1.50

1977-79 Sportscaster Series 29
COMPLETE SET (24) 17.50 35.00
2902 The Perfect Game 2.00 4.00
2922 At-A-Glance 1.00 2.00

1977-79 Sportscaster Series 30
COMPLETE SET (24) 12.50 25.00
3003 Triple Crown 1.25 2.50
3016 Ron Cey .75 1.50

1977-79 Sportscaster Series 31
COMPLETE SET (24) 12.50 25.00
3101 Instruction 1.25 2.50

1977-79 Sportscaster Series 32
COMPLETE SET (24) 17.50 35.00
3201 The 3000 Hit Club 10.00 20.00
3204 Tommy John .75 1.50
3217 Cy Young Award 1.25 2.50

1977-79 Sportscaster Series 33
COMPLETE SET (24) 10.00 20.00
3305 Keeping Score .25 .50

1977-79 Sportscaster Series 34
COMPLETE SET (24) 15.00 30.00
3402 Four Home Runs In 4.00 8.00
3419 All-Star Game 1.25 2.50
3424 Greg Luzinski .50 1.00

1977-79 Sportscaster Series 35
COMPLETE SET (24) 15.00 30.00
3502 Infield Fly Rule .75 1.50
3504 John Candelaria .75 1.50
3515 Interference 1.50 3.00

1977-79 Sportscaster Series 36
COMPLETE SET (24) 15.00 30.00
3601 Ron LeFlore .50 1.00

1977-79 Sportscaster Series 37
Please note that cards number 4 and 17 are not listed. Any information on the two missing cards is very appreciated.
COMPLETE SET (24) 12.50 25.00
3709 Pickoff .75 1.50
3722 NCAA Tournament .50 1.00

1977-79 Sportscaster Series 38
COMPLETE SET (24) 20.00 40.00
3809 George Brett 7.50 15.00
3810 Jim Rice 1.00 2.00

1977-79 Sportscaster Series 39
COMPLETE SET (24) 7.50 15.00
3902 Rundown .75 1.50
3904 Measurements .25 .50

1977-79 Sportscaster Series 40
COMPLETE SET (24) 10.00 20.00
4001 Garry Templeton .50 1.00
4002 Jeff Burroughs .50 1.00

1977-79 Sportscaster Series 41
COMPLETE SET (24) 20.00 40.00
4103 Relief Pitching .50 1.00
4107 Triple Play .50 1.00

1977-79 Sportscaster Series 42
COMPLETE SET (24) 15.00 30.00
4208 Dave Parker .75 1.50
4209 Bert Blyleven .75 1.50

1977-79 Sportscaster Series 43
COMPLETE SET (24) 12.50 25.00
4307 Rick Reuschel .50 1.00

1977-79 Sportscaster Series 44
COMPLETE SET (24) 12.50 25.00
4417 Hidden Ball Trick .75 1.50

1977-79 Sportscaster Series 45
Card number 11 is not in our checklist. Any information on this missing card is greatly appreciated.
COMPLETE SET (24) 20.00 40.00
4517 Hit and Run .75 1.50
4522 Hitting the Cutoff .75 1.50

1977-79 Sportscaster Series 46
COMPLETE SET (24) 12.50 25.00
4622 Amateur Draft .50 1.00

1977-79 Sportscaster Series 47
COMPLETE SET (24) 17.50 35.00
4702 Great Moments 1.00 2.00
4705 Great Moments 1.25 2.50

1977-79 Sportscaster Series 50
COMPLETE SET (24) 15.00 30.00
5007 Dennis Eckersley 2.00 4.00

1977-79 Sportscaster Series 51
COMPLETE SET (24) 20.00 40.00
5102 The Double Steal .75 1.50
5103 Cy Young 1.50 3.00

1977-79 Sportscaster Series 52
COMPLETE SET (24) 10.00 20.00
5202 Gene Tenace .50 1.00
5209 Great Moments .75 1.50

1977-79 Sportscaster Series 53
COMPLETE SET (24) 15.00 30.00
5307 Andre Thornton .50 1.00

1977-79 Sportscaster Series 54
COMPLETE SET (24) 15.00 30.00
5408 Great Moments 1.25 2.50
5409 Freddie Patek .50 1.00

1977-79 Sportscaster Series 55
COMPLETE SET (24) 12.50 25.00
5503 Lyman Bostock .75 1.50

1977-79 Sportscaster Series 56
COMPLETE SET (24) 37.50 75.00
5613 Carlton Fisk 5.00 10.00

1977-79 Sportscaster Series 57
COMPLETE SET (24) 40.00 80.00
5702 Dave Winfield 6.00 12.00

1977-79 Sportscaster Series 58
COMPLETE SET (24) 25.00 50.00
5801 Shea Stadium 1.00 2.00
5802 Busch Memorial 1.00 2.00
5805 Fenway Park 2.50 5.00
5812 Baltimore Memorial 1.00 2.00
5814 Yankee Stadium 2.50 5.00
5818 Candlestick Park 2.00 4.00
5821 Veterans Stadium 1.00 2.00
5823 Dodger Stadium 1.00 2.00

1977-79 Sportscaster Series 59
COMPLETE SET (24) 50.00 100.00
5920 Frank Robinson 4.00 8.00

1977-79 Sportscaster Series 60
COMPLETE SET (24) 37.50 75.00
6023 Sandy Koufax 5.00 10.00

1977-79 Sportscaster Series 61
COMPLETE SET (24) 50.00 100.00
6102 Ron Guidry 2.00 4.00
6116 Roberto Clemente 12.50 25.00

1977-79 Sportscaster Series 62
COMPLETE SET (24) 40.00 80.00
6204 Don Larsen's 2.50 5.00

1977-79 Sportscaster Series 63
COMPLETE SET (24) 30.00 60.00
6318 Gil Hodges 4.00 8.00

1977-79 Sportscaster Series 65
COMPLETE SET (24) 40.00 80.00
6518 Vida Blue 1.50 3.00

1977-79 Sportscaster Series 66
COMPLETE SET (24) 37.50 75.00
6615 Designated Hitter 2.50 5.00

1977-79 Sportscaster Series 67
COMPLETE SET (24) 40.00 80.00
6701 Steve Garvey 2.50 5.00
6715 The Presidential 2.50 5.00

1977-79 Sportscaster Series 68
COMPLETE SET (24) 40.00 80.00
6810 7th Game of the 2.00 4.00
6818 Babe Ruth Baseball 2.00 4.00

1977-79 Sportscaster Series 69
COMPLETE SET (24) 40.00 80.00
6906 Roy Campanella 5.00 10.00
6917 Little League To 2.00 4.00

1977-79 Sportscaster Series 70
COMPLETE SET (24) 30.00 60.00
7013 The Dean Brothers 2.50 5.00

1977-79 Sportscaster Series 71
COMPLETE SET (24) 40.00 80.00
7103 J.R. Richard 2.00 4.00

1977-79 Sportscaster Series 72
COMPLETE SET (24) 50.00 100.00
7209 High School Record 2.00 4.00
7213 Hitting Pitchers 4.00 8.00

1977-79 Sportscaster Series 73
COMPLETE SET (24) 40.00 80.00
7315 Emmett Ashford 2.00 4.00

1977-79 Sportscaster Series 74
COMPLETE SET (24) 200.00 400.00
7401 Forever Blowing 2.50 5.00
7410 Phil Niekro 4.00 8.00
7423 The Forsch Brothers 2.00 4.00

1977-79 Sportscaster Series 75
COMPLETE SET (24) 30.00 60.00
7509 Tommy Lasorda 4.00 8.00
7513 Fellowship of 2.00 4.00
7515 Hack Wilson 2.50 5.00
7524 The Firemen 4.00 8.00

1977-79 Sportscaster Series 76
COMPLETE SET (24) 30.00 60.00
7611 Iron Mike 1.00 2.00
7619 Training Camps 1.00 2.00

1977-79 Sportscaster Series 77
COMPLETE SET (24) 150.00 300.00
7708 Monty Stratton 2.50 5.00
7713 Ron Taylor 2.00 4.00

1977-79 Sportscaster Series 78
COMPLETE SET (24) 150.00 300.00
7816 Willie McCovey 4.00 8.00

1977-79 Sportscaster Series 79
COMPLETE SET (24) 60.00 120.00
7911 Craig Swan 1.50 3.00

1977-79 Sportscaster Series 80
COMPLETE SET (24) 62.50 125.00
8021 Umpires Strike 2.50 5.00

1977-79 Sportscaster Series 81
COMPLETE SET (24) 62.50 125.00
8124 Wrigley Marathlon 7.50 15.00

1977-79 Sportscaster Series 82
COMPLETE SET (24) 50.00 100.00
8219 Bobby Bonds 3.00 6.00

1977-79 Sportscaster Series 83
COMPLETE SET (24) 62.50 125.00
8309 Billy Martin 4.00 8.00
8321 Brother vs. Brother 3.00 6.00

1977-79 Sportscaster Series 84
COMPLETE SET (24) 60.00 120.00
8408 Triple Play 3.00 6.00
8415 The Money Game 4.00 8.00
8418 Clemente Award 3.00 6.00

1977-79 Sportscaster Series 85
COMPLETE SET (24) 62.50 125.00
8504 Like Father 2.50 5.00
8513 Walkie-Talkie 6.00 12.00

1977-79 Sportscaster Series 86
COMPLETE SET (24) 50.00 100.00
8608 Danny Ainge 15.00 40.00

1977-79 Sportscaster Series 87
This series contains two cards numbered 4.
COMPLETE SET (24) 60.00 120.00
8712 Lee Mazzilli 3.00 6.00
8718 Steve Dembowski 2.00 4.00
8720 Hutch Award 7.50 15.00

1977-79 Sportscaster Series 88
COMPLETE SET (24) 50.00 100.00
8803 Dave Winfield 7.50 15.00
8824 Cape Cod League 2.50 5.00

1977-79 Sportscaster Series 101
COMPLETE SET (24) 62.50 125.00
10122 400-Homer Club 4.00 8.00

1977-79 Sportscaster Series 102
COMPLETE SET (24) 75.00 150.00
10201 Mike Flanagan 3.00 6.00
10210 Boston's Fenway 3.00 6.00
10224 Jim Piersall 3.00 6.00

1984-85 Sports Design Products West
This 48-card standard-sized set was issued in two series and featured the drawings of sports artist Doug West. The set was produced and distributed by Sports Design Products (Charlie Mandel).
COMPLETE SET (48) 12.00 30.00
1 Jackie Robinson .60 1.50
2 Luis Aparicio .20 .50
3 Roberto Clemente .60 1.50
4 Mickey Mantle .75 2.00
5 Joe DiMaggio .75 2.00
6 Willie Stargell .20 .50
7 Brooks Robinson .30 .75
8 Ty Cobb .60 1.50
9 Don Drysdale .20 .50
10 Bob Feller .30 .75
11 Stan Musial .40 1.00
12 Al Kaline .20 .50
13 Willie Mays .60 1.50
14 Willie McCovey .20 .50
15 Thurman Munson .08 .25
16 Charlie Gehringer .20 .50
17 Eddie Mathews .20 .50
18 Carl Yastrzemski .20 .50
19 Warren Spahn .20 .50
20 Ted Williams .60 1.50
21 Ernie Banks .30 .75
22 Roy Campanella .30 .75
23 Harmon Killebrew .20 .50
24 Duke Snider .20 .50
25 Lou Gehrig .60 1.50
26 Hoyt Wilhelm .20 .50
27 Enos Slaughter .20 .50
28 Lou Brock .20 .50
29 Mickey Cochrane .20 .50
30 Gil Hodges .20 .50
31 Yogi Berra .40 1.00
32 Carl Hubbell .20 .50
33 Hank Greenberg .20 .50
34 Pee Wee Reese .40 1.00
35 Casey Stengel MG .40 1.00
36 Ralph Kiner .20 .50
37 Satchel Paige .60 1.50
38 Richie Ashburn UER .40 1.00
Spelled Ritchie
39 Connie Mack MG .20 .50
40 Dick Groat .08 .25
41 Tony Oliva .08 .25
42 Honus Wagner .40 1.00
43 Denny McLain .08 .25
44 Johnny Mize .20 .50
45 Bob Lemon .20 .50
46 Ferguson Jenkins .20 .50
47 Babe Ruth 1.00 2.50
48 Ted Kluszewski .20 .50

1986 Sports Design J.D. McCarthy
This 24-card standard-size set features the photography of J.D. McCarthy. The fronts have a similar design to the 1969 Topps issue, while the back identifies the player.
COMPLETE SET (24) 3.00 8.00
1 J.D. McCarthy .40 1.00
Ted Williams
2 Lou Brock .30 .75
3 Carl Yastrzemski .30 .75
4 Mickey Mantle 1.00 2.50
5 Roger Maris .60 1.50
6 Walter Alston .08 .25
7 Ernie Banks .40 1.00
8 Billy Williams .30 .75
9 Hank Aaron .75 2.00
10 Brooks Robinson .40 1.00
11 Joe DiMaggio .75 2.00
12 Casey Stengel .30 .75
13 Juan Marichal .40 1.00
14 Jim Bunning .30 .75
15 Matty Alou .08 .25
16 Eddie Mathews .20 .50
17 Sandy Koufax .60 1.50
18 Roberto Clemente .75 2.00
19 Gil Hodges .30 .75
Ernie Banks
20 Duke Snider .30 .75
21 Robin Roberts .20 .50
22 Willie Mays .75 2.00
23 Willie Stargell .20 .50
24 Whitey Ford .30 .75

1946-49 Sports Exchange W603
These cards measuring approximately 7" by 10" were issued by Sports Exchange between 1946 and 1949. The cards are numbered but we have sequenced them alphabetically within series. This set is considered one of the first "collector-issued" sets as many copies were sold through what was then considered a small group of dedicated collectors.
COMPLETE SET (117) 1250.00 2500.00
1-1A Phil Cavaretta 7.50 15.00
1-1B Bill Dickey 25.00 50.00
2-Jan John 'Al' Benton 6.00 12.00
3-Jan Harry Brecheen 7.50 15.00
4-Jan Jimmy Foxx 30.00 60.00
(Jimmie)
5-Jan Edwin Dyer 6.00 12.00
6-Jan Ewell Blackwell 7.50 15.00
7-Jan Floyd Bevens 6.00 12.00
8-Jan Nick Altrock 6.00 12.00
9-Jan George Case 6.00 12.00
10-Jan Lu Blue 6.00 12.00
11-Jan Ralph Branca- 7.50 15.00
Ken Keltner
12-Jan Gene Bearden 6.00 12.00
2-1A Walker Cooper 6.00 12.00
2-1B Bob Doerr 10.00 20.00
2-Feb Lou Boudreau 20.00 40.00
3-Feb Dom DiMaggio 10.00 20.00
4-Feb Frank Frisch 20.00 40.00
5-Feb Charlie Grimm 7.50 15.00
6-Feb Jimmy Outlaw 6.00 12.00
7-Feb Hugh Casey 6.00 12.00
8-Feb Mark Christman 6.00 12.00
9-Feb Jake Early 6.00 12.00
10-Feb Bruce Edwards 6.00 12.00
11-Feb Mickey Cochrane- 10.00 20.00
Bob Dillinger
12-Feb Ben Chapman 6.00 12.00
3-1A Dave Ferriss 6.00 12.00
3-1B Bob Feller 20.00 40.00
2-Mar Spud Chandler 7.50 15.00
3-Mar Del Ennis 7.50 15.00
4-Mar Lou Gehrig 125.00 250.00
5-Mar William Herman 12.50 25.00
6-Mar Andy Pafko 7.50 15.00
7-Mar Sam Chapman 6.00 12.00
8-Mar Earle Combs 12.50 25.00
9-Mar Carl Furillo 10.00 20.00
10-Mar Elbie Fletcher 6.00 12.00
11-Mar Dizzy Dean- 12.50 25.00
Edwin Joost
12-Mar Steve Gromek 6.00 12.00
4-1A George Kurowski 6.00 12.00
4-1B Hank Greenberg 12.50 25.00
2-Apr Jeff Heath 6.00 12.00
3-Apr Al Evans 6.00 12.00
4-Apr Lefty Grove 30.00 60.00
5-Apr Ted Lyons 12.50 25.00
6-Apr Pee Wee Reese 12.50 25.00
7-Apr Joe DiMaggio 100.00 200.00
8-Apr Travis Jackson 10.00 20.00
9-Apr Augie Galan 6.00 12.00
10-Apr Joe Gordon 7.50 15.00
11-Apr Joe Jackson- 75.00 150.00
Wally Westlake
12-Apr Jim Hegan 6.00 12.00
5-1A Marty Marion 7.50 15.00
5-1B George McQuinn 6.00 12.00
2-May Kirby Higbe 6.00 12.00
3-May John Lindell 6.00 12.00
4-May Bill Hallahan 6.00 12.00
5-May Lefty O'Doul 7.50 15.00
6-May Phil Rizzuto 25.00 50.00
7-May Tommy Henrich 7.50 15.00
8-May Bob Muncrief 6.00 12.00
9-May Berthold Haas 6.00 12.00
10-May Tommy Holmes 7.50 15.00
11-May Larry Jansen- 12.50 25.00
Yogi Berra
12-May Bob Lemon 12.50 25.00
6-1A Truett'Rip' Sewell 6.00 12.00
6-1B Ray Mueller 6.00 12.00
2-Jun Tex Hughson 6.00 12.00
3-Jun John Mize 12.50 25.00
4-Jun Rogers Hornsby 30.00 60.00
5-Jun Steve O'Neil 6.00 12.00
6-Jun Buddy Rosar 6.00 12.00
7-Jun Ralph Kiner 12.50 25.00
9-Jun John Hopp 6.00 12.00
10-Jun Bill Johnson 6.00 12.00
11-Jun Harry Lowrey- 7.50 15.00
Heinie Manush
12-Jun Billy Meyer 6.00 12.00
7-1A Ed Stanky 7.50 15.00
7-1B Hal Newhouser 10.00 20.00
2-Jul Stan Musial 50.00 100.00
3-Jul Johnny Pesky 7.50 15.00
4-Jul Carl Hubbell 12.50 25.00
5-Jul Herb Pennock 12.50 25.00
6-Jul Johnny Sain 7.50 15.00
7-Jul Harry Lavagetto 7.50 15.00
8-Jul Joe Page 7.50 15.00
9-Jul John 'Buddy' Kelly 6.00 12.00
10-Jul Phil Masi 6.00 12.00
12-Jul Dale Mitchell 6.00 12.00
8-1A Fred'Dixie' Walker 6.00 12.00
8-1B Dick Wakefield 6.00 12.00
2-Aug Howie Pollet 6.00 12.00
3-Aug Harold Reiser 7.50 15.00
4-Aug Babe Ruth 150.00 300.00
5-Aug Luke Sewell 7.50 15.00
6-Aug Dizzy Trout 6.00 12.00
7-Aug Vic Lombardi 6.00 12.00
8-Aug Honus Wagner 50.00 100.00
9-Aug Ray Lamanno 6.00 12.00
10-Aug George Munger 6.00 12.00
12-Aug Red Rolfe 6.00 12.00
9-1B Ted Williams 75.00 150.00
2-Sep Enos Slaughter 12.50 25.00
3-Sep Aaron Robinson 6.00 12.00
4-Sep Hack Wilson 12.50 25.00
5-Sep William Southworth 6.00 12.00
6-Sep Harry Walker 6.00 12.00
7-Sep Cecil Travis 6.00 12.00
8-Sep Mickey Witek 6.00 12.00
9-Sep Warren Spahn 20.00 40.00
10-Sep Vern Stephens 6.00 12.00
12-Sep Sibbi Sisti 6.00 12.00
3-Oct Bos. Red Sox-1946 7.50 15.00
12-Oct Zach Taylor 6.00 12.00
3-Nov St.L.Cardinals-1946 7.50 15.00
12-Nov Earl Torgeson 6.00 12.00
12-Dec Mickey Vernon 7.50 15.00

1977 Sports Illustrated Ad Cards
This set is a multi-sport set and features cards with action player photos from various sports as they appeared on different covers of Sports Illustrated Magazine. The cards measure approximately 3 1/2" by 4 3/4" with the backs displaying the player's name and team name and information on how to subscribe to the magazine at a special rate. It was issued by Mrs. Carter Breads.
COMPLETE SET 12.50 25.00
1 George Brett 4.00 10.00
2 George Foster 1.50 3.00
3 Bump Wills 1.50 3.00

1997 Sports Illustrated
The 1997 Sports Illustrated set (created by Fleer) was issued in one series totalling 180 cards. Each pack contained six cards and carried a $1.99 SRP. The fronts feature Sports Illustrated action player photos with player stories on the backs. The set contains the topical subsets: Fresh Faces (1-27), Season Highlights (28-36), Inside Baseball (37-54), S.I.BER Vision 55-72) and Classic Covers (169-180). An unnumbered Jose Cruz Jr. foldout checklist was also seeded in approximately 1:4 packs.
COMPLETE SET (180) 15.00 40.00
SUBSET CARDS HALF VALUE OF BASE CARDS
1 Bob Abreu .20 .50
2 Jaime Bluma .10 .30
3 Emil Brown RC .10 .30
4 Jose Cruz Jr. RC .20 .50
5 Jason Dickson .10 .30
6 Nomar Garciaparra .50 1.25
7 Todd Greene .10 .30
8 Vladimir Guerrero .30 .75
9 Wilton Guerrero .10 .30
10 Jose Guillen .10 .30
11 Hideki Irabu RC .20 .50
12 Russ Johnson .10 .30
13 Andruw Jones .20 .50
14 Damon Mashore .10 .30
15 Jason McDonald .10 .30
16 Ryan McGuire .10 .30
17 Matt Morris .10 .30
18 Kevin Orie .10 .30
19 Dante Powell .10 .30
20 Pokey Reese .10 .30
21 Joe Roa RC .10 .30
22 Scott Rolen .20 .50
23 Glendon Rusch .10 .30
24 Scott Spiezio .10 .30
25 Bubba Trammell RC .20 .50
26 Todd Walker .10 .30
27 Jamey Wright .10 .30
28 Ken Griffey Jr. SH .40 1.00

29 Tino Martinez SH .10 .30
30 Roger Clemens SH .30 .75
31 Hideki Irabu SH .10 .30
32 Kevin Brown SH .10 .30
33 C.Ripken .40 1.00
C.Jones SH
34 Sandy Alomar Jr. SH .10 .30
35 Ken Caminiti SH .10 .30
36 Randy Johnson SH .20 .50
37 Andy Ashby IB .10 .30
38 Jay Buhner IB .10 .30
39 Joe Carter IB .10 .30
40 Darren Daulton IB .10 .30
41 Jeff Fassero IB .10 .30
42 Andres Galarraga IB .10 .30
43 Rusty Greer IB .10 .30
44 Marquis Grissom IB .10 .30
45 Joey Hamilton IB .10 .30
46 Jimmy Key IB .10 .30
47 Ryan Klesko IB .10 .30
48 Eddie Murray IB .20 .50
49 Charles Nagy IB .10 .30
50 Dave Nilsson IB .10 .30
51 Ricardo Rincon IB RC .10 .30
52 Billy Wagner IB .10 .30
53 Dan Wilson IB .10 .30
54 Dmitri Young IB .10 .30
55 Roberto Alomar SIV .10 .30
56 Sandy Alomar Jr. SIV .10 .30
57 Scott Brosius SIV .10 .30
58 Tony Clark SIV .10 .30
59 Carlos Delgado SIV .10 .30
60 Jermaine Dye SIV .10 .30
61 Darin Erstad SIV .10 .30
62 Derek Jeter SIV .40 1.00
63 Jason Kendall SIV .10 .30
64 Hideo Nomo SIV .10 .30
65 Rey Ordonez SIV .10 .30
66 Andy Pettitte SIV .10 .30
67 Manny Ramirez SIV .10 .30
68 Edgar Renteria SIV .10 .30
69 Shane Reynolds SIV .10 .30
70 Alex Rodriguez SIV .30 .75
71 Ivan Rodriguez SIV .10 .30
72 Jose Rosado SIV .10 .30
73 John Smoltz .20 .50
74 Tom Glavine .20 .50
75 Greg Maddux .50 1.25
76 Chipper Jones .30 .75
77 Kenny Lofton .10 .30
78 Fred McGriff .20 .50
79 Kevin Brown .10 .30
80 Alex Fernandez .10 .30
81 Al Leiter .10 .30
82 Bobby Bonilla .10 .30
83 Gary Sheffield .10 .30
84 Moises Alou .10 .30
85 Henry Rodriguez .10 .30
86 Mark Grudzielanek .10 .30
87 Pedro Martinez .20 .50
88 Todd Hundley .10 .30
89 Bernard Gilkey .10 .30
90 Bobby Jones .10 .30
91 Curt Schilling .10 .30
92 Ricky Bottalico .10 .30
93 Mike Lieberthal .10 .30
94 Sammy Sosa .30 .75
95 Ryne Sandberg .50 1.25
96 Mark Grace .20 .50
97 Deion Sanders .20 .50
98 Reggie Sanders .10 .30
99 Barry Larkin .20 .50
100 Craig Biggio .20 .50
101 Jeff Bagwell .20 .50
102 Derek Bell .10 .30
103 Brian Jordan .10 .30
104 Ray Lankford .10 .30
105 Ron Gant .10 .30
106 Al Martin .10 .30
107 Kevin Elster .10 .30
108 Jermaine Allensworth .10 .30
109 Vinny Castilla .10 .30
110 Dante Bichette .10 .30
111 Larry Walker .10 .30
112 Mike Piazza .50 1.25
113 Eric Karros .10 .30
114 Todd Hollandsworth .10 .30
115 Raul Mondesi .10 .30
116 Hideo Nomo .30 .75
117 Ramon Martinez .10 .30
118 Ken Caminiti .10 .30
119 Tony Gwynn .40 1.00
120 Steve Finley .10 .30
121 Barry Bonds .75 2.00
122 J.T. Snow .10 .30
123 Rod Beck .10 .30
124 Cal Ripken 1.00 2.50
125 Mike Mussina .20 .50
126 Brady Anderson .10 .30
127 Bernie Williams .20 .50
128 Derek Jeter .75 2.00
129 Tino Martinez .20 .50
130 Andy Pettitte .20 .50
131 David Cone .10 .30
132 Mariano Rivera .30 .75
133 Roger Clemens .60 1.50
134 Pat Hentgen .10 .30
135 Juan Guzman .10 .30
136 Bob Higginson .10 .30
137 Tony Clark .10 .30
138 Travis Fryman .10 .30
139 Mo Vaughn .10 .30
140 Tim Naehring .10 .30
141 John Valentin .10 .30
142 Matt Williams .10 .30
143 David Justice .10 .30
144 Jim Thome .20 .50
145 Chuck Knoblauch .10 .30
146 Paul Molitor .10 .30
147 Marty Cordova .10 .30
148 Frank Thomas .30 .75
149 Albert Belle .10 .30
150 Robin Ventura .10 .30
151 John Jaha .10 .30
152 Jeff Cirillo .10 .30
153 Jose Valentin .10 .30
154 Jay Bell .10 .30
155 Jeff King .10 .30
156 Kevin Appier .10 .30
157 Ken Griffey Jr. .60 1.50
158 Alex Rodriguez .50 1.25
159 Randy Johnson .30 .75
160 Juan Gonzalez .10 .30
161 Will Clark .20 .50
162 Dean Palmer .10 .30
163 Tim Salmon .20 .50
164 Jim Edmonds .10 .30
165 Jim Leyritz .10 .30
166 Jose Canseco .20 .50
167 Jason Giambi .10 .30
168 Mark McGwire .75 2.00
169 Barry Bonds CC .40 1.00
170 Alex Rodriguez CC .30 .75
171 Roger Clemens CC .30 .75
172 Ken Griffey Jr. CC .40 1.00
173 Greg Maddux CC .30 .75
174 Mike Piazza CC .30 .75
175 M.McGwire .30 .75
W.Clark CC
176 Hideo Nomo CC .10 .30
177 Cal Ripken CC .50 1.25
178 K.Griffey Jr. .40 1.00
F.Thomas CC
179 A.Rodriguez .50 1.25
D.Jeter CC
180 John Wetteland CC .10 .30
P158 Alex Rodriguez Promo .60 1.50
NNO Jose Cruz Jr. CL .08 .25

1997 Sports Illustrated Extra Edition

*STARS: 6X TO 15X BASIC CARDS
*ROOKIES: 3X TO 8X BASIC CARDS
RANDOM INSERTS IN PACKS
STATED PRINT RUN 500 SERIAL #'d SETS

1997 Sports Illustrated Autographed Mini-Covers

1 Alex Rodriguez 30.00 80.00
2 Cal Ripken 25.00 60.00
3 Kirby Puckett 60.00 120.00
4 Willie Mays 100.00 250.00
5 Frank Robinson 20.00 50.00
6 Hank Aaron 125.00 200.00

1997 Sports Illustrated Cooperstown Collection

COMPLETE SET (12) 25.00 60.00
STATED ODDS 1:12
1 Hank Aaron 4.00 10.00
2 Yogi Berra 2.50 6.00
3 Lou Brock 2.00 5.00
4 Rod Carew 2.00 5.00
5 Juan Marichal 2.00 5.00
6 Al Kaline 2.50 6.00
7 Joe Morgan 2.00 5.00
8 Brooks Robinson 2.00 5.00
9 Willie Stargell 2.00 5.00
10 Kirby Puckett 2.00 5.00
11 Willie Mays 5.00 12.00
12 Frank Robinson 2.00 5.00

1997 Sports Illustrated Great Shots

COMPLETE SET (25) 3.00 8.00
STATED ODDS ONE PER PACK
1 Chipper Jones .20 .50
2 Ryan Klesko .07 .20
3 Kenny Lofton .07 .20
4 Greg Maddux .30 .75
5 John Smoltz .10 .30
6 Roberto Alomar .07 .20
7 Cal Ripken .60 1.50
8 Mo Vaughn .07 .20
9 Albert Belle .07 .20
10 Frank Thomas .20 .50
11 Ryne Sandberg .30 .75
12 Deion Sanders .10 .30
13 V.Castilla .07 .20
A.Galarraga
14 Eric Karros .07 .20
15 Mike Piazza .30 .75
16 Derek Jeter .50 1.25
17 Mark McGwire .50 1.25
18 Darren Daulton .07 .20
19 Andy Ashby .07 .20
20 Barry Bonds .50 1.25
21 Jay Buhner .07 .20
22 Randy Johnson .20 .50
23 Alex Rodriguez .30 .75
24 Juan Gonzalez .07 .20
25 Ken Griffey Jr. .40 1.00

1998 Sports Illustrated

The 1998 Sports Illustrated set (created by Fleer) was issued in one series totalling 200 cards and was distributed in six-card packs with a suggested retail price of $1.99. The cards feature exclusive Sports Illustrated photography and commentary. The set contains the topical subsets: Baseball's Best (129-148), One to Watch (149-176/201), and 97 in Review (177-200). A Travis Lee One to Watch subset card (number 201) was inserted into the product just before going to press. Though official numbers were never released, it appears the card was seeded into approximately one in every four boxes, making it about two times tougher to pull than any of the other regular issue cards. Notable Rookie Cards include Magglio Ordonez. Also, a 3 1/2" by 5" Alex Rodriguez bonus card was randomly inserted one in every six packs displaying an action color player photo with the complete Sports Illustrated checklist printed on the card. In addition a promotional card featuring Alex Rodriguez was distributed to dealers and hobby media severia weeks prior to the products release. The "Promotional Sample" text running diagonally across the front and back of the card makes it easy to distinguish.

COMPLETE SET (200) 10.00 25.00
COMP.SET DOES NOT INCLUDE SP 201
1 Edgardo Alfonzo .10 .30
2 Roberto Alomar .20 .50
3 Sandy Alomar Jr. .10 .30
4 Moises Alou .10 .30
5 Brady Anderson .10 .30
6 Garret Anderson .10 .30
7 Kevin Appier .10 .30
8 Jeff Bagwell .20 .50
9 Jay Bell .10 .30
10 Albert Belle .10 .30
11 Dante Bichette .10 .30
12 Craig Biggio .20 .50
13 Barry Bonds .75 2.00
14 Bobby Bonilla .10 .30
15 Kevin Brown .20 .50
16 Jay Buhner .10 .30
17 Ellis Burks .10 .30
18 Mike Cameron .10 .30
19 Ken Caminiti .10 .30
20 Jose Canseco .20 .50
21 Joe Carter .10 .30
22 Vinny Castilla .10 .30
23 Jeff Cirillo .10 .30
24 Tony Clark .10 .30
25 Will Clark .20 .50
26 Roger Clemens .60 1.50
27 David Cone .10 .30
28 Jose Cruz Jr. .10 .30
29 Carlos Delgado .10 .30
30 Jason Dickson .10 .30
31 Dennis Eckersley .10 .30
32 Jim Edmonds .10 .30
33 Scott Erickson .10 .30
34 Darin Erstad .10 .30
35 Shawn Estes .10 .30
36 Jeff Fassero .10 .30
37 Alex Fernandez .10 .30
38 Chuck Finley .10 .30
39 Steve Finley .10 .30
40 Travis Fryman .10 .30
41 Andres Galarraga .10 .30
42 Ron Gant .10 .30
43 Nomar Garciaparra .50 1.25
44 Jason Giambi .10 .30
45 Tom Glavine .20 .50
46 Juan Gonzalez .10 .30
47 Mark Grace .20 .50
48 Willie Greene .10 .30
49 Rusty Greer .10 .30
50 Ben Grieve .10 .30
51 Ken Griffey Jr. .60 1.50
52 Mark Grudzielanek .10 .30
53 Vladimir Guerrero .30 .75
54 Juan Guzman .10 .30
55 Tony Gwynn .40 1.00
56 Joey Hamilton .10 .30
57 Rickey Henderson .30 .75
58 Pat Hentgen .10 .30
59 Livan Hernandez .10 .30
60 Bobby Higginson .10 .30
61 Todd Hundley .10 .30
62 Hideki Irabu .10 .30
63 John Jaha .10 .30
64 Derek Jeter .75 2.00
65 Charles Johnson .10 .30
66 Randy Johnson .30 .75
67 Andruw Jones .20 .50
68 Bobby Jones .10 .30
69 Chipper Jones .30 .75
70 Brian Jordan .10 .30
71 David Justice .10 .30
72 Eric Karros .10 .30
73 Jeff Kent .10 .30
74 Jimmy Key .10 .30
75 Darryl Kile .10 .30
76 Jeff King .10 .30
77 Ryan Klesko .10 .30
78 Chuck Knoblauch .10 .30
79 Ray Lankford .10 .30
80 Barry Larkin .20 .50
81 Kenny Lofton .10 .30
82 Greg Maddux .50 1.25
83 Al Martin .10 .30
84 Edgar Martinez .20 .50
85 Pedro Martinez .20 .50
86 Tino Martinez .20 .50
87 Mark McGwire .75 2.00
88 Paul Molitor .10 .30
89 Raul Mondesi .10 .30
90 Jamie Moyer .10 .30
91 Mike Mussina .20 .50
92 Tim Naehring .10 .30
93 Charles Nagy .10 .30
94 Denny Neagle .10 .30
95 Dave Nilsson .10 .30
96 Hideo Nomo .30 .75
97 Rey Ordonez .10 .30
98 Dean Palmer .10 .30
99 Rafael Palmeiro .20 .50
100 Andy Pettitte .20 .50
101 Mike Piazza .50 1.25
102 Brad Radke .10 .30
103 Manny Ramirez .20 .50
104 Edgar Renteria .10 .30
105 Cal Ripken 1.00 2.50
106 Alex Rodriguez .50 1.25
107 Henry Rodriguez .10 .30
108 Ivan Rodriguez .20 .50
109 Scott Rolen .20 .50
110 Tim Salmon .20 .50
111 Curt Schilling .10 .30
112 Gary Sheffield .10 .30
113 John Smoltz .20 .50
114 J.T. Snow .10 .30
115 Sammy Sosa .30 .75
116 Matt Stairs .10 .30
117 Shannon Stewart .10 .30
118 Frank Thomas .30 .75
119 Jim Thome .20 .50
120 Justin Thompson .10 .30
121 Mo Vaughn .10 .30
122 Robin Ventura .10 .30
123 Larry Walker .10 .30
124 Rondell White .10 .30
125 Bernie Williams .20 .50
126 Matt Williams .10 .30
127 Tony Womack .10 .30
128 Jaret Wright .10 .30
129 Edgar Renteria BB .10 .30
130 Kenny Lofton BB .10 .30
131 Tony Gwynn BB .20 .50
132 Mark McGwire BB .40 1.00
133 Craig Biggio BB .10 .30
134 Charles Johnson BB .10 .30
135 J.T. Snow BB .10 .30
136 Ken Caminiti BB .10 .30
137 Vladimir Guerrero BB .20 .50
138 Jim Edmonds BB .10 .30
139 Randy Johnson BB .20 .50
140 Darryl Kile BB .10 .30
141 John Smoltz BB .10 .30
142 Greg Maddux BB .30 .75
143 Andy Pettitte BB .10 .30
144 Ken Griffey Jr. BB .40 1.00
145 Mike Piazza BB .30 .75
146 Todd Greene BB .10 .30
147 Vinny Castilla BB .10 .30
148 Derek Jeter BB .40 1.00
149 Robert Machado OW RC .10 .30
150 Mike Gulan OW RC .10 .30
151 Randall Simon OW .10 .30
152 Michael Coleman OW .10 .30
153 Brian Rose OW .10 .30
154 Scott Eyre OW .10 .30
155 Magglio Ordonez OW RC 1.00 2.50
156 Todd Helton OW .20 .50
157 Juan Encarnacion OW .10 .30
158 Mark Kotsay OW .10 .30
159 Josh Booty OW .10 .30
160 Melvin Rosario OW .10 .30
161 Shane Halter OW .10 .30
162 Paul Konerko OW .10 .30
163 Henry Blanco OW .10 .30
164 Antone Williamson OW .10 .30
165 Brad Fullmer OW .10 .30
166 Ricky Ledee OW .10 .30
167 Ben Grieve OW .10 .30
168 Frank Catalanotto OW RC .20 .50
169 Bobby Estalella OW .10 .30
170 Dennis Reyes OW .10 .30
171 Kevin Polcovich OW .10 .30
172 Jacob Cruz OW .10 .30
173 Ken Cloude OW .10 .30
174 Eli Marrero OW .10 .30
175 Fernando Tatis OW .10 .30
176 Tom Evans OW .10 .30
177 R.Palmeiro .20 .50
C.Jones '97
178 Eric Davis '97 .10 .30
179 Roger Clemens '97 .30 .75
180 B.Butler .20 .50
E.Murray '97
181 Frank Thomas '97 .20 .50
182 Curt Schilling '97 .10 .30
183 Jeff Bagwell '97 .10 .30
184 K.Griffey Jr. .40 1.00
M.McGwire '97
185 Kevin Brown '97 .10 .30
186 M.Cordova .10 .30
R.Rincon '97
187 Charles Johnson '97 .10 .30
188 Hideki Irabu '97 .10 .30
189 Tony Gwynn '97 .20 .50
190 Sandy Alomar Jr. '97 .10 .30
191 Ken Griffey Jr. '97 .40 1.00
192 Larry Walker '97 .10 .30
193 Roger Clemens '97 .30 .75
194 Pedro Martinez '97 .20 .50
195 Nomar Garciaparra '97 .30 .75
196 Scott Rolen '97 .10 .30
197 Brian Anderson '97 .10 .30
198 Tony Saunders '97 .10 .30
199 Florida Celebration '97 .10 .30
200 Livan Hernandez '97 .10 .30
201 Travis Lee OW SP .75 2.00
P106 Alex Rodriguez PROMO .75 2.00
NNO Alex Rodriguez CL .20 .50

1998 Sports Illustrated Extra Edition

*STARS: 6X TO 15X BASIC CARDS
*ROOKIES: 4X TO 10X BASIC CARDS
RANDOM INSERTS IN PACKS
STATED PRINT RUN 250 SERIAL #'d SETS

1998 Sports Illustrated Autographs

RANDOM INSERTS IN PACKS
PRINT RUNS LISTED BELOW
EXCHANGE DEADLINE: 11/1/99
1 Lou Brock/500 12.00 30.00
2 Jose Cruz Jr./250 6.00 15.00
3 Rollie Fingers/500 6.00 15.00
4 Ben Grieve/250 6.00 15.00
5 Paul Konerko/250 10.00 25.00
6 Brooks Robinson/500 10.00 25.00

1998 Sports Illustrated Covers

COMPLETE SET (10) 10.00 25.00
STATED ODDS 1:9
C1 K.Griffey 2.00 5.00
M.Piazza
C2 Derek Jeter 2.50 6.00
C3 Ken Griffey Jr. 2.00 5.00
C4 Cal Ripken 3.00 8.00
C5 Manny Ramirez .60 1.50
C6 Jay Buhner .40 1.00
C7 Matt Williams .40 1.00
C8 Randy Johnson 1.00 2.50
C9 Deion Sanders .40 1.00
C10 Jose Canseco .60 1.50

1998 Sports Illustrated Editor's Choice

COMPLETE SET (10) 30.00 80.00
STATED ODDS 1:24
EC1 Ken Griffey Jr. 5.00 12.00
EC2 Alex Rodriguez 4.00 10.00
EC3 Frank Thomas 2.50 6.00
EC4 Mark McGwire 6.00 15.00
EC5 Greg Maddux 4.00 10.00
EC6 Derek Jeter 6.00 15.00
EC7 Cal Ripken 8.00 20.00
EC8 Nomar Garciaparra 4.00 10.00
EC9 Jeff Bagwell 1.50 4.00
EC10 Jose Cruz Jr. 1.00 2.50

1998 Sports Illustrated Opening Day Mini Posters

COMPLETE SET (30) 4.00 10.00
OD1 Tim Salmon .10 .30
OD2 Matt Williams .07 .20
OD3 J.Smoltz .30 .75
G.Maddux
OD4 Cal Ripken .60 1.50
OD5 Nomar Garciaparra .30 .75
OD6 Sammy Sosa .20 .50
OD7 Frank Thomas .20 .50
OD8 Barry Larkin .10 .30
OD9 David Justice .07 .20
OD10 Larry Walker .07 .20
OD11 Tony Clark .07 .20
OD12 Livan Hernandez .07 .20
OD13 Jeff Bagwell .10 .30
OD14 Kevin Appier .07 .20
OD15 Mike Piazza .30 .75
OD16 Fernando Vina .07 .20
OD17 Paul Molitor .07 .20
OD18 Vladimir Guerrero .20 .50
OD19 Rey Ordonez .07 .20
OD20 Bernie Williams .10 .30
OD21 Matt Stairs .07 .20
OD22 Curt Schilling .07 .20
OD23 Tony Womack .07 .20
OD24 Mark McGwire .50 1.25
OD25 Tony Gwynn .25 .60
OD26 Barry Bonds .50 1.25
OD27 Ken Griffey Jr. .40 1.00
OD28 Fred McGriff .10 .30
OD29 J.Gonzalez .10 .30
I.Rodriguez
OD30 Roger Clemens .40 1.00

1999 Sports Illustrated

Released in mid-March, 1999, this set was produced by Fleer/SkyBox. Each pack contained six cards and carried an SRP of $1.99. The 180-card basic set features full-bleed action player photos printed on thick 20-pt. stock and contains the following subsets: Post-Season (1-9), Award Winners (10-20), Season Highlights (21-41), Prospects 2000 (42-71) and Checklists (179-180). In addition, a Kerry Wood sample card was distributed to dealers and hobby media a few months prior to the product's release. The card can be easily identified by the bold "SAMPLE" text running diagonally across the back.

COMPLETE SET (180) 20.00 50.00
COMMON RC .08 .25
1 Yankees POST .50 1.25
Derek Jeter
2 Scott Brosius POST .07 .20
3 David Wells POST .07 .20
4 Sterling Hitchcock POST .07 .20
5 David Justice POST .07 .20
6 David Cone POST .07 .20
7 Greg Maddux POST .30 .75
8 Jim Leyritz POST .07 .20
9 Gary Gaetti POST .07 .20
10 M.McGwire .40 1.00
K.Griffey Jr. AW
11 S.Sosa .10 .30
J.Gonzalez AW
12 L.Walker .10 .30
B.Williams AW
13 T.Womack .20 .50
R.Henderson AW
14 Glav .10 .30
Clem
Cone
Helling AW
15 C.Schilling .20 .50
R.Clemens AW
16 G.Maddux .30 .75
R.Clemens AW
17 T.Hoffman .10 .30
T.Gordon AW
18 K.Wood .07 .20
B.Grieve AW
19 T.Glavine .20 .50
R.Clemens AW
20 S.Sosa .10 .30
J.Gonzalez AW
21 Travis Lee SH .07 .20
22 Roberto Alomar SH .10 .30
23 Roger Clemens SH .30 .75
24 Barry Bonds SH .40 1.00
25 Paul Molitor SH .07 .20
26 Todd Stottlemyre SH .07 .20
27 Chris Hoiles SH .07 .20
28 Albert Belle SH .07 .20
29 Tony Clark SH .07 .20
30 Kerry Wood SH .07 .20
31 David Wells SH .07 .20
32 Dennis Eckersley SH .10 .30
33 Mark McGwire SH .40 1.00
34 Cal Ripken SH .50 1.25
35 Ken Griffey Jr. SH .40 1.00
36 Alex Rodriguez SH .30 .75
37 Craig Biggio SH .10 .30
38 Sammy Sosa SH .20 .50
39 Dennis Martinez SH .07 .20
40 Curt Schilling SH .07 .20
41 Orlando Hernandez SH .07 .20
42 Ben Molina RC .30 .75
T.Glaus
43 M.Meluskey .07 .20
D.Ward
M.Grzanich RC
44 Eric Chavez .10 .30
45 R.Halladay .30 .75
K.Witt
46 B.Chen .07 .20
G.Lombard
47 R.Roque RC .07 .20
R.Belliard
V. de los Santos
48 J.D. Drew .10 .30
49 Jose Nieves RC .07 .20
50 Mike Duvall RC .07 .20
51 Bryan Corey RC .07 .20
52 P.LoDuca .10 .30
A.Pena
J.Kubenka
53 Fernando Seguignol .07 .20
54 R.Martinez RC .07 .20
W.Delgado
A.Rios
55 J.Cabrera RC .07 .20
Branyan
Rakers
56 C.Guillen .10 .30
D.Holdridge RC
G.Guevara RC
57 A.Gonzalez .07 .20
J.Fontenot
P.Wilson
58 M.Kinkade .07 .20
J.Payton
M.Yoshii
59 C.Pickering .07 .20
R.Minor
60 B.Davis .07 .20
M.Clement
61 M.Anderson .07 .20
G.Bennett RC
62 Aramis Ramirez .10 .30
63 Robert Sasser RC .07 .20
64 K.Glauber .07 .20
G.Garcia
E.Priest
65 B.Barkley .07 .20
J.Ho Cho
D.Sadler
66 D.Gibson .07 .20
M.Strittmatter
E.Clemente
67 Je.Giambi .07 .20
D.Brown
68 Gabe Kapler .10 .30
69 C.Koskie .10 .30
A.J.Pierzynski
B.Sampson
70 B.Simmons .07 .20
M.Johnson
C.Wilson
71 R.Bradley .10 .30
M.Lowell
J.Tessmer
72 Ben Grieve .07 .20
73 Shawn Green .10 .30
74 Rafael Palmeiro .20 .50
75 Juan Gonzalez .10 .30
76 Mike Piazza .50 1.25
77 Devon White .10 .30
78 Jim Thome .20 .50
79 Barry Larkin .20 .50
80 Scott Rolen .20 .50
81 Raul Mondesi .10 .30
82 Jason Giambi .10 .30
83 Jose Canseco .20 .50
84 Tony Gwynn .40 1.00
85 Cal Ripken 1.00 2.50
86 Andy Pettitte .20 .50
87 Carlos Delgado .10 .30
88 Jeff Cirillo .10 .30
89 Bret Saberhagen .10 .30
90 John Olerud .10 .30
91 Ron Coomer .07 .20
92 Todd Helton .20 .50
93 Ray Lankford .10 .30
94 Tim Salmon .20 .50
95 Fred McGriff .20 .50
96 Matt Stairs .07 .20
97 Ken Griffey Jr. .60 1.50
98 Chipper Jones .30 .75
99 Mark Grace .20 .50
100 Ivan Rodriguez .20 .50
101 Jeromy Burnitz .10 .30
102 Kenny Rogers .10 .30
103 Kevin Millwood .10 .30
104 Vinny Castilla .10 .30
105 Jim Edmonds .10 .30
106 Craig Biggio .20 .50
107 Andres Galarraga .10 .30
108 Sammy Sosa .30 .75
109 Juan Encarnacion .07 .20
110 Larry Walker .10 .30
111 John Smoltz .20 .50
112 Randy Johnson .30 .75
113 Bobby Higginson .10 .30
114 Albert Belle .10 .30
115 Jaret Wright .07 .20
116 Edgar Renteria .10 .30
117 Andruw Jones .20 .50
118 Barry Bonds .75 2.00
119 Rondell White .10 .30
120 Jamie Moyer .10 .30
121 Darin Erstad .10 .30
122 Al Leiter .10 .30
123 Mark McGwire .75 2.00
124 Mo Vaughn .10 .30
125 Livan Hernandez .10 .30
126 Jason Kendall .10 .30
127 Frank Thomas .30 .75
128 Denny Neagle .07 .20
129 Johnny Damon .20 .50
130 Derek Bell .07 .20
131 Jeff Kent .10 .30
132 Tony Womack .07 .20
133 Trevor Hoffman .10 .30
134 Gary Sheffield .10 .30
135 Tino Martinez .20 .50
136 Travis Fryman .10 .30
137 Rolando Arrojo .07 .20
138 Dante Bichette .10 .30
139 Nomar Garciaparra .50 1.25
140 Moises Alou .10 .30
141 Chuck Knoblauch .10 .30
142 Robin Ventura .10 .30
143 Scott Erickson .07 .20
144 David Cone .10 .30
145 Greg Vaughn .07 .20
146 Wade Boggs .20 .50
147 Mike Mussina .20 .50
148 Tony Clark .07 .20
149 Alex Rodriguez .50 1.25
150 Javy Lopez .10 .30
151 Bartolo Colon .10 .30
152 Derek Jeter .75 2.00
153 Greg Maddux .50 1.25
154 Kevin Brown .20 .50
155 Curt Schilling .10 .30
156 Jeff King .07 .20
157 Bernie Williams .20 .50
158 Roberto Alomar .20 .50
159 Travis Lee .07 .20
160 Kerry Wood .10 .30
161 Jeff Bagwell .20 .50
162 Roger Clemens .60 1.50
163 Matt Williams .10 .30
164 Chan Ho Park .10 .30
165 Damion Easley .07 .20
166 Manny Ramirez .20 .50
167 Quinton McCracken .07 .20
168 Todd Walker .07 .20
169 Eric Karros .10 .30
170 Will Clark .20 .50
171 Edgar Martinez .20 .50
172 Cliff Floyd .10 .30
173 Vladimir Guerrero .30 .75
174 Tom Glavine .20 .50
175 Pedro Martinez .20 .50
176 Chuck Finley .10 .30
177 Dean Palmer .10 .30
178 Omar Vizquel .20 .50
179 Checklist .07 .20
180 Checklist .07 .20
S160 Kerry Wood Sample .40 1.00

1999 Sports Illustrated Diamond Dominators

COMPLETE SET (10) 40.00 100.00
STATED ODDS 1:90 PITCHER/1:180 HITTER
1 Kerry Wood 2.00 5.00
2 Roger Clemens 6.00 15.00
3 Randy Johnson 5.00 12.00
4 Greg Maddux 6.00 15.00
5 Pedro Martinez 3.00 8.00
6 Ken Griffey Jr. 10.00 25.00
7 Sammy Sosa 5.00 12.00
8 Nomar Garciaparra 3.00 8.00
9 Mark McGwire 8.00 20.00
10 Alex Rodriguez 6.00 15.00

1999 Sports Illustrated Fabulous 40's

COMPLETE SET (13) 25.00 60.00
STATED ODDS 1:20
1 Mark McGwire 5.00 12.00
2 Sammy Sosa 2.00 5.00
3 Ken Griffey Jr. 4.00 10.00
4 Greg Vaughn .50 1.25
5 Albert Belle .75 2.00
6 Jose Canseco 1.25 3.00
7 Vinny Castilla .75 2.00
8 Juan Gonzalez .75 2.00
9 Manny Ramirez 1.25 3.00
10 Andres Galarraga .75 2.00
11 Rafael Palmeiro 1.25 3.00
12 Alex Rodriguez 3.00 8.00
13 Mo Vaughn .75 2.00

1999 Sports Illustrated Fabulous 40's Extra

RANDOM INSERTS IN PACKS
PRINT RUNS BASED ON HR'S HIT IN 1998
1 Mark McGwire/70 30.00 60.00
2 Sammy Sosa/66 10.00 25.00
3 Ken Griffey Jr./56 300.00 500.00
4 Greg Vaughn/50 4.00 10.00
5 Albert Belle/49 4.00 10.00
6 Jose Canseco/46 6.00 15.00
7 Vinny Castilla/46 4.00 10.00
8 Juan Gonzalez/45 4.00 10.00
9 Manny Ramirez/45 6.00 15.00
10 Andres Galarraga/44 4.00 10.00
11 Rafael Palmeiro/43 6.00 15.00
12 Alex Rodriguez/42 15.00 40.00
13 Mo Vaughn/40 4.00 10.00

1999 Sports Illustrated Headliners

COMPLETE SET (25) 15.00 40.00
STATED ODDS 1:4
1 Vladimir Guerrero .60 1.50
2 Randy Johnson .60 1.50
3 Mo Vaughn .25 .60
4 Chipper Jones .60 1.50
5 Jeff Bagwell .40 1.00
6 Juan Gonzalez .25 .60
7 Mark McGwire 1.50 4.00
8 Cal Ripken 2.00 5.00
9 Frank Thomas .60 1.50
10 Manny Ramirez .40 1.00
11 Ken Griffey Jr. 1.25 3.00
12 Scott Rolen .40 1.00
13 Alex Rodriguez 1.00 2.50
14 Barry Bonds 1.50 4.00
15 Roger Clemens 1.25 3.00
16 Darin Erstad .25 .60
17 Nomar Garciaparra 1.00 2.50
18 Mike Piazza 1.00 2.50
19 Greg Maddux 1.00 2.50
20 Ivan Rodriguez .40 1.00
21 Derek Jeter 1.50 4.00
22 Sammy Sosa .60 1.50
23 Andruw Jones .40 1.00
24 Pedro Martinez .40 1.00
25 Kerry Wood .25 .60

1999 Sports Illustrated One's To Watch

COMPLETE SET (15) 8.00 20.00
STATED ODDS 1:12
DREW AU RANDOM INSERT IN PACKS
1 J.D. Drew .60 1.50
2 Marlon Anderson .40 1.00
3 Roy Halladay 1.50 4.00
4 Ben Grieve .40 1.00
5 Todd Helton 1.00 2.50
6 Gabe Kapler .60 1.50
7 Troy Glaus 1.50 4.00
8 Ben Davis .40 1.00
9 Eric Chavez .60 1.50
10 Richie Sexson .60 1.50
11 Fernando Seguignol .40 1.00
12 Kerry Wood .60 1.50
13 Bobby Smith .40 1.00
14 Ryan Minor .40 1.00
15 Jeremy Giambi .40 1.00
NNO J.D. Drew AU/250 5.00 12.00

1999 Sports Illustrated Greats of the Game

The 1999 Sports Illustrated Greats of the Game (created by Fleer) was issued in one series totalling 90 cards and was distributed in seven-card packs with a suggested retail price of $15. The fronts feature color photos of some of Baseball's greatest players (including reproductions of numerous SI front covers). The backs carry player information.

COMPLETE SET (90) 30.00 80.00
1 Jimmie Foxx .60 1.50
2 Red Schoendienst .40 1.00
3 Babe Ruth 2.00 5.00
4 Lou Gehrig 1.25 3.00
5 Mel Ott .60 1.50
6 Stan Musial 1.00 2.50
7 Mickey Mantle 2.50 6.00
8 Carl Yastrzemski 1.00 2.50
9 Enos Slaughter .25 .60
10 Andre Dawson .25 .60
11 Luis Aparicio .25 .60
12 Ferguson Jenkins .25 .60
13 Christy Mathewson .60 1.50
14 Ernie Banks .60 1.50
15 Johnny Podres .25 .60
16 George Foster .25 .60
17 Jerry Koosman .25 .60
18 Curt Simmons .15 .40
19 Bob Feller .25 .60
20 Frank Robinson .40 1.00
21 Gary Carter .25 .60
22 Frank Thomas .15 .40
23 Bill Lee .25 .60
24 Willie Mays 1.25 3.00
25 Tommie Agee .25 .60
26 Boog Powell .25 .60
27 Jim Wynn .25 .60
28 Sparky Lyle .25 .60
29 Bo Belinsky .15 .40
30 Maury Wills .25 .60
31 Bill Buckner .25 .60
32 Steve Carlton .25 .60
33 Harmon Killebrew .60 1.50
34 Nolan Ryan 1.50 4.00
35 Randy Jones .15 .40
36 Robin Roberts .25 .60
37 Al Oliver .25 .60
38 Rico Petrocelli .15 .40
39 Dave Parker .25 .60
40 Eddie Mathews .60 1.50
41 Earl Weaver .25 .60
42 Jackie Robinson .60 1.50
43 Lou Brock .40 1.00
44 Reggie Jackson .40 1.00
45 Bob Gibson .40 1.00
46 Jeff Burroughs .15 .40
47 Jim Bouton .25 .60
48 Bob Forsch .15 .40
49 Ron Guidry .25 .60
50 Ty Cobb 1.00 2.50
51 Roy White .25 .60
52 Joe Rudi .25 .60
53 Moose Skowron .25 .60
54 Goose Gossage .25 .60
55 Ed Kranepool .15 .40
56 Paul Blair .15 .40
57 Kent Hrbek .25 .60
58 Orlando Cepeda .25 .60
59 Buck O'Neill .25 .60
60 Al Kaline .60 1.50
61 Vida Blue .25 .60
62 Sam McDowell .15 .40
63 Jesse Barfield .15 .40
64 Dave Kingman .25 .60
65 Ron Santo .40 1.00
66 Steve Garvey .25 .60
67 Gaylord Perry .25 .60
68 Darrell Evans .25 .60
69 Rollie Fingers .25 .60
70 Walter Johnson .60 1.50
71 Al Hrabosky .25 .60
72 Mickey Rivers .15 .40
73 Mike Torrez .15 .40
74 Hank Bauer .25 .60
75 Tug McGraw .25 .60
76 David Clyde .15 .40
77 Jim Lonborg .15 .40
78 Clete Boyer .25 .60
79 Harry Walker .15 .40
80 Cy Young .60 1.50
81 Bud Harrelson .15 .40
82 Paul Splittorff .15 .40
83 Bert Campaneris .25 .60
84 Joe Niekro .25 .60
85 Bob Horner .25 .60
86 Jerry Royster .15 .40
87 Tommy John .25 .60
88 Mark Fidrych .25 .60
89 Dick Williams .25 .60
90 Graig Nettles .25 .60

1999 Sports Illustrated Greats of the Game Autographs

ONE CARD PER PACK
NNO CARDS LISTED IN ALPHABETICAL ORDER
1 Tommie Agee 5.00 12.00
2 Luis Aparicio 6.00 15.00
3 Ernie Banks 30.00 80.00
4 Jesse Barfield 5.00 12.00
5 Hank Bauer 8.00 20.00
6 Bo Belinsky 5.00 12.00
7 Paul Blair 5.00 12.00
8 Vida Blue 5.00 12.00
9 Jim Bouton 5.00 12.00
10 Clete Boyer 5.00 12.00
11 Lou Brock 10.00 25.00
12 Bill Buckner 12.00 30.00
13 Jeff Burroughs 5.00 12.00
14 Bert Campaneris 5.00 12.00
15 Steve Carlton 8.00 20.00
16 Gary Carter 15.00 40.00
17 Orlando Cepeda 6.00 15.00
18 David Clyde 5.00 12.00
19 Andre Dawson 10.00 25.00
20 Darrell Evans 5.00 12.00
21 Bob Feller 6.00 15.00
22 Mark Fidrych 20.00 50.00
23 Rollie Fingers 5.00 12.00
24 Bob Forsch 6.00 15.00
25 George Foster 5.00 12.00
26 Steve Garvey 5.00 12.00
27 Bob Gibson 20.00 50.00
28 Goose Gossage 5.00 12.00
29 Ron Guidry 5.00 12.00
30 Bud Harrelson 5.00 12.00
31 Bob Horner 5.00 12.00
32 Al Hrabosky 5.00 12.00
33 Kent Hrbek 6.00 15.00
34A Reggie Jackson 75.00 150.00
34B R.Jackson Mr. October 125.00 200.00
34C R.Jackson HOF 93 150.00 250.00
35 Ferguson Jenkins 5.00 12.00
36 Tommy John 5.00 12.00
37 Randy Jones 5.00 12.00
38 Al Kaline 25.00 50.00
39 Harmon Killebrew 8.00 20.00
40 Dave Kingman 6.00 15.00
41 Jerry Koosman 5.00 12.00
42 Ed Kranepool 5.00 12.00
43 Bill Lee 6.00 15.00
44 Jim Lonborg 5.00 12.00
45 Sparky Lyle 5.00 12.00
46 Eddie Mathews 20.00 50.00
47 Willie Mays 150.00 250.00
48 Sam McDowell 5.00 12.00
49 Tug McGraw 5.00 12.00
50 Stan Musial 40.00 100.00
51 Graig Nettles 6.00 15.00
52 Joe Niekro 5.00 12.00
53 Buck O'Neill 15.00 40.00
54 Al Oliver 5.00 12.00
55 Dave Parker 10.00 25.00
56 Gaylord Perry 8.00 20.00
57 Rico Petrocelli 5.00 12.00
58 Johnny Podres 5.00 12.00
59 Boog Powell 5.00 12.00
60 Mickey Rivers 8.00 20.00
61 Robin Roberts 8.00 20.00
62 Frank Robinson 15.00 40.00
63 Jerry Royster 5.00 12.00
64 Joe Rudi 5.00 12.00
65 Nolan Ryan 50.00 120.00
66 Ron Santo 12.00 30.00
67 Red Schoendienst 5.00 12.00
68 Curt Simmons 5.00 12.00
69 Moose Skowron 5.00 12.00
70 Enos Slaughter 6.00 15.00
71 Paul Splittorff 5.00 12.00
72 Frank Thomas 5.00 12.00
73 Mike Torrez 5.00 12.00
74 Harry Walker 5.00 12.00
75 Earl Weaver 6.00 15.00
76 Roy White 5.00 12.00
77 Dick Williams 6.00 15.00
78 Maury Wills 5.00 12.00
79 Jim Wynn 5.00 12.00
80 Carl Yastrzemski 25.00 60.00

1999 Sports Illustrated Greats of the Game Cover Collection

COMPLETE SET (50) 25.00 60.00
ONE PER PACK
1 Johnny Podres .40 1.00
2 Mickey Mantle 4.00 10.00
3 Stan Musial 1.50 4.00
4 Eddie Mathews 1.00 2.50
5 Frank Thomas .25 .60
6 Willie Mays 2.00 5.00
7 Red Schoendienst .60 1.50
8 Luis Aparicio .40 1.00
9 Mickey Mantle 4.00 10.00
10 Al Kaline 1.00 2.50
11 Maury Wills .40 1.00
12 Sam McDowell .25 .60
13 Harry Walker .25 .60
14 Carl Yastrzemski 1.50 4.00
15 Carl Yastrzemski 1.50 4.00
16 Lou Brock .60 1.50
17 Ron Santo .60 1.50
18 Reggie Jackson .60 1.50
19 Frank Robinson .60 1.50
20 Jerry Koosman .40 1.00
21 Bud Harrelson .25 .60
22 Vida Blue .40 1.00
23 Ferguson Jenkins .40 1.00
24 Sparky Lyle .40 1.00
25 Steve Carlton .40 1.00
26 Bert Campaneris .40 1.00
27 Jim Wynn .40 1.00
28 Steve Garvey .40 1.00
29 Nolan Ryan 2.50 6.00
30 Randy Jones .25 .60
31 Reggie Jackson .60 1.50
32 Joe Rudi .40 1.00
33 Reggie Jackson .60 1.50
34 Dave Parker .40 1.00
35 Mark Fidrych .40 1.00
36 Earl Weaver .40 1.00
37 Nolan Ryan 2.50 6.00
38 Steve Carlton .40 1.00
39 Reggie Jackson .60 1.50
40 Rollie Fingers .40 1.00
41 Gary Carter .40 1.00
42 Graig Nettles .40 1.00
43 Gaylord Perry .40 1.00
44 Kent Hrbek .40 1.00
45 Gary Carter .40 1.00
46 Steve Garvey .40 1.00
47 Steve Carlton .40 1.00
48 Nolan Ryan 2.50 6.00
49 Nolan Ryan 2.50 6.00
50 Mickey Mantle 4.00 10.00

1999 Sports Illustrated Greats of the Game Record Breakers

COMPLETE SET (10) 60.00 120.00
STATED ODDS 1:12
*GOLD: 2X TO 5X BASIC RB'S
GOLD STATED ODDS 1:120
1 Mickey Mantle 12.50 30.00
2 Stan Musial 5.00 12.00
3 Babe Ruth 10.00 25.00
4 Christy Mathewson 3.00 8.00
5 Cy Young 3.00 8.00
6 Nolan Ryan 8.00 20.00
7 Jackie Robinson 3.00 8.00
8 Lou Gehrig 6.00 15.00
9 Ty Cobb 5.00 12.00
10 Walter Johnson 3.00 8.00

1999 Sports Illustrated Greats of the Game Record Breakers Gold

*GOLD: 2X TO 5X BASIC RB'S
STATED ODDS 1:120

1989 Sports Illustrated for Kids I

Since its debut issue in January 1989, SI for Kids has included a perforated sheet of nine standard-size cards bound into each magazine. The cards were consecutively numbered 1-324 through December 1991. The athletes featured represent an extremely wide spectrum of sports. Each card features color photos with variously colored borders. The borders are as follows: aqua (1-108), green (109-207), woodgrain (208-216), red (217-315), marble (316-324). The player's name is printed in a white bar at the top, while his or her sport appears at the bottom. The backs carry biographical information, career highlights, and a trivia question with answer. The cards' magazine issue date appears on the back in very small type. Although originally distributed in sheet form, the cards are frequently traded as singles. Thus, they are priced individually. The value of an intact sheet is equal to the sum of the nine cards plus a premium of up to 20%.

5 Orel Hershiser BB .40 1.00
11 Jose Canseco BB .75 2.00
20 Darryl Strawberry BB .40 1.00
31 Mike Greenwell BB .40 1.00
33 Tony Gwynn BB .75 2.00
35 Frank Viola BB .40 1.00
37 Don Mattingly BB 1.25 3.00
43 Ozzie Smith BB .75 2.00
46 Rickey Henderson BB .75 2.00
48 Chris Sabo BB .40 1.00
52 Andre Dawson BB .40 1.00
56 Alan Trammell BB .40 1.00
60 Roger Clemens BB 1.25 3.00
63 Andres Galarraga BB .40 1.00
64 John Franco BB .40 1.00
69 Cal Ripken Jr. BB 3.00 8.00
70 Will Clark BB .50 1.25
75 Bo Jackson BB .75 2.00
81 Nolan Ryan BB 2.00 5.00
90 Mike Schmidt BB .60 1.50

1990 Sports Illustrated for Kids I

112 Kevin Mitchell BB .20 .50
121 Ryne Sandberg BB 1.25 3.00
127 Robin Yount BB .75 2.00
133 Dave Stewart BB .40 1.00
140 Eric Davis BB .20 .50
144 Mike Scott BB .20 .50
146 Mark McGwire BB 1.25 3.00
151 Dwight Gooden BB .40 1.00
158 Ken Griffey Jr. BB 2.50 6.00
162 George Brett BB 1.25 3.00
165 Ruben Sierra BB .20 .50
167 Kirby Puckett BB .75 2.00
171 Carlton Fisk BB .60 1.50
172 Fred McGriff BB .60 1.50
176 Wade Boggs BB .60 1.50
178 Tim Raines BB .20 .50
181 Bobby Bonilla BB .20 .50
189 Kelly Gruber BB .10 .30
197 Dennis Eckersley BB .30 .75
205 Cecil Fielder BB .40 1.00
212 Jackie Robinson BB .75 2.00
216 George (Babe) Ruth BB 1.50 4.00

1991 Sports Illustrated for Kids I

229 Barry Bonds BB 1.25 3.00
240 Jose Rijo BB .10 .30
248 Sandy Alomar Jr. BB .20 .50
251 Ron Gant BB .20 .50
259 David Justice BB .60 1.50
261 Bob Welch BB .20 .50
266 Doug Drabek BB .10 .30
268 Rafael Palmeiro BB .50 1.25
271 Paul Molitor BB .40 1.00
275 Bobby Thigpen BB .20 .50
279 Edgar Martinez BB .50 1.25
282 Dave Winfield BB .40 1.00
283 Mark Grace BB .30 .75
288 Dwight Evans BB .10 .30
289 Dave Henderson BB .10 .30
294 Lee Smith BB .20 .50
303 Ramon Martinez BB .10 .30
320 Jim Thorpe .60 1.50
Track and Field
Football

Baseball
321 Ty Cobb BB .75 2.00

1992 Sports Illustrated for Kids II

Since its debut issue in January 1989, SI for Kids has included a perforated sheet of nine standard-size cards bound into each magazine. In January 1992, the card numbers started over again at 1. This listing comprises the cards contained from that magazine through the last 2000 issue. The athletes featured represent an extremely wide spectrum of sports. Each card features color photos with borders of various designs and colors. The borders are as follows: navy (1-9, 19-99), clouds (10-18, 55-63, 226-234), marble (100-108, 208-216, 316-324), pink (109-207), purple (217-225), blue (235-315), gold/silver (325-486), clouds (487-495) and gold/silver (496-621). The athlete's name is printed at the top while his or her sport appears at the bottom. The backs carry biographical information, career highlights, and a trivia question with answer. The cards' magazine issue date appears on the back in very small type. Although originally distributed in sheet form, the cards are frequently traded as singles. Thus, they are priced individually. The value of an intact sheet is equal to the sum of the nine cards plus a premium of up to 20 percent. The cards labeled as "MC" were issued in SI for Kids as part of a milk promotion.

24 Terry Pendleton BB .20 .50
29 Kirby Puckett BB .40 1.00
36 Roger Clemens BB .75 2.00
40 Tom Glavine BB .30 .75
45 Frank Thomas BB .40 1.00
50 Jim Abbott BB .20 .50
54 Roberto Alomar BB .30 .75
64 Matt Williams BB .20 .50
68 Bobby Bonilla BB .20 .50
72 Chuck Finley BB .20 .50
75 Danny Tartabull BB .20 .50
81 Jack Morris BB .20 .50
86 Will Clark BB .30 .75
108 Lou Gehrig BB .75 2.00

1993 Sports Illustrated for Kids II

121 Juan Gonzalez BB .20 .50
132 Cal Ripken Jr. BB 1.50 4.00
136 Jack McDowell BB .20 .50
144 Marquis Grissom BB .20 .50
145 Andy Van Slyke BB .20 .50
152 Dennis Eckersley BB .20 .50
157 Barry Bonds BB .75 2.00
162 Greg Maddux BB .60 1.50
168 Nolan Ryan BB 1.25 3.00
170 Dave Winfield BB .20 .50
173 Ken Griffey Jr. BB 1.50 4.00
178 Wade Boggs BB .30 .75
185 Kirk Gibson BB .20 .50
187 Albert Belle BB .20 .50
190 John Burkett BB .20 .50
196 John Kruk BB .20 .50
199 Randy Johnson BB .40 1.00
204 Lou Whitaker BB .20 .50
212 Yogi Berra BB .40 1.00

1994 Sports Illustrated for Kids II

236 Lenny Dykstra BB .20 .50
244 Carlos Baerga BB .20 .50
254 Joe Carter BB .20 .50
266 Chuck Carr BB .20 .50
268 Julie Croteau BB .20 .50
270 Michael Jordan BB 2.00 5.00
274 Andres Galarraga BB .20 .50
278 Jeff Bagwell BB .30 .75
281 John Olerud BB .20 .50
288 Tony Gwynn BB .40 1.00
292 Gregg Jefferies BB .20 .50
297 Mo Vaughn BB .20 .50
298 Moises Alou BB .20 .50
305 Jimmy Key BB .20 .50
311 Mike Mussina BB .30 .75
313 Mike Piazza BB .40 1.00
320 Stan Musial BB .40 1.00

1996 Sports Illustrated for Kids II

433 Chuck Knoblauch BB .20 .50
447 Chipper Jones BB .40 1.00
451 Tom Glavine BB .20 .50
kid photo
455 Cal Ripken BB 1.25 3.00
kid photo
462 Jeff Conine BB .20 .50
470 Hideo Nomo BB .40 1.00
475 Bernie Williams BB .30 .75
478 Craig Biggio BB .30 .75
485 Jose Mesa BB .20 .50
497 Roberto Alomar BB .30 .75
503 John Smoltz BB .30 .75
505 Henry Rodriguez BB .20 .50
513 Rey Ordonez BB .20 .50
516 Ellis Burks BB .20 .50
518 Ivan Rodriguez BB .30 .75

1997 Sports Illustrated for Kids II

543 Alex Rodriguez BB 1.25 3.00
553 Mo Vaughn BB .20 .50
561 Andy Pettitte BB .30 .75
562 Barry Bonds BB .75 2.00
572 Anfernee Hardaway .50 1.25
Ken Griffey Jr.
April Fool
582 Andruw Jones BB .30 .75
588 Brian Jordan BB .20 .50
589 Derek Jeter BB 1.50 4.00
596 Juan Gonzalez BB .20 .50
598 Andres Galarraga BB .20 .50
608 Mark McGwire BB .75 2.00
611 Pat Hentgen BB .20 .50
613 Tino Martinez BB .30 .75
617 Deion Sanders BB .30 .75
627 Cal Ripken BB .75 2.00
cartoon
634 Sandy Alomar BB .20 .50
641 Brady Anderson BB .20 .50

1998 Sports Illustrated for Kids II

652 Jeff Bagwell BB .30 .75
669 Larry Walker BB .20 .50
673 Roger Clemens BB .40 1.00
685 Frank Thomas BB .40 1.00
693 Denny Neagle BB .20 .50
695 Tony Gywnn BB .40 1.00
697 Mike Piazza BB .40 1.00
703 Kenny Lofton BB .20 .50
708 Moises Alou BB .20 .50
712 Dante Bichette BB .20 .50
720 John Wetteland BB .20 .50
721 Curt Schilling BB .20 .50
725 Nomar Garciaparra BB .40 1.00
734 Ken Griffey Jr. BB 1.00 2.50
737 Greg Maddux BB .40 1.00
743 Sammy Sosa BB .40 1.00
749 David Wells BB .20 .50

1999 Sports Illustrated for Kids II

758 Pedro Martinez BB .30 .75
768 Ila Borders BB .20 .50
770 David Cone BB .20 .50
784 Mike Piazza BB .40 1.00
790 Mark McGwire BB .75 2.00
795 Craig Biggio BB .30 .75
796 Tom Glavine BB .30 .75
802 Alex Rodriguez BB .75 2.00
804 Trevor Hoffman BB .20 .50
813 Rickey Henderson BB .40 1.00
815 Mo Vaughn BB .20 .50
817 Vinny Castilla BB .20 .50
820 John Smoltz BB .30 .75
825 Jose Canseco BB .30 .75
831 Matt Williams BB .20 .50
833 Derek Jeter BB .75 2.00
840 Ivan Rodriguez BB .30 .75
841 Roger Clemens BB .40 1.00
846 Ken Caminiti BB .20 .50
849 Roberto Alomar BB .30 .75
856 Randy Johnson BB .40 1.00

1999 Sports Illustrated for Kids Fall-Winter

GM Greg Maddux .40 1.00
KG Ken Griffey Jr. .50 1.25

2000 Sports Illustrated for Kids II

866 Babe Ruth BB .75 2.00
869 Mickey Mantle BB 2.00 5.00
870 Jackie Robinson BB .40 1.00
882 Mark McGwire BB .75 2.00
884 Mariano Rivera BB .30 .75
901 Kevin Millwood BB .20 .50
906 Manny Ramirez BB .30 .75
910 Bernie Williams BB .30 .75
914 Larry Walker BB .20 .50
920 Ken Griffey Jr BB 1.00 2.50
922 David Wells BB .20 .50
929 Chipper Jones BB .40 1.00
935 Carlos Beltran BB .30 .75
941 Vladimir Guerrero BB .40 1.00
945 Andres Galarraga BB .20 .50
953 Jason Kendall BB .20 .50
955 Pedro Martinez BB .30 .75
962 Todd Helton BB .30 .75

2001 Sports Illustrated for Kids

COMPLETE SET (108) 25.00 50.00
8 Gary Sheffield BB .08 .25
10 Carlos Delgado BB .20 .50
24 Jason Giambi BB .20 .50
30 Kazuhiro Sasaki BB .40 1.00
34 Jeff Kent BB .10 .30
39 Randy Johnson BB .40 1.00
40 Rafael Furcal BB .20 .50
50 Nomar Garciaparra BB .40 1.00
54 Darin Erstad BB .20 .50
57 Edgar Martinez BB .30 .75
62 Andruw Jones BB .20 .50
68 Edgardo Alfonzo BB .20 .50
72 Tim Hudson BB .20 .50
74 Barry Bonds BB .75 2.00
80 Juan Gonzalez BB .20 .50
85 Kevin Brown BB .20 .50
87 Luis Gonzalez BB .20 .50
92 Bret Boone BB .10 .30
98 Mike Hampton BB .20 .50
101 Mike Piazza BB .40 1.00

2002 Sports Illustrated for Kids

110 Alex Rodriguez BB .40 1.00
122 Sammy Sosa BB .40 1.00
131 Ichiro Suzuki BB .75 2.00
141 Curt Schilling BB .20 .50
144 Albert Pujols BB .75 2.00
152 Derek Jeter BB .60 1.50
157 Mariano Rivera BB .30 .75
162 Juan Pierre BB .20 .50
164 Robb Nen BB .20 .50
169 Jim Thome BB .15 .40
174 Ken Griffey Jr BB .50 1.25
176 Hideo Nomo BB .40 1.00
182 Pedro Martinez BB .30 .75
186 Tino Martinez BB .30 .75
191 Lance Berkman BB .20 .50
195 Omar Vizquel BB .30 .75
199 Tom Glavine BB .30 .75
207 Torii Hunter BB .20 .50
209 Luis Castillo BB .20 .50
216 Jorge Posada BB .30 .75
221 Barry Zito BB .20 .50

2003 Sports Illustrated for Kids

228 Manny Ramirez BB .30 .75
237 Troy Glaus BB .20 .50
246 Scott Rolen BB .30 .75
248 Alex Rodriguez BB .40 1.00
255 Eric Hinske BB .20 .50
257 John Smoltz BB .30 .75
267 Alfonso Soriano BB .20 .50
269 Derek Lowe BB .20 .50
271 Roy Oswalt BB .20 .50
276 Miguel Tejada BB .20 .50

2004 Sports Illustrated for Kids

ONE NINE-CARD SHEET PER MAGAZINE
339 Barry Bonds BB .75 2.00
347 Ivan Rodriguez BB .10 .30
352 Eric Gagne BB .20 .50
356 Hideki Matsui BB .40 1.00
361 Todd Helton BB .20 .50
366 Kerry Wood BB .20 .50
374 Carlos Delgado BB .20 .50
376 Tim Hudson BB .20 .50
381 Jim Thome BB .20 .50
383 Josh Beckett BB .30 .75
388 Andruw Jones BB .30 .75
393 Bill Mueller BB .20 .50
398 Sean Casey BB .20 .50
402 Dontrelle Willis BB .20 .50
406 Jennie Finch Softball .30 .75
408 Vladimir Guerrero BB .40 1.00
410 Randy Johnson BB .40 1.00
417 Ichiro Suzuki BB .40 1.00
422 Ben Sheets BB .20 .50
429 Eric Chavez BB .20 .50
430 Russ Ortiz BB .20 .50
434 Johan Santana BB .30 .75

2005 Sports Illustrated for Kids

442 Adrian Beltre BB .20 .50
447 Curt Schilling BB .30 .75
453 Francisco Cordero BB .20 .50
455 Derek Jeter BB .60 1.50
462 Jason Schmidt BB .20 .50
466 Adam Dunn BB .20 .50
470 Joe Nathan BB .20 .50
472 Jason Bay BB .20 .50
479 Roger Clemens BB .40 1.00
483 Melvin Mora BB .20 .50
488 Gary Sheffield BB .20 .50
490 C.C. Sabathia BB .20 .50
497 Miguel Cabrera BB .30 .75
505 Paul Konerko BB .20 .50
509 Pedro Martinez BB .30 .75
514 Derrek Lee BB .20 .50
521 Chris Carpenter BB .20 .50
523 Mark Teixeira BB .30 .75
527 Chad Cordero BB .20 .50
536 Tim Wakefield BB .20 .50
538 Carlos Lee BB .20 .50

2006 Sports Illustrated for Kids

5 Bartolo Colon BB .07 .20
7 Andruw Jones BB .07 .20
10 Roy Oswalt BB .08 .25
15 Alex Rodriguez BB .30 .75
20 Jermaine Dye BB .07 .20
25 Jake Peavy BB .07 .20
30 David Ortiz BB .08 .25
34 Huston Street BB .07 .20
39 Chone Figgins BB .07 .20
40 Cliff Lee BB .08 .25
48 Dontrelle Willis .07 .20
53 Jim Edmonds BB .08 .25
55 Lance Berkman BB .08 .25
59 Mark Buehrle BB .07 .20
68 Albert Pujols BB .50 1.25
72 Scott Kazmir BB .07 .20
77 Greg Maddux BB .30 .75
79 Michael Young BB .08 .25
83 Mike Mussina BB .08 .25
87 Nomar Garciaparra BB .08 .25
93 Magglio Ordonez BB .08 .25
95 Jon Papelbon BB .08 .25
100 Carlos Beltran BB .07 .20
104 Joe Mauer BB .10 .30

2007 Sports Illustrated for Kids

ONE NINE-CARD SHEET PER MAGAZINE
110 Alex Rodriguez BB .30 .75
119 Michael Main HS BB .07 .20
123 Justin Jackson HS BB .07 .20
128 Justin Verlander .08 .25
135 Paul LoDuca BB .07 .20
138 Scott Rolen BB .08 .25
143 Chien-Ming Wang BB .08 .25
149 Johan Santana BB .10 .30
151 Craig Biggio BB .08 .25
156 Aramis Ramirez BB .07 .20
160 Feliz Hernandez BB .08 .25
165 David Wright BB .25 .60
171 C.C. Sabathia BB .08 .25
172 J.J. Hardy BB .07 .20
176 Roy Halladay BB .10 .30
179 Monica Abbott BB .07 .20
181 Justin Morneau BB .08 .25
185 John Smoltz BB .08 .25
191 Carlos Guillen BB .07 .20
196 Brandon Webb BB .07 .20
202 John Maine BB .07 .20
206 Mike Lowell BB .07 .20
213 Matt Holliday BB .08 .25

2008 Sports Illustrated for Kids

228 Dustin Pedroia BB .20 .50
236 Fausto Carmona BB .20 .50
242 Russell Martin BB .20 .50
246 Joba Chamberlain BB
248 Jimmy Rollins BB
257 Prince Fielder BB
259 John Lackey BB
264 Grady Sizemore BB
268 Brad Penny BB
273 Ryan Braun BB
278 Mariano Rivera BB
282 Scott Kazmir BB
284 Chase Utley BB
292 Josh Hamilton BB
297 Edinson Volquez BB
299 Tim Lincecum BB
306 Tommy Mendonca BB
314 Derek Jeter BB
316 Daisuke Matsuzaka BB
320 Manny Ramirez BB

2009 Sports Illustrated for Kids

336 Jorge Posada BB
341 Mike Schmidt BB
345 David Ortiz ART BB
354 Cliff Lee BB
358 Adrian Gonzalez BB
363 Carlos Quentin BB
365 Brad Lidge BB
374 Albert Pujols BB
376 Joakim Soria BB
384 Francisco Rodriguez BB
385 Miguel Cabrera BB
392 Torii Hunter BB
396 Yovani Gallardo BB
398 Carl Crawford BB
405 Matt Cain BB
410 Hanley Ramirez BB
412 Felix Hernandez BB
419 Joe Mauer BB
423 Adam Wainwright BB
428 Ryan Howard BB
430 Andrew Bailey BB

2010 Sports Illustrated for Kids

438 Zack Greinke BB
443 Chris Carpenter BB
445 Chris Coghlan BB
451 Jonathan Papelbon BB
455 Ichiro Suzuki BB
464 Mark Teixeira BB
466 Dan Haren BB
473 CC Sabathia BB
477 Jason Heyward BB
482 Ubaldo Jimenez BB
486 Andre Ethier BB
489 Robinson Cano BB
491 Stephen Strasburg BB
496 Joey Votto BB
501 Jered Weaver BB
507 David Price BB
508 Juan Pierre BB
516 Jose Bautista BB
527 Roy Halladay BB

2011 Sports Illustrated for Kids

6 Matt Cain BB
12 Felix Hernandez BB
13 Josh Hamilton BB
21 Carlos Gonzalez BB
22 Josh Johnson BB
32 Brian Wilson BB
34 Vladimir Guerrero BB
39 Prince Fielder BB
44 Jeremy Guthrie BB
50 Justin Verlander BB
54 Lance Berkman BB
55 Cole Hamels BB
60 Jose Reyes BB
66 Adrian Gonzalez BB
67 Jair Jurrjens BB
73 Ian Kennedy BB
81 Bryce Harper BB
84 Curtis Granderson BB
88 Johnny Cueto BB
99 Nelson Cruz BB

2012 Sports Illustrated for Kids

102 David Freese BB
123 Clayton Kershaw BB
131 Roy Halladay BB
135 Dustin Pedroia BB
140 Albert Pujols BB
142 John Axford BB
147 Josh Hamilton BB
155 C.J. Wilson BB
159 Andrew McCutchen BB
165 Matt Cain BB
167 Ryan Braun BB
172 Gio Gonzalez BB
177 Mike Trout BB
183 R.A. Dickey BB
190 Jim Johnson BB
195 Miguel Cabrera BB

2013 Sports Illustrated for Kids

201 Pablo Sandoval BB
208 David Price BB
213 Buster Posey BB
219 Bryce Harper BB
223 Yadier Molina BB
228 Felix Hernandez BB
229 Edwin Encarnacion BB
241 Yu Darvish BB
248 Justin Upton BB
253 Mark Appel BB
257 Robinson Cano BB
262 Keilani Ricketts Softball
266 Yasiel Puig BB
268 Matt Harvey BB
283 Jose Fernandez BB
288 Paul Goldschmidt BB
293 Big Puppy BB
Dog head caricature

2015 Sports Illustrated for Kids

389 Madison Bumgarner BB
401 Clayton Kershaw BB
409 Jose Abreu BB
422 Corey Kluber BB
431 Jacob deGrom BB
435 Matt Carpenter BB
445 Josh Sborz BB
447 Jason Kipnis BB
452 Dallas Keuchel BB
457 Sierra Romero Softball
463 Gerrit Cole BB
474 Billy Hamilton BB
480 Bryce Harper BB
All-Star

1998 Sports Illustrated Then and Now

The 1998 Sports Illustrated Then and Now set (created by Fleer) was issued in one series totalling 150 cards and was distributed in six-card packs containing five cards and one mini-poster with a suggested retail price of $1.99. The fronts feature color photos of active and retired players plus 1998 rookies and prospects. The backs carry ratings for each player in key skill areas. The set contains the topical subset: A Place in History (37-53) which displays statistical compairson between current players and retired greats. Notable Rookie Cards include Magglio Ordonez. An Alex Rodriguez checklist mini-poster was randomly seeded into 1:12 packs. In addition, an Alex Rodriguez promo card was distributed to dealers and hobby media several weeks to the product's release.

COMPLETE SET (150) 10.00 25.00
1 Luis Aparicio .10 .30
2 Richie Ashburn .20 .50
3 Ernie Banks .30 .75
4 Yogi Berra .30 .75
5 Lou Boudreau .10 .30
6 Lou Brock .20 .50
7 Jim Bunning .10 .30
8 Rod Carew .20 .50
9 Bob Feller .10 .30
10 Rollie Fingers .10 .30
11 Bob Gibson .20 .50
12 Ferguson Jenkins .10 .30

13 Al Kaline	.30	.75
14 George Kell	.10	.30
15 Harmon Killebrew	.30	.75
16 Ralph Kiner	.10	.30
17 Tommy Lasorda	.10	.30
18 Juan Marichal	.10	.30
19 Eddie Mathews	.30	.75
20 Willie Mays	.60	1.50
21 Willie McCovey	.10	.30
22 Joe Morgan	.10	.30
23 Gaylord Perry	.10	.30
24 Kirby Puckett	.30	.75
25 Pee Wee Reese	.20	.50
26 Phil Rizzuto	.20	.50
27 Robin Roberts	.10	.30
28 Brooks Robinson	.20	.50
29 Frank Robinson	.20	.50
30 Red Schoendienst	.10	.30
31 Enos Slaughter	.10	.30
32 Warren Spahn	.20	.50
33 Willie Stargell	.20	.50
34 Earl Weaver	.10	.30
35 Billy Williams	.10	.30
36 Early Wynn	.10	.30
37 Rickey Henderson HIST	.20	.50
38 Greg Maddux HIST	.30	.75
39 Mike Mussina HIST	.10	.30
40 Cal Ripken HIST	.50	1.25
41 Albert Belle HIST	.10	.30
42 Frank Thomas HIST	.20	.50
43 Jeff Bagwell HIST	.10	.30
44 Paul Molitor HIST	.10	.30
45 Chuck Knoblauch HIST	.10	.30
46 Todd Hundley HIST	.10	.30
47 Bernie Williams HIST	.10	.30
48 Tony Gwynn HIST	.20	.50
49 Barry Bonds HIST	.40	1.00
50 Ken Griffey Jr. HIST	.40	1.00
51 Randy Johnson HIST	.20	.50
52 Mark McGwire HIST	.40	1.00
53 Roger Clemens HIST	.30	.75
54 Jose Cruz Jr. HIST	.10	.30
55 Roberto Alomar	.20	.50
56 Sandy Alomar Jr.	.10	.30
57 Brady Anderson	.10	.30
58 Kevin Appier	.10	.30
59 Jeff Bagwell	.20	.50
60 Albert Belle	.10	.30
61 Dante Bichette	.10	.30
62 Craig Biggio	.20	.50
63 Barry Bonds	.75	2.00
64 Kevin Brown	.20	.50
65 Jay Buhner	.10	.30
66 Ellis Burks	.10	.30
67 Ken Caminiti	.10	.30
68 Jose Canseco	.20	.50
69 Joe Carter	.10	.30
70 Vinny Castilla	.10	.30
71 Tony Clark	.10	.30
72 Roger Clemens	.60	1.50
73 David Cone	.10	.30
74 Jose Cruz Jr.	.10	.30
75 Jason Dickson	.10	.30
76 Jim Edmonds	.10	.30
77 Scott Erickson	.10	.30
78 Darin Erstad	.10	.30
79 Alex Fernandez	.10	.30
80 Steve Finley	.10	.30
81 Travis Fryman	.10	.30
82 Andres Galarraga	.10	.30
83 Nomar Garciaparra	.50	1.25
84 Tom Glavine	.20	.50
85 Juan Gonzalez	.10	.30
86 Mark Grace	.20	.50
87 Willie Greene	.10	.30
88 Ken Griffey Jr.	.60	1.50
89 Vladimir Guerrero	.30	.75
90 Tony Gwynn	.40	1.00
91 Livan Hernandez	.10	.30
92 Bobby Higginson	.10	.30
93 Derek Jeter	.75	2.00
94 Charles Johnson	.10	.30
95 Randy Johnson	.30	.75
96 Andruw Jones	.20	.50
97 Chipper Jones	.30	.75
98 David Justice	.10	.30
99 Eric Karros	.10	.30
100 Jason Kendall	.10	.30
101 Jimmy Key	.10	.30
102 Darryl Kile	.10	.30
103 Chuck Knoblauch	.10	.30
104 Ray Lankford	.10	.30
105 Barry Larkin	.20	.50
106 Kenny Lofton	.10	.30
107 Greg Maddux	.50	1.25
108 Al Martin	.10	.30
109 Edgar Martinez	.20	.50
110 Pedro Martinez	.20	.50
111 Ramon Martinez	.10	.30
112 Tino Martinez	.20	.50
113 Mark McGwire	.75	2.00
114 Raul Mondesi	.10	.30
115 Matt Morris	.10	.30
116 Charles Nagy	.10	.30
117 Denny Neagle	.10	.30
118 Hideo Nomo	.30	.75
119 Dean Palmer	.10	.30
120 Andy Pettitte	.20	.50
121 Mike Piazza	.50	1.25
122 Manny Ramirez	.20	.50
123 Edgar Renteria	.10	.30
124 Cal Ripken	1.00	2.50
125 Alex Rodriguez	.50	1.25
126 Henry Rodriguez	.10	.30
127 Ivan Rodriguez	.20	.50
128 Scott Rolen	.20	.50
129 Tim Salmon	.20	.50
130 Curt Schilling	.10	.30
131 Gary Sheffield	.10	.30
132 John Smoltz	.20	.50
133 Sammy Sosa	.30	.75
134 Frank Thomas	.30	.75
135 Jim Thome	.20	.50
136 Mo Vaughn	.10	.30
137 Robin Ventura	.10	.30
138 Larry Walker	.10	.30
139 Bernie Williams	.20	.50
140 Matt Williams	.10	.30
141 Jaret Wright	.10	.30
142 Michael Coleman	.10	.30
143 Juan Encarnacion	.10	.30
144 Brad Fullmer	.10	.30
145 Ben Grieve	.10	.30
146 Todd Helton	.20	.50
147 Paul Konerko	.10	.30
148 Derrek Lee	.20	.50
149 Magglio Ordonez RC	1.00	2.50
150 Enrique Wilson	.10	.30
P125 Alex Rodriguez PROMO	.75	2.00
NNO Alex Rodriguez CL	.20	.50

1998 Sports Illustrated Then and Now Extra Edition

*STARS: 4X TO 10X BASIC CARDS
*ROOKIES: 3X TO 8X BASIC CARDS
RANDOM INSERTS IN PACKS
STATED PRINT RUN 500 SERIAL #'d SETS

1998 Sports Illustrated Then and Now Art of the Game

COMPLETE SET (8)	8.00	20.00
STATED ODDS 1:9		
AG1 Ken Griffey Jr.	1.25	3.00
AG2 Alex Rodriguez	1.25	3.00
AG3 Mike Piazza	1.25	3.00
AG4 Brooks Robinson	.50	1.25
AG5 David Justice	.30	.75
AG6 Cal Ripken	2.50	6.00
AG7 Prospect 'n Prospector	.30	.75
AG8 Barry Bonds	2.00	5.00

1998 Sports Illustrated Then and Now Autographs

ONE CARD VIA MAIL PER RDMP.CARD
SERIAL #'d PRINT RUNS LISTED BELOW
EXCHANGE RANDOM INSERTS IN PACKS
EXCHANGE DEADLINE: 11/01/99

1 Roger Clemens/250	50.00	100.00
2 Bob Gibson/500	15.00	40.00
3 Tony Gwynn/250	30.00	60.00
4 Harmon Killebrew/500	20.00	50.00
5 Willie Mays/250	75.00	150.00
6 Scott Rolen/250	8.00	20.00

1998 Sports Illustrated Then and Now Autograph Redemptions

*EXCHANGE CARDS: .1X TO .25X BASIC AU'S
RANDOM INSERTS IN PACKS
SERIAL #'d PRINT RUNS LISTED BELOW
EXCHANGE DEADLINE: 11/1/99

1 Roger Clemens/250	10.00	25.00
2 Bob Gibson/500	4.00	10.00
3 Tony Gwynn/250	6.00	15.00
4 Harmon Killebrew/500	4.00	10.00
5 Willie Mays/250	15.00	40.00
6 Scott Rolen/250	4.00	10.00

1998 Sports Illustrated Then and Now Covers

COMPLETE SET (12)	30.00	80.00
STATED ODDS 1:18		
C1 Lou Brock	1.25	3.00
C2 Kirby Puckett	2.00	5.00
C3 Harmon Killebrew	2.00	5.00
C4 Eddie Mathews	2.00	5.00
C5 Willie Mays	4.00	10.00
C6 Frank Robinson	1.25	3.00
C7 Cal Ripken	6.00	15.00
C8 Roger Clemens	4.00	10.00
C9 Ken Griffey Jr.	4.00	10.00
C10 Mark McGwire	5.00	12.00
C11 Tony Gwynn	2.50	6.00
C12 Ivan Rodriguez	1.25	3.00

1998 Sports Illustrated Then and Now Great Shots

COMPLETE SET (25)	4.00	10.00
1 Ken Griffey Jr.	.40	1.00
2 Frank Thomas	.20	.50
3 Alex Rodriguez	.30	.75
4 Andruw Jones	.10	.30
5 Chipper Jones	.20	.50
6 Cal Ripken	.60	1.50
7 Mark McGwire	.50	1.25
8 Derek Jeter	.50	1.25
9 Greg Maddux	.30	.75
10 Jeff Bagwell	.10	.30
11 Mike Piazza	.30	.75
12 Scott Rolen	.10	.30
13 Nomar Garciaparra	.30	.75
14 Jose Cruz Jr.	.07	.20
15 Charles Johnson	.07	.20
16 Fergie Jenkins	.07	.20
17 Lou Brock	.10	.30
18 Bob Gibson	.10	.30
19 Harmon Killebrew	.20	.50
20 Juan Marichal	.07	.20
21 B.Robinson	.10	.30
F.Robinson		
22 Rod Carew	.10	.30
23 Yogi Berra	.20	.50
24 Willie Mays	.40	1.00
25 Kirby Puckett	.20	.50

1998 Sports Illustrated Then and Now Road to Cooperstown

COMPLETE SET (10)	30.00	80.00
STATED ODDS 1:24		
RC1 Barry Bonds	6.00	15.00
RC2 Roger Clemens	5.00	12.00
RC3 Ken Griffey Jr.	5.00	12.00
RC4 Tony Gwynn	3.00	8.00
RC5 Rickey Henderson	1.50	4.00
RC6 Greg Maddux	4.00	10.00
RC7 Paul Molitor	1.00	2.50
RC8 Mike Piazza	4.00	10.00
RC9 Cal Ripken	8.00	20.00
RC10 Frank Thomas	2.50	6.00

1998 Sports Illustrated World Series Fever Postcard Promo

1 Mark McGwire	2.00	5.00

1998 Sports Illustrated World Series Fever

The 1998 Sports Illustrated World Series Fever set (created by Fleer) was issued in one series totalling 150 cards. The set contains the topical subsets: Covers (1-20), and Magnificent Moments (21-30). Notable Rookie Cards include Orlando Hernandez and Magglio Ordonez. A Cal Ripken promo card was distributed to dealers and hobby media to preview the brand a few month's before th product's national release. The promo is similar in design to the basic Ripken except for the text "PROMOTIONAL SAMPLE" running diagonally across the front and back of the card.

COMPLETE SET (150)	10.00	25.00
1 Mickey Mantle COV	1.25	3.00
2 W.S. Preview COV	.10	.30
3 W.S. Preview COV	.10	.30
4 Chicago (AL) COV	.10	.30
5 W.S. Preview COV	.10	.30
6 Lou Brock COV	.10	.30
7 Brooks Robinson COV	.10	.30
8 Frank Robinson COV	.10	.30
9 L.A. Oakland COV	.10	.30
10 Reggie Jackson COV	.10	.30
11 Kansas City COV	.10	.30
12 Minnesota COV	.10	.30
13 Orel Hershiser COV	.10	.30
14 Rickey Henderson COV	.20	.50
15 Minnesota COV	.10	.30
16 Toronto COV	.10	.30
17 Joe Carter COV	.10	.30
18 Atlanta COV	.10	.30
19 New York Yankees COV	.10	.30
20 Edgar Renteria COV	.10	.30
21 Bill Mazeroski MM	.10	.30
22 Joe Carter MM	.10	.30
23 Carlton Fisk MM	.10	.30
24 Bucky Dent MM	.10	.30
25 Mookie Wilson MM	.10	.30
26 Enos Slaughter MM	.10	.30
27 Mickey Lolich MM	.10	.30
28 Bobby Richardson MM	.10	.30
29 Kirk Gibson MM	.10	.30
30 Edgar Renteria MM	.10	.30
31 Albert Belle	.10	.30
32 Kevin Brown	.20	.50
33 Brian Rose	.10	.30
34 Ron Gant	.10	.30
35 Jeromy Burnitz	.10	.30
36 Andres Galarraga	.10	.30
37 Jim Edmonds	.10	.30
38 Jose Cruz Jr.	.10	.30
39 Mark Grudzielanek	.10	.30
40 Shawn Estes	.10	.30
41 Mark Grace	.20	.50
42 Nomar Garciaparra	.50	1.25
43 Juan Gonzalez	.10	.30
44 Tom Glavine	.20	.50
45 Brady Anderson	.10	.30
46 Tony Clark	.10	.30
47 Jeff Cirillo	.10	.30
48 Dante Bichette	.10	.30
49 Ben Grieve	.10	.30
50 Ken Griffey Jr.	.60	1.50
51 Edgardo Alfonzo	.10	.30
52 Roger Clemens	.60	1.50
53 Pat Hentgen	.10	.30
54 Todd Helton	.20	.50
55 Andy Benes	.10	.30
56 Tony Gwynn	.40	1.00
57 Andruw Jones	.20	.50
58 Bobby Higginson	.10	.30
59 Bobby Jones	.10	.30
60 Darryl Kile	.10	.30
61 Chan Ho Park	.10	.30
62 Charles Johnson	.10	.30
63 Rusty Greer	.10	.30
64 Travis Fryman	.10	.30
65 Derek Jeter	.75	2.00
66 Jay Buhner	.10	.30
67 Chuck Knoblauch	.10	.30
68 David Justice	.10	.30
69 Brian Hunter	.10	.30
70 Eric Karros	.10	.30
71 Edgar Martinez	.20	.50
72 Chipper Jones	.30	.75
73 Barry Larkin	.20	.50
74 Mike Lansing	.10	.30
75 Craig Biggio	.20	.50
76 Al Martin	.10	.30
77 Barry Bonds	.75	2.00
78 Randy Johnson	.30	.75
79 Ryan Klesko	.10	.30
80 Mark McGwire	.75	2.00
81 Fred McGriff	.20	.50
82 Javy Lopez	.10	.30
83 Kenny Lofton	.10	.30
84 Sandy Alomar Jr.	.10	.30
85 Matt Morris	.10	.30
86 Paul Konerko	.10	.30
87 Ray Lankford	.10	.30
88 Kerry Wood	.15	.40
89 Roberto Alomar	.20	.50
90 Greg Maddux	.50	1.25
91 Travis Lee	.10	.30
92 Moises Alou	.10	.30
93 Dean Palmer	.10	.30
94 Hideo Nomo	.30	.75
95 Ken Caminiti	.10	.30
96 Pedro Martinez	.20	.50
97 Raul Mondesi	.10	.30
98 Denny Neagle	.10	.30
99 Tino Martinez	.20	.50
100 Mike Mussina	.20	.50
101 Kevin Appier	.10	.30
102 Vinny Castilla	.10	.30
103 Jeff Bagwell	.20	.50
104 Paul O'Neill	.20	.50
105 Rey Ordonez	.10	.30
106 Vladimir Guerrero	.30	.75
107 Rafael Palmeiro	.20	.50
108 Alex Rodriguez	.50	-1.25
109 Andy Pettitte	.20	.50
110 Carl Pavano	.10	.30
111 Henry Rodriguez	.10	.30
112 Gary Sheffield	.10	.30
113 Curt Schilling	.10	.30
114 John Smoltz	.20	.50
115 Reggie Sanders	.10	.30
116 Scott Rolen	.20	.50
117 Mike Piazza	.50	1.25
118 Manny Ramirez	.20	.50
119 Cal Ripken	1.00	2.50
120 Brad Radke	.10	.30
121 Tim Salmon	.20	.50
122 Brett Tomko	.10	.30
123 Robin Ventura	.10	.30
124 Mo Vaughn	.10	.30
125 A.J. Hinch	.10	.30
126 Derrek Lee	.20	.50
127 Orlando Hernandez RC	.50	1.25
128 Aramis Ramirez	.10	.30
129 Frank Thomas	.30	.75
130 J.T. Snow	.10	.30
131 Magglio Ordonez RC	1.00	2.50
132 Bobby Bonilla	.10	.30
133 Marquis Grissom	.10	.30
134 Jim Thome	.20	.50
135 Justin Thompson	.10	.30
136 Matt Williams	.10	.30
137 Matt Stairs	.10	.30
138 Wade Boggs	.20	.50
139 Chuck Finley	.10	.30
140 Jaret Wright	.10	.30
141 Ivan Rodriguez	.20	.50
142 Brad Fullmer	.10	.30
143 Bernie Williams	.20	.50
144 Jason Giambi	.10	.30
145 Larry Walker	.10	.30
146 Tony Womack	.10	.30
147 Sammy Sosa	.30	.75
148 Rondell White	.10	.30
149 Todd Stottlemyre	.10	.30
150 Shane Reynolds	.10	.30
P8 Cal Ripken Promo	.75	2.00

1998 Sports Illustrated World Series Fever Extra Edition

*STARS: 10X TO 25X BASIC CARDS
*ROOKIES: 8X TO 20X BASIC CARDS
RANDOM INSERTS IN PACKS
STATED PRINT RUN 98 SERIAL #'d SETS

1998 Sports Illustrated World Series Fever Autumn Excellence

COMPLETE SET (10)	25.00	60.00
STATED ODDS 1:24		
GOLD STATED ODDS 1:240		
1 Willie Mays	3.00	8.00
2 Kirby Puckett	1.50	4.00
3 Babe Ruth	4.00	10.00
4 Reggie Jackson	1.00	2.50
5 Whitey Ford	1.00	2.50
6 Lou Brock	1.00	2.50
7 Mickey Mantle	6.00	15.00
8 Yogi Berra	1.50	4.00
9 Bob Gibson	1.00	2.50
10 Don Larsen	.60	1.50

1998 Sports Illustrated World Series Fever MVP Collection

COMPLETE SET (10)	3.00	8.00
STATED ODDS 1:4		
1 Frank Robinson	.50	1.25
2 Brooks Robinson	.50	1.25
3 Willie Stargell	.50	1.25
4 Bret Saberhagen	.30	.75
5 Rollie Fingers	.30	.75
6 Orel Hershiser	.30	.75
7 Paul Molitor	.30	.75
8 Tom Glavine	.50	1.25
9 John Wetteland	.30	.75
10 Livan Hernandez	.30	.75

1998 Sports Illustrated World Series Fever Reggie Jackson's Picks

COMPLETE SET (15)	15.00	40.00
STATED ODDS 1:12		
1 Paul O'Neill	.60	1.50
2 Barry Bonds	2.50	6.00
3 Ken Griffey Jr.	2.00	5.00
4 Juan Gonzalez	.40	1.00
5 Greg Maddux	1.50	4.00
6 Mike Piazza	1.50	4.00
7 Larry Walker	.40	-1.00
8 Mo Vaughn	.40	1.00
9 Roger Clemens	2.00	5.00
10 John Smoltz	.60	1.50
11 Alex Rodriguez	1.50	4.00
12 Frank Thomas	1.00	2.50
13 Mark McGwire	2.50	6.00
14 Jeff Bagwell	.60	1.50
15 Randy Johnson	1.00	2.50

1968 Sports Memorabilia All-Time Greats

This 15-card standard-size set features some of the leading players of all-time. The fronts have crude drawings of the players, while the backs have a player biography. The drawings were done by sports artist Art Ouellette.

COMPLETE SET (15)	50.00	100.00
1 Checklist	2.00	5.00
2 Connie Mack	3.00	8.00
3 Walter Johnson	4.00	10.00
4 Warren Spahn	3.00	8.00
5 Christy Mathewson	4.00	10.00
6 Lefty Grove	3.00	8.00
7 Mickey Cochrane	2.00	5.00
8 Bill Dickey	2.00	5.00
9 Tris Speaker	3.00	8.00
10 Ty Cobb	6.00	15.00
11 Babe Ruth	10.00	25.00
12 Lou Gehrig	6.00	15.00
13 Rogers Hornsby	4.00	10.00
14 Honus Wagner	4.00	10.00
15 Pie Traynor	2.00	5.00

1987 Sports Reading

These 9" by 14" cards were issued to promote education and sports. They are part of of a reading series for schools. These cards all feature various fun facts about major leaguers. The cards have photos on both sides along with history about a specific event.

COMPLETE SET	60.00	120.00
1 Carlos May	.40	1.00
2 Babe Ruth	8.00	20.00
3 Eddie Gaedel	1.00	2.50
4 Cesar Gutierrez	.40	1.00
5 Ted Williams	6.00	15.00
6 Pete Gray	1.00	2.50
7 Hank Aaron	5.00	12.00
8 Virgil Trucks	.40	1.00
9 Bob Gibson	2.00	5.00
10 Johnny Vander Meer	.40	1.00
11 Ron Hansen	.40	1.00
12 Roger Clemens	2.50	6.00
13 Dwight Gooden	.50	1.25
14 Jimmy Piersall	.40	1.00
15 Dale Long	.40	1.00
16 Herb Score	.40	1.00
17 Dizzy Dean	.50	1.25
Paul Dean		
18 Stan Musial	4.00	10.00
19 Pete Rose	5.00	12.00
20 Cy Young	2.00	5.00
21 Don Mattingly	4.00	10.00
22 Pete Rose	5.00	12.00
Tom Seaver		
Nolan Ryan		
Phil Niekro		
23 Minnie Minoso	.50	1.25
24 Walker Cooper	.40	1.00
Mort Cooper		
25 Jim Thorpe	3.00	8.00
26 Robert Moses Grove	2.00	5.00
27 Roberto Clemente	6.00	15.00
28 Lou Gehrig	6.00	15.00
29 Shea Stadium, 1969	.40	1.00
30 Yankee Stadium	.40	1.00
31 Carl Hubbell	1.50	4.00
32 Wade Boggs	1.50	4.00
33 Harvey Haddix	.40	1.00
34 Harold Reiser	.40	1.00
35 Jackie Robinson	6.00	15.00
36 Walter Johnson	2.00	5.00
37 The Hall of Fame	.40	1.00
38 Lou Boudreau	.75	2.00
39 Hank Greenberg	1.50	4.00
40 Fernando Valenzuela	.50	1.25

1973 Sports Scoop HOF Candidates

This 14-card set measures approximately 3 1/2" by 5 1/2" and features borderless black-and-white photos of National Baseball Hall of Fame Nominees according to Sports Scoop. The backs display the players name and why he might be considered for the Hall of Fame. The cards are unnumbered and checklisted below in alphabetical order.

COMPLETE SET (14)	5.00	12.00
1 Earl Averill/(Batting)	.40	1.00
2 Earl Averill/(Holding bat)	.40	1.00
3 Earl Averill/(Ready to catch ball)	.40	1.00
4 George Burns	.20	.50
5 Jack Fournier	.20	.50
6 Jeff Heath	.20	.50
7 Joe Jackson	1.50	4.00
8 Fred Lindstrom/(Holding bat)	.40	1.00
9 Fred Lindstrom/(Portrait)	.40	1.00
10 Fred Lindstrom/(Sitting)	.40	1.00
11 Barney McCoskey	.20	.50
12 Johnny Mize/(Holding bat in front)	.60	1.50
13 Johnny Mize/(Kneeling with bat)	.60	1.50
14 Johnny Mize/(Swinging bat)	.60	1.50

1976 Sportstix

This set features color action photos of some of the favorite sport stars printed on various geometric shaped stickers with peel off backing. These are all that are known to date -- however, other groups may surface -- if so -- any additions to this checklist are appreciated.

COMMON PLAYER (1-10)	60.00	120.00
1 Dave Kingman	4.00	10.00
2 Steve Busby	2.00	5.00
3 Bill Madlock	2.50	6.00
4 Jeff Burroughs	2.00	5.00
5 Ted Simmons	3.00	8.00
6 Randy Jones	2.00	5.00
7 Buddy Bell	2.50	6.00
8 Dave Cash	2.00	5.00
9 Jerry Grote	2.00	5.00
10 Dave Lopes	2.00	5.00
A Willie Mays	6.00	15.00
B Roberto Clemente	20.00	50.00
C Mickey Mantle	12.50	35.00

1986 Springhill Offset

This five card set, which measures approximately 2 5/8" by 4 1/8" features a few retired players as well varying information about some information about what Springhill Offset could do. Since these cards are not numbered, we have sequenced them in alphabetical order

COMPLETE SET (5)	3.00	8.00
1 Grover C. Alexander	.60	1.50
2 John McGraw	.60	1.50
3 Honus Wagner	1.00	2.50
4 Cy Young	1.00	2.50
5 Header Card	.08	.25

2007 SP Rookie Edition

COMP.SET w/o RC's (100)	6.00	15.00
COMMON CARD (1-100)	.12	.30
COMMON RC (101-142)	.25	.60
COMMON SP (143-234)	.40	1.00
SP ODDS 1:2		
COMMON CARD (235-284)	.25	.60
1 Chipper Jones	.30	.75
2 Andruw Jones	.12	.30
3 Jeff Francoeur	.30	.75
4 Stephen Drew	.12	.30
5 Randy Johnson	.30	.75
6 Brandon Webb	.20	.50
7 Alfonso Soriano	.20	.50
8 Derrek Lee	.12	.30
9 Aramis Ramirez	.12	.30
10 Carlos Zambrano	.20	.50
11 Ken Griffey Jr.	.60	1.50
12 Adam Dunn	.20	.50
13 Bronson Arroyo	.12	.30
14 Todd Helton	.20	.50
15 Jeff Francis	.12	.30
16 Matt Holliday	.30	.75
17 Hanley Ramirez	.20	.50
18 Dontrelle Willis	.12	.30
19 Miguel Cabrera	.30	.75
20 Lance Berkman	.20	.50
21 Roy Oswalt	.20	.50
22 Carlos Lee	.12	.30
23 Nomar Garciaparra	.20	.50
24 Jason Schmidt	.12	.30
25 Juan Pierre	.12	.30
26 Rafael Furcal	.12	.30
27 Rickie Weeks	.12	.30
28 Prince Fielder	.20	.50
29 Ben Sheets	.12	.30
30 David Wright	.25	.60
31 Jose Reyes	.20	.50
32 Pedro Martinez	.20	.50
33 Carlos Beltran	.20	.50
34 Cole Hamels	.25	.60
35 Jimmy Rollins	.20	.50
36 Ryan Howard	.25	.60
37 Jason Bay	.20	.50
38 Freddy Sanchez	.12	.30
39 Zach Duke	.12	.30
40 Jake Peavy	.12	.30
41 Greg Maddux	.40	1.00
42 Trevor Hoffman	.20	.50
43 Matt Cain	.20	.50
44 Barry Zito	.20	.50
45 Omar Vizquel	.20	.50
46 Albert Pujols	.40	1.00
47 Chris Carpenter	.20	.50
48 Jim Edmonds	.20	.50
49 Scott Rolen	.20	.50
50 Ryan Zimmerman	.20	.50
51 Felipe Lopez	.12	.30
52 Austin Kearns	.12	.30
53 Miguel Tejada	.20	.50
54 Erik Bedard	.12	.30
55 Chris Ray	.12	.30
56 David Ortiz	.30	.75
57 Curt Schilling	.20	.50
58 Manny Ramirez	.30	.75
59 Jonathan Papelbon	.30	.75
60 Jim Thome	.20	.50
61 Paul Konerko	.20	.50
62 Bobby Jenks	.12	.30
63 Grady Sizemore	.20	.50
64 Victor Martinez	.20	.50
65 C.C. Sabathia	.20	.50
66 Ivan Rodriguez	.20	.50
67 Justin Verlander	.30	.75
68 Joel Zumaya	.12	.30
69 Jeremy Bonderman	.12	.30
70 Gil Meche	.12	.30
71 Mike Sweeney	.12	.30
72 Mark Teahen	.12	.30
73 Vladimir Guerrero	.20	.50
74 Howie Kendrick	.12	.30
75 Francisco Rodriguez	.20	.50
76 Johan Santana	.20	.50
77 Justin Morneau	.20	.50
78 Joe Mauer	.25	.60
79 Joe Nathan	.12	.30
80 Alex Rodriguez	.40	1.00
81 Derek Jeter	.75	2.00
82 Johnny Damon	.20	.50
83 Mariano Rivera	.40	1.00
84 Rich Harden	.12	.30
85 Mike Piazza	.30	.75
86 Nick Swisher	.20	.50
87 Ichiro Suzuki	.40	1.00
88 Felix Hernandez	.20	.50
89 Kenji Johjima	.30	.75
90 Richie Sexson	.12	.30
91 Carl Crawford	.20	.50
92 Scott Kazmir	.20	.50
93 B.J. Upton	.12	.30
94 Michael Young	.12	.30
95 Mark Teixeira	.20	.50
96 Eric Gagne	.12	.30
97 Hank Blalock	.12	.30
98 Vernon Wells	.12	.30
99 Roy Halladay	.20	.50
100 Frank Thomas	.30	.75
101 Joaquin Arias (RC)	.25	.60
102 Jeff Baker (RC)	.25	.60
103 Brian Barden RC	.25	.60
104 Michael Bourn (RC)	.40	1.00
105 Kevin Slowey (RC)	.60	1.50
106 Chase Wright RC	.60	1.50
107 Kory Casto (RC)	.25	.60
108 Matt Chico (RC)	.25	.60
109 Matt DeSalvo (RC)	.25	.60
110 Homer Bailey (RC)	.40	1.00
111 Ryan Braun (RC)	1.25	3.00
112 Felix Pie (RC)	.25	.60
113 Jesus Flores RC	.25	.60
114 Ryan Sweeney (RC)	.25	.60
115 Ryan Z. Braun RC	.25	.60
116 Alex Gordon RC	.75	2.00
117 Josh Hamilton (RC)	.75	2.00
118 Sean Henn (RC)	.25	.60
119 Kei Igawa RC	.60	1.50
120 Akinori Iwamura RC	.60	1.50
121 Andy LaRoche (RC)	.25	.60
122 Kevin Kouzmanoff (RC)	.25	.60
123 Matt Lindstrom (RC)	.25	.60
124 Tim Lincecum RC	1.25	3.00
125 Daisuke Matsuzaka RC	1.00	2.50
126 Gustavo Molina RC	.25	.60
127 Miguel Montero (RC)	.25	.60
128 Brandon Morrow RC	1.25	3.00
129 Hideki Okajima RC	1.25	3.00
130 Adam Lind (RC)	.25	.60
131 Mike Rabelo RC	.25	.60
132 Micah Owings (RC)	.25	.60
133 Brandon Wood (RC)	.25	.60
134 Alexi Casilla RC	.40	1.00
135 Joe Smith RC	.25	.60
136 Hunter Pence (RC)	.75	2.00
137 Glen Perkins (RC)	.25	.60
138 Chris Stewart RC	.25	.60
139 Troy Tulowitzki (RC)	.75	2.00
140 Billy Butler (RC)	.40	1.00
141 Delmon Young (RC)	.40	1.00
142 Phil Hughes (RC)	.60	1.50
143 Joaquin Arias 95	.40	1.00
144 Jeff Baker 95	.40	1.00
145 Brian Barden 95	.40	1.00
146 Michael Bourn 95	.60	1.50
147 Kevin Slowey 95	1.00	2.50
148 Chase Wright 95	1.00	2.50
149 Kory Casto 95	.40	1.00
150 Matt Chico 95	.40	1.00
151 Shawn Riggans 95	.40	1.00
152 Juan Salas 95	.40	1.00
153 Ryan Braun 95	2.00	5.00
154 Felix Pie 95	.40	1.00
155 Jesus Flores 95	.40	1.00
156 Ryan Sweeney 95	.40	1.00
157 Ryan Z. Braun 95	.40	1.00
158 Alex Gordon 95	1.25	3.00
159 Josh Hamilton 95	1.25	3.00
160 Sean Henn 95	.40	1.00
161 Kei Igawa 95	1.00	2.50
162 Akinori Iwamura 95	1.00	2.50
163 Andy LaRoche 95	.40	1.00
164 Kevin Kouzmanoff 95	.40	1.00
165 Matt Lindstrom 95	.40	1.00
166 Tim Lincecum 95	2.00	5.00
167 Daisuke Matsuzaka 95	1.50	4.00
168 Gustavo Molina 95	.40	1.00
169 Miguel Montero 95	.40	1.00
170 Brandon Morrow 95	2.00	5.00
171 Hideki Okajima 95	2.00	5.00
172 Adam Lind 95	.40	1.00
173 Mike Rabelo 95	.40	1.00
174 Micah Owings 95	.40	1.00
175 Brandon Wood 95	.40	1.00
176 Alexi Casilla 95	.60	1.50
177 Joe Smith 95	.40	1.00
178 Hunter Pence 95	1.25	3.00
179 Glen Perkins 95	.40	1.00
180 Chris Stewart 95	.40	1.00
181 Troy Tulowitzki 95	1.25	3.00
182 Billy Butler 95	.60	1.50
183 Delmon Young 95	.60	1.50
184 Phil Hughes 95	1.00	2.50
185 Joaquin Arias 93	.40	1.00
186 Jeff Baker 93	.40	1.00
187 Mark Reynolds 93	1.25	3.00
188 Joseph Bisenius 93	.40	1.00
189 Michael Bourn 93	.60	1.50
190 Zack Segovia 93	.40	1.00
191 Kevin Slowey 93	1.00	2.50
192 Chase Wright 93	1.00	2.50
193 Rocky Cherry 93	1.00	2.50
194 Danny Putnam 93	.40	1.00
195 Kory Casto 93	.40	1.00
196 Matt Chico 93	.40	1.00
197 John Danks 93	.60	1.50
198 Homer Bailey 93	.60	1.50
199 Ryan Braun 93	2.00	5.00
200 Felix Pie 93	.40	1.00
201 Jesus Flores 93	.40	1.00
202 Andy Gonzalez 93	.40	1.00
203 Ryan Sweeney 93	.40	1.00
204 Jarrod Saltalamacchia 93	.60	1.50
205 Alex Gordon 93	1.25	3.00
206 Josh Hamilton 93	1.25	3.00
207 Sean Henn 93	.40	1.00
208 Kei Igawa 93	1.00	2.50
209 Akinori Iwamura 93	1.00	2.50
210 Andy LaRoche 93	.40	1.00
211 Rick Vanden Hurk 93	.40	1.00
212 Kevin Kouzmanoff 93	.40	1.00
213 Matt Lindstrom 93	.40	1.00
214 Tim Lincecum 93	2.00	5.00
215 Daisuke Matsuzaka 93	1.50	4.00
216 Gustavo Molina 93	.40	1.00
217 Miguel Montero 93	.40	1.00
218 Brandon Morrow 93	2.00	5.00
219 Hideki Okajima 93	2.00	5.00
220 Adam Lind 93	.40	1.00
221 Mike Rabelo 93	.40	1.00
222 Brian Burres 93	.40	1.00
223 Micah Owings 93	.40	1.00
224 Brandon Wood 93	.40	1.00
225 Alexi Casilla 93	.60	1.50
226 Joe Smith 93	.40	1.00
227 Hunter Pence 93	1.25	3.00
228 Glen Perkins 93	.40	1.00
229 Chris Stewart 93	.40	1.00
230 Ben Francisco 93	.40	1.00
231 Troy Tulowitzki 93	1.25	3.00
232 Billy Butler 93	.60	1.50
233 Delmon Young 93	.60	1.50
234 Phil Hughes 93	1.00	2.50
235 Joaquin Arias 96	.25	.60
236 Jeff Baker 96	.25	.60
237 Mark Reynolds 96	.75	2.00
238 Joseph Bisenius 96	.25	.60
239 Michael Bourn 96	.40	1.00
240 Zack Segovia 96	.25	.60
241 Travis Buck 96	.25	.60
242 Chase Wright 96	.60	1.50
243 Rocky Cherry 96	.60	1.50
244 Danny Putnam 96	.25	.60
245 Kory Casto 96	.25	.60
246 Matt Chico 96	.25	.60
247 John Danks 96	.40	1.00
248 Juan Salas 96	.25	.60
249 Ryan Braun 96	1.25	3.00
250 Felix Pie 96	.25	.60
251 Jesus Flores 96	.25	.60
252 Andy Gonzalez 96	.25	.60
253 Ryan Sweeney 96	.25	.60
254 Jarrod Saltalamacchia 96	.40	1.00
255 Alex Gordon 96	.75	2.00
256 Josh Hamilton 96	.75	2.00
257 Sean Henn 96	.25	.60
258 Kei Igawa 96	.60	1.50
259 Akinori Iwamura 96	.60	1.50
260 Andy LaRoche 96	.25	.60
261 Rick Vanden Hurk 96	.25	.60
262 Kevin Kouzmanoff 96	.25	.60
263 Matt Lindstrom 96	.25	.60
264 Tim Lincecum 96	1.25	3.00
265 Daisuke Matsuzaka 96	1.00	2.50
266 Gustavo Molina 96	.25	.60
267 Miguel Montero 96	.25	.60
268 Brandon Morrow 96	1.25	3.00
269 Hideki Okajima 96	1.25	3.00
270 Adam Lind 96	.25	.60
271 Mike Rabelo 96	.25	.60
272 Brian Burres 96	.25	.60
273 Micah Owings 96	.25	.60
274 Brandon Wood 96	.25	.60
275 Alexi Casilla 96	.40	1.00
276 Joe Smith 96	.25	.60
277 Hunter Pence 96	.75	2.00
278 Glen Perkins 96	.25	.60
279 Chris Stewart 96	.25	.60
280 Ben Francisco 96	.25	.60
281 Troy Tulowitzki 96	.75	2.00
282 Billy Butler 96	.40	1.00

283 Delmon Young 96 .40 1.00
284 Phil Hughes 96 .60 1.50

2007 SP Rookie Edition Autographs

STATED ODDS 1:7
EXCH DEADLINE 8/17/2009
NO SP PRICING DUE TO SCARCITY
101 Joaquin Arias 3.00 8.00
102 Jeff Baker 3.00 8.00
103 Brian Barden 3.00 8.00
104 Michael Bourn 3.00 8.00
105 Kevin Slowey 6.00 15.00
106 Chase Wright 6.00 15.00
107 Kory Casto 3.00 8.00
108 Matt Chico 3.00 8.00
109 Matt DeSalvo 5.00 12.00
110 Homer Bailey 6.00 15.00
111 Ryan Braun 12.50 30.00
112 Felix Pie 3.00 8.00
113 Jesus Flores 3.00 8.00
114 Ryan Sweeney 4.00 10.00
115 Ryan Z. Braun 5.00 12.00
117 Josh Hamilton 15.00 40.00
118 Sean Henn 3.00 8.00
121 Andy LaRoche 4.00 10.00
122 Kevin Kouzmanoff 3.00 8.00
123 Matt Lindstrom 3.00 8.00
126 Gustavo Molina 4.00 10.00
127 Miguel Montero 3.00 8.00
128 Brandon Morrow 6.00 15.00
130 Adam Lind 4.00 10.00
131 Mike Rabelo 3.00 8.00
132 Micah Owings 4.00 10.00
133 Brandon Wood 6.00 15.00
134 Alexi Casilla 4.00 10.00
135 Joe Smith 3.00 8.00
137 Glen Perkins 3.00 8.00
138 Chris Stewart 3.00 8.00
140 Billy Butler 6.00 15.00
143 Joaquin Arias 95 3.00 8.00
144 Jeff Baker 95 3.00 8.00
145 Brian Barden 95 3.00 8.00
146 Michael Bourn 95 3.00 8.00
147 Kevin Slowey 95 6.00 15.00
148 Chase Wright 95 6.00 15.00
149 Kory Casto 95 3.00 8.00
150 Matt Chico 95 3.00 8.00
151 Shawn Riggans 95 3.00 8.00
152 Juan Salas 95 3.00 8.00
153 Ryan Braun 95 12.50 30.00
154 Felix Pie 95 5.00 12.00
155 Jesus Flores 95 3.00 8.00
156 Ryan Sweeney 95 4.00 10.00
157 Ryan Z. Braun 95 5.00 12.00
159 Josh Hamilton 95 15.00 40.00
160 Sean Henn 95 3.00 8.00
163 Andy LaRoche 95 4.00 10.00
164 Kevin Kouzmanoff 95 3.00 8.00
165 Matt Lindstrom 95 3.00 8.00
168 Gustavo Molina 95 3.00 8.00
169 Miguel Montero 95 3.00 8.00
170 Brandon Morrow 95 3.00 8.00
172 Adam Lind 95 4.00 10.00
173 Mike Rabelo 95 3.00 8.00
174 Micah Owings 95 4.00 10.00
175 Brandon Wood 95 6.00 15.00
176 Alexi Casilla 95 4.00 10.00
177 Joe Smith 95 4.00 10.00
178 Hunter Pence 95 10.00 25.00
179 Glen Perkins 95 3.00 8.00
180 Chris Stewart 95 3.00 8.00
181 Troy Tulowitzki 95 15.00 40.00
182 Billy Butler 95 6.00 15.00
185 Joaquin Arias 93 3.00 8.00
186 Jeff Baker 93 3.00 8.00
188 Joseph Bisenius 93 3.00 8.00
189 Michael Bourn 93 3.00 8.00
190 Zack Segovia 93 3.00 8.00
191 Kevin Slowey 93 6.00 15.00
192 Chase Wright 93 6.00 15.00
193 Rocky Cherry 93 10.00 25.00
194 Danny Putnam 93 8.00 20.00
195 Kory Casto 93 3.00 8.00
196 Matt Chico 93 3.00 8.00
197 John Danks 93 3.00 8.00
198 Homer Bailey 93 6.00 15.00
200 Felix Pie 93 5.00 12.00
201 Jesus Flores 93 4.00 10.00
202 Andy Gonzalez 93 4.00 10.00
204 Jarrod Saltalamacchia 93 5.00 12.00
207 Sean Henn 93 3.00 8.00
210 Andy LaRoche 93 4.00 10.00
211 Rick Vanden Hurk 93 3.00 8.00
212 Kevin Kouzmanoff 93 4.00 10.00
213 Matt Lindstrom 93 3.00 8.00
216 Gustavo Molina 93 4.00 10.00
217 Miguel Montero 93 3.00 8.00
218 Brandon Morrow 93 5.00 12.00
220 Adam Lind 93 4.00 10.00
221 Mike Rabelo 93 3.00 8.00
222 Brian Burres 93 3.00 8.00
223 Micah Owings 93 4.00 10.00
225 Alexi Casilla 93 4.00 10.00
226 Joe Smith 93 4.00 10.00
228 Glen Perkins 93 3.00 8.00
229 Chris Stewart 93 3.00 8.00
230 Ben Francisco 93 3.00 8.00
235 Joaquin Arias 96 3.00 8.00
236 Jeff Baker 96 3.00 8.00
238 Joseph Bisenius 96 3.00 8.00
239 Michael Bourn 96 3.00 8.00
240 Zack Segovia 96 3.00 8.00
242 Chase Wright 96 6.00 15.00
243 Rocky Cherry 96 10.00 25.00
244 Danny Putnam 96 8.00 20.00
245 Kory Casto 96 3.00 8.00
246 Matt Chico 96 3.00 8.00
247 John Danks 96 3.00 8.00
248 Juan Salas 96 3.00 8.00
250 Felix Pie 96 5.00 12.00
251 Jesus Flores 96 4.00 10.00
252 Andy Gonzalez 96 4.00 10.00
253 Ryan Sweeney 96 4.00 10.00
256 Josh Hamilton 96 20.00 50.00
257 Sean Henn 96 3.00 8.00
260 Andy LaRoche 96 4.00 10.00
261 Rick Vanden Hurk 96 3.00 8.00
262 Kevin Kouzmanoff 96 4.00 10.00
263 Matt Lindstrom 96 3.00 8.00
266 Gustavo Molina 96 4.00 10.00
267 Miguel Montero 96 3.00 8.00
268 Brandon Morrow 96 5.00 12.00
270 Adam Lind 96 4.00 10.00
271 Mike Rabelo 96 3.00 8.00
272 Brian Burres 96 3.00 8.00
273 Micah Owings 96 4.00 10.00
274 Brandon Wood 96 6.00 15.00
275 Alexi Casilla 96 4.00 10.00
276 Joe Smith 96 4.00 10.00
278 Glen Perkins 96 3.00 8.00
279 Chris Stewart 3.00 8.00
280 Ben Francisco 3.00 8.00

2007 SP Rookie Edition Promos

SPRC1 Daisuke Matsuzaka 1.00 2.50
SPRC2 Justin Upton .75 2.00
SPRC3 Joba Chamberlain .40 1.00
SPRC4 Andrew Miller 1.00 2.50
SPRC5 Yunel Escobar .25 .60
SPRC6 Cameron Maybin .40 1.00

1996 SPx

This 1996 SPx set (produced by Upper Deck) was issued in one series totalling 60 cards. The one-card packs had a suggested retail price of $3.49. Printed on 32 pt. card stock with Holoview technology and a perimeter diecut design, the set features color player photos with a Holography background on the fronts and decorative foil stamping on the back. Two special cards are included in the set: a Ken Griffey Jr. Commemorative card was inserted one in every 75 packs and a Mike Piazza Tribute card inserted one in every 95 packs. An autographed version of each of these cards was inserted at the rate of one in 2,000.

COMPLETE SET (60) 12.50 30.00
GRIFFEY KG1 STATED ODDS 1:75
PIAZZA MP1 STATED ODDS 1:95
GRIFFEY AUTO STATED ODDS 1:2000
PIAZZA AUTO STATED ODDS 1:2000
1 Greg Maddux 1.25 3.00
2 Chipper Jones .75 2.00
3 Fred McGriff .50 1.25
4 Tom Glavine .50 1.25
5 Cal Ripken 2.50 6.00
6 Roberto Alomar .50 1.25
7 Rafael Palmeiro .50 1.25
8 Jose Canseco .50 1.25
9 Roger Clemens 1.50 4.00
10 Mo Vaughn .30 .75
11 Jim Edmonds .30 .75
12 Tim Salmon .50 1.25
13 Sammy Sosa .75 2.00
14 Ryne Sandberg 1.25 3.00
15 Mark Grace .50 1.25
16 Frank Thomas .75 2.00
17 Barry Larkin .50 1.25
18 Kenny Lofton .30 .75
19 Albert Belle .30 .75
20 Eddie Murray .75 2.00
21 Manny Ramirez .50 1.25
22 Dante Bichette .30 .75
23 Larry Walker .30 .75
24 Vinny Castilla .30 .75
25 Andres Galarraga .30 .75
26 Cecil Fielder .30 .75
27 Gary Sheffield .30 .75
28 Craig Biggio .50 1.25
29 Jeff Bagwell .50 1.25
30 Derek Bell .30 .75
31 Johnny Damon .50 1.25
32 Eric Karros .30 .75
33 Mike Piazza 1.25 3.00
34 Raul Mondesi .30 .75
35 Hideo Nomo .75 2.00
36 Kirby Puckett .75 2.00
37 Paul Molitor .30 .75
38 Marty Cordova .30 .75
39 Rondell White .30 .75
40 Jason Isringhausen .30 .75
41 Paul Wilson .30 .75
42 Rey Ordonez .30 .75
43 Derek Jeter 2.00 5.00
44 Wade Boggs .50 1.25
45 Mark McGwire 2.00 5.00
46 Jason Kendall .30 .75
47 Ron Gant .30 .75
48 Ozzie Smith 1.25 3.00
49 Tony Gwynn 1.00 2.50
50 Ken Caminiti .30 .75
51 Barry Bonds 2.00 5.00
52 Matt Williams .30 .75
53 Osvaldo Fernandez .30 .75
54 Jay Buhner .30 .75
55 Ken Griffey Jr. 1.50 4.00
56 Randy Johnson .75 2.00
57 Alex Rodriguez 1.50 4.00
58 Juan Gonzalez .30 .75
59 Joe Carter .30 .75
60 Carlos Delgado .30 .75
KG1 Ken Griffey Jr. Comm. 2.50 6.00
MP1 Mike Piazza Trib. 2.50 6.00
KGA1 Ken Griffey Jr. Auto. 60.00 120.00
MPA1 Mike Piazza Auto. 60.00 120.00
KG Ken Griffey Jr. Promo 1.25 3.00

1996 SPx Gold

*STARS: 1.25X TO 3X BASIC CARDS
STATED ODDS 1:7

1996 SPx Bound for Glory

COMPLETE SET (10) 30.00 80.00
STATED ODDS 1:24
1 Ken Griffey Jr. 4.00 10.00
2 Frank Thomas 2.00 5.00
3 Barry Bonds 5.00 12.00
4 Cal Ripken 6.00 15.00
5 Greg Maddux 3.00 8.00
6 Chipper Jones 2.00 5.00
7 Roberto Alomar 1.25 3.00
8 Manny Ramirez 1.25 3.00
9 Tony Gwynn 2.50 6.00
10 Mike Piazza 3.00 8.00

1997 SPx

The 1997 SPx set (produced by Upper Deck) was issued in one series totalling 50 cards and was distributed in three-card hobby only packs with a suggested retail price of $5.99. The fronts feature color player images on a Holoview perimeter die cut design. The backs carry a player photo, player information, and career statistics. A sample card featuring Ken Griffey Jr. was distributed to dealers and hobby media several weeks prior to the products release.

COMPLETE SET (50) 20.00 50.00
1 Eddie Murray .60 1.50
2 Darin Erstad .25 .60
3 Tim Salmon .40 1.00
4 Andruw Jones .40 1.00
5 Chipper Jones .60 1.50
6 John Smoltz .40 1.00
7 Greg Maddux 1.00 2.50
8 Kenny Lofton .25 .60
9 Roberto Alomar .40 1.00
10 Rafael Palmeiro .40 1.00
11 Brady Anderson .25 .60
12 Cal Ripken 2.00 5.00
13 Nomar Garciaparra 1.00 2.50
14 Mo Vaughn .25 .60
15 Ryne Sandberg 1.00 2.50
16 Sammy Sosa .60 1.50
17 Frank Thomas .60 1.50
18 Albert Belle .25 .60
19 Barry Larkin .40 1.00
20 Deion Sanders .40 1.00
21 Manny Ramirez .40 1.00
22 Jim Thome .40 1.00
23 Dante Bichette .25 .60
24 Andres Galarraga .25 .60
25 Larry Walker .25 .60
26 Gary Sheffield .25 .60
27 Jeff Bagwell .40 1.00
28 Raul Mondesi .25 .60
29 Hideo Nomo .60 1.50
30 Mike Piazza 1.00 2.50
31 Paul Molitor .25 .60
32 Todd Walker .25 .60
33 Vladimir Guerrero .60 1.50
34 Todd Hundley .25 .60
35 Andy Pettitte .40 1.00
36 Derek Jeter 1.50 4.00
37 Jose Canseco .40 1.00
38 Mark McGwire 1.50 4.00
39 Scott Rolen .40 1.00
40 Ron Gant .25 .60
41 Ken Caminiti .25 .60
42 Tony Gwynn .75 2.00
43 Barry Bonds 1.50 4.00
44 Jay Buhner .25 .60
45 Ken Griffey Jr. 1.25 3.00
46 Alex Rodriguez 1.00 2.50
47 Jose Cruz Jr. RC .40 1.00
48 Juan Gonzalez .25 .60
49 Ivan Rodriguez .40 1.00
50 Roger Clemens 1.25 3.00
S45 Ken Griffey Jr. Sample 1.00 2.50

1997 SPx Bronze

COMPLETE SET (50) 75.00 150.00
*STARS: 1X TO 2.5X BASIC CARDS
*ROOKIES: .6X TO 1.5X BASIC CARDS
RANDOM INSERTS IN PACKS

1997 SPx Gold

*STARS: 2.5X TO 6X BASIC CARDS
*ROOKIES: 1.5X TO 4X BASIC CARDS
STATED ODDS 1:17

1997 SPx Grand Finale

*STARS: 12.5X TO 30X BASIC CARDS
*ROOKIES: 5X TO 12X BASIC CARDS
RANDOM INSERTS IN PACKS
STATED PRINT RUN 50 SETS

1997 SPx Silver

*STARS: 1.5X TO 4X BASIC CARDS
*ROOKIES: 1X TO 2.5X BASIC CARDS
RANDOM INSERTS IN PACKS

1997 SPx Steel

COMPLETE SET (50) 40.00 100.00
*STARS: .6X TO 1.5X BASIC CARDS
*ROOKIES: .5X TO 1.2X BASIC CARDS
RANDOM INSERTS IN PACKS

1997 SPx Bound for Glory

COMPLETE SET (20) 40.00 100.00
RANDOM INSERTS IN PACKS
STATED PRINT RUN 1500 SERIAL #'d SETS
1 Andruw Jones 1.00 2.50
2 Chipper Jones 2.50 6.00
3 Greg Maddux 4.00 10.00
4 Kenny Lofton 1.00 2.50
5 Cal Ripken 8.00 20.00
6 Mo Vaughn 1.00 2.50
7 Frank Thomas 2.50 6.00
8 Albert Belle 1.00 2.50
9 Manny Ramirez 1.50 4.00
10 Gary Sheffield 1.00 2.50
11 Jeff Bagwell 1.50 4.00
12 Mike Piazza 2.50 6.00
13 Derek Jeter 6.00 15.00
14 Mark McGwire 4.00 10.00
15 Tony Gwynn 2.50 6.00
16 Ken Caminiti 1.00 2.50
17 Barry Bonds 4.00 10.00
18 Alex Rodriguez 3.00 8.00
19 Ken Griffey Jr. 5.00 12.00
20 Juan Gonzalez 1.00 2.50

1997 SPx Bound for Glory Supreme Signatures

RANDOM INSERTS IN PACKS
STATED PRINT RUN 250 SERIAL #'d SETS
1 Jeff Bagwell 40.00 80.00
2 Ken Griffey Jr. 75.00 150.00
3 Andruw Jones 10.00 25.00
4 Alex Rodriguez 50.00 120.00
5 Gary Sheffield 10.00 25.00

1997 SPx Cornerstones of the Game

COMPLETE SET (10) 50.00 100.00
RANDOM INSERTS IN PACKS
STATED PRINT RUN 500 SERIAL #'d SETS
1 K.Griffey Jr. / B.Bonds 8.00 20.00
2 F.Thomas / A.Belle 4.00 10.00
3 G.Maddux / C.Jones 6.00 15.00
4 T.Gwynn / P.Molitor 4.00 10.00
5 V.Guerrero / A.Jones 2.50 6.00
6 J.Bagwell / R.Sandberg 6.00 15.00
7 M.Piazza / I.Rodriguez 4.00 10.00
8 C.Ripken / E.Murray 12.00 30.00
9 M.McGwire / M.Vaughn 6.00 15.00
10 A.Rodriguez / D.Jeter 10.00 25.00

1998 SPx Finite Sample

1 Ken Griffey Jr. 2.50 6.00
2 Ken Griffey Jr. 2.50 6.00

1998 SPx Finite

The 1998 SPx Finite set contains a total of 180 cards, all serial numbered based upon specific subsets. The three-card packs retailed for $5.99 each and hit the market in June, 1998. The subsets and serial numbering are as follows: Youth Movement (1-30) - 5000 of each card, Power Explosion (31-50) - 4000 of each card, Basic Cards (51-140) - 9000 of each card, Star Focus (141-170) - 7000 of each card, Heroes of the Game (171-180) - 2000 of each card, Youth Movement (181-210) - 5000 of each card, Power Passion (211-240) - 7000 of each card, Basic Cards (241-330) - 9000 of each card, Tradewinds (331-350) - 4000 of each card and Cornerstones of the Game (351-360) -2000 of each card. Notable Rookie Cards include Kevin Millwood and Magglio Ordonez.

COMP.YM SER.1 (30) 8.00 20.00
COMMON YM (1-30) .30 .75
YM 1-30 PRINT RUN 5000 SERIAL #'d SETS
COMP.PE SER.1 (20) 8.00 20.00
COMMON PE (31-50) .30 .75
PE 31-50 PRINT RUN 4000 SERIAL #'d SETS
COMP.BASIC SER.1 (90) 20.00 50.00
COMMON CARD (51-140) .25 .60
BASIC 51-140 PR.RUN 9000 SERIAL #'d SETS
COMP.SF SER.1 (30) 12.00 30.00
COMMON SF (141-170) .25 .60
SF 141-170 PRINT RUN 7000 SERIAL #'d SETS
COMP.HG SER.1 (10) 10.00 25.00
COMMON HG (171-180) .40 1.00
HG 171-180 PRINT RUN 2000 #'d SETS
COMP.YM SER.2 (30) 8.00 20.00
COMMON YM (181-210) .30 .75
YM 181-210 PR.RUN 5000 SERIAL #'d SETS
COMP.PP SER.2 (30) 8.00 20.00
COMMON PP (211-240) .25 .60
PP 211-240 PRINT RUN 7000 SERIAL #'d SETS
COMP.BASIC SER.2 (90) 15.00 40.00
COMMON CARD (241-330) .25 .60
BASIC 241-330 PR.RUN 9000 SERIAL #'d SETS
COMP.TW SER.2 (20) 5.00 12.00
COMMON TW (331-350) .30 .75
TW 331-350 PR.RUN 4000 SERIAL #'d SETS
COMP.CG SER.2 (10) 8.00 20.00
COMMON CG (351-360) .40 1.00
CG 351-360 PRINT RUN 2000 #'d SETS
1 Nomar Garciaparra YM .50 1.25
2 Miguel Tejada YM .75 2.00
3 Mike Cameron YM .30 .75
4 Ken Cloude YM .30 .75
5 Jaret Wright YM .30 .75
6 Mark Kotsay YM .30 .75
7 Craig Counsell YM .30 .75
8 Jose Guillen YM .30 .75
9 Neifi Perez YM .30 .75
10 Jose Cruz Jr. YM .30 .75
11 Brett Tomko YM .30 .75
12 Matt Morris YM .30 .75
13 Justin Thompson YM .30 .75
14 Jeremi Gonzalez YM .30 .75
15 Scott Rolen YM .50 1.25
16 Vladimir Guerrero YM .50 1.25
17 Brad Fullmer YM .30 .75
18 Brian Giles YM .30 .75
19 Todd Dunwoody YM .30 .75
20 Ben Grieve YM .30 .75
21 Juan Encarnacion YM .30 .75
22 Aaron Boone YM .30 .75
23 Richie Sexson YM .30 .75
24 Richard Hidalgo YM .30 .75
25 Andruw Jones YM .30 .75
26 Todd Helton YM .50 1.25
27 Paul Konerko YM .30 .75
28 Dante Powell YM .30 .75
29 Elli Marrero YM .30 .75
30 Derek Jeter YM 2.00 5.00
31 Mike Piazza PE .75 2.00
32 Tony Clark PE .30 .75
33 Larry Walker PE .50 1.25
34 Jim Thome PE .50 1.25
35 Juan Gonzalez PE .30 .75
36 Jeff Bagwell PE .50 1.25
37 Jay Buhner PE .30 .75
38 Tim Salmon PE .30 .75
39 Albert Belle PE .30 .75
40 Mark McGwire PE 1.25 3.00
41 Sammy Sosa PE .75 2.00
42 Mo Vaughn PE .30 .75
43 Manny Ramirez PE .75 2.00
44 Tino Martinez PE .30 .75
45 Frank Thomas PE .75 2.00
46 Nomar Garciaparra PE .50 1.25
47 Alex Rodriguez PE 1.00 2.50
48 Chipper Jones PE .75 2.00
49 Barry Bonds PE 1.25 3.00
50 Ken Griffey Jr. PE 1.50 4.00
51 Jason Dickson .25 .60
52 Jim Edmonds .40 1.00
53 Darin Erstad .25 .60
54 Tim Salmon .40 1.00
55 Chipper Jones .60 1.50
56 Ryan Klesko .25 .60
57 Tom Glavine .40 1.00
58 Denny Neagle .25 .60
59 John Smoltz .40 1.00
60 Javy Lopez .25 .60
61 Roberto Alomar .40 1.00
62 Rafael Palmeiro .40 1.00
63 Mike Mussina .40 1.00
64 Cal Ripken 2.00 5.00
65 Mo Vaughn .25 .60
66 Tim Naehring .25 .60
67 John Valentin .25 .60
68 Mark Grace .40 1.00
69 Kevin Orie .25 .60
70 Sammy Sosa .60 1.50
71 Albert Belle .25 .60
72 Frank Thomas .60 1.50
73 Robin Ventura .25 .60
74 David Justice .25 .60
75 Kenny Lofton .25 .60
76 Omar Vizquel .40 1.00
77 Manny Ramirez .60 1.50
78 Jim Thome .40 1.00
79 Dante Bichette .25 .60
80 Larry Walker .40 1.00
81 Vinny Castilla .25 .60
82 Ellis Burks .25 .60
83 Bobby Higginson .25 .60
84 Brian Hunter .25 .60
85 Tony Clark .25 .60
86 Mike Hampton .25 .60
87 Jeff Bagwell .40 1.00
88 Craig Biggio .40 1.00
89 Derek Bell .25 .60
90 Mike Piazza .60 1.50
91 Ramon Martinez .25 .60
92 Raul Mondesi .25 .60
93 Hideo Nomo .60 1.50
94 Eric Karros .25 .60
95 Paul Molitor .60 1.50
96 Marty Cordova .25 .60
97 Brad Radke .25 .60
98 Mark Grudzielanek .25 .60
99 Carlos Perez .25 .60
100 Rondell White .25 .60
101 Todd Hundley .25 .60
102 Edgardo Alfonzo .25 .60
103 John Franco .25 .60
104 John Olerud .25 .60
105 Tino Martinez .25 .60
106 David Cone .25 .60
107 Paul O'Neill .40 1.00
108 Andy Pettitte .40 1.00
109 Bernie Williams .40 1.00
110 Rickey Henderson .60 1.50
111 Jason Giambi .25 .60
112 Matt Stairs .25 .60
113 Gregg Jefferies .25 .60
114 Rico Brogna .25 .60
115 Curt Schilling .40 1.00
116 Jason Schmidt .25 .60
117 Jose Guillen .25 .60
118 Kevin Young .25 .60
119 Ray Lankford .25 .60
120 Mark McGwire 1.00 2.50
121 Delino DeShields .25 .60
122 Ken Caminiti .25 .60
123 Tony Gwynn .60 1.50
124 Trevor Hoffman .40 1.00
125 Barry Bonds 1.00 2.50
126 Jeff Kent .25 .60
127 Shawn Estes .25 .60
128 J.T. Snow .25 .60
129 Jay Buhner .25 .60
130 Ken Griffey Jr. 1.25 3.00
131 Dan Wilson .25 .60
132 Edgar Martinez .40 1.00
133 Alex Rodriguez .75 2.00
134 Rusty Greer .25 .60
135 Juan Gonzalez .25 .60
136 Fernando Tatis .25 .60
137 Ivan Rodriguez .40 1.00
138 Carlos Delgado .25 .60
139 Pat Hentgen .25 .60
140 Roger Clemens .75 2.00
141 Chipper Jones SF .60 1.50
142 Greg Maddux SF .75 2.00
143 Rafael Palmeiro SF .40 1.00
144 Mike Mussina SF .40 1.00
145 Cal Ripken SF 2.00 5.00
146 Nomar Garciaparra SF .40 1.00
147 Mo Vaughn SF .25 .60
148 Sammy Sosa SF .60 1.50
149 Albert Belle SF .25 .60
150 Frank Thomas SF .60 1.50
151 Jim Thome SF .40 1.00
152 Kenny Lofton SF .25 .60
153 Manny Ramirez SF .60 1.50
154 Larry Walker SF .40 1.00
155 Jeff Bagwell SF .40 1.00
156 Craig Biggio SF .40 1.00
157 Mike Piazza SF .60 1.50
158 Paul Molitor SF .60 1.50
159 Derek Jeter SF 1.50 4.00
160 Tino Martinez SF .25 .60
161 Curt Schilling SF .40 1.00
162 Mark McGwire SF 1.00 2.50
163 Tony Gwynn SF .60 1.50
164 Barry Bonds SF 1.00 2.50
165 Ken Griffey Jr. SF 1.25 3.00
166 Randy Johnson SF .60 1.50
167 Alex Rodriguez SF .75 2.00
168 Juan Gonzalez SF .25 .60
169 Ivan Rodriguez SF .40 1.00
170 Roger Clemens SF .75 2.00
171 Greg Maddux HG 1.25 3.00
172 Cal Ripken HG 3.00 8.00
173 Frank Thomas HG 1.00 2.50
174 Jeff Bagwell HG .60 1.50
175 Mike Piazza HG 1.00 2.50
176 Mark McGwire HG 1.50 4.00
177 Barry Bonds HG 1.50 4.00
178 Ken Griffey Jr. HG 2.00 5.00
179 Alex Rodriguez HG 1.25 3.00
180 Roger Clemens HG 1.25 3.00
181 Mike Caruso YM .30 .75
182 David Ortiz YM 1.00 2.50
183 Gabe Alvarez YM .30 .75
184 Gary Matthews Jr. YM RC .30 .75
185 Kerry Wood YM .30 .75
186 Carl Pavano YM .30 .75
187 Alex Gonzalez YM .30 .75
188 Masato Yoshii YM RC .30 .75
189 Larry Sutton YM .30 .75
190 Russell Branyan YM .30 .75
191 Bruce Chen YM .30 .75
192 Rolando Arrojo YM RC .30 .75
193 Ryan Christenson YM RC .30 .75
194 Cliff Politte YM .30 .75
195 A.J. Hinch YM .30 .75
196 Kevin Witt YM .30 .75
197 Daryle Ward YM .30 .75
198 Corey Koskie YM RC .30 .75
199 Mike Lowell YM RC 3.00 8.00
200 Travis Lee YM .30 .75
201 Kevin Millwood YM RC .75 2.00
202 Robert Smith YM .30 .75
203 Magglio Ordonez YM RC 1.25 3.00
204 Eric Milton YM .30 .75
205 Geoff Jenkins YM .30 .75
206 Rich Butler YM RC .30 .75
207 Mike Kinkade YM RC .30 .75
208 Braden Looper YM .30 .75
209 Matt Clement YM .30 .75
210 Derrek Lee YM .30 .75
211 Randy Johnson PP .60 1.50
212 John Smoltz PP .40 1.00
213 Roger Clemens PP .75 2.00
214 Curt Schilling PP .40 1.00
215 Pedro Martinez PP .40 1.00
216 Vinny Castilla PP .25 .60
217 Jose Cruz Jr. PP .25 .60
218 Jim Thome PP .40 1.00
219 Alex Rodriguez PP .75 2.00
220 Frank Thomas PP .60 1.50
221 Tim Salmon PP .25 .60
222 Larry Walker PP .40 1.00
223 Albert Belle PP .25 .60
224 Manny Ramirez PP .60 1.50
225 Mark McGwire PP 1.00 2.50
226 Mo Vaughn PP .25 .60
227 Andres Galarraga PP .40 1.00
228 Scott Rolen PP .40 1.00
229 Travis Lee PP .25 .60
230 Mike Piazza PP .60 1.50
231 Nomar Garciaparra PP .40 1.00
232 Andruw Jones PP .25 .60
233 Barry Bonds PP 1.00 2.50
234 Jeff Bagwell PP .40 1.00
235 Juan Gonzalez PP .25 .60
236 Tino Martinez PP .25 .60
237 Vladimir Guerrero PP .40 1.00
238 Rafael Palmeiro PP .40 1.00
239 Russell Branyan PP .25 .60
240 Ken Griffey Jr. PP 1.25 3.00
241 Cecil Fielder .25 .60
242 Chuck Finley .25 .60
243 Jay Bell .25 .60
244 Andy Benes .25 .60
245 Matt Williams .25 .60
246 Brian Anderson .25 .60
247 David Dellucci RC .40 1.00
248 Andres Galarraga .25 .60
249 Andruw Jones .25 .60
250 Greg Maddux .75 2.00
251 Brady Anderson .25 .60
252 Joe Carter .25 .60
253 Eric Davis .25 .60
254 Pedro Martinez .40 1.00
255 Nomar Garciaparra .40 1.00
256 Dennis Eckersley .40 1.00
257 Henry Rodriguez .25 .60
258 Jeff Blauser .25 .60
259 Jaime Navarro .25 .60
260 Ray Durham .25 .60
261 Chris Stynes .25 .60
262 Willie Greene .25 .60
263 Reggie Sanders .25 .60
264 Bret Boone .25 .60
265 Barry Larkin .40 1.00
266 Travis Fryman .25 .60
267 Charles Nagy .25 .60
268 Sandy Alomar Jr. .25 .60
269 Darryl Kile .25 .60
270 Mike Lansing .25 .60
271 Pedro Astacio .25 .60
272 Damion Easley .25 .60
273 Joe Randa .25 .60
274 Luis Gonzalez .25 .60
275 Mike Piazza .60 1.50
276 Todd Zeile .25 .60
277 Edgar Renteria .25 .60
278 Livan Hernandez .25 .60
279 Cliff Floyd .25 .60
280 Moises Alou .25 .60
281 Billy Wagner .25 .60
282 Jeff King .25 .60
283 Hal Morris .25 .60
284 Johnny Damon .40 1.00
285 Dean Palmer .25 .60
286 Tim Belcher .25 .60
287 Eric Young .25 .60
288 Bobby Bonilla .25 .60
289 Gary Sheffield .25 .60
290 Chan Ho Park .40 1.00
291 Charles Johnson .25 .60
292 Jeff Cirillo .25 .60
293 Jeromy Burnitz .25 .60
294 Jose Valentin .25 .60
295 Marquis Grissom .25 .60
296 Todd Walker .25 .60
297 Terry Steinbach .25 .60
298 Rick Aguilera .25 .60
299 Vladimir Guerrero .40 1.00
300 Rey Ordonez .25 .60
301 Butch Huskey .25 .60
302 Bernard Gilkey .25 .60
303 Mariano Rivera .40 1.00
304 Chuck Knoblauch .25 .60
305 Derek Jeter 1.50 4.00
306 Ricky Bottalico .25 .60
307 Bob Abreu .25 .60
308 Scott Rolen .40 1.00
309 Al Martin .25 .60
310 Jason Kendall .25 .60
311 Brian Jordan .25 .60
312 Ron Gant .25 .60
313 Todd Stottlemyre .25 .60
314 Greg Vaughn .25 .60
315 Kevin Brown .25 .60
316 Wally Joyner .25 .60
317 Robb Nen .25 .60
318 Orel Hershiser .25 .60
319 Russ Davis .25 .60
320 Randy Johnson .60 1.50
321 Quinton McCracken .25 .60
322 Tony Saunders .25 .60
323 Wilson Alvarez .25 .60
324 Wade Boggs .40 1.00
325 Fred McGriff .40 1.00
326 Lee Stevens .25 .60
327 John Wetteland .25 .60
328 Jose Canseco .40 1.00
329 Randy Myers .25 .60
330 Jose Cruz Jr. .25 .60
331 Matt Williams TW .30 .75
332 Andres Galarraga TW .50 1.25
333 Walt Weiss TW .30 .75
334 Joe Carter TW .30 .75
335 Pedro Martinez TW .50 1.25
336 Henry Rodriguez TW .30 .75
337 Travis Fryman TW .30 .75
338 Darryl Kile TW .30 .75
339 Mike Lansing TW .30 .75
340 Mike Piazza TW .75 2.00
341 Moises Alou TW .30 .75
342 Charles Johnson TW .30 .75
343 Chuck Knoblauch TW .30 .75
344 Rickey Henderson TW .75 2.00
345 Kevin Brown TW .30 .75
346 Orel Hershiser TW .30 .75
347 Wade Boggs TW .50 1.25
348 Fred McGriff TW .50 1.25
349 Jose Canseco TW .50 1.25
350 Gary Sheffield TW .30 .75
351 Travis Lee CG .40 1.00
352 Nomar Garciaparra CG .60 1.50
353 Frank Thomas CG 1.00 2.50
354 Cal Ripken CG 3.00 8.00
355 Mark McGwire CG 1.50 4.00
356 Mike Piazza CG 1.00 2.50
357 Alex Rodriguez CG 1.25 3.00
358 Barry Bonds CG 1.50 4.00
359 Tony Gwynn CG 1.00 2.50
360 Ken Griffey Jr. CG 2.00 5.00

1998 SPx Finite Radiance

*YM RADIANCE: .5X TO 1.2X BASIC YM
YM 1-30 PRINT RUN 2500 SERIAL #'d SETS
*PE RADIANCE: .6X TO 1.5X BASIC PE
PE 31-50 PRINT RUN 1000 SERIAL #'d SETS
EXCH.CARDS MADE FOR #'s 39/40/41/46
EXCHANGE DEADLINE WAS 6/2/99
*BASIC RADIANCE: .5X TO 1.22X BASIC CARDS
BASIC 51-140 PR.RUN 4500 SERIAL #'d SETS
*SF RADIANCE: .5X TO 1.2X BASIC SF
SF 141-170 PRINT RUN 3500 SERIAL #'d SETS
*HG RADIANCE: 4X TO 10X BASIC HG
HG 171-180 PRINT RUN 100 SERIAL #'d SETS
*YM RADIANCE: .5X TO 1.2X BASIC YM
*YM RADIANCE RC's: .5X TO 1.2X BASIC YM
YM 181-210 PR.RUN 2500 SERIAL #'d SETS
*PP RADIANCE: .5X TO 1.2X BASIC PP
PP 211-240 PRINT RUN 3500 SERIAL #'d SETS
*BASIC RADIANCE: .5X TO 1.2X BASIC CARDS
BASIC 241-330 PR.RUN 4500 SERIAL #'d SETS
*TW RADIANCE: .6X TO 1.5X BASIC TW
TW 331-350 PRINT RUN 1000 SERIAL #'d SETS
*CG RADIANCE: 4X TO 10X BASIC CG
CG 351-360 PRINT RUN 100 SERIAL #'d SETS
RANDOM INSERTS IN PACKS

1998 SPx Finite Spectrum

*YM SPECTRUM: 1X TO 2.5X BASIC YM
YM 1-30 PRINT RUN 1250 SERIAL #'d SETS
*PE SPECTRUM: 5X TO 12X BASIC PE
PE 31-50 PRINT RUN 50 SERIAL #'d SETS
*BASIC SPECTRUM: 1.25X TO 3X BASIC
BASIC 51-140 PR.RUN 2250 SERIAL #'d SETS
*SF SPECTRUM: 1.25X TO 3X BASIC SF
SF 141-170 PRINT RUN 1750 SERIAL #'d SETS
HG 171-180 PRINT RUN 1 SERIAL #'d SET
HG NOT PRICED DUE TO SCARCITY
*YM SPECTRUM: .75X TO 2X BASIC YM
*YM SPEC. RC's: .5X TO 1.2X BASIC YM
YM 181-210 PR.RUN 1250 SERIAL #'d SETS
*PP SPECTRUM: 1.25X TO 3X BASIC PP
PP 211-240 PRINT RUN 1750 SERIAL #'d SETS
*BASIC SPECTRUM: 1.25X TO 3X BASIC
BASIC 241-330 PR.RUN 2250 SERIAL #'d SETS
*TW SPECTRUM: 5X TO 12X BASIC TW
TW 331-350 PRINT RUN 50 SERIAL #'d SETS
CG 351-360 PRINT RUN 1 SERIAL #'d SET
CG NOT PRICED DUE TO SCARCITY
RANDOM INSERTS IN PACKS

1998 SPx Finite Home Run Hysteria

RANDOM INSERTS IN SER.2 PACKS
STATED PRINT RUN 62 SERIAL #'d SETS
HR1 Ken Griffey Jr. 150.00 400.00
HR2 Mark McGwire 30.00 80.00
HR3 Sammy Sosa 20.00 50.00
HR4 Albert Belle 8.00 20.00
HR5 Alex Rodriguez 25.00 60.00
HR6 Greg Vaughn 8.00 20.00
HR7 Andres Galarraga 12.00 30.00
HR8 Vinny Castilla 8.00 20.00
HR9 Juan Gonzalez 8.00 20.00
HR10 Chipper Jones 20.00 50.00

1999 SPx

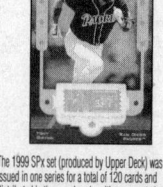

The 1999 SPx set (produced by Upper Deck) was issued in one series for a total of 120 cards and distributed in thee-card packs with a suggested retail price of $5.99. The set features color photos of 80 MLB veteran players (1-80) with 40 top rookies on subset cards (81-120) numbered to 1,999. J.D. Drew and Gabe Kapler autographed all 1,999 of their respective rookie cards. A Ken Griffey Jr. Sample card was distributed to dealers and hobby media several weeks prior to the product's release. This card is serial numbered "0000/0000" on front, has the word "SAMPLE" pasted across the back in red ink and is oddly numbered "24 East" on back (even though the basic cards have no regional references). Also, 350 Willie Mays A Piece of History 500 Home Run bat cards were randomly seeded into packs. Mays personally signed an additional 24 cards (matching his jersey number) - all of which were then serial numbered by hand and randomly seeded into packs. Pricing for these bat cards can be referenced under 1999 Upper Deck A Piece of History 500 Club.

COMP.SET w/o SP's (80) 10.00 25.00
COMMON MCGWIRE (1-10) .60 1.50
COMMON CARD (11-80) .20 .50
COMMON SP (81-120) 4.00 10.00
81-120 RANDOM INSERTS IN PACKS
81-120 PRINT RUN 1999 SERIAL #'d SETS
W.MAYS BAT LISTED W/UD APH 500 CLUB
1 Mark McGwire 61 1.25 3.00
2 Mark McGwire 62 1.25 3.00
3 Mark McGwire 63 .60 1.50
4 Mark McGwire 64 .60 1.50
5 Mark McGwire 65 .60 1.50
6 Mark McGwire 66 .60 1.50
7 Mark McGwire 67 .60 1.50
8 Mark McGwire 68 .60 1.50
9 Mark McGwire 69 .60 1.50
10 Mark McGwire 70 1.50 4.00
11 Mo Vaughn .20 .50
12 Darin Erstad .20 .50
13 Travis Lee .20 .50
14 Randy Johnson .50 1.25
15 Matt Williams .20 .50
16 Chipper Jones .50 1.25
17 Greg Maddux .75 2.00
18 Andruw Jones .30 .75
19 Andres Galarraga .20 .50
20 Cal Ripken 1.50 4.00
21 Albert Belle .20 .50
22 Mike Mussina .30 .75
23 Nomar Garciaparra .75 2.00
24 Pedro Martinez .30 .75
25 John Valentin .20 .50
26 Kerry Wood .20 .50
27 Sammy Sosa .50 1.25
28 Mark Grace .30 .75
29 Frank Thomas .50 1.25
30 Mike Caruso .20 .50
31 Barry Larkin .30 .75
32 Sean Casey .20 .50
33 Jim Thome .30 .75
34 Kenny Lofton .20 .50
35 Manny Ramirez .30 .75
36 Larry Walker .20 .50
37 Todd Helton .30 .75
38 Vinny Castilla .20 .50
39 Tony Clark .20 .50
40 Derrek Lee .30 .75
41 Mark Kotsay .20 .50
42 Jeff Bagwell .30 .75
43 Craig Biggio .30 .75
44 Moises Alou .20 .50
45 Larry Sutton .20 .50
46 Johnny Damon .30 .75
47 Gary Sheffield .20 .50
48 Raul Mondesi .20 .50
49 Jeromy Burnitz .20 .50
50 Todd Walker .20 .50
51 David Ortiz .50 1.25
52 Vladimir Guerrero .50 1.25
53 Rondell White .20 .50
54 Mike Piazza .75 2.00
55 Derek Jeter 1.25 3.00
56 Tino Martinez .30 .75
57 Roger Clemens 1.00 2.50
58 Ben Grieve .20 .50
59 A.J. Hinch .20 .50
60 Scott Rolen .30 .75
61 Doug Glanville .20 .50
62 Aramis Ramirez .20 .50
63 Jose Guillen .20 .50
64 Tony Gwynn .60 1.50
65 Greg Vaughn .20 .50
66 Ruben Rivera .20 .50
67 Barry Bonds 1.25 3.00
68 J.T. Snow .20 .50
69 Alex Rodriguez .75 2.00
70 Ken Griffey Jr. 1.00 2.50
71 Jay Buhner .20 .50
72 Mark McGwire 1.25 3.00
73 Fernando Tatis .20 .50
74 Quinton McCracken .20 .50
75 Wade Boggs .30 .75
76 Ivan Rodriguez .30 .75
77 Juan Gonzalez .20 .50
78 Rafael Palmeiro .30 .75
79 Jose Cruz Jr. .20 .50
80 Carlos Delgado .20 .50
81 Troy Glaus SP 6.00 15.00
82 Vladimir Nunez SP 4.00 10.00
83 George Lombard SP 4.00 10.00
84 Bruce Chen SP 4.00 10.00
85 Ryan Minor SP 4.00 10.00
86 Calvin Pickering SP 4.00 10.00
87 Jin Ho Cho SP 4.00 10.00
88 Russ Branyan SP 4.00 10.00
89 Derrick Gibson SP 4.00 10.00
90 Gabe Kapler SP AU 6.00 15.00
91 Matt Anderson SP 4.00 10.00
92 Robert Fick SP 4.00 10.00
93 Juan Encarnacion SP 4.00 10.00
94 Preston Wilson SP 4.00 10.00
95 Alex Gonzalez SP 4.00 10.00
96 Carlos Beltran SP 6.00 15.00
97 Jeremy Giambi SP 4.00 10.00
98 Dee Brown SP 4.00 10.00
99 Adrian Beltre SP 4.00 10.00
100 Alex Cora SP 4.00 10.00
101 Angel Pena SP 4.00 10.00
102 Geoff Jenkins SP 4.00 10.00
103 Ronnie Belliard SP 4.00 10.00
104 Corey Koskie SP 4.00 10.00
105 A.J. Pierzynski SP 4.00 10.00
106 Michael Barrett SP 4.00 10.00
107 Fernando Seguignol SP 4.00 10.00
108 Mike Kinkade SP 4.00 10.00
109 Mike Lowell SP 4.00 10.00
110 Ricky Ledee SP 4.00 10.00
111 Eric Chavez SP 4.00 10.00
112 Abraham Nunez SP 4.00 10.00
113 Matt Clement SP 4.00 10.00
114 Ben Davis SP 4.00 10.00
115 Mike Darr SP 4.00 10.00
116 Ramon E.Martinez SP RC 4.00 10.00
117 Carlos Guillen SP 4.00 10.00
118 Shane Monahan SP 4.00 10.00
119 J.D. Drew SP AU 4.00 10.00
120 Kevin Witt SP 4.00 10.00
24EAST Ken Griffey Jr. Sample 1.00 2.50

1999 SPx Finite Radiance

*RADIANCE 1-10: 5X TO 12X BASIC 1-10
*RADIANCE 11-80: 8X TO 20X BASIC 11-80
*RADIANCE 81-120: .75X TO 2X BASIC 81-120
THREE CARDS PER RADIANCE HOT PACK
STATED PRINT RUN 100 SERIAL #'D SETS
90 Gabe Kapler AU 10.00 25.00
119 J.D. Drew AU 10.00 25.00

1999 SPx Dominance

COMPLETE SET (20) 15.00 40.00
STATED ODDS 1:17
FB1 Chipper Jones 1.00 2.50
FB2 Greg Maddux 1.25 3.00
FB3 Cal Ripken 3.00 8.00
FB4 Nomar Garciaparra .60 1.50
FB5 Mo Vaughn .40 1.00
FB6 Sammy Sosa 1.00 2.50
FB7 Albert Belle .40 1.00
FB8 Frank Thomas 1.00 2.50
FB9 Jim Thome .60 1.50
FB10 Jeff Bagwell .60 1.50
FB11 Vladimir Guerrero .60 1.50
FB12 Mike Piazza 1.00 2.50
FB13 Derek Jeter 2.50 6.00
FB14 Tony Gwynn 1.00 2.50
FB15 Barry Bonds 1.50 4.00
FB16 Ken Griffey Jr. 2.00 5.00
FB17 Alex Rodriguez 1.25 3.00
FB18 Mark McGwire 1.50 4.00
FB19 J.D. Drew .40 1.00
FB20 Juan Gonzalez .40 1.00

1999 SPx Power Explosion

COMPLETE SET (30) 15.00 40.00
STATED ODDS 1:3
PE1 Troy Glaus .50 1.25
PE2 Mo Vaughn .30 .75
PE3 Travis Lee .30 .75
PE4 Chipper Jones .75 2.00
PE5 Andres Galarraga .30 .75
PE6 Brady Anderson .30 .75
PE7 Albert Belle .30 .75
PE8 Nomar Garciaparra 1.25 3.00
PE9 Sammy Sosa .75 2.00
PE10 Frank Thomas .75 2.00
PE11 Jim Thome .50 1.25
PE12 Manny Ramirez .50 1.25
PE13 Larry Walker .30 .75
PE14 Tony Clark .30 .75
PE15 Jeff Bagwell .50 1.25
PE16 Moises Alou .30 .75
PE17 Ken Caminiti .30 .75
PE18 Vladimir Guerrero .75 2.00
PE19 Mike Piazza 1.25 3.00
PE20 Tino Martinez .50 1.25
PE21 Ben Grieve .30 .75
PE22 Scott Rolen .50 1.25
PE23 Greg Vaughn .30 .75
PE24 Barry Bonds 2.00 5.00
PE25 Ken Griffey Jr. 1.50 4.00
PE26 Alex Rodriguez 1.25 3.00
PE27 Mark McGwire 2.00 5.00
PE28 J.D. Drew .30 .75
PE29 Juan Gonzalez .30 .75
PE30 Ivan Rodriguez .50 1.25

1999 SPx Premier Stars

COMP. SET (PS1-PS30) 30.00 80.00
STATED ODDS 1:17
PS1 Mark McGwire 2.50 6.00
PS2 Sammy Sosa 1.50 4.00
PS3 Frank Thomas 1.50 4.00
PS4 J.D. Drew .60 1.50
PS5 Kerry Wood .60 1.50
PS6 Moises Alou .60 1.50
PS7 Kenny Lofton .60 1.50
PS8 Jeff Bagwell 1.00 2.50
PS9 Tony Clark .60 1.50
PS10 Roberto Alomar 1.00 2.50
PS11 Cal Ripken 5.00 12.00
PS12 Derek Jeter 4.00 10.00
PS13 Mike Piazza 1.50 4.00
PS14 Jose Cruz Jr. .60 1.50
PS15 Chipper Jones 1.50 4.00
PS16 Nomar Garciaparra 1.00 2.50
PS17 Greg Maddux 2.00 5.00
PS18 Scott Rolen 1.00 2.50
PS19 Vladimir Guerrero 1.00 2.50
PS20 Albert Belle .60 1.50
PS21 Ken Griffey Jr. 3.00 8.00
PS22 Alex Rodriguez 2.00 5.00
PS23 Ben Grieve .60 1.50
PS24 Juan Gonzalez .60 1.50
PS25 Barry Bonds 2.50 6.00
PS26 Roger Clemens 2.00 5.00
PS27 Tony Gwynn 1.50 4.00
PS28 Randy Johnson 1.50 4.00
PS29 Travis Lee .60 1.50
PS30 Mo Vaughn .60 1.50

1999 SPx Star Focus

COMPLETE SET (30) 60.00 120.00
STATED ODDS 1:8
SF1 Chipper Jones 2.00 5.00
SF2 Greg Maddux 3.00 8.00
SF3 Cal Ripken 6.00 15.00
SF4 Nomar Garciaparra 1.00 2.50
SF5 Mo Vaughn .75 2.00
SF6 Sammy Sosa 2.00 5.00
SF7 Albert Belle .75 2.00
SF8 Frank Thomas 2.00 5.00
SF9 Jim Thome 1.25 3.00
SF10 Kenny Lofton .75 2.00
SF11 Manny Ramirez 1.25 3.00
SF12 Larry Walker .75 2.00
SF13 Jeff Bagwell 1.25 3.00
SF14 Craig Biggio 1.25 3.00
SF15 Randy Johnson 2.00 5.00
SF16 Vladimir Guerrero 2.00 5.00
SF17 Mike Piazza 3.00 8.00
SF18 Derek Jeter 5.00 12.00
SF19 Tino Martinez 1.25 3.00
SF20 Bernie Williams 2.00 5.00
SF21 Curt Schilling .75 2.00
SF22 Tony Gwynn 2.50 6.00
SF23 Barry Bonds 5.00 12.00
SF24 Ken Griffey Jr. 4.00 10.00
SF25 Alex Rodriguez 3.00 8.00
SF26 Mark McGwire 5.00 12.00
SF27 J.D. Drew .75 2.00
SF28 Juan Gonzalez .75 2.00
SF29 Ivan Rodriguez 1.25 3.00
SF30 Ben Grieve .75 2.00

1999 SPx Winning Materials

STATED ODDS 1:251
IR Ivan Rodriguez 6.00 15.00
JD J.D. Drew 6.00 15.00
JR Ken Griffey Jr. 25.00 60.00
TG Tony Gwynn 6.00 15.00
TH Todd Helton 6.00 15.00
TL Travis Lee 4.00 10.00
VC Vinny Castilla 6.00 15.00
VG Vladimir Guerrero 6.00 15.00

2000 SPx

COMP.BASIC w/o SP's (90) 10.00 25.00
COMP.UPDATE w/o SP's (30) 4.00 10.00
COMMON CARD (1-90) .20 .50
COMMON AU/1500 (91-120) 4.00 10.00
COMMON NO AU/1000 (91-120) .60 1.50
NO AU/1000 SEMIS 91-120 1.00 2.50
NO.AU/1000 UNLISTED 91-120 1.50 4.00
91-120 RANDOM INSERTS IN PACKS
TIER 1 UNSIGNED 1000 SERIAL #'d SETS
TIER 2 SIGNED 1500 SERIAL #'d SETS
TIER 3 SIGNED 500 SERIAL #'d SETS
EXCHANGE DEADLINE 01/24/01
COMMON (121-135/182-196) .60 1.50
121-135/182-196 PRINT RUN 1600 #'d SETS
COMMON CARD (136-151) 4.00 10.00
136-151 PRINT RUN 1500 SERIAL #'d SETS
COMMON CARD (152-181) .30 .75
121-196 DISTRIBUTED IN ROOKIE UPD.PACKS
TY COBB 3K LISTED W/UD 3000 CLUB
1 Troy Glaus .20 .50
2 Mo Vaughn .20 .50
3 Ramon Ortiz .20 .50
4 Jeff Bagwell .30 .75
5 Moises Alou .20 .50
6 Craig Biggio .30 .75
7 Jose Lima .20 .50
8 Jason Giambi .20 .50
9 John Jaha .20 .50
10 Matt Stairs .20 .50
11 Chipper Jones .50 1.25
12 Greg Maddux .60 1.50
13 Andres Galarraga .20 .50
14 Andruw Jones .20 .50
15 Jeromy Burnitz .20 .50
16 Ron Belliard .20 .50
17 Carlos Delgado .20 .50
18 David Wells .20 .50
19 Tony Batista .20 .50
20 Shannon Stewart .20 .50
21 Sammy Sosa .50 1.25
22 Mark Grace .30 .75
23 Henry Rodriguez .20 .50
24 Mark McGwire .75 2.00
25 J.D. Drew .20 .50
26 Luis Gonzalez .20 .50
27 Randy Johnson .50 1.25
28 Matt Williams .20 .50
29 Steve Finley .20 .50
30 Shawn Green .20 .50
31 Kevin Brown .20 .50
32 Gary Sheffield .20 .50
33 Jose Canseco .30 .75
34 Greg Vaughn .20 .50
35 Vladimir Guerrero .30 .75
36 Michael Barrett .20 .50
37 Russ Ortiz .20 .50
38 Barry Bonds .75 2.00
39 Jeff Kent .20 .50
40 Richie Sexson .20 .50
41 Manny Ramirez .50 1.25
42 Jim Thome .30 .75
43 Roberto Alomar .30 .75
44 Edgar Martinez .30 .75
45 Alex Rodriguez .60 1.50
46 John Olerud .20 .50
47 Alex Gonzalez .20 .50
48 Cliff Floyd .20 .50
49 Mike Piazza .50 1.25
50 Al Leiter .20 .50
51 Robin Ventura .20 .50
52 Edgardo Alfonzo .20 .50
53 Albert Belle .20 .50
54 Cal Ripken 1.50 4.00
55 B.J. Surhoff .20 .50
56 Tony Gwynn .50 1.25
57 Trevor Hoffman .30 .75
58 Brian Giles .20 .50
59 Jason Kendall .20 .50
60 Kris Benson .20 .50
61 Bob Abreu .20 .50
62 Scott Rolen .30 .75
63 Curt Schilling .20 .50
64 Mike Lieberthal .20 .50
65 Sean Casey .20 .50
66 Dante Bichette .20 .50
67 Ken Griffey Jr. 1.00 2.50
68 Pokey Reese .20 .50
69 Mike Sweeney .20 .50
70 Carlos Febles .20 .50
71 Ivan Rodriguez .30 .75
72 Ruben Mateo .20 .50
73 Rafael Palmeiro .30 .75
74 Larry Walker .20 .50
75 Todd Helton .30 .75
76 Nomar Garciaparra .30 .75
77 Pedro Martinez .30 .75
78 Troy O'Leary .20 .50
79 Jacque Jones .20 .50
80 Corey Koskie .20 .50
81 Juan Gonzalez .20 .50
82 Dean Palmer .20 .50
83 Juan Encarnacion .20 .50
84 Frank Thomas .50 1.25
85 Magglio Ordonez .30 .75
86 Paul Konerko .20 .50
87 Bernie Williams .30 .75
88 Derek Jeter 1.25 3.00
89 Roger Clemens .60 1.50
90 Orlando Hernandez .20 .50
91 Vernon Wells AU/1500 6.00 15.00
92 Rick Ankiel AU/1500 6.00 15.00
93 Eric Chavez AU/1500 8.00 20.00
94 Alfonso Soriano AU/1500 8.00 20.00
95 Eric Gagne AU/1500 6.00 15.00
96 Rob Bell AU/1500 4.00 10.00
97 Matt Riley AU/1500 4.00 10.00
98 Josh Beckett AU/1500 8.00 20.00
99 Ben Petrick AU/1500 4.00 10.00
100 Rob Ramsay AU/1500 4.00 10.00
101 Scott Williamson AU/1500 4.00 10.00
102 Doug Davis AU/1500 6.00 15.00
103 Eric Munson AU/1500 4.00 10.00
104 Pat Burrell AU/500 8.00 20.00
105 Jim Morris AU/1500 15.00 40.00
106 Gabe Kapler AU/500 4.00 10.00
107 Lance Berkman/1000 1.00 2.50
108 Erubiel Durazo AU/1500 4.00 10.00
109 Tim Hudson AU/1500 6.00 15.00
110 Ben Davis AU/1500 4.00 10.00
111 Nick Johnson AU/1500 6.00 15.00
112 Octavio Dotel AU/1500 4.00 10.00
113 Jerry Hairston/1000 .60 1.50
114 Ruben Mateo/1000 .60 1.50
115 Chris Singleton/1000 .60 1.50
116 Bruce Chen AU/1500 4.00 10.00
117 Derrick Gibson/1000 .60 1.50
118 Carlos Beltran AU/500 12.00 30.00
119 Freddy Garcia AU/1500 6.00 15.00
120 Preston Wilson AU/1500 6.00 15.00
121 Brad Wilkerson/1600 RC 1.50 4.00
122 Roy Oswalt/1600 RC 10.00 25.00
123 Wascar Serrano/1600 RC .60 1.50
124 Sean Burnett/1600 RC .60 1.50
125 Alex Cabrera/1600 RC .60 1.50
126 Timo Perez/1600 RC 1.00 2.50
127 Juan Pierre/1600 RC 3.00 8.00
128 Daylan Holt/1600 RC .60 1.50
129 Tomokazu Ohka/1600 RC .60 1.50
130 Kazuhiro Sasaki/1600 RC 1.50 4.00
131 Kurt Ainsworth/1600 RC .60 1.50
132 Brent Abernathy/1600 RC .60 1.50
133 Danys Baez/1600 RC .60 1.50
134 Brad Cresse/1600 RC .60 1.50
135 Ryan Franklin/1600 RC .60 1.50
136 Mike Lamb AU/1500 RC 6.00 15.00
137 David Espinosa AU/1500 RC 4.00 10.00
138 Matt Wheatland AU/1500 RC 4.00 10.00
139 Xavier Nady AU/1500 RC 8.00 20.00
140 Scott Heard AU/1500 RC 4.00 10.00
141 P.Coco AU/1500 UER54 RC 4.00 10.00
142 Justin Miller AU/1500 RC 4.00 10.00
143 Dave Krynzel AU/1500 RC 4.00 10.00
144 Dane Sardinha AU/1500 RC 4.00 10.00
145 Ben Sheets AU/1500 RC 6.00 15.00
146 Leo Estrella AU/1500 RC 4.00 10.00
147 Ben Diggins AU/1500 RC 4.00 10.00
148 Barry Zito AU/1500 RC 6.00 15.00
149 Joe Torres AU/1500 RC 4.00 10.00
150 Mike Meyers AU/1500 RC 4.00 10.00
151 Kris Wilson AU/1500 RC 4.00 10.00
152 Darin Erstad .30 .75
153 Richard Hidalgo .30 .75
154 Eric Chavez .30 .75
155 B.J. Surhoff .30 .75
156 Richie Sexson .30 .75
157 Raul Mondesi .30 .75
158 Rondell White .30 .75
159 Jim Edmonds .30 .75
160 Curt Schilling .30 .75
161 Tom Goodwin .30 .75
162 Fred McGriff .50 1.25
163 Jose Vidro .30 .75
164 Ellis Burks .30 .75
165 David Segui .30 .75
166 Aaron Sele .30 .75
167 Henry Rodriguez .30 .75
168 Mike Bordick .30 .75
169 Mike Mussina .50 1.25
170 Ryan Klesko .30 .75
171 Kevin Young .30 .75
172 Travis Lee .30 .75
173 Aaron Boone .30 .75
174 Jermaine Dye .30 .75
175 Ricky Ledee .30 .75
176 Jeffrey Hammonds .30 .75
177 Carl Everett .30 .75
178 Matt Lawton .30 .75
179 Bobby Higginson .30 .75
180 Charles Johnson .30 .75
181 David Justice .30 .75
182 Joey Nation/1600 RC .60 1.50
183 Rico Washington/1600 RC .60 1.50
184 Luis Matos/1600 RC .60 1.50
185 Chris Wakeland/1600 RC .60 1.50
186 Sun Woo Kim/1600 RC .60 1.50
187 Keith Ginter/1600 RC .60 1.50
188 Geraldo Guzman/1600 RC .60 1.50
189 Jay Spurgeon/1600 RC .60 1.50
190 Jace Brewer/1600 RC .60 1.50
191 Juan Guzman/1600 RC .60 1.50
192 Ross Gload/1600 RC .60 1.50
193 Paxton Crawford/1600 RC .60 1.50
194 Ryan Kohlmeier/1600 RC .60 1.50
195 Julio Zuleta/1600 RC .60 1.50
196 Matt Ginter/1600 RC .60 1.50

2000 SPx Radiance

*RADIANCE 1-90: 6X TO 15X BASIC
COMMON CARD (91-120) 3.00 8.00
SEMISTARS 91-120 5.00 12.00
UNLISTED STARS 91-120 8.00 20.00
STATED PRINT RUN 100 SERIAL #'d SETS
DUPE VERSIONS EXIST FOR 98/103/106
91 Vernon Wells 3.00 8.00
92 Rick Ankiel 5.00 12.00
93 Eric Chavez 5.00 12.00
94 Alfonso Soriano 8.00 20.00
95 Eric Gagne 3.00 8.00
96 Rob Bell 3.00 8.00
97 Matt Riley 3.00 8.00
98 Josh Beckett 6.00 15.00
98A John Bale * 3.00 8.00
98B Alex Escobar * 3.00 8.00
98C Joe Mays * 3.00 8.00
98D Calvin Pickering * 3.00 8.00
98E Dave Roberts * 5.00 12.00
98F Jared Sandberg * 3.00 8.00
98G Dernell Stenson * 3.00 8.00
98H Reggie Taylor * 3.00 8.00
98I Ed Yarnall * 3.00 8.00
99 Ben Petrick 3.00 8.00
100 Rob Ramsay 3.00 8.00
101 Scott Williamson 3.00 8.00
102 Doug Davis 3.00 8.00
103 Eric Munson 3.00 8.00
103A Tony Armas Jr. * 3.00 8.00
103B Travis Dawkins * 3.00 8.00
103C Mike Lamb * 3.00 8.00
103D Rico Washington * 3.00 8.00
104 Pat Burrell 3.00 8.00
105 Jim Morris 8.00 20.00
106 Gabe Kapler 3.00 8.00
106A Adam Piatt * 3.00 8.00
106B Mark Quinn * 3.00 8.00
107 Lance Berkman 5.00 12.00
108 Erubiel Durazo 3.00 8.00
109 Tim Hudson 5.00 12.00
110 Ben Davis 3.00 8.00
111 Nick Johnson 3.00 8.00
112 Octavio Dotel 3.00 8.00
113 Jerry Hairston 3.00 8.00
114 Ruben Mateo 3.00 8.00
115 Chris Singleton 3.00 8.00
116 Bruce Chen 3.00 8.00
117 Derrick Gibson 3.00 8.00
118 Carlos Beltran 5.00 12.00
119 Freddy Garcia 3.00 8.00
120 Preston Wilson 3.00 8.00

2000 SPx Foundations

COMPLETE SET (10) 10.00 25.00
STATED ODDS 1:32
F1 Ken Griffey Jr. 2.00 5.00
F2 Nomar Garciaparra .60 1.50
F3 Cal Ripken 3.00 8.00
F4 Chipper Jones 1.00 2.50
F5 Mike Piazza 1.00 2.50
F6 Derek Jeter 2.50 6.00
F7 Manny Ramirez 1.00 2.50
F8 Jeff Bagwell .60 1.50
F9 Tony Gwynn 1.00 2.50
F10 Larry Walker .60 1.50

2000 SPx Heart of the Order

COMPLETE SET (20) 12.50 30.00
STATED ODDS 1:8
H1 Bernie Williams .60 1.50
H2 Mike Piazza 1.00 2.50
H3 Ivan Rodriguez .60 1.50
H4 Mark McGwire 1.50 4.00
H5 Manny Ramirez 1.00 2.50
H6 Ken Griffey Jr. 2.00 5.00
H7 Matt Williams .40 1.00
H8 Sammy Sosa 1.00 2.50
H9 Mo Vaughn .40 1.00
H10 Carlos Delgado .40 1.00
H11 Brian Giles .40 1.00
H12 Chipper Jones 1.00 2.50
H13 Sean Casey .40 1.00
H14 Tony Gwynn 1.00 2.50
H15 Barry Bonds 1.50 4.00
H16 Carlos Beltran .60 1.50
H17 Scott Rolen .60 1.50
H18 Juan Gonzalez .40 1.00
H19 Larry Walker .60 1.50
H20 Vladimir Guerrero .60 1.50

2000 SPx Highlight Heroes

COMPLETE SET (10) 6.00 15.00
STATED ODDS 1:16
HH1 Pedro Martinez .60 1.50
HH2 Ivan Rodriguez .60 1.50
HH3 Carlos Beltran .60 1.50
HH4 Nomar Garciaparra .60 1.50
HH5 Ken Griffey Jr. 2.00 5.00
HH6 Randy Johnson 1.00 2.50
HH7 Chipper Jones 1.00 2.50
HH8 Scott Williamson .40 1.00
HH9 Larry Walker .60 1.50
HH10 Mark McGwire 1.50 4.00

2000 SPx Power Brokers

COMPLETE SET (20) 10.00 25.00
STATED ODDS 1:8
PB1 Rafael Palmeiro .60 1.50
PB2 Carlos Delgado .40 1.00
PB3 Ken Griffey Jr. 2.00 5.00
PB4 Matt Stairs .40 1.00
PB5 Mike Piazza 1.00 2.50
PB6 Vladimir Guerrero .60 1.50
PB7 Chipper Jones 1.00 2.50
PB8 Mark McGwire 1.50 4.00
PB9 Matt Williams .40 1.00
PB10 Juan Gonzalez .40 1.00
PB11 Shawn Green .40 1.00
PB12 Sammy Sosa 1.00 2.50
PB13 Brian Giles .40 1.00
PB14 Jeff Bagwell .60 1.50
PB15 Alex Rodriguez 1.25 3.00
PB16 Frank Thomas 1.00 2.50
PB17 Larry Walker .60 1.50
PB18 Albert Belle .40 1.00
PB19 Dean Palmer .40 1.00
PB20 Mo Vaughn .40 1.00

2000 SPx Signatures

STATED ODDS 1:179
EXCHANGE DEADLINE 02/03/01
XBB Barry Bonds 50.00 120.00
XCJ Chipper Jones 30.00 60.00
XCR Cal Ripken 50.00 100.00
XDJ Derek Jeter 100.00 200.00
XIR Ivan Rodriguez 15.00 30.00
XJB Jeff Bagwell 15.00 40.00
XJC Jose Canseco 10.00 25.00
XKG Ken Griffey Jr. 100.00 250.00
XMR Manny Ramirez 12.00 25.00
XOH Orlando Hernandez 60.00 120.00
XRC Roger Clemens 25.00 60.00
XSC Sean Casey 6.00 15.00
XSR Scott Rolen 4.00 10.00
XTG Tony Gwynn 25.00 60.00
XVG Vladimir Guerrero 6.00 15.00

2000 SPx SPXcitement

COMPLETE SET (20) 12.50 30.00
STATED ODDS 1:4
XC1 Nomar Garciaparra .60 1.50
XC2 Mark McGwire 1.50 4.00
XC3 Derek Jeter 2.50 6.00
XC4 Cal Ripken 3.00 8.00
XC5 Barry Bonds 1.50 4.00
XC6 Alex Rodriguez 1.25 3.00
XC7 Scott Rolen .60 1.50
XC8 Pedro Martinez .60 1.50
XC9 Sean Casey .40 1.00
XC10 Sammy Sosa 1.00 2.50
XC11 Randy Johnson 1.00 2.50
XC12 Ivan Rodriguez .60 1.50
XC13 Frank Thomas 1.00 2.50
XC14 Greg Maddux 1.25 3.00
XC15 Tony Gwynn 1.00 2.50
XC16 Ken Griffey Jr. 2.00 5.00
XC17 Carlos Beltran .60 1.50
XC18 Mike Piazza 1.00 2.50
XC19 Chipper Jones 1.00 2.50
XC20 Craig Biggio .60 1.50

2000 SPx Untouchable Talents

COMPLETE SET (10) 15.00 40.00
STATED ODDS 1:96
UT1 Mark McGwire 4.00 10.00
UT2 Ken Griffey Jr. 5.00 12.00
UT3 Shawn Green 1.00 2.50
UT4 Ivan Rodriguez 1.50 4.00
UT5 Sammy Sosa 2.50 6.00
UT6 Derek Jeter 6.00 15.00
UT7 Sean Casey 1.00 2.50
UT8 Chipper Jones 2.50 6.00
UT9 Pedro Martinez 1.50 4.00
UT10 Vladimir Guerrero 1.50 4.00

2000 SPx Winning Materials

BAT-JERSEY STATED ODDS 1:112
OTHER CARDS RANDOM INSERTS IN PACKS
SERIAL #'d PRINT RUNS FROM 50-250 PER
AU SERIAL #'d PRINT RUNS FROM 2-25 PER
NO PRICING ON QTY OF 25 OR LESS
EXCHANGE DEADLINE 12/31/00
AR1 A.Rodriguez Bat-Jsy 10.00 25.00
AR2 A.Rodriguez Cap-Jsy/100 10.00 25.00
AR3 A.Rodriguez Ball-Jsy/50 30.00 60.00
BB1 B.Bonds Bat-Jsy 5.00 12.00
BB2 B.Bonds Cap-Jsy/100 15.00 40.00
BW B.Williams Bat-Jsy 6.00 15.00
DJ1 D.Jeter Bat-Jsy 20.00 50.00
DJ2 D.Jeter Ball-Jsy/50 50.00 100.00
EC1 E.Chavez Bat-Jsy 4.00 10.00
EC2 E.Chavez Cap-Jsy/100 6.00 15.00
GM G.Maddux Bat-Jsy 10.00 25.00
IR I.Rodriguez Bat-Jsy 6.00 15.00
JB1 J.Bagwell Bat-Jsy 6.00 15.00
JB2 J.Bagwell Ball-Jsy/50 15.00 40.00
JC J.Canseco Bat-Jsy 6.00 15.00
JL1 J.Lopez Bat-Jsy 4.00 10.00
JL2 J.Lopez Cap-Jsy 6.00 15.00
KG1 K.Griffey Jr. Bat-Jsy 10.00 25.00
KG2 K.Griffey Jr. Ball-Jsy/50 30.00 60.00
MM1 McGwire Ball-Base/250 12.50 30.00
MM2 McGwire Ball-Base/250 12.50 30.00
MR1 M.Ramirez Bat-Jsy 6.00 15.00
MW M.Williams Bat-Jsy 4.00 10.00
PM P.Martinez Cap-Jsy/100 10.00 25.00
PO P.O'Neill Bat-Jsy 6.00 15.00
VG1 V.Guerrero Bat-Jsy 6.00 15.00
VG2 V.Guerrero Cap-Jsy/100 10.00 25.00
VG3 V.Guerrero Ball-Jsy/50 15.00 40.00
GL T.Glaus Bat-Jsy 4.00 10.00
TGW1 T.Gwynn Bat-Jsy 6.00 15.00
TGW2 T.Gwynn Ball-Jsy/50 20.00 50.00
TGW3 T.Gwynn Cap-Jsy/100 12.50 30.00

2000 SPx Winning Materials Update

MKGD T.Dawkins M.Kinkade 1.25 3.00
BAAE B.Abernathy A.Everett 1.25 3.00
BWEY B.Wilkerson E.Young 3.00 8.00
CRTG C.Ripken T.Gwynn 10.00 25.00
DJAR D.Jeter A.Rodriguez 8.00 20.00
DJNG D.Jeter N.Garciaparra 8.00 20.00
FTMO F.Thomas M.Ordonez 3.00 8.00
GSR Griffey/Sosa/A-Rod 6.00 15.00
GWBS Ben Sheets 3.00 8.00
GWDM Doug Mientkiewicz 1.25 3.00
GWEY Ernie Young 1.25 3.00
GWJC John Cotton 1.25 3.00
GWMN Mike Neill 1.25 3.00
GWSB Sean Burroughs 1.25 3.00
IRRP I.Rodriguez R.Palmeiro 2.00 5.00
JGR Jeter/Nomar/A-Rod 8.00 20.00
JBCB J.Bagwell C.Biggio 2.00 5.00
JCBB J.Canseco B.Bonds 5.00 12.00
KGSS K.Griffey Jr. S.Sosa 6.00 15.00
MMKG M.McGwire K.Griffey Jr. 6.00 15.00
MMRA M.McGwire R.Ankiel 5.00 12.00
MMSS M.McGwire S.Sosa 5.00 12.00
MPRV M.Piazza R.Ventura 3.00 8.00
NGPM Nomar Pedro 2.00 5.00
RCPM R.Clemens P.Martinez 4.00 10.00
SBBS S.Burroughs B.Sheets 3.00 8.00

2000 SPx Winning Materials Update Numbered

STATED PRINT RUN 50 SERIAL #'d SETS
CBG Canseco/Bonds/Griffey 60.00 120.00
GSM Griffey/Sosa/McGwire 30.00 60.00
JGR Jeter/Nomar/A-Rod 50.00 100.00

2001 SPx

COMP.BASIC w/o SP's (90) 10.00 25.00
COMP.UPDATE w/o SP's (30) 4.00 10.00
COMMON CARD (1-90) .20 .50
COMMON YS (91-120) 2.00 5.00
YS 91-120 RANDOM INSERTS IN PACKS
YS 91-120 PRINT RUN 2000 SERIAL #'d SETS
COMMON JSY (121-135) 3.00 8.00
JSY 121-135 STATED ODDS 1:18
COMMON JSY AU (136-150) 4.00 10.00
JSY AU STATED ODDS 1:36
ICHIRO 4X SCARCER THAN OTHER JSY AU'S
COMMON CARD (151-180) .30 .75
COMMON CARD (181-205) 2.00 5.00
181-210 RANDOM IN ROOKIE UPD.PACKS
181-210 PRINT RUN 1500 SERIAL #'d SETS
151-210 DISTRIBUTED IN ROOKIE UPD.PACKS
EXCHANGE DEADLINE 12/10/04
1 Darin Erstad .20 .50
2 Troy Glaus .20 .50
3 Mo Vaughn .20 .50
4 Johnny Damon .30 .75
5 Jason Giambi .20 .50
6 Tim Hudson .20 .50
7 Miguel Tejada .20 .50
8 Carlos Delgado .20 .50
9 Raul Mondesi .20 .50
10 Tony Batista .20 .50
11 Ben Grieve .20 .50
12 Greg Vaughn .20 .50
13 Juan Gonzalez .20 .50
14 Jim Thome .30 .75
15 Roberto Alomar .30 .75
16 John Olerud .20 .50
17 Edgar Martinez .30 .75
18 Albert Belle .20 .50
19 Cal Ripken 1.50 4.00
20 Ivan Rodriguez .30 .75
21 Rafael Palmeiro .30 .75
22 Alex Rodriguez .60 1.50
23 Nomar Garciaparra .75 2.00
24 Pedro Martinez .30 .75
25 Manny Ramirez Sox .30 .75
26 Jermaine Dye .20 .50
27 Mark Quinn .20 .50
28 Carlos Beltran .20 .50
29 Tony Clark .20 .50
30 Bobby Higginson .20 .50
31 Eric Milton .20 .50
32 Matt Lawton .20 .50
33 Frank Thomas .50 1.25
34 Magglio Ordonez .20 .50
35 Ray Durham .20 .50
36 David Wells .20 .50
37 Derek Jeter 1.25 3.00
38 Bernie Williams .30 .75
39 Roger Clemens 1.00 2.50
40 David Justice .20 .50
41 Jeff Bagwell .30 .75
42 Richard Hidalgo .20 .50
43 Moises Alou .20 .50
44 Chipper Jones .50 1.25
45 Andruw Jones .20 .50
46 Greg Maddux .75 2.00
47 Rafael Furcal .20 .50
48 Jeromy Burnitz .20 .50
49 Geoff Jenkins .20 .50
50 Mark McGwire 1.25 3.00
51 Jim Edmonds .20 .50
52 Rick Ankiel .20 .50
53 Edgar Renteria .20 .50
54 Sammy Sosa .50 1.25
55 Kerry Wood .20 .50
56 Rondell White .20 .50
57 Randy Johnson .50 1.25
58 Steve Finley .20 .50
59 Matt Williams .20 .50
60 Luis Gonzalez .20 .50
61 Kevin Brown .20 .50
62 Gary Sheffield .20 .50
63 Shawn Green .20 .50
64 Vladimir Guerrero .50 1.25
65 Jose Vidro .20 .50
66 Barry Bonds 1.25 3.00
67 Jeff Kent .20 .50
68 Livan Hernandez .20 .50
69 Preston Wilson .20 .50
70 Charles Johnson .20 .50
71 Cliff Floyd .20 .50
72 Mike Piazza .75 2.00
73 Edgardo Alfonzo .20 .50
74 Jay Payton .20 .50
75 Robin Ventura .20 .50
76 Tony Gwynn .60 1.50
77 Phil Nevin .20 .50
78 Ryan Klesko .20 .50
79 Scott Rolen .30 .75
80 Pat Burrell .20 .50
81 Bob Abreu .20 .50
82 Brian Giles .20 .50
83 Kris Benson .20 .50
84 Jason Kendall .20 .50
85 Ken Griffey Jr. 1.00 2.50
86 Barry Larkin .30 .75
87 Sean Casey .20 .50
88 Todd Helton .30 .75
89 Larry Walker .20 .50
90 Mike Hampton .20 .50
91 Billy Sylvester YS RC 2.00 5.00
92 Josh Towers YS RC 3.00 8.00
93 Zach Day YS RC 2.00 5.00
94 Martin Vargas YS RC 2.00 5.00
95 Adam Pettyjohn YS RC 2.00 5.00
96 Andres Torres YS RC 2.00 5.00
97 Kris Keller YS RC 2.00 5.00
98 Blaine Neal YS RC 2.00 5.00
99 Kyle Kessel YS RC 2.00 5.00
100 Greg Miller YS RC 2.00 5.00
101 Shawn Sonnier YS 2.00 5.00
102 Alexis Gomez YS RC 2.00 5.00
103 Grant Balfour YS RC 2.00 5.00
104 Henry Mateo YS RC 2.00 5.00
105 Wilken Ruan YS RC 2.00 5.00
106 Nick Maness YS RC 2.00 5.00
107 Jason Michaels YS RC 2.00 5.00
108 Esix Snead YS RC 2.00 5.00

109 William Ortega YS RC	2.00	5.00
110 David Elder YS RC	2.00	5.00
111 Jackson Melian YS RC	2.00	5.00
112 Nate Teut YS RC	2.00	5.00
113 Jason Smith YS RC	2.00	5.00
114 Mike Penney YS RC	2.00	5.00
115 Jose Mieses YS RC	2.00	5.00
116 Juan Pena YS	2.00	5.00
117 Brian Lawrence YS RC	2.00	5.00
118 Jeremy Owens YS RC	2.00	5.00
119 Carlos Valderrama YS RC	2.00	5.00
120 Rafael Soriano YS RC	2.00	5.00
121 Horacio Ramirez JSY RC	4.00	10.00
122 Ricardo Rodriguez JSY RC	3.00	8.00
123 Juan Diaz JSY RC	3.00	8.00
124 Donnie Bridges JSY	3.00	8.00
125 Tyler Walker JSY RC	3.00	8.00
126 Erick Almonte JSY RC	3.00	8.00
127 Jesus Colome JSY	3.00	8.00
128 Ryan Freel JSY RC	4.00	10.00
129 Elpidio Guzman JSY RC	3.00	8.00
130 Jack Cust JSY	3.00	8.00
131 Eric Hinske JSY RC	4.00	10.00
132 Josh Fogg JSY RC	3.00	8.00
133 Juan Uribe JSY RC	4.00	10.00
134 Bert Snow JSY RC	3.00	8.00
135 Pedro Feliz JSY	3.00	8.00
136 Wilson Betemit JSY AU RC	4.00	10.00
137 Sean Douglass JSY AU RC	4.00	10.00
138 Dernell Stenson JSY AU	4.00	10.00
139 Brandon Inge JSY AU	4.00	10.00
140 Mor.Ensberg JSY AU RC	4.00	10.00
141 Brian Cole JSY AU	6.00	15.00
142 A.Hernandez JSY AU RC	4.00	10.00
143 B.Duckworth JSY AU RC	4.00	10.00
144 Jack Wilson JSY AU RC	4.00	10.00
145 Travis Hafner JSY AU RC	4.00	10.00
146 Carlos Pena JSY AU	6.00	15.00
147 Corey Patterson JSY AU	4.00	10.00
148 Xavier Nady JSY AU	4.00	10.00
149 Jason Hart JSY AU	4.00	10.00
150 I.Suzuki JSY AU RC	750.00	2000.00
151 Garret Anderson	.30	.75
152 Jermaine Dye	.30	.75
153 Shannon Stewart	.30	.75
154 Toby Hall	.30	.75
155 C.C. Sabathia	.30	.75
156 Bret Boone	.30	.75
157 Tony Batista	.30	.75
158 Gabe Kapler	.30	.75
159 Carl Everett	.30	.75
160 Mike Sweeney	.30	.75
161 Dean Palmer	.30	.75
162 Doug Mientkiewicz	.30	.75
163 Carlos Lee	.30	.75
164 Mike Mussina	.50	1.25
165 Lance Berkman	.30	.75
166 Ken Caminiti	.30	.75
167 Ben Sheets	.50	1.25
168 Matt Morris	.30	.75
169 Fred McGriff	.50	1.25
170 Curt Schilling	.30	.75
171 Paul LoDuca	.30	.75
172 Javier Vazquez	.30	.75
173 Rich Aurilia	.30	.75
174 A.J. Burnett	.30	.75
175 Al Leiter	.30	.75
176 Mark Kotsay	.30	.75
177 Jimmy Rollins	.30	.75
178 Aramis Ramirez	.30	.75
179 Aaron Boone	.30	.75
180 Jeff Cirillo	.30	.75
181 Johnny Estrada YS RC	3.00	8.00
182 Dave Williams YS RC	2.00	5.00
183 Donaldo Mendez YS RC	2.00	5.00
184 Junior Spivey YS RC	3.00	8.00
185 Jay Gibbons YS RC	3.00	8.00
186 Kyle Lohse YS RC	5.00	12.00
187 Willie Harris YS RC	2.00	5.00
188 Juan Cruz YS RC	2.00	5.00
189 Joe Kennedy YS RC	3.00	8.00
190 Duaner Sanchez YS RC	2.00	5.00
191 Jorge Julio YS RC	2.00	5.00
192 Cesar Crespo YS RC	2.00	5.00
193 Casey Fossum YS RC	2.00	5.00
194 Brian Roberts YS RC	6.00	15.00
195 Troy Mattes YS RC	2.00	5.00
196 Rob Mackowiak YS RC	3.00	8.00
197 Tsuyoshi Shinjo YS RC	3.00	8.00
198 Nick Punto YS RC	2.00	5.00
199 Wilmy Caceres YS RC	2.00	5.00
200 Jeremy Affeldt YS RC	2.00	5.00
201 Bret Prinz YS RC	2.00	5.00
202 Delvin James YS RC	2.00	5.00
203 Luis Pineda YS RC	2.00	5.00
204 Matt White YS RC	2.00	5.00
205 Brandon Knight YS RC	2.00	5.00
206 Albert Pujols YS AU RC	250.00	600.00
207 Mark Teixeira YS AU RC	12.50	30.00
208 Mark Prior YS AU RC	8.00	20.00
209 Dewon Brazelton YS AU RC	6.00	15.00
210 Bud Smith YS AU RC	6.00	15.00

2001 SPx Spectrum

*STARS 1-90: 12.5X TO 30X BASIC CARDS
*YS 91-120: 1X TO 2.5X BASIC CARDS
STATED PRINT RUN 50 SERIAL #'d SETS

2001 SPx Foundations

COMPLETE SET (12)	20.00	50.00
STATED ODDS 1:8		
F1 Mark McGwire	3.00	8.00
F2 Jeff Bagwell	.75	2.00
F3 Alex Rodriguez	1.50	4.00
F4 Ken Griffey Jr.	2.50	6.00
F5 Andruw Jones	.75	2.00
F6 Cal Ripken	4.00	10.00
F7 Barry Bonds	3.00	8.00
F8 Derek Jeter	3.00	8.00
F9 Frank Thomas	1.25	3.00
F10 Sammy Sosa	1.25	3.00
F11 Tony Gwynn	1.50	4.00
F12 Vladimir Guerrero	1.25	3.00

2001 SPx SPXcitement

COMPLETE SET (12)	20.00	50.00
STATED ODDS 1:8		
X1 Alex Rodriguez	1.50	4.00
X2 Jason Giambi	.75	2.00
X3 Ken Griffey Jr.	2.50	6.00
X4 Sammy Sosa	1.25	3.00
X5 Frank Thomas	1.25	3.00
X6 Todd Helton	.75	2.00
X7 Mark McGwire	3.00	8.00
X8 Mike Piazza	2.00	5.00
X9 Derek Jeter	3.00	8.00
X10 Vladimir Guerrero	1.25	3.00
X11 Carlos Delgado	.75	2.00
X12 Chipper Jones	1.25	3.00

2001 SPx Untouchable Talents

COMPLETE SET (6)	15.00	40.00
STATED ODDS 1:15		
UT1 Ken Griffey Jr.	2.50	6.00
UT2 Mike Piazza	2.00	5.00
UT3 Mark McGwire	3.00	8.00
UT4 Alex Rodriguez	1.50	4.00
UT5 Sammy Sosa	2.00	5.00
UT6 Derek Jeter	3.00	8.00

2001 SPx Winning Materials Ball-Base

STATED PRINT RUN 250 SERIAL #'d SETS		
BAJ Andruw Jones	10.00	25.00
BAR Alex Rodriguez	10.00	25.00
BBB Barry Bonds	20.00	50.00
BCJ Chipper Jones	10.00	25.00
BDJ Derek Jeter	20.00	50.00
BFT Frank Thomas	10.00	25.00
BKG Ken Griffey Jr.	15.00	40.00
BMM Mark McGwire	12.00	30.00
BMP Mike Piazza	10.00	25.00
BNG Nomar Garciaparra	10.00	25.00
BPM Pedro Martinez	10.00	25.00
BSS Sammy Sosa	10.00	25.00
BVG Vladimir Guerrero	10.00	25.00

2001 SPx Winning Materials Base Duos

STATED PRINT RUN 50 SERIAL #'d SETS		
B2GJ N.Garciaparra/D.Jeter	12.50	30.00
B2JG D.Jeter/J.Giambi	10.00	25.00
B2JP D.Jeter/M.Piazza	12.50	30.00
B2MG M.McGwire/K.Grif	10.00	25.00
B2MR M.McGwire/A.Rod	10.00	25.00
B2MS M.McGwire/S.Sosa	12.50	30.00
B2PB M.Piazza/B.Bonds	12.50	30.00
B2PM M.Piazza/M.McGwire	10.00	25.00
B2RJ A.Rodriguez/D.Jeter	10.00	25.00
B2TR F.Thomas/A.Rodriguez	10.00	25.00

2001 SPx Winning Materials Bat-Jersey

STATED ODDS 1:18		
ASTERISKS PERCEIVED SHORTER SUPPLY		
AJ1 Andruw Jones AS	2.50	6.00
AJ2 Andruw Jones	2.50	6.00
AR1 Alex Rodriguez AS	5.00	12.00
AR2 Alex Rodriguez AS	5.00	12.00
BB1 Barry Bonds AS	6.00	15.00
BB2 Barry Bonds	6.00	15.00
CD Carlos Delgado AS *	1.50	4.00
CJ1 Chipper Jones AS	4.00	10.00
CJ2 Chipper Jones	4.00	10.00
CR Cal Ripken	12.00	30.00
FT Frank Thomas	4.00	10.00
IR1 Ivan Rodriguez AS	2.50	6.00
IR2 Ivan Rodriguez	2.50	6.00
JD Joe DiMaggio	40.00	100.00
JE Jim Edmonds *	2.50	6.00
KG1 Ken Griffey Jr. AS	8.00	20.00
KG2 Ken Griffey Jr.	8.00	20.00
RA Rick Ankiel *	1.50	4.00
RJ1 Randy Johnson AS	4.00	10.00
RJ2 Randy Johnson	4.00	10.00
SS Sammy Sosa	2.50	6.00

2001 SPx Winning Materials Jersey Duos

STATED PRINT RUN 50 SERIAL #'d SETS		
AJCJ A.Jones/C.Jones	15.00	40.00
ARCR A.Rod/C.Ripken	50.00	100.00
BBSS B.Bonds/S.Sosa	30.00	60.00
CJDW C.Jones/D.Wells	15.00	40.00
IRAR I.Rod/A.Rod	40.00	80.00
KGAR K.Griffey Jr./A.Rod AS	40.00	80.00
KGBB K.Griffey/B.Bonds AS	50.00	100.00
KGJD Griffey Jr./DiMaggio	40.00	80.00
KGKG Griffey Jr./Griffey Jr. AS	40.00	80.00
KGRJ Griffey Jr./Johnson AS	15.00	40.00
KGSS K.Griffey Jr./S.Sosa	40.00	80.00
SSCD S.Sosa/C.Delgado	15.00	40.00
SSFT S.Sosa/F.Thomas	15.00	40.00

2001 SPx Winning Materials Update Duos

STATED ODDS 1:15		
GOLD RANDOM INSERTS IN PACKS		
GOLD PRINT RUN 25 SERIAL #'d SETS		
NO GOLD PRICING DUE TO SCARCITY		
EACH CARD FEATURES DUAL JSY SWATCH		
APJE A.Pujols/J.Edmonds	12.00	30.00
ASKS A.Sele/K.Sasaki	1.50	4.00
BBLG B.Bonds/L.Gonzalez	6.00	15.00
BWMR B.Williams/M.Rivera	4.00	10.00
BWRJ B.Williams/R.Jackson	3.00	8.00
CPBK C.Park/B.Kim	2.50	6.00
CPFV C.Park/F.Valenzuela	8.00	20.00
CREM C.Ripken/E.Murray	8.00	20.00
CRX2 C.Ripken/C.Ripken	8.00	20.00
CSRJ C.Schilling/R.Johnson	4.00	10.00
EMJM E.Milton/J.Mays	1.50	4.00
FTMO F.Thomas/M.Ordonez	4.00	10.00
GSSG G.Sheffield/S.Green	1.50	4.00
HNMY H.Nomo/M.Yoshii	4.00	10.00
IRAR I.Rodriguez/A.Rodriguez	5.00	12.00
JBCB J.Bagwell/C.Biggio	2.50	6.00
JBRY J.Burnitz/R.Yount	4.00	10.00
JGBB J.Giambi/B.Bonds	6.00	15.00
KGSC K.Griffey Jr./S.Casey	5.00	12.00
LWTH L.Walker/T.Helton	2.50	6.00
MPEA M.Piazza/E.Alfonzo	4.00	10.00
MRJG M.Ramirez Sox/J.Gonzalez	4.00	10.00
PMGM P.Martinez/G.Maddux	6.00	15.00
PMRJ P.Martinez/R.Johnson	4.00	10.00
SRBA S.Rolen/B.Abreu	2.50	6.00
SSEB S.Sosa/E.Banks	4.00	10.00
SSJG S.Sosa/J.Giambi	2.50	6.00
TGCR T.Gwynn/C.Ripken	10.00	25.00
TGDW T.Gwynn/D.Winfield	4.00	10.00
TGX2 T.Gwynn/T.Gwynn	4.00	10.00
TSHN T.Shinjo/H.Nomo	4.00	10.00

2001 SPx Winning Materials Update Trios

STATED ODDS 1:15		
GOLD RANDOM INSERTS IN PACKS		
GOLD PRINT RUN 25 SERIAL #'d SETS		
NO GOLD PRICING DUE TO SCARCITY		
ALL FEATURE THREE JSY SWATCHES		
BGG Bonds/L.Gonz/Griffey	12.00	30.00
BTD Bagwell/Thomas/Delgado	6.00	15.00
CHN Clemens/Hudson/Nomo	10.00	25.00
DEA Drew/Edmonds/Abreu	4.00	10.00
DOP Delgado/M.Ordonez/Pujols	12.00	30.00
GWS L.Gonz/M.Will/Schilling	4.00	10.00
GZH Giambi/Zito/Hudson	4.00	10.00
HDG Helton/Delgado/Giambi	6.00	15.00
JAF C.Jones/A.Jones/Furcal	6.00	15.00
KBA Kent/Bonds/Aurilia	10.00	25.00
MGJ Maddux/Glavine/A.Jones	10.00	25.00
PPV Payton/Piazza/Ventura	8.00	20.00
PWO Pettitte/B.Williams/O'Neill	6.00	15.00
RPK I.Rod/Piazza/Kendall	8.00	20.00
RRK A.Rod/I.Rod/Kapler	8.00	20.00
SJC Schilling/R.John/Clemens	8.00	20.00
SKB Sheffield/Karros/K.Brown	4.00	10.00
SSM Sele/Ichiro/E.Martinez	15.00	40.00
SYN Sasaki/Yoshii/Nomo	6.00	15.00
TDK Thomas/Durham/Konerko	6.00	15.00
TGA Thome/J.Gonz/R.Alomar	4.00	10.00
VRF Vizquel/A.Rod/Furcal	8.00	20.00

2002 SPx

COMP.LOW w/o SP's (90)	10.00	25.00
COMP.UPDATE w/o SP's (30)	4.00	10.00
91-120 RANDOM INSERTS IN PACKS		
91-120 ACTION 1800 SERIAL #'d SETS		
91-120 PORTRAIT 1800 SERIAL #'d SETS		
91-120 ACTION/PORTRAIT EQUAL VALUE		
121-150 STATED ODDS 1:18		
151-190 RANDOM INSERTS IN PACKS		
151-190 PR.RUN 700-800 SER.#'d OF EACH		
221-250 RANDOM IN ROOKIE UPD.PACKS		
221-250 PRINT RUN 825 SERIAL #'d SETS		
191-250 ISSUED IN ROOKIE UPDATE PACKS		
1 Troy Glaus	.20	.50
2 Darin Erstad	.20	.50
3 David Justice	.20	.50
4 Tim Hudson	.20	.50
5 Miguel Tejada	.20	.50
6 Barry Zito	.20	.50
7 Carlos Delgado	.20	.50
8 Shannon Stewart	.20	.50
9 Greg Vaughn	.20	.50
10 Toby Hall	.20	.50
11 Jim Thome	.30	.75
12 C.C. Sabathia	.20	.50
13 Ichiro Suzuki	1.00	2.50
14 Edgar Martinez	.30	.75
15 Freddy Garcia	.20	.50
16 Mike Cameron	.20	.50
17 Jeff Conine	.20	.50
18 Tony Batista	.20	.50
19 Alex Rodriguez	.60	1.50
20 Rafael Palmeiro	.30	.75
21 Ivan Rodriguez	.30	.75
22 Carl Everett	.20	.50
23 Pedro Martinez	.30	.75
24 Manny Ramirez	.30	.75
25 Nomar Garciaparra	.75	2.00
26 Johnny Damon Sox	.30	.75
27 Mike Sweeney	.20	.50
28 Carlos Beltran	.20	.50
29 Dmitri Young	.20	.50
30 Joe Mays	.20	.50
31 Doug Mientkiewicz	.20	.50
32 Cristian Guzman	.20	.50
33 Corey Koskie	.20	.50
34 Frank Thomas	.50	1.25
35 Magglio Ordonez	.20	.50
36 Mark Buehrle	.20	.50
37 Bernie Williams	.30	.75
38 Roger Clemens	1.00	2.50
39 Derek Jeter	1.25	3.00
40 Jason Giambi	.20	.50
41 Mike Mussina	.30	.75
42 Lance Berkman	.20	.50
43 Jeff Bagwell	.30	.75
44 Roy Oswalt	.20	.50
45 Greg Maddux	.75	2.00
46 Chipper Jones	.50	1.25
47 Andruw Jones	.30	.75
48 Gary Sheffield	.20	.50
49 Geoff Jenkins	.20	.50
50 Richie Sexson	.20	.50
51 Ben Sheets	.20	.50
52 Albert Pujols	1.00	2.50
53 J.D. Drew	.20	.50
54 Jim Edmonds	.20	.50
55 Sammy Sosa	.50	1.25
56 Moises Alou	.20	.50
57 Kerry Wood	.20	.50
58 Jon Lieber	.20	.50
59 Fred McGriff	.30	.75
60 Randy Johnson	.50	1.25
61 Luis Gonzalez	.20	.50
62 Curt Schilling	.20	.50
63 Kevin Brown	.20	.50
64 Hideo Nomo	.50	1.25
65 Shawn Green	.20	.50
66 Vladimir Guerrero	.50	1.25
67 Jose Vidro	.20	.50
68 Barry Bonds	1.25	3.00
69 Jeff Kent	.20	.50
70 Rich Aurilia	.20	.50
71 Cliff Floyd	.20	.50
72 Josh Beckett	.20	.50
73 Preston Wilson	.20	.50
74 Mike Piazza	.75	2.00
75 Mo Vaughn	.20	.50
76 Jeromy Burnitz	.20	.50
77 Roberto Alomar	.30	.75
78 Phil Nevin	.20	.50
79 Ryan Klesko	.20	.50
80 Scott Rolen	.30	.75
81 Bobby Abreu	.20	.50
82 Jimmy Rollins	.20	.50
83 Brian Giles	.20	.50
84 Aramis Ramirez	.20	.50
85 Ken Griffey Jr.	1.00	2.50
86 Sean Casey	.20	.50
87 Barry Larkin	.30	.75
88 Mike Hampton	.20	.50
89 Larry Walker	.20	.50
90 Todd Helton	.30	.75
91A Ron Calloway YS RC	3.00	8.00
91P Ron Calloway YS RC	3.00	8.00
92A Joe Orloski YS RC	3.00	8.00
92P Joe Orloski YS RC	3.00	8.00
93A Anderson Machado YS RC	3.00	8.00
93P Anderson Machado YS RC	3.00	8.00
94A Eric Good YS RC	3.00	8.00
94P Eric Good YS RC	3.00	8.00
95A Reed Johnson YS RC	4.00	10.00
95P Reed Johnson YS RC	4.00	10.00
96A Brendan Donnelly YS RC	3.00	8.00
96P Brendan Donnelly YS RC	3.00	8.00
97A Chris Baker YS RC	3.00	8.00
97P Chris Baker YS RC	3.00	8.00
98A Wilson Valdez YS RC	3.00	8.00
98P Wilson Valdez YS RC	3.00	8.00
99A Scotty Layfield YS RC	3.00	8.00
99P Scotty Layfield YS RC	3.00	8.00
100A P.J. Bevis YS RC	3.00	8.00
100P P.J. Bevis YS RC	3.00	8.00
101A Edwin Almonte YS RC	3.00	8.00
101P Edwin Almonte YS RC	3.00	8.00
102A Francis Beltran YS RC	3.00	8.00
102P Francis Beltran YS RC	3.00	8.00
103A Val Pascucci YS	3.00	8.00
103P Val Pascucci YS	3.00	8.00
104A Nelson Castro YS RC	3.00	8.00
104P Nelson Castro YS RC	3.00	8.00
105A Michael Crudale YS RC	3.00	8.00
105P Michael Crudale YS RC	3.00	8.00
106A Colin Young YS RC	3.00	8.00
106P Colin Young YS RC	3.00	8.00
107A Todd Donovan YS RC	3.00	8.00
107P Todd Donovan YS RC	3.00	8.00
108A Felix Escalona YS RC	3.00	8.00
108P Felix Escalona YS RC	3.00	8.00
109A Brandon Backe YS RC	4.00	10.00
109P Brandon Backe YS RC	4.00	10.00
110A Corey Thurman YS RC	3.00	8.00
110P Corey Thurman YS RC	3.00	8.00
111A Kyle Kane YS RC	3.00	8.00
111P Kyle Kane YS RC	3.00	8.00
112A Allan Simpson YS RC	3.00	8.00
112P Allan Simpson YS RC	3.00	8.00
113A Jose Valverde YS RC	3.00	8.00
113P Jose Valverde YS RC	6.00	15.00
114A Chris Booker YS RC	3.00	8.00
114P Chris Booker YS RC	3.00	8.00
115A Brandon Puffer YS RC	3.00	8.00
115P Brandon Puffer YS RC	3.00	8.00
116A John Foster YS RC	3.00	8.00
116P John Foster YS RC	3.00	8.00
117A Cliff Bartosh YS RC	3.00	8.00
117P Cliff Bartosh YS RC	3.00	8.00
118A Gustavo Chacin YS RC	4.00	10.00
118P Gustavo Chacin YS RC	4.00	10.00
119A Steve Kent YS RC	3.00	8.00
119P Steve Kent YS RC	3.00	8.00
120A Nate Field YS RC	3.00	8.00
120P Nate Field YS RC	3.00	8.00
121 Victor Alvarez AU RC	4.00	10.00
122 Steve Bechler AU RC	4.00	10.00
123 Adrian Burnside AU RC	4.00	10.00
124 Marlon Byrd AU	6.00	15.00
125 Jaime Cerda AU RC	4.00	10.00
126 Brandon Claussen AU	6.00	15.00
127 Mark Corey AU RC	4.00	10.00
128 Doug Devore AU RC	4.00	10.00
129 Kazuhisa Ishii AU SP RC	4.00	10.00
130 John Ennis AU RC	4.00	10.00
131 Kevin Frederick AU RC	4.00	10.00
132 Josh Hancock AU RC	8.00	20.00
133 Ben Howard AU RC	4.00	10.00
134 Orlando Hudson AU	6.00	15.00
135 Hansel Izquierdo AU RC	4.00	10.00
136 Eric Junge AU RC	4.00	10.00
137 Austin Kearns AU	6.00	15.00
138 Victor Martinez AU	8.00	20.00
139 Luis Martinez AU RC	4.00	10.00
140 Danny Mota AU RC	4.00	10.00
141 Jorge Padilla AU RC	4.00	10.00
142 Andy Pratt AU RC	4.00	10.00
143 Rene Reyes AU RC	4.00	10.00
144 Rodrigo Rosario AU RC	4.00	10.00
145 Tom Shearn AU RC	4.00	10.00
146 So Taguchi AU SP RC	6.00	15.00
147 Dennis Tankersley AU	6.00	15.00
148 Matt Thornton AU RC	4.00	10.00
149 Jeremy Ward AU RC	4.00	10.00
150 Mitch Wylie AU RC	4.00	10.00
151 Pedro Martinez JSY/800	2.50	6.00
152 Cal Ripken JSY/800	12.00	30.00
153 Roger Clemens JSY/800	5.00	12.00
154 Bernie Williams JSY/800	2.50	6.00
155 Jason Giambi JSY/700	1.50	4.00
156 Robin Ventura JSY/800	1.50	4.00
157 Carlos Delgado JSY/800	1.50	4.00
158 Frank Thomas JSY/800	4.00	10.00
159 Magglio Ordonez JSY/800	2.50	6.00
160 Jim Thome JSY/800	2.50	6.00
161 Darin Erstad JSY/800	1.50	4.00
162 Tim Salmon JSY/800	1.50	4.00
163 Tim Hudson JSY/800	2.50	6.00
164 Barry Zito JSY/800	1.50	4.00
165 Ichiro Suzuki JSY/800	5.00	12.00
166 Edgar Martinez JSY/800	2.50	6.00
167 Alex Rodriguez JSY/800	5.00	12.00
168 Ivan Rodriguez JSY/800	2.50	6.00
169 Juan Gonzalez JSY/800	1.50	4.00
170 Greg Maddux JSY/800	6.00	15.00
171 Chipper Jones JSY/800	4.00	10.00
172 Andruw Jones JSY/800	1.50	4.00
173 Tom Glavine JSY/800	2.50	6.00
174 Mike Piazza JSY/800	4.00	10.00
175 Roberto Alomar JSY/800	2.50	6.00
176 Scott Rolen JSY/800	2.50	6.00
177 Sammy Sosa JSY/800	4.00	10.00
178 Moises Alou JSY/800	1.50	4.00
179 Ken Griffey Jr. JSY/700	8.00	20.00
180 Jeff Bagwell JSY/800	2.50	6.00
181 Jim Edmonds JSY/800	2.50	6.00
182 J.D. Drew JSY/800	1.50	4.00
183 Brian Giles JSY/800	1.50	4.00
184 Randy Johnson JSY/800	4.00	10.00
185 Curt Schilling JSY/800	2.50	6.00
186 Luis Gonzalez JSY/800	1.50	4.00
187 Todd Helton JSY/800	2.50	6.00
188 Shawn Green JSY/800	1.50	4.00
189 David Wells JSY/800	1.50	4.00
190 Jeff Kent JSY/800	1.50	4.00
191 Tom Glavine	.50	1.25
192 Cliff Floyd	.30	.75
193 Mark Prior	.50	1.25
194 Corey Patterson	.30	.75
195 Paul Konerko	.30	.75
196 Adam Dunn	.30	.75
197 Joe Borchard	.30	.75
198 Carlos Pena	.30	.75
199 Juan Encarnacion	.30	.75
200 Luis Castillo	.30	.75
201 Torii Hunter	.30	.75
202 Hee Seop Choi	.30	.75
203 Bartolo Colon	.30	.75
204 Raul Mondesi	.30	.75
205 Jeff Weaver	.30	.75
206 Eric Munson	.30	.75
207 Alfonso Soriano	.30	.75
208 Ray Durham	.30	.75
209 Eric Chavez	.30	.75
210 Brett Myers	.30	.75
211 Jeremy Giambi	.30	.75
212 Vicente Padilla	.30	.75
213 Felipe Lopez	.30	.75
214 Sean Burroughs	.30	.75
215 Kenny Lofton	.30	.75
216 Scott Rolen	.50	1.25
217 Carl Crawford	.30	.75
218 Juan Gonzalez	.30	.75
219 Orlando Hudson	.30	.75
220 Eric Hinske	.30	.75
221 Adam Walker AU RC	4.00	10.00
222 Aaron Cook AU RC	6.00	15.00
223 Cam Esslinger AU RC	4.00	10.00
224 Kirk Saarloos AU RC	4.00	10.00
225 Jose Diaz AU RC	4.00	10.00
226 David Ross AU RC	60.00	150.00
227 Jayson Durocher AU RC	4.00	10.00
228 Brian Mallette AU RC	4.00	10.00
229 Aaron Guiel AU RC	4.00	10.00
230 Jorge Nunez AU RC	4.00	10.00
231 Satoru Komiyama AU RC	6.00	15.00
232 Tyler Yates AU RC	4.00	10.00
233 Pete Zamora AU RC	4.00	10.00
234 Mike Gonzalez AU RC	4.00	10.00
235 Oliver Perez AU RC	4.00	10.00
236 Julius Matos AU RC	6.00	15.00
237 Andy Shibilo AU RC	4.00	10.00
238 Jason Simontacchi AU RC	4.00	10.00
239 Ron Chiavacci AU	4.00	10.00
240 Deivis Santos AU	4.00	10.00
241 Travis Driskill AU RC	4.00	10.00
242 Jorge De La Rosa AU RC	4.00	10.00
243 Anastacio Martinez AU RC	4.00	10.00
244 Earl Snyder AU RC	4.00	10.00
245 Freddy Sanchez AU RC	12.00	30.00
246 Miguel Asencio AU RC	4.00	10.00
247 Juan Brito AU RC	4.00	10.00
248 Franklyn German AU RC	4.00	10.00
249 Chris Snelling AU RC	6.00	15.00
250 Ken Huckaby AU RC	4.00	10.00

2002 SPx SuperStars Swatches Gold

*GOLD JSY: .6X TO 1.5X BASIC JSY
RANDOM INSERTS IN PACKS
STATED PRINT RUN 150 SERIAL #'d SETS

2002 SPx SuperStars Swatches Silver

*SILVER JSY: .4X TO 1X BASIC JSY
RANDOM INSERTS IN PACKS
STATED PRINT RUN 400 SERIAL #'d SETS

2002 SPx Winning Materials 2-Player Base Combos

RANDOM INSERTS IN PACKS		
STATED PRINT RUN 200 SERIAL #'d SETS		
BBG B.Bonds S.Green	10.00	25.00
BGR Troy Glaus Alex Rodriguez	8.00	20.00
BGS Ken Griffey Jr. Sammy Sosa	12.00	30.00
BIM Ichiro Suzuki Edgar Martinez	8.00	20.00
BPE Mike Piazza Jim Edmonds	6.00	15.00
BPI Albert Pujols Ichiro Suzuki	12.00	30.00
BRJ Alex Rodriguez Derek Jeter	10.00	25.00
BSG Sammy Sosa Luis Gonzalez	6.00	15.00
BSR Kazuhiro Sasaki Mariano Rivera	6.00	15.00
BWJ Bernie Williams Derek Jeter	12.00	30.00

2002 SPx Winning Materials 2-Player Jersey Combos

STATED ODDS 1:18		
SP INFO PROVIDED BY UPPER DECK		
DP PERCEIVED AS LARGER SUPPLY		
WMAR A.Rodriguez I.Rodriguez	6.00	15.00
WMBA J.Burnitz/E.Alfonzo	2.00	5.00
WMBG J.Bagwell/J.Gonzalez	3.00	8.00
WMBR J.Bagwell/A.Rodriguez DP	6.00	15.00
WMDH J.Dye/T.Hudson	3.00	8.00
WMDS C.Delgado/S.Stewart	2.00	5.00
WMED J.Edmonds/J.Drew	3.00	8.00
WMGC K.Griffey Jr./S.Casey SP	10.00	25.00
WMGK S.Green/E.Karros	2.00	5.00
WMGR J.Gonzalez/I.Rodriguez	3.00	8.00
WMHW M.Hampton/L.Walker	3.00	8.00
WMJJ C.Jones/A.Jones	5.00	12.00
WMJS R.Johnson/C.Schilling	5.00	12.00
WMKG J.Kendall/B.Giles	2.00	5.00
WMLH A.Leiter/M.Hampton	2.00	5.00
WMMC E.Martinez/M.Cameron	3.00	8.00
WMMJ G.Maddux/C.Jones	8.00	20.00
WMNM H.Nomo/P.Martinez SP	5.00	12.00
WMPA M.Piazza/R.Alomar DP	5.00	12.00
WMRA S.Rolen/B.Abreu	3.00	8.00
WMRP I.Rodriguez/C.Park	3.00	8.00
WMSE A.Sele/D.Erstad	2.00	5.00
WMSH K.Sasaki/S.Hasegawa	2.00	5.00
WMSP S.Sosa/C.Patterson	5.00	12.00
WMTO F.Thomas/M.Ordonez	5.00	12.00
WMTS J.Thome/C.Sabathia DP	3.00	8.00
WMVR O.Vizquel/A.Rodriguez	6.00	15.00
WMWG B.Williams/J.Giambi DP	3.00	8.00
WMWP D.Wells/J.Posada DP	3.00	8.00

2002 SPx Winning Materials USA Jersey Combos

RANDOM INSERTS IN PACKS		
STATED PRINT RUN 150 SERIAL #'d SETS		
USAAH B.Abernathy/O.Hudson	6.00	15.00
USAAW M.Anderson/J.Weaver	6.00	15.00
USABT S.Burroughs/M.Teixeira	10.00	25.00
USAGB J.Giambi/S.Burroughs	6.00	15.00
USAGT J.Giambi/M.Teixeira	10.00	25.00
USAHD O.Hudson/J.Deardorff	6.00	15.00
USAHP D.Hermanson/M.Prior	6.00	15.00
USAJC J.Jones/M.Cuddyer	6.00	15.00
USAKB A.Kearns/S.Burroughs	6.00	15.00
USAKC A.Kearns/M.Cuddyer	6.00	15.00
USAMG D.Mientk/J.Giambi	6.00	15.00
USAMO M.Morris/R.Oswalt	6.00	15.00
USAMP M.Morris/M.Prior	6.00	15.00
USAMW M.Morris/J.Weaver	6.00	15.00
USAPB M.Prior/D.Brazelton	6.00	15.00
USARE B.Roberts/A.Everett	6.00	15.00
USASD M.Kotsay/S.Burroughs	6.00	15.00
USATB B.Abernathy/D.Braz	6.00	15.00
USATP M.Teixeira/M.Prior	10.00	25.00
USAWB J.Weaver/D.Brazelton	6.00	15.00
USAWH J.Weaver/D.Hermanson	6.00	15.00
USAHOU R.Oswalt/A.Everett	6.00	15.00
USAMIN D.Mientk/M.Cuddyer	6.00	15.00

2003 SPx

COMP.LO SET w/o SP's (100)	10.00	25.00
COMP.LO SET w/ SP's (125)	20.00	50.00
COMMON CARD (1-125)	.20	.50
COMMON SP (1-125)	.60	1.50
SP: 4/9/13/20/22/26/35/53/60/64/70/72		
SP: 79/82-84/91/94/101/105/108/111		
SP: 114/116/125		
COMMON CARD (126-160)	1.00	2.50
126-160 PRINT RUN 999 SERIAL #'d SETS		
COMMON CARD (161-178)	6.00	15.00
CARD 161 PRINT RUN 864 SERIAL #'d COPIES		
CARD 162 PRINT RUN 800 SERIAL #'d COPIES		
163-178 PRINT RUN 1224 SERIAL #'d SETS		
126-178 RANDOM INSERTS IN SPx PACKS		
COMMON CARD (179-193)	2.50	6.00
179-193 RANDOM IN UD FINITE BONUS PACK		
179-193 PRINT RUN 150 SERIAL #'d SETS		
COMMON CARD (381-387)	6.00	15.00
381-387 RANDOM IN UD FINITE BONUS PACK		
381-387 PRINT RUN 355 SERIAL #'d SETS		
1 Darin Erstad	.20	.50
2 Garret Anderson	.20	.50
3 Tim Salmon	.20	.50
4 Troy Glaus SP	.60	1.50
5 Luis Gonzalez	.20	.50
6 Randy Johnson	.50	1.25
7 Curt Schilling	.30	.75
8 Lyle Overbay	.20	.50
9 Andruw Jones SP	.60	1.50
10 Gary Sheffield	.20	.50
11 Rafael Furcal	.20	.50
12 Greg Maddux	.60	1.50
13 Chipper Jones SP	1.50	4.00
14 Tony Batista	.20	.50
15 Rodrigo Lopez	.20	.50
16 Jay Gibbons	.20	.50
17 Byung-Hyun Kim	.20	.50
18 Johnny Damon	.30	.75
19 Derek Lowe	.20	.50
20 Nomar Garciaparra SP	1.00	2.50
21 Pedro Martinez	.30	.75
22 Manny Ramirez SP	1.50	4.00
23 Mark Prior	.30	.75
24 Kerry Wood	.20	.50
25 Corey Patterson	.20	.50
26 Sammy Sosa SP	1.50	4.00
27 Moises Alou	.20	.50
28 Magglio Ordonez	.30	.75
29 Frank Thomas	.50	1.25
30 Paul Konerko	.30	.75
31 Bartolo Colon	.20	.50
32 Adam Dunn	.30	.75
33 Austin Kearns	.20	.50
34 Aaron Boone	.20	.50
35 Ken Griffey Jr. SP	3.00	8.00
36 Omar Vizquel	.30	.75
37 C.C. Sabathia	.30	.75
38 Jason Davis	.20	.50
39 Travis Hafner	.20	.50
40 Brandon Phillips	.20	.50
41 Larry Walker	.30	.75
42 Preston Wilson	.20	.50
43 Jay Payton	.20	.50
44 Todd Helton	.30	.75
45 Carlos Pena	.30	.75
46 Eric Munson	.20	.50
47 Ivan Rodriguez	.30	.75
49 Alex Gonzalez	.20	.50
50 Roy Oswalt	.30	.75
51 Craig Biggio	.30	.75
52 Jeff Bagwell	.30	.75
53 Dontrelle Willis SP	.60	1.50
54 Mike Sweeney	.20	.50
55 Carlos Beltran	.30	.75
56 Brent Mayne	.20	.50
57 Hideo Nomo	.50	1.25
58 Rickey Henderson	.50	1.25
59 Adrian Beltre	.50	1.25
60 Miguel Cabrera SP	8.00	20.00
61 Kazuhisa Ishii	.20	.50
62 Ben Sheets	.20	.50
63 Richie Sexson	.20	.50
64 Torii Hunter SP	.60	1.50
65 Jacque Jones	.20	.50
66 Joe Mays	.20	.50
67 Corey Koskie	.20	.50
68 A.J. Pierzynski	.20	.50
69 Jose Vidro	.20	.50
70 Vladimir Guerrero SP	1.00	2.50
71 Tom Glavine	.30	.75
72 Jose Reyes SP	1.50	4.00
73 Aaron Heilman	.20	.50
74 Mike Piazza	.50	1.25
75 Jorge Posada	.30	.75
77 Robin Ventura	.20	.50
78 Mariano Rivera	.60	1.50
79 Roger Clemens SP	2.00	5.00
80 Jason Giambi	.20	.50
81 Bernie Williams	.30	.75
82 Alfonso Soriano SP	1.00	2.50
83 Derek Jeter SP	4.00	10.00
84 Miguel Tejada SP	1.00	2.50
85 Eric Chavez	.20	.50
86 Tim Hudson	.30	.75
87 Barry Zito	.30	.75
88 Mark Mulder	.20	.50
89 Erubiel Durazo	.20	.50
90 Pat Burrell	.20	.50
91 Jim Thome SP	1.00	2.50
92 Bobby Abreu	.20	.50
93 Brian Giles	.20	.50
94 Reggie Sanders SP	.60	1.50
95 Kenny Lofton	.20	.50
96 Ryan Klesko	.20	.50
97 Sean Burroughs	.20	.50
98 Edgardo Alfonzo	.20	.50
99 Rich Aurilia	.20	.50
100 Jose Cruz Jr.	.20	.50
101 Barry Bonds SP	2.50	6.00
102 Mike Cameron	.20	.50
103 Kazuhiro Sasaki	.20	.50
104 Bret Boone	.20	.50
105 Ichiro Suzuki SP	2.00	5.00
106 J.D. Drew	.20	.50
107 Jim Edmonds	.30	.75
108 Scott Rolen SP	1.00	2.50
109 Matt Morris	.20	.50
110 Tino Martinez	.20	.50
111 Albert Pujols SP	2.00	5.00
112 Damian Rolls	.20	.50
113 Carl Crawford	.30	.75
114 Rocco Baldelli SP	.60	1.50
115 Hank Blalock	.20	.50
116 Alex Rodriguez SP	2.00	5.00
117 Kevin Mench	.20	.50
118 Rafael Palmeiro	.30	.75
119 Mark Teixeira	.30	.75
120 Shannon Stewart	.20	.50
121 Vernon Wells	.20	.50
122 Josh Phelps	.20	.50
123 Eric Hinske	.20	.50
124 Orlando Hudson	.20	.50
125 Carlos Delgado SP	.60	1.50
126 Jason Roach ROO RC	1.00	2.50
127 Dan Haren ROO RC	5.00	12.00
128 Luis Ayala ROO RC	1.00	2.50
129 Bo Hart ROO RC	1.00	2.50
130 Wilfredo Ledezma ROO RC	1.00	2.50
131 Rick Roberts ROO RC	1.00	2.50
132 Miguel Ojeda ROO RC	1.00	2.50
133 Aquilino Lopez ROO RC	1.00	2.50
134 Roger Deago ROO RC	1.00	2.50
135 Arnie Munoz ROO RC	1.00	2.50
136 Brent Hoard ROO RC	1.00	2.50
137 Termel Sledge ROO RC	1.00	2.50
138 Ryan Cameron ROO RC	1.00	2.50
139 Prentice Redman ROO RC	1.00	2.50
140 Clint Barmes ROO RC	2.50	6.00
141 Jeremy Griffiths ROO RC	1.00	2.50
142 Jon Leicester ROO RC	1.00	2.50
143 Brandon Webb ROO RC	3.00	8.00
144 Todd Wellemeyer ROO RC	1.00	2.50
145 Felix Sanchez ROO RC	1.00	2.50
146 Anthony Ferrari ROO RC	1.00	2.50
147 Ian Ferguson ROO RC	1.00	2.50
148 Michael Nakamura ROO RC	1.00	2.50
149 Lew Ford ROO RC	1.00	2.50
150 Nate Bland ROO RC	1.00	2.50
151 David Matranga ROO RC	1.00	2.50
152 Edgar Gonzalez ROO RC	1.00	2.50
153 Carlos Mendez ROO RC	1.00	2.50
154 Jason Gilfillan ROO RC	1.00	2.50
155 Mike Neu ROO RC	1.00	2.50
156 Jason Shiell ROO RC	1.00	2.50
157 Jeff Duncan ROO RC	1.00	2.50
158 Oscar Villarreal ROO RC	1.00	2.50
159 Diegomar Markwell ROO RC	1.00	2.50
160 Joe Valentine ROO RC	1.00	2.50
161 Hideki Matsui AU JSY RC	100.00	200.00
162 Jose Contreras AU RC	20.00	40.00
163 Willie Eyre AU JSY RC	6.00	15.00
164 Matt Bruback AU JSY RC	6.00	15.00
165 Rett Johnson AU JSY RC	6.00	15.00
166 Jeremy Griffiths AU JSY	6.00	15.00
167 Fran Cruceta AU JSY RC	6.00	15.00
168 Fern Cabrera AU JSY RC	6.00	15.00
169 Jhonny Peralta AU JSY	6.00	15.00
170 Shane Bazzell AU JSY RC	6.00	15.00
171 Bob Madritsch AU JSY RC	10.00	25.00
172 Phil Seibel AU JSY RC	6.00	15.00
173 J.Willingham AU JSY RC	6.00	15.00
174 Rob Hammock AU JSY RC	6.00	15.00
175 A.Machado AU JSY RC	6.00	15.00
176 David Sanders AU JSY RC	6.00	15.00
177 Matt Kata AU JSY RC	6.00	15.00
178 Heath Bell AU JSY RC	6.00	15.00
179 Chad Gaudin ROO RC	2.50	6.00
180 Chris Capuano ROO RC	2.50	6.00
181 Danny Garcia ROO RC	2.50	6.00
182 Delmon Young ROO	15.00	40.00
183 Edwin Jackson ROO RC	4.00	10.00
184 Greg Jones ROO RC	2.50	6.00
185 Jeremy Bonderman ROO RC	10.00	25.00
186 Jorge DePaula ROO	2.50	6.00

187 Khalil Greene ROO 4.00 10.00
188 Chad Cordero ROO RC 2.50 6.00
189 Miguel Cabrera ROO 20.00 50.00
190 Rich Harden ROO 4.00 10.00
191 Rickie Weeks ROO 8.00 20.00
192 Rosman Garcia ROO RC 2.50 6.00
193 Tom Gregorio ROO RC 2.50 6.00
381 Andrew Brown AU JSY RC 6.00 15.00
382 Delm Young AU JSY RC 12.50 30.00
383 Colin Porter AU JSY RC 6.00 15.00
385 Rick. Weeks AU JSY RC 10.00 25.00
386 David Matranga AU JSY RC 6.00 15.00
387 Bo Hart AU JSY 6.00 15.00

2003 SPx Spectrum

*SPECTRUM 1-125 p/r 51-75: 5X TO 12X
*SPECTRUM 1-125 p/r 36-50: 6X TO 15X
*SPECTRUM 1-125 p/r 26-35: 8X TO 20X
*SPECTRUM 1-125 p/r 51-75: 1.25X TO 3X SP
*SPECTRUM 1-125 p/r 36-50: 1.5X TO 4X SP
*SPECTRUM 1-125 p/r 26-35: 2X TO 5X SP
1-125 PRINT RUNS B/WN 1-75 COPIES PER
*SPECTRUM 126-160: 2X TO 5X BASIC
126-160 PRINT RUN 125 SERIAL #'d SETS
161-178 PRINT RUN 25 SERIAL #'d SETS
161-178 NO PRICING DUE TO SCARCITY

2003 SPx Game Used Combos

PRINT RUNS B/WN 10-90 COPIES PER
NO PRICING ON QTY OF 25 OR LESS
BK J.Bagwell/J.Kent/90 15.00 40.00
BM B.Bonds/R.Maris/50 30.00 60.00
BT B.Bonds/T.Williams/50 125.00 250.00
CA C.Ripken/A.Rodriguez/50 125.00 200.00
CC J.Contreras/R.Clemens/50 20.00 50.00
CL C.Ripken/L.Gehrig/90 150.00 300.00
CM J.Contreras/P.Martinez/90 15.00 40.00
ED D.Erstad/T.Glaus/90 10.00 25.00
FC C.Fisk/G.Carter/90 15.00 40.00
GC G.Maddux/C.Jones/90 20.00 50.00
GD K.Griffey Jr./A.Dunn/90 30.00 60.00
GR K.Griffey Jr./S.Sosa/90 30.00 60.00
GS J.Giambi/A.Soriano/90 10.00 25.00
HJ H.Matsui/J.Giambi/50 50.00 100.00
IA I.Suzuki/A.Pujols/50 150.00 250.00
JJ C.Jones/A.Jones/90 15.00 40.00
MB M.Mantle/B.Bonds/50 50.00 120.00
MD M.Mantle/D.Jeter/50 150.00 250.00
MG P.Martinez/Nomar/90 30.00 60.00
MJ H.Matsui/D.Jeter/90 60.00 120.00
MS H.Matsui/I.Suzuki/50 250.00 400.00
MW M.Mantle/T.Williams/50 75.00 150.00
NI H.Nomo/K.Ishii/50 40.00 80.00
PM R.Palmeiro/F.McGriff/90 15.00 40.00
RC N.Ryan/R.Clemens/90 20.00 50.00
RG A.Rod/N.Garciaparra/90 30.00 60.00
RR C.Ripken/S.Rolen/90 25.00 60.00
RS N.Ryan/T.Seaver/90 75.00 150.00
RT A.Rodriguez/M.Tejada/90 20.00 50.00
SB S.Sosa/B.Bonds/90 30.00 60.00
SJ C.Schilling/R.Johnson/90 15.00 40.00
SN I.Suzuki/H.Nomo/90 125.00 200.00
SP S.Sosa/R.Palmeiro/90 15.00 40.00

2003 SPx Stars Autograph Jersey

PRINT RUNS B/WN 195-790 COPIES PER
SPECTRUM PRINT RUN 1 SERIAL #'d SET
NO SPECTRUM PRICING DUE TO SCARCITY
CJ0 Chipper Jones/195 40.00 80.00
CS Curt Schilling/490 15.00 40.00
JG Jason Giambi/315 15.00 40.00
KG Ken Griffey Jr./690 30.00 80.00
LB Lance Berkman/590 6.00 15.00
LG Luis Gonzalez/790 6.00 15.00
MP Mark Prior/490 8.00 20.00
NM Nomar Garciaparra/195 15.00 40.00
PB Pat Burrell/590 10.00 25.00
TG Troy Glaus/490 6.00 15.00
VG Vladimir Guerrero/390 10.00 25.00

2003 SPx Winning Materials 375

LOGO'S CONSECUTIVELY #'d FROM 41-375
NUMBERS CONSECUTIVELY #'d FROM 1-40
CARDS CUMULATIVELY SERIAL #'d TO 375
*WIN.MAT.250: .5X TO 1.2X WIN.MAT.375
NUMBERS CONSECUTIVELY #'d FROM 1-28
LOGOS CONSECUTIVELY #'d FROM 29-250
WM 250 CUMULATIVELY SERIAL #'d TO 250
LOGO/NUMBER PRINTS PROVIDED BY UD
AJ1A Andruw Jones Logo 1.50 4.00
AJ1B Andruw Jones Num 3.00 8.00
AP1A Albert Pujols Logo 5.00 12.00
AP1B Albert Pujols Num 10.00 25.00
AR1A Alex Rodriguez Logo 5.00 12.00
AR1B Alex Rodriguez Num 10.00 25.00
AS1A Alfonso Soriano Logo 2.50 6.00
AS1B Alfonso Soriano Num 5.00 12.00
BW1A Bernie Williams Logo 2.50 6.00
BW1B Bernie Williams Num 5.00 12.00
BZ1A Barry Zito Logo 2.50 6.00
BZ1B Barry Zito Num 5.00 12.00
CD1A Carlos Delgado Logo 1.50 4.00
CD1B Carlos Delgado Num 3.00 8.00
CJ1A Chipper Jones Logo 4.00 10.00
CJ1B Chipper Jones Num 8.00 20.00
CS1A Curt Schilling Logo 2.50 6.00
CS1B Curt Schilling Num 5.00 12.00
FT1A Frank Thomas Logo 4.00 10.00
FT1B Frank Thomas Num 8.00 20.00
GM1A Greg Maddux Logo 5.00 12.00
GM1B Greg Maddux Num 10.00 25.00
GS1A Gary Sheffield Logo 1.50 4.00
GS1B Gary Sheffield Num 3.00 8.00
HM1A Hideki Matsui Logo 8.00 20.00
HM1B Hideki Matsui Num 15.00 40.00
HN1A Hideo Nomo Logo 4.00 10.00
HN1B Hideo Nomo Num 8.00 20.00
IR1A Ivan Rodriguez Logo 2.50 6.00
IR1B Ivan Rodriguez Num 5.00 12.00
IS1A Ichiro Suzuki Logo 5.00 12.00
IS1B Ichiro Suzuki Num 10.00 25.00
JB1A Jeff Bagwell Logo 2.50 6.00
JB1B Jeff Bagwell Num 5.00 12.00
JG1A Jason Giambi Logo 1.50 4.00
JG1B Jason Giambi Num 3.00 8.00
JK1A Jeff Kent Logo 1.50 4.00
JK1B Jeff Kent Num 3.00 8.00
JT1A Jim Thome Logo 2.50 6.00
JT1B Jim Thome Num 5.00 12.00
KG1A Ken Griffey Jr. Logo 8.00 20.00
KG1B Ken Griffey Jr. Num 15.00 40.00
LB1A Lance Berkman Logo 2.50 6.00
LB1B Lance Berkman Num 5.00 12.00
LG1A Luis Gonzalez Logo 1.50 4.00
LG1B Luis Gonzalez Num 3.00 8.00
MA1A Mark Prior Logo 2.50 6.00
MA1B Mark Prior Num 5.00 12.00
MP1A Mike Piazza Logo 4.00 10.00
MP1B Mike Piazza Num 8.00 20.00
MR1A Manny Ramirez Logo 4.00 10.00
MR1B Manny Ramirez Num 8.00 20.00
MT1A Miguel Tejada Logo 2.50 6.00
MT1B Miguel Tejada Num 5.00 12.00
PB1A Pat Burrell Logo 1.50 4.00
PB1B Pat Burrell Num 3.00 8.00
PM1A Pedro Martinez Logo 2.50 6.00
PM1B Pedro Martinez Num 5.00 12.00
RA1A Roberto Alomar Logo 2.50 6.00
RA1B Roberto Alomar Num 5.00 12.00
RC1A Roger Clemens Logo 5.00 12.00
RC1B Roger Clemens Num 10.00 25.00
RF1A Rafael Furcal Logo 1.50 4.00
RF1B Rafael Furcal Num 3.00 8.00
RJ1A Randy Johnson Logo 4.00 10.00
RJ1B Randy Johnson Num 8.00 20.00
SG1A Shawn Green Logo 1.50 4.00
SG1B Shawn Green Num 3.00 8.00
SS1A Sammy Sosa Logo 4.00 10.00
SS1B Sammy Sosa Num 8.00 20.00
TG1A Tom Glavine Logo 2.50 6.00
TG1B Tom Glavine Num 5.00 12.00
TH1A Torii Hunter Logo 1.50 4.00
TH1B Torii Hunter Num 3.00 8.00
TO1A Todd Helton Logo 2.50 6.00
TO1B Todd Helton Num 5.00 12.00
TR1A Troy Glaus Logo 1.50 4.00
TR1B Troy Glaus Num 3.00 8.00
VG1A Vladimir Guerrero Logo 2.50 6.00
VG1B Vladimir Guerrero Num 5.00 12.00

2003 SPx Winning Materials 175

NUMBERS CONSECUTIVELY #'d FROM 1-20
LOGOS CONSECUTIVELY #'d FROM 21-175
CARDS CUMULATIVELY SERIAL #'d TO 175
*WM LOGO 50: .5X TO 1.2X WM LOGO 175
WM 50 NUMBERS CONSECUTIVELY #'d 1-10
WM 50 LOGOS CONSECUTIVELY #'d 11-50
WM 50 CUMULATIVELY SERIAL #'d TO 50
NO NUMBER PRICING DUE TO SCARCITY
LOGO/NUMBER PRINTS PROVIDED BY UD
AJ2A Andruw Jones Logo 2.00 5.00
AP2A Albert Pujols Logo 6.00 15.00
AR2A Alex Rodriguez Logo 6.00 15.00
AS2A Alfonso Soriano Logo 3.00 8.00
BW2A Bernie Williams Logo 3.00 8.00
BZ2A Barry Zito Logo 3.00 8.00
CD2A Carlos Delgado Logo 2.00 5.00
CJ2A Chipper Jones Logo 5.00 12.00
CS2A Curt Schilling Logo 3.00 8.00
FT2A Frank Thomas Logo 5.00 12.00
GM2A Greg Maddux Logo 6.00 15.00
GS2A Gary Sheffield Logo 2.00 5.00
HM2A Hideki Matsui Logo 10.00 25.00
HN2A Hideo Nomo Logo 5.00 12.00
IR2A Ivan Rodriguez Logo 3.00 8.00
IS2A Ichiro Suzuki Logo 6.00 15.00
JB2A Jeff Bagwell Logo 3.00 8.00
JG2A Jason Giambi Logo 2.00 5.00
JK2A Jeff Kent Logo 2.00 5.00
JT2A Jim Thome Logo 3.00 8.00
KG2A Ken Griffey Jr. Logo 10.00 25.00
LB2A Lance Berkman Logo 3.00 8.00
LG2A Luis Gonzalez Logo 2.00 5.00
MM2A M.Mantle Pants Logo 60.00 150.00
MP2RA Mark Prior Logo 3.00 8.00
MP2A Mike Piazza Logo 5.00 12.00
MR2A Manny Ramirez Logo 5.00 12.00
MT2A Miguel Tejada Logo 3.00 8.00
PB2A Pat Burrell Logo 2.00 5.00
PM2A Pedro Martinez Logo 3.00 8.00
RA2A Roberto Alomar Logo 3.00 8.00
RC2A Roger Clemens Logo 6.00 15.00
RF2A Rafael Furcal Logo 2.00 5.00
RJ2A Randy Johnson Logo 5.00 12.00
SG2A Shawn Green Logo 2.00 5.00
SS2A Sammy Sosa Logo 5.00 12.00
TGL2A Troy Glaus Logo 2.00 5.00
TG2A Tom Glavine Logo 3.00 8.00
THE2A Todd Helton Logo 3.00 8.00
TH2A Torii Hunter Logo 2.00 5.00
TW2A T.Williams Pants Logo 20.00 50.00
VG2A Vladimir Guerrero Logo 3.00 8.00

2003 SPx Young Stars Autograph Jersey

PRINT RUNS B/WN 355-1460 COPIES PER
SPECTRUM PRINT RUN 25 SERIAL #'d SETS
NO SPECTRUM PRICING DUE TO SCARCITY
EXCHANGE DEADLINE 08/15/06
AD Adam Dunn/1295 6.00 15.00
AK Austin Kearns/964 6.00 15.00
BM Brett Myers/1295 6.00 15.00
BP Brandon Phillips/1295 6.00 15.00
CG Chris George/1260 6.00 15.00
DW Dontrelle Willis/355 12.50 30.00
EH Eric Hinske/1295 6.00 15.00
HB Hank Blalock/1295 6.00 15.00
JA Jason Jennings/1295 6.00 15.00
JBA Josh Bard/1295 6.00 15.00
JJ Jacque Jones/1260 6.00 15.00
JP Josh Phelps/1295 6.00 15.00
KA Kurt Ainsworth/1460 6.00 15.00
KG Khalil Greene/355 20.00 50.00
KS Kirk Saarloos/1295 6.00 15.00
MD Michael Cuddyer/1156 6.00 15.00
MK Mike Kinkade/1295 6.00 15.00
MT Mark Teixeira/1295 10.00 25.00
NJ Nick Johnson/1295 6.00 15.00
RB Rocco Baldelli/1295 6.00 15.00
RH Rich Harden/355 6.00 15.00
RO Roy Oswalt/1295 6.00 15.00
SB Sean Burroughs/1295 6.00 15.00

2004 SPx

COMP.SET w/o SP's (100) 10.00 25.00
COMMON CARD (1-100) .20 .50
COMMON CARD (101-110) .60 1.50
101-110 STATED ODDS 1:18
COMMON CARD (111-145) .60 1.50
111-145 PRINT RUN 1599 SERIAL #'d SETS
COMMON CARD (146-154) 1.50 4.00
146-154 PRINT RUN 499 SERIAL #'d SETS
COMMON CARD (155-160) 1.50 4.00
155-160 PRINT RUN 299 SERIAL #'d SETS
111-160 ODDS W/SPECTRUM 1:9
COMMON CARD (161-202) 6.00 15.00
161-202 ODDS W/SPECTRUM 1:18
161-202 PRINT RUN 799 SERIAL #'d SETS
EXCHANGE DEADLINE 12/03/07
MASTER PLATE ODDS 1:2500
MASTER PLATE PRINT RUN 1 #'d SET
NO PLATE PRICING DUE TO SCARCITY
1 Alfonso Soriano .30 .75
2 Todd Helton .30 .75
3 Andruw Jones .20 .50
4 Eric Gagne .20 .50
5 Craig Wilson .20 .50
6 Brian Giles .20 .50
7 Miguel Tejada .30 .75
8 Kevin Brown .20 .50
9 Shawn Green .20 .50
10 Ben Sheets .20 .50
11 John Smoltz .50 1.25
12 Tim Hudson .30 .75
13 Jason Schmidt .20 .50
14 Paul Konerko .30 .75
15 Randy Johnson .50 1.25
16 Roy Oswalt .30 .75
17 Mike Lowell .20 .50
18 Carlos Lee .20 .50
19 Sean Burroughs .20 .50
20 Edgar Renteria .20 .50
21 Michael Young .20 .50
22 Jose Vidro .20 .50
23 Scott Rolen .30 .75
24 Rafael Furcal .20 .50
25 Tom Glavine .30 .75
26 Scott Podsednik .20 .50
27 Gary Sheffield .20 .50
28 Eric Chavez .20 .50
29 Mark Prior .30 .75
30 Chipper Jones .50 1.25
31 Frank Thomas .50 1.25
32 Victor Martinez .30 .75
33 Jake Peavy .20 .50
34 Carlos Beltran .30 .75
35 Roy Halladay .30 .75
36 Mark Teixeira .30 .75
37 Jacque Jones .20 .50
38 Mike Sweeney .20 .50
39 Troy Glaus .20 .50
40 Pat Burrell .20 .50
41 Ichiro Suzuki .60 1.50
42 Vladimir Guerrero .30 .75
43 Bobby Abreu .20 .50
44 Jim Edmonds .30 .75
45 Garret Anderson .20 .50
46 J.D. Drew .20 .50
47 C.C. Sabathia .30 .75
48 Joe Mauer .40 1.00
49 Phil Nevin .20 .50
50 Hank Blalock .20 .50
51 Carlos Zambrano .30 .75
52 Mike Piazza .50 1.25
53 Manny Ramirez .50 1.25
54 Lance Berkman .30 .75
55 Delmon Young .30 .75
56 Nomar Garciaparra .30 .75
57 Alex Rodriguez .60 1.50
58 Rickie Weeks .20 .50
59 Adrian Beltre .50 1.25
60 Albert Pujols .60 1.50
61 Richie Sexson .20 .50
62 Magglio Ordonez .30 .75
63 Derrek Lee .20 .50
64 Sammy Sosa .50 1.25
65 Jason Giambi .20 .50
66 Curt Schilling .30 .75
67 Jorge Posada .30 .75
68 Rafael Palmeiro .30 .75
69 Jeff Kent .20 .50
70 Jose Reyes .20 .50
71 David Ortiz .50 1.25
72 Aubrey Huff .20 .50
73 Jim Thome .30 .75
74 Andy Pettitte .30 .75
75 Barry Zito .30 .75
76 Carlos Delgado .20 .50
77 Hideki Matsui .75 2.00
78 Sean Casey .20 .50
79 Luis Gonzalez .20 .50
80 Marcus Giles .20 .50
81 Preston Wilson .20 .50
82 Javy Lopez .20 .50
83 Mark Mulder .20 .50
84 Derek Jeter 1.25 3.00
85 Miguel Cabrera .50 1.25
86 Vernon Wells .20 .50
87 Roger Clemens .60 1.50
88 Lyle Overbay .20 .50
89 Bret Boone .20 .50
90 Melvin Mora .20 .50
91 Greg Maddux .60 1.50
92 Kerry Wood .20 .50
93 Ivan Rodriguez .30 .75
94 Pedro Martinez .30 .75
95 Jeff Bagwell .30 .75
96 Torii Hunter .20 .50
97 Ken Griffey Jr. 1.00 2.50
98 Mike Mussina .30 .75
99 Oliver Perez .20 .50
100 Josh Beckett .20 .50
101 Bob Gibson LGD 1.00 2.50
102 Cal Ripken LGD 5.00 12.00
103 Ted Williams LGD 3.00 8.00
104 Nolan Ryan LGD 5.00 12.00
105 Mickey Mantle LGD 5.00 12.00
106 Ernie Banks LGD 1.50 4.00
107 Joe DiMaggio LGD 3.00 8.00
108 Stan Musial LGD 2.50 6.00
109 Tom Seaver LGD 1.00 2.50
110 Mike Schmidt LGD 2.50 6.00
111 Jerry Gil T1 RC .60 1.50
112 Dioner Navarro T1 RC 1.00 2.50
113 Bartolome Fortunato T1 RC .60 1.50
114 Carlos Hines T1 RC .60 1.50
115 Franklyn Gracesqui T1 RC .60 1.50
116 Aarom Baldiris T1 RC .60 1.50
117 Casey Daigle T1 RC .60 1.50
118 Joey Gathright T1 RC .60 1.50
119 William Bergolla T1 RC .60 1.50
120 Jeff Bennett T1 RC .60 1.50
121 Lincoln Holdzkom T1 RC .60 1.50
122 Jorge Vasquez T1 RC .60 1.50
123 Donnie Kelly T1 RC 1.00 2.50
124 Yadier Molina T1 RC 40.00 100.00
125 Ryan Wing T1 RC .60 1.50
126 Justin Germano T1 RC .60 1.50
127 Freddy Guzman T1 RC .60 1.50
128 Onil Joseph T1 RC .60 1.50
129 Roman Colon T1 RC .60 1.50
130 Roberto Novoa T1 RC .60 1.50
131 Renyel Pinto T1 RC .60 1.50
132 Evan Rust T1 RC .60 1.50
133 Orlando Rodriguez T1 RC .60 1.50
134 Edwardo Sierra T1 RC .60 1.50
135 Mike Rose T1 RC .60 1.50
136 Phil Stockman T1 RC .60 1.50
137 Greg Dobbs T1 RC .60 1.50
138 Brad Halsey T1 RC .60 1.50
139 David Aardsma T1 RC .60 1.50
140 Joe Hietpas T1 RC .60 1.50
141 Josh Labandeira T1 RC .60 1.50
142 Mariano Gomez T1 RC .60 1.50
143 Jeff Bajenaru T1 RC .60 1.50
144 Travis Blackley T1 RC .60 1.50
145 Abe Alvarez T1 RC .60 1.50
146 Ramon Ramirez T2 RC 1.50 4.00
147 Edwin Moreno T2 RC 1.50 4.00
148 Ronny Cedeno T2 RC 1.50 4.00
149 Hector Gimenez T2 RC 1.50 4.00
150 Carlos Vasquez T2 RC 1.50 4.00
151 Jesse Crain T2 RC 2.50 6.00
152 Logan Kensing T2 RC 1.50 4.00
153 Sean Henn T2 RC 1.50 4.00
154 Rusty Tucker T2 RC 1.50 4.00
155 Justin Lehr T3 RC 1.50 4.00
156 Ian Snell T3 RC 1.50 4.00
157 Merkin Valdez T3 RC 1.50 4.00
158 Scott Proctor T3 RC 1.50 4.00
159 Jose Capellan T3 RC 1.50 4.00
160 Kazuo Matsui T3 RC 2.50 6.00
161 Chris Oxspring AU JSY RC 6.00 15.00
162 Jimmy Serrano AU JSY RC 6.00 15.00
163 Jeff Keppinger AU JSY RC 8.00 20.00
164 B.Medders AU JSY RC 6.00 15.00
165 Brian Dallimore AU JSY RC 6.00 15.00
166 Chad Bentz AU JSY RC 6.00 15.00
167 Chris Aguila AU JSY RC 6.00 15.00
168 Chris Saenz AU JSY RC 6.00 15.00
169 Frank Francisco AU JSY RC 6.00 15.00
170 Colby Miller AU JSY RC 6.00 15.00
172 Charles Thomas AU JSY RC 6.00 15.00
173 Dennis Sarfate AU JSY RC 6.00 15.00
174 Lance Cormier AU JSY RC 6.00 15.00
175 Joe Horgan AU JSY RC 6.00 15.00
176 Fernando Nieve AU JSY RC 6.00 15.00
177 Jake Woods AU JSY RC 6.00 15.00
178 Matt Treanor AU JSY RC 6.00 15.00
179 Jerome Gamble AU JSY RC 6.00 15.00
180 John Gall AU JSY RC 10.00 25.00
181 Jorge Sequea AU JSY RC 6.00 15.00
182 Justin Hampson AU JSY RC 6.00 15.00
183 Justin Huisman AU JSY RC 6.00 15.00
184 Justin Knoedler AU JSY RC 6.00 15.00
185 Justin Leone AU JSY RC 10.00 25.00
186 Scott Atchison AU JSY RC 6.00 15.00
187 Jon Knott AU JSY RC 6.00 15.00
188 Kevin Cave AU JSY RC 6.00 15.00
189 Jason Frasor AU JSY RC 6.00 15.00
190 George Sherrill AU JSY RC 6.00 15.00
191 Mike Gosling AU JSY RC 6.00 15.00
192 Mike Johnston AU JSY RC 6.00 15.00
193 Mike Rouse AU JSY RC 6.00 15.00
194 Nick Regilio AU JSY RC 6.00 15.00
195 Ryan Meaux AU JSY RC 6.00 15.00
196 Scott Dohmann AU JSY RC 6.00 15.00
197 Shawn Camp AU JSY RC 6.00 15.00
198 Shawn Hill AU JSY RC 6.00 15.00
199 Shingo Takatsu AU JSY RC 6.00 15.00
200 Tim Bausher AU JSY RC 6.00 15.00
201 Tim Bittner AU JSY RC 6.00 15.00
202 Scott Kazmir AU JSY RC 10.00 25.00

2004 SPx Spectrum

*SPEC 1-100: 6X TO 15X BASIC
*SPEC 101-110: 2X TO 5X
1-110 STATED ODDS 1:252
111-160 W/BASIC OVERALL ODDS 1:9
161-202 W/BASIC OVERALL ODDS 1:18
STATED PRINT RUN 25 SERIAL #'d SETS
111-202 NO PRICING DUE TO SCARCITY
EXCHANGE DEADLINE 12/03/07

2004 SPx SuperScripts Rookies

OVERALL SUPERSCRIPT ODDS 1:18
EXCHANGE DEADLINE 12/03/07
AS Alfredo Simon 4.00 10.00
CH Carlos Hines 4.00 10.00
CV Carlos Vasquez 6.00 15.00
DK Donnie Kelly 10.00 25.00
ES Edwardo Sierra 6.00 15.00
IO Ivan Ochoa 4.00 10.00
IS Ian Snell 8.00 20.00
JL Justin Lehr 4.00 10.00
LA Josh Labandeira 4.00 10.00
LH Lincoln Holdzkom 4.00 10.00
MG Mariano Gomez 4.00 10.00
MV Merkin Valdez 4.00 10.00
PS Phil Stockman 4.00 10.00
RR Ramon Ramirez 4.00 10.00
RU Evan Rust 4.00 10.00
SH Sean Henn 4.00 10.00
SP Scott Proctor 6.00 15.00
VE Michael Vento 6.00 15.00

2004 SPx SuperScripts Stars

OVERALL SUPERSCRIPT ODDS 1:18
SP INFO PROVIDED BY UPPER DECK
AP Albert Pujols SP 60.00 150.00
CR Cal Ripken SP 40.00 100.00
DJ Derek Jeter SP 75.00 200.00
EC Eric Chavez 6.00 15.00
JB Josh Beckett 8.00 20.00
KG Ken Griffey Jr. 30.00 80.00
MP Mark Prior 6.00 15.00
NG Nomar Garciaparra SP 12.00 30.00
NR Nolan Ryan SP 30.00 80.00
TE Miguel Tejada 6.00 15.00

2004 SPx SuperScripts Young Stars

OVERALL SUPERSCRIPT ODDS 1:18
BC Bobby Crosby 6.00 15.00
BW Brandon Webb 6.00 15.00
DW Dontrelle Willis 6.00 15.00
DY Delmon Young 6.00 15.00
EJ Edwin Jackson 6.00 15.00
JM Joe Mauer 12.00 30.00
JR Jose Reyes 6.00 15.00
MC Miguel Cabrera 20.00 50.00
MT Mark Teixeira 10.00 25.00
RH Rich Harden 6.00 15.00
RO Roy Oswalt 6.00 15.00
RW Rickie Weeks 6.00 15.00

2004 SPx Swatch Supremacy Signatures Stars

STATED PRINT RUN 275 SERIAL #'d SETS
*SPECTRUM: .75X TO 1.5X BASIC
SPECTRUM PRINT RUN 25 #'d SETS
OVERALL SWATCH SUP.ODDS 1:18
AP Albert Pujols 75.00 200.00
CR Cal Ripken 40.00 100.00
DJ Derek Jeter 125.00 300.00
DL Derrek Lee 10.00 25.00
EC Eric Chavez 6.00 15.00
GA Garret Anderson 10.00 25.00
KG Ken Griffey Jr. 60.00 150.00
MP Mark Prior 15.00 40.00
NG Nomar Garciaparra 15.00 40.00
NR Nolan Ryan 60.00 120.00

2004 SPx Swatch Supremacy Signatures Young Stars

STATED PRINT RUN 999 SERIAL #'d SETS
*SPECTRUM: .6X TO 1.5X BASIC
SPECTRUM PRINT RUN 25 #'d SETS
OVERALL SWATCH SUP.ODDS 1:18
AB Angel Berroa 4.00 10.00
AE Adam Eaton 4.00 10.00
BC Bobby Crosby 4.00 10.00
BS Ben Sheets 4.00 10.00
BW Brandon Webb 4.00 10.00
CC Chad Cordero 4.00 10.00
CK Casey Kotchman 4.00 10.00
CL Cliff Lee 4.00 10.00
CP Corey Patterson 4.00 10.00
DW Dontrelle Willis 4.00 10.00
GR Khalil Greene 4.00 10.00
HB Hank Blalock 4.00 10.00
HR Horacio Ramirez 4.00 10.00
JB Josh Beckett 4.00 10.00
JM Joe Mauer 12.00 30.00
JP Jake Peavy 4.00 10.00
JR Jose Reyes 6.00 15.00
JW Jerome Williams 4.00 10.00
LO Lyle Overbay 4.00 10.00
MC Miguel Cabrera 20.00 50.00
MG Marcus Giles 4.00 10.00
MT Mark Teixeira 6.00 15.00
MY Michael Young 6.00 15.00
RB Rocco Baldelli 4.00 10.00
RH Rich Harden 4.00 10.00
RO Roy Oswalt 4.00 10.00
RW Rickie Weeks 4.00 10.00
SB Sean Burroughs 4.00 10.00
SP Scott Podsednik 4.00 10.00

2004 SPx Winning Materials Dual Jersey

*SPECTRUM: .6X TO 1.5X BASIC
SPECTRUM PRINT RUN 25 #'d SETS
OVERALL WINNING MTL.ODDS 1:18
ALL HAVE GAME-WORN & BP SWATCHES
AP Albert Pujols 6.00 15.00
BE Josh Beckett 2.00 5.00
CD Carlos Delgado 2.00 5.00
CJ Chipper Jones 5.00 12.00
DJ Derek Jeter 12.00 30.00
EC Eric Chavez 2.00 5.00
GM Greg Maddux 6.00 15.00
GS Gary Sheffield 2.00 5.00
HB Hank Blalock 2.00 5.00
HM Hideki Matsui 8.00 20.00
IS Ichiro Suzuki 6.00 15.00
JB Jeff Bagwell 3.00 8.00
JG Jason Giambi 2.00 5.00
JP Jorge Posada 3.00 8.00
JR Jose Reyes 3.00 8.00
JT Jim Thome 3.00 8.00
KB Kevin Brown 2.00 5.00
MM Mike Mussina 3.00 8.00
MP Mark Prior 3.00 8.00
MR Manny Ramirez 5.00 12.00
PI Mike Piazza 5.00 12.00
RC Roger Clemens 6.00 15.00
RP Rafael Palmeiro 3.00 8.00
SG Shawn Green 2.00 5.00
SR Scott Rolen 3.00 8.00
SS Sammy Sosa 5.00 12.00
TE Miguel Tejada 3.00 8.00
TG Troy Glaus 2.00 5.00
VG Vladimir Guerrero 3.00 8.00

2005 SPx

COMP.BASIC SET (100) 10.00 25.00
COMMON CARD (1-100) .15 .40
COMMON RC (1-100) .25 .60
1-100 ISSUED IN 05 SP COLLECTION PACKS
COMMON AUTO (101-180) 4.00 10.00
101-180 ODDS APPX 1:8 '05 UD UPDATE
101-180 PRINT RUN 185 SERIAL #'d SETS
105, 117, 139, 149, 155, 172 DO NOT EXIST
175, 178, 180 DO NOT EXIST
1 Aaron Harang .15 .40
2 Aaron Rowand .15 .40
3 Aaron Miles .15 .40
4 Adrian Gonzalez .30 .75
5 Alex Rios .15 .40
6 Angel Berroa .15 .40
7 B.J. Upton .25 .60
8 Brandon Claussen .15 .40
9 Andy Marte .15 .40
10 Brandon Webb .25 .60
11 Bronson Arroyo .15 .40
12 Casey Kotchman .15 .40
13 Cesar Izturis .15 .40
14 Chad Cordero .15 .40
15 Chad Tracy .15 .40
16 Charles Thomas .15 .40
17 Chase Utley .25 .60
18 Chone Figgins .15 .40
19 Chris Burke .15 .40
20 Cliff Lee .25 .60
21 Clint Barmes .15 .40
22 Coco Crisp .15 .40
23 Bill Hall .15 .40
24 Dallas McPherson .15 .40
25 Brad Halsey .15 .40
26 Daniel Cabrera .15 .40
27 Danny Haren .15 .40
28 Dave Bush .15 .40
29 David DeJesus .15 .40
30 D.J. Houlton RC .25 .60
31 Derek Jeter 1.00 2.50
32 Dewon Brazelton .15 .40
33 Edwin Jackson .15 .40
34 Brad Hawpe .15 .40
35 Brandon Inge .15 .40
36 Brett Myers .15 .40
37 Garrett Atkins .15 .40
38 Gavin Floyd .15 .40
39 Grady Sizemore .25 .60
40 Guillermo Mota .15 .40
41 Carlos Guillen .15 .40
42 Gustavo Chacin .15 .40
43 Huston Street .15 .40
44 Chris Duffy .15 .40
45 J.D. Closser .15 .40
46 J.J. Hardy .15 .40
47 Jason Bartlett .15 .40
48 Jason DuBois .15 .40
49 Chris Shelton .15 .40
50 Jason Lane .15 .40
51 Jayson Werth .25 .60
52 Jeff Baker .15 .40
53 Jeff Francis .15 .40
54 Jeremy Bonderman .15 .40
55 Jeremy Reed .15 .40
56 Jerome Williams .15 .40
57 Jesse Crain .15 .40
58 Chris Young .25 .60
59 Jhonny Peralta .15 .40
60 Joe Blanton .15 .40
61 Joe Crede .15 .40
62 Joel Pineiro .15 .40
63 Joey Gathright .15 .40
64 John Buck .15 .40
65 Jonny Gomes .15 .40
66 Jorge Cantu .15 .40
67 Dan Johnson .15 .40
68 Jose Valverde .15 .40
69 Ervin Santana .15 .40
70 Justin Morneau .25 .60
71 Keiichi Yabu RC .25 .60
72 Ken Griffey Jr. .75 2.00
73 Jason Repko .15 .40
74 Kevin Youkilis .15 .40
75 Koyie Hill .15 .40
76 Laynce Nix .15 .40
77 Luke Scott RC .60 1.50
78 Juan Rivera .15 .40
79 Justin Duchscherer .15 .40
80 Mark Teahen .15 .40
81 Lance Niekro .15 .40
82 Michael Cuddyer .15 .40
83 Nick Swisher .25 .60
84 Noah Lowry .15 .40
85 Matt Holliday .40 1.00
86 Reed Johnson .15 .40
87 Rich Harden .15 .40
88 Robb Quinlan .15 .40
89 Nick Johnson .15 .40
90 Ryan Howard .30 .75
91 Nook Logan .15 .40
92 Steve Schmoll RC .25 .60
93 Tadahito Iguchi RC .40 1.00
94 Willy Taveras .15 .40
95 Wily Mo Pena .15 .40
96 Xavier Nady .15 .40
97 Yadier Molina 8.00 20.00
98 Yhency Brazoban .15 .40
99 Ryan Freel .15 .40
100 Zack Greinke .50 1.25
101 Adam Shabala AU RC 4.00 10.00
102 Ambiorix Burgos AU RC 4.00 10.00
103 Ambiorix Concepcion AU RC 4.00 10.00
104 Anibal Sanchez AU RC 6.00 15.00
106 Brandon McCarthy AU RC 6.00 15.00
107 Brian Burres AU RC 4.00 10.00
108 Carlos Ruiz AU RC 8.00 20.00
109 Casey Rogowski AU RC 4.00 10.00
110 Chad Orvella AU RC 4.00 10.00
111 Chris Resop AU RC 6.00 15.00
112 Chris Roberson AU RC 4.00 10.00
113 Chris Seddon AU RC 4.00 10.00
114 Colter Bean AU RC 6.00 15.00
115 Dave Gassner AU RC 4.00 10.00
116 Brian Anderson AU RC 6.00 15.00
118 Devon Lowery AU RC 4.00 10.00
119 Enrique Gonzalez AU RC 6.00 15.00
120 Eude Brito AU RC 4.00 10.00
121 Francisco Butto AU RC 4.00 10.00
122 Franquelis Osoria AU RC 4.00 10.00
123 Garrett Jones AU RC 10.00 25.00
124 Geovany Soto AU RC 10.00 25.00
125 Hayden Penn AU RC 6.00 15.00
126 Ismael Ramirez AU RC 4.00 10.00
127 Jared Gothreaux AU RC 4.00 10.00
128 Jason Hammel AU RC 10.00 25.00
129 Jeff Miller AU RC 4.00 10.00
130 Jeff Niemann AU RC 5.00 12.00
131 Joel Peralta AU RC 4.00 10.00
132 John Hattig AU RC 4.00 10.00
133 Jorge Campillo AU RC 4.00 10.00
134 Juan Morillo AU RC 4.00 10.00
135 Justin Verlander AU RC 75.00 200.00
136 Ryan Garko AU RC 4.00 10.00
137 Kendry Morales AU RC 10.00 25.00
138 Luis Hernandez AU RC 4.00 10.00
140 Luis O.Rodriguez AU RC 4.00 10.00
141 Mark Woodyard AU RC 4.00 10.00
142 Matt A.Smith AU RC 4.00 10.00
143 Matthew Lindstrom AU RC 4.00 10.00
144 Miguel Negron AU RC 6.00 15.00
145 Mike Morse AU RC 6.00 15.00
146 Nate McLouth AU RC 6.00 15.00
147 Nelson Cruz AU RC 60.00 150.00
148 Nick Masset AU RC 4.00 10.00
150 Paulino Reynoso AU RC 4.00 10.00
151 Pedro Lopez AU RC 4.00 10.00
152 Philip Humber AU RC 6.00 15.00
153 Prince Fielder AU RC 12.00 30.00
154 Randy Messenger AU RC 4.00 10.00
156 Raul Tablado AU RC 4.00 10.00
157 Ronny Paulino AU RC 6.00 15.00
158 Russ Rohlicek AU RC 4.00 10.00
159 Russell Martin AU RC 10.00 25.00
160 Scott Baker AU RC 6.00 15.00
161 Scott Munter AU RC 4.00 10.00
162 Sean Thompson AU RC 4.00 10.00
163 Sean Tracey AU RC 4.00 10.00
164 Shane Costa AU RC 4.00 10.00
165 Stephen Drew AU RC 12.50 30.00
166 Tony Giarratano AU RC 4.00 10.00
167 Tony Pena AU RC 4.00 10.00
168 Travis Bowyer AU RC 4.00 10.00
169 Ubaldo Jimenez AU RC 10.00 25.00
170 Wladimir Balentien AU RC 6.00 15.00
171 Yorman Bazardo AU RC 4.00 10.00
173 Ryan Zimmerman AU RC 20.00 50.00
174 Chris Denorfia AU RC 6.00 15.00
176 Jermaine Van Buren AU 4.00 10.00
177 Mark McLemore AU RC 4.00 10.00
179 Ryan Speier AU RC 4.00 10.00

2005 SPx Jersey

STATED PRINT RUN 199 SERIAL #'d SETS
*SPECTRUM: .5X TO 1.2X BASIC
SPECTRUM PRINT RUN 99 SERIAL #'d SETS
ISSUED IN 05 SP COLLECTION PACKS
OVERALL GAME-USED ODDS 1:10
1 Aaron Harang 2.00 5.00
2 Aaron Rowand 2.00 5.00
3 Aaron Miles 2.00 5.00
4 Adrian Gonzalez 2.00 5.00
5 Alex Rios 2.00 5.00
6 Angel Berroa 2.00 5.00
7 B.J. Upton 2.00 5.00
8 Brandon Claussen 2.00 5.00
9 Andy Marte 2.00 5.00
10 Brandon Webb 2.00 5.00
11 Bronson Arroyo 2.00 5.00
12 Casey Kotchman 2.00 5.00
13 Cesar Izturis 2.00 5.00
14 Chad Cordero 2.00 5.00
15 Chad Tracy 2.00 5.00
16 Charles Thomas 2.00 5.00
17 Chase Utley 3.00 8.00
18 Chone Figgins 2.00 5.00
19 Chris Burke 2.00 5.00
20 Cliff Lee 2.00 5.00
21 Clint Barmes 2.00 5.00
22 Coco Crisp 2.00 5.00
23 Bill Hall 2.00 5.00
24 Dallas McPherson 2.00 5.00
25 Brad Halsey 2.00 5.00
26 Daniel Cabrera 2.00 5.00
27 Danny Haren 2.00 5.00
28 Dave Bush 2.00 5.00
29 David DeJesus 2.00 5.00
30 D.J. Houlton 2.00 5.00
31 Derek Jeter Pants 8.00 20.00
32 Dewon Brazelton 2.00 5.00
33 Edwin Jackson 2.00 5.00
34 Brad Hawpe 2.00 5.00
35 Brandon Inge 2.00 5.00
36 Brett Myers 2.00 5.00
37 Garrett Atkins 2.00 5.00
38 Gavin Floyd 2.00 5.00
39 Grady Sizemore 3.00 8.00
40 Guillermo Mota 2.00 5.00
41 Carlos Guillen 2.00 5.00
42 Gustavo Chacin 2.00 5.00
43 Huston Street 3.00 8.00
44 Chris Duffy 2.00 5.00
45 J.D. Closser 2.00 5.00
46 J.J. Hardy 2.00 5.00
47 Jason Bartlett 2.00 5.00
48 Jason DuBois 2.00 5.00
49 Chris Shelton 4.00 10.00
50 Jason Lane 2.00 5.00
51 Jayson Werth 2.00 5.00
52 Jeff Baker 2.00 5.00
53 Jeff Francis 2.00 5.00
54 Jeremy Bonderman 2.00 5.00
55 Jeremy Reed 2.00 5.00
56 Jerome Williams 2.00 5.00
57 Jesse Crain 2.00 5.00
58 Chris Young 2.00 5.00
59 Jhonny Peralta 2.00 5.00
60 Joe Blanton 2.00 5.00
61 Joe Crede 2.00 5.00
62 Joel Pineiro 2.00 5.00
63 Joey Gathright 2.00 5.00
64 John Buck 2.00 5.00
65 Jonny Gomes 2.00 5.00
66 Jorge Cantu 2.00 5.00
67 Dan Johnson 2.00 5.00
68 Jose Valverde 2.00 5.00
69 Ervin Santana 2.00 5.00
70 Justin Morneau 2.00 5.00
71 Keiichi Yabu 2.00 5.00
72 Ken Griffey Jr. 6.00 15.00

73 Jason Repko 2.00 5.00
74 Kevin Youkilis 2.00 5.00
75 Koyie Hill 2.00 5.00
76 Laynce Nix 2.00 5.00
77 Luke Scott 4.00 10.00
78 Juan Rivera 2.00 5.00
79 Justin Duchscherer 2.00 5.00
80 Mark Teahen 2.00 5.00
81 Lance Niekro 2.00 5.00
82 Michael Cuddyer 2.00 5.00
83 Nick Swisher 2.00 5.00
84 Noah Lowry 2.00 5.00
85 Matt Holliday 2.50 6.00
86 Reed Johnson 2.00 5.00
87 Rich Harden 2.00 5.00
88 Robb Quinlan 2.00 5.00
89 Nick Johnson 2.00 5.00
90 Ryan Howard 10.00 25.00
91 Nook Logan 2.00 5.00
92 Steve Schmoll 2.00 5.00
93 Tadahito Iguchi 12.50 30.00
94 Willy Taveras 2.00 5.00
95 Wily Mo Pena 2.00 5.00
96 Xavier Nady 2.00 5.00
97 Yadier Molina 4.00 10.00
98 Yhency Brazoban 2.00 5.00
99 Ryan Freel 2.00 5.00
100 Zack Greinke 2.00 5.00

2005 SPx Signature

PRINT RUNS B/WN 50-350 COPIES PER
SPECTRUM PRINT RUN 10 SERIAL #'d SETS
NO SPECTRUM PRICING DUE TO SCARCITY
OVERALL AUTO ODDS 1:10
1 Aaron Harang/350 6.00 15.00
2 Aaron Rowand/150 10.00 25.00
4 Adrian Gonzalez/225 10.00 25.00
6 Angel Berroa/150 4.00 10.00
7 B.J. Upton/50 8.00 20.00
8 Brandon Claussen/350 4.00 10.00
9 Andy Marte/350 4.00 10.00
11 Bronson Arroyo/350 6.00 15.00
12 Casey Kotchman/225 6.00 15.00
13 Cesar Izturis/150 4.00 10.00
14 Chad Cordero/350 6.00 15.00
15 Chad Tracy/350 4.00 10.00
16 Charles Thomas/350 4.00 10.00
17 Chase Utley/50 10.00 25.00
18 Chone Figgins/150 6.00 15.00
19 Chris Burke/350 4.00 10.00
20 Cliff Lee/225 12.50 30.00
21 Clint Barmes/350 6.00 15.00
22 Coco Crisp/225 10.00 25.00
23 Bill Hall/350 4.00 10.00
24 Dallas McPherson/150 4.00 10.00
25 Brad Halsey/350 4.00 10.00
26 Daniel Cabrera/350 4.00 10.00
27 Danny Haren/225 4.00 10.00
28 Dave Bush/350 4.00 10.00
29 David DeJesus/225 4.00 10.00
30 D.J. Houlton/350 4.00 10.00
31 Derek Jeter/50 90.00 150.00
32 Dewon Brazelton/225 4.00 10.00
33 Edwin Jackson/150 4.00 10.00
34 Brad Hawpe/350 10.00 25.00
35 Brandon Inge/350 4.00 10.00
36 Brett Myers/150 6.00 15.00
37 Garrett Atkins/350 4.00 10.00
38 Gavin Floyd/150 4.00 10.00
39 Grady Sizemore/350 12.50 30.00
40 Guillermo Mota/225 4.00 10.00
41 Carlos Guillen/150 6.00 15.00
42 Gustavo Chacin/350 6.00 15.00
43 Huston Street/350 10.00 25.00
44 Chris Duffy/225 4.00 10.00
45 J.D. Closser/350 4.00 10.00
46 J.J. Hardy/350 20.00 50.00
47 Jason Bartlett/350 4.00 10.00
48 Jason DuBois/350 4.00 10.00
50 Jason Lane/350 4.00 10.00
51 Jayson Werth/350 4.00 10.00
52 Jeff Baker/350 4.00 10.00
53 Jeff Francis/150 4.00 10.00
54 Jeremy Bonderman/50 8.00 20.00
55 Jeremy Reed/150 6.00 15.00
56 Jerome Williams/50 8.00 20.00
57 Jesse Crain/350 4.00 10.00
59 Jhonny Peralta/350 6.00 15.00
60 Joe Blanton/350 4.00 10.00
61 Joe Crede/350 10.00 25.00
62 Joel Pineiro/150 6.00 15.00
63 Joey Gathright/350 4.00 10.00
64 John Buck/350 4.00 10.00
65 Jonny Gomes/350 6.00 15.00
66 Jorge Cantu/350 6.00 15.00
67 Dan Johnson/350 6.00 15.00
68 Jose Valverde/350 4.00 10.00
69 Ervin Santana/350 6.00 15.00
70 Justin Morneau/50 8.00 20.00
71 Keiichi Yabu/350 6.00 15.00
73 Jason Repko/350 10.00 25.00
74 Kevin Youkilis/225 8.00 20.00
75 Koyie Hill/350 4.00 10.00
76 Laynce Nix/150 4.00 10.00
77 Luke Scott/350 20.00 50.00
78 Juan Rivera/225 4.00 10.00
79 Justin Duchscherer/350 4.00 10.00
80 Mark Teahen/350 4.00 10.00
81 Lance Niekro/350 4.00 10.00
82 Michael Cuddyer/350 4.00 10.00
84 Noah Lowry/150 6.00 15.00
85 Matt Holliday/225 6.00 15.00
86 Reed Johnson/350 4.00 10.00
88 Robb Quinlan/350 4.00 10.00
89 Nick Johnson/150 6.00 15.00
90 Ryan Howard/225 10.00 25.00
91 Nook Logan/350 4.00 10.00
92 Steve Schmoll/350 4.00 10.00
93 Tadahito Iguchi/50 125.00 200.00
95 Wily Mo Pena/150 6.00 15.00
96 Xavier Nady/150 4.00 10.00
98 Yhency Brazoban/350 4.00 10.00
100 Zack Greinke/150 10.00 25.00

2005 SPx SPxtreme Stats

ISSUED IN 05 SP COLLECTION PACKS
OVERALL INSERT ODDS 1:10
STATED PRINT RUN 299 SERIAL #'d SETS
AB Adrian Beltre 1.50 4.00
AD Adam Dunn 1.00 2.50
AJ Andruw Jones .60 1.50
AP Albert Pujols 2.00 5.00
AR Aramis Ramirez .60 1.50
BA Bobby Abreu .60 1.50
BC Bobby Crosby .60 1.50
BS Ben Sheets .60 1.50
CB Craig Biggio 1.00 2.50
CC Carl Crawford 1.00 2.50
CP Corey Patterson .60 1.50
CZ Carlos Zambrano 1.00 2.50
DJ Derek Jeter 4.00 10.00
DL Derrek Lee .60 1.50
DO David Ortiz 1.50 4.00
DW David Wright 1.25 3.00
EC Eric Chavez .60 1.50
EG Eric Gagne .60 1.50
ER Edgar Renteria .60 1.50
GM Greg Maddux 2.00 5.00
GR Khalil Greene .60 1.50
GS Gary Sheffield .60 1.50
HB Hank Blalock .60 1.50
HU Torii Hunter .60 1.50
JD J.D. Drew .60 1.50
JM Joe Mauer 1.25 3.00
JP Jake Peavy .60 1.50
JR Jose Reyes 1.00 2.50
KG Ken Griffey Jr. 3.00 8.00
KW Kerry Wood .60 1.50
MC Miguel Cabrera 1.50 4.00
MM Mark Mulder .60 1.50
MO Melvin Mora .60 1.50
MP Mark Prior 1.00 2.50
MT Mark Teixeria 1.00 2.50
MY Michael Young .60 1.50
OP Oliver Perez .60 1.50
PI Mike Piazza 1.50 4.00
RC Roger Clemens 2.00 5.00
RJ Randy Johnson 1.50 4.00
RO Roy Oswalt 1.00 2.50
RP Rafael Palmeiro 1.00 2.50
SA Johan Santana 1.00 2.50
SC Sean Casey .60 1.50
SM John Smoltz 1.50 4.00
SR Scott Rolen 1.00 2.50
TE Miguel Tejada 1.00 2.50
TH Tim Hudson 1.00 2.50
VG Vladimir Guerrero 1.00 2.50
VM Victor Martinez 1.00 2.50

2005 SPx SPxtreme Stats Jersey

ISSUED IN 05 SP COLLECTION PACKS
OVERALL PREMIUM AU-GU ODDS 1:20
STATED PRINT RUN 130 SERIAL #'d SETS
AB Adrian Beltre 2.00 5.00
AD Adam Dunn 2.00 5.00
AJ Andruw Jones 3.00 8.00
AP Albert Pujols 6.00 15.00
AR Aramis Ramirez 2.00 5.00
BA Bobby Abreu 2.00 5.00
BC Bobby Crosby 2.00 5.00
BS Ben Sheets 2.00 5.00
CB Craig Biggio 3.00 8.00
CC Carl Crawford 2.00 5.00
CP Corey Patterson 2.00 5.00
CZ Carlos Zambrano 2.00 5.00
DJ Derek Jeter Pants 8.00 20.00
DL Derrek Lee 3.00 8.00
DO David Ortiz 3.00 8.00
DW David Wright 4.00 10.00
EC Eric Chavez 2.00 5.00
EG Eric Gagne 2.00 5.00
ER Edgar Renteria 2.00 5.00
GM Greg Maddux 4.00 10.00
GR Khalil Greene 3.00 8.00
GS Gary Sheffield 2.00 5.00
HB Hank Blalock 2.00 5.00
HU Torii Hunter 2.00 5.00
JD J.D. Drew 2.00 5.00
JM Joe Mauer 4.00 10.00
JP Jake Peavy 2.00 5.00
JR Jose Reyes 2.00 5.00
KG Ken Griffey Jr. 6.00 15.00
KW Kerry Wood 2.00 5.00
MC Miguel Cabrera 3.00 8.00
MM Mark Mulder 2.00 5.00
MO Melvin Mora 2.00 5.00
MP Mark Prior 3.00 8.00
MT Mark Teixeria 3.00 8.00
MY Michael Young 2.00 5.00
OP Oliver Perez 2.00 5.00
PI Mike Piazza 4.00 10.00
RC Roger Clemens Pants 4.00 10.00
RJ Randy Johnson 4.00 10.00
RO Roy Oswalt 2.00 5.00
RP Rafael Palmeiro 3.00 8.00
SA Johan Santana 4.00 10.00
SC Sean Casey 2.00 5.00
SM John Smoltz 3.00 8.00
SR Scott Rolen 3.00 8.00
TE Miguel Tejada 2.00 5.00
TH Tim Hudson 2.00 5.00
VG Vladimir Guerrero 4.00 10.00
VM Victor Martinez 2.00 5.00

2006 SPx

COMP.BASIC SET (100) 10.00 25.00
COMMON CARD (1-100) .15 .40
COMMON AU p/r 659-999 4.00 10.00
COMMON AU p/r 350-500 4.00 10.00
OVERALL 101-161 AU ODDS 1:9
101-161 AU EXCH DEADLINE 09/07/08
101-161 AU PRINT RUN B/WN 190-999 PER
101-161 PRINTING PLATE ODDS 1:224
101-161 PLATES PRINT RUN 1 SET PER CLR
101-161 PLATES FEATURE AUTOS
BLACK-CYAN-MAGENTA-YELLOW ISSUED
NO PLATE PRICING DUE TO SCARCITY
EXQUISITE EXCH ODDS 1:36
EXQUISITE EXCH DEADLINE 07/27/07
1 Luis Gonzalez .15 .40
2 Chad Tracy .15 .40
3 Brandon Webb .25 .60
4 Andruw Jones .15 .40
5 Chipper Jones .40 1.00
6 John Smoltz .40 1.00
7 Tim Hudson .25 .60
8 Miguel Tejada .25 .60
9 Brian Roberts .15 .40
10 Ramon Hernandez .15 .40
11 Curt Schilling .25 .60
12 David Ortiz .40 1.00
13 Manny Ramirez .40 1.00
14 Jason Varitek .40 1.00
15 Josh Beckett .15 .40
16 Greg Maddux .50 1.25
17 Derrek Lee .15 .40
18 Mark Prior .25 .60
19 Aramis Ramirez .15 .40
20 Jim Thome .25 .60
21 Paul Konerko .25 .60
22 Scott Podsednik .15 .40
23 Jose Contreras .15 .40
24 Ken Griffey Jr. .75 2.00
25 Adam Dunn .25 .60
26 Felipe Lopez .15 .40
27 Travis Hafner .15 .40
28 Victor Martinez .25 .60
29 Grady Sizemore .25 .60
30 Jhonny Peralta .15 .40
31 Todd Helton .25 .60
32 Garrett Atkins .15 .40
33 Clint Barmes .15 .40
34 Ivan Rodriguez .25 .60
35 Chris Shelton .15 .40
36 Jeremy Bonderman .15 .40
37 Miguel Cabrera .40 1.00
38 Dontrelle Willis .15 .40
39 Lance Berkman .25 .60
40 Morgan Ensberg .15 .40
41 Roy Oswalt .25 .60
42 Reggie Sanders .15 .40
43 Mike Sweeney .15 .40
44 Vladimir Guerrero .25 .60
45 Bartolo Colon .15 .40
46 Chone Figgins .15 .40
47 Nomar Garciaparra .25 .60
48 Jeff Kent .15 .40
49 J.D. Drew .15 .40
50 Carlos Lee .15 .40
51 Ben Sheets .15 .40
52 Rickie Weeks .15 .40
53 Johan Santana .25 .60
54 Torii Hunter .15 .40
55 Joe Mauer .25 .60
56 Pedro Martinez .25 .60
57 David Wright .30 .75
58 Carlos Beltran .25 .60
59 Carlos Delgado .15 .40
60 Jose Reyes .25 .60
61 Derek Jeter 1.00 2.50
62 Alex Rodriguez .50 1.25
63 Randy Johnson .40 1.00
64 Hideki Matsui .40 1.00
65 Gary Sheffield .15 .40
66 Rich Harden .15 .40
67 Eric Chavez .15 .40
68 Huston Street .15 .40
69 Bobby Crosby .15 .40
70 Bobby Abreu .15 .40
71 Ryan Howard .30 .75
72 Chase Utley .25 .60
73 Pat Burrell .15 .40
74 Jason Bay .15 .40
75 Sean Casey .15 .40
76 Mike Piazza .40 1.00
77 Jake Peavy .15 .40
78 Brian Giles .15 .40
79 Milton Bradley .15 .40
80 Omar Vizquel .25 .60
81 Jason Schmidt .15 .40
82 Ichiro Suzuki .50 1.25
83 Felix Hernandez .25 .60
84 Richie Sexson .15 .40
85 Albert Pujols .50 1.25
86 Chris Carpenter .25 .60
87 Scott Rolen .25 .60
88 Jim Edmonds .25 .60
89 Carl Crawford .25 .60
90 Jonny Gomes .15 .40
91 Scott Kazmir .25 .60
92 Mark Teixeira .25 .60
93 Michael Young .15 .40
94 Phil Nevin .15 .40
95 Vernon Wells .15 .40
96 Roy Halladay .25 .60
97 Troy Glaus .15 .40
98 Alfonso Soriano .25 .60
99 Nick Johnson .15 .40
100 Jose Vidro .15 .40
101 Conor Jackson AU/999 (RC) 6.00 15.00
102 J.Weaver AU/299 (RC) EXCH 8.00 20.00
103 Macay McBride AU/999 (RC) 4.00 10.00
104 Aaron Rakers AU/499 (RC) 4.00 10.00
105 J.Papelbon AU/499 (RC) 5.00 12.00
106 J.Bergmann AU/999 RC 4.00 10.00
107 S.Drew AU/350 (RC) 6.00 15.00
108 Chris Denorfia AU/999 (RC) 4.00 10.00
109 Kelly Shoppach AU/999 (RC) 4.00 10.00
110 Ryan Shealy AU/999 (RC) 4.00 10.00
111 Josh Wilson AU/999 (RC) 4.00 10.00
112 Brian Anderson AU/999 (RC) 4.00 10.00
113 J.Verlander AU/749 (RC) 25.00 60.00
114 J.Hermida AU/999 (RC) 6.00 15.00
115 M.Jacobs AU/999 (RC) 6.00 15.00
116 Josh Johnson AU/999 (RC) 8.00 20.00
117 Hanley Ramirez AU/659 (RC) 6.00 15.00
118 Chris Resop AU/999 (RC) 4.00 10.00
119 J.Willingham AU/999 (RC) 4.00 10.00
120 Cole Hamels AU/499 (RC) 10.00 25.00
121 Matt Cain AU/999 (RC) 10.00 25.00
122 Steve Stemle AU/999 RC 4.00 10.00
123 Tim Hamulack AU/999 (RC) 4.00 10.00
124 Choo Freeman AU/999 (RC) 4.00 10.00
125 H.Kuo AU/999 (RC) 8.00 20.00
126 Cody Ross AU/999 (RC) 4.00 10.00
127 Jose Capellan AU/999 (RC) 4.00 10.00
128 Prince Fielder AU/190 (RC) 15.00 40.00
129 David Gassner AU/999 (RC) 4.00 10.00
130 Jason Kubel AU/999 (RC) 4.00 10.00
131 F.Liriano AU/299 (RC) 6.00 15.00
132 A.Hernandez AU/999 (RC) 6.00 15.00
133 Joey Devine AU/499 RC 4.00 10.00
134 Chris Booker AU/999 (RC) 4.00 10.00
135 Matt Capps AU/999 (RC) 4.00 10.00
136 Paul Maholm AU/999 (RC) 4.00 10.00
137 N.McLouth AU/999 (RC) 6.00 15.00
138 J.Van Benschoten AU/999 (RC) 4.00 10.00
139 Jeff Harris AU/999 RC 4.00 10.00
140 Ben Johnson AU/999 (RC) 4.00 10.00
141 Wil Nieves AU/999 (RC) 4.00 10.00
142 G.Quiroz AU/999 (RC) 4.00 10.00
143 Josh Rupe AU/500 (RC) 4.00 10.00
144 Skip Schumaker AU/999 (RC) 4.00 10.00
145 Jack Taschner AU/999 (RC) 4.00 10.00
146 A.Wainwright AU/999 (RC) 6.00 15.00
147 Alay Soler AU/499 RC 4.00 10.00
148 Kendry Morales AU/999 (RC) 6.00 15.00
149 Ian Kinsler AU/999 (RC) 8.00 20.00
150 Jason Hammel AU/999 (RC) 4.00 10.00
151 C.Billingsley AU/499 (RC) 12.00 30.00
152 Boof Bonser AU/999 (RC) 6.00 15.00
153 Peter Moylan AU/999 RC 4.00 10.00
154 Chris Britton AU/999 RC 4.00 10.00
155 Takashi Saito AU/999 RC 6.00 15.00
156 Scott Dunn AU/999 (RC) 4.00 10.00
157 J.Zumaya AU/299 (RC) EXCH 4.00 10.00
158 Dan Uggla AU/999 (RC) 6.00 15.00
159 Taylor Buchholz AU/999 (RC) 4.00 10.00

2006 SPx Spectrum

*SPECTRUM 1-100: 2X TO 5X BASIC
STATED ODDS 1:3

2006 SPx Next In Line

STATED ODDS 1:9
AW Adam Wainwright 1.00 2.50
BA Brian Anderson .60 1.50
BB Brian Bannister .60 1.50
BJ Ben Johnson .60 1.50
CJ Conor Jackson 1.00 2.50
DU Dan Uggla 1.00 2.50
FH Felix Hernandez 1.00 2.50
FL Francisco Liriano 1.50 4.00
HR Hanley Ramirez 1.00 2.50
HS Huston Street .60 1.50
IK Ian Kinsler 2.00 5.00
JB Josh Barfield .60 1.50
JE Jered Weaver 2.00 5.00
JH Jeremy Hermida .60 1.50
JL James Loney 1.00 2.50
JP Jonathan Papelbon 3.00 8.00
JS Jeremy Sowers .60 1.50
JV Justin Verlander 5.00 12.00
JW Josh Willingham 1.00 2.50
LE Jon Lester 2.50 6.00
MC Matt Cain 4.00 10.00
MJ Mike Jacobs .60 1.50
AS Alay Soler .60 1.50
PF Prince Fielder 3.00 8.00
RC Ryan Church .60 1.50
RH Ryan Howard 1.25 3.00
RZ Ryan Zimmerman 2.00 5.00
SO Scott Olsen .60 1.50
TB Taylor Buchholz .60 1.50
TI Travis Ishikawa 1.00 2.50

2006 SPx SPxtra Info

STATED ODDS 1:9
AJ Andruw Jones .60 1.50
AP Albert Pujols 2.00 5.00
BA Bobby Abreu .60 1.50
BG Brian Giles .60 1.50
CC Carl Crawford 1.00 2.50
CL Carlos Lee .60 1.50
DJ Derek Jeter 4.00 10.00
DL Derrek Lee .60 1.50
DO David Ortiz 1.50 4.00
DW Dontrelle Willis .60 1.50
EC Eric Chavez .60 1.50
HE Todd Helton 1.00 2.50
IR Ivan Rodriguez 1.00 2.50
IS Ichiro Suzuki 2.00 5.00
JB Jason Bay .60 1.50
JK Jeff Kent .60 1.50
JS Johan Santana 1.00 2.50
JT Jim Thome 1.00 2.50
KG Ken Griffey Jr. 3.00 8.00
LG Luis Gonzalez .60 1.50
MT Miguel Tejada 1.00 2.50
NJ Nick Johnson .60 1.50
PM Pedro Martinez 1.00 2.50
RO Roy Oswalt 1.00 2.50
RS Reggie Sanders .60 1.50
SC Jason Schmidt .60 1.50
TE Mark Teixeira 1.00 2.50
TH Travis Hafner .60 1.50
VG Vladimir Guerrero 1.00 2.50
VW Vernon Wells .60 1.50

2006 SPx SPxciting Signature

RANDOM INSERTS IN PACKS
PRINT RUNS B/WN 10-30 COPIES PER
NO PRICING ON MOST DUE TO SCARCITY
JP Jonathan Papelbon/30 10.00 25.00
MC Matt Cain/30 40.00 80.00
PE Jake Peavy/30 6.00 15.00

2006 SPx SPxtreme Team

STATED ODDS 1:9
AD Adam Dunn 1.00 2.50
AJ Andruw Jones .60 1.50
AP Albert Pujols 2.00 5.00
AR Alex Rodriguez 2.00 5.00
AS Alfonso Soriano 1.00 2.50
BA Bobby Abreu .60 1.50
CC Chris Carpenter 1.00 2.50
CD Carlos Delgado .60 1.50
CL Carlos Lee .60 1.50
CR Carl Crawford 1.00 2.50
DJ Derek Jeter 4.00 10.00
DL Derrek Lee .60 1.50
DO David Ortiz 1.50 4.00
DW David Wright 1.25 3.00
GS Grady Sizemore 1.00 2.50
HA Travis Hafner .60 1.50
HM Hideki Matsui 1.50 4.00
HO Ryan Howard 1.25 3.00
IS Ichiro Suzuki 2.00 5.00
JB Jason Bay .60 1.50
JK Jeff Kent .60 1.50
JP Jake Peavy .60 1.50
JR Jose Reyes 1.00 2.50
JS Johan Santana 1.00 2.50
JT Jim Thome 1.00 2.50
KG Ken Griffey Jr. 3.00 8.00
LB Lance Berkman 1.00 2.50
MC Miguel Cabrera 1.50 4.00
MR Manny Ramirez 1.50 4.00
MT Mark Teixeira 1.00 2.50
MY Michael Young .60 1.50
PF Prince Fielder 3.00 8.00
PK Paul Konerko 1.00 2.50
PM Pedro Martinez 1.00 2.50
RH Rich Harden .60 1.50
TE Miguel Tejada 1.00 2.50
TH Todd Helton 1.00 2.50
VG Vladimir Guerrero 1.00 2.50
VM Victor Martinez 1.00 2.50
VW Vernon Wells .60 1.50

2006 SPx WBC All-World Team

STATED ODDS 1:9
1 Brett Willemburg .60 1.50
2 Bradley Harman 1.00 2.50
3 Adam Stern .60 1.50
4 Jason Bay .60 1.50
5 Adam Loewen .60 1.50
6 Wei Wang .60 1.50
7 Yi Feng .60 1.50
8 Yung Chi Chen 1.00 2.50
9 Chin-Lung Hu .60 1.50
10 Wei-Lun Pan 1.50 4.00
11 Yoandy Garlobo .60 1.50
12 Frederich Cepeda .60 1.50
13 Osmany Urrutia .60 1.50
14 Yulieski Gourriel 2.00 5.00
15 Yadel Marti .60 1.50
16 Pedro Luis Lazo 1.00 2.50
17 Adrian Beltre 1.50 4.00
18 David Ortiz 1.50 4.00
19 Albert Pujols 2.00 5.00
20 Bartolo Colon .60 1.50
21 Miguel Tejada 1.00 2.50
22 Mike Piazza 1.50 4.00
23 Jason Grilli .60 1.50
24 Nobuhiko Matsunaka 1.00 2.50
25 Tomoya Satozaki 1.00 2.50
26 Ichiro Suzuki 2.00 5.00
27 Hitoshi Tamura 1.00 2.50
28 Daisuke Matsuzaka 2.00 5.00
29 Koji Uehara 2.00 5.00
30 Jong Beom Lee .60 1.50
31 Seung Yeop Lee 1.00 2.50
32 Jae Seo .60 1.50
33 Min Han Son .60 1.50
34 Chan Ho Park 1.00 2.50
35 Jorge Cantu .60 1.50
36 Miguel Ojeda .60 1.50
37 Andruw Jones .60 1.50
38 Shairon Martis .60 1.50
39 Carlos Lee .60 1.50
40 Carlos Beltran 1.00 2.50
41 Javy Lopez .60 1.50
42 Javier Vazquez .60 1.50
43 Ken Griffey Jr. 3.00 8.00
44 Derek Jeter 4.00 10.00
45 Alex Rodriguez 2.00 5.00
46 Derrek Lee .60 1.50
47 Roger Clemens 2.00 5.00
48 Miguel Cabrera 1.50 4.00
49 Victor Martinez 1.00 2.50
50 Johan Santana 1.00 2.50

2006 SPx Winning Big Materials

STATED ODDS 1:252
PRINT RUNS B/WN 5-40 COPIES PER
NO PRICING ON QTY 26 OR LESS
PRICING IS FOR 2-3 CLR PATCHES
AB Adrian Beltre/40 50.00 100.00
AI Akinori Iwamura/30 200.00 300.00
AJ Andruw Jones/40 50.00 100.00
AP Ariel Pestano/30 50.00 100.00
AR Alex Rios/55 30.00 60.00
AS Alfonso Soriano/40 50.00 100.00
BA Bobby Abreu/40 50.00 100.00
BW Bernie Williams/40 75.00 120.00
CB Carlos Beltran/40 50.00 100.00
CD Carlos Delgado/40 30.00 60.00
CL Carlos Lee/40 30.00 60.00
CZ Carlos Zambrano/40 75.00 150.00
DL Derrek Lee/40 50.00 100.00
DO David Ortiz/30 30.00 60.00
EB Erik Bedard/40 30.00 60.00
EP Eduardo Paret/30 30.00 60.00
FC Frederich Cepeda/30 50.00 100.00
GY Guogan Yang/52 30.00 60.00
HC Hee Seop Choi/32 50.00 100.00
HT Hitoshi Tamura/30 200.00 300.00
IR Ivan Rodriguez/40 30.00 60.00
JB Jason Bay/40 50.00 100.00
JD Johnny Damon/40 50.00 100.00
JF Jeff Francis/40 30.00 60.00
JS Johan Santana/40 50.00 100.00
JV Jason Varitek/40 50.00 100.00
KU Koji Uehara/30 250.00 400.00
LO Javy Lopez/40 30.00 60.00
MA Moises Alou/53 30.00 60.00
MC Miguel Cabrera/40 50.00 100.00
ME Michel Enriquez/30 50.00 100.00
MF Maikel Folch/30 50.00 100.00
MK Munenori Kawasaki/30 250.00 400.00
MO Michihiro Ogasawara/30 300.00 400.00
MP Mike Piazza/40 60.00 150.00
MT Miguel Tejada/40 50.00 100.00
NM Nobuhiko Matsunaka/30 225.00 350.00
NS Naoyuki Shimizu/30 150.00 300.00
OU Osmany Urrutia/30 30.00 60.00
PE Wily Mo Pena/60 30.00 60.00
PL Pedro Luis Lazo/30 50.00 100.00
SW Shunsuke Watanabe/30 200.00 300.00
TN Tsuyoshi Nishioka/30 250.00 400.00
TW Tsuyoshi Wada/30 150.00 300.00
VM Victor Martinez/40 50.00 100.00
VO Vicyohandry Odelin/30 50.00 100.00
WL Wei-Chu Lin/45 200.00 400.00
WP Wei-Lun Pan/38 200.00 300.00
YG Yulieski Gourriel/30 50.00 100.00
YM Yunieski Maya/30 50.00 100.00

2006 SPx Winning Materials

STATED ODDS 1:18
AI Akinori Iwamura 8.00 20.00
AJ Andruw Jones 4.00 10.00
AP Ariel Pestano 3.00 8.00
AR Alex Rodriguez 6.00 15.00
AS Alfonso Soriano 3.00 8.00
BA Bobby Abreu 3.00 8.00
CB Carlos Beltran 3.00 8.00
CD Carlos Delgado 3.00 8.00
DL Derrek Lee 3.00 8.00
DO David Ortiz 4.00 10.00
EP Eduardo Paret 3.00 8.00
FC Frederich Cepeda 3.00 8.00
HC Hee Seop Choi 3.00 8.00
HT Hitoshi Tamura 8.00 20.00
IS Ichiro Suzuki 15.00 40.00
JB Jason Bay 3.00 8.00
JD Johnny Damon 3.00 8.00
JL Jong Beom Lee 3.00 8.00
JS Johan Santana 4.00 10.00
KG Ken Griffey Jr. 6.00 15.00
KU Koji Uehara 8.00 20.00
MC Miguel Cabrera 4.00 10.00
ME Michel Enriquez 3.00 8.00
MF Maikel Folch 3.00 8.00
MK Munenori Kawasaki 10.00 25.00
MO Michihiro Ogasawara 8.00 20.00
MP Mike Piazza 4.00 10.00
MS Min Han Son 4.00 10.00
MT Miguel Tejada 3.00 8.00
NM Nobuhiko Matsunaka 6.00 15.00
NS Naoyuki Shimizu 6.00 15.00
OU Osmany Urrutia 3.00 8.00
PL Pedro Luis Lazo 4.00 10.00
PU Albert Pujols 8.00 20.00
RC Roger Clemens 6.00 15.00
SW Shunsuke Watanabe 8.00 20.00
TN Tsuyoshi Nishioka 8.00 20.00
TW Tsuyoshi Wada 10.00 25.00
VM Victor Martinez 3.00 8.00
VO Vicyohandry Odelin 4.00 10.00
YG Yulieski Gourriel 3.00 8.00
YM Yunieski Maya 3.00 8.00

2007 SPx

COMMON CARD (1-100) .30 .75
COMMON AU RC (101-150) 3.00 8.00
OVERALL 101-150 AU RC ODDS 1:3
101-150 AU RC EXCH DEADLINE 05/10/2010
ASTERISK EQUALS PARTIAL EXCH
APPX.PRINTING PLATE ODDS 2 PER CASE
PLATES PRINT RUN 1 SET PER COLOR
BLACK-CYAN-MAGENTA-YELLOW ISSUED
NO PLATE PRICING DUE TO SCARCITY
1 Miguel Tejada .50 1.25
2 Brian Roberts .30 .75
3 Melvin Mora .30 .75
4 David Ortiz .75 2.00
5 Manny Ramirez .75 2.00
6 Jason Varitek .75 2.00
7 Curt Schilling .50 1.25
8 Jim Thome .50 1.25
9 Paul Konerko .50 1.25
10 Jermaine Dye .30 .75
11 Travis Hafner .30 .75
12 Victor Martinez .50 1.25
13 Grady Sizemore .50 1.25
14 C.C. Sabathia .50 1.25
15 Ivan Rodriguez .50 1.25
16 Magglio Ordonez .50 1.25
17 Carlos Guillen .30 .75
18 Justin Verlander .75 2.00
19 Shane Costa .30 .75
20 Emil Brown .30 .75
21 Mark Teahen .30 .75
22 Vladimir Guerrero .50 1.25
23 Jered Weaver .50 1.25
24 Juan Rivera .30 .75
25 Justin Morneau .50 1.25
26 Joe Mauer .60 1.50
27 Torii Hunter .30 .75
28 Johan Santana .50 1.25
29 Derek Jeter 2.00 5.00
30 Alex Rodriguez 1.00 2.50
31 Johnny Damon .50 1.25
32 Jason Giambi .30 .75
33 Bobby Crosby .30 .75
34 Nick Swisher .50 1.25
35 Eric Chavez .30 .75
36 Ichiro Suzuki 1.00 2.50
37 Raul Ibanez .50 1.25
38 Richie Sexson .30 .75
39 Carl Crawford .50 1.25
40 Rocco Baldelli .30 .75
41 Scott Kazmir .50 1.25
42 Michael Young .30 .75
43 Mark Teixeira .50 1.25
44 Ian Kinsler .50 1.25
45 Troy Glaus .30 .75
46 Vernon Wells .30 .75
47 Roy Halladay .50 1.25
48 Lyle Overbay .30 .75
49 Brandon Webb .50 1.25
50 Conor Jackson .30 .75
51 Stephen Drew .30 .75
52 Chipper Jones .75 2.00
53 Andruw Jones .30 .75
54 Adam LaRoche .30 .75
55 John Smoltz .75 2.00
56 Derrek Lee .30 .75
57 Aramis Ramirez .30 .75
58 Carlos Zambrano .50 1.25
59 Ken Griffey Jr. 1.50 4.00
60 Adam Dunn .50 1.25
61 Aaron Harang .30 .75
62 Todd Helton .50 1.25
63 Matt Holliday .75 2.00
64 Garrett Atkins .30 .75
65 Miguel Cabrera .75 2.00
66 Hanley Ramirez .50 1.25
67 Dontrelle Willis .30 .75
68 Lance Berkman .50 1.25
69 Roy Oswalt .50 1.25
70 Craig Biggio .50 1.25
71 J.D. Drew .30 .75
72 Nomar Garciaparra .50 1.25
73 Rafael Furcal .30 .75
74 Jeff Kent .30 .75
75 Prince Fielder .50 1.25
76 Bill Hall .30 .75
77 Rickie Weeks .30 .75
78 Jose Reyes .50 1.25
79 David Wright .60 1.50
80 Carlos Delgado .30 .75
81 Carlos Beltran .50 1.25
82 Ryan Howard .60 1.50
83 Chase Utley .50 1.25
84 Jimmy Rollins .50 1.25
85 Jason Bay .50 1.25
86 Freddy Sanchez .30 .75
87 Zach Duke .30 .75
88 Trevor Hoffman .50 1.25
89 Adrian Gonzalez .60 1.50
90 Chris Young .30 .75
91 Ray Durham .30 .75
92 Omar Vizquel .50 1.25
93 Jason Schmidt .30 .75
94 Albert Pujols 1.00 2.50
95 Scott Rolen .50 1.25
96 Jim Edmonds .50 1.25
97 Chris Carpenter .50 1.25
98 Alfonso Soriano .50 1.25
99 Ryan Zimmerman .50 1.25
100 Nick Johnson .30 .75
101 Delmon Young AU (RC) 8.00 20.00
102 A.Miller AU RC EXCH * 3.00 8.00
103 Troy Tulowitzki AU (RC) 4.00 10.00
104 Jeff Fiorentino AU (RC) 3.00 8.00
105 David Murphy AU (RC) 3.00 8.00
106 T.Lincecum AU RC 10.00 25.00
107 P.Hughes AU (RC) EXCH 6.00 15.00
108 K.Kouzmanoff AU (RC) EXCH 6.00 15.00
109 A.Lind AU (RC) EXCH * 3.00 8.00
110 M.Reynolds AU RC EXCH 8.00 20.00
111 Kevin Hooper AU (RC) 3.00 8.00
112 Mitch Maier AU RC 3.00 8.00
113 Homey Bailey AU (RC) 5.00 12.00
114 Dennis Sarfate AU (RC) 3.00 8.00
115 Drew Anderson AU RC 3.00 8.00
116 Miguel Montero AU (RC) 3.00 8.00
117 G.Perkins AU (RC) EXCH 3.00 8.00
119 Tim Gradoville AU RC 3.00 8.00
120 Ryan Braun AU (RC) 6.00 15.00
121 Chris Narveson AU (RC) 3.00 8.00
122 P.Misch AU (RC) EXCH * 3.00 8.00
123 Juan Salas AU (RC) 3.00 8.00
124 Beltran Perez AU (RC) 3.00 8.00
125 Joaquin Arias AU (RC) 3.00 8.00
126 Philip Humber AU (RC) 3.00 8.00
127 Kei Igawa AU RC 10.00 25.00
128 Daisuke Matsuzaka AU RC 20.00 50.00
129 Andy Cannizaro AU RC 6.00 15.00
130 Ubaldo Jimenez AU (RC) 5.00 12.00
131 Fred Lewis AU (RC) 6.00 15.00
132 Ryan Sweeney AU (RC) 3.00 8.00
133 Jeff Baker AU (RC) 3.00 8.00
134 Michael Bourn AU (RC) 3.00 8.00
135 Akinori Iwamura AU RC 6.00 15.00
136 Oswaldo Navarro AU RC 3.00 8.00
137 Hunter Pence AU (RC) 6.00 15.00
138 Jon Knott AU (RC) 3.00 8.00
139 J.Hampson AU (RC) EXCH 3.00 8.00
140 J.Salazar AU (RC) EXCH 3.00 8.00
141 Juan Morillo AU (RC) 3.00 8.00
142 Delwyn Young AU (RC) 3.00 8.00
143 Brian Burres AU (RC) 5.00 12.00
144 Chris Stewart AU RC 3.00 8.00
145 Eric Stults AU RC 3.00 8.00
146 Carlos Maldonado AU (RC) 3.00 8.00
147 Angel Sanchez AU RC 3.00 8.00
148 Cesar Jimenez AU RC 3.00 8.00
149 Shawn Riggans AU (RC) 3.00 8.00
150 John Nelson AU (RC) 3.00 8.00

2007 SPx Autofacts Preview

ONE PER HOBBY BOX TOPPER
EXCH DEADLINE 05/10/2010
AI Akinori Iwamura 15.00 40.00
AL Adam Lind 5.00 12.00
AS Angel Sanchez 3.00 8.00
BP Beltran Perez 3.00 8.00
BR Jeremy Brown 3.00 8.00
CM Carlos Maldonado 3.00 8.00
CN Chris Narveson 3.00 8.00
DS Dennis Sarfate 3.00 8.00
DW Dewayne Wise 5.00 12.00
DY Delmon Young 6.00 15.00
ES Eric Stults 3.00 8.00
FL Fred Lewis 5.00 12.00
GP Glen Perkins 3.00 8.00
JA Joaquin Arias 3.00 8.00
JB Jeff Baker 3.00 8.00
JH Justin Hampson 3.00 8.00
JK Jon Knott 3.00 8.00
JM Juan Morillo 3.00 8.00
JN John Nelson 3.00 8.00
JS Juan Salas 3.00 8.00
JW Jason Wood 3.00 8.00
KH Kevin Hooper 3.00 8.00
KI Kei Igawa 6.00 15.00
KK Kevin Kouzmanoff 5.00 12.00
MB Michael Bourn 5.00 12.00
MM Miguel Montero 3.00 8.00
PH Philip Humber 5.00 12.00
PM Patrick Misch 3.00 8.00
SA Jeff Salazar 3.00 8.00
SR Shawn Riggans 3.00 8.00
ST Chris Stewart 3.00 8.00

TT Troy Tulowitzki 10.00 25.00
YO Delwyn Young 3.00 8.00

2007 SPx Iron Man

COMMON CARD 1.50 4.00
APPX.ODDS 1:3
STATED PRINT RUN 699 SER.#'d SETS
APPX.PRINTING PLATE ODDS 2 PER CASE
PLATES PRINT RUN 1 SET PER COLOR
BLACK-CYAN-MAGENTA-YELLOW ISSUED
NO PLATE PRICING DUE TO SCARCITY

2007 SPx Iron Man Platinum

COMMON CARD 15.00 40.00
RANDOM INSERTS IN PACKS
STATED PRINT RUN 1 SER.#'d SET

2007 SPx Iron Man Memorabilia

COMMON CARD 10.00 25.00
APPX. SIX GAME-USED PER BOX
STATED PRINT RUN 25 SER.#'d SETS

2007 SPx Iron Man Signatures

COMMON CARD 150.00 300.00
RANDOM INSERTS IN PACKS
STATED PRINT RUN 1 SER.#'d SET

2007 SPx Winning Materials 199 Bronze

APPX. SIX GAME-USED PER BOX
STATED PRINT RUN 199 SER.#'d SETS
APPX.PRINTING PLATE ODDS 2 PER CASE
PLATES PRINT RUN 1 SET PER COLOR
BLACK-CYAN-MAGENTA-YELLOW ISSUED
NO PLATE PRICING DUE TO SCARCITY
AB A.J. Burnett/199 3.00 8.00
AD Adam Dunn/199 3.00 8.00
AE Andre Ethier/199 3.00 8.00
AJ Andruw Jones/199 3.00 8.00
AL Adam LaRoche/199 3.00 8.00
AP Albert Pujols/199 6.00 15.00
AR Aramis Ramirez/199 3.00 8.00
AS Anibal Sanchez/199 3.00 8.00
BA Bobby Abreu/199 4.00 10.00
BG Brian Giles/199 3.00 8.00
BL Joe Blanton/199 3.00 8.00
BM Brian McCann/199 3.00 8.00
BO Jeremy Bonderman/199 3.00 8.00
BR Brian Roberts/199 3.00 8.00
BS Ben Sheets/199 3.00 8.00
BU B.J. Upton/199 3.00 8.00
CA Miguel Cabrera/199 3.00 8.00
CB Craig Biggio/199 4.00 10.00
CC Chris Carpenter/199 3.00 8.00
CF Chone Figgins/199 3.00 8.00
CH Cole Hamels/199 4.00 10.00
CJ Chipper Jones/199 4.00 10.00
CL Roger Clemens/199 6.00 15.00
CN Robinson Cano/199 4.00 10.00
CR Carl Crawford/199 3.00 8.00
CU Chase Utley/199 4.00 10.00
CW Chien-Ming Wang/199 6.00 15.00
DJ Derek Jeter/199 8.00 20.00
DJ2 Derek Jeter/199 8.00 20.00
DL Derrek Lee/199 3.00 8.00
DO David Ortiz/199 4.00 10.00
DU Dan Uggla/199 3.00 8.00
DW Dontrelle Willis/199 3.00 8.00
EC Eric Chavez/199 3.00 8.00
FH Felix Hernandez/199 4.00 10.00
FL Francisco Liriano/199 3.00 8.00
FS Freddy Sanchez/199 3.00 8.00
FT Frank Thomas/199 4.00 10.00
GA Garrett Atkins/199 3.00 8.00
HA Travis Hafner/199 3.00 8.00
HE Todd Helton/199 4.00 10.00
HI Rich Hill/199 3.00 8.00
HK Howie Kendrick/199 3.00 8.00
HN Rich Harden/199 3.00 8.00
HR Hanley Ramirez/199 4.00 10.00
HS Huston Street/199 3.00 8.00
IK Ian Kinsler/199 3.00 8.00
IR Ivan Rodriguez/199 4.00 10.00
JB Jason Bay/199 3.00 8.00
JE Jim Edmonds/199 3.00 8.00
JF Jeff Francoeur/199 4.00 10.00
JJ Josh Johnson/199 3.00 8.00
JL Chad Billingsley/199 3.00 8.00
JM Joe Mauer/199 4.00 10.00
JN Joe Nathan/199 3.00 8.00
JP Jake Peavy/199 3.00 8.00
JR Jose Reyes/199 3.00 8.00
JS Jeremy Sowers/199 3.00 8.00
JT Jim Thome/199 3.00 8.00
JV Justin Verlander/199 4.00 10.00
JW Jered Weaver/199 3.00 8.00
JZ Joel Zumaya/199 3.00 8.00
KG Ken Griffey Jr./199 6.00 15.00
KG2 Ken Griffey Jr./199 6.00 15.00
KH Khalil Greene/199 4.00 10.00
KU Hong-Chih Kuo/199 8.00 20.00
LE Jon Lester/199 4.00 10.00
LG Luis Gonzalez/199 3.00 8.00
MC Matt Cain/199 3.00 8.00
ME Melky Cabrera/199 3.00 8.00
MH Matt Holliday/199 4.00 10.00
MO Justin Morneau/199 3.00 8.00
MT Mark Teixeira/199 3.00 8.00
NM Nick Markakis/199 4.00 10.00
NS Nick Swisher/199 3.00 8.00
PA Jonathan Papelbon/199 4.00 10.00
PF Prince Fielder/199 4.00 10.00
PL Paul LoDuca/199 3.00 8.00
RC Cal Ripken /199 6.00 15.00
RI Alex Rios/199 3.00 8.00
RJ Randy Johnson/199 3.00 8.00
RO Roy Oswalt/199 3.00 8.00
RW Rickie Weeks/199 3.00 8.00
RZ Ryan Zimmerman/199 3.00 8.00
SA Alfonso Soriano/199 3.00 8.00
SD Stephen Drew/199 3.00 8.00
SH James Shields/199 3.00 8.00
SK Scott Kazmir/199 3.00 8.00
SM John Smoltz/199 4.00 10.00
SO Scott Olsen/199 3.00 8.00
SR Scott Rolen/199 4.00 10.00
TE Miguel Tejada/199 3.00 8.00
TG Tom Glavine/199 4.00 10.00
TH Trevor Hoffman/199 3.00 8.00
TO Torii Hunter/199 3.00 8.00
VG Vladimir Guerrero/199 4.00 10.00
VM Victor Martinez/199 3.00 8.00
WE David Wells/199 3.00 8.00
WI Josh Willingham/199 3.00 8.00
YB Yuniesky Betancourt/199 3.00 8.00

2007 SPx Winning Materials 199 Gold

*199 GOLD: .4X TO 1X 199 BRONZE
APPX. SIX GAME-USED PER BOX
STATED PRINT RUN 199 SER.#'d SETS

2007 SPx Winning Materials 199 Silver

*199 SILVER: .4X TO 1X 199 BRONZE
APPX. SIX GAME-USED PER BOX
STATED PRINT RUN 199 SER.#'d SETS

2007 SPx Winning Materials 175 Blue

*175 BLUE: .4X TO 1X 199 BRONZE
APPX. SIX GAME-USED PER BOX
STATED PRINT RUN 175 SER.#'d SETS

2007 SPx Winning Materials 175 Green

*175 GREEN: .4X TO 1X 199 BRONZE
APPX. SIX GAME-USED PER BOX
STATED PRINT RUN 175 SER.#'d SETS

2007 SPx Winning Materials 99 Gold

*99 GOLD: .5X TO 1.2X 199 BRONZE
APPX. SIX GAME-USED PER BOX
STATED PRINT RUN 99 SER.#'d SETS

2007 SPx Winning Materials 99 Silver

*99 SILVER: .5X TO 1.2X 199 BRONZE
APPX. SIX GAME-USED PER BOX
STATED PRINT RUN 99 SER.#'d SETS

2007 SPx Winning Materials Dual Gold

APPX. SIX GAME-USED PER BOX
STATED PRINT RUN 50 SER.#'d SETS
AB A.J. Burnett/50 5.00 12.00
AD Adam Dunn/50 5.00 12.00
AE Andre Ethier/50 5.00 12.00
AJ Andruw Jones/50 5.00 12.00
AL Adam LaRoche/50 5.00 12.00
AP Albert Pujols/50 10.00 25.00
AR Aramis Ramirez/50 5.00 12.00
AS Anibal Sanchez/50 5.00 12.00
BA Bobby Abreu/50 6.00 15.00
BG Brian Giles/50 5.00 12.00
BL Joe Blanton/50 5.00 12.00
BM Brian McCann/50 5.00 12.00
BO Jeremy Bonderman/50 5.00 12.00
BR Brian Roberts/50 5.00 12.00
BS Ben Sheets/50 5.00 12.00
BU B.J. Upton/50 5.00 12.00
CA Miguel Cabrera/50 5.00 12.00
CB Craig Biggio/50 6.00 15.00
CC Chris Carpenter/50 5.00 12.00
CF Chone Figgins/50 5.00 12.00
CH Cole Hamels/50 6.00 15.00
CJ Chipper Jones/50 6.00 15.00
CL Roger Clemens/50 10.00 25.00
CN Robinson Cano/50 6.00 15.00
CR Carl Crawford/50 5.00 12.00
CU Chase Utley/50 6.00 15.00
CW Chien-Ming Wang/50 10.00 25.00
DJ Derek Jeter/50 12.50 30.00
DJ2 Derek Jeter/50 12.50 30.00
DL Derrek Lee/50 5.00 12.00
DO David Ortiz/50 6.00 15.00
DU Dan Uggla/50 6.00 15.00
DW Dontrelle Willis/50 5.00 12.00
EC Eric Chavez/50 5.00 12.00
FH Felix Hernandez/50 6.00 15.00
FL Francisco Liriano/50 5.00 12.00
FS Freddy Sanchez/50 5.00 12.00
FT Frank Thomas/50 6.00 15.00
GA Garrett Atkins/50 5.00 12.00
HA Travis Hafner/50 5.00 12.00
HE Todd Helton/50 6.00 15.00
HI Rich Hill/50 5.00 12.00
HK Howie Kendrick/50 5.00 12.00
HN Rich Harden/50 5.00 12.00
HR Hanley Ramirez/50 6.00 15.00
HS Huston Street/50 5.00 12.00
IK Ian Kinsler/50 5.00 12.00
IR Ivan Rodriguez/50 6.00 15.00
JB Jason Bay/50 5.00 12.00
JE Jim Edmonds/50 5.00 12.00
JF Jeff Francoeur/50 6.00 15.00
JJ Josh Johnson/50 5.00 12.00
JL Chad Billingsley/50 5.00 12.00
JM Joe Mauer/50 6.00 15.00
JN Joe Nathan/50 5.00 12.00
JP Jake Peavy/50 5.00 12.00
JR Jose Reyes/50 5.00 12.00
JS Jeremy Sowers/50 5.00 12.00
JT Jim Thome/50 5.00 12.00
JV Justin Verlander/50 6.00 15.00
JW Jered Weaver/50 5.00 12.00
JZ Joel Zumaya/50 5.00 12.00
KG Ken Griffey Jr./50 10.00 25.00
KG2 Ken Griffey Jr./50 10.00 25.00
KH Khalil Greene/50 6.00 15.00
KU Hong-Chih Kuo/50 12.50 30.00
LE Jon Lester/50 6.00 15.00
LG Luis Gonzalez/50 5.00 12.00
MC Matt Cain/50 5.00 12.00
ME Melky Cabrera/50 5.00 12.00
MH Matt Holliday/50 6.00 15.00
MO Justin Morneau/50 5.00 12.00
MT Mark Teixeira/50 5.00 12.00
NM Nick Markakis/50 6.00 15.00
NS Nick Swisher/50 5.00 12.00
PA Jonathan Papelbon/50 6.00 15.00
PF Prince Fielder/50 6.00 15.00
PL Paul LoDuca/50 5.00 12.00
RC Cal Ripken /50 10.00 25.00
RI Alex Rios/50 5.00 12.00
RJ Randy Johnson/50 5.00 12.00
RO Roy Oswalt/50 5.00 12.00
RW Rickie Weeks/50 5.00 12.00
RZ Ryan Zimmerman/50 5.00 12.00
SA Alfonso Soriano/50 5.00 12.00
SD Stephen Drew/50 5.00 12.00
SH James Shields/50 5.00 12.00
SK Scott Kazmir/50 5.00 12.00
SM John Smoltz/50 5.00 12.00
SO Scott Olsen/50 5.00 12.00
SR Scott Rolen/50 5.00 12.00
TE Miguel Tejada/50 5.00 12.00
TG Tom Glavine/50 5.00 12.00
TH Trevor Hoffman/50 5.00 12.00
TO Torii Hunter/50 5.00 12.00
VG Vladimir Guerrero/50 6.00 15.00
VM Victor Martinez/50 5.00 12.00
WE David Wells/50 5.00 12.00
WI Josh Willingham/50 5.00 12.00
YB Yuniesky Betancourt/50 5.00 12.00

2007 SPx Winning Materials Dual Silver

*DUAL SILVER: .4X TO 1X DUAL GOLD
APPX. SIX GAME-USED PER BOX
STATED PRINT RUN 50 SER.#'d SETS

2007 SPx Winning Materials Patches Gold

APPX. SIX GAME-USED PER BOX
PRINT RUNS B/WN 3-99 COPIES PER
NO VERLANDER PRICING DUE TO SCARCITY
AB A.J. Burnett/99 4.00 10.00
AD Adam Dunn/99 4.00 10.00
AE Andre Ethier/99 5.00 12.00
AJ Andruw Jones/99 5.00 12.00
AL Adam LaRoche/99 4.00 10.00
AP Albert Pujols/99 15.00 40.00
AR Aramis Ramirez/99 4.00 10.00
AS Anibal Sanchez/54 4.00 10.00
BA Bobby Abreu/99 6.00 15.00
BG Brian Giles/99 4.00 10.00
BL Joe Blanton/99 4.00 10.00
BM Brian McCann/99 6.00 15.00
BO Jeremy Bonderman/99 6.00 15.00
BR Brian Roberts/99 4.00 10.00
BS Ben Sheets/99 4.00 10.00
BU B.J. Upton/99 10.00 25.00
CA Miguel Cabrera/99 5.00 12.00
CB Craig Biggio/99 6.00 15.00
CC Chris Carpenter/99 5.00 12.00
CF Chone Figgins/99 4.00 10.00
CH Cole Hamels/99 6.00 15.00
CJ Chipper Jones/99 6.00 15.00
CL Roger Clemens/99 15.00 40.00
CN Robinson Cano/99 6.00 15.00
CR Carl Crawford/99 5.00 12.00
CU Chase Utley/99 6.00 15.00
CW Chien-Ming Wang/99 15.00 40.00
DJ Derek Jeter/99 20.00 50.00
DJ2 Derek Jeter/99 20.00 50.00
DL Derrek Lee/99 4.00 10.00
DO David Ortiz/99 6.00 15.00
DU Dan Uggla/99 4.00 10.00
DW Dontrelle Willis/99 4.00 10.00
EC Eric Chavez/99 4.00 10.00
FH Felix Hernandez/99 5.00 12.00
FL Francisco Liriano/99 6.00 15.00
FS Freddy Sanchez/99 4.00 10.00
FT Frank Thomas/99 10.00 25.00
GA Garrett Atkins/99 4.00 10.00
HA Travis Hafner/99 4.00 10.00
HE Todd Helton/99 5.00 12.00
HI Rich Hill/99 4.00 10.00
HK Howie Kendrick/34 6.00 15.00
HN Rich Harden/99 4.00 10.00
HR Hanley Ramirez/99 5.00 12.00
HS Huston Street/99 4.00 10.00
IK Ian Kinsler/99 4.00 10.00
IR Ivan Rodriguez/99 5.00 12.00
JB Jason Bay/99 5.00 12.00
JE Jim Edmonds/99 5.00 12.00
JF Jeff Francoeur/99 10.00 25.00
JJ Josh Johnson/99 4.00 10.00
JL Chad Billingsley/99 4.00 10.00
JM Joe Mauer/99 5.00 12.00
JN Joe Nathan/99 4.00 10.00
JP Jake Peavy/99 4.00 10.00
JR Jose Reyes/99 6.00 15.00
JS Jeremy Sowers/99 4.00 10.00
JT Jim Thome/99 5.00 12.00
JW Jered Weaver/99 5.00 12.00
JZ Joel Zumaya/99 5.00 12.00
KG Ken Griffey Jr./99 12.50 30.00
KG2 Ken Griffey Jr./99 12.50 30.00
KH Khalil Greene/99 5.00 12.00
KU Hong-Chih Kuo/99 5.00 12.00
LE Jon Lester/99 5.00 12.00
LG Luis Gonzalez/99 4.00 10.00
MC Matt Cain/99 5.00 12.00
ME Melky Cabrera/99 4.00 10.00
MH Matt Holliday/99 5.00 12.00
MO Justin Morneau/99 4.00 10.00
MT Mark Teixeira/99 5.00 12.00
NM Nick Markakis/99 10.00 25.00
NS Nick Swisher/99 6.00 15.00
PA Jonathan Papelbon/99 6.00 15.00
PF Prince Fielder/99 6.00 15.00
PL Paul LoDuca/99 5.00 12.00
RC Cal Ripken /99 12.50 30.00
RI Alex Rios/99 4.00 10.00
RJ Randy Johnson/99 6.00 15.00
RO Roy Oswalt/99 5.00 12.00
RW Rickie Weeks/99 4.00 10.00
RZ Ryan Zimmerman/99 10.00 25.00
SA Alfonso Soriano/99 5.00 12.00
SD Stephen Drew/99 5.00 12.00
SH James Shields/99 4.00 10.00
SK Scott Kazmir/99 5.00 12.00
SM John Smoltz/99 10.00 25.00
SO Scott Olsen/99 4.00 10.00
SR Scott Rolen/99 4.00 10.00
TE Miguel Tejada/99 4.00 10.00
TG Tom Glavine/99 6.00 15.00
TH Trevor Hoffman/99 5.00 12.00
TO Torii Hunter/99 5.00 12.00
VG Vladimir Guerrero/99 10.00 25.00
VM Victor Martinez/99 4.00 10.00
WE David Wells/99 4.00 10.00
WI Josh Willingham/99 4.00 10.00
YB Yuniesky Betancourt/99 4.00 10.00

2007 SPx Winning Materials Patches Silver

*PATCH SILVER: .4X TO 1X PATCH GOLD
APPX. SIX GAME-USED PER BOX
PRINT RUN B/WN 3-99 COPIES PER
NO PRICING ON QTY 27 OR LESS
JV Justin Verlander/99 6.00 15.00
LE Jon Lester/37 6.00 15.00

2007 SPx Winning Materials Patches Bronze

*PATCH BRONZE: .5X TO 1.2X PATCH GOLD
APPX. SIX GAME-USED PER BOX
STATED PRINT RUN 50 SER.#'d SETS
AR Aramis Ramirez/50 4.00 10.00
LE Jon Lester/50 6.00 15.00
MH Matt Holliday/50 5.00 12.00

2007 SPx Winning Trios Bronze

*BRONZE: .5X TO 1.2X GOLD
APPX. SIX GAME-USED PER BOX
STATED PRINT RUN 30 SER.#'d SETS

2007 SPx Winning Trios Gold

APPX. SIX GAME-USED PER BOX
STATED PRINT RUN 75 SER.#'d SETS
WT1 Griffey Jr./Pujols/Jeter 20.00 50.00
WT2 Uggla/Hanley/Willingham 10.00 25.00
WT3 Willis/J.Johnson/Anibal 6.00 15.00
WT4 Berkman/Papi/Hafner 10.00 25.00
WT5 Peavy/Oswalt/Sheets 6.00 15.00
WT6 Verlander/Bonderman/Pudge 10.00 25.00
WT7 J.Reyes/Hanley/S.Drew 10.00 25.00
WT8 Mig.Cabrera/Zimmerman/B.Upton 10.00 25.00
WT9 Jer.Weaver/Verlander/Papelbon 10.00 25.00
WT10 Jeter/Big Unit/Abreu 10.00 25.00
WT11 Ensberg/Biggio/Berkman 6.00 15.00
WT12 Francoeur/LaRoche/ McCann 10.00 25.00
WT13 Mauer/McCann/V.Martinez 10.00 25.00
WT14 Crawford/Sizemore/J.Reyes 10.00 25.00
WT15 F.Garcia/Zambrano/Santana 6.00 15.00
WT16 Vlad/Abreu/Soriano 10.00 25.00
WT17 Morneau/Mauer/Santana 10.00 25.00
WT18 Delgado/J.Reyes/Beltran 6.00 15.00
WT19 Billingsley/Ethier/Kemp 10.00 25.00
WT20 Thome/Dye/Iguchi 10.00 25.00
WT21 Utley/Rowand/Rollins 10.00 25.00
WT22 Ordonez/Pudge/Granderson 15.00 40.00
WT23 Pujols/Carpenter/Rolen 15.00 40.00
WT24 Shields/B.Upton/Crawford 6.00 15.00
WT25 Kendrick/Jer.Weaver/Napoli 6.00 15.00
WT26 Uggla/Kendrick/Kinsler 6.00 15.00
WT27 Roberts/Mig.Tejada/Markakis 10.00 25.00
WT28 Jer.Weaver/Verlander/Pelfrey 10.00 25.00
WT29 Hamels/Hill/Liriano 10.00 25.00
WT30 Anibal/Lowe/Big Unit 6.00 15.00
WT31 Zimmerman/Prince/Uggla 10.00 25.00
WT32 Hoffman/Nathan/Street 6.00 15.00
WT33 Burnett/Rios/Wells 6.00 15.00
WT34 Weeks/Prince/Sheets 10.00 25.00
WT35 Betancourt/Beltre/F.Hernandez 10.00 25.00
WT36 Verlander/Zumaya/Bonderman 10.00 25.00
WT37 Wagner/J.Reyes/Lo Duca 6.00 15.00
WT38 Sowers/Sabathia/Martinez 6.00 15.00
WT39 S.Drew/Webb/C.Jackson 6.00 15.00
WT40 F.Hernandez/Jer.Weaver/Verlander 10.00 25.00
WT41 Griffey Jr./Big Hurt/Pudge 10.00 25.00
WT42 Jeter/Ripken Jr./J.Reyes 10.00 25.00

2007 SPx Winning Trios Silver

*SILVER: .4X TO 1X GOLD
APPX. SIX GAME-USED PER BOX
STATED PRINT RUN 50 SER.#'d SETS

2007 SPx Young Stars Signatures

STATED ODDS 1:12
EXCH DEADLINE 05/10/2010
APPX.PRINTING PLATE ODDS 2 PER CASE
PLATES PRINT RUN 1 SET PER COLOR
BLACK-CYAN-MAGENTA-YELLOW ISSUED
NO PLATE PRICING DUE TO SCARCITY
AE Andre Ethier 3.00 8.00
AG Adrian Gonzalez 6.00 15.00
AM Andrew Miller 10.00 25.00
AS Anibal Sanchez 3.00 8.00
BU B.J. Upton 6.00 15.00
CA Matt Cain 8.00 20.00
CH Cole Hamels 6.00 15.00
CQ Carlos Quentin 3.00 8.00
DJ Derek Jeter EXCH 125.00 300.00
DU Dan Uggla 6.00 15.00
DY Delmon Young 6.00 15.00
FH Felix Hernandez 10.00 25.00
FL Francisco Liriano 4.00 10.00
HA Rich Harden 5.00 12.00
HI Rich Hill 6.00 15.00
HK Howie Kendrick 6.00 15.00
HR Hanley Ramirez 4.00 10.00
JB Jeremy Brown 3.00 8.00
JJ Josh Johnson 8.00 20.00
JL Jon Lester 6.00 15.00
JM Joe Mauer 12.00 30.00
JP Jonathan Papelbon 6.00 15.00
JR Jose Reyes 4.00 10.00
JS Jeremy Sowers 3.00 8.00
JV Justin Verlander 25.00 60.00
JW Jered Weaver 3.00 8.00
JZ Joel Zumaya 4.00 10.00
KG Ken Griffey Jr. 50.00 120.00
KU Hong-Chih Kuo 4.00 10.00
LO James Loney 3.00 8.00
MO Justin Morneau 6.00 15.00
NM Nick Markakis 10.00 25.00
PH Philip Humber 5.00 12.00
RW Rickie Weeks 5.00 12.00
RZ Ryan Zimmerman EXCH 3.00 8.00
SD Stephen Drew EXCH 4.00 10.00
ST Scott Thorman 5.00 12.00
TT Troy Tulowitzki 6.00 15.00*
WI Josh Willingham 3.00 8.00

2008 SPx

OVERALL AU ODDS FOUR PER BOX
1 Brandon Webb .40 1.00
2 Chris B. Young .25 .60
3 Eric Byrnes .25 .60
4 Dan Haren .25 .60
5 Mark Teixeira .40 1.00
6 Chipper Jones .60 1.50
7 John Smoltz .60 1.50
8 Erik Bedard .25 .60
9 Nick Markakis .50 1.25
10 Brian Roberts .25 .60
11 David Ortiz .60 1.50
12 Curt Schilling .40 1.00
13 Manny Ramirez .60 1.50
14 Daisuke Matsuzaka .40 1.00
15 Josh Beckett .25 .60
16 Derrek Lee .25 .60
17 Alfonso Soriano .40 1.00
18 Carlos Zambrano .40 1.00
19 Aramis Ramirez .25 .60
20 Jermaine Dye .25 .60
21 Jim Thome .40 1.00
22 Nick Swisher .40 1.00
23 Ken Griffey Jr. 1.25 3.00
24 Adam Dunn .40 1.00
25 Brandon Phillips .25 .60
26 Grady Sizemore .40 1.00
27 Victor Martinez .40 1.00
28 C.C. Sabathia .40 1.00
29 Travis Hafner .25 .60
30 Matt Holliday .60 1.50
31 Todd Helton .40 1.00
32 Troy Tulowitzki .60 1.50
33 Magglio Ordonez .40 1.00
34 Gary Sheffield .25 .60
35 Justin Verlander .60 1.50
36 Curtis Granderson .40 1.00
37 Miguel Cabrera .60 1.50
38 Hanley Ramirez .40 1.00
39 Dan Uggla .25 .60
40 Miguel Tejada .40 1.00
41 Lance Berkman .40 1.00
42 Hunter Pence .40 1.00
43 Carlos Lee .25 .60
44 Alex Gordon .40 1.00
45 David DeJesus .25 .60
46 Vladimir Guerrero .40 1.00
47 Jered Weaver .40 1.00
48 Torii Hunter .25 .60
49 Andruw Jones .25 .60
50 Rafael Furcal .25 .60
51 Russell Martin .25 .60
52 Brad Penny .25 .60
53 Ryan Braun .40 1.00
54 Prince Fielder .40 1.00
55 J.J. Hardy .25 .60
56 Justin Morneau .40 1.00
57 Johan Santana .40 1.00
58 Joe Mauer .50 1.25
59 Delmon Young .40 1.00
60 Jose Reyes .40 1.00
61 David Wright .40 1.00
62 Carlos Beltran .40 1.00
63 Pedro Martinez .40 1.00
64 Chien-Ming Wang .40 1.00
65 Alex Rodriguez .75 2.00
66 Derek Jeter 1.50 4.00
67 Robinson Cano .40 1.00
68 Hideki Matsui .60 1.50
69 Joe Blanton .25 .60
70 Jack Cust .25 .60
71 Cole Hamels .50 1.25
72 Jimmy Rollins .40 1.00
73 Ryan Howard .40 1.00
74 Chase Utley .40 1.00
75 Jason Bay .40 1.00
76 Freddy Sanchez .25 .60
77 Jake Peavy .25 .60
78 Greg Maddux .75 2.00
79 Adrian Gonzalez .40 1.00
80 Barry Zito .40 1.00
81 Omar Vizquel .40 1.00
82 Tim Lincecum .40 1.00
83 Ichiro Suzuki .75 2.00
84 Felix Hernandez .40 1.00
85 Kenji Johjima .25 .60
86 Albert Pujols .75 2.00
87 Scott Rolen .40 1.00
88 Chris Carpenter .40 1.00
89 Rick Ankiel .25 .60
90 Scott Kazmir .40 1.00
91 Carl Crawford .40 1.00
92 B.J. Upton .40 1.00
93 Michael Young .25 .60
94 Josh Hamilton .40 1.00
95 Hank Blalock .25 .60
96 Roy Halladay .40 1.00
97 Vernon Wells .25 .60
98 Alex Rios .25 .60
99 Ryan Zimmerman .40 1.00
100 Dmitri Young .25 .60
101 Bill Murphy AU (RC) 3.00 8.00
102 Emilio Bonifacio AU RC 5.00 12.00
103 Brandon Jones AU RC 3.00 8.00
104 Clint Sammons AU (RC) 3.00 8.00
105 Clay Buchholz AU (RC) 8.00 20.00
106 Kevin Hart AU (RC) 3.00 8.00
107 Donny Lucy AU (RC) 3.00 8.00
108 Lance Broadway AU (RC) 3.00 8.00
109 Joey Votto AU (RC) 40.00 100.00
110 Ryan Hanigan AU RC 4.00 10.00
111 Joe Koshansky AU (RC) 3.00 8.00
112 Josh Newman AU RC 3.00 8.00
113 Seth Smith AU (RC) 3.00 8.00
114 Chris Seddon AU (RC) 3.00 8.00
115 Harvey Garcia AU (RC) 3.00 8.00
116 Felipe Paulino AU RC 3.00 8.00
117 J.R. Towles AU RC 4.00 10.00
118 Josh Anderson AU (RC) 3.00 8.00
119 Troy Patton AU (RC) 3.00 8.00
120 Billy Buckner AU (RC) 3.00 8.00
121 Luke Hochevar AU RC 3.00 8.00
122 Chin-Lung Hu AU (RC) 6.00 15.00
124 Jose Morales AU (RC) 6.00 15.00
126 Alberto Gonzalez AU RC 3.00 8.00
127 Bronson Sardinha AU (RC) 3.00 8.00
128 Ian Kennedy AU RC 6.00 15.00
129 Ross Ohlendorf AU RC 3.00 8.00
130 Daric Barton AU (RC) 6.00 15.00
131 Jerry Blevins AU RC 3.00 8.00
132 Dave Davidson AU RC 3.00 8.00
133 Nyjer Morgan AU (RC) 3.00 8.00
134 Steve Pearce AU RC 6.00 15.00
135 Colt Morton AU RC 3.00 8.00
136 Eugenio Velez AU RC 3.00 8.00
138 Rob Johnson AU (RC) 3.00 8.00
139 Wladimir Balentien AU (RC) 3.00 8.00
140 Justin Ruggiano AU RC 3.00 8.00
141 Bill White AU RC 3.00 8.00
142 Luis Mendoza AU (RC) 3.00 8.00
143 Jonathan Albaladejo AU RC 3.00 8.00
145 Ross Detwiler AU RC 6.00 15.00
146 J.Bruce AU (RC) UER 6.00 15.00
147 C.Gonzalez AU (RC) 20.00 50.00
148 E.Longoria AU RC 10.00 25.00
150 M.Scherzer AU RC 100.00 250.00
151 C.Kershaw AU RC 125.00 300.00
152 A.Ramirez AU RC 4.00 10.00

2008 SPx Silver

*SILVER AU: .4X TO 1X BASIC AU RC
RANDOM INSERT IN BOX TOPPER PACK
CARDS 146-150 DO NOT EXIST

2008 SPx Babe Ruth American Legend

COMMON RUTH 20.00 50.00
OVERALL ODDS ONE PER CASE
STATED PRINT RUN 1 SER.#'d SET

2008 SPx Ken Griffey Jr. American Hero

COMMON GRIFFEY 1.25 3.00
RANDOM INSERTS IN PACKS
STATED PRINT RUN 725 SER.#'d SETS

2008 SPx Ken Griffey Jr. American Hero Boxscore

COMMON GRIFFEY 12.00 30.00
OVERALL ODDS ONE PER CASE
STATED PRINT RUN 1 SER.#'d SET

2008 SPx Ken Griffey Jr. American Hero Memorabilia

COMMON GRIFFEY 12.50 30.00
OVERALL MEM ODDS SIX PER BOX
STATED PRINT RUN 25 SER.#'d SETS

2008 SPx Ken Griffey Jr. American Hero Signature

COMMON GRIFFEY 100.00 200.00
OVERALL AU ODDS FOUR PER BOX
STATED PRINT RUN 3 SER.#'d SETS

2008 SPx Superstar Signatures

OVERALL AU ODDS FOUR PER BOX
EXCHANGE DEADLINE 4/28/2010
BW Brandon Webb 6.00 15.00
DJ Derek Jeter 100.00 175.00
DM Daisuke Matsuzaka 20.00 50.00
DU Dan Uggla 6.00 15.00
HR Hanley Ramirez 8.00 20.00
KG Ken Griffey Jr. 30.00 60.00
MH Matt Holliday 10.00 25.00
MT Mark Teixeira 10.00 25.00
PF Prince Fielder 4.00 10.00
SR Scott Rolen 5.00 12.00
TG Tom Glavine 10.00 25.00
TH Travis Hafner 5.00 12.00
VG Vladimir Guerrero 8.00 20.00
VM Victor Martinez 4.00 10.00

2008 SPx Winning Materials SPx 150

OVERALL GU ODDS SIX PER BOX
STATED PRINT RUN 150 SER.#'d SETS
AB A.J. Burnett 3.00 8.00
AE Andre Ethier 3.00 8.00
AG Adrian Gonzalez 3.00 8.00
AH Aaron Harang 3.00 8.00
AJ Andruw Jones 3.00 8.00
AK Austin Kearns 3.00 8.00
AL Adam LaRoche 3.00 8.00
AP Albert Pujols 5.00 12.00
AP Andy Pettitte 4.00 10.00
AR Aaron Rowand 3.00 8.00
AS Alfonso Soriano 3.00 8.00
BA Bobby Abreu 3.00 8.00
BC Bartolo Colon 3.00 8.00
BE Adrian Beltre 3.00 8.00
BG Brian Giles 3.00 8.00
BM Brian McCann 3.00 8.00
BS Ben Sheets 3.00 8.00
BU B.J. Upton 3.00 8.00
BW Billy Wagner 4.00 10.00
CA Chris Carpenter 3.00 8.00
CB Carlos Beltran 3.00 8.00
CC Chad Cordero 3.00 8.00
CD Carlos Delgado 3.00 8.00
CG Carlos Guillen 3.00 8.00
CH Chris Burke 3.00 8.00
CK Casey Kotchman 3.00 8.00
CL Carlos Lee 3.00 8.00
CS Curt Schilling 3.00 8.00
CU Chase Utley 5.00 12.00
CZ Carlos Zambrano 3.00 8.00
DH Dan Haren 3.00 8.00
DJ Derek Jeter 10.00 25.00
DL Derrek Lee 3.00 8.00
DO David Ortiz 3.00 8.00
DU Dan Uggla 3.00 8.00
DW Dontrelle Willis 3.00 8.00
DY Jermaine Dye 3.00 8.00
EC Eric Chavez 3.00 8.00
FH Felix Hernandez 3.00 8.00
FL Francisco Liriano 3.00 8.00
GA Garret Anderson 3.00 8.00
GA Garrett Atkins 3.00 8.00
GJ Geoff Jenkins 3.00 8.00
GM Greg Maddux 5.00 12.00
GO Alex Gordon 5.00 12.00
GR Curtis Granderson 3.00 8.00
GS Grady Sizemore 3.00 8.00
HA Cole Hamels 3.00 8.00
HB Hank Blalock 3.00 8.00
HE Todd Helton 3.00 8.00
HO Trevor Hoffman 3.00 8.00
HR Hanley Ramirez 3.00 8.00
HU Torii Hunter 3.00 8.00
IR Ivan Rodriguez 4.00 10.00
JA Conor Jackson 3.00 8.00
JB Josh Barfield 3.00 8.00
JD J.D. Drew 3.00 8.00
JE Jim Edmonds 4.00 10.00
JF Jeff Francoeur 4.00 10.00
JG Jason Giambi 3.00 8.00
JH Jhonny Peralta 3.00 8.00
JJ J.J. Hardy 3.00 8.00
JK Jeff Kent 3.00 8.00
JM Joe Mauer 3.00 8.00
JN Joe Nathan 3.00 8.00
JO Josh Beckett 4.00 10.00
JP Jake Peavy 3.00 8.00
JR Jose Reyes 3.00 8.00
JS Johan Santana 3.00 8.00
JT Jim Thome 3.00 8.00
JV Jason Varitek 4.00 10.00
KJ Kenji Johjima 3.00 8.00
KY Kevin Youkilis 4.00 10.00
LB Lance Berkman 3.00 8.00
LG Luis Gonzalez 3.00 8.00
MC Miguel Cabrera 3.00 8.00
MH Matt Holliday 3.00 8.00
MO Justin Morneau 3.00 8.00
MR Manny Ramirez 4.00 10.00
MT Mark Teixeira 3.00 8.00
MY Michael Young 3.00 8.00
OR Magglio Ordonez 3.00 8.00
PA Jonathan Papelbon 4.00 10.00
PF Prince Fielder 4.00 10.00
PM Pedro Martinez 3.00 8.00
PO Jorge Posada 3.00 8.00
RA Aramis Ramirez 3.00 8.00
RH Roy Halladay 3.00 8.00
RJ Randy Johnson 3.00 8.00
RO Roy Oswalt 3.00 8.00
SM John Smoltz 4.00 10.00
TE Miguel Tejada 3.00 8.00
TH Tim Hudson 3.00 8.00
TR Travis Hafner 3.00 8.00
VE Justin Verlander 3.00 8.00
VG Vladimir Guerrero 3.00 8.00
VW Vernon Wells 3.00 8.00

2008 SPx Winning Materials Baseball 99

*BB 99: .4X TO 1X WM SPX 150
OVERALL GU ODDS SIX PER BOX
STATED PRINT RUN 99 SER.#'d SETS
KG Ken Griffey Jr. 5.00 12.00
RF Rafael Furcal 3.00 8.00

2008 SPx Winning Materials Dual Jersey Number

*DUAL JN: .5X TO 1.2X WM SPX 150
OVERALL GU ODDS SIX PER BOX
PRINT RUNS B/WN 35-46 COPIES PER
CJ Chipper Jones/46 5.00 12.00

2008 SPx Winning Materials Dual Limited Patch SPx

*DUAL LTD PATCH: .6X TO 1.5X LTD PATCH SPX
OVERALL GU ODDS SIX PER BOX
PRINT RUNS B/WN 23-50 COPIES PER
NO PRICING ON QTY 25 OR LESS
KG Ken Griffey Jr. 15.00 40.00

2008 SPx Winning Materials Dual SPx

*DUAL SPX: .5X TO 1.2X WM SPX 150
OVERALL GU ODDS SIX PER BOX
STATED PRINT RUN 50 SER.#'d SETS

2008 SPx Winning Materials Jersey Number 125

*JN 125: .4X TO 1X WM SPX 150
OVERALL GU ODDS SIX PER BOX
STATED PRINT RUN 125 SER.#'d SETS
RF Rafael Furcal 3.00 8.00

2008 SPx Winning Materials Limited Patch SPx

OVERALL GU ODDS SIX PER BOX
PRINT RUNS B/WN 72-99 COPIES PER
AB A.J. Burnett 4.00 10.00
AE Andre Ethier 4.00 10.00
AG Adrian Gonzalez 4.00 10.00
AH Aaron Harang 4.00 10.00
AJ Andruw Jones 4.00 10.00
AK Austin Kearns 4.00 10.00
AL Adam LaRoche 4.00 10.00
AP Albert Pujols 10.00 25.00
AR Aaron Rowand 4.00 10.00
AS Alfonso Soriano 4.00 10.00
AT Garrett Atkins 4.00 10.00
BA Bobby Abreu 4.00 10.00
BC Bartolo Colon 4.00 10.00
BE Adrian Beltre 4.00 10.00
BG Brian Giles 4.00 10.00
BM Brian McCann/72 4.00 10.00
BS Ben Sheets/97 4.00 10.00
BU B.J. Upton 4.00 10.00
BW Billy Wagner 5.00 12.00
CA Chris Carpenter 4.00 10.00
CB Carlos Beltran 4.00 10.00
CC Chad Cordero 4.00 10.00
CD Carlos Delgado 4.00 10.00
CG Carlos Guillen 4.00 10.00
CH Chris Burke 4.00 10.00
CJ Chipper Jones 5.00 12.00
CK Casey Kotchman 4.00 10.00
CL Carlos Lee 4.00 10.00
CS Curt Schilling 4.00 10.00
CU Chase Utley 5.00 12.00
CZ Carlos Zambrano 4.00 10.00
DH Dan Haren 4.00 10.00
DJ Derek Jeter/76 15.00 40.00
DL Derrek Lee 4.00 10.00
DO David Ortiz 5.00 12.00
DU Dan Uggla 4.00 10.00
DW Dontrelle Willis 4.00 10.00
DY Jermaine Dye 4.00 10.00
EC Eric Chavez 4.00 10.00
FH Felix Hernandez 4.00 10.00
FL Francisco Liriano 4.00 10.00
GA Garret Anderson 4.00 10.00
GJ Geoff Jenkins 4.00 10.00
GM Greg Maddux 6.00 15.00
GO Alex Gordon 6.00 15.00
GR Curtis Granderson 4.00 10.00
GS Grady Sizemore 4.00 10.00
HA Cole Hamels 4.00 10.00
HB Hank Blalock 4.00 10.00
HE Todd Helton 4.00 10.00
HO Trevor Hoffman 4.00 10.00
HR Hanley Ramirez 4.00 10.00
HU Torii Hunter 4.00 10.00
IR Ivan Rodriguez 5.00 12.00
JA Conor Jackson/80 4.00 10.00
JB Josh Barfield 4.00 10.00
JD J.D. Drew 4.00 10.00
JE Jim Edmonds 5.00 12.00
JF Jeff Francoeur 5.00 12.00
JG Jason Giambi 4.00 10.00

JH Jhonny Peralta 4.00 10.00
JJ J.J. Hardy 4.00 10.00
JK Jeff Kent 4.00 10.00
JM Joe Mauer 4.00 10.00
JN Joe Nathan 4.00 10.00
JO Josh Beckett 5.00 12.00
JP Jake Peavy 4.00 10.00
JR Jose Reyes 4.00 10.00
JS Johan Santana 4.00 10.00
JT Jim Thome 4.00 10.00
JV Jason Varitek 5.00 12.00
KG Ken Griffey Jr. 6.00 15.00
KJ Kenji Johjima 4.00 10.00
KY Kevin Youkilis 5.00 12.00
LB Lance Berkman 4.00 10.00
LG Luis Gonzalez 4.00 10.00
MC Miguel Cabrera 4.00 10.00
MH Matt Holliday 4.00 10.00
MO Justin Morneau 4.00 10.00
MR Manny Ramirez 5.00 12.00
MT Mark Teixeira 4.00 10.00
MY Michael Young 4.00 10.00
OR Magglio Ordonez 4.00 10.00
PA Jonathan Papelbon 5.00 12.00
PE Andy Pettitte 4.00 10.00
PF Prince Fielder 5.00 12.00
PM Pedro Martinez 4.00 10.00
PO Jorge Posada 4.00 10.00
RA Aramis Ramirez 4.00 10.00
RF Rafael Furcal 4.00 10.00
RH Roy Halladay 4.00 10.00
RJ Randy Johnson 4.00 10.00
RO Roy Oswalt 4.00 10.00
SM John Smoltz 5.00 12.00
TE Miguel Tejada/83 4.00 10.00
TH Tim Hudson 4.00 10.00
TR Travis Hafner 4.00 10.00
VE Justin Verlander 4.00 10.00
VG Vladimir Guerrero 4.00 10.00
VW Vernon Wells 4.00 10.00

2008 SPx Winning Materials Limited Patch Team Initials

*LTD PATCH TI: .5X TO 1.2X LTD PATCH SPX
OVERALL GU ODDS SIX PER BOX
PRINT RUNS B/WN 40-50 COPIES PER

2008 SPx Winning Materials MLB 125

*MLB 125: .4X TO 1X WM SPX 150
OVERALL GU ODDS SIX PER BOX
STATED PRINT RUN 125 SER.#'d SETS
RF Rafael Furcal 3.00 8.00

2008 SPx Winning Materials Position 75

*POS 75: .4X TO 1X WM SPX 150
OVERALL GU ODDS SIX PER BOX
STATED PRINT RUN 75 SER.#'d SETS

2008 SPx Winning Materials SPx Die Cut 150

*SPX DC 150: .4X TO 1X SPX 150
OVERALL GU ODDS SIX PER BOX
STATED PRINT RUN 150 SER.#'d SETS

2008 SPx Winning Materials Team Initials 99

*TI 99: .4X TO 1X WM SPX 150
OVERALL GU ODDS SIX PER BOX
STATED PRINT RUN 99 SER.#'d SETS
KG Ken Griffey Jr. 5.00 12.00
RF Rafael Furcal 3.00 8.00

2008 SPx Winning Materials UD Logo

*LOGO 99: .4X TO 1X WM SPX 150
OVERALL GU ODDS SIX PER BOX
PRINT RUNS B/WN 26-99 COPIES PER
KG Ken Griffey Jr./26 8.00 20.00
RF Rafael Furcal 3.00 8.00

2008 SPx Winning Trios

OVERALL GU ODDS SIX PER BOX
STATED PRINT RUN 75 SER.#'d SETS
GOLD 25 PRINT RUN 25 SER.#'d SETS
NO GOLD 25 PRICING DUE TO SCARCITY
GOLD 15 PRINT RUN 15 SER.#'d SETS
NO GOLD 15 PRICING DUE TO SCARCITY
LTD.PATCH PRINT RUN 25 SER.#'d SETS
NO LTD.PATCH PRICING DUE TO SCARCITY
AGK Anderson/Vlad/Kotchman 4.00 10.00
BHJ Beltre/Hernandez/Johjima 4.00 10.00
BSS Beckett/Santana/Sabathia 4.00 10.00
CRP Carpenter/Rolen/Pujols 6.00 15.00
CRU Cabrera/Ramirez/Uggla 4.00 10.00
DBR Delgado/Beltran/Reyes 4.00 10.00
DOP Delgado/Papi/Pujols 8.00 20.00
GHL Gallardo/Hughes/Lincecum 6.00 15.00
GIB Gordon/Iwamura/Braun 20.00 50.00
GJP Griffey Jr./Jeter/Pujols 15.00 40.00
GMW Glavine/Pedro/Wagner 8.00 20.00
HAH Helton/Atkins/Holliday 5.00 12.00
HDF Hafner/Dunn/Fielder 5.00 12.00
HFB Hardy/Prince/Braun 8.00 20.00
HRR Hardy/Reyes/Ramirez 4.00 10.00
HSS Hafner/Siemore/Sabathia 4.00 10.00
JBH Jones/Beltran/Hunter 4.00 10.00
JDY Jackson/Drew/Young 4.00 10.00
JRR Jones/Rolen/Ramirez 5.00 12.00
JST Chipper/Smoltz/Teixeira 6.00 15.00
KFE Kent/Furcal/Ethier 5.00 12.00
KUY Kazmir/Upton/Young 4.00 10.00
LBO Lee/Berkamn/Oswalt 4.00 10.00
LCL Lowry/Cain/Lincecum 6.00 15.00
LSZ Lee/Soriano/Zambrano 6.00 15.00
MGS Maddux/Glavine/Smoltz 15.00 40.00
MHP Maddux/Hoffman/Peavy 6.00 15.00
MPB VMart/Peralta/Barfield 4.00 10.00
MSM Morneau/Santana/Mauer 5.00 12.00
OGV Ordonez/Grander/Verland 10.00 25.00
PJP Pettitte/Jeter/Posada 10.00 25.00
RJC ARod/Jeter/Cano 30.00 60.00
RMM IRod/VMart/Mauer 5.00 12.00
SBP Schilling/Beckett/Papelbon 6.00 15.00
SOH Sheets/Oswalt/Harang 4.00 10.00
SRG Sheffield/IRod/Guillen 6.00 15.00
TDB Thome/Dye/Buehrle 5.00 12.00
UHR Utley/Hamels/Rowand 6.00 15.00
UKU Utley/Insler/Uggla 4.00 10.00
VOY Varitek/Papi/Youkilis 12.50 30.00
WHB Wells/Halladay/Burnett 5.00 12.00
ZPH Zambrano/Peavy/Harang 4.00 10.00

2008 SPx Young Star Signatures

OVERALL AU ODDS FOUR PER BOX
EXCHANGE DEADLINE 4/28/2010
AC Alexi Casilla 3.00 8.00
AE Andre Ethier 3.00 8.00
BB Brian Bannister 4.00 10.00
BM Brian McCann 4.00 10.00
BU Brian Burres 4.00 10.00
CD Chris Duncan 6.00 15.00
CH Cole Hamels 8.00 20.00
CY Chris B. Young 5.00 12.00
FC Fausto Carmona 4.00 10.00
FL Francisco Liriano 4.00 10.00
IK Ian Kinsler 3.00 8.00
JA Joaquin Arias 3.00 8.00
JD John Danks 3.00 8.00
JJ Josh Johnson 5.00 12.00
JL James Loney 6.00 15.00
JS Jarrod Saltalamacchia 3.00 8.00
JV Justin Verlander 10.00 25.00
JW Josh Willingham 3.00 8.00
JZ Joel Zumaya 3.00 8.00
KK Kevin Kouzmanoff 3.00 8.00
MA Nick Markakis 8.00 20.00
MC Matt Chico 3.00 8.00
MF Mike Fontenot 5.00 12.00
MO Micah Owings 4.00 10.00
MR Mark Reynolds 5.00 12.00
NM Nate McLouth 3.00 8.00
PH Phil Hughes 3.00 8.00
RB Ryan Braun 5.00 12.00
RG Ryan Garko 3.00 8.00
RM Russell Martin 6.00 15.00
SD Stephen Drew 4.00 10.00
SH James Shields 5.00 12.00
TB Travis Buck 4.00 10.00
TG Tom Gorzelanny 3.00 8.00
TT Troy Tulowitzki 4.00 10.00

2009 SPx

COMP.SET w/o AU's (100) 12.50 30.00
COMMON CARD (1-100) .20 .50
COMMON AU RC (101-123) 4.00 10.00
OVERALL AUTO ODDS 1:18
AU RC PRINT RUN 99 SER.#'d SETS
1 Ichiro Suzuki .60 1.50
2 Rick Ankiel .20 .50
3 Garrett Atkins .20 .50
4 Jason Bay .30 .75
5 Josh Beckett .20 .50
6 Erik Bedard .20 .50
7 Carlos Beltran .30 .75
8 Lance Berkman .30 .75
9 Ryan Braun .30 .75
10 Jay Bruce .30 .75
11 Miguel Cabrera .50 1.25
12 Matt Cain .30 .75
13 Joba Chamberlain .20 .50
14 Carl Crawford .30 .75
15 Jack Cust .20 .50
16 Joe DiMaggio 1.00 2.50
17 Ryan Doumit .20 .50
18 Justin Duchscherer .20 .50
19 Adam Dunn .30 .75
20 Prince Fielder .30 .75
21 Kosuke Fukudome .30 .75
22 Troy Glaus .20 .50
23 Tom Glavine .30 .75
24 Adrian Gonzalez .40 1.00
25 Alex Gordon .30 .75
26 Zack Greinke .50 1.25
27 Ken Griffey Jr. 1.00 2.50
28 Vladimir Guerrero .30 .75
29 Travis Hafner .20 .50
30 Roy Halladay .30 .75
31 Cole Hamels .40 1.00
32 Josh Hamilton .30 .75
33 Rich Harden .20 .50
34 Dan Haren .20 .50
35 Felix Hernandez .30 .75
36 Trevor Hoffman .30 .75
37 Matt Holliday .50 1.25
38 Ryan Howard .40 1.00
39 Torii Hunter .20 .50
40 Derek Jeter 1.25 3.00
41 Randy Johnson .50 1.25
42 Chipper Jones .50 1.25
43 Scott Kazmir .20 .50
44 Matt Kemp .40 1.00
45 Clayton Kershaw .75 2.00
46 Ian Kinsler .30 .75
47 John Lackey .30 .75
48 Carlos Lee .20 .50
49 Derrek Lee .20 .50
50 Tim Lincecum .30 .75
51 Evan Longoria .30 .75
52 Nick Markakis .40 1.00
53 Russell Martin .20 .50
54 Victor Martinez .30 .75
55 Hideki Matsui .50 1.25
56 Daisuke Matsuzaka .30 .75
57 Joe Mauer .40 1.00
58 Brian McCann .30 .75
59 Nate McLouth .20 .50
60 Lastings Milledge .20 .50
61 Justin Morneau .30 .75
62 Magglio Ordonez .30 .75
63 David Ortiz .50 1.25
64 Roy Oswalt .30 .75
65 Jonathan Papelbon .30 .75
66 Jake Peavy .20 .50
67 Dustin Pedroia .50 1.25
68 Brandon Phillips .20 .50
69 Albert Pujols .60 1.50
70 Carlos Quentin .20 .50
71 Aramis Ramirez .20 .50
72 Hanley Ramirez .30 .75
73 Manny Ramirez .50 1.25
74 Jose Reyes .30 .75
75 Alex Rios .20 .50
76 Mariano Rivera .60 1.50
77 Brian Roberts .20 .50
78 Alex Rodriguez .60 1.50
79 Ivan Rodriguez .30 .75
80 Jimmy Rollins .30 .75
81 CC Sabathia .30 .75
82 Johan Santana .30 .75
83 Grady Sizemore .30 .75
84 John Smoltz .50 1.25
85 Alfonso Soriano .30 .75
86 Mark Teixeira .30 .75
87 Miguel Tejada .30 .75
88 Jim Thome .30 .75
89 Troy Tulowitzki .50 1.25
90 Dan Uggla .20 .50
91 B.J. Upton .30 .75
92 Chase Utley .30 .75
93 Edinson Volquez .20 .50
94 Chien-Ming Wang .30 .75
95 Brandon Webb .30 .75
96 Vernon Wells .20 .50
97 David Wright .40 1.00
98 Michael Young .20 .50
99 Carlos Zambrano .30 .75
100 Ryan Zimmerman .30 .75
101 David Price AU RC 20.00 50.00
102 A.Cunningham AU RC 12.50 30.00
103 A.Salome AU (RC) 10.00 25.00
104 C.Gillaspie AU RC 10.00 25.00
105 C.Lambert AU (RC) 8.00 20.00
106 D.Fowler AU (RC) 10.00 25.00
107 F.Cervelli AU RC EXCH 10.00 25.00
108 G.Golson AU (RC) 8.00 20.00
109 Josh Geer AU (RC) 4.00 10.00
110 J.Outman AU RC 4.00 10.00
111 James Parr AU (RC) 8.00 20.00
112 K.Ka'aihue AU (RC) 6.00 15.00
113 Luis Cruz AU RC 10.00 25.00
114 L.Marson AU (RC) 15.00 40.00
115 M.Antonelli AU RC 4.00 10.00
116 M.Bowden AU (RC) 4.00 10.00
117 Mat Gamel AU RC 15.00 40.00
118 Tuiasosopo AU (RC) 15.00 40.00
119 Phil Coke AU RC 12.50 30.00
120 J.McDonald AU RC 10.00 25.00
121 S.Martis AU RC EXCH 4.00 10.00
122 Travis Snider AU RC 8.00 20.00
123 Wade LeBlanc AU RC 4.00 10.00
124 Matt Wieters AU RC 15.00 40.00
125 Colby Rasmus AU (RC) 4.00 10.00
126 Josh Reddick AU RC 4.00 10.00
127 Mat Latos AU RC 4.00 10.00
128 A.McCutchen AU (RC) 50.00 120.00
129 Chris Tillman AU RC 6.00 15.00
130 Koji Uehara AU RC 20.00 50.00

2009 SPx Flashback Fabrics

OVERALL MEM ODDS 4 PER BOX
FFAG Adrian Gonzalez 3.00 8.00
FFAJ Andruw Jones 3.00 8.00
FFAP Andy Pettitte 3.00 8.00
FFBA Bobby Abreu 3.00 8.00
FFCC Coco Crisp 3.00 8.00
FFCD Carlos Delgado 3.00 8.00
FFCL Carlos Lee 3.00 8.00
FFCS Curt Schilling 3.00 8.00
FFDA Johnny Damon 3.00 8.00
FFFT Frank Thomas 4.00 10.00
FFGJ Geoff Jenkins 3.00 8.00
FFIR Ivan Rodriguez 4.00 10.00
FFJE Jim Edmonds 3.00 8.00
FFJV Jose Valverde 3.00 8.00
FFKM Kevin Millwood 3.00 8.00
FFLG Luis Gonzalez Pants 3.00 8.00
FFMA Moises Alou 3.00 8.00
FFMG Magglio Ordonez 3.00 8.00
FFMR Manny Ramirez 5.00 12.00
FFMT Mark Teixeira 4.00 10.00
FFOC Orlando Cabrera 3.00 8.00
FFPM Pedro Martinez 3.00 8.00
FFRJ Randy Johnson Pants 3.00 8.00
FFSR Scott Rolen 3.00 8.00
FFVG Vladimir Guerrero 3.00 8.00

2009 SPx Game Jersey

OVERALL MEM ODDS 4 PER BOX
GJBU B.J. Upton 3.00 8.00
GJCZ Carlos Zambrano 3.00 8.00
GJDJ Derek Jeter 10.00 25.00
GJDL Derrek Lee 3.00 8.00
GJDO David Ortiz 3.00 8.00
GJFL Francisco Liriano 3.00 8.00
GJGJ Geoff Jenkins 3.00 8.00
GJHR Hanley Ramirez 3.00 8.00
GJJD Jermaine Dye 3.00 8.00
GJJL John Lackey 3.00 8.00
GJJS John Smoltz 3.00 8.00
GJJT Jim Thome 3.00 8.00
GJJV Justin Verlander 3.00 8.00
GJKF Kosuke Fukudome 4.00 10.00
GJKW Kerry Wood 3.00 8.00
GJMR Manny Ramirez 3.00 8.00
GJMT Miguel Tejada 3.00 8.00
GJRH Roy Halladay 3.00 8.00
GJSA Johan Santana 3.00 8.00
GJTH Travis Hafner 3.00 8.00
GJTT Troy Tulowitzki 3.00 8.00

2009 SPx Game Jersey Autographs

OVERALL AUTO ODDS 1:18
GJAAE Andre Ethier 8.00 20.00
GJAAK Austin Kearns 4.00 10.00
GJAAL Adam LaRoche 4.00 10.00
GJAAM Andrew Miller 10.00 25.00
GJAAR Aaron Rowand 8.00 20.00
GJAAX Alex Romero 4.00 10.00
GJABA Brian Barton 4.00 10.00
GJABC Bobby Crosby 4.00 10.00
GJABE Josh Beckett 15.00 40.00
GJABG Brian Giles 4.00 10.00
GJABH Bill Hall 4.00 10.00
GJABM Brian McCann 5.00 12.00
GJABP Brandon Phillips 6.00 15.00
GJABR Brian Roberts 15.00 40.00
GJABW Brandon Webb 10.00 25.00
GJACB Chad Billingsley 8.00 20.00
GJACC Chris Carpenter 10.00 25.00
GJACD Chris Duncan 10.00 25.00
GJACF Chone Figgins 6.00 15.00
GJACH Cole Hamels 30.00 60.00
GJACJ Chipper Jones 50.00 100.00
GJACL Clay Buchholz 10.00 25.00
GJACR Coco Crisp 8.00 20.00
GJADL Derrek Lee 10.00 25.00
GJADS Denard Span 10.00 25.00
GJADU Dan Uggla 5.00 12.00
GJAEC Eric Chavez 4.00 10.00
GJAEM Evan Meek 4.00 10.00
GJAEV Edinson Volquez 6.00 15.00
GJAFC Fausto Carmona 4.00 10.00
GJAFH Felix Hernandez 12.50 30.00
GJAFL Francisco Liriano 5.00 12.00
GJAFP Felix Pie 4.00 10.00
GJAFT Frank Thomas 40.00 80.00
GJAGJ Geoff Jenkins 4.00 10.00
GJAHA Craig Hansen 4.00 10.00
GJAHC Hong-Chih Kuo 10.00 25.00
GJAHK Howie Kendrick 5.00 12.00
GJAHR Hanley Ramirez 8.00 20.00
GJAIK Ian Kinsler 10.00 25.00
GJAJB Jason Bay 10.00 25.00
GJAJC Johnny Cueto 6.00 15.00
GJAJH Jeremy Hermida 4.00 10.00
GJAJJ Josh Johnson 6.00 15.00
GJAJL John Lackey 5.00 12.00
GJAJN Joe Nathan 8.00 20.00
GJAJP Jonathan Papelbon 4.00 10.00
GJAJR J.R. Towles 4.00 10.00
GJAJV Joey Votto 15.00 40.00
GJAJZ Joel Zumaya 4.00 10.00
GJALA Andy LaRoche 4.00 10.00
GJALE Jon Lester 15.00 40.00
GJALS Luke Scott 4.00 10.00
GJAML Mark Loretta 4.00 10.00
GJAMO Justin Morneau 8.00 20.00
GJANS Nick Swisher 6.00 15.00
GJAPF Prince Fielder 12.50 30.00
GJAPH Phil Hughes 8.00 20.00
GJARA Aramis Ramirez 6.00 15.00
GJARH Ramon Hernandez 8.00 20.00
GJASD Stephen Drew 8.00 20.00
GJATH Travis Hafner 4.00 10.00
GJATT Troy Tulowitzki 8.00 20.00
GJAVE Justin Verlander 15.00 40.00
GJAVM Victor Martinez 5.00 12.00
GJAWI Josh Willingham 4.00 10.00
GJAZG Zack Greinke 12.50 30.00

2009 SPx Game Patch

OVERALL MEM ODDS 4 PER BOX
PRINT RUNS B/WN 50-99 COPIES PER
PRICING FOR 1-2 COLOR PATCHES
GJBU B.J. Upton 5.00 12.00
GJCZ Carlos Zambrano 6.00 15.00
GJDJ Derek Jeter/50 30.00 60.00
GJDL Derrek Lee 6.00 15.00
GJDO David Ortiz 5.00 12.00
GJFL Francisco Liriano 6.00 15.00
GJGJ Geoff Jenkins 5.00 12.00
GJHR Hanley Ramirez 6.00 15.00
GJJD Jermaine Dye 5.00 12.00
GJJL John Lackey 5.00 12.00
GJJS John Smoltz 8.00 20.00
GJJT Jim Thome 5.00 12.00
GJJV Justin Verlander 5.00 12.00
GJKF Kosuke Fukudome 8.00 20.00
GJKW Kerry Wood 5.00 12.00
GJMR Manny Ramirez 6.00 15.00
GJMT Miguel Tejada 5.00 12.00
GJRH Roy Halladay 6.00 15.00
GJSA Johan Santana 6.00 15.00
GJTH Travis Hafner 5.00 12.00
GJTT Troy Tulowitzki 5.00 12.00

2009 SPx Joe DiMaggio Career Highlights

COMMON DIMAGGIO (1-100) 3.00 8.00
STATED PRINT RUN 425 SER.#'d SETS
JD1 Joe DiMaggio 2.50 6.00
JD2 Joe DiMaggio 2.50 6.00
JD3 Joe DiMaggio 2.50 6.00
JD4 Joe DiMaggio 2.50 6.00
JD5 Joe DiMaggio 2.50 6.00
JD6 Joe DiMaggio 2.50 6.00
JD7 Joe DiMaggio 2.50 6.00
JD8 Joe DiMaggio 2.50 6.00
JD9 Joe DiMaggio 2.50 6.00
JD10 Joe DiMaggio 2.50 6.00
JD11 Joe DiMaggio 2.50 6.00
JD12 Joe DiMaggio 2.50 6.00
JD13 Joe DiMaggio 2.50 6.00
JD14 Joe DiMaggio 2.50 6.00
JD15 Joe DiMaggio 2.50 6.00
JD16 Joe DiMaggio 2.50 6.00
JD17 Joe DiMaggio 2.50 6.00
JD18 Joe DiMaggio 2.50 6.00
JD19 Joe DiMaggio 2.50 6.00
JD20 Joe DiMaggio 2.50 6.00
JD21 Joe DiMaggio 2.50 6.00
JD22 Joe DiMaggio 2.50 6.00
JD23 Joe DiMaggio 2.50 6.00
JD24 Joe DiMaggio 2.50 6.00
JD25 Joe DiMaggio 2.50 6.00
JD26 Joe DiMaggio 2.50 6.00
JD27 Joe DiMaggio 2.50 6.00
JD28 Joe DiMaggio 2.50 6.00
JD29 Joe DiMaggio 2.50 6.00
JD30 Joe DiMaggio 2.50 6.00
JD31 Joe DiMaggio 2.50 6.00
JD32 Joe DiMaggio 2.50 6.00
JD33 Joe DiMaggio 2.50 6.00
JD34 Joe DiMaggio 2.50 6.00
JD35 Joe DiMaggio 2.50 6.00
JD36 Joe DiMaggio 2.50 6.00
JD37 Joe DiMaggio 2.50 6.00
JD38 Joe DiMaggio 2.50 6.00
JD39 Joe DiMaggio 2.50 6.00
JD40 Joe DiMaggio 2.50 6.00
JD41 Joe DiMaggio 2.50 6.00
JD42 Joe DiMaggio 2.50 6.00
JD43 Joe DiMaggio 2.50 6.00
JD44 Joe DiMaggio 2.50 6.00
JD45 Joe DiMaggio 2.50 6.00
JD46 Joe DiMaggio 2.50 6.00
JD47 Joe DiMaggio 2.50 6.00
JD48 Joe DiMaggio 2.50 6.00
JD49 Joe DiMaggio 2.50 6.00
JD50 Joe DiMaggio 2.50 6.00
JD51 Joe DiMaggio 2.50 6.00
JD52 Joe DiMaggio 2.50 6.00
JD53 Joe DiMaggio 2.50 6.00
JD54 Joe DiMaggio 2.50 6.00
JD55 Joe DiMaggio 2.50 6.00
JD56 Joe DiMaggio 2.50 6.00
JD57 Joe DiMaggio 2.50 6.00
JD58 Joe DiMaggio 2.50 6.00
JD59 Joe DiMaggio 2.50 6.00
JD60 Joe DiMaggio 2.50 6.00
JD61 Joe DiMaggio 2.50 6.00
JD62 Joe DiMaggio 2.50 6.00
JD63 Joe DiMaggio 2.50 6.00
JD64 Joe DiMaggio 2.50 6.00
JD65 Joe DiMaggio 2.50 6.00
JD66 Joe DiMaggio 2.50 6.00
JD67 Joe DiMaggio 2.50 6.00
JD68 Joe DiMaggio 2.50 6.00
JD69 Joe DiMaggio 2.50 6.00
JD70 Joe DiMaggio 2.50 6.00
JD71 Joe DiMaggio 2.50 6.00
JD72 Joe DiMaggio 2.50 6.00
JD73 Joe DiMaggio 2.50 6.00
JD74 Joe DiMaggio 2.50 6.00
JD75 Joe DiMaggio 2.50 6.00
JD76 Joe DiMaggio 2.50 6.00
JD77 Joe DiMaggio 2.50 6.00
JD78 Joe DiMaggio 2.50 6.00
JD79 Joe DiMaggio 2.50 6.00
JD80 Joe DiMaggio 2.50 6.00
JD81 Joe DiMaggio 2.50 6.00
JD82 Joe DiMaggio 2.50 6.00
JD83 Joe DiMaggio 2.50 6.00
JD84 Joe DiMaggio 2.50 6.00
JD85 Joe DiMaggio 2.50 6.00
JD86 Joe DiMaggio 2.50 6.00
JD87 Joe DiMaggio 2.50 6.00
JD88 Joe DiMaggio 2.50 6.00
JD89 Joe DiMaggio 2.50 6.00
JD90 Joe DiMaggio 2.50 6.00
JD91 Joe DiMaggio 2.50 6.00
JD92 Joe DiMaggio 2.50 6.00
JD93 Joe DiMaggio 2.50 6.00
JD94 Joe DiMaggio 2.50 6.00
JD95 Joe DiMaggio 2.50 6.00
JD96 Joe DiMaggio 2.50 6.00
JD97 Joe DiMaggio 2.50 6.00
JD98 Joe DiMaggio 2.50 6.00
JD99 Joe DiMaggio 2.50 6.00
JD100 Joe DiMaggio 2.50 6.00

2009 SPx Mystery Rookie Redemption

RANDOM INSERTS IN PACKS
EXCHANGE DEADLINE 6/30/2011
NNO EXCH Card 20.00 50.00

2009 SPx Winning Materials

OVERALL MEM ODDS 4 PER BOX
WMAS Alfonso Soriano 3.00 8.00
WMCJ Chipper Jones 4.00 10.00
WMCW Chien-Ming Wang 4.00 10.00
WMDJ Derek Jeter 6.00 15.00
WMDM Daisuke Matsuzaka 6.00 15.00
WMJB Josh Beckett 3.00 8.00
WMJM Justin Morneau 3.00 8.00
WMJP Jake Peavy 3.00 8.00
WMJR Jose Reyes 3.00 8.00
WMLB Lance Berkman 3.00 8.00
WMMC Miguel Cabrera 3.00 8.00
WMMH Matt Holliday 3.00 8.00
WMMR Mariano Rivera 6.00 15.00
WMMT Mark Teixeira 4.00 10.00
WMPF Prince Fielder 3.00 8.00
WMRA Manny Ramirez 3.00 8.00
WMRB Ryan Braun 4.00 10.00
WMRL Ryan Ludwick 4.00 10.00
WMSK Scott Kazmir 3.00 8.00
WMTL Tim Lincecum 5.00 12.00

2009 SPx Winning Materials Patch

OVERALL MEM ODDS 4 PER BOX
PRINT RUNS B/WN 59-99 COPIES PER
PRICING FOR 1-2 COLOR PATCHES
WMAS Alfonso Soriano 6.00 15.00
WMCJ Chipper Jones 10.00 25.00
WMCW Chien-Ming Wang 8.00 20.00
WMDJ Derek Jeter 20.00 50.00
WMJB Josh Beckett 6.00 15.00
WMJM Justin Morneau 5.00 12.00
WMJP Jake Peavy 5.00 12.00
WMJR Jose Reyes 10.00 25.00
WMLB Lance Berkman 5.00 12.00
WMMC Miguel Cabrera 5.00 12.00
WMMH Matt Holliday 5.00 12.00
WMMR Mariano Rivera 12.50 30.00
WMMT Mark Teixeira 5.00 12.00
WMPF Prince Fielder 5.00 12.00
WMRA Manny Ramirez 6.00 15.00
WMRB Ryan Braun/59 10.00 25.00
WMRL Ryan Ludwick 6.00 15.00
WMSK Scott Kazmir 5.00 12.00
WMTL Tim Lincecum 6.00 15.00

2009 SPx Winning Materials Dual

OVERALL MEM ODDS 4 PER BOX
BH A.Burnett/R.Halladay 3.00 8.00
GE K.Griffey/J.Edmonds 5.00 12.00
GR K.Greene/J.Reyes 4.00 10.00
GS R.Sexson/J.Giambi 3.00 8.00
HB J.Baker/M.Holliday 3.00 8.00
JD J.DiMaggio/D.Jeter 40.00 80.00
JY R.Johnson/C.Young 4.00 10.00
KT P.Konerko/J.Thome 3.00 8.00
LL A.LaRoche/A.LaRoche 3.00 8.00
ML Matsuzaka/Lincecum 5.00 12.00
PS J.Peavy/C.Sabathia 4.00 10.00
RB J.Bay/M.Ramirez 4.00 10.00
RO D.Ortiz/M.Ramirez 4.00 10.00
RP Papelbon/M.Rivera 4.00 10.00

2009 SPx Winning Materials Quad

OVERALL MEM ODDS 4 PER BOX
BDBM Braun/Duncan/Bald/Markakis 8.00 20.00
BUUB Ryan Braun/Dan Uggla/Chase Utley
Lance Berkman 4.00 10.00
DJCP DiMaggio/Jeter/Cano/Posada 30.00 60.00
DTGS Dye/Thome/Grif/Swisher 5.00 12.00
HFBS Hardy/Prince/Hall/Sheets 5.00 12.00
HHBN Matt Holliday/Todd Helton
Jeff Baker/Jayson Nix 4.00 10.00
HRBB Matt Holliday/Manny Ramirez
Pat Burrell/Ryan Braun 4.00 10.00
HRNB Trevor Hoffman/Mariano Rivera/Joe
Nathan/Brad Lidge 4.00 10.00
HSLC Trevor Hoffman/Takashi Saito
Brad Lidge/Chad Cordero 4.00 10.00
JTJF Chipper/Teix/Andruw/Furcal 6.00 15.00
KFSK Matt Kemp/Rafael Furcal
Takashi Saito/Hong-Chih Kuo 4.00 10.00
MMPV Brian McCann/Joe Mauer
Jorge Posada/Jason Varitek 4.00 10.00
OEYV Papi/Ellsbury/Youkilis/Varitek 10.00 25.00
OGDF David Ortiz/Jason Giambi/Carlos
Delgado/Prince Fielder 4.00 10.00
OGTS David Ortiz/Jason Giambi/Jim Thome/Gary
Sheffield 4.00 10.00
PCLZ Pujols/Carp/D.Lee/Zambrano 8.00 20.00
PLKL Peavy/Lince/Kazmir/Liriano 8.00 20.00
PMSL Papel/DiceK/Schilling/Lester 20.00 50.00
PRMV Posada/Pudge/Mauer/Varitek 5.00 12.00
RGBN Manny/Grif/Bay/Nady 5.00 12.00
RLZW Aramis/D.Lee/Zambrano/Wood 6.00 15.00
RRTD Reyes/Hanley/Tulo/S.Drew 6.00 15.00
RUJC Hanley/Uggla/Jeter/Cano 10.00 25.00
SZCO Ben Sheets/Carlos Zambrano/Chris
Carpenter/Roy Oswalt 4.00 10.00
UPRI Utley/Phillips/Roberts/Iwamura 5.00 12.00
VGSZ Verland/Grand/Shef/Zumaya 6.00 15.00

2009 SPx Winning Materials Triple

OVERALL MEM ODDS 4 PER BOX
AKD Garrett Atkins 4.00 10.00
Kevin Kouzmanoff
Blake DeWitt
BCM Brian Barton 4.00 10.00
Chris Carpenter
Mark Mulder
CGV Cabrera/Grand/Verlander 8.00 20.00
DOF Jermaine Dye 4.00 10.00
Magglio Ordonez
Jeff Francoeur
FJH Prince Fielder 4.00 10.00
J.J. Hardy
Bill Hall
KCM Paul Konerko 4.00 10.00
Miguel Cabrera
Justin Morneau
KIB Scott Kazmir 4.00 10.00
Akinori Iwamura
Rocco Baldelli
KSB Jeff Kent 4.00 10.00
Freddy Sanchez
Josh Barfield
KSK Kuroda/Saito/Kuo 6.00 15.00
MBK Kevin Millwood 4.00 10.00
Hank Blalock
Ian Kinsler
MLY Mauer/Liriano/Delmon 6.00 15.00
NLB Joe Nathan 4.00 10.00
Francisco Liriano
Scott Baker
PCS Jonathan Papelbon 4.00 10.00
Chad Cordero
Joakim Soria
PJG Andy Pettitte 4.00 10.00
Randy Johnson
Tom Glavine
PKD Penny/Kent/DeWitt 5.00 12.00
RBE Manny/Bay/Ellsbury 6.00 15.00
RMD Manny/Pedro/Damon 8.00 20.00
SBM Schilling/Beckett/Matsuzaka 5.00 12.00
TCB Thomas/Crosby/Buck 10.00 25.00
TGB Teahen/Greinke/Butler 5.00 12.00
WNP Kerry Wood 4.00 10.00
Joe Nathan
Jonathan Papelbon

1981 Squirt

The cards in this 22-panel set consist of 33 different individual cards, each measuring the standard-size. The set was also available as two-card panels measuring approximately 2 1/2" by 10 1/2". Cards numbered 1-11 appear twice, whereas cards 12-33 appear only once in the 22-panel set. The pattern for pairings was 1/12 and 1/23, 2/13 and 2/24, 3/14 and 3/25, and so forth on up to 11/22 and 11/33. Two card panels have a value equal to the sum of the individual cards on the panel. Supposedly panels 4/15, 4/26, 5/27, and 6/28 are more difficult to find than the other panels and are marked as SP in the checklist below.

COMPLETE PANEL SET 10.00 20.00
COMPLETE IND. SET 5.00 12.00
COMMON PANEL .20 .50
COMMON CARD (1-11) DP .10 .25
COMMON CARD (12-33) .10 .25
COMMON SP .30 .75
COMMON DP .10 .25
1 George Brett DP 1.00 2.50
2 George Foster DP .15 .40
3 Ben Oglivie DP .08 .25
4 Steve Garvey DP .20 .50
5 Reggie Jackson DP .25 .60
6 Bill Buckner DP .15 .40
7 Jim Rice DP .15 .40
8 Mike Schmidt DP .60 1.50
9 Rod Carew DP .25 .60
10 Dave Parker DP .15 .40
11 Pete Rose DP .60 1.50
12 Garry Templeton .08 .25
13 Rick Burleson .08 .25
14 Dave Kingman .15 .40
15 Eddie Murray SP 2.50 6.00
16 Don Sutton .30 .75
17 Dusty Baker .15 .40
18 Jack Clark .08 .25
19 Dave Winfield .40 1.00
20 Johnny Bench .50 1.25
21 Lee Mazzilli .08 .25
22 Al Oliver .15 .40
23 Jerry Mumphrey .08 .25
24 Tony Armas .08 .25
25 Fred Lynn .15 .40
26 Ron LeFlore SP .30 .75
27 Steve Kemp SP .30 .75
28 Rickey Henderson SP 4.00 10.00
29 John Castino .08 .25
30 Cecil Cooper .08 .25
31 Bruce Bochte .08 .25
32 Joe Charboneau .15 .40
33 Chet Lemon .08 .25

1982 Squirt

The cards in this 22-card set measure the standard size. Although the 1982 "Exclusive Limited Edition" was prepared for Squirt by Topps, the format and pictures are completely different from the regular Topps cards of this year. Each color picture is obliquely cut and the word Squirt is printed in red in the top left corner. The cards are numbered 1 through 22 and the reverses are yellow and black on white. The cards were issued on four types of panels: (1) yellow attachment card at top with picture card in center and scratch-off game at bottom; (2) yellow attachment card at top with scratch-off game in center and picture card at bottom; (3) white attachment card at top with "Collect all 22" panel in center and picture card at bottom; (4) two card panel with attachment card at top. The two card panels have parallel cards; that is, numbers 1 and 12 together, numbers 2 and 13 together, etc. Two card panels have a value equal to the sum of the individual cards on the panel. The two types (1 and 2) with the scratch-off games are more slightly difficult to obtain than the other two types and hence command prices double those below.

COMPLETE SET (22) 5.00 12.00
1 Cecil Cooper .15 .40
2 Jerry Remy .08 .25
3 George Brett 1.00 2.50
4 Alan Trammell .20 .50
5 Reggie Jackson .40 1.00
6 Kirk Gibson .20 .50
7 Dave Winfield .40 1.00
8 Carlton Fisk .50 1.25
9 Ron Guidry .15 .40
10 Dennis Leonard .08 .25
11 Rollie Fingers .40 1.00
12 Pete Rose .50 1.25
13 Phil Garner .15 .40
14 Mike Schmidt .50 1.25
15 Dave Concepcion .15 .40
16 George Hendrick .08 .25
17 Andre Dawson .30 .75
18 George Foster .15 .40
19 Gary Carter .40 1.00
20 Fernando Valenzuela .15 .40
21 Tom Seaver .40 1.00
22 Bruce Sutter .30 .75

1975 SSPC 18

This 18-card promo standard-size set was released the year before the 1976 SSPC 630-card set. Like the 1976 "Pure Card" set, the cards feature white-bordered color player photos on their otherwise plain fronts. The back carries the player's position, team, and biography in red lettering at the upper right. The player's uniform number appears in red within a black-lettered circle formed by the words "Sample Card 1976" at the upper left. Shown below are the player's full name and his career highlights in black lettering. The card number appears on the back at the bottom, as does the copyright date, 1975. These cards were also included as inserts in the Winter 1975 issue of Collectors Quarterly.

COMPLETE SET (18) 8.00 20.00
1 Harry Parker .25 .60
2 Jim Bibby .25 .60
3 Mike Wallace .25 .60
4 Tony Muser .25 .60
5 Yogi Berra MG 3.00 8.00
6 Preston Gomez MG .25 .60
7 Jack McKeon MG .25 .60
8 Sam McDowell .50 1.25
9 Gaylord Perry 2.50 6.00
10 Fred Scherman .25 .60
11 Willie Davis .25 .60
12 Don Hopkins .25 .60
13 Whitey Herzog MG .50 1.25
14 Ray Sadecki .25 .60
15 Stan Bahnsen .25 .60
16 Bob Oliver .25 .60
17 Denny Doyle .25 .60
18 Deron Johnson .25 .60

1975 SSPC 42

This 42-card standard-size set features posed color player photos with white borders. The horizontal backs are plain white card stock and carry the player's name, biographical information, career highlights, and statistics.

COMPLETE SET (42) 40.00 80.00
1 Wilbur Wood .25 .60
2 Johnny Sain CO .50 1.25
3 Bill Melton .25 .60
4 Dick Allen .75 2.00
5 Jim Palmer 2.50 6.00
6 Brooks Robinson 3.00 8.00
7 Tommy Davis .50 1.25
8 Frank Robinson MG 2.50 6.00
9 Vada Pinson .50 1.25
10 Nolan Ryan 12.50 30.00
11 Reggie Jackson 4.00 10.00
12 Vida Blue .50 1.25
13 Sal Bando .50 1.25
14 Bert Campaneris .50 1.25
15 Tom Seaver 3.00 8.00
16 Bud Harrelson .50 1.25
17 Jerry Koosman .50 1.25
18 David Nelson .25 .60
19 Ted Williams 5.00 12.00
20 Tony Oliva .75 2.00
21 Mickey Lolich .50 1.25
22 Amos Otis .25 .60
23 Carl Yastrzemski 2.50 6.00
24 Mike Cuellar .50 1.25
25 Doc Medich .25 .60
26 Cesar Cedeno .25 .60
27 Jeff Burroughs .50 1.25
28 Sparky Lyle and Ted Williams 2.50 6.00
29 Johnny Bench 3.00 8.00
30 Gaylord Perry 2.00 5.00

Card	Low	High
31 John Mayberry	.25	.60
32 Rod Carew	2.50	6.00
33 Whitey Ford CO	2.50	6.00
34 Al Kaline	2.50	6.00
35 Willie Mays CO	5.00	12.00
36 Warren Spahn	2.50	6.00
37 Mickey Mantle	10.00	25.00
38 Norm Cash	.75	2.00
39 Steve Busby	.25	.60
40 Yogi Berra MG	2.50	6.00
41 Harvey Kuenn CO	.25	.60
42 The Alou Brothers	.50	1.25
Felipe Alou		
Matty Alou		
Jesus		

1975 SSPC Puzzle Back

The 24 cards in this set measure approximately 3 1/2" by 4 1/4" and feature posed color player photos with white borders on the front. The player's name, position, and team are printed at the bottom. The backs are the pieces of a puzzle that shows a 17" by 21" black-and-white photo of Nolan Ryan and Catfish Hunter. When the puzzle is assembled, the player's names appear at the bottom. The name and address of Sports Stars Publishing Company is printed around the left, top, and right edges. The cards are unnumbered and checklisted below in alphabetical order.

Card	Low	High
COMPLETE SET (24)	12.50	30.00
1 Hank Aaron	2.50	6.00
2 Johnny Bench	1.25	3.00
3 Bobby Bonds	.40	1.00
4 Jeff Burroughs	.10	.25
5 Rod Carew	.75	2.00
6 Dave Cash	.10	.25
7 Cesar Cedeno	.10	.25
8 Bucky Dent	.40	1.00
9 Rollie Fingers	.60	1.50
10 Steve Garvey	.40	1.00
11 John Grubb	.10	.25
12 Reggie Jackson	2.00	5.00
13 Jim Kaat	.40	1.00
14 Greg Luzinski	.20	.50
15 Fred Lynn	.40	1.00
16 Bill Madlock	.20	.50
17 Andy Messersmith	.10	.25
18 Thurman Munson	.75	2.00
19 Jim Palmer	1.00	2.50
20 Dave Parker	.60	1.50
21 Jim Rice	.40	1.00
22 Pete Rose	1.25	3.00
23 Tom Seaver	1.25	3.00
24 Chris Speier	.10	.25

1975 SSPC Samples

This six-card standard-size set features posed color player photos with white borders. The backs are white card stock and have either a horizontal or vertical format. Each card carries the player's name, biographical information, and career highlights. The horizontal backs also carry statistics. The cards are unnumbered, and checklisted below in alphabetical order.

Card	Low	High
COMPLETE SET (6)	12.50	30.00
1 Hank Aaron	4.00	10.00
2 Catfish Hunter	1.25	3.00
3 Dave Kingman	.50	1.25
4 Mickey Mantle	8.00	20.00
5 Willie Mays	4.00	10.00
6 Tom Seaver	2.50	6.00

1976 SSPC Promos

These standard-size cards were issued by SSPC/TCMA to promote their first (and would prove to be their only) major set. These cards feature the photos used in the 1975 SSPC Samples set on the front. The only difference between this set and the 1975 SSPC Samples set are the card backs. There might be additions to this checklist so any additional information would be appreciated. These cards are not numbered, so we have sequenced them in alphabetical order.

Card	Low	High
COMPLETE SET	12.50	30.00
1 Hank Aaron	6.00	15.00
2 Jim Hunter	6.00	15.00
3 Dave Kingman	6.00	15.00
4 Mickey Mantle	8.00	20.00
5 Willie Mays	6.00	15.00
6 Tom Seaver	6.00	15.00

1976 SSPC

The cards in this 630-card set measure 2 1/2" by 3 1/2". The 1976 "Pure Card" set issued by TCMA derives its name from the lack of borders, logos, signatures, etc., which often clutter up the picture areas of some baseball sets. It differs from other sets produced by this company in that it cannot be re-issued due to an agreement entered into by the manufacturer. Thus, while not technically a legitimate issue, it is significant because it cannot be reprinted, unlike other collector issues. The cards are numbered in team groups, i.e., Atlanta (1-21), Cincinnati (22-46), Houston (47-65), Los Angeles (66-91), San Francisco (92-113), San Diego (114-133), Chicago White Sox (134-158), Kansas City (159-185), California (186-204), Minnesota (205-225), Milwaukee (226-251), Texas (252-273), St. Louis (274-300), Chicago Cubs (301-321), Montreal (322-351), Detroit (352-373), Baltimore (374-401), Boston (402-424), New York Yankees (425-455), Philadelphia (456-477), Oakland (478-503), Cleveland (504-532), New York Mets (533-560), and Pittsburgh (561-586). The rest of the numbers are filled in with checklists (589-595), miscellaneous players, and a heavy dose of coaches. There are a few instances in the set where the team identified on the back is different from the team shown on the front due to trades made after the completion of the 1975 season. The set features rookie year cards of Dennis Eckersley and Willie Randolph as well as early cards of George Brett, Gary Carter, and Robin Yount. The card backs were edited by Keith Olbermann, prior to his network broadcasting days. Although some of these cards were copyrighted in 1975, they were not released until spring of 1976 and have always been considered cards from 1976 within the hobby. These cards were originally available directly from SSPC for $10.99 per set.

Card	Low	High
COMPLETE SET (630)	40.00	80.00
1 Buzz Capra	.08	.20
2 Tom House	.08	.20
3 Max Leon	.08	.20
4 Carl Morton	.08	.20
5 Phil Niekro	1.50	4.00
6 Mike Thompson	.08	.20
7 Elias Sosa	.08	.20
8 Larvell Blanks	.08	.20
9 Darrell Evans	.08	.20
10 Rod Gilbreath	.08	.20
11 Mike Lum	.08	.20
12 Craig Robinson	.08	.20
13 Earl Williams	.08	.20
14 Vic Correll	.08	.20
15 Biff Pocoroba	.08	.20
16 Dusty Baker	.12	.30
17 Ralph Garr	.08	.20
18 Cito Gaston	.08	.20
19 Dave May	.08	.20
20 Rowland Office	.08	.20
21 Bob Beall	.08	.20
22 Sparky Anderson MG	.30	.75
23 Jack Billingham	.08	.20
24 Pedro Borbon	.08	.20
25 Clay Carroll	.08	.20
26 Pat Darcy	.08	.20
27 Don Gullett	.08	.20
28 Clay Kirby	.08	.20
29 Gary Nolan	.08	.20
30 Fred Norman	.08	.20
31 Johnny Bench	2.50	6.00
32 Bill Plummer	.08	.20
33 Darrel Chaney	.08	.20
34 Dave Concepcion	.12	.30
35 Terry Crowley	.08	.20
36 Dan Driessen	.08	.20
37 Doug Flynn	.08	.20
38 Joe Morgan	1.25	3.00
39 Tony Perez	1.00	2.50
40 Ken Griffey	.40	1.00
41 Pete Rose	3.00	8.00
42 Ed Armbrister	.08	.20
43 John Vukovich	.08	.20
44 George Foster	.20	.50
45 Cesar Geronimo	.08	.20
46 Merv Rettenmund	.08	.20
47 Jim Crawford	.08	.20
48 Ken Forsch	.08	.20
49 Doug Konieczny	.08	.20
50 Joe Niekro	.08	.20
51 Cliff Johnson	.08	.20
52 Skip Jutze	.08	.20
53 Milt May	.08	.20
54 Rob Andrews	.08	.20
55 Ken Boswell	.08	.20
56 Tommy Helms	.08	.20
57 Roger Metzger	.08	.20
58 Larry Milbourne	.08	.20
59 Doug Rader	.08	.20
60 Bob Watson	.12	.30
61 Enos Cabell	.08	.20
62 Jose Cruz	.08	.20
63 Cesar Cedeno	.08	.20
64 Greg Gross	.08	.20
65 Wilbur Howard	.08	.20
66 Al Downing	.08	.20
67 Burt Hooton	.08	.20
68 Charlie Hough	.12	.30
69 Tommy John	.30	.75
70 Andy Messersmith	.08	.20
71 Doug Rau	.08	.20
72 Rick Rhoden	.08	.20
73 Don Sutton	1.00	2.50
74 Rick Auerbach	.08	.20
75 Ron Cey	.12	.30
76 Ivan DeJesus	.08	.20
77 Steve Garvey	.60	1.50
78 Lee Lacy	.08	.20
79 Dave Lopes	.08	.20
80 Ken McMullen	.08	.20
81 Joe Ferguson	.08	.20
82 Paul Powell	.08	.20
83 Steve Yeager	.08	.20
84 Willie Crawford	.08	.20
85 Henry Cruz	.08	.20
86 Charlie Manuel	.08	.15
87 Manny Mota	.08	.20
88 Tom Paciorek	.08	.20
89 Jim Wynn	.08	.20
90 Walt Alston MG	.30	.75
91 Bill Buckner	.12	.30
92 Jim Barr	.08	.20
93 Mike Caldwell	.08	.20
94 John D'Acquisto	.08	.20
95 Dave Heaverlo	.08	.20
96 Gary Lavelle	.08	.20
97 John Montefusco	.08	.20
98 Charlie Williams	.08	.20
99 Chris Arnold	.08	.20
100 Marc Hill	.08	.20
101 Dave Rader	.08	.20
102 Bruce Miller	.08	.20
103 Willie Montanez	.08	.20
104 Steve Ontiveros	.08	.20
105 Chris Speier	.08	.20
106 Derrel Thomas	.08	.20
107 Gary Thomasson	.08	.20
108 Glenn Adams	.08	.20
109 Von Joshua	.08	.20
110 Gary Matthews	.08	.20
111 Bobby Murcer	.12	.30
112 Horace Speed	.08	.20
113 Wes Westrum MG	.08	.20
114 Rich Folkers	.08	.20
115 Alan Foster	.08	.20
116 Dave Freisleben	.08	.20
117 Dan Frisella	.08	.20
118 Randy Jones	.08	.20
119 Dan Spillner	.08	.20
120 Larry Hardy	.08	.20
121 Randy Hundley	.08	.20
122 Fred Kendall	.08	.20
123 John McNamara MG	.08	.20
124 Tito Fuentes	.08	.20
125 Enzo Hernandez	.08	.20
126 Steve Huntz	.08	.20
127 Mike Ivie	.08	.20
128 Hector Torres	.08	.20
129 Ted Kubiak	.08	.20
130 John Grubb	.08	.20
131 John Scott	.08	.20
132 Bob Tolan	.08	.20
133 Dave Winfield	5.00	12.00
134 Bill Gogolewski	.08	.20
135 Dan Osborn	.08	.20
136 Jim Kaat	.30	.75
137 Claude Osteen	.08	.20
138 Cecil Upshaw	.08	.20
139 Wilbur Wood	.08	.20
140 Lloyd Allen	.08	.20
141 Brian Downing	.08	.20
142 Jim Essian	.08	.20
143 Bucky Dent	.08	.20
144 Jorge Orta	.08	.20
145 Lee Richard	.08	.20
146 Bill Stein	.08	.20
147 Ken Henderson	.08	.20
148 Carlos May	.08	.20
149 Nyls Nyman	.08	.20
150 Bob Coluccio	.08	.20
151 Chuck Tanner MG	.08	.20
152 Pat Kelly	.08	.20
153 Jerry Hairston	.08	.20
154 Pete Varney	.08	.20
155 Bill Melton	.08	.20
156 Goose Gossage	.50	1.25
157 Terry Forster	.08	.20
158 Rich Hinton	.08	.20
159 Nelson Briles	.08	.20
160 Al Fitzmorris	.08	.20
161 Steve Mingori	.08	.20
162 Marty Pattin	.08	.20
163 Paul Splittorff	.08	.20
164 Dennis Leonard	.08	.20
165 Buck Martinez	.08	.20
166 Bob Stinson	.08	.20
167 George Brett	8.00	20.00
168 Harmon Killebrew	1.25	3.00
169 John Mayberry	.08	.20
170 Fred Patek	.08	.20
171 Cookie Rojas	.08	.20
172 Rodney Scott	.08	.20
173 Tony Solaita	.08	.20
174 Frank White	.12	.30
175 Al Cowens	.08	.20
176 Hal McRae	.12	.30
177 Amos Otis	.08	.20
178 Vada Pinson	.12	.30
179 Jim Wohlford	.08	.20
180 Doug Bird	.08	.20
181 Mark Littell	.08	.20
182 Bob McClure	.08	.20
183 Steve Busby	.08	.20
184 Fran Healy	.08	.20
185 Whitey Herzog MG	.08	.20
186 Andy Hassler	.08	.20
187 Nolan Ryan	10.00	25.00
188 Bill Singer	.08	.20
189 Frank Tanana	.12	.30
190 Ed Figueroa	.08	.20
191 Dave Collins	.08	.20
192 Dick Williams MG	.08	.20
193 Ellie Rodriguez	.08	.20
194 Dave Chalk	.08	.20
195 Winston Llenas	.08	.20
196 Rudy Meoli	.08	.20
197 Orlando Ramirez	.08	.20
198 Jerry Remy	.08	.20
199 Billy Smith	.08	.20
200 Bruce Bochte	.08	.20
201 Joe Lahoud	.08	.20
202 Morris Nettles	.08	.20
203 Mickey Rivers	.08	.20
204 Leroy Stanton	.08	.20
205 Vic Albury	.08	.20
206 Tom Burgmeier	.08	.20
207 Bill Butler	.08	.20
208 Bill Campbell	.08	.20
209 Ray Corbin	.08	.20
210 Joe Decker	.08	.20
211 Jim Hughes	.08	.20
212 Ed Bane UER/(Photo actually Mike Pazik)	.08	.20
213 Glenn Borgmann	.08	.20
214 Rod Carew	2.00	5.00
215 Steve Brye	.08	.20
216 Dan Ford	.08	.20
217 Tony Oliva	.30	.75
218 Dave Goltz	.08	.20
219 Bert Blyleven	.20	.50
220 Larry Hisle	.08	.20
221 Steve Braun	.08	.20
222 Jerry Terrell	.08	.20
223 Eric Soderholm	.08	.20
224 Phil Roof	.08	.20
225 Danny Thompson	.08	.20
226 Jim Colborn	.08	.20
227 Tom Murphy	.08	.20
228 Ed Rodriguez	.08	.20
229 Jim Slaton	.08	.20
230 Ed Sprague	.08	.20
231 Charlie Moore	.08	.20
232 Darrell Porter	.08	.20
233 Kurt Bevacqua	.08	.20
234 Pedro Garcia	.08	.20
235 Mike Hegan	.08	.20
236 Don Money	.08	.20
237 George Scott	.08	.20
238 Robin Yount	5.00	12.00
239 Hank Aaron	4.00	10.00
240 Rob Ellis	.08	.20
241 Sixto Lezcano	.08	.20
242 Bob Mitchell	.08	.20
243 Gorman Thomas	.08	.20
244 Bill Travers	.08	.20
245 Pete Broberg	.08	.20
246 Bill Sharp	.08	.20
247 Bobby Darwin	.08	.20
248 Rick Austin UER/(Photo actually Larry Anderson)	.08	.20
249 Larry Anderson UER/(Photo actually Rick Austin)	.08	.20
250 Tom Bianco	.08	.20
251 Lafayette Currence	.08	.20
252 Steve Foucault	.08	.20
253 Bill Hands	.08	.20
254 Steve Hargan	.08	.20
255 Fergie Jenkins	1.25	3.00
256 Bob Sheldon	.08	.20
257 Jim Umbarger	.08	.20
258 Clyde Wright	.08	.20
259 Bill Fahey	.08	.20
260 Jim Sundberg	.08	.20
261 Leo Cardenas	.08	.20
262 Jim Fregosi	.08	.20
263 Mike Hargrove	.08	.20
264 Toby Harrah	.08	.20
265 Roy Howell	.08	.20
266 Lenny Randle	.08	.20
267 Roy Smalley	.08	.20
268 Jim Spencer	.08	.20
269 Jeff Burroughs	.08	.20
270 Tom Grieve	.08	.20
271 Joe Lovitto	.08	.20
272 Frank Lucchesi MG	.08	.20
273 Dave Nelson	.08	.20
274 Ted Simmons	.30	.75
275 Lou Brock	1.50	4.00
276 Ron Fairly	.08	.20
277 Bake McBride	.08	.20
278 Reggie Smith	.08	.20
279 Willie Davis	.08	.20
280 Ken Reitz	.08	.20
281 Buddy Bradford	.08	.20
282 Luis Melendez	.08	.20
283 Mike Tyson	.08	.20
284 Ted Sizemore	.08	.20
285 Mario Guerrero	.08	.20
286 Larry Lintz	.08	.20
287 Ken Rudolph	.08	.20
288 Dick Billings	.08	.20
289 Jerry Mumphrey	.08	.20
290 Mike Wallace	.08	.20
291 Al Hrabosky	.08	.20
292 Ken Reynolds	.08	.20
293 Mike Garman	.08	.20
294 Bob Forsch	.08	.20
295 John Denny	.08	.20
296 Harry Rasmussen	.08	.20
297 Lynn McGlothen	.08	.20
298 Mike Barlow	.08	.20
299 Greg Terlecky	.08	.20
300 Red Schoendienst MG	.20	.50
301 Rick Reuschel	.08	.20
302 Steve Stone	.08	.20
303 Bill Bonham	.08	.20
304 Oscar Zamora	.08	.20
305 Ken Frailing	.08	.20
306 Milt Wilcox	.08	.20
307 Darold Knowles	.08	.20
308 Jim Marshall MG	.08	.20
309 Bill Madlock	.20	.50
310 Jose Cardenal	.08	.20
311 Rick Monday	.08	.20
312 Jerry Morales	.08	.20
313 Tim Hosley	.08	.20
314 Gene Hiser	.08	.20
315 Don Kessinger	.08	.20
316 Manny Trillo	.08	.20
317 Pete LaCock	.08	.20
318 George Mitterwald	.08	.20
319 Steve Swisher	.08	.20
320 Rob Sperring	.08	.20
321 Vic Harris	.08	.20
322 Ron Dunn	.08	.20
323 Jose Morales	.08	.20
324 Pete Mackanin	.08	.20
325 Jim Cox	.08	.20
326 Larry Parrish	.08	.20
327 Mike Jorgensen	.08	.20
328 Tim Foli	.08	.20
329 Hal Breeden	.08	.20
330 Nate Colbert	.08	.20
331 Pepe Frias	.08	.20
332 Pat Scanlon	.08	.20
333 Bob Bailey	.08	.20
334 Gary Carter	2.00	5.00
335 Pepe Mangual	.08	.20
336 Larry Biittner	.08	.20
337 Jim Lyttle	.08	.20
338 Gary Roenicke	.08	.20
339 Tony Scott	.08	.20
340 Jerry White	.08	.20
341 Jim Dwyer	.08	.20
342 Ellis Valentine	.08	.20
343 Fred Scherman	.08	.20
344 Dennis Blair	.08	.20
345 Woodie Fryman	.08	.20
346 Chuck Taylor	.08	.20
347 Dan Warthen	.08	.20
348 Dan Carrithers	.08	.20
349 Steve Rogers	.08	.20
350 Dale Murray	.08	.20
351 Duke Snider CO	.75	2.00
352 Ralph Houk MG	.08	.20
353 John Hiller	.08	.20
354 Mickey Lolich	.12	.30
355 Dave Lemancyzk	.08	.20
356 Lerrin LaGrow	.08	.20
357 Fred Arroyo	.08	.20
358 Joe Coleman	.08	.20
359 Ben Oglivie	.08	.20
360 Willie Horton	.08	.20
361 John Knox	.08	.20
362 Leon Roberts	.08	.20
363 Ron LeFlore	.08	.20
364 Gary Sutherland	.08	.20
365 Dan Meyer	.08	.20
366 Aurelio Rodriguez	.08	.20
367 Tom Veryzer	.08	.20
368 Jack Pierce	.08	.20
369 Gene Michael	.08	.20
370 Billy Baldwin	.08	.20
371 Gates Brown	.08	.20
372 Mickey Stanley	.08	.20
373 Terry Humphrey	.08	.20
374 Doyle Alexander	.08	.20
375 Mike Cuellar	.08	.20
376 Wayne Garland	.08	.20
377 Ross Grimsley	.08	.20
378 Grant Jackson	.08	.20
379 Dyar Miller	.08	.20
380 Jim Palmer	1.50	4.00
381 Mike Torrez	.08	.20
382 Mike Willis	.08	.20
383 Dave Duncan	.08	.20
384 Ellie Hendricks	.08	.20
385 Jim Hutto	.08	.20
386 Bob Bailor	.08	.20
387 Doug DeCinces	.08	.20
388 Bob Grich	.08	.20
389 Lee May	.08	.20
390 Tony Muser	.08	.20
391 Tim Nordbrook	.08	.20
392 Brooks Robinson	1.50	4.00
393 Royle Stillman	.08	.20
394 Don Baylor	.30	.75
395 Paul Blair	.08	.20
396 Al Bumbry	.08	.20
397 Larry Harlow	.08	.20
398 Tommy Davis	.08	.20
399 Jim Northrup	.08	.20
400 Ken Singleton	.08	.20
401 Tom Shopay	.08	.20
402 Fred Lynn	.30	.75
403 Carlton Fisk	2.00	5.00
404 Cecil Cooper	.12	.30
405 Jim Rice	.75	2.00
406 Juan Beniquez	.08	.20
407 Denny Doyle	.08	.20
408 Dwight Evans	.40	1.00
409 Carl Yastrzemski	2.00	5.00
410 Rick Burleson	.08	.20
411 Bernie Carbo	.08	.20
412 Doug Griffin	.08	.20
413 Rico Petrocelli	.08	.20
414 Bob Montgomery	.08	.20
415 Tim Blackwell	.08	.20
416 Rick Miller	.08	.20
417 Darrell Johnson MG	.08	.20
418 Jim Burton	.08	.20
419 Jim Willoughby	.08	.20
420 Rogelio Moret	.08	.20
421 Bill Lee	.08	.20
422 Dick Drago	.08	.20
423 Diego Segui	.08	.20
424 Luis Tiant	.12	.30
425 Jim Hunter	1.25	3.00
426 Rick Sawyer	.08	.20
427 Rudy May	.08	.20
428 Dick Tidrow	.08	.20
429 Sparky Lyle	.12	.30
430 Doc Medich	.08	.20
431 Pat Dobson	.08	.20
432 Dave Pagan	.08	.20
433 Thurman Munson	1.25	3.00
434 Chris Chambliss	.12	.30
435 Roy White	.08	.20
436 Walt Williams	.08	.20
437 Graig Nettles	.20	.50
438 Rick Dempsey	.08	.20
439 Bobby Bonds	.30	.75
440 Ed Herrmann	.08	.20
441 Sandy Alomar	.08	.20
442 Fred Stanley	.08	.20
443 Terry Whitfield	.08	.20
444 Rich Bladt	.08	.20
445 Lou Piniella	.20	.50
446 Rich Coggins	.08	.20
447 Ed Brinkman	.08	.20
448 Jim Mason	.08	.20
449 Larry Murray	.08	.20
450 Ron Blomberg	.08	.20
451 Elliott Maddox	.08	.20
452 Kerry Dineen	.08	.20
453 Billy Martin MG	.30	.75
454 Dave Bergman	.08	.20
455 Otto Velez	.08	.20
456 Joe Hoerner	.08	.20
457 Tug McGraw	.12	.30
458 Gene Garber	.08	.20
459 Steve Carlton	2.00	5.00
460 Larry Christenson	.08	.20
461 Tom Underwood	.08	.20
462 Jim Lonborg	.08	.20
463 Jay Johnstone	.08	.20
464 Larry Bowa	.08	.20
465 Dave Cash	.08	.20
466 Ollie Brown	.08	.20
467 Greg Luzinski	.12	.30
468 Johnny Oates	.08	.20
469 Mike Anderson	.08	.20
470 Mike Schmidt	6.00	15.00
471 Bob Boone	.20	.50
472 Tom Hutton	.08	.20
473 Rich Allen	.30	.75
474 Tony Taylor	.08	.20
475 Jerry Martin	.08	.20
476 Danny Ozark MG	.08	.20
477 Dick Ruthven	.08	.20
478 Jim Todd	.08	.20
479 Paul Lindblad	.08	.20
480 Rollie Fingers	1.25	3.00
481 Vida Blue	.08	.20
482 Ken Holtzman	.08	.20
483 Dick Bosman	.08	.20
484 Sonny Siebert	.08	.20
485 Glenn Abbott	.08	.20
486 Stan Bahnsen	.08	.20
487 Mike Norris	.08	.20
488 Alvin Dark MG	.08	.20
489 Claudell Washington	.08	.20
490 Joe Rudi	.08	.20
491 Bill North	.08	.20
492 Bert Campaneris	.08	.20
493 Gene Tenace	.08	.20
494 Reggie Jackson	3.00	8.00
495 Phil Garner	.20	.50
496 Billy Williams	1.25	3.00
497 Sal Bando	.08	.20
498 Jim Holt	.08	.20
499 Ted Martinez	.08	.20
500 Ray Fosse	.08	.20
501 Matt Alexander	.08	.20
502 Larry Haney	.08	.20
503 Angel Mangual	.08	.20
504 Fred Beene	.08	.20
505 Tom Buskey	.08	.20
506 Dennis Eckersley	5.00	12.00
507 Roric Harrison	.08	.20
508 Don Hood	.08	.20
509 Jim Kern	.08	.20
510 Dave LaRoche	.08	.20
511 Fritz Peterson	.08	.20
512 Jim Strickland	.08	.20
513 Rick Waits	.08	.20
514 Alan Ashby	.08	.20
515 John Ellis	.08	.20
516 Rick Cerone	.08	.20
517 Buddy Bell	.08	.20
518 Jack Brohamer	.08	.20
519 Rico Carty	.08	.20
520 Ed Crosby	.08	.20
521 Frank Duffy	.08	.20
522 Duane Kuiper UER/(Photo actually Rick Manning)	.08	.20
523 Joe Lis	.08	.20
524 Boog Powell	.40	1.00
525 Frank Robinson	1.50	4.00
526 Oscar Gamble	.08	.20
527 George Hendrick	.08	.20
528 John Lowenstein	.08	.20
529 Rick Manning UER/(Photo actually Duane Kuiper)	.08	.20
530 Tommy Smith	.08	.20
531 Charlie Spikes	.08	.20
532 Steve Kline	.08	.20
533 Ed Kranepool	.08	.20
534 Mike Vail	.08	.20
535 Del Unser	.08	.20
536 Felix Millan	.08	.20
537 Rusty Staub	.12	.30
538 Jesus Alou	.08	.20
539 Wayne Garrett	.08	.20
540 Mike Phillips	.08	.20
541 Joe Torre	.20	.50
542 Dave Kingman	.20	.50
543 Gene Clines	.08	.20
544 Jack Heidemann	.08	.20
545 Bud Harrelson	.08	.20
546 John Stearns	.08	.20
547 John Milner	.08	.20
548 Bob Apodaca	.08	.20
549 Skip Lockwood	.08	.20
550 Ken Sanders	.08	.20
551 Tom Seaver	2.50	6.00
552 Rick Baldwin	.08	.20
553 Jon Matlack	.08	.20
554 Hank Webb	.08	.20
555 Randy Tate	.08	.20
556 Tom Hall	.08	.20
557 George Stone	.08	.20
558 Craig Swan	.08	.20
559 Jerry Cram	.08	.20
560 Roy Staiger	.08	.20
561 Kent Tekulve	.12	.30
562 Jerry Reuss	.08	.20
563 John Candelaria	.08	.20
564 Larry Demery	.08	.20
565 Dave Giusti	.08	.20
566 Jim Rooker	.08	.20
567 Ramon Hernandez	.08	.20
568 Bruce Kison	.08	.20
569 Ken Brett	.08	.20
570 Bob Moose	.08	.20
571 Manny Sanguillen	.08	.20
572 Dave Parker	1.00	2.50
573 Willie Stargell	1.25	3.00
574 Richie Zisk	.08	.20
575 Rennie Stennett	.08	.20
576 Al Oliver	.20	.50
577 Bill Robinson	.08	.20
578 Bob Robertson	.08	.20
579 Rich Hebner	.08	.20
580 Ed Kirkpatrick	.08	.20
581 Duffy Dyer	.08	.20
582 Craig Reynolds	.08	.20
583 Frank Taveras	.08	.20
584 Willie Randolph	1.25	3.00
585 Art Howe	.08	.20
586 Danny Murtaugh MG	.08	.20
587 Rick McKinney	.08	.20
588 Ed Goodson	.08	.20
589 George Brett / Al Cowens CL	1.50	4.00
590 Keith Hernandez / Lou Brock CL	.40	1.00
591 Jerry Koosman / Duke Snider CL	.40	1.00
592 Maury Wills / John Knox CL	.08	.20
593A Checklist 5 ERR / Jim Hunter / Nolan Ryan/(Noland o	6.00	15.00
593B Jim Hunter / Nolan Ryan CL COR	2.00	5.00
594 Checklist 6 / Ralph Branca / Carl Erskine / Pee Wee R	.08	.20
595 Willie Mays / Herb Score CL	.60	1.50
596 Larry Cox	.08	.20
597 Gene Mauch MG	.08	.20
598 Whitey Wietelmann CO	.08	.20
599 Wayne Simpson	.08	.20
600 Erskine Thomason	.08	.20
601 Ike Hampton	.08	.20
602 Ken Crosby	.08	.20
603 Ralph Rowe	.08	.20
604 Jim Tyrone	.08	.20
605 Mick Kelleher	.08	.20
606 Mario Mendoza	.08	.20
607 Mike Rogodzinski	.08	.20
608 Bob Gallagher	.08	.20
609 Jerry Koosman	.08	.20
610 Joe Frazier MG	.08	.20
611 Karl Kuehl MG	.08	.20
612 Frank LaCorte	.08	.20
613 Ray Bare	.08	.20
614 Billy Muffett CO	.08	.20
615 Bill Laxton	.08	.20
616 Willie Mays CO	3.00	8.00
617 Phil Cavarretta CO	.08	.20
618 Ted Kluszewski CO	.12	.30
619 Elston Howard CO	.08	.20
620 Alex Grammas CO	.08	.20
621 Mickey Vernon CO	.08	.20
622 Dick Sisler CO	.08	.20
623 Harvey Haddix CO	.08	.20
624 Bobby Winkles CO	.08	.20
625 John Pesky CO	.08	.20
626 Jim Davenport CO	.08	.20
627 Dave Tomlin	.08	.20
628 Roger Craig CO	.08	.20
629 Joe Amalfitano CO	.08	.20
630 Jim Reese CO	.12	.30

1976 SSPC 1887 World Series

This 18-card standard-size set was inserted into the Fall 1976 Collectors Quarterly issue. Many of the players featured have few cards issued of them during their career. The fronts feature drawings while the backs talk about the 1887 World Series.

Card	Low	High
COMPLETE SET (18)	5.00	12.00
1 Bob Caruthers	.30	.75
2 Dave Foutz	.20	.50
3 Arlie Latham	.30	.75
4 Charlie Getzein	.20	.50
5 Jack Rowe	.20	.50
6 Fred Dunlap	.20	.50
7 Tip O'Neill	.30	.75
8 Curt Welch	.30	.75
9 Kid Gleason	.40	1.00
10 Sam Thompson	.60	1.50
11 Ned Hanlon	.60	1.50
12 Dan Brouthers	.60	1.50
13 Doc Bushong	.20	.50
14 Charles Comiskey	1.25	3.00
15 Yank Robinson	.20	.50
16 Charlie Bennett	.30	.75
17 Hardy Richardson	.20	.50
18 Deacon White	.30	.75

1976 SSPC Yankees Old-Timers Day

These nine standard-size cards were inserted in the Collectors Quarterly Spring 1976 edition. The cards feature the player's photo and his name on the bottom. The backs form a puzzle of four Yankee greats: Billy Martin, Joe DiMaggio, Whitey Ford and Mickey Mantle. The cards are unnummbered and thus sequenced in alphabetical order.

Card	Low	High
COMPLETE SET (9)	3.00	8.00
1 Earl Averill	.30	.75
2 Joe DiMaggio	1.25	3.00
3 Tommy Henrich	.20	.50
4 Billy Herman	.30	.75
5 Monte Irvin	.30	.75
6 Jim Konstanty	.10	.25
7 Mickey Mantle	1.25	3.00
8 Pee Wee Reese	.40	1.00
9 Bobby Thomson	.20	.50

1978 SSPC 270

This 270-card set was issued as magazine (All-Star Gallery) inserts in sets of three panels, with each panel measuring approximately 7 1/4" by 10 3/4". Each of the three panels contains nine cards. If cut, the individual cards would measure the standard size (2 1/2" by 3 1/2"). The fronts display color posed and action player photos with thin black inner borders and white outer borders. The backs carry the player's name, biographical information, and career summary. The cards are checklisted below alphabetically according to teams as follows: New York Yankees (1-27)), Philadelphia Phillie (28-54), Los Angeles Dodgers (55-81), Texas Rangers (82-108), Cincinnati Reds (109-135), Chicago White Sox (136-162), Boston Red Sox (163-189), California Angels (190-216), Kansas City Royals (217-243), and Chicago Cubs (244-270). The pricing below is for individual cards.

Card	Low	High
COMPLETE SET (270)	50.00	100.00
1 Thurman Munson	.75	2.00
2 Cliff Johnson	.08	.20
3 Lou Piniella	.15	.40
4 Dell Alston	.08	.20
5 Yankee Stadium	.08	.20
6 Ken Holtzman	.08	.20
7 Chris Chambliss	.12	.30
8 Roy White	.08	.20
9 Ed Figueroa	.08	.20
10 Dick Tidrow	.08	.20
11 Sparky Lyle	.12	.30
12 Fred Stanley	.08	.20
13 Mickey Rivers	.08	.20
14 Billy Martin MG	.15	.40
15 George Zeber	.08	.20
16 Ken Clay	.08	.20
17 Ron Guidry	.12	.30
18 Don Gullett	.08	.20
19 Fran Healy	.08	.20
20 Paul Blair	.08	.20
21 Mickey Klutts	.08	.20
22 Yankees Team Photo	.08	.20
23 Catfish Hunter	.75	2.00
24 Bucky Dent	.08	.20
25 Graig Nettles	.15	.40
26 Reggie Jackson	1.50	4.00
27 Willie Randolph	.12	.30
28 Garry Maddox	.08	.20
29 Steve Carlton	1.25	3.00
30 Ron Reed	.08	.20
31 Greg Luzinski	.12	.30
32 Bobby Wine CO	.08	.20
33 Bob Boone	.12	.30
34 Carroll Beringer CO	.08	.20
35 Richie Hebner	.08	.20
36 Ray Rippelmeyer CO	.08	.20
37 Terry Harmon	.08	.20
38 Gene Garber	.08	.20
39 Ted Sizemore	.08	.20
40 Barry Foote	.08	.20
41 Tony Taylor CO	.08	.20
42 Tug McGraw	.15	.40
43 Jay Johnstone	.12	.30
44 Randy Lerch	.08	.20
45 Billy DeMars CO	.08	.20
46 Mike Schmidt	2.00	5.00

47 Larry Christenson .08 .20
48 Tim McCarver .15 .40
49 Larry Bowa .12 .30
50 Danny Ozark MG .08 .20
51 Jerry Martin .08 .20
52 Jim Lonborg .08 .20
53 Bake McBride .08 .20
54 Warren Brusstar .08 .20
55 Burt Hooton .08 .20
56 Bill Russell .08 .20
57 Dusty Baker .12 .30
58 Reggie Smith .12 .30
59 Rick Rhoden .08 .20
60 Jerry Grote .08 .20
61 Bill Butler .08 .20
62 Ron Cey .12 .30
63 Tom Lasorda MG .30 .75
64 Teddy Martinez .08 .20
65 Ed Goodson .08 .20
66 Vic Davalillo .08 .20
67 Davey Lopes .08 .20
68 Terry Forster .08 .20
69 Lee Lacy .08 .20
70 Mike Garman .08 .20
71 Steve Garvey .30 .75
72 Johnny Oates .08 .20
73 Steve Yeager .08 .20
74 Rafael Landestoy .08 .20
75 Tommy John .15 .40
76 Glenn Burke .08 .20
77 Rick Monday .08 .20
78 Doug Rau .08 .20
79 Manny Mota .08 .20
80 Don Sutton .40 1.00
81 Charlie Hough .12 .30
82 Mike Hargrove .08 .20
83 Jim Sundberg .08 .20
84 Fergie Jenkins .60 1.50
85 Paul Lindblad .08 .20
86 Sandy Alomar .08 .20
87 John Lowenstein .08 .20
88 Claudell Washington .08 .20
89 Toby Harrah .08 .20
90 Jim Umbarger .08 .20
91 Len Barker .08 .20
92 Dave May .08 .20
93 Kurt Bevacqua .08 .20
94 Jim Mason .08 .20
95 Bump Wills .08 .20
96 Dock Ellis .08 .20
97 Bill Fahey .08 .20
98 Richie Zisk .08 .20
99 Jon Matlack .08 .20
100 John Ellis .08 .20
101 Bert Campaneris .08 .20
102 Doc Medich .08 .20
103 Juan Beniquez .08 .20
104 Billy Hunter MG .08 .20
105 Doyle Alexander .08 .20
106 Roger Moret .08 .20
107 Mike Jorgensen .08 .20
108 Al Oliver .12 .30
109 Fred Norman .08 .20
110 Ray Knight .15 .40
111 Pedro Borbon .08 .20
112 Bill Bonham .08 .20
113 George Foster .15 .40
114 Doug Bair .08 .20
115 Cesar Geronimo .08 .20
116 Tom Seaver 1.00 2.50
117 Mario Soto .08 .20
118 Ken Griffey .12 .30
119 Mike Lum .08 .20
120 Tom Hume .08 .20
121 Joe Morgan .75 2.00
122 Manny Sarmiento .08 .20
123 Dan Driessen .08 .20
124 Ed Armbrister .08 .20
125 Champ Summers .08 .20
126 Rick Auerbach .08 .20
127 Doug Capilla .08 .20
128 Johnny Bench 1.00 2.50
129 Sparky Anderson MG .15 .40
130 Raul Ferreyra .08 .20
131 Dale Murray .08 .20
132 Pete Rose 1.25 3.00
133 Dave Concepcion .12 .30
134 Junior Kennedy .08 .20
135 Dave Collins .08 .20
136 Mike Eden .08 .20
137 Lamar Johnson .08 .20
138 Ron Schueler .08 .20
139 Bob Lemon MG .15 .40
140 Bobby Bonds .15 .40
141 Thad Bosley .08 .20
142 Jorge Orta .08 .20
143 Wilbur Wood .08 .20
144 Francisco Barrios .08 .20
145 Greg Prior .08 .20
146 Chet Lemon .08 .20
147 Mike Squires .08 .20
148 Eric Soderholm .08 .20
149 Reggie Sanders .08 .20
150 Kevin Bell .08 .20
151 Alan Bannister .08 .20
152 Henry Cruz .08 .20
153 Larry Doby CO .15 .40
154 Don Kessinger .08 .20
155 Ralph Garr .08 .20
156 Bill Nahorodny .08 .20
157 Ron Blomberg .08 .20
158 Bob Molinaro .08 .20
159 Junior Moore .08 .20
160 Minnie Minoso CO .12 .30
161 Lerrin LaGrow .08 .20
162 Wayne Nordhagen .08 .20
163 Ramon Aviles .08 .20
164 Bob Stanley .12 .30
165 Reggie Cleveland .08 .20
166 Jack Brohamer .08 .20
167 Bill Lee .08 .20
168 Jim Burton .08 .20
169 Bill Campbell .08 .20
170 Mike Torrez .08 .20
171 Dick Drago .08 .20
172 Butch Hobson .08 .20
173 Bob Bailey .08 .20
174 Fred Lynn .08 .20
175 Rick Burleson .08 .20
176 Luis Tiant .12 .30
177 Ted Williams CO 3.00 8.00
178 Dennis Eckersley 1.50 4.00
179 Don Zimmer MG .08 .20
180 Carlton Fisk 1.50 4.00
181 Dwight Evans .15 .40
182 Fred Kendall .08 .20
183 George Scott .08 .20
184 Frank Duffy .08 .20
185 Bernie Carbo .08 .20
186 Jerry Remy .08 .20
187 Carl Yastrzemski 1.50 4.00
188 Allen Ripley .08 .20
189 Jim Rice .40 1.00
190 Ken Landreaux .08 .20
191 Paul Hartzell .08 .20
192 Ken Brett .08 .20
193 Dave Garcia MG .08 .20
194 Bobby Grich .12 .30
195 Lyman Bostock Jr. .12 .30
196 Ike Hampton .08 .20
197 Dave LaRoche .08 .20
198 Dave Chalk .08 .20
199 Rick Miller .08 .20
200 Floyd Rayford .08 .20
201 Willie Aikens .08 .20
202 Balor Moore .08 .20
203 Nolan Ryan 8.00 20.00
204 Danny Goodwin .08 .20
205 Ron Fairly .08 .20
206 Dyar Miller .08 .20
207 Carney Lansford .15 .40
208 Don Baylor .15 .40
209 Gil Flores .08 .20
210 Terry Humphrey .08 .20
211 Frank Tanana .15 .40
212 Chris Knapp .08 .20
213 Ron Jackson .08 .20
214 Joe Rudi .08 .20
215 Tony Solaita .08 .20
216 Rance Mulliniks .08 .20
217 George Brett 6.00 15.00
218 Doug Bird .08 .20
219 Hal McRae .15 .40
220 Dennis Leonard .08 .20
221 Darrell Porter .08 .20
222 Randy McGilberry .08 .20
223 Pete LaCock .08 .20
224 Whitey Herzog MG .12 .30
225 Andy Hassler .08 .20
226 Joe Lahoud .08 .20
227 Amos Otis .08 .20
228 Al Hrabosky .08 .20
229 Clint Hurdle .15 .40
230 Paul Splittorff .08 .20
231 Marty Pattin .08 .20
232 Frank White .12 .30
233 John Wathan .08 .20
234 Freddie Patek .08 .20
235 Rich Gale .08 .20
236 U.L. Washington .08 .20
237 Larry Gura .08 .20
238 Jim Colborn .08 .20
239 Tom Poquette .08 .20
240 Al Cowens .08 .20
241 Willie Wilson .15 .40
242 Steve Mingori .08 .20
243 Jerry Terrell .08 .20
244 Larry Biittner .08 .20
245 Rick Reuschel .08 .20
246 Dave Rader .08 .20
247 Paul Reuschel .08 .20
248 Heity Cruz .08 .20
249 Woodie Fryman .08 .20
250 Steve Ontiveros .08 .20
251 Mike Gordon .08 .20
252 Dave Kingman .15 .40
253 Gene Clines .08 .20
254 Bruce Sutter .30 .75
255 Willie Hernandez .08 .20
256 Ivan DeJesus .08 .20
257 Greg Gross .08 .20
258 Larry Cox .08 .20
259 Joe Wallis .08 .20
260 Dennis Lamp .08 .20
261 Ray Burris .08 .20
262 Bill Caudill .08 .20
263 Donnie Moore .08 .20
264 Bill Buckner .12 .30
265 Bobby Murcer .12 .30
266 Dave Roberts .08 .20
267 Mike Krukow .08 .20
268 Herman Franks MG .08 .20
269 Mike Kelleher .08 .20
270 Rudy Meoli .08 .20

1980-87 SSPC HOF

The 1980 SSPC set was commonly known as the Baseball Immortals set. This standard-size set honored all of the members of the Hall of Fame. When the set was first issued the first 10,000 sets made indicated first printing on the back. This set continued to be issued as new additions were inducted into the Hall of Fame. Baseball writers Bill Madden and Fred McMane wrote the text used on the backs.

COMPLETE SET (199) 40.00 80.00
1 Babe Ruth .75 2.00
2 Ty Cobb .60 1.50
3 Walter Johnson .30 .75
4 Christy Mathewson .30 .75
5 Honus Wagner 1.00
6 Morgan Bulkeley .05
7 Ban Johnson .05
8 Larry Lajoie .20 .50
9 Connie Mack .08 .25
10 John McGraw .08 .25
11 Tris Speaker .08 .25
12 George Wright .05
13 Cy Young .30 .75
14 Grover Alexander .30 .75
15 Alexander Cartwright .05
16 Henry Chadwick .05
17 Cap Anson .08 .25
18 Eddie Collins .05 .15
19 Charles Comiskey .05
20 Candy Cummings .05
21 Buck Ewing .05
22 Lou Gehrig .60 1.50
23 Willie Keeler .05
24 Hoss Radbourne .05
25 George Sisler .05 .15
26 Albert Spalding .05
27 Rogers Hornsby .30 .75
28 Judge Landis .05
29 Roger Bresnahan .05
30 Dan Brouthers .05
31 Fred Clarke .05
32 James Collins .05
33 Ed Delahanty .05
34 Hugh Duffy .05
35 Hughie Jennings .05
36 Mike King Kelly .05 .15
37 James O'Rourke .05
38 Wilbert Robinson .05
39 Jesse Burkett .05
40 Frank Chance .05 .15
41 Jack Chesbro .05
42 John Evers .05 .15
43 Clark Griffith .05
44 Thomas McCarthy .05
45 Joe McGinnity .05
46 Eddie Plank .05 .15
47 Joe Tinker .05 .15
48 Rube Waddell .05
49 Ed Walsh .05
50 Mickey Cochrane .05 .15
51 Frankie Frisch .05 .15
52 Lefty Grove .05 .15
53 Carl Hubbell .08 .25
54 Herb Pennock .05
55 Pie Traynor .05 .15
56 Three Finger Brown .05
57 Charlie Gehringer .05 .15
58 Kid Nichols .05
59 Jimmie Foxx .30 .75
60 Mel Ott .20 .50
61 Harry Heilmann .05
62 Paul Waner .05 .15
63 Ed Barrow .05
64 Chief Bender .05
65 Tom Connolly .05
66 Dizzy Dean .30 .75
67 Bill Klem .05
68 Al Simmons .05 .15
69 Bobby Wallace .05
70 Harry Wright .05
71 Bill Dickey .08 .25
72 Rabbit Maranville .05
73 Bill Terry .05 .15
74 Home Run Baker .05 .15
75 Joe DiMaggio .60 1.50
76 Gabby Hartnett .05
77 Ted Lyons .05
78 Ray Schalk .05
79 Dazzy Vance .05
80 Joe Cronin .05 .15
81 Hank Greenberg .05 .15
82 Sam Crawford .05
83 Joe McCarthy .05
84 Zack Wheat .05
85 Max Carey .05
86 Billy Hamilton .05
87 Bob Feller .30 .75
88 Bill McKechnie .05
89 Jackie Robinson 1.00
90 Ed Roush .05
91 John Clarkson .05
92 Elmer Flick .05
93 Sam Rice .05
94 Eppa Rixey .05
95 Luke Appling .05
96 Red Faber .05
97 Burleigh Grimes .05
98 Miller Huggins .05
99 Tim Keefe .05
100 Heinie Manush .05
101 John Ward .05
102 Pud Galvin .05
103 Casey Stengel .08 .25
104 Ted Williams 1.00
105 Branch Rickey .05 .15
106 Red Ruffing .05
107 Lloyd Waner .05
108 Kiki Cuyler .05
109 Goose Goslin .05
110 Joe Medwick .05
111 Roy Campanella .20 .50
112 Stan Coveleski .05
113 Waite Hoyt .05
114 Stan Musial .30 .75
115 Lou Boudreau .05
116 Earle Combs .05
117 Ford Frick .05
118 Jesse Haines .05
119 Dave Bancroft .05
120 Jake Beckley .05
121 Chick Hafey .05
122 Harry Hooper .05
123 Joe Kelley .05
124 Rube Marquard .05
125 Satchel Paige .20 .50
126 George Weiss .05
127 Yogi Berra .20 .50
128 Josh Gibson .20 .50
129 Lefty Gomez .05 .15
130 Will Harridge .05
131 Sandy Koufax .30 .75
132 Buck Leonard .05 .15
133 Early Wynn .05 .15
134 Ross Youngs .05
135 Roberto Clemente 1.00
136 Billy Evans .05
137 Monte Irvin .05 .15
138 George Kelly .05
139 Warren Spahn .05 .15
140 Mickey Welch .05
141 Cool Papa Bell .05 .15
142 Jim Bottomley .05
143 Jocko Conlan .05
144 Whitey Ford .08 .25
145 Mickey Mantle .60 1.50
146 Sam Thompson .05
147 Earl Averill .05
148 Bucky Harris .05
149 Billy Herman .05
150 Judy Johnson .05
151 Ralph Kiner .05 .15
152 Oscar Charleston .05
153 Roger Connor .05
154 Cal Hubbard .05
155 Bob Lemon .05
156 Fred Lindstrom .05
157 Robin Roberts .05 .15
158 Ernie Banks .20 .50
159 Martin Dihigo .05
160 John Henry Lloyd .05
161 Al Lopez .05
162 Amos Rusie .05
163 Joe Sewell .05
164 Addie Joss .05
165 Larry McPhail .05
166 Eddie Mathews .20 .50
167 Warren Giles .05
168 Willie Mays 1.00
169 Hack Wilson .05
170 Duke Snider .40 1.00
171 Al Kaline .40 1.00
172 Chuck Klein .05
173 Tom Yawkey .05
174 Bob Gibson .30 .75
175 Rube Foster .05
176 Johnny Mize .05
177 Hank Aaron .75 2.00
178 Frank Robinson .30 .75
179 Happy Chandler .05
180 Travis Jackson .05
181 Brooks Robinson .08 .25
182 Juan Marichal .08 .25
183 George Kell .05 .15
184 Walter Alston .05
185 Harmon Killebrew .08 .25
186 Luis Aparicio .05 .15
187 Don Drysdale .05 .15
188 Pee Wee Reese .08 .25
189 Rick Ferrell .05
190 Willie McCovey .08 .25
191 Ernie Lombardi .05
192 Bobby Doerr .05
193 Arky Vaughan .05
194 Enos Slaughter .20 .50
195 Lou Brock .20 .50
196 Hoyt Wilhelm .20 .50
197 Billy Williams .20 .50
198 Jim Hunter .20 .50
199 Ray Dandridge .05 .15

1992 St. Vincent HOF Heroes Stamps

This 12-card standard-size set was issued by the St. Vincent Philatelic Services, Ltd. The peel-away stamps are official legal postage in St. Vincent and the Grenadines. The fronts have a head shot of various HOFers in sepia tones on a gold background that fades to red. The borders have a stamp edge design with an inner border of green. A blue banner across the top carries the words Baseball Hall of Fame Heroes and is placed over a baseball. The card's stamp value of $4.00 is shown in the top right. The lower margin carries the year the player entered the major leagues, his name and final year in the majors. The backs carry the player's name, biography and career statistics.

COMPLETE SET (12) 4.00 10.00
1 Ty Cobb .60 1.50
2 Dizzy Dean .20 .50
3 Bob Feller .20 .50
4 Whitey Ford .20 .50
5 Lou Gehrig 1.25 3.00
6 Rogers Hornsby .20 .50
7 Mel Ott .20 .50
8 Satchel Paige .30 .75
9 Babe Ruth 1.25 3.00
10 Casey Stengel .20 .50
11 Honus Wagner .40 1.00
12 Cy Young .30 .75

1997 St. Vincent HOF Heroes Stamps

This 17-card set commemorates the 50th anniversary of Jackie Robinson breaking Baseball's color barrier. The set features color head portraits of 16 different Black Hall of Famers on 1 3/16" by 1 9/16" $1 stamps. The player's name and year he entered the Hall of Fame are printed down the left. The last stamp listed in the checklist is a $6 stamp and honors Jackie Robinson. It measures approximately 2 3/4" by 4 1/8". The stamps were designed to be placed in a 9" by 8" album with a black-and-white picture of Jackie Robinson in action on the cover. The stamps are unnumbered and checklisted below in alphabetical order.

COMPLETE SET (17) 5.00 12.00
1 Hank Aaron .60 1.50
2 Ernie Banks .30 .75
3 Lou Brock .20 .50
4 Roy Campanella .30 .75
5 Rod Carew .20 .50
6 Roberto Clemente 1.25 3.00
7 Bob Gibson .20 .50
8 Monte Irvin .20 .50
9 Reggie Jackson .30 .75
10 Ferguson Jenkins .20 .50
11 Willie McCovey .20 .50
12 Joe Morgan .20 .50
13 Satchel Paige .30 .75
14 Frank Robinson .30 .75
15 Willie Stargell .20 .50
16 Billy Williams .20 .50
17 Jackie Robinson 2.00 5.00

1991 Stadium Club Pre-Production

The exact origins of this scarce 50-card set is unclear, but speculation is that Topps distributed single cards or uncut strips to its employees and/or major candy wholesale accounts. The card fronts are very similar to the player's corresponding regular Stadium Club cards with the addition of an extra horizontal gold foil stripe at the bottom. The backs of all 50 cards are identical -- unnumbered with a reproduction of Jose Canseco's 1986 Topps Traded card.

COMPLETE SET (50) 75.00 150.00
1 Allan Anderson 3.00 8.00
2 Steve Balboni 3.00 8.00
3 Jeff Ballard 3.00 8.00
4 Jesse Barfield 3.00 8.00
5 Andy Benes 3.00 8.00
6 Bobby Bonilla 3.00 8.00
7 Chris Bosio 3.00 8.00
8 Daryl Boston 3.00 8.00
9 Chuck Cary 3.00 8.00
10 Pat Combs 3.00 8.00
11 Delino DeShields 3.00 8.00
12 Shawon Dunston 3.00 8.00
13 Alvaro Espinoza 3.00 8.00
14 Sid Fernandez 3.00 8.00
15 Bob Geren 3.00 8.00
16 Brian Holman 3.00 8.00
17 Jay Howell 3.00 8.00
18 Stan Javier 3.00 8.00
19 Dave Johnson 3.00 8.00
20 Howard Johnson 3.00 8.00
21 Kevin Maas 3.00 8.00
22 Shane Mack 3.00 8.00
23 Joe Magrane 3.00 8.00
24 Denny Martinez 3.00 8.00
25 Don Mattingly 15.00 40.00
26 Ben McDonald 3.00 8.00
27 Eddie Murray 5.00 12.00
28 Matt Nokes 3.00 8.00
29 Greg Olson 3.00 8.00
30 Gregg Olson 3.00 8.00
31 Jose Oquendo 3.00 8.00
32 Tony Phillips 3.00 8.00
33 Rafael Ramirez 3.00 8.00
34 Dennis Rasmussen 3.00 8.00
35 Billy Ripken 3.00 8.00
36 Nolan Ryan 12.00 60.00
37 Bill Sampen 3.00 8.00
38 Steve Sax 3.00 8.00
39 Mike Scioscia 5.00 12.00
40 David Segui 3.00 8.00
41 Zane Smith 3.00 8.00
42 B.J. Surhoff 3.00 8.00
43 Bobby Thigpen 3.00 8.00
44 Alan Trammell 5.00 12.00
45 Fernando Valenzuela 5.00 12.00
46 Andy Van Slyke 3.00 8.00
47 Hector Villanueva 3.00 8.00
48 Larry Walker 5.00 12.00
49 Walt Weiss 3.00 8.00
50 Bob Walk 3.00 8.00

1991 Stadium Club

This 600-card standard size set marked Topps first premium quality set. The set was issued in two separate series of 300 cards each. Cards were distributed in plastic wrapped packs. Series II cards were also available at McDonald's restaurants in the Northeast at three cards per pack. The set created a stir in the hobby upon release with dazzling full-color borderless photos and slick, glossy card stock. The back of each card has the basic biographical information as well as making use of the Fastball BARS system and an inset photo of the player's Topps rookie card. Notable Rookie Cards include Jeff Bagwell.

COMPLETE SET (600) 12.00 30.00
COMPLETE SERIES 1 (300) 8.00 20.00
COMPLETE SERIES 2 (300) 8.00 20.00
1 Dave Stewart Tuxedo .20 .50
2 Wally Joyner .20 .50
3 Shawon Dunston .08 .25
4 Darren Daulton .20 .50
5 Will Clark .30 .75
6 Sammy Sosa .50 1.25
7 Dan Plesac .08 .25
8 Marquis Grissom .20 .50
9 Erik Hanson .08 .25
10 Geno Petralli .08 .25
11 Jose Rijo .08 .25
12 Carlos Quintana .08 .25
13 Junior Ortiz .08 .25
14 Bob Walk .08 .25
15 Mike Macfarlane .08 .25
16 Eric Yelding .08 .25
17 Bryn Smith .08 .25
18 Bip Roberts .08 .25
19 Mike Scioscia .08 .25
20 Mark Williamson .08 .25
21 Don Mattingly 1.25 3.00
22 John Franco .20 .50
23 Chet Lemon .08 .25
24 Tom Henke .08 .25
25 Jerry Browne .08 .25
26 Dave Justice .20 .50
27 Mark Langston .08 .25
28 Damon Berryhill .08 .25
29 Kevin Bass .08 .25
30 Scott Fletcher .08 .25
31 Moises Alou .20 .50
32 Dave Valle .08 .25
33 Jody Reed .08 .25
34 Dave West .08 .25
35 Kevin McReynolds .08 .25
36 Pat Combs .08 .25
37 Eric Davis .20 .50
38 Bret Saberhagen .20 .50
39 Stan Javier .08 .25
40 Chuck Cary .08 .25
41 Tony Phillips .08 .25
42 Lee Smith .20 .50
43 Tim Teufel .08 .25
44 Lance Dickson RC .15 .40
45 Greg Litton .08 .25
46 Ted Higuera .08 .25
47 Edgar Martinez .30 .75
48 Steve Avery .08 .25
49 Walt Weiss .08 .25
50 David Segui .08 .25
51 Andy Benes .08 .25
52 Karl Rhodes .08 .25
53 Neal Heaton .08 .25
54 Danny Gladden .08 .25
55 Luis Rivera .08 .25
56 Kevin Brown .20 .50
57 Frank Thomas .50 1.25
58 Terry Mulholland .08 .25
59 Dick Schofield .08 .25
60 Ron Darling .08 .25
61 Sandy Alomar Jr. .08 .25
62 Dave Stieb .08 .25
63 Alan Trammell .20 .50
64 Matt Nokes .08 .25
65 Lenny Harris .08 .25
66 Milt Thompson .08 .25
67 Storm Davis .08 .25
68 Joe Oliver .08 .25
69 Andres Galarraga .20 .50
70 Ozzie Guillen .20 .50
71 Ken Howell .08 .25
72 Garry Templeton .08 .25
73 Derrick May .08 .25
74 Xavier Hernandez .08 .25
75 Dave Parker .20 .50
76 Rick Aguilera .20 .50
77 Robby Thompson .08 .25
78 Pete Incaviglia .08 .25
79 Bob Welch .08 .25
80 Randy Milligan .08 .25
81 Chuck Finley .20 .50
82 Alvin Davis .08 .25
83 Tim Naehring .08 .25
84 Jay Bell .20 .50
85 Joe Magrane .08 .25
86 Howard Johnson .08 .25
87 Jack McDowell .08 .25
88 Kevin Seitzer .08 .25
89 Bruce Ruffin .08 .25
90 Fernando Valenzuela .20 .50
91 Terry Kennedy .08 .25
92 Barry Larkin .30 .75
93 Larry Walker .50 1.25
94 Luis Salazar .08 .25
95 Gary Sheffield .20 .50
96 Bobby Witt .08 .25
97 Lonnie Smith .08 .25
98 Bryan Harvey .08 .25
99 Mookie Wilson .20 .50
100 Dwight Gooden .20 .50
101 Lou Whitaker .20 .50
102 Ron Karkovice .08 .25
103 Jesse Barfield .08 .25
104 Jose DeJesus .08 .25
105 Benito Santiago .20 .50
106 Brian Holman .08 .25
107 Rafael Ramirez .08 .25
108 Ellis Burks .20 .50
109 Mike Bielecki .08 .25
110 Kirby Puckett .50 1.25
111 Terry Shumpert .08 .25
112 Chuck Crim .08 .25
113 Todd Benzinger .08 .25
114 Brian Barnes RC .15 .40
115 Carlos Baerga .08 .25
116 Kal Daniels .08 .25
117 Dave Johnson .08 .25
118 Andy Van Slyke .30 .75
119 John Burkett .08 .25
120 Rickey Henderson .50 1.25
121 Tim Jones .08 .25
122 Daryl Irvine RC .08 .25
123 Ruben Sierra .20 .50
124 Jim Abbott .30 .75
125 Daryl Boston .08 .25
126 Greg Maddux .75 2.00
127 Von Hayes .08 .25
128 Mike Fitzgerald .08 .25
129 Wayne Edwards .08 .25
130 Greg Briley .08 .25
131 Rob Dibble .20 .50
132 Gene Larkin .08 .25
133 David Wells .20 .50
134 Steve Balboni .08 .25
135 Greg Vaughn .08 .25
136 Mark Davis .08 .25
137 Dave Rhode .08 .25
138 Eric Show .08 .25
139 Bobby Bonilla .20 .50
140 Dana Kiecker .08 .25
141 Gary Pettis .08 .25
142 Dennis Boyd .08 .25
143 Mike Benjamin .08 .25
144 Luis Polonia .08 .25
145 Doug Jones .08 .25
146 Al Newman .08 .25
147 Alex Fernandez .08 .25
148 Bill Doran .08 .25
149 Kevin Elster .08 .25
150 Len Dykstra .20 .50
151 Mike Gallego .08 .25
152 Tim Belcher .08 .25
153 Jay Buhner .20 .50
154 Ozzie Smith UER .75 2.00
155 Jose Canseco .30 .75
156 Gregg Olson .08 .25
157 Charlie O'Brien .08 .25
158 Frank Tanana .08 .25
159 George Brett 1.25 3.00
160 Jeff Huson .08 .25
161 Kevin Tapani .08 .25
162 Jerome Walton .08 .25
163 Charlie Hayes .08 .25
164 Chris Bosio .08 .25
165 Chris Sabo .08 .25
166 Lance Parrish .20 .50
167 Don Robinson .08 .25
168 Manny Lee .08 .25
169 Dennis Rasmussen .08 .25
170 Wade Boggs .30 .75
171 Bob Geren .08 .25
172 Mackey Sasser .08 .25
173 Julio Franco .20 .50
174 Otis Nixon .08 .25
175 Bert Blyleven .20 .50
176 Craig Biggio .30 .75
177 Eddie Murray .50 1.25
178 Randy Tomlin RC .15 .40
179 Tino Martinez .50 1.25
180 Carlton Fisk .30 .75
181 Dwight Smith .08 .25
182 Scott Garrelts .08 .25
183 Jim Gantner .08 .25
184 Dickie Thon .08 .25
185 John Farrell .08 .25
186 Cecil Fielder .20 .50
187 Glenn Braggs .08 .25
188 Allan Anderson .08 .25
189 Kurt Stillwell .08 .25
190 Jose Oquendo .08 .25
191 Joe Orsulak .08 .25
192 Ricky Jordan .08 .25
193 Kelly Downs .08 .25
194 Delino DeShields .08 .25
195 Omar Vizquel .30 .75
196 Mark Carreon .08 .25
197 Mike Harkey .08 .25
198 Jack Howell .08 .25
199 Lance Johnson .08 .25
200 Nolan Ryan TUX 2.00 5.00
201 John Marzano .08 .25
202 Doug Drabek .08 .25
203 Mark Lemke .08 .25
204 Steve Sax .08 .25
205 Greg Harris .08 .25
206 B.J. Surhoff .20 .50
207 Todd Burns .08 .25
208 Jose Gonzalez .08 .25
209 Mike Scott .08 .25
210 Dave Magadan .08 .25
211 Dante Bichette .20 .50
212 Trevor Wilson .08 .25
213 Hector Villanueva .08 .25
214 Dan Pasqua .08 .25
215 Greg Colbrunn RC .25 .60
216 Mike Jeffcoat .08 .25
217 Harold Reynolds .20 .50
218 Paul O'Neill .30 .75
219 Mark Guthrie .08 .25
220 Barry Bonds 1.50 4.00
221 Jimmy Key .20 .50
222 Billy Ripken .08 .25
223 Tom Pagnozzi .08 .25
224 Bo Jackson .50 1.25
225 Sid Fernandez .08 .25
226 Mike Marshall .08 .25
227 John Kruk .20 .50
228 Mike Fetters .08 .25
229 Eric Anthony .08 .25
230 Ryne Sandberg .75 2.00
231 Carney Lansford .20 .50
232 Melido Perez .08 .25
233 Jose Lind .08 .25
234 Darryl Hamilton .08 .25
235 Tom Browning .08 .25
236 Spike Owen .08 .25
237 Juan Gonzalez .50 1.25
238 Felix Fermin .08 .25
239 Keith Miller .08 .25
240 Mark Gubicza .08 .25
241 Kent Anderson .08 .25
242 Alvaro Espinoza .08 .25
243 Dale Murphy .30 .75
244 Orel Hershiser .20 .50
245 Paul Molitor .20 .50
246 Eddie Whitson .08 .25
247 Joe Girardi .08 .25
248 Kent Hrbek .20 .50
249 Bill Sampen .08 .25
250 Kevin Mitchell .08 .25
251 Mariano Duncan .08 .25
252 Scott Bradley .08 .25
253 Mike Greenwell .08 .25
254 Tom Gordon .08 .25
255 Todd Zeile .08 .25
256 Bobby Thigpen .08 .25
257 Gregg Jefferies .08 .25
258 Kenny Rogers .20 .50
259 Shane Mack .08 .25
260 Zane Smith .08 .25
261 Mitch Williams .08 .25
262 Jim Deshaies .08 .25
263 Dave Winfield .20 .50
264 Ben McDonald .08 .25
265 Randy Ready .08 .25
266 Pat Borders .08 .25
267 Jose Uribe .08 .25
268 Derek Lilliquist .08 .25
269 Greg Brock .08 .25
270 Ken Griffey Jr. 1.25 3.00
271 Jeff Gray RC .08 .25
272 Danny Tartabull .08 .25
273 Dennis Martinez .20 .50
274 Robin Ventura .20 .50
275 Randy Myers .20 .50
276 Jack Daugherty .08 .25
277 Greg Gagne .08 .25
278 Jay Howell .08 .25
279 Mike LaValliere .08 .25
280 Rex Hudler .08 .25
281 Mike Simms RC .08 .25
282 Kevin Maas .08 .25
283 Jeff Ballard .08 .25
284 Dave Henderson .08 .25
285 Pete O'Brien .08 .25
286 Brook Jacoby .08 .25
287 Mike Henneman .08 .25
288 Greg Olson .08 .25
289 Greg Myers .08 .25
290 Mark Grace .30 .75
291 Shawn Abner .08 .25
292 Frank Viola .20 .50
293 Lee Stevens .08 .25
294 Jason Grimsley .08 .25
295 Matt Williams .20 .50
296 Ron Robinson .08 .25
297 Tom Brunansky .08 .25
298 Checklist 1-100 .08 .25
299 Checklist 101-200 .08 .25
300 Checklist 201-300 .08 .25
301 Darryl Strawberry .20 .50
302 Bud Black .08 .25
303 Harold Baines .20 .50
304 Roberto Alomar .30 .75
305 Norm Charlton .08 .25
306 Gary Thurman .08 .25
307 Mike Felder .08 .25
308 Tony Gwynn .60 1.50
309 Roger Clemens 1.50 4.00
310 Andre Dawson .20 .50
311 Scott Radinsky .08 .25

312 Bob Melvin .08 .25
313 Kirk McCaskill .08 .25
314 Pedro Guerrero .20 .50
315 Walt Terrell .08 .25
316 Sam Horn .08 .25
317 Wes Chamberlain UER RC .25 .60
318 Pedro Munoz RC .15 .40
319 Roberto Kelly .08 .25
320 Mark Portugal .08 .25
321 Tim McIntosh .08 .25
322 Jesse Orosco .08 .25
323 Gary Green .08 .25
324 Greg Harris .08 .25
325 Hubie Brooks .08 .25
326 Chris Nabholz .08 .25
327 Terry Pendleton .20 .50
328 Eric King .08 .25
329 Chili Davis .20 .50
330 Anthony Telford RC .08 .25
331 Kelly Gruber .08 .25
332 Dennis Eckersley .20 .50
333 Mel Hall .08 .25
334 Bob Kipper .08 .25
335 Willie McGee .20 .50
336 Steve Olin .08 .25
337 Steve Buechele .08 .25
338 Scott Leius .08 .25
339 Hal Morris .08 .25
340 Jose Offerman .08 .25
341 Kent Mercker .08 .25
342 Ken Griffey Sr. .20 .50
343 Pete Harnisch .08 .25
344 Kirk Gibson .20 .50
345 Dave Smith .08 .25
346 Dave Martinez .08 .25
347 Atlee Hammaker .08 .25
348 Brian Downing .08 .25
349 Todd Hundley .08 .25
350 Candy Maldonado .08 .25
351 Dwight Evans .30 .75
352 Steve Searcy .08 .25
353 Gary Gaetti .20 .50
354 Jeff Reardon .20 .50
355 Travis Fryman .20 .50
356 Dave Righetti .20 .50
357 Fred McGriff .30 .75
358 Don Slaught .08 .25
359 Gene Nelson .08 .25
360 Billy Spiers .08 .25
361 Lee Guetterman .08 .25
362 Darren Lewis .08 .25
363 Duane Ward .08 .25
364 Lloyd Moseby .08 .25
365 John Smoltz .30 .75
366 Felix Jose .08 .25
367 David Cone .20 .50
368 Wally Backman .08 .25
369 Jeff Montgomery .08 .25
370 Rich Garces RC .15 .40
371 Billy Hatcher .08 .25
372 Bill Swift .08 .25
373 Jim Eisenreich .08 .25
374 Rob Ducey .08 .25
375 Tim Crews .08 .25
376 Steve Finley .20 .50
377 Jeff Blauser .08 .25
378 Willie Wilson .08 .25
379 Gerald Perry .08 .25
380 Jose Mesa .08 .25
381 Pat Kelly RC .25 .60
382 Matt Merullo .08 .25
383 Ivan Calderon .08 .25
384 Scott Chiamparino .08 .25
385 Lloyd McClendon .08 .25
386 Dave Bergman .08 .25
387 Ed Sprague .08 .25
388 Jeff Bagwell RC 1.25 3.00
389 Brett Butler .20 .50
390 Larry Andersen .08 .25
391 Glenn Davis .08 .25
392 Alex Cole UER .08 .25
Front photo actually
Otis Nixon
393 Mike Heath .08 .25
394 Danny Darwin .08 .25
395 Steve Lake .08 .25
396 Tim Layana .08 .25
397 Terry Leach .08 .25
398 Bill Wegman .08 .25
399 Mark McGwire 1.50 4.00
400 Mike Boddicker .08 .25
401 Steve Howe .08 .25
402 Bernard Gilkey .08 .25
403 Thomas Howard .08 .25
404 Rafael Belliard .08 .25
405 Tom Candiotti .08 .25
406 Rene Gonzales .08 .25
407 Chuck McElroy .08 .25
408 Paul Sorrento .08 .25
409 Randy Johnson .60 1.50
410 Brady Anderson .20 .50
411 Dennis Cook .08 .25
412 Mickey Tettleton .08 .25
413 Mike Stanton .08 .25
414 Ken Oberkfell .08 .25
415 Rick Honeycutt .08 .25
416 Nelson Santovenia .08 .25
417 Bob Tewksbury .08 .25
418 Brent Mayne .08 .25
419 Steve Farr .08 .25
420 Phil Stephenson .08 .25
421 Jeff Russell .08 .25
422 Chris James .08 .25
423 Tim Leary .08 .25
424 Gary Carter .20 .50
425 Glenallen Hill .08 .25
426 Matt Young UER .08 .25
427 Sid Bream .08 .25
428 Greg Swindell .08 .25
429 Scott Aldred .08 .25
430 Cal Ripken 1.50 4.00
431 Bill Landrum .08 .25
432 Earnest Riles .08 .25
433 Danny Jackson .08 .25
434 Casey Candaele .08 .25
435 Ken Hill .08 .25
436 Jaime Navarro .08 .25
437 Lance Blankenship .08 .25
438 Randy Velarde .08 .25
439 Frank DiPino .08 .25
440 Carl Nichols .08 .25
441 Jeff M. Robinson .08 .25
442 Deion Sanders .30 .75
443 Vicente Palacios .08 .25
444 Devon White .20 .50
445 John Cerutti .08 .25
446 Tracy Jones .08 .25
447 Jack Morris .20 .50
448 Mitch Webster .08 .25
449 Bob Ojeda .08 .25
450 Oscar Azocar .08 .25
451 Luis Aquino .08 .25
452 Mark Whiten .08 .25
453 Stan Belinda .08 .25
454 Ron Gant .20 .50
455 Jose DeLeon .08 .25
456 Mark Salas UER .08 .25
Back has 85T photo,
but calls it 86T
457 Junior Felix .08 .25
458 Wally Whitehurst .08 .25
459 Phil Plantier RC .25 .60
460 Juan Berenguer .08 .25
461 Franklin Stubbs .08 .25
462 Joe Boever .08 .25
463 Tim Wallach .08 .25
464 Mike Moore .08 .25
465 Albert Belle .20 .50
466 Mike Witt .08 .25
467 Craig Worthington .08 .25
468 Jerald Clark .08 .25
469 Scott Terry .08 .25
470 Milt Cuyler .08 .25
471 John Smiley .08 .25
472 Charles Nagy .08 .25
473 Alan Mills .08 .25
474 John Russell .08 .25
475 Bruce Hurst .08 .25
476 Andujar Cedeno .08 .25
477 Dave Eiland .08 .25
478 Brian McRae RC .25 .60
479 Mike LaCoss .08 .25
480 Chris Gwynn .08 .25
481 Jamie Moyer .20 .50
482 John Olerud .20 .50
483 Efrain Valdez RC .08 .25
484 Sil Campusano .08 .25
485 Pascual Perez .08 .25
486 Gary Redus .08 .25
487 Andy Hawkins .08 .25
488 Cory Snyder .08 .25
489 Chris Hoiles .08 .25
490 Ron Hassey .08 .25
491 Gary Wayne .08 .25
492 Mark Lewis .08 .25
493 Scott Coolbaugh .08 .25
494 Gerald Young .08 .25
495 Juan Samuel .08 .25
496 Willie Fraser .08 .25
497 Jeff Treadway .08 .25
498 Vince Coleman .08 .25
499 Cris Carpenter .08 .25
500 Jack Clark .20 .50
501 Kevin Appier .20 .50
502 Rafael Palmeiro .30 .75
503 Hensley Meulens .08 .25
504 George Bell .08 .25
505 Tony Pena .08 .25
506 Roger McDowell .08 .25
507 Luis Sojo .08 .25
508 Mike Schooler .08 .25
509 Robin Yount .75 2.00
510 Jack Armstrong .08 .25
511 Rick Cerone .08 .25
512 Curt Wilkerson .08 .25
513 Joe Carter .20 .50
514 Tim Burke .08 .25
515 Tony Fernandez .08 .25
516 Ramon Martinez .08 .25
517 Tim Hulett .08 .25
518 Terry Steinbach .08 .25
519 Pete Smith .08 .25
520 Ken Caminiti .20 .50
521 Shawn Boskie .08 .25
522 Mike Pagliarulo .08 .25
523 Tim Raines .20 .50
524 Alfredo Griffin .08 .25
525 Henry Cotto .08 .25
526 Mike Stanley .08 .25
527 Charlie Leibrandt .08 .25
528 Jeff King .08 .25
529 Eric Plunk .08 .25
530 Tom Lampkin .08 .25
531 Steve Bedrosian .08 .25
532 Tom Herr .08 .25
533 Craig Lefferts .08 .25
534 Jeff Reed .08 .25
535 Mickey Morandini .08 .25
536 Greg Cadaret .08 .25
537 Ray Lankford .20 .50
538 John Candelaria .08 .25
539 Rob Deer .08 .25
540 Brad Arnsberg .08 .25
541 Mike Sharperson .08 .25
542 Jeff D. Robinson .08 .25
543 Mo Vaughn .20 .50
544 Jeff Parrett .08 .25
545 Willie Randolph .20 .50
546 Herm Winningham .08 .25
547 Jeff Innis .08 .25
548 Chuck Knoblauch .20 .50
549 Tommy Greene UER .08 .25
Born in North Carolina,
not South Carolina
550 Jeff Hamilton .08 .25
551 Barry Jones .08 .25
552 Ken Dayley .08 .25
553 Rick Dempsey .08 .25
554 Greg Smith .08 .25
555 Mike Devereaux .08 .25
556 Keith Comstock .08 .25
557 Paul Faries RC .08 .25
558 Tom Glavine .30 .75
559 Craig Grebeck .08 .25
560 Scott Erickson .08 .25
561 Joel Skinner .08 .25
562 Mike Morgan .08 .25
563 Dave Gallagher .08 .25
564 Todd Stottlemyre .08 .25
565 Rich Rodriguez RC .08 .25
566 Craig Wilson RC .08 .25
567 Jeff Brantley .08 .25
568 Scott Kamieniecki RC .25 .60
569 Steve Decker RC .15 .40
570 Juan Agosto .08 .25
571 Tommy Gregg .08 .25
572 Kevin Wickander .08 .25
573 Jamie Quirk UER .08 .25
Rookie card is 1976,
but card back is 1990
574 Jerry Don Gleaton .08 .25
575 Chris Hammond .08 .25
576 Luis Gonzalez RC .60 1.50
577 Russ Swan .08 .25
578 Jeff Conine RC .40 1.00
579 Charlie Hough .20 .50
580 Jeff Kunkel .08 .25
581 Darrel Akerfelds .08 .25
582 Jeff Manto .08 .25
583 Alejandro Pena .08 .25
584 Mark Davidson .08 .25
585 Bob MacDonald RC .15 .40
586 Paul Assenmacher .08 .25
587 Dan Wilson RC .25 .60
588 Tom Bolton .08 .25
589 Brian Harper .08 .25
590 John Habyan .08 .25
591 John Orton .08 .25
592 Mark Gardner .08 .25
593 Turner Ward RC .25 .60
594 Bob Patterson .08 .25
595 Ed Nunez .08 .25
596 Gary Scott UER RC .15 .40
597 Scott Bankhead .08 .25
598 Checklist 301-400 .08 .25
599 Checklist 401-500 .08 .25
600 Checklist 501-600 .08 .25

1991 Stadium Club Charter Member

This 50-card multi-sport standard-size set was sent to charter members in the Topps Stadium Club. The sports represented in the set are baseball (1-32), football (33-41), and hockey (42-50). The cards feature on the fronts full-bleed posed and action glossy color player photos. The player's name is shown in the light blue stripe that intersects the Stadium Club logo near the bottom of the picture. The words "Charter Member" are printed in gold foil lettering immediately below the stripe. The back design features a newspaper-like masthead (The Stadium Club Herald) complete with a headline announcing a major event in the player's season with copy below providing more information about the event. The cards are unnumbered and arranged below alphabetically within sports. Topps apparently made two printings of this set, which are most easily identifiable by the small asterisks on the bottom left of the card backs. The first printing cards have one asterisk, the second printing cards have two. The display box that contained the cards also included a Nolan Ryan bronze metallic card and a key chain. Very early members of the Stadium Club received a large size bronze metallic Nolan Ryan 1990 Topps card. It is valued below as well as the normal size Ryan metallic card. A third varation on the Ryan medallion has been found. This is another version of the 1991 Stadium Club charter member bronze medallion, except this one has a 24K logo on it. It is suspected that this might be a Home Shopping Newtork variety. No pricing is provided at this time for this piece due to lack of market information.

COMP.FACT SET (50) 6.00 15.00
1 Sandy Alomar .10 .30
2 George Brett .60 1.50
3 Barry Bonds .40 1.00
4 Ellis Burks .10 .30
5 Eric Davis .10 .30
6 Delino DeShields .07 .20
7 Doug Drabek .07 .20
8 Cecil Fielder .10 .30
9 Carlton Fisk .20 .50
10 Ken Griffey Jr. 1.50 4.00
Ken Griffey Sr.
11 Billy Hatcher .07 .20
12 Andy Hawkins .07 .20
13 Rickey Henderson .20 .50
A.L. Recognizes
Rickey As MVP
14 Rickey Henderson .20 .50
Rickey is A.L.'s
Leading Thief
15 Randy Johnson .30 .75
16 Dave Justice .30 .75
17 Mark Langston .07 .20
Mike Witt
18 Kevin Maas .07 .20
19 Ramon Martinez .10 .30
20 Willie McGee .07 .20
21 Terry Mulholland .07 .20
22 Jose Offerman .07 .20
23 Melido Perez .07 .20
24 Nolan Ryan 1.25 3.00
A No-Hitter For
The Ages
25 Nolan Ryan 1.25 3.00
Nolan Ryan Earns/300th Career Win
26 Ryne Sandberg .60 1.50
27 Dave Stewart .10 .30
28 Dave Stieb .07 .20
29 Bobby Thigpen .07 .20
30 Fernando Valenzuela .10 .30
31 Frank Viola .07 .20
32 Bob Welch .10 .30
NNO Nolan Ryan Bronze Medal. 6.00 15.00
NNO N.Ryan Bronze Medal. Lge. 80.00 200.00
NNO Nolan Ryan Bronze .75 2.00
Medallion small/1991 Stadium C

1991 Stadium Club Members Only

This 50-card multi-sport standard-size set was sent in three installments to members in the Topps Stadium Club. The first and second installments featured baseball players (card numbers 1-10 and 11-30), while the third spotlighted football (31-37) and hockey (38-50) players. The cards feature on the fronts full-bleed posed and action glossy color player photos. The player's name is shown in the light blue stripe that intersects the Stadium Club logo near the bottom of the picture. The words "Members Only" are printed in gold foil lettering immediately below the stripe. The back design features a newspaper-like masthead (The Stadium Club Herald) complete with a headline announcing a major event in the player's season with copy below providing more information about the event. The cards are unnumbered and arranged below alphabetically according to and within installments.

COMPLETE SET (50) 6.00 15.00
1 Wilson Alvarez .07 .20
2 Andy Ashby .07 .20
3 Tommy Greene .07 .20
4 Rickey Henderson .20 .50
Rickey Is Top
Thief in History
5 Denny Martinez .07 .20
6 Paul Molitor .30 .75
7 Nolan Ryan 1.25 3.00
Ryan Extends Record
With 7th No-Hitte
8 Robby Thompson .07 .20
9 Dave Winfield .30 .75
10 Orioles No-Hitter .07 .20
Bob Milacki
Mike Flanagan
Mar
11 Jeff Bagwell 1.25 3.00
12 Roger Clemens .50 1.25
13 David Cone .08 .25
14 Carlton Fisk .20 .50
15 Julio Franco .07 .20
16 Tom Glavine .08 .25
17 Pete Harnisch .07 .20
18 Rickey Henderson .20 .50
Rickey Leads A.L. In
Thefts For
19 Howard Johnson .07 .20
20 Chuck Knoblauch .07 .20
21 Ray Lankford .07 .20
22 Jack Morris .08 .25
23 Terry Pendleton .08 .25
NL's Leading Batsman
24 Terry Pendleton .08 .25
Close MVP Race
Favors Terry
25 Jeff Reardon .07 .20
26 Cal Ripken 1.25 3.00
27 Nolan Ryan 1.25 3.00
Ryan's 22nd Straight
Year With Over/
28 Bret Saberhagen .07 .20
29 Cecil Fielder .15 .40
Jose Canseco
30 Braves No Hitter .07 .20
Kent Mercker
Mark Wohlers
Alej

1992 Stadium Club Dome

The 1992 Stadium Club Dome set (issued by Topps) features 100 top draft picks, 56 1991 All-Star Game cards, 25 1991 Team U.S.A. cards, and 19 1991 Championship and World Series cards, all packaged in a factory set box inside a molded-plastic SkyDome display. Topps actually references this set as a 1991 set and the copyright lines on the card backs say 1991, but the set was released well into 1992. Rookie Cards in this set include Shawn Green and Manny Ramirez.

COMP.FACT.SET (200) 6.00 15.00
ORIGINALLY INTENDED AS A 1991 RELEASE
1 Terry Adams RC .20 .50
2 Tommy Adams RC .08 .25
3 Rick Aguilera .05 .15
4 Ron Allen RC .08 .25
5 Roberto Alomar .08 .25
6 Sandy Alomar Jr. .02 .10
7 Greg Anthony RC .08 .25
8 James Austin RC .08 .25
9 Steve Avery .02 .10
10 Harold Baines .05 .15
11 Brian Barber RC .08 .25
12 Jon Barnes RC .08 .25
13 George Bell .02 .10
14 Doug Bennett RC .08 .25
15 Sean Bergman RC .20 .50
16 Craig Biggio .08 .25
17 Bill Bliss RC .08 .25
18 Wade Boggs .08 .25
19 Bobby Bonilla .05 .15
20 Russell Brock RC .08 .25
21 Tarrik Brock RC .08 .25
22 Tom Browning .02 .10
23 Brett Butler .05 .15
24 Ivan Calderon .02 .10
25 Joe Carter .05 .15
26 Joe Caruso RC .08 .25
27 Dan Cholowsky RC .08 .25
28 Will Clark .08 .25
29 Roger Clemens .40 1.00
30 Shawn Curran RC .08 .25
31 Chris Curtis RC .08 .25
32 Chili Davis .05 .15
33 Andre Dawson .05 .15
34 Joe DeBerry RC .08 .25
35 John Dettmer .02 .10
36 Rob Dibble .05 .15
37 John Donati RC .08 .25
38 Dave Doorneweerd RC .08 .25
39 Darren Dreifort .02 .10
40 Mike Durant RC .08 .25
41 Chris Durkin RC .08 .25
42 Dennis Eckersley .05 .15
43 Brian Edmondson RC .08 .25
44 Vaughn Eshelman RC .08 .25
45 Shawn Estes RC .20 .50
46 Jorge Fabregas RC .20 .50
47 Jon Farrell RC .08 .25
48 Cecil Fielder .05 .15
49 Carlton Fisk .08 .25
50 Tim Flannelly RC .08 .25
51 Cliff Floyd RC .60 1.50
52 Julio Franco .05 .15
53 Greg Gagne .02 .10
54 Chris Gambs RC .08 .25
55 Ron Gant .05 .15
56 Brent Gates RC .08 .25
57 Dwayne Gerald RC .08 .25
58 Jason Giambi .40 1.00
59 Benji Gil RC .20 .50
60 Mark Gipner RC .08 .25
61 Danny Gladden .02 .10
62 Tom Glavine .08 .25
63 Jimmy Gonzalez RC .08 .25
64 Jeff Granger .02 .10
65 Dan Grapenthien RC .08 .25
66 Dennis Gray RC .08 .25
67 Shawn Green RC .75 2.00
68 Tyler Green RC .08 .25
69 Todd Greene .02 .10
70 Ken Griffey Jr. .40 1.00
71 Kelly Gruber .02 .10
72 Ozzie Guillen .05 .15
73 Tony Gwynn .25 .60
74 Shane Halter RC .08 .25
75 Jeffrey Hammonds .05 .15
76 Larry Hanlon RC .08 .25
77 Pete Harnisch .02 .10
78 Mike Harrison RC .08 .25
79 Bryan Harvey .02 .10
80 Scott Hatteberg RC .20 .50
81 Rick Helling .02 .10
82 Dave Henderson .02 .10
83 Rickey Henderson .20 .50
84 Tyrone Hill RC .08 .25
85 Todd Hollandsworth RC .20 .50
86 Brian Holliday RC .08 .25
87 Terry Horn RC .08 .25
88 Jeff Hostetler RC .08 .25
89 Kent Hrbek .05 .15
90 Mark Hubbard RC .08 .25
91 Charles Johnson .05 .15
92 Howard Johnson .02 .10
93 Todd Johnson .02 .10
94 Bobby Jones RC .20 .50
95 Dan Jones RC .08 .25
96 Felix Jose .02 .10
97 David Justice .02 .10
98 Jimmy Key .05 .15
99 Marc Kroon RC .08 .25
100 John Kruk .05 .15
101 Mark Langston .02 .10
102 Barry Larkin .08 .25
103 Mike LaValliere .02 .10
104 Scott Leius .02 .10
105 Mark Lemke .02 .10
106 Donnie Leshnock .02 .10
107 Jimmy Lewis RC .08 .25
108 Shane Livesy RC .08 .25
109 Ryan Long RC .08 .25
110 Trevor Mallory RC .08 .25
111 Dennis Martinez .05 .15
112 Justin Mashore RC .08 .25
113 Jason McDonald .02 .10
114 Jack McDowell .02 .10
115 Tom McKinnon RC .08 .25
116 Billy McMillon .02 .10
117 Buck McNabb RC .08 .25
118 Jim Mecir RC .08 .25
119 Dan Melendez .08 .25
120 Shawn Miller RC .08 .25
121 Trever Miller RC .08 .25
122 Paul Molitor .05 .15
123 Vincent Moore RC .08 .25
124 Mike Morgan .02 .10
125 Jack Morris WS .02 .10
126 Jack Morris AS .02 .10
127 Sean Mulligan RC .08 .25
128 Eddie Murray AS .20 .50
129 Mike Neill RC .20 .50
130 Phil Nevin .40 1.00
131 Mark O'Brien RC .08 .25
132 Alex Ochoa RC .08 .25
133 Chad Ogea RC .08 .25
134 Greg Olson .02 .10
135 Paul O'Neill .08 .25
136 Jared Osentowski RC .08 .25
137 Mike Pagliarulo .02 .10
138 Rafael Palmeiro .08 .25
139 Rodney Pedraza RC .08 .25
140 Tony Phillips P .02 .10
141 Scott Pisciotta RC .08 .25
142 Chris Pritchett RC .08 .25
143 Jason Pruitt RC .08 .25
144 Kirby Puckett WS UER .20 .50
Championship series
AB and BA is wrong
145 Kirby Puckett AS .20 .50
146 Manny Ramirez RC 2.50 6.00
147 Eddie Ramos RC .08 .25
148 Mark Ratekin RC .08 .25
149 Jeff Reardon .05 .15
150 Sean Rees RC .08 .25
151 Pokey Reese RC .20 .50
152 Desmond Relaford RC .08 .25
153 Eric Richardson RC .08 .25
154 Cal Ripken .60 1.50
155 Chris Roberts .02 .10
156 Mike Robertson RC .08 .25
157 Steve Rodriguez .02 .10
158 Mike Rossiter RC .08 .25
159 Scott Ruffcorn RC .08 .25
160 Chris Sabo .02 .10
161 Juan Samuel .02 .10
162 Ryne Sandberg UER .30 .75
163 Scott Sanderson .02 .10
164 Benny Santiago .05 .15
165 Gene Schall RC .08 .25
166 Chad Schoenvogel RC .08 .25
167 Chris Seelbach RC .08 .25
168 Aaron Sele RC .20 .50
169 Basil Shabazz RC .08 .25
170 Al Shirley RC .08 .25
171 Paul Shuey .02 .10
172 Ruben Sierra .02 .10
173 John Smiley .02 .10
174 Lee Smith .05 .15
175 Ozzie Smith .30 .75
176 Tim Smith RC .08 .25
177 Zane Smith .02 .10
178 John Smoltz .08 .25
179 Scott Stahoviak RC .08 .25
180 Kennie Steenstra .02 .10
181 Kevin Stocker RC .08 .25
182 Chris Stynes RC .20 .50
183 Danny Tartabull .02 .10
184 Brien Taylor RC .20 .50
185 Todd Taylor .02 .10
186 Larry Thomas RC .08 .25
187 Ozzie Timmons RC .08 .25
See also 188
188 David Tuttle UER .02 .10
Mistakenly numbered
as 187 on card
189 Andy Van Slyke .08 .25
190 Frank Viola .05 .15
191 Michael Walkden RC .08 .25
192 Jeff Ware .02 .10
193 Allen Watson RC .08 .25
194 Steve Whitaker RC .08 .25
195 Jerry Willard .02 .10
196 Craig Wilson .02 .10
197 Chris Wimmer .02 .10
198 Steve Wojciechowski RC .08 .25
199 Joel Wolfe RC .08 .25
200 Ivan Zweig .02 .10

1992 Stadium Club

The 1992 Stadium Club baseball card set consists of 900 standard-size cards issued in three series of 300 cards each. Cards were issued in plastic wrapped packs. A card-like application form for membership in Topps Stadium Club was inserted in each pack. Card numbers 591-610 form a "Members Choice" subset.

COMPLETE SET (900) 20.00 50.00
COMPLETE SERIES 1 (300) 6.00 15.00
COMPLETE SERIES 2 (300) 6.00 15.00
COMPLETE SERIES 3 (300) 6.00 15.00
1 Cal Ripken UER .60 1.50
2 Eric Yelding .02 .10
3 Geno Petralli .02 .10
4 Wally Backman .02 .10
5 Milt Cuyler .02 .10
6 Kevin Bass .02 .10
7 Dante Bichette .05 .15
8 Ray Lankford .05 .15
9 Mel Hall .02 .10
10 Joe Carter .05 .15
11 Juan Samuel .02 .10
12 Jeff Montgomery .02 .10
13 Glenn Braggs .02 .10
14 Henry Cotto .02 .10
15 Deion Sanders .08 .25
16 Dick Schofield .02 .10
17 David Cone .05 .15
18 Chili Davis .05 .15
19 Tom Foley .02 .10
20 Ozzie Guillen .05 .15
21 Luis Salazar .02 .10
22 Terry Steinbach .02 .10
23 Chris James .02 .10
24 Jeff King .02 .10
25 Carlos Quintana .02 .10
26 Mike Maddux .02 .10
27 Tommy Greene .02 .10
28 Jeff Russell .02 .10
29 Steve Finley .05 .15
30 Mike Flanagan .02 .10
31 Darren Lewis .02 .10
32 Mark Lee .02 .10
33 Willie Fraser .02 .10
34 Mike Henneman .02 .10
35 Kevin Maas .02 .10
36 Dave Hansen .02 .10
37 Erik Hanson .02 .10
38 Bill Doran .02 .10
39 Mike Boddicker .02 .10
40 Vince Coleman .02 .10
41 Devon White .05 .15
42 Mark Gardner .02 .10
43 Scott Lewis .02 .10
44 Juan Berenguer .02 .10
45 Carney Lansford .05 .15
46 Curt Wilkerson .02 .10
47 Shane Mack .02 .10
48 Bip Roberts .02 .10
49 Greg A. Harris .02 .10
50 Ryne Sandberg .30 .75
51 Mark Whiten .02 .10
52 Jack McDowell .02 .10
53 Jimmy Jones .02 .10
54 Steve Lake .02 .10
55 Bud Black .02 .10
56 Dave Valle .02 .10
57 Kevin Reimer .02 .10
58 Rich Gedman UER .02 .10
Wrong BARS chart used
59 Travis Fryman .05 .15
60 Steve Avery .02 .10
61 Francisco de la Rosa .02 .10
62 Scott Hemond .02 .10
63 Hal Morris .02 .10
64 Hensley Meulens .02 .10
65 Frank Castillo .02 .10
66 Gene Larkin .02 .10
67 Jose DeLeon .02 .10
68 Al Osuna .02 .10
69 Dave Cochrane .02 .10
70 Robin Ventura .05 .15
71 John Cerutti .02 .10
72 Kevin Gross .02 .10
73 Ivan Calderon .02 .10
74 Mike Macfarlane .02 .10
75 Stan Belinda .02 .10
76 Shawn Hillegas .02 .10
77 Pat Borders .02 .10
78 Jim Vatcher .02 .10
79 Bobby Rose .02 .10
80 Roger Clemens .40 1.00
81 Craig Worthington .02 .10
82 Jeff Treadway .02 .10
83 Jamie Quirk .02 .10
84 Randy Bush .02 .10
85 Anthony Young .02 .10
86 Trevor Wilson .02 .10
87 Jaime Navarro .02 .10
88 Les Lancaster .02 .10
89 Pat Kelly .02 .10
90 Alvin Davis .02 .10
91 Larry Andersen .02 .10
92 Rob Deer .02 .10
93 Mike Sharperson .02 .10
94 Lance Parrish .05 .15
95 Cecil Espy .02 .10
96 Tim Spehr .02 .10
97 Dave Stieb .02 .10
98 Terry Mulholland .02 .10
99 Dennis Boyd .02 .10
100 Barry Larkin .08 .25
101 Ryan Bowen .02 .10
102 Felix Fermin .02 .10
103 Luis Alicea .02 .10
104 Tim Hulett .02 .10
105 Rafael Belliard .02 .10
106 Mike Gallego .02 .10
107 Dave Righetti .05 .15
108 Jeff Schaefer .02 .10
109 Ricky Bones .02 .10
110 Scott Erickson .02 .10
111 Matt Nokes .02 .10
112 Bob Scanlan .02 .10
113 Tom Candiotti .02 .10
114 Sean Berry .02 .10
115 Kevin Morton .02 .10
116 Scott Fletcher .02 .10
117 B.J. Surhoff .05 .15
118 Dave Magadan UER .02 .10
Born Tampa, not Tamps
119 Bill Gullickson .02 .10
120 Marquis Grissom .05 .15
121 Lenny Harris .02 .10
122 Wally Joyner .05 .15
123 Kevin Brown .02 .10
124 Braulio Castillo .02 .10
125 Eric King .02 .10
126 Mark Portugal .02 .10
127 Calvin Jones .02 .10
128 Mike Heath .02 .10
129 Todd Van Poppel .02 .10
130 Benny Santiago .05 .15
131 Gary Thurman .02 .10
132 Joe Girardi .02 .10
133 Dave Eiland .02 .10
134 Orlando Merced .02 .10
135 Joe Orsulak .02 .10
136 John Burkett .02 .10
137 Ken Dayley .02 .10
138 Ken Hill .02 .10
139 Walt Terrell .02 .10
140 Mike Scioscia .02 .10
141 Junior Felix .02 .10
142 Ken Caminiti .05 .15
143 Carlos Baerga .02 .10
144 Tony Fossas .02 .10
145 Craig Grebeck .02 .10
146 Scott Bradley .02 .10
147 Kent Mercker .02 .10
148 Derrick May .02 .10
149 Jerald Clark .02 .10
150 George Brett .50 1.25
151 Luis Quinones .02 .10
152 Mike Pagliarulo .02 .10
153 Jose Guzman .02 .10
154 Charlie O'Brien .02 .10
155 Darren Holmes .02 .10
156 Joe Boever .02 .10
157 Rich Monteleone .02 .10
158 Reggie Harris .02 .10
159 Roberto Alomar .08 .25
160 Robby Thompson .02 .10
161 Chris Hoiles .02 .10
162 Tom Pagnozzi .02 .10
163 Omar Vizquel .08 .25
164 John Candelaria .02 .10
165 Terry Shumpert .02 .10
166 Andy Mota .02 .10
167 Scott Bailes .02 .10
168 Jeff Blauser .02 .10
169 Steve Olin .02 .10
170 Doug Drabek .02 .10
171 Dave Bergman .02 .10
172 Eddie Whitson .02 .10
173 Gilberto Reyes .02 .10
174 Mark Grace .08 .25
175 Paul O'Neill .08 .25
176 Greg Cadaret .02 .10
177 Mark Williamson .02 .10
178 Casey Candaele .02 .10
179 Candy Maldonado .02 .10
180 Lee Smith .05 .15
181 Harold Reynolds .05 .15
182 David Justice .05 .15
183 Lenny Webster .02 .10
184 Donn Pall .02 .10
185 Gerald Alexander .02 .10
186 Jack Clark .05 .15
187 Stan Javier .02 .10
188 Ricky Jordan .02 .10
189 Franklin Stubbs .02 .10
190 Dennis Eckersley .05 .15
191 Danny Tartabull .02 .10
192 Pete O'Brien .02 .10
193 Mark Lewis .02 .10
194 Mike Felder .02 .10
195 Mickey Tettleton .02 .10
196 Dwight Smith .02 .10
197 Shawn Abner .02 .10
198 Jim Leyritz UER .02 .10
Career totals less
than 1991 totals
199 Mike Devereaux .02 .10
200 Craig Biggio .08 .25
201 Kevin Elster .02 .10
202 Rance Mulliniks .02 .10
203 Tony Fernandez .02 .10
204 Allan Anderson .02 .10
205 Herm Winningham .02 .10
206 Tim Jones .02 .10

207 Ramon Martinez .02 .10
208 Teddy Higuera .02 .10
209 John Kruk .05 .15
210 Jim Abbott .08 .25
211 Dean Palmer .05 .15
212 Mark Davis .02 .10
213 Jay Buhner .05 .15
214 Jesse Barfield .02 .10
215 Kevin Mitchell .02 .10
216 Mike LaValliere .02 .10
217 Mark Wohlers .02 .10
218 Dave Henderson .02 .10
219 Dave Smith .02 .10
220 Albert Belle .05 .15
221 Spike Owen .02 .10
222 Jeff Gray .02 .10
223 Paul Gibson .02 .10
224 Bobby Thigpen .02 .10
225 Mike Mussina .20 .50
226 Darrin Jackson .02 .10
227 Luis Gonzalez .05 .15
228 Greg Briley .02 .10
229 Brent Mayne .02 .10
230 Paul Molitor .05 .15
231 Al Leiter .05 .15
232 Andy Van Slyke .08 .25
233 Ron Tingley .02 .10
234 Bernard Gilkey .02 .10
235 Kent Hrbek .05 .15
236 Eric Karros .05 .15
237 Randy Velarde .02 .10
238 Andy Allanson .02 .10
239 Willie McGee .05 .15
240 Juan Gonzalez .08 .25
241 Karl Rhodes .02 .10
242 Luis Mercedes .02 .10
243 Bill Swift .02 .10
244 Tommy Gregg .02 .10
245 David Howard .02 .10
246 Dave Hollins .02 .10
247 Kip Gross .02 .10
248 Walt Weiss .02 .10
249 Mackey Sasser .02 .10
250 Cecil Fielder .05 .15
251 Jerry Browne .02 .10
252 Doug Dascenzo .02 .10
253 Darryl Hamilton .02 .10
254 Dann Bilardello .02 .10
255 Luis Rivera .02 .10
256 Larry Walker .08 .25
257 Ron Karkovice .02 .10
258 Bob Tewksbury .02 .10
259 Jimmy Key .05 .15
260 Bernie Williams .08 .25
261 Gary Wayne .02 .10
262 Mike Simms UER .02 .10
Reversed negative
263 John Orton .02 .10
264 Marvin Freeman .02 .10
265 Mike Jeffcoat .02 .10
266 Roger Mason .02 .10
267 Edgar Martinez .08 .25
268 Henry Rodriguez .02 .10
269 Sam Horn .02 .10
270 Brian McRae .02 .10
271 Kirt Manwaring .02 .10
272 Mike Bordick .02 .10
273 Chris Sabo .02 .10
274 Jim Olander .02 .10
275 Greg W. Harris .02 .10
276 Dan Gakeler .02 .10
277 Bill Sampen .02 .10
278 Joel Skinner .02 .10
279 Curt Schilling .08 .25
280 Dale Murphy .08 .25
281 Lee Stevens .02 .10
282 Lonnie Smith .02 .10
283 Manuel Lee .02 .10
284 Shawn Boskie .02 .10
285 Kevin Seitzer .02 .10
286 Stan Royer .02 .10
287 John Dopson .02 .10
288 Scott Bullett RC .02 .10
289 Ken Patterson .02 .10
290 Todd Hundley .02 .10
291 Tim Leary .02 .10
292 Brett Butler .05 .15
293 Gregg Olson .02 .10
294 Jeff Brantley .02 .10
295 Brian Holman .02 .10
296 Brian Harper .02 .10
297 Brian Bohanon .02 .10
298 Checklist 1-100 .02 .10
299 Checklist 101-200 .02 .10
300 Checklist 201-300 .02 .10
301 Frank Thomas .20 .50
302 Lloyd McClendon .02 .10
303 Brady Anderson .05 .15
304 Julio Valera .02 .10
305 Mike Aldrete .02 .10
306 Joe Oliver .02 .10
307 Todd Stottlemyre .02 .10
308 Rey Sanchez RC .05 .15
309 Gary Sheffield UER .05 .15
310 Andujar Cedeno .02 .10
311 Kenny Rogers .05 .15
312 Bruce Hurst .02 .10
313 Mike Schooler .02 .10
314 Mike Benjamin .02 .10
315 Chuck Finley .05 .15
316 Mark Lemke .02 .10
317 Scott Livingstone .02 .10
318 Chris Nabholz .02 .10
319 Mike Humphreys .02 .10
320 Pedro Guerrero .05 .15
321 Willie Banks .02 .10
322 Tom Goodwin .02 .10
323 Hector Wagner .02 .10
324 Wally Ritchie .02 .10
325 Mo Vaughn .05 .15
326 Joe Klink .02 .10
327 Cal Eldred .02 .10
328 Daryl Boston .02 .10
329 Mike Huff .02 .10
330 Jeff Bagwell .20 .50
331 Bob Milacki .02 .10
332 Tom Prince .02 .10
333 Pat Tabler .02 .10
334 Ced Landrum .02 .10
335 Reggie Jefferson .02 .10
336 Mo Sanford .02 .10
337 Kevin Ritz .02 .10
338 Gerald Perry .02 .10
339 Jeff Hamilton .02 .10
340 Tim Wallach .02 .10
341 Jeff Huson .02 .10
342 Jose Melendez .02 .10
343 Willie Wilson .02 .10
344 Mike Stanton .02 .10
345 Joel Johnston .02 .10
346 Lee Guetterman .02 .10
347 Francisco Oliveras .02 .10
348 Dave Burba .02 .10
349 Tim Crews .02 .10
350 Scott Leius .02 .10
351 Danny Cox .02 .10
352 Wayne Housie .02 .10
353 Chris Donnels .02 .10
354 Chris George .02 .10
355 Gerald Young .02 .10
356 Roberto Hernandez .02 .10
357 Neal Heaton .02 .10
358 Todd Frohwirth .02 .10
359 Jose Vizcaino .02 .10
360 Jim Thome .20 .50
361 Craig Wilson .02 .10
362 Dave Haas .02 .10
363 Billy Hatcher .02 .10
364 John Barfield .02 .10
365 Luis Aquino .02 .10
366 Charlie Leibrandt .02 .10
367 Howard Farmer .02 .10
368 Bryn Smith .02 .10
369 Mickey Morandini .02 .10
370 Jose Canseco .08 .25
See also 597
371 Jose Uribe .02 .10
372 Bob MacDonald .02 .10
373 Luis Sojo .02 .10
374 Craig Shipley .02 .10
375 Scott Bankhead .02 .10
376 Greg Gagne .02 .10
377 Scott Cooper .02 .10
378 Jose Offerman .02 .10
379 Bill Spiers .02 .10
380 John Smiley .02 .10
381 Jeff Carter .02 .10
382 Heathcliff Slocumb .02 .10
383 Jeff Tackett .02 .10
384 John Kiely .02 .10
385 John Vander Wal .02 .10
386 Omar Olivares .02 .10
387 Ruben Sierra .05 .15
388 Tom Gordon .02 .10
389 Charles Nagy .02 .10
390 Dave Stewart .05 .15
391 Pete Harnisch .02 .10
392 Tim Burke .02 .10
393 Roberto Kelly .02 .10
394 Freddie Benavides .02 .10
395 Tom Glavine .08 .25
396 Wes Chamberlain .02 .10
397 Eric Gunderson .02 .10
398 Dave West .02 .10
399 Ellis Burks .05 .15
400 Ken Griffey Jr. .40 1.00
401 Thomas Howard .02 .10
402 Juan Guzman .02 .10
403 Mitch Webster .02 .10
404 Matt Merullo .02 .10
405 Steve Buechele .02 .10
406 Danny Jackson .02 .10
407 Felix Jose .02 .10
408 Doug Piatt .02 .10
409 Jim Eisenreich .02 .10
410 Bryan Harvey .02 .10
411 Jim Austin .02 .10
412 Jim Poole .02 .10
413 Glenallen Hill .02 .10
414 Gene Nelson .02 .10
415 Ivan Rodriguez .20 .50
416 Frank Tanana .02 .10
417 Steve Decker .02 .10
418 Jason Grimsley .02 .10
419 Tim Layana .02 .10
420 Don Mattingly .50 1.25
421 Jerome Walton .02 .10
422 Rob Ducey .02 .10
423 Andy Benes .02 .10
424 John Marzano .02 .10
425 Gene Harris .02 .10
426 Tim Raines .05 .15
427 Bret Barberie .02 .10
428 Harvey Pulliam .02 .10
429 Cris Carpenter .02 .10
430 Howard Johnson .02 .10
431 Orel Hershiser .05 .15
432 Brian Hunter .02 .10
433 Kevin Tapani .02 .10
434 Rick Reed .02 .10
435 Ron Witmeyer RC .02 .10
436 Gary Gaetti .05 .15
437 Alex Cole .02 .10
438 Chito Martinez .02 .10
439 Greg Litton .02 .10
440 Julio Franco .05 .15
441 Mike Munoz .02 .10
442 Erik Pappas .02 .10
443 Pat Combs .02 .10
444 Lance Johnson .02 .10
445 Ed Sprague .02 .10
446 Mike Greenwell .02 .10
447 Milt Thompson .02 .10
448 Mike Magnante RC .02 .10
449 Chris Haney .02 .10
450 Robin Yount .30 .75
451 Rafael Ramirez .02 .10
452 Gino Minutelli .02 .10
453 Tom Lampkin .02 .10
454 Tony Perezchica .02 .10
455 Dwight Gooden .05 .15
456 Mark Guthrie .02 .10
457 Jay Howell .02 .10
458 Gary DiSarcina .02 .10
459 John Smoltz .08 .25
460 Will Clark .08 .25
461 Dave Otto .02 .10
462 Rob Maurer RC .02 .10
463 Dwight Evans .08 .25
464 Tom Brunansky .02 .10
465 Shawn Hare RC .02 .10
466 Geronimo Pena .02 .10
467 Alex Fernandez .02 .10
468 Greg Myers .02 .10
469 Jeff Fassero .02 .10
470 Len Dykstra .05 .15
471 Jeff Johnson .02 .10
472 Russ Swan .02 .10
473 Archie Corbin .02 .10
474 Chuck McElroy .02 .10
475 Mark McGwire .50 1.25
476 Wally Whitehurst .02 .10
477 Tim McIntosh .02 .10
478 Sid Bream .02 .10
479 Jeff Juden .02 .10
480 Carlton Fisk .08 .25
481 Jeff Plympton .02 .10
482 Carlos Martinez .02 .10
483 Jim Gott .02 .10
484 Bob McClure .02 .10
485 Tim Teufel .02 .10
486 Vicente Palacios .02 .10
487 Jeff Reed .02 .10
488 Tony Phillips .02 .10
489 Mel Rojas .02 .10
490 Ben McDonald .02 .10
491 Andres Santana .02 .10
492 Chris Beasley .02 .10
493 Mike Timlin .02 .10
494 Brian Downing .02 .10
495 Kirk Gibson .05 .15
496 Scott Sanderson .02 .10
497 Nick Esasky .02 .10
498 Johnny Guzman RC .02 .10
499 Mitch Williams .02 .10
500 Kirby Puckett .20 .50
501 Mike Harkey .02 .10
502 Jim Gantner .02 .10
503 Bruce Egloff .02 .10
504 Josias Manzanillo RC .02 .10
505 Delino DeShields .02 .10
506 Rheal Cormier .02 .10
507 Jay Bell .05 .15
508 Rich Rowland RC .02 .10
509 Scott Servais .02 .10
510 Terry Pendleton .05 .15
511 Rich DeLucia .02 .10
512 Warren Newson .02 .10
513 Paul Faries .02 .10
514 Kal Daniels .02 .10
515 Jarvis Brown .02 .10
516 Rafael Palmeiro .08 .25
517 Kelly Downs .02 .10
518 Steve Chitren .02 .10
519 Moises Alou .05 .15
520 Wade Boggs .08 .25
521 Pete Schourek .02 .10
522 Scott Terry .02 .10
523 Kevin Appier .05 .15
524 Gary Redus .02 .10
525 George Bell .02 .10
526 Jeff Kaiser .02 .10
527 Alvaro Espinoza .02 .10
528 Luis Polonia .02 .10
529 Darren Daulton .05 .15
530 Norm Charlton .02 .10
531 John Olerud .05 .15
532 Dan Plesac .02 .10
533 Billy Ripken .02 .10
534 Rod Nichols .02 .10
535 Joey Cora .02 .10
536 Harold Baines .05 .15
537 Bob Ojeda .02 .10
538 Mark Leonard .02 .10
539 Danny Darwin .02 .10
540 Shawon Dunston .02 .10
541 Pedro Munoz .02 .10
542 Mark Gubicza .02 .10
543 Kevin Baez .02 .10
544 Todd Zeile .02 .10
545 Don Slaught .02 .10
546 Tony Eusebio .05 .15
547 Alonzo Powell .02 .10
548 Gary Pettis .02 .10
549 Brian Barnes .02 .10
550 Lou Whitaker .05 .15
551 Keith Mitchell .02 .10
552 Oscar Azocar .02 .10
553 Stu Cole RC .02 .10
554 Steve Wapnick .02 .10
555 Derek Bell .05 .15
556 Luis Lopez .02 .10
557 Anthony Telford .02 .10
558 Tim Mauser .02 .10
559 Glen Sutko .02 .10
560 Darryl Strawberry .05 .15
561 Tom Bolton .02 .10
562 Cliff Young .02 .10
563 Bruce Walton .02 .10
564 Chico Walker .02 .10
565 John Franco .05 .15
566 Paul McClellan .02 .10
567 Paul Abbott .02 .10
568 Gary Varsho .02 .10
569 Carlos Maldonado RC .02 .10
570 Kelly Gruber .02 .10
571 Jose Oquendo .02 .10
572 Steve Frey .02 .10
573 Tino Martinez .08 .25
574 Bill Haselman .02 .10
575 Eric Anthony .02 .10
576 John Habyan .02 .10
577 Jeff McNeely .02 .10
578 Chris Bosio .02 .10
579 Joe Grahe .02 .10
580 Fred McGriff .08 .25
581 Rick Honeycutt .02 .10
582 Matt Williams .05 .15
583 Cliff Brantley .02 .10
584 Rob Dibble .05 .15
585 Skeeter Barnes .02 .10
586 Greg Hibbard .02 .10
587 Randy Milligan .02 .10
588 Checklist 301-400 .02 .10
589 Checklist 401-500 .02 .10
590 Checklist 501-600 .02 .10
591 Frank Thomas MC .08 .25
592 David Justice MC .02 .10
593 Roger Clemens MC .20 .50
594 Steve Avery MC .02 .10
595 Cal Ripken MC .30 .75
596 Barry Larkin MC UER .05 .15
Ranked in AL,
should be NL
597 Jose Canseco MC UER .05 .15
Mistakenly numbered
370 on card back
598 Will Clark MC .05 .15
599 Cecil Fielder MC .02 .10
600 Ryne Sandberg MC .20 .50
601 Chuck Knoblauch MC .02 .10
602 Dwight Gooden MC .02 .10
603 Ken Griffey Jr. MC .25 .60
604 Barry Bonds MC .40 1.00
605 Nolan Ryan MC .30 .75
606 Jeff Bagwell MC .08 .25
607 Robin Yount MC .20 .50
608 Bobby Bonilla MC .02 .10
609 George Brett MC .25 .60
610 Howard Johnson MC .02 .10
611 Esteban Beltre .02 .10
612 Mike Christopher .02 .10
613 Troy Afenir .02 .10
614 Mariano Duncan .02 .10
615 Doug Henry RC .02 .10
616 Doug Jones .02 .10
617 Alvin Davis .02 .10
618 Craig Lefferts .02 .10
619 Kevin McReynolds .02 .10
620 Barry Bonds .60 1.50
621 Turner Ward .02 .10
622 Joe Magrane .02 .10
623 Mark Parent .02 .10
624 Tom Browning .02 .10
625 John Smiley .02 .10
626 Steve Wilson .02 .10
627 Mike Gallego .02 .10
628 Sammy Sosa .20 .50
629 Rico Rossy .02 .10
630 Royce Clayton .02 .10
631 Clay Parker .02 .10
632 Pete Smith .02 .10
633 Jeff McKnight .02 .10
634 Jack Daugherty .02 .10
635 Steve Sax .02 .10
636 Joe Hesketh .02 .10
637 Vince Horsman .02 .10
638 Eric King .02 .10
639 Joe Boever .02 .10
640 Jack Morris .05 .15
641 Arthur Rhodes .02 .10
642 Bob Melvin .02 .10
643 Rick Wilkins .02 .10
644 Scott Scudder .02 .10
645 Bip Roberts .02 .10
646 Julio Valera .02 .10
647 Kevin Campbell .02 .10
648 Steve Searcy .02 .10
649 Scott Kamieniecki .02 .10
650 Kurt Stillwell .02 .10
651 Bob Welch .02 .10
652 Andres Galarraga .05 .15
653 Mike Jackson .02 .10
654 Bo Jackson .20 .50
655 Sid Fernandez .02 .10
656 Mike Bielecki .02 .10
657 Jeff Reardon .05 .15
658 Wayne Rosenthal .02 .10
659 Eric Bullock .02 .10
660 Eric Davis .05 .15
661 Randy Tomlin .02 .10
662 Tom Edens .02 .10
663 Rob Murphy .02 .10
664 Leo Gomez .02 .10
665 Greg Maddux .30 .75
666 Greg Vaughn .02 .10
667 Wade Taylor .02 .10
668 Brad Arnsberg .02 .10
669 Mike Moore .02 .10
670 Mark Langston .02 .10
671 Barry Jones .02 .10
672 Bill Landrum .02 .10
673 Greg Swindell .02 .10
674 Wayne Edwards .02 .10
675 Greg Olson .02 .10
676 Bill Pulsipher RC .02 .10
677 Bobby Witt .02 .10
678 Mark Carreon .02 .10
679 Patrick Lennon .02 .10
680 Ozzie Smith .30 .75
681 John Briscoe .02 .10
682 Matt Young .02 .10
683 Jeff Conine .05 .15
684 Phil Stephenson .02 .10
685 Ron Darling .02 .10
686 Bryan Hickerson RC .02 .10
687 Dale Sveum .02 .10
688 Kirk McCaskill .02 .10
689 Rich Amaral .02 .10
690 Danny Tartabull .02 .10
691 Donald Harris .02 .10
692 Doug Davis .02 .10
693 John Farrell .02 .10
694 Paul Gibson .02 .10
695 Kenny Lofton .08 .25
696 Mike Fetters .02 .10
697 Rosario Rodriguez .02 .10
698 Chris Jones .02 .10
699 Jeff Manto .02 .10
700 Rick Sutcliffe .05 .15
701 Scott Bankhead .02 .10
702 Donnie Hill .02 .10
703 Todd Worrell .02 .10
704 Rene Gonzales .02 .10
705 Rick Cerone .02 .10
706 Tony Pena .02 .10
707 Paul Sorrento .02 .10
708 Gary Scott .02 .10
709 Junior Noboa .02 .10
710 Wally Joyner .05 .15
711 Charlie Hayes .02 .10
712 Rich Rodriguez .02 .10
713 Rudy Seanez .02 .10
714 Jim Bullinger .02 .10
715 Jeff M. Robinson .02 .10
716 Jeff Branson .02 .10
717 Andy Ashby .02 .10
718 Dave Burba .02 .10
719 Rich Gossage .05 .15
720 Randy Johnson .20 .50
721 David Wells .05 .15
722 Paul Kilgus .02 .10
723 Dave Martinez .02 .10
724 Denny Neagle .05 .15
725 Andy Stankiewicz .02 .10
726 Rick Aguilera .05 .15
727 Junior Ortiz .02 .10
728 Storm Davis .02 .10
729 Don Robinson .02 .10
730 Ron Gant .05 .15
731 Paul Assenmacher .02 .10
732 Mike Gardiner .02 .10
733 Milt Hill .02 .10
734 Jeremy Hernandez RC .02 .10
735 Ken Hill .02 .10
736 Xavier Hernandez .02 .10
737 Gregg Jefferies .02 .10
738 Dick Schofield .02 .10
739 Ron Robinson .02 .10
740 Sandy Alomar Jr. .02 .10
741 Mike Stanley .02 .10
742 Butch Henry RC .02 .10
743 Floyd Bannister .02 .10
744 Brian Drahman .02 .10
745 Dave Winfield .05 .15
746 Bob Walk .02 .10
747 Chris James .02 .10
748 Don Prybylinski RC .02 .10
749 Dennis Rasmussen .02 .10
750 Rickey Henderson .20 .50
751 Chris Hammond .02 .10
752 Bob Kipper .02 .10
753 Dave Rohde .02 .10
754 Hubie Brooks .02 .10
755 Bret Saberhagen .05 .15
756 Jeff D. Robinson .02 .10
757 Pat Listach RC .05 .15
758 Bill Wegman .02 .10
759 John Wetteland .05 .15
760 Phil Plantier .02 .10
761 Wilson Alvarez .02 .10
762 Scott Aldred .02 .10
763 Armando Reynoso RC .05 .15
764 Todd Benzinger .02 .10
765 Kevin Mitchell .02 .10
766 Gary Sheffield .05 .15
767 Allan Anderson .02 .10
768 Rusty Meacham .02 .10
769 Rick Parker .02 .10
770 Nolan Ryan .75 2.00
771 Jeff Ballard .02 .10
772 Cory Snyder .02 .10
773 Denis Boucher .02 .10
774 Jose Gonzalez .02 .10
775 Juan Guerrero .02 .10
776 Ed Nunez .02 .10
777 Scott Ruskin .02 .10
778 Terry Leach .02 .10
779 Carl Willis .02 .10
780 Bobby Bonilla .05 .15
781 Duane Ward .02 .10
782 Joe Slusarski .02 .10
783 David Segui .02 .10
784 Kirk Gibson .05 .15
785 Frank Viola .05 .15
786 Keith Miller .02 .10
787 Mike Morgan .02 .10
788 Kim Batiste .02 .10
789 Sergio Valdez .02 .10
790 Eddie Taubensee RC .05 .15
791 Jack Armstrong .02 .10
792 Scott Fletcher .02 .10
793 Steve Farr .02 .10
794 Dan Pasqua .02 .10
795 Eddie Murray .20 .50
796 John Morris .02 .10
797 Francisco Cabrera .02 .10
798 Mike Perez .02 .10
799 Ted Wood .02 .10
800 Jose Rijo .02 .10
801 Danny Gladden .02 .10
802 Archi Cianfrocco RC .02 .10
803 Monty Fariss .02 .10
804 Roger McDowell .02 .10
805 Randy Myers .02 .10
806 Kirk Dressendorfer .02 .10
807 Zane Smith .02 .10
808 Glenn Davis .02 .10
809 Torey Lovullo .02 .10
810 Andre Dawson .05 .15
811 Bill Pecota .02 .10
812 Ted Power .02 .10
813 Willie Blair .02 .10
814 Dave Fleming .02 .10
815 Chris Gwynn .02 .10
816 Jody Reed .02 .10
817 Mark Dewey .02 .10
818 Kyle Abbott .02 .10
819 Tom Henke .02 .10
820 Kevin Seitzer .02 .10
821 Al Newman .02 .10
822 Tim Sherrill .02 .10
823 Chuck Crim .02 .10
824 Darren Reed .02 .10
825 Tony Gwynn .25 .60
826 Steve Foster .02 .10
827 Steve Howe .02 .10
828 Brook Jacoby .02 .10
829 Rodney McCray .02 .10
830 Chuck Knoblauch .05 .15
831 John Wehner .02 .10
832 Scott Garrelts .02 .10
833 Alejandro Pena .02 .10
834 Jeff Parrett UER .02 .10
Kentucy
835 Juan Bell .02 .10
836 Lance Dickson .02 .10
837 Darryl Kile .05 .15
838 Efrain Valdez .02 .10
839 Bob Zupcic RC .02 .10
840 George Bell .02 .10
841 Dave Gallagher .02 .10
842 Tim Belcher .02 .10
843 Jeff Shaw .02 .10
844 Mike Fitzgerald .02 .10
845 Gary Carter .05 .15
846 John Russell .02 .10
847 Eric Hillman RC .02 .10
848 Mike Witt .02 .10
849 Curt Wilkerson .02 .10
850 Alan Trammell .05 .15
851 Rex Hudler .02 .10
852 Mike Walkden RC .02 .10
853 Kevin Ward .02 .10
854 Tim Naehring .02 .10
855 Bill Swift .02 .10
856 Damon Berryhill .02 .10
857 Mark Eichhorn .02 .10
858 Hector Villanueva .02 .10
859 Jose Lind .02 .10
860 Dennis Martinez .05 .15
861 Bill Krueger .02 .10
862 Mike Kingery .02 .10
863 Jeff Innis .02 .10
864 Derek Lilliquist .02 .10
865 Reggie Sanders .05 .15
866 Ramon Garcia .02 .10
867 Bruce Ruffin .02 .10
868 Dickie Thon .02 .10
869 Melido Perez .02 .10
870 Ruben Amaro .02 .10
871 Alan Mills .02 .10
872 Matt Sinatro .02 .10
873 Eddie Zosky .02 .10
874 Pete Incaviglia .02 .10
875 Tom Candiotti .02 .10
876 Bob Patterson .02 .10
877 Neal Heaton .02 .10
878 Terrel Hansen RC .02 .10
879 Dave Eiland .02 .10
880 Von Hayes .02 .10
881 Tim Scott .02 .10
882 Otis Nixon .02 .10
883 Herm Winningham .02 .10
884 Dion James .02 .10
885 Dave Wainhouse .02 .10
886 Frank DiPino .02 .10
887 Dennis Cook .02 .10
888 Jose Mesa .02 .10
889 Mark Leiter .02 .10
890 Willie Randolph .05 .15
891 Craig Colbert .02 .10
892 Dwayne Henry .02 .10
893 Jim Lindeman .02 .10
894 Charlie Hough .05 .15
895 Gil Heredia RC .05 .15
896 Scott Chiamparino .02 .10
897 Lance Blankenship .02 .10
898 Checklist 601-700 .02 .10
899 Checklist 701-800 .02 .10
900 Checklist 801-900 .02 .10

1992 Stadium Club First Draft Picks

RANDOM INSERTS IN SER.3 PACKS
ONE CARD SENT TO EACH ST.CLUB MEMBER
1 Chipper Jones 2.00 5.00
2 Brien Taylor .75 2.00
3 Phil Nevin .75 2.00

1992 Stadium Club Master Photos

COMPLETE SET (15) 8.00 20.00
1 Wade Boggs .50 1.25
2 Barry Bonds .75 2.00
3 Jose Canseco .50 1.25
4 Will Clark .40 1.00
5 Cecil Fielder .20 .50
6 Dwight Gooden .20 .50
7 Ken Griffey Jr. 1.25 3.00
8 Rickey Henderson .60 1.50
9 Lance Johnson .08 .25
10 Cal Ripken 2.00 5.00
11 Nolan Ryan 2.00 5.00
12 Deion Sanders .40 1.00
13 Darryl Strawberry .20 .50
14 Danny Tartabull .08 .25
15 Frank Thomas .60 1.50

1992 Stadium Club East Coast National

These cards were selected from the regular Stadium Club series and were printed for the Gloria Rothstein's East Coast National Convention. The fronts feature borderless color player photos with the East Coast National Convention logo printed in gold foil in a top corner while the backs display a mini reprint of the player's rookie card and "BARS" (Baseball Analysis and Reporting System) statistics. The cards are checklisted below according to their numbers in the regular series.

COMPLETE SET (100) 100.00 200.00
601 Chuck Knoblauch MC 2.00 5.00
602 Doc Gooden MC .75 2.00
603 Ken Griffey Jr. MC 12.50 30.00
604 Barry Bonds MC 8.00 20.00
605 Nolan Ryan MC 20.00 50.00
606 Jeff Bagwell MC 6.00 15.00
607 Robin Yount MC 3.00 8.00
608 Bobby Bonilla MC .40 1.00
609 George Brett MC 10.00 25.00
610 Howard Johnson MC .40 1.00
611 Esteban Beltre .40 1.00
612 Mike Christopher .40 1.00
613 Troy Afenir .40 1.00
619 Kevin McReynolds .40 1.00
620 Barry Bonds 8.00 20.00
622 Joe Magrane .40 1.00
623 Mark Parent .40 1.00
626 Steve Wilson .40 1.00
629 Rico Rossy .40 1.00
631 Clay Parker .40 1.00
633 Jeff McKnight .40 1.00
637 Vince Horsman .40 1.00
638 Eric King .40 1.00
639 Joe Boever .40 1.00
641 Arthur Rhodes .40 1.00
647 Kevin Campbell .40 1.00
653 Mike Jackson .40 1.00
661 Randy Tomlin .40 1.00
665 Greg Maddux 12.50 30.00
668 Brad Arnsberg .40 1.00
671 Barry Jones .40 1.00
672 Bill Landrum .40 1.00
673 Greg Swindell .40 1.00
676 Bill Pulsipher .40 1.00
679 Patrick Lennon .40 1.00
681 John Briscoe .40 1.00
684 Phil Stephenson .40 1.00
685 Ron Darling .40 1.00
686 Bryan Hickerson .40 1.00
688 Kirk McCaskill .40 1.00
689 Rich Amaral .40 1.00
692 Doug Davis .40 1.00
693 John Farrell .40 1.00
700 Rick Sutcliffe .75 2.00
704 Rene Gonzalez .40 1.00
713 Rudy Seanez .40 1.00
714 Jim Bullinger .40 1.00
716 Jeff Branson .40 1.00
717 Andy Ashby .40 1.00
725 Andy Stankiewicz .40 1.00
733 Milt Hill .40 1.00
739 Ron Robinson .40 1.00
742 Butch Henry .40 1.00
747 Chris James .40 1.00
749 Dennis Rasmussen .40 1.00
753 Dave Rohde .40 1.00
757 Pat Listach .40 1.00
758 Bill Wegman .40 1.00
763 Armando Reynoso .40 1.00
765 Kevin Mitchell .40 1.00
766 Gary Sheffield 3.00 8.00
769 Rick Parker .40 1.00
771 Jeff Ballard .40 1.00
772 Cory Snyder .40 1.00
774 Jose Gonzalez .40 1.00
775 Juan Guerrero .40 1.00
776 Ed Nunez .40 1.00
778 Terry Leach .40 1.00
782 Joe Slusarski .40 1.00
784 Kirk Gibson .75 2.00
788 Kim Batiste .40 1.00
802 Archi Cianfrocco .40 1.00
806 Kirk Dressendorfer .40 1.00
807 Zane Smith .40 1.00
814 Dave Fleming .40 1.00
815 Chris Gwynn .40 1.00
817 Mark Dewey .40 1.00
819 Tom Henke .75 2.00
822 Tim Sherrill .40 1.00
826 Steve Foster .40 1.00
831 John Wehner .40 1.00
832 Scott Garrelts .40 1.00
840 George Bell .40 1.00
841 Dave Gallagher .40 1.00
846 John Russell .40 1.00
847 Eric Hillman .40 1.00
852 Mike Walkden .40 1.00
855 Bill Swift .40 1.00
864 Derek Lilliquist .40 1.00
876 Bob Patterson .40 1.00
878 Terrel Hansen .40 1.00
881 Tim Scott .40 1.00
886 Frank DiPino .40 1.00
891 Craig Colbert .40 1.00
892 Dwayne Henry .40 1.00
893 Jim Lindeman .40 1.00
895 Gil Heredia .40 1.00
898 Checklist .40 1.00
899 Checklist .40 1.00
900 Checklist .40 1.00

1992 Stadium Club Members Only

This 50-card standard-size set was sent to 1992 Stadium Club members in four installments. In addition to the Stadium Club cards, the first installment included one "Top Draft Picks of the '90s" card (as a bonus) and a randomly chosen "Master Photo" printed on 5" by 7" white card stock. The third and fourth installments included hockey and football players in addition to baseball players. The cards feature full-bleed glossy color player photos. The fronts of the regular cards have the words "Members Only" printed in gold foil at the bottom along with the player's name and the Stadium Club logo. The backs feature a stadium scene with the scoreboard displaying, in yellow neon, a career highlight. The cards are unnumbered and checklisted below alphabetically, with the two-player cards listed at the end.

COMPLETE SET (50) 12.00 30.00
1 Carlos Baerga .07 .20
2 Wade Boggs .20 .50
3 Barry Bonds .30 .75
4 Bret Boone .07 .20
5 Pat Borders .07 .20
6 George Brett .40 1.00
7 George Brett .40 1.00
8 Jim Bullinger .07 .20
9 Gary Carter .15 .40
10 Andujar Cedeno .07 .20
11 Roger Clemens .50 1.25
Matt Young
12 Dennis Eckersley .15 .40
13 Dennis Eckersley .15 .40
14 Dave Eiland .07 .20
15 Ken Griffey Jr. 1.50 4.00
16 Kevin Gross .07 .20
17 Bo Jackson .20 .50
18 Eric Karros .07 .20
19 Pat Listach .07 .20
20 Greg Maddux .75 2.00
21 Mickey Morandini .07 .20
22 Jack Morris .15 .40
23 Eddie Murray .20 .50
24 Eddie Murray .20 .50
25 Bip Roberts .07 .20
26 Nolan Ryan/27 Seasons 1.00 2.50
27 Nolan Ryan/1993 Seasons His Finale 1.00 2.50
28 Gary Sheffield .15 .40
Dwight Gooden
29 Gary Sheffield .15 .40
Fred McGriff
30 Lee Smith .15 .40
31 Ozzie Smith/(2,000th Hit) .50 1.25
32 Ozzie Smith/(7,000th Career Assist) .50 1.25
33 Ozzie Smith .50 1.25
34 Bobby Thigpen .07 .20

35 Dave Winfield .20 .50
36 Robin Yount .20 .50

1992 Stadium Club National Convention

These cards were selected from the regular Stadium Club series and were printed for the National Convention in Atlanta. The fronts feature borderless color player photos with the National Convention logo printed in gold foil in a top corner while the backs display a mini reprint of the player's rookie card and "BARS" (Baseball Analysis and Reporting System) statistics. The cards are checklisted below according to their numbers in the regular series.

COMPLETE SET (100) 75.00 150.00
616 Doug Jones .75 2.00
617 Alvin Davis .40 1.00
618 Craig Lefferts .40 1.00
621 Turner Ward .40 1.00
625 John Smiley .40 1.00
627 Mike Gallego .40 1.00
630 Royce Clayton .40 1.00
634 Jack Daugherty .40 1.00
635 Steve Sax .40 1.00
636 Joe Hesketh .40 1.00
643 Rick Wilkins .40 1.00
644 Scott Scudder .40 1.00
645 Bip Roberts .40 1.00
650 Kurt Stillwell .40 1.00
652 Andres Galarraga 2.00 5.00
657 Jeff Reardon .75 2.00
660 Eric Davis .75 2.00
662 Tom Edens .40 1.00
675 Greg Olson .40 1.00
678 Mark Carreon .40 1.00
680 Ozzie Smith 25.00 60.00
682 Matt Young .40 1.00
690 Danny Tartabull .40 1.00
691 Donald Harris .40 1.00
695 Kenny Lofton 3.00 8.00
697 Rosario Rodriguez .40 1.00
701 Scott Bankhead .40 1.00
705 Rick Cerone .40 1.00
706 Tony Pena .40 1.00
709 Junior Noboa .40 1.00
710 Wally Joyner .75 2.00
711 Charlie Hayes .40 1.00
712 Rich Rodriguez .40 1.00
721 David Wells 1.25 3.00
723 Dave Martinez .40 1.00
726 Rick Aguilera .75 2.00
727 Junior Ortiz .40 1.00
729 Don Robinson .40 1.00
730 Ron Gant .75 2.00
731 Paul Assenmacher .40 1.00
732 Mark Gardiner .40 1.00
735 Ken Hill .40 1.00
736 Xavier Hernandez .40 1.00
737 Gregg Jefferies .40 1.00
740 Sandy Alomar .40 1.00
741 Mike Stanley .40 1.00
744 Brian Drahman .40 1.00
746 Bob Walk .40 1.00
751 Chris Hammond .40 1.00
759 John Wetteland .75 2.00
760 Phil Plantier .40 1.00
761 Wilson Alvarez .75 2.00
773 Dennis Boucher .40 1.00
777 Scott Ruskin .40 1.00
779 Carl Willis .40 1.00
783 David Segui .40 1.00
786 Keith Miller .40 1.00
790 Eddie Taubensee .40 1.00
791 Jack Armstrong .40 1.00
792 Scott Fletcher .40 1.00
793 Steve Farr .40 1.00
794 Dan Pasqua .40 1.00
797 Francisco Cabrera .40 1.00
798 Mike Perez .40 1.00
801 Danny Gladden .40 1.00
803 Monty Fariss .40 1.00
804 Roger McDowell .40 1.00
805 Randy Myers .75 2.00
808 Glenn Davis .40 1.00
809 Torey Lovullo .40 1.00
816 Jody Reed .40 1.00
825 Tony Gwynn 10.00 25.00
827 Steve Howe .40 1.00
828 Brook Jacoby .40 1.00
829 Rodney McCray .40 1.00
830 Chuck Knoblauch 3.00 8.00
835 Juan Bell .40 1.00
836 Lance Dickson .40 1.00
837 Darryl Kile .40 1.00
842 Tim Belcher .40 1.00
843 Jeff Shaw .40 1.00
844 Mike Fitzgerald .40 1.00
845 Gary Carter 5.00 12.00
850 Alan Trammell 1.25 3.00
851 Rex Hudler .75 2.00
856 Damon Berryhill .40 1.00
857 Mark Eichhorn .40 1.00
858 Hector Villanueva .40 1.00
860 Denny Martinez .75 2.00
865 Reggie Sanders .75 2.00
869 Melido Perez .40 1.00
874 Pete Incaviglia .40 1.00
875 Tom Candiotti .40 1.00
877 Neal Heaton .40 1.00
879 Dave Eiland .40 1.00
882 Otis Nixon .40 1.00
883 Herm Winningham .40 1.00
884 Dion James .40 1.00
887 Dennis Cook .40 1.00
894 Charlie Hough .75 2.00

1993 Stadium Club Murphy

This 200-card boxed set features 1992 All-Star Game cards, 1992 Team USA cards, and 1992 Championship and World Series cards. Topps actually refers to this set as a 1992 issue, but the set was released in 1993. This set is housed in a replica of San Diego's Jack Murphy Stadium, site of the 1992 All-Star Game. Production was limited to 8,000 cases, with 16 boxes per case. The set includes 100 Draft Pick cards, 56 All-Star cards, 25 Team USA cards, and 19 cards commemorating the 1992 National and American League Championship Series and the World Series. Notable Rookie Cards in this set include Derek Jeter, Jason Kendall, Shannon Stewart and Preston Wilson. A second year Team USA Nomar Garciaparra is featured in this set as well.

COMP.FACT.SET (212) 75.00 150.00
COMPLETE SET (200) 60.00 120.00
COMMON CARD (1-200) .05 .15
COMMON RC .05 .15
STATED PRINT RUN 128,000 SETS
1 Dave Winfield WS .05 .15
2 Juan Guzman AS .05 .15
3 Tony Gwynn AS .40 1.00
4 Chris Roberts USA .05 .15
5 Benny Santiago .10 .30
6 Sherard Clinkscales RC .05 .15
7 Jon Nunnally RC .20 .50
8 Chuck Knoblauch .10 .30
9 Bob Wolcott RC .05 .15
10 Steve Rodriguez USA .05 .15
11 Mark Williams RC .05 .15
12 Danny Clyburn RC .05 .15
13 Darren Dreifort USA .05 .15
14 Andy Van Slyke .20 .50
15 Wade Boggs AS .20 .50
16 Scott Patton RC .05 .15
17 Gary Sheffield AS .10 .30
18 Ron Villone USA .05 .15
19 Roberto Alomar ALCS .20 .50
20 Marc Valdes USA .05 .15
21 Daron Kirkreit USA .05 .15
22 Jeff Granger USA .05 .15
23 Levon Largusa RC .05 .15
24 Jimmy Key .10 .30
25 Kevin Pearson RC .05 .15
26 Michael Moore RC .05 .15
27 Preston Wilson RC .60 1.50
28 Kirby Puckett AS .30 .75
29 Tim Crabtree RC .05 .15
30 Bip Roberts .05 .15
31 Kelly Gruber .05 .15
32 Tony Fernandez .05 .15
33 Jason Angel RC .05 .15
34 Calvin Murray USA .05 .15
35 Chad McConnell .05 .15
36 Jason Moler USA .05 .15
37 Mark Lemke .05 .15
38 Tom Knauss RC .05 .15
39 Larry Mitchell RC .05 .15
40 Doug Mirabelli RC .20 .50
41 Everett Stull RC .05 .15
42 Chris Wimmer USA .05 .15
43 Dan Serafini RC .05 .15
44 Ryne Sandberg AS .50 1.25
45 Steve Lyons RC .05 .15
46 Ryan Freeburg RC .05 .15
47 Ruben Sierra .10 .30
48 David Mysel RC .05 .15
49 Joe Hamilton RC .05 .15
50 Steve Rodriguez .05 .15
51 Tim Wakefield .30 .75
52 Scott Gentile RC .05 .15
53 Doug Jones .05 .15
54 Willie Brown RC .05 .15
55 Chad Mottola RC .20 .50
56 Ken Griffey Jr. AS .60 1.50
57 Jon Lieber RC 1.00 2.50
58 Dennis Martinez .10 .30
59 Joe Petcka RC .05 .15
60 Benji Simonton RC .05 .15
61 Brett Backlund RC .05 .15
62 Damon Berryhill .05 .15
63 Juan Guzman ALCS .05 .15
64 Doug Hecker RC .05 .15
65 Jamie Arnold RC .05 .15
66 Bob Tewksbury .05 .15
67 Tim Leger RC .05 .15
68 Todd Etler RC .05 .15
69 Lloyd McClendon .05 .15
70 Kurt Ehmann RC .05 .15
71 Rick Magdaleno RC .05 .15
72 Tom Pagnozzi .05 .15
73 Jeffrey Hammonds USA .05 .15
74 Joe Carter AS .10 .30
75 Chris Holt RC .10 .30
76 Charles Johnson USA .10 .30
77 Bob Walk .05 .15
78 Fred McGriff AS .20 .50
79 Tom Evans RC .05 .15
80 Scott Klingenbeck RC .05 .15
81 Chad McConnell USA .05 .15
82 Chris Eddy RC .05 .15
83 Phil Nevin USA .10 .30
84 John Kruk .10 .30
85 Tony Sheffield RC .05 .15
86 John Smoltz .20 .50
87 Trevor Humphry RC .05 .15
88 Charles Nagy .05 .15
89 Sean Runyan RC .05 .15
90 Mike Gulan RC .05 .15
91 Darren Daulton .10 .30
92 Otis Nixon .05 .15
93 Nomar Garciaparra USA 2.00 5.00
94 Larry Walker AS .10 .30
95 Hut Smith RC .05 .15
96 Rick Helling USA .05 .15
97 Roger Clemens AS .60 1.50
98 Ron Gant .10 .30
99 Kenny Felder RC .05 .15
100 Steve Murphy RC .05 .15
101 Mike Smith RC .05 .15
102 Terry Pendleton .10 .30
103 Tim Davis USA .05 .15
104 Jeff Patzké RC .05 .15
105 Craig Wilson USA .05 .15
106 Tom Glavine AS .20 .50
107 Mark Langston .05 .15
108 Mark Thompson RC .05 .15
109 Eric Owens RC .05 .15
110 Keith Johnson RC .05 .15
111 Robin Ventura AS .10 .30
112 Ed Sprague .05 .15
113 Jeff Schmidt RC .05 .15
114 Don Wengert RC .05 .15
115 Craig Biggio .20 .50
116 Kenny Carlyle RC .05 .15
117 Derek Jeter RC 60.00 150.00
118 Manuel Lee .05 .15
119 Jeff Haas RC .05 .15
120 Roger Bailey RC .05 .15
121 Sean Lowe RC .05 .15
122 Rick Aguilera .05 .15
123 Sandy Alomar Jr. .05 .15
124 Derek Wallace RC .05 .15
125 B.J.Wallace USA .05 .15
126 Greg Maddux AS .50 1.25
127 Tim Moore RC .05 .15
128 Lee Smith .10 .30
129 Todd Steverson RC .05 .15
130 Chris Widger RC .20 .50
131 Paul Molitor AS .10 .30
132 Chris Smith RC .05 .15
133 Chris Gomez RC .20 .50
134 Jimmy Baron RC .05 .15
135 John Smoltz .20 .50
136 Pat Borders .05 .15
137 Donnie Leshnock .05 .15
138 Gus Gandarillas RC .05 .15
139 Will Clark .20 .50
140 Ryan Luzinski RC .05 .15
141 Cal Ripken AS 1.00 2.50
142 B.J.Wallace .05 .15
143 Trey Beamon RC .20 .50
144 Norm Charlton .05 .15
145 Mike Mussina AS .20 .50
146 Billy Owens RC .05 .15
147 Ozzie Smith AS .50 1.25
148 Jason Kendall RC .60 1.50
149 Mike Matthews RC .05 .15
150 David Spykstra RC .05 .15
151 Benji Grigsby RC .05 .15
152 Sean Smith RC .05 .15
153 Mark McGwire AS .75 2.00
154 David Cone .10 .30
155 Shon Walker RC .05 .15
156 Jason Giambi USA .40 1.00
157 Jack McDowell AS .05 .15
158 Paxton Briley RC .05 .15
159 Edgar Martinez .20 .50
160 Brian Sackinsky RC .05 .15
161 Barry Bonds AS .75 2.00
162 Roberto Kelly .05 .15
163 Jeff Alkire .05 .15
164 Mike Sharperson .05 .15
165 Jamie Taylor RC .05 .15
166 John Saffer UER RC .05 .15
167 Jerry Browne .05 .15
168 Travis Fryman AS .10 .30
169 Brady Anderson .10 .30
170 Chris Roberts .05 .15
171 Lloyd Peever RC .05 .15
172 Francisco Cabrera .05 .15
173 Ramiro Martinez RC .05 .15
174 Jeff Alkire USA .05 .15
175 Ivan Rodriguez AS .20 .50
176 Kevin Brown .10 .30
177 Chad Roper RC .05 .15
178 Rod Henderson RC .05 .15
179 Dennis Eckersley .10 .30
180 Shannon Stewart RC .60 1.50
181 DeShawn Warren RC .05 .15
182 Lonnie Smith .05 .15
183 Willie Adams USA .05 .15
184 Jeff Montgomery .05 .15
185 Damon Hollins RC .20 .50
186 Byron Mathews RC .05 .15
187 Harold Baines .10 .30
188 Rick Greene USA .05 .15
189 Carlos Baerga AS .05 .15
190 Brandon Cromer RC .05 .15
191 Roberto Alomar AS .20 .50
192 Rich Ireland RC .05 .15
193 Steve Montgomery RC .05 .15
194 Brant Brown RC .05 .15
195 Ritchie Moody RC .05 .15
196 Michael Tucker USA .05 .15
197 Jason Varitek USA 2.00 5.00
198 David Manning RC .05 .15
199 Marquis Riley RC .05 .15
200 Jason Giambi .40 1.00

1993 Stadium Club Murphy Master Photos

COMPLETE SET (12) 2.00 5.00
ONE MP SET PER MURPHY FACTORY SET
STATED PRINT RUN 128,000 SETS
UNNUMBERED LARGE CARDS
1 Sandy Alomar Jr. AS .05 .15
2 Tom Glavine AS .20 .50
3 Ken Griffey Jr. AS .60 1.50
4 Tony Gwynn AS .40 1.00
5 Chuck Knoblauch AS .10 .30
6 Chad Mottola .20 .50
7 Kirby Puckett AS .30 .75
8 Chris Roberts USA .05 .15
9 Ryne Sandberg AS .50 1.25
10 Gary Sheffield AS .10 .30
11 Larry Walker AS .10 .30
12 Preston Wilson .75 2.00

1993 Stadium Club

The 1993 Stadium Club baseball set consists of 750 standard-size cards issued in three series of 300, 300, and 150 cards respectively. Each series closes with a Members Choice subset (291-300, 591-600, and 746-750.

COMPLETE SET (750) 12.50 30.00
COMPLETE SERIES 1 (300) 5.00 12.00
COMPLETE SERIES 2 (300) 5.00 12.00
COMPLETE SERIES 3 (150) 4.00 10.00
1 Pat Borders .05 .15
2 Greg Maddux .50 1.25
3 Daryl Boston .05 .15
4 Bob Ayrault .05 .15
5 Tony Phillips IF .05 .15
6 Damion Easley .05 .15
7 Kip Gross .05 .15
8 Jim Thome .20 .50
9 Tim Belcher .05 .15
10 Gary Wayne .05 .15
11 Sam Militello .05 .15
12 Mike Magnante .05 .15
13 Tim Wakefield .30 .75
14 Tim Hulett .05 .15
15 Rheal Cormier .05 .15
16 Juan Guerrero .05 .15
17 Rich Gossage .10 .30
18 Tim Laker RC .05 .15
19 Darrin Jackson .05 .15
20 Jack Clark .10 .30
21 Roberto Hernandez .05 .15
22 Dean Palmer .10 .30
23 Harold Reynolds .10 .30
24 Dan Plesac .05 .15
25 Brent Mayne .05 .15
26 Pat Hentgen .05 .15
27 Luis Sojo .05 .15
28 Ron Gant .10 .30
29 Paul Gibson .05 .15
30 Bip Roberts .05 .15
31 Mickey Tettleton .05 .15
32 Randy Velarde .05 .15
33 Brian McRae .05 .15
34 Wes Chamberlain .05 .15
35 Wayne Kirby .05 .15
36 Rey Sanchez .05 .15
37 Jesse Orosco .05 .15
38 Mike Stanton .05 .15
39 Royce Clayton .05 .15
40 Cal Ripken UER 1.00 2.50
41 John Dopson .05 .15
42 Gene Larkin .05 .15
43 Tim Raines .10 .30
44 Randy Myers .05 .15
45 Clay Parker .05 .15
46 Mike Scioscia .05 .15
47 Pete Incaviglia .05 .15
48 Todd Van Poppel .05 .15
49 Ray Lankford .10 .30
50 Eddie Murray .30 .75
51 Barry Bonds COR .75 2.00
51A Barry Bonds ERR .75 2.00
52 Gary Thurman .05 .15
53 Bob Wickman .05 .15
54 Joey Cora .05 .15
55 Kenny Rogers .10 .30
56 Mike Devereaux .05 .15
57 Kevin Seitzer .05 .15
58 Rafael Belliard .05 .15
59 David Wells .10 .30
60 Mark Clark .05 .15
61 Carlos Baerga .05 .15
62 Scott Brosius .10 .30
63 Jeff Grotewold .05 .15
64 Rick Wrona .05 .15
65 Kurt Knudsen .05 .15
66 Lloyd McClendon .05 .15
67 Omar Vizquel .20 .50
68 Jose Vizcaino .05 .15
69 Rob Ducey .05 .15
70 Casey Candaele .05 .15
71 Ramon Martinez .05 .15
72 Todd Hundley .05 .15
73 John Marzano .05 .15
74 Derek Parks .05 .15
75 Jack McDowell .05 .15
76 Tim Scott .05 .15
77 Mike Mussina .20 .50
78 Delino DeShields .05 .15
79 Chris Bosio .05 .15
80 Mike Bordick .05 .15
81 Rod Beck .05 .15
82 Ted Power .05 .15
83 John Kruk .10 .30
84 Steve Shifflett .05 .15
85 Danny Tartabull .05 .15
86 Mike Greenwell .05 .15
87 Jose Melendez .05 .15
88 Craig Wilson .05 .15
89 Melvin Nieves .05 .15
90 Ed Sprague .05 .15
91 Willie McGee .10 .30
92 Joe Orsulak .05 .15
93 Jeff King .05 .15
94 Dan Pasqua .05 .15
95 Brian Harper .05 .15
96 Joe Oliver .05 .15
97 Shane Turner .05 .15
98 Lenny Harris .05 .15
99 Jeff Parrett .05 .15
100 Luis Polonia .05 .15
101 Kent Bottenfield .05 .15
102 Albert Belle .10 .30
103 Mike Maddux .05 .15
104 Randy Tomlin .05 .15
105 Andy Stankiewicz .05 .15
106 Rico Rossy .05 .15
107 Joe Hesketh .05 .15
108 Dennis Powell .05 .15
109 Derrick May .05 .15
110 Pete Harnisch .05 .15
111 Kent Mercker .05 .15
112 Scott Fletcher .05 .15
113 Rex Hudler .05 .15
114 Chico Walker .05 .15
115 Rafael Palmeiro .20 .50
116 Mark Leiter .05 .15
117 Pedro Munoz .05 .15
118 Jim Bullinger .05 .15
119 Ivan Calderon .05 .15
120 Mike Timlin .05 .15
121 Rene Gonzales .05 .15
122 Greg Vaughn .05 .15
123 Mike Flanagan .05 .15
124 Mike Hartley .05 .15
125 Jeff Montgomery .05 .15
126 Mike Gallego .05 .15
127 Don Slaught .05 .15
128 Charlie O'Brien .05 .15
129 Jose Offerman .05 .15
Can be found with home town missing on back
130 Mark Wohlers .05 .15
131 Eric Fox .05 .15
132 Doug Strange .05 .15
133 Jeff Frye .05 .15
134 Wade Boggs UER .20 .50
Redundantly lists lefty breakdown
135 Lou Whitaker .10 .30
136 Craig Grebeck .05 .15
137 Rich Rodriguez .05 .15
138 Jay Bell .10 .30
139 Felix Fermin .05 .15
140 Dennis Martinez .10 .30
141 Eric Anthony .05 .15
142 Roberto Alomar .20 .50
143 Darren Lewis .05 .15
144 Mike Blowers .05 .15
145 Scott Bankhead .05 .15
146 Jeff Reboulet .05 .15
147 Frank Viola .10 .30
148 Bill Pecota .05 .15
149 Carlos Hernandez .05 .15
150 Bobby Witt .05 .15
151 Sid Bream .05 .15
152 Todd Zeile .05 .15
153 Dennis Cook .05 .15
154 Brian Bohanon .05 .15
155 Pat Kelly .05 .15
156 Milt Cuyler .05 .15
157 Juan Bell .05 .15
158 Randy Milligan .05 .15
159 Mark Gardner .05 .15
160 Pat Tabler .05 .15
161 Jeff Reardon .10 .30
162 Ken Patterson .05 .15
163 Bobby Bonilla .10 .30
164 Tony Pena .05 .15
165 Greg Swindell .05 .15
166 Kirk McCaskill .05 .15
167 Doug Drabek .05 .15
168 Franklin Stubbs .05 .15
169 Ron Tingley .05 .15
170 Willie Banks .05 .15
171 Sergio Valdez .05 .15
172 Mark Lemke .05 .15
173 Robin Yount .50 1.25
174 Storm Davis .05 .15
175 Dan Walters .05 .15
176 Steve Farr .05 .15
177 Curt Wilkerson .05 .15
178 Luis Alicea .05 .15
179 Russ Swan .05 .15
180 Mitch Williams .05 .15
181 Wilson Alvarez .05 .15
182 Carl Willis .05 .15
183 Craig Biggio .20 .50
184 Sean Berry .05 .15
185 Trevor Wilson .05 .15
186 Jeff Tackett .05 .15
187 Ellis Burks .10 .30
188 Jeff Branson .05 .15
189 Matt Nokes .05 .15
190 John Smiley .05 .15
191 Danny Gladden .05 .15
192 Mike Boddicker .05 .15
193 Roger Pavlik .05 .15
194 Paul Sorrento .05 .15
195 Vince Coleman .05 .15
196 Gary DiSarcina .05 .15
197 Rafael Bournigal .05 .15
198 Mike Schooler .05 .15
199 Scott Ruskin .05 .15
200 Frank Thomas .30 .75
201 Kyle Abbott .05 .15
202 Mike Perez .05 .15
203 Andre Dawson .10 .30
204 Bill Swift .05 .15
205 Alejandro Pena .05 .15
206 Dave Winfield .10 .30
207 Andujar Cedeno .05 .15
208 Terry Steinbach .05 .15
209 Chris Hammond .05 .15
210 Todd Burns .05 .15
211 Hipolito Pichardo .05 .15
212 John Kiely .05 .15
213 Tim Teufel .05 .15
214 Lee Guetterman .05 .15
215 Geronimo Pena .05 .15
216 Brett Butler .10 .30
217 Bryan Hickerson .05 .15
218 Rick Trlicek .05 .15
219 Lee Stevens .05 .15
220 Roger Clemens .60 1.50
221 Carlton Fisk .20 .50
222 Chili Davis .10 .30
223 Walt Terrell .05 .15
224 Jim Eisenreich .05 .15
225 Ricky Bones .05 .15
226 Henry Rodriguez .05 .15
227 Ken Hill .05 .15
228 Rick Wilkins .05 .15
229 Ricky Jordan .05 .15
230 Bernard Gilkey .05 .15
231 Tim Fortugno .05 .15
232 Geno Petralli .05 .15
233 Jose Rijo .05 .15
234 Jim Leyritz .05 .15
235 Kevin Campbell .05 .15
236 Al Osuna .05 .15
237 Pete Smith .05 .15
238 Pete Schourek .05 .15
239 Moises Alou .10 .30
240 Donn Pall .05 .15
241 Denny Neagle .10 .30
242 Dan Peltier .05 .15
243 Scott Scudder .05 .15
244 Juan Guzman .05 .15
245 Dave Burba .05 .15
246 Rick Sutcliffe .10 .30
247 Tony Fossas .05 .15
248 Mike Munoz .05 .15
249 Tim Salmon .20 .50
250 Rob Murphy .05 .15
251 Roger McDowell .05 .15
252 Lance Parrish .10 .30
253 Cliff Brantley .05 .15
254 Scott Leius .05 .15
255 Carlos Martinez .05 .15
256 Vince Horsman .05 .15
257 Oscar Azocar .05 .15
258 Craig Shipley .05 .15
259 Ben McDonald .05 .15
260 Jeff Brantley .05 .15
261 Damon Berryhill .05 .15
262 Joe Grahe .05 .15
263 Dave Hansen .05 .15
264 Rich Amaral .05 .15
265 Tim Pugh RC .05 .15
266 Dion James .05 .15
267 Frank Tanana .05 .15
268 Stan Belinda .05 .15
269 Jeff Kent .30 .75
270 Bruce Ruffin .05 .15
271 Xavier Hernandez .05 .15
272 Darrin Fletcher .05 .15
273 Tino Martinez .20 .50
274 Benny Santiago .10 .30
275 Scott Radinsky .05 .15
276 Mariano Duncan .05 .15
277 Kenny Lofton .10 .30
278 Dwight Smith .05 .15
279 Joe Carter .10 .30
280 Tim Jones .05 .15
281 Jeff Huson .05 .15
282 Phil Plantier .05 .15
283 Kirby Puckett .30 .75
284 Johnny Guzman .05 .15
285 Mike Morgan .05 .15
286 Chris Sabo .05 .15
287 Matt Williams .10 .30
288 Checklist 1-100 .05 .15
289 Checklist 101-200 .05 .15
290 Checklist 201-300 .05 .15
291 Dennis Eckersley MC .10 .30
292 Eric Karros MC .05 .15
293 Pat Listach MC .05 .15
294 Andy Van Slyke MC .10 .30
295 Robin Ventura MC .05 .15
296 Tom Glavine MC .10 .30
297 Juan Gonzalez MC UER .05 .15
Misspelled Gonzales
298 Travis Fryman MC .05 .15
299 Larry Walker MC .10 .30
300 Gary Sheffield MC .05 .15
301 Chuck Finley .10 .30
302 Luis Gonzalez .10 .30
303 Darryl Hamilton .05 .15
304 Bien Figueroa .05 .15
305 Ron Darling .05 .15
306 Jonathan Hurst .05 .15
307 Mike Sharperson .05 .15
308 Mike Christopher .05 .15
309 Marvin Freeman .05 .15
310 Jay Buhner .10 .30
311 Butch Henry .05 .15
312 Greg W. Harris .05 .15
313 Darren Daulton .10 .30
314 Chuck Knoblauch .10 .30
315 Greg A. Harris .05 .15
316 John Franco .10 .30
317 John Wehner .05 .15
318 Donald Harris .05 .15
319 Benny Santiago .10 .30
320 Larry Walker .10 .30
321 Randy Knorr .05 .15
322 Ramon Martinez RC .05 .15
323 Mike Stanley .05 .15
324 Bill Wegman .05 .15
325 Tom Candiotti .05 .15
326 Glenn Davis .05 .15
327 Chuck Crim .05 .15
328 Scott Livingstone .05 .15
329 Eddie Taubensee .05 .15
330 George Bell .05 .15
331 Edgar Martinez .20 .50
332 Paul Assenmacher .05 .15
333 Steve Hosey .05 .15
334 Mo Vaughn .10 .30
335 Bret Saberhagen .10 .30
336 Mike Trombley .05 .15
337 Mark Lewis .05 .15
338 Terry Pendleton .10 .30
339 Dave Hollins .05 .15
340 Jeff Conine .10 .30
341 Bob Tewksbury .05 .15
342 Billy Ashley .05 .15
343 Zane Smith .05 .15
344 John Wetteland .10 .30
345 Chris Hoiles .05 .15
346 Frank Castillo .05 .15
347 Bruce Hurst .05 .15
348 Kevin McReynolds .05 .15
349 Dave Henderson .05 .15
350 Ryan Bowen .05 .15
351 Sid Fernandez .05 .15
352 Mark Whiten .05 .15
353 Nolan Ryan 1.25 3.00
354 Rick Aguilera .05 .15
355 Mark Langston .05 .15
356 Jack Morris .10 .30
357 Rob Deer .05 .15
358 Dave Fleming .05 .15
359 Lance Johnson .05 .15
360 Joe Millette .05 .15
361 Wil Cordero .05 .15
362 Chito Martinez .05 .15
363 Scott Servais .05 .15
364 Bernie Williams .20 .50
365 Pedro Martinez .60 1.50
366 Ryne Sandberg .50 1.25
367 Brad Ausmus .30 .75
368 Scott Cooper .05 .15
369 Rob Dibble .10 .30
370 Walt Weiss .05 .15
371 Mark Davis .05 .15
372 Orlando Merced .05 .15
373 Mike Jackson .05 .15
374 Kevin Appier .10 .30
375 Esteban Beltre .05 .15
376 Joe Slusarski .05 .15
377 William Suero .05 .15
378 Pete O'Brien .05 .15
379 Alan Embree .05 .15
380 Lenny Webster .05 .15
381 Eric Davis .10 .30
382 Duane Ward .05 .15
383 John Habyan .05 .15
384 Jeff Bagwell .20 .50
385 Ruben Amaro .05 .15
386 Julio Valera .05 .15
387 Robin Ventura .10 .30
388 Archi Cianfrocco .05 .15
389 Skeeter Barnes .05 .15
390 Tim Costo .05 .15
391 Luis Mercedes .05 .15
392 Jeremy Hernandez .05 .15
393 Shawon Dunston .05 .15
394 Andy Van Slyke .20 .50
395 Kevin Maas .05 .15
396 Kevin Brown .10 .30
397 J.T. Bruett .05 .15
398 Darryl Strawberry .10 .30
399 Tom Pagnozzi .05 .15
400 Sandy Alomar Jr. .05 .15
401 Keith Miller .05 .15
402 Rich DeLucia .05 .15
403 Shawn Abner .05 .15
404 Howard Johnson .05 .15
405 Mike Benjamin .05 .15
406 Roberto Mejia RC .05 .15
407 Mike Butcher .05 .15
408 Deion Sanders UER .20 .50
Braves on front and Yankees on back
409 Todd Stottlemyre .05 .15
410 Scott Kamieniecki .05 .15
411 Doug Jones .05 .15
412 John Burkett .05 .15
413 Lance Blankenship .05 .15
414 Jeff Parrett .05 .15
415 Barry Larkin .20 .50
416 Alan Trammell .10 .30
417 Mark Kiefer .05 .15
418 Gregg Olson .05 .15
419 Mark Grace .20 .50
420 Shane Mack .05 .15
421 Bob Walk .05 .15
422 Curt Schilling .10 .30
423 Erik Hanson .05 .15
424 George Brett .75 2.00
425 Reggie Jefferson .05 .15
426 Mark Portugal .05 .15
427 Ron Karkovice .05 .15
428 Matt Young .05 .15
429 Troy Neel .05 .15
430 Hector Fajardo .05 .15
431 Dave Righetti .10 .30
432 Pat Listach .05 .15
433 Jeff Innis .05 .15
434 Bob MacDonald .05 .15
435 Brian Jordan .10 .30
436 Jeff Blauser .05 .15
437 Mike Myers RC .05 .15
438 Frank Seminara .05 .15
439 Rusty Meacham .05 .15
440 Greg Briley .05 .15
441 Derek Lilliquist .05 .15
442 John Vander Wal .05 .15
443 Scott Erickson .05 .15
444 Bob Scanlan .05 .15
445 Todd Frohwirth .05 .15
446 Tom Goodwin .05 .15
447 William Pennyfeather .05 .15
448 Travis Fryman .10 .30
449 Mickey Morandini .05 .15
450 Greg Olson .05 .15
451 Trevor Hoffman .30 .75
452 Dave Magadan .05 .15
453 Shawn Jeter .05 .15
454 Andres Galarraga .10 .30
455 Ted Wood .05 .15
456 Freddie Benavides .05 .15
457 Junior Felix .05 .15
458 Alex Cole .05 .15
459 John Orton .05 .15
460 Eddie Zosky .05 .15
461 Dennis Eckersley .10 .30
462 Lee Smith .10 .30
463 John Smoltz .20 .50
464 Ken Caminiti .10 .30
465 Melido Perez .05 .15
466 Tom Marsh .05 .15
467 Jeff Nelson .05 .15
468 Jesse Levis .05 .15
469 Chris Nabholz .05 .15
470 Mike Macfarlane .05 .15
471 Reggie Sanders .10 .30
472 Chuck McElroy .05 .15
473 Kevin Gross .05 .15
474 Matt Whiteside RC .05 .15
475 Cal Eldred .05 .15
476 Dave Gallagher .05 .15
477 Len Dykstra .10 .30
478 Mark McGwire .75 2.00
479 David Segui .05 .15
480 Mike Henneman .05 .15
481 Bret Barberie .05 .15
482 Steve Sax .05 .15
483 Dave Valle .05 .15
484 Danny Darwin .05 .15
485 Devon White .10 .30
486 Eric Plunk .05 .15
487 Jim Gott .05 .15
488 Scooter Tucker .05 .15
489 Omar Olivares .05 .15
490 Greg Myers .05 .15
491 Brian Hunter .05 .15
492 Kevin Tapani .05 .15
493 Rich Monteleone .05 .15
494 Steve Buechele .05 .15
495 Bo Jackson .30 .75
496 Mike LaValliere .05 .15
497 Mark Leonard .05 .15
498 Daryl Boston .05 .15
499 Jose Canseco .20 .50
500 Brian Barnes .05 .15
501 Randy Johnson .30 .75
502 Tim McIntosh .05 .15
503 Cecil Fielder .10 .30
504 Derek Bell .05 .15
505 Kevin Koslofski .05 .15
506 Darren Holmes .05 .15
507 Brady Anderson .10 .30
508 John Valentin .05 .15
509 Jerry Browne .05 .15
510 Fred McGriff .20 .50
511 Pedro Astacio .05 .15

512 Gary Gaetti .10 .30
513 John Burke RC .05 .15
514 Dwight Gooden .10 .30
515 Thomas Howard .05 .15
516 Darrell Whitmore RC UER .05 .15
11 games played in 1992; should be 121
517 Ozzie Guillen .10 .30
518 Darryl Kile .10 .30
519 Rich Rowland .05 .15
520 Carlos Delgado .30 .75
521 Doug Henry .05 .15
522 Greg Colbrunn .05 .15
523 Tom Gordon .05 .15
524 Ivan Rodriguez .20 .50
525 Kent Hrbek .10 .30
526 Eric Young .05 .15
527 Rod Brewer .05 .15
528 Eric Karros .10 .30
529 Marquis Grissom .10 .30
530 Rico Brogna .05 .15
531 Sammy Sosa .30 .75
532 Bret Boone .10 .30
533 Luis Rivera .05 .15
534 Hal Morris .05 .15
535 Monty Fariss .05 .15
536 Leo Gomez .05 .15
537 Wally Joyner .10 .30
538 Tony Gwynn .40 1.00
539 Mike Williams .05 .15
540 Juan Gonzalez .10 .30
541 Ryan Klesko .10 .30
542 Ryan Thompson .05 .15
543 Chad Curtis .05 .15
544 Orel Hershiser .10 .30
545 Carlos Garcia .05 .15
546 Bob Welch .05 .15
547 Vinny Castilla .30 .75
548 Ozzie Smith .50 1.25
549 Luis Salazar .05 .15
550 Mark Guthrie .05 .15
551 Charles Nagy .05 .15
552 Alex Fernandez .05 .15
553 Mel Rojas .05 .15
554 Orestes Destrade .05 .15
555 Mark Gubicza .05 .15
556 Steve Finley .10 .30
557 Don Mattingly .75 2.00
558 Rickey Henderson .30 .75
559 Tommy Greene .05 .15
560 Arthur Rhodes .05 .15
561 Alfredo Griffin .05 .15
562 Will Clark .20 .50
563 Bob Zupcic .05 .15
564 Chuck Carr .05 .15
565 Henry Cotto .05 .15
566 Billy Spiers .05 .15
567 Jack Armstrong .05 .15
568 Kurt Stillwell .05 .15
569 David McCarty .05 .15
570 Joe Vitiello .05 .15
571 Gerald Williams .05 .15
572 Dale Murphy .20 .50
573 Scott Aldred .05 .15
574 Bill Gullickson .05 .15
575 Bobby Thigpen .05 .15
576 Glenallen Hill .05 .15
577 Dwayne Henry .05 .15
578 Calvin Jones .05 .15
579 Al Martin .05 .15
580 Ruben Sierra .10 .30
581 Andy Benes .05 .15
582 Anthony Young .05 .15
583 Shawn Boskie .05 .15
584 Scott Pose RC .05 .15
585 Mike Piazza 1.25 3.00
586 Donovan Osborne .05 .15
587 Jim Austin .05 .15
588 Checklist 301-400 .05 .15
589 Checklist 401-500 .05 .15
590 Checklist 501-600 .05 .15
591 Ken Griffey Jr. MC .40 1.00
592 Ivan Rodriguez MC .10 .30
593 Carlos Baerga MC .05 .15
594 Fred McGriff MC .10 .30
595 Mark McGwire MC .40 1.00
596 Roberto Alomar MC .10 .30
597 Kirby Puckett MC .20 .50
598 Marquis Grissom MC .05 .15
599 John Smoltz MC .10 .30
600 Ryne Sandberg MC .30 .75
601 Wade Boggs .20 .50
602 Jeff Reardon .10 .30
603 Billy Ripken .05 .15
604 Bryan Harvey .05 .15
605 Carlos Quintana .05 .15
606 Greg Hibbard .05 .15
607 Ellis Burks .10 .30
608 Greg Swindell .05 .15
609 Dave Winfield .10 .30
610 Charlie Hough .10 .30
611 Chili Davis .10 .30
612 Jody Reed .05 .15
613 Mark Williamson .05 .15
614 Phil Plantier .05 .15
615 Jim Abbott .20 .50
616 Dante Bichette .10 .30
617 Mark Eichhorn .05 .15
618 Gary Sheffield .10 .30
619 Richie Lewis RC .05 .15
620 Joe Girardi .05 .15
621 Jaime Navarro .05 .15
622 Willie Wilson .05 .15
623 Scott Fletcher .05 .15
624 Bud Black .05 .15
625 Tom Brunansky .05 .15
626 Steve Avery .05 .15
627 Paul Molitor .10 .30
628 Gregg Jefferies .05 .15
629 Dave Stewart .10 .30
630 Javier Lopez .20 .50
631 Greg Gagne .05 .15
632 Roberto Kelly .05 .15
633 Mike Fetters .05 .15
634 Ozzie Canseco .05 .15
635 Jeff Russell .05 .15
636 Pete Incaviglia .05 .15
637 Tom Henke .05 .15
638 Chipper Jones .30 .75
639 Jimmy Key .10 .30
640 Dave Martinez .05 .15
641 Dave Stieb .05 .15
642 Milt Thompson .05 .15
643 Alan Mills .05 .15
644 Tony Fernandez .05 .15
645 Randy Bush .05 .15
646 Joe Magrane .05 .15
647 Ivan Calderon .05 .15
648 Jose Guzman .05 .15
649 John Olerud .10 .30
650 Tom Glavine .20 .50
651 Julio Franco .10 .30
652 Armando Reynoso .05 .15
653 Felix Jose .05 .15
654 Ben Rivera .05 .15
655 Andre Dawson .10 .30
656 Mike Harkey .05 .15
657 Kevin Seitzer .05 .15
658 Lonnie Smith .05 .15
659 Norm Charlton .05 .15
660 David Justice .10 .30
661 Fernando Valenzuela .10 .30
662 Dan Wilson .10 .30
663 Mark Gardner .05 .15
664 Doug Dascenzo .05 .15
665 Greg Maddux .50 1.25
666 Harold Baines .10 .30
667 Randy Myers .05 .15
668 Harold Reynolds .10 .30
669 Candy Maldonado .05 .15
670 Al Leiter .10 .30
671 Jerald Clark .05 .15
672 Doug Drabek .05 .15
673 Kirk Gibson .10 .30
674 Steve Reed RC .05 .15
675 Mike Felder .05 .15
676 Ricky Gutierrez .05 .15
677 Spike Owen .05 .15
678 Otis Nixon .05 .15
679 Scott Sanderson .05 .15
680 Mark Carreon .05 .15
681 Troy Percival .20 .50
682 Kevin Stocker .05 .15
683 Jim Converse RC .05 .15
684 Barry Bonds .75 2.00
685 Greg Gohr .05 .15
686 Tim Wallach .05 .15
687 Matt Mieske .05 .15
688 Robby Thompson .05 .15
689 Brien Taylor .05 .15
690 Kirt Manwaring .05 .15
691 Mike Lansing RC .10 .30
692 Steve Decker .05 .15
693 Mike Moore .05 .15
694 Kevin Mitchell .05 .15
695 Phil Hiatt .05 .15
696 Tony Tarasco RC .05 .15
697 Benji Gil .05 .15
698 Jeff Juden .05 .15
699 Kevin Reimer .05 .15
700 Andy Ashby .05 .15
701 John Jaha .05 .15
702 Tim Bogar RC .05 .15
703 David Cone .10 .30
704 Willie Greene .05 .15
705 David Hulse RC .05 .15
706 Cris Carpenter .05 .15
707 Ken Griffey Jr. .60 1.50
708 Steve Bedrosian .05 .15
709 Dave Nilsson .05 .15
710 Paul Wagner .05 .15
711 B.J. Surhoff .10 .30
712 Rene Arocha RC .10 .30
713 Manuel Lee .05 .15
714 Brian Williams .05 .15
715 Sherman Obando RC .05 .15
716 Terry Mulholland .05 .15
717 Paul O'Neill .20 .50
718 David Nied .05 .15
719 J.T. Snow RC .20 .50
720 Nigel Wilson .05 .15
721 Mike Bielecki .05 .15
722 Kevin Young .10 .30
723 Charlie Leibrandt .05 .15
724 Frank Bolick .05 .15
725 Jon Shave RC .05 .15
726 Steve Cooke .05 .15
727 Domingo Martinez RC .05 .15
728 Todd Worrell .05 .15
729 Jose Lind .05 .15
730 Jim Tatum RC .05 .15
731 Mike Hampton .10 .30
732 Mike Draper .05 .15
733 Henry Mercedes .05 .15
734 John Johnstone RC .05 .15
735 Mitch Webster .05 .15
736 Russ Springer .05 .15
737 Rob Natal .05 .15
738 Steve Howe .05 .15
739 Darrell Sherman RC .05 .15
740 Pat Mahomes .05 .15
741 Alex Arias .05 .15
742 Damon Buford .05 .15
743 Charlie Hayes .05 .15
744 Guillermo Velasquez .05 .15
745 CL 601-750 UER .05 .15
650 Tom Glavine
746 Frank Thomas MC .20 .50
747 Barry Bonds MC .40 1.00
748 Roger Clemens MC .30 .75
749 Joe Carter MC .05 .15
750 Greg Maddux MC .30 .75

1993 Stadium Club First Day Issue

*STARS: 8X TO 20X BASIC CARDS
STATED ODDS 1:24 H/R, 1:15 JUMBO
BEWARE OF TRANSFERRED FDI LOGOS

1993 Stadium Club Members Only Parallel

COMPLETE FACT.SET (760) 75.00 150.00
*COMMON CARD (1-750) .20 .50
*STARS: 2X TO 4X BASIC CARDS
*ROOKIES: 1.5X to 3X BASIC CARDS
MA1 Robin Yount 1.50 4.00
MA2 George Brett 3.00 8.00
MA3 David Nied .60 1.50
MA4 Nigel Wilson .60 1.50
MB1 W.Clark 3.00 8.00
M.McGwire
MB2 D.Gooden 1.50 4.00
D.Mattingly
MB3 R.Sandberg 2.00 5.00
F.Thomas
MB4 D.Strawberry 2.50 6.00
K.Griffey
MC1 David Nied .60 1.50
MC2 Charlie Hough .60 1.50

1993 Stadium Club Inserts

COMPLETE SET (10) 5.00 12.00
COMPLETE SERIES 1 (4) .75 2.00
COMPLETE SERIES 2 (4) 4.00 10.00
COMPLETE SERIES 3 (2) .20 .50
COMMON SER.1 CARD (A1-A4) .10 .30
COMMON SER.2 CARD (B1-B4) .10 .30
COMMON SER.3 CARD (C1-C2) .10 .30
A1-A4 SER.1 STATED ODDS 1:15
B1-B4 SER.2 STATED ODDS 1:15
C1-C2 SER.3 STATED ODDS 1:15
A1 Robin Yount 1.00 2.50
A2 George Brett 1.50 4.00
A3 David Nied .10 .30
A4 Nigel Wilson .10 .30
B1 M.McGwire 1.50 4.00
W.Clark
B2 D.Gooden 1.50 4.00
D.Mattingly
B3 F.Thomas .60 1.50
R.Sandberg
B4 K.Griffey Jr. 1.25 3.00
D.Strawberry
C1 David Nied .10 .30
C2 Charlie Hough .25 .60

1993 Stadium Club Master Photos

COMPLETE SET (30) 10.00 25.00
COMPLETE SERIES 1 (12) 2.50 6.00
COMPLETE SERIES 2 (12) 3.00 8.00
COMPLETE SERIES 3 (6) 4.00 10.00
STATED ODDS 1:24 HOB/RET, 1:15 JUM
THREE JUMBOS VIA MAIL PER WINNER CARD
ONE JUMBO PER HOBBY BOX
1 Carlos Baerga .08 .25
2 Delino DeShields .08 .25
3 Brian McRae .08 .25
4 Sam Militello .08 .25
5 Joe Oliver .08 .25
6 Kirby Puckett .50 1.25
7 Cal Ripken 1.50 4.00
8 Bip Roberts .08 .25
9 Mike Scioscia .08 .25
10 Rick Sutcliffe .20 .50
11 Danny Tartabull .08 .25
12 Tim Wakefield .50 1.25
13 George Brett 1.25 3.00
14 Jose Canseco .30 .75
15 Will Clark .30 .75
16 Travis Fryman .20 .50
17 Dwight Gooden .20 .50
18 Mark Grace .30 .75
19 Rickey Henderson .50 1.25
20 Mark McGwire 1.25 3.00
21 Nolan Ryan 2.00 5.00
22 Ruben Sierra .20 .50
23 Darryl Strawberry .20 .50
24 Larry Walker .20 .50
25 Barry Bonds 1.25 3.00
26 Ken Griffey Jr. 1.00 2.50
27 Greg Maddux .75 2.00
28 David Nied .08 .25
29 J.T.Snow .30 .75
30 Brien Taylor .08 .25

1993 Stadium Club Master Photos Members Only Parallel

*MEMBERS ONLY: .5X TO 1.2X BASIC

1993 Stadium Club Ultra-Pro

The ten cards in this set measure the standard size and were available singly as limited edition random inserts in the Topps Stadium Club Ultra-Pro Platinum collector pages refill packs (1-6) and individual semi-rigid card protector packs (7-10). In light of a marketing partnership with the Rembrandt Company, this ten-card set was produced by Stadium Club to mark the launch of a new accessory line of premium card storage accessory products. Reportedly no more than 150,000 sets were produced. Willie Mays is Barry Bonds' godfather.

COMPLETE SET (10) 8.00 20.00
1 Barry Bonds 1.00 2.50
Willie Mays
Bobby Bonds
2 Willie Mays 1.25 3.00
Leaning on bat
3 Bobby Bonds .40 1.00
Kneeling, leaning on bat
4 Barry Bonds .75 2.00
Bat extended
5 Barry Bonds .75 2.00
Bobby Bonds
6 Willie Mays 1.25 3.00
Squatting posture, glove in hand
7 Barry Bonds .75 2.00
Dressed in suit
8 Bobby Bonds .75 2.00
Willie Mays
9 Willie Mays 1.25 3.00
Kneeling, bat in right hand
10 Barry Bonds .75 2.00
Dressed in tuxedo

1993 Stadium Club Members Only

This 59-card standard-size set was mailed out to Stadium Club Members in four separate mailings. Each box contained several sports. The fronts have full-bleed color action player photos with the words "Members Only" printed in gold foil at the bottom along with the player's name and the Stadium Club logo. On a multi-colored background, the horizontal backs carry player information and a computer generated drawing of a baseball player. The cards are unnumbered and checklisted below alphabetically according to sport as follows: baseball (1-28), basketball (29-44), football (45-53), and hockey (54-59).

COMPLETE SET (59) 10.00 20.00
1 Jim Abbott .08 .25
2 Barry Bonds .30 .75
3 Chris Bosio .07 .20
4 George Brett .50 1.25
5 Jay Buhner .08 .25
6 Joe Carter .08 .25
Belts 3 for Fifth
Time in Career
7 Joe Carter .08 .25
Carter's Dramatics
Give Jays Series C
8 Carlton Fisk .15 .40
9 Travis Fryman .07 .20
10 Mark Grace .08 .25
11 Ken Griffey Jr. 1.50 4.00
12 Darryl Kile .07 .20
13 Darren Lewis .07 .20
14 Greg Maddux .75 2.00
15 Jack McDowell .07 .20
16 Paul Molitor .25 .60
17 Eddie Murray .25 .60
18 Mike Piazza 1.25 3.00
Home Run Record
for Rookie Catchers
19 Mike Piazza 1.25 3.00
NL Rookie Honors
20 Kirby Puckett .50 1.25
21 Jeff Reardon .08 .25
22 Tim Salmon .08 .25
23 Curt Schilling .25 .60
24 Lee Smith .08 .25
25 Dave Stewart .08 .25
26 Frank Thomas 1.00 2.50
27 Mark Whiten .07 .20
28 Dave Winfield .25 .60

1994 Stadium Club Pre-Production

COMPLETE SET (9) 2.50 6.00
6 Al Martin .20 .50
15 Junior Ortiz .20 .50
36 Tim Salmon .50 1.25
56 Jerry Spradlin .20 .50
122 Tom Pagnozzi .20 .50
123 Ron Gant .30 .75
125 Dennis Eckersley .60 1.50
135 Jose Lind .20 .50
238 Barry Bonds 1.00 2.50

1994 Stadium Club

The 720 standard-size cards comprising this set were issued two series of 270 and a third series of 180. There are a number of subsets including Home Run Club (258-268), Tale of Two Players (525/526), Division Leaders (527-532), Quick Starts (533-538), Career Contributors (541-543), Rookie Rocker (626-630), Rookie Rocket (631-634) and Fantastic Finishes (714-719). Rookie Cards include Jeff Cirillo and Chan Ho Park.

COMPLETE SET (720) 25.00 60.00
COMPLETE SERIES 1 (270) 8.00 20.00
COMPLETE SERIES 2 (270) 8.00 20.00
COMPLETE SERIES 3 (180) 6.00 15.00
SUBSET CARDS HALF VALUE OF BASE CARDS
1 Robin Yount .50 1.25
2 Rick Wilkins .05 .15
3 Steve Scarsone .05 .15
4 Gary Sheffield .10 .30
5 George Brett .75 2.00
6 Al Martin .05 .15
7 Joe Oliver .05 .15
8 Stan Belinda .05 .15
9 Denny Hocking .05 .15
10 Roberto Alomar .20 .50
11 Luis Polonia .05 .15
12 Scott Hemond .05 .15
13 Jody Reed .05 .15
14 Mel Rojas .05 .15
15 Junior Ortiz .05 .15
16 Harold Baines .10 .30
17 Brad Pennington .05 .15
18 Jay Bell .10 .30
19 Tom Henke .05 .15
20 Jeff Branson .05 .15
21 Roberto Mejia .05 .15
22 Pedro Munoz .05 .15
23 Matt Nokes .05 .15
24 Jack McDowell .05 .15
25 Cecil Fielder .10 .30
26 Tony Fossas .05 .15
27 Jim Eisenreich .05 .15
28 Anthony Young .05 .15
29 Chuck Carr .05 .15
30 Jeff Treadway .05 .15
31 Chris Nabholz .05 .15
32 Tom Candiotti .05 .15
33 Mike Maddux .05 .15
34 Nolan Ryan 1.25 3.00
35 Luis Gonzalez .10 .30
36 Tim Salmon .20 .50
37 Mark Whiten .05 .15
38 Roger McDowell .05 .15
39 Royce Clayton .05 .15
40 Troy Neel .05 .15
41 Mike Harkey .05 .15
42 Darrin Fletcher .05 .15
43 Wayne Kirby .05 .15
44 Rich Amaral .05 .15
45 Robb Nen UER .10 .30
46 Tim Teufel .05 .15
47 Steve Cooke .05 .15
48 Jeff McNeely .05 .15
49 Jeff Montgomery .05 .15
50 Skeeter Barnes .05 .15
51 Scott Stahoviak .05 .15
52 Pat Kelly .05 .15
53 Brady Anderson .10 .30
54 Mariano Duncan .05 .15
55 Brian Bohanon .05 .15
56 Jerry Spradlin .05 .15
57 Ron Karkovice .05 .15
58 Jeff Gardner .05 .15
59 Bobby Bonilla .10 .30
60 Tino Martinez .20 .50
61 Todd Benzinger .05 .15
62 Steve Trachsel .05 .15
63 Brian Jordan .10 .30
64 Steve Bedrosian .05 .15
65 Brent Gates .05 .15
66 Shawn Green .30 .75
67 Sean Berry .05 .15
68 Joe Klink .05 .15
69 Fernando Valenzuela .10 .30
70 Andy Tomberlin .05 .15
71 Tony Pena .05 .15
72 Eric Young .05 .15
73 Chris Gomez .05 .15
74 Paul O'Neill .20 .50
75 Ricky Gutierrez .05 .15
76 Brad Holman .05 .15
77 Lance Painter .05 .15
78 Mike Butcher .05 .15
79 Sid Bream .05 .15
80 Sammy Sosa .30 .75
81 Felix Fermin .05 .15
82 Todd Hundley .05 .15
83 Kevin Higgins .05 .15
84 Todd Pratt .05 .15
85 Ken Griffey Jr. .60 1.50
86 John O'Donoghue .05 .15
87 Rick Renteria .05 .15
88 John Burkett .05 .15
89 Jose Vizcaino .05 .15
90 Kevin Seitzer .05 .15
91 Bobby Witt .05 .15
92 Chris Turner .05 .15
93 Omar Vizquel .20 .50
94 David Justice .10 .30
95 David Segui .05 .15
96 Dave Hollins .05 .15
97 Doug Strange .05 .15
98 Jerald Clark .05 .15
99 Mike Moore .05 .15
100 Joey Cora .05 .15
101 Scott Kamieniecki .05 .15
102 Andy Benes .05 .15
103 Chris Bosio .05 .15
104 Rey Sanchez .05 .15
105 John Jaha .05 .15
106 Otis Nixon .05 .15
107 Rickey Henderson .30 .75
108 Jeff Bagwell .20 .50
109 Gregg Jefferies .05 .15
110 Alomar .10 .30
Molitor
Olerud
111 Gant .10 .30
Justice
McGriff
112 Gonzalez .20 .50
Palmeiro
Palmer
113 Greg Swindell .05 .15
114 Bill Haselman .05 .15
115 Phil Plantier .05 .15
116 Ivan Rodriguez .20 .50
117 Kevin Tapani .05 .15
118 Mike LaValliere .05 .15
119 Tim Costo .05 .15
120 Mickey Morandini .05 .15
121 Brett Butler .10 .30
122 Tom Pagnozzi .05 .15
123 Ron Gant .10 .30
124 Damion Easley .05 .15
125 Dennis Eckersley .10 .30
126 Matt Mieske .05 .15
127 Cliff Floyd .10 .30
128 Julian Tavarez RC .10 .30
129 Arthur Rhodes .05 .15
130 Dave West .05 .15
131 Tim Naehring .05 .15
132 Freddie Benavides .05 .15
133 Paul Assenmacher .05 .15
134 David McCarty .05 .15
135 Jose Lind .05 .15
136 Reggie Sanders .10 .30
137 Don Slaught .05 .15
138 Andujar Cedeno .05 .15
139 Rob Deer .05 .15
140 Mike Piazza .60 1.50
141 Moises Alou .10 .30
142 Tom Foley .05 .15
143 Benito Santiago .10 .30
144 Sandy Alomar Jr. .05 .15
145 Carlos Hernandez .05 .15
146 Luis Alicea .05 .15
147 Tom Lampkin .05 .15
148 Ryan Klesko .10 .30
149 Juan Guzman .05 .15
150 Scott Servais .05 .15
151 Tony Gwynn .40 1.00
152 Tim Wakefield .20 .50
153 David Nied .05 .15
154 Chris Haney .05 .15
155 Danny Bautista .05 .15
156 Randy Velarde .05 .15
157 Darrin Jackson .05 .15
158 J.R. Phillips .05 .15
159 Greg Gagne .05 .15
160 Luis Aquino .05 .15
161 John Vander Wal .05 .15
162 Randy Myers .05 .15
163 Ted Power .05 .15
164 Scott Brosius .10 .30
165 Len Dykstra .10 .30
166 Jacob Brumfield .05 .15
167 Bo Jackson .30 .75
168 Eddie Taubensee .05 .15
169 Carlos Baerga .05 .15
170 Tim Bogar .05 .15
171 Jose Canseco .20 .50
172 Greg Blosser UER/(Gregg on front) .05 .15
173 Chili Davis .10 .30
174 Randy Knorr .05 .15
175 Mike Perez .05 .15
176 Henry Rodriguez .05 .15
177 Brian Turang RC .05 .15
178 Roger Pavlik .05 .15
179 Aaron Sele .05 .15
180 F.McGriff .20 .50
G.Sheffield
181 J.T.Snow .20 .50
T.Salmon
182 Roberto Hernandez .05 .15
183 Jeff Reboulet .05 .15
184 John Doherty .05 .15
185 Danny Sheaffer .05 .15
186 Bip Roberts .05 .15
187 Dennis Martinez .10 .30
188 Darryl Hamilton .05 .15
189 Eduardo Perez .05 .15
190 Pete Harnisch .05 .15
191 Rich Gossage .10 .30
192 Mickey Tettleton .05 .15
193 Lenny Webster .05 .15
194 Lance Johnson .05 .15
195 Don Mattingly .75 2.00
196 Gregg Olson .05 .15
197 Mark Gubicza .05 .15
198 Scott Fletcher .05 .15
199 Jon Shave .05 .15
200 Tim Mauser .05 .15
201 Jeromy Burnitz .10 .30
202 Rob Dibble .10 .30
203 Will Clark .20 .50
204 Steve Buechele .05 .15
205 Brian Williams .05 .15
206 Carlos Garcia .05 .15
207 Mark Clark .05 .15
208 Rafael Palmeiro .20 .50
209 Eric Davis .10 .30
210 Pat Meares .05 .15
211 Chuck Finley .10 .30
212 Jason Bere .05 .15
213 Gary DiSarcina .05 .15
214 Tony Fernandez .05 .15
215 B.J. Surhoff .10 .30
216 Lee Guetterman .05 .15
217 Tim Wallach .05 .15
218 Kirt Manwaring .05 .15
219 Albert Belle .10 .30
220 Dwight Gooden .10 .30
221 Archi Cianfrocco .05 .15
222 Terry Mulholland .05 .15
223 Hipolito Pichardo .05 .15
224 Kent Hrbek .10 .30
225 Craig Grebeck .05 .15
226 Todd Jones .05 .15
227 Mike Bordick .05 .15
228 John Olerud .10 .30
229 Jeff Blauser .05 .15
230 Alex Arias .05 .15
231 Bernard Gilkey .05 .15
232 Denny Neagle .10 .30
233 Pedro Borbon .05 .15
234 Dick Schofield .05 .15
235 Matias Carrillo .05 .15
236 Juan Bell .05 .15
237 Mike Hampton .10 .30
238 Barry Bonds .75 2.00
239 Cris Carpenter .05 .15
240 Eric Karros .10 .30
241 Greg McMichael .05 .15
242 Pat Hentgen .05 .15
243 Tim Pugh .05 .15
244 Vinny Castilla .10 .30
245 Charlie Hough .10 .30
246 Bobby Munoz .05 .15
247 Kevin Baez .05 .15
248 Todd Frohwirth .05 .15
249 Charlie Hayes .05 .15
250 Mike Macfarlane .05 .15
251 Danny Darwin .05 .15
252 Ben Rivera .05 .15
253 Dave Henderson .05 .15
254 Steve Avery .05 .15
255 Tim Belcher .05 .15
256 Dan Plesac .05 .15
257 Jim Thome .20 .50
258 Albert Belle HR .05 .15
259 Barry Bonds HR .40 1.00
260 Ron Gant HR .05 .15
261 Juan Gonzalez HR .05 .15
262 Ken Griffey Jr. HR .40 1.00
263 David Justice HR .05 .15
264 Fred McGriff HR .10 .30
265 Rafael Palmeiro HR .10 .30
266 Mike Piazza HR .30 .75
267 Frank Thomas HR .20 .50
268 Matt Williams HR .05 .15
269 Checklist 1-135 .05 .15
270 Checklist 136-270 .05 .15
271 Mike Stanley .05 .15
272 Tony Tarasco .05 .15
273 Teddy Higuera .05 .15
274 Ryan Thompson .05 .15
275 Rick Aguilera .05 .15
276 Ramon Martinez .05 .15
277 Orlando Merced .05 .15
278 Guillermo Velasquez .05 .15
279 Mark Hutton .05 .15
280 Larry Walker .10 .30
281 Kevin Gross .05 .15
282 Jose Offerman .05 .15
283 Jim Leyritz .05 .15
284 Jamie Moyer .10 .30
285 Frank Thomas .30 .75
286 Derek Bell .05 .15
287 Derrick May .05 .15
288 Dave Winfield .10 .30
289 Curt Schilling .10 .30
290 Carlos Quintana .05 .15
291 Bob Natal .05 .15
292 David Cone .10 .30
293 Al Osuna .05 .15
294 Bob Hamelin .05 .15
295 Chad Curtis .05 .15
296 Danny Jackson .05 .15
297 Bob Welch .05 .15
298 Felix Jose .05 .15
299 Jay Buhner .10 .30
300 Joe Carter .10 .30
301 Kenny Lofton .10 .30
302 Kirk Rueter .05 .15
303 Kim Batiste .05 .15
304 Mike Morgan .05 .15
305 Pat Borders .05 .15
306 Rene Arocha .05 .15
307 Ruben Sierra .10 .30
308 Steve Finley .10 .30
309 Travis Fryman .10 .30
310 Zane Smith .05 .15
311 Willie Wilson .05 .15
312 Trevor Hoffman .20 .50
313 Terry Pendleton .10 .30
314 Salomon Torres .05 .15
315 Robin Ventura .10 .30
316 Randy Tomlin .05 .15
317 Dave Stewart .10 .30
318 Mike Benjamin .05 .15
319 Matt Turner .05 .15
320 Manny Ramirez .30 .75
321 Kevin Young .05 .15
322 Ken Caminiti .10 .30
323 Joe Girardi .05 .15
324 Jeff McKnight .05 .15
325 Gene Harris .05 .15
326 Devon White .10 .30
327 Darryl Kile .10 .30
328 Craig Paquette .05 .15
329 Cal Eldred .05 .15
330 Bill Swift .05 .15
331 Alan Trammell .10 .30
332 Armando Reynoso .05 .15
333 Brent Mayne .05 .15
334 Chris Donnels .05 .15
335 Darryl Strawberry .10 .30
336 Dean Palmer .10 .30
337 Frank Castillo .05 .15
338 Jeff King .05 .15
339 John Franco .10 .30
340 Kevin Appier .10 .30
341 Lance Blankenship .05 .15
342 Mark McLemore .05 .15
343 Pedro Astacio .05 .15
344 Rich Batchelor .05 .15
345 Ryan Bowen .05 .15
346 Terry Steinbach .05 .15
347 Troy O'Leary .05 .15
348 Willie Blair .05 .15
349 Wade Boggs .20 .50
350 Tim Raines .10 .30
351 Scott Livingstone .05 .15
352 Rod Correia .05 .15
353 Ray Lankford .10 .30
354 Pat Listach .05 .15
355 Milt Thompson .05 .15
356 Miguel Jimenez .05 .15
357 Marc Newfield .05 .15
358 Mark McGwire .75 2.00
359 Kirby Puckett .30 .75
360 Kent Mercker .05 .15
361 John Kruk .10 .30
362 Jeff Kent .20 .50
363 Hal Morris .05 .15
364 Edgar Martinez .20 .50
365 Dave Magadan .05 .15
366 Dante Bichette .10 .30
367 Chris Hammond .05 .15
368 Bret Saberhagen .10 .30
369 Billy Ripken .05 .15
370 Bill Gullickson .05 .15
371 Andre Dawson .10 .30
372 Roberto Kelly .05 .15
373 Cal Ripken 1.00 2.50
374 Craig Biggio .20 .50
375 Dan Pasqua .05 .15
376 Dave Nilsson .05 .15
377 Duane Ward .05 .15
378 Greg Vaughn .05 .15
379 Jeff Fassero .05 .15
380 Jerry DiPoto .05 .15
381 John Patterson .05 .15
382 Kevin Brown .10 .30
383 Kevin Roberson .05 .15
384 Joe Orsulak .05 .15
385 Hilly Hathaway .05 .15
386 Mike Greenwell .05 .15
387 Orestes Destrade .05 .15
388 Mike Gallego .05 .15
389 Ozzie Guillen .10 .30
390 Raul Mondesi .10 .30
391 Scott Lydy .05 .15
392 Tom Urbani .05 .15
393 Wil Cordero .05 .15
394 Tony Longmire .05 .15
395 Todd Zeile .05 .15
396 Scott Cooper .05 .15
397 Ryne Sandberg .50 1.25
398 Ricky Bones .05 .15
399 Phil Clark .05 .15
400 Orel Hershiser .10 .30
401 Mike Henneman .05 .15
402 Mark Lemke .05 .15
403 Mark Grace .20 .50
404 Ken Ryan .05 .15
405 John Smoltz .20 .50
406 Jeff Conine .10 .30
407 Greg Harris .05 .15
408 Doug Drabek .05 .15
409 Dave Fleming .05 .15
410 Danny Tartabull .05 .15
411 Chad Kreuter .05 .15
412 Brad Ausmus .20 .50

413 Ben McDonald .05 .15
414 Barry Larkin .20 .50
415 Bret Barberie .05 .15
416 Chuck Knoblauch .10 .30
417 Ozzie Smith .50 1.25
418 Ed Sprague .05 .15
419 Matt Williams .10 .30
420 Jeremy Hernandez .05 .15
421 Jose Bautista .05 .15
422 Kevin Mitchell .05 .15
423 Manuel Lee .05 .15
424 Mike Devereaux .05 .15
425 Omar Olivares .05 .15
426 Rafael Belliard .05 .15
427 Richie Lewis .05 .15
428 Ron Darling .05 .15
429 Shane Mack .05 .15
430 Tim Hulett .05 .15
431 Wally Joyner .10 .30
432 Wes Chamberlain .05 .15
433 Tom Browning .05 .15
434 Scott Radinsky .05 .15
435 Rondell White .10 .30
436 Rod Beck .05 .15
437 Rheal Cormier .05 .15
438 Randy Johnson .30 .75
439 Pete Schourek .05 .15
440 Mo Vaughn .10 .30
441 Mike Timlin .05 .15
442 Mark Langston .05 .15
443 Lou Whitaker .10 .30
444 Kevin Stocker .05 .15
445 Ken Hill .05 .15
446 John Wetteland .10 .30
447 J.T. Snow .10 .30
448 Erik Pappas .05 .15
449 David Hulse .05 .15
450 Darren Daulton .10 .30
451 Chris Hoiles .05 .15
452 Bryan Harvey .05 .15
453 Darren Lewis .05 .15
454 Andres Galarraga .10 .30
455 Joe Hesketh .05 .15
456 Jose Valentin .05 .15
457 Dan Peltier .05 .15
458 Joe Boever .05 .15
459 Kevin Rogers .05 .15
460 Craig Shipley .05 .15
461 Alvaro Espinoza .05 .15
462 Wilson Alvarez .05 .15
463 Cory Snyder .05 .15
464 Candy Maldonado .05 .15
465 Blas Minor .05 .15
466 Rod Bolton .05 .15
467 Kenny Rogers .10 .30
468 Greg Myers .05 .15
469 Jimmy Key .10 .30
470 Tony Castillo .05 .15
471 Mike Stanton .05 .15
472 Deion Sanders .20 .50
473 Tito Navarro .05 .15
474 Mike Gardiner .05 .15
475 Steve Reed .05 .15
476 John Roper .05 .15
477 Mike Trombley .05 .15
478 Charles Nagy .05 .15
479 Larry Casian .05 .15
480 Eric Hillman .05 .15
481 Bill Wertz .05 .15
482 Jeff Schwarz .05 .15
483 John Valentin .05 .15
484 Carl Willis .05 .15
485 Gary Gaetti .10 .30
486 Bill Pecota .05 .15
487 John Smiley .05 .15
488 Mike Mussina .20 .50
489 Mike Ignasiak .05 .15
490 Billy Brewer .05 .15
491 Jack Voigt .05 .15
492 Mike Munoz .05 .15
493 Lee Tinsley .05 .15
494 Bob Wickman .05 .15
495 Roger Salkeld .05 .15
496 Thomas Howard .05 .15
497 Mark Davis .05 .15
498 Dave Clark .05 .15
499 Turk Wendell .05 .15
500 Rafael Bournigal .05 .15
501 Chip Hale .05 .15
502 Matt Whiteside .05 .15
503 Brian Koelling .05 .15
504 Jeff Reed .05 .15
505 Paul Wagner .05 .15
506 Torey Lovullo .05 .15
507 Curt Leskanic .05 .15
508 Derek Lilliquist .05 .15
509 Joe Magrane .05 .15
510 Mackey Sasser .05 .15
511 Lloyd McClendon .05 .15
512 Jayhawk Owens .05 .15
513 Woody Williams .05 .15
514 Gary Redus .05 .15
515 Tim Spehr .05 .15
516 Jim Abbott .20 .50
517 Lou Frazier .05 .15
518 Erik Plantenberg RC .05 .15
519 Tim Worrell .05 .15
520 Brian McRae .05 .15
521 Chan Ho Park RC .30 .75
522 Mark Wohlers .05 .15
523 Geronimo Pena .05 .15
524 Andy Ashby .05 .15
525 T.Raines .05 .15
A.Dawson TALE
526 Paul Molitor TALE .05 .15
527 Joe Carter DL .05 .15
528 Frank Thomas DL .20 .50
529 Ken Griffey Jr. DL .40 1.00
530 David Justice DL .05 .15
531 Gregg Jefferies DL .05 .15
532 Barry Bonds DL .40 1.00
533 John Kruk QS .05 .15
534 Roger Clemens QS .30 .75
535 Cecil Fielder QS .05 .15
536 Ruben Sierra QS .05 .15
537 Tony Gwynn QS .20 .50
538 Tom Glavine QS .10 .30
539 Checklist 271-405 UER
(number on back is 269) .05 .15
540 Checklist 406-540 UER
(numbered 270 on back) .05 .15
541 Ozzie Smith CC .30 .75
542 Eddie Murray ATL .20 .50
543 Lee Smith ATL .05 .15
544 Greg Maddux .50 1.25
545 Denis Boucher .05 .15
546 Mark Gardner .05 .15
547 Bo Jackson .30 .75
548 Eric Anthony .05 .15
549 Delino DeShields .05 .15
550 Turner Ward .05 .15
551 Scott Sanderson .05 .15
552 Hector Carrasco .05 .15
553 Tony Phillips .05 .15
554 Melido Perez .05 .15
555 Mike Felder .05 .15
556 Jack Morris .10 .30
557 Rafael Palmeiro .20 .50
558 Shane Reynolds .05 .15
559 Pete Incaviglia .05 .15
560 Greg Harris .05 .15
561 Matt Walbeck .05 .15
562 Todd Van Poppel .05 .15
563 Todd Stottlemyre .05 .15
564 Ricky Bones .05 .15
565 Mike Jackson .05 .15
566 Kevin McReynolds .05 .15
567 Melvin Nieves .05 .15
568 Juan Gonzalez .10 .30
569 Frank Viola .10 .30
570 Vince Coleman .05 .15
571 Brian Anderson RC .10 .30
572 Omar Vizquel .20 .50
573 Bernie Williams .20 .50
574 Tom Glavine .20 .50
575 Mitch Williams .05 .15
576 Shawon Dunston .05 .15
577 Mike Lansing .05 .15
578 Greg Pirkl .05 .15
579 Sid Fernandez .05 .15
580 Doug Jones .05 .15
581 Walt Weiss .05 .15
582 Tim Belcher .05 .15
583 Alex Fernandez .05 .15
584 Alex Cole .05 .15
585 Greg Cadaret .05 .15
586 Bob Tewksbury .05 .15
587 Dave Hansen .05 .15
588 Kurt Abbott RC .05 .15
589 Rick White RC .05 .15
590 Kevin Bass .05 .15
591 Geronimo Berroa .05 .15
592 Jaime Navarro .05 .15
593 Steve Farr .05 .15
594 Jack Armstrong .05 .15
595 Steve Howe .05 .15
596 Jose Rijo .05 .15
597 Otis Nixon .05 .15
598 Robby Thompson .05 .15
599 Kelly Stinnett RC .10 .30
600 Carlos Delgado .20 .50
601 Brian Johnson RC .05 .15
602 Gregg Olson .05 .15
603 Jim Edmonds .30 .75
604 Mike Blowers .05 .15
605 Lee Smith .10 .30
606 Pat Rapp .05 .15
607 Mike Magnante .05 .15
608 Karl Rhodes .05 .15
609 Jeff Juden .05 .15
610 Rusty Meacham .05 .15
611 Pedro Martinez .30 .75
612 Todd Worrell .05 .15
613 Stan Javier .05 .15
614 Mike Hampton .10 .30
615 Jose Guzman .05 .15
616 Xavier Hernandez .05 .15
617 David Wells .10 .30
618 John Habyan .05 .15
619 Chris Nabholz .05 .15
620 Bobby Jones .05 .15
621 Chris James .05 .15
622 Ellis Burks .10 .30
623 Erik Hanson .05 .15
624 Pat Meares .05 .15
625 Harold Reynolds .10 .30
626 Bob Hamelin RR .05 .15
627 Manny Ramirez RR .20 .50
628 Ryan Klesko RR .05 .15
629 Carlos Delgado RR .10 .30
630 Javier Lopez RR .10 .30
631 Steve Karsay RR .05 .15
632 Rick Helling RR .05 .15
633 Steve Trachsel RR .05 .15
634 Hector Carrasco RR .05 .15
635 Andy Stankiewicz .05 .15
636 Paul Sorrento .05 .15
637 Scott Erickson .05 .15
638 Chipper Jones .30 .75
639 Luis Polonia .05 .15
640 Howard Johnson .05 .15
641 John Dopson .05 .15
642 Jody Reed .05 .15
643 Lonnie Smith UER .05 .15
Card numbered 543
644 Mark Portugal .05 .15
645 Paul Molitor .10 .30
646 Paul Assenmacher .05 .15
647 Hubie Brooks .05 .15
648 Gary Wayne .05 .15
649 Sean Berry .05 .15
650 Roger Clemens .60 1.50
651 Brian R. Hunter .05 .15
652 Wally Whitehurst .05 .15
653 Allen Watson .05 .15
654 Rickey Henderson .30 .75
655 Sid Bream .05 .15
656 Dan Wilson .05 .15
657 Ricky Jordan .05 .15
658 Sterling Hitchcock .05 .15
659 Darrin Jackson .05 .15
660 Junior Felix .05 .15
661 Tom Brunansky .05 .15
662 Jose Vizcaino .05 .15
663 Mark Leiter .05 .15
664 Gil Heredia .05 .15
665 Fred McGriff .20 .50
666 Will Clark .20 .50
667 Al Leiter .10 .30
668 James Mouton .05 .15
669 Billy Bean .05 .15
670 Scott Leius .05 .15
671 Bret Boone .10 .30
672 Darren Holmes .05 .15
673 Dave Weathers .05 .15
674 Eddie Murray .30 .75
675 Felix Fermin .05 .15
676 Chris Sabo .05 .15
677 Billy Spiers .05 .15
678 Aaron Sele .05 .15
679 Juan Samuel .05 .15
680 Julio Franco .10 .30
681 Heathcliff Slocumb .05 .15
682 Dennis Martinez .10 .30
683 Jerry Browne .05 .15
684 Pedro A.Martinez RC .05 .15
685 Rex Hudler .05 .15
686 Willie McGee .10 .30
687 Andy Van Slyke .20 .50
688 Pat Mahomes .05 .15
689 Dave Henderson .05 .15
690 Tony Eusebio .05 .15
691 Rick Sutcliffe .10 .30
692 Willie Banks .05 .15
693 Alan Mills .05 .15
694 Jeff Treadway .05 .15
695 Alex Gonzalez .05 .15
696 David Segui .05 .15
697 Rick Helling .05 .15
698 Bip Roberts .05 .15
699 Jeff Cirillo RC .10 .30
700 Terry Mulholland .05 .15
701 Marvin Freeman .05 .15
702 Jason Bere .05 .15
703 Javier Lopez .10 .30
704 Greg Hibbard .05 .15
705 Tommy Greene .05 .15
706 Marquis Grissom .10 .30
707 Brian Harper .05 .15
708 Steve Karsay .05 .15
709 Jeff Brantley .05 .15
710 Jeff Russell .05 .15
711 Bryan Hickerson .05 .15
712 Jim Pittsley RC .05 .15
713 Bobby Ayala .05 .15
714 John Smoltz .20 .50
715 Jose Rijo .05 .15
716 Greg Maddux FAN .30 .75
717 Matt Williams FAN .05 .15
718 Frank Thomas FAN .20 .50
719 Ryne Sandberg FAN .30 .75
720 Checklist .05 .15

1994 Stadium Club First Day Issue

COMPLETE SET (720) 1500.00 2500.00
*STARS: 8X TO 20X BASIC CARDS
*ROOKIES: 6X TO 15X BASIC CARDS
STATED ODDS 1:24 H/R, 1:15 JUMBO
STATED PRINT RUN 2000 SETS
BEWARE OF TRANSFERRED FDI LOGOS

1994 Stadium Club Golden Rainbow

COMPLETE SET (720) 75.00 150.00
COMPLETE SERIES 1 (270) 25.00 60.00
COMPLETE SERIES 2 (270) 25.00 60.00
COMPLETE SERIES 3 (180) 15.00 40.00
*STARS: 1.25X TO 3X BASIC CARDS
*ROOKIES: 1X TO 2.5X BASIC CARDS
ONE PER PACK/TWO PER JUMBO

1994 Stadium Club Members Only Parallel

COMPLETE FACT.SET (770) 100.00 200.00
*1ST SERIES MEMBERS ONLY: 4X BASIC CARDS
2ND AND 3RD SERIES STARS: 6X BASIC CARDS
F1 Jeff Bagwell 1.50 4.00
F2 Albert Belle .60 1.50
F3 Barry Bonds 3.00 8.00
F4 Juan Gonzalez 1.25 3.00
F5 Ken Griffey Jr. 6.00 15.00
F6 Marquis Grissom .40 1.00
F7 David Justice 1.25 3.00
F8 Mike Piazza 3.00 8.00
F9 Tim Salmon 1.25 3.00
F10 Frank Thomas 2.50 6.00
DD1 Mike Piazza 3.00 8.00
DD2 Dave Winfield 1.25 3.00
DD3 John Kruk .60 1.50
DD4 Cal Ripken 6.00 15.00
DD5 Jack McDowell 2.50 6.00
DD6 Barry Bonds 3.00 8.00
DD7 Ken Griffey Jr. 6.00 15.00
DD8 Tim Salmon 1.25 3.00
DD9 Frank Thomas 2.00 5.00
DD10 Jeff Kent 1.25 3.00
DD11 Randy Johnson 1.50 4.00
DD12 Darren Daulton .60 1.50
ST1 Atlanta Braves D .30 .75
L
WS
ST2 Chicago Cubs .60 1.50
ST3 Cin.Reds .40 1.00
R.Sand
Lark D
ST4 Colorado Rockies .20 .50
ST5 Florida Marlins .20 .50
ST6 Houston Astros .30 .75
ST7 L.A.Dodgers 2.00 5.00
Piazza D
ST8 Montreal Expos .30 .75
ST9 New York Mets .20 .50
ST10 Philadelphia Phillies .20 .50
ST11 Pittsburgh Pirates .30 .75
ST12 St.Louis Cardinals .20 .50
ST13 San Diego Padres .20 .50
ST14 S.F.Giants .40 1.00
M.Williams
ST15 Baltimore Orioles 2.50 6.00
Ripken
ST16 Boston Red Sox D .20 .50
ST17 California Angels .60 1.50
ST18 Chicago White Sox .20 .50
ST19 Cle.Indians .40 1.00
Bel
Bae
Lof D
L
ST20 Detroit Tigers .30 .75
ST21 Kansas City Royals .20 .50
ST22 Milwaukee Brewers .20 .50
ST23 Minnesota Twins 1.25 3.00
Puckett
ST24 N.Y.Yankees 1.25 3.00
Mattingly
ST25 Oakland Athletics .20 .50
ST26 Seattle Mariners D .40 1.00
ST27 Tex.Rangers .60 1.50
Cans
Gonz
ST28 Toronto Blue Jays .20 .50

1994 Stadium Club Dugout Dirt

COMPLETE SET (12) 4.00 10.00
COMPLETE SERIES 1 (4) 2.00 5.00
COMPLETE SERIES 2 (4) 1.25 3.00
COMPLETE SERIES 3 (4) 1.25 3.00
STATED ODDS 1:6 H/R, 1:3 JUM
1 Mike Piazza .60 1.50
2 Dave Winfield .10 .30
3 John Kruk .10 .30
4 Cal Ripken 1.00 2.50
5 Jack McDowell .05 .15
6 Barry Bonds .75 2.00
7 Ken Griffey Jr. .60 1.50
8 Tim Salmon .20 .50
9 Frank Thomas .30 .75
10 Jeff Kent .20 .50
11 Randy Johnson .30 .75
12 Darren Daulton .10 .30

1994 Stadium Club Finest

COMPLETE SET (10) 10.00 25.00
SER.3 STATED ODDS 1:6
*JUMBOS: .6X TO 1.5X BASIC SC FINEST
JUMBOS DISTRIBUTED IN RETAIL PACKS
F1 Jeff Bagwell .60 1.50
F2 Albert Belle .40 1.00
F3 Barry Bonds 2.50 6.00
F4 Juan Gonzalez .40 1.00
F5 Ken Griffey Jr. 2.00 5.00
F6 Marquis Grissom .40 1.00
F7 David Justice .40 1.00
F8 Mike Piazza 2.00 5.00
F9 Tim Salmon .60 1.50
F10 Frank Thomas 1.00 2.50

1994 Stadium Club Super Teams

COMPLETE SET (28) 20.00 50.00
SER.1 STAT.ODDS 1:24 HOB/RET, 1:15 JUM
CONTEST APPLIED TO 1995 SEASON
WINNERS LISTED UNDER 1995 STAD.CLUB
ST1 Atlanta DLWS 1.00 2.50
ST2 Chicago Cubs .40 1.00
ST3 Cincinnati .60 1.50
B.Larkin D
ST4 Colorado Rockies .40 1.00
ST5 Florida Marlins .40 1.00
ST6 Houston Astros .40 1.00
ST7 Los Angeles 2.00 5.00
M.Piazza D
ST8 Montreal Expos .40 1.00
ST9 New York Mets .40 1.00
ST10 Philadelphia Phillies .40 1.00
ST11 Pittsburgh Pirates .60 1.50
ST12 St.Louis Cardinals .40 1.00
ST13 San Diego Padres .40 1.00
ST14 San Francisco .40 1.00
M.Williams
ST15 Baltimore 3.00 8.00
C.Ripken
ST16 Boston .40 1.00
J.Valentin D
ST17 California Angels .40 1.00
ST18 Chicago White Sox .40 1.00
ST19 Cleveland .40 1.00
Belle
Lofton DL
ST20 Detroit Tigers .40 1.00
ST21 Kansas City Royals .40 1.00
ST22 Milwaukee Brewers .40 1.00
ST23 Minnesota 1.00 2.50
K.Puckett
ST24 New York 2.50 6.00
D.Mattingly
ST25 Oakland Athletics .40 1.00
ST26 Seattle .40 1.00
J.Buhner D
ST27 Texas .40 1.00
J.Gonzalez
ST28 Toronto Blue Jays .40 1.00

1994 Stadium Club Superstar Samplers

4 Gary Sheffield 2.00 5.00
10 Roberto Alomar 1.25 3.00
24 Jack McDowell .40 1.00
25 Cecil Fielder .60 1.50
36 Tim Salmon .60 1.50
59 Bobby Bonilla .60 1.50
85 Ken Griffey Jr. 4.00 10.00
94 David Justice 1.25 3.00
108 Jeff Bagwell 2.00 5.00
109 Gregg Jefferies .40 1.00
127 Cliff Floyd 1.00 2.50
140 Mike Piazza 3.00 8.00
151 Tony Gwynn 3.00 8.00
165 Len Dykstra .40 1.00
169 Carlos Baerga .40 1.00
171 Jose Canseco 2.00 5.00
195 Don Mattingly 1.50 4.00
203 Will Clark 1.25 3.00
208 Rafael Palmeiro 1.50 4.00
219 Albert Belle .60 1.50
228 John Olerud .60 1.50
238 Barry Bonds 3.00 8.00
280 Larry Walker 1.50 4.00
285 Frank Thomas 2.00 5.00
300 Joe Carter .60 1.50
320 Manny Ramirez 2.00 5.00
359 Kirby Puckett 2.00 5.00
373 Cal Ripken 6.00 15.00
390 Raul Mondesi .60 1.50
397 Ryne Sandberg 2.50 6.00
403 Mark Grace 1.00 2.50
414 Barry Larkin 1.25 3.00
419 Matt Williams 1.00 2.50
438 Randy Johnson 2.50 6.00
440 Mo Vaughn .60 1.50
450 Darren Daulton .60 1.50
454 Andres Galarraga 1.25 3.00
544 Greg Maddux 4.00 10.00
568 Juan Gonzalez 1.25 3.00
574 Tom Glavine 1.50 4.00
645 Paul Molitor 1.50 4.00
650 Roger Clemens 3.00 8.00
665 Fred McGriff 1.00 2.50
687 Andy Van Slyke .40 1.00
706 Marquis Grissom .60 1.50

1994 Stadium Club Members Only 50

Issued to Stadium Club members, this 50-card standard-size set features 45 regular Stadium Club cards as well as five Stadium Club Finest cards.

COMPLETE SET (50) 8.00 20.00
1 Juan Gonzalez .30 .75
2 Tom Henke .02 .10
3 John Kruk .08 .25
4 Paul Molitor .30 .75
5 David Justice .08 .25
6 Rafael Palmeiro .25 .60
7 John Smoltz .25 .60
8 Matt Williams .15 .40
9 John Olerud .08 .25
10 Mark Grace .15 .40
11 Joe Carter .08 .25
12 Wilson Alvarez .08 .25
13 Len Dykstra .08 .25
14 Kevin Appier .08 .25
15 Andres Galarraga .25 .60
16 Mark Langston .02 .10
17 Ken Griffey Jr. 1.00 2.50
18 Albert Belle .08 .25
19 Gregg Jefferies .02 .10
20 Duane Ward .02 .10
21 Jack McDowell .02 .10
22 Randy Johnson .30 .75
23 Tom Glavine .25 .60
24 Barry Bonds .60 1.50
25 Chuck Carr .02 .10
26 Ron Gant .08 .25
27 Kenny Lofton .15 .40
28 Mike Piazza .60 1.50
29 Frank Thomas .40 1.00
30 Fred McGriff .15 .40
31 Bryan Harvey .02 .10
32 John Burkett .02 .10
33 Roberto Alomar .25 .60
34 Cecil Fielder .08 .25
35 Marquis Grissom .08 .25
36 Randy Myers .02 .10
37 Tony Phillips .02 .10
38 Rickey Henderson .30 .75
39 Luis Polonia .02 .10
40 Jose Rijo .02 .10
41 Jeff Montgomery .02 .10
42 Greg Maddux .75 2.00
43 Tony Gwynn .60 1.50
44 Rod Beck .02 .10
45 Carlos Baerga .08 .25
46 Wil Cordero FIN .20 .50
47 Tim Salmon FIN .75 2.00
48 Mike Lansing FIN .20 .50
49 J.T. Snow FIN .20 .50
50 Jeff Conine FIN .30 .75

1994 Stadium Club Team

This 360-card standard-size set features 30 players from 12 teams. The cards are checklisted alphabetically according to teams.

COMPLETE SET (360) 15.00 40.00
1 Barry Bonds .75 2.00
2 Royce Clayton .02 .10
3 Kirt Manwaring .02 .10
4 J.R. Phillips .02 .10
5 Robby Thompson .02 .10
6 Willie McGee .07 .20
7 Steve Hosey .02 .10
8 Dave Burba .02 .10
9 Steve Scarsone .02 .10
10 Salomon Torres .02 .10
11 Bryan Hickerson .02 .10
12 Mike Benjamin .02 .10
13 Mark Carreon .02 .10
14 Rich Monteleone .02 .10
15 Dave Martinez .02 .10
16 Bill Swift .02 .10
17 Jeff Reed .02 .10
18 John Patterson .02 .10
19 Darren Lewis .02 .10
20 Mark Portugal .02 .10
21 Trevor Wilson .02 .10
22 Matt Williams .15 .40
23 Kevin Rogers .02 .10
24 Luis Mercedes .02 .10
25 Mike Jackson .02 .10
26 Steve Frey .02 .10
27 Tony Menendez .02 .10
28 John Burkett .02 .10
29 Todd Benzinger .02 .10
30 Rod Beck .02 .10
31 Greg Maddux 1.00 2.50
32 Steve Avery .02 .10
33 Milt Hill .02 .10
34 Charlie O'Brien .02 .10
35 John Smoltz .07 .20
36 Jarvis Brown .02 .10
37 Dave Gallagher .02 .10
38 Ryan Klesko .15 .40
39 Kent Mercker .02 .10
40 Terry Pendleton .02 .10
41 Ron Gant .07 .20
42 Pedro Borbon Jr. .02 .10
43 Steve Bedrosian .02 .10
44 Ramon Caraballo .02 .10
45 Tyler Houston .02 .10
46 Mark Lemke .02 .10
47 Fred McGriff .15 .40
48 Jose Oliva .02 .10
49 David Justice .25 .60
50 Chipper Jones .75 2.00
51 Tony Tarasco .02 .10
52 Javier Lopez .15 .40
53 Mark Wohlers .02 .10
54 Deion Sanders .25 .60
55 Greg McMichael .02 .10
56 Tom Glavine .40 1.00
57 Bill Pecota .02 .10
58 Mike Stanton .02 .10
59 Rafael Belliard .02 .10
60 Jeff Blauser .02 .10
61 Bryan Harvey .02 .10
62 Bret Barberie .02 .10
63 Rick Renteria .02 .10
64 Chris Hammond .02 .10
65 Pat Rapp .02 .10
66 Nigel Wilson .02 .10
67 Gary Sheffield .40 1.00
68 Jerry Browne .02 .10
69 Charlie Hough .07 .20
70 Orestes Destrade .07 .20
71 Mario Diaz .02 .10
72 Ryan Bowen .02 .10
73 Carl Everett .07 .20
74 Richie Lewis .02 .10
75 Bob Natal .02 .10
76 Rich Rodriguez .02 .10
77 Darrell Whitmore .02 .10
78 Matt Turner .02 .10
79 Benito Santiago .07 .20
80 Robb Nen .07 .20
81 Dave Magadan .02 .10
82 Brian Drahman .02 .10
83 Mark Gardner .02 .10
84 Chuck Carr .02 .10
85 Alex Arias .02 .10
86 Kurt Abbott .02 .10
87 Joe Klink .02 .10
88 Jeff Mutis .02 .10
89 Dave Weathers .02 .10
90 Jeff Conine .07 .20
91 Andres Galarraga .25 .60
92 Vinny Castilla .07 .20
93 Roberto Mejia .02 .10
94 Darrell Sherman .02 .10
95 Mike Harkey .02 .10
96 Danny Sheaffer .02 .10
97 Pedro Castellano .02 .10
98 Walt Weiss .02 .10
99 Greg W. Harris .02 .10
100 Jayhawk Owens .02 .10
101 Bruce Ruffin .02 .10
102 Mike Munoz .02 .10
103 Armando Reynoso .02 .10
104 Eric Young .07 .20
105 Dante Bichette .07 .20
106 Marvin Freeman .02 .10
107 Joe Girardi .07 .20
108 Kent Bottenfield .02 .10
109 Howard Johnson .02 .10
110 Nelson Liriano .02 .10
111 David Nied .02 .10
112 Steve Reed .02 .10
113 Eric Wedge .07 .20
114 Charlie Hayes .02 .10
115 Ellis Burks .15 .40
116 Willie Blair .02 .10
117 Darren Holmes .02 .10
118 Curtis Leskanic .02 .10
119 Lance Painter .02 .10
120 Jim Tatum .02 .10
121 Frank Thomas .50 1.25
122 Jack McDowell .02 .10
123 Ron Karkovice .02 .10
124 Mike LaValliere .02 .10
125 Scott Radinsky .02 .10
126 Robin Ventura .15 .40
127 Scott Ruffcorn .02 .10
128 Steve Sax .02 .10
129 Roberto Hernandez .07 .20
130 Jose DeLeon .02 .10
131 Rod Bolton .02 .10
132 Wilson Alvarez .02 .10
133 Craig Grebeck .02 .10
134 Lance Johnson .02 .10
135 Kirk McCaskill .02 .10
136 Tim Raines .07 .20
137 Jeff Schwarz .02 .10
138 Warren Newson .02 .10
139 Norberto Martin .02 .10
140 Mike Huff .02 .10
141 Ozzie Guillen .15 .40
142 Alex Fernandez .02 .10
143 Joey Cora .02 .10
144 Jason Bere .02 .10
145 James Baldwin .07 .20
146 Esteban Beltre .02 .10
147 Julio Franco .07 .20
148 Matt Merullo .02 .10
149 Dan Pasqua .02 .10
150 Darrin Jackson .02 .10
151 Joe Carter .07 .20
152 Danny Cox .02 .10
153 Roberto Alomar .25 .60
154 Woody Williams .15 .40
155 Duane Ward .02 .10
156 Ed Sprague .02 .10
157 Domingo Martinez .02 .10
158 Pat Hentgen .07 .20
159 Shawn Green .40 1.00
160 Dick Schofield .02 .10
161 Paul Molitor .40 1.00
162 Darnell Coles .02 .10
163 Willie Canate .02 .10
164 Domingo Cedeno .02 .10
165 Pat Borders .02 .10
166 Greg Cadaret .02 .10
167 Tony Castillo .02 .10
168 Carlos Delgado .40 1.00
169 Scott Brow .02 .10
170 Juan Guzman .02 .10
171 Al Leiter .07 .20
172 John Olerud .15 .40
173 Todd Stottlemyre .02 .10
174 Devon White .07 .20
175 Paul Spoljaric .02 .10
176 Randy Knorr .02 .10
177 Huck Flener .02 .10
178 Rob Butler .02 .10
179 Dave Stewart .07 .20
180 Mike Timlin .02 .10
181 Don Mattingly .75 2.00
182 Mark Hutton .02 .10
183 Mike Gallego .02 .10
184 Jim Abbott .07 .20
185 Paul Gibson .02 .10
186 Scott Kamieniecki .02 .10
187 Sam Horn .02 .10
188 Melido Perez .02 .10
189 Randy Velarde .02 .10
190 Gerald Williams .02 .10
191 Dave Silvestri .02 .10
192 Jim Leyritz .02 .10
193 Steve Howe .02 .10
194 Russ Davis .02 .10
195 Paul Assenmacher .02 .10
196 Pat Kelly .02 .10
197 Mike Stanley .02 .10
198 Bernie Williams .30 .75
199 Paul O'Neill .25 .60
200 Donn Pall .02 .10
201 Xavier Hernandez .02 .10
202 Jim Austin .02 .10
203 Sterling Hitchcock .07 .20
204 Wade Boggs .40 1.00
205 Jimmy Key .07 .20
206 Matt Nokes .02 .10
207 Bobby Munoz .02 .10
208 Luis Polonia .02 .10
209 Danny Tartabull .07 .20
210 Bob Wickman .02 .10
211 Len Dykstra .07 .20
212 Kim Batiste .02 .10
213 Tony Longmire .02 .10
214 Terry Mulholland .02 .10
215 Pete Incaviglia .02 .10
216 Doug Jones .07 .20
217 Mariano Duncan .02 .10
218 Jeff Juden .02 .10
219 Milt Thompson .02 .10
220 Dave West .02 .10
221 Roger Mason .02 .10
222 Tommy Greene .02 .10
223 Larry Andersen .02 .10
224 Jim Eisenreich .02 .10
225 Dave Hollins .02 .10
226 John Kruk .07 .20
227 Todd Pratt .02 .10
228 Ricky Jordan .02 .10
229 Curt Schilling .60 1.50
230 Mike Williams .02 .10
231 Heathcliff Slocumb .02 .10
232 Ben Rivera .02 .10
233 Mike Lieberthal .07 .20
234 Mickey Morandini .02 .10
235 Danny Jackson .02 .10
236 Kevin Foster .02 .10
237 Darren Daulton .07 .20
238 Wes Chamberlain .02 .10
239 Tyler Green .02 .10
240 Kevin Stocker .02 .10
241 Juan Gonzalez .30 .75
242 Rick Honeycutt .02 .10
243 Bruce Hurst .02 .10
244 Steve Dreyer .02 .10
245 Brian Bohanon .02 .10
246 Benji Gil .02 .10
247 Jon Shave .02 .10
248 Manuel Lee .02 .10
249 Donald Harris .02 .10
250 Jose Canseco .30 .75
251 David Hulse .02 .10
252 Kenny Rogers .02 .10
253 Jeff Huson .02 .10
254 Dan Peltier .02 .10
255 Mike Scioscia .07 .20
256 Jack Armstrong .02 .10
257 Rob Ducey .02 .10
258 Will Clark .25 .60
259 Cris Carpenter .02 .10
260 Kevin Brown .15 .40
261 Jeff Frye .02 .10
262 Jay Howell .02 .10
263 Roger Pavlik .02 .10
264 Gary Redus .02 .10
265 Ivan Rodriguez .40 1.00
266 Matt Whiteside .02 .10
267 Doug Strange .02 .10
268 Billy Ripken .02 .10
269 Dean Palmer .07 .20
270 Tom Henke .02 .10
271 Cal Ripken 1.50 4.00
272 Mark McLemore .07 .20
273 Sid Fernandez .07 .20
274 Sherman Obando .02 .10
275 Paul Carey .02 .10
276 Mike Oquist .02 .10
277 Alan Mills .02 .10
278 Harold Baines .07 .20
279 Mike Mussina .40 1.00
280 Arthur Rhodes .02 .10
281 Kevin McGehee .02 .10
282 Mark Eichhorn .02 .10
283 Damon Buford .02 .10
284 Ben McDonald .02 .10
285 David Segui .02 .10
286 Brad Pennington .02 .10
287 Jamie Moyer .15 .40
288 Chris Hoiles .02 .10
289 Mike Cook .02 .10
290 Brady Anderson .07 .20
291 Chris Sabo .02 .10
292 Jack Voigt .02 .10
293 Jim Poole .02 .10
294 Jeff Tackett .02 .10
295 Rafael Palmeiro .30 .75
296 Alex Ochoa .02 .10
297 John O'Donoghue .02 .10
298 Tim Hulett .02 .10
299 Mike Devereaux .02 .10
300 Manny Alexander .02 .10
301 Ozzie Smith .40 1.00
302 Omar Olivares .02 .10
303 Rheal Cormier .02 .10
304 Donovan Osborne .02 .10
305 Mark Whiten .02 .10
306 Todd Zeile .07 .20
307 Geronimo Pena .02 .10
308 Brian Jordan .07 .20

309 Luis Alicea .02 .10
310 Ray Lankford .07 .20
311 Stan Royer .02 .10
312 Bob Tewksbury .02 .10
313 Jose Oquendo .02 .10
314 Steve Dixon .02 .10
315 Rene Arocha .02 .10
316 Bernard Gilkey .02 .10
317 Gregg Jefferies .02 .10
318 Rob Murphy .02 .10
319 Tom Pagnozzi .02 .10
320 Mike Perez .02 .10
321 Tom Urbani .02 .10
322 Allen Watson .02 .10
323 Erik Pappas .02 .10
324 Paul Kilgus .02 .10
325 John Habyan .02 .10
326 Rod Brewer .02 .10
327 Rich Batchelor .02 .10
328 Tripp Cromer .02 .10
329 Gerald Perry .02 .10
330 Les Lancaster .02 .10
331 Ryne Sandberg .75 2.00
332 Derrick May .02 .10
333 Steve Buechele .02 .10
334 Willie Banks .02 .10
335 Larry Luebbers .02 .10
336 Tommy Shields .02 .10
337 Eric Yelding .02 .10
338 Rey Sanchez .02 .10
339 Mark Grace .15 .40
340 Jose Bautista .02 .10
341 Frank Castillo .02 .10
342 Jose Guzman .02 .10
343 Rafael Novoa .02 .10
344 Karl Rhodes .02 .10
345 Steve Trachsel .02 .10
346 Rick Wilkins .02 .10
347 Sammy Sosa .60 1.50
348 Kevin Roberson .02 .10
349 Mark Parent .02 .10
350 Randy Myers .07 .20
351 Glenallen Hill .02 .10
352 Lance Dickson .02 .10
353 Shawn Boskie .02 .10
354 Shawon Dunston .07 .20
355 Dan Plesac .02 .10
356 Jose Vizcaino .02 .10
357 Willie Wilson .02 .10
358 Turk Wendell .02 .10
359 Mike Morgan .02 .10
360 Jim Bullinger .02 .10

1994 Stadium Club Team First Day Issue

*FIRST DAY: 5X to 12X BASIC CARDS
RANDOM INSERTS IN PACKS

1994 Stadium Club Team Finest

COMPLETE SET (12) 12.50 30.00
1 Roberto Alomar .75 2.00
2 Barry Bonds 2.00 5.00
3 Len Dykstra .40 1.00
4 Andres Galarraga .75 2.00
5 Juan Gonzalez .75 2.00
6 David Justice .75 2.00
7 Don Mattingly 1.50 4.00
8 Cal Ripken 4.00 10.00
9 Ryne Sandberg 2.00 5.00
10 Gary Sheffield 1.00 2.50
11 Ozzie Smith 1.50 4.00
12 Frank Thomas .75 2.00

1994 Stadium Club Draft Picks

This 90-card standard-size set features players chosen in the June 1994 MLB draft and photographed in their major league uniforms. Each 24-pack box included four First Day Issue Draft Pick cards randomly packed, one in every six packs. Early cards of Nomar Garciaparra, Ben Grieve and Terrence Long are featured in this set.

COMPLETE SET (90) 4.00 10.00
1 Jacob Shumate XRC .08 .25
2 C.J. Nitkowski XRC .08 .25
3 Doug Million XRC .08 .25
4 Matt Smith XRC .08 .25
5 Kevin Lovinger XRC .08 .25
6 Alberto Castillo XRC .08 .25
7 Mike Russell XRC .08 .25
8 Dan Lock XRC .08 .25
9 Tom Szimanski XRC .08 .25
10 Aaron Boone XRC .20 .50
11 Jayson Peterson XRC .08 .25
12 Mark Johnson XRC .08 .25
13 Cade Gaspar XRC .08 .25
14 George Lombard XRC .08 .25
15 Russ Johnson .08 .25
16 Travis Miller XRC .08 .25
17 Jay Payton XRC .20 .50
18 Brian Buchanan XRC .08 .25
19 Jacob Cruz XRC .15 .40
20 Gary Rath XRC .08 .25
21 Ramon Castro XRC .08 .25
22 Tommy Davis XRC .08 .25
23 Tony Terry XRC .08 .25
24 Jerry Whittaker XRC .08 .25
25 Mike Darr XRC .08 .25
26 Doug Webb XRC .08 .25
27 Jason Camilli XRC .08 .25
28 Brad Rigby XRC .08 .25
29 Ryan Nye XRC .08 .25
30 Carl Dale XRC .08 .25
31 Andy Taulbee XRC .08 .25
32 Trey Moore XRC .08 .25
33 John Crowther XRC .08 .25
34 Joe Giuliano XRC .08 .25
35 Brian Rose XRC .08 .25
36 Paul Failla XRC .08 .25
37 Brian Meadows XRC .08 .25
38 Oscar Robles XRC .15 .40
39 Mike Metcalfe XRC .08 .25
40 Larry Barnes XRC .08 .25
41 Paul Ottavinia XRC .08 .25
42 Chris McBride XRC .08 .25
43 Ricky Stone XRC .08 .25
44 Billy Blythe XRC .08 .25
45 Eddie Priest XRC .08 .25
46 Scott Forster XRC .08 .25
47 Eric Pickett XRC .08 .25
48 Matt Beaumont .08 .25
49 Darrell Nicholas XRC .08 .25
50 Mike A. Hampton XRC .08 .25
51 Paul O'Malley XRC .08 .25
52 Steve Shoemaker XRC .08 .25
53 Jason Sikes XRC .08 .25
54 Bryan Farson XRC .08 .25
55 Yates Hall XRC .08 .25
56 Troy Brohawn XRC .08 .25
57 Dan Hower XRC .08 .25
58 Clay Caruthers XRC .08 .25
59 Pepe McNeal XRC .08 .25
60 Ray Ricken XRC .08 .25
61 Scott Shores XRC .08 .25
62 Eddie Brooks XRC .08 .25
63 Dave Kauflin XRC .08 .25
64 David Meyer XRC .08 .25
65 Geoff Blum XRC .20 .50
66 Roy Marsh XRC .08 .25
67 Ryan Beeney XRC .08 .25
68 Derek Dukart XRC .08 .25
69 Nomar Garciaparra 1.25 3.00
70 Jason Kelly XRC .08 .25
71 Jesse Ibarra XRC .08 .25
72 Bucky Buckles XRC .08 .25
73 Mark Little XRC .08 .25
74 Heath Murray XRC .08 .25
75 Greg Morris XRC .08 .25
76 Mike Halperlin XRC .08 .25
77 Wes Helms XRC .15 .40
78 Ray Brown XRC .08 .25
79 Kevin L.Brown XRC .15 .40
80 Paul Konerko XRC 2.00 5.00
81 Mike Thurman XRC .08 .25
82 Paul Wilson .08 .25
83 Terrence Long XRC .15 .40
84 Ben Grieve XRC .15 .40
85 Mark Farris XRC .08 .25
86 Bret Wagner .08 .25
87 Dustin Hermanson .08 .25
88 Kevin Witt XRC .15 .40
89 Corey Pointer XRC .08 .25
90 Tim Grieve XRC .08 .25

1994 Stadium Club Draft Picks First Day Issue

COMPLETE SET (90) 60.00 120.00
*FIRST DAY: 1.25X TO 3X BASIC CARDS
RANDOM INSERTS IN PACKS

1994 Stadium Club Draft Picks Members Only

*MEMBERS ONLY: 1.25X TO 3X BASIC CARD

1995 Stadium Club

The 1995 Stadium Club baseball card set was issued in three series of 270, 225 and 135 standard-size cards for a total of 630. The cards were distributed in 14-card packs at a suggested retail price of $2.50 and contained 24 packs per box. Notable Rookie Cards include Mark Grudzielanek, Bobby Higginson and Hideo Nomo.

COMPLETE SET (630) 12.50 30.00
COMPLETE SERIES 1 (270) 5.00 12.00
COMPLETE SERIES 2 (225) 4.00 10.00
COMPLETE SERIES 3 (135) 3.00 8.00
SUBSET CARDS HALF VALUE OF BASE CARDS
1 Cal Ripken 1.00 2.50
2 Bo Jackson .30 .75
3 Bryan Harvey .05 .15
4 Curt Schilling .10 .30
5 Bruce Ruffin .05 .15
6 Travis Fryman .10 .30
7 Jim Abbott .20 .50
8 David McCarty .05 .15
9 Gary Gaetti .10 .30
10 Roger Clemens .60 1.50
11 Carlos Garcia .05 .15
12 Lee Smith .10 .30
13 Bobby Ayala .05 .15
14 Charles Nagy .05 .15
15 Lou Frazier .05 .15
16 Rene Arocha .05 .15
17 Carlos Delgado .10 .30
18 Steve Finley .10 .30
19 Ryan Klesko .10 .30
20 Cal Eldred .05 .15
21 Rey Sanchez .05 .15
22 Ken Hill .05 .15
23 Benito Santiago .10 .30
24 Julian Tavarez .05 .15
25 Jose Vizcaino .05 .15
26 Andy Benes .05 .15
27 Mariano Duncan .05 .15
28 Checklist A .05 .15
29 Shawon Dunston .05 .15
30 Rafael Palmeiro .20 .50
31 Dean Palmer .10 .30
32 Andres Galarraga .10 .30
33 Joey Cora .05 .15
34 Mickey Tettleton .05 .15
35 Barry Larkin .20 .50
36 Carlos Baerga .05 .15
37 Orel Hershiser .10 .30
38 Jody Reed .05 .15
39 Paul Molitor .10 .30
40 Jim Edmonds .20 .50
41 Bob Tewksbury .05 .15
42 John Patterson .05 .15
43 Ray McDavid .05 .15
44 Zane Smith .05 .15
45 Bret Saberhagen SE .05 .15
46 Greg Maddux SE .30 .75
47 Frank Thomas SE .20 .50
48 Carlos Baerga SE .05 .15
49 Billy Spiers .05 .15
50 Stan Javier .05 .15
51 Rex Hudler .05 .15
52 Denny Hocking .05 .15
53 Todd Worrell .05 .15
54 Mark Clark .05 .15
55 Hipolito Pichardo .05 .15
56 Bob Wickman .05 .15
57 Raul Mondesi .10 .30
58 Steve Cooke .05 .15
59 Rod Beck .05 .15
60 Tim Davis .05 .15
61 Jeff Kent .10 .30
62 John Valentin .05 .15
63 Alex Arias .05 .15
64 Steve Reed .05 .15
65 Ozzie Smith .50 1.25
66 Terry Pendleton .10 .30
67 Kenny Rogers .10 .30
68 Vince Coleman .05 .15
69 Tom Pagnozzi .05 .15
70 Roberto Alomar .20 .50
71 Darrin Jackson .05 .15
72 Dennis Eckersley .10 .30
73 Jay Buhner .10 .30
74 Darren Lewis .05 .15
75 Dave Weathers .05 .15
76 Matt Walbeck .05 .15
77 Brad Ausmus .10 .30
78 Danny Bautista .05 .15
79 Bob Hamelin .05 .15
80 Steve Trachsel .05 .15
81 Ken Ryan .05 .15
82 Chris Turner .05 .15
83 David Segui .05 .15
84 Ben McDonald .05 .15
85 Wade Boggs .20 .50
86 John Vander Wal .05 .15
87 Sandy Alomar Jr. .06 .15
88 Ron Karkovice .05 .15
89 Doug Jones .05 .15
90 Gary Sheffield .10 .30
91 Ken Caminiti .10 .30
92 Chris Bosio .05 .15
93 Kevin Tapani .05 .15
94 Walt Weiss .05 .15
95 Erik Hanson .05 .15
96 Ruben Sierra .10 .30
97 Nomar Garciaparra .75 2.00
98 Terrence Long .05 .15
99 Jacob Shumate .05 .15
100 Paul Wilson .05 .15
101 Kevin Witt .05 .15
102 Paul Konerko .40 1.00
103 Ben Grieve .05 .15
104 Mark Johnson RC .15 .40
105 Cade Gaspar RC .05 .15
106 Mark Farris .05 .15
107 Dustin Hermanson .05 .15
108 Scott Elarton RC .15 .40
109 Doug Million .05 .15
110 Matt Smith .05 .15
111 Brian Buchanan RC .05 .15
112 Jayson Peterson RC .05 .15
113 Bret Wagner .05 .15
114 C.J. Nitkowski RC .15 .40
115 Ramon Castro RC .15 .40
116 Rafael Bournigal .05 .15
117 Jeff Fassero .05 .15
118 Bobby Bonilla .10 .30
119 Ricky Gutierrez .05 .15
120 Roger Pavlik .05 .15
121 Mike Greenwell .05 .15
122 Deion Sanders .20 .50
123 Charlie Hayes .05 .15
124 Paul O'Neill .20 .50
125 Jay Bell .10 .30
126 Royce Clayton .05 .15
127 Willie Banks .05 .15
128 Mark Wohlers .05 .15
129 Todd Jones .05 .15
130 Todd Stottlemyre .05 .15
131 Will Clark .20 .50
132 Wilson Alvarez .05 .15
133 Chili Davis .10 .30
134 Dave Burba .05 .15
135 Chris Hoiles .05 .15
136 Jeff Blauser .05 .15
137 Jeff Reboulet .05 .15
138 Bret Saberhagen .10 .30
139 Kirk Rueter .05 .15
140 Dave Nilsson .05 .15
141 Pat Borders .05 .15
142 Ron Darling .05 .15
143 Derek Bell .05 .15
144 Dave Hollins .05 .15
145 Juan Gonzalez .10 .30
146 Andre Dawson .10 .30
147 Jim Thome .20 .50
148 Larry Walker .10 .30
149 Mike Piazza .50 1.25
150 Mike Perez .05 .15
151 Steve Avery .05 .15
152 Dan Wilson .05 .15
153 Andy Van Slyke .20 .50
154 Junior Felix .05 .15
155 Jack McDowell .05 .15
156 Danny Tartabull .05 .15
157 Willie Blair .05 .15
158 Wm.VanLandingham .05 .15
159 Robb Nen .10 .30
160 Lee Tinsley .05 .15
161 Ismael Valdes .05 .15
162 Juan Guzman .05 .15
163 Scott Servais .05 .15
164 Cliff Floyd .10 .30
165 Allen Watson .05 .15
166 Eddie Taubensee .05 .15
167 Scott Hemond .05 .15
168 Jeff Tackett .05 .15
169 Chad Curtis .05 .15
170 Rico Brogna .05 .15
171 Luis Polonia .05 .15
172 Checklist B .05 .15
173 Lance Johnson .05 .15
174 Sammy Sosa .30 .75
175 Mike Macfarlane .05 .15
176 Darryl Hamilton .05 .15
177 Rick Aguilera .05 .15
178 Dave West .05 .15
179 Mike Gallego .05 .15
180 Marc Newfield .05 .15
181 Steve Buechele .05 .15
182 David Wells .10 .30
183 Tom Glavine .20 .50
184 Joe Girardi .05 .15
185 Craig Biggio .20 .50
186 Eddie Murray .30 .75
187 Kevin Gross .05 .15
188 Sid Fernandez .05 .15
189 John Franco .10 .30
190 Bernard Gilkey .05 .15
191 Matt Williams .10 .30
192 Darrin Fletcher .05 .15
193 Jeff Conine .10 .30
194 Ed Sprague .05 .15
195 Eduardo Perez .05 .15
196 Scott Livingstone .05 .15
197 Ivan Rodriguez .20 .50
198 Orlando Merced .05 .15
199 Ricky Bones .05 .15
200 Javier Lopez .10 .30
201 Miguel Jimenez .05 .15
202 Terry McGriff .05 .15
203 Mike Lieberthal .10 .30
204 David Cone .10 .30
205 Todd Hundley .05 .15
206 Ozzie Guillen .10 .30
207 Alex Cole .05 .15
208 Tony Phillips .05 .15
209 Jim Eisenreich .05 .15
210 Greg Vaughn BES .05 .15
211 Barry Larkin BES .10 .30
212 Don Mattingly BES .40 1.00
213 Mark Grace BES .10 .30
214 Jose Canseco BES .10 .30
215 Joe Carter BES .05 .15
216 David Cone BES .05 .15
217 Sandy Alomar Jr. BES .05 .15
218 Al Martin BES .05 .15
219 Roberto Kelly BES .05 .15
220 Paul Sorrento .05 .15
221 Tony Fernandez .05 .15
222 Stan Belinda .05 .15
223 Mike Stanley .05 .15
224 Doug Drabek .05 .15
225 Todd Van Poppel .05 .15
226 Matt Mieske .05 .15
227 Tino Martinez .20 .50
228 Andy Ashby .05 .15
229 Midre Cummings .05 .15
230 Jeff Frye .05 .15
231 Hal Morris .05 .15
232 Jose Lind .05 .15
233 Shawn Green .10 .30
234 Rafael Belliard .05 .15
235 Randy Myers .05 .15
236 Frank Thomas CE .20 .50
237 Darren Daulton CE .05 .15
238 Sammy Sosa CE .20 .50
239 Cal Ripken CE .50 1.25
240 Jeff Bagwell CE .10 .30
241 Ken Griffey Jr. .60 1.50
242 Brett Butler .10 .30
243 Derrick May .05 .15
244 Pat Listach .05 .15
245 Mike Bordick .05 .15
246 Mark Langston .05 .15
247 Randy Velarde .05 .15
248 Julio Franco .10 .30
249 Chuck Knoblauch .10 .30
250 Bill Gullickson .05 .15
251 Dave Henderson .05 .15
252 Bret Boone .10 .30
253 Al Martin .05 .15
254 Armando Benitez .05 .15
255 Wil Cordero .05 .15
256 Al Leiter .10 .30
257 Luis Gonzalez .10 .30
258 Charlie O'Brien .05 .15
259 Tim Wallach .05 .15
260 Scott Sanders .05 .15
261 Tom Henke .05 .15
262 Otis Nixon .05 .15
263 Darren Daulton .10 .30
264 Manny Ramirez .20 .50
265 Bret Barberie .05 .15
266 Mel Rojas .05 .15
267 John Burkett .05 .15
268 Brady Anderson .10 .30
269 John Roper .05 .15
270 Shane Reynolds .05 .15
271 Barry Bonds .75 2.00
272 Alex Fernandez .05 .15
273 Brian McRae .05 .15
274 Todd Zeile .05 .15
275 Greg Swindell .05 .15
276 Johnny Ruffin .05 .15
277 Troy Neel .05 .15
278 Eric Karros .10 .30
279 John Hudek .05 .15
280 Thomas Howard .05 .15
281 Joe Carter .10 .30
282 Mike Devereaux .05 .15
283 Butch Henry .05 .15
284 Reggie Jefferson .05 .15
285 Mark Lemke .05 .15
286 Jeff Montgomery .05 .15
287 Ryan Thompson .05 .15
288 Paul Shuey .05 .15
289 Mark McGwire .75 2.00
290 Bernie Williams .20 .50
291 Mickey Morandini .05 .15
292 Scott Leius .05 .15
293 David Hulse .05 .15
294 Greg Gagne .05 .15
295 Moises Alou .10 .30
296 Geronimo Berroa .05 .15
297 Eddie Zambrano .05 .15
298 Alan Trammell .10 .30
299 Don Slaught .05 .15
300 Jose Rijo .05 .15
301 Joe Ausanio .05 .15
302 Tim Raines .10 .30
303 Melido Perez .05 .15
304 Kent Mercker .05 .15
305 James Mouton .05 .15
306 Luis Lopez .05 .15
307 Mike Kingery .05 .15
308 Willie Greene .05 .15
309 Cecil Fielder .10 .30
310 Scott Kamieniecki .05 .15
311 Mike Greenwell BES .05 .15
312 Bobby Bonilla BES .05 .15
313 Andres Galarraga BES .05 .15
314 Cal Ripken BES .50 1.25
315 Matt Williams BES .05 .15
316 Tom Pagnozzi BES .05 .15
317 Len Dykstra BES .05 .15
318 Frank Thomas BES .20 .50
319 Kirby Puckett BES .30 .75
320 Mike Piazza BES .30 .75
321 Jason Jacome .05 .15
322 Brian Hunter .05 .15
323 Brent Gates .05 .15
324 Jim Converse .05 .15
325 Damion Easley .05 .15
326 Dante Bichette .10 .30
327 Kurt Abbott .05 .15
328 Scott Cooper .05 .15
329 Mike Henneman .05 .15
330 Orlando Miller .05 .15
331 John Kruk .10 .30
332 Jose Oliva .05 .15
333 Reggie Sanders .10 .30
334 Omar Vizquel .20 .50
335 Devon White .10 .30
336 Mike Morgan .05 .15
337 J.R. Phillips .05 .15
338 Gary DiSarcina .05 .15
339 Joey Hamilton .05 .15
340 Randy Johnson .30 .75
341 Jim Leyritz .05 .15
342 Bobby Jones .05 .15
343 Jaime Navarro .05 .15
344 Bip Roberts .05 .15
345 Steve Karsay .05 .15
346 Kevin Stocker .05 .15
347 Jose Canseco .20 .50
348 Bill Wegman .05 .15
349 Rondell White .10 .30
350 Mo Vaughn .10 .30
351 Joe Orsulak .05 .15
352 Pat Meares .05 .15
353 Albie Lopez .05 .15
354 Edgar Martinez .20 .50
355 Brian Jordan .10 .30
356 Tommy Greene .05 .15
357 Chuck Carr .05 .15
358 Pedro Astacio .05 .15
359 Russ Davis .05 .15
360 Chris Hammond .05 .15
361 Gregg Jefferies .05 .15
362 Shane Mack .05 .15
363 Fred McGriff .20 .50
364 Pat Rapp .05 .15
365 Bill Swift .05 .15
366 Checklist .05 .15
367 Robin Ventura .10 .30
368 Bobby Witt .05 .15
369 Karl Rhodes .05 .15
370 Eddie Williams .05 .15
371 John Jaha .05 .15
372 Steve Howe .05 .15
373 Leo Gomez .05 .15
374 Hector Fajardo .05 .15
375 Jeff Bagwell .20 .50
376 Mark Acre .05 .15
377 Wayne Kirby .05 .15
378 Mark Portugal .05 .15
379 Jesus Tavarez .05 .15
380 Jim Lindeman .05 .15
381 Don Mattingly .75 2.00
382 Trevor Hoffman .10 .30
383 Chris Gomez .05 .15
384 Garret Anderson .10 .30
385 Bobby Munoz .05 .15
386 Jon Lieber .05 .15
387 Rick Helling .05 .15
388 Marvin Freeman .05 .15
389 Juan Castillo .05 .15
390 Jeff Cirillo .05 .15
391 Sean Berry .05 .15
392 Hector Carrasco .05 .15
393 Mark Grace .20 .50
394 Pat Kelly .05 .15
395 Tim Naehring .05 .15
396 Greg Pirkl .05 .15
397 John Smoltz .20 .50
398 Robby Thompson .05 .15
399 Rick White .05 .15
400 Frank Thomas .30 .75
401 Jeff Conine CS .05 .15
402 Jose Valentin CS .05 .15
403 Carlos Baerga CS .05 .15
404 Rick Aguilera CS .05 .15
405 Wilson Alvarez CS .05 .15
406 Juan Gonzalez CS .05 .15
407 Barry Larkin CS .10 .30
408 Ken Hill CS .05 .15
409 Chuck Carr CS .05 .15
410 Tim Raines CS .05 .15
411 Bryan Eversgerd .05 .15
412 Phil Plantier .05 .15
413 Josias Manzanillo .05 .15
414 Roberto Kelly .05 .15
415 Rickey Henderson .30 .75
416 John Smiley .05 .15
417 Kevin Brown .10 .30
418 Jimmy Key .10 .30
419 Wally Joyner .10 .30
420 Roberto Hernandez .05 .15
421 Felix Fermin .05 .15
422 Checklist .05 .15
423 Greg Vaughn .05 .15
424 Ray Lankford .10 .30
425 Greg Maddux .50 1.25
426 Mike Mussina .20 .50
427 Geronimo Pena .05 .15
428 David Nied .05 .15
429 Scott Erickson .05 .15
430 Kevin Mitchell .05 .15
431 Mike Lansing .05 .15
432 Brian Anderson .05 .15
433 Jeff King .05 .15
434 Ramon Martinez .05 .15
435 Kevin Seitzer .05 .15
436 Salomon Torres .05 .15
437 Brian L.Hunter .05 .15
438 Melvin Nieves .05 .15
439 Mike Kelly .05 .15
440 Marquis Grissom .10 .30
441 Chuck Finley .10 .30
442 Len Dykstra .10 .30
443 Ellis Burks .10 .30
444 Harold Baines .10 .30
445 Kevin Appier .10 .30
446 David Justice .10 .30
447 Darryl Kile .10 .30
448 John Olerud .10 .30
449 Greg McMichael .05 .15
450 Kirby Puckett .30 .75
451 Jose Valentin .05 .15
452 Rick Wilkins .05 .15
453 Arthur Rhodes .05 .15
454 Pat Hentgen .05 .15
455 Tom Gordon .05 .15
456 Tom Candiotti .05 .15
457 Jason Bere .05 .15
458 Wes Chamberlain .05 .15
459 Greg Colbrunn .05 .15
460 John Doherty .05 .15
461 Kevin Foster .05 .15
462 Mark Whiten .05 .15
463 Terry Steinbach .05 .15
464 Aaron Sele .05 .15
465 Kirt Manwaring .05 .15
466 Darren Hall .05 .15
467 Delino DeShields .05 .15
468 Andujar Cedeno .05 .15
469 Billy Ashley .05 .15
470 Kenny Lofton .10 .30
471 Pedro Munoz .05 .15
472 John Wetteland .10 .30
473 Tim Salmon .20 .50
474 Denny Neagle .10 .30
475 Tony Gwynn .40 1.00
476 Vinny Castilla .10 .30
477 Steve Dreyer .05 .15
478 Jeff Shaw .05 .15
479 Chad Ogea .05 .15
480 Scott Ruffcorn .05 .15
481 Lou Whitaker .10 .30
482 J.T. Snow .10 .30
483 Rich Rowland .05 .15
484 Denny Martinez .10 .30
485 Pedro Martinez .20 .50
486 Rusty Greer .10 .30
487 Dave Fleming .05 .15
488 John Dettmer .05 .15
489 Albert Belle .10 .30
490 Ravelo Manzanillo .05 .15
491 Henry Rodriguez .05 .15
492 Andrew Lorraine .05 .15
493 Dwayne Hosey .05 .15
494 Mike Blowers .05 .15
495 Turner Ward .05 .15
496 Fred McGriff EC .10 .30
497 Sammy Sosa EC .20 .50
498 Barry Larkin EC .10 .30
499 Andres Galarraga EC .05 .15
500 Gary Sheffield EC .05 .15
501 Jeff Bagwell EC .10 .30
502 Mike Piazza EC .30 .75
503 Moises Alou EC .05 .15
504 Bobby Bonilla EC .05 .15
505 Darren Daulton EC .05 .15
506 Jeff King EC .05 .15
507 Ray Lankford EC .05 .15
508 Tony Gwynn EC .20 .50
509 Barry Bonds EC .40 1.00
510 Cal Ripken EC .50 1.25
511 Mo Vaughn EC .05 .15
512 Tim Salmon EC .10 .30
513 Frank Thomas EC .20 .50
514 Albert Belle EC .05 .15
515 Cecil Fielder EC .05 .15
516 Kevin Appier EC .05 .15
517 Greg Vaughn EC .05 .15
518 Kirby Puckett EC .20 .50
519 Paul O'Neill EC .10 .30
520 Ruben Sierra EC .05 .15
521 Ken Griffey Jr. EC .40 1.00
522 Will Clark EC .10 .30
523 Joe Carter EC .05 .15
524 Antonio Osuna .05 .15
525 Glenallen Hill .05 .15
526 Alex Gonzalez .05 .15
527 Dave Stewart .10 .30
528 Ron Gant .10 .30
529 Jason Bates .05 .15
530 Mike Macfarlane .05 .15
531 Esteban Loaiza .05 .15
532 Joe Randa .10 .30
533 Dave Winfield .10 .30
534 Danny Darwin .05 .15
535 Pete Harnisch .05 .15
536 Joey Cora .05 .15
537 Jaime Navarro .05 .15
538 Marty Cordova .05 .15
539 Andujar Cedeno .05 .15
540 Mickey Tettleton .05 .15
541 Andy Van Slyke .20 .50
542 Carlos Perez RC .15 .40
543 Chipper Jones .30 .75
544 Tony Fernandez .05 .15
545 Tom Henke .05 .15
546 Pat Borders .05 .15
547 Chad Curtis .05 .15
548 Ray Durham .10 .30
549 Joe Oliver .05 .15
550 Jose Mesa .05 .15
551 Steve Finley .10 .30
552 Otis Nixon .05 .15
553 Jacob Brumfield .05 .15
554 Bill Swift .05 .15
555 Quilvio Veras .05 .15
556 Hideo Nomo RC 1.00 2.50
557 Joe Vitiello .05 .15
558 Mike Perez .05 .15
559 Charlie Hayes .05 .15
560 Brad Radke RC .30 .75
561 Darren Bragg .05 .15
562 Orel Hershiser .10 .30
563 Edgardo Alfonzo .05 .15
564 Doug Jones .05 .15
565 Andy Pettitte .20 .50
566 Benito Santiago .10 .30
567 John Burkett .05 .15
568 Brad Clontz .05 .15
569 Jim Abbott .20 .50
570 Joe Rosselli .05 .15
571 Mark Grudzielanek RC .30 .75
572 Dustin Hermanson .05 .15
573 Benji Gil .05 .15
574 Mark Whiten .05 .15
575 Mike Ignasiak .05 .15
576 Kevin Ritz .05 .15
577 Paul Quantrill .05 .15
578 Andre Dawson .10 .30
579 Jerald Clark .05 .15
580 Frank Rodriguez .05 .15
581 Mark Kiefer .05 .15
582 Trevor Wilson .05 .15
583 Gary Wilson RC .05 .15
584 Andy Stankiewicz .05 .15
585 Felipe Lira .05 .15
586 Michael Mimbs RC .05 .15
587 Jon Nunnally .05 .15
588 Tomas Perez RC .05 .15
589 Chad Fonville .05 .15
590 Todd Hollandsworth .05 .15
591 Roberto Petagine .05 .15
592 Mariano Rivera .75 2.00
593 Mark McLemore .05 .15
594 Bobby Witt .05 .15
595 Jose Offerman .05 .15
596 Jason Christiansen RC .05 .15
597 Jeff Manto .05 .15
598 Jim Dougherty RC .05 .15
599 Juan Acevedo RC .05 .15
600 Troy O'Leary .05 .15
601 Ron Villone .05 .15
602 Tripp Cromer .05 .15
603 Steve Scarsone .05 .15
604 Lance Parrish .10 .30
605 Ozzie Timmons .05 .15
606 Ray Holbert .05 .15
607 Tony Phillips .05 .15
608 Phil Plantier .05 .15
609 Shane Andrews .05 .15
610 Heathcliff Slocumb .05 .15
611 Bob Higginson RC .30 .75
612 Bob Tewksbury .05 .15
613 Terry Pendleton .10 .30
614 Scott Cooper TA .05 .15
615 John Wetteland TA .05 .15
616 Ken Hill TA .05 .15
617 Marquis Grissom TA .05 .15
618 Larry Walker TA .05 .15
619 Derek Bell TA .05 .15
620 David Cone TA .05 .15
621 Ken Caminiti TA .05 .15
622 Jack McDowell TA .05 .15
623 Vaughn Eshelman TA .05 .15
624 Brian McRae TA .05 .15
625 Gregg Jefferies TA .05 .15
626 Kevin Brown TA .05 .15
627 Lee Smith TA .05 .15
628 Tony Tarasco TA .05 .15
629 Brett Butler TA .05 .15
630 Jose Canseco TA .10 .30

1995 Stadium Club First Day Issue

COMPLETE SET (270) 125.00 250.00
COMMON CARD (1-270) .75 2.00
*STARS: 5X TO 12X BASIC CARDS
*ROOKIES: 3X TO 8X BASIC CARDS
*DP STARS: 1.25X TO 3X BASIC CARDS
RANDOM INSERTS IN TOPPS SER.2 PACKS
TEN PER TOPPS FACTORY SET
DPs INSERTED IN TOPPS SER.1 & 2 PACKS
BEWARE OF TRANSFERRED FDI LOGOS

1995 Stadium Club Members Only Parallel

COMP.SET w/o VR (755) 125.00 250.00
*MEM.ONLY 1-630: 1.5X TO 4X BASIC CARDS
CB1 Chipper Jones 3.00 8.00
CB2 Dustin Hermanson .30 .75
CB3 Ray Durham .60 1.50
CB4 Phil Nevin .30 .75
CB5 Billy Ashley .08 .25
CB6 Shawn Green .75 2.00
CB7 Jason Bates .08 .25
CB8 Benji Gil .08 .25
CB9 Marty Cordova .08 .25
CB10 Quilvio Veras .30 .75
CB11 Mark Grudzielanek .30 .75
CB12 Ruben Rivera .08 .25
CB13 Bill Pulsipher .08 .25
CB14 Derek Jeter 6.00 15.00
CB15 LaTroy Hawkins .08 .25
CC1 Mike Piazza 3.00 8.00
CC2 Ruben Sierra .08 .25
CC3 Tony Gwynn 3.00 8.00
CC4 Frank Thomas 2.50 6.00
CC5 Fred McGriff .60 1.50
CC6 Rafael Palmeiro .75 2.00
CC7 Bobby Bonilla .08 .25
CC8 Chili Davis .30 .75
CC9 Hal Morris .08 .25
CC10 Jose Canseco 1.25 3.00
CC11 Jay Bell .30 .75
CC12 Kirby Puckett 2.50 6.00
CC13 Gary Sheffield .75 2.00
CC14 Bob Hamelin .08 .25
CC15 Jeff Bagwell 1.25 3.00
CC16 Albert Belle .30 .75
CC17 Sammy Sosa 3.00 8.00
CC18 Ken Griffey Jr. 6.00 15.00
CC19 Todd Zeile .30 .75
CC20 Mo Vaughn .30 .75
CC21 Moises Alou .30 .75
CC22 Paul O'Neill .30 .75
CC23 Andres Galarraga .75 2.00
CC24 Greg Vaughn .30 .75
CC25 Len Dykstra .30 .75
CC26 Joe Carter .30 .75
CC27 Barry Bonds 3.00 8.00
CC28 Cecil Fielder .30 .75
PZ1 Jeff Bagwell 1.25 3.00
PZ2 Albert Belle .30 .75

PZ3 Barry Bonds 3.00 8.00
PZ4 Joe Carter .30 .75
PZ5 Cecil Fielder .30 .75
PZ6 Andres Galarraga .75 2.00
PZ7 Ken Griffey Jr. 6.00 15.00
PZ8 Paul Molitor .75 2.00
PZ9 Fred McGriff .60 1.50
PZ10 Rafael Palmeiro .75 2.00
PZ11 Frank Thomas 2.50 6.00
PZ12 Matt Williams .60 1.50
RL1 Jeff Bagwell 1.25 3.00
RL2 Mark McGwire 5.00 12.00
RL3 Ozzie Smith 2.50 6.00
RL4 Paul Molitor .75 2.00
RL5 Darryl Strawberry .08 .25
RL6 Eddie Murray .75 2.00
RL7 Tony Gwynn 3.00 8.00
RL8 Jose Canseco 1.25 3.00
RL9 Howard Johnson .08 .25
RL10 Andre Dawson .60 1.50
RL11 Matt Williams .60 1.50
RL12 Tim Raines .30 .75
RL13 Fred McGriff .60 1.50
RL14 Ken Griffey Jr. 6.00 15.00
RL15 Gary Sheffield .75 2.00
RL16 Dennis Eckersley .30 .75
RL17 Kevin Mitchell .08 .25
RL18 Will Clark .75 2.00
RL19 Darren Daulton .30 .75
RL20 Paul O'Neill .75 2.00
RL21 Julio Franco .08 .25
RL22 Albert Belle .30 .75
RL23 Juan Gonzalez 1.25 3.00
RL24 Kirby Puckett 2.50 6.00
RL25 Joe Carter .30 .75
RL26 Frank Thomas 2.50 6.00
RL27 Cal Ripken 6.00 15.00
RL28 John Olerud .30 .75
RL29 Ruben Sierra .30 .75
RL30 Barry Bonds 3.00 8.00
RL31 Cecil Fielder .30 .75
RL32 Roger Clemens 3.00 8.00
RL33 Don Mattingly 3.00 8.00
RL34 Terry Pendleton .08 .25
RL35 Rickey Henderson 1.25 3.00
RL36 Dave Winfield 1.25 3.00
RL37 Edgar Martinez .60 1.50
RL38 Wade Boggs 1.25 3.00
RL39 Willie McGee .30 .75
RL40 Andres Galarraga .75 2.00
SS1 Roberto Alomar .75 2.00
SS2 Barry Bonds 3.00 8.00
SS3 Jay Buhner .30 .75
SS4 Chuck Carr .08 .25
SS5 Don Mattingly 3.00 8.00
SS6 Raul Mondesi .60 1.50
SS7 Tim Salmon .75 2.00
SS8 Deion Sanders .30 .75
SS9 Devon White .08 .25
SS10 Mark Whiten .08 .25
SS11 Ken Griffey Jr. 6.00 15.00
SS12 Marquis Grissom .08 .25
SS13 Paul O'Neill .30 .75
SS14 Kenny Lofton .08 .25
SS15 Larry Walker .75 2.00
SS16 Scott Cooper .08 .25
SS17 Barry Larkin .75 2.00
SS18 Matt Williams .60 1.50
SS19 John Wetteland .30 .75
SS20 Randy Johnson 1.25 3.00
VRE1 Barry Bonds 3.00 8.00
VRE2 Ken Griffey Jr. 6.00 15.00
VRE3 Jeff Bagwell 1.25 3.00
VRE4 Albert Belle .30 .75
VRE5 Frank Thomas 2.50 6.00
VRE6 Tony Gwynn 3.00 8.00
VRE7 Kenny Lofton .30 .75
VRE8 Deion Sanders .75 2.00
VRE9 Ken Hill .08 .25
VRE10 Jimmy Key .08 .25

1995 Stadium Club Super Team Division Winners

COMP.BRAVES SET (11) 3.00 8.00
COMP.DODGERS SET (11) 3.00 8.00
COMP.INDIANS SET (11) 2.50 6.00
COMP.MARINERS SET (11) 3.00 8.00
COMP.REDS SET (11) 1.25 3.00
COMP.RED SOX SET (11) 2.50 6.00
COMMON SUPER TEAM .40 1.00
ONE TEAM SET PER '94 SUPER TEAM WINNER
B1T Braves DW Super Team .40 1.00
B19 Ryan Klesko .25 .60
B128 Mark Wohlers .10 .30
B151 Steve Avery .10 .30
B183 Tom Glavine .40 1.00
B200 Javy Lopez .25 .60
B393 Fred McGriff .40 1.00
B397 John Smoltz .40 1.00
B425 Greg Maddux 1.00 2.50
B446 Dave Justice .25 .60
B543 Chipper Jones .60 1.50
D7T Dodgers DW Super Team .40 1.00
D57 Raul Mondesi .25 .60
D149 Mike Piazza 1.00 2.50
D161 Ismael Valdes .10 .30
D242 Brett Butler .25 .60
D259 Tim Wallach .10 .30
D278 Eric Karros .25 .60
D434 Ramon Martinez .10 .30
D456 Tom Candiotti .10 .30
D467 Delino Deshields .10 .30
D556 Hideo Nomo 2.00 5.00
I19T Indians DW Super Team .40 1.00
I36 Carlos Baerga .10 .30
I147 Jim Thome .40 1.00
I186 Eddie Murray .60 1.50
I264 Manny Ramirez .40 1.00
I334 Omar Vizquel .40 1.00
I470 Kenny Lofton .25 .60
I484 Dennis Martinez .25 .60
I489 Albert Belle .25 .60
I550 Jose Mesa .10 .30
I562 Orel Hershiser .25 .60
M26T Mariners DW Super Team .40 1.00
M73 Jay Buhner .25 .60
M92 Chris Bosio .10 .30
M152 Dan Wilson .10 .30
M227 Tino Martinez .40 1.00
M241 Ken Griffey Jr. 1.25 3.00
M340 Randy Johnson .60 1.50
M354 Edgar Martinez .40 1.00
M421 Felix Fermin .10 .30
M494 Mike Blowers .10 .30
M536 Joey Cora .10 .30
RE3T Reds DW Super Team
RE35 Barry Larkin .40 1.00
RE231 Hal Morris .10 .30
RE252 Bret Boone .25 .60
RE280 Thomas Howard .10 .30
RE300 Jose Rijo .10 .30
RE333 Reggie Sanders .25 .60
RE392 Hector Carrasco .10 .30
RE416 John Smiley .10 .30
RE528 Ron Gant .25 .60
RE566 Benito Santiago .25 .60
RS1T Red Sox DW Super Team .40 1.00
RS10 Roger Clemens 1.25 3.00
RS62 John Valentin .10 .30
RS121 Mike Greenwell .10 .30
RS160 Lee Tinsley .10 .30
RS347 Jose Canseco .40 1.00
RS350 Mo Vaughn .25 .60
RS395 Tim Naehring .10 .30
RS464 Aaron Sele .10 .30
RS530 Mike Macfarlane .10 .30
RS600 Troy O'Leary .10 .30

1995 Stadium Club Super Team Master Photos

COMP.BRAVES SET (10) 4.00 10.00
COMP.INDIANS SET (10) 3.00 8.00
ONE TEAM SET PER '94 SUPER TEAM WINNER
1 Steve Avery .15 .40
2 Tom Glavine .50 1.25
3 Chipper Jones .75 2.00
4 Dave Justice .30 .75
5 Ryan Klesko .30 .75
6 Javy Lopez .30 .75
7 Greg Maddux 1.25 3.00
8 Fred McGriff .50 1.25
9 John Smoltz .50 1.25
10 Mark Wohlers .15 .40
11 Carlos Baerga .15 .40
12 Albert Belle .30 .75
13 Orel Hershiser .30 .75
14 Kenny Lofton .30 .75
15 Dennis Martinez .30 .75
16 Jose Mesa .15 .40
17 Eddie Murray .75 2.00
18 Manny Ramirez .50 1.25
19 Jim Thome .50 1.25
20 Omar Vizquel .50 1.25

1995 Stadium Club Super Team World Series

COMP.WS SET (585) 50.00 120.00
COMP.EC/TA SET (45) 6.00 15.00
*STARS: .6X TO 1.5X BASIC CARDS
*ROOKIES: .6X TO 1.5X BASIC CARDS
ONE SET VIA MAIL PER 1994 BRAVES SUP.TM
SER.3 EC AND TA SUBSETS SHIPPED LATER

1995 Stadium Club Virtual Reality

COMPLETE SET (270) 40.00 100.00
COMPLETE SERIES 1 (135) 20.00 50.00
COMPLETE SERIES 2 (135) 20.00 50.00
*STARS: .75X TO 2X BASIC CARDS
ONE PER PACK/TWO PER RACK PACK

1995 Stadium Club Virtual Reality Members Only

COMPLETE FACT.SET (270) 40.00 100.00
*MEMBERS ONLY: 2X BASIC CARDS

1995 Stadium Club Clear Cut

COMPLETE SET (28) 30.00 80.00
COMPLETE SERIES 1 (14) 15.00 40.00
COMPLETE SERIES 2 (14) 15.00 40.00
STATED ODDS 1:24 HOB/RET,1:10 RACK
CC1 Mike Piazza 4.00 10.00
CC2 Ruben Sierra 1.00 2.50
CC3 Tony Gwynn 3.00 8.00
CC4 Frank Thomas 2.50 6.00
CC5 Fred McGriff 1.50 4.00
CC6 Rafael Palmeiro 1.50 4.00
CC7 Bobby Bonilla 1.00 2.50
CC8 Chili Davis 1.00 2.50
CC9 Hal Morris .50 1.25
CC10 Jose Canseco 1.50 4.00
CC11 Jay Bell 1.00 2.50
CC12 Kirby Puckett 2.50 6.00
CC13 Gary Sheffield 1.00 2.50
CC14 Bob Hamelin .50 1.25
CC15 Jeff Bagwell 1.50 4.00
CC16 Albert Belle 1.00 2.50
CC17 Sammy Sosa 2.50 6.00
CC18 Ken Griffey Jr. 5.00 12.00
CC19 Todd Zeile .50 1.25
CC20 Mo Vaughn 1.00 2.50
CC21 Moises Alou 1.00 2.50
CC22 Paul O'Neill 1.50 4.00
CC23 Andres Galarraga 1.00 2.50
CC24 Greg Vaughn .50 1.25
CC25 Len Dykstra 1.00 2.50
CC26 Joe Carter 1.00 2.50
CC27 Barry Bonds 6.00 15.00
CC28 Cecil Fielder 1.00 2.50

1995 Stadium Club Crunch Time

COMPLETE SET (20) 20.00 50.00
ONE PER SER.1 RACK PACK
1 Jeff Bagwell .75 2.00
2 Kirby Puckett 1.25 3.00
3 Frank Thomas 1.25 3.00
4 Albert Belle .50 1.25
5 Julio Franco .50 1.25
6 Jose Canseco .75 2.00
7 Paul Molitor .50 1.25
8 Joe Carter .50 1.25
9 Ken Griffey Jr. 2.50 6.00
10 Larry Walker .50 1.25
11 Dante Bichette .50 1.25
12 Carlos Baerga .25 .60
13 Fred McGriff .75 2.00
14 Ruben Sierra .50 1.25
15 Will Clark .75 2.00
16 Moises Alou .50 1.25
17 Rafael Palmeiro .75 2.00
18 Travis Fryman .50 1.25
19 Barry Bonds 3.00 8.00
20 Cal Ripken 4.00 10.00

1995 Stadium Club Crystal Ball

COMPLETE SET (15) 30.00 80.00
SER.3 STATED ODDS 1:24
CB1 Chipper Jones 4.00 10.00
CB2 Dustin Hermanson .75 2.00
CB3 Ray Durham 1.50 4.00
CB4 Phil Nevin 1.50 4.00
CB5 Billy Ashley .75 2.00
CB6 Shawn Green 1.50 4.00
CB7 Jason Bates .75 2.00
CB8 Benji Gil .75 2.00
CB9 Marty Cordova .75 2.00
CB10 Quilvio Veras .75 2.00
CB11 Mark Grudzielanek 2.50 6.00
CB12 Ruben Rivera .75 2.00
CB13 Bill Pulsipher .75 2.00
CB14 Derek Jeter 15.00 40.00
CB15 LaTroy Hawkins .75 2.00

1995 Stadium Club Phone Cards

COMPLETE REGULAR SET (13) 8.00 20.00
COMMON REGULAR CARD 1.00 2.00
COMPLETE SILVER SET (13) 15.00 30.00
COMMON SILVER CARD 2.00 4.00
COMPLETE GOLD SET (13) 30.00 75.00
COMMON GOLD CARD 4.00 8.00
*PIN NUMBER REVEALED: .25X to .50X HI

1995 Stadium Club Power Zone

COMPLETE SET (12) 20.00 50.00
SER.3 STATED ODDS 1:24
PZ1 Jeff Bagwell 1.50 4.00
PZ2 Albert Belle 1.00 2.50
PZ3 Barry Bonds 6.00 15.00
PZ4 Joe Carter 1.00 2.50
PZ5 Cecil Fielder 1.00 2.50
PZ6 Andres Galarraga 1.00 2.50
PZ7 Ken Griffey Jr. 5.00 12.00
PZ8 Paul Molitor 1.00 2.50
PZ9 Fred McGriff 1.50 4.00
PZ10 Rafael Palmeiro 1.50 4.00
PZ11 Frank Thomas 2.50 6.00
PZ12 Matt Williams 1.00 2.50

1995 Stadium Club Ring Leaders

COMPLETE SET (40) 40.00 100.00
COMPLETE SERIES 1 (20) 20.00 50.00
COMPLETE SERIES 2 (20) 20.00 50.00
STATED ODDS 1:24 HOB/RET,1:10 RACK
ONE SET VIA MAIL PER PHONE WINNER
RL1 Jeff Bagwell 1.25 3.00
RL2 Mark McGwire 5.00 12.00
RL3 Ozzie Smith 3.00 8.00
RL4 Paul Molitor .75 2.00
RL5 Darryl Strawberry .75 2.00
RL6 Eddie Murray 2.00 5.00
RL7 Tony Gwynn 2.50 6.00
RL8 Jose Canseco 1.25 3.00
RL9 Howard Johnson .75 2.00
RL10 Andre Dawson .75 2.00
RL11 Matt Williams .75 2.00
RL12 Tim Raines .75 2.00
RL13 Fred McGriff 1.25 3.00
RL14 Ken Griffey Jr. 4.00 10.00
RL15 Gary Sheffield .75 2.00
RL16 Dennis Eckersley .75 2.00
RL17 Kevin Mitchell .75 2.00
RL18 Will Clark 1.25 3.00
RL19 Darren Daulton .75 2.00
RL20 Paul O'Neill 1.25 3.00
RL21 Julio Franco .75 2.00
RL22 Albert Belle .75 2.00
RL23 Juan Gonzalez .75 2.00
RL24 Kirby Puckett 2.00 5.00
RL25 Joe Carter .75 2.00
RL26 Frank Thomas 2.00 5.00
RL27 Cal Ripken 6.00 15.00
RL28 John Olerud .75 2.00
RL29 Ruben Sierra .75 2.00
RL30 Barry Bonds 5.00 12.00
RL31 Cecil Fielder .75 2.00
RL32 Roger Clemens 4.00 10.00
RL33 Don Mattingly 5.00 12.00
RL34 Terry Pendleton .75 2.00
RL35 Rickey Henderson 2.00 5.00
RL36 Dave Winfield .75 2.00
RL37 Edgar Martinez 1.25 3.00
RL38 Wade Boggs 1.25 3.00
RL39 Willie McGee .75 2.00
RL40 Andres Galarraga .75 2.00

1995 Stadium Club Super Skills

COMPLETE SET (20) 30.00 80.00
COMPLETE SERIES 1 (9) 12.50 30.00
COMPLETE SERIES 2 (11) 15.00 40.00
STATED ODDS 1:24 HOBBY
SS1 Roberto Alomar 1.50 4.00
SS2 Barry Bonds 6.00 15.00
SS3 Jay Buhner .75 2.00
SS4 Chuck Carr .50 1.25
SS5 Don Mattingly 6.00 15.00
SS6 Raul Mondesi .75 2.00
SS7 Tim Salmon 1.50 4.00
SS8 Deion Sanders 1.50 4.00
SS9 Devon White 1.00 2.50
SS10 Mark Whiten .50 1.25
SS11 Ken Griffey Jr. 5.00 12.00
SS12 Marquis Grissom 1.00 2.50
SS13 Paul O'Neill 1.50 4.00
SS14 Kenny Lofton 1.00 2.50
SS15 Larry Walker 1.00 2.50
SS16 Scott Cooper .50 1.25
SS17 Barry Larkin 1.50 4.00
SS18 Matt Williams 1.00 2.50
SS19 John Wetteland 1.00 2.50
SS20 Randy Johnson 2.50 6.00

1995 Stadium Club Virtual Extremists

COMPLETE SET (10) 30.00 80.00
SER.2 STATED ODDS 1:10 RACK
VRE1 Barry Bonds 10.00 25.00
VRE2 Ken Griffey Jr. 8.00 20.00
VRE3 Jeff Bagwell 2.50 6.00
VRE4 Albert Belle 1.50 4.00
VRE5 Frank Thomas 4.00 10.00
VRE6 Tony Gwynn 5.00 12.00
VRE7 Kenny Lofton 1.50 4.00
VRE8 Deion Sanders 2.50 6.00
VRE9 Ken Hill .75 2.00
VRE10 Jimmy Key 1.50 4.00

1995 Stadium Club Members Only 50

Topps produced a 50-card boxed set for each of the four major sports. With their club membership, members received one set of their choice and had the option of purchasing additional sets for $10.00 each. Player section was based on 1994 leaders from both leagues in various statistical categories. The five Finest cards (46-50) represent Topps' selection of the top rookies of 1994. The color action photos on the fronts have brightly-colored backgrounds and carry the distinctive Topps Stadium Club Members Only gold foil seal. The backs present a second color photo and player profile.

COMP. FACT SET (50) 8.00 20.00
1 Moises Alou .08 .25
2 Jeff Bagwell .40 1.00
3 Albert Belle .08 .25
4 Andy Benes .02 .10
5 Dante Bichette .08 .25
6 Craig Biggio .20 .50
7 Wade Boggs .40 1.00
8 Barry Bonds .60 1.50
9 Brett Butler .08 .25
10 Jose Canseco .40 1.00
11 Joe Carter .08 .25
12 Vince Coleman .02 .10
13 Jeff Conine .02 .10
14 Cecil Fielder .08 .25
15 John Franco .08 .25
16 Julio Franco .08 .25
17 Travis Fryman .08 .25
18 Andres Galarraga .30 .75
19 Ken Griffey Jr. 1.25 3.00
20 Marquis Grissom .02 .10
21 Tony Gwynn .75 2.00
22 Ken Hill .02 .10
23 Randy Johnson .50 1.25
24 Lance Johnson .02 .10
25 Jimmy Key .08 .25
26 Chuck Knoblauch .20 .50
27 Ray Lankford .08 .25
28 Darren Lewis .02 .10
29 Kenny Lofton .20 .50
30 Greg Maddux 1.00 2.50
31 Fred McGriff .20 .50
32 Kevin Mitchell .02 .10
33 Paul Molitor .40 1.00
34 Hal Morris .02 .10
35 Paul O'Neill .08 .25
36 Rafael Palmeiro .30 .75
37 Tony Phillips .02 .10
38 Mike Piazza 1.00 2.50
39 Kirby Puckett .50 1.25
40 Cal Ripken 1.50 4.00
41 Deion Sanders .30 .75
42 Lee Smith .08 .25
43 Frank Thomas .50 1.25
44 Larry Walker .30 .75
45 Matt Williams .20 .50
46 Manny Ramirez .40 1.00
47 Joey Hamilton .02 .10
48 Raul Mondesi .20 .50
49 Bob Hamelin .02 .10
50 Ryan Klesko .08 .25

1995 Stadium Club Members Only Finest Bronze

COMPLETE SET (4) 20.00 50.00
1 Bob Hamelin 1.25 3.00
2 Greg Maddux 15.00 40.00
3 David Cone 2.00 5.00
4 Raul Mondesi 2.00 5.00

1996 Stadium Club

The 1996 Stadium Club set consists of 450 cards with cards 1-225 in first series packs and 226-450 in second series packs. The product was primarily distributed in first and second series foil-wrapped packs.There was also a factory set, which included the Mantle insert cards, packaged in mini-cereal box type cartons and made available through retail outlets. The set includes a Team TSC subset (181-270). These subset cards were slightly shortprinted in comparison to the other cards in the set. Though not confirmed by the manufacturer, it is believed that card number 22 (Roberto Hernandez) is a short-print.

COMPLETE SET (450) 25.00 60.00
COMP.CEREAL SET (454) 25.00 60.00
COMPLETE SERIES 1 (225) 12.50 30.00
COMPLETE SERIES 2 (225) 12.50 30.00
COMMON (1-180/271-450) .10 .30
COMMON TSC SP (181-270) .20 .50
SILVER FOIL: ONLY IN CEREAL SETS
1 Hideo Nomo .30 .75
2 Paul Molitor .10 .30
3 Garret Anderson .10 .30
4 Jose Mesa .10 .30
5 Vinny Castilla .10 .30
6 Mike Mussina .20 .50
7 Ray Durham .10 .30
8 Jack McDowell .10 .30
9 Juan Gonzalez .10 .30
10 Chipper Jones .30 .75
11 Deion Sanders .20 .50
12 Rondell White .10 .30
13 Tom Henke .10 .30
14 Derek Bell .10 .30
15 Randy Myers .10 .30
16 Randy Johnson .30 .75
17 Len Dykstra .10 .30
18 Bill Pulsipher .10 .30
19 Greg Colbrunn .10 .30
20 David Wells .10 .30
21 Chad Curtis .10 .30
22 Roberto Hernandez SP 2.00 5.00
23 Kirby Puckett .30 .75
24 Joe Vitiello .10 .30
25 Roger Clemens .60 1.50
26 Al Martin .10 .30
27 Chad Ogea .10 .30
28 David Segui .10 .30
29 Joey Hamilton .10 .30
30 Dan Wilson .10 .30
31 Chad Fonville .10 .30
32 Bernard Gilkey .10 .30
33 Kevin Seitzer .10 .30
34 Shawn Green .10 .30
35 Rick Aguilera .10 .30
36 Gary DiSarcina .10 .30
37 Jaime Navarro .10 .30
38 Doug Jones .10 .30
39 Brent Gates .10 .30
40 Dean Palmer .10 .30
41 Pat Rapp .10 .30
42 Tony Clark .10 .30
43 Bill Swift .10 .30
44 Randy Velarde .10 .30
45 Matt Williams .10 .30
46 John Mabry .10 .30
47 Mike Fetters .10 .30
48 Orlando Miller .10 .30
49 Tom Glavine .20 .50
50 Delino DeShields .10 .30
51 Scott Erickson .10 .30
52 Andy Van Slyke .20 .50
53 Jim Bullinger .10 .30
54 Lyle Mouton .10 .30
55 Bret Saberhagen .10 .30
56 Benito Santiago .10 .30
57 Dan Miceli .10 .30
58 Carl Everett .10 .30
59 Rod Beck .10 .30
60 Phil Nevin .10 .30
61 Jason Giambi .10 .30
62 Paul Menhart .10 .30
63 Eric Karros .10 .30
64 Allen Watson .10 .30
65 Jeff Cirillo .10 .30
66 Lee Smith .10 .30
67 Sean Berry .10 .30
68 Luis Sojo .10 .30
69 Jeff Montgomery .10 .30
70 Todd Hundley .10 .30
71 John Burkett .10 .30
72 Mark Gubicza .10 .30
73 Don Mattingly .75 2.00
74 Jeff Brantley .10 .30
75 Matt Walbeck .10 .30
76 Steve Parris .10 .30
77 Ken Caminiti .10 .30
78 Kirt Manwaring .10 .30
79 Greg Vaughn .10 .30
80 Pedro Martinez .20 .50
81 Benji Gil .10 .30
82 Heathcliff Slocumb .10 .30
83 Joe Girardi .10 .30
84 Sean Bergman .10 .30
85 Matt Karchner .10 .30
86 Butch Huskey .10 .30
87 Mike Morgan .10 .30
88 Todd Worrell .10 .30
89 Mike Bordick .10 .30
90 Bip Roberts .10 .30
91 Mike Hampton .10 .30
92 Troy O'Leary .10 .30
93 Wally Joyner .10 .30
94 Dave Stevens .10 .30
95 Cecil Fielder .10 .30
96 Wade Boggs .20 .50
97 Hal Morris .10 .30
98 Mickey Tettleton .10 .30
99 Jeff Kent .10 .30
100 Denny Martinez .10 .30
101 Luis Gonzalez .10 .30
102 John Jaha .10 .30
103 Javier Lopez .10 .30
104 Mark McGwire .75 2.00
105 Ken Griffey Jr. .60 1.50
106 Darren Daulton .10 .30
107 Bryan Rekar .10 .30
108 Mike Macfarlane .10 .30
109 Gary Gaetti .10 .30
110 Shane Reynolds .10 .30
111 Pat Meares .10 .30
112 Jason Schmidt .20 .50
113 Otis Nixon .10 .30
114 John Franco .10 .30
115 Marc Newfield .10 .30
116 Andy Benes .10 .30
117 Ozzie Guillen .10 .30
118 Brian Jordan .10 .30
119 Terry Pendleton .10 .30
120 Chuck Finley .10 .30
121 Scott Stahoviak .10 .30
122 Sid Fernandez .10 .30
123 Derek Jeter .75 2.00
124 John Smiley .10 .30
125 David Bell .10 .30
126 Brett Butler .10 .30
127 Doug Drabek .10 .30
128 J.T. Snow .10 .30
129 Joe Carter .10 .30
130 Dennis Eckersley .10 .30
131 Marty Cordova .10 .30
132 Greg Maddux .50 1.25
133 Tom Goodwin .10 .30
134 Andy Ashby .10 .30
135 Paul Sorrento .10 .30
136 Ricky Bones .10 .30
137 Shawon Dunston .10 .30
138 Moises Alou .10 .30
139 Mickey Morandini .10 .30
140 Ramon Martinez .10 .30
141 Royce Clayton .10 .30
142 Brad Ausmus .10 .30
143 Kenny Rogers .10 .30
144 Tim Naehring .10 .30
145 Chris Gomez .10 .30
146 Bobby Bonilla .10 .30
147 Wilson Alvarez .10 .30
148 Johnny Damon .20 .50
149 Pat Hentgen .10 .30
150 Andres Galarraga .10 .30
151 David Cone .10 .30
152 Lance Johnson .10 .30
153 Carlos Garcia .10 .30
154 Doug Johns .10 .30
155 Midre Cummings .10 .30
156 Steve Sparks .10 .30
157 Sandy Martinez .10 .30
158 Wm. Van Landingham .10 .30
159 David Justice .10 .30
160 Mark Grace .20 .50
161 Robb Nen .10 .30
162 Mike Greenwell .10 .30
163 Brad Radke .10 .30
164 Edgardo Alfonzo .10 .30
165 Mark Leiter .10 .30
166 Walt Weiss .10 .30
167 Mel Rojas .10 .30
168 Bret Boone .10 .30
169 Ricky Bottalico .10 .30
170 Bobby Higginson .10 .30
171 Trevor Hoffman .10 .30
172 Jay Bell .10 .30
173 Gabe White .10 .30
174 Curtis Goodwin .10 .30
175 Tyler Green .10 .30
176 Roberto Alomar .20 .50
177 Sterling Hitchcock .10 .30
178 Ryan Klesko .10 .30
179 Donne Wall .10 .30
180 Brian McRae .10 .30
181 Will Clark TSC SP .30 .75
182 Frank Thomas TSC SP .40 1.00
183 Jeff Bagwell TSC SP .30 .75
184 Mo Vaughn TSC SP .20 .50
185 Tino Martinez TSC SP .30 .75
186 Craig Biggio TSC SP .30 .75
187 Chuck Knoblauch TSC SP .20 .50
188 Carlos Baerga TSC SP .20 .50
189 Quilvio Veras TSC SP .20 .50
190 Luis Alicea TSC SP .20 .50
191 Jim Thome TSC SP .30 .75
192 Mike Blowers TSC SP .20 .50
193 Robin Ventura TSC SP .20 .50
194 Jeff King TSC SP .20 .50
195 Tony Phillips TSC SP .20 .50
196 John Valentin TSC SP .20 .50
197 Barry Larkin TSC SP .30 .75
198 Cal Ripken TSC SP 1.25 3.00
199 Omar Vizquel TSC SP .30 .75
200 Kurt Abbott TSC SP .20 .50
201 Albert Belle TSC SP .20 .50
202 Barry Bonds TSC SP 1.00 2.50
203 Ron Gant TSC SP .20 .50
204 Dante Bichette TSC SP .20 .50
205 Jeff Conine TSC SP .20 .50
206 Jim Edmonds TSC SP .20 .50
207 Stan Javier TSC SP .20 .50
208 Kenny Lofton TSC SP .20 .50
209 Ray Lankford TSC SP .20 .50
210 Bernie Williams TSC SP .30 .75
211 Jay Buhner TSC SP .20 .50
212 Paul O'Neill TSC SP .30 .75
213 Tim Salmon TSC SP .30 .75
214 Reggie Sanders TSC SP .20 .50
215 Manny Ramirez TSC SP .30 .75
216 Mike Piazza TSC SP .60 1.50
217 Mike Stanley TSC SP .20 .50
218 Tony Eusebio TSC SP .20 .50
219 Chris Hoiles TSC SP .20 .50
220 Ron Karkovice TSC SP .20 .50
221 Edgar Martinez TSC SP .30 .75
222 Chili Davis TSC SP .20 .50
223 Jose Canseco TSC SP .30 .75
224 Eddie Murray TSC SP .40 1.00
225 Geronimo Berroa TSC SP .20 .50
226 Chipper Jones TSC SP .40 1.00
227 Garret Anderson TSC SP .20 .50
228 Marty Cordova TSC SP .20 .50
229 Jon Nunnally TSC SP .20 .50
230 Brian L.Hunter TSC SP .20 .50
231 Shawn Green TSC SP .20 .50
232 Ray Durham TSC SP .20 .50
233 Alex Gonzalez TSC SP .20 .50
234 Bobby Higginson TSC SP .20 .50
235 Randy Johnson TSC SP .40 1.00
236 Al Leiter TSC SP .20 .50
237 Tom Glavine TSC SP .30 .75
238 Kenny Rogers TSC SP .20 .50
239 Mike Hampton TSC SP .20 .50
240 David Wells TSC SP .20 .50
241 Jim Abbott TSC SP .30 .75
242 Denny Neagle TSC SP .20 .50
243 Wilson Alvarez TSC SP .20 .50
244 John Smiley TSC SP .20 .50
245 Greg Maddux TSC SP .75 2.00
246 Andy Ashby TSC SP .20 .50
247 Hideo Nomo TSC SP .40 1.00
248 Pat Rapp TSC SP .20 .50
249 Tim Wakefield TSC SP .20 .50
250 John Smoltz TSC SP .30 .75
251 Joey Hamilton TSC SP .20 .50
252 Frank Castillo TSC SP .20 .50
253 Denny Martinez TSC SP .20 .50
254 Jaime Navarro TSC SP .20 .50
255 Karim Garcia TSC SP .20 .50
256 Bob Abreu TSC SP .40 1.00
257 Butch Huskey TSC SP .20 .50
258 Ruben Rivera TSC SP .20 .50
259 Johnny Damon TSC SP .30 .75
260 Derek Jeter TSC SP 1.00 2.50
261 Dennis Eckersley TSC SP .20 .50
262 Jose Mesa TSC SP .20 .50
263 Tom Henke TSC SP .20 .50
264 Rick Aguilera TSC SP .20 .50
265 Randy Myers TSC SP .20 .50
266 John Franco TSC SP .20 .50
267 Jeff Brantley TSC SP .20 .50
268 John Wetteland TSC SP .20 .50
269 Mark Wohlers TSC SP .20 .50
270 Rod Beck TSC SP .20 .50
271 Barry Larkin .20 .50
272 Paul O'Neill .20 .50
273 Bobby Jones .10 .30
274 Will Clark .20 .50
275 Steve Avery .10 .30
276 Jim Edmonds .10 .30
277 John Olerud .10 .30
278 Carlos Perez .10 .30
279 Chris Hoiles .10 .30
280 Jeff Conine .10 .30
281 Jim Eisenreich .10 .30
282 Jason Jacome .10 .30
283 Ray Lankford .10 .30
284 John Wasdin .10 .30
285 Frank Thomas .30 .75
286 Jason Isringhausen .10 .30
287 Glenallen Hill .10 .30
288 Esteban Loaiza .10 .30
289 Bernie Williams .20 .50
290 Curtis Leskanic .10 .30
291 Scott Cooper .10 .30
292 Curt Schilling .10 .30
293 Eddie Murray .30 .75
294 Rick Krivda .10 .30
295 Domingo Cedeno .10 .30
296 Jeff Fassero .10 .30
297 Albert Belle .10 .30
298 Craig Biggio .20 .50
299 Fernando Vina .10 .30
300 Edgar Martinez .20 .50
301 Tony Gwynn .40 1.00
302 Felipe Lira .10 .30
303 Mo Vaughn .10 .30
304 Alex Fernandez .10 .30
305 Keith Lockhart .10 .30
306 Roger Pavlik .10 .30
307 Lee Tinsley .10 .30
308 Omar Vizquel .20 .50
309 Scott Servais .10 .30
310 Danny Tartabull .10 .30
311 Chili Davis .10 .30
312 Cal Eldred .10 .30
313 Roger Cedeno .10 .30
314 Chris Hammond .10 .30
315 Rusty Greer .10 .30
316 Brady Anderson .10 .30
317 Ron Villone .10 .30
318 Mark Carreon .10 .30
319 Larry Walker .10 .30
320 Pete Harnisch .10 .30
321 Robin Ventura .10 .30
322 Tim Belcher .10 .30
323 Tony Tarasco .10 .30
324 Juan Guzman .10 .30
325 Kenny Lofton .10 .30
326 Kevin Foster .10 .30
327 Wil Cordero .10 .30
328 Troy Percival .10 .30
329 Turk Wendell .10 .30
330 Thomas Howard .10 .30
331 Carlos Baerga .10 .30
332 B.J. Surhoff .10 .30
333 Jay Buhner .10 .30
334 Andujar Cedeno .10 .30
335 Jeff King .10 .30
336 Dante Bichette .10 .30
337 Alan Trammell .10 .30
338 Scott Leius .10 .30
339 Chris Snopek .10 .30
340 Roger Bailey .10 .30
341 Jacob Brumfield .10 .30
342 Jose Canseco .20 .50
343 Rafael Palmeiro .20 .50
344 Quilvio Veras .10 .30
345 Darrin Fletcher .10 .30
346 Carlos Delgado .10 .30
347 Tony Eusebio .10 .30
348 Ismael Valdes .10 .30
349 Terry Steinbach .10 .30
350 Orel Hershiser .10 .30
351 Kurt Abbott .10 .30
352 Jody Reed .10 .30
353 David Howard .10 .30
354 Ruben Sierra .10 .30
355 John Ericks .10 .30
356 Buck Showalter .10 .30
357 Jim Thome .20 .50
358 Geronimo Berroa .10 .30
359 Robby Thompson .10 .30
360 Jose Vizcaino .10 .30
361 Jeff Frye .10 .30
362 Kevin Appier .10 .30
363 Pat Kelly .10 .30
364 Ron Gant .10 .30
365 Luis Alicea .10 .30
366 Armando Benitez .10 .30
367 Rico Brogna .10 .30
368 Manny Ramirez .20 .50
369 Mike Lansing .10 .30
370 Sammy Sosa .30 .75
371 Don Wengert .10 .30
372 Dave Nilsson .10 .30
373 Sandy Alomar Jr. .10 .30
374 Joey Cora .10 .30
375 Larry Thomas .10 .30
376 John Valentin .10 .30
377 Kevin Ritz .10 .30
378 Steve Finley .10 .30
379 Frank Rodriguez .10 .30
380 Ivan Rodriguez .20 .50
381 Alex Ochoa .10 .30
382 Mark Lemke .10 .30
383 Scott Brosius .10 .30
384 James Mouton .10 .30
385 Mark Langston .10 .30
386 Ed Sprague .10 .30
387 Joe Oliver .10 .30
388 Steve Ontiveros .10 .30
389 Rey Sanchez .10 .30
390 Mike Henneman .10 .30

391 Jose Valentin .10 .30
392 Tom Candiotti .10 .30
393 Damon Buford .10 .30
394 Erik Hanson .10 .30
395 Mark Smith .10 .30
396 Pete Schourek .10 .30
397 John Flaherty .10 .30
398 Dave Martinez .10 .30
399 Tommy Greene .10 .30
400 Gary Sheffield .10 .30
401 Glenn Dishman .10 .30
402 Barry Bonds .75 2.00
403 Tom Pagnozzi .10 .30
404 Todd Stottlemyre .10 .30
405 Tim Salmon .20 .50
406 John Hudek .10 .30
407 Fred McGriff .20 .50
408 Orlando Merced .10 .30
409 Brian Barber .10 .30
410 Ryan Thompson .10 .30
411 Mariano Rivera .60 1.50
412 Eric Young .10 .30
413 Chris Bosio .10 .30
414 Chuck Knoblauch .10 .30
415 Jamie Moyer .10 .30
416 Chan Ho Park .10 .30
417 Mark Portugal .10 .30
418 Tim Raines .10 .30
419 Antonio Osuna .10 .30
420 Todd Zeile .10 .30
421 Steve Wojciechowski .10 .30
422 Marquis Grissom .10 .30
423 Norm Charlton .10 .30
424 Cal Ripken 1.00 2.50
425 Gregg Jefferies .10 .30
426 Mike Stanton .10 .30
427 Tony Fernandez .10 .30
428 Jose Rijo .10 .30
429 Jeff Bagwell .20 .50
430 Raul Mondesi .10 .30
431 Travis Fryman .10 .30
432 Ron Karkovice .10 .30
433 Alan Benes .10 .30
434 Tony Phillips .10 .30
435 Reggie Sanders .10 .30
436 Andy Pettitte .20 .50
437 Matt Lawton RC .10 .30
438 Jeff Blauser .10 .30
439 Michael Tucker .10 .30
440 Mark Loretta .10 .30
441 Charlie Hayes .10 .30
442 Mike Piazza .50 1.25
443 Shane Andrews .10 .30
444 Jeff Suppan .10 .30
445 Steve Rodriguez .10 .30
446 Mike Matheny .10 .30
447 Trenidad Hubbard .10 .30
448 Denny Hocking .10 .30
449 Mark Grudzielanek .10 .30
450 Joe Randa .10 .30
NNO Roger Clemens 2.00 5.00
Extreme Gold PROMO

1996 Stadium Club Members Only Parallel

COMP.SET W/INSERTS (555) 250.00 500.00
COMPLETE BASE SET (450) 100.00 200.00
COMMON CARD (1-450) .10 .25
COMMON MANTLE (MMA1-MMA19) 2.00 5.00
*MEMBERS ONLY: 6X BASIC CARDS
M1 Jeff Bagwell 1.50 4.00
M2 Barry Bonds 4.00 10.00
M3 Jose Canseco 1.50 4.00
M4 Roger Clemens 4.00 10.00
M5 Dennis Eckersley .60 1.50
M6 Greg Maddux 5.00 12.00
M7 Cal Ripken 8.00 20.00
M8 Frank Thomas 3.00 8.00
BB1 Sammy Sosa 4.00 10.00
BB2 Barry Bonds 4.00 10.00
BB3 Reggie Sanders .40 1.00
BB4 Craig Biggio .75 2.00
BB5 Raul Mondesi .75 2.00
BB6 Ron Gant .40 1.00
BB7 Ray Lankford .60 1.50
BB8 Glenallen Hill .40 1.00
BB9 Chad Curtis .40 1.00
BB10 John Valentin .60 1.50
MH1 Frank Thomas 3.00 8.00
MH2 Ken Griffey Jr. 8.00 20.00
MH3 Hideo Nomo 1.50 4.00
MH4 Ozzie Smith 1.50 4.00
MH5 Will Clark 1.25 3.00
MH6 Jack McDowell .40 1.00
MH7 Andres Galarraga 1.25 3.00
MH8 Roger Clemens 4.00 10.00
MH9 Deion Sanders .60 1.50
MH10 Mo Vaughn .60 1.50
MM1 H.Nomo 2.00 5.00
R.Johnson
MM2 M.Piazza 5.00 12.00
I.Rodriguez
MM3 F.McGriff 3.00 8.00
F.Thomas
MM4 C.Biggio .75 2.00
C.Baerga
MM5 V.Castilla 1.50 4.00
W.Boggs
MM6 B.Larkin 8.00 20.00
C.Ripken
MM7 B.Bonds 3.00 8.00
A.Belle
MM8 L.Dykstra .60 1.50
K.Lofton
MM9 T.Gwynn 4.00 10.00
K.Puckett
MM10 R.Gant .75 2.00
E.Martinez
PC1 Albert Belle .60 1.50
PC2 Barry Bonds 1.50 4.00
PC3 Ken Griffey Jr. 8.00 20.00
PC4 Tony Gwynn 4.00 10.00
PC5 Edgar Martinez .75 2.00
PC6 Rafael Palmeiro 1.25 3.00
PC7 Mike Piazza 4.00 10.00
PC8 Frank Thomas 3.00 8.00
PP1 Albert Belle .60 1.50
PP2 Mark McGwire 6.00 15.00
PP3 Jose Canseco 1.50 4.00
PP4 Mike Piazza 4.00 10.00
PP5 Ron Gant .60 1.50
PP6 Ken Griffey Jr. 8.00 20.00
PP7 Mo Vaughn .60 1.50
PP8 Cecil Fielder .60 1.50
PP9 Tim Salmon 1.25 3.00
PP10 Frank Thomas 3.00 8.00
PP11 Juan Gonzalez 1.50 4.00
PP12 Andres Galarraga 1.25 3.00
PP13 Fred McGriff .75 2.00
PP14 Jay Buhner .60 1.50
PP15 Dante Bichette .60 1.50
PS1 Randy Johnson 1.50 4.00
PS2 Hideo Nomo 2.00 5.00
PS3 Albert Belle .60 1.50
PS4 Dante Bichette .60 1.50
PS5 Jay Buhner .60 1.50
PS6 Frank Thomas 3.00 8.00
PS7 Mark McGwire 6.00 15.00
PS8 Rafael Palmeiro 1.25 3.00
PS9 Mo Vaughn .60 1.50
PS10 Sammy Sosa 4.00 10.00
PS11 Larry Walker 1.25 3.00
PS12 Gary Gaetti .60 1.50
PS13 Tim Salmon 1.25 3.00
PS14 Barry Bonds 4.00 10.00
PS15 Jim Edmonds 1.25 3.00
TSCA1 Cal Ripken 8.00 20.00
TSCA2 Albert Belle .60 1.50
TSCA3 Tom Glavine 1.25 3.00
TSCA4 Jeff Conine .40 1.00
TSCA5 Ken Griffey Jr. 8.00 20.00
TSCA6 Hideo Nomo 1.50 4.00
TSCA7 Greg Maddux 4.00 10.00
TSCA8 Chipper Jones 4.00 10.00
TSCA9 Randy Johnson 1.50 4.00
TSCA10 Jose Mesa .40 1.00

1996 Stadium Club Bash and Burn

COMPLETE SET (10) 15.00 40.00
SER.2 STATED ODDS 1:48 HOB, 1:24 RET
BB1 Sammy Sosa 4.00 10.00
BB2 Barry Bonds 10.00 25.00
BB3 Reggie Sanders 1.50 4.00
BB4 Craig Biggio 2.50 6.00
BB5 Raul Mondesi 1.50 4.00
BB6 Ron Gant 1.50 4.00
BB7 Ray Lankford 1.50 4.00
BB8 Glenallen Hill 1.50 4.00
BB9 Chad Curtis 1.50 4.00
BB10 John Valentin 1.50 4.00

1996 Stadium Club Extreme Players Bronze

COMP.BRONZE SET (180) 125.00 250.00
COMP.BRONZE SER.1 (90) 50.00 120.00
COMP.BRONZE SER.2 (90) 50.00 120.00
*BRONZE: 2X TO 5X BASE CARD HI
BRONZE STATED ODDS 1:12
*SILVER SINGLES: .6X TO 1.5X BRONZE
*SILVER WIN: .6X TO 1.5X BRONZE WIN
SILVER STATED ODDS 1:24
*GOLD SINGLES: 1.25X TO 3X BRONZE
*GOLD WIN: 1.25X TO 3X BRONZE WIN
GOLD STATED ODDS 1:48
BRONZE WINNERS LISTED BELOW
SKIP-NUMBERED 179-CARD SET
77 Ken Caminiti W 1.50 4.00
88 Todd Worrell W .60 1.50
105 Ken Griffey Jr. W 6.00 15.00
132 Greg Maddux W 5.00 12.00
150 Andres Galarraga W 1.50 4.00
271 Barry Larkin W 1.50 4.00
400 Gary Sheffield W 2.00 5.00
402 Barry Bonds W 8.00 20.00
414 Chuck Knoblauch W 1.25 3.00
442 Mike Piazza W 5.00 12.00

1996 Stadium Club Extreme Winners Bronze

COMPLETE SET (10) 10.00 25.00
ONE SET VIA MAIL PER BRONZE WINNER
*SILVER: 1.25X TO 3X BRONZE WINNER
ONE SILV.SET VIA MAIL PER SILV.WINNER
*GOLD: 5X TO 12X BRONZE WINNERS
ONE GOLD CARD VIA MAIL PER GOLD WNR.
EW1 Greg Maddux 1.50 4.00
EW2 Mike Piazza 1.50 4.00
EW3 Andres Galarraga .40 1.00
EW4 Chuck Knoblauch .40 1.00
EW5 Ken Caminiti .40 1.00
EW6 Barry Larkin .60 1.50
EW7 Barry Bonds 2.50 6.00
EW8 Ken Griffey Jr. 2.00 5.00
EW9 Gary Sheffield .40 1.00
EW10 Todd Worrell .40 1.00

1996 Stadium Club Mantle

COMPLETE SET (19) 30.00 60.00
COMPLETE SERIES 1 (9) 15.00 40.00
COMMON CARD (MM1-MM9) 2.00 5.00
COMMON CARD (MM10-MM19) 1.25 3.00
SER.1 STATED ODDS 1:24
SER.2 STATED ODDS 1:12

1996 Stadium Club Megaheroes

COMPLETE SET (10) 15.00 40.00
SER.1 STATED ODDS 1:48 HOB, 1:24 RET
MH1 Frank Thomas 2.00 5.00
MH2 Ken Griffey Jr. 4.00 10.00
MH3 Hideo Nomo 2.00 5.00
MH4 Ozzie Smith 2.00 5.00
MH5 Will Clark 1.25 3.00
MH6 Jack McDowell .75 2.00
MH7 Andres Galarraga .75 2.00
MH8 Roger Clemens 4.00 10.00
MH9 Deion Sanders 1.25 3.00
MH10 Mo Vaughn .75 2.00

1996 Stadium Club Metalists

COMPLETE SET (8) 15.00 40.00
SER.2 STATED ODDS 1:48 HOB, 1:96 RET
M1 Jeff Bagwell 1.00 2.50
M2 Barry Bonds 4.00 10.00
M3 Jose Canseco 1.00 2.50
M4 Roger Clemens 3.00 8.00
M5 Dennis Eckersley .60 1.50
M6 Greg Maddux 2.50 6.00
M7 Cal Ripken 5.00 12.00
M8 Frank Thomas 1.50 4.00

1996 Stadium Club Midsummer Matchups

COMPLETE SET (10) 25.00 60.00
SER.1 STATED ODDS 1:48 HOB, 1:24 RET
M1 H.Nomo 2.00 5.00
R.Johnson
M2 M.Piazza 3.00 8.00
I.Rodriguez
M3 F.Thomas 2.00 5.00
F.McGriff
M4 C.Biggio 1.25 3.00
C.Baerga
M5 V.Castilla 1.25 3.00
W.Boggs
M6 C.Ripken 6.00 15.00
B.Larkin
M7 B.Bonds 5.00 12.00
A.Belle
M8 K.Lofton .75 2.00
L.Dykstra
M9 T.Gwynn 2.50 6.00
K.Puckett
M10 R.Gant 1.25 3.00
E.Martinez

1996 Stadium Club Power Packed

COMPLETE SET (15) 25.00 60.00
SER.2 STATED ODDS 1:48 RETAIL
PP1 Albert Belle 1.00 2.50
PP2 Mark McGwire 6.00 15.00
PP3 Jose Canseco 1.50 4.00
PP4 Mike Piazza 4.00 10.00
PP5 Ron Gant 1.00 2.50
PP6 Ken Griffey Jr. 5.00 12.00
PP7 Mo Vaughn 1.00 2.50
PP8 Cecil Fielder 1.00 2.50
PP9 Tim Salmon 1.50 4.00
PP10 Frank Thomas 2.50 6.00
PP11 Juan Gonzalez 1.00 2.50
PP12 Andres Galarraga 1.00 2.50
PP13 Fred McGriff 1.50 4.00
PP14 Jay Buhner 1.00 2.50
PP15 Dante Bichette 1.00 2.50

1996 Stadium Club Power Streak

COMPLETE SET (15) 25.00 60.00
SER.1 STATED ODDS 1:24 HOB, 1:48 RET
PS1 Randy Johnson 2.50 6.00
PS2 Hideo Nomo 2.50 6.00
PS3 Albert Belle 1.00 2.50
PS4 Dante Bichette 1.00 2.50
PS5 Jay Buhner 1.00 2.50
PS6 Frank Thomas 2.50 6.00
PS7 Mark McGwire 6.00 15.00
PS8 Rafael Palmeiro 1.50 4.00
PS9 Mo Vaughn 1.00 2.50
PS10 Sammy Sosa 2.50 6.00
PS11 Larry Walker 1.00 2.50
PS12 Gary Gaetti 1.00 2.50
PS13 Tim Salmon 1.50 4.00
PS14 Barry Bonds 6.00 15.00
PS15 Jim Edmonds 1.00 2.50

1996 Stadium Club Prime Cuts

COMPLETE SET (8) 20.00 50.00
SER.1 STATED ODDS 1:36 HOB, 1:72 RET
PC1 Albert Belle .75 2.00
PC2 Barry Bonds 5.00 12.00
PC3 Ken Griffey Jr. 4.00 10.00
PC4 Tony Gwynn 2.50 6.00
PC5 Edgar Martinez 1.25 3.00
PC6 Rafael Palmeiro 1.25 3.00
PC7 Mike Piazza 3.00 8.00
PC8 Frank Thomas 2.00 5.00

1996 Stadium Club TSC Awards

COMPLETE SET (10) 15.00 40.00
SER.2 STATED ODDS 1:48 HOB, 1:24 RET
1 Cal Ripken 5.00 12.00
2 Albert Belle .60 1.50
3 Tom Glavine 1.00 2.50
4 Jeff Conine .60 1.50
5 Ken Griffey Jr. 3.00 8.00
6 Hideo Nomo 1.50 4.00
7 Greg Maddux 2.50 6.00
8 Chipper Jones 1.50 4.00
9 Randy Johnson 1.50 4.00
10 Jose Mesa .60 1.50

1996 Stadium Club Members Only 50

This 50-card set features color player photos of Topps' selection of 45 (numbers 1-45) of the top 1995 American and National League players. The set includes five Finest Cards (numbers 46-50) which represent Topps' selection of the top rookies from 1995. The backs carry information about the player.

COMP. FACT SET (50) 8.00 20.00
1 Carlos Baerga .02 .10
2 Derek Bell .02 .10
3 Albert Belle .08 .25
4 Dante Bichette .08 .25
5 Craig Biggio .15 .40
6 Wade Boggs .30 .75
7 Barry Bonds .50 1.25
8 Jay Buhner .08 .25
9 Vinny Castilla .08 .25
10 Jeff Conine .02 .10
11 Jim Edmonds .25 .60
12 Steve Finley .08 .25
13 Andres Galarraga .25 .60
14 Mark Grace .15 .40
15 Tony Gwynn .60 1.50
16 Lance Johnson .02 .10
17 Randy Johnson .30 .75
18 Eric Karros .08 .25
19 Chuck Knoblauch .15 .40
20 Barry Larkin .25 .60
21 Kenny Lofton .15 .40
22 Greg Maddux .75 2.00
23 Edgar Martinez .15 .40
24 Tino Martinez .08 .25
25 Mark McGwire .60 1.50
26 Brian McRae .02 .10
27 Jose Mesa .02 .10
28 Eddie Murray .30 .75
29 Mike Mussina .25 .60
30 Randy Myers .02 .10
31 Hideo Nomo .30 .75
32 Rafael Palmeiro .30 .75
33 Tony Phillips .02 .10
34 Mike Piazza .75 2.00
35 Kirby Puckett .40 1.00
36 Manny Ramirez .30 .75
37 Tim Salmon .15 .40
38 Reggie Sanders .02 .10
39 Sammy Sosa .50 1.25
40 Frank Thomas .30 .75
41 Jim Thome .30 .75
42 John Valentin .02 .10
43 Mo Vaughn .08 .25
44 Quilvio Veras .02 .10
45 Larry Walker .30 .75
46 Hideo Nomo FIN .60 1.50
47 Marty Cordova FIN .08 .25
48 Chipper Jones FIN 1.25 3.00
49 Garret Anderson FIN .40 1.00
50 Andy Pettitte FIN .25 .60

1997 Stadium Club Pre-Production

Each Topps wholesale account received one of these three Pre-Production sample cards along with their order forms for 1997 Stadium Club Series 1 baseball. The cards were designed to provide wholesale customers with a sneak preview of the upcoming Stadium Club release. The design parallels the regular issue cards excpt for the PP-prefixed numbering. In addition, the term "Pre-Production Sample" replaces the line of 1996 statistics on back.

COMPLETE SET (3) 2.00 5.00
PP1 Chipper Jones 1.25 3.00
PP2 Kenny Lofton .40 1.00
PP3 Gary Sheffield 1.00 2.50

1997 Stadium Club

Cards from this 390 card set were distributed in eight-card hobby and retail packs (SRP $3) and 13-card hobby collector packs (SRP $5). Card fronts feature color action player photos printed on 20 pt. card stock with Topps Super Color processing, Hi-gloss laminating, embossing and double foil stamping. The backs carry player information and statistics. In addition to the standard selection of major leaguers, the set contains a 15-card TSC 2000 subset (181-195) featuring a selection of top young prospects. These subset cards were inserted one in every two eight-card first series packs and one per 13-card first series pack. First series cards were released in February, 1997. The 195-card Series two set was issued in six-card retail packs with a suggested retail price of $2 and in nine-card hobby packs with a suggested retail price of $3. The second series set features a 15-card Stadium Sluggers subset (376-390) with an insertion rate of one in every two hobby and three retail Series 2 packs. Second series cards were released in April, 1997. Please note that cards 361 and 374 do not exist. Due to an error at the manufacturer both Mike Sweeney and Tom Pagnozzi had their cards numbered as 274. In addition, Jermaine Dye and Brant Brown both had their cards numbered as 351. These numbering errors were never corrected and no premiums in value are associated.

COMPLETE SET (390) 30.00 60.00
COMPLETE SERIES 1 (195) 12.50 30.00
COMPLETE SERIES 2 (195) 12.50 30.00
COMMON (1-180/196-375) .10 .30
COM.SP (181-195/376-390) .30 .75
181-195 SER.1 ODDS 1:2 HOB/RET, 1:1 HTA
376-390 SER.2 ODDS 1:2 HOB, 1:3 RET
CARDS 361 AND 374 DON'T EXIST
SWEENEY AND PAGNOZZI NUMBERED 274
J.DYE AND B.BROWN NUMBERED 351
1 Chipper Jones .30 .75
2 Gary Sheffield .10 .30
3 Kenny Lofton .10 .30
4 Brian Jordan .10 .30
5 Mark McGwire .75 2.00
6 Charles Nagy .10 .30
7 Tim Salmon .20 .50
8 Cal Ripken 1.00 2.50
9 Jeff Conine .10 .30
10 Paul Molitor .10 .30
11 Mariano Rivera .30 .75
12 Pedro Martinez .20 .50
13 Jeff Bagwell .20 .50
14 Bobby Bonilla .10 .30
15 Barry Bonds .75 2.00
16 Ryan Klesko .10 .30
17 Barry Larkin .20 .50
18 Jim Thome .20 .50
19 Jay Buhner .10 .30
20 Juan Gonzalez .10 .30
21 Mike Mussina .20 .50
22 Kevin Appier .10 .30
23 Eric Karros .10 .30
24 Steve Finley .10 .30
25 Ed Sprague .10 .30
26 Bernard Gilkey .10 .30
27 Tony Phillips .10 .30
28 Henry Rodriguez .10 .30
29 John Smoltz .20 .50
30 Dante Bichette .10 .30
31 Mike Piazza .50 1.25
32 Paul O'Neill .20 .50
33 Billy Wagner .10 .30
34 Reggie Sanders .10 .30
35 John Jaha .10 .30
36 Eddie Murray .30 .75
37 Eric Young .10 .30
38 Roberto Hernandez .10 .30
39 Pat Hentgen .10 .30
40 Sammy Sosa .30 .75
41 Todd Hundley .10 .30
42 Mo Vaughn .10 .30
43 Robin Ventura .10 .30
44 Mark Grudzielanek .10 .30
45 Shane Reynolds .10 .30
46 Andy Pettitte .20 .50
47 Fred McGriff .20 .50
48 Rey Ordonez .10 .30
49 Will Clark .20 .50
50 Ken Griffey Jr. .60 1.50
51 Todd Worrell .10 .30
52 Rusty Greer .10 .30
53 Mark Grace .20 .50
54 Tom Glavine .20 .50
55 Derek Jeter .75 2.00
56 Rafael Palmeiro .20 .50
57 Bernie Williams .20 .50
58 Marty Cordova .10 .30
59 Andres Galarraga .10 .30
60 Ken Caminiti .10 .30
61 Garret Anderson .10 .30
62 Denny Martinez .10 .30
63 Mike Greenwell .10 .30
64 David Segui .10 .30
65 Julio Franco .10 .30
66 Rickey Henderson .30 .75
67 Ozzie Guillen .10 .30
68 Pete Harnisch .10 .30
69 Chan Ho Park .10 .30
70 Harold Baines .10 .30
71 Mark Clark .10 .30
72 Steve Avery .10 .30
73 Brian Hunter .10 .30
74 Pedro Astacio .10 .30
75 Jack McDowell .10 .30
76 Gregg Jefferies .10 .30
77 Jason Kendall .10 .30
78 Todd Walker .10 .30
79 B.J. Surhoff .10 .30
80 Moises Alou .10 .30
81 Fernando Vina .10 .30
82 Darryl Strawberry .10 .30
83 Jose Rosado .10 .30
84 Chris Gomez .10 .30
85 Chili Davis .10 .30
86 Alan Benes .10 .30
87 Todd Hollandsworth .10 .30
88 Jose Vizcaino .10 .30
89 Edgardo Alfonzo .10 .30
90 Ruben Rivera .10 .30
91 Donovan Osborne .10 .30
92 Doug Glanville .10 .30
93 Gary DiSarcina .10 .30
94 Brooks Kieschnick .10 .30
95 Bobby Jones .10 .30
96 Raul Casanova .10 .30
97 Jermaine Allensworth .10 .30
98 Kenny Rogers .10 .30
99 Mark McLemore .10 .30
100 Jeff Fassero .10 .30
101 Sandy Alomar Jr. .10 .30
102 Chuck Finley .10 .30
103 Eric Owens .10 .30
104 Billy McMillon .10 .30
105 Dwight Gooden .10 .30
106 Sterling Hitchcock .10 .30
107 Doug Drabek .10 .30
108 Paul Wilson .10 .30
109 Chris Snopek .10 .30
110 Al Leiter .10 .30
111 Bob Tewksbury .10 .30
112 Todd Greene .10 .30
113 Jose Valentin .10 .30
114 Delino DeShields .10 .30
115 Mike Bordick .10 .30
116 Pat Meares .10 .30
117 Mariano Duncan .10 .30
118 Steve Trachsel .10 .30
119 Luis Castillo .10 .30
120 Andy Benes .10 .30
121 Donne Wall .10 .30
122 Alex Gonzalez .10 .30
123 Dan Wilson .10 .30
124 Omar Vizquel .20 .50
125 Devon White .10 .30
126 Darryl Hamilton .10 .30
127 Orlando Merced .10 .30
128 Royce Clayton .10 .30
129 William VanLandingham .10 .30
130 Terry Steinbach .10 .30
131 Jeff Blauser .10 .30
132 Jeff Cirillo .10 .30
133 Roger Pavlik .10 .30
134 Danny Tartabull .10 .30
135 Jeff Montgomery .10 .30
136 Bobby Higginson .10 .30
137 Mike Grace .10 .30
138 Kevin Elster .10 .30
139 Brian Giles RC .60 1.50
140 Rod Beck .10 .30
141 Ismael Valdes .10 .30
142 Scott Brosius .10 .30
143 Mike Fetters .10 .30
144 Gary Gaetti .10 .30
145 Mike Lansing .10 .30
146 Glenallen Hill .10 .30
147 Shawn Green .10 .30
148 Mel Rojas .10 .30
149 Joey Cora .10 .30
150 John Smiley .10 .30
151 Marvin Benard .10 .30
152 Curt Schilling .10 .30
153 Dave Nilsson .10 .30
154 Edgar Renteria .10 .30
155 Joey Hamilton .10 .30
156 Carlos Garcia .10 .30
157 Nomar Garciaparra .50 1.25
158 Kevin Ritz .10 .30
159 Keith Lockhart .10 .30
160 Justin Thompson .10 .30
161 Terry Adams .10 .30
162 Jamey Wright .10 .30
163 Otis Nixon .10 .30
164 Michael Tucker .10 .30
165 Mike Stanley .10 .30
166 Ben McDonald .10 .30
167 John Mabry .10 .30
168 Troy O'Leary .10 .30
169 Mel Nieves .10 .30
170 Bret Boone .10 .30
171 Mike Timlin .10 .30
172 Scott Rolen .20 .50
173 Reggie Jefferson .10 .30
174 Neifi Perez .10 .30
175 Brian McRae .10 .30
176 Tom Goodwin .10 .30
177 Aaron Sele .10 .30
178 Benito Santiago .10 .30
179 Frank Rodriguez .10 .30
180 Eric Davis .10 .30
181 Andruw Jones 2000 SP .30 .75
182 Todd Walker 2000 SP .30 .75
183 Wes Helms 2000 SP .30 .75
184 N.Figueroa 2000 SP RC .30 .75
185 Vlad.Guerrero 2000 SP .50 1.25
186 Billy McMillon 2000 SP .30 .75
187 Todd Helton 2000 SP .50 1.25
188 N.Garciaparra 2000 SP 1.00 2.50
189 Katsuhiro Maeda 2000 SP .30 .75
190 Russell Branyan 2000 SP .30 .75
191 Glendon Rusch 2000 SP .30 .75
192 Bartolo Colon 2000 SP .30 .75
193 Scott Rolen 2000 SP .30 .75
194 Angel Echevarria 2000 SP .30 .75
195 Bob Abreu 2000 SP .30 .75
196 Greg Maddux .50 1.25
197 Joe Carter .10 .30
198 Alex Ochoa .10 .30
199 Ellis Burks .10 .30
200 Ivan Rodriguez .20 .50
201 Marquis Grissom .10 .30
202 Trevor Hoffman .10 .30
203 Matt Williams .10 .30
204 Carlos Delgado .10 .30
205 Ramon Martinez .10 .30
206 Chuck Knoblauch .10 .30
207 Juan Guzman .10 .30
208 Derek Bell .10 .30
209 Roger Clemens .60 1.50
210 Vladimir Guerrero .30 .75
211 Cecil Fielder .10 .30
212 Hideo Nomo .30 .75
213 Frank Thomas .30 .75
214 Greg Vaughn .10 .30
215 Javy Lopez .10 .30
216 Raul Mondesi .10 .30
217 Wade Boggs .20 .50
218 Carlos Baerga .10 .30
219 Tony Gwynn .40 1.00
220 Tino Martinez .20 .50
221 Vinny Castilla .10 .30
222 Lance Johnson .10 .30
223 David Justice .10 .30
224 Rondell White .10 .30
225 Dean Palmer .10 .30
226 Jim Edmonds .10 .30
227 Albert Belle .10 .30
228 Alex Fernandez .10 .30
229 Ryne Sandberg .50 1.25
230 Jose Mesa .10 .30
231 David Cone .10 .30
232 Troy Percival .10 .30
233 Edgar Martinez .20 .50
234 Jose Canseco .20 .50
235 Kevin Brown .10 .30
236 Ray Lankford .10 .30
237 Karim Garcia .10 .30
238 J.T. Snow .10 .30
239 Dennis Eckersley .10 .30
240 Roberto Alomar .20 .50
241 John Valentin .10 .30
242 Ron Gant .10 .30
243 Geronimo Berroa .10 .30
244 Manny Ramirez .20 .50
245 Travis Fryman .10 .30
246 Denny Neagle .10 .30
247 Randy Johnson .30 .75
248 Darin Erstad .10 .30
249 Mark Wohlers .10 .30
250 Ken Hill .10 .30
251 Larry Walker .10 .30
252 Craig Biggio .20 .50
253 Brady Anderson .10 .30
254 John Wetteland .10 .30
255 Andruw Jones .20 .50
256 Turk Wendell .10 .30
257 Jason Isringhausen .10 .30
258 Jaime Navarro .10 .30
259 Sean Berry .10 .30
260 Albie Lopez .10 .30
261 Jay Bell .10 .30
262 Bobby Witt .10 .30
263 Tony Clark .10 .30
264 Tim Wakefield .10 .30
265 Brad Radke .10 .30
266 Tim Belcher .10 .30
267 Nerio Rodriguez RC .10 .30
268 Roger Cedeno .10 .30
269 Tim Naehring .10 .30
270 Kevin Tapani .10 .30
271 Joe Randa .10 .30
272 Randy Myers .10 .30
273 Dave Burba .10 .30
274 Mike Sweeney .10 .30
275 Danny Graves .10 .30
276 Chad Mottola .10 .30
277 Ruben Sierra .10 .30
278 Norm Charlton .10 .30
279 Scott Servais .10 .30
280 Jacob Cruz .10 .30
281 Mike Macfarlane .10 .30
282 Rich Becker .10 .30
283 Shannon Stewart .10 .30
284 Gerald Williams .10 .30
285 Jody Reed .10 .30
286 Jeff D'Amico .10 .30
287 Walt Weiss .10 .30
288 Jim Leyritz .10 .30
289 Francisco Cordova .10 .30
290 F.P. Santangelo .10 .30
291 Scott Erickson .10 .30
292 Hal Morris .10 .30
293 Ray Durham .10 .30
294 Andy Ashby .10 .30
295 Darryl Kile .10 .30
296 Jose Paniagua .10 .30
297 Mickey Tettleton .10 .30
298 Joe Girardi .10 .30
299 Rocky Coppinger .10 .30
300 Bob Abreu .20 .50
301 John Olerud .10 .30
302 Paul Shuey .10 .30
303 Jeff Brantley .10 .30
304 Bob Wells .10 .30
305 Kevin Seitzer .10 .30
306 Shawon Dunston .10 .30
307 Jose Herrera .10 .30
308 Butch Huskey .10 .30
309 Jose Offerman .10 .30
310 Rick Aguilera .10 .30
311 Greg Gagne .10 .30
312 John Burkett .10 .30
313 Mark Thompson .10 .30
314 Alvaro Espinoza .10 .30
315 Todd Stottlemyre .10 .30
316 Al Martin .10 .30
317 James Baldwin .10 .30
318 Cal Eldred .10 .30
319 Sid Fernandez .10 .30
320 Mickey Morandini .10 .30
321 Robb Nen .10 .30
322 Mark Lemke .10 .30
323 Pete Schourek .10 .30
324 Marcus Jensen .10 .30
325 Rich Aurilia .10 .30
326 Jeff King .10 .30
327 Scott Stahoviak .10 .30
328 Ricky Otero .10 .30
329 Antonio Osuna .10 .30
330 Chris Hoiles .10 .30
331 Luis Gonzalez .10 .30
332 Wil Cordero .10 .30
333 Johnny Damon .20 .50
334 Mark Langston .10 .30
335 Orlando Miller .10 .30
336 Jason Giambi .10 .30
337 Damian Jackson .10 .30
338 David Wells .10 .30
339 Bip Roberts .10 .30
340 Matt Ruebel .10 .30
341 Tom Candiotti .10 .30
342 Wally Joyner .10 .30
343 Jimmy Key .10 .30
344 Tony Batista .10 .30
345 Paul Sorrento .10 .30
346 Ron Karkovice .10 .30
347 Wilson Alvarez .10 .30
348 John Flaherty .10 .30
349 Rey Sanchez .10 .30
350 John Vander Wal .10 .30
351 Jermaine Dye .10 .30
352 Mike Hampton .10 .30
353 Greg Colbrunn .10 .30
354 Heathcliff Slocumb .10 .30
355 Ricky Bottalico .10 .30
356 Marty Janzen .10 .30
357 Orel Hershiser .10 .30
358 Rex Hudler .10 .30
359 Amaury Telemaco .10 .30
360 Darrin Fletcher .10 .30
361 Brant Brown UER .10 .30
362 Russ Davis .10 .30
363 Allen Watson .10 .30
364 Mike Lieberthal .10 .30
365 Dave Stevens .10 .30
366 Jay Powell .10 .30
367 Tony Fossas .10 .30
368 Bob Wolcott .10 .30
369 Mark Loretta .10 .30
370 Shawn Estes .10 .30
371 Sandy Martinez .10 .30
372 Wendell Magee Jr. .10 .30
373 John Franco .10 .30
374 Tom Pagnozzi UER .10 .30
375 Willie Adams .10 .30
376 Chipper Jones SS SP .50 1.25
377 Mo Vaughn SS SP .30 .75
378 Frank Thomas SS SP .50 1.25
379 Albert Belle SS SP .30 .75
380 Andres Galarraga SS SP .30 .75
381 Gary Sheffield SS SP .30 .75
382 Jeff Bagwell SS SP .30 .75
383 Mike Piazza SS SP 1.00 2.50
384 Mark McGwire SS SP 1.50 4.00
385 Ken Griffey Jr. SS SP 1.25 3.00
386 Barry Bonds SS SP 1.50 4.00
387 Juan Gonzalez SS SP .30 .75
388 Brady Anderson SS SP .30 .75
389 Ken Caminiti SS SP .30 .75
390 Jay Buhner SS SP .30 .75

1997 Stadium Club Matrix

*STARS: 4X TO 10X BASIC CARDS
STATED ODDS 1:12 H/R, 1:18 ANCO, 1:6 HCP
CARDS 1-60 DISTRIBUTED IN SERIES 1
CARDS 196-255 DISTRIBUTED IN SERIES 2

1997 Stadium Club Members Only Parallel

COMP.FACT SET (497) 200.00 400.00
COMPLETE SERIES 1 (235) 100.00 200.00
COMPLETE SERIES 2 (242) 100.00 200.00
COMMON CARD .10 .25
*MEMBERS ONLY: 6X BASIC CARDS
I1 Eddie Murray 1.50 4.00
I2 Paul Molitor 1.50 4.00
I3 Todd Hundley .75 2.00
I4 Roger Clemens 4.00 10.00
I5 Barry Bonds 2.00 5.00
I6 Mark McGwire 10.00 25.00
I7 Brady Anderson .75 2.00
I8 Barry Larkin 1.50 4.00
I9 Ken Caminiti 1.25 3.00
I10 Hideo Nomo 1.50 4.00
I11 Bernie Williams 1.50 4.00
I12 Juan Gonzalez 1.50 4.00
I13 Andy Pettitte 1.25 3.00
I14 Albert Belle .75 2.00
I15 John Smoltz .75 2.00
I16 Brian Jordan .40 1.00
I17 Derek Jeter 10.00 25.00
I18 Ken Caminiti .75 2.00
I19 John Wetteland .75 2.00
I20 Brady Anderson .75 2.00
I21 Andruw Jones 2.00 5.00
I22 Jim Leyritz .40 1.00
M1 Derek Jeter 10.00 25.00

M2 Mark Grudzielanek .75 2.00
M3 Jacob Cruz .40 1.00
M4 Ray Durham 1.25 3.00
M5 Tony Clark .75 2.00
M6 Chipper Jones 5.00 12.00
M7 Luis Castillo .75 2.00
M8 Carlos Delgado 2.00 5.00
M9 Brant Brown .40 1.00
M10 Jason Kendall 1.25 3.00
M11 Alan Benes .40 1.00
M12 Rey Ordonez .40 1.00
M13 Justin Thompson .40 1.00
M14 Jermaine Allensworth .40 1.00
M15 Brian L. Hunter .40 1.00
M16 Marty Cordova .40 1.00
M17 Edgar Renteria .40 1.00
M18 Karim Garcia .40 1.00
M19 Todd Greene .40 1.00
M20 Paul Wilson .40 1.00
M21 Andruw Jones 2.00 5.00
M22 Todd Walker .40 1.00
M23 Alex Ochoa .40 1.00
M24 Bartolo Colon 1.50 4.00
M25 Wendell Magee Jr. .40 1.00
M26 Jose Rosado .40 1.00
M27 Katsuhiro Maeda .40 1.00
M28 Bob Abreu 1.50 4.00
M29 Brooks Kieschnick .40 1.00
M30 Derrick Gibson .40 1.00
M31 Mike Sweeney 2.00 5.00
M32 Jeff D'Amico .40 1.00
M33 Chad Mottola .40 1.00
M34 Chris Snopek .40 1.00
M35 Jaime Bluma .40 1.00
M36 Vladimir Guerrero 3.00 8.00
M37 Nomar Garciaparra 6.00 15.00
M38 Scott Rolen 1.50 4.00
M39 Dmitri Young .75 2.00
M40 Neifi Perez .40 1.00
FB1 Jeff Bagwell 2.00 5.00
FB2 Albert Belle .75 2.00
FB3 Barry Bonds 5.00 12.00
FB4 Andres Galarraga 1.50 4.00
FB5 Ken Griffey Jr. 10.00 25.00
FB6 Brady Anderson .75 2.00
FB7 Mark McGwire 8.00 20.00
FB8 Chipper Jones 5.00 12.00
FB9 Frank Thomas 3.00 8.00
FB10 Mike Piazza 6.00 15.00
FB11 Mo Vaughn .75 2.00
FB12 Juan Gonzalez 2.00 5.00
PG1 Brady Anderson .75 2.00
PG2 Albert Belle .75 2.00
PG3 Dante Bichette .75 2.00
PG4 Barry Bonds 5.00 12.00
PG5 Jay Buhner .75 2.00
PG6 Tony Gwynn 5.00 12.00
PG7 Chipper Jones 5.00 12.00
PG8 Mark McGwire 8.00 20.00
PG9 Gary Sheffield 1.50 4.00
PG10 Frank Thomas 4.00 10.00
PG11 Juan Gonzalez 2.00 5.00
PG12 Ken Caminiti .75 2.00
PG13 Kenny Lofton .75 2.00
PG14 Jeff Bagwell 2.00 5.00
PG15 Ken Griffey Jr. 10.00 25.00
PG16 Cal Ripken 10.00 25.00
PG17 Mo Vaughn .75 2.00
PG18 Mike Piazza 5.00 12.00
PG19 Derek Jeter 10.00 25.00
PG20 Andres Galarraga 1.50 4.00
PL1 Ivan Rodriguez 2.00 5.00
PL2 Ken Caminiti .75 2.00
PL3 Barry Bonds 5.00 12.00
PL4 Ken Griffey Jr. 10.00 25.00
PL5 Greg Maddux 6.00 15.00
PL6 Craig Biggio 1.25 3.00
PL7 Andres Galarraga 1.50 4.00
PL8 Kenny Lofton .75 2.00
PL9 Barry Larkin 1.50 4.00
PL10 Mark Grace 1.50 4.00
PL11 Rey Ordonez .40 1.00
PL12 Roberto Alomar 1.50 4.00
PL13 Derek Jeter 10.00 25.00

1997 Stadium Club Co-Signers

STATED ODDS 1:168 HOBBY, 1:96 HCP
CO1 D.Jeter/A.Pettitte 125.00 250.00
CO2 P.Wilson/T.Hundley 6.00 15.00
CO3 J.Dye/M.Wohlers 12.50 30.00
CO4 S.Rolen/G.Jefferies 8.00 20.00
CO5 J.Kendall/T.Holland 6.00 15.00
CO6 R.Ventura/A.Benes 10.00 25.00
CO7 R.Mondesi/E.Karros 6.00 15.00
CO8 N.Garciaparra/R.Ordon 20.00 50.00
CO9 R.White/M.Cordova 6.00 15.00
CO10 T.Gwynn/K.Garcia 12.50 30.00

1997 Stadium Club Firebrand Redemption

SER.1 STAT.ODDS 1:24 HOB/RET,1:36 ANCO
*WOOD: 5X TO 1.2X BASIC FIREBRAND
ONE WOOD CARD VIA MAIL PER EXCH.CARD
F1 Jeff Bagwell 1.50 4.00
F2 Albert Belle 1.00 2.50
F3 Barry Bonds 6.00 15.00
F4 Andres Galarraga 1.00 2.50
F5 Ken Griffey Jr. 5.00 12.00
F6 Brady Anderson 1.00 2.50
F7 Mark McGwire 6.00 15.00
F8 Chipper Jones 2.50 6.00
F9 Frank Thomas 2.50 6.00
F10 Mike Piazza 4.00 10.00
F11 Mo Vaughn 1.00 2.50
F12 Juan Gonzalez 1.00 2.50

1997 Stadium Club Instavision

COMPLETE SET (22) 20.00 50.00
COMPLETE SERIES 1 (10) 10.00 25.00
COMPLETE SERIES 2 (12) 10.00 25.00
STATED ODDS 1:24 HOB/RET, 1:36 ANCO
I1 Eddie Murray 1.50 4.00
I2 Paul Molitor .60 1.50
I3 Todd Hundley .60 1.50
I4 Roger Clemens 3.00 8.00
I5 Barry Bonds 4.00 10.00
I6 Mark McGwire 4.00 10.00
I7 Brady Anderson .60 1.50
I8 Barry Larkin 1.00 2.50
I9 Ken Caminiti .60 1.50
I10 Hideo Nomo 1.50 4.00
I11 Bernie Williams 1.00 2.50
I12 Juan Gonzalez .60 1.50
I13 Andy Pettitte 1.00 2.50
I14 Albert Belle .60 1.50
I15 John Smoltz 1.00 2.50
I16 Brian Jordan .60 1.50
I17 Derek Jeter 4.00 10.00
I18 Ken Caminiti .60 1.50
I19 John Wetteland .60 1.50
I20 Brady Anderson .60 1.50
I21 Andruw Jones 1.00 2.50
I22 Jim Leyritz .60 1.50

1997 Stadium Club Millennium

COMPLETE SET (40) 60.00 120.00
COMPLETE SERIES 1 (20) 20.00 50.00
COMPLETE SERIES 2 (20) 30.00 80.00
STATED ODDS 1:24H/R, 1:36ANCO, 1:12HCP
M1 Derek Jeter 8.00 20.00
M2 Mark Grudzielanek .60 1.50
M3 Jacob Cruz .60 1.50
M4 Ray Durham 1.00 2.50
M5 Tony Clark .60 1.50
M6 Chipper Jones 2.50 6.00
M7 Luis Castillo .60 1.50
M8 Carlos Delgado 1.00 2.50
M9 Brant Brown .60 1.50
M10 Jason Kendall 1.00 2.50
M11 Alan Benes .60 1.50
M12 Rey Ordonez .60 1.50
M13 Justin Thompson .60 1.50
M14 Jermaine Allensworth .60 1.50
M15 Brian Hunter .60 1.50
M16 Marty Cordova .60 1.50
M17 Edgar Renteria 1.00 2.50
M18 Karim Garcia .60 1.50
M19 Todd Greene .60 1.50
M20 Paul Wilson .60 1.50
M21 Andruw Jones 1.50 4.00
M22 Todd Walker .60 1.50
M23 Alex Ochoa .60 1.50
M24 Bartolo Colon 1.00 2.50
M25 Wendell Magee Jr. .60 1.50
M26 Jose Rosado .60 1.50
M27 Katsuhiro Maeda .60 1.50
M28 Bob Abreu .60 1.50
M29 Brooks Kieschnick .60 1.50
M30 Derrick Gibson .60 1.50
M31 Mike Sweeney 1.00 2.50
M32 Jeff D'Amico .60 1.50
M33 Chad Mottola .60 1.50
M34 Chris Snopek .60 1.50
M35 Jaime Bluma .60 1.50
M36 Vladimir Guerrero 2.50 6.00
M37 Nomar Garciaparra 5.00 12.00
M38 Scott Rolen 1.50 4.00
M39 Dmitri Young 1.00 2.50
M40 Neifi Perez .60 1.50

1997 Stadium Club Patent Leather

COMPLETE SET (13) 60.00 120.00
SER.2 STATED ODDS 1:36 RETAIL
PL1 Ivan Rodriguez 2.50 6.00
PL2 Ken Caminiti 1.50 4.00
PL3 Barry Bonds 10.00 25.00
PL4 Ken Griffey Jr. 8.00 20.00
PL5 Greg Maddux 6.00 15.00
PL6 Craig Biggio 2.50 6.00
PL7 Andres Galarraga 1.50 4.00
PL8 Kenny Lofton 1.50 4.00
PL9 Barry Larkin 2.50 6.00
PL10 Mark Grace 2.50 6.00
PL11 Rey Ordonez 1.50 4.00
PL12 Roberto Alomar 2.50 6.00
PL13 Derek Jeter 10.00 25.00

1997 Stadium Club Pure Gold

COMPLETE SET (20) 100.00 200.00
COMPLETE SERIES 1 (10) 50.00 120.00
COMPLETE SERIES 2 (10) 100.00 200.00
STATED ODDS 1:72H/R, 1:108ANCO, 1:36HCP
PG1 Brady Anderson 1.25 3.00
PG2 Albert Belle 1.25 3.00
PG3 Dante Bichette 1.25 3.00
PG4 Barry Bonds 8.00 20.00
PG5 Jay Buhner 1.25 3.00
PG6 Tony Gwynn 4.00 10.00
PG7 Chipper Jones 3.00 8.00
PG8 Mark McGwire 8.00 20.00
PG9 Gary Sheffield 1.25 3.00
PG10 Frank Thomas 3.00 8.00
PG11 Juan Gonzalez 1.25 3.00
PG12 Ken Caminiti 1.25 3.00
PG13 Kenny Lofton 1.25 3.00
PG14 Jeff Bagwell 2.00 5.00
PG15 Ken Griffey Jr. 6.00 15.00
PG16 Cal Ripken 10.00 25.00
PG17 Mo Vaughn 1.25 3.00
PG18 Mike Piazza 5.00 12.00
PG19 Derek Jeter 8.00 20.00
PG20 Andres Galarraga 1.25 3.00

1998 Stadium Club

The 1998 Stadium Club set was issued in two separate 200-card series and distributed in six-card retail packs for $2, nine-card hobby packs for $3, and 15-card Home Team Advantage packs for $5. The card fronts feature action color player photos with player information displayed on the backs. The series one set included odd numbered cards only and series two included even numbered cards only. The set contains the topical subsets: Future Stars (odd-numbered 361-379), Draft Picks (odd-numbered 381-399) and Traded (even-numbered 356-400). Two separate Cal Ripken Sound Chip cards were distributed as chiptoppers in Home Team Advantage boxes. The second series features a 23-card Transaction subset (356-400). Second series cards were released in April, 1998. Rookie Cards include Jack Cust, Kevin Millwood and Magglio Ordonez.

COMPLETE SET (400) 30.00 80.00
COMPLETE SERIES 1 (200) 15.00 40.00
COMPLETE SERIES 2 (200) 15.00 40.00
ODD CARDS DISTRIBUTED IN SER.1 PACKS
EVEN CARDS DISTRIBUTED IN SER.2 PACKS
ONE RIPKEN SOUND CHIP PER HTA BOX
1 Chipper Jones .30 .75
2 Frank Thomas .30 .75
3 Vladimir Guerrero .30 .75
4 Ellis Burks .10 .30
5 John Franco .10 .30
6 Paul Molitor .10 .30
7 Rusty Greer .10 .30
8 Todd Hundley .10 .30
9 Brett Tomko .10 .30
10 Eric Karros .10 .30
11 Mike Cameron .10 .30
12 Jim Edmonds .10 .30
13 Bernie Williams .20 .50
14 Denny Neagle .10 .30
15 Jason Dickson .10 .30
16 Sammy Sosa .30 .75
17 Brian Jordan .10 .30
18 Jose Vidro .10 .30
19 Scott Spiezio .10 .30
20 Jay Buhner .10 .30
21 Jim Thome .20 .50
22 Sandy Alomar Jr. .10 .30
23 Livan Hernandez .10 .30
24 Roberto Alomar .20 .50
25 Chris Gomez .10 .30
26 John Wetteland .10 .30
27 Willie Greene .10 .30
28 Gregg Jefferies .10 .30
29 Johnny Damon .20 .50
30 Barry Larkin .20 .50
31 Chuck Knoblauch .10 .30
32 Mo Vaughn .10 .30
33 Tony Clark .10 .30
34 Marty Cordova .10 .30
35 Vinny Castilla .10 .30
36 Jeff King .10 .30
37 Reggie Jefferson .10 .30
38 Mariano Rivera .30 .75
39 Jermaine Allensworth .10 .30
40 Livan Hernandez .10 .30
41 Heathcliff Slocumb .10 .30
42 Jacob Cruz .10 .30
43 Barry Bonds .75 2.00
44 Dave Magadan .10 .30
45 Chan Ho Park .10 .30
46 Jeremi Gonzalez .10 .30
47 Jeff Cirillo .10 .30
48 Delino DeShields .10 .30
49 Craig Biggio .20 .50
50 Benito Santiago .10 .30
51 Mark Clark .10 .30
52 Fernando Vina .10 .30
53 F.P. Santangelo .10 .30
54 Pep Harris .10 .30
55 Edgar Renteria .10 .30
56 Jeff Bagwell .20 .50
57 Jimmy Key .10 .30
58 Bartolo Colon .10 .30
59 Curt Schilling .10 .30
60 Steve Finley .10 .30
61 Andy Ashby .10 .30
62 John Burkett .10 .30
63 Orel Hershiser .10 .30
64 Pokey Reese .10 .30
65 Scott Servais .10 .30
66 Todd Jones .10 .30
67 Javy Lopez .10 .30
68 Robin Ventura .10 .30
69 Miguel Tejada .30 .75
70 Raul Casanova .10 .30
71 Reggie Sanders .10 .30
72 Edgardo Alfonzo .10 .30
73 Dean Palmer .10 .30
74 Todd Stottlemyre .10 .30
75 David Wells .10 .30
76 Troy Percival .10 .30
77 Albert Belle .10 .30
78 Pat Hentgen .10 .30
79 Brian Hunter .10 .30
80 Richard Hidalgo .10 .30
81 Darren Oliver .10 .30
82 Mark Wohlers .10 .30
83 Cal Ripken 1.00 2.50
84 Hideo Nomo .30 .75
85 Derrek Lee .20 .50
86 Stan Javier .10 .30
87 Rey Ordonez .10 .30
88 Randy Johnson .30 .75
89 Jeff Kent .10 .30
90 Brian McRae .10 .30
91 Manny Ramirez .20 .50
92 Trevor Hoffman .10 .30
93 Doug Glanville .10 .30
94 Todd Walker .10 .30
95 Andy Benes .10 .30
96 Jason Schmidt .10 .30
97 Mike Matheny .10 .30
98 Tim Naehring .10 .30
99 Keith Lockhart .10 .30
100 Jose Rosado .10 .30
101 Roger Clemens .60 1.50
102 Pedro Astacio .10 .30
103 Mark Bellhorn .10 .30
104 Paul O'Neill .20 .50
105 Darin Erstad .10 .30
106 Mike Lieberthal .10 .30
107 Wilson Alvarez .10 .30
108 Mike Mussina .20 .50
109 George Williams .10 .30
110 Cliff Floyd .10 .30
111 Shawn Estes .10 .30
112 Mark Grudzielanek .10 .30
113 Tony Gwynn .40 1.00
114 Alan Benes .10 .30
115 Terry Steinbach .10 .30
116 Greg Maddux .50 1.25
117 Andy Pettitte .20 .50
118 Dave Nilsson .10 .30
119 Deivi Cruz .10 .30
120 Carlos Delgado .10 .30
121 Scott Hatteberg .10 .30
122 John Olerud .10 .30
123 Todd Dunwoody .10 .30
124 Garret Anderson .10 .30
125 Royce Clayton .10 .30
126 Dante Powell .10 .30
127 Tom Glavine .20 .50
128 Gary DiSarcina .10 .30
129 Terry Adams .10 .30
130 Raul Mondesi .10 .30
131 Dan Wilson .10 .30
132 Al Martin .10 .30
133 Mickey Morandini .10 .30
134 Rafael Palmeiro .20 .50
135 Juan Encarnacion .10 .30
136 Jim Pittsley .10 .30
137 Magglio Ordonez RC 1.25 3.00
138 Will Clark .20 .50
139 Todd Helton .20 .50
140 Kelvim Escobar .10 .30
141 Esteban Loaiza .10 .30
142 John Jaha .10 .30
143 Jeff Fassero .10 .30
144 Harold Baines .10 .30
145 Butch Huskey .10 .30
146 Pat Meares .10 .30
147 Brian Giles .10 .30
148 Ramiro Mendoza .10 .30
149 John Smoltz .20 .50
150 Felix Martinez .10 .30
151 Jose Valentin .10 .30
152 Brad Rigby .10 .30
153 Ed Sprague .10 .30
154 Mike Hampton .10 .30
155 Carlos Perez .10 .30
156 Ray Lankford .10 .30
157 Bobby Bonilla .10 .30
158 Bill Mueller .10 .30
159 Jeffrey Hammonds .10 .30
160 Charles Nagy .10 .30
161 Rich Loiselle RC .10 .30
162 Al Leiter .10 .30
163 Larry Walker .10 .30
164 Chris Hoiles .10 .30
165 Jeff Montgomery .10 .30
166 Francisco Cordova .10 .30
167 James Baldwin .10 .30
168 Mark McLemore .10 .30
169 Kevin Appier .10 .30
170 Jamey Wright .10 .30
171 Nomar Garciaparra .50 1.25
172 Matt Franco .10 .30
173 Armando Benitez .10 .30
174 Jeromy Burnitz .10 .30
175 Ismael Valdes .10 .30
176 Lance Johnson .10 .30
177 Paul Sorrento .10 .30
178 Rondell White .10 .30
179 Kevin Elster .10 .30
180 Jason Giambi .10 .30
181 Carlos Baerga .10 .30
182 Russ Davis .10 .30
183 Ryan McGuire .10 .30
184 Eric Young .10 .30
185 Ron Gant .10 .30
186 Manny Alexander .10 .30
187 Scott Karl .10 .30
188 Brady Anderson .10 .30
189 Randall Simon .10 .30
190 Tim Belcher .10 .30
191 Jaret Wright .10 .30
192 Dante Bichette .10 .30
193 John Valentin .10 .30
194 Darren Bragg .10 .30
195 Mike Sweeney .10 .30
196 Craig Counsell .10 .30
197 Jaime Navarro .10 .30
198 Todd Dunn .10 .30
199 Ken Griffey Jr. .60 1.50
200 Juan Gonzalez .10 .30
201 Billy Wagner .10 .30
202 Tino Martinez .20 .50
203 Mark McGwire .75 2.00
204 Jeff D'Amico .10 .30
205 Rico Brogna .10 .30
206 Todd Hollandsworth .10 .30
207 Chad Curtis .10 .30
208 Tom Goodwin .10 .30
209 Neifi Perez .10 .30
210 Derek Bell .10 .30
211 Quilvio Veras .10 .30
212 Greg Vaughn .10 .30
213 Kirk Rueter .10 .30
214 Arthur Rhodes .10 .30
215 Cal Eldred .10 .30
216 Bill Taylor .10 .30
217 Todd Greene .10 .30
218 Mario Valdez .10 .30
219 Ricky Bottalico .10 .30
220 Frank Rodriguez .10 .30
221 Rich Becker .10 .30
222 Roberto Duran RC .10 .30
223 Ivan Rodriguez .20 .50
224 Mike Jackson .10 .30
225 Deion Sanders .20 .50
226 Tony Womack .10 .30
227 Mark Kotsay .10 .30
228 Steve Trachsel .10 .30
229 Ryan Klesko .10 .30
230 Ken Cloude .10 .30
231 Luis Gonzalez .10 .30
232 Gary Gaetti .10 .30
233 Michael Tucker .10 .30
234 Shawn Green .10 .30
235 Ariel Prieto .10 .30
236 Kirt Manwaring .10 .30
237 Omar Vizquel .20 .50
238 Matt Beech .10 .30
239 Justin Thompson .10 .30
240 Bret Boone .10 .30
241 Derek Jeter .75 2.00
242 Ken Caminiti .10 .30
243 Jose Offerman .10 .30
244 Kevin Tapani .10 .30
245 Jason Kendall .10 .30
246 Jose Guillen .10 .30
247 Mike Bordick .10 .30
248 Dustin Hermanson .10 .30
249 Darrin Fletcher .10 .30
250 Dave Hollins .10 .30
251 Ramon Martinez .10 .30
252 Hideki Irabu .10 .30
253 Mark Grace .20 .50
254 Jason Isringhausen .10 .30
255 Jose Cruz Jr. .10 .30
256 Brian Johnson .10 .30
257 Brad Ausmus .10 .30
258 Andruw Jones .20 .50
259 Doug Jones .10 .30
260 Jeff Shaw .10 .30
261 Chuck Finley .10 .30
262 Gary Sheffield .10 .30
263 David Segui .10 .30
264 John Smiley .10 .30
265 Tim Salmon .20 .50
266 J.T. Snow .10 .30
267 Alex Fernandez .10 .30
268 Matt Stairs .10 .30
269 B.J. Surhoff .10 .30
270 Keith Foulke .10 .30
271 Edgar Martinez .20 .50
272 Shannon Stewart .10 .30
273 Eduardo Perez .10 .30
274 Wally Joyner .10 .30
275 Kevin Young .10 .30
276 Eli Marrero .10 .30
277 Brad Radke .10 .30
278 Jamie Moyer .10 .30
279 Joe Girardi .10 .30
280 Troy O'Leary .10 .30
281 Jeff Frye .10 .30
282 Jose Offerman .10 .30
283 Scott Erickson .10 .30
284 Sean Berry .10 .30
285 Shigetoshi Hasegawa .10 .30
286 Felix Heredia .10 .30
287 Willie McGee .10 .30
288 Alex Rodriguez .50 1.25
289 Ugueth Urbina .10 .30
290 Jon Lieber .10 .30
291 Fernando Tatis .10 .30
292 Chris Stynes .10 .30
293 Bernard Gilkey .10 .30
294 Joey Hamilton .10 .30
295 Matt Karchner .10 .30
296 Paul Wilson .10 .30
297 Damion Easley .10 .30
298 Kevin Millwood RC .40 1.00
299 Ellis Burks .10 .30
300 Jerry DiPoto .10 .30
301 Jermaine Dye .10 .30
302 Travis Lee .10 .30
303 Ron Coomer .10 .30
304 Matt Williams .10 .30
305 Bobby Higginson .10 .30
306 Jorge Fabregas .10 .30
307 Jon Nunnally .10 .30
308 Jay Bell .10 .30
309 Jason Schmidt .10 .30
310 Andy Benes .10 .30
311 Sterling Hitchcock .10 .30
312 Jeff Suppan .10 .30
313 Shane Reynolds .10 .30
314 Willie Blair .10 .30
315 Scott Rolen .20 .50
316 Wilson Alvarez .10 .30
317 David Justice .10 .30
318 Fred McGriff .20 .50
319 Bobby Jones .10 .30
320 Wade Boggs .20 .50
321 Tim Wakefield .10 .30
322 Tony Saunders .10 .30
323 David Cone .10 .30
324 Roberto Hernandez .10 .30
325 Jose Canseco .20 .50
326 Kevin Stocker .10 .30
327 Gerald Williams .10 .30
328 Quinton McCracken .10 .30
329 Mark Gardner .10 .30
330 Ben Grieve .10 .30
331 Kevin Brown .20 .50
332 Mike Lowell RC .60 1.50
333 Jed Hansen .10 .30
334 Abraham Nunez .10 .30
335 John Thomson .10 .30
336 Masato Yoshii RC .15 .40
337 Mike Piazza .50 1.25
338 Brad Fullmer .10 .30
339 Ray Durham .10 .30
340 Kerry Wood .15 .40
341 Kevin Polcovich .10 .30
342 Russ Johnson .10 .30
343 Darryl Hamilton .10 .30
344 David Ortiz .40 1.00
345 Kevin Orie .10 .30
346 Mike Caruso .10 .30
347 Juan Guzman .10 .30
348 Ruben Rivera .10 .30
349 Rick Aguilera .10 .30
350 Bobby Estalella .10 .30
351 Bobby Witt .10 .30
352 Paul Konerko .10 .30
353 Matt Morris .10 .30
354 Carl Pavano .10 .30
355 Todd Zeile .10 .30
356 Kevin Brown TR .20 .50
357 Alex Gonzalez .10 .30
358 Chuck Knoblauch TR .10 .30
359 Joey Cora .10 .30
360 Mike Lansing TR .10 .30
361 Adrian Beltre .10 .30
362 Dennis Eckersley TR .10 .30
363 A.J. Hinch .10 .30
364 Kenny Lofton TR .10 .30
365 Alex Gonzalez .10 .30
366 Henry Rodriguez TR .10 .30
367 Mike Stoner RC .10 .30
368 Darryl Kile TR .10 .30
369 Kevin McGlinchy .10 .30
370 Walt Weiss TR .10 .30
371 Kris Benson .10 .30
372 Cecil Fielder TR .10 .30
373 Dermal Brown .10 .30
374 Rod Beck TR .10 .30
375 Eric Milton .10 .30
376 Travis Fryman TR .10 .30
377 Preston Wilson .10 .30
378 Chili Davis TR .10 .30
379 Travis Lee .10 .30
380 Jim Leyritz TR .10 .30
381 Vernon Wells .10 .30
382 Joe Carter TR .10 .30
383 J.J. Davis .10 .30
384 Marquis Grissom TR .10 .30
385 Mike Cuddyer RC .40 1.00
386 Rickey Henderson TR .30 .75
387 Chris Enochs RC .10 .30
388 Andres Galarraga TR .10 .30
389 Jason Dellaero .10 .30
390 Robb Nen TR .10 .30
391 Mark Mangum .10 .30
392 Jeff Blauser TR .10 .30
393 Adam Kennedy .10 .30
394 Bob Abreu TR .10 .30
395 Jack Cust RC .75 2.00
396 Jose Vizcaino TR .10 .30
397 Jon Garland .10 .30
398 Pedro Martinez TR .20 .50
399 Aaron Akin .10 .30
400 Jeff Conine TR .10 .30
NNO Cal Ripken Sound Chip 1 6.00 15.00
NNO Cal Ripken Sound Chip 2 6.00 15.00

1998 Stadium Club First Day Issue

*STARS: 6X TO 15X BASIC CARDS
*ROOKIES: 6X TO 15X BASIC CARDS
SER.1 STATED ODDS 1:42 RETAIL PACKS
SER.2 STATED ODDS 1:47 RETAIL PACKS
STATED PRINT RUN 200 SERIAL #'d SETS

1998 Stadium Club One Of A Kind

*STARS: 8X TO 20X BASIC CARDS
*ROOKIES: 8X TO 20X BASIC CARDS
SER.1 STATED ODDS 1:21 HOB, 1:13 HTA
SER.2 STATED ODDS 1:24 HOB, 1:14 HTA
STATED PRINT RUN 150 SERIAL #'d SETS

1998 Stadium Club Co-Signers

SER.1 A ODDS 1:4372 HOB, 1:2623 HTA
SER.2 A ODDS 1:4702 HOB, 1:2821 HTA
SER.1 B ODDS 1:1457 HOB, 1:874 HTA
SER.2 B ODDS 1:1567 HOB, 1:940 HTA
SER.1 C ODDS 1:121 HOB, 1:73 HTA
SER.2 C ODDS 1:131 HOB, 1: 78 HTA
CS1 N.Garciaparra/S.Rolen A 60.00 120.00
CS2 N.Garciaparra/D.Jeter B 175.00 300.00
CS3 N.Garciaparra/E.Karros C 20.00 50.00
CS4 S.Rolen/D.Jeter C 100.00 200.00
CS5 S.Rolen/E.Karros B 6.00 15.00
CS6 D.Jeter/E.Karros A 75.00 150.00
CS7 T.Lee/J.Cruz Jr. B 6.00 15.00
CS8 T.Lee/M.Kotsay C 6.00 15.00
CS9 T.Lee/P.Konerko A 40.00 80.00
CS10 J.Cruz Jr./M.Kotsay A 20.00 50.00
CS11 J.Cruz Jr./P.Konerko C 6.00 15.00
CS12 M.Kotsay/P.Konerko B 10.00 25.00
CS13 T.Gwynn/L.Walker A 150.00 300.00
CS14 T.Gwynn/M.Grudz. C 15.00 40.00
CS15 T.Gwynn/A.Galarraga B 60.00 120.00
CS16 L.Walker/M.Grudz. B 40.00 80.00
CS17 L.Walker/A.Galarraga C 15.00 40.00
CS18 A.Galarraga/M.Grudz. A 20.00 50.00
CS19 S.Alomar/R.Alomar A 15.00 40.00
CS20 S.Alomar/A.Pettitte C 15.00 40.00
CS21 S.Alomar/T.Martinez B 30.00 60.00
CS22 R.Alomar/A.Pettitte B 8.00 20.00
CS23 R.Alomar/T.Martinez C 20.00 50.00
CS24 A.Pettitte/T.Martinez A 60.00 120.00
CS25 T.Clark/T.Hundley A 20.00 50.00
CS26 T.Clark/T.Salmon B 20.00 50.00
CS27 T.Clark/R.Ventura C 6.00 15.00
CS28 T.Hundley/T.Salmon C 6.00 15.00
CS29 T.Hundley/R.Ventura B 15.00 40.00
CS30 T.Salmon/R.Ventura A 40.00 80.00
CS31 R.Clemens/R.Johnson B 100.00 200.00
CS32 R.Clemens/J.Wright A 75.00 150.00
CS33 R.Clemens/M.Morris C 20.00 50.00
CS34 R.Johnson/J.Wright C 30.00 80.00
CS35 R.Johnson/M.Morris A 20.00 50.00
CS36 J.Wright/M.Morris B 15.00 40.00

1998 Stadium Club In The Wings

COMPLETE SET (15) 15.00 40.00
SER.1 STATED ODDS 1:36 H/R, 1:12 HTA
W1 Juan Encarnacion 1.50 4.00
W2 Brad Fullmer 1.50 4.00
W3 Ben Grieve 1.50 4.00
W4 Todd Helton 2.50 6.00
W5 Richard Hidalgo 1.50 4.00
W6 Russ Johnson 1.50 4.00
W7 Paul Konerko 1.50 4.00
W8 Mark Kotsay 1.50 4.00
W9 Derrek Lee 2.50 6.00
W10 Travis Lee 1.50 4.00
W11 Eli Marrero 1.50 4.00
W12 David Ortiz 5.00 12.00
W13 Randall Simon 1.50 4.00
W14 Shannon Stewart 1.50 4.00
W15 Fernando Tatis 1.50 4.00

1998 Stadium Club Never Compromise

COMPLETE SET (20) 30.00 80.00
SER.1 STATED ODDS 1:12 H/R, 1:4 HTA
NC1 Cal Ripken 4.00 10.00
NC2 Ivan Rodriguez .75 2.00
NC3 Ken Griffey Jr. 2.50 6.00
NC4 Frank Thomas 1.25 3.00
NC5 Tony Gwynn 1.50 4.00
NC6 Mike Piazza 2.00 5.00
NC7 Randy Johnson 1.25 3.00
NC8 Greg Maddux 2.00 5.00
NC9 Roger Clemens 2.50 6.00
NC10 Derek Jeter 3.00 8.00
NC11 Chipper Jones 1.25 3.00
NC12 Barry Bonds 3.00 8.00
NC13 Larry Walker .50 1.25
NC14 Jeff Bagwell .75 2.00
NC15 Barry Larkin .75 2.00
NC16 Ken Caminiti .50 1.25
NC17 Mark McGwire 3.00 8.00
NC18 Manny Ramirez .75 2.00
NC19 Tim Salmon .75 2.00
NC20 Paul Molitor .50 1.25

1998 Stadium Club Playing With Passion

COMPLETE SET (10) 10.00 25.00
SER.2 STATED ODDS 1:12 H/R, 1:4 HTA
P1 Bernie Williams .60 1.50
P2 Jim Edmonds .40 1.00
P3 Chipper Jones 1.00 2.50
P4 Cal Ripken 3.00 8.00
P5 Craig Biggio .60 1.50
P6 Juan Gonzalez .40 1.00
P7 Alex Rodriguez 1.50 4.00
P8 Tino Martinez .60 1.50
P9 Mike Piazza 1.50 4.00
P10 Ken Griffey Jr. 2.00 5.00

1998 Stadium Club Royal Court

COMPLETE SET (15) 20.00 50.00
SER.2 STATED ODDS 1:36 H/R, 1:12 HTA
RC1 Ken Griffey Jr. 4.00 10.00
RC2 Frank Thomas 2.00 5.00
RC3 Mike Piazza 2.00 5.00
RC4 Chipper Jones 2.00 5.00
RC5 Mark McGwire 3.00 8.00
RC6 Cal Ripken 6.00 15.00
RC7 Jeff Bagwell 1.25 3.00
RC8 Barry Bonds 3.00 8.00
RC9 Juan Gonzalez .75 2.00
RC10 Alex Rodriguez 2.50 6.00
RC11 Travis Lee .75 2.00
RC12 Paul Konerko .75 2.00
RC13 Todd Helton 1.25 3.00
RC14 Ben Grieve .75 2.00
RC15 Mark Kotsay .75 2.00

1998 Stadium Club Triumvirate Luminous

STATED ODDS 1:48 RETAIL
*LUMINESCENT: 1.25X TO 3X LUMINOUS
LUMINESCENT STATED ODDS 1:192 RETAIL
*ILLUMINATOR: 2X TO 5X LUMINOUS
ILLUMINATOR STATED ODDS 1:384 RETAIL
T1A Chipper Jones 2.50 6.00
T1B Andruw Jones 1.50 4.00
T1C Kenny Lofton 1.00 2.50
T2A Derek Jeter 6.00 15.00
T2B Bernie Williams 1.50 4.00
T2C Tino Martinez 1.50 4.00
T3A Jay Buhner 1.00 2.50
T3B Edgar Martinez 1.50 4.00
T3C Ken Griffey Jr. 5.00 12.00
T4A Albert Belle 1.00 2.50
T4B Robin Ventura 1.00 2.50
T4C Frank Thomas 2.50 6.00
T5A Brady Anderson 1.00 2.50
T5B Cal Ripken 8.00 20.00
T5C Rafael Palmeiro 1.50 4.00
T6A Mike Piazza 4.00 10.00
T6B Raul Mondesi 1.00 2.50
T6C Eric Karros 1.00 2.50
T7A Vinny Castilla 1.00 2.50
T7B Andres Galarraga 1.00 2.50
T7C Larry Walker 1.00 2.50
T8A Jim Thome 1.50 4.00
T8B Manny Ramirez 1.50 4.00
T8C David Justice 1.00 2.50
T9A Mike Mussina 1.50 4.00
T9B Greg Maddux 4.00 10.00
T9C Randy Johnson 2.50 6.00
T10A Mike Piazza 4.00 10.00
T10B Sandy Alomar Jr. 1.00 2.50
T10C Ivan Rodriguez 1.50 4.00
T11A Mark McGwire 6.00 15.00
T11B Tino Martinez 1.50 4.00
T11C Frank Thomas 2.50 6.00
T12A Roberto Alomar 1.50 4.00
T12B Chuck Knoblauch 1.00 2.50
T12C Craig Biggio 1.50 4.00
T13A Cal Ripken 8.00 20.00
T13B Chipper Jones 2.50 6.00
T13C Ken Caminiti 1.00 2.50
T14A Derek Jeter 6.00 15.00
T14B Nomar Garciaparra 4.00 10.00
T14C Alex Rodriguez 4.00 10.00
T15A Barry Bonds 6.00 15.00
T15B David Justice 1.00 2.50
T15C Albert Belle 1.00 2.50
T16A Bernie Williams 1.50 4.00
T16B Ken Griffey Jr. 5.00 12.00
T16C Ray Lankford 1.00 2.50
T17A Tim Salmon 1.50 4.00
T17B Larry Walker 1.00 2.50
T17C Tony Gwynn 3.00 8.00
T18A Paul Molitor 1.00 2.50
T18B Edgar Martinez 1.50 4.00
T18C Juan Gonzalez 1.00 2.50

1999 Stadium Club

This 355-card set of 1999 Stadium Club cards was distributed in two separate series of 170 and 185 cards respectively. Six-card hobby and six-card retail packs each carried a suggested retail price of $2. 15-card Home Team Advantage packs (SRP of $5) were also distributed. All pack types contained a trifold/checklist info card. The card fronts feature color action player photos printed on 20 pt. card stock. The backs carry player information and career statistics. Draft Pick and Future Stars cards 141-160 and 336-355 were shortprinted at the following rates: 1:3 hobby/retail packs, one per HTA pack. Key Rookie Cards include Pat Burrell, Nick Johnson and Austin Kearns.

COMPLETE SET (355) 30.00 60.00
COMPLETE SERIES 1 (170) 12.50 30.00
COMP.SER.1 w/o SP's (150) 6.00 15.00
COMPLETE SERIES 2 (185) 12.50 30.00
COMP.SER.2 w/o SP's (165) 6.00 15.00
COMMON (1-140/161-170) .10 .30
COMMON CARD (171-335) .10 .30
COMM.SP (141-160/336-355) .75 2.00
SP ODDS 1:3 HOB/RET, 1 PER HTA
1 Alex Rodriguez .50 1.25
2 Chipper Jones .30 .75
3 Rusty Greer .10 .30
4 Jim Edmonds .10 .30
5 Ron Gant .10 .30
6 Kevin Polcovich .10 .30
7 Darryl Strawberry .10 .30
8 Bill Mueller .10 .30

9 Vinny Castilla .10 .30
10 Wade Boggs .20 .50
11 Jose Lima .10 .30
12 Darren Dreifort .10 .30
13 Jay Bell .10 .30
14 Ben Grieve .10 .30
15 Shawn Green .10 .30
16 Andres Galarraga .10 .30
17 Bartolo Colon .10 .30
18 Francisco Cordova .10 .30
19 Paul O'Neill .20 .50
20 Trevor Hoffman .10 .30
21 Darren Oliver .10 .30
22 John Franco .10 .30
23 Eli Marrero .10 .30
24 Roberto Hernandez .10 .30
25 Craig Biggio .20 .50
26 Brad Fullmer .10 .30
27 Scott Erickson .10 .30
28 Tom Gordon .10 .30
29 Brian Hunter .10 .30
30 Raul Mondesi .10 .30
31 Rick Reed .10 .30
32 Jose Canseco .20 .50
33 Robb Nen .10 .30
34 Turner Ward .10 .30
35 Orlando Hernandez .10 .30
36 Jeff Shaw .10 .30
37 Matt Lawton .10 .30
38 David Wells .10 .30
39 Bob Abreu .10 .30
40 Jeromy Burnitz .10 .30
41 Deivi Cruz .10 .30
42 Derek Bell .10 .30
43 Rico Brogna .10 .30
44 Dmitri Young .10 .30
45 Chuck Knoblauch .10 .30
46 Johnny Damon .20 .50
47 Brian Meadows .10 .30
48 Jeromi Gonzalez .10 .30
49 Gary DiSarcina .10 .30
50 Frank Thomas .30 .75
51 F.P. Santangelo .10 .30
52 Tom Candiotti .10 .30
53 Shane Reynolds .10 .30
54 Rod Beck .10 .30
55 Rey Ordonez .10 .30
56 Todd Helton .20 .50
57 Mickey Morandini .10 .30
58 Jorge Posada .20 .50
59 Mike Mussina .20 .50
60 Al Leiter .10 .30
61 David Segui .10 .30
62 Brian McRae .10 .30
63 Fred McGriff .20 .50
64 Brett Tomko .10 .30
65 Derek Jeter .75 2.00
66 Sammy Sosa .30 .75
67 Kenny Rogers .10 .30
68 Dave Nilsson .10 .30
69 Eric Young .10 .30
70 Mark McGwire .75 2.00
71 Kenny Lofton .10 .30
72 Tom Glavine .20 .50
73 Joey Hamilton .10 .30
74 John Valentin .10 .30
75 Mariano Rivera .30 .75
76 Ray Durham .10 .30
77 Tony Clark .10 .30
78 Livan Hernandez .10 .30
79 Rickey Henderson .30 .75
80 Vladimir Guerrero .30 .75
81 J.T. Snow .10 .30
82 Juan Guzman .10 .30
83 Darryl Hamilton .10 .30
84 Matt Anderson .10 .30
85 Travis Lee .10 .30
86 Joe Randa .10 .30
87 Dave Dellucci .10 .30
88 Moises Alou .10 .30
89 Alex Gonzalez .10 .30
90 Tony Womack .10 .30
91 Neifi Perez .10 .30
92 Travis Fryman .10 .30
93 Masato Yoshii .10 .30
94 Woody Williams .10 .30
95 Ray Lankford .10 .30
96 Roger Clemens .60 1.50
97 Dustin Hermanson .10 .30
98 Joe Carter .10 .30
99 Jason Schmidt .10 .30
100 Greg Maddux .50 1.25
101 Kevin Tapani .10 .30
102 Charles Johnson .10 .30
103 Derrek Lee .20 .50
104 Pete Harnisch .10 .30
105 Dante Bichette .10 .30
106 Scott Brosius .10 .30
107 Mike Caruso .10 .30
108 Eddie Taubensee .10 .30
109 Jeff Fassero .10 .30
110 Marquis Grissom .10 .30
111 Jose Hernandez .10 .30
112 Chan Ho Park .10 .30
113 Wally Joyner .10 .30
114 Bobby Estalella .10 .30
115 Pedro Martinez .20 .50
116 Shawn Estes .10 .30
117 Walt Weiss .10 .30
118 John Mabry .10 .30
119 Brian Johnson .10 .30
120 Jim Thome .20 .50
121 Bill Spiers .10 .30
122 John Olerud .10 .30
123 Jeff King .10 .30
124 Tim Belcher .10 .30
125 John Wetteland .10 .30
126 Tony Gwynn .40 1.00
127 Brady Anderson .10 .30
128 Randy Winn .10 .30
129 Andy Fox .10 .30
130 Eric Karros .10 .30
131 Kevin Millwood .10 .30
132 Andy Benes .10 .30
133 Andy Ashby .10 .30
134 Ron Coomer .10 .30
135 Juan Gonzalez .10 .30
136 Randy Johnson .30 .75
137 Aaron Sele .10 .30
138 Edgardo Alfonzo .10 .30
139 B.J. Surhoff .10 .30
140 Jose Vizcaino .10 .30
141 Chad Moeller SP RC .75 2.00
142 Mike Zywica SP RC .75 2.00
143 Angel Pena SP .75 2.00
144 Nick Johnson SP RC 1.00 2.50
145 G.Chiaramonte SP RC .75 2.00
146 Kit Pellow SP RC .75 2.00
147 Clayton Andrews SP RC .75 2.00
148 Jerry Hairston Jr. SP .75 2.00
149 Jason Tyner SP RC .75 2.00
150 Chip Ambres SP RC .75 2.00
151 Pat Burrell SP RC 1.50 4.00
152 Josh McKinley SP RC .75 2.00
153 Choo Freeman SP RC .75 2.00
154 Rick Elder SP RC .75 2.00
155 Eric Valent SP RC .75 2.00
156 Jeff Winchester SP RC .75 2.00
157 Mike Nannini SP RC .75 2.00
158 Mamon Tucker SP RC .75 2.00
159 Nate Bump SP RC .75 2.00
160 Andy Brown SP RC .75 2.00
161 Troy Glaus .20 .50
162 Adrian Beltre .10 .30
163 Mitch Meluskey .10 .30
164 Alex Gonzalez .10 .30
165 George Lombard .10 .30
166 Eric Chavez .10 .30
167 Ruben Mateo .10 .30
168 Calvin Pickering .10 .30
169 Gabe Kapler .10 .30
170 Bruce Chen .10 .30
171 Darin Erstad .10 .30
172 Sandy Alomar Jr. .10 .30
173 Miguel Cairo .10 .30
174 Jason Kendall .10 .30
175 Cal Ripken 1.00 2.50
176 Darryl Kile .10 .30
177 David Cone .10 .30
178 Mike Sweeney .10 .30
179 Royce Clayton .10 .30
180 Curt Schilling .10 .30
181 Barry Larkin .20 .50
182 Eric Milton .10 .30
183 Ellis Burks .10 .30
184 A.J. Hinch .10 .30
185 Garret Anderson .10 .30
186 Sean Bergman .10 .30
187 Shannon Stewart .10 .30
188 Bernard Gilkey .10 .30
189 Jeff Blauser .10 .30
190 Andruw Jones .20 .50
191 Omar Daal .10 .30
192 Jeff Kent .10 .30
193 Mark Kotsay .10 .30
194 Dave Burba .10 .30
195 Bobby Higginson .10 .30
196 Hideki Irabu .10 .30
197 Jamie Moyer .10 .30
198 Doug Glanville .10 .30
199 Quinton McCracken .10 .30
200 Ken Griffey Jr. .60 1.50
201 Mike Lieberthal .10 .30
202 Carl Everett .10 .30
203 Omar Vizquel .20 .50
204 Mike Lansing .10 .30
205 Manny Ramirez .20 .50
206 Ryan Klesko .10 .30
207 Jeff Montgomery .10 .30
208 Chad Curtis .10 .30
209 Rick Helling .10 .30
210 Justin Thompson .10 .30
211 Tom Goodwin .10 .30
212 Todd Dunwoody .10 .30
213 Kevin Young .10 .30
214 Tony Saunders .10 .30
215 Gary Sheffield .10 .30
216 Jaret Wright .10 .30
217 Quilvio Veras .10 .30
218 Marty Cordova .10 .30
219 Tino Martinez .20 .50
220 Scott Rolen .20 .50
221 Fernando Tatis .10 .30
222 Damion Easley .10 .30
223 Aramis Ramirez .10 .30
224 Brad Radke .10 .30
225 Nomar Garciaparra .50 1.25
226 Magglio Ordonez .10 .30
227 Andy Pettitte .20 .50
228 David Ortiz .30 .75
229 Todd Jones .10 .30
230 Larry Walker .10 .30
231 Tim Wakefield .10 .30
232 Jose Guillen .10 .30
233 Gregg Olson .10 .30
234 Ricky Gutierrez .10 .30
235 Todd Walker .10 .30
236 Abraham Nunez .10 .30
237 Sean Casey .10 .30
238 Greg Norton .10 .30
239 Bret Saberhagen .10 .30
240 Bernie Williams .20 .50
241 Tim Salmon .20 .50
242 Jason Giambi .10 .30
243 Fernando Vina .10 .30
244 Darrin Fletcher .10 .30
245 Mike Bordick .10 .30
246 Dennis Reyes .10 .30
247 Hideo Nomo .30 .75
248 Kevin Stocker .10 .30
249 Mike Hampton .10 .30
250 Kerry Wood .10 .30
251 Ismael Valdes .10 .30
252 Pat Hentgen .10 .30
253 Scott Spiezio .10 .30
254 Chuck Finley .10 .30
255 Troy Glaus .20 .50
256 Bobby Jones .10 .30
257 Wayne Gomes .10 .30
258 Rondell White .10 .30
259 Todd Zeile .10 .30
260 Matt Williams .10 .30
261 Henry Rodriguez .10 .30
262 Matt Stairs .10 .30
263 Jose Valentin .10 .30
264 David Justice .10 .30
265 Javy Lopez .10 .30
266 Matt Morris .10 .30
267 Steve Trachsel .10 .30
268 Edgar Martinez .20 .50
269 Al Martin .10 .30
270 Ivan Rodriguez .20 .50
271 Carlos Delgado .10 .30
272 Mark Grace .20 .50
273 Ugueth Urbina .10 .30
274 Jay Buhner .10 .30
275 Mike Piazza .50 1.25
276 Rick Aguilera .10 .30
277 Javier Valentin .10 .30
278 Brian Anderson .10 .30
279 Cliff Floyd .10 .30
280 Barry Bonds .75 2.00
281 Troy O'Leary .10 .30
282 Seth Greisinger .10 .30
283 Mark Grudzielanek .10 .30
284 Jose Cruz Jr. .10 .30
285 Jeff Bagwell .20 .50
286 John Smoltz .20 .50
287 Jeff Cirillo .10 .30
288 Richie Sexson .10 .30
289 Charles Nagy .10 .30
290 Pedro Martinez .20 .50
291 Juan Encarnacion .10 .30
292 Phil Nevin .10 .30
293 Terry Steinbach .10 .30
294 Miguel Tejada .10 .30
295 Dan Wilson .10 .30
296 Chris Peters .10 .30
297 Brian Moehler .10 .30
298 Jason Christiansen .10 .30
299 Kelly Stinnett .10 .30
300 Dwight Gooden .10 .30
301 Randy Velarde .10 .30
302 Kirt Manwaring .10 .30
303 Jeff Abbott .10 .30
304 Dave Hollins .10 .30
305 Kerry Ligtenberg .10 .30
306 Aaron Boone .10 .30
307 Carlos Hernandez .10 .30
308 Mike Difelice .10 .30
309 Brian Meadows .10 .30
310 Tim Bogar .10 .30
311 Greg Vaughn TR .10 .30
312 Brant Brown TR .10 .30
313 Steve Finley TR .10 .30
314 Bret Boone TR .10 .30
315 Albert Belle TR .10 .30
316 Robin Ventura TR .10 .30
317 Eric Davis TR .10 .30
318 Todd Hundley TR .10 .30
319 Roger Clemens TR .60 1.50
320 Kevin Brown TR .10 .30
321 Jose Offerman TR .10 .30
322 Brian Jordan TR .10 .30
323 Mike Cameron TR .10 .30
324 Bobby Bonilla TR .10 .30
325 Roberto Alomar TR .20 .50
326 Ken Caminiti TR .10 .30
327 Todd Stottlemyre TR .10 .30
328 Randy Johnson TR .30 .75
329 Luis Gonzalez TR .10 .30
330 Rafael Palmeiro TR .20 .50
331 Devon White TR .10 .30
332 Will Clark TR .20 .50
333 Dean Palmer TR .10 .30
334 Gregg Jefferies TR .10 .30
335 Mo Vaughn TR .10 .30
336 Brad Lidge SP RC 1.50 4.00
337 Chris George SP RC .75 2.00
338 Austin Kearns SP RC 1.50 4.00
339 Matt Belisle SP RC .75 2.00
340 Nate Cornejo SP RC .75 2.00
341 Matt Holliday SP RC 3.00 8.00
342 J.M. Gold SP RC .75 2.00
343 Matt Roney SP RC .75 2.00
344 Seth Etherton SP RC .75 2.00
345 Adam Everett SP RC .75 2.00
346 Marlon Anderson SP .75 2.00
347 Ron Belliard SP .75 2.00
348 Fernando Seguignol SP .75 2.00
349 Michael Barrett SP .75 2.00
350 Dernell Stenson SP .75 2.00
351 Ryan Anderson SP .75 2.00
352 Ramon Hernandez SP .75 2.00
353 Jeremy Giambi SP .75 2.00
354 Ricky Ledee SP .75 2.00
355 Carlos Lee SP .75 2.00

1999 Stadium Club First Day Issue

*STARS: 6X TO 15X BASIC CARDS
*SP 141-160/336-355: 2X TO 5X BASIC SP
SER.1 STATED ODDS 1:75 RETAIL
SER.2 STATED ODDS 1:60 RETAIL
SER.1 PRINT RUN 170 SERIAL #'d SETS
SER.2 PRINT RUN 200 SERIAL #'d SETS

1999 Stadium Club One of a Kind

*STARS: 6X TO 15X BASIC CARDS
*SP'S 141-160/336-355: 2X TO 5X BASIC
SER.1 STATED ODDS 1:53 HOBBY, 1:21 HTA
SER.2 STATED ODDS 1:48 HOBBY, 1:19 HTA
STATED PRINT RUN 150 SERIAL #'d SETS

1999 Stadium Club Autographs

SER.1 STATED ODDS 1:1107 RETAIL
SER.2 STATED ODDS 1:877 RETAIL
CARDS 1-5 IN SER.1, 6-10 IN SER.2
SCA1 Alex Rodriguez 40.00 80.00
SCA2 Chipper Jones 20.00 50.00
SCA3 Barry Bonds 100.00 175.00
SCA4 Tino Martinez 10.00 25.00
SCA5 Ben Grieve 6.00 15.00
SCA6 Juan Gonzalez 10.00 25.00
SCA7 Vladimir Guerrero 8.00 20.00
SCA8 Albert Belle 6.00 15.00
SCA9 Kerry Wood 10.00 25.00
SCA10 Todd Helton 10.00 25.00

1999 Stadium Club Chrome

COMPLETE SET (40) 60.00 120.00
COMPLETE SERIES 1 (20) 30.00 60.00
COMPLETE SERIES 2 (20) 25.00 60.00
STATED ODDS 1:24 HOB/RET, 1:6 HTA
*REFRACTORS: 1X TO 2.5X BASIC CHROME
REFRACTOR ODDS 1:96 HOB/RET, 1:24 HTA
SCC1 Nomar Garciaparra 2.50 6.00
SCC2 Kerry Wood .60 1.50
SCC3 Jeff Bagwell 1.00 2.50
SCC4 Ivan Rodriguez 1.00 2.50
SCC5 Albert Belle .60 1.50
SCC6 Gary Sheffield .60 1.50
SCC7 Andruw Jones 1.00 2.50
SCC8 Kevin Brown .60 1.50
SCC9 David Cone .60 1.50
SCC10 Darin Erstad .60 1.50
SCC11 Manny Ramirez 1.00 2.50
SCC12 Larry Walker .60 1.50
SCC13 Mike Piazza 2.50 6.00
SCC14 Cal Ripken 5.00 12.00
SCC15 Pedro Martinez 1.00 2.50
SCC16 Greg Vaughn .60 1.50
SCC17 Barry Bonds 4.00 10.00
SCC18 Mo Vaughn .60 1.50
SCC19 Bernie Williams 1.00 2.50
SCC20 Ken Griffey Jr. 3.00 8.00
SCC21 Alex Rodriguez 2.50 6.00
SCC22 Chipper Jones 1.50 4.00
SCC23 Ben Grieve .60 1.50
SCC24 Frank Thomas 1.50 4.00
SCC25 Derek Jeter 4.00 10.00
SCC26 Sammy Sosa 1.50 4.00
SCC27 Mark McGwire 4.00 10.00
SCC28 Vladimir Guerrero 1.50 4.00
SCC29 Greg Maddux 2.50 6.00
SCC30 Juan Gonzalez .60 1.50
SCC31 Troy Glaus 1.00 2.50
SCC32 Adrian Beltre .60 1.50
SCC33 Mitch Meluskey .60 1.50
SCC34 Alex Gonzalez .60 1.50
SCC35 George Lombard .60 1.50
SCC36 Eric Chavez .60 1.50
SCC37 Ruben Mateo .60 1.50
SCC38 Calvin Pickering .60 1.50
SCC39 Gabe Kapler .60 1.50
SCC40 Bruce Chen .60 1.50

1999 Stadium Club Co-Signers

SER.1 A ODDS 1:45213 HOB, 1:18085 HTA
SER.2 A ODDS 1:43639 HOB, 1:18171 HTA
SER.1 B ODDS 1:9043 HOB, 1:3617 HTA
SER.2 B ODDS 1:8984 HOB, 1:3533 HTA
SER.1 C ODDS 1:3104 HOB, 1:1006 HTA
SER.2 C ODDS 1:2975 HOB, 1:1189 HTA
SER.1 D ODDS 1:254 HOB, 1:102 HTA
SER.2 D ODDS 1:251 HOB, 1:100 HTA
NO GROUP A PRICING DUE TO SCARCITY
NO SER.2 GROUP B PRICING AVAILABLE
CS1 B.Grieve/R.Sexson D 8.00 20.00
CS2 T.Helton/T.Glaus D 8.00 20.00
CS3 A.Rodriguez/S.Rolen D 30.00 60.00
CS4 D.Jeter/C.Jones D 300.00 400.00
CS5 C.Floyd/E.Marrero D 8.00 20.00
CS6 J.Buhner/K.Young D 8.00 20.00
CS7 B.Grieve/T.Glaus C 15.00 40.00
CS8 T.Helton/R.Sexson C 15.00 40.00
CS9 A.Rodriguez/C.Jones C 90.00 150.00
CS10 D.Jeter/S.Rolen C 125.00 250.00
CS11 C.Floyd/K.Young C 8.00 20.00
CS12 J.Buhner/E.Marrero B 8.00 20.00
CS13 B.Grieve/T.Helton B 30.00 60.00
CS14 R.Sexson/T.Glaus B 30.00 60.00
CS15 A.Rodriguez/D.Jeter B 250.00 500.00
CS16 C.Jones/S.Rolen B 60.00 120.00
CS17 C.Floyd/J.Buhner B 15.00 40.00
CS18 E.Marrero/K.Young B 8.00 20.00
CS19 Grieve/Helton/Sexson/Glaus A
CS20 A.Rod/Jeter/Jones/Rolen A
CS21 Floyd/Buhner/Marrero/Young A
CS22 E.Alfonzo/J.Guillen D 8.00 20.00
CS23 M.Lowell/R.Rincon D 8.00 20.00
CS24 J.Gonzalez/V.Castilla D 8.00 20.00
CS25 M.Alou/R.Clemens D 15.00 40.00
CS26 S.Spiezio/T.Womack D 6.00 15.00
CS27 F.Vina/Q.Veras D 6.00 15.00
CS28 E.Alfonzo/R.Rincon C 8.00 20.00
CS29 J.Guillen/M.Lowell C 8.00 20.00
CS30 J.Gonzalez/M.Alou C 8.00 20.00
CS31 R.Clemens/V.Castilla C 30.00 60.00
CS32 S.Spiezio/F.Vina C 6.00 15.00
CS33 T.Womack/Q.Veras B 8.00 20.00
CS34 E.Alfonzo/M.Lowell B 15.00 40.00
CS35 J.Guillen/R.Rincon B 15.00 40.00
CS36 J.Gonzalez/R.Clemens B 150.00 250.00
CS37 M.Alou/V.Castilla B 30.00 60.00
CS38 S.Spiezio/Q.Veras B 8.00 20.00
CS39 T.Womack/F.Vina B 8.00 20.00
CS40 Alfonzo/Guillen/Lowell/Rincon A
CS41 Gonzalez/Alou/Clemens/Castilla A
CS42 Spiezio/Womack/Vina/Veras A

1999 Stadium Club Never Compromise

COMPLETE SET (20) 20.00 50.00
COMPLETE SERIES 1 (10) 15.00 40.00
COMPLETE SERIES 2 (10) 8.00 20.00
STATED ODDS 1:12 HOB/RET, 1:4 HTA
NC1 Mark McGwire 2.00 5.00
NC2 Sammy Sosa .75 2.00
NC3 Ken Griffey Jr. 1.50 4.00
NC4 Greg Maddux 1.25 3.00
NC5 Barry Bonds 2.00 5.00
NC6 Alex Rodriguez 1.25 3.00
NC7 Darin Erstad .30 .75
NC8 Roger Clemens 1.50 4.00
NC9 Nomar Garciaparra 1.25 3.00
NC10 Derek Jeter 2.00 5.00
NC11 Cal Ripken 2.50 6.00
NC12 Mike Piazza 1.25 3.00
NC13 Kerry Wood .30 .75
NC14 Andres Galarraga .30 .75
NC15 Vinny Castilla .30 .75
NC16 Jeff Bagwell .50 1.25
NC17 Chipper Jones .75 2.00
NC18 Eric Chavez .30 .75
NC19 Orlando Hernandez .30 .75
NC20 Troy Glaus .50 1.25

1999 Stadium Club Triumvirate Luminous

COMPLETE SET (48) 150.00 300.00
COMPLETE SERIES 1 (24) 60.00 120.00
COMPLETE SERIES 2 (24) 75.00 150.00
STATED ODDS 1:36 H, 1:48 R, 1:18 HTA
*ILLUMINATOR: 2X TO 5X LUMINOUS
ILLUM.ODDS 1:288 H, 1:384 R, 1:144 HTA
*LUMINESCENT: 1X TO 2.5X LUMINOUS
L'SCENT.ODDS 1:144 H, 1:192 R, 1:72 HTA
T1A Greg Vaughn .75 2.00
T1B Ken Caminiti .75 2.00
T1C Tony Gwynn 2.50 6.00
T2A Andruw Jones 1.25 3.00
T2B Chipper Jones 2.00 5.00
T2C Andres Galarraga .75 2.00
T3A Jay Buhner .75 2.00
T3B Ken Griffey Jr. 4.00 10.00
T3C Alex Rodriguez 3.00 8.00
T4A Derek Jeter 5.00 12.00
T4B Tino Martinez 1.25 3.00
T4C Bernie Williams 1.25 3.00
T5A Brian Jordan .75 2.00
T5B Ray Lankford .75 2.00
T5C Mark McGwire 5.00 12.00
T6A Jeff Bagwell 1.25 3.00
T6B Craig Biggio 1.25 3.00
T6C Randy Johnson 2.00 5.00
T7A Nomar Garciaparra 3.00 8.00
T7B Pedro Martinez 1.25 3.00
T7C Mo Vaughn .75 2.00
T8A Sammy Sosa 2.00 5.00
T8B Mark Grace 1.25 3.00
T8C Kerry Wood .75 2.00
T9A Alex Rodriguez 3.00 8.00
T9B Nomar Garciaparra 3.00 8.00
T9C Derek Jeter 5.00 12.00
T10A Todd Helton 1.25 3.00
T10B Travis Lee .75 2.00
T10C Pat Burrell 1.25 3.00
T11A Greg Maddux 3.00 8.00
T11B Kerry Wood .75 2.00
T11C Tom Glavine 1.25 3.00
T12A Chipper Jones 2.00 5.00
T12B Vinny Castilla .75 2.00
T12C Scott Rolen 1.25 3.00
T13A Juan Gonzalez .75 2.00
T13B Ken Griffey Jr. 10.00 25.00
T13C Ben Grieve .75 2.00
T14A Sammy Sosa 2.00 5.00
T14B Vladimir Guerrero 2.00 5.00
T14C Barry Bonds 5.00 12.00
T15A Frank Thomas 2.00 5.00
T15B Jim Thome 1.25 3.00
T15C Tino Martinez 1.25 3.00
T16A Mark McGwire 5.00 12.00
T16B Andres Galarraga .75 2.00
T16C Jeff Bagwell 1.25 3.00

1999 Stadium Club Video Replay

COMPLETE SET (5) 5.00 12.00
SER.2 STATED ODDS 1:12 HOB/RET, 1:4 HTA
VR1 Mark McGwire 1.50 4.00
VR2 Sammy Sosa .60 1.50
VR3 Ken Griffey Jr. 1.25 3.00
VR4 Kerry Wood .25 .60
VR5 Alex Rodriguez 1.00 2.50

2000 Stadium Club Pre-Production

COMPLETE SET (3) 1.25 3.00
PP1 Ivan Rodriguez .60 1.50
PP2 Magglio Ordonez .60 1.50
PP3 Craig Biggio .60 1.50

2000 Stadium Club

COMPLETE SET (250) 50.00 120.00
COMP.SET w/o SP'S (200) 12.50 30.00
COMMON CARD (1-200) .12 .30
COMMON SP (201-250) .75 2.00
SP 201-250 ODDS 1:5 HOB/RET, 1:1 HTC
1 Nomar Garciaparra .20 .50
2 Brian Jordan .12 .30
3 Mark Grace .20 .50
4 Jeromy Burnitz .12 .30
5 Shane Reynolds .12 .30
6 Alex Gonzalez .12 .30
7 Jose Offerman .12 .30
8 Orlando Hernandez .12 .30
9 Mike Caruso .12 .30
10 Tony Clark .12 .30
11 Sean Casey .12 .30
12 Johnny Damon .20 .50
13 Dante Bichette .12 .30
14 Kevin Young .12 .30
15 Juan Gonzalez .12 .30
16 Chipper Jones .30 .75
17 Quilvio Veras .12 .30
18 Trevor Hoffman .20 .50
19 Roger Cedeno .12 .30
20 Ellis Burks .12 .30
21 Richie Sexson .12 .30
22 Gary Sheffield .12 .30
23 Delino DeShields .12 .30
24 Wade Boggs .20 .50
25 Ray Lankford .12 .30
26 Kevin Appier .12 .30
27 Roy Halladay .20 .50
28 Harold Baines .20 .50
29 Todd Zeile .12 .30
30 Barry Larkin .20 .50
31 Ron Coomer .12 .30
32 Jorge Posada .20 .50
33 Magglio Ordonez .20 .50
34 Brian Giles .12 .30
35 Jeff Kent .12 .30
36 Henry Rodriguez .12 .30
37 Fred McGriff .20 .50
38 Shawn Green .12 .30
39 Derek Bell .12 .30
40 Ben Grieve .12 .30
41 Dave Nilsson .12 .30
42 Mo Vaughn .12 .30
43 Rondell White .12 .30
44 Doug Glanville .12 .30
45 Paul O'Neill .20 .50
46 Carlos Lee .12 .30
47 Vinny Castilla .12 .30
48 Mike Sweeney .12 .30
49 Rico Brogna .12 .30
50 Alex Rodriguez .40 1.00
51 Luis Castillo .12 .30
52 Kevin Brown .12 .30
53 Jose Vidro .12 .30
54 John Smoltz .30 .75
55 Garret Anderson .12 .30
56 Matt Stairs .12 .30
57 Omar Vizquel .20 .50
58 Tom Goodwin .12 .30
59 Scott Brosius .12 .30
60 Robin Ventura .12 .30
61 B.J. Surhoff .12 .30
62 Andy Ashby .12 .30
63 Chris Widger .12 .30
64 Tim Hudson .20 .50
65 Javy Lopez .12 .30
66 Tim Salmon .12 .30
67 Warren Morris .12 .30
68 John Wetteland .12 .30
69 Gabe Kapler .12 .30
70 Bernie Williams .20 .50
71 Rickey Henderson .30 .75
72 Andruw Jones .12 .30
73 Eric Young .12 .30
74 Bob Abreu .12 .30
75 David Cone .12 .30
76 Rusty Greer .12 .30
77 Ron Belliard .12 .30
78 Troy Glaus .12 .30
79 Mike Hampton .12 .30
80 Miguel Tejada .20 .50
81 Jeff Cirillo .12 .30
82 Todd Hundley .12 .30
83 Roberto Alomar .20 .50
84 Charles Johnson .12 .30
85 Rafael Palmeiro .20 .50
86 Doug Mientkiewicz .12 .30
87 Mariano Rivera .40 1.00
88 Neifi Perez .12 .30
89 Jermiane Dye .12 .30
90 Ivan Rodriguez .20 .50
91 Jay Buhner .12 .30
92 Pokey Reese .12 .30
93 John Olerud .12 .30
94 Brady Anderson .12 .30
95 Manny Ramirez .30 .75
96 Keith Osik RC .12 .30
97 Mickey Morandini .12 .30
98 Matt Williams .12 .30
99 Eric Karros .12 .30
100 Ken Griffey Jr. .60 1.50
101 Bret Boone .12 .30
102 Ryan Klesko .12 .30
103 Craig Biggio .20 .50
104 John Jaha .12 .30
105 Vladimir Guerrero .20 .50
106 Devon White .12 .30
107 Tony Womack .12 .30
108 Marvin Benard .12 .30
109 Kenny Lofton .12 .30
110 Preston Wilson .12 .30
111 Al Leiter .12 .30
112 Reggie Sanders .12 .30
113 Scott Williamson .12 .30
114 Deivi Cruz .12 .30
115 Carlos Beltran .20 .50
116 Ray Durham .12 .30
117 Ricky Ledee .12 .30
118 Torii Hunter .12 .30
119 John Valentin .12 .30
120 Scott Rolen .20 .50
121 Jason Kendall .12 .30
122 Dave Martinez .12 .30
123 Jim Thome .20 .50
124 David Bell .12 .30
125 Jose Canseco .20 .50
126 Jose Lima .12 .30
127 Carl Everett .12 .30
128 Kevin Millwood .12 .30
129 Bill Spiers .12 .30
130 Omar Daal .12 .30
131 Miguel Cairo .12 .30
132 Mark Grudzielanek .12 .30
133 David Justice .12 .30
134 Russ Ortiz .12 .30
135 Mike Piazza .30 .75
136 Brian Meadows .12 .30
137 Tony Gwynn .30 .75
138 Cal Ripken 1.00 2.50
139 Kris Benson .12 .30
140 Larry Walker .20 .50
141 Cristian Guzman .12 .30
142 Tino Martinez .12 .30
143 Chris Singleton .12 .30
144 Lee Stevens .12 .30
145 Rey Ordonez .12 .30
146 Russ Davis .12 .30
147 J.T. Snow .12 .30
148 Luis Gonzalez .12 .30
149 Marquis Grissom .12 .30
150 Greg Maddux .40 1.00
151 Fernando Tatis .12 .30
152 Jason Giambi .12 .30
153 Carlos Delgado .12 .30
154 Joe McEwing .12 .30
155 Raul Mondesi .12 .30
156 Rich Aurilia .12 .30
157 Alex Fernandez .12 .30
158 Albert Belle .12 .30
159 Pat Meares .12 .30
160 Mike Lieberthal .12 .30
161 Mike Cameron .12 .30
162 Juan Encarnacion .12 .30
163 Chuck Knoblauch .12 .30
164 Pedro Martinez .20 .50
165 Randy Johnson .30 .75
166 Shannon Stewart .12 .30
167 Jeff Bagwell .20 .50
168 Edgar Renteria .12 .30
169 Barry Bonds .50 1.25
170 Steve Finley .12 .30
171 Brian Hunter .12 .30
172 Tom Glavine .20 .50
173 Mark Kotsay .12 .30
174 Tony Fernandez .12 .30
175 Sammy Sosa .30 .75
176 Geoff Jenkins .12 .30
177 Adrian Beltre .30 .75
178 Jay Bell .12 .30
179 Mike Bordick .12 .30
180 Ed Sprague .12 .30
181 Dave Roberts .20 .50
182 Greg Vaughn .12 .30
183 Brian Daubach .12 .30
184 Damion Easley .12 .30
185 Carlos Febles .12 .30
186 Kevin Tapani .12 .30
187 Frank Thomas .30 .75
188 Roger Clemens .40 1.00
189 Mike Benjamin .12 .30
190 Curt Schilling .20 .50
191 Edgardo Alfonzo .12 .30
192 Mike Mussina .20 .50
193 Todd Helton .20 .50
194 Todd Jones .12 .30
195 Dean Palmer .12 .30
196 John Flaherty .12 .30
197 Derek Jeter .75 2.00
198 Todd Walker .12 .30
199 Brad Ausmus .12 .30
200 Mark McGwire .50 1.25
201 Erubiel Durazo SP .75 2.00
202 Nick Johnson SP .75 2.00
203 Ruben Mateo SP .75 2.00
204 Lance Berkman SP 1.25 3.00
205 Pat Burrell SP .75 2.00
206 Pablo Ozuna SP .75 2.00
207 Roosevelt Brown SP .75 2.00
208 Alfonso Soriano SP 2.00 5.00
209 A.J. Burnett SP .75 2.00
210 Rafael Furcal SP 1.25 3.00
211 Scott Morgan SP .75 2.00
212 Adam Piatt SP .75 2.00
213 Dee Brown SP .75 2.00
214 Corey Patterson SP .75 2.00
215 Mickey Lopez SP .75 2.00
216 Rob Ryan SP .75 2.00
217 Sean Burroughs SP .75 2.00
218 Jack Cust SP .75 2.00
219 John Patterson SP .75 2.00
220 Kit Pellow SP .75 2.00
221 Chad Hermansen SP .75 2.00
222 Daryle Ward SP .75 2.00
223 Jayson Werth SP 1.25 3.00
224 Jason Standridge SP .75 2.00
225 Mark Mulder SP .75 2.00
226 Peter Bergeron SP .75 2.00
227 Willi Mo Pena SP .75 2.00
228 Aramis Ramirez SP .75 2.00
229 John Sneed SP RC .75 2.00
230 Wilton Veras SP .75 2.00
231 Josh Hamilton 2.50 6.00
232 Eric Munson SP .75 2.00
233 Bobby Bradley SP RC .75 2.00
234 Larry Bigbie SP RC .75 2.00
235 B.J. Garbe SP RC .75 2.00
236 Brett Myers SP RC 2.50 6.00
237 Jason Stumm SP RC .75 2.00
238 Corey Myers SP RC .75 2.00
239 Ryan Christianson SP RC .75 2.00
240 David Walling SP .75 2.00
241 Josh Girdley SP .75 2.00
242 Omar Ortiz SP .75 2.00
243 Jason Jennings SP .75 2.00
244 Kyle Snyder SP .75 2.00
245 Jay Gehrke SP .75 2.00
246 Mike Paradis SP .75 2.00
247 Chance Caple SP RC .75 2.00
248 Ben Christensen SP RC .75 2.00
249 Brad Baker SP RC .75 2.00
250 Rick Asadoorian SP RC .75 2.00

2000 Stadium Club First Day Issue

*1ST DAY: 10X TO 25X BASIC
*SP'S 201-250: 1.5X TO 4X BASIC
STATED ODDS 1:36 RETAIL
STATED PRINT RUN 150 SERIAL #'d SETS

2000 Stadium Club One of a Kind

*ONE.KIND 1-250: 10X TO 25X BASIC
*ONE 201-250: 1.5X TO 4X BASIC
STATED ODDS 1:27 HOBBY, 1:11 HTC
STATED PRINT RUN 150 SERIAL #'d SETS

2000 Stadium Club Bats of Brilliance

COMPLETE SET (10) 8.00 20.00
STATED ODDS 1:12 HOB, 1:15 RET, 1:6 HTC
*DIE CUTS: 1.25X TO 3X BASIC BATS
DIE CUT ODDS 1:60 HOB, 1:75 RET, 1:30 HTC
BB1 Mark McGwire 1.50 4.00
BB2 Sammy Sosa .60 1.50
BB3 Jose Canseco .40 1.00
BB4 Jeff Bagwell .40 1.00
BB5 Ken Griffey Jr. 1.25 3.00
BB6 Nomar Garciaparra 1.00 2.50
BB7 Mike Piazza 1.00 2.50
BB8 Alex Rodriguez 1.00 2.50
BB9 Vladimir Guerrero .60 1.50
BB10 Chipper Jones .60 1.50

2000 Stadium Club Capture the Action

COMPLETE SET (20) 15.00 40.00
STATED ODDS 1:12 HOB/RET, 1:6 HTC
*GAME VIEW: 5X TO 12X BASIC CAPTURE
GAME VIEW ODDS 1:508 HOB, 1:203 HTC
GAME VIEW PRINT RUN 100 SERIAL #'d SETS
CA1 Josh Hamilton 1.25 3.00
CA2 Pat Burrell .40 1.00
CA3 Erubiel Durazo .40 1.00
CA4 Alfonso Soriano 1.00 2.50
CA5 A.J. Burnett .40 1.00
CA6 Alex Rodriguez 1.25 3.00
CA7 Sean Casey .40 1.00
CA8 Derek Jeter 2.50 6.00
CA9 Vladimir Guerrero .60 1.50
CA10 Nomar Garciaparra .60 1.50
CA11 Mike Piazza 1.00 2.50
CA12 Ken Griffey Jr. 2.00 5.00

CA13 Sammy Sosa 1.00 2.50
CA14 Juan Gonzalez .40 1.00
CA15 Mark McGwire 1.50 4.00
CA16 Ivan Rodriguez .60 1.50
CA17 Barry Bonds 1.50 4.00
CA18 Wade Boggs .60 1.50
CA19 Tony Gwynn 1.00 2.50
CA20 Cal Ripken 3.00 8.00

2000 Stadium Club Chrome Preview

COMPLETE SET (20) 20.00 50.00
STATED ODDS 1:24 HOB/RET, 1:12 HTC
*REFRACTOR: 1.25X TO 3X BASIC CHR.PREV.
REFRACTOR ODDS 1:120 HOB/RET, 1:60 HTC
SCC1 Nomar Garciaparra 1.00 2.50
SCC2 Juan Gonzalez .60 1.50
SCC3 Chipper Jones 1.50 4.00
SCC4 Alex Rodriguez 2.00 5.00
SCC5 Ivan Rodriguez 1.00 2.50
SCC6 Manny Ramirez 1.50 4.00
SCC7 Ken Griffey Jr. 3.00 8.00
SCC8 Vladimir Guerrero 1.00 2.50
SCC9 Mike Piazza 1.50 4.00
SCC10 Pedro Martinez 1.00 2.50
SCC11 Jeff Bagwell 1.00 2.50
SCC12 Barry Bonds 2.50 6.00
SCC13 Sammy Sosa 1.50 4.00
SCC14 Derek Jeter 4.00 10.00
SCC15 Mark McGwire 2.50 6.00
SCC16 Erubiel Durazo .60 1.50
SCC17 Nick Johnson .60 1.50
SCC18 Pat Burrell .60 1.50
SCC19 Alfonso Soriano 1.50 4.00
SCC20 Adam Piatt .60 1.50

2000 Stadium Club Co-Signers

A ODDS 1:10,184 HOB, 1:4060 HTC
B ODDS 1:5,092 HOB, 1:2,030 HTC
C ODDS 1:508 HOB, 1:203 HTC
CO1 A.Rodriguez/D.Jeter A 300.00 600.00
CO2 D.Jeter/O.Vizquel B 150.00 300.00
CO3 A.Rodriguez/R.Ordonez B 90.00 150.00
CO4 D.Jeter/R.Ordonez B 100.00 175.00
CO5 O.Vizquel/A.Rodriguez B 90.00 150.00
CO6 R.Ordonez/O.Vizquel C 15.00 40.00
CO7 W.Boggs/R.Ventura C 15.00 40.00
CO8 R.Johnson/M.Mussina C 30.00 80.00
CO9 P.Burrell/M.Ordonez C 10.00 25.00
CO10 C.Hermansen/P.Burrell C 6.00 15.00
CO11 M.Ordonez/C.Herm C 10.00 25.00
CO12 J.Hamilton/C.Myers C 12.00 30.00
CO13 B.Garbe/J.Hamilton C 40.00 80.00
CO14 C.Myers/B.Garbe C 6.00 15.00
CO15 T.Martinez/F.McGriff C 20.00 50.00

2000 Stadium Club Lone Star Signatures

G1 ODDS 1:1,979 HOB, 1:1981 RET, 1:792 HTC
G2 ODDS 1:2,374 HOB,1:2,421 RET,1:946 HTC
G3 ODDS 1:1,979 HOB, 1:1981 RET, 1:792 HTC
G4 ODDS 1:424 HOB, 1:423 RET, 1:169 HTC
LS1 Derek Jeter G1 150.00 400.00
LS2 Alex Rodriguez G1 40.00 80.00
LS3 Wade Boggs G1 20.00 50.00
LS4 Robin Ventura G1 10.00 25.00
LS5 Randy Johnson G2 40.00 80.00
LS6 Mike Mussina G2 10.00 25.00
LS7 Tino Martinez G3 20.00 50.00
LS8 Fred McGriff G3 6.00 15.00
LS9 Omar Vizquel G4 12.50 30.00
LS10 Rey Ordonez G4 4.00 10.00
LS11 Pat Burrell G4 6.00 15.00
LS12 Chad Hermansen G4 4.00 10.00
LS13 Magglio Ordonez G4 6.00 15.00
LS14 Josh Hamilton 30.00 60.00
LS15 Corey Myers G4 4.00 10.00
LS16 B.J. Garbe G4 4.00 10.00

2000 Stadium Club Onyx Extreme

COMPLETE SET (10) 8.00 20.00
STATED ODDS 1:12 HOB, 1:15 RET, 1:6 HTC
*DIE CUTS: 1.25X TO 3X BASIC ONYX
DIE CUT ODDS 1:60 HOB, 1:75 RET, 1:30 HTC
OE1 Ken Griffey Jr. 2.00 5.00
OE2 Derek Jeter 2.50 6.00
OE3 Vladimir Guerrero .60 1.50
OE4 Nomar Garciaparra .60 1.50
OE5 Barry Bonds 1.50 4.00
OE6 Alex Rodriguez 1.25 3.00
OE7 Sammy Sosa 1.00 2.50
OE8 Ivan Rodriguez .60 1.50
OE9 Larry Walker .60 1.50
OE10 Andruw Jones .40 1.00

2000 Stadium Club Scenes

COMPLETE SET (8) 10.00 25.00
ONE PER HOBBY/HTC BOX CHIP-TOPPER
SCS1 Mark McGwire 1.50 4.00
SCS2 Alex Rodriguez 1.25 3.00
SCS3 Cal Ripken 3.00 8.00
SCS4 Sammy Sosa 1.00 2.50
SCS5 Derek Jeter 2.50 6.00
SCS6 Ken Griffey Jr. 2.00 5.00
SCS7 Nomar Garciaparra .60 1.50
SCS8 Chipper Jones 1.00 2.50

2000 Stadium Club Souvenir

STATED ODDS 1:339 HOB, 1:136 HTC
S1 Wade Boggs 10.00 25.00
S2 Edgardo Alfonzo 4.00 10.00
S3 Robin Ventura 6.00 15.00

2000 Stadium Club 3 X 3 Luminous

COMPLETE SET (30) 25.00 50.00
STATED ODDS 1:18 HOB, 1:24 RET, 1:9 HTC
*ILLUMINATOR: 1.5X TO 4X LUMINOUS
ILLUM ODDS 1:144 HOB, 1:192 RET, 1:72 HTC
*L'SCENT: .75X TO 2X LUMINOUS
L'SCENT ODDS 1:72 HOB, 1:96 RET, 1:36 HTC
1A Randy Johnson 1.50 4.00
1B Pedro Martinez 1.00 2.50
1C Greg Maddux 2.00 5.00
2A Mike Piazza 1.50 4.00
2B Ivan Rodriguez 1.00 2.50
2C Mike Lieberthal .60 1.50
3A Mark McGwire 2.50 6.00
3B Jeff Bagwell 1.00 2.50
3C Sean Casey .60 1.50
4A Craig Biggio 1.00 2.50
4B Roberto Alomar 1.00 2.50
4C Jay Bell .60 1.50
5A Chipper Jones 1.50 4.00
5B Matt Williams .60 1.50
5C Robin Ventura .60 1.50
6A Alex Rodriguez 2.00 5.00
6B Derek Jeter 4.00 10.00
6C Nomar Garciaparra 1.00 2.50
7A Barry Bonds 2.50 6.00
7B Luis Gonzalez .60 1.50
7C Dante Bichette .60 1.50
8A Ken Griffey Jr. 3.00 8.00
8B Bernie Williams 1.00 2.50
8C Andruw Jones .60 1.50
9A Manny Ramirez 1.50 4.00
9B Sammy Sosa 1.50 4.00
9C Juan Gonzalez .60 1.50
10A Jose Canseco 1.00 2.50
10B Frank Thomas 1.50 4.00
10C Rafael Palmeiro 1.00 2.50

2001 Stadium Club Pre-Production

COMPLETE SET (3) 1.20 3.00
PP1 Andruw Jones .60 1.50
PP2 Jorge Posada .30 .75
PP3 Jeff Bagwell .60 1.50

2001 Stadium Club

COMPLETE SET (200) 50.00 120.00
COMP.SET w/o SP's (175) 10.00 25.00
SP STATED ODDS 1:6
SP's: 153/156-157/161-162/166-170/186-200
1 Nomar Garciaparra .20 .50
2 Chipper Jones .30 .75
3 Jeff Bagwell .20 .50
4 Chad Kreuter .12 .30
5 Randy Johnson .30 .75
6 Mike Hampton .12 .30
7 Barry Larkin .20 .50
8 Bernie Williams .20 .50
9 Chris Singleton .12 .30
10 Larry Walker .20 .50
11 Brad Ausmus .12 .30
12 Ron Coomer .12 .30
13 Edgardo Alfonzo .12 .30
14 Delino DeShields .12 .30
15 Tony Gwynn .30 .75
16 Andruw Jones .20 .50
17 Raul Mondesi .12 .30
18 Troy Glaus .12 .30
19 Ben Grieve .12 .30
20 Sammy Sosa .20 .50
21 Fernando Vina .12 .30
22 Jeromy Burnitz .12 .30
23 Jay Bell .12 .30
24 Pete Harnisch .12 .30
25 Barry Bonds .50 1.25
26 Eric Karros .12 .30
27 Alex Gonzalez .12 .30
28 Mike Lieberthal .12 .30
29 Juan Encarnacion .12 .30
30 Derek Jeter .75 2.00
31 Luis Sojo .12 .30
32 Eric Milton .12 .30
33 Aaron Boone .12 .30
34 Roberto Alomar .20 .50
35 John Olerud .12 .30
36 Orlando Cabrera .12 .30
37 Shawn Green .12 .30
38 Roger Cedeno .12 .30
39 Garret Anderson .12 .30
40 Jim Thome .20 .50
41 Gabe Kapler .12 .30
42 Mo Vaughn .12 .30
43 Sean Casey .12 .30
44 Preston Wilson .12 .30
45 Javy Lopez .12 .30
46 Ryan Klesko .12 .30
47 Ray Durham .12 .30
48 Dean Palmer .12 .30
49 Jorge Posada .20 .50
50 Alex Rodriguez .40 1.00
51 Tom Glavine .20 .50
52 Ray Lankford .12 .30
53 Jose Canseco .20 .50
54 Tim Salmon .20 .50
55 Cal Ripken 1.00 2.50
56 Bob Abreu .12 .30
57 Robin Ventura .12 .30
58 Damion Easley .12 .30
59 Paul O'Neill .20 .50
60 Ivan Rodriguez .20 .50
61 Carl Everett .12 .30
62 Doug Glanville .12 .30
63 Jeff Kent .12 .30
64 Jay Buhner .12 .30
65 Cliff Floyd .12 .30
66 Rick Ankiel .12 .30
67 Mark Grace .20 .50
68 Brian Jordan .12 .30
69 Craig Biggio .20 .50
70 Carlos Delgado .12 .30
71 Brad Radke .12 .30
72 Greg Maddux .50 1.25
73 Al Leiter .12 .30
74 Pokey Reese .12 .30
75 Todd Helton .20 .50
76 Mariano Rivera .30 .75
77 Shane Spencer .12 .30
78 Jason Kendall .12 .30
79 Chuck Knoblauch .12 .30
80 Scott Rolen .20 .50
81 Jose Offerman .12 .30
82 J.T. Snow .12 .30
83 Pat Meares .12 .30
84 Quilvio Veras .12 .30
85 Edgar Renteria .12 .30
86 Luis Matos .12 .30
87 Adrian Beltre .30 .75
88 Luis Gonzalez .12 .30
89 Rickey Henderson .30 .75
90 Brian Giles .12 .30
91 Carlos Febles .12 .30
92 Tino Martinez .20 .50
93 Magglio Ordonez .12 .30
94 Rafael Furcal .12 .30
95 Mike Mussina .20 .50
96 Gary Sheffield .12 .30
97 Kenny Lofton .12 .30
98 Fred McGriff .20 .50
99 Ken Caminiti .12 .30
100 Mark McGwire .50 1.25
101 Tom Goodwin .12 .30
102 Mark Grudzielanek .12 .30
103 Derek Bell .12 .30
104 Mike Lowell .12 .30
105 Jeff Cirillo .12 .30
106 Orlando Hernandez .12 .30
107 Jose Valentin .12 .30
108 Warren Morris .12 .30
109 Mike Williams .12 .30
110 Greg Zaun .12 .30
111 Jose Vidro .12 .30
112 Omar Vizquel .20 .50
113 Vinny Castilla .12 .30
114 Gregg Jefferies .12 .30
115 Kevin Brown .12 .30
116 Shannon Stewart .12 .30
117 Marquis Grissom .12 .30
118 Manny Ramirez .30 .75
119 Albert Belle .12 .30
120 Bret Boone .12 .30
121 Johnny Damon .20 .50
122 Juan Gonzalez .12 .30
123 David Justice .12 .30
124 Jeffrey Hammonds .12 .30
125 Ken Griffey Jr. .60 1.50
126 Mike Sweeney .12 .30
127 Tony Clark .12 .30
128 Todd Zeile .12 .30
129 Mark Johnson .12 .30
130 Matt Williams .12 .30
131 Geoff Jenkins .12 .30
132 Jason Giambi .12 .30
133 Steve Finley .12 .30
134 Derrek Lee .12 .30
135 Royce Clayton .12 .30
136 Joe Randa .12 .30
137 Rafael Palmeiro .20 .50
138 Kevin Young .12 .30
139 Mike Redmond .12 .30
140 Vladimir Guerrero .30 .75
141 Greg Vaughn .12 .30
142 Jermaine Dye .12 .30
143 Roger Clemens .50 1.25
144 Denny Hocking .12 .30
145 Frank Thomas .30 .75
146 Carlos Beltran .12 .30
147 Eric Young .12 .30
148 Pat Burrell .12 .30
149 Pedro Martinez .20 .50
150 Mike Piazza .30 .75
151 Adrian Gonzalez 1.25 3.00
152 Adam Johnson .20 .50
153 Luis Montanez SP RC 1.25 3.00
154 Mike Stodolka .20 .50
155 Phil Dumatrait .20 .50
156 Sean Burnett SP 1.25 3.00
157 Dominic Rich SP RC 1.25 3.00
158 Adam Wainwright .30 .75
159 Scott Thorman .20 .50
160 Scott Heard SP 1.25 3.00
161 Chad Petty SP RC 1.25 3.00
162 Matt Wheatland .20 .50
163 Bryan Digby .20 .50
164 Rocco Baldelli .20 .50
165 Grady Sizemore .75 2.00
166 Brian Sellier SP RC 1.25 3.00
167 Rick Brosseau SP RC 1.25 3.00
168 Shawn Fagan SP RC 1.25 3.00
169 Sean Smith SP 1.25 3.00
170 Chris Bass SP RC 1.25 3.00
171 Corey Patterson .20 .50
172 Sean Burroughs .20 .50
173 Ben Petrick .20 .50
174 Mike Glendenning .20 .50
175 Barry Zito .30 .75
176 Milton Bradley .20 .50
177 Bobby Bradley .20 .50
178 Jason Hart .20 .50
179 Ryan Anderson .20 .50
180 Ben Sheets .20 .50
181 Adam Everett .20 .50
182 Alfonso Soriano .30 .75
183 Josh Hamilton .30 .75
184 Eric Munson .20 .50
185 Chin-Feng Chen .20 .50
186 Tim Christman SP RC 1.25 3.00
187 J.R. House SP 1.25 3.00
188 Brandon Parker SP RC 1.25 3.00
189 Sean Fesh SP RC 1.25 3.00
190 Joel Pineiro SP 1.25 3.00
191 Oscar Ramirez SP RC 1.25 3.00
192 Alex Santos SP RC 1.25 3.00
193 Eddy Reyes SP RC 1.25 3.00
194 Mike Jacobs SP RC 3.00 8.00
195 Erick Almonte SP RC 1.25 3.00
196 Brandon Claussen SP RC 1.25 3.00
197 Kris Keller SP RC 1.25 3.00
198 Wilson Betemit SP RC 2.00 5.00
199 Andy Phillips SP RC 3.00 8.00
200 Adam Pettyjohn SP RC 1.25 3.00

2001 Stadium Club Beam Team

STATED ODDS 1:175 HOB, 1:68 HTA
STATED PRINT RUN 500 SERIAL #'d SETS
BT1 Sammy Sosa 5.00 12.00
BT2 Mark McGwire 12.50 30.00
BT3 Vladimir Guerrero 5.00 12.00
BT4 Chipper Jones 5.00 12.00
BT5 Manny Ramirez 3.00 8.00
BT6 Derek Jeter 15.00 40.00
BT7 Alex Rodriguez 6.00 15.00
BT8 Cal Ripken 15.00 40.00
BT9 Ken Griffey Jr. 10.00 25.00
BT10 Greg Maddux 8.00 20.00
BT11 Barry Bonds 12.50 30.00
BT12 Pedro Martinez 3.00 8.00
BT13 Nomar Garciaparra 8.00 20.00
BT14 Randy Johnson 5.00 12.00
BT15 Frank Thomas 5.00 12.00
BT16 Ivan Rodriguez 3.00 8.00
BT17 Jeff Bagwell 3.00 8.00
BT18 Mike Piazza 8.00 20.00
BT19 Todd Helton 3.00 8.00
BT20 Shawn Green 2.00 5.00
BT21 Juan Gonzalez 2.00 5.00
BT22 Larry Walker 2.00 5.00
BT23 Tony Gwynn 8.00 20.00
BT24 Pat Burrell 2.00 5.00
BT25 Rafael Furcal 2.00 5.00
BT26 Corey Patterson 2.00 5.00
BT27 Chin-Feng Chen 2.00 5.00
BT28 Sean Burroughs 2.00 5.00
BT29 Ryan Anderson 2.00 5.00
BT30 Josh Hamilton 4.00 10.00

2001 Stadium Club Capture the Action

COMPLETE SET (15) 8.00 20.00
STATED ODDS 1:8 HOB/RET, 1:2 HTA
*GAME VIEW: 10X TO 25X BASIC CAPTURE
GAME VIEW ODDS 1:577 HOBBY, 1:224 HTA
GAME VIEW PRINT RUN 100 SERIAL #'d SETS
CA1 Cal Ripken 1.50 4.00
CA2 Alex Rodriguez .60 1.50
CA3 Mike Piazza .75 2.00
CA4 Mark McGwire 1.25 3.00
CA5 Greg Maddux .75 2.00
CA6 Derek Jeter 1.25 3.00
CA7 Chipper Jones .50 1.25
CA8 Pedro Martinez .40 1.00
CA9 Ken Griffey Jr. 1.00 2.50
CA10 Nomar Garciaparra .75 2.00
CA11 Randy Johnson .50 1.25
CA12 Sammy Sosa .50 1.25
CA13 Vladimir Guerrero .50 1.25
CA14 Barry Bonds 1.25 3.00
CA15 Ivan Rodriguez .40 1.00

2001 Stadium Club Co-Signers

STATED ODDS 1:962 HOB, 1:374 HTA
CO1 N.Garciaparra D.Jeter 250.00 400.00
CO2 R.Alomar/E.Alfonzo 20.00 50.00
CO3 R.Ankiel/K.Millwood 15.00 40.00
CO4 C.Jones/T.Glaus 40.00 80.00
CO5 M.Ordonez/B.Abreu 15.00 40.00
CO6 A.Piatt/S.Burroughs 10.00 25.00
CO7 C.Patterson/N.Johnson 15.00 40.00
CO8 A.Gonzalez/R.Baldelli 20.00 50.00
CO9 A.Johnson/M.Stodolka 10.00 25.00

2001 Stadium Club Diamond Pearls

COMPLETE SET (20) 12.50 30.00
STATED ODDS 1:8 HOB/RET, 1:3 HTA
DP1 Ken Griffey Jr. 1.50 4.00
DP2 Alex Rodriguez 1.00 2.50
DP3 Derek Jeter 2.00 5.00
DP4 Chipper Jones .75 2.00
DP5 Nomar Garciaparra 1.25 3.00
DP6 Vladimir Guerrero .75 2.00
DP7 Jeff Bagwell .60 1.50
DP8 Cal Ripken 2.50 6.00
DP9 Sammy Sosa .75 2.00
DP10 Mark McGwire 2.00 5.00
DP11 Frank Thomas .75 2.00
DP12 Pedro Martinez .60 1.50
DP13 Manny Ramirez .60 1.50
DP14 Randy Johnson .75 2.00
DP15 Barry Bonds 2.00 5.00
DP16 Ivan Rodriguez .60 1.50
DP17 Greg Maddux 1.25 3.00
DP18 Mike Piazza 1.25 3.00
DP19 Todd Helton .60 1.50
DP20 Shawn Green .60 1.50

2001 Stadium Club King of the Hill Dirt Relic

STATED ODDS 1:20 HTA
KH1 Pedro Martinez 4.00 10.00
KH2 Randy Johnson 4.00 10.00
KH3 Greg Maddux ERR 4.00 10.00
KH4 Rick Ankiel ERR 3.00 8.00
KH5 Kevin Brown 3.00 8.00

2001 Stadium Club Lone Star Signatures

GROUP A ODDS 1:937 H/R 1:364 HTA
GROUP B ODDS 1:1010 H/R 1:392 HTA
GROUP C ODDS 1:1541 H/R 1:600 HTA
GROUP D ODDS 1:354 H/R 1:138 HTA
OVERALL ODDS 1:181 H/R, 1:70 HTA
LS1 Nomar Garciaparra A 20.00 50.00
LS2 Derek Jeter A 100.00 250.00
LS3 Edgardo Alfonzo A 10.00 25.00
LS4 Roberto Alomar A 10.00 25.00
LS5 Magglio Ordonez A 10.00 25.00
LS6 Bobby Abreu A 6.00 15.00
LS7 Chipper Jones A 30.00 60.00
LS8 Troy Glaus A 15.00 40.00
LS9 Nick Johnson B 6.00 15.00
LS10 Adam Piatt B 6.00 15.00
LS11 Sean Burroughs B 4.00 10.00
LS12 Corey Patterson B 4.00 10.00
LS13 Rick Ankiel C 10.00 25.00
LS14 Kevin Millwood C 6.00 15.00
LS15 Adrian Gonzalez D 8.00 20.00
LS16 Adam Johnson D 4.00 10.00
LS17 Rocco Baldelli D 6.00 15.00
LS18 Mike Stodolka D 4.00 10.00

2001 Stadium Club Play at the Plate Dirt Relic

STATED ODDS 1:10 HTA
CARD NUMBER PP9 DOES NOT EXIST
PP1 Mark McGwire ERR 15.00 40.00
PP2 Sammy Sosa ERR 2.50 6.00
PP3 Vladimir Guerrero 4.00 10.00
PP4 Ken Griffey Jr. ERR 8.00 20.00
PP5 Mike Piazza 4.00 10.00
PP6 Jeff Bagwell ERR 2.50 6.00
PP6 Chipper Jones ERR 4.00 10.00
PP7 Barry Bonds 6.00 15.00
PP8 Alex Rodriguez 5.00 12.00
PP10 N.Garciaparra ERR 2.50 6.00

2001 Stadium Club Prospect Performance

STATED ODDS 1:262 HOB/RET, 1:102 HTA
PRP1 Chin-Feng Chen 40.00 80.00
PRP2 Bobby Bradley 3.00 8.00
PRP3 Tomokazu Ohka 4.00 10.00
PRP4 Kurt Ainsworth 3.00 8.00
PRP5 Craig Anderson 3.00 8.00
PRP6 Josh Hamilton 6.00 15.00
PRP7 Felipe Lopez 4.00 10.00
PRP8 Ryan Anderson 3.00 8.00
PRP9 Alex Escobar 3.00 8.00
PRP10 Ben Sheets 6.00 15.00
PRP11 Ntema Ndungidi 3.00 8.00
PRP12 Eric Munson 3.00 8.00
PRP13 Aaron Myette 3.00 8.00
PRP14 Jack Cust 3.00 8.00
PRP15 Julio Zuleta 3.00 8.00
PRP16 Corey Patterson 3.00 8.00
PRP17 Carlos Pena 3.00 8.00
PRP18 Marcus Giles 4.00 10.00
PRP19 Travis Wilson 3.00 8.00
PRP20 Barry Zito 6.00 15.00

2001 Stadium Club Souvenirs

GROUP A BAT ODDS 1:849 H/R, 1:330 HTA
GROUP B BAT ODDS 1:2164 H/R, 1:847 HTA
JERSEY ODDS 1:216 H/R, 1:84 HTA
OVERALL ODDS 1:160 HOB, 1:62 HTA
SCS1 S.Rolen Bat A ERR 6.00 15.00
SCS2 Larry Walker Bat B 6.00 15.00
SCS3 Rafael Furcal Bat A 6.00 15.00
SCS4 Darin Erstad Bat A 6.00 15.00
SCS5 Mike Sweeney Jsy 4.00 10.00
SCS6 Matt Lawton Jsy ERR 4.00 10.00
SCS7 Jose Vidro Jsy ERR 4.00 10.00
SCS8 Pat Burrell Jsy ERR 4.00 10.00

2002 Stadium Club

COMP.SET w/o SP's (100) 12.50 30.00
COMMON CARD (1-100) .10 .30
COMMON CARD (101-125) 10.00 25.00
101-125 PRINT RUN 2999 SERIAL #'d SETS
101-115 ODDS 1:42 HOB, 1:50 RET, 1:7 HTA
116-125 ODDS 1:60 HOB, 1:74 RET, 1:11 HTA
BONDS AU BALL ODDS 1:147 HTA
BONDS AU BALL PRINT RUN 500
BONDS AU BALL EXCH.DEADLINE 11/30/03
1 Pedro Martinez .20 .50
2 Derek Jeter .75 2.00
3 Chipper Jones .30 .75
4 Roberto Alomar .20 .50
5 Albert Pujols 5.00 12.00
6 Bret Boone .10 .30
7 Alex Rodriguez .40 1.00
8 Jose Cruz Jr. .10 .30
9 Mike Hampton .10 .30
10 Vladimir Guerrero .30 .75
11 Jim Edmonds .10 .30
12 Luis Gonzalez .10 .30
13 Jeff Kent .10 .30
14 Mike Piazza .50 1.25
15 Ben Sheets .10 .30
16 Tsuyoshi Shinjo .10 .30
17 Pat Burrell - Rolen Photo .10 .30
18 Jermaine Dye .10 .30
19 Rafael Furcal .10 .30
20 Randy Johnson .30 .75
21 Carlos Delgado .10 .30
22 Roger Clemens .60 1.50
23 Eric Chavez .10 .30
24 Nomar Garciaparra .50 1.25
25 Ivan Rodriguez .20 .50
26 Juan Gonzalez .10 .30
27 Reggie Sanders .10 .30
28 Jeff Bagwell .20 .50
29 Kazuhiro Sasaki .10 .30
30 Larry Walker .10 .30
31 Ben Grieve .10 .30
32 David Justice .10 .30
33 David Wells .10 .30
34 Kevin Brown .10 .30
35 Miguel Tejada .10 .30
36 Jorge Posada .20 .50
37 Javy Lopez .10 .30
38 Cliff Floyd .10 .30
39 Carlos Lee .10 .30
40 Manny Ramirez .20 .50
41 Jim Thome .20 .50
42 Pokey Reese .10 .30
43 Scott Rolen .20 .50
44 Richie Sexson .10 .30
45 Dean Palmer .10 .30
46 Rafael Palmeiro .20 .50
47 Alfonso Soriano .10 .30
48 Craig Biggio .20 .50
49 Troy Glaus .10 .30
50 Andruw Jones .20 .50
51 Ichiro Suzuki .60 1.50
52 Kenny Lofton .10 .30
53 Hideo Nomo .30 .75
54 Magglio Ordonez .10 .30
55 Brad Penny .10 .30
56 Omar Vizquel .20 .50
57 Mike Sweeney .10 .30
58 Gary Sheffield .10 .30
59 Ken Griffey Jr. .60 1.50
60 Curt Schilling .10 .30
61 Bobby Higginson .10 .30
62 Terrence Long .10 .30
63 Moises Alou .10 .30
64 Sandy Alomar Jr. .10 .30
65 Cristian Guzman .10 .30
66 Sammy Sosa .30 .75
67 Jose Vidro .10 .30
68 Edgar Martinez .20 .50
69 Jason Giambi .10 .30
70 Mark McGwire .75 2.00
71 Barry Bonds .75 2.00
72 Greg Vaughn .10 .30
73 Phil Nevin .10 .30
74 Jason Kendall .10 .30
75 Greg Maddux .50 1.25
76 Jeromy Burnitz .10 .30
77 Mike Mussina .20 .50
78 Johnny Damon .20 .50
79 Shawn Green .10 .30
80 Jimmy Rollins .10 .30
81 Edgardo Alfonzo .10 .30
82 Barry Larkin .20 .50
83 Raul Mondesi .10 .30
84 Preston Wilson .10 .30
85 Mike Lieberthal .10 .30
86 J.D. Drew .10 .30
87 Ryan Klesko .10 .30
88 David Segui .10 .30
89 Derek Bell .10 .30
90 Bernie Williams .20 .50
91 Doug Mientkiewicz .10 .30
92 Rich Aurilia .10 .30
93 Ellis Burks .10 .30
94 Placido Polanco .10 .30
95 Darin Erstad .10 .30
96 Brian Giles .10 .30
97 Geoff Jenkins .10 .30
98 Kerry Wood .10 .30
99 Mariano Rivera .30 .75
100 Todd Helton .20 .50
101 Adam Dunn FS 10.00 25.00
102 Grant Balfour FS 10.00 25.00
103 Jae Seo FS 10.00 25.00
104 Hank Blalock FS 10.00 25.00
105 Chris George FS 10.00 25.00
106 Jack Cust FS 10.00 25.00
107 Juan Cruz FS 10.00 25.00
108 Adrian Gonzalez FS 10.00 25.00
109 Nick Johnson FS 10.00 25.00
110 Jeff DaVanon FS 10.00 25.00
111 Juan Diaz FS 10.00 25.00
112 Brandon Duckworth FS 10.00 25.00
113 Jason Lane FS 10.00 25.00
114 Seung Song FS 10.00 25.00
115 Morgan Ensberg FS 10.00 25.00
116 Marlyn Tisdale FY RC 10.00 25.00
117 Jason Botts FY RC 6.00 15.00
118 Henry Pichardo FY RC 10.00 25.00
119 John Rodriguez FY RC 10.00 25.00
120 Mike Peeples FY RC 10.00 25.00
121 Rob Bowen EFY RC 10.00 25.00
122 Jeremy Affeldt EFY 10.00 25.00
123 Jorge Buret EFY RC 10.00 25.00
124 Manny Ravelo EFY RC 10.00 25.00
125 Eudy Lajara EFY RC 10.00 25.00
NNO B.Bonds AU Ball 50.00 100.00

2002 Stadium Club All-Star Relics

GROUP 1 ODDS 1:477 H, 1:548 R, 1:80 HTA
GROUP 1 PRINT RUN 400 SERIAL #'d SETS
GROUP 2 ODDS 1:795 H, 1:915 R, 1:133 HTA
GROUP 2 PRINT RUN 800 SERIAL #'d SETS
GROUP 3 ODDS 1:199 H, 1:247 R, 1:33 HTA
GROUP 3 PRINT RUN 1200 SERIAL #'d SETS
GROUP 4 ODDS 1:199 H, 1:247 R, 1:33 HTA
GROUP 4 PRINT RUN 2400 SERIAL #'d SETS
GROUP 5 ODDS 1:265 H, 1:305 R, 1:44 HTA
GROUP 5 PRINT RUN 3600 SERIAL #'d SETS
GROUP 6 ODDS 1:397 H, 1:457 R, 1:67 HTA
GROUP 6 PRINT RUN 4800 SERIAL #'d SETS
SCASAP Albert Pujols Bat G2 6.00 15.00
SCASBB Barry Bonds Uni G6 12.50 30.00
SCASBG Brian Giles Bat G2 4.00 10.00
SCASCF Cliff Floyd Bat G1 4.00 10.00
SCASCG C.Guzman Bat G1 4.00 10.00
SCASCJ Chipper Jones Jsy G3 6.00 15.00
SCASEM Edgar Martinez Jsy G3 6.00 15.00
SCASIR Ivan Rodriguez Uni G4 6.00 15.00
SCASJG Juan Gonzalez Bat G1 4.00 10.00
SCASJK Jeff Kent Bat G1 4.00 10.00
SCASJO John Olerud Jsy G3 4.00 10.00
SCASJP Jorge Posada Bat G1 6.00 15.00
SCASKS Kaz Sasaki Jsy G3 4.00 10.00
SCASLW Larry Walker Jsy G4 4.00 10.00
SCASMA Moises Alou Bat G1 4.00 10.00
SCASMC Mike Cameron Bat G1 4.00 10.00
SCASMO Magg Ordonez Bat G1 4.00 10.00
SCASMP Mike Piazza Uni G3 15.00 40.00
SCASMR M.Ramirez Uni G5 6.00 15.00
SCASMS Mike Sweeney Bat G1 4.00 10.00
SCASRA Roberto Alomar Uni G5 4.00 10.00
SCASRJ Randy Johnson Jsy G4 6.00 15.00
SCASRK Ryan Klesko Jsy G3 4.00 10.00
SCASSC Sean Casey Bat G1 4.00 10.00
SCASTG Tony Gwynn Jsy G4 8.00 20.00
SCASTH Todd Helton Jsy G3 6.00 15.00
SCASBRB Bret Boone Bat G3 4.00 10.00
SCASLG3 Luis Gonzalez Bat G2 4.00 10.00

2002 Stadium Club Chasing 500-500

DUAL ODDS 1:3209 HOBBY, 1:1290 HTA
JSY ODDS 1:1072 HOBBY, 1:427 HTA
MULTIPLE ODDS 1:3209 HOBBY, 1:1290 HTA
C55BB1 Barry Bonds Dual 10.00 25.00
C55BB2 Barry Bonds Jsy/600 8.00 20.00
C55BB3 Barry Bonds Mult/200 15.00 40.00

2002 Stadium Club Passport to the Majors

BAT ODDS 1:795 HOB, 1:915 RET, 1:133 HTA
JSY/UNI ODDS 1:84 HOB, 1:96 RET, 1:14 HTA
BAT PRINT RUNS LISTED BELOW
JSY/UNI PRINT RUN 1200 SERIAL #'d SETS
PTMAG Andres Galarraga Jsy/1200 4.00 10.00
PTMAJ Andruw Jones Jsy/1200 6.00 15.00
PTMAP Albert Pujols Bat/450 20.00 50.00
PTMAS Alf Soriano Bat/400 4.00 10.00
PTMBA Bob Abreu Bat/450 4.00 10.00
PTMBC Bartolo Colon Uni/1200 4.00 10.00
PTMCL Carlos Lee Jsy/1200 4.00 10.00
PTMCP Chan Ho Park Jsy/1200 4.00 10.00
PTMEA Edgardo Alfonzo Jsy/1200 4.00 10.00
PTMIR Ivan Rodriguez Uni/1200 6.00 15.00
PTMJG Juan Gonzalez Jsy/1200 4.00 10.00
PTMJL Javier Lopez Jsy/1200 4.00 10.00
PTMKS Kazuhiro Sasaki Jsy/1200 4.00 10.00
PTMLW Larry Walker Jsy/1200 4.00 10.00
PTMMO Magglio Ordonez Jsy/1200 4.00 10.00
PTMMR Manny Ramirez Jsy/1200 6.00 15.00
PTMMT Miguel Tejada Bat/375 4.00 10.00
PTMPM Pedro Martinez Jsy/1200 6.00 15.00
PTMRA Roberto Alomar Uni/1200 6.00 15.00
PTMRF Rafael Furcal Jsy/1200 4.00 10.00
PTMRM Raul Mondesi Jsy/1200 4.00 10.00
PTMRP Rafael Palmeiro Jsy/1200 6.00 15.00
PTMSH Shig Hasegawa Jsy/1200 4.00 10.00
PTMTS Tsuy Shinjo Bat/400 4.00 10.00
PTMWB Wilson Betemit Bat/325 4.00 10.00

2002 Stadium Club Reel Time

COMPLETE SET (20) 15.00 40.00
STATED ODDS 1:8 H/R, 1:4 HTA
RT1 Luis Gonzalez .75 2.00
RT2 Derek Jeter 2.50 6.00
RT3 Ken Griffey Jr. 2.00 5.00
RT4 Alex Rodriguez 1.25 3.00
RT5 Barry Bonds 2.50 6.00
RT6 Ichiro Suzuki 2.00 5.00
RT7 Carlos Delgado .75 2.00
RT8 Manny Ramirez .75 2.00
RT9 Mike Piazza 1.50 4.00
RT10 Mark McGwire 2.50 6.00
RT11 Todd Helton .75 2.00
RT12 Vladimir Guerrero 1.00 2.50
RT13 Jim Thome .75 2.00
RT14 Rich Aurilia .75 2.00
RT15 Bret Boone .75 2.00
RT16 Roberto Alomar .75 2.00
RT17 Jason Giambi .75 2.00
RT18 Chipper Jones 1.00 2.50
RT19 Albert Pujols 2.00 5.00
RT20 Sammy Sosa 1.00 2.50

2002 Stadium Club Stadium Shots

COMPLETE SET (10) 10.00 25.00
STATED ODDS 1:12 H/R, 1:6 HTA
SS1 Sammy Sosa 1.00 2.50
SS2 Manny Ramirez 1.00 2.50
SS3 Jason Giambi 1.00 2.50
SS4 Mike Piazza 1.50 4.00
SS5 Barry Bonds 2.50 6.00
SS6 Ken Griffey Jr. 2.00 5.00
SS7 Juan Gonzalez 1.00 2.50
SS8 Jeff Bagwell 1.00 2.50
SS9 Jim Thome 1.00 2.50
SS10 Mark McGwire 2.50 6.00

2002 Stadium Club Stadium Slices Barrel Relics

GROUP A ODDS 1:4289 HOBBY, 1:1700 HTA
GROUP B ODDS 1:6768 HOBBY, 1:2680 HTA
GROUP C ODDS 1:6465 HOBBY, 1:2581 HTA
GROUP D ODDS 1:6101 HOBBY, 1:2489 HTA
SCSSAP Albert Pujols B/95 15.00 40.00
SCSSBB Barry Bonds C/100 40.00 80.00
SCSSBW Bern Williams A/100 12.50 30.00
SCSSIR Ivan Rodriguez D/105 12.50 30.00
SCSSLG Luis Gonzalez A/75 12.50 30.00

2002 Stadium Club Stadium Slices Handle Relics

GROUP A ODDS 1:3671 HOBBY, 1:1483 HTA
GROUP B ODDS 1:3580 HOBBY, 1:1422 HTA
GROUP C ODDS 1:3384 HOBBY, 1:1366 HTA
GROUP D ODDS 1:3209 HOBBY, 1:1290 HTA
GROUP E ODDS 1:3050 HOBBY, 1:1222 HTA
SCSSAP Albert Pujols C/190 10.00 25.00
SCSSBB Barry Bonds A/175 12.50 30.00
SCSSBW Bernie Williams E/210 8.00 20.00
SCSSIR Ivan Rodriguez B/180 8.00 20.00
SCSSLG Luis Gonzalez D/200 8.00 20.00

2002 Stadium Club Stadium Slices Trademark Relics

GROUP A ODDS 1:6101 HOBBY, 1:2489 HTA
GROUP B ODDS 1:5853 HOBBY, 1:2323 HTA
GROUP C ODDS 1:4922 HOBBY, 1:1991 HTA
GROUP D ODDS 1:4559 HOBBY, 1:1834 HTA
GROUP E ODDS 1:3800 HOBBY, 1:1515 HTA
PRINT RUNS B/WN 105-170 COPIES PER
PRINT RUN INFO PROVIDED BY TOPPS
SCSSAP Albert Pujols C/130 12.00 30.00
SCSSBB Barry Bonds A/105 20.00 50.00
SCSSBW Bernie Williams B/110 10.00 25.00
SCSSIR Ivan Rodriguez E/170 10.00 25.00
SCSSLG Luis Gonzalez D/140 10.00 25.00

2002 Stadium Club World Champion Relics

BAT ODDS 1:94 H, 1:108 R, 1:16 HTA
JERSEY ODDS 1:106 H, 1:122 R, 1:18 HTA
PANTS ODDS 1:795 H, 1:1022 R, 1:133 HTA
SPIKES 1:38,400 H, 1:51,696 R, 1:6335 HTA
WCAB Al Bumbry Bat 4.00 10.00
WCAL Al Leiter Jsy 6.00 15.00
WCAT Alan Trammell Bat 6.00 15.00
WCBB Bert Blyleven Jsy 6.00 15.00
WCBD Bucky Dent Bat 6.00 15.00
WCBM Bill Madlock Bat 6.00 15.00
WCBW Bernie Williams Bat 8.00 20.00
WCBRB Bob Boone Jsy 6.00 15.00
WCCC Chris Chambliss Bat 6.00 15.00
WCCJ Chipper Jones Bat 10.00 25.00
WCCK Chuck Knoblauch Bat 6.00 15.00
WCDB Don Baylor Bat 6.00 15.00
WCDC Dave Concepcion Bat 6.00 15.00
WCDJ David Justice Bat 6.00 15.00
WCDL Dave Lopes Bat 6.00 15.00
WCDP Dave Parker Bat 6.00 15.00
WCDW Dave Winfield Bat 6.00 15.00
WCED Eric Davis Bat 6.00 15.00
WCES Ed Sprague Jsy 4.00 10.00
WCEM1 Eddie Murray Bat 10.00 25.00
WCEM2 Eddie Murray Jsy 10.00 25.00
WCFM Fred McGriff Jsy 8.00 20.00
WCFV Fernando Valenzuela Bat 6.00 15.00
WCGB George Brett Bat 12.00 30.00
WCGF George Foster Bat 6.00 15.00
WCGH George Hendrick Bat 6.00 15.00
WCGL Greg Luzinski Bat 6.00 15.00
WCGM Greg Maddux Jsy 12.50 30.00
WCGC1 Gary Carter Bat 6.00 15.00
WCGC2 Gary Carter Jsy 6.00 15.00
WCHM Hal McRae Bat 6.00 15.00
WCJB Johnny Bench Bat 10.00 25.00
WCJC Joe Carter Jsy 6.00 15.00
WCJL Javy Lopez Bat 6.00 15.00
WCJO John Olerud Jsy 6.00 15.00
WCJP Jorge Posada Bat 8.00 20.00
WCJS John Smoltz Jsy 8.00 20.00
WCJV Jose Vizcaino Bat 4.00 10.00
WCJC1 Jose Canseco Yank Bat 8.00 20.00
WCJC2 Jose Canseco A's Bat 8.00 20.00
WCKG Ken Griffey Sr. Bat 8.00 20.00
WCKH Keith Hernandez Bat 6.00 15.00
WCKP Kirby Puckett Bat 15.00 40.00

WCKG1 Kirk Gibson Bat 6.00 15.00
WCKG2 Kirk Gibson Jsy 6.00 15.00
WCLW Lou Whitaker Bat 6.00 15.00
WCLVP Lou Piniella Bat 6.00 15.00
WCMA Moises Alou Bat 6.00 15.00
WCMS Mike Scioscia Bat 6.00 15.00
WCMW Mookie Wilson Bat 6.00 15.00
WCMJS Mike Schmidt Bat 10.00 25.00
WCOH Orel Hershiser Jsy 6.00 15.00
WCOS Ozzie Smith Bat 15.00 40.00
WCPG Phil Garner Bat 6.00 15.00
WCPM Paul Molitor Bat 6.00 15.00
WCPO Paul O'Neill Pants 8.00 20.00
WCRA Roberto Alomar Pants 8.00 20.00
WCRC Ron Cey Bat 6.00 15.00
WCRJ Reggie Jackson Bat 8.00 20.00
WCSB Scott Brosius Bat 6.00 15.00
WCTG Tom Glavine Jsy 8.00 20.00
WCTM Thurman Munson Bat 30.00 60.00
WCTP Tony Perez Bat 6.00 15.00
WCTLM Tino Martinez Bat 8.00 20.00
WCWB Wade Boggs Bat 8.00 20.00
WCWH Willie Hernandez Jsy 6.00 15.00
WCWR Willie Randolph Bat 6.00 15.00
WCWS Willie Stargell Bat 8.00 20.00

2003 Stadium Club

COMP.MASTER SET (150) 30.00 60.00
COMPLETE SET (125) 20.00 40.00
COMMON CARD (1-100) .12 .30
COMMON CARD (101-115) .20 .50
COMMON CARD (116-125) .40 1.00
1 Rafael Furcal .12 .30
2 Randy Winn .12 .30
3 Eric Chavez .12 .30
4 Fernando Vina .12 .30
5 Pat Burrell .12 .30
6 Derek Jeter .75 2.00
7 Ivan Rodriguez .20 .50
8 Eric Hinske .12 .30
9 Roberto Alomar .20 .50
10 Tony Batista .12 .30
11 Jacque Jones .12 .30
12 Alfonso Soriano .20 .50
13 Omar Vizquel .20 .50
14 Paul Konerko .20 .50
15 Shawn Green .12 .30
16 Garret Anderson .12 .30
17 Darin Erstad .12 .30
18 Johnny Damon .20 .50
19 Juan Gonzalez .12 .30
20 Luis Gonzalez .12 .30
21 Sean Burroughs .12 .30
22 Mark Prior .20 .50
23 Javier Vazquez .12 .30
24 Shannon Stewart .12 .30
25 Jay Gibbons .12 .30
26 A.J. Pierzynski .12 .30
27 Vladimir Guerrero .20 .50
28 Austin Kearns .12 .30
29 Shea Hillenbrand .12 .30
30 Magglio Ordonez .20 .50
31 Mike Cameron .12 .30
32 Tim Salmon .12 .30
33 Brian Jordan .12 .30
34 Moises Alou .12 .30
35 Rich Aurilia .12 .30
36 Nick Johnson .12 .30
37 Junior Spivey .12 .30
38 Curt Schilling .20 .50
39 Jose Vidro .12 .30
40 Orlando Cabrera .12 .30
41 Jeff Bagwell .20 .50
42 Mo Vaughn .12 .30
43 Luis Castillo .12 .30
44 Vicente Padilla .12 .30
45 Pedro Martinez .20 .50
46 John Olerud .12 .30
47 Tom Glavine .20 .50
48 Torii Hunter .12 .30
49 J.D. Drew .12 .30
50 Alex Rodriguez .40 1.00
51 Randy Johnson .30 .75
52 Richie Sexson .12 .30
53 Jimmy Rollins .20 .50
54 Cristian Guzman .12 .30
55 Tim Hudson .20 .50
56 Mark Buehrle .20 .50
57 Paul Lo Duca .12 .30
58 Aramis Ramirez .12 .30
59 Todd Helton .20 .50
60 Lance Berkman .20 .50
61 Josh Beckett .12 .30
62 Bret Boone .12 .30
63 Miguel Tejada .20 .50
64 Nomar Garciaparra .20 .50
65 Albert Pujols .40 1.00
66 Chipper Jones .30 .75
67 Scott Rolen .20 .50
68 Kerry Wood .12 .30
69 Jorge Posada .20 .50
70 Ichiro Suzuki .40 1.00
71 Jeff Kent .12 .30
72 David Eckstein .12 .30
73 Phil Nevin .12 .30
74 Brian Giles .12 .30
75 Barry Zito .20 .50
76 Andruw Jones .12 .30
77 Jim Thome .20 .50
78 Robert Fick .12 .30
79 Rafael Palmeiro .20 .50
80 Barry Bonds .50 1.25
81 Gary Sheffield .12 .30
82 Jim Edmonds .20 .50
83 Kazuhisa Ishii .12 .30
84 Jose Hernandez .12 .30
85 Jason Giambi .12 .30
86 Mark Mulder .12 .30
87 Roger Clemens .40 1.00
88 Troy Glaus .12 .30
89 Carlos Delgado .12 .30
90 Mike Sweeney .12 .30
91 Ken Griffey Jr. .60 1.50
92 Manny Ramirez .30 .75
93 Ryan Klesko .12 .30
94 Larry Walker .20 .50
95 Adam Dunn .20 .50
96 Raul Ibanez .20 .50
97 Preston Wilson .12 .30
98 Roy Oswalt .20 .50
99 Sammy Sosa .30 .75
100 Mike Piazza .30 .75
101H Jose Reyes FS .50 1.25
101R Jose Reyes FS .50 1.25
102H Ed Rogers FS .20 .50
102R Ed Rogers FS .20 .50
103H Hank Blalock FS .20 .50
103R Hank Blalock FS .20 .50
104H Mark Teixeira FS .30 .75
104R Mark Teixeira FS .30 .75
105H Orlando Hudson FS .20 .50
105R Orlando Hudson FS .20 .50
106H Drew Henson FS .20 .50
106R Drew Henson FS .20 .50
107H Joe Mauer FS .50 1.25
107R Joe Mauer FS .50 1.25
108H Carl Crawford FS .30 .75
108R Carl Crawford FS .30 .75
109H Marlon Byrd FS .20 .50
109R Marlon Byrd FS .20 .50
110H Jason Stokes FS .20 .50
110R Jason Stokes FS .20 .50
111H Miguel Cabrera FS 2.50 6.00
111R Miguel Cabrera FS 2.50 6.00
112H Wilson Betemit FS .20 .50
112R Wilson Betemit FS .20 .50
113H Jerome Williams FS .20 .50
113R Jerome Williams FS .20 .50
114H Walter Young FYP .20 .50
114R Walter Young FYP .20 .50
115H Juan Camacho FYP RC .40 1.00
115R Juan Camacho FYP RC .40 1.00
116H Chris Duncan FYP RC 1.25 3.00
116R Chris Duncan FYP RC 1.25 3.00
117H Franklin Gutierrez FYP RC 1.00 2.50
117R Franklin Gutierrez FYP RC 1.00 2.50
118H Adam LaRoche FYP .40 1.00
118R Adam LaRoche FYP .40 1.00
119H Manuel Ramirez FYP RC .40 1.00
119R Manuel Ramirez FYP RC .40 1.00
120H Il Kim FYP RC .40 1.00
120R Il Kim FYP RC .40 1.00
121H Wayne Lydon FYP RC .40 1.00
121R Wayne Lydon FYP RC .40 1.00
122H Daryl Clark FYP RC .40 1.00
122R Daryl Clark FYP RC .40 1.00
123H Sean Pierce FYP .40 1.00
123R Sean Pierce FYP .40 1.00
124H Andy Marte FYP RC .40 1.00
124R Andy Marte FYP RC .40 1.00
125H Matthew Peterson FYP RC .40 1.00
125R Matthew Peterson FYP RC .40 1.00

2003 Stadium Club Photographer's Proof

*PROOF 1-100: 4X TO 10X BASIC
*PROOF 101-115: 2.5X TO 6X BASIC
*PROOF 116-125: 1.25X TO 3X BASIC
1-100 ODDS 1:39 H, 1:23 HTA, 1:34 R
101-125 ODDS 1:61 H, 1:17 HTA, 1:92 R
STATED PRINT RUN 299 SERIAL #'d SETS

2003 Stadium Club Royal Gold

*GOLD 1-100: 1X TO 2.5X BASIC
*GOLD 101-115: 1X TO 2.5X BASIC
*GOLD 116-125: .75X TO 2X BASIC
STATED ODDS 1:1 HOB, 1:1 HTA
101-125 HOB/RET PHOTOS EQUAL VALUE

2003 Stadium Club Beam Team

STATED ODDS 1:12 HOB/RET, 1:2 HTA
BT1 Lance Berkman .60 1.50
BT2 Barry Bonds 1.50 4.00
BT3 Carlos Delgado .40 1.00
BT4 Adam Dunn .60 1.50
BT5 Nomar Garciaparra .60 1.50
BT6 Jason Giambi .40 1.00
BT7 Brian Giles .40 1.00
BT8 Shawn Green .40 1.00
BT9 Vladimir Guerrero .60 1.50
BT10 Todd Helton .60 1.50
BT11 Derek Jeter 2.50 6.00
BT12 Chipper Jones 1.00 2.50
BT13 Jeff Kent .40 1.00
BT14 Mike Piazza 1.00 2.50
BT15 Alex Rodriguez 1.25 3.00
BT16 Ivan Rodriguez .60 1.50
BT17 Sammy Sosa 1.00 2.50
BT18 Ichiro Suzuki 1.25 3.00
BT19 Miguel Tejada .60 1.50
BT20 Larry Walker .60 1.50

2003 Stadium Club Born in the USA Relics

BAT ODDS 1:76 H, 1:23 HTA, 1:89 R
JERSEY ODDS 1:52 H, 1:15 HTA, 1:61 R
UNIFORM ODDS 1:413 H, 1:126 HTA, 1:484 R
AB A.J. Burnett Jsy 4.00 10.00
AD Adam Dunn Bat 4.00 10.00
AR Alex Rodriguez Bat 10.00 25.00
BB Bret Boone Jsy 4.00 10.00
BF Brad Fullmer Bat 4.00 10.00
BL Barry Larkin Jsy 6.00 15.00
CB Craig Biggio Jsy 6.00 15.00
CF Cliff Floyd Bat 4.00 10.00
CJ Chipper Jones Jsy 6.00 15.00
CP Corey Patterson Bat 4.00 10.00
EC Eric Chavez Uni 4.00 10.00
EM Eric Milton Jsy 4.00 10.00
FT Frank Thomas Bat 6.00 15.00
GM Greg Maddux Jsy 6.00 15.00
GS Gary Sheffield Bat 4.00 10.00
JB Jeff Bagwell Jsy 6.00 15.00
JD Johnny Damon Bat 6.00 15.00
JDD J.D. Drew Bat 4.00 10.00
JE Jim Edmonds Jsy 4.00 10.00
JH Josh Hamilton 8.00 20.00
JNB Jeromy Burnitz Bat 4.00 10.00
JO John Olerud Jsy 4.00 10.00
JS John Smoltz Jsy 6.00 15.00
JT Jim Thome Jsy 6.00 15.00
KW Kerry Wood Bat 4.00 10.00
LG Luis Gonzalez Bat 4.00 10.00
MG Mark Grace Jsy 6.00 15.00
MP Mike Piazza Jsy 6.00 15.00
MV Mo Vaughn Bat 4.00 10.00
MW Matt Williams Bat 4.00 10.00
NG Nomar Garciaparra Bat 10.00 25.00
PB Pat Burrell Bat 4.00 10.00
PK Paul Konerko Bat 4.00 10.00
PW Preston Wilson Jsy 4.00 10.00
RA Rich Aurilia Jsy 4.00 10.00
RH Rickey Henderson Bat 6.00 15.00
RJ Randy Johnson Bat 6.00 15.00
RK Ryan Klesko Bat 4.00 10.00
RS Richie Sexson Bat 4.00 10.00
RV Robin Ventura Bat 4.00 10.00
SB Sean Burroughs Bat 4.00 10.00
SG Shawn Green Bat 4.00 10.00
SR Scott Rolen Bat 6.00 15.00
TC Tony Clark Bat 4.00 10.00
TH Todd Helton Bat 6.00 15.00
TJH Toby Hall Bat 4.00 10.00
TL Terrence Long Uni 4.00 10.00
TM Tino Martinez Bat 6.00 15.00
TRL Travis Lee Bat 4.00 10.00
WM Willie Mays Bat 12.50 30.00

2003 Stadium Club Clubhouse Exclusive

JSY ODDS 1:488 H, 1:178 HTA
BAT-JSY ODDS 1:2073 H, 1:758 HTA
BAT-JSY-SPK ODDS 1:2750 H, 1:1016 HTA
BAT-HAT-JSY-SPK ODDS 1:1016 HTA
CE1 Albert Pujols Jsy 8.00 20.00
CE2 Albert Pujols Bat-Jsy 15.00 40.00
CE3 Albert Pujols Bat-Jsy-Spike 50.00 100.00

2003 Stadium Club Co-Signers

GROUP A STATED ODDS 1: 339 HTA
GROUP B STATED ODDS 1:1016 HTA
MURAKAMI AU 50% ENGLISH/50% JAPAN
AM H.Aaron/W.Mays A 300.00 600.00
MI M.Murakami/K.Ishii B 175.00 300.00

2003 Stadium Club License to Drive Bat Relics

STATED ODDS 1:98 H, 1:29 HTA, 1:114 R
AB Adrian Beltre 4.00 10.00
AD Adam Dunn 4.00 10.00
AJ Andruw Jones 6.00 15.00
ANR Aramis Ramirez 4.00 10.00
AP Albert Pujols 8.00 20.00
AR Alex Rodriguez 10.00 25.00
BW Bernie Williams 6.00 15.00
CJ Chipper Jones 6.00 15.00
EC Eric Chavez 4.00 10.00
FT Frank Thomas 6.00 15.00
GS Gary Sheffield 4.00 10.00
IR Ivan Rodriguez 6.00 15.00
JG Juan Gonzalez 4.00 10.00
LB Lance Berkman 4.00 10.00
LG Luis Gonzalez 4.00 10.00
LW Larry Walker 4.00 10.00
MA Moises Alou 4.00 10.00
MP Mike Piazza 10.00 25.00
NG Nomar Garciaparra 10.00 25.00
RA Roberto Alomar 6.00 15.00
RP Rafael Palmeiro 6.00 15.00
SG Shawn Green 4.00 10.00
SR Scott Rolen 6.00 15.00
TH Todd Helton 6.00 15.00
TM Tino Martinez 6.00 15.00

2003 Stadium Club MLB Match-Up Dual Relics

STATED ODDS 1:485 H, 1:148 HTA, 1:570 R
AJ Andruw Jones 2.50 6.00
AP Albert Pujols 8.00 20.00
BB Bret Boone 2.50 6.00
GM Greg Maddux 8.00 20.00
TH Todd Helton 4.00 10.00

2003 Stadium Club Shots

STATED ODDS 1:24 HOB/RET, 1:4 HTA
SS1 Lance Berkman .60 1.50
SS2 Barry Bonds 1.50 4.00
SS3 Jason Giambi .40 1.00
SS4 Shawn Green .40 1.00
SS5 Miguel Tejada .60 1.50
SS6 Paul Konerko .60 1.50
SS7 Mike Piazza 1.00 2.50
SS8 Alex Rodriguez 1.25 3.00
SS9 Sammy Sosa 1.00 2.50
SS10 Gary Sheffield .40 1.00

2003 Stadium Club Stadium Slices Barrel Relics

AJ Andruw Jones 15.00 40.00
AP Albert Pujols 20.00 50.00
AR Alex Rodriguez 30.00 60.00
CD Carlos Delgado 10.00 25.00
GS Gary Sheffield 10.00 25.00
MP Mike Piazza 30.00 60.00
NG Nomar Garciaparra 12.50 30.00
RA Roberto Alomar 10.00 25.00
RP Rafael Palmeiro 15.00 40.00
TH Todd Helton 15.00 40.00

2003 Stadium Club Stadium Slices Handle Relics

STATED ODDS 1:237 HOB, 1:86 HTA
AJ Andruw Jones 8.00 20.00
AP Albert Pujols 10.00 25.00
AR Alex Rodriguez 12.50 30.00
CD Carlos Delgado 5.00 12.00
GS Gary Sheffield 5.00 12.00
MP Mike Piazza 12.50 30.00
NG Nomar Garciaparra 15.00 40.00
RA Roberto Alomar 8.00 20.00
RP Rafael Palmeiro 8.00 20.00
TH Todd Helton 8.00 20.00

2003 Stadium Club Stadium Slices Trademark Relics

STATED ODDS 1:415 HOB, 1:151 HTA
AJ Andruw Jones 10.00 25.00
AP Albert Pujols 12.50 30.00
AR Alex Rodriguez 15.00 40.00
CD Carlos Delgado 6.00 15.00
GS Gary Sheffield 6.00 15.00
MP Mike Piazza 15.00 40.00
NG Nomar Garciaparra 20.00 50.00
RA Roberto Alomar 10.00 25.00
RP Rafael Palmeiro 10.00 25.00
TH Todd Helton 10.00 25.00

2003 Stadium Club World Stage Relics

BAT ODDS 1:809 H, 1:246 HTA, 1:950 R
JSY ODDS 1:118 H, 1:36 HTA, 1:138 R
AB Adrian Beltre Jsy 3.00 8.00
AP Albert Pujols Jsy 8.00 20.00
AS Alfonso Soriano Bat 4.00 10.00
BK Byung-Hyun Kim Jsy 4.00 10.00
HN Hideo Nomo Bat 10.00 25.00
IR Ivan Rodriguez Jsy 4.00 10.00
KI Kazuhisa Ishii Jsy 3.00 8.00
KS Kazuhiro Sasaki Jsy 3.00 8.00
MT Miguel Tejada Jsy 3.00 8.00
TS Tsuyoshi Shinjo Bat 4.00 10.00

2008 Stadium Club

COMMON CARD(1-100) .40 1.00
COMMON 999 (1-100) .75 2.00
COMMON RC (1-150) .40 1.00
COMMON RC 999 (1-150) .60 1.50
COMMON AU RC (151-185) 4.00 10.00
AU RC A ODDS 1:3
AU RC B ODDS 1:8
EXCHANGE DEADLINE 10/31/2010
PRINTING PLATE ODDS 1:85 HOBBY
PRINT.PLATE AUTO ODDS 1:198 HOBBY
PLATE PRINT RUN 1 SET PER COLOR
BLACK-CYAN-MAGENTA-YELLOW ISSUED
NO PLATE PRICING DUE TO SCARCITY
1 Chase Utley .60 1.50
2 Tim Lincecum .60 1.50
3 Ryan Zimmerman/999 1.00 2.50
4 Todd Helton .60 1.50
5 Russell Martin .40 1.00
6 Curtis Granderson/999 1.00 2.50
7 Torii Hunter .40 1.00
8 Mark Teixeira .60 1.50
9 Alfonso Soriano/999 1.00 2.50
10 C.C. Sabathia .60 1.50
11 David Ortiz 1.00 2.50
12 Miguel Tejada/999 1.00 2.50
13 Alex Rodriguez 1.25 3.00
14 Prince Fielder .60 1.50
15 Alex Gordon/999 1.00 2.50
16 Jake Peavy .40 1.00
17 B.J. Upton .60 1.50
18 Michael Young/999 .60 1.50
19 Jason Bay .60 1.50
20 Jorge Posada .60 1.50
21 Jacoby Ellsbury/999 1.25 3.00
22 Nick Markakis .75 2.00
23 Tom Glavine .60 1.50
24 Justin Upton/999 1.00 2.50
25 Edinson Volquez .40 1.00
26 Miguel Cabrera 1.00 2.50
27 Carlos Lee/999 .60 1.50
28 Ryan Church .40 1.00
29 Delmon Young .60 1.50
30 Carlos Quentin/999 .60 1.50
31 Carl Crawford .60 1.50
32 Roy Halladay .60 1.50
33 Brandon Webb/999 1.00 2.50
34 Brian Roberts .40 1.00
35 Ken Griffey Jr. 2.00 5.00
36 Troy Tulowitzki/999 1.50 4.00
37 Hanley Ramirez .60 1.50
38 Hunter Pence .60 1.50
39 Johnny Damon/999 1.00 2.50
40 Eric Chavez .40 1.00
41 Adrian Gonzalez .60 1.50
42 Carlos Pena/999 1.00 2.50
43 Felix Hernandez .60 1.50
44 Magglio Ordonez .60 1.50
45 Josh Beckett/999 .60 1.50
46 Fausto Carmona .40 1.00
47 Chris Young .40 1.00
48 John Lackey/999 1.00 2.50
49 John Smoltz 1.00 2.50
50 David Wright .60 1.50
51 Ichiro Suzuki/999 2.00 5.00
52 Vernon Wells .40 1.00
53 Josh Hamilton .60 1.50
54 Albert Pujols/999 2.00 5.00
55 Dustin Pedroia 1.00 2.50
56 Garrett Atkins .40 1.00
57 Roy Oswalt/999 1.00 2.50
58 Jose Reyes .60 1.50
59 Derek Jeter 2.50 6.00
60 Scott Kazmir/999 1.00 2.50
61 Vladimir Guerrero .60 1.50
62 Joba Chamberlain .40 1.00
63 Kevin Youkilis/999 .60 1.50
64 Victor Martinez .60 1.50
65 Nick Swisher .60 1.50
66 Carlos Beltran/999 1.00 2.50
67 Joe Mauer .75 2.00
68 Gary Sheffield .40 1.00
69 Cole Hamels/999 1.25 3.00
70 Brian McCann .60 1.50
71 Grady Sizemore .60 1.50
72 Robinson Cano/999 1.00 2.50
73 Greg Maddux 1.25 3.00
74 Rich Harden .40 1.00
75 Ryan Howard/999 1.00 2.50
76 Johan Santana .60 1.50
77 Dan Uggla .40 1.00
78 Justin Verlander/999 1.50 4.00
79 Derrek Lee .40 1.00
80 Ryan Braun .60 1.50
81 Lance Berkman/999 1.00 2.50
82 Manny Ramirez 1.00 2.50
83 Chipper Jones 1.00 2.50
84 Daisuke Matsuzaka/999 1.00 2.50
85 Matt Holliday 1.00 2.50
86 Justin Morneau .60 1.50
87 Jimmy Rollins/999 1.00 2.50
88 Hideki Matsui 1.00 2.50
89 Pedro Martinez .60 1.50
90 Carlos Zambrano/999 1.00 2.50
91 Jackie Robinson 1.00 2.50
92 Mickey Mantle 3.00 8.00
93 Ty Cobb/999 2.50 6.00
94 J.DiMaggio Cut Out
95 Honus Wagner 1.00 2.50
96 Babe Ruth/999 4.00 10.00
97 Nolan Ryan 3.00 8.00
98 Roberto Clemente 2.50 6.00
99 Ted Williams/999 3.00 8.00
100 Tom Seaver .60 1.50
101a Luke Hochevar RC .60 1.50
101b Luke Hochevar VAR/999 1.00 2.50
102a Daric Barton/999 (RC) .60 1.50
102b Daric Barton VAR/999 (RC) .60 1.50
103a Nick Adenhart (RC) .40 1.00
103b Nick Adenhart VAR/999 .60 1.50
104a Gregor Blanco (RC) .40 1.00
104b Gregor Blanco VAR/999 .60 1.50
105a Chris Carter/999 (RC) 1.00 2.50
105b Chris Carter VAR/999 (RC) 1.00 2.50
106a Eric Hurley (RC) .40 1.00
106b Eric Hurley VAR/999 .60 1.50
107a Clayton Kershaw RC 12.00 30.00
107b Clayton Kershaw VAR/999 20.00 50.00
108a Evan Longoria/999 RC 2.50 6.00
108b Evan Longoria VAR/999 RC 2.50 6.00
109a Garrett Mock (RC) .40 1.00
109b Garrett Mock VAR/999 .60 1.50
110a David Purcey (RC) .40 1.00
110b David Purcey VAR/999 .60 1.50
111a Ryan Tucker/999 (RC) .60 1.50
111b Ryan Tucker VAR/999 (RC) .60 1.50
112a Joey Votto (RC) 3.00 8.00
112b Joey Votto VAR/999 5.00 12.00
113a Jeff Clement (RC) .60 1.50
113b Jeff Clement VAR/999 1.00 2.50
114a Michael Aubrey/999 RC 1.00 2.50
114b Michael Aubrey VAR RC/999 1.00 2.50
115a Brandon Boggs .60 1.50
115b Brandon Boggs VAR/999 1.00 2.50
116a Johnny Cueto RC 1.00 2.50
116b Johnny Cueto VAR/999 1.50 4.00
117a Hernan Iribarren/999 (RC) 1.00 2.50
117b Hernan Iribarren VAR/999 (RC) 1.00 2.50
118a Masahide Kobayashi RC .60 1.50
118b Masahide Kobayashi VAR/999 1.00 2.50
119a Jed Lowrie (RC) .40 1.00
119b Jed Lowrie VAR/999 .60 1.50
120a Greg Reynolds/999 RC 1.00 2.50
120b Greg Reynolds VAR/999 RC 1.00 2.50
121a Matt Tolbert RC .60 1.50
121b Matt Tolbert VAR/999 1.00 2.50
122a Jonathan Herrera RC .60 1.50
122b Jonathan Herrera VAR/999 1.00 2.50
123a J.R. Towles/999 RC 1.00 2.50
123b J.R. Towles VAR/999 RC 1.00 2.50
124a Armando Galarraga RC .60 1.50
124b Armando Galarraga VAR/999 1.00 2.50
125a Josh Banks (RC) .40 1.00
125b Josh Banks VAR/999 .60 1.50
126a Mitch Boggs/999 (RC) .60 1.50
126b Mitch Boggs VAR/999 (RC) .60 1.50
127a Blake DeWitt (RC) .60 1.50
127b Blake DeWitt VAR/999 1.00 2.50
128a Carlos Gonzalez (RC) 1.00 2.50
128b Carlos Gonzalez VAR/999 1.50 4.00
129a Elliot Johnson/999 (RC) .60 1.50
129b Elliot Johnson VAR/999 (RC) .60 1.50
130a Brian Barton RC .60 1.50
130b Brian Barton VAR/999 1.00 2.50
131a Sean Rodriguez (RC) .40 1.00
131b Sean Rodriguez VAR/999 .60 1.50
132a Kosuke Fukudome/999 RC 2.00 5.00
132b Kosuke Fukudome VAR/999 RC 2.00 5.00
133a Chin-Lung Hu (RC) .40 1.00
133b Chin-Lung Hu VAR/999 .60 1.50
134a Wladimir Balentien (RC) .40 1.00
134b Wladimir Balentien VAR/999 .60 1.50
135a Jeff Niemann/999 (RC) .60 1.50
135b Jeff Niemann VAR/999 (RC) .60 1.50
136a Jay Bruce (RC) 1.25 3.00
136b Jay Bruce VAR/999 2.00 5.00
137a Brandon Jones RC 1.00 2.50
137b Brandon Jones VAR/999 1.50 4.00
138a Justin Masterson/999 RC 1.50 4.00
138b Justin Masterson VAR/999 RC 1.50 4.00
139a Jayson Nix (RC) .40 1.00
139b Jayson Nix VAR/999 .60 1.50
140a Max Scherzer RC 4.00 10.00
140b Max Scherzer VAR/999 6.00 15.00
141a Mike Aviles/999 RC 1.00 2.50
141b Mike Aviles VAR/999 RC 1.00 2.50
142a Greg Smith RC .40 1.00
142b Greg Smith VAR/999 .60 1.50
143a Nick Blackburn RC .60 1.50
143b Nick Blackburn VAR/999 1.00 2.50
144a Justin Ruggiano/999 RC 1.00 2.50
144b Justin Ruggiano VAR/999 RC 1.00 2.50
145a Clay Buchholz .60 1.50
145b Clay Buchholz VAR/999 (RC) 1.00 2.50
146a German Duran RC .60 1.50
146b German Duran VAR/999 1.00 2.50
147a Radhames Liz/999 RC 1.00 2.50
147b Radhames Liz VAR/999 RC 1.00 2.50
148a Chris Perez RC .60 1.50
148b Chris Perez VAR/999 1.00 2.50
149a Hiroki Kuroda RC 1.00 2.50
149b Hiroki Kuroda VAR/999 1.50 4.00
150a Gregorio Petit RC .60 1.50
150b Gregorio Petit VAR/999 1.00 2.50
151 Emmanuel Burriss AU RC EXCH A 4.00 10.00
152 Elliot Johnson AU A 4.00 10.00
153 Jonathan Van Every AU RC A 4.00 10.00
154 Darren O'Day AU RC A 4.00 10.00
155 Matt Joyce AU RC A 6.00 15.00
156 Burke Badenhop AU RC A 4.00 10.00
157 Brent Lillibridge AU (RC) A 4.00 10.00
158 Johnny Cueto AU A 8.00 20.00
159 Jeff Niemann AU A 4.00 10.00
160 John Bowker AU (RC) A 4.00 10.00
161 Brandon Boggs AU A 4.00 10.00
162 Justin Masterson AU A 6.00 15.00
163 Masahide Kobayashi AU A 5.00 12.00
164 Nick Adenhart AU A 4.00 10.00
165 Chris Perez AU EXCH A 4.00 10.00
166 Gregor Blanco AU A 4.00 10.00
167 Travis Denker AU RC A 4.00 10.00
168 Jeff Clement AU EXCH A 4.00 10.00
169 Evan Longoria AU A 10.00 25.00
170 Greg Smith AU A 4.00 10.00
171 Jay Bruce AU (RC) B 6.00 15.00
172 Brian Barton AU B 6.00 15.00
173 Max Scherzer AU B 75.00 200.00
174 Blake DeWitt AU B 4.00 10.00
175 Jed Lowrie AU B 6.00 15.00
176 Clayton Kershaw AU B 75.00 200.00
177 Jonathan Albaladejo AU RC B 4.00 10.00
178 Josh Banks AU B 4.00 10.00
179 Brian Horwitz AU RC B 4.00 10.00
180 Micah Hoffpauir AU RC B 8.00 20.00
181 Robinzon Diaz AU (RC) B 4.00 10.00
182 Nick Evans AU RC B 6.00 15.00
183 J.Mather AU RC EXCH B 5.00 12.00
184 Danny Herrera AU RC B 4.00 10.00
185 Eugenio Velez AU RC B 4.00 10.00

2008 Stadium Club First Day Issue

*1ST DAY VET 1-100: .6X TO 1.5X BASIC
*1ST DAY RC 101-150: .6X TO 1.5X BASIC
APPX. ODDS TEN PER HOBBY BOX
STATED PRINT RUN 599 SER.#'d SETS

2008 Stadium Club First Day Issue Unnumbered

*1ST UNUM VET 1-100: .5X TO 1.2X BAS
*1ST UNUM RC 101-150: .5X TO 1.2X BAS
RANDOM INSERTS IN RETAIL BACKS

2008 Stadium Club Photographer's Proof Blue

*BLUE VET 1-100: 1X TO 2.5X BASIC
*BLUE 999 1-100: .6X TO 1.5X BASIC
*BLUE RC 101-150: 1X TO 2.5X BASIC
*BLUE 999 101-150: .6X TO 1.5X BASIC
NON-AU BLUE ODDS 1:5 HOBBY
*BLUE AU: .5X TO 1.2X BASIC
AU BLUE ODDS 1:29 HOBBY
BLUE PRINT RUN 99 SER.#'d SETS

2008 Stadium Club Photographer's Proof Gold

*GLD VET 1-100: 1.2X TO 3X BASIC
*GLD 999 1-100: .75X TO 2X BASIC
*GLD RC 101-150: 1.2X TO 3X BASIC
*GLD 999 101-150: .75X TO 2X BASIC
NON-AU GOLD ODDS 1:9 HOBBY
*GLD AU: .6X TO 1.5X BASIC
AU GOLD ODDS 1:62 HOBBY
GOLD PRINT RUN 50 SER.#'d SETS

2008 Stadium Club Beam Team Autographs

GROUP A ODDS 1:13 HOBBY
GROUP B ODDS 1:6 HOBBY
GROUP C ODDS 1:11 HOBBY
PRINTING PLATE ODDS 1:198 HOBBY
PLATE PRINT RUN 1 SET PER COLOR
BLACK-CYAN-MAGENTA-YELLOW ISSUED
NO PLATE PRICING DUE TO SCARCITY
EXCHANGE DEADLINE 10/31/2010
AG Adrian Gonzalez C 6.00 15.00
BH Brad Hawpe C 4.00 10.00
BP Brandon Phillips B 4.00 10.00
BT Brad Thompson C 8.00 20.00
CC Carl Crawford C 6.00 15.00
CCR Callix Crabbe C 4.00 10.00
CD Carlos Delgado C 6.00 15.00
CF Chone Figgins B 4.00 10.00
CM Carlos Marmol C 4.00 10.00
CMO Craig Monroe B 4.00 10.00
CP Carlos Pena C 6.00 15.00
CV Claudio Vargas C 4.00 10.00
CVI Carlos Villanueva B 4.00 10.00
CW C.J. Wilson B 4.00 10.00
DH Dan Haren C 6.00 15.00
DS Darryl Strawberry B 8.00 20.00
DY Delwyn Young A 4.00 10.00
ER Edwar Ramirez C 4.00 10.00
FL Francisco Liriano C 5.00 12.00
FP Felix Pie B 4.00 10.00
FS Freddy Sanchez C 4.00 10.00
GC Gary Carter C 10.00 25.00
GD German Duran B 4.00 10.00
GP Glen Perkins B 4.00 10.00
GS Gary Sheffield C 6.00 15.00
GSM Greg Smith C 4.00 10.00
JB Jason Bartlett C 4.00 10.00
JC Jack Cust C 5.00 12.00
JCR Jesse Crain A 4.00 10.00
JGA Joey Gathright C 4.00 10.00
JGU Jeremy Guthrie C 4.00 10.00
JH Josh Hamilton B 4.00 10.00
JJ Jair Jurrjens C 5.00 12.00
JL John Lackey B 5.00 12.00
JN Jayson Nix A 4.00 10.00
JP Jonathan Papelbon C 8.00 20.00
JPO Johnny Podres B 4.00 10.00
JR Jose Reyes C 8.00 20.00
JS Jeff Salazar B 4.00 10.00
KS Kevin Slowey B 5.00 12.00
LM Lastings Milledge B 4.00 10.00
ME Mark Ellis C 4.00 10.00
MK Mark Kotsay C 4.00 10.00
MN Mike Napoli C 4.00 10.00
MT Marcus Thames C 4.00 10.00
MTO Matt Tolbert A 4.00 10.00
NR Nate Robertson B 4.00 10.00
RC Robinson Cano B 6.00 15.00
RP Ronny Paulino B 4.00 10.00
TG Tom Gorzelanny C 4.00 10.00
TJ Todd Jones B 4.00 10.00
YP Yusmeiro Petit A 4.00 10.00

2008 Stadium Club Beam Team Autographs Black and White

*B AND W: .5X TO 1.2X BASIC
STATED ODDS 1:19 HOBBY
STATED PRINT RUN 99 SER.#'d SETS
EXCHANGE DEADLINE 10/31/2010

2008 Stadium Club Beam Team Autographs Gold

*GOLD: .5X TO 1.2X BASIC
STATED ODDS 1:40 HOBBY
STATED PRINT RUN 50 SER.#'d SETS
EXCHANGE DEADLINE 10/31/2010

2008 Stadium Club Ceremonial Cuts

STATED ODDS 1:34 HOBBY
STATED PRINT RUN 199 SER.#'d SETS
BR Babe Ruth 15.00 40.00
GB George Bush 10.00 25.00
JF Jimmie Foxx 8.00 20.00
JR Jackie Robinson 12.50 30.00
LG Lou Gehrig 15.00 40.00
MO Mel Ott 8.00 20.00
RH Rogers Hornsby 8.00 20.00
TC Ty Cobb 12.50 30.00
TW Ted Williams 12.50 30.00

2008 Stadium Club Ceremonial Cuts Photographer's Proof Blue

*BLUE: .5X TO 1.2X BASIC
STATED ODDS 1:28 HOBBY
STATED PRINT RUN 99 SER.#'d SETS

2008 Stadium Club Stadium Slices

STATED ODDS 1:23 HOBBY
PRINT RUNS B/WN 89-428 COPIES PER
AP Albert Pujols/428 10.00 25.00
AR Alex Rodriguez/89 30.00 60.00
DM Daisuke Matsuzaka/428 5.00 12.00
DO David Ortiz/428 4.00 10.00
GG Goose Gossage/89 15.00 40.00
HM Hideki Matsui/428 6.00 15.00
IS Ichiro Suzuki/428 10.00 25.00
JT Joe Torre/89 15.00 40.00
LP Lou Piniella/89 8.00 20.00
MM Mickey Mantle/89 15.00 40.00
MR Mariano Rivera/428 6.00 15.00
RJ Reggie Jackson/89 10.00 25.00
TM Thurman Munson/89 30.00 60.00
WF Whitey Ford/89 20.00 50.00
YB Yogi Berra/89 20.00 50.00

2008 Stadium Club Stadium Slices Photographer's Proof Blue

*BLUE: .5X TO 1.2X BASIC
STATED ODDS 1:28 HOBBY
PRINT RUNS B/WN 25-99 SER.#'d SETS
NO PRICING ON QTY 25 OR LESS

2008 Stadium Club Stadium Slices Photographer's Proof Gold

*GOLD: .5X TO 1.2X BASIC
STATED ODDS 1:55 HOBBY
PRINT RUNS B/WN 5-50 SER.#'d SETS
NO PRICING ON QTY 5 OR LESS

2008 Stadium Club Triumvirate Memorabilia Autographs

STATED ODDS 1:26 HOBBY
PRINT RUNS B/WN 49-99 SER.#'d SETS
EXCHANGE DEADLINE 10/31/2010
AD Adam Dunn 8.00 20.00
AP Albert Pujols 100.00 200.00
AR Aramis Ramirez 12.00 30.00
ARI Alex Rios 6.00 15.00
AS Alfonso Soriano 15.00 40.00
BU B.J. Upton 6.00 15.00
CC Carl Crawford 12.00 30.00
CL Carlos Lee 6.00 15.00
CW Chien-Ming Wang 30.00 60.00
DL Derrek Lee 12.00 30.00
DO David Ortiz 30.00 60.00
HR Hanley Ramirez 10.00 25.00
JF Jeff Francoeur 10.00 25.00
JM Justin Morneau 15.00 40.00
JP Jake Peavy 6.00 15.00
JPA Jonathan Papelbon 15.00 40.00
JU Justin Upton 8.00 20.00
MH Matt Holliday 12.00 30.00
MO Magglio Ordonez/49 6.00 15.00
MR Mariano Rivera 75.00 150.00
MT Miguel Tejada 10.00 25.00
RM Russ Martin 8.00 20.00
SK Scott Kazmir 8.00 20.00
TH Torii Hunter 12.00 30.00
TLH Todd Helton 10.00 25.00
TT Troy Tulowitzki 6.00 15.00
VG Vladimir Guerrero 12.00 30.00
VW Vernon Wells 10.00 25.00

2014 Stadium Club

COMPLETE SET (200) 25.00 60.00
1 Ken Griffey Jr. 1.00 2.50
2 Matt Holliday .50 1.25
3 Babe Ruth 1.25 3.00
4 Jon Singleton RC .40 1.00
5 Curtis Granderson .40 1.00
6 Shane Victorino .40 1.00
7 Adrian Gonzalez .40 1.00
8 Stephen Strasburg .50 1.25
9 Hisashi Iwakuma .40 1.00
10 Sergio Romo .30 .75
11 Max Scherzer .50 1.25
12 Gio Gonzalez .40 1.00
13 Stan Musial .75 2.00
14 Travis d'Arnaud RC .40 1.00
15 Mark Trumbo .30 .75
16 Nolan Arenado .75 2.00
17 Michael Cuddyer .30 .75
18 Derek Jeter 2.50 6.00
19 Jered Weaver .40 1.00
20 Ivan Rodriguez .40 1.00
21 Roy Halladay .40 1.00
22 Matt Adams .30 .75
23 John Smoltz .50 1.25
24 Anthony Rizzo .60 1.50
25 Edwin Encarnacion .50 1.25
26 Elvis Andrus .40 1.00
27 Lou Gehrig 1.00 2.50
28 Giancarlo Stanton .50 1.25
29 Jose Reyes .40 1.00
30 Andrew McCutchen .50 1.25

31 Todd Helton .40 1.00
32 Ernie Banks .50 1.25
33 Tony Cingrani .40 1.00
34 Jordan Zimmermann .40 1.00
35 Brian Dozier .40 1.00
36 Randy Johnson .50 1.25
37 Hunter Pence .40 1.00
38 Robinson Cano .40 1.00
39 Chase Utley .40 1.00
40 Justin Verlander .50 1.25
41 Shin-Soo Choo .40 1.00
42 Jackie Robinson .50 1.25
43 Pedro Martinez .40 1.00
44 Hank Aaron 1.00 2.50
45 Gregory Polanco RC .50 1.25
46 Rickey Henderson .50 1.25
47 Oscar Taveras RC .40 1.00
48 Jacoby Ellsbury .40 1.00
49 Michael Choice RC .30 .75
50 Mike Trout 2.50 6.00
51 Chris Davis .30 .75
52 Manny Machado .50 1.25
53 Willie Mays 1.00 2.50
54 Wil Myers .30 .75
55 Andrew Heaney RC .30 .75
56 Nick Castellanos RC 1.00 2.50
57 Jayson Werth .40 1.00
58 Zack Wheeler .40 1.00
59 Jonathan Schoop RC .30 .75
60 Albert Pujols .60 1.50
61 Alex Guerrero RC .40 1.00
62 Starling Marte .40 1.00
63 Billy Butler .30 .75
64 Tim Lincecum .40 1.00
65 Yu Darvish .50 1.25
66 Matt Cain .40 1.00
67 Ozzie Smith .60 1.50
68 Adrian Beltre .50 1.25
69 Freddie Freeman .60 1.50
70 Justin Upton .40 1.00
71 Ian Kinsler .40 1.00
72 Ty Cobb .75 2.00
73 Matt Carpenter .50 1.25
74 Josh Donaldson .40 1.00
75 Pablo Sandoval .40 1.00
76 Taijuan Walker RC .30 .75
77 Al Kaline .50 1.25
78 Josh Hamilton .40 1.00
79 Brandon Phillips .30 .75
80 Roger Clemens .60 1.50
81 Anibal Sanchez .30 .75
82 Evan Longoria .40 1.00
83 Brooks Robinson .40 1.00
84 Aroldis Chapman .50 1.25
85 Kolten Wong RC .40 1.00
86 David Wright .40 1.00
87 Joey Votto .50 1.25
88 Wilmer Flores RC .40 1.00
89 Yordano Ventura RC .40 1.00
90 Jose Altuve .40 1.00
91 Miguel Cabrera .50 1.25
92 CC Sabathia .40 1.00
93 Chris Owings RC .30 .75
94 George Springer RC 1.25 3.00
95 Mark McGwire 1.00 2.50
96 Johnny Cueto .40 1.00
97 Yasiel Puig .50 1.25
98 Victor Martinez .40 1.00
99 Trevor Rosenthal .40 1.00
100 Jose Abreu RC 2.50 6.00
101 Mike Napoli .30 .75
102 Adam Jones .40 1.00
103 Adam Eaton .30 .75
104 Nolan Ryan 1.50 4.00
105 Troy Tulowitzki .50 1.25
106 Eric Hosmer .40 1.00
107 Zack Greinke .50 1.25
108 Pedro Alvarez .30 .75
109 Jeff Bagwell .40 1.00
110 Xander Bogaerts RC 1.00 2.50
111 Duke Snider .40 1.00
112 Albert Belle .30 .75
113 Johnny Bench .50 1.25
114 Bob Feller .40 1.00
115 Jason Heyward .40 1.00
116 Andrelton Simmons .30 .75
117 Don Mattingly 1.00 2.50
118 Alex Gordon .40 1.00
119 Sonny Gray .40 1.00
120 Jose Bautista .40 1.00
121 Carlos Gonzalez .40 1.00
122 Craig Kimbrel .40 1.00
123 Andre Dawson .40 1.00
124 Billy Hamilton RC .40 1.00
125 Madison Bumgarner .40 1.00
126 Torii Hunter .30 .75
127 Roberto Clemente 1.25 3.00
128 Marcus Stroman RC .50 1.25
129 Hanley Ramirez .40 1.00
130 Starlin Castro .30 .75
131 Dustin Pedroia .50 1.25
132 Wilin Rosario .30 .75
133 Ted Williams 1.00 2.50
134 Carlos Beltran .40 1.00
135 Eddie Butler RC .30 .75
136 Jason Kipnis .40 1.00
137 Julio Teheran .40 1.00
138 Wade Boggs .40 1.00
139 Koji Uehara .30 .75
140 Mookie Betts RC 25.00 60.00
141 Evan Gattis .30 .75
142 Matt Harvey .40 1.00
143 Jean Segura .40 1.00
144 Yoenis Cespedes .50 1.25
145 Matt Kemp .40 1.00
146 Jay Bruce .40 1.00
147 Bo Jackson .50 1.25
148 Salvador Perez .40 1.00
149 Mike Piazza .50 1.25
150 Clayton Kershaw .75 2.00
151 Sandy Koufax 1.00 2.50
152 Nelson Cruz .50 1.25
153 Bryce Harper .75 2.00
154 Chris Sale .50 1.25
155 Michael Wacha .40 1.00
156 Prince Fielder .40 1.00
157 Jurickson Profar .40 1.00
158 Hyun-Jin Ryu .40 1.00
159 Mariano Rivera .60 1.50
160 Joe Mauer .40 1.00
161 Tony Gwynn .50 1.25
162 Jose Canseco .40 1.00
163 Masahiro Tanaka RC 1.00 2.50
164 Ryan Braun .40 1.00
165 Cole Hamels .40 1.00
166 Mat Latos .40 1.00
167 Domonic Brown .40 1.00
168 Adam Wainwright .40 1.00
169 Shelby Miller .40 1.00
170 Ryan Howard .40 1.00
171 Robin Yount .50 1.25
172 Arismendy Alcantara RC .30 .75
173 Mike Schmidt .75 2.00
174 Yadier Molina .60 1.50
175 Jose Fernandez .50 1.25
176 Jeff Samardzija .30 .75
177 Eddie Murray .40 1.00
178 Greg Maddux .60 1.50
179 Felix Hernandez .40 1.00
180 Ian Desmond .30 .75
181 C.J. Cron RC .30 .75
182 David Ortiz .50 1.25
183 Carlos Gomez .30 .75
184 Cliff Lee .40 1.00
185 Buster Posey .60 1.50
186 Carl Crawford .40 1.00
187 Christian Yelich .60 1.50
188 George Brett 1.00 2.50
189 David Price .40 1.00
190 Todd Frazier .30 .75
191 Gerrit Cole .50 1.25
192 Brett Lawrie .40 1.00
193 R.A. Dickey .40 1.00
194 Tom Seaver .40 1.00
195 Chris Archer .30 .75
196 Ryan Zimmerman .40 1.00
197 Cal Ripken Jr. 1.50 4.00
198 Carlos Santana .40 1.00
199 Paul Goldschmidt .50 1.25
200 Joe DiMaggio 1.00 2.50

2014 Stadium Club Electric Foil

*ELECTRIC: 1.5X TO 4X BASIC
*ELECTRIC RC: 1.5X TO 4X BASIC
STATED ODDS 1:9 MINI BOX
1 Ken Griffey Jr. 6.00 15.00
18 Derek Jeter 20.00 50.00
29 Jose Reyes 5.00 12.00
67 Ozzie Smith 6.00 15.00
100 Jose Abreu 8.00 20.00
104 Nolan Ryan 10.00 25.00
117 Don Mattingly 8.00 20.00
127 Roberto Clemente 6.00 15.00
159 Mariano Rivera 8.00 20.00
161 Tony Gwynn 5.00 12.00
173 Mike Schmidt 6.00 15.00
188 George Brett 6.00 15.00
197 Cal Ripken Jr. 6.00 15.00

2014 Stadium Club Foilboard

*FOILBOARD: 4X TO 10X BASIC
*FOILBOARD RC: 4X TO 10X BASIC
STATED ODDS 1:11 MINI BOX
STATED PRINT RUN 25 SER.#'d SETS
1 Ken Griffey Jr. 20.00 50.00
18 Derek Jeter 50.00 120.00
29 Jose Reyes 8.00 20.00
37 Hunter Pence 6.00 15.00
67 Ozzie Smith 8.00 20.00
86 David Wright 10.00 25.00
90 Jose Altuve 12.00 30.00
95 Mark McGwire 15.00 40.00
97 Yasiel Puig 20.00 50.00
100 Jose Abreu 15.00 40.00
104 Nolan Ryan 25.00 60.00
117 Don Mattingly 15.00 40.00
127 Roberto Clemente 15.00 40.00
159 Mariano Rivera 15.00 40.00
161 Tony Gwynn 10.00 25.00
173 Mike Schmidt 10.00 25.00
178 Greg Maddux 10.00 25.00
188 George Brett 10.00 25.00
197 Cal Ripken Jr. 30.00 80.00

2014 Stadium Club Gold

*GOLD: 1.2X TO 3X BASIC
*GOLD RC: 1.2X TO 3X BASIC
STATED ODDS 1:3 MINI BOX
18 Derek Jeter 15.00 40.00
29 Jose Reyes 5.00 12.00
67 Ozzie Smith 5.00 12.00
100 Jose Abreu 6.00 15.00
104 Nolan Ryan 8.00 20.00
117 Don Mattingly 6.00 15.00
127 Roberto Clemente 5.00 12.00
159 Mariano Rivera 6.00 15.00
161 Tony Gwynn 4.00 10.00
173 Mike Schmidt 5.00 12.00
188 George Brett 5.00 12.00
197 Cal Ripken Jr. 5.00 12.00

2014 Stadium Club Rainbow

*RAINBOW: .6X TO 1.5X BASIC
*RAINBOW RC: .6X TO 1.5X BASIC
RANDOM INSERTS IN PACKS
18 Derek Jeter 10.00 25.00

2014 Stadium Club Autographs

OVERALL ONE AUTO PER MINI BOX
EXCHANGE DEADLINE 9/30/2017
SCAAA Arismendy Alcantara 2.50 6.00
SCAAE Adam Eaton 2.50 6.00
SCAAH Andrew Heaney 2.50 6.00
SCACA Chase Anderson 2.50 6.00
SCACBL Charlie Blackmon 8.00 20.00
SCACCR C.J. Cron 2.50 6.00
SCACF Cliff Floyd 2.50 6.00
SCACO Chris Owings 2.50 6.00
SCACY Christian Yelich 10.00 25.00
SCADA Dean Anna 2.50 6.00
SCADS Danny Salazar 4.00 10.00
SCAEG Evan Gattis 2.50 6.00
SCAEJ Erik Johnson 2.50 6.00
SCAGP Gregory Polanco 4.00 10.00
SCAGS George Springer 12.00 30.00
SCAJA Jose Abreu 15.00 40.00
SCAJJ James Jones 2.50 6.00
SCAJK Joe Kelly 2.50 6.00
SCAJL Junior Lake 2.50 6.00
SCAJM Jake Marisnick 2.50 6.00
SCAJSA Jarrod Saltalamacchia 2.50 6.00
SCAJSC Jonathan Schoop 5.00 12.00
SCAJSE Jean Segura 3.00 8.00
SCAJT Julio Teheran 3.00 8.00
SCAKU Koji Uehara 25.00 60.00
SCAKW Kolten Wong 3.00 8.00
SCALH Livan Hernandez 2.50 6.00
SCALS Luis Sardinas 2.50 6.00
SCAMA Matt Adams 2.50 6.00
SCAMBE Mookie Betts 100.00 250.00
SCAMCA Matt Carpenter 8.00 20.00
SCAMH Mario Hollands 3.00 8.00
SCAMST Marcus Stroman 5.00 12.00
SCAMW Maury Wills 4.00 10.00
SCAMZ Mike Zunino 2.50 6.00
SCAOT Oscar Taveras 3.00 8.00
SCAOV Omar Vizquel 15.00 40.00
SCARE Roenis Elias 2.50 6.00
SCARM Rafael Montero 2.50 6.00
SCASG Sonny Gray 6.00 15.00
SCASM Shelby Miller 10.00 25.00
SCASMA Starling Marte 5.00 12.00
SCASR Stefen Romero 2.50 6.00
SCATC Tony Cingrani 3.00 8.00
SCATW Taijuan Walker 2.50 6.00
SCAYS Yangervis Solarte 2.50 6.00
SCAZW Zack Wheeler 8.00 20.00

2014 Stadium Club Autographs Gold

*GOLD: .75X TO 2X BASIC
STATED ODDS 1:30 MINI BOX
STATED PRINT RUN 25 SER.#'d SETS
EXCHANGE DEADLINE 9/30/2017
SCAAB Albert Belle 20.00 50.00
SCAAD Andre Dawson 12.00 30.00
SCACR Cal Ripken Jr. 150.00 300.00
SCAFM Fred McGriff 40.00 100.00
SCAGM Greg Maddux 150.00 250.00
SCAJC Jose Canseco EXCH 25.00 60.00
SCAJG Juan Gonzalez 15.00 40.00
SCAJS John Smoltz 50.00 120.00
SCAJV Joey Votto 30.00 80.00
SCAKG Ken Griffey Jr. 150.00 250.00
SCAMN Mike Napoli 30.00 80.00
SCAMS Mike Schmidt 40.00 100.00
SCAMT Mike Trout 200.00 300.00
SCAPG Paul Goldschmidt 20.00 50.00
SCARP Rafael Palmeiro 20.00 50.00
SCATP Terry Pendleton 10.00 25.00
SCATT Troy Tulowitzki 30.00 80.00
SCAYP Yasiel Puig 125.00 250.00

2014 Stadium Club Autographs Rainbow

*RAINBOW: .6X TO 1.5X BASIC
STATED ODDS 1:18 MINI BOX
STATED PRINT RUN 50 SER.#'d SETS
EXCHANGE DEADLINE 9/30/2017
SCAAB Albert Belle 10.00 25.00
SCACK Clayton Kershaw 90.00 150.00
SCACSA Chris Sale 12.00 30.00
SCAJC Jose Canseco EXCH 20.00 50.00
SCAJG Juan Gonzalez 12.00 30.00
SCAMM Mike Minor 4.00 10.00
SCAMN Mike Napoli 25.00 60.00
SCAPG Paul Goldschmidt 15.00 40.00
SCATP Terry Pendleton 8.00 20.00

2014 Stadium Club Beam Team

STATED ODDS 1:3 MINI BOX
BT1 Miguel Cabrera 1.25 3.00
BT2 Max Scherzer 1.25 3.00
BT3 Clayton Kershaw 2.00 5.00
BT4 Wil Myers .75 2.00
BT5 Jose Fernandez 1.25 3.00
BT6 Troy Tulowitzki 1.25 3.00
BT7 Mike Trout 6.00 15.00
BT8 Joey Votto 1.25 3.00
BT9 Adam Jones 1.00 2.50
BT10 David Wright 1.00 2.50
BT11 Dustin Pedroia 1.25 3.00
BT12 Yadier Molina 1.50 4.00
BT13 Manny Machado 1.25 3.00
BT14 Evan Longoria 1.00 2.50
BT15 Yu Darvish 1.25 3.00
BT16 David Ortiz 1.25 3.00
BT17 Derek Jeter 4.00 10.00
BT18 Andrew McCutchen 1.25 3.00
BT19 Bryce Harper 2.00 5.00
BT20 Felix Hernandez 1.00 2.50
BT21 Robinson Cano 1.00 2.50
BT22 Jacoby Ellsbury 1.00 2.50
BT23 Adam Wainwright 1.00 2.50
BT24 Masahiro Tanaka 3.00 8.00
BT25 Dylan Bundy 1.00 2.50

2014 Stadium Club Beam Team Gold

*GOLD: 2.5X TO 6X BASIC
STATED ODDS 1:36 MINI BOX
BT17 Derek Jeter 50.00 120.00

2014 Stadium Club Field Access

RANDOM INSERTS IN PACKS
FA1 Mike Trout 6.00 15.00
FA2 Andrew McCutchen 1.25 3.00
FA3 Buster Posey 1.50 4.00
FA4 Bryce Harper 2.00 5.00
FA5 Willie Mays 2.50 6.00
FA6 Babe Ruth 3.00 8.00
FA7 David Wright 1.00 2.50
FA8 Hank Aaron 2.50 6.00
FA9 Roger Clemens 1.50 4.00
FA10 Stan Musial 2.00 5.00
FA11 Greg Maddux 1.50 4.00
FA12 Rickey Henderson 1.25 3.00
FA13 Randy Johnson 1.25 3.00
FA14 Miguel Cabrera 1.25 3.00
FA15 Yasiel Puig 1.25 3.00
FA16 Johnny Bench 1.25 3.00
FA17 Joe Mauer 1.00 2.50
FA18 Clayton Kershaw 2.00 5.00
FA19 Ken Griffey Jr. 2.50 6.00
FA20 Nolan Ryan 4.00 10.00
FA21 Justin Verlander 1.25 3.00
FA22 Derek Jeter 3.00 8.00
FA23 Jose Fernandez 1.25 3.00
FA24 Mark McGwire 2.50 6.00
FA25 Robinson Cano 1.00 2.50

2014 Stadium Club Field Access Electric Foil

*ELECTRIC FOIL: 1X TO 2.5X BASIC
STATED ODDS 1:88 MINI BOX
STATED PRINT RUN 25 SER.#'D SETS
FA1 Mike Trout 15.00 40.00
FA3 Buster Posey 12.00 30.00
FA13 Randy Johnson 10.00 25.00
FA18 Clayton Kershaw 12.00 30.00
FA19 Ken Griffey Jr. 25.00 60.00
FA20 Nolan Ryan 30.00 80.00
FA22 Derek Jeter 25.00 60.00

2014 Stadium Club Field Access Gold

*GOLD: .75X TO 2X BASIC
STATED ODDS 1:44 MINI BOX
STATED PRINT RUN 50 SER.#'D SETS

2014 Stadium Club Field Access Rainbow

*RAINBOW: .6X TO 1.5X BASIC
STATED ODDS 1:23 MINI BOX
STATED PRINT RUN 99 SER.#'D SETS
FA19 Ken Griffey Jr. 10.00 25.00
FA20 Nolan Ryan 10.00 25.00
FA22 Derek Jeter 10.00 25.00

2014 Stadium Club Future Stars Die Cut

STATED ODDS 1:3 MINI BOX
FS1 Jose Fernandez .75 2.00
FS2 Gerrit Cole .75 2.00
FS3 Michael Wacha .60 1.50
FS4 Wil Myers .50 1.25
FS5 Yasiel Puig .75 2.00
FS6 Xander Bogaerts 1.50 4.00
FS7 Billy Hamilton .60 1.50
FS8 Jose Abreu 4.00 10.00
FS9 Masahiro Tanaka 1.50 4.00
FS10 George Springer 2.00 5.00

2014 Stadium Club Future Stars Die Cut Gold

*GOLD: 2X TO 5X BASIC
STATED ODDS 1:218 MINI BOX
STATED PRINT RUN 25 SER.#'d SETS
FS7 Billy Hamilton 10.00 25.00

2014 Stadium Club Legends Die Cut

STATED ODDS 1:3 MINI BOX
LDC1 Stan Musial 1.50 4.00
LDC2 Greg Maddux 1.25 3.00
LDC3 Rickey Henderson 1.00 2.50
LDC4 Randy Johnson 1.00 2.50
LDC5 Johnny Bench 1.00 2.50
LDC6 George Brett 2.00 5.00
LDC7 Cal Ripken Jr. 3.00 8.00
LDC8 Ken Griffey Jr. 2.00 5.00
LDC9 Nolan Ryan 3.00 8.00
LDC10 Sandy Koufax 2.00 5.00

2014 Stadium Club Legends Die Cut Gold

*GOLD: 3X TO 8X BASIC
STATED ODDS 1:218 MINI BOX
STATED PRINT RUN 25 SER.#'d SETS
LDC4 Randy Johnson 12.00 30.00
LDC8 Ken Griffey Jr. 30.00 80.00

2014 Stadium Club Lone Star Signatures

STATED ODDS 1:219 MINI BOX
EXCHANGE DEADLINE 9/30/2017
LSSCK Clayton Kershaw EXCH 100.00 200.00
LSSHA Hank Aaron EXCH 100.00 200.00
LSSIR Ivan Rodriguez 20.00 50.00
LSSMM Mark McGwire 150.00 250.00
LSSMS Max Scherzer 40.00 100.00
LSSMW Michael Wacha EXCH 20.00 50.00
LSSNR Nolan Ryan EXCH 100.00 200.00
LSSRC Roger Clemens EXCH 50.00 120.00
LSSWM Willie Mays EXCH 125.00 250.00
LSSYD Yu Darvish EXCH 60.00 150.00

2014 Stadium Club Triumvirates Luminous

STATED ODDS 1:3 MINI BOX
T1A Hanley Ramirez 1.50 4.00
T1B Clayton Kershaw 3.00 8.00
T1C Yasiel Puig 2.00 5.00
T2A Albert Pujols 2.50 6.00
T2B Derek Jeter 5.00 12.00
T2C David Ortiz 2.00 5.00
T3A Adam Jones 1.50 4.00
T3B Mike Trout 10.00 25.00
T3C Giancarlo Stanton 2.00 5.00
T4A Stephen Strasburg 2.00 5.00
T4B Justin Verlander 2.00 5.00
T4C Adam Wainwright 1.50 4.00
T5A Troy Tulowitzki 2.00 5.00
T5B Miguel Cabrera 2.00 5.00
T5C Robinson Cano 1.50 4.00
T6A Andrew McCutchen 2.00 5.00
T6B Bryce Harper 3.00 8.00
T6C Carlos Gonzalez 1.50 4.00
T7A Yu Darvish 2.00 5.00
T7B Masahiro Tanaka 4.00 10.00
T7C Hyun-Jin Ryu 1.50 4.00
T8A Buster Posey 2.50 6.00
T8B Yadier Molina 2.50 6.00
T8C Joe Mauer 1.50 4.00
T9A Evan Longoria 1.50 4.00
T9B Manny Machado 2.00 5.00
T9C David Wright 1.50 4.00
T10A Xander Bogaerts 4.00 10.00
T10B Jose Abreu 6.00 15.00
T10C George Springer 5.00 12.00

2014 Stadium Club Triumvirates Illuminator

*ILLUMINATOR: 1X TO 2.5X BASIC
STATED ODDS 1:36 MINI BOX
T1B Clayton Kershaw 20.00 50.00
T2B Derek Jeter 50.00 120.00
T3B Mike Trout 40.00 100.00
T8A Buster Posey 12.00 30.00
T10B Jose Abreu 60.00 150.00

2014 Stadium Club Triumvirates Luminescent

*LUMINESCENT: .6X TO 1.5X BASIC
STATED ODDS 1:12 MINI BOX
T2B Derek Jeter 12.00 30.00

2015 Stadium Club

COMPLETE SET (300) 40.00 80.00
1 Fernando Valenzuela .25 .60
2 Sonny Gray .30 .75
3 David Cone .25 .60
4 Huston Street .25 .60
5 Anthony Ranaudo RC .50 1.25
6 J.J. Hardy .25 .60
7 Brandon Moss .25 .60
8 Mark Reynolds .25 .60
9 Rick Porcello .30 .75
10 Zach Britton .30 .75
11 Mark Buehrle .30 .75
12 Giancarlo Stanton .40 1.00
13 Ernie Banks .40 1.00
14 Mark Teixeira .30 .75
15 Adrian Beltre .40 1.00
16 Robinson Cano .30 .75
17 Jacoby Ellsbury .30 .75
18 Zack Wheeler .30 .75
19 Scott Kazmir .25 .60
20 Eric Chavez .25 .60
21 Patrick Corbin .30 .75
22 Ivan Rodriguez .30 .75
23 Ozzie Smith .50 1.25
24 Dale Murphy .40 1.00
25 Matt Holliday .40 1.00
26 Juan Lagares .25 .60
27 Carlos Santana .30 .75
28 Dallas Keuchel .30 .75
29 Trevor Rosenthal .30 .75
30 Dilson Herrera RC .60 1.50
31 Albert Belle .25 .60
32 Nolan Arenado .60 1.50
33 Cal Ripken Jr. 1.25 3.00
34 Mariano Rivera .50 1.25
35 Ryne Sandberg .75 2.00
36 Frank Robinson .30 .75
37 Carlos Ruiz .25 .60
38 Jonathan Lucroy .30 .75
39 Josh Donaldson .30 .75
40 Josh Hamilton .30 .75
41 Gregory Polanco .30 .75
42 Jordan Zimmermann .30 .75
43 Jose Bautista .30 .75
44 Todd Frazier .25 .60
45 Matt Shoemaker .30 .75
46 Yonder Alonso .25 .60
47 Michael Brantley .30 .75
48 Steven Moya .30 .75
49 Kurt Suzuki .25 .60
50 Ender Inciarte RC .50 1.25
51 Miguel Cabrera .40 1.00
52 Jake Marisnick .25 .60
53 Chipper Jones .40 1.00
54 Bip Roberts .25 .60
55 Lucas Duda .30 .75
56 Hunter Pence .30 .75
57 Marcus Stroman .30 .75
58 Jason Giambi .25 .60
59 Adrian Gonzalez .30 .75
60 James Shields .25 .60
61 Joe Mauer .30 .75
62 Paul Goldschmidt .40 1.00
63 Matt Adams .25 .60
64 Brett Gardner .30 .75
65 Jackie Robinson .40 1.00
66 Seth Smith .25 .60
67 Don Mattingly .75 2.00
68 Brooks Robinson .30 .75
69 Chris Sale .40 1.00
70 James McCann RC .75 2.00
71 Curtis Granderson .30 .75
72 Madison Bumgarner .30 .75
73 Starling Marte .30 .75
74 Adam Wainwright .30 .75
75 Lou Brock .30 .75
76 Bo Jackson .40 1.00
77 Marcell Ozuna .40 1.00
78 Juan Gonzalez .25 .60
79 Bartolo Colon .25 .60
80 Andrew Heaney .25 .60
81 Monte Irvin .30 .75
82 Deion Sanders .30 .75
83 Sean Doolittle .25 .60
84 Andrelton Simmons .25 .60
85 Joey Votto .40 1.00
86 Wily Peralta .25 .60
87 Christian Yelich .50 1.25
88 Chris Davis .25 .60
89 Joc Pederson RC 2.00 5.00
90 Justin Morneau .30 .75
91 Dusty Baker .25 .60
92 Jorge Soler RC .75 2.00
93 Andy Van Slyke .25 .60
94 Wei-Yin Chen .25 .60
95 Rob Dibble .25 .60
96 Jonathan Papelbon .30 .75
97 Evan Gattis .25 .60
98 Jim Rice .30 .75
99 Chase Utley .30 .75
100 Alex Cobb .25 .60
101 Mookie Betts .75 2.00
102 Cliff Lee .30 .75
103 Kennys Vargas .25 .60
104 Billy Hamilton .30 .75
105 Devin Mesoraco .25 .60
106 Shin-Soo Choo .30 .75
107 Ron Gant .25 .60
108 Buster Posey .50 1.25
109 David Price .30 .75
110 Terry Pendleton .25 .60
111 Whitey Ford .30 .75
112 Paul Konerko .30 .75
113 Buck Farmer RC .50 1.25
114 Gary Sheffield .25 .60
115 Jason Heyward .30 .75
116 Maikel Franco RC .60 1.50
117 Lenny Dykstra .25 .60
118 Yasiel Puig .40 1.00
119 Pedro Alvarez .25 .60
120 Victor Martinez .30 .75
121 Luis Aparicio .30 .75
122 Mike Minor .25 .60
123 Lenny Harris .25 .60
124 Cliff Floyd .25 .60
125 Jake Arrieta .30 .75
126 Rougned Odor .30 .75
127 Alfredo Simon .25 .60
128 Cory Spangenberg .25 .60
129 Adam Eaton .25 .60
130 John Olerud .25 .60
131 Phil Hughes .25 .60
132 Jered Weaver .30 .75
133 Kenley Jansen .30 .75
134 Mitch Moreland .25 .60
135 Mike Trout 2.00 5.00
136 Reggie Jackson .30 .75
137 Rondell White .25 .60
138 Ben Zobrist .30 .75
139 Andrew McCutchen .40 1.00
140 Jay Bruce .30 .75
141 Edwin Escobar .25 .60
142 Anthony Rendon .40 1.00
143 Mickey Tettleton .25 .60
144 Prince Fielder .30 .75
145 R.A. Dickey .30 .75
146 Mike Mussina .30 .75
147 Henderson Alvarez .25 .60
148 Kevin Gausman .40 1.00
149 Orlando Cepeda .30 .75
150 Jacob deGrom .75 2.00
151 Andrew Cashner .25 .60
152 Jose Abreu .40 1.00
153 Mark McGwire .60 1.50
154 J.D. Martinez .40 1.00
155 Nick Swisher .30 .75
156 Chris Carter .25 .60
157 Orlando Hernandez .25 .60
158 Eric Hosmer .30 .75
159 Torii Hunter .25 .60
160 Elvis Andrus .30 .75
161 Ryan Braun .30 .75
162 Craig Kimbrel .30 .75
163 C.J. Wilson .25 .60
164 Carlton Fisk .30 .75
165 Willie Stargell .30 .75
166 Ian Kinsler .30 .75
167 Edwin Encarnacion .40 1.00
168 Carlos Baerga .25 .60
169 Brock Holt .25 .60
170 Albert Pujols .50 1.25
171 Jimmy Rollins .30 .75
172 Yoenis Cespedes .30 .75
173 Gary Brown RC .50 1.25
174 George Springer .30 .75
175 Drew Stubbs .25 .60
176 Matt Barnes RC .50 1.25
177 Guilder Rodriguez RC .50 1.25
178 Steve Pearce .40 1.00
179 Bud Norris .25 .60
180 Adam LaRoche .25 .60
181 Alcides Escobar .30 .75
182 Clayton Kershaw .60 1.50
183 Travis Ishikawa .25 .60
184 David Ortiz .40 1.00
185 Josh Harrison .25 .60
186 Lou Gehrig .75 2.00
187 Xander Bogaerts .40 1.00
188 Jhonny Peralta .25 .60
189 Jeurys Familia .30 .75
190 Stan Musial .60 1.50
191 Joe Panik .30 .75
192 Kolten Wong .30 .75
193 David Wright .30 .75
194 Carlos Gomez .25 .60
195 Yan Gomes .25 .60
196 Brandon Finnegan RC .50 1.25
197 Dalton Pompey RC .60 1.50
198 Cole Hamels .30 .75
199 Ryan Howard .30 .75
200 Mike Morse .25 .60
201 Rafael Montero .25 .60
202 Stephen Strasburg .40 1.00
203 Javier Baez RC 4.00 10.00
204 Raul Ibanez .30 .75
205 Jose Altuve .30 .75
206 Julio Teheran .30 .75
207 Doug Fister .25 .60
208 Masahiro Tanaka .30 .75
209 Mike Zunino .25 .60
210 George Brett .75 2.00
211 Justin Verlander .40 1.00
212 Rusney Castillo RC .60 1.50
213 Kyle Seager .25 .60
214 Brandon Crawford .30 .75
215 Adam Jones .30 .75
216 Bryce Harper .60 1.50
217 Yu Darvish .40 1.00
218 Nelson Cruz .40 1.00
219 C.J. Cron .25 .60
220 Jake Peavy .25 .60
221 Nick Castellanos .40 1.00
222 Tanner Roark .25 .60
223 Lorenzo Cain .25 .60
224 Kendall Graveman RC .50 1.25
225 Kristopher Negron RC .50 1.25
226 Dennis Eckersley .30 .75
227 Jon Singleton .30 .75
228 Chris Sabo .25 .60
229 Dayan Viciedo .25 .60
230 Billy Butler .25 .60
231 Joe Morgan .30 .75
232 Corey Dickerson .25 .60
233 Felix Hernandez .30 .75
234 Brandon Guyer .25 .60
235 Johnny Cueto .30 .75
236 Yusmeiro Petit .25 .60
237 Mike Moustakas .30 .75
238 Roberto Alomar .30 .75
239 Roger Clemens .50 1.25
240 Josh Beckett .25 .60
241 Garrett Richards .30 .75
242 Troy Tulowitzki .40 1.00
243 Salvador Perez .30 .75
244 Daniel Norris .25 .60
245 Edgar Martinez .30 .75
246 Adam Dunn .30 .75
247 Matt Williams .25 .60
248 Alex Gordon .30 .75
249 Daniel Murphy .30 .75
250 Manny Machado .40 1.00
251 Jayson Werth .30 .75
252 Tom Glavine .30 .75
253 Hisashi Iwakuma .30 .75
254 Evan Longoria .30 .75
255 Dellin Betances .30 .75
256 David Robertson .30 .75
257 Paul Molitor .40 1.00
258 Zack Greinke .40 1.00
259 Greg Maddux .50 1.25
260 Ken Griffey Jr. .75 2.00
261 Jake Odorizzi .25 .60
262 Luis Gonzalez .25 .60
263 Anthony Rizzo .50 1.25
264 Alex Rodriguez .50 1.25
265 Tony Gwynn .40 1.00
266 Derek Jeter 1.00 2.50
267 Corey Kluber .30 .75
268 Matt Carpenter .40 1.00
269 Angel Pagan .25 .60
270 Kevin Kiermaier .30 .75
271 Russell Martin .25 .60
272 Alexander Guerrero (RC) .60 1.50
273 Mike Piazza .40 1.00
274 Tim Hudson .30 .75
275 Freddie Freeman .50 1.25
276 Jonathan Schoop .25 .60
277 Oswaldo Arcia .25 .60
278 Omar Vizquel .30 .75
279 Joe DiMaggio .75 2.00
280 Rymer Liriano RC .50 1.25
281 Yordano Ventura .30 .75
282 Fred McGriff .30 .75
283 Aaron Sanchez .60 1.50
284 Jose Fernandez .40 1.00
285 Hanley Ramirez .30 .75
286 Tyson Ross .25 .60
287 Pablo Sandoval .30 .75
288 David Peralta .25 .60
289 Danny Santana .25 .60
290 Dwight Gooden .25 .60
291 Arismendy Alcantara .25 .60
292 Fernando Rodney .25 .60
293 Trevor May RC .50 1.25
294 Wil Myers .30 .75
295 Michael Taylor .25 .60
296 Max Scherzer .40 1.00
297 Wade Davis .25 .60
298 Larry Doby .30 .75
299 Jake Lamb RC .75 2.00
300 Kris Bryant RC 10.00 25.00

2015 Stadium Club Black

*BLACK: 3X TO 8X BASIC
*BLACK RC: 1.5X TO 4X BASIC RC
STATED ODDS 1:8 HOBBY
ANNCD PRINT RUN 201 SETS

2015 Stadium Club Black and White

*B/W: 8X TO 20X BASIC
*B/W RC: 4X TO 10X BASIC RC
STATED ODDS 1:46 HOBBY
ANNCD PRINT RUN 17 SETS
89 Joc Pederson 60.00 150.00
266 Derek Jeter 60.00 150.00
300 Kris Bryant 100.00 250.00

2015 Stadium Club Foilboard

*FOIL: 6X TO 15X BASIC
*FOIL RC: 3X TO 8X BASIC RC
STATED ODDS 1:65 HOBBY
STATED PRINT RUN 25 SER.#'d SETS
89 Joc Pederson 50.00 120.00
266 Derek Jeter 50.00 120.00
300 Kris Bryant 75.00 200.00

2015 Stadium Club Gold

*GOLD: 1.5X TO 4X BASIC
*GOLD RC: .75X TO 2X BASIC RC
STATED ODDS 1:3 HOBBY

2015 Stadium Club Autographs

STATED ODDS 1:10 HOBBY
EXCHANGE DEADLINE 5/31/2018
SCAAA Arismendy Alcantara 3.00 8.00
SCAAB Archie Bradley 3.00 8.00
SCAAC Alex Cobb 3.00 8.00
SCAARZ Anthony Rizzo 15.00 40.00
SCAASZ Aaron Sanchez 4.00 10.00
SCABFN Brandon Finnegan 3.00 8.00
SCACB Carlos Baerga 8.00 20.00
SCACC C.J. Cron 3.00 8.00
SCACF Cliff Floyd 3.00 8.00
SCACKR Corey Kluber 5.00 12.00
SCACR Carlos Rodon 8.00 20.00
SCACS Chris Sale 5.00 12.00
SCACW Christian Walker 6.00 15.00
SCACY Christian Yelich 12.00 30.00
SCADB Dellin Betances 5.00 12.00
SCADC David Cone 10.00 25.00
SCADH Dilson Herrera 4.00 10.00
SCADN Daniel Norris 3.00 8.00
SCADP Dalton Pompey 5.00 12.00
SCAED Eric Davis 8.00 20.00
SCAEG Evan Gattis 3.00 8.00
SCAGR Garrett Richards 4.00 10.00
SCAGS George Springer 12.00 30.00
SCAJB Javier Baez 8.00 50.00
SCAJC Jarred Cosart 3.00 8.00
SCAJDM Jacob deGrom 40.00 100.00
SCAJF Jose Fernandez 20.00 50.00
SCAJH Jason Heyward 30.00 80.00
SCAJK Jung-Ho Kang 40.00 100.00
SCAJLS Juan Lagares 3.00 8.00
SCAJPA Joe Panik 4.00 10.00
SCAJPN Joc Pederson 12.00 30.00
SCAKB Kris Bryant 100.00 250.00
SCAKGA Kevin Gausman 5.00 12.00
SCAKGN Kendall Graveman 3.00 8.00
SCAKS Kyle Seager 3.00 8.00
SCAKV Kennys Vargas 3.00 8.00
SCALH Livan Hernandez 3.00 8.00
SCAMA Matt Adams 4.00 10.00
SCAMB Matt Barnes 3.00 8.00
SCAMCR Matt Carpenter 8.00 20.00
SCAMFO Maikel Franco 4.00 10.00
SCAMS Matt Shoemaker 4.00 10.00
SCAMST Marcus Stroman 4.00 10.00
SCAMTR Michael Taylor 3.00 8.00
SCAMW Matt Williams 3.00 8.00
SCANS Noah Syndergaard 20.00 50.00
SCAOV Omar Vizquel 8.00 20.00
SCARL Rymer Liriano 3.00 8.00

SCASG Sonny Gray 4.00 10.00
SCASM Starling Marte 4.00 10.00
SCATR Tyson Ross 3.00 8.00
SCATW Taijuan Walker 3.00 8.00
SCAWM Wil Myers 6.00 15.00
SCAYT Yasmany Tomas 20.00 50.00
SCAZW Zack Wheeler 8.00 20.00

2015 Stadium Club Autographs Black

*BLACK: .6X TO 1.5X BASIC
STATED ODDS 1:87 HOBBY
STATED PRINT RUN 50 SER.#'d SETS
EXCHANGE DEADLINE 5/31/2018
SCACKW Clayton Kershaw EXCH 60.00 150.00
SCAJDN Josh Donaldson 12.00 30.00
SCAJS Jorge Soler 10.00 25.00
SCAPG Paul Goldschmidt 25.00 60.00

2015 Stadium Club Autographs Gold

*GOLD: .75X TO 2X BASIC
STATED ODDS 1:142 HOBBY
STATED PRINT RUN 25 SER.#'d SETS
EXCHANGE DEADLINE 5/31/2018
SCABH Bryce Harper 250.00 350.00
SCABP Buster Posey 100.00 200.00
SCACKW Clayton Kershaw EXCH 75.00 200.00
SCADO David Ortiz 90.00 150.00
SCADW David Wright 50.00 120.00
SCAEL Evan Longoria 25.00 60.00
SCAFF Freddie Freeman 20.00 50.00
SCAFV Fernando Valenzuela 30.00 80.00
SCAJA Jose Abreu 40.00 100.00
SCAJDN Josh Donaldson 15.00 40.00
SCAJH Jason Heyward 50.00 120.00
SCAJS Jorge Soler 12.00 30.00
SCAJV Joey Votto 50.00 120.00
SCAMP Mike Piazza 90.00 150.00
SCAMR Mariano Rivera 100.00 250.00
SCAPG Paul Goldschmidt 30.00 80.00

2015 Stadium Club Contact Sheet

COMPLETE SET (25) 15.00 40.00
STATED ODDS 1:8 HOBBY
*WHITE/99: .6X TO 1.5X BASIC
*GOLD/50: 1.5X TO 4X BASIC
*ORANGE/25: 2.5X TO 6X BASIC
CS1 Mike Trout 5.00 12.00
CS2 Andrew McCutchen 1.00 2.50
CS3 Buster Posey 1.25 3.00
CS4 Giancarlo Stanton 1.00 2.50
CS5 Troy Tulowitzki 1.00 2.50
CS6 Josh Donaldson .75 2.00
CS7 Miguel Cabrera 1.00 2.50
CS8 Evan Longoria .75 2.00
CS9 Jose Bautista .75 2.00
CS10 Yasiel Puig 1.00 2.50
CS11 Robinson Cano .75 2.00
CS12 Manny Machado 1.00 2.50
CS13 Adrian Beltre 1.00 2.50
CS14 Paul Goldschmidt 1.00 2.50
CS15 Jason Heyward .75 2.00
CS16 Anthony Rendon 1.00 2.50
CS17 Dustin Pedroia 1.00 2.50
CS18 Anthony Rizzo 1.25 3.00
CS19 Alex Gordon .75 2.00
CS20 Carlos Gomez .60 1.50
CS21 Joey Votto 1.00 2.50
CS22 Bryce Harper 1.50 4.00
CS23 David Wright .75 2.00
CS24 Jose Abreu 1.00 2.50
CS25 Jacoby Ellsbury .75 2.00

2015 Stadium Club Crystal Ball

STATED ODDS 1:355 HOBBY
STATED PRINT RUN 70 SER.#'d SETS
*GOLD/30: .5X TO 1.2X BASIC
CB01 Mike Trout 80.00 200.00
CB02 Bryce Harper 25.00 60.00
CB03 Jorge Soler 15.00 40.00
CB04 Yordano Ventura 12.00 30.00
CB05 George Springer 12.00 30.00
CB06 Mookie Betts 30.00 80.00
CB07 Javier Baez 80.00 200.00
CB08 Taijuan Walker 10.00 25.00
CB09 Jacob deGrom 30.00 80.00
CB10 Daniel Norris 10.00 25.00

2015 Stadium Club Legends Die Cut

COMPLETE SET (10) 10.00 25.00
RANDOM INSERTS IN PACKS
*GOLD/25: 2.5X TO 6X BASIC
LDC01 Babe Ruth 2.50 6.00
LDC02 Ty Cobb 1.50 4.00
LDC03 Jackie Robinson 1.00 2.50
LDC04 Willie Mays 2.00 5.00
LDC05 Ted Williams 2.00 5.00
LDC06 Roberto Clemente 2.50 6.00
LDC07 Nolan Ryan 3.00 8.00
LDC08 Randy Johnson 1.00 2.50
LDC09 Roger Clemens 1.25 3.00
LDC10 Tony Gwynn 1.00 2.50

2015 Stadium Club Lone Star Signatures

STATED ODDS 1:2244 HOBBY
STATED PRINT RUN 25 SER.#'d SETS
EXCHANGE DEADLINE 5/31/2018
LSSAJ Adam Jones 20.00 50.00
LSSCH Cole Hamels 20.00 50.00
LSSGS Giancarlo Stanton EXCH 50.00 120.00
LSSJA Jose Abreu 25.00 60.00
LSSJD Josh Donaldson 20.00 50.00
LSSMR Mariano Rivera 100.00 250.00
LSSMT Mike Trout 200.00 400.00
LSSPG Paul Goldschmidt 40.00 100.00
LSSRC Robinson Cano 20.00 50.00
LSSRJ Randy Johnson 90.00 150.00
LSSTT Troy Tulowitzki 30.00 80.00

2015 Stadium Club Triumvirates Luminous

STATED ODDS 1:16 HOBBY
*LUMINESCENT: .6X TO 1.5X BASIC
*ILLUMINATOR: 1.5X TO 4X BASIC
T1A David Price 1.25 3.00
T1B Miguel Cabrera 1.50 4.00
T1C Victor Martinez 1.25 3.00
T2A Matt Harvey 1.25 3.00
T2B Jacob deGrom 3.00 8.00
T2C Zack Wheeler 1.25 3.00
T3A Adam Wainwright 1.25 3.00
T3B Jason Heyward 1.25 3.00
T3C Yadier Molina 2.00 5.00
T4A Jorge Soler 1.50 4.00
T4B Javier Baez 8.00 20.00
T4C Starlin Castro 1.00 2.50
T5A Jose Fernandez 1.50 4.00
T5B Giancarlo Stanton 1.50 4.00
T5C Christian Yelich 2.00 5.00
T6A Bryce Harper 2.50 6.00
T6B Stephen Strasburg 1.50 4.00
T6C Anthony Rendon 1.50 4.00
T7A Andrew McCutchen 1.50 4.00
T7B Starling Marte 1.25 3.00
T7C Gregory Polanco 1.25 3.00
T8A Eric Hosmer 1.25 3.00
T8B Salvador Perez 1.25 3.00
T8C Alex Gordon 1.25 3.00
T9A Josh Donaldson 1.25 3.00
T9B Evan Longoria 1.25 3.00
T9C Pablo Sandoval 1.25 3.00
T10A Yasiel Puig 1.50 4.00
T10B Jose Abreu 1.50 4.00
T10C Rusney Castillo 1.25 3.00

2015 Stadium Club True Colors

STATED ODDS 1:16 HOBBY
*REF: .6X TO 1.5X BASIC
*GOLD REF: .75X TO 2X BASIC
*ELEC.REF/25: 4X TO 10X BASIC
TCAAG Adrian Gonzalez .75 2.00
TCAAP Albert Pujols 1.25 3.00
TCABH Bryce Harper 1.50 4.00
TCABP Buster Posey 1.25 3.00
TCACK Clayton Kershaw 1.50 4.00
TCADO David Ortiz 1.00 2.50
TCAFV Fernando Valenzuela .60 1.50
TCAGS Giancarlo Stanton 1.00 2.50
TCAJA Jose Abreu 1.00 2.50
TCAJM Joe Mauer .75 2.00
TCAJP Joe Panik .75 2.00
TCALG Luis Gonzalez .60 1.50
TCAMB Madison Bumgarner .75 2.00
TCAMC Miguel Cabrera 1.00 2.50
TCAMM Mike Mussina .75 2.00
TCAMP Mike Piazza 1.00 2.50
TCAMR Mariano Rivera 1.25 3.00
TCAMT Mike Trout 5.00 12.00
TCAPG Paul Goldschmidt 1.00 2.50
TCARB Ryan Braun .75 2.00
TCARC Roger Clemens 1.25 3.00
TCATS Tom Seaver .75 2.00
TCAWM Willie Mays 2.00 5.00
TCAYD Yu Darvish 1.00 2.50
TCAYP Yasiel Puig 1.00 2.50

2016 Stadium Club

COMP.SET w/o SP's (300) 40.00 100.00
1 Gary Sanchez RC 1.50 4.00
2 Garrett Richards .30 .75
3 Matt Kemp .30 .75
4 Kevin Kiermaier .30 .75
5 Jay Bruce .30 .75
6 Brandon Phillips .25 .60
7 Edwin Encarnacion .40 1.00
8 Stephen Vogt .30 .75
9 Addison Russell .40 1.00
10 Jose Altuve .30 .75
11 Todd Frazier .25 .60
12 Jon Lester .30 .75
13 Sandy Koufax .75 2.00
14 Chris Davis .25 .60
15 Ozzie Smith .50 1.25
16 Greg Holland .25 .60
17 Raul Mondesi RC 1.00 2.50
18 Willie McCovey .30 .75
19 Marco Estrada .25 .60
20A Al Leiter .25 .60
20B Al Leiter SP 6.00 15.00
Holding head
21 Carson Smith .25 .60
22 Matt Reynolds .25 .60
23 Nolan Arenado .60 1.50
24 Michael Reed RC .50 1.25
25 Chris Archer .25 .60
26 Steven Matz .25 .60
27 Anthony Gose .25 .60
28 Dee Gordon .25 .60
29 Rob Refsnyder RC .60 1.50
30 Jose Bautista .30 .75
31 Brett Gardner .30 .75
32 Bob Feller .30 .75
33 Mitch Moreland .25 .60
34 Santiago Casilla .25 .60
35 Kendrys Morales .25 .60
36 Nomar Mazara RC .75 2.00
37 Yadier Molina .50 1.25
38 Frank Thomas .40 1.00
39 Michael Brantley .30 .75
40 Kyle Waldrop .30 .75
41 Reggie Jackson .30 .75
42 Francisco Lindor .75 2.00
43 Joc Pederson .30 .75
44 Mark Melancon .25 .60
45 Craig Biggio .30 .75
46 Greg Bird RC .60 1.50
47 Brandon Crawford .30 .75
48 Harold Baines .30 .75
49 Brett Anderson .25 .60
50 Whitey Ford .30 .75
51 Ken Griffey Jr. .75 2.00
52 Yangervis Solarte .25 .60
53 Chris Heston .25 .60
54 Matt Duffy .25 .60
55 Stephen Strasburg .40 1.00
56A Yordano Ventura .30 .75
56B Yordano Ventura SP 8.00 20.00
Sunglasses
57 Huston Street .25 .60
58 Eddie Murray .30 .75
59 Ken Giles .25 .60
60 Carl Yastrzemski .60 1.50
61 Miguel Almonte RC .50 1.25
62 Luke Jackson RC .50 1.25
63 Orlando Cepeda .30 .75
64 Lucas Duda .30 .75
65 Ender Inciarte .25 .60
66 Catfish Hunter .30 .75
67 Yu Darvish .40 1.00
68 Raisel Iglesias .30 .75
69A Clayton Kershaw .60 1.50
69B Kershaw SP Batting 20.00 50.00
70 Dennis Eckersley .30 .75
71 Luis Gonzalez .30 .75
72 Tom Murphy RC .50 1.25
73 Chris Tillman .25 .60
74 Maikel Franco .30 .75
75 Hank Aaron .75 2.00
76 Tyson Ross .25 .60
77 Tyler White RC .50 1.25
78A James Shields .25 .60
78B James Shields SP 6.00 15.00
Brown jersey
79 Marquis Grissom .25 .60
80A Nolan Ryan 1.25 3.00
80B Ryan SP HOF 30.00 80.00
81A Miguel Sano RC .75 2.00
81B Sano SP Dugout 10.00 25.00
82 Blake Swihart .30 .75
83 Tom Seaver .30 .75
84 Logan Forsythe .25 .60
85 J.J. Hardy .25 .60
86 Andrew Miller .30 .75
87 Lou Gehrig .75 2.00
88 Devin Mesoraco .25 .60
89 Erick Aybar .25 .60
90 Jason Kipnis .30 .75
91 Kenta Maeda RC 1.00 2.50
92 Max Scherzer .40 1.00
93 C.J. Wilson .25 .60
94 Adrian Beltre .40 1.00
95 Francisco Cervelli .25 .60
96 Adam Eaton .25 .60
97 Eric Hosmer .30 .75
98 Ian Kinsler .30 .75
99 Justin Turner .40 1.00
100 Carlos Gonzalez .30 .75
101 Archie Bradley .25 .60
102 Ichiro Suzuki .50 1.25
103 Mark McGwire .60 1.50
104 Cole Hamels .30 .75
105 Bryce Harper .60 1.50
106 Sonny Gray .30 .75
107 Jake Arrieta .30 .75
108 Omar Vizquel .30 .75
109 Josh Reddick .25 .60
110 Salvador Perez .30 .75
111 Matt Carpenter .40 1.00
112 Curt Schilling .30 .75
113 Andrew McCutchen .40 1.00
114 David Ortiz .40 1.00
115 Paul Goldschmidt .40 1.00
116 J.T. Realmuto .40 1.00
117 Charlie Blackmon .40 1.00
118 Brian Dozier .30 .75
119 Mark Teixeira .30 .75
120A Mike Moustakas .30 .75
120B Mike Moustakas SP 8.00 20.00
w/Dog
121A Masahiro Tanaka .30 .75
121B Masahiro Tanaka SP 8.00 20.00
Batting
122A Greg Maddux .50 1.25
122B Maddux SP w/Chipper 15.00 40.00
123 Willie Stargell .30 .75
124 Felix Hernandez .30 .75
125A Corey Kluber .30 .75
125B Corey Kluber SP 8.00 20.00
Batting
126 Roberto Clemente 1.00 2.50
127 Max Kepler RC .75 2.00
128 Dallas Keuchel .30 .75
129 Adam Jones .30 .75
130 Jason Heyward .30 .75
131 Gerrit Cole .40 1.00
132 Carlos Correa .40 1.00
133 David Price .30 .75
134 Adrian Gonzalez .30 .75
135 Phil Niekro .30 .75
136 Derek Norris .25 .60
137A Josh Harrison .25 .60
137B Josh Harrison SP 10.00 25.00
Throwing
138 Shawn Tolleson .25 .60
139 Matt Harvey .30 .75
140 Gio Gonzalez .30 .75
141 Mookie Betts .75 2.00
142A Corey Seager RC 5.00 12.00
142B Seager SP Helmet 25.00 60.00
143 Jim Abbott .25 .60
144 Kole Calhoun .25 .60
145 Carl Edwards Jr. RC .60 1.50
146 Johnny Bench .40 1.00
147A Henry Owens RC .60 1.50
147B Henry Owens SP 8.00 20.00
Green jersey
148 Danny Salazar .30 .75
149 Jeurys Familia .30 .75
150 Jorge De La Rosa .25 .60
151A Stephen Piscotty RC .75 2.00
151B Stephen Piscotty SP 10.00 25.00
w/Bat
152 Albert Pujols .50 1.25
153 Yovani Gallardo .25 .60
154 Yoenis Cespedes .40 1.00
155 Marcus Semien .40 1.00
156 Randal Grichuk .25 .60
157 Mike Leake .25 .60
158 Gary Carter .30 .75
159 Trevor Story RC 2.50 6.00
160 Miguel Cabrera .40 1.00
161 Alex Rodriguez .50 1.25
162 T.J. House .25 .60
163 Billy Hamilton .30 .75
164 DJ LeMahieu .40 1.00
165 Zach Lee RC .50 1.25
166 Freddy Galvis .25 .60
167 Micah Johnson .25 .60
168 Javier Baez .50 1.25
169 Kevin Pillar .25 .60
170 Colby Lewis .25 .60
171 Randy Johnson .40 1.00
172 Buster Posey .50 1.25
173 Nathan Eovaldi .30 .75
174 Victor Martinez .30 .75
175 Frankie Montas RC .60 1.50
176 Alex Colome .25 .60
177 Monte Irvin .30 .75
178 Brandon Drury RC .75 2.00
179 Lou Brock .30 .75
180 George Brett .75 2.00
181 Manny Banuelos .40 1.00
182 Ryan Braun .30 .75
183 Brad Ziegler .25 .60
184 Byron Buxton .40 1.00
185 Jorge Soler .40 1.00
186 A.J. Ramos .25 .60
187 Johnny Cueto .30 .75
188 Colin Rea RC .50 1.25
189 Chris Sale .40 1.00
190 Erasmo Ramirez .25 .60
191 Frank Viola .25 .60
192 Delino DeShields .25 .60
193 Melvin Upton Jr. .30 .75
194 Willie Mays .75 2.00
195 Hisashi Iwakuma .30 .75
196 Adam Wainwright .30 .75
197 Zack Greinke .40 1.00
198 Roberto Osuna .25 .60
199 Hector Rondon .25 .60
200A Jose Fernandez .40 1.00
200B Jose Fernandez SP 6.00 15.00
Batting
201 Nelson Cruz .40 1.00
202 Daniel Murphy .30 .75
203A Alex Gordon .30 .75
203B Alex Gordon SP 8.00 20.00
Sunglasses
204 Andre Ethier .30 .75
205 Christian Yelich .50 1.25
206 Josh Hamilton .30 .75
207 Anthony Rizzo .50 1.25
208 Edgar Martinez .30 .75
209A Julio Teheran .30 .75
209B Julio Teheran SP 8.00 20.00
Batting
210 Luis Severino RC .60 1.50
211 Didi Gregorius .30 .75
212 Jonathan Lucroy .30 .75
213 Fernando Valenzuela .25 .60
214A Madison Bumgarner .30 .75
214B Bumgarner SP Batting 20.00 50.00
215 Jimmy Paredes .25 .60
216 Noah Syndergaard .30 .75
217 Carlos Santana .30 .75
218 Brandon Belt .30 .75
219 Kevin Plawecki .25 .60
220 Jung Ho Kang .25 .60
221 Jacob deGrom .75 2.00
222 Evan Longoria .30 .75
223 Nomar Garciaparra .30 .75
224 David Wright .30 .75
225 Trea Turner RC 1.50 4.00
226 Scott Kazmir .25 .60
227 Robin Yount .40 1.00
228 Jeremy Hellickson .25 .60
229 Babe Ruth 1.00 2.50
230 Jayson Werth .30 .75
231 Starlin Castro .25 .60
232 Sean Doolittle .25 .60
233 Robinson Cano .30 .75
234 Kyle Gibson .30 .75
235 Russell Martin .25 .60
236 Kris Bryant .50 1.25
237 Richie Shaffer RC .50 1.25
238 Jhonny Peralta .25 .60
239 Shelby Miller .30 .75
240 Brock Holt .25 .60
241 Rick Porcello .30 .75
242 Collin McHugh .25 .60
243 Hunter Pence .30 .75
244 Andres Galarraga .30 .75
245 Ketel Marte RC 1.00 2.50
246 Josh Donaldson .30 .75
247 Cameron Rupp .25 .60
248 Ted Williams .75 2.00
249 Yasmany Tomas .25 .60
250A Bartolo Colon .25 .60
250B Bartolo Colon SP 6.00 15.00
Batting
251 Jon Gray .25 .60
252 Phil Hughes .25 .60
253 Paul Molitor .40 1.00
254 Dustin Pedroia .40 1.00
255 Wade Davis .25 .60
256 Rusney Castillo .25 .60
257 Joe Morgan .30 .75
258 Jose Peraza RC .60 1.50
259 Aroldis Chapman .40 1.00
260 Ryan Howard .30 .75
261 Johnny Damon .30 .75
262 Joey Votto .40 1.00
263 J.D. Martinez .40 1.00
264A A.J. Pollock .25 .60
264B A.J. Pollock SP 6.00 15.00
Batting
265A Hector Olivera RC .60 1.50
265B Hector Olivera SP 8.00 20.00
w/Bat
266 Edinson Volquez .25 .60
267 John Smoltz .40 1.00
268 Jordan Zimmermann .30 .75
269 Hector Santiago .25 .60
270 Prince Fielder .30 .75
271 Martin Prado .25 .60
272A Michael Conforto .30 .75
272B Conforto SP Gray jrsy 8.00 20.00
273 Brian Johnson RC .50 1.25
274 Giancarlo Stanton .40 1.00
275 David Peralta .25 .60
276 Francisco Liriano .25 .60
277A Kyle Schwarber RC 1.50 4.00
277B Schwarber SP Blue jrsy 20.00 50.00
278 Khris Davis .40 1.00
279 Joe Panik .30 .75
280A Mike Trout 2.00 5.00
280B Trout SP w/Bag 50.00 125.00
281 Peter O'Brien RC .50 1.25
282 Joe Mauer .30 .75
283 Rougned Odor .30 .75
284 Freddie Freeman .50 1.25
285 Trevor May .25 .60
286 Harmon Killebrew .40 1.00
287 Blake Snell RC .60 1.50
288 Jose Abreu .40 1.00
289 Anthony DeSclafani .25 .60
290 Manny Machado .40 1.00
291 George Springer .30 .75
292 Shin-Soo Choo .30 .75
293 Cal Ripken Jr. 1.25 3.00
294 Jackie Robinson .40 1.00
295A Aaron Nola RC 1.00 2.50
295B Aaron Nola SP 12.00 30.00
Red jersey
296 Byung-Ho Park RC .60 1.50
297 Wade Boggs .30 .75
298 Curtis Granderson .30 .75
299 Kyle Seager .25 .60
300 Matt Wisler .25 .60

2016 Stadium Club Black

*BLACK: 2.5X TO 6X BASIC
*BLACK RC: 1.2X TO 3X BASIC RC

2016 Stadium Club Black and White

*B/W: 8X TO 20X BASIC
*B/W RC: 4X TO 10X BASIC RC

2016 Stadium Club Foilboard

*FOIL: 8X TO 20X BASIC
*FOIL RC: 4X TO 10X BASIC RC

2016 Stadium Club Gold

*GOLD: 1.5X TO 4X BASIC
*GOLD RC: .75X TO 2X BASIC RC

2016 Stadium Club Autographs

EXCHANGE DEADLINE 6/30/2018
SCAAC Alex Colome 3.00 8.00
SCAAGA Andres Galarraga 5.00 12.00
SCAAN Aaron Nola 6.00 15.00
SCAAP A.J. Pollock 3.00 8.00
SCAAR Addison Russell
SCABB Brandon Belt 4.00 10.00
SCABC Brandon Crawford 15.00 40.00
SCABD Brandon Drury 5.00 12.00
SCABHP Byung-Ho Park 4.00 10.00
SCABJ Brian Johnson 3.00 8.00
SCABP Buster Posey
SCACC Carlos Correa
SCACE Carl Edwards Jr. 4.00 10.00
SCACH Chris Heston 3.00 8.00
SCACK Clayton Kershaw
SCACRA Colin Rea 3.00 8.00
SCACRJ Cal Ripken Jr.
SCACSE Chris Sale
SCACSH Carson Smith 3.00 8.00
SCACSR Corey Seager
SCADK Dallas Keuchel
SCADL DJ LeMahieu 10.00 25.00
SCAFL Francisco Lindor 12.00 30.00
SCAFV Fernando Valenzuela
SCAGB Greg Bird 4.00 10.00
SCAGH Greg Holland 3.00 8.00
SCAGM Greg Maddux
SCAHB Harold Baines 5.00 12.00
SCAHOA Hector Olivera 4.00 10.00
SCAHOS Henry Owens 4.00 10.00
SCAI Ichiro Suzuki
SCAJA Jose Altuve
SCAJG Jon Gray
SCAJPK Joe Panik 10.00 25.00
SCAJPS Jimmy Paredes 3.00 8.00
SCAJR J.T. Realmuto 10.00 25.00
SCAKB Kris Bryant
SCAKC Kole Calhoun 5.00 12.00
SCAKG Ken Griffey Jr.
SCAKM Ketel Marte 6.00 15.00
SCAKMA Kenta Maeda 30.00 80.00
SCAKP Kevin Plawecki 3.00 8.00
SCAKS Kyle Schwarber 25.00 60.00
SCAKW Kyle Waldrop 4.00 10.00
SCALG Luis Gonzalez
SCALJ Luke Jackson 3.00 8.00
SCALS Luis Severino 6.00 15.00
SCAMA Miguel Almonte 3.00 8.00
SCAMC Michael Conforto
SCAMM Mark McGwire
SCAMR Michael Reed 3.00 8.00
SCAMS Miguel Sano 10.00 25.00
SCAMT Mike Trout
SCAMW Matt Wisler 3.00 8.00
SCANG Nomar Garciaparra
SCANM Nomar Mazara 30.00 80.00
SCANS Noah Syndergaard
SCAOV Omar Vizquel 4.00 10.00
SCAPM Paul Molitor
SCAPN Phil Niekro
SCAPO Peter O'Brien 3.00 8.00
SCARCA Robinson Cano
SCARM Raul Mondesi 6.00 15.00
SCARR Rob Refsnyder 4.00 10.00
SCARS Richie Shaffer 3.00 8.00
SCASK Sandy Koufax
SCASMR Shelby Miller
SCASMZ Steven Matz 6.00 15.00
SCASP Stephen Piscotty 5.00 12.00
SCATH T.J. House 3.00 8.00
SCATMA Trevor May 3.00 8.00
SCATMY Tom Murphy 3.00 8.00
SCATS Trevor Story EXCH 20.00 50.00
SCATTR Trea Turner 20.00 50.00
SCAWD Wade Davis 3.00 8.00
SCAZL Zach Lee 3.00 8.00

2016 Stadium Club Autographs Black

*BLACK: .5X TO 1.2X BASIC
STATED PRINT RUN 50 SER.#'d SETS
EXCHANGE DEADLINE 6/30/2018
SCAAR Addison Russell 20.00 50.00
SCABP Buster Posey 50.00 120.00
SCACC Carlos Correa
SCACK Clayton Kershaw
SCACRJ Cal Ripken Jr. 50.00 120.00
SCACSE Chris Sale 15.00 40.00
SCACSR Corey Seager 50.00 120.00
SCADK Dallas Keuchel 10.00 25.00
SCAFV Fernando Valenzuela 20.00 50.00
SCAGM Greg Maddux
SCAJA Jose Altuve 25.00 60.00
SCAJG Jon Gray 10.00 25.00
SCAKB Kris Bryant 75.00 200.00
SCALG Luis Gonzalez 6.00 15.00
SCAMC Michael Conforto 15.00 40.00
SCAMM Mark McGwire
SCAMT Mike Trout
SCANG Nomar Garciaparra
SCANS Noah Syndergaard 30.00 80.00
SCAPM Paul Molitor 15.00 40.00
SCAPN Phil Niekro 10.00 25.00
SCARCA Robinson Cano
SCASK Sandy Koufax
SCASMR Shelby Miller 5.00 12.00

2016 Stadium Club Autographs Gold

*GOLD: .75X TO 2X BASIC
STATED PRINT RUN 25 SER.#'d SETS
EXCHANGE DEADLINE 6/30/2018
SCAAR Addison Russell 25.00 60.00
SCABP Buster Posey 75.00 200.00
SCACC Carlos Correa 150.00 250.00
SCACK Clayton Kershaw 125.00 250.00
SCACRJ Cal Ripken Jr. 75.00 200.00
SCACSE Chris Sale 25.00 60.00
SCACSR Corey Seager 75.00 200.00
SCADK Dallas Keuchel 15.00 40.00
SCAFV Fernando Valenzuela 30.00 80.00
SCAGM Greg Maddux 60.00 150.00
SCAJA Jose Altuve 40.00 100.00
SCAJG Jon Gray 15.00 40.00
SCAKB Kris Bryant 125.00 300.00
SCALG Luis Gonzalez 10.00 25.00
SCAMC Michael Conforto 20.00 50.00
SCAMM Mark McGwire 75.00 200.00
SCAMT Mike Trout 200.00 400.00
SCANG Nomar Garciaparra 50.00 120.00
SCANS Noah Syndergaard 50.00 120.00
SCAPM Paul Molitor 25.00 60.00
SCAPN Phil Niekro 15.00 40.00
SCARCA Robinson Cano 25.00 60.00
SCASK Sandy Koufax 300.00 500.00
SCASMR Shelby Miller 8.00 20.00

2016 Stadium Club Beam Team

COMPLETE SET (25) 25.00 60.00
*GOLD/25: 1X TO 2.5X BASIC
BT01 Carlos Correa 2.00 5.00
BT02 Kris Bryant 2.50 6.00
BT03 Mike Trout 10.00 25.00
BT04 Yu Darvish 2.00 5.00
BT05 Omar Vizquel 1.50 4.00
BT06 Don Mattingly 4.00 10.00
BT07 Robinson Cano 1.50 4.00
BT08 Yoenis Cespedes 2.00 5.00
BT09 Hector Olivera 1.50 4.00
BT10 Aaron Nola 2.50 6.00
BT11 Nomar Garciaparra 1.50 4.00
BT12 Miguel Sano 2.00 5.00
BT13 Noah Syndergaard 1.50 4.00
BT14 Corey Seager 12.00 30.00
BT15 Matt Harvey 1.50 4.00
BT16 Yadier Molina 2.50 6.00
BT17 Madison Bumgarner 1.50 4.00
BT18 Buster Posey 2.50 6.00
BT19 Bryce Harper 3.00 8.00
BT20 David Wright 1.50 4.00
BT21 Clayton Kershaw 3.00 8.00
BT22 David Ortiz 2.00 5.00
BT23 Jose Abreu 2.00 5.00
BT24 Giancarlo Stanton 2.00 5.00
BT25 Andrew McCutchen 2.00 5.00

2016 Stadium Club Contact Sheet

COMPLETE SET (10) 4.00 10.00
*WHITE/99: .75X TO 2X BASIC
*GOLD/50: 1.2X TO 3X BASIC
*ORANGE/25: 5X TO 12X BASIC
CS1 Bryce Harper 1.00 2.50
CS2 Mike Trout 3.00 8.00
CS3 Josh Donaldson .50 1.25
CS4 Albert Pujols .75 2.00
CS5 Michael Conforto .50 1.25
CS6 Kris Bryant .75 2.00
CS7 Miguel Cabrera .60 1.50
CS8 Buster Posey .75 2.00
CS9 Carlos Correa .60 1.50
CS10 Nolan Arenado 1.00 2.50

2016 Stadium Club Instavision

*GOLD/25: .6X TO 1.5X BASIC
IV1 Mike Trout 30.00 80.00
IV2 Kris Bryant 8.00 20.00
IV3 Buster Posey 8.00 20.00
IV4 Clayton Kershaw 10.00 25.00
IV5 Bryce Harper 10.00 25.00
IV6 Matt Harvey 5.00 12.00
IV7 Andrew McCutchen 6.00 15.00
IV8 Josh Donaldson 5.00 12.00
IV9 Carlos Correa 6.00 15.00
IV10 Yadier Molina 8.00 20.00

2016 Stadium Club ISOmetrics

COMPLETE SET (25) 15.00 40.00
*GOLD/50: 1X TO 2.5X BASIC
I1 Josh Donaldson .75 2.00
I2 Mike Trout 5.00 12.00
I3 Kevin Kiermaier .75 2.00
I4 Dallas Keuchel .75 2.00
I5 Manny Machado 1.00 2.50
I6 Ian Kinsler .75 2.00
I7 Adrian Beltre 1.00 2.50
I8 Nelson Cruz 1.00 2.50
I9 Mookie Betts 2.00 5.00
I10 Miguel Cabrera 1.00 2.50
I11 Bryce Harper 1.50 4.00
I12 Zack Greinke 1.00 2.50
I13 Jake Arrieta .75 2.00
I14 Kris Bryant 1.25 3.00
I15 Clayton Kershaw 1.50 4.00
I16 Carlos Correa 1.00 2.50
I17 Paul Goldschmidt 1.00 2.50
I18 Joey Votto 1.00 2.50
I19 Max Scherzer 1.00 2.50
I20 Dee Gordon .60 1.50
I21 David Price .75 2.00
I22 Chris Sale 1.00 2.50
I23 A.J. Pollock .60 1.50
I24 Buster Posey 1.25 3.00
I25 Nolan Arenado 1.50 4.00

2016 Stadium Club Legends Die Cut

COMPLETE SET (10) 15.00 40.00
*GOLD/25: 4X TO 10X BASIC
LDC1 Robin Yount 1.00 2.50
LDC2 Robin Roberts .75 2.00
LDC3 Willie McCovey .75 2.00
LDC4 Johnny Bench 1.00 2.50
LDC5 Brooks Robinson .75 2.00
LDC6 Lou Gehrig 2.00 5.00
LDC7 Whitey Ford .75 2.00
LDC8 Tom Seaver .75 2.00
LDC9 Ozzie Smith 1.25 3.00
LDC10 Reggie Jackson .75 2.00

2016 Stadium Club Lone Star Signatures

EXCHANGE DEADLINE 6/30/2018
LSSBH Bryce Harper 75.00 200.00
LSSBP Buster Posey 25.00 60.00
LSSCC Carlos Correa 60.00 150.00
LSSCK Clayton Kershaw 60.00 150.00
LSSCR Cal Ripken Jr. 60.00 150.00
LSSCS Chris Sale 25.00 60.00
LSSDW David Wright
LSSKB Kris Bryant
LSSMP Mike Piazza 50.00 120.00
LSSOV Omar Vizquel
LSSPN Phil Niekro 20.00 50.00
LSSRC Robinson Cano 20.00 50.00
LSSYD Yu Darvish 30.00 80.00

2016 Stadium Club Triumvirates Luminous

*LUMINESCENT: .6X TO 1.5X BASIC
*ILLUMINATOR: 1.5X TO 4X BASIC
T1A Buster Posey 2.00 5.00
T1B Madison Bumgarner 1.25 3.00
T1C Hunter Pence 1.25 3.00
T2A Aroldis Chapman 1.50 4.00
T2B Andrew Miller 1.25 3.00
T2C Dellin Betances 1.25 3.00
T3A Lorenzo Cain 1.00 2.50
T3B Salvador Perez 1.25 3.00
T3C Kendrys Morales 1.00 2.50
T4A Jacob deGrom 3.00 8.00
T4B Noah Syndergaard 1.25 3.00
T4C Matt Harvey 1.25 3.00
T5A Kris Bryant 2.00 5.00
T5B Kyle Schwarber 3.00 8.00
T5C Addison Russell 1.50 4.00
T6A Miguel Sano 1.50 4.00
T6B Francisco Lindor 1.50 4.00
T6C Carlos Correa 1.50 4.00
T7A Mike Trout 8.00 20.00
T7B Josh Donaldson 1.25 3.00
T7C Bryce Harper 2.50 6.00
T8A Zack Greinke 1.50 4.00
T8B Jake Arrieta 1.25 3.00
T8C Dallas Keuchel 1.25 3.00
T9A Adrian Beltre 1.50 4.00
T9B Prince Fielder 1.25 3.00
T9C Mitch Moreland 1.00 2.50
T10A Michael Wacha 1.25 3.00
T10B Adam Wainwright 1.25 3.00
T10C Trevor Rosenthal 1.25 3.00

2017 Stadium Club

COMP.SET w/o SP's (300) 40.00 100.00
SP VAR ODDS 1:72 HOBBY
1 Albert Almora .25 .60
2 Mike Moustakas .30 .75
3 Noah Syndergaard .30 .75
4A Nelson Cruz .40 1.00
4B Nelson Cruz SP w/ bat 8.00 20.00
5 Aroldis Chapman .40 1.00
6 Adam Jones .30 .75
7 C.J. Cron .25 .60
8A Yu Darvish .40 1.00
8B Clayton Kershaw SP portrait w ball in hand 8.00 20.00
9 Greg Maddux .50 1.25
10 Danny Santana .25 .60
11 Harmon Killebrew .40 1.00
12 JaCoby Jones RC .50 1.25
13 Jake Thompson .25 .60
14A Ben Zobrist .30 .75
14B Zbrst SP WS trophy 10.00 25.00
15 Jorge Soler .40 1.00
16 Matt Harvey .30 .75
17 Didi Gregorius .30 .75
18 Fernando Rodney .25 .60
19 DJ LeMahieu .40 1.00
20A Dansby Swanson RC 1.00 2.50
20B Swnsn SP Glv on hat 12.00 30.00
21 Randy Johnson .40 1.00
22 Adam Duvall .30 .75
23 Yasmany Tomas .25 .60
24 Zack Greinke .40 1.00
25 Mark Melancon .25 .60
26 Eric Hosmer .30 .75
27 David Peralta .25 .60
28 Joe Mauer .30 .75
29 John Smoltz .40 1.00
30 Danny Duffy .25 .60
31A Salvador Perez .30 .75
31B Salvador Perez SP wearing catcher's gear 8.00 20.00
32A Brandon Phillips .25 .60
32B Brandon Phillips SP front of jersey visible 6.00 15.00
33 Yadier Molina .50 1.25
34 Greg Bird .30 .75
35 Nomar Mazara .25 .60
36 Willson Contreras .40 1.00
37A Jose Bautista .30 .75
37B Jose Bautista SP w/ cigar and goggles 8.00 20.00
38 Robert Gsellman .25 .60
39A Bryce Harper .60 1.50
39B Hrpr SP Hat over heart 12.00 30.00
40 Jose Peraza .30 .75
41A Kris Bryant .50 1.25
41B Bryant SP w/WWE belt 10.00 25.00
42A Justin Verlander .40 1.00
42B Justin Verlander SP in batting cage 8.00 20.00
43 Jharel Cotton RC .40 1.00
44 Jacoby Ellsbury .30 .75
45 Kyle Seager .25 .60

46 Trayce Thompson .30 .75
47 Ryan Braun .30 .75
48 Tanner Roark .25 .60
49 Masahiro Tanaka .30 .75
50 Todd Frazier .25 .60
51 Travis Jankowski .25 .60
52 Jason Varitek .40 1.00
53A Anthony Rizzo .50 1.25
53B Rizzo SP WS parade 12.00 30.00
54 Kevin Pillar .25 .60
55 Hank Aaron .75 2.00
56 Ian Kinsler .30 .75
57 Josh Bell RC 1.00 2.50
58 Christian Friedrich .25 .60
59 Josh Donaldson .30 .75
60 Clay Buchholz .25 .60
61 Rod Carew .30 .75
62 Mark Trumbo .25 .60
63A Jason Heyward .30 .75
63B Jason Heyward SP unbuttoned jersey 6.00 15.00
64 Aaron Judge RC 5.00 12.00
65 Zach Britton .30 .75
66 Teoscar Hernandez RC 1.50 4.00
67 Whitey Ford .30 .75
68 Braden Shipley .25 .60
69 Jay Bruce .30 .75
70 Ken Griffey Jr. .75 2.00
71 J.T. Realmuto .40 1.00
72 Johnny Damon .30 .75
73 Julio Teheran .30 .75
74 Andrew Miller .30 .75
75A Eduardo Nunez .25 .60
75B Eduardo Nunez SP sitting down 5.00 12.00
76 Hunter Pence .30 .75
77 Rick Porcello .30 .75
78 Denard Span .25 .60
79 Matt Olson 1.25 3.00
80 Henry Owens .25 .60
81 Carlos Rodon .40 1.00
82 Mitch Moreland .25 .60
83 Matt Strahm .25 .60
84 Chad Pinder RC .40 1.00
85 Matt Duffy .25 .60
86 Ichiro .50 1.25
87 Tony Cingrani .25 .60
88 Rickey Henderson .40 1.00
89 Hunter Renfroe RC .50 1.25
90 Matt Wieters .40 1.00
91 Pat Neshek .25 .60
92 Alex Gordon .30 .75
93 Brad Miller .30 .75
94A Carlos Correa .40 1.00
94B Correa SP w/Altuve 8.00 20.00
95 Corey Dickerson .25 .60
96 Adam Conley .25 .60
97 Troy Tulowitzki .40 1.00
98 Stephen Piscotty .30 .75
99A Paul Goldschmidt .40 1.00
99B Gldschmdt SP Pntng bat 10.00 25.00
100 Brian Dozier .40 1.00
101 Lucas Giolito .30 .75
102 Billy Wagner .25 .60
103 Gabriel Ynoa .25 .60
104 Ryon Healy RC .50 1.25
105 Ty Blach .25 .60
106 Brandon Belt .30 .75
107 Alex Reyes RC .50 1.25
108 Jorge Alfaro RC .50 1.25
109 Mallex Smith .25 .60
110 Michael Conforto .30 .75
111 Yoan Moncada RC 1.25 3.00
112 Michael Lorenzen .25 .60
113 David Price .30 .75
114A Nolan Arenado .60 1.50
114B Nolan Arenado SP face visible 12.00 30.00
115 Logan Forsythe .25 .60
116A Jose Altuve .50 1.25
116B Altuve SP Portrait 12.00 30.00
117A Wil Myers .30 .75
117B Wil Myers SP standing w
bat in hands 8.00 20.00
118 Yandy Diaz RC .75 2.00
119 David Wright .30 .75
120A Jon Lester .30 .75
120B Jon Lester SP holding up
World Series trophy 8.00 20.00
121 Tim Anderson .40 1.00
122 Adrian Gonzalez .30 .75
123A Kyle Hendricks .40 1.00
123B Kyle Hendricks SP no hat 8.00 20.00
124 Shawn O'Malley .25 .60
125 Randal Grichuk .25 .60
126 Brooks Robinson .30 .75
127 J.J. Hardy .25 .60
128 Luis Severino .30 .75
129 Jason Kipnis .25 .60
130A Jonathan Villar .25 .60
130B Jonathan Villar SP
looking towards the sky 8.00 20.00
131A Manny Machado .40 1.00
131B Machado SP In dugout 12.00 30.00
132 Scooter Gennett .30 .75
133A Jeff Bagwell .30 .75
133B Jeff Bagwell SP signing autographs 6.00 15.00
134 Carlos Gonzalez .30 .75
135 Jameson Taillon .30 .75
136 Trey Mancini RC .75 2.00
137 Derek Jeter 1.00 2.50
138 Renato Nunez RC .75 2.00
139 Marcus Stroman .30 .75
140 Miguel Cabrera .40 1.00
141 Omar Vizquel .30 .75
142 Frank Thomas .40 1.00
143 Carlos Beltran .30 .75
144 Joey Votto .40 1.00
145 Aledmys Diaz .30 .75
146 Byron Buxton .40 1.00
147 Kyle Zimmer RC .40 1.00
148 Carson Fulmer RC .40 1.00
149A Andrew Benintendi RC 1.50 4.00
149B Bnntndi SP w/C.Yng 15.00 40.00
150 Felix Hernandez .30 .75
151A Tim Raines .30 .75
151B Tim Raines SP hitting off of a tee 6.00 15.00
152 Gregory Polanco .30 .75
153 Roy Oswalt .30 .75
154 Lou Gehrig .75 2.00
155 Corey Seager .40 1.00
156 Lucas Duda .30 .75
157 Gerrit Cole .40 1.00
158A Francisco Lindor .40 1.00
158B Lindor SP No hat 8.00 20.00
159 Johnny Bench .40 1.00
160 Julio Urias .40 1.00
161 Tyler Glasnow RC 1.50 4.00
162 Andrew McCutchen .40 1.00
163 Don Mattingly .75 2.00
164 Kenta Maeda .30 .75
165A Addison Russell .40 1.00
165B Addison Russell
SP World Series hat on 8.00 20.00
166 Javier Lopez .25 .60
167 Tommy Joseph .40 1.00
168 Sandy Koufax .75 2.00
169A Matt Carpenter .40 1.00
169B Matt Carpenter SP w/ bat 8.00 20.00
170 Ryne Sandberg .75 2.00
171 Manuel Margot RC .40 1.00
172 Brandon Crawford .30 .75
173 Steven Matz .25 .60
174A Aaron Nola .30 .75
174B Aaron Nola SP stretching 6.00 15.00
175 Mark McGwire .60 1.50
176A Dustin Pedroia .40 1.00
176B Dustin Pedroia SP red jersey 8.00 20.00
177 Robinson Cano .30 .75
178 Zach McAllister .25 .60
179 Brad Ziegler .25 .60
180 A.J. Reed .25 .60
181 Nolan Ryan 1.25 3.00
182 Kevin Kiermaier .30 .75
183A Jose Abreu .40 1.00
183B Jose Abreu SP portrait w/ bat 8.00 20.00
184 Cameron Maybin .25 .60
185 Gary Carter .30 .75
186 Kendrys Morales .25 .60
187 Dexter Fowler .30 .75
188 Reynaldo Lopez RC .40 1.00
189 Justin Upton .30 .75
190 Xander Bogaerts .40 1.00
191 Cole Hamels .30 .75
192 A.J. Pollock .25 .60
193 Jackie Robinson .40 1.00
194 Andres Galarraga .30 .75
195A Alex Bregman RC 2.00 5.00
195B Bregman SP w/Correa 25.00 60.00
196 Victor Martinez .30 .75
197 Tyler Skaggs .25 .60
198 Ryan Schimpf .25 .60
199 Roman Quinn .25 .60
200 Dave Winfield .30 .75
201A Trea Turner .30 .75
201B Turner SP Blue jrsy 6.00 15.00
202 Alex Colome .25 .60
203A Hernan Perez .25 .60
203B Hernan Perez SP w/ Scooter Gennett 5.00 12.00
204A Kyle Schwarber .30 .75
204B Schwrbr SP WS hat 8.00 20.00
205 Warren Spahn .30 .75
206 Duke Snider .30 .75
207 Charlie Blackmon .40 1.00
208 J.A. Happ .30 .75
209 Hisashi Iwakuma .30 .75
210 Garrett Richards .30 .75
211 Zach Davies .25 .60
212 Christian Yelich .50 1.25
213 Jonathan Lucroy .30 .75
214 Max Scherzer .40 1.00
215 Willie Stargell .30 .75
216 Odubel Herrera .30 .75
217 Ender Inciarte .25 .60
218 Ozzie Smith .50 1.25
219 Aaron Sanchez .30 .75
220A Jose Berrios .30 .75
220B Jose Berrios SP standing in hallway 6.00 15.00
221 Cal Ripken Jr. 1.25 3.00
222 Miguel Sano .30 .75
223A Jake Arrieta .30 .75
223B Jake Arrieta SP w/ David Ross 6.00 15.00
224 Drew Pomeranz .30 .75
225 Yangervis Solarte .25 .60
226 Mookie Betts .75 2.00
227 Jose Canseco .30 .75
228 Gavin Cecchini RC .40 1.00
229 Jordan Zimmermann .30 .75
230A Clayton Kershaw .60 1.50
230B Krshw SP Ball in hand 12.00 30.00
231A Giancarlo Stanton .40 1.00
231B Giancarlo Stanton SP sitting 6.00 15.00
232 Joe Musgrove RC 1.25 3.00
233A Mike Trout 2.00 5.00
233B Trout SP Petting dog 40.00 100.00
234 Bo Jackson .40 1.00
235 Yulieski Gurriel RC .60 1.50
236 Bobby Abreu .25 .60
237 Ervin Santana .25 .60
238A Sonny Gray .30 .75
238B Gray SP w/Hahn 10.00 25.00
239 Chris Davis .25 .60
240 Andrelton Simmons .25 .60
241 Elvis Andrus .30 .75
242 Carl Yastrzemski .60 1.50
243 Jose De Leon RC .40 1.00
244 Raimel Tapia RC .50 1.25
245 Chris Sale .40 1.00
246A Javier Baez .50 1.25
246B Baez SP WS trophy 10.00 25.00
247A Gary Sanchez .40 1.00
247B Sanchez SP Towel 8.00 20.00
248 David Ortiz .40 1.00
249 Chipper Jones .40 1.00
250 Dee Gordon .25 .60
251 Tyler Naquin .40 1.00
252 Luke Weaver RC .60 1.50
253A Evan Longoria .30 .75
253B Evan Longoria SP w/ David Ortiz 8.00 20.00
254 Maikel Franco .30 .75
255 Seth Lugo RC .40 1.00
256 Michael Fulmer .25 .60
257 Daniel Murphy .30 .75
258 Stephen Vogt .30 .75
259 Adrian Beltre .40 1.00
260 Ted Williams .75 2.00
261 Luis Perdomo .25 .60
262 Joc Pederson .30 .75
263 Freddie Freeman .50 1.25
264 Rougned Odor .30 .75
265 Matt Shoemaker .30 .75
266A Starling Marte .30 .75
266B Starling Marte SP Gregory Polanco 8.00 20.00
Andrew McCutchen
267 Hunter Dozier RC .40 1.00
268A Jacob deGrom .75 2.00
268B Jacob deGrom SP
spining iPad on finger 15.00 40.00
269A Albert Pujols .50 1.25
269B Pujols SP w/Cabrera 10.00 25.00
270 Steven Wright .25 .60
271 Joe Panik .30 .75
272 Jeremy Hazelbaker .30 .75
273 A.J. Ramos .25 .60
274 Ian Desmond .25 .60
275 Stephen Strasburg .40 1.00
276 Martin Prado .25 .60
277A Billy Hamilton .30 .75
277B Billy Hamilton SP
getting cooler dumped 8.00 20.00
278A Buster Posey .50 1.25
278B Posey SP Sitting 10.00 25.00
279 Trevor Story .40 1.00
280 Ken Giles .25 .60
281 Edwin Encarnacion .40 1.00
282 Max Kepler .30 .75
283 Willie McCovey .30 .75
284 Chase Anderson .25 .60
285A Orlando Arcia RC .60 1.50
285B Orlando Arcia SP sitting w/ bat 8.00 20.00
286 David Ross .25 .60
287 Derrek Lee .25 .60
288 Tyler Austin .30 .75
289 Reggie Jackson .30 .75
290 Jon Gray .25 .60
291 Jimmy Nelson .25 .60
292 Alex Dickerson .25 .60
293 David Dahl RC .50 1.25
294 George Springer .30 .75
295 Jayson Werth .30 .75
296 Shelby Miller .30 .75
297 Curtis Granderson .30 .75
298 Dan Vogelbach .40 1.00
299 Corey Kluber .30 .75
300 Eddie Rosario .30 .75

2017 Stadium Club Black and White Orange Foil

*BW ORNG: 5X TO 12X BASIC
*BW ORNG RC: 3X TO 8X BASIC RC
STATED ODDS 1:48 HOBBY
64 Aaron Judge 60.00 150.00
70 Ken Griffey Jr. 25.00 60.00
137 Derek Jeter 40.00 100.00
181 Nolan Ryan 20.00 50.00
221 Cal Ripken Jr. 25.00 60.00
233 Mike Trout 25.00 60.00

2017 Stadium Club Black Foil

*BLK FOIL: 1.5X TO 4X BASIC
*BLK FOIL RC: 1X TO 2.5X BASIC RC
STATED ODDS 1:8 HOBBY
64 Aaron Judge 15.00 40.00

2017 Stadium Club Gold Foil

*GLD FOIL: 1X TO 2.5X BASIC
*GLD FOIL RC: .6X TO 1.5X BASIC RC
STATED ODDS 1:3 HOBBY
64 Aaron Judge 10.00 25.00

2017 Stadium Club Rainbow Foil

*RAINBOW: 8X TO 20X BASIC
*RAINBOW RC: 5X TO 12X BASIC RC
STATED ODDS 1:96 HOBBY
STATED PRINT RUN 25 SER.#'d SETS
41 Kris Bryant 40.00 100.00
64 Aaron Judge 100.00 250.00
86 Ichiro 30.00 80.00
116 Jose Altuve 20.00 50.00
137 Derek Jeter 60.00 150.00
163 Don Mattingly 25.00 60.00
168 Sandy Koufax 40.00 100.00
181 Nolan Ryan 40.00 100.00
221 Cal Ripken Jr. 40.00 100.00
233 Mike Trout 40.00 100.00

2017 Stadium Club Sepia

*SEPIA: 1.5X TO 4X BASIC
*SEPIA RC: 1X TO 2.5X BASIC RC
INSERTED IN RETAIL PACKS
64 Aaron Judge 15.00 40.00
137 Derek Jeter 12.00 30.00
163 Don Mattingly 12.00 30.00
181 Nolan Ryan 8.00 20.00
221 Cal Ripken Jr. 15.00 40.00

2017 Stadium Club Chrome

STATED ODDS 1:16 HOBBY
SCC1 Sandy Koufax 2.50 6.00
SCC2 Hank Aaron 2.50 6.00
SCC3 Mike Trout 6.00 15.00
SCC4 Ichiro 1.50 4.00
SCC5 Bryce Harper 2.00 5.00
SCC6 Ken Griffey Jr. 2.50 6.00
SCC7 Greg Maddux 1.50 4.00
SCC8 Randy Johnson 1.25 3.00
SCC9 Buster Posey 1.50 4.00
SCC10 Cal Ripken Jr. 4.00 10.00
SCC11 Bo Jackson 1.25 3.00
SCC12 Carl Yastrzemski 2.00 5.00
SCC13 Mark McGwire 2.00 5.00
SCC14 Nolan Ryan 4.00 10.00
SCC15 Reggie Jackson 1.00 2.50
SCC16 Rickey Henderson 1.25 3.00
SCC17 Kris Bryant 1.50 4.00
SCC18 Chipper Jones 1.25 3.00
SCC19 David Ortiz 1.25 3.00
SCC20 Ryne Sandberg 2.50 6.00
SCC21 Carlos Correa 1.25 3.00
SCC22 Clayton Kershaw 2.00 5.00
SCC23 Don Mattingly 2.50 6.00
SCC24 Frank Thomas 1.25 3.00
SCC25 Ryan Braun 1.00 2.50
SCC26 David Wright 1.00 2.50
SCC27 Corey Seager 1.25 3.00
SCC28 Bobby Abreu .75 2.00
SCC29 John Smoltz 1.25 3.00
SCC30 Ozzie Smith 1.50 4.00
SCC31 David Price 1.00 2.50
SCC32 Dustin Pedroia 1.25 3.00
SCC33 Manny Machado 1.25 3.00
SCC34 Yoan Moncada 2.50 6.00
SCC35 Freddie Freeman 1.50 4.00
SCC36 Chris Sale 1.25 3.00
SCC37 Jacob deGrom 2.50 6.00
SCC38 Kenta Maeda 1.00 2.50
SCC39 Anthony Rizzo 1.50 4.00
SCC40 Nolan Arenado 2.00 5.00
SCC41 Julio Urias 1.25 3.00
SCC42 Kyle Schwarber 1.25 3.00
SCC43 Noah Syndergaard 1.00 2.50
SCC44 Addison Russell 1.25 3.00
SCC45 Albert Almora .75 2.00
SCC46 Dexter Fowler 1.00 2.50
SCC47 Francisco Lindor 1.25 3.00
SCC48 Jose Altuve 1.00 2.50
SCC49 Matt Carpenter 1.25 3.00
SCC50 Dansby Swanson 2.00 5.00
SCC51 Yulieski Gurriel 1.25 3.00
SCC52 Sonny Gray 1.00 2.50
SCC53 Jameson Taillon 1.00 2.50
SCC54 Lucas Giolito 1.00 2.50
SCC55 Miguel Sano 1.00 2.50
SCC56 Joc Pederson 1.00 2.50
SCC57 Alex Bregman 4.00 10.00
SCC58 Hunter Dozier .75 2.00
SCC59 Andres Galarraga .75 2.00
SCC60 Kyle Seager .75 2.00
SCC61 Omar Vizquel 1.00 2.50
SCC62 George Springer 1.00 2.50
SCC63 Kendrys Morales .75 2.00
SCC64 Starling Marte 1.00 2.50
SCC65 Trevor Story 1.25 3.00
SCC66 David Dahl 1.00 2.50
SCC67 Alex Reyes 1.00 2.50
SCC68 Tyler Glasnow 3.00 8.00
SCC69 Roy Oswalt 1.00 2.50
SCC70 Steven Matz .75 2.00
SCC71 Trea Turner 1.00 2.50
SCC72 Willson Contreras 1.25 3.00
SCC73 Stephen Piscotty 1.00 2.50
SCC74 Greg Bird 1.00 2.50
SCC75 Randal Grichuk .75 2.00
SCC76 Aaron Judge 10.00 25.00
SCC77 Andrew Benintendi 2.50 6.00
SCC78 Luke Weaver 1.25 3.00
SCC79 Jose De Leon .75 2.00
SCC80 Aaron Nola 1.00 2.50
SCC81 Aledmys Diaz 1.00 2.50
SCC82 Gavin Cecchini .75 2.00
SCC83 Jharel Cotton .75 2.00
SCC84 Joe Musgrove 2.50 6.00
SCC85 Jose Canseco 1.00 2.50
SCC86 Tim Anderson 1.25 3.00
SCC87 Ryon Healy 1.00 2.50
SCC88 Michael Fulmer .75 2.00
SCC89 Jeff Bagwell 1.00 2.50
SCC90 Tim Raines 1.00 2.50

2017 Stadium Club Chrome Refractors

*REF: 1X TO 2.5X BASIC
STATED ODDS 1:64 HOBBY
SCC76 Aaron Judge 25.00 60.00

2017 Stadium Club Contact Sheet

COMPLETE SET (15) 8.00 20.00
STATED ODDS 1:8 HOBBY
*GOLD: .75X TO 2X BASIC
*BLACK/99: 1.2X TO 3X BASIC
*ORANGE/50: 2.5X TO 6X BASIC
CSAB Alex Bregman 2.00 5.00
CSAR Addison Russell .60 1.50
CSCC Carlos Correa .60 1.50
CSDL DJ LeMahieu .60 1.50
CSDM Daniel Murphy .50 1.25
CSGS Giancarlo Stanton .60 1.50
CSI Ichiro .75 2.00
CSJA Jose Altuve .50 1.25
CSJB Jose Bautista .50 1.25
CSJD Josh Donaldson .50 1.25
CSJV Joey Votto .60 1.50
CSMB Mookie Betts 1.25 3.00
CSMC Miguel Cabrera .60 1.50
CSMT Mike Trout 3.00 8.00
CSRC Robinson Cano .50 1.25

2017 Stadium Club Instavision

STATED ODDS 1:256 HOBBY
*GOLD/50: .6X TO 1.5X BASIC
*BLACK/25: .75X TO 2X BASIC
IAJ Aaron Judge 30.00 80.00
IBH Bryce Harper 6.00 15.00
ICK Clayton Kershaw 6.00 15.00
IDJ Derek Jeter 12.00 30.00
IFL Francisco Lindor 4.00 10.00
IHA Hank Aaron 8.00 20.00
IKB Kris Bryant 15.00 40.00
IMB Mookie Betts 6.00 15.00
IMF Michael Fulmer 6.00 15.00
IMT Mike Trout 15.00 40.00

2017 Stadium Club Lone Star Signatures

STATED ODDS 1:1593 HOBBY
PRINT RUNS B/WN 10-25 COPIES PER
NO PRICING ON QTY 15 OR LESS
EXCHANGE DEADLINE 5/31/2019
LSSAG Andres Galarraga/25
LSSAR Anthony Rizzo/25 25.00 60.00
LSSCS Corey Seager/25 50.00 120.00
LSSDO David Ortiz
LSSJC Jose Canseco/25 25.00 60.00
LSSKB Kris Bryant EXCH
LSSOV Omar Vizquel/25 10.00 25.00

2017 Stadium Club Power Zone

STATED ODDS 1:8 HOBBY
*GOLD: .75X TO 2X BASIC
*BLACK/99: 1.2X TO 3X BASIC
*ORANGE/50: 2.5X TO 6X BASIC
PZAB Adrian Beltre .60 1.50
PZAG Andres Galarraga .50 1.25
PZAP Albert Pujols .75 2.00
PZAR Anthony Rizzo .75 2.00
PZBH Bryce Harper 1.00 2.50
PZBJ Bo Jackson .60 1.50
PZCJ Chipper Jones .60 1.50
PZCS Corey Seager .60 1.50
PZDO David Ortiz .60 1.50
PZEE Edwin Encarnacion .60 1.50
PZFF Freddie Freeman .75 2.00
PZFT Frank Thomas .60 1.50
PZGS Giancarlo Stanton .60 1.50
PZJC Jose Canseco .50 1.25
PZJD Josh Donaldson .50 1.25
PZJV Joey Votto .60 1.50
PZKB Kris Bryant .75 2.00
PZKG Ken Griffey Jr. 1.25 3.00
PZMC Miguel Cabrera .60 1.50
PZMM Manny Machado .60 1.50
PZMMC Mark McGwire 1.00 2.50
PZMT Mike Trout 3.00 8.00
PZNA Nolan Arenado 1.00 2.50
PZRB Ryan Braun .50 1.25
PZRC Robinson Cano .50 1.25
PZYC Yoenis Cespedes .60 1.50

2017 Stadium Club Scoreless Streak

COMPLETE SET (25) 10.00 25.00
STATED ODDS 1:8 HOBBY
*GOLD: .75X TO 2X BASIC
*BLACK/99: 1.2X TO 3X BASIC
*ORANGE/50: 2.5X TO 6X BASIC
SSAC Aroldis Chapman .60 1.50
SSAN Aaron Nola .50 1.25
SSAR Alex Reyes .50 1.25
SSCK Clayton Kershaw 1.00 2.50
SSCKR Corey Kluber .50 1.25
SSCM Carlos Martinez .50 1.25
SSCS Chris Sale .60 1.50
SSDP David Price .50 1.25
SSFH Felix Hernandez .50 1.25
SSJA Jake Arrieta .50 1.25
SSJC Johnny Cueto .50 1.25
SSJD Jacob deGrom 1.25 3.00
SSJL Jon Lester .50 1.25
SSJU Julio Urias .60 1.50
SSJV Justin Verlander .60 1.50
SSKM Kenta Maeda .50 1.25
SSMF Michael Fulmer .40 1.00
SSMS Max Scherzer .60 1.50
SSMSN Marcus Stroman .50 1.25
SSMT Masahiro Tanaka .50 1.25
SSNS Noah Syndergaard .50 1.25
SSSG Sonny Gray .50 1.25
SSSS Stephen Strasburg .60 1.50
SSYD Yu Darvish .60 1.50
SSZG Zack Greinke .60 1.50

2017 Stadium Club Autographs

STATED ODDS 1:10 HOBBY
EXCHANGE DEADLINE 5/31/2019
SCAAB Andrew Benintendi 25.00 60.00
SCAABN Alex Bregman 12.00 30.00
SCAAD Aledmys Diaz 4.00 10.00
SCAAGA Andres Galarraga 4.00 10.00
SCAAJE Aaron Judge 75.00 200.00
SCAAN Aaron Nola 5.00 12.00
SCAAR Alex Reyes 5.00 12.00
SCAARD A.J. Reed 3.00 8.00
SCABA Bobby Abreu 6.00 15.00
SCABH Bryce Harper
SCABP Buster Posey
SCABS Braden Shipley EXCH 3.00 8.00
SCABW Billy Wagner 5.00 12.00
SCACA Christian Arroyo EXCH 15.00 40.00
SCACC Carlos Correa
SCACF Carson Fulmer 3.00 8.00
SCACS Corey Seager
SCADJ Derek Jeter
SCADL Derrek Lee 3.00 8.00
SCADS Dansby Swanson
SCADV Dan Vogelbach 5.00 12.00
SCAFL Francisco Lindor 15.00 40.00
SCAGB Greg Bird 4.00 10.00
SCAGC Gavin Cecchini 3.00 8.00
SCAHA Hank Aaron
SCAHD Hunter Dozier 5.00 12.00
SCAHO Henry Owens 3.00 8.00
SCAI Ichiro
SCAJA Jose Altuve EXCH 25.00 60.00
SCAJAO Jorge Alfaro 4.00 10.00
SCAJBZ Javier Baez 12.00 30.00
SCAJC Jharel Cotton 3.00 8.00
SCAJCO Jose Canseco 6.00 15.00
SCAJDN Johnny Damon
SCAJH Jeremy Hazelbaker 4.00 10.00
SCAJM Joe Musgrove 10.00 25.00
SCAJTN Jake Thompson 3.00 8.00
SCAJU Julio Urias EXCH 6.00 15.00
SCAJV Jason Varitek
SCAKB Kris Bryant
SCAKS Kyle Schwarber EXCH
SCAKSR Kyle Seager 3.00 8.00
SCALW Luke Weaver 4.00 10.00
SCAMC Matt Carpenter 8.00 20.00
SCAMO Matt Olson EXCH 10.00 25.00
SCAMSM Matt Strahm 3.00 8.00
SCAMT Mike Trout
SCAOV Omar Vizquel 5.00 12.00
SCARGN Robert Gsellman 3.00 8.00
SCARHY Ryon Healy 4.00 10.00
SCARL Reynaldo Lopez 3.00 8.00
SCARO Roy Oswalt 12.00 30.00
SCARQ Roman Quinn 3.00 8.00
SCARSF Ryan Schimpf 3.00 8.00
SCART Raimel Tapia 4.00 10.00
SCASK Sandy Koufax
SCASL Seth Lugo 3.00 8.00
SCASW Steven Wright 3.00 8.00
SCATA Tyler Austin 4.00 10.00
SCATAN Tim Anderson 5.00 12.00
SCATB Ty Blach 3.00 8.00
SCATC Tim Cooney 3.00 8.00
SCATG Tyler Glasnow EXCH 10.00 25.00
SCATH Teoscar Hernandez 12.00 30.00
SCATM Trey Mancini 6.00 15.00
SCATN Tyler Naquin 5.00 12.00
SCAYG Yulieski Gurriel 10.00 25.00
SCAYMA Yoan Moncada

2017 Stadium Club Autographs Black Foil

*BLACK: .75X TO 2X BASIC
STATED ODDS 1:256 HOBBY
STATED PRINT RUN 25 SER.#'d SETS
EXCHANGE DEADLINE 5/31/2019
SCACS Corey Seager 40.00 100.00

2017 Stadium Club Autographs Gold Foil

*GOLD: .5X TO 1.2X BASIC
STATED ODDS 1:140 HOBBY
STATED PRINT RUN 50 SER.#'d SETS
EXCHANGE DEADLINE 5/31/2019
SCADS Dansby Swanson 40.00 100.00
SCAFL Francisco Lindor 25.00 60.00

2017 Stadium Club Autographs Mystery Redemption

EXCHANGE DEADLINE 5/31/2019
SCACB Cody Bellinger 75.00 200.00
SCAIH Ian Happ 75.00 200.00

2017 Stadium Club Beam Team

STATED ODDS 1:16 HOBBY
*GOLD: 1X TO 2.5X BASIC
*BLACK/99: 1.2X TO 3X BASIC
*ORANGE/50: 2.5X TO 6X BASIC
BTAB Andrew Benintendi 1.50 4.00
BTAR Anthony Rizzo 1.00 2.50
BTARL Addison Russell .75 2.00
BTBH Bryce Harper 1.25 3.00
BTBP Buster Posey 1.00 2.50
BTCC Carlos Correa .75 2.00
BTCK Clayton Kershaw 1.25 3.00
BTCS Corey Seager .75 2.00
BTDJ Derek Jeter 2.00 5.00
BTDP Dustin Pedroia .75 2.00
BTDS Dansby Swanson 1.25 3.00
BTFF Freddie Freeman 1.00 2.50
BTFL Francisco Lindor .75 2.00
BTGS Gary Sanchez .75 2.00
BTJA Jose Altuve .60 1.50
BTJD Jacob deGrom 1.50 4.00
BTJU Julio Urias .75 2.00
BTJV Justin Verlander .75 2.00
BTKB Kris Bryant 1.00 2.50
BTKS Kyle Schwarber .75 2.00
BTMM Manny Machado .75 2.00
BTMT Mike Trout 4.00 10.00
BTNA Nolan Arenado 1.25 3.00
BTNS Noah Syndergaard .60 1.50
BTRC Robinson Cano .60 1.50

2018 Stadium Club

COMPLETE SET (300) 25.00 60.00
1 Sandy Alcantara RC .20 .50
2 Miguel Cabrera .30 .75
3 Clint Frazier RC .60 1.50
4 Darryl Strawberry .20 .50
5 Johnny Cueto .25 .60
6 Carlos Gonzalez .25 .60
7 Alex Mejia RC .30 .75
8 Starlin Castro .20 .50
9 Zack Godley .20 .50
10 Matt Kemp .25 .60
11 Tzu-Wei Lin .20 .50
12 Andrew McCutchen .30 .75
13 Justin Bour .20 .50
14 Daniel Murphy .25 .60
15 Hanley Ramirez .25 .60
16 Carlos Rodon .25 .60
17 Zack Granite RC .30 .75
18 Christian Villanueva RC .30 .75
19 Garrett Richards .25 .60
20 Stephen Strasburg .30 .75
21 Robinson Cano .25 .60
22 Kevin Kiermaier .25 .60
23 Carlos Martinez .25 .60
24 Carlos Santana .25 .60
25 Marcell Ozuna .30 .75
26 Niko Goodrum RC .50 1.25
27 Michael Conforto .25 .60
28 Billy Hamilton .25 .60
29 Johnny Bench .30 .75
30 Javier Baez .40 1.00
31 Jose Quintana .20 .50
32 Carlos Correa .30 .75
33 Evan Longoria .25 .60
34 Manny Margot .20 .50
35 Marcus Stroman .25 .60
36 Gerrit Cole .30 .75
37 Victor Robles RC .75 2.00
38 Jake Arrieta .25 .60
39 Wil Myers .25 .60
40 Justin Smoak .20 .50
41 Corey Kluber .25 .60
42 Jacob deGrom .60 1.50
43 Michael Fulmer .20 .50
44 Matt Olson .25 .60
45 J.P. Crawford RC .30 .75
46 Dallas Keuchel .25 .60
47 Matt Carpenter .30 .75
48 Mike Trout 1.50 4.00
49 Mike Moustakas .25 .60
50 Adam Jones .25 .60
51 Taijuan Walker .20 .50
52 Paul Goldschmidt .30 .75
53 Jake Lamb .25 .60
54 Masahiro Tanaka .25 .60
55 Lucas Giolito .25 .60
56 Jon Lester .25 .60
57 Luiz Gohara RC .30 .75
58 Francisco Lindor .30 .75
59 Yonder Alonso .20 .50
60 Aaron Altherr .20 .50
61 Anthony Rendon .30 .75
62 Tyler Glasnow .30 .75
63 Ian Kinsler .20 .50
64 Ender Inciarte .20 .50
65 Andrelton Simmons .20 .50
66 Jose Ramirez .25 .60
67 A.J. Minter RC .40 1.00
68 Ozzie Smith .40 1.00
69 Max Scherzer .30 .75
70 Noah Syndergaard .25 .60
71 Chris Sale .30 .75
72 Bo Jackson .30 .75
73 George Springer .25 .60
74 Ichiro .40 1.00
75 Ryne Sandberg .60 1.50
76 Eddie Rosario .30 .75
77 Paul Blackburn RC .30 .75
78 Yoenis Cespedes .30 .75
79 Mike Clevinger .25 .60
80 Andy Pettitte .25 .60
81 Will Clark .25 .60
82 Felix Jorge RC .30 .75
83 Joey Votto .30 .75
84 Nicky Delmonico RC .30 .75
85 Josh Reddick .20 .50
86 Dansby Swanson .30 .75
87 Nicholas Castellanos .30 .75
88 Andrew Stevenson RC .30 .75
89 Brandon Woodruff RC 1.00 2.50
90 Jose Canseco .25 .60
91 Dustin Fowler RC .30 .75
92 Kyle Farmer RC .30 .75
93 Nick Williams RC .40 1.00
94 Justin Upton .25 .60
95 Yasiel Puig .30 .75
96 J.D. Martinez .30 .75
97 Miguel Sano .25 .60
98 Jon Gray .20 .50
99 Jay Bruce .25 .60
100 Cam Gallagher RC .30 .75
101 Jack Flaherty RC 1.25 3.00
102 Richard Urena RC .30 .75
103 Tim Raines .25 .60
104 Hunter Renfroe .25 .60
105 Tomas Nido RC .30 .75
106 Austin Barnes .25 .60
107 Keon Broxton .20 .50
108 Erick Fedde RC .30 .75
109 Whit Merrifield .30 .75
110 Ozzie Albies RC 1.00 2.50
111 Cody Bellinger .60 1.50
112 Robbie Ray .20 .50
113 Tommy Pham .20 .50
114 Victor Caratini RC .40 1.00
115 Greg Allen RC .30 .75
116 Rougned Odor .25 .60
117 Rafael Devers RC 1.00 2.50
118 Xander Bogaerts .30 .75
119 Mitch Haniger .25 .60
120 Breyvic Valera RC .30 .75
121 Ryder Jones RC .30 .75
122 Chris Davis .20 .50
123 Craig Kimbrel .25 .60
124 Trevor Bauer .40 1.00
125 Chipper Jones .30 .75
126 Max Kepler .25 .60
127 Yadier Molina .40 1.00
128 Jose Berrios .25 .60
129 Manny Machado .30 .75
130 Eric Hosmer .25 .60
131 Matt Chapman .30 .75
132 Tyler Mahle RC .40 1.00
133 Nolan Ryan 1.00 2.50
134 Lucas Sims RC .30 .75
135 Chance Sisco RC .40 1.00
136 Christian Yelich .40 1.00
137 Josh Harrison .20 .50
138 Shohei Ohtani RC 8.00 20.00
139 Garrett Cooper RC .30 .75
140 Miguel Andujar RC 1.25 3.00
141 Jim Thome .25 .60
142 Chris Taylor .30 .75
143 Tim Locastro RC .30 .75
144 Luis Castillo .25 .60
145 Giancarlo Stanton .30 .75
146 Lance McCullers .20 .50
147 Ryan McMahon RC .75 2.00
148 Todd Frazier .20 .50
149 John Smoltz .25 .60
150 Justin Verlander .30 .75
151 Justin Turner .30 .75
152 Dwight Gooden .20 .50
153 Cameron Maybin .20 .50
154 Brandon Crawford .25 .60
155 Francisco Mejia RC .40 1.00
156 German Marquez .20 .50
157 Brett Gardner .25 .60
158 Dillon Maples RC .30 .75
159 Trey Mancini .25 .60
160 Cal Ripken Jr. 1.00 2.50
161 Rickey Henderson .30 .75
162 Brad Ziegler .20 .50
163 Ryan Zimmerman .25 .60
164 Barry Larkin .25 .60
165 Anthony Rizzo .40 1.00
166 Wade Boggs .25 .60
167 Dexter Fowler .25 .60
168 Chris Archer .20 .50
169 Trea Turner .25 .60
170 J.D. Davis RC .40 1.00
171 Don Mattingly .60 1.50
172 CC Sabathia .25 .60
173 Anthony Banda RC .30 .75
174 Kenley Jansen .25 .60
175 Mookie Betts .60 1.50
176 Dennis Eckersley .25 .60
177 Sean Newcomb .25 .60
178 Andrew Benintendi .30 .75
179 Bryce Harper .50 1.25
180 Ted Williams .60 1.50
181 Roberto Clemente .75 2.00
182 Aroldis Chapman .25 .60
183 Elvis Andrus .25 .60
184 Jeff Bagwell .25 .60
185 Jose Abreu .25 .60
186 Greg Bird .25 .60
187 Dustin Pedroia .25 .60
188 Bob Gibson .25 .60
189 Lewis Brinson .20 .50
190 Ian Happ .25 .60
191 Raisel Iglesias .25 .60
192 Buster Posey .40 1.00
193 Joc Pederson .25 .60
194 Joe Mauer .25 .60
195 Sonny Gray .25 .60
196 Pat Neshek .20 .50
197 Rhys Hoskins RC 1.25 3.00
198 Keury Mella RC .30 .75
199 Joey Gallo .25 .60
200 Jackie Robinson .30 .75
201 Kris Bryant .40 1.00
202 Yoan Moncada .30 .75
203 Zack Cozart .20 .50
204 Charlie Blackmon .30 .75
205 Austin Hays RC .50 1.25
206 Cole Hamels .25 .60
207 Nelson Cruz .30 .75
208 Greg Maddux .40 1.00
209 Dillon Peters RC .25 .60

210 Victor Arano RC .30 .75
211 Luis Severino .25 .60
212 Corey Seager .30 .75
213 Didi Gregorius .25 .60
214 Parker Bridwell RC .30 .75
215 Willson Contreras .30 .75
216 Anthony Santander RC .30 .75
217 Max Fried RC 1.25 3.00
218 Jimmie Sherfy RC .30 .75
219 Josh Donaldson .25 .60
220 Walker Buehler RC 1.50 4.00
221 Ryan Braun .25 .60
222 Domingo Santana .25 .60
223 Hank Aaron .60 1.50
224 Josh Hader .25 .60
225 Lorenzo Cain .20 .50
226 Starling Marte .25 .60
227 Andrew Miller .25 .60
228 Frank Thomas .30 .75
229 Paul DeJong .30 .75
230 Archie Bradley .20 .50
231 Julio Urias .30 .75
232 Freddie Freeman .40 1.00
233 Troy Scribner RC .30 .75
234 Adrian Beltre .30 .75
235 Orlando Arcia .20 .50
236 Albert Pujols .40 1.00
237 Kyle Seager .20 .50
238 Zach Davies .20 .50
239 Edwin Encarnacion .30 .75
240 David Price .25 .60
241 Aaron Judge .75 2.00
242 George Brett .60 1.50
243 Adam Duvall .25 .60
244 Yu Darvish .30 .75
245 Byron Buxton .30 .75
246 Alex Bregman .30 .75
247 Josh Bell .25 .60
248 Mariano Rivera .40 1.00
249 Nomar Mazara .20 .50
250 Mike Foltynewicz .20 .50
251 Dee Gordon .20 .50
252 Felix Hernandez .25 .60
253 Aaron Nola .25 .60
254 Jorge Alfaro .20 .50
255 Gregory Polanco .25 .60
256 Reggie Jackson .25 .60
257 Gary Sanchez .30 .75
258 Kenta Maeda .25 .60
259 Eric Thames .20 .50
260 Amed Rosario RC .40 1.00
261 Hunter Pence .25 .60
262 Randy Johnson .30 .75
263 Willie Calhoun RC .50 1.25
264 Alex Wood .20 .50
265 Travis Shaw .20 .50
266 Alex Verdugo RC .50 1.25
267 Avisail Garcia .25 .60
268 A.J. Pollock .20 .50
269 Zack Greinke .30 .75
270 Carlos Carrasco .20 .50
271 Jose Altuve .25 .60
272 Salvador Perez .25 .60
273 Kyle Schwarber .30 .75
274 Dominic Smith RC .40 1.00
275 Derek Jeter .75 2.00
276 Clayton Kershaw .50 1.25
277 Yuli Gurriel .25 .60
278 Marwin Gonzalez .20 .50
279 Brian Anderson RC .40 1.00
280 Harrison Bader RC .50 1.25
281 Brian Dozier .25 .60
282 Mark McGwire .50 1.25
283 Jonathan Schoop .20 .50
284 Tyler Wade RC .40 1.00
285 Mike Piazza .30 .75
286 Addison Russell .25 .60
287 J.T. Realmuto .30 .75
288 Sandy Koufax .60 1.50
289 Jason Heyward .25 .60
290 Nolan Arenado .50 1.25
291 Edwin Diaz .25 .60
292 Jen-Ho Tseng RC .30 .75
293 Jackie Bradley Jr. .30 .75
294 Sean Manaea .20 .50
295 Mitch Garver RC .30 .75
296 Jackson Stephens RC .30 .75
297 Khris Davis .30 .75
298 Tim Beckham .25 .60
299 Trevor Story .30 .75
300 Hideki Matsui .30 .75

2018 Stadium Club Black and White Orange Foil

*BW ORNG: 5X TO 12X BASIC
*BW ORNG RC: 3X TO 8X BASIC RC
STATED ODDS 1:48 HOBBY

2018 Stadium Club Black Foil

*BLK FOIL: 1.5X TO 4X BASIC
*BLK FOIL RC: 1X TO 2.5X BASIC RC
STATED ODDS 1:8 HOBBY

2018 Stadium Club Rainbow Foil

*RAINBOW: 8X TO 20X BASIC
*RAINBOW RC: 5X TO 12X BASIC RC
STATED ODDS 1:145 HOBBY
STATED PRINT RUN 25 SER.#'d SETS

2018 Stadium Club Red Foil

*RED FOIL: 1X TO 2.5X BASIC
*RED FOIL RC: .6X TO 1.5X BASIC RC
STATED ODDS 1:3 HOBBY

2018 Stadium Club Sepia

*SEPIA: 2X TO 5X BASIC
*SEPIA RC: 1.2X TO 3X BASIC RC
INSERTED IN RETAIL PACKS

2018 Stadium Club Photo Variations

STATED ODDS 1:109 HOBBY
3 Frazier Jumping 10.00 25.00
32 Correa WS Celebrtn 8.00 20.00
37 Robles Bat 12.00 30.00
48 Trout Running 40.00 100.00
52 Gldschmdt Wht jsy 8.00 20.00
58 Lindor Diving 25.00 60.00
69 Scherzer Red jsy 15.00 40.00
70 Syndergaard Throwing 6.00 15.00
71 Sale Bullpen 20.00 50.00
72 Jackson Brkng Bat 25.00 60.00
81 Clark Jsy back 30.00 80.00
83 Votto Fielding 8.00 20.00
100 Ripken w Mascot 60.00 150.00
111 Bellinger Running 15.00 40.00
117 Devers Red jsy 15.00 40.00
125 Jones Bubble 8.00 20.00
129 Machado Towel 8.00 20.00
133 Ryan Wht jsu 25.00 60.00
138 Ohtani Pitching 40.00 100.00
145 Stanton Cage 8.00 20.00
150 Vrlndr Jsy back 8.00 20.00
165 Rizzo Fielding 15.00 40.00
169 Turner Bunting 10.00 25.00
171 Mtngly Gray jsy 12.00 30.00
175 Betts Flag 25.00 60.00
178 Benintendi Catching 8.00 20.00
179 Harper High-five 25.00 60.00
180 Williams Color 15.00 40.00
181 Clemente Elastic 15.00 40.00
192 Posey Sliding 10.00 25.00
197 Hoskins Sunglasses 20.00 50.00
200 Robinson Running 8.00 20.00
201 Bryant Batting 15.00 40.00
213 Gleyber Torres 100.00 250.00
223A Aaron Running 15.00 40.00
223B Ronald Acuna 100.00 250.00
228 Thomas Cage 8.00 20.00
241 Judge Bat 50.00 120.00
242 Brett Blue jsy 25.00 60.00
244 Darvish Pnstrp jsy 8.00 20.00
248 Rivera Ball 10.00 25.00
260 Rosario Batting 20.00 50.00
262 Johnson Batting 15.00 40.00
271 Altuve Batting 6.00 15.00
275 Jeter Jumping 30.00 80.00
276 Kershaw w Kids 12.00 30.00
282 McGwire Grn jsy 12.00 30.00
285 Piazza Gear 8.00 20.00
288 Koufax Color 40.00 100.00
290 Arenado Pstripe jsy 12.00 30.00

2018 Stadium Club Autographs

STATED ODDS 1:10 HOBBY
EXCHANGE DEADLINE 5/30/2020
*RED/50: .5X TO 1.2X BASIC
*BLACK/25: .6X TO 1.5X BASIC
SCAAA Aaron Altherr 4.00 10.00
SCAAB Anthony Banda 3.00 8.00
SCAABA Austin Barnes 4.00 10.00
SCAAH Austin Hays 6.00 15.00
SCAAME Alex Mejia 3.00 8.00
SCAAMI A.J. Minter 4.00 10.00
SCAAR Anthony Rizzo 20.00 50.00
SCAARO Amed Rosario 4.00 10.00
SCAAS Anthony Santander 3.00 8.00
SCAAST Andrew Stevenson 3.00 8.00
SCAAW Alex Wood 3.00 8.00
SCABH Bryce Harper
SCABJ Bo Jackson
SCABV Breyvic Valera 3.00 8.00
SCABW Brandon Woodruff 10.00 25.00
SCACG Cam Gallagher 3.00 8.00
SCACS Carlos Santana 6.00 15.00
SCACT Chris Taylor 4.00 10.00
SCACV Christian Villanueva 3.00 8.00
SCADF Dustin Fowler 3.00 8.00
SCADG Dwight Gooden 8.00 20.00
SCADJ Derek Jeter
SCADM Don Mattingly 60.00 150.00
SCADMA Dillon Maples 3.00 8.00
SCADSM Dominic Smith 4.00 10.00
SCADST Darryl Strawberry 10.00 25.00
SCAFL Francisco Lindor 15.00 40.00
SCAFM Francisco Mejia 6.00 15.00
SCAFT Frank Thomas 40.00 100.00
SCAGA Greg Allen 3.00 8.00
SCAGC Garrett Cooper 3.00 8.00
SCAGT Gleyber Torres 75.00 200.00
SCAHA Hank Aaron 100.00 250.00
SCAHB Harrison Bader 8.00 20.00
SCAIH Ian Happ 8.00 20.00
SCAI Ichiro
SCAJA Jose Altuve 40.00 100.00
SCAJBE Jose Berrios 4.00 10.00
SCAJBO Justin Bour 3.00 8.00
SCAJC Jose Canseco 10.00 25.00
SCAJD J.D. Davis 4.00 10.00
SCAJF Jack Flaherty 15.00 40.00
SCAJR Jose Ramirez 10.00 25.00
SCAJS Jimmie Sherfy 3.00 8.00
SCAJST Jackson Stephens 3.00 8.00
SCAJV Joey Votto 40.00 100.00
SCAKB Kris Bryant
SCAKBR Keon Broxton 5.00 12.00
SCAKD Khris Davis 6.00 15.00
SCAKF Kyle Farmer 3.00 8.00
SCAKM Keury Mella 3.00 8.00
SCAKS Kyle Schwarber 10.00 25.00
SCALC Luis Castillo 4.00 10.00
SCAMA Miguel Andujar 10.00 25.00
SCAMFR Max Fried 6.00 15.00
SCAMIG Miguel Gomez 3.00 8.00
SCAMM Manny Machado 25.00 60.00
SCAMMC Mark McGwire 30.00 80.00
SCAMO Matt Olson 5.00 12.00
SCAMT Mike Trout 250.00 400.00
SCAND Nicky Delmonico 3.00 8.00
SCANG Niko Goodrum 5.00 12.00
SCANR Nolan Ryan 75.00 200.00
SCANSY Noah Syndergaard 15.00 40.00
SCAOA Ozzie Albies 20.00 50.00
SCAPB Paul Blackburn 3.00 8.00
SCAPD Paul DeJong 5.00 12.00
SCAPE Phillip Evans 3.00 8.00
SCAPG Paul Goldschmidt 20.00 50.00
SCARA Ronald Acuna 600.00 1200.00
SCARD Rafael Devers 30.00 80.00
SCARH Rhys Hoskins 15.00 40.00
SCARJ Ryder Jones 3.00 8.00
SCARR Randy Read 3.00 8.00
SCARU Richard Urena 3.00 8.00
SCASA Sandy Alcantara 3.00 8.00
SCASG Sonny Gray 10.00 25.00
SCASN Sean Newcomb 4.00 10.00
SCASO Shohei Ohtani EXCH 200.00 400.00
SCATB Tim Beckham 4.00 10.00
SCATL Tzu-Wei Lin 4.00 10.00
SCATLO Tim Locastro 3.00 8.00
SCATMA Trey Mancini 4.00 10.00
SCATN Tomas Nido 3.00 8.00
SCATP Tommy Pham 3.00 8.00
SCATS Troy Scribner 3.00 8.00
SCATW Tyler Wade 4.00 10.00
SCAVA Victor Arano 3.00 8.00
SCAVC Victor Caratini 4.00 10.00
SCAVR Victor Robles 10.00 25.00
SCAWCO Willson Contreras 10.00 25.00
SCAWM Whit Merrifield 8.00 20.00
SCAYA Yonder Alonso 3.00 8.00

2018 Stadium Club Beam Team

STATED ODDS 1:16 HOBBY
BTAB Andrew Benintendi .75 2.00
BTAJ Aaron Judge 2.00 5.00
BTAR Anthony Rizzo 1.00 2.50
BTARO Amed Rosario .60 1.50
BTBH Bryce Harper 1.25 3.00
BTCB Cody Bellinger 1.50 4.00
BTCC Carlos Correa .75 2.00
BTCF Clint Frazier 1.00 2.50
BTCK Clayton Kershaw 1.25 3.00
BTCS Corey Seager .75 2.00
BTDJ Derek Jeter 2.00 5.00
BTFL Francisco Lindor .75 2.00
BTGS Gary Sanchez .75 2.00
BTGST Giancarlo Stanton .75 2.00
BTJA Jose Altuve .60 1.50
BTJV Joey Votto .75 2.00
BTKB Kris Bryant 1.00 2.50
BTMB Mookie Betts 1.50 4.00
BTMM Manny Machado .75 2.00
BTMT Mike Trout 4.00 10.00
BTNS Noah Syndergaard .60 1.50
BTPG Paul Goldschmidt .75 2.00
BTRD Rafael Devers 1.50 4.00
BTRH Rhys Hoskins 2.00 5.00
BTSO Shohei Ohtani 12.00 30.00

2018 Stadium Club Beam Team Black

*BLACK: 1.2X TO 3X BASIC
STATED ODDS 1:438 HOBBY
STATED PRINT RUNT 99 SER.#'d SETS
BTSO Shohei Ohtani 30.00 80.00

2018 Stadium Club Beam Team Orange

*ORANGE: 3X TO 8X BASIC
STATED ODDS 1:868 HOBBY
STATED PRINT RUNT 50 SER.#'d SETS
BTSO Shohei Ohtani 60.00 150.00

2018 Stadium Club Beam Team Red

*RED: 1X TO 2.5X BASIC
STATED ODDS 1:256 HOBBY
BTSO Shohei Ohtani 20.00 50.00

2018 Stadium Club Chrome

STATED ODDS 1:16 HOBBY
*REF: .6X TO 1.5X BASIC
*GOLD MINT: 2.5X TO 6X BASIC
SCC3 Clint Frazier 1.50 4.00
SCC4 Darryl Strawberry .75 2.00
SCC12 Andrew McCutchen 1.25 3.00
SCC21 Robinson Cano 1.00 2.50
SCC27 Michael Conforto 1.00 2.50
SCC29 Johnny Bench 1.25 3.00
SCC30 Javier Baez 1.50 4.00
SCC32 Carlos Correa 1.25 3.00
SCC37 Victor Robles 2.00 5.00
SCC45 J.P. Crawford .75 2.00
SCC48 Mike Trout 8.00 20.00
SCC54 Masahiro Tanaka 1.00 2.50
SCC58 Francisco Lindor 1.25 3.00
SCC68 Ozzie Smith 1.50 4.00
SCC69 Max Scherzer 1.25 3.00
SCC70 Noah Syndergaard 1.00 2.50
SCC71 Chris Sale 1.25 3.00
SCC72 Bo Jackson 1.25 3.00
SCC73 George Springer 1.00 2.50
SCC74 Ichiro 1.50 4.00
SCC75 Ryne Sandberg 2.50 6.00
SCC80 Andy Pettitte 1.00 2.50
SCC83 Joey Votto 1.25 3.00
SCC84 Nicky Delmonico .75 2.00
SCC90 Jose Canseco 1.00 2.50
SCC93 Nick Williams 1.00 2.50
SCC97 Miguel Sano 1.00 2.50
SCC100 Cal Ripken Jr. 4.00 10.00
SCC101 Jack Flaherty 3.00 8.00
SCC104 Hunter Renfroe .75 2.00
SCC110 Ozzie Albies 2.50 6.00
SCC111 Cody Bellinger 2.50 6.00
SCC117 Rafael Devers 2.50 6.00
SCC125 Chipper Jones 1.25 3.00
SCC128 Jose Berrios 1.00 2.50
SCC129 Manny Machado 1.25 3.00
SCC132 Tyler Mahle 1.00 2.50
SCC133 Nolan Ryan 4.00 10.00
SCC138 Shohei Ohtani 10.00 25.00
SCC141 Jim Thome 1.00 2.50
SCC145 Giancarlo Stanton 1.25 3.00
SCC149 John Smoltz 1.00 2.50
SCC152 Dwight Gooden .75 2.00
SCC155 Francisco Mejia 1.00 2.50
SCC159 Trey Mancini 1.00 2.50
SCC161 Rickey Henderson 1.25 3.00
SCC164 Barry Larkin 1.00 2.50
SCC165 Anthony Rizzo 1.50 4.00
SCC166 Wade Boggs 1.00 2.50
SCC169 Trea Turner 1.00 2.50
SCC171 Don Mattingly 2.50 6.00
SCC176 Dennis Eckersley 1.00 2.50
SCC178 Andrew Benintendi 1.25 3.00
SCC179 Bryce Harper 2.00 5.00
SCC190 Ian Happ 1.00 2.50
SCC192 Buster Posey 1.50 4.00
SCC195 Sonny Gray 1.00 2.50
SCC197 Rhys Hoskins 3.00 8.00
SCC201 Kris Bryant 1.50 4.00
SCC205 Austin Hays 1.25 3.00
SCC208 Greg Maddux 1.50 4.00
SCC211 Luis Severino 1.00 2.50
SCC212 Corey Seager 1.25 3.00
SCC215 Willson Contreras 1.25 3.00
SCC220 Walker Buehler 4.00 10.00
SCC223 Hank Aaron 2.50 6.00
SCC228 Frank Thomas 1.25 3.00
SCC232 Freddie Freeman 1.50 4.00
SCC241 Aaron Judge 3.00 8.00
SCC244 Yu Darvish 1.25 3.00
SCC245 Byron Buxton 1.25 3.00
SCC246 Alex Bregman 1.25 3.00
SCC248 Mariano Rivera 1.50 4.00
SCC256 Reggie Jackson 1.00 2.50
SCC257 Gary Sanchez 1.25 3.00
SCC260 Amed Rosario 1.00 2.50
SCC262 Randy Johnson 1.25 3.00
SCC263 Willie Calhoun 1.25 3.00
SCC266 Alex Verdugo 1.25 3.00
SCC271 Jose Altuve 1.00 2.50
SCC273 Kyle Schwarber 1.25 3.00
SCC274 Dominic Smith 1.00 2.50
SCC275 Derek Jeter 3.00 8.00
SCC276 Clayton Kershaw 2.00 5.00
SCC280 Harrison Bader 1.25 3.00
SCC282 Mark McGwire 2.00 5.00
SCC286 Addison Russell 1.00 2.50
SCC288 Sandy Koufax 2.50 6.00
SCC290 Nolan Arenado 2.00 5.00
SCC300 Hideki Matsui 1.25 3.00

2018 Stadium Club Instavision

STATED ODDS 1:321 HOBBY
*RED/50: .5X TO 1.2X BASIC
*BLACK/25: .75X TO 2X BASIC
IAJ Aaron Judge 12.00 30.00
IBH Bryce Harper 8.00 20.00
IBP Buster Posey 6.00 15.00
ICB Cody Bellinger 10.00 25.00
ICC Carlos Correa 5.00 12.00
IGS Giancarlo Stanton 5.00 12.00
IKB Kris Bryant 6.00 15.00
IMT Mike Trout 25.00 60.00
IRD Rafael Devers 10.00 25.00
ISO Shohei Ohtani 80.00 200.00

2018 Stadium Club Lone Star Signatures

STATED ODDS 1:2363 HOBBY
PRINT RUNS B/WN 5-25 COPIES PER
NO PRICING ON QTY 10 OR LESS
EXCHANGE DEADLINE 5/30/2020
LSSAJ Aaron Judge EXCH
LSSAR Amed Rosario/25 8.00 20.00
LSSBH Bryce Harper
LSSDJ Derek Jeter
LSSFL Francisco Lindor EXCH 60.00 150.00
LSSFT Frank Thomas
LSSKB Kris Bryant
LSSNS Noah Syndergaard/25 8.00 20.00
LSSRD Rafael Devers EXCH 25.00 60.00

2018 Stadium Club Never Compromise

STATED ODDS 1:8 HOBBY
*RED: .75X TO 2X BASIC
*BLACK/99: 1.5X TO 4X BASIC
*ORANGE/50: 3X TO 8X BASIC
NCAB Andrew Benintendi .50 1.25
NCAJ Aaron Judge 1.25 3.00
NCAR Anthony Rizzo .60 1.50
NCARO Amed Rosario .40 1.00
NCBH Bryce Harper .75 2.00
NCCB Cody Bellinger 1.00 2.50
NCCC Carlos Correa .50 1.25
NCCF Clint Frazier .60 1.50
NCCJ Chipper Jones .50 1.25
NCCR Cal Ripken Jr. 1.50 4.00
NCDJ Derek Jeter 1.25 3.00
NCFL Francisco Lindor .50 1.25
NCFT Frank Thomas .50 1.25
NCGS Giancarlo Stanton .50 1.25
NCJA Jose Altuve .40 1.00
NCJS John Smoltz .50 1.25
NCJV Joey Votto .50 1.25
NCKB Kris Bryant .60 1.50
NCMM Manny Machado .50 1.25
NCMMC Mark McGwire .75 2.00
NCMT Mike Trout 2.50 6.00
NCNS Noah Syndergaard .40 1.00
NCRD Rafael Devers 1.00 2.50
NCRH Rhys Hoskins 1.25 3.00
NCSO Shohei Ohtani 8.00 20.00

2018 Stadium Club Power Zone

STATED ODDS 1:8 HOBBY
*RED: .75X TO 2X BASIC
*BLACK/99: 1.5X TO 4X BASIC
*ORANGE/50: 3X TO 8X BASIC
PZAJ Aaron Judge 1.25 3.00
PZAM Andrew McCutchen .50 1.25
PZAR Anthony Rizzo .60 1.50
PZBH Bryce Harper .75 2.00
PZCB Cody Bellinger 1.00 2.50
PZCC Carlos Correa .50 1.25
PZGS Gary Sanchez .50 1.25
PZGSP George Springer .40 1.00
PZJD Josh Donaldson .40 1.00
PZJG Joey Gallo .40 1.00
PZJM J.D. Martinez .50 1.25
PZJU Justin Upton .40 1.00
PZJV Joey Votto .50 1.25
PZKB Kris Bryant .60 1.50
PZKD Khris Davis .50 1.25
PZKS Kyle Schwarber .50 1.25
PZMM Manny Machado .50 1.25
PZMO Marcell Ozuna .50 1.25
PZMT Mike Trout 2.50 6.00
PZNA Nolan Arenado .75 2.00
PZNC Nelson Cruz .50 1.25
PZPG Paul Goldschmidt .50 1.25
PZRD Rafael Devers 1.00 2.50
PZRH Rhys Hoskins 1.25 3.00
PZSO Shohei Ohtani 8.00 20.00

2018 Stadium Club Special Forces

STATED ODDS 1:8 HOBBY
*RED: .75X TO 2X BASIC
*BLACK/99: 1.5X TO 4X BASIC
*ORANGE/50: 3X TO 8X BASIC
SFAJ Aaron Judge 1.25 3.00
SFAR Anthony Rizzo .60 1.50
SFBH Bryce Harper .75 2.00
SFBP Buster Posey .60 1.50
SFCB Cody Bellinger 1.00 2.50
SFCC Carlos Correa .50 1.25
SFCK Clayton Kershaw .75 2.00
SFGS Giancarlo Stanton .50 1.25
SFJA Jose Altuve .40 1.00
SFJV Justin Verlander .50 1.25
SFJVO Joey Votto .50 1.25
SFKB Kris Bryant .60 1.50
SFMS Max Scherzer .50 1.25
SFMT Mike Trout 2.50 6.00
SFSO Shohei Ohtani 8.00 20.00

2019 Stadium Club

1 Mookie Betts .60 1.50
2 Kyle Schwarber .30 .75
3 Touki Toussaint RC .40 1.00
4 Josh Donaldson .25 .60
5 David Dahl .20 .50
6 Kyle Wright RC .50 1.25
7 David Fletcher RC 1.00 2.50
8 Max Scherzer .30 .75
9 David Price .25 .60
10 Javier Baez .40 1.00
11 Andrew Benintendi .30 .75
12 Brooks Robinson .25 .60
13 Ted Williams .60 1.50
14 Cedric Mullins RC .60 1.50
15 Zack Greinke .30 .75
16 Fred McGriff .25 .60
17 Jackie Bradley Jr. .30 .75
18 Willson Contreras .25 .60
19 Albert Almora Jr. .25 .60
20 Eugenio Suarez .25 .60
21 Charlie Blackmon .30 .75
22 Giancarlo Stanton .30 .75
23 Jose Peraza .25 .60
24 Frank Thomas .30 .75
25 Ernie Banks .30 .75
26 Cal Ripken Jr. 1.00 2.50
27 Freddie Freeman .40 1.00
28 Eddie Murray .25 .60
29 Christy Mathewson .30 .75
30 Carlos Correa .30 .75
31 Lance McCullers Jr. .20 .50
32 Trey Mancini .25 .60
33 Jake Lamb .25 .60
34 Trevor Bauer .40 1.00
35 Francisco Lindor .30 .75
36 J.D. Martinez .30 .75
37 Carlos Carrasco .20 .50
38 Ryne Sandberg .60 1.50
39 Rafael Devers .40 1.00
40 Ender Inciarte .20 .50
41 A.J. Pollock .20 .50
42 Luis Castillo .25 .60
43 Carlos Santana .25 .60
44 Alex Bregman .30 .75
45 Albert Pujols .40 1.00
46 Michael Kopech RC 1.00 2.50
47 Scooter Gennett .25 .60
48 Tim Anderson .30 .75
49 Bryse Wilson RC .40 1.00
50 Mike Foltynewicz .20 .50
51 Robbie Ray .20 .50
52 DJ Stewart RC .40 1.00
53 Nolan Arenado .50 1.25
54 Hank Aaron .60 1.50
55 Cole Hamels .25 .60
56 Ronald Acuna Jr. 1.50 4.00
57 Carlos Rodon .30 .75
58 Joey Votto .30 .75
59 Tony Gwynn .30 .75
60 Mike Trout 1.50 4.00
61 Jim Palmer .25 .60
62 Barry Larkin .25 .60
63 Dustin Pedroia .30 .75
64 Jon Lester .25 .60
65 Yoan Moncada .30 .75
66 Shohei Ohtani .50 1.25
67 Justin Verlander .30 .75
68 Carl Yastrzemski .50 1.25
69 David Peralta .20 .50
70 Jackie Robinson .30 .75
71 Kris Bryant .40 1.00
72 Shane Bieber UER 8.00 20.00
73 Yasiel Puig .30 .75
74 Jake Bauers RC .50 1.25
75 Mark Trumbo .20 .50
76 Chris Sale .30 .75
77 Jose Abreu .30 .75
78 Chipper Jones .30 .75
79 Eloy Jimenez RC 1.25 3.00
80 Matt Kemp .25 .60
81 Jose Ramirez .25 .60
82 Dansby Swanson .30 .75
83 Justin Upton .25 .60
84 Andrelton Simmons .20 .50
85 Xander Bogaerts .30 .75
86 Johnny Bench .30 .75
87 Christian Yelich .40 1.00
88 Fernando Tatis Jr. RC 10.00 25.00
89 Kole Calhoun .20 .50
90 Eddie Mathews .30 .75
91 Yu Darvish .30 .75
92 Corey Kluber .25 .60
93 Matt Harvey .25 .60
94 Adam Jones .25 .60
95 Archie Bradley .20 .50
96 Ketel Marte .25 .60
97 Ozzie Albies .30 .75
98 Dale Murphy .30 .75
99 Wade Boggs .25 .60
100 Anthony Rizzo .40 1.00
101 Max Muncy .25 .60
102 Andrew McCutchen .30 .75
103 Enrique Hernandez .30 .75
104 Corbin Burnes RC 2.50 6.00
105 Nicholas Castellanos .30 .75
106 Kyle Tucker RC .75 2.00
107 Miguel Sano .25 .60
108 Williams Astudillo .20 .50
109 Khris Davis .30 .75
110 Jean Segura .30 .75
111 Gerrit Cole .30 .75
112 Michael Conforto .25 .60
113 Brandon Nimmo .25 .60
114 Justin Turner .30 .75
115 Roberto Clemente .75 2.00
116 Walker Buehler .40 1.00
117 Brian Anderson .20 .50
118 Trevor Richards RC .30 .75
119 Luis Severino .25 .60
120 Mike Piazza .30 .75
121 Jorge Alfaro .20 .50
122 Yuli Gurriel .25 .60
123 Miguel Andujar .30 .75
124 Orlando Arcia .20 .50
125 Michael Fulmer .20 .50
126 Billy Hamilton .25 .60
127 Jake Arrieta .25 .60
128 Jose Berrios .25 .60
129 Josh James RC .50 1.25
130 Jeff McNeil RC .75 2.00
131 Reggie Jackson .25 .60
132 Rickey Henderson .30 .75
133 Jacob deGrom .60 1.50
134 Jeff Bagwell .25 .60
135 Eddie Rosario .25 .60
136 Ryan Braun .25 .60
137 Gary Sanchez .30 .75
138 Miguel Cabrera .30 .75
139 Darryl Strawberry .20 .50
140 Myles Straw RC .50 1.25
141 Derek Jeter .75 2.00
142 Adalberto Mondesi .25 .60
143 Kenley Jansen .25 .60
144 Josh Hader .25 .60
145 Mark McGwire .50 1.25
146 Cody Bellinger .60 1.50
147 Julio Urias .30 .75
148 Dallas Keuchel .25 .60
149 Alex Gordon .25 .60
150 Lewis Brinson .20 .50
151 Ramon Laureano RC .60 1.50
152 Aaron Nola .25 .60
153 Gleyber Torres .60 1.50
154 Didi Gregorius .25 .60
155 Rhys Hoskins .40 1.00
156 George Springer .25 .60
157 Don Mattingly .60 1.50
158 Joc Pederson .30 .75
159 Noah Syndergaard .25 .60
160 Jesus Aguilar .25 .60
161 Clayton Kershaw .50 1.25
162 Stephen Piscotty .20 .50
163 Matthew Boyd .20 .50
164 Matt Chapman .30 .75
165 Ryan O'Hearn RC .30 .75
166 J.T. Realmuto .30 .75
167 Robinson Cano .25 .60
168 Christin Stewart RC .40 1.00
169 Nelson Cruz .30 .75
170 Jose Altuve .25 .60
171 Eric Thames .20 .50
172 Lorenzo Cain .20 .50
173 Mariano Rivera .40 1.00
174 Dennis Eckersley .25 .60
175 Corey Seager .30 .75
176 Matt Olson .30 .75
177 Whit Merrifield .30 .75
178 Bo Jackson .30 .75
179 Max Kepler .25 .60
180 Jonathan Schoop .20 .50
181 Masahiro Tanaka .25 .60
182 Robin Yount .30 .75
183 Amed Rosario .25 .60
184 Odubel Herrera .25 .60
185 Jose Canseco .25 .60
186 George Brett .60 1.50
187 Todd Frazier .20 .50
188 Brad Keller RC .30 .75
189 Starlin Castro .20 .50
190 Niko Goodrum .25 .60
191 Nick Martini RC .30 .75
192 Sandy Koufax .60 1.50
193 Byron Buxton .30 .75
194 Aaron Judge .75 2.00
195 Hyun-Jin Ryu .30 .75
196 Travis Shaw .20 .50
197 Hideki Matsui .30 .75
198 Salvador Perez .25 .60
199 Edwin Diaz .25 .60
200 Chris Taylor .30 .75
201 Harmon Killebrew .30 .75
202 Wil Myers .25 .60
203 Johnny Mize .25 .60
204 Mel Ott .30 .75
205 Warren Spahn .30 .75
206 Roy Halladay .25 .60
207 Patrick Wisdom RC .30 .75
208 Carlton Fisk .25 .60
209 Felix Hernandez .25 .60
210 Franmil Reyes .30 .75
211 Jack Flaherty .30 .75
212 Starling Marte .25 .60
213 Blake Snell .25 .60
214 Victor Robles .40 1.00
215 Ty Cobb .50 1.25
216 Justus Sheffield RC .50 1.25
217 Trevor Story .30 .75
218 Marcus Stroman .25 .60
219 Ryan Zimmerman .30 .75
220 Stephen Strasburg .30 .75
221 Danny Jansen RC .30 .75
222 Johnny Cueto .25 .60
223 Edgar Martinez .25 .60
224 Mitch Haniger .25 .60
225 Juan Marichal .30 .75
226 Manny Machado .30 .75
227 Yadier Molina .40 1.00
228 Mike Moustakas .25 .60
229 Josh Bell .25 .60
230 Reese McGuire RC .50 1.25
231 Pee Wee Reese .30 .75
232 Lourdes Gurriel Jr. .25 .60
233 Sammy Sosa .30 .75
234 Dereck Rodriguez .20 .50
235 Anthony Rendon .30 .75
236 Honus Wagner .30 .75
237 Justin Smoak .20 .50
238 Steven Duggar RC .40 1.00
239 Luis Urias RC .50 1.25
240 Joey Gallo .25 .60
241 Shin-Soo Choo .25 .60
242 Kevin Kramer RC .40 1.00
243 Ichiro .40 1.00
244 Buster Posey .40 1.00
245 Lou Gehrig .60 1.50
246 Juan Soto 1.00 2.50
247 Austin Meadows .30 .75
248 Willie Calhoun .20 .50
249 Jeff Samardzija .20 .50
250 Duke Snider .25 .60
251 Nolan Ryan 1.00 2.50
252 Dee Gordon .20 .50
253 Jameson Taillon .25 .60
254 Sean Reid-Foley RC .30 .75
255 Paul DeJong .30 .75
256 Roger Maris .30 .75
257 Ken Griffey Jr. .60 1.50
258 Roberto Alomar .25 .60
259 Babe Ruth .75 2.00
260 German Marquez .20 .50
261 Brian Dozier .25 .60
262 Bob Feller .25 .60
263 Brandon Crawford .25 .60
264 Felipe Vazquez .20 .50
265 Edwin Encarnacion .30 .75
266 Bob Gibson .25 .60
267 Kevin Newman RC .50 1.25
268 Vladimir Guerrero .25 .60
269 Francisco Mejia .25 .60
270 Craig Kimbrel .25 .60
271 Kyle Freeland .25 .60
272 Pete Alonso RC 2.50 6.00
273 Rogers Hornsby .25 .60
274 Yusei Kikuchi RC .50 1.25
275 Adrian Beltre .30 .75
276 Ozzie Smith .40 1.00
277 Carlos Martinez .25 .60
278 Al Kaline .30 .75
279 Rougned Odor .25 .60
280 Trea Turner .30 .75
281 David Ortiz .30 .75
282 Marcell Ozuna .30 .75
283 Eric Hosmer .25 .60
284 Matt Carpenter .30 .75
285 Paul Goldschmidt .30 .75
286 Todd Helton .25 .60
287 Kevin Kiermaier .25 .60
288 Rod Carew .25 .60
289 Ian Kinsler .25 .60
290 Stan Musial .50 1.25
291 Bryce Harper .50 1.25
292 Chris Archer .20 .50
293 Rowdy Tellez RC .50 1.25
294 Evan Longoria .25 .60
295 Tommy Pham .20 .50
296 Hunter Renfroe .20 .50
297 Nomar Mazara .20 .50
298 Harrison Bader .25 .60
299 Elvis Andrus .25 .60
300 Will Clark .25 .60
301 Vladimir Guerrero Jr. RC 5.00 12.00

2019 Stadium Club Black and White

*BW: 5X TO 12X BASIC
*BW RC: 3X TO 8X BASIC RC
STATED ODDS 1:48 HOBBY
79 Eloy Jimenez 15.00 40.00
272 Pete Alonso 30.00 80.00

2019 Stadium Club Black Foil

*BLK FOIL: 1.5X TO 4X BASIC
*BLK FOIL RC: 1X TO 2.5X BASIC RC
STATED ODDS 1:8 HOBBY
272 Pete Alonso 10.00 25.00

2019 Stadium Club Rainbow Foil

*RAINBOW: 8X TO 20X BASIC
*RAINBOW RC: 5X TO 12X BASIC RC
STATED ODDS 1:147 HOBBY
STATED PRINT RUN 25 SER.#'d SETS
79 Eloy Jimenez 20.00 50.00
272 Pete Alonso 50.00 120.00

2019 Stadium Club Red Foil

*RED FOIL: 1X TO 2.5X BASIC
*RED FOIL RC: .6X TO 1.5X BASIC RC
STATED ODDS 1:3 HOBBY
272 Pete Alonso 6.00 15.00

2019 Stadium Club Sepia

*SEPIA: 2X TO 5X BASIC
*SEPIA RC: 1.2X TO 3X BASIC RC
STATED ODDS 1:8 BLASTER
79 Eloy Jimenez 6.00 15.00
272 Pete Alonso 15.00 40.00

2019 Stadium Club Photo Variations

STATED ODDS 1:110 HOBBY
1 Mookie Betts 12.00 30.00
8 Max Scherzer 6.00 15.00
10 Javier Baez 8.00 20.00
11 Andrew Benintendi 6.00 15.00
24 Frank Thomas 6.00 15.00
26 Cal Ripken Jr. 20.00 50.00
27 Freddie Freeman 8.00 20.00
30 Carlos Correa 6.00 15.00
35 Francisco Lindor 6.00 15.00
38 Ryne Sandberg 12.00 30.00
44 Alex Bregman 6.00 15.00
54 Hank Aaron 12.00 30.00
56 Ronald Acuna Jr. 30.00 80.00
58 Joey Votto 6.00 15.00
60 Mike Trout 40.00 100.00
66 Shohei Ohtani 10.00 25.00
67 Justin Verlander 6.00 15.00
71 Kris Bryant 10.00 25.00
76 Chris Sale 6.00 15.00
78 Chipper Jones 6.00 15.00
79 Eloy Jimenez 15.00 40.00
87 Christian Yelich 8.00 20.00
88 Fernando Tatis Jr. 60.00 150.00
100 Anthony Rizzo 8.00 20.00
102 Andrew McCutchen 6.00 15.00
106 Kyle Tucker 10.00 25.00
123 Miguel Andujar 6.00 15.00
131 Reggie Jackson 5.00 12.00
132 Rickey Henderson 10.00 25.00
137 Gary Sanchez 6.00 15.00
141 Derek Jeter 15.00 40.00
145 Mark McGwire 10.00 25.00
155 Rhys Hoskins 8.00 20.00
157 Don Mattingly 12.00 30.00
161 Clayton Kershaw 10.00 25.00
170 Jose Altuve 5.00 12.00
173 Mariano Rivera 8.00 20.00
192 Sandy Koufax 12.00 30.00

194 Aaron Judge 15.00 40.00
197 Hideki Matsui 6.00 15.00
Holding key
206 Roy Halladay 5.00 12.00
227 Yadier Molina 8.00 20.00
243 Ichiro 8.00 20.00
244 Buster Posey 8.00 20.00
246 Juan Soto 20.00 50.00
257 Ken Griffey Jr. 12.00 30.00
272 Pete Alonso 30.00 80.00
274 Yusei Kikuchi 6.00 15.00
285 Paul Goldschmidt 6.00 15.00
291 Bryce Harper 10.00 25.00

2019 Stadium Club Autographs

STATED ODDS 1:10 HOBBY
EXCHANGE DEADLINE 5/31/2021
SCAAC Adam Cimber 6.00 15.00
SCAAD Austin Dean 3.00 8.00
SCAAG Adolis Garcia 15.00 40.00
SCABG Bob Gibson 25.00 60.00
SCABJ Bo Jackson EXCH
SCABK Brad Keller 3.00 8.00
SCABL Brandon Lowe 10.00 25.00
SCABN Brandon Nimmo 4.00 10.00
SCABS Blake Snell 6.00 15.00
SCABW Bryse Wilson 4.00 10.00
SCACA Chance Adams 3.00 8.00
SCACB Corbin Burnes 15.00 40.00
SCACD Corey Dickerson 3.00 8.00
SCACH Cesar Hernandez 3.00 8.00
SCACR Cal Ripken Jr. 50.00 120.00
SCACS Chris Shaw 3.00 8.00
SCADD Dean Deetz 3.00 8.00
SCADF David Fletcher 6.00 15.00
SCADH Dakota Hudson 4.00 10.00
SCADJ David Justice 10.00 25.00
SCADM Dale Murphy 40.00 100.00
SCADR Dereck Rodriguez 3.00 8.00
SCADS Darryl Strawberry 12.00 30.00
SCAEJ Eloy Jimenez 30.00 80.00
SCAEM Edgar Martinez 20.00 50.00
SCAFA Francisco Arcia 5.00 12.00
SCAFL Francisco Lindor 20.00 50.00
SCAFP Freddy Peralta 5.00 12.00
SCAI Ichiro
SCAJH Josh Hader 4.00 10.00
SCAJR Josh Rogers 3.00 8.00
SCAJS Juan Soto 40.00 100.00
SCAKA Kolby Allard 5.00 12.00
SCAKB Kris Bryant
SCAKK Kevin Kramer 4.00 10.00
SCAKN Kevin Newman 5.00 12.00
SCAKT Kyle Tucker 15.00 40.00
SCAKW Kyle Wright 5.00 12.00
SCALO Luis Ortiz 3.00 8.00
SCALV Luke Voit 25.00 60.00
SCAMC Matt Chapman 10.00 25.00
SCAMF Mike Foltynewicz 5.00 12.00
SCAMK Michael Kopech 10.00 25.00
SCAMM Miles Mikolas 5.00 12.00
SCAMS Myles Straw 5.00 12.00
SCAMT Mike Trout
SCANB Nick Burdi 3.00 8.00
SCANC Nicholas Ciuffo 3.00 8.00
SCANM Nick Martini 3.00 8.00
SCANR Nolan Ryan
SCANS Noah Syndergaard 4.00 10.00
SCAOA Ozzie Albies 10.00 25.00
SCAOH Odubel Herrera 4.00 10.00
SCAPA Peter Alonso 50.00 120.00
SCAPG Paul Goldschmidt 20.00 50.00
SCAPW Patrick Wisdom 3.00 8.00
SCARA Ronald Acuna Jr. 60.00 150.00
SCARB Ray Black 3.00 8.00
SCARH Rhys Hoskins 15.00 40.00
SCARL Ramon Laureano 5.00 12.00
SCARO Ryan O'Hearn 3.00 8.00
SCART Rowdy Tellez 5.00 12.00
SCASG Scooter Gennett 4.00 10.00
SCASR Sean Reid-Foley 3.00 8.00
SCAST Stephen Tarpley 4.00 10.00
SCATB Trevor Bauer 6.00 15.00
SCATR Trevor Richards 3.00 8.00
SCATS Tyler Skaggs 6.00 15.00
SCATT Touki Toussaint 4.00 10.00
SCATW Taylor Ward 3.00 8.00
SCAVG Vladimir Guerrero Jr. 75.00 200.00
SCAWA Willians Astudillo 10.00 25.00
SCAWC Will Clark 40.00 100.00
SCAYM Yadier Molina 30.00 80.00
SCACMU Cedric Mullins 10.00 25.00
SCACST Christin Stewart 4.00 10.00
SCADJA Danny Jansen 3.00 8.00
SCADMA Don Mattingly 50.00 120.00
SCADPO Daniel Poncedeleon 5.00 12.00
SCADSA Dennis Santana 3.00 8.00
SCADST DJ Stewart 4.00 10.00
SCAFTA Fernando Tatis Jr. 100.00 250.00
SCAFVA Framber Valdez 6.00 15.00
SCAJAL Jose Altuve 15.00 40.00
SCAJBA Jake Bauers 5.00 12.00
SCAJBE Jalen Beeks 3.00 8.00
SCAJBR Jose Briceno 3.00 8.00
SCAJCA Jake Cave 4.00 10.00
SCAJMA Juan Marichal 15.00 40.00
SCAJSH Justus Sheffield 5.00 12.00
SCAJSP Jeffrey Springs 3.00 8.00
SCAMMG Mark McGwire 40.00 25.00
SCAMMU Max Muncy 8.00 20.00
SCARBO Ryan Borucki 3.00 8.00
SCARMC Reese McGuire 5.00 12.00

2019 Stadium Club Autographs Black Foil

*BLACK FOIL: .6X TO 1.5X BASIC
STATED ODDS 1:274 HOBBY
STATED PRINT RUN 25 SER.#'d SETS
EXCHANGE DEADLINE 5/31/2021
SCAMK Michael Kopech 15.00 40.00
SCAOA Ozzie Albies 25.00 60.00
SCAPA Peter Alonso 100.00 250.00
SCAPG Paul Goldschmidt 40.00 100.00
SCAVG Vladimir Guerrero Jr. 150.00 400.00

2019 Stadium Club Autographs Red Foil

*RED FOIL: .5X TO 1.2X BASIC
STATED ODDS 1:152 HOBBY
STATED PRINT RUN 50 SER.#'d SETS
EXCHANGE DEADLINE 5/31/2021
SCAOA Ozzie Albies 20.00 50.00
SCAPA Peter Alonso 75.00 200.00
SCAVG Vladimir Guerrero Jr. 125.00 300.00

2019 Stadium Club Beam Team

STATED ODDS 1:16 HOBBY
*RED: 1X TO 2.5X BASIC
*BLACK/99: 1.2X TO 3X BASIC
*ORANGE/50: 3X TO 8X BASIC
BT1 Javier Baez 1.00 2.50
BT2 Derek Jeter 2.00 5.00
BT3 Mike Trout 4.00 10.00
BT4 Shohei Ohtani 1.25 3.00
BT5 Ichiro 1.00 2.50
BT6 Bryce Harper 1.25 3.00
BT7 Aaron Judge 2.00 5.00
BT8 Cal Ripken Jr. 2.50 6.00
BT9 Kris Bryant 1.00 2.50
BT10 Joey Votto .75 2.00
BT11 Manny Machado .75 2.00
BT12 Anthony Rizzo 1.00 2.50
BT13 Jose Altuve .60 1.50
BT14 Paul Goldschmidt .75 2.00
BT15 Francisco Lindor .75 2.00
BT16 Yadier Molina 1.00 2.50
BT17 Jacob deGrom 1.50 4.00
BT18 Ronald Acuna Jr. 4.00 10.00
BT19 Alex Bregman .75 2.00
BT20 Gleyber Torres 1.50 4.00
BT21 Chris Sale .75 2.00
BT22 Christian Yelich 1.00 2.50
BT23 Ken Griffey Jr. 1.50 4.00
BT24 Tony Gwynn .75 2.00
BT25 Juan Soto 2.50 6.00

2019 Stadium Club Chrome

STATED ODDS 1:16 HOBBY
SCC1 Sandy Koufax 4.00 10.00
SCC2 Derek Jeter 3.00 8.00
SCC3 Hank Aaron 2.50 6.00
SCC4 Mike Trout 6.00 15.00
SCC5 Shohei Ohtani 2.00 5.00
SCC6 Ichiro 1.50 4.00
SCC7 Mariano Rivera 1.50 4.00
SCC8 Bryce Harper 2.00 5.00
SCC9 Aaron Judge 3.00 8.00
SCC10 Buster Posey 1.50 4.00
SCC11 Clayton Kershaw 2.00 5.00
SCC12 Cal Ripken Jr. 4.00 10.00
SCC13 Johnny Bench 1.25 3.00
SCC14 Nolan Ryan 4.00 10.00
SCC15 Bo Jackson 1.25 3.00
SCC16 Masahiro Tanaka 1.00 2.50
SCC17 Hideki Matsui 1.25 3.00
SCC18 Reggie Jackson 1.00 2.50
SCC19 Rickey Henderson 1.25 3.00
SCC20 Mark McGwire 2.00 5.00
SCC21 Chipper Jones 1.25 3.00
SCC22 Kris Bryant 1.50 4.00
SCC23 Wade Boggs 1.00 2.50
SCC24 Ryne Sandberg 2.50 6.00
SCC25 Anthony Rizzo 1.50 4.00
SCC26 Frank Thomas 1.25 3.00
SCC27 Joey Votto 1.25 3.00
SCC28 Manny Machado 1.25 3.00
SCC29 Barry Larkin 1.00 2.50
SCC30 Jose Altuve 1.00 2.50
SCC31 Don Mattingly 2.50 6.00
SCC32 Jose Ramirez 1.00 2.50
SCC33 Gary Sanchez 1.25 3.00
SCC34 Ozzie Smith 1.50 4.00
SCC35 Andrew McCutchen 1.25 3.00
SCC36 Gleyber Torres 2.50 6.00
SCC37 Chris Sale 1.25 3.00
SCC38 George Springer 1.00 2.50
SCC39 Freddie Freeman 1.50 4.00
SCC40 Francisco Lindor 1.25 3.00
SCC41 Noah Syndergaard 1.00 2.50
SCC42 Miguel Andujar 1.25 3.00
SCC43 Yadier Molina 1.50 4.00
SCC44 Bob Gibson 1.00 2.50
SCC45 Andrew Benintendi 1.25 3.00
SCC46 Willson Contreras 1.00 2.50
SCC47 Luis Severino 1.00 2.50
SCC48 Jacob deGrom 2.50 6.00
SCC49 Kyle Schwarber 1.25 3.00
SCC50 Alex Bregman 1.25 3.00
SCC51 Darryl Strawberry .75 2.00
SCC52 Dennis Eckersley 1.00 2.50
SCC53 Ronald Acuna Jr. 6.00 15.00
SCC54 Rafael Devers 1.50 4.00
SCC55 Rhys Hoskins 1.50 4.00
SCC56 Juan Soto 4.00 10.00
SCC57 Charlie Blackmon 1.25 3.00
SCC58 Trevor Bauer 1.50 4.00
SCC59 Victor Robles 1.50 4.00
SCC60 Christian Yelich 1.50 4.00
SCC61 Ken Griffey Jr. 2.50 6.00
SCC62 Sammy Sosa 1.25 3.00
SCC63 Ozzie Albies 1.25 3.00
SCC64 Jose Canseco 1.00 2.50
SCC65 Blake Snell 1.00 2.50
SCC66 Khris Davis 1.25 3.00
SCC67 Roy Halladay 1.00 2.50
SCC68 Jack Flaherty 1.25 3.00
SCC69 Whit Merrifield 1.25 3.00
SCC70 Michael Kopech 2.50 6.00
SCC71 Justus Sheffield 1.25 3.00
SCC72 Eloy Jimenez 3.00 8.00
SCC73 Kyle Wright 1.25 3.00
SCC74 Kyle Tucker 2.00 5.00
SCC75 Touki Toussaint 1.00 2.50
SCC76 Pete Alonso 10.00 25.00
SCC77 Nolan Arenado 2.00 5.00
SCC78 Jeff McNeil 2.00 5.00
SCC79 Ryan O'Hearn .75 2.00
SCC80 Fernando Tatis Jr. 20.00 50.00
SCC81 Albert Pujols 1.50 4.00
SCC82 Giancarlo Stanton 1.25 3.00
SCC83 Mookie Betts 2.50 6.00
SCC84 Carlos Correa 1.25 3.00
SCC85 Max Scherzer 1.25 3.00
SCC86 J.D. Martinez 1.25 3.00
SCC87 Trea Turner 1.00 2.50
SCC88 Javier Baez 1.50 4.00
SCC89 Corey Seager 1.25 3.00
SCC90 Cody Bellinger 2.50 6.00

2019 Stadium Club Chrome Gold Mint

*GOLD MINT: 2.5X TO 6X BASIC
STATED ODDS 1:257 HOBBY
SCC2 Derek Jeter 40.00 100.00
SCC4 Mike Trout 50.00 120.00
SCC53 Ronald Acuna Jr. 40.00 100.00
SCC76 Pete Alonso 75.00 200.00
SCC80 Fernando Tatis Jr. 125.00 300.00

2019 Stadium Club Chrome Orange Refractors

*ORNG: 1.2X TO 3X BASIC
STATED ODDS 1:124 HOBBY
STATED PRINT RUN 99 SER.#'d SETS
SCC2 Derek Jeter 20.00 50.00
SCC4 Mike Trout 25.00 60.00
SCC53 Ronald Acuna Jr. 20.00 50.00
SCC76 Pete Alonso 40.00 100.00

2019 Stadium Club Chrome Refractors

*REF: .6X TO 1.5X BASIC
STATED ODDS 1:64 HOBBY
SCC4 Mike Trout 15.00 40.00
SCC53 Ronald Acuna Jr. 10.00 25.00
SCC76 Pete Alonso 20.00 50.00

2019 Stadium Club Emperors of the Zone

STATED ODDS 1:8 HOBBY
*RED: .75X TO 2X BASIC
*BLACK/99: 1.5X TO 4X BASIC
*ORANGE/50: 3X TO 8X BASIC
EZ1 Shohei Ohtani .75 2.00
EZ2 Pedro Martinez .40 1.00
EZ3 Clayton Kershaw .75 2.00
EZ4 Masahiro Tanaka .40 1.00
EZ5 Nolan Ryan 1.50 4.00
EZ6 Andy Pettitte .40 1.00
EZ7 Tom Glavine .40 1.00
EZ8 Zack Greinke .50 1.25
EZ9 John Smoltz .50 1.25
EZ10 Chris Sale .50 1.25
EZ11 Corey Kluber .40 1.00
EZ12 Trevor Bauer .60 1.50
EZ13 Noah Syndergaard .40 1.00
EZ14 Gerrit Cole .50 1.25
EZ15 Jacob deGrom 1.00 2.50
EZ16 Luis Severino .40 1.00
EZ17 Stephen Strasburg .50 1.25
EZ18 Dennis Eckersley .40 1.00
EZ19 Aaron Nola .40 1.00
EZ20 Blake Snell .40 1.00
EZ21 Walker Buehler .60 1.50
EZ22 Mariano Rivera .60 1.50
EZ23 Yusei Kikuchi .50 1.25
EZ24 Justin Verlander .50 1.25
EZ25 Max Scherzer .50 1.25

2019 Stadium Club Instavision

STATED ODDS 1:321 HOBBY
*RED/50: .5X TO 1.2X BASIC
*BLACK/25: .75X TO 2X BASIC
IV1 Cal Ripken Jr. 15.00 40.00
IV2 Javier Baez 6.00 15.00
IV3 Ken Griffey Jr. 10.00 25.00
IV4 Justin Verlander 5.00 12.00
IV5 Mark McGwire 8.00 20.00
IV6 Manny Machado 5.00 12.00
IV7 Bryce Harper 8.00 20.00
IV8 Mike Trout 25.00 60.00
IV9 Aaron Judge 12.00 30.00
IV10 Ichiro 6.00 15.00

2019 Stadium Club Lone Star Signatures

STATED ODDS 1:2138 HOBBY
PRINT RUNS B/WN 5-25 COPIES PER
NO PRICING ON QTY 15 OR LESS
EXCHANGE DEADLINE 5/31/2021
LSABG Bob Gibson/25 25.00
LSACS Chris Sale/25 10.00 25.00
LSADJ Derek Jeter
LSAEJ Eloy Jimenez/25 40.00 100.00
LSAFL Francisco Lindor/25
LSAJd Jacob deGrom/25 30.00 80.00
LSASO Shohei Ohtani
LSAVG Vladimir Guerrero Jr./25 125.00 300.00
LSAWC Will Clark/25 30.00 80.00
LSAYM Yadier Molina/25 30.00 80.00

2019 Stadium Club Oversized Box Toppers

INSERTED IN HOBBY BOXES
OBVI Ichiro 2.00 5.00
OBVAJ Aaron Judge 4.00 10.00
OBVAR Anthony Rizzo 2.00 5.00
OBVBG Bob Gibson 1.25 3.00
OBVBH Bryce Harper 2.50 6.00
OBVBJ Bo Jackson 1.50 4.00
OBVBP Buster Posey 2.00 5.00
OBVBR Babe Ruth 4.00 10.00
OBVCB Charlie Blackmon 1.50 4.00
OBVCF Carlton Fisk 1.25 3.00
OBVCJ Chipper Jones 1.50 4.00
OBVCK Clayton Kershaw 2.50 6.00
OBVCR Cal Ripken Jr. 5.00 12.00
OBVCS Chris Sale 1.50 4.00
OBVDJ Derek Jeter 4.00 10.00
OBVDM Don Mattingly 6.00 15.00
OBVDO David Ortiz 1.50 4.00
OBVFL Francisco Lindor 1.50 4.00
OBVHA Hank Aaron 3.00 8.00
OBVJA Jose Altuve 1.25 3.00
OBVJB Javier Baez 2.00 5.00
OBVJM Juan Marichal 1.25 3.00
OBVJR Jackie Robinson 1.50 4.00
OBVJS Juan Soto 5.00 12.00
OBVJV Joey Votto 1.50 4.00
OBVKB Kris Bryant 2.00 5.00
OBVKD Khris Davis 1.50 4.00
OBVKS Kyle Schwarber 1.50 4.00
OBVLG Lou Gehrig 3.00 8.00
OBVMB Mookie Betts 3.00 8.00
OBVMC Matt Carpenter 1.50 4.00
OBVMM Manny Machado 1.50 4.00
OBVMR Mariano Rivera 2.00 5.00
OBVMS Max Scherzer 1.50 4.00
OBVMT Mike Trout 8.00 20.00
OBVNA Nolan Arenado 2.50 6.00
OBVNR Nolan Ryan 5.00 12.00
OBVNS Noah Syndergaard 1.25 3.00
OBVOA Ozzie Albies 1.50 4.00
OBVRA Ronald Acuna Jr. 8.00 20.00
OBVRC Roberto Clemente 4.00 10.00
OBVRH Rhys Hoskins 2.00 5.00
OBVSK Sandy Koufax 5.00 12.00
OBVSO Shohei Ohtani 2.50 6.00
OBVTW Ted Williams 3.00 8.00
OBVYM Yadier Molina 2.00 5.00
OBVABE Andrew Benintendi 1.50 4.00
OBVABR Alex Bregman 1.50 4.00
OBVMMC Mark McGwire 2.50 6.00
OBVRHE Rickey Henderson 1.50 4.00

2019 Stadium Club Power Zone

STATED ODDS 1:8 HOBBY
*RED: .75X TO 2X BASIC
*BLACK/99: 1.5X TO 4X BASIC
*ORANGE/50: 3X TO 8X BASIC
PZ1 Shohei Ohtani .75 2.00
PZ2 Mike Trout 2.50 6.00
PZ3 Bryce Harper .75 2.00
PZ4 Aaron Judge 1.25 3.00
PZ5 Mark McGwire .75 2.00
PZ6 Cal Ripken Jr. 1.50 4.00
PZ7 Hideki Matsui .50 1.25
PZ8 Kris Bryant .60 1.50
PZ9 Chipper Jones .50 1.25
PZ10 Will Clark .40 1.00
PZ11 Francisco Lindor .50 1.25
PZ12 Miguel Andujar .50 1.25
PZ13 Todd Helton .40 1.00
PZ14 Alex Bregman .50 1.25
PZ15 Ronald Acuna Jr. 2.50 6.00
PZ16 Kyle Schwarber .50 1.25
PZ17 Rhys Hoskins .60 1.50
PZ18 Christian Yelich .60 1.50
PZ19 Khris Davis .50 1.25
PZ20 Gleyber Torres 1.00 2.50
PZ21 Mike Piazza .50 1.25
PZ22 Bo Jackson .50 1.25
PZ23 Matt Carpenter .50 1.25
PZ24 Vladimir Guerrero .40 1.00
PZ25 Ken Griffey Jr. 1.00 2.50

2019 Stadium Club Warp Speed

STATED ODDS 1:8 HOBBY
*RED: .75X TO 2X BASIC
*BLACK/99: 1.5X TO 4X BASIC
*ORANGE/50: 3X TO 8X BASIC
WS1 Ronald Acuna Jr. 2.50 6.00
WS2 Trea Turner .40 1.00
WS3 Francisco Lindor .50 1.25
WS4 Billy Hamilton .40 1.00
WS5 Harrison Bader .40 1.00
WS6 Adalberto Mondesi .40 1.00
WS7 Trevor Story .50 1.25
WS8 Victor Robles .60 1.50
WS9 Mike Trout 2.50 6.00
WS10 Whit Merrifield .50 1.25
WS11 Amed Rosario .40 1.00
WS12 Mookie Betts 1.00 2.50
WS13 Dee Gordon .30 .75
WS14 Javier Baez .60 1.50
WS15 Byron Buxton .50 1.25

2020 Stadium Club

1 Mike Trout 1.50 4.00
2 Nelson Cruz .30 .75
3 Babe Ruth .75 2.00
4 Justus Sheffield .30 .75
5 Bobby Bradley RC .30 .75
6 Abraham Toro RC .40 1.00
7 Michel Baez RC .30 .75
8 Michael Conforto .25 .60
9 Jameson Taillon .25 .60
10 Chris Sale .30 .75
11 Matt Olson .30 .75
12 David Dahl .20 .50
13 Yadier Molina .40 1.00
14 Anthony Rizzo .40 1.00
15 DJ LeMahieu .30 .75
16 Michael Chavis .25 .60
17 J.T. Realmuto .30 .75
18 Giancarlo Stanton .30 .75
19 Eddie Rosario .25 .60
20 Mitch Garver .20 .50
21 Xander Bogaerts .30 .75
22 Jose Ramirez .25 .60
23 Dylan Cease RC .50 1.25
24 Walker Buehler .40 1.00
25 Yasmani Grandal .20 .50
26 Sean Murphy RC .50 1.25
27 Mike Clevinger .25 .60
28 Max Muncy .25 .60
29 Lorenzo Cain .20 .50
30 Bryce Harper .50 1.25
31 John Means .30 .75
32 Yuli Gurriel .25 .60
33 Albert Pujols .40 1.00
34 Anthony Kay RC .30 .75
35 Lou Gehrig .60 1.50
36 Aristides Aquino RC .75 2.00
37 Mark Canha .20 .50
38 Eugenio Suarez .25 .60
39 Ryan Zimmerman .25 .60
40 Blake Snell .25 .60
41 Jonathan Villar .20 .50
42 Michael Brantley .25 .60
43 Byron Buxton .30 .75
44 Tommy Edman .30 .75
45 Justin Turner .30 .75
46 Joey Gallo .30 .75
47 Robel Garcia RC .30 .75
48 George Springer .25 .60
49 Josh VanMeter .30 .75
50 Mike Moustakas .25 .60
51 Adbert Alzolay RC .40 1.00
52 Mike Schmidt .50 1.25
53 Brusdar Graterol RC .50 1.25
54 David Wright .25 .60
55 Lucas Giolito .25 .60
56 Robinson Cano .25 .60
57 Shun Yamaguchi RC .40 1.00
58 Jason Varitek .30 .75
59 Sean Doolittle .20 .50
60 Josh Donaldson .25 .60
61 Dale Murphy .30 .75
62 Austin Meadows .30 .75
63 Yoan Moncada .30 .75
64 Yoshi Tsutsugo RC .75 2.00
65 Dario Agrazal RC .40 1.00
66 Aaron Hicks .25 .60
67 Ted Williams .60 1.50
68 Paul Goldschmidt .30 .75
69 Yordan Alvarez RC 3.00 8.00
70 Bob Feller .25 .60
71 Carl Yastrzemski .50 1.25
72 Zack Collins RC .40 1.00
73 Ketel Marte .25 .60
74 Brandon Woodruff .30 .75
75 Nolan Ryan 1.00 2.50
76 Mike Soroka .30 .75
77 Andrew McCutchen .30 .75
78 Sean Manaea .20 .50
79 Jose Abreu .30 .75
80 Mike Brosseau RC .60 1.50
81 Randal Grichuk .20 .50
82 Kirby Yates .20 .50
83 Max Kepler .25 .60
84 Adrian Morejon RC .30 .75
85 Kyle Hendricks .30 .75
86 Yu Chang RC .50 1.25
87 Clayton Kershaw .50 1.25
88 Starling Marte .25 .60
89 Adalberto Mondesi .25 .60
90 Tommy La Stella .20 .50
91 Max Scherzer .30 .75
92 Luke Voit .40 1.00
93 Kwang-Hyun Kim RC .60 1.50
94 Masahiro Tanaka .30 .75
95 Jesus Luzardo RC .60 1.50
96 Mark McGwire .50 1.25
97 Brendan Rodgers .30 .75
98 Sam Hilliard RC .50 1.25
99 Nomar Garciaparra .25 .60
100 Javier Baez .40 1.00
101 James Marvel RC .30 .75
102 Barry Larkin .25 .60
103 Hideki Matsui .30 .75
104 Juan Soto 1.00 2.50
105 Junior Fernandez RC .30 .75
106 Cal Ripken Jr. 1.00 2.50
107 Kris Bryant .40 1.00
108 Yusei Kikuchi .25 .60
109 Trey Mancini .30 .75
110 Ernie Banks .30 .75
111 Luis Severino .25 .60
112 Bo Bichette RC 6.00 15.00
113 Darryl Strawberry .20 .50
114 Robbie Ray .20 .50
115 Ramon Laureano .25 .60
116 Ronald Acuna Jr. 1.25 3.00
117 Miguel Cabrera .30 .75
118 Jacob deGrom .60 1.50
119 Derek Dietrich .25 .60
120 Nolan Arenado .50 1.25
121 Nick Markakis .25 .60
122 Carter Kieboom .25 .60
123 Carlos Correa .30 .75
124 Keston Hiura .40 1.00
125 Sonny Gray .25 .60
126 Travis Demeritte RC .50 1.25
127 Miguel Sano .25 .60
128 Lourdes Gurriel Jr. .25 .60
129 Alex Young RC .30 .75
130 Cody Bellinger .60 1.50
131 Joey Votto .30 .75
132 Jeff McNeil .25 .60
133 Victor Robles .40 1.00
134 Didi Gregorius .25 .60
135 J.D. Martinez .30 .75
136 Zack Greinke .30 .75
137 Hyun-Jin Ryu .25 .60
138 Aaron Judge .75 2.00
139 Trevor Story .30 .75
140 Willie Mays .60 1.50
141 Danny Jansen .20 .50
142 Adam Wainwright .25 .60
143 Will Smith .30 .75
144 Lewis Thorpe RC .30 .75
145 Shohei Ohtani .50 1.25
146 Jose Canseco .25 .60
147 Gleyber Torres .60 1.50
148 Honus Wagner .30 .75
149 Jose Urquidy RC .40 1.00
150 Rod Carew .25 .60
151 Nick Solak RC 1.25 3.00
152 Trent Grisham RC 1.25 3.00
153 Roberto Alomar .25 .60
154 Brian Anderson .20 .50
155 Joey Lucchesi .20 .50
156 Matt Thaiss RC .40 1.00
157 Marcell Ozuna .30 .75
158 Noah Syndergaard .25 .60
159 Roberto Clemente .75 2.00
160 Tony Gwynn .30 .75
161 Manny Machado .30 .75
162 Jaylin Davis RC .50 1.25
163 Nomar Mazara .20 .50
164 Pete Alonso .75 2.00
165 Stephen Strasburg .30 .75
166 Ozzie Smith .40 1.00
167 Trevor Bauer .40 1.00
168 Ryne Sandberg .60 1.50
169 Chris Paddack .30 .75
170 Seth Brown RC .30 .75
171 Tim Lincecum .25 .60
172 Jeff Bagwell .25 .60
173 Freddie Freeman .40 1.00
174 Gio Urshela .30 .75
175 Justin Dunn RC .40 1.00
176 Dallas Keuchel .25 .60
177 Yasiel Puig .30 .75
178 Barry Zito .25 .60
179 Marcus Semien .30 .75
180 Josh Bell .25 .60
181 Josh Hader .25 .60
182 Aroldis Chapman .30 .75
183 Andres Munoz RC .50 1.25
184 Brandon Lowe .25 .60
185 Buster Posey .40 1.00
186 Austin Nola RC .50 1.25
187 Stan Musial .50 1.25
188 Fernando Tatis Jr. 1.50 4.00
189 Jorge Posada .25 .60
190 Dakota Hudson .25 .60
191 Francisco Lindor .30 .75
192 Hank Aaron .60 1.50
193 Jack Flaherty .30 .75
194 Matt Chapman .30 .75
195 Andrew Benintendi .30 .75
196 Marcus Stroman .25 .60
197 Mike Yastrzemski .50 1.25
198 Shed Long .25 .60
199 David Ortiz .30 .75
200 Will Clark .25 .60
201 Kerry Wood .20 .50
202 Patrick Corbin .25 .60
203 Chipper Jones .30 .75
204 Patrick Sandoval RC .50 1.25
205 Corey Kluber .25 .60
206 Salvador Perez .25 .60
207 Shane Bieber .30 .75
208 Domingo Leyba RC .40 1.00
209 Charlie Morton .30 .75
210 Eduardo Escobar .20 .50
211 Lance McCullers Jr. .20 .50
212 Jorge Soler .30 .75
213 Josh Rojas RC .30 .75
214 Ty Cobb .50 1.25
215 Gary Sanchez .30 .75
216 Rhys Hoskins .40 1.00
217 Logan Webb RC .50 1.25
218 Mookie Betts .60 1.50
219 Hunter Harvey RC .50 1.25
220 Paul DeJong .30 .75
221 Dan Vogelbach .20 .50
222 Elvis Andrus .25 .60
223 Matthew Boyd .20 .50
224 Edgar Martinez .25 .60
225 Nick Senzel .30 .75
226 Hunter Dozier .20 .50
227 Justin Verlander .30 .75
228 Khris Davis .30 .75
229 Tim Anderson .30 .75
230 Jordan Yamamoto RC .30 .75
231 Al Kaline .30 .75
232 Jake Fraley RC .40 1.00
233 Nick Castellanos .30 .75
234 Rafael Devers .40 1.00
235 Carlos Santana .25 .60
236 Alex Bregman .30 .75
237 Brendan McKay RC .50 1.25
238 Amed Rosario .25 .60
239 Austin Hays .30 .75
240 A.J. Puk RC .50 1.25
241 Kyle Tucker .30 .75
242 George Brett .60 1.50
243 Aaron Nola .25 .60
244 Ichiro .40 1.00
245 Willi Castro RC .50 1.25
246 Trea Turner .25 .60
247 Gerrit Cole .50 1.25
248 Yu Darvish .30 .75
249 Kyle Lewis RC 3.00 8.00
250 Tyler Glasnow .30 .75
251 Luis Arraez .40 1.00
252 Brock Burke RC .30 .75
253 Nico Hoerner RC 1.25 3.00
254 Jose Berrios .25 .60
255 Dustin May RC 1.00 2.50
256 Bryan Reynolds .25 .60
257 Frank Thomas .30 .75
258 Isan Diaz RC .50 1.25
259 Joc Pederson .25 .60
260 Willie Calhoun .20 .50
261 Charlie Blackmon .30 .75
262 Zac Gallen RC .75 2.00
263 Corey Seager .30 .75
264 Cavan Biggio .40 1.00
265 Christian Walker .25 .60
266 Kolten Wong .25 .60
267 Mitch Keller .30 .75
268 Luis Castillo .25 .60
269 Aaron Civale RC .60 1.50
270 Ken Griffey Jr. .60 1.50
271 Logan Allen RC .30 .75
272 Don Mattingly .60 1.50
273 Austin Riley .40 1.00
274 Felix Hernandez .25 .60
275 Bubba Starling RC .60 1.50
276 Kyle Schwarber .30 .75
277 Johnny Bench .30 .75
278 Jose Altuve .25 .60
279 Mitch Haniger .25 .60
280 Dansby Swanson .30 .75
281 Josh Staumont RC .30 .75
282 Sheldon Neuse RC .40 1.00
283 Anthony Rendon .30 .75
284 James Karinchak RC .50 1.25
285 Shogo Akiyama .30 .75
286 Ozzie Albies .30 .75
287 Tommy Pham .20 .50
288 Vladimir Guerrero Jr. .50 1.25
289 Luis Robert RC 6.00 15.00
290 Sandy Koufax .60 1.50
291 Willson Contreras .30 .75
292 Christian Yelich .40 1.00
293 Randy Johnson .30 .75
294 T.J. Zeuch RC .30 .75
295 Jake Rogers RC .30 .75
296 Eduardo Rodriguez .20 .50
297 Mauricio Dubon RC .40 1.00
298 Gavin Lux RC 2.50 6.00
299 Randy Arozarena RC 3.00 8.00
300 Eloy Jimenez .60 1.50

2020 Stadium Club Black and White

*BW: 5X TO 12X BASIC
*BW RC: 3X TO 8X BASIC RC
STATED ODDS 1:48 HOBBY

2020 Stadium Club Black Foil

*BLACK: 1.5X TO 4X BASIC
*BLACK RC: 1X TO 2.5X BASIC RC
STATED ODDS 1:8 RETAIL

2020 Stadium Club Blue Foil

*BLUE/50: 6X TO 15X BASIC
*BLUE RC/50: 4X TO 10X BASIC RC
STATED ODDS 1:95 HOBBY
STATED PRINT RUN 50 SER.#'d SETS
69 Yordan Alvarez 20.00 50.00
104 Juan Soto 20.00 50.00
138 Aaron Judge 20.00 50.00
188 Fernando Tatis Jr. 25.00 60.00
192 Hank Aaron 25.00 60.00
244 Ichiro 12.00 30.00
270 Ken Griffey Jr. 40.00 100.00
290 Sandy Koufax 20.00 50.00

2020 Stadium Club Rainbow Foil

*RAINBOW/25: 8X TO 20X BASIC
*RAINBOW RC/25: 5X TO 1X BASIC RC
STATED ODDS 1:188 HOBBY
STATED PRINT RUN 25 SER.#'d SETS
1 Mike Trout 60.00 150.00
3 Babe Ruth 25.00 60.00
69 Yordan Alvarez 40.00 100.00
71 Carl Yastrzemski 15.00 40.00
104 Juan Soto 25.00 60.00
138 Aaron Judge 40.00 100.00
188 Fernando Tatis Jr. 40.00 100.00
192 Hank Aaron 30.00 80.00
244 Ichiro 15.00 40.00
270 Ken Griffey Jr. 50.00 120.00
290 Sandy Koufax 25.00 60.00
298 Gavin Lux 60.00 150.00

2020 Stadium Club Red Foil

*RED: 1X TO 2.5X BASIC
*RED RC: .6X TO 1.5X BASIC RC
STATED ODDS 1:3 HOBBY

2020 Stadium Club Sepia

*SEPIA: 2X TO 5X BASIC
*SEPIA RC: 1.2X TO 3X BASIC RC
STATED ODDS 1:8 RETAIL

2020 Stadium Club Autographs

STATED ODDS 1:9 HOBBY
EXCHANGE DEADLINE 7/31/22
AS Mike Schmidt
AAA Aristides Aquino 6.00 15.00
AAJ Aaron Judge 150.00 400.00
AAM Andres Munoz 5.00 12.00
AAN Austin Nola 5.00 12.00
AAT Abraham Toro 4.00 10.00
AAY Alex Young 3.00 8.00
ABB Bo Bichette EXCH 200.00 500.00
ABG Brusdar Graterol 5.00 12.00
ABH Bryce Harper
ABL Brandon Lowe 4.00 10.00
ABR Bryan Reynolds 4.00 10.00
ABZ Barry Zito 8.00 20.00
ACB Cavan Biggio 10.00 25.00
ACJ Chipper Jones 60.00 150.00
ACK Carter Kieboom 6.00 15.00
ACY Christian Yelich
ADL Domingo Leyba 4.00 10.00
ADM Dustin May 20.00 50.00
ADS Darryl Strawberry 25.00 60.00
ADV Dan Vogelbach 3.00 8.00
ADW David Wright 50.00 120.00
AEJ Eloy Jimenez 15.00 40.00
AEM Edgar Martinez 25.00 60.00
AGL Gavin Lux EXCH 25.00 60.00
AGT Gleyber Torres 30.00 80.00
AGU Gio Urshela 12.00 30.00
AJC Jose Canseco 15.00 40.00
AJD Justin Dunn 4.00 10.00
AJF Junior Fernandez 3.00 8.00
AJK James Karinchak 12.00 30.00
AJL Jesus Luzardo 6.00 15.00
AJM James Marvel 3.00 8.00
AJR Jake Rogers 3.00 8.00
AJS Josh Staumont 3.00 8.00
AJU Jose Urquidy 4.00 10.00
AJV Josh VanMeter 5.00 12.00
AJY Jordan Yamamoto 3.00 8.00
AKB Kris Bryant
AKL Kyle Lewis 40.00 100.00
AKY Kirby Yates 6.00 15.00
ALR Luis Robert 75.00 200.00
AMB Mike Brosseau 6.00 15.00
AMD Mauricio Dubon 4.00 10.00
AMG Mitch Garver 3.00 8.00
AMO Matt Olson 6.00 15.00
AMT Matt Thaiss 4.00 10.00
AMY Mike Yastrzemski 20.00 50.00
ANH Nico Hoerner 12.00 30.00
ANS Nick Solak 6.00 15.00
APA Pete Alonso 30.00 80.00
ARA Randy Arozarena 50.00 120.00
ARG Robel Garcia 3.00 8.00
ARH Rhys Hoskins 15.00 40.00
ASH Sam Hilliard 8.00 20.00
ASL Shed Long 4.00 10.00
ASM Sean Murphy 5.00 12.00
ASN Sheldon Neuse 4.00 10.00
ATA Tim Anderson 10.00 25.00
ATD Travis Demeritte 5.00 12.00
ATG Trent Grisham 15.00 40.00
ATL Tim Lincecum 40.00 100.00
ATZ T.J. Zeuch 3.00 8.00
AVG Vladimir Guerrero Jr. 40.00 100.00
AVR Victor Robles 10.00 25.00
AWC Willi Castro 10.00 25.00
AWS Will Smith 8.00 20.00
AXB Xander Bogaerts 25.00 60.00
AYA Yordan Alvarez 30.00 80.00
AYG Yasmani Grandal 5.00 12.00
AZC Zack Collins 4.00 10.00
AZG Zac Gallen 10.00 25.00
AAKA Anthony Kay 3.00 8.00
AAME Austin Meadows 6.00 15.00
ABBR Bobby Bradley 3.00 8.00
ABBU Brock Burke 3.00 8.00
ADCE Dylan Cease 5.00 12.00
ADMA Don Mattingly 75.00 200.00
AJAL Jose Altuve 15.00 40.00
AJDA Jaylin Davis 5.00 12.00
AJdG Jacob deGrom 125.00 300.00
AJFR Jake Fraley 4.00 10.00
AJME John Means 40.00 100.00
AJMN Jeff McNeil 12.00 30.00
AJRO Josh Rojas 3.00 8.00
AJSO Jorge Soler 5.00 12.00
AJST Juan Soto 75.00 200.00
AJVA Jason Varitek 40.00 100.00
AKHE Kyle Hendricks 10.00 25.00
AKHI Keston Hiura 10.00 25.00
ALGI Lucas Giolito 10.00 25.00
AMBA Michel Baez 3.00 8.00
AMMC Mark McGwire 50.00 120.00

AMMU Max Muncy 6.00 15.00
AMSO Mike Soroka 15.00 40.00
AMTR Mike Trout 400.00 800.00
ARAJ Ronald Acuna Jr. 60.00 150.00
ARAL Roberto Alomar 40.00 100.00
ARLA Ramon Laureano 6.00 15.00
ATLS Tommy La Stella 3.00 8.00
AWCL Will Clark 30.00 80.00

2020 Stadium Club Autographs Black

*BLACK/25: .6X TO 1.5X BASIC
STATED ODDS 1:754 HOBBY
STATED PRINT RUN 25 SER.#'d SETS
EXCHANGE DEADLINE 7/31/22
AAN Austin Nola 15.00 40.00
AGL Gavin Lux EXCH 125.00 300.00
AKL Kyle Lewis 75.00 200.00
ALR Luis Robert 250.00 600.00

2020 Stadium Club Autographs Red

*RED/50: .5X TO 1.2X BASIC
STATED ODDS 1:388 HOBBY
STATED PRINT RUN 50 SER.#'d SETS
EXCHANGE DEADLINE 7/31/22
AGL Gavin Lux EXCH 100.00 250.00
ALR Luis Robert 200.00 500.00

2020 Stadium Club Bash and Burn

STATED ODDS 1:8 HOBBY
*RED: .6X TO 1.5X BASIC
BAB1 Ronald Acuna Jr. 2.50 6.00
BAB2 Mike Trout 3.00 8.00
BAB3 Shohei Ohtani 1.00 2.50
BAB4 Christian Yelich .75 2.00
BAB5 Vladimir Guerrero Jr. 1.00 2.50
BAB6 Juan Soto 2.00 5.00
BAB7 Fernando Tatis Jr. 3.00 8.00
BAB8 Bryce Harper 1.00 2.50
BAB9 Rickey Henderson .60 1.50
BAB10 Victor Robles .75 2.00
BAB11 Ken Griffey Jr. 1.25 3.00
BAB12 Gavin Lux 2.00 5.00
BAB13 Jose Altuve .50 1.25
BAB14 Bo Bichette 3.00 8.00
BAB15 Mookie Betts 1.25 3.00

2020 Stadium Club Bash and Burn Black

*BLACK/99: .8X TO 2X BASIC
STATED ODDS 1:952 HOBBY
STATED PRINT RUN 99 SER.#'d SETS
BAB11 Ken Griffey Jr. 8.00 20.00

2020 Stadium Club Bash and Burn Orange

*ORANGE/50: 1.5X TO 4X BASIC
STATED ODDS 1:1883 HOBBY
STATED PRINT RUN 50 SER.#'d SETS
BAB11 Ken Griffey Jr. 15.00 40.00

2020 Stadium Club Chrome Insert

STATED ODDS 1:6 HOBBY
1 Mike Trout 6.00 15.00
13 Yadier Molina 1.50 4.00
14 Anthony Rizzo 1.50 4.00
18 Giancarlo Stanton 1.25 3.00
21 Xander Bogaerts 1.25 3.00
23 Dylan Cease 1.25 3.00
24 Walker Buehler 1.50 4.00
26 Sean Murphy 1.25 3.00
30 Bryce Harper 2.00 5.00
33 Albert Pujols 1.50 4.00
34 Anthony Kay .75 2.00
36 Aristides Aquino 2.00 5.00
47 Robel Garcia .75 2.00
48 George Springer 1.00 2.50
51 Adbert Alzolay 1.00 2.50
54 David Wright 1.00 2.50
68 Paul Goldschmidt 1.25 3.00
69 Yordan Alvarez 8.00 20.00
72 Zack Collins 1.00 2.50
75 Nolan Ryan 4.00 10.00
77 Andrew McCutchen 1.25 3.00
87 Clayton Kershaw 2.00 5.00
91 Max Scherzer 1.25 3.00
94 Masahiro Tanaka 1.25 3.00
95 Jesus Luzardo 1.50 4.00
96 Mark McGwire 2.00 5.00
100 Javier Baez 1.50 4.00
102 Barry Larkin 1.00 2.50
103 Hideki Matsui 1.25 3.00
104 Juan Soto 5.00 12.00
106 Cal Ripken Jr. 4.00 10.00
107 Kris Bryant 1.50 4.00
112 Bo Bichette 12.00 30.00
113 Darryl Strawberry .75 2.00
116 Ronald Acuna Jr. 5.00 12.00
118 Jacob deGrom 2.50 6.00
120 Nolan Arenado 2.00 5.00
123 Carlos Correa 1.25 3.00
124 Keston Hiura 1.50 4.00
130 Cody Bellinger 2.50 6.00
131 Joey Votto 1.25 3.00
138 Aaron Judge 3.00 8.00
139 Trevor Story 1.25 3.00
145 Shohei Ohtani 2.00 5.00
147 Gleyber Torres 2.50 6.00
151 Nick Solak 3.00 8.00
158 Noah Syndergaard 1.00 2.50
160 Tony Gwynn 1.25 3.00
161 Manny Machado 1.25 3.00
162 Jaylin Davis 1.25 3.00
164 Pete Alonso 3.00 8.00
165 Stephen Strasburg 1.25 3.00
173 Freddie Freeman 1.50 4.00
180 Josh Bell 1.00 2.50
185 Buster Posey 1.50 4.00
188 Fernando Tatis Jr. 6.00 15.00
191 Francisco Lindor 1.25 3.00
192 Hank Aaron 2.50 6.00
193 Jack Flaherty 1.25 3.00
199 David Ortiz 1.25 3.00
200 Will Clark 1.00 2.50
203 Chipper Jones 1.25 3.00
216 Rhys Hoskins 1.50 4.00
218 Mookie Betts 2.50 6.00
227 Justin Verlander 1.25 3.00
233 Nick Castellanos 1.25 3.00
234 Rafael Devers 1.50 4.00
236 Alex Bregman 1.25 3.00
237 Brendan McKay 1.25 3.00
240 A.J. Puk 1.25 3.00
244 Ichiro 1.50 4.00
247 Gerrit Cole 2.00 5.00
249 Kyle Lewis 8.00 20.00
253 Nico Hoerner 3.00 8.00
255 Dustin May 2.50 6.00
257 Frank Thomas 1.25 3.00
262 Zac Gallen 2.00 5.00
270 Ken Griffey Jr. 2.50 6.00
272 Don Mattingly 2.50 6.00
278 Jose Altuve 1.00 2.50
283 Anthony Rendon 1.25 3.00
286 Ozzie Albies 1.25 3.00
288 Vladimir Guerrero Jr. 2.00 5.00
290 Sandy Koufax 2.50 6.00
291 Willson Contreras 1.25 3.00
292 Christian Yelich 1.50 4.00
293 Randy Johnson 1.25 3.00
295 Jake Rogers .75 2.00
298 Gavin Lux 4.00 10.00
300 Eloy Jimenez 2.50 6.00

2020 Stadium Club Chrome Insert Gold Mint

*GOLD MINT: 2X TO 5X BASIC
STATED ODDS 1:256 HOBBY
1 Mike Trout 60.00 150.00
69 Yordan Alvarez 50.00 120.00
104 Juan Soto 30.00 80.00
188 Fernando Tatis Jr. 50.00 120.00
249 Kyle Lewis 60.00 150.00
270 Ken Griffey Jr. 50.00 120.00
298 Gavin Lux 50.00 120.00

2020 Stadium Club Chrome Insert Orange Refractors

*ORANGE/99: 1.2X TO 3X BASIC
STATED ODDS 1:159 HOBBY
STATED PRINT RUN 99 SER.#'d SETS
1 Mike Trout 40.00 100.00
69 Yordan Alvarez 30.00 80.00
104 Juan Soto 20.00 50.00
188 Fernando Tatis Jr. 30.00 80.00
249 Kyle Lewis 40.00 100.00
270 Ken Griffey Jr. 30.00 80.00

2020 Stadium Club Chrome Insert Refractors

*REF: .8X TO 2X BASIC
STATED ODDS 1:64 HOBBY
1 Mike Trout 25.00 60.00
249 Kyle Lewis 25.00 60.00
270 Ken Griffey Jr. 20.00 50.00

2020 Stadium Club Emperors of the Zone

STATED ODDS 1:16 HOBBY
*RED: .6X TO 1.5X BASIC
EOZ1 Mike Soroka .60 1.50
EOZ2 Chris Paddack .60 1.50
EOZ3 Lucas Giolito .50 1.25
EOZ4 Shohei Ohtani 1.00 2.50
EOZ5 Sonny Gray .50 1.25
EOZ6 Mike Clevinger .50 1.25
EOZ7 Shane Bieber .60 1.50
EOZ8 Gerrit Cole 1.00 2.50
EOZ9 Justin Verlander .60 1.50
EOZ10 Zack Greinke .60 1.50
EOZ11 Clayton Kershaw 1.00 2.50
EOZ12 Walker Buehler .75 2.00
EOZ13 Jacob deGrom 1.25 3.00
EOZ14 Jack Flaherty .60 1.50
EOZ15 Max Scherzer .60 1.50
EOZ16 Brendan McKay .60 1.50
EOZ17 Aaron Nola .50 1.25
EOZ18 Stephen Strasburg .60 1.50
EOZ19 Chris Sale .60 1.50
EOZ20 Noah Syndergaard .50 1.25
EOZ21 Luis Severino .50 1.25
EOZ22 Blake Snell .50 1.25
EOZ23 Tyler Glasnow .60 1.50
EOZ24 Jose Berrios .50 1.25
EOZ25 Patrick Corbin .50 1.25

2020 Stadium Club Emperors of the Zone Black

*BLACK/99: .8X TO 2X BASIC
STATED ODDS 1:571 HOBBY
EOZ11 Clayton Kershaw 5.00 12.00

2020 Stadium Club Emperors of the Zone Orange

*ORANGE/50: 1.5X TO 4X BASIC
STATED ODDS 1:1131 HOBBY
STATED PRINT RUN 50 SER.#'d SETS
EOZ11 Clayton Kershaw 10.00 25.00

2020 Stadium Club In the Wings

STATED ODDS 1:16 HOBBY
*RED: .6X TO 1.5X BASIC
ITW1 Ronald Acuna Jr. 2.50 6.00
ITW2 Vladimir Guerrero Jr. 1.00 2.50
ITW3 Juan Soto 2.00 5.00
ITW4 Fernando Tatis Jr. 3.00 8.00
ITW5 Victor Robles .75 2.00
ITW6 Bo Bichette 3.00 8.00
ITW7 Aristides Aquino 1.00 2.50
ITW8 Gavin Lux 2.00 5.00
ITW9 Gleyber Torres 1.25 3.00
ITW10 Kyle Tucker .60 1.50
ITW11 Ozzie Albies .60 1.50
ITW12 Yordan Alvarez 4.00 10.00
ITW13 Pete Alonso 1.50 4.00
ITW14 Keston Hiura .75 2.00
ITW15 Rafael Devers .75 2.00
ITW16 Shane Bieber .60 1.50
ITW17 Jack Flaherty .60 1.50
ITW18 Shohei Ohtani 1.00 2.50
ITW19 Walker Buehler .75 2.00
ITW20 Chris Paddack .60 1.50
ITW21 Mike Soroka .60 1.50
ITW22 Eloy Jimenez 1.25 3.00
ITW23 Cody Bellinger 1.25 3.00
ITW24 Jesus Luzardo .75 2.00
ITW25 Nico Hoerner 1.50 4.00

2020 Stadium Club In the Wings Black

*BLACK/99: .8X TO 2X BASIC
STATED ODDS 1:571 HOBBY
STATED PRINT RUN 99 SER.#'d SETS
ITW9 Gleyber Torres 6.00 15.00

2020 Stadium Club In the Wings Orange

*ORANGE/50: 1.5X TO 4X BASIC
STATED ODDS 1:1131 HOBBY
STATED PRINT RUN 50 SER.#'d SETS
ITW9 Gleyber Torres 12.00 30.00

2020 Stadium Club Instavision

STATED ODDS 1:256 HOBBY
IVC1 Ronald Acuna Jr. 6.00 15.00
IVC2 Vladimir Guerrero Jr. 4.00 10.00
IVC3 Fernando Tatis Jr. 12.00 30.00
IVC4 Peter Alonso 6.00 15.00
IVC5 Mike Trout 8.00 20.00
IVC6 Bryce Harper 6.00 15.00
IVC7 Luis Robert 12.00 30.00
IVC8 Gavin Lux 5.00 12.00
IVC9 Yordan Alvarez 5.00 12.00
IVC10 Bo Bichette 12.00 30.00

2020 Stadium Club Instavision Black

*BLACK/25: .8X TO 2X BASIC
STATED ODDS 1:5630 HOBBY
STATED PRINT RUN 25 SER.#'d SETS
IVC3 Fernando Tatis Jr. 40.00 100.00
IVC4 Peter Alonso 20.00 50.00
IVC5 Mike Trout 40.00 100.00
IVC7 Luis Robert 125.00 300.00
IVC10 Bo Bichette 30.00 80.00

2020 Stadium Club Instavision Red

*RED/50: .5X TO 1.2X BASIC
STATED ODDS 1:2828 HOBBY
STATED PRINT RUN 50 SER.#'d SETS
IVC3 Fernando Tatis Jr. 20.00 50.00
IVC4 Peter Alonso 12.00 30.00
IVC5 Mike Trout 25.00 60.00
IVC7 Luis Robert 75.00 200.00
IVC10 Bo Bichette 20.00 50.00

2020 Stadium Club Lone Star Signatures

STATED ODDS 1:4471 HOBBY
PRINT RUNS B/WN 10-25 COPIES PER
NO PRICING ON QTY 15 OR LESS
EXCHANGE DEADLINE 7/31/22
LSSBH Bryce Harper
LSSCY Christian Yelich/25 EXCH 50.00 120.00
LSSDJ Derek Jeter/25
LSSDW David Wright/25 60.00 150.00
LSSFT Frank Thomas/25 50.00 120.00
LSSGL Gavin Lux/25 EXCH 100.00 250.00
LSSJS Juan Soto/25 60.00 150.00
LSSPA Pete Alonso/25 60.00 150.00
LSSYA Yordan Alvarez/25 60.00 150.00
LSSBBI Bo Bichette/25 EXCH 60.00 150.00
LSSKGJ Ken Griffey Jr.
LSSRAJ Ronald Acuna Jr./25

2020 Stadium Club Oversized Box Toppers

STATED ODDS 1 PER HOBBY BOX
OBB Barry Bonds 2.50 6.00
OBS Mike Schmidt 2.50 6.00
OBAA Aristides Aquino 2.50 6.00
OBAJ Aaron Judge 10.00 25.00
OBBB Bo Bichette 8.00 20.00
OBBH Bryce Harper 2.50 6.00
OBBZ Barry Zito 1.25 3.00
OBCI Ichiro 5.00 12.00
OBCJ Chipper Jones 1.50 4.00
OBCR Cal Ripken Jr. 5.00 12.00
OBCY Christian Yelich 2.00 5.00
OBDM Dale Murphy 1.50 4.00
OBDS Darryl Strawberry 1.00 2.50
OBEM Edgar Martinez 1.25 3.00
OBFL Francisco Lindor 1.50 4.00
OBFT Fernando Tatis Jr. 8.00 20.00
OBGL Gavin Lux 5.00 12.00
OBGT Gleyber Torres 3.00 8.00
OBHA Hank Aaron 3.00 8.00
OBHM Hideki Matsui 1.50 4.00
OBJd Jacob deGrom 3.00 8.00
OBJL Jesus Luzardo 2.00 5.00
OBJS Juan Soto 5.00 12.00
OBJV Jason Varitek 1.50 4.00
OBKB Kris Bryant 2.00 5.00
OBKG Ken Griffey Jr. 6.00 15.00
OBKL Kyle Lewis 8.00 20.00
OBMM Mark McGwire 8.00 20.00
OBMS Max Scherzer 1.50 4.00
OBNA Nolan Arenado 2.50 6.00
OBNR Nolan Ryan 8.00 20.00
OBOA Ozzie Albies 1.50 4.00
OBPA Pete Alonso 4.00 10.00
OBPG Paul Goldschmidt 1.50 4.00
OBRA Roberto Alomar 1.25 3.00
OBRH Rhys Hoskins 2.00 5.00
OBRJ Randy Johnson 1.50 4.00
OBSB Shane Bieber 1.50 4.00
OBSO Shohei Ohtani 2.50 6.00
OBTL Tim Lincecum 1.25 3.00
OBVG Vladimir Guerrero Jr. 2.50 6.00
OBVR Victor Robles 2.00 5.00
OBWC Will Clark 1.25 3.00
OBXB Xander Bogaerts 1.50 4.00
OBYA Yordan Alvarez 10.00 25.00
OBDMA Dustin May 3.00 8.00
OBDMT Don Mattingly 3.00 8.00
OBFTH Frank Thomas 1.50 4.00
OBJCO Jose Canseco 1.25 3.00
OBRAJ Ronald Acuna Jr. 6.00 15.00

2020 Stadium Club Oversized Widevision

STATED ODDS 1 PER BLASTER BOX
30 Bryce Harper 8.00 20.00
68 Paul Goldschmidt 1.25 3.00
69 Yordan Alvarez 8.00 20.00
75 Nolan Ryan 8.00 20.00
96 Mark McGwire 2.00 5.00
100 Javier Baez 1.50 4.00
104 Juan Soto 10.00 25.00
107 Kris Bryant 1.50 4.00
3 Ronald Acuna Jr. 2.00 5.00
118 Jacob deGrom 5.00 12.00
120 Nolan Arenado 2.00 5.00
130 Cody Bellinger 2.50 6.00
138 Aaron Judge 3.00 8.00
147 Gleyber Torres 2.50 6.00
164 Pete Alonso 3.00 8.00
188 Fernando Tatis Jr. 12.00 30.00
192 Hank Aaron 2.50 6.00
218 Mookie Betts 2.50 6.00
227 Justin Verlander 1.25 3.00
244 Ichiro 1.50 4.00
249 Kyle Lewis 6.00 15.00
288 Vladimir Guerrero Jr. 2.00 5.00
290 Sandy Koufax 2.50 6.00
292 Christian Yelich 1.50 4.00
298 Gavin Lux 4.00 10.00

2020 Stadium Club Power Zone

STATED ODDS 1:16 HOBBY
*RED: .6X TO 1.5X BASIC
PZ1 Darryl Strawberry .40 1.00
PZ2 Pete Alonso 1.50 4.00
PZ3 Mike Trout 3.00 8.00
PZ4 Shohei Ohtani 1.00 2.50
PZ5 Christian Yelich .75 2.00
PZ6 Chipper Jones .60 1.50
PZ7 Ronald Acuna Jr. 2.50 6.00
PZ8 Vladimir Guerrero Jr. 1.00 2.50
PZ9 Juan Soto 2.00 5.00
PZ10 Fernando Tatis Jr. 3.00 8.00
PZ11 Mark McGwire 1.00 2.50
PZ12 Rhys Hoskins .75 2.00
PZ13 Bryce Harper 1.00 2.50
PZ14 Aaron Judge 1.50 4.00
PZ15 Jeff Bagwell .50 1.25
PZ16 Francisco Lindor .60 1.50
PZ17 Frank Thomas .60 1.50
PZ18 Eloy Jimenez 1.25 3.00
PZ19 Kris Bryant .75 2.00
PZ20 Anthony Rizzo .75 2.00
PZ21 David Wright .50 1.25
PZ22 Nolan Arenado 1.00 2.50
PZ23 Gleyber Torres 1.25 3.00
PZ24 Yordan Alvarez 4.00 10.00
PZ25 Ken Griffey Jr. 1.25 3.00

2020 Stadium Club Power Zone Black

*BLACK/99: .8X TO 2X BASIC
STATED ODDS 1:571 HOBBY
STATED PRINT RUN 99 SER.#'d SETS
PZ25 Ken Griffey Jr. 10.00 25.00

2020 Stadium Club Power Zone Orange

*ORANGE/50: 1.5X TO 4X BASIC
STATED ODDS 1:1131 HOBBY
STATED PRINT RUN 50 SER.#'d SETS
PZ14 Aaron Judge 15.00 40.00
PZ25 Ken Griffey Jr. 20.00 50.00

2000 Stadium Club Chrome

COMPLETE SET (250) 20.00 50.00
COMMON CARD (1-250) .20 .50
COMMON RC .30 .75
FUTURE STARS/PROSPECTS ARE NOT SP'S!
1 Nomar Garciaparra .30 .75
2 Brian Jordan .20 .50
3 Mark Grace .30 .75
4 Jeromy Burnitz .20 .50
5 Shane Reynolds .20 .50
6 Alex Gonzalez .20 .50
7 Jose Offerman .20 .50
8 Orlando Hernandez .20 .50
9 Mike Caruso .20 .50
10 Tony Clark .20 .50
11 Sean Casey .20 .50
12 Johnny Damon .30 .75
13 Dante Bichette .20 .50
14 Kevin Young .20 .50
15 Juan Gonzalez .20 .50
16 Chipper Jones .50 1.25
17 Quilvio Veras .20 .50
18 Trevor Hoffman .30 .75
19 Roger Cedeno .20 .50
20 Ellis Burks .20 .50
21 Richie Sexson .20 .50
22 Gary Sheffield .20 .50
23 Delino DeShields .20 .50
24 Wade Boggs .30 .75
25 Ray Lankford .20 .50
26 Kevin Appier .20 .50
27 Roy Halladay .30 .75
28 Harold Baines .30 .75
29 Todd Zeile .20 .50
30 Barry Larkin .30 .75
31 Ron Coomer .20 .50
32 Jorge Posada .30 .75
33 Magglio Ordonez .30 .75
34 Brian Giles .20 .50
35 Jeff Kent .20 .50
36 Henry Rodriguez .20 .50
37 Fred McGriff .30 .75
38 Shawn Green .20 .50
39 Derek Bell .20 .50
40 Ben Grieve .20 .50
41 Dave Nilsson .20 .50
42 Mo Vaughn .20 .50
43 Rondell White .20 .50
44 Doug Glanville .20 .50
45 Paul O'Neill .30 .75
46 Carlos Lee .20 .50
47 Vinny Castilla .20 .50
48 Mike Sweeney .20 .50
49 Rico Brogna .20 .50
50 Alex Rodriguez .60 1.50
51 Luis Castillo .20 .50
52 Kevin Brown .20 .50
53 Jose Vidro .20 .50
54 John Smoltz .50 1.25
55 Garret Anderson .20 .50
56 Matt Stairs .20 .50
57 Omar Vizquel .30 .75
58 Tom Goodwin .20 .50
59 Scott Brosius .20 .50
60 Robin Ventura .20 .50
61 B.J. Surhoff .20 .50
62 Andy Ashby .20 .50
63 Chris Widger .20 .50
64 Tim Hudson .30 .75
65 Javy Lopez .20 .50
66 Tim Salmon .20 .50
67 Warren Morris .20 .50
68 John Wetteland .20 .50
69 Gabe Kapler .20 .50
70 Bernie Williams .30 .75
71 Rickey Henderson .50 1.25
72 Andruw Jones .20 .50
73 Eric Young .20 .50
74 Bob Abreu .20 .50
75 David Cone .20 .50
76 Rusty Greer .20 .50
77 Ron Belliard .20 .50
78 Troy Glaus .20 .50
79 Mike Hampton .20 .50
80 Miguel Tejada .30 .75
81 Jeff Cirillo .20 .50
82 Todd Hundley .20 .50
83 Roberto Alomar .30 .75
84 Charles Johnson .20 .50
85 Rafael Palmeiro .30 .75
86 Doug Mientkiewicz .20 .50
87 Mariano Rivera .60 1.50
88 Neifi Perez .20 .50
89 Jermiane Dye .20 .50
90 Ivan Rodriguez .30 .75
91 Jay Buhner .20 .50
92 Pokey Reese .20 .50
93 John Olerud .20 .50
94 Brady Anderson .20 .50
95 Manny Ramirez .50 1.25
96 Keith Osik RC .30 .75
97 Mickey Morandini .20 .50
98 Matt Williams .20 .50
99 Eric Karros .20 .50
100 Ken Griffey Jr. 1.00 2.50
101 Bret Boone .20 .50
102 Ryan Klesko .20 .50
103 Craig Biggio .30 .75
104 John Jaha .20 .50
105 Vladimir Guerrero .30 .75
106 Devon White .20 .50
107 Tony Womack .20 .50
108 Marvin Benard .20 .50
109 Kenny Lofton .20 .50
110 Preston Wilson .20 .50
111 Al Leiter .20 .50
112 Reggie Sanders .20 .50
113 Scott Williamson .20 .50
114 Deivi Cruz .20 .50
115 Carlos Beltran .30 .75
116 Ray Durham .20 .50
117 Ricky Ledee .20 .50
118 Torii Hunter .20 .50
119 John Valentin .20 .50
120 Scott Rolen .30 .75
121 Jason Kendall .20 .50
122 Dave Martinez .20 .50
123 Jim Thome .30 .75
124 David Bell .20 .50
125 Jose Canseco .30 .75
126 Jose Lima .20 .50
127 Carl Everett .20 .50
128 Kevin Millwood .20 .50
129 Bill Spiers .20 .50
130 Omar Daal .20 .50
131 Miguel Cairo .20 .50
132 Mark Grudzielanek .20 .50
133 David Justice .20 .50
134 Russ Ortiz .20 .50
135 Mike Piazza .50 1.25
136 Brian Meadows .20 .50
137 Tony Gwynn .50 1.25
138 Cal Ripken 1.50 4.00
139 Kris Benson .20 .50
140 Larry Walker .30 .75
141 Cristian Guzman .20 .50
142 Tino Martinez .20 .50
143 Chris Singleton .20 .50
144 Lee Stevens .20 .50
145 Rey Ordonez .20 .50
146 Russ Davis .20 .50
147 J.T. Snow .20 .50
148 Luis Gonzalez .20 .50
149 Marquis Grissom .20 .50
150 Greg Maddux .60 1.50
151 Fernando Tatis .20 .50
152 Jason Giambi .20 .50
153 Carlos Delgado .20 .50
154 Joe McEwing .20 .50
155 Raul Mondesi .20 .50
156 Rich Aurilia .20 .50
157 Alex Fernandez .20 .50
158 Albert Belle .20 .50
159 Pat Meares .20 .50
160 Mike Lieberthal .20 .50
161 Mike Cameron .20 .50
162 Juan Encarnacion .20 .50
163 Chuck Knoblauch .20 .50
164 Pedro Martinez .30 .75
165 Randy Johnson .50 1.25
166 Shannon Stewart .20 .50
167 Jeff Bagwell .30 .75
168 Edgar Renteria .20 .50
169 Barry Bonds .75 2.00
170 Steve Finley .20 .50
171 Brian Hunter .20 .50
172 Tom Glavine .30 .75
173 Mark Kotsay .20 .50
174 Tony Fernandez .20 .50
175 Sammy Sosa .50 1.25
176 Geoff Jenkins .20 .50
177 Adrian Beltre .50 1.25
178 Jay Bell .20 .50
179 Mike Bordick .20 .50
180 Ed Sprague .20 .50
181 Dave Roberts .30 .75
182 Greg Vaughn .20 .50
183 Brian Daubach .20 .50
184 Damion Easley .20 .50
185 Carlos Febles .20 .50
186 Kevin Tapani .20 .50
187 Frank Thomas .50 1.25
188 Roger Clemens .60 1.50
189 Mike Benjamin .20 .50
190 Curt Schilling .30 .75
191 Edgardo Alfonzo .20 .50
192 Mike Mussina .30 .75
193 Todd Helton .30 .75
194 Todd Jones .20 .50
195 Dean Palmer .20 .50
196 John Flaherty .20 .50
197 Derek Jeter 1.25 3.00
198 Todd Walker .20 .50
199 Brad Ausmus .20 .50
200 Mark McGwire .75 2.00
201 Erubiel Durazo .20 .50
202 Nick Johnson .20 .50
203 Ruben Mateo .20 .50
204 Lance Berkman .30 .75
205 Pat Burrell .20 .50
206 Pablo Ozuna .20 .50
207 Roosevelt Brown .20 .50
208 Alfonso Soriano .50 1.25
209 A.J. Burnett .20 .50
210 Rafael Furcal .30 .75
211 Scott Morgan .20 .50
212 Adam Piatt .20 .50
213 Dee Brown .20 .50
214 Corey Patterson .20 .50
215 Mickey Lopez .20 .50
216 Rob Ryan .20 .50
217 Sean Burroughs .20 .50
218 Jack Cust .20 .50
219 John Patterson .20 .50
220 Kit Pellow .20 .50
221 Chad Hermansen .20 .50
222 Daryle Ward .20 .50
223 Jayson Werth .30 .75
224 Jason Standridge .20 .50
225 Mark Mulder .20 .50
226 Peter Bergeron .20 .50
227 Willi Mo Pena .20 .50
228 Aramis Ramirez .20 .50
229 John Sneed RC .30 .75
230 Wilton Veras .20 .50
231 Josh Hamilton .60 1.50
232 Eric Munson .20 .50
233 Bobby Bradley RC .30 .75
234 Larry Bigbie RC .30 .75
235 B.J. Garbe RC .30 .75
236 Brett Myers RC 1.00 2.50
237 Jason Stumm RC .30 .75
238 Corey Myers RC .30 .75
239 Ryan Christianson RC .30 .75
240 David Walling .20 .50
241 Josh Girdley .20 .50
242 Omar Ortiz .20 .50
243 Jason Jennings .20 .50
244 Kyle Snyder .20 .50
245 Jay Gehrke .20 .50
246 Mike Paradis .20 .50
247 Chance Caple RC .30 .75
248 Ben Christensen RC .30 .75
249 Brad Baker RC .30 .75
250 Rick Asadoorian RC .30 .75

2000 Stadium Club Chrome First Day Issue

*1ST DAY: 4X TO 10X BASIC
*ROOKIES: 2.5X TO 6X BASIC CARDS
STATED ODDS 1:33 HOB/RET
STATED PRINT RUN 100 SERIAL #'d SETS

2000 Stadium Club Chrome First Day Issue Refractors

*1ST REF: 15X TO 40X BASIC
STATED ODDS 1:131
STATED PRINT RUN 25 SERIAL #'d SETS
NO PRICING ON ROOKIES

2000 Stadium Club Chrome Refractors

*REF: 2.5X TO 6X BASIC
*REF RC: 1.5X TO 4X BASIC
STATED ODDS 1:12

2000 Stadium Club Chrome Capture the Action

COMPLETE SET (20) 15.00 40.00
STATED ODDS 1:18
*REFRACTORS: 1X TO 2.5X BASIC CAPTURE
REFRACTOR STATED ODDS 1:90
CA1 Josh Hamilton 1.25 3.00
CA2 Pat Burrell .40 1.00
CA3 Erubiel Durazo .40 1.00
CA4 Alfonso Soriano 1.00 2.50
CA5 A.J. Burnett .40 1.00
CA6 Alex Rodriguez 1.25 3.00
CA7 Sean Casey .40 1.00
CA8 Derek Jeter 2.50 6.00
CA9 Vladimir Guerrero .60 1.50
CA10 Nomar Garciaparra .60 1.50
CA11 Mike Piazza 1.00 2.50
CA12 Ken Griffey Jr. 2.00 5.00
CA13 Sammy Sosa 1.00 2.50
CA14 Juan Gonzalez .40 1.00
CA15 Mark McGwire 1.50 4.00
CA16 Ivan Rodriguez .60 1.50
CA17 Barry Bonds 1.50 4.00
CA18 Wade Boggs .60 1.50
CA19 Tony Gwynn 1.00 2.50
CA20 Cal Ripken 3.00 8.00

2000 Stadium Club Chrome Clear Shots

COMPLETE SET (10) 8.00 20.00
STATED ODDS 1:24
*REFRACTORS: 1X TO 2.5X BASIC CLEAR
REFRACTOR ODDS 1:120
CS1 Derek Jeter 2.50 6.00
CS2 Bernie Williams .60 1.50
CS3 Roger Clemens 1.25 3.00
CS4 Chipper Jones 1.00 2.50
CS5 Greg Maddux 1.25 3.00
CS6 Andruw Jones .40 1.00
CS7 Juan Gonzalez .40 1.00
CS8 Manny Ramirez 1.00 2.50
CS9 Ken Griffey Jr. 2.00 5.00
CS10 Josh Hamilton 1.25 3.00

2000 Stadium Club Chrome Eyes of the Game

COMPLETE SET (10) 10.00 25.00
STATED ODDS 1:16
*REFRACTORS: 1X TO 2.5X BASIC EYES
REFRACTOR ODDS 1:80
EG1 Randy Johnson 1.50 4.00
EG2 Mike Piazza 1.50 4.00
EG3 Nomar Garciaparra 1.00 2.50
EG4 Mark McGwire 2.50 6.00
EG5 Alex Rodriguez 2.00 5.00
EG6 Derek Jeter 4.00 10.00
EG7 Tony Gwynn 1.50 4.00
EG8 Sammy Sosa 1.50 4.00
EG9 Larry Walker 1.00 2.50
EG10 Ken Griffey Jr. 3.00 8.00

2000 Stadium Club Chrome True Colors

COMPLETE SET (10) 10.00 25.00
STATED ODDS 1:32
*REFRACTORS: 1X TO 2.5X BASIC TRUE
REFRACTOR ODDS 1:160
TC1 Sammy Sosa 1.00 2.50
TC2 Nomar Garciaparra .60 1.50
TC3 Alex Rodriguez 1.25 3.00
TC4 Derek Jeter 2.50 6.00
TC5 Mark McGwire 1.50 4.00
TC6 Chipper Jones 1.00 2.50
TC7 Mike Piazza 1.00 2.50
TC8 Ken Griffey Jr. 2.00 5.00
TC9 Manny Ramirez 1.00 2.50
TC10 Vladimir Guerrero .60 1.50

2000 Stadium Club Chrome Visionaries

COMPLETE SET (20) 8.00 20.00
STATED ODDS 1:18
*REF: .75X TO 2X BASIC VISIONARIES
REFRACTOR ODDS 1:90
V1 Alfonso Soriano 1.00 2.50
V2 Josh Hamilton 1.25 3.00
V3 A.J. Burnett .40 1.00
V4 Pat Burrell .40 1.00
V5 Ruben Salazar .40 1.00
V6 Aaron Rowand 2.00 5.00
V7 Adam Piatt .40 1.00
V8 Nick Johnson .40 1.00
V9 Brett Myers 1.25 3.00
V10 Jack Cust .40 1.00
V11 Corey Patterson .40 1.00
V12 Sean Burroughs .40 1.00
V13 Pablo Ozuna .40 1.00
V14 Dee Brown .40 1.00
V15 John Patterson .40 1.00
V16 Willi Mo Pena .40 1.00
V17 Mark Mulder .40 1.00
V18 Eric Munson .40 1.00
V19 Alex Escobar .40 1.00
V20 Rick Asadoorian .40 1.00

2020 Stadium Club Chrome

1 Mike Trout 4.00 10.00
2 Nelson Cruz .60 1.50
3 Babe Ruth 1.50 4.00
4 Justus Sheffield .60 1.50
5 Bobby Bradley RC .60 1.50
6 Abraham Toro RC .75 2.00
7 Michel Baez RC .60 1.50
8 Michael Conforto .50 1.25
9 Jameson Taillon .50 1.25
10 Chris Sale .60 1.50
11 Matt Olson .60 1.50
12 David Dahl .40 1.00
13 Yadier Molina .75 2.00
14 Anthony Rizzo .75 2.00
15 DJ LeMahieu .60 1.50
16 Michael Chavis .50 1.25
17 J.T. Realmuto .60 1.50
18 Giancarlo Stanton .60 1.50
19 Eddie Rosario .50 1.25
20 Mitch Garver .40 1.00
21 Xander Bogaerts .60 1.50
22 Jose Ramirez .50 1.25
23 Dylan Cease RC 1.00 2.50
24 Walker Buehler .75 2.00
25 Yasmani Grandal .40 1.00
26 Sean Murphy RC 1.00 2.50
27 Mike Clevinger .50 1.25
28 Max Muncy .50 1.25
29 Lorenzo Cain .40 1.00
30 Bryce Harper 1.00 2.50
31 John Means .60 1.50
32 Yuli Gurriel .50 1.25
33 Albert Pujols .75 2.00
34 Anthony Kay RC .60 1.50
35 Lou Gehrig 1.25 3.00
36 Aristides Aquino RC 1.50 4.00
37 Mark Canha .40 1.00
38 Eugenio Suarez .50 1.25
39 Ryan Zimmerman .50 1.25
40 Blake Snell .50 1.25
41 Jonathan Villar .40 1.00
42 Michael Brantley .50 1.25
43 Byron Buxton .60 1.50
44 Tommy Edman .60 1.50
45 Justin Turner .60 1.50
46 Joey Gallo .60 1.50
47 Robel Garcia RC .60 1.50
48 George Springer .50 1.25
49 Josh VanMeter .60 1.50
50 Mike Moustakas .50 1.25
51 Adbert Alzolay RC .75 2.00
52 Mike Schmidt 1.00 2.50
53 Brusdar Graterol RC 1.00 2.50
54 David Wright .50 1.25
55 Lucas Giolito .50 1.25
56 Robinson Cano .50 1.25
57 Shun Yamaguchi RC .75 2.00
58 Jason Varitek .60 1.50
59 Sean Doolittle .40 1.00
60 Josh Donaldson .50 1.25
61 Dale Murphy .60 1.50

62 Austin Meadows .60 1.50
63 Yoan Moncada .60 1.50
64 Yoshi Tsutsugo RC 1.50 4.00
65 Dario Agrazal RC .75 2.00
66 Aaron Hicks .50 1.25
67 Ted Williams 1.25 3.00
68 Paul Goldschmidt .60 1.50
69 Yordan Alvarez RC 6.00 15.00
70 Bob Feller .50 1.25
71 Carl Yastrzemski 1.00 2.50
72 Zack Collins RC .75 2.00
73 Ketel Marte .50 1.25
74 Brandon Woodruff .60 1.50
75 Nolan Ryan 2.50 6.00
76 Mike Soroka .60 1.50
77 Andrew McCutchen .60 1.50
78 Sean Manaea .40 1.00
79 Jose Abreu .60 1.50
80 Mike Brosseau RC 1.25 3.00
81 Randal Grichuk .40 1.00
82 Kirby Yates .40 1.00
83 Max Kepler .50 1.25
84 Adrian Morejon RC .60 1.50
85 Kyle Hendricks .60 1.50
86 Yu Chang RC 1.00 2.50
87 Clayton Kershaw 1.00 2.50
88 Starling Marte .50 1.25
89 Adalberto Mondesi .50 1.25
90 Tommy La Stella .40 1.00
91 Max Scherzer .60 1.50
92 Luke Voit .75 2.00
93 Kwang-Hyun Kim RC 1.25 3.00
94 Masahiro Tanaka .60 1.50
95 Jesus Luzardo RC 1.25 3.00
96 Mark McGwire 1.00 2.50
97 Brendan Rodgers .60 1.50
98 Sam Hilliard RC 1.00 2.50
99 Nomar Garciaparra .50 1.25
100 Javier Baez .75 2.00
101 James Marvel RC .60 1.50
102 Barry Larkin .50 1.25
103 Hideki Matsui .60 1.50
104 Juan Soto 3.00 7.00
105 Junior Fernandez RC .60 1.50
106 Cal Ripken Jr. 2.00 5.00
107 Kris Bryant .75 2.00
108 Yusei Kikuchi .50 1.25
109 Trey Mancini .60 1.50
110 Ernie Banks .60 1.50
111 Luis Severino .50 1.25
112 Bo Bichette RC 6.00 15.00
113 Darryl Strawberry .40 1.00
114 Robbie Ray .40 1.00
115 Ramon Laureano .50 1.25
116 Ronald Acuna Jr. 4.00 10.00
117 Miguel Cabrera .60 1.50
118 Jacob deGrom 1.25 3.00
119 Derek Dietrich .50 1.25
120 Nolan Arenado 1.00 2.50
121 Nick Markakis .50 1.25
122 Carter Kieboom .50 1.25
123 Carlos Correa .60 1.50
124 Keston Hiura .75 2.00
125 Sonny Gray .50 1.25
126 Travis Demeritte RC 1.00 2.50
127 Miguel Sano .50 1.25
128 Lourdes Gurriel Jr. .50 1.25
129 Alex Young RC .60 1.50
130 Cody Bellinger 1.25 3.00
131 Joey Votto .60 1.50
132 Jeff McNeil .50 1.25
133 Victor Robles .75 2.00
134 Didi Gregorius .50 1.25
135 J.D. Martinez .60 1.50
136 Zack Greinke .60 1.50
137 Hyun-Jin Ryu .50 1.25
138 Aaron Judge 1.50 4.00
139 Trevor Story .60 1.50
140 Willie Mays 1.25 3.00
141 Danny Jansen .40 1.00
142 Adam Wainwright .50 1.25
143 Will Smith .60 1.50
144 Lewis Thorpe RC .60 1.50
145 Shohei Ohtani 1.00 2.50
146 Jose Canseco .50 1.25
147 Gleyber Torres 1.25 3.00
148 Honus Wagner .60 1.50
149 Jose Urquidy RC .75 2.00
150 Rod Carew .50 1.25
151 Nick Solak RC 2.50 6.00
152 Trent Grisham RC 2.50 6.00
153 Roberto Alomar .50 1.25
154 Brian Anderson .40 1.00
155 Joey Lucchesi .40 1.00
156 Matt Thaiss RC .75 2.00
157 Marcell Ozuna .60 1.50
158 Noah Syndergaard .50 1.25
159 Roberto Clemente 1.50 4.00
160 Tony Gwynn .60 1.50
161 Manny Machado .60 1.50
162 Jaylin Davis RC 1.00 2.50
163 Nomar Mazara .40 1.00
164 Pete Alonso 1.50 4.00
165 Stephen Strasburg .60 1.50
166 Ozzie Smith .75 2.00
167 Trevor Bauer .75 2.00
168 Ryne Sandberg 1.25 3.00
169 Chris Paddack .60 1.50
170 Seth Brown RC .60 1.50
171 Tim Lincecum .50 1.25
172 Jeff Bagwell .50 1.25
173 Freddie Freeman .75 2.00
174 Gio Urshela .60 1.50
175 Justin Dunn RC .75 2.00
176 Dallas Keuchel .50 1.25
177 Yasiel Puig .60 1.50
178 Barry Zito .50 1.25
179 Marcus Semien .60 1.50
180 Josh Bell .50 1.25
181 Josh Hader .50 1.25
182 Aroldis Chapman .60 1.50
183 Andres Munoz RC 1.00 2.50
184 Brandon Lowe .50 1.25
185 Buster Posey .75 2.00
186 Austin Nola RC 1.00 2.50
187 Stan Musial 1.00 2.50
188 Fernando Tatis Jr. 3.00 8.00
189 Jorge Posada .50 1.25
190 Dakota Hudson .50 1.25
191 Francisco Lindor .60 1.50
192 Hank Aaron 1.25 3.00
193 Jack Flaherty .60 1.50
194 Matt Chapman .60 1.50
195 Andrew Benintendi .60 1.50
196 Marcus Stroman .50 1.25
197 Mike Yastrzemski 1.00 2.50
198 Shed Long RC .75 2.00
199 David Ortiz .60 1.50
200 Will Clark .50 1.25
201 Kerry Wood .40 1.00
202 Patrick Corbin .50 1.25
203 Chipper Jones .60 1.50
204 Patrick Sandoval RC 1.00 2.50
205 Corey Kluber .50 1.25
206 Salvador Perez .50 1.25
207 Shane Bieber .60 1.50
208 Domingo Leyba RC .75 2.00
209 Charlie Morton .60 1.50
210 Eduardo Escobar .40 1.00
211 Lance McCullers Jr. .40 1.00
212 Jorge Soler .60 1.50
213 Josh Rojas RC .60 1.50
214 Ty Cobb 1.00 2.50
215 Gary Sanchez .60 1.50
216 Rhys Hoskins .75 2.00
217 Logan Webb RC 1.00 2.50
218 Mookie Betts 1.25 3.00
219 Hunter Harvey RC 1.00 2.50
220 Paul DeJong .60 1.50
221 Dan Vogelbach .40 1.00
222 Elvis Andrus .50 1.25
223 Matthew Boyd .40 1.00
224 Edgar Martinez .50 1.25
225 Nick Senzel .60 1.50
226 Hunter Dozier .40 1.00
227 Justin Verlander .60 1.50
228 Khris Davis .60 1.50
229 Tim Anderson .60 1.50
230 Jordan Yamamoto RC .60 1.50
231 Al Kaline .60 1.50
232 Jake Fraley RC .75 2.00
233 Nick Castellanos .60 1.50
234 Rafael Devers .75 2.00
235 Carlos Santana .50 1.25
236 Alex Bregman .60 1.50
237 Brendan McKay RC 1.00 2.50
238 Amed Rosario .50 1.25
239 Austin Hays .60 1.50
240 A.J. Puk RC 1.00 2.50
241 Kyle Tucker .60 1.50
242 George Brett 1.25 3.00
243 Aaron Nola .50 1.25
244 Ichiro .75 2.00
245 Willi Castro RC 1.00 2.50
246 Trea Turner .50 1.25
247 Gerrit Cole 1.00 2.50
248 Yu Darvish .60 1.50
249 Kyle Lewis RC 5.00 12.00
250 Tyler Glasnow .60 1.50
251 Luis Arraez .75 2.00
252 Brock Burke RC .60 1.50
253 Nico Hoerner RC 2.50 6.00
254 Jose Berrios .50 1.25
255 Dustin May RC 2.00 5.00
256 Bryan Reynolds .50 1.25
257 Frank Thomas .60 1.50
258 Isan Diaz RC 1.00 2.50
259 Joc Pederson .50 1.25
260 Willie Calhoun .40 1.00
261 Charlie Blackmon .60 1.50
262 Zac Gallen RC 1.50 4.00
263 Corey Seager .60 1.50
264 Cavan Biggio .75 2.00
265 Christian Walker .50 1.25
266 Kolten Wong .50 1.25
267 Mitch Keller .60 1.50
268 Luis Castillo .50 1.25
269 Aaron Civale RC 1.25 3.00
270 Ken Griffey Jr. 2.00 5.00
271 Logan Allen RC .60 1.50
272 Don Mattingly 1.25 3.00
273 Austin Riley .75 2.00
274 Felix Hernandez .50 1.25
275 Bubba Starling RC 1.25 3.00
276 Kyle Schwarber .60 1.50
277 Johnny Bench .60 1.50
278 Jose Altuve .50 1.25
279 Mitch Haniger .50 1.25
280 Dansby Swanson .60 1.50
281 Josh Staumont RC .60 1.50
282 Sheldon Neuse RC .75 2.00
283 Anthony Rendon .60 1.50
284 James Karinchak RC 1.00 2.50
285 Shogo Akiyama RC 1.00 2.50
286 Ozzie Albies .60 1.50
287 Tommy Pham .40 1.00
288 Vladimir Guerrero Jr. 1.00 2.50
289 Luis Robert RC 12.00 30.00
290 Sandy Koufax 1.25 3.00
291 Willson Contreras .60 1.50
292 Christian Yelich .75 2.00
293 Randy Johnson .60 1.50
294 T.J. Zeuch RC .60 1.50
295 Jake Rogers RC .60 1.50
296 Eduardo Rodriguez .40 1.00
297 Mauricio Dubon RC .75 2.00
298 Gavin Lux RC 3.00 8.00
299 Randy Arozarena RC 5.00 12.00
300 Eloy Jimenez 1.25 3.00
301 David Price .50 1.25
302 Derek Jeter 1.50 4.00
303 Dylan Bundy .50 1.25
304 Renato Nunez .50 1.25
305 Hanser Alberto .40 1.00
306 Carlton Fisk .50 1.25
307 Wade Boggs .50 1.25
308 Roger Clemens .75 2.00
309 Cole Hamels .50 1.25
310 Jon Lester .50 1.25
311 Franmil Reyes .40 1.00
312 Carlos Carrasco .40 1.00
313 Ryan McMahon .60 1.50
314 Ryan Braun .50 1.25
315 Robin Yount .60 1.50
316 Brandon Nimmo .50 1.25
317 Gary Carter .50 1.25
318 Miguel Andujar .60 1.50
319 Eric Hosmer .50 1.25
320 Hunter Renfroe .40 1.00
321 Wil Myers .50 1.25
322 Jeff Samardzija .40 1.00
323 Evan Longoria .50 1.25
324 J.P. Crawford .40 1.00
325 Dee Gordon .40 1.00
326 Luis Urias .50 1.25
327 Francisco Mejia .50 1.25
328 Zach Wheeler .50 1.25
329 Danny Mendick RC .75 2.00
330 Rangel Ravelo RC .75 2.00
331 Tim Lopes RC .75 2.00
332 Dom Nunez RC .75 2.00
333 Tony Gonsolin RC 2.50 6.00
334 Tyler Alexander RC 1.00 2.50
335 Yonathan Daza RC .75 2.00
336 Randy Dobnak RC 1.25 3.00
337 Bryan Abreu RC .60 1.50
338 Clint Frazier .50 1.25
339 Frankie Montas .40 1.00
340 Eric Thames .40 1.00
341 Alex Verdugo .50 1.25
342 Max Fried .60 1.50
343 Ian Happ .50 1.25
344 Jason Heyward .50 1.25
345 Kenley Jansen .50 1.25
346 Jorge Polanco .50 1.25
347 Dinelson Lamet .40 1.00
348 Mike Minor .40 1.00
349 Edwin Encarnacion .60 1.50
350 Danny Santana .40 1.00
351 Kenta Maeda .50 1.25
352 Justin Upton .50 1.25
353 Jake Odorizzi .40 1.00
354 J.D. Davis .40 1.00
355 Chris Archer .40 1.00
356 Miles Mikolas .40 1.00
357 Starlin Castro .40 1.00
358 Michael Kopech .75 2.00
359 Willy Adames .40 1.00
360 Johnny Cueto .50 1.25
361 Kyle Seager .40 1.00
362 Kole Calhoun .40 1.00
363 Justin Smoak .40 1.00
364 Domingo Santana .50 1.25
365 Julio Teheran .50 1.25
366 Jesus Aguilar .50 1.25
367 Kevin Pillar .40 1.00
368 Howie Kendrick .40 1.00
369 Lewis Brinson .40 1.00
370 Yoenis Cespedes .60 1.50
371 Hunter Pence .50 1.25
372 Ryan O'Hearn .40 1.00
373 Alex Gordon .50 1.25
374 David Bednar RC .60 1.50
375 Jon Berti RC .60 1.50
376 Ryan McBroom RC .75 2.00
377 Chad Wallach RC .60 1.50
378 Scott Heineman RC .60 1.50
379 Edwin Rios RC 1.50 4.00
380 Brian O'Grady RC .60 1.50
381 Jack Mayfield RC .60 1.50
382 Lamonte Wade Jr. RC 1.00 2.50
383 Kyle Garlick RC 1.00 2.50
384 Seth Mejias-Brean RC .60 1.50
385 Garrett Stubbs RC .60 1.50
386 Kean Wong RC 1.00 2.50
387 Tyrone Taylor RC .60 1.50
388 Jose Rodriguez RC .60 1.50
389 Tom Eshelman RC .75 2.00
390 Robert Dugger RC .60 1.50
391 Emmanuel Clase RC 1.00 2.50
392 Jonathan Hernandez RC .60 1.50
393 Rogelio Armenteros RC .75 2.00
394 Danny Hultzen RC .75 2.00
395 Kevin Ginkel RC .60 1.50
396 Mariano Rivera .75 2.00
397 Vladimir Guerrero .50 1.25
398 Mike Piazza .60 1.50
399 Rickey Henderson .60 1.50
400 Jackie Robinson .60 1.50

2020 Stadium Club Chrome Gold Refractors

*GOLD REF.: 2X TO 5X BASIC
*GOLD REF.RC: 1.2X TO 3X BASIC RC
STATED ODDS 1:27 HOBBY
STATED PRINT RUN 50 SER.#'d SETS
1 Mike Trout 60.00 150.00
3 Babe Ruth 15.00 40.00
67 Ted Williams 15.00 40.00
69 Yordan Alvarez 25.00 60.00
104 Juan Soto 40.00 100.00
112 Bo Bichette 40.00 100.00
244 Ichiro 15.00 40.00
270 Ken Griffey Jr. 50.00 120.00
299 Randy Arozarena 50.00 120.00
302 Derek Jeter 40.00 100.00

2020 Stadium Club Chrome Orange Refractors

*ORNG REF.: 3X TO 8X BASIC
*ORNG REF.RC: 2X TO 5X BASIC RC
STATED ODDS 1:31 HOBBY
STATED PRINT RUN 25 SER.#'d SETS
1 Mike Trout 100.00 250.00
3 Babe Ruth 25.00 60.00
67 Ted Williams 12.00 30.00
69 Yordan Alvarez 40.00 100.00
104 Juan Soto 60.00 150.00
112 Bo Bichette 125.00 300.00
244 Ichiro 25.00 60.00
270 Ken Griffey Jr. 75.00 200.00
272 Don Mattingly 50.00 120.00
299 Randy Arozarena 75.00 200.00
302 Derek Jeter 60.00 150.00

2020 Stadium Club Chrome Refractors

*REF.: 1.2X TO 3X BASIC
*REF.RC: .8X TO 2X BASIC RC
STATED ODDS 1:2 HOBBY
1 Mike Trout 15.00 40.00
69 Yordan Alvarez 12.00 30.00
104 Juan Soto 12.00 30.00
112 Bo Bichette 20.00 50.00
270 Ken Griffey Jr. 8.00
299 Randy Arozarena 15.00 40.00

2020 Stadium Club Chrome X-Fractors

*XFRAC.: 1.5X TO 5X BASIC
*XFRAC.RC: 1X TO 2.5X BASIC RC
STATED ODDS 4 PER BLASTER
1 Mike Trout 20.00 50.00
69 Yordan Alvarez 15.00 40.00
104 Juan Soto 15.00 40.00
112 Bo Bichette 25.00 60.00
244 Ichiro 10.00 25.00
270 Ken Griffey Jr. 15.00 40.00
299 Randy Arozarena 20.00 50.00
302 Derek Jeter 10.00 25.00

2020 Stadium Club Chrome Autographs

STATED ODDS 1:17 HOBBY
EXCHANGE DEADLINE 10/31/2022
CAAB Abraham Toro 4.00 10.00
CAAK Anthony Kay 3.00 8.00
CAAQ Aristides Aquino 15.00 40.00
CABH Bryce Harper 150.00 400.00
CABO Bo Bichette EXCH
CABS Blake Snell 15.00 40.00
CADC Dylan Cease 8.00 20.00
CADM Dustin May 15.00 40.00
CAEJ Eloy Jimenez
CAGL Gavin Lux
CAGT Gleyber Torres 40.00 100.00
CAJA Jake Rogers 3.00 8.00
CAJD Jaylin Davis 5.00 12.00
CAJF Jack Flaherty 20.00 50.00
CAJL Jesus Luzardo 10.00 25.00
CAJN Junior Fernandez 3.00 8.00
CAJS Juan Soto 250.00 600.00
CAJU Justin Dunn 4.00 10.00
CAJY Jordan Yamamoto 3.00 8.00
CAKH Keston Hiura 6.00 15.00
CAKL Kyle Lewis 50.00 120.00
CALW Logan Webb 5.00 12.00
CAMC Brendan McKay 8.00 20.00
CAMS Mike Soroka 20.00 50.00
CAMY Mike Yastrzemski 15.00 40.00
CANA Nolan Arenado
CANH Nico Hoerner 12.00 30.00
CANS Nick Solak 15.00 40.00
CAPA Pete Alonso 40.00 100.00
CAPG Paul Goldschmidt 25.00 60.00
CARA Ronald Acuna Jr. 100.00 250.00
CARG Robel Garcia 3.00 8.00
CASB Seth Brown 3.00 8.00
CASM Sean Murphy 6.00 15.00
CASO Shohei Ohtani 150.00 400.00
CAVG Vladimir Guerrero Jr. 40.00 100.00
CAYA Yordan Alvarez EXCH 125.00 300.00
CAZC Zack Collins 4.00 10.00
UAAM Andres Munoz 5.00 12.00
UAAR Austin Riley 15.00 40.00
UABA Bryan Abreu 3.00 8.00
UACB Cody Bellinger EXCH
UADJ Derek Jeter
UADL Domingo Leyba 4.00 10.00
UADN Dom Nunez 4.00 10.00
UAJF Jake Fraley 4.00 10.00
UAJR Josh Rojas 6.00 15.00
UAJS Josh Staumont 3.00 8.00
UAJU Jose Urquidy 4.00 10.00
UALR Luis Robert EXCH
UAMD Mauricio Dubon 4.00 10.00
UAMR Mike Brosseau 6.00 15.00
UAMT Matt Thaiss 4.00 10.00
UARA Randy Arozarena 60.00 150.00
UARD Randy Dobnak 6.00 15.00
UATA Tyler Alexander 5.00 12.00
UATD Travis Demeritte 5.00 12.00
UATE Tommy Edman 10.00 25.00
UATG Tony Gonsolin EXCH 12.00 30.00
UATL Tim Lopes 4.00 10.00
UAWC Willi Castro 15.00 40.00
UAYD Yonathan Daza 4.00 10.00

2020 Stadium Club Chrome Autographs Gold Refractors

*GOLD REF.: .5X TO 1.2X BASIC
STATED ODDS 1:171 HOBBY
STATED PRINT RUN 50 SER.#'d SETS
EXCHANGE DEADLINE 10/31/2022
CAKH Keston Hiura 15.00 40.00
UAWC Willi Castro 40.00 100.00

2020 Stadium Club Chrome Autographs Orange Refractors

*ORANGE REF.: .6X TO 1.5X BASIC
STATED ODDS 1:185 HOBBY
STATED PRINT RUN 25 SER.#'d SETS
EXCHANGE DEADLINE 10/31/2022
CAEJ Eloy Jimenez 40.00 100.00
CAJS Juan Soto 800.00 1500.00
CAKH Keston Hiura 20.00 50.00
UAWC Willi Castro 50.00 120.00

2020 Stadium Club Chrome Beam Team

STATED ODDS 1:4 HOBBY
BT1 Pete Alonso 3.00 8.00
BT2 Mike Trout 8.00 20.00
BT3 Shohei Ohtani 2.00 5.00
BT4 Christian Yelich 1.50 4.00
BT5 Ronald Acuna Jr. 5.00 12.00
BT6 Vladimir Guerrero Jr. 2.00 5.00
BT7 Juan Soto 4.00 10.00
BT8 Ken Griffey Jr. 4.00 10.00
BT9 Fernando Tatis Jr. 6.00 15.00
BT10 Bryce Harper 2.00 5.00
BT11 Aaron Judge 3.00 8.00
BT12 Luis Robert 10.00 25.00
BT13 Yordan Alvarez 8.00 20.00
BT14 Bo Bichette 6.00 15.00
BT15 Gavin Lux 4.00 10.00
BT16 Francisco Lindor 1.25 3.00
BT17 Clayton Kershaw 2.00 5.00
BT18 Walker Buehler 1.50 4.00
BT19 Max Scherzer 1.25 3.00
BT20 Kris Bryant 1.50 4.00
BT21 Cody Bellinger 2.50 6.00
BT22 Rafael Devers 1.50 4.00
BT23 Justin Verlander 1.25 3.00
BT24 Mookie Betts 2.50 6.00
BT25 Gleyber Torres 2.50 6.00

2020 Stadium Club Chrome Beam Team Gold Refractors

*GOLD REF.: 1.5X TO 4X BASIC
STATED ODDS 1:423 HOBBY
STATED PRINT RUN 50 SER.#'d SETS
BT2 Mike Trout 75.00 200.00
BT5 Ronald Acuna Jr. 40.00 100.00
BT7 Juan Soto 40.00 100.00
BT9 Fernando Tatis Jr. 40.00 100.00
BT10 Bryce Harper 12.00 30.00
BT12 Luis Robert 50.00 120.00
BT13 Yordan Alvarez 30.00 80.00
BT24 Mookie Betts 30.00 80.00

2020 Stadium Club Chrome Beam Team Orange Refractors

*ORANGE REF.: 2X TO 5X BASIC
STATED ODDS 1:482 HOBBY
STATED PRINT RUN 25 SER.#'d SETS
BT2 Mike Trout 100.00 250.00
BT5 Ronald Acuna Jr. 50.00 120.00
BT7 Juan Soto 50.00 120.00
BT9 Fernando Tatis Jr. 50.00 120.00
BT10 Bryce Harper 25.00 60.00
BT12 Luis Robert 100.00 250.00
BT13 Yordan Alvarez 40.00 100.00
BT24 Mookie Betts 40.00 100.00

2020 Stadium Club Chrome Emperors of the Zone

STATED ODDS 1:14 HOBBY
*GOLD REF.: 1.5X TO 4X BASIC
*ORANGE REF.: 2X TO 5X BASIC
EOZ1 Mike Soroka 1.25 3.00
EOZ2 Chris Paddack 1.25 3.00
EOZ3 Lucas Giolito 1.00 2.50
EOZ4 Shohei Ohtani 2.00 5.00
EOZ5 Sonny Gray 1.00 2.50
EOZ6 Mike Clevinger 1.00 2.50
EOZ7 Shane Bieber 1.25 3.00
EOZ8 Gerrit Cole 2.00 5.00
EOZ9 Justin Verlander 1.25 3.00
EOZ10 Zack Greinke 1.25 3.00
EOZ11 Clayton Kershaw 2.00 5.00
EOZ12 Walker Buehler 1.50 4.00
EOZ13 Jacob deGrom 2.50 6.00
EOZ14 Jack Flaherty 1.25 3.00
EOZ15 Max Scherzer 1.25 3.00
EOZ16 Brendan McKay 1.25 3.00
EOZ17 Aaron Nola 1.00 2.50
EOZ18 Stephen Strasburg 1.25 3.00
EOZ19 Chris Sale 1.25 3.00
EOZ20 Noah Syndergaard 1.00 2.50
EOZ21 Luis Severino 1.00 2.50
EOZ22 Blake Snell 1.00 2.50
EOZ23 Tyler Glasnow 1.25 3.00
EOZ24 Jose Berrios 1.00 2.50
EOZ25 Patrick Corbin 1.00 2.50

2020 Stadium Club Chrome Lone Star Signatures

STATED ODDS 1:2086 HOBBY
PRINT RUNS B/WN 10-25 COPIES PER
NO PRICING QTY 15 OR LESS
EXCHANGE DEADLINE 10/31/2022
LSSGL Gavin Lux 30.00 80.00
LSSHA Hank Aaron
LSSMT Mike Trout
LSSPA Pete Alonso 40.00 100.00
LSSFTJ Fernando Tatis Jr. 125.00 300.00
LSSRAJ Ronald Acuna Jr.
LSSVGJ Vladimir Guerrero Jr. 40.00 100.00

2020 Stadium Club Chrome Power Zone

STATED ODDS 1:14 HOBBY
PZ1 Darryl Strawberry .75 2.00
PZ2 Pete Alonso 3.00 8.00
PZ3 Mike Trout 6.00 15.00
PZ4 Shohei Ohtani 2.00 5.00
PZ5 Christian Yelich 1.50 4.00
PZ6 Chipper Jones 1.25 3.00
PZ7 Ronald Acuna Jr. 5.00 12.00
PZ8 Vladimir Guerrero Jr. 2.00 5.00
PZ9 Juan Soto 4.00 10.00
PZ10 Fernando Tatis Jr. 6.00 15.00
PZ11 Mark McGwire 2.00 5.00
PZ12 Rhys Hoskins 1.50 4.00
PZ13 Bryce Harper 2.00 5.00
PZ14 Aaron Judge 3.00 8.00
PZ15 Jeff Bagwell 1.00 2.50
PZ16 Francisco Lindor 1.25 3.00
PZ17 Frank Thomas 1.25 3.00
PZ18 Eloy Jimenez 2.50 6.00
PZ19 Kris Bryant 1.50 4.00
PZ20 Anthony Rizzo 1.50 4.00
PZ21 David Wright 1.00 2.50
PZ22 Nolan Arenado 2.00 5.00
PZ23 Gleyber Torres 2.50 6.00
PZ24 Yordan Alvarez 8.00 20.00
PZ25 Ken Griffey Jr. 2.50 6.00

2020 Stadium Club Chrome Power Zone Gold Refractors

*GOLD REF.: 1.5X TO 4X BASIC
STATED ODDS 1:423 HOBBY
STATED PRINT RUN 50 SER.#'d SETS
PZ3 Mike Trout 30.00 80.00
PZ9 Juan Soto 25.00 60.00

1996 Stadum Club Porcelain

These six cards were available through the Topps catalog at an issue price of $79. The six players in the set each represent a key player from each year of the Stadium Club brand history. A special display which cost an additional $19.95 was also available for this set.
1 Ken Griffey Jr 12.50 30.00
2 Frank Thomas 10.00 25.00
3 Kenny Lofton 8.00 20.00
4 Barry Bonds 12.50 30.00
5 Paul Molitor 8.00 20.00
6 Randy Johnson 10.00 25.00

1953 Stahl Meyer

The cards in this nine-card set measure approximately 3 1/4" by 4 1/2". The 1953 Stahl Meyer set of full color, unnumbered cards includes three players from each of the three New York teams. The cards have white borders. The Lockman card is the most plentiful of any card in the set. Some batting and fielding statistics and short biography are included on the back. The cards are ordered in the checklist below by alphabetical order without regard to team affiliation. A promotional kit, titled a "Baseball Kit" was also issued and sent to stores to promote this set. Information about the cards and a checklist was included in that kit.
COMPLETE SET (9) 7500.00 15000.00
1 Hank Bauer 250.00 500.00
2 Roy Campanella 1000.00 2000.00
3 Gil Hodges 250.00 500.00
4 Monte Irvin 300.00 600.00
5 Whitey Lockman 200.00 400.00
6 Mickey Mantle 4000.00 8000.00
7 Phil Rizzuto 500.00 1000.00
8 Duke Snider 1000.00 2000.00
9 Bobby Thomson 250.00 500.00

1954 Stahl Meyer

The cards in this 12-card set measure approximately 3 1/4" by 4 1/2". The 1954 Stahl Meyer set of full color, unnumbered cards includes four players from each of the three New York teams. The cards have yellow borders and the backs, oriented horizontally, include an ad for a baseball kit and the player's statistics. No player biography is included on the back. The cards are ordered in the checklist below by alphabetical order without regard to team affiliation.
COMPLETE SET (12) 7500.00 15000.00
1 Hank Bauer 250.00 500.00
2 Carl Erskine 250.00 500.00
3 Gil Hodges 400.00 800.00
4 Monte Irvin 300.00 600.00
5 Whitey Lockman 200.00 400.00
6 Mickey Mantle 4000.00 8000.00
7 Willie Mays 2000.00 4000.00
8 Gil McDougald 250.00 500.00
9 Don Mueller 200.00 400.00
10 Don Newcombe 250.00 500.00
11 Phil Rizzuto 400.00 800.00
12 Duke Snider 750.00 1500.00

1955 Stahl Meyer

The cards in this 12-card set measure approximately 3 1/4" by 4 1/2". The 1955 Stahl Meyer set of full color, unnumbered cards contains four players each from the three New York teams. As in the 1954 set, the cards have yellow borders; however, the back of the cards contain a sketch of Mickey Mantle with an ad for a baseball cap or a pennant. The cards are ordered in the checklist below by alphabetical order without regard to team affiliation.
COMPLETE SET (12) 6000.00 12000.00
1 Hank Bauer 250.00 500.00
2 Carl Erskine 250.00 500.00
3 Gil Hodges 400.00 800.00
4 Monte Irvin 300.00 600.00
5 Whitey Lockman 200.00 400.00
6 Mickey Mantle 4000.00 8000.00
7 Gil McDougald 250.00 500.00
8 Don Mueller 200.00 400.00
9 Don Newcombe 250.00 500.00
10 Dusty Rhodes 200.00 400.00
11 Phil Rizzuto 400.00 800.00
12 Duke Snider 750.00 1500.00

1910 Standard Caramel E93

The cards in this 30-card set measure 1 1/2" by 2 3/4". The E93 set was distributed by Standard Caramel in 1910. It consists of black and white player photos which were tinted and placed against solid color backgrounds. A checklist, starting with Ames, is printed in brown ink on the reverse. Some blank backs are known and all poses also appear in W555. Listed pricing for raw cards references "VgEx" condition.
COMPLETE SET (30) 60000.00 120000.00
1 Red Ames 250.00 400.00
2 Chief Bender 350.00 600.00
3 Mordecai Brown 500.00 800.00
4 Frank Chance 350.00 600.00
5 Hal Chase 250.00 400.00
6 Ty Cobb 2500.00 4000.00
7 Eddie Collins 300.00 500.00
8 Harry Coveleskie (Coveleski) 250.00 400.00
9 Fred Clarke 300.00 500.00
10 Jim Delehanty 250.00 400.00
11 Bill Donovan 250.00 400.00
12 Red Dooin 250.00 400.00
13 Johnny Evers 350.00 600.00
14 George Gibson 250.00 400.00
15 Clark Griffith 300.00 500.00
16 Hugh Jennings 300.00 500.00
17 Davy Jones 250.00 400.00
18 Addie Joss 350.00 600.00
19 Napoleon Lajoie 500.00 800.00
20 Tommy Leach 250.00 400.00
21 Christy Mathewson 1500.00 2500.00
22 John McGraw 300.00 500.00
23 Jim Pastorius 250.00 400.00
24 Deacon Phillippe 250.00 400.00
25 Eddie Plank 500.00 800.00
26 Joe Tinker 300.00 500.00
27 Rube Waddell 300.00 500.00
28 Honus Wagner 2500.00 4000.00
29 Hooks Wiltse 250.00 400.00
30 Cy Young 1500.00 2500.00

1952 Star Cal Large

Type One of the Star Cal Decal set, issued in 1952, contains the cards listed in the checklist below. Each decal sheet measures 4 1/8" by 6 1/8". When the decal is taken from the paper wrapper, a checklist of existing decals is revealed on the wrapper. The set was issued by the Meyercord Company of Chicago and carries a catalog designation of W625-1.
COMPLETE SET (70) 4000.00 8000.00
70A Allie Reynolds 30.00 60.00
70B Ed Lopat 30.00 60.00
70C Yogi Berra 100.00 200.00
70D Vic Raschi 25.00 50.00
70E Jerry Coleman 25.00 50.00
70F Phil Rizzuto 60.00 120.00
70G Mickey Mantle 1000.00 2000.00
71A Mel Parnell 25.00 50.00
71B Ted Williams 250.00 500.00
71C Ted Williams 250.00 500.00
71D Vern Stephens 25.00 50.00
71E Billy Goodman 25.00 50.00
71F Dom DiMaggio 30.00 60.00
71G Dick Gernert 20.00 40.00
71H Hoot Evers 100.00 200.00
72A George Kell 60.00 120.00
72B Hal Newhouser 50.00 100.00
72C Hoot Evers 20.00 40.00
72D Vic Wertz 20.00 40.00
72E Fred Hutchinson 25.00 50.00
72F Johnny Groth 20.00 40.00
73A Al Zarilla 20.00 40.00
73B Billy Pierce 30.00 60.00
73C Eddie Robinson 20.00 40.00
73D Chico Carrasquel 25.00 50.00
73E Minnie Minoso 40.00 80.00
73F Jim Busby 20.00 40.00
73G Nellie Fox 50.00 100.00
73H Sam Mele 100.00 200.00
74A Larry Doby 50.00 100.00
74B Al Rosen 30.00 60.00
74C Bob Lemon 50.00 100.00
74D Jim Hegan 20.00 40.00
74E Bob Feller 100.00 200.00
74F Dale Mitchell 25.00 50.00
75A Ned Garver 20.00 40.00
76A Gus Zernial 25.00 50.00
76B Ferris Fain 20.00 40.00
76C Bobby Shantz 100.00 200.00
77A Richie Ashburn 50.00 100.00
77B Ralph Kiner 60.00 120.00
77C Curt Simmons 100.00 200.00
78A Bobby Thomson 25.00 50.00
78B Alvin Dark 25.00 50.00
78C Sal Maglie 25.00 50.00
78D Larry Jansen 20.00 40.00
78E Willie Mays 400.00 800.00
78F Monte Irvin 60.00 120.00
78G Whitey Lockman 20.00 40.00
79A Gil Hodges 60.00 120.00
79B Pee Wee Reese 75.00 150.00
79C Roy Campanella 200.00 400.00
79D Don Newcombe 40.00 80.00
79E Duke Snider 125.00 250.00
79F Preacher Roe 30.00 60.00
79G Jackie Robinson 250.00 500.00
80A Eddie Miksis 20.00 40.00
80B Dutch Leonard 20.00 40.00
80C Randy Jackson 20.00 40.00
80D Bob Rush 20.00 40.00
80E Hank Sauer 20.00 40.00
80F Phil Cavarretta 25.00 50.00
80G Warren Hacker 20.00 40.00
81A Red Schoendienst 50.00 100.00
81B Wally Westlake 20.00 40.00
81C Cliff Chambers 20.00 40.00
81D Enos Slaughter 50.00 100.00
81E Stan Musial 150.00 300.00
81F Stan Musial 150.00 300.00
81G Gerry Staley 20.00 40.00

1952 Star Cal Small

Type Two of the Star Cal Decal set features a decal package half the size of the W625-1 set, each sheet contains two decals, each of which is approximately half the size of the large decal found in the W625-1 set. Each decal package (sheet) measures 3 1/16" by 4 1/8". The set was issued by the Meyercord Company of Chicago and carries a catalog designation of W625-2. The checklist below features two players per "card".
COMPLETE SET (32) 750.00 1500.00
84A A. Reynolds / V. Raschi 25.00 50.00
84B E. Lopat / Y. Berra 40.00 80.00
84C P. Rizzuto / J. Coleman 30.00 60.00
85A T. Williams / T. Williams 250.00 500.00
85B D. DiMaggio / M. Parnell 25.00 50.00
85C V. Stephens / B. Goodman 20.00 40.00
86A G. Kell / H. Newhouser 40.00 80.00
86B H. Evers / V. Wertz 20.00 40.00
86C J. Groth / F. Hutchinson 20.00 40.00
87A E. Robinson / E. Robinson 20.00 40.00
87B C. Carrasquel / M. Minoso 25.00 50.00
87C B. Pierce / N. Fox 60.00 120.00
87D A. Zarilla / J. Busby 20.00 40.00
88A B. Lemon / J. Hegan 25.00 50.00
88B L. Doby / B. Feller 50.00 100.00
88C D. Mitchell / A. Rosen 25.00 50.00
89A N. Garver / N. Garver 20.00 40.00
89B F. Fain / G. Zernial 20.00 40.00
89C R. Ashburn / R. Ashburn 40.00 80.00
89D R. Kiner / R. Kiner 50.00 100.00
90A W. Mays / M. Irvin 150.00 300.00
90B L. Jansen / S. Maglie 25.00 50.00

90C B. Thomson	25.00	50.00
A. Dark		
91A G. Hodges	75.00	150.00
P. Reese		
91B R. Campanella	150.00	300.00
J. Robinson		
91C D. Snider	50.00	100.00
P. Roe		
92A P. Cavarretta	20.00	40.00
D. Leonard		
92B R. Jackson	20.00	40.00
E. Miksis		
92C B. Rush	20.00	40.00
H. Sauer		
93A S. Musial	200.00	400.00
S. Musial		
93B R. Schoendienst	30.00	60.00
E. Slaughter		
93C C. Chambers	20.00	40.00
W. Westlake		

1983 Star Schmidt

This 15-card standard-size set features Phillies great Mike Schmidt. This was the first baseball set issued by the Star Company, who had the NBA contract in the mid-1980's. Star company products are usually sold in complete set form.

COMPLETE SET	12.50	30.00
COMMON PLAYER	.80	2.00

1984 Star Brett

This 24 card standard-size set features long time Kansas City Royals star George Brett. This set was issued in complete set form.

COMPLETE SET (24)	8.00	20.00
COMMON CARD (1-24)	.40	1.00

1984 Star Carlton

This 24-card standard-size set features another Philly great, Steve Carlton. The set was issued in complete form and can be dated by the "Star 84" notation.

COMPLETE SET	8.00	20.00
COMMON PLAYER	.40	1.00

1984 Star Garvey

This 36 card standard-size set features San Diego and Los Angeles star Steve Garvey. Garvey, who established a consecutive game streak in the National League, led the Padres to the 1984 National League Pennant. These card trace his career.

COMPLETE SET (36)	8.00	20.00
COMMON CARD (1-36)	.24	.60

1984 Star Strawberry

This 12-card standard-size set features then Met phenom Darryl Strawberry. This set was issued by the Star company and takes the collector through the early part of Strawberry's career. The set is dated with the "Star 84" logo in the upper right corner.

COMPLETE SET (12)	3.00	8.00
COMMON CARD (1-12)	.30	.75

1984 Star Yastrzemski

This 24 card standard-size set feature the long career of Red Sox star Carl Yastrzemski. These cards which have pictures of Yaz career surrounded by red borders traces his career from the beginning through the end in 1983.

COMPLETE SET (24)	8.00	20.00
COMMON CARD (1-24)	.40	1.00
4 Carl Yastrzemski	.75	2.00
George Brett		
World Series Stats		
9 Carl Yastrzemksi	.50	1.25
Joe Cronin		
Seven Times Gold Glo		
13 Carl Yastrzemski	.50	1.25
Gaylord Perry		
Milestone Hits		
19 Carl Yastrzemski	.75	2.00
Johnny Bench		
Red Sox Club Recor		

1985 Star Carew

This 24 card standard-size set features all time great hitter Rod Carew from his early days with the Minnesota Twins until near the end of his career.

COMPLETE SET	8.00	20.00
COMMON CARD	.30	.75

1985 Star Reggie Jackson

This 24-card standard-size set features California Angels star, Reggie Jackson. These cards trace Reggie's career beginning with his early days. The set is dated by the "Star 85" logo in the top right.

COMPLETE SET (24)	8.00	20.00
COMMON CARD (1-24)	.40	1.00

1986 Star Boggs

This 12-card standard-size set features then Boston Red Sox hitting star Wade Boggs. The set traces Boggs through the early part of his career. There was also a yellow sticker set issued which has the same value as these red bordered cards. This set was originally issued as eight 3 card panels. The backs of the not listed four panels form an action picture of Boggs.

COMPLETE SET (12)	2.00	5.00
COMMON CARD (1-12)	.20	.50

1986 Star Canseco

This 15-card standard-size set was issued by the Star Company to honor young star Jose Canseco. Since many of the cards are titled "His Era Begins," we have given pose descriptions to those cards.

COMPLETE SET (15)	4.00	10.00
COMMON CARD (1-15)	.30	.75

1986 Star Joyner Red

The year 1986 was a big year for young major league players. Wally Joyner, another star rookie in this class is featured in this 15-card standard-size set issued by the Star Company. We have called this the "red" set since the borders are red in color.

COMPLETE SET (15)	2.50	6.00
COMMON CARD (1-15)	.20	.50

1986 Star Murphy

The Star company featured Dale Murphy, twice the National League MVP in this 12-card standard-size set. These cards trace the career of Murphy from his early days to the middle of his career.

COMPLETE SET (12)	2.00	5.00
COMMON CARD (1-12)	.20	.50

1986 Star Rice

This 12-card standard-size set features Red Sox slugger Jim Rice. The set was issued by the Star company and has the traditional "Star 86" logo in the upper right corner.

COMPLETE SET (12)	2.00	5.00
COMMON CARD (1-12)	.20	.50

1986 Star Ryan

This 12-card standard-size set features photos of pitching great, Nolan Ryan. These cards trace Ryan's career beginning with his early days to the present. Twelve Puzzle Back cards were also issued for this set

COMPLETE SET (24)	15.00	40.00
COMMON CARD (1-24)	.80	2.00

1986 Star Seaver

This 12-card standard-size set features Hall of Fame pitcher to be Tom Seaver. These cards trace Seaver's career from his early days in the Mets organization through the end of his career. This set, similar to the Boggs set was originally issued as eight panels. The backs form an action picture of Seaver when properly arranged.

COMPLETE SET (12)	2.00	5.00
COMMON CARD (1-12)	.20	.50

1986 Star Stickers Canseco

This 15-card standard-size set features young star Jose Canseco. This set displays the same photos as the regular Star set but these items are blank-backed.

COMPLETE SET (15)	2.50	6.00
COMMON CARD (1-15)	.20	.50

1986 Star Stickers Joyner Blue

The same photos as in the 1986 Star Joyner Red set are featured. The difference between this set and the cards are the blank backed stickers and the blue borders for these cards.

COMPLETE SET (15)	2.50	6.00
COMMON CARD (1-15)	.16	.40

1987 Star Award Winners

These five standard-size cards feature Jose Canseco and Wade Boggs who won various honors during the 1986 season.

COMPLETE SET (5)	.75	2.00
1 Jose Canseco/1986 A.L. Top Rookie	.20	.50
2 Jose Canseco/1986 Stats	.20	.50
3 Jose Canseco	.20	.50
Rookie Voting		
4 Wade Boggs/1986 A.L. Batting Champ	.20	.50
5 Wade Boggs/1986 A.L. Batting Champ/(Portrait)	.20	.50

1987 Star Gary Carter

This 14-card standard-size set features long-time star catcher Gary Carter. These cards have a "Star 87" logo in the upper right corner.

COMPLETE SET (14)	2.00	5.00
COMMON CARD (1-14)	.16	.40

1987 Star Clemens

This 12-card standard-size set features Roger Clemens, who was in the process of winning consecutive Cy Young Awards. Clemens' career is traced from the beginning to his sensational 1986 season.

COMPLETE SET (12)	4.00	10.00
COMMON CARD (1-12)	.40	1.00

1987 Star Clemens II

These five standard-size cards update the first Roger Clemens set issued earlier in 1987. These cards have a pink border as compared to the red border in the regular issue.

COMPLETE SET (5)	1.25	3.00
COMMON CARD (1-5)	.30	.75

1987 Star Keith Hernandez

This 13-card standard-size set features Keith Hernandez. These cards trace Hernandez' career from its beginnings to the time of issue.

COMPLETE SET (13)	2.00	5.00
COMMON CARD (1-13)	.16	.40

1987 Star Mattingly

This 12-card standard-size set features Yankee great, Don Mattingly. These cards trace Mattingly's career beginning with his early days to the present. The set is dated by the "Star 87" logo in the top right.

COMPLETE SET (12)	4.00	10.00
COMMON CARD (1-12)	.40	1.00

1987 Star Mattingly Blankback

These six cards feature Yankee great Don Mattingly. These cards are differentiated from the other Mattingly cards because of the blank back

COMPLETE SET (6)	1.00	2.50
COMMON CARD (1-6)	.20	.50

1987 Star Raines

This 12-card standard-size set features baseball star Tim Raines. The "Star '87" logo in the upper right dates the set which traces his career from its beginnings to the present day.

COMPLETE SET (12)	1.50	4.00
COMMON CARD (1-12)	.16	.40

1987 Star Valenzuela

These 13 standard-size cards feature highlights in the career of Fernando Valuenzuela. These cards trace his career from its beginnings to the present day.

COMPLETE SET (13)	2.00	5.00
COMMON CARD (1-13)	.16	.40

1987 Star Sticker Mattingly

These 24 standard-size stickers feature Yankee great Don Mattingly. These stickers are blank backed and trace his career from the minors to the present day.

COMPLETE SET (24)	4.00	10.00
COMMON CARD (1-24)	.20	.50

1987 Star Sticker Valenzuela

These 10 standard-size sticker set is different from the regular cards issued by Star about Valenzuela. These cards have blank backs and also feature highlights in Valenzuela's career.

COMPLETE SET (10)	1.50	4.00
COMMON CARD (1-10)	.16	.40

1988 Star Jorge Bell

These 11 standard-size cards feature highlights in the career of George Bell, 1987 American League MVP. The cards are dated by the 1988 copyright on the back..

COMPLETE SET (11)	1.50	4.00
COMMON CARD (1-11)	.16	.40

1988 Star Boggs

This 11-card set of Wade Boggs features color player photos in a red border. The player's name, team, and card title are printed in the bottom margin while the top contains the word, "Star," in the upper right margin. The backs carry the information indicated by the card title.

COMPLETE SET (11)	2.00	5.00
COMMON CARD (1-11)	.20	.50

1988 Star Boggs Glossy

This 10 card standard-size set features the career of then Red Sox hitting star Wade Boggs from the beginning of his career through the 1987 season. These cards feature shots of Wade Boggs surrounded by a yellow border.

COMPLETE SET (10)	4.00	10.00
COMMON CARD (1-10)	.40	1.00

1988 Star Boggs Hitman

These 11 standard-size cards feature highlights in the career of Boston Red Sox hitting star, Wade Boggs. These cards are dated by the 1988 copyright on the back. Various highlights of Boggs' career are noted.

COMPLETE SET (11)	2.00	5.00
COMMON CARD (1-11)	.20	.50

1988 Star Boggs Silver

COMPLETE SET (9)	3.00	8.00
COMMON BOGGS	.40	1.00

1988 Star Boggs/Gwynn

Two of baseball's best hitters: Wade Boggs and Tony Gwynn are featured in this 11-card standard-size set. Other than the checklist card on which both players are pictured, the set alternates between Boggs and Gwynn cards.

COMPLETE SET (11)	2.00	5.00
COMMON BOGGS (1-11)	.20	.50
COMMON GWYNN		.75
1 Wade Boggs	.30	.75
Tony Gwynn CL		

1988 Star Brett Platinum

This 10 card standard-size set features highlights from the career of long time Kansas City Royal superstar George Brett. These cards have a glossy front and came with a note that there were 1,000 sets produced.

COMPLETE SET	4.00	10.00
COMMON CARD	.40	1.00

1988 Star Canseco

This 11-card standard-size set features highlights in the career of Jose Canseco. The set is dated to 1988 with the 1988 copyright on the back.

COMPLETE SET (11)	3.00	8.00
COMMON CARD (1-11)	.30	.75

1988 Star Gary Carter

These 11 standard-size set, features yet again, Mets catcher Gary Carter. These cards trace his career from the beginning to the present day. The set is dated by the 1988 copyright on the back.

COMPLETE SET (11)	2.00	5.00
COMMON CARD (1-11)	.20	.50

1988 Star Will Clark

These 11 standard-size cards feature highlights in the career of former Olympian and current star, Will Clark. These cards are dated by the1988 copyright on the back.

COMPLETE SET (11)	2.00	5.00
COMMON CARD (1-11)	.20	.50

1988 Star Clemens

This 10 card standard-size set features the career of then Red Sox fireballer Roger Clemens. This set traces his career from the beginning through the 1987 season.

COMPLETE SET (10)	4.00	10.00
COMMON CARD	.40	1.00

1988 Star Clemens Platinum

This 10-card set, issued as part of Star's platinum player format, features Red Sox ace Roger Clemens.

COMPLETE SET (10)		
COMMON CARD (111-120)		

1988 Star Clemens/Gooden

Two pitchers with very parallel careers: Dwight Gooden and Roger Clemens are featured in this set. Other than the checklist card in which pictures of both players are found, the set alternates between cards of Clemens and Gooden.

COMPLETE SET (11)	2.00	5.00
COMMON GOODEN (1-11)	.20	.50
COMMON CLEMENS		1.00
1 Roger Clemens	.40	1.00
Dwight Gooden CL		

1988 Star Cone

These 11 standard-size cards feature New York Mets star pitcher David Cone. These cards trace his career from the beginning through his breakthrough season in 1988.

COMPLETE SET (11)	1.50	4.00
COMMON CARD (1-11)	.16	.40

1988 Star Eric Davis

Eric Daivs is featured in this 12-card standard-size set. The cards trace his career from the minors through the present day. The set is dated by the 1988 copyright on the back.

COMPLETE SET (12)	1.50	4.00
COMMON CARD (1-12)	.16	.40

1988 Star Eric Davis Gold

This 10 card standard-size set, which had a print run to 1,500 featured then up and coming Reds star Eric Davis. One can tell the set is the "gold" variety by the lettering on the front.

COMPLETE SET	8.00	20.00
COMMON CARD	.80	2.00

1988 Star Davis/McGwire

This 11-card standard-size set features cards of Eric Davis and Mark McGwire. Other than the checklist card, the set features a picture of either Davis or McGwire.

COMPLETE SET (11)	2.50	6.00
COMMON DAVIS (1-11)	.16	.40
COMMON MCGWIRE		1.00
1 Eric Davis	.40	1.00
Mark McGwire CL		

1988 Star Dawson

This 11-card standard-size set feature 1987 NL MVP Andre Dawson. Dawson's career is traced from its start to the time of issue. The set is dated with a 1988 copyright on the back.

COMPLETE SET (11)	1.50	4.00
COMMON CARD (1-11)	.16	.40

1988 Star Gooden Blue

This 12-card set features color photos of Dwight Gooden inside a thin white and red border surrounded by a wider blue border. The card title is printed in the bottom margin with "Star '88" in the top margin. The backs carry the information as indicated by the card title on the front.

COMPLETE SET (12)	2.00	5.00
COMMON CARD (1-12)	.20	.50

1988 Star Gooden Orange

This 11-card standard-size set traces Dwight Gooden's career. These cards are dated by the 1988 copyright on the back. These cards are usually sold as a complete set but we have identified each card from this issue. The fronts feature orange-bordered color phots of Dwight Gooden with his name and card name printed in the bottom margin. The word, "Star," is printed in the top margin. The backs lists the information that identifies the card on the front.

COMPLETE SET (11)	2.00	5.00
COMMON CARD (1-11)	.20	.50

1988 Star Grace

This 11 card standard-size set features then Cub rookie star, Mark Grace. This set takes the collector from the beginning of his professional career through 1988.

COMPLETE SET (11)	4.00	10.00
COMMON CARD (1-11)	.40	1.00

1988 Star Grace Gold

This 10 card standard-size set features then Cub Rookie Mark Grace. This set features Grace at the beginning of his career. And according to the set information, the print run was limited to 1,500 sets.

COMPLETE SET (10)	12.50	30.00
COMMON CARD	2.00	5.00

1988 Star Greenwell Purple

Mike Greenwell, Boston Red Sox outfielder, is the focus of this 11-card standard-size set. This set traces Greenwell's career from its beginnings to his breakthrough as a major leaguer. The set is dated by the 1988 copyright on the back. The fronts feature color player phots in a border of various shades of purple. The backs carry the information that the front card title indicates.

COMPLETE SET (11)	1.50	4.00
COMMON CARD (1-11)	.16	.40

1988 Star Greenwell Red

Mike Greenwell, Boston Red Sox outfielder, is the focus of this 11-card standard-size set. This set traces Greenwell's career from its beginnings to his breakthrough as a major leaguer. The set is dated by the 1988 copyright on the back. The fronts feature color player phots in a border of various shades of red. The backs carry the information that the front card title indicates.

COMPLETE SET (11)	1.50	4.00
COMMON CARD (1-11)	.16	.40

1988 Star Gwynn

This 11-card standard-size set features highlights of Tony Gwynn's career. The set is dated with a 1988 copyright on the back.

COMPLETE SET (11)	2.00	5.00
COMMON CARD (1-11)	.20	.50

1988 Star Hershiser

Issued after the 1988 World Series, this set focuses on Dodger star Orel Hershiser. This 11-card standard-size set includes career highlights such as his consecutive scoreless inning streak and his dominant 1988 post season.

COMPLETE SET (11)	1.50	4.00
COMMON CARD (1-11)	.16	.40

1988 Star Horn

Soon to be failed Red Sox prospect, Sam Horn is featured in this set. These cards were issued after Horn tore up the American League in a late season call up in 1987. These 11 standard-size cards take the collectors through Horn's career highlights.

COMPLETE SET (11)	.75	2.00
COMMON CARD (1-11)	.10	.25

1988 Star Bo Jackson

This 16-card standard-size set features two sport star Bo Jackson. The first 12 cards of the set feature him playing baseball while the final four cards feature him in an Auburn uniform, playing football and are blank-backed.

COMPLETE SET (16)	6.00	15.00
COMMON CARD (1-16_	.40	1.00

1988 Star Jefferies

Two time minor league player of the year, Gregg Jefferies is feature in this set. As the hottest prospect entering the 1988 season, this set took a person through Jefferies' minor league career. These 11 standard-size cards were issued with the 1988 copyright on the back.

COMPLETE SET (11)	2.00	5.00
COMMON CARD (1-11)	.20	.50

1988 Star Jordan

After having a great rookie half season for the Philadelphia Phillies, Ricky Jordan is featured in this 11-card standard-size set. Sold in complete set form, we have described all of these cards individually.

COMPLETE SET (11)	.75	2.00
COMMON CARD (1-11)	.10	.25

1988 Star Mattingly

Yankee superstar Don Mattingly is featured in this 11-card standard-size set. The 1988 copyright date is located on the back. That is how this set can be differentiated from other Mattingly Star sets. Numbered to 1000.

COMPLETE SET (11)	2.00	5.00
COMMON CARD (1-11)	.20	.50

1988 Star Mattingly/Schmidt

This 11-card standard-size set features East Coast stars: Don Mattingly and Mike Schmidt. Other than the first card in the set, either Mattingly or Schmidt is featured.

COMPLETE SET (11)	2.00	5.00
COMMON CARD (1-11)	.20	.50
1 Don Mattingly	.40	1.00
Mike Schmidt		
Baseball's Best		

1988 Star McGwire

This 11-card standard-size set feature Oakland A's slugger Mark McGwire. This set is differentated from the other Star McGwire issues by the 1988 copyright on the back.

COMPLETE SET (11)	6.00	15.00
COMMON CARD (1-11)	.60	1.50

1988 Star McGwire Green

This 11-card standard-size set features Oakland A's slugger Mark McGwire. This set is differentiated from the other McGwire sets by the green borders.

COMPLETE SET (11)	6.00	15.00
COMMON CARD (1-11)	.60	1.50

1988 Star McGwire Yellow

This 12-card standard-size set features slugger Mark McGwire at the beginning of his career. The cards have yellow borders.

COMPLETE SET (12)	6.00	15.00
COMMON CARD (1-12)	.60	1.50
10 Mark McGwire	1.00	2.50
Jose Canseco		
Carney Lansford		
Caree		

1988 Star McReynolds

These 11 standard-size cards feature New York Mets outfielder Kevin McReynolds. These cards take McReynolds from his beginnings to the present day.

COMPLETE SET (11)	1.25	3.00
COMMON CARD (1-11)	.12	.30

1988 Star Murphy Platinum

This 10-card standard-size set was issued by Star to honor the career of two-time NL MVP Dale Murphy. Unlike the regular sets issued by Star, these sets clearly say platinum on the front.

COMPLETE SET (10)	12.50	30.00
COMMON CARD (1-10)	1.20	3.00

1988 Star Nokes

This 11-card standard-size set features Matt Nokes. These cards were printed after Nokes' 30 homer rookie season. They were designed to take advantage of Nokes' popularity.

COMPLETE SET (11)	1.25	3.00
COMMON CARD (1-11)	.12	.30

1988 Star Puckett

This 11-card standard-size set features Minnesota Twins superstar Kirby Puckett. The cards trace Puckett's career from the beginning through the present day.

COMPLETE SET (11)	2.00	5.00
COMMON CARD (1-11)	.20	.50

1988 Star Puckett Ad Card

This one card standard-size red bordered set featured a photo of Kirby Puckett on the front along with ad information about Star Company products on the back.

1 Kirby Puckett	1.25	3.00

1988 Star Scott

These 11 standard-size cards feature Houston Astros star pitcher Mike Scott. These cards trace Scott's career from the beginning through the present day. The cards are dated in the back by a 1988 copyright.

COMPLETE SET (11)	1.25	3.00
COMMON CARD (1-11)	.12	.30

1988 Star Seitzer

This 11-card standard-size set features young Royals player Kevin Seitzer. These cards take Seitzer's career from its beginning through the present day. The cards are notated on the back with a 1988 copyright.

COMPLETE SET (11)	1.50	4.00
COMMON CARD (1-11)	.16	.40

1988 Star Snyder

Former Olympian Cory Snyder is featured in this 11-card standard-size set. These cards trace Snyder's career from its beginnings through 1988. The cards are dated on the back with a 1988 copyright date.

COMPLETE SET (11)	1.25	3.00
COMMON CARD (1-11)	.12	.30

1988 Star Strawberry

This 11-card standard-size set again features Mets player Darryl Strawberry. This set is differentiated from other Strawberry sets by the 1988 copyright date on the back and was issued with two different color borders--one violet and the other blue. The corresponding fronts of each set display different color photos of Darryl Strawberry while the backs carry the same information on the corresponding violet and blue bordered cards.

COMPLETE SET (11)	1.50	4.00
COMMON CARD (1-11)	.16	.40

1988 Star Trammell

Long term Detroit Tiger star Alan Trammell is featured in this set. These 11 standard-sized cards trace his career from the minors through his major league career. These cards are dated by the 1988 copyright date on the back.

COMPLETE SET (11)	1.50	4.00
COMMON CARD (1-11)	.16	.40

1988 Star Trammell Platinum

This 10 card standard-size set features Detroit Tiger star Alan Trammell. The set has a glossy feel to it and production was limited to 1,000 sets.

COMPLETE SET	12.50	30.00
COMMON CARD	1.20	3.00

1988 Star Ventura

These 11 standard-size cards feature Robin Ventura. Ventura, who had established a consecutive-game hitting streak at Oklahoma State, was a highly regarded prospect. These cards feature highlights of his pre-White Sox career.

COMPLETE SET (11)	2.00	5.00
COMMON CARD (1-11)	.20	.50

1988 Star Winfield

These 12 standard-size cards feature highlights in the career of Dave Winfield. These cards are dated by the 1988 copyright date on the back. Even though these issues are usually sold in complete set form we have noted all the individual cards.

COMPLETE SET (12)	2.00	5.00
COMMON CARD (1-12)	.20	.50

1988 Star Stickers George Bell

These 10 standard-size stickers feature Toronto slugging outfielder, George Bell. These stickers are blank backed and the fronts describe various career highlights.

COMPLETE SET (10)	1.00	2.50
COMMON CARD (1-10)	.10	.25

1988 Star Stickers Snyder

These stickers, which are not the same as the regular card issue, feature Cleveland Indians outfielder Cory Snyder. These standard-sized stickers are blank backed and have various career highlights.

COMPLETE SET (8)	.75	2.00
COMMON CARD (1-8)	.10	.25

1988 Star Stickers Winfield

These 10 standard-sized stickers feature Yankee outfielder Dave Winfield. Various highlights from Winfield's career are featured in this set.

COMPLETE SET (10)	2.00	5.00
COMMON CARD (1-10)	.20	.50

1989 Star Canseco Platinum

This 10 card standard-size set was issued to honor the career of the first 40 homer/40 stolen base player, Jose Canseco. The set was limited to a production run of 1,000 sets.

COMPLETE SET	20.00	50.00
COMMON CARD	2.00	5.00

1989 Star Gordon

These 11 standard-sized cards feature Tom "Flash" Gordon, rookie pitcher for the Kansas City Royals. This set was issued as Gordon had an excellent rookie season and became very popular in the hobby.

COMPLETE SET (11)	2.00	5.00
COMMON CARD (1-11)	.20	.50

1989 Star Greenwell Gold

This 10 card standard-size set features highlights from the career of Red Sox slugger Mike Greenwell. Fifteen hundred of these sets were produced.

COMPLETE SET	6.00	15.00
COMMON CARD	.60	1.50

1989 Star Greenwell Platinum

This set has the same checklist as the Star Greenwell Gold set but uses different photos and is limited to 1,000 sets produced.

COMPLETE SET	8.00	20.00
COMMON CARD	.80	2.00

1989 Star Griffey Jr.

This 11 card standard-size set details Ken Griffey Jr.'s career as it was beginning on the major league level. Like the other Star sets, it was issued in its own individual bag.

COMPLETE SET (11)	8.00	20.00
COMMON CARD (1-11)	.80	2.00
7 Ken Griffey Jr.	1.25	3.00
Ken Griffey Sr.		
Father		
Son		

1989 Star Hershiser Gold

This 10 card standard-size set features Orel Hershisher just after the end of his greatest major league season. These cards, which feature highlights of his career, was limited to 1,000 sets produced

COMPLETE SET (10)	8.00	20.00
COMMON CARD	.80	2.00

1989 Star Mitchell

Kevin Mitchell, the 1989 NL MVP is featured in this 11 card standard-sized set. These cards trace Mitchell's career from his earliest days to the present. These cards are dated on the back and are arranged that way.

COMPLETE SET (11)	1.50	4.00
COMMON CARD (1-11)	.16	.40

1989 Star Mitchell/Clark

This 11 card standard-sized set features San Francisco Giant sluggers: Kevin Mitchell and Will Clark. Other than the first card, either Mitchell or Clark is pictured seperately.

COMPLETE SET (11)	1.50	4.00
COMMON MITCHELL (1-11)	.12	.30
COMMON CLARK		.75
1 Kevin Mitchell	.30	.75
Will Clark CL		

1989 Star Puckett Platinum

This 10 card standard-size set features highlights from the career of the Minnesota Twins superstar Kirby Puckett. The set was limited to 1,000 sets produced

COMPLETE SET	20.00	50.00
COMMON CARD	2.00	5.00

1989 Star Strawberry Platinum

This 10 card standard-size set features highlights from the career of Darryl Strawberry. The set was limited to 1,000 sets produced.

COMPLETE SET	8.00	20.00
COMMON CARD	.80	2.00

1989 Star Santiago

This 11 card standard-sized set features Benito Santiago. The set can be dated thanks to the 1989 copyright date on the back. This set traces Santiago's career from the earliest days through the 1988 season.

COMPLETE SET (11)	1.25	3.00
COMMON CARD (1-11)	.12	.30

1989 Star Walton

Jerome Walton is featured in this 11-card standard-size set. Walton, the 1989 NL Rookie of the Year, has his career highlighted in this set. The set is dated by the 1989 copyright on the back.

COMPLETE SET (11)	1.00	2.50
COMMON CARD (1-11)	.10	.25

1989 Star Walton/Olson

This 11 card standard-size set features Gregg Olson and Jerome Walton, the 1989 Rookies of the Year. Other than the 1st checklist card, either Walton or Olson are only featured in this set.

COMPLETE SET (11)	1.00	2.50
1 Jerome Walton	.08	.25
Gregg Olson CL		

1990 Star Abbott

This 11-card standard-size set features highlights in the career of inspirational player, Jim Abbott. Abbott, who only has one hand, became a sucsessful major league pitcher. These cards are dated by the 1990 copyright on the back.

COMPLETE SET (11)	1.50	4.00
COMMON CARD (1-11)	.16	.40

1990 Star Sandy Alomar

This 11-card standard-size set features Sandy Alomar Jr. While this set (as well as all Star products) are usually sold in complete set form, we have broken down this set into its individual components. The set is dated by the 1990 copyright on the back.

COMPLETE SET (11)	1.50	4.00
COMMON CARD (1-11)	.15	.40

1990 Star Alomar Brothers

This 11-card standard-size set features the Alomar Brothers. These players, sons of former major league second basemall Sandy Alomar, each came up with the San Diego Padres. The brothers are only pictured together on card number 1.

COMPLETE SET (11)	1.50	4.00
COMMON S. ALOMAR (1-11)	.12	.30
COMMON R. ALOMAR (1-11)		.75
1 Roberto Alomar CL	.30	.75
Sandy Alomar Jr.		

1990 Star Benes

This 11-card standard-size set features former number one overall draft pick Andy Benes. These cards have highlights of Benes' career and is dated by the 1990 copyright date on the back.

COMPLETE SET (11)	1.00	2.50
COMMON CARD (1-11)	.10	.25

1990 Star Bonds

This 11-card standard-size set was issued by Star Co. in honor of Pittsburgh Pirates superstar Barry Bonds. The cards have on the fronts a mix of action and non-action color shots, with purple borders and white lettering. The horizontally oriented backs are also in purple print and have player information.

COMPLETE SET (11)	4.00	10.00
COMMON CARD		1.00

1990 Star Clark/Grace

The two competing first baseman in the 1989 NL Championship series are featured in this set. These 11 standard-sized cards, other than the first card, feature either Will Clark or Mark Grace and we have identified which player is pictured.

COMPLETE SET (11)	2.00	5.00
COMMON CARD (1-11)	.20	.50
1 Will Clark	.20	.50
Mark Grace CL		

1990 Star Clemens Nova

109 Roger Clemens
110 Roger Clemens
111 Roger Clemens
112 Roger Clemens
113 Roger Clemens
114 Roger Clemens
115 Roger Clemens
116 Roger Clemens
117 Roger Clemens
NNO Roger Clemens

1990 Star Clemens Platinum

This 10-card set is part of the Star Platinum card series. These ten cards feature highlights of Roger Clemens' career.

COMPLETE SET (9)		
COMMON CARD (46-54)		

1990 Star Fielder

This 11-card standard-size set features homerun specialist Cecil Fielder. After playing in Japan, Fielder came back to the American League and hit 50 homers in the 1990 season. This set was issued soon after that season to take advantage of Fielder's popularity.

COMPLETE SET (11)	2.00	5.00
COMMON CARD (1-11)	.20	.50

1990 Star Griffey Jr.

Ken Griffey Jr. is the featured player in this 11-card standard-sized set. These cards, dated by the copyright date on the back, feature highlights from the early part of his career.

COMPLETE SET (11)	6.00	15.00
COMMON CARD (1-11)	.60	1.50
9 Ken Griffey, Jr.	1.00	2.50
Ken Griffey Sr.		
Father		
Son		

1990 Star Rickey Henderson

Rickey Henderson, perhaps the finest lead-off hitter ever, is featured in this 11-card standard-size set. These cards take the collector from the beginnings of Henderson's career to the present day.

COMPLETE SET (11)	4.00	10.00
COMMON CARD (1-11)	.40	1.00

1990 Star Justice

After the Atlanta Braves traded Dale Murphy, David Justice got a chance to play every day. By responding in fine fashion, collectors took notice of this young right fielder. After his rookie season, the Star Company issued this set to honor Justice.

COMPLETE SET (11)	2.00	5.00
COMMON CARD (1-11)	.20	.50

1990 Star Barry Larkin

This 11-card standard-size set features highlights from the career of Cincinnati Reds shortstop Barry Larkin. These cards take the collector from the beginnings of Larkin's career to the present day.

COMPLETE SET (11)	2.00	5.00
COMMON CARD (1-11)	.20	.50

1990 Star Maas

This 11-card standard-size set features highlights from the meteoric career of Yankee first baseman, Kevin Maas. Maas, who established a record for hitting his first 20 homers in the shortest number of at bats

became very popular in the hobby. The Star Company issued this set to capitalize on that popularity.
COMPLETE SET (11) 1.00 2.50
COMMON CARD (1-11) .10 .25

1990 Star Matt Williams
Matt Williams, slugging third baseman for the San Francisco Giants, is featured in this 11-card standard-size set. These cards display various highlights (noted explicitly below) from his career.
COMPLETE SET (11) 2.00 5.00
COMMON CARD (1-11) .20 .50

1990 Star McDonald
This 11-card standard-size set features young Baltimore Oriole pitcher Ben McDonald. McDonald, who was drafted first overall in 1989, has his career traced from his earliest days to the present.
COMPLETE SET (11) 1.00 2.50
COMMON CARD (1-11) .10 .25

1990 Star Mitchell/Yount
Kevin Mitchell and Robin Yount won MVP awards in 1989. This set features Mitchell and Yount on various cards. Other than the first card in the set, only one of the players is pictured.
COMPLETE SET (11) 1.50 4.00
COMMON MITCHELL (1-11) .12 .30
COMMON YOUNT .75
1 Kevin Mitchell .20 .50
Robin Yount CL

1990 Star Ripken
This 11-card standard-size set covers various highlights of Cal Ripken's Jr. career.
COMPLETE SET (11) 4.00 10.00
COMMON CARD (1-11) .40 1.00

1990 Star Ryan
This 12-card standard-size set was issued by Star Co. in honor of Texas Rangers' pitching ace Nolan Ryan. The cards have on the fronts a mix of action and non-action color shots, with blue borders and white lettering. The horizontally oriented backs are in blue print and have player information.
COMPLETE SET (11) 4.00 10.00
COMMON PLAYER (1-11) .40 1.00

1990 Star Saberhagen/Davis
Bret Saberhagen and Mark Davis won their respective leagues Cy Young award in 1989. The Star Company than issued an 11-card standard-size set to honor these pitchers. Other than the first card, either Davis or Saberhagen appears on the card and we have noted who is portrayed on the card.
COMPLETE SET (11) 1.25 3.00
COMMON DAVIS (1-11) .10 .25
COMMON SABERHAGEN
1 Bret Saberhagen .10 .30
Mark Davis CL

1990 Star Sandberg
This 11-card standard-size set features highlights from the career of Chicago Cub second baseman Ryne Sandberg. These cards trace Sandberg's career from its earliest days through major league stardom.
COMPLETE SET (11) 2.00 5.00
COMMON CARD (1-11) .20 .50

1990 Star Yount
This 11-card standard-size set features highlights from the career of long-time Milwaukee Brewers star Robin Yount. These cards cover some of the best moments from his major league career. The set is dated by the 1990 copyright on the back.
COMPLETE SET (11) 2.00 5.00
COMMON CARD (1-11) .20 .50

1991 Star Belle Rookie Guild
This 11-card set features Albert Belle of the Cleveland Indians. The fronts display color photos while the backs carry either statistics, career or personal information. Only 5,000 of this set were produced.
COMPLETE SET (11) 2.00 5.00
COMMON CARD (1-11) .20 .50

1991 Star Clemen
This 11-card set features highlights from the career of Roger Clemens, who would continue his career and win more than 300 games in his career.
COMPLETE SET (11) 4.00 10.00
COMMON CLEMENS .40 1.00

1991 Star Gonzalez Rookie Guild
This 11-card set features Juan Gonzalez of the Texas Rangers. The fronts display color photos while the backs carry either statistics, career or personal information. Only 5,000 of this set were produced.
COMPLETE SET (11) 2.00 5.00
COMMON CARD (1-11) .20 .50

1991 Star Griffeys
Both Ken Griffey Sr. and Ken Griffey Jr. are featured in this set. Only the first card in the set features both Griffeys. Otherwise, we have listed only which Griffey is pictured on the card.
COMPLETE SET (11) 3.00 8.00
COMMON GRIFFEY SR (1-11) .16 .40
COMMON GRIFFEY JR 1.50
1 Ken Griffey Jr. .50 1.25
Ken Griffey Sr. CL

1991 Star Knoblauch Rookie Guild
COMPLETE SET (11) 2.50 6.00
12 Chuck Knoblauch .30 .75
Checklist
13 Chuck Knoblauch .30 .75
Career Stats
14 Chuck Knoblauch .30 .75
1989 season
15 Chuck Knoblauch .30 .75
1990 season
16 Chuck Knoblauch .30 .75
1991 season
17 Chuck Knoblauch .30 .75
pro info
18 Chuck Knoblauch .30 .75
personal data
19 Chuck Knoblauch .30 .75
personal info
20 Chuck Knoblauch .30 .75
Minnesota Twins
21 Chuck Knoblauch .30 .75
Minnesota Twins
22 Chuck Knoblauch .30 .75
Minnesota Twins

1991 Star Rickey Henderson
The only difference with this set as opposed to the 1990 Star Rickey Henderson set is the copyright date on the back. These cards are dated with a 1991 copyright.
COMPLETE SET (11) 2.50 6.00
COMMON CARD (1-11) .30 .75

1991 Star Mark Lewis Rookie Guild
This 11-card set features Mark Lewis of the Cleveland Indians. The fronts display color photos while the backs carry either statistics, career or personal information. Only 5,000 of this set were produced.
COMPLETE SET (11) 1.00 2.50
COMMON CARD (1-11) .10 .25

1991 Star Ryan
This 11-card set was issued by Star Co. in honor of Texas Rangers' pitching ace Nolan Ryan. The fronts feature a mix of action and non-action color photos, with red-and-gray borders. The backs carry player information printed in red.
COMPLETE SET (11) 4.00 10.00
COMMON CARD (1-11) .40 1.00

1991 Star Strawberry
This 11-card standard-size set features outfielder Darryl Strawberry. This set can be dated to 1991 by his appearence as an Los Angeles Dodger.
COMPLETE SET (11) 1.50 4.00
COMMON CARD (1-11) .16 .40

1991 Star Thomas Rookie Guild
This 11-card set features Frank Thomas of the Chicago White Sox. The fronts display color photos while the backs carry either statistics, career or personal information. Only 5,000 of this set were produced.
COMPLETE SET (11) 3.00 8.00
COMMON CARD (1-11) .30 .75
P1 Frank Thomas Promo .40 1.00
Card has glossy front and is blank-backed

1992 Star Promos
These 11 standard-size cards were issued separately. The purpose of these cards was to promote some upcoming 1992 Star Company issues.
COMPLETE SET (11) 8.00 20.00
1 Roberto Alomar 1.00 2.50
2 Steve Avery .40 1.00
3 Jeff Bagwell 1.25 3.00
4 Rickey Henderson 1.25 3.00
5 Eric Karros .75 2.00
6 Kevin Maas .40 1.00
7 Don Mattingly 2.00 5.00
8 Benito Santiago .60 1.50
9 Darryl Strawberry .60 1.50
10 Frank Thomas 1.25 3.00
11 Jerome Walton .40 1.00

1992 Star Avery
This 11-card standard-size set features Atlanta Braves pitcher Steve Avery. These cards were issued after Avery's sensational post season pitching efforts. These cards trace Avery's career from its beginnings to major league stardom.
COMPLETE SET (11) 1.00 2.50
COMMON PLAYER (1-11) .10 .25

1992 Star Bagwell
These 11 standard-size cards feature Houston Astros star player Jeff Bagwell. These cards trace Bagwell's career from his minor league days through his rookie season.
COMPLETE SET (11) 2.00 5.00
COMMON PLAYER (1-11) .20 .50

1992 Star Belle
Cleveland Indians outfielder Albert Belle is featured in this 11-card standard-size set. These cards take Belle's career from his earliest days to the present day.
COMPLETE SET (11) 1.50 4.00
COMMON PLAYER (1-11) .15 .40

1992 Star Will Clark
These 11 standard-size cards feature San Francisco Giants first baseman Will.Clark. Clark's career is traced from its earliest days through the present day. These cards are dated by the 1992 copyright on the back.
COMPLETE SET (11) 2.00 5.00
COMMON PLAYER (1-11) .20 .50

1992 Star Erickson
COMPLETE SET (11) 2.00 5.00
COMMON ERICKSON .20 .50

1992 Star Gant
These 11 standard-sized cards feature outfielder Ron Gant. These cards are dated by the 1992 copyright on the back. These cards trace Gant's career from his minor league days to the present.
COMPLETE SET (11) 1.50 4.00
COMMON PLAYER (1-11) .16 .40

1992 Star Griffey Jr.
This set, like many others issued, feature Ken Griffey Jr. These 11 standard-size cards take the collector through various highlights of Griffey's career.
COMPLETE SET (11) 4.00 10.00
COMMON PLAYER (1-11) .40 1.00

1992 Star Bo Jackson
These 11 standard-size cards feature two sport star Bo Jackson. These cards basically cover only Bo's baseball career.
COMPLETE SET (11) 2.00 5.00
COMMON PLAYER (1-11) .20 .50

1992 Star Justice
This is another set issued by Star Company about David Justice. These cards are differentiated from the first set as it had different cards as well as a 1992 copyright date.
COMPLETE SET (11) 1.50 4.00
COMMON PLAYER (1-11) .16 .40

1992 Star Knoblauch
Chuck Knoblauch, second baseman for the Minnesota Twins is featured in this set. These standard-size cards take the collector from his earliest playing days to the present day.
COMPLETE SET (11) 2.00 5.00
COMMON PLAYER (1-11) .20 .50

1992 Star Palmer
Dean Palmer, young third baseman for the Texas Rangers is featured in this set. These 11 standard-size cards take Palmer's career from its beginning to the present day.
COMPLETE SET (11) 1.25 3.00
COMMON PLAYER (1-11) .10 .30

1992 Star Plantier
As the 1991 season ended Phil Plantier was one of the hottest players in the game. To take advantage of his popularity, Star Company issued this 11 card standard-size set featuring highlights from Plantier's career.
COMPLETE SET (11) 1.00 2.50
COMMON PLAYER (1-11) .10 .25

1992 Star Puckett
This 1992 Star Kirby Puckett set consists of 11 standard-sized cards. These cards are broken down by subject and pertain to various highlights in his career. The set is dated by the 1992 copyright on the back.
COMPLETE SET (11) 2.00 5.00
COMMON PLAYER (1-11) .20 .50

1992 Star Sandberg
These 11 standard-size cards feature highlights in the career of Cubs second baseman Ryne Sandberg. These cards trace his career from his earliest days through the present.
COMPLETE SET (11) 2.00 5.00
COMMON PLAYER (1-11) .20 .50

1992 Star Tartabull
Danny Tartabull is featured in this 11-card standard-size set. These cards trace Tartabull's career from its beginnings to the present day. The set is dated by the 1992 copyright on the back. Also, Star Company sets are usually sold in complete set form.
COMPLETE SET (11) 1.25 3.00
COMMON PLAYER (1-11) .12 .30

1992 Star Van Poppel
The 1992 Star Todd Van Poppel card set consists of 11 standard-size cards. The fronts display color action shots of Van Poppel with a border that fades from green to gray. The card title is printed in green lettering at the lower right corner. The horizontal backs are yellow with green lettering. In the upper left corner is a color head shot photo of Van Poppel. The backs also contain career statistics, 1990 highlights and biography.
COMPLETE SET (10) .75 2.00
COMMON PLAYER (1-10) .10 .25

1993 Star Autographs
These cards features players on 1993 Star cards which have been autographed. The card features a Certificate of Authenticity issued by Star.
COMPLETE SET 2.00 8.00
1 Andy Benes 1.50 4.00
2 Eric Karros 2.00 5.00

1995 Star Ripken 80
This 80-card set commemorates the 2,131 Consecutive Games Played Record set by Cal Ripken Jr. The fronts feature color action pictures of Ripken while the backs carry facts about his career.
COMPLETE SET (80) 4.00 10.00
COMMON CARD (1-80) .06 .15

1995 Star Ripken 110
This 110-card standard-size set came in its own special box. These cards are basically an update of the previously issued 80-card set issued earlier in the year. Please note that these cards have glossy fronts and discuss highlights of Cal's career. The backs provide either statistical or factual information.
COMPLETE SET 10.00 25.00
COMMON CARD .10 .25

1928 Star Player Candy
This set is presumed to have been inserts to a candy box named "Star Player Candy" produced by Dockman and Sons candy company. The cards are sepia colored and measure approximately 1 7/8" by 2 7/8" with blank backs. The fronts feature full length action shots except for Dave Bancroft which is a portrait. The player's name is printed in brown capital letters in the bottom border. A second version of some cards in this set were recently discovered as part of a multi-sport product (issued by Dockman and Son) entitled "Headliners and Gum." This version features card numbers and bios on the backs and the baseball players were issued with golfers and aviators.
COMPLETE SET 60000.00 120000.00
1 Dave Bancroft 1500.00 3000.00
2 Emile Barnes 500.00 1000.00
3 Lu Blue 500.00 1000.00
4 Garland Buckeye 500.00 1000.00
5 George Burns 500.00 1000.00
6 Guy Bush 500.00 1000.00
7 Owen Carroll 500.00 1000.00
8 Bud Cissell 500.00 1000.00
9 Ty Cobb 12500.00 25000.00
10 Mickey Cochrane 1500.00 3000.00
11 Richard Coffman 500.00 1000.00
12 Eddie Collins 2500.00 5000.00
13 Stan Coveleskie 1500.00 3000.00
14 Hugh Critz 500.00 1000.00
15 Kiki Cuyler 1500.00 3000.00
16 Chuck Dressen 600.00 1200.00
17 Joe Dugan 600.00 1200.00
18 Woody English 500.00 1000.00
19 Bibb Falk 500.00 1000.00
20 Ira Flagstead 500.00 1000.00
21 Bob Fothergill 500.00 1000.00
22 Frank Frisch 1500.00 3000.00
23 Foster Ganzel 500.00 1000.00
24 Lou Gehrig 6000.00 12000.00
25 Charley Gehringer 1500.00 3000.00
26 George Gerken 500.00 1000.00
27 Grant Gillis 500.00 1000.00
28 Mike Gonzales 500.00 1000.00
29 Sam Gray 500.00 1000.00
30 Charlie Grimm 750.00 1500.00
31 Lefty Grove 2000.00 4000.00
32 Chick Hafey 1500.00 3000.00
33 Jesse Haines 1500.00 3000.00
34 Gabby Hartnett 1500.00 3000.00
35 Clifton Heathcote 500.00 1000.00
36 Harry Heilmann 1500.00 3000.00
37 John Heving 500.00 1000.00
38 Waite Hoyt 1000.00 2000.00
39 Charles Jamieson 500.00 1000.00
40 Joe Judge 500.00 1000.00
41 Willie Kamm 500.00 1000.00
42 George Kelly 1000.00 2000.00
43 Tony Lazzeri 1000.00 2000.00
44 Adolfo Luque 750.00 1500.00
45 Ted Lyons 1000.00 2000.00
46 Hugh McMullen 500.00 1000.00
47 Bob Meusel 750.00 1500.00
48 Wilcy Moore 500.00 1000.00
49 Ed Morgan 500.00 1000.00
50 Buddy Myer 600.00 1200.00
51 Herb Pennock 1000.00 2000.00
52 Everett Purdy 500.00 1000.00
53 William Regan 500.00 1000.00
54 Eppa Rixey 1000.00 2000.00
55 Charles Root 500.00 1000.00
56 Jack Rothrock 500.00 1000.00
57 Muddy Ruel 500.00 1000.00
58 Babe Ruth 12500.00 25000.00
59 Wally Schang 500.00 1000.00
60 Joe Sewell 1000.00 2000.00
61 Luke Sewell 500.00 1000.00
62 Joe Shaute 500.00 1000.00
63 George Sisler 750.00 1500.00
64 Tris Speaker 2000.00 4000.00
65 Riggs Stephenson 750.00 1500.00
66 Jack Tavener 500.00 1000.00
67 Al Thomas 500.00 1000.00
68 Pie Traynor 1000.00 2000.00
69 George Uhle 500.00 1000.00
70 Dazzy Vance 1000.00 2000.00
71 Cy Williams 600.00 1200.00
72 Ken Williams 600.00 1200.00
73 Hack Wilson 1000.00 2000.00

1983 Stargell Junior Watson Dinner
This one card set featured retired Pirate great Willie Stargell and was handed out at the Junior Watson dinner. The front has black borders and features a head shot of Stargell. The horizontal back has career statistics.
1 Willie Stargell 2.00 5.00

1990 Starline Long John Silver
The 1990 Starline Long John Silver set was issued over an eight-week promotion, five cards at a time within a cello pack. The set was initially available only through the Long John Silver seafood fast-food chain with one pack being given to each customer who ordered a meal with a 32-ounce Coke. This 40-card, standard-size set featured the best of today's players. There are several cards for some of the players in the set. After the promotion at Long John Silver had been completed, there were reportedly more than 100,000 sets left over that were released into the organized hobby.
COMPLETE SET (40) 2.50 6.00
1 Don Mattingly .30 .75
2 Mark Grace .10 .30
3 Eric Davis .02 .10
4 Tony Gwynn .30 .75
5 Bobby Bonilla .01 .05
6 Wade Boggs .15 .40
7 Frank Viola .01 .05
8 Ruben Sierra .02 .10
9 Mark McGwire .30 .75
10 Alan Trammell .07 .20
11 Mark McGwire .30 .75
12 Gregg Jefferies .01 .05
13 Nolan Ryan .60 1.50
14 John Smoltz .02 .10
15 Glenn Davis .01 .05
16 Mark Grace .10 .30
17 Wade Boggs .15 .40
18 Frank Viola .01 .05
19 Bret Saberhagen .02 .10
20 Chris Sabo .01 .05
21 Darryl Strawberry .02 .10
22 Wade Boggs .15 .40
23 Tim Raines .02 .10
24 Alan Trammell .07 .20
25 Chris Sabo .01 .05
26 Nolan Ryan .60 1.50
27 Mark McGwire .30 .75
28 Don Mattingly .30 .75
29 Tony Gwynn .30 .75
30 Glenn Davis .01 .05
31 Bobby Bonilla .01 .05
32 Gregg Jefferies .01 .05
33 Ruben Sierra .02 .10
34 John Smoltz .02 .10
35 Don Mattingly .30 .75
36 Bret Saberhagen .02 .10
37 Darryl Strawberry .02 .10
38 Eric Davis .02 .10
39 Tim Raines .02 .10
40 Mark Grace .10 .30

1991 Starline Prototypes
This five-card set measures approximately 2 11/16" by 3 11/16". Sixty of each card were produced and submitted to Major League Baseball for approval to be offered to prospective sponsors. The cards are unnumbered and checklisted below in alphabetical order.
COMPLETE SET (5) 100.00 200.00
1 George Bell 10.00 25.00
2 Bobby Bonilla 10.00 25.00
3 Roger Clemens 40.00 100.00
4 Tim Raines 12.50 30.00
5 Darryl Strawberry 12.50 30.00

1988 Starting Lineup All-Stars
This set measures approximately 2 5/8" by 3" and were included in the Starting Lineup game. The fronts have a player photo while the back has recent seasonal stats and some personal information.
COMPLETE SET (39) 8.00 25.00
1 Buddy Bell .20 .50
2 George Bell .08 .25
3 Wade Boggs .60 1.50
4 George Brett 1.00 2.50
5 Gary Carter .60 1.50
6 Jack Clark .20 .50
7 Roger Clemens 1.00 2.50
8 Eric Davis .20 .50
9 Jody Davis .08 .25
10 Andre Dawson .40 1.00
11 Carlton Fisk .60 1.50
12 Dwight Gooden .20 .50
13 Tony Gwynn 1.00 2.50
14 Rickey Henderson .60 1.50
15 Keith Hernandez .20 .50
16 Terry Kennedy .08 .25
17 Don Mattingly 1.25 3.00
18 Jack Morris .20 .50
19 Dale Murphy .30 .75
20 Eddie Murray .60 1.50
21 Kirby Puckett .75 2.00
22 Dan Quisenberry .08 .25
23 Tim Raines .20 .50
24 Willie Randolph .08 .25
25 Dave Righetti .08 .25
26 Cal Ripken 2.00 5.00
27 Nolan Ryan 2.00 5.00
28 Ryne Sandberg .75 2.00
29 Steve Sax .08 .25
30 Mike Schmidt .60 1.50
31 Mike Scott .08 .25
32 Ozzie Smith .60 1.50
33 Darryl Strawberry .20 .50
34 Fernando Valenzuela .20 .50
35 Lou Whitaker .20 .50
36 Dave Winfield .60 1.50
37 Todd Worrell .08 .25
38 Robin Yount .60 1.50
39 Game card and Help 2 .08 .25

1988 Starting Lineup Angels
This 21-card set of the California Angels measures approximately 2 5/8" by 3" and features colored drawings of the players on the fronts while the backs carry the player's statistics. The cards are unnumbered and checklisted below in alphabetical order.
COMPLETE SET (21) 2.00 5.00
1 Bob Boone .30 .75
2 Bill Buckner .20 .50
3 DeWayne Buice .08 .25
4 Chili Davis .30 .75
5 Brian Downing .08 .25
6 Chuck Finley .40 1.00
7 Willie Frasier .08 .25
8 George Hendrick .08 .25
9 Jack Howell .08 .25
10 Ruppert Jones .08 .25
11 Wally Joyner .40 1.00
12 Kirk McCaskill .08 .25
13 Mark McLemore .08 .25
14 Darrell Miller .08 .25
15 Greg Minton .08 .25
16 Gary Pettis .08 .25
17 Johnny Ray .08 .25
18 Dick Schofield .08 .25
19 Devon White .40 1.00
20 Mike Witt .08 .25
21 Team Checklist .08 .25

1988 Starting Lineup A's
This 21-card set of the Oakland A's measures approximately 2 5/8" by 3" and features colored drawings of the players on the fronts while the backs carry the player's statistics. The cards are unnumbered and checklisted below in alphabetical order.
COMPLETE SET (21) 3.00 8.00
1 Tony Bernazard .08 .25
2 Jose Canseco .75 2.00
3 Mike Davis .08 .25
4 Dennis Eckersley .60 1.50
5 Mike Gallego .08 .25
6 Alfredo Griffin .08 .25
7 Dave Henderson .08 .25
8 Reggie Jackson .60 1.50
9 Carney Lansford .20 .50
10 Mark McGwire 1.50 4.00
11 Steve Ontiveros .08 .25
12 Dave Parker .30 .75
13 Tony Phillips .08 .25
14 Luis Polonia .08 .25
15 Terry Steinbach .20 .50
16 Dave Stewart .30 .75
17 Mickey Tettleton .20 .50
18 Bob Welch .20 .50
19 Curt Young .08 .25
20 Matt Young .08 .25
21 Team Checklist .08 .25

1988 Starting Lineup Astros
These cards feature members of the 1988 Houston Astros. These cards measure approximately 2 5/8" by 3" and have player photos on the front. The backs have recent seasonal statistics and some personal information. Ken Caminiti is featured in his Rookie Card season.
COMPLETE SET (21) 4.00 10.00
1 Juan Agosto .08 .25
2 Larry Andersen .08 .25
3 Alan Ashby .08 .25
4 Kevin Bass .08 .25
5 Ken Caminiti .40 1.00
6 Jose Cruz .20 .50
7 Danny Darwin .08 .25
8 Glenn Davis .08 .25
9 Bill Doran .08 .25
10 Billy Hatcher .08 .25
11 Jim Pankovitz .08 .25
12 Terry Puhl .08 .25
13 Rafael Ramirez .08 .25
14 Craig Reynolds .08 .25
15 Nolan Ryan 3.00 8.00
16 Mike Scott .30 .75
17 Dave Smith .08 .25
18 Marc Sullivan .08 .25
19 Denny Walling .08 .25
20 Gerald Young .08 .25
21 Team Checklist .08 .25

1988 Starting Lineup Blue Jays
These cards feature members of the 1988 Toronto Blue Jays. These cards measure approximately 2 5/8" by 3" and have player photos on the front. The backs have recent seasonal statistics and some personal information.
COMPLETE SET (21) 2.00 5.00
1 Jesse Barfield .20 .50
2 George Bell .20 .50
3 Juan Beniquez .08 .25
4 Jim Clancy .08 .25
5 Mark Eichhorn .08 .25
6 Tony Fernandez .30 .75
7 Cecil Fielder .08 .25
8 Tom Henke .08 .25
9 Garth Iorg .08 .25
10 Jimmy Key .40 1.00
11 Rick Leach .08 .25
12 Manuel Lee .08 .25
13 Nelson Liriano .08 .25
14 Fred McGriff .75 2.00
15 Lloyd Moseby .08 .25
16 Rance Mulliniks .08 .25
17 Jeff Musselman .08 .25
18 Dave Stieb .20 .50
19 Willie Upshaw .08 .25
20 Ernie Whitt .08 .25
21 Team Checklist .08 .25

1988 Starting Lineup Braves
These cards feature members of the 1988 Atlanta Braves. These cards measure approximately 2 5/8" by 3" and have player photos on the front. The backs have recent seasonal statistics and some personal information. Jeff Blauser, Ron Gant and Tom Glavine are all featured in their Rookie Card season.
COMPLETE SET (21) 3.00 8.00
1 Jim Acker .08 .25
2 Paul Assenmacher .08 .25
3 Jeff Blauser .40 1.00
4 Jeff Dedman .08 .25
5 Ron Gant .60 1.50
6 Tom Glavine 1.50 4.00
7 Ken Griffey .20 .50
8 Albert Hall .08 .25
9 Glenn Hubbard .08 .25
10 Dion James .08 .25
11 Rick Mahler .08 .25
12 Dale Murphy .60 1.50
13 Ken Oberkfell .08 .25
14 Gerald Perry .08 .25
15 Gary Roenicke .08 .25
16 Paul Runge .08 .25
17 Ted Simmons .20 .50
18 Zane Smith .08 .25
19 Andres Thomas .08 .25
20 Ozzie Virgil .08 .25
21 Team Checklist .08 .25

1988 Starting Lineup Brewers
These cards feature members of the 1988 Milwaukee Brewers. These cards measure approximately 2 5/8" by 3" and have player photos on the front. The backs have recent seasonal statistics and some personal information.
COMPLETE SET (21) 2.00 5.00
1 Chris Bosio .08 .25
2 Glenn Braggs .08 .25
3 Greg Brock .08 .25
4 Juan Castillo .08 .25
5 Chuck Crim .08 .25
6 Rob Deer .08 .25
7 Mike Felder .08 .25
8 Jim Gantner .08 .25
9 Ted Higuera .08 .25
10 Steve Kiefer .08 .25
11 Paul Molitor .60 1.50
12 Juan Nieves .08 .25
13 Dan Plesac .08 .25
14 Ernest Riles .08 .25
15 Billy Jo Robidoux .08 .25
16 Bill Schroeder .08 .25
17 B. J. Surhoff .30 .75
18 Dale Sveum .08 .25
19 Bill Wegman .08 .25
20 Robin Yount .60 1.50
21 Team Checklist .08 .25

1988 Starting Lineup Cardinals
These cards feature members of the 1988 St. Louis Cardinals. These cards measure approximately 2 5/8" by 3" and have player photos on the front. The backs have recent seasonal statistics and some personal information.
COMPLETE SET (21) 2.50 6.00
1 Rob Booker .08 .25
2 Jack Clark .20 .50
3 Vince Coleman .20 .50
4 Danny Cox .08 .25
5 Ken Dayley .08 .25
6 Curt Ford .08 .25
7 Tommy Herr .08 .25
8 Bob Horner .20 .50
9 Ricky Horton .08 .25
10 Lance Johnson .40 1.00
11 Steve Lake .08 .25
12 Jim Lindeman .08 .25
13 Greg Mathews .08 .25
14 Willie McGee .40 1.00
15 Jose Oquendo .08 .25
16 Tony Pena .08 .25
17 Terry Pendleton .30 .75
18 Ozzie Smith 1.50 4.00
19 John Tudor .08 .25
20 Todd Worrell .20 .50
21 Team Checklist .08 .25

1988 Starting Lineup Cubs
These cards feature members of the 1988 Chicago Cubs. These cards measure approximately 2 5/8" by 3" and have player photos on the front. The backs have recent seasonal statistics and some personal information.
COMPLETE SET (14) 2.50 6.00
1 Jody Davis .08 .25
2 Andre Dawson .60 1.50
3 Bob Dernier .08 .25
4 Frank DiPino .08 .25
5 Leon Durham .08 .25
6 Dave Martinez .08 .25
7 Keith Moreland .08 .25
8 Jamie Moyer .40 1.00
9 Jerry Mumphrey .08 .25
10 Ryne Sandberg 1.00 2.50
11 Scott Sanderson .08 .25
12 Calvin Schiraldi .08 .25
13 Lee Smith .30 .75
14 Jim Sundberg .08 .25
15 Rick Sutcliffe .20 .50
16 Manny Trillo .08 .25

1988 Starting Lineup Dodgers
This 21-card set of the Los Angeles Dodgers measures approximately 2 5/8" by 3" and features colored drawings of the players on the fronts while the backs carry the player's statistics. The cards are unnumbered and checklisted below in alphabetical order.
COMPLETE SET (21) 1.50 4.00
1 Dave Anderson .08 .25
2 Mike Davis .08 .25
3 Mariano Duncan .08 .25
4 Kirk Gibson .40 1.00
5 Alfredo Griffin .08 .25
6 Pedro Guerrero .30 .75
7 Mickey Hatcher .08 .25
8 Orel Hershiser .40 1.00
9 Glenn Hoffman .08 .25
10 Brian Holton .08 .25
11 Mike Marshall .08 .25
12 Jesse Orosco .20 .50
13 Alejandro Pena .08 .25
14 Steve Sax .30 .75
15 Mike Scioscia .30 .75
16 John Shelby .08 .25
17 Franklin Stubbs .08 .25
18 Don Sutton .40 1.00
19 Alex Trevino .08 .25
20 Fernando Valenzuela .30 .75
21 Team Checklist .08 .25

1988 Starting Lineup Expos
This 21-card set of the Montreal Expos measures approximately 2 5/8" by 3" and features colored drawings of the players on the fronts while the backs carry the player's statistics. The cards are unnumbered and checklisted below in alphabetical order.
COMPLETE SET (21) 2.00 5.00
1 Hubie Brooks .08 .25
2 Tim Burke .08 .25
3 Casey Candaele .08 .25
4 Mike Fitzgerald .08 .25
5 Tom Foley .08 .25
6 Andres Galarraga .60 1.50
7 Neal Heaton .08 .25
8 Wallace Johnson .08 .25
9 Vance Law .08 .25
10 Bob McClure .08 .25
11 Andy McGaffigan .08 .25
12 Alonzo Powell .08 .25
13 Tim Raines .40 1.00
14 Jeff Reed .08 .25
15 Luis Rivera .08 .25
16 Bryn Smith .08 .25
17 Tim Wallach .20 .50
18 Mitch Webster .08 .25
19 Herm Winningham .08 .25
20 Floyd Youmans .08 .25
21 Team Checklist .08 .25

1988 Starting Lineup Giants
These cards feature members of the 1988 San Francisco Giants. These cards measure approximately 2 5/8" by 3" and have player photos on the front. The backs have recent seasonal statistics and some personal information. An early card of Matt Williams is included in this set.
COMPLETE SET (21) 3.00 8.00
1 Mike Aldrete .08 .25
2 Bob Brenly .08 .25
3 Brett Butler .20 .50
4 Will Clark .75 2.00
5 Chili Davis .30 .75
6 Dave Dravecky .20 .50
7 Scott Garrelts .08 .25
8 Atlee Hammaker .08 .25
9 Craig Lefferts .08 .25
10 Jeffrey Leonard .08 .25
11 Candy Maldonado .08 .25
12 Bob Melvin .20 .50
13 Kevin Mitchell .20 .50
14 Rick Reuschel .20 .50
15 Don Robinson .08 .25
16 Chris Speier .08 .25
17 Harry Spilman .08 .25
18 Robby Thompson .20 .50
19 Jose Uribe .08 .25
20 Matt Williams 1.00 2.50
21 Team Checklist .08 .25

1988 Starting Lineup Indians
This 21-card set of the Cleveland Indians measures approximately 2 5/8" by 3" and features colored drawings of the players on the fronts while the backs carry the player's statistics. The cards are unnumbered and checklisted below in alphabetical order.
COMPLETE SET (21) 2.00 5.00
1 Andy Allanson .08 .25
2 Scott Bailes .08 .25
3 Chris Bando .08 .25
4 Jay Bell .40 1.00
5 Brett Butler .20 .50
6 Tom Candiotti .08 .25
7 Joe Carter .60 1.50
8 Carmen Castillo .08 .25
9 Dave Clark .08 .25
10 John Farrell .08 .25
11 Julio Franco .20 .50
12 Mel Hall .08 .25
13 Tommy Hinzo .08 .25
14 Brook Jacoby .08 .25
15 Doug Jones .08 .25
16 Junior Noboa .08 .25
17 Ken Schrom .08 .25
18 Cory Snyder .08 .25
19 Greg Swindell .08 .25
20 Pat Tabler .08 .25
21 Team Checklist .08 .25

1988 Starting Lineup Mariners
This 21-card set of the Seattle Mariners measures approximately 2 5/8" by 3" and features colored

drawings of the players on the fronts while the backs carry the player's statistics. The cards are unnumbered and checklisted below in alphabetical order.
COMPLETE SET (21) 1.50 4.00
1 Phil Bradley .08 .25
2 Scott Bradley .08 .25
3 Mickey Brantley .08 .25
4 Mike Campbell .08 .25
5 Henry Cotto .08 .25
6 Alvin Davis .20 .50
7 Mike Kingery .08 .25
8 Mark Langston .30 .75
9 Mike Moore .08 .25
10 John Moses .08 .25
11 Otis Nixon .08 .25
12 Edwin Nunez .08 .25
13 Ken Phelps .08 .25
14 Jim Presley .08 .25
15 Rey Quinones .08 .25
16 Jerry Reed .08 .25
17 Harold Reynolds .20 .50
18 Dave Valle .08 .25
19 Bill Wilkinson .08 .25
20 Glenn Wilson .08 .25
21 Team Checklist .08 .25

1988 Starting Lineup Mets

This 21-card set of the New York Mets measures approximately 2 5/8" by 3" and features colored drawings of the players on the fronts while the backs carry the player's statistics. The cards are unnumbered and checklisted below in alphabetical order.
COMPLETE SET (21) 2.00 5.00
1 Bill Almon .08 .25
2 Wally Backman .08 .25
3 Gary Carter .60 1.50
4 Dave Cone .75 2.00
(David)
5 Ron Darling .20 .50
6 Len Dykstra .30 .75
7 Sid Fernandez .20 .50
8 Dwight Gooden .40 1.00
9 Keith Hernandez .30 .75
10 Howard Johnson .20 .50
11 Barry Lyons .08 .25
12 Dave Magadan .08 .25
13 Lee Mazzilli .08 .25
14 Roger McDowell .08 .25
15 Kevin McReynolds .20 .50
16 Jesse Orosco .20 .50
17 Rafael Santana .08 .25
18 Darryl Strawberry .40 1.00
19 Tim Teufel .08 .25
20 Mookie Wilson .20 .50
21 Team Checklist .08 .25

1988 Starting Lineup Orioles

This 21-card set of the Baltimore Orioles measures approximately 2 5/8" by 3" and features colored drawings of the players on the fronts while the backs carry the player's statistics. The cards are unnumbered and checklisted below in alphabetical order.
COMPLETE SET (21) 3.00 8.00
1 Eric Bell .08 .25
2 Mike Boddicker .08 .25
3 Jim Dwyer .08 .25
4 Ken Gerhart .08 .25
5 Rene Gonzales .08 .25
6 Terry Kennedy .08 .25
7 Ray Knight .08 .25
8 Lee Lacy .08 .25
9 Fred Lynn .30 .75
10 Eddie Murray .60 1.50
11 Tom Niedenfuer .08 .25
12 Billy Ripken .08 .25
13 Cal Ripken 2.50 6.00
14 Dave Schmidt .08 .25
15 Larry Sheets .08 .25
16 Steve Stanicek .08 .25
17 Mark Thurmond .08 .25
18 Ron Washington .08 .25
19 Mark Williamson .08 .25
20 Mike Young .08 .25
21 Team Checklist .08 .25

1988 Starting Lineup Padres

These cards feature members of the 1988 San Diego Padres. These cards measure approximately 2 5/8" by 3" and have player photos on the front. The backs have recent seasonal statistics and some personal information. Roberto Alomar has a card in his rookie season in this set.
COMPLETE SET 3.00 8.00
1 Shawn Abner .08 .25
2 Roberto Alomar 1.50 4.00
3 Chris Brown .08 .25
4 Joey Cora .08 .25
5 Mark Davis .08 .25
6 Tim Flannery .08 .25
7 Goose Gossage .30 .75
8 Mark Grant .08 .25
9 Tony Gwynn 1.50 4.00
10 Stan Jefferson .08 .25
11 John Kruk .40 1.00
12 Shane Mack .08 .25
13 Carmelo Martinez .08 .25
14 Lance McCullers .08 .25
15 Randy Ready .08 .25
16 Benito Santiago .20 .50
17 Eric Show .08 .25
18 Ed Whitson .08 .25
19 Marvell Wynne .08 .25

1988 Starting Lineup Phillies

This 21-card set of the Philadelphia Phillies measures approximately 2 5/8" by 3" and features colored drawings of the players on the fronts while the backs carry the player's statistics. The cards are unnumbered and checklisted below in alphabetical order.
COMPLETE SET (21) 2.00 5.00
1 Luis Aguayo .08 .25
2 Steve Bedrosian .08 .25
3 Phil Bradley .08 .25
4 Jeff Calhoun .08 .25
5 Don Carman .08 .25
6 Darren Daulton .40 1.00
7 Bob Dernier .08 .25
8 Greg Gross .08 .25
9 Von Hayes .08 .25
10 Chris James .08 .25
11 Steve Jeltz .08 .25
12 Lance Parrish .20 .50
13 Shane Rawley .08 .25
14 Bruce Ruffin .08 .25
15 Juan Samuel .08 .25
16 Mike Schmidt .75 2.00
17 Rick Schu .08 .25
18 Kent Tekulve .20 .50
19 Milt Thompson .08 .25
20 Glenn Wilson .08 .25
21 Team Checklist .08 .25

1988 Starting Lineup Pirates

This 21-card set of the Pittsburgh Pirates measures approximately 2 5/8" by 3" and features colored drawings of the players on the fronts while the backs carry the player's statistics. The cards are unnumbered and checklisted below in alphabetical order.
COMPLETE SET (21) 2.50 6.00
1 Rafael Belliard .08 .25
2 Barry Bonds 1.50 4.00
3 Bobby Bonilla .20 .50
4 Sid Bream .08 .25
5 John Cangelosi .08 .25
6 Darnell Coles .08 .25
7 Mike Diaz .08 .25
8 Doug Drabek .20 .50
9 Mike Dunne .08 .25
10 Felix Fermin .08 .25
11 Brian Fisher .08 .25
12 Jim Gott .08 .25
13 Mike LaValliere .08 .25
14 Jose Lind .08 .25
15 Junior Ortiz .08 .25
16 Al Pedrique .08 .25
17 R.J. Reynolds .08 .25
18 Jeff Robinson .08 .25
19 John Smiley .20 .50
20 Andy Van Slyke .30 .75
21 Team Checklist .08 .25

1988 Starting Lineup Rangers

This 21-card set of the Texas Rangers measures approximately 2 5/8" by 3" and features colored drawings of the players on the fronts while the backs carry the player's statistics. The cards are unnumbered and checklisted below in alphabetical order.
COMPLETE SET (21) 1.50 4.00
1 Bob Brower .08 .25
2 Jerry Browne .08 .25
3 Steve Buechele .08 .25
4 Scott Fletcher .08 .25
5 Jose Guzman .08 .25
6 Charlie Hough .20 .50
7 Pete Incaviglia .20 .50
8 Oddibe McDowell .08 .25
9 Dale Mohorcic .08 .25
10 Pete O'Brien .08 .25
11 Tom O'Malley .08 .25
12 Larry Parrish .08 .25
13 Geno Petralli .08 .25
14 Jeff Russell .08 .25
15 Ruben Sierra .20 .50
16 Don Slaught .08 .25
17 Mike Stanley .08 .25
18 Curt Wilkerson .08 .25
19 Mitch Williams .20 .50
20 Bobby Witt .20 .50
21 Title Card .08 .25
Batting Order

1988 Starting Lineup Red Sox

This 21-card set of the Boston Red Sox measures approximately 2 5/8" by 3" and features colored drawings of the players on the fronts while the backs carry the player's statistics. The cards are unnumbered and checklisted below in alphabetical order.
COMPLETE SET (21) 2.50 6.00
1 Marty Barrett .08 .25
2 Todd Benzinger .08 .25
3 Wade Boggs .60 1.50
4 Oil Can Boyd .08 .25
5 Ellis Burks .60 1.50
6 Roger Clemens 1.50 4.00
7 Dwight Evans .40 1.00
8 Wes Gardner .08 .25
9 Rich Gedman .08 .25
10 Mike Greenwell .20 .50
11 Sam Horn .08 .25
12 Bruce Hurst .08 .25
13 John Marzano .08 .25
14 Spike Owen .08 .25
15 Jody Reed .08 .25
16 Jim Rice .30 .75
17 Ed Romero .08 .25
18 Kevin Romine .08 .25
19 Lee Smith .20 .50
20 Bob Stanley .08 .25
21 Team Checklist .08 .25

1988 Starting Lineup Reds

This 21-card set of the Cincinnati Reds measures approximately 2 5/8" by 3" and features colored drawings of the players on the fronts while the backs carry the player's statistics. The cards are unnumbered and checklisted below in alphabetical order.
COMPLETE SET (21) 2.00 5.00
1 Buddy Bell .20 .50
2 Tom Browning .08 .25
3 Dave Collins .08 .25
4 Dave Concepcion .30 .75
5 Kal Daniels .08 .25
6 Eric Davis .40 1.00
7 Bo Diaz .08 .25
8 Nick Esasky .08 .25
9 John Franco .40 1.00
10 Terry Francona .20 .50
11 Tracy Jones .08 .25
12 Barry Larkin .60 1.50
13 Bob Murphy .08 .25
14 Paul O'Neill .40 1.00
15 Dave Parker .30 .75
16 Ted Power .08 .25
17 Dennis Rasmussen .08 .25
18 Kurt Stillwell .08 .25
19 Jeff Treadway .08 .25
20 Frank Williams .08 .25
21 Team Checklist .08 .25

1988 Starting Lineup Royals

This 21-card set of the Kansas City Royals measures approximately 2 5/8" by 3" and features colored drawings of the players on the fronts while the backs carry the player's statistics. The cards are unnumbered and checklisted below in alphabetical order.
COMPLETE SET (21) 2.50 6.00
1 Steve Balboni .08 .25
2 George Brett 1.00 2.50
3 Jim Eisenreich .20 .50
4 Gene Garber .20 .50
5 Jerry Don Gleaton .08 .25
6 Mark Gubicza .08 .25
7 Bo Jackson .40 1.00
8 Charlie Leibrandt .08 .25
9 Mike MacFarlane .08 .25
10 Larry Owen .08 .25
11 Bill Pecota .08 .25
12 Jamie Quirk .08 .25
13 Dan Quisenberry .20 .50
14 Bret Saberhagen .30 .75
15 Kevin Seitzer .20 .50
16 Kurt Stillwell .08 .25
17 Danny Tartabull .20 .50
18 Gary Thurman .08 .25
19 Frank White .20 .50
20 Willie Wilson .20 .50
21 Team Checklist .08 .25

1988 Starting Lineup Tigers

This 21-card set of the Detroit Tigers measures approximately 2 5/8" by 3" and features colored drawings of the players on the fronts while the backs carry the player's statistics. The cards are unnumbered and checklisted below in alphabetical order.
COMPLETE SET (21) 2.00 5.00
1 Doyle Alexander .08 .25
2 Dave Bergman .08 .25
3 Tom Brookens .08 .25
4 Darrell Evans .20 .50
5 Kirk Gibson .40 1.00
6 Mike Heath .08 .25
7 Mike Henneman .30 .75
8 Guillermo Willie Hernandez .08 .25
9 Larry Herndon .08 .25
10 Eric King .08 .25
11 Ray Knight .08 .25
12 Chet Lemon .08 .25
13 Bill Madlock .20 .50
14 Jack Morris .40 1.00
15 Jim Morrison .08 .25
16 Matt Nokes .20 .50
17 Pat Sheridan .08 .25
18 Frank Tanana .20 .50
19 Alan Trammell .60 1.50
20 Lou Whitaker .40 1.00
21 Team Checklist .08 .25

1988 Starting Lineup Twins

This 21-card set of the Minnesota Twins measures approximately 2 5/8" by 3" and features colored drawings of the players on the fronts while the backs carry the player's statistics. The cards are unnumbered and checklisted below in alphabetical order.
COMPLETE SET (21) 2.00 5.00
1 Don Baylor .20 .50
2 Juan Berenguer .08 .25
3 Bert Blyleven .30 .75
4 Tom Brunansky .20 .50
5 Randy Bush .08 .25
6 Mark Davidson .08 .25
7 Gary Gaetti .30 .75
8 Greg Gagne .08 .25
9 Dan Gladden .08 .25
10 Kent Hrbek .40 1.00
11 Gene Larkin .20 .50
12 Tim Laudner .08 .25
13 Steve Lombardozzi .08 .25
14 Al Newman .08 .25
15 Kirby Puckett .75 2.00
16 Jeff Reardon .20 .50
17 Dan Schatzeder .08 .25
18 Roy Smalley .08 .25
19 Les Straker .08 .25
20 Frank Viola .30 .75
21 Team Checklist .08 .25

1988 Starting Lineup White Sox

These cards feature members of the 1988 San Diego Padres. These cards measure approximately 2 5/8" by 3" and have player photos on the front. The backs have recent seasonal statistics and some personal information. The cards are unnumbered and checklisted below in alphabetical order.
COMPLETE SET (21) 1.50 4.00
1 Harold Baines .30 .75
2 Floyd Bannister .08 .25
3 Daryl Boston .08 .25
4 Ivan Calderon .08 .25
5 Jose DeLeon .08 .25
6 Rich Dotson .08 .25
7 Carlton Fisk .60 1.50
8 Ozzie Guillen .40 1.00
9 Jerry Hairston .08 .25
10 Donnie Hill .08 .25
11 Dave LaPoint .08 .25
12 Steve Lyons .20 .50
13 Fred Manrique .08 .25
14 Dan Pasqua .08 .25
15 Gary Redus .08 .25
16 Mark Salas .08 .25
17 Ray Searage .08 .25
18 Bobby Thigpen .08 .25
19 Greg Walker .08 .25
20 Ken Williams .40 1.00
21 Team Checklist .08 .25

1988 Starting Lineup Yankees

This 21-card set of the New York Yankees measures approximately 2 5/8" by 3" and features colored drawings of the players on the fronts while the backs carry the player's statistics. The cards are unnumbered and checklisted below in alphabetical order.
COMPLETE SET (21) 2.50 6.00
1 Rick Cerone .08 .25
2 Jack Clark .20 .50
3 Pat Clements .08 .25
4 Mike Easler .08 .25
5 Ron Guidry .30 .75
6 Rickey Henderson .75 2.00
7 Tommy John .30 .75
8 Don Mattingly 1.50 4.00
9 Bobby Meacham .08 .25
10 Mike Pagliarulo .08 .25
11 Willie Randolph .20 .50
12 Rick Rhoden .08 .25
13 Dave Righetti .20 .50
14 Jerry Royster .08 .25
15 Don Slaught .08 .25
16 Tim Stoddard .08 .25
17 Wayne Tolleson .08 .25
18 Gary Ward .08 .25
19 Claudell Washington .08 .25
20 Dave Winfield .60 1.50
21 Team Checklist .08 .25

1985 George Steinbrenner Menu

Issued in the mid 1980's these cards honored some all-time Yankee greats. These cards were issued to promote George Steinbrenner's restaurant in Tampa, Florida, spring training home of the New York Yankees. Steinbrenner has also been the Yankees owner for more than two decades.
COMPLETE SET (8) 12.50 30.00
1 Yogi Berra 1.00 2.50
2 Lou Gehrig 2.00 5.00
3 Whitey Ford 1.00 2.50
4 Elston Howard .40 1.00
5 Mickey Mantle 3.00 8.00
6 Roger Maris 1.50 4.00
7 Thurman Munson .75 2.00
8 Babe Ruth 3.00 8.00

1965 Stengel Dugan Brothers

This one card set was issued to commemorate the retirement of Casey Stengel from baseball. The black and white front features him in a Mets uniform while the back contains biographical information.
1 Casey Stengel 75.00 150.00

1992 Sterling Dravecky

This Heroes of Life set measures the standard size. According to serious Dravecky collectors, so far only cards numbered 2 and 12 are known. If other cards are discovered, please let us know.
COMPLETE SET (2) 4.00 10.00
COMMON PLAYER (2/12) 2.00 5.00

1995 Stouffer Pop-ups

This five-card set was distributed by Stouffer's Frozen Foods and features small color photos of great baseball players set on a ball and glove background. When the tab at the top of the card is pulled, the player's image "pops" out. The backs carry another player photo with player information.
COMPLETE SET (5) 6.00 15.00
1 Yogi Berra 1.50 4.00
1A Yogi Berra • 25.00 60.00
Certified Auto
2 Gary Carter .75 2.00
3 Don Drysdale 1.50 4.00
4 Bob Feller 1.50 4.00
5 Willie Stargell 1.25 3.00

1997 Strat-O-Matic All-Stars

This 62-card set features small color action photos of all the players from the 1997 All-Star Game with player statistics printed on perforated cards measuring approximately 3" by 5 1/2". The backs are blank. The cards are unnumbered and checklisted below in alphabetical order.
COMPLETE SET (62) 12.50 30.00
1 Roberto Alomar .40 1.00
2 Sandy Alomar .08 .25
3 Moises Alou .30 .75
4 Brady Anderson .20 .50
5 Jeff Bagwell .50 1.25
6 Rod Beck .08 .25
7 Albert Belle .20 .50
8 Craig Biggio .40 1.00
9 Jeff Blauser .08 .25
10 Barry Bonds .75 2.00
11 Kevin Brown .30 .75
12 Ken Caminiti .40 1.00
13 Jeff Cirillo .08 .25
14 Royce Clayton .08 .25
15 Roger Clemens 1.00 2.50
16 David Cone .30 .75
17 Joey Cora .08 .25
18 Jason Dickson .08 .25
19 Shawn Estes .08 .25
20 Steve Finley .20 .50
21 Andres Galarraga .40 1.00
22 Nomar Garciaparra 1.25 3.00
23 Tom Glavine .50 1.25
24 Mark Grace .30 .75
25 Ken Griffey Jr. 1.50 4.00
26 Tony Gwynn 1.00 2.50
27 Pat Hentgen .20 .50
28 Todd Hundley .20 .50
29 Charles Johnson .08 .25
30 Randy Johnson .60 1.50
31 Bobby Jones .08 .25
32 Chipper Jones 1.00 2.50
33 Dave Justice .40 1.00
34 Jimmy Key .20 .50
35 Darryl Kile .08 .25
36 Chuck Knoblauch .40 1.00
37 Ray Lankford .20 .50
38 Barry Larkin .40 1.00
39 Kenny Lofton .30 .75
40 Javy Lopez .20 .50
41 Greg Maddux 1.25 3.00
42 Edgar Martinez .30 .75
43 Pedro Martinez .50 1.25
44 Tino Martinez .40 1.00
45 Mark McGwire 1.00 2.50
46 Mike Mussina .40 1.00
47 Randy Myers .08 .25
48 Denny Neagle .08 .25
49 Paul O'Neill .20 .50
50 Mike Piazza 1.25 3.00
51 Cal Ripken 2.00 5.00
52 Mariano Rivera .50 1.25
53 Alex Rodriguez 1.25 3.00
54 Ivan Rodriguez .50 1.25
55 Jose Rosado .08 .25
56 Curt Schilling .50 1.25
57 Frank Thomas .50 1.25
58 Jim Thome .50 1.25
59 Justin Thompson .08 .25
60 Larry Walker .50 1.25
61 Bernie Williams .40 1.00
62 Tony Womack .08 .25

1987 Stuart Panels

Subtitled "Super Stars" in English and French, this set consists of 28 four-part perforated panels each featuring three players from the same team and a contest entry card. All 26 teams are included at least once; the Montreal Expos and Toronto Blue Jays each have two panels. Printed on white stock, the four-part panels measure 10 1/8" by 3 7/16"; each card measures 2 1/2" by 3 7/16". The fronts feature color player headshots with white stars on a blue field on each side of the photo. The player's name, along with bilingual team name and position, appear at the bottom, below a crossed bats and baseballs icon. The plain white back carries the player's bilingual biography and 1986 statistics. Team insignias are not shown on the cards because the set was licensed only by the Major League Baseball Players Association. The set is priced below as panels because that is the way the cards are typically found and because the three player cards on each panel carry the same number (No. X de/of 28) on the back.
COMPLETE SET (28) 40.00 100.00
1 Darryl Strawberry 2.00 5.00
Keith Hernandez
Gary Carter
2 Bruce Benedict 1.25 3.00
Ken Griffey Sr.
Dale Murphy
3 Leon Durham 1.25 3.00
Jody Davis
Andre Dawson
4 Buddy Bell 1.25 3.00
Dave Parker
Eric Davis
5 Mike Scott 4.00 10.00
Nolan Ryan
Glenn Davis
6 Mike Marshall .75 2.00
Fernando Valenzuela
Pedro Guerrero
7 Mitch Webster 1.25 3.00
Tim Wallach
Tim Raines
8 Bryn Smith .75 2.00
Hubie Brooks
Floyd Youmans
9 Juan Samuel 1.50 4.00
Shane Rawley
Mike Schmidt
10 Jim Morrison .75 2.00
R.J. Reynolds
Johnny Ray
11 Ozzie Smith 3.00 8.00
Vince Coleman
Jack Clark
12 John Kruk 3.00 8.00
Tony Gwynn
Steve Garvey
13 Robby Thompson 1.25 3.00
Jeffrey Leonard
Chili Davis
14 Fred Lynn 4.00 10.00
Eddie Murray
Cal Ripken
15 Roger Clemens 3.00 8.00
Wade Boggs
Don Baylor
16 Mike Witt .75 2.00
Wally Joyner
Doug DeCinces
17 Ozzie Guillen 1.50 4.00
Carlton Fisk
Harold Baines
18 Joe Carter .75 2.00
Julio Franco
Pat Tabler
19 Kirk Gibson 1.50 4.00
Alan Trammell
Jack Morris
20 Willie Wilson 3.00 8.00
Bret Saberhagen
George Brett
21 Paul Molitor 3.00 8.00
Robin Yount
Cecil Cooper
22 Kirby Puckett 3.00 8.00
Kent Hrbek
Tom Brunansky
23 Dave Winfield 4.00 10.00
Don Mattingly
Rickey Henderson
24 Alfredo Griffin 1.25 3.00
Carney Lansford
Jose Canseco
25 Mark Langston .75 2.00
Phil Bradley
Alvin Davis
26 Larry Parrish .75 2.00
Pete O'Brien
Pete Incaviglia
27 George Bell 1.25 3.00
Tony Fernandez
Jesse Barfield
28 Ernie Whitt 1.25 3.00
Lloyd Moseby
Dave Stieb

1991 Studio Previews

COMPLETE SET (18) 12.50 30.00
FOUR PER DONRUSS RETAIL FACT.SET
1 Juan Bell .40 1.00
2 Roger Clemens 6.00 15.00
3 Dave Parker .75 2.00
4 Tim Raines .75 2.00
5 Kevin Seitzer .40 1.00
6 Ted Higuera .40 1.00
7 Bernie Williams 2.50 6.00
8 Harold Baines .75 2.00
9 Gary Pettis .40 1.00
10 David Justice .75 2.00
11 Eric Davis .75 2.00
12 Andujar Cedeno .40 1.00
13 Tom Foley .40 1.00
14 Dwight Gooden .75 2.00
15 Doug Drabek .40 1.00
16 Steve Decker .40 1.00
17 Joe Torre MG .75 2.00
NNO Title Card .40 1.00

1991 Studio

The 1991 Studio set, issued by Donruss/Leaf, contains 264 standard-size cards issued in one series. Cards were distributed in foil packs each of which contained one of 21 different Rod Carew puzzle panels. The Studio card fronts feature posed black and white head-and-shoulders player photos with mauve borders. The team logo, player's name, and position appear along the bottom of the card face. The cards are ordered alphabetically within and according to teams for each league with American League teams preceding National League. Rookie Cards in the set include Jeff Bagwell, Jeff Conine and Brian McRae.
COMPLETE SET (264) 8.00 20.00
1 Glenn Davis .02 .10
2 Dwight Evans .08 .25
3 Leo Gomez .02 .10
4 Chris Hoiles .02 .10
5 Sam Horn .02 .10
6 Ben McDonald .02 .10
7 Randy Milligan .02 .10
8 Gregg Olson .02 .10
9 Cal Ripken .60 1.50
10 David Segui .02 .10
11 Wade Boggs .08 .25
12 Ellis Burks .05 .15
13 Jack Clark .05 .15
14 Roger Clemens .60 1.50
15 Mike Greenwell .02 .10
16 Tim Naehring .02 .10
17 Tony Pena .02 .10
18 Phil Plantier RC .02 .10
19 Jeff Reardon .05 .15
20 Mo Vaughn .05 .15
21 Jimmie Reese CO .05 .15
22 Jim Abbott UER .08 .25
Born in 1967, not 1969
23 Bert Blyleven .05 .15
24 Chuck Finley .05 .15
25 Gary Gaetti .05 .15
26 Wally Joyner .05 .15
27 Mark Langston .02 .10
28 Kirk McCaskill .02 .10
29 Lance Parrish .05 .15
30 Dave Winfield .05 .15
31 Alex Fernandez .02 .10
32 Carlton Fisk .08 .25
33 Scott Fletcher .02 .10
34 Greg Hibbard .02 .10
35 Charlie Hough .05 .15
36 Jack McDowell .02 .10
37 Tim Raines .05 .15
38 Sammy Sosa .20 .50
39 Bobby Thigpen .02 .10
40 Frank Thomas .20 .50
41 Sandy Alomar Jr. .02 .10
42 John Farrell .02 .10
43 Glenallen Hill .02 .10
44 Brook Jacoby .02 .10
45 Chris James .02 .10
46 Doug Jones .02 .10
47 Eric King .02 .10
48 Mark Lewis .02 .10
49 Greg Swindell UER .02 .10
Photo actually
Turner Ward
50 Mark Whiten .02 .10
51 Milt Cuyler .02 .10
52 Rob Deer .02 .10
53 Cecil Fielder .05 .15
54 Travis Fryman .05 .15
55 Bill Gullickson .02 .10
56 Lloyd Moseby .02 .10
57 Frank Tanana .02 .10
58 Mickey Tettleton .02 .10
59 Alan Trammell .05 .15
60 Lou Whitaker .05 .15
61 Mike Boddicker .02 .10
62 George Brett .50 1.25
63 Jeff Conine RC .20 .50
64 Warren Cromartie .02 .10
65 Storm Davis .02 .10
66 Kirk Gibson .05 .15
67 Mark Gubicza .02 .10
68 Brian McRae RC .05 .15
69 Bret Saberhagen .05 .15
70 Kurt Stillwell .02 .10
71 Tim McIntosh .02 .10
72 Candy Maldonado .02 .10
73 Paul Molitor .05 .15
74 Willie Randolph .05 .15
75 Ron Robinson .02 .10
76 Gary Sheffield .05 .15
77 Franklin Stubbs .02 .10
78 B.J. Surhoff .05 .15
79 Greg Vaughn .02 .10
80 Robin Yount .30 .75
81 Rick Aguilera .05 .15
82 Steve Bedrosian .02 .10
83 Scott Erickson .02 .10
84 Greg Gagne .02 .10
85 Dan Gladden .02 .10
86 Brian Harper .02 .10
87 Kent Hrbek .05 .15
88 Shane Mack .02 .10
89 Jack Morris .05 .15
90 Kirby Puckett .20 .50
91 Jesse Barfield .02 .10
92 Steve Farr .02 .10
93 Steve Howe .02 .10
94 Roberto Kelly .02 .10
95 Tim Leary .02 .10
96 Kevin Maas .02 .10
97 Don Mattingly .50 1.25
98 Hensley Meulens .02 .10
99 Scott Sanderson .02 .10
100 Steve Sax .02 .10
101 Jose Canseco .08 .25
102 Dennis Eckersley .05 .15
103 Dave Henderson .02 .10
104 Rickey Henderson .20 .50
105 Rick Honeycutt .02 .10
106 Mark McGwire .60 1.50
107 Dave Stewart UER .05 .15
No-hitter against
Toronto& not Texas
108 Eric Show .02 .10
109 Todd Van Poppel RC .02 .10
110 Bob Welch .02 .10
111 Alvin Davis .02 .10
112 Ken Griffey Jr. .50 1.25
113 Ken Griffey Sr. .05 .15
114 Erik Hanson UER .02 .10
Misspelled Eric
115 Brian Holman .02 .10
116 Randy Johnson .25 .60
117 Edgar Martinez .08 .25
118 Tino Martinez .20 .50
119 Harold Reynolds .05 .15
120 David Valle .02 .10
121 Kevin Belcher RC .02 .10
122 Scott Chiamparino .02 .10
123 Julio Franco .05 .15
124 Juan Gonzalez .20 .50
125 Rich Gossage .05 .15
126 Jeff Kunkel .02 .10
127 Rafael Palmeiro .08 .25
128 Nolan Ryan .75 2.00
129 Ruben Sierra .05 .15
130 Bobby Witt .02 .10
131 Roberto Alomar .08 .25
132 Tom Candiotti .02 .10
133 Joe Carter .05 .15
134 Ken Dayley .02 .10
135 Kelly Gruber .02 .10
136 John Olerud .05 .15
137 Dave Stieb .02 .10
138 Turner Ward RC .05 .15
139 Devon White .05 .15
140 Mookie Wilson .05 .15
141 Steve Avery .02 .10
142 Sid Bream .02 .10
143 Nick Esasky UER .02 .10
Homers abbreviated RH
144 Ron Gant .05 .15
145 Tom Glavine .08 .25
146 David Justice .05 .15
147 Kelly Mann .02 .10
148 Terry Pendleton .05 .15
149 John Smoltz .08 .25
150 Jeff Treadway .02 .10
151 George Bell .02 .10
152 Shawn Boskie .02 .10
153 Andre Dawson .05 .15
154 Lance Dickson RC .02 .10
155 Shawon Dunston .02 .10
156 Joe Girardi .02 .10
157 Mark Grace .08 .25
158 Ryne Sandberg .30 .75
159 Gary Scott RC .02 .10
160 Dave Smith .02 .10
161 Tom Browning .02 .10
162 Eric Davis .05 .15
163 Rob Dibble .05 .15
164 Mariano Duncan .02 .10
165 Chris Hammond .02 .10
166 Billy Hatcher .02 .10
167 Barry Larkin .08 .25
168 Hal Morris .02 .10
169 Paul O'Neill .08 .25
170 Chris Sabo .02 .10
171 Eric Anthony .02 .10
172 Jeff Bagwell RC 1.00 2.50
173 Craig Biggio .08 .25
174 Ken Caminiti .05 .15
175 Jim Deshaies .02 .10
176 Steve Finley .05 .15
177 Pete Harnisch .02 .10
178 Darryl Kile .05 .15
179 Curt Schilling .20 .50
180 Mike Scott .02 .10
181 Brett Butler .05 .15
182 Gary Carter .05 .15
183 Orel Hershiser .05 .15
184 Ramon Martinez .02 .10
185 Eddie Murray .20 .50
186 Jose Offerman .02 .10
187 Bob Ojeda .02 .10
188 Juan Samuel .02 .10
189 Mike Scioscia .02 .10
190 Darryl Strawberry .05 .15
191 Moises Alou .05 .15
192 Brian Barnes RC .02 .10
193 Oil Can Boyd .02 .10
194 Ivan Calderon .02 .10
195 Delino DeShields .05 .15
196 Mike Fitzgerald .02 .10
197 Andres Galarraga .05 .15
198 Marquis Grissom .05 .15
199 Bill Sampen .02 .10
200 Tim Wallach .02 .10
201 Daryl Boston .02 .10
202 Vince Coleman .02 .10
203 John Franco .05 .15
204 Dwight Gooden .05 .15
205 Tom Herr .02 .10
206 Gregg Jefferies .02 .10
207 Howard Johnson .02 .10
208 Dave Magadan UER .02 .10
Born 1862&
should be 1962
209 Kevin McReynolds .02 .10
210 Frank Viola .05 .15
211 Wes Chamberlain RC .02 .10
212 Darren Daulton .05 .15
213 Len Dykstra .05 .15
214 Charlie Hayes .02 .10
215 Ricky Jordan .02 .10
216 Steve Lake .02 .10
Pictured with parrot
on his shoulder

217 Roger McDowell .02 .10
218 Mickey Morandini .02 .10
219 Terry Mulholland .02 .10
220 Dale Murphy .08 .25
221 Jay Bell .05 .15
222 Barry Bonds .60 1.50
223 Bobby Bonilla .05 .15
224 Doug Drabek .02 .10
225 Bill Landrum .02 .10
226 Mike LaValliere .02 .10
227 Jose Lind .02 .10
228 Don Slaught .02 .10
229 John Smiley .02 .10
230 Andy Van Slyke .08 .25
231 Bernard Gilkey .02 .10
232 Pedro Guerrero .05 .15
233 Rex Hudler .02 .10
234 Ray Lankford .05 .15
235 Joe Magrane .02 .10
236 Jose Oquendo .02 .10
237 Lee Smith .05 .15
238 Ozzie Smith .30 .75
239 Milt Thompson .02 .10
240 Todd Zeile .02 .10
241 Larry Andersen .02 .10
242 Andy Benes .02 .10
243 Paul Faries RC .02 .10
244 Tony Fernandez .02 .10
245 Tony Gwynn .25 .60
246 Atlee Hammaker .02 .10
247 Fred McGriff .08 .25
248 Bip Roberts .02 .10
249 Benito Santiago .05 .15
250 Ed Whitson .02 .10
251 Dave Anderson .02 .10
252 Mike Benjamin .02 .10
253 John Burkett UER .02 .10
Front photo actually
Trevor Wilson
254 Will Clark .08 .25
255 Scott Garrelts .02 .10
256 Willie McGee .05 .15
257 Kevin Mitchell .02 .10
258 Dave Righetti .05 .15
259 Matt Williams .05 .15
260 Bud Black .02 .10
Steve Decker
261 S.Anderson MG CL .05 .15
262 Tom Lasorda MG CL .08 .25
263 Tony LaRussa MG CL .05 .15
NNO Title Card .02 .10

1992 Studio Previews

COMPLETE SET (22) 100.00 200.00
COMMON PLAYER (1-22) .80 2.00
COMMON SP
1 Ruben Sierra 1.25 3.00
2 Kirby Puckett 4.00 10.00
3 Ryne Sandberg 5.00 12.00
4 John Kruk 1.25 3.00
5 Cal Ripken 12.50 30.00
6 Robin Yount 3.00 8.00
7 Dwight Gooden 1.25 3.00
8 David Justice 2.00 5.00
9 Don Mattingly 6.00 15.00
10 Wally Joyner 1.25 3.00
11 Will Clark 2.00 5.00
12 Rob Dibble 1.25 3.00
13 Roberto Alomar SP 8.00 20.00
14 Wade Boggs 3.00 8.00
15 Barry Bonds 6.00 15.00
16 Jeff Bagwell 3.00 8.00
17 Mark McGwire 6.00 15.00
18 Frank Thomas 3.00 8.00
19 Brett Butler 1.25 3.00
20 Ozzie Smith SP 10.00 25.00
21 Jim Abbott 1.25 3.00
22 Tony Gwynn 6.00 15.00

1992 Studio

The 1992 Studio set consists of ten players from each of the 26 major league teams, three checklists, and an introduction card for a total of 264 standard-size cards. The key Rookie Cards in this set are Chad Curtis and Brian Jordan.

COMPLETE SET (264) 6.00 15.00
1 Steve Avery .02 .10
2 Sid Bream .02 .10
3 Ron Gant .05 .15
4 Tom Glavine .08 .25
5 David Justice .08 .25
6 Mark Lemke .02 .10
7 Greg Olson .02 .10
8 Terry Pendleton .05 .15
9 Deion Sanders .08 .25
10 John Smoltz .08 .25
11 Doug Dascenzo .02 .10
12 Andre Dawson .05 .15
13 Joe Girardi .02 .10
14 Mark Grace .08 .25
15 Greg Maddux .25 .60
16 Chuck McElroy .02 .10
17 Mike Morgan .02 .10
18 Ryne Sandberg .25 .60
19 Gary Scott .02 .10
20 Sammy Sosa .15 .40
21 Norm Charlton .02 .10
22 Rob Dibble .05 .15
23 Barry Larkin .08 .25
24 Hal Morris .02 .10
25 Paul O'Neill .08 .25
26 Jose Rijo .02 .10
27 Bip Roberts .02 .10
28 Chris Sabo .02 .10
29 Reggie Sanders .05 .15
30 Greg Swindell .02 .10
31 Jeff Bagwell .15 .40
32 Craig Biggio .08 .25
33 Ken Caminiti .05 .15
34 Andujar Cedeno .02 .10
35 Steve Finley .05 .15
36 Pete Harnisch .02 .10
37 Butch Henry RC .02 .10
38 Doug Jones .02 .10
39 Darryl Kile .05 .15
40 Eddie Taubensee RC .08 .25
41 Brett Butler .05 .15
42 Tom Candiotti .02 .10
43 Eric Davis .05 .15
44 Orel Hershiser .05 .15
45 Eric Karros .05 .15
46 Ramon Martinez .02 .10
47 Jose Offerman .02 .10
48 Mike Scioscia .02 .10
49 Mike Sharperson .02 .10
50 Darryl Strawberry .05 .15
51 Bret Barberie .02 .10
52 Ivan Calderon .02 .10
53 Gary Carter .05 .15
54 Delino DeShields .02 .10
55 Marquis Grissom .05 .15
56 Ken Hill .02 .10
57 Dennis Martinez .05 .15
58 Spike Owen .02 .10
59 Larry Walker .08 .25
60 Tim Wallach .02 .10
61 Bobby Bonilla .05 .15
62 Tim Burke .02 .10
63 Vince Coleman .02 .10
64 John Franco .05 .15
65 Dwight Gooden .05 .15
66 Todd Hundley .05 .15
67 Howard Johnson .02 .10
68 Eddie Murray .15 .40
69 Bret Saberhagen .05 .15
70 Anthony Young .02 .10
71 Kim Batiste .02 .10
72 Wes Chamberlain .02 .10
73 Darren Daulton .05 .15
74 Mariano Duncan .02 .10
75 Len Dykstra .05 .15
76 John Kruk .05 .15
77 Mickey Morandini .02 .10
78 Terry Mulholland .02 .10
79 Dale Murphy .08 .25
80 Mitch Williams .02 .10
81 Jay Bell .05 .15
82 Barry Bonds .60 1.50
83 Steve Buechele .02 .10
84 Doug Drabek .02 .10
85 Mike LaValliere .02 .10
86 Jose Lind .02 .10
87 Denny Neagle .05 .15
88 Randy Tomlin .02 .10
89 Andy Van Slyke .08 .25
90 Gary Varsho .02 .10
91 Pedro Guerrero .05 .15
92 Rex Hudler .02 .10
93 Brian Jordan RC .20 .50
94 Felix Jose .02 .10
95 Donovan Osborne .02 .10
96 Tom Pagnozzi .02 .10
97 Lee Smith .05 .15
98 Ozzie Smith .25 .60
99 Todd Worrell .02 .10
100 Todd Zeile .02 .10
101 Andy Benes .02 .10
102 Jerald Clark .02 .10
103 Tony Fernandez .02 .10
104 Tony Gwynn .20 .50
105 Greg W. Harris .02 .10
106 Fred McGriff .08 .25
107 Benito Santiago .05 .15
108 Gary Sheffield .05 .15
109 Kurt Stillwell .02 .10
110 Tim Teufel .02 .10
111 Kevin Bass .02 .10
112 Jeff Brantley .02 .10
113 John Burkett .02 .10
114 Will Clark .08 .25
115 Royce Clayton .02 .10
116 Mike Jackson .02 .10
117 Darren Lewis .02 .10
118 Bill Swift .02 .10
119 Robby Thompson .02 .10
120 Matt Williams .05 .15
121 Brady Anderson .05 .15
122 Glenn Davis .02 .10
123 Mike Devereaux .02 .10
124 Chris Hoiles .02 .10
125 Sam Horn .02 .10
126 Ben McDonald .02 .10
127 Mike Mussina .15 .40
128 Gregg Olson .02 .10
129 Cal Ripken .50 1.25
130 Rick Sutcliffe .05 .15
131 Wade Boggs .08 .25
132 Roger Clemens .30 .75
133 Greg A. Harris .02 .10
134 Tim Naehring .02 .10
135 Tony Pena .02 .10
136 Phil Plantier .02 .10
137 Jeff Reardon .05 .15
138 Jody Reed .02 .10
139 Mo Vaughn .05 .15
140 Frank Viola .05 .15
141 Jim Abbott .08 .25
142 Hubie Brooks .02 .10
143 Chad Curtis RC .08 .25
144 Gary DiSarcina .02 .10
145 Chuck Finley .05 .15
146 Bryan Harvey .02 .10
147 Von Hayes .02 .10
148 Mark Langston .02 .10
149 Lance Parrish .05 .15
150 Lee Stevens .02 .10
151 George Bell .02 .10
152 Alex Fernandez .02 .10
153 Greg Hibbard .02 .10
154 Lance Johnson .02 .10
155 Kirk McCaskill .02 .10
156 Tim Raines .05 .15
157 Steve Sax .02 .10
158 Bobby Thigpen .02 .10
159 Frank Thomas .15 .40
160 Robin Ventura .05 .15
161 Sandy Alomar Jr. .02 .10
162 Jack Armstrong .02 .10
163 Carlos Baerga .02 .10
164 Albert Belle .05 .15
165 Alex Cole .02 .10
166 Glenallen Hill .02 .10
167 Mark Lewis .02 .10
168 Kenny Lofton .08 .25
169 Paul Sorrento .02 .10
170 Mark Whiten .02 .10
171 Milt Cuyler .02 .10
172 Rob Deer .02 .10
173 Cecil Fielder .05 .15
174 Travis Fryman .05 .15
175 Mike Henneman .02 .10
176 Tony Phillips .02 .10
177 Frank Tanana .02 .10
178 Mickey Tettleton .02 .10
179 Alan Trammell .05 .15
180 Lou Whitaker .05 .15
181 George Brett .40 1.00
182 Tom Gordon .02 .10
183 Mark Gubicza .02 .10
184 Gregg Jefferies .02 .10
185 Wally Joyner .05 .15
186 Brent Mayne .02 .10
187 Brian McRae .02 .10
188 Kevin McReynolds .02 .10
189 Keith Miller .02 .10
190 Jeff Montgomery .02 .10
191 Dante Bichette .05 .15
192 Ricky Bones .02 .10
193 Scott Fletcher .02 .10
194 Paul Molitor .05 .15
195 Jaime Navarro .02 .10
196 Franklin Stubbs .02 .10
197 B.J. Surhoff .05 .15
198 Greg Vaughn .02 .10
199 Bill Wegman .02 .10
200 Robin Yount .25 .60
201 Rick Aguilera .05 .15
202 Scott Erickson .02 .10
203 Greg Gagne .02 .10
204 Brian Harper .02 .10
205 Kent Hrbek .05 .15
206 Scott Leius .02 .10
207 Shane Mack .02 .10
208 Pat Mahomes RC .08 .25
209 Kirby Puckett .15 .40
210 John Smiley .02 .10
211 Mike Gallego .02 .10
212 Charlie Hayes .02 .10
213 Pat Kelly .02 .10
214 Roberto Kelly .02 .10
215 Kevin Maas .02 .10
216 Don Mattingly .40 1.00
217 Matt Nokes .02 .10
218 Melido Perez .02 .10
219 Scott Sanderson .02 .10
220 Danny Tartabull .02 .10
221 Harold Baines .05 .15
222 Jose Canseco .08 .25
223 Dennis Eckersley .05 .15
224 Dave Henderson .02 .10
225 Carney Lansford .05 .15
226 Mark McGwire .40 1.00
227 Mike Moore .02 .10
228 Randy Ready .02 .10
229 Terry Steinbach .02 .10
230 Dave Stewart .05 .15
231 Jay Buhner .05 .15
232 Ken Griffey Jr. .30 .75
233 Erik Hanson .02 .10
234 Randy Johnson .15 .40
235 Edgar Martinez .08 .25
236 Tino Martinez .08 .25
237 Kevin Mitchell .02 .10
238 Pete O'Brien .02 .10
239 Harold Reynolds .05 .15
240 David Valle .02 .10
241 Julio Franco .05 .15
242 Juan Gonzalez .08 .25
243 Jose Guzman .02 .10
244 Rafael Palmeiro .08 .25
245 Dean Palmer .05 .15
246 Ivan Rodriguez .15 .40
247 Jeff Russell .02 .10
248 Nolan Ryan .60 1.50
249 Ruben Sierra .05 .15
250 Dickie Thon .02 .10
251 Roberto Alomar .08 .25
252 Derek Bell .05 .15
253 Pat Borders .02 .10
254 Joe Carter .05 .15
255 Kelly Gruber .02 .10
256 Juan Guzman .02 .10
257 Jack Morris .05 .15
258 John Olerud .05 .15
259 Devon White .05 .15
260 Dave Winfield .05 .15
261 Checklist .02 .10
262 Checklist .02 .10
263 Checklist .02 .10
264 History Card .02 .10

1992 Studio Heritage

COMPLETE SET (14) 10.00 25.00
COMP.FOIL SET (8) 6.00 15.00
COMP.JUMBO SET (6) 4.00 10.00
FOIL: RAND.INSERTS IN FOIL PACKS
JUMBO'S: ONE PER JUMBO PACK
BC1 Ryne Sandberg 1.25 3.00
BC2 Carlton Fisk .75 2.00
BC3 Wade Boggs .50 1.25
BC4 Jose Canseco .50 1.25
BC5 Don Mattingly 2.00 5.00
BC6 Darryl Strawberry .30 .75
BC7 Cal Ripken 2.50 6.00
BC8 Will Clark .50 1.25
BC9 Andre Dawson .30 .75
BC10 Andy Van Slyke/1960 Pirates .50 1.25
BC11 Paul Molitor .30 .75
BC12 Jeff Bagwell .75 2.00
BC13 Darren Daulton .30 .75
BC14 Kirby Puckett .75 2.00

1993 Studio Promo

COMPLETE SET 2.00 5.00
176 Ryne Sandberg 2.00 5.00

1993 Studio

The 220 standard-size cards comprising this set feature borderless fronts with posed color player photos that are cut out and superposed upon a closeup of an embroidered team logo. The key Rookie Card in this set is J.T. Snow.

COMPLETE SET (220) 6.00 15.00
1 Dennis Eckersley .08 .25
2 Chad Curtis .05 .15
3 Eric Anthony .05 .15
4 Roberto Alomar .15 .40
5 Steve Avery .05 .15
6 Cal Eldred .05 .15
7 Bernard Gilkey .05 .15
8 Steve Buechele .05 .15
9 Brett Butler .08 .25
10 Terry Mulholland .05 .15
11 Moises Alou .08 .25
12 Barry Bonds .60 1.50
13 Sandy Alomar Jr. .05 .15
14 Chris Bosio .05 .15
15 Scott Sanderson .05 .15
16 Bobby Bonilla .08 .25
17 Brady Anderson .08 .25
18 Derek Bell .05 .15
19 Wes Chamberlain .05 .15
20 Jay Bell .08 .25
21 Kevin Brown .08 .25
22 Roger Clemens .50 1.25
23 Roberto Kelly .05 .15
24 Dante Bichette .08 .25
25 George Brett .60 1.50
26 Rob Deer .05 .15
27 Brian Harper .05 .15
28 George Bell .05 .15
29 Jim Abbott .15 .40
30 Dave Henderson .05 .15
31 Wade Boggs .15 .40
32 Chili Davis .08 .25
33 Ellis Burks .08 .25
34 Jeff Bagwell .15 .40
35 Kent Hrbek .08 .25
36 Pat Borders .05 .15
37 Cecil Fielder .08 .25
38 Sid Bream .05 .15
39 Greg Gagne .05 .15
40 Darryl Hamilton .05 .15
41 Jerald Clark .05 .15
42 Mark Grace .15 .40
43 Barry Larkin .15 .40
44 John Burkett .05 .15
45 Scott Cooper .05 .15
46 Mike Lansing RC .08 .25
47 Jose Canseco .15 .40
48 Will Clark .15 .40
49 Carlos Garcia .05 .15
50 Carlos Baerga .05 .15
51 Darren Daulton .08 .25
52 Jay Buhner .08 .25
53 Andy Benes .05 .15
54 Jeff Conine .08 .25
55 Mike Devereaux .05 .15
56 Vince Coleman .05 .15
57 Terry Steinbach .05 .15
58 J.T.Snow RC .15 .40
59 Greg Swindell .05 .15
60 Devon White .08 .25
61 John Smoltz .15 .40
62 Todd Zeile .05 .15
63 Rick Wilkins .05 .15
64 Tim Wallach .05 .15
65 John Wetteland .08 .25
66 Matt Williams .08 .25
67 Paul Sorrento .05 .15
68 David Valle .05 .15
69 Walt Weiss .05 .15
70 John Franco .08 .25
71 Nolan Ryan 1.00 2.50
72 Frank Viola .08 .25
73 Chris Sabo .05 .15
74 David Nied .05 .15
75 Kevin McReynolds .05 .15
76 Lou Whitaker .08 .25
77 Dave Winfield .08 .25
78 Robin Ventura .08 .25
79 Spike Owen .05 .15
80 Cal Ripken .75 2.00
81 Dan Walters .05 .15
82 Mitch Williams .05 .15
83 Tim Wakefield .25 .60
84 Rickey Henderson .25 .60
85 Gary DiSarcina .05 .15
86 Craig Biggio .15 .40
87 Joe Carter .08 .25
88 Ron Gant .08 .25
89 John Jaha .05 .15
90 Gregg Jefferies .05 .15
91 Jose Guzman .05 .15
92 Eric Karros .08 .25
93 Wil Cordero .05 .15
94 Royce Clayton .05 .15
95 Albert Belle .08 .25
96 Ken Griffey Jr. .50 1.25
97 Orestes Destrade .05 .15
98 Tony Fernandez .05 .15
99 Leo Gomez .05 .15
100 Tony Gwynn .30 .75
101 Len Dykstra .08 .25
102 Jeff King .05 .15
103 Julio Franco .08 .25
104 Andre Dawson .08 .25
105 Randy Milligan .05 .15
106 Alex Cole .05 .15
107 Phil Hiatt .05 .15
108 Travis Fryman .08 .25
109 Chuck Knoblauch .08 .25
110 Bo Jackson .25 .60
111 Pat Kelly .05 .15
112 Bret Saberhagen .08 .25
113 Ruben Sierra .08 .25
114 Tim Salmon .15 .40
115 Doug Jones .05 .15
116 Ed Sprague .05 .15
117 Terry Pendleton .08 .25
118 Robin Yount .40 1.00
119 Mark Whiten .05 .15
120 Checklist 1-110 .05 .15
121 Sammy Sosa .25 .60
122 Darryl Strawberry .08 .25
123 Larry Walker .08 .25
124 Robby Thompson .05 .15
125 Carlos Martinez .05 .15
126 Edgar Martinez .15 .40
127 Benito Santiago .08 .25
128 Howard Johnson .05 .15
129 Harold Reynolds .08 .25
130 Craig Shipley .05 .15
131 Curt Schilling .08 .25
132 Andy Van Slyke .15 .40
133 Ivan Rodriguez .15 .40
134 Mo Vaughn .08 .25
135 Bip Roberts .05 .15
136 Charlie Hayes .05 .15
137 Brian McRae .05 .15
138 Mickey Tettleton .05 .15
139 Frank Thomas .25 .60
140 Paul O'Neill .15 .40
141 Mark McGwire .60 1.50
142 Damion Easley .05 .15
143 Ken Caminiti .08 .25
144 Juan Guzman .05 .15
145 Tom Glavine .15 .40
146 Pat Listach .05 .15
147 Lee Smith .08 .25
148 Derrick May .05 .15
149 Ramon Martinez .05 .15
150 Delino DeShields .05 .15
151 Kirt Manwaring .05 .15
152 Reggie Jefferson .05 .15
153 Randy Johnson .25 .60
154 Dave Magadan .05 .15
155 Dwight Gooden .08 .25
156 Chris Hoiles .05 .15
157 Fred McGriff .15 .40
158 Dave Hollins .05 .15
159 Al Martin .05 .15
160 Juan Gonzalez .08 .25
161 Mike Greenwell .05 .15
162 Kevin Mitchell .05 .15
163 Andres Galarraga .08 .25
164 Wally Joyner .08 .25
165 Kirk Gibson .08 .25
166 Pedro Munoz .05 .15
167 Ozzie Guillen .08 .25
168 Jimmy Key .08 .25
169 Kevin Seitzer .05 .15
170 Luis Polonia .05 .15
171 Luis Gonzalez .08 .25
172 Paul Molitor .08 .25
173 David Justice .08 .25
174 B.J. Surhoff .08 .25
175 Ray Lankford .08 .25
176 Ryne Sandberg .40 1.00
177 Jody Reed .05 .15
178 Marquis Grissom .08 .25
179 Willie McGee .08 .25
180 Kenny Lofton .08 .25
181 Junior Felix .05 .15
182 Jose Offerman .08 .25
183 John Kruk .08 .25
184 Orlando Merced .05 .15
185 Rafael Palmeiro .15 .40
186 Billy Hatcher .05 .15
187 Joe Oliver .05 .15
188 Joe Girardi .05 .15
189 Jose Lind .05 .15
190 Harold Baines .08 .25
191 Mike Pagliarulo .05 .15
192 Lance Johnson .05 .15
193 Don Mattingly .60 1.50
194 Doug Drabek .05 .15
195 John Olerud .08 .25
196 Greg Maddux .40 1.00
197 Greg Vaughn .05 .15
198 Tom Pagnozzi .05 .15
199 Willie Wilson .05 .15
200 Jack McDowell .05 .15
201 Mike Piazza 1.25 3.00
202 Mike Mussina .15 .40
203 Charles Nagy .05 .15
204 Tino Martinez .15 .40
205 Charlie Hough .08 .25
206 Todd Hundley .05 .15
207 Gary Sheffield .08 .25
208 Mickey Morandini .05 .15
209 Don Slaught .05 .15
210 Dean Palmer .08 .25
211 Jose Rijo .05 .15
212 Vinny Castilla .25 .60
213 Tony Phillips .05 .15
214 Kirby Puckett .25 .60
215 Tim Raines .08 .25
216 Otis Nixon .05 .15
217 Ozzie Smith .40 1.00
218 Jose Vizcaino .05 .15
219 Randy Tomlin .05 .15
220 Checklist 111-220 .05 .15

1993 Studio Heritage

COMPLETE SET (12) 12.50 30.00
RANDOM INSERTS IN ALL PACKS
1 George Brett 4.00 10.00
2 Juan Gonzalez .60 1.50
3 Roger Clemens 3.00 8.00
4 Mark McGwire 4.00 10.00
5 Mark Grace 1.00 2.50
6 Ozzie Smith 2.50 6.00
7 Barry Larkin 1.00 2.50
8 Frank Thomas 1.50 4.00
9 Carlos Baerga .40 1.00
10 Eric Karros .60 1.50
11 J.T.Snow 1.00 2.50
12 John Kruk .60 1.50

1993 Studio Silhouettes

COMPLETE SET (10) 10.00 25.00
ONE PER JUMBO PACK
1 Frank Thomas .75 2.00
2 Barry Bonds 2.00 5.00
3 Jeff Bagwell .50 1.25
4 Juan Gonzalez .30 .75
5 Travis Fryman .30 .75
6 J.T.Snow .50 1.25
7 John Kruk .30 .75
8 Jeff Blauser .20 .50
9 Mike Piazza 4.00 10.00
10 Nolan Ryan 3.00 8.00

1993 Studio Superstars on Canvas

COMPLETE SET (10) 15.00 40.00
RANDOM INSERTS IN HOBBY/RETAIL PACKS
1 Ken Griffey Jr. 3.00 8.00
2 Jose Canseco 1.00 2.50
3 Mark McGwire 4.00 10.00
4 Mike Mussina 1.00 2.50
5 Joe Carter .60 1.50
6 Frank Thomas 1.50 4.00
7 Darren Daulton .60 1.50
8 Mark Grace 1.00 2.50
9 Andres Galarraga .60 1.50
10 Barry Bonds 4.00 10.00

1993 Studio Thomas

COMPLETE SET (5) 3.00 8.00
COMMON THOMAS (1-5) .75 2.00
RANDOM INSERTS IN ALL PACKS

1994 Studio Promos

COMPLETE SET (3) 2.50 6.00
83 Barry Bonds 1.50 4.00
154 Juan Gonzalez 1.25 3.00
209 Frank Thomas 1.25 3.00

1994 Studio

The 1994 Studio set consists of 220 full-bleed, standard-size cards. Card fronts offer a player photo with his jersey hanging in a locker room setting in the background. The set is grouped alphabetically within teams.

COMPLETE SET (220) 10.00 25.00
1 Dennis Eckersley .10 .30
2 Brent Gates .05 .15
3 Rickey Henderson .30 .75
4 Mark McGwire .75 2.00
5 Troy Neel .05 .15
6 Ruben Sierra .10 .30
7 Terry Steinbach .05 .15
8 Chad Curtis .05 .15
9 Chili Davis .10 .30
10 Gary DiSarcina .05 .15
11 Damion Easley .05 .15
12 Bo Jackson .30 .75
13 Mark Langston .05 .15
14 Eduardo Perez .05 .15
15 Tim Salmon .20 .50
16 Jeff Bagwell .20 .50
17 Craig Biggio .20 .50
18 Ken Caminiti .10 .30
19 Andujar Cedeno .05 .15
20 Doug Drabek .05 .15
21 Steve Finley .10 .30
22 Luis Gonzalez .10 .30
23 Darryl Kile .10 .30
24 Roberto Alomar .20 .50
25 Pat Borders .05 .15
26 Joe Carter .10 .30
27 Carlos Delgado .20 .50
28 Pat Hentgen .05 .15
29 Paul Molitor .10 .30
30 John Olerud .10 .30
31 Ed Sprague .05 .15
32 Devon White .10 .30
33 Steve Avery .05 .15
34 Tom Glavine .20 .50
35 David Justice .10 .30
36 Roberto Kelly .05 .15
37 Ryan Klesko .10 .30
38 Javier Lopez .10 .30
39 Greg Maddux .50 1.25
40 Fred McGriff .20 .50
41 Terry Pendleton .10 .30
42 Ricky Bones .05 .15
43 Darryl Hamilton .05 .15
44 Brian Harper .05 .15
45 John Jaha .05 .15
46 Dave Nilsson .05 .15
47 Kevin Seitzer .05 .15
48 Greg Vaughn .05 .15
49 Turner Ward .05 .15
50 Bernard Gilkey .05 .15
51 Gregg Jefferies .05 .15
52 Ray Lankford .10 .30
53 Tom Pagnozzi .05 .15
54 Ozzie Smith .50 1.25
55 Bob Tewksbury .05 .15
56 Mark Whiten .05 .15
57 Todd Zeile .05 .15
58 Steve Buechele .05 .15
59 Shawon Dunston .05 .15
60 Mark Grace .20 .50
61 Derrick May .05 .15
62 Karl Rhodes .05 .15
63 Ryne Sandberg .50 1.25
64 Sammy Sosa .30 .75
65 Rick Wilkins .05 .15
66 Brett Butler .10 .30
67 Delino DeShields .05 .15
68 Orel Hershiser .10 .30
69 Eric Karros .10 .30
70 Raul Mondesi .10 .30
71 Jose Offerman .05 .15
72 Mike Piazza .60 1.50
73 Tim Wallach .05 .15
74 Moises Alou .10 .30
75 Sean Berry .05 .15
76 Wil Cordero .05 .15
77 Cliff Floyd .10 .30
78 Marquis Grissom .10 .30
79 Ken Hill .05 .15
80 Larry Walker .10 .30
81 John Wetteland .10 .30
82 Rod Beck .05 .15
83 Barry Bonds .75 2.00
84 Royce Clayton .05 .15
85 Darren Lewis .05 .15
86 Willie McGee .10 .30
87 Bill Swift .05 .15
88 Robby Thompson .05 .15
89 Matt Williams .10 .30
90 Sandy Alomar Jr. .05 .15
91 Carlos Baerga .05 .15
92 Albert Belle .10 .30
93 Kenny Lofton .10 .30
94 Eddie Murray .30 .75
95 Manny Ramirez .30 .75
96 Paul Sorrento .05 .15
97 Jim Thome .20 .50
98 Rich Amaral .05 .15
99 Eric Anthony .05 .15
100 Jay Buhner .10 .30
101 Ken Griffey Jr. .60 1.50
102 Randy Johnson .30 .75
103 Edgar Martinez .20 .50
104 Tino Martinez .20 .50
105 Kurt Abbott RC .05 .15
106 Bret Barberie .05 .15
107 Chuck Carr .05 .15
108 Jeff Conine .10 .30
109 Chris Hammond .05 .15
110 Bryan Harvey .05 .15
111 Benito Santiago .10 .30
112 Gary Sheffield .10 .30
113 Bobby Bonilla .10 .30
114 Dwight Gooden .10 .30
115 Todd Hundley .05 .15
116 Bobby Jones .05 .15
117 Jeff Kent .20 .50
118 Kevin McReynolds .05 .15
119 Bret Saberhagen .10 .30
120 Ryan Thompson .05 .15
121 Harold Baines .10 .30
122 Mike Devereaux .05 .15
123 Jeffrey Hammonds .05 .15
124 Ben McDonald .05 .15
125 Mike Mussina .20 .50
126 Rafael Palmeiro .20 .50
127 Cal Ripken 1.00 2.50
128 Lee Smith .10 .30
129 Brad Ausmus .20 .50
130 Derek Bell .05 .15
131 Andy Benes .05 .15
132 Tony Gwynn .40 1.00
133 Trevor Hoffman .20 .50
134 Scott Livingstone .05 .15
135 Phil Plantier .05 .15
136 Darren Daulton .10 .30
137 Mariano Duncan .05 .15
138 Lenny Dykstra .05 .15
139 Dave Hollins .05 .15
140 Pete Incaviglia .05 .15
141 Danny Jackson .05 .15
142 John Kruk .10 .30
143 Kevin Stocker .05 .15
144 Jay Bell .10 .30
145 Carlos Garcia .05 .15
146 Jeff King .05 .15
147 Al Martin .05 .15
148 Orlando Merced .05 .15
149 Don Slaught .05 .15
150 Andy Van Slyke .20 .50
151 Kevin Brown .10 .30
152 Jose Canseco .20 .50
153 Will Clark .20 .50
154 Juan Gonzalez .10 .30
155 David Hulse .05 .15
156 Dean Palmer .10 .30
157 Ivan Rodriguez .20 .50
158 Kenny Rogers .10 .30
159 Roger Clemens .60 1.50
160 Scott Cooper .05 .15
161 Andre Dawson .10 .30
162 Mike Greenwell .05 .15
163 Otis Nixon .05 .15
164 Aaron Sele .05 .15
165 John Valentin .05 .15
166 Mo Vaughn .10 .30
167 Bret Boone .10 .30
168 Barry Larkin .20 .50
169 Kevin Mitchell .05 .15
170 Hal Morris .05 .15
171 Jose Rijo .05 .15
172 Deion Sanders .20 .50
173 Reggie Sanders .05 .15
174 John Smiley .05 .15
175 Dante Bichette .10 .30
176 Ellis Burks .10 .30
177 Andres Galarraga .10 .30
178 Joe Girardi .05 .15
179 Charlie Hayes .05 .15
180 Roberto Mejia .05 .15
181 Walt Weiss .05 .15
182 David Cone .10 .30
183 Gary Gaetti .10 .30
184 Greg Gagne .05 .15
185 Felix Jose .05 .15
186 Wally Joyner .10 .30
187 Mike Macfarlane .05 .15
188 Brian McRae .05 .15
189 Eric Davis .10 .30
190 Cecil Fielder .10 .30
191 Travis Fryman .10 .30
192 Tony Phillips .05 .15
193 Mickey Tettleton .05 .15
194 Alan Trammell .10 .30
195 Lou Whitaker .10 .30
196 Kent Hrbek .10 .30
197 Chuck Knoblauch .10 .30
198 Shane Mack .05 .15
199 Pat Meares .05 .15
200 Kirby Puckett .30 .75
201 Matt Walbeck .05 .15
202 Dave Winfield .10 .30
203 Wilson Alvarez .05 .15
204 Alex Fernandez .05 .15
205 Julio Franco .10 .30
206 Ozzie Guillen .10 .30
207 Jack McDowell .05 .15
208 Tim Raines .10 .30
209 Frank Thomas .30 .75
210 Robin Ventura .10 .30
211 Jim Abbott .20 .50
212 Wade Boggs .20 .50
213 Pat Kelly .05 .15
214 Jimmy Key .10 .30
215 Don Mattingly .75 2.00
216 Paul O'Neill .20 .50
217 Mike Stanley .05 .15
218 Danny Tartabull .05 .15
219 Checklist .05 .15
220 Checklist .05 .15

1994 Studio Editor's Choice

COMPLETE SET (8) 12.50 30.00
STATED ODDS 1:36

1 Barry Bonds 4.00 10.00
2 Frank Thomas 1.50 4.00
3 Ken Griffey Jr. 3.00 8.00
4 Andres Galarraga .60 1.50
5 Juan Gonzalez .60 1.50
6 Tim Salmon 1.00 2.50
7 Paul O'Neill 1.00 2.50
8 Mike Piazza 3.00 8.00

1994 Studio Heritage

COMPLETE SET (8) 5.00 12.00
STATED ODDS 1:9
1 Barry Bonds 2.00 5.00
2 Frank Thomas .75 2.00
3 Joe Carter .30 .75
4 Don Mattingly 2.00 5.00
5 Ryne Sandberg 1.25 3.00
6 Javier Lopez .30 .75
7 Gregg Jefferies .15 .40
8 Mike Mussina .50 1.25

1994 Studio Series Stars

COMPLETE SET (10) 60.00 120.00
STATED ODDS 1:60
STATED PRINT RUN 10,000 SETS
*GOLD: .75X TO 2X BASIC SERIES STARS
GOLD STATED ODDS 1:120
GOLD PRINT RUN 5000 SERIAL #'d SETS
1 Tony Gwynn 2.00 5.00
2 Barry Bonds 4.00 10.00
3 Frank Thomas 2.00 5.00
4 Ken Griffey Jr. 4.00 10.00
5 Joe Carter 1.25 3.00
6 Mike Piazza 2.00 5.00
7 Cal Ripken 6.00 15.00
8 Greg Maddux 3.00 8.00
9 Juan Gonzalez 1.25 3.00
10 Don Mattingly 4.00 10.00

1995 Studio

This 200-card horizontal set was issued by Donruss for the fifth consecutive year. Using a different design than past Studio issues, these cards were designed similarly to credit cards. The cards were issued in five-card packs with a suggested retail price of $1.49. There are no Rookie Cards in this set.

COMPLETE SET (200) 20.00 50.00
1 Frank Thomas .40 1.00
2 Jeff Bagwell .25 .60
3 Don Mattingly 1.00 2.50
4 Mike Piazza .60 1.50
5 Ken Griffey Jr. .75 2.00
6 Greg Maddux .60 1.50
7 Barry Bonds 1.00 2.50
8 Cal Ripken 1.25 3.00
9 Jose Canseco .25 .60
10 Paul Molitor .15 .40
11 Kenny Lofton .15 .40
12 Will Clark .25 .60
13 Tim Salmon .25 .60
14 Joe Carter .15 .40
15 Albert Belle .15 .40
16 Roger Clemens .75 2.00
17 Roberto Alomar .25 .60
18 Alex Rodriguez 1.00 2.50
19 Raul Mondesi .15 .40
20 Deion Sanders .25 .60
21 Juan Gonzalez .15 .40
22 Kirby Puckett .40 1.00
23 Fred McGriff .25 .60
24 Matt Williams .15 .40
25 Tony Gwynn .50 1.25
26 Cliff Floyd .15 .40
27 Travis Fryman .15 .40
28 Shawn Green .15 .40
29 Mike Mussina .25 .60
30 Bob Hamelin .07 .20
31 David Justice .15 .40
32 Manny Ramirez .25 .60
33 David Cone .15 .40
34 Marquis Grissom .15 .40
35 Moises Alou .15 .40
36 Carlos Baerga .07 .20
37 Barry Larkin .25 .60
38 Robin Ventura .15 .40
39 Mo Vaughn .15 .40
40 Jeffrey Hammonds .07 .20
41 Ozzie Smith .60 1.50
42 Andres Galarraga .15 .40
43 Carlos Delgado .15 .40
44 Lenny Dykstra .15 .40
45 Cecil Fielder .15 .40
46 Wade Boggs .25 .60
47 Gregg Jefferies .07 .20
48 Randy Johnson .40 1.00
49 Rafael Palmeiro .25 .60
50 Craig Biggio .25 .60
51 Steve Avery .07 .20
52 Ricky Bottalico .07 .20
53 Chris Gomez .07 .20
54 Carlos Garcia .07 .20
55 Brian Anderson .07 .20
56 Wilson Alvarez .07 .20
57 Roberto Kelly .07 .20
58 Larry Walker .15 .40
59 Dean Palmer .15 .40
60 Rick Aguilera .07 .20
61 Javier Lopez .15 .40
62 Shawon Dunston .07 .20
63 Wm. VanLandingham .07 .20
64 Jeff Kent .15 .40
65 David McCarty .07 .20
66 Armando Benitez .07 .20
67 Brett Butler .15 .40
68 Bernard Gilkey .07 .20
69 Joey Hamilton .07 .20
70 Chad Curtis .07 .20
71 Dante Bichette .15 .40
72 Chuck Carr .07 .20
73 Pedro Martinez .25 .60
74 Ramon Martinez .07 .20
75 Rondell White .15 .40
76 Alex Fernandez .07 .20
77 Dennis Martinez .15 .40
78 Sammy Sosa .40 1.00
79 Bernie Williams .25 .60
80 Lou Whitaker .15 .40
81 Kurt Abbott .07 .20
82 Tino Martinez .25 .60
83 Willie Greene .07 .20
84 Garret Anderson .15 .40
85 Jose Rijo .07 .20
86 Jeff Montgomery .07 .20
87 Mark Langston .07 .20
88 Reggie Sanders .15 .40
89 Rusty Greer .15 .40
90 Delino DeShields .07 .20
91 Jason Bere .07 .20
92 Lee Smith .15 .40
93 Devon White .15 .40
94 John Wetteland .15 .40
95 Luis Gonzalez .15 .40
96 Greg Vaughn .07 .20
97 Lance Johnson .07 .20
98 Alan Trammell .15 .40
99 Bret Saberhagen .15 .40
100 Jack McDowell .07 .20
101 Trevor Hoffman .15 .40
102 Dave Nilsson .07 .20
103 Bryan Harvey .07 .20
104 Chuck Knoblauch .15 .40
105 Bobby Bonilla .15 .40
106 Hal Morris .07 .20
107 Mark Whiten .07 .20
108 Phil Plantier .07 .20
109 Ryan Klesko .15 .40
110 Greg Gagne .07 .20
111 Ruben Sierra .15 .40
112 J.R. Phillips .07 .20
113 Terry Steinbach .07 .20
114 Jay Buhner .15 .40
115 Ken Caminiti .15 .40
116 Gary DiSarcina .07 .20
117 Ivan Rodriguez .25 .60
118 Bip Roberts .07 .20
119 Jay Bell .15 .40
120 Ken Hill .07 .20
121 Mike Greenwell .07 .20
122 Rick Wilkins .07 .20
123 Rickey Henderson .40 1.00
124 Dave Hollins .07 .20
125 Terry Pendleton .15 .40
126 Rich Becker .07 .20
127 Billy Ashley .07 .20
128 Derek Bell .07 .20
129 Dennis Eckersley .15 .40
130 Andujar Cedeno .07 .20
131 John Jaha .07 .20
132 Chuck Finley .15 .40
133 Steve Finley .15 .40
134 Danny Tartabull .07 .20
135 Jeff Conine .15 .40
136 Jon Lieber .07 .20
137 Jim Abbott .25 .60
138 Steve Trachsel .07 .20
139 Bret Boone .15 .40
140 Charles Johnson .15 .40
141 Mark McGwire 1.00 2.50
142 Eddie Murray .40 1.00
143 Doug Drabek .07 .20
144 Steve Cooke .07 .20
145 Kevin Seitzer .07 .20
146 Rod Beck .07 .20
147 Eric Karros .15 .40
148 Tim Raines .15 .40
149 Joe Girardi .07 .20
150 Aaron Sele .07 .20
151 Robby Thompson .07 .20
152 Chan Ho Park .15 .40
153 Ellis Burks .15 .40
154 Brian McRae .07 .20
155 Jimmy Key .15 .40
156 Rico Brogna .07 .20
157 Ozzie Guillen .15 .40
158 Chili Davis .15 .40
159 Darren Daulton .15 .40
160 Chipper Jones .40 1.00
161 Walt Weiss .07 .20
162 Paul O'Neill .25 .60
163 Al Martin .07 .20
164 John Valentin .07 .20
165 Tim Wallach .07 .20
166 Scott Erickson .07 .20
167 Ryan Thompson .07 .20
168 Todd Zeile .07 .20
169 Scott Cooper .07 .20
170 Matt Mieske .07 .20
171 Allen Watson .07 .20
172 Brian L.Hunter .07 .20
173 Kevin Stocker .07 .20
174 Cal Eldred .07 .20
175 Tony Phillips .07 .20
176 Ben McDonald .07 .20
177 Mark Grace .25 .60
178 Midre Cummings .07 .20
179 Orlando Merced .07 .20
180 Jeff King .07 .20
181 Gary Sheffield .15 .40
182 Tom Glavine .25 .60
183 Edgar Martinez .25 .60
184 Steve Karsay .07 .20
185 Pat Listach .07 .20
186 Wil Cordero .07 .20
187 Brady Anderson .15 .40
188 Bobby Jones .07 .20
189 Andy Benes .07 .20
190 Ray Lankford .15 .40
191 John Doherty .07 .20
192 Wally Joyner .15 .40
193 Jim Thome .25 .60
194 Royce Clayton .07 .20
195 John Olerud .15 .40
196 Steve Buechele .07 .20
197 Harold Baines .15 .40
198 Geronimo Berroa .07 .20
199 Checklist .07 .20
200 Checklist .07 .20

1995 Studio Gold Series

COMPLETE SET (50) 12.50 30.00
*GOLD: .5X TO 1.2X BASIC CARDS
ONE PER PACK

1995 Studio Platinum Series

*PLATINUM: 2.5X TO 6X BASIC CARDS
STATED ODDS 1:10

1996 Studio

The 1996 Studio set was issued in one series totalling 150 cards and was distributed in seven-card packs. The fronts feature color action player photos with a player portrait in the background.

COMPLETE SET (150) 6.00 15.00
1 Cal Ripken .75 2.00
2 Alex Gonzalez .08 .25
3 Roger Cedeno .08 .25
4 Todd Hollandsworth .08 .25
5 Gregg Jefferies .08 .25
6 Ryne Sandberg .40 1.00
7 Eric Karros .08 .25
8 Jeff Conine .08 .25
9 Rafael Palmeiro .15 .40
10 Bip Roberts .08 .25
11 Roger Clemens .50 1.25
12 Tom Glavine .15 .40
13 Jason Giambi .08 .25
14 Rey Ordonez .08 .25
15 Chan Ho Park .08 .25
16 Vinny Castilla .08 .25
17 Butch Huskey .08 .25
18 Greg Maddux .40 1.00
19 Bernard Gilkey .08 .25
20 Marquis Grissom .08 .25
21 Chuck Knoblauch .08 .25
22 Ozzie Smith .40 1.00
23 Garret Anderson .08 .25
24 J.T. Snow .08 .25
25 John Valentin .08 .25
26 Barry Larkin .15 .40
27 Bobby Bonilla .08 .25
28 Todd Zeile .08 .25
29 Roberto Alomar .15 .40
30 Ramon Martinez .08 .25
31 Jeff King .08 .25
32 Dennis Eckersley .08 .25
33 Derek Jeter .60 1.50
34 Edgar Martinez .15 .40
35 Geronimo Berroa .08 .25
36 Hal Morris .08 .25
37 Troy Percival .08 .25
38 Jason Isringhausen .08 .25
39 Greg Vaughn .08 .25
40 Robin Ventura .08 .25
41 Craig Biggio .15 .40
42 Will Clark .15 .40
43 Sammy Sosa .25 .60
44 Bernie Williams .15 .40
45 Kenny Lofton .08 .25
46 Wade Boggs .15 .40
47 Javy Lopez .08 .25
48 Reggie Sanders .08 .25
49 Jeff Bagwell .15 .40
50 Fred McGriff .15 .40
51 Charles Johnson .08 .25
52 Darren Daulton .08 .25
53 Jose Canseco .15 .40
54 Cecil Fielder .08 .25
55 Hideo Nomo .25 .60
56 Tim Salmon .15 .40
57 Carlos Delgado .08 .25
58 David Cone .08 .25
59 Tim Raines .08 .25
60 Lyle Mouton .08 .25
61 Wally Joyner .08 .25
62 Bret Boone .08 .25
63 Raul Mondesi .08 .25
64 Gary Sheffield .08 .25
65 Alex Rodriguez .50 1.25
66 Russ Davis .08 .25
67 Checklist .08 .25
68 Marty Cordova .08 .25
69 Ruben Sierra .08 .25
70 Jose Mesa .08 .25
71 Matt Williams .08 .25
72 Chipper Jones .25 .60
73 Randy Johnson .25 .60
74 Kirby Puckett .25 .60
75 Jim Edmonds .08 .25
76 Barry Bonds .60 1.50
77 David Segui .08 .25
78 Larry Walker .08 .25
79 Jason Kendall .08 .25
80 Mike Piazza .40 1.00
81 Brian L.Hunter .08 .25
82 Julio Franco .08 .25
83 Jay Bell .08 .25
84 Kevin Seitzer .08 .25
85 John Smoltz .15 .40
86 Joe Carter .08 .25
87 Ray Durham .08 .25
88 Carlos Baerga .08 .25
89 Ron Gant .08 .25
90 Orlando Merced .08 .25
91 Lee Smith .08 .25
92 Pedro Martinez .15 .40
93 Frank Thomas .25 .60
94 Al Martin .08 .25
95 Chad Curtis .08 .25
96 Eddie Murray .25 .60
97 Rusty Greer .08 .25
98 Jay Buhner .08 .25
99 Rico Brogna .08 .25
100 Todd Hundley .08 .25
101 Moises Alou .08 .25
102 Chili Davis .08 .25
103 Ismael Valdes .08 .25
104 Mo Vaughn .08 .25
105 Juan Gonzalez .08 .25
106 Mark Grudzielanek .08 .25
107 Derek Bell .08 .25
108 Shawn Green .08 .25
109 David Justice .08 .25
110 Paul O'Neill .15 .40
111 Kevin Appier .08 .25
112 Ray Lankford .08 .25
113 Travis Fryman .08 .25
114 Manny Ramirez .15 .40
115 Brooks Kieschnick .08 .25
116 Ken Griffey Jr. .50 1.25
117 Jeffrey Hammonds .08 .25
118 Mark McGwire .60 1.50
119 Denny Neagle .08 .25
120 Quilvio Veras .08 .25
121 Alan Benes .08 .25
122 Rondell White .08 .25
123 Osvaldo Fernandez RC .08 .25
124 Andres Galarraga .08 .25
125 Johnny Damon .15 .40
126 Lenny Dykstra .08 .25
127 Jason Schmidt .15 .40
128 Mike Mussina .15 .40
129 Ken Caminiti .08 .25
130 Michael Tucker .08 .25
131 LaTroy Hawkins .08 .25
132 Checklist .08 .25
133 Delino DeShields .08 .25
134 Dave Nilsson .08 .25
135 Jack McDowell .08 .25
136 Joey Hamilton .08 .25
137 Dante Bichette .08 .25
138 Paul Molitor .08 .25
139 Ivan Rodriguez .15 .40
140 Mark Grace .15 .40
141 Paul Wilson .08 .25
142 Orel Hershiser .08 .25
143 Albert Belle .08 .25
144 Tino Martinez .15 .40
145 Tony Gwynn .30 .75
146 George Arias .08 .25
147 Brian Jordan .08 .25
148 Brian McRae .08 .25
149 Rickey Henderson .25 .60
150 Ryan Klesko .08 .25

1996 Studio Bronze Press Proofs

*STARS: 5X TO 12X BASIC CARDS
STATED ODDS 1:6
STATED PRINT RUN 2000 SETS
33 Derek Jeter 12.50 30.00

1996 Studio Gold Press Proofs

*STARS: 12.5X TO 30X BASIC CARDS
STATED ODDS 1:24
STATED PRINT RUN 500 SETS
33 Derek Jeter 40.00 80.00

1996 Studio Silver Press Proofs

*STARS: 25X TO 60X BASIC CARDS
RANDOM INSERTS IN MAGAZINE PACKS
STATED PRINT RUN 100 SETS
33 Derek Jeter 75.00 150.00

1996 Studio Hit Parade

COMPLETE SET (10) 25.00 60.00
STATED ODDS 1:48 HOBBY
STATED PRINT RUN 5000 SERIAL #'d SETS
1 Tony Gwynn 3.00 8.00
2 Ken Griffey Jr. 5.00 12.00
3 Frank Thomas 2.50 6.00
4 Jeff Bagwell 1.50 4.00
5 Kirby Puckett 2.50 6.00
6 Mike Piazza 4.00 10.00
7 Barry Bonds 6.00 15.00
8 Albert Belle 1.00 2.50
9 Tim Salmon 1.50 4.00
10 Mo Vaughn 1.00 2.50

1996 Studio Masterstrokes Samples

COMPLETE SET (8) 15.00 40.00
1 Tony Gwynn 2.00 5.00
2 Mike Piazza 2.50 6.00
3 Jeff Bagwell 1.50 4.00
4 Manny Ramirez 1.25 3.00
5 Cal Ripken 4.00 10.00
6 Frank Thomas 1.25 3.00
7 Ken Griffey Jr. 3.00 8.00
8 Greg Maddux 2.00 5.00

1996 Studio Masterstrokes

COMPLETE SET (8) 10.00 25.00
STATED ODDS 1:96
STATED PRINT RUN 5000 SERIAL #'d SETS
1 Tony Gwynn 1.25 3.00
2 Mike Piazza 1.25 3.00
3 Jeff Bagwell .75 2.00
4 Manny Ramirez .75 2.00
5 Cal Ripken 4.00 10.00
6 Frank Thomas 1.25 3.00
7 Ken Griffey Jr. 2.50 6.00
8 Greg Maddux 2.00 5.00

1996 Studio Stained Glass Stars

COMPLETE SET (12) 10.00 25.00
STATED ODDS 1:24
1 Cal Ripken 3.00 8.00
2 Ken Griffey Jr. 2.00 5.00
3 Frank Thomas 1.00 2.50
4 Greg Maddux 1.50 4.00
5 Chipper Jones 1.00 2.50
6 Mike Piazza 1.00 2.50
7 Albert Belle .40 1.00
8 Jeff Bagwell .60 1.50
9 Hideo Nomo 1.00 2.50
10 Barry Bonds 1.50 4.00
11 Manny Ramirez .60 1.50
12 Kenny Lofton .40 1.00

1997 Studio

The 1997 Studio set was issued in one series totalling 165 cards and was distributed in five-card packs with an 8x10 Studio Portrait for a suggested retail price of $2.49. The fronts feature color player portraits, while the backs carry player information. It is believed that the following cards: 112, 133, 137, 147 and 161 were short printed.

COMPLETE SET (165) 25.00 60.00
SP'S REPORTED BY CASE DEALERS
SP'S NOT CONFIRMED BY MANUFACTURER
SP CL: 112/133/137/147/161
1 Frank Thomas .30 .75
2 Gary Sheffield .10 .30
3 Jason Isringhausen .10 .30
4 Ron Gant .10 .30
5 Andy Pettitte .20 .50
6 Todd Hollandsworth .10 .30
7 Troy Percival .10 .30
8 Mark McGwire .75 2.00
9 Barry Larkin .20 .50
10 Ken Caminiti .10 .30
11 Paul Molitor .10 .30
12 Travis Fryman .10 .30
13 Kevin Brown .10 .30
14 Robin Ventura .10 .30
15 Andres Galarraga .10 .30
16 Ken Griffey Jr. .60 1.50
17 Roger Clemens .60 1.50
18 Alan Benes .10 .30
19 Dave Justice .10 .30
20 Damon Buford .10 .30
21 Mike Piazza .50 1.25
22 Ray Durham .10 .30
23 Billy Wagner .10 .30
24 Dean Palmer .10 .30
25 David Cone .10 .30
26 Ruben Sierra .10 .30
27 Henry Rodriguez .10 .30
28 Ray Lankford .10 .30
29 Jamey Wright .10 .30
30 Brady Anderson .10 .30
31 Tino Martinez .20 .50
32 Manny Ramirez .20 .50
33 Jeff Conine .10 .30
34 Dante Bichette .10 .30
35 Jose Canseco .20 .50
36 Mo Vaughn .10 .30
37 Sammy Sosa .30 .75
38 Mark Grudzielanek .10 .30
39 Mike Mussina .20 .50
40 Bill Pulsipher .10 .30
41 Ryne Sandberg .50 1.25
42 Rickey Henderson .30 .75
43 Alex Rodriguez .50 1.25
44 Eddie Murray .30 .75
45 Ernie Young .10 .30
46 Joey Hamilton .10 .30
47 Wade Boggs .20 .50
48 Rusty Greer .10 .30
49 Carlos Delgado .10 .30
50 Ellis Burks .10 .30
51 Cal Ripken 1.00 2.50
52 Alex Fernandez .10 .30
53 Wally Joyner .10 .30
54 James Baldwin .10 .30
55 Juan Gonzalez .10 .30
56 John Smoltz .20 .50
57 Omar Vizquel .20 .50
58 Shane Reynolds .10 .30
59 Barry Bonds .75 2.00
60 Jason Kendall .10 .30
61 Marty Cordova .10 .30
62 Charles Johnson .10 .30
63 John Jaha .10 .30
64 Chan Ho Park .10 .30
65 Jermaine Allensworth .10 .30
66 Mark Grace .20 .50
67 Tim Salmon .20 .50
68 Edgar Martinez .20 .50
69 Marquis Grissom .10 .30
70 Craig Biggio .20 .50
71 Bobby Higginson .10 .30
72 Kevin Seitzer .10 .30
73 Hideo Nomo .30 .75
74 Dennis Eckersley .10 .30
75 Bobby Bonilla .10 .30
76 Dwight Gooden .10 .30
77 Jeff Cirillo .10 .30
78 Brian McRae .10 .30
79 Chipper Jones .30 .75
80 Jeff Fassero .10 .30
81 Fred McGriff .20 .50
82 Garret Anderson .10 .30
83 Eric Karros .10 .30
84 Derek Bell .10 .30
85 Kenny Lofton .10 .30
86 John Mabry .10 .30
87 Pat Hentgen .10 .30
88 Greg Maddux .50 1.25
89 Jason Giambi .10 .30
90 Al Martin .10 .30
91 Derek Jeter .75 2.00
92 Rey Ordonez .10 .30
93 Will Clark .20 .50
94 Kevin Appier .10 .30
95 Roberto Alomar .20 .50
96 Joe Carter .10 .30
97 Bernie Williams .20 .50
98 Albert Belle .10 .30
99 Greg Vaughn .10 .30
100 Tony Clark .10 .30
101 Matt Williams .10 .30
102 Jeff Bagwell .20 .50
103 Reggie Sanders .10 .30
104 Mariano Rivera .30 .75
105 Larry Walker .10 .30
106 Shawn Green .10 .30
107 Alex Ochoa .10 .30
108 Ivan Rodriguez .20 .50
109 Eric Young .10 .30
110 Javier Lopez .10 .30
111 Brian Hunter .10 .30
112 Raul Mondesi SP 1.50 4.00
113 Randy Johnson .30 .75
114 Tony Phillips .10 .30
115 Carlos Garcia .10 .30
116 Moises Alou .10 .30
117 Paul O'Neill .20 .50
118 Jim Thome .20 .50
119 Jermaine Dye .10 .30
120 Wilson Alvarez .10 .30
121 Rondell White .10 .30
122 Michael Tucker .10 .30
123 Mike Lansing .10 .30
124 Tony Gwynn .40 1.00
125 Ryan Klesko .10 .30
126 Jim Edmonds .10 .30
127 Chuck Knoblauch .10 .30
128 Rafael Palmeiro .20 .50
129 Jay Buhner .10 .30
130 Tom Glavine .20 .50
131 Julio Franco .10 .30
132 Cecil Fielder .10 .30
133 Paul Wilson SP 1.50 4.00
134 Deion Sanders .20 .50
135 Alex Gonzalez .10 .30
136 Charles Nagy .10 .30
137 Andy Ashby SP 1.50 4.00
138 Edgar Renteria .10 .30
139 Pedro Martinez .20 .50
140 Brian Jordan .10 .30
141 Todd Hundley .10 .30
142 Marc Newfield .10 .30
143 Darryl Strawberry .10 .30
144 Dan Wilson .10 .30
145 Brian Giles RC .60 1.50
146 F.P. Santangelo .10 .30
147 Shannon Stewart SP 1.50 4.00
148 Scott Spiezio .10 .30
149 Andruw Jones .20 .50
150 Karim Garcia .10 .30
151 Vladimir Guerrero .30 .75
152 George Arias .10 .30
153 Brooks Kieschnick .10 .30
154 Todd Walker .10 .30
155 Scott Rolen .20 .50
156 Todd Greene .10 .30
157 Dmitri Young .10 .30
158 Ruben Rivera .10 .30
159 Bartolo Colon .10 .30
160 Nomar Garciaparra .50 1.25
161 Bob Abreu SP 2.50 6.00
162 Darin Erstad .10 .30
163 Ken Griffey Jr. CL .40 1.00
164 Frank Thomas CL .20 .50
165 Alex Rodriguez CL .30 .75

1997 Studio Gold Press Proofs

*STARS: 8X TO 20X BASIC CARDS
*SP'S: .6X TO 1.5X BASIC CARDS
*ROOKIES: 2.5X TO 6X BASIC CARDS
RANDOM INSERTS IN PACKS
STATED PRINT RUN 500 SETS

1997 Studio Silver Press Proofs

*STARS: 4X TO 10X BASIC CARDS
*SP'S: .3X TO .8X BASIC CARDS
*ROOKIES: 1.25X TO 3X BASIC CARDS
RANDOM INSERTS IN PACKS
STATED PRINT RUN 1500 SETS

1997 Studio Autographs

COMPLETE SET (3) 40.00 100.00
RANDOM INSERTS IN PACKS
PRINT RUNS B/WN 500-1250 PER
SKIP-NUMBERED 3-CARD SET
1ST 100 CARDS ALL SIGNED IN BLUE INK
12 Todd Walker/1250 6.00 15.00
21 Vladimir Guerrero/500 15.00 40.00
24 Scott Rolen/1000 10.00 25.00

1997 Studio Hard Hats Samples

COMPLETE SET (24) 25.00 60.00
1 Ivan Rodriguez 1.00 2.50
2 Albert Belle .40 1.00
3 Ken Griffey Jr. 3.00 8.00
4 Chuck Knoblauch .50 1.25
5 Frank Thomas 1.25 3.00
6 Cal Ripken 4.00 10.00
7 Todd Walker .50 1.25
8 Alex Rodriguez 2.00 5.00
9 Jim Thome 1.00 2.50
10 Mike Piazza 2.50 6.00
11 Barry Larkin .75 2.00
12 Chipper Jones 2.00 5.00
13 Derek Jeter 4.00 10.00
14 Matt Williams .60 1.50
15 Jason Giambi 1.25 3.00
16 Tim Salmon .50 1.25
17 Brady Anderson .50 1.25
18 Rondell White .50 1.25
19 Bernie Williams .75 2.00
20 Juan Gonzalez 1.00 2.50
21 Karim Garcia .50 1.25
22 Scott Rolen 1.25 3.00
23 Darin Erstad 1.25 3.00
24 Brian Jordan .50 1.25

1997 Studio Hard Hats

COMPLETE SET (24) 20.00 50.00
1 Ivan Rodriguez 1.00 2.50
2 Albert Belle .60 1.50
3 Ken Griffey Jr. 10.00 25.00
4 Chuck Knoblauch .60 1.50
5 Frank Thomas 1.50 4.00
6 Cal Ripken 5.00 12.00
7 Todd Walker .60 1.50
8 Alex Rodriguez 2.00 5.00
9 Jim Thome 1.00 2.50
10 Mike Piazza 1.50 4.00
11 Barry Larkin 1.00 2.50
12 Chipper Jones 1.50 4.00
13 Derek Jeter 4.00 10.00
14 Matt Williams .60 1.50
15 Jason Giambi .60 1.50
16 Tim Salmon .60 1.50
17 Brady Anderson .60 1.50
18 Rondell White .60 1.50
19 Bernie Williams 1.00 2.50
20 Juan Gonzalez .60 1.50
21 Karim Garcia .60 1.50
22 Scott Rolen 1.00 2.50
23 Darin Erstad .60 1.50
24 Brian Jordan .60 1.50

1997 Studio Master Strokes

RANDOM INSERTS IN PACKS
STATED PRINT RUN 2000 SERIAL #'d SETS
8 X 10: RANDOM INSERTS IN PACKS
8 X 10 PRINT RUN 5000 SERIAL #'d SETS
1 Derek Jeter 10.00 25.00
2 Jeff Bagwell 1.00 2.50
3 Ken Griffey Jr. 3.00 8.00
4 Barry Bonds 2.50 6.00
5 Frank Thomas 1.50 4.00
6 Andy Pettitte 1.00 2.50
7 Mo Vaughn .60 1.50
8 Alex Rodriguez 2.00 5.00
9 Andruw Jones .60 1.50
10 Kenny Lofton .60 1.50
11 Cal Ripken 5.00 12.00
12 Greg Maddux 2.50 6.00
13 Manny Ramirez 1.00 2.50
14 Mike Piazza 1.50 4.00
15 Vladimir Guerrero 1.00 2.50
16 Albert Belle .60 1.50
17 Chipper Jones 1.50 4.00
18 Hideo Nomo 1.00 2.50
19 Sammy Sosa 1.00 2.50
20 Tony Gwynn 1.50 4.00
21 Gary Sheffield .60 1.50
22 Mark McGwire 2.50 6.00
23 Juan Gonzalez .60 1.50
24 Paul Molitor 1.50 4.00

1997 Studio Portraits 8 x 10

COMPLETE SET (24) 10.00 25.00
1 Ken Griffey Jr. 1.25 3.00
2 Frank Thomas .60 1.50
3 Alex Rodriguez 1.00 2.50
4 Andruw Jones .40 1.00
5 Cal Ripken 2.00 5.00
6 Greg Maddux 1.00 2.50
7 Mike Piazza 1.00 2.50
8 Chipper Jones .60 1.50
9 Albert Belle .25 .60
10 Derek Jeter 1.50 4.00
11 Juan Gonzalez .25 .60
12 Todd Walker .25 .60
13 Mark McGwire 1.50 4.00
14 Barry Bonds 1.50 4.00
15 Jeff Bagwell .40 1.00
16 Manny Ramirez .40 1.00
17 Kenny Lofton .25 .60
18 Mo Vaughn .25 .60
19 Hideo Nomo .60 1.50
20 Tony Gwynn .75 2.00
21 Vladimir Guerrero .60 1.50
22 Gary Sheffield .25 .60
23 Ryne Sandberg 1.00 2.50
24 Scott Rolen .40 1.00

1998 Studio 8 x 10 Samples

COMPLETE SET (3) 2.00 5.00
1 Travis Lee .40 1.00
2 Todd Helton 1.25 3.00
3 Ben Grieve .60 1.50

1998 Studio

The 1998 Studio set consists of 220 cards. The eight-card packs retailed for $2.99 each. Each pack contains 1-8"x10" card and seven standard size cards. The fronts feature candid head/shoulder player photos with game action photography in the background. The player's name lines the bottom border and the Donruss logo sits in the upper left corner. The release date was June, 1998.

COMPLETE SET (220) 20.00 50.00
1 Tony Clark .10 .30
2 Jose Cruz Jr. .10 .30
3 Ivan Rodriguez .20 .50
4 Mo Vaughn .10 .30
5 Kenny Lofton .10 .30
6 Will Clark .20 .50
7 Barry Larkin .20 .50
8 Jay Bell .10 .30
9 Kevin Young .10 .30
10 Francisco Cordova .10 .30
11 Justin Thompson .10 .30
12 Paul Molitor .10 .30
13 Jeff Bagwell .20 .50
14 Jose Canseco .20 .50
15 Scott Rolen .20 .50
16 Wilton Guerrero .10 .30
17 Shannon Stewart .10 .30
18 Hideki Irabu .10 .30
19 Michael Tucker .10 .30
20 Joe Carter .10 .30
21 Gabe Alvarez .10 .30
22 Ricky Ledee .10 .30
23 Karim Garcia .10 .30
24 Eli Marrero .10 .30
25 Scott Elarton .10 .30
26 Mario Valdez .10 .30
27 Ben Grieve .10 .30
28 Paul Konerko .10 .30
29 Esteban Yan RC .15 .40
30 Esteban Loaiza .10 .30
31 Delino DeShields .10 .30
32 Bernie Williams .20 .50
33 Joe Randa .10 .30
34 Randy Johnson .30 .75
35 Brett Tomko .10 .30
36 Todd Erdos RC .10 .30
37 Bobby Higginson .10 .30
38 Jason Kendall .10 .30
39 Ray Lankford .10 .30
40 Mark Grace .20 .50
41 Andy Pettitte .20 .50
42 Alex Rodriguez .50 1.25
43 Hideo Nomo .30 .75
44 Sammy Sosa .30 .75
45 J.T. Snow .10 .30
46 Jason Varitek .30 .75
47 Vinny Castilla .10 .30
48 Neifi Perez .10 .30
49 Todd Walker .10 .30
50 Mike Cameron .10 .30
51 Jeffrey Hammonds .10 .30
52 Deivi Cruz .10 .30
53 Brian Hunter .10 .30
54 Al Martin .10 .30
55 Ron Coomer .10 .30
56 Chan Ho Park .10 .30
57 Pedro Martinez .20 .50
58 Darin Erstad .10 .30
59 Albert Belle .10 .30
60 Nomar Garciaparra .50 1.25
61 Tony Gwynn .40 1.00
62 Mike Piazza .50 1.25
63 Todd Helton .20 .50
64 David Ortiz .40 1.00
65 Todd Dunwoody .10 .30
66 Orlando Cabrera .10 .30
67 Ken Cloude .10 .30
68 Andy Benes .10 .30
69 Mariano Rivera .30 .75
70 Cecil Fielder .10 .30
71 Brian Jordan .10 .30
72 Darryl Kile .10 .30
73 Reggie Jefferson .10 .30
74 Shawn Estes .10 .30
75 Bobby Bonilla .10 .30
76 Denny Neagle .10 .30
77 Robin Ventura .10 .30

78 Omar Vizquel .20 .50
79 Craig Biggio .20 .50
80 Moises Alou .10 .30
81 Garret Anderson .10 .30
82 Eric Karros .10 .30
83 Dante Bichette .10 .30
84 Charles Johnson .10 .30
85 Rusty Greer .10 .30
86 Travis Fryman .10 .30
87 Fernando Tatis .10 .30
88 Wilson Alvarez .10 .30
89 Carl Pavano .10 .30
90 Brian Rose .10 .30
91 Geoff Jenkins .10 .30
92 Magglio Ordonez RC 1.00 2.50
93 David Segui .10 .30
94 David Cone .10 .30
95 John Smoltz .20 .50
96 Jim Thome .20 .50
97 Gary Sheffield .10 .30
98 Barry Bonds .75 2.00
99 Andres Galarraga .10 .30
100 Brad Fullmer .10 .30
101 Bobby Estalella .10 .30
102 Enrique Wilson .10 .30
103 Frank Catalanotto RC .25 .60
104 Mike Lowell RC .60 1.50
105 Kevin Orie .10 .30
106 Matt Morris .10 .30
107 Pokey Reese .10 .30
108 Shawn Green .10 .30
109 Tony Womack .10 .30
110 Ken Caminiti .10 .30
111 Roberto Alomar .20 .50
112 Ken Griffey Jr. .60 1.50
113 Cal Ripken 1.00 2.50
114 Lou Collier .10 .30
115 Larry Walker .10 .30
116 Fred McGriff .20 .50
117 Jim Edmonds .10 .30
118 Edgar Martinez .20 .50
119 Matt Williams .10 .30
120 Ismael Valdes .10 .30
121 Bartolo Colon .10 .30
122 Jeff Cirillo .10 .30
123 Steve Woodard .10 .30
124 Kevin Millwood RC .40 1.00
125 Derrick Gibson .10 .30
126 Jacob Cruz .10 .30
127 Russell Branyan .10 .30
128 Sean Casey .10 .30
129 Derrek Lee .20 .50
130 Paul O'Neill .20 .50
131 Brad Radke .10 .30
132 Kevin Appier .10 .30
133 John Olerud .10 .30
134 Alan Benes .10 .30
135 Todd Greene .10 .30
136 Carlos Mendoza RC .10 .30
137 Wade Boggs .20 .50
138 Jose Guillen .10 .30
139 Tino Martinez .20 .50
140 Aaron Boone .10 .30
141 Abraham Nunez .10 .30
142 Preston Wilson .10 .30
143 Randall Simon .10 .30
144 Dennis Reyes .10 .30
145 Mark Kotsay .10 .30
146 Richard Hidalgo .10 .30
147 Travis Lee .10 .30
148 Hanley Frias RC .10 .30
149 Ruben Rivera .10 .30
150 Rafael Medina .10 .30
151 Dave Nilsson .10 .30
152 Curt Schilling .10 .30
153 Brady Anderson .10 .30
154 Carlos Delgado .10 .30
155 Jason Giambi .10 .30
156 Pat Hentgen .10 .30
157 Tom Glavine .20 .50
158 Ryan Klesko .10 .30
159 Chipper Jones .30 .75
160 Juan Gonzalez .10 .30
161 Mark McGwire .75 2.00
162 Vladimir Guerrero .30 .75
163 Derek Jeter .75 2.00
164 Manny Ramirez .20 .50
165 Mike Mussina .20 .50
166 Rafael Palmeiro .20 .50
167 Henry Rodriguez .10 .30
168 Jeff Suppan .10 .30
169 Eric Milton .10 .30
170 Scott Spiezio .10 .30
171 Wilson Delgado .10 .30
172 Bubba Trammell .10 .30
173 Ellis Burks .10 .30
174 Jason Dickson .10 .30
175 Butch Huskey .10 .30
176 Edgardo Alfonzo .10 .30
177 Eric Young .10 .30
178 Marquis Grissom .10 .30
179 Lance Johnson .10 .30
180 Kevin Brown .20 .50
181 Sandy Alomar Jr. .10 .30
182 Todd Hundley .10 .30
183 Rondell White .10 .30
184 Javier Lopez .10 .30
185 Damian Jackson .10 .30
186 Raul Mondesi .10 .30
187 Rickey Henderson .30 .75
188 David Justice .10 .30
189 Jay Buhner .10 .30
190 Jaret Wright .10 .30
191 Miguel Tejada .30 .75
192 Ron Wright .10 .30
193 Livan Hernandez .10 .30
194 A.J. Hinch .10 .30
195 Richie Sexson .10 .30
196 Bob Abreu .10 .30
197 Luis Castillo .10 .30
198 Michael Coleman .10 .30
199 Greg Maddux .50 1.25
200 Frank Thomas .30 .75
201 Andruw Jones .20 .50
202 Roger Clemens .60 1.50
203 Tim Salmon .20 .50
204 Chuck Knoblauch .10 .30
205 Wes Helms .10 .30
206 Juan Encarnacion .10 .30
207 Russ Davis .10 .30
208 John Valentin .10 .30
209 Tony Saunders .10 .30
210 Mike Sweeney .10 .30
211 Steve Finley .10 .30
212 Dave Dellucci RC .25 .60
213 Edgar Renteria .10 .30
214 Jeremi Gonzalez .10 .30
CL1 Jeff Bagwell CL .10 .30
CL2 Mike Piazza CL .30 .75
CL3 Greg Maddux CL .30 .75
CL4 Cal Ripken CL .50 1.25
CL5 Frank Thomas CL .20 .50
CL6 Ken Griffey Jr. CL .40 1.00

1998 Studio Gold Press Proofs

*STARS: 4X TO 10X BASIC CARDS
*ROOKIES: 4X TO 10X BASIC CARDS
RANDOM INSERTS IN PACKS
STATED PRINT RUN 300 SERIAL #'d SETS

1998 Studio Silver Press Proofs

COMMON (1-214/CL1-CL6) .75 2.00
*STARS: 2X TO 5X BASIC CARDS
*ROOKIES: 2X TO 5X BASIC CARDS
RANDOM INSERTS IN PACKS
STATED PRINT RUN 1000 SETS

1998 Studio Autographs 8 x 10

RANDOM INSERTS IN PACKS
PRINT RUNS B/WN 500-1000 COPIES PER
1 Travis Lee/500 4.00 10.00
2 Todd Helton/1000 10.00 25.00
3 Ben Grieve/1000 4.00 10.00

1998 Studio Freeze Frame

COMPLETE SET (30) 75.00 150.00
STATED PRINT RUN 3500 SERIAL #'d SETS
DIE CUT PRINT RUN 500 SERIAL #'d SETS
RANDOM INSERTS IN PACKS
1 Ken Griffey Jr. 5.00 12.00
2 Derek Jeter 6.00 15.00
3 Ben Grieve 1.00 2.50
4 Cal Ripken 8.00 20.00
5 Alex Rodriguez 4.00 10.00
6 Greg Maddux 4.00 10.00
7 David Justice 1.00 2.50
8 Mike Piazza 4.00 10.00
9 Chipper Jones 2.50 6.00
10 Randy Johnson 2.50 6.00
11 Jeff Bagwell 1.50 4.00
12 Nomar Garciaparra 4.00 10.00
13 Andruw Jones 1.50 4.00
14 Frank Thomas 2.50 6.00
15 Scott Rolen 1.50 4.00
16 Barry Bonds 6.00 15.00
17 Kenny Lofton 1.00 2.50
18 Ivan Rodriguez 1.50 4.00
19 Chuck Knoblauch 1.00 2.50
20 Jose Cruz Jr. 1.00 2.50
21 Bernie Williams 1.50 4.00
22 Tony Gwynn 3.00 8.00
23 Juan Gonzalez 1.00 2.50
24 Gary Sheffield 1.00 2.50
25 Roger Clemens 5.00 12.00
26 Travis Lee 1.00 2.50
27 Brad Fullmer 1.00 2.50
28 Tim Salmon 1.50 4.00
29 Raul Mondesi 1.00 2.50
30 Roberto Alomar 1.50 4.00

1998 Studio Hit Parade

COMPLETE SET (20) 20.00 50.00
RANDOM INSERTS IN PACKS
STATED PRINT RUN 5000 SERIAL #'d SETS
1 Tony Gwynn 2.00 5.00
2 Larry Walker 1.25 3.00
3 Mike Piazza 2.00 5.00
4 Frank Thomas 2.00 5.00
5 Manny Ramirez 2.00 5.00
6 Ken Griffey Jr. 4.00 10.00
7 Todd Helton 1.25 3.00
8 Vladimir Guerrero 1.25 3.00
9 Albert Belle .75 2.00
10 Jeff Bagwell 1.25 3.00
11 Juan Gonzalez .75 2.00
12 Jim Thome 1.25 3.00
13 Scott Rolen 1.25 3.00
14 Tino Martinez .75 2.00
15 Mark McGwire 3.00 8.00
16 Barry Bonds 3.00 8.00
17 Tony Clark .75 2.00
18 Mo Vaughn .75 2.00
19 Darin Erstad .75 2.00
20 Paul Konerko .75 2.00

1998 Studio Masterstrokes

COMPLETE SET (20) 75.00 150.00
STATED PRINT RUN 1000 SERIAL #'d SETS
1 Travis Lee 2.00 5.00
2 Kenny Lofton 2.00 5.00
3 Mo Vaughn 2.00 5.00
4 Ivan Rodriguez 3.00 8.00
5 Roger Clemens 10.00 25.00
6 Mark McGwire 12.50 30.00
7 Hideo Nomo 5.00 12.00
8 Andruw Jones 3.00 8.00
9 Nomar Garciaparra 8.00 20.00
10 Juan Gonzalez 2.00 5.00
11 Jeff Bagwell 3.00 8.00
12 Derek Jeter 12.50 30.00
13 Tony Gwynn 6.00 15.00
14 Chipper Jones 5.00 12.00
15 Mike Piazza 8.00 20.00
16 Greg Maddux 8.00 20.00
17 Alex Rodriguez 8.00 20.00
18 Cal Ripken 15.00 40.00
19 Frank Thomas 5.00 12.00
20 Ken Griffey Jr. 10.00 25.00

1998 Studio Portraits 8 x 10

COMPLETE SET (36) 15.00 40.00
ONE PER PACK
GOLD: RANDOM INSERTS IN PACKS
GOLD PRINT RUN 300 SERIAL #'d SETS
1 Travis Lee .20 .50
2 Todd Helton .30 .75
3 Ben Grieve .20 .50
4 Paul Konerko .20 .50
5 Jeff Bagwell .30 .75
6 Derek Jeter 1.25 3.00
7 Ivan Rodriguez .30 .75
8 Cal Ripken 1.50 4.00
9 Mike Piazza .75 2.00
10 Chipper Jones .50 1.25
11 Frank Thomas .50 1.25
12 Tony Gwynn .60 1.50
13 Nomar Garciaparra .75 2.00
14 Juan Gonzalez .20 .50
15 Greg Maddux .75 2.00
16 Hideo Nomo .50 1.25
17 Scott Rolen .30 .75
18 Barry Bonds 1.25 3.00
19 Ken Griffey Jr. 1.00 2.50
20 Alex Rodriguez .75 2.00
21 Roger Clemens 1.00 2.50
22 Mark McGwire 1.25 3.00
23 Jose Cruz Jr. .20 .50
24 Andruw Jones .30 .75
25 Tino Martinez .30 .75
26 Mo Vaughn .20 .50
27 Vladimir Guerrero .50 1.25
28 Tony Clark .20 .50
29 Andy Pettitte .30 .75
30 Jaret Wright .20 .50
31 Paul Molitor .20 .50
32 Darin Erstad .20 .50
33 Larry Walker .20 .50
34 Chuck Knoblauch .20 .50
35 Barry Larkin .30 .75
36 Kenny Lofton .20 .50

2001 Studio

COMP.SET w/o SP's (150) 15.00 40.00
COMMON CARD (1-150) .20 .50
COMMON CARD (151-200) 3.00 8.00
151-200 RANDOM INSERTS IN PACKS
151-200 PRINT RUN 700 SERIAL #'d SETS
1 Alex Rodriguez .60 1.50
2 Barry Bonds 1.25 3.00
3 Cal Ripken 1.50 4.00
4 Chipper Jones .50 1.25
5 Derek Jeter 1.25 3.00
6 Troy Glaus .20 .50
7 Frank Thomas .50 1.25
8 Greg Maddux .75 2.00
9 Ivan Rodriguez .30 .75
10 Jeff Bagwell .30 .75
11 Mark Quinn .20 .50
12 Todd Helton .30 .75
13 Ken Griffey Jr. 1.00 2.50
14 Manny Ramirez Sox .30 .75
15 Mark McGwire 1.25 3.00
16 Mike Piazza .75 2.00
17 Nomar Garciaparra .75 2.00
18 Robin Ventura .20 .50
19 Aramis Ramirez .20 .50
20 J.T. Snow .20 .50
21 Pat Burrell .20 .50
22 Curt Schilling .20 .50
23 Carlos Delgado .20 .50
24 J.D. Drew .20 .50
25 Cliff Floyd .20 .50
26 Brian Jordan .20 .50
27 Roberto Alomar .30 .75
28 Barry Zito .30 .75
29 Harold Baines .20 .50
30 Brad Penny .20 .50
31 Jose Cruz Jr. .20 .50
32 Andy Pettitte .30 .75
33 Jim Edmonds .20 .50
34 Darin Erstad .20 .50
35 Jason Giambi .20 .50
36 Tom Glavine .30 .75
37 Juan Gonzalez .20 .50
38 Mark Grace .30 .75
39 Shawn Green .20 .50
40 Tim Hudson .20 .50
41 Andruw Jones .30 .75
42 Jeff Kent .20 .50
43 Barry Larkin .30 .75
44 Rafael Furcal .20 .50
45 Mike Mussina .30 .75
46 Hideo Nomo .50 1.25
47 Rafael Palmeiro .30 .75
48 Scott Rolen .30 .75
49 Gary Sheffield .20 .50
50 Bernie Williams .30 .75
51 Bob Abreu .20 .50
52 Edgardo Alfonzo .20 .50
53 Edgar Martinez .30 .75
54 Magglio Ordonez .20 .50
55 Kerry Wood .20 .50
56 Matt Morris .20 .50
57 Lance Berkman .20 .50
58 Kevin Brown .20 .50
59 Sean Casey .20 .50
60 Eric Chavez .20 .50
61 Bartolo Colon .20 .50
62 Johnny Damon .30 .75
63 Jermaine Dye .20 .50
64 Juan Encarnacion .20 .50
65 Carl Everett .20 .50
66 Brian Giles .20 .50
67 Mike Hampton .20 .50
68 Richard Hidalgo .20 .50
69 Geoff Jenkins .20 .50
70 Jacque Jones .20 .50
71 Jason Kendall .20 .50
72 Ryan Klesko .20 .50
73 Chan Ho Park .20 .50
74 Richie Sexson .20 .50
75 Mike Sweeney .20 .50
76 Fernando Tatis .20 .50
77 Miguel Tejada .20 .50
78 Jose Vidro .20 .50
79 Larry Walker .75 2.00
80 Preston Wilson .20 .50
81 Craig Biggio .30 .75
82 Fred McGriff .30 .75
83 Jim Thome .30 .75
84 Garret Anderson .20 .50
85 Mark Mulder .20 .50
86 Tony Batista .20 .50
87 Terrence Long .20 .50
88 Brad Fullmer .20 .50
89 Rusty Greer .20 .50
90 Orlando Hernandez .20 .50
91 Gabe Kapler .20 .50
92 Paul Konerko .20 .50
93 Carlos Lee .20 .50
94 Kenny Lofton .20 .50
95 Raul Mondesi .20 .50
96 Jorge Posada .30 .75
97 Tim Salmon .30 .75
98 Greg Vaughn .20 .50
99 Mo Vaughn .20 .50
100 Omar Vizquel .30 .75
101 Ben Grieve .20 .50
102 Luis Gonzalez .20 .50
103 Ray Durham .20 .50
104 Ryan Dempster .20 .50
105 Eric Karros .20 .50
106 David Justice .20 .50
107 Pedro Martinez .30 .75
108 Randy Johnson .50 1.25
109 Rick Ankiel .20 .50
110 Rickey Henderson .50 1.25
111 Roger Clemens 1.00 2.50
112 Sammy Sosa .50 1.25
113 Tony Gwynn .60 1.50
114 Vladimir Guerrero .50 1.25
115 Kazuhiro Sasaki .20 .50
116 Phil Nevin .20 .50
117 Ruben Mateo .20 .50
118 Shannon Stewart .20 .50
119 Matt Williams .20 .50
120 Tino Martinez .30 .75
121 Ken Caminiti .20 .50
122 Edgar Renteria .20 .50
123 Charles Johnson .20 .50
124 Aaron Sele .20 .50
125 Javy Lopez .20 .50
126 Mariano Rivera .50 1.25
127 Shea Hillenbrand .20 .50
128 Jeff D'Amico .20 .50
129 Brady Anderson .20 .50
130 Kevin Millwood .20 .50
131 Trot Nixon .20 .50
132 Mike Lieberthal .20 .50
133 Juan Pierre .20 .50
134 Russ Ortiz .20 .50
135 Jose Macias .20 .50
136 John Smoltz .30 .75
137 Jason Varitek .50 1.25
138 Dean Palmer .20 .50
139 Jeff Cirillo .20 .50
140 Paul O'Neill .30 .75
141 Andres Galarraga .20 .50
142 David Wells .20 .50
143 Brad Radke .20 .50
144 Wade Miller .20 .50
145 John Olerud .20 .50
146 Moises Alou .20 .50
147 Carlos Beltran .20 .50
148 Jeromy Burnitz .20 .50
149 Steve Finley .20 .50
150 Joe Mays .20 .50
151 Alex Escobar ROO 3.00 8.00
152 Johnny Estrada ROO RC 4.00 10.00
153 Pedro Feliz ROO 3.00 8.00
154 Nate Frese ROO RC 3.00 8.00
155 Dee Brown ROO 3.00 8.00
156 Brandon Larson ROO RC 3.00 8.00
157 Alexis Gomez ROO RC 3.00 8.00
158 Jason Hart ROO 3.00 8.00
159 C.C. Sabathia ROO 3.00 8.00
160 Josh Towers ROO RC 4.00 10.00
161 Christian Parker ROO RC 3.00 8.00
162 Jackson Melian ROO RC 3.00 8.00
163 Joe Kennedy ROO RC 4.00 10.00
164 Adrian Hernandez ROO RC 3.00 8.00
165 Jimmy Rollins ROO 3.00 8.00
166 Jose Mieses ROO RC 3.00 8.00
167 Roy Oswalt ROO 4.00 10.00
168 Eric Munson ROO 3.00 8.00
169 Xavier Nady ROO 3.00 8.00
170 Horacio Ramirez ROO RC 4.00 10.00
171 Abraham Nunez ROO 3.00 8.00
172 Jose Ortiz ROO 3.00 8.00
173 Jeremy Owens ROO RC 3.00 8.00
174 Claudio Vargas ROO RC 3.00 8.00
175 Corey Patterson ROO 3.00 8.00
176 Carlos Pena ROO 3.00 8.00
177 Bud Smith ROO RC 3.00 8.00
178 Adam Dunn ROO 4.00 10.00
179 Adam Pettyjohn ROO RC 3.00 8.00
180 Elpidio Guzman ROO RC 3.00 8.00
181 Jay Gibbons ROO RC 4.00 10.00
182 Wilkin Ruan ROO RC 3.00 8.00
183 Tsuyoshi Shinjo ROO RC 4.00 10.00
184 Alfonso Soriano ROO 4.00 10.00
185 Marcus Giles ROO 3.00 8.00
186 Ichiro Suzuki ROO RC 40.00 100.00
187 Juan Uribe ROO RC 4.00 10.00
188 David Williams ROO RC 3.00 8.00
189 Carlos Valderrama ROO RC 3.00 8.00
190 Matt White ROO RC 3.00 8.00
191 Albert Pujols ROO RC 75.00 200.00
192 Donaldo Mendez ROO RC 3.00 8.00
193 Cory Aldridge ROO RC 3.00 8.00
194 Endy Chavez ROO RC 3.00 8.00
195 Josh Beckett ROO 4.00 10.00
196 Wilson Betemit ROO RC 4.00 10.00
197 Ben Sheets ROO 4.00 10.00
198 Andres Torres ROO RC 3.00 8.00
199 Aubrey Huff ROO 3.00 8.00
200 Jack Wilson ROO RC 4.00 10.00

2001 Studio Diamond Collectio

CARDS 24, 35 AND 44 DO NOT EXIST
DC1 Vladimir Guerrero 4.00 10.00
DC2 Barry Bonds 6.00 15.00
DC3 Cal Ripken 10.00 25.00
DC4 Nomar Garciaparra 4.00 10.00
DC5 Greg Maddux 4.00 10.00
DC6 Frank Thomas 4.00 10.00
DC7 Roger Clemens 6.00 15.00
DC8 Luis Gonzalez SP 4.00 10.00
DC9 Tony Gwynn 4.00 10.00
DC10 Carlos Lee SP 4.00 10.00
DC11 Troy Glaus 2.50 6.00
DC12 Randy Johnson 4.00 10.00
DC13 Manny Ramirez SP 6.00 15.00
DC14 Pedro Martinez 4.00 10.00
DC15 Todd Helton 4.00 10.00
DC16 Jeff Bagwell 4.00 10.00
DC17 Rickey Henderson 4.00 10.00
DC18 Kazuhiro Sasaki 2.50 6.00
DC19 Albert Pujols SP 25.00 50.00
DC20 Ivan Rodriguez 4.00 10.00
DC21 Darin Erstad 2.50 6.00
DC22 Andruw Jones 4.00 10.00
DC23 Roberto Alomar 4.00 10.00
DC25 Juan Gonzalez 2.50 6.00
DC26 Shawn Green 2.50 6.00
DC27 Lance Berkman 2.50 6.00
DC28 Scott Rolen 4.00 10.00
DC29 Rafael Palmeiro 4.00 10.00
DC30 J.D. Drew 2.50 6.00
DC31 Kerry Wood 2.50 6.00
DC32 Jim Edmonds 2.50 6.00
DC33 Tom Glavine SP 6.00 15.00
DC34 Hideo Nomo SP 6.00 15.00
DC36 Tim Hudson 2.50 6.00
DC37 Miguel Tejada 2.50 6.00
DC38 Chipper Jones 4.00 10.00
DC39 Edgar Martinez SP 6.00 15.00
DC40 Chan Ho Park 2.50 6.00
DC41 Magglio Ordonez 2.50 6.00
DC42 Sean Casey 2.50 6.00
DC43 Larry Walker 2.50 6.00
DC45 Cliff Floyd 2.50 6.00
DC46 Mike Sweeney 2.50 6.00
DC47 Kevin Brown 2.50 6.00
DC48 Richie Sexson 2.50 6.00
DC49 Jermaine Dye 2.50 6.00
DC50 Craig Biggio 4.00 10.00

2001 Studio Leather and Lumber

CARDS 4, 22 AND 39 DO NOT EXIST
COMBOS PRINT RUN 25 #'d SETS
NO COMBO PRICING DUE TO SCARCITY
LL1 Barry Bonds 10.00 25.00
LL2 Cal Ripken 15.00 40.00
LL3 Miguel Tejada 4.00 10.00
LL5 Frank Thomas 6.00 15.00
LL6 Greg Maddux 6.00 15.00
LL7 Ivan Rodriguez 6.00 15.00
LL8 Jeff Bagwell SP 10.00 25.00
LL9 Sean Casey SP 6.00 15.00
LL10 Todd Helton 6.00 15.00
LL11 Cliff Floyd 4.00 10.00
LL12 Hideo Nomo 6.00 15.00
LL13 Chipper Jones 6.00 15.00
LL14 Rickey Henderson 6.00 15.00
LL15 Richard Hidalgo 4.00 10.00
LL16 Mike Piazza 6.00 15.00
LL17 Larry Walker 4.00 10.00
LL18 Tony Gwynn 6.00 15.00
LL19 Vladimir Guerrero 6.00 15.00
LL20 Rafael Furcal 4.00 10.00
LL21 Roberto Alomar SP 10.00 25.00
LL23 Albert Pujols 25.00 60.00
LL24 Raul Mondesi 4.00 10.00
LL25 J.D. Drew 4.00 10.00
LL26 Jim Edmonds 4.00 10.00
LL27 Darin Erstad SP 6.00 15.00
LL28 Craig Biggio 6.00 15.00
LL29 Kenny Lofton 4.00 10.00
LL30 Juan Gonzalez 4.00 10.00
LL31 John Olerud 4.00 10.00
LL32 Shawn Green 4.00 10.00
LL33 Andruw Jones SP 10.00 25.00
LL34 Moises Alou 4.00 10.00
LL35 Jeff Kent 4.00 10.00
LL36 Ryan Klesko 4.00 10.00
LL37 Luis Gonzalez 4.00 10.00
LL38 Rafael Palmeiro 6.00 15.00
LL40 Scott Rolen 6.00 15.00
LL41 Carlos Lee 4.00 10.00
LL42 Bob Abreu 4.00 10.00
LL43 Edgardo Alfonzo 4.00 10.00
LL44 Bernie Williams 6.00 15.00
LL45 Brian Giles 4.00 10.00
LL46 Jermaine Dye 4.00 10.00
LL47 Lance Berkman 4.00 10.00
LL48 Edgar Martinez 6.00 15.00
LL49 Richie Sexson 4.00 10.00
LL50 Magglio Ordonez 4.00 10.00

2001 Studio Masterstrokes

STATED PRINT RUN 200 SERIAL #'d SETS
CARDS 13 AND 15 DO NOT EXIST
MS1 Tony Gwynn 10.00 25.00
MS2 Ivan Rodriguez 10.00 25.00
MS3 J.D. Drew 6.00 15.00
MS4 Cal Ripken 30.00 60.00
MS5 Hideo Nomo 10.00 25.00
MS6 Darin Erstad 6.00 15.00
MS7 Frank Thomas 10.00 25.00
MS8 Andruw Jones 10.00 25.00
MS9 Roberto Alomar 10.00 25.00
MS10 Larry Walker 6.00 15.00
MS11 Vladimir Guerrero 10.00 25.00
MS12 Barry Bonds 10.00 25.00
MS14 Luis Gonzalez 6.00 15.00
MS16 Juan Gonzalez 6.00 15.00
MS17 Todd Helton 10.00 25.00
MS18 Jeff Bagwell 10.00 25.00
MS19 Albert Pujols 50.00 120.00
MS20 Shawn Green 6.00 15.00
MS21 Magglio Ordonez 6.00 15.00
MS22 Scott Rolen 10.00 25.00
MS23 Rafael Palmeiro 10.00 25.00
MS24 Sean Casey 6.00 15.00
MS25 Jim Edmonds 6.00 15.00
MS26 Chipper Jones 10.00 25.00
MS27 Cliff Floyd 6.00 15.00
MS28 Carlos Lee 6.00 15.00
MS29 Edgar Martinez 10.00 25.00

2001 Studio Private Signings 5 x 7

ONE PER SEALED BOX
SP's ARE NOT SERIAL NUMBERED
SP PRINT RUNS PROVIDED BY DONRUSS
NO PRICING ON QTY OF 25 OR LESS
1 Bob Abreu 6.00 15.00
2 Roberto Alomar SP/200 * 10.00 25.00
3 Rick Ankiel 6.00 15.00
4 Josh Beckett 10.00 25.00
5 Lance Berkman 6.00 15.00
6 Wilson Betemit 10.00 25.00
7 Barry Bonds SP/95 * 100.00 175.00
8 Sean Casey 6.00 15.00
9 Roger Clemens SP/200 * 40.00 80.00
10 Adam Dunn 10.00 25.00
12 Alex Escobar 4.00 10.00
13 Cliff Floyd 6.00 15.00
14 Jason Giambi SP/250 * 6.00 15.00
15 Brian Giles 6.00 15.00
16 Troy Glaus 10.00 25.00
17 Tom Glavine 15.00 40.00
18 Luis Gonzalez 6.00 15.00
19 Shawn Green SP/190 * 10.00 25.00
20 Vladimir Guerrero 6.00 15.00
21 Tony Gwynn SP/190 * 12.00 30.00
22 Todd Helton SP/125 * 10.00 25.00
23 Andruw Jones SP/250 * 10.00 25.00
24 Gabe Kapler 6.00 15.00
25 Ryan Klesko 6.00 15.00
26 Carlos Lee 6.00 15.00
27 Greg Maddux SP/200 * 50.00 100.00
28 Edgar Martinez 15.00 40.00
29 Mike Mussina SP/144 * 15.00 40.00
30 Magglio Ordonez 6.00 15.00
31 Rafael Palmeiro SP/250 * 20.00 50.00
32 Corey Patterson 4.00 10.00
33 Brad Penny 4.00 10.00
34 Albert Pujols SP/50 * 600.00 1500.00
35 Manny Ramirez Sox SP/115 * 12.50 30.00
36 Cal Ripken SP/50 * 150.00 250.00
37 Alex Rodriguez 20.00 50.00
38 Ivan Rodriguez SP/150 * 15.00 40.00
39 Scott Rolen 10.00 25.00
40 C.C. Sabathia 6.00 15.00
41 Curt Schilling 8.00 20.00
42 Ben Sheets 10.00 25.00
43 Alfonso Soriano 10.00 25.00
44 Mike Sweeney 6.00 15.00
45 Miguel Tejada 10.00 25.00
46 Frank Thomas 15.00 40.00
47 Kerry Wood 10.00 25.00
48 Barry Zito 6.00 15.00

2001 Studio Warning Track

OFF THE WALL 25 SERIAL #'D SETS
OFF THE WALL: NO PRICING DUE TO SCARCITY
CARD 26 DOES NOT EXIST
WT1 Andruw Jones 4.00 10.00
WT2 Rafael Palmeiro 4.00 10.00
WT3 Gary Sheffield 3.00 8.00
WT4 Larry Walker 3.00 8.00
WT5 Shawn Green 3.00 8.00
WT6 Mike Piazza 6.00 15.00
WT7 Barry Bonds 10.00 25.00
WT8 J.D. Drew 3.00 8.00
WT9 Magglio Ordonez 3.00 8.00
WT10 Todd Helton 4.00 10.00
WT11 Juan Gonzalez 3.00 8.00
WT12 Pat Burrell 3.00 8.00
WT13 Mark McGwire 12.50 30.00
WT14 Frank Robinson 4.00 10.00
WT15 Manny Ramirez 4.00 10.00
WT16 Lance Berkman 3.00 8.00
WT17 Kirby Puckett 4.00 10.00
WT18 Johnny Bench 4.00 10.00
WT19 Chipper Jones 4.00 10.00
WT20 Mike Schmidt 8.00 20.00
WT21 Vladimir Guerrero 4.00 10.00
WT22 Sammy Sosa 4.00 10.00
WT23 Cal Ripken 12.50 30.00
WT24 Roberto Alomar 4.00 10.00
WT25 Willie Stargell 4.00 10.00
WT27 Scott Rolen 4.00 10.00
WT28 Roberto Clemente SP 20.00 50.00
WT29 Tony Gwynn 6.00 15.00
WT30 Ivan Rodriguez 4.00 10.00
WT31 Sean Casey 3.00 8.00
WT32 Frank Thomas 4.00 10.00
WT33 Jeff Bagwell 4.00 10.00
WT34 Jeff Kent 3.00 8.00
WT35 Reggie Jackson 4.00 10.00

2002 Studio Samples

*SAMPLES: 1.5X TO 4X BASIC CARDS
ONE PER ICHIRO BBCM 210
*GOLD: 1.5X TO 4X BASIC SAMPLES
GOLD: ISSUED IN 10% OF TOTAL RUN

2002 Studio

COMP.LOW SET w/o SP's (200) 20.00 50.00
COMMON CARD (1-200) .20 .50
COMMON ROOKIE (1-200) .20 .50
COMMON CARD (201-275) 1.50 4.00
201-250 RANDOM IN STUDIO PACKS
251-275 RANDOM IN DONRUSS ROOK.PACKS
201-275 PRINT RUN 1500 SERIAL #'d SETS
1 Vladimir Guerrero .50 1.25
2 Chipper Jones .50 1.25
3 Bob Abreu .20 .50
4 Barry Zito .20 .50
5 Larry Walker .20 .50
6 Miguel Tejada .20 .50
7 Mike Sweeney .20 .50
8 Shannon Stewart .20 .50
9 Sammy Sosa .50 1.25
10 Bud Smith .20 .50
11 Wilson Betemit .20 .50
12 Kevin Brown .20 .50
13 Ellis Burks .20 .50
14 Pat Burrell .20 .50
15 Cliff Floyd .20 .50
16 Marcus Giles .20 .50
17 Troy Glaus .20 .50
18 Barry Larkin .30 .75
19 Carlos Lee .20 .50
20 Brian Lawrence .20 .50
21 Paul Lo Duca .20 .50
22 Ben Grieve .20 .50
23 Shawn Green .20 .50
24 Mike Cameron .20 .50
25 Roger Clemens 1.00 2.50
26 Joe Crede .20 .50
27 Jose Cruz Jr. .20 .50
28 Jeremy Affeldt .20 .50
29 Adrian Beltre .20 .50
30 Josh Beckett .20 .50
31 Roberto Alomar .30 .75
32 Toby Hall .20 .50
33 Mike Hampton .20 .50
34 Eric Milton .20 .50
35 Eric Munson .20 .50
36 Trot Nixon .20 .50
37 Roy Oswalt .20 .50
38 Chan Ho Park .20 .50
39 Charles Johnson .20 .50
40 Nick Johnson .20 .50
41 Tim Hudson .20 .50
42 Cristian Guzman .20 .50
43 Drew Henson .20 .50
44 Mark Grace .30 .75
45 Luis Gonzalez .20 .50
46 Pedro Martinez .30 .75
47 Joe Mays .20 .50
48 Jorge Posada .30 .75
49 Aramis Ramirez .20 .50
50 Kip Wells .20 .50
51 Moises Alou .20 .50
52 Omar Vizquel .30 .75
53 Ichiro Suzuki 1.00 2.50
54 Jimmy Rollins .20 .50
55 Freddy Garcia .20 .50
56 Steve Green .20 .50
57 Brian Jordan .20 .50
58 Paul Konerko .20 .50
59 Jack Cust .20 .50
60 Sean Casey .20 .50
61 Bret Boone .20 .50
62 Hideo Nomo .50 1.25
63 Magglio Ordonez .20 .50
64 Frank Thomas .50 1.25
65 Josh Towers .20 .50
66 Javier Vazquez .20 .50
67 Robin Ventura .20 .50
68 Aubrey Huff .20 .50
69 Richard Hidalgo .20 .50
70 Brandon Claussen .20 .50
71 Bartolo Colon .20 .50
72 John Buck .20 .50
73 Dee Brown .20 .50
74 Barry Bonds 1.25 3.00
75 Jason Giambi .20 .50
76 Erick Almonte .20 .50
77 Ryan Dempster .20 .50
78 Jim Edmonds .20 .50
79 Jay Gibbons .20 .50
80 Shigetoshi Hasegawa .20 .50
81 Todd Helton .30 .75
82 Erik Bedard .20 .50
83 Carlos Beltran .20 .50
84 Rafael Soriano .20 .50
85 Gary Sheffield .20 .50
86 Richie Sexson .20 .50
87 Mike Rivera .20 .50
88 Jose Ortiz .20 .50
89 Abraham Nunez .20 .50
90 Dave Williams .20 .50
91 Preston Wilson .20 .50
92 Jason Jennings .20 .50
93 Juan Diaz .20 .50
94 Steve Smyth .20 .50
95 Phil Nevin .20 .50
96 John Olerud .20 .50
97 Brad Penny .20 .50
98 Andy Pettitte .30 .75
99 Juan Pierre .20 .50
100 Manny Ramirez .30 .75
101 Edgardo Alfonzo .20 .50
102 Michael Cuddyer .20 .50
103 Johnny Damon Sox .30 .75
104 Carlos Zambrano .20 .50
105 Jose Vidro .20 .50
106 Tsuyoshi Shinjo .20 .50
107 Ed Rogers .20 .50
108 Scott Rolen .30 .75
109 Mariano Rivera .50 1.25
110 Tim Redding .20 .50
111 Josh Phelps .20 .50
112 Gabe Kapler .20 .50
113 Edgar Martinez .30 .75
114 Fred McGriff .30 .75
115 Raul Mondesi .20 .50
116 Wade Miller .20 .50
117 Mike Mussina .30 .75
118 Rafael Palmeiro .30 .75
119 Adam Johnson .20 .50
120 Rickey Henderson .50 1.25
121 Bill Hall .20 .50
122 Ken Griffey Jr. 1.00 2.50
123 Geronimo Gil .20 .50
124 Robert Fick .20 .50
125 Darin Erstad .20 .50
126 Brandon Duckworth .20 .50
127 Garret Anderson .20 .50
128 Pedro Feliz .20 .50
129 Jeff Cirillo .20 .50
130 Brian Giles .20 .50
131 Craig Biggio .30 .75
132 Willie Harris .20 .50
133 Doug Davis .20 .50
134 Jeff Kent .20 .50
135 Terrence Long .20 .50
136 Carlos Delgado .20 .50
137 Tino Martinez .30 .75
138 Donaldo Mendez .20 .50
139 Sean Douglass .20 .50
140 Eric Chavez .20 .50
141 Rick Ankiel .20 .50
142 Jeremy Giambi .20 .50
143 Juan Pena .20 .50
144 Bernie Williams .30 .75
145 Craig Wilson .20 .50
146 Ricardo Rodriguez .20 .50
147 Albert Pujols 1.00 2.50
148 Antonio Perez .20 .50
149 Russ Ortiz .20 .50
150 Corky Miller .20 .50
151 Rich Aurilia .20 .50
152 Kerry Wood .20 .50
153 Joe Thurston .20 .50
154 Jeff Deardorff .20 .50
155 Jermaine Dye .20 .50

156 Andruw Jones .30 .75
157 Victor Martinez .50 1.25
158 Nick Neugebauer .20 .50
159 Matt Morris .20 .50
160 Casey Fossum .20 .50
161 J.D. Drew .20 .50
162 Matt Childers .20 .50
163 Mark Buehrle .20 .50
164 Jeff Bagwell .30 .75
165 Kazuhiro Sasaki .20 .50
166 Ben Sheets .20 .50
167 Alex Rodriguez .60 1.50
168 Adam Pettyjohn .20 .50
169 Chris Snelling RC .50 1.25
170 Robert Person .20 .50
171 Juan Uribe .20 .50
172 Mo Vaughn .20 .50
173 Alfredo Amezaga .20 .50
174 Ryan Drese .20 .50
175 Corey Thurman RC .20 .50
176 Jim Thome .30 .75
177 Orlando Cabrera .20 .50
178 Eric Cyr .20 .50
179 Greg Maddux .75 2.00
180 Earl Snyder RC .20 .50
181 C.C. Sabathia .20 .50
182 Mark Mulder .20 .50
183 Jose Mieses .20 .50
184 Joe Kennedy .20 .50
185 Randy Johnson .50 1.25
186 Tom Glavine .30 .75
187 Eric Junge RC .20 .50
188 Mike Piazza .75 2.00
189 Corey Patterson .20 .50
190 Carlos Pena .20 .50
191 Curt Schilling .20 .50
192 Nomar Garciaparra .75 2.00
193 Lance Berkman .20 .50
194 Ryan Klesko .20 .50
195 Ivan Rodriguez .30 .75
196 Alfonso Soriano .20 .50
197 Derek Jeter 1.25 3.00
198 David Justice .20 .50
199 Juan Gonzalez .20 .50
200 Adam Dunn .20 .50
201 Victor Alvarez ROO RC 1.50 4.00
202 Miguel Asencio ROO RC 1.50 4.00
203 Brandon Backe ROO RC 2.00 5.00
204 Chris Baker ROO RC 1.50 4.00
205 Steve Bechler ROO RC 1.50 4.00
206 Francis Beltran ROO RC 1.50 4.00
207 Angel Berroa ROO 1.50 4.00
208 Hank Blalock ROO 2.00 5.00
209 Dewon Brazelton ROO 1.50 4.00
210 Sean Burroughs ROO 1.50 4.00
211 Marlon Byrd ROO 1.50 4.00
212 Raul Chavez ROO RC 1.50 4.00
213 Juan Cruz ROO 1.50 4.00
214 Jorge De La Rosa ROO RC 1.50 4.00
215 Doug Devore ROO RC 1.50 4.00
216 John Ennis ROO RC 1.50 4.00
217 Felix Escalona ROO RC 1.50 4.00
218 Morgan Ensberg ROO 1.50 4.00
219 Cam Esslinger ROO RC 1.50 4.00
220 Kevin Frederick ROO RC 1.50 4.00
221 Franklyn German ROO RC 1.50 4.00
222 Eric Hinske ROO 1.50 4.00
223 Ben Howard ROO RC 1.50 4.00
224 Orlando Hudson ROO 1.50 4.00
225 Travis Hughes ROO RC 1.50 4.00
226 Kazuhisa Ishii ROO RC 2.00 5.00
227 Ryan Jamison ROO 1.50 4.00
228 Reed Johnson ROO RC 2.00 5.00
229 Kyle Kane ROO RC 1.50 4.00
230 Austin Kearns ROO 1.50 4.00
231 Satoru Komiyama ROO RC 1.50 4.00
232 Jason Lane ROO 1.50 4.00
233 Jeremy Lambert ROO RC 1.50 4.00
234 Anderson Machado ROO RC 1.50 4.00
235 Brian Mallette ROO RC 1.50 4.00
236 Takahito Nomura ROO RC 1.50 4.00
237 Jorge Padilla ROO RC 1.50 4.00
238 Luis Ugueto ROO RC 1.50 4.00
239 Mark Prior ROO 2.00 5.00
240 Rene Reyes ROO RC 1.50 4.00
241 Deivis Santos ROO 1.50 4.00
242 Elio Serrano ROO RC 1.50 4.00
243 Tom Shearn ROO RC 1.50 4.00
244 Allan Simpson ROO RC 1.50 4.00
245 So Taguchi ROO RC 2.00 5.00
246 Dennis Tankersley ROO 1.50 4.00
247 Mark Teixeira ROO 2.00 5.00
248 Matt Thornton ROO RC 1.50 4.00
249 Bobby Hill ROO 1.50 4.00
250 Ramon Vazquez ROO 1.50 4.00
251 Freddy Sanchez ROO RC 2.00 5.00
252 Josh Bard ROO RC 1.50 4.00
253 Trey Hodges ROO RC 1.50 4.00
254 Jorge Sosa ROO RC 2.00 5.00
255 Ben Kozlowski ROO RC 1.50 4.00
256 Eric Good ROO RC 1.50 4.00
257 Brian Tallet ROO RC 1.50 4.00
258 P.J. Bevis ROO RC 1.50 4.00
259 Rodrigo Rosario ROO RC 1.50 4.00
260 Kirk Saarloos ROO RC 1.50 4.00
261 Runelvys Hernandez ROO RC 1.50 4.00
262 Josh Hancock ROO RC 2.00 5.00
263 Tim Kalita ROO RC 1.50 4.00
264 Jason Simontacchi ROO RC 1.50 4.00
265 Clay Condrey ROO RC 1.50 4.00
266 Cliff Lee ROO RC 5.00 12.00
267 Aaron Guiel ROO RC 1.50 4.00
268 Andy Pratt ROO RC 1.50 4.00
269 Wilson Valdez ROO RC 1.50 4.00
270 Oliver Perez ROO RC 2.00 5.00
271 Joe Borchard ROO 1.50 4.00
272 Jeriome Robertson ROO RC 1.50 4.00
273 Aaron Cook ROO RC 1.50 4.00
274 Kevin Cash ROO RC 1.50 4.00
275 Chone Figgins ROO RC 2.00 5.00

2002 Studio Private Signings

1-250 RANDOM INSERTS IN STUDIO PACKS
251-275 RANDOM IN DONRUSS ROOK.PACKS
STATED PRINT RUNS LISTED BELOW
NO PRICING ON QTY OF 25 OR LESS
SKIP-NUMBERED 210-CARD SET
3 Bob Abreu/50 10.00 25.00
6 Miguel Tejada/50 15.00 40.00
7 Mike Sweeney/50 10.00 25.00
8 Shannon Stewart/50 10.00 25.00
10 Bud Smith/100 6.00 15.00
11 Wilson Betemit/250 4.00 10.00
15 Cliff Floyd/50 10.00 25.00
16 Marcus Giles/250 6.00 15.00
17 Troy Glaus/50 6.00 15.00
20 Brian Lawrence/250 4.00 10.00
21 Paul Lo Duca/50 10.00 25.00
26 Joe Crede/250 6.00 15.00
28 Jeremy Affeldt/250 4.00 10.00
32 Toby Hall/250 4.00 10.00
37 Roy Oswalt/50 10.00 25.00
40 Nick Johnson/250 6.00 15.00
43 Drew Henson/150 4.00 10.00
47 Joe Mays/100 6.00 15.00
49 Aramis Ramirez/50 10.00 25.00
50 Kip Wells/250 4.00 10.00
55 Freddy Garcia/50 10.00 25.00
56 Steve Green/250 4.00 10.00
59 Jack Cust/250 4.00 10.00
60 Sean Casey/50 10.00 25.00
65 Josh Towers/250 4.00 10.00
66 Javier Vazquez/100 8.00 20.00
68 Aubrey Huff/250 6.00 15.00
70 Brandon Claussen/250 4.00 10.00
72 John Buck/250 4.00 10.00
73 Dee Brown/250 4.00 10.00
76 Erick Almonte/250 4.00 10.00
79 Jay Gibbons/250 4.00 10.00
82 Erik Bedard/250 6.00 15.00
84 Rafael Soriano/250 4.00 10.00
86 Richie Sexson/50 10.00 25.00
87 Mike Rivera/250 4.00 10.00
88 Jose Ortiz/250 4.00 10.00
89 Abraham Nunez/250 4.00 10.00
90 Dave Williams/250 4.00 10.00
92 Jason Jennings/250 4.00 10.00
93 Juan Diaz/250 4.00 10.00
94 Steve Smyth/250 4.00 10.00
97 Brad Penny/80 6.00 15.00
99 Juan Pierre/100 8.00 20.00
102 Michael Cuddyer/250 4.00 10.00
104 Carlos Zambrano/250 6.00 15.00
105 Jose Vidro/100 6.00 15.00
107 Ed Rogers/250 4.00 10.00
110 Tim Redding/250 4.00 10.00
111 Josh Phelps/250 4.00 10.00
112 Gabe Kapler/100 8.00 20.00
113 Edgar Martinez/50 20.00 50.00
116 Wade Miller/250 4.00 10.00
121 Bill Hall/250 6.00 15.00
123 Geronimo Gil/250 4.00 10.00
124 Robert Fick/150 4.00 10.00
126 Brandon Duckworth/250 4.00 10.00
128 Pedro Feliz/250 4.00 10.00
132 Willie Harris/250 4.00 10.00
133 Doug Davis/250 4.00 10.00
135 Terrence Long/50 10.00 25.00
138 Donaldo Mendez/250 4.00 10.00
139 Sean Douglass/250 4.00 10.00
141 Rick Ankiel/250 6.00 15.00
142 Jeremy Giambi/100 6.00 15.00
143 Juan Pena/250 4.00 10.00
145 Craig Wilson/250 4.00 10.00
146 Ricardo Rodriguez/250 4.00 10.00
148 Antonio Perez/250 4.00 10.00
150 Corky Miller/250 4.00 10.00
153 Joe Thurston/250 4.00 10.00
154 Jeff Deardorff/250 4.00 10.00
157 Victor Martinez/250 6.00 15.00
158 Nick Neugebauer/150 4.00 10.00
160 Casey Fossum/250 4.00 10.00
162 Matt Childers/250 4.00 10.00
163 Mark Buehrle/150 12.50 30.00
166 Ben Sheets/100 8.00 20.00
168 Adam Pettyjohn/250 4.00 10.00
169 Chris Snelling/250 5.00 12.00
170 Robert Person/250 4.00 10.00
171 Juan Uribe/250 4.00 10.00
173 Alfredo Amezaga/250 4.00 10.00
175 Corey Thurman/250 4.00 10.00
178 Eric Cyr/250 4.00 10.00
180 Earl Snyder/250 4.00 10.00
181 C.C. Sabathia/50 10.00 25.00
182 Mark Mulder/50 10.00 25.00
183 Jose Mieses/250 4.00 10.00
184 Joe Kennedy/250 4.00 10.00
187 Eric Junge/250 4.00 10.00
189 Corey Patterson/205 4.00 10.00
190 Carlos Pena/200 4.00 10.00
196 Alfonso Soriano/50 10.00 25.00
201 Victor Alvarez ROO/250 4.00 10.00
203 Brandon Backe ROO/250 6.00 15.00
204 Chris Baker ROO/250 4.00 10.00
205 Steve Bechler ROO/250 4.00 10.00
206 Francis Beltran ROO/250 4.00 10.00
207 Angel Berroa ROO/250 4.00 10.00
208 Hank Blalock ROO/100 8.00 20.00
209 Dewon Brazelton ROO/200 4.00 10.00
210 Sean Burroughs ROO/50 10.00 25.00
211 Marlon Byrd ROO/200 4.00 10.00
212 Raul Chavez ROO/250 4.00 10.00
213 Juan Cruz ROO/50 10.00 25.00
214 Jorge De La Rosa ROO/250 4.00 10.00
215 Doug Devore ROO/250 4.00 10.00
216 John Ennis ROO/250 4.00 10.00
217 Felix Escalona ROO/250 4.00 10.00
218 Morgan Ensberg ROO/250 6.00 15.00
219 Cam Esslinger ROO/250 4.00 10.00
220 Kevin Frederick ROO/250 4.00 10.00
221 Franklyn German ROO/250 4.00 10.00
222 Eric Hinske ROO/250 4.00 10.00
223 Ben Howard ROO/250 4.00 10.00
224 Orlando Hudson ROO/250 4.00 10.00
225 Travis Hughes ROO/250 4.00 10.00
226 Kazuhisa Ishii ROO/50 15.00 40.00
227 Ryan Jamison ROO/250 4.00 10.00
228 Reed Johnson ROO/250 6.00 15.00
229 Kyle Kane ROO/250 4.00 10.00
230 Austin Kearns ROO/250 4.00 10.00
231 Satoru Komiyama ROO/50 15.00 40.00
232 Jason Lane ROO/200 6.00 15.00
233 Jeremy Lambert ROO/250 4.00 10.00
234 And Machado ROO/200 4.00 10.00
235 Brian Mallette ROO/250 4.00 10.00
236 Takahito Nomura ROO/100 10.00 25.00
237 Jorge Padilla ROO/200 4.00 10.00
238 Luis Ugueto ROO/250 4.00 10.00
239 Mark Prior ROO/100 8.00 20.00
240 Rene Reyes ROO/250 4.00 10.00
241 Deivis Santos ROO/250 4.00 10.00
242 Elio Serrano ROO/250 4.00 10.00
243 Tom Shearn ROO/250 4.00 10.00
244 Allan Simpson ROO/250 4.00 10.00
245 So Taguchi ROO/100 10.00 25.00
246 Dennis Tankersley ROO/100 6.00 15.00
247 Mark Teixeira ROO/50 20.00 50.00
248 Matt Thornton ROO/250 4.00 10.00
249 Bobby Hill ROO/100 6.00 15.00
250 Ramon Vazquez ROO/250 4.00 10.00
252 Josh Bard ROO/100 4.00 10.00
253 Trey Hodges ROO/250 4.00 10.00
255 Ben Kozlowski ROO/200 4.00 10.00
256 Eric Good ROO/200 4.00 10.00
257 Brian Tallet ROO/100 4.00 10.00
258 P.J. Bevis ROO/50 10.00 25.00
259 Rodrigo Rosario ROO/250 4.00 10.00
260 Kirk Saarloos ROO/100 4.00 10.00
263 Tim Kalita ROO/50 6.00 15.00
266 Cliff Lee ROO/100 20.00 50.00
268 Andy Pratt ROO/250 4.00 10.00
269 Wilson Valdez ROO/200 4.00 10.00
271 Joe Borchard ROO/100 6.00 15.00
274 Kevin Cash ROO/100 4.00 10.00
275 Chone Figgins ROO/100 10.00 25.00

2002 Studio Proofs

*PROOFS 1-200: 4X TO 10X BASIC
*PROOFS RC'S 1-200: 3X TO 8X BASIC
*PROOFS 201-275: .75X TO 2X BASIC
1-250 RANDOM INSERTS IN STUDIO PACKS
251-275 RANDOM IN DONRUSS ROOK.PACKS
STATED PRINT RUN 100 SERIAL #'d SETS
201 Victor Alvarez ROO 3.00 8.00
202 Miguel Asencio ROO 3.00 8.00
203 Brandon Backe ROO 4.00 10.00
204 Chris Baker ROO 3.00 8.00
205 Steve Bechler ROO 3.00 8.00
206 Francis Beltran ROO 3.00 8.00
207 Angel Berroa ROO 3.00 8.00
208 Hank Blalock ROO 4.00 10.00
209 Dewon Brazelton ROO 3.00 8.00
210 Sean Burroughs ROO 3.00 8.00
211 Marlon Byrd ROO 3.00 8.00
212 Raul Chavez ROO 3.00 8.00
213 Juan Cruz ROO 3.00 8.00
214 Jorge De La Rosa ROO 3.00 8.00
215 Doug Devore ROO 3.00 8.00
216 John Ennis ROO 3.00 8.00
217 Felix Escalona ROO 3.00 8.00
218 Morgan Ensberg ROO 3.00 8.00
219 Cam Esslinger ROO 3.00 8.00
220 Kevin Frederick ROO 3.00 8.00
221 Franklyn German ROO 3.00 8.00
222 Eric Hinske ROO 3.00 8.00
223 Ben Howard ROO 3.00 8.00
224 Orlando Hudson ROO 3.00 8.00
225 Travis Hughes ROO 3.00 8.00
226 Kazuhisa Ishii ROO 4.00 10.00
227 Ryan Jamison ROO 3.00 8.00
228 Reed Johnson ROO 4.00 10.00
229 Kyle Kane ROO 3.00 8.00
230 Austin Kearns ROO 3.00 8.00
231 Satoru Komiyama ROO 3.00 8.00
232 Jason Lane ROO 3.00 8.00
233 Jeremy Lambert ROO 3.00 8.00
234 Anderson Machado ROO 3.00 8.00
235 Brian Mallette ROO 3.00 8.00
236 Takahito Nomura ROO 3.00 8.00
237 Jorge Padilla ROO 3.00 8.00
238 Luis Ugueto ROO 3.00 8.00
239 Mark Prior ROO 4.00 10.00
240 Rene Reyes ROO 3.00 8.00
241 Deivis Santos ROO 3.00 8.00
242 Elio Serrano ROO 3.00 8.00
243 Tom Shearn ROO 3.00 8.00
244 Allan Simpson ROO 3.00 8.00
245 So Taguchi ROO 4.00 10.00
246 Dennis Tankersley ROO 3.00 8.00
247 Mark Teixeira ROO 4.00 10.00
248 Matt Thornton ROO 3.00 8.00
249 Bobby Hill ROO 3.00 8.00
250 Ramon Vazquez ROO 3.00 8.00
251 Freddy Sanchez ROO 4.00 10.00
252 Josh Bard ROO 3.00 8.00
253 Trey Hodges ROO 3.00 8.00
254 Jorge Sosa ROO 4.00 10.00
255 Ben Kozlowski ROO 3.00 8.00
256 Eric Good ROO 3.00 8.00
257 Brian Tallet ROO 3.00 8.00
258 P.J. Bevis ROO 3.00 8.00
259 Rodrigo Rosario ROO 3.00 8.00
260 Kirk Saarloos ROO 3.00 8.00
261 Runelvys Hernandez ROO 3.00 8.00
262 Josh Hancock ROO 4.00 10.00
263 Tim Kalita ROO 3.00 8.00
264 Jason Simontacchi ROO 3.00 8.00
265 Clay Condrey ROO 3.00 8.00
266 Cliff Lee ROO 8.00 20.00
267 Aaron Guiel ROO 3.00 8.00
268 Andy Pratt ROO 3.00 8.00
269 Wilson Valdez ROO 3.00 8.00
270 Oliver Perez ROO 4.00 10.00
271 Joe Borchard ROO 3.00 8.00
272 Jeriome Robertson ROO 3.00 8.00
273 Aaron Cook ROO 3.00 8.00
274 Kevin Cash ROO 3.00 8.00
275 Chone Figgins ROO 4.00 10.00

2002 Studio Classic

COMPLETE SET (25) 75.00 150.00
RANDOM INSERTS IN PACKS
STATED PRINT RUN 1000 SERIAL #'d SETS
*1ST BALLOT: 1X TO 2.5X BASIC CLASSIC
1ST BALLOT PRINT RUN BASED ON HOF YR
1 Kirby Puckett 3.00 8.00
2 George Brett 5.00 12.00
3 Nolan Ryan 6.00 15.00
4 Mike Schmidt 5.00 12.00
5 Steve Carlton 2.00 5.00
6 Reggie Jackson 2.00 5.00
7 Tom Seaver 2.00 5.00
8 Joe Morgan 2.00 5.00
9 Jim Palmer 2.00 5.00
10 Johnny Bench 3.00 8.00
11 Willie McCovey 2.00 5.00
12 Brooks Robinson 2.00 5.00
13 Al Kaline 3.00 8.00
14 Stan Musial 4.00 10.00
15 Ozzie Smith 4.00 10.00
16 Dave Winfield 2.00 5.00
17 Robin Yount 3.00 8.00
18 Rod Carew 2.00 5.00
19 Willie Stargell 2.00 5.00
20 Lou Brock 2.00 5.00
21 Ernie Banks 3.00 8.00
22 Ted Williams 5.00 12.00
23 Jackie Robinson 3.00 8.00
24 Roberto Clemente 6.00 15.00
25 Lou Gehrig 6.00 15.00

2002 Studio Diamond Collection

COMPLETE SET (25) 60.00 120.00
STATED ODDS 1:17
1 Todd Helton 1.50 4.00
2 Chipper Jones 1.50 4.00
3 Lance Berkman 1.50 4.00
4 Derek Jeter 4.00 10.00
5 Hideo Nomo 1.50 4.00
6 Kazuhisa Ishii 1.50 4.00
7 Barry Bonds 4.00 10.00
8 Alex Rodriguez 2.00 5.00
9 Ichiro Suzuki 3.00 8.00
10 Mike Piazza 2.50 6.00
11 Jim Thome 1.50 4.00
12 Greg Maddux 2.50 6.00
13 Jeff Bagwell 1.50 4.00
14 Vladimir Guerrero 1.50 4.00
15 Ken Griffey Jr. 3.00 8.00
16 Jason Giambi 1.50 4.00
17 Nomar Garciaparra 2.50 6.00
18 Albert Pujols 3.00 8.00
19 Manny Ramirez 1.50 4.00
20 Pedro Martinez 1.50 4.00
21 Roger Clemens 3.00 8.00
22 Randy Johnson 1.50 4.00
23 Mark Prior 1.50 4.00
24 So Taguchi 1.50 4.00
25 Sammy Sosa 1.50 4.00

2002 Studio Diamond Collection Artist's Proofs

RANDOM INSERTS IN PACKS
STATED PRINT RUNS LISTED BELOW
1 Todd Helton Jsy/200 6.00 15.00
2 Chipper Jones Jsy/150 6.00 15.00
3 Lance Berkman Jsy/200 4.00 10.00
4 Derek Jeter Base/200 10.00 25.00
5 Hideo Nomo Jsy/150 30.00 80.00
6 Kazuhisa Ishii Jsy/150 6.00 15.00
7 Barry Bonds Base/200 10.00 25.00
8 Alex Rodriguez Jsy/150 8.00 20.00
9 Ichiro Suzuki Base/200 10.00 25.00
10 Mike Piazza Jsy/150 6.00 15.00
11 Jim Thome Jsy/150 6.00 15.00
12 Greg Maddux Jsy/150 6.00 15.00
13 Jeff Bagwell Jsy/150 6.00 15.00
14 Vladimir Guerrero Jsy/200 6.00 15.00
15 Ken Griffey Jr. Base/200 6.00 15.00
16 Jason Giambi Base/200 4.00 10.00
17 Nomar Garciaparra Jsy/150 8.00 20.00
18 Albert Pujols Base/200 6.00 15.00
19 Manny Ramirez Jsy/150 6.00 15.00
20 Pedro Martinez Jsy/150 6.00 15.00
21 Roger Clemens Jsy/150 10.00 25.00
22 Randy Johnson Jsy/150 6.00 15.00
24 So Taguchi Jsy/200 6.00 15.00
25 Sammy Sosa Base/200 6.00 15.00

2002 Studio Heroes Icons Texans

RANDOM INSERTS IN PACKS
STATED PRINT RUNS LISTED BELOW
HIT2 Nolan Ryan 4.00 10.00
HIT2 Nolan Ryan/500 6.00 15.00
HIT2 Nolan Ryan/100 20.00 50.00
HIT2 Nolan Ryan AU/32 150.00 250.00

2002 Studio Leather and Lumber

COMPLETE SET (25)
STATED PRINT RUNS LISTED BELOW
*AP: .75X TO 2X BASIC
1 Nomar Garciaparra/200 3.00 8.00
2 Jeff Bagwell/150 3.00 8.00
3 Alex Rodriguez/200 6.00 15.00
4 Vladimir Guerrero/100 4.00 10.00
5 Luis Gonzalez/200 2.00 5.00
6 Chipper Jones/200 5.00 12.00
7 Shawn Green/200 2.00 5.00
8 Kirby Puckett/100 25.00 60.00
9 Juan Gonzalez/200 2.00 5.00
10 Troy Glaus/200 2.00 5.00
11 Don Mattingly/100 12.00 30.00
12 Todd Helton/200 3.00 8.00
13 Jim Thome/200 3.00 8.00
14 Rickey Henderson/200 5.00 12.00
15 Mike Schmidt/100 10.00 25.00
16 Adam Dunn/100 4.00 10.00
17 Ivan Rodriguez/200 3.00 8.00
18 Manny Ramirez/150 3.00 8.00
19 Tsuyoshi Shinjo/200 2.00 5.00
20 Andruw Jones/150 2.50 6.00
21 Roberto Alomar/200 4.00 10.00
22 Lance Berkman/200 4.00 10.00
23 Derek Jeter Ball/50 15.00 40.00
24 Ichiro Suzuki Ball/50 8.00 20.00
25 Mike Piazza/200 6.00 15.00

2002 Studio Masterstrokes

COMPLETE SET (25) 50.00 100.00
STATED ODDS 1:17
1 Vladimir Guerrero 1.50 4.00
2 Frank Thomas 1.50 4.00
3 Alex Rodriguez 2.00 5.00
4 Manny Ramirez 1.50 4.00
5 Jeff Bagwell 1.50 4.00
6 Jim Thome 1.50 4.00
7 Ichiro Suzuki 3.00 8.00
8 Andruw Jones 1.50 4.00
9 Troy Glaus 1.50 4.00
10 Chipper Jones 1.50 4.00
11 Juan Gonzalez 1.50 4.00
12 Lance Berkman 1.50 4.00
13 Mike Piazza 2.50 6.00
14 Darin Erstad 1.50 4.00
15 Albert Pujols 3.00 8.00
16 Kazuhisa Ishii 1.50 4.00
17 Shawn Green 1.50 4.00
18 Rafael Palmeiro 1.50 4.00
19 Todd Helton 1.50 4.00
20 Carlos Delgado 1.50 4.00
21 Ivan Rodriguez 1.50 4.00
22 Luis Gonzalez 1.50 4.00
23 Derek Jeter 4.00 10.00
24 Nomar Garciaparra 2.50 6.00
25 J.D. Drew 1.50 4.00

2002 Studio Masterstrokes Artist's Proofs

STATED PRINT RUNS LISTED BELOW
ALL BAT-JSY CARDS EXCEPT #'s 7/15/23
7/15/23 ARE BALL-BASE CARDS
1 Vladimir Guerrero/200 8.00 20.00
2 Frank Thomas/200 8.00 20.00
3 Alex Rodriguez/100 15.00 40.00
4 Manny Ramirez/200 8.00 20.00
5 Jeff Bagwell/150 8.00 20.00
6 Jim Thome/200 8.00 20.00
7 Ichiro Suzuki/100 30.00 60.00
8 Andruw Jones/200 8.00 20.00
9 Troy Glaus/200 6.00 15.00
10 Chipper Jones/200 8.00 20.00
11 Juan Gonzalez/200 6.00 15.00
12 Lance Berkman/200 6.00 15.00
13 Mike Piazza/200 15.00 40.00
14 Darin Erstad/200 6.00 15.00
15 Albert Pujols/100 15.00 40.00
16 Kazuhisa Ishii/150 8.00 20.00
17 Shawn Green/200 6.00 15.00
18 Rafael Palmeiro/200 8.00 20.00
19 Todd Helton/200 8.00 20.00
20 Carlos Delgado/200 6.00 15.00
21 Ivan Rodriguez/200 8.00 20.00
22 Luis Gonzalez/200 6.00 15.00
23 Derek Jeter/100 12.00 30.00
24 Nomar Garciaparra/150 15.00 40.00
25 J.D. Drew/150 6.00 15.00

2002 Studio Spirit of the Game

COMPLETE SET (50) 60.00 120.00
STATED ODDS 1:9
1 Alex Rodriguez 2.00 5.00
2 Curt Schilling 1.00 2.50
3 Hideo Nomo 1.50 4.00
4 Derek Jeter 4.00 10.00
5 Mike Sweeney 1.00 2.50
6 Mike Piazza 2.50 6.00
7 Roger Clemens 3.00 8.00
8 Shawn Green 1.00 2.50
9 Vladimir Guerrero 1.50 4.00
10 Carlos Lee 1.00 2.50
11 Edgar Martinez 1.00 2.50
12 Albert Pujols 3.00 8.00
13 Mark Prior 1.00 2.50
14 Mark Buehrle 1.00 2.50
15 Chipper Jones 1.50 4.00
16 Paul Lo Duca 1.00 2.50
17 Frank Thomas 1.50 4.00
18 Randy Johnson 1.50 4.00
19 Cliff Floyd 1.00 2.50
20 Todd Helton 1.00 2.50
21 Luis Gonzalez 1.00 2.50
22 Brandon Duckworth 1.00 2.50
23 Jason Giambi 1.00 2.50
24 Juan Uribe 1.00 2.50
25 Dewon Brazelton 1.00 2.50
26 J.D. Drew 1.00 2.50
27 Troy Glaus 1.00 2.50
28 Wade Miller 1.00 2.50
29 Darin Erstad 1.00 2.50
30 Brian Giles 1.00 2.50
31 Lance Berkman 1.00 2.50
32 Shannon Stewart 1.00 2.50
33 Kazuhisa Ishii 1.00 2.50
34 Corey Patterson 1.00 2.50
35 Rafael Palmeiro 1.00 2.50
36 Roy Oswalt 1.00 2.50
37 Jason Lane 1.00 2.50
38 Andruw Jones 1.00 2.50
39 Brad Penny 1.00 2.50
40 Bud Smith 1.00 2.50
41 Carlos Beltran 1.00 2.50
42 Magglio Ordonez 1.00 2.50
43 Craig Biggio 1.00 2.50
44 Hank Blalock 1.00 2.50
45 Jeff Bagwell 1.00 2.50
46 Josh Beckett 1.00 2.50
47 Juan Cruz 1.00 2.50
48 Kerry Wood 1.00 2.50
49 Brandon Berger 1.00 2.50
50 Juan Pierre 1.00 2.50

2002 Studio Spirit of the Game Hats Off

STATED PRINT RUN 100 SERIAL #'d SETS
SKIP-NUMBERED 24-CARD SET
MLB LOGO PRINT RUN 1 SERIAL #'d SET
NO MLB LOGO PRICING DUE TO SCARCITY
USA FLAG PRINT RUN 1 SERIAL #'d SET
NO USA FLAG PRICING DUE TO SCARCITY
10 Carlos Lee 10.00 25.00
14 Mark Buehrle 10.00 25.00
16 Paul Lo Duca 10.00 25.00
22 Brandon Duckworth 6.00 15.00
26 J.D. Drew 10.00 25.00
28 Wade Miller 6.00 15.00
30 Brian Giles 10.00 25.00
31 Lance Berkman 10.00 25.00
32 Shannon Stewart 10.00 25.00
33 Kazuhisa Ishii SP/50 10.00 25.00
35 Rafael Palmeiro 15.00 40.00
36 Roy Oswalt 10.00 25.00
37 Jason Lane 10.00 25.00
38 Andruw Jones 15.00 40.00
39 Brad Penny 6.00 15.00
40 Bud Smith 6.00 15.00
41 Carlos Beltran 10.00 25.00
42 Magglio Ordonez 10.00 25.00
43 Craig Biggio 15.00 40.00
45 Jeff Bagwell 15.00 40.00
47 Juan Cruz 6.00 15.00
48 Kerry Wood 10.00 25.00
49 Brandon Berger 6.00 15.00
50 Juan Pierre 6.00 15.00

2002 Studio Stars

COMPLETE SET (50) 50.00 100.00
GOLD PRINT RUN 250 SERIAL #'d SETS
PLATINUM PRINT RUN 50 SERIAL #'d SETS
1 Mike Piazza 1.50 4.00
2 Ivan Rodriguez .75 2.00
3 Albert Pujols 2.00 5.00
4 Scott Rolen .75 2.00
5 Alex Rodriguez 1.25 3.00
6 Curt Schilling .75 2.00
7 Vladimir Guerrero .75 2.00
8 Jim Thome .75 2.00
9 Derek Jeter 2.50 6.00
10 C.C. Sabathia .75 2.00
11 Sammy Sosa .75 2.00
12 Adam Dunn .75 2.00
13 Bernie Williams .75 2.00
14 Ichiro Suzuki 2.00 5.00
15 Barry Bonds 2.50 6.00
16 Rickey Henderson .75 2.00
17 Ken Griffey Jr. 2.00 5.00
18 Kazuhisa Ishii .75 2.00
19 Kerry Wood .75 2.00
20 Todd Helton .75 2.00
21 Hideo Nomo .75 2.00
22 Frank Thomas .75 2.00
23 Manny Ramirez .75 2.00
24 Luis Gonzalez .75 2.00
25 Rafael Palmeiro .75 2.00
26 Mike Mussina .75 2.00
27 Roy Oswalt .75 2.00
28 Darin Erstad .75 2.00
29 Barry Larkin .75 2.00
30 Randy Johnson .75 2.00
31 Tom Glavine .75 2.00
32 Lance Berkman .75 2.00
33 Juan Gonzalez .75 2.00
34 Shawn Green .75 2.00
35 Nomar Garciaparra 1.50 4.00
36 Troy Glaus .75 2.00
37 Tim Hudson .75 2.00
38 Carlos Delgado .75 2.00
39 Jason Giambi .75 2.00
40 Andruw Jones .75 2.00
41 Roberto Alomar .75 2.00
42 Greg Maddux 1.50 4.00
43 Pedro Martinez .75 2.00
44 Tony Gwynn 1.25 3.00
45 Alfonso Soriano .75 2.00
46 Chipper Jones .75 2.00
47 J.D. Drew .75 2.00
48 Roger Clemens 2.00 5.00
49 Barry Zito .75 2.00
50 Jeff Bagwell .75 2.00

2003 Studio

COMP.LO SET (200) 20.00 50.00
COMMON CARD (1-190) .20 .50
COMMON RC (1-190) .20 .50
COMMON CARD (191-200) .20 .50
COMMON CARD (201-211) 1.50 4.00
201-211 PRINT RUN 1500 SERIAL #'d SETS
1 Darin Erstad .20 .50
2 David Eckstein .20 .50
3 Garret Anderson .20 .50
4 Jarrod Washburn .20 .50
5 Tim Salmon .20 .50
6 Troy Glaus .20 .50
7 Jay Gibbons .20 .50
8 Melvin Mora .20 .50
9 Rodrigo Lopez .20 .50
10 Tony Batista .20 .50
11 Freddy Sanchez .20 .50
12 Derek Lowe .20 .50
13 Johnny Damon .30 .75
14 Manny Ramirez .50 1.25
15 Nomar Garciaparra .30 .75
16 Pedro Martinez .30 .75
17 Rickey Henderson .50 1.25
18 Shea Hillenbrand .20 .50
19 Carlos Lee .20 .50
20 Frank Thomas .50 1.25
21 Magglio Ordonez .30 .75
22 Bartolo Colon .20 .50
23 Paul Konerko .30 .75
24 Josh Stewart RC .20 .50
25 C.C. Sabathia .30 .75
26 Jeremy Guthrie .20 .50
27 Ellis Burks .20 .50
28 Omar Vizquel .30 .75
29 Victor Martinez .30 .75
30 Cliff Lee 1.25 3.00
31 Jhonny Peralta .20 .50
32 Brian Tallet .20 .50
33 Bobby Higginson .20 .50
34 Carlos Pena .30 .75
35 Nook Logan RC .20 .50
36 Steve Sparks .20 .50
37 Travis Chapman .20 .50
38 Carlos Beltran .30 .75
39 Joe Randa .20 .50
40 Mike Sweeney .20 .50
41 Jimmy Gobble .20 .50
42 Michael Tucker .20 .50
43 Runelvys Hernandez .20 .50
44 Brad Radke .20 .50
45 Corey Koskie .20 .50
46 Cristian Guzman .20 .50
47 J.C. Romero .20 .50
48 Doug Mientkiewicz .20 .50
49 Lew Ford RC .20 .50
50 Jacque Jones .20 .50
51 Torii Hunter .20 .50
52 Alfonso Soriano .30 .75
53 Nick Johnson .20 .50
54 Bernie Williams .30 .75
55 Jose Contreras RC .50 1.25
56 Derek Jeter 1.25 3.00
57 Jason Giambi .20 .50
58 Brandon Claussen .20 .50
59 Jorge Posada .30 .75
60 Mike Mussina .30 .75
61 Roger Clemens .60 1.50
62 Hideki Matsui RC 1.00 2.50
63 Barry Zito .30 .75
64 Adam Morrissey .20 .50
65 Eric Chavez .20 .50
66 Jermaine Dye .20 .50
67 Mark Mulder .20 .50
68 Miguel Tejada .30 .75
69 Joe Valentine RC .20 .50
70 Tim Hudson .30 .75
71 Bret Boone .20 .50
72 Chris Snelling .20 .50
73 Edgar Martinez .30 .75
74 Freddy Garcia .20 .50
75 Ichiro Suzuki .60 1.50
76 Jamie Moyer .20 .50
77 John Olerud .20 .50
78 Kazuhiro Sasaki .20 .50
79 Aubrey Huff .20 .50
80 Joe Kennedy .20 .50
81 Dewon Brazelton .20 .50
82 Pete LaForest RC .20 .50
83 Alex Rodriguez .60 1.50
84 Chan Ho Park .30 .75
85 Hank Blalock .20 .50
86 Juan Gonzalez .20 .50
87 Kevin Mench .20 .50
88 Rafael Palmeiro .30 .75
89 Carlos Delgado .20 .50
90 Eric Hinske .20 .50
91 Josh Phelps .20 .50
92 Roy Halladay .30 .75
93 Shannon Stewart .20 .50
94 Vernon Wells .20 .50
95 Vinny Chulk .20 .50
96 Curt Schilling .30 .75
97 Junior Spivey .20 .50
98 Luis Gonzalez .20 .50
99 Mark Grace .30 .75
100 Randy Johnson .50 1.25
101 Andruw Jones .20 .50
102 Chipper Jones .50 1.25
103 Gary Sheffield .20 .50
104 Greg Maddux .60 1.50
105 John Smoltz .50 1.25
106 Mike Hampton .20 .50
107 Adam LaRoche .20 .50
108 Michael Hessman RC .20 .50
109 Corey Patterson .20 .50
110 Kerry Wood .20 .50
111 Mark Prior .30 .75
112 Moises Alou .20 .50
113 Sammy Sosa .50 1.25
114 Adam Dunn .30 .75
115 Austin Kearns .20 .50
116 Barry Larkin .30 .75
117 Ken Griffey Jr. 1.00 2.50
118 Sean Casey .20 .50
119 Jason Jennings .20 .50
120 Jay Payton .20 .50
121 Larry Walker .30 .75
122 Todd Helton .30 .75
123 Jeff Baker .20 .50
124 Clint Barmes RC .50 1.25
125 Ivan Rodriguez .30 .75
126 Josh Beckett .20 .50
127 Juan Encarnacion .20 .50
128 Mike Lowell .20 .50
129 Craig Biggio .30 .75
130 Jason Lane .20 .50
131 Jeff Bagwell .30 .75
132 Lance Berkman .30 .75
133 Roy Oswalt .30 .75
134 Jeff Kent .20 .50
135 Hideo Nomo .50 1.25
136 Kazuhisa Ishii .20 .50
137 Kevin Brown .20 .50
138 Odalis Perez .20 .50
139 Paul Lo Duca .20 .50
140 Shawn Green .20 .50
141 Adrian Beltre .50 1.25
142 Ben Sheets .20 .50
143 Bill Hall .20 .50
144 Jeffrey Hammonds .20 .50
145 Richie Sexson .20 .50
146 Termel Sledge RC .20 .50
147 Brad Wilkerson .20 .50
148 Javier Vazquez .20 .50
149 Jose Vidro .20 .50
150 Michael Barrett .20 .50
151 Vladimir Guerrero .30 .75
152 Al Leiter .20 .50
153 Mike Piazza .50 1.25
154 Mo Vaughn .20 .50
155 Cliff Floyd .20 .50
156 Roberto Alomar .30 .75
157 Roger Cedeno .20 .50
158 Tom Glavine .30 .75
159 Prentice Redman RC .20 .50
160 Bobby Abreu .20 .50
161 Jimmy Rollins .30 .75
162 Mike Lieberthal .20 .50
163 Pat Burrell .20 .50
164 Vicente Padilla .20 .50
165 Jim Thome .30 .75
166 Kevin Millwood .20 .50
167 Aramis Ramirez .20 .50
168 Brian Giles .20 .50
169 Jason Kendall .20 .50
170 Josh Fogg .20 .50
171 Kip Wells .20 .50
172 Jose Castillo .20 .50
173 Mark Kotsay .20 .50
174 Oliver Perez .20 .50
175 Phil Nevin .20 .50
176 Ryan Klesko .20 .50
177 Sean Burroughs .20 .50
178 Brian Lawrence .20 .50
179 Shane Victorino RC .60 1.50
180 Barry Bonds .75 2.00
181 Benito Santiago .20 .50
182 Ray Durham .20 .50
183 Rich Aurilla .20 .50
184 Damian Moss .20 .50

185 Albert Pujols .60 1.50
186 J.D. Drew .20 .50
187 Jim Edmonds .30 .75
188 Matt Morris .20 .50
189 Tino Martinez .20 .50
190 Scott Rolen .30 .75
191 T.Glaus .20 .50
T.Salmon
192 B.Zito .30 .75
T.Hudson
193 C.Lee .50 1.25
F.Thomas
194 L.Berkman .30 .75
J.Kent
195 J.Contreras .60 1.50
M.Rivera
196 A.Rodriguez .60 1.50
J.Gonzalez
197 A.Pettitte .30 .75
D.Wells
198 S.Green .30 .75
D.Roberts
199 M.Lieberthal .30 .75
J.Rollins
200 M.Mussina 1.00 2.50
H.Matsui
201 Adam Loewen ROO RC .60 1.50
202 Jeremy Bonderman ROO RC 2.50 6.00
203 Brandon Webb ROO RC 2.00 5.00
204 Chien-Ming Wang ROO RC 2.50 6.00
205 Chad Gaudin ROO RC .60 1.50
206 Ryan Wagner ROO RC .60 1.50
207 Hong-Chih Kuo ROO RC 3.00 8.00
208 Dan Haren ROO RC 3.00 8.00
209 Rickie Weeks ROO RC 2.00 5.00
210 Ramon Nivar ROO RC .60 1.50
211 Delmon Young ROO RC 4.00 10.00

2003 Studio Private Signings

1-200 RANDOM INSERTS IN PACKS
PRINT RUNS B/WN 5-200 COPIES PER
NO PRICING ON QTY OF 35 OR LESS
7 Jay Gibbons/100 6.00 15.00
11 Freddy Sanchez/150 6.00 15.00
24 Josh Stewart/200 4.00 10.00
26 Jeremy Guthrie/125 4.00 10.00
29 Victor Martinez/200 10.00 25.00
30 Cliff Lee/150 6.00 15.00
31 Jhonny Peralta/200 6.00 15.00
35 Nook Logan/100 6.00 15.00
37 Travis Chapman/150 4.00 10.00
41 Jimmy Gobble/200 4.00 10.00
47 J.C. Romero/200 4.00 10.00
49 Lew Ford/200 6.00 15.00
51 Torii Hunter/50 10.00 25.00
53 Nick Johnson/100 8.00 20.00
55 Jose Contreras/100 12.50 30.00
58 Brandon Claussen/200 4.00 10.00
69 Joe Valentine/200 4.00 10.00
79 Aubrey Huff/50 10.00 25.00
81 Dewon Brazelton/75 6.00 15.00
82 Pete LaForest/200 4.00 10.00
85 Hank Blalock/50 10.00 25.00
87 Kevin Mench/200 6.00 15.00
90 Eric Hinske/125 4.00 10.00
95 Vinny Chulk/100 6.00 15.00
97 Junior Spivey/50 6.00 15.00
107 Adam LaRoche/200 4.00 10.00
108 Michael Hessman/200 4.00 10.00
111 Mark Prior/50 15.00 40.00
119 Jason Jennings/50 6.00 15.00
123 Jeff Baker/75 6.00 15.00
124 Clint Barmes/200 6.00 15.00
130 Jason Lane/100 8.00 20.00
139 Paul Lo Duca/75 8.00 20.00
143 Bill Hall/50 6.00 15.00
146 Terrmel Sledge/125 4.00 10.00
149 Jose Vidro/50 6.00 15.00
159 Prentice Redman/200 4.00 10.00
160 Bobby Abreu/50 10.00 25.00
171 Kip Wells/100 6.00 15.00
172 Jose Castillo/175 4.00 10.00
178 Brian Lawrence/100 6.00 15.00
179 Shane Victorino/200 12.50 30.00
201 Adam Loewen ROO/100 10.00 25.00
202 Jeremy Bonderman ROO/50 30.00 60.00
203 Brandon Webb ROO/100 10.00 25.00
204 C.Wang ROO/50 60.00 120.00
206 Ryan Wagner ROO/100 4.00 10.00
208 Dan Haren ROO/100 5.00 12.00
210 Ramon Nivar ROO/100 4.00 10.00

2003 Studio Proofs

*PROOFS 1-190: 4X TO 10X BASIC
*PROOFS RC's 1-190: 4X TO 10X BASIC
*PROOFS 191-200: 4X TO 10X BASIC
*PROOFS 201-211: 1.25X TO 3X BASIC
1-200 RANDOM INSERTS IN PACKS
201-211 RANDOM IN DLP R/T PACKS
STATED PRINT RUN 100 SERIAL #'d SETS

2003 Studio Big League Challenge

STATED PRINT RUN 400 SERIAL #'d SETS
*PROOFS: 1.5X TO 4X BASIC BLC
PROOFS PRINT RUN 25 SERIAL #'d SETS
NO PROOFS PRICING DUE TO SCARCITY
DUPE PLAYER CARDS VALUED EQUALLY
1 Jose Canseco 00 WIN 1.00 2.50
2 Magglio Ordonez 03 WIN 1.00 2.50
3 Alex Rodriguez 03 2.00 5.00
4 Lance Berkman 03 1.00 2.50
5 Rafael Palmeiro 03 1.00 2.50
6 Nomar Garciaparra 00 1.00 2.50
7 Nomar Garciaparra 00 1.00 2.50
8 Nomar Garciaparra 00 1.00 2.50
9 Troy Glaus 02 WIN .60 1.50
10 Mark McGwire 00 2.50 6.00
11 Mark McGwire 00 2.50 6.00
12 Mark McGwire 00 2.50 6.00
13 Jim Thome 02 1.00 2.50
14 Chipper Jones 00 1.50 4.00
15 Shawn Green 02 .60 1.50
16 Alex Rodriguez 00 2.00 5.00
17 Alex Rodriguez 00 2.00 5.00
18 Alex Rodriguez 00 2.00 5.00
19 Alex Rodriguez 00 2.00 5.00
20 Jason Giambi 01 .60 1.50
21 Pat Burrell 03 .60 1.50
22 Mike Piazza 01 1.50 4.00
23 Mike Piazza 01 1.50 4.00
24 Mike Piazza 01 1.50 4.00
25 Frank Thomas 01 1.50 4.00
26 Rafael Palmeiro 01 WIN 1.00 2.50
27 Todd Helton 01 1.00 2.50
28 Jose Canseco 01 1.00 2.50
29 Albert Pujols 03 2.00 5.00
30 Troy Glaus 01 .60 1.50
31 Barry Bonds 01 2.50 6.00
32 Barry Bonds 01 2.50 6.00
33 Barry Bonds 01 2.50 6.00
34 Todd Helton 02 1.00 2.50
35 Rafael Palmeiro 02 1.00 2.50
36 Jim Thome 02 1.00 2.50
37 Ozzie Smith 02 2.00 5.00
38 Troy Glaus 02 WIN .60 1.50
39 Shawn Green 02 .60 1.50
40 Barry Bonds 02 2.50 6.00
41 Barry Bonds 02 2.50 6.00
42 Barry Bonds 02 2.50 6.00
43 Magglio Ordonez 03 WIN 1.00 2.50
44 Alex Rodriguez 03 2.00 5.00
45 Alex Rodriguez 03 2.00 5.00
46 Alex Rodriguez 03 2.00 5.00
47 Lance Berkman 03 1.00 2.50
48 Rafael Palmeiro 03 1.00 2.50
49 Pat Burrell 03 .60 1.50
50 Albert Pujols 03 2.00 5.00

2003 Studio Big League Challenge Materials

STATED ODDS 1:20
*PRIME 100: 1X TO 2.5X BASIC MATERIAL
*PRIME 50: 1.5X TO 4X BASIC MATERIAL
PRIME RANDOM INSERTS IN PACKS
PRIME PRINT RUN B/WN 50-100 COPIES PER
2 Magglio Ordonez 03 BP Jsy 3.00 8.00
3 Alex Rodriguez 03 BP Jsy 6.00 15.00
4 Lance Berkman 03 Jsy 3.00 8.00
15 Shawn Green 02 BP Jsy 3.00 8.00
29 Albert Pujols 03 Jsy 10.00 25.00
36 Jim Thome 02 BP Jsy 3.00 8.00
39 Shawn Green 02 Pants 3.00 8.00
40 Barry Bonds 02 Base 6.00 15.00
41 Barry Bonds 02 Base 6.00 15.00
42 Barry Bonds 02 Plate 6.00 15.00
43 Magglio Ordonez 03 Jsy 3.00 8.00
45 Alex Rodriguez 03 Jsy 6.00 15.00
46 Alex Rodriguez 03 Pants 6.00 15.00
47 Lance Berkman 03 BP Jsy 3.00 8.00
48 Rafael Palmeiro 03 BP Jsy 3.00 8.00
50 Albert Pujols 03 Pants 6.00 15.00

2003 Studio Enshrinement

STATED PRINT RUN 750 SERIAL #'d SETS
PROOFS PRINT RUN B/WN 20-21 COPIES PER
NO PROOFS PRICING DUE TO SCARCITY
1 Gary Carter 1.00 2.50
2 Ozzie Smith 2.00 5.00
3 Kirby Puckett 1.50 4.00
4 Carlton Fisk 1.00 2.50
5 Tony Perez 1.00 2.50
6 Nolan Ryan 5.00 12.00
7 George Brett 3.00 8.00
8 Robin Yount 1.50 4.00
9 Orlando Cepeda 1.00 2.50
10 Phil Niekro 1.00 2.50
11 Mike Schmidt 2.50 6.00
12 Richie Ashburn 1.00 2.50
13 Steve Carlton 1.00 2.50
14 Phil Rizzuto 1.00 2.50
15 Reggie Jackson 1.00 2.50
16 Tom Seaver 1.00 2.50
17 Rollie Fingers 1.00 2.50
18 Rod Carew 1.00 2.50
19 Gaylord Perry 1.00 2.50
20 Fergie Jenkins 1.00 2.50
21 Jim Palmer 1.00 2.50
22 Joe Morgan 1.00 2.50
23 Johnny Bench 1.50 4.00
24 Willie Stargell 1.00 2.50
25 Billy Williams 1.00 2.50
26 Catfish Hunter 1.00 2.50
27 Willie McCovey 1.00 2.50
28 Bobby Doerr 1.00 2.50
29 Lou Brock 1.00 2.50
30 Enos Slaughter 1.00 2.50
31 Hoyt Wilhelm 1.00 2.50
32 Harmon Killebrew 1.50 4.00
33 Pee Wee Reese 1.00 2.50
34 Luis Aparicio 1.00 2.50
35 Brooks Robinson 1.00 2.50
36 Juan Marichal 1.00 2.50
37 Frank Robinson 1.00 2.50
38 Bob Gibson 1.00 2.50
39 Al Kaline 1.00 2.50
40 Duke Snider 1.00 2.50
41 Eddie Mathews 1.50 4.00
42 Robin Roberts 1.00 2.50
43 Ralph Kiner 1.00 2.50
44 Whitey Ford 1.00 2.50
45 Roberto Clemente 4.00 10.00
46 Warren Spahn 1.00 2.50
47 Yogi Berra 1.50 4.00
48 Early Wynn 1.00 2.50
49 Stan Musial 2.50 6.00
50 Bob Feller 1.00 2.50

2003 Studio Enshrinement Autographs

PRINT RUNS B/WN 1-100 COPIES PER CARD
NO PRICING ON QTY OF 25 OR FEWER
1 Gary Carter/50 20.00 50.00
5 Tony Perez/50 12.50 30.00
9 Orlando Cepeda/50 10.00 25.00
10 Phil Niekro/50 8.00 20.00
13 Steve Carlton/50 12.50 30.00
20 Fergie Jenkins/50 12.50 30.00
28 Bobby Doerr/100 10.00 25.00
31 Hoyt Wilhelm/50 20.00 50.00
34 Luis Aparicio/100 10.00 25.00
50 Bob Feller/100 10.00 25.00

2003 Studio Leather and Lumber

COMMON CARD p/r 300-400 3.00 8.00
PRINT RUNS B/WN 100-400 COPIES PER
1 Adam Dunn Bat/400 3.00 8.00
2 Alex Rodriguez Bat/250 8.00 20.00
3 Alfonso Soriano Bat/250 4.00 10.00
4 Andruw Jones Bat/400 4.00 10.00
5 Austin Kearns Bat/400 3.00 8.00
6 Chipper Jones Bat/400 4.00 10.00
7 Derek Jeter Ball/100 15.00 40.00
8 Don Mattingly Bat/100 15.00 40.00
9 Edgar Martinez Bat/400 4.00 10.00
10 Frank Thomas Bat/400 4.00 10.00
11 Fred McGriff Bat/400 4.00 10.00
13 Greg Maddux Bat/150 6.00 15.00
14 Hideki Matsui Ball/100 10.00 25.00
15 Hideo Nomo Bat/150 8.00 20.00
16 Ichiro Suzuki Ball/100 15.00 40.00
17 Ivan Rodriguez Bat/250 6.00 15.00
18 Jason Giambi Bat/400 3.00 8.00
19 Jeff Bagwell Bat/400 4.00 10.00
20 Jim Edmonds Bat/150 4.00 10.00
21 Jim Thome Bat/400 4.00 10.00
22 Juan Gonzalez Bat/400 3.00 8.00
23 Kerry Wood Bat/250 4.00 10.00
24 Kirby Puckett Bat/100 10.00 25.00
25 Lance Berkman Bat/400 3.00 8.00
26 Magglio Ordonez Bat/400 3.00 8.00
27 Manny Ramirez Bat/250 6.00 15.00
28 Mark Prior Bat/400 4.00 10.00
29 Miguel Tejada Bat/200 4.00 10.00
30 Mike Piazza Bat/400 4.00 10.00
31 Mike Schmidt Bat/200 15.00 40.00
32 Nomar Garciaparra Bat/400 6.00 15.00
33 Pat Burrell Bat/400 3.00 8.00
34 Pedro Martinez Bat/150 6.00 15.00
36 Randy Johnson Bat/250 6.00 15.00
37 Rickey Henderson Bat/175 6.00 15.00
38 Sammy Sosa Bat/300 4.00 10.00
39 Shawn Green Bat/400 3.00 8.00
40 Vladimir Guerrero Bat/400 4.00 10.00

2003 Studio Leather and Lumber Combos

RANDOM INSERTS IN PACKS
PRINT RUNS B/WN 25-50 COPIES PER
NO PRICING ON QTY OF 25 OR LESS
1 Adam Dunn Bat-Btg Glv/50 10.00 25.00
2 Alex Rodriguez Bat-Fld Glv/50 15.00 40.00
4 Andruw Jones Bat-Fld Glv/50 15.00 40.00
5 Austin Kearns Bat-Shoe/50 10.00 25.00
10 Frank Thomas Bat-Btg Glv/50 15.00 40.00
13 Greg Maddux Bat-Shoe/50 10.00 25.00
17 Ivan Rodriguez Bat-Btg Glv/50 15.00 40.00
20 Jim Edmonds Bat-Shoe/50 10.00 25.00
23 Kerry Wood Bat-Fld Glv/50 10.00 25.00
25 Lance Berkman Bat-Fld Glv/50 10.00 25.00

2003 Studio Masterstrokes

RANDOM INSERTS IN PACKS
STATED PRINT RUN 1000 SERIAL #'d SETS
1 Adam Dunn 1.00 2.50
2 Albert Pujols 2.00 5.00
3 Alex Rodriguez 2.00 5.00
4 Alfonso Soriano 1.00 2.50
5 Andruw Jones .60 1.50
6 Chipper Jones 1.50 4.00
7 Derek Jeter 4.00 10.00
8 Greg Maddux 2.00 5.00
9 Hideki Matsui 3.00 8.00
10 Hideo Nomo 1.50 4.00
11 Ivan Rodriguez 1.00 2.50
12 Jason Giambi .60 1.50
13 Jeff Bagwell 1.00 2.50
14 Juan Gonzalez .60 1.50
15 Ken Griffey Jr. 3.00 8.00
16 Lance Berkman 1.00 2.50
17 Magglio Ordonez 1.00 2.50
18 Manny Ramirez 1.50 4.00
19 Mark Prior 1.00 2.50
20 Miguel Tejada 1.00 2.50
21 Mike Piazza 1.50 4.00
22 Nomar Garciaparra 1.00 2.50
23 Pat Burrell .60 1.50
24 Sammy Sosa 1.50 4.00
25 Vladimir Guerrero 1.00 2.50

2003 Studio Masterstrokes Proofs

RANDOM INSERTS IN PACKS
STATED PRINT RUN 50 SERIAL #'d SETS
1 Adam Dunn Bat-Jsy 8.00 20.00
2 Albert Pujols Bat-Jsy 25.00 60.00
3 Alex Rodriguez Bat-Jsy 25.00 60.00
4 Alfonso Soriano Bat-Jsy 8.00 20.00
5 Andruw Jones Bat-Jsy 12.50 30.00
6 Chipper Jones Bat-Jsy 12.50 30.00
7 Derek Jeter Base-Ball 15.00 40.00
8 Greg Maddux Bat-Jsy 15.00 40.00
9 Hideki Matsui Base-Ball 40.00 80.00
10 Hideo Nomo Bat-Jsy 60.00 120.00
11 Ivan Rodriguez Bat-Jsy 12.50 30.00
12 Jason Giambi Bat-Jsy 8.00 20.00
13 Jeff Bagwell Bat-Jsy 12.50 30.00
14 Juan Gonzalez Bat-Jsy 8.00 20.00
15 Ken Griffey Jr. Base-Base 20.00 50.00
16 Lance Berkman Bat-Jsy 8.00 20.00
17 Magglio Ordonez Bat-Jsy 8.00 20.00
18 Manny Ramirez Bat-Jsy 12.50 30.00
19 Mark Prior Bat-Jsy 12.50 30.00
20 Miguel Tejada Bat-Jsy 8.00 20.00
21 Mike Piazza Bat-Jsy 15.00 40.00
22 Nomar Garciaparra Bat-Jsy 20.00 50.00
23 Pat Burrell Bat-Jsy 8.00 20.00
24 Sammy Sosa Bat-Jsy 12.50 30.00
25 Vladimir Guerrero Bat-Jsy 12.50 30.00

2003 Studio Recollection Autographs 5 x 7

ONE PER SEALED HOBBY CASE
PRINT RUNS B/WN 1-200 COPIES PER
NO PRICING ON QTY OF 25 OR LESS
ALL CARDS ARE 2001 STUDIO BUYBACKS
3 Sean Casey/125 8.00 20.00
5 Troy Glaus/82 12.50 30.00
8 Vladimir Guerrero/125 15.00 40.00
10 Todd Helton/55 15.00 40.00
12 Ryan Klesko/75 8.00 20.00
18 Ivan Rodriguez/50 20.00 50.00
19 C.C. Sabathia/50 10.00 25.00
20 Curt Schilling/75 20.00 50.00
23 Mike Sweeney/42 10.00 25.00
24 Miguel Tejada/44 15.00 40.00
26 Kerry Wood/200 10.00 25.00
27 Barry Zito/200 10.00 25.00

2003 Studio Spirit of the Game

RANDOM INSERTS IN PACKS
STATED PRINT RUN 1250 SERIAL #'d SETS
1 Garret Anderson .60 1.50
2 Nomar Garciaparra 1.00 2.50
3 Pedro Martinez 1.00 2.50
4 Rickey Henderson 1.50 4.00
5 Magglio Ordonez 1.00 2.50
6 Torii Hunter .60 1.50
7 Alfonso Soriano 1.00 2.50
8 Jose Contreras 1.50 4.00
9 Derek Jeter 4.00 10.00
10 Jason Giambi .60 1.50
11 Roger Clemens 2.00 5.00
12 Hideki Matsui 3.00 8.00
13 Barry Zito 1.00 2.50
14 Ichiro Suzuki 2.00 5.00
15 Alex Rodriguez 2.00 5.00
16 Curt Schilling 1.00 2.50
17 Randy Johnson 1.50 4.00
18 Andruw Jones .60 1.50
19 Chipper Jones 1.50 4.00
20 Greg Maddux 2.00 5.00
21 Sammy Sosa 1.50 4.00
22 Adam Dunn 1.00 2.50
23 Ken Griffey Jr. 3.00 8.00
24 Todd Helton 1.00 2.50
25 Ivan Rodriguez 1.00 2.50
26 Lance Berkman 1.00 2.50
27 Hideo Nomo 1.50 4.00
28 Shawn Green .60 1.50
29 Vladimir Guerrero 1.00 2.50
30 Mike Piazza 1.50 4.00
31 Roberto Alomar 1.00 2.50
32 Jim Thome 1.00 2.50
33 Barry Bonds 2.50 6.00
34 Albert Pujols 2.00 5.00
35 Scott Rolen 1.00 2.50

2003 Studio Spirit of MLB

STATED PRINT RUN 1 SERIAL #'d SET

2003 Studio Stars

STATED ODDS 1:5
*GOLD: 1X TO 2.5X BASIC STARS
GOLD PRINT RUN 100 SERIAL #'d SETS
PLATINUM PRINT RUN 25 SERIAL #'d SETS
NO PLATINUM PRICING DUE TO SCARCITY
1 Troy Glaus .40 1.00
2 Manny Ramirez 1.00 2.50
3 Nomar Garciaparra .60 1.50
4 Pedro Martinez .60 1.50
5 Rickey Henderson 1.00 2.50
6 Torii Hunter .40 1.00
7 Frank Thomas 1.00 2.50
8 Magglio Ordonez .60 1.50
9 Alfonso Soriano .60 1.50
10 Jose Contreras 1.00 2.50
11 Derek Jeter 2.50 6.00
12 Jason Giambi .40 1.00
13 Roger Clemens 1.25 3.00
14 Mike Mussina .60 1.50
15 Barry Zito .60 1.50
16 Miguel Tejada .60 1.50
17 Ichiro Suzuki 1.25 3.00
18 Alex Rodriguez 1.25 3.00
19 Juan Gonzalez .40 1.00
20 Rafael Palmeiro .60 1.50
21 Hank Blalock .40 1.00
22 Curt Schilling .60 1.50
23 Randy Johnson 1.00 2.50
24 Junior Spivey .40 1.00
25 Andruw Jones .40 1.00
26 Chipper Jones 1.00 2.50
27 Greg Maddux 1.25 3.00
28 Kerry Wood .40 1.00
29 Mark Prior .60 1.50
30 Sammy Sosa 1.00 2.50
31 Adam Dunn .60 1.50
32 Ken Griffey Jr. 2.00 5.00
33 Austin Kearns .40 1.00
34 Larry Walker .60 1.50
35 Todd Helton .60 1.50
36 Ivan Rodriguez .60 1.50
37 Jeff Bagwell .60 1.50
38 Lance Berkman .60 1.50
39 Craig Biggio .60 1.50
40 Hideo Nomo 1.00 2.50
41 Shawn Green .40 1.00
42 Vladimir Guerrero .60 1.50
43 Mike Piazza 1.00 2.50
44 Tom Glavine .60 1.50
45 Roberto Alomar .60 1.50
46 Pat Burrell .40 1.00
47 Jim Thome .60 1.50
48 Barry Bonds 1.50 4.00
49 Albert Pujols 1.25 3.00
50 Scott Rolen .60 1.50

2004 Studio

COMP.SET w/o SP's (200) 20.00 50.00
COMMON ACTIVE (1-200) .15 .40
COMMON RETIRED (1-200) .15 .40
COMMON RC (1-200) .15 .40
COMMON AU p/r 766-800 3.00 8.00
COMMON AU p/r 400-550 4.00 10.00
AU'S RANDOM INSERTS IN PACKS
AU PRINT RUNS B/WN 400-800 COPIES PER
COMMON CARD (226-241) .40 1.00
COMMON CARD (242-275) 1.50 4.00
226-275 ODDS 1:23 '05 DONRUSS
CARDS 220/222-225 DO NOT EXIST
1 Bartolo Colon .15 .40
2 Garret Anderson .15 .40
3 Tim Salmon .15 .40
4 Troy Glaus .15 .40
5 Vladimir Guerrero .25 .60
6 Brandon Webb .15 .40
7 Brian Bruney .15 .40
8 Casey Fossum .15 .40
9 Luis Gonzalez .15 .40
10 Randy Johnson .40 1.00
11 Richie Sexson .15 .40
12 Robby Hammock .15 .40
13 Roberto Alomar .25 .60
14 Shea Hillenbrand .15 .40
15 Steve Finley .15 .40
16 Adam LaRoche .15 .40
17 Andruw Jones .15 .40
18 Bubba Nelson .15 .40
19 Chipper Jones .40 1.00
20 Dale Murphy .40 1.00
21 J.D. Drew .15 .40
22 Marcus Giles .15 .40
23 Michael Hessman .15 .40
24 Rafael Furcal .15 .40
25 Warren Spahn .25 .60
26 Adam Loewen .15 .40
27 Cal Ripken 1.25 3.00
28 Javy Lopez .15 .40
29 Jay Gibbons .15 .40
30 Luis Matos .15 .40
31 Miguel Tejada .25 .60
32 Rafael Palmeiro .25 .60
33 Curt Schilling .25 .60
34 Jason Varitek .40 1.00
35 Kevin Youkilis .15 .40
36 Manny Ramirez .40 1.00
37 Nomar Garciaparra .25 .60
38 Pedro Martinez .25 .60
39 Trot Nixon .15 .40
40 Aramis Ramirez .15 .40
41 Brendan Harris .15 .40
42 Derrek Lee .15 .40
43 Ernie Banks .40 1.00
44 Greg Maddux .50 1.25
45 Kerry Wood .15 .40
46 Mark Prior .25 .60
47 Ryne Sandberg .75 2.00
48 Sammy Sosa .40 1.00
49 Todd Wellemeyer .15 .40
50 Carlos Lee .15 .40
51 Edwin Almonte .15 .40
52 Frank Thomas .40 1.00
53 Joe Borchard .15 .40
54 Joe Crede .15 .40
55 Magglio Ordonez .25 .60
56 Adam Dunn .25 .60
57 Austin Kearns .15 .40
58 Barry Larkin .25 .60
59 Brandon Larson .15 .40
60 Ken Griffey Jr. .75 2.00
61 Ryan Wagner .15 .40
62 Sean Casey .15 .40
63 Brian Tallet .15 .40
64 C.C. Sabathia .25 .60
65 Jeremy Guthrie .15 .40
66 Jody Gerut .15 .40
67 Travis Hafner .15 .40
68 Clint Barmes .25 .60
69 Jeff Baker .15 .40
70 Joe Kennedy .15 .40
71 Larry Walker .25 .60
72 Preston Wilson .15 .40
73 Todd Helton .25 .60
74 Dmitri Young .15 .40
75 Ivan Rodriguez .25 .60
76 Jeremy Bonderman .15 .40
77 Preston Larrison .15 .40
78 Dontrelle Willis .15 .40
79 Josh Beckett .15 .40
80 Juan Pierre .15 .40
81 Luis Castillo .15 .40
82 Miguel Cabrera .40 1.00
83 Mike Lowell .15 .40
84 Andy Pettitte .25 .60
85 Chris Burke .15 .40
86 Craig Biggio .25 .60
87 Jeff Bagwell .25 .60
88 Jeff Kent .15 .40
89 Lance Berkman .25 .60
90 Morgan Ensberg .15 .40
91 Richard Hidalgo .15 .40
92 Roger Clemens .50 1.25
93 Roy Oswalt .25 .60
94 Wade Miller .15 .40
95 Angel Berroa .15 .40
96 Byron Gettis .15 .40
97 Carlos Beltran .25 .60
98 Juan Gonzalez .15 .40
99 Mike Sweeney .15 .40
100 Duke Snider .25 .60
101 Edwin Jackson .15 .40
102 Eric Gagne .15 .40
103 Hideo Nomo .40 1.00
104 Hong-Chih Kuo .15 .40
105 Kazuhisa Ishii .15 .40
106 Paul Lo Duca .15 .40
107 Robin Ventura .15 .40
108 Shawn Green .15 .40
109 Junior Spivey .15 .40
110 Lyle Overbay .15 .40
111 Rickie Weeks .15 .40
112 Scott Podsednik .15 .40
113 J.D. Durbin .15 .40
114 Jacque Jones .15 .40
115 Jason Kubel .15 .40
116 Johan Santana .25 .60
117 Shannon Stewart .15 .40
118 Torii Hunter .15 .40
119 Brad Wilkerson .15 .40
120 Jose Vidro .15 .40
121 Nick Johnson .15 .40
122 Orlando Cabrera .15 .40
123 Zach Day .15 .40
124 Gary Carter .25 .60
125 Jae Weong Seo .15 .40
126 Kazuo Matsui RC .25 .60
127 Mike Piazza .40 1.00
128 Tom Glavine .25 .60
129 Alex Rodriguez Yanks .50 1.25
130 Bernie Williams .25 .60
131 Chien-Ming Wang .60 1.50
132 Derek Jeter 1.00 2.50
133 Don Mattingly .75 2.00
134 Gary Sheffield .15 .40
135 Hideki Matsui .60 1.50
136 Jason Giambi .15 .40
137 Javier Vazquez .15 .40
138 Jorge Posada .25 .60
139 Jose Contreras .15 .40
140 Kevin Brown .15 .40
141 Mariano Rivera .50 1.25
142 Mike Mussina .25 .60
143 Whitey Ford .25 .60
144 Barry Zito .25 .60
145 Eric Chavez .15 .40
146 Mark Mulder .15 .40
147 Rich Harden .15 .40
148 Tim Hudson .25 .60
149 Bobby Abreu .15 .40
150 Jim Thome .25 .60
151 Kevin Millwood .15 .40
152 Marlon Byrd .15 .40
153 Mike Schmidt .60 1.50
154 Ryan Howard .30 .75
155 Jack Wilson .15 .40
156 Jason Kendall .15 .40
157 Akinori Otsuka RC .15 .40
158 Brian Giles .15 .40
159 David Wells .15 .40
160 Jay Payton .15 .40
161 Phil Nevin .15 .40
162 Ryan Klesko .15 .40
163 Sean Burroughs .15 .40
164 A.J. Pierzynski .15 .40
165 J.T. Snow .15 .40
166 Jason Schmidt .15 .40
167 Jerome Williams .15 .40
168 Merkin Valdez RC .15 .40
169 Will Clark .25 .60
170 Bret Boone .15 .40
171 Chris Snelling .15 .40
172 Edgar Martinez .25 .60
173 Ichiro Suzuki .50 1.25
174 Jamie Moyer .15 .40
175 Randy Winn .15 .40
176 Rich Aurilia .15 .40
177 Shigetoshi Hasegawa .15 .40
178 Albert Pujols .50 1.25
179 Dan Haren .15 .40
180 Edgar Renteria .15 .40
181 Jim Edmonds .25 .60
182 Matt Morris .15 .40
183 Scott Rolen .25 .60
184 Stan Musial .60 1.50
185 Aubrey Huff .15 .40
186 Chad Gaudin .15 .40
187 Delmon Young .25 .60
188 Fred McGriff .15 .40
189 Rocco Baldelli .15 .40
190 Alfonso Soriano .25 .60
191 Hank Blalock .15 .40
192 Mark Teixeira .25 .60
193 Nolan Ryan 1.25 3.00
194 Alexis Rios .15 .40
195 Carlos Delgado .15 .40
196 Dustin McGowan .15 .40
197 Guillermo Quiroz .15 .40
198 Josh Phelps .15 .40
199 Roy Halladay .25 .60
200 Vernon Wells .15 .40
201 Mike Gosling AU/400 RC 4.00 10.00
202 Ronny Cedeno AU/766 RC 6.00 15.00
203 Ron Belisario AU/400 RC 4.00 10.00
204 Justin Hampson AU/800 RC 3.00 8.00
205 Carlos Vasquez AU/800 RC 3.00 8.00
206 Linc.Holdzkom AU/800 RC 3.00 8.00
207 Casey Daigle AU/550 RC 4.00 10.00
208 Jason Bartlett AU/800 RC 4.00 10.00
209 Mariano Gomez AU/800 RC 3.00 8.00
210 Mike Rouse AU/800 RC 3.00 8.00
211 Chris Shelton AU/800 RC 3.00 8.00
212 Dennis Sarfate AU/800 RC 3.00 8.00
213 Shingo Takatsu AU/400 RC 6.00 15.00
214 Justin Leone AU/800 RC 4.00 10.00
215 Cory Sullivan AU/800 RC 3.00 8.00
216 Michael Wuertz AU/800 RC 4.00 10.00
217 Tim Bausher AU/800 RC 3.00 8.00
218 Jesse Harper AU/800 RC 3.00 8.00
219 Ryan Meaux AU/800 RC 3.00 8.00
221 Kevin Cave AU/800 RC 3.00 8.00
226 Abe Alvarez XRC .40 1.00
227 Carlos Hines XRC .40 1.00
228 Charles Thomas XRC .40 1.00
229 Frankie Francisco XRC .40 1.00
230 Greg Dobbs XRC .40 1.00
231 Hector Gimenez XRC .40 1.00
232 Jesse Crain XRC .60 1.50
233 Joey Gathright XRC .40 1.00
234 Justin Knoedler XRC .40 1.00
235 Kazuhito Tadano XRC .40 1.00
236 Lance Cormier XRC .40 1.00
237 Scott Proctor XRC .40 1.00
238 Tim Bittner XRC .40 1.00
239 Travis Blackley XRC .40 1.00
240 Mike Johnston XRC .40 1.00
241 Yadier Molina XRC 30.00 80.00
242 B.J. Upton 2.50 6.00
243 Ben Sheets 1.50 4.00
244 Bobby Crosby 1.50 4.00
245 Brad Penny 1.50 4.00
246 Carl Crawford 2.50 6.00
247 Carlos Beltran 2.50 6.00
248 Carlos Guillen 1.50 4.00
249 Carlos Zambrano 2.50 6.00
250 Casey Kotchman 1.50 4.00
251 Chase Utley 2.50 6.00
252 Craig Wilson 1.50 4.00
253 Danny Graves 1.50 4.00
254 Danny Kolb 1.50 4.00
255 David Wright 3.00 8.00
256 Eric Milton 1.50 4.00
257 Esteban Loaiza 1.50 4.00
258 Francisco Cordero 1.50 4.00
259 Francisco Rodriguez 2.50 6.00
260 Jake Peavy 1.50 4.00
261 Jason Bay 2.50 6.00
262 Jermaine Dye 1.50 4.00
263 Joe Nathan 1.50 4.00
264 John Lackey 2.50 6.00
265 Ken Harvey 1.50 4.00
266 Khalil Greene 2.50 6.00
267 Lew Ford 1.50 4.00
268 Livan Hernandez 1.50 4.00
269 Milton Bradley 1.50 4.00
270 Nomar Garciaparra 2.50 6.00
271 Orlando Cabrera Sox 1.50 4.00
272 Paul Lo Duca 1.50 4.00
273 Richard Hidalgo 1.50 4.00
274 Steve Finley 1.50 4.00
275 Victor Martinez 2.50 6.00

2004 Studio Proofs Gold

*GOLD 1-200: 5X TO 12X BASIC ACTIVE
*GOLD 1-200: 5X TO 12X BASIC RETIRED
*GOLD 1-200: 5X TO 12X BASIC RC'S
COMMON CARD (201-221) 2.00 5.00
SEMISTARS 3.00 8.00
UNLISTED STARS 5.00 12.00
COMMON (220/222-225) 2.00 5.00
SEMIS 220/222-225 3.00 8.00
UNLISTED 220/222-225 5.00 12.00
1-225 RANDOM INSERTS IN PACKS
220/222-225 EXIST ONLY IN PARALLEL SET
*GOLD 226-241: 2X TO 5X BASIC
*GOLD 242-275: .6X TO 1.5X BASIC
226-275 RANDOM IN '05 DONRUSS
STATED PRINT RUN 50 SERIAL #'d SETS
201 Mike Gosling 2.00 5.00
202 Ronny Cedeno 2.00 5.00
203 Ronald Belisario 2.00 5.00
204 Justin Hampson 2.00 5.00
205 Carlos Vasquez 2.00 5.00
206 Lincoln Holdzkom 2.00 5.00
207 Casey Daigle 2.00 5.00
208 Jason Bartlett 6.00 15.00
209 Mariano Gomez 2.00 5.00
210 Mike Rouse 2.00 5.00
211 Chris Shelton 2.00 5.00
212 Dennis Sarfate 2.00 5.00
213 Shingo Takatsu 2.00 5.00
214 Justin Leone 2.00 5.00
215 Cory Sullivan 2.00 5.00
216 Michael Wuertz 2.00 5.00
217 Tim Bausher 2.00 5.00
218 Jesse Harper 2.00 5.00
219 Ryan Meaux 2.00 5.00
220 David Aardsma 2.00 5.00
221 Kevin Cave 2.00 5.00
222 Mike Johnston 2.00 5.00
223 Jason Szuminski 2.00 5.00
224 Shawn Camp 2.00 5.00
225 Colby Miller 2.00 5.00

2004 Studio Proofs Silver

*SILVER 1-200: 3X TO 8X BASIC ACTIVE
*SILVER 1-200: 3X TO 8X BASIC RETIRED
*SILVER 1-200: 3X TO 8X BASIC RC'S
COMMON CARD (201-221) 1.25 3.00
SEMISTARS 2.00 5.00
UNLISTED STARS 3.00 8.00
COMMON (220/222-225) 1.25 3.00
SEMIS 220/222-225 2.00 5.00
UNLISTED 220/222-225 3.00 8.00
1-225 RANDOM INSERTS IN PACKS
*SILVER 226-241: 1.25X TO 3X BASIC
*SILVER 242-275: .5X TO 1.2X BASIC
226-275 RANDOM IN '05 DONRUSS
STATED PRINT RUN 100 SERIAL #'d SETS
220/222-225 EXIST ONLY IN PARALLEL SET
201 Mike Gosling 1.25 3.00
202 Ronny Cedeno 1.25 3.00
203 Ronald Belisario 1.25 3.00
204 Justin Hampson 1.25 3.00
205 Carlos Vasquez 1.25 3.00
206 Lincoln Holdzkom 1.25 3.00
207 Casey Daigle 1.25 3.00
208 Jason Bartlett 4.00 10.00
209 Mariano Gomez 1.25 3.00
210 Mike Rouse 1.25 3.00
211 Chris Shelton 1.25 3.00
212 Dennis Sarfate 1.25 3.00
213 Shingo Takatsu 1.25 3.00
214 Justin Leone 1.25 3.00
215 Cory Sullivan 1.25 3.00
216 Michael Wuertz 1.25 3.00
217 Tim Bausher 1.25 3.00
218 Jesse Harper 1.25 3.00
219 Ryan Meaux 1.25 3.00
220 David Aardsma 1.25 3.00
222 Mike Johnston 1.25 3.00
223 Jason Szuminski 1.25 3.00
224 Shawn Camp 1.25 3.00
225 Colby Miller 1.25 3.00

2004 Studio Private Signings Gold

PRINT RUNS B/WN 1-100 COPIES PER
NO PRICING ON QTY OF 12 OR LESS
NO RC YR PRICING ON QTY OF 25 OR LESS
2 Garret Anderson/16 15.00 40.00
6 Brandon Webb/55 6.00 15.00
7 Brian Bruney/100 4.00 10.00
14 Shea Hillenbrand/28 10.00 25.00
16 Adam LaRoche/25 8.00 20.00
18 Bubba Nelson/100 4.00 10.00
22 Marcus Giles/25 12.50 30.00
23 Michael Hessman/25 8.00 20.00
29 Jay Gibbons/25 8.00 20.00
30 Luis Matos/100 4.00 10.00
34 Jason Varitek/33 30.00 60.00
35 Kevin Youkilis/100 6.00 15.00
40 Aramis Ramirez/16 15.00 40.00
41 Brendan Harris/75 4.00 10.00
46 Mark Prior/22 15.00 40.00
49 Todd Wellemeyer/50 5.00 12.00
50 Carlos Lee/45 8.00 20.00
51 Edwin Almonte/56 5.00 12.00
53 Joe Borchard/25 8.00 20.00
54 Joe Crede/24 12.50 30.00
57 Austin Kearns/28 6.00 15.00
59 Brandon Larson/16 10.00 25.00
61 Ryan Wagner/38 5.00 12.00
63 Brian Tallet/50 5.00 12.00
65 Jeremy Guthrie/67 4.00 10.00
66 Jody Gerut/25 8.00 20.00
67 Travis Hafner/34 10.00 25.00
68 Clint Barmes/36 8.00 20.00
69 Jeff Baker/62 4.00 10.00
70 Joe Kennedy/37 5.00 12.00
73 Todd Helton/17 30.00 60.00
77 Preston Larrison/56 5.00 12.00
78 Dontrelle Willis/35 15.00 40.00

82 Miguel Cabrera/24 30.00 60.00
85 Chris Burke/46 8.00 20.00
89 Lance Berkman/17 30.00 60.00
90 Morgan Ensberg/25 12.50 30.00
96 Byron Gettis/100 4.00 10.00
97 Carlos Beltran/25 12.50 30.00
98 Juan Gonzalez/22 12.50 30.00
100 Duke Snider/25 20.00 50.00
101 Edwin Jackson/50 5.00 12.00
104 Hong-Chih Kuo/100 12.00 30.00
105 Kazuhisa Ishii/17 15.00 40.00
106 Paul Lo Duca/16 15.00 40.00
107 Robin Ventura/25 20.00 50.00
108 Shawn Green/15 30.00 60.00
109 Junior Spivey/37 5.00 12.00
112 Scott Podsednik/20 20.00 50.00
113 J.D. Durbin/31 6.00 15.00
114 Jacque Jones/25 12.50 30.00
116 Johan Santana/57 12.50 30.00
117 Shannon Stewart/23 8.00 20.00
121 Nick Johnson/21 12.50 30.00
122 Orlando Cabrera/18 12.50 30.00
124 Gary Carter/25 12.50 30.00
125 Jae Weong Seo/25 12.50 30.00
131 Chien-Ming Wang/100 25.00 60.00
147 Rich Harden/53 8.00 20.00
152 Marlon Byrd/29 6.00 15.00
154 Ryan Howard/100 15.00 40.00
160 Jay Payton/17 10.00 25.00
167 Jerome Williams/50 5.00 12.00
168 Merkin Valdez/100 4.00 10.00
171 Chris Snelling/32 6.00 15.00
177 Shigetoshi Hasegawa/17 60.00 120.00
179 Dan Haren/100 4.00 10.00
184 Stan Musial/25 40.00 80.00
185 Aubrey Huff/19 15.00 40.00
186 Chad Gaudin/100 4.00 10.00
187 Delmon Young/73 10.00 25.00
192 Mark Teixeira/25 20.00 50.00
194 Alexis Rios/50 8.00 20.00
196 Dustin McGowan/50 5.00 12.00
198 Josh Phelps/17 10.00 25.00
226 Abe Alvarez/50 6.00 15.00
227 Carlos Hines/50 4.00 10.00
228 Charles Thomas/50 5.00 12.00
229 Frankie Francisco/50 4.00 10.00
231 Hector Gimenez/50 4.00 10.00
232 Jesse Crain/50 8.00 20.00
233 Joey Gathright/50 6.00 15.00
234 Justin Knoedler/50 4.00 10.00
236 Lance Cormier/50 4.00 10.00
237 Scott Proctor/50 6.00 15.00
238 Tim Bittner/50 4.00 10.00
239 Travis Blackley/50 4.00 10.00
240 Mike Johnston/50 4.00 10.00
241 Yadier Molina/50 200.00 500.00

2004 Studio Private Signings Silver

PRINT RUNS B/WN 1-250 COPIES PER
NO PRICING ON QTY OF 10 OR LESS
NO RC YR PRICING ON QTY OF 25 OR LESS
2 Garret Anderson/25 12.50 30.00
6 Brandon Webb/25 10.00 25.00
7 Brian Bruney/200 4.00 10.00
8 Casey Fossum/63 4.00 10.00
14 Shea Hillenbrand/25 12.50 30.00
16 Adam LaRoche/26 6.00 15.00
18 Bubba Nelson/250 4.00 10.00
22 Marcus Giles/25 12.50 30.00
23 Michael Hessman/95 4.00 10.00
24 Rafael Furcal/25 12.50 30.00
26 Adam Loewen/25 8.00 20.00
29 Jay Gibbons/50 5.00 12.00
30 Luis Matos/250 4.00 10.00
35 Kevin Youkilis/250 6.00 15.00
39 Trot Nixon/25 12.50 30.00
40 Aramis Ramirez/25 12.50 30.00
41 Brendan Harris/100 4.00 10.00
43 Ernie Banks/25 40.00 80.00
48 Sammy Sosa/21 50.00 100.00
49 Todd Wellemeyer/92 4.00 10.00
50 Carlos Lee/25 12.50 30.00
51 Edwin Almonte/227 4.00 10.00
53 Joe Borchard/100 4.00 10.00
59 Brandon Larson/100 4.00 10.00
61 Ryan Wagner/50 5.00 12.00
63 Brian Tallet/250 4.00 10.00
65 Jeremy Guthrie/89 4.00 10.00
66 Jody Gerut/100 4.00 10.00
67 Travis Hafner/100 6.00 15.00
68 Clint Barmes/100 6.00 15.00
69 Jeff Baker/50 5.00 12.00
70 Joe Kennedy/100 4.00 10.00
72 Preston Wilson/25 12.50 30.00
77 Preston Larrison/100 4.00 10.00
81 Luis Castillo/25 8.00 20.00
82 Miguel Cabrera/25 30.00 60.00
85 Chris Burke/100 4.00 10.00
90 Morgan Ensberg/50 8.00 20.00
96 Byron Gettis/250 4.00 10.00
97 Carlos Beltran/50 8.00 20.00
100 Duke Snider/50 12.50 30.00
101 Edwin Jackson/100 4.00 10.00
104 Hong-Chih Kuo/250 12.00 30.00
106 Paul Lo Duca/25 12.50 30.00
107 Robin Ventura/25 20.00 50.00
109 Junior Spivey/50 5.00 12.00
112 Scott Podsednik/100 10.00 25.00
113 J.D. Durbin/250 4.00 10.00
114 Jacque Jones/50 8.00 20.00
115 Jason Kubel/100 4.00 10.00
116 Johan Santana/25 20.00 50.00
117 Shannon Stewart/25 8.00 20.00
120 Jose Vidro/15 10.00 25.00
122 Orlando Cabrera/15 12.50 30.00
124 Gary Carter/50 8.00 20.00
131 Chien-Ming Wang/243 20.00 50.00
133 Don Mattingly/25 50.00 100.00
134 Gary Sheffield/25 12.50 30.00
147 Rich Harden/200 6.00 15.00
154 Ryan Howard/250 12.50 30.00
160 Jay Payton/50 5.00 12.00
167 Jerome Williams/57 5.00 12.00
168 Merkin Valdez/250 3.00 8.00
169 Will Clark/25 20.00 50.00
171 Chris Snelling/200 4.00 10.00
177 Shigetoshi Hasegawa/25 60.00 120.00
179 Dan Haren/250 4.00 10.00
184 Stan Musial/25 30.00 60.00
185 Aubrey Huff/250 6.00 15.00
186 Chad Gaudin/100 4.00 10.00
187 Delmon Young/25 20.00 50.00
192 Mark Teixeira/23 10.00 25.00
193 Nolan Ryan/34 60.00 120.00
194 Alexis Rios/250 6.00 15.00
196 Dustin McGowan/115 4.00 10.00
197 Guillermo Quiroz/120 4.00 10.00
226 Abe Alvarez/100 5.00 12.00
227 Carlos Hines/100 3.00 8.00
228 Charles Thomas/100 4.00 10.00
229 Frankie Francisco/100 3.00 8.00
230 Greg Dobbs/40 3.00 8.00
231 Hector Gimenez/100 3.00 8.00
232 Jesse Crain/100 6.00 15.00
233 Joey Gathright/100 5.00 12.00
234 Justin Knoedler/100 3.00 8.00
236 Lance Cormier/100 3.00 8.00
237 Scott Proctor/100 5.00 12.00
238 Tim Bittner/100 3.00 8.00
239 Travis Blackley/100 3.00 8.00
240 Mike Johnston/100 3.00 8.00
241 Yadier Molina/100 150.00 400.00

2004 Studio Big League Challenge

STATED PRINT RUN 999 SERIAL #'d SETS
*DIE CUT: .6X TO 1.5X BASIC
DIE CUT PRINT RUN 500 SERIAL #'d SETS
*GOLD: .6X TO 1.5X BASIC
GOLD PRINT RUN 499 SERIAL #'d SETS
1 Albert Pujols Left 1.50 4.00
2 Albert Pujols Right 1.50 4.00
3 Alex Rodriguez Rgr Left 1.50 4.00
4 Alex Rodriguez Rgr Right 1.50 4.00
5 Magglio Ordonez .75 2.00
6 Rafael Palmeiro .75 2.00
7 Troy Glaus Follow .50 1.25
8 Troy Glaus Start .50 1.25
9 Albert Pujols Bat Up 1.50 4.00
10 Alex Rodriguez Rgr Bat Up 1.50 4.00

2004 Studio Big League Challenge Material

STATED PRINT RUN 100 SERIAL #'d SETS
*COMBO: .75X TO 2X BASIC
COMBO PRINT RUN 50 SERIAL #'d SETS
RANDOM INSERTS IN PACKS
1 Albert Pujols Jsy 6.00 15.00
2 Albert Pujols Pants 6.00 15.00
3 Alex Rodriguez Rgr Jsy 4.00 10.00
4 Alex Rodriguez Rgr Pants 4.00 10.00
5 Magglio Ordonez Jsy 3.00 8.00
6 Rafael Palmeiro Jsy 4.00 10.00
7 Troy Glaus Jsy 3.00 8.00
8 Troy Glaus Pants 3.00 8.00
9 Albert Pujols Hat 8.00 20.00
10 Alex Rodriguez Rgr Hat 6.00 15.00

2004 Studio Diamond Cuts Material Bat

RANDOM INSERTS IN PACKS
PRINT RUNS B/WN 100-200 COPIES PER
1 Derek Jeter/100 10.00 25.00
2 Greg Maddux/100 5.00 12.00
3 Nomar Garciaparra/200 4.00 10.00
4 Miguel Cabrera/200 3.00 8.00
5 Mark Mulder/200 2.00 5.00
6 Rafael Furcal/200 2.00 5.00
7 Mark Prior/200 3.00 8.00
8 Roy Oswalt/200 2.00 5.00
9 Dontrelle Willis/100 4.00 10.00
10 Jay Gibbons/200 2.00 5.00
11 Josh Beckett/200 2.00 5.00
12 Angel Berroa/200 2.00 5.00
13 Adam Dunn/200 2.00 5.00
14 Hank Blalock/200 2.00 5.00
15 Carlos Beltran/200 2.00 5.00
16 Shannon Stewart/200 2.00 5.00
17 Aubrey Huff/200 2.00 5.00
18 Jeff Bagwell/200 3.00 8.00
19 Trot Nixon/200 2.00 5.00
21 Tony Gwynn/200 5.00 12.00
22 Andre Dawson/200 3.00 8.00
23 Don Mattingly/200 6.00 15.00
24 Dale Murphy/200 4.00 10.00
25 Gary Carter/200 3.00 8.00

2004 Studio Diamond Cuts Material Jersey

PRINT RUNS B/WN 200-250 COPIES PER
PRIME PRINT RUN B/WN 5-10 COPIES PER
NO PRIME PRICING DUE TO SCARCITY
1 Derek Jeter/250 8.00 20.00
2 Greg Maddux/250 4.00 10.00
3 Nomar Garciaparra/200 4.00 10.00
4 Miguel Cabrera/250 3.00 8.00
5 Mark Mulder/250 2.00 5.00
6 Rafael Furcal/250 2.00 5.00
7 Mark Prior/250 3.00 8.00
8 Roy Oswalt/250 2.00 5.00
9 Dontrelle Willis/250 3.00 8.00
10 Jay Gibbons/250 2.00 5.00
11 Josh Beckett/250 2.00 5.00
12 Angel Berroa/250 2.00 5.00
13 Adam Dunn/250 2.00 5.00
14 Hank Blalock/250 2.00 5.00
15 Carlos Beltran/250 2.00 5.00
16 Shannon Stewart/250 2.00 5.00
17 Aubrey Huff/250 2.00 5.00
18 Jeff Bagwell/250 3.00 8.00
19 Trot Nixon/250 2.00 5.00
20 Nolan Ryan Jacket/250 10.00 25.00
21 Tony Gwynn/250 6.00 15.00
22 Andre Dawson/250 3.00 8.00
23 Don Mattingly Jacket/250 6.00 15.00
24 Dale Murphy/250 4.00 10.00
25 Gary Carter/250 3.00 8.00

2004 Studio Diamond Cuts Combo Material

PRINT RUNS B/WN 25-50 COPIES PER
PRIME PRINT RUN 5 SERIAL #'d SETS
NO PRIME PRICING DUE TO SCARCITY
RANDOM INSERTS IN PACKS
1 Derek Jeter Bat-Jsy/50 20.00 50.00
2 Greg Maddux Bat-Jsy/50 10.00 25.00
4 Miguel Cabrera Bat-Jsy/50 8.00 20.00
5 Mark Mulder Bat-Jsy/50 5.00 12.00
6 Rafael Furcal Bat-Jsy/50 5.00 12.00
7 Mark Prior Bat-Jsy/50 8.00 20.00
8 Roy Oswalt Bat-Jsy/50 5.00 12.00
10 Jay Gibbons Bat-Jsy/50 5.00 12.00
11 Josh Beckett Bat-Jsy/50 5.00 12.00
12 Angel Berroa Bat-Jsy/50 5.00 12.00
13 Adam Dunn Bat-Jsy/50 5.00 12.00
14 Hank Blalock Bat-Jsy/50 5.00 12.00
15 Carlos Beltran Bat-Jsy/50 5.00 12.00
16 Shannon Stewart Bat-Jsy/50 5.00 12.00
17 Aubrey Huff Bat-Jsy/50 5.00 12.00
18 Jeff Bagwell Bat-Jsy/50 8.00 20.00
19 Trot Nixon Bat-Jsy/50 5.00 12.00
20 Nolan Ryan Jacket-Jsy/50 15.00 40.00
21 Tony Gwynn Bat-Jsy/50 15.00 40.00
22 Andre Dawson Bat-Jsy/50 6.00 15.00
23 D.Mattingly Bat-Jacket/50 20.00 50.00
24 Dale Murphy Bat-Jsy/50 10.00 25.00
25 Gary Carter Bat-Jsy/50 6.00 15.00

2004 Studio Fans of the Game

RANDOM INSERTS IN PACKS
216 Regis Philbin 1.50 4.00
217 Denis Leary 1.25 3.00
218 Bode Miller 1.50 4.00
219 Steve Schirripa .75 2.00
220 Adam Mesh .75 2.00

2004 Studio Fans of the Game Autographs

RANDOM INSERTS IN PACKS
SP PRINT RUNS PROVIDED BY DONRUSS
SP'S ARE NOT SERIAL-NUMBERED
216 Regis Philbin 12.50 30.00
217 Denis Leary 12.00 30.00
218 Bode Miller SP/250 15.00 40.00
219 Steve Schirripa 6.00 15.00
220 Adam Mesh SP/300 10.00 25.00

2004 Studio Game Day Souvenirs

*SOUV: .4X TO 1X NUMBER p/r 150-300
*SOUV: .25X TO .6X NUMBER p/r 75-100
*SOUV: .2X TO .5X NUMBER p/r 50
*SOUV: .12X TO .3X NUMBER p/r 25
DISTRIBUTED BY MLBPA AND PROPERTIES

2004 Studio Game Day Souvenirs Number

PRINT RUNS B/WN 25-300 COPIES PER
*POSITION: .4X TO 1X BASIC
POSITION PRINT B/WN 25-300 COPIES PER
1 Garret Anderson Jsy/300 2.00 5.00
2 Troy Glaus Jsy/300 2.00 5.00
3 Vladimir Guerrero Jsy/300 3.00 8.00
4 Steve Finley Jsy/250 2.00 5.00
5 Luis Gonzalez Jsy/25 6.00 15.00
6 Richie Sexson Jsy/250 2.00 5.00
7 Andruw Jones Jsy/300 3.00 8.00
8 Chipper Jones Jsy/250 3.00 8.00
9 Rafael Furcal Jsy/250 2.00 5.00
13 Curt Schilling Jsy/300 3.00 8.00
14 Pedro Martinez Jsy/300 3.00 8.00
15 David Ortiz Jsy/300 3.00 8.00
16 Sammy Sosa Jsy/300 3.00 8.00
17 Corey Patterson Jsy/250 2.00 5.00
18 Moises Alou Jsy/300 2.00 5.00
19 Magglio Ordonez Jsy/250 2.00 5.00
20 Paul Konerko Jsy/300 2.00 5.00
21 Frank Thomas Jsy/300 3.00 8.00
22 Austin Kearns Jsy/50 4.00 10.00
23 Sean Casey Jsy/200 2.00 5.00
24 Adam Dunn Jsy/200 2.00 5.00
25 Omar Vizquel Jsy/250 3.00 8.00
26 C.C. Sabathia Jsy/300 2.00 5.00
27 Jody Gerut Jsy/250 2.00 5.00
28 Todd Helton Jsy/300 3.00 8.00
29 Vinny Castilla Jsy/300 2.00 5.00
30 Jeromy Burnitz Jsy/300 2.00 5.00
31 Fernando Vina Jsy/150 2.00 5.00
32 Ivan Rodriguez Jsy/300 3.00 8.00
33 Jeremy Bonderman Jsy/300 2.00 5.00
34 Mike Lowell Jsy/225 2.00 5.00
35 Luis Castillo Jsy/250 2.00 5.00
36 Miguel Cabrera Jsy/250 3.00 8.00
37 Roger Clemens Jsy/300 4.00 10.00
38 Andy Pettitte Jsy/300 3.00 8.00
39 Jeff Bagwell Jsy/300 3.00 8.00
40 Mike Sweeney Jsy/150 2.00 5.00
41 Carlos Beltran Jsy/200 2.00 5.00
42 Angel Berroa Jsy/100 3.00 8.00
43 Paul Lo Duca Jsy/75 3.00 8.00
44 Shawn Green Jsy/300 2.00 5.00
45 Adrian Beltre Jsy/150 2.00 5.00
46 Ben Sheets Jsy/300 2.00 5.00
47 Geoff Jenkins Jsy/250 2.00 5.00
48 Junior Spivey Jsy/300 2.00 5.00
49 Doug Mientkiewicz Jsy/100 3.00 8.00
50 Shannon Stewart Jsy/100 3.00 8.00
51 Torii Hunter Jsy/300 2.00 5.00
52 Livan Hernandez Jsy/300 2.00 5.00
53 Jose Vidro Jsy/200 2.00 5.00
54 Orlando Cabrera Jsy/300 2.00 5.00
55 Mike Piazza Jsy/250 3.00 8.00
56 Mike Cameron Jsy/250 2.00 5.00
57 Kazuo Matsui Jsy/200 3.00 8.00
58 Derek Jeter Jsy/50 10.00 25.00
59 Jason Giambi Jsy/50 4.00 10.00
61 Barry Zito Jsy/200 2.00 5.00
62 Eric Chavez Jsy/150 2.00 5.00
63 Eric Byrnes Jsy/150 2.00 5.00
65 Jim Thome Jsy/300 3.00 8.00
66 Jimmy Rollins Jsy/250 2.00 5.00
67 Jason Kendall Jsy/250 2.00 5.00
68 Craig Wilson Jsy/250 2.00 5.00
69 Jack Wilson Jsy/250 2.00 5.00
70 Ryan Klesko Jsy/300 2.00 5.00
71 Brian Giles Jsy/300 2.00 5.00
72 Sean Burroughs Jsy/300 2.00 5.00
73 A.J. Pierzynski Jsy/300 2.00 5.00
74 J.T. Snow Jsy/300 2.00 5.00
75 Michael Tucker Jsy/300 2.00 5.00
77 Edgar Martinez Jsy/50 6.00 15.00
79 Scott Rolen Jsy/300 3.00 8.00
80 Albert Pujols Jsy/300 6.00 15.00
81 Jim Edmonds Jsy/300 2.00 5.00
82 Aubrey Huff Jsy/100 3.00 8.00
83 Tino Martinez Jsy/100 5.00 12.00
84 Rocco Baldelli Jsy/100 2.00 5.00
85 Alfonso Soriano Jsy/200 2.00 5.00
86 Michael Young Jsy/250 2.00 5.00
87 Hank Blalock Jsy/200 2.00 5.00
88 Eric Hinske Jsy/200 2.00 5.00
89 Carlos Delgado Jsy/300 2.00 5.00
90 Vernon Wells Jsy/250 2.00 5.00

2004 Studio Heritage

STATED PRINT RUN 999 SERIAL #'d SETS
*DIE CUT: 1.25X TO 3X BASIC
DIE CUT PRINT RUN 100 SERIAL #'d SETS
*GOLD: .6X TO 1.5X BASIC
GOLD PRINT RUN 499 SERIAL #'d SETS
1 George Brett 2.50 6.00
2 Nolan Ryan 4.00 10.00
3 Cal Ripken 4.00 10.00
4 Mike Schmidt 2.00 5.00
5 Roberto Clemente 3.00 8.00
6 Don Mattingly 2.50 6.00
7 Dale Murphy 1.25 3.00
8 Ryne Sandberg 2.50 6.00
9 Harmon Killebrew 1.25 3.00
10 Stan Musial 2.00 5.00

2004 Studio Heritage Material Bat

RANDOM INSERTS IN PACKS
STATED PRINT RUN 50 SERIAL #'d SETS
1 George Brett 10.00 25.00
3 Cal Ripken 30.00 60.00
4 Mike Schmidt 10.00 25.00
5 Roberto Clemente 50.00 100.00
6 Don Mattingly 10.00 25.00
7 Dale Murphy 8.00 20.00
8 Ryne Sandberg 15.00 40.00
9 Harmon Killebrew 8.00 20.00
10 Stan Musial 15.00 40.00

2004 Studio Heritage Material Jersey

PRINT RUNS B/WN 50-200 COPIES PER
PRIME PRINT RUN B/WN 3-10 COPIES PER
NO PRIME PRICING DUE TO SCARCITY
RANDOM INSERTS IN PACKS
1 George Brett/200 6.00 15.00
2 Nolan Ryan Jacket/200 10.00 25.00
3 Cal Ripken/200 8.00 20.00
4 Mike Schmidt Pants/200 6.00 15.00
5 Roberto Clemente/50 50.00 100.00
6 Don Mattingly Jacket/200 6.00 15.00
7 Dale Murphy/200 4.00 10.00
8 Ryne Sandberg/200 10.00 25.00
9 Harmon Killebrew Pants/200 6.00 15.00
10 Stan Musial/100 10.00 25.00

2004 Studio Heroes of the Hall

STATED PRINT RUN 999 SERIAL #'d SETS
*DIE CUT: .6X TO 1.5X BASIC
DIE CUT PRINT RUN 500 SERIAL #'d SETS
*GOLD: .6X TO 1.5X BASIC
GOLD PRINT RUN 499 SERIAL #'d SETS
1 Fergie Jenkins .75 2.00
2 Gary Carter .75 2.00
3 Gaylord Perry .75 2.00
4 George Brett 2.50 6.00
5 Jim Palmer .75 2.00
6 Nolan Ryan 4.00 10.00
7 Paul Molitor 1.25 3.00
8 Rod Carew .75 2.00
9 Steve Carlton .75 2.00
10 Robin Yount 1.25 3.00

2004 Studio Heroes of the Hall Material Bat

RANDOM INSERTS IN PACKS
STATED PRINT RUN 100 SERIAL #'d SETS
2 Gary Carter 3.00 8.00
4 George Brett 10.00 25.00
7 Paul Molitor 3.00 8.00
8 Rod Carew 4.00 10.00
9 Steve Carlton 3.00 8.00
10 Robin Yount 4.00 10.00

2004 Studio Heroes of the Hall Material Jersey

STATED PRINT RUN 200 SERIAL #'d SETS
PRIME PRINT RUN 10 SERIAL #'d SETS
NO PRIME PRICING DUE TO SCARCITY
1 Fergie Jenkins Pants/200 3.00 8.00
2 Gary Carter/200 3.00 8.00
3 Gaylord Perry/100 3.00 8.00
4 George Brett/200 6.00 15.00
5 Jim Palmer/200 3.00 8.00
6 Nolan Ryan/200 10.00 25.00
7 Paul Molitor/200 3.00 8.00
8 Rod Carew/200 4.00 10.00
9 Steve Carlton/200 3.00 8.00
10 Robin Yount/200 4.00 10.00

2004 Studio Masterstrokes Material Bat

RANDOM INSERTS IN PACKS
STATED PRINT RUN 200 SERIAL #'d SETS
1 Todd Helton 3.00 8.00
2 Jose Vidro .75 2.00
3 Edgar Renteria 2.00 5.00
4 Mike Lowell 2.00 5.00
5 Gary Sheffield 2.00 5.00
6 Albert Pujols 6.00 15.00
7 Javy Lopez 2.00 5.00
8 Carlos Delgado 2.00 5.00
9 Bret Boone 2.00 5.00
10 Alex Rodriguez Rgr 4.00 10.00
11 Vernon Wells 2.00 5.00
12 Manny Ramirez 3.00 8.00
13 Jorge Posada 3.00 8.00
14 Edgar Martinez 3.00 8.00
15 Bernie Williams 3.00 8.00
16 Magglio Ordonez 2.00 5.00
17 Garret Anderson 2.00 5.00
18 Eric Chavez 2.00 5.00
19 Alfonso Soriano 2.00 5.00
20 Jason Giambi 2.00 5.00
21 Jeff Kent 2.00 5.00
22 Scott Rolen 3.00 8.00
23 Vladimir Guerrero 3.00 8.00
24 Sammy Sosa 3.00 8.00
25 Mike Piazza 4.00 10.00

2004 Studio Masterstrokes Material Jersey

PRINT RUNS B/WN 150-250 COPIES PER
PRIME PRINT RUN 5 SERIAL #'d SETS
NO PRIME PRICING DUE TO SCARCITY
RANDOM INSERTS IN PACKS
1 Todd Helton/250 3.00 8.00
2 Jose Vidro/250 2.00 5.00
3 Edgar Renteria/250 2.00 5.00
4 Mike Lowell/250 2.00 5.00
5 Gary Sheffield/250 2.00 5.00
6 Albert Pujols/250 6.00 15.00
7 Javy Lopez/250 2.00 5.00
8 Carlos Delgado/250 2.00 5.00
9 Bret Boone/250 2.00 5.00
10 Alex Rodriguez Rgr/250 4.00 10.00
11 Vernon Wells/250 2.00 5.00
12 Manny Ramirez/250 3.00 8.00
13 Jorge Posada/250 3.00 8.00
14 Edgar Martinez/250 3.00 8.00
15 Bernie Williams/250 3.00 8.00
16 Magglio Ordonez/250 2.00 5.00
17 Garret Anderson/250 2.00 5.00
18 Eric Chavez/250 2.00 5.00
19 Alfonso Soriano/150 2.00 5.00
20 Jason Giambi/250 2.00 5.00
21 Jeff Kent/250 2.00 5.00
22 Scott Rolen/250 3.00 8.00
23 Vladimir Guerrero/250 3.00 8.00
24 Sammy Sosa/250 3.00 8.00
25 Mike Piazza/250 4.00 10.00

2004 Studio Masterstrokes Combo Material

STATED PRINT RUN 50 SERIAL #'d SETS
PRIME PRINT RUN 5 SERIAL #'d SETS
NO PRIME PRICING DUE TO SCARCITY
RANDOM INSERTS IN PACKS
1 Todd Helton Bat-Jsy/50 8.00 20.00
2 Jose Vidro Bat-Jsy/50 5.00 12.00
3 Edgar Renteria Bat-Jsy/50 5.00 12.00
4 Mike Lowell Bat-Jsy/50 5.00 12.00
5 Gary Sheffield Bat-Jsy/50 5.00 12.00
6 Albert Pujols Bat-Jsy/50 15.00 40.00
7 Javy Lopez Bat-Jsy/50 5.00 12.00
8 Carlos Delgado Bat-Jsy/50 5.00 12.00
9 Bret Boone Bat-Jsy/50 5.00 12.00
10 A.Rodriguez Rgr Bat-Jsy/50 10.00 25.00
11 Vernon Wells Bat-Jsy/50 5.00 12.00
12 Manny Ramirez Bat-Jsy/50 8.00 20.00
13 Jorge Posada Bat-Jsy/50 8.00 20.00
14 Edgar Martinez Bat-Jsy/50 8.00 20.00
15 Bernie Williams Bat-Jsy/50 8.00 20.00
16 Magglio Ordonez Bat-Jsy/50 5.00 12.00
17 Garret Anderson Bat-Jsy/50 5.00 12.00
18 Eric Chavez Bat-Jsy/50 5.00 12.00
19 Alfonso Soriano Bat-Jsy/50 5.00 12.00
20 Jason Giambi Bat-Jsy/50 5.00 12.00
22 Scott Rolen Bat-Jsy/50 8.00 20.00
23 Vladimir Guerrero Bat-Jsy/50 8.00 20.00
24 Sammy Sosa Bat-Jsy/50 8.00 20.00
25 Mike Piazza Bat-Jsy/50 12.50 30.00

2004 Studio Players Collection Jersey

*STUDIO PC: .4X TO 1X PRESTIGE PC
STATED PRINT RUN 150 SERIAL #'d SETS
*STUDIO PC PLAT: .75X TO 2X PRESTIGE PC
PLATINUM PRINT RUN 50 SERIAL #'d SETS
RANDOM INSERTS IN PACKS

2004 Studio Rally Caps

STATED PRINT RUN 999 SERIAL #'d SETS
*DIE CUT: .6X TO 1.5X BASIC
DIE CUT PRINT RUN 500 SERIAL #'d SETS
*GOLD: .6X TO 1.5X BASIC
GOLD PRINT RUN 499 SERIAL #'d SETS
1 Adam Dunn .75 2.00
2 Adrian Beltre 1.25 3.00
3 Albert Pujols 1.50 4.00
4 Alex Rodriguez 1.50 4.00
5 Andruw Jones .50 1.25
6 Angel Berroa .50 1.25
7 Aubrey Huff .50 1.25
8 Austin Kearns .50 1.25
9 Ben Sheets .50 1.25
10 Brad Penny .50 1.25
11 Carlos Beltran .75 2.00
12 Carlos Lee .50 1.25
13 Casey Fossum .50 1.25
14 Eric Hinske .50 1.25
15 Geoff Jenkins .50 1.25
16 Jack Wilson .50 1.25
17 Jason Jennings .50 1.25
18 Joe Kennedy .50 1.25
19 Lance Berkman .75 2.00
20 Magglio Ordonez .75 2.00
21 Kerry Wood .50 1.25
22 Mark Buehrle .75 2.00
23 Mark Prior .75 2.00
24 Mark Teixeira .75 2.00
25 Michael Cuddyer .50 1.25
26 Jeff Conine .50 1.25
27 Mike Mussina .75 2.00
28 Mike Piazza 1.25 3.00
29 Jose Reyes .75 2.00
30 Paul Lo Duca .50 1.25
31 Pedro Martinez .75 2.00
32 Roy Oswalt .75 2.00
33 Ryan Klesko .50 1.25
34 Sammy Sosa 1.25 3.00
35 Tim Hudson .75 2.00
36 Todd Helton .75 2.00
37 Torii Hunter .50 1.25
38 Vernon Wells .50 1.25
39 Craig Wilson .50 1.25
40 Edgar Renteria .50 1.25

2004 Studio Spirit of the Game

STATED PRINT RUN 999 SERIAL #'d SETS
*DIE CUT: .6X TO 1.5X BASIC
DIE CUT PRINT RUN 500 SERIAL #'d SETS
RANDOM INSERTS IN PACKS
1 Sammy Sosa 1.25 3.00
2 Alex Rodriguez Rgr 1.50 4.00
3 Nomar Garciaparra .75 2.00
4 Derek Jeter 3.00 8.00
5 Albert Pujols 1.50 4.00
6 Roger Clemens 1.50 4.00
7 Mark Prior .75 2.00
8 Randy Johnson 1.25 3.00
9 Pedro Martinez .75 2.00
10 Vladimir Guerrero .75 2.00
11 Todd Helton .75 2.00
12 Jeff Bagwell .75 2.00
13 Mike Mussina .75 2.00
14 Josh Beckett .50 1.25
15 Hideo Nomo 1.25 3.00
16 Mike Piazza 1.25 3.00
17 Don Mattingly 2.50 6.00
18 George Brett 2.50 6.00
19 Nolan Ryan 4.00 10.00
20 Cal Ripken 4.00 10.00

2004 Studio Spirit of the Game Material Bat

RANDOM INSERTS IN PACKS
PRINT RUNS B/WN 10-100 COPIES PER
NO PRICING ON QTY OF 10 OR LESS
1 Sammy Sosa/100 4.00 10.00
2 Alex Rodriguez Rgr/100 5.00 12.00
3 Nomar Garciaparra/100 5.00 12.00
4 Derek Jeter/100 12.00 30.00
5 Albert Pujols/100 8.00 20.00
6 Roger Clemens/50 10.00 25.00
7 Mark Prior/100 4.00 10.00
8 Randy Johnson/100 4.00 10.00
10 Vladimir Guerrero/100 4.00 10.00
11 Todd Helton/100 4.00 10.00
12 Jeff Bagwell/100 4.00 10.00
13 Mike Mussina/50 4.00 10.00
14 Josh Beckett/100 3.00 8.00
15 Hideo Nomo/100 4.00 10.00
16 Mike Piazza/100 5.00 12.00
17 Don Mattingly/100 10.00 25.00
18 George Brett/100 10.00 25.00
20 Cal Ripken/50 30.00 60.00

2004 Studio Spirit of the Game Material Jersey

PRINT RUNS B/WN 100-200 COPIES PER
PRIME PRINT RUNS B/WN 1-5 COPIES PER
NO PRIME PRICING DUE TO SCARCITY
1 Sammy Sosa/200 3.00 8.00
2 Alex Rodriguez Rgr/200 4.00 10.00
3 Nomar Garciaparra/100 5.00 12.00
4 Derek Jeter/200 8.00 20.00
5 Albert Pujols/100 8.00 20.00
7 Mark Prior/200 3.00 8.00
8 Randy Johnson/100 4.00 10.00
9 Pedro Martinez/200 3.00 8.00
11 Todd Helton/100 4.00 10.00
12 Jeff Bagwell/200 3.00 8.00
13 Mike Mussina/200 3.00 8.00
14 Josh Beckett/200 2.00 5.00
15 Hideo Nomo/200 3.00 8.00
16 Mike Piazza/200 4.00 10.00
17 Don Mattingly Jacket/200 6.00 15.00
18 George Brett/200 6.00 15.00
19 Nolan Ryan/100 15.00 40.00
20 Cal Ripken/100 20.00 50.00

2004 Studio Stars

STATED ODDS 1:5
*GOLD: 1.25X TO 3X BASIC
GOLD PRINT RUN 100 SERIAL #'d SETS
*PLAT: 2.5X TO 6X BASIC
PLATINUM PRINT RUN 25 SERIAL #'d SETS
GOLD/PLATINUM RANDOM IN PACKS
1 Albert Pujols 1.25 3.00
2 Alex Rodriguez Yanks 1.25 3.00
3 Alfonso Soriano .60 1.50
4 Andy Pettitte .60 1.50
5 Angel Berroa .40 1.00
6 Aubrey Huff .40 1.00
7 Austin Kearns .40 1.00
8 Barry Zito .60 1.50
9 Brian Giles .40 1.00
10 Carlos Delgado .40 1.00
11 Chipper Jones 1.00 2.50
12 Craig Biggio .60 1.50
13 Curt Schilling .60 1.50
14 Derek Jeter 2.50 6.00
15 Edgar Martinez .60 1.50
16 Eric Gagne .40 1.00
17 Frank Thomas 1.00 2.50
18 Hank Blalock .40 1.00
19 Hideki Matsui 1.50 4.00
20 Hideo Nomo 1.00 2.50
21 Ichiro Suzuki 1.25 3.00
22 Ivan Rodriguez .60 1.50
23 Jason Kendall .40 1.00
24 Jason Schmidt .40 1.00
25 Jeff Bagwell .60 1.50
26 Jim Edmonds .60 1.50
27 Jim Thome .60 1.50
28 Josh Beckett .40 1.00
29 Kazuo Matsui .60 1.50
30 Ken Griffey Jr. 2.00 5.00
31 Larry Walker .60 1.50
32 Magglio Ordonez .60 1.50
33 Manny Ramirez 1.00 2.50
34 Mark Mulder .40 1.00
35 Mark Prior .60 1.50
36 Mark Teixeira .60 1.50
37 Miguel Tejada .60 1.50
38 Mike Mussina .60 1.50
39 Mike Piazza 1.00 2.50
40 Pedro Martinez .60 1.50
41 Randy Johnson 1.00 2.50
42 Roger Clemens 1.25 3.00
43 Roy Halladay .60 1.50
44 Russ Ortiz .40 1.00
45 Sammy Sosa 1.00 2.50
46 Scott Podsednik .40 1.00
47 Tim Hudson .60 1.50
48 Todd Helton .60 1.50
49 Vernon Wells .40 1.00
50 Vladimir Guerrero .60 1.50

2005 Studio

COMPLETE SET (300) 30.00 60.00
COMMON CARD (1-300) .15 .40
COMMON RC .15 .40
1 Casey Kotchman .15 .40
2 Chone Figgins .15 .40
3 Dallas McPherson .15 .40
4 Darin Erstad .15 .40
5 Ervin Santana .15 .40
6 Garret Anderson .15 .40
7 Norihiro Nakamura RC .15 .40
8 John Lackey .25 .60
9 Orlando Cabrera .15 .40
10 Robb Quinlan .15 .40
11 Steve Finley .15 .40
12 Tim Salmon .15 .40
13 Vladimir Guerrero .25 .60
14 Brandon Webb .25 .60
15 Craig Counsell .15 .40
16 Javier Vazquez .15 .40
17 Luis Gonzalez .15 .40
18 Tony Pena RC .15 .40
19 Russ Ortiz .15 .40
20 Scott Hairston .15 .40
21 Shawn Green .15 .40
22 Jose Cruz Jr. .15 .40
23 Troy Glaus .15 .40
24 Adam LaRoche .15 .40
25 Andruw Jones .15 .40
26 Chipper Jones .40 1.00
27 Danny Kolb .15 .40
28 John Smoltz .40 1.00
29 Johnny Estrada .15 .40
30 Marcus Giles .15 .40
31 Nick Green .15 .40
32 Rafael Furcal .15 .40
33 Tim Hudson .25 .60
34 Brian Roberts .15 .40
35 Javy Lopez .15 .40
36 Jay Gibbons .15 .40
37 Melvin Mora .15 .40
38 Miguel Tejada .25 .60
39 Rafael Palmeiro .25 .60
40 Rodrigo Lopez .15 .40
41 Sidney Ponson .15 .40
42 Abe Alvarez .15 .40
43 Bill Mueller .15 .40
44 Curt Schilling .25 .60
45 David Ortiz .40 1.00
46 David Wells .15 .40
47 Edgar Renteria .15 .40
48 Jason Varitek .40 1.00
49 Jay Payton .15 .40
50 Johnny Damon .25 .60
51 Juan Cedeno .15 .40
52 Manny Ramirez .40 1.00
53 Matt Clement .15 .40
54 Trot Nixon .15 .40
55 Wade Miller .15 .40
56 Aramis Ramirez .15 .40
57 Carlos Zambrano .25 .60
58 Corey Patterson .15 .40
59 Derrek Lee .15 .40
60 Greg Maddux .50 1.25
61 Kerry Wood .15 .40
62 Mark Prior .25 .60
63 Nomar Garciaparra .25 .60
64 Sammy Sosa .40 1.00
65 Todd Walker .15 .40
66 A.J. Pierzynski .15 .40
67 Aaron Rowand .15 .40
68 Frank Thomas .40 1.00
69 Freddy Garcia .15 .40
70 Jermaine Dye .15 .40
71 Mark Buehrle .25 .60
72 Paul Konerko .25 .60
73 Tadahito Iguchi RC .25 .60
74 Pedro Lopez RC .15 .40
75 Scott Podsednik .15 .40
76 Shingo Takatsu .15 .40
77 Adam Dunn .25 .60
78 Austin Kearns .15 .40
79 Barry Larkin .25 .60
80 Bubba Nelson .15 .40
81 Danny Graves .15 .40
82 Eric Milton .15 .40
83 Ken Griffey Jr. .75 2.00
84 Ryan Wagner .15 .40
85 Sean Casey .15 .40
86 C.C. Sabathia .25 .60
87 Cliff Lee .25 .60
88 Fausto Carmona .15 .40
89 Grady Sizemore .25 .60
90 Jake Westbrook .15 .40
91 Jody Gerut .15 .40
92 Juan Gonzalez .15 .40
93 Kazuhito Tadano .15 .40
94 Travis Hafner .15 .40
95 Victor Martinez .25 .60
96 Charles Johnson .15 .40
97 Clint Barmes .15 .40
98 Cory Sullivan .15 .40
99 Jeff Baker .15 .40
100 Jeff Francis .15 .40
101 Jeff Salazar .15 .40
102 Jeromy Burnitz .15 .40
103 Joe Kennedy .15 .40
104 Matt Holliday .40 1.00
105 Preston Wilson .15 .40
106 Todd Helton .25 .60
107 Ubaldo Jimenez RC .40 1.00
108 Brandon Inge .15 .40
109 Carlos Guillen .15 .40
110 Carlos Pena .25 .60
111 Craig Monroe .15 .40
112 Ivan Rodriguez .25 .60
113 Jeremy Bonderman .15 .40
114 Justin Verlander RC 3.00 8.00
115 Magglio Ordonez .25 .60
116 Troy Percival .15 .40
117 Vance Wilson .15 .40
118 A.J. Burnett .15 .40
119 Al Leiter .15 .40
120 Dontrelle Willis .15 .40
121 Josh Beckett .15 .40
122 Juan Pierre .15 .40
123 Miguel Cabrera .40 1.00
124 Mike Lowell .15 .40
125 Paul Lo Duca .15 .40
126 Randy Messenger RC .15 .40
127 Yorman Bazardo RC .15 .40

128 Andy Pettitte .25 .60
129 Brad Lidge .15 .40
130 Chris Burke .15 .40
131 Craig Biggio .25 .60
132 Fernando Nieve .15 .40
133 Jason Lane .15 .40
134 Jeff Bagwell .25 .60
135 Lance Berkman .25 .60
136 Morgan Ensberg .15 .40
137 Roger Clemens .50 1.25
138 Roy Oswalt .25 .60
139 Ambiorix Burgos RC .15 .40
140 David DeJesus .15 .40
141 Jeremy Affeldt .15 .40
142 Jose Lima .15 .40
143 Ken Harvey .15 .40
144 Mike MacDougal .15 .40
145 Mike Sweeney .15 .40
146 Terrence Long .15 .40
147 Zack Greinke .50 1.25
148 Brad Penny .15 .40
149 Derek Lowe .15 .40
150 Dioner Navarro .15 .40
151 Edwin Jackson .15 .40
152 Eric Gagne .15 .40
153 Hee Seop Choi .15 .40
154 Hideo Nomo .40 1.00
155 J.D. Drew .15 .40
156 Jeff Kent .15 .40
157 Jeff Weaver .15 .40
158 Milton Bradley .15 .40
159 Yhency Brazoban .15 .40
160 Ben Sheets .15 .40
161 Bill Hall .15 .40
162 Carlos Lee .15 .40
163 Gustavo Chacin .15 .40
164 Geoff Jenkins .15 .40
165 Jose Capellan .15 .40
166 Lyle Overbay .15 .40
167 Rickie Weeks .15 .40
168 Jacque Jones .15 .40
169 Joe Mauer .30 .75
170 Joe Nathan .15 .40
171 Johan Santana .25 .60
172 Justin Morneau .25 .60
173 Lew Ford .15 .40
174 Michael Cuddyer .15 .40
175 Shannon Stewart .15 .40
176 Torii Hunter .15 .40
177 Brad Radke .15 .40
178 Ambiorix Concepcion RC .15 .40
179 Carlos Beltran .25 .60
180 David Wright .30 .75
181 Jose Reyes .25 .60
182 Kazuo Matsui .15 .40
183 Kris Benson .15 .40
184 Mike Piazza .40 1.00
185 Pedro Martinez .25 .60
186 Phil Humber RC .40 1.00
187 Tom Glavine .25 .60
188 Alex Rodriguez .50 1.25
189 Carl Pavano .15 .40
190 Derek Jeter 1.00 2.50
191 Yuniesky Betancourt RC .60 1.50
192 Hideki Matsui .60 1.50
193 Jorge Posada .25 .60
194 Kevin Brown .15 .40
195 Mariano Rivera .50 1.25
196 Mike Mussina .25 .60
197 Randy Johnson .40 1.00
198 Scott Proctor .15 .40
199 Tom Gordon .15 .40
200 Barry Zito .25 .60
201 Bobby Crosby .15 .40
202 Dan Haren .15 .40
203 Eric Chavez .15 .40
204 Keiichi Yabu RC .15 .40
205 Jason Kendall .15 .40
206 Joe Blanton .15 .40
207 Mark Kotsay .15 .40
208 Nick Swisher .25 .60
209 Octavio Dotel .15 .40
210 Rich Harden .15 .40
211 Billy Wagner .15 .40
212 Bobby Abreu .15 .40
213 Chase Utley .25 .60
214 Gavin Floyd .15 .40
215 Jim Thome .25 .60
216 Jimmy Rollins .25 .60
217 Jon Lieber .15 .40
218 Kenny Lofton .15 .40
219 Mike Lieberthal .15 .40
220 Pat Burrell .15 .40
221 Randy Wolf .15 .40
222 Craig Wilson .15 .40
223 Jack Wilson .15 .40
224 Jason Bay .15 .40
225 John Van Benschoten .15 .40
226 Jose Castillo .15 .40
227 Kip Wells .15 .40
228 Matt Lawton .15 .40
229 Akinori Otsuka .15 .40
230 Brian Giles .15 .40
231 Freddy Guzman .15 .40
232 Jake Peavy .15 .40
233 Khalil Greene .15 .40
234 Mark Loretta .15 .40
235 Sean Burroughs .15 .40
236 Trevor Hoffman .25 .60
237 Woody Williams .15 .40
238 Armando Benitez .15 .40
239 Edgardo Alfonzo .15 .40
240 Erick Threets RC .15 .40
241 Jason Schmidt .15 .40
242 Marquis Grissom .15 .40
243 Merkin Valdez .15 .40
244 Michael Tucker .15 .40
245 Moises Alou .15 .40
246 Omar Vizquel .25 .60
247 Adrian Beltre .40 1.00
248 Bret Boone .15 .40
249 Bucky Jacobsen .15 .40
250 Clint Nageotte .15 .40
251 Ichiro Suzuki .50 1.25
252 J.J. Putz .15 .40
253 Jeremy Reed .15 .40
254 Miguel Olivo .15 .40
255 Mike Morse RC .50 1.25
256 Richie Sexson .15 .40
257 Wladimir Balentien RC .25 .60
258 Albert Pujols .50 1.25
259 Jason Isringhausen .15 .40
260 Jeff Suppan .15 .40
261 Jim Edmonds .25 .60
262 Larry Walker .25 .60
263 Mark Mulder .15 .40
264 Rick Ankiel .15 .40
265 Scott Rolen .25 .60
266 Yadier Molina 1.50 4.00
267 Aubrey Huff .15 .40
268 B.J. Upton .25 .60
269 Carl Crawford .25 .60
270 Chris Seddon RC .15 .40
271 Delmon Young .40 1.00
272 Dewon Brazelton .15 .40
273 Jeff Niemann RC .40 1.00
274 Rocco Baldelli .15 .40
275 Scott Kazmir .40 1.00
276 Adrian Gonzalez .30 .75
277 Alfonso Soriano .25 .60
278 Francisco Cordero .15 .40
279 Hank Blalock .15 .40
280 Kameron Loe .15 .40
281 Kenny Rogers .15 .40
282 Laynce Nix .15 .40
283 Mark Teixeira .25 .60
284 Michael Young .15 .40
285 Corey Koskie .15 .40
286 Dave Bush .15 .40
287 Frank Catalanotto .15 .40
288 Gabe Gross .15 .40
289 Raul Tablado RC .15 .40
290 Roy Halladay .25 .60
291 Shea Hillenbrand .15 .40
292 Vernon Wells .15 .40
293 Chad Cordero .15 .40
294 Cristian Guzman .15 .40
295 Jose Guillen .15 .40
296 Jose Vidro .15 .40
297 Josh Karp .15 .40
298 Livan Hernandez .15 .40
299 Nick Johnson .15 .40
300 Vinny Castilla .15 .40

2005 Studio Proofs Gold

*GOLD: 6X TO 15X BASIC
OVERALL INSERT ODDS 1:1 HOBBY
STATED PRINT RUN 25 SERIAL #'d SETS
NO RC YR PRICING DUE TO SCARCITY

2005 Studio Proofs Silver

*SILVER: 2.5X TO 6X BASIC
*SILVER: 2X TO 5X BASIC RC's
OVERALL INSERT ODDS 1:1 HOBBY
STATED PRINT RUN 100 SERIAL #'d SETS

2005 Studio Autographs

OVERALL AU-GU ODDS 1:8 HOBBY
SP INFO PROVIDED BY DONRUSS
NO SP PRICING DUE TO SCARCITY
CARDS LACK PRIVATE SIGNINGS LOGO
1 Casey Kotchman 4.00 10.00
3 Dallas McPherson 4.00 10.00
5 Ervin Santana 4.00 10.00
8 John Lackey 4.00 10.00
18 Tony Pena 4.00 10.00
31 Nick Green 4.00 10.00
51 Juan Cedeno 4.00 10.00
80 Bubba Nelson 4.00 10.00
88 Fausto Carmona 6.00 15.00
93 Kazuhito Tadano 6.00 15.00
101 Jeff Salazar 4.00 10.00
103 Joe Kennedy 4.00 10.00
108 Brandon Inge 4.00 10.00
111 Craig Monroe 4.00 10.00
113 Jeremy Bonderman 6.00 15.00
117 Vance Wilson 4.00 10.00
126 Randy Messenger 4.00 10.00
127 Yorman Bazardo 4.00 10.00
150 Dioner Navarro 4.00 10.00
159 Yhency Brazoban 4.00 10.00
161 Bill Hall 4.00 10.00
170 Joe Nathan 6.00 15.00
178 Ambiorix Concepcion 4.00 10.00
191 Yuniesky Betancourt 15.00 30.00
198 Scott Proctor 4.00 10.00
223 Jack Wilson 6.00 15.00
226 Jose Castillo 4.00 10.00
231 Freddy Guzman 4.00 10.00
250 Clint Nageotte 4.00 10.00
252 J.J. Putz 4.00 10.00
257 Wladimir Balentien 6.00 15.00
260 Jeff Suppan 6.00 15.00
276 Adrian Gonzalez 6.00 15.00
280 Kameron Loe 4.00 10.00
282 Laynce Nix 4.00 10.00
297 Josh Karp 4.00 10.00

2005 Studio Private Signings Gold

*GOLD: .5X TO 1.2X SILVER
*GOLD RC YR: .5X TO 1.2X SILVER RC YR
OVERALL AU-GU ODDS 1:8 HOBBY
STATED PRINT RUN 50 SERIAL #'d SETS
6 Garret Anderson 8.00 20.00
10 Robb Quinlan 5.00 12.00
11 Steve Finley 8.00 20.00
14 Brandon Webb 5.00 12.00
29 Johnny Estrada 5.00 12.00
32 Rafael Furcal 8.00 20.00
40 Rodrigo Lopez 5.00 12.00
47 Edgar Renteria 8.00 20.00
53 Matt Clement 8.00 20.00
54 Trot Nixon 8.00 20.00
59 Derrek Lee 20.00 50.00
71 Mark Buehrle 15.00 40.00
72 Paul Konerko 12.50 30.00
76 Shingo Takatsu 8.00 20.00
78 Austin Kearns 5.00 12.00
93 Kazuhito Tadano 8.00 20.00
116 Troy Percival 8.00 20.00
123 Miguel Cabrera 15.00 40.00
148 Brad Penny 5.00 12.00
168 Jacque Jones 8.00 20.00
175 Shannon Stewart 8.00 20.00
199 Tom Gordon 5.00 12.00
229 Akinori Otsuka 8.00 20.00
235 Sean Burroughs 5.00 12.00
243 Merkin Valdez 5.00 12.00
246 Omar Vizquel 12.50 30.00
249 Bucky Jacobsen 5.00 12.00
254 Miguel Olivo 5.00 12.00
266 Yadier Molina 125.00 300.00
267 Aubrey Huff 8.00 20.00
268 B.J. Upton 8.00 20.00
269 Carl Crawford 8.00 20.00
271 Delmon Young 12.50 30.00
272 Dewon Brazelton 5.00 12.00
284 Michael Young 8.00 20.00
299 Nick Johnson 8.00 20.00

2005 Studio Private Signings Silver

OVERALL AU-GU ODDS 1:8 HOBBY
STATED PRINT RUN 100 SERIAL #'d SETS
1 Casey Kotchman 6.00 15.00
2 Chone Figgins 4.00 10.00
5 Ervin Santana 4.00 10.00
9 Orlando Cabrera 6.00 15.00
12 Tim Salmon 10.00 25.00
18 Tony Pena 4.00 10.00
19 Russ Ortiz 4.00 10.00
24 Adam LaRoche 4.00 10.00
27 Danny Kolb 4.00 10.00
31 Nick Green 6.00 15.00
34 Brian Roberts 6.00 15.00
36 Jay Gibbons 4.00 10.00
49 Jay Payton 4.00 10.00
51 Juan Cedeno 4.00 10.00
55 Wade Miller 4.00 10.00
57 Carlos Zambrano 10.00 25.00
65 Todd Walker 6.00 15.00
70 Jermaine Dye 6.00 15.00
80 Bubba Nelson 4.00 10.00
81 Danny Graves 4.00 10.00
84 Ryan Wagner 4.00 10.00
87 Cliff Lee 6.00 15.00
88 Fausto Carmona 6.00 15.00
91 Jody Gerut 4.00 10.00
94 Travis Hafner 6.00 15.00
98 Cory Sullivan 4.00 10.00
101 Jeff Salazar 4.00 10.00
103 Joe Kennedy 4.00 10.00
108 Brandon Inge 6.00 15.00
111 Craig Monroe 4.00 10.00
113 Jeremy Bonderman 6.00 15.00
117 Vance Wilson 4.00 10.00
127 Yorman Bazardo 4.00 10.00
133 Jason Lane 6.00 15.00
136 Morgan Ensberg 6.00 15.00
141 Jeremy Affeldt 4.00 10.00
143 Ken Harvey 4.00 10.00
150 Dioner Navarro 6.00 15.00
151 Edwin Jackson 4.00 10.00
158 Milton Bradley 6.00 15.00
159 Yhency Brazoban 4.00 10.00
161 Bill Hall 4.00 10.00
162 Carlos Lee 6.00 15.00
166 Lyle Overbay 4.00 10.00
170 Joe Nathan 6.00 15.00
173 Lew Ford 4.00 10.00
191 Yuniesky Betancourt 20.00 40.00
198 Scott Proctor 4.00 10.00
201 Bobby Crosby 6.00 15.00
202 Dan Haren 4.00 10.00
209 Octavio Dotel 4.00 10.00
210 Rich Harden 6.00 15.00
219 Mike Lieberthal 6.00 15.00
221 Randy Wolf 4.00 10.00
222 Craig Wilson 4.00 10.00
223 Jack Wilson 6.00 15.00
224 Jason Bay 6.00 15.00
226 Jose Castillo 4.00 10.00
231 Freddy Guzman 4.00 10.00
232 Jake Peavy 6.00 15.00
234 Mark Loretta 4.00 10.00
250 Clint Nageotte 4.00 10.00
252 J.J. Putz 4.00 10.00
260 Jeff Suppan 6.00 15.00
276 Adrian Gonzalez 6.00 15.00
278 Francisco Cordero 6.00 15.00
280 Kameron Loe 4.00 10.00
282 Laynce Nix 4.00 10.00
291 Shea Hillenbrand 4.00 10.00
293 Chad Cordero 6.00 15.00
295 Jose Guillen 6.00 15.00
297 Josh Karp 4.00 10.00
298 Livan Hernandez 10.00 25.00

2005 Studio Diamond Cuts

STATED PRINT RUN 1250 SERIAL #'d SETS
*DIE CUT: .6X TO 1.5X BASIC
DIE CUT PRINT RUN 250 #'d SETS
*DC GOLD: 1X TO 2.5X BASIC
DC GOLD PRINT RUN 75 #'d SETS
OVERALL INSERT ODDS 1:1 HOBBY
1 Roger Clemens 1.50 4.00
2 Manny Ramirez 1.25 3.00
3 Francisco Rodriguez .75 2.00
4 Brian Roberts .50 1.25
5 Javy Lopez .50 1.25
6 Vernon Wells .50 1.25
7 Johan Santana .75 2.00
8 Torii Hunter .50 1.25
9 Mike Mussina .75 2.00
10 Sammy Sosa 1.25 3.00
11 Ryan Wagner .50 1.25
12 Jack Wilson .50 1.25
13 Ichiro Suzuki 1.50 4.00
14 Greg Maddux 1.50 4.00
15 Albert Pujols 1.50 4.00
16 Jeremy Bonderman .50 1.25
17 Johnny Estrada .50 1.25
18 Mark Buehrle .75 2.00
19 Jorge Posada .75 2.00
20 Carl Crawford .75 2.00
21 Paul Konerko .75 2.00
22 Victor Martinez .75 2.00
23 Jose Vidro .50 1.25
24 Jim Thome .75 2.00
25 Andruw Jones .50 1.25

2005 Studio Diamond Cuts Bat

*BAT p/r 200-300: .4X TO 1X JSY p/r 175-250
*BAT p/r 200-300: .15X TO .4X JSY p/r 15
*BAT p/r 50: .6X TO 1.5X JSY p/r 175-250
*BAT p/r 50: .5X TO 1.2X JSY p/r 125
*BAT p/r 25: .75X TO 2X JSY p/r 175-250
OVERALL AU-GU ODDS 1:8 HOBBY
PRINT RUNS B/WN 5-300 COPIES PER
NO PRICING ON QTY OF 10 OR LESS

2005 Studio Diamond Cuts Jersey

PRINT RUNS B/WN 15-250 COPIES PER
PRIME PRINT RUNS B/WN 5-10 COPIES PER
NO PRIME PRICING DUE TO SCARCITY
OVERALL AU-GU ODDS 1:8 HOBBY
1 Roger Clemens/125 5.00 12.00
2 Manny Ramirez/250 2.50 6.00
3 Francisco Rodriguez/250 2.00 5.00
4 Brian Roberts/250 2.00 5.00
5 Javy Lopez/250 2.00 5.00
6 Vernon Wells/250 2.00 5.00
7 Johan Santana/175 3.00 8.00
8 Torii Hunter/250 2.00 5.00
9 Mike Mussina/250 2.50 6.00
10 Sammy Sosa/250 3.00 8.00
11 Ryan Wagner/250 2.00 5.00
12 Jack Wilson/15 5.00 12.00
14 Greg Maddux/250 4.00 10.00
15 Albert Pujols/250 6.00 15.00
16 Jeremy Bonderman/250 2.00 5.00
17 Johnny Estrada/250 2.00 5.00
18 Mark Buehrle/250 2.00 5.00
19 Jorge Posada/250 2.50 6.00
20 Carl Crawford/250 2.00 5.00
21 Paul Konerko/250 2.00 5.00
22 Victor Martinez/250 2.00 5.00
23 Jose Vidro/175 2.00 5.00
24 Jim Thome/250 2.50 6.00
25 Andruw Jones/250 2.50 6.00

2005 Studio Diamond Cuts Combo

*COMBO p/r 50: .75X TO 2X JSY p/r 175-250
*COMBO p/r 50: .6X TO 1.5X JSY p/r 125
*COMBO p/r 50: .3X TO .8X JSY p/r 15
PRINT RUNS B/WN 5-50 COPIES PER
PRIME PRINT RUN 10 SERIAL #'d SETS
NO PRIME PRICING DUE TO SCARCITY
OVERALL AU-GU ODDS 1:8 HOBBY

2005 Studio Diamond Cuts Signature Combo

PRINT RUNS B/WN 25-50 COPIES PER
PRIME PRINT 10 SERIAL #'d SETS
NO PRIME PRICING DUE TO SCARCITY
OVERALL AU-GU ODDS 1:8 HOBBY
3 F.Rodriguez Jsy-Jsy/25 20.00 50.00
6 Vernon Wells Jsy-Jsy/25 12.50 30.00
8 Torii Hunter Bat-Jsy/50 10.00 25.00
11 Ryan Wagner Jsy-Jsy/50 6.00 15.00
12 Jack Wilson Bat-Jsy/50 10.00 25.00
16 J.Bonderman Jsy-Jsy/50 10.00 25.00
17 J.Estrada Fld Glv-Jsy/50 6.00 15.00
21 Paul Konerko Jsy-Jsy/25 20.00 50.00

2005 Studio Heritage

STATED PRINT RUN 1000 SERIAL #'d SETS
*DIE CUT: .6X TO 1.5X BASIC
DIE CUT PRINT RUN 200 #'d SETS
*DC GOLD: 1.25X TO 3X BASIC
DC GOLD PRINT RUN 50 #'d SETS
OVERALL INSERT ODDS 1:1 HOBBY
1 Rickey Henderson 1.25 3.00
2 Jeff Bagwell .75 2.00
3 Steve Garvey .50 1.25
4 Albert Pujols 1.50 4.00
5 Don Mattingly 2.50 6.00
6 Frank Thomas 1.25 3.00
7 Tony Gwynn 1.50 4.00
8 Gary Sheffield .50 1.25
9 Dale Murphy 1.25 3.00
10 Kerry Wood .50 1.25
11 Cal Ripken 4.00 10.00
12 Miguel Cabrera 1.25 3.00
13 Dwight Gooden .50 1.25
14 Barry Zito .75 2.00
15 Darryl Strawberry .50 1.25

2005 Studio Heritage Bat

*BAT: .4X TO 1X JSY p/r 250
*BAT: .25X TO .6X JSY p/r 50
OVERALL AU-GU ODDS 1:8 HOBBY
STATED PRINT RUN 150 SERIAL #'d SETS
8 Gary Sheffield 2.00 5.00

2005 Studio Heritage Jersey

PRINT RUNS B/WN 50-250 COPIES PER
PRIME PRINT RUN 10 SERIAL #'d SETS
NO PRIME PRICING DUE TO SCARCITY
OVERALL AU-GU ODDS 1:8 HOBBY
1 Rickey Henderson/250 4.00 10.00
2 Jeff Bagwell/250 2.50 6.00
3 Steve Garvey/250 1.50 4.00
4 Albert Pujols/250 5.00 12.00
5 Don Mattingly/250 6.00 15.00
6 Frank Thomas/250 4.00 10.00
7 Tony Gwynn/250 5.00 12.00
9 Dale Murphy/250 4.00 10.00
10 Kerry Wood/250 1.50 4.00
11 Cal Ripken/250 8.00 20.00
12 Miguel Cabrera/50 4.00 10.00
13 Dwight Gooden/250 1.50 4.00
14 Barry Zito/250 2.50 6.00
15 Darryl Strawberry/250 1.50 4.00

2005 Studio Heritage Combo

*COMBO p/r 50: .75X TO 2X JSY p/r 250
*COMBO p/r 50: .5X TO 1.2X JSY p/r 50
*COMBO p/r 25: 1X TO 2.5X JSY p/r 250
PRINT RUNS B/WN 10-50 COPIES PER
NO PRICING ON QTY OF 10
PRIME PRINT RUN 10 SERIAL #'d SETS
NO PRIME PRICING DUE TO SCARCITY
OVERALL AU-GU ODDS 1:8 HOBBY
8 Gary Sheffield Bat-Jsy/50 4.00 10.00

2005 Studio Heritage Signature Combo

PRINT RUNS B/WN 10-50 COPIES PER
NO PRICING ON QTY OF 10
PRIME PRINT RUNS B/WN 5-10 COPIES PER
NO PRIME PRICING DUE TO SCARCITY
OVERALL AU-GU ODDS 1:8 HOBBY
3 Steve Garvey Bat-Jsy/50 10.00 25.00
5 Don Mattingly Bat-Jsy/25 40.00 80.00
7 Tony Gwynn Bat-Jsy/15 50.00 100.00
9 Dale Murphy Bat-Jsy/25 20.00 50.00
11 Cal Ripken Bat-Jsy/50 50.00 120.00
12 Miguel Cabrera Bat-Jsy/25 30.00 60.00
13 Dwight Gooden Bat-Jsy/25 12.50 30.00
15 D.Strawberry Bat-Jsy/25 12.50 30.00

2005 Studio Heroes of the Hall

STATED PRINT RUN 350 SERIAL #'d SETS
*DIE CUT: .6X TO 1.5X BASIC
DIE CUT PRINT RUN 75 #'d SETS
*DC GOLD: 1.25X TO 3X BASIC
DC GOLD PRINT RUN 25 #'d SETS
OVERALL INSERT ODDS 1:1 HOBBY
1 Luis Aparicio 1.25 3.00
2 Dennis Eckersley 1.25 3.00
3 Brooks Robinson 1.25 3.00
4 Carlton Fisk 1.25 3.00
5 Tom Seaver 1.25 3.00
6 Paul Molitor 2.00 5.00
7 Rod Carew 1.25 3.00
8 George Brett 4.00 10.00
9 Nolan Ryan 6.00 15.00
10 Mike Schmidt 3.00 8.00
11 Willie Mays 4.00 10.00
12 Gary Carter 1.25 3.00
13 Lou Brock 1.25 3.00
14 Steve Carlton 1.25 3.00
15 Harmon Killebrew 2.00 5.00

2005 Studio Heroes of the Hall Bat

*BAT p/r 150: .4X TO 1X JSY p/r 150
*BAT p/r 150: .25X TO .6X JSY p/r 50
*BAT p/r 100-125: .5X TO 1.2X JSY p/r 150
*BAT p/r 100-125: .4X TO 1X JSY p/r 100
*BAT p/r 100-125: .3X TO .8X JSY p/r 50
OVERALL AU-GU ODDS 1:8 HOBBY
PRINT RUNS B/WN 100-150 COPIES PER
13 Lou Brock/150 3.00 8.00

2005 Studio Heroes of the Hall Jersey

PRINT RUNS B/WN 50-150 COPIES PER
PRIME PRINT RUNS B/WN 5-10 COPIES PER
NO PRIME PRICING DUE TO SCARCITY
OVERALL AU-GU ODDS 1:8 HOBBY
1 Luis Aparicio/150 2.50 6.00
2 Dennis Eckersley/150 2.50 6.00
3 Brooks Robinson/50 5.00 12.00
4 Carlton Fisk/150 3.00 8.00
5 Tom Seaver/150 3.00 8.00
6 Paul Molitor/150 2.50 6.00
7 Rod Carew/150 3.00 8.00
8 George Brett/150 5.00 12.00
9 Nolan Ryan/100 8.00 20.00
10 Mike Schmidt/100 6.00 15.00
11 Willie Mays/50 12.00 30.00
12 Gary Carter/150 2.50 6.00
14 Steve Carlton/150 2.50 6.00
15 Harmon Killebrew/150 4.00 10.00

2005 Studio Heroes of the Hall Combo

*COMBO p/r 50: .75X TO 2X JSY p/r 150
*COMBO p/r 50: .6X TO 1.5X JSY p/r 100
*COMBO p/r 25: .6X TO 1.5X JSY p/r 50
PRINT RUNS B/WN 25-50 COPIES PER
PRIME PRINT RUNS B/WN 5-10 COPIES PER
NO PRIME PRICING DUE TO SCARCITY
OVERALL AU-GU ODDS 1:8 HOBBY
13 Lou Brock Bat-Jkt/50 6.00 15.00

2005 Studio Heroes of the Hall Signature Combo

PRINT RUNS B/WN 5-50 COPIES PER
NO PRICING ON QTY OF 10 OR LESS
PRIME PRINT RUNS B/WN 5-10 COPIES PER
NO PRIME PRICING DUE TO SCARCITY
OVERALL AU-GU ODDS 1:8 HOBBY
1 Luis Aparicio Bat-Jsy/50 10.00 25.00
2 D.Eckersley Jsy-Pants/25 12.50 30.00
4 Carlton Fisk Bat-Jsy/25 20.00 50.00
5 Tom Seaver Jsy-Pants/15 40.00 100.00
6 Paul Molitor Bat-Jsy/25 12.50 30.00
12 Gary Carter Jsy-Pants/15 20.00 50.00
14 Steve Carlton Bat-Jsy/25 12.50 30.00
15 H.Killebrew Bat-Jsy/25 40.00 80.00

2005 Studio Masterstrokes

STATED PRINT RUN 750 SERIAL #'d SETS
*DIE CUT: .6X TO 1.5X BASIC
DIE CUT PRINT RUN 150 #'d SETS
*DC GOLD: 1X TO 2.5X BASIC
DC GOLD PRINT RUN 50 #'d SETS
OVERALL INSERT ODDS 1:1 HOBBY
1 Hideki Matsui 2.50 6.00
2 David Ortiz 1.50 4.00
3 Aramis Ramirez .60 1.50
4 Lance Berkman 1.00 2.50
5 Ichiro Suzuki 2.00 5.00
6 Mike Piazza 1.50 4.00
7 Ivan Rodriguez 1.00 2.50
8 Hideo Nomo 1.50 4.00
9 Jeff Bagwell 1.00 2.50
10 Travis Hafner .60 1.50
11 Casey Kotchman .60 1.50
12 Jim Edmonds 1.00 2.50
13 Michael Young .60 1.50
14 Lyle Overbay .60 1.50
15 Eric Chavez .60 1.50
16 Jason Bay .60 1.50
17 Hank Blalock .60 1.50
18 Frank Thomas 1.50 4.00
19 Craig Biggio 1.00 2.50
20 Miguel Cabrera 1.50 4.00
21 Vladimir Guerrero 1.00 2.50
22 Sammy Sosa 1.50 4.00
23 Chipper Jones 1.50 4.00
24 Rafael Palmeiro 1.00 2.50
25 Adam Dunn 1.00 2.50

2005 Studio Masterstrokes Bat

*BAT p/r 200-250: .4X TO 1X JSY p/r 150-250
*BAT p/r 200-250: .25X TO .6X JSY p/r 40-50
*BAT p/r 100: .5X TO 1.2X JSY p/r 150-250
*BAT p/r 50: .6X TO 1.5X JSY p/r 150-250
*BAT p/r 25: .75X TO 2X JSY p/r 150-250
OVERALL AU-GU ODDS 1:8 HOBBY
PRINT RUNS B/WN 25-250 COPIES PER

2005 Studio Masterstrokes Jersey

PRINT RUNS B/WN 40-250 COPIES PER
PRIME PRINT RUN 10 SERIAL #'d SETS
NO PRIME PRICING DUE TO SCARCITY
OVERALL AU-GU ODDS 1:8 HOBBY
1 Hideki Matsui/250 10.00 25.00
2 David Ortiz/250 2.50 6.00
3 Aramis Ramirez/250 2.00 5.00
4 Lance Berkman/250 2.00 5.00
6 Mike Piazza/250 3.00 8.00
7 Ivan Rodriguez/250 2.50 6.00
8 Hideo Nomo/250 3.00 8.00
9 Jeff Bagwell/250 2.50 6.00
10 Travis Hafner/200 2.00 5.00
11 Casey Kotchman/250 2.00 5.00
12 Jim Edmonds/250 2.00 5.00
13 Michael Young/150 2.00 5.00
14 Lyle Overbay/250 2.00 5.00
15 Eric Chavez/250 2.00 5.00
16 Jason Bay/150 2.00 5.00
17 Hank Blalock/250 2.00 5.00
18 Frank Thomas/250 3.00 8.00
19 Craig Biggio/250 2.50 6.00
20 Miguel Cabrera/250 2.50 6.00
21 Vladimir Guerrero/50 5.00 12.00
22 Sammy Sosa/250 3.00 8.00
23 Chipper Jones/225 3.00 8.00
24 Rafael Palmeiro/40 4.00 10.00
25 Adam Dunn/250 2.00 5.00

2005 Studio Masterstrokes Combo

*COMBO p/r 50: .75X TO 2X JSY p/r 150-250
*COMBO p/r 50: .5X TO 1.2X JSY p/r 40-50
*COMBO p/r 15: 1.25X TO 3X JSY p/r 150-250
PRINT RUNS B/WN 15-50 COPIES PER
PRIME PRINT RUN 10 SERIAL #'d SETS
NO PRIME PRICING DUE TO SCARCITY
OVERALL AU-GU ODDS 1:8 HOBBY

2005 Studio Masterstrokes Signature Combo

PRINT RUNS B/WN 5-50 COPIES PER
NO PRICING ON QTY OF 10 OR LESS
PRIME PRINT RUNS B/WN 5-10 COPIES PER
NO PRIME PRICING DUE TO SCARCITY
OVERALL AU-GU ODDS 1:8 HOBBY
10 Travis Hafner Bat-Jsy/50 10.00 25.00
11 C.Kotchman Bat-Jsy/50 10.00 25.00
14 Lyle Overbay Bat-Jsy/50 6.00 15.00
15 Eric Chavez Bat-Jsy/25 12.50 30.00
16 Jason Bay Bat-Jsy/50 10.00 25.00
17 Hank Blalock Jsy-Jsy/25 12.50 30.00
20 Miguel Cabrera Bat-Jsy/25 30.00 60.00

2005 Studio Portraits Zenith White

STATED PRINT RUN 70 SERIAL #'d SETS
*PARALLEL #'d OF 50-60: .4X TO 1X
*PARALLEL #'d OF 40-45: .5X TO 1.2X
*PARALLEL #'d OF 30-35: .6X TO 1.5X
*PARALLEL #'d OF 20-25: .75X TO 2X
*PARALLEL #'d OF 15: 1X TO 2.5X
PARALLELS #'d FROM 5-60 COPIES PER
NO PRICING ON QTY OF 10 OR LESS
OVERALL PORTRAITS ODDS 1:3 HOBBY
1 Ozzie Smith 2.00 5.00
2 Derek Jeter 4.00 10.00
3 Eric Chavez .60 1.50
4 Duke Snider 1.00 2.50
5 Albert Pujols 2.00 5.00
6 Stan Musial 2.50 6.00
7 Ivan Rodriguez 1.00 2.50
8 Cal Ripken 5.00 12.00
9 Hank Blalock .60 1.50
10 Chipper Jones 1.50 4.00
11 Gary Sheffield .60 1.50
12 Alfonso Soriano 1.00 2.50
13 Carl Crawford 1.00 2.50
14 Lou Brock 1.00 2.50
15 Jim Edmonds 1.00 2.50
16 Bo Jackson 1.50 4.00
17 Todd Helton 1.00 2.50
18 Javy Lopez .60 1.50
19 Tony Gwynn 2.00 5.00
20 Mark Mulder .60 1.50
21 Sammy Sosa 1.50 4.00
22 Roger Clemens 2.00 5.00
23 Don Mattingly 3.00 8.00
24 Willie Mays 3.00 8.00
25 Andruw Jones .60 1.50
26 Steve Garvey .60 1.50
27 Scott Rolen 1.00 2.50
28 George Brett 3.00 8.00
29 Rod Carew 1.00 2.50
30 Ken Griffey Jr. 3.00 8.00
31 Mike Piazza 1.50 4.00
32 Steve Carlton 1.00 2.50
33 Larry Walker 1.00 2.50
34 Kerry Wood .60 1.50
35 Frank Thomas 1.50 4.00
36 Lance Berkman 1.00 2.50
37 Nomar Garciaparra 1.00 2.50
38 Curt Schilling 1.00 2.50
39 Carl Yastrzemski 2.00 5.00
40 Mark Grace 1.00 2.50
41 Tom Seaver 1.00 2.50
42 Mariano Rivera 2.00 5.00
43 Carlos Beltran 1.00 2.50
44 Reggie Jackson 1.00 2.50
45 Pedro Martinez 1.00 2.50
46 Richie Sexson .60 1.50
47 Tom Glavine 1.00 2.50
48 Torii Hunter .60 1.50
49 Ron Guidry .60 1.50
50 Michael Young .60 1.50
51 Ichiro Suzuki 2.00 5.00
52 C.C. Sabathia 1.00 2.50
53 Johnny Bench 1.50 4.00
54 Mark Teixeira 1.00 2.50
55 Hideki Matsui 2.50 6.00
56 Mike Mussina 1.00 2.50
57 Johan Santana 1.00 2.50
58 Fergie Jenkins 1.00 2.50
59 Hideo Nomo 1.50 4.00
60 Nolan Ryan 5.00 12.00
61 Whitey Ford 1.00 2.50
62 Jim Thome 1.00 2.50
63 Gary Carter 1.00 2.50
64 Randy Johnson 1.50 4.00
65 Vladimir Guerrero 1.00 2.50
66 Harmon Killebrew 1.50 4.00
67 Tim Hudson 1.00 2.50
68 Josh Beckett .60 1.50
69 Eddie Murray 1.00 2.50
70 Greg Maddux 2.00 5.00
71 J.D. Drew .60 1.50
72 Bob Feller 1.00 2.50
73 Adrian Beltre 1.50 4.00
74 Wade Boggs 1.00 2.50
75 Barry Zito 1.00 2.50
76 David Ortiz 1.50 4.00
77 Mike Schmidt 2.50 6.00
78 Miguel Cabrera 1.50 4.00
79 Carlos Delgado .60 1.50
80 Andre Dawson 1.00 2.50
81 Garret Anderson .60 1.50
82 Rickey Henderson 1.50 4.00
83 Shawn Green .60 1.50
84 Dale Murphy 1.50 4.00
85 Alex Rodriguez 2.00 5.00
86 Mark Prior 1.00 2.50
87 Paul Molitor 1.50 4.00
88 Jeff Bagwell 1.00 2.50
89 Eric Gagne .60 1.50
90 Troy Glaus .60 1.50
91 Robin Yount 1.50 4.00
92 Miguel Tejada 1.00 2.50
93 Kirk Gibson .60 1.50
94 Manny Ramirez 1.50 4.00
95 Rafael Palmeiro 1.00 2.50
96 Maury Wills .60 1.50
97 Craig Biggio 1.00 2.50
98 Jim Palmer 1.00 2.50
99 Adam Dunn 1.00 2.50
100 Carlton Fisk 1.00 2.50

2005 Studio Spirit of the Game

STATED PRINT RUN 600 SERIAL #'d SETS
*DIE CUT: .6X TO 1.5X BASIC
DIE CUT PRINT RUN 125 #'d SETS
*DC GOLD: 1.5X TO 4X BASIC
DC GOLD PRINT RUN 25 #'d SETS
OVERALL INSERT ODDS 1:1 HOBBY
1 Mark Prior 1.25 3.00
2 Sean Casey .75 2.00
3 Ichiro Suzuki 2.50 6.00
4 Andruw Jones .75 2.00
5 Francisco Cordero .75 2.00
6 Ben Sheets .75 2.00
7 Rocco Baldelli .75 2.00
8 Rafael Furcal .75 2.00
9 Angel Berroa .75 2.00
10 Roy Oswalt 1.25 3.00
11 Jose Reyes 1.25 3.00
12 Shannon Stewart .75 2.00
13 Greg Maddux 2.50 6.00
14 Alfonso Soriano 1.25 3.00
15 Curt Schilling 1.25 3.00
16 Jody Gerut .75 2.00
17 Brandon Webb 1.25 3.00
18 Josh Beckett .75 2.00
19 Laynce Nix .75 2.00
20 Scott Rolen 1.25 3.00

2005 Studio Spirit of the Game Bat

*BAT p/r 225-300: .4X TO 1X JSY p/r 250
*BAT p/r 225-300: .3X TO .8X JSY p/r 125
*BAT p/r 75: .5X TO 1.2X JSY p/r 250
OVERALL AU-GU ODDS 1:8 HOBBY
PRINT RUNS B/WN 75-300 COPIES PER

2005 Studio Spirit of the Game Jersey

PRINT RUNS B/WN 125-250 COPIES PER
PRIME PRINT RUN 10 SERIAL #'d SETS
NO PRIME PRICING DUE TO SCARCITY
OVERALL AU-GU ODDS 1:8 HOBBY
1 Mark Prior/250 2.50 6.00
2 Sean Casey/250 2.00 5.00
4 Andruw Jones/250 2.50 6.00
5 Francisco Cordero/250 2.50 6.00
6 Ben Sheets/250 2.00 5.00
7 Rocco Baldelli/250 2.00 5.00
8 Rafael Furcal/250 2.00 5.00
10 Roy Oswalt/250 2.00 5.00
11 Jose Reyes/250 2.00 5.00
12 Shannon Stewart/250 2.00 5.00
13 Greg Maddux/250 4.00 10.00
14 Alfonso Soriano/250 2.00 5.00
15 Curt Schilling/250 2.50 6.00
16 Jody Gerut/125 2.50 6.00
18 Josh Beckett/250 2.00 5.00
19 Laynce Nix/250 2.00 5.00
20 Scott Rolen/250 2.50 6.00

2005 Studio Spirit of the Game Combo

*COMBO: .75X TO 2X JSY p/r 250
*COMBO: .6X TO 1.5X JSY p/r 125
STATED PRINT RUN 50 SERIAL #'d SETS
PRIME PRINT RUN 10 SERIAL #'d SETS
NO PRIME PRICING DUE TO SCARCITY
OVERALL AU-GU ODDS 1:8 HOBBY

2005 Studio Spirit of the Game Signature Combo

PRINT RUNS B/WN 10-25 COPIES PER
NO PRICING ON QTY OF 10
PRIME PRINT RUNS B/WN 5-10 COPIES PER
NO PRIME PRICING DUE TO SCARCITY
OVERALL AU-GU ODDS 1:8 HOBBY
1 Mark Prior Bat-Jsy/15 20.00 50.00
2 Sean Casey Jsy-Jsy/25 12.50 30.00
8 Rafael Furcal Bat-Jsy/25 12.50 30.00
12 S.Stewart Jsy-Jsy/25 12.50 30.00
14 A.Soriano Jsy-Jsy/15 15.00 40.00
16 Jody Gerut Bat-Jsy/25 8.00 20.00
19 Laynce Nix Bat-Jsy/25 8.00 20.00

2005 Studio Stars

STATED ODDS 1:6
*GOLD: .75X TO 2X BASIC
GOLD PRINT RUN 500 #'d SETS
*PLATINUM: 1.5X TO 4X BASIC
PLATINUM PRINT RUN 50 #'d SETS
OVERALL INSERT ODDS 1:1 HOBBY
1 Carlos Beltran .60 1.50
2 Sean Casey .40 1.00
3 Ichiro Suzuki 1.25 3.00
4 Vladimir Guerrero .60 1.50
5 Tim Hudson .60 1.50

6 Alex Rodriguez 1.25 3.00
7 Miguel Tejada .60 1.50
8 Curt Schilling .60 1.50
9 Roger Clemens 1.25 3.00
10 Ben Sheets .40 1.00
11 Todd Helton .60 1.50
12 Mark Mulder .40 1.00
13 Scott Podsednik .40 1.00
14 Victor Martinez .60 1.50
15 Mark Prior .60 1.50
16 Ivan Rodriguez .60 1.50
17 Dontrelle Willis .40 1.00
18 Andy Pettitte .60 1.50
19 Khalil Greene .40 1.00
20 Jeff Kent .40 1.00
21 Paul Konerko .60 1.50
22 Joe Mauer .75 2.00
23 Bobby Crosby .40 1.00
24 Pedro Martinez .60 1.50
25 John Smoltz 1.00 2.50
26 Derek Jeter 2.50 6.00
27 Moises Alou .40 1.00
28 Rich Harden .40 1.00
29 Jim Thome .60 1.50
30 Jason Bay .40 1.00
31 Aramis Ramirez .40 1.00
32 Carlos Lee .40 1.00
33 B.J. Upton .60 1.50
34 Nomar Garciaparra .60 1.50
35 Ken Griffey Jr. 2.00 5.00
36 Darin Erstad .40 1.00
37 Larry Walker .60 1.50
38 Jose Vidro .40 1.00
39 Zack Greinke 1.25 3.00
40 Michael Young .40 1.00
41 David Wright .75 2.00
42 Albert Pujols 1.25 3.00
43 Vernon Wells .40 1.00
44 Mark Teixeira .60 1.50
45 Jacque Jones .40 1.00
46 Brian Giles .40 1.00
47 Austin Kearns .40 1.00
48 Omar Vizquel .60 1.50
49 Randy Johnson 1.00 2.50
50 Jason Varitek 1.00 2.50

2018 Studio

1 Chance Sisco RC .30 .75
2 Dustin Fowler RC .25 .60
3 Shohei Ohtani RC 6.00 15.00
4 Clint Frazier RC .50 1.25
5 Amed Rosario RC .30 .75
6 Rhys Hoskins RC 1.00 2.50
7 Rafael Devers RC .75 2.00
8 Ozzie Albies RC .75 2.00
9 J.P. Crawford RC .25 .60
10 Victor Robles RC .60 1.50
11 Austin Hays RC .40 1.00
12 J.D. Davis RC .30 .75
13 Luiz Gohara RC .25 .60
14 Nicky Delmonico RC .25 .60
15 Brian Anderson RC .30 .75
16 Walker Buehler RC 1.25 3.00
17 Manny Machado .25 .60
18 Aaron Judge .60 1.50
19 Ronald Acuna Jr. RC 8.00 20.00
20 Gleyber Torres RC 2.50 6.00

2018 Studio Signatures

RANDOM INSERTS IN PACKS
13 Luiz Gohara 3.00 8.00
14 Nicky Delmonico 3.00 8.00

2018 Studio Signatures Gold

*GOLD/25: .75X TO 2X BASIC
RANDOM INSERTS IN PACKS
PRINT RUNS B/WN 3-25 COPIES PER
NO PRICING ON QTY 10 OR LESS
11 Austin Hays/25 8.00 20.00

1985 Subway Discs

This set is parallel to the 1985 Thom McAn discs. While the same design was used, it was distributed in outlets of the sandwhich chain. Thi s set is much easier than the Thom McAn set.

COMPLETE SET (46) 40.00 100.00
1 Benny Ayala .08 .25
2 Buddy Bell .20 .50
3 Juan Beniquez .08 .25
4 Tony Bernazard .08 .25
5 Mike Boddicker .08 .25
6 Bill Buckner .08 .25
7 Rod Carew 4.00 10.00
8 Onix Concepcion .08 .25
9 Cecil Cooper .20 .50
10 Al Cowens .08 .25
11 Ron Guidry .20 .50
12 Mike Hargrove .20 .50
13 Kent Hrbek .20 .50
14 Rick Langford .08 .25
15 Jack Morris .20 .50
16 Dan Quisenberry .08 .25
17 Cal Ripken 12.50 30.00
18 Ed Romero .08 .25
19 Tom Seaver 4.00 10.00
20 Alan Trammell .40 1.00
21 Greg Walker .08 .25
22 Willie Wilson .08 .25
23 Dave Winfield 4.00 10.00
24 Geoff Zahn .08 .25
25 Steve Carlton 4.00 10.00
26 Cesar Cedeno .08 .25
27 Jose Cruz .08 .25
28 Ivan DeJesus .08 .25
29 Luis DeLeon .08 .25
30 Rich Gossage .20 .50
31 Pedro Guerrero .08 .25
32 Tony Gwynn 10.00 25.00
33 Keith Hernandez .20 .50
34 Bob Horner .08 .25
35 Jeff Leonard .08 .25
36 Willie McGee .20 .50
37 Jesse Orosco .20 .50
38 Junior Ortiz .08 .25
39 Terry Puhl .08 .25
40 Johnny Ray .08 .25
41 Ryne Sandberg 6.00 15.00
42 Mike Schmidt 4.00 10.00
43 Rick Sutcliffe .20 .50
44 Bruce Sutter 2.00 5.00
45 Fernando Valenzuela .20 .50
46 Ozzie Virgil .08 .25

1994 Sucker Saver

These sucker saver lollipops were produced by Innovative Confections. The actual discs were issued by Michael Schechter Associates, and one disc was included with each sucker. It is reported that sales of this confectionary product were so poor that it was discontinued. Each disc measures 2 5/8" in diameter. Inside a red ring, the fronts display a color player headshot within a diamond design. The player's name appears in black lettering on a yellow stripe across the top of the disc. The backs of the discs are printed in blue and are numbered "X of 20."

COMPLETE SET (20) 20.00 50.00
1 Rickey Henderson 1.50 4.00
2 Ken Caminiti .75 2.00
3 Terry Pendleton .20 .50
4 Tim Raines .40 1.00
5 Joe Carter .40 1.00
6 Benito Santiago .40 1.00
7 Jim Abbott .40 1.00
8 Ozzie Smith 3.00 8.00
9 Don Slaught .20 .50
10 Tony Gwynn 3.00 8.00
11 Mark Langston .20 .50
12 Darryl Strawberry .40 1.00
13 Dave Justice .75 2.00
14 Cecil Fielder .40 1.00
15 Cal Ripken 6.00 15.00
16 Jeff Bagwell 1.50 4.00
17 Mike Piazza 4.00 10.00
18 Bobby Bonilla .20 .50
19 Barry Bonds 2.50 6.00
20 Roger Clemens 3.00 8.00

1995 Summit Samples

COMPLETE SET (9) 3.00 8.00
10 Barry Larkin .40 1.00
11 Albert Belle .20 .50
79 Cal Ripken 2.00 5.00
80 David Cone .20 .50
125 Alex Gonzalez .08 .25
130 Charles Johnson .08 .25
BB12 Jose Canseco .50 1.25
BB17 Fred McGriff .30 .75
NNO Title Card .08 .25

1995 Summit

This set contains 200 standard-size cards and was sold in seven-card retail packs for a suggested price of $1.99. This set is a premium product issued by Pinnacle Brands and produced on thicker paper than the regular set. Subsets featured are Rookies (112-173), Bat Speed (174-188) and Special Delivery (189-193). Notable Rookie Cards in this set include Bobby Higginson and Hideo Nomo.

COMPLETE SET (200) 8.00 20.00
SUBSET CARDS HALF VALUE OF BASE CARDS
1 Ken Griffey Jr. .50 1.25
2 Alex Fernandez .05 .15
3 Fred McGriff .15 .40
4 Ben McDonald .05 .15
5 Rafael Palmeiro .15 .40
6 Tony Gwynn .30 .75
7 Jim Thome .15 .40
8 Ken Hill .05 .15
9 Barry Bonds .60 1.50
10 Barry Larkin .15 .40
11 Albert Belle .08 .25
12 Billy Ashley .05 .15
13 Matt Williams .08 .25
14 Andy Benes .05 .15
15 Midre Cummings .05 .15
16 J.R. Phillips .05 .15
17 Edgar Martinez .15 .40
18 Manny Ramirez .15 .40
19 Jose Canseco .15 .40
20 Chili Davis .08 .25
21 Don Mattingly .60 1.50
22 Bernie Williams .15 .40
23 Tom Glavine .15 .40
24 Robin Ventura .08 .25
25 Jeff Conine .08 .25
26 Mark Grace .15 .40
27 Mark McGwire .60 1.50
28 Carlos Delgado .08 .25
29 Greg Colbrunn .05 .15
30 Greg Maddux .40 1.00
31 Craig Biggio .15 .40
32 Kirby Puckett .25 .60
33 Derek Bell .05 .15
34 Lenny Dykstra .08 .25
35 Tim Salmon .15 .40
36 Deion Sanders .15 .40
37 Moises Alou .08 .25
38 Ray Lankford .08 .25
39 Willie Greene .05 .15
40 Ozzie Smith .40 1.00
41 Roger Clemens .50 1.25
42 Andres Galarraga .08 .25
43 Gary Sheffield .08 .25
44 Sammy Sosa .25 .60
45 Larry Walker .08 .25
46 Kevin Appier .08 .25
47 Raul Mondesi .08 .25
48 Kenny Lofton .08 .25
49 Darryl Hamilton .05 .15
50 Roberto Alomar .15 .40
51 Hal Morris .05 .15
52 Cliff Floyd .08 .25
53 Brent Gates .05 .15
54 Rickey Henderson .25 .60
55 John Olerud .08 .25
56 Gregg Jefferies .05 .15
57 Cecil Fielder .08 .25
58 Paul Molitor .08 .25
59 Bret Boone .08 .25
60 Greg Vaughn .05 .15
61 Wally Joyner .08 .25
62 Jeffrey Hammonds .05 .15
63 James Mouton .05 .15
64 Omar Vizquel .15 .40
65 Wade Boggs .15 .40
66 Terry Steinbach .05 .15
67 Wil Cordero .05 .15
68 Joey Hamilton .05 .15
69 Rico Brogna .05 .15
70 Darren Daulton .08 .25
71 Chuck Knoblauch .08 .25
72 Bob Hamelin .05 .15
73 Carl Everett .08 .25
74 Joe Carter .08 .25
75 Dave Winfield .08 .25
76 Bobby Bonilla .08 .25
77 Paul O'Neill .15 .40
78 Javier Lopez .08 .25
79 Cal Ripken .75 2.00
80 David Cone .08 .25
81 Bernard Gilkey .05 .15
82 Ivan Rodriguez .15 .40
83 Dean Palmer .08 .25
84 Jason Bere .05 .15
85 Will Clark .15 .40
86 Scott Cooper .05 .15
87 Royce Clayton .05 .15
88 Mike Piazza .40 1.00
89 Ryan Klesko .08 .25
90 Juan Gonzalez .08 .25
91 Travis Fryman .08 .25
92 Frank Thomas .25 .60
93 Eduardo Perez .05 .15
94 Mo Vaughn .08 .25
95 Jay Bell .08 .25
96 Jeff Bagwell .15 .40
97 Randy Johnson .25 .60
98 Jimmy Key .08 .25
99 Dennis Eckersley .08 .25
100 Carlos Baerga .05 .15
101 Eddie Murray .25 .60
102 Mike Mussina .15 .40
103 Brian Anderson .05 .15
104 Jeff Cirillo .05 .15
105 Dante Bichette .08 .25
106 Bret Saberhagen .08 .25
107 Jeff Kent .08 .25
108 Ruben Sierra .08 .25
109 Kirk Gibson .08 .25
110 Steve Karsay .05 .15
111 David Justice .08 .25
112 Benji Gil .05 .15
113 Vaughn Eshelman .05 .15
114 Carlos Perez RC .15 .40
115 Chipper Jones .25 .60
116 Shane Andrews .05 .15
117 Orlando Miller .05 .15
118 Scott Ruffcorn .05 .15
119 Jose Oliva .05 .15
120 Joe Vitiello .05 .15
121 Jon Nunnally .05 .15
122 Garret Anderson .08 .25
123 Curtis Goodwin .05 .15
124 Mark Grudzielanek RC .30 .75
125 Alex Gonzalez .05 .15
126 David Bell .05 .15
127 Dustin Hermanson .05 .15
128 Dave Nilsson .05 .15
129 Wilson Heredia .05 .15
130 Charles Johnson .08 .25
131 Frank Rodriguez .05 .15
132 Alex Ochoa .05 .15
133 Alex Rodriguez .60 1.50
134 Bob Higginson RC .30 .75
135 Edgardo Alfonzo .05 .15
136 Armando Benitez .05 .15
137 Rich Aude .05 .15
138 Tim Naehring .05 .15
139 Joe Randa .08 .25
140 Quilvio Veras .05 .15
141 Hideo Nomo RC .75 2.00
142 Ray Holbert .05 .15
143 Michael Tucker .05 .15
144 Chad Mottola .05 .15
145 John Valentin .05 .15
146 James Baldwin .05 .15
147 Esteban Loaiza .05 .15
148 Marty Cordova .05 .15
149 Juan Acevedo RC .05 .15
150 Tim Unroe RC UER .05 .15
151 Brad Clontz UER .05 .15
152 Steve Rodriguez UER .05 .15
153 Rudy Pemberton UER .05 .15
154 Ozzie Timmons UER .05 .15
155 Ricky Otero .05 .15
156 Allen Battle .05 .15
157 Joe Rosselli .05 .15
158 Roberto Petagine .05 .15
159 Todd Hollandsworth .05 .15
160 Shannon Penn UER .05 .15
161 Antonio Osuna UER .05 .15
162 Russ Davis UER .05 .15
163 Jason Giambi UER .15 .40
164 Terry Bradshaw .05 .15
165 Ray Durham .08 .25
166 Todd Steverson .05 .15
167 Tim Belk .05 .15
168 Andy Pettitte .15 .40
169 Roger Cedeno .05 .15
170 Jose Parra .05 .15
171 Scott Sullivan .05 .15
172 LaTroy Hawkins .05 .15
173 Jeff McCurry .05 .15
174 Ken Griffey Jr. BAT .30 .75
175 Frank Thomas BAT .15 .40
176 Cal Ripken BAT .40 1.00
177 Jeff Bagwell BAT .08 .25
178 Mike Piazza BAT .25 .60
179 Barry Bonds BAT .30 .75
180 Matt Williams BAT .05 .15
181 Don Mattingly BAT .40 1.00
182 Will Clark BAT .08 .25
183 Tony Gwynn BAT .15 .40
184 Kirby Puckett BAT .15 .40
185 Jose Canseco BAT .08 .25
186 Paul Molitor BAT .05 .15
187 Albert Belle BAT .05 .15
188 Joe Carter BAT .05 .15
189 Greg Maddux SPD .25 .60
190 Roger Clemens SD .25 .60
191 David Cone SD .05 .15
192 Mike Mussina SD .08 .25
193 Randy Johnson SPD .15 .40
194 Frank Thomas CL .15 .40
195 Ken Griffey Jr. CL .30 .75
196 Cal Ripken CL .40 1.00
197 Jeff Bagwell CL .08 .25
198 Mike Piazza CL .25 .60
199 Barry Bonds CL .30 .75
200 M.Vaughn .05 .15
M.Williams CL

1995 Summit Nth Degree

COMPLETE SET (200) 200.00 400.00
*STARS: 3X TO 8X BASIC CARDS
*ROOKIES: 2.5X TO 6X BASIC CARDS
STATED ODDS 1:4

1995 Summit Big Bang

COMPLETE SET (20) 40.00 100.00
STATED ODDS 1:72
BB1 Ken Griffey Jr. 6.00 15.00
BB2 Frank Thomas 3.00 8.00
BB3 Cal Ripken 10.00 25.00
BB4 Jeff Bagwell 2.00 5.00
BB5 Mike Piazza 3.00 8.00
BB6 Barry Bonds 5.00 12.00
BB7 Matt Williams 1.25 3.00
BB8 Don Mattingly 6.00 15.00
BB9 Will Clark 1.25 3.00
BB10 Tony Gwynn 3.00 8.00
BB11 Kirby Puckett 3.00 8.00
BB12 Jose Canseco 2.00 5.00
BB13 Paul Molitor 3.00 8.00
BB14 Albert Belle 1.25 3.00
BB15 Joe Carter 1.25 3.00
BB16 Rafael Palmeiro 2.00 5.00
BB17 Fred McGriff 2.00 5.00
BB18 David Justice 1.25 3.00
BB19 Tim Salmon 1.25 3.00
BB20 Mo Vaughn 1.25 3.00

1995 Summit New Age

COMPLETE SET (15) 15.00 40.00
STATED ODDS 1:18
NA1 Cliff Floyd .75 2.00
NA2 Manny Ramirez 1.25 3.00
NA3 Raul Mondesi .75 2.00
NA4 Alex Rodriguez 5.00 12.00
NA5 Billy Ashley .40 1.00
NA6 Alex Gonzalez .40 1.00
NA7 Michael Tucker .40 1.00
NA8 Charles Johnson .75 2.00
NA9 Carlos Delgado .75 2.00
NA10 Benji Gil .40 1.00
NA11 Chipper Jones 2.00 5.00
NA12 Todd Hollandsworth .40 1.00
NA13 Frankie Rodriguez .40 1.00
NA14 Shawn Green .75 2.00
NA15 Ray Durham .75 2.00

1995 Summit 21 Club

COMPLETE SET (9) 10.00 25.00
STATED ODDS 1:36
TC1 Bob Abreu 3.00 8.00
TC2 Pokey Reese .75 2.00
TC3 Edgardo Alfonzo .75 2.00
TC4 Jim Pittsley .75 2.00
TC5 Ruben Rivera .75 2.00
TC6 Chan Ho Park 1.25 3.00
TC7 Julian Tavarez .75 2.00
TC8 Ismael Valdes .75 2.00
TC9 Dmitri Young 1.25 3.00

1996 Summit

The 1996 Summit set was issued in one series totalling 200 cards. The seven-card packs had a suggested retail of $2.99 each. The fronts feature color player photos on a gold striped black background. The backs carry another player photo with player information and statistics.

COMPLETE SET (200) 10.00 25.00
SUBSET CARDS HALF VALUE OF BASE CARDS
1 Mike Piazza .50 1.25
2 Matt Williams .10 .30
3 Tino Martinez .20 .50
4 Reggie Sanders .10 .30
5 Ray Durham .10 .30
6 Brad Radke .10 .30
7 Jeff Bagwell .20 .50
8 Ron Gant .10 .30
9 Lance Johnson .10 .30
10 Kevin Seitzer .10 .30
11 Dante Bichette .10 .30
12 Ivan Rodriguez .20 .50
13 Jim Abbott .20 .50
14 Greg Colbrunn .10 .30
15 Rondell White .10 .30
16 Shawn Green .10 .30
17 Gregg Jefferies .10 .30
18 Omar Vizquel .20 .50
19 Cal Ripken 1.00 2.50
20 Mark McGwire .75 2.00
21 Wally Joyner .10 .30
22 Chili Davis .10 .30
23 Jose Canseco .20 .50
24 Royce Clayton .10 .30
25 Jay Bell .10 .30
26 Travis Fryman .10 .30
27 Jeff King .10 .30
28 Todd Hundley .10 .30
29 Joe Vitiello .10 .30
30 Russ Davis .10 .30
31 Mo Vaughn .10 .30
32 Raul Mondesi .10 .30
33 Ray Lankford .10 .30
34 Mike Stanley .10 .30
35 B.J. Surhoff .10 .30
36 Greg Vaughn .10 .30
37 Todd Stottlemyre .10 .30
38 Carlos Delgado .10 .30
39 Kenny Lofton .10 .30
40 Hideo Nomo .30 .75
41 Sterling Hitchcock .10 .30
42 Pete Schourek .10 .30
43 Edgardo Alfonzo .10 .30
44 Ken Hill .10 .30
45 Ken Caminiti .10 .30
46 Bobby Higginson .10 .30
47 Michael Tucker .10 .30
48 David Cone .10 .30
49 Cecil Fielder .10 .30
50 Brian L. Hunter .10 .30
51 Charles Johnson .10 .30
52 Bobby Bonilla .10 .30
53 Eddie Murray .30 .75
54 Kenny Rogers .10 .30
55 Jim Edmonds .10 .30
56 Trevor Hoffman .10 .30
57 Kevin Mitchell UER .10 .30
58 Ruben Sierra .10 .30
59 Benji Gil .10 .30
60 Juan Gonzalez .10 .30
61 Larry Walker .10 .30
62 Jack McDowell .10 .30
63 Shawon Dunston .10 .30
64 Andy Benes .10 .30
65 Jay Buhner .10 .30
66 Rickey Henderson .30 .75
67 Alex Gonzalez .10 .30
68 Mike Kelly .10 .30
69 Fred McGriff .20 .50
70 Ryne Sandberg .50 1.25
71 Ernie Young .10 .30
72 Kevin Appier .10 .30
73 Moises Alou .10 .30
74 John Jaha .10 .30
75 J.T. Snow .10 .30
76 Jim Thome .20 .50
77 Kirby Puckett .30 .75
78 Hal Morris .10 .30
79 Robin Ventura .10 .30
80 Ben McDonald .10 .30
81 Tim Salmon .20 .50
82 Albert Belle .10 .30
83 Marquis Grissom .10 .30
84 Alex Rodriguez .60 1.50
85 Manny Ramirez .20 .50
86 Ken Griffey Jr. .60 1.50
87 Sammy Sosa .30 .75
88 Frank Thomas .30 .75
89 Lee Smith .10 .30
90 Marty Cordova .10 .30
91 Greg Maddux .50 1.25
92 Lenny Dykstra .10 .30
93 Butch Huskey .10 .30
94 Garret Anderson .10 .30
95 Mike Bordick .10 .30
96 Dave Justice .10 .30
97 Chad Curtis .10 .30
98 Carlos Baerga .10 .30
99 Jason Isringhausen .10 .30
100 Gary Sheffield .10 .30
101 Roger Clemens .60 1.50
102 Ozzie Smith .50 1.25
103 Ramon Martinez .10 .30
104 Paul O'Neill .20 .50
105 Will Clark .20 .50
106 Tom Glavine .20 .50
107 Barry Bonds .75 2.00
108 Barry Larkin .20 .50
109 Derek Bell .10 .30
110 Randy Johnson .30 .75
111 Jeff Conine .10 .30
112 John Mabry .10 .30
113 Julian Tavarez .10 .30
114 Gary DiSarcina .10 .30
115 Andres Galarraga .10 .30
116 Marc Newfield .10 .30
117 Frank Rodriguez .10 .30
118 Brady Anderson .10 .30
119 Mike Mussina .20 .50
120 Orlando Merced .10 .30
121 Melvin Nieves .10 .30
122 Brian Jordan .10 .30
123 Rafael Palmeiro .20 .50
124 Johnny Damon .20 .50
125 Wil Cordero .10 .30
126 Chipper Jones .30 .75
127 Eric Karros .10 .30
128 Darren Daulton .10 .30
129 Vinny Castilla .10 .30
130 Joe Carter .10 .30
131 Bernie Williams .20 .50
132 Bernard Gilkey .10 .30
133 Bret Boone .10 .30
134 Tony Gwynn .40 1.00
135 Dave Nilsson .10 .30
136 Ryan Klesko .10 .30
137 Paul Molitor .10 .30
138 John Olerud .10 .30
139 Craig Biggio .20 .50
140 John Valentin .10 .30
141 Chuck Knoblauch .10 .30
142 Edgar Martinez .20 .50
143 Rico Brogna .10 .30
144 Dean Palmer .10 .30
145 Mark Grace .20 .50
146 Roberto Alomar .20 .50
147 Alex Fernandez .10 .30
148 Andre Dawson .10 .30
149 Wade Boggs .20 .50
150 Mark Lewis .10 .30
151 Gary Gaetti .10 .30
152 P.Wilson .30 .75
R.Clemens
153 R.Ordonez .20 .50
O.Smith
154 C.Ripken .50 1.25
D.Jeter
155 A.Benes .10 .30
A.Benes
156 M.Piazza .30 .75
J.Kendall
157 F.Thomas .20 .50
R.Klesko
158 K.Griffey Jr. .40 1.00
J.Damon
159 S.Sosa .20 .50
K.Garcia
160 R.Mondesi .20 .50
T.Salmon
161 C.Jones .20 .50
M.Williams
162 Rey Ordonez .10 .30
163 Bob Wolcott .10 .30
164 Brooks Kieschnick .10 .30
165 Steve Gibralter .10 .30
166 Bob Abreu .30 .75
167 Greg Zaun .10 .30
168 Tavo Alvarez .10 .30
169 Sal Fasano .10 .30
170 George Arias .10 .30
171 Derek Jeter 1.00 2.50
172 Livan Hernandez RC .40 1.00
173 Alan Benes .10 .30
174 George Williams .10 .30
175 John Wasdin .10 .30
176 Chan Ho Park .10 .30
177 Paul Wilson .10 .30
178 Jeff Suppan .10 .30
179 Quinton McCracken .10 .30
180 Wilton Guerrero RC .10 .30
181 Eric Owens .10 .30
182 Felipe Crespo .10 .30
183 LaTroy Hawkins .10 .30
184 Jason Schmidt .20 .50
185 Terrell Wade .10 .30
186 Mike Grace RC .10 .30
187 Chris Snopek .10 .30
188 Jason Kendall .10 .30
189 Todd Hollandsworth .10 .30
190 Jim Pittsley .10 .30
191 Jermaine Dye .10 .30
192 Mike Busby RC .10 .30
193 Richard Hidalgo .10 .30
194 Tyler Houston .10 .30
195 Jimmy Haynes .10 .30
196 Karim Garcia .10 .30
197 Ken Griffey Jr. CL .40 1.00
198 Frank Thomas CL .20 .50
199 Greg Maddux CL .30 .75
200 Cal Ripken CL .50 1.25

1996 Summit Above and Beyond

*STARS: 4X TO 10X BASIC CARDS
*ROOKIES: 2.5X TO 6X BASIC CARDS
STATED ODDS 1:4
154 D.Jeter 10.00 25.00
C.Ripken

1996 Summit Artist's Proofs

*STARS: 10X TO 25X BASIC CARDS
*ROOKIES: 6X TO 15X BASIC CARDS
STATED ODDS 1:36

1996 Summit Foil

COMPLETE SET (200) 20.00 50.00
*STARS: .6X TO 1.5X BASIC CARDS
FOIL DISTRIBUTED IN RETAIL SUPER PACKS

1996 Summit Ballparks

COMPLETE SET (18) 40.00 100.00
STATED ODDS 1:18
STATED PRINT RUN 8000 SERIAL #'d SETS
1 Cal Ripken 8.00 20.00
2 Albert Belle 1.00 2.50
3 Dante Bichette 1.00 2.50
4 Mo Vaughn 1.00 2.50
5 Ken Griffey Jr. 5.00 12.00
6 Derek Jeter 6.00 15.00
7 Juan Gonzalez 1.00 2.50
8 Greg Maddux* 4.00 10.00
9 Frank Thomas 2.50 6.00
10 Ryne Sandberg 4.00 10.00
11 Mike Piazza 4.00 10.00
12 Johnny Damon 1.50 4.00
13 Barry Bonds 6.00 15.00
14 Jeff Bagwell 1.50 4.00
15 Paul Wilson 1.00 2.50
16 Tim Salmon 1.50 4.00
17 Kirby Puckett 2.50 6.00
18 Tony Gwynn 3.00 8.00

1996 Summit Big Bang

COMPLETE SET (16) 50.00 100.00
STATED ODDS 1:72
STATED PRINT RUN 600 SERIAL #'d SETS
MIRAGE STATED ODDS 1:72
MIRAGE PRINT RUN 600 SERIAL #'d SETS
1 Frank Thomas 4.00 10.00
2 Ken Griffey Jr. 12.50 30.00
3 Albert Belle 1.50 4.00
4 Mo Vaughn 1.50 4.00
5 Barry Bonds 6.00 15.00
6 Cal Ripken 12.00 30.00
7 Jeff Bagwell 2.50 6.00
8 Mike Piazza 4.00 10.00
9 Ryan Klesko 1.50 4.00
10 Manny Ramirez 2.50 6.00
11 Tim Salmon 1.50 4.00
12 Dante Bichette 1.50 4.00
13 Sammy Sosa 4.00 10.00
14 Raul Mondesi 1.50 4.00
15 Chipper Jones 4.00 10.00
16 Garret Anderson 1.50 4.00

1996 Summit Hitters Inc.

COMPLETE SET (16) 15.00 40.00
STATED ODDS 1:36
STATED PRINT RUN 4000 SERIAL #'d SETS
1 Tony Gwynn 1.50 4.00
2 Mo Vaughn .60 1.50
3 Tim Salmon .60 1.50
4 Ken Griffey Jr. 3.00 8.00
5 Sammy Sosa 1.50 4.00
6 Frank Thomas 1.50 4.00
7 Wade Boggs 1.00 2.50
8 Albert Belle .60 1.50
9 Cal Ripken 5.00 12.00
10 Manny Ramirez 1.00 2.50
11 Ryan Klesko .60 1.50
12 Dante Bichette .60 1.50
13 Mike Piazza 1.50 4.00
14 Chipper Jones 1.50 4.00
15 Ryne Sandberg 2.50 6.00
16 Matt Williams .60 1.50
S11 Ryan Klesko Sample .60 1.50

1996 Summit Positions

COMPLETE SET (9) 150.00 300.00
STATED ODDS 1:50 MAGAZINE
1 F.Thomas 6.00 15.00
Bagwell
Mo
2 C.Biggio 6.00 15.00
R.Alomar
Knobl
3 C.Jones 6.00 15.00
Thome
Williams
4 C.Ripken 30.00 60.00
A.Rodriguez
Larkin
5 M.Piazza 10.00 25.00
I.Rod.
C.Johnson
6 G.Maddux 10.00 25.00
Nomo
R.Johnson
7 B.Bonds 20.00 40.00
Belle
Klesko
8 K.Griffey 12.50 30.00
Edmonds
Damon
9 S.Sosa 6.00 15.00
M.Ramirez
Sheff

1990 Sunflower Seeds

This 24-card, standard-size set is an attractive set which frames the players photo by solid blue borders. This set was issued by Stagi and Scriven Farms Inc. with the cooperation of Michael Schechter Associates (MSA) and features some of the big-name stars in baseball at the time of printing of the set. The set was an attempt by the company to promote sunflower seeds as an alternative to chewing tobacco in the dugout. Three cards were available as an insert in each specially marked bag of Jumbo California Sunflower Seeds.

COMPLETE SET (24) 6.00 15.00
1 Kevin Mitchell .02 .10
2 Ken Griffey Jr. 1.50 4.00
3 Howard Johnson .02 .10
4 Bo Jackson .30 .75
5 Kirby Puckett .50 1.25
6 Robin Yount .50 1.25
7 Dave Stieb .08 .25
8 Don Mattingly 1.00 2.50
9 Barry Bonds .75 2.00
10 Pedro Guerrero .02 .10
11 Tony Gwynn 1.00 2.50
12 Von Hayes .02 .10
13 Rickey Henderson .50 1.25
14 Tim Raines .08 .25
15 Alan Trammell .20 .50
16 Dave Stewart .08 .25
17 Will Clark .30 .75
18 Roger Clemens 1.00 2.50
19 Wally Joyner .08 .25
20 Ryne Sandberg .75 2.00
21 Eric Davis .08 .25
22 Mike Scott .02 .10
23 Cal Ripken 2.00 5.00
24 Eddie Murray .50 1.25

1991 Sunflower Seeds

This 24-card, standard-size set was sponsored by Jumbo California Sunflower Seeds. The set was again issued by Stagi and Scriven Farms Inc. with the cooperation of Michael Schechter Associates (MSA). The set was another attempt by the company to promote sunflower seeds as an alternative to chewing tobacco in the dugout. Two cards were available as an insert in each specially marked bag of Jumbo California Sunflower Seeds.

COMPLETE SET (24) 4.00 10.00
1 Ozzie Smith .60 1.50
2 Wade Boggs .40 1.00
3 Bobby Bonilla .08 .25
4 George Brett .75 2.00
5 Kal Daniels .02 .10
6 Glenn Davis .02 .10
7 Chuck Finley .08 .25
8 Cecil Fielder .08 .25
9 Len Dykstra .08 .25
10 Dwight Gooden .08 .25
11 Ken Griffey Jr. 1.25 3.00
12 Kelly Gruber .02 .10
13 Kent Hrbek .08 .25
14 Andre Dawson .30 .75
15 Dave Justice .30 .75
16 Barry Larkin .30 .75
17 Ben McDonald .02 .10
18 Mark McGwire 1.00 2.50
19 Roberto Alomar .30 .75
20 Nolan Ryan 1.50 4.00
21 Sandy Alomar Jr. .08 .25
22 Bobby Thigpen .02 .10
23 Tim Wallach .02 .10
24 Matt Williams .20 .50

1992 Sunflower Seeds

This 24-card, standard-size set was sponsored by Jumbo California Sunflower Seeds and produced by Michael Schechter Associates (MSA). The posed color player photos are framed in white and bright blue on a white background. The company log appears in the upper left corner. The words "Autograph Series III" are printed in red at the top.

COMPLETE SET (24) 4.00 10.00
1 Jeff Reardon .08 .25
2 Bill Gullickson .02 .10
3 Todd Zeile .08 .25
4 Terry Mulholland .02 .10
5 Kirby Puckett .50 1.25
6 Howard Johnson .02 .10
7 Terry Pendleton .02 .10
8 Will Clark .30 .75
9 Cal Ripken 1.50 4.00
10 Chris Sabo .02 .10
11 Jim Abbott .08 .25
12 Joe Carter .08 .25
13 Paul Molitor .40 1.00
14 Ken Griffey Jr. 1.00 2.50
15 Randy Johnson .50 1.25
16 Bobby Bonilla .02 .10
17 John Smiley .02 .10
18 Jose Canseco .40 1.00
19 Tom Glavine .40 1.00
20 Darryl Strawberry .08 .25
21 Brett Butler .08 .25
22 Devon White .02 .10

23 Scott Erickson .02 .10
24 Willie McGee .08 .25

2001 Sunoco Dream Team

COMPLETE SET (12) 3.20 8.00
1 W.Stargell .40 1.00
B.Mazeroski
2 M.Schmidt .60 1.50
S.Carlton
3 T.Perez .40 1.00
J.Morgan
4 D.Mattingly .60 1.50
Y.Berra
5 J.Palmer .40 1.00
F.Robinson
6 L.Tiant .30 .75
C.Fisk
7 F.Lynn .20 .50
J.Rice
8 S.Anderson .40 1.00
A.Kaline
9 R.Roberts .50 1.25
R.Ashburn
10 T.McGraw .10 .25
G.Carter
11 L.Boudreau .20 .50
B.Feller
12 R.Maris .40 1.00
C.Hunter

1994 SuperSlam McDowell Promos

Although difficult to obtain, these 5 1/2" by 7 1/2" framed versions of 3 1/2 by 5" color cutouts were issued late in 1994. These cards can be unfolded and stood up. The creator of this concept was also one of the founders of the Upper Deck company. Our checklist is incomplete on these cards and all additions are appreciated.

COMPLETE SET (2) 4.00 10.00
COMMON CARD (1-2) 2.00 5.00
1 Jeff Bagwell
3 Frank Thomas
2 Mike Piazza
P1 Jack McDowell 2.00 5.00
Silver border
P2 Jack McDowell 2.00 5.00
Gold border

1962 Sugardale

The 1962 Sugardale Meats set of 22 black and white, numbered and lettered cards featuring the Cleveland Indians and Pittsburgh Pirates. The Indians are numbered while the Pirates are lettered. The backs, in red print, give player tips. The Bob Nieman card is considered to be scarce. The catalog numbering for this set is F174-1.

COMPLETE SET (22) 1500.00 3000.00
COMMON CARD (1-22) 40.00 100.00
COMMON SP 200.00 400.00
1 Barry Latman 40.00 100.00
2 Gary Bell 40.00 100.00
3 Dick Donovan 40.00 100.00
4 Frank Funk 40.00 100.00
5 Jim Perry 60.00 120.00
7 John Romano 40.00 100.00
8 Ty Cline 40.00 100.00
9 Tito Francona 40.00 100.00
10 Bob Nieman SP 200.00 400.00
11 Willie Kirkland 40.00 100.00
12 Woody Held 40.00 100.00
13 Jerry Kindall 40.00 100.00
14 Bubba Phillips 40.00 100.00
15 Mel Harder CO 60.00 120.00
16 Salty Parker CO 40.00 100.00
17 Ray Katt CO 40.00 100.00
18 Mel McGaha MG 40.00 100.00
19 Pedro Ramos 40.00 100.00
A Dick Groat 75.00 150.00
B Roberto Clemente 1000.00 2000.00
C Don Hoak 40.00 100.00
D Dick Stuart 40.00 100.00

1963 Sugardale

The 1963 Sugardale Meats set of 31 black and white, numbered and lettered cards, features the Cleveland Indians and Pittsburgh Pirates. The Indians cards are numbered while the Pirates cards are lettered. The backs are printed in red and give player tips. The 1963 Sugardale set can be distinguished from the 1962 set by examing the biographies on the card for mentions of the 1962 season. The Perry and Skinner cards were withdrawn after June trades and are quite scarce

COMPLETE SET (31) 3000.00 6000.00
COMMON CARD 100.00 200.00
COMMON SP 200.00 400.00
1 Barry Latman 100.00 200.00
2 Gary Bell 100.00 200.00
3 Dick Donovan 100.00 200.00
4 Joe Adcock 150.00 300.00
5 Jim Perry SP 200.00 400.00
7 John Romano 100.00 200.00
8 Mike de la Hoz 100.00 200.00
9 Tito Francona 100.00 200.00
10 Gene Green 100.00 200.00
11 Willie Kirkland 100.00 200.00
12 Woody Held 100.00 200.00
13 Jerry Kindall 100.00 200.00
14 Max Alvis 100.00 200.00
15 Mel Harder CO 125.00 250.00
16 George Strickland CO 100.00 200.00
17 Elmer Valo CO 100.00 200.00
18 Birdie Tebbetts MG 100.00 200.00
19 Pedro Ramos 100.00 200.00
20 Al Luplow 100.00 200.00
23 Jim Grant 100.00 200.00
24 Vic Davalillo 100.00 200.00
25 Jerry Walker 100.00 200.00
26 Sam McDowell 200.00 400.00
27 Fred Whitfield 100.00 200.00
28 Jack Kralick 100.00 200.00
33 Bob Allen 100.00 200.00
A Don Cardwell 100.00 200.00
B Bob Skinner SP 200.00 400.00
C Don Schwall 100.00 200.00
D Jim Pagliaroni 100.00 200.00
E Dick Schofield 100.00 200.00

1962 Swan-Virdon Postcard

This one-card postcard set features Bill Virdon in which the front is a portrait shot of Virdon and the back promotes the Swan-Virdon company of Missouri. Like so many other postcards at that time, the photo was taken by noted sports photographer J.D. McCarthy.

1 Bill Virdon 6.00 15.00

2001 Sweet Spot

COMP.BASIC w/o SP's (60) 8.00 20.00
COMP.UPDATE w/o SP's (30) 4.00 10.00
COMMON CARD (1-60) .15 .40
COMMON CARD (61-90) 4.00 10.00
61-90 SB PRINT RUN 1000 SERIAL #'d CARDS
61-90 SB RANDOM INSERTS IN PACKS
COMMON CARD (91-120) .25 .60
COMMON CARD (121-150) 2.00 5.00
121-150 RANDOM IN ROOKIE UPD.PACKS
121-150 PRINT RUN 1500 SERIAL #'d SETS
91-150 DISTRIBUTED IN ROOKIE UPD.PACKS
1 Troy Glaus .15 .40
2 Darin Erstad .15 .40
3 Jason Giambi .15 .40
4 Tim Hudson .15 .40
5 Ben Grieve .15 .40
6 Carlos Delgado .15 .40
7 David Wells .15 .40
8 Greg Vaughn .15 .40
9 Roberto Alomar .25 .60
10 Jim Thome .25 .60
11 John Olerud .15 .40
12 Edgar Martinez .25 .60
13 Cal Ripken 1.25 3.00
14 Albert Belle .15 .40
15 Ivan Rodriguez .25 .60
16 Alex Rodriguez Rangers 1.00 2.50
17 Pedro Martinez .25 .60
18 Nomar Garciaparra .60 1.50
19 Manny Ramirez .25 .60
20 Jermaine Dye .15 .40
21 Juan Gonzalez .15 .40
22 Dean Palmer .15 .40
23 Matt Lawton .15 .40
24 Eric Milton .15 .40
25 Frank Thomas .40 1.00
26 Magglio Ordonez .15 .40
27 Derek Jeter 1.00 2.50
28 Bernie Williams .25 .60
29 Roger Clemens .75 2.00
30 Jeff Bagwell .25 .60
31 Richard Hidalgo .15 .40
32 Chipper Jones .40 1.00
33 Greg Maddux .60 1.50
34 Richie Sexson .15 .40
35 Jeromy Burnitz .15 .40
36 Mark McGwire 1.00 2.50
37 Jim Edmonds .15 .40
38 Sammy Sosa .40 1.00
39 Randy Johnson .40 1.00
40 Steve Finley .15 .40
41 Gary Sheffield .15 .40
42 Shawn Green .15 .40
43 Vladimir Guerrero .40 1.00
44 Jose Vidro .15 .40
45 Barry Bonds 1.00 2.50
46 Jeff Kent .15 .40
47 Preston Wilson .15 .40
48 Luis Castillo .15 .40
49 Mike Piazza .60 1.50
50 Edgardo Alfonzo .15 .40
51 Tony Gwynn .50 1.25
52 Ryan Klesko .15 .40
53 Scott Rolen .25 .60
54 Bob Abreu .15 .40
55 Jason Kendall .15 .40
56 Brian Giles .15 .40
57 Ken Griffey Jr. .75 2.00
58 Barry Larkin .25 .60
59 Todd Helton .25 .60
60 Mike Hampton UER .15 .40
61 Corey Patterson SB 4.00 10.00
62 Ichiro Suzuki SB RC 50.00 120.00
63 Jason Grilli SB 4.00 10.00
64 Brian Cole SB 4.00 10.00
65 Juan Pierre SB 4.00 10.00
66 Matt Ginter SB 4.00 10.00
67 Jimmy Rollins SB 4.00 10.00
68 Jason Smith SB RC 4.00 10.00
69 Israel Alcantara SB 4.00 10.00
70 Adam Pettyjohn SB RC 4.00 10.00
71 Luke Prokopec SB 4.00 10.00
72 Barry Zito SB 5.00 12.00
73 Keith Ginter SB 4.00 10.00
74 Sun Woo Kim SB 4.00 10.00
75 Ross Gload SB 4.00 10.00
76 Matt Wise SB 4.00 10.00
77 Aubrey Huff SB 4.00 10.00
78 Ryan Franklin SB 4.00 10.00
79 Brandon Inge SB 4.00 10.00
80 Wes Helms SB 4.00 10.00
81 Junior Spivey SB RC 5.00 12.00
82 Ryan Vogelsong SB 4.00 10.00
83 John Parrish SB 4.00 10.00
84 Joe Crede SB 5.00 12.00
85 Damian Rolls SB 4.00 10.00
86 Esix Snead SB RC 4.00 10.00
87 Rocky Biddle SB 4.00 10.00
88 Brady Clark SB 4.00 10.00
89 Timo Perez SB 4.00 10.00
90 Jay Spurgeon SB 4.00 10.00
91 Garret Anderson .25 .60
92 Jermaine Dye .25 .60
93 Shannon Stewart .25 .60
94 Ben Grieve .25 .60
95 Juan Gonzalez .25 .60
96 Brett Boone .25 .60
97 Tony Batista .25 .60
98 Rafael Palmeiro .40 1.00
99 Carl Everett .25 .60
100 Mike Sweeney .25 .60
101 Tony Clark .25 .60
102 Doug Mientkiewicz .25 .60
103 Jose Canseco .40 1.00
104 Mike Mussina .40 1.00
105 Lance Berkman .25 .60
106 Andruw Jones .40 1.00
107 Geoff Jenkins .25 .60
108 Matt Morris .25 .60
109 Fred McGriff .40 1.00
110 Luis Gonzalez .25 .60
111 Kevin Brown .25 .60
112 Tony Armas Jr. .25 .60
113 John Vander Wal .25 .60
114 Cliff Floyd .25 .60
115 Matt Lawton .25 .60
116 Phil Nevin .25 .60
117 Pat Burrell .25 .60
118 Aramis Ramirez .25 .60
119 Sean Casey .25 .60
120 Larry Walker .25 .60
121 Albert Pujols SB RC 40.00 100.00
122 Johnny Estrada SB RC 2.00 5.00
123 Wilson Betemit SB RC 3.00 8.00
124 Adrian Hernandez SB RC 2.00 5.00
125 Morgan Ensberg SB RC 3.00 8.00
126 Horacio Ramirez SB RC 2.00 5.00
127 Josh Towers SB RC 2.00 5.00
128 Juan Uribe SB RC 2.00 5.00
129 Wilken Ruan SB RC 2.00 5.00
130 Andres Torres SB RC 2.00 5.00
131 Brian Lawrence SB RC 2.00 5.00
132 Ryan Freel SB RC 2.00 5.00
133 Brandon Duckworth SB RC 2.00 5.00
134 Juan Diaz SB RC 2.00 5.00
135 Rafael Soriano SB RC 2.00 5.00
136 Ricardo Rodriguez SB RC 2.00 5.00
137 Bud Smith SB RC 2.00 5.00
138 Mark Teixeira SB RC 6.00 15.00
139 Mark Prior SB RC 3.00 8.00
140 Jackson Melian SB RC 2.00 5.00
141 Dewon Brazelton SB RC 2.00 5.00
142 Greg Miller SB RC 2.00 5.00
143 Billy Sylvester SB RC 2.00 5.00
144 Elpidio Guzman SB RC 2.00 5.00
145 Jack Wilson SB RC 2.00 5.00
146 Jose Mieses SB RC 2.00 5.00
147 Brandon Lyon SB RC 2.00 5.00
148 Tsuyoshi Shinjo SB RC 2.00 5.00
149 Juan Cruz SB RC 2.00 5.00
150 Jay Gibbons SB RC 2.00 5.00

2001 Sweet Spot Big League Challenge

COMPLETE SET (20) 30.00 60.00
STATED ODDS 1:6
BL1 Mark McGwire 3.00 8.00
BL2 Richard Hidalgo .75 2.00
BL3 Alex Rodriguez 1.50 4.00
BL4 Shawn Green .75 2.00
BL5 Frank Thomas 1.25 3.00
BL6 Chipper Jones 1.25 3.00
BL7 Rafael Palmeiro .75 2.00
BL8 Troy Glaus .75 2.00
BL9 Mike Piazza 2.00 5.00
BL10 Andruw Jones .75 2.00
BL11 Todd Helton .75 2.00
BL12 Jason Giambi .75 2.00
BL13 Sammy Sosa 1.25 3.00
BL14 Carlos Delgado .75 2.00
BL15 Barry Bonds 3.00 8.00
BL16 Jose Canseco .75 2.00
BL17 Jim Edmonds .75 2.00
BL18 Manny Ramirez .75 2.00
BL19 Gary Sheffield .75 2.00
BL20 Nomar Garciaparra 2.00 5.00

2001 Sweet Spot Game Base Duos

AUTO OR BASE STATED ODDS 1:18
B1BD Bagwell/Dye 6.00 15.00
B1BH Bonds/Helton 10.00 25.00
B1CP Clemens/Piazza 6.00 15.00
B1GD V.Guerrero/C.Delgado 6.00 15.00
B1HG Hammonds/Glaus 4.00 10.00
B1JG C.Jones/Garciaparra 6.00 15.00
B1JP Piazza/Jeter 12.00 30.00
B1MG McGwire/Griffey Jr. 10.00 25.00
B1MP McGwire/T.Perez 20.00 50.00
B1RJ A.Rodriguez/Jeter 10.00 25.00
B1RR Rolen/Ripken 10.00 25.00
B1SR Sheffield/A.Rodriguez 6.00 15.00
B1ST Sosa/Thomas 6.00 15.00
B1GRA Griffey/Ramirez 12.50 30.00
B1GRO Gwynn/I.Rodriguez 4.00 10.00
B1JGI R.Johnson/Giambi 6.00 15.00

2001 Sweet Spot Game Base Trios

STATED PRINT RUN 50 SERIAL #'d SETS
BDH Bagwell/Dye/Hidalgo 15.00 40.00
BHK Bonds/Helton/Kent 40.00 80.00
GDM Vlad/Delga/Mond 15.00 40.00
GRP Gwynn/I-Rod/Palmeiro 15.00 40.00
GRT Griffey/Ramirez/Thome 10.00 25.00
HGH Hammo/Glaus/Helton 15.00 40.00
JGC R.John/Giambi/Chavez 15.00 40.00
JGJ Chipper/Nomar/Andruw 20.00 50.00
MGE McGwire/Griffey/Edm 50.00 100.00
PJW Piazza/Jeter/B.Will 40.00 80.00
RRB Rolen/Ripken/Belle 30.00 60.00
SRM Sheffield/A-Rod/Edgar 15.00 40.00
STO Sosa/Thomas/Ordonez 15.00 40.00

2001 Sweet Spot Game Bat

STATED ODDS 1:18
BAJ Andruw Jones 2.00 5.00
BAR Alex Rodriguez 4.00 10.00
BBB Barry Bonds 5.00 12.00
BCR Cal Ripken 6.00 15.00
BFT Frank Thomas 3.00 8.00
BGS Gary Sheffield 1.25 3.00
BHA Hank Aaron 15.00 40.00
BIR Ivan Rodriguez 2.00 5.00
BJC Jose Canseco 2.00 5.00
BJD Joe DiMaggio 25.00 60.00
BKG Ken Griffey Jr. 6.00 15.00
BMM Mickey Mantle 25.00 60.00
BNR Nolan Ryan 10.00 25.00
BRA Rick Ankiel 1.25 3.00
BRJ Reggie Jackson 2.50 6.00
BSM Stan Musial 15.00 40.00
BSS Sammy Sosa 2.00 5.00
BTC Ty Cobb 30.00 80.00
BWM Willie Mays 12.00 30.00

2001 Sweet Spot Game Jersey

STATED ODDS 1:18
JAJ Andruw Jones 6.00 15.00
JAR Alex Rodriguez 6.00 15.00
JBB Barry Bonds 10.00 25.00
JCJ Chipper Jones 6.00 15.00
JCR Cal Ripken 10.00 25.00
JDS Duke Snider 6.00 15.00
JFT Frank Thomas 6.00 15.00
JIR Ivan Rodriguez 6.00 15.00
JIS Ichiro Suzuki 25.00 60.00
JJC Jose Canseco 6.00 15.00
JJD Joe DiMaggio 20.00 50.00
JKG Ken Griffey Jr. 6.00 15.00
JMM Mickey Mantle 40.00 100.00
JNR Nolan Ryan 12.00 30.00
JRC Roberto Clemente 30.00 60.00
JRC Roger Clemens 6.00 15.00
JRJ Randy Johnson 6.00 15.00
JSM Stan Musial 12.50 30.00
JSS Sammy Sosa 6.00 15.00
JWM Willie Mays 10.00 25.00

2001 Sweet Spot Players Party

COMPLETE SET (10) 25.00 50.00
STATED ODDS 1:12
PP1 Derek Jeter 3.00 8.00
PP2 Randy Johnson 1.25 3.00
PP3 Frank Thomas 1.25 3.00
PP4 Nomar Garciaparra 2.00 5.00
PP5 Ken Griffey Jr. 2.50 6.00
PP6 Carlos Delgado .75 2.00
PP7 Mike Piazza 2.00 5.00
PP8 Barry Bonds 3.00 8.00
PP9 Sammy Sosa 1.25 3.00
PP10 Pedro Martinez .75 2.00

2001 Sweet Spot Signatures

AUTO OR BASE STATED ODDS 1:18
ASTERISK IS 50% EXCH-50% IN-PACK AU
NO ASTERISK MEANS 100% EXCHANGE
40 OF 150 DIMAGGIO AU'S SAY CLIPPER
NO PRICING ON QTY OF 10 OR LESS
SAB Albert Belle 8.00 20.00
SAH Art Howe 10.00 25.00
SAJ Andruw Jones 6.00 15.00
SAR Alex Rodriguez SP/154 * 60.00 150.00
SAT Alan Trammell 10.00 25.00
SBB Buddy Bell 6.00 15.00
SBM Bill Madlock 6.00 15.00
SBV Bobby Valentine 8.00 20.00
SCB Chris Chambliss 8.00 20.00
SCD Carlos Delgado 8.00 20.00
SCJ Chipper Jones 30.00 60.00
SDB Dusty Baker 30.00 60.00
SDB Don Baylor 8.00 20.00
SDE Darin Erstad 6.00 15.00
SDJ Davey Johnson 6.00 15.00
SDL Davey Lopes 6.00 15.00
SFT Frank Thomas 50.00 100.00
SGS Gary Sheffield 10.00 25.00
SHM Hal McRae 6.00 15.00
SIR Ivan Rodriguez SP/150 * 30.00 80.00
SJB Jeff Bagwell SP/214 * 40.00 80.00
SJC Jose Canseco 30.00 60.00
SJD Joe DiMaggio SP/110 * 400.00 600.00
SJDa DiMag Clipper SP/40 * 600.00 1000.00
SJG Joe Garagiola 20.00 50.00
SJG Jason Giambi 6.00 15.00
SJR Jim Rice 15.00 40.00
SKG Ken Griffey Jr. SP/100 * 200.00 300.00
SLP Lou Piniella 15.00 40.00
SMB Milton Bradley 6.00 15.00
SML Mike Lamb 10.00 25.00
SMW Matt Williams 10.00 25.00
SNR Nolan Ryan 40.00 80.00
SPB Pat Burrell 6.00 15.00
SPO Paul O'Neill 12.00 30.00
SRAl Roberto Alomar 15.00 40.00
SRAN Rick Ankiel 6.00 15.00
SRC Roger Clemens 30.00 60.00
SRF Rafael Furcal 6.00 15.00
SRJ Randy Johnson 40.00 80.00
SRV Robin Ventura 10.00 25.00
SSG Shawn Green 6.00 15.00
SSM Stan Musial 90.00 150.00
SSS Sammy Sosa SP/148 * 30.00 60.00
STGL Troy Glaus 8.00 20.00
STGW Tony Gwynn 15.00 40.00
STH Tim Hudson 6.00 15.00
STL Tony LaRussa 15.00 40.00
SWM Willie Mays 150.00 250.00

2002 Sweet Spot

COMP.SET w/o SP's (90) 8.00 20.00
COMMON CARD (1-90) .15 .40
COMMON CARD (91-130) 1.50 4.00
91-130 RANDOM INSERTS IN PACKS
91-130 PRINT RUN 1300 SERIAL #'d SETS
COMMON TIER 1 AU (131-145) 6.00 15.00
COMMON TIER 2 AU (131-145) 10.00 25.00
COMMON CARD (146-175) 4.00 10.00
146-175 STATED ODDS 1:24
GAME FACE FEATURES GRAY PORTRAITS
MCGWIRE AU EXCH.RANDOM IN PACKS
MCGWIRE AU EXCH.DEADLINE 09/12/03
1 Troy Glaus .15 .40
2 Darin Erstad .15 .40
3 Tim Hudson .15 .40
4 Eric Chavez .15 .40
5 Barry Zito .15 .40
6 Miguel Tejada .15 .40
7 Carlos Delgado .15 .40
8 Eric Hinske .15 .40
9 Ben Grieve .15 .40
10 Jim Thome .25 .60
11 C.C. Sabathia .15 .40
12 Omar Vizquel .25 .60
13 Ichiro Suzuki .75 2.00
14 Edgar Martinez .25 .60
15 Bret Boone .15 .40
16 Freddy Garcia .15 .40
17 Tony Batista .15 .40
18 Geronimo Gil .15 .40
19 Alex Rodriguez .50 1.50
20 Rafael Palmeiro .25 .60
21 Ivan Rodriguez .25 .60
22 Hank Blalock .25 .60
23 Juan Gonzalez .15 .40
24 Nomar Garciaparra .60 1.50
25 Pedro Martinez .25 .60
26 Manny Ramirez .25 .60
27 Mike Sweeney .15 .40
28 Carlos Beltran .15 .40
29 Dmitri Young .15 .40
30 Torii Hunter .15 .40
31 Eric Milton .15 .40
32 Corey Koskie .15 .40
33 Frank Thomas .40 1.00
34 Mark Buehrle .15 .40
35 Magglio Ordonez .15 .40
36 Roger Clemens .75 2.00
37 Derek Jeter 1.00 2.50
38 Jason Giambi .15 .40
39 Alfonso Soriano .15 .40
40 Bernie Williams .25 .60
41 Jeff Bagwell .25 .60
42 Roy Oswalt .15 .40
43 Lance Berkman .15 .40
44 Greg Maddux .60 1.50
45 Chipper Jones .40 1.00
46 Gary Sheffield .15 .40
47 Andruw Jones .25 .60
48 Richie Sexson .15 .40
49 Ben Sheets .15 .40
50 Albert Pujols .75 2.00
51 Matt Morris .15 .40
52 J.D. Drew .15 .40
53 Sammy Sosa .40 1.00
54 Kerry Wood .15 .40
55 Mark Prior .25 .60
56 Moises Alou .15 .40
57 Corey Patterson .15 .40
58 Randy Johnson .40 1.00
59 Luis Gonzalez .15 .40
60 Curt Schilling .15 .40
61 Shawn Green .15 .40
62 Kevin Brown .15 .40
63 Paul Lo Duca .15 .40
64 Adrian Beltre .15 .40
65 Vladimir Guerrero .40 1.00
66 Jose Vidro .15 .40
67 Javier Vazquez .15 .40
68 Barry Bonds 1.00 2.50
69 Jeff Kent .15 .40
70 Rich Aurilia .15 .40
71 Mike Lowell .15 .40
72 Josh Beckett .15 .40
73 Brad Penny .15 .40
74 Roberto Alomar .25 .60
75 Mike Piazza .60 1.50
76 Jeromy Burnitz .15 .40
77 Mo Vaughn .15 .40
78 Phil Nevin .15 .40
79 Sean Burroughs .15 .40
80 Jeremy Giambi .15 .40
81 Bobby Abreu .15 .40
82 Jimmy Rollins .15 .40
83 Pat Burrell .15 .40
84 Brian Giles .15 .40
85 Aramis Ramirez .15 .40
86 Ken Griffey Jr. .75 2.00
87 Adam Dunn .15 .40
88 Austin Kearns .15 .40
89 Todd Helton .25 .60
90 Larry Walker .15 .40
91 Earl Snyder SB RC 1.50 4.00
92 Jorge Padilla SB RC 1.50 4.00
93 Felix Escalona SB RC 1.50 4.00
94 John Foster SB RC 1.50 4.00
95 Brandon Puffer SB RC 1.50 4.00
96 Steve Bechler SB RC 1.50 4.00
97 Hansel Izquierdo SB RC 1.50 4.00
98 Chris Baker SB RC 1.50 4.00
99 Jeremy Ward SB RC 1.50 4.00
100 Kevin Frederick SB RC 1.50 4.00
101 Josh Hancock SB RC 2.00 5.00
102 Allan Simpson SB RC 1.50 4.00
103 Mitch Wylie SB RC 1.50 4.00
104 Mark Corey SB RC 1.50 4.00
105 Victor Alvarez SB RC 1.50 4.00
106 Todd Donovan SB RC 1.50 4.00
107 Nelson Castro SB RC 1.50 4.00
108 Chris Booker SB RC 1.50 4.00
109 Corey Thurman SB RC 1.50 4.00
110 Kirk Saarloos SB RC 1.50 4.00
111 Michael Crudale SB RC 1.50 4.00
112 Jason Simontacchi SB RC 1.50 4.00
113 Ron Calloway SB RC 1.50 4.00
114 Brandon Backe SB RC 2.00 5.00
115 Tom Shearn SB RC 1.50 4.00
116 Oliver Perez SB RC 2.00 5.00
117 Kyle Kane SB RC 1.50 4.00
118 Francis Beltran SB RC 1.50 4.00
119 So Taguchi SB RC 2.00 5.00
120 Doug Devore SB RC 1.50 4.00
121 Juan Brito SB RC 1.50 4.00
122 Cliff Bartosh SB RC 1.50 4.00
123 Eric Junge SB RC 1.50 4.00
124 Joe Orloski SB RC 1.50 4.00
125 Scotty Layfield SB RC 1.50 4.00
126 Jorge Sosa SB RC 2.00 5.00
127 Satoru Komiyama SB RC 1.50 4.00
128 Edwin Almonte SB RC 1.50 4.00
129 Takahito Nomura SB RC 1.50 4.00
130 John Ennis SB RC 1.50 4.00
131 Kazuhisa Ishii T2 AU RC 12.00 30.00
132 Ben Howard T2 AU RC 10.00 25.00
133 Aaron Cook T1 AU RC 8.00 20.00
134 Andy Machado T1 AU RC 6.00 15.00
135 Luis Ugueto T1 AU RC 6.00 15.00
136 Tyler Yates T1 AU RC 6.00 15.00
137 Rodrigo Rosario T1 AU RC 6.00 15.00
138 Jaime Cerda T1 AU RC 6.00 15.00
139 Luis Martinez T1 AU RC 6.00 15.00
140 Rene Reyes T1 AU RC 6.00 15.00
141 Eric Good T1 AU RC 6.00 15.00
142 Matt Thornton T2 AU RC 10.00 25.00
143 Steve Kent T1 AU RC 6.00 15.00
144 Jose Valverde T1 AU RC 6.00 15.00
145 Adrian Burnside T1 AU RC 6.00 15.00
146 Barry Bonds GF 10.00 25.00
147 Ken Griffey Jr. GF 8.00 20.00
148 Alex Rodriguez GF 5.00 12.00
149 Jason Giambi GF 1.50 4.00
150 Chipper Jones GF 4.00 10.00
151 Nomar Garciaparra GF 6.00 15.00
152 Mike Piazza GF 6.00 15.00
153 Sammy Sosa GF 4.00 10.00
154 Derek Jeter GF 10.00 25.00
155 Jeff Bagwell GF 4.00 10.00
156 Albert Pujols GF 6.00 15.00
157 Ichiro Suzuki GF 6.00 15.00
158 Randy Johnson GF 4.00 10.00
159 Frank Thomas GF 4.00 10.00
160 Greg Maddux GF 6.00 15.00
161 Jim Thome GF 4.00 10.00
162 Scott Rolen GF 4.00 10.00
163 Shawn Green GF 4.00 10.00
164 Vladimir Guerrero GF 4.00 10.00
165 Troy Glaus GF 4.00 10.00
166 Carlos Delgado GF 4.00 10.00
167 Luis Gonzalez GF 4.00 10.00
168 Roger Clemens GF 8.00 20.00
169 Todd Helton GF 4.00 10.00
170 Eric Chavez GF 4.00 10.00
171 Rafael Palmeiro GF 4.00 10.00
172 Pedro Martinez GF 4.00 10.00
173 Lance Berkman GF 4.00 10.00
174 Josh Beckett GF 4.00 10.00
175 Sean Burroughs GF 4.00 10.00

2002 Sweet Spot Game Face Blue Portraits

*GAME FACE: .6X TO 1.5X BASIC CARDS
RANDOM INSERTS IN PACKS
STATED PRINT RUN 100 SERIAL #'d SETS

2002 Sweet Spot Legendary Signatures

STATED ODDS 1:72
STATED PRINT RUNS LISTED BELOW
PRINT RUN INFO PROVIDED BY UD
AK Al Kaline/835 * 15.00 40.00
AT Alan Trammell/843 * 6.00 15.00
BP Boog Powell/944 * 6.00 15.00
BR Brooks Robinson 12.50 30.00
CR Cal Ripken/194 * 25.00 60.00
FJ Ferguson Jenkins/857 * 6.00 15.00
FL Fred Lynn/853 * 6.00 15.00
GP Gaylord Perry/921 * 6.00 15.00
JD Joe DiMaggio/50 * 500.00 800.00
KH Keith Hernandez/906 * 6.00 15.00
LA Luis Aparicio/485 * 12.00 30.00
MM Mark McGwire/90 * 150.00 300.00
PM Paul Molitor/852 * 6.00 15.00
RF Rollie Fingers/866 * 6.00 15.00
SG Steve Garvey/871 * 8.00 20.00
SK Sandy Koufax/485 * 175.00 300.00

2002 Sweet Spot Signatures

STATED ODDS 1:72
AD Adam Dunn/291 6.00 15.00
AJ Andruw Jones/291 6.00 15.00
AR Alex Rodriguez/291 40.00 100.00
BB Barry Bonds/380 50.00 120.00
BG Brian Giles/291 6.00 15.00
BZ Barry Zito/291 6.00 15.00
CD Carlos Delgado/291 6.00 15.00
FG Freddy Garcia/145 6.00 15.00
FT Frank Thomas/291 40.00 80.00
HB Hank Blalock/291 6.00 15.00
IS Ichiro Suzuki/145 150.00 300.00
JB Jeromy Burnitz/291 6.00 15.00
JG Jason Giambi/291 6.00 15.00
JT Jim Thome/291 10.00 25.00
KG Ken Griffey Jr./291 30.00 80.00
LB Lance Berkman/291 10.00 25.00
LG Luis Gonzalez/291 10.00 25.00
MPR Mark Prior/291 6.00 15.00
MS Mike Sweeney/291 6.00 15.00
RC Roger Clemens/194 25.00 60.00
RO Roy Oswalt/291 6.00 15.00
SB Sean Burroughs/291 6.00 15.00
SR Scott Rolen/291 6.00 15.00
SS Sammy Sosa/145 20.00 50.00
TG Tom Glavine/291 20.00 50.00

2002 Sweet Spot Swatches

STATED ODDS 1:12
JBE Josh Beckett 4.00 10.00
SAR Alex Rodriguez 6.00 15.00
SBG Brian Giles 4.00 10.00
SBW Bernie Williams 4.00 10.00
SCJ Chipper Jones 4.00 10.00
SDE Darin Erstad 4.00 10.00
SEC Eric Chavez 4.00 10.00
SFT Frank Thomas 4.00 10.00
SGM Greg Maddux 6.00 15.00
SIR Ivan Rodriguez 4.00 10.00
SIS Ichiro Suzuki 20.00 50.00
SJE Jim Edmonds 4.00 10.00
SKG Ken Griffey Jr. 6.00 15.00
SKI Kazuhisa Ishii 4.00 10.00
SLG Luis Gonzalez 4.00 10.00
SMP Mike Piazza 6.00 15.00
SOV Omar Vizquel 4.00 10.00
SPM Pedro Martinez 4.00 10.00
SSB Sean Burroughs 4.00 10.00
SSG Shawn Green 4.00 10.00
SSR Scott Rolen 4.00 10.00
SSS Sammy Sosa 4.00 10.00
SJBS Jeff Bagwell 4.00 10.00
SJGI Jason Giambi 4.00 10.00
SJGO Juan Gonzalez 4.00 10.00

2002 Sweet Spot USA Jerseys

STATED ODDS 1:12
USAAE Adam Everett 3.00 8.00
USAAK Adam Kennedy 3.00 8.00
USABA Brent Abernathy 3.00 8.00
USADB Dewon Brazelton 3.00 8.00
USADG Danny Graves 3.00 8.00
USADM Doug Mientkiewicz 3.00 8.00
USAEM Eric Munson 3.00 8.00
USAJG Jake Gautreau 3.00 8.00
USAJK Josh Karp 3.00 8.00
USAJM Joe Mauer 12.00 30.00
USAJR Jon Rauch 3.00 8.00
USAJW Justin Wayne 3.00 8.00
USAMP Mark Prior 4.00 10.00
USAMT Mark Teixeira 4.00 10.00
USARO Roy Oswalt 3.00 8.00
USATB Tagg Bozied 4.00 10.00
USAXN Xavier Nady 3.00 8.00

2003 Sweet Spot

COMP.SET w/o SP's (100) 8.00 20.00
COMP.SET w/SP's (130) 60.00 120.00
COMMON CARD (1-130) .20 .50
COMMON SP (1-130) .60 1.50
SP 1-130 STATED ODDS 1:4
SP's: 9-13/18-23/78-85/101-105/111-116
COMMON CARD (131-190) .75 2.00
131-190 STATED ODDS 1:3
131-190 PRINT RUN 2003 SERIAL #'d SETS
COMMON P1 (191-232) 2.00 5.00
P1 191-232 PRINT RUN 500 SERIAL #'d SETS
COMMON P2-P3 (191-232) .75 2.00
P2 191-232 PRINT RUN 1200 SERIAL #'d SETS
P3 191-232 PRINT RUN 1430 SERIAL #'d SETS
191-232 STATED ODDS 1:9
CARD 217 DOES NOT EXIST
1 Darin Erstad .20 .50
2 Garret Anderson .20 .50
3 Tim Salmon .20 .50
4 Troy Glaus .20 .50
5 Luis Gonzalez .20 .50
6 Randy Johnson .50 1.25
7 Curt Schilling .30 .75
8 Lyle Overbay .20 .50
9 Andruw Jones SP .60 1.50
10 Gary Sheffield SP .60 1.50
11 Rafael Furcal SP .60 1.50
12 Greg Maddux SP 2.00 5.00
13 Chipper Jones SP 1.50 4.00
14 Tony Batista .20 .50
15 Rodrigo Lopez .20 .50
16 Jay Gibbons .20 .50
17 Jason Johnson .20 .50
18 Byung-Hyun Kim SP .60 1.50
19 Johnny Damon SP 1.00 2.50
20 Derek Lowe SP .60 1.50
21 Nomar Garciaparra SP 1.00 2.50
22 Pedro Martinez SP 1.00 2.50
23 Manny Ramirez SP 1.50 4.00
24 Mark Prior .30 .75
25 Kerry Wood .20 .50
26 Corey Patterson .20 .50
27 Sammy Sosa .50 1.25
28 Moises Alou .20 .50
29 Magglio Ordonez .30 .75
30 Frank Thomas .50 1.25
31 Paul Konerko .30 .75
32 Roberto Alomar .30 .75
33 Adam Dunn .30 .75
34 Austin Kearns .20 .50
35 Ryan Wagner RC .20 .50
36 Ken Griffey Jr. 1.00 2.50
37 Sean Casey .20 .50
38 Omar Vizquel .30 .75
39 C.C. Sabathia .30 .75
40 Jason Davis .20 .50
41 Travis Hafner .20 .50
42 Brandon Phillips .20 .50
43 Larry Walker .30 .75
44 Preston Wilson .20 .50
45 Jay Payton .20 .50
46 Todd Helton .30 .75
47 Carlos Pena .30 .75
48 Eric Munson .20 .50
49 Ivan Rodriguez .30 .75
50 Josh Beckett .20 .50
51 Alex Gonzalez .20 .50
52 Roy Oswalt .30 .75
53 Craig Biggio .30 .75
54 Jeff Bagwell .30 .75
55 Lance Berkman .30 .75
56 Mike Sweeney .20 .50
57 Carlos Beltran .30 .75
58 Brent Mayne .20 .50
59 Mike MacDougal .20 .50
60 Hideo Nomo .50 1.25
61 Dave Roberts .30 .75
62 Adrian Beltre .50 1.25
63 Shawn Green .20 .50
64 Kazuhisa Ishii .20 .50
65 Rickey Henderson .50 1.25
66 Richie Sexson .20 .50
67 Torii Hunter .20 .50
68 Jacque Jones .20 .50
69 Joe Mays .20 .50
70 Corey Koskie .20 .50
71 A.J. Pierzynski .20 .50
72 Jose Vidro .20 .50
73 Vladimir Guerrero .30 .75
74 Tom Glavine .30 .75
75 Mike Piazza .50 1.25
76 Jose Reyes .50 1.25

77 Jae Weong Seo .20 .50
78 Jorge Posada SP 1.00 2.50
79 Mike Mussina SP 1.00 2.50
80 Robin Ventura SP .60 1.50
81 Mariano Rivera SP 2.00 5.00
82 Roger Clemens SP 2.00 5.00
83 Jason Giambi SP .60 1.50
84 Bernie Williams SP 1.00 2.50
85 Alfonso Soriano SP 1.00 2.50
86 Derek Jeter 1.25 3.00
87 Miguel Tejada .30 .75
88 Eric Chavez .20 .50
89 Tim Hudson .30 .75
90 Barry Zito .30 .75
91 Mark Mulder .20 .50
92 Erubiel Durazo .20 .50
93 Pat Burrell .20 .50
94 Jim Thome .30 .75
95 Bobby Abreu .20 .50
96 Brian Giles .20 .50
97 Reggie Sanders .20 .50
98 Jose Hernandez .20 .50
99 Ryan Klesko .20 .50
100 Sean Burroughs .20 .50
101 Edgardo Alfonzo SP .60 1.50
102 Rich Aurilia SP .60 1.50
103 Jose Cruz Jr. SP .60 1.50
104 Barry Bonds SP 2.50 6.00
105 Andres Galarraga SP 1.00 2.50
106 Mike Cameron .20 .50
107 Kazuhiro Sasaki .20 .50
108 Bret Boone .20 .50
109 Ichiro Suzuki .60 1.50
110 John Olerud .20 .50
111 J.D. Drew SP .60 1.50
112 Jim Edmonds SP 1.00 2.50
113 Scott Rolen SP 1.00 2.50
114 Matt Morris SP .60 1.50
115 Tino Martinez SP .60 1.50
116 Albert Pujols SP 2.00 5.00
117 Jared Sandberg .20 .50
118 Carl Crawford .30 .75
119 Rafael Palmeiro .30 .75
120 Hank Blalock .20 .50
121 Alex Rodriguez SP 2.00 5.00
122 Kevin Mench .20 .50
123 Juan Gonzalez .20 .50
124 Mark Teixeira .30 .75
125 Shannon Stewart .20 .50
126 Vernon Wells .20 .50
127 Josh Phelps .20 .50
128 Eric Hinske .20 .50
129 Orlando Hudson .20 .50
130 Carlos Delgado .20 .50
131 Jason Shiell SB RC .75 2.00
132 Kevin Tolar SB RC .75 2.00
133 Nathan Bland SB RC .75 2.00
134 Brent Hoard SB RC .75 2.00
135 Jon Pridie SB RC .75 2.00
136 Mike Ryan SB RC .75 2.00
137 Francisco Rosario SB RC .75 2.00
138 Runelvys Hernandez SB .75 2.00
139 Guillermo Quiroz SB RC .75 2.00
140 Chin-Hui Tsao SB .75 2.00
141 Rett Johnson SB RC .75 2.00
142 Colin Porter SB RC .75 2.00
143 Jose Castillo SB .75 2.00
144 Chris Waters SB RC .75 2.00
145 Jeremy Guthrie SB .75 2.00
146 Pedro Liriano SB .75 2.00
147 Joe Borowski SB .75 2.00
148 Felix Sanchez SB RC .75 2.00
149 Todd Wellemeyer SB RC .75 2.00
150 Gerald Laird SB .75 2.00
151 Brandon Webb SB RC 2.50 6.00
152 Tommy Whiteman SB .75 2.00
153 Carlos Rivera SB .75 2.00
154 Rick Roberts SB RC .75 2.00
155 Terrmel Sledge SB RC .75 2.00
156 Jeff Duncan SB RC .75 2.00
157 Craig Brazell SB RC .75 2.00
158 Bernie Castro SB RC .75 2.00
159 Cory Stewart SB RC .75 2.00
160 Brandon Villafuerte SB .75 2.00
161 Tommy Phelps SB .75 2.00
162 Josh Hall SB RC .75 2.00
163 Ryan Cameron SB RC .75 2.00
164 Garret Atkins SB .75 2.00
165 Brian Stokes SB RC .75 2.00
166 Rafael Betancourt SB RC .75 2.00
167 Jaime Cerda SB .75 2.00
168 D.J. Carrasco SB RC .75 2.00
169 Ian Ferguson SB RC .75 2.00
170 Jorge Cordova SB RC .75 2.00
171 Eric Munson SB .75 2.00
172 Nook Logan SB RC .75 2.00
173 Jeremy Bonderman SB RC 3.00 8.00
174 Kyle Snyder SB .75 2.00
175 Rich Harden SB 1.25 3.00
176 Kevin Ohme SB RC .75 2.00
177 Roger Deago SB RC .75 2.00
178 Marlon Byrd SB .75 2.00
179 Dontrelle Willis SB .75 2.00
180 Bobby Hill SB .75 2.00
181 Jesse Foppert SB .75 2.00
182 Andrew Good SB .75 2.00
183 Chase Utley SB 1.25 3.00
184 Bo Hart SB RC .75 2.00
185 Dan Haren SB RC 4.00 10.00
186 Tim Olson SB RC .75 2.00
187 Joe Thurston SB .75 2.00
188 Jason Anderson SB .75 2.00
189 Jason Gilfillan SB RC .75 2.00
190 Rickie Weeks SB RC 2.50 6.00
191 Hideki Matsui SB P1 RC 10.00 25.00
192 Jose Contreras SB P3 RC 2.00 5.00
193 Willie Eyre SB P3 RC .75 2.00
194 Matt Bruback SB P3 RC .75 2.00
195 Heath Bell SB P3 RC 1.25 3.00
196 Lew Ford SB P3 RC .75 2.00
197 Jeremy Griffiths SB P3 RC .75 2.00
198 Oscar Villarreal SB P1 RC 2.00 5.00
199 Francisco Cruceta SB P3 RC .75 2.00
200 Fern Cabrera SB P3 RC .75 2.00
201 Jhonny Peralta SB P3 .75 2.00
202 Shane Bazzell SB P3 RC .75 2.00
203 Bobby Madritsch SB P1 RC 2.00 5.00
204 Phil Seibel SB P3 RC .75 2.00
205 Josh Willingham SB P3 RC 2.50 6.00
206 Rob Hammock SB P1 RC 2.00 5.00
207 Alejandro Machado SB P3 RC .75 2.00
208 David Sanders SB P3 RC .75 2.00
209 Mike Neu SB P1 RC 2.00 5.00
210 Andrew Brown SB P3 RC .75 2.00
211 Nate Robertson SB P3 RC 2.50 6.00
212 Miguel Ojeda SB P3 RC .75 2.00
213 Beau Kemp SB P3 RC .75 2.00
214 Aaron Looper SB P3 RC .75 2.00
215 Alfredo Gonzalez SB P3 RC .75 2.00
216 Rich Fischer SB P1 RC 2.00 5.00
218 Jeremy Wedel SB P3 RC .75 2.00
219 Prentice Redman SB P3 RC .75 2.00
220 Michel Hernandez SB P3 RC .75 2.00
221 Rocco Baldelli SB P1 2.00 5.00
222 Luis Ayala SB P3 RC .75 2.00
223 Arnaldo Munoz SB P3 RC .75 2.00
224 Wilfredo Ledezma SB P3 RC .75 2.00
225 Chris Capuano SB P3 RC .75 2.00
226 Aquilino Lopez SB P3 RC .75 2.00
227 Joe Valentine SB P1 RC 2.00 5.00
228 Matt Kata SB P2 RC .75 2.00
229 Diegomar Markwell SB P2 RC .75 2.00
230 Clint Barmes SB P2 RC 2.00 5.00
231 Mike Nicolas SB P1 RC 2.00 5.00
232 Jon Leicester SB P2 RC .75 2.00

2003 Sweet Spot Sweet Beginnings 75

*SB 75: .5X TO 1.2X BASIC P1
*SB 75 MATSUI: .75X TO 1.5X BASIC MATSUI
*SB 75: 1.25X TO 3X BASIC P2-P3
RANDOM INSERTS IN PACKS
STATED PRINT RUN 75 SERIAL #'d SETS
CARDS ARE NOT GAME-USED MATERIAL

2003 Sweet Spot Sweet Beginnings Game Used 25

RANDOM INSERTS IN PACKS
STATED PRINT RUN 25 SERIAL #'d SETS
NO PRICING DUE TO SCARCITY

2003 Sweet Spot Instant Win Redemptions

ONE OR MORE CARDS PER CASE
PRINT RUNS B/WN 1-350 COPIES PER
PRICES BELOW REFER ONLY TO TRADE CARD
PRICES BELOW DO NOT REFER TO LIVE ITEM
NO PRICING ON QTY OF 28 OR LESS
EXCHANGE DEADLINE 09/16/06

2003 Sweet Spot Patches

*PATCH 75: .75X TO 2X BASIC
PATCH 75 PRINT RUN 75 SERIAL #'d SETS
CUMULATIVE PATCHES ODDS 1:8
CARDS ARE NOT GAME-USED MATERIAL
AD1 Adam Dunn 1.50 4.00
AJ1 Andruw Jones 1.00 2.50
AP1 Albert Pujols 3.00 8.00
AR1 Alex Rodriguez 3.00 8.00
AS1 Alfonso Soriano 1.50 4.00
BB1 Barry Bonds 4.00 10.00
BW1 Bernie Williams 1.50 4.00
BZ1 Barry Zito 1.50 4.00
CD1 Carlos Delgado 1.00 2.50
CJ1 Chipper Jones 2.50 6.00
CP1 Corey Patterson 1.00 2.50
CS1 Curt Schilling 1.50 4.00
DE1 Darin Erstad 1.00 2.50
DJ1 Derek Jeter 6.00 15.00
GM1 Greg Maddux 3.00 8.00
GS1 Gary Sheffield 1.00 2.50
HN1 Hideo Nomo 2.50 6.00
IS1 Ichiro Suzuki 3.00 8.00
JB1 Jeff Bagwell 1.50 4.00
JE1 Jim Edmonds 1.50 4.00
JG1 Jason Giambi 1.00 2.50
JK1 Jeff Kent 1.00 2.50
JT1 Jim Thome 1.50 4.00
KG1 Ken Griffey Jr. 5.00 12.00
KI1 Kazuhisa Ishii 1.00 2.50
LB1 Lance Berkman 1.50 4.00
LG1 Luis Gonzalez 1.00 2.50
MA1 Mark Prior 1.50 4.00
MO1 Magglio Ordonez 1.50 4.00
MP1 Mike Piazza 2.50 6.00
MT1 Miguel Tejada 1.50 4.00
NG1 Nomar Garciaparra 1.50 4.00
PB1 Pat Burrell 1.00 2.50
PM1 Pedro Martinez 1.50 4.00
RC1 Roger Clemens 3.00 8.00
RJ1 Randy Johnson 2.50 6.00
SG1 Shawn Green 1.00 2.50
SS1 Sammy Sosa 2.50 6.00
TG1 Troy Glaus 1.00 2.50
TH1 Torii Hunter 1.00 2.50
TO1 Tom Glavine 1.50 4.00
VG1 Vladimir Guerrero 1.50 4.00

2003 Sweet Spot Signatures Black Ink

CUMULATIVE AUTO ODDS 1:24
SP PRINT RUNS PROVIDED BY UPPER DECK
SP'S ARE NOT SERIAL-NUMBERED
ADAU Adam Dunn 6.00 15.00
AKAU Austin Kearns 6.00 15.00
BHAU Bo Hart 6.00 15.00
BPAU Brandon Phillips 10.00 25.00
BWAU Brandon Webb 6.00 15.00
CRAU Cal Ripken SP/122 60.00 150.00
CSAU Curt Schilling 10.00 25.00
DHAU Drew Henson 6.00 15.00
DWAU Dontrelle Willis 6.00 15.00
GLAU Tom Glavine 10.00 25.00
GSAU Gary Sheffield 6.00 15.00
HAAU Travis Hafner 6.00 15.00
HBAU Hank Blalock 10.00 25.00
HMAU Hideki Matsui SP/147 175.00 300.00
JCAU Jose Contreras 6.00 15.00
JGAU Jason Giambi SP 6.00 15.00
JRAU Jose Reyes 10.00 25.00
JTAU Jim Thome 25.00 60.00
JWAU Jerome Williams 6.00 15.00
KIAU Kazuhisa Ishii SP 20.00 50.00
LOAU Lyle Overbay 6.00 15.00
MPAU Mark Prior 8.00 20.00
MTAU Mark Teixeira 12.50 30.00
NGAU Nomar Garciaparra 15.00 40.00
NRAU Nolan Ryan SP 50.00 100.00
PBAU Pat Burrell 10.00 25.00
RCAU Roger Clemens SP/73 40.00 80.00
ROAU Roy Oswalt 10.00 25.00
THAU Todd Helton SP/45 20.00 50.00
TRAU Troy Glaus 6.00 15.00
TSAU Tim Salmon 6.00 15.00
VGAU Vladimir Guerrero 12.50 30.00
KGJAU Ken Griffey Jr. 40.00 80.00
KGSAU Ken Griffey Sr. 6.00 15.00

2003 Sweet Spot Signatures Blue Ink

CUMULATIVE AUTO ODDS 1:24
STATED PRINT RUN 40 SERIAL #'d SETS
T.GWYNN CARD NOT SERIAL-NUMBERED
T.GWYNN AU IN FAR GREATER SUPPLY
M.MANTLE PRINT RUN 7 SERIAL #'d CARDS
T.WILLIAMS PRINT RUN 9 SERIAL #'d CARDS
NO M.MANTLE PRICING DUE TO SCARCITY
NO T.WILLIAMS PRICING DUE TO SCARCITY
ADAU Adam Dunn 10.00 25.00
AKAU Austin Kearns 10.00 25.00
BHAU Bo Hart 10.00 25.00
BPAU Brandon Phillips 10.00 25.00
BWAU Brandon Webb 15.00 40.00
CRAU Cal Ripken 50.00 100.00
CSAU Curt Schilling 40.00 80.00
DHAU Drew Henson 10.00 25.00
DWAU Dontrelle Willis 15.00 40.00
GLAU Tom Glavine 40.00 80.00
GSAU Gary Sheffield 10.00 25.00
HAAU Travis Hafner 15.00 40.00
HBAU Hank Blalock 15.00 40.00
HMAU Hideki Matsui 250.00 400.00
ISAU Ichiro Suzuki 200.00 400.00
JCAU Jose Contreras 20.00 50.00
JGAU Jason Giambi 15.00 40.00
JRAU Jose Reyes 15.00 40.00
JTAU Jim Thome 40.00 100.00
JWAU Jerome Williams 10.00 25.00
KIAU Kazuhisa Ishii 10.00 25.00
LOAU Lyle Overbay 10.00 25.00
MPAU Mark Prior 20.00 50.00
MTAU Mark Teixeira 10.00 25.00
NGAU Nomar Garciaparra 15.00 40.00
NRAU Nolan Ryan 60.00 120.00
PBAU Pat Burrell 15.00 40.00
RCAU Roger Clemens 125.00 200.00
ROAU Roy Oswalt 15.00 40.00
RWAU Rickie Weeks/100 10.00 25.00
SSAU Sammy Sosa 60.00 120.00
TGAU Tony Gwynn NNO 20.00 50.00
THAU Todd Helton 30.00 60.00
TRAU Troy Glaus 30.00 60.00
TSAU Tim Salmon 15.00 40.00
VGAU Vladimir Guerrero 12.50 30.00
KGJAU Ken Griffey Jr. 60.00 120.00
KGSAU Ken Griffey Sr. 15.00 40.00

2003 Sweet Spot Signatures Red Ink

CUMULATIVE AUTO ODDS 1:24
PRINT RUNS B/WN 9-35 COPIES PER
GWYNN CARD NOT SERIAL-NUMBERED
NO PRICING ON QTY OF 10 OR LESS

2003 Sweet Spot Signatures Barrel

CUMULATIVE AUTO ODDS 1:24
PRINT RUNS B/WN 49-445 COPIES PER
CARDS ARE NOT GAME-USED MATERIAL
AUAD Adam Dunn/345 6.00 15.00
AUCR Cal Ripken/149 60.00 120.00
AUHB Hank Blalock/420 6.00 15.00
AUHM Hideki Matsui/124 200.00 400.00
AUJT Jim Thome/345 30.00 60.00
AUKG Ken Griffey Jr./295 50.00 100.00
AUNR Nolan Ryan/445 30.00 60.00
AUPB Pat Burrell/345 6.00 15.00
AURC Roger Clemens/49 150.00 250.00
AUTG Tom Glavine/345 12.50 30.00
AUTR Troy Glaus/345 6.00 15.00

2003 Sweet Spot Swatches

SP INFO PROVIDED BY UPPER DECK
SP'S ARE NOT SERIAL-NUMBERED
*SWATCH 75: .6X TO 1.5X BASIC
*SWATCH 75: .5X TO 1.2X BASIC SP
*SWATCH 75: .4X TO 1X BASIC SP p/r 75-100
*SWATCH 75 MATSUI: .5X TO 1.2X BASIC
SWATCH 75 PRINT RUN 75 #'d SETS
CUMULATIVE SWATCHES ODDS 1:20
AJ Andruw Jones 3.00 8.00
AK Austin Kearns 2.00 5.00
AP Albert Pujols 8.00 20.00
AR Alex Rodriguez 4.00 10.00
AS Alfonso Soriano SP/81 4.00 10.00
BW Bernie Williams SP 6.00 15.00
BZ Barry Zito SP 4.00 10.00
CJ Chipper Jones 3.00 8.00
CS Curt Schilling 2.00 5.00
FT Frank Thomas 3.00 8.00
GM Greg Maddux 4.00 10.00
GS Gary Sheffield SP 4.00 10.00
HM Hideki Matsui SP/150 15.00 40.00
IS Ichiro Suzuki 10.00 25.00
JG Jason Giambi 2.00 5.00
JT Jim Thome 3.00 8.00
KG Ken Griffey Jr. 6.00 15.00
LG Luis Gonzalez 2.00 5.00
MM Mantle Pants UER SP/100 30.00 80.00
MP Mike Piazza 4.00 10.00
MP Mark Prior SP 6.00 15.00
MT Miguel Tejada 2.00 5.00
PB Pat Burrell 2.00 5.00
RA Roberto Alomar SP 6.00 15.00
RC Roger Clemens 4.00 10.00
RJ Randy Johnson SP 6.00 15.00
RO Roy Oswalt 2.00 5.00
SS Sammy Sosa 3.00 8.00
TG Troy Glaus 2.00 5.00
TG Tom Glavine SP 6.00 15.00
TH Torii Hunter 2.00 5.00
TW Ted Williams Pants SP/100 15.00 40.00
VG Vladimir Guerrero 3.00 8.00

2004 Sweet Spot

COMP.SET w/o SP's (90) 8.00 20.00
COMMON CARD (1-90) .20 .50
COMMON (91-170/261-262) .60 1.50
91-170/261-262 STATED ODDS 1:12
91-170/261-262 PRINT RUN 799 #'d SETS
COMMON CARD (171-230) .75 2.00
171-230 PRINT RUN 399 SERIAL #'d SETS
COMMON CARD (231-250) .75 2.00
231-250 PRINT RUN 299 SERIAL #'d SETS
COMMON CARD (251-260) 1.00 2.50
251-260 PRINT RUN 199 SERIAL #'d SETS
171-260/Ltd 10/W99 OVERALL ODDS 1:12
OVERALL PLATES ODDS 1:360 HOBBY
PLATES PRINT RUN 1 SET PER COLOR
BLACK-CYAN-MAGENTA-YELLOW ISSUED
NO PLATES PRICING DUE TO SACRCITY
1 Albert Pujols .60 1.50
2 Alex Rodriguez .60 1.50
3 Alfonso Soriano .30 .75
4 Andruw Jones .20 .50
5 Andy Pettitte .30 .75
6 Aubrey Huff .20 .50
7 Austin Kearns .20 .50
8 Barry Zito .30 .75
9 Bobby Abreu .20 .50
10 Brandon Webb .20 .50
11 Bret Boone .20 .50
12 Brian Giles .20 .50
13 C.C. Sabathia .30 .75
14 Carlos Beltran .30 .75
15 Carlos Delgado .20 .50
16 Chipper Jones .50 1.25
17 Cliff Floyd .20 .50
18 Curt Schilling .30 .75
19 Delmon Young .30 .75
20 Derek Jeter 1.25 3.00
21 Dontrelle Willis .20 .50
22 Edgar Martinez .30 .75
23 Edgar Renteria .20 .50
24 Eric Chavez .20 .50
25 Eric Gagne .20 .50
26 Frank Thomas .50 1.25
27 Garret Anderson .20 .50
28 Gary Sheffield .20 .50
29 Geoff Jenkins .20 .50
30 Greg Maddux .60 1.50
31 Hank Blalock .20 .50
32 Hideo Nomo .50 1.25
33 Ichiro Suzuki .60 1.50
34 Ivan Rodriguez .30 .75
35 Jacque Jones .20 .50
36 Jason Giambi .20 .50
37 Jason Schmidt .20 .50
38 Javier Vazquez .20 .50
39 Javy Lopez .20 .50
40 Jeff Bagwell .30 .75
41 Jim Edmonds .30 .75
42 Jim Thome .30 .75
43 Joe Mauer .40 1.00
44 John Smoltz .50 1.25
45 Jose Cruz Jr. .20 .50
46 Jose Reyes .30 .75
47 Jose Vidro .20 .50
48 Josh Beckett .20 .50
49 Ken Griffey Jr. 1.00 2.50
50 Kerry Wood .20 .50
51 Kevin Brown .20 .50
52 Larry Walker .30 .75
53 Magglio Ordonez .30 .75
54 Manny Ramirez .50 1.25
55 Mark Mulder .20 .50
56 Mark Prior .30 .75
57 Mark Teixeira .30 .75
58 Miguel Cabrera .50 1.25
59 Miguel Tejada .30 .75
60 Mike Lowell .20 .50
61 Mike Mussina .30 .75
62 Mike Piazza .50 1.25
63 Nomar Garciaparra .30 .75
64 Orlando Cabrera .20 .50
65 Pat Burrell .20 .50
66 Pedro Martinez .30 .75
67 Phil Nevin .20 .50
68 Preston Wilson .20 .50
69 Rafael Furcal .20 .50
70 Rafael Palmeiro .30 .75
71 Randy Johnson .50 1.25
72 Craig Wilson .20 .50
73 Rich Harden .20 .50
74 Richie Sexson .20 .50
75 Rickie Weeks .20 .50
76 Rocco Baldelli .20 .50
77 Roger Clemens .60 1.50
78 Roy Halladay .30 .75
79 Roy Oswalt .30 .75
80 Ryan Klesko .20 .50
81 Sammy Sosa .50 1.25
82 Scott Podsednik .20 .50
83 Scott Rolen .30 .75
84 Shawn Green .20 .50
85 Tim Hudson .30 .75
86 Todd Helton .30 .75
87 Torii Hunter .20 .50
88 Troy Glaus .20 .50
89 Vernon Wells .20 .50
90 Vladimir Guerrero .30 .75
91 Aarom Baldiris SB RC .75 2.00
92 Akinori Otsuka SB RC .75 2.00
93 Andres Blanco SB RC .75 2.00
94 Angel Chavez SB RC .75 2.00
95 Brian Dallimore SB RC .75 2.00
96 Carlos Hines SB RC .75 2.00
97 Carlos Vasquez SB RC .75 2.00
98 Casey Daigle SB RC .75 2.00
99 Chad Bentz SB RC .75 2.00
100 Chris Aguila SB RC .75 2.00
101 Chris Oxspring SB RC .75 2.00
102 Chris Saenz SB RC .75 2.00
103 Chris Shelton SB RC .75 2.00
104 Colby Miller SB RC .75 2.00
105 Dave Crouthers SB RC .75 2.00
106 David Aardsma SB RC .75 2.00
107 Dennis Sarfate SB RC .75 2.00
108 Donnie Kelly SB RC 1.25 3.00
109 Eddy Rodriguez SB RC .75 2.00
110 Eduardo Villacis SB RC .75 2.00
111 Edwin Moreno SB RC .75 2.00
112 Enemencio Pacheco SB RC .75 2.00
113 Fernando Nieve SB RC .75 2.00
114 Franklyn Gracesqui SB RC .75 2.00
115 Freddy Guzman SB RC .75 2.00
116 Greg Dobbs SB RC .75 2.00
117 Hector Gimenez SB RC .75 2.00
118 Ian Snell SB RC .75 2.00
119 Ivan Ochoa SB RC .75 2.00
120 Jake Woods SB RC .75 2.00
121 Jamie Brown SB RC .75 2.00
122 Jason Bartlett SB RC 2.50 6.00
123 Jason Frasor SB RC .75 2.00
124 Jeff Bennett SB RC .75 2.00
125 Jerome Gamble SB RC .75 2.00
126 Jerry Gil SB RC .75 2.00
127 Brandon Medders SB RC .75 2.00
128 Ryan Meaux SB RC .75 2.00
129 John Gall SB RC .75 2.00
130 Jorge Sequea SB RC .75 2.00
131 Jorge Vasquez SB RC .75 2.00
132 Jose Capellan SB RC .75 2.00
133 Josh Labandeira SB RC .75 2.00
134 Justin Germano SB RC .75 2.00
135 Justin Hampson SB RC .75 2.00
136 Justin Huisman SB RC .75 2.00
137 Justin Knoedler SB RC .75 2.00
138 Justin Leone SB RC .75 2.00
139 Kazuhito Tadano SB RC .75 2.00
140 Kazuo Matsui SB RC 1.25 3.00
141 Kevin Cave SB RC .75 2.00
142 Lincoln Holdzkom SB RC .75 2.00
143 Lino Urdaneta SB RC .75 2.00
144 Luis A. Gonzalez SB RC .75 2.00
145 Mariano Gomez SB RC .75 2.00
146 Merkin Valdez SB RC .75 2.00
147 Michael Vento SB RC .75 2.00
148 Michael Wuertz SB RC .75 2.00
149 Mike Gosling SB RC .75 2.00
150 Mike Johnston SB RC .75 2.00
151 Mike Rouse SB RC .75 2.00
152 Nick Regilio SB RC .75 2.00
153 Onil Joseph SB RC .75 2.00
154 Orlando Rodriguez SB RC .75 2.00
155 Ramon Ramirez SB RC .75 2.00
156 Renyel Pinto SB RC .75 2.00
157 Roberto Novoa SB RC .75 2.00
158 Roman Colon SB RC .75 2.00
159 Ronald Belisario SB RC .75 2.00
160 Ronny Cedeno SB RC .75 2.00
161 Rusty Tucker SB RC .75 2.00
162 Ryan Wing SB RC .75 2.00
163 Scott Dohmann SB RC .75 2.00
164 Scott Proctor SB RC .75 2.00
165 Sean Henn SB RC .75 2.00
166 Shawn Camp SB RC .75 2.00
167 Shawn Hill SB RC .75 2.00
168 Shingo Takatsu SB RC .75 2.00
169 Tim Hamulack SB RC .75 2.00
170 William Bergolla SB RC .75 2.00
171 Adam Dunn SF 1.25 3.00
172 Albert Pujols SF 2.50 6.00
173 Alex Rodriguez SF 2.50 6.00
174 Alfonso Soriano SF 1.25 3.00
175 Andruw Jones SF .75 2.00
176 Bret Boone SF .75 2.00
177 Brian Giles SF .75 2.00
178 Carlos Delgado SF .75 2.00
179 Derrek Lee SF .75 2.00
180 Eric Chavez SF .75 2.00
181 Frank Thomas SF 2.00 5.00
182 Garret Anderson SF .75 2.00
183 Gary Sheffield SF .75 2.00
184 Hank Blalock SF .75 2.00
185 Jason Giambi SF .75 2.00
186 Javy Lopez SF .75 2.00
187 Jeff Bagwell SF 1.25 3.00
188 Jim Edmonds SF 1.25 3.00
189 Jim Thome SF 1.25 3.00
190 Ken Griffey Jr. SF 4.00 10.00
191 Lance Berkman SF 1.25 3.00
192 Magglio Ordonez SF 1.25 3.00
193 Manny Ramirez SF 2.00 5.00
194 Mike Lowell SF .75 2.00
195 Mike Piazza SF 2.00 5.00
196 Preston Wilson SF .75 2.00
197 Rafael Palmeiro SF 1.25 3.00
198 Richie Sexson SF .75 2.00
199 Sammy Sosa SF 2.00 5.00
200 Scott Rolen SF 1.25 3.00
201 Shawn Green SF .75 2.00
202 Todd Helton SF 1.25 3.00
203 Troy Glaus SF .75 2.00
204 Vernon Wells SF .75 2.00
205 Vladimir Guerrero SF 1.25 3.00
206 G.Anderson 1.25 3.00
V.Guerrero SL
207 L.Gonzalez .75 2.00
R.Sexson SL
208 A.Jones 2.00 5.00
C.Jones SL
209 J.Lopez 1.25 3.00
M.Tejada SL
210 M.Ramirez 2.00 5.00
D.Ortiz SL
211 D.Lee 2.00 5.00
S.Sosa SL
212 F.Thomas 2.00 5.00
M.Ordonez SL
213 A.Kearns 4.00 10.00
K.Griffey Jr. SL
214 P.Wilson 1.25 3.00
T.Helton SL
215 D.Young 1.25 3.00
I.Rodriguez SL
216 M.Cabrera 2.00 5.00
M.Lowell SL
217 J.Bagwell 1.25 3.00
L.Berkman SL
218 L.Overbay .75 2.00
G.Jenkins SL
219 A.Beltre 2.00 5.00
S.Green SL
220 J.Jones .75 2.00
T.Hunter SL
221 J.Vidro .75 2.00
N.Johnson SL
222 K.Matsui 2.00 5.00
M.Piazza SL
223 A.Rodriguez 2.50 6.00
J.Giambi SL
224 E.Chavez .75 2.00
J.Dye SL
225 J.Thome 1.25 3.00
P.Burrell SL
226 B.Giles .75 2.00
P.Nevin SL
227 B.Boone 2.50 6.00
I.Suzuki SL
228 A.Pujols 2.50 6.00
S.Rolen SL
229 H.Blalock 1.25 3.00
M.Teixeira SL
230 C.Delgado .75 2.00
V.Wells SL
231 Albert Pujols PD 2.50 6.00
232 Alex Rodriguez PD 2.50 6.00
233 Chipper Jones PD 2.00 5.00
234 Craig Biggio PD 1.25 3.00
235 Curt Schilling PD 1.25 3.00
236 Derek Jeter PD 5.00 12.00
237 Ivan Rodriguez PD 1.25 3.00
238 Jeff Bagwell PD 1.25 3.00
239 Jim Edmonds PD 1.25 3.00
240 Jim Thome PD 1.25 3.00
241 Josh Beckett PD .75 2.00
242 Kerry Wood PD .75 2.00
243 Kevin Brown PD .75 2.00
244 Mark Prior PD 1.25 3.00
245 Miguel Tejada PD 1.25 3.00
246 Mike Mussina PD 1.25 3.00
247 Nomar Garciaparra PD 1.25 3.00
248 Pedro Martinez PD 1.25 3.00
249 Randy Johnson PD 2.00 5.00
250 Roger Clemens PD 2.50 6.00
251 A.Rodriguez 6.00 15.00
D.Jeter DD
252 A.Soriano 1.50 4.00
H.Blalock DD
253 B.Abreu 1.00 2.50
P.Burrell DD
254 E.Renteria 1.50 4.00
S.Rolen DD
255 G.Anderson 1.50 4.00
V.Guerrero DD
256 J.Bagwell 1.50 4.00
J.Kent DD
257 J.Reyes 1.50 4.00
K.Matsui DD
258 K.Greene 1.50 4.00
S.Burroughs DD
259 M.Giles 1.00 2.50
R.Furcal DD
260 M.Ramirez 2.50 6.00
J.Damon DD
261 Tim Bausher SB RC .60 1.50
262 Tim Bittner SB RC .60 1.50

2004 Sweet Spot Limited

Basic 171-260/Ltd 10/Wood 99 ODDS 1:12
STATED PRINT RUN 10 SERIAL #'d SETS
NO PRICING DUE TO SCARCITY

2004 Sweet Spot Wood

*WOOD 91-170/261-262: .6X TO 1.5X BASIC
*WOOD 171-230: .6X TO 1.5X BASIC
*WOOD 231-250: .6X TO 1.5X BASIC
*WOOD 251-260: .5X TO 1.2X BASIC
Wood 99/Basic 171-260/Ltd 10 ODDS 1:12
STATED PRINT RUN 99 SERIAL #'d SETS
OVERALL PLATES ODDS 1:360 HOBBY
PLATES PRINT RUN 1 SET PER COLOR
BLACK-CYAN-MAGENTA-YELLOW ISSUED
NO PLATES PRICING DUE TO SCARCITY

2004 Sweet Spot Diamond Champs Jersey

STATED PRINT RUN 150 SERIAL #'d SETS
PATCH PRINT RUN 10 SERIAL #'d SETS
A-ROD PATCH PRINT RUN 1 #'d CARD
NO PATCH PRICING DUE TO SCARCITY
OVERALL GAME-USED ODDS 1:6
RJ Randy Johnson 4.00 10.00
DCAP Albert Pujols 8.00 20.00
DCAR Alex Rodriguez Yanks 6.00 15.00
DCBZ Barry Zito 3.00 8.00
DCCJ Chipper Jones 4.00 10.00
DCCS Curt Schilling 6.00 15.00
DCDJ Derek Jeter 10.00 25.00
DCEG Eric Gagne 3.00 8.00
DCGA Garret Anderson 3.00 8.00
DCGM Greg Maddux 6.00 15.00
DCIR Ivan Rodriguez 4.00 10.00
DCIS Ichiro Suzuki 12.50 30.00
DCJB Josh Beckett 3.00 8.00
DCKG Ken Griffey Jr. 8.00 20.00
DCMP Mike Piazza 6.00 15.00
DCMT Miguel Tejada 3.00 8.00
DCPE Andy Pettitte 4.00 10.00
DCPM Pedro Martinez 4.00 10.00
DCRC Roger Clemens 6.00 15.00
DCRH Roy Halladay 3.00 8.00

2004 Sweet Spot Home Run Heroes Jersey

STATED PRINT RUN 199 SERIAL #'d SETS
*1-2 COLOR PATCH: .75X TO 2X BASIC
*3-4 COLOR PATCH: 1.25X TO 3X BASIC
PATCH PRINT RUN 55 SERIAL #'d SETS
A-ROD PATCH PRINT RUN 10 #'d CARDS
NO A-ROD PATCH PRICING AVAILABLE
OVERALL GAME-USED ODDS 1:6
HRAB Adrian Beltre 3.00 8.00
HRAD Adam Dunn 3.00 8.00
HRAJ Andruw Jones 4.00 10.00
HRAP Albert Pujols 8.00 20.00
HRAR A.Rod Yanks Bat Up 6.00 15.00
HRAS Alfonso Soriano 3.00 8.00
HRBB Bret Boone 3.00 8.00
HRBG Brian Giles 3.00 8.00
HRBW Bernie Williams 4.00 10.00
HRCB Carlos Beltran 3.00 8.00
HRCD Carlos Delgado 3.00 8.00
HRCJ Chipper Jones 4.00 10.00
HRDJ Derek Jeter 10.00 25.00
HRDL Derrek Lee 4.00 10.00
HRDO David Ortiz 4.00 10.00
HREC Eric Chavez 3.00 8.00
HRFM Fred McGriff 4.00 10.00
HRFT Frank Thomas 4.00 10.00
HRGA Garret Anderson 3.00 8.00
HRGS Gary Sheffield 3.00 8.00
HRHA Travis Hafner 3.00 8.00
HRHB Hank Blalock 3.00 8.00
HRHM Hideki Matsui 12.50 30.00
HRIR Ivan Rodriguez 4.00 10.00
HRJB Jeff Bagwell 4.00 10.00
HRJD J.D. Drew 3.00 8.00
HRJE Jim Edmonds 3.00 8.00
HRJG Jason Giambi 3.00 8.00
HRJK Jeff Kent 3.00 8.00
HRJM Joe Mauer 4.00 10.00
HRJP Jorge Posada 4.00 10.00
HRJT Jim Thome 4.00 10.00
HRKG Ken Griffey Jr. Bat Up 6.00 15.00
HRLB Lance Berkman 3.00 8.00
HRLG Luis Gonzalez 3.00 8.00
HRMC Miguel Cabrera 4.00 10.00
HRML Mike Lowell 3.00 8.00
HRMO Magglio Ordonez 3.00 8.00
HRMP Mike Piazza 6.00 15.00
HRMR Manny Ramirez 4.00 10.00
HRMT Mark Teixeira 4.00 10.00
HRPB Pat Burrell 3.00 8.00
HRPW Preston Wilson 3.00 8.00
HRRP Rafael Palmeiro 4.00 10.00
HRRS Richie Sexson 3.00 8.00
HRSG Shawn Green 3.00 8.00
HRSR Scott Rolen 4.00 10.00
HRSS Sammy Sosa 4.00 10.00
HRTE Miguel Tejada 3.00 8.00
HRTG Troy Glaus 3.00 8.00
HRTH Todd Helton 4.00 10.00
HRVG Vladimir Guerrero 4.00 10.00
HRVW Vernon Wells 3.00 8.00
HRAR1 A.Rod Yanks Swing 6.00 15.00
HRKG1 Ken Griffey Jr. Swing 6.00 15.00

2004 Sweet Spot Marquee Attractions Jersey

STATED PRINT RUN 199 SERIAL #'d SETS
*1-2 COLOR PATCH: 1X TO 2.5X BASIC
*3-4 COLOR PATCH: 1.5X TO 4X BASIC
*5+ COLOR PATCH: 2X TO 5X BASIC
PATCH PRINT RUN 35 SERIAL #'d SETS
A-ROD PATCH PRINT RUN 5 #'d CARDS
NO A-ROD PATCH PRICING AVAILABLE
OVERALL GAME-USED ODDS 1:6
MAAJ Andruw Jones 4.00 10.00
MAAP Albert Pujols 8.00 20.00
MAAR Alex Rodriguez Yanks 6.00 15.00
MABG Brian Giles 3.00 8.00
MABS Ben Sheets 3.00 8.00
MACD Carlos Delgado 3.00 8.00
MACS Curt Schilling 4.00 10.00
MADJ Derek Jeter 10.00 25.00
MAEC Eric Chavez 3.00 8.00
MAEG Eric Gagne 3.00 8.00
MAFT Frank Thomas 4.00 10.00
MAHB Hank Blalock 3.00 8.00
MAHU Torii Hunter 3.00 8.00
MAIR Ivan Rodriguez 4.00 10.00
MAIS Ichiro Suzuki 12.50 30.00
MAJS Jason Schmidt 3.00 8.00
MAJT Jim Thome 4.00 10.00
MAKG Ken Griffey Jr. 6.00 15.00
MAMC Miguel Cabrera 4.00 10.00
MAMP Mark Prior 4.00 10.00
MAMS Mike Sweeney 3.00 8.00
MAMT Miguel Tejada 3.00 8.00
MAPI Mike Piazza 6.00 15.00
MARC Roger Clemens 6.00 15.00
MARJ Randy Johnson 4.00 10.00
MATH Todd Helton 4.00 10.00
MAVG Vladimir Guerrero 4.00 10.00

2004 Sweet Spot Signatures

TIER 4 PRINT RUNS 201 COPIES AND UP
TIER 3 PRINT RUNS B/WN 101-200 PER
TIER 2 PRINT RUNS B/WN 51-100 PER
TIER 1 PRINT RUNS B/WN 27-34 PER
TIER 1 PRINT RUNS PROVIDED BY UD
OVERALL AU ODDS 1:12
TIER INFO PROVIDED BY UPPER DECK
CARDS ARE NOT SERIAL-NUMBERED
BASIC SIGNATURES FEATURE RED STITCH
SSAB Angel Berroa T4 6.00 15.00
SSAD Adam Dunn T4 6.00 15.00
SSAK Austin Kearns T4 6.00 15.00
SSAP Albert Pujols T3 75.00 150.00
SSBB Bret Boone T4 6.00 15.00
SSBE Josh Beckett T3 6.00 15.00
SSBG Brian Giles T4 6.00 15.00
SSBS Ben Sheets T4 6.00 15.00
SSBW Brandon Webb T4 6.00 15.00
SSCB Carlos Beltran T3 10.00 25.00
SSCL Carlos Lee T4 6.00 15.00
SSCP Corey Patterson T2 6.00 15.00
SSCR Cal Ripken T2/100 * 40.00 80.00
SSCZ Carlos Zambrano T3 6.00 15.00
SSDJ Derek Jeter T2 125.00 200.00
SSDL Derrek Lee T4 6.00 15.00
SSDM Don Mattingly T4 30.00 80.00
SSDW Dontrelle Willis T4 6.00 15.00
SSDY Delmon Young T4 6.00 15.00
SSEC Eric Chavez T4 6.00 15.00
SSEL Esteban Loaiza T4 6.00 15.00
SSEM Edgar Martinez T3 12.50 30.00
SSFT Frank Thomas T3 40.00 80.00
SSGA Garret Anderson T4 6.00 15.00
SSGJ Geoff Jenkins T4 6.00 15.00
SSGL Tom Glavine T2 12.00 30.00
SSGS Gary Sheffield T4 8.00 20.00
SSHA Roy Halladay T3 15.00 40.00
SSHB Hank Blalock T4 6.00 15.00
SSHI Richard Hidalgo T4 6.00 15.00
SSHO Trevor Hoffman T4 6.00 15.00
SSHU Torii Hunter T4 6.00 15.00

SSIR Ivan Rodriguez T2 20.00 50.00
SSIS Ichiro Suzuki T4 100.00 250.00
SSJD J.D. Drew T3 6.00 15.00
SSJG Juan Gonzalez T2 12.50 30.00
SSJJ Jacque Jones T4 6.00 15.00
SSJM Joe Mauer T4 12.50 30.00
SSJR Jose Reyes T4 6.00 15.00
SSJS Jason Schmidt T4 6.00 15.00
SSJV Javier Vazquez T4 6.00 15.00
SSKG Ken Griffey Jr. T4 50.00 120.00
SSKW Kerry Wood T4 6.00 15.00
SSLG Luis Gonzalez T2 6.00 15.00
SSLO Mike Lowell T3 10.00 25.00
SSMA Mike Marshall T1/34 * 125.00 250.00
SSMC Miguel Cabrera T4 20.00 50.00
SSMG Marcus Giles T4 6.00 15.00
SSML Mike Lieberthal T4 12.50 30.00
SSMM Mike Mussina T3 15.00 40.00
SSMP Mark Prior T3 6.00 15.00
SSMR Manny Ramirez T2 25.00 60.00
SSMT Mark Teixeira T4 8.00 20.00
SSMU Mark Mulder T4 6.00 15.00
SSNG Nomar Garciaparra T4 10.00 25.00
SSNR Nolan Ryan T2 40.00 80.00
SSOP Odalis Perez T4 6.00 15.00
SSPB Pat Burrell T2 12.50 30.00
SSPI Mike Piazza T2 60.00 120.00
SSRB Rocco Baldelli T2 12.50 30.00
SSRC Roger Clemens T2 30.00 60.00
SSRH Rich Harden T4 6.00 15.00
SSRK Ryan Klesko T4 6.00 15.00
SSRO Roy Oswalt T4 6.00 15.00
SSRS Ryne Sandberg T2 20.00 50.00
SSRW Randy Wolf T4 6.00 15.00
SSSA Johan Santana T4 10.00 25.00
SSSB Sean Burroughs T4 6.00 15.00
SSSM John Smoltz T3 12.00 30.00
SSSP Scott Podsednik T4 6.00 15.00
SSSR Scott Rolen T4 6.00 15.00
SSTE Miguel Tejada T3 15.00 40.00
SSTG Tony Gwynn T3 30.00 60.00
SSTH Todd Helton T2 20.00 50.00
SSTI Tim Hudson T2 6.00 15.00
SSTS Tom Seaver T3 30.00 80.00
SSVG Vladimir Guerrero T2 12.50 30.00
SSWA Billy Wagner T4 6.00 15.00
SSWC Will Clark T4 10.00 25.00
SSWE Rickie Weeks T4 6.00 15.00

2004 Sweet Spot Signatures Red-Blue Stitch

BLK/RED-BLUE/DUAL/HIST AU ODDS 1:180
PRINT RUNS B/WN 10-55 COPIES PER
NO PRICING ON QTY OF 10 OR LESS
EXCHANGE DEADLINE 11/22/07
SSAP Albert Pujols/45 75.00 150.00
SSCR Cal Ripken/35* 75.00 150.00
SSDJ Derek Jeter/35 200.00 350.00
SSIS Ichiro Suzuki/25 400.00 600.00
SSNR Nolan Ryan/40 125.00 200.00
SSPI Mike Piazza/20 150.00 250.00
SSRC Roger Clemens/30 * 125.00 200.00

2004 Sweet Spot Signatures Barrel

OVERALL AU ODDS 1:12
PRINT RUNS B/WN 13-74 COPIES PER
CARDS ARE NOT SERIAL-NUMBERED
PRINT RUNS PROVIDED BY UPPER DECK
NO PRICING ON QTY OF 14 OR LESS
EXCHANGE DEADLINE 11/22/07
SSAB Angel Berroa/64 * 12.50 30.00
SSAD Adam Dunn/74 * 8.00 20.00
SSAK Austin Kearns/64 * 12.50 30.00
SSAP Albert Pujols/64 * 75.00 200.00
SSAR Alex Rodriguez/28 * 50.00 120.00
SSBB Bret Boone/64 * 20.00 50.00
SSBE Josh Beckett/65 * 20.00 50.00
SSBG Brian Giles/64 * 15.00 40.00
SSBS Ben Sheets/64 * 15.00 40.00
SSBW Brandon Webb/64 * 12.00 30.00
SSCB Carlos Beltran/55 * 30.00 80.00
SSCL Carlos Lee/64 * 15.00 40.00
SSCR Cal Ripken/38 * 30.00 80.00
SSCZ Carlos Zambrano/38 * 30.00 60.00
SSDJ Derek Jeter/53 * 125.00 300.00
SSDL Derrek Lee/64 * 6.00 15.00
SSDM Don Mattingly/38 * 40.00 100.00
SSDW Dontrelle Willis/64 * 20.00 50.00
SSDY Delmon Young/74 * 20.00 50.00
SSEC Eric Chavez/74 * 6.00 15.00
SSEL Esteban Loaiza/64 * 12.50 30.00
SSEM Edgar Martinez/64 * 25.00 60.00
SSGA Garret Anderson/74 * 15.00 40.00
SSGJ Geoff Jenkins/64 * 15.00 40.00
SSGL Tom Glavine/64 * 20.00 50.00
SSGS Gary Sheffield/38 * 15.00 40.00
SSHA Roy Halladay/64 * 15.00 40.00
SSHB Hank Blalock/74 * 6.00 15.00
SSHI Richard Hidalgo/64 * 12.50 30.00
SSHO Trevor Hoffman/68 * 15.00 40.00
SSHU Torii Hunter/64 * 15.00 40.00
SSIR Ivan Rodriguez/64 * 20.00 50.00
SSIS Ichiro Suzuki/64 * 400.00 600.00
SSJJ Jacque Jones/64 * 15.00 40.00
SSJM Joe Mauer/72 * 25.00 60.00
SSJR Jose Reyes/49 * 20.00 50.00
SSJS Jason Schmidt/64 * 15.00 40.00
SSJV Javier Vazquez/64 * 15.00 40.00
SSKG Ken Griffey Jr./64 * 60.00 150.00
SSKW Kerry Wood/64 * 20.00 50.00
SSLO Mike Lowell/64 * 15.00 40.00
SSMC Miguel Cabrera/64 * 50.00 120.00
SSMG Marcus Giles/64 * 6.00 15.00
SSML Mike Lieberthal/64 * 10.00 25.00
SSMM Mike Mussina/64 * 15.00 40.00
SSMP Mark Prior/64 * 6.00 15.00
SSMR Manny Ramirez/63 * 30.00 60.00
SSMT Mark Teixeira/64 * 20.00 50.00
SSMU Mark Mulder/64 * 15.00 40.00
SSNG Nomar Garciaparra/38 * 15.00 40.00
SSNR Nolan Ryan/38 * 25.00 60.00
SSOP Odalis Perez/64 * 12.50 30.00
SSPI Mike Piazza/38 * 50.00 120.00
SSRB Rocco Baldelli/19 * 30.00 60.00
SSRH Rich Harden/64 * 15.00 40.00
SSRK Ryan Klesko/64 * 15.00 40.00
SSRO Roy Oswalt/64 * 15.00 40.00
SSRW Randy Wolf/64 * 12.50 30.00
SSSA Johan Santana/64 * 12.00 30.00
SSSB Sean Burroughs/64 * 12.50 30.00
SSSP Scott Podsednik/64 * 6.00 15.00
SSTE Miguel Tejada/64 * 20.00 50.00
SSTH Todd Helton/38 * 25.00 60.00
SSTI Tim Hudson/64 * 12.00 30.00
SSTS Tom Seaver/38 * 40.00 100.00
SSVG Vladimir Guerrero/38 * 30.00 80.00
SSVW Vernon Wells/33 * 20.00 50.00
SSWA Billy Wagner/64 * 20.00 50.00
SSWE Rickie Weeks/64 * 15.00 40.00

2004 Sweet Spot Signatures Glove

OVERALL AU ODDS 1:12
PRINT RUNS B/WN 5-25 #'d COPIES PER
NO PRICING ON QTY OF 5 OR LESS
EXCHANGE DEADLINE 11/22/07
SSAB Angel Berroa/25 20.00 50.00
SSAD Adam Dunn/25 12.50 30.00
SSAK Austin Kearns/25 20.00 50.00
SSAP Albert Pujols/25 60.00 120.00
SSBB Bret Boone/25 40.00 80.00
SSBE Josh Beckett/25 40.00 80.00
SSBG Brian Giles/25 30.00 60.00
SSBS Ben Sheets/25 30.00 60.00
SSBW Brandon Webb/25 20.00 50.00
SSCB Carlos Beltran/25 30.00 60.00
SSCL Carlos Lee/25 30.00 60.00
SSCR Cal Ripken/25 40.00 80.00
SSCZ Carlos Zambrano/15 50.00 10.00
SSDL Derrek Lee/25 40.00 80.00
SSDM Don Mattingly/25 50.00 120.00
SSDW Dontrelle Willis/25 40.00 80.00
SSDY Delmon Young/25 40.00 80.00
SSEC Eric Chavez/25 20.00 50.00
SSEL Esteban Loaiza/25 20.00 50.00
SSEM Edgar Martinez/25 30.00 60.00
SSFT Frank Thomas/15 50.00 100.00
SSGA Garret Anderson/25 30.00 60.00
SSGJ Geoff Jenkins/25 30.00 60.00
SSGL Tom Glavine/25 30.00 60.00
SSGS Gary Sheffield/20 50.00 100.00
SSHA Roy Halladay/24 75.00 150.00
SSHB Hank Blalock/25 30.00 60.00
SSHI Richard Hidalgo/15 30.00 60.00
SSHO Trevor Hoffman/15 40.00 80.00
SSHU Torii Hunter/25 30.00 60.00
SSJG Juan Gonzalez/25 15.00 40.00
SSJJ Jacque Jones/25 30.00 60.00
SSJM Joe Mauer/25 50.00 100.00
SSJR Jose Reyes/25 30.00 60.00
SSJS Jason Schmidt/25 30.00 60.00
SSJV Javier Vazquez/25 30.00 60.00
SSKG Ken Griffey Jr./25 100.00 250.00
SSKW Kerry Wood/25 40.00 80.00
SSLG Luis Gonzalez/25 10.00 25.00
SSMA Mike Marshall/25 20.00 50.00
SSMC Miguel Cabrera/25 20.00 50.00
SSMG Marcus Giles/25 30.00 60.00
SSML Mike Lieberthal/25 30.00 60.00
SSMM Mike Mussina/25 50.00 100.00
SSMP Mark Prior/25 30.00 60.00
SSMR Manny Ramirez/25 60.00 120.00
SSMT Mark Teixeira/25 20.00 50.00
SSMU Mark Mulder/25 30.00 60.00
SSNG Nomar Garciaparra/25 20.00 50.00
SSNR Nolan Ryan/25 175.00 300.00
SSOP Odalis Perez/25 20.00 50.00
SSPB Pat Burrell/15 40.00 80.00
SSRB Rocco Baldelli/25 30.00 60.00
SSRH Rich Harden/25 30.00 60.00
SSRK Ryan Klesko/15 40.00 80.00
SSRO Roy Oswalt/25 30.00 60.00
SSRS Ryne Sandberg/20 75.00 150.00
SSRW Randy Wolf/15 30.00 60.00
SSSA Johan Santana/25 10.00 25.00
SSSB Sean Burroughs/25 20.00 50.00
SSSP Scott Podsednik/25 6.00 15.00
SSTE Miguel Tejada/25 40.00 80.00
SSTG Tony Gwynn/25 60.00 120.00
SSTH Todd Helton/25 30.00 60.00
SSTI Tim Hudson/25 10.00 25.00
SSTS Tom Seaver/15 25.00 60.00
SSVG Vladimir Guerrero/25 60.00 120.00
SSWA Billy Wagner/25 40.00 80.00
SSWC Will Clark/25 75.00 150.00
SSWE Rickie Weeks/25 30.00 60.00

2004 Sweet Spot Signatures Dual

BLK/RED-BLUE/DUAL/HIST AU ODDS 1:180
STATED PRINT RUN 10 SERIAL #'d SETS
NO PRICING DUE TO SCARCITY
EXCHANGE DEADLINE 11/22/07

2004 Sweet Spot Sweet Sticks

OVERALL GAME-USED ODDS 1:6
STATED PRINT RUN 199 SERIAL #'d SETS
SSSAB Adrian Beltre 3.00 8.00
SSSAD Adam Dunn 3.00 8.00
SSSAJ Andruw Jones 4.00 10.00
SSSAP Albert Pujols 8.00 20.00
SSSAR Alex Rodriguez 6.00 15.00
SSSAS Alfonso Soriano 3.00 8.00
SSSBA Bobby Abreu 3.00 8.00
SSSBB Bret Boone 3.00 8.00
SSSBE Carlos Beltran 3.00 8.00
SSSBG Brian Giles 3.00 8.00
SSSCB Craig Biggio 4.00 10.00
SSSCD Carlos Delgado 3.00 8.00
SSSCJ Chipper Jones 4.00 10.00
SSSCR Cal Ripken 12.50 30.00
SSSCS Curt Schilling 4.00 10.00
SSSDJ Derek Jeter 10.00 25.00
SSSDL Derrek Lee 4.00 10.00
SSSEC Eric Chavez 3.00 8.00
SSSER Edgar Renteria 3.00 8.00
SSSFT Frank Thomas 4.00 10.00
SSSGA Garret Anderson 3.00 8.00
SSSGL Tom Glavine 4.00 10.00
SSSGM Greg Maddux 6.00 15.00
SSSGS Gary Sheffield 3.00 8.00
SSSHB Hank Blalock 3.00 8.00
SSSHM Hideki Matsui 12.50 30.00
SSSIR Ivan Rodriguez 4.00 10.00
SSSIS Ichiro Suzuki 12.50 30.00
SSSJB Jeff Bagwell 4.00 10.00
SSSJD J.D. Drew 3.00 8.00
SSSJE Jim Edmonds 3.00 8.00
SSSJG Jason Giambi 3.00 8.00
SSSJK Jeff Kent 3.00 8.00
SSSJR Jose Reyes 3.00 8.00
SSSJT Jim Thome 4.00 10.00
SSSKG Ken Griffey Jr. 8.00 20.00
SSSKM Kazuo Matsui 3.00 8.00
SSSLB Lance Berkman 4.00 10.00
SSSLG Luis Gonzalez 3.00 8.00
SSSLW Larry Walker Cards 4.00 10.00
SSSMA Moises Alou 3.00 8.00
SSSMC Miguel Cabrera 4.00 10.00
SSSMG Marcus Giles 3.00 8.00
SSSML Mike Lowell 3.00 8.00
SSSMO Magglio Ordonez 3.00 8.00
SSSMP Mike Piazza 6.00 15.00
SSSMR Manny Ramirez 4.00 10.00
SSSMT Mark Teixeira 4.00 10.00
SSSNG Nomar Garciaparra 6.00 15.00
SSSPB Pat Burrell 3.00 8.00
SSSPR Mark Prior 4.00 10.00
SSSPW Preston Wilson 3.00 8.00
SSSRC Roger Clemens 6.00 15.00
SSSRF Rafael Furcal 3.00 8.00
SSSRJ Randy Johnson 4.00 10.00
SSSRP Rafael Palmeiro 4.00 10.00
SSSRS Richie Sexson 3.00 8.00
SSSSG Shawn Green 3.00 8.00
SSSSR Scott Rolen 4.00 10.00
SSSSS Sammy Sosa 4.00 10.00
SSSTE Miguel Tejada 3.00 8.00
SSSTG Troy Glaus 3.00 8.00
SSSTH Todd Helton 4.00 10.00
SSSTW Ted Williams 10.00 25.00
SSSVG Vladimir Guerrero 4.00 10.00

2004 Sweet Spot Sweet Sticks Dual

OVERALL GAME-USED ODDS 1:6
STATED PRINT RUN 100 SERIAL #'d SETS
SSDBT H.Blalock/M.Teixeira 6.00 15.00
SSDCL M.Cabrera/M.Lowell 6.00 15.00
SSDJC R.Johnson/R.Clemens 12.50 30.00
SSDJG D.Jeter/N.Garciaparra 15.00 40.00
SSDJM J.Reyes/K.Matsui 6.00 15.00
SSDMM H.Matsui/K.Matsui 10.00 25.00
SSDPR A.Pujols/S.Rolen 15.00 40.00
SSDRJ A.Rodriguez/D.Jeter 30.00 60.00
SSDRP I.Rodriguez/M.Piazza 6.00 15.00
SSDTB J.Thome/P.Burrell 6.00 15.00
SSDWP K.Wood/M.Prior 6.00 15.00
SSSRG M.Ramirez/N.Garciaparra 10.00 25.00

2004 Sweet Spot Sweet Sticks Triple

OVERALL GAME-USED ODDS 1:6
STATED PRINT RUN 50 SERIAL #'d SETS
SSSGPS Griffey Jr./Palmeiro/Sosa 20.00 50.00
SSSJJD Andruw/Chipper/Drew 12.00 30.00
SSSJSG Jeter/Ichiro/Griffey Jr. 40.00 80.00
SSSMWP Maddux/Wood/Prior 20.00 50.00
SSSRJG A.Rod/Jeter/Giambi 12.00 30.00

2004 Sweet Spot Sweet Sticks Quad

OVERALL GAME-USED ODDS 1:6
STATED PRINT RUN 25 SERIAL #'d SETS
SSSPRSG Pujols/A.Rod/Ichiro/Grif 100.00 200.00
SSSRGDM Ruth/Gehr/DiMag/Mant 600.00 1000.00

2004 Sweet Spot Sweet Threads

*1-2 COLOR PATCH: .75X TO 2X BASIC
*3-4 COLOR PATCH: 1.25X TO 3X BASIC
*1-2 COLOR PATCH: .6X TO 1.5X BASIC SP
*3-4 COLOR PATCH: 1X TO 2.5X BASIC SP
PATCH PRINT RUN 85 SERIAL #'d SETS
MAUER PATCH PRINT RUN 70 #'d CARDS
OVERALL GAME-USED ODDS 1:6
PLATES PRINT RUN 4 SERIAL #'d SETS
BLACK-CYAN-MAGENTA-YELLOW EXIST
NO PLATES PRICING DUE TO SCARCITY
STSAS Alfonso Soriano 2.00 5.00
STSBB Bret Boone 2.00 5.00
STSBC Bartolo Colon 2.00 5.00
STSBG Brian Giles 2.00 5.00
STSCB Carlos Beltran 2.00 5.00
STSCD Carlos Delgado 2.00 5.00
STSDW Dontrelle Willis 3.00 8.00
STSDY Delmon Young 3.00 8.00
STSEC Eric Chavez 2.00 5.00
STSEM Edgar Martinez 3.00 8.00
STSFT Frank Thomas 3.00 8.00
STSGS Gary Sheffield 2.00 5.00
STSHB Hank Blalock 2.00 5.00
STSHE Todd Helton 3.00 8.00
STSHN Hideo Nomo 3.00 8.00
STSJB Jeff Bagwell 3.00 8.00
STSJG Jason Giambi 2.00 5.00
STSJM Joe Mauer 3.00 8.00
STSJR Jose Reyes 2.00 5.00
STSJS Jason Schmidt 2.00 5.00
STSJT Jim Thome 3.00 8.00
STSKM Kazuo Matsui SP 4.00 10.00
STSKW Kerry Wood 2.00 5.00
STSLB Lance Berkman 2.00 5.00
STSMC Miguel Cabrera 3.00 8.00
STSML Mike Lowell 2.00 5.00
STSMM Mark Mulder 2.00 5.00
STSMO Magglio Ordonez 2.00 5.00
STSMP Mark Prior 3.00 8.00
STSMR Manny Ramirez 3.00 8.00
STSMT Mark Teixeira 3.00 8.00
STSPW Preston Wilson 2.00 5.00
STSRH Rich Harden 2.00 5.00
STSRO Roy Oswalt 2.00 5.00
STSRS Richie Sexson 2.00 5.00
STSRW Rickie Weeks 2.00 5.00
STSSG Shawn Green 2.00 5.00
STSSS Sammy Sosa 3.00 8.00
STSTG Troy Glaus 2.00 5.00
STSTH Tim Hudson 2.00 5.00
STSVG Vladimir Guerrero 3.00 8.00
STSVW Vernon Wells 2.00 5.00

2004 Sweet Spot Sweet Threads Dual

OVERALL GAME-USED ODDS 1:6
STATED PRINT RUN 150 SERIAL #'d SETS
STDBP A.Berroa/S.Podsednik 4.00 10.00
STDBT H.Blalock/M.Teixeira 6.00 15.00
STDCK C.Schilling/K.Brown 6.00 15.00
STDCS R.Clemens/S.Sosa 8.00 20.00
STDDT C.Delgado/J.Thome 6.00 15.00
STDGH E.Gagne/R.Halladay 4.00 10.00
STDHG T.Hudson/V.Guerrero 4.00 10.00
STDJC R.Johnson/R.Clemens 10.00 25.00
STDJH A.Jones/T.Hunter 6.00 15.00
STDJJ A.Jones/C.Jones 6.00 15.00
STDMM H.Matsui/K.Matsui 4.00 10.00
STDMP J.Mauer/M.Prior 6.00 15.00
STDPC A.Pettitte/R.Clemens 8.00 20.00
STDPP J.Posada/M.Piazza 6.00 15.00
STDPS A.Pujols/I.Suzuki 12.50 30.00
STDPW A.Pujols/K.Wood 8.00 20.00
STDRJ A.Rodriguez/D.Jeter 10.00 25.00
STDRM J.Reyes/K.Matsui 4.00 10.00
STDSB A.Soriano/B.Boone 4.00 10.00
STDSM G.Sheffield/P.Martinez 6.00 15.00
STDWP K.Wood/M.Prior 6.00 15.00
STDYW D.Young/R.Weeks 6.00 15.00

2004 Sweet Spot Sweet Threads Dual Patch

*PATCHES: 1X TO 2.5X BASIC
OVERALL GAME-USED ODDS 1:6
STATED PRINT RUN 60 SERIAL #'d SETS
A.ROD-JETER PRINT RUN 10 #'d CARDS
NO A.ROD-JETER PRICING AVAILABLE

2004 Sweet Spot Sweet Threads Triple

OVERALL GAME-USED ODDS 1:6
STATED PRINT RUN 99 SERIAL #'d SETS
STTAGG Garret/Glaus/Guerrero 10.00 25.00
STTBKE Bagwell/Kent/Ensberg 6.00 15.00
STTBLR Beltre/Lowell/Rolen 6.00 15.00
STTBMS Boone/Edgar/Ichiro 30.00 60.00
STTBWC Beckett/Wood/Clemens 12.50 30.00
STTCMM Crosby/Mauer/Kazuo 10.00 25.00
STTDHW Delgado/Halladay/Wells 6.00 15.00
STTDKG Dunn/Kearns/Griffey Jr. 10.00 25.00
STTDMJ DiMaggio/Mantle/Jeter 40.00 80.00
STTDMJ DiMag/Mantle/Williams 200.00 350.00
STTDRN Damon/Manny/Nixon 20.00 50.00
STTFRP Foulke/Rivera/Percival 10.00 25.00
STTGPS Griffey/Palmeiro/Sosa 15.00 40.00
STTJJD Andruw/Chipper/Drew 10.00 25.00
STTJTG Jeter/Tejada/Nomar 12.50 30.00
STTJWH Edwin/Jerome/Harden 6.00 15.00
STTKVG Kent/Vidro/Giles 6.00 15.00
STTLTO C.Lee/Thomas/Magglio 10.00 25.00
STTLTP Javy/Tejada/Palmeiro 6.00 15.00
STTMCF Kazuo/Cabrera/Furcal 10.00 25.00
STTMMH Mussina/Pedro/Hudson 10.00 25.00
STTMSH Mauer/Johan/Torii 10.00 25.00
STTMWP Maddux/Wood/Prior 15.00 40.00
STTPAS Patterson/Alou/Sosa 10.00 25.00
STTPCO Pettitte/Clemens/Oswalt 6.00 15.00
STTPRR Pujols/Renteria/Rolen 15.00 40.00
STTPTH Pujols/Thome/Helton 10.00 25.00
STTRCB A.Rod/Chavez/Blalock 10.00 25.00
STTRGJ A.Rod/Griffey Jr./Randy 30.00 60.00
STTRGW Reyes/Khalil/Weeks 10.00 25.00
STTRJG A.Rod/Jeter/Giambi 30.00 60.00
STTRMP Reyes/Kazuo/Piazza 15.00 40.00
STTSBK Soriano/Boone/Kenn 6.00 15.00
STTSBP J.Schmidt/Beckett/Prior 10.00 25.00
STTSBT Soriano/Blalock/Teix 10.00 25.00
STTSLM Schilling/Lowe/Pedro 20.00 50.00
STTVBM Vazq/Brown/Mussina 6.00 15.00
STTWBP Webb/Beckett/Prior 10.00 25.00
STTWGS Wagner/Gagne/Smoltz 10.00 25.00
STTWRC Wood/Ryan/Clemens 40.00 80.00
STTYCW Delmon/Cabrera/Weeks 10.00 25.00
STTZMH Zito/Mulder/Hudson 6.00 15.00

2004 Sweet Spot Sweet Threads Triple Patch

*PATCH p/r 20-25: 1.5X TO 3X BASIC
OVERALL GAME-USED ODDS 1:6
PRINT RUNS B/WN 5-25 COPIES PER
NO PRICING ON QTY OF 5 OR LESS
STTFRP Foulke/Rivera/Percival/25 30.00 60.00
STTGPS Griffey/Palmeiro/Sosa/25 40.00 80.00
STTJTG Jeter/Tejada/Nomar/25 40.00 80.00
STTWRC Wood/Ryan/Clem/25 100.00 200.00

2004 Sweet Spot Sweet Threads Quad

OVERALL GAME-USED ODDS 1:6
STATED PRINT RUN 99 SERIAL #'d SETS
STQBADH Beltran/And/Damon/Tor 15.00 40.00
STQBBGS Berr/Beltran/Gonz/Swe 10.00 25.00
STQBPJC Beck/Prior/Randy/Clem 10.00 25.00
STQBWRC Beck/Wood/Ryan/Clem 40.00 80.00
STQCAGG Colon/And/Glaus/Vlad 15.00 40.00
STQDHHW Delg/Hinske/Hal/Wells 10.00 25.00
STQDOGP Delg/Ortiz/Giam/Raffy 15.00 40.00
STQGNKB Giles/Nevin/Klesko/Burr 10.00 25.00
STQGNLG Gagn/Nomo/LoD/Green 10.00 25.00
STQJBGB Chip/Berk/Luis/Burrell 10.00 25.00
STQJEGW Andruw/Edm/Grif/P.Wil 15.00 40.00
STQJJDF Andr/Chip/Drew/Furc 15.00 40.00
STQJMSH Jacq/Mauer/Stew/Torii 12.50 30.00
STQJRMT Jeter/Rent/Kaz/Tejada 20.00 50.00
STQKGCS Kearns/Giles/Cab/Sosa 15.00 40.00
STQLMRS Lee/Hideki/Manny/Ste 30.00 60.00
STQLTOK Lee/Thomas/Magg/Kon 15.00 40.00
STQLTPP Javy/Teja/Raffy/Pons 15.00 40.00
STQMMMH Muld/Muss/Pedro/Hal 10.00 25.00
STQMTTS Edgar/Thom/Teix/Swe 15.00 40.00
STQNSGH Nev/Sexs/Green/Helt 10.00 25.00
STQPBBC Pett/Bigg/Bag/Clemens 20.00 50.00
STQPLBT Pujols/Lee/Bag/Thome 15.00 40.00
STQPRER Pujols/Rent/Edm/Rolen 15.00 40.00
STQPWPS Patt/Wood/Prior/Sosa 15.00 40.00
STQRCBG Alex/Chav/Blal/Glaus 10.00 25.00
STQRDRW Alex/DiMag/Manny/Ted 40.00 80.00
STQRJDM Alex/Jeter/DiMag/Mantle 125.00 250.00
STQRJGP Alex/Jeter/Giam/Posa 15.00 40.00
STQRLPM I.Rod/Javy/Posa/Mauer 15.00 40.00
STQRMPG Reyes/Kaz/Piaz/Glav 15.00 40.00
STQSBKV Sor/Boone/Kent/Vidro 10.00 25.00
STQSBMM Schill/Brow/Mus/Pedro 15.00 40.00
STQSDRM Sch/Dam/Manny/Pedro 50.00 100.00
STQSSOG Shef/Ichiro/Magg/Vlad 30.00 60.00
STQVCBM Vazq/Cont/Brown/Muss 10.00 25.00
STQWATM Wag/Abreu/Thome/Mill 15.00 40.00
STQWBCL Willis/Beck/Cab/Lowell 15.00 40.00
STQWGJS Webb/Luis/Randy/Sexs 10.00 25.00
STQZMHH Zito/Muld/Harden/Hud 15.00 40.00

2004 Sweet Spot Sweet Threads Quad Patch

*PATCH: 1.5X TO 3X BASIC
OVERALL GAME-USED ODDS 1:6
PRINT RUNS B/WN 1-15 #'d COPIES PER
NO PRICING ON QTY OF 10 OR LESS
STQBWRC Bec/Woo/Ryan/Clem/15 40.00 80.00
STQLMRS Lee/Mats/Manny/Ste/15 125.00 200.00
STQPRER Pujols/Rent/Edm/Rol/15 125.00 200.00
STQPWPS Pat/Wood/Prior/Sosa/15 60.00 120.00
STQSBMM Sch/Brow/Mus/Pedro/15 40.00 80.00
STQSDRM Sch/Dam/Man/Pedro/15 175.00 300.00

2005 Sweet Spot

COMP.BASIC SET (90) 8.00 20.00
COMP.UPDATE SET (84) 10.00 25.00
COMMON CARD (1-90) .20 .50
COMMON RC 1-90 .20 .50
COMMON CARD (91-174) .20 .50
91-174 ONE PER '05 UD UPDATE PACK
1 Magglio Ordonez .30 .75
2 Craig Biggio .30 .75
3 Hank Blalock .20 .50
4 Nomar Garciaparra .30 .75
5 Ken Griffey Jr. 1.00 2.50
6 Khalil Greene .20 .50
7 Andruw Jones .20 .50
8 Ichiro Suzuki .60 1.50
9 Philip Humber RC .50 1.25
10 Vladimir Guerrero .30 .75
11 Carlos Delgado .20 .50
12 Jeff Niemann RC .50 1.25
13 Chipper Jones .50 1.25
14 Jose Vidro .20 .50
15 Miguel Cabrera .50 1.25
16 Albert Pujols .60 1.50
17 Tadahito Iguchi RC .30 .75
18 Norihiro Nakamura RC .20 .50
19 Jeff Bagwell .30 .75
20 Troy Glaus .20 .50
21 Scott Rolen .30 .75
22 Derek Lowe .20 .50
23 Mark Prior .30 .75
24 Bobby Abreu .20 .50
25 David Wright .40 1.00
26 Barry Zito .30 .75
27 Livan Hernandez .20 .50
28 Mark Teixeira .30 .75
29 Manny Ramirez .50 1.25
30 Paul Konerko .30 .75
31 Victor Martinez .30 .75
32 Greg Maddux .60 1.50
33 Jim Thome .30 .75
34 Miguel Tejada .30 .75
35 Ivan Rodriguez .30 .75
36 Carlos Beltran .30 .75
37 Steve Finley .20 .50
38 Torii Hunter .20 .50
39 Bobby Crosby .20 .50
40 Jorge Posada .30 .75
41 Ben Sheets .20 .50
42 Mike Piazza .50 1.25
43 Luis Gonzalez .20 .50
44 Joe Mauer .40 1.00
45 Shawn Green .20 .50
46 Eric Gagne .20 .50
47 Kerry Wood .20 .50
48 Derek Jeter 1.25 3.00
49 Josh Beckett .20 .50
50 Alex Rodriguez .60 1.50
51 Aubrey Huff .20 .50
52 Eric Chavez .20 .50
53 Sammy Sosa .50 1.25
54 Roger Clemens .60 1.50
55 Mike Mussina .30 .75
56 Mike Sweeney .20 .50
57 Oliver Perez .20 .50
58 Tim Hudson .30 .75
59 Justin Verlander RC 4.00 10.00
60 Johan Santana .30 .75
61 Hideki Matsui .75 2.00
62 Mark Mulder .20 .50
63 Jake Peavy .20 .50
64 Adam Dunn .30 .75
65 Dallas McPherson .20 .50
66 Jeff Kent .20 .50
67 Pedro Martinez .30 .75
68 J.D. Drew .20 .50
69 Frank Thomas .50 1.25
70 Kazuo Matsui .20 .50
71 Travis Hafner .20 .50
72 John Smoltz .50 1.25
73 Jason Schmidt .20 .50
74 Carlos Lee .20 .50
75 Todd Helton .30 .75
76 David Ortiz .50 1.25
77 Roy Oswalt .30 .75
78 Brian Giles .20 .50
79 Gary Sheffield .20 .50
80 Jason Bay .20 .50
81 Alfonso Soriano .30 .75
82 Randy Johnson .50 1.25
83 Tom Glavine .30 .75
84 Richie Sexson .20 .50
85 Curt Schilling .30 .75
86 Adrian Beltre .50 1.25
87 Jim Edmonds .30 .75
88 Roy Halladay .30 .75
89 Johnny Damon .30 .75
90 Lance Berkman .30 .75
91 Adam Shabala SB RC .20 .50
92 Ambiorix Burgos SB RC .20 .50
93 Ambiorix Concepcion SB RC .20 .50
94 Anibal Sanchez SB RC .75 2.00
95 Bill McCarthy SB RC .20 .50
96 Brandon McCarthy SB RC .30 .75
97 Brian Burres SB RC .20 .50
98 Carlos Ruiz SB RC .30 .75
99 Casey Rogowski SB RC .30 .75
100 Chad Orvella SB RC .20 .50
101 Chris Resop SB RC .20 .50
102 Chris Roberson SB RC .20 .50
103 Chris Seddon SB RC .20 .50
104 Colter Bean SB RC .20 .50
105 Dae-Sung Koo SB RC .20 .50
106 Ryan Zimmerman SB RC 1.00 2.50
107 Dave Gassner SB RC .20 .50
108 Brian Anderson SB RC .30 .75
109 D.J. Houlton SB RC .20 .50
110 Derek Wathan SB RC .20 .50
111 Devon Lowery SB RC .20 .50
112 Enrique Gonzalez SB RC .20 .50
113 Chris Denorfia SB RC .20 .50
114 Eude Brito SB RC .20 .50
115 Francisco Butto SB RC .20 .50
116 Franquelis Osoria SB RC .20 .50
117 Garrett Jones SB RC .30 .75
118 Geovany Soto SB RC 1.00 2.50
119 Hayden Penn SB RC .20 .50
120 Ismael Ramirez SB RC .20 .50
121 Jared Gothreaux SB RC .20 .50
122 Jason Hammel SB RC .50 1.25
123 Dana Eveland SB RC .20 .50
124 Jeff Miller SB RC .20 .50
125 Jermaine Van Buren SB .20 .50
126 Joel Peralta SB RC .20 .50
127 John Hattig SB RC .20 .50
128 Jorge Campillo SB RC .20 .50
129 Juan Morillo SB RC .20 .50
130 Ryan Garko SB RC .20 .50
131 Keiichi Yabu SB RC .20 .50
132 Kendry Morales SB RC .50 1.25
133 Luis Hernandez SB RC .20 .50
134 Mark McLemore SB RC .20 .50
135 Luis Pena SB RC .20 .50
136 Luis O.Rodriguez SB RC .20 .50
137 Luke Scott SB RC .50 1.25
138 Marcos Carvajal SB RC .20 .50
139 Mark Woodyard SB RC .20 .50
140 Matt A.Smith SB RC .20 .50
141 Matthew Lindstrom SB RC .20 .50
142 Miguel Negron SB RC .30 .75
143 Mike Morse SB RC .60 1.50
144 Nate McLouth SB RC .30 .75
145 Nelson Cruz SB RC 2.50 6.00
146 Nick Masset SB RC .20 .50
147 Ryan Spilborghs SB RC .50 1.25
148 Oscar Robles SB RC .20 .50
149 Paulino Reynoso SB RC .20 .50
150 Pedro Lopez SB RC .20 .50
151 Pete Orr SB RC .30 .75
152 Prince Fielder SB RC 1.00 2.50
153 Randy Messenger SB RC .20 .50
154 Randy Williams SB RC .20 .50
155 Raul Tablado SB RC .20 .50
156 Ronny Paulino SB RC .30 .75
157 Russ Rohlicek SB RC .20 .50
158 Russell Martin SB RC .60 1.50
159 Scott Baker SB RC .30 .75
160 Scott Munter SB RC .20 .50
161 Sean Thompson SB RC .20 .50
162 Sean Tracey SB RC .20 .50
163 Shane Costa SB RC .20 .50
164 Stephen Drew SB RC .60 1.50
165 Steve Schmoll SB RC .20 .50
166 Ryan Speier SB RC .20 .50
167 Tadahito Iguchi SB .30 .75
168 Tony Giarratano SB RC .20 .50
169 Tony Pena SB RC .20 .50
170 Travis Bowyer SB RC .20 .50
171 Ubaldo Jimenez SB RC .50 1.25
172 Wladimir Balentien SB RC .30 .75
173 Yorman Bazardo SB RC .20 .50
174 Yuniesky Betancourt SB RC .75 2.00

2005 Sweet Spot Gold

*GOLD 1-90: 1.25X TO 3X BASIC
*GOLD 1-90: 1X TO 2.5X BASIC RC
1-90 OVERALL PARALLEL ODDS 1:6
1-90 PRINT RUN 599 SERIAL #'d SETS
*GOLD 91-174: 1X TO 2.5X BASIC
91-174 ISSUED IN '05 UD UPDATE PACKS
91-174 ONE #'d CARD OR AU PER PACK
91-174 PRINT RUN 399 SERIAL #'d SETS

2005 Sweet Spot Platinum

*PLATINUM 1-90: 2X TO 5X BASIC
*PLATINUM 1-90: 1.25X TO 3X BASIC RC
1-90 OVERALL PARALLEL ODDS 1:6
*PLATINUM 91-174: 1.5X TO 4X BASIC
91-174 ISSUED IN '05 UD UPDATE PACKS
91-174 ONE #'d CARD OR AU PER PACK
STATED PRINT RUN 99 SERIAL #'d SETS

2005 Sweet Spot Majestic Materials

*GOLD: .6X TO 1.5X BASIC
GOLD PRINT RUN 75 SERIAL #'d SETS
PLATINUM PRINT RUN 10 SERIAL #'d SETS
NO PLATINUM PRICING DUE TO SCARCITY
PLUTONIUM PRINT RUN 1 SERIAL #'d SET
NO PLUTONIUM PRICING DUE TO SCARCITY
OVERALL 1-PIECE GU ODDS 1:6
*PATCH: 1.5X TO 4X BASIC
OVERALL PATCH ODDS 1:96
PATCH PRINT RUN 35 SERIAL #'d SETS
PRICES ARE FOR 2-3 COLOR PATCHES
REDUCE 20% FOR 1-COLOR PATCH
ADD 20% FOR 4-COLOR PATCH
ADD 50% FOR 5-COLOR+ PATCH
MMAD Adam Dunn 2.00 5.00
MMAJ Andruw Jones 3.00 8.00
MMAP Andy Pettitte 3.00 8.00
MMBA Bobby Abreu 2.00 5.00
MMBB Bret Boone 2.00 5.00
MMBC Bobby Crosby 2.00 5.00
MMBE Josh Beckett 2.00 5.00
MMBG Brian Giles 2.00 5.00
MMBS Ben Sheets 2.00 5.00
MMBU B.J. Upton 2.00 5.00
MMBZ Barry Zito 2.00 5.00
MMCB Craig Biggio 3.00 8.00
MMCD Carlos Delgado 2.00 5.00
MMDM Dallas McPherson 2.00 5.00
MMDW David Wright 4.00 10.00
MMER Edgar Renteria 2.00 5.00
MMGS Gary Sheffield 2.00 5.00
MMHA Travis Hafner 2.00 5.00
MMHU Torii Hunter 2.00 5.00
MMJB Jason Bay 2.00 5.00
MMJD J.D. Drew 2.00 5.00
MMJE Jim Edmonds 2.00 5.00
MMJG Jason Giambi 2.00 5.00
MMJK Jeff Kent 2.00 5.00
MMJM Joe Mauer 3.00 8.00
MMJP Jake Peavy 2.00 5.00
MMJR Jose Reyes 2.00 5.00
MMJS Jason Schmidt 2.00 5.00
MMJV Jose Vidro 2.00 5.00
MMKG Khalil Greene 3.00 8.00
MMKM Kazuo Matsui 2.00 5.00
MMLB Lance Berkman 2.00 5.00
MMLG Luis Gonzalez 2.00 5.00
MMMA Moises Alou 2.00 5.00
MMMM Mark Mulder 2.00 5.00
MMMO Magglio Ordonez 2.00 5.00
MMMU Mike Mussina 3.00 8.00
MMOP Oliver Perez 2.00 5.00
MMPO Jorge Posada 3.00 8.00
MMRH Roy Halladay 2.00 5.00
MMRO Roy Oswalt 2.00 5.00
MMRS Richie Sexson 2.00 5.00
MMSG Shawn Green 2.00 5.00
MMSK Scott Kazmir 2.00 5.00
MMST Shingo Takatsu 2.00 5.00
MMTG Troy Glaus 2.00 5.00
MMTH Tim Hudson 2.00 5.00
MMTI Tadahito Iguchi 6.00 15.00
MMVM Victor Martinez 2.00 5.00
MMVW Vernon Wells 2.00 5.00

2005 Sweet Spot Majestic Materials Dual

STATED PRINT RUN 25 SERIAL #'d SETS
GOLD PRINT RUN 5 SERIAL #'d SETS
NO GOLD PRICING DUE TO SCARCITY
PLUTONIUM PRINT RUN 1 SERIAL #'d SET
NO PLUTONIUM PRICING DUE TO SCARCITY
OVERALL COMBO GU ODDS 1:192
OVERALL PATCH ODDS 1:96
PATCH PRINT RUN 5 SERIAL #'d SETS
NO PATCH PRICING DUE TO SCARCITY
MMDBB C.Biggio/J.Bagwell 8.00 20.00
MMDBP J.Bay/O.Perez 6.00 15.00
MMDBS A.Beltre/R.Sexson 6.00 15.00
MMDBT H.Blalock/M.Teixeira 8.00 20.00
MMDCC B.Crosby/E.Chavez 6.00 15.00
MMDDG A.Dunn/K.Griffey Jr. 15.00 40.00
MMDDK J.Drew/J.Kent 6.00 15.00
MMDDR J.Damon/M.Ramirez 8.00 20.00
MMDGG S.Green/T.Glaus 6.00 15.00
MMDGR E.Gagne/M.Rivera 10.00 25.00
MMDHM T.Hafner/V.Martinez 6.00 15.00
MMDJJ A.Jones/C.Jones 10.00 25.00
MMDMC D.Mattingly/W.Clark 15.00 40.00
MMDMW D.McPherson/D.Wright 10.00 25.00
MMDPC A.Pujols/M.Cabrera 15.00 40.00
MMDPG J.Peavy/K.Greene 8.00 20.00
MMDPL A.Pujols/D.Lee 15.00 40.00
MMDRM J.Reyes/K.Matsui 6.00 15.00
MMDRO I.Rodriguez/M.Ordonez 8.00 20.00
MMDRT B.Roberts/M.Tejada 6.00 15.00
MMDSH J.Smoltz/T.Hudson 8.00 20.00
MMDSM J.Mauer/J.Santana 8.00 20.00
MMDTI S.Takatsu/T.Iguchi 12.50 30.00
MMDUK B.Upton/S.Kazmir 6.00 15.00
MMDWC D.Wright/M.Cabrera 12.50 30.00

2005 Sweet Spot Majestic Materials Triple

STATED PRINT RUN 25 SERIAL #'d SETS
GOLD PRINT RUN 5 SERIAL #'d SETS
NO GOLD PRICING DUE TO SCARCITY
PLUTONIUM PRINT RUN 1 SERIAL #'d SET
NO PLUTONIUM PRICING DUE TO SCARCITY
OVERALL COMBO GU ODDS 1:192
OVERALL PATCH ODDS 1:96
PATCH PRINT RUN 5 SERIAL #'d SETS
NO PATCH PRICING DUE TO SCARCITY
BPO Beckett/Prior/Oswalt 10.00 25.00
BSB Brett/Schmidt/Boggs 30.00 60.00
BTH Bagwell/Thome/Helton 10.00 25.00
HRG Torii/Manny/Vlad 10.00 25.00
JCG Andruw/M.Cabrera/Vlad 10.00 25.00
JRT Jeter/Renteria/Tejada 15.00 40.00
MMP Maddux/Pedro/Peavy 15.00 40.00
MSG Maddux/Smoltz/Glavine 30.00 60.00
OGP Ortiz/Giambi/Raffy 10.00 25.00
PBC Pujols/Beltran/M.Cabrera 15.00 40.00
RBW Ryan/Beckett/Wood 30.00 60.00
RGB Ripken/Gwynn/Boggs 40.00 80.00
SSJ Schilling/Santana/Randy 10.00 25.00
VPP Varitek/Posada/Piazza 10.00 25.00
WRG Wright/Rolen/Glaus 12.50 30.00

2005 Sweet Spot Majestic Materials Quad

STATED PRINT RUN 25 SERIAL #'d SETS
GOLD PRINT RUN 5 SERIAL #'d SETS
NO GOLD PRICING DUE TO SCARCITY
PLUTONIUM PRINT RUN 1 SERIAL #'d SET
NO PLUTONIUM PRICING DUE TO SCARCITY
OVERALL COMBO GU ODDS 1:192
OVERALL PATCH ODDS 1:96
PATCH PRINT RUN 5 SERIAL #'d SETS
NO PATCH PRICING DUE TO SCARCITY

JJSH Andruw/Chip/Smoltz/Hud 20.00 50.00
JSJP Jeter/Shef/Randy/Posada 50.00 100.00
OVDR Ortiz/Varit/Damon/Manny 30.00 60.00
PEWR Pujols/Edm/Walk/Rolen 40.00 80.00
ZMWP Zam/Maddux/Wood/Prior 20.00 50.00

2005 Sweet Spot Signatures Red Stitch Black Ink

OVERALL AU ODDS 1:12
PRINT RUNS B/WN 58-350 COPIES PER
EXCHANGE DEADLINE 09/15/08

AD Adam Dunn/175 12.50 30.00
AH Aubrey Huff/350 6.00 15.00
AJ Andruw Jones/175 10.00 25.00
AP Albert Pujols/175 75.00 150.00
AR Aramis Ramirez/350 6.00 15.00
BC Bobby Crosby/350 6.00 15.00
BJ Bo Jackson/175 40.00 80.00
BL Barry Larkin/175 15.00 40.00
BU B.J. Upton/350 8.00 20.00
CA Miguel Cabrera/175 25.00 60.00
CC Carl Crawford/350 6.00 15.00
CR Cal Ripken/175 25.00 60.00
CZ Carlos Zambrano/350 10.00 25.00
DA Andre Dawson/175 8.00 20.00
DJ Derek Jeter/175 110.00 175.00
DW David Wright/350 12.00 30.00
EM Edgar Martinez/175 12.50 30.00
GF Gavin Floyd/350 6.00 15.00
GR Khalil Greene/350 10.00 25.00
HB Hank Blalock/175 8.00 20.00
HO Ryan Howard/350 10.00 25.00
JB Jason Bay/350 6.00 15.00
JN Jeff Niemann/350 8.00 20.00
JP Jake Peavy/350 10.00 25.00
JV Justin Verlander/350 20.00 50.00
KG Ken Griffey Jr./175 50.00 100.00
KH Keith Hernandez/350 6.00 15.00
LO Lyle Overbay/350 6.00 15.00
MA Don Mattingly/175 40.00 80.00
MG Marcus Giles/350 6.00 15.00
MM Mark Mulder/350 6.00 15.00
MO Justin Morneau/350 8.00 20.00
MP Mark Prior/175 8.00 20.00
MS Mike Schmidt/175 30.00 60.00
MT Mark Teixeira/175 12.50 30.00
NG Nomar Garciaparra/175 40.00 80.00
NR Nolan Ryan/175 30.00 80.00
PH Phillip Humber/350 6.00 15.00
PI Mike Piazza/175 50.00 100.00
PM Paul Molitor/175 8.00 20.00
RC Roger Clemens/175 60.00 120.00
RE Jose Reyes/350 10.00 25.00
RH Rich Harden/350 6.00 15.00
RJ Randy Johnson/175 30.00 60.00
RO Roy Oswalt/350 6.00 15.00
RS Ryne Sandberg/175 30.00 60.00
RY Robin Yount/175 20.00 50.00
SC Steve Carlton/58 10.00 25.00
SE Sean Casey/350 6.00 15.00
SK Scott Kazmir/350 8.00 20.00
WB Wade Boggs/175 15.00 40.00
WC Will Clark/175 12.50 30.00

2005 Sweet Spot Signatures Red Stitch Blue Ink

*BLUE p/r 135: .5X TO 1.2X BLK p/r 350
*BLUE p/r135: .5X TO 1.2X BLK RC YR p/r350
*BLUE p/r 75: .5X TO 1.2X BLK p/r 175
*BLUE p/r 75: .4X TO 1X BLK p/r 58
OVERALL AU ODDS 1:12
PRINT RUNS B/WN 75-135 COPIES PER
EXCHANGE DEADLINE 09/15/08

AP Albert Pujols/75 100.00 200.00
CP Corey Patterson/135 8.00 20.00
CR Cal Ripken/75 60.00 120.00
DJ Derek Jeter/75 125.00 200.00
GL Tom Glavine/135 12.50 30.00
HA Travis Hafner/135 8.00 20.00
NR Nolan Ryan/75 50.00 100.00
PI Mike Piazza/75 60.00 120.00
RC Roger Clemens/75 30.00 60.00

2005 Sweet Spot Signatures Red Stitch Red Ink

*RED p/r 35: .75X TO 2X BLK p/r 350
*RED p/r 35: .75X TO 2X BLK RC YR p/r 350
*RED p/r 15: .75X TO 2X BLK p/r 175
*RED p/r 15: .6X TO 1.5X BLK p/r 58
OVERALL AU ODDS 1:12
PRINT RUNS B/WN 15-35 COPIES PER
EXCHANGE DEADLINE 09/15/08

AP Albert Pujols/15 150.00 250.00
CP Corey Patterson/35 12.00 30.00
CR Cal Ripken/15 100.00 200.00
DJ Derek Jeter/15 250.00 400.00
GL Tom Glavine/35 20.00 50.00
HA Travis Hafner/35 12.00 30.00
NR Nolan Ryan/15 30.00 80.00
PI Mike Piazza/15 110.00 175.00
RC Roger Clemens/15 100.00 200.00

2005 Sweet Spot Signatures Red-Blue Stitch Black Ink

*BLK p/r 50: .6X TO 1.5X BLK p/r 350
*BLK p/r 50: .6X TO 1.5X BLK RC YR p/r 350
*BLK p/r 25: .6X TO 1.5X BLK p/r 175
*BLK p/r 25: .5X TO 1.2X BLK p/r 58
OVERALL AU ODDS 1:12
PRINT RUNS B/WN 25-50 COPIES PER
EXCHANGE DEADLINE 09/15/08

AP Albert Pujols/25 100.00 200.00
CR Cal Ripken/25 50.00 120.00
DJ Derek Jeter/25 175.00 300.00
JS Johan Santana/25 40.00 80.00
NR Nolan Ryan/25 75.00 125.00
PI Mike Piazza/25 90.00 150.00
RC Roger Clemens/25 90.00 150.00

2005 Sweet Spot Signatures Red-Blue Stitch Blue Ink

*BLUE p/r 30: .75X TO 2X BLK p/r 350
*BLUE p/r 30: .75X TO 2X BLK RC YR p/r 350
*BLUE p/r 15: .75X TO 2X BLK p/r 175
*BLUE p/r 15: .6X TO 1.5X BLK p/r 58
OVERALL AU ODDS 1:12
PRINT RUNS B/WN 15-30 COPIES PER
EXCHANGE DEADLINE 09/15/08

AP Albert Pujols/15 150.00 300.00
CR Cal Ripken/15 100.00 200.00
GL Tom Glavine/30 20.00 50.00
HA Travis Hafner/30 12.00 30.00
JS Johan Santana/15 40.00 80.00
NR Nolan Ryan/15 90.00 150.00
RC Roger Clemens/15 100.00 200.00

2005 Sweet Spot Signatures Red-Blue Stitch Red Ink

OVERALL AU ODDS 1:12
PRINT RUNS B/WN 5-10 SERIAL #'d SETS
NO PRICING DUE TO SCARCITY
EXCHANGE DEADLINE 09/15/08

2005 Sweet Spot Signatures Barrel Black Ink

*BLK p/r 50: .6X TO 1.5X BLK p/r 350
*BLK p/r 50: .6X TO 1.5X BLK RC YR p/r 350
*BLK p/r 25: .6X TO 1.5X BLK p/r 175
*BLK p/r 25: .5X TO 1.2X BLK p/r 58
OVERALL AU ODDS 1:12
PRINT RUNS B/WN 25-50 COPIES PER
EXCHANGE DEADLINE 09/15/08

SSAP Albert Pujols/25 150.00 250.00
SSDJ Derek Jeter/25 200.00 400.00
SSGL Tom Glavine/50 15.00 40.00
SSHA Travis Hafner/50 10.00 25.00

2005 Sweet Spot Signatures Barrel Blue Ink

*BLUE p/r 30: .75X TO 2X BLK p/r 350
*BLUE p/r 30: .75X TO 2X BLK RC YR p/r 350
*BLUE p/r 15: .75X TO 2X BLK p/r 175
*BLUE p/r 15: .6X TO 1.5X BLK p/r 58
OVERALL AU ODDS 1:12
PRINT RUNS B/WN 15-30 COPIES PER
EXCHANGE DEADLINE 09/15/08

SSAP Albert Pujols/15 175.00 300.00
SSCP Corey Patterson/30 12.00 30.00
SSCR Cal Ripken/15 150.00 250.00
SSDJ Derek Jeter/15 300.00 500.00
SSGL Tom Glavine/30 20.00 50.00
SSHA Travis Hafner/30 12.00 30.00
SSNR Nolan Ryan/15 90.00 150.00
SSPH Phillip Humber/30 20.00 50.00
SSPI Mike Piazza/15 110.00 175.00
SSRC Roger Clemens/15 125.00 200.00

2005 Sweet Spot Signatures Barrel Red Ink

OVERALL AU ODDS 1:12
PRINT RUNS B/WN 5-10 COPIES PER
NO PRICING DUE TO SCARCITY
EXCHANGE DEADLINE 09/15/08

2005 Sweet Spot Signatures Glove Black Ink

*BLK p/r 30: 1X TO 2.5X BLK p/r 350
*BLK p/r 30: 1X TO 2.5X BLK RC YR p/r 350
*BLK p/r 15: 1X TO 2.5X BLK p/r 175
*BLK p/r 15: .75X TO 2X BLK p/r 58
OVERALL AU ODDS 1:12
PRINT RUNS B/WN 15-30 COPIES PER
EXCHANGE DEADLINE 09/15/08

AP Albert Pujols/15 250.00 400.00
BJ Bo Jackson/15 125.00 200.00
CP Corey Patterson/30 15.00 40.00
CR Cal Ripken/15 175.00 300.00
DJ Derek Jeter/15 300.00 500.00
GL Tom Glavine/30 25.00 60.00
HA Travis Hafner/30 15.00 40.00
NR Nolan Ryan/15 75.00 200.00
PI Mike Piazza/15 150.00 250.00

2005 Sweet Spot Signatures Dual Red Stitch

OVERALL DUAL AU ODDS 1:196
STATED PRINT RUN 25 SERIAL #'d SETS
EXCHANGE DEADLINE 09/15/08

BJ Bobby Crosby / Jason Bay 30.00 60.00
DC A.Dunn/S.Casey 10.00 25.00
GL K.Greene/M.Loretta 10.00 25.00
NH J.Niemann/P.Humber 30.00 60.00
PB J.Bay/O.Perez 30.00 60.00
PC A.Pujols/M.Cabrera 250.00 400.00
PO J.Peavy/R.Oswalt 30.00 60.00
SB R.Sandberg/W.Boggs 60.00 120.00
SG N.Garciaparra/R.Sandberg 125.00 200.00
SP B.Sheets/J.Peavy 30.00 60.00
WC D.Wright/M.Cabrera 100.00 200.00
WR D.Wright/J.Reyes 150.00 250.00

2005 Sweet Spot Sweet Threads

*GOLD: .6X TO 1.5X BASIC
GOLD PRINT RUN 75 SERIAL #'d SETS
PLATINUM PRINT RUN 10 SERIAL #'d SETS
NO PLATINUM PRICING DUE TO SCARCITY
PLUTONIUM PRINT RUN 1 SERIAL #'d SET
NO PLUTONIUM PRICING DUE TO SCARCITY
OVERALL 1-PIECE GU ODDS 1:6
*PATCH: 1.5X TO 4X BASIC
OVERALL PATCH ODDS 1:96
PATCH PRINT RUN 35 SERIAL #'d SETS
PRICES ARE FOR 2-3 COLOR PATCHES
REDUCE 20% FOR 1-COLOR PATCH
ADD 20% FOR 4-COLOR PATCH
ADD 50% FOR 5-COLOR+ PATCH

STAB Adrian Beltre 2.00 5.00
STAP Albert Pujols 6.00 15.00
STAS Alfonso Soriano 2.00 5.00
STBC Bartolo Colon 2.00 5.00
STBJ Bo Jackson 4.00 10.00
STBW Bernie Williams 3.00 8.00
STCB Carlos Beltran 2.00 5.00
STCJ Chipper Jones 4.00 10.00
STCL Carlos Lee 2.00 5.00
STCR Cal Ripken 8.00 20.00
STCS Curt Schilling 3.00 8.00
STDJ Derek Jeter 10.00 25.00
STDM Don Mattingly 5.00 12.00
STDO David Ortiz 4.00 10.00
STEC Eric Chavez 2.00 5.00
STEG Eric Gagne 2.00 5.00
STFT Frank Thomas 4.00 10.00
STGB George Brett 5.00 12.00
STGM Greg Maddux 4.00 10.00
STGW Tony Gwynn 4.00 10.00
STHB Hank Blalock 2.00 5.00
STHO Trevor Hoffman 2.00 5.00
STIR Ivan Rodriguez 3.00 8.00
STJB Jeff Bagwell 3.00 8.00
STJD Johnny Damon 3.00 8.00
STJS Johan Santana 4.00 10.00
STJT Jim Thome 3.00 8.00
STJV Jason Varitek 6.00 15.00
STKG Ken Griffey Jr. 6.00 15.00
STKW Kerry Wood 2.00 5.00
STMC Miguel Cabrera 3.00 8.00
STMP Mark Prior 3.00 8.00
STMR Manny Ramirez 3.00 8.00
STMS Mike Schmidt 5.00 12.00
STMT Mark Teixeira 3.00 8.00
STNR Nolan Ryan 8.00 20.00
STPI Mike Piazza 4.00 10.00
STPM Pedro Martinez 3.00 8.00
STRJ Randy Johnson 4.00 10.00
STRP Rafael Palmeiro 3.00 8.00
STRS Ryne Sandberg 5.00 12.00
STSM John Smoltz 3.00 8.00
STSR Scott Rolen 3.00 8.00
STSS Sammy Sosa 4.00 10.00
STTE Miguel Tejada 2.00 5.00
STTG Tom Glavine 3.00 8.00
STTH Todd Helton 3.00 8.00
STVG Vladimir Guerrero 4.00 10.00
STWB Wade Boggs 3.00 8.00
STWC Will Clark 3.00 8.00

2005 Sweet Spot Sweet Threads Dual

STATED PRINT RUN 25 SERIAL #'d SETS
GOLD PRINT RUN 5 SERIAL #'d SETS
NO GOLD PRICING DUE TO SCARCITY
PLUTONIUM PRINT RUN 1 SERIAL #'d SET
NO PLUTONIUM PRICING DUE TO SCARCITY
OVERALL COMBO GU ODDS 1:192
OVERALL PATCH ODDS 1:96
PATCH PRINT RUN 5 SERIAL #'d SETS
NO PATCH PRICING DUE TO SCARCITY

STDBG C.Beltran/K.Griffey Jr. 15.00 40.00
STDBM C.Beltran/P.Martinez 8.00 20.00
STDDC C.Delgado/M.Cabrera 8.00 20.00
STDGC K.Griffey Jr./M.Cabrera 15.00 40.00
STDGM D.McPherson/V.Guerrero 10.00 25.00
STDJB B.Jackson/G.Brett 15.00 40.00
STDJJ R.Johnson/D.Jeter 20.00 50.00
STDJM D.Jeter/D.Mattingly 30.00 60.00
STDJS J.Thome/M.Schmidt 15.00 40.00
STDMG G.Maddux/T.Glavine 15.00 40.00
STDMJ M.Mussina/R.Johnson 10.00 25.00
STDMP G.Maddux/M.Prior 15.00 40.00
STDOR D.Ortiz/M.Ramirez 8.00 20.00
STDPO A.Pettitte/R.Oswalt 8.00 20.00
STDPR P.Martinez/R.Johnson 10.00 25.00
STDPS R.Palmeiro/S.Sosa 10.00 25.00
STDPW D.Wright/M.Piazza 15.00 40.00
STDRJ C.Ripken/D.Jeter 40.00 80.00
STDRP A.Pujols/S.Rolen 15.00 40.00
STDRT C.Ripken/M.Tejada 30.00 60.00
STDSB R.Sandberg/W.Boggs 15.00 40.00
STDSJ C.Schilling/R.Johnson 10.00 25.00
STDSV C.Schilling/J.Varitek 10.00 25.00
STDWP K.Wood/M.Prior 8.00 20.00

2005 Sweet Spot Sweet Threads Triple

STATED PRINT RUN 25 SERIAL #'d SETS
GOLD PRINT RUN 5 SERIAL #'d SETS
NO GOLD PRICING DUE TO SCARCITY
PLUTONIUM PRINT RUN 1 SERIAL #'d SET
NO PLUTONIUM PRICING DUE TO SCARCITY
OVERALL COMBO GU ODDS 1:192
OVERALL PATCH ODDS 1:96
PATCH PRINT RUN 5 SERIAL #'d SETS
NO PATCH PRICING DUE TO SCARCITY

BBB Biggio/Bagwell/Berkman 10.00 25.00
BWP Beltran/Wright/Piazza 15.00 40.00
GGG L.Gonz/S.Green/Glaus 8.00 20.00
JMB Randy/Mussina/K.Brown 10.00 25.00
JWS Jeter/Bernie/Sheffield 30.00 60.00
KGD Kearns/Griffey Jr./Dunn 15.00 40.00
LOP Lidge/Oswalt/Pettitte 10.00 25.00
ODR D.Ortiz/Damon/Manny 10.00 25.00
PER Pujols/Edmonds/Rolen 15.00 40.00
PWM Prior/Wood/Maddux 15.00 40.00
RDN Manny/Damon/Nixon 15.00 40.00
SBT Soriano/Blalock/Teixeira 10.00 25.00
SMJ Schilling/Pedro/Randy 10.00 25.00
TPS Tejada/Rafty/Sosa 10.00 25.00

2005 Sweet Spot Sweet Threads Quad

STATED PRINT RUN 25 SERIAL #'d SETS
GOLD PRINT RUN 5 SERIAL #'d SETS
NO GOLD PRICING DUE TO SCARCITY
PLUTONIUM PRINT RUN 1 SERIAL #'d SET
NO PLUTONIUM PRICING DUE TO SCARCITY
OVERALL COMBO GU ODDS 1:192
OVERALL PATCH ODDS 1:96
PATCH PRINT RUN 5 SERIAL #'d SETS
NO PATCH PRICING DUE TO SCARCITY

STQBMCB Belt/McPher/Chav/Blal 15.00 40.00
STQBRGG Beltran/Manny/Grif/Vlad 30.00 60.00
STQPOTH Pujols/Ortiz/Thome/Helt 30.00 60.00
STQRBGB Rip/Brett/Gwynn/Boggs 60.00 120.00
STQRVMP Ivan/Varit/Mauer/Posa 20.00 50.00

2006 Sweet Spot

COMP.SET w/o AU's (100) 10.00 25.00
COMMON CARD (1-100) .20 .50
OVERALL AU ODDS 1:12
AU PRINT RUNS B/WN 45-275 PER
EXCHANGE DEADLINE 05/25/08
ASTERISK = PARTIAL EXCHANGE

1 Bartolo Colon .20 .50
2 Garret Anderson .20 .50
3 Francisco Rodriguez .30 .75
4 Dallas McPherson .20 .50
5 Andy Pettitte .30 .75
6 Lance Berkman .30 .75
7 Willy Taveras .20 .50
8 Bobby Crosby .20 .50
9 Dan Haren .20 .50
10 Nick Swisher .30 .75
11 Vernon Wells .20 .50
12 Orlando Hudson .20 .50
13 Roy Halladay .30 .75
14 Andruw Jones .20 .50
15 Chipper Jones .50 1.25
16 Jeff Francoeur .50 1.25
17 John Smoltz .50 1.25
18 Carlos Lee .20 .50
19 Rickie Weeks .20 .50
20 Bill Hall .20 .50
21 Jim Edmonds .30 .75
22 David Eckstein .20 .50
23 Mark Mulder .20 .50
24 Aramis Ramirez .20 .50
25 Greg Maddux .60 1.50
26 Nomar Garciaparra .30 .75
27 Carlos Zambrano .30 .75
28 Scott Kazmir .30 .75
29 Jorge Cantu .20 .50
30 Carl Crawford .30 .75
31 Luis Gonzalez .20 .50
32 Troy Glaus .20 .50
33 Shawn Green .20 .50
34 Jeff Kent .20 .50
35 Milton Bradley .20 .50
36 Cesar Izturis .20 .50
37 Omar Vizquel .30 .75
38 Moises Alou .20 .50
39 Randy Winn .20 .50
40 Jason Schmidt .20 .50
41 Coco Crisp .20 .50
42 C.C. Sabathia .30 .75
43 Cliff Lee .30 .75
44 Ichiro Suzuki .60 1.50
45 Richie Sexson .20 .50
46 Jeremy Reed .20 .50
47 Carlos Delgado .20 .50
48 Miguel Cabrera .50 1.25
49 Luis Castillo .20 .50
50 Carlos Beltran .30 .75
51 Tom Glavine .30 .75
52 David Wright .40 1.00
53 Cliff Floyd .20 .50
54 Chad Cordero .20 .50
55 Jose Vidro .20 .50
56 Jose Guillen .20 .50
57 Nick Johnson .20 .50
58 Miguel Tejada .30 .75
59 Melvin Mora .20 .50
60 Javy Lopez .20 .50
61 Khalil Greene .20 .50
62 Brian Giles .20 .50
63 Trevor Hoffman .30 .75
64 Bobby Abreu .20 .50
65 Jimmy Rollins .30 .75
66 Pat Burrell .20 .50
67 Billy Wagner .20 .50
68 Jack Wilson .20 .50
69 Zach Duke .20 .50
70 Craig Wilson .20 .50
71 Mark Teixeira .30 .75
72 Hank Blalock .20 .50
73 David Dellucci .20 .50
74 Manny Ramirez .50 1.25
75 Johnny Damon .30 .75
76 Jason Varitek .50 1.25
77 Trot Nixon .20 .50
78 Adam Dunn .30 .75
79 Felipe Lopez .20 .50
80 Brandon Claussen .20 .50
81 Sean Casey .20 .50
82 Todd Helton .30 .75
83 Clint Barmes .20 .50
84 Matt Holliday .50 1.25
85 Mike Sweeney .20 .50
86 Zack Greinke .50 1.25
87 David DeJesus .20 .50
88 Ivan Rodriguez .30 .75
89 Jeremy Bonderman .20 .50
90 Magglio Ordonez .30 .75
91 Torii Hunter .20 .50
92 Joe Nathan .20 .50
93 Michael Cuddyer .20 .50
94 Paul Konerko .30 .75
95 Jermaine Dye .20 .50
96 Jon Garland .20 .50
97 Alex Rodriguez .60 1.50
98 Hideki Matsui .50 1.25
99 Jason Giambi .20 .50
100 Mariano Rivera .60 1.50
101 Adrian Beltre AU/99 10.00 25.00
102 Matt Cain AU/275 (RC) 20.00 50.00
103 Craig Biggio AU/99 30.00 60.00
104 Eric Chavez AU/99 12.50 30.00
105 J.D. Drew AU/99 12.50 30.00
106 Eric Gagne AU/99 8.00 20.00
107 Tim Hudson AU/99 10.00 25.00
108 Tom Glavine AU/275 20.00 50.00
109 David Ortiz AU/99 20.00 50.00
110 Scott Rolen AU/275 8.00 20.00
111 Johan Santana AU/99 20.00 50.00
112 Curt Schilling AU/96 15.00 40.00
113 John Smoltz AU/99 30.00 60.00
114 Alfonso Soriano AU/99 1.50 30.00
115 Kerry Wood AU/99 8.00 20.00
116 Edwin Jackson AU/99 8.00 20.00
117 Felix Hernandez AU/125 10.00 25.00
118 Prince Fielder AU/99 (RC) 20.00 50.00
119 Vladimir Guerrero AU/86 30.00 60.00
120 Roger Clemens AU/99 30.00 60.00
121 Albert Pujols AU/45 100.00 200.00
122 Chris Carpenter AU/99 20.00 50.00
123 Derrek Lee AU/99 15.00 40.00
124 Dontrelle Willis AU/99 12.50 30.00
125 Roy Oswalt AU/99 15.00 40.00
126 Ryan Garko AU/275 (RC) 10.00 25.00
127 Tadahito Iguchi AU/275 10.00 25.00
128 Hank Blalock AU/99 10.00 25.00
129 Joe Mauer AU/275 12.00 30.00
130 Victor Martinez AU/275 6.00 15.00
131 Wily Mo Pena AU/275 10.00 25.00
132 Oliver Perez AU/274 6.00 15.00
134 Ben Sheets AU/275 10.00 25.00
135 Michael Young AU/275 10.00 25.00
136 Jonny Gomes AU/275 6.00 15.00
137 Derek Jeter AU/99 125.00 250.00
138 Ken Griffey Jr. AU/37
138 Ken Griffey Jr. AU/275 75.00 200.00
139 R.Zimmerman AU/275 (RC) 10.00 25.00
140 Scott Baker AU/275 (RC) 6.00 15.00
141 Huston Street AU/275 10.00 25.00
142 Jason Bay AU/275 5.00 12.00
143 Ryan Howard AU/275 10.00 25.00
145 Travis Hafner AU/275 10.00 25.00
146 Brian Myrow AU/275 RC 6.00 15.00
147 Scott Podsednik AU/275 10.00 25.00
148 Brian Roberts AU/275 10.00 25.00
149 Grady Sizemore AU/135 5.00 12.00
150 Chris Demaria AU/275 RC 6.00 15.00
151 Jonah Bayliss AU/275 RC 6.00 15.00
152 Geovany Soto AU/275 (RC) 8.00 20.00
153 Lyle Overbay AU/275 6.00 15.00
154 Joey Devine AU/275 RC 6.00 15.00
155 A.Freire AU/275 RC 6.00 15.00
156 Conor Jackson AU/275 (RC) 10.00 25.00
157 Danny Sandoval AU/275 RC 6.00 15.00
158 Chase Utley AU/275 10.00 25.00
159 Jeff Harris AU/275 RC 6.00 15.00
160 Ron Flores AU/275 RC 6.00 15.00
161 Scott Feldman AU/275 RC 6.00 15.00
162 Yadier Molina AU/275 15.00 40.00
163 Tim Corcoran AU/275 RC 6.00 15.00
164 Craig Hansen AU/275 RC 6.00 15.00
165 Jason Bergmann AU/275 RC 6.00 15.00
166 Craig Breslow AU/275 RC 6.00 15.00
167 Jhonny Peralta AU/275 6.00 15.00
168 J.Hermida AU/275 (RC) 10.00 25.00
169 Scott Kazmir AU/275 10.00 25.00
170 Bobby Crosby AU/99 12.50 30.00
171 Rich Harden AU/275 6.00 15.00
172 Casey Kotchman AU/275 6.00 15.00
173 Tim Hamulack AU/275 (RC) 6.00 15.00
174 Justin Morneau AU/275 6.00 15.00
175 Jake Peavy AU/275 6.00 15.00
176 Y.Betancourt AU/275 10.00 25.00
177 Jeremy Accardo AU/275 RC 6.00 15.00
178 Jorge Cantu AU/200 10.00 25.00
179 Marlon Byrd AU/275 6.00 15.00
180 R.Jorgensen AU/275 RC 6.00 15.00
181 C.Denorfia AU/275 (RC) 6.00 15.00
182 Steve Stemle AU/275 RC 6.00 15.00
183 Robert Andino AU/275 RC 6.00 15.00
184 Chris Heintz AU/275 RC 6.00 15.00

2006 Sweet Spot Signatures Red Stitch Blue Ink

*RS BLUE p/r 114-150: .4X TO 1X p/r 125-275
*RS BLUE p/r 114-150: .3X TO .8X p/r 99
*RS BLUE p/r 75-100: .5X TO 1.2X p/r 125-275
*RS BLUE p/r 40: .6X TO 1.5X p/r 125-275
OVERALL AUTO ODDS 1:12
PRINT RUNS B/WN 15-150 COPIES PER
NO PRICING ON QTY OF 25 OR LESS
EXCHANGE DEADLINE 05/25/08

144 Mike Piazza/100 50.00 100.00

2006 Sweet Spot Signatures Red-Blue Stitch Black Ink

*RBS BLK p/r 50-99: .5X TO 1.2X p/r 125-275
*RBS BLACK p/r 50-99: .4X TO 1X p/r 86-99
*RBS BLACK p/r 45-49: .5X TO 1.2X p/r 86-99
OVERALL AUTO ODDS 1:12
PRINT RUNS B/WN 25-99 COPIES PER
NO PRICING ON QTY OF 25 OR LESS
EXCHANGE DEADLINE 05/25/08

2006 Sweet Spot Signatures Red-Blue Stitch Blue Ink

*RBS BLUE p/r 50: .5X TO 1.2X p/r 125-275
*RBS BLUE p/r 50: .4X TO 1X p/r 86-99
*RBS BLUE p/r 30-49: .6X TO 1.5X p/r 125-275
OVERALL AUTO ODDS 1:12
PRINT RUNS B/WN 5-50 COPIES PER
NO PRICING ON QTY OF 25 OR LESS
EXCHANGE DEADLINE 05/25/08

144 Mike Piazza/50 60.00 120.00

2006 Sweet Spot Super Sweet Swatch

OVERALL GU ODDS 1:12
PRINT RUNS B/WN 5-299 COPIES PER
NO PRICING ON QTY OF 9 OR LESS

SWAD Adam Dunn Jsy/299 4.00 10.00
SWAE Adam Eaton Jsy/299 3.00 8.00
SWAJ Andruw Jones Jsy/299 5.00 12.00
SWAN Andy Pettitte Jsy/299 5.00 12.00
SWAP Albert Pujols Jsy/299 10.00 25.00
SWAT Garrett Atkins Jsy/299 3.00 8.00
SWBA Bobby Abreu Jsy/299 4.00 10.00
SWBC Brandon Claussen Jsy/299 3.00 8.00
SWBE Josh Beckett Jsy/299 4.00 10.00
SWBG Brian Giles Jsy/299 3.00 8.00
SWBS Ben Sheets Jsy/299 4.00 10.00
SWBW Bernie Williams Bat/299 5.00 12.00
SWBZ Barry Zito Jsy/299 4.00 10.00
SWCB Craig Biggio Jsy/299 5.00 12.00
SWCD Carlos Delgado Bat/299 5.00 12.00
SWCJ Chipper Jones Jsy/299 5.00 12.00
SWCR Bobby Crosby Bat/136 4.00 10.00
SWCS Curt Schilling Jsy/299 5.00 12.00
SWDJ Derek Jeter Bat/299 15.00 40.00
SWDL Derrek Lee Jsy/299 4.00 10.00
SWDO David Ortiz Jsy/299 6.00 15.00
SWDW Dontrelle Willis Jsy/299 4.00 10.00
SWDY Jermaine Dye Jsy/299 4.00 10.00
SWEC Eric Chavez Jsy/299 3.00 8.00
SWED Jim Edmonds Bat/257 5.00 12.00
SWEG Eric Gagne Jsy/299 4.00 10.00
SWFG Freddy Garcia Jsy/299 4.00 10.00
SWFH Felix Hernandez Jsy/299 5.00 12.00
SWFR Jeff Francoeur Jsy/299 10.00 25.00
SWFT Frank Thomas Jsy/299 6.00 15.00
SWGA Garret Anderson Jsy/299 4.00 10.00
SWGL Tom Glavine Jsy/299 5.00 12.00
SWGR Grady Sizemore Jsy/299 6.00 15.00
SWGS Gary Sheffield Bat/189 4.00 10.00
SWHA Travis Hafner Jsy/299 4.00 10.00
SWHB Hank Blalock Jsy/299 4.00 10.00
SWHE Ramon Hernandez Bat/272 3.00 8.00
SWHO Trevor Hoffman Jsy/299 4.00 10.00
SWHU Torii Hunter Bat/287 4.00 10.00
SWHY Roy Halladay Jsy/299 4.00 10.00
SWIR Ivan Rodriguez Jsy/299 5.00 12.00
SWJA Jay Payton Bat/193 3.00 8.00
SWJB Jason Bay Jsy/299 4.00 10.00
SWJE Johnny Estrada Jsy/299 3.00 8.00
SWJG Jason Giambi Jsy/299 6.00 15.00
SWJJ Jacque Jones Jsy/299 4.00 10.00
SWJL Jeff Bagwell Jsy/299 5.00 12.00
SWJM Joe Mauer Jsy/299 5.00 12.00
SWJO John Smoltz Jsy/299 5.00 12.00
SWJP Jorge Posada Jsy/299 8.00 20.00
SWJR Jose Reyes Jsy/299 4.00 10.00
SWJS Jason Schmidt Jsy/299 4.00 10.00
SWJU Justin Morneau Jsy/299 4.00 10.00
SWJV Jason Varitek Jsy/299 6.00 15.00
SWJW Jack Wilson Jsy/299 3.00 8.00
SWKG Ken Griffey Jr. Jsy/299 15.00 40.00
SWKO Paul Konerko Jsy/299 4.00 10.00
SWKW Kerry Wood Jsy/299 4.00 10.00
SWLB Lance Berkman Bat/299 4.00 10.00
SWMA Matt Cain Jsy/299 5.00 12.00
SWMC Matt Clement Jsy/299 4.00 10.00
SWMG Marcus Giles Jsy/299 3.00 8.00
SWMI Miguel Cabrera Jsy/299 5.00 12.00
SWML Mark Loretta Bat/267 3.00 8.00
SWMM Mark Mulder Jsy/299 4.00 10.00
SWMP Mark Prior Jsy/299 4.00 10.00
SWMR Manny Ramirez Jsy/299 5.00 12.00
SWMS Mike Sweeney Jsy/299 3.00 8.00
SWMT Miguel Tejada Jsy/299 4.00 10.00
SWMY Michael Young Bat/221 4.00 10.00
SWNJ Nick Johnson Jsy/299 3.00 8.00
SWNL Noah Lowry Jsy/299 3.00 8.00
SWNS Nick Swisher Jsy/299 4.00 10.00
SWPE Jake Peavy Jsy/299 4.00 10.00
SWPF Prince Fielder Jsy/299 6.00 15.00
SWPI Mike Piazza Jsy/299 6.00 15.00
SWPM Pedro Martinez Jsy/299 5.00 12.00
SWRB Rocco Baldelli Jsy/299 3.00 8.00
SWRH Ryan Howard Jsy/299 12.50 30.00
SWRK Ryan Klesko Jsy/299 3.00 8.00
SWRO Roy Oswalt Jsy/299 4.00 10.00
SWRS Richie Sexson Jsy/299 3.00 8.00
SWRW Rickie Weeks Jsy/299 4.00 10.00
SWRZ Ryan Zimmerman Jsy/299 6.00 15.00
SWSA Johan Santana Jsy/299 5.00 12.00
SWSK Scott Kazmir Jsy/299 4.00 10.00
SWSR Scott Rolen Jsy/299 5.00 12.00
SWST Huston Street Jsy/299 4.00 10.00
SWTG Troy Glaus Bat/160 4.00 10.00
SWTH Tim Hudson Jsy/299 4.00 10.00
SWTN Trot Nixon Jsy/299 5.00 12.00
SWTO Todd Helton Bat/232 5.00 12.00
SWTX Mark Teixeira Jsy/299 4.00 10.00
SWVG Vladimir Guerrero Jsy/299 6.00 15.00
SWVM Victor Martinez Jsy/299 4.00 10.00
SWVW Vernon Wells Jsy/299 4.00 10.00
SWWE David Wells Jsy/299 3.00 8.00
SWZD Zach Duke Jsy/299 3.00 8.00

2006 Sweet Spot Super Sweet Swatch Gold

*GOLD: .5X TO 1.2X BASIC
OVERALL GU ODDS 1:12
STATED PRINT RUN 75 SERIAL #'d SETS

SWMO Magglio Ordonez Bat 5.00 12.00
SWSF Steve Finley Bat 5.00 12.00

2006 Sweet Spot Super Sweet Swatch Platinum

*PLATINUM: .6X TO 1.5X BASIC
OVERALL GU ODDS 1:12
STATED PRINT RUN 45 SERIAL #'d SETS

SWMO Magglio Ordonez Bat 6.00 15.00
SWSF Steve Finley Bat 6.00 15.00

2007 Sweet Spot

COMMON CARD (1-100) .75 2.00
STATED PRINT RUN 850 SER.#'d SETS
TWO BASE CARDS PER TIN
COMMON AU RC (101-142) 3.00 8.00
OVERALL AU ODDS ONE PER TIN
EXCHANGE DEADLINE 11/9/2009

1 Adam Dunn 1.25 3.00
2 Adrian Beltre 2.00 5.00
3 Albert Pujols 2.50 6.00
4 Alex Rios .75 2.00
5 Alex Rodriguez 2.50 6.00
6 Alfonso Soriano 1.25 3.00
7 Andruw Jones .75 2.00
8 Aramis Ramirez .75 2.00
9 B.J. Upton .75 2.00
10 Barry Zito .75 2.00
11 Bartolo Colon .75 2.00
12 Ben Sheets .75 2.00
13 Bill Hall .75 2.00
14 Brad Penny .75 2.00
15 Brandon Webb 1.25 3.00
16 C.C. Sabathia 1.25 3.00
17 Carl Crawford 1.25 3.00
18 Carlos Beltran 1.25 3.00
19 Carlos Guillen .75 2.00
20 Carlos Lee .75 2.00
21 Chase Utley 1.25 3.00
22 Chien-Ming Wang 1.25 3.00
23 Chipper Jones 2.00 5.00
24 Chris Carpenter 1.25 3.00
25 Cole Hamels 1.50 4.00
26 Craig Biggio 1.25 3.00
27 Curt Schilling 1.25 3.00
28 Dan Haren .75 2.00
29 David Ortiz 2.00 5.00
30 David Wright 1.50 4.00
31 Delmon Young 1.25 3.00
32 Derek Jeter 5.00 12.00
33 Derrek Lee .75 2.00
34 Dontrelle Willis .75 2.00
35 Felix Hernandez 1.25 3.00
36 Frank Thomas 2.00 5.00
37 Gil Meche .75 2.00
38 Grady Sizemore 1.25 3.00
39 Greg Maddux 2.50 6.00
40 Ian Kinsler 1.25 3.00
41 Ichiro Suzuki 2.50 6.00
42 Ivan Rodriguez 1.25 3.00
43 Jake Peavy .75 2.00
44 Jason Bay 1.25 3.00
45 Jason Varitek 2.00 5.00
46 Jeff Kent .75 2.00
47 Jermaine Dye .75 2.00
48 Jim Edmonds 1.25 3.00
49 Jim Thome 1.25 3.00
50 Jimmy Rollins 1.25 3.00
51 Joe Mauer 1.50 4.00
52 Johan Santana 1.25 3.00
53 John Smoltz 2.00 5.00
54 Jonathan Papelbon 2.00 5.00
55 Jorge Posada 1.25 3.00
56 Jose Reyes 1.25 3.00
57 Josh Beckett .75 2.00
58 Justin Morneau 1.25 3.00
59 Justin Verlander 2.00 5.00
60 Ken Griffey Jr. 4.00 10.00
61 Kenji Johjima 2.00 5.00
62 Lance Berkman 1.25 3.00
63 Magglio Ordonez 1.25 3.00
64 Manny Ramirez 1.25 3.00
65 Mariano Rivera 2.50 6.00
66 Mark Buehrle 1.25 3.00
67 Mark Teixeira 1.25 3.00
68 Matt Holliday 2.00 5.00
69 Matt Morris .75 2.00
70 Melvin Mora .75 2.00
71 Michael Young .75 2.00
72 Miguel Cabrera 2.00 5.00
73 Miguel Tejada 1.25 3.00
74 Mike Lowell .75 2.00
75 Mike Mussina 2.00 5.00
76 Mike Piazza 2.00 5.00
77 Nick Swisher 1.25 3.00
78 Orlando Hudson .75 2.00
79 Paul Konerko 1.25 3.00
80 Paul Lo Duca .75 2.00
81 Pedro Martinez 1.25 3.00
82 Prince Fielder 1.25 3.00
83 Randy Johnson 2.00 5.00
84 Rickie Weeks .75 2.00
85 Roger Clemens 2.50 6.00
86 Roy Halladay 1.25 3.00
87 Roy Oswalt 1.25 3.00
88 Russell Martin .75 2.00
89 Ryan Howard 1.50 4.00
90 Ryan Zimmerman 1.25 3.00
91 Sammy Sosa 2.00 5.00
92 Scott Rolen 1.25 3.00
93 Shawn Green .75 2.00
94 Todd Helton 1.25 3.00
95 Tom Glavine 1.25 3.00
96 Torii Hunter .75 2.00
97 Travis Hafner .75 2.00
98 Vernon Wells .75 2.00
99 Victor Martinez 1.25 3.00
100 Vladimir Guerrero 1.25 3.00
101 Adam Lind AU (RC) 3.00 8.00
102 Akinori Iwamura AU SP RC 5.00 12.00
103 Alex Gordon AU RC 10.00 25.00
104 Alexi Casilla AU RC 6.00 15.00
105 Andy LaRoche AU (RC) 6.00 15.00
106 Billy Butler AU (RC) 6.00 15.00
107 Ryan Rowland-Smith AU RC 3.00 8.00
108 Brandon Wood AU (RC) 6.00 15.00
109 Brian Burres AU (RC) 3.00 8.00
110 Chase Wright AU RC 4.00 10.00
111 Chris Stewart AU RC 3.00 8.00
112 D.Matsuzaka AU SP RC 20.00 50.00
113 Delmon Young AU SP (RC) 6.00 15.00
114 Andy Sonnanstine AU RC 6.00 15.00
116 Fred Lewis AU (RC) 4.00 10.00
117 Glen Perkins AU SP (RC) 10.00 25.00
118 David Murphy AU (RC) 3.00 8.00
119 Hunter Pence AU (RC) 4.00 10.00
120 Jarrod Saltalamacchia AU (RC) 6.00 15.00
121 Jeff Baker AU SP (RC) 6.00 15.00
122 Jesus Flores AU SP RC 5.00 12.00
123 Joakim Soria AU SP RC 10.00 25.00
124 Joe Smith AU RC 4.00 10.00
125 Jon Knott AU (RC) 3.00 8.00
126 Josh Hamilton AU (RC) 12.50 30.00
127 Justin Hampson AU (RC) 3.00 8.00
128 Kei Igawa AU SP RC 10.00 25.00
129 Kevin Cameron AU RC 3.00 8.00
130 Matt Chico AU (RC) 4.00 10.00
131 Matt DeSalvo AU (RC) 4.00 10.00
132 Micah Owings AU SP (RC) 10.00 25.00
133 Michael Bourn AU (RC) 4.00 10.00
134 Miguel Montero AU (RC) 3.00 8.00
135 Phil Hughes AU SP (RC) 6.00 15.00
136 Rick Vanden Hurk AU RC 3.00 8.00
139 Travis Buck AU (RC) 4.00 10.00
140 T.Tulowitzki AU SP (RC) 12.50 30.00
141 Sean Henn AU (RC) 4.00 10.00
142 Zack Segovia AU (RC) 3.00 8.00
NNO Michael Buysner 15.00 40.00

2007 Sweet Spot Sweet Swatch Memorabilia

OVERALL MEM ODDS TWO PER TIN

SWAD Adam Dunn 3.00 8.00
SWAJ Andruw Jones 3.00 8.00
SWAP Albert Pujols 6.00 15.00
SWAS Alfonso Soriano 3.00 8.00
SWAT Garrett Atkins 3.00 8.00
SWBA Bobby Abreu 3.00 8.00
SWBE Josh Beckett 4.00 10.00
SWBG Brian Giles 3.00 8.00
SWBI Craig Biggio 3.00 8.00
SWBO Jeremy Bonderman 3.00 8.00
SWBR Brian Roberts 3.00 8.00
SWBU B.J. Upton 3.00 8.00

SWBW Billy Wagner 3.00 8.00
SWCA Chris Carpenter 3.00 8.00
SWCB Carlos Beltran 3.00 8.00
SWCC Carl Crawford 3.00 8.00
SWCD Carlos Delgado 3.00 8.00
SWCH Cole Hamels 3.00 8.00
SWCJ Chipper Jones 4.00 10.00
SWCL Carlos Lee 3.00 8.00
SWCS Curt Schilling 4.00 10.00
SWCU Chase Utley 4.00 10.00
SWDJ Derek Jeter 8.00 20.00
SWDM Daisuke Matsuzaka 6.00 15.00
SWDO David Ortiz 5.00 12.00
SWDW Dontrelle Willis 3.00 8.00
SWEB Erik Bedard 3.00 8.00
SWEC Eric Chavez 3.00 8.00
SWFG Freddy Garcia 3.00 8.00
SWFH Felix Hernandez 3.00 8.00
SWFL Francisco Liriano 3.00 8.00
SWFT Frank Thomas 5.00 12.00
SWGA Garret Anderson 3.00 8.00
SWGM Greg Maddux 5.00 12.00
SWGR Khalil Greene 3.00 8.00
SWGS Grady Sizemore 3.00 8.00
SWHA Roy Halladay 3.00 8.00
SWHB Hank Blalock 3.00 8.00
SWHE Todd Helton 3.00 8.00
SWHO Trevor Hoffman 3.00 8.00
SWHR Hanley Ramirez 3.00 8.00
SWHS Huston Street 3.00 8.00
SWHU Torii Hunter 3.00 8.00
SWIK Ian Kinsler 3.00 8.00
SWIR Ivan Rodriguez 3.00 8.00
SWJB Jason Bay 3.00 8.00
SWJD Jermaine Dye 3.00 8.00
SWJE Jim Edmonds 4.00 10.00
SWJF Jeff Francoeur 4.00 10.00
SWJG Jason Giambi 3.00 8.00
SWJK Jeff Kent 3.00 8.00
SWJM Joe Mauer 3.00 8.00
SWJN Joe Nathan 3.00 8.00
SWJP Jake Peavy 3.00 8.00
SWJR Jimmy Rollins 3.00 8.00
SWJS Jason Schmidt 3.00 8.00
SWJT Jim Thome 3.00 8.00
SWJV Jason Varitek 5.00 12.00
SWJW Jered Weaver 3.00 8.00
SWJZ Joel Zumaya 3.00 8.00
SWKG Ken Griffey Jr. 6.00 15.00
SWKM Kendry Morales 3.00 8.00
SWLB Lance Berkman 3.00 8.00
SWLG Luis Gonzalez 3.00 8.00
SWMC Miguel Cabrera 3.00 8.00
SWMM Mike Mussina 3.00 8.00
SWMO Justin Morneau 3.00 8.00
SWMR Manny Ramirez 4.00 10.00
SWMT Mark Teixeira 3.00 8.00
SWMY Michael Young 3.00 8.00
SWOR Magglio Ordonez 3.00 8.00
SWOS Roy Oswalt 3.00 8.00
SWPA Jonathan Papelbon 5.00 12.00
SWPB Pat Burrell 3.00 8.00
SWPE Jhonny Peralta 3.00 8.00
SWPF Prince Fielder 3.00 8.00
SWPM Pedro Martinez 3.00 8.00
SWPO Jorge Posada 3.00 8.00
SWRC Robinson Cano 4.00 10.00
SWRE Jose Reyes 5.00 12.00
SWRH Rich Harden 3.00 8.00
SWRI Mariano Rivera 3.00 8.00
SWRJ Randy Johnson 3.00 8.00
SWRO Roger Clemens 6.00 15.00
SWRW Rickie Weeks 3.00 8.00
SWRZ Ryan Zimmerman 5.00 12.00
SWSA Johan Santana 3.00 8.00
SWSD Stephen Drew 3.00 8.00
SWSK Scott Kazmir 3.00 8.00
SWSM John Smoltz 4.00 10.00
SWSR Scott Rolen 3.00 8.00
SWTE Miguel Tejada 3.00 8.00
SWTG Tom Glavine 3.00 8.00
SWTH Tim Hudson 3.00 8.00
SWTR Travis Hafner 3.00 8.00
SWVE Justin Verlander 4.00 10.00
SWVG Vladimir Guerrero 3.00 8.00
SWVM Victor Martinez 3.00 8.00
SWVW Vernon Wells 3.00 8.00

2007 Sweet Spot Sweet Swatch Memorabilia Patch

OVERALL MEM ODDS TWO PER TIN
STATED PRINT RUN 25 SER.#'d SETS
NO PRICING DUE TO SCARCITY

2007 Sweet Spot Signatures Red Stitch Blue Ink

OVERALL AU ODDS ONE PER TIN
PRINT RUNS B/WN 99-350 COPIES PER
EXCHANGE DEADLINE 11/9/2009
SSAD Adam Dunn/99 12.50 30.00
SSAG Adrian Gonzalez/350 8.00 20.00
SSAI Akinori Iwamura/99 8.00 20.00
SSAK Austin Kearns/299 4.00 10.00
SSAL Adam LaRoche/350 4.00 10.00
SSAM Andrew Miller/99 5.00 12.00
SSAX Alex Gordon/99 6.00 15.00
SSBB Boof Bonser/299 4.00 10.00
SSBP Brandon Phillips/99 10.00 25.00
SSBR Brian Bruney/299 4.00 10.00
SSBW Brandon Wood/350 6.00 15.00
SSCA Carl Crawford/99 6.00 15.00
SSCB Chad Billingsley/299 4.00 10.00
SSCC Chris Capuano/299 4.00 10.00
SSCH Cole Hamels/99 8.00 20.00
SSCJ Conor Jackson/299 4.00 10.00
SSCK Casey Kotchman/99 6.00 15.00
SSCL Cliff Lee/299 30.00 60.00
SSCQ Carlos Quentin/299 5.00 12.00
SSCY Chris Young/350 4.00 10.00
SSDC Daniel Cabrera/299 4.00 10.00
SSDH Dan Haren/299 6.00 15.00
SSDR Darrel Rasner/299 4.00 10.00
SSDY Delmon Young/99 10.00 25.00
SSEA Erick Aybar/299 4.00 10.00
SSFH Felix Hernandez/99 15.00 40.00
SSFP Felix Pie/99 10.00 25.00
SSGP Glen Perkins/350 4.00 10.00
SSHA Travis Hafner/99 6.00 15.00
SSHK Howie Kendrick/350 4.00 10.00
SSHP Hunter Pence/350 8.00 20.00
SSHS Huston Street/99 6.00 15.00
SSJA Jeremy Accardo/299 4.00 10.00
SSJH Josh Hamilton/350 12.50 30.00
SSJK Jason Kubel/299 4.00 10.00
SSJL Jon Lester/99 10.00 25.00
SSJN Joe Nathan/299 4.00 10.00
SSJP Jonathan Papelbon/99 6.00 15.00
SSJS Jeremy Sowers/99 6.00 15.00
SSJV Jason Varitek/99 20.00 50.00
SSJW Josh Willingham/299 4.00 10.00
SSKA Jeff Karstens/299 4.00 10.00
SSKS Kurt Suzuki/299 4.00 10.00
SSLI Adam Lind/299 4.00 10.00
SSLO Lyle Overbay/299 4.00 10.00
SSMC Matt Cain/299 6.00 15.00
SSMM Melvin Mora/99 6.00 15.00
SSNS Nick Swisher/299 6.00 15.00
SSPH Phil Hughes/99 6.00 15.00
SSPK Paul Konerko/99 10.00 25.00
SSRC Roger Clemens/99 50.00 100.00
SSRH Rich Hill/299 6.00 15.00
SSRI Rich Harden/99 6.00 15.00
SSRW Rickie Weeks/99 6.00 15.00
SSRZ Ryan Zimmerman/99 12.50 30.00
SSSE Sergio Mitre/299 4.00 10.00
SSSK Scott Kazmir/99 10.00 25.00
SSTB Travis Buck/299 6.00 15.00
SSTG Tom Glavine/99 12.50 30.00
SSTL Tim Lincecum/99 50.00 100.00
SSVE Justin Verlander/99 20.00 50.00
SSVM Victor Martinez/99 6.00 15.00
SSYG Chris B. Young/299 6.00 15.00
SSNNO 756 Asterisk

2007 Sweet Spot Signatures Red-Blue Stitch Red Ink

OVERALL AU ODDS ONE PER TIN
PRINT RUNS B/WN 5-15 COPIES PER
NO PRICING DUE TO SCARCITY
EXCHANGE DEADLINE 11/9/2009

2007 Sweet Spot Signatures Black-Silver Stitch Silver Ink

OVERALL AU ODDS ONE PER TIN
STATED PRINT RUN 1 SER.#'d SET
NO PRICING DUE TO SCARCITY
EXCHANGE DEADLINE 11/9/2009

2007 Sweet Spot Signatures Gold Stitch Gold Ink

OVERALL AU ODDS ONE PER TIN
PRINT RUNS B/WN 25-99 COPIES PER
NO PRICING ON QTY 25 OR LESS
EXCHANGE DEADLINE 11/9/2009
SPSAG Adrian Gonzalez/99 12.50 30.00
SPSAK Austin Kearns/99 6.00 15.00
SPSAL Adam LaRoche/99 6.00 15.00
SSBB Boof Bonser/99 6.00 15.00
SSBR Brian Bruney/99 6.00 15.00
SSBW Brandon Wood/99 10.00 25.00
SSCB Chad Billingsley/99 6.00 15.00
SSCC Chris Capuano/99 6.00 15.00
SSCJ Conor Jackson/99 6.00 15.00
SSCL Cliff Lee/99 40.00 80.00
SSCQ Carlos Quentin/99 8.00 20.00
SSCY Chris Young/99 6.00 15.00
SSDC Daniel Cabrera/99 6.00 15.00
SSDH Dan Haren/99 6.00 15.00
SSDR Darrel Rasner/99 12.50 30.00
SSEA Erick Aybar/99 6.00 15.00
SSGP Glen Perkins/99 6.00 15.00
SSHK Howie Kendrick/99 6.00 15.00
SSHP Hunter Pence/99 6.00 15.00
SSJH Josh Hamilton/99 12.50 30.00
SSJK Jason Kubel/99 6.00 15.00
SSJN Joe Nathan/99 6.00 15.00
SSJW Josh Willingham/99 6.00 15.00
SSKA Jeff Karstens/99 6.00 15.00
SSKS Kurt Suzuki/99 6.00 15.00
SSLI Adam Lind/99 6.00 15.00
SSLO Lyle Overbay/99 6.00 15.00
SSMC Matt Cain/99 15.00 40.00
SSNS Nick Swisher/99 10.00 25.00
SSRH Rich Hill/99 6.00 15.00
SSSE Sergio Mitre/99 6.00 15.00
SSTB Travis Buck/99 10.00 25.00
SSYG Chris B. Young/99 10.00 25.00

2007 Sweet Spot Signatures Silver Stitch Silver Ink

OVERALL AU ODDS ONE PER TIN
PRINT RUNS B/WN 1-99 COPIES PER
NO PRICING ON QTY 25 OR LESS
EXCHANGE DEADLINE 11/9/2009
SPSAD Adam Dunn/44 15.00 40.00
SPSAM Andrew Miller/48 20.00 50.00
SSBB Boof Bonser/26 8.00 20.00
SSBP Brandon Phillips/99 10.00 25.00
SSBR Brian Bruney/99 6.00 15.00
SSCB Chad Billingsley/58 10.00 25.00
SSCC Chris Capuano/39 8.00 20.00
SSCH Cole Hamels/35 20.00 50.00
SSCK Casey Kotchman/99 6.00 15.00
SSCL Cliff Lee/31 30.00 60.00
SSCY Chris Young/32 8.00 20.00
SSDC Daniel Cabrera/35 8.00 20.00
SSDR Darrel Rasner/27 8.00 20.00
SSDY Delmon Young/26 12.50 30.00
SSEA Erick Aybar/32 8.00 20.00
SSFH Felix Hernandez/34 20.00 50.00
SSFP Felix Pie/99 10.00 25.00
SSGP Glen Perkins/60 6.00 15.00
SSHA Travis Hafner/48 8.00 20.00
SSHK Howie Kendrick/47 8.00 20.00
SSJH Josh Hamilton/33 30.00 60.00
SSJL Jon Lester/31 12.50 30.00
SSJN Joe Nathan/36 8.00 20.00
SSJP Jonathan Papelbon/58 20.00 50.00
SSJS Jeremy Sowers/45 8.00 20.00
SSJV Jason Varitek/33 30.00 60.00
SSKS Kurt Suzuki/99 6.00 15.00
SSLI Adam Lind/99 6.00 15.00
SSNS Nick Swisher/33 12.50 30.00
SSPH Phil Hughes/65 12.50 30.00
SSPK Paul Konerko/99 10.00 25.00
SSRH Rich Hill/51 10.00 25.00
SSRI Rich Harden/40 8.00 20.00
SSSE Sergio Mitre/99 6.00 15.00
SSTG Tom Glavine/47 20.00 50.00
SSTH Torii Hunter/48 8.00 20.00
SSTL Tim Lincecum/55 100.00 175.00
SSVE Justin Verlander/35 30.00 60.00
SSVM Victor Martinez/41 8.00 20.00

2007 Sweet Spot Signatures Bat Barrel Blue Ink

OVERALL AU ODDS ONE PER TIN
PRINT RUNS B/WN 1-99 COPIES PER
NO PRICING ON QTY 25 OR LESS
EXCHANGE DEADLINE 11/9/2009
SSAD Adam Dunn/44 10.00 25.00
SSAM Andrew Miller/48 4.00 10.00
SSBB Boof Bonser/26 4.00 10.00
SSBP Brandon Phillips/99 10.00 25.00
SSBR Brian Bruney/99 4.00 10.00
SSCB Chad Billingsley/58 10.00 25.00
SSCC Chris Capuano/39 4.00 10.00
SSCH Cole Hamels/35 12.50 30.00
SSCK Casey Kotchman/99 4.00 10.00
SSCL Cliff Lee/31 12.50 30.00
SSCY Chris Young/32 4.00 10.00
SSDC Daniel Cabrera/35 4.00 10.00
SSDR Darrel Rasner/27 4.00 10.00
SSDY Delmon Young/26 12.50 30.00
SSFH Felix Hernandez/34 20.00 50.00
SSFP Felix Pie/99 10.00 25.00
SSGP Glen Perkins/60 4.00 10.00
SSHA Travis Hafner/48 4.00 10.00
SSHK Howie Kendrick/47 4.00 10.00
SSJH Josh Hamilton/33 20.00 50.00
SSJL Jon Lester/31 20.00 50.00
SSJN Joe Nathan/36 10.00 25.00
SSJP Jonathan Papelbon/58 20.00 50.00
SSJS Jeremy Sowers/45 4.00 10.00
SSJV Jason Varitek/33 30.00 60.00
SSKS Kurt Suzuki/99 4.00 10.00
SSLI Adam Lind/99 4.00 10.00
SSNS Nick Swisher/33 12.50 30.00
SSPH Phil Hughes/65 12.50 30.00
SSPK Paul Konerko/99 10.00 25.00
SSRH Rich Hill/53 10.00 25.00
SSRM Russell Martin/55 4.00 10.00
SSSE Sergio Mitre/99 4.00 10.00
SSTG Tom Glavine/47 20.00 50.00
SSTL Tim Lincecum/55 50.00 120.00
SSVE Justin Verlander/35 30.00 60.00
SSVM Victor Martinez/41 10.00 25.00

2007 Sweet Spot Signatures Glove Leather Black Ink

OVERALL AU ODDS ONE PER TIN
PRINT RUNS B/WN 25-75 COPIES PER
NO PRICING DUE TO SCARCITY
EXCHANGE DEADLINE 11/9/2009
SSAG Adrian Gonzalez/75 6.00 15.00
SSAK Austin Kearns/75 6.00 15.00
SSAL Adam LaRoche/75 6.00 15.00
SSBB Boof Bonser/75 6.00 15.00
SSBR Brian Bruney/75 6.00 15.00
SSBW Brandon Wood/75 10.00 25.00
SSCB Chad Billingsley/75 10.00 25.00
SSCC Chris Capuano/75 6.00 15.00
SSCJ Conor Jackson/75 6.00 15.00
SSCL Cliff Lee/75 10.00 25.00
SSCQ Carlos Quentin/75 8.00 20.00
SSCY Chris Young/75 6.00 15.00
SSDC Daniel Cabrera/75 6.00 15.00
SSDH Dan Haren/75 6.00 15.00
SSDR Darrel Rasner/75 6.00 15.00
SSEA Erick Aybar/75 6.00 15.00
SSGP Glen Perkins/75 6.00 15.00
SSHK Howie Kendrick/75 6.00 15.00
SSHP Hunter Pence/75 40.00 80.00
SSJH Josh Hamilton/75 12.00 30.00
SSJK Jason Kubel/75 6.00 15.00
SSJN Joe Nathan/75 6.00 15.00
SSJW Josh Willingham/75 6.00 15.00
SSKA Jeff Karstens/75 6.00 15.00
SSKS Kurt Suzuki/75 6.00 15.00
SSLO Lyle Overbay/75 6.00 15.00
SSMC Matt Cain/75 12.50 30.00
SSNS Nick Swisher/75 10.00 25.00
SSRH Rich Hill/75 10.00 25.00
SSRM Russell Martin/75 15.00 40.00
SSSE Sergio Mitre/75 6.00 15.00
SSTB Travis Buck/75 10.00 25.00
SSYG Chris B. Young/75 10.00 25.00

2007 Sweet Spot Dual Signatures Gold Stitch Gold Ink

OVERALL AU ODDS ONE PER TIN
PRINT RUNS B/WN 5-10 COPIES PER
NO PRICING DUE TO SCARCITY
EXCHANGE DEADLINE 11/9/2009

2007 Sweet Spot Dual Signatures Silver Stitch Silver Ink

OVERALL AU ODDS ONE PER TIN
STATED PRINT RUN 5 SER.#'d SETS
NO PRICING DUE TO SCARCITY
EXCHANGE DEADLINE 11/9/2009

2008 Sweet Spot

COMMON CARD (1-100) .40 1.00
COMMON AUTO (101-150) 3.00 8.00
AU PRINT RUNS B/WN 199-699 COPIES PER
OVERALL AUTO ODDS 1:3 PACKS
EXCH DEADLINE 11/10/2010
1 Aaron Harang .40 1.00
2 Aaron Rowand .40 1.00
3 Adam Dunn .60 1.50
4 Albert Pujols 1.25 3.00
5 Alex Gordon .60 1.50
6 Alex Rios .40 1.00
7 Alex Rodriguez 1.25 3.00
8 Alfonso Soriano .60 1.50
9 Andruw Jones .40 1.00
10 Aramis Ramirez .40 1.00
11 B.J. Upton .60 1.50
12 Barry Zito .60 1.50
13 Billy Butler .40 1.00
14 Brandon Phillips .40 1.00
15 Brandon Webb .60 1.50
16 Brian McCann .60 1.50
17 Brian Roberts .40 1.00
18 CC Sabathia .60 1.50
19 Carl Crawford .60 1.50
20 Carlos Beltran .60 1.50
21 Carlos Lee .40 1.00
22 Carlos Pena .60 1.50
23 Carlos Zambrano .60 1.50
24 Chase Utley .60 1.50
25 Chipper Jones 1.00 2.50
26 Chris B. Young .40 1.00
27 Chris Carpenter .60 1.50
28 Cole Hamels .75 2.00
29 Daisuke Matsuzaka .60 1.50
30 Dan Haren .40 1.00
31 Dan Uggla .40 1.00
32 David Ortiz 1.00 2.50
33 David Wright .60 1.50
34 Derek Jeter 2.50 6.00
35 Dontrelle Willis .40 1.00
36 Dustin Pedroia 1.00 2.50
37 Erik Bedard .40 1.00
38 Felix Hernandez .60 1.50
39 Frank Thomas 1.00 2.50
40 Freddy Sanchez .40 1.00
41 Gary Sheffield .40 1.00
42 Grady Sizemore .60 1.50
43 Greg Maddux 1.25 3.00
44 Hanley Ramirez .60 1.50
45 Hideki Matsui 1.00 2.50
46 Hunter Pence .60 1.50
47 Ichiro Suzuki 1.25 3.00
48 Ivan Rodriguez .60 1.50
49 Jake Peavy .40 1.00
50 Jason Bay .60 1.50
51 Jeff Francoeur .60 1.50
52 Jeff Kent .40 1.00
53 Jim Thome .60 1.50
54 Jimmy Rollins .60 1.50
55 Joba Chamberlain .40 1.00
56 Joe Blanton .40 1.00
57 Joe Mauer .75 2.00
58 Johan Santana .60 1.50
59 John Smoltz 1.00 2.50
60 Jonathan Papelbon .60 1.50
61 Jose Reyes .60 1.50
62 Josh Beckett .40 1.00
63 Josh Hamilton .60 1.50
64 Justin Morneau .60 1.50
65 Justin Verlander 1.00 2.50
66 Ken Griffey Jr. 2.00 5.00
67 Lance Berkman .60 1.50
68 Lastings Milledge .40 1.00
69 Magglio Ordonez .60 1.50
70 Manny Ramirez 1.00 2.50
71 Mariano Rivera 1.25 3.00
72 Mark Teixeira .60 1.50
73 Matt Holliday 1.00 2.50
74 Michael Young .40 1.00
75 Miguel Cabrera 1.00 2.50
76 Miguel Tejada .60 1.50
77 Mike Lowell .40 1.00
78 Nick Markakis .75 2.00
79 Nick Swisher .60 1.50
80 Paul Konerko .60 1.50
81 Pedro Martinez .60 1.50
82 Phil Hughes .40 1.00
83 Prince Fielder .60 1.50
84 Randy Johnson 1.00 2.50
85 Rich Harden .40 1.00
86 Robinson Cano .60 1.50
87 Roy Oswalt .60 1.50
88 Russell Martin .40 1.00
89 Ryan Braun .60 1.50
90 Ryan Howard .60 1.50
91 Ryan Zimmerman .60 1.50
92 Scott Rolen .60 1.50
93 Tom Glavine .60 1.50
94 Torii Hunter .40 1.00
95 Travis Hafner .40 1.00
96 Trevor Hoffman .60 1.50
97 Troy Tulowitzki 1.00 2.50
98 Vernon Wells .40 1.00
99 Victor Martinez .60 1.50
100 Vladimir Guerrero .60 1.50
101 Alex Romero AU/499 (RC) 3.00 8.00
102 Alexei Ramirez AU/399 RC 10.00 25.00
103 Bobby Korecky AU/399 RC 3.00 8.00
104 Bobby Wilson AU/499 RC 3.00 8.00
105 Brad Harman AU/699 RC 3.00 8.00
106 Brandon Boggs AU/699 (RC) 3.00 8.00
107 Brent Lillibridge AU/399 (RC) 4.00 10.00
108 Brian Barton AU/699 RC 3.00 8.00
109 Brian Bass AU/699 (RC) 3.00 8.00
110 Brian Bixler AU/699 (RC) 3.00 8.00
111 Brian Bocock AU/399 RC 3.00 8.00
112 Burke Badenhop AU/699 RC 3.00 8.00
113 Chin-Lung Hu AU/199 (RC) 12.50 30.00
114 Clay Buchholz AU/199 (RC) 12.50 30.00
115 Clay Timpner AU/699 (RC) 3.00 8.00
116 Cory Wade AU/699 (RC) 3.00 8.00
117 Daric Barton AU/399 (RC) 3.00 8.00
118 Eider Torres AU/699 (RC) 3.00 8.00
119 Jonathan Van Every AU/399 RC 3.00 8.00
120 Emmanuel Burriss AU/399 RC 3.00 8.00
121 Evan Longoria AU/249 RC 60.00 120.00
122 Felipe Paulino AU/499 RC 3.00 8.00
123 Fernando Hernandez AU/499 RC 3.00 8.00
124 German Duran AU/499 RC 3.00 8.00
125 Greg Smith AU/399 RC 3.00 8.00
126 Hernan Iribarren AU/699 (RC) EXCH 3.00 8.00
127 Kennedy AU/249 RC EXCH 8.00 20.00
128 Jed Lowrie AU/349 (RC) 5.00 12.00
129 Jeff Clement AU/199 (RC) 15.00 40.00
130 Jesse Carlson AU/649 RC 3.00 8.00
131 Johnny Cueto AU/249 RC 20.00 50.00
133 C.Kershaw AU/199 RC 100.00 250.00
134 Josh Newman AU/699 RC 3.00 8.00
135 J.Masterson AU/399 RC 6.00 15.00
136 Kevin Hart AU/399 (RC) 3.00 8.00
137 Luke Hochevar AU/199 RC 6.00 15.00
138 Jay Bruce AU/399 (RC) 8.00 20.00
139 Max Scherzer AU/299 RC 60.00 150.00
140 Nick Adenhart AU/399 (RC) 8.00 20.00
141 Nick Blackburn AU/399 RC 4.00 10.00
142 Nyjer Morgan AU/399 (RC) 3.00 8.00
143 Ramon Troncoso AU/699 RC 3.00 8.00
144 Randor Bierd AU/499 RC 3.00 8.00
145 Rich Thompson AU/399 RC 3.00 8.00
146 Robinzon Diaz AU/699 (RC) 3.00 8.00
147 Ross Ohlendorf AU/399 RC 3.00 8.00
148 Steve Holm AU/699 RC 3.00 8.00
149 Wesley Wright AU/499 RC 3.00 8.00
150 W.Balentien AU/399 (RC) 6.00 15.00

2008 Sweet Spot Rookie Signatures 50

OVERALL AU ODDS 1:3 PACKS
STATED PRINT RUN 50 SER.#'d SETS
EXCH DEADLINE 11/10/2010
101 Alex Romero AU 5.00 12.00
102 Alexei Ramirez AU 15.00 40.00
103 Bobby Korecky AU 5.00 12.00
104 Bobby Wilson AU 5.00 12.00
105 Brad Harman AU 5.00 12.00
106 Brandon Boggs AU 5.00 12.00
107 Brent Lillibridge AU 6.00 15.00
108 Brian Barton AU 5.00 12.00
109 Brian Bass AU 5.00 12.00
110 Brian Bixler AU 5.00 12.00
111 Brian Bocock AU 5.00 12.00
112 Burke Badenhop AU 5.00 12.00
113 Chin-Lung Hu AU 20.00 50.00
114 Clay Buchholz AU 8.00 20.00
115 Clay Timpner AU 5.00 12.00
116 Cory Wade AU 5.00 12.00
117 Daric Barton AU 5.00 12.00
118 Eider Torres AU 5.00 12.00
119 Jonathan Van Every AU 5.00 12.00
120 Emmanuel Burriss AU 5.00 12.00
121 Evan Longoria AU 75.00 150.00
122 Felipe Paulino AU 5.00 12.00
123 Fernando Hernandez AU 5.00 12.00
124 German Duran AU 5.00 12.00
125 Greg Smith AU 5.00 12.00
126 Hernan Iribarren AU 5.00 12.00
127 Ian Kennedy AU 12.50 30.00
128 Jed Lowrie AU 8.00 20.00
129 Jeff Clement AU 30.00 60.00
130 Jesse Carlson AU 5.00 12.00
131 Johnny Cueto AU 25.00 60.00
133 Clayton Kershaw AU 150.00 300.00
134 Josh Newman AU 5.00 12.00
135 Justin Masterson AU 20.00 50.00
136 Kevin Hart AU 5.00 12.00
137 Luke Hochevar AU 10.00 25.00
138 Jay Bruce AU 6.00 15.00
139 Max Scherzer AU 60.00 150.00
140 Nick Adenhart AU 12.50 30.00
141 Nick Blackburn AU 6.00 15.00
142 Nyjer Morgan AU 5.00 12.00
143 Ramon Troncoso AU 5.00 12.00
144 Randor Bierd AU 5.00 12.00
145 Rich Thompson AU 5.00 12.00
146 Robinzon Diaz AU 5.00 12.00
147 Ross Ohlendorf AU 5.00 12.00
148 Steve Holm AU 5.00 12.00
149 Wesley Wright AU 5.00 12.00
150 Wladimir Balentien AU 5.00 12.00

2008 Sweet Spot Signatures Bat Barrel Black Ink

OVERALL AU ODDS 1:3 PACKS
PRINT RUNS B/WN 1-51 COPIES PER
NO PRICING ON QTY 25 OR LESS
EXCH DEADLINE 11/10/2010
SJR Jose Reyes/51 12.50 30.00

2008 Sweet Spot Signatures Bat Barrel Blue Ink

OVERALL AU ODDS 1:3 PACKS
PRINT RUNS B/WN 1-75 COPIES PER
NO PRICING ON QTY 25 OR LESS
EXCH DEADLINE 11/10/2010
SJR Jose Reyes/30 30.00 60.00
SRC Roger Clemens/28 50.00 100.00
STG Tony Gwynn/75 25.00 60.00

2008 Sweet Spot Signatures Bat Barrel Silver Ink

OVERALL AU ODDS 1:3 PACKS
PRINT RUNS B/WN 1-50 COPIES PER
NO PRICING ON QTY 10 OR LESS
EXCH DEADLINE 11/10/2010
STG Tony Gwynn/50 40.00 80.00

2008 Sweet Spot Signatures Black Glove Leather Silver Ink

OVERALL AU ODDS 1:3 PACKS
PRINT RUNS B/WN 3-250 COPIES PER
NO PRICING ON QTY 16 OR LESS
EXCH DEADLINE 11/10/2010
SBD Bucky Dent/250 12.00 30.00
SBG Bob Gibson/150 20.00 50.00
SBH Bill Hall/250 6.00 15.00
SBO Bobby Richardson/250 8.00 20.00
SCB Chad Billingsley/246 6.00 15.00
SCW Chien-Ming Wang/250 30.00 60.00
SDB Don Baylor/100 8.00 20.00
SDL Don Larsen/150 12.00 30.00
SJH Josh Hamilton/250 6.00 15.00
SLB Lance Berkman/99 20.00 50.00
SMK Matt Kemp/245 10.00 25.00
SSK Bill Skowron/250 10.00 25.00

2008 Sweet Spot Signatures Brown Glove Leather

OVERALL AU ODDS 1:3 PACKS
PRINT RUNS B/WN 10-150 COPIES PER
NO PRICING ON QTY 15 OR LESS
EXCH DEADLINE 11/10/2010
SBG Bob Gibson/100 20.00 50.00
SDB Don Baylor Blk Leather/150 8.00 20.00

2008 Sweet Spot Signatures Brown Glove Leather Black Ink

OVERALL AU ODDS 1:3 PACKS
PRINT RUNS B/WN 7-100 COPIES PER
NO PRICING ON QTY 20 OR LESS
EXCH DEADLINE 11/10/2010
SEE Edwin Encarnacion/100 6.00 15.00
SJR Jose Reyes/30 30.00 60.00
SKJ Kelly Johnson/100 6.00 15.00

2008 Sweet Spot Signatures Brown Glove Leather Silver Ink

OVERALL AU ODDS 1:3 PACKS
PRINT RUNS B/WN 1-150 COPIES PER
NO PRICING ON QTY 4 OR LESS
EXCH DEADLINE 11/10/2010
SEE Edwin Encarnacion/150 6.00 15.00
SKJ Kelly Johnson/150 6.00 15.00
STG Tony Gwynn/50 30.00 60.00

2008 Sweet Spot Signatures Gold Stitch Black Ink

OVERALL AU ODDS 1:3 PACKS
STATED PRINT RUN 15 SER.#'d SETS
NO PRICING DUE TO SCARCITY

2008 Sweet Spot Signatures Ken Griffey Jr.

OVERALL AU ODDS 1:3 PACKS
PRINT RUNS B/WN 15-30 COPIES PER
NO PRICING ON QTY 15 OR LESS
EXCH DEADLINE 11/10/2010
SKG1 K.Griffey Jr. Bat/230 50.00 120.00
SKG2 K.Griffey Jr. Bat/230 50.00 120.00
SKG3 K.Griffey Jr. Bat/230 50.00 120.00
SKG4 K.Griffey Jr. Bat/230 50.00 120.00
SKG5 K.Griffey Jr. Bat/243 50.00 120.00
SKG6 K.Griffey Jr. 97 AL MVP/300 50.00 120.00
SKG7 K.Griffey Jr. 92 ASG MVP/135 50.00 120.00

2008 Sweet Spot Signatures Red Stitch Black Ink

OVERALL AU ODDS 1:3 PACKS
PRINT RUNS B/WN 1-366 COPIES PER
NO PRICING ON QTY 25 OR LESS
EXCH DEADLINE 11/10/2010
SAB Adrian Beltre/84 6.00 15.00
SBD Bucky Dent/145 8.00 20.00
SBG Bob Gibson/250 15.00 40.00
SBH Bill Hall/125 6.00 15.00
SBO Bobby Richardson/250 12.50 30.00
SCB Chad Billingsley/250 8.00 20.00
SCW Chien-Ming Wang/95 25.00 60.00
SDB Don Baylor/250 6.00 15.00
SDO David Ortiz/56 20.00 50.00
SEC Eric Chavez/59 10.00 25.00
SEE Edwin Encarnacion/250 6.00 15.00
SEG Eric Gagne/59 5.00 12.00
SJD J.D. Drew/45 20.00 50.00
SJH Josh Hamilton/250 10.00 25.00
SJR Jim Rice/99 8.00 20.00
SJR Jose Reyes/27 30.00 60.00
SJS John Smoltz/59 30.00 60.00
SJS Johan Santana/32 30.00 60.00
SJT Jim Thome/358 20.00 50.00
SKJ Kelly Johnson/248 5.00 12.00
SKW Kerry Wood/58 10.00 25.00
SLO Lyle Overbay/366 5.00 12.00
SMA Daisuke Matsuzaka/250 50.00 100.00
SMK Matt Kemp/250 10.00 25.00
SMY Michael Young/38 15.00 40.00
SOP Oliver Perez/43 6.00 15.00
SRS Ryne Sandberg/226 20.00 50.00
SSK Bill Skowron/250 8.00 20.00
SSR Scott Rolen/207 5.00 12.00
STG Tom Glavine/222 15.00 40.00
STH Tim Hudson/57 10.00 25.00
STH Travis Hafner/171 6.00 15.00
SBPA Brandon Phillips/299 8.00 20.00
SBPB Brandon Phillips/200 8.00 20.00
SRS2 Ryne Sandberg/265 20.00 50.00

2008 Sweet Spot Signatures Red Stitch Blue Ink

OVERALL AU ODDS 1:3 PACKS
PRINT RUNS B/WN 1-315 COPIES PER
NO PRICING ON QTY 15 OR LESS
EXCH DEADLINE 11/10/2010
SAB Adrian Beltre/74 8.00 20.00
SAE Andre Ethier/250 10.00 25.00
SAP Albert Pujols/45 100.00 200.00
SAW Adam Wainwright/135 12.00 30.00
SBB Boof Bonser/300 5.00 12.00
SBR Brian Roberts/290 5.00 12.00
SBR Brooks Robinson/48 20.00 50.00
SCH Cole Hamels/300 10.00 25.00
SCQ Carlos Quentin/315 6.00 15.00
SCR Cal Ripken Jr./275 50.00 100.00
SCR Cal Ripken Jr./275 50.00 100.00
SCY Carl Yastrzemski/50 20.00 50.00
SDL Don Larsen/250 8.00 20.00
SDO David Ortiz/49 30.00 60.00
SDW Dontrelle Willis/174 5.00 12.00
SEC Eric Chavez/49 12.00 30.00
SEG Eric Gagne/49 6.00 15.00
SFL Francisco Liriano/190 6.00 15.00
SHK Hong-Chih Kuo/300 6.00 15.00
SHK Harmon Killebrew/229 30.00 60.00
SHR Hanley Ramirez/300 6.00 15.00
SHS Huston Street/225 5.00 12.00
SIK Ian Kinsler/150 12.00 30.00
SJD J.D. Drew/49 20.00 50.00
SJJ Josh Johnson/180 5.00 12.00
SJK Jason Kubel/300 5.00 12.00
SJN Joe Nathan/225 5.00 12.00
SJS Johan Santana/38 30.00 60.00
SJV Justin Verlander/299 25.00 60.00
SKW Kerry Wood/73 10.00 25.00
SMM Mark Mulder/124 6.00 15.00
SPM Paul Molitor/250 12.00 30.00
SRS Ryne Sandberg/60 20.00 50.00
STG Tony Gwynn/105 8.00 20.00
STH Tim Hudson/49 10.00 25.00
STS Takashi Saito/300 6.00 15.00
SWC Will Clark/200 12.00 30.00
SCR3 Cal Ripken Jr./258 40.00 80.00

2008 Sweet Spot Signatures Red Stitch Red Ink

OVERALL AU ODDS 1:3 PACKS
PRINT RUNS B/WN 1-35 COPIES PER
NO PRICING ON QTY 25 OR LESS
EXCH DEADLINE 11/10/2010
SJR Jose Reyes/35 15.00 40.00

2008 Sweet Spot Signatures Red-Blue Stitch Black Ink

OVERALL AU ODDS 1:3 PACKS
PRINT RUNS B/WN 1-126 COPIES PER
NO PRICING ON QTY 25 OR LESS
EXCH DEADLINE 11/10/2010
STH Travis Hafner/126 6.00 15.00

2008 Sweet Spot Signatures Red-Blue Stitch Blue Ink

OVERALL AU ODDS 1:3 PACKS
PRINT RUNS B/WN 3-100 COPIES PER
NO PRICING ON QTY 25 OR LESS
EXCH DEADLINE 11/10/2010
SCQ Carlos Quentin/35 15.00 40.00
SCU Chase Utley/100 75.00 150.00

2008 Sweet Spot Signatures Red-Blue Stitch Red Ink

OVERALL AU ODDS 1:3 PACKS
PRINT RUNS B/WN 5-304 COPIES PER
NO PRICING ON QTY 18 OR LESS
EXCH DEADLINE 11/10/2010
SAE Andre Ethier/50 6.00 15.00
SAW Adam Wainwright/50 15.00 40.00
SBB Boof Bonser/50 6.00 15.00
SBR Brian Roberts/199 6.00 15.00
SDW Dontrelle Willis/73 6.00 15.00
SFL Francisco Liriano/48 10.00 25.00
SHK Hong-Chih Kuo/50 30.00 60.00
SHR Hanley Ramirez/50 15.00 40.00
SHS Huston Street/199 5.00 12.00
SJK Jason Kubel/50 6.00 15.00
SJL Jon Lester/90 12.00 30.00
SJN Joe Nathan/202 5.00 12.00
SJP Jonathan Papelbon/304 8.00 20.00
SJS John Smoltz/291 20.00 50.00
SJT Jim Thome/50 15.00 40.00
SJV Justin Verlander/125 25.00 80.00

2008 Sweet Spot Swatches

OVERALL MEM ODDS 2:3 PACKS
SSAP Albert Pujols 5.00 12.00
SSAS Alfonso Soriano 3.00 8.00
SSBU B.J. Upton 3.00 8.00
SSCA Miguel Cabrera 3.00 8.00
SSCF Carlton Fisk 3.00 8.00
SSCJ Chipper Jones 3.00 8.00
SSCM Chien-Ming Wang 4.00 10.00
SSCR Cal Ripken Jr. 8.00 20.00
SSCU Chase Utley 3.00 8.00
SSCY Carl Yastrzemski 4.00 10.00
SSCZ Carlos Zambrano 3.00 8.00
SSDH Dan Haren 3.00 8.00
SSDJ Derek Jeter 8.00 20.00
SSDM Daisuke Matsuzaka 4.00 10.00
SSDO David Ortiz 3.00 8.00
SSDW Dontrelle Willis 3.00 8.00
SSEM Eddie Murray 3.00 8.00
SSFH Felix Hernandez 3.00 8.00
SSFL Francisco Liriano 3.00 8.00
SSFT Frank Thomas 4.00 10.00
SSGS Grady Sizemore 3.00 8.00
SSHR Hanley Ramirez 3.00 8.00
SSIR Ivan Rodriguez 3.00 8.00
SSJB Jeremy Bonderman 3.00 8.00
SSJM Joe Mauer 3.00 8.00
SSJP Jake Peavy 3.00 8.00
SSJS Johan Santana 3.00 8.00
SSJT Jim Thome 3.00 8.00
SSMA Don Mattingly 6.00 15.00
SSMO Joe Morgan 3.00 8.00
SSMR Manny Ramirez 4.00 10.00
SSMS Mike Schmidt 5.00 12.00
SSMT Mark Teixeira 3.00 8.00
SSNM Nick Markakis 3.00 8.00
SSNR Nolan Ryan 8.00 20.00
SSOS Ozzie Smith 6.00 15.00
SSPF Prince Fielder 3.00 8.00
SSPM Pedro Martinez 3.00 8.00
SSRA Roberto Alomar 3.00 8.00
SSRG Ron Guidry 4.00 10.00
SSRJ Reggie Jackson 3.00 8.00
SSRS Ryne Sandberg 5.00 12.00
SSRY Robin Yount 5.00 12.00
SSSM John Smoltz 3.00 8.00
SSTG Tony Gwynn 4.00 10.00
SSTH Travis Hafner 3.00 8.00
SSTR Tim Raines 3.00 8.00
SSVG Vladimir Guerrero 3.00 8.00
SSWB Wade Boggs 4.00 10.00
SSWI Dave Winfield 3.00 8.00

2008 Sweet Spot Swatches Dual

OVERALL MEM ODDS 2:3 PACKS
DSBM J.Beckett/D.Matsuzaka 6.00 15.00
DSBT Lance Berkman 4.00 10.00
Mark Teixeira
DSCW Miguel Cabrera 4.00 10.00
Dontrelle Willis
DSDR A.Dawson/T.Raines 5.00 12.00
DSFB P.Fielder/R.Braun 6.00 15.00
DSGS K.Griffey Jr./G.Sizemore 6.00 15.00
DSHM Travis Hafner 4.00 10.00
Justin Morneau
DSJH D.Jeter/H.Ramirez 8.00 20.00
DSJR N.Ryan/R.Johnson 8.00 20.00
DSJZ C.Jones/R.Zimmerman 5.00 12.00
DSLP A.Pujols/D.Lee 5.00 12.00
DSMJ D.Mattingly/D.Jeter 12.00 30.00
DSMM J.Mauer/J.Morneau 5.00 12.00
DSMS Johan Santana 4.00 10.00
Pedro Martinez
DSMW D.Winfield/D.Mattingly 10.00 25.00
DSOZ Roy Oswalt 4.00 10.00
Carlos Zambrano
DSPL Jake Peavy 5.00 12.00
Tim Lincecum
DSRC Robinson Cano 4.00 10.00
Brian Roberts
DSRM C.Ripken Jr./E.Murray 15.00 40.00
DSRO Manny Ramirez 4.00 10.00
David Ortiz
DSRP Jonathan Papelbon 4.00 10.00
Mariano Rivera
DSSH Alfonso Soriano 4.00 10.00
Matt Holliday
DSUH C.Utley/C.Hamels 4.00 10.00
DSVH Felix Hernandez 4.00 10.00
Justin Verlander
DSWM C.Wang/D.Matsuzaka 5.00 12.00

2008 Sweet Spot Swatches Triple

OVERALL MEM ODDS 2:3 PACKS
TSBOP Lance Berkman 4.00 10.00
Roy Oswalt
Hunter Pence

TSFPB Ryan Braun 4.00 10.00
Hunter Pence
Jeff Francoeur
TSGBY Gwynn/Boggs/Yount 15.00 40.00
TSGOO Vladimir Guerrero 4.00 10.00
David Ortiz
Magglio Ordonez
TSJMH Pedro/Hoffman/Big Unit 5.00 12.00
TSJMJ Reggie/Mattingly/Jeter 10.00 25.00
TSLHW Felix Hernandez 4.00 10.00
Jered Weaver
Francisco Liriano
TSLPF Pujols/Prince/D.Lee 6.00 15.00
TSMCH Maddux/Carpenter/Halladay 15.00 40.00
TSPMM Mauer/R.Martin/Posada 5.00 12.00
TSSPM Dice-K/Schilling/Papelbon 8.00 20.00
TSSRJ Ozzie/Ripken/Jeter 10.00 25.00
TSSSP Peavy/Johan/Smoltz 6.00 15.00
TSTGT Miguel Tejada 4.00 10.00
Troy Tulowitzki
Khalil Greene
TSWHS Grady Sizemore 4.00 10.00
Torii Hunter
Vernon Wells

2008 Sweet Spot Swatches Quad

OVERALL MEM ODDS 2:3 PACKS
QSBSPS Johan Santana/Jake Peavy/CC Sabathia/Josh Beckett 5.00 12.00
QSGLPC Pujols/Vlad/Mig.Cab./C.Lee 6.00 15.00
QSGTTR Grif/Hurt/Thome/Manny 12.50 30.00
QSJYRR Han/Rollins/Jeter/Young 8.00 20.00
QSLRSZ Sori/Aram/Lee/Zamb 6.00 15.00
QSMJJC Matt/Reggie/Jeter/Cano 20.00 50.00
QSOCGV Miguel Cabrera/Justin Verlander/Magglio Ordonez/Curtis Granderson 5.00 12.00
QSRSOM Papi/Manny/Dice-K/Schil 6.00 15.00
QSSCSS Schmidt/Ozzie/Ryno/W.Clark 20.00 50.00
QSTGHO David Ortiz/Travis Hafner/Jim Thome/Jason Giambi 5.00 12.00

2008 Sweet Spot USA Signatures Black Glove Leather

OVERALL AU ODDS 1:3 PACKS
PRINT RUNS B/WN 29-32 COPIES PER
EXCH DEADLINE 11/10/2010
USAAG A.J. Griffin/32 6.00 15.00
USAAO Andrew Oliver/32 10.00 25.00
USABS Blake Smith/30 8.00 20.00
USACC Christian Colon/32 40.00 80.00
USACH Chris Hernandez/30 6.00 15.00
USAKG Kyle Gibson/32 6.00 15.00
USAKR Kevin Rhoderick/32 6.00 15.00
USAKV Kendal Volz/32 10.00 25.00
USAML Mike Leake/32 40.00 80.00
USAMM Mike Minor/32 20.00 50.00
USARJ Ryan Jackson/32 6.00 15.00
USASS Stephen Strasburg/32 100.00 250.00

2008 Sweet Spot USA Signatures Red-Blue Stitch Black Ink

OVERALL AU ODDS 1:3 PACKS
PRINT RUNS B/WN 16-40 COPIES PER
NO PRICING ON QTY 16
EXCH DEADLINE 11/10/2010
USAAG A.J. Griffin/37 8.00 20.00
USAAO Andrew Oliver/37 10.00 25.00
USABS Blake Smith/37 12.50 30.00
USADD Derek Dietrich/37 20.00 50.00
USAKR Kevin Rhoderick/37 6.00 15.00
USAKV Kendal Volz/40 6.00 15.00
USAML Mike Leake/37 40.00 80.00
USARJ Ryan Jackson/37 8.00 20.00
USASS Stephen Strasburg/37 100.00 250.00
USATL Tyler Lyons/37 12.50 30.00

2008 Sweet Spot USA Signatures Red Stitch Black Ink

OVERALL AU ODDS 1:3 PACKS
PRINT RUNS B/WN 140-260 COPIES PER
EXCH DEADLINE 11/10/2010
USAAG A.J. Griffin Blk Glv/230 8.00 20.00
USAAO Andrew Oliver Blk Glv/220 6.00 15.00
USABS Blake Smith/219 4.00 10.00
USACC Christian Colon/230 8.00 20.00
USACH Chris Hernandez/220 6.00 15.00
USADD Derek Dietrich/200 10.00 25.00
USAHM Hunter Morris Blk Glv/219 6.00 15.00
USAJF Josh Fellhauer/230 4.00 10.00
USAKD Kentrail Davis/200 15.00 40.00
USAKG Kyle Gibson/198 5.00 12.00
USAKR Kevin Rhoderick/200 6.00 15.00
USAKV Kendal Volz/140 6.00 15.00
USAMD Matt den Dekker/200 6.00 15.00
USAMG Micah Gibbs/200 5.00 12.00
USAML Mike Leake/189 8.00 20.00
USAMM Mike Minor/219 8.00 20.00
USARJ Ryan Jackson/222 5.00 12.00
USARL Ryan Lipkin/218 5.00 12.00
USASS Stephen Strasburg/260 25.00 60.00
USATL Tyler Lyons/215 4.00 10.00

2009 Sweet Spot

COMP.SET w/o AU's (100) 12.50 30.00
COMMON CARD (1-100) .25 .60
COMMON AU RC (101-130) 3.00 8.00
OVERALL AUTO ODDS 1:3 HOBBY
AU PRINT RUN B/WN 99-699 COPIES PER
EXCHANGE DEADLINE 10/7/2011
1 A.J. Burnett .25 .60
2 Adam Dunn .40 1.00
3 Adam Jones .40 1.00
4 Adrian Gonzalez .50 1.25
5 Albert Pujols .75 2.00
6 Alex Rodriguez .75 2.00
7 Alfonso Soriano .40 1.00
8 B.J. Upton .40 1.00
9 Brian McCann .40 1.00
10 Brian Roberts .25 .60
11 Carl Crawford .40 1.00
12 Carlos Beltran .40 1.00
13 Carlos Quentin .25 .60
14 Carlos Zambrano .40 1.00
15 CC Sabathia .40 1.00
16 Chad Billingsley .40 1.00
17 Chase Utley .40 1.00
18 Chien-Ming Wang .40 1.00
19 Chipper Jones .60 1.50
20 Chris Carpenter .40 1.00
21 Clayton Kershaw 1.00 2.50
22 Cliff Lee .40 1.00
23 Cole Hamels .50 1.25
24 Curtis Granderson .50 1.25
25 Daisuke Matsuzaka .40 1.00
26 David Ortiz .60 1.50
27 David Wright .50 1.25
28 Derek Jeter 1.50 4.00
29 Dustin Pedroia .60 1.50
30 Evan Longoria .40 1.00
31 Felix Hernandez .40 1.00
32 Francisco Rodriguez .40 1.00
33 Freddy Sanchez .25 .60
34 Geovany Soto .40 1.00
35 Grady Sizemore .40 1.00
36 Hanley Ramirez .40 1.00
37 Hideki Matsui .60 1.50
38 Hideki Okajima .25 .60
39 Hiroki Kuroda .25 .60
40 Hunter Pence .40 1.00
41 Ian Kinsler .40 1.00
42 Ichiro Suzuki .75 2.00
43 Jake Peavy .25 .60
44 Pedro Martinez .40 1.00
45 Jason Varitek .60 1.50
46 Javier Vazquez .25 .60
47 Jay Bruce .40 1.00
48 Jeff Samardzija .40 1.00
49 Jermaine Dye .25 .60
50 Jim Thome .40 1.00
51 Jimmy Rollins .40 1.00
52 Joba Chamberlain .25 .60
53 Joe Mauer .50 1.25
54 Joey Votto .60 1.50
55 Johan Santana .40 1.00
56 Shin-Soo Choo .40 1.00
57 Johnny Cueto .40 1.00
58 Johnny Damon .40 1.00
59 Jon Lester .40 1.00
60 Jose Reyes .40 1.00
61 Josh Beckett .25 .60
62 Josh Hamilton .40 1.00
63 Josh Johnson .40 1.00
64 Justin Morneau .40 1.00
65 Justin Upton .40 1.00
66 Justin Verlander .60 1.50
67 Ken Griffey Jr. 1.25 3.00
68 Kevin Youkilis .25 .60
69 Kosuke Fukudome .40 1.00
70 Lance Berkman .40 1.00
71 Manny Ramirez .60 1.50
72 Mariano Rivera .75 2.00
73 Mark Teixeira .40 1.00
74 Matt Holliday .60 1.50
75 Matt Kemp .50 1.25
76 Max Scherzer .60 1.50
77 Michael Young .25 .60
78 Miguel Cabrera .60 1.50
79 Miguel Tejada .40 1.00
80 Nate McLouth .25 .60
81 Nick Markakis .50 1.25
82 Nomar Garciaparra .40 1.00
83 Prince Fielder .40 1.00
84 Randy Johnson .60 1.50
85 Raul Ibanez .40 1.00
86 Roy Halladay .40 1.00
87 Roy Oswalt .40 1.00
88 Russell Martin .25 .60
89 Ryan Braun .40 1.00
90 Ryan Howard .50 1.25
91 Ryan Ludwick .40 1.00
92 Ryan Zimmerman .40 1.00
93 Stephen Drew .25 .60
94 Tim Lincecum .40 1.00
95 Todd Helton .40 1.00
96 Troy Tulowitzki .60 1.50
97 Victor Martinez .40 1.00
98 Vladimir Guerrero .40 1.00
99 Yovani Gallardo .25 .60
100 Zack Greinke .60 1.50
101 B.Parnell AU/699 RC 6.00 15.00
102 B.Anderson AU/650 RC 5.00 12.00
103 B.Gardner AU/699 10.00 25.00
104 C.Rasmus AU/350 (RC) 5.00 12.00
105 D.Price AU/299 RC 12.50 30.00
106 D.Fowler AU/699 (RC) 6.00 15.00
107 D.Veal AU/650 RC 4.00 10.00
108 E.Andrus AU/350 RC 10.00 25.00
109 E.Cabrera AU/699 RC 5.00 12.00
110 F.Martinez AU/300 RC 6.00 15.00
111 G.Beckham AU/99 RC 8.00 20.00
112 James McDonald AU/699 RC 3.00 8.00
113 James Parr AU/699 (RC) 3.00 8.00
114 J.Motte AU/699 (RC) 6.00 15.00
115 J.Schafer AU/350 (RC) 4.00 10.00
116 J.Zimmermann AU/699 RC 6.00 15.00
117 K.Kawakami AU/350 RC 8.00 20.00
118 Kevin Jepsen AU/699 (RC) 3.00 8.00
119 K.Uehara AU/300 RC 8.00 20.00
120 Luis Perdomo AU/699 RC 3.00 8.00
121 Matt Tuiasosopo AU/699 (RC) 3.00 8.00
122 M.Wieters AU/350 RC 15.00 40.00
123 P.Sandoval AU/550 3.00 8.00
124 P.Coke AU/699 RC 4.00 10.00
125 R.Porcello AU/550 RC 6.00 15.00
126 R.Perry AU/199 RC 8.00 20.00
127 Shairon Martis AU/699 RC 3.00 8.00
128 T.Hanson AU/199 RC 20.00 50.00
129 T.Snider AU/300 RC 10.00 25.00
130 T.Cahill AU/499 RC 3.00 8.00

2009 Sweet Spot Rookie Signatures Silver

OVERALL AUTO ODDS 1:3 HOBBY
STATED PRINT RUN 65 SER.#'d SETS
EXCHANGE DEADLINE 10/7/2011
101 Bobby Parnell AU 4.00 10.00
102 Brett Anderson AU 6.00 15.00
103 Brett Gardner AU 20.00 50.00
104 Colby Rasmus AU 12.50 30.00
105 David Price AU 12.50 30.00
106 Dexter Fowler AU 10.00 25.00
107 Donald Veal AU 5.00 12.00
108 Elvis Andrus AU 15.00 40.00
109 Everth Cabrera AU 8.00 20.00
110 Fernando Martinez AU 10.00 25.00
111 Gordon Beckham AU 6.00 15.00
112 James McDonald AU 10.00 25.00
113 James Parr AU 4.00 10.00
114 Jason Motte AU 10.00 25.00
115 Jordan Schafer AU 5.00 12.00
116 Jordan Zimmermann AU 6.00 15.00
117 Kenshin Kawakami AU 6.00 15.00
118 Kevin Jepsen AU 4.00 10.00
119 Koji Uehara AU 30.00 60.00
120 Luis Perdomo AU 4.00 10.00
121 Matt Tuiasosopo AU 8.00 20.00
122 Matt Wieters AU 40.00 80.00
123 Pablo Sandoval AU 40.00 80.00
124 Phil Coke AU 8.00 20.00
125 Rick Porcello AU 30.00 60.00
126 Ryan Perry AU 10.00 25.00
127 Shairon Martis AU 4.00 10.00
128 Tommy Hanson AU 10.00 25.00
129 Travis Snider AU 10.00 25.00
130 Trevor Cahill AU 6.00 15.00

2009 Sweet Spot Classic Patches

OVERALL MEM ODDS 2:3 HOBBY
PRINT RUNS B/WN 9-52 COPIES PER
NO PRICING ON QTY 22 OR LESS
BJ Bo Jackson/48 75.00 150.00
BW Billy Williams/52 40.00 80.00
CH Catfish Hunter/27 60.00 120.00
EM Eddie Mathews/41 200.00 300.00
MA Edgar Martinez/44 50.00 100.00
RC Rod Carew/49 60.00 120.00
RF Rollie Fingers/47 90.00 150.00
RJ Reggie Jackson/44 75.00 150.00
RS Ryne Sandberg/50 60.00 120.00
SA Sparky Anderson/46 90.00 150.00

2009 Sweet Spot Classic Signatures Bat Barrel Black Ink

OVERALL AUTO ODDS 1:3 HOBBY
PRINT RUNS B/WN 1-40 COPIES PER
NO PRICING ON QTY 25 OR LESS
EXCHANGE DEADLINE 10/7/2011
SCEM Edgar Martinez/40 20.00 50.00

2009 Sweet Spot Classic Signatures Black Baseball Black Stitch Silver Ink

OVERALL AUTO ODDS 1:3 HOBBY
PRINT RUNS B/WN 1-34 COPIES PER
NO PRICING ON QTY 23 OR LESS
EXCHANGE DEADLINE 10/7/2011
SCNR Nolan Ryan/34 75.00 150.00
SCTR Tim Raines/30 15.00 40.00

2009 Sweet Spot Classic Signatures Black Bat Barrel Silver Ink

OVERALL AUTO ODDS 1:3 HOBBY
PRINT RUNS B/WN 5-50 COPIES PER
NO PRICING ON QTY 25 OR LESS
EXCHANGE DEADLINE 10/7/2011
SCKG Ken Griffey Sr./25 8.00 20.00

2009 Sweet Spot Classic Signatures Red-Blue Stitch Blue Ink

OVERALL AUTO ODDS 1:3 HOBBY
STATED PRINT RUN 40 SER.#'d SETS
EXCHANGE DEADLINE 10/7/2011
SCRY Robin Yount/40 20.00 50.00

2009 Sweet Spot Classic Signatures Red Stitch Black Ink

OVERALL AUTO ODDS 1:3 HOBBY
PRINT RUNS B/WN 5-250 COPIES PER
NO PRICING ON QTY 25 OR LESS
EXCHANGE DEADLINE 10/7/2011
SCKG Ken Griffey Sr./250 6.00 15.00
SCKH Kent Hrbek/50 10.00 25.00
SCOC Dennis Boyd/99 10.00 25.00

2009 Sweet Spot Classic Signatures Red Stitch Blue Ink

OVERALL AUTO ODDS 1:3 HOBBY
PRINT RUNS B/WN 1-199 COPIES PER
NO PRICING ON QTY 25 OR LESS
EXCHANGE DEADLINE 10/7/2011
SCAK Al Kaline/99 20.00 50.00
SCBW Billy Williams/50 8.00 20.00
SCCR Cal Ripken Jr./199 60.00 150.00
SCDA Dick Allen/50 15.00 40.00
SCGP Gaylord Perry/50 10.00 25.00
SCJP Jim Palmer/49 10.00 25.00
SCKH Kent Hrbek/99 10.00 25.00
SCRY Robin Yount/50 20.00 50.00
SCTR Tim Raines/99 12.00 30.00

2009 Sweet Spot Classic Signatures Red Stitch Green Ink

OVERALL AUTO ODDS 1:3 HOBBY
ANNOUNCED PRINT RUNS LISTED
PRINT RUN INFO PROVIDED BY UD
EXCHANGE DEADLINE 10/7/2011
SCAK Al Kaline/100 * 25.00 50.00
SCBJ Bo Jackson/26 * 90.00 150.00
SCBR Brooks Robinson/58 * 30.00 60.00
SCCF Carlton Fisk/81 * 10.00 25.00
SCCR Cal Ripken Jr./55 * 50.00 120.00
SCEM Edgar Martinez/46 * 12.00 30.00
SCNR Nolan Ryan/61 * 60.00 120.00

2009 Sweet Spot Classic Signatures Red Stitch Red Ink

OVERALL AUTO ODDS 1:3 HOBBY
PRINT RUNS B/WN 1-47 COPIES PER
NO PRICING ON QTY 25 OR LESS
EXCHANGE DEADLINE 10/7/2011
SCBR Brooks Robinson/47 15.00 40.00
SCJP Jim Palmer/47 10.00 25.00

2009 Sweet Spot Immortal Signatures

OVERALL AUTO ODDS 1:3 HOBBY
PRINT RUNS B/WN 1-32 COPIES PER
NO PRICING ON QTY 19 OR LESS
EXCHANGE DEADLINE 10/7/2011
DC Dolph Camilli/26 90.00 150.00
FC Frank Crosetti/32 15.00 40.00
HS Hank Sauer/31 25.00 60.00
JP Johnny Podres/30 20.00 50.00

2009 Sweet Spot Signatures Bat Barrel Black Ink

OVERALL AUTO ODDS 1:3 HOBBY
PRINT RUNS B/WN 1-50 COPIES PER
NO PRICING ON QTY 25 OR LESS
EXCHANGE DEADLINE 10/7/2011
SDJ Derek Jeter/50 150.00 300.00
SML Mark Loretta/35 6.00 15.00

2009 Sweet Spot Signatures Bat Barrel Blue Ink

OVERALL AUTO ODDS 1:3 HOBBY
PRINT RUNS B/WN 1-199 COPIES PER
NO PRICING ON QTY 25 OR LESS
EXCHANGE DEADLINE 10/7/2011
SJR Ken Griffey Jr./199 75.00 200.00

2009 Sweet Spot Signatures Black Baseball Black Stitch Silver Ink

OVERALL AUTO ODDS 1:3 HOBBY
PRINT RUNS B/WN 1-60 COPIES PER
NO PRICING ON QTY 25 OR LESS
EXCHANGE DEADLINE 10/7/2011
SCB Chad Billingsley/58 4.00 10.00
SCL Carlos Lee/45 8.00 20.00
SFH Felix Hernandez/34 40.00 80.00
SJB Jay Bruce/32 30.00 60.00
SJN Joe Nathan/36 10.00 25.00
SMK Matt Kemp/27 50.00 100.00
STC Trevor Cahill/60 3.00 8.00

2009 Sweet Spot Signatures Black Bat Barrel Silver Ink

OVERALL AUTO ODDS 1:3 HOBBY
PRINT RUN B/WN 5-60 COPIES PER
NO PRICING ON QTY 25 OR LESS
EXCHANGE DEADLINE 10/7/2011
SCB Chad Billingsley/50 4.00 10.00
SDJ Derek Jeter/50 200.00 300.00
SGP Glen Perkins/50 5.00 12.00
SJB Jay Bruce/50 15.00 40.00
SJN Joe Nathan/50 8.00 20.00
SJR Ken Griffey Jr./60 60.00 150.00
SJW Josh Willingham/50 8.00 20.00
SMC Matt Cain/50 8.00 20.00
SMK Matt Kemp/50 60.00 120.00
SMN Nick Markakis/50 10.00 25.00

2009 Sweet Spot Signatures Black Glove Leather Silver Ink

OVERALL AUTO ODDS 1:3 HOBBY
PRINT RUNS B/WN 1-30 COPIES PER
NO PRICING ON QTY 25 OR LESS
EXCHANGE DEADLINE 10/7/2011
SCB Chad Billingsley/30 6.00 15.00
SDJ Derek Jeter/30 300.00 600.00
SJB Jay Bruce/30 40.00 80.00
SJN Joe Nathan/30 8.00 20.00
SJR Ken Griffey Jr./30 150.00 250.00
SMC Matt Cain/30 15.00 40.00
SMN Nick Markakis/30 20.00 50.00

2009 Sweet Spot Signatures Glove Leather Black Ink

OVERALL AUTO ODDS 1:3 HOBBY
PRINT RUNS B/WN 10-30 COPIES PER
NO PRICING ON QTY 15 OR LESS
EXCHANGE DEADLINE 10/7/2011
SYM Yadier Molina/30 30.00 80.00

2009 Sweet Spot Signatures Red-Blue Stitch Blue Ink

OVERALL AUTO ODDS 1:3 HOBBY
PRINT RUNS B/WN 10-50 COPIES PER
NO PRICING ON QTY 25 OR LESS
EXCHANGE DEADLINE 10/7/2011
SHR Hanley Ramirez/50 15.00 40.00

2009 Sweet Spot Signatures Red-Blue Stitch Red Ink

OVERALL AUTO ODDS 1:3 HOBBY
PRINT RUNS B/WN 5-50 COPIES PER
NO PRICING ON QTY 5 OR LESS
EXCHANGE DEADLINE 10/7/2011
SCR Cody Ross/50 6.00 15.00
SDU Dan Uggla/50 5.00 12.00
SJP James Shields/50 10.00 25.00
SKS Kelly Shoppach/50 5.00 12.00
SNM Nate McLouth/50 5.00 12.00
SSM Sean Marshall/49 8.00 20.00

2009 Sweet Spot Signatures Red Stitch Black Ink

OVERALL AUTO ODDS 1:3 HOBBY
PRINT RUNS B/WN 1-120 COPIES PER
NO PRICING ON QTY 25 OR LESS
EXCHANGE DEADLINE 10/7/2011
SCB Chad Billingsley/50 5.00 12.00
SDJ Derek Jeter/150 150.00 300.00
SDP David Price/50 20.00 50.00
SGP Glen Perkins/99 6.00 15.00
SGS Grady Sizemore/75 12.50 30.00
SJB Jay Bruce/150 12.50 30.00
SJN Joe Nathan/50 5.00 12.00
SJR Ken Griffey Jr./199 50.00 100.00
SJW Josh Willingham/99 5.00 12.00
SMB Marlon Byrd/350 4.00 10.00
SMK Matt Kemp/99 12.50 30.00
SMN Nick Markakis/99 4.00 10.00
SMU David Murphy/99 4.00 10.00
SPK Paul Konerko/50 15.00 40.00
STC Trevor Cahill/50 6.00 15.00
STG Tom Glavine/50 15.00 40.00
STT Troy Tulowitzki/199 12.00 30.00
SVM Victor Martinez/120 8.00 20.00
SYM Yadier Molina/37 40.00 80.00

2009 Sweet Spot Signatures Red Stitch Blue Ink

OVERALL AUTO ODDS 1:3 HOBBY
PRINT RUNS B/WN 2-199 COPIES PER
NO PRICING ON QTY 25 OR LESS
EXCHANGE DEADLINE 10/7/2011
SBU B.J. Upton/50 8.00 20.00
SCB Chad Billingsley/199 5.00 12.00
SCJ Chipper Jones/50 60.00 120.00
SCR Cody Ross/299 10.00 25.00
SDJ Derek Jeter/299 150.00 300.00
SDP David Price/99 12.50 30.00
SDU Dan Uggla/35 10.00 25.00
SEJ Edwin Jackson/350 10.00 25.00
SFC Fausto Carmona/300 8.00 20.00
SFH Felix Hernandez/50 30.00 60.00
SGP Glen Perkins/199 5.00 12.00
SHR Hanley Ramirez/300 6.00 15.00
SIK Ian Kinsler/150 6.00 15.00
SJB Jay Bruce/299 6.00 15.00
SJN Joe Nathan/299 5.00 12.00
SJP James Shields/300 8.00 20.00
SJW Josh Willingham/199 5.00 12.00
SJW Jered Weaver/100 10.00 25.00
SKS Kelly Shoppach/300 5.00 12.00
SKU Koji Uehara/50 30.00 60.00
SLJ LeBron James/15 150.00 300.00
SMJ Mike Jacobs/199 5.00 12.00
SMK Matt Kemp/199 20.00 50.00
SMN Nick Markakis/199 12.50 30.00
SMU David Murphy/199 5.00 12.00
SNM Nate McLouth/300 5.00 12.00
SPK Paul Konerko/99 12.50 30.00
SPM Paul Maholm/200 5.00 12.00
SRB Rocco Baldelli/99 6.00 15.00
SSM Sean Marshall/250 6.00 15.00
STC Trevor Cahill/99 12.50 30.00
STS Travis Snider/50 15.00 40.00
STT Troy Tulowitzki/99 12.00 30.00
SVW Vernon Wells/63 10.00 25.00
SZG Zack Greinke/50 15.00 40.00

2009 Sweet Spot Signatures Red Stitch Green Ink

OVERALL AUTO ODDS 1:3 HOBBY
ANNOUNCED PRINT RUNS LISTED
PRINT RUN INFO PROVIDED BY UD
EXCHANGE DEADLINE 10/7/2011
SBU B.J. Upton/96 * 10.00 25.00
SCJ Chipper Jones/96 * 40.00 80.00
SCL Carlos Lee/98 * 8.00 20.00
SCW Chien-Ming Wang/49 * 90.00 150.00
SEJ Evan Longoria/77 * 20.00 50.00
SLJ LeBron James/25 * 125.00 250.00
SVM Victor Martinez/98 * 20.00 50.00

2009 Sweet Spot Signatures Red Stitch Red Ink

OVERALL AUTO ODDS 1:3 HOBBY
PRINT RUNS B/WN 1-100 COPIES PER
NO PRICING ON QTY 25 OR LESS
EXCHANGE DEADLINE 10/7/2011
SDJ Derek Jeter/50 200.00 300.00
SJB Jay Bruce/50 15.00 40.00
SMC Matt Cain/100 10.00 25.00
SML Mark Loretta/35 10.00 25.00
SMY Michael Young/56 15.00 40.00
SPM Paul Maholm/50 6.00 15.00
SYM Yadier Molina/35 15.00 40.00

2009 Sweet Spot Swatch Patches

OVERALL MEM ODDS 2:3 HOBBY
PRINT RUNS B/WN 10-30 COPIES PER
NO PRICING ON QTY 25 OR LESS
SSAP Albert Pujols/30 15.00 40.00
SSCD Carlos Delgado/30 6.00 15.00
SSCL Carlos Lee/30 6.00 15.00
SSDO David Ortiz/30 6.00 15.00
SSFS Freddy Sanchez/30 6.00 15.00
SSGS Grady Sizemore/30 10.00 25.00
SSIK Ian Kinsler/30 6.00 15.00

2009 Sweet Spot Swatches

OVERALL MEM ODDS 2:3 HOBBY
SSAJ Adam Jones 3.00 8.00
SSAP Albert Pujols 5.00 12.00
SSAR Aramis Ramirez 3.00 8.00
SSBB Billy Butler 3.00 8.00
SSCB Clay Buchholz 3.00 8.00
SSCD Carlos Delgado 3.00 8.00
SSCG Curtis Granderson 3.00 8.00
SSCL Carlos Lee 3.00 8.00
SSCY Carl Yastrzemski 3.00 8.00
SSDO David Ortiz 3.00 8.00
SSDW Dave Winfield 3.00 8.00
SSGS Grady Sizemore 3.00 8.00
SSHK Howie Kendrick 3.00 8.00
SSIK Ian Kinsler 3.00 8.00
SSJB Jason Bay 3.00 8.00
SSJH Josh Hamilton 3.00 8.00
SSJP Jake Peavy 3.00 8.00
SSJW Jered Weaver 3.00 8.00
SSKW Kerry Wood 3.00 8.00
SSLE Cliff Lee 3.00 8.00
SSNM Nick Markakis 3.00 8.00
SSRG Ryan Garko 3.00 8.00
SSRH Roy Halladay 3.00 8.00
SSRP Rick Porcello 3.00 8.00
SSSC Steve Carlton 3.00 8.00
SSSH Shin-Soo Choo 3.00 8.00
SSTH Trevor Hoffman 3.00 8.00
SSVW Vernon Wells 3.00 8.00
SSZG Zack Greinke 3.00 8.00

2009 Sweet Spot Swatches Dual

OVERALL MEM ODDS 2:3 HOBBY
DSBB J.Bench/Y.Berra 10.00 25.00
DSBM Josh Beckett 4.00 10.00
Daisuke Matsuzaka
DSBS Schoendienst/Brock 10.00 25.00
DSBV J.Bruce/J.Votto 12.00 30.00
DSGJ K.Griffey Jr./D.Jeter 10.00 25.00
DSHP J.Hamilton/A.Pujols 8.00 20.00
DSJP D.Jeter/J.Posada 12.00 30.00
DSMJ Kenji Johjima 4.00 10.00
Daisuke Matsuzaka
DSMM J.Mauer/J.Morneau 6.00 15.00
DSMW Daisuke Matsuzaka 4.00 10.00
Chien-Ming Wang
DSPV Jake Peavy 4.00 10.00
Justin Verlander
DSRH J.Hamilton/N.Ryan 6.00 15.00
DSSP A.Pujols/O.Smith 12.00 30.00
DSSR O.Smith/J.Reyes 10.00 25.00
DSSW R.Sandberg/B.Williams 8.00 20.00
DSUW Justin Upton 4.00 10.00
Brandon Webb
DSVO David Ortiz 4.00 10.00
Jason Varitek
DSWL Tim Lincecum 4.00 10.00
Brandon Webb
DSYC Carl Yastrzemski 4.00 10.00
Orlando Cepeda
DSYJ F.Jenkins/C.Yaz 6.00 15.00

2009 Sweet Spot Swatches Quad

OVERALL MEM ODDS 2:3 HOBBY
QSCNR Schm/Fielder/C.Jones/Murray 10.00 25.00
QSCST Matsu/Jenk/Linc/Perry 12.50 30.00
QSGNY Linc/Jones/Reyes/Ham 8.00 20.00
QSNYC Reggie/DiMag/Yogi/Jeter 40.00 80.00
QSPHI Hamel/Carlton/Utley/Schmidt 12.50 30.00
QSTOP Hamilton/Pujols/Jeter/Griff Jr. 8.00 20.00
QSVEN Felix Hernandez/Johan Santana/Magglio Ordonez/Miguel Cabrera 5.00 12.00
QSVET Billy Wagner/Roy Halladay/Tom Glavine/Josh Beckett 5.00 12.00

2009 Sweet Spot Swatches Triple

OVERALL MEM ODDS 2:3 HOBBY
TSATL Tom Glavine 4.00 10.00
Tim Hudson
Phil Niekro
TSBPL Beck/Lince/Peavy 6.00 15.00
TSFMM Brian McCann 4.00 10.00
Carlton Fisk
Joe Mauer
TSJPN Fuk/Johjima/Dice-K 5.00 12.00
TSLMR Reyes/McCann/Lester 5.00 12.00
TSMIL Hall/Fielder/Braun 6.00 15.00
TSMIN Francisco Liriano 4.00 10.00
Joe Mauer
Justin Morneau
TSNYC Damon/Jeter/Jackson 10.00 25.00
TSNYY Jeter/Berra/DiMaggio 30.00 60.00
TSODF David Ortiz 4.00 10.00
Carlos Delgado
Prince Fielder
TSSFG Marichal/Lincecum/McCovey 6.00 15.00
TSSSC Cepeda/Sandberg/Schmidt 12.50 30.00

2002 Sweet Spot Classics

COMPLETE SET (90) 15.00 40.00
1 Mickey Mantle 2.50 6.00
2 Joe DiMaggio 1.25 3.00
3 Babe Ruth 2.00 5.00
4 Ty Cobb 1.00 2.50
5 Nolan Ryan 1.50 4.00
6 Sandy Koufax 1.25 3.00
7 Cy Young .60 1.50
8 Roberto Clemente 1.50 4.00
9 Lefty Grove .40 1.00
10 Lou Gehrig 1.25 3.00
11 Walter Johnson .60 1.50
12 Honus Wagner .75 2.00
13 Christy Mathewson .60 1.50
14 Jackie Robinson .60 1.50
15 Joe Morgan .40 1.00
16 Reggie Jackson .40 1.00
17 Eddie Collins .40 1.00
18 Cal Ripken 2.00 5.00
19 Hank Greenberg .60 1.50
20 Harmon Killebrew .60 1.50
21 Johnny Bench .60 1.50
22 Ernie Banks .60 1.50
23 Willie McCovey .40 1.00
24 Mel Ott .60 1.50
25 Tom Seaver .40 1.00
26 Tony Gwynn .75 2.00
27 Dave Winfield .40 1.00
28 Willie Stargell .40 1.00
29 Mark McGwire 1.50 4.00
30 Al Kaline .60 1.50
31 Jimmie Foxx .60 1.50
32 Satchel Paige .60 1.50
33 Eddie Murray .60 1.50
34 Lou Boudreau .40 1.00
35 Joe Jackson 1.25 3.00
36 Luke Appling .40 1.00
37 Ralph Kiner .40 1.00
38 Robin Yount .60 1.50
39 Paul Molitor .40 1.00
40 Juan Marichal .40 1.00
41 Brooks Robinson .40 1.00
42 Wade Boggs .40 1.00
43 Kirby Puckett .60 1.50
44 Yogi Berra .60 1.50
45 George Sisler .40 1.00
46 Buck Leonard .40 1.00
47 Billy Williams .40 1.00
48 Duke Snider .40 1.00
49 Don Drysdale .40 1.00
50 Bill Mazeroski .40 1.00
51 Tony Oliva .40 1.00
52 Luis Aparicio .40 1.00
53 Carlton Fisk .40 1.00
54 Kirk Gibson .40 1.00
55 Catfish Hunter .40 1.00
56 Joe Carter .40 1.00
57 Gaylord Perry .40 1.00
58 Don Mattingly 1.25 3.00
59 Eddie Mathews .60 1.50
60 Fergie Jenkins .40 1.00
61 Roy Campanella .60 1.50
62 Orlando Cepeda .40 1.00
63 Tony Perez .40 1.00
64 Dave Parker .40 1.00
65 Richie Ashburn .40 1.00
66 Andre Dawson .40 1.00
67 Dwight Evans .40 1.00
68 Rollie Fingers .40 1.00
69 Dale Murphy .40 1.00
70 Ron Santo .40 1.00
71 Steve Garvey .40 1.00
72 Monte Irvin .40 1.00
73 Alan Trammell .40 1.00
74 Ryne Sandberg 1.00 2.50
75 Gary Carter .40 1.00
76 Fred Lynn .40 1.00
77 Maury Wills .40 1.00
78 Ozzie Smith 1.00 2.50
79 Bobby Bonds .40 1.00
80 Mickey Cochrane .40 1.00
81 Dizzy Dean .60 1.50
82 Graig Nettles .40 1.00
83 Keith Hernandez .40 1.00
84 Boog Powell .40 1.00
85 Jack Clark .40 1.00
86 Dave Stewart .40 1.00
87 Tommy Lasorda .40 1.00
88 Dennis Eckersley .40 1.00
89 Ken Griffey Sr. .40 1.00
90 Bucky Dent .40 1.00

2002 Sweet Spot Classics Game Bat

STATED ODDS 1:8
SP INFO PROVIDED BY UPPER DECK
SP'S ARE NOT SERIAL-NUMBERED
ASTERISKS PERCEIVED AS LARGER SUPPLY
GOLD RANDOM INSERTS IN PACKS
GOLD PRINT RUN 25 SERIAL #'d SETS
GOLD NO PRICING DUE TO SCARCITY
BAK Al Kaline 6.00 15.00
BBBO Bob Boone 4.00 10.00
BBBU Bill Buckner 4.00 10.00
BBD Bucky Dent 4.00 10.00
BBM Bill Madlock 4.00 10.00
BBR Brooks Robinson 6.00 15.00
BBW Billy Williams 4.00 10.00
BCR Cal Ripken DP 6.00 15.00
BDE Dwight Evans 6.00 15.00
BDM Don Mattingly 10.00 25.00
BDP Dave Parker 4.00 10.00
BDW Dave Winfield DP 4.00 10.00
BFJ Fergie Jenkins 4.00 10.00
BFL Fred Lynn 4.00 10.00
BGC Gary Carter 4.00 10.00
BGN Graig Nettles 4.00 10.00
BHG Hank Greenberg SP 30.00 60.00
BJB Johnny Bench 6.00 15.00
BKG Ken Griffey Sr. DP 4.00 10.00
BKP Kirby Puckett DP 6.00 15.00
BNR Nolan Ryan 6.00 15.00
BPM Paul Molitor 4.00 10.00
BRC Roberto Clemente 15.00 40.00
BRJ Reggie Jackson 6.00 15.00
BSG Steve Garvey 4.00 10.00
BTG Tony Gwynn DP 6.00 15.00
BTM Thurman Munson 10.00 25.00
BWB Wade Boggs DP 6.00 15.00
BYB Yogi Berra 10.00 25.00

2002 Sweet Spot Classics Game Jersey

STATED ODDS 1:8
SP INFO PROVIDED BY UPPER DECK
SP'S ARE NOT SERIAL-NUMBERED
ASTERISKS PERCEIVED AS LARGER SUPPLY
GOLD RANDOM INSERTS IN PACKS
GOLD PRINT RUN 25 SERIAL #'d SETS
GOLD NO PRICING DUE TO SCARCITY
JBM Bill Madlock 4.00 10.00
JBW Billy Williams 4.00 10.00
JCR Cal Ripken DP 10.00 25.00
JDM Don Mattingly DP 10.00 25.00
JDP Dave Parker 4.00 10.00
JDSN Duke Snider SP/53 * 15.00 40.00
JDST Dave Stewart 4.00 10.00
JEM Eddie Murray 6.00 15.00
JGC Gary Carter 6.00 15.00
JGN Graig Nettles 4.00 10.00
JJC Joe Carter 4.00 10.00
JJD Joe DiMaggio SP/53 * 100.00 200.00
JJMA Juan Marichal 4.00 10.00
JMM Mickey Mantle SP/53 * 150.00 250.00
JNR Nolan Ryan DP 15.00 40.00
JOS Ozzie Smith 6.00 15.00
JPM Paul Molitor DP 4.00 10.00
JRF Rollie Fingers 4.00 10.00
JRJ Reggie Jackson 6.00 15.00
JRS Ryne Sandberg 6.00 15.00
JRY Robin Yount DP 6.00 15.00
JSG Steve Garvey 4.00 10.00
JSK Sandy Koufax SP 30.00 60.00
JTG Tony Gwynn DP 6.00 15.00
JTS Tom Seaver 6.00 15.00
JWB Wade Boggs 6.00 15.00
JWS Willie Stargell 6.00 15.00

2002 Sweet Spot Classics Signatures

STATED ODDS 1:24
SP INFO PROVIDED BY UPPER DECK
SP'S ARE NOT SERIAL-NUMBERED
DP PERCEIVED AS LARGER SUPPLY
GOLD RANDOM INSERTS IN PACKS
GOLD PRINT RUN 25 SERIAL #'d SETS
GOLD NO PRICING DUE TO SCARCITY
SAD Andre Dawson SP/100 * 30.00 60.00
SAK Al Kaline 15.00 40.00
SAT Alan Trammell 8.00 20.00
SBD Bucky Dent 6.00 15.00
SBM Bill Mazeroski 12.50 30.00

Card	Low	High
SBP Boog Powell	6.00	15.00
SBR Brooks Robinson	12.00	30.00
SCF Carlton Fisk SP/100 *	30.00	60.00
SCR Cal Ripken	30.00	80.00
SDAM Dale Murphy	10.00	25.00
SDAS Dave Stewart	6.00	15.00
SDEE Dennis Eckersley	8.00	20.00
SDOM Don Mattingly DP	30.00	80.00
SDW Dave Winfield SP/70 *	30.00	60.00
SEB Ernie Banks	30.00	60.00
SFJ Fergie Jenkins	6.00	15.00
SFL Fred Lynn	6.00	15.00
SGP Gaylord Perry	8.00	20.00
SJB Johnny Bench	30.00	60.00
SJM Joe Morgan	15.00	40.00
SKG Kirk Gibson SP	12.50	30.00
SKH Keith Hernandez	6.00	15.00
SKP Kirby Puckett SP/74 *	75.00	150.00
SNR Nolan Ryan SP/74 *	225.00	350.00
SOS Ozzie Smith SP/137 *	30.00	60.00
SPM Paul Molitor	10.00	25.00
SRF Rollie Fingers	8.00	20.00
SRJ Reggie Jackson SP *	20.00	50.00
SSG Steve Garvey	6.00	15.00
SSK Sandy Koufax SP *	150.00	300.00
STL Tommy Lasorda	40.00	100.00
STS Tom Seaver	30.00	80.00
SWM Willie McCovey SP *	15.00	40.00
SYB Yogi Berra SP/100 *	50.00	120.00

2003 Sweet Spot Classics

Card	Low	High
COMP.SET w/o SP's (89)	15.00	40.00
COMMON (1-74/76-90)	.30	.75
COMMON CARD (91-120)	3.00	8.00
91-120 PRINT RUN 1941 SERIAL #'d SETS		
COMMON CARD (121-150)	.75	2.00
121-150 PRINT RUN 1500 SERIAL #'d SETS		
91-150 RANDOM INSERTS IN PACKS		
CAREW 75B NOT INTENDED FOR RELEASE		
1 Al Hrabosky	.30	.75
2 Al Lopez	.30	.75
3 Andre Dawson	.50	1.25
4 Bill Buckner	.30	.75
5 Billy Williams	.50	1.25
6 Bob Feller	.50	1.25
7 Bob Lemon	.50	1.25
8 Bobby Doerr	.50	1.25
9 Cecil Cooper	.30	.75
10 Cal Ripken	2.50	6.00
11 Carlton Fisk	.50	1.25
12 Catfish Hunter	.50	1.25
13 Chris Chambliss	.30	.75
14 Dale Murphy	.75	2.00
15 Gaylord Perry	.50	1.25
16 Dave Kingman	.30	.75
17 Dave Parker	.30	.75
18 Dave Stewart	.30	.75
19 David Cone	.30	.75
20 Dennis Eckersley	.50	1.25
21 Don Baylor	.30	.75
22 Don Sutton	.50	1.25
23 Duke Snider	.50	1.25
24 Dwight Evans	.30	.75
25 Dwight Gooden	.30	.75
26 Earl Weaver MG	.50	1.25
27 Early Wynn	.50	1.25
28 Eddie Mathews	.75	2.00
29 Enos Slaughter	.50	1.25
30 Ernie Banks	.75	2.00
31 Fred Lynn	.30	.75
32 Fred Stanley	.30	.75
33 Gary Carter	.50	1.25
34 George Foster	.30	.75
35 Hal Newhouser	.50	1.25
36 George Kell	.50	1.25
37 Harmon Killebrew	.75	2.00
38 Hoyt Wilhelm	.50	1.25
39 Jack Morris	.50	1.25
40 Jim Bunning	.50	1.25
41 Jim Gilliam	.30	.75
42 Jim Leyritz	.30	.75
43 Jimmy Key	.30	.75
44 Joe Carter	.30	.75
45 Joe Morgan	.50	1.25
46 John Montefusco	.30	.75
47 Johnny Bench	.75	2.00
48 Johnny Podres	.30	.75
49 Jose Canseco	.50	1.25
50 Juan Marichal	.50	1.25
51 Keith Hernandez	.30	.75
52 Ken Griffey Sr.	1.50	4.00
53 Kirby Puckett	.75	2.00
54 Kirk Gibson	.30	.75
55 Larry Doby	.50	1.25
56 Lee May	.30	.75
57 Lee Mazzilli	.30	.75
58 Lou Boudreau	.50	1.25
59 Mark McGwire	1.25	3.00
60 Maury Wills	.30	.75
61 Mike Pagliarulo	.30	.75
62 Monte Irvin	.50	1.25
63 Nolan Ryan	2.50	6.00
64 Orlando Cepeda	.50	1.25
65 Ozzie Smith	1.00	2.50
66 Paul O'Neill	.50	1.25
67 Pee Wee Reese	.50	1.25
68 Phil Niekro	.50	1.25
69 Ralph Kiner	.50	1.25
70 Red Schoendienst	.50	1.25
71 Richie Ashburn	.50	1.25
72 Rick Ferrell	.30	.75
73 Robin Roberts	.50	1.25
74 Robin Yount	.75	2.00
75 Hideki Matsui/1999 XRC	6.00	15.00
75B Rod Carew ERR	.50	1.25
76 Rollie Fingers	.50	1.25
77 Ron Cey	.30	.75
78 Tom Seaver	.50	1.25
79 Sparky Anderson MG	.50	1.25
80 Stan Musial	1.25	3.00
81 Steve Garvey	.30	.75
82 Ted Williams	1.50	4.00
83 Tommy Lasorda	.50	1.25
84 Tony Gwynn	.75	2.00
85 Tony Perez	.50	1.25
86 Vida Blue	.30	.75
87 Warren Spahn	.50	1.25
88 Bob Gibson	.50	1.25
89 Willie McCovey	.50	1.25
90 Willie Stargell	.50	1.25
91 Ted Williams TB	2.50	6.00
92 Ted Williams TB	2.50	6.00
93 Ted Williams TB	2.50	6.00
94 Ted Williams TB	2.50	6.00
95 Ted Williams TB	2.50	6.00
96 Ted Williams TB	2.50	6.00
97 Ted Williams TB	2.50	6.00
98 Ted Williams TB	2.50	6.00
99 Ted Williams TB	2.50	6.00
100 Ted Williams TB	2.50	6.00
101 Ted Williams TB	2.50	6.00
102 Ted Williams TB	2.50	6.00
103 Ted Williams TB	2.50	6.00
104 Ted Williams TB	2.50	6.00
105 Ted Williams TB	2.50	6.00
106 Ted Williams TB	2.50	6.00
106B Ted Williams TB	2.50	6.00
107 Ted Williams TB	2.50	6.00
108 Ted Williams TB	2.50	6.00
109 Ted Williams TB	2.50	6.00
110 Ted Williams TB	2.50	6.00
111 Ted Williams TB	2.50	6.00
112 Ted Williams TB	2.50	6.00
113 Ted Williams TB	2.50	6.00
114 Ted Williams TB	2.50	6.00
115 Ted Williams TB	2.50	6.00
117 Ted Williams TB	2.50	6.00
118 Ted Williams TB	2.50	6.00
119 Ted Williams TB	2.50	6.00
120 Ted Williams TB	2.50	6.00
121 Babe Ruth YH	5.00	12.00
122 Bucky Dent YH	.75	2.00
123 Casey Stengel YH	1.25	3.00
124 Dave Righetti YH	.75	2.00
125 Dave Winfield YH	1.25	3.00
126 Dick Tidrow YH	.75	2.00
127 Dock Ellis YH	.75	2.00
128 Don Mattingly YH	4.00	10.00
129 Hank Bauer YH	.75	2.00
130 Jim Bouton YH	.75	2.00
131 Jim Kaat YH	.75	2.00
132 Joe DiMaggio YH	4.00	10.00
133 Joe Torre YH	1.25	3.00
134 Lou Piniella YH	.75	2.00
135 Mel Stottlemyre YH	.75	2.00
136 Mickey Mantle YH	6.00	15.00
137 Mickey Rivers YH	.75	2.00
138 Phil Rizzuto YH	1.25	3.00
139 Ralph Branca YH	.75	2.00
140 Ralph Houk YH	.75	2.00
141 Roger Maris YH	2.00	5.00
142 Ron Guidry YH	.75	2.00
143 Ruben Amaro Sr. YH	.75	2.00
144 Sparky Lyle YH	.75	2.00
145 Thurman Munson YH	2.00	5.00
146 Tommy Henrich YH	.75	2.00
147 Tommy John YH	.75	2.00
148 Tony Kubek YH	.75	2.00
149 Whitey Ford YH	1.25	3.00
150 Yogi Berra YH	2.00	5.00

2003 Sweet Spot Classics Matsui Parallel

RANDOM INSERTS IN PACKS
STATED PRINT RUNS LISTED BELOW
NO PRICING ON 75C DUE TO SCARCITY

Card	Low	High
75A Hideki Matsui Red/500	6.00	15.00
75B Hideki Matsui Blue/250	8.00	20.00

2003 Sweet Spot Classics Autographs Black Ink

ONE AUTO CUMULATIVELY PER 24 PACKS
STATED PRINT RUNS LISTED BELOW
ALL MCGWIRE'S INSCRIBED MARIS 61

Card	Low	High
CGAD Andre Dawson/75	12.50	30.00
CGAH Al Hrabosky/100	15.00	40.00
CGAT Alan Trammell/173	12.00	30.00
CGBB Bill Buckner/85	20.00	50.00
CGBW Billy Williams/173	6.00	15.00
CGCR Cal Ripken/38	50.00	120.00
CGDB Don Baylor/50	25.00	60.00
CGDE Dwight Evans/100	12.50	30.00
CGDP Dave Parker/113	6.00	15.00
CGDS Don Sutton/123	10.00	25.00
CGDS Duke Snider/100	40.00	80.00
CGEB Ernie Banks/73	60.00	120.00
CGGC Gary Carter/173	15.00	40.00
CGGF George Foster/173	6.00	15.00
CGHK Harmon Killebrew/73	15.00	40.00
CGJB Johnny Bench/73	30.00	60.00
CGJC Joe Carter/123	20.00	50.00
CGJM Joe Morgan/169	15.00	40.00
CGJM Jack Morris/123	15.00	40.00
CGJP Johnny Podres/173	6.00	15.00
CGKG Kirk Gibson/173	15.00	40.00
CGKH Keith Hernandez/173	6.00	15.00
CGKP Kirby Puckett/174	100.00	200.00
CGMM Mark McGwire/73	175.00	350.00
CGMW Maury Wills/173	10.00	25.00
CGPN Phil Niekro/173	12.50	30.00
CGRF Rollie Fingers/73	12.00	30.00
CGRR Robin Roberts/173	12.00	30.00
CGRY Robin Yount/73	30.00	60.00
CGSG Steve Garvey/173	12.00	30.00
CGTG Tony Gwynn/101	12.00	30.00
CGTP Tony Perez/51	40.00	80.00
CGTS Tom Seaver/74	40.00	100.00
CGKGS Ken Griffey Sr./100	12.00	30.00

2003 Sweet Spot Classics Autographs Blue Ink

ONE AUTO CUMULATIVELY PER 24 PACKS
SP INFO PROVIDED BY UPPER DECK
ASTERISKS PERCEIVED AS LARGER SUPPLY

Card	Low	High
CGAD Andre Dawson	12.00	30.00
CGAH Al Hrabosky SP	10.00	25.00
CGBB Bill Buckner SP	12.00	30.00
CGCF Carlton Fisk	15.00	40.00
CGCR Cal Ripken	40.00	80.00
CGDB Don Baylor SP	12.00	30.00
CGDE Dennis Eckersley	10.00	25.00
CGDE Dwight Evans *	6.00	15.00
CGDM Dale Murphy	12.50	30.00
CGDS Duke Snider	15.00	40.00
CGKP Kirby Puckett	100.00	200.00
CGOC Orlando Cepeda *	6.00	15.00
CGTG Tony Gwynn	20.00	50.00
CGDST Dave Stewart	10.00	25.00
CGKGS Ken Griffey Sr.	10.00	25.00

2003 Sweet Spot Classics Autographs Yankee Greats Black Ink

ONE AUTO CUMULATIVELY PER 24 PACKS
STATED PRINT RUNS LISTED BELOW
NO PRICING ON QTY OF 25 OR LESS

Card	Low	High
YGCC Chris Chambliss/101	30.00	60.00
YGDC David Cone/74	40.00	80.00
YGDE Dock Ellis/174	10.00	25.00
YGDG Dwight Gooden/74	30.00	60.00
YGDK Dave Kingman/100	30.00	60.00
YGDM Don Mattingly/74	75.00	150.00
YGDR Dave Righetti/173	20.00	50.00
YGDT Dick Tidrow/101	15.00	40.00
YGFS Fred Stanley/101	15.00	40.00
YGGU Ron Guidry/100	40.00	80.00
YGHB Hank Bauer/75	6.00	15.00
YGJB Jim Bouton/100	15.00	40.00
YGJC Jose Canseco/73	40.00	80.00
YGJK Jim Kaat/100	10.00	25.00
YGJK Jimmy Key/100	10.00	25.00
YGJL Jim Leyritz/100	15.00	40.00
YGJM John Montefusco/100	6.00	15.00
YGJT Joe Torre/73	40.00	80.00
YGLM Lee Mazzilli/100	15.00	40.00
YGLP Lou Piniella/100	15.00	40.00
YGMP Mike Pagliarulo/99	15.00	40.00
YGMR Mickey Rivers/73	30.00	60.00
YGMS Mel Stottlemyre/73	30.00	60.00
YGPO Paul O'Neill/100	40.00	80.00
YGPR Phil Rizzuto/173	40.00	80.00
YGRA Ruben Amaro Sr./100	6.00	15.00
YGRB Ralph Branca/100	10.00	25.00
YGRH Ralph Houk/100	10.00	25.00
YGSL Sparky Lyle/100	15.00	40.00
YGTH Tommy Henrich/100	15.00	40.00
YGTJ Tommy John/100	15.00	40.00
YGTK Tony Kubek/123	20.00	50.00
YGYB Yogi Berra/73	60.00	150.00

2003 Sweet Spot Classics Autographs Yankee Greats Blue Ink

ONE AUTO CUMULATIVELY PER 24 PACKS
SP INFO PROVIDED BY UPPER DECK
ASTERISKS PERCEIVED AS LARGER SUPPLY

Card	Low	High
YGBD Bucky Dent *	10.00	25.00
YGCC Chris Chambliss SP	10.00	25.00
YGDK Dave Kingman	10.00	25.00
YGDT Dick Tidrow	10.00	25.00
YGFS Fred Stanley	10.00	25.00
YGGU Ron Guidry	10.00	25.00
YGHB Hank Bauer SP	15.00	40.00
YGJB Jim Bouton	10.00	25.00
YGJK Jim Kaat	10.00	25.00
YGJK Jimmy Key	10.00	25.00
YGJL Jim Leyritz	10.00	25.00
YGJM John Montefusco	10.00	25.00
YGLM Lee Mazzilli	10.00	25.00
YGLP Lou Piniella SP	15.00	40.00
YGMP Mike Pagliarulo	10.00	25.00
YGPO Paul O'Neill	20.00	50.00
YGRA Ruben Amaro Sr.	10.00	25.00
YGRB Ralph Branca	10.00	25.00
YGRH Ralph Houk	10.00	25.00
YGSL Sparky Lyle SP	15.00	40.00
YGTH Tommy Henrich SP	15.00	40.00
YGTJ Tommy John	10.00	25.00

2003 Sweet Spot Classics Game Jersey

STATED ODDS 1:16

Card	Low	High
AD Andre Dawson SP	3.00	8.00
CC Cecil Cooper	2.00	5.00
CF Carlton Fisk	3.00	8.00
CR Cal Ripken	10.00	25.00
DM Dale Murphy	5.00	12.00
DP0 Dave Parker Pants	2.00	5.00
DS Duke Snider SP	3.00	8.00
EB Ernie Banks SP	5.00	12.00
FL Fred Lynn	2.00	5.00
GC Gary Carter SP	6.00	15.00
GF George Foster	2.00	5.00
HK Harmon Killebrew	5.00	12.00
JB Johnny Bench	5.00	12.00
JC Jose Canseco	3.00	8.00
JG Jim Gilliam	2.00	5.00
JM0 Joe Morgan Pants	3.00	8.00
JP Johnny Podres	2.00	5.00
KP Kirby Puckett	5.00	12.00
LM Lee May	2.00	5.00
MM Mark McGwire	8.00	20.00
NR Nolan Ryan	15.00	40.00
OS Ozzie Smith	6.00	15.00
RC Ron Cey	2.00	5.00
RF Rollie Fingers	3.00	8.00
RY Robin Yount	5.00	12.00
SG Steve Garvey	2.00	5.00
SM Stan Musial SP	15.00	40.00
TG Tony Gwynn	5.00	12.00
TW Ted Williams SP	20.00	50.00
WS Willie Stargell SP	3.00	8.00

2003 Sweet Spot Classics Patch Cards

STATED ODDS 1:6
STATED PRINT RUNS LISTED BELOW
NO PRICING ON QTY OF 40 OR LESS

Card	Low	High
BR1 Babe Ruth Red Sox/350	8.00	20.00
BR2 Babe Ruth Yankees	10.00	25.00
BR3 Babe Ruth 27 WS/150	8.00	20.00
BW1 Billy Williams	1.25	3.00
CF1 Carlton Fisk Red Sox	1.25	3.00
CF2 Carlton Fisk White Sox/150	2.00	5.00
CH1 Catfish Hunter A's/350	1.50	4.00
CH2 Catfish Hunter Yankees	1.25	3.00
CH3 Catfish Hunter A's GU/39	15.00	40.00
CH4 Catfish Hunter 72 WS/50	2.50	6.00
CR1 Cal Ripken	6.00	15.00
CR2 Cal Ripken GU/75	75.00	150.00
CR3 Cal Ripken 83 WS/150	10.00	25.00
DS1 Duke Snider	1.25	3.00
DS2 Duke Snider LA/150	2.00	5.00
DS3 Duke Snider Mets/350	1.50	4.00
DS5 Duke Snider Brooklyn/150	2.00	5.00
DS6 Duke Snider 59 WS/150	2.00	5.00
EB1 Ernie Banks	2.00	5.00
FL1 Fred Lynn Red Sox	.75	2.00
FL2 Fred Lynn Angels/350	1.00	2.50
FL3 Fred Lynn O's/150	1.25	3.00
FL4 Fred Lynn Tigers/50	1.50	4.00
GF1 George Foster Mets/350	1.00	2.50
GF2 George Foster Reds	.75	2.00
HM1 Hideki Matsui	4.00	10.00
JB1 Johnny Bench	2.00	5.00
JB2 Johnny Bench GU/150	20.00	50.00
JB3 Johnny Bench 76 WS/150	3.00	8.00
JD1 Joe DiMaggio	4.00	10.00
JD2 Joe DiMaggio 47 WS/50	8.00	20.00
JD3 Joe DiMaggio 37 WS/350	5.00	12.00
JD4 Joe DiMaggio 39 WS/150	6.00	15.00
JM1 Joe Morgan Reds	1.25	3.00
JM2 Joe Morgan Astros/350	1.50	4.00
JM3 Joe Morgan Giants/150	2.00	5.00
JM4 Joe Morgan Reds GU/150	15.00	40.00
JM5 Joe Morgan 76 WS/100	2.00	5.00
KG1 Kirk Gibson Dodgers	.75	2.00
KG2 Kirk Gibson Tigers/350	1.00	2.50
KP1 Kirby Puckett	2.00	5.00
KP2 Kirby Puckett GU/40	40.00	80.00
MC1 Mark McGwire A's	3.00	8.00
MC2 Mark McGwire Cards/350	4.00	10.00
MM1 Mickey Mantle	10.00	25.00
MM2 M.Mantle 52 WS/150	10.00	25.00
MM3 M.Mantle 56 WS/150	10.00	25.00
MM4 M.Mantle 60 WS/150	10.00	25.00
NR1 Nolan Ryan Astros	6.00	15.00
NR2 Nolan Ryan Rangers/350	8.00	20.00
NR3 Nolan Ryan Angels/150	10.00	25.00
NR4 N.Ryan Astros GU/105	60.00	120.00
OS1 Ozzie Smith Cards	2.50	6.00
OS2 Ozzie Smith Padres/350	3.00	8.00
OS3 Ozzie Smith Cards GU/150	30.00	60.00
OS4 Ozzie Smith 82 WS/100	4.00	10.00
OS5 Ozzie Smith 85 WS/100	4.00	10.00
RM1 Roger Maris Yankees	2.00	5.00
RM2 Roger Maris Cards/350	2.50	6.00
RM3 Roger Maris 62 WS/150	3.00	8.00
RM4 Roger Maris 67 WS/50	4.00	10.00
RY1 Robin Yount	2.00	5.00
RY2 Robin Yount GU/150	20.00	50.00
RY3 Robin Yount 82 WS/350	2.50	6.00
SG1 Steve Garvey Dodgers	.75	2.00
SG2 Steve Garvey Padres/350	1.00	2.50
SG3 S.Garvey Dodgers GU/150	15.00	40.00
SG4 Steve Garvey 77 WS/50	1.50	4.00
SG5 Steve Garvey 81 WS/50	1.50	4.00
TG1 Tony Gwynn	2.00	5.00
TG2 Tony Gwynn GU/150	40.00	80.00
TG3 Tony Gwynn 84 WS/350	2.50	6.00
TW1 Ted Williams	4.00	10.00
TW2 Ted Williams 46 WS/350	5.00	12.00
WS1 Willie Stargell	1.25	3.00
WS2 Willie Stargell GU/137	15.00	40.00
WS3 Willie Stargell 71 WS/150	2.00	5.00
WS4 Willie Stargell 79 WS/50	2.50	6.00
YB1 Yogi Berra	2.00	5.00
YB2 Yogi Berra 53 WS/350	2.50	6.00
YB3 Yogi Berra 56 WS/150	3.00	8.00

2003 Sweet Spot Classics Pinstripes

STATED ODDS 1:40

Card	Low	High
SPBR Babe Ruth Pants SP	150.00	300.00
SPCS Casey Stengel	6.00	15.00
SPDE Bucky Dent	4.00	10.00
SPDG Dwight Gooden Pants	4.00	10.00
SPDM Don Mattingly Pants	15.00	40.00
SPDR Dave Righetti	4.00	10.00
SPJB Jim Bouton	4.00	10.00
SPJD Joe DiMaggio SP	60.00	120.00
SPMM Mickey Mantle SP	25.00	60.00
SPPR Phil Rizzuto	8.00	20.00
SPTM Thurman Munson SP	15.00	40.00
SPYB Yogi Berra	8.00	20.00

2004 Sweet Spot Classic

Card	Low	High
COMP.SET w/o SP'S (90)	15.00	40.00
COMMON CARD (1-90)	.30	.75
COMMON CARD (91-161)	1.25	3.00
91-161 STATED ODDS 1:3		
91-161 PRINTS B/WN 1910-1999 COPIES PER		
CARDS 143 AND 148 DO NOT EXIST		
1 Al Kaline	.75	2.00
2 Andre Dawson	.50	1.25
3 Bert Blyleven	.50	1.25
4 Bill Dickey	.30	.75
5 Bill Mazeroski	.50	1.25
6 Billy Martin	.50	1.25
7 Bob Feller	.50	1.25
8 Bob Gibson	.50	1.25
9 Bob Lemon	.50	1.25
10 George Kell	.50	1.25
11 Bobby Doerr	.50	1.25
12 Brooks Robinson	.50	1.25
13 Cal Ripken	2.50	6.00
14 Carl Hubbell	.50	1.25
15 Carl Yastrzemski	.75	2.00
16 Charlie Keller	.30	.75
17 Chuck Dressen	.30	.75
18 Cy Young	.50	1.25
19 Dave Winfield	.50	1.25
20 Dizzy Dean	.50	1.25
21 Don Drysdale	.50	1.25
22 Don Larsen	.30	.75
23 Don Mattingly	1.50	4.00
24 Don Newcombe	.30	.75
25 Duke Snider	.50	1.25
26 Early Wynn	.50	1.25
27 Eddie Mathews	.75	2.00
28 Elston Howard	.30	.75
29 Frank Robinson	.50	1.25
30 Gary Carter	.50	1.25
31 Gil Hodges	.50	1.25
32 Gil McDougald	.30	.75
33 Hank Greenberg	.75	2.00
34 Harmon Killebrew	.75	2.00
35 Harry Caray	.50	1.25
36 Honus Wagner	.75	2.00
37 Hoyt Wilhelm	.50	1.25
38 Jackie Robinson	.75	2.00
39 Jim Bunning	.50	1.25
40 Jim Palmer	.50	1.25
41 Jimmie Foxx	.75	2.00
42 Jimmy Wynn	.30	.75
43 Joe DiMaggio	1.50	4.00
44 Joe Torre	.50	1.25
45 Johnny Mize	.50	1.25
46 Juan Marichal	.50	1.25
47 Larry Doby	.50	1.25
48 Lefty Gomez	.30	.75
49 Lefty Grove	.50	1.25
50 Leo Durocher	.30	.75
51 Lou Boudreau	.50	1.25
52 Lou Brock	.50	1.25
53 Lou Gehrig	1.50	4.00
54 Luis Aparicio	.50	1.25
55 Maury Wills	.30	.75
56 Mel Allen	.30	.75
57 Mel Ott	.75	2.00
58 Mickey Cochrane	.50	1.25
59 Mickey Mantle	2.50	6.00
60 Mike Schmidt	1.25	3.00
61 Monte Irvin	.50	1.25
62 Nolan Ryan	2.50	6.00
63 Pee Wee Reese	.50	1.25
64 Phil Rizzuto	.50	1.25
65 Ralph Kiner	.50	1.25
66 Richie Ashburn	.50	1.25
67 Rick Ferrell	.30	.75
68 Roberto Clemente	2.00	5.00
69 Robin Roberts	.50	1.25
70 Robin Yount	.75	2.00
71 Rogers Hornsby	.50	1.25
72 Rollie Fingers	.50	1.25
73 Roy Campanella	.75	2.00
74 Ryne Sandberg	1.50	4.00
75 Tony Gwynn	.75	2.00
76 Satchel Paige	.75	2.00
77 Shoeless Joe Jackson	1.00	2.50
78 Stan Musial	1.25	3.00
79 Ted Williams	1.50	4.00
80 Thurman Munson	.75	2.00
81 Tom Seaver	.50	1.25
82 Tommy Henrich	.30	.75
83 Tony Perez	.50	1.25
84 Tris Speaker	.50	1.25
85 Vida Blue	.30	.75
86 Wade Boggs	.50	1.25
87 Walter Johnson	.50	1.25
88 Warren Spahn	.50	1.25
89 Whitey Ford	.50	1.25
90 Willie McCovey	.50	1.25
91 Andre Dawson FF/1987	2.00	5.00
92 Andre Dawson FF/1990	2.00	5.00
93 Ernie Banks FF/1958	3.00	8.00
94 Bob Lemon FF/1948	2.00	5.00
95 Cal Ripken FF/1982	6.00	15.00
96 Cal Ripken FF/1995	6.00	15.00
97 Carl Yastrzemski FF/1979	3.00	8.00
98 Carlton Fisk FF/1972	2.00	5.00
99 Cy Young FF/1910	2.00	5.00
100 Don Larsen FF/1956	1.25	3.00
101 Don Newcombe FF/1949	1.25	3.00
102 Don Newcombe FF/1956	1.25	3.00
103 Dwight Evans FF/1986	1.25	3.00
104 Elston Howard FF/1955	1.25	3.00
105 Frank Robinson FF/1956	2.00	5.00
106 Frank Robinson FF/1966	2.00	5.00
107 Frank Robinson FF/1973	2.00	5.00
108 Gil McDougald FF/1951	1.25	3.00
109 Hank Greenberg FF/1941	3.00	8.00
110 Harmon Killebrew FF/1964	3.00	8.00
111 Hoyt Wilhelm FF/1952	2.00	5.00
112 Hoyt Wilhelm FF/1958	2.00	5.00
113 Jackie Robinson FF/1946	3.00	8.00
114 J.Robinson FF Black/1947	3.00	8.00
115 J.Robinson FF ROY/1947	3.00	8.00
116 Jackie Robinson FF/1997	3.00	8.00
117 Jim Bunning FF/1964	2.00	5.00
118 J.DiMaggio FF Bench/1950	4.00	10.00
119 Joe Morgan FF/1976	2.00	5.00
120 Johnny Mize FF/1939	2.00	5.00
121 Johnny Mize FF/1947	2.00	5.00
122 Juan Marichal FF/1968	2.00	5.00
123 Ken Griffey Sr. FF/1990	1.25	3.00
124 Larry Doby FF/1947	2.00	5.00
125 Lefty Gomez FF/1933	1.25	3.00
126 Lou Boudreau FF/1946	2.00	5.00
127 Lou Gehrig FF Lineup/1939	4.00	10.00
128 Lou Gehrig FF Number/1939	4.00	10.00
129 Mark McGwire FF/1989	4.00	10.00
130 Mark McGwire FF/1998	4.00	10.00
131 Maury Wills FF/1962	1.25	3.00
132 Mel Ott FF/1946	3.00	8.00
133 Mike Schmidt FF/1980	4.00	10.00
134 Nolan Ryan FF/1973	5.00	12.00
135 Nolan Ryan FF/1989	5.00	12.00
136 Pee Wee Reese FF/1955	2.00	5.00
137 Nolan Ryan FF/1979	5.00	12.00
138 Richie Ashburn FF/1962	2.00	5.00
139 Roberto Clemente FF/1971	8.00	20.00
140 Roberto Clemente FF/1973	8.00	20.00
141 Robin Roberts FF/1956	2.00	5.00
142 Robin Yount FF/1982	3.00	8.00
144 Rollie Fingers FF/1975	2.00	5.00
145 Rollie Fingers FF/1981	2.00	5.00
146 Roy Campanella FF/1953	3.00	8.00
147 Ryne Sandberg FF/1990	3.00	8.00
149 Satchel Paige FF/1948	3.00	8.00
150 Stan Musial FF/1952	3.00	8.00
151 Stan Musial FF/1954	3.00	8.00
152 Stan Musial FF/1963	3.00	8.00
153 Ted Williams FF/1947	4.00	10.00
154 Ted Williams FF/1957	4.00	10.00
155 Tom Seaver FF/1970	2.00	5.00
156 Tom Seaver FF/1975	2.00	5.00
157 Wade Boggs FF/1999	2.00	5.00
158 Warren Spahn FF/1957	2.00	5.00
159 Warren Spahn FF/1958	2.00	5.00
160 Joe DiMaggio FF AS/1950	4.00	10.00
161 Yogi Berra FF/1947	3.00	8.00

2004 Sweet Spot Classic Barrel Signatures

OVERALL AUTO ODDS 1:24
PRINT RUNS B/WN 24-203 COPIES PER
NO PRICING ON QTY OF 25 OR LESS
EXCHANGE DEADLINE 01/27/07

Card	Low	High
BW Billy Williams/200	10.00	25.00
HB Harold Baines/200	20.00	50.00
RS Ron Santo/203	15.00	40.00
WB Wade Boggs/200	15.00	40.00

2004 Sweet Spot Classic Game Used Memorabilia

OVERALL GU MEMORABILIA ODDS 1:24
STATED PRINT RUN 275 SERIAL #'d SETS

Card	Low	High
SSAD Andre Dawson Expos Jsy	4.00	10.00
SSBB Bert Blyleven Jsy	4.00	10.00
SSBM Billy Martin Pants	6.00	15.00
SSCD Chuck Dressen Pants	4.00	10.00
SSCK Charlie Keller Jsy	6.00	15.00
SSCR Cal Ripken Jsy	15.00	40.00
SSCY Carl Yastrzemski Jsy	10.00	25.00
SSDM Don Mattingly Jsy	10.00	25.00
SSEH Elston Howard Jsy	6.00	15.00
SSEM Eddie Mathews Jsy	6.00	15.00
SSFR Frank Robinson Jsy	4.00	10.00
SSGC Gary Carter Pants	4.00	10.00
SSGM Gil McDougald Jsy	6.00	15.00
SSJB Jim Bunning Pants	6.00	15.00
SSJD Joe DiMaggio Pants	15.00	40.00
SSJM Juan Marichal Pants	4.00	10.00
SSJO Johnny Mize Pants	6.00	15.00
SSJP Jim Palmer Jsy	4.00	10.00
SSJR Jackie Robinson Pants	15.00	40.00
SSJT Joe Torre Jsy	6.00	15.00
SSKG Ken Griffey Sr. Jsy	4.00	10.00
SSML Mickey Lolich Jsy	4.00	10.00
SSMM Mickey Mantle Pants	60.00	120.00
SSMW Maury Wills Pants	4.00	10.00
SSNR Nolan Ryan Jsy	10.00	25.00
SSOS Ozzie Smith Jsy	6.00	15.00
SSPR Phil Rizzuto Pants	6.00	15.00
SSRB Ron Blomberg Jsy	4.00	10.00
SSRC Roberto Clemente Pants	20.00	50.00
SSRM Roger Maris Pants	10.00	25.00
SSRY Robin Yount Jsy	6.00	15.00
SSSA Sparky Anderson Jsy	4.00	10.00
SSSB Sal Bando Jsy	4.00	10.00
SSSM Stan Musial Pants	15.00	40.00
SSTG Tony Gwynn Pants	6.00	15.00
SSTM Thurman Munson Jsy	12.50	30.00
SSTS Tom Seaver Pants	6.00	15.00
SSTW Ted Williams Pants	12.50	30.00
SSWB Wade Boggs Sox Pants	6.00	15.00
SSAD1 Andre Dawson Cubs Jsy	4.00	10.00
SSWB1 Wade Boggs Yanks Pants	6.00	15.00

2004 Sweet Spot Classic Game Used Memorabilia Silver Rainbow

*SILVER RBW: .75X TO 2X BASIC SWATCH
OVERALL GU MEMORABILIA ODDS 1:24
STATED PRINT RUN 50 SERIAL #'d SETS

Card	Low	High
SSJD Joe DiMaggio Pants	20.00	50.00
SSMM Mickey Mantle Pants	125.00	200.00
SSRC Roberto Clemente Pants	25.00	60.00
SSTW Ted Williams Pants	15.00	40.00

2004 Sweet Spot Classic Game Used Patch

PRINT RUNS B/WN 17-176 COPIES PER
NO PRICING ON QTY OF 23 OR LESS
SILVER RAINBOW PRINT RUN 10 #'d SETS
NO SILV.RAIN.PRICING DUE TO SCARCITY
RANDOM INSERTS IN PACKS

Card	Low	High
GUAD Andre Dawson/100	10.00	25.00
GUBB Bert Blyleven/113	10.00	25.00
GUCK Charlie Keller/55	15.00	40.00
GUDM Don Mattingly/176	15.00	40.00
GUFR Frank Robinson/50	15.00	40.00
GUGM Gil McDougald/31	20.00	50.00
GUML Mickey Lolich/115	10.00	25.00
GUMW Maury Wills/78	10.00	25.00
GUNR Nolan Ryan/96	50.00	100.00
GURY Robin Yount/100	20.00	50.00
GUTG Tony Gwynn/100	30.00	60.00
GUTM Thurman Munson/100	30.00	60.00
GUTS Tom Seaver/94	15.00	40.00
GUWB Wade Boggs/90	15.00	40.00

2004 Sweet Spot Classic Patch 300

STATED PRINT RUN 300 SERIAL #'d SETS
*PATCH 230: .4X TO 1X BASIC
PATCH 230 PRINT RUN 230 SERIAL #'d SETS
*PATCH 200: .4X TO 1X BASIC
PATCH 200 PRINT RUN 200 SERIAL #'d SETS
*PATCH 150: .5X TO 1.2X BASIC
PATCH 150 PRINT RUN 150 SERIAL #'d SETS
*PATCH 125: .5X TO 1.2X BASIC
PATCH 125 PRINT RUN 125 SERIAL #'d SETS
*PATCH 75: .6X TO 1.5X BASIC
PATCH 75 PRINT RUN 75 SERIAL #'d SETS
*PATCH 50: .75X TO 2X BASIC
PATCH 50 PRINT RUN 50 SERIAL #'d SETS
PATCH 25 PRINT RUN 25 SERIAL #'d SETS
NO PATCH 25 PRICING DUE TO SCARCITY
PATCH 10 PRINT RUN 10 SERIAL #'d SETS
NO PATCH 10 PRICING DUE TO SCARCITY
OVERALL PATCH ODDS 1:3

Card	Low	High
SSPAD Andre Dawson Cubs	4.00	10.00
SSPAK Al Kaline Tigers	8.00	20.00
SSPAL Mel Allen Yanks	4.00	10.00
SSPBD Bill Dickey Yanks	6.00	15.00
SSPBF Bob Feller Indians	4.00	10.00
SSPBG Bob Gibson Cards	6.00	15.00
SSPBL Bob Lemon Indians	4.00	10.00
SSPBM Billy Martin Yanks	6.00	15.00
SSPBR Lou Brock Cards	6.00	15.00
SSPCA Roy Campanella Dodgers	6.00	15.00
SSPCG Charlie Gehringer Tigers	4.00	10.00
SSPCH Carl Hubbell Giants	6.00	15.00
SSPCM Christy Mathewson Giants	6.00	15.00
SSPCO Mickey Cochrane Tigers	4.00	10.00
SSPCR Cal Ripken AS	15.00	40.00
SSPCY Cy Young Indians	6.00	15.00
SSPDD Dizzy Dean Cards	6.00	15.00
SSPDL Don Larsen Yanks	4.00	10.00
SSPDM Don Mattingly Yanks	10.00	25.00
SSPDN Don Newcombe Dodgers	4.00	10.00
SSPDO Bobby Doerr Red Sox	4.00	10.00
SSPDR Don Drysdale Dodgers	6.00	15.00
SSPDS Duke Snider AS	6.00	15.00
SSPDU Leo Durocher Dodgers	4.00	10.00
SSPDW Dave Winfield Yanks	4.00	10.00
SSPEM Eddie Mathews Braves	6.00	15.00
SSPES Enos Slaughter Cards	4.00	10.00
SSPEW Early Wynn Indians	4.00	10.00
SSPFF Frankie Frisch Cards	4.00	10.00
SSPFI Rollie Fingers A's	4.00	10.00
SSPFJ Ferguson Jenkins Cubs	4.00	10.00
SSPFR Frank Robinson Reds	4.00	10.00
SSPGC Gary Carter Mets	4.00	10.00
SSPGE Lou Gehrig Yanks	12.50	30.00
SSPGH Gil Hodges Dodgers	6.00	15.00
SSPGP Gaylord Perry Giants	4.00	10.00
SSPGR Lefty Grove A's	6.00	15.00
SSPHC Harry Caray Cubs	4.00	10.00
SSPHG Hank Greenberg Tigers	6.00	15.00
SSPHK Harmon Killebrew Twins	8.00	20.00
SSPHW Honus Wagner Pirates	6.00	15.00
SSPIR Monte Irvin Giants	4.00	10.00
SSPJB Jim Bunning Phils	6.00	15.00
SSPJD Joe DiMaggio AS	8.00	20.00
SSPJF Jimmie Foxx A's	6.00	15.00
SSPJJ Shoeless Joe Jackson Sox	8.00	20.00
SSPJM Johnny Mize Cards	4.00	10.00
SSPJP Jim Palmer O's	4.00	10.00
SSPJR Jackie Robinson Dodgers	6.00	15.00
SSPJT Joe Torre Braves	4.00	10.00
SSPLA Luis Aparicio White Sox	4.00	10.00
SSPLB Lou Boudreau Indians	4.00	10.00
SSPLD Larry Doby Indians	4.00	10.00
SSPLG Lefty Gomez Yanks	6.00	15.00
SSPMA Juan Marichal Giants	4.00	10.00
SSPMI Mickey Mantle AS	10.00	25.00
SSPML Mickey Lolich Tigers	4.00	10.00
SSPMO Mel Ott Giants	6.00	15.00
SSPMS Mike Schmidt Phils	10.00	25.00
SSPMW Maury Wills Dodgers	4.00	10.00
SSPNR Nolan Ryan Mets	12.50	30.00
SSPPR Pee Wee Reese Dodgers	6.00	15.00
SSPRA Richie Ashburn Phils	6.00	15.00
SSPRC Roberto Clemente Pirates	12.50	30.00
SSPRF Rick Ferrell Red Sox	4.00	10.00
SSPRH Rogers Hornsby Cards	6.00	15.00
SSPRI Phil Rizzuto Yanks	6.00	15.00
SSPRK Ralph Kiner Pirates	4.00	10.00
SSPRO Brooks Robinson O's	6.00	15.00
SSPRR Robin Roberts Phils	4.00	10.00
SSPRS Ryne Sandberg Cubs	10.00	25.00
SSPRU Babe Ruth AS	12.50	30.00
SSPSK Bill Skowron Yanks	4.00	10.00
SSPSM Stan Musial Cards	8.00	20.00
SSPSP Satchel Paige Indians	6.00	15.00
SSPTC Ty Cobb Tigers	8.00	20.00
SSPTH Tommy Henrich Yanks	4.00	10.00
SSPTL Tommy Lasorda Dodgers	4.00	10.00
SSPTM Thurman Munson Yanks	6.00	15.00
SSPTP Tony Perez Reds	4.00	10.00
SSPTR Tris Speaker Red Sox	6.00	15.00
SSPTS Tom Seaver Mets	6.00	15.00
SSPTW Ted Williams AS	10.00	25.00
SSPWB Wade Boggs Red Sox	6.00	15.00
SSPWF Whitey Ford Yanks	6.00	15.00
SSPWI Hoyt Wilhelm White Sox	4.00	10.00
SSPWJ Walter Johnson Senators	6.00	15.00
SSPWM Willie McCovey Giants	4.00	10.00
SSPWS Warren Spahn Braves	6.00	15.00
SSPYA Carl Yastrzemski Red Sox	10.00	25.00

2004 Sweet Spot Classic Signatures Black

OVERALL AUTO ODDS 1:24
PRINT RUNS B/WN 25-275 COPIES PER
NO PRICING ON QTY OF 25 OR LESS
EXCHANGE DEADLINE 01/27/07

Card	Low	High
SSA2 Preacher Roe/225	10.00	25.00
SSA4 Bob Feller/65	10.00	25.00
SSA5 Bob Gibson/50	20.00	50.00
SSA6 Harry Kalas/100	75.00	150.00
SSA7 Bobby Doerr/100	15.00	40.00
SSA8 Cal Ripken/50	100.00	175.00
SSA10 Carlton Fisk/100	10.00	25.00
SSA11 Chuck Tanner/150	10.00	25.00
SSA12 Cito Gaston/150	10.00	25.00
SSA13 Danny Ozark/150	10.00	25.00
SSA14 Dave Winfield/80	15.00	40.00
SSA15 Davey Johnson/175	15.00	40.00
SSA16 Ernie Harwell/100	40.00	80.00
SSA17 Dick Williams/150	10.00	25.00
SSA19 Don Newcombe/40	20.00	50.00
SSA20 Duke Snider/35	15.00	40.00
SSA21 Steve Carlton/150	15.00	40.00
SSA22 Felipe Alou/175	6.00	15.00
SSA23 Frank Robinson/65	20.00	50.00
SSA24 Gary Carter/100	15.00	40.00
SSA25 Gene Mauch/225	10.00	25.00
SSA26 George Bamberger/225	10.00	25.00
SSA28 Gus Suhr/100	15.00	40.00
SSA30 Harmon Killebrew/50	20.00	50.00
SSA31 Jack McKeon/225	6.00	15.00
SSA32 Jim Bunning/100	15.00	40.00
SSA33 Jimmy Piersall/212	10.00	25.00
SSA35 Johnny Bench/50	50.00	100.00
SSA36 Juan Marichal/50	20.00	50.00
SSA37 Lou Brock/50	20.00	50.00
SSA38 George Kell/40	10.00	25.00
SSA39 Maury Wills/40	20.00	50.00
SSA41 Mike Schmidt/40	30.00	60.00
SSA43 Ozzie Smith/65	50.00	100.00
SSA44 Eddie Mayo/140	10.00	25.00
SSA45 Phil Rizzuto/50	30.00	60.00
SSA47 Lonny Frey/114	10.00	25.00
SSA48 Bill Mazeroski/50	12.50	30.00
SSA49 Robin Roberts/40	40.00	80.00
SSA50 Robin Yount/40	50.00	100.00
SSA55 Tony Perez/40	20.00	50.00
SSA56 Sparky Anderson/175	15.00	40.00
SSA58 Ted Radcliffe/225	10.00	25.00
SSA62 Tony LaRussa/275	12.00	30.00
SSA63 Tony Oliva/150	10.00	25.00
SSA64 Tony Pena/150	10.00	25.00
SSA66 Whitey Ford/45	40.00	80.00
SSA67 Yogi Berra/65	50.00	120.00

2004 Sweet Spot Classic Signatures Black Holo-Foil

OVERALL AUTO ODDS 1:24
PRINT RUNS B/WN 10-100 COPIES PER
NO PRICING ON QTY OF 25 OR LESS
EXCHANGE DEADLINE 01/27/07
MOST CARDS FEATURE INSCRIPTIONS

Card	Low	High
SSA11 Chuck Tanner/100	10.00	25.00
SSA12 Cito Gaston/100	10.00	25.00

SSA13 Danny Ozark/100 10.00 25.00
SSA15 Davey Johnson/50 20.00 50.00
SSA17 Dick Williams/100 10.00 25.00
SSA22 Felipe Alou/50 12.50 30.00
SSA24 Gary Carter/50 30.00 60.00
SSA52 Roger Craig/50 20.00 50.00
SSA56 Sparky Anderson/50 20.00 50.00
SSA62 Tony LaRussa/50 30.00 60.00
SSA63 Tony Oliva/100 10.00 25.00
SSA64 Tony Pena/100 10.00 25.00

2004 Sweet Spot Classic Signatures Blue

OVERALL AUTO ODDS 1:24
PRINT RUNS B/WN 15-150 COPIES PER
NO PRICING ON QTY OF 25 OR LESS
SSA2 Preacher Roe/150 15.00 40.00
SSA4 Bob Feller/50 20.00 50.00
SSA6 Harry Kalas/50 60.00 120.00
SSA7 Bobby Doerr/50 20.00 50.00
SSA10 Carlton Fisk/50 40.00 80.00
SSA11 Chuck Tanner/125 10.00 25.00
SSA12 Cito Gaston/125 6.00 15.00
SSA13 Danny Ozark/125 10.00 25.00
SSA14 Dave Winfield/35 40.00 80.00
SSA15 Davey Johnson/150 15.00 40.00
SSA17 Dick Williams/125 10.00 25.00
SSA21 Steve Carlton/100 15.00 40.00
SSA22 Felipe Alou/150 10.00 25.00
SSA23 Frank Robinson/50 8.00 20.00
SSA24 Gary Carter/75 15.00 40.00
SSA25 Gene Mauch/150 10.00 25.00
SSA26 George Bamberger/150 10.00 25.00
SSA28 Gus Suhr/85 20.00 50.00
SSA31 Jack McKeon/150 10.00 25.00
SSA32 Jim Bunning/65 12.50 30.00
SSA33 Jimmy Piersall/150 6.00 15.00
SSA43 Ozzie Smith/50 50.00 100.00
SSA44 Eddie Mayo/50 12.50 30.00
SSA47 Lonny Frey/75 12.50 30.00
SSA52 Roger Craig/150 10.00 25.00
SSA56 Sparky Anderson/150 15.00 40.00
SSA58 Ted Radcliffe/150 40.00 80.00
SSA62 Tony LaRussa/145 15.00 40.00
SSA63 Tony Oliva/125 15.00 40.00
SSA64 Tony Pena/115 10.00 25.00
SSA67 Yogi Berra/50 50.00 120.00

2004 Sweet Spot Classic Signatures Red

OVERALL AUTO ODDS 1:24
PRINT RUNS B/WN 2-86 COPIES PER
NO PRICING ON QTY OF 25 OR LESS
EXCHANGE DEADLINE 01/27/07
ALL BUT DIMAGGIO/WILLIAMS ARE RED INK
DIMAGGIO/T.WILLIAMS ARE BLUE INK
APPX.25% OF DIMAGGIO'S = YANKEE CLIPPER
SSA34 Joe DiMaggio/86 600.00 900.00

2005 Sweet Spot Classic

COMPLETE SET (100) 15.00 40.00
COMMON CARD (1-100) .30 .75
1 Al Kaline .75 2.00
2 Al Rosen .30 .75
3 Babe Ruth 2.00 5.00
4 Bill Mazeroski .50 1.25
5 Dilly Williams .50 1.25
6 Bob Feller .50 1.25
7 Bob Gibson .50 1.25
8 Bobby Doerr .50 1.25
9 Brooks Robinson .50 1.25
10 Cal Ripken 2.50 6.00
11 Carl Yastrzemski 1.00 2.50
12 Carlton Fisk .50 1.25
13 Casey Stengel .50 1.25
14 Christy Mathewson .75 2.00
15 Cy Young .50 1.25
16 Dale Murphy .75 2.00
17 Dave Winfield .50 1.25
18 Dennis Eckersley .50 1.25
19 Dizzy Dean .50 1.25
20 Don Drysdale .50 1.25
21 Don Mattingly 1.50 4.00
22 Don Newcombe .30 .75
23 Don Sutton .30 .75
24 Duke Snider .50 1.25
25 Dwight Evans .50 1.25
26 Eddie Mathews .75 2.00
27 Eddie Murray .50 1.25
28 Enos Slaughter .50 1.25
29 Ernie Banks .75 2.00
30 Frank Howard .30 .75
31 Frank Robinson .50 1.25
32 Gary Carter .50 1.25
33 Gaylord Perry .50 1.25
34 George Brett 1.50 4.00
35 George Kell .50 1.25
36 George Sisler .50 1.25
37 Larry Doby .50 1.25
38 Harmon Killebrew .75 2.00
39 Honus Wagner .50 1.25
40 Jackie Robinson .50 1.25
41 Jim Bunning .50 1.25
42 Jim Palmer .50 1.25
43 Jim Rice .50 1.25
44 Jimmie Foxx .50 1.25
45 Joe DiMaggio 1.50 4.00
46 Joe Morgan .50 1.25
47 Johnny Bench .75 2.00
48 Johnny Mize .50 1.25
49 Johnny Podres .30 .75
50 Juan Marichal .50 1.25
51 Keith Hernandez .30 .75
52 Kirby Puckett .75 2.00
53 Lefty Grove .50 1.25
54 Lou Brock .50 1.25
55 Lou Gehrig 1.50 4.00
56 Luis Aparicio .50 1.25
57 Fergie Jenkins .50 1.25
58 Maury Wills .30 .75
59 Mel Ott .75 2.00
60 Mickey Cochrane .50 1.25
61 Mickey Mantle 2.50 6.00
62 Mike Schmidt 1.25 3.00
63 Monte Irvin .50 1.25
64 Nolan Ryan 2.50 6.00
65 Orlando Cepeda .50 1.25
66 Ozzie Smith 1.00 2.50
67 Paul Molitor .75 2.00
68 Pee Wee Reese .50 1.25
69 Phil Niekro .50 1.25
70 Phil Rizzuto .50 1.25
71 Ralph Kiner .50 1.25
72 Richie Ashburn .50 1.25
73 Roberto Clemente 2.00 5.00
74 Robin Roberts .50 1.25
75 Robin Yount .75 2.00
76 Rocky Colavito .50 1.25
77 Rod Carew .50 1.25
78 Rogers Hornsby .30 .75
79 Rollie Fingers .50 1.25
80 Roy Campanella .50 1.25
81 Bob Lemon .50 1.25
82 Red Schoendienst .50 1.25
83 Satchel Paige .75 2.00
84 Stan Musial 1.25 3.00
85 Steve Carlton .50 1.25
86 Ted Williams 1.50 4.00
87 Thurman Munson .50 1.25
88 Tom Seaver .50 1.25
89 Tony Gwynn 1.00 2.50
90 Tony Perez .50 1.25
91 Ty Cobb 1.25 3.00
92 Wade Boggs .50 1.25
93 Walter Johnson .50 1.25
94 Warren Spahn .50 1.25
95 Whitey Ford .50 1.25
96 Will Clark .50 1.25
97 Catfish Hunter .50 1.25
98 Willie McCovey .50 1.25
99 Willie Stargell .50 1.25
100 Yogi Berra .75 2.00

2005 Sweet Spot Classic Gold

*GOLD: 2.5X TO 6X BASIC
STATED ODDS 1:120 HOBBY
STATED PRINT RUN 50 SERIAL #'d SETS

2005 Sweet Spot Classic Silver

*SILVER: X TO X BASIC
RANDOM INSERTS IN RETAIL PACKS
STATED PRINT RUN 100 SERIAL #'d SETS

2005 Sweet Spot Classic Materials

OVERALL GAME-USED ODDS 1:6
SP INFO PROVIDED BY UPPER DECK
STARGELL PRINT RUN PROVIDED BY UD
NO STARGELL PRICING DUE TO SCARCITY
CMAD Andre Dawson Jsy 3.00 8.00
CMAK Al Kaline Jsy 6.00 15.00
CMBE Johnny Bench Jsy 6.00 15.00
CMBF Bob Feller Jsy 4.00 10.00
CMBG Bob Gibson Jsy 4.00 10.00
CMBM Bill Mazeroski Jsy 4.00 10.00
CMBR Babe Ruth Pants SP 300.00 500.00
CMCA Rod Carew Jsy 4.00 10.00
CMCF Carlton Fisk Jsy 4.00 10.00
CMCH Catfish Hunter Pants 4.00 10.00
CMCO Rocky Colavito Jsy 4.00 10.00
CMCP Roy Campanella Pants 6.00 15.00
CMCR C.Ripken Hitting Jsy 8.00 20.00
CMCY Carl Yastrzemski Jsy 6.00 15.00
CMDC David Cone Jsy 3.00 8.00
CMDD Don Drysdale Pants 6.00 15.00
CMDM D.Mattingly Pose Jsy 6.00 15.00
CMDS Don Sutton Dgr Jsy 3.00 8.00
CMDW D.Winfield Yanks Jsy 3.00 8.00
CMED Eddie Murray O's Jsy 6.00 15.00
CMEM Eddie Mathews Pants 6.00 15.00
CMEW Early Wynn Pants 4.00 10.00
CMFJ Fergie Jenkins Jsy 3.00 8.00
CMFR Frank Robinson Jsy 4.00 10.00
CMFV Fernando Valenzuela Jsy 4.00 10.00
CMGB G.Brett Sunglass Jsy 6.00 15.00
CMGC Gary Carter Expos Jsy 3.00 8.00
CMGP Gaylord Perry Jsy 3.00 8.00
CMHK Harmon Killebrew Jsy 8.00 20.00
CMJB Jim Bunning Jsy 4.00 10.00
CMJD Joe DiMaggio Jsy 30.00 60.00
CMJM Joe Morgan Reds Pants 3.00 8.00
CMJP Jim Palmer Jsy 3.00 8.00
CMJR Jackie Robinson Jsy 20.00 50.00
CMLB Lou Brock Jsy 4.00 10.00
CMLG Lou Gehrig Pants SP 75.00 200.00
CMMA Juan Marichal Jsy 3.00 8.00
CMMG Mark Grace Jsy 4.00 10.00
CMMM Mickey Mantle Jsy SP 40.00 80.00
CMMS M.Schmidt Hitting Jsy 6.00 15.00
CMMU Dale Murphy Jsy 4.00 10.00
CMMW Maury Wills Dgr Jsy 3.00 8.00
CMNR Nolan Ryan Astros Jsy 12.50 30.00
CMOC Orlando Cepeda Jsy 3.00 8.00
CMOS Ozzie Smith Jsy SP 50.00 100.00
CMPM Paul Molitor Brewers Jsy 3.00 8.00
CMPN Phil Niekro Jsy 3.00 8.00
CMPR Phil Rizzuto Pants 6.00 15.00
CMRC Roberto Clemente Pants 25.00 60.00
CMRE Pee Wee Reese Jsy SP 20.00 50.00
CMRG Ron Guidry Jsy 3.00 8.00
CMRI Jim Rice Jsy 3.00 8.00
CMRO Brooks Robinson Jsy 6.00 15.00
CMRR Robin Roberts Pants 8.00 20.00
CMRY Robin Yount Jsy 6.00 15.00
CMSC Steve Carlton Pants 3.00 8.00
CMSD Red Schoendienst Jsy 3.00 8.00
CMSM Stan Musial Pants SP 30.00 60.00
CMSN Duke Snider Pants 6.00 15.00
CMSP Satchel Paige Pants 40.00 80.00
CMTC Ty Cobb Pants SP 300.00 600.00
CMTG Tony Gwynn Jsy 6.00 15.00
CMTM Thurman Munson Jsy SP 10.00 25.00
CMTP Tony Perez Jsy 4.00 10.00
CMTS Tom Seaver Reds Jsy 4.00 10.00
CMTW Ted Williams Jsy SP 30.00 60.00
CMWB Wade Boggs Jsy 4.00 10.00
CMWC Will Clark Giants Jsy 4.00 10.00
CMWI Willie McCovey Jsy 4.00 10.00
CMWS Warren Spahn Jsy 6.00 15.00
CMYB Yogi Berra Pants 8.00 20.00
CMCR1 C.Ripken Fielding Pants 8.00 20.00
CMDM1 D.Mattingly Hitting Jsy 6.00 15.00
CMDS1 Don Sutton Astros Jsy 3.00 8.00
CMDW1 D.Winfield Padres Jsy 3.00 8.00
CMED1 Eddie Murray Dgr Jsy 6.00 15.00
CMGB1 G.Brett Hitting Jsy 6.00 15.00
CMJM1 Joe Morgan Astros Jsy 3.00 8.00
CMMS1 M.Schmidt Running Jsy 6.00 15.00
CMMW1 Maury Wills Pirates Jsy 3.00 8.00
CMNR1 Nolan Ryan Rgr Jsy 12.50 30.00
CMWC1 Will Clark Rgr Jsy 4.00 10.00

2005 Sweet Spot Classic Patches

OVERALL GAME-USED ODDS 1:6
PRINT RUNS B/WN 1-50 COPIES PER
NO PRICING ON QTY OF 19 OR LESS
LISTED PRICES ARE 2-3 COLOR PATCH
*1-COLOR PATCH: DROP 20-50% DISCOUNT
*4-5-COLOR PATCH: ADD 20-50% PREMIUM
LOGO PATCHES TOO VOLATILE TO PRICE
BE Johnny Bench/32 250.00 500.00
BS Bruce Sutter/50 75.00 150.00
CF1 Carlton Fisk/50 125.00 250.00
CR C.Ripken Hitting/34 250.00 500.00
CR1 C.Ripken Fielding/34 400.00 800.00
CY Carl Yastrzemski/35 200.00 400.00
DC David Cone/39 100.00 175.00
DS Don Sutton Dgr/34 40.00 80.00
DS1 Don Sutton Astros/50 40.00 80.00
DW1 D.Winfield Padres/50 100.00 175.00
ED Eddie Murray O's/34 100.00 175.00
ED1 Eddie Murray Dgr/50 100.00 175.00
FH Frank Howard/34 200.00 400.00
FJ Fergie Jenkins/34 100.00 175.00
FR Frank Robinson/34 125.00 250.00
GB G.Brett Pose/38 175.00 350.00
GB1 G.Brett Action/50 175.00 350.00
GC Gary Carter Expos/47 75.00 150.00
GC1 Gary Carter Mets/34 75.00 150.00
GP Gaylord Perry/34 75.00 150.00
JD Joe DiMaggio/38 400.00 800.00
JM Joe Morgan Reds/50 125.00 250.00
LB Lou Brock/34 100.00 175.00
MU Dale Murphy/34 100.00 175.00
MW Maury Wills Dgr/50 100.00 175.00
MW1 Maury Wills Pirates/47 100.00 200.00
OC Orlando Cepeda/40 75.00 150.00
OS Ozzie Smith/34 125.00 250.00
PN Phil Niekro/44 75.00 150.00
PO Johnny Podres/50 100.00 175.00
RG Ron Guidry/30 75.00 150.00
RI Jim Rice/34 100.00 175.00
RO B.Robinson Color/50 150.00 300.00
RO1 B.Robinson B
W/43 150.00 300.00
RY R.Yount Bat Back/34 125.00 250.00
SC Steve Carlton/50 100.00 200.00
SD Red Schoendienst/42 75.00 150.00
ST Willie Stargell/50 100.00 175.00
TG T.Gwynn Blue Uni/34 125.00 250.00
TG1 T.Gwynn Camo Uni/30 125.00 250.00
TP Tony Perez/34 125.00 250.00
TS Tom Seaver Reds/50 100.00 175.00
TS1 Tom Seaver Mets/50 100.00 175.00
WB Wade Boggs Sox/25 100.00 175.00
WB1 Wade Boggs Yanks/34 100.00 175.00
WI Willie McCovey/50 100.00 200.00

2005 Sweet Spot Classic Signatures

OVERALL AUTO ODDS 1:12
TIER 1 PRINT RUNS B/WN 25-99 PER
TIER 2 PRINT RUNS B/WN 125-230 PER
TIER 3 PRINT RUNS 250 OR MORE PER
CARDS ARE NOT SERIAL-NUMBERED
TIER 1-3 INFO PROVIDED BY UPPER DECK
NO DIMAGGIO PRICING DUE TO SCARCITY
EXCHANGE DEADLINE 01/28/08
AD Andre Dawson T3 10.00 25.00
AK Al Kaline T3 15.00 40.00
AR Al Rosen T3 6.00 20.00
BD Bobby Doerr T3 10.00 25.00
BE Johnny Bench T2 30.00 60.00
BF Bob Feller T3 12.50 30.00
BG Bob Gibson T3 20.00 50.00
BJ Bo Jackson T2 30.00 60.00
BM Bill Mazeroski T3 12.50 30.00
BR Brooks Robinson T3 15.00 40.00
BW Billy Williams T3 10.00 25.00
CA Rod Carew T2 20.00 50.00
CF Carlton Fisk T2 20.00 50.00
CR Cal Ripken T2 30.00 80.00
CY Carl Yastrzemski T2 50.00 120.00
DC David Cone T3 6.00 15.00
DE Dennis Eckersley T3 10.00 25.00
DJ Dave Justice T3 12.50 30.00
DM Don Mattingly T2 20.00 50.00
DN Don Newcombe T2 12.50 30.00
DS Don Sutton T2 12.50 30.00
EB Ernie Banks T2 30.00 60.00
EV Dwight Evans T3 6.00 20.00
FH Frank Howard T3 10.00 25.00
FR Frank Robinson T2 12.50 30.00
FV Fernando Valenzuela T3 25.00 60.00
GB George Brett T2 75.00 150.00
GC Gary Carter T3 15.00 40.00
GK George Kell T3 12.50 30.00
GP Gaylord Perry T3 10.00 25.00
HB Harold Baines T3 6.00 15.00
HK Harmon Killebrew T3 15.00 40.00
JB Jim Bunning T3 10.00 25.00
JC Jose Canseco T2 20.00 50.00
JM Joe Morgan T1/99 15.00 40.00
JP Jim Palmer T3 10.00 25.00
JR Jim Rice T3 10.00 25.00
KA Harry Kalas T3 60.00 120.00
KH Keith Hernandez T3 8.00 20.00
LA Luis Aparicio T3 6.00 15.00
LT Luis Tiant T3 6.00 15.00
MA Juan Marichal T3 10.00 25.00
MC Willie McCovey T1/99 40.00 80.00
MG Mark Grace T3 10.00 25.00
MI Monte Irvin T3 6.00 15.00
MS Mike Schmidt T2 20.00 50.00
MU Dale Murphy T3 12.50 30.00
MW Matt Williams T3 6.00 15.00
NR Nolan Ryan T2 40.00 80.00
OC Orlando Cepeda T3 10.00 25.00
OS Ozzie Smith T2 30.00 60.00
PM Paul Molitor T3 10.00 25.00
PN Phil Niekro T2 12.50 30.00
PO Johnny Podres T3 10.00 25.00
PR Phil Rizzuto T2 20.00 50.00
RE Red Schoendienst T2 15.00 40.00
RF Rollie Fingers T3 8.00 20.00
RK Ralph Kiner T1/99 10.00 25.00
RR Robin Roberts T2 12.50 30.00
RS Ron Santo T3 15.00 40.00
SC Steve Carlton T2 15.00 40.00
SM Stan Musial T2 60.00 120.00
SN Duke Snider T2 15.00 40.00
ST Rusty Staub T3 6.00 15.00
SU Bruce Sutter T3 8.00 20.00
TG Tony Gwynn T2 20.00 50.00
TP Tony Perez T2 10.00 25.00
TS Tom Seaver T2 30.00 80.00
WB Wade Boggs T2 15.00 40.00
WC Will Clark T3 10.00 25.00
WF Whitey Ford T2 20.00 50.00
WI Maury Wills T3 6.00 15.00
YB Yogi Berra T1/99 30.00 80.00

2005 Sweet Spot Classic Signatures Red-Blue Stitch

*R/B: .6X TO 1.5X TIER 3
*R/B: .5X TO 1.2X TIER 2
*R/B: .5X TO 1.2X TIER 1 p/r 99
*R/B: .4X TO 1X TIER 1 p/r 50-56
OVERALL AUTO ODDS 1:12
STATED PRINT RUN 40 SERIAL #'d SETS
BO JACKSON PRINT RUN 36 #'d CARDS
EXCHANGE DEADLINE 01/28/08
BJ Bo Jackson/36 75.00 150.00
CR Cal Ripken 100.00 200.00
DM Don Mattingly 60.00 120.00
GB George Brett 60.00 120.00
HB Harold Baines 15.00 40.00
JC Jose Canseco 30.00 80.00
LT Luis Tiant 15.00 40.00
MS Mike Schmidt 60.00 120.00
MU Dale Murphy 25.00 60.00
NR Nolan Ryan 60.00 120.00
SM Stan Musial 60.00 120.00
ST Rusty Staub 15.00 40.00
SU Bruce Sutter 25.00 60.00

2005 Sweet Spot Classic Signature Sticks

*STICKS: .75X TO 2X TIER 3
*STICKS: .6X TO 1.5X TIER 2
*STICKS: .6X TO 1.5X TIER 1 p/r 99
*STICKS: .5X TO 1.2X TIER 1 p/r 50-56
OVERALL AUTO ODDS 1:12
STATED PRINT RUN 35 SERIAL #'d SETS
BJ Bo Jackson 90.00 180.00
CR Cal Ripken 175.00 300.00
DM Don Mattingly 75.00 150.00
FH Frank Howard 10.00 25.00
GB George Brett 75.00 150.00
HB Harold Baines 20.00 50.00
JC Jose Canseco 40.00 100.00
LT Luis Tiant 20.00 50.00
MS Mike Schmidt 75.00 150.00
MU Dale Murphy 30.00 80.00
NR Nolan Ryan 100.00 200.00
RC Rocky Colavito 75.00 150.00
SM Stan Musial 75.00 150.00
ST Rusty Staub 20.00 50.00
SU Bruce Sutter 30.00 80.00

2005 Sweet Spot Classic Signatures Sweet Leather

*LEATHER: 1.25X TO 2.5X TIER 3
*LEATHER: 1X TO 2X TIER 2
*LEATHER: 1X TO 2X TIER 1 p/r 99
*LEATHER: .75X TO 1.5X TIER 1 p/r 50-56
OVERALL AUTO ODDS 1:12
STATED PRINT RUN 25 SERIAL #'d SETS
EXCHANGE DEADLINE 01/28/08
BJ Bo Jackson 100.00 200.00
CR Cal Ripken 200.00 350.00
DM Don Mattingly 90.00 180.00
GB George Brett 90.00 180.00
HB Harold Baines 30.00 60.00
JC Jose Canseco 60.00 120.00
LT Luis Tiant 30.00 60.00
MS Mike Schmidt 90.00 180.00
MU Dale Murphy 50.00 100.00
NR Nolan Ryan 150.00 250.00
SM Stan Musial 100.00 200.00
ST Rusty Staub 30.00 60.00
SU Bruce Sutter 50.00 100.00

2005 Sweet Spot Classic Wingfield Classics Collection

ONE PER SEALED HOBBY BOX
50 Yogi Berra 4.00 10.00
WCC1 Al Kaline 4.00 10.00
WCC2 Pee Wee Reese 2.50 6.00
WCC3 S.Musial
T.Williams 8.00 20.00
WCC4 Bill Dickey 1.50 4.00
WCC5 Frank Robinson 2.50 6.00
WCC6 Billy Martin 2.50 6.00
WCC7 J.DiMaggio
C.Stengel 8.00 20.00
WCC8 D.Eisenhower
B.Feller 2.50 6.00
WCC9 Duke Snider 2.50 6.00
WCC10 Carl Yastrzemski 5.00 12.00
WCC11 Honus Wagner 2.50 6.00
WCC12 C.Griffith
D.Eisenhower 1.50 4.00
WCC13 M.Mantle
J.DiMaggio 12.00 30.00
WCC14 Don Drysdale 2.50 6.00
WCC15 Ted Williams 8.00 20.00
WCC16 M.Mantle
A.Kaline 12.00 30.00
WCC17 Ernie Banks 4.00 10.00
WCC18 Lou Boudreau 2.50 6.00
WCC19 G.Sisler
H.Killebrew 4.00 10.00
WCC20 Gil Hodges 2.50 6.00
WCC21 Rogers Hornsby 1.50 4.00
WCC22 Luis Aparicio 2.50 6.00
WCC23 Jackie Robinson 2.50 6.00
WCC24 Joe Morgan 2.50 6.00
WCC25 Enos Slaughter 2.50 6.00
WCC26 Joe DiMaggio 8.00 20.00
WCC27 M.Mantle
T.Kluszewski 12.00 30.00
WCC28 John F. Kennedy 4.00 10.00
WCC29 Johnny Bench 4.00 10.00
WCC30 Juan Marichal 2.50 6.00
WCC31 Larry Doby 2.50 6.00
WCC32 D.Newcombe
E.Howard 1.50 4.00
WCC33 D.Eisenhower
H.Killebrew 4.00 10.00
WCC34 R.Maris
M.Mantle 12.00 30.00
WCC35 S.Musial
M.Mantle 12.00 30.00
WCC36 Williams
Berra
Mantle 12.00 30.00
WCC37 Nellie Fox 2.50 6.00
WCC38 Richie Ashburn 2.50 6.00
WCC39 Roberto Clemente 10.00 25.00
WCC40 S.Musial
R.Roberts 6.00 15.00
WCC41 J.DiMaggio
T.Henrich 8.00 20.00
WCC42 Roy Campanella 2.50 6.00
WCC43 R.Colavito
H.Killebrew 4.00 10.00
WCC44 Steve Carlton 2.50 6.00
WCC45 Thurman Munson 2.50 6.00
WCC46 E.Banks
L.Aparicio 4.00 10.00
WCC47 Eisenhower
Hodges
Berra 4.00 10.00
WCC48 Whitey Ford 2.50 6.00
WCC49 Berra
Mantle
DiMaggio 12.00 30.00

2007 Sweet Spot Classic

COMMON CARD .60 1.50
STATED PRINT RUN 575 SER.#'d SETS
1 Phil Niekro 1.00 2.50
2 Fred McGriff 1.00 2.50
3 Bob Horner .60 1.50
4 Earl Weaver 1.00 2.50
5 Boog Powell .60 1.50
6 Eddie Murray 1.00 2.50
7 Fred Lynn .60 1.50
8 Dwight Evans .60 1.50
9 Jim Rice 1.00 2.50
10 Carlton Fisk 1.00 2.50
11 Luis Tiant .60 1.50
12 Robin Yount 1.50 4.00
13 Bobby Doerr 1.00 2.50
14 Ryne Sandberg 3.00 8.00
15 Billy Williams 1.00 2.50
16 Andre Dawson 1.00 2.50
17 Mark Grace 1.00 2.50
18 Ron Santo 1.00 2.50
19 Shawon Dunston .60 1.50
20 Harold Baines 1.00 2.50
21 Carlton Fisk 1.00 2.50
22 Sparky Anderson 1.00 2.50
23 George Foster .60 1.50
24 Dave Parker .60 1.50
25 Ken Griffey Sr. .60 1.50
26 Dave Concepcion .60 1.50
27 Rafael Palmeiro 1.00 2.50
28 Al Rosen .60 1.50
29 Kirk Gibson .60 1.50
30 Alan Trammell 1.00 2.50
31 Jack Morris 1.00 2.50
32 Willie Horton .60 1.50
33 JR Richard .60 1.50
34 Jose Cruz .60 1.50
36 Willie Wilson .60 1.50
37 Bo Jackson 1.50 4.00
38 Nolan Ryan 5.00 12.00
39 Don Baylor .60 1.50
40 Maury Wills .60 1.50
41 Tommy John .60 1.50
42 Ron Cey .60 1.50
43 Davey Lopes .60 1.50
44 Tommy Lasorda 1.00 2.50
45 Burt Hooton .60 1.50
46 Reggie Smith .60 1.50
47 Rollie Fingers 1.00 2.50
48 Cecil Cooper .60 1.50
49 Paul Molitor 1.50 4.00
50 Vern Stephens .60 1.50
51 Tony Oliva .60 1.50
52 Andres Galarraga 1.00 2.50
53 Tim Raines 1.00 2.50
54 Dennis Martinez .60 1.50
55 Lee Mazzilli .60 1.50
56 Rusty Staub .60 1.50
57 David Cone .60 1.50
58 Reggie Jackson 1.00 2.50
59 Ron Guidry .60 1.50
60 Tino Martinez .60 1.50
61 Don Mattingly 3.00 8.00
62 Chris Chambliss .60 1.50
63 Sparky Lyle .60 1.50
64 Goose Gossage 1.00 2.50
65 Dave Righetti .60 1.50
66 Phil Garner .60 1.50
67 Bill Madlock .60 1.50
68 Kent Hrbek .60 1.50
69 Al Oliver .60 1.50
70 John Kruk .60 1.50
71 Greg Luzinski .60 1.50
72 Dick Allen .60 1.50
73 Richie Ashburn 1.00 2.50
74 Gary Matthews .60 1.50
76 Mike Schmidt 2.50 6.00
77 Waite Hoyt .60 1.50
78 Bruce Sutter 1.00 2.50
79 Roger Maris 1.50 4.00
80 Joe Torre 1.00 2.50
81 Kevin Mitchell .60 1.50
82 John Montefusco .60 1.50
83 Rick Reuschel .60 1.50
84 Will Clark 1.00 2.50
85 Jack Clark .60 1.50
86 Matt Williams .60 1.50
87 Steve Garvey .60 1.50
88 Dave Winfield 1.00 2.50
89 Jay Buhner .60 1.50
90 Edgar Martinez 1.00 2.50
91 Carney Lansford .60 1.50
92 Sal Bando .60 1.50
93 Dave Stewart .60 1.50
94 Dennis Eckersley 1.00 2.50
95 Jose Canseco 1.00 2.50
96 Dennis Eckersley 1.00 2.50
97 Roberto Alomar 1.00 2.50
98 George Bell .60 1.50
99 Joe Carter .60 1.50
100 Frank Howard .60 1.50
101 Brooks Robinson 1.00 2.50
102 Frank Robinson 1.00 2.50
103 Jim Palmer 1.00 2.50
104 Cal Ripken Jr. 5.00 12.00
105 Warren Spahn 1.00 2.50
106 Cy Young 1.50 4.00
107 Waite Hoyt .60 1.50
108 Carl Yastrzemski 2.50 6.00
109 Johnny Pesky .60 1.50
110 Wade Boggs 1.00 2.50
111 Jackie Robinson 1.50 4.00
112 Roy Campanella 1.50 4.00
113 Pee Wee Reese 1.00 2.50
114 Don Newcombe .60 1.50
115 Rod Carew 1.00 2.50
116 Ernie Banks 1.50 4.00
117 Fergie Jenkins 1.00 2.50
118 Al Lopez .60 1.50
119 Luis Aparicio 1.00 2.50
120 Toby Harrah .60 1.50
121 Joe Morgan 1.00 2.50
122 Johnny Bench 1.50 4.00
123 Tony Perez 1.00 2.50
124 Ted Kluszewski 1.00 2.50
125 Bob Feller 1.00 2.50
126 Bob Lemon 1.00 2.50
127 Larry Doby 1.00 2.50
128 Lou Boudreau 1.00 2.50
129 George Kell 1.00 2.50
130 Hal Newhouser 1.00 2.50
131 Al Kaline 1.50 4.00
132 Ty Cobb 2.50 6.00
133 Denny McLain .60 1.50
134 Buck Leonard .60 1.50
135 Dean Chance .60 1.50
136 Don Drysdale 1.00 2.50
137 Don Sutton 1.00 2.50
138 Eddie Mathews 1.50 4.00
139 Paul Molitor 1.50 4.00
140 Kirby Puckett 1.50 4.00
141 Rod Carew 1.00 2.50
142 Harmon Killebrew 1.50 4.00
143 Monte Irvin 1.00 2.50
144 Mel Ott .60 1.50
145 Christy Mathewson 1.50 4.00
146 Hoyt Wilhelm 1.00 2.50
147 Tom Seaver 1.00 2.50
148 Joe McCarthy .60 1.50
149 Joe DiMaggio 3.00 8.00
150 Lou Gehrig 3.00 8.00
151 Babe Ruth 4.00 10.00
152 Casey Stengel 1.00 2.50
153 Phil Rizzuto 1.00 2.50
154 Thurman Munson 1.50 4.00
155 Johnny Mize .60 1.50
156 Yogi Berra 1.50 4.00
157 Roger Maris 1.50 4.00
158 Don Larsen .60 1.50
159 Bill Skowron .60 1.50
160 Lou Piniella .60 1.50
161 Joe Pepitone .60 1.50
162 Ray Dandridge .60 1.50
163 Rollie Fingers 1.00 2.50
165 Reggie Jackson 1.00 2.50
166 Mickey Cochrane 1.00 2.50
167 Jimmie Foxx 1.50 4.00
168 Lefty Grove 1.00 2.50
169 Gus Zernial .60 1.50
170 Jim Bunning 1.00 2.50
171 Steve Carlton 1.00 2.50
172 Robin Roberts 1.00 2.50
173 Ralph Kiner 1.00 2.50
174 Willie Stargell 1.00 2.50
175 Roberto Clemente 4.00 10.00
176 Bill Mazeroski 1.00 2.50
177 Honus Wagner 1.50 4.00
178 Pie Traynor 1.00 2.50
179 Elroy Face .60 1.50
180 Dick Groat .60 1.50
181 Tony Gwynn 1.50 4.00
182 Willie McCovey 1.00 2.50
183 Gaylord Perry 1.00 2.50
184 Juan Marichal 1.00 2.50
185 Orlando Cepeda 1.00 2.50
186 Satchel Paige 1.50 4.00
187 George Sisler 1.00 2.50
188 Rogers Hornsby 1.00 2.50
189 Stan Musial 2.50 6.00
190 Dizzy Dean 1.00 2.50
191 Bob Gibson 1.00 2.50
192 Red Schoendienst 1.00 2.50
193 Lou Brock 1.00 2.50
194 Enos Slaughter .60 1.50
195 Nolan Ryan 5.00 12.00
196 Mickey Vernon .60 1.50
197 Walter Johnson 1.50 4.00
198 Rick Ferrell .60 1.50
199 Roy Sievers .60 1.50
200 Judy Johnson .60 1.50

2007 Sweet Spot Classic Classic Cuts

RANDOM INSERTS IN TINS
PRINT RUNS B/WN 1-103
NO PRICING ON MOST DUE TO SCARCITY
CARDS LISTED ALPHABETICALLY
CHECKLIST MAY BE INCOMPLETE
MYSTERY EXCHANGE RANDOMLY INSERTED
EXCHANGE DEADLINE 8/3/2009
SSCCC Pappy Boyington/52 100.00 200.00
SSCCC Art Carney/34 30.00 60.00
SSCCC Gerald Ford/61 125.00 250.00
SSCCC Alex Haley/103 12.50 30.00

2007 Sweet Spot Classic Classic Memorabilia

RANDOM INSERTS IN TINS
CMAD Andre Dawson Pants 3.00 8.00
CMAK Al Kaline 4.00 10.00
CMAO Al Oliver 3.00 8.00
CMBE Johnny Bench Pants 5.00 12.00
CMBJ Bo Jackson 5.00 12.00
CMBM Bill Madlock Bat 3.00 8.00
CMBO Wade Boggs Yanks 4.00 10.00
CMBR Babe Ruth Bat 300.00 500.00
CMBS Bruce Sutter Cubs Pants 3.00 8.00
CMCL Roberto Clemente 15.00 40.00
CMCM Christy Mathewson Pants 60.00 120.00
CMCR Cal Ripken Jr. 6.00 15.00
CMCS Casey Stengel 6.00 15.00
CMCY Carl Yastrzemski 4.00 10.00
CMDD Dizzy Dean 15.00 40.00
CMDE Dennis Eckersley 3.00 8.00
CMDM Don Mattingly 6.00 15.00
CMDP Dave Parker Reds 3.00 8.00
CMDR Don Drysdale Pants 4.00 10.00
CMDS Don Sutton 3.00 8.00
CMDW Dave Winfield 3.00 8.00
CMED Eddie Murray Pants 3.00 8.00
CMEM Eddie Mathews Pants 6.00 15.00
CMEV Dwight Evans 3.00 8.00
CMEW Early Wynn Pants 4.00 10.00
CMFG Fred McGriff Jsy 3.00 8.00
CMFI Rollie Fingers Mil 3.00 8.00
CMFR Frank Robinson 6.00 15.00
CMGF George Foster 3.00 8.00
CMGG Goose Gossage 3.00 8.00
CMGI Kirk Gibson 3.00 8.00
CMGP Gaylord Perry 3.00 8.00
CMGW Tony Gwynn 5.00 12.00
CMHB Harold Baines Bat 3.00 8.00
CMHK Harmon Killebrew 15.00 40.00
CMJB Jim Bunning Pants 3.00 8.00
CMJD Joe DiMaggio Pants 30.00 60.00
CMJI Jim Rice Bat 3.00 8.00
CMJM Jack Morris 3.00 8.00
CMJP Jim Palmer 3.00 8.00
CMJU Juan Marichal 5.00 12.00
CMKG Ken Griffey Sr. 3.00 8.00
CMKH Kent Hrbek 3.00 8.00
CMKP Kirby Puckett 5.00 12.00
CMLA Luis Aparicio 3.00 8.00
CMLB Lou Brock 4.00 10.00
CMLG Lou Gehrig Pants 50.00 120.00
CMMA Don Mattingly Pants 5.00 12.00
CMME Eddie Murray Pants 3.00 8.00
CMMG Mark Grace 3.00 8.00
CMMP Paul Molitor Mil 3.00 8.00
CMMR Edgar Martinez 3.00 8.00
CMMS Mike Schmidt 5.00 12.00
CMMW Maury Wills Pants 3.00 8.00
CMNR Nolan Ryan Hou 6.00 15.00
CMPA Dave Parker Brewers 3.00 8.00
CMPE Tony Perez Sox 3.00 8.00
CMPM Paul Molitor Twins Pants 3.00 8.00
CMPN Phil Niekro 3.00 8.00
CMPR Pee Wee Reese Bat 5.00 12.00
CMRF Rollie Fingers Oak 3.00 8.00
CMRG Ron Guidry Pants 10.00 25.00
CMRH Rogers Hornsby Pants 12.50 30.00
CMRK Ralph Kiner Bat 6.00 15.00
CMRM Roger Maris Pants 12.50 30.00
CMRO Roy Campanella Pants 10.00 25.00
CMRS Ron Santo Bat 40.00 80.00
CMRY Nolan Ryan Tex 8.00 20.00
CMSC Red Schoendienst Bat 3.00 8.00
CMSG Steve Garvey 3.00 8.00
CMST Steve Carlton Bat 3.00 8.00
CMSU Bruce Sutter Cards 3.00 8.00
CMTG Tony Gwynn Bat 4.00 10.00
CMTM Thurman Munson Pants 10.00 25.00
CMTO Tony Oliva 3.00 8.00
CMTP Tony Perez Reds 3.00 8.00
CMTR Tim Raines 3.00 8.00
CMWB Wade Boggs Sox 4.00 10.00
CMWM Willie McCovey Pants 4.00 10.00
CMWS Willie Stargell Bat 8.00 20.00
CMYO Robin Yount Bat 4.00 10.00
CMCF1 Carlton Fisk Red Sox 4.00 10.00
CMCF2 Carlton Fisk ChiSox 4.00 10.00
CMFR1 Frank Robinson 6.00 15.00
CMMI1 Johnny Mize NYG Pants 6.00 15.00
CMMI1 Johnny Mize Yanks Bat 4.00 10.00
CMMO1 Mel Ott 12.50 30.00
CMRC1 Rod Carew Twins 3.00 8.00
CMRC2 Rod Carew Angels Pants 3.00 8.00
CMRJ1 Reggie Jackson Oakland 4.00 10.00

CMRJ2 Reggie Jackson Angels 4.00 10.00
CMRJ3 Reggie Jackson Yanks 4.00 10.00
CMWC1 Will Clark Bat 3.00 8.00
CMWC2 Will Clark Jsy 4.00 10.00

2007 Sweet Spot Classic Classic Memorabilia Patch

RANDOM INSERTS IN TINS
STATED PRINT RUNS B/WN 10-55 COPIES PER
NO PRICING ON QTY UNDER 28
PRICING FOR NON-PREMIUM PATCHES
CMAD Andre Dawson/55 12.50 30.00
CMAK Al Kaline/55 10.00 25.00
CMAO Al Oliver/55 5.00 12.00
CMBE Johnny Bench/55 30.00 60.00
CMBJ Bo Jackson/55 10.00 25.00
CMBM Bill Madlock/55 5.00 12.00
CMBO Wade Boggs/55 15.00 40.00
CMBS Bruce Sutter/55 8.00 20.00
CMCL Roberto Clemente/55 100.00 200.00
CMCR Cal Ripken Jr./55 30.00 60.00
CMCS Casey Stengel/55 30.00 60.00
CMCY Carl Yastrzemski/55 12.50 30.00
CMDE Dennis Eckersley/55 6.00 15.00
CMDM Don Mattingly/55 12.50 30.00
CMDP Dave Parker/55 5.00 12.00
CMDR Don Drysdale/55 40.00 80.00
CMDS Don Sutton/55 6.00 15.00
CMDW Dave Winfield/55 10.00 25.00
CMED Eddie Murray/55 6.00 15.00
CMEV Dwight Evans/55 8.00 20.00
CMFI Rollie Fingers/55 8.00 20.00
CMFR Frank Robinson/28 15.00 40.00
CMGF George Foster/55 5.00 12.00
CMGG Goose Gossage/55 5.00 12.00
CMGI Kirk Gibson/55 8.00 20.00
CMGP Gaylord Perry/55 5.00 12.00
CMGW Tony Gwynn/55 10.00 25.00
CMHB Harold Baines/55 6.00 15.00
CMJI Jim Rice/55 20.00 50.00
CMJM Jack Morris/55 6.00 15.00
CMJP Jim Palmer/55 6.00 15.00
CMKG Ken Griffey Sr./55 5.00 12.00
CMKP Kirby Puckett/55 15.00 40.00
CMLA Luis Aparicio/55 12.50 30.00
CMLB Lou Brock/55 10.00 25.00
CMMA Don Mattingly/55 30.00 60.00
CMME Eddie Murray/55 6.00 15.00
CMMG Mark Grace/55 10.00 25.00
CMMP Paul Molitor/55 15.00 40.00
CMMS Mike Schmidt/55 10.00 25.00
CMMW Maury Wills/55 6.00 15.00
CMPA Dave Parker/55 6.00 15.00
CMPE Tony Perez/55 10.00 25.00
CMPM Paul Molitor/55 15.00 40.00
CMPN Phil Niekro/55 20.00 50.00
CMPR Pee Wee Reese/55 15.00 40.00
CMRA Roberto Alomar/55 12.00 30.00
CMRF Rollie Fingers/55 8.00 20.00
CMRG Ron Guidry/55 15.00 40.00
CMRM Roger Maris/55 40.00 80.00
CMRY Nolan Ryan/55 30.00 60.00
CMSC Red Schoendienst/55 40.00 80.00
CMSG Steve Garvey/55 10.00 25.00
CMSU Bruce Sutter/55 8.00 20.00
CMTG Tony Gwynn/55 10.00 25.00
CMTO Tony Oliva/55 6.00 15.00
CMTP Tony Perez/55 10.00 25.00
CMTR Tim Raines/55 8.00 20.00
CMWI Dave Winfield/55 10.00 25.00
CMWM Willie McCovey/55 8.00 20.00
CMYO Robin Yount/55 12.50 30.00
CMCF1 Carlton Fisk/55 8.00 20.00
CMCF2 Carlton Fisk/55 8.00 20.00
CMFR1 Frank Robinson/28 15.00 40.00
CMRC1 Rod Carew/55 5.00 12.00
CMRC2 Rod Carew/55 5.00 12.00
CMRJ1 Reggie Jackson/55 50.00 100.00
CMRJ2 Reggie Jackson/55 8.00 20.00
CMRJ3 Reggie Jackson/55 12.50 30.00
CMWC1 Will Clark/55 8.00 20.00

2007 Sweet Spot Classic Dual Signatures Red Stitch Blue Ink

RANDOM INSERTS IN TINS
STATED PRINT RUN 50 SER.#'d SETS
EXCHANGE DEADLINE 8/3/2009
AG L.Aparicio/O.Guillen 30.00 60.00
BC B.Robinson/C.Ripken 100.00 150.00
BF C.Fisk/J.Bench 15.00 40.00
BG H.Baines/O.Guillen 10.00 25.00
BR J.Bunning/R.Roberts 10.00 25.00
CO R.Carew/T.Oliva 15.00 40.00
FE R.Fingers/D.Eckersley 30.00 60.00
FG E.Face/D.Groat 20.00 50.00
FM F.Robinson/M.Schmidt 40.00 80.00
FR C.Fisk/J.Rice 40.00 80.00
GR B.Gibson/J.Richard 15.00 40.00
GS S.Garvey/R.Smith 20.00 50.00
GW T.Gwynn/D.Winfield 20.00 50.00
HK W.Horton/A.Kaline 40.00 100.00
KM R.Kiner/B.Mazeroski 10.00 25.00
MC W.McCovey/J.Clark 40.00 80.00
MG J.Marichal/B.Gibson 20.00 50.00
MK S.Musial/A.Kaline 40.00 100.00
MM D.Mattingly/T.Martinez 50.00 100.00
OH T.Oliva/K.Hrbek 10.00 25.00
RR J.Richard/N.Ryan 60.00 120.00
RS C.Ripken/M.Schmidt EXCH 30.00 60.00
SB R.Santo/E.Banks 40.00 80.00
SC M.Schmidt/S.Carlton 30.00 60.00
SD R.Sandberg/S.Dunston 50.00 100.00
SS R.Santo/R.Sandberg 60.00 120.00
SV R.Sievers/M.Vernon 20.00 50.00
YP Yastrzemski/Pesky 20.00 50.00

2007 Sweet Spot Classic Dual Signatures Gold Stitch Black Ink

RANDOM INSERTS IN TINS
STATED PRINT RUN 15 SER.#'d SETS
NO PRICING DUE TO SCARCITY
EXCHANGE DEADLINE 8/3/2009

2007 Sweet Spot Classic Immortal Signatures

RANDOM INSERTS IN TINS
PRINT RUNS B/WN 1-126 COPIES PER
NO PRICING ON QTY 25 OR LESS
EXCHANGE DEADLINE 8/3/2009
AB Al Barlick/43 30.00 60.00
BH Billy Herman/49 20.00 50.00
BL Bob Lemon/58 30.00 60.00
BO Buck O'Neil/126 30.00 60.00
EM Eddie Mathews/35 150.00 250.00
ES Enos Slaughter/80 40.00 80.00
EW Early Wynn/26 40.00 80.00
HC Happy Chandler/29 30.00 60.00
HN Hal Newhouser/33 60.00 100.00
HW Hoyt Wilhelm/33 20.00 50.00
JM Johnny Mize/48 60.00 100.00
JV Johnny Vander Meer/49 75.00 120.00
LA Luke Appling/31 75.00 120.00
LB Lou Boudreau/47 30.00 60.00
MH Mel Harder/37 30.00 60.00
PR Pee Wee Reese/37 60.00 120.00
RA Richie Ashburn/29 100.00 200.00
RF Rick Ferrell/52 20.00 50.00
ST Willie Stargell/30 150.00 200.00
WS Warren Spahn/102 40.00 80.00

2007 Sweet Spot Classic Legendary Lettermen

E.BANKS p/r 25 10.00 25.00
E.BANKS TWO p/r 15 10.00 25.00
J.BENCH p/r 25 30.00 60.00
R.CAMPANELLA p/r 10 30.00 60.00
T.COBB p/r 25 20.00 50.00
T.COBB PEACH p/r 5 30.00 60.00
D.DEAN p/r 25 30.00 60.00
D.DRYSDALE p/r 25 15.00 40.00
C.FISK p/r 20 30.00 60.00
J.FOXX p/r 25 30.00 60.00
L.GEHRIG p/r 15 100.00 150.00
B.GIBSON p/r 25 15.00 40.00
T.GWYNN p/r 25 15.00 40.00
R.HORNSBY p/r 25 10.00 25.00
R.JACKSON p/r 25 20.00 50.00
B.JACKSON p/r 25 20.00 50.00
B.JACKSON KNOWS p/r 15 20.00 50.00
W.JOHNSON p/r 15 15.00 40.00
W.JOHNSON TRAIN p/r 10 20.00 50.00
A.KALINE p/r 25 15.00 40.00
S.KOUFAX p/r 25 225.00 300.00
C.MATHEWSON p/r 10 30.00 60.00
D.MATTINGLY p/r 15 30.00 60.00
B.MAZEROSKI p/r 15 10.00 25.00
T.MUNSON p/r 25 12.50 30.00
T.MUNSON CAPTAIN p/r 10 15.00 40.00
S.MUSIAL p/r 25 15.00 40.00
S.MUSIAL MAN p/r 25 15.00 40.00
M.OTT p/r 25 15.00 40.00
S.PAIGE p/r 25 10.00 25.00
C.RIPKEN p/r 25 30.00 60.00
C.RIPKEN IRON p/r 25 30.00 60.00
J.ROBINSON p/r 10 15.00 40.00
J.ROBINSON PIONEER p/r 10 15.00 40.00
B.RUTH p/r 25 15.00 40.00
B.RUTH SULTAN p/r 15 60.00 120.00
N.RYAN p/r 20 30.00 60.00
N.RYAN EXPRESS p/r 15 30.00 60.00
R.SANDBERG p/r 25 30.00 60.00
M.SCHMIDT p/r 25 30.00 60.00
H.WAGNER p/r 25 20.00 50.00
C.YASTRZEMSKI p/r 15 30.00 60.00
RANDOM INSERTS IN TINS
PRINT RUNS B/WN 5-25 COPIES PER
LL1H Babe Ruth H/25 15.00 40.00
LL1R Babe Ruth R/25 15.00 40.00
LL1T Babe Ruth T/25 15.00 40.00
LL1U Babe Ruth U/25 15.00 40.00
LL2B Ty Cobb B/25 20.00 50.00
LL2B Ty Cobb B/25 20.00 50.00
LL2C Ty Cobb C/25 20.00 50.00
LL2O Ty Cobb O/25 20.00 50.00
LL3A Christy Mathewson A/10 30.00 60.00
LL3E Christy Mathewson E/10 30.00 60.00
LL3H Christy Mathewson H/10 30.00 60.00
LL3M Christy Mathewson M/10 30.00 60.00
LL3N Christy Mathewson N/10 30.00 60.00
LL3O Christy Mathewson O/10 30.00 60.00
LL3S Christy Mathewson S/10 30.00 60.00
LL3T Christy Mathewson T/10 30.00 60.00
LL3W Christy Mathewson W/10 30.00 60.00
LL4B Jackie Robinson B/10 15.00 40.00
LL4I Jackie Robinson I/10 15.00 40.00
LL4N Jackie Robinson N/10 15.00 40.00
LL4N Jackie Robinson N/10 15.00 40.00
LL4O Jackie Robinson O/10 15.00 40.00
LL4O Jackie Robinson O/10 15.00 40.00
LL4R Jackie Robinson R/10 15.00 40.00
LL4S Jackie Robinson S/10 15.00 40.00
LL5A Roy Campanella A/10 30.00 60.00
LL5A Roy Campanella A/10 30.00 60.00
LL5A Roy Campanella A/10 30.00 60.00
LL5C Roy Campanella C/10 30.00 60.00
LL5E Roy Campanella E/10 30.00 60.00
LL5L Roy Campanella L/10 30.00 60.00
LL5L Roy Campanella L/10 30.00 60.00
LL5M Roy Campanella M/10 30.00 60.00
LL5N Roy Campanella N/10 30.00 60.00
LL5P Roy Campanella P/10 30.00 60.00
LL6E Lou Gehrig E/15 100.00 150.00
LL6G Lou Gehrig G/15 100.00 150.00
LL6G Lou Gehrig G/15 100.00 150.00
LL6H Lou Gehrig H/15 100.00 150.00
LL6I Lou Gehrig I/15 100.00 150.00
LL6R Lou Gehrig R/15 100.00 150.00
LL7O Mel Ott O/25 15.00 40.00
LL7T Mel Ott T/25 15.00 40.00
LL7T Mel Ott T/25 15.00 40.00
LL8F Jimmie Foxx F/25 30.00 60.00
LL8O Jimmie Foxx O/25 30.00 60.00
LL8X Jimmie Foxx X/25 30.00 60.00
LL8X Jimmie Foxx X/25 30.00 60.00
LL9A Satchel Paige A/25 10.00 25.00
LL9E Satchel Paige E/25 10.00 25.00
LL9G Satchel Paige G/25 10.00 25.00
LL9I Satchel Paige I/25 10.00 25.00
LL9P Satchel Paige P/25 10.00 25.00
LL10A Don Drysdale A/25 15.00 40.00
LL10D Don Drysdale D/25 15.00 40.00
LL10D Don Drysdale D/25 15.00 40.00
LL10E Don Drysdale E/25 15.00 40.00
LL10L Don Drysdale L/25 15.00 40.00
LL10R Don Drysdale R/25 15.00 40.00
LL10S Don Drysdale S/25 15.00 40.00
LL10Y Don Drysdale Y/25 15.00 40.00
LL11B Rogers Hornsby B/25 10.00 25.00
LL11H Rogers Hornsby H/25 10.00 25.00
LL11N Rogers Hornsby N/25 10.00 25.00
LL11O Rogers Hornsby O/25 10.00 25.00
LL11R Rogers Hornsby R/25 10.00 25.00
LL11S Rogers Hornsby S/25 10.00 25.00
LL11Y Rogers Hornsby Y/25 10.00 25.00
LL12A Honus Wagner A/25 20.00 50.00
LL12E Honus Wagner E/25 20.00 50.00
LL12G Honus Wagner G/25 20.00 50.00
LL12N Honus Wagner N/25 20.00 50.00
LL12R Honus Wagner R/25 20.00 50.00
LL12W Honus Wagner W/25 20.00 50.00
LL13A Babe Ruth A/15 60.00 120.00
LL13B Babe Ruth B/15 60.00 120.00
LL13B Babe Ruth B/15 60.00 120.00
LL13I Babe Ruth I/15 60.00 120.00
LL13M Babe Ruth M/15 60.00 120.00
LL13N Babe Ruth N/15 60.00 120.00
LL13O Babe Ruth O/15 60.00 120.00
LL14A Dizzy Dean A/25 30.00 60.00
LL14D Dizzy Dean D/25 30.00 60.00
LL14E Dizzy Dean E/25 30.00 60.00
LL14N Dizzy Dean N/25 30.00 60.00
LL15A Ty Cobb A/5 30.00 60.00
LL15A Ty Cobb A/5 30.00 60.00
LL15C Ty Cobb C/5 30.00 60.00
LL15E Ty Cobb E/5 30.00 60.00
LL15E Ty Cobb E/5 30.00 60.00
LL15G Ty Cobb G/5 30.00 60.00
LL15G Ty Cobb G/5 30.00 60.00
LL15H Ty Cobb H/5 30.00 60.00
LL15I Ty Cobb I/5 30.00 60.00
LL15O Ty Cobb O/5 30.00 60.00
LL15P Ty Cobb P/5 30.00 60.00
LL15R Ty Cobb R/5 30.00 60.00
LL16H Walter Johnson H/15 15.00 40.00
LL16J Walter Johnson J/15 15.00 40.00
LL16N Walter Johnson N/15 15.00 40.00
LL16N Walter Johnson N/15 15.00 40.00
LL16O Walter Johnson O/15 15.00 40.00
LL16O Walter Johnson O/15 15.00 40.00
LL16S Walter Johnson S/15 15.00 40.00
LL17A Walter Johnson A/10 20.00 50.00
LL17B Walter Johnson B/10 20.00 50.00
LL17G Walter Johnson G/10 20.00 50.00
LL17I Walter Johnson I/10 20.00 50.00
LL17I Walter Johnson I/10 20.00 50.00
LL17N Walter Johnson N/10 20.00 50.00
LL17R Walter Johnson R/10 20.00 50.00
LL17T Walter Johnson T/10 20.00 50.00
LL18E Cal Ripken Jr. E/25 30.00 60.00
LL18I Cal Ripken Jr. I/25 30.00 60.00
LL18K Cal Ripken Jr. K/25 30.00 60.00
LL18N Cal Ripken Jr. N/25 30.00 60.00
LL18P Cal Ripken Jr. P/25 30.00 60.00
LL18R Cal Ripken Jr. R/25 30.00 60.00
LL19A Sandy Koufax A/25 225.00 300.00
LL19F Sandy Koufax F/25 225.00 300.00
LL19K Sandy Koufax K/25 225.00 300.00
LL19O Sandy Koufax O/25 225.00 300.00
LL19U Sandy Koufax U/25 225.00 300.00
LL19X Sandy Koufax X/25 225.00 300.00
LL20M Thurman Munson M/25 12.50 30.00
LL20N Thurman Munson N/25 12.50 30.00
LL20N Thurman Munson N/25 12.50 30.00
LL20O Thurman Munson O/25 12.50 30.00
LL20S Thurman Munson S/25 12.50 30.00
LL20U Thurman Munson U/25 12.50 30.00
LL21A Thurman Munson A/10 15.00 40.00
LL21A Thurman Munson A/10 15.00 40.00
LL21C Thurman Munson C/10 15.00 40.00
LL21I Thurman Munson I/10 15.00 40.00
LL21N Thurman Munson N/10 15.00 40.00
LL21P Thurman Munson P/10 15.00 40.00
LL21T Thurman Munson T/10 15.00 40.00
LL22A Cal Ripken Jr. A/25 20.00 50.00
LL22I Cal Ripken Jr. I/25 20.00 50.00
LL22M Cal Ripken Jr. M/25 20.00 50.00
LL22N Cal Ripken Jr. N/25 20.00 50.00
LL22N Cal Ripken Jr. N/25 20.00 50.00
LL22O Cal Ripken Jr. O/25 20.00 50.00
LL22R Cal Ripken Jr. R/25 20.00 50.00
LL23G Tony Gwynn G/25 15.00 40.00
LL23N Tony Gwynn N/25 15.00 40.00
LL23N Tony Gwynn N/25 15.00 40.00
LL23W Tony Gwynn W/25 15.00 40.00
LL23Y Tony Gwynn Y/25 15.00 40.00
LL24A Nolan Ryan A/20 30.00 60.00
LL24N Nolan Ryan N/20 30.00 60.00
LL24R Nolan Ryan R/20 30.00 60.00
LL24Y Nolan Ryan Y/20 30.00 60.00
LL25A Nolan Ryan A/15 30.00 60.00
LL25E Nolan Ryan E/15 30.00 60.00
LL25E Nolan Ryan E/15 30.00 60.00
LL25N Nolan Ryan N/15 30.00 60.00
LL25P Nolan Ryan P/15 30.00 60.00
LL25R Nolan Ryan R/15 30.00 60.00
LL25R Nolan Ryan R/15 30.00 60.00
LL25S Nolan Ryan S/15 30.00 60.00
LL25S Nolan Ryan S/15 30.00 60.00
LL25X Nolan Ryan X/15 30.00 60.00
LL25Y Nolan Ryan Y/15 30.00 60.00
LL26E Jackie Robinson E/10 15.00 40.00
LL26E Jackie Robinson E/10 15.00 40.00
LL26I Jackie Robinson I/10 15.00 40.00
LL26N Jackie Robinson N/10 15.00 40.00
LL26O Jackie Robinson O/10 15.00 40.00
LL26P Jackie Robinson P/10 15.00 40.00
LL26R Jackie Robinson R/10 15.00 40.00
LL27F Carlton Fisk F/20 30.00 60.00
LL27I Carlton Fisk I/20 30.00 60.00
LL27K Carlton Fisk K/20 30.00 60.00
LL27S Carlton Fisk S/20 30.00 60.00
LL28A Carl Yastrzemski A/15 20.00 50.00
LL28E Carl Yastrzemski E/15 20.00 50.00
LL28I Carl Yastrzemski I/15 20.00 50.00
LL28K Carl Yastrzemski K/15 20.00 50.00
LL28M Carl Yastrzemski M/15 20.00 50.00
LL28R Carl Yastrzemski R/15 20.00 50.00
LL28S Carl Yastrzemski S/15 20.00 50.00
LL28S Carl Yastrzemski S/15 20.00 50.00
LL28T Carl Yastrzemski T/15 20.00 50.00
LL28Y Carl Yastrzemski Y/15 20.00 50.00
LL28Z Carl Yastrzemski Z/15 20.00 50.00
LL29B Johnny Bench B/25 30.00 60.00
LL29C Johnny Bench C/25 30.00 60.00
LL29E Johnny Bench E/25 30.00 60.00
LL29H Johnny Bench H/25 30.00 60.00
LL29N Johnny Bench N/25 30.00 60.00
LL30A Ryne Sandberg A/25 30.00 60.00
LL30B Ryne Sandberg B/25 30.00 60.00
LL30D Ryne Sandberg D/25 30.00 60.00
LL30E Ryne Sandberg E/25 30.00 60.00
LL30G Ryne Sandberg G/25 30.00 60.00
LL30N Ryne Sandberg N/25 30.00 60.00
LL30R Ryne Sandberg R/25 30.00 60.00
LL30S Ryne Sandberg S/25 30.00 60.00
LL31A Don Mattingly A/15 30.00 60.00
LL31G Don Mattingly G/15 30.00 60.00
LL31I Don Mattingly I/15 30.00 60.00
LL31L Don Mattingly L/15 30.00 60.00
LL31M Don Mattingly M/15 30.00 60.00
LL31N Don Mattingly N/15 30.00 60.00
LL31T Don Mattingly T/15 30.00 60.00
LL31T Don Mattingly T/15 30.00 60.00
LL31Y Don Mattingly Y/15 30.00 60.00
LL32A Ernie Banks A/25 10.00 25.00
LL32B Ernie Banks B/25 10.00 25.00
LL32K Ernie Banks K/25 10.00 25.00
LL32N Ernie Banks N/25 10.00 25.00
LL32S Ernie Banks S/25 10.00 25.00
LL33A Bill Mazeroski A/15 10.00 25.00
LL33E Bill Mazeroski E/15 10.00 25.00
LL33I Bill Mazeroski I/15 10.00 25.00
LL33K Bill Mazeroski K/15 10.00 25.00
LL33M Bill Mazeroski M/15 10.00 25.00
LL33O Bill Mazeroski O/15 10.00 25.00
LL33R Bill Mazeroski R/15 10.00 25.00
LL33S Bill Mazeroski S/15 10.00 25.00
LL33Z Bill Mazeroski Z/15 10.00 25.00
LL34A Ernie Banks A/15 10.00 25.00
LL34E Ernie Banks E/15 10.00 25.00
LL34L Ernie Banks L/15 10.00 25.00
LL34L Ernie Banks L/15 10.00 25.00
LL34O Ernie Banks O/15 10.00 25.00
LL34P Ernie Banks P/15 10.00 25.00
LL34S Ernie Banks S/15 10.00 25.00
LL34T Ernie Banks T/15 10.00 25.00
LL34T Ernie Banks T/15 10.00 25.00
LL34W Ernie Banks W/15 10.00 25.00
LL34Y Ernie Banks Y/15 10.00 25.00
LL35B Bob Gibson B/25 15.00 40.00
LL35G Bob Gibson G/25 15.00 40.00
LL35I Bob Gibson I/25 15.00 40.00
LL35N Bob Gibson N/25 15.00 40.00
LL35O Bob Gibson O/25 15.00 40.00
LL35S Bob Gibson S/25 15.00 40.00
LL36C Mike Schmidt C/25 30.00 60.00
LL36D Mike Schmidt D/25 30.00 60.00
LL36H Mike Schmidt H/25 30.00 60.00
LL36I Mike Schmidt I/25 30.00 60.00
LL36M Mike Schmidt M/25 30.00 60.00
LL36S Mike Schmidt S/25 30.00 60.00
LL36T Mike Schmidt T/25 30.00 60.00
LL37A Al Kaline A/25 12.50 30.00
LL37E Al Kaline E/25 12.50 30.00
LL37I Al Kaline I/25 12.50 30.00
LL37K Al Kaline K/25 12.50 30.00
LL37L Al Kaline L/25 12.50 30.00
LL37N Al Kaline N/25 12.50 30.00
LL38A Reggie Jackson A/25 20.00 50.00
LL38C Reggie Jackson C/25 20.00 50.00
LL38J Reggie Jackson J/25 20.00 50.00
LL38K Reggie Jackson K/25 20.00 50.00
LL38N Reggie Jackson N/25 20.00 50.00
LL38O Reggie Jackson O/25 20.00 50.00
LL38S Reggie Jackson S/25 20.00 50.00
LL39A Stan Musial A/25 30.00 60.00
LL39I Stan Musial I/25 30.00 60.00
LL39L Stan Musial L/25 30.00 60.00
LL39M Stan Musial M/25 30.00 60.00
LL39S Stan Musial S/25 30.00 60.00
LL39U Stan Musial U/25 30.00 60.00
LL40A Bo Jackson A/25 20.00 50.00
LL40C Bo Jackson C/25 20.00 50.00
LL40J Bo Jackson J/25 20.00 50.00
LL40K Bo Jackson K/25 20.00 50.00
LL40N Bo Jackson N/25 20.00 50.00
LL40O Bo Jackson O/25 20.00 50.00
LL40S Bo Jackson S/25 20.00 50.00
LL41B Bo Jackson B/15 20.00 50.00
LL41K Bo Jackson K/15 20.00 50.00
LL41N Bo Jackson N/15 20.00 50.00
LL41O Bo Jackson O/15 20.00 50.00
LL41O Bo Jackson O/15 20.00 50.00
LL41S Bo Jackson S/15 20.00 50.00
LL41W Bo Jackson W/15 20.00 50.00
LL42A Stan Musial A/25 15.00 40.00
LL42E Stan Musial E/25 15.00 40.00
LL42H Stan Musial H/25 15.00 40.00
LL42M Stan Musial M/25 15.00 40.00
LL42N Stan Musial N/25 15.00 40.00
LL42T Stan Musial T/25 15.00 40.00

2007 Sweet Spot Classic Signatures Red Stitch Black Ink

RANDOM INSERTS IN TINS
PRINT RUNS B/WN 35-175 COPIES PER
EXCHANGE DEADLINE 8/3/2009
SPSAG Andres Galarraga/175 6.00 15.00
SPSAK Al Kaline/175 15.00 40.00
SPSAO Al Oliver/175 6.00 15.00
SPSBJ Bo Jackson/175 20.00 50.00
SPSBM Bill Mazeroski/175 10.00 25.00
SPSBO Wade Boggs/75 15.00 40.00
SPSBR Brooks Robinson/175 10.00 25.00
SPSBS Bruce Sutter/75 12.50 30.00
SPSBW Billy Williams/175 6.00 15.00
SPSCF Carlton Fisk/75 15.00 40.00
SPSCL Carney Lansford/175 6.00 15.00
SPSCO Dave Concepcion/175 10.00 25.00
SPSCY Carl Yastrzemski/75 30.00 60.00
SPSDA Dick Allen/175 6.00 15.00
SPSDG Dick Groat/175 6.00 15.00
SPSDL Don Larsen/175 6.00 15.00
SPSDM Don Mattingly/75 30.00 60.00
SPSDS Don Sutton/175 6.00 15.00
SPSDW Dave Winfield/75 20.00 50.00
SPSEB Ernie Banks/75 30.00 60.00
SPSEC Dennis Eckersley/175 10.00 25.00
SPSEF Elroy Face/175 6.00 15.00
SPSEM Edgar Martinez/175 6.00 15.00
SPSEV Dwight Evans/175 8.00 20.00
SPSFL Fred Lynn/175 8.00 20.00
SPSFM Fred McGriff/175 10.00 25.00
SPSFR Frank Robinson Blue/75 8.00 20.00
SPSGI Bob Gibson/175 12.50 30.00
SPSGP Gaylord Perry/175 6.00 15.00
SPSHB Harold Baines/175 6.00 15.00
SPSJB Johnny Bench/75 20.00 50.00
SPSJI Jim Bunning/175 10.00 25.00
SPSJK John Kruk/175 6.00 15.00
SPSJP Johnny Pesky/175 20.00 50.00
SPSJR Jim Rice/175 6.00 15.00
SPSKG Ken Griffey Sr./175 6.00 15.00
SPSLA Luis Aparicio/175 6.00 15.00
SPSLB Lou Brock/75 15.00 40.00
SPSMA Juan Marichal/175 10.00 25.00
SPSMG Mark Grace/175 6.00 15.00
SPSMO Jack Morris/175 6.00 15.00
SPSMS Mike Schmidt/75 15.00 40.00
SPSMU Stan Musial/75 40.00 80.00
SPSMV Mickey Vernon/75 6.00 15.00
SPSNR Nolan Ryan/75 50.00 100.00
SPSOG Ozzie Guillen/175 6.00 15.00
SPSOS Ozzie Smith/75 20.00 50.00
SPSPN Phil Niekro/175 6.00 15.00
SPSRA Roberto Alomar/175 20.00 50.00
SPSRC Rod Carew/75 12.50 30.00
SPSRF Rollie Fingers/175 6.00 15.00
SPSRI Jim Rice/175 6.00 15.00
SPSRJ Reggie Jackson/75 30.00 60.00
SPSRK Ralph Kiner/75 10.00 25.00
SPSRR Robin Roberts/175 10.00 25.00
SPSRS Ryne Sandberg/75 20.00 50.00
SPSRY Robin Yount/75 15.00 40.00
SPSSA Ron Santo/175 12.50 30.00
SPSSC Steve Carlton/175 8.00 20.00
SPSSD Shawon Dunston/175 6.00 15.00
SPSSG Steve Garvey/175 8.00 20.00
SPSSK Bill Skowron/175 6.00 15.00
SPSSM Reggie Smith/175 6.00 15.00
SPSTG Tony Gwynn/75 30.00 60.00
SPSTH Toby Harrah/175 6.00 15.00
SPSTM Tino Martinez/175 10.00 25.00
SPSTO Tony Oliva/175 6.00 15.00
SPSTP Tony Perez/175 6.00 15.00
SPSTR Tim Raines/175 6.00 15.00
SPSWB Wade Boggs/75 8.00 20.00
SPSWD Willie Davis/75 10.00 25.00
SPSWH Willie Horton/175 6.00 15.00
SPSWM Willie McCovey/75 15.00 40.00
SPSYB Yogi Berra/75 15.00 40.00

2007 Sweet Spot Classic Signatures Red Stitch Blue Ink

*BLUE p/r 75-125: .5X TO 1.2X BLK p/r 175
*BLUE p/r 75-125: .4X TO 1X BLK p/r 75
*BLUE p/r 35: .6X TO 1.5X BLK p/r 175
*BLUE p/r 35: .5X TO 1.2X BLK p/r 75
RANDOM INSERTS IN TINS
PRINT RUNS B/WN 35-125 COPIES PER
EXCHANGE DEADLINE 8/3/2009
SPSBM Bill Mazeroski/125 8.00 20.00
SPSDG Dick Groat/125 8.00 20.00
SPSMV Mickey Vernon/125 8.00 20.00
SPSNR Nolan Ryan/35 30.00 60.00
SPSRR Robin Roberts/125 8.00 20.00
SPSYB Yogi Berra/35 20.00 50.00

2007 Sweet Spot Classic Signatures Gold Stitch Black Ink

RANDOM INSERTS IN TINS
PRINT RUNS B/WN 25-99 COPIES PER
NO PRICING ON QTY 25 OR LESS
BLUE RANDOMLY INSERTED IN TINS
BLUE PRINT RUN B/WN 15-50 PER
EXCHANGE DEADLINE 8/3/2009
N.RYAN/25 SIGNED IN GOLD INK
SPSAG Andres Galarraga/99 6.00 15.00
SPSAK Al Kaline/99 12.00 30.00
SPSAO Al Oliver/99 6.00 15.00
SPSBJ Bo Jackson/99 EXCH 30.00 60.00
SPSBM Bill Mazeroski/99 6.00 15.00
SPSBR Brooks Robinson/99 6.00 15.00
SPSBW Billy Williams/99 6.00 15.00
SPSCL Carney Lansford/99 6.00 15.00
SPSCO Dave Concepcion/99 EXCH 10.00 25.00
SPSDA Dick Allen/99 EXCH 6.00 15.00
SPSDG Dick Groat/99 6.00 15.00
SPSDL Don Larsen/99 12.50 30.00
SPSDS Don Sutton/99 6.00 15.00
SPSEB Ernie Banks/99 40.00 80.00
SPSEC Dennis Eckersley/99 10.00 25.00
SPSEF Elroy Face/99 6.00 15.00
SPSEM Edgar Martinez/99 6.00 15.00
SPSEV Dwight Evans/99 6.00 15.00
SPSFL Fred Lynn/99 6.00 15.00
SPSFM Fred McGriff/99 15.00 40.00
SPSGI Bob Gibson/99 20.00 50.00
SPSGP Gaylord Perry/99 6.00 15.00
SPSHB Harold Baines/99 6.00 15.00
SPSJI Jim Bunning/99 10.00 25.00
SPSJK John Kruk/99 6.00 15.00
SPSJP Johnny Pesky/99 12.50 30.00
SPSJR Jim Rice/99 10.00 25.00
SPSKG Ken Griffey Sr./99 6.00 15.00
SPSLA Luis Aparicio/99 6.00 15.00
SPSMA Juan Marichal/99 10.00 25.00
SPSMG Mark Grace/99 8.00 20.00
SPSMO Jack Morris/99 6.00 15.00
SPSMV Mickey Vernon/99 6.00 15.00
SPSOG Ozzie Guillen/99 6.00 15.00
SPSPN Phil Niekro/99 10.00 25.00
SPSRA Roberto Alomar/99 15.00 40.00
SPSRF Rollie Fingers/99 10.00 25.00
SPSRI Jim Rice/99 10.00 25.00
SPSRR Robin Roberts/99 6.00 15.00
SPSSA Ron Santo/99 15.00 40.00
SPSSC Steve Carlton/99 15.00 40.00
SPSSD Shawon Dunston/99 6.00 15.00
SPSSG Steve Garvey/99 10.00 25.00
SPSSK Bill Skowron/99 6.00 15.00
SPSSM Reggie Smith/99 6.00 15.00
SPSTH Toby Harrah/99 6.00 15.00
SPSTM Tino Martinez/99 15.00 40.00
SPSTO Tony Oliva/99 8.00 20.00
SPSTP Tony Perez/99 10.00 25.00
SPSTR Tim Raines/99 6.00 15.00
SPSWH Willie Horton/99 10.00 25.00

2007 Sweet Spot Classic Signatures Gold Stitch Blue Ink

*BLUE: .5X TO 1.2X BLACK INK
RANDOM INSERTS IN TINS
PRINT RUNS B/WN 15-50 COPIES PER
NO PRICING ON QTY 25 OR LESS
EXCHANGE DEADLINE 8/3/2009
SPSCY Carl Yastrzemski/50 30.00 60.00
SPSDW Dave Winfield/50 12.50 30.00
SPSEF Elroy Face/50 8.00 20.00
SPSJP Johnny Pesky/50 6.00 15.00
SPSMU Stan Musial/50 20.00 50.00
SPSRF Rollie Fingers/50 10.00 25.00
SPSRY Robin Yount/50 20.00 50.00

2007 Sweet Spot Classic Signatures Sepia Black Ink

RANDOM INSERTS IN TINS
PRINT RUNS B/WN 16-199 COPIES PER
NO PRICING ON QTY 25 OR LESS
EXCHANGE DEADLINE 8/3/2009
SPSCF Carlton Fisk/124 12.50 30.00
SPSCY Carl Yastrzemski/124 20.00 50.00
SPSDM Don Mattingly/124 20.00 50.00
SPSDS Duke Snider/30 15.00 40.00
SPSJM Juan Marichal/124 10.00 25.00
SPSJR Jim Rice/85 10.00 25.00
SPSMU Dale Murphy/183 20.00 50.00
SPSNR Nolan Ryan/123 50.00 100.00
SPSOS Ozzie Smith/183 20.00 50.00
SPSRS Ryne Sandberg/199 20.00 50.00
SPSTG Tony Gwynn/199 20.00 50.00

2007 Sweet Spot Classic Signatures Sepia Blue Ink

RANDOM INSERTS IN TINS
PRINT RUNS B/WN 15-200 COPIES PER
NO PRICING ON QTY 25 OR LESS
EXCHANGE DEADLINE 8/3/2009
SPSAK Al Kaline/199 20.00 50.00
SPSBR Brooks Robinson/200 10.00 25.00
SPSBW Billy Williams/199 10.00 25.00
SPSCF Carlton Fisk/78 15.00 40.00
SPSCR Cal Ripken Jr./199 60.00 100.00
SPSCY Carl Yastrzemski/90 30.00 60.00
SPSDM Don Mattingly/78 20.00 50.00
SPSDS Duke Snider/199 12.50 30.00
SPSEM Edgar Martinez/74 12.50 30.00
SPSJM Juan Marichal/84 12.50 30.00
SPSJP Jim Palmer/200 10.00 25.00
SPSJR Jim Rice/75 10.00 25.00
SPSLM Lee Mazzilli/199 10.00 25.00
SPSMU Dale Murphy/75 25.00 60.00
SPSNR Nolan Ryan/80 60.00 120.00
SPSOS Ozzie Smith/75 30.00 60.00
SPSRC Rocky Colavito/199 30.00 60.00
SPSRY Robin Yount/35 30.00 60.00
SPSTG Tony Gwynn/199 20.00 50.00
SPSWC Will Clark/199 10.00 25.00

2007 Sweet Spot Classic Signatures Silver Stitch Blue Ink

RANDOM INSERTS IN TINS
PRINT RUNS B/WN 16-199 COPIES PER
NO PRICING ON QTY 25 OR LESS
EXCHANGE DEADLINE 8/3/2009
SPSBW Billy Williams/26 12.50 30.00
SPSDW Dave Winfield/31 10.00 25.00
SPSEC Dennis Eckersley/43 10.00 25.00
SPSFM Fred McGriff/27 6.00 15.00
SPSGI Bob Gibson/45 30.00 60.00
SPSGP Gaylord Perry/36 12.00 30.00
SPSJK John Kruk/29 6.00 25.00
SPSKG Ken Griffey Sr./30 12.00 30.00
SPSMA Juan Marichal/27 12.00 30.00
SPSMO Jack Morris/47 10.00 25.00
SPSNR Nolan Ryan/30 40.00 80.00
SPSPN Phil Niekro/35 12.00 30.00
SPSRC Rod Carew/29 12.00 30.00
SPSRF Rollie Fingers/34 10.00 25.00
SPSRJ Reggie Jackson/44 30.00 60.00
SPSRR Robin Roberts/36 6.00 15.00
SPSSC Steve Carlton/32 12.00 30.00
SPSTR Tim Raines/30 40.00 80.00
SPSWB Wade Boggs/26 20.00 50.00
SPSWM Willie McCovey/44 30.00 60.00

2007 Sweet Spot Classic Signatures Barrel Black Ink

*BLUE: .5X TO 1.2X BLACK INK
RANDOM INSERTS IN TINS
STATED PRINT RUN B/WN 15-50 PER
NO BLUE PRICING ON QTY 25 OR LESS
EXCHANGE DEADLINE 8/3/2009
SPSRR Robin Roberts Blue/50 20.00 50.00

2007 Sweet Spot Classic Signatures Barrel Blue Ink

RANDOM INSERTS IN TINS
PRINT RUNS B/WN 25-75 COPIES PER
NO PRICING ON QTY 25 OR LESS
*BLUE: .5X TO 1.2X BLACK INK
BLUE RANDOMLY INSERTED IN TINS
BLUE PRINT RUN B/WN 15-50 PER
NO BLUE PRICING ON QTY 25 OR LESS
EXCHANGE DEADLINE 8/3/2009
SPSAG Andres Galarraga/75 6.00 15.00
SPSAK Al Kaline/75 20.00 50.00
SPSAO Al Oliver/75 8.00 20.00
SPSBJ Bo Jackson/75 30.00 60.00
SPSBM Bill Mazeroski/75 10.00 25.00
SPSBR Brooks Robinson/75 30.00 60.00
SPSBW Billy Williams/75 12.50 30.00
SPSCL Carney Lansford/75 8.00 20.00
SPSDA Dick Allen/75 10.00 25.00
SPSDG Dick Groat/75 10.00 25.00
SPSDL Don Larsen/75 10.00 25.00
SPSDS Don Sutton/75 10.00 25.00
SPSEC Dennis Eckersley/75 10.00 25.00
SPSEF Elroy Face/75 6.00 15.00
SPSEM Edgar Martinez/75 10.00 25.00
SPSEV Dwight Evans/75 10.00 25.00
SPSFL Fred Lynn/75 8.00 20.00
SPSFM Fred McGriff/75 8.00 20.00
SPSGP Gaylord Perry/75 6.00 15.00
SPSHB Harold Baines/75 6.00 15.00
SPSJI Jim Bunning/75 6.00 15.00
SPSJK John Kruk/75 8.00 20.00
SPSJP Johnny Pesky/75 12.50 30.00
SPSKG Ken Griffey Sr./75 10.00 25.00
SPSLA Luis Aparicio/75 10.00 25.00
SPSMA Juan Marichal/75 15.00 40.00
SPSMG Mark Grace/75 15.00 40.00
SPSMO Jack Morris/75 8.00 20.00
SPSMV Mickey Vernon/75 6.00 15.00
SPSOG Ozzie Guillen/75 10.00 25.00
SPSPN Phil Niekro/75 6.00 15.00
SPSRA Roberto Alomar/75 30.00 60.00
SPSRF Rollie Fingers/75 8.00 20.00
SPSRI Jim Rice/75 12.50 30.00
SPSRR Robin Roberts/50 6.00 15.00
SPSSA Ron Santo/75 20.00 50.00
SPSSC Steve Carlton/75 20.00 50.00
SPSSD Shawon Dunston/75 10.00 25.00
SPSSG Steve Garvey/75 10.00 25.00
SPSSK Bill Skowron/75 6.00 15.00
SPSSM Reggie Smith/75 6.00 15.00
SPSTH Toby Harrah/75 6.00 15.00
SPSTM Tino Martinez/75 12.50 30.00
SPSTO Tony Oliva/75 10.00 25.00
SPSTP Tony Perez/75 12.50 30.00
SPSTR Tim Raines/75 10.00 25.00
SPSWH Willie Horton/75 10.00 25.00

2007 Sweet Spot Classic Signatures Black Barrel Silver Ink

RANDOM INSERTS IN TINS
PRINT RUNS B/WN 1-47 COPIES PER
NO PRICING ON QTY 25 OR LESS
EXCHANGE DEADLINE 8/3/2009
SPSBW Billy Williams/26 20.00 50.00
SPSEC Dennis Eckersley/43 12.50 30.00
SPSEF Elroy Face/26 20.00 50.00
SPSFM Fred McGriff/27 15.00 40.00
SPSGP Gaylord Perry/36 10.00 25.00
SPSJK John Kruk/29 12.50 30.00
SPSKG Ken Griffey Sr./30 15.00 40.00
SPSMA Juan Marichal/27 10.00 25.00
SPSMO Jack Morris/47 10.00 25.00
SPSPN Phil Niekro/35 15.00 40.00
SPSRF Rollie Fingers/34 10.00 25.00
SPSRR Robin Roberts/36 20.00 50.00
SPSSC Steve Carlton/32 20.00 50.00
SPSTR Tim Raines/30 30.00 60.00

2007 Sweet Spot Classic Signatures Black Leather Silver Ink

RANDOM INSERTS IN TINS
PRINT RUNS B/WN 1-47 COPIES PER
NO PRICING ON QTY 25 OR LESS
EXCHANGE DEADLINE 8/3/2009
SPSBS Bruce Sutter/42 12.50 30.00
SPSBW Billy Williams/26 15.00 40.00
SPSCF Carlton Fisk/27 20.00 50.00
SPSDW Dave Winfield/31 12.50 30.00
SPSEC Dennis Eckersley/43 8.00 20.00
SPSEF Elroy Face/26 10.00 25.00
SPSFM Fred McGriff/27 15.00 40.00
SPSGI Bob Gibson/45 12.50 30.00
SPSGP Gaylord Perry/36 10.00 25.00
SPSJK John Kruk/29 12.50 30.00
SPSKG Ken Griffey Sr./30 15.00 40.00
SPSMA Juan Marichal/27 30.00 60.00
SPSMO Jack Morris/47 12.50 30.00
SPSNR Nolan Ryan/30 75.00 150.00
SPSPN Phil Niekro/35 15.00 40.00
SPSRC Rod Carew/29 20.00 50.00
SPSRF Rollie Fingers/34 12.50 30.00
SPSRJ Reggie Jackson/44 30.00 60.00
SPSRR Robin Roberts/36 10.00 25.00
SPSSC Steve Carlton/32 20.00 50.00
SPSTR Tim Raines/30 30.00 60.00
SPSWB Wade Boggs/26 30.00 60.00
SPSWM Willie McCovey/44 30.00 60.00

2007 Sweet Spot Classic Signatures Leather Blue Ink

RANDOM INSERTS IN TINS
PRINT RUNS B/WN 25-75 COPIES PER
NO PRICING ON QTY 25 OR LESS
GOLD RANDOMLY INSERTED IN TINS
GOLD PRINT RUN B/WN 15-50 PER
EXCHANGE DEADLINE 8/3/2009
SPSAG Andres Galarraga/75 6.00 15.00
SPSAK Al Kaline/75 20.00 50.00
SPSAO Al Oliver/75 8.00 20.00
SPSBJ Bo Jackson/75 30.00 60.00
SPSBM Bill Mazeroski/75 10.00 25.00
SPSBR Brooks Robinson/75 12.50 30.00
SPSBW Billy Williams/75 12.50 30.00
SPSCL Carney Lansford/75 8.00 20.00
SPSDA Dick Allen/75 10.00 25.00
SPSDG Dick Groat/75 10.00 25.00
SPSDL Don Larsen/75 12.50 30.00
SPSEC Dennis Eckersley/75 10.00 25.00
SPSEF Elroy Face/75 6.00 15.00
SPSEM Edgar Martinez/75 20.00 50.00
SPSEV Dwight Evans/75 10.00 25.00
SPSFL Fred Lynn/75 8.00 20.00
SPSFM Fred McGriff/75 15.00 40.00
SPSGP Gaylord Perry/75 10.00 25.00
SPSHB Harold Baines/75 10.00 25.00
SPSJI Jim Bunning/75 10.00 25.00
SPSJK John Kruk/75 8.00 20.00
SPSJP Johnny Pesky/75 12.50 30.00
SPSKG Ken Griffey Sr./75 12.50 30.00
SPSLA Luis Aparicio/75 10.00 25.00
SPSLB Lou Brock/75 15.00 40.00
SPSMA Juan Marichal/75 15.00 40.00
SPSMG Mark Grace/75 15.00 40.00
SPSMO Jack Morris/75 8.00 20.00
SPSMV Mickey Vernon/75 8.00 20.00
SPSOG Ozzie Guillen/75 10.00 25.00
SPSRA Roberto Alomar/75 30.00 60.00
SPSRC Rod Carew/75 12.50 30.00

SPSRF Rollie Fingers/75	8.00	20.00
SPSRI Jim Rice/75	10.00	25.00
SPSRR Robin Roberts/75	10.00	25.00
SPSRS Ryne Sandberg/75	20.00	50.00
SPSSA Ron Santo/75	30.00	60.00
SPSSC Steve Carlton/75	20.00	50.00
SPSSD Shawon Dunston/75	10.00	25.00
SPSSG Steve Garvey/75	10.00	25.00
SPSSK Bill Skowron/75	10.00	25.00
SPSSM Reggie Smith/75	6.00	15.00
SPSTH Toby Harrah/75	6.00	15.00
SPSTM Tino Martinez/75	12.50	30.00
SPSTO Tony Oliva/75	10.00	25.00
SPSTP Tony Perez/75	12.50	30.00
SPSTR Tim Raines/75	6.00	15.00
SPSWH Willie Horton/75	10.00	25.00

2007 Sweet Spot Classic Signatures Leather Gold Ink

*GOLD: .5X TO 1.2X BLUE INK
GOLD RANDOMLY INSERTED IN TINS
GOLD PRINT RUN B/WN 15-50 PER
NO GOLD PRICING ON QTY 25 OR LESS
EXCHANGE DEADLINE 8/3/2009

SPSPN Phil Niekro/50	10.00	25.00

2006 Sweet Spot Update

COMP.SET w/o AU's (100)	10.00	25.00
COMMON CARD (1-100)	.20	.50
COMMON AU p/r 399-499	3.00	8.00
COMMON AU p/r 150-240	4.00	10.00
COMMON AU p/r 98-125	4.00	10.00
OVERALL AU ODDS 1:6		
AU PRINT RUNS B/WN 98-499 PER		
EXCHANGE DEADLINE 12/19/09		
1 Luis Gonzalez	.20	.50
2 Chad Tracy	.20	.50
3 Brandon Webb	.30	.75
4 Andruw Jones	.20	.50
5 Chipper Jones	.50	1.25
6 John Smoltz	.50	1.25
7 Tim Hudson	.30	.75
8 Miguel Tejada	.30	.75
9 Brian Roberts	.20	.50
10 Ramon Hernandez	.20	.50
11 Curt Schilling	.30	.75
12 David Ortiz	.50	1.25
13 Manny Ramirez	.50	1.25
14 Jason Varitek	.50	1.25
15 Josh Beckett	.20	.50
16 Greg Maddux	.60	1.50
17 Derrek Lee	.20	.50
18 Mark Prior	.30	.75
19 Aramis Ramirez	.20	.50
20 Jim Thome	.30	.75
21 Paul Konerko	.30	.75
22 Scott Podsednik	.20	.50
23 Jose Contreras	.20	.50
24 Ken Griffey Jr.	1.00	2.50
25 Adam Dunn	.30	.75
26 Felipe Lopez	.20	.50
27 Travis Hafner	.20	.50
28 Victor Martinez	.30	.75
29 Grady Sizemore	.30	.75
30 Jhonny Peralta	.20	.50
31 Todd Helton	.30	.75
32 Garrett Atkins	.20	.50
33 Clint Barmes	.20	.50
34 Ivan Rodriguez	.30	.75
35 Chris Shelton	.20	.50
36 Jeremy Bonderman	.20	.50
37 Miguel Cabrera	.50	1.25
38 Dontrelle Willis	.20	.50
39 Lance Berkman	.30	.75
40 Morgan Ensberg	.20	.50
41 Roy Oswalt	.30	.75
42 Reggie Sanders	.20	.50
43 Mike Sweeney	.20	.50
44 Vladimir Guerrero	.30	.75
45 Bartolo Colon	.20	.50
46 Chone Figgins	.20	.50
47 Nomar Garciaparra	.30	.75
48 Jeff Kent	.20	.50
49 J.D. Drew	.20	.50
50 Carlos Lee	.20	.50
51 Ben Sheets	.20	.50
52 Rickie Weeks	.20	.50
53 Johan Santana	.30	.75
54 Torii Hunter	.20	.50
55 Joe Mauer	.30	.75
56 Pedro Martinez	.30	.75
57 David Wright	.40	1.00
58 Carlos Beltran	.30	.75
59 Carlos Delgado	.20	.50
60 Jose Reyes	.30	.75
61 Derek Jeter	1.25	3.00
62 Alex Rodriguez	.60	1.50
63 Randy Johnson	.50	1.25
64 Hideki Matsui	.50	1.25
65 Gary Sheffield	.20	.50
66 Rich Harden	.20	.50
67 Eric Chavez	.20	.50
68 Huston Street	.20	.50
69 Bobby Crosby	.20	.50
70 Bobby Abreu	.20	.50
71 Ryan Howard	.40	1.00
72 Chase Utley	.30	.75
73 Pat Burrell	.20	.50
74 Jason Bay	.20	.50
75 Sean Casey	.20	.50
76 Mike Piazza	.50	1.25
77 Jake Peavy	.20	.50
78 Brian Giles	.20	.50
79 Milton Bradley	.20	.50
80 Omar Vizquel	.30	.75
81 Jason Schmidt	.20	.50
82 Ichiro Suzuki	.60	1.50
83 Felix Hernandez	.30	.75
84 Kenji Johjima RC	.50	1.25
85 Albert Pujols	.60	1.50
86 Chris Carpenter	.30	.75
87 Scott Rolen	.30	.75
88 Jim Edmonds	.30	.75
89 Carl Crawford	.30	.75
90 Jonny Gomes	.20	.50
91 Scott Kazmir	.30	.75
92 Mark Teixeira	.30	.75
93 Michael Young	.20	.50
94 Phil Nevin	.20	.50
95 Vernon Wells	.20	.50
96 Roy Halladay	.30	.75
97 Troy Glaus	.20	.50
98 Alfonso Soriano	.30	.75
99 Nick Johnson	.20	.50
100 Jose Vidro	.20	.50
101 A.Wainwright AU/100 (RC)	15.00	40.00
102 A.Hernandez AU/100 (RC)	6.00	15.00
103 A.Ethier AU/150 (RC)	8.00	20.00
104 J.Botts AU/100 (RC) EXCH	4.00	10.00
105 B.Johnson AU/400 (RC)	3.00	8.00
106 B.Bonser AU/100 (RC)	6.00	15.00
107 B.Logan AU/200 RC	4.00	10.00
108 B.Anderson AU/200 (RC)	4.00	10.00
109 B.Bannister AU/100 (RC)	8.00	20.00
110 C.Denorfia AU/100 (RC)	4.00	10.00
111 A.Montero AU/100 (RC)	6.00	15.00
112 C.Ross AU/100 (RC)	20.00	50.00
113 C.Hamels AU/399 (RC)	10.00	25.00
114 C.Jackson AU/400 (RC)	4.00	10.00
115 D.Uggla AU/125 (RC)	8.00	20.00
116 D.Gassner AU/100 (RC)	4.00	10.00
117 C.Wilson AU/150 (RC)	8.00	20.00
118 E.Reed AU/150 (RC)	4.00	10.00
119 F.Carmona AU/99 (RC)	10.00	25.00
120 F.Nieve AU/100 (RC)	4.00	10.00
121 F.Liriano AU/499 (RC)	6.00	15.00
122 F.Bynum AU/100 (RC)	4.00	10.00
123 H.Ramirez AU/100 (RC)	10.00	25.00
124 H.Kuo AU/100 (RC)	10.00	25.00
125 I.Kinsler AU/100 (RC)	10.00	25.00
126 C.Marmol AU/100 RC	6.00	15.00
127 B.Keppel AU/200 (RC)	4.00	10.00
128 J.Kubel AU/100 (RC)	6.00	15.00
129 J.Harris AU/100 RC	4.00	10.00
130 A.Soler AU/100 RC	6.00	15.00
131 J.Weaver AU/100 (RC)	40.00	80.00
132 C.Quentin AU/100 (RC)	12.00	30.00
133 J.Hermida AU/100 (RC)	6.00	15.00
134 J.Zumaya AU/100 (RC)	10.00	25.00
135 J.Devine AU/100 RC	6.00	15.00
136 J.Koronka AU/98 (RC)	4.00	10.00
137 J.Papelbon AU/399 (RC)	5.00	12.00
138 J.Capellan AU/240 (RC)	12.00	30.00
139 J.Johnson AU/100 (RC)	6.00	15.00
141 J.Willingham AU/100 (RC)	4.00	10.00
143 J.Verlander AU/100 (RC)	25.00	60.00
144 K.Shoppach AU/100 (RC)	6.00	15.00
146 K.Thompson AU/100 (RC)	4.00	10.00
147 M.McBride AU/100 (RC)	4.00	10.00
149 M.Cain AU/150 (RC)	30.00	60.00
150 C.Hensley AU/100 (RC)	4.00	10.00
151 T.Taubenheim AU/100 RC	10.00	25.00
152 M.Jacobs AU/200 (RC)	4.00	10.00
153 S.Rivera AU/100 (RC)	4.00	10.00
154 M.Thompson AU/100 RC	4.00	10.00
155 N.McLouth AU/100 (RC)	10.00	25.00
156 M.Vento AU/100 (RC)	4.00	10.00
157 P.Maholm AU/200 (RC)	4.00	10.00
159 R.Abercrombie AU/100 (RC)	4.00	10.00
160 M.Rouse AU/100 (RC)	4.00	10.00
161 K.Ray AU/100 (RC)	4.00	10.00
162 R.Flores AU/100 RC	4.00	10.00
163 R.Zimmerman AU/100 (RC)	10.00	25.00
164 E.Aybar AU/100 (RC)	6.00	15.00
165 S.Marshall AU/150 (RC)	8.00	20.00
167 T.Buchholz AU/100 (RC)	4.00	10.00
168 M.Murton AU/100 (RC)	12.00	30.00
170 W.Nieves AU/100 (RC)	6.00	15.00
171 J.Shields AU/100 RC	8.00	20.00
172 J.Lester AU/399 RC	10.00	25.00
173 C.Hansen AU/100 RC EXCH	6.00	15.00
174 A.Rakers AU/100 (RC)	4.00	10.00
175 B.Livingston AU/100 (RC)	6.00	15.00
176 B.Harris AU/100 (RC)	4.00	10.00
177 Z.Jackson AU/100 (RC)	6.00	15.00
178 C.Britton AU/100 RC	4.00	10.00
179 H.Kendrick AU/399 (RC)	6.00	15.00
180 Z.Miner AU/100 (RC)	6.00	15.00
181 K.Frandsen AU/100 (RC)	4.00	10.00
182 M.Capps AU/100 (RC)	4.00	10.00
183 P.Moylan AU/100 RC	4.00	10.00

2006 Sweet Spot Update Rookie Signatures Red-Blue Stitch Red Ink

*RB p/r 175-225:.5X TO 1.2X RC p/r 399-499
*RB p/r 100: .6X TO 1.5X RC p/r 399-499
*RB p/r 100: .5X TO 1.2X RC p/r 150-240
*RB p/r 100: .4X TO 1X RC p/r 98-125
*RB p/r 50: .6X TO 1.5X RC p/r 150-240
*RB p/r 50: .5X TO 1.2X RC p/r 98-125
OVERALL AUTO ODDS 1:6
PRINT RUNS B/WN 50-225 COPIES PER
EXCHANGE DEADLINE 12/19/09
ASTERISK = PARTIAL EXCHANGE

124 Hong-Chih Kuo/50	15.00	40.00
164 Erick Aybar/50	10.00	25.00
172 Jon Lester/175	20.00	50.00

2006 Sweet Spot Update Rookie Signatures Bat Barrel Black Ink

*BLK p/r 34-35:1X TO 2.5X RC p/r 399-499
*BLK p/r 70: .5X TO 1.2X RC p/r 150-240
*BLK p/r 34-35: .75X TO 2X RC p/r 150-240
*BLK p/r 70: .6X TO 1.5X RC p/r 399-499
*BLK p/r 34-35: .6X TO 1.5X RC p/r 98-125
OVERALL AUTO ODDS 1:6
PRINT RUNS B/WN 34-70 COPIES PER
EXCHANGE DEADLINE 12/19/09

101 Adam Wainwright/35	20.00	50.00
119 Fausto Carmona/35	20.00	50.00
124 Hong-Chih Kuo/35	15.00	40.00
137 Jonathan Papelbon/70	30.00	60.00

2006 Sweet Spot Update Rookie Signatures Glove Leather Black Ink

OVERALL AUTO ODDS 1:6
PRINT RUNS B/WN 20-40 PER
NO PRICING ON QTY OF 25 OR LESS
EXCHANGE DEADLINE 12/19/09
ASTERISK = PARTIAL EXCHANGE

121 Francisco Liriano/40	15.00	40.00
137 Jonathan Papelbon/40	8.00	20.00
172 Jon Lester/40	50.00	100.00
179 Howie Kendrick/40	15.00	40.00

2006 Sweet Spot Update Announcer Signatures

OVERALL AUTO ODDS 1:6
PRINT RUNS B/WN 25-50 PER

CB Chris Berman/50	20.00	50.00
DP Dan Patrick/50	30.00	60.00
LC Linda Cohn/50	15.00	40.00
PG Peter Gammons/25	30.00	60.00
SS Stuart Scott/50	20.00	50.00

2006 Sweet Spot Update Dual Signatures

OVERALL AUTO ODDS 1:6
PRINT RUNS B/WN 1-55 PER
NO PRICING ON QTY OF 25 OR LESS
EXCHANGE DEADLINE 12/19/09

SS2BN T.Buchholz/F.Nieve/55	8.00	20.00
SS2CK C.Crawford/S.Kazmir/50	8.00	20.00
SS2CU C.Crawford/B.Upton/45	12.50	30.00
SS2CZ Cabrera/Zimmer./35	20.00	50.00
SS2EG A.Ethier/T.Gwynn Jr./35	8.00	20.00
SS2GG Griffey Jr./Vlad/35 EXCH	60.00	120.00
SS2GT K.Griffey Jr./J.Thome/35	75.00	150.00
SS2HK J.Kubel/J.Hermida/55	8.00	20.00
SS2HM T.Hafner/V.Martinez/35	8.00	20.00
SS2HW J.Willingham/J.Hermida/55	8.00	20.00
SS2JW J.Johnson/D.Willis/55 EXCH	12.00	30.00
SS2KU S.Kazmir/B.Upton/55	8.00	20.00
SS2KW S.Kazmir/D.Willis/35	8.00	20.00
SS2LN F.Liriano/J.Nathan/35	40.00	80.00
SS2MM J.Morneau/J.Mauer/35	100.00	200.00
SS2MO J.Morneau/L.Overbay/35	8.00	20.00
SS2PZ J.Papelbon/J.Zumaya/35	8.00	20.00
SS2SN H.Street/J.Nathan/35	8.00	20.00
SS2TJ Travis Hafner Jeremy Sowers/35	8.00	20.00
SS2UH C.Utley/C.Hamels/35	125.00	250.00
SS2UU C.Utley/D.Uggla/35	20.00	50.00
SS2UW Uggla/Willing./55 EXCH	8.00	20.00

2006 Sweet Spot Update Spokesmen Signatures

OVERALL AUTO ODDS 1:6
UNPRICED AU PRINT RUN 5-20

4 Michael Jordan/20	2000.00	4000.00

2006 Sweet Spot Update Sweet Beginnings Swatches

OVERALL GU ODDS 1:12
NO SP PRICING DUE TO SCARCITY

SWAB Adrian Beltre	3.00	8.00
SWAI Akinori Iwamura	12.50	30.00
SWAJ Andruw Jones	4.00	10.00
SWAP Ariel Pestano	3.00	8.00
SWAR Alex Rios	3.00	8.00
SWAS Alfonso Soriano	3.00	8.00
SWBA Bobby Abreu	4.00	10.00
SWBB Brian Bannister	3.00	8.00
SWBI Chad Billingsley	4.00	10.00
SWBW Bernie Williams	4.00	10.00
SWCA Miguel Cabrera	6.00	15.00
SWCB Carlos Beltran	4.00	10.00
SWCD Carlos Delgado	3.00	8.00
SWCH Chin-Lung Hu	20.00	50.00
SWCJ Conor Jackson	4.00	10.00
SWCL Carlos Lee	3.00	8.00
SWCM Matt Cain	4.00	10.00
SWCU Chris Duncan	4.00	10.00
SWCZ Carlos Zambrano	3.00	8.00
SWDL Derrek Lee	3.00	8.00
SWDO David Ortiz	6.00	15.00
SWEB Erik Bedard	3.00	8.00
SWEP Eduardo Paret	3.00	8.00
SWFA Fausto Carmona	3.00	8.00
SWFC Frederich Cepeda	3.00	8.00
SWGY Guogang Yang	3.00	8.00
SWHA Cole Hamels	6.00	15.00
SWHC Hee Seop Choi	3.00	8.00
SWHT Hitoshi Tamura	12.50	30.00
SWIK Ian Kinsler	6.00	15.00
SWIR Ivan Rodriguez	6.00	15.00
SWIS Ichiro Suzuki	50.00	100.00
SWJB Jason Bay	6.00	15.00
SWJD Johnny Damon	4.00	10.00
SWJF Jeff Francis	3.00	8.00
SWJH Jeremy Hermida	3.00	8.00
SWJL Jong Beom Lee	3.00	8.00
SWJM Justin Morneau	6.00	15.00
SWJP Jin Man Park	3.00	8.00
SWJS Johan Santana	6.00	15.00
SWJV Jason Varitek	10.00	25.00
SWJZ Joel Zumaya	10.00	25.00
SWKE Matt Kemp	4.00	10.00
SWKG Ken Griffey Jr.	10.00	25.00
SWKU Koji Uehara	12.50	30.00
SWLO Javy Lopez	3.00	8.00
SWMA Moises Alou	3.00	8.00
SWMC Michael Collins	4.00	10.00
SWME Michel Enriquez	3.00	8.00
SWMF Maikel Folch	3.00	8.00
SWMJ Mike Jacobs	3.00	8.00
SWMK Munenori Kawasaki	30.00	60.00
SWMN Mike Napoli	4.00	10.00
SWMO Michihiro Ogasawara	12.50	30.00
SWMP Mike Piazza	8.00	20.00
SWMS Min Han Son	4.00	10.00
SWMT Miguel Tejada	3.00	8.00
SWNM Nobuhiko Matsunaka	12.50	30.00
SWNS Naoyuki Shimizu	12.50	30.00
SWOU Osmany Urrutia	3.00	8.00
SWPL Pedro Luis Lazo	3.00	8.00
SWPU Albert Pujols	12.50	30.00
SWRO Alex Rodriguez	8.00	20.00
SWSH James Shields	3.00	8.00
SWSW Shunsuke Watanabe	12.50	30.00
SWTN Tsuyoshi Nishioka	15.00	40.00
SWTW Tsuyoshi Wada	15.00	40.00
SWVE Justin Verlander	6.00	15.00
SWVM Victor Martinez	6.00	15.00
SWVO Vicyohandry Odelin	3.00	8.00
SWWI Josh Willingham	3.00	8.00
SWWL Wei-Chu Lin	30.00	60.00
SWYG Yulieski Gourriel	6.00	15.00
SWYM Yunieski Maya	3.00	8.00

2006 Sweet Spot Update Sweet Beginnings Patches

OVERALL GU ODDS 1:12
PRICING FOR NON-LOGO PATCHES
NO SP PRICING DUE TO SCARCITY

SWAB Adrian Beltre	30.00	60.00
SWAE Andre Ethier	20.00	50.00
SWAJ Andruw Jones	20.00	50.00
SWAP Ariel Pestano	20.00	50.00
SWAS Alfonso Soriano	60.00	120.00
SWBA Bobby Abreu	30.00	60.00
SWBB Brian Bannister	20.00	50.00
SWBI Chad Billingsley	20.00	50.00
SWBW Bernie Williams	60.00	120.00
SWCA Miguel Cabrera	30.00	60.00
SWCB Carlos Beltran	30.00	60.00
SWCD Carlos Delgado	40.00	80.00
SWCJ Conor Jackson	30.00	60.00
SWCL Carlos Lee	20.00	50.00
SWCM Matt Cain	40.00	80.00
SWCU Chris Duncan	20.00	50.00
SWCZ Carlos Zambrano	40.00	80.00
SWDL Derrek Lee	40.00	80.00
SWDO David Ortiz	40.00	80.00
SWDU Dan Uggla	20.00	50.00
SWEB Erik Bedard	30.00	60.00
SWEP Eduardo Paret	20.00	50.00
SWFA Fausto Carmona	10.00	25.00
SWFC Frederich Cepeda	20.00	50.00
SWFL Francisco Liriano	20.00	50.00
SWHA Cole Hamels	20.00	50.00
SWHK Hong-Chih Kuo	175.00	300.00
SWJB Jason Bay	20.00	50.00
SWJD Johnny Damon	20.00	50.00
SWJF Jeff Francis	20.00	50.00
SWJH Jeremy Hermida	20.00	50.00
SWJJ Josh Johnson	20.00	50.00
SWJO Josh Barfield	20.00	50.00
SWJS Johan Santana	50.00	100.00
SWJV Jason Varitek	20.00	50.00
SWJZ Joel Zumaya	30.00	60.00
SWKE Matt Kemp	20.00	50.00
SWKJ Kenji Johjima	125.00	250.00
SWLE Jon Lester	30.00	60.00
SWLO Javy Lopez	20.00	50.00
SWMC Michael Collins	20.00	50.00
SWME Michel Enriquez	10.00	25.00
SWMF Maikel Folch	20.00	50.00
SWMJ Mike Jacobs	20.00	50.00
SWMK Munenori Kawasaki	200.00	300.00
SWMN Mike Napoli	20.00	50.00
SWMO Michihiro Ogasawara	150.00	250.00
SWMP Mike Piazza	60.00	120.00
SWNI Nick Markakis	30.00	60.00
SWNM Nobuhiko Matsunaka	40.00	80.00
SWOU Osmany Urrutia	30.00	60.00
SWPA Jonathan Papelbon	10.00	25.00
SWPE Mike Pelfrey	50.00	100.00
SWPL Pedro Luis Lazo	30.00	60.00
SWRM Russell Martin	30.00	60.00
SWRN Ricky Nolasco	20.00	50.00
SWRZ Ryan Zimmerman	30.00	60.00
SWTW Tsuyoshi Wada	150.00	300.00
SWVE Justin Verlander	30.00	60.00
SWVM Victor Martinez	30.00	60.00
SWVO Vicyohandry Odelin	20.00	50.00
SWWF Jered Weaver	20.00	50.00
SWWI Josh Willingham	20.00	50.00
SWYG Yulieski Gourriel	50.00	100.00
SWYM Yunieski Maya	20.00	50.00

2006 Sweet Spot Update Veteran Signatures Red Stitch Blue Ink

OVERALL AUTO ODDS 1:6
PRINT RUNS B/WN 30-525 COPIES PER
EXCHANGE DEADLINE 12/19/09
ASTERISK = PARTIAL EXCHANGE

SSAG Tony Gwynn Jr./425	6.00	15.00
SSAH Aaron Harang/425	5.00	12.00
SSAP Albert Pujols/30	175.00	300.00
SSAZ Aramis Ramirez/225	6.00	15.00
SSBJ B.J. Upton/193	10.00	25.00
SSBR Brian Roberts/300	6.00	15.00
SSCC Carl Crawford/425	6.00	15.00
SSCU Chase Utley/425	10.00	25.00
SSDJ Derek Jeter/75	125.00	250.00
SSDW Dontrelle Willis/125	8.00	20.00
SSHS Huston Street/200	6.00	15.00
SSJB Jason Bay/425	8.00	20.00
SSJN Joe Nathan/200	6.00	15.00
SSJS Jeremy Sowers/425	6.00	15.00
SSJT Jim Thome/75	30.00	60.00
SSKG Ken Griffey Jr./50	50.00	120.00
SSKG Ken Griffey Jr./115	50.00	120.00
SSKY Kevin Youkilis/425	8.00	20.00
SSLO Lyle Overbay/525	6.00	15.00
SSMC Miguel Cabrera/525	12.00	30.00
SSMO Justin Morneau/425	10.00	25.00
SSRC Roger Clemens/30	75.00	150.00
SSSD Stephen Drew/525	6.00	15.00
SSSK Scott Kazmir/522	8.00	20.00
SSSM John Smoltz/507	15.00	40.00
SSSP Scott Podsednik/247	5.00	12.00
SSSS Mark Mulder/300	5.00	12.00
SSTH Travis Hafner/525	6.00	15.00
SSTI Tadahito Iguchi/425	4.00	10.00
SSKG2 Ken Griffey Jr./358	50.00	120.00

2006 Sweet Spot Update Veteran Signatures Red-Blue Stitch Red Ink

*RBS: .5X TO 1.2X RED STITCH AU
OVERALL AUTO ODDS 1:6
PRINT RUNS B/WN 5-299 COPIES PER
NO PRICING ON QTY OF 25 OR LESS
EXCHANGE DEADLINE 12/19/09
ASTERISK = PARTIAL EXCHANGE

SSKG Ken Griffey Jr./38	50.00	100.00
SSMC Miguel Cabrera/299	30.00	60.00
SSKG2 Ken Griffey Jr./37	50.00	100.00

2006 Sweet Spot Update Veteran Signatures Bat Barrel Black Ink

COMMON CARD	12.50	30.00
OVERALL AUTO ODDS 1:6		
PRINT RUNS B/WN 10-35 COPIES PER		
NO PRICING ON QTY OF 25 OR LESS		
EXCHANGE DEADLINE 12/19/09		
SSAG Tony Gwynn Jr./35	12.50	30.00
SSAH Aaron Harang/35	12.50	30.00
SSAZ Aramis Ramirez/35	12.50	30.00
SSBJ B.J. Upton/35	10.00	25.00
SSBR Brian Roberts/35	12.50	30.00
SSCC Carl Crawford/35	12.50	30.00
SSCU Chase Utley/35	20.00	50.00
SSHS Huston Street/35	12.50	30.00
SSJB Jason Bay/35	12.50	30.00
SSJN Joe Nathan/35	12.50	30.00
SSJS Jeremy Sowers/35	12.50	30.00
SSKG Ken Griffey Jr./28	75.00	150.00
SSKY Kevin Youkilis/35	20.00	50.00
SSLO Lyle Overbay/35	12.50	30.00
SSMC Miguel Cabrera/35	25.00	60.00
SSMO Justin Morneau/35	12.50	30.00
SSSD Stephen Drew/35	30.00	60.00
SSSK Scott Kazmir/33	12.50	30.00
SSSM John Smoltz/35	20.00	50.00
SSSP Scott Podsednik/35	12.50	30.00
SSSS Mark Mulder/35	12.50	30.00
SSTH Travis Hafner/35	20.00	50.00
SSTI Tadahito Iguchi/35	30.00	60.00
SSVM Victor Martinez/35	12.50	30.00

1948 Swell Sport Thrills

The cards in this 20-card set measure approximately 2 7/16" by 3". The 1948 Swell Gum Sports Thrills set of black and white, numbered cards highlights events from baseball history. The cards have picture framed borders with the title "Sports Thrills Highlights in the World of Sport" on the front. The backs of the cards give the story of the event pictured on the front and most of the cards also promote the then recently printed "How to Pitch" book written by Bob Feller. Cards numbered 9, 11, 16, and 20 are more difficult to obtain than the other cards in this set. The catalog designation is R448. These cards were issued as one card packaged with two pieces of gum.

COMPLETE SET (20)	500.00	1000.00
1 Greatest Single Inning Athletics' 10 Run Rally	17.50	35.00
2 Amazing Record: Pete Reiser's Debut With Dodgers	12.50	25.00
3 Dramatic Debut: Jackie Robinson ROY	75.00	150.00
4 Greatest Pitcher of Them All: Walter Johnson	30.00	60.00
5 Three Strikes Not Out: Lost Third Strike Changes	12.50	25.00
6 Home Run Wins Series: Bill Dickey's Last Home Ru	20.00	40.00
7 Never Say Die Pitcher: Hal Schumacher Pitching	12.50	25.00
8 Five Strikeouts: Nationals Lose All Star Game/(	20.00	40.00
9 Greatest Catch: Al Gionfriddo's Catch	15.00	30.00
10 No Hits No Runs: Johnny VanderMeer Comes Back	15.00	30.00
11 Bases Loaded:/(Grover C.) Alexander The Great	20.00	40.00
12 Most Dramatic Homer: Babe Ruth Points	100.00	200.00
13 Winning Run: Tommy Bridges' Pitching and Goose G	12.50	25.00
14 Great Slugging: Lou Gehrig's Four Homers	60.00	120.00
15 Four Men To Stop Him: Joe DiMaggio's Bat Streak	17.50	35.00
16 Three Run Homer in Ninth: Ted Williams' Homer	100.00	200.00
17 Football Block: Johnny Lindell's Football Block	12.50	25.00
18 Home Run To Fame: PeeWee Reese's Grand Slam	20.00	40.00
19 Strikeout Record: Bob Feller Whiffs Five	20.00	40.00
20 Rifle Arm: Carl Furillo	17.50	35.00

1989 Swell Baseball Greats

The 1989 Swell Baseball Greats set contains 135 standard-size cards. The fronts have vintage color photos with beige, red and white borders. The horizontally oriented backs are white and scarlet, and feature career highlights and lifetime stats. The set was produced by Philadelphia Chewing Gum Corporation.

COMPLETE SET (135)	10.00	25.00
1 Babe Ruth	1.25	3.00
2 Ty Cobb	1.00	2.50
3 Walter Johnson	.30	.75
4 Honus Wagner	.30	.75
5 Cy Young	.30	.75
6 Joe Adcock	.02	.10
7 Jim Bunning	.08	.25
8 Orlando Cepeda	.07	.20
9 Harvey Kuenn	.02	.10
10 Jim Hunter	.08	.25
11 Johnny VanderMeer	.05	.15
12 Tony Oliva	.07	.20
13 Harvey Haddix UER/(Reverse negative)	.02	.10
14 Dick McAuliffe	.02	.10
15 Lefty Grove	.08	.25
16 Bo Belinsky	.05	.15
17 Claude Osteen	.02	.10
18 Doc Medich	.02	.10
19 Del Ennis	.02	.10
20 Rogers Hornsby	.30	.75
21 Bob Buhl	.02	.10
22 Phil Niekro	.08	.25
23 Don Zimmer	.02	.10
24 Greg Luzinski	.05	.15
25 Lou Gehrig	1.00	2.50
26 Ken Singleton	.02	.10
27 Bob Allison	.02	.10
28 Ed Kranepool	.02	.10
29 Manny Sanguillen	.02	.10
30 Luke Appling	.08	.25
31 Ralph Terry	.02	.10
32 Smoky Burgess	.02	.10
33 Gil Hodges	.08	.25
34 Harry Walker	.02	.10
35 Edd Roush	.08	.25
36 Ron Santo	.07	.20
37 Jim Perry	.02	.10
38 Jose Morales	.02	.10
39 Stan Bahnsen	.02	.10
40 Al Kaline	.30	.75
41 Mel Harder	.02	.10
42 Ralph Houk	.02	.10
43 Jack Billingham	.02	.10
44 Carl Erskine	.05	.15
45 Hoyt Wilhelm	.08	.25
46 Dick Radatz	.02	.10
47 Roy Sievers	.02	.10
48 Jim Lonborg	.02	.10
49 Bobby Richardson	.05	.15
50 Whitey Ford	.30	.75
51 Roy Face	.02	.10
52 Tom Tresh	.02	.10
53 Joe Nuxhall	.02	.10
54 Mickey Vernon	.02	.10
55 Johnny Mize	.08	.25
56 Scott McGregor	.02	.10
57 Billy Pierce	.05	.15
58 Dave Giusti	.02	.10
59 Minnie Minoso	.07	.20
60 Early Wynn	.08	.25
61 Jose Cardenal	.02	.10
62 Sam Jethroe	.05	.15
63 Sal Bando	.02	.10
64 Elrod Hendricks	.02	.10
65 Enos Slaughter	.08	.25
66 Jim Bouton	.05	.15
67 Bill Mazeroski	.07	.20
68 Tony Kubek	.05	.15
69 Joe Black	.02	.10
70 Harmon Killebrew	.08	.25
71 Sam McDowell	.02	.10
72 Bucky Dent	.02	.10
73 Virgil Trucks	.02	.10
74 Andy Pafko	.02	.10
75 Bob Feller	.30	.75
76 Tito Francona	.02	.10
77 Al Dark	.02	.10
78 Larry Dierker	.05	.15
79 Nellie Briles	.02	.10
80 Lou Boudreau	.08	.25
81 Wally Moon	.02	.10
82 Hank Bauer	.05	.15
83 Jim Piersall	.05	.15
84 Jim Grant	.02	.10
85 Richie Ashburn	.08	.25
86 Bob Friend	.02	.10
87 Ken Keltner	.02	.10
88 Jim Kaat	.05	.15
89 Dean Chance	.02	.10
90 Al Lopez	.08	.25
91 Dick Groat	.05	.15
92 Johnny Blanchard	.02	.10
93 Chuck Hinton	.02	.10
94 Clete Boyer	.05	.15
95 Steve Carlton	.30	.75
96 Tug McGraw	.05	.15
97 Mickey Lolich	.05	.15
98 Earl Weaver MG	.08	.25
99 Sal Maglie	.02	.10
100 Ted Williams	1.00	2.50
101 Allie Reynolds UER/(Photo actually Marius Russo)	.05	.15
102 Gene Woodling UER/(Photo actually Irv Noren)	.02	.10
103 Moe Drabowsky	.02	.10
104 Mickey Stanley	.02	.10
105 Jim Palmer	.30	.75
106 Bill Freehan	.05	.15
107 Bob Robertson	.02	.10
108 Walt Dropo	.02	.10
109 Jerry Koosman	.05	.15
110 Bobby Doerr	.08	.25
111 Phil Rizzuto	.30	.75
112 Don Kessinger	.02	.10
113 Milt Pappas	.02	.10
114 Herb Score	.05	.15
115 Larry Doby	.08	.25
116 Glenn Beckert	.02	.10
117 Andre Thornton	.02	.10
118 Gary Matthews	.02	.10
119 Bill Virdon	.02	.10
120 Billy Williams	.08	.25
121 Johnny Sain	.02	.10
122 Don Newcombe	.05	.15
123 Rico Petrocelli	.05	.15
124 Dick Bosman	.02	.10
125 Roberto Clemente	1.00	2.50
126 Rocky Colavito	.07	.20
127 Wilbur Wood	.02	.10
128 Duke Sims	.02	.10
129 Ken Holtzman	.02	.10
130 Casey Stengel	.08	.25
131 Bobby Shantz	.02	.10
132 Del Crandall	.02	.10
133 Bobby Thomson	.05	.15
134 Brooks Robinson	.30	.75
135 Checklist Card	.02	.10

1990 Swell Baseball Greats

The 1990 Swell Baseball Greats set is a standard-size 135-card set. The words Baseball Greats is boldly proclaimed on the top of the card. This set was issued by Swell in both complete set form and in 10-card wax packs.

COMPLETE SET (135)	8.00	20.00
1 Tom Seaver	.30	.75
2 Hank Aaron	1.00	2.50
3 Mickey Cochrane	.08	.25
4 Rod Carew	.30	.75
5 Carl Yastrzemski	.30	.75
6 Dizzy Dean	.30	.75
7 Sal Bando	.02	.10
8 Whitey Ford	.30	.75
9 Bill White	.05	.15
10 Babe Ruth	1.25	3.00
11 Robin Roberts	.08	.25
12 Warren Spahn	.08	.25
13 Billy Williams	.08	.25
14 Joe Garagiola	.05	.15
15 Ty Cobb	1.00	2.50
16 Boog Powell	.07	.20
17 Tom Tresh	.02	.10
18 Luke Appling	.08	.25
19 Tommie Agee	.02	.10
20 Roberto Clemente	1.00	2.50
21 Bobby Thomson	.05	.15
22 Charlie Keller	.02	.10
23 George Bamberger	.02	.10
24 Eddie Lopat	.05	.15
25 Lou Gehrig	1.00	2.50
26 Manny Mota	.02	.10
27 Steve Stone	.02	.10
28 Orlando Cepeda	.07	.20
29 Al Bumbry	.02	.10
30 Grover Alexander	.08	.25
31 Lou Boudreau	.08	.25
32 Herb Score	.05	.15
33 Harry Walker	.02	.10
34 Deron Johnson	.02	.10
35 Edd Roush	.08	.25
36 Carl Erskine	.05	.15
37 Ken Forsch	.02	.10
38 Sal Maglie	.02	.10
39 Al Rosen	.05	.15
40 Casey Stengel	.08	.25
41 Cesar Cedeno	.02	.10
42 Roy White	.02	.10
43 Larry Doby	.08	.25
44 Rod Kanehl	.02	.10
45 Tris Speaker	.08	.25
46 Ralph Garr	.02	.10
47 Andre Thornton	.02	.10
48 Frankie Crosetti	.05	.15
49 Dick Groat	.05	.15
50 Honus Wagner	.30	.75
51 Rogers Hornsby	.30	.75
52 Ken Brett	.02	.10
53 Lenny Randle	.02	.10
54 Enos Slaughter	.08	.25
55 Mel Ott	.08	.25
56 Rico Petrocelli	.05	.15
57 Walt Dropo	.02	.10
58 Bob Grich	.02	.10
59 Billy Herman	.08	.25
60 Bob Feller	.30	.75
61 Davey Johnson	.05	.15
62 Don Drysdale	.08	.25
63 Lary Sorensen	.02	.10
64 Ron Santo	.07	.20
65 Eddie Mathews	.08	.25
66 Gaylord Perry	.08	.25
67 Lee May	.02	.10
68 Johnnie LeMaster	.02	.10
69 Don Kessinger	.02	.10
70 Lefty Grove	.08	.25
71 Lou Brock	.08	.25
72 Don Cardwell	.02	.10
73 Harvey Haddix	.02	.10
74 Frank Torre	.02	.10
75 Walter Johnson	.30	.75
76 Don Newcombe	.05	.15
77 Marv Throneberry	.05	.15
78 Jim Northrup	.02	.10
79 Fritz Peterson	.02	.10
80 Ralph Kiner	.08	.25
81 Mickey Lolich	.05	.15
82 Donn Clendenon	.02	.10
83 Pete Vuckovich	.02	.10
84 Lefty Gomez	.08	.25
85 Monte Irvin	.08	.25
86 Rick Ferrell	.08	.25
87 Tommy Hutton	.02	.10
88 Julio Cruz	.02	.10
89 Vida Blue	.05	.15
90 Johnny Mize	.08	.25
91 Rusty Staub	.05	.15
92 Jimmy Piersall	.05	.15
93 Bill Mazeroski	.07	.20
94 Lee Lacy	.02	.10
95 Ernie Banks	.30	.75
96 Bobby Doerr	.08	.25
97 George Foster	.05	.15
98 Eric Soderholm	.02	.10
99 Johnny Vander Meer	.05	.15
100 Cy Young	.30	.75
101 Jimmie Foxx	.30	.75
102 Clete Boyer	.05	.15
103 Steve Garvey	.07	.20
104 Johnny Podres	.05	.15
105 Yogi Berra	.30	.75
106 Bill Monbouquette	.02	.10
107 Milt Pappas	.02	.10
108 Dave LaRoche	.02	.10

109 Elliott Maddox .02 .10
110 Steve Carlton .30 .75
111 Bud Harrelson .02 .10
112 Mark Littell .02 .10
113 Frank Thomas .02 .10
114 Bill Robinson .02 .10
115 Satchel Paige .60 1.50
116 John Denny .02 .10
117 Clyde King .02 .10
118 Billy Sample .02 .10
119 Rocky Colavito .07 .20
120 Bob Gibson .30 .75
121 Bert Campaneris .05 .15
122 Mark Fidrych .07 .20
123 Ed Charles .02 .10
124 Jim Lonborg .02 .10
125 Ted Williams 1.00 2.50
126 Manny Sanguillen .02 .10
127 Matt Keough .02 .10
128 Vern Ruhle .02 .10
129 Bob Skinner .02 .10
130 Joe Torre .07 .20
131 Ralph Houk .02 .10
132 Gil Hodges .08 .25
133 Ralph Branca .05 .15
134 Christy Mathewson .30 .75
135 Checklist Card .02 .10

1991 Swell Baseball Greats

This set marks the third year Philadelphia Chewing Gum (using the Swell trade name) issued a set honoring retired players. The front of the cards feature yellow and red borders framing the full-color photo of the player(where full color was available) The cards were issued with cooperation from Impel Marketing. This 150-card standard-size set is sequenced in alphabetical orders within several seperate categories.

COMPLETE SET (150) 5.00 12.00
1 Tommie Agee .02 .10
2 Matty Alou .02 .10
3 Luke Appling .08 .25
4 Richie Ashburn .08 .25
5 Ernie Banks .30 .75
6 Don Baylor .07 .20
7 Buddy Bell .05 .15
8 Yogi Berra .30 .75
9 Joe Black .05 .15
10 Vida Blue .05 .15
11 Bobby Bonds .05 .15
12 Lou Boudreau .08 .25
13 Lou Brock .08 .25
14 Ralph Branca .05 .15
15 Bobby Brown .05 .15
16 Lou Burdette .05 .15
17 Steve Carlton .30 .75
18 Rico Carty .05 .15
19 Jerry Coleman .05 .15
20 Frankie Crosetti .05 .15
21 Julio Cruz .02 .10
22 Alvin Dark .05 .15
23 Doug DeCinces .02 .10
24 Larry Doby .08 .25
25 Bobby Doerr .08 .25
26 Don Drysdale .08 .25
27 Carl Erskine .05 .15
28 Roy Face .02 .10
29 Rick Ferrell .08 .25
30 Rollie Fingers .08 .25
31 Joe Garagiola .05 .15
32 Steve Garvey .07 .20
33 Bob Gibson .30 .75
34 Mudcat Grant .02 .10
35 Dick Groat .05 .15
36 Jerry Grote .02 .10
37 Toby Harrah .02 .10
38 Bud Harrelson .02 .10
39 Billy Herman .08 .25
40 Ken Holtzman .02 .10
41 Willie Horton .02 .10
42 Ralph Houk .02 .10
43 Al Hrabosky .02 .10
44 Monte Irvin .08 .25
45 Fergie Jenkins .08 .25
46 Davey Johnson .05 .15
47 George Kell .08 .25
48 Charlie Keller .02 .10
49 Harmon Killebrew .08 .25
50 Ralph Kiner .08 .25
51 Clyde King .02 .10
52 Dave Kingman .05 .15
53 Al Kaline .30 .75
54 Clem Labine .02 .10
55 Vern Law .02 .10
56 Mickey Lolich .05 .15
57 Jim Lonborg .02 .10
58 Eddie Lopat .05 .15
59 Sal Maglie .02 .10
60 Bill Mazeroski .07 .20
61 Johnny VanderMeer .05 .15
62 Johnny Mize .08 .25
63 Manny Mota .02 .10
64 Wally Moon .02 .10
65 Rick Monday .02 .10
66 Tom Tresh .02 .10
67 Graig Nettles .07 .20
68 Don Newcombe .05 .15
69 Milt Pappas .02 .10
70 Gaylord Perry .08 .25
71 Rico Petrocelli .05 .15
72 Jimmy Piersall .05 .15
73 Johnny Podres .05 .15
74 Boog Powell .07 .20
75 Bobby Richardson .05 .15
76 Vern Ruhle .02 .10
77 Robin Roberts .08 .25
78 Al Rosen .05 .15
79 Billy Sample .02 .10
80 Manny Sanguillen .02 .10
81 Ron Santo .07 .20
82 Herb Score .05 .15
83 Bobby Shantz .02 .10
84 Enos Slaughter .08 .25
85 Eric Soderholm .02 .10
86 Warren Spahn .08 .25
87 Rusty Staub .05 .15
88 Bobby Thomson .05 .15
89 Marv Throneberry .05 .15
90 Luis Tiant .05 .15
91 Frank Torre .02 .10
92 Joe Torre .07 .20
93 Bill Virdon .02 .10
94 Harry Walker MG .02 .10
95 Earl Weaver .08 .25
96 Bill White .05 .15
97 Roy White .02 .10
98 Billy Williams .08 .25
99 Dick Williams .02 .10
100 Ted Williams 1.00 2.50
101 Gene Woodling .02 .10
102 Hank Aaron 1.00 2.50
103 Rod Carew .30 .75
104 Cesar Cedeno .02 .10
105 Orlando Cepeda .07 .20
106 Willie Mays 1.00 2.50
107 Tom Seaver .30 .75
108 Carl Yastrzemski .30 .75
109 Clete Boyer .05 .15
110 Bert Campaneris .05 .15
111 Walt Dropo .02 .10
112 George Foster .05 .15
113 Phil Garner .02 .10
114 Harvey Haddix .02 .10
115 Don Kessinger .02 .10
116 Rocky Colavito .07 .20
117 Bobby Murcer .05 .15
118 Mel Parnell .02 .10
119 Ken Reitz .02 .10
120 Earl Wilson .02 .10
121 Wilbur Wood .02 .10
122 Ed Yost .02 .10
123 Jim Bouton .05 .15
124 Babe Ruth 1.25 3.00
125 Lou Gehrig 1.00 2.50
126 Honus Wagner .30 .75
127 Ty Cobb 1.00 2.50
128 Grover C. Alexander .30 .75
129 Lefty Gomez .08 .25
130 Walter Johnson .30 .75
131 Gil Hodges .08 .25
132 Roberto Clemente 1.00 2.50
133 Satchel Paige .60 1.50
134 Edd Roush .08 .25
135 Cy Young .30 .75
136 Casey Stengel .08 .25
137 Rogers Hornsby .30 .75
138 Dizzy Dean .30 .75
139 Lefty Grove .08 .25
140 Tris Speaker .08 .25
141 Christy Mathewson .30 .75
142 Mickey Cochrane .08 .25
143 Jimmie Foxx .30 .75
144 Mel Ott .08 .25
145 Bob Feller .30 .75
146 Brooks Robinson .30 .75
147 Eddie Mathews .08 .25
148 Pie Traynor .08 .25
149 Thurman Munson .07 .20
150 Checklist Card .02 .10

1957 Swift Meats

The cards in this 18-card set measure approximately 3 1/2" by 4". These full color, numbered cards issued in 1957 by the Swift Company are die-cut and have rounded corners. Each card consists of several pieces which can be punched out and assembled to form a stand-up model of the player. The cards and a game board were available directly from the company. The company-direct set consisted of three panels each containing six cards; sets found in this "uncut" state carry a value 25 percent higher than the values listed below. The catalog designation for this set is F162. Rocky Colavito appears in his Rookie Card year.

COMPLETE SET (18) 750.00 1500.00
1 John Podres 30.00 60.00
2 Gus Triandos 25.00 50.00
3 Dale Long 25.00 50.00
4 Billy Pierce 30.00 60.00
5 Ed Bailey 25.00 50.00
6 Vic Wertz 25.00 50.00
7 Nelson Fox 75.00 150.00
8 Ken Boyer 40.00 80.00
9 Gil McDougald 30.00 60.00
10 Junior Gilliam 30.00 60.00
11 Eddie Yost 25.00 50.00
12 Johnny Logan 25.00 50.00
13 Hank Aaron 200.00 400.00
14 Bill Tuttle 25.00 50.00
15 Jackie Jensen 40.00 80.00
16 Frank Robinson 250.00
17 Richie Ashburn 75.00 150.00
18 Rocky Colavito 60.00 120.00

1988 T/M Umpires

This set of 64 standard-size color cards was distributed as a small boxed set featuring Major League umpires exclusively. The box itself is blank, white, and silver. The set was produced by T and M Sports under licenses from Major League Baseball and the Major League Umpires Association. Card backs are printed in black on light blue. All the cards are black bordered, but the American Leaguers have a red thin inner border, whereas the National Leaguers have a green thin inner border. A short biographical sketch is given on the back for each umpire. The cards are numbered on the back; the number on the front of each card refers to the umpire's uniform number.

COMP. FACT SET (64) 4.00 10.00
1 Doug Harvey .25 .60
2 Lee Weyer .08 .25
3 Billy Williams .08 .25
4 John Kibler .08 .25
5 Bob Engel .25 .60
6 Harry Wendelstedt .15 .40
7 Larry Barnett .08 .25
8 Don Denkinger .15 .40
9 Dave Phillips .15 .40
10 Larry McCoy .08 .25
11 Bruce Froemming .15 .40
12 John McSherry .30 .75
13 Jim Evans .08 .25
14 Frank Pulli .08 .25
15 Joe Brinkman .08 .25
16 Terry Tata .08 .25
17 Paul Runge .08 .25
18 Dutch Rennert .08 .25
19 Nick Bremigan .08 .25
20 Jim McKean .08 .25
21 Terry Cooney .08 .25
22 Rich Garcia .08 .25
23 Dale Ford .08 .25
24 Al Clark .08 .25
25 Greg Kosc .08 .25
26 Jim Quick .08 .25
27 Ed Montague .08 .25
28 Jerry Crawford .08 .25
29 Steve Palermo .30 .75
30 Durwood Merrill .15 .40
31 Ken Kaiser .15 .40
32 Vic Voltaggio .08 .25
33 Mike Reilly .08 .25
34 Eric Gregg .25 .60
35 Ted Hendry .08 .25
36 Joe West .08 .25
37 Dave Pallone .15 .40
38 Fred Brocklander .08 .25
39 John Shulock .08 .25
40 Derryl Cousins .08 .25
41 Charlie Williams .08 .25
42 Rocky Roe .08 .25
43 Randy Marsh .08 .25
44 Bob Davidson .08 .25
45 Drew Coble .08 .25
46 Tim McClelland .08 .25
47 Dan Morrison .08 .25
48 Rick Reed .08 .25
49 Steve Rippley .08 .25
50 John Hirschbeck .25 .60
51 Mark Johnson .08 .25
52 Gerry Davis .08 .25
53 Dana DeMuth .08 .25
54 Larry Young .08 .25
55 Tim Welke .08 .25
56 Greg Bonin .08 .25
57 Tom Hallion .08 .25
58 Dale Scott .08 .25
59 Tim Tschida .08 .25
60 Dick Stello MEM .08 .25
61 All-Star Game .08 .25
62 World Series .08 .25
63 Jocko Conlan HOF .30 .75
64 Checklist Card .08 .25

1989 T/M Umpires

The 1989 Umpires set contains 63 standard-size cards. The fronts have borderless color photos with AL or NL logos. The backs are grey and include biographical information. The cards were distributed as a boxed set along with a custom album.

COMP. FACT SET (63) 3.00 8.00
1 Doug Harvey .25 .60
2 John Kibler .08 .25
3 Bob Engel .25 .60
4 Harry Wendelstedt .15 .40
5 Larry Barnett .08 .25
6 Don Denkinger .15 .40
7 Dave Phillips .15 .40
8 Larry McCoy .08 .25
9 Bruce Froemming .15 .40
10 John McSherry .30 .75
11 Jim Evans .08 .25
12 Frank Pulli .08 .25
13 Joe Brinkman .08 .25
14 Terry Tata .08 .25
15 Nick Bremigan .08 .25
16 Jim McKean .08 .25
17 Paul Runge .08 .25
18 Dutch Rennert .08 .25
19 Terry Cooney .08 .25
20 Rich Garcia .08 .25
21 Dale Ford .08 .25
22 Al Clark .08 .25
23 Greg Kosc .08 .25
24 Jim Quick .08 .25
25 Eddie Montague .08 .25
26 Jerry Crawford .08 .25
27 Steve Palermo .30 .75
28 Durwood Merrill .15 .40
29 Ken Kaiser .15 .40
30 Vic Voltaggio .08 .25
31 Mike Reilly .08 .25
32 Eric Gregg .25 .60
33 Ted Hendry .08 .25
34 Joe West .08 .25
35 Dave Pallone .15 .40
36 Fred Brocklander .08 .25
37 John Shulock .08 .25
38 Derryl Cousins .08 .25
39 Charlie Williams .08 .25
40 Rocky Roe .08 .25
41 Randy Marsh .08 .25
42 Bob Davidson .08 .25
43 Drew Coble .08 .25
44 Tim McClelland .08 .25
45 Dan Morrison .08 .25
46 Rick Reed .08 .25
47 Steve Rippley .08 .25
48 John Hirschbeck .25 .60
49 Mark Johnson .08 .25
50 Gerry Davis .08 .25
51 Dana DeMuth .08 .25
52 Larry Young .08 .25
53 Tim Welke .08 .25
54 Greg Bonin .08 .25
55 Tom Hallion .08 .25
56 Dale Scott .08 .25
57 Tim Tschida .08 .25
58 Gary Darling .08 .25
59 Mark Hirschbeck .08 .25
60 All Star Game .08 .25
Randy Marsh
Terry Tata
Frank Pull
61 World Series .08 .25
62 Lee Weyer .08 .25
63 Tommy Connolly and .30 .75
Bill Klem

1989-90 T/M Senior League

The 1989-90 T/M Senior League set contains 120 standard-size cards depicting members of the Senior League. The fronts are borderless, with full color photos and black bands at the bottom with player names and positions. The vertically oriented backs are gray and red, and show career major league totals and highlights. The cards were distributed as a boxed set with a checklist card and eight card-sized puzzle pieces. The set ordering is essentially alphabetical according to the player's name.

COMP. FACT SET (121) 4.00 10.00
1 Curt Flood COMM .08 .25
2 Willie Aikens .01 .05
3 Gary Allenson .01 .05
4 Stan Bahnsen .01 .05
5 Alan Bannister .01 .05
6 Juan Beniquez .01 .05
7 Jim Bibby .01 .05
8 Paul Blair .01 .05
9 Vida Blue .02 .10
10 Bobby Bonds .08 .25
11 Pedro Borbon .01 .05
12 Clete Boyer .02 .10
13 Gates Brown .01 .05
14 Al Bumbry .01 .05
15 Sal Butera .01 .05
16 Bert Campaneris .02 .10
17 Bill Campbell .01 .05
18 Bernie Carbo .01 .05
19 Dave Cash .01 .05
20 Cesar Cedeno .02 .10
21 Gene Clines .01 .05
22 Dave Collins .01 .05
23 Cecil Cooper .02 .10
24 Doug Corbett .01 .05
25 Al Cowens .01 .05
26 Jose Cruz .02 .10
27 Mike Cuellar .02 .10
28 Pat Dobson .01 .05
29 Dick Drago .01 .05
30 Dan Driessen .01 .05
31 Jamie Easterly .01 .05
32 Juan Eichelberger .01 .05
33 Dock Ellis .01 .05
34 Ed Figueroa .01 .05
35 Rollie Fingers .20 .50
36 George Foster .08 .25
37 Oscar Gamble .02 .10
38 Wayne Garland .01 .05
39 Wayne Garrett .01 .05
40 Ross Grimsley .01 .05
41 Jerry Grote .02 .10
42 Johnny Grubb .01 .05
43 Mario Guerrero .01 .05
44 Toby Harrah .02 .10
45 Steve Henderson .01 .05
46 George Hendrick .02 .10
47 Butch Hobson .01 .05
48 Roy Howell .01 .05
49 Al Hrabosky .02 .10
50 Clint Hurdle .02 .10
51 Garth Iorg .01 .05
52 Tim Ireland .01 .05
53 Grant Jackson .01 .05
54 Ron Jackson .01 .05
55 Ferguson Jenkins .20 .50
56 Odell Jones .01 .05
57 Mike Kekich .01 .05
58 Steve Kemp .01 .05
59 Dave Kingman .08 .25
60 Bruce Kison .01 .05
61 Lee Lacy .01 .05
62 Rafael Landestoy .01 .05
63 Ken Landreaux .01 .05
64 Tito Landrum .01 .05
65 Dave LaRoche .01 .05
66 Bill Lee .02 .10
67 Ron LeFlore .02 .10
68 Dennis Leonard .01 .05
69 Bill Madlock .05 .15
70 Mickey Mahler .01 .05
71 Rich Manning .01 .05
72 Tippy Martinez .01 .05
73 Jon Matlack .01 .05
74 Bake McBride .01 .05
75 Steve McCatty .01 .05
76 Hal McRae .02 .10
77 Dan Meyer .01 .05
78 Felix Millan .01 .05
79 Paul Mirabella .01 .05
80 Omar Moreno .01 .05
81 Jim Morrison .01 .05
82 Graig Nettles .05 .15
83 Al Oliver .05 .15
84 Amos Otis .02 .10
85 Tom Paciorek .01 .05
86 Lowell Palmer .01 .05
87 Pat Putnam .01 .05
88 Lenny Randle .01 .05
89 Ken Reitz .01 .05
90 Gene Richards .01 .05
91 Mickey Rivers .02 .10
92 Leon Roberts .01 .05
93 Joe Sambito .01 .05
94 Rodney Scott .01 .05
95 Bob Shirley .01 .05
96 Jim Slaton .01 .05
97 Elias Sosa .01 .05
98 Fred Stanley .01 .05
99 Bill Stein .01 .05
100 Rennie Stennett .01 .05
101 Sammy Stewart .01 .05
102 Tim Stoddard .01 .05
103 Champ Summers .01 .05
104 Derrel Thomas .01 .05
105 Luis Tiant .05 .15
106 Bobby Tolan MG .01 .05
107 Bill Travers .01 .05
108 Tom Underwood .01 .05
109 Rick Waits .01 .05
110 Ron Washington .01 .05
111 U.L. Washington .01 .05
112 Earl Weaver MG .20 .50
113 Jerry White .01 .05
114 Milt Wilcox .01 .05
115 Dick Williams MG .02 .10
116 Walt Williams .01 .05
117 Rick Wise .01 .05
118 Favorite Suns .02 .10
Luis Tiant
Cesar Cedeno
119 Home Run Legends .08 .25
George Foster
Bobby Bonds
120 Sunshine Skippers .05 .15
Earl Weaver
Dick Williams
NNO Checklist 1-120 .01 .05

1990 T/M Umpires

The 1990 T/M Umpires set is a standard-size set which features a picture of each umpire on the front of the card with a baseball rules question on the back of the card. The set was issued as a boxed set as well as in packs.

COMP. FACT SET (70) 3.00 8.00
1 Doug Harvey .15 .40
2 John Kibler .07 .20
3 Bob Engel .15 .40
4 Harry Wendelstedt .10 .30
5 Larry Barnett .07 .20
6 Don Denkinger .10 .30
7 Dave Phillips .10 .30
8 Larry McCoy .07 .20
9 Bruce Froemming .10 .30
10 John McSherry .20 .50
11 Jim Evans .07 .20
12 Frank Pulli .07 .20
13 Joe Brinkman .07 .20
14 Terry Tata .07 .20
15 Jim McKean .07 .20
16 Dutch Rennert .07 .20
17 Paul Runge .07 .20
18 Terry Cooney .07 .20
19 Rich Garcia .07 .20
20 Dale Ford .07 .20
21 Al Clark .07 .20
22 Greg Kosc .07 .20
23 Jim Quick .07 .20
24 Eddie Montague .07 .20
25 Jerry Crawford .07 .20
26 Steve Palermo .20 .50
27 Durwood Merrill .10 .30
28 Ken Kaiser .10 .30
29 Vic Voltaggio .07 .20
30 Mike Reilly .07 .20
31 Eric Gregg .15 .40
32 Ted Hendry .07 .20
33 Joe West .07 .20
34 Fred Brocklander .07 .20
35 John Shulock .07 .20
36 Derryl Cousins .07 .20
37 Charlie Williams .07 .20
38 Rocky Roe .07 .20
39 Randy Marsh .07 .20
40 Bob Davidson .07 .20
41 Drew Coble .07 .20
42 Tim McClelland .07 .20
43 Dan Morrison .07 .20
44 Rick Reed .07 .20
45 Steve Rippley .07 .20
46 John Hirschbeck .15 .40
47 Mark Johnson .07 .20
48 Gerry Davis .07 .20
49 Dana DeMuth .07 .20
50 Larry Young .07 .20
51 Tim Welke .07 .20
52 Greg Bonin .07 .20
53 Tom Hallion .07 .20
54 Dale Scott .07 .20
55 Tim Tschida .07 .20
56 Gary Darling .07 .20
57 Mark Hirschbeck .07 .20
58 Jerry Layne .07 .20
59 Jim Joyce .07 .20
60 Bill Hohn .07 .20
61 All-Star Game .07 .20
62 World Series .07 .20
63 Nick Bremigan .07 .20
64 The Runges .10 .30
65 Bart Giamatti MEM .20 .50
66 Puzzle Piece 1 .07 .20
67 Puzzle Piece 2 .07 .20
68 Puzzle Piece 3 .07 .20
69 Puzzle Piece 4 .07 .20
70 Checklist Card .07 .20
71 Al Barlick HOF .20 .50

1911 T205 Gold Border

The cards in this 218-card set measure approximately 1 1/2" by 2 5/8". The T205 set (catalog designation), also known as the "Gold Border" set, was issued in 1911 in packages of the following cigarette brands: American Beauty, Broadleaf, Cycle, Drum, Hassan, Honest Long Cut, Piedmont, Polar Bear, Sovereign and Sweet Caporal. All the above were products of the American Tobacco Company, and the ads for the various brands appear below the biographical section on the back of each card. There are pose variations noted in the checklist (which is alphabetized and numbered for reference) and there are 12 minor league cards of a more ornate design which are somewhat scarce. The numbers below correspond to alphabetical order within category, i.e., major leaguers and minor leaguers are alphabetized separately. The gold borders of T205 cards chip easily and they are hard to find in "Mint" or even "Near Mint" condition, due to this there is a high premium on these high condition cards. Listed pricing for raw cards references "EX" condition.

COMPLETE SET (218) 15000.00 40000.00
COMMON MAJOR (1-186) 90.00 150.00
COM. MINOR (187-198) 150.00 300.00
1 Ed Abbaticchio 60.00 100.00
2 Merle (Doc) Adkins 125.00 200.00
3 Red Ames 60.00 100.00
4 Jimmy Archer 60.00 100.00
5 Jimmy Austin 60.00 100.00
6 Bill Bailey 60.00 100.00
7 Frank Baker 175.00 300.00
8 Neal Ball 60.00 100.00
9 Cy Barger Full B 60.00 100.00
10 Cy Barger Part B 250.00 400.00
11 Jack Barry 60.00 100.00
12 Emil Batch 125.00 200.00
13 Johnny Bates 60.00 100.00
14 Fred Beck 60.00 100.00
15 Beals Becker 60.00 100.00
16 George Bell 60.00 100.00
17 Chief Bender 175.00 300.00
18 Bill Bergen 60.00 100.00
19 Bob Bescher 60.00 100.00
20 Joe Birmingham 60.00 100.00
21 Russ Blackburne 60.00 100.00
22 Kitty Bransfield 60.00 100.00
23 R.Bresnahan Closed 175.00 300.00
24 R.Bresnahan Open 300.00 500.00
25 Al Bridwell 60.00 100.00
26 Mordecai Brown 175.00 300.00
27 Bobby Byrne 60.00 100.00
28 Hick Cady 150.00 250.00
29 Howie Camnitz 60.00 100.00
30 Bill Carrigan 60.00 100.00
31 Frank Chance 175.00 300.00
32A Hal Chase Both - Ends 125.00 200.00
32B Hal Chase Both - Extends 125.00 200.00
33 Hal Chase Left Ear 300.00 500.00
34 Eddie Cicotte 250.00 400.00
35 Fred Clarke 150.00 250.00
36 Ty Cobb 2500.00 4000.00
37 E.Collins Mouth Closed 175.00 300.00
38 E.Collins Mouth Open 350.00 600.00
39 Jimmy Collins 250.00 400.00
40 Frank Corridon 60.00 100.00
41A Otis Crandall (Otis) 150.00 250.00
41B Otis Crandall (Olis) 90.00 150.00
42 Lou Criger 60.00 100.00
43 Bill Dahlen 250.00 400.00
44 Jake Daubert 60.00 100.00
45 Jim Delahanty 60.00 100.00
46 Art Devlin 60.00 100.00
47 Josh Devore 60.00 100.00
48 Walt Dickson 60.00 100.00
49 Jiggs Donohue 250.00 400.00
50 Red Dooin 60.00 100.00
51 Mickey Doolan 60.00 100.00
52A Patsy Dougherty Red 150.00 250.00
52B Patsy Dougherty White 150.00 250.00
53 Tom Downey 60.00 100.00
54 Larry Doyle 60.00 100.00
55 Hugh Duffy 175.00 300.00
56 Jack Dunn 175.00 300.00
57 Jimmy Dygert 60.00 100.00
58 Dick Egan 60.00 100.00
59 Kid Elberfeld 60.00 100.00
60 Clyde Engle 60.00 100.00
61 Steve Evans 60.00 100.00
62 Johnny Evers 300.00 500.00
63 Bob Ewing 60.00 100.00
64 George Ferguson 60.00 100.00
65 Ray Fisher 175.00 300.00
66 Art Fletcher 60.00 100.00
67 John Flynn 60.00 100.00
68 Russ Ford Dark Cap 60.00 100.00
69 Russ Ford Light Cap 250.00 400.00
70 Bill Foxen 60.00 100.00
71 James Frick 150.00 250.00
72 Art Fromme 60.00 100.00
73 Earl Gardner 60.00 100.00
74 Harry Gaspar 60.00 100.00
75 George Gibson 60.00 100.00
76 Wilbur Good 60.00 100.00
77 P.Graham Cubs 250.00 400.00
78 P.Graham Rustlers 60.00 100.00
79 Eddie Grant 250.00 400.00
80A Dolly Gray w/o Stats 150.00 250.00
80B Dolly Gray w/Stats 600.00 1000.00
81 Clark Griffith 175.00 300.00
82 Bob Groom 60.00 100.00
83 Charles Hanford 150.00 250.00
84 Robert Harmon 60.00 100.00
Both ears
85 Robert Harmon 250.00 400.00
Left ear only
86 Topsy Hartsel 60.00 100.00
87 Arnold Hauser 60.00 100.00
88 Charlie Hemphill 60.00 100.00
89 Buck Herzog 60.00 100.00
90A D.Hoblitzell No Stats 7000.00 12000.00
90B D.Hoblitzell w/CIN 90.00 150.00
90C D.Hoblitzell (Hoblitzel) 350.00 600.00
90D D.Hoblitzell w/o CIN 350.00 600.00
91 Danny Hoffman 60.00 100.00
92 Miller Huggins 175.00 300.00
93 John Hummell 60.00 100.00
94 Fred Jacklitsch 60.00 100.00
95 Hughie Jennings MG 175.00 300.00
96 Walter Johnson 1000.00 1800.00
97 Davy Jones 60.00 100.00
98 Tom Jones 60.00 100.00
99 Addie Joss 900.00 1500.00
100 Ed Karger 250.00 400.00
101 Ed Killian 60.00 100.00
102 Red Kleinow 250.00 400.00
103 John Kling 60.00 100.00
104 John Knight 60.00 100.00
105 Ed Konetchy 60.00 100.00
106 Harry Krause 60.00 100.00
107 Rube Kroh 60.00 100.00
108 Frank Lang 60.00 100.00
109 Frank LaPorte 60.00 100.00
110A Arlie Latham (A.) 125.00 200.00
110B Arlie Latham (W.A.) 250.00 400.00
111 Tommy Leach 60.00 100.00
112 Wyatt Lee 90.00 150.00
113 Sam Leever 60.00 100.00
114A Lefty Leifield (A.) 150.00 250.00
114B Lefty Leifield (A.P.) 250.00 400.00
115 Ed Lennox 60.00 100.00
116 Paddy Livingston 60.00 100.00
117 Hans Lobert 60.00 100.00
118 Bris Lord 60.00 100.00
119 Harry Lord 60.00 100.00
120 John Lush 60.00 100.00
121 Nick Maddox 60.00 100.00
122 Sherry Magee 60.00 100.00
123 Rube Marquard 175.00 300.00
124 Christy Mathewson 1000.00 1800.00
125 Al Mattern 60.00 100.00
126 Lewis McAllister 90.00 150.00
127 George McBride 60.00 100.00
128 Amby McConnell 60.00 100.00
129 Pryor McElveen 60.00 100.00
130 John McGraw MG 175.00 300.00
131 Harry McIntire 60.00 100.00
132 Matty McIntyre 60.00 100.00
133 Larry McLean 60.00 100.00
134 Fred Merkle 60.00 100.00
135 George Merritt 150.00 250.00
136 Chief Meyers 60.00 100.00
137 Clyde Milan 60.00 100.00
138 Dots Miller 60.00 100.00
139 Mike Mitchell 60.00 100.00
140A Pat Moran Extra Stat 900.00 1500.00
140B Pat Moran 60.00 100.00
141 George Moriarity 60.00 100.00
142 George Mullin 60.00 100.00
143 Danny Murphy 60.00 100.00
144 Red Murray 60.00 100.00
145 John Nee 150.00 250.00
146 Tom Needham 60.00 100.00
147 Rebel Oakes 60.00 100.00
148 Rube Oldring 60.00 100.00
149 Charley O'Leary 60.00 100.00
150 Fred Olmstead 60.00 100.00
151 Orval Overall 60.00 100.00
152 Freddy Parent 60.00 100.00
153 Dode Paskert 60.00 100.00
154 Fred Payne 60.00 100.00
155 Barney Pelty 60.00 100.00
156 Jack Pfiester 60.00 100.00
157 James Phelan 150.00 250.00
158 Ed Phelps 60.00 100.00
159 Decon Phillippe 60.00 100.00
160 Jack Quinn 60.00 100.00
161 Bugs Raymond 250.00 400.00
162 Ed Reulbach 60.00 100.00
163 Lewis Richie 60.00 100.00
164 Jack Rowan 175.00 300.00
165 Nap Rucker 60.00 100.00
166 Doc Scanlan 250.00 400.00
167 Germany Schaefer 60.00 100.00
168 Admiral Schlei 60.00 100.00
169 Boss Schmidt 60.00 100.00
170 Wildfire Schulte 60.00 100.00
171 Jim Scott 60.00 100.00
172 Bayard Sharpe 60.00 100.00
173 David Shean 175.00 300.00
Chicago Cubs
174 David Shean 60.00 100.00
Boston Rustlers
175 Jimmy Sheckard 60.00 100.00
176 Hack Simmons 60.00 100.00
177 Tony Smith 60.00 100.00
178 Fred Snodgrass 60.00 100.00
179 Tris Speaker 500.00 800.00
180 Jake Stahl 60.00 100.00
181 Oscar Stanage 60.00 100.00
182 Harry Steinfeldt 60.00 100.00
183 George Stone 60.00 100.00
184 George Stovall 60.00 100.00
185 Gabby Street 60.00 100.00
186 George Suggs 250.00 400.00
187 Ed Summers 60.00 100.00
188 Jeff Sweeney 250.00 400.00
189 Lee Tannehill 60.00 100.00
190 Ira Thomas 60.00 100.00
191 Joe Tinker 175.00 300.00
192 John Titus 60.00 100.00
193 Terry Turner 250.00 400.00
194 Hippo Vaughn 300.00 500.00
195 Heinie Wagner 175.00 300.00
196 B.Wallace w/cap 150.00 250.00
197A B.Wallace w/o Cap 1 Line 1200.00 2000.00
197B B.Wallace w/o Cap 2 Lines 700.00 1200.00
198 Ed Walsh 500.00 800.00
199 Zach Wheat 175.00 300.00
200 Doc White 60.00 100.00
201 Kirby White 250.00 400.00
202A Irvin K. Wilhelm 350.00 600.00
202B Irvin K. Wilhelm Missing Letter 175.00 300.00
203 Ed Willett 60.00 100.00
204 Owen Wilson 60.00 100.00
205 H.Wiltse Both Ears 60.00 100.00
206 H.Wiltse Right Ear 250.00 400.00
207 Harry Wolter 60.00 100.00
208 Cy Young 1000.00 1800.00

1909-11 T206

The T206 set was and is the most popular of all the tobacco issues. The set was issued from 1909 to 1911 with sixteen different brands of cigarettes: American Beauty, Broadleaf, Cycle, Carolina Brights, Drum, El Principe de Gales, Hindu, Lenox, Old Mill, Piedmont, Polar Bear, Sovereign, Sweet Caporal, Tolstoi, and Uzit. There was also an extremely rare Ty Cobb back version for the Ty Cobb Red Portrait that it's believed was issued as a promotional card. Pricing for the Cobb back card is unavailable and it's typically not considered part of the complete 524-card set. The minor league cards are supposedly slightly more difficult to obtain than the cards of the major leaguers, with the Southern League player cards being definitively more difficult. Minor League players were obtained from the American Association and the Eastern league. Southern League players were obtained from a variety of leagues including the following: South

Atlantic League, Southern League, Texas League, and Virginia League. Series 150 (notated as such on the card backs) was issued between February 1909 thru the end of May, 1909. Series 350 was issued from the end of May, 1909 thru April, 1910. The last series 350 to 460 was issued in late December 1910 through early 1911. The set price below does not include ultra-expensive Wagner, Plank, Magie error, or Doyle variation. The Wagner card is one of the most sought after cards in the hobby. This card was pulled from circulation almost immediately after being issued. Estimates of how many Wagners are in existence generally settle on around 50 to 60 copies. The backs vary in scarcity as follows: Exceedingly Rare: Ty Cobb; Rare: Drum, Uzit, Lenox, Broadleaf 460 and Hindu; Scarce: Broadleaf 350, Carolina brights, Hindu Red; Less Common: American Beauty, Cycle and Tolstoi; Readily Available: El Principe de Gales, Old Mill, Polar Bear and Sovereign and Common: Piedmont and Sweet Caporal. Listed prices refer to the Piedmont and Sweet caporal backs in raw "EX" condition. Of note, the O'Hara St. Louis and Demmitt St. Louis cards were only issued with Polar Bear backs and are are priced as such. Pricing is unavailable for the unbelieveably rare Joe Doyle Nat'l variation (perhaps a dozen or fewer copies exist) in addition to the Bud Shappe and Fred nodgrass printing variaitons. Finally, unlike the other cards in this set, listed raw pricing for the famed Honus Wagner references "Good" condition insetad of "EX".

COMPLETE SET (520) 30000.00 60000.00
COMMON MAJOR (1-389) 50.00 100.00
COMMON MINOR (390-475) 50.00 100.00
COM. SO. LEA. (476-523) 125.00 250.00
CARDS PRICED IN EXMT CONDITION
HONUS WAGNER PRICED IN GOOD CONDITION
1 Ed Abbaticchio Blue 85.00 135.00
2 Ed Abbaticchio Brown 85.00 135.00
3 Fred Abbott 60.00 100.00
4 Bill Abstein 60.00 100.00
5 Doc Adkins 125.00 200.00
6 Whitey Alperman 60.00 100.00
7 Red Ames Hands at 150.00 250.00
8 Red Ames Hands over 60.00 100.00
9 Red Ames Portrait 60.00 100.00
10 John Anderson 60.00 100.00
11 Frank Arellanes 60.00 100.00
12 Herman Armbruster 60.00 100.00
13 Harry Arndt 70.00 120.00
14 Jake Atz 60.00 100.00
15 Home Run Baker 250.00 400.00
16 Neal Ball Cleveland 60.00 100.00
17 Neal Ball New York 60.00 100.00
18 Jap Barbeau 60.00 100.00
19 Cy Barger 60.00 100.00
20 Jack Barry 60.00 100.00
21 Shad Barry 60.00 100.00
22 Jack Bastian 175.00 300.00
23 Emil Batch 60.00 100.00
24 Johnny Bates 60.00 100.00
25 Harry Bay 175.00 300.00
26 Ginger Beaumont 60.00 100.00
27 Fred Beck 60.00 100.00
28 Beals Becker 60.00 100.00
29 Jake Beckley 175.00 300.00
30 George Bell Follow 60.00 100.00
31 George Bell Hands above 60.00 100.00
32 Chief Bender Pitching 250.00 400.00
33 Chief Bender Pitching Trees in Back 250.00 400.00
34 Chief Bender Portrait 300.00 500.00
35 Bill Bergen Batting 60.00 100.00
36 Bill Bergen Catching 60.00 100.00
37 Heinie Berger 60.00 100.00
38 Bill Bernhard 175.00 300.00
39 Bob Bescher Hands 60.00 100.00
40 Bob Bescher Portrait 60.00 100.00
41 Joe Birmingham 90.00 150.00
42 Lena Blackburne 60.00 100.00
43 Jack Bliss 60.00 100.00
44 Frank Bowerman 60.00 100.00
45 Bill Bradley with Bat 60.00 100.00
46 Bill Bradley Portrait 60.00 100.00
47 David Brain 60.00 100.00
48 Kitty Bransfield 60.00 100.00
49 Roy Brashear 60.00 100.00
50 Ted Breitenstein 175.00 300.00
51 Roger Bresnahan Portrait 175.00 300.00
52 Roger Bresnahan with Bat 175.00 300.00
53 Al Bridwell No Cap 60.00 100.00
54 Al Bridwell with Cap 60.00 100.00
55 George Brown Chicago 125.00 200.00
56 George Brown Washington 300.00 500.00
57 Mordecai Brown Chicago 200.00 350.00
58 Mordecai Brown Cubs 350.00 600.00
59 Mordecai Brown Portrait 300.00 500.00
60 Al Burch Batting 125.00 200.00
61 Al Burch Fielding 60.00 100.00
62 Fred Burchell 60.00 100.00
63 Jimmy Burke 60.00 100.00
64 Bill Burns 60.00 100.00
65 Donie Bush 60.00 100.00
66 John Butler 60.00 100.00
67 Bobby Byrne 60.00 100.00
68 Howie Camnitz Arm at Side 60.00 100.00
69 Howie Camnitz Folded 60.00 100.00
70 Howie Camnitz Hands 60.00 100.00
71 Billy Campbell 60.00 100.00
72 Scoops Carey 175.00 300.00
73 Charley Carr 60.00 100.00
74 Bill Carrigan 60.00 100.00
75 Doc Casey 60.00 100.00
76 Peter Cassidy 60.00 100.00
77 Frank Chance Batting 250.00 400.00
78 F.Chance Portrait Red 300.00 500.00
79 F.Chance Portrait Yel 250.00 400.00
80 Bill Chappelle 60.00 100.00
81 Chappie Charles 60.00 100.00
82 Hal Chase Dark Cap 90.00 150.00
83 Hal Chase Holding Trophy 150.00 250.00
84 Hal Chase Portrait Blue 90.00 150.00
85 Hal Chase Portrait Pink 250.00 400.00
86 Hal Chase White Cap 125.00 200.00
87 Jack Chesbro 250.00 400.00
88 Ed Cicotte 175.00 300.00
89 Bill Clancy (Clancey) 60.00 100.00
90 Fred Clarke Holding Bat 250.00 400.00
91 Fred Clarke Portrait 250.00 400.00
92 Josh Clark (Clarke) ML 60.00 100.00
93 J.J. (Nig) Clarke 60.00 100.00
94 Bill Clymer 60.00 100.00
95 Ty Cobb Bat off Shoulder 1500.00 2500.00
96 Ty Cobb Bat on Shoulder 1500.00 2500.00
97 Ty Cobb Portrait Green 3500.00 5000.00
98 Ty Cobb Portrait Red 1200.00 2000.00
99 Cad Coles 175.00 300.00
100 Eddie Collins 200.00 350.00
101 Jimmy Collins 175.00 300.00
102 Bunk Congalton ML 60.00 100.00
103 Wid Conroy Fielding 60.00 100.00
104 Wid Conroy with Bat 60.00 100.00
105 Harry Covaleski (Coveleski) 60.00 100.00
106 Doc Crandall No Cap 60.00 100.00
107 Doc Crandall with Cap 60.00 100.00
108 Bill Cranston 175.00 300.00
109 Gavvy Cravath 60.00 100.00
110 Sam Crawford Throwing 250.00 400.00
111 Sam Crawford with Bat 250.00 400.00
112 Birdie Cree 60.00 100.00
113 Lou Criger 60.00 100.00
114 Dode Criss UER 60.00 100.00
115 Monte Cross 60.00 100.00
116 Bill Dahlen Boston 90.00 150.00
117 Bill Dahlen Brooklyn 300.00 500.00
118 Paul Davidson 60.00 100.00
119 George Davis 175.00 300.00
120 Harry Davis Davis on Front 60.00 100.00
121 Harry Davis H.Davis on Front 60.00 100.00
122 Frank Delehanty 60.00 100.00
123 Jim Delehanty 60.00 100.00
124 Ray Demmitt New York 70.00 120.00
125 Ray Demmitt St. Louis 6000.00 10000.00
126 Rube Dessau 85.00 135.00
127 Art Devlin 60.00 100.00
128 Josh Devore 60.00 100.00
129 Bill Dineen 60.00 100.00
130 Mike Donlin Fielding 125.00 200.00
131 Mike Donlin Sitting 60.00 100.00
132 Mike Donlin with Bat 60.00 100.00
133 Jiggs Donahue (Donohue) 60.00 100.00
134 Wild Bill Donovan Portrait 60.00 100.00
135 Wild Bill Donovan Throwing 60.00 100.00
136 Red Dooin 60.00 100.00
137 Mickey Doolan Batting 60.00 100.00
138 Mickey Doolan Fielding 60.00 100.00
139 Mickey Doolin Portrait (Doolan) 60.00 100.00
140 Gus Dorner ML 60.00 100.00
141 Gus Dorner Card Spelled Dopner on Back
142 Patsy Dougherty Arm in Air 60.00 100.00
143 Patsy Dougherty Portrait 60.00 100.00
144 Tom Downey Batting 60.00 100.00
145 Tom Downey Fielding 60.00 100.00
146 Jerry Downs 60.00 100.00
147 Joe Doyle 350.00 600.00
148 Joe Doyle Nat'l
149 Larry Doyle Portrait 60.00 100.00
150 Larry Doyle Throwing 60.00 100.00
151 Larry Doyle with Bat 60.00 100.00
152 Jean Dubuc 60.00 100.00
153 Hugh Duffy 175.00 300.00
154 Jack Dunn Baltimore 60.00 100.00
155 Joe Dunn Brooklyn 60.00 100.00
156 Bull Durham 60.00 100.00
157 Jimmy Dygert 60.00 100.00
158 Ted Easterly 60.00 100.00
159 Dick Egan 90.00 150.00
160 Kid Elberfeld Fielding 60.00 100.00
161 Kid Elberfeld Port NY 60.00 100.00
162 Kid Elberfeld Port Wash 1800.00 3000.00
163 Roy Ellam 175.00 300.00
164 Clyde Engle 60.00 100.00
165 Steve Evans 60.00 100.00
166 J.Evers Portrait 350.00 600.00
167 J.Evers Chi Shirt 250.00 400.00
168 J.Evers Cubs Shirt 500.00 800.00
169 Bob Ewing 60.00 100.00
170 Cecil Ferguson 60.00 100.00
171 Hobe Ferris 60.00 100.00
172 Lou Fiene Portrait 60.00 100.00
173 Lou Fiene Throwing 60.00 100.00
174 Steamer Flanagan 60.00 100.00
175 Art Fletcher 60.00 100.00
176 Elmer Flick 175.00 300.00
177 Russ Ford 60.00 100.00
178 Ed Foster 175.00 300.00
179 Jerry Freeman 60.00 100.00
180 John Frill 60.00 100.00
181 Charlie Fritz 175.00 300.00
182 Art Fromme 60.00 100.00
183 Chick Gandil 175.00 300.00
184 Bob Ganley 60.00 100.00
185 John Ganzel 60.00 100.00
186 Harry Gasper (Gaspar) 60.00 100.00
187 Rube Geyer 60.00 100.00
188 George Gibson 60.00 100.00
189 Billy Gilbert 60.00 100.00
190 Wilbur Goode (Good) 60.00 100.00
191 Bill Graham St. Louis 60.00 100.00
192 Peaches Graham 70.00 120.00
193 Dolly Gray 60.00 100.00
194 Ed Greminger 175.00 300.00
195 Clark Griffith Batting 175.00 300.00
196 Clark Griffith Portrait 175.00 300.00
197 Moose Grimshaw 60.00 100.00
198 Bob Groom 60.00 100.00
199 Tom Guiheen 175.00 300.00
200 Ed Hahn 60.00 100.00
201 Bob Hall 60.00 100.00
202 Bill Hallman 60.00 100.00
203 Jack Hannifan (Hannifin) 60.00 100.00
204 Bill Hart Little Rock 175.00 300.00
205 Jimmy Hart Montgomery 175.00 300.00
206 Topsy Hartsel 60.00 100.00
207 Jack Hayden 60.00 100.00
208 J.Ross Helm 175.00 300.00
209 Charlie Hemphill 60.00 100.00
210 Buck Herzog Boston 60.00 100.00
211 Buck Herzog New York 60.00 100.00
212 Gordon Hickman 175.00 300.00
213 Bill Hinchman 60.00 100.00
214 Harry Hinchman 60.00 100.00
215 Doc Hoblitzell 60.00 100.00
216 Danny Hoffman St. Louis 60.00 100.00
217 Izzy Hoffman Providence 60.00 100.00
218 Solly Hofman 60.00 100.00
219 Buck Hooker 175.00 300.00
220 Del Howard Chicago 60.00 100.00
221 Ernie Howard Savannah 175.00 300.00
222 Harry Howell Hand at Waist 60.00 100.00
223 Harry Howell Portrait 60.00 100.00
224 M.Huggins Mouth 175.00 300.00
225 M.Huggins Portrait 175.00 300.00
226 Rudy Hulswitt 60.00 100.00
227 John Hummel 60.00 100.00
228 George Hunter 60.00 100.00
229 Frank Isbell 60.00 100.00
230 Fred Jacklitsch 60.00 100.00
231 Jimmy Jackson 60.00 100.00
232 H.Jennings Both 175.00 300.00
233 H.Jennings One 175.00 300.00
234 H.Jennings Portrait 175.00 300.00
235 Walter Johnson Hands 700.00 1200.00
236 Walter Johnson Port 1000.00 1800.00
237 Davy Jones Detroit 60.00 100.00
238 Fielder Jones Hands at Hips 60.00 100.00
239 Fielder Jones Portrait 60.00 100.00
240 Tom Jones St. Louis 60.00 100.00
241 Dutch Jordan Atlanta 175.00 300.00
242 Tim Jordan Batting 60.00 100.00
243 Tim Jordan Portrait 60.00 100.00
244 Addie Joss Pitching 175.00 300.00
245 Addie Joss Portrait 250.00 400.00
246 Ed Karger 60.00 100.00
247 Willie Keeler Portrait 350.00 600.00
248 Willie Keeler Batting 350.00 600.00
249 Joe Kelley 150.00 250.00
250 J.F. Kiernan 300.00 500.00
251 Ed Killian Pitching 60.00 100.00
252 Ed Killian Portrait 60.00 100.00
253 Frank King 175.00 300.00
254 Rube Kisinger (Kissinger) 60.00 100.00
255 Red Kleinow Boston 300.00 500.00
256 Red Kleinow NY Catch 60.00 100.00
257 Red Kleinow NY Bat 60.00 100.00
258 Johnny Kling 60.00 100.00
259 Otto Knabe 60.00 100.00
260 Jack Knight Portrait 60.00 100.00
261 Jack Knight with Bat 60.00 100.00
262 Ed Konetchy Glove Lo 60.00 100.00
263 Ed Konetchy Glove Hi 60.00 100.00
264 Harry Krause Pitching 60.00 100.00
265 Harry Krause Portrait 60.00 100.00
266 Rube Kroh 60.00 100.00
267 Otto Kruger (Krueger) 60.00 100.00
268 James LaFitte 175.00 300.00
269 Nap Lajoie Portrait 500.00 800.00
270 Nap Lajoie Throwing 400.00 700.00
271 Nap Lajoie with Bat 400.00 700.00
272 Joe Lake NY 60.00 100.00
273 Joe Lake Stl No Ball 60.00 100.00
274 Joe Lake Stl with Ball 60.00 100.00
275 Frank LaPorte 60.00 100.00
276 Arlie Latham 60.00 100.00
277 Bill Lattimore 60.00 100.00
278 Jimmy Lavender 60.00 100.00
279 Tommy Leach Bending Over 60.00 100.00
280 Tommy Leach Portrait 60.00 100.00
281 Lefty Leifield Batting 60.00 100.00
282 Lefty Leifield Pitching 60.00 100.00
283 Ed Lennox 60.00 100.00
284 Harry Lentz (Sentz) SL 250.00 400.00
285 Glenn Liebhardt 60.00 100.00
286 Vive Lindaman 60.00 100.00
287 Perry Lipe 175.00 300.00
288 Paddy Livingstone (Livingston) 60.00 100.00
289 Hans Lobert 60.00 100.00
290 Harry Lord 60.00 100.00
291 Harry Lumley 60.00 100.00
292 Carl Lundgren Chicago 500.00 800.00
293 Carl Lundgren Kansas City 125.00 200.00
294 Nick Maddox 60.00 100.00
294 Sherry Magie Portrait ERR 15000.00 25000.00
295 Sherry Magee with Bat 60.00 100.00
296 Sherry Magee Portrait 150.00 250.00
298 Bill Malarkey 60.00 100.00
299 Bill Maloney 60.00 100.00
300 George Manion 175.00 300.00
301 Rube Manning Batting 60.00 100.00
302 Rube Manning Pitching 60.00 100.00
303 R.Marquard Follow 175.00 300.00
304 R.Marquard Hands 175.00 300.00
305 R.Marquard Portrait 200.00 350.00
306 Doc Marshall 60.00 100.00
307 C.Mathewson Drk Cap 700.00 1200.00
308 C.Mathewson Portrait 900.00 1500.00
309 C.Mathewson Wht Cap 900.00 1500.00
310 Al Mattern 60.00 100.00
311 John McAleese 60.00 100.00
312 George McBride 60.00 100.00
313 Pat McCauley 175.00 300.00
314 Moose McCormick 60.00 100.00
315 Pryor McElveen 60.00 100.00
316 Dennis McGann 60.00 100.00
317 Jim McGinley 60.00 100.00
318 Iron Man McGinnity 175.00 300.00
319 Stoney McGlynn 60.00 100.00
320 J.McGraw Finger 250.00 400.00
321 J.McGraw Glove-Hip 250.00 400.00
322 J.McGraw w/o Cap 250.00 400.00
323 J.McGraw w/Cap 250.00 400.00
324 Harry McIntyre Brooklyn 60.00 100.00
325 Harry McIntyre Brooklyn-Chicago 60.00 100.00
326 Matty McIntyre Detroit 60.00 100.00
327 Larry McLean 60.00 100.00
328 George McQuillan Ball in Hand 60.00 100.00
329 George McQuillan with Bat 60.00 100.00
330 Fred Merkle Portrait 70.00 120.00
331 Fred Merkle Throwing 90.00 150.00
332 George Merritt 60.00 100.00
333 Chief Meyers 60.00 100.00
334 Chief Myers Batting (Meyers) 70.00 120.00
335 Chief Myers Fielding (Meyers) 60.00 100.00
336 Clyde Milan 60.00 100.00
337 Molly Miller Dallas 175.00 300.00
338 Dots Miller Pittsburgh 60.00 100.00
339 Bill Milligan 60.00 100.00
340 Fred Mitchell Toronto 60.00 100.00
341 Mike Mitchell Cincinnati 60.00 100.00
342 Dan Moeller 60.00 100.00
343 Carleton Molesworth 175.00 300.00
344 Herbie Moran Providence 60.00 100.00
345 Pat Moran Chicago 60.00 100.00
346 George Moriarty 60.00 100.00
347 Mike Mowrey 60.00 100.00
348 Dom Mullaney 175.00 300.00
349 George Mullen (Mullin) 60.00 100.00
350 George Mullin with Bat 60.00 100.00
351 George Mullin Throwing 60.00 100.00
352 Danny Murphy Batting 60.00 100.00
353 Danny Murphy Throwing 60.00 100.00
354 Red Murray Batting 60.00 100.00
355 Red Murray Portrait 60.00 100.00
356 Billy Nattress 60.00 100.00
357 Tom Needham 60.00 100.00
358 Simon Nicholls Hands on Knees 60.00 100.00
359 Simon Nichols Batting (Nicholls) 60.00 100.00
360 Harry Niles 60.00 100.00
361 Rebel Oakes 60.00 100.00
362 Frank Oberlin 60.00 100.00
363 Peter O'Brien 60.00 100.00
364 Bill O'Hara NY 60.00 100.00
365 Bill O'Hara Stl 6000.00 10000.00
366 Rube Oldring Batting 60.00 100.00
367 Rube Oldring Fielding 60.00 100.00
368 Charley O'Leary Hands on Knees 60.00 100.00
369 Charley O'Leary Portrait 60.00 100.00
370 William O'Neil 150.00 250.00
371 Albert Orth 175.00 300.00
372 William Otey 175.00 300.00
373 Orval Overall Hand at Face 60.00 100.00
374 Orval Overall Hands at Waist 60.00 100.00
375 Orval Overall Portrait 60.00 100.00
376 Frank Owen (Owens) 60.00 100.00
377 George Paige 175.00 300.00
378 Freddy Parent 60.00 100.00
379 Dode Paskert 60.00 100.00
380 Jim Pastorius 60.00 100.00
381 Harry Pattee 60.00 100.00
382 Fred Payne 60.00 100.00
383 Barney Pelty Horizontal 60.00 100.00
384 Barney Pelty Vertical 60.00 100.00
385 Hub Perdue 175.00 300.00
386 George Perring 60.00 100.00
387 Arch Persons 175.00 300.00
388 Jeff Pfeffer 60.00 100.00
389 Jeff Pfeffer ERR Chicago
390 Jake Pfeister Seated (Pfiester) 60.00 100.00
391 Jake Pfeister Throwing (Pfiester) 60.00 100.00
392 Jimmy Phelan 60.00 100.00
393 Ed Phelps 60.00 100.00
394 Deacon Phillippe. 60.00 100.00
395 Ollie Pickering 60.00 100.00
396 Eddie Plank 45000.00 60000.00
397 Phil Poland 60.00 100.00
398 Jack Powell 60.00 100.00
399 Mike Powers 60.00 100.00
400 Billy Purtell 60.00 100.00
401 Ambrose Puttman (Puttmann) 85.00 135.00
402 Lee Quillen (Quillin) 60.00 100.00
403 Jack Quinn 60.00 100.00
404 Newt Randall 60.00 100.00
405 Bugs Raymond 60.00 100.00
406 Ed Reagan 175.00 300.00
407 Ed Reulbach Glove 60.00 100.00
408 Ed Reulbach No Glove 70.00 120.00
409 Dutch Revelle 175.00 300.00
410 Bob Rhoades Hands 60.00 100.00
411 Bob Rhoades Right 60.00 100.00
412 Charlie Rhodes 60.00 100.00
413 Claude Ritchey 60.00 100.00
414 Lou Ritter 60.00 100.00
415 Ike Rockenfeld 175.00 300.00
416 Claude Rossman 60.00 100.00
417 Nap Rucker Portrait 60.00 100.00
418 Nap Rucker Throwing 60.00 100.00
419 Dick Rudolph 60.00 100.00
420 Ray Ryan 175.00 300.00
421 Germany Schaefer Det 60.00 100.00
422 Germany Schaefer Wash 60.00 100.00
423 George Schirm 85.00 135.00
424 Larry Schlafly 60.00 100.00
425 Admiral Schlei Batting 60.00 100.00
426 Admiral Schlei Catching 60.00 100.00
427 Admiral Schlei Portrait 60.00 100.00
428 Boss Schmidt Portrait 60.00 100.00
429 Boss Schmidt Throwing 60.00 100.00
430 Ossee Schreck (Schreckengost) 70.00 120.00
431 Wildfire Schulte Back View 60.00 100.00
432 Wildfire Schulte Front View 175.00 300.00
433 Jim Scott 60.00 100.00
434 Charles Seitz 175.00 300.00
435 Cy Seymour Batting 60.00 100.00
436 Cy Seymour Portrait 60.00 100.00
437 Cy Seymour Throwing 60.00 100.00
438 Spike Shannon 60.00 100.00
439 Bud Sharpe 60.00 100.00
440 Bud Shappe ERR (Sharpe) ML
441 Frank Shaughnessy SL 175.00 300.00
442 Al Shaw St. Louis 60.00 100.00
443 Hunky Shaw Providence 60.00 100.00
444 Jimmy Sheckard Glove 60.00 100.00
445 Jimmy Sheckard No Glove 60.00 100.00
446 Bill Shipke 60.00 100.00
447 Jimmy Slagle 60.00 100.00
448 Carlos Smith Shreveport 175.00 300.00
449 Frank Smith Chi-Bos 350.00 600.00
450 Frank Smith Chi F.Smith 60.00 100.00
451 Frank Smith Chi Whit Cap 60.00 100.00
452 Heinie Smith Buffalo 60.00 100.00
453 Happy Smith Brooklyn 60.00 100.00
454 Sid Smith Atlanta 175.00 300.00
455 F.Snodgrass Batting 60.00 100.00
456 F.nodgrass Batting ERR
457 F.Snodgrass Catching 60.00 100.00
458 Bob Spade 60.00 100.00
459 Tris Speaker 600.00 1000.00
460 Tubby Spencer 60.00 100.00
461 Jake Stahl Glove 85.00 135.00
462 Jake Stahl No Glove 60.00 100.00
463 Oscar Stanage 60.00 100.00
464 Dolly Stark 175.00 300.00
465 Charlie Starr 60.00 100.00
466 Harry Steinfeldt with Bat 60.00 100.00
467 Harry Steinfeldt Portrait 60.00 100.00
468 Jim Stephens 60.00 100.00
469 George Stone 60.00 100.00
470 George Stovall Batting 60.00 100.00
471 George Stovall Portrait 60.00 100.00
472 Sam Strang 60.00 100.00
473 Gabby Street Catching 60.00 100.00
474 Gabby Street Portrait 60.00 100.00
475 Billy Sullivan 60.00 100.00
476 Ed Summers 60.00 100.00
477 Bill Sweeney Boston 60.00 100.00
478 Jeff Sweeney New York 60.00 100.00
479 Jesse Tannehill Washington 60.00 100.00
480 Lee Tannehill Chi L.Tannehill 60.00 100.00
481 Lee Tannehill Chi Tannehill 60.00 100.00
482 Dummy Taylor 60.00 100.00
483 Fred Tenney 60.00 100.00
484 Tony Thebo 175.00 300.00
485 Jake Thielman 90.00 150.00
486 Ira Thomas 60.00 100.00
487 Woodie Thornton 175.00 300.00
488 J.Tinker Bat off Shldr 250.00 400.00
489 J.Tinker Bat on Shldr 400.00 800.00
490 J.Tinker Hand-Knee 350.00 600.00
491 J.Tinker Portrait 350.00 600.00
492 John Titus 60.00 100.00
493 Terry Turner 60.00 100.00
494 Bob Unglaub 60.00 100.00
495 Juan Violat (Viola) 175.00 300.00
496 R.Waddell Portrait 250.00 400.00
497 R.Waddell Throwing 250.00 400.00
498 Heinie Wagner on Left 60.00 100.00
499 Heinie Wagner on Right 60.00 100.00
500 Honus Wagner 800000.001500000.00
501 Bobby Wallace 175.00 300.00
502 Ed Walsh 250.00 400.00
503 Jack Warhop 60.00 100.00
504 Jake Weimer 60.00 100.00
505 James Westlake 175.00 300.00
506 Zack Wheat 200.00 350.00
507 Doc White Pitching 60.00 100.00
508 Doc White Portrait 60.00 100.00
509 Foley White Houston 175.00 300.00
510 Jack White Buffalo 60.00 100.00
511 Kaiser Wilhelm Hands 60.00 100.00
512 Kaiser Wilhelm with Bat 60.00 100.00
513 Ed Willett with Bat 60.00 100.00
514 Ed Willetts Throwing (Willett) 60.00 100.00
515 Jimmy Williams 60.00 100.00
516 Vic Willis Pitt 200.00 350.00
517 Vic Willis Stl Throw 175.00 300.00
518 Vic Willis Stl Bat 175.00 300.00
519 Owen Wilson 60.00 100.00
520 Hooks Wiltse Pitching 60.00 100.00
521 Hooks Wiltse Portrait 60.00 100.00
522 Hooks Wiltse Sweater 60.00 100.00
523 Lucky Wright 60.00 100.00
524 Cy Young Bare Hand 700.00 1200.00
525 Cy Young w/Glove 700.00 1200.00
526 Cy Young Portrait 1000.00 1800.00
527 Irv Young Minneapolis 70.00 120.00
528 Heinie Zimmerman: 60.00 100.00

1909-11 T206 Ty Cobb Back

1 Ty Cobb Portrait

1912 T207 Brown Background

The cards in this 207-card set measure approximately 1 1/2" by 2 5/8". The T207 set, also known as the "Brown Background" set was issued beginning in May with Broadleaf, Cycle, Napoleon, Recruit and anonymous (Factories no. 2, 3 or 25) backs in 1912. Broadleaf, Cycle and anonymous backs are difficult to obtain. Although many scarcities and cards with varying degrees of difficulty to obtain exist (see prices below), the Loudermilk, Lewis (Boston NL) and Miller (Chicago NL) cards are the rarest, followed by Saier and Tyler. The cards are numbered below for reference in alphabetical order by player's name. The complete set price below does include the Lewis variation missing the Braves patch on the sleeve. Listed pricing references raw "VgEx" condition.

COMPLETE SET (208) 15000.00 30000.00
1 Bert Adams 175.00 300.00
2 Eddie Ainsmith 30.00 50.00
3 Rafael Almeida 125.00 200.00
4 Jimmy Austin Insignia 30.00 50.00
5 Jimmy Austin No Insignia 60.00 100.00
6 Neal Ball 30.00 50.00
7 Cy Barger 30.00 50.00
8 Jack Barry 30.00 50.00
9 Paddy Bauman 125.00 200.00
10 Beals Becker 30.00 50.00
11 Chief Bender 90.00 150.00
12 Joe Benz 125.00 200.00
13 Bob Bescher 30.00 50.00
14 Joe Birmingham 125.00 200.00
15 Lena Blackburne 60.00 100.00
16 Fred Blanding 90.00 150.00
17 Bruno Block 60.00 100.00
18 Ping Bodie 35.00 60.00
19 Hugh Bradley 30.00 50.00
20 Roger Bresnahan 90.00 150.00
21 Jack Bushelman 125.00 200.00
22 Hank Butcher 90.00 150.00
23 Bobby Byrne 30.00 50.00
24 Nixey Callahan 30.00 50.00
25 Howie Camnitz 30.00 50.00
26 Max Carey 150.00 250.00
27 Bill Carrigan Correct Back 30.00 50.00
28 Bill Carrigan Wagner Back 60.00 100.00
29 George Chalmers 30.00 50.00
30 Frank Chance 90.00 150.00
31 Eddie Cicotte 300.00 500.00
32 Tommy Clarke 30.00 50.00
33 King Cole 30.00 50.00
34 Shano Collins 30.00 50.00
35 Bob Coulson 30.00 50.00
36 Tex Covington 30.00 50.00
37 Doc Crandall 30.00 50.00
38 Bill Cunningham 90.00 150.00
39 Dave Danforth 30.00 50.00
40 Bert Daniels 30.00 50.00
41 Jake Daubert 60.00 100.00
42 Harry Davis 30.00 50.00
43 Jim Delahanty 30.00 50.00
44 Claud Derrick 30.00 50.00
45 Art Devlin 30.00 50.00
46 Josh Devore 30.00 50.00
47 Mike Donlin 90.00 150.00
48 Ed Donnelly 60.00 100.00
49 Red Dooin 30.00 50.00
50 Tom Downey 125.00 200.00
51 Larry Doyle 30.00 50.00
52 Dellos Drake 35.00 60.00
53 Ted Easterly 30.00 50.00
54 Rube Ellis 90.00 150.00
55 Clyde Engle 50.00 80.00
56 Tex Erwin 35.00 60.00
57 Steve Evans 30.00 50.00
58 Jack Ferry 30.00 50.00
59 Ray Fisher Blue Cap 60.00 100.00
60 Ray Fisher White Cap 60.00 100.00
61 Art Fletcher 30.00 50.00
62 Jack Fournier 125.00 200.00
63 Art Fromme 30.00 50.00
64 Del Gainor 30.00 50.00
65 Larry Gardner 30.00 50.00
66 Lefty George 30.00 50.00
67 Roy Golden 30.00 50.00
68 Hank Gowdy 35.00 60.00
69 Peaches Graham 60.00 100.00
70 Jack Graney 35.00 60.00
71 Vean Gregg 60.00 100.00
72 Casey Hageman 30.00 50.00
73 Sea Lion Hall 30.00 50.00
74 Ed Hallinan 35.00 60.00
75 Earl Hamilton 30.00 50.00
76 Bob Harmon 30.00 50.00
77 Grover Hartley 60.00 100.00
78 Olaf Henriksen 30.00 50.00
79 John Henry 60.00 100.00
80 Buck Herzog 90.00 150.00
81 Bob Higgins 35.00 60.00
82 Red Hoff 70.00 120.00
83 Willie Hogan 35.00 60.00
84 Harry Hooper 300.00 500.00
85 Ben Houser 90.00 150.00
86 Ham Hyatt 70.00 120.00
87 Walter Johnson 350.00 600.00
88 George Kaler (Kahler) 30.00 50.00
89 Billy Kelly 60.00 100.00
90 Jay Kirke 70.00 120.00
91 Johnny Kling 90.00 150.00
92 Otto Knabe 30.00 50.00
93 Elmer Knetzer 30.00 50.00
94 Ed Konetchy 30.00 50.00
95 Harry Krause 30.00 50.00
96 Walt Kuhn 90.00 150.00
97 Joe Kutina 90.00 150.00
98 Frank Lange 60.00 100.00
99 Jack Lapp 35.00 60.00
100 Arlie Latham 30.00 50.00
101 Tommy Leach 30.00 50.00
102 Lefty Leifield 35.00 60.00
103 Ed Lennox 30.00 50.00
104 Duffy Lewis Boston 125.00 200.00
105A Irving Lewis Emblem on Sleeve 3500.006000.00
105B Irving Lewis No Emblem on Sleeve 3500.00 6000.00
106 Jack Lively 30.00 50.00
107 Paddy Livingston A on Shirt 125.00 200.00
108 Paddy Livingston Big C on Shirt 70.00 120.00
109 Paddy Livingston c Shirt 50.00 80.00
110 Bris Lord Philadelphia 35.00 60.00
111 Harry Lord Chicago 35.00 60.00
112 Louis Lowdermilk 2500.00 4000.00
113 Rube Marquard 90.00 150.00
114 Armando Marsans 60.00 100.00
115 George McBride 30.00 50.00
116 Alex McCarthy 125.00 200.00
117 Ed McDonald 30.00 50.00
118 John McGraw 90.00 150.00
119 Harry McIntire 30.00 50.00
120 Matty McIntyre 35.00 60.00
121 Bill McKechnie 300.00 500.00
122 Larry McLean 30.00 50.00
123 Clyde Milan 30.00 50.00
124 Doc Miller Boston 175.00 300.00
125 Dots Miller Pittsburgh 30.00 50.00
126 Otto Miller Brooklyn 60.00 100.00
127 Ward Miller Chicago 1200.00 2000.00
128 Mike Mitchell Cincinnati 35.00 60.00
129 Willie Mitchell Cleveland 30.00 50.00
130 George Mogridge 60.00 100.00
131 Earl Moore 60.00 100.00
132 Pat Moran 30.00 50.00
133 Cy Morgan Philadelphia 50.00 80.00
134 Ray Morgan Washington 50.00 80.00
135 George Moriarty 70.00 120.00
136 George Mullin D Cap 60.00 100.00
137 George Mullin d Cap 70.00 120.00
138 Tom Needham 30.00 50.00
139 Red Nelson 90.00 150.00
140 Hub Northen 30.00 50.00
141 Les Nunamaker 30.00 50.00
142 Rebel Oakes 30.00 50.00
143 Buck O'Brien 30.00 50.00
144 Rube Oldring 30.00 50.00
145 Ivy Olson 30.00 50.00
146 Marty O'Toole 30.00 50.00

147 Dode Paskert 30.00 50.00
148 Barney Pelty 90.00 150.00
149 Hub Perdue 30.00 50.00
150 Rube Peters 35.00 60.00
151 Art Phelan 90.00 150.00
152 Jack Quinn 30.00 50.00
153 Pat Ragan 175.00 300.00
154 Rasmussen 175.00 300.00
155 Morrie Rath 125.00 200.00
156 Ed Reulbach 30.00 50.00
157 Nap Rucker 60.00 100.00
158 Bud Ryan 150.00 250.00
159 Vic Saier 600.00 1000.00
160 Doc Scanlon (Scanlan) 30.00 50.00
161 Germany Schaefer 30.00 50.00
162 Bill Schardt 50.00 80.00
163 Frank Schulte 50.00 80.00
164 Jim Scott 60.00 100.00
165 Hank Severeid 30.00 50.00
166 Mike Simon 30.00 50.00
167 Frank Smith Cincinnati 35.00 60.00
168 Wally Smith St. Louis 35.00 60.00
169 Fred Snodgrass 30.00 50.00
170 Tris Speaker 500.00 800.00
171 Harry Spratt 30.00 50.00
172 Eddie Stack 35.00 60.00
173 Oscar Stanage 30.00 50.00
174 Bill Steele 90.00 150.00
175 Harry Steinfeldt 35.00 60.00
176 George Stovall 30.00 50.00
177 Gabby Street 30.00 50.00
178 Amos Strunk 35.00 60.00
179 Billy Sullivan 35.00 60.00
180 Bill Sweeney 90.00 150.00
181 Lee Tannehill 30.00 50.00
182 Claude Thomas 90.00 150.00
183 Joe Tinker 125.00 200.00
184 Bert Tooley 30.00 50.00
185 Terry Turner 30.00 50.00
186 Lefty Tyler 350.00 600.00
187 Hippo Vaughn 60.00 100.00
188 Heine Wagner Correct Back 60.00 100.00
189 Dixie Walker 30.00 50.00
190 Bobby Wallace 125.00 200.00
191 Jack Warhop 30.00 50.00
192 Buck Weaver 900.00 1500.00
193 Zack Wheat 125.00 200.00
194 Doc White 35.00 60.00
195 Dewey Wilie 30.00 50.00
196 Bob Williams 50.00 80.00
197 Art Wilson New York 35.00 60.00
198 Chief Wilson Pittsburgh 30.00 50.00
199 Hooks Wiltse 30.00 50.00
200 Ivey Wingo 50.00 80.00
201 Harry Wolverton 30.00 50.00
202 Joe Wood 500.00 800.00
203 Gene Woodburn 125.00 200.00
204 Ralph Works 300.00 500.00
205 Steve Yerkes 50.00 80.00
206 Rollie Zeider 50.00 80.00

1912 T227 Series of Champions

The cards in this four-card set measure approximately 2 5/16" by 3 3/8". Actually these four baseball players are but a small part of a larger set featuring a total of 21 other "Champions." The set was produced in 1912. These cards are unnumbered; the players have been alphabetized and numbered for reference in the checklist below. Card backs can be found with either Miners Extra or Honest Long Cut. The complete set price refers only to the four subjects listed immediately below and does not include any non-baseball subjects that may be in the set.

COMPLETE SET (4) 10000.00 20000.00
1 Frank Baker 1500.00 3000.00
2 Chief Bender 1250.00 2500.00
3 Ty Cobb 7500.00 15000.00
4 Rube Marquard 1250.00 2500.00

1916 Tango Brand Eggs

This 20-card set of 1916 Tango Brand Eggs Baseball cards was issued by the L. Frank Company in New Orleans as a promotion to increase egg sales. Less than 500 examples are known to exist, with some of the cards having quantities of less than 10 copies found. The cards have a glazed finish, a process used in several other sets of this vintage (E106, D303, T213 and T216). The fronts display a player color photo in a mix of poses (portrait, throwing, fielding, and batting). The player's name, position, and team are printed below the photo. Some of the cards are off center and poorly cut. The backs carry promotional information for the Tango Brand Eggs. The cards do not carry the Federal League designation since the league dissolved in 1915 and players moved back to the National and American League teams. One irregularity is the fact that Demmitt, Dooin, Jacklitsch, and Tinker of the E106 set appear as cards of Meyer, Morgan, Meyer, and Weaver in the Tango Brand Egg set. The set can be dated 1916, as "Germany" Schaefer appears in the set as a Brooklyn player, and prior to that year he played for Neward of the Federal League. During the 1916 season he was sold to the New York Americans, making that the only year he played for Brooklyn. The cards are unnumbered and checklisted below alphabetically.

COMPLETE SET (20) 12500.00 25000.00
1 Bob Bescher 250.00 500.00
2 Roger Bresnahan 400.00 800.00
3 Al Bridwell 250.00 500.00
4 Hal Chase 400.00 800.00
5 Ty Cobb 5000.00 10000.00
6 Eddie Collins 1250.00 2500.00
7 Sam Crawford 1250.00 2500.00
8 Red Dooin 25.00 500.00
9 Johnny Evers 500.00 1000.00
10 Hap Felsch 500.00 1000.00
Photo of Ray Demmitt
11 Hugh Jennings 400.00 800.00
12 George McQuillen 250.00 500.00
13 Billy Meyer 300.00 600.00
Photo of Fred Jacklitsch
14 Ray Morgan 300.00 600.00
Photo of Red Dooin
15 Eddie Murphy 250.00 500.00
16 Germany Schaefer 300.00 600.00
17 Joe Tinker 500.00 1000.00
18 Honus Wagner 750.00 1500.00
19 Buck Weaver 1500.00 3000.00
Photo of Joe Tinker
20 Heinie Zimmerman 250.00 500.00

1934 Tarzan Thoro Bread D382

These cards measuring approximately 2 1/2"" by 3 1/8"and featuring attractive black and white photos were issued with Tarzan Thoro Bread. The players name is in the upper right hand corner. Since the cards are unnumbered, we have sequenced them in alphabetical order. New additions have been found in recent years to our checklist; therefore, more additions if found are appeciated.

COMPLETE SET 3750.00 7500.00
1 Sparky Adams 750.00 1500.00
2 Walter Betts 750.00 1500.00
3 George Blaeholder 750.00 1500.00
4 Edward Brandt 750.00 1500.00
5 Tommy Bridges 1000.00 2000.00
6 Irving 'Jack' Burns 750.00 1500.00
7 Bruce Campbell 750.00 1500.00
8 Tex Carleton 750.00 1500.00
9 Dick Coffman 750.00 1500.00
10 George Connally 750.00 1500.00
11 Tony Cuccinello 750.00 1500.00
12 Debs Garms 750.00 1500.00
13 Alex Gaston 750.00 1500.00
14 Bill Hallahan 750.00 1500.00
15 Myril Hoag 750.00 1500.00
16 Chief Hogsett 750.00 1500.00
17 Arndt Jorgens 750.00 1500.00
18 Willie Kamm 1000.00 2000.00
19 Dutch Leonard 750.00 1500.00
20 Clyde Manion 750.00 1500.00
21 Eric McNair 750.00 1500.00
22 Oscar Mellilo 750.00 1500.00
23 Randy Moore 750.00 1500.00
24 Bob O'Farrell 750.00 1500.00
25 Gus Suhr 750.00 1500.00
26 Evar Swanson 750.00 1500.00
27 Billy Urbanski 750.00 1500.00
28 Johnny Vergez 750.00 1500.00
29 Red Worthington 750.00 1500.00
30 Tom Zachary 750.00 1500.00

1969 Tasco Associates

These oversized crude caricatures were issued by Tasco Associates and featured some of the leading players in baseball. It is presumed that the set was skewed towards the more popular teams since certain teams have many more players known to exist than other less popular teams. This checklist may be incomplete so any additions are appreciated. We have sequenced this set in alphabetical order.

COMPLETE SET 150.00 300.00
1 Hank Aaron 6.00 15.00
2 Richie Allen 4.00 10.00
3 Mike Andrews 2.00 5.00
4 Luis Aparicio 5.00 12.00
5 Ernie Banks 5.00 12.00
6 Glenn Beckert 2.00 5.00
7 Johnny Bench 8.00 20.00
8 Norm Cash 4.00 10.00
9 Danny Cater 2.00 5.00
10 Tony Conigliaro 4.00 10.00
11 Ray Culp 2.00 5.00
12 Don Drysdale 5.00 12.00
13 Bill Freehan 2.50 6.00
14 Jim Fregosi 2.00 5.00
15 Bob Gibson 5.00 12.00
16 Bill Hands 2.00 5.00
17 Ken Holtzman 2.00 5.00
18 Frank Howard 2.50 6.00
19 Randy Hundley 2.00 5.00
20 Ferguson Jenkins 5.00 12.00
21 Jerry Koosman 3.00 8.00
22 Juan Marichal 5.00 12.00
23 Willie Mays 8.00 20.00
24 Bill Mazeroski 5.00 12.00
25 Dick McAuliffe 2.00 5.00
26 Dave McNally 2.00 5.00
27 Jim Northrup 2.00 5.00
28 Tony Oliva 4.00 10.00
29 Rico Petrocelli 2.00 5.00
30 Adolpho Phillips 2.00 5.00
31 Brooks Robinson 5.00 12.00
32 Pete Rose 8.00 20.00
33 Ron Santo 4.00 10.00
34 George Scott 2.00 5.00
35 Reggie Smith 2.50 6.00
36 Mel Stottlemyre 2.00 5.00
37 Luis Tiant 2.50 6.00
38 Billy Williams 5.00 12.00
39 Carl Yastrzemski 6.00 15.00

1978 Tastee-Freez Discs

This set of 26 discs were given out at participating Big T and Tastee-Freez restaurants. The discs measure 3 3/8" in diameter and were produced by MSA. The front design features a black and white headshot inside a white baseball diamond pattern. Four red stars adorn the top of the discs, and the white diamond is bordered by various colors on different discs. The backs are printed in red and blue on white and provide the disc number, player's name, his batting average or won/loss record, and sponsors' advertisements.

COMPLETE SET (26) 15.00 40.00
1 Buddy Bell .40 1.00
2 Jim Palmer 1.50 4.00
3 Steve Garvey .60 1.50
4 Jeff Burroughs .20 .50
5 Greg Luzinski .40 1.00
6 Lou Brock 1.25 3.00
7 Thurman Munson .75 2.00
8 Rod Carew 1.25 3.00
9 George Brett 4.00 10.00
10 Tom Seaver 1.50 4.00
11 Willie Stargell 1.25 3.00
12 Jerry Koosman .20 .50
13 Bill North .20 .50
14 Richie Zisk .20 .50
15 Bill Madlock .40 1.00
16 Carl Yastrzemski 1.25 3.00
17 Dave Cash .20 .50
18 Bob Watson .40 1.00
19 Dave Kingman .75 2.00
20 Gene Tenace .20 .50
21 Ralph Garr .20 .50
22 Mark Fidrych 1.25 3.00
23 Frank Tanana .40 1.00
24 Larry Hisle .20 .50
25 Bruce Bochte .20 .50
26 Bob Bailor .20 .50

1933 Tattoo Orbit

The cards in this 60-card set measure 2" by 2 1/4". The 1933 Tatoo Orbit set contains unnumbered, color cards. Blaeholder and Hadley, and to a lesser degree Andrews and Hornsby are considered more difficult to obtain than the other cards in this set. The cards are ordered and numbered below alphabetically by the player's name.

COMPLETE SET (60) 7500.00 15000.00
1 Dale Alexander 100.00 200.00
2 Ivy Andrews 300.00 600.00
3 Earl Averill 200.00 400.00
4 Dick Bartell 100.00 200.00
5 Wally Berger 100.00 200.00
6 George Blaeholder 500.00 1000.00
7 Irving Burns 100.00 200.00
8 Guy Bush 100.00 200.00
9 Bruce Campbell 100.00 200.00
10 Chalmers Cissell 100.00 200.00
11 Watson Clark 100.00 200.00
12 Mickey Cochrane 300.00 600.00
13 Phil Collins 100.00 200.00
14 Kiki Cuyler 200.00 400.00
15 Dizzy Dean 500.00 1000.00
16 Jimmy Dykes 125.00 250.00
17 George Earnshaw 100.00 200.00
18 Woody English 100.00 200.00
19 Lou Fonseca 100.00 200.00
20 Jimmy Foxx 400.00 800.00
(Jimmie)
21 Burleigh Grimes 200.00 400.00
22 Charlie Grimm 150.00 300.00
23 Lefty Grove 300.00 600.00
24 Frank Grube 100.00 200.00
25 George Haas 100.00 200.00
26 Bump Hadley 500.00 1000.00
27 Chick Hafey 200.00 400.00
28 Jess Haines 200.00 400.00
29 Bill Hallahan 100.00 200.00
30 Mel Harder 125.00 250.00
31 Gabby Hartnett 200.00 400.00
32 Babe Herman 150.00 300.00
33 Billy Herman 200.00 400.00
34 Rogers Hornsby 600.00 1200.00
35 Roy Johnson 100.00 200.00
36 Smead Jolley 100.00 200.00
37 Billy Jurges 100.00 200.00
38 Willie Kamm 100.00 200.00
39 Mark Koenig 100.00 200.00
40 Jim Levey 100.00 200.00
41 Ernie Lombardi 200.00 400.00
42 Red Lucas 100.00 200.00
43 Ted Lyons 200.00 400.00
44 Connie Mack MG 250.00 500.00
45 Pat Malone 100.00 200.00
46 Pepper Martin 150.00 300.00
47 Marty McManus 100.00 200.00
48 Lefty O'Doul 150.00 300.00
49 Dick Porter 100.00 200.00
50 Carl N. Reynolds 100.00 200.00
51 Charlie Root 125.00 250.00
52 Bob Seeds 100.00 200.00
53 Al Simmons 200.00 400.00
54 Riggs Stephenson 125.00 250.00
55 Lyle Tinning 100.00 200.00
56 Joe Vosmik 100.00 200.00
57 Rube Walberg 100.00 200.00
58 Paul Waner 200.00 400.00
59 Lon Warneke 100.00 200.00
60 Arthur Whitney 100.00 200.00

1933 Tattoo Orbit Self Develop R308

These very small (1 1/4" by 1 7/8") cards are very scarce. They were produced by Tattoo Orbit around 1933. The set is presumed to include the numbers between 151 and 210; a few of the numbers are still unknown at this time. Badly over exposed cards are very difficult to identify and are considered (graded) fair at best. Two types of these cards are known: A larger card (of which only very few are known) and are very rare, and a smaller type -- which is considered the normal card. We are pricing the smaller cards. The larger cards are valued at approximately 5X the listed prices. An album is known for these cards

COMPLETE SET 2000.00 4000.00
151 Vernon Gomez 150.00 300.00
152 Kiki Cuyler 125.00 250.00
153 Jimmy Foxx 400.00 800.00
(Jimmie)
154 Al Simmons 150.00 300.00
155 Gordon Cochrane 150.00 300.00
156 Woody English 75.00 150.00
157 Chuck Klein 125.00 250.00
158 Dick Bartell 75.00 150.00
159 Pepper Martin 100.00 200.00
160 Earl Averill 125.00 250.00
161 William Dickey 150.00 300.00
162 Wesley Ferrell 100.00 200.00
163 Oral Hildebrand 75.00 150.00
164 Willie Kamm 75.00 150.00
165 Earl Whitehill 75.00 150.00
166 Charles Fullis 75.00 150.00
167 Jimmy Dykes 75.00 150.00
168 Ben Cantwell 75.00 150.00
169 George Earnshaw 75.00 150.00
170 Jackson Stephenson 100.00 200.00
171 Randy Moore 75.00 150.00
172 Ted Lyons 125.00 250.00
173 Goose Goslin 125.00 250.00
174 Evar Swanson 75.00 150.00
175 Leroy Mahaffey 75.00 150.00
176 Joe Cronin 150.00 300.00
177 Tom Bridges 75.00 150.00
178 Henry Manush 125.00 250.00
179 Walter Stewart 75.00 150.00
180 Frank Pytlak 75.00 150.00
181 Dale Alexander 75.00 150.00
182 Robert Grove 200.00 400.00
183 Charles Gehringer 150.00 300.00
184 Lewis Fonseca 75.00 150.00
185 Alvin Crowder 75.00 150.00
186 Mickey Cochrane 150.00 300.00
187 Max Bishop 75.00 150.00
188 Connie Mack MG 150.00 300.00
189 Guy Bush 75.00 150.00
190 Charlie Root 75.00 150.00
191 Burleigh Grimes 125.00 250.00
Gabby Hartnett
192 Pat Malone 75.00 150.00
193 Woody English 75.00 150.00
194 Lonnie Warneke 75.00 150.00
195 Babe Herman 100.00 200.00
200 Gabby Hartnett 125.00 250.00
201 Paul Waner 150.00 300.00
202 Dizzy Dean 400.00 800.00
205 Jim Bottomley 125.00 250.00
207 Charles Hafey 125.00 250.00
XX Album 25.00 50.00

1976 Taylor/Schmierer Bowman 47

This set which measures 2 1/16" by 2 1/2" was issued by show promoters Bob Schmierer and Ted Taylor to promote what would become their long running EPSCC shows in the Philadelphia area. The set is designed in the style of the 1948 Bowman set and according to printed stories even some of the same paper stock was used for these sets as was used in 1948. The first series (1-49) cards sell for considerably more than the later two series. A reprint card of the T-206 Wagner along with a card of show promoter and long time hobbyist Ted Taylor were also produced. They are not considered part of the complete set. Each series was available from the producers at the time of issue for $4.50 each.

COMPLETE SET (113) 100.00 200.00
COMMON CARD (1-49) .40 1.00
COMMON CARD (50-113) .10 .25
1 Bobby Doerr 1.50 4.00
2 Stan Musial 4.00 10.00
3 Babe Ruth 8.00 20.00
4 Joe DiMaggio 6.00 15.00
5 Andy Pafko .40 1.00
6 Johnny Pesky .75 2.00
7 Gil Hodges 3.00 8.00
8 Tommy Holmes .40 1.00
9 Ralph Kiner 3.00 8.00
10 Yogi Berra 4.00 10.00
11 Bob Feller 1.50 4.00
12 Sid Gordon .40 1.00
13 Eddie Joost .40 1.00
14 Del Ennis .40 1.00
15 Johnny Mize 3.00 8.00
16 Pee Wee Reese 4.00 10.00
17 Jackie Robinson 6.00 15.00
18 Enos Slaughter 1.50 4.00
19 Vern Stephens .40 1.00
20 Bobby Thomson .75 2.00
21 Ted Williams 6.00 15.00
22 Bob Elliott .40 1.00
23 Mickey Vernon .40 1.00
24 Ewell Blackwell .40 1.00
25 Lou Boudreau 1.50 4.00
26 Ralph Branca .40 1.00
27 Harry Breechen .40 1.00
28 Dom DiMaggio 1.25 3.00
29 Bruce Edwards .40 1.00
30 Sam Chapman .40 1.00
31 George Kell 1.50 4.00
32 Jack Kramer .40 1.00
33 Hal Newhouser 1.50 4.00
34 Charlie Keller .40 1.00
35 Ken Keltner .40 1.00
36 Hank Greenberg 3.00 8.00
37 Howie Pollet .40 1.00
38 Luke Appling 1.50 4.00
39 Pete Suder .40 1.00
40 Johnny Sain 1.25 3.00
41 Phil Cavaretta .75 2.00
42 Johnny Vander Meer .75 2.00
43 Mel Ott 3.00 8.00
44 Walker Cooper .40 1.00
45 Birdie Tebbetts .40 1.00
46 Snuffy Stirnweiss .40 1.00
47 Connie Mack MG 1.50 4.00
48 Jimmie Foxx 3.00 8.00
49 Joe DiMaggio 6.00 15.00
Babe Ruth
Checklist Back
50 Schoolboy Rowe .10 .25
51 Andy Seminick .10 .25
52 Dixie Walker .10 .25
53 Virgil Trucks .10 .25
54 Dizzy Trout .10 .25
55 Hoot Evers .10 .25
56 Thurman Tucker .10 .25
57 Fritz Ostermuller .10 .25
58 Augie Galan .10 .25
59 Babe Young .10 .25
60 Skeeter Newsome .10 .25
61 Jack Lohrke .10 .25
62 Rudy York .20 .50
63 Tex Hughson .10 .25
64 Sam Mele .10 .25
65 Fred Hutchinson .20 .50
66 Don Black .10 .25
67 Les Fleming .10 .25
68 George McQuinn .10 .25
69 Mike McCormick .10 .25
70 Mickey Witek .10 .25
71 Blix Donnelly .10 .25
72 Elbie Fletcher .10 .25
73 Hal Gregg .10 .25
74 Dick Whitman .10 .25
75 Johnny Neun MG .10 .25
76 Doyle Lade .10 .25
77 Ron Northey .10 .25
78 Mort Cooper .10 .25
79 Warren Spahn 1.25 3.00
80 Happy Chandler COMM .40 1.00
81 Connie Mack .40 1.00
Roy Mack
Connie Mack III
Checklist
82 Earle Mack Asst MG .10 .25
83 Buddy Rosar .10 .25
84 Walt Judnich .10 .25
85 Bob Kennedy .10 .25
86 Tom Tresh .10 .25
87 Sid Hudson .10 .25
88 Gene Thompson .10 .25
89 Bill Nicholson .10 .25
90 Stan Hack .10 .25
91 Terry Moore .20 .50
92 Ted Lyons MG .40 1.00
93 Barney McCoskey .10 .25
94 Stan Spence .10 .25
95 Larry Jensen .10 .25
96 Whitey Kurowski .10 .25
97 Honus Wagner CO 1.50 4.00
98 Billy Herman MG .40 1.00
99 Jim Tabor .10 .25
100 Phil Marchidon .10 .25
101 Dave Ferriss .10 .25
102 Al Zarilla .10 .25
103 Bob Dillinger .20 .50
104 Bob Lemon .75 2.00
105 Jim Hegan .10 .25
106 Johnny Lindell .10 .25
107 Williard Marshall .10 .25
108 Walt Masterson .10 .25
109 Carl Scheib .10 .25
110 Bobby Brown .30 .75
111 Cy Block .10 .25
112 Sid Gordon .20 .50
113 Ty Cobb 3.00 8.00
Babe Ruth
Tris Speaker
Checklist Back
NNO Honus Wagner 2.00 5.00
NNO Ted Taylor .10 .25

1972 TCMA the 1930's Panels

This set consists of two 9" by 12" panels of 12 uncut cards each which feature black-and-white photos of players who played during the 1930's. The photos measure approximately 2 1/16" by 2 7/8" each. One panel contains cards #169-180, while the other panel consists of cards #193-204.

COMPLETE SET 12.50 30.00
169 Alvin Crowder .40 1.00
170 August Suhr .40 1.00
171 Monty Stratton .75 2.00
172 Louis Berger .40 1.00
173 John Whitehead .40 1.00
174 Joe Heving .40 1.00
175 Mervyn Shea .40 1.00
176 Ed Durham .40 1.00
177 Buddy Myer .75 2.00
178 Carl Whitehill .40 1.00
179 Joe Cronin 1.50 4.00
180 Zeke Bonura .75 2.00
193 George Myatt .40 1.00
194 Bill Werber .75 2.00
195 Red Lucas .40 1.00
196 Hal Luby .40 1.00
197 Vic Sorell .40 1.00
198 Mickey Cochrane 1.50 4.00
199 Rudy York 1.00 2.00
200 Ray Mack .40 1.00
201 Vince DiMaggio .75 2.00
202 Mel Ott 1.50 4.00
203 John Lucadello .40 1.00
204 Debs Garms .40 1.00

1972 TCMA's the 30's

This 120-card set features borderless black-and-white photos of players who played during the 1930's and measures approximately 2" by 2 7/8". The backs carry the player's name, team and years during the 1930's in which he played. Cards numbered 1-72 are unnumbered and checklisted below alphabetically. Cards numbered 73-120 are listed according to the number on their backs.

COMPLETE SET (120) 50.00 100.00
1 Beau Bell .20 .50
2 Max Bishop .20 .50
3 Robert Boken .20 .50
4 Cliff Bolton .20 .50
5 John Broaca .20 .50
6 Bill Brubaker .20 .50
7 Slick Castleman .20 .50
8 Dick Coffman .20 .50
9 Philip Collins .20 .50
10 Earle Combs .75 2.00
11 Doc Cramer .40 1.00
12 Joseph Cronin .75 2.00
13 Jack Crouch .20 .50
14 Anthony Cuccinello .20 .50
15 Babe Dahlgren .40 1.00
16 Spud Davis .20 .50
17 Daffy Dean .40 1.00
18 Dizzy Dean 1.25 3.00
19 Bill Dickey .75 2.00
20 Joe DiMaggio 3.00 8.00
21 George Earnshaw .20 .50
22 Woody English/(Portrait) .20 .50
23 Woody English/(Batting) .20 .50
24 Harold Finney .20 .50
25 Freddie Fitzsimmons .40 1.00
Hadley Fitzsimmons
26 Tony Freitas .20 .50
27 Frank Frisch .75 2.00
28 Milt Gaston .20 .50
29 Sidney Gautreaux .20 .50
30 Charles Gehringer .75 2.00
31 Charles Gelbert .20 .50
32 Lefty Gomez .75 2.00
33 Lefty Grove .75 2.00
34 Charles Hafey .60 1.50
35 Jesse Haines .60 1.50
36 William Hallahan .40 1.00
37 Bucky Harris .75 2.00
38 Edward Heusser .20 .50
39 Carl Hubbell/(Portrait) .75 2.00
40 Carl Hubbell/(Throwing) .75 2.00
41 James Jordan .20 .50
42 Joseph Judge .40 1.00
43 Leonard Koenecke .20 .50
44 Mark Koenig .40 1.00
45 Cookie Lavagetto .40 1.00
46 Alfred Lawson .20 .50
47 Tony Lazzeri .75 2.00
48 Gus Mancuso .20 .50
49 John McCarthy .20 .50
50 Joe Medwick .75 2.00
51 Clifford Melton .20 .50
52 Terry Moore .60 1.50
53 John Murphy .40 1.00
54 Ken O'Dea .20 .50
55 Robert O'Farrell .20 .50
56 Manuel Onis .20 .50
57 Marcellus Pearson .20 .50
58 Paul Richards .40 1.00
59 Max Rosenfeld .20 .50
60 Red Ruffing/(Side view throwing) .75 2.00
61 Red Ruffing/(Front view throwing) .75 2.00
62 Harold Schumacher .40 1.00
63 George Selkirk .20 .50
64 Joseph Shaute .20 .50
65 Gordon Slade .20 .50
66 Lindo Storti .20 .50
67 Stephen Sundra .20 .50
68 Bill Terry .75 2.00
69 John Tising .20 .50
70 Joseph Vance .20 .50
71 Rube Walberg .40 1.00
72 Samuel West .40 1.00
73 Vic Tamulis .20 .50
74 Kemp Wicker .20 .50
75 Robert Seeds .20 .50
76 Jack Saltzgaver .20 .50
77 Walter Brown .20 .50
78 Spud Chandler .40 1.00
79 Myril Hoag .20 .50
80 Joseph Glenn .20 .50
81 Lefty Gomez .75 2.00
82 Art Jorgens .20 .50
83 Jesse Hill .20 .50
84 Red Rolfe .60 1.50
85 Wesley Ferrell .60 1.50
86 Joseph Morrissey .20 .50
87 Anthony Piet .20 .50
88 Fred Walker .60 1.50
89 William Dietrich .20 .50
90 Lynford Lary/(Portrait) .20 .50
91 Lynford Lary/(Batting) .20 .50
92 Lynford Lary
(Batting in striped uniform) .20 .50
93 Lynford Lary/(Batting facing forward) .20 .50
94 Ralph Boyle .20 .50
95 Tony Malinosky .20 .50
96 Al Lopez .75 2.00
97 Lonny Frey .20 .50
98 Anthony Malinosky .20 .50
99 Owen Carroll .20 .50
100 John Hassett .20 .50
101 Gib Brack .20 .50
102 Samuel Leslie .20 .50
103 Fred Heimach .20 .50
104 Burleigh Grimes .75 2.00
105 Ray Benge .20 .50
106 Joseph Stripp .20 .50
107 Joseph Becker .20 .50
108 Oscar Melillo .20 .50
109 Charles O'Leary CO .75 2.00
Roger Hornsby MG
110 Luke Appling .75 2.00
111 Stanley Hack .40 1.00
112 Raymond Hayworth .20 .50
113 Charles Wilson .20 .50
114 Hal Trosky .60 1.50
115 Wes Ferrell .60 1.50
116 Lyn Lary/(Throwing) .20 .50
117 Nathaniel Gaston .20 .50
118 Eldon Auker .40 1.00
119 Heinie Manush .75 2.00
120 James Foxx 2.00 5.00

1973-79 TCMA All-Time Greats

This set eatures black-and-white photos of some of the greatest baseball players of all time. These cards measure approximately 3 1/2" by 5 1/2". The cards are unnumbered and checklisted below in alphabetical order in order of the series they were released in. The Cy Young card in 1st series of 1973 did not have the 1973 information on the back.

COMPLETE SET 125.00 250.00
1 Luke Appling .40 1.00
2 Mickey Cochrane .75 2.00
3 Eddie Collins 1.00 2.50
4 Kiki Cuyler .40 1.00
5 Bill Dickey .60 1.50
6 Joe DiMaggio 4.00 10.00
7 Bob Feller 1.50 4.00
8 Frankie Frisch .60 1.50
9 Lou Gehrig 2.50 6.00
10 Goose Goslin .40 1.00
11 Chick Hafey .40 1.00
12 Gabby Hartnett .60 1.50
13 Rogers Hornsby 1.00 2.50
14 Ted Lyons .40 1.00
15 Connie Mack .60 1.50
16 Heinie Manush .40 1.00
17 Rabbit Maranville .40 1.00
18 Joe Medwick .40 1.00
19 Al Simmons .60 1.50
20 Bill Terry .60 1.50
21 Pie Traynor .60 1.50
22 Dazzy Vance .40 1.00
23 Cy Young 1.50 4.00
24 Gabby Hartnett 2.00 5.00
Babe Ruth
25 Roger Bresnahan .40 1.00
26 Dizzy Dean .75 2.00
27 Buck Ewing .40 1.00
Mascot
28 Jimmy Foxx 1.00 2.50
(Jimmie)
29 Hank Greenberg 1.00 2.50
30 Burleigh Grimes .40 1.00
31 Harry Heilman .40 1.00
32 Waite Hoyt .40 1.00
33 Walter Johnson 1.00 2.50
34 George Kelly .40 1.00
35 Stan Musial 2.00 5.00
36 Christy Mathewson 1.00 2.50
37 John McGraw .60 1.50
38 Mel Ott 1.00 2.50
39 Satchel Paige 1.00 2.50
40 Sam Rice .40 1.00
41 Edd Roush .40 1.00
42 Red Ruffing .40 1.00
43 Casey Stengel .75 2.00
44 Harry Wright .40 1.00
45 Paul Waner .60 1.50
46 Honus Wagner 1.00 2.50
47 Lloyd Waner .40 1.00
48 Ross Youngs .40 1.00
49 Frank Baker .60 1.50
50 Chief Bender .60 1.50
51 Jim Bottomley .40 1.00
52 Lou Boudreau .60 1.50
53 Mordecai Brown .75 2.00
54 Roy Campanella 1.00 2.50
55 Max Carey .40 1.00
56 Ty Cobb 2.00 5.00
57 Earle Combs .60 1.50
58 Jocko Conlan .40 1.00
59 Hugh Duffy .40 1.00
60 Red Faber .40 1.00
61 Lefty Grove 1.00 2.50
62 Kennesaw M. Landis .40 1.00
63 Eddie Plank .60 1.50
64 Hoss Radbourne .40 1.00
Sic, spelled without an E
65 Eppa Rixey .40 1.00
66 Jackie Robinson 2.50 6.00
67 Babe Ruth 4.00 10.00
68 George Sisler .60 1.50
69 Zack Wheat .60 1.50
70 Ted Williams 3.00 8.00
71 Mel Ott 2.50 6.00
Babe Ruth
72 Tris Speaker 1.00 2.50
Wilbert Robinson
73 Grover C. Alexander 1.25 3.00
74 Cap Anson 1.25 3.00
75 Earl Averill .60 1.50
76 Ed Barrow .40 1.00
77 Yogi Berra 1.00 2.50
78 Roberto Clemente 2.00 5.00
79 Jimmy Collins .60 1.50
80 Whitey Ford 1.00 2.50
81 Ford Frick .40 1.00
82 Lefty Gomez .75 2.00
83 Bucky Harris .60 1.50
84 Billy Herman .60 1.50
85 Carl Hubbell 1.00 2.50
86 Miller Huggins .60 1.50
87 Monte Irvin .60 1.50
88 Bill Klem .40 1.00
89 Sandy Koufax 1.50 4.00
90 Napoleon Lajoie 1.00 2.50
91 Bob Lemon .60 1.50
92 Ralph Kiner .75 2.00
93 Mickey Mantle 2.50 6.00
94 Rube Marquard .60 1.50
95 Joe McCarthy .40 1.00
96 Bill McKechnie .40 1.00
97 Herb Pennock .60 1.50
98 Warren Spahn 1.00 2.50
99 Joe Tinker 1.00 2.50
100 Early Wynn .75 2.00
101 Joe Cronin 1.00 2.50
Honus Wagner
Bill Terry
102 Jimmie Foxx 1.25 3.00
Lou Gehrig
103 Hank Greenberg 1.00 2.50
Ralph Kiner
104 Walter Johnson 1.00 2.50
Connie Mack
105 Connie Mack 1.00 2.50
Bob Feller
106 Mel Ott 1.25 3.00
Lou Gehrig
107 Al Simmons 1.25 3.00
Tris Speaker
Ty Cobb
108 Ted Williams 1.25 3.00
Lou Boudreau
109 Dave Bancroft .40 1.00
110 Ernie Banks 1.25 3.00
111 Frank Chance 1.00 2.50
112 Stan Covaleskie .40 1.00
113 Billy Evans .40 1.00
114 Clark Griffith .60 1.50
115 Jesse Haines .40 1.00
116 Will Harridge .40 1.00
117 Harry Hooper .40 1.00
118 Cal Hubbard .40 1.00
119 Hugh Jennings .60 1.50
120 Willie Keeler 1.00 2.50
121 Fred Lindstrom .40 1.00
122 John Henry Lloyd .75 2.00
123 Al Lopez .40 1.00
124 Robin Roberts 1.00 2.50
125 Amos Rusie .40 1.00
126 Ray Schalk .40 1.00
127 Joe Sewell .40 1.00
128 Rube Waddell .60 1.50
129 George Weiss .40 1.00
130 Dizzy Dean .60 1.50
Gabby Hartnett
131 Joe DiMaggio 4.00 10.00
Mickey Mantle
132 Ted Williams 4.00 10.00
Joe DiMaggio
133 Jack Chesbro .40 1.00
134 Tom Connolly .40 1.00
135 Sam Crawford .60 1.50
136 Elmer Flick .40 1.00
137 Charlie Gehringer .60 1.50
138 Warren Giles .40 1.00
139 Ban Johnson .40 1.00
140 Addie Joss .40 1.00
141 Al Kaline 1.25 3.00
142 Willie Mays 2.00 5.00
143 Joe McGinnity .40 1.00
144 Larry MacPhail .40 1.00
145 Branch Rickey .40 1.00

146 Wilbert Robinson .40 1.00
147 Duke Snider 1.50 4.00
148 Tris Speaker 1.00 2.50
149 Bobby Wallace .40 1.00
150 Hack Wilson .40 1.00
151 Yogi Berra 2.00 5.00
Casey Stengel
152 Warren Giles 2.00 5.00
Roberto Clemente
153 Mickey Mantle 4.00 10.00
Willie Mays
154 John McGraw 2.50 6.00
Babe Ruth
155 Satchel Paige 2.50 6.00
Bob Feller
156 Paul Waner 2.00 5.00
Lloyd Waner

1973 TCMA Autograph Series

These blank-backs cards measure 3.5 x 5.5 and feature black and white photos. Below the player's photo is a white strip where collectors could have the player sign the card. These were quite popular with collectors, and finding a complete, unsigned set, is quite rare. Prices listed are for unsigned cards.

COMPLETE CARD (36) 50.00 100.00
1 Stachel Paige 2.00 5.00
2 Phil Rizzuto 1.25 3.00
3 Sid Gordon .75 2.00
4 Ernie Lombardi .75 2.00
5 Jesse Haines .75 2.00
6 Joe Gordon .75 2.00
7 Billy Terry .75 2.00
8 Bill Dickey 1.25 3.00
9 Joe DiMaggio 6.00 15.00
10 Carl Hubbell 2.00 5.00
11 Freddie Lindstrom .75 2.00
12 Ted Lyons .75 2.00
13 Red Ruffing .75 2.00
14 Joe Gordon .75 2.00
15 Bob Feller 3.00 8.00
16 Yogi Berra 2.00 5.00
17 Whitey Ford/Ford Frick 2.00 5.00
18 Sandy Koufax 3.00 8.00
19 Ted Williams 5.00 12.00
20 Warren Spahn 2.00 5.00
21 Al Rosen .75 2.00
22 Luke Appling .75 2.00
23 Joe Bush .75 2.00
24 Joe Medwick .75 2.00
25 Lou Boudreau 1.25 3.00
26 Ralph Kiner 2.00 5.00
27 Lloyd Waner .75 2.00
28 Pee Wee Reese 1.25 3.00
29 Duke Snider 3.00 8.00
30 Sal Maglie .75 2.00
31 Monte Irvin 1.25 3.00
32 Lefty Gomez 2.00 5.00
33 George Kelly .75 2.00
34 Joe Adcock .75 2.00
35 Max Carey .75 2.00
36 Rube Marquard 1.25 3.00

1973 TCMA Drawings

These postcards measure 3.5 by 5.5 and feature black and white player illustrations and a facsimile signature.

1 Mickey Cochrane .75 2.00
2 Christy Mathewson 1.00 2.50
3 Roberto Clemente 20.00 50.00
4 Rogers Hornsby 1.00 2.50
5 Pie Traynor .60 1.50
6 Frank Frisch .60 1.50
7 Ty Cobb 2.00 5.00
8 Connie Mack .60 1.50
9 Babe Ruth 4.00 10.00
10 Lou Gehrig 2.50 6.00
11 Gil Hodges 1.00 2.50
12 Jackie Robinson 2.50 6.00

1974 TCMA Nicknames

This 27-card set features black-and-white player photos with red printing and measures approximately 2 1/4" by 3 1/2". The backs carry player information.

COMPLETE SET (27) 12.50 30.00
1 Bob Feller 1.00 2.50
2 Babe Dahlgren .40 1.00
3 Spud Chandler .60 1.50
4 Ducky Medwick 1.00 2.50
5 Cal Benge .40 1.00
6 Goose Goslin 1.00 2.50
7 Mule Haas .40 1.00
8 Dizzy Dean 1.00 2.50
9 Ray Harrell .40 1.00
10 Ralph Boyle .40 1.00
11 Curtis Davis .40 1.00
12 Moose Solters .40 1.00
13 Sam Jones .40 1.00
14 Bad News Hale .40 1.00
15 Bucky Harris 1.00 2.50
16 Jim Jordan .40 1.00
17 Zeke Bonura .60 1.50
18 Tom Hafey .40 1.00
19 Virgil Davis .40 1.00
20 Bing Miller .40 1.00
21 Preacher Roe .60 1.50
22 Bill Hallahan .40 1.00
23 Bob Johnson .40 1.00
24 Joe Gordon .60 1.50
25 Tot Presnell .40 1.00
26 Luke Hamlin .40 1.00
27 Tommy Henrich .75 2.00

1975 TCMA All-Time Greats

This 36-card set measures approximately 2 3/8" by 3 3/4". The first printing of the set features blue and white player photos, while the second printing features black and white. The cards were issued in six-card strips, with six different strips in all. Reportedly, each strip had spot in the upper-right hand corner for retail pricing.The pictures are framed in blue with a bat and ball in each top corner. The card name and player's name are in the top and bottom margins respectively. The backs carry the player's name, position, team name and career stats. The cards are unnumbered and checklisted below in alphabetical order.

COMPLETE SET (36) 20.00 50.00
1 Earl Averill .40 1.00
2 Jim Bottomley .40 1.00
3 Lou Boudreau .40 1.00
4 Fred Clarke .40 1.00
5 Roberto Clemente 2.00 5.00
6 Ty Cobb 2.00 5.00
7 Jocko Conlon .40 1.00
8 Hugh Duffy .40 1.00
9 Red Faber .40 1.00
10 Whitey Ford 1.00 2.50
11 Jimmy Foxx 1.00 2.50
(Jimmie)
12 Burleigh Grimes .40 1.00
13 Lefty Grove .75 2.00
14 Bucky Harris .40 1.00
15 Billy Herman .40 1.00
16 Miller Huggins .40 1.00
17 Monte Irvin .40 1.00
18 Ralph Kiner .75 2.00
19 Sandy Koufax 1.00 2.50
20 Judge Landis .40 1.00
21 Mickey Mantle 2.00 5.00
22 Joe McCarthy .40 1.00
23 John McGraw .40 1.00
24 Bill McKechnie .40 1.00
25 Ducky Medwick .40 1.00
26 Hoss Radborn .40 1.00
27 Sam Rice .40 1.00
28 Jackie Robinson 2.00 5.00
29 Wilbert Robinson .40 1.00
30 Babe Ruth 3.00 8.00
31 Babe Ruth/(Closer head photo) 3.00 8.00
32 George Sisler .40 1.00
33 Tris Speaker .40 1.00
34 Zack Wheat .40 1.00
35 Ted Williams 2.00 5.00
36 Ross Youngs .40 1.00

1975 TCMA Guam

This 18-card set measures approximately 3 1/2" by 5 1/2" and features black and white photos of baseball players who served in the Navy in Guam during World War II. The backs display an on-going story about the team by Harrington Crissey.

COMPLETE SET (18) 8.00 20.00
1 Phil Rizzuto 1.00 2.50
Terry Moore
2 Gab Gab Guam 1945 .40 1.00
3 Team Photo .40 1.00
4 Merrill May .75 2.00
Pee Wee Reese
Johnny Vander Meer
5 Team Photo .40 1.00
6 Team Photo .40 1.00
7 Del Ennis .60 1.50
8 Mace Brown .60 1.50
9 Pee Wee Reese 1.00 2.50
Joe Gordon
Bill Dickey
10 Glenn McQuillen .40 1.00
11 Mike Budnick .40 1.00
12 Team Photo .40 1.00
13 Skeets Dickey .40 1.00
14 Connie Ryan .40 1.00
15 Hal White .40 1.00
16 Mickey Cochrane 1.00 2.50
17 Barney McCosky .40 1.00
18 Ben Huffman .40 1.00

1975 TCMA House of Jazz

This 35-card set features black-and-white player photos printed on thin card stock and measuring approximately 2 3/8" by 3 1/2". The cards are unnumbered and checklisted below in alphabetical order.

COMPLETE SET (35) 30.00 60.00
1 John Antonelli .20 .50
2 Richie Ashburn .75 2.00
3 Ernie Banks 1.25 3.00
4 Hank Bauer .40 1.00
5 Joe DiMaggio 2.00 5.00
6 Bobby Doerr .20 .50
7 Herman Franks .20 .50
8 Lou Gehrig 2.00 5.00
9 Granny Hamner .20 .50
10 Al Kaline .75 2.00
11 Harmon Killebrew .75 2.00
12 Jim Konstanty .20 .50
13 Bob Lemon .60 1.50
14 Ed Lopat .20 .50
15 Stan Lopata .20 .50
16 Peanuts Lowrey .20 .50
17 Mickey Mantle 3.00 8.00
18 Phil Marchildon .20 .50
19 Walt Masterson .20 .50
20 Ed Mathews .75 2.00
21 Willie Mays 2.00 5.00
22 Don Newcombe .40 1.00
23 Joe Nuxhall .20 .50
24 Satchel Paige 1.50 4.00
25 Roy Partee .20 .50
26 Jackie Robinson 2.00 5.00
27 Babe Ruth 3.00 8.00
28 Carl Scheib .20 .50
29 Bobby Shantz .20 .50
30 Burt Shotten .20 .50
31 Duke Snider .75 2.00
32 Warren Spahn .75 2.00
33 Johnny Temple .20 .50
34 Ted Williams 2.00 5.00
35 Early Wynn .75 2.00

1975 TCMA Larry French Postcards

This six-card set features black-and-white pictures of Larry French printed in a postcard format. The backs when put together become a life story of French. It is written by French as told to Harrington Crissey.

COMPLETE SET (6) 8.00 20.00
COMMON CARD (1-6) 1.50 4.00
3 Bill Lee 1.50 4.00
Charlie Root
Larry French
Tuck Stainba
4 Larry French 1.50 4.00
Charlie Grimm
Fred Lindstrom
6 Larry French 1.50 4.00
Mickey Owen

1976 TCMA Umpires

This three-card set was produced by TCMA for the three umpires pictured on the cards and was distributed through the umpires themselves. The cards are unnumbered and checklisted below in alphabetical order.

COMPLETE SET (8) 2.00 5.00
1 Larry Barnett .75 2.00
2 Al Clark .75 2.00
3 Nick Colosi .75 2.00
4 Don Denkinger .75 2.00
5 Art Frantz .75 2.00
6 Marty Springstead .75 2.00
7 Ed Sudol .75 2.00
8 Bill Williams .75 2.00

1977-80 TCMA The War Years

This standard-size set features players who stayed at home and played major league baseball during the Second World War. The set was released in two 45-card series. Cards 1-45 were issued as Series 1 in 1977. Series 2, cards 46-90, were released in 1980. Reportedly, Series 1 cards are available in shorter supply.

COMPLETE SET (90) 20.00 50.00
1 Sam Narron .20 .50
2 Ray Mack .20 .50
3 Mickey Owen .20 .50
4 John Gaston Peacock .20 .50
5 Dizzy Trout .20 .50
6 Birdie Tebbetts .20 .50
7 Alfred Todd .20 .50
8 Harland Clift .20 .50
9 Don Gilberto Nunez .20 .50
Gil Torres
10 Al Lopez .50 1.25
11 Tony Lupien .20 .50
12 Luke Appling .50 1.25
13 Pat Seerey .20 .50
14 Phil Masi .20 .50
15 Thomas Turner .20 .50
16 Nicholas Picciuto .20 .50
17 Mel Ott 1.00 2.50
18 Red Treadway .20 .50
19 Samuel Naham .20 .50
20 Rip Sewell .20 .50
21 Roy Partee .20 .50
22 Richard Siebert .20 .50
23 Red Barrett .20 .50
24 Lefty O'Dea .20 .50
25 Louis Parisse .20 .50
26 Martin Marion .40 1.00
27 Eugene Moore Jr. .20 .50
28 Walter Boom Boom Beck .20 .50
29 Donald Manno .20 .50
30 Hal Newhouser .50 1.25
31 Gus Mancuso .20 .50
32 Pinky May .20 .50
33 Gerald Priddy .20 .50
34 Herman Besse .20 .50
35 Luis Olmo .20 .50
36 Robert O'Neill .20 .50
37 John Barrett .20 .50
38 Gordon Maltzberger .20 .50
39 William Nicholson .30 .75
40 Ron Northey .20 .50
41 Howard Pollet .20 .50
42 Aloysius Piechota .20 .50
43 Robert Shepard .20 .50
44 Alfred Anderson .20 .50
45 Damon Phillips .20 .50
46 Herman Franks .20 .50
47 Aldon Wilkie .20 .50
48 Max Macon .20 .50
49 Lester Webber .20 .50
50 Robert Swift .20 .50
51 Philip Weintraub .20 .50
52 Nicholas Strincevich .20 .50
53 Michael Tresh .20 .50
54 William Trotter .20 .50
55 1943 New York Yankees .40 1.00
Starting World Series
Line
56 Johnny Sturm .20 .50
57 Silas Johnson .20 .50
58 Don Kolloway .20 .50
59 Cecil Porter Vaughan .20 .50
60 St. Louis Browns .20 .50
Belters
George McQuinn
Chet La
61 Harold Wagner .20 .50
62 Alva Javery .20 .50
63 Boston Bees Rookie .30 .75
Pitchers
George Barnicle
Bob
64 Dolf Camilli .40 1.00
65 Mike McCormick .20 .50
66 Dick Wakefield .20 .50
67 Mickey Vernon .40 1.00
68 John Vander Meer .40 1.00
69 Mack McDonnell .20 .50
70 Thomas Jordan .20 .50
71 Maurice Van Robays .20 .50
72 Charles Stanceu .20 .50
73 Samuel Zoldak .20 .50
74 Ray Starr .20 .50
75 Roger Wolff .20 .50
76 Cecil Travis .30 .75
77 Arthur Johnson .20 .50
78 Louis Riggs .20 .50
79 Peter Suder .20 .50
80 Thomas Warren .20 .50
81 John Welaj .20 .50
82 Gee Walker .20 .50
83 Dee Williams .20 .50
84 Leonard Merullo .20 .50
85 Swede Johnson .20 .50
86 Junior Thompson .20 .50
87 William Zuber .20 .50
88 Earl Johnson .20 .50
89 Babe Young .20 .50
90 Jim Wallace .20 .50

1978 TCMA 60'S I

The TCMA Stars of the 60's consists of 293 standard-size cards. This set was issued through hobby dealers at the time and was TCMA's second set of retired players. The set uses many photos from Mike Aronstein's library of photos. Many of the great and not so great players of the 60's are featured. No card numbers 43 or 98 were printed.

COMPLETE SET (293) 40.00 80.00
1 Smoky Burgess .20 .50
2 Juan Marichal 1.25 3.00
3 Don Drysdale 1.25 3.00
4 Jim Gentile .10 .25
5 Roy Face .20 .50
6 Joe Pepitone .20 .50
7 Joe Christopher .10 .25
8 Wayne Causey .10 .25
9 Frank Bolling .10 .25
10 Jim Maloney .20 .50
11 Roger Maris 1.50 4.00
12 Bill White .30 .75
13 Roberto Clemente 4.00 10.00
14 Bob Saverine .10 .25
15 Barney Schultz .10 .25
16 Albie Pearson .10 .25
17 Denny LeMaster .10 .25
18 Ernie Broglio .10 .25
19 Bobby Klaus .10 .25
20 Tony Cloninger .10 .25
21 Whitey Ford 1.25 3.00
22 Ron Santo .30 .75
23 Jim Duckworth .10 .25
24 Willie Davis .20 .50
25 Ed Charles .10 .25
26 Bob Allison .20 .50
27A Fritz Ackley .30 .75
27B Gary Kroll .30 .75
28 Ruben Amaro .10 .25
29 Johnny Callison .20 .50
30 Greg Bollo .10 .25
31 Felix Millan .10 .25
32 Camilo Pascual .20 .50
33 Jackie Brandt .10 .25
34 Don Lock .10 .25
35 Chico Ruiz .10 .25
36 Joe Azcue .10 .25
37 Ed Bailey .10 .25
38 Pete Ramos .10 .25
39 Eddie Bressoud .10 .25
40 Al Kaline 1.50 4.00
41 Ron Brand .10 .25
42 Bob Lillis .10 .25
44 Buster Narum .10 .25
45 Junior Gilliam .30 .75
46 Claude Raymond .10 .25
47 Billy Bryan .10 .25
48 Marshall Bridges .10 .25
49 Norm Cash .30 .75
50 Orlando Cepeda .60 1.50
51 Lee Maye .10 .25
52 Andy Rodgers .10 .25
53 Ken Berry .10 .25
54 Don Mincher .10 .25
55 Jerry Lumpe .10 .25
56 Milt Pappas .10 .25
57 Steve Barber .10 .25
58 Dennis Menke .10 .25
59 Larry Maxie .10 .25
60 Bob Gibson 1.25 3.00
61 Larry Bearnarth .10 .25
62 Bill Mazeroski .60 1.50
63 Bob Rodgers .10 .25
64 Jerry Arrigo .10 .25
65 Joe Nuxhall .20 .50
66 Dean Chance .20 .50
67 Ken Boyer .30 .75
68 John Odom .10 .25
69 Chico Cardenas .10 .25
70 Maury Wills .30 .75
71 Tony Oliva .30 .75
72 Don Nottebart .10 .25
73 Joe Adcock .20 .50
74 Felipe Alou .30 .75
75 Matty Alou .20 .50
76 Dick Radatz .10 .25
77 Jim Bouton .30 .75
78 John Blanchard .10 .25
79 Juan Pizarro .10 .25
80 Boog Powell .30 .75
81 Earl Robinson .10 .25
82 Bob Chance .10 .25
83 Max Alvis .10 .25
84 Don Blasingame .10 .25
85 Tom Cheney .10 .25
86 Jerry Arrigo .10 .25
87 Tommy Davis .20 .50
88 Steve Boros .10 .25
89 Don Cardwell .10 .25
90 Harmon Killebrew .75 2.00
91 Jim Pagliaroni .10 .25
92 Jim O'Toole .10 .25
93 Dennis Bennett .10 .25
94 Dick McAuliffe .20 .50
95 Dick Brown .10 .25
96 Joe Amalfitano .10 .25
97 Phil Linz .10 .25
99 Dave Nicholson .10 .25
100 Hoyt Wilhelm .60 1.50
101 Don Leppert .10 .25
102 Jose Pagan .10 .25
103 Sam McDowell .20 .50
104 Jack Baldschun .10 .25
105 Jim Perry .20 .50
106 Hal Reniff .10 .25
107 Lee Maye .10 .25
108 Joe Adcock .20 .50
109 Bob Bolin .10 .25
110 Don Leppert .10 .25
111 Bill Monbouquette .10 .25
112 Bobby Richardson .30 .75
113 Earl Battey .10 .25
114 Bob Veale .10 .25
115 Lou Jackson .10 .25
116 Frank Kreutzer .10 .25
117 Jerry Zimmerman .10 .25
118 Don Schwall .10 .25
119 Rich Rollins .10 .25
120 Pete Ward .10 .25
121 Moe Drabowsky .10 .25
122 Jesse Gonder .10 .25
123 Hal Woodeschick .10 .25
124 John Herrnstein .10 .25
125A Leon Wagner .30 .75
125B Gary Peters .30 .75
126 Dwight Siebler .10 .25
127 Gary Kroll .10 .25
128 Tony Horton .10 .25
129 John DeMerit .10 .25
130 Sandy Koufax 2.50 6.00
131 Jim Davenport .10 .25
132 Wes Covington .10 .25
133 Tony Taylor .20 .50
134 Jack Kralick .10 .25
135 Bill Pleis .10 .25
136 Russ Snyder .10 .25
137 Joe Torre .30 .75
138 Ted Wills .10 .25
139 Wes Stock .10 .25
140 Frank Robinson 1.25 3.00
141 Dave Stenhouse .10 .25
142 Ron Hansen .10 .25
143 Don Elston .10 .25
144 Del Crandall .10 .25
145 Bennie Daniels .10 .25
146 Vada Pinson .20 .50
147 Bill Spanswick .10 .25
148 Earl Wilson .10 .25
149 Ty Cline .10 .25
150 Dick Groat .20 .50
151 Jim Duckworth .10 .25
152 Jim Schaffer .10 .25
153 George Thomas .10 .25
154 Wes Stock .10 .25
155 Mike White .10 .25
156 John Podres .20 .50
157 Willie Crawford .10 .25
158 Fred Gladding .10 .25
159 John Wyatt .10 .25
160 Bob Friend .10 .25
161 Ted Uhlaender .10 .25
162 Dick Stigman .10 .25
163 Don Wert .10 .25
164 Eddie Bressoud .10 .25
165A Ed Roebuck .30 .75
165B Leon Wagner .30 .75
166 Al Spangler .10 .25
167 Bob Sadowski .10 .25
168 Ralph Terry .10 .25
169 Jim Schaffer .10 .25
170 Jim Fregosi .20 .50
170 Dick Hall .10 .25
171 Al Spangler .10 .25
172 Bob Tillman .10 .25
173 Ed Bailey .10 .25
174 Cesar Tovar .10 .25
175 Morrie Stevens .10 .25
176 Floyd Weaver .10 .25
177 Frank Malzone .10 .25
178 Norm Siebern .10 .25
179 Dick Phillips .10 .25
181 Bobby Wine .10 .25
182 Masanori Murakami 1.50 4.00
183 Chuck Schilling .10 .25
184 Jim Schaffer .10 .25
185 John Roseboro .20 .50
186 Jake Wood .10 .25
187 Dallas Green .20 .50
188 Tom Haller .10 .25
189 Chuck Cottier .10 .25
190 Brooks Robinson 1.25 3.00
191 Ty Cline .10 .25
192 Bubba Phillips .10 .25
193 Al Jackson .10 .25
194 Herm Starrette .10 .25
195 Dave Wickersham .10 .25
196 Vic Power .10 .25
197 Ray Culp .10 .25
198 Don Demeter .10 .25
199 Dick Schofield .10 .25
200 Mudcat Grant .10 .25
201 Roger Craig .20 .50
202 Dick Farrell .10 .25
203 Clay Dalrymple .10 .25
204 Jim Duffalo .10 .25
205 Tito Francona .10 .25
206 Tony Conigliaro .30 .75
207 Jim King .10 .25
208 Joel Gibson .10 .25
209 Arnold Earley .10 .25
210 Denny McLain .30 .75
211 Don Larsen .20 .50
212 Ron Hunt .10 .25
213 Deron Johnson .10 .25
214 Harry Bright .10 .25
215 Ernie Fazio .10 .25
216 Joey Jay .10 .25
217 Jim Coates .10 .25
218 Jerry Kindall .10 .25
219 Joe Gibbon .10 .25
220 Frank Howard .30 .75
221 Howie Koplitz .10 .25
222 Larry Jackson .10 .25
223 Dale Long .10 .25
224 Jimmy Dykes MG .20 .50
225 Hank Aguirre .10 .25
226 Earl Francis .10 .25
227 Vic Wertz .10 .25
228 Larry Haney .10 .25
229 Tony LaRussa .30 .75
230 Moose Skowron .20 .50
231 Lee Thomas .10 .25
231 Tito Francona .10 .25
232 Ken Johnson .10 .25
233 Dick Howser .10 .25
234 Bobby Knoop .10 .25
236 Elston Howard .30 .75
237 Donn Clendenon .10 .25
238 Jesse Gonder .10 .25
239 Vern Law .20 .50
240 Curt Flood .30 .75
241 Dal Maxvill .10 .25
242 Roy Sievers .20 .50
243 Jim Brewer .10 .25
244 Harry Craft MG .10 .25
245 Dave Eilers .10 .25
246 Dave DeBusschere .30 .75
247 Ken Harrelson .20 .50
248 Jim Duffalo UER .10 .25
Card #'d 249
249 Ed Kasko .10 .25
250 Luis Aparicio .60 1.50
251 Ron Kline .10 .25
252 Chuck Hinton .10 .25
253 Frank Lary .10 .25
254 Stu Miller .10 .25
255 Ernie Banks 1.50 4.00
256 Dick Farrell .10 .25
257 Bud Daley .10 .25
258 Luis Arroyo .10 .25
259 Bob Del Greco .10 .25
260 Ted Williams 4.00 10.00
261 Mike Epstein .10 .25
262 Mickey Mantle 6.00 15.00
263 Jim LeFebvre .10 .25
264 Pat Jarvis .10 .25
265 Chuck Hinton .10 .25
266 Don Larsen .30 .75
267 Jim Coates .10 .25
268 Gary Kolb .10 .25
269 Jim Hart .10 .25
270 Dave McNally .20 .50
271 Jerry Kindall .10 .25
272 Hector Lopez .10 .25
273 Claude Osteen .10 .25
274 Jack Aker .10 .25
275 Mike Shannon .20 .50
276 Lew Burdette .20 .50
277 Mack Jones .10 .25
278 Art Shamsky .10 .25
279 Bob Johnson .10 .25
280 Willie Mays 3.00 8.00
281 Rich Nye .10 .25
282 Bill Cowan .10 .25
283 Gary Kolb .10 .25
284 Woody Held .10 .25
285 Bill Freehan .20 .50
286 Larry Jackson .10 .25
287 Mike Hershberger .10 .25
288 Julian Javier .10 .25
289 Charley Smith .10 .25
290 Hank Aaron 3.00 8.00
291 John Boccabella .10 .25
292 Charley James .10 .25
293 Sammy Ellis .10 .25

1979 TCMA 50'S

The TCMA Stars of the 50's set contains 291 standard-size cards featuring the players of the 50's. The set features a good mix of superstars and not so important players of the era. This set was TCMA's attempt at issuing cards after Topps successfully enjoined them from issuing current players. Using the style which was typical of most of the TCMA issues, the fronts are clear with an informative biography on the back. The Hutchinson and Wertz cards were also issued with the word "SAMPLE" stamped on the back.

COMPLETE SET (291) 40.00 80.00
1 Joe DiMaggio 4.00 10.00
2 Yogi Berra 1.50 4.00
3 Warren Spahn 1.25 3.00
4 Robin Roberts .60 1.50
5 Ernie Banks 1.50 4.00
6 Willie Mays 3.00 8.00
7 Mickey Mantle 6.00 15.00
8 Roy Campanella 1.50 4.00
9 Stan Musial 2.00 5.00
10 Ted Williams 4.00 10.00
11 Ed Bailey .10 .25
12 Ted Kluszewski .40 1.00
13 Ralph Kiner .60 1.50
14 Dick Littlefield .10 .25
15 Nellie Fox .60 1.50
16 Billy Pierce .20 .50
17 Richie Ashburn .60 1.50
18 Del Ennis .20 .50
19 Bob Lemon .60 1.50
20 Early Wynn .60 1.50
21 Joe Collins .10 .25
22 Hank Bauer .20 .50
23 Roberto Clemente 4.00 10.00
24 Frank Thomas .20 .50
25 Alvin Dark .20 .50
26 Whitey Lockman .10 .25
27 Larry Doby .60 1.50
28 Bob Feller 1.50 4.00
29 Willie Jones .10 .25
30 Granny Hamner .10 .25
31 Clem Labine .20 .50
32 Ralph Branca .20 .50
33 Jack Harshman .10 .25
34 Dick Donovan .10 .25
35 Tommy Henrich .30 .75
36 Jerry Coleman .20 .50
37 Billy Hoeft .10 .25
38 Johnny Groth .10 .25
39 Harvey Haddix .20 .50
40 Gerry Staley .10 .25
41 Dale Long .10 .25
42 Vernon Law .20 .50
43 Dodger Power .75 2.00
44 Sam Jethroe .20 .50
45 Vic Wertz .20 .50
45A Vic Wertz .20 .50
Sample Back
46 Wes Westrum .10 .25
47 Dee Fondy .10 .25
48 Gene Baker .10 .25
49 Sandy Koufax 2.00 5.00
50 Billy Loes .10 .25
51 Chuck Diering .10 .25
52 Joe Ginsberg .10 .25
53 Jim Konstanty .20 .50
54 Curt Simmons .20 .50
55 Alex Kellner .10 .25
56 Charlie Dressen MG .20 .50
57 Frank Sullivan .10 .25
58 Mel Parnell .10 .25
59 Bobby Hofman .10 .25
60 Bill Connelly .10 .25
61 Corky Valentine .10 .25
62 Johnny Klippstein .10 .25
63 Chuck Tanner .20 .50
64 Dick Drott .10 .25
65 Dean Stone .10 .25
66 Jim Busby .10 .25
67 Sid Gordon .10 .25
68 Del Crandall .20 .50
69 Walker Cooper .10 .25
70 Hank Sauer .20 .50
71 Gil Hodges .40 1.00
72 Duke Snider 1.50 4.00
73 Sherman Lollar .10 .25
74 Chico Carrasquel .10 .25
75 Gus Triandos .20 .50
76 Bob Harrison .10 .25
77 Eddie Waitkus .10 .25
78 Ken Heintzelman .10 .25
79 Harry Simpson .10 .25
80 Luke Easter .20 .50
81 Ed Dick .10 .25
82 Jim DePalo .10 .25
83 Billy Cox .20 .50
84 Pee Wee Reese 1.25 3.00
85 Virgil Trucks .10 .25
86 George Kell .40 1.00
87 Mickey Vernon .20 .50
88 Eddie Yost .10 .25
89 Gus Bell .10 .25
91 Eddie Lopat .20 .50
92 Dick Wakefield .10 .25
93 Solly Hemus .10 .25
94 Al Schoendienst .60 1.50
95 Sammy White .10 .25
96 Billy Goodman .10 .25
97 Jim Hearn .10 .25
98 Ruben Gomez .10 .25
99 Marty Marion .20 .50
100 Bill Virdon .20 .50
101 Chuck Stobbs .10 .25
102 Ron Samford .10 .25
103 Bill Tuttle .10 .25
104 Harvey Kuenn .20 .50
105 Joe Cunningham .20 .50
106 Bill Sarni .10 .25
107 Jack Kramer .10 .25
108 Eddie Stanky .20 .50
109 Carmen Mauro .10 .25
110 Wayne Belardi .10 .25
111 Preston Ward .10 .25
112 Jack Shepard .10 .25
113 Buddy Kerr .10 .25
114 Vern Bickford .10 .25
115 Ellis Kinder .10 .25
116 Walt Dropo .10 .25
117 Duke Maas .10 .25
118 Billy Hunter .10 .25
119 Ewell Blackwell .20 .50
120 Hershell Freeman .10 .25
121 Freddie Martin .10 .25
122 Erv Dusak .10 .25
123 Roy Hartsfield .10 .25
124 Willard Marshall .10 .25
125 Jack Sanford .10 .25
126 Herman Wehmeier .10 .25
127 Hal Smith .10 .25
128 Jim Finigan .10 .25
129 Bob Hale .10 .25
130 Jim Wilson .10 .25
131 Bill Wight .10 .25
132 Mike Fornieles .10 .25
133 Steve Gromek .10 .25
134 Herb Score .20 .50
135 Ryne Duren .20 .50
136 Bob Turley .20 .50
137 Wally Moon .20 .50
138 Fred Hutchinson .20 .50
138A Fred Hutchinson .20 .50
Sample Back
139 Jim Hegan .10 .25
140 Dale Mitchell .10 .25
141 Walt Moryn .10 .25
142 Cal Neeman .10 .25
143 Billy Martin .40 1.00
144 Phil Rizzuto 1.25 3.00
145 Preacher Roe .30 .75
146 Carl Erskine .30 .75
147 Vic Power .10 .25
148 Elmer Valo .10 .25
149 Don Mueller .20 .50
150 Hank Thompson .10 .25
151 Stan Lopata .10 .25
152 Dick Sisler .10 .25
153 Willard Schmidt .10 .25
154 Roy McMillan .10 .25
155 Gil McDougald .20 .50
156 Gene Woodling .20 .50
157 Eddie Mathews .75 2.00
158 Johnny Logan .20 .50
159 Dan Bankhead .10 .25
160 Joe Black .20 .50
161 Roger Maris 2.00 5.00
162 Bob Cerv .10 .25
163 Paul Minner .10 .25
164 Bob Rush .10 .25
165 Gene Hermanski .10 .25
166 Harry Brecheen .10 .25
167 Davey Williams .10 .25
168 Monte Irvin .60 1.50
169 Clint Courtney .10 .25
170 Sandy Consuegra .10 .25
171 Bobby Shantz .20 .50

172 Harry Byrd .10 .25
173 Marv Throneberry .20 .50
174 Woody Held .10 .25
175 Al Rosen .30 .75
176 Rance Pless .10 .25
177 Steve Bilko .10 .25
178 Joe Presko .10 .25
179 Ray Boone .10 .25
180 Jim Lemon .10 .25
181 Andy Pafko .20 .50
182 Don Newcombe .30 .75
183 Frank Lary .10 .25
184 Al Kaline 1.50 4.00
185 Allie Reynolds .30 .75
186 Vic Raschi .20 .50
187 Dodger Braintrust .30 .75
188 Jimmy Piersall .20 .50
189 George Wilson .10 .25
190 Dusty Rhodes .10 .25
191 Duane Pillette .10 .25
192 Dave Philley .10 .25
193 Bobby Morgan .10 .25
194 Russ Meyer .10 .25
195 Hector Lopez .10 .25
196 Arnie Portocarrero .10 .25
197 Joe Page .20 .50
198 Tommy Byrne .10 .25
199 Ray Monzant .30 .75
200 John McCall .10 .25
201 Leo Durocher .40 1.00
202 Bobby Thomson .30 .75
203 Jack Banta .10 .25
204 Joe Pignatano .10 .25
205 Carlos Paula .10 .25
206 Roy Sievers .20 .50
207 Mickey McDermott .10 .25
208 Ray Scarborough .10 .25
209 Bill Miller .10 .25
210 Bill Skowron .30 .75
211 Bob Nieman .10 .25
212 Al Pilarcik .10 .25
213 Jerry Priddy .10 .25
214 Frank House .10 .25
215 Don Mossi .20 .50
216 Rocky Colavito .40 1.00
217 Brooks Lawrence .10 .25
218 Ted Wilks .10 .25
219 Zack Monroe .10 .25
220 Art Ditmar .10 .25
221 Cal McLish .10 .25
222 Gene Bearden .10 .25
223 Norm Siebern .10 .25
224 Bob Wiesler .10 .25
225 Foster Castleman .10 .25
226 Daryl Spencer .10 .25
227 Dick Williams .20 .50
228 Don Zimmer .20 .50
229 Jackie Jensen .20 .50
230 Billy Johnson .10 .25
231 Dave Koslo .10 .25
232 Al Corwin .10 .25
233 Erv Palica .10 .25
234 Bob Milliken .10 .25
235 Ray Kaat .10 .25
236 Sammy Calderone .10 .25
237 Don Demeter .10 .25
238 Karl Spooner .10 .25
239 Preacher Roe .20 .50
Johnny Podres
240 Enos Slaughter .40 1.00
241 Dick Kryhoski .10 .25
242 Art Houtteman .10 .25
243 Andy Carey .10 .25
244 Tony Kubek .30 .75
245 Mike McCormick .10 .25
246 Bob Schmidt .10 .25
247 Nelson King .10 .25
248 Bob Skinner .10 .25
249 Dick Bokelmann .10 .25
250 Eddie Kazak .10 .25
251 Billy Klaus .10 .25
252 Norm Zauchin .10 .25
253 Art Schult .10 .25
254 Bob Martyn .10 .25
255 Larry Jansen .10 .25
256 Sal Maglie .20 .50
257 Bob Darnell .10 .25
258 Ken Lehman .10 .25
259 Jim Blackburn .10 .25
260 Bob Purkey .10 .25
261 Harry Walker .10 .25
262 Joe Garagiola .40 1.00
263 Gus Zernial .10 .25
264 Walter Evers .10 .25
265 Mark Freeman .10 .25
266 Charlie Silvera .10 .25
267 Johnny Podres .30 .75
268 Jim Hughes .10 .25
269 Al Worthington .10 .25
270 Hoyt Wilhelm .40 1.00
271 Elston Howard .40 1.00
272 Don Larsen .30 .75
273 Don Hoak .10 .25
274 Chico Fernandez .10 .25
275 Gail Harris .10 .25
276 Valmy Thomas .10 .25
277 George Shuba .10 .25
278 Al Walker .10 .25
279 Willard Ramsdell .10 .25
280 Lindy McDaniel .10 .25
281 Bob Wilson .10 .25
282 Chuck Templeton .10 .25
283 Eddie Robinson .10 .25
284 Bob Porterfield .10 .25
285 Larry Miggins .10 .25
286 Minnie Minoso .40 1.00
287 Lou Boudreau .40 1.00
288 Jim Davenport .10 .25
289 Bob Miller .10 .25
290 Jim Gilliam .30 .75
291 Jackie Robinson 4.00 10.00
BC1 1955 Brooklyn Dodgers .30 .75
Bonus Card
BC2 1957 Milwaukee Braves .30 .75
Bonus Card

1981 TCMA 60's II

The cards in this 189-card set measure approximately 2 1/2" by 3 1/2". This set was actually a continuation of the prior TCMA Stars of the 1960's set and includes 189 additional cards for which the numbering sequence begins at number 294. They are similar in format to the first series, however, many new and different players are featured. The set was produced in 1981 and was only issued in complete set form. No card number 319 was made and there are two cards numbered at 399. The set was available upon release from the manufacturer for $9.99.

COMPLETE SET (189) 75.00 150.00
294 Fritz Brickell .50 1.25
295 Craig Anderson .50 1.25
296 Cliff Cook .50 1.25
297 Pumpsie Green .50 1.25
298 ChooChoo Coleman .50 1.25
299 Don Buford .50 1.25
300 Sparky Anderson 1.50 4.00
301 John Anderson .50 1.25
302 Ted Beard .50 1.25
303 Mickey Mantle 4.00 10.00
Roger Maris
304 Gene Freese .50 1.25
305 Don Wilkinson .50 1.25
306 Walter Alston MG 1.50 4.00
307 George Bamberger .50 1.25
308 Nelson Briles .50 1.25
309 Dave Baldwin .50 1.25
310 Bob Bailey .50 1.25
311 Paul Blair .50 1.25
312 Ken Boswell .50 1.25
313 Sam Bowens .50 1.25
314 Ray Barker .50 1.25
315 Gil Hodges MG 1.25 3.00
Tommie Agee
316 Elmer Valo .50 1.25
317 Ken Walters .50 1.25
318 Joel Horlen .50 1.25
320 Charlie Maxwell .50 1.25
321 Joe Foy .50 1.25
322 Cleon Jones .50 1.25
Tommie Agee
Ron Swoboda
323 Paul Foytack .50 1.25
324 Ron Fairly .75 2.00
325 Wilbur Wood .75 2.00
326 Don Wilson .50 1.25
327 Felix Mantilla .50 1.25
328 Ed Bouchee .50 1.25
329 Sandy Valdespino .50 1.25
330 Al Ferrara .50 1.25
331 Jose Tartabull .50 1.25
332 Dick Kenworthy .50 1.25
333 Don Pavletich .50 1.25
334 Jim Fairey .50 1.25
335 Rico Petrocelli .75 2.00
336 Garry Roggenburk .50 1.25
337 Rick Reichardt .50 1.25
338 Ken McMullen .50 1.25
339 Dooley Womack .50 1.25
340 Joe Moock .50 1.25
341 Lou Brock 3.00 8.00
342 Hector Torres .50 1.25
343 Ted Savage .50 1.25
344 Hobie Landrith .50 1.25
345 Ed Lopat MG .75 2.00
346 Mel Nelson .50 1.25
347 Mickey Lolich 1.25 3.00
348 Al Lopez MG 1.50 4.00
349 ChiChi Olivo .50 1.25
350 Bob Moose .50 1.25
351 Bill McCool .50 1.25
352 Ernie Bowman .50 1.25
353 Tommy McCraw .50 1.25
354 Sam Mele MG .50 1.25
355 Len Boehmer .50 1.25
356 Hank Aaron 4.00 10.00
357 Ron Hunt .50 1.25
358 Luis Aparicio 2.00 5.00
359 Gene Mauch MG .75 2.00
360 Barry Moore .50 1.25
361 John Buzhardt .50 1.25
362 Solly Hemus MG .75 2.00
Gussie Busch OWN
Bill Lewis CO
Johnny Grodzicki CO
363 Duke Snider 3.00 8.00
364 Billy Martin 1.25 3.00
365 Wes Parker .75 2.00
366 Dick Stuart .75 2.00
367 Glenn Beckert .50 1.25
368 Ollie Brown .50 1.25
369 Stan Bahnsen .50 1.25
370 Wesley(Lee) Bales .50 1.25
371 Johnny Keane MG .50 1.25
372 Wally Moon .75 2.00
373 Larry Miller .50 1.25
374 Fred Newman .50 1.25
375 John Orsino .50 1.25
376 Joe Pactwa .50 1.25
377 John O'Donoghue .50 1.25
378 Jim Ollom .50 1.25
379 Ray Oyler .50 1.25
380 Ron Nischwitz .50 1.25
381 Ron Paul .50 1.25
382 Roger Maris 3.00 8.00
Yogi Berra
Johnny Blanchard
383 Jim McKnight .50 1.25
384 Gene Michael .75 2.00
385 Dave May .50 1.25
386 Tim McCarver 1.50 4.00
387 Larry Mason .50 1.25
388 Don Hoak .50 1.25
389 Nate Oliver .50 1.25
390 Phil Ortega .50 1.25
391 Billy Madden .50 1.25
392 John Miller .50 1.25
393 Danny Murtaugh MG .75 2.00
394 Nelson Mathews .50 1.25
395 Red Schoendienst 1.50 4.00
396 Roger Nelson .50 1.25
397 Tom Matchick .50 1.25
398 Dennis Musgraves .50 1.25
399 Tommy Harper .75 2.00
399 Chet Trail .50 1.25
400 Francis Peters .50 1.25
401 Tony Pierce .50 1.25
402 Billy Williams 2.00 5.00
403 Dave Boswell .50 1.25
404 Ray Washburn .50 1.25
405 Al Worthington .50 1.25
406 Jesus Alou .50 1.25
407 Gil Hodges MG 1.50 4.00
Yogi Berra CO
Eddie Yost CO
Rube Walker CO
Joe Pignatano CO
408 Wally Bunker .50 1.25
409 Jim Brenneman .50 1.25
410 Bobby Bragan MG .50 1.25
411 Cal McLish .50 1.25
412 Curt Blefary .50 1.25
413 Jim Bethke .50 1.25
414 Bill White .75 2.00
Julian Javier
Dick Groat
Ken Boyer
415 Richie Allen 1.25 3.00
416 Larry Brown .50 1.25
417 Mike Andrews .50 1.25
418 Don Mossi .75 2.00
419 J.C. Martin .50 1.25
420 Dick Rustek .50 1.25
421 Elly Rodriguez .50 1.25
422 Casey Stengel MG 3.00 8.00
423 Gil Hodges MG 1.25 3.00
Ed Vargo UMP
424 Johnny Briggs .50 1.25
425 Bud Harrelson .50 1.25
Al Weis
426 Doc Edwards .50 1.25
427 Joe Hague .50 1.25
428 Lee Elia .50 1.25
429 Billy Moran .50 1.25
430 Al Moran .50 1.25
431 Pete Mikkelsen .50 1.25
432 Aurelio Monteagudo .50 1.25
433 Ken Mackenzie .50 1.25
434 Dick Egan .50 1.25
435 Al McBean .50 1.25
436 Mike Ferraro .50 1.25
437 Gary Wagner .50 1.25
438 Jerry Grote .50 1.25
J.C. Martin
439 Ted Kluszewski 1.50 4.00
440 Jerry Johnson .50 1.25
441 Ross Moschitto .50 1.25
442 Zoilo Versalles .50 1.25
443 Dennis Ribant .50 1.25
444 Ted Williams 4.00 10.00
445 Steve Whitaker .50 1.25
446 Frank Bertaina .50 1.25
447 Bo Belinsky 1.25 3.00
448 Joe Moeller .50 1.25
449 Ron Taylor .50 1.25
Don Shaw
450 Al Downing 1.25 3.00
Mel Stottlemyre
Fritz Peterson
Whitey Ford CO
451 Jack Tracy .50 1.25
452 Tony Curry .50 1.25
453 Roy White .75 2.00
454 Jim Bunning 2.00 5.00
455 Ralph Houk MG .75 2.00
456 Bobby Shantz .75 2.00
457 Bill Rigney MG .50 1.25
458 Roger Repoz .50 1.25
459 Bob Turley .75 2.00
Robin Roberts
460 Gordon Richardson .50 1.25
461 Dick Tracewski .50 1.25
462 Thad Tillotson .50 1.25
463 Bobo Osborne .50 1.25
464 Larry Burright .50 1.25
465 Alan Foster .50 1.25
466 Ron Taylor .50 1.25
467 Fred Talbot .50 1.25
468 Bob Miller .50 1.25
469 Frank Tepedino .75 2.00
470 Danny Frisella .50 1.25
471 Cecil Perkins UER .50 1.25
Rich Beck pictured
472 Danny Napoleon .50 1.25
473 John Upham .50 1.25
474 Roger Maris 4.00 10.00
Yogi Berra
Mickey Mantle
Elston Howard
Moose Skowron
Johnny Blanchard
475 Al Weis .50 1.25
476 Rich Beck UER .50 1.25
Cecil Perkins pictured
477 Clete Boyer 1.50 4.00
Tony Kubek
Bobby Richardson
Joe Pepitone
478 Jack Fisher .50 1.25
479 Archie Moore .50 1.25
480 Ralph Terry .50 1.25
481 Jim Hegan CO .75 2.00
Wally Moses CO
Ralph Houk MG
Frank Crosetti CO
Johnny Sain CO
482 Gil Hodges 2.50 6.00
Clem Labine
Cookie Lavagetto CO
Roger Craig
Don Zimmer
Charlie Neal
Casey Stengel MG

1982 TCMA Greatest Pitchers

This-45 card set honors Baseball's greatest pitchers and features both color and black-and-white player photos with either thin red or green borders printed on white. The backs carry player information and career statistics.

COMPLETE SET (45) 8.00 20.00
1 Bob Feller .60 1.50
2 Bob Lemon .40 1.00
3 Whitey Ford .60 1.50
4 Joe Page .08 .25
5 Wilbur Wood .08 .25
6 Robin Roberts .40 1.00
7 Warren Spahn .60 1.50
8 Sandy Koufax .75 2.00
9 Juan Marichal .40 1.00
10 Don Newcombe .20 .50
11 Hoyt Wilhelm .30 .75
12 Roy Face .08 .25
13 Allie Reynolds .20 .50
14 Don Drysdale .40 1.00
15 Bob Gibson .40 1.00
16 Cy Young .75 2.00
17 Walter Johnson .75 2.00
18 Grover Alexander .60 1.50
19 Jack Chesbro .08 .25
20 Lefty Gomez .40 1.00
21 Wes Ferrel .08 .25
22 Hal Newhouser .20 .50
23 Early Wynn .40 1.00
24 Denny McLain .20 .50
25 Catfish Hunter .40 1.00
26 Jim Lonborg .08 .25
27 Frank Lary .08 .25
28 Red Ruffing .40 1.00
29 Lefty Grove .60 1.50
30 Herb Pennock .08 .25
31 Satchel Paige .08 .25
32 Joe McGinnity .40 1.00
33 Christy Mathewson .60 1.50
34 Mordecai Three Finger Brown .40 1.00
35 Eppa Rixey .30 .75
36 Dizzy Dean .40 1.00
37 Carl Hubbell .50 1.25
38 Dazzy Vance .40 1.00
39 Jim Bunning .40 1.00
40 Joe Wood .30 .75
41 Freddie Fitzsimmons .20 .50
42 Rube Waddell .40 1.00
43 Addie Joss .40 1.00
44 Burleigh Grimes .40 1.00
45 Chief Bender .40 1.00

1982 TCMA Greatest Hitters

This-45 card set honors some of Baseball's greatest hitters and features both color and black-and-white player photos with either thin red or green borders printed on white. The backs carry player information and career statistics. All the "greatest" sets were available from TCMA for $4 each.

COMPLETE SET (45) 10.00 25.00
1 Ted Williams 1.25 3.00
2 Stan Musial 1.00 2.50
3 Joe DiMaggio 1.25 3.00
4 Roberto Clemente 1.25 3.00
5 Jackie Robinson 1.25 3.00
6 Willie Mays 1.25 3.00
7 Lou Brock .40 1.00
8 Al Kaline .40 1.00
9 Richie Ashburn .40 1.00
10 Tony Oliva .20 .50
11 Harvey Kuenn .08 .25
12 Mickey Vernon .08 .25
13 Tommy Davis .08 .25
14 Ty Cobb 1.25 3.00
15 Rogers Hornsby .40 1.00
16 Joe Jackson .75 2.00
17 Willie Keeler .08 .25
18 Tris Speaker .20 .50
19 Babe Ruth 2.00 5.00
20 Harry Heilmann .08 .25
21 Bill Terry .20 .50
22 George Sisler .20 .50
23 Lou Gehrig 1.25 3.00
24 Nap Lajoie .40 1.00
25 Riggs Stephenson .08 .25
26 Al Simmons .40 1.00
27 Cap Anson .40 1.00
28 Paul Waner .40 1.00
29 Eddie Collins .40 1.00
30 Heinie Manush .40 1.00
31 Honus Wagner .40 1.00
32 Earle Combs .08 .25
33 Sam Rice .08 .25
34 Charlie Gehringer .40 1.00
35 Chick Hafey .20 .50
36 Zack Wheat .40 1.00
37 Frankie Frisch .40 1.00
38 Bill Dickey .40 1.00
39 Ernie Lombardi .40 1.00
40 Joe Cronin .40 1.00
41 Lefty O'Doul .20 .50
42 Luke Appling .40 1.00
43 Ferris Fain .08 .25
44 Arky Vaughan .30 .75
45 Joe Medwick .40 1.00

1982 TCMA Greatest Sluggers

This-45 card set honors some of Baseball's greatest sluggers and features both color and black-and-white player photos with either thin red or green borders printed on white. The backs carry player information and career statistics.

COMPLETE SET (45) 10.00 25.00
1 Harmon Killebrew .40 1.00
2 Roger Maris .40 1.00
3 Mickey Mantle 2.00 5.00
4 Hank Aaron 1.25 3.00
5 Ralph Kiner .40 1.00
6 Willie McCovey .40 1.00
7 Eddie Matthews .40 1.00
8 Ernie Banks .40 1.00
9 Duke Snider .40 1.00
10 Frank Howard .20 .50
11 Ted Kluszewski .30 .75
12 Frank Robinson .40 1.00
13 Billy Williams .40 1.00
14 Gil Hodges .30 .75
15 Yogi Berra .40 1.00
16 Richie Allen .30 .75
17 Joe Adcock .08 .25
18 Babe Ruth 2.00 5.00
19 Lou Gehrig 1.25 3.00
20 Jimmie Foxx .40 1.00
21 Rogers Hornsby .40 1.00
22 Ted Williams 1.25 3.00
23 Hack Wilson .40 1.00
24 Al Simmons .40 1.00
25 John Mize .40 1.00
26 Chuck Klein .30 .75
27 Hank Greenberg .40 1.00
28 Babe Herman .20 .50
29 Norm Cash .08 .25
30 Rudy York .08 .25
31 Gavvy Cravath .08 .25
32 Mel Ott .40 1.00
33 Orlando Cepeda .20 .50
34 Dolph Camilli .08 .25
35 Frank Baker .30 .75
36 Larry Doby .40 1.00
37 Jim Gentile .08 .25
38 Harry Davis .08 .25
39 Rocco Colavito .40 1.00
40 Cy Williams .20 .50
41 Roy Seivers .08 .25
42 Boog Powell .20 .50
43 Willie Mays 1.25 3.00
44 Joe Dimaggio 1.25 3.00
45 Earl Averill .40 1.00

1982 TCMA Stars of the 50's

This 20-card set features color photos of great Baseball stars of the 1950s printed in a postcard format and measuring approximately 3 3/4" by 5 3/4".

COMPLETE SET (20) 10.00 25.00
1 Roberto Clemente 2.00 5.00
2 Sandy Koufax 1.00 2.50
3 Phil Rizzuto .60 1.50
4 Bob Feller .60 1.50
5 Duke Snider 1.00 2.50
6 Hank Aaron 1.50 4.00
7 Eddie Mathews .60 1.50
8 Roy Campanella 1.00 2.50
9 Willie Mays 1.50 4.00
10 Robin Roberts .40 1.00
11 Nellie Fox .40 1.00
12 Early Wynn .40 1.00
13 Ted Williams 1.50 4.00
14 Warren Spahn .40 1.00
15 Jackie Robinson 2.00 5.00
16 Joe DiMaggio 2.00 5.00
17 Frank Robinson .40 1.00
18 Yogi Berra .75 2.00
19 Mickey Mantle 2.50 6.00
20 Stan Musial 1.50 4.00

1983 TCMA Playball 1942

This 45-card standard-size set was printed in 1983 by TCMA and features sepia-tone posed and action player photos with white borders. A black-outline banner at the bottom contains the player's name and is accented with a baseball glove, bat, ball, and catchers mask icons. The backs are cardboard with navy blue print and display biography, player profile, and a Playball advertisement. All the TCMA Playball sets were available directly from TCMA for $4 each.

COMPLETE SET (45) 15.00 40.00
1 Joe Gordon .30 .75
2 Joe DiMaggio 4.00 10.00
3 Bill Dickey .60 1.50
4 Joe McCarthy MG .60 1.50
5 Tex Hughson .20 .50
6 Ted Williams 4.00 10.00
7 Walt Judnich .20 .50
8 Vern Stephens .30 .75
9 Denny Galehouse .20 .50
10 Lou Boudreau P .60 1.50
MG
11 Ken Keltner .30 .75
12 Jim Bagby .20 .50
13 Rudy York .20 .50
14 Barney McCosky .20 .50
15 Schoolboy Rowe .20 .50
16 Luke Appling .60 1.50
17 Taffy Wright .20 .50
18 Ted Lyons .60 1.50
19 Mickey Vernon .30 .75
20 George Case .20 .50
21 Bobo Newsom .30 .75
22 Bob Johnson .20 .50
23 Buddy Blair .20 .50
24 Pete Suder .20 .50
25 Terry Moore .20 .50
26 Stan Musial 2.00 5.00
27 Marty Marion .40 1.00
28 Pee Wee Reese 1.25 3.00
29 Arky Vaughan .60 1.50
30 Larry French .20 .50
31 Johnny Mize .60 1.50
32 Mel Ott P .60 1.50
MG
33 Willard Marshall .20 .50
34 Carl Hubbell .60 1.50
35 Frank McCormick .20 .50
36 Linus Frey .20 .50
37 Bob Elliott .30 .75
38 Vince DiMaggio .20 .50
39 Al Lopez .60 1.50
40 Stan Hack .30 .75
41 Lou Novikoff .20 .50
42 Casey Stengel MG .60 1.50
43 Tommy Holmes .30 .75
44 Ron Northey .20 .50
45 Rube Melton .20 .50

1983 TCMA Playball 1943

This 45-card standard-size set was printed in 1983 by TCMA and features sepia-tone posed and action player photos with white borders. A black-outline banner at the bottom contains the player's name and is accented with a baseball glove, bat, ball, and catchers mask icons. The backs are cardboard with navy blue print and display biography, player profile, and a Playball advertisement.

COMPLETE SET (45) 8.00 20.00
1 Spud Chandler .30 .75
2 Frank Crosetti .30 .75
3 Johnny Lindell .20 .50
4 Dutch Leonard .20 .50
5 Stan Spence .20 .50
6 Ray Mack .20 .50
7 Hank Edwards .20 .50
8 Al Smith .20 .50
9 Mike Tresh .20 .50
10 Don Kolloway .20 .50
11 Orval Grove .20 .50
12 Doc Cramer .30 .75
13 Mike Higgins .20 .50
14 Dick Wakefield .20 .50
15 Harland Clift .20 .50
16 Chet Laabs .20 .50
17 George McQuinn .20 .50
18 Tony Lupien .20 .50
19 Oscar Judd .20 .50
20 Roy Partee .20 .50
21 Lum Harris .20 .50
22 Roger Wolf .20 .50
23 Dick Siebert .20 .50
24 Walker Cooper .30 .75
25 Mort Cooper .30 .75
26 Whitey Kurowski .20 .50
27 Eddie Miller .20 .50
28 Elmer Riddle .20 .50
29 Bucky Walters .30 .75
30 Whitlow Wyatt .30 .75
31 Dolph Camilli .30 .75
32 Elbie Fletcher .20 .50
33 Frank Gustine .20 .50
34 Rip Sewell .20 .50
35 Phil Cavarretta .30 .75
36 Bill(Swish) Nicholson .30 .75
37 Peanuts Lowery .20 .50
38 Phil Masi .20 .50
39 Al Javery .20 .50
40 Jim Tobin .20 .50
41 Glen Stewart .20 .50
42 Mickey Livingston .20 .50
43 Ace Adams .20 .50
44 Joe Medwick .60 1.50
45 Sid Gordon .30 .75

1983 TCMA Playball 1944

This 45-card standard-size set was printed in 1983 by TCMA and features black and white posed and action player photos with white borders. A blue-outline banner at the bottom contains the player's name and is accented with a baseball glove, bat, ball and catchers mask icons. The backs are cardboard with black print and display biography, player profile, and a Playball advertisement.

COMPLETE SET (45) 8.00 20.00
1 Don Gutteridge .20 .50
2 Mark Christman .20 .50
3 Mike Kreevich .20 .50
4 Jimmy Outlaw .20 .50
5 Paul Richards .30 .75
6 Hal Newhouser .50 1.25
7 Bud Metheny .20 .50
8 Mike Garbark .20 .50
9 Hersh Martin .20 .50
10 Bob Johnson .20 .50
11 Mike Ryba .20 .50
12 Oris Hockett .20 .50
13 Ed Klieman .20 .50
14 Ford Garrison .20 .50
15 Irv Hall .20 .50
16 Ed Busch .20 .50
17 Ralph Hodgin .20 .50
18 Thurman Tucker .20 .50
19 Bill Dietrich .20 .50
20 Rick Ferrell .50 1.25
21 John Sullivan .20 .50
22 Mickey Haefner .20 .50
23 Ray Sanders .20 .50
24 Johnny Hopp .20 .50
25 Ted Wilks .20 .50
26 John Barrett .20 .50
27 Jim Russell .20 .50
28 Nick Strincevich .20 .50
29 Eric Tipton .20 .50
30 Jim Konstanty .30 .75
31 Gee Walker .20 .50
32 Dom Dellessandro .20 .50
33 Bob Chipman .20 .50
34 Hank Wyse .20 .50
35 Phil Weintraub .20 .50
36 George Hausmann .20 .50
37 Bill Voiselle .20 .50
38 Whitey Wietelman .20 .50
39 Clyde Kluttz .20 .50
40 Connie Ryan .20 .50
41 Eddie Stanky .30 .75
42 Augie Galan .30 .75
43 Mickey Owen .20 .50
44 Charlie Schanz .20 .50
45 Bob Finley .20 .50

1983 TCMA Playball 1945

This 45-card standard-size set was printed in 1983 by TCMA and features black and white posed and action player photos with white borders. A blue-outline banner at the bottom contains the player's name and is accented with a baseball glove, bat, ball, and catchers mask icons. The backs are cardboard with black print and display biography, player profile, and a Playball advertisement.

COMPLETE SET (45) 8.00 20.00
1 Eddie Mayo .20 .50
2 Dizzy Trout .30 .75
3 Roy Cullenbine .20 .50
4 Joe Kuhel .20 .50
5 George Binks .20 .50
6 Roger Wolff .20 .50
7 Gene Moore .20 .50
8 Frank Mancuso .20 .50
9 Bob Muncrief .20 .50
10 Tuck Stainback .20 .50
11 Bill Bevens .20 .50
12 Snuffy Stirnweiss .30 .75
13 Don Ross .20 .50
14 Felix Mackiewicz .20 .50
15 Jeff Heath .30 .75
16 Johnny Dickshot .20 .50
17 Ed Lopat .40 1.00
18 Skeeter Newsom .20 .50
19 Eddie Lake .20 .50
20 John Lazor .20 .50
21 Hal Peck .20 .50
22 Al Brancato .20 .50
23 Paul Derringer .30 .75
24 Stan Hack .20 .50
25 Lenny Merullo .20 .50
26 Emil Verban .20 .50
27 Ken O'Dea .20 .50
28 Red Barrett .20 .50
29 Eddie Basinski .20 .50
30 Dixie Walker .30 .75
31 Goody Rosen .20 .50
32 Preacher Roe .30 .75
33 Pete Coscarart .20 .50
34 Frankie Frisch MG .50 1.25
35 Nap Reyes .20 .50
36 Danny Gardella .20 .50
37 Buddy Kerr .20 .50
38 Dick Culler .20 .50
39 Tommy Holmes .30 .75
40 Al Libke .20 .50
41 Howie Fox .20 .50
42 Johnny Riddle .20 .50
43 Andy Seminick .30 .75
44 Andy Karl .20 .50
45 Rene Monteguedo .20 .50

1983 TCMA Ruth

This six-card set features borderless black-and-white photos of Babe Ruth with other players and measures approximately 2 5/8" by 4". The backs display a postcard format and carry a cancelled Babe Ruth 20 cent postage stamp dated July 6, 1983, the first day of issue. The cards are unnumbered and checklisted below in alphabetical order.

COMPLETE SET (6) 8.00 20.00
1 Earl Averill 1.50 4.00
Ben Chapman
Heinie Manush
Babe Rut
2 Lou Gehrig 1.50 4.00
Joe McCarthy
Babe Ruth
3 Miller Huggins MG 1.50 4.00
Babe Ruth
4 Walter Johnson 1.50 4.00
Babe Ruth
5 Tony Lazzari 1.50 4.00
Babe Ruth CO
6 Babe Ruth 1.50 4.00
Bill Terry

1984 TCMA All-Time All Stars

These standard-size cards were issued by TCMA and feature players who did exceptionally well in All-Star Games. The fronts have a player photo in a specially colored frame surrounded by white borders. The frames are red for National League players and blue for American League players. The player's name is in white against the blue frame. The back has information about the reason for this set as well as the player's All-Star game career record. Since these cards are unnumbered, we have sequenced them in alphabetical order.

COMPLETE SET 4.00 10.00
1 Ernie Banks .50 1.25
2 Lou Boudreau .30 .75
3 Ken Boyer .20 .50
4 Roberto Clemente 1.25 3.00
5 Rocky Colavito .30 .75
6 Bill Dickey .20 .50
7 Nellie Fox .30 .75
8 Jimmie Foxx .50 1.25
9 Dick Groat .20 .50
10 Mel Harder .20 .50
11 Billy Herman .20 .50
12 Al Kaline .50 1.25
13 Ernie Lombardi .20 .50
14 Juan Marichal .30 .75
15 Willie Mays 1.00 2.50
16 Stan Musial .75 2.00
17 Brooks Robinson .30 .75
18 Ted Williams 1.00 2.50

1984 TCMA Bruce Stark Postcards

This five-card set features artwork of great players by Bruce Stark measuring approximately 3 3/4" by 5 3/4" and printed in a postcard format.

COMPLETE SET (5) 6.00 15.00
BS1 Joe DiMaggio 2.00 5.00
BS2 Ted Williams 2.00 5.00
BS3 Ted Kluzewski UER .75 2.00
misspelled Kluszewski
BS4 Mickey Vernon .40 1.00
BS5 Stan Musial 1.50 4.00

1984 TCMA HOF Induction Postcards

These two postcards feature some of the players who were inducted into Cooperstown in 1984. These cards are unnumbered so we have sequenced them in alphabetical order.

COMPLETE SET (2) 1.25 3.00
1 Luis Aparicio .40 1.00
2 Pee Wee Reese .75 2.00

1984 TCMA Playball 1946

This 45-card standard-size set was printed in 1984 by TCMA and features black and white posed and action player photos with white borders. A green-outline banner at the bottom contains the player's name and is accented with a baseball glove, bat, ball, and catchers mask icons. The backs are cardboard with black print and display biography, player profile, and a Playball advertisement.

COMPLETE SET (45) 12.50 30.00
1 Dom DiMaggio .30 .75
2 Boo Ferriss .08 .25
3 Johnny Pesky .20 .50
4 Hank Greenberg .75 2.00
5 George Kell .40 1.00
6 Virgil Trucks .08 .25
7 Phil Rizzuto .75 2.00
8 Charlie Keller .20 .50
9 Tommy Henrich .30 .75
10 Cecil Travis .08 .25
11 Al Evans .08 .25
12 Buddy Lewis .08 .25
13 Edgar Smith .08 .25
14 Dario Lodigiani .08 .25
15 Earl Caldwell .08 .25
16 Jim Hegan .08 .25
17 Bob Feller .75 2.00
18 John Berardino .20 .50
19 Jack Kramer .08 .25
20 John Lucadello .08 .25
21 Hank Majeski .08 .25
22 Elmer Valo .08 .25
23 Buddy Rosar .08 .25
24 Red Schoendienst .40 1.00
25 Dick Sisler .08 .25
26 Johnny Beazley .08 .25
27 Vic Lombardi .08 .25
28 Dick Whitman .08 .25
29 Carl Furillo .30 .75
30 Billy Jurges .08 .25
31 Marv Rickert .08 .25
32 Clyde McCullough .08 .25
33 Johnny Hopp .08 .25
34 Mort Cooper .08 .25
35 Johnny Sain .20 .50
36 Del Ennis .20 .50
37 Roy Hughes .08 .25
38 Bert Haas .08 .25
39 Grady Hatton .08 .25
40 Ed Bahr .08 .25
41 Billy Cox .20 .50
42 Lee Handley .08 .25
43 Bill Rigney .08 .25
44 Babe Young .08 .25
45 Buddy Blattner .08 .25

1985 TCMA AL MVP

COMPLETE SET (10) 4.00 10.00
1 Richie Allen .30 .75
2 Yogi Berra .60 1.50
3 Elston Howard .40 1.00
4 Jackie Jensen .30 .75
5 Harmon Killebrew .50 1.25
6 Mickey Mantle 1.25 3.00
7 Roger Maris .60 1.50
8 Boog Powell .30 .75
9 Brooks Robinson .50 1.25
10 Carl Yastrzemski .40 1.00

1985 TCMA Cy Young Award

This 10-card set features color photos of past greats who won the Cy Young Award. The cards were printed with an orange border at the top and bottom and are unnumbered and checklisted below in alphabetical order.

COMPLETE SET (10) 4.00 10.00
1 Don Drysdale .60 1.50
2 Whitey Ford .60 1.50
3 Bob Gibson .60 1.50
4 Catfish Hunter .40 1.00
5 Sandy Koufax .75 2.00
6 Vernon Law .30 .75
7 Sparky Lyle .30 .75
8 Denny McLain .40 1.00
9 Jim Palmer .40 1.00
10 Warren Spahn .40 1.00

1985 TCMA Home Run Champs

This 10-card set features color photos of players who hit home runs regularly in white borders with brown sun borders. The cards are unnumbered and checklisted below in alphabetical order.

COMPLETE SET (10) 4.00 10.00
1 Hank Aaron 1.25 3.00
2 Orlando Cepeda .40 1.00
3 Joe DiMaggio 1.25 3.00
4 Larry Doby .40 1.00
5 Ralph Kiner .40 1.00
6 Eddie Mathews .40 1.00
7 Willie McCovey .40 1.00
8 Al Rosen .30 .75
9 Duke Snider .40 1.00
10 Ted Williams 1.25 3.00

1985 TCMA NL MVP

COMPLETE SET (10) 5.00 12.00
1 Ernie Banks .50 1.25
2 Johnny Bench .60 1.50
3 Roy Campanella .40 1.00
4 Roberto Clemente .75 2.00
5 Dick Groat .30 .75
6 Willie Mays 1.00 2.50
7 Frank Robinson .50 1.25
7 Stan Musial .50 1.25
8 Willie Stargell .40 1.00
10 Maury Wills .40 1.00

1985 TCMA Photo Classics

This 40-card set features black-and-white photos of great Baseball players and measures approximately 3 1/2" by 5 1/2".

COMPLETE SET (40) 20.00 50.00
1 Warren Spahn .60 1.50
Johnny Sain
2 Jackie Robinson 2.00 5.00
3 President Eisenhowser .75 2.00
Meeting the Yankees
4 Babe Ruth 3.00 8.00
5 Yankees Dugout 1.00 2.50
Joe McCarthy MG
Lou Gehrig MG
Jo
6 Bob Feller 1.00 2.50
7 Johnny Lindell .40 1.00
Johnny Murphy
8 Babe Ruth 1.50 4.00
Claire Ruth
9 Babe Ruth 1.50 4.00
Joe Cook
10 Bobo Newsom .40 1.00
11 Johnny Antonelli .40 1.00
Robin Roberts
12 Joe Adcock .60 1.50
Eddie Mathews
13 Al Lopez MG .40 1.00
Mike Garcia
Bob Lemon
Early Wynn
14 Gil McDougald .75 2.00
Roy Campanella
15 Ralph Branca .40 1.00
Bobby Thomson
16 Lou Gehrig .40 1.00
17 John Mize .75 2.00
Bill Rigney
Mel Ott
18 Jorgeson 1.00 2.50
Pee Wee Reese
Eddie Stanky
Jackie Robi
19 Tommy Holmes .40 1.00
Earl Torgeson
Jeff Heath
Connie Ry
20 Ted Williams 1.00 2.50
Bobby Doerr
Dom DiMaggio
Vern Step
21 Chuck Shilling .60 1.50
Carl Yasztremski
22 Roger Maris 1.50 4.00
Mickey Mantle
23 Rogers Hornsby 1.00 2.50
Gil McDougald
24 Jim Gentle .40 1.00
Gus Triandos
25 Bobby Avila 1.00 2.50
Willie Mays
26 Joe Garagiola .75 2.00
Ralph Kiner
27 Jim Gentile 1.00 2.50
Willie Mays
28 Red Schoendienst .60 1.50
Marty Marion
29 Charlie Keller .40 1.00
30 House of David team .40 1.00
31 Harvey Kuenn .40 1.00
Al Kaline
32 Hank Sauer .40 1.00
33 Enos Slaughter .40 1.00
34 Stan Musial 1.00 2.50
35 Willie Mays 2.00 5.00
36 William Bendix 1.50 4.00
Babe Ruth
37 Lockman .40 1.00
Williams
Thompson
Dark Mueller
Mays
I
38 Pete Runnels .40 1.00
Vic Wertz
39 Stan Musial 1.00 2.50
40 Dom DiMaggio .40 1.00

1985 TCMA Playball 1947

This 45-card standard-size set was printed in 1985 by TCMA and features black and white posed and action player photos with white borders. A blue-outline banner at the bottom contains the player's name and is accented with a baseball glove, bat, ball, and catchers mask icons. The backs are cardboard with black print and display biography, player profile, and a Playball advertisement.

COMPLETE SET (45) 20.00 50.00
1 Hal Wagner .30 .75
2 Jake Jones .30 .75
3 Bobby Doerr 1.25 3.00
4 Fred Hutchinson .60 1.50
5 Bob Swift .30 .75
6 Pat Mullin .30 .75
7 Joe Page .60 1.50
8 Allie Reynolds .60 1.50
9 Billy Johnson .30 .75
10 Early Wynn 1.25 3.00
11 Eddie Yost .30 .75
12 Floyd Baker .30 .75
13 Dave Philley .30 .75
14 George Dickey .30 .75
15 Dale Mitchell .60 1.50
16 Bob Lemon 1.25 3.00
17 Jerry Witte .30 .75
18 Paul Lehner .30 .75
19 Sam Zoldak .30 .75
20 Sam Chapman .30 .75
21 Eddie Joost .60 1.50
22 Ferris Fain .60 1.50
23 Erv Dusak .30 .75
24 Joe Garagiola 1.00 2.50
25 Vernal Nippy Jones .30 .75
26 Bobby Bragan .30 .75
27 Jackie Robinson 4.00 10.00
28 Spider Jorgensen .30 .75
29 TCMA Playball 1947 .30 .75
Bob Scheffing
30 Johnny Schmitz .30 .75
31 Doyle Lade .30 .75
32 Earl Torgeson .30 .75
33 Warren Spahn 1.25 3.00
34 Walt Lanfranconi .30 .75
35 Johnny Wyrostek .30 .75
36 Oscar Judd .30 .75
37 Ewell Blackwell .60 1.50
38 Eddie Lukon .30 .75
39 Benny Zientara .30 .75
40 Gene Woodling .60 1.50
41 Ernie Bonham .30 .75
42 Hank Greenberg 1.25 3.00
43 Bobby Thomson 1.00 2.50
44 Jack Lucky Lohrke .30 .75
45 Dave Koslo .30 .75

1985 TCMA Playball 1948

This 45-card set was printed in 1985 by TCMA and measures approximately 2 1/2" by 3 1/8". The fronts feature player photos with red trimming. The backs are cardboard with black print and display biography, player profile, and a Playball advertisement.

COMPLETE SET (45) 30.00 60.00
1 Murry Dickson .60 1.50
2 Enos Slaugther 1.50 4.00
3 Don Lang .60 1.50
4 Joe Hatten .60 1.50
5 Gil Hodges 1.50 4.00
6 Gene Hermanski .60 1.50
7 Eddie Waitkus 1.00 2.50
8 Jesse Dobernic .60 1.50
9 Andy Pafko 1.00 2.50
10 Vern Bickford .60 1.50
11 Mike McCormick .60 1.50
12 Harry Walker 1.00 2.50
13 Putsy Caballero .60 1.50
14 Dutch Leonard .60 1.50
15 Frank Baumholtz .60 1.50
16 Ted Kluszewski 1.50 4.00
17 Virgil Stallcup .60 1.50
18 Bob Chesnes .60 1.50
19 Ted Beard .60 1.50
20 Wes Westrum .60 1.50
21 Clint Hartung .60 1.50
22 Whitey Lockman 1.00 2.50
23 Billy Goodman .60 1.50
24 Jack Kramer .60 1.50
25 Mel Parnell 1.00 2.50
26 George Vico .60 1.50
27 Walter Evers .60 1.50
28 Vic Wertz .60 1.50
29 Yogi Berra 3.00 8.00
30 Joe DiMaggio 4.00 10.00
31 Tommy Byrne .60 1.50
32 Al Kozar .60 1.50
33 Jake Early .60 1.50
34 Gil Coan .60 1.50
35 Pat Seerey .60 1.50
36 Ralph Hodgin .60 1.50
37 Allie Clark .60 1.50
38 Gene Bearden .60 1.50
39 Steve Gromek .60 1.50
40 Al Zarilla .60 1.50
41 Fred Sanford .60 1.50
42 Les Moss .60 1.50
43 Don White .60 1.50
44 Carl Scheib .60 1.50
45 Lou Brissie .60 1.50

1985 TCMA Playball 1949

This 45-card set was printed in 1985 by TCMA and measures approximately 2 1/2" by 3 1/8". The fronts feature player photos with red trimming. The backs are cardboard with black print and display biography, player profile, and a Playball advertisement.

COMPLETE SET (45) 8.00 20.00
1 Al Brazle .08 .25
2 Harry Brecheen .08 .25
3 Howie Pollet .08 .25
4 Cal Abrams .08 .25
5 Ralph Branca .20 .50
6 Duke Snider 1.25 3.00
7 Charlie Grimm .20 .50
8 Clarence Maddern .08 .25
9 Hal Jeffcoat .08 .25
10 John Antonelli .20 .50
11 Alvin Dark .30 .75
12 Nelson Potter .08 .25
13 Granny Hamner .20 .50
14 Willie Jones .20 .50
15 Robin Roberts .75 2.00
16 Lloyd Merriman .08 .25
17 Bobby Adams .08 .25
18 Herm Wehmeier .08 .25
19 Ralph Kiner .75 2.00
20 Dino Restelli .08 .25
21 Larry Jansen .20 .50
22 Sheldon Jones .08 .25
23 Red Webb .08 .25
24 Vern Stephens .20 .50
25 Tex Hughson .08 .25
26 Ellis Kinder .08 .25
27 Neil Berry .08 .25
28 Johnny Groth .08 .25
29 Art Houteman .08 .25
30 Hank Bauer .20 .50
31 Vic Raschi .20 .50
32 Bobby Brown .20 .50
33 Joe Haynes .08 .25
34 Eddie Robinson .08 .25
35 Sam Dente .08 .25
36 Herb Adams .08 .25
37 Don Wheeler .08 .25
38 Randy Gumpert .08 .25
39 Ray Boone .08 .25
40 Larry Doby .40 1.00
41 Jack Graham .08 .25
42 Bob Dillinger .20 .50
43 Dick Kokos .08 .25
44 Wally Moses .08 .25
45 Mike Guerra .08 .25

1985 TCMA Rookies of the Year

COMPLETE SET (10) 6.00 15.00
1 Jackie Robinson
2 Don Newcombe
3 Thurman Munson
4 Frank Howard
5 Billy Williams
6 Herb Score
7 Harvey Kuenn
8 Tony Oliva
9 Luis Aparicio
10 Tommie Agee

1986 TCMA

The 1986 TCMA set is comprised of 20 cards measure 2 5/16" by 3 1/2". The cards were styled after the 1953 Bowman Black and White set. The fronts feature posed and action black-and-white photos within a white outer border and an inner fine black line. The player's name does not appear on the front. The horizontal white backs contain biography within a red stripe, player profile and lifetime statistics are printed below. The card number appears in the top left corner on a diamond icon. The cards are numbered on the back.

COMPLETE SET (20) 6.00 15.00
1 Roberto Clemente .75 2.00
2 Duke Snider .40 1.00
3 Sandy Koufax .60 1.50
4 Carl Hubbell .20 .50
5 Ty Cobb .75 2.00
6 Willie Mays .75 2.00
7 Jackie Robinson .75 2.00
8 Joe DiMaggio .75 2.00
9 Stan Musial .40 1.00
10 Pie Traynor .20 .50
11 Yogi Berra .40 1.00
12 Babe Ruth .75 2.00
13 Brooks Robinson .20 .50
14 Walter Johnson .40 1.00
15 Ted Williams .60 1.50
16 Bill Dickey .20 .50
17 Lou Gehrig .75 2.00
18 Hank Aaron .60 1.50
19 Eddie Mathews .20 .50
20 Mickey Mantle .75 2.00

1986 TCMA Limited Autographs

Thess cards were issued by TCMA as a premium for collectors who purchased other product from TCMA. The front features a glossy photo along with an autograph signed in blue sharpie. The back has a "message" from the player thanking them for their purchase along with the player's 1985 statistics. There may be other cards in this set so any additions are appreciated.

COMPLETE SET 75.00 150.00
2 Tony Gwynn 40.00 80.00
1 Gary Carter 40.00 80.00

1986 TCMA Superstars Simon

These 50 cards mesaure 2 3/4" by 3 1/2". The cards feature drawings from sports artist Robert Stephen Simon on the front. The backs have vital statistics and biographical information.

COMPLETE SET (50) 6.00 15.00
1 Carl Erskine .08 .25
2 Babe Ruth .40 1.00
Hank Aaron
3 Ted Williams .75 2.00
4 Mickey Mantle 1.00 2.50
5 Gil Hodges .20 .50
6 Roberto Clemente .75 2.00
7 Mickey Mantle 1.00 2.50
8 Walter Johnson .30 .75
9 Superstar Card Set .60 1.50
Yanks of Yesteryear
10 Carl Yatrzemski .20 .50
Ted Williams
11 Mickey Mantle 1.00 2.50
12 Harmon Killebrew .30 .75
13 Warren Spahn .30 .75
14 Ralph Kiner .40 1.00
Babe Ruth
15 Bob Gibson .30 .75
16 Pee Wee Reese .30 .75
17 Billy Martin .20 .50
18 Joe DiMaggio .75 2.00
Mickey Mantle
19 Phil Rizzuto .30 .75
20 Sandy Koufax .40 1.00
21 Jackie Robinson .75 2.00
22 Don Drysdale .30 .75
23 Mickey Mantle 1.00 2.50
24 Mickey Mantle 1.00 2.50
25 Joe DiMaggio .75 2.00
26 Robin Roberts .30 .75
27 Lou Brock .30 .75
28 Lou Gehrig .75 2.00
29 Willie Mays .60 1.50
30 Brooks Robinson .30 .75
31 Thurman Munson .20 .50
32 Roger Maris .40 1.00
33 Jim Palmer .30 .75
34 Stan Musial .40 1.00
35 Roy Campanella .40 1.00
36 Joe Pepitone .08 .25
37 Ebbetts Field .08 .25
38 Honus Wagner .30 .75
39 Yogi Berra .40 1.00
40 Eddie Mathews .30 .75
41 Carl Yastrzemski .30 .75
42 Babe Ruth 1.00 2.50
43 Babe Ruth 1.00 2.50
44 Pete Reiser .08 .25
45 Don Larsen .08 .25
46 Ernie Banks .30 .75
47 Casey Stengel .40 1.00
48 Jackie Robinson .75 2.00
49 Duke Snider .40 1.00
50 Duke Snider CL .20 .50

1996 Team Out

This 101-card set makes up a Baseball card game and is distributed in boxes of 60-card decks with a suggested retail of $12.95 a box. Each deck contains 34 player photo cards and 23 cartoon player cards. A total of 91 different player cards and 10 cartoon cards are available. The backs carry the name of the card game printed on a picture of a section of a baseball. The cards are unnumbered and checklisted below in alphabetical order with the last 10 cards being the cartoon cards and listed with a "C" prefix.

COMPLETE SET (101) 40.00 80.00
1 Roberto Alomar .30 .75
2 Brady Anderson .08 .25
3 Kevin Appier .02 .10
4 Carlos Baerga .02 .10
5 Jeff Bagwell .40 1.00
6 Albert Belle .08 .25
7 Dante Bichette .08 .25
8 Craig Biggio .30 .75
9 Wade Boggs .40 1.00
10 Barry Bonds .60 1.50
11 Kevin Brown .20 .50
12 Jay Buhner .08 .25
13 Ellis Burks .08 .25
14 Ken Caminiti .30 .75
15 Joe Carter .08 .25
16 Vinny Castilla .08 .25
17 Jeff Cirillo .02 .10
18 Will Clark .30 .75
19 Jeff Conine .08 .25
20 Joey Cora .02 .10
21 Marty Cordova .02 .10
22 Eric Davis .08 .25
23 Ray Durham .08 .25
24 Jim Edmonds .30 .75
25 Cecil Fielder .08 .25
26 Travis Fryman .08 .25
27 Jason Giambi .30 .75
28 Bernard Gilkey .02 .10
29 Tom Glavine .40 1.00
30 Juan Gonzalez .30 .75
31 Mark Grace .20 .50
32 Ken Griffey Jr. 1.00 2.50
33 Marquis Grissom .08 .25
34 Mark Grudzielanek .02 .10
35 Ozzie Guillen .20 .50
36 Tony Gwynn .75 2.00
37 Bobby Higginson .08 .25
38 Todd Hundley .08 .25
39 Derek Jeter 20.00 50.00
40 Lance Johnson .02 .10
41 Randy Johnson .40 1.00
42 Chipper Jones .75 2.00
43 Brian Jordan .08 .25
44 Wally Joyner .08 .25
45 Mike Lansing .02 .10
46 Chuck Knoblauch .08 .25
47 Ray Lankford .08 .25
48 Mike Lansing .02 .10
49 Barry Larkin .30 .75
50 Kenny Lofton .08 .25
51 Javier Lopez .20 .50
52 Mike MacFarlane .02 .10
53 Greg Maddux .75 2.00
54 Al Martin .02 .10
55 Mark McGwire .75 2.00
56 Brian McRae .02 .10
57 Raul Mondesi .08 .25
58 Denny Neagle .02 .10
59 Hideo Nomo .30 .75
60 John Olerud .20 .50
61 Rey Ordonez .02 .10
62 Troy Percival .08 .25
63 Andy Pettitte .20 .50
64 Mike Piazza 1.00 2.50
65 Manny Ramirez .40 1.00
66 Cal Ripken 1.50 4.00
67 Alex Rodriguez 1.00 2.50
68 Ivan Rodriguez .40 1.00
69 Tim Salmon .30 .75
70 Ryne Sandberg .40 1.00
71 Benito Santiago .08 .25
72 Kevin Seitzer .02 .10
73 Scott Servais .02 .10
74 Gary Sheffield .40 1.00
75 Ozzie Smith .75 2.00
76 John Smoltz .08 .25
77 Sammy Sosa .50 1.25
78 Mike Stanley .02 .10
79 Terry Steinbach .02 .10
80 Frank Thomas .40 1.00
81 Steve Trachsel .02 .10
82 Jose Valentin .02 .10
83 Mo Vaughn .08 .25
84 Robin Ventura .20 .50
85 Jose Vizcaino .02 .10
86 Larry Walker .30 .75
87 Walt Weiss .02 .10
88 Bernie Williams .30 .75
89 Matt Williams .20 .50
90 Eric Young .02 .10
91 Todd Zeile .08 .25
C92 Roberto Alomar .25 .60
C93 Albert Belle .08 .25
Raul Mondesi
C94 Barry Bonds/ .25 .60
C95 Ken Griffey .75 2.00
Sammy Sosa
C96 Greg Maddux .25 .60
C97 Mark McGwire .60 1.50
Ozzie Smith
Mo Vaughn
C98 Mike Piazza .15 .40
Matt Williams
C99 Alex Rodriguez .50 1.25
Cal Ripken
C100 Frank Thomas .50 1.25
C101 G.T. Roped .02 .10

1993 Ted Williams Promos

COMPLETE SET (3) 12.50 30.00
1 Ted Williams 6.00 15.00
115 Satchell Paige 2.50 6.00
160 Juan Gonzalez 4.00 10.00
The Measure of a Hitter

1993 Ted Williams

This set of 160 cards marks the inaugural effort of the Ted Williams Card Company. The standard-size cards are UV-coated, and bear the company's embossed logo. The card designs vary from subset to subset, and since the borderless cards feature players of the past (with only two exceptions), some of the photos on the fronts are black-and-white, some are color, and still others are sepia-toned. Generally, the backs carry Williams' comments on each player's abilities and career highlights. All the cards are grouped according to team. This set features these subsets: The Negro Leagues (97-115), All-American Girls' Professional Baseball League (116-120), Ted's Greatest Hitters (121-130), Barrier Breakers (131-140), Goin' North (141-150), and Dawning of a Legacy (151-160), which features cards of Juan Gonzalez and Jeff Bagwell, the only two current players in the set. Ted Williams personally signed 406 of his Locklear Collection insert card for this set and Juan Gonzalez signed 172 cards (43 each of his four different regular cards in this set) as well. Also, two POGs, or milk bottle caps, were inserted in each pack. These feature illustrations of former major and Negro league players, logos of their teams, and reproductions of selected signatures of former major league players.

COMPLETE SET (160) 6.00 15.00
1 Ted Williams .75 2.00
2 Rick Ferrell .08 .25
3 Jim Lonborg .01 .05
4 Mel Parnell .01 .05
5 Jim Piersall .02 .10
6 Luis Tiant .02 .10
7 Carl Yastrzemski .20 .50
8 Ralph Branca .02 .10
9 Roy Campanella .30 .75
10 Ron Cey .02 .10
11 Tommy Davis .02 .10
12 Don Drysdale .15 .40
13 Carl Erskine .02 .10
14 Steve Garvey .05 .15
15 Don Newcombe .05 .15
16 Duke Snider .30 .75
17 Maury Wills .05 .15
18 Jim Fregosl .02 .10
19 Bobby Grich .02 .10
20 Bill Buckner .02 .10
21 Billy Herman UER/(Ted Williams .08 .25
stats on back)
22 Ferguson Jenkins .08 .25
23 Ron Santo .05 .15
24 Billy Williams .08 .25
25 Luis Aparicio .08 .25
26 Luke Appling .08 .25
27 Minnie Minoso .05 .15
28 Johnny Bench .20 .50
29 George Foster .02 .10
30 Joe Morgan .08 .25
31 Buddy Bell .02 .10
32 Lou Boudreau .08 .25
33 Rocky Colavito .05 .15
34 Jim(Mudcat) Grant .01 .05
35 Tris Speaker .08 .25
36 Ray Boone .01 .05
37 Darrell Evans .02 .10
38 Al Kaline .20 .50
39 George Kell .08 .25
40 Mickey Lolich .05 .15
41 Cesar Cedeno .02 .10
42 Sal Bando .01 .05
43 Vida Blue .02 .10
44 Bert Campaneris .01 .05
45 Ken Holtzman .01 .05
46 Lew Burdette .02 .10
47 Bob Horner .01 .05
48 Warren Spahn .08 .25
49 Cecil Cooper .02 .10
50 Tony Oliva .05 .15
51 Bobby Bonds .05 .15
52 Alvin Dark .02 .10
53 Dave Dravecky .02 .10
54 Monte Irvin .08 .25
55 Willie Mays .40 1.00
56 Bud Harrelson .02 .10
57 Dave Kingman UER
(Darrell Evans has/414 homers a .02 .10
58 Yogi Berra .20 .50
59 Don Baylor .05 .15
60 Jim Bouton .02 .10
61 Bobby Brown .02 .10
62 Whitey Ford .20 .50
63 Lou Gehrig .60 1.50
64 Charlie Keller .02 .10
65 Eddie Lopat .02 .10
66 Johnny Mize .08 .25
67 Bobby Murcer .02 .10
68 Graig Nettles .05 .15
69 Bobby Shantz .01 .05
70 Richie Ashburn .08 .25
71 Larry Bowa .02 .10
72 Steve Carlton .15 .40
73 Robin Roberts .08 .25
74 Matty Alou .01 .05
75 Harvey Haddix .01 .05
76 Ralph Kiner .08 .25
77 Bill Madlock .02 .10
78 Bill Mazeroski .05 .15
79 Al Oliver .02 .10
80 Manny Sanguillen .01 .05
81 Willie Stargell .08 .25
82 Al Bumbry .01 .05
83 Davey Johnson .02 .10
84 Boog Powell .05 .15
85 Earl Weaver MG .05 .15
86 Lou Brock .08 .25
87 Orlando Cepeda UER
(Born in Puerto Rico& .05 .15
not Dom
88 Curt Flood .02 .10
89 Joe Garagiola .05 .15
90 Bob Gibson .08 .25
91 Rogers Hornsby UER
(Misspelled Rodgers .08 .25
on card f
92 Enos Slaughter .08 .25
93 Joe Torre .05 .15
94 Gaylord Perry .08 .25
95 Checklist .01 .05
96 Checklist .01 .05
97 Cool Papa Bell .08 .25
98 Garnett Blair .02 .10
99 Gene Benson .05 .15
100 Lyman Bostock Sr. .02 .10
101 Marlin Carter .02 .10
102 Oscar Charleston .08 .25
103 Ray Dandridge .08 .25
104 Mahlon Duckett .02 .10
105 Josh Gibson .30 .75
106 Cowan(Bubber) Hyde .02 .10
107 William(Judy) Johnson .08 .25
108 Buck Leonard .08 .25
109 John Henry Lloyd .08 .25
110 Lester Lockett .02 .10
111 Max Manning .02 .10
112 Satchel Paige .30 .75
113 Armando Vazquez .02 .10
114 Joe(Smokey) Williams .08 .25
115 Checklist .01 .05
116 Alice(Lefty) Hohlmeyer .08 .25
117 Dotty Kamenshek .08 .25
118 Lavonne(Pepper) Davis .08 .25
119 Marge Wenzell .08 .25
120 Checklist .01 .05
121 Babe Ruth 1.00 2.50
122 Lou Gehrig .60 1.50
123 Jimmie Foxx .20 .50
124 Rogers Hornsby .20 .50
125 Ty Cobb .60 1.50
126 Willie Mays .40 1.00
127 Ralph Kiner .15 .40
128 Tris Speaker .15 .40
129 Johnny Mize .08 .25
130 Checklist .01 .05
131 Satchel Paige .20 .50
132 Joe Black .02 .10
133 Roy Campanella .20 .50
134 Larry Doby UER/(Misspelled Dolby.05 .15
on card back)
135 Jim Gilliam .05 .15
136 Monte Irvin .15 .40
137 Sam Jethroe .02 .10
138 Willie Mays .40 1.00
139 Don Newcombe .02 .10
140 Checklist .01 .05
141 Roy Campanella .20 .50
142 Bob Gibson .08 .25
143 Boog Powell .05 .15
144 Willie Mays .40 1.00
145 Johnny Mize .08 .25
146 Monte Irvin .08 .25
147 Earl Weaver MG .05 .15
148 Ted Williams .60 1.50
149 Jim Gilliam .02 .10
150 Checklist .01 .05
151 Juan Gonzalez .20 .50
Footsteps to Greatness
152 Juan Gonzalez .20 .50
Sign 'em Up
153 Juan Gonzalez .20 .50
The Road to Success
154 Juan Gonzalez .20 .50
Looking Ahead
155 Checklist 151-155 .01 .05
156 Jeff Bagwell .20 .50
Born with Red Sox Blood
157 Jeff Bagwell .20 .50
Movin' Up Then Out
158 Jeff Bagwell .20 .50
Year 1
159 Jeff Bagwell .20 .50
Year 2
160 Checklist 156-160 .01 .05
AU151 Juan Gonzalez AU
(Certified autograph) 100.00 250.00
Footsteps
AU152 Juan Gonzalez AU
(Certified autograph) 100.00 250.00
Sign 'em
AU153 Juan Gonzalez AU
(Certified autograph) 100.00 250.00
The Road
AU154 Juan Gonzalez AU
(Certified autograph) 100.00 250.00
Looking A

1993 Ted Williams Brooks Robinson

COMPLETE SET (10) 6.00 15.00
COMMON CARD (1-10) .60 1.50
AU Brooks Robinson AU 8.00 20.00

1993 Ted Williams Locklear Collection

COMPLETE SET (10) 15.00 40.00
1 Yogi Berra 2.50 6.00
2 Lou Brock 1.25 3.00
3 Willie Mays 3.00 8.00
4 Johnny Mize 1.25 3.00
5 Satchel Paige 2.50 6.00
6 Babe Ruth 3.00 8.00
7 Enos Slaughter 1.25 3.00
8 Carl Yastrzemski 2.00 5.00
9 Ted Williams 3.00 8.00
10 Checklist 1.25 3.00
AU9 Ted Williams AU/406
(Certified autograph) 200.00 500.00

1993 Ted Williams Memories

COMPLETE SET (20) 15.00 40.00
1 Roy Campanella 2.00 5.00
2 Jim Gilliam .75 2.00
3 Gil Hodges 1.25 3.00
4 Duke Snider 2.00 5.00
5 1955 Brooklyn .60 1.50
Dodgers Checklist
6 Don Drysdale 1.25 3.00
7 Tommy Davis .60 1.50
8 Johnny Podres .60 1.50
9 Maury Wills 1.25 3.00
10 1963 Los Angeles .60 1.50
Dodgers Checklist
11 Roberto Clemente 3.00 8.00
12 Al Oliver .75 2.00
13 Manny Sanguillen .60 1.50
14 Willie Stargell 1.25 3.00
15 1971 Pittsburgh .60 1.50
Pirates Checklist
16 Johnny Bench 1.25 3.00
17 George Foster .75 2.00
18 Joe Morgan 1.25 3.00
19 Tony Perez 1.25 3.00
20 1975 Cincinnati .60 1.50
Reds Checklist

1993 Ted Williams POG Cards

Card	Low	High
COMPLETE SET (26)	2.50	6.00
1 Atlanta Black Crackers	.08	.25
Baltimore Elite Giants		
2 Atlanta Braves	.08	.25
New York Mets		
3 Baltimore Orioles		
1993 All-Star Game/1993 World	.08	.25
4 Birmingham Black Barons	.08	.25
New York Cuban Stars		
5 Chicago Cubs	.08	.25
Detroit Tigers		
6 Cincinnati Reds	.08	.25
Kansas City Royals/1969-1993		
7 Classic Teams	.08	.25
The Negro Leagues		
Negro League		
Ba		
8 Cleveland Buckeyes	.08	.25
Detroit Stars		
9 Cleveland Indians	.08	.25
Kansas City Athletics		
10 Houston Colt .45s	.08	.25
New York Yankees		
11 Florida Marlins/1993 Inaugural Year	.08	.25
Colorado Roc		
12 Indianapolis ABCs	.08	.25
New York Harlem Stars		
13 Louisville Black Caps	.08	.25
Philadelphia Stars		
14 Minnesota Twins	.08	.25
Boston Red Sox		
15 Montreal Expos/1969-1993	.08	.25
San Diego Padres/1969-		
16 New York Black Yankees	.08	.25
Homestead Grays		
17 New York Giants	.08	.25
Milwaukee Braves		
18 Oakland A's/21 (Clemente's number)	.08	.25
19 Pittsburgh Pirates	.08	.25
St. Louis Cardinals		
20 St. Louis Browns	.08	.25
Brooklyn Dodgers		
21 Yogi Berra	.40	1.00
Roy Campanella		
22 Brooklyn Dodgers	.30	.75
Roy Campanella		
23 Lou Gehrig	.75	2.00
Ted Williams		
24 Lou Gehrig	.40	1.00
New York Yankees		
25 Tommy Davis	.20	.50
George Foster		
26 Ted Williams/1941 - .406	.40	1.00
Ted Williams		

1993 Ted Williams Etched in Stone Clemente

Card	Low	High
COMPLETE SET (10)	4.00	10.00
COMMON CARD (1-10)	.40	1.00

1994 Ted Williams

The 1994 Ted Williams set comprises 162 standard-size cards distributed in 12-card packs. The series features former major league baseball players, players from the All-American Girls Professional Baseball League, 17 Negro League stars, and 17 current top prospects. Topical subsets featured are Women in Baseball (93-99), The Negro League (100-117), The Campaign (118-135), Goin' North (136-144), Swinging for the Fences (145-153), and Dawning of a Legacy (154-162). A red foil version of the Ted Williams (LP1) and Larry Bird (LP2) insert cards were also produced. The values are the same as those listed below. Leon Day signed some cards for release in the packs. Packs of the football card product from the same year included a Ted Willams "Teddy Football" card and a numbered signed version of the same card seeded randomly. We've included pricing on those two cards below.

Card	Low	High
COMPLETE SET (162)	4.00	10.00
1 Ted Williams	.40	1.00
2 Bernie Carbo	.01	.05
3 Bobby Doerr	.08	.25
4 Fred Lynn	.02	.10
5 John Pesky	.02	.10
6 Rico Petrocelli	.02	.10
7 Cy Young	.20	.50
8 Paul Blair	.01	.05
9 Andy Etchebarren	.01	.05
10 Brooks Robinson	.08	.25
11 Gil Hodges	.05	.15
12 Tommy John	.02	.10
13 Rick Monday	.01	.05
14 Dean Chance	.01	.05
15 Doug DeCinces	.01	.05
16 Gabby Hartnett	.08	.25
17 Don Kessinger	.01	.05
18 Bruce Sutter	.08	.25
19 Eddie Collins Sr.	.05	.15
20 Nellie Fox	.08	.25
21 Carlos May	.01	.05
22 Ted Kluszewski	.05	.15
23 Vada Pinson	.02	.10
24 Johnny Vander Meer	.02	.10
25 Bob Feller	.08	.25
26 Mike Garcia	.01	.05
27 Sam McDowell	.01	.05
28 Al Rosen	.02	.10
29 Norm Cash	.02	.10
30 Ty Cobb	.30	.75
31 Mark Fidrych	.02	.10
32 Hank Greenberg	.08	.25
33 Dennis McLain	.02	.10
34 Virgil Trucks	.01	.05
35 Enos Cabell	.01	.05
36 Mike Scott	.01	.05
37 Bob Watson	.02	.10
38 Amos Otis	.01	.05
39 Frank White	.02	.10
40 Joe Adcock	.02	.10
41 Rico Carty	.01	.05
42 Ralph Garr	.01	.05
43 Ed Mathews	.08	.25
44 Ben Oglivie	.01	.05
45 Gorman Thomas	.01	.05
46 Earl Battey	.01	.05
47 Rod Carew	.08	.25
48 Jim Kaat	.02	.10
49 Harmon Killebrew	.08	.25
50 Gary Carter	.08	.25
51 Steve Rogers	.01	.05
52 Rusty Staub	.02	.10
53 Sal Maglie	.02	.10
54 Juan Marichal	.08	.25
55 Mel Ott	.08	.25
56 Bobby Thomson	.05	.15
57 Tommie Agee	.01	.05
58 Tug McGraw	.02	.10
59 Elston Howard	.05	.15
60 Sparky Lyle	.02	.10
61 Billy Martin	.02	.10
62 Thurman Munson	.05	.15
63 Bobby Richardson	.02	.10
64 Bill Skowron	.02	.10
65 Mickey Cochrane	.08	.25
66 Rollie Fingers	.08	.25
67 Lefty Grove	.08	.25
68 James Hunter	.08	.25
69 Connie Mack MG	.08	.25
70 Al Simmons	.02	.10
71 Dick Allen	.05	.15
72 Bob Boone	.02	.10
73 Del Ennis	.01	.05
74 Chuck Klein	.08	.25
75 Mike Schmidt	.08	.25
76 Dock Ellis	.01	.05
77 Roy Face	.01	.05
78 Phil Garner	.02	.10
79 Bill Mazeroski	.08	.25
80 Pie Traynor	.08	.25
81 Honus Wagner	.08	.25
82 Dizzy Dean	.08	.25
83 Red Schoendienst	.08	.25
84 Randy Jones	.01	.05
85 Nate Colbert	.01	.05
86 Jeff Burroughs	.01	.05
87 Jim Sundberg	.01	.05
88 Frank Howard	.02	.10
89 Walter Johnson	.08	.25
90 Eddie Yost	.01	.05
91 Checklist 1	.01	.05
92 Checklist 2	.01	.05
93 Faye Dancer	.05	.15
94 Snookie Dayle	.02	.10
95 Maddy English	.02	.10
96 Nickie Fox	.02	.10
97 Sophie Kurys	.08	.25
98 Alma Ziegler	.02	.10
99 Checklist	.01	.05
100 Newton Allen	.02	.10
101 Willard Brown	.02	.10
102 Larry Brown	.02	.10
103 Leon Day	.08	.25
104 John Donaldson	.02	.10
105 Rube Foster	.05	.15
106 John Fowler	.02	.10
107 Elander Harris	.02	.10
108 Webster McDonald	.02	.10
109 Buck O'Neil	.08	.25
110 Ted Double Duty Radcliffe	.08	.25
111 Wilber Rogan	.02	.10
112 Marcenia Stone	.02	.10
113 James Taylor	.02	.10
114 Fleetwood Walker	.05	.15
115 George Wilson	.02	.10
116 Judson Wilson	.02	.10
117 Checklist	.01	.05
118 Howard Battle	.01	.05
119 John Burke	.01	.05
120 Brian Dubose	.01	.05
121 Alex Gonzalez	.05	.15
122 Jose Herrera	.01	.05
123 Jason Giambi	.40	1.00
124 Derek Jeter	1.50	4.00
125 Charles Johnson	.02	.10
126 Daron Kirkreit	.01	.05
127 Jason Moler	.01	.05
128 Vince Moore	.01	.05
129 Chad Mottola	.01	.05
130 Jose Silva	.01	.05
131 Mac Suzuki	.01	.05
132 Brien Taylor	.01	.05
133 Michael Tucker	.02	.10
134 Billy Wagner	.40	1.00
135 Checklist	.01	.05
136 Gary Carter	.08	.25
137 Tony Conigliaro	.02	.10
138 Sparky Lyle	.02	.10
139 Roger Maris	.05	.15
140 Vada Pinson	.02	.10
141 Mike Schmidt	.08	.25
142 Frank White	.02	.10
143 Ted Williams	.30	.75
144 Checklist	.01	.05
145 Joe Adcock	.01	.05
146 Rocky Colavito	.05	.15
147 Lou Gehrig	.40	1.00
148 Gil Hodges	.02	.10
149 Bob Horner	.01	.05
150 Willie Mays	.40	1.00
151 Mike Schmidt	.08	.25
152 Pat Seerey	.01	.05
153 Checklist	.01	.05
154 Cliff Floyd	.10	.30
The Honors Begin		
155 Cliff Floyd	.10	.30
The Top Polecat		
156 Cliff Floyd	.10	.30
Minor League Team		
of the Year		
157 Cliff Floyd	.10	.30
Major League Debut		
158 Tim Salmon	.10	.30
Award Winner		
159 Tim Salmon	.10	.30
Early Professional		
Career		
160 Tim Salmon	.10	.30
An MVP Season		
161 Tim Salmon	.10	.30
Rookie of the Year		
162 Checklist	.01	.05
P1 Ted Williams Promo	.75	2.00
LP1A Larry Bird	.75	2.00
Brown		
LP1B Larry Bird	1.50	4.00
Red		
LP2A Ted Williams	4.00	10.00
Brown		
LP2B Ted Williams	2.00	5.00
Red		
TW1 Ted Williams	.75	2.00
TW1AU Ted Williams AU/54	300.00	500.00
NNO Leon Day AU	30.00	60.00
Certified Autograph		

1994 Ted Williams 500 Club

Card	Low	High
COMPLETE SET (9)	8.00	20.00
1 Hank Aaron	1.50	4.00
2 Reggie Jackson	1.25	3.00
3 Harmon Killebrew	.50	1.25
4 Mickey Mantle	3.00	8.00
5 Jimmie Foxx	1.25	3.00
6 Babe Ruth	2.50	6.00
7 Mike Schmidt	2.00	5.00
8 Ted Williams	2.50	6.00
9 Checklist	.40	1.00

1994 Ted Williams Dan Gardiner Collection

Card	Low	High
COMPLETE SET (9)	12.50	30.00
DG1 Michael Jordan	6.00	15.00
DG2 Michael Tucker	.75	2.00
DG3 Derek Jeter	6.00	15.00
DG4 Charles Johnson	.40	1.00
DG5 Howard Battle	.30	.75
DG6 Quilvio Veras	.40	1.00
DG7 Brian L. Hunter	.30	.75
DG8 Brien Taylor	.30	.75
DG9 Checklist	.75	2.00

1994 Ted Williams Locklear Collection

Card	Low	High
COMPLETE SET (9)	8.00	20.00
LC11 Ty Cobb	2.00	5.00
LC12 Bob Feller	1.00	2.50
LC13 Lou Gehrig	3.00	8.00
LC14 Josh Gibson	1.25	3.00
LC15 Walter Johnson	1.25	3.00
LC16 Casey Stengel	1.25	3.00
LC17 Honus Wagner	2.50	6.00
LC18 Cy Young	1.25	3.00
LC19 Checklist	.60	1.50

1994 Ted Williams Memories

Card	Low	High
COMPLETE SET (17)	15.00	40.00
M21 Monte Irvin	1.00	2.50
M22 Sal Maglie	.75	2.00
M23 Dusty Rhodes	.60	1.50
M24 Hank Thompson	.60	1.50
M25 Yogi Berra	2.00	5.00
M26 Elston Howard	1.50	4.00
M27 Roger Maris	2.40	6.00
M28 Bobby Richardson	.75	2.00
M29 Norm Cash	.75	2.00
M30 Al Kaline	2.50	6.00
M31 Mickey Lolich	.75	2.00
M32 Denny McLain	.75	2.00
M33 Bernie Carbo	.60	1.50
M34 Fred Lynn	.75	2.00
M35 Rico Petrocelli	.60	1.50
M36 Luis Tiant	.75	2.00
M37 Checklist	.40	1.00

1994 Ted Williams Mike Schmidt

Card	Low	High
COMPLETE SET (9)	3.00	8.00
COMMON CARD (MS1-MS9)	.40	1.00

1994 Ted Williams Roger Maris

Card	Low	High
COMPLETE SET (9)	5.00	12.00
COMMON CARD (ES1-ES8)	.60	1.50

1994 Ted Williams Trade for Babe

Card	Low	High
COMPLETE SET (9)	20.00	50.00
COMMON CARD (T1-T8)	2.50	6.00
T9 Babe Ruth	2.00	5.00
Checklist		
NNO0 Trade Card	2.00	5.00

1988 Tetley Tea Discs

These discs, which are parallel to the 1988 MSA Iced Tea Discs, say Tetley Tea on the front. They are valued the same as the regular discs.

Card	Low	High
COMPLETE SET (20)	4.00	10.00
1 Wade Boggs	.60	1.00
2 Ellis Burks	.30	.75
3 Don Mattingly	.75	2.00
4 Mark McGwire	.75	2.00
5 Matt Nokes	.02	.10
6 Kirby Puckett	.80	1.00
7 Billy Ripken	.02	.10
8 Kevin Seitzer	.02	.10
9 Roger Clemens	.75	2.00
10 Will Clark	.30	.75
11 Vince Coleman	.02	.10
12 Eric Davis	.08	.25
13 Dave Magadan	.02	.10
14 Dale Murphy	.20	.50
15 Benito Santiago	.08	.25
16 Mike Schmidt	.30	1.00
17 Darryl Strawberry	.08	.25
18 Steve Bedrosian	.02	.10
19 Dwight Gooden	.08	.25
20 Fernando Valenzuela	.08	.25

1989 Tetley Tea Discs

For the second year, Tetlea tea was one of the companies distributing the MSA Iced Tea Discs. These Discs say Tetley on the front and are valued the same as the MSA Iced Tea Discs.

Card	Low	High
COMPLETE SET (20)	20.00	50.00
1 Don Mattingly	2.50	6.00
2 Dave Cone	.20	.50
(David)		
3 Mark McGwire	2.50	6.00
4 Will Clark	.75	2.00
5 Darryl Strawberry	.40	1.00
6 Dwight Gooden	.40	1.00
7 Wade Boggs	1.25	3.00
8 Roger Clemens	2.50	6.00
9 Benito Santiago	.40	1.00
10 Orel Hershiser	.40	1.00
11 Eric Davis	.40	1.00
12 Kirby Puckett	2.00	5.00
13 Dave Winfield	1.25	3.00
14 Andre Dawson	.75	2.00
15 Steve Bedrosian	.20	.50
16 Cal Ripken	5.00	12.00
17 Andy Van Slyke	.20	.50
18 Jose Canseco	1.00	2.50
19 Jose Oquendo	.20	.50
20 Dale Murphy	.60	1.50

1914 Texas Tommy E224

There are two types of these cards:Type I are 1-50 and Type II are 51-64. The type one cards measure 2 3/8" by 3 1/2" while the type two cards measure 1 7/8" by 3". The type one cards have stats on the back while the type 2 cards have blank backs. Harry Hooper and Rube Marquard only exist in type two fashion. Some more cards were recently discovered and as it is currently the only one known there is no pricing on this card at this time

Card	Low	High
COMPLETE SET	50000.00	100000.00
COMMON CARD (1-51)	200.00	400.00
COMMON CARD (52-66)	500.00	1000.00
1 Jimmy Archer	4000.00	8000.00
2 Jimmy Austin	4000.00	8000.00
3 Frank Baker	7500.00	15000.00
4 Chief Bender	7500.00	15000.00
5 Bob Bescher	4000.00	8000.00
6 Ping Bodie	5000.00	10000.00
7 Donie Bush	4000.00	8000.00
8 Bobby Byrne	4000.00	8000.00
9 Nixey Callahan	4000.00	8000.00
10 Howie Camnitz	4000.00	8000.00
11 Frank Chance	7500.00	15000.00
12 Hal Chase	7500.00	15000.00
13 Ty Cobb	50000.00	100000.00
14 Jack Coombs	5000.00	10000.00
15 Sam Crawford	7500.00	15000.00
16 Birdie Cree	4000.00	8000.00
17 Al Demaree	4000.00	8000.00
18 Red Dooin	5000.00	10000.00
19 Larry Doyle	7500.00	15000.00
20 Johnny Evers	7500.00	15000.00
21 Vean Gregg	4000.00	8000.00
22 Bob Harmon	4000.00	8000.00
23 Joe Jackson	60000.00	120000.00
24 Walter Johnson	12500.00	25000.00
25 Otto Knabe	4000.00	8000.00
26 Nap Lajoie	7500.00	15000.00
27 Harry Lord	4000.00	8000.00
28 Connie Mack MG	7500.00	15000.00
29 Armando Marsans	4000.00	8000.00
30 Christy Mathewson	12500.00	25000.00
31 George McBride	4000.00	8000.00
32 John McGraw MG	15000.00	30000.00
33 Snuffy McInnis	5000.00	10000.00
34 Chief Meyers	5000.00	10000.00
35 Earl Moore	4000.00	8000.00
36 Mike Mowrey	4000.00	8000.00
37 Rebel Oakes	4000.00	8000.00
38 Marty O'Toole	4000.00	8000.00
39 Eddie Plank	7500.00	15000.00
40 Buddy Ryan	4000.00	8000.00
41 Tris Speaker	12500.00	25000.00
42 Jake Stahl	4000.00	8000.00
43 Oscar Stanage	4000.00	8000.00
44 Bill Sweeney	4000.00	8000.00
45 Honus Wagner	30000.00	60000.00
46 Ed Walsh	7500.00	15000.00
47 Zack Wheat	4000.00	8000.00
48 Harry Wolter	4000.00	8000.00
49 Joe Wood	7500.00	15000.00
50 Steve Yerkes	6000.00	12000.00
51 Heinie Zimmerman	5000.00	10000.00
52 Ping Bodie	6000.00	12000.00
53 Larry Doyle	10000.00	20000.00
54 Vean Gregg	6000.00	12000.00
55 Harry Hooper	12500.00	25000.00
56 Walter Johnson	30000.00	60000.00
57 Connie Mack MG	12500.00	25000.00
58 Rube Marquard	12500.00	25000.00
59 Christy Mathewson	12500.00	25000.00
60 John McGraw MG	12500.00	25000.00
61 Chief Meyers	7500.00	15000.00
62 Fred Snodgrass	7500.00	15000.00
63 Jake Stahl	6000.00	12000.00
64 Honus Wagner	50000.00	100000.00
65 Joe Wood	12500.00	25000.00
66 Steve Yerkes	6000.00	12000.00

1948 Thom McAn Feller

This one-card set was distributed by Thom McAn Shoe Stores and features a black-and-white picture of Bob Feller of the Cleveland Indians with a facsimile autograph. The back carrys a Baseball Quiz with the answers to the questions at the bottom.

Card	Low	High
1 Bob Feller	40.00	80.00

1985 Thom McAn Discs

MSA (Michael Schechter Associates) produced this 46-disc set for Thom McAn to promote a specially developed line of boys' and young men's JOX all-turf cleat shoes. The give-away consisted of a set of 10 discs with every pair of shoes purchased. The production of the discs was discontinued when a decision was made to replace this line of shoes with a newer one. The discs measure 2 3/4" in diameter. The front design resembles a baseball, with a black and white headshot sandwiched between the two rows of stitching. Four stars appear above the player's picture, and the two ovals created by the stitching are colored yellow, green, red, or mustard. In addition, at least 8 players (Cedeno, Cooper, Cowens, Hargrove, Leonard, Valenzuela, Walker, and Zahn) had their photo and information printed in two different colors. The back of the discs are printed in black on white and have a Thom McAn advertisement. The discs are unnumbered and checklisted below alphabetically according to AL (1-24) and NL players (25-46).

Card	Low	High
COMPLETE SET (46)	175.00	350.00
1 Benny Ayala	.40	1.00
2 Buddy Bell	.75	2.00
3 Juan Beniquez	.40	1.00
4 Tony Bernazard	.40	1.00
5 Mike Boddicker	.40	1.00
6 Bill Buckner	.40	1.00
7 Rod Carew	15.00	40.00
8 Onix Concepcion	.40	1.00
9 Cecil Cooper	.75	2.00
10 Al Cowens	.40	1.00
11 Ron Guidry	.75	2.00
12 Mike Hargrove	.75	2.00
13 Kent Hrbek	.75	2.00
14 Rick Langford	.40	1.00
15 Jack Morris	.75	2.00
16 Dan Quisenberry	.40	1.00
17 Cal Ripken	40.00	80.00
18 Ed Romero	.40	1.00
19 Tom Seaver	15.00	40.00
20 Alan Trammell	1.25	3.00
21 Greg Walker	.40	1.00
22 Willie Wilson	.40	1.00
23 Dave Winfield	15.00	40.00
24 Geoff Zahn	.40	1.00
25 Steve Carlton	15.00	40.00
26 Cesar Cedeno	.40	1.00
27 Jose Cruz	.40	1.00
28 Ivan DeJesus	.40	1.00
29 Luis DeLeon	.40	1.00
30 Rich Gossage	.75	2.00
31 Pedro Guerrero	.40	1.00
32 Tony Gwynn	25.00	60.00
33 Keith Hernandez	.75	2.00
34 Bob Horner	.40	1.00
35 Jeff Leonard	.40	1.00
36 Willie McGee	.75	2.00
37 Jesse Orosco	.75	2.00
38 Junior Ortiz	.40	1.00
39 Terry Puhl	.40	1.00
40 Johnny Ray	.40	1.00
41 Ryne Sandberg	20.00	50.00
42 Mike Schmidt	15.00	40.00
43 Rick Sutcliffe	.40	1.00
44 Bruce Sutter	4.00	10.00
45 Fernando Valenzuela	.75	2.00
46 Ozzie Virgil	.40	1.00

1994 Frank Thomas Ameritech

This phone card, with a $1 denomination, was issued in 1994. The front has a "Big Hurt" logo on the left with a full color photo next to it. The back has information on how to use the card. The cards are serial numbered to 40,000.

Card	Low	High
1 Frank Thomas	2.00	5.00

1996 Thome Buick Postcard

Measuring approximately 4 1/2" by 6", this one card set featured star third baseman Jim Thome and was issued to promoted sales of Buicks in Northern Ohio. The front features a photo of Thome while the back has promotional information about various Buick automobiles.

Card	Low	High
1 Jim Thome	1.25	3.00

1937 Thrilling Moments

Doughnut Company of America produced these cards and distributed them on the outside of doughnut boxes twelve per box. The cards were to be cut from the boxes and affixed to an album that housed the set. The set's full name is Thrilling Moments in the Lives of Famous Americans. Only seven athletes were included among 65-other famous non-sport American figures. Each blankbacked card measures roughly 1 7/8" by 2 7/8" when neatly trimmed. The set was produced in four different colored backgrounds: blue, green, orange, and yellow with each subject being printed in only one background color.

Card	Low	High
59 Babe Ruth Y BB	800.00	1200.00

2004 Throwback Threads

Card	Low	High
COMP.SET w/o SP's (200)	15.00	40.00
COMMON CARD (1-200)	.10	.30
COMMON RETIRED (201-224)	.50	1.25
COMMON ROOKIE (225-250)	.60	1.50
201-250 RANDOM INSERTS IN PACKS		
201-250 PRINT RUN 1000 SERIAL #'d SETS		
1 Bartolo Colon	.12	.30
2 Darin Erstad	.12	.30
3 David Eckstein	.12	.30
4 Garret Anderson	.12	.30
5 Tim Salmon	.12	.30
6 Troy Glaus	.12	.30
7 Vladimir Guerrero	.20	.50
8 Brandon Webb	.12	.30
9 Luis Gonzalez	.12	.30
10 Randy Johnson	.30	.75
11 Richie Sexson	.12	.30
12 Roberto Alomar	.20	.50
13 Shea Hillenbrand	.12	.30
14 Steve Finley	.12	.30
15 Adam LaRoche	.12	.30
16 Andruw Jones	.12	.30
17 Chipper Jones	.30	.75
18 J.D. Drew	.12	.30
19 John Smoltz	.30	.75
20 Rafael Furcal	.12	.30
21 Russ Ortiz	.12	.30
22 Javy Lopez	.12	.30
23 Jay Gibbons	.12	.30
24 Larry Bigbie	.12	.30
25 Luis Matos	.12	.30
26 Melvin Mora	.12	.30
27 Miguel Tejada	.20	.50
28 Rafael Palmeiro	.20	.50
29 Curt Schilling	.20	.50
30 David Ortiz	.30	.75
31 Derek Lowe	.12	.30
32 Jason Varitek	.30	.75
33 Johnny Damon	.20	.50
34 Manny Ramirez	.30	.75
35 Nomar Garciaparra	.20	.50
36 Pedro Martinez	.20	.50
37 Trot Nixon	.12	.30
38 Aramis Ramirez	.12	.30
39 Corey Patterson	.12	.30
40 Derrek Lee	.12	.30
41 Greg Maddux	.40	1.00
42 Kerry Wood	.12	.30
43 Mark Prior	.20	.50
44 Sammy Sosa	.30	.75
45 Carlos Lee	.12	.30
46 Esteban Loaiza	.12	.30
47 Frank Thomas	.30	.75
48 Joe Borchard	.12	.30
49 Magglio Ordonez	.20	.50
50 Mark Buehrle	.20	.50
51 Paul Konerko	.20	.50
52 Adam Dunn	.20	.50
53 Austin Kearns	.12	.30
54 Barry Larkin	.20	.50
55 Brandon Larson	.12	.30
56 Ken Griffey Jr.	.60	1.50
57 Ryan Wagner	.12	.30
58 Sean Casey	.12	.30
59 C.C. Sabathia	.20	.50
60 Jody Gerut	.12	.30
61 Omar Vizquel	.20	.50
62 Travis Hafner	.12	.30
63 Victor Martinez	.20	.50
64 Charles Johnson	.12	.30
65 Garrett Atkins	.12	.30
66 Jason Jennings	.12	.30
67 Joe Kennedy	.12	.30
68 Larry Walker	.20	.50
69 Preston Wilson	.12	.30
70 Todd Helton	.20	.50
71 Ivan Rodriguez	.20	.50
72 Jeremy Bonderman	.12	.30
73 A.J. Burnett	.12	.30
74 Brad Penny	.12	.30
75 Dontrelle Willis	.12	.30
76 Josh Beckett	.12	.30
77 Juan Pierre	.12	.30
78 Luis Castillo	.12	.30
79 Miguel Cabrera	.30	.75
80 Mike Lowell	.12	.30
81 Andy Pettitte	.20	.50
82 Craig Biggio	.20	.50
83 Jeff Bagwell	.20	.50
84 Jeff Kent	.12	.30
85 Lance Berkman	.20	.50
86 Morgan Ensberg	.12	.30
87 Richard Hidalgo	.12	.30
88 Roger Clemens	.40	1.00
89 Roy Oswalt	.20	.50
90 Wade Miller	.12	.30
91 Angel Berroa	.12	.30
92 Carlos Beltran	.20	.50
93 Juan Gonzalez	.12	.30
94 Ken Harvey	.12	.30
95 Mike Sweeney	.12	.30
96 Runelvys Hernandez	.12	.30
97 Adrian Beltre	.30	.75
98 Edwin Jackson	.12	.30
99 Eric Gagne	.12	.30
100 Hideo Nomo	.30	.75
101 Hong-Chih Kuo	.12	.30
102 Kazuhisa Ishii	.12	.30
103 Paul Lo Duca	.12	.30
104 Shawn Green	.12	.30
105 Ben Sheets	.12	.30
106 Geoff Jenkins	.12	.30
107 Junior Spivey	.12	.30
108 Rickie Weeks	.12	.30
109 Scott Podsednik	.12	.30
110 Corey Koskie	.12	.30
111 Doug Mientkiewicz	.12	.30
112 Jacque Jones	.12	.30
113 Joe Mays	.12	.30
114 Johan Santana	.20	.50
115 Shannon Stewart	.12	.30
116 Torii Hunter	.12	.30
117 Brad Wilkerson	.12	.30
118 Carl Everett	.12	.30
119 Chad Cordero	.12	.30
120 Jose Vidro	.12	.30
121 Nick Johnson	.12	.30
122 Orlando Cabrera	.12	.30
123 Al Leiter	.12	.30
124 Cliff Floyd	.12	.30
125 Jae Weong Seo	.12	.30
126 Jose Reyes	.20	.50
127 Mike Cameron	.12	.30
128 Mike Piazza	.30	.75
129 Tom Glavine	.20	.50
130 Alex Rodriguez	.40	1.00
131 Bernie Williams	.20	.50
132 Chien-Ming Wang	.50	1.25
133 Derek Jeter	.75	2.00
134 Gary Sheffield	.12	.30
135 Hideki Matsui	.50	1.25
136 Jason Giambi	.12	.30
137 Javier Vazquez	.12	.30
138 Jorge Posada	.20	.50
139 Jose Contreras	.12	.30
140 Kevin Brown	.12	.30
141 Mariano Rivera	.40	1.00
142 Mike Mussina	.20	.50
143 Barry Zito	.20	.50
144 Bobby Crosby	.12	.30
145 Eric Chavez	.12	.30
146 Erubial Durazo	.12	.30
147 Jermaine Dye	.12	.30
148 Mark Kotsay	.12	.30
149 Mark Mulder	.12	.30
150 Rich Harden	.12	.30
151 Tim Hudson	.20	.50
152 Billy Wagner	.12	.30
153 Bobby Abreu	.12	.30
154 Brett Myers	.12	.30
155 Jim Thome	.20	.50
156 Jimmy Rollins	.20	.50
157 Kevin Millwood	.12	.30
158 Marlon Byrd	.12	.30
159 Pat Burrell	.12	.30
160 Jason Bay	.20	.50
161 Jason Kendall	.12	.30
162 Brian Giles	.12	.30
163 Jay Payton	.12	.30
164 Ryan Klesko	.12	.30
165 Edgardo Alfonzo	.12	.30
166 Jason Schmidt	.12	.30
167 Jerome Williams	.12	.30
168 Todd Linden	.12	.30
169 Bret Boone	.12	.30
170 Edgar Martinez	.20	.50
171 Freddy Garcia	.12	.30
172 Ichiro Suzuki	.40	1.00
173 Jamie Moyer	.12	.30
174 John Olerud	.12	.30
175 Shigetoshi Hasegawa	.12	.30
176 Albert Pujols	.40	1.00
177 Dan Haren	.12	.30
178 Edgar Renteria	.12	.30
179 Jim Edmonds	.20	.50
180 Matt Morris	.12	.30
181 Scott Rolen	.20	.50
182 Aubrey Huff	.12	.30
183 Carl Crawford	.20	.50
184 Chad Gaudin	.12	.30
185 Delmon Young	.20	.50
186 Dewon Brazelton	.12	.30
187 Fred McGriff	.12	.30
188 Rocco Baldelli	.12	.30
189 Alfonso Soriano	.20	.50
190 Hank Blalock	.12	.30
191 Laynce Nix	.12	.30
192 Mark Teixeira	.20	.50
193 Michael Young	.12	.30
194 Carlos Delgado	.12	.30
195 Eric Hinske	.12	.30
196 Frank Catalanotto	.12	.30
197 Josh Phelps	.12	.30
198 Orlando Hudson	.12	.30
199 Roy Halladay	.20	.50
200 Vernon Wells	.12	.30
201 Dale Murphy RET	1.25	3.00
202 Cal Ripken RET	4.00	10.00
203 Fred Lynn RET	.50	1.25
204 Wade Boggs RET	.75	2.00
205 Nolan Ryan RET	4.00	10.00
206 Rod Carew RET	.75	2.00
207 Andre Dawson RET	.75	2.00
208 Ernie Banks RET	1.25	3.00
209 Ryne Sandberg RET	2.50	6.00
210 Bo Jackson RET	1.25	3.00
211 Carlton Fisk RET	.75	2.00
212 Dave Concepcion RET	.50	1.25
213 Alan Trammell RET	.75	2.00
214 George Brett RET	2.50	6.00
215 Robin Yount RET	1.25	3.00
216 Gary Carter RET	.75	2.00
217 Darryl Strawberry RET	.50	1.25
218 Dwight Gooden RET	.50	1.25
219 Babe Ruth RET	3.00	8.00
220 Don Mattingly RET	2.50	6.00
221 Reggie Jackson RET	.75	2.00
222 Mike Schmidt RET	2.00	5.00
223 Tony Gwynn RET	1.25	3.00
224 Keith Hernandez RET	.50	1.25
225 Hector Gimenez ROO RC	.60	1.50
226 Graham Koonce ROO	.60	1.50
227 John Gall ROO RC	.60	1.50
228 Jerry Gil ROO RC	.60	1.50
229 Jason Frasor ROO RC	.60	1.50
230 Justin Knoedler ROO RC	.60	1.50
231 Ivan Ochoa ROO RC	.60	1.50
232 Greg Dobbs ROO RC	.60	1.50
233 Ronald Belisario ROO RC	.60	1.50
234 Jerome Gamble ROO RC	.60	1.50
235 Roberto Novoa ROO RC	.60	1.50
236 Sean Henn ROO RC	.60	1.50
237 Willy Taveras ROO RC	1.50	4.00
238 Ramon Ramirez ROO RC	.60	1.50
239 Kazuo Matsui ROO RC	1.00	2.50
240 Akinori Otsuka ROO RC	.60	1.50
241 Jason Bartlett ROO RC	2.00	5.00
242 Fernando Nieve ROO RC	.60	1.50
243 Freddy Guzman ROO RC	.60	1.50
244 Aarom Baldiris ROO RC	.60	1.50
245 Merkin Valdez ROO RC	.60	1.50
246 Mike Gosling ROO RC	.60	1.50
247 Shingo Takatsu ROO RC	.60	1.50
248 William Bergolla ROO RC	.60	1.50
249 Shawn Hill ROO RC	.60	1.50
250 Justin Germano ROO RC	.60	1.50

2004 Throwback Threads Gold Proof

*GOLD 1-200: 3X TO 8X BASIC
*GOLD 201-224: .75X TO 2X BASIC
*GOLD 225-250: .6X TO 1.5X BASIC
RANDOM INSERTS IN PACKS
STATED PRINT RUN 100 SERIAL #'d SETS

2004 Throwback Threads Green Proof

*GREEN 1-200: 8X TO 20X BASIC
*GREEN 201-224: 2X TO 5X BASIC
RANDOM INSERTS IN RETAIL PACKS
STATED PRINT RUN 25 SERIAL #'d SETS
NO PRICING ON 225-250 DUE TO SCARCITY

2004 Throwback Threads Silver Proof

*SILVER 1-200: 3X TO 8X BASIC
*SILVER 201-224: .75X TO 2X BASIC
*SILVER 225-250: .6X TO 1.5X BASIC
RANDOM INSERTS IN RETAIL PACKS
STATED PRINT RUN 100 SERIAL #'d SETS

2004 Throwback Threads Material

OVERALL AU-GU ODDS 1:8
PRINT RUNS B/WN 25-100 COPIES PER

Card	Low	High
2 Darin Erstad Jsy/100	2.00	5.00
4 Garret Anderson Jsy/100	2.00	5.00
5 Tim Salmon Jsy/100	3.00	8.00
6 Troy Glaus Jsy/100	2.00	5.00
7 Vladimir Guerrero Bat/100	4.00	10.00
8 Brandon Webb Pants/100	2.00	5.00
9 Luis Gonzalez Jsy/100	2.00	5.00
10 Randy Johnson Jsy/100	4.00	10.00
11 Richie Sexson Bat/50	3.00	8.00
12 Roberto Alomar Bat/100	3.00	8.00
14 Steve Finley Jsy/100	2.00	5.00
15 Adam LaRoche Bat/100	2.00	5.00

16 Andruw Jones Jsy/100 3.00 8.00
17 Chipper Jones Jsy/100 4.00 10.00
18 J.D. Drew Bat/100 2.00 5.00
19 John Smoltz Jsy/100 3.00 8.00
20 Rafael Furcal Jsy/100 2.00 5.00
22 Javy Lopez Bat/100 2.00 5.00
23 Jay Gibbons Jsy/100 2.00 5.00
24 Larry Bigbie Jsy/100 2.00 5.00
25 Luis Matos Jsy/100 2.00 5.00
26 Melvin Mora Jsy/100 2.00 5.00
27 Miguel Tejada Bat/100 2.00 5.00
28 Rafael Palmeiro Jsy/100 3.00 8.00
29 Curt Schilling Bat/100 3.00 8.00
30 David Ortiz Bat/100 4.00 10.00
32 Jason Varitek Jsy/100 4.00 10.00
33 Johnny Damon Bat/100 3.00 8.00
34 Manny Ramirez Jsy/100 3.00 8.00
35 Nomar Garciaparra Jsy/100 5.00 12.00
36 Pedro Martinez Jsy/100 3.00 8.00
37 Trot Nixon Bat/100 2.00 5.00
38 Aramis Ramirez Jsy/100 2.00 5.00
39 Corey Patterson Pants/100 2.00 5.00
41 Greg Maddux Bat/100 5.00 12.00
42 Kerry Wood Pants/100 2.00 5.00
43 Mark Prior Jsy/100 3.00 8.00
44 Sammy Sosa Jsy/100 4.00 10.00
45 Carlos Lee Jsy/100 2.00 5.00
47 Frank Thomas Pants/100 4.00 10.00
48 Joe Borchard Jsy/100 2.00 5.00
49 Magglio Ordonez Jsy/100 2.00 5.00
50 Mark Buehrle Jsy/100 2.00 5.00
51 Paul Konerko Jsy/100 2.00 5.00
52 Adam Dunn Jsy/100 2.00 5.00
53 Austin Kearns Jsy/100 2.00 5.00
54 Barry Larkin Jsy/100 3.00 8.00
55 Brandon Larson Fld Glv/100 2.00 5.00
58 Sean Casey Jsy/100 2.00 5.00
59 C.C. Sabathia Jsy/100 2.00 5.00
60 Jody Gerut Jsy/100 2.00 5.00
61 Omar Vizquel Jsy/100 3.00 8.00
62 Travis Hafner Jsy/100 2.00 5.00
63 Victor Martinez Bat/100 2.00 5.00
64 Charles Johnson Bat/100 2.00 5.00
65 Garrett Atkins Jsy/100 2.00 5.00
66 Jason Jennings Jsy/100 2.00 5.00
67 Joe Kennedy Bat/100 2.00 5.00
68 Larry Walker Jsy/100 2.00 5.00
69 Preston Wilson Jsy/100 2.00 5.00
70 Todd Helton Jsy/100 3.00 8.00
71 Ivan Rodriguez Bat/100 3.00 8.00
72 Jeremy Bonderman Jsy/100 2.00 5.00
73 A.J. Burnett Jsy/100 2.00 5.00
74 Brad Penny Jsy/100 2.00 5.00
75 Dontrelle Willis Jsy/100 3.00 8.00
76 Josh Beckett Jsy/100 2.00 5.00
77 Juan Pierre Bat/100 2.00 5.00
78 Luis Castillo Jsy/100 2.00 5.00
79 Miguel Cabrera Jsy/100 3.00 8.00
80 Mike Lowell Jsy/50 3.00 8.00
81 Andy Pettitte Bat/100 3.00 8.00
82 Craig Biggio Jsy/100 3.00 8.00
83 Jeff Bagwell Jsy/100 3.00 8.00
84 Jeff Kent Jsy/100 2.00 5.00
85 Lance Berkman Jsy/100 2.00 5.00
86 Morgan Ensberg Jsy/100 2.00 5.00
87 Richard Hidalgo Pants/100 2.00 5.00
88 Roger Clemens Bat/50 8.00 20.00
89 Roy Oswalt Jsy/100 2.00 5.00
90 Wade Miller Jsy/100 2.00 5.00
91 Angel Berroa Pants/100 2.00 5.00
92 Carlos Beltran Jsy/100 2.00 5.00
93 Juan Gonzalez Bat/100 2.00 5.00
94 Ken Harvey Bat/100 2.00 5.00
95 Mike Sweeney Jsy/100 2.00 5.00
96 Runelvys Hernandez Jsy/100 2.00 5.00
97 Adrian Beltre Jsy/100 2.00 5.00
98 Edwin Jackson Jsy/100 2.00 5.00
100 Hideo Nomo Jsy/100 4.00 10.00
101 Hong-Chih Kuo Bat/100 2.00 5.00
102 Kazuhisa Ishii Jsy/100 2.00 5.00
103 Paul Lo Duca Jsy/100 2.00 5.00
104 Shawn Green Jsy/100 2.00 5.00
105 Ben Sheets Jsy/100 2.00 5.00
106 Geoff Jenkins Jsy/100 2.00 5.00
107 Junior Spivey Bat/50 3.00 8.00
108 Rickie Weeks Bat/50 3.00 8.00
111 Doug Mientkiewicz Bat/100 2.00 5.00
112 Jacque Jones Jsy/100 2.00 5.00
113 Joe Mays Jsy/100 2.00 5.00
114 Johan Santana Jsy/100 3.00 8.00
115 Shannon Stewart Jsy/100 2.00 5.00
116 Torii Hunter Jsy/100 2.00 5.00
117 Brad Wilkerson Bat/100 2.00 5.00
118 Carl Everett Bat/100 2.00 5.00
120 Jose Vidro Jsy/100 2.00 5.00
121 Nick Johnson Bat/100 2.00 5.00
122 Orlando Cabrera Jsy/100 2.00 5.00
123 Al Leiter Jsy/100 2.00 5.00
124 Cliff Floyd Bat/100 2.00 5.00
125 Jae Weong Seo Jsy/100 2.00 5.00
126 Jose Reyes Jsy/100 2.00 5.00
128 Mike Piazza Jsy/100 5.00 12.00
129 Tom Glavine Jsy/100 3.00 8.00
130 Alex Rodriguez Bat/100 5.00 12.00
131 Bernie Williams Jsy/100 3.00 8.00
133 Derek Jeter Jsy/100 10.00 25.00
134 Gary Sheffield Bat/100 2.00 5.00
135 Hideki Matsui Jsy/100 12.50 30.00
136 Jason Giambi Jsy/100 2.00 5.00
138 Jorge Posada Jsy/100 3.00 8.00
141 Mariano Rivera Jsy/50 6.00 15.00
142 Mike Mussina Jsy/100 3.00 8.00
143 Barry Zito Jsy/100 2.00 5.00
145 Eric Chavez Jsy/100 2.00 5.00
146 Erubiel Durazo Bat/100 2.00 5.00
147 Jermaine Dye Bat/100 2.00 5.00
149 Mark Mulder Jsy/100 2.00 5.00
150 Rich Harden Jsy/100 2.00 5.00
151 Tim Hudson Jsy/100 2.00 5.00
153 Bobby Abreu Jsy/100 2.00 5.00
154 Brett Myers Jsy/100 2.00 5.00
155 Jim Thome Jsy/100 3.00 8.00
157 Kevin Millwood Jsy/100 2.00 5.00
158 Marlon Byrd Jsy/100 2.00 5.00
159 Pat Burrell Jsy/100 2.00 5.00
161 Jason Kendall Jsy/100 2.00 5.00
162 Brian Giles Bat/100 2.00 5.00
164 Ryan Klesko Jsy/100 2.00 5.00
165 Edgardo Alfonzo Bat/100 2.00 5.00
167 Jerome Williams Jsy/100 2.00 5.00
170 Edgar Martinez Jsy/100 3.00 8.00
171 Freddy Garcia Jsy/100 2.00 5.00
173 Jamie Moyer Jsy/100 2.00 5.00
174 John Olerud Jsy/100 2.00 5.00
176 Albert Pujols Jsy/100 8.00 20.00
177 Dan Haren Jsy/100 2.00 5.00
178 Edgar Renteria Jsy/100 2.00 5.00
179 Jim Edmonds Jsy/100 2.00 5.00
180 Matt Morris Jsy/100 2.00 5.00
181 Scott Rolen Jsy/100 3.00 8.00
182 Aubrey Huff Jsy/100 2.00 5.00
183 Carl Crawford Jsy/100 2.00 5.00
184 Chad Gaudin Jsy/100 2.00 5.00
185 Delmon Young Bat/100 3.00 8.00
186 Dewon Brazelton Jsy/100 2.00 5.00
187 Fred McGriff Jsy/100 3.00 8.00
188 Rocco Baldelli Jsy/100 2.00 5.00
189 Alfonso Soriano Bat/100 2.00 5.00
190 Hank Blalock Jsy/100 2.00 5.00
191 Laynce Nix Bat/100 2.00 5.00
192 Mark Teixeira Jsy/23 8.00 20.00
193 Michael Young Bat/100 2.00 5.00
194 Carlos Delgado Jsy/100 2.00 5.00
195 Eric Hinske Jsy/100 2.00 5.00
196 Frank Catalanotto Jsy/100 2.00 5.00
197 Josh Phelps Jsy/100 2.00 5.00
198 Orlando Hudson Jsy/100 2.00 5.00
199 Roy Halladay Jsy/100 2.00 5.00
200 Vernon Wells Jsy/100 2.00 5.00
201 Dale Murphy RET Jsy/100 5.00 12.00
202 Cal Ripken RET Jsy/100 15.00 40.00
203 Fred Lynn RET Bat/100 3.00 8.00
204 Wade Boggs RET Jsy/100 5.00 12.00
205 Nolan Ryan RET Jkt/100 10.00 25.00
206 Rod Carew RET Jkt/100 5.00 12.00
207 A.Dawson RET Pants/100 3.00 8.00
208 Ernie Banks RET Pants/50 8.00 20.00
209 Ryne Sandberg RET Jsy/50 12.50 30.00
210 Bo Jackson RET Jsy/100 6.00 15.00
211 Carlton Fisk RET Jkt/100 5.00 12.00
212 D.Concepcion RET Jsy/100 3.00 8.00
213 Alan Trammell RET Bat/100 3.00 8.00
214 George Brett RET Jsy/100 8.00 20.00
215 Robin Yount RET Jsy/100 4.00 10.00
216 Gary Carter RET Jsy/100 3.00 8.00
217 D.Straw RET Pants/100 3.00 8.00
218 Dwight Gooden RET Jsy/50 4.00 10.00
219 Babe Ruth RET Jsy/25 450.00 600.00
220 Don Mattingly RET Jkt/100 6.00 15.00
221 R.Jackson RET Jkt/100 5.00 12.00
222 Mike Schmidt RET Jkt/100 8.00 20.00
223 Tony Gwynn RET Jsy/100 6.00 15.00
224 K.Hernandez RET Jsy/100 3.00 8.00

2004 Throwback Threads Material Prime

*PRIME p/r 25: 1.25X TO 3X BASIC p/r 100
*PRIME p/r 25: .75X TO 2X BASIC p/r 50
OVERALL AU-GU ODDS 1:8
PRINT RUNS B/WN 5-25 COPIES PER
NO PRICING ON QTY OF 10 OR LESS

2004 Throwback Threads Material Combo

*COMBO p/r 50: .75X TO 2X BASIC p/r 100
*COMBO p/r 50: .6X TO 1.5X BASIC p/r 50
*COMBO p/r 50: .4X TO 1X BASIC p/r 23-29
*COMBO p/r 25: 1X TO 2.5X BASIC p/r 100
*COMBO p/r 25: .75X TO 2X BASIC p/r 50
OVERALL AU-GU ODDS 1:8
PRINT RUNS B/WN 10-50 COPIES PER
NO PRICING ON QTY OF 10 OR LESS
MOST COMBOS FEATURE BAT-JSY

2004 Throwback Threads Material Combo Prime

*COMBO PR p/r 24-25: 1.5X TO 4X p/r 100
*COMBO PR p/r 24-25: 1X TO 2.5X p/r 23
*COMBO PR p/r 15-17: 2X TO 5X p/r 100
OVERALL AU-GU ODDS 1:8
PRINT RUNS B/WN 5-25 COPIES PER
NO PRICING ON QTY OF 12 OR LESS

2004 Throwback Threads Signature Marks

OVERALL AU-GU ODDS 1:8
PRINT RUNS B/WN 5-200 COPIES PER
1-224 NO PRICING ON QTY OF 10 OR LESS
225-250 NO PRICING ON QTY OF 25 OR LESS
4 Garret Anderson/25 10.00 25.00
8 Brandon Webb/50 5.00 12.00
13 Shea Hillenbrand/50 8.00 20.00
15 Adam LaRoche/50 5.00 12.00
20 Rafael Furcal/25 10.00 25.00
23 Jay Gibbons/50 5.00 12.00
24 Larry Bigbie/50 8.00 20.00
25 Luis Matos/50 5.00 12.00
26 Melvin Mora/50 8.00 20.00
30 David Ortiz/25 30.00 60.00
40 Derrek Lee/25 15.00 40.00
43 Mark Prior/25 12.00 30.00
45 Carlos Lee/50 8.00 20.00
46 Esteban Loaiza/50 6.00 15.00
49 Joe Borchard/25 6.00 15.00
50 Mark Buehrle/25 10.00 25.00
53 Austin Kearns/25 6.00 15.00
55 Brandon Larson/25 6.00 15.00
60 Jody Gerut/50 5.00 12.00
62 Travis Hafner/50 5.00 12.00
63 Victor Martinez/50 5.00 12.00
69 Preston Wilson/50 5.00 12.00
74 Brad Penny/50 5.00 12.00
79 Miguel Cabrera/25 20.00 50.00
80 Mike Lowell/25 10.00 25.00
86 Morgan Ensberg/50 5.00 12.00
91 Angel Berroa/25 6.00 15.00
92 Carlos Beltran/25 10.00 25.00
98 Edwin Jackson/50 6.00 15.00
101 Hong-Chih Kuo/50 20.00 50.00
109 Scott Podsednik/50 12.00 30.00
112 Jacque Jones/50 8.00 20.00
114 Johan Santana/25 6.00 15.00
115 Shannon Stewart/25 10.00 25.00
116 Torii Hunter/25 10.00 25.00
119 Chad Cordero/50 8.00 20.00
120 Jose Vidro/25 6.00 15.00
122 Orlando Cabrera/50 8.00 20.00
132 Chien-Ming Wang/25 125.00 200.00
147 Jermaine Dye/50 8.00 20.00
160 Jason Bay/50 8.00 20.00
163 Jay Payton/50 5.00 12.00
168 Todd Linden/50 5.00 12.00
175 Shigetoshi Hasegawa/25 40.00 80.00
181 Scott Rolen/25 15.00 40.00
182 Aubrey Huff/50 8.00 20.00
184 Chad Gaudin/50 5.00 12.00
186 Dewon Brazelton/50 5.00 12.00
187 Fred McGriff/25 30.00 60.00
189 Alfonso Soriano/25 8.00 20.00
193 Michael Young/50 8.00 20.00
203 Fred Lynn RET/50 5.00 12.00
207 Andre Dawson RET/50 8.00 20.00
216 Gary Carter RET/25 10.00 25.00
217 Darryl Strawberry RET/50 8.00 20.00
218 Dwight Gooden RET/50 8.00 20.00
224 Keith Hernandez RET/50 8.00 20.00
225 Hector Gimenez ROO/100 3.00 8.00
226 Graham Koonce ROO/100 3.00 8.00
228 Jerry Gil ROO/100 4.00 10.00
229 Jason Frasor ROO/100 4.00 10.00
230 Justin Knoedler ROO/50 6.00 15.00
233 Ronald Belisario ROO/200 4.00 10.00
234 Jerome Gamble ROO/200 3.00 8.00
235 Roberto Novoa ROO/200 3.00 8.00
236 Sean Henn ROO/200 4.00 10.00
237 Willy Taveras ROO/100 12.00 30.00
238 Ramon Ramirez ROO/200 4.00 10.00
248 William Bergolla ROO/100 4.00 10.00
249 Shawn Hill ROO/100 4.00 10.00
250 Justin Germano ROO/100 4.00 10.00

2004 Throwback Threads Blast From the Past

STATED PRINT RUN 1500 SERIAL #'d SETS
*SPECTRUM: .75X TO 2X BASIC
SPECTRUM PRINT RUN 100 #'d SETS
RANDOM INSERTS IN PACKS
1 Albert Pujols 1.25 3.00
2 Alex Rodriguez 1.25 3.00
3 Babe Ruth 2.50 6.00
4 Cal Ripken 3.00 8.00
5 Carlton Fisk .60 1.50
6 Eddie Mathews 1.00 2.50
7 Eddie Murray .60 1.50
8 Ernie Banks 1.00 2.50
9 Frank Robinson .60 1.50
10 George Foster .40 1.00
11 Harmon Killebrew 1.00 2.50
12 Jim Rice .60 1.50
13 Jim Thome .60 1.50
14 Johnny Bench 1.00 2.50
15 Jose Canseco .60 1.50
16 Juan Gonzalez .40 1.00
17 Ken Griffey Jr. 2.00 5.00
18 Mike Piazza 1.00 2.50
19 Mike Schmidt 1.50 4.00
20 Reggie Jackson .60 1.50
21 Roger Maris 1.00 2.50
22 Sammy Sosa 1.00 2.50
23 Stan Musial 1.50 4.00
24 Willie McCovey .60 1.50
25 Willie Stargell .60 1.50

2004 Throwback Threads Blast From the Past Material Bat

OVERALL AU-GU ODDS 1:8
PRINT RUNS B/WN 50-250 COPIES PER
1 Albert Pujols/250 6.00 15.00
2 Alex Rodriguez/250 4.00 10.00
3 Babe Ruth/50 100.00 200.00
4 Cal Ripken/250 12.50 30.00
5 Carlton Fisk/250 4.00 10.00
6 Eddie Mathews/250 4.00 10.00
7 Eddie Murray/250 4.00 10.00
8 Ernie Banks/250 4.00 10.00
9 Frank Robinson/250 3.00 8.00
10 George Foster/250 3.00 8.00
11 Harmon Killebrew/250 4.00 10.00
12 Jim Rice/250 3.00 8.00
13 Jim Thome/250 3.00 8.00
14 Johnny Bench/250 4.00 10.00
15 Jose Canseco/100 5.00 12.00
16 Juan Gonzalez/250 2.00 5.00
18 Mike Piazza/250 4.00 10.00
19 Mike Schmidt/250 6.00 15.00
20 Reggie Jackson/250 4.00 10.00
21 Roger Maris/250 10.00 25.00
22 Sammy Sosa/250 4.00 10.00
23 Stan Musial/250 8.00 20.00
24 Willie McCovey/250 4.00 10.00
25 Willie Stargell/250 4.00 10.00

2004 Throwback Threads Century Collection Material

PRINT RUNS B/WN 25-250 COPIES PER
*COMBO p/r 50: .75X TO 2X p/r 150-250
*COMBO p/r 50: .75X TO 2X p/r 100
*COMBO p/r 50: .6X TO 1.5X p/r 50
*COMBO p/r 50: .4X TO 1X p/r 25
*COMBO p/r 20-25: 1X TO 2.5X p/r 250
*COMBO p/r 20-25: .5X TO 1.2X p/r 25
*COMBO p/r 15: 1.25X TO 3X p/r 250
COMBO PRINT RUNS B/WN 5-50 PER
NO COMBO PRICING ON QTY OF 5 OR LESS
OVERALL AU-GU ODDS 1:8
1 Alan Trammell Jsy/250 3.00 8.00
2 Alex Rodriguez Jsy/250 4.00 10.00
3 Alfonso Soriano Jsy/250 2.00 5.00
4 Andre Dawson Jsy/250 3.00 8.00
5 Andy Pettitte Jsy/250 3.00 8.00
6 Bert Blyleven Jsy/250 3.00 8.00
7 Bo Jackson Jsy/250 6.00 15.00
8 Bobby Doerr Jsy/250 3.00 8.00
9 Brooks Robinson Jsy/25 10.00 25.00
10 Carl Yastrzemski Jsy/250 8.00 20.00
11 Carlos Delgado Jsy/250 2.00 5.00
12 Carlton Fisk Jkt/250 4.00 10.00
13 Curt Schilling Jsy/250 3.00 8.00
14 Darryl Strawberry Jsy/250 3.00 8.00
15 Dave Concepcion Jsy/250 3.00 8.00
16 Dave Parker Jsy/100 3.00 8.00
17 Dennis Eckersley Jsy/250 4.00 10.00
18 Don Sutton Jsy/250 3.00 8.00
19 Duke Snider Jsy/250 6.00 15.00
20 Dwight Gooden Jsy/250 3.00 8.00
21 Eddie Mathews Jsy/25 15.00 40.00
22 Enos Slaughter Jsy/100 6.00 15.00
23 Ernie Banks Pants/250 4.00 10.00
24 Frankie Frisch Jkt/250 6.00 15.00
25 Frank Robinson Jsy/250 4.00 10.00
26 Frank Thomas Jsy/250 4.00 10.00
27 Garret Anderson Jsy/250 2.00 5.00
28 Gary Carter Jsy/250 3.00 8.00
29 Gary Sheffield Jsy/250 2.00 5.00
30 Harmon Killebrew Jsy/250 8.00 20.00
31 Harold Baines Jsy/250 3.00 8.00
32 Hideo Nomo Jsy/250 4.00 10.00
33 Jack Morris Jsy/250 3.00 8.00
34 Jason Giambi Jsy/250 2.00 5.00
35 Jeff Kent Jsy/250 2.00 5.00
36 Catfish Hunter Jsy/250 4.00 10.00
37 Jim Palmer Jsy/50 4.00 10.00
38 Jim Rice Jsy/250 3.00 8.00
39 Jim Thome Jsy/250 3.00 8.00
40 John Smoltz Jsy/250 3.00 8.00
41 Johnny Mize Pants/250 4.00 10.00
42 Jose Canseco Jsy/250 4.00 10.00
43 Juan Gonzalez Jsy/250 2.00 5.00
44 Juan Marichal Jsy/250 3.00 8.00
45 Keith Hernandez Jsy/250 3.00 8.00
46 Kerry Wood Jsy/250 2.00 5.00
47 Kevin Brown Jsy/250 2.00 5.00
48 Lance Berkman Jsy/250 2.00 5.00
49 Larry Walker Jsy/250 2.00 5.00
50 Lee Smith Jsy/250 3.00 8.00
51 Lenny Dykstra Bat/250 3.00 8.00
52 Luis Tiant Jsy/250 3.00 8.00
53 Magglio Ordonez Jsy/250 2.00 5.00
54 Manny Ramirez Jsy/250 3.00 8.00
55 Mariano Rivera Jsy/100 4.00 10.00
56 Mark Grace Jsy/250 4.00 10.00
57 Mark Mulder Jsy/250 2.00 5.00
58 Mark Teixeira Jsy/150 3.00 8.00
59 Marty Marion Jsy/25 6.00 15.00
60 Mike Mussina Pants/250 3.00 8.00
61 Mike Piazza Jsy/250 4.00 10.00
62 Nellie Fox Bat/250 8.00 20.00
63 Nolan Ryan Jkt/250 10.00 25.00
65 Ozzie Smith Jsy/250 5.00 12.00
66 Pedro Martinez Jsy/250 3.00 8.00
67 Pee Wee Reese Bat/250 4.00 10.00
68 Phil Niekro Jsy/250 3.00 8.00
69 Phil Rizzuto Pants/250 4.00 10.00
70 Rafael Palmeiro Jsy/250 3.00 8.00
71 Ralph Kiner Bat/250 4.00 10.00
72 Randy Johnson Jsy/250 4.00 10.00
73 Reggie Jackson Jkt/250 4.00 10.00
74 Rickey Henderson Jsy/250 4.00 10.00
75 Roberto Alomar Jsy/250 3.00 8.00
76 Robin Ventura Jsy/250 2.00 5.00
77 Rod Carew Jsy/250 4.00 10.00
78 Roger Clemens Jsy/250 4.00 10.00
79 Ron Santo Bat/250 4.00 10.00
80 Scott Rolen Jsy/250 3.00 8.00
81 Shawn Green Jsy/250 2.00 5.00
82 Steve Garvey Jsy/250 3.00 8.00
83 Tim Hudson Jsy/250 2.00 5.00
84 Tom Glavine Jsy/250 3.00 8.00
85 Tom Seaver Jsy/25 10.00 25.00
86 Adam Dunn Jsy/250 2.00 5.00
87 Tommy John Jsy/250 3.00 8.00
88 Tommy Lasorda Jsy/250 3.00 8.00
89 Tony Oliva Jsy/250 3.00 8.00
90 Tony Perez Bat/250 3.00 8.00
91 Torii Hunter Jsy/250 2.00 5.00
92 Troy Glaus Jsy/250 2.00 5.00
93 Vernon Wells Jsy/250 2.00 5.00
94 Vladimir Guerrero Jsy/250 4.00 10.00
95 Wade Boggs Jsy/250 4.00 10.00
96 Warren Spahn Jsy/100 6.00 15.00
97 Will Clark Bat/250 4.00 10.00
98 Willie McCovey Jsy/250 4.00 10.00
99 Willie Stargell Jsy/250 4.00 10.00
100 George Foster Jsy/250 3.00 8.00

2004 Throwback Threads Century Collection Material Prime

*PRIME p/r 20-25: 1.25X TO 3X p/r 150-250
*PRIME p/r 20-25: 1.25X TO 3X p/r 100
*PRIME p/r 20-25: .75X TO 2X p/r 50
*PRIME p/r 15: 1.5X TO 4X BASIC p/r 250
OVERALL AU-GU ODDS 1:8
PRINT RUNS B/WN 10-25 COPIES PER
NO PRICING ON QTY OF 10 OR LESS
7 Bo Jackson Jsy/25 30.00 60.00
63 Nolan Ryan Jkt/25 50.00 100.00
65 Ozzie Smith Jsy/25 30.00 60.00

2004 Throwback Threads Century Collection Material Combo Prime

*COMBO PR p/r 25: 1.5X TO 4X p/r 150-250
*COMBO PR p/r 25: 1.5X TO 4X p/r 100
*COMBO PR p/r 25: 1X TO 2.5X p/r 50
*COMBO PR p/r 15: 2X TO 5X p/r 250
OVERALL AU-GU ODDS 1:8
PRINT RUNS B/WN 4-25 COPIES PER
NO PRICING ON QTY OF 10 OR LESS
7 Bo Jackson Bat-Jsy/25 30.00 60.00
32 Hideo Nomo Bat-Jsy/25 15.00 40.00
63 Nolan Ryan Jkt-Jsy/25 50.00 100.00
65 Ozzie Smith Bat-Jsy/25 30.00 60.00

2004 Throwback Threads Century Collection Signature Material

PRINT RUNS B/WN 10-50 COPIES PER
NO PRICING ON QTY OF 10 OR LESS
PRIME PRINT RUNS B/WN 5-10 COPIES PER
NO PRIME PRICING DUE TO SCARCITY
*COMBO p/r 25: .6X TO 1.5X BASIC p/r 50
*COMBO p/r 25: .5X TO 1.2X BASIC p/r 25
COMBO PRINT RUN B/WN 5-25 COPIES PER
NO COMBO PRICE ON QTY OF 10 OR LESS
COMBO PRIME PRINT RUN B/WN 4-10 PER
NO COMBO PR PRICING DUE TO SCARCITY
OVERALL AU-GU ODDS 1:8
1 Alan Trammell Jsy/50 10.00 25.00
3 Alfonso Soriano Jsy/25 15.00 40.00
4 Andre Dawson Jsy/50 10.00 25.00
6 Bert Blyleven Jsy/50 12.50 30.00
8 Bobby Doerr Jsy/50 10.00 25.00
14 Darryl Strawberry Jsy/50 10.00 25.00
15 Dave Concepcion Jsy/50 10.00 25.00
16 Dave Parker Jsy/50 10.00 25.00
17 Dennis Eckersley Jsy/50 15.00 40.00
18 Don Sutton Jsy/50 10.00 25.00
19 Duke Snider Jsy/25 10.00 25.00
20 Dwight Gooden Jsy/50 10.00 25.00
27 Garret Anderson Jsy/50 10.00 25.00
28 Gary Carter Jsy/50 15.00 40.00
29 Gary Sheffield Jsy/25 10.00 25.00
31 Harold Baines Jsy/50 10.00 25.00
33 Jack Morris Jsy/50 6.00 15.00
37 Jim Palmer Jsy/25 12.50 30.00
38 Jim Rice Jsy/50 10.00 25.00
42 Jose Canseco Jsy/25 20.00 50.00
44 Juan Marichal Jsy/50 10.00 25.00
45 Keith Hernandez Jsy/50 10.00 25.00
50 Lee Smith Jsy/50 6.00 15.00
51 Lenny Dykstra Bat/50 10.00 25.00
52 Luis Tiant Jsy/50 6.00 15.00
53 Magglio Ordonez Jsy/50 10.00 25.00
56 Mark Grace Jsy/50 15.00 40.00
57 Mark Mulder Jsy/25 12.50 30.00
58 Mark Teixeira Jsy/25 10.00 25.00
59 Marty Marion Jsy/50 6.00 15.00
68 Phil Niekro Jsy/50 10.00 25.00
71 Ralph Kiner Bat/50 15.00 40.00
75 Roberto Alomar Jsy/25 12.00 30.00
76 Robin Ventura Jsy/50 10.00 25.00
82 Steve Garvey Jsy/50 15.00 40.00
87 Tommy John Jsy/50 6.00 15.00
90 Tony Perez Bat/25 30.00 60.00
91 Torii Hunter Jsy/25 12.50 30.00
93 Vernon Wells Jsy/25 12.50 30.00
94 Vladimir Guerrero Jsy/50 20.00 50.00
100 George Foster Jsy/50 6.00 15.00

2004 Throwback Threads Century Stars

STATED PRINT RUN 1500 SERIAL #'d SETS
*SPECTRUM: .75X TO 2X BASIC
SPECTRUM PRINT RUN 100 #'d SETS
RANDOM INSERTS IN PACKS
1 Al Kaline 1.00 2.50
2 Albert Pujols 1.25 3.00
3 Alex Rodriguez 1.25 3.00
4 Barry Larkin .60 1.50
5 Barry Zito .60 1.50
6 Billy Williams .60 1.50
7 Bob Feller .60 1.50
8 Bob Gibson .60 1.50
9 Cal Ripken 3.00 8.00
10 Chipper Jones 1.00 2.50
11 Curt Schilling .60 1.50
12 Dale Murphy 1.00 2.50
13 Dave Parker .40 1.00
14 Derek Jeter 2.50 6.00
15 Don Drysdale .60 1.50
16 Don Mattingly 2.00 5.00
17 Eddie Murray .60 1.50
18 Fergie Jenkins .60 1.50
19 Gary Carter .60 1.50
20 George Brett 2.00 5.00
21 Greg Maddux 1.25 3.00
22 Ivan Rodriguez .60 1.50
23 Jeff Bagwell .60 1.50
24 Joe Morgan .60 1.50
25 Johnny Bench 1.00 2.50
26 Kirby Puckett 1.00 2.50
27 Lou Boudreau .60 1.50
28 Lou Brock .60 1.50
29 Luis Aparicio .60 1.50
30 Manny Ramirez 1.00 2.50
31 Mark Prior .60 1.50
32 Miguel Tejada .60 1.50
33 Mike Mussina .60 1.50
34 Mike Piazza 1.00 2.50
35 Mike Schmidt 1.50 4.00
36 Nolan Ryan 3.00 8.00
37 Nomar Garciaparra .60 1.50
38 Ozzie Smith 1.25 3.00
39 Paul Molitor 1.00 2.50
40 Pedro Martinez .60 1.50
41 Rafael Palmeiro .60 1.50
42 Randy Johnson 1.00 2.50
43 Red Schoendienst .60 1.50
44 Reggie Jackson .60 1.50
45 Rickey Henderson 1.00 2.50
46 Roberto Alomar .60 1.50
47 Roberto Clemente 2.50 6.00
48 Robin Yount 1.00 2.50
49 Rod Carew .60 1.50
50 Roger Clemens 1.25 3.00
51 Ryne Sandberg 2.00 5.00
52 Sammy Sosa 1.00 2.50
53 Stan Musial 1.50 4.00
54 Steve Carlton .60 1.50
55 Todd Helton .60 1.50
56 Tom Glavine .60 1.50
57 Tom Seaver .60 1.50
58 Tony Gwynn 1.00 2.50
59 Wade Boggs .60 1.50
60 Whitey Ford .60 1.50

2004 Throwback Threads Century Stars Material

PRINT RUNS B/WN 10-50 COPIES PER
NO PRICING ON QTY OF 10 OR LESS
PRIME PRINT RUN 5 SERIAL #'d SETS
NO PRIME PRICING DUE TO SCARCITY
OVERALL AU-GU ODDS 1:8
1 Al Kaline Pants/25 15.00 40.00
2 Albert Pujols Jsy/50 12.50 30.00
4 Barry Larkin Jsy/50 5.00 12.00
5 Barry Zito Jsy/50 3.00 8.00
6 Billy Williams Jsy/50 4.00 10.00
8 Bob Gibson Jsy/25 10.00 25.00
9 Cal Ripken Jsy/25 25.00 60.00
10 Chipper Jones Jsy/50 6.00 15.00
11 Curt Schilling Jsy/50 3.00 8.00
12 Dale Murphy Jsy/50 6.00 15.00
13 Dave Parker Jsy/50 4.00 10.00
14 Derek Jeter Jsy/50 15.00 40.00
15 Don Drysdale Jsy/50 8.00 20.00
16 Don Mattingly Jkt/50 12.50 30.00
17 Eddie Murray Jsy/50 4.00 10.00
18 Fergie Jenkins Pants/25 6.00 15.00
19 Gary Carter Pants/50 4.00 10.00
20 George Brett Jsy/50 12.50 30.00
21 Greg Maddux Jsy/50 8.00 20.00
22 Ivan Rodriguez Jsy/50 5.00 12.00
23 Jeff Bagwell Jsy/50 5.00 12.00
24 Joe Morgan Jsy/50 6.00 15.00
25 Johnny Bench Jsy/50 8.00 20.00
26 Kirby Puckett Jsy/50 8.00 20.00
27 Lou Boudreau Jsy/50 4.00 10.00
28 Lou Brock Jsy/25 10.00 25.00
29 Luis Aparicio Pants/50 4.00 10.00
30 Manny Ramirez Jsy/50 5.00 12.00
31 Mark Prior Jsy/50 5.00 12.00
32 Miguel Tejada Jsy/50 3.00 8.00
33 Mike Mussina Jsy/50 5.00 12.00
34 Mike Piazza Jsy/50 8.00 20.00
35 Mike Schmidt Jsy/50 12.50 30.00
36 Nolan Ryan Jsy/50 10.00 25.00
37 Nomar Garciaparra Jsy/50 8.00 20.00
38 Ozzie Smith Jsy/50 10.00 25.00
40 Pedro Martinez Jsy/50 5.00 12.00
41 Rafael Palmeiro Jsy/25 8.00 20.00
42 Randy Johnson Jsy/50 6.00 15.00
43 Red Schoendienst Jsy/50 4.00 10.00
44 Reggie Jackson Pants/50 6.00 15.00
45 Rickey Henderson Jsy/50 8.00 20.00
46 Roberto Alomar Jsy/50 5.00 12.00
48 Robin Yount Jsy/50 8.00 20.00
49 Rod Carew Jkt/50 6.00 15.00
50 Roger Clemens Jsy/50 8.00 20.00
51 Ryne Sandberg Jsy/50 12.50 30.00
52 Sammy Sosa Jsy/50 6.00 15.00
54 Steve Carlton Jsy/25 6.00 15.00
55 Todd Helton Jsy/50 5.00 12.00
56 Tom Glavine Jsy/50 5.00 12.00
57 Tom Seaver Jsy/50 6.00 15.00
58 Tony Gwynn Jsy/50 8.00 20.00
59 Wade Boggs Jsy/50 6.00 15.00

2004 Throwback Threads Century Stars Signature

PRINT RUNS B/WN 5-25 COPIES PER
NO PRICING ON QTY OF 10 OR LESS
SIG.MATERIAL PRINT RUN 5 #'d SETS
NO SIG.MTL.PRICING DUE TO SCARCITY
SIG.MATERIAL PRIME PRINT RUN 5 #'d SETS
NO SIG.MTL.PR.PRICING DUE TO SCARCITY
OVERALL AU-GU ODDS 1:8
1 Al Kaline/25 30.00 80.00
6 Billy Williams/25 10.00 25.00
7 Bob Feller/25 15.00 40.00
8 Bob Gibson/25 15.00 40.00
12 Dale Murphy/25 10.00 25.00
13 Dave Parker/25 10.00 25.00
18 Fergie Jenkins/25 10.00 25.00
19 Gary Carter/25 10.00 25.00
24 Joe Morgan/25 10.00 25.00
28 Lou Brock/25 15.00 40.00
29 Luis Aparicio/25 10.00 25.00
31 Mark Prior/25 12.50 30.00
35 Mike Schmidt/25 30.00 60.00
39 Paul Molitor/25 40.00 80.00
53 Stan Musial/25 25.00 60.00

2004 Throwback Threads Dynasty

STATED PRINT RUN 1500 SERIAL #'d SETS
*SPECTRUM: .75X TO 2X BASIC
SPECTRUM PRINT RUN 100 #'d SETS
RANDOM INSERTS IN PACKS
1 P.Rizzuto .60 1.50
W.Ford
2 Reese .60 1.50
Snider
Lasorda
3 C.Hunter .60 1.50
R.Jackson
4 R.Maris 1.00 2.50
W.Ford
5 Slaughter 1.50 4.00
Marion
Musial
6 Gooden .60 1.50
Carter
Straw
Hern
7 Bench 1.00 2.50
Perez
Morgan
Foster
8 Jeter 2.50 6.00
Posa
Bernie
Pettitte
9 F.Rob .60 1.50
Brooks
Palmer
10 Stargell .60 1.50
Parker
Madlock
11 Gibson .60 1.50
Brock
Boyer
12 Hend 1.00 2.50
Moli
Carter
Alomar

2004 Throwback Threads Dynasty Material

PRINT RUNS B/WN 5-50 COPIES PER
NO PRICING ON QTY OF 10 OR LESS
ALL ARE JSY SWATCHES UNLESS NOTED
PRIME PRINT RUN 5 SERIAL #'d SETS
NO PRIME PRICING DUE TO SCARCITY
OVERALL AU-GU ODDS 1:8
3 C.Hunter/R.Jackson/25 10.00 25.00
6 Dwight Gooden Jsy 10.00 25.00
Gary Carter Jsy
Darryl Strawberry Pants
Keith Hernandez Bat/50
7 Ben/Per Bat/Morg/Fost/25 60.00 120.00
8 Jeter/Posa/Bernie/Pett/50 30.00 60.00
10 Starg 15.00 40.00
Park
Madlock Bat/25
11 Gibson 15.00 40.00
Brock
Boyer/25
12 Rickey Henderson Jsy 20.00 50.00
Paul Molitor Bat
Joe Carter Jsy
Roberto Alomar Bat/25

2004 Throwback Threads Fans of the Game

STATED ODDS 1:24
1 Emilio Estevez 1.25 3.00
2 Shannon Elizabeth 1.25 3.00
3 Joe Mantegna UER .75 2.00
4 Jamie-Lynn DiScala 1.25 3.00
5 Jonathan Silverman .75 2.00

2004 Throwback Threads Fans of the Game Autographs

RANDOM INSERTS IN PACKS
1 Emilio Estevez 20.00 50.00
2 Shannon Elizabeth 30.00 60.00
3 Joe Mantegna UER 10.00 25.00
4 Jamie-Lynn DiScala 10.00 25.00
5 Jonathan Silverman 6.00 15.00

2004 Throwback Threads Generations

STATED PRINT RUN 1500 SERIAL #'d SETS
*SPECTRUM: .75X TO 2X BASIC
SPECTRUM PRINT RUN 100 #'d SETS
RANDOM INSERTS IN PACKS
1 G.Brett 2.00 5.00
A.Pujols
2 W.Boggs .60 1.50
A.Huff
3 C.Hunter .60 1.50
T.Hudson
4 S.Garvey .40 1.00
S.Green
5 T.Gwynn 1.00 2.50
G.Anderson
6 F.Jenkins .60 1.50
M.Prior
7 R.Yount 1.00 2.50
R.Weeks
8 W.Spahn 1.25 3.00
G.Maddux
9 Brooks 3.00 8.00
Ripken
Tejada
10 Doerr 1.00 2.50
Yaz
Manny
11 Kaline 1.00 2.50
Trammell
I.Rod
12 Seaver .60 1.50
Gooden
Glavine
13 Musial 1.50 4.00
Brock
Edmonds
14 Foster .40 1.00
Parker
Kearns
15 Mathews 1.00 2.50
Murphy
Chipper
16 Sutton 3.00 8.00
Ryan
Clemens
17 B.Williams 1.00 2.50
Dawson
Sosa
18 Ford .60 1.50
John
Pettitte
19 Fisk 1.25 3.00
Clemens
Nomar
20 Marion 1.25 3.00
Ozzie
Renteria
21 Reggie 1.00 2.50
Rickey
Chavez
22 Ruth 2.50 6.00
Mattingly
Jeter
23 Clemente 2.50 6.00
Reggie
Sosa
24 Feller 1.25 3.00
Seaver
Clemens
25 Banks 3.00 8.00
Ripken
A.Rod
26 Reese 2.50 6.00
Ozzie
Jeter
27 Killebrew 1.50 4.00
Schmidt
A.Rod
28 Gibson .60 1.50
Gooden
Beckett

2004 Throwback Threads Generations Material

PRINT RUNS B/WN 5-50 COPIES PER
NO PRICING ON QTY OF 10 OR LESS
ALL ARE JSY SWATCHES UNLESS NOTED
PRIME PRINT RUN 5 SERIAL #'d SETS
NO PRIME PRICING DUE TO SCARCITY
OVERALL AU-GU ODDS 1:8
1 G.Brett/A.Pujols/50 15.00 40.00
4 W.Boggs/A.Huff/50 6.00 15.00
3 C.Hunter/T.Hudson/25 8.00 20.00
5 T.Gwynn/G.Anderson/50 10.00 25.00
6 F.Jenkins Pants/M.Prior/25 8.00 20.00
7 R.Yount/R.Weeks Bat/50 8.00 20.00
8 Spahn Pants/Maddux/25 15.00 40.00
11 Kalin Pant 20.00 50.00
Tram
Ivan Bat/25

14 Foster Parker Kearns/25 10.00 25.00
16 Sutt Ryan Jkt Clem Bat/50 20.00 50.00
17 B.Will Dawson Sosa/50 10.00 25.00
18 Ford John Pettitte/25 15.00 40.00
19 Fisk Clemens Nomar/50 15.00 40.00
20 Marion Ozzie Renteria/25 30.00 60.00
21 Reggie Jkt Rickey Chav/50 15.00 40.00
24 Feller Seaver Clemens/25 15.00 40.00
25 Banks Pant Rip A.Rod/50 40.00 80.00
26 Reese Ozzie Jeter/25 30.00 60.00
27 Kill Schmidt A.Rod Bat/25 30.00 60.00
28 Gibson Gooden Beckett/25 15.00 40.00

2004 Throwback Threads Player Threads

STATED PRINT RUN 250 SERIAL #'d SETS
CARD 57 PRINT RUN 25 SERIAL #'d COPIES
ALL ARE JSY SWATCHES UNLESS NOTED
*PRIME p/r 25: 1.25X TO 3X BASIC
PRIME PRINT RUNS B/WN 10-25 PER
NO PRIME PRICING ON QTY OF 10 OR LESS
OVERALL AU-GU ODDS 1:8
1 Aaron Boone 2.00 5.00
2 Alex Rodriguez M's-Rgr 6.00 15.00
3 A.Gala Braves-Giants-Rgr 6.00 15.00
4 Aramis Ramirez 2.00 5.00
5 Bartolo Colon 2.00 5.00
6 Ben Grieve A's-D'Rays 3.00 8.00
7 Brad Fullmer 2.00 5.00
8 Bret Boone Braves-M's 3.00 8.00
9 Brian Giles 2.00 5.00
10 Brian Jordan 2.00 5.00
11 Byung-Hyun Kim 2.00 5.00
12 Casey Fossum 2.00 5.00
13 Cesar Izturis Pants 2.00 5.00
14 Chan Ho Park 2.00 5.00
15 Charles Johnson 2.00 5.00
16 Cliff Floyd 2.00 5.00
17 D.Straw Dgr-Met-Ynk Pant 4.00 10.00
18 David Ortiz 5.00 12.00
19 David Wells Jays-Yanks 3.00 8.00
20 Derrek Lee 3.00 8.00
21 Dmitri Young 2.00 5.00
22 Edgardo Alfonzo 2.00 5.00
23 Ellis Burks 2.00 5.00
24 G.Shef Braves-Brew-Dgr 4.00 10.00
25 Hee Seop Choi 2.00 5.00
26 I.Rodriguez Marlins-Rgr 4.00 10.00
27 J.D. Drew 2.00 5.00
28 Javier Vazquez 2.00 5.00
29 Jay Payton 2.00 5.00
30 Jeff Kent Astros-Giants-Jays 4.00 10.00
31 Jeromy Burnitz 2.00 5.00
32 Jim Thome Indians-Phils 4.00 10.00
33 Joe Kennedy 2.00 5.00
34 Joe Torre 3.00 8.00
35 Jose Cruz Jr. 2.00 5.00
36 Juan Encarnacion 2.00 5.00
37 Juan Gonzalez Indians-Rgr 3.00 8.00
38 Juan Pierre 2.00 5.00
39 Junior Spivey 2.00 5.00
40 K.Loft Brave Glv-Tribe Hat 4.00 10.00
41 Kevin Millwood Braves-Phils 3.00 8.00
42 Manny Ramirez Indians-Sox 4.00 10.00
43 Mark Grace Cubs-D'backs 4.00 10.00
44 Mike Hampton 2.00 5.00
45 M.Piazza Dgr-Marlins-Mets 8.00 20.00
46 Milton Bradley 2.00 5.00
47 Moises Alou 2.00 5.00
48 Nick Johnson 2.00 5.00
49 N.Ryan Ang Jkt-Ast Jkt-Rgr 20.00 50.00
50 P.Wilson Marlins-Rockies 3.00 8.00
51 Rafael Palmeiro O's-Rgr 4.00 10.00
52 Ray Durham 2.00 5.00
53 R.Jack A's Jkt-Ang-Yank 6.00 15.00
54 Reggie Sanders 2.00 5.00
55 Rich Aurilia 2.00 5.00
56 Richie Sexson 2.00 5.00
57 R.Hend A's-M's-Yanks/25 20.00 50.00
58 R.Hend Dgr-Mets-Padres 6.00 15.00
59 Robert Fick 2.00 5.00
60 Roberto Alomar Mets-Sox 4.00 10.00
61 Roberto Alomar Indians-O's 4.00 10.00
62 R.Ventura Mets-Sox-Yanks 4.00 10.00
63 Rondell White Cubs-Expos 3.00 8.00
64 Ryan Klesko Braves-Padres 3.00 8.00
65 Sean Casey 2.00 5.00
66 S.Stewart Jays-Twins 3.00 8.00
67 Shawn Green Jays-Dgr 3.00 8.00
68 Shea Hillenbrand 2.00 5.00
69 Steve Carlton Giants-Sox 3.00 8.00
70 Terrence Long 2.00 5.00
71 Tony Batista 2.00 5.00
72 Travis Hafner Indians-Rgr 3.00 8.00
73 Travis Lee 2.00 5.00
74 Vladimir Guerrero 4.00 10.00
75 Wes Helms 2.00 5.00

2004 Throwback Threads Player Threads Signature

OVERALL AU-GU ODDS 1:8
PRINT RUNS B/WN 3-25 COPIES PER
NO PRICING ON QTY OF 11 OR LESS
ALL ARE JSY SWATCHES UNLESS NOTED
4 Aramis Ramirez/25 12.50 30.00
17 D.Straw Dgr-Met-Ynk Pnt/25 20.00 50.00
24 G.Shef Brave-Brw-Dgr/25 20.00 50.00
28 Javier Vazquez/25 12.50 30.00
29 Jay Payton/25 8.00 20.00
37 J.Gonzalez Indians-Rgr/25 15.00 40.00
39 Junior Spivey/25 8.00 20.00
50 P.Wilson Marlins-Rockies/25 15.00 40.00
55 Rich Aurilia/25 8.00 20.00
62 R.Vent Mets-Sox-Yanks/25 20.00 50.00
74 Vladimir Guerrero/25 30.00 60.00

2005 Throwback Threads

COMP.SET w/o RUTH (299) 35.00 60.00
COMMON CARD (1-277) .10 .30
COMMON RC (1-277) .15 .40
COMMON RET (278-299) .15 .40
CARD 300 RUTH SP RANDOM IN PACKS
1 Luis Castillo .12 .30
2 Derek Jeter .75 2.00
3 Eric Chavez .12 .30
4 Angel Berroa .12 .30
5 Jeff Bagwell .20 .50
6 J.T. Snow .12 .30
7 Craig Biggio .20 .50
8 Michael Barrett .12 .30
9 Hank Blalock .12 .30
10 Chipper Jones .30 .75
11 Jacque Jones .12 .30
12 Mark Teixeira .20 .50
13 Omar Vizquel .20 .50
14 Paul Lo Duca .12 .30
15 Jim Edmonds .20 .50
16 Aramis Ramirez .12 .30
17 Lance Berkman .20 .50
18 Javy Lopez .12 .30
19 Adam LaRoche .12 .30
20 Jorge Posada .20 .50
21 Sean Casey .12 .30
22 Mark Prior .20 .50
23 Phil Nevin .12 .30
24 Manny Ramirez .30 .75
25 Andruw Jones .12 .30
26 Matt Lawton .12 .30
27 Vladimir Guerrero .20 .50
28 Austin Kearns .12 .30
29 John Smoltz .30 .75
30 Ken Griffey Jr. .60 1.50
31 Mike Piazza .30 .75
32 Jason Jennings .12 .30
33 Jason Varitek .30 .75
34 David Ortiz .30 .75
35 Mike Mussina .20 .50
36 Joe Nathan .12 .30
37 Kenny Rogers .12 .30
38 Carlos Zambrano .20 .50
39 Eric Byrnes .12 .30
40 Clint Barmes .12 .30
41 Danny Kolb .12 .30
42 Mariano Rivera .40 1.00
43 Joey Gathright .12 .30
44 Adam Dunn .20 .50
45 Carlos Lee .12 .30
46 Yhency Brazoban .12 .30
47 Roy Oswalt .20 .50
48 Torii Hunter .12 .30
49 Scott Podsednik .12 .30
50 Jason Hammel RC .40 1.00
51 Ichiro Suzuki .40 1.00
52 C.C. Sabathia .20 .50
53 Bobby Abreu .12 .30
54 Jon Garland .12 .30
55 Brandon Webb .20 .50
56 Mark Buehrle .20 .50
57 Johan Santana .20 .50
58 Mike Sweeney .12 .30
59 Tadahito Iguchi RC .25 .60
60 Edgar Renteria .12 .30
61 Aaron Rowand .12 .30
62 Craig Wilson .12 .30
63 J.D. Drew .12 .30
64 Bobby Crosby .12 .30
65 Justin Morneau .20 .50
66 Scott Rolen .20 .50
67 Jose Vidro .12 .30
68 Carlos Beltran .20 .50
69 Jeff Weaver .12 .30
70 Jason Schmidt .12 .30
71 Brad Wilkerson .12 .30
72 Yuniesky Betancourt RC .60 1.50
73 Octavio Dotel .12 .30
74 Mike Cameron .12 .30
75 Barry Zito .20 .50
76 Woody Williams .12 .30
77 Russ Rohlicek RC .15 .40
78 Mark Kotsay .12 .30
79 Jeff Suppan .12 .30
80 Eric Gagne .12 .30
81 Tim Salmon .12 .30
82 Troy Glaus .12 .30
83 Kevin Mench .12 .30
84 Ivan Rodriguez .20 .50
85 Sean Burroughs .12 .30
86 Dallas McPherson .12 .30
87 Jamie Moyer .12 .30
88 Orlando Cabrera .12 .30
89 Wladimir Balentien RC .25 .60
90 Phil Humber RC .40 1.00
91 Francisco Cordero .12 .30
92 Danny Graves .12 .30
93 Bucky Jacobsen .12 .30
94 Cliff Lee .20 .50
95 Oliver Perez .12 .30
96 Jake Peavy .12 .30
97 Doug Mientkiewicz .12 .30
98 Brad Radke .12 .30
99 Jeremy Reed .12 .30
100 Garret Anderson .12 .30
101 Rafael Furcal .12 .30
102 Jack Wilson .12 .30
103 Bernie Williams .20 .50
104 Josh Beckett .12 .30
105 Albert Pujols .40 1.00
106 Ubaldo Jimenez RC .40 1.00
107 Richard Hidalgo .12 .30
108 Luke Scott RC .40 1.00
109 Hideo Nomo .30 .75
110 Vernon Wells .12 .30
111 Richie Sexson .12 .30
112 Chad Cordero .12 .30
113 Alex Rodriguez .40 1.00
114 Paul Konerko .20 .50
115 Carlos Guillen .12 .30
116 Francisco Rodriguez .20 .50
117 Johnny Damon .20 .50
118 David Wright .25 .60
119 Lyle Overbay .12 .30
120 Brian Roberts .12 .30
121 Sammy Sosa .30 .75
122 Roger Clemens .40 1.00
123 Rickie Weeks .12 .30
124 Larry Bigbie .12 .30
125 Rafael Palmeiro .20 .50
126 Jason Giambi .12 .30
127 Hideki Matsui .50 1.25
128 Brad Lidge .12 .30
129 Jeremy Affeldt .12 .30
130 Mike MacDougal .12 .30
131 Troy Percival .12 .30
132 Matt Morris .12 .30
133 Dave Gassner RC .15 .40
134 Kerry Wood .12 .30
135 Dontrelle Willis .12 .30
136 Michael Young .12 .30
137 Andy Pettitte .20 .50
138 Kris Benson .12 .30
139 Miguel Negron RC .25 .60
140 Rich Harden .12 .30
141 Bret Boone .12 .30
142 Danny Rueckel RC .15 .40
143 Jeff Niemann RC .40 1.00
144 Randy Messenger RC .15 .40
145 Pedro Martinez .20 .50
146 Kazuhisa Ishii .12 .30
147 Carlos Delgado .12 .30
148 Tom Glavine .20 .50
149 Russ Ortiz .12 .30
150 Gavin Floyd .12 .30
151 Randy Johnson .30 .75
152 Prince Fielder RC .75 2.00
153 Nomar Garciaparra .20 .50
154 Pat Burrell .12 .30
155 Melvin Mora .12 .30
156 Jose Reyes .20 .50
157 Trot Nixon .12 .30
158 B.J. Upton .20 .50
159 Jody Gerut .12 .30
160 Juan Pierre .12 .30
161 Miguel Tejada .20 .50
162 Barry Larkin .20 .50
163 Carl Crawford .20 .50
164 Ben Sheets .12 .30
165 Tim Hudson .20 .50
166 Darin Erstad .12 .30
167 Todd Helton .20 .50
168 Luis Gonzalez .12 .30
169 Mark Mulder .12 .30
170 David Dellucci .12 .30
171 Marcus Giles .12 .30
172 Shannon Stewart .12 .30
173 Zack Greinke .40 1.00
174 Miguel Cabrera .30 .75
175 Nick Johnson .12 .30
176 Derrek Lee .12 .30
177 Jim Thome .20 .50
178 Ken Harvey .12 .30
179 Ambiorix Concepcion RC .15 .40
180 Roy Halladay .20 .50
181 Larry Walker .20 .50
182 Greg Maddux .40 1.00
183 Frank Thomas .30 .75
184 Travis Hafner .12 .30
185 Matt Holliday .30 .75
186 Victor Martinez .20 .50
187 Jason Isringhausen .12 .30
188 Bill Mueller .12 .30
189 Dewon Brazelton .12 .30
190 Adrian Beltre .30 .75
191 Tim Wakefield .20 .50
192 Alexis Rios .12 .30
193 Alfonso Soriano .20 .50
194 Fernando Vina .12 .30
195 Armando Benitez .12 .30
196 Bartolo Colon .12 .30
197 A.J. Burnett .12 .30
198 Milton Bradley .12 .30
199 Brad Penny .12 .30
200 Rocco Baldelli .12 .30
201 Curt Schilling .20 .50
202 Ryan Wagner .12 .30
203 Preston Wilson .12 .30
204 Akinori Otsuka .12 .30
205 Bill McCarthy RC .15 .40
206 Edgardo Alfonzo .12 .30
207 Mike Lieberthal .12 .30
208 Shea Hillenbrand .12 .30
209 Tom Gordon .12 .30
210 Kip Wells .12 .30
211 Frank Catalanotto .12 .30
212 Casey Kotchman .12 .30
213 Justin Verlander RC 3.00 8.00
214 Brandon Inge .12 .30
215 Termel Sledge .12 .30
216 Gary Sheffield .12 .30
217 Steve Finley .12 .30
218 Kenny Lofton .12 .30
219 Chris Carpenter .20 .50
220 Dan Haren .12 .30
221 Brett Myers .12 .30
222 Joe Mauer .25 .60
223 David Wells .12 .30
224 Brian Giles .12 .30
225 Moises Alou .12 .30
226 Casey Rogowski RC .25 .60
227 Chase Utley .20 .50
228 Corey Koskie .12 .30
229 Derek Lowe .12 .30
230 Erick Threets RC .15 .40
231 Grady Sizemore .20 .50
232 Jason Lane .12 .30
233 Jeremy Bonderman .12 .30
234 Livan Hernandez .12 .30
235 Ryan Klesko .12 .30
236 Sidney Ponson .12 .30
237 Jimmy Rollins .20 .50
238 Eric Milton .12 .30
239 Shingo Takatsu .12 .30
240 Scott Kazmir .30 .75
241 Shawn Green .12 .30
242 Nick Swisher .20 .50
243 Shawn Chacon .12 .30
244 Javier Vazquez .12 .30
245 Mark Loretta .12 .30
246 Dmitri Young .12 .30
247 Charles Johnson .12 .30
248 Magglio Ordonez .20 .50
249 Sean Thompson RC .15 .40
250 Jared Gothreaux RC .15 .40
251 Kevin Millwood .12 .30
252 Mike Lowell .12 .30
253 Cristian Guzman .12 .30
254 Nate McLouth RC .25 .60
255 Delmon Young .30 .75
256 Jeromy Burnitz .12 .30
257 Garrett Atkins .12 .30
258 Junior Spivey .12 .30
259 Morgan Ensberg .12 .30
260 Chone Figgins .12 .30
261 Hayden Penn RC .15 .40
262 Jason Bay .12 .30
263 Jose Cruz Jr. .12 .30
264 Khalil Greene .12 .30
265 Ray Durham .12 .30
266 Juan Gonzalez .12 .30
267 Jeff Kent .12 .30
268 Dioner Navarro .12 .30
269 Rodrigo Lopez .12 .30
270 Geoff Jenkins .12 .30
271 Jermaine Dye .12 .30
272 Orlando Hudson .12 .30
273 Jose Lima .12 .30
274 Jeff Francis .12 .30
275 Luis Matos .12 .30
276 Jason Kendall .12 .30
277 Mike Hampton .12 .30
278 Al Kaline RET .40 1.00
279 Bert Blyleven RET .25 .60
280 Bill Madlock RET .15 .40
281 Cal Ripken RET 1.25 3.00
282 Dale Murphy RET .40 1.00
283 Gary Carter RET .25 .60
284 George Brett RET .75 2.00
285 Harmon Killebrew RET .40 1.00
286 Harold Baines RET .25 .60
287 John Kruk RET .15 .40
288 Keith Hernandez RET .15 .40
289 Willie Mays RET .75 2.00
290 Matt Williams RET .25 .60
291 Nolan Ryan RET 1.25 3.00
292 Paul Molitor RET .40 1.00
293 Reggie Jackson RET .25 .60
294 Rickey Henderson RET .40 1.00
295 Ron Cey RET .15 .40
296 Ryne Sandberg RET .75 2.00
297 Ted Williams RET .75 2.00
298 Tom Seaver RET .25 .60
299 Tony Gwynn RET .50 1.25
300 Babe Ruth RET SP 8.00 20.00

2005 Throwback Threads Blue Century Proof

*BLUE 1-277: 3X TO 8X BASIC
*BLUE 1-277: 2X TO 5X BASIC RC
*BLUE 278-300: 2.5X TO 6X BASIC
OVERALL INSERT ODDS 1:2
STATED PRINT RUN 150 SERIAL #'d SETS
300 Babe Ruth RET 5.00 12.00

2005 Throwback Threads Gold Century Proof

*GOLD 1-277: 3X TO 8X BASIC
*GOLD 1-277: 2X TO 5X BASIC RC
*GOLD 278-300: 2.5X TO 6X BASIC
OVERALL INSERT ODDS 1:2
STATED PRINT RUN 100 SERIAL #'d SETS
300 Babe Ruth RET 5.00 12.00

2005 Throwback Threads Green Century Proof

*GREEN 1-277: 3X TO 8X BASIC
*GREEN 1-277: 2X TO 5X BASIC RC
*GREEN 278-300: 2.5X TO 6X BASIC
RANDOM INSERTS IN BLASTER PACKS
300 Babe Ruth RET 5.00 12.00

2005 Throwback Threads Material Bat

*1-277 p/r 150-250: .4X TO 1X JSYp/r150-250
*1-277 p/r 150-250: .3X TO .8X JSY p/r 75-100
*1-277 p/r 150-250: .25X TO .6X JSY p/r 40-50
*1-277 p/r 150-250: .2X TO .5X JSY p/r 20-35
*1-277 p/r 100: .3X TO .8X JSY p/r 40-50
*1-277 p/r 50: .6X TO 1.5X JSY p/r 150-250
*1-277 p/r 50: .5X TO 1.2X JSY p/r 75-100
*1-277 p/r 20-35: .75X TO 2X JSY p/r 150-250
*1-277 p/r 20-35: .4X TO 1X JSY p/r 20-35
*1-277 p/r 20-35: .3X TO .8X JSY p/r 15
*1-277 p/r 15: 1X TO 2.5X JSY p/r 150-250
*278-300 p/r 150-250: .25X TO .6X JSY p/r 50
*278-300 p/r 50: .4X TO 1X JSYp/r 50
*278-300 p/r 25: .5X TO 1.2X JSYp/r 50
*278-300 p/r 25: .4X TO 1X JSYp/r 25
OVERALL AU-GU ODDS 1:8
PRINT RUNS B/WN 5-250 COPIES PER
NO PRICING ON QTY OF 10 OR LESS
4 Angel Berroa/250 1.50 4.00
14 Paul Lo Duca/250 1.50 4.00
26 Matt Lawton/250 1.50 4.00
33 Jason Varitek/50 5.00 12.00
55 Brandon Webb/250 1.50 4.00
63 J.D. Drew/250 2.50 6.00
68 Carlos Beltran/250 2.50 6.00
81 Tim Salmon/250 4.00 10.00
82 Troy Glaus/250 2.50 6.00
88 Orlando Cabrera/15 4.00 10.00
107 Richard Hidalgo/250 1.50 4.00
111 Richie Sexson/100 2.00 5.00
121 Sammy Sosa/50 5.00 12.00
123 Rickie Weeks/25 3.00 8.00
153 Nomar Garciaparra/150 3.00 8.00
160 Juan Pierre/250 1.50 4.00
165 Tim Hudson/50 2.50 6.00
169 Mark Mulder/35 3.00 8.00
175 Nick Johnson/250 1.50 4.00
192 Alexis Rios/50 2.50 6.00
206 Edgardo Alfonzo/250 1.50 4.00
215 Termel Sledge/250 1.50 4.00
218 Kenny Lofton/150 1.50 4.00
225 Moises Alou/250 1.50 4.00
241 Shawn Green/250 1.50 4.00
247 Charles Johnson/250 1.50 4.00
248 Magglio Ordonez/250 1.50 4.00
255 Delmon Young/250 2.50 6.00
265 Ray Durham/200 1.50 4.00
266 Juan Gonzalez/250 1.50 4.00
267 Jeff Kent/250 1.50 4.00
280 Bill Madlock RET/100 2.50 6.00
288 Keith Hernandez RET/25 4.00 10.00
300 Babe Ruth RET/25 125.00 200.00

2005 Throwback Threads Material Combo

*1-277 p/r 85-100: .6X TO 1.5X JSYp/r150-250
*1-277 p/r 85-100: .5X TO 1.2X JSY p/r 75-100
*1-277 p/r 85-100: .4X TO 1X JSY p/r 40-50
*1-277 p/r 40-65: .75X TO 2X JSY p/r 150-250
*1-277 p/r 40-65: .6X TO 1.5X JSY p/r 75-100
*1-277 p/r 40-65: .4X TO 1X JSY p/r 20-35
*1-277 p/r 40-65: .3X TO .8X JSY p/r 15
*1-277 p/r 25-30: 1X TO 2.5X JSY p/r 150-250
*1-277 p/r 25-30: .75X TO 2X JSY p/r 75-100
*1-277 p/r 25-30: .6X TO 1.5X JSY p/r 40-50
*1-277 p/r 25-30: .5X TO 1.2X JSY p/r 20-35
*1-277 p/r 15: 1.25X TO 3X JSY p/r 150-250
*278-300 p/r 50: .5X TO 1.2X JSY p/r 50
*278-300 p/r 25: .6X TO 1.5X JSY p/r 50
*278-300 p/r 25: .5X TO 1.2X JSY p/r 25
OVERALL AU-GU ODDS 1:8
PRINT RUNS B/WN 10-100 COPIES PER
NO PRICING ON QTY OF 10
55 B.Webb Bat-Pants/100 2.50 6.00
85 Sean Burroughs Bat-Jsy/15 5.00 12.00
160 Juan Pierre Bat-Fld Glv/95 2.50 6.00
183 Frank Thomas Hat-Jsy/25 8.00 20.00
218 K.Lofton Bat-Fld Glv/100 2.50 6.00
288 K.Hern RET Bat-Jsy/25 5.00 12.00
300 Babe Ruth RET Bat-Jsy/25 250.00 400.00

2005 Throwback Threads Material Combo Prime

*1-277 p/r 20-25: 1.25X TO 3X JSYp/r150-250
*1-277 p/r 20-25: 1X TO 2.5X JSY p/r 75-100
*1-277 p/r 20-25: .75X TO 2X JSY p/r 40-50
*1-277 p/r 20-25: .6X TO 1.5X JSY p/r 20-35
*1-277 p/r 20-25: .5X TO 1.2X JSY p/r 15
*1-277 p/r 15: 1.5X TO 4X JSY p/r 150-250
*1-277 p/r 15: 1X TO 2.5X JSY p/r 40-50
*278-300 p/r 25: .75X TO 2X JSY p/r 50
*278-300 p/r 25: .6X TO 1.5X JSY p/r 25
OVERALL AU-GU ODDS 1:8
PRINT RUNS B/WN 5-40 COPIES PER
NO PRICING ON QTY OF 10 OR LESS
4 Angel Berroa Bat-Jsy/25 5.00 12.00
81 Tim Salmon Bat-Jsy/25 8.00 20.00
183 Frank Thomas Hat-Jsy/15 12.50 30.00
266 Juan Gonzalez Bat-Jsy/40 4.00 10.00
288 K.Hern RET Bat-Jsy/25 6.00 15.00

2005 Throwback Threads Material Jersey

OVERALL AU-GU ODDS 1:8
PRINT RUNS B/WN 5-250 COPIES PER
NO PRICING ON QTY OF 10 OR LESS
1 Luis Castillo/45 2.50 6.00
3 Eric Chavez/250 1.50 4.00
5 Jeff Bagwell/250 2.50 6.00
6 J.T. Snow/250 1.50 4.00
7 Craig Biggio/50 4.00 10.00
9 Hank Blalock/25 3.00 8.00
10 Chipper Jones/250 3.00 8.00
11 Jacque Jones/250 1.50 4.00
12 Mark Teixeira/150 2.50 6.00
15 Jim Edmonds/250 1.50 4.00
16 Aramis Ramirez/250 1.50 4.00
17 Lance Berkman/250 1.50 4.00
18 Javy Lopez/250 1.50 4.00
20 Jorge Posada/250 2.50 6.00
21 Sean Casey/250 1.50 4.00
22 Mark Prior/50 4.00 10.00
23 Phil Nevin/50 2.50 6.00
24 Manny Ramirez/250 2.50 6.00
25 Andruw Jones/250 2.50 6.00
27 Vladimir Guerrero/250 3.00 8.00
28 Austin Kearns/250 1.50 4.00
29 John Smoltz/250 2.50 6.00
31 Mike Piazza/250 3.00 8.00
32 Jason Jennings/250 1.50 4.00
34 David Ortiz/250 2.50 6.00
35 Mike Mussina/250 2.50 6.00
38 Carlos Zambrano/250 1.50 4.00
42 Mariano Rivera/50 5.00 12.00
43 Joey Gathright/100 2.00 5.00
44 Adam Dunn/250 1.50 4.00
47 Roy Oswalt/250 1.50 4.00
48 Torii Hunter/100 2.00 5.00
52 C.C. Sabathia/250 1.50 4.00
53 Bobby Abreu/250 1.50 4.00
56 Mark Buehrle/250 1.50 4.00
57 Johan Santana/250 3.00 8.00
58 Mike Sweeney/75 2.00 5.00
62 Craig Wilson/250 1.50 4.00
64 Bobby Crosby/100 2.00 5.00
66 Scott Rolen/250 2.50 6.00
67 Jose Vidro/75 2.00 5.00
74 Mike Cameron/250 1.50 4.00
75 Barry Zito/250 1.50 4.00
83 Kevin Mench/250 1.50 4.00
84 Ivan Rodriguez/250 2.50 6.00
87 Jamie Moyer/50 2.50 6.00
91 Francisco Cordero/250 1.50 4.00
94 Cliff Lee/250 1.50 4.00
98 Brad Radke/250 1.50 4.00
100 Garret Anderson/50 2.50 6.00
101 Rafael Furcal/100 2.00 5.00
102 Jack Wilson/15 4.00 10.00
103 Bernie Williams/250 2.50 6.00
104 Josh Beckett/25 3.00 8.00
105 Albert Pujols/250 6.00 15.00
109 Hideo Nomo/250 3.00 8.00
110 Vernon Wells/250 1.50 4.00
114 Paul Konerko/250 1.50 4.00
116 Francisco Rodriguez/250 1.50 4.00
117 Johnny Damon/250 2.50 6.00
118 David Wright/250 4.00 10.00
119 Lyle Overbay/250 1.50 4.00
120 Brian Roberts/100 2.00 5.00
122 Roger Clemens/100 5.00 12.00
124 Larry Bigbie/200 1.50 4.00
125 Rafael Palmeiro/250 2.50 6.00
126 Jason Giambi/250 1.50 4.00
127 Hideki Matsui/250 6.00 15.00
132 Matt Morris/20 3.00 8.00
134 Kerry Wood/250 1.50 4.00
135 Dontrelle Willis/250 1.50 4.00
136 Michael Young/250 1.50 4.00
137 Andy Pettitte/250 2.50 6.00
141 Bret Boone/250 1.50 4.00
146 Kazuhisa Ishii/250 1.50 4.00
147 Carlos Delgado/250 1.50 4.00
148 Tom Glavine/250 2.50 6.00
154 Pat Burrell/250 1.50 4.00
155 Melvin Mora/250 1.50 4.00
156 Jose Reyes/200 1.50 4.00
157 Trot Nixon/250 1.50 4.00
158 B.J. Upton/250 1.50 4.00
159 Jody Gerut/100 2.00 5.00
161 Miguel Tejada/35 3.00 8.00
162 Barry Larkin/40 4.00 10.00
163 Carl Crawford/40 2.50 6.00
164 Ben Sheets/250 1.50 4.00
166 Darin Erstad/25 3.00 8.00
167 Todd Helton/150 2.50 6.00
168 Luis Gonzalez/250 1.50 4.00
170 David Dellucci/150 1.50 4.00
171 Marcus Giles/15 4.00 10.00
172 Shannon Stewart/250 1.50 4.00
174 Miguel Cabrera/100 3.00 8.00
176 Derrek Lee/250 2.50 6.00
177 Jim Thome/250 2.50 6.00
178 Ken Harvey/150 1.50 4.00
180 Roy Halladay/250 1.50 4.00
182 Greg Maddux/250 4.00 10.00
186 Victor Martinez/250 1.50 4.00
189 Dewon Brazelton/250 1.50 4.00
190 Adrian Beltre/250 1.50 4.00
193 Alfonso Soriano/250 1.50 4.00
197 A.J. Burnett/250 1.50 4.00
200 Rocco Baldelli/250 1.50 4.00
201 Curt Schilling/250 2.50 6.00
202 Ryan Wagner/250 1.50 4.00
203 Preston Wilson/250 1.50 4.00
211 Frank Catalanotto/250 1.50 4.00
212 Casey Kotchman/250 1.50 4.00
214 Brandon Inge/250 1.50 4.00
221 Brett Myers/50 2.50 6.00
224 Brian Giles/20 3.00 8.00
232 Jason Lane/95 2.00 5.00
233 Jeremy Bonderman/250 1.50 4.00
234 Livan Hernandez/250 1.50 4.00
235 Ryan Klesko/250 1.50 4.00
237 Jimmy Rollins/35 3.00 8.00
252 Mike Lowell/250 1.50 4.00
257 Garrett Atkins/250 1.50 4.00
258 Junior Spivey/250 1.50 4.00
259 Morgan Ensberg/150 1.50 4.00
260 Chone Figgins/250 1.50 4.00
262 Jason Bay/250 1.50 4.00
269 Rodrigo Lopez/250 1.50 4.00
270 Geoff Jenkins/250 1.50 4.00
272 Orlando Hudson/20 3.00 8.00
275 Luis Matos/250 1.50 4.00
279 Bert Blyleven RET/50 3.00 8.00
281 Cal Ripken RET/50 15.00 40.00
282 Dale Murphy RET/25 6.00 15.00
283 Gary Carter RET/50 3.00 8.00
284 George Brett RET/50 8.00 20.00
285 Harmon Killebrew RET/25 8.00 20.00
286 Harold Baines RET/50 3.00 8.00
287 John Kruk RET/50 5.00 12.00
289 Willie Mays RET Pants/25 20.00 50.00
290 Matt Williams RET/50 5.00 12.00
291 Nolan Ryan RET/50 15.00 40.00
292 Paul Molitor RET/50 3.00 8.00
293 Reggie Jackson RET/25 6.00 15.00
294 Rickey Henderson RET/50 6.00 15.00
295 Ron Cey RET/50 3.00 8.00
296 Ryne Sandberg RET/50 8.00 20.00
297 Ted Williams RET/25 30.00 60.00
298 Tom Seaver RET/25 6.00 15.00
299 Tony Gwynn RET/50 6.00 15.00
300 Babe Ruth RET/25 200.00 300.00

2005 Throwback Threads Material Jersey Prime

*1-277 p/r 75-100: .75X TO 2X JSYp/r150-250
*1-277 p/r 75-100: .6X TO 1.5X JSY p/r 75-100
*1-277 p/r 75-100: .5X TO 1.2X JSY p/r 40-50
*1-277 p/r 75-100: .4X TO 1X JSY p/r 20-35
*1-277 p/r 75-100: .3X TO .8X JSY p/r 15
*1-277 p/r 40-50: 1X TO 2.5X JSY p/r 150-250
*1-277 p/r 40-50: .75X TO 2X JSY p/r 75-100
*1-277 p/r 40-50: .6X TO 1.5X JSY p/r 40-50
*1-277 p/r 40-50: .5X TO 1.2X JSY p/r 20-35
*1-277 p/r 20-35: 1.25X TO 3X JSYp/r150-250
*1-277 p/r 20-35: 1X TO 2.5X JSY p/r 75-100
*1-277 p/r 20-35: .75X TO 2X JSY p/r 40-50
*278-300 p/r 100: .4X TO 1X JSY p/r 25
*278-300 p/r 50: .6X TO 1.5X JSY p/r 50
*278-300 p/r 25: .75X TO 2X JSY p/r 50
*278-300 p/r 25: .6X TO 1.5X JSY p/r 25
OVERALL AU-GU ODDS 1:8
PRINT RUNS B/WN 10-100 COPIES PER
NO PRICING ON QTY OF 10
4 Angel Berroa/50 4.00 10.00
39 Eric Byrnes/100 3.00 8.00
55 Brandon Webb/25 5.00 12.00
81 Tim Salmon/30 8.00 20.00
85 Sean Burroughs/100 3.00 8.00
140 Rich Harden/40 4.00 10.00
183 Frank Thomas/100 6.00 15.00
184 Travis Hafner/35 5.00 12.00
194 Fernando Vina/100 3.00 8.00
266 Juan Gonzalez/50 4.00 10.00
288 Keith Hernandez RET/100 4.00 10.00

2005 Throwback Threads Signature Marks

OVERALL AU-GU ODDS 1:8
PRINT RUNS B/WN 5-1000 COPIES PER
NO PRICING ON QTY OF 10 OR LESS
4 Angel Berroa/25 6.00 15.00
11 Jacque Jones/15 12.50 30.00
13 Omar Vizquel/15 20.00 50.00
19 Adam LaRoche/50 5.00 12.00
21 Sean Casey/15 12.50 30.00
28 Austin Kearns/15 8.00 20.00
36 Joe Nathan/25 10.00 25.00
38 Carlos Zambrano/25 15.00 40.00
39 Eric Byrnes/50 5.00 12.00
41 Danny Kolb/25 6.00 15.00
45 Carlos Lee/25 10.00 25.00
47 Roy Oswalt/15 12.50 30.00
48 Torii Hunter/15 12.50 30.00
49 Scott Podsednik/20 15.00 40.00
52 C.C. Sabathia/25 10.00 25.00
56 Mark Buehrle/25 20.00 50.00
62 Craig Wilson/50 5.00 12.00
64 Bobby Crosby/100 6.00 15.00
67 Jose Vidro/25 6.00 15.00
73 Octavio Dotel/25 6.00 15.00
77 Russ Rohlicek/250 3.00 8.00
81 Tim Salmon/50 12.50 30.00
85 Sean Burroughs/25 6.00 15.00
87 Jamie Moyer/25 10.00 25.00
88 Orlando Cabrera/25 10.00 25.00
90 Phil Humber/50 10.00 25.00
91 Francisco Cordero/50 5.00 12.00
92 Danny Graves/25 6.00 15.00
93 Bucky Jacobsen/64 5.00 12.00
94 Cliff Lee/50 12.50 30.00
96 Jake Peavy/25 15.00 40.00
100 Garret Anderson/15 12.50 30.00
101 Rafael Furcal/25 10.00 25.00
102 Jack Wilson/100 6.00 15.00
108 Luke Scott/250 12.50 30.00
110 Vernon Wells/25 10.00 25.00
112 Chad Cordero/25 10.00 25.00
114 Paul Konerko/25 15.00 40.00
116 Francisco Rodriguez/25 10.00 25.00
118 David Wright/25 40.00 80.00
119 Lyle Overbay/25 6.00 15.00
120 Brian Roberts/100 6.00 15.00
123 Rickie Weeks/15 12.50 30.00
124 Larry Bigbie/75 4.00 10.00
129 Jeremy Affeldt/50 5.00 12.00
131 Troy Percival/25 10.00 25.00
133 Dave Gassner/1000 3.00 8.00
136 Michael Young/25 10.00 25.00
139 Miguel Negron/250 4.00 10.00
140 Rich Harden/50 8.00 20.00
142 Danny Rueckel/250 3.00 8.00
144 Randy Messenger/500 3.00 8.00
149 Russ Ortiz/25 6.00 15.00
157 Trot Nixon/25 10.00 25.00
158 B.J. Upton/25 10.00 25.00
159 Jody Gerut/25 6.00 15.00
164 Ben Sheets/15 12.50 30.00
170 David Dellucci/50 8.00 20.00
172 Shannon Stewart/25 10.00 25.00
174 Miguel Cabrera/15 30.00 60.00
175 Nick Johnson/25 10.00 25.00
176 Derrek Lee/25 15.00 40.00
178 Ken Harvey/50 5.00 12.00
179 Ambiorix Concepcion/500 3.00 8.00
184 Travis Hafner/50 8.00 20.00
189 Dewon Brazelton/66 4.00 10.00
192 Alexis Rios/25 10.00 25.00
198 Milton Bradley/100 6.00 15.00
199 Brad Penny/25 6.00 15.00
202 Ryan Wagner/25 6.00 15.00
204 Akinori Otsuka/25 10.00 25.00
207 Mike Lieberthal/25 10.00 25.00
208 Shea Hillenbrand/25 10.00 25.00
209 Tom Gordon/25 6.00 15.00
212 Casey Kotchman/100 6.00 15.00
213 Justin Verlander/50 40.00 80.00
217 Steve Finley/15 12.50 30.00
220 Dan Haren/25 10.00 25.00
226 Casey Rogowski/250 4.00 10.00
230 Erick Threets/500 3.00 8.00
232 Jason Lane/25 10.00 25.00
233 Jeremy Bonderman/50 8.00 20.00
234 Livan Hernandez/25 10.00 25.00
239 Shingo Takatsu/25 10.00 25.00
245 Mark Loretta/25 6.00 15.00
248 Magglio Ordonez/15 12.50 30.00
250 Jared Gothreaux/1000 3.00 8.00
254 Nate McLouth/1000 6.00 15.00
258 Junior Spivey/25 6.00 15.00
259 Morgan Ensberg/25 10.00 25.00
260 Chone Figgins/50 5.00 12.00
262 Jason Bay/186 6.00 15.00
266 Juan Gonzalez/15 12.50 30.00
268 Dioner Navarro/75 4.00 10.00
271 Jermaine Dye/25 10.00 25.00
272 Orlando Hudson/100 4.00 10.00
275 Luis Matos/50 5.00 12.00
278 Al Kaline RET/15 30.00 80.00
279 Bert Blyleven RET/25 10.00 25.00
280 Bill Madlock RET/50 8.00 20.00
281 Cal Ripken RET/25 100.00 175.00
282 Dale Murphy RET/25 10.00 25.00
285 Harmon Killebrew RET/15 15.00 40.00
286 Harold Baines RET/25 10.00 25.00
288 Keith Hernandez RET/25 10.00 25.00
290 Matt Williams RET/25 15.00 40.00
295 Ron Cey RET/15 12.50 30.00

2005 Throwback Threads Century Stars

*SPECTRUM: 1X TO 2.5X BASIC
SPECTRUM PRINT RUN 100 #'d SETS
OVERALL INSERT ODDS 1:2
1 Bobby Doerr .60 1.50
2 Derek Jeter 2.50 6.00
3 Harmon Killebrew 1.00 2.50
4 Paul Molitor 1.00 2.50
5 Brooks Robinson .60 1.50
6 Steve Garvey .40 1.00
7 Ivan Rodriguez .60 1.50
8 Carl Yastrzemski 1.25 3.00
9 Nomar Garciaparra .60 1.50
10 Miguel Tejada .60 1.50

11 Edgar Martinez .60 1.50
12 Kevin Brown .40 1.00
13 Alex Rodriguez 1.25 3.00
14 Carlton Fisk .60 1.50
15 Craig Biggio .60 1.50
16 Dwight Gooden .40 1.00
17 Jim Palmer .60 1.50
18 Ken Griffey Jr. 2.00 5.00
19 Bob Feller .60 1.50
20 Don Sutton .60 1.50
21 Al Kaline 1.00 2.50
22 Roger Clemens 1.25 3.00
23 Kirk Gibson .40 1.00
24 Willie Mays 2.00 5.00
25 Frank Robinson .60 1.50
26 Randy Johnson 1.00 2.50
27 Catfish Hunter .60 1.50
28 Austin Kearns .40 1.00
29 John Smoltz 1.00 2.50
30 Nolan Ryan 3.00 8.00
31 Duke Snider .60 1.50
32 Bernie Williams .60 1.50
33 David Wells .40 1.00
34 Bo Jackson 1.00 2.50
35 Mike Mussina .60 1.50
36 Gaylord Perry .60 1.50
37 Andre Dawson .60 1.50
38 Curt Schilling .60 1.50
39 Darryl Strawberry .40 1.00
40 Willie McCovey .60 1.50
41 Tom Seaver .60 1.50
42 Mariano Rivera 1.25 3.00
43 Dennis Eckersley .60 1.50
44 David Cone .40 1.00
45 Bret Boone .40 1.00
46 Will Clark .60 1.50
47 Jack Morris .60 1.50
48 Ichiro Suzuki 1.25 3.00
49 Alan Trammell .60 1.50
50 Cal Ripken 3.00 8.00

2005 Throwback Threads Century Stars Material

PRINT RUNS B/WN 20-50 COPIES PER
PRIME PRINT RUN 5 SERIAL #'d SETS
NO PRIME PRICING DUE TO SCARCITY
OVERALL AU-GU ODDS 1:8
1 Bobby Doerr Pants/50 3.00 8.00
3 Harmon Killebrew Jsy/50 6.00 15.00
4 Paul Molitor Jsy/50 3.00 8.00
5 Brooks Robinson Bat/50 5.00 12.00
6 Steve Garvey Jsy/50 3.00 8.00
7 Ivan Rodriguez Jsy/50 4.00 10.00
8 Carl Yastrzemski Jsy/50 6.00 15.00
10 Miguel Tejada Jsy/50 2.50 6.00
11 Edgar Martinez Jsy/50 5.00 12.00
12 Kevin Brown Jsy/50 2.50 6.00
14 Carlton Fisk Jsy/50 5.00 12.00
15 Craig Biggio Jsy/50 4.00 10.00
16 Dwight Gooden Jsy/50 3.00 8.00
17 Jim Palmer Jsy/50 3.00 8.00
19 Bob Feller Pants/20 4.00 10.00
20 Don Sutton Jsy/50 3.00 8.00
21 Al Kaline Bat/50 6.00 15.00
22 Roger Clemens Jsy/50 6.00 15.00
23 Kirk Gibson Jsy/50 3.00 8.00
24 Willie Mays Jsy/20 20.00 50.00
25 Frank Robinson Bat/50 3.00 8.00
26 Randy Johnson Jsy/50 5.00 12.00
27 Catfish Hunter Jsy/20 4.00 10.00
28 Austin Kearns Jsy/50 2.50 6.00
29 John Smoltz Jsy/50 4.00 10.00
30 Nolan Ryan Jkt/50 10.00 25.00
31 Duke Snider Pants/20 6.00 15.00
32 Bernie Williams Jsy/50 4.00 10.00
33 David Wells Jsy/50 2.50 6.00
34 Bo Jackson Jsy/50 6.00 15.00
35 Mike Mussina Jsy/50 4.00 10.00
36 Gaylord Perry Jsy/50 3.00 8.00
37 Andre Dawson Jsy/50 3.00 8.00
38 Curt Schilling Jsy/50 4.00 10.00
39 Darryl Strawberry Jsy/50 3.00 8.00
40 Willie McCovey Jsy/50 5.00 12.00
41 Tom Seaver Jsy/20 6.00 15.00
42 Mariano Rivera Jsy/50 5.00 12.00
43 Dennis Eckersley Jsy/50 3.00 8.00
44 David Cone Jsy/50 3.00 8.00
45 Bret Boone Jsy/50 2.50 6.00
46 Will Clark Jsy/20 6.00 15.00
47 Jack Morris Jsy/50 3.00 8.00
49 Alan Trammell Jsy/50 3.00 8.00
50 Cal Ripken Jsy/50 15.00 40.00

2005 Throwback Threads Dynasty

*SPECTRUM: 1X TO 2.5X BASIC
SPECTRUM PRINT RUN 100 #'d SETS
OVERALL INSERT ODDS 1:2
1 Reggie .60 1.50
Catfish
Lyle
2 Ripken 3.00 8.00
Palmer
Murray
3 Gooden .60 1.50
Carter
Straw
4 Rickey 1.00 2.50
Eck
Canseco
5 Chipper 1.25 3.00
Maddux
Just
6 Clemens 1.25 3.00
Soriano
Bernie
7 Randy 1.00 2.50
Schilling
M.Will
8 Glaus .60 1.50
Garret
F.Rod
9 Beckett 1.00 2.50
Cabrera
Lowell
10 Schilling 1.00 2.50
Manny
Varitek

2005 Throwback Threads Dynasty Material

PRINT RUNS B/WN 20-50 COPIES PER
PRIME PRINT RUN 5 SERIAL #'d SETS
NO PRIME PRICING DUE TO SCARCITY
OVERALL AU-GU ODDS 1:8
1 Reggie P 8.00 20.00
Hunt P
Lyle P/50
2 Ripken J 20.00 50.00
Palm J
Murr J/50
3 Good J 6.00 15.00
Cart J
Straw P/20
4 Rickey J 20.00 50.00
Eck P
Cans J/50
5 Chip J 12.50 30.00
Maddux J
Just J/50
6 Clem J 12.50 30.00
A.Sor J
Bernie J/50
7 Randy J 10.00 25.00
Schil J
M.Will J/50
8 Glaus J 5.00 12.00
Garret J
F.Rod J/50
9 Beck J 6.00 15.00
M.Cab J
Low J/20
10 Schil J 15.00 40.00
Manny J
Varit J/50

2005 Throwback Threads Generations

*SPECTRUM: 1X TO 2.5X BASIC
SPECTRUM PRINT RUN 100 #'d SETS
OVERALL INSERT ODDS 1:2
1 Snider 1.00 2.50
Reggie
Sosa
2 Carew .60 1.50
Kruk
Chavez
3 Bo 1.00 2.50
Deion
B.Jordan
4 Brett 2.00 5.00
Gwynn
Helton
5 Ruth 2.50 6.00
Williams
Mays
6 Rickey 1.25 3.00
Dykstra
Ichiro
7 K.Hern 2.00 5.00
Mattingly
Kotch
8 Boggs .60 1.50
Grace
Blalock
9 G.Carter .60 1.50
I.Rod
V.Mart
10 Perry 1.25 3.00
Morris
Maddux
11 Morgan 2.00 5.00
Ryno
Soriano
12 Marichal .60 1.50
Tiant
Pedro
13 Musial 1.50 4.00
Yaz
Berkman
14 Bench 1.00 2.50
Fisk
Piazza
15 Killebrew 3.00 8.00
Ripken
Pujols
16 F.Rob .60 1.50
Dawson
Sheff
17 Feller 1.25 3.00
Clemens
Wood
18 Carlton .60 1.50
Glavine
Zito
19 Murray .60 1.50
Raffy
Teixeira
20 Brooks 1.50 4.00
Schmidt
Rolen
21 Aparicio .60 1.50
Vizquel
Furcal
22 Sutton .60 1.50
Cone
Oswalt
23 Lynn 1.00 2.50
Murphy
Edmonds
24 Ozzie 1.25 3.00
Larkin
Upton
25 Gibson 3.00 8.00
Ryan
Prior

2005 Throwback Threads Generations Material

PRINT RUNS B/WN 20-50 COPIES PER
PRIME PRINT RUN 10 SERIAL #'d SETS
NO PRIME PRICING DUE TO SCARCITY
OVERALL AU-GU ODDS 1:8
1 Snider P/Regg J/Sosa J/20 15.00 40.00
2 Carew J/Kruk J/Chav J/50 8.00 20.00
3 Bo J/Deion J/B.Jord J/50 12.50 30.00
4 Brett J/Gwynn J/Helt J/50 12.50 30.00
5 Ruth J/T.Will J/Mays J/20 250.00 400.00
7 K.Hern J/Matt P/Kotch J/20 15.00 40.00
8 Boggs J/Grace J/Blal J/50 8.00 20.00
9 G.Cart J/I.Rod J/Mart J/50 8.00 20.00
10 Perry J/Morris J/Madd J/50 12.50 30.00
11 Morg J/Ryno J/A.Sor J/50 8.00 20.00
12 Mari P/Tiant P/Pedro J/50 8.00 20.00
13 Musial P/Yaz P/Berk J/20 20.00 50.00
14 Bench P/Fisk J/Piaz J/50 15.00 40.00
15 Kill J/Ripken J/Pujols J/50 30.00 60.00
16 F.Rob B/Daws J/Shef J/20 6.00 15.00
17 Fell P/Clem J/Wood J/20 15.00 40.00
18 Carlton J/Glav J/Zito J/50 8.00 20.00
19 Murray J/Raffy J/Teix J/50 10.00 25.00
20 B.Rob J/Schm J/Rolen J/20 15.00 40.00
21 Apar J/Vizq J/Furcal J/20 10.00 25.00
22 Sutt J/Cone J/Oswalt J/20 6.00 15.00
23 Lynn J/Murphy J/Edm J/50 8.00 20.00
24 Ozzie J/Lark J/Upton B/20 12.50 30.00
25 Gibson J/Ryan J/Prior J/50 20.00 50.00

2005 Throwback Threads Player Timelines

*SPECTRUM: 1X TO 2.5X BASIC
SPECTRUM PRINT RUN 100 #'d SETS
OVERALL INSERT ODDS 1:2
1 D.Murphy Braves-Phils 1.00 2.50
2 G.Maddux Braves-Cubs 1.25 3.00
3 T.Glavine Braves-Mets .60 1.50
4 D.Ortiz Twins-Sox 1.00 2.50
5 B.Jackson Royals-Sox 1.00 2.50
6 L.Overbay D'backs-Brew .40 1.00
7 T.John Yanks-Angels .40 1.00
8 S.Green Jays-Dgr .40 1.00
9 A.Ramirez Pirates-Cubs .40 1.00
10 J.Lopez Braves-O's .40 1.00
11 V.Guerrero Expos-Angels .60 1.50
12 T.Hafner Rgr-Indians .40 1.00
13 J.Spivey D'backs-Brew .40 1.00
14 A.Soriano Yanks-Rgr .60 1.50
15 A.Dawson Expos-Cubs-Sox .60 1.50
16 S.Sosa Sox-Cubs 1.00 2.50
17 A.Pettitte Yanks-Astros .60 1.50
18 J.Edmonds Angels-Cards .60 1.50
19 W.McCovey Giants-Padres .60 1.50
20 S.Rolen Phils-Cards .60 1.50
21 J.Dye Royals-A's .40 1.00
22 P.Martinez Dgr-Expos-Sox .60 1.50
23 D.Sutton Dgr-Astros-Angels .60 1.50
24 R.Johnson Expos-M's-Astro 1.00 2.50
25 N.Ryan Mets-Angels-Astros 3.00 8.00
26 D.Eckersley Sox-A's-Cards .60 1.50
27 R.Jackson A's-Yanks-Angel .60 1.50
28 D.Sanders Yank-Brave-Red .60 1.50
29 C.Schilling Phil-D'back-Sox .60 1.50
30 R.Hend Yanks-Padres-Dgr 1.00 2.50
31 M.Piazza Dgr-M's-Mets 1.00 2.50
32 G.Carter Expos-Mets-Dgr .60 1.50
33 R.Alomar O's-Indians-Mets .60 1.50
34 H.Nomo Dgr-Mets-Sox 1.00 2.50
35 A.Galarraga Brv-Rgr-Giant .60 1.50
36 J.Gonzalez Rgr-Ind-Royal .40 1.00
37 R.Clemens Sox-Yank-Astr 1.25 3.00
38 J.Kent Jays-Giants-Astros .40 1.00
39 S.Carlton Phils-Sox-Giants .60 1.50
40 W.Boggs Sox-Yanks-Rays .60 1.50

2005 Throwback Threads Player Timelines Material

OVERALL AU-GU ODDS 1:8
PRINT RUNS B/WN 25-250 COPIES PER
1 D.Murphy Braves-Phils/50 6.00 15.00
2 G.Maddux Braves-Cub/100 5.00 12.00
3 T.Glavine Braves-Mets/50 5.00 12.00
4 D.Ortiz Twins-Sox/250 3.00 8.00
5 B.Jackson Royals-Sox/100 6.00 15.00
6 L.Over D'back-Brew/250 2.00 5.00
7 T.John Yank Pnt-Angel/250 2.50 6.00
8 S.Green Jays-Dgr/100 2.50 6.00
9 A.Ramirez Pirates-Cubs/250 2.00 5.00
10 J.Lopez Braves-O's/100 2.50 6.00
11 V.Guerrero Expo-Angels/25 8.00 20.00
12 T.Hafner Rgr-Indians/25 4.00 10.00
13 J.Spivey D'backs-Brew/250 2.00 5.00
14 A.Soriano Yanks-Rgr/100 2.50 6.00
16 S.Sosa Sox-Cubs/250 4.00 10.00
17 A.Pettitte Yanks-Astros/100 4.00 10.00
18 J.Edmonds Angel-Card/100 2.50 6.00
19 McCov Giant Pnt-Padre/50 6.00 15.00
20 S.Rolen Phils-Cards/50 5.00 12.00
21 J.Dye Royals-A's/100 2.50 6.00
22 P.Mart Dgr-Expos-Sox/50 6.00 15.00
23 D.Sutton Dgr-Astr-Angel/25 6.00 15.00
24 R.Johnson Exp-M's-Astr/50 8.00 20.00
25 Ryan Met-Angel Jkt-Astr/50 20.00 50.00
27 R.Jack A's-Yank P-Angel/50 8.00 20.00
28 D.Sand Yank-Brv-Red/25 10.00 25.00
29 C.Schill Phil-D'back-Sox/50 4.00 10.00
30 Hend Ynk P-Pdr P-Dgr/100 8.00 20.00
31 M.Piazza Dgr-M's-Mets/50 8.00 20.00
32 G.Cart Exp-Met-Dgr C P/50 5.00 12.00
33 R.Alomar O's-Ind-Met/250 5.00 12.00
34 H.Nomo Dgr-Mets-Sox/50 8.00 20.00
35 A.Gala Brv-Rgr-Giant/250 3.00 8.00
36 J.Gon Rgr-Ind-Royals/25 5.00 12.00
37 R.Clem Sox-Yank-Astr/25 15.00 40.00
38 J.Kent Jays-Giants-Astr/50 4.00 10.00

2005 Throwback Threads Player Timelines Signature Material

PRINT RUNS B/WN 5-50 COPIES PER
NO PRICING ON QTY OF 10 OR LESS
PRIME PRINT RUNS B/WN 5-10 COPIES PER
NO PRIME PRICING DUE TO SCARCITY
OVERALL AU-GU ODDS 1:8
1 D.Murphy Braves-Phils/50 15.00 40.00
6 L.Overbay D'back-Brew/50 6.00 15.00
7 T.John Yank Pnt-Angel/50 10.00 25.00
12 T.Hafner Rgr-Indians/25 12.50 30.00
13 J.Spivey D'backs-Brew/50 6.00 15.00
15 A.Daws Expos-Cub-Sox/25 12.50 30.00
21 J.Dye Royals-A's/50 10.00 25.00
23 D.Sutton Dgr-Astr-Angel/25 12.50 30.00
32 G.Cart Exp-Met-Dgr C P/50 15.00 40.00
36 J.Gon Rgr-Ind-Royals/25 12.50 30.00
40 W.Boggs Sox-Ynk-Ray/15 30.00 60.00

2005 Throwback Threads Polo Grounds 85 HIT Long Fly

STATED PRINT RUN 85 SERIAL #'d SETS
*PARALLEL #'d OF 50-75: .4X TO 1X
*PARALLEL #'d OF 40-45: .5X TO 1.2X
*PARALLEL #'d OF 30-35: .6X TO 1.5X
*PARALLEL #'d OF 20-25: .75X TO 2X
*PARALLEL #'d OF 15: 1X TO 2.5X
PARALLELS #'d FROM 5-75 COPIES PER
NO PRICING ON QTY OF 5
OVERALL INSERT ODDS 1:2
1 Ken Griffey Jr. 4.00 10.00
2 Roger Clemens 2.50 6.00
3 Barry Zito 1.25 3.00
4 Alex Rodriguez 2.50 6.00
5 Melvin Mora .75 2.00
6 Kevin Brown .75 2.00
7 Chipper Jones 2.00 5.00
8 Scott Kazmir 2.00 5.00
9 Kip Wells .75 2.00
10 Khalil Greene .75 2.00
11 Kevin Millwood .75 2.00
12 Kerry Wood .75 2.00
13 Mark Kotsay .75 2.00
14 Jeff Bagwell 1.25 3.00
15 Hank Blalock .75 2.00
16 Scott Rolen 1.25 3.00
17 Lance Berkman 1.25 3.00
18 Mike Mussina 1.25 3.00
19 Jim Edmonds 1.25 3.00
20 Jorge Posada 1.25 3.00
21 Curt Schilling 1.25 3.00
22 Vernon Wells .75 2.00
23 Pedro Martinez 1.25 3.00
24 Jeremy Reed .75 2.00
25 Hideki Matsui 3.00 8.00
26 Steve Finley .75 2.00
27 Gavin Floyd .75 2.00
28 Darin Erstad .75 2.00
29 Bernie Williams 1.25 3.00
30 Mark Mulder .75 2.00
31 Rafael Palmeiro 1.25 3.00
32 Andruw Jones .75 2.00
33 Roy Halladay 1.25 3.00
34 Dontrelle Willis .75 2.00
35 Bret Boone .75 2.00
36 Andy Pettitte 1.25 3.00
37 Vladimir Guerrero 1.25 3.00
38 Randy Johnson 2.00 5.00
39 Michael Young .75 2.00
40 Frank Thomas 2.00 5.00
41 Todd Helton 1.25 3.00
42 Johan Santana 1.25 3.00
43 Mark Teixeira 1.25 3.00
44 Justin Morneau 1.25 3.00
45 Brad Radke .75 2.00
46 Dallas McPherson .75 2.00
47 Tim Hudson 1.25 3.00
48 Carl Crawford 1.25 3.00
49 Eric Gagne .75 2.00
50 Mark Prior 1.25 3.00
51 Tom Glavine 1.25 3.00
52 Craig Biggio 1.25 3.00
53 John Smoltz 2.00 5.00
54 Manny Ramirez 2.00 5.00
55 Ivan Rodriguez 1.25 3.00
56 Gary Sheffield .75 2.00
57 Josh Beckett .75 2.00
58 Miguel Tejada 1.25 3.00
59 Bobby Abreu .75 2.00
60 Ichiro Suzuki 2.50 6.00
61 Sammy Sosa 2.00 5.00
62 Garret Anderson .75 2.00
63 Sean Casey .75 2.00
64 Troy Glaus .75 2.00
65 Larry Walker 1.25 3.00
66 Alfonso Soriano 1.25 3.00
67 Luis Gonzalez .75 2.00
68 Eric Chavez .75 2.00
69 Adrian Beltre 2.00 5.00
70 Miguel Cabrera 2.00 5.00
71 Carlos Beltran 1.25 3.00
72 Jim Thome 1.25 3.00
73 David Ortiz 2.00 5.00
74 Adam Dunn 1.25 3.00
75 Jacque Jones .75 2.00
76 Shawn Green .75 2.00
77 Victor Martinez 1.25 3.00
78 Torii Hunter .75 2.00
79 Carlos Lee .75 2.00
80 C.C. Sabathia 1.25 3.00
81 Joe Mauer 1.50 4.00
82 Kris Benson .75 2.00
83 Zack Greinke 2.50 6.00
84 Greg Maddux 2.50 6.00
85 David Wright 1.50 4.00
86 Mike Piazza 2.00 5.00
87 Johnny Damon 1.25 3.00
88 Derek Jeter 5.00 12.00
89 B.J. Upton 1.25 3.00
90 Albert Pujols 2.50 6.00
91 Cal Ripken 6.00 15.00
92 Nolan Ryan 6.00 15.00
93 George Brett 4.00 10.00
94 Don Mattingly 4.00 10.00
95 Ryne Sandberg 4.00 10.00
96 Rickey Henderson 2.00 5.00
97 Robin Yount 2.00 5.00
98 Mike Schmidt 3.00 8.00
99 Tony Gwynn 2.50 6.00
100 Willie Mays 4.00 10.00

2005 Throwback Threads Throwback Collection

*SPECTRUM: 1X TO 2.5X BASIC
SPECTRUM PRINT RUN 100 #'d SETS
OVERALL INSERT ODDS 1:2
1 Billy Martin .60 1.50
2 Tony Gwynn 1.25 3.00
3 Babe Ruth 2.50 6.00
4 Angel Berroa .40 1.00
5 Jeff Bagwell .60 1.50
6 Tony Oliva .40 1.00
7 Ivan Rodriguez .60 1.50
8 Gary Carter .60 1.50
9 Ted Williams 2.00 5.00
10 Chipper Jones 1.00 2.50
11 Al Oliver .40 1.00
12 Roberto Alomar .60 1.50
13 Omar Vizquel .60 1.50
14 Ernie Banks 1.00 2.50
15 Carlos Beltran .60 1.50
16 Garret Anderson .40 1.00
17 Mark Grace .60 1.50
18 Jason Giambi .40 1.00
19 Dave Righetti .40 1.00
20 Mike Schmidt 1.50 4.00
21 Roger Clemens 1.25 3.00
22 Juan Gonzalez .40 1.00
23 Carlos Delgado .40 1.00
24 Manny Ramirez 1.00 2.50
25 Jim Thome .60 1.50
26 Wade Boggs .60 1.50
27 Luis Tiant .40 1.00
28 Kerry Wood .40 1.00
29 Rod Carew .60 1.50
30 Dwight Evans .60 1.50
31 Mike Piazza 1.00 2.50
32 Billy Williams .60 1.50
33 Larry Walker .60 1.50
34 Nolan Ryan 3.00 8.00
35 Edgar Renteria .40 1.00
36 Greg Maddux 1.25 3.00
37 Gaylord Perry .60 1.50
38 Curt Schilling .60 1.50
39 Dave Parker .40 1.00
40 Andruw Jones .40 1.00
41 Orlando Cepeda .60 1.50
42 Fergie Jenkins .60 1.50
43 Kirby Puckett 1.00 2.50
44 Reggie Jackson .60 1.50
45 Bob Gibson .60 1.50
46 Rickey Henderson 1.00 2.50
47 Lee Smith .40 1.00
48 Lou Brock .60 1.50
49 Fred Lynn .40 1.00
50 Lance Berkman .60 1.50
51 Shawn Green .40 1.00
52 Hoyt Wilhelm .60 1.50
53 Sammy Sosa 1.00 2.50
54 Tim Hudson .60 1.50
55 Matt Williams .60 1.50
56 Marty Marion .40 1.00
57 Eric Chavez .40 1.00
58 Rafael Palmeiro .60 1.50
59 Randy Johnson 1.00 2.50
60 David Ortiz 1.00 2.50
61 Hank Blalock .40 1.00
62 Jim Rice .60 1.50
63 Mark Mulder .40 1.00
64 Kazuo Matsui .40 1.00
65 Pedro Martinez .60 1.50
66 Sean Casey .40 1.00
67 Carlos Lee .40 1.00
68 Stan Musial 1.50 4.00
69 Fred McGriff .60 1.50
70 Darryl Strawberry .40 1.00
71 Tommy John .40 1.00
72 Hideo Nomo 1.00 2.50
73 Johnny Bench 1.00 2.50
74 Cal Ripken 3.00 8.00
75 Harold Baines .60 1.50

2005 Throwback Threads Throwback Collection Material

OVERALL AU-GU ODDS 1:8
PRINT RUNS B/WN 5-500 COPIES PER
NO PRICING ON QTY OF 5
1 Billy Martin Pants/250 3.00 8.00
2 Tony Gwynn Jsy/250 4.00 10.00
3 Babe Ruth Pants/20 175.00 300.00
4 Angel Berroa Pants/100 2.00 5.00
5 Jeff Bagwell Jsy/250 2.50 6.00
6 Tony Oliva Jsy/250 2.00 5.00
7 Ivan Rodriguez Jsy/500 2.50 6.00
8 Gary Carter Pants/250 2.00 5.00
9 Ted Williams Jsy/20 30.00 60.00
10 Chipper Jones Jsy/250 3.00 8.00
11 Al Oliver Jsy/250 2.00 5.00
12 Roberto Alomar Jsy/500 3.00 8.00
13 Omar Vizquel Jsy/500 2.50 6.00
14 Ernie Banks Jsy/20 10.00 25.00
15 Carlos Beltran Jsy/100 2.00 5.00
16 Garret Anderson Jsy/50 2.50 6.00
17 Mark Grace Jsy/250 3.00 8.00
18 Jason Giambi Jsy/500 1.50 4.00
19 Dave Righetti Jsy/250 2.00 5.00
20 Mike Schmidt Jsy/20 10.00 25.00
21 Roger Clemens Jsy/250 4.00 10.00
22 Juan Gonzalez Jsy/150 1.50 4.00
23 Carlos Delgado Jsy/150 1.50 4.00
24 Manny Ramirez Jsy/50 4.00 10.00
25 Jim Thome Jsy/500 2.50 6.00
26 Wade Boggs Jsy/250 3.00 8.00
27 Luis Tiant Pants/500 2.00 5.00
28 Kerry Wood Jsy/50 2.50 6.00
29 Rod Carew Jkt/250 3.00 8.00
30 Dwight Evans Jsy/50 5.00 12.00
31 Mike Piazza Jsy/250 3.00 8.00
32 Billy Williams Jsy/100 2.50 6.00
33 Larry Walker Jsy/500 2.50 6.00
34 Nolan Ryan Pants/100 8.00 20.00
35 Edgar Renteria Jsy/500 1.50 4.00
36 Greg Maddux Jsy/375 4.00 10.00
37 Gaylord Perry Jsy/250 2.00 5.00
38 Curt Schilling Jsy/500 1.50 4.00
39 Dave Parker Jsy/50 3.00 8.00
40 Andruw Jones Jsy/500 2.50 6.00
41 Orlando Cepeda Pants/250 2.00 5.00
42 Fergie Jenkins Jsy/250 2.00 5.00
43 Kirby Puckett Jsy/400 4.00 10.00
44 Reggie Jackson Jsy/250 3.00 8.00
45 Bob Gibson Jsy/100 4.00 10.00
46 Rickey Henderson Jsy/500 4.00 10.00
47 Lee Smith Jsy/250 2.00 5.00
49 Fred Lynn Jsy/250 2.00 5.00
50 Lance Berkman Jsy/500 1.50 4.00
51 Shawn Green Jsy/500 1.50 4.00
52 Hoyt Wilhelm Jsy/250 2.00 5.00
53 Sammy Sosa Jsy/500 3.00 8.00
54 Tim Hudson Jsy/500 1.50 4.00
55 Matt Williams Jsy/250 3.00 8.00
57 Eric Chavez Jsy/500 1.50 4.00
58 Rafael Palmeiro Jsy/500 2.50 6.00
59 Randy Johnson Jsy/250 3.00 8.00
60 David Ortiz Jsy/500 2.50 6.00
61 Hank Blalock Jsy/50 2.50 6.00
62 Jim Rice Pants/250 2.00 5.00
63 Mark Mulder Jsy/100 2.00 5.00
64 Kazuo Matsui Jsy/500 1.50 4.00
65 Pedro Martinez Jsy/250 2.50 6.00
66 Sean Casey Jsy/500 1.50 4.00
67 Carlos Lee Jsy/500 1.50 4.00
68 Stan Musial Pants/100 8.00 20.00
69 Fred McGriff Jsy/500 3.00 8.00
70 Darryl Strawberry Jsy/250 2.00 5.00
71 Tommy John Jsy/250 2.00 5.00
72 Hideo Nomo Jsy/500 3.00 8.00
73 Johnny Bench Pants/100 5.00 12.00
74 Cal Ripken Jsy/250 10.00 25.00
75 Harold Baines Jsy/250 2.00 5.00

2005 Throwback Threads Throwback Collection Material Prime

*PRIME p/r 25: 1.25X TO 3X MTL p/r 150+
*PRIME p/r 25: 1X TO 2.5X MTL p/r 100
*PRIME p/r 25: .75X TO 2X MTL p/r 50
*PRIME p/r 25: .6X TO 1.5X MTL p/r 20
OVERALL AU-GU ODDS 1:8
PRINT RUNS B/WN 5-25 COPIES PER
NO PRICING ON QTY OF 5
48 Lou Brock Jsy/25 10.00 25.00

2005 Throwback Threads Throwback Collection Material Combo

*COMBO p/r 100: .6X TO 1.5X MTL p/r 150+
*COMBO p/r 100: .5X TO 1.2X MTL p/r 100
*COMBO p/r 50: .75X TO 2X MTL p/r 150+
*COMBO p/r 50: .5X TO 1.2X MTL p/r 50
*COMBO p/r 20-25: .75X TO 2X MTL p/r 100
*COMBO p/r 20-25: .6X TO 1.5X MTL p/r 50
*COMBO p/r 20-25: .5X TO 1.2X MTL p/r 20
OVERALL AU-GU ODDS 1:8
PRINT RUNS B/WN 5-100 COPIES PER
NO PRICING ON QTY OF 10 OR LESS
3 Babe Ruth Bat-Pants/20 250.00 400.00

2005 Throwback Threads Throwback Collection Material Combo Prime

*COM.PRIMEp/r25: 1.25X TO 3X MTLp/r150+
*COM.PRIME p/r 25: 1X TO 2.5X MTL p/r 100
*COM.PRIME p/r 25: .75X TO 2X MTL p/r 50
OVERALL AU-GU ODDS 1:8
PRINT RUNS B/WN 5-25 COPIES PER
NO PRICING ON QTY OF 5
48 Lou Brock Bat-Jsy/25 10.00 25.00

2005 Throwback Threads Throwback Collection Signature Material

OVERALL AU-GU ODDS 1:8
PRINT RUNS B/WN 5-50 COPIES PER
NO PRICING ON QTY OF 10 OR LESS
2 Tony Gwynn Jsy/50 20.00 50.00
4 Angel Berroa Pants/50 6.00 15.00
5 Jeff Bagwell Jsy/20 30.00 60.00
6 Tony Oliva Jsy/50 10.00 25.00
8 Gary Carter Pants/50 10.00 25.00
10 Chipper Jones Jsy/20 30.00 60.00
12 Roberto Alomar Jsy/50 15.00 40.00
13 Omar Vizquel Jsy/50 15.00 40.00
14 Ernie Banks Jsy/20 30.00 60.00
15 Carlos Beltran Jsy/50 10.00 25.00
16 Garret Anderson Jsy/20 12.50 30.00
17 Mark Grace Jsy/50 15.00 40.00
19 Dave Righetti Jsy/50 10.00 25.00
26 Wade Boggs Jsy/50 15.00 40.00
27 Luis Tiant Pants/50 10.00 25.00
28 Kerry Wood Jsy/20 20.00 50.00
29 Rod Carew Jkt/50 15.00 40.00
30 Dwight Evans Jsy/25 20.00 50.00
32 Billy Williams Jsy/50 10.00 25.00
34 Nolan Ryan Pants/20 50.00 100.00
35 Edgar Renteria Jsy/50 10.00 25.00
37 Gaylord Perry Jsy/50 10.00 25.00
39 Dave Parker Jsy/50 10.00 25.00
41 Orlando Cepeda Pants/25 12.50 30.00
42 Fergie Jenkins Jsy/50 10.00 25.00
44 Reggie Jackson Jsy/25 30.00 60.00
45 Bob Gibson Jsy/25 20.00 50.00
49 Fred Lynn Jsy/50 10.00 25.00
54 Tim Hudson Jsy/25 12.50 30.00
55 Matt Williams Jsy/50 15.00 40.00
56 Marty Marion Jsy/20 12.50 30.00
57 Eric Chavez Jsy/50 10.00 25.00
62 Jim Rice Pants/50 10.00 25.00
63 Mark Mulder Jsy/50 10.00 25.00
66 Sean Casey Jsy/50 10.00 25.00
67 Carlos Lee Jsy/50 10.00 25.00
68 Stan Musial Pants/25 40.00 80.00
70 Darryl Strawberry Jsy/50 10.00 25.00
71 Tommy John Jsy/50 10.00 25.00
73 Johnny Bench Pants/25 30.00 60.00
75 Harold Baines Jsy/50 10.00 25.00

2005 Throwback Threads Throwback Collection Signature Material Prime

*PRIME p/r 25: .6X TO 1.5X SIG.MTL p/r 50
*PRIME p/r 25: .5X TO 1.2X SIG.MTL p/r 20-25
OVERALL AU-GU ODDS 1:8
PRINT RUNS B/WN 5-25 COPIES PER
NO PRICING ON QTY OF 10 OR LESS
20 Mike Schmidt Jsy/25 50.00 100.00
48 Lou Brock Jsy/25 30.00 60.00

2005 Throwback Threads Throwback Collection Signature Material Combo

*COMBOp/r20-25: .5X TO 1.2X SIG.MTLp/r50
*COMBOp/r20-25: .4X TO 1X SIG.MTLp/r20-25
*COMBO p/r 15: .6X TO 1.5X SIG.MTL p/r 50
PRINT RUNS B/WN 5-25 COPIES PER
NO PRICING ON QTY OF 10 OR LESS
PRIME PRINT RUN B/WN 5-10 COPIES PER
NO PRIME PRICING DUE TO SCARCITY
OVERALL AU-GU ODDS 1:8

1907-09 Tigers A.C. Dietsche Postcards PC765

These postcards were issued over a three year period. The cards numbered from 1 through 15 are known as series one and issued in 1907 with a 1907 copyright. Cards numbered from 16 to 29 are known as series two and have 1908 or 1909 copyrights. An oversize team card has been rumored to exist but it has never been verified.

COMPLETE SET (29) 750.00 1500.00
1 Ty Cobb 150.00 300.00
2 William Coughlin 30.00 60.00
3 Sam Crawford 60.00 120.00
4 Bill Donovan 40.00 80.00
5 Jerome W. Downs 30.00 60.00
6 Hugh Jennings MG 60.00 120.00
7 Davy Jones 30.00 60.00
8 Ed Killian 30.00 60.00
9 George Mullin 30.00 60.00
10 Charles O'Leary 30.00 60.00
11 Fred T. Payne 30.00 60.00
12 Claude Rossman 30.00 60.00
13 Germany Schaefer 40.00 80.00
14 Boss Schmidt 30.00 60.00
15 Edward Siever 30.00 60.00
16 Henry Beckendorf 08 30.00 60.00
17 Owen Bush 08 30.00 60.00
18 Ty Cobb 08 Batting 150.00 300.00
19 James Delehanty 09 30.00 60.00
20 Bill Donovan 08 40.00 80.00
21 Hugh Jennings MG 08 60.00 120.00
22 Tom Jones 09 30.00 60.00
23 Matthew McIntrye 08 30.00 60.00
24 George Moriarty 08 30.00 60.00
25 Oscar Stanage 08 30.00 60.00
26 Oren Edgar Summers 08 30.00 60.00
27 Edgar Willett 08 30.00 60.00
28 Ralph Works 09 30.00 60.00
29 Team Picture 09 50.00 100.00

1908 Tigers Fred G.Wright Postcard

Fred G. Wright was the photographer for several cards including the Detroit Tigers set produced by H.M. Taylor, established his own company. The only card positively identified is one of "Wild Bill" Donovan, a star pitcher for the Tigers. All additions to this checklist are appreciated.

1 Bill Donovan 125.00 250.00

1909-11 Tigers H.M. Taylor PC773-2

The H.M. Taylor postcard set measures 3 1/2" by 5 1/2" and was issued during the 1909-11 time period and features Detroit Tigers players only. The cards are black and white with a rather large border around the card. The H.M Taylor identification is presented on the back of the card.

COMPLETE SET (9) 1375.00 2750.00
1 Ty Cobb At Bat 750.00 1500.00
2 Bill Coughlin 100.00 200.00
Batting
3 Sam Crawford 150.00 300.00
Ready for the ball
4 Detroit Team Card 400.00 800.00
5 Wild Bill Donovan/ 100.00 200.00
6 Wild Bill Donovan 100.00 200.00
Batting
7 Hugh Jennings 200.00 400.00
Wee Ah; Yours Truly
8 Wild Bill Donovan 100.00 200.00
Hugh Jennings
Frank Chance
9 Hugh Jennings MG 150.00 300.00
and his Tigers
Caraciture

1909-10 Tigers Topping and Company PC773-1

This set of Detroit Tiger stars is believed to have been issued in late 1909 and early 1910. This distinctive set features yellow bands at the top and bottom and a face shot of the player in a center of a six-pointed star, which also contains a yellow outline. The words "Tiger Stars" are printed in the upper yellow band whereas the player's name and position appears in the lower band. Topping and Publishers Company, Detroit, is identified on the reverse.

COMPLETE SET (20) 2250.00 4500.00
1 Henry Beckendorf 100.00 200.00
2 Donie Bush 100.00 200.00
3 Ty Cobb 1250.00 2500.00
4 Sam Crawford 200.00 400.00
5 Jim Delahanty 100.00 200.00
6 Bill Donovan 100.00 200.00
7 Hugh Jennings MG 200.00 400.00
8 Davy Jones 100.00 200.00
9 Tom Jones 100.00 200.00
10 Ed Killian 100.00 200.00
11 Matty McIntyre 100.00 200.00
12 George Moriarty 100.00 200.00
13 George Mullin 125.00 250.00
14 Charlie O'Leary 100.00 200.00
15 Charlie Schmidt 100.00 200.00
16 George Speer 100.00 200.00
17 Oscar Stanage 100.00 200.00
18 Eddie Summers 100.00 200.00
19 Edgar Willet 100.00 200.00
20 Ralph Works 100.00 200.00

1909 Tigers Wolverine News Postcards PC773-3

The Wolverine News Company features Detroit Tigers. Two poses each of Ty Cobb and Sam Crawford highlight this black and white set. The Wolverine News Company identification is printed on the back of the card.

COMPLETE SET 1000.00 2000.00
1 Ty Cobb at bat 400.00 800.00
2 Ty Cobb Portrait 400.00 800.00
3 Bill Coughlin Capt. 40.00 80.00
and Third Baseman
4 Sam Crawford 75.00 150.00
Bunting
5 Sam Crawford 75.00 150.00
Center Field
6 Wild Bill Donovan 50.00 100.00
Pitcher
7 Wild Bill Donovan 50.00 100.00
At the Water Wagon
8 Jerry Downs 40.00 80.00
Utility
9 Hugh Jennings MG 75.00 150.00
On the Coaching Line HOR
10 Hugh (ey) Jennings 75.00 150.00
Manager
11 Davy Jones 40.00 80.00

Left Fielder
12 Ed Killian 40.00 80.00
Pitcher
13 George Mullin 40.00 80.00
Pitcher
14 Charlie O'Leary 40.00 80.00
Short Stop
15 Fred Payne 40.00 80.00
Catcher
16 Claude Rossman/1st Baseman 40.00 80.00
17 Herman Schaefer/2d. Baseman 40.00 80.00
18 Schaefer and O'Leary 50.00 100.00
working double play HOR
19 Charlie Schmidt 40.00 80.00
Catcher
20 Eddie Siever 40.00 80.00
Pitcher

1910 Tigers Brush Postcards

These postcards, which measure 3 1/2" by 5 1/2" feature members of the then three-time defending American League champions Detroit Tigers. The fronts have a photo of players posed with Brush automobiles along with a poetic description of the player. The backs have traditional post-card markings. Since these cards are unnumbered; we have sequenced them in alphabetical order. It is possible there are more postcards in this set so any help is greatly appreciated.

1 Ty Cobb 2500.00 5000.00
3 George Mullin 500.00 1000.00
2 Hugh Jennings MG 1000.00 2000.00

1934 Tigers Annis Furs

These 23 photos, which measure approximately 3 1/2" by 5 1/2" features members of the 1934 Tigers. This set has recently been identified as being produced by Annis Furs as some discovered promotional material matches these cards. The set's year is identifiable by the Frank Doljack photo who only played for the Tigers in 1934. The player's name and position is located in the upper left corner. This set is also known as W-UNC.

COMPLETE SET (23) 400.00 800.00
1 Eldon Auker 15.00 40.00
2 Del Baker CO 15.00 40.00
3 Tommy Bridges 30.00 60.00
4 Mickey Cochrane 60.00 120.00
5 Alvin Crowder 15.00 40.00
6 Frank Doljack 15.00 40.00
7 Carl Fischer 15.00 40.00
8 Pete Fox 15.00 40.00
9 Charlie Gehringer 60.00 120.00
10 Goose Goslin 40.00 80.00
11 Hank Greenberg 75.00 150.00
12 Luke Hamlin 15.00 40.00
13 Ray Hayworth 15.00 40.00
14 Chief Hogsett 15.00 40.00
15 Firpo Marberry 15.00 40.00
16 Marv Owen 15.00 40.00
17 Cy Perkins CO 15.00 40.00
18 Bill Rogell 15.00 40.00
19 Schoolboy Rowe 15.00 40.00
20 Heinie Schuble 15.00 40.00
21 Vic Sorrell 15.00 40.00
22 Gee Walker 15.00 40.00
23 Jo Jo White 15.00 40.00

1939 Tigers Sportservice

These cards which measure 6 3/8"" by 4 1/8" are sepia toned and feature members of the 1939 Detroit Tigers. The fronts feature a player photo as well as a short biography. There may be more cards so any additions are appreciated.

COMPLETE SET 75.00 150.00
1 Earl Averill 20.00 40.00
2 Beau Bell 10.00 20.00
3 Tommy Bridges 10.00 20.00
4 Pinky Higgins 10.00 20.00
5 Red Kress 10.00 20.00
6 Barney McCoskey 10.00 20.00
7 Bobo Newsom 10.00 20.00
8 Birdie Tebbetts 10.00 20.00

1953 Tigers Glendale

The cards in this 28-card set measure approximately 2 5/8" by 3 3/4". The 1953 Glendale Meats set of full-color, unnumbered cards features Detroit Tiger ballplayers exclusively and was distributed one per package of Glendale Meats in the Detroit area. The back contains the complete major and minor league record through the 1952 season. The scarcer cards of the set command higher prices, with the Houtteman card being the most difficult to find. There is an album associated with the set (which also is quite scarce now). The catalog designation for this scarce regional set is F151. Since the cards are unnumbered, they are ordered below alphabetically.

COMPLETE SET (28) 7500.00 15000.00
COMMON CARD (1-28) 100.00 200.00
COMMON SP 150.00 300.00
1 Matt Batts 200.00 400.00
2 Johnny Bucha 200.00 400.00
3 Frank Carswell 200.00 400.00
4 Jim Delsing 200.00 400.00
5 Walt Dropo 250.00 500.00
6 Hal Erickson 200.00 400.00
7 Paul Foytack 200.00 400.00
8 Owen Friend 200.00 400.00
9 Ned Garver 250.00 500.00
10 Joe Ginsberg SP 600.00 1200.00
11 Ted Gray 200.00 400.00
12 Fred Hatfield 200.00 400.00
13 Ray Herbert 200.00 400.00
14 Billy Hitchcock 200.00 400.00
15 Billy Hoeft SP 300.00 600.00
16 Art Houtteman SP 2500.00 5000.00
17 Milt Jordan 200.00 400.00
18 Harvey Kuenn 600.00 1200.00
19 Don Lund 200.00 400.00
20 Dave Madison 200.00 400.00
21 Dick Marlowe 200.00 400.00
22 Pat Mullin 200.00 400.00
23 Bob Nieman 200.00 400.00
24 Johnny Pesky 250.00 500.00
25 Jerry Priddy 200.00 400.00
26 Steve Souchock 200.00 400.00
27 Russ Sullivan 200.00 400.00
28 Bill Wight 200.00 400.00

1959 Tigers Graphic Arts Service PC749

The Graphic Art Service postcards were issued in the late 1950's and early 60's in Cincinnati, Ohio. Despite being issued in Cincinnati, the players featured are all Detroit Tigers. These black and white, unnumbered cards feature facsimile autographs on the front. Two poses of Reno Bertoia exist.

COMPLETE SET (16) 37.50 75.00
1 Al Aber 1.50 3.00
2 Hank Aguirre 2.50 5.00
3 Reno Bertoia (2) 1.50 3.00
4 Frank Bolling 1.50 3.00
5 Jim Bunning 7.50 15.00
6 Paul Foytack 1.50 3.00
7 Jim Hegan 1.50 3.00
8 Tom Heinrich CO 5.00 10.00
9 Bill Hoeft 1.50 3.00
10 Frank House 1.50 3.00
11 Harvey Kuenn 2.50 5.00
12 Billy Martin 5.00 10.00
13 Tom Morgan 2.50 5.00
14 Bob Shaw 1.50 3.00
15 Lou Slater 1.50 3.00
16 Tim Thompson 1.50 3.00

1960 Tigers Jay Publishing

This 12-card set of the Detroit Tigers measures approximately 5" by 7" and features black-and-white player photos in a white border. These cards were packaged 12 to a packet. The backs are blank. The cards are unnumbered and checklisted below in alphabetical order.

COMPLETE SET (12) 20.00 50.00
1 Lou Berberet 1.00 2.50
2 Frank Bolling 1.00 2.50
3 Rocky Bridges 1.00 2.50
4 Jim Bunning 3.00 8.00
5 Rocky Colavito 2.00 5.00
6 Paul Foytack 1.00 2.50
7 Al Kaline 5.00 12.00
8 Frank Lary 1.00 2.50
9 Charlie Maxwell 1.00 2.50
10 Don Mossi 1.25 3.00
11 Ray Narleski 1.00 2.50
12 Eddie Yost 1.00 2.50

1961 Tigers Jay Publishing

This 12-card set of the Detroit Tigers measures approximately 5" by 7". The fronts feature black-and-white posed player photos with the player's and team name printed below in the white border. These cards were packaged 12 in a packet. The backs are blank. The cards are unnumbered and checklisted below in alphabetical order.

COMPLETE SET (12) 15.00 40.00
1 Steve Boros 1.00 2.50
2 Dick Brown 1.00 2.50
3 Bill Bruton 1.00 2.50
4 Jim Bunning 3.00 8.00
5 Norm Cash 1.50 4.00
6 Rocky Colavito 2.00 5.00
7 Chuck Cottier 1.00 2.50
8 Dick Gernert 1.00 2.50
9 Al Kaline 5.00 12.00
10 Frank Lary 1.00 2.50
11 Charlie Maxwell 1.00 2.50
12 Bob Sheffing MG 1.00 2.50

1962 Tigers Jay Publishing

This 12-card set of the Detroit Tigers measures approximately 5" by 7". The fronts feature black-and-white posed player photos with the player's and team name printed below in the white border. These cards were packaged 12 in a packet. The backs are blank. The cards are unnumbered and checklisted below in alphabetical order.

COMPLETE SET (12) 20.00 50.00
1 Steve Boros 1.00 2.50
2 Dick Brown 1.00 2.50
3 Jim Bunning 3.00 8.00
4 Norm Cash 2.00 5.00
5 Rocky Colavito 3.00 8.00
6 Chico Fernandez 1.00 2.50
7 Al Kaline 5.00 12.00
8 Frank Lary 1.00 2.50
9 Charley Maxwell 1.00 2.50
10 Don Mossi 1.25 3.00
11 Bob Scheffing MG 1.00 2.50
12 Jake Wood 1.00 2.50

1962 Tigers Post Cards Ford

These postcards feature members of the 1962 Detroit Tigers. They are unnumbered and we have sequenced them in alphabetical order. These cards are usually seen with real autographs.

COMPLETE SET 500.00 1000.00
1 Hank Aguirre 40.00 80.00
2 Steve Boros 30.00 60.00
3 Dick Brown 30.00 60.00
4 Jim Bunning 100.00 200.00
5 Phil Cavarretta CO 40.00 80.00
6 Rocky Colavito 75.00 150.00
7 Terry Fox 30.00 60.00
8 Purnal Goldy 30.00 60.00
9 Jack Hommel TR 30.00 60.00
10 Dave Jolley 30.00 60.00
11 Ron Kline 30.00 60.00
12 Don Mossi 40.00 80.00
13 George Myatt CO 40.00 80.00
14 Ron Nischwitz 30.00 60.00
15 Larry Osborne 30.00 60.00
16 Phil Regan 30.00 60.00
17 Mike Roarke 30.00 60.00

1963 Tigers Jay Publishing

This 12-card set of the Detroit Tigers measures approximately 5" by 7". The fronts feature black-and-white posed player photos with the player's and team name printed below in the white border. These cards were packaged 12 in a packet. The backs are blank. The cards are unnumbered and checklisted below in alphabetical order.

COMPLETE SET (12) 15.00 40.00
1 Hank Aguirre .75 2.00
2 Bill Bruton .75 2.00
3 Jim Bunning 3.00 8.00
4 Norm Cash 1.50 4.00
5 Rocky Colavito 2.50 6.00
6 Chico Fernandez .75 2.00
7 Paul Foytack .75 2.00
8 Al Kaline 5.00 12.00
9 Frank Lary 1.00 2.50
10 Bob Sheffing MG .75 2.00
11 Gus Triandos 1.00 2.50
12 Jake Wood .75 2.00

1964 Tigers Jay Publishing

This 12-card set of the Detroit Tigers measures approximately 5" by 7". The fronts feature black-and-white posed player photos with the player's and team name printed below in the white border. These cards were packaged 12 in a packet. The backs are blank. The cards are unnumbered and checklisted below in alphabetical order.

COMPLETE SET (12) 15.00 40.00
1 Hank Aguirre .75 2.00
2 Bill Bruton .75 2.00
3 Norm Cash 1.50 4.00
4 Chuck Dressen MG 1.00 2.50
5 Bill Freehan 1.50 4.00
6 Al Kaline 5.00 12.00
7 Frank Lary 1.00 2.50
8 Jerry Lumpe .75 2.00
9 Ed Rakow .75 2.00
10 Phil Regan .75 2.00
11 Mike Roarke .75 2.00
12 Jake Wood .75 2.00

1964 Tigers Lids

This set of 14 lids was produced in 1964 and features members of the Detroit Tigers. The catalog designation for this set is F96-5. These lids are actually milk bottle caps. Each lid is blank backed and measures approximately 1 1/4" in diameter. Since the lids are unnumbered, they are ordered below in alphabetical order. The players are drawn on the lids in blue and the player's name is written in orange. The lids say "Visit Tiger Stadium" at the top and "See the Tigers More in '64" at the bottom of every lid.

COMPLETE SET 100.00 200.00
1 Hank Aguirre 5.00 12.00
2 Billy Bruton 5.00 12.00
3 Norm Cash 15.00 40.00
4 Don Demeter 5.00 12.00
5 Chuck Dressen MG 6.00 15.00
6 Bill Freehan 10.00 25.00
7 Al Kaline 50.00 100.00
8 Frank Lary 6.00 15.00
9 Jerry Lumpe 5.00 12.00
10 Dick McAuliffe 6.00 15.00
11 Bubba Phillips 5.00 12.00
12 Ed Rakow 5.00 12.00
13 Phil Regan 5.00 12.00
14 Dave Wickersham 5.00 12.00

1965 Tigers Jay Publishing

These blank-backed photos measure approximately 5" by 7" and feature white-bordered black-and-white posed player photos. The photos are printed on thin paper stock. The player's name and team appear below the photo within the bottom margin. The cards are unnumbered and checklisted below in alphabetical order. More than 12 photos are listed since the players were changed during the season

COMPLETE SET (19) 15.00 40.00
1 Hank Aguirre .75 2.00
2 Gates Brown .75 2.00
3 Norm Cash 1.50 4.00
4 Don Demeter .75 2.00
5 Charlie Dressen MG 1.00 2.50
6 Bill Faul .75 2.00
7 Bill Freehan 1.25 3.00
8 Al Kaline 5.00 12.00
9 Mickey Lolich 1.50 4.00
10 Jerry Lumpe .75 2.00
11 Dick McAuliffe 1.00 2.50
12 Bubba Phillips .75 2.00
13 Ed Rakow .75 2.00
14 Phil Regan .75 2.00
15 Larry Sherry .75 2.00
16 George Thomas .75 2.00
17 Don Wert .75 2.00
18 Dave Wickersham .75 2.00
19 Jake Wood .75 2.00

1966 Tigers Team Issue

This 24 card issue measures 9 13/16" by 7 11/16" and features full color photos of members of the 1966 Detroit Tigers. Since the cards are unnumbered, we have sequenced them in alphabetical order.

COMPLETE SET (24) 30.00 60.00
1 Hank Aguirre .75 2.00
2 Gates Brown .75 2.00
3 Norm Cash 2.00 5.00
4 Don Demeter .75 2.00
5 Chuck Dressen MG .75 2.00
6 Bill Freehan 1.50 4.00
7 Fred Gladding .75 2.00
8 Willie Horton 1.25 3.00
9 Al Kaline 4.00 10.00
10 Mickey Lolich 2.00 5.00
11 Jerry Lumpe .75 2.00
12 Dick McAuliffe 1.25 3.00
13 Denny McLain 2.50 6.00
14 Bill Monbouquette .75 2.00
15 Jim Northrup 1.25 3.00
16 Ray Oyler .75 2.00
17 Orlando Pena .75 2.00
18 Larry Sherry .75 2.00
19 Joe Sparma .75 2.00
20 Mickey Stanley 1.25 3.00
21 Dick Tracewski .75 2.00
22 Don Wert .75 2.00
23 Dave Wickersham .75 2.00
24 Jake Wood .75 2.00

1967 Tigers Dexter Press

This set, which features 11 photo cards that measure approximately 5 1/2" by 7", has white-bordered posed color player photos on its fronts. The set was produced by Dexter Press located in West Nyack, New York and features Detroit Tigers' players. A facsimile autograph is printed across the top of the picture. The white backs carry a short biography printed in blue ink, with only one line providing statistics for the 1966 season. The cards are unnumbered and checklisted below in alphabetical order.

COMPLETE SET (11) 12.50 30.00
1 Norm Cash 2.00 5.00
2 Bill Freehan 1.50 4.00
3 Willie Horton 1.25 3.00
4 Al Kaline 3.00 8.00
5 Jerry Lumpe 1.00 2.50
6 Dick McAuliffe 1.25 3.00
7 Johnny Podres 1.25 3.00
8 Joe Sparma 1.00 2.50
9 Don Wert 1.00 2.50
10 Dave Wickersham 1.00 2.50
11 Earl Wilson 1.00 2.50

1968 Tigers Detroit Free Press Bubblegumless

This set features members of the World Champion 1968 Detroit Tigers. The cards are unnumbered so we have sequenced them in alphabetical order.

COMPLETE SET 30.00 60.00
1 Gates Brown .60 1.50
2 Norm Cash 2.00 5.00
3 Tony Cuccinello CO .60 1.50
4 Pat Dobson .60 1.50
5 Bill Freehan 2.00 5.00
6 John Hiller .60 1.50
7 Willie Horton 1.00 2.50
8 Al Kaline 4.00 10.00
9 Fred Lasher .60 1.50
10 Mickey Lolich 2.00 5.00
11 Dick McAuliffe .75 2.00
12 Denny McLain 2.00 5.00
13 Don McMahon .60 1.50
14 Tom Matchick .60 1.50
15 Wally Moses CO .60 1.50
16 Jim Northrup .75 2.00
17 Ray Oyler .60 1.50
18 Jim Price .60 1.50
19 Daryl Patterson .60 1.50
20 Johnny Sain CO 1.00 2.50
21 Mayo Smith MG .60 1.50
22 Joe Sparma .60 1.50
23 Mickey Stanley .75 2.00
24 Dick Tracewski .60 1.50
25 Jon Warden .60 1.50
26 Don Wert .60 1.50
27 Earl Wilson .60 1.50
28 John Wyatt .60 1.50

1968 Tigers News Super Posters

Issued to commemorate the Detroit Tigers would championship in 1968, these posters which measure approximately 13 1/2" by 23" feature all the players who participated in the World Series that year. Since these are unnumbered, we have sequenced them in alphabetical order.

COMPLETE SET (26) 75.00 150.00
1 Gates Brown 2.00 5.00
2 Norm Cash 3.00 8.00
3 Wayne Comer 2.00 5.00
4 Pat Dobson 2.00 5.00
5 Bill Freehan 2.50 6.00
6 John Hiller 2.00 5.00
7 Willie Horton 2.50 6.00
8 Al Kaline 6.00 15.00
9 Fred Lasher 2.00 5.00
10 Mickey Lolich 2.50 6.00
11 Tom Matchick 2.00 5.00
12 Eddie Mathews 5.00 12.00
13 Dick McAuliffe 2.50 6.00
14 Denny McLain 4.00 10.00
15 Don McMahon 2.00 5.00
16 Jim Northrup 2.50 6.00
17 Ray Oyler 2.00 5.00
18 Daryl Patterson 2.00 5.00
19 Jim Price 2.00 5.00
20 Mayo Smith MG 2.00 5.00
21 Joe Sparma 2.00 5.00
22 Mickey Stanley 2.50 6.00
23 Dick Tracewski 2.00 5.00
24 Jon Warden 2.00 5.00
25 Don Wert 2.00 5.00
26 Earl Wilson 2.00 5.00
27 John Wyatt 2.00 5.00
28 Detroit Tigers team 2.50 6.00

1968 Tigers Team Issue

These blank-backed cards, which measure approximately 5" by 7" feature members of the World Champion Detroit Tigers. Since these cards are unnumbered, we have sequenced them in alphabetical order. Since different players were substituted during the season -- there are more than 12 players in this set.

COMPLETE SET (12) 12.50 30.00
1 Norm Cash 1.50 4.00
2 Bill Freehan 1.25 3.00
3 Willie Horton 1.00 2.50
4 Al Kaline 3.00 8.00
5 Mike Kilkenny .75 2.00
6 Eddie Mathews 2.00 5.00
7 Dick McAuliffe .75 2.00
8 Denny McLain 1.50 4.00
9 Jim Northrup 1.00 2.50
10 Mayo Smith MG .75 2.00
11 Mickey Stanley .75 2.00
12 Don Wert .75 2.00
13 Earl Wilson .75 2.00

1969 Tigers Farmer Jack

This set features six-inch iron-on transfers of player faces of the 1969 Detroit Tigers team and was distributed by Farmer Jack's Supermarket. An iron-on facsimile autograph is printed below the head. The transfers are unnumbered and checklisted below in alphabetical order. The checklist may be incomplete and additions are welcomed.

COMPLETE SET 30.00 60.00
1 Gates Brown 2.00 5.00
2 Norm Cash 4.00 10.00
3 Bill Freehan 3.00 8.00
4 Willie Horton 2.50 6.00
5 Al Kaline 10.00 25.00
6 Mickey Lolich 4.00 10.00
7 Dick McAuliffe 2.00 5.00
8 Denny McLain 4.00 10.00
9 Jim Northrup 2.50 6.00
10 Joe Sparma 2.00 5.00
11 Mickey Stanley 2.50 6.00
12 Earl Wilson 2.00 5.00

1969 Tigers Strip-Posters

Inserted into each Sunday issue of the Detroit Free Press were these "strip-posters" which featured various members of the Detroit Tigers. When properly cut out of the paper, these color drawings (by Dick Mayer) measure 4: by 15". Please note that this checklist is far from complete and any additions are greatly appreciated.

COMPLETE SET 12.50 30.00
1 Bill Freehan 5.00 12.00
2 Denny McLain 6.00 15.00
3 Jim Northrup 4.00 10.00
4 Mickey Stanley 3.00 8.00

1969 Tigers Team Issue

This 12-card set of the Detroit Tigers measures approximately 4 1/4" by 7". The fronts display black-and-white player portraits bordered in white. The player's name and team are printed in the top margin. The backs are blank. The cards are unnumbered and checklisted below in alphabetical order.

COMPLETE SET (12) 10.00 25.00
1 Norm Cash 1.25 3.00
2 Bill Freehan 1.25 3.00
3 Willie Horton .75 2.00
4 Al Kaline 2.50 6.00
5 Mike Kilkenny .60 1.50
6 Mickey Lolich 1.25 3.00
7 Dick McAuliffe .75 2.00
8 Denny McLain 1.25 3.00
9 Jim Northrup 1.00 2.50
10 Mayo Smith MG .60 1.50
11 Mickey Stanley .60 1.50
12 Don Wert .60 1.50

1969 Tigers Team Issue Color

This 20-card set of the Detroit Tigers measures approximately 7" by 8 3/4" with the fronts featuring white-bordered color player photos. The player's name and team is printed in black in the white margin below the picture. The backs are blank. The cards are unnumbered and checklisted below in alphabetical order.

COMPLETE SET (20) 20.00 50.00
1 Gates Brown .75 2.00
2 Norm Cash 1.50 4.00
3 Pat Dobson .75 2.00
4 Bill Freehan 1.50 4.00
5 John Hiller .75 2.00
6 Willie Horton 1.00 2.50
7 Al Kaline 4.00 10.00
8 Fred Lasher .75 2.00
9 Mickey Lolich 1.50 4.00
10 Tom Matchick .75 2.00
11 Dick McAuliffe 1.00 2.50
12 Denny McLain 1.50 4.00
13 Jim Northrup 1.25 3.00
14 Jim Price .75 2.00
15 Mayo Smith .75 2.00
16 Joe Sparma .75 2.00
17 Mickey Stanley 1.00 2.50
18 Dick Tracewski .75 2.00
19 Don Wert .75 2.00
20 Earl Wilson .75 2.00

1972 Tigers Team Issue

This 12-card set of the Detroit Tigers measures approximately 4 1/4" by 7". The fronts display black-and-white player portraits bordered in white. The player's name and team are printed in the top margin. The backs are blank. The cards are unnumbered and checklisted below in alphabetical order.

COMPLETE SET (12) 8.00 20.00
1 Ed Brinkman .40 1.00
2 Norm Cash 1.00 2.50
3 Joe Coleman .40 1.00
4 Bill Freehan .75 2.00
5 Willie Horton .60 1.50
6 Al Kaline 2.00 5.00
7 Mickey Lolich 1.00 2.50
8 Billy Martin MG 1.25 3.00
9 Dick McAuliffe .60 1.50
10 Jim Northrup .60 1.50
11 Aurelio Rodriguez .40 1.00
12 Mickey Stanley .40 1.00

1973 Tigers Jewel

This 20-card set of the Detroit Tigers was produced by Jewel Food Stores and was issued in two series of ten cards each. Measuring approximately 7" by 8 3/4", the set features color posed player photos with white borders with blank backs. The cards are unnumbered and checklisted below in alphabetical order.

COMPLETE SET (20) 40.00 80.00
1 Ed Brinkman 1.50 4.00
2 Gates Brown 1.50 4.00
3 Ike Brown 1.50 4.00
4 Les Cain 1.50 4.00
5 Norman Cash 3.00 8.00
6 Joe Coleman 1.50 4.00
7 Bill Freehan 3.00 8.00
8 Tom Haller 1.50 4.00
9 Willie Horton 2.50 6.00
10 Al Kaline 6.00 15.00
11 Mickey Lolich 2.50 6.00
12 Billy Martin 3.00 8.00
13 Dick McAuliffe 2.00 5.00
14 Joe Niekro 2.00 5.00
15 Jim Northrup 2.00 5.00
16 Aurelio Rodriguez 1.50 4.00
17 Red Scherman 1.50 4.00
18 Mickey Stanley 2.50 6.00
19 Tony Taylor 1.50 4.00
20 Tom Timmerman 1.50 4.00

1974 Tigers

This 12-piece set of photos are blank-backed, white-bordered and 7" X 8 3/4". The player's name and team in black are within lower margin. The photos are unnumbered and checklisted below in alphabetical order.

COMPLETE SET (12) 8.00 20.00
1 Gates Brown .75 2.00
2 Ron Cash .60 1.50
3 Joe Coleman .60 1.50
4 Bill Freehan 1.25 3.00
5 John Hiller .60 1.50
6 Al Kaline 2.00 5.00
7 John Knox .60 1.50
8 Jim Northrup .75 2.00
9 Ben Oglivie .75 2.00
10 Jim Ray .60 1.50
11 Chuck Seelbach .60 1.50
12 Dick Sharon .60 1.50

1974 Tigers TCMA 1934-35 AL Champions

This 36-card set of the 1934-35 American League Champion Detroit Tigers features black-and-white player photos measuring approximately 2 1/8" by 3 11/16". The backs carry 1934 and 1935 player statistics. The cards are unnumbered and checklisted below in alphabetical order with cards 35 and 36 being jumbo cards.

COMPLETE SET (36) 10.00 25.00
1 Elden Auker .20 .50
2 Del Baker CO .20 .50
3 Tommy Bridges .20 .50
4 Flea Clifton .20 .50
5 Mickey Cochrane .75 2.00
6 Alvin Crowder .20 .50
7 Frank Doljack .20 .50
8 Carl Fisher .20 .50
9 Pete Fox .20 .50
10 Vic Frasier .20 .50
11 Charles Gehringer .75 2.00
12 Goose Goslin .75 2.00
13 Hank Greenberg 1.25 3.00
14 Luke Hamlin .20 .50
15 Clyde Hatter .20 .50
16 Ray Hayworth .20 .50
17 Chief Hogsett .20 .50
18 Roxie Lawson .20 .50
19 Fred Marberry .20 .50
20 Chet Morgan .20 .50
21 Marv Owen .20 .50
22 Cy Perkins CO .20 .50
23 Red Phillips .20 .50
24 Frank Reiber .20 .50
25 Bill Rogell .20 .50
26 Schoolboy Rowe .60 1.50
27 Henry Schuble .20 .50
28 Hugh Shelly .20 .50
29 Vic Sorrell .20 .50
30 Joe Sullivan .20 .50
31 Gee Walker .20 .50
32 Harvey Walker .20 .50
33 Jo Jo White .20 .50
34 Rudy York .40 1.00
35 Elden Auker .75 2.00
Firpo Marberry
Tommy Bridges
School
36 Goose Goslin .75 2.00
Jo Jo White
Pete Fox

1975 Tigers Postcards

This 36-card set of the Detroit Tigers features player photos on postcard-size cards. The cards are unnumbered and checklisted below in alphabetical order.

COMPLETE SET (36) 8.00 20.00
1 Fred Arroyo .20 .50
2 Billy Baldwin .20 .50
3 Ray Bare .20 .50
4 Gates Brown .30 .75
5 Nate Colbert .20 .50
6 Joe Coleman .20 .50
7 Bill Freehan .40 1.00
8 Steve Hamilton CO .20 .50
9 Jim Hegan CO .20 .50
10 John Hiller .30 .75
11 Ralph Houk MG .30 .75
12 Willie Horton .60 1.50
13 Terry Humphrey .20 .50
14 Art James .20 .50
15 John Knox .20 .50
16 Lerrin LaGrow .20 .50
17 Gene Lamont .20 .50
18 Ron LeFlore .40 1.00
19 Dave Lemanczyk .20 .50
20 Mickey Lolich .60 1.50
21 Dan Meyer .20 .50
22 Gene Michael .30 .75
23 Ben Oglivie .30 .75
24 Gene Pentz .20 .50
25 Jack Pierce .20 .50
26 Bob Reynolds .20 .50
27 Leon Roberts .20 .50
28 Aurelio Rodriguez .20 .50
29 Vern Ruhle .20 .50
30 Joe Schultz CO .20 .50
31 Mickey Stanley .20 .50
32 Gary Sutherland .20 .50
33 Dick Tracewski .20 .50
34 Tom Veryzer .20 .50
35 Tom Walker .20 .50
36 John Wockenfuss .20 .50

1976 Tigers Old-Timers Troy Show

This 23-card set was available at the 7th Annual Midwest Sports Collectors Convention held July 16-18, 1976 in Troy-Hilton, Michigan. The cards measure 2 3/8" by 2 7/8" and feature portrait and action black-and-white illustrations of players. The player's name is near the top as is a small paragraph giving career history. A box at the bottom contains unusual personal facts. The backs carry information about the card show. The cards are unnumbered and checklisted below in alphabetical order.

COMPLETE SET (23) 3.00 8.00
1 Elden Auker .10 .25
2 Tommy Bridges .30 .75
3 Flea Clifton .10 .25
4 Mickey Cochrane .40 1.00
5 General Crowder .10 .25
6 Frank Doljack .10 .25
7 Carl Fischer .10 .25
8 Pete Fox .10 .25
9 Charles Gehringer .40 1.00
10 Goose Goslin .40 1.00
11 Hank Greenberg .40 1.00
12 Luke Hamlin .10 .25
13 Ray Hayworth .10 .25
14 Chief Hogsett .10 .25
15 Firpo Marberry .10 .25
16 Marvin Owen .30 .75
17 Cy Perkins .10 .25
18 Bill Rogell .10 .25
19 Schoolboy Rowe .40 1.00
20 Heinie Schuble .10 .25
21 Vic Sorrell .10 .25
22 Gerald Walker .10 .25
23 Jo Jo White .10 .25

1976 Tigers Postcards

This 35-card set of the Detroit Tigers features player photos on postcard-size cards. The cards are unnumbered and checklisted below in alphabetical order.

COMPLETE SET (35) 8.00 20.00
1 Ray Bare .20 .50
2 Joe Coleman .20 .50
3 Jim Crawford .20 .50
4 Mark Fidrych 1.50 4.00
5 Bill Freehan .40 1.00
6 Pedro Garcia .20 .50
7 Fred Gladding CO .20 .50
8 Steve Grilli .20 .50
9 Jim Hegan CO .20 .50
10 John Hiller .30 .75
11 Willie Horton .40 1.00
12 Ralph Houk MG .30 .75
13 Alex Johnson .20 .50
14 Bruce Kimm .20 .50
15 Bill Laxton .20 .50
16 Ron LeFlore .30 .75
17 Dave Lemanczyk .20 .50
18 Frank MacCormack .20 .50
19 Jerry Manuel .20 .50
20 Milt May .20 .50
21 Dan Meyer .20 .50
22 Ben Oglivie .30 .75
23 Dave Roberts .20 .50
24 Aurelio Rodriguez .20 .50
25 Vern Ruhle .20 .50
26 Joe Schultz CO .20 .50
27 Chuck Scrivener .20 .50
28 Mickey Stanley .20 .50
29 Rusty Staub .40 1.00
30 Gary Sutherland .20 .50
31 Jason Thompson .60 1.50
32 Dick Tracewski CO .20 .50
33 Tom Veryzer .20 .50
34 John Wockenfuss .20 .50
35 Tiger Stadium .20 .50

1977 Tigers Burger King

This four-card set was issued in 1977 by Burger King and features Detroit Tigers. The photo cards measure approximately 8" by 10" and carry posed player color portraits. The backs are blank and the set is checklisted below in alphabetical order.

COMPLETE SET (4) 4.00 10.00
1 Mark Fidyrich 1.50 4.00
2 Ron LeFlore 1.00 2.50
3 Dave Rozema .75 2.00
4 Mickey Stanley 1.00 2.50

1978 Tigers Burger King

The cards in this 23-card set measure 2 1/2" by 3 1/2". Twenty-three color cards, 22 players and one numbered checklist, comprise the 1978 Burger King Tigers set issued in the Detroit area. The cards marked with an asterisk contain photos different from those appearing on the Topps regular issue cards of that year. For example, Jack Morris, Alan Trammell, and Lou Whitaker (in the 1978 Topps regular issue cards) each appear on rookie prospect cards with three other young players; whereas in this Burger King set, each has his own individual card.

COMPLETE SET (23) 20.00 50.00
1 Ralph Houk MG .30 .75
2 Milt May .10 .25
3 John Wockenfuss .10 .25
4 Mark Fidrych .30 .75
5 Dave Rozema .10 .25
6 Jack Billingham * .10 .25
7 Jim Slaton * .10 .25
8 Jack Morris * 6.00 15.00
9 John Hiller .20 .50
10 Steve Foucault .10 .25
11 Milt Wilcox .10 .25
12 Jason Thompson .30 .75
13 Lou Whitaker * 12.00 30.00
14 Aurelio Rodriguez .10 .25
15 Alan Trammell * 12.00 30.00
16 Steve Dillard * .10 .25
17 Phil Mankowski .10 .25
18 Steve Kemp .10 .25
19 Ron LeFlore .30 .75
20 Tim Corcoran .10 .25
21 Mickey Stanley .30 .75
22 Rusty Staub .40 1.00
NNO Checklist Card TP .08 .15

1978-80 Tigers Dearborn Card Show

These 2 5/8" by 3 5/8" cards were issued in conjunction with the annual Detroit area Dearborn card show. They feature Tiger greats from the past. For the 1978 set, 1,200 of each set were printed; 900 for promotional purposes and 300 for collector sales. For the 1980 set (issued in 1979), 1000 sets were produced; 600 for promotional purposes and 400 for collector sales. The first 18 cards were originally available for $2 per set.

COMPLETE SET 12.50 30.00
1 Rocky Colavito .75 2.00
2 Ervin Fox .30 .75
3 Schoolboy Rowe .30 .75
4 Gerald Walker .30 .75

5 Leon Goslin .60 1.50
6 Harvey Kuenn .40 1.00
7 Frank Howard .40 1.00
8 Woodie Fryman .30 .75
9 Don Wert .30 .75
10 Jim Perry .40 1.00
11 Mayo Smith MG .30 .75
12 Al Kaline 1.25 3.00
13 Norm Cash .60 1.50
14 Mickey Cochrane .40 1.00
15 Fred Marberry .30 .75
16 Bill Freehan .40 1.00
17 Charley Gehringer .60 1.50
18 Jim Northrup .30 .75
19 Slick Coffman .30 .75
20 Bruce Campbell .30 .75
21 Jack Burns .30 .75
22 Herman Flea Clifton .30 .75
23 Vic Frasier .30 .75
24 Pete Fox .30 .75
25 Al Simmons .75 2.00
26 Woodrow Davis .30 .75
27 Dick Conger .30 .75
28 John Corsica .30 .75
29 Frank Croucher .30 .75
30 Hank Greenberg 1.25 3.00
31 Tommy Bridges .30 .75
32 William Hargrave .30 .75
33 Chad Kimsey .30 .75
34 Harry Eisenstat .30 .75
35 Gene Desaultels .30 .75
36 Dizzy Trout .40 1.00

1978 Tigers Team Issue

These 3" by 5" photos feature the members of the 1978 Detroit Tigers. They are unnumbered so we have sequenced them in alphabetical order. Photos of Alan Trammell, Lou Whitaker, Jack Morris and Lance Parrish are included in their rookie season.

COMPLETE SET 15.00 40.00
1 Fernando Arroyo .20 .50
2 Steve Baker .20 .50
3 Jack Billingham .20 .50
4 Gates Brown CO .20 .50
5 Tim Corcoran .20 .50
6 Jim Crawford .20 .50
7 Steve Dillard .20 .50
8 Mark Fidrych .60 1.50
9 Steve Foucault .20 .50
10 Fred Gladding CO .20 .50
11 Fred Hatfield CO .20 .50
12 Steve Hackett .20 .50
13 Jim Hegan CO .20 .50
14 John Hiller .20 .50
15 Ralph Houk MG .20 .50
16 Steve Kemp .30 .75
17 Ron LeFlore .30 .75
18 Phil Mankowski .20 .50
19 Milt May .20 .50
20 Jack Morris 3.00 8.00
21 Lance Parrish 1.50 4.00
22 Aurelio Rodriguez .20 .50
23 Dave Rozema .20 .50
24 Jim Slaton .20 .50
25 Charlie Spikes .20 .50
26 Mickey Stanley .20 .50
27 Rusty Staub .40 1.00
28 Bob Sykes .20 .50
29 Bruce Taylor .20 .50
30 Jason Thompson .20 .50
31 Dick Tracewski CO .20 .50
32 Alan Trammell 4.00 10.00
33 Mark Wayne .20 .50
34 Lou Whitaker 3.00 8.00
35 Milt Wilcox .20 .50
36 John Wockenfuss .20 .50
37 Tiger Stadium .20 .50

1979 Tigers Free Press

These 10" by 15" posters was published in the Detroit Free Press Newspaper and displays a black-and-white player photo with player information and statistics including a printed feature on the player with his career highlights. There may be even more posters and all additions to the checklist are welcomed.

COMPLETE SET 6.00 15.00
1 Jason Thompson 1.25 3.00
4 Ron LeFlore 1.25 3.00
5 Dave Rozema 1.25 3.00
6 Mickey Stanley 1.50 4.00
8 Milt May 1.25 3.00
9 Jim Slaton 1.25 3.00

1979 Tigers Team Issue

These cards, which originally sold from the Tigers directly for 20 cents each, feature members of the 1979 Detroit Tigers. This list consists solely of the new members of the 1979 Tigers that season and since they are unnumbered are sequenced in alphabetical order. Please note that there are 2 different manager cards as Sparky Anderson replaced Les Moss early in the 1979 season.

COMPLETE SET 4.00 10.00
1 Sparky Anderson MG 1.00 2.50
2 Steve Baker .20 .50
3 Tom Brookens .20 .50
4 Sheldon Burnside .20 .50
5 Steve Baker .20 .50
6 Mike Chris .20 .50
7 Billy Consolo CO .20 .50
8 Tim Corcoran .20 .50
9 Danny Gonzalez .20 .50
10 Al Greene .20 .50
11 John Grodzicki CO .20 .50
12 John Hiller .30 .75
13 Lynn Jones .20 .50
14 Aurelio Lopez .20 .50
15 Dave Machemer .20 .50
16 Milt May .20 .50
17 Jerry Morales .20 .50
18 Les Moss MG .30 .75
19 Dan Petry .30 .75
20 Ed Putnam .20 .50
21 Bruce Robbins .20 .50
22 Champ Summers .20 .50
23 Dave Tobik .20 .50
24 Pat Underwood .20 .50
25 Kip Young .20 .50

1980 Tigers Greats TCMA

This 12-card standard-size set features some of the best Detroit Tigers of all time. The fronts have a black-and-white player photo while the horizontal backs have vital statistics, a biography and career statistics.

COMPLETE SET (12) 2.50 6.00
1 George Kell .20 .50
2 Billy Rogell .08 .25
3 Ty Cobb .60 1.50
4 Hank Greenberg .40 1.00
5 Al Kaline .40 1.00
6 Charlie Gehringer .30 .75
7 Harry Heilmann .20 .50
8 Hal Newhouser .20 .50
9 Steve O'Neill MG .08 .25
10 Denny McLain .20 .50
11 Mickey Cochrane .30 .75
12 John Hiller .08 .25

1981 Tigers Detroit News

This 135-card, standard-size set was issued in 1981 to celebrate the centennial of professional baseball in Detroit. This set features black and white photos surrounded by solid red borders, while the back provides information about either the player or event featured on the front of the card. This set was issued by the Detroit newspaper, the Detroit News and covered players from the nineteenth century right up to players and other personnel active at the time of issue.

COMPLETE SET (135) 8.00 20.00
1 Detroit's Boys of Summer 100th Anniversary .20 .50
2 Charles W. Bennett .02 .10
3 Mickey Cochrane .30 .75
4 Harry Heilmann .20 .50
5 Walter O. Briggs OWN .02 .10
6 Mark Fidrych .20 .50
7 1887 Tigers .02 .10
8 Tiger Stadium .02 .10
9 Rudy York .02 .10
10 George Kell .30 .75
11 Steve O'Neill MG .02 .10
12 John Hiller .02 .10
13 1934 Tigers .02 .10
14 Charlie Gehringer .30 .75
15 Denny McLain .20 .50
16 Billy Rogell .02 .10
17 Ty Cobb 1.25 3.00
18 Sparky Anderson MG .20 .50
19 Davy Jones .02 .10
20 Kirk Gibson .30 .75
21 Pat Mullin .02 .10
22 1972 Tigers .02 .10
23 What A Night .02 .10
24 Doc Cramer .02 .10
25 Mickey Stanley .02 .10
26 John Lipon .02 .10
27 Jo Jo White .02 .10
28 Recreation Park .02 .10
29 Wild Bill Donovan .02 .10
30 Ray Oyler .02 .10
31 Earl Whitehill .02 .10
32 Billy Hoeft .02 .10
33 Johnny Groth .02 .10
34 Hughie Jennings P-MG .20 .50
35 Mayo Smith MG .02 .10
36 Bennett Park .02 .10
37 Tigers Win .02 .10
38 Donie Bush P-MG .02 .10
39 Harry Coveleski .02 .10
40 Paul Richards .02 .10
41 Jonathon Stone .02 .10
42 Bob Swift .02 .10
43 Roy Cullenbine .02 .10
44 Hoot Evers .02 .10
45 Tigers Win Series .02 .10
46 Art Houtteman .02 .10
47 Aurelio Rodriguez .02 .10
48 Fred Hutchinson P MG .02 .10
49 Don Mossi .08 .25
50 Lou Gehrig Streak Ends in Detroit At 2130 Games .30 .75
51 Earl Wilson .02 .10
52 Jim Northrup .02 .10
53 1907 Tigers .02 .10
54 Hank Greenberg Hits 2 Homers to Draw Even With Ruth .30 .75
55 Mickey Lolich .20 .50
56 Tommy Bridges .02 .10
57 Al Benton .02 .10
58 Del Baker MG .02 .10
59 Lou Whitaker .08 .25
60 Navin Field .02 .10
61 1945 Tigers .02 .10
62 Ernie Harwell ANN .20 .50
63 Tigers League Champs .02 .10
64 Bobo Newsom .08 .25
65 Don Wert .02 .10
66 Ed Summers .02 .10
67 Billy Martin MG .30 .75
68 Alan Trammell .50 1.25
69 Dale Alexander .02 .10
70 Ed Brinkman .02 .10
71 Right Man in Right Place in Right Park Wins Game .02 .10
72 Bill Freehan .08 .25
73A Norm Cash Red border .20 .50
73B Norm Cash Black border .20 .50
74 George Dauss .02 .10
75 Aurelio Lopez .02 .10
76 Charlie Maxwell .02 .10
77 Ed Barrow MG .08 .25
78 Willie Horton .08 .25
79 Denny McLain Sets Record 31 Wins .20 .50
80 Dan Brouthers .30 .75
81 John E. Fetzer OWN .02 .10
82A Heinie Manush Red border .20 .50
82B Heinie Manush Black border .20 .50
83 1935 Tigers .02 .10
84 Ray Boone .08 .25
85 Bob Fothergill .02 .10
86 Steve Kemp .02 .10
87 Ed Killian .02 .10
88 Floyd Giebell Is Ineligible for Series But ... .02 .10
89 Pinky Higgins .02 .10
90 Lance Parrish .08 .25
91 Eldon Auker .02 .10
92 Birdie Tebbetts .02 .10
93 Schoolboy Rowe .08 .25
94 Tiger Rally Gives Denny McLain 30 .20 .50
95 1909 Tigers .02 .10
96 Harvey Kuenn .20 .50
97 Jim Bunning .20 .50
98 1940 Tigers .02 .10
99 Rocky Colavito .20 .50
100 Al Kaline Enters Hall Of Fame .50 1.25
101 Billy Bruton .02 .10
102 Germany Schaefer .08 .25
103 Frank Bolling .02 .10
104 Briggs Stadium .02 .10
105 Bucky Harris P-MG .08 .25
106 Gates Brown .02 .10
107 Billy Martin Made the Difference .20 .50
108 1908 Tigers .02 .10
109 Gee Walker .02 .10
110 Pete Fox .02 .10
111 Virgil Trucks .02 .10
112 1968 Tigers .08 .25
113 Dizzy Trout .02 .10
114 Barney McCosky .02 .10
115 Lu Blue .02 .10
116 Hal Newhouser .30 .75
117 Tigers Are Home To Prepare For World's Champions .02 .10
118 Bobby Veach .02 .10
119 George Mullin .02 .10
120 Reggie Jackson's Super Homer Ignites A.L. .30 .75
121 Sam Crawford .20 .50
122 Hank Aguirre .02 .10
123 Vic Wertz .08 .25
124 Goose Goslin .20 .50
125 Frank Lary .08 .25
126 Joe Coleman .02 .10
127 Ed Katalinas Scout .02 .10
128 Jack Morris .30 .75
129 Tigers Picked As Winners Of Pirate Battle .02 .10
130 James A. Campbell GM .08 .25
131 Ted Gray .02 .10
132 Al Kaline 1.00 2.50
133 Hank Greenberg .30 .75
134 Dick McAuliffe .08 .25
135 Ozzie Virgil .02 .10

1981 Tigers Pepsi Trammell

This one-card set produced by Pepsi-Cola features a small color photo of Detroit Tigers player, Alan Trammell, and was an invitation to kids to join the Pepsi-Tiger Fan Club. The back displays the official application form.

1 Alan Trammell 2.00 5.00

1981 Tigers Second National Plymouth

This set was issued in conjuction with the Second National Sports Collectors Convention held in Plymouth, Michigan. The fronts have a photo, the player's name and his years as a Tiger. The backs are blank.

COMPLETE SET (32) 8.00 20.00
1 Ty Cobb 1.25 3.00
2 Hughie Jennings MG .60 1.50
3 Heinie Manush .60 1.50
4 George Mullin .30 .75
5 Donie Bush .20 .50
6 Bobby Veach .20 .50
7 Wild Bill Donovan .20 .50
8 Harry Heilmann .40 1.00
9 Sam Crawford .40 1.00
10 Lu Blue .20 .50
11 Bob Fothergill .20 .50
12 Harry Coveleski .20 .50
13 Dale Alexander .20 .50
14 Charlie Gehringer .60 1.50
15 Tommy Bridges .30 .75
16 Detroit Tigers/1935 Team Photo .20 .50
17 Hank Greenberg .60 1.50
18 Goose Goslin .40 1.00
19 Firpo Marberry .20 .50
20 Hal Newhouser .40 1.00
21 Schoolboy Rowe .30 .75
22 Mickey Cochrane .40 1.00
23 Gee Walker .20 .50
24 Marv Owen .20 .50
25 Barney McCosky .20 .50
26 Rudy York .30 .75
27 Pete Fox .20 .50
28 Al Benton .20 .50
29 Billy Rogell .20 .50
30 JoJo White .20 .50
31 Dizzy Trout .20 .50
32 Detroit Tigers/1945 Team Photo .20 .50

1983 Tigers Postcards

This set features members of the 1983 Detroit Tigers. Since these cards are unnumbered we have checklisted them below in alphabetical order.

COMPLETE SET (32) 4.00 10.00
1 Sparky Anderson MG .30 .75
2 Sal Butera .08 .25
3 Howard Bailey .08 .25
4 Juan Berenguer .08 .25
5 Tom Brookens .08 .25
6 Gates Brown CO .08 .25
7 Enos Cabell .08 .25
8 Bill Consolo CO .08 .25
9 Roger Craig CO .08 .25
10 Bill Fahey .08 .25
11 Kirk Gibson .75 2.00
12 Alex Grammas CO .08 .25
13 John Grubb .08 .25
14 Larry Herndon .08 .25
15 Mike Ivie .08 .25
16 Howard Johnson .40 1.00
17 Lynn Jones .08 .25
18 Rick Leach .08 .25
19 Chet Lemon .20 .50
20 Aurelio Lopez .08 .25
21 Jack Morris .40 1.00
22 Lance Parrish .30 .75
23 Larry Pashnick .08 .25
24 Dan Petry .08 .25
25 Dave Rozema .08 .25
26 Dave Rucker .08 .25
27 Dick Tracewski CO .08 .25
28 Alan Trammell .75 2.00
29 Jerry Ujdur .08 .25
30 Pat Underwood .08 .25
31 Lou Whitaker .40 1.00
32 Milt Wilcox .08 .25
33 Glenn Wilson .08 .25
34 John Wockenfuss .08 .25
35 Tiger Stadium .08 .25

1983 Tigers Al Kaline Story

This 72-card set was issued in 1983 to celebrate Al Kaline's thirtieth year of association with the Detroit Tigers. The set was issued in its own orange box and most of the cards in the series have orange borders. There are some cards which have black borders and those cards are the cards in the set which feature color photos. The set is basically in chronological order and covers events crucial to Kaline's career and the backs of the cards give further details about the picture on the front. The set was produced by Homeplate Sports Cards.

COMPLETE SET (73) 8.00 20.00
COMMON CARD (1-72) .10 .25
COMMON CARD COLOR .16 .40
1A Autographed Title Card/(Color) 5.00 12.00
1B Al Kaline I'd play for nothing/(Color) .25 .60
7 Al Kaline Louise Kaline .15 .40
8 Al Kaline Pat Mullin .08 .25
12 Al Kaline George Stark .08 .25
13 Al watching Gordie Howe (Howe taking batting pra .60 1.50
14 Al Kaline Mickey Mantle 1.00 2.50
15 1958 Group Photo/(Jim Hegan& Billy.25 .60
Martin& Ray B
16 AL All-Stars Billy Martin& Al Kaline& Harvey Kue .60 1.50
18 Bill Skowron Al Kaline .25 .60
19 1960 Tigers Stars/(Norm Cash& Rocky.30 .75
Colavito& Al
20 Kaline Slides Under Fox/(Al Kaline and.30 .75
Nellie Fo
21 Al Kaline/1961 Gold Glove .15 .40
22 1962 Tigers Al Kaline& Jim Campbell GM& Norm C .15 .40
24 Japanese Tour 1962/(Jim Bunning& Al.25 .60
Kaline& Norm
26 Receiving Awards (Ernie Harwell ANN& Al Kaline&# .30 .75
28 Family Game 1964/(Al& Michael& and.08 .25
Mark Kaline)
29 Al Kaline Charlie Dressen MG .08 .25
30 George Kell Al Kaline .25 .60
31 Al Kaline Hal Newhouser .25 .60
32 The Kaline Family/(Michael& Louise&.08 .25
Al& and Mark
33 Receiving Gold Glove (Al Kaline& Charlie Gehring .30 .75
34 Al Kaline Rapping a Hit, 1967 Color .25 .60
35 Mickey Mantle Al Kaline 1.00 2.50
39 1969 All-Time Tigers (Hank Greenberg& Hal Newhou .25 .60
41 Al Kaline Family Portrait, Color .25 .60
43 Billy Martin Al Kaline .25 .60
44 First 100&000 Tiger (With John Fetzer OWN and Ji .15 .40
45 Al Kaline On Deck, 1972; Color .25 .60
48 Al Kaline Hit Number 3,000 .15 .40
51 Al Kaline Orlando Cepeda .25 .60
52 1968 World Series Celebration/(Al Kaline& John/ .15 .40
53 Al Kaline Day; Color .25 .60
54 3&000 Hit Day/(Al Kaline& Father and Mother& Lee .15 .40
57 Al Kaline George Kell Color .30 .75
58 Al Kaline George Kell .25 .60
59 Al Kaline Tiger Record Setter; Color .25 .60
60 Al Kaline Last All-Star Team; Color .25 .60
61 Pat Mullin Al Kaline .08 .25
62 Al Kaline Mickey Lolich Color .25 .60
64 Al Kaline Bowie Kuhn COMM Color .25 .60
65 Al and Parents/(Nicholas and Naomi Kaline) (colo .15 .40
66 Al Kaline Kaline Family at Hall; color .15 .40
67 Stan Musial Al Kaline .30 .75
68 Ted Williams Al Kaline .60 1.50
69 Al Kaline Brooks Robinson color .30 .75
70 Al Kaline Pat Underwood .08 .25
72 Al Kaline A Tiger Forever; Color .30 .75

1984 Tigers Detroit News

These newspaper clippings, which measure approximately 13 1/2" by 8" feature the members of the 1984 World Champion Detroit Tigers. These newspaper clippings feature a large color photo of the featured player along with a box with biographical and personal information about the featured player. Since these are unnumbered, we have sequenced them in alphabetical order.

COMPLETE SET 20.00 50.00
1 Sparky Anderson MG 1.25 3.00
2 Doug Bair .75 2.00
3 Doug Baker .75 2.00
4 Dave Bergman .75 2.00
5 Tom Brookens .75 2.00
6 Marty Castillo .75 2.00
7 Darrell Evans 1.00 2.50
8 Barbero Garbey .75 2.00
9 Kirk Gibson 1.50 4.00
10 John Grubb .75 2.00
11 Willie Hernandez 1.00 2.50
12 Larry Herndon .75 2.00
13 Howard Johnson 1.00 2.50
14 Ruppert Jones .75 2.00
15 Rusty Kuntz .75 2.00
16 Chet Lemon .75 2.00
17 Sid Monge .75 2.00
18 Jack Morris 1.50 4.00
19 Lance Parrish 1.25 3.00
20 Dan Petry .75 2.00
21 Dave Rozema .75 2.00
22 Bill Scherrer .75 2.00
23 Alan Trammell 1.50 4.00
24 Lou Whitaker 1.25 3.00

1984 Tigers Farmer Jack

These 16 photo cards were sponsored by the Farmer Jack grocery store chain in the upper Midwest in 1984, to honor the 1984 World Champion Detroit Tigers. The photos were a promotional item given away singly with a purchase. The cards measure approximately 6" by 9" and are printed on photographic paper stock. The white bordered fronts feature color player portraits with an autograph facsimile superimposed on the photo. The backs are blank. The cards are unnumbered and are checklisted alphabetically below.

COMPLETE SET (16) 5.00 12.00
1 Dave Bergman .20 .50
2 Darrell Evans .40 1.00
3 Barbaro Garbey .20 .50
4 Kirk Gibson .60 1.50
5 John Grubb .20 .50
6 Willie Hernandez .30 .75
7 Larry Herndon .20 .50
8 Howard Johnson .40 1.00
9 Chet Lemon .20 .50
10 Jack Morris .60 1.50
11 Lance Parrish .40 1.00
12 Dan Petry .30 .75
13 Dave Rozema .20 .50
14 Alan Trammell 1.25 3.00
15 Lou Whitaker 1.00 2.50
16 Milt Wilcox .20 .50

1984 Tigers Team Issue

These photos were issued by the Detroit Tigers during the 1984 season and featured the players who would go to become the World Champions. The photos are unnumbered so we have sequenced them in alphabetical order

COMPLETE SET 5.00 12.00
1 Tiger Stadium .20 .50
2 Detroit Tigers .20 .50
3 Glenn Abbott .20 .50
4 Rod Allen .20 .50
5 Doug Bair .20 .50
6 Juan Berenguer .20 .50
7 Dave Bergman .20 .50
8 Tom Brookens .20 .50
9 Gates Brown CO .20 .50
10 Marty Castillo .20 .50
11 Billy Consolo CO .20 .50
12 Roger Craig MG .20 .50
13 Darrell Evans .30 .75
14 Barbaro Garbey .20 .50
15 Kirk Gibson .60 1.50
16 Alex Grammas CO .20 .50
17 John Grubb .20 .50
18 Larry Herndon .20 .50
19 Willie Hernandez .30 .75
20 Howard Johnson .30 .75
21 Rusty Kuntz .20 .50
22 Chet Lemon .20 .50
23 Aurelio Lopez .20 .50
24 Dwight Lowry .20 .50
25 Jack Morris .60 1.50
26 Lance Parrish .40 1.00
27 Dan Petry .20 .50
28 Dave Rozema .20 .50
29 Dick Tracewski CO .20 .50
30 Alan Trammell .60 1.50
31 Lou Whitaker .40 1.00
32 Milt Wilcox .20 .50

1984 Tigers Wave Postcards

During the 1984 Tigers World Championship season, these post cards were issued by Batter-Up, Inc. The fronts have two drawings; one of which is a head shot while the other one is an action pose. These cards are unnumbered and we have sequenced them in alphabetical order.

COMPLETE SET (35) 6.00 15.00
1 Sparky Anderson MG .40 1.00
2 Glenn Abbott .20 .50
3 Doug Bair .20 .50
4 Doug Baker .20 .50
5 Bill Behm .20 .50
6 Juan Berenguer .20 .50
7 Dave Bergman .20 .50
8 Tom Brookens .20 .50
9 Gates Brown CO .20 .50
10 Marty Castillo .20 .50
11 Billy Consolo CO .20 .50
12 Roger Craig CO .30 .75
13 Pio DiSalvo .20 .50
14 Darrell Evans .30 .75
15 Barbaro Garbey .20 .50
16 Kirk Gibson .60 1.50
17 Alex Grammas CO .20 .50
18 John Grubb .20 .50
19 Willie Hernandez .30 .75
20 Larry Herndon .20 .50
21 Howard Johnson .40 1.00
22 Ruppert Jones .20 .50
23 Chet Lemon .20 .50
24 Rusty Kuntz .20 .50
25 Aurelio Lopez .20 .50
26 Sid Monge .20 .50
27 Jack Morris .60 1.50
28 Lance Parrish .30 .75
29 Dan Petry .20 .50
30 Dave Rozema .20 .50
31 Jim Schmakel .20 .50
32 Dick Tracewski CO .20 .50
33 Alan Trammell 1.25 3.00
34 Lou Whitaker .60 1.50
35 Milt Wilcox .20 .50

1985 Tigers Cain's Discs

This set of discs was distributed by Cain's Potato Chips in 1985 to commemorate the Tigers' World Championship in 1984. Each disc measures 2 3/4" in diameter. Each disc has a distinctive yellow border on the front. Inside this yellow border is a full color photo of the player with his hat on. The statistics on back of the disc give the player's 1984 pitching or hitting record as well as his vital statistics. The discs are not numbered; hence they are listed below in alphabetical order.

COMPLETE SET (20) 15.00 40.00
1 Doug Bair .40 1.00
2 Juan Berenguer .40 1.00
3 Dave Bergman .40 1.00
4 Tom Brookens .40 1.00
5 Marty Castillo .40 1.00
6 Darrell Evans 1.00 2.50
7 Barbaro Garbey .40 1.00
8 Kirk Gibson 2.00 5.00
9 John Grubb .40 1.00
10 Willie Hernandez .60 1.50
11 Larry Herndon .40 1.00
12 Chet Lemon .60 1.50
13 Aurelio Lopez .40 1.00
14 Jack Morris 1.50 4.00
15 Lance Parrish 1.00 2.50
16 Dan Petry .40 1.00
17 Bill Scherrer .40 1.00
18 Alan Trammell 2.50 6.00
19 Lou Whitaker 2.00 5.00
20 Milt Wilcox .40 1.00

1985 Tigers Wendy's/Coke

This 22-card standard-size set features Detroit Tigers. The set was co-sponsored by Wendy's and Coca-Cola and was distributed in the Detroit metropolitan area. Coca-Cola purchasers were given a pack which contained three Tiger cards plus a header card. The orange-bordered player photos are different from those used by Topps in their regular set. The cards were produced by Topps as evidenced by the similarity of the card backs with the Topps regular set backs. The set is numbered on the back; the order corresponds to the alphabetical order of the player's names.

COMPLETE SET (22) 2.50 6.00
1 Sparky Anderson MG/(Checklist back).20 .50
2 Doug Bair .02 .10
3 Juan Berenguer .02 .10
4 Dave Bergman .02 .10
5 Tom Brookens .02 .10
6 Marty Castillo .02 .10
7 Darrell Evans .10 .30
8 Barbaro Garbey .02.109 Kirk
Gibson .50 1.25
10 Johnny Grubb .02 .10
11 Willie Hernandez .07 .20
12 Larry Herndon .02 .10
13 Rusty Kuntz .02 .10
14 Chet Lemon .07 .20
15 Aurelio Lopez .02 .10
16 Jack Morris .50 1.25
17 Lance Parrish .20 .50
18 Dan Petry .07 .20
19 Bill Scherrer .02 .10
20 Alan Trammell 1.00 2.50
21 Lou Whitaker .60 1.50
22 Milt Wilcox .02 .10

1986 Tigers Cain's Discs

This set of 20 discs was distributed by Cain's Potato Chips in 1986 and consists solely of Detroit Tigers. Each disc measures 2 3/4" in diameter. The statistics on back of the disc give the player's 1985 pitching or hitting record as well as his vital statistics.

COMPLETE SET (20) 15.00 40.00
1 Tom Brookens .40 1.00
2 Willie Hernandez .60 1.50
3 Dave Bergman .40 1.00
4 Lou Whitaker 2.00 5.00
5 Dave LaPoint .40 1.00
6 Lance Parrish 1.00 2.50
7 Randy O'Neal .40 1.00
8 Nelson Simmons .40 1.00
9 Larry Herndon .40 1.00
10 Doug Flynn .40 1.00
11 Jack Morris 1.50 4.00
12 Dan Petry .40 1.00
13 Walt Terrell .40 1.00
14 Chet Lemon .40 1.00
15 Frank Tanana .60 1.50
16 Kirk Gibson 2.00 5.00
17 Darrell Evans 1.00 2.50
18 Dave Collins .40 1.00
19 John Grubb .40 1.00
20 Alan Trammell 2.50 6.00

1986 Tigers Sports Design

This 22-card standard-size set displays an unknown artist's portrait of "All-Time Great Tigers." The fronts are bordered in white with an inner black border. The player's name is printed across the bottom with a blue line above and below. The horizontal backs are printed in blue over a light gray background with a ghosted design that includes several bats and balls. Player statistics, biography and career summary are included.

COMPLETE SET (22) 3.00 8.00
1 Ty Cobb .60 1.50
2 Hughie Jennings .30 .75
3 Harry Heilmann .30 .75
4 Charlie Gehringer .30 .75
5 Mickey Cochrane .30 .75
6 Hank Greenberg .40 1.00
7 Billy Rogell .08 .25
8 Schoolboy Rowe .08 .25
9 Hal Newhouser .30 .75
10 George Kell .30 .75
11 Harvey Kuenn .20 .50
12 Al Kaline .40 1.00
13 Jim Bunning .30 .75
14 Norm Cash .20 .50
15 Mickey Stanley .08 .25
16 Jim Northrup .08 .25
17 Bill Freehan .20 .50
18 Gates Brown .08 .25
19 Willie Horton .20 .50
20 Mickey Lolich .20 .50
21 Denny McLain .20 .50
22 John Hiller .08 .25

1987 Tigers Cain's Discs

This set of 20 discs was distributed by Cain's Potato Chips in 1987 and consists solely of Detroit Tigers. Each disc measures 2 3/4" in diameter. The statistics on back of the disc give the player's 1986 pitching or hitting record as well as his vital statistics. The discs are numbered on the back and have a distinctive orange border on the front of the disc.

COMPLETE SET (20) 10.00 25.00
1 Tom Brookens .40 1.00
2 Darnell Coles .40 1.00
3 Mike Heath .40 1.00
4 Dave Bergman .40 1.00
5 Dwight Lowry .40 1.00
6 Darrell Evans .60 1.50
7 Alan Trammell 2.00 5.00
8 Lou Whitaker 1.50 4.00
9 Kirk Gibson 1.50 4.00
10 Chet Lemon .40 1.00
11 Larry Herndon .40 1.00
12 John Grubb .40 1.00
13 Willie Hernandez .60 1.50
14 Jack Morris 1.00 2.50
15 Dan Petry .40 1.00
16 Walt Terrell .40 1.00
17 Mark Thurmond .40 1.00
18 Pat Sheridan .40 1.00
19 Eric King .40 1.00
20 Frank Tanana .60 1.50

1987 Tigers Coke

Coca-Cola, in collaboration with S. Abraham and Sons, issued a set of 18 cards featuring the Detroit Tigers. The cards are numbered on the back. The cards are distinguished by the bright yellow border framing the full-color picture of the player on the front. The cards were issued in panels of four: three player cards and a team logo card. The cards measure the standard size and were produced by MSA, Mike Schechter Associates.

COMPLETE SET (18) 2.50 6.00
1 Kirk Gibson .50 1.25
2 Larry Herndon .02 .10
3 Walt Terrell .02 .10
4 Alan Trammell .75 2.00
5 Frank Tanana .08 .25
6 Pat Sheridan .02 .10
7 Jack Morris .50 1.25
8 Mike Heath .02 .10
9 Dave Bergman .02 .10
10 Chet Lemon .08 .25
11 Dwight Lowry .02 .10
12 Dan Petry .02 .10
13 Darrell Evans .20 .50
14 Darnell Coles .02 .10
15 Willie Hernandez .08 .25
16 Lou Whitaker .60 1.50
17 Tom Brookens .02 .10
18 John Grubb .02 .10

1988 Tigers Domino's

This rather unattractive set commemorates the 20th anniversary of the Detroit Tigers' World Championship season in 1968. The card stock used is rather thin. The cards measure approximately 2 1/2" by 3 1/2". There are a number of errors in the set including biographical errors, misspellings, and photo misidentifications. Players are pictured in black and white inside a red and blue horseshoe. The numerous factual errors in the set detract from the set's collectibility in the eyes of many collectors. The set numbering is in alphabetical order by player's name.

COMPLETE SET (28) 1.50 4.00
1 Gates Brown .08 .25
2 Norm Cash .20 .50
3 Wayne Comer .02 .10
4 Pat Dobson .08 .25
5 Bill Freehan .20 .50
6 Ernie Harwell ANN .20 .50
7 John Hiller .08 .25
8 Willie Horton .08 .25

9 Al Kaline .50 1.25
10 Fred Lasher .02 .10
11 Mickey Lolich .20 .50
12 Tom Matchick .02 .10
13 Ed Mathews .40 1.00
14 Dick McAuliffe .08 .25
15 Denny McLain .30 .75
16 Don McMahon .02 .10
17 Jim Northrup .08 .25
18 Ray Oyler .02 .10
19 Daryl Patterson .02 .10
20 Jim Price .02 .10
21 Joe Sparma .02 .10
22 Mickey Stanley .08 .25
23 Dick Tracewski .02 .10
24 Jon Warden .02 .10
25 Don Wert .02 .10
26 Earl Wilson .02 .10
27 Pizza Buck Coupon .02 .10
28 Title Card .02 .10
Old Timers Game 1988

1988 Tigers Pepsi/Kroger

This set of 25 cards features members of the Detroit Tigers and was sponsored by Pepsi Cola and Kroger. The cards are in full color on the fronts and measure approximately 2 7/8" by 4 1/4". The card backs contain complete Major and Minor League season-by-season statistics. The cards are unnumbered so they are listed below by uniform number, which is given on the card.

COMPLETE SET (25) 5.00 12.00
1 Lou Whitaker .75 2.00
2 Alan Trammell 1.25 3.00
8 Mike Heath .08 .25
11 Sparky Anderson MG .40 1.00
12 Luis Salazar .08 .25
14 Dave Bergman .08 .25
15 Pat Sheridan .08 .25
16 Tom Brookens .08 .25
19 Doyle Alexander .20 .50
21 Willie Hernandez .20 .50
22 Ray Knight .08 .25
24 Gary Pettis .08 .25
25 Eric King .08 .25
26 Frank Tanana .20 .50
31 Larry Herndon .08 .25
32 Jim Walewander .08 .25
33 Matt Nokes .30 .75
34 Chet Lemon .20 .50
35 Walt Terrell .08 .25
39 Mike Henneman .40 1.00
41 Darrell Evans .20 .50
44 Jeff M. Robinson .08 .25
47 Jack Morris .40 1.00
48 Paul Gibson .08 .25
NNO Tigers Coaches .08 .25
Billy Consolo
Alex Grammas
Billy

1988 Tigers Police

This set was sponsored by the Michigan State Police and the Detroit Tigers organization. There are 14 blue-bordered cards in the set; each card measures approximately 2 1/2" by 3 1/2". The cards are completely unnumbered as there is not even any reference to uniform numbers on the cards; the cards are listed below in alphabetical order.

COMPLETE SET (14) 12.50 30.00
1 Doyle Alexander .60 1.50
2 Sparky Anderson MG 1.25 3.00
3 Dave Bergman .60 1.50
4 Tom Brookens .60 1.50
5 Darrell Evans 1.00 2.50
6 Larry Herndon .60 1.50
7 Chet Lemon .60 1.50
8 Jack Morris 3.00 8.00
9 Matt Nokes 1.00 2.50
10 Jeff M. Robinson .60 1.50
11 Frank Tanana .75 2.00
12 Walt Terrell .60 1.50
13 Alan Trammell 5.00 12.00
14 Lou Whitaker 3.00 8.00

1989 Tigers Marathon

The 1989 Marathon Tigers set features 28 cards measuring approximately 2 3/4" by 4 1/2". The set features color photos surrounded by blue borders and a white background. The Tigers logo is featured prominently under the photo and then the players uniform number name and position is underneath the Tiger logo. The horizontally oriented backs show career stats. The set was given away at the July 15, 1989 Tigers home game against the Seattle Mariners. The cards are numbered by the players' uniform numbers.

COMPLETE SET (28) 4.00 10.00
1 Lou Whitaker .75 2.00
3 Alan Trammell 1.00 2.50
8 Mike Heath .08 .25
9 Fred Lynn .20 .50
10 Keith Moreland .08 .25
11 Sparky Anderson MG .30 .75
12 Mike Brumley .08 .25
14 Dave Bergman .08 .25
15 Pat Sheridan .08 .25
17 Al Pedrique .08 .25
18 Ramon Pena .08 .25
19 Doyle Alexander .08 .25
21 Willie Hernandez .20 .50
23 Torey Lovullo .08 .25
24 Gary Pettis .08 .25
25 Ken Williams .20 .50
26 Frank Tanana .30 .75
27 Charles Hudson .08 .25
32 Gary Ward .08 .25
33 Matt Nokes .30 .75
34 Chet Lemon .20 .50
35 Rick Schu .08 .25
36 Frank Williams .08 .25
39 Mike Henneman .30 .75
44 Jeff M. Robinson .08 .25
47 Jack Morris .40 1.00
48 Paul Gibson .08 .25
NNO Tiger Coaches .08 .25
Billy Consolo
Alex Grammas
Billy

1989 Tigers Police

The 1989 Police Detroit Tigers set contains 14 standard-size cards. The fronts have color photos with blue and orange borders; the backs feature safety tips. These unnumbered cards were given away by the Michigan state police. The cards are numbered below according to uniform number.

COMPLETE SET (14) 5.00 12.00
1 Lou Whitaker 1.25 3.00
3 Alan Trammell 1.50 4.00
9 Fred Lynn .40 1.00
14 Dave Bergman .20 .50
15 Pat Sheridan .20 .50
19 Doyle Alexander .20 .50
21 Willie Hernandez .30 .75
26 Frank Tanana .40 1.00
33 Matt Nokes .30 .75
34 Chet Lemon .30 .75
39 Mike Henneman .40 1.00
44 Jeff M. Robinson .20 .50
47 Jack Morris .60 1.50
NNO Sparky Anderson MG .60 1.50

1990 Tigers Coke/Kroger

The 1990 Coke/Kroger Detroit Tigers set contains 28 cards, measuring approximately 2 7/8" by 4 1/4", which was used as a giveaway at the July 14th Detroit Tigers home game. The player photo is surrounded by green borders with complete career statistical information printed on the back of each card. This set is checklisted alphabetically in the listings below.

COMPLETE SET (28) 3.00 8.00
1 Sparky Anderson MG .30 .75
2 Dave Bergman .08 .25
3 Brian DuBois .08 .25
4 Cecil Fielder .20 .50
5 Paul Gibson .08 .25
6 Jerry Don Gleaton .08 .25
7 Mike Heath .08 .25
8 Mike Henneman .20 .50
9 Tracy Jones .08 .25
10 Chet Lemon .20 .50
11 Urbano Lugo .08 .25
12 Jack Morris .40 1.00
13 Lloyd Moseby .08 .25
14 Matt Nokes .20 .50
15 Edwin Nunez .08 .25
16 Dan Petry .08 .25
17 Tony Phillips .08 .25
18 Kevin Ritz .08 .25
19 Jeff M. Robinson .08 .25
20 Ed Romero .08 .25
21 Mark Salas .08 .25
22 Larry Sheets .08 .25
23 Frank Tanana .30 .75
24 Alan Trammell .75 2.00
25 Gary Ward .08 .25
26 Lou Whitaker .60 1.50
27 Ken Williams .20 .50
28 Tigers Coaches .20 .50
Billy Consolo
Alex Grammas
Billy

1990 Tigers Milk Henneman

This eight-card standard-size set was a collector series issued by Real Milk Co. The set includes a title card and a membership card that enabled the consumer to mail in the card and become a Tiger Clubhouse Member. All the cards picture Mike Henneman and a carton of Real milk. The cards are numbered on the back and front.

COMPLETE SET (8) 3.00 8.00
COMMON PLAYER (1-6) .30 .75
COMMON HENNEMAN .80 2.00
NNO Title card .30 .75
NNO Membership card .30 .75

1991 Tigers Coke/Kroger

The 1991 Coke/Kroger Tigers set contains 27 cards measuring approximately 2 7/8" by 4 1/4". The set is skip-numbered by uniform number and checklisted accordingly. The Mike Dalton card (number 42) exists. However, most were produced with a stain on his face and were pulled from circulation. We are calling this card a SP and are not including it in the complete set price.

COMPLETE SET (27) 4.00 10.00
COMMON SP 2.00 5.00
1 Lou Whitaker .40 1.00
3 Alan Trammell .75 2.00
4 Tony Phillips .08 .25
10 Andy Allanson .08 .25
11 Sparky Anderson MG .30 .75
14 Dave Bergman .08 .25
15 Lloyd Moseby .08 .25
19 Jerry Don Gleaton .08 .25
20 Mickey Tettleton .40 1.00
22 Milt Cuyler .08 .25
23 Mark Leiter .08 .25
24 Travis Fryman .40 1.00
25 John Shelby .08 .25
26 Frank Tanana .30 .75
27 Mark Salas .08 .25
29 Pete Incaviglia .20 .50
31 Kevin Ritz .08 .25
35 Walt Terrell .08 .25
36 Bill Gullickson .08 .25
39 Mike Henneman .20 .50
42 Mike Dalton SP 2.00 5.00
44 Rob Deer .08 .25
45 Cecil Fielder .40 1.00
46 Dan Petry .08 .25
48 Paul Gibson .08 .25
49 Steve Searcy .08 .25
55 John Cerutti .08 .25
NNO Coaches Card .08 .25
Billy Consolo
Jim Davenport
Alex G

1991 Tigers Police

This 14-card standard-sized set was sponsored by the Michigan State Police, HSP, and Team Michigan, and their sponsor logos appear on the backs. The cards feature a mix of posed and action color player photos. The player's name appears in blue lettering in an orange stripe above the picture, while a second orange stripe below the picture intersects the team logo at the lower right corner. The backs contain safety tips. The cards are unnumbered and checklisted below in alphabetical order.

COMPLETE SET (14) 10.00 25.00
1 Sparky Anderson MG 1.00 2.50
2 Dave Bergman .40 1.00
3 Cecil Fielder 1.00 2.50
4 Travis Fryman 3.00 8.00
5 Paul Gibson .40 1.00
6 Jerry Don Gleaton .40 1.00
7 Lloyd Moseby .40 1.00
8 Dan Petry .40 1.00
9 Tony Phillips .40 1.00
10 Mark Salas .40 1.00
11 John Shelby .40 1.00
12 Frank Tanana .60 1.50
13 Alan Trammell 3.00 8.00
14 Lou Whitaker 1.50 4.00

1992 Tigers Kroger

This 28-card set measures approximately 2 7/8" by 4 1/4" and features color action photos of the 1992 Detroit Tigers with white borders. The backs display player information and career statistics. The cards are unnumbered and checklisted below in alphabetical order.

COMPLETE SET (28) 4.00 10.00
1 Sparky Anderson MG .40 1.00
2 Skeeter Barnes .08 .25
3 Dave Bergman .08 .25
4 Mark Carreon .08 .25
5 Milt Cuyler .08 .25
6 Rob Deer .08 .25
7 John Doherty .08 .25
8 Cecil Fielder .60 1.50
9 Travis Fryman .40 1.00
10 Dan Gladden .08 .25
11 Bill Gullickson .08 .25
12 Mike Henneman .20 .50
13 John Kiely .08 .25
14 Kurt Knudsen .08 .25
15 Chad Kreuter .08 .25
16 Mark Leiter .08 .25
17 Les Lancaster .08 .25
18 Scott Livingstone .08 .25
19 Mike Munoz .08 .25
20 Gary Pettis .08 .25
21 Tony Phillips .08 .25
22 Kevin Ritz .08 .25
23 Frank Tanana .20 .50
24 Walt Terrell .08 .25
25 Mickey Tettleton .30 .75
26 Alan Trammell .75 2.00
27 Lou Whitaker .40 1.00
28 Billy Consolo CO .08 .25
Larry Herndon CO
Billy Muffett

1993 Tigers Gatorade

Sponsored by Gatorade, this 28-card set measures approximately 2 7/8" by 4 1/4". The cards are unnumbered and checklisted below in alphabetical order.

COMPLETE SET (28) 3.00 8.00
1 Sparky Anderson MG .40 1.00
2 Skeeter Barnes .08 .25
3 Tom Bolton .08 .25
4 Milt Cuyler .08 .25
5 Rob Deer .08 .25
6 John Doherty .08 .25
7 Cecil Fielder .40 1.00
8 Travis Fryman .40 1.00
9 Kirk Gibson .30 .75
10 Dan Gladden .08 .25
11 Buddy Groom .08 .25
12 Bill Gullickson .08 .25
13 David Haas .08 .25
14 Mike Henneman .20 .50
15 Kurt Knudsen .08 .25
16 Chad Kreuter .08 .25
17 Bill Krueger .08 .25
18 Mark Leiter .08 .25
19 Scott Livingstone .08 .25
20 Bob MacDonald .08 .25
21 Mike Moore .08 .25
22 Tony Phillips .08 .25
23 Mickey Tettleton .30 .75
24 Gary Thurman .08 .25
25 Alan Trammell .60 1.50
26 David Wells .30 .75
27 Lou Whitaker .40 1.00
28 Coaches Card .08 .25
Dick Tracewski
Billy Muffett
Larry

1993 Tigers Little Caesars

Issued as a seven-card/pin set, the '93 Tigers Little Caesars set spotlights the Tigers' World Series victories. The cards measure 2 1/2" by 5 1/4", are printed on thin white card stock, and have black-and-white or color photos on their fronts. The backs carry information regarding the particular Tigers team that won that World Series. The brass pins are affixed to the cards near the bottom. Cards 1-4 are numbered as such on their backs; cards 5-7 are unnumbered and so are checklisted below in chronological order.

COMPLETE SET (7) 4.00 10.00
1 1935 World Champions .60 1.50
2 1945 World Champions .60 1.50
3 1968 World Champions .60 1.50
4 1984 World Champions .60 1.50
5 Denny McLain/31 Win Season 1.25 3.00
6 1968 Tigers Celebration .60 1.50
7 Mickey Lolich 1.25 3.00
World Series MVP

1996 Tigers Hebrew National

This 25-card set measures approximately 2 7/8" by 4 1/4" and features color photos of the Detroit Tigers in white borders. The backs carry biographical information and career statistics. Cards numbers 4 and 6 were supposed to be Chad Curtis and Cecil Fielder, but they do not exist. There is no card number 5. Card 3, Tony Clark, and card 28, the Coaches card, were not issued at the same time as the rest of the set.

COMPLETE SET (25) 3.00 8.00
1 Kimera Bartee .08 .25
2 Jose Lima .08 .25
3 Tony Clark .60 1.50
7 Bobby Higginson .20 .50
8 Greg Keagle .08 .25
9 Mark Lewis .08 .25
10 Richie Lewis .08 .25
11 Felipe Lira .08 .25
12 Mike Myers .08 .25
13 Melvin Nieves .08 .25
14 Alan Trammell .60 1.50
15 Tom Urbani .08 .25
16 Brian Williams .08 .25
17 Eddie Williams .08 .25
18 Curtis Pride .08 .25
19 Mark Parent .08 .25
20 Raul Casanova .08 .25
21 Omar Olivares .08 .25
22 Gregg Olson .20 .50
23 Justin Thompson .08 .25
24 Brad Ausmus .20 .50
25 Andujar Cedeno .08 .25
26 Buddy Bell MG .20 .50
27 Paws(Mascot) .08 .25
28 Glenn Ezell CO .08 .25
Terry Francona CO
Larry Herndon C

1996 Tigers Postcards

These 38 cards, which measure approximately 3 34/" by 5 1/4" and are blank backed feature members of the 1996 Detroit Tigers. Some of these cards also appear with a "coke" emblem. Since these cards are unnumbered, we have sequenced them in alphabetical order.

COMPLETE SET 8.00 20.00
1 Rick Adair CO .20 .50
2 Scott Aldred .20 .50
3 Brad Ausmus .20 .50
4 Kimera Bartee .20 .50
5 Danny Bautista .20 .50
6 Buddy Bell MG .30 .75
Has the Coke emblem
7 Doug Brocail .20 .50
8 Raul Casanova .20 .50
9 Mike Christopher .20 .50
10 Chad Curtis .20 .50
11 Glenn Ezell CO .20 .50
12 Cecil Fielder .60 1.50
13 John Flaherty .20 .50
14 Terry Francona CO .20 .50
15 Travis Fryman .40 1.00
16 Greg Gohr .20 .50
17 Chris Gomez .20 .50
18 Larry Herndon CO .20 .50
19 Bobby Higginson .30 .75
20 Greg Keagle .20 .50
21 Fred Kendall CO .20 .50
22 Mark Lewis .20 .50
23 Richie Lewis .20 .50
24 Jose Lima .20 .50
25 Felipe Lira .20 .50
26 Jon Matlack CO .20 .50
27 Mike Myers .20 .50
28 Melvin Nieves .20 .50
29 C.J. Nitkowski .20 .50
30 Ron Oester CO .20 .50
31 Omar Olivares .20 .50
32 Mark Parent .20 .50
33 Curtis Pride .20 .50
Has the Coke Emblem
34 Justin Thompson .20 .50
Has the Coke Emblem
35 Alan Trammell CO .40 1.00
36 Randy Veres .20 .50
37 Brian Williams .20 .50
38 Eddie Williams .20 .50

1997 Tigers Hebrew National

This 28 standard-size card set features members of the 1997 Detroit Tigers. The full-bleed borders have the player photo in the middle with the Detroit Tigers name on the top and the players name, small inset photo and position on the bottom. The horizontal backs have the players vital stats as well as their career records.

COMPLETE SET (28) 6.00 15.00
1 Jose Bautista .20 .50
2 Willie Blair .20 .50
3 Doug Brocail .20 .50
4 Raul Casanova .20 .50
5 Tony Clark .75 2.00
6 Deivi Cruz .20 .50
7 John Cummings .20 .50
8 Damion Easley .20 .50
9 Travis Fryman .40 1.00
10 Bobby Higginson .30 .75
11 Brian L. Hunter .20 .50
12 Brian Johnson .20 .50
13 Todd Jones .20 .50
14 Felipe Lira .20 .50
15 Dan Miceli .20 .50
16 Brian Moehler .20 .50
17 Mike Myers .20 .50
18 Phil Nevin .60 1.50
19 Melvin Nieves .20 .50
20 Omar Oliveres .20 .50
21 Curtis Pride .20 .50
22 A.J. Sager .20 .50
23 Justin Thompson .20 .50
24 Matt Walbeck .20 .50
25 Jody Reed .20 .50
26 Bob Hamelin .20 .50
27 Buddy Bell MG .20 .50
28 Rick Adair CO .20 .50
Larry Herndon CO
Perry Hill CO
Fred Kendall CO
Larry Parrish CO
Jerry White CO

1997 Tigers Postcards

These 33 blank-backed postcards, which measure approximately 3 3/4" by 5 1/4", feature members of the 1997 Detroit Tigers. Since these cards are not numbered, we have sequenced them in alphabetical order.

COMPLETE SET 6.00 15.00
1 Rick Adair CO .20 .50
2 Buddy Bell MG .30 .75
3 Willie Blair .20 .50
4 Doug Brocail .20 .50
5 Tony Clark .75 2.00
6 Deivi Cruz .20 .50
7 John Cummings .20 .50
8 Damion Easley .20 .50
9 Travis Fryman .20 .50
10 Bob Hamelin .20 .50
11 Larry Herndon CO .20 .50
12 Bobby Higginson .60 1.50
13 Perry Hill CO .20 .50
14 Brian Hunter .20 .50
15 Brian Johnson .20 .50
16 Todd Jones .20 .50
17 Fred Kendall CO .20 .50
18 Felipe Lira .20 .50
19 Dan Miceli .20 .50
20 Orlando Miller .20 .50
21 Brian Moehler .20 .50
22 Mike Myers .20 .50
23 Phil Nevin .60 1.50
24 Melvin Nieves .20 .50
25 Omar Olivares .20 .50
26 Larry Parrish CO .20 .50
27 Curtis Pride .20 .50
28 Jody Reed .20 .50
29 A.J. Sager .20 .50
30 Justin Thompson .20 .50
31 Bubba Trammell .30 .75
32 Matt Walbeck .20 .50
33 Jerry White CO .20 .50

1998 Tigers Ball Park

This 26 card standard-size set features members of the 1998 Detroit Tigers. The fronts have the players name and position on the left side and the rest of the white bordered card has an action photo of the player. The horizontal backs have complete statistics along with biographical information and a brief blurb with a highlight from the players 1997 season. In additon, the Ball Park Franks logo is in the lower right on the back.

COMPLETE SET (26) 2.50 6.00
1 Gabe Alvarez .08 .25
2 Matt Anderson .08 .25
3 Paul Bako .08 .25
4 Trey Beamon .08 .25
5 Buddy Bell MG .20 .50
6 Geronimo Berroa .08 .25
7 Doug Bochtler .08 .25
8 Doug Brocail .08 .25
9 Raul Casanova .08 .25
10 Frank Castillo .08 .25
11 Frank Catalanotto .60 1.50
12 Tony Clark .50 1.25
13 Dean Crow .08 .25
14 Deivi Cruz .08 .25
15 Damion Easley .08 .25
16 Bryce Florie .08 .25
17 Luis Gonzalez .50 1.25
18 Seth Greisinger .08 .25
19 Bobby Higginson .20 .50
20 Brian Hunter .08 .25
21 Todd Jones .20 .50
22 Brian Moehler .08 .25
23 Brian Powell .08 .25
24 Joe Randa .30 .75
25 Sean Runyan .08 .25
26 Justin Thompson .08 .25

1998 Tigers Postcards

These blank-backed 3 3/4" by 5 1/4" postcards featuring members of the 1998 Detroit Tigers and were issued with black and white photos. We have split this checklist into three sections; of which all are in alphabetical order by group: The first 20 postcards have new poses for 1998; the next nine have the same pose as 1997 and the final 11 were late season additions

COMPLETE SET (39) 8.00 20.00
1 Willie Blair .20 .50
2 Raul Casanova .20 .50
3 Frank Castillo .20 .50
4 Frank Catalanotto .75 2.00
5 Tony Clark .75 2.00
6 Deivi Cruz .20 .50
7 Damion Easley .20 .50
8 Bryce Florie .20 .50
9 Luis Gonzalez .75 2.00
10 Bobby Higginson .30 .75
11 Perry Hill CO .20 .50
12 Brian L. Hunter .20 .50
13 Todd Jones .30 .75
14 Greg Keagle .20 .50
15 Joe Oliver .20 .50
16 Joe Randa .40 1.00
17 Bill Ripken .20 .50
18 Bip Roberts .20 .50
19 Sean Runyan .20 .50
20 Justin Thompson .20 .50
21 Tim Worrell .20 .50
22 Rick Adair CO .20 .50
23 Buddy Bell MG .30 .75
24 Doug Brocail .20 .50
25 Larry Herndon CO .20 .50
26 Fred Kendall CO .20 .50
27 Brian Moehler .20 .50
28 Larry Parrish CO .20 .50
29 A.J. Sager .20 .50
30 Jerry White CO .20 .50
31 Gabe Alvarez .20 .50
32 Matt Anderson .20 .50
33 Paul Bako .20 .50
34 Trey Beamon .20 .50
35 Kimera Bartee .20 .50
36 Geronino Berroa .20 .50
37 Dean Crow .20 .50
38 Seth Greisinger .20 .50
39 Brian Powell .20 .50
40 Roberto Duran .20 .50

1999 Tigers Pop Secret

This 26 card standard-size set features members of the 1999 Detroit Tigers. The cards have a black and blue stripes going down the side with the player name and position printed in the black stripe. The rest of the borderless card features an action player photo. The back has a player portrait, biographical information and complete career stats. The cards are unnumbered except for the uniform number so we have sequenced them in alphabetical order.

COMPLETE SET (26) 3.00 8.00
1 Matt Anderson .08 .25
2 Brad Ausmus .08 .25
3 Willie Blair .08 .25
4 Doug Brocail .08 .25
5 Frank Catalanotto .30 .75
6 Tony Clark .40 1.00
7 Deivi Cruz .08 .25
8 Damion Easley .08 .25
9 Juan Encarnacion .40 1.00
10 Karim Garcia .08 .25
11 Seth Greisinger .08 .25
12 Bill Haselman .08 .25
13 Bobby Higginson .20 .50
14 Gregg Jefferies .08 .25
15 Todd Jones .20 .50
16 Gabe Kapler .08 .25
17 Masao Kida .08 .25
18 Dave Mlicki .08 .25
19 Brian Moehler .08 .25
20 C.J. Nitkowski .08 .25
21 Dean Palmer .20 .50
22 Larry Parrish MG .08 .25
23 Luis Polonia .08 .25
24 Justin Thompson .08 .25
25 Jeff Weaver .50 1.25
26 The Corner .08 .25
Tiger Stadium

1999 Tigers Postcards

These blank backed postcards measure 3 3/4" by 5 1/4" and feature members of the 1999 Detroit Tigers. The cards are unnumbered so we have sequenced them in alphabetical order.

COMPLETE SET 4.00 10.00
1 Rick Adair CO .08 .25
2 Gabe Alvarez .08 .25
3 Matt Anderson .08 .25
4 Brad Ausmus .08 .25
5 Willie Blair .08 .25
6 Doug Brocail .08 .25
7 Will Brunson .08 .25
8 Frank Catalanotto .30 .75
9 Tony Clark .40 1.00
10 Deivi Cruz .08 .25
11 Nelson Cruz .08 .25
12 Damion Easley .08 .25
13 Juan Encarnacion .40 1.00
14 Bryce Florie .08 .25
15 Karim Garcia .08 .25
16 Seth Greisinger .08 .25
17 Bill Haselman .08 .25
18 Bobby Higginson .20 .50
19 Perry Hill CO .08 .25
20 Gregg Jefferies .08 .25
21 Jeff Jones CO .08 .25
22 Todd Jones .20 .50
23 Gabe Kapler .08 .25
24 Masao Kida .08 .25
25 Dave Mlicki .08 .25
26 Brian Moehler .08 .25
27 C.J. Nitkowski .08 .25
28 Dean Palmer .20 .50
29 Lance Parrish CO .08 .25
30 Larry Parrish MG .08 .25
31 Dean Palmer .20 .50
32 Luis Polonia .08 .25
33 Sean Runyan .08 .25
34 Justin Thompson .08 .25
35 Alan Trammell CO .30 .75
36 Jeff Weaver .50 1.25
37 Jason Wood .08 .25

2000 Tigers Postcards

COMPLETE SET 4.80 12.00
1 Matt Anderson .10 .25
2 Brad Ausmus .20 .50
3 Rich Becker .10 .25
4 Willie Blair .10 .25
5 Dave Borkowski .10 .25
6 Doug Brocail .10 .25
7 Javier Cardona .10 .25
8 Tony Clark .40 1.00
9 Deivi Cruz .10 .25
10 Nelson Cruz .10 .25
11 Damion Easley .10 .25
12 Juan Encarnacion .40 1.00
14 Phil Garner MG .10 .25
14 Robert Fick .10 .25
15 Juan Gonzalez .40 1.00
16 Seth Greisinger .10 .25
17 Shane Halter .10 .25
18 Bobby Higginson .20 .50
19 Chris Holt .10 .25
20 Gregg Jefferies .10 .25
21 Mark Johnson .10 .25
22 Todd Jones .20 .50
23 Jose Macias .10 .25
24 Bill Madlock .20 .50
25 Doug Mansolino CO .10 .25
26 Allen McDill .10 .25
27 Wendell MaGee .10 .25
28 Dave Mlicki .10 .25
29 Brian Moehler .10 .25
30 Eric Munson .10 .25
31 C.J. Nitkowski .10 .25
32 Hideo Nomo .80 2.00
33 Dean Palmer .20 .50
34 Danny Patterson .10 .25
35 Lance Parrish CO .20 .50
36 Luis Polonia .10 .25
37 Juan Samuel CO .10 .25
38 Dan Warthen CO .10 .25
39 Jeff Weaver .30 .75

2000 Tigers Upper Deck Pepsi

COMPLETE SET .75 2.00
1 Damion Easley .10 .25
2 Dave Mlicki .10 .25
3 Jeff Weaver .10 .25
4 Deivi Cruz .10 .25
5 Juan Encarnacion .10 .25
6 Brian Moehler .10 .25
7 Robert Fick .10 .25
8 Phil Garner MG .10 .25
9 Juan Gonzalez .10 .25
10 Brad Ausmus .10 .25
11 Todd Jones .10 .25
12 Bobby Higginson .10 .25
13 Tony Clark .10 .25
14 Dean Palmer .10 .25
15 Doug Brocail .10 .25

2001 Tigers Postcards

COMPLETE SET 4.80 12.00
1 Matt Anderson .10 .25
2 Frank Beckerman ANN .10 .25
3 Adam Bernero .10 .25
4 Javier Cardona .10 .25
5 Roger Cedeno .10 .25
6 Tony Clark .20 .50
7 Deivi Cruz .10 .25
8 Damion Easley .10 .25
9 Juan Encarnacion .20 .50
10 Robert Fick .10 .25
11 Phil Garner MG .10 .25
12 Shane Halter .10 .25
13 Ernie Harwell ANN .40 1.00
14 Bobby Higginson .20 .50
15 Brandon Inge .10 .25
16 Ryan Jackson .10 .25
17 Al Kaline ANN .80 2.00
18 Bill Madlock .20 .50
19 Doug Mansolino .10 .25
20 Wendell Magee .10 .25
21 Billy McMillon .10 .25
22 Mitch Meluskey .10 .25
23 Brian Moehler .10 .25
24 Heath Murray .10 .25
25 C.J. Nitkowski .10 .25
26 Ed Ott CO .10 .25
27 Dean Palmer .20 .50
28 Lance Parrish CO .20 .50
29 Danny Patterson .10 .25
30 Adam Pettyjohn .10 .25
31 Jim Price ANN .10 .25
32 Juan Samuel .10 .25
33 Victor Santos .10 .25
34 Randall Simon .10 .25
35 Randy Smith GM .10 .25
36 Steve Sparks .10 .25
37 Dan Warthen CO .10 .25
38 Jeff Weaver .30 .75
39 Matt Wheatland .10 .25

2002 Tigers Team Issue

COMPLETE SET 6.00 15.00
1 Juan Acevedo .20 .50
2 Felipe Alou CO .30 .75
3 Matt Anderson .20 .50
4 Dave Borkowski .20 .50
5 Nate Cornejo .20 .50
6 Jacob Cruz .20 .50
7 David Dombrowski GM .20 .50
8 Damion Easley .20 .50
9 Jeff Farnsworth .20 .50
10 Robert Fick .20 .50
11 Seth Greisinger .20 .50
12 Shane Halter .20 .50
13 Bobby Higginson .30 .75
14 Damian Jackson .20 .50
15 Ryan Jackson .20 .50
16 Jeff Jones .20 .50
17 Al Kaline 1.25 3.00
18 Rafael Landestoy .20 .50
19 Jose Lima .20 .50
20 Wendell Magee .20 .50
21 Mitch Meluskey .20 .50
22 Steve McCatty CO .20 .50
23 Eric Munson .20 .50
24 Dean Palmer .30 .75
25 Jose Paniagua .20 .50
26 Lance Parrish CO .20 .50
27 Adam Pettyjohn .20 .50
28 Craig Paquette .20 .50
29 Luis Pujols MG .20 .50
30 Mark Redman .20 .50
31 Merv Rettenmund CO .20 .50
32 Michael Rivera .20 .50
33 Juan Samuel CO .20 .50
34 Randall Simon .20 .50
35 Steve Sparks .20 .50
36 Dmitri Young .40 1.00

2003 Tigers Team Issue

COMPLETE SET 4.00 10.00
1 Nate Cornejo .20 .50
2 Kirk Gibson CO .60 1.50
3 Shane Halter .20 .50
4 Bobby Higginson .30 .75
5 Brandon Inge .20 .50
6 Mick Kelleher CO .20 .50
7 Mike Maroth .20 .50
8 Craig Monroe .60 1.50
9 Eric Munson .20 .50
10 Lance Parrish CO .30 .75
11 Carlos Pena .40 1.00
12 Matt Roney .20 .50
13 Juan Samuel CO .20 .50
14 Ramon Santiago .20 .50
15 Andres Torres .20 .50
16 Alan Trammell MG .60 1.50
17 Matt Walbeck .20 .50
18 Jamie Walker .20 .50

2004 Tigers Team Issue

COMPLETE SET
1 Rod Allen .20 .50

2 Matt Anderson .20 .50
3 Kenny Baugh .20 .50
4 Frank Beckman .20 .50
5 Jeremy Bonderman .40 1.00
6 Mike Bumatay .20 .50
7 Adrian Burnside .20 .50
8 Nate Cornejo .20 .50
9 Dan Dickerson .20 .50
10 Eric Eckenstahler .20 .50
11 Dave Espinosa .20 .50
12 Bruce Fields .20 .50
13 Bob Henkel .20 .50
14 Bobby Higginson .30 .75
15 Willie Horton .40 1.00
16 Mario Impemba .20 .50
17 Brandon Inge .20 .50
18 Jason Johnson .20 .50
19 Al Kaline 1.00 2.50
20 Tim Kalita .20 .50
21 Don Kelly .20 .50
22 Gary Knotts .20 .50
23 Preston Larrison .20 .50
24 Wil Ledezma .20 .50
25 Al Levine .20 .50
26 Nook Logan .60 1.50
27 Shane Loux .20 .50
28 Mike Maroth .20 .50
29 Chris Mears .20 .50
30 Craig Monroe .60 1.50
31 Eric Munson .20 .50
32 Jim Price .20 .50
33 Ryan Raburn .20 .50
34 Nate Robertson .20 .50
35 Fernando Rodney .20 .50
36 Matt Roney .20 .50
37 Cody Ross .20 .50
38 Juan Samuel .20 .50
39 Alex Sanchez .20 .50
40 Chris Shelton .20 .50
41 Chris Spurling .20 .50
42 Alan Trammell MG .40 1.00
43 Andy Van Hekken .20 .50
44 Jamie Walker .20 .50
45 Rondell White .40 1.00
46 Dmitri Young .40 1.00

2006 Tigers Topps

COMPLETE SET (14) 3.00 8.00
DET1 Ivan Rodriguez .20 .50
DET2 Dmitri Young .12 .30
DET3 Carlos Guillen .12 .30
DET4 Magglio Ordonez .20 .50
DET5 Curtis Granderson .25 .60
DET6 Nook Logan .12 .30
DET7 Brandon Inge .12 .30
DET8 Placido Polanco .12 .30
DET9 Kenny Rogers .12 .30
DET10 Todd Jones .12 .30
DET11 Mike Maroth .12 .30
DET12 Troy Percival .12 .30
DET13 Jeremy Bonderman .12 .30
DET14 Chris Shelton .12 .30

2007 Tigers Topps

COMPLETE SET (14) 3.00 8.00
DET1 Ivan Rodriguez .20 .50
DET2 Craig Monroe .12 .30
DET3 Justin Verlander .30 .75
DET4 Nate Robertson .12 .30
DET5 Joel Zumaya .12 .30
DET6 Placido Polanco .12 .30
DET7 Jeremy Bonderman .12 .30
DET8 Kenny Rogers .12 .30
DET9 Brandon Inge .12 .30
DET10 Curtis Granderson .25 .60
DET11 Sean Casey .12 .30
DET12 Gary Sheffield .12 .30
DET13 Carlos Guillen .12 .30
DET14 Magglio Ordonez .20 .50

2008 Tigers Topps

COMPLETE SET (14) 3.00 8.00
DET1 Miguel Cabrera .30 .75
DET2 Dontrelle Willis .12 .30
DET3 Justin Verlander .30 .75
DET4 Kenny Rogers .12 .30
DET5 Joel Zumaya .12 .30
DET6 Placido Polanco .12 .30
DET7 Jeremy Bonderman .12 .30
DET8 Ivan Rodriguez .20 .50
DET9 Edgar Renteria .12 .30
DET10 Curtis Granderson .20 .50
DET11 Jacque Jones .12 .30
DET12 Gary Sheffield .12 .30
DET13 Carlos Guillen .12 .30
DET14 Magglio Ordonez .20 .50

2009 Tigers Topps

DET1 Miguel Cabrera .40 1.00
DET2 Armando Galarraga .15 .40
DET3 Curtis Granderson .30 .75
DET4 Justin Verlander .40 1.00
DET5 Magglio Ordonez .25 .60
DET6 Jeremy Bonderman .15 .40
DET7 Marcus Thames .15 .40
DET8 Dontrelle Willis .15 .40
DET9 Placido Polanco .15 .40
DET10 Fernando Rodney .15 .40
DET11 Gary Sheffield .15 .40
DET12 Gerald Laird .15 .40
DET13 Carlos Guillen .15 .40
DET14 Brandon Inge .15 .40
DET15 Paws .15 .40

2010 Tigers Topps

DET1 Miguel Cabrera .40 1.00
DET2 Jarrod Washburn .15 .40
DET3 Clete Thomas .15 .40
DET4 Rick Porcello .25 .60
DET5 Brandon Inge .25 .60
DET6 Nate Robertson .15 .40
DET7 Magglio Ordonez .25 .60
DET8 Jeremy Bonderman .15 .40
DET9 Marcus Thames .15 .40
DET10 Wilkin Ramirez .15 .40
DET11 Phil Coke .15 .40
DET12 Justin Verlander .40 1.00
DET13 Joel Zumaya .15 .40
DET14 Robinzon Diaz .15 .40
DET15 Carlos Guillen .15 .40
DET16 Max Scherzer .40 1.00
DET17 Daniel Schlereth .15 .40

2011 Tigers Topps

DET1 Miguel Cabrera .40 1.00
DET2 Magglio Ordonez .25 .60
DET3 Brandon Inge .15 .40
DET4 Max Scherzer .40 1.00
DET5 Brad Penny .15 .40
DET6 Ryan Raburn .15 .40
DET7 Carlos Guillen .15 .40
DET8 Austin Jackson .15 .40
DET9 Jhonny Peralta .15 .40
DET10 Rick Porcello .25 .60
DET11 Brennan Boesch .25 .60
DET12 Joaquin Benoit .15 .40
DET13 Justin Verlander .40 1.00
DET14 Jose Valverde .15 .40
DET15 Alex Avila .25 .60
DET16 Victor Martinez .25 .60
DET17 Comerica Park .15 .40

2012 Tigers Topps

DET1 Prince Fielder .30 .75
DET2 Ryan Raburn .25 .60
DET3 Brennan Boesch .25 .60
DET4 Alex Avila .25 .60
DET5 Miguel Cabrera .40 1.00
DET6 Doug Fister .25 .60
DET7 Delmon Young .30 .75
DET8 Brandon Inge .25 .60
DET9 Victor Martinez .30 .75
DET10 Justin Verlander .40 1.00
DET11 Max Scherzer .40 1.00
DET12 Austin Jackson .30 .75
DET13 Jhonny Peralta .25 .60
DET14 Jacob Turner .30 .75
DET15 Rick Porcello .25 .60
DET16 Jose Valverde .30 .75
DET17 Comerica Park .15 .40

2013 Tigers Topps

COMPLETE SET (17) 3.00 8.00
DET1 Justin Verlander .25 .60
DET2 Miguel Cabrera .25 .60
DET3 Doug Fister .15 .40
DET4 Max Scherzer .40 1.00
DET5 Andy Dirks .15 .40
DET6 Drew Smyly .15 .40
DET7 Omar Infante .25 .60
DET8 Jhonny Peralta .15 .40
DET9 Phil Coke .15 .40
DET10 Austin Jackson .15 .40
DET11 Joaquin Benoit .15 .40
DET12 Alex Avila .20 .50
DET13 Victor Martinez .30 .75
DET14 Prince Fielder .30 .75
DET15 Anibal Sanchez .25 .60
DET16 Torii Hunter .15 .40
DET17 Comerica Park .15 .40

2014 Tigers Topps

COMPLETE SET (17) 3.00 8.00
DET1 Justin Verlander .25 .60
DET2 Miguel Cabrera .25 .60
DET3 Drew Smyly .15 .40
DET4 Max Scherzer .25 .60
DET5 Andy Dirks .15 .40
DET6 Nick Castellanos .50 1.25
DET7 Ian Kinsler .20 .50
DET8 Rick Porcello .20 .50
DET9 Jose Iglesias .20 .50
DET10 Austin Jackson .15 .40
DET11 Joe Nathan .15 .40
DET12 Alex Avila .20 .50
DET13 Victor Martinez .20 .50
DET14 Bruce Rondon .15 .40
DET15 Anibal Sanchez .15 .40
DET16 Torii Hunter .15 .40
DET17 Comerica Park .15 .40

2015 Tigers Topps

COMPLETE SET (17) 3.00 8.00
DT1 Miguel Cabrera .25 .60
DT2 Alex Avila .20 .50
DT3 Al Alburquerque .15 .40
DT4 Ian Kinsler .20 .50
DT5 J.D. Martinez .25 .60
DT6 Anibal Sanchez .15 .40
DT7 Jose Iglesias .20 .50
DT8 Yoenis Cespedes .20 .50
DT9 Joe Nathan .15 .40
DT10 Anthony Gose .15 .40
DT11 Nick Castellanos .25 .60
DT12 James McCann .25 .60
DT13 Steven Moya .20 .50
DT14 Joakim Soria .15 .40
DT15 Victor Martinez .20 .50
DT16 David Price .20 .50
DT17 Justin Verlander .25 .60

2016 Tigers Topps

COMPLETE SET (17) 3.00 8.00
DET1 Miguel Cabrera .25 .60
DET2 James McCann .20 .50
DET3 Ian Kinsler .20 .50
DET4 Jose Iglesias .20 .50
DET5 Nick Castellanos .25 .60
DET6 Anthony Gose .15 .40
DET7 J.D. Martinez .25 .60
DET8 Victor Martinez .20 .50
DET9 Justin Verlander .25 .60
DET10 Francisco Rodriguez .20 .50
DET11 Cameron Maybin .15 .40
DET12 Jordan Zimmermann .20 .50
DET13 Mike Pelfrey .15 .40
DET14 Anibal Sanchez .15 .40
DET15 Daniel Norris .15 .40
DET16 Justin Upton .20 .50
DET17 Mark Lowe .15 .40

2017 Tigers Topps

COMPLETE SET (17) 3.00 8.00
DET1 Miguel Cabrera .25 .60
DET2 Jordan Zimmermann .20 .50
DET3 Anibal Sanchez .15 .40
DET4 Daniel Norris .15 .40
DET5 Ian Kinsler .20 .50
DET6 J.D. Martinez .25 .60
DET7 Tyler Collins .15 .40
DET8 Victor Martinez .20 .50
DET9 Michael Fulmer .15 .40
DET10 Justin Verlander .25 .60
DET11 Jose Iglesias .20 .50
DET12 Nick Castellanos .25 .60
DET13 Mike Pelfrey .15 .40
DET14 Francisco Rodriguez .20 .50
DET15 James McCann .20 .50
DET16 Justin Upton .20 .50
DET17 Alex Avila .20 .50

2018 Tigers Topps

COMPLETE SET (17) 2.00 5.00
DT1 Miguel Cabrera .25 .60
DT2 Jose Iglesias .20 .50
DT3 James McCann .20 .50
DT4 Michael Fulmer .15 .40
DT5 Daniel Norris .15 .40
DT6 Jordan Zimmermann .20 .50
DT7 Buck Farmer .15 .40
DT8 Jeimer Candelario .20 .50
DT9 JaCoby Jones .20 .50
DT10 Victor Martinez .20 .50
DT11 Mikie Mahtook .15 .40
DT12 Dixon Machado .15 .40
DT13 Shane Greene .15 .40
DT14 Nick Castellanos .25 .60
DT15 John Hicks .15 .40
DT16 Joe Jimenez .15 .40
DT17 Matthew Boyd .15 .40

2019 Tigers Topps

COMPLETE SET (17) 2.00 5.00
DT1 Miguel Cabrera .25 .60
DT2 Nicholas Castellanos .25 .60
DT3 Jeimer Candelario .15 .40
DT4 Ronny Rodriguez .15 .40
DT5 Dawel Lugo .25 .60
DT6 Matt Boyd .15 .40
DT7 Michael Fulmer .15 .40
DT8 Niko Goodrum .20 .50
DT9 Christin Stewart .20 .50
DT10 JaCoby Jones .20 .50
DT11 Jordan Zimmermann .20 .50
DT12 Daniel Norris .15 .40
DT13 Spencer Turnbull .25 .60
DT14 Shane Greene .15 .40
DT15 Joe Jimenez .15 .40
DT16 Mikie Mahtook .15 .40
DT17 John Hicks .15 .40

2020 Tigers Topps

DET1 Miguel Cabrera .25 .60
DET2 Dawel Lugo .15 .40
DET3 Jake Rogers .15 .40
DET4 Matthew Boyd .15 .40
DET5 Travis Demeritte .25 .60
DET6 Joe Jimenez .15 .40
DET7 Spencer Turnbull .15 .40
DET8 Christin Stewart .15 .40
DET9 Daniel Norris .15 .40
DET10 Niko Goodrum .20 .50
DET11 Willi Castro .25 .60
DET12 Jordan Zimmermann .20 .50
DET13 JaCoby Jones .20 .50
DET14 Victor Reyes .15 .40
DET15 Comerica Park .15 .40
DET16 Brandon Dixon .15 .40
DET17 Jeimer Candelario .15 .40

2017 Tigers Topps National Baseball Card Day

COMPLETE SET (10) 6.00 15.00
DET1 Miguel Cabrera 1.00 2.50
DET2 Jordan Zimmermann .75 2.00
DET3 Nicholas Castellanos 1.00 2.50
DET4 Michael Fulmer .60 1.50
DET5 J.D. Martinez 1.00 2.50
DET6 Victor Martinez .75 2.00
DET7 James McCann .75 2.00
DET8 Justin Verlander 1.00 2.50
DET9 Ian Kinsler .75 2.00
DET10 Al Kaline 1.00 2.50

2008 Tigers Topps Gift Set

1 Jim Leyland MG .15 .40
2 Curtis Granderson 20-20-20-20 .25 .60
3 Magglio Ordonez .25 .60
4 Magglio Ordonez/Gary Sheffield/Curtis Granderson .25 .60
5 Justin Verlander .40 1.00
6 Ivan Rodriguez .25 .60
7 Dontrelle Willis .15 .40
8 Miguel Cabrera .40 1.00
9 Magglio Ordonez/Placido Polanco .25 .60
10 Verlander/Durbin/Robertson .40 1.00
11 Nate Robertson .15 .40
12 Carlos Guillen .15 .40
13 IRod/Verlander/Ordonez .40 1.00
14 Kenny Rogers .15 .40
15 Ryan Raburn .15 .40
16 Justin Verlander No-Hitter .40 1.00
17 Placido Polanco .15 .40
18 Jeremy Bonderman .15 .40
19 Verlander/Bonderman/Robertson .40 1.00
20 Curtis Granderson .25 .60
21 Curtis Granderson/Carlos Guillen .25 .60
22 Joel Zumaya .15 .40
23 Magglio Ordonez/Placido Polanco/Curtis Granderson .25 .60
24 Curtis Granderson POTW .25 .60
25 Edgar Renteria .15 .40
26 Andy Van Slyke CO .15 .40
27 Todd Jones .15 .40
28 Magglio Ordonez Wins Al Batting Title.25 .60
29 Gary Sheffield .15 .40
30 Fernando Rodney .15 .40
31 Verlander/Bonderman/Robertson .40 1.00
32 Vance Wilson .15 .40
33 Bobby Seay .15 .40
34 Gene Lamont CO .15 .40
35 Magglio Ordonez POTM .25 .60
36 Matt Joyce .40 1.00
37 Zach Miner .15 .40
38 Magglio Ordonez/Placido Polanco/Curtis Granderson .25 .60
39 Brandon Inge .15 .40
40 Macay McBride .15 .40
41 Chuck Hernandez CO .15 .40
42 Ivan Rodriguez/Placido Polanco .25 .60
43 Marcus Thames .15 .40
44 Jason Grilli .15 .40
45 Verlander/Robertson/Bonderman .40 1.00
46 Curtis Granderson Triples .25 .60
47 Magglio Ordonez/Carlos Guillen/Gary Sheffield .25 .60
48 Ramon Santiago .15 .40
49 Cabrera/Guillen/Polanco/Renteria .40 1.00
50 Armando Galarraga .25 .60
51 Lloyd McClendon CO .15 .40
52 Ivan Rodriguez/Kenny Rogers .25 .60
53 Magglio Ordonez Doubles .25 .60
54 Paws .15 .40
55 Comerica Park .15 .40

2003 Timeless Treasures

COMMON CARD (1-100) .50 1.25
COMMON RC .60 1.50
STATED PRINT RUN 900 SERIAL #'d SETS
PRODUCED BY DONRUSS/PLAYOFF
1 Adam Dunn .75 2.00
2 Al Kaline .75 2.00
3 Alan Trammell .75 2.00
4 Albert Pujols 1.50 4.00
5 Alex Rodriguez 1.50 4.00
6 Alfonso Soriano .75 2.00
7 Andre Dawson .75 2.00
8 Andruw Jones .50 1.25
9 Austin Kearns .50 1.25
10 Babe Ruth 3.00 8.00
11 Barry Bonds 2.00 5.00
12 Barry Larkin .75 2.00
13 Barry Zito .75 2.00
14 Bernie Williams .75 2.00
15 Bo Jackson 1.25 3.00
16 Brooks Robinson .75 2.00
17 Cal Ripken 4.00 10.00
18 Carlton Fisk .75 2.00
19 Chipper Jones 1.25 3.00
20 Curt Schilling .75 2.00
21 Dale Murphy 1.25 3.00
22 Derek Jeter 3.00 8.00
23 Don Mattingly 2.50 6.00
24 Duke Snider .75 2.00
25 Eddie Mathews 1.25 3.00
26 Frank Robinson .75 2.00
27 Frank Thomas 1.25 3.00
28 Garret Anderson .50 1.25
29 Gary Carter .75 2.00
30 George Brett 2.50 6.00
31 Greg Maddux 1.50 4.00
32 Harmon Killebrew 1.25 3.00
33 Hideki Matsui RC 2.50 6.00
34 Hideo Nomo 1.25 3.00
35 Ichiro Suzuki 1.50 4.00
36 Ivan Rodriguez .75 2.00
37 Jackie Robinson 1.25 3.00
38 Jason Giambi .50 1.25
39 Jeff Bagwell .75 2.00
40 Jim Edmonds .75 2.00
41 Jim Palmer .75 2.00
42 Jim Thome .75 2.00
43 Joe Morgan .75 2.00
44 Jorge Posada .75 2.00
45 Jose Contreras RC 1.25 3.00
46 Juan Gonzalez .50 1.25
47 Kazuhisa Ishii .50 1.25
48 Ken Griffey Jr. 2.50 6.00
49 Kerry Wood .50 1.25
50 Kirby Puckett 1.25 3.00
51 Lance Berkman .75 2.00
52 Larry Walker .75 2.00
53 Lou Brock .75 2.00
54 Lou Gehrig 2.50 6.00
55 Magglio Ordonez .75 2.00
56 Mark Prior .75 2.00
57 Miguel Tejada .75 2.00
58 Mike Mussina .75 2.00
59 Mike Piazza 1.25 3.00
60 Mike Schmidt 2.00 5.00
61 Nolan Ryan 4.00 10.00
62 Nomar Garciaparra .75 2.00
63 Ozzie Smith 1.50 4.00
64 Pat Burrell .50 1.25
65 Pedro Martinez .75 2.00
66 Pee Wee Reese .75 2.00
67 Phil Rizzuto .75 2.00
68 Rafael Palmeiro .75 2.00
69 Randy Johnson 1.25 3.00
70 Reggie Jackson .75 2.00
71 Richie Ashburn .75 2.00
72 Rickey Henderson 1.25 3.00
73 Roberto Alomar .75 2.00
74 Roberto Clemente 3.00 8.00
75 Robin Yount 1.25 3.00
76 Rod Carew .75 2.00
77 Roger Clemens 1.50 4.00
78 Rogers Hornsby .75 2.00
79 Roy Oswalt .75 2.00
80 Ryan Klesko .50 1.25
81 Ryne Sandberg 2.50 6.00
82 Sammy Sosa 1.25 3.00
83 Scott Rolen .75 2.00
84 Shawn Green .50 1.25
85 Stan Musial 2.00 5.00
86 Steve Carlton .75 2.00
87 Thurman Munson 1.25 3.00
88 Todd Helton .75 2.00
89 Tom Glavine .75 2.00
90 Tom Seaver .75 2.00
91 Tony Gwynn 1.25 3.00
92 Tony Perez .75 2.00
93 Torii Hunter .50 1.25
94 Troy Glaus .50 1.25
95 Ty Cobb 2.00 5.00
96 Vernon Wells .50 1.25
97 Vladimir Guerrero .75 2.00
98 Warren Spahn .75 2.00
99 Willie McCovey .75 2.00
100 Yogi Berra 1.25 3.00

2003 Timeless Treasures Silver

*ACTIVE STARS: 1.25X TO 3X BASIC
*RETIRED POST-WAR STARS: 1.25X TO 3X
*RETIRED PRE-WAR STARS: 1.25X TO 3X
*ROOKIES: 1.25X TO 3X BASIC
STATED PRINT RUN 50 SERIAL #'d SETS

2003 Timeless Treasures Award

PRINT RUNS B/WN 50-100 COPIES PER CARD
1 Ivan Rodriguez Bat/100 8.00 20.00
2 Mike Schmidt Bat-Jsy/50 75.00 150.00
3 Roberto Clemente Bat/50 60.00 120.00
4 Roger Clemens Jsy/50 30.00 60.00
5 Randy Johnson Jsy/100 8.00 20.00
6 Pedro Martinez Jsy/100 8.00 20.00
7 Ivan Rodriguez Chest/100 8.00 20.00
8 Jeff Bagwell Pants/100 8.00 20.00
9 Frank Thomas Jsy/100 8.00 20.00
10 Cal Ripken Bat/75 10.00 25.00
11 Tom Seaver Jsy/50 15.00 40.00

2003 Timeless Treasures Award Autographs

PRINT RUNS B/WN 5-15 COPIES PER CARD
NO PRICING DUE TO SCARCITY

2003 Timeless Treasures Award Prime

PRINT RUNS B/WN 15-50 COPIES PER CARD
NO PRICING ON QTY OF 30 OR LESS
6 Pedro Martinez Jsy/50 20.00 50.00
9 Frank Thomas Jsy/50 30.00 60.00

2003 Timeless Treasures Classic Combos

STATED PRINT RUN 100 SERIAL #'d SETS
1 Jason Giambi Hat-Jsy 2.50 6.00
2 Adrian Beltre Hat-Shoes 6.00 15.00
3 Alex Rodriguez Bat-Jsy 8.00 20.00
4 Alfonso Soriano Bat-Jsy 4.00 10.00
5 Andruw Jones Fld Glv-Jsy 2.50 6.00
6 Andre Dawson ST Bat-Jsy 4.00 10.00
7 Barry Larkin Bat-Jsy 4.00 10.00
8 Barry Zito Fld Glv-Jsy 4.00 10.00
9 Cal Ripken Bat-Jsy 20.00 50.00
10 Chipper Jones Bat-Jsy 6.00 15.00
11 Don Mattingly Bat-Jsy 12.00 30.00
12 Eric Chavez Bat-Jsy 2.50 6.00
13 Frank Thomas Bat-Jsy 6.00 15.00
14 Greg Maddux Bat-Jsy 8.00 20.00
15 Ivan Rodriguez Fld Glv-Jsy 4.00 10.00
16 Jeff Bagwell Bat-Jsy 4.00 10.00
17 Jim Thome Bat-Jsy 4.00 10.00
18 Juan Gonzalez Bat-Jsy 2.50 6.00
19 Kazuhisa Ishii Bat-Jsy 2.50 6.00
20 Kerry Wood Jsy-Shoes 2.50 6.00
21 Lance Berkman Fld Glv-Jsy 4.00 10.00
22 Magglio Ordonez Bat-Jsy 4.00 10.00
23 Manny Ramirez Bat-Jsy 6.00 15.00
24 Miguel Tejada Hat-Jsy 4.00 10.00
25 Mike Piazza Bat-Jsy 6.00 15.00
26 Nomar Garciaparra Bat-Jsy 4.00 10.00
27 Pedro Martinez Bat-Jsy 4.00 10.00
28 Randy Johnson Bat-Jsy 6.00 15.00
29 Rickey Henderson Bat-Jsy 6.00 15.00
30 Ryne Sandberg Bat-Jsy 12.00 30.00
31 Sammy Sosa Bat-Jsy 6.00 15.00
32 Shawn Green Bat-Jsy 2.50 6.00
33 Todd Helton Bat-Jsy 4.00 10.00
34 Tony Gwynn Bat-Jsy 6.00 15.00
35 Vladimir Guerrero Bat-Jsy 4.00 10.00

2003 Timeless Treasures Classic Combos Autographs

PRINT RUNS B/WN 5-50 COPIES PER CARD
NO PRICING ON QTY OF 25 OR LESS
6 Andre Dawson Bat-ST Jsy/50 30.00 60.00
30 Ryne Sandberg Bat-Jsy/50 40.00 80.00
35 Vladimir Guerrero Bat-Jsy/50 50.00 100.00

2003 Timeless Treasures Game Day

BAT-HAT-JSY PRINT RUN 100 #'d SETS
BALL PRINT RUN 20 SERIAL #'d SETS
NO BALL PRICING DUE TO SCARCITY
1 Tony Gwynn Bat 5.00 12.00
2 Magglio Ordonez Hat 3.00 8.00
3 George Brett Bat 10.00 25.00
4 Rickey Henderson Jsy 5.00 12.00
5 Billy Williams Bat 3.00 8.00
6 Frank Thomas Bat 5.00 12.00
7 Tony Gwynn Jsy 10.00 25.00
10 Ryne Sandberg Bat 10.00 25.00
11 Miguel Tejada Jsy 3.00 8.00

2003 Timeless Treasures Game Day Prime

PRINT RUNS B/WN 5-75 COPIES PER CARD
NO PRICING ON QTY OF 25 OR LESS
4 Rickey Henderson Jsy/75 20.00 50.00
7 Tony Gwynn Jsy/75 40.00 80.00
11 Miguel Tejada Jsy/75 12.50 30.00

2003 Timeless Treasures HOF Combos

PRINT RUNS B/WN 25-100 COPIES PER CARD
NO PRICING ON QTY 25 OR LESS
1 Al Kaline Bat-Jsy/50 10.00 25.00
3 Eddie Mathews Bat-Jsy/50 15.00 40.00
4 Kirby Puckett Bat-Hat/75 20.00 50.00
6 Mike Schmidt Bat-Jsy/100 10.00 25.00
7 Nolan Ryan Fld Glv-Jsy/50 75.00 150.00
8 Phil Rizzuto Bat-Jsy/50 10.00 25.00
11 Rod Carew Bat-Jsy/100 20.00 50.00
14 George Brett Bat-Hat/50 75.00 150.00
15 Carlton Fisk Bat-Jsy/100 20.00 50.00

2003 Timeless Treasures HOF Logos

PRINT RUNS B/WN 1-35 COPIES PER CARD
NO PRICING ON QTY OF 25 OR LESS
29 Eddie Mathews/35 40.00 80.00
36 Nolan Ryan Angels/35 40.00 80.00
37 Nolan Ryan Astros/35 40.00 80.00
43 Robin Yount/35 40.00 80.00
44 Rod Carew/35 30.00 60.00

2003 Timeless Treasures HOF Materials

PRINT RUNS B/WN 25-100 COPIES PER CARD
NO PRICING ON QTY OF 25 OR LESS
1 Al Kaline Bat/100 15.00 40.00
2 Babe Ruth Bat/75 60.00 120.00
3 Carlton Fisk Bat/100 10.00 25.00
4 Eddie Mathews Bat/100 15.00 40.00
5 Gary Carter Bat/100 8.00 20.00
6 George Brett Bat/100 20.00 50.00
7 Harmon Killebrew Bat/100 15.00 40.00
8 Joe Morgan Bat/100 8.00 20.00
9 Kirby Puckett Bat/100 10.00 25.00
10 Lou Gehrig Bat/100 50.00 100.00
11 Luis Aparicio Bat/100 8.00 20.00
12 Mike Schmidt Bat/100 20.00 50.00
13 Ozzie Smith Bat/100 15.00 40.00
14 Phil Rizzuto Bat/100 10.00 25.00
15 Reggie Jackson Bat/100 10.00 25.00
16 Richie Ashburn Bat/100 10.00 25.00
17 Roberto Clemente Bat/100 30.00 80.00
18 Robin Yount Bat/100 10.00 25.00
19 Rod Carew Bat/100 10.00 25.00
20 Rogers Hornsby Bat/100 8.00 20.00
21 Stan Musial Bat/100 10.00 25.00
22 Ty Cobb Bat/100 30.00 80.00
23 Willie McCovey Bat/100 8.00 20.00
24 Yogi Berra Bat/100 10.00 25.00
25 Al Kaline Jsy/100 15.00 40.00
26 Babe Ruth Jsy/50 250.00 400.00
27 Bobby Doerr Jsy/100 8.00 20.00
28 Brooks Robinson Jsy/100 10.00 25.00
29 Eddie Mathews Jsy/100 15.00 40.00
30 Harmon Killebrew Jsy/100 15.00 40.00
31 Ty Cobb Pants/50 100.00 200.00
32 Joe Morgan Jsy/100 8.00 20.00
33 Lou Brock Jsy/100 10.00 25.00
34 Lou Gehrig Jsy/50 75.00 150.00
35 Mike Schmidt Jsy/100 20.00 50.00
36 Nolan Ryan Angels Jsy/100 12.50 30.00
37 Nolan Ryan Astros Jsy/100 12.50 30.00
38 Nolan Ryan Rangers Jsy/100 12.50 30.00
39 Phil Rizzuto Jsy/100 10.00 25.00
41 Reggie Jackson A's Jsy/100 10.00 25.00
42 Roberto Clemente Jsy/50 75.00 150.00
43 Robin Yount Jsy/100 10.00 25.00
44 Rod Carew Jsy/100 10.00 25.00
45 Stan Musial Jsy/100 10.00 25.00
46 Tom Seaver Jsy/100 10.00 25.00
47 Steve Carlton Jsy/100 8.00 20.00
48 Carlton Fisk Jsy/100 10.00 25.00
49 Pee Wee Reese Jsy/100 10.00 25.00
50 Jackie Robinson Jsy/50 50.00 100.00

2003 Timeless Treasures HOF Materials Autographs

PRINT RUNS B/WN 5-50 COPIES PER CARD
NO PRICING ON QTY OF 25 OR LESS
30 Harmon Killebrew Jsy/50 20.00 50.00
33 Lou Brock Jsy/50 20.00 50.00
45 Stan Musial Jsy/50 60.00 120.00

2003 Timeless Treasures HOF Numbers

PRINT RUNS B/WN 5-50 COPIES PER CARD
NO PRICING ON QTY OF 30 OR LESS
29 Eddie Mathews/35 40.00 80.00
35 Mike Schmidt/50 50.00 100.00
36 Nolan Ryan Angels/35 30.00 60.00
43 Robin Yount/35 40.00 80.00
46 Tom Seaver/35 30.00 60.00
47 Steve Carlton/40 20.00 50.00
48 Carlton Fisk/35 30.00 60.00

2003 Timeless Treasures Home Run

BAT-JSY PRINT RUN 100 SERIAL #'d SETS
BALL PRINT RUN 20 SERIAL #'d SETS
NO BALL PRICING DUE TO SCARCITY
1 Harmon Killebrew HR 570 Bat 15.00 40.00
2 Harmon Killebrew HR 565 Bat 15.00 40.00
3 Jose Canseco HR 311 Bat 15.00 40.00
4 Magglio Ordonez 00 HR 17 Bat 6.00 15.00
5 Rafael Palmeiro HR 425 Bat 8.00 20.00
6 Rafael Palmeiro HR 440 Bat 8.00 20.00
7 Rafael Palmeiro HR 448 Jsy 8.00 20.00
8 Alex Rodriguez 00 HR 36 Bat 10.00 25.00
9 Alex Rodriguez 00 HR 37 Bat 10.00 25.00
10 Alex Rodriguez 00 HR 33 Bat 10.00 25.00
12 Adam Dunn 00 HR 9 Jsy 6.00 15.00

2003 Timeless Treasures Material Ink

COMMON CARD 10.00 25.00
PRINT RUNS B/WN 25-100 COPIES PER CARD
NO PRICING ON QTY OF 25 OR LESS
1 Adam Dunn/50 10.00 25.00
2 Alan Trammell/100 15.00 40.00
5 Andre Dawson/100 10.00 25.00
6 Barry Zito/50 40.00 80.00
7 Bo Jackson/100 40.00 80.00
9 Bobby Doerr/50 12.50 30.00
11 Cal Ripken No Sleeve/50 40.00 80.00
12 Cal Ripken Black Sleeve/50 75.00 150.00
14 Dale Murphy/50 40.00 80.00
15 Dave Parker/75 15.00 40.00
16 David Cone/100 10.00 25.00
17 Don Mattingly/100 40.00 80.00
19 Edgar Martinez/50 12.00 30.00
20 Gary Carter/100 12.00 30.00
21 Harmon Killebrew/75 30.00 60.00
23 Jim Thome/50 40.00 80.00
24 Joe Carter/100 15.00 40.00
25 Jose Canseco/50 40.00 80.00
26 Jose Vidro/100 15.00 40.00
27 Kazuhisa Ishii/100 10.00 25.00
28 Kerry Wood/50 40.00 80.00
29 Lance Berkman/50 12.50 30.00
31 Mark Prior/50 20.00 50.00
32 Mike Schmidt/50 75.00 150.00
33 Nick Johnson/100 15.00 40.00
37 Paul LoDuca/100 15.00 40.00
38 Paul Molitor/50 30.00 60.00
41 Roberto Alomar Mets/50 12.00 30.00
42 Roberto Alomar Indians/100 10.00 25.00
43 Robin Yount/50 75.00 150.00
47 Ryan Klesko/75 10.00 25.00
52 Steve Carlton Giants/100 15.00 40.00
53 Steve Carlton Sox/100 15.00 40.00
54 Todd Helton/50 10.00 25.00
55 Tom Seaver/50 20.00 50.00
57 Torii Hunter/100 10.00 25.00
58 Vladimir Guerrero/100 10.00 25.00
59 Will Clark/50 15.00 40.00

2003 Timeless Treasures Milestone

JSY PRINT RUN 100 SERIAL #'d SETS
BALL PRINT RUN 24 SERIAL #'d SETS
NO BALL PRICING DUE TO SCARCITY
3 R.Henderson Padres Jsy/100 10.00 25.00
4 Gaylord Perry Jsy/100 8.00 20.00
5 R.Henderson A's Jsy/100 10.00 25.00

2003 Timeless Treasures Past and Present

STATED PRINT RUN 100 SERIAL #'d SETS
1 Alex Rodriguez 15.00 40.00
2 Hideo Nomo 10.00 25.00
3 Jason Giambi 8.00 20.00
4 Juan Gonzalez 8.00 20.00
5 Mike Piazza 15.00 40.00
6 Pedro Martinez 10.00 25.00
7 Randy Johnson 10.00 25.00
8 Rickey Henderson 10.00 25.00
9 Roberto Alomar 10.00 25.00
10 Roger Clemens 15.00 40.00
11 Sammy Sosa 10.00 25.00

2003 Timeless Treasures Past and Present Letters

PRINT RUNS B/WN 25-75 COPIES PER CARD
NO PRICING ON QTY OF 25 OR LESS
1 Alex Rodriguez/75 40.00 80.00
4 Juan Gonzalez/50 15.00 40.00
6 Pedro Martinez/75 15.00 40.00
7 Randy Johnson/75 20.00 50.00

2003 Timeless Treasures Past and Present Logos

PRINT RUNS B/WN 5-75 COPIES PER CARD
NO PRICING ON QTY OF 25 OR LESS
1 Alex Rodriguez/60 12.50 30.00
3 Jason Giambi/75 12.50 30.00
5 Mike Piazza/50 40.00 80.00
10 Roger Clemens/35 50.00 100.00

2003 Timeless Treasures Past and Present Numbers

PRINT RUNS B/WN 5-75 COPIES PER CARD
NO PRICING ON QTY OF 25 OR LESS
1 Alex Rodriguez/35 12.50 30.00
3 Jason Giambi/75 12.50 30.00
6 Pedro Martinez/50 20.00 50.00
7 Randy Johnson/50 30.00 60.00

2003 Timeless Treasures Post Season

PRINT RUNS B/WN 25-100 COPIES PER CARD
NO PRICING ON QTY OF 25 OR LESS
1 Ozzie Smith Jsy/100 15.00 40.00
2 Tom Glavine Jsy/50 15.00 40.00
3 Bernie Williams Bat/100 8.00 20.00
4 Roger Clemens Jsy/100 15.00 40.00
6 Christy Mathewson Seat/100 20.00 50.00

2003 Timeless Treasures Post Season Prime

PRINT RUNS B/WN 5-75 COPIES PER CARD
NO PRICING ON QTY OF 25 OR LESS
1 Ozzie Smith Jsy/75 30.00 60.00

2003 Timeless Treasures Prime Ink

PRINT RUNS B/WN 5-50 COPIES PER CARD
NO PRICING ON QTY OF 25 OR LESS
2 Alan Trammell/50 15.00 40.00
7 Bo Jackson/50 30.00 60.00
20 Gary Carter/50 30.00 60.00
24 Joe Carter/50 15.00 40.00
27 Kazuhisa Ishii/50 15.00 40.00
33 Nick Johnson/50 15.00 40.00
52 Steve Carlton Giants/50 15.00 40.00
53 Steve Carlton Sox/50 15.00 40.00
57 Torii Hunter/50 15.00 40.00
58 Vladimir Guerrero/50 30.00 60.00

2003 Timeless Treasures Rookie Year

COMMON ACTIVE p/r 100 4.00 10.00
COMMON RETIRED p/r 100 6.00 15.00
PRINT RUNS B/WN 50-100 COPIES PER CARD
*PARALLEL p/r 75-100: .4X TO 1X BASIC RY
*PARALLEL p/r 61-68: .5X TO 1.2X BASIC RY
*PARALLEL p/r 42-47: .6X TO 1.5X BASIC RY
PARALLEL PRINT B/WN 42-100 COPIES PER
1 Cal Ripken Bat/100 15.00 40.00
2 Mike Schmidt Bat/50 30.00 60.00
3 Rafael Palmeiro Bat/100 6.00 15.00
4 Nomar Garciaparra Jsy/100 15.00 40.00
5 Sean Casey Jsy/100 4.00 10.00
6 Stan Musial Jsy/100 20.00 50.00
7 Yogi Berra Jsy/100 15.00 40.00
8 Bernie Williams Bat/100 6.00 15.00
9 Ivan Rodriguez Jsy/100 6.00 15.00
10 J.D. Drew Jsy/100 4.00 10.00
11 Scott Rolen Jsy/100 6.00 15.00
12 Vladimir Guerrero Jsy/100 6.00 15.00
13 Johnny Bench Bat/100 10.00 25.00
14 Ivan Rodriguez Bat/100 6.00 15.00
15 Andruw Jones Jsy/100 6.00 15.00
16 Andruw Jones Bat/100 6.00 15.00
17 Fred Lynn Jsy/100 6.00 15.00
18 Jeff Kent Jsy/100 4.00 10.00
19 Gary Sheffield Jsy/100 4.00 10.00
20 Ron Santo Bat/100 10.00 25.00
21 Juan Gonzalez Jsy/100 4.00 10.00
22 Alfonso Soriano Jsy/100 4.00 10.00
23 Ryan Klesko Jsy/100 4.00 10.00
24 Adam Dunn Btg Glv/100 4.00 10.00
25 Hideo Nomo Jsy/100 6.00 15.00
26 Mark Prior Jsy/100 6.00 15.00
27 Pat Burrell Bat/50 10.00 25.00
28 Magglio Ordonez Bat/100 4.00 10.00
29 Kirby Puckett Bat/100 15.00 40.00
30 Albert Pujols Jsy/100 15.00 40.00
31 Albert Pujols Bat/100 15.00 40.00

2003 Timeless Treasures Rookie Year Combos
PRINT RUNS B/WN 25-50 COPIES PER CARD
NO PRICJNG ON QTY OF 25 OR LESS
3 Andruw Jones Bat-Jsy/50 15.00 40.00
4 Ivan Rodriguez Bat-Jsy/50 15.00 40.00
6 Mark Prior Hat-Jsy/50 15.00 40.00
7 Albert Pujols Bat-Jsy/50 12.00 30.00

2003 Timeless Treasures Rookie Year Letters
PRINT RUNS B/WN 15-35 COPIES PER CARD
NO PRICING ON QTY OF 25 OR LESS
4 Nomar Garciaparra/35 30.00 60.00
9 Ivan Rodriguez/35 20.00 50.00
12 Vladimir Guerrero/35 20.00 50.00

2003 Timeless Treasures Rookie Year Logos
PRINT RUNS B/WN 10-50 COPIES PER CARD
NO PRICING ON QTY OF 25 OR LESS
5 Sean Casey/50 15.00 40.00
10 J.D. Drew/50 15.00 40.00
11 Scott Rolen/50 20.00 50.00
12 Vladimir Guerrero/50 20.00 50.00
15 Andruw Jones/50 20.00 50.00
18 Jeff Kent/50 15.00 40.00
19 Gary Sheffield/50 15.00 40.00
23 Ryan Klesko/50 15.00 40.00
30 Albert Pujols/50 50.00 100.00

2003 Timeless Treasures Rookie Year Numbers
PRINT RUNS B/WN 15-50 COPIES PER CARD
NO PRICING ON QTY OF 30 OR LESS
12 Vladimir Guerrero/50 15.00 40.00
15 Andruw Jones/50 15.00 40.00
22 Alfonso Soriano/35 10.00 25.00
23 Ryan Klesko/35 10.00 25.00
26 Mark Prior/35 15.00 40.00

2003 Timeless Treasures Rookie Year Parallel
*PARALLEL p/r 75-99: .4X TO 1X BASIC RYM
*PARALLEL p/r 61-68: .5X TO 1.2X BASIC RYM
*PARALLEL p/r 42-47: .4X TO 1X BASIC RYM
PRINT RUNS B/WN 42-99 COPIES PER CARD
1 Cal Ripken Bat/82 15.00 40.00
3 Rafael Palmeiro Bat/86 6.00 15.00
5 Sean Casey Jsy/97 4.00 10.00
6 Stan Musial Jsy/42 30.00 80.00
7 Yogi Berra Jsy/47 25.00 60.00
8 Bernie Williams Bat/91 6.00 15.00
9 Ivan Rodriguez Jsy/91 6.00 15.00
10 J.D. Drew Jsy/99 4.00 10.00
11 Scott Rolen Jsy/96 6.00 15.00
12 Vladimir Guerrero Jsy/97 8.00 20.00
13 Johnny Bench Bat/68 10.00 25.00
14 Ivan Rodriguez Bat/91 6.00 15.00
15 Andruw Jones Jsy/96 6.00 15.00
16 Andruw Jones Bat/96 6.00 15.00
17 Fred Lynn Jsy/75 6.00 15.00
18 Jeff Kent Jsy/92 4.00 10.00
19 Gary Sheffield Jsy/89 4.00 10.00
20 Ron Santo Bat/61 12.50 30.00
21 Juan Gonzalez Jsy/89 4.00 10.00
23 Ryan Klesko Jsy/92 4.00 10.00
25 Hideo Nomo Jsy/95 6.00 15.00
27 Pat Burrell Bat/99 10.00 25.00
28 Magglio Ordonez Bat/98 4.00 10.00
29 Kirby Puckett Bat/84 15.00 40.00

2004 Timeless Treasures
COMPLETE SET (100) 50.00 100.00
STATED PRINT RUN 999 SERIAL #'d SETS
1 Albert Pujols 1.50 4.00
2 Garret Anderson .50 1.25
3 Randy Johnson 1.25 3.00
4 Alex Rodriguez Yanks 1.50 4.00
5 Manny Ramirez 1.25 3.00
6 Mark Prior .75 2.00
7 Roberto Alomar .75 2.00
8 Barry Larkin .75 2.00
9 Todd Helton .75 2.00
10 Ivan Rodriguez .75 2.00
11 Jacque Jones .50 1.25
12 Jeff Kent .50 1.25
13 Mike Sweeney .50 1.25
14 Shawn Green .50 1.25
15 Richie Sexson .50 1.25
16 Mike Piazza 1.25 3.00
17 Vladimir Guerrero .75 2.00
18 Mike Mussina .75 2.00
19 Barry Zito .75 2.00
20 Don Mattingly 2.50 6.00
21 Ichiro Suzuki 1.50 4.00
22 Rocco Baldelli .50 1.25
23 Rafael Palmeiro .75 2.00
24 Carlos Delgado .50 1.25
25 Roger Clemens 1.50 4.00
26 Luis Gonzalez .50 1.25
27 Gary Sheffield .50 1.25
28 Jay Gibbons .50 1.25
29 Nomar Garciaparra .75 2.00
30 Aramis Ramirez .50 1.25
31 Frank Thomas 1.25 3.00
32 Ryan Wagner .50 1.25
33 Preston Wilson .50 1.25
34 Hideki Matsui 2.00 5.00
35 Roy Oswalt .75 2.00
36 Angel Berroa .50 1.25
37 Kazuhisa Ishii .50 1.25
38 Scott Podsednik .50 1.25
39 Torii Hunter .50 1.25
40 Tom Glavine .75 2.00
41 Jason Giambi .50 1.25
42 Eric Chavez .50 1.25
43 Jim Thome .75 2.00
44 Tony Gwynn 1.25 3.00
45 Edgar Martinez .75 2.00
46 Jim Edmonds .75 2.00
47 Delmon Young .75 2.00
48 Hank Blalock .50 1.25
49 Vernon Wells .50 1.25
50 Curt Schilling .75 2.00
51 Chipper Jones 1.25 3.00
52 Cal Ripken 4.00 10.00
53 Jason Varitek 1.25 3.00
54 Kerry Wood .50 1.25
55 Magglio Ordonez .75 2.00
56 Adam Dunn .75 2.00
57 Jay Payton .50 1.25
58 Josh Beckett .50 1.25
59 Jeff Bagwell .75 2.00
60 Carlos Beltran .75 2.00
61 Hideo Nomo 1.25 3.00
62 Rickie Weeks .50 1.25
63 Alfonso Soriano .75 2.00
64 Miguel Tejada .75 2.00
65 Bret Boone .50 1.25
66 Scott Rolen .75 2.00
67 Aubrey Huff .50 1.25
68 Juan Gonzalez .50 1.25
69 Roy Halladay .75 2.00
70 Brandon Webb .50 1.25
71 Andruw Jones .50 1.25
72 Pedro Martinez .75 2.00
73 Carlos Lee .50 1.25
74 Lance Berkman .75 2.00
75 Paul LoDuca .50 1.25
76 Jorge Posada .75 2.00
77 Tim Hudson .75 2.00
78 Stan Musial 2.00 5.00
79 Mark Teixeira .75 2.00
80 Trot Nixon .50 1.25
81 Fred McGriff .50 1.25
82 Nick Johnson .50 1.25
83 Nolan Ryan 4.00 10.00
84 Ken Griffey Jr. 2.50 6.00
85 Mariano Rivera 1.50 4.00
86 Mark Mulder .50 1.25
87 Bob Gibson .75 2.00
88 Dale Murphy UER 1.25 3.00
89 Bernie Williams .75 2.00
90 Carl Yastrzemski 1.25 3.00
91 Sammy Sosa 1.25 3.00
92 Miguel Cabrera 1.25 3.00
93 Craig Biggio .75 2.00
94 George Brett 2.50 6.00
95 Rickey Henderson 1.25 3.00
96 Derek Jeter 3.00 8.00
97 Greg Maddux 1.50 4.00
98 Bob Abreu .50 1.25
99 Troy Glaus .50 1.25
100 Dontrelle Willis .50 1.25

2004 Timeless Treasures Bronze
*BRONZE ACTIVE: 1.2X TO 3X BASIC
*BRONZE RETIRED: 1.2X TO 3X BASIC
STATED PRINT RUN 100 SERIAL #'d SETS

2004 Timeless Treasures Silver
*SILVER ACTIVE: 2X TO 5X BASIC
*SILVER RETIRED: 2X TO 5X BASIC
STATED PRINT RUN 25 SERIAL #'d SETS

2004 Timeless Treasures Signature Bronze
RANDOM INSERTS IN PACKS
PRINT RUNS B/WN 1-73 COPIES PER
NO PRICING ON QTY OF 11 OR LESS
1 Albert Pujols/25 75.00 150.00
2 Garret Anderson/16 15.00 40.00
4 Alex Rodriguez/25 30.00 80.00
5 Manny Ramirez/24 30.00 60.00
6 Mark Prior/50 12.50 30.00
8 Barry Larkin/25 30.00 60.00
9 Todd Helton/17 30.00 60.00
14 Shawn Green/15 30.00 60.00
17 Vladimir Guerrero/50 20.00 50.00
20 Don Mattingly/50 40.00 80.00
23 Rafael Palmeiro/25 30.00 60.00
27 Gary Sheffield/50 12.50 30.00
37 Kazuhisa Ishii/17 15.00 40.00
40 Tom Glavine/25 20.00 50.00
42 Eric Chavez/25 12.50 30.00
44 Tony Gwynn/50 30.00 60.00
46 Jim Edmonds/15 30.00 60.00
47 Delmon Young/73 6.00 15.00
49 Vernon Wells/25 12.50 30.00
50 Curt Schilling/38 30.00 60.00
53 Jason Varitek/33 30.00 60.00
56 Adam Dunn/25 20.00 50.00
58 Josh Beckett/21 20.00 50.00
59 Jeff Bagwell/25 30.00 60.00
60 Carlos Beltran/15 10.00 25.00
68 Juan Gonzalez/25 12.50 30.00
71 Andruw Jones/25 12.50 30.00
76 Jorge Posada/25 75.00 150.00
77 Tim Hudson/15 12.50 30.00
78 Stan Musial/50 30.00 60.00
79 Mark Teixeira/23 12.50 30.00
83 Nolan Ryan/50 60.00 120.00
87 Bob Gibson/25 20.00 50.00
88 Dale Murphy UER/50 12.50 30.00
90 Carl Yastrzemski/25 40.00 80.00
91 Sammy Sosa/50 40.00 100.00
92 Miguel Cabrera/24 30.00 60.00
94 George Brett/25 75.00 150.00
95 Rickey Henderson/25 60.00 120.00
97 Greg Maddux/31 60.00 120.00
100 Dontrelle Willis/35 4.00 10.00

2004 Timeless Treasures Signature Silver
RANDOM INSERTS IN PACKS
PRINT RUNS B/WN 1-34 COPIES PER
NO PRICING ON QTY OF 13 OR LESS
6 Mark Prior/22 15.00 40.00
17 Vladimir Guerrero/27 30.00 60.00
20 Don Mattingly/23 60.00 120.00
27 Gary Sheffield/25 20.00 50.00
44 Tony Gwynn/19 50.00 100.00
47 Delmon Young/25 12.50 30.00
76 Jorge Posada/20 75.00 150.00
78 Stan Musial/25 50.00 100.00
83 Nolan Ryan/34 50.00 120.00
88 Dale Murphy UER/25 20.00 50.00
91 Sammy Sosa/21 50.00 100.00

2004 Timeless Treasures Award Materials
PRINT RUNS B/WN 9-99 COPIES PER
NO PRICING ON QTY OF 9 OR LESS
*NBR p/r 45-51: .5X TO 1.2X BASIC p/r 97
*NBR p/r 45-51: .4X TO 1X BASIC p/r 68
*NBR p/r 45-51: .3X TO .8X BASIC p/r 25
*NBR p/r 33-35: .6X TO 1.5X BASIC p/r 88-94
*NBR p/r 20-22: .75X TO 2X BASIC p/r 80-81
*NBR p/r 20-22: .6X TO 1.5X BASIC p/r 50
*NBR p/r 19: .75X TO 2X BASIC p/r 75
*NBR p/r 19: .4X TO 1X BASIC p/r 19
NUMBER PRINT RUNS B/WN 3-51 PER
NO NUMBER PRICING ON QTY 14 OR LESS
*PRIME p/r 25: 1X TO 2.5X BASIC p/r 78-97
*PRIME p/r 25: 1X TO 2.5X BASIC p/r 50-68
*PRIME p/r 25: .75X TO 2X BASIC p/r 25
PRIME PRINT RUNS B/WN 1-25 COPIES PER
NO PRIME PRICING ON QTY OF 10 OR LESS
2 Stan Musial Jsy/43 15.00 40.00
3 Lou Boudreau Jsy/19 8.00 20.00
4 Roger Maris Pants/61 20.00 50.00
5 Roger Maris Bat/61 20.00 50.00
6 Roberto Clemente Bat/66 30.00 60.00
7 Bob Gibson 68 CY Jsy/68 6.00 15.00
8 Bob Gibson 68 MVP Jsy/68 6.00 15.00
9 Tom Seaver Jsy/19 10.00 25.00
10 Fred Lynn Jsy/75 4.00 10.00
11 Jim Rice Jsy/78 4.00 10.00
12 M.Schmidt 80 MVP Jsy/80 8.00 20.00
13 M.Schmidt 80 MVP Pants/80 8.00 20.00
14 M.Schmidt 80 MVP Stir/80 8.00 20.00
15 M.Schmidt 81 MVP Jsy/81 8.00 20.00
16 M.Schmidt 81 MVP Bat/81 8.00 20.00
17 Dale Murphy Jsy/82 6.00 15.00
18 M.Schmidt 86 MVP Hat/19 20.00 50.00
19 M.Schmidt 86 MVP Shoe/19 20.00 50.00
20 M.Schmidt 86 MVP Bat/86 8.00 20.00
21 M.Schmidt 86 MVP Stir/19 20.00 50.00
22 Jose Canseco Jsy/88 6.00 15.00
23 F.Thomas 93 MVP Bat/93 6.00 15.00
24 F.Thomas 93 MVP Jsy/93 6.00 15.00
25 Jeff Bagwell Pants/94 6.00 15.00
26 F.Thomas 94 MVP Jsy/94 6.00 15.00
27 F.Thomas 94 MVP Pants/94 6.00 15.00
28 Jeff Bagwell Bat/94 6.00 15.00
29 Pedro Martinez 97 CY Jsy/97 6.00 15.00
30 Ivan Rodriguez Bat/99 6.00 15.00
31 R.Johnson 00 CY Jsy/25 8.00 20.00
32 P.Martinez 00 CY Jsy/25 8.00 20.00
33 Roger Clemens Jsy/50 10.00 25.00
34 R.Johnson 02 CY Jsy/25 8.00 20.00
35 Miguel Tejada Jsy/25 6.00 15.00

2004 Timeless Treasures Award Materials Signature
PRINT RUNS B/WN 1-78 COPIES PER
NO PRICING ON QTY OF 9 OR LESS
*NBR p/r 19: .75X TO 2X BASIC p/r 75
NUMBER PRINT RUNS B/WN 1-19 PER
NO NUMBER PRICES ON QTY OF 14 OR LESS
PRIME PRINT RUNS B/WN 1-14 COPIES PER
NO PRIME PRICING DUE TO SCARCITY
RANDOM INSERTS IN PACKS
7 Bob Gibson 68 CY Jsy/19 10.00 25.00
8 Bob Gibson 68 MVP Jsy/19 12.00 30.00
10 Fred Lynn Jsy/75 8.00 20.00
11 Jim Rice Jsy/78 10.00 25.00

2004 Timeless Treasures Award Materials Combos
PRINT RUNS B/WN 25-50 COPIES PER
*PRIME: .6X TO 1.5X BASIC p/r 25
PRIME PRINT RUN 19 SERIAL #'d SETS
4 Roger Maris Bat-Pants/25 40.00 80.00
12 M.Schmidt 80M Jsy-Pant/25 20.00 50.00
13 Mike Schmidt 80M Pant-Stir/50 15.00 40.00
14 Mike Schmidt 80M Jsy-Stir/50 15.00 40.00
15 Mike Schmidt 81M Bat-Jsy/25 20.00 50.00
16 Mike Schmidt 81M Bat-Stir/50 15.00 40.00
18 Mike Schmidt 86M Hat-Shoe/50 15.00 40.00
19 Mike Schmidt 86M Hat-Bat/50 15.00 40.00
20 Mike Schmidt 86M Hat-Stir/50 15.00 40.00
21 Mike Schmidt 86M Bat-Shoe/50 15.00 40.00
23 Frank Thomas 93M Bat-Jsy/25 12.50 30.00
25 Jeff Bagwell Bat-Jsy/25 12.50 30.00
26 Frank Thomas 94M Bat-Jsy/25 12.50 30.00
35 Miguel Tejada Bat-Jsy/25 8.00 20.00

2004 Timeless Treasures Game Day Materials
RANDOM INSERTS IN PACKS
PRINT RUNS B/WN 8-99 COPIES PER
NO PRICING ON QTY OF 9 OR LESS
1 Nellie Fox Bat/58 30.00 60.00
2 Frank Robinson Bat/61 6.00 15.00
3 George Brett Bat/77 10.00 25.00
4 George Brett Hat/82 15.00 40.00
5 Nolan Ryan Hat/19 60.00 120.00
6 Cal Ripken Hat/85 15.00 40.00
7 Rod Carew Hat/19 12.50 30.00
8 Ryne Sandberg Bat/91 10.00 25.00
9 Kirby Puckett Bat/92 8.00 20.00
10 Frank Thomas Bat/93 6.00 15.00
12 Tony Gwynn Pants/99 6.00 15.00
13 Vladimir Guerrero Bat/99 6.00 15.00
14 Tony Gwynn Hat/99 12.50 30.00
15 Magglio Ordonez Hat/15 10.00 25.00
16 Rickey Henderson Bat/50 6.00 15.00

2004 Timeless Treasures Game Day Materials Signature
PRINT RUNS B/WN 8-25 COPIES PER
NO PRICING ON QTY OF 10 OR LESS
2 Frank Robinson Bat/25 30.00 60.00
15 Magglio Ordonez Hat/25 20.00 50.00

2004 Timeless Treasures HOF Materials Signature
RANDOM INSERTS IN PACKS
PRINT RUNS B/WN 1-34 COPIES PER
NO PRICING ON QTY OF 11 OR LESS
1 Al Kaline/25 30.00 80.00
3 Bob Feller/25 12.50 30.00
5 Brooks Robinson/25 12.50 30.00
7 Carlton Fisk/27 20.00 50.00
9 Duke Snider/25 20.00 50.00
11 Ernie Banks/25 30.00 60.00
12 Fergie Jenkins/31 12.50 30.00
13 Frank Robinson/20 20.00 50.00
15 Hoyt Wilhelm/25 20.00 50.00
17 Jim Palmer/22 12.50 30.00
20 Juan Marichal/27 12.50 30.00
21 Kirby Puckett/34 75.00 150.00
22 Lou Brock/20 20.00 50.00
26 Orlando Cepeda/30 12.50 30.00
28 Phil Rizzuto/25 20.00 50.00
29 Red Schoendienst/25 12.50 30.00
32 Paul Molitor/25 12.50 30.00
34 Warren Spahn/21 30.00 60.00
35 Willie McCovey/25 20.00 50.00

2004 Timeless Treasures HOF Materials Bat
PRINT RUNS B/WN 5-50 COPIES PER
NO PRICING ON QTY OF 5 OR LESS
1 Al Kaline/25 15.00 40.00
2 Babe Ruth/50 75.00 150.00
4 Bobby Doerr/25 6.00 15.00
5 Brooks Robinson/25 10.00 25.00
6 Carl Yastrzemski/25 15.00 40.00
7 Carlton Fisk/25 10.00 25.00
8 Dave Winfield/25 8.00 20.00
10 Eddie Murray/25 15.00 40.00
11 Ernie Banks/25 10.00 25.00
13 Frank Robinson/25 10.00 25.00
18 Joe Morgan/25 8.00 20.00
19 Johnny Bench/25 15.00 40.00
21 Kirby Puckett/25 15.00 40.00
22 Lou Brock/25 10.00 25.00
23 Lou Gehrig/50 40.00 100.00
24 Luis Aparicio/25 6.00 15.00
25 Mel Ott/25 20.00 50.00
26 Orlando Cepeda/25 8.00 20.00
27 Pee Wee Reese/25 10.00 25.00
28 Phil Rizzuto/25 10.00 25.00
29 Red Schoendienst/25 8.00 20.00
30 Roberto Clemente/25 20.00 50.00
31 Roy Campanella/25 15.00 40.00
32 Paul Molitor/25 8.00 20.00
33 Ty Cobb/25 75.00 200.00
35 Willie McCovey/25 8.00 20.00
36 Willie Stargell/25 10.00 25.00

2004 Timeless Treasures HOF Materials Bat Signature
RANDOM INSERTS IN PACKS
PRINT RUNS B/WN 10-50 COPIES PER
NO PRICING ON QTY OF 10 OR LESS
1 Al Kaline/50 25.00 50.00
4 Bobby Doerr/50 10.00 25.00
5 Brooks Robinson/50 12.00 30.00
11 Ernie Banks/25 40.00 80.00
13 Frank Robinson/50 15.00 40.00
18 Joe Morgan/25 15.00 40.00
19 Johnny Bench/25 40.00 80.00
22 Lou Brock/50 15.00 40.00
24 Luis Aparicio/50 10.00 25.00
26 Orlando Cepeda/50 12.50 30.00
28 Phil Rizzuto/50 15.00 40.00
29 Red Schoendienst/50 12.50 30.00
32 Paul Molitor/25 15.00 40.00

2004 Timeless Treasures HOF Materials Jersey
PRINT RUNS B/WN 5-50 COPIES PER
NO PRICING ON QTY OF 10 OR LESS
PRIME PRINT RUNS B/WN 1-10 COPIES PER
NO PRIME PRICING DUE TO SCARCITY
RANDOM INSERTS IN PACKS
2 Babe Ruth/25 300.00 500.00
3 Bob Feller/50 6.00 15.00
4 Bobby Doerr/25 6.00 15.00
5 Brooks Robinson/50 8.00 20.00
6 Carl Yastrzemski/50 12.50 30.00
7 Carlton Fisk/50 8.00 20.00
8 Dave Winfield/50 6.00 15.00
10 Eddie Murray/25 15.00 40.00
13 Frank Robinson/25 20.00 50.00
14 Hal Newhouser/50 6.00 15.00
15 Hoyt Wilhelm/50 6.00 15.00
17 Jim Palmer/50 6.00 15.00
18 Joe Morgan/50 6.00 15.00
20 Juan Marichal/50 6.00 15.00
21 Kirby Puckett/50 10.00 25.00
22 Lou Brock/25 10.00 25.00
23 Lou Gehrig/25 60.00 150.00
24 Luis Aparicio/25 6.00 15.00
25 Mel Ott/25 20.00 50.00
27 Pee Wee Reese/50 8.00 20.00
28 Phil Rizzuto/50 8.00 20.00
30 Roberto Clemente/50 40.00 80.00
32 Paul Molitor/50 6.00 15.00
34 Warren Spahn/50 10.00 25.00
35 Willie McCovey/50 6.00 15.00
36 Willie Stargell/50 8.00 20.00

2004 Timeless Treasures HOF Materials Jersey Number
*NUMBER p/r 44: .4X TO 1X BASIC p/r 50
*NUMBER p/r 27-34: .5X TO 1.2X BASIC p/r 50
*NUMBER p/r 27-34: .4X TO 1X BASIC p/r 25
*NUMBER p/r 20-22: .6X TO 1.5X BASIC p/r 50
*NUMBER p/r 20-22: .4X TO 1X BASIC p/r 25
*NUMBER p/r 16-19: .6X TO 1.5X BASIC p/r 50
RANDOM INSERTS IN PACKS
PRINT RUNS B/WN 1-44 COPIES PER
NO PRICING ON QTY OF 14 OR LESS
3 Bob Feller/19 10.00 25.00
16 Jackie Robinson/42 30.00 60.00

2004 Timeless Treasures HOF Materials Jersey Signature
PRINT RUNS B/WN 5-50 COPIES PER
NO PRICING ON QTY OF 10 OR LESS
PRIME PRINT RUNS B/WN 1-10 COPIES PER
NO PRIME PRICING DUE TO SCARCITY
1 Al Kaline/25 25.00 50.00
4 Bobby Doerr/50 10.00 25.00
5 Brooks Robinson/25 20.00 50.00
13 Frank Robinson/50 12.00 30.00
15 Hoyt Wilhelm/25 20.00 50.00
17 Jim Palmer/50 12.50 30.00
18 Joe Morgan/25 10.00 25.00
20 Juan Marichal/50 12.50 30.00
22 Lou Brock/50 15.00 40.00
24 Luis Aparicio/50 10.00 25.00
26 Orlando Cepeda/25 10.00 25.00
28 Phil Rizzuto/50 15.00 40.00
29 Red Schoendienst/50 12.50 30.00
32 Paul Molitor/50 12.50 30.00
34 Warren Spahn/25 20.00 50.00

2004 Timeless Treasures HOF Materials Jersey Signature Number
*NUMBER p/r 25: .5X TO 1.2X BASIC p/r 50
*NUMBER p/r 25: .4X TO 1X BASIC p/r 25
PRINT RUNS B/WN 10-25 COPIES PER
NO PRICING ON QTY OF 10 OR LESS
12 Fergie Jenkins Pants/25 15.00 40.00

2004 Timeless Treasures HOF Materials Pants
PRINT RUNS B/WN 25-50 COPIES PER
1 Al Kaline/25 15.00 40.00
2 Babe Ruth/50 100.00 200.00
12 Fergie Jenkins/25 8.00 20.00
23 Lou Gehrig/50 40.00 100.00
24 Luis Aparicio/25 6.00 15.00
25 Mel Ott/25 20.00 50.00
31 Roy Campanella/25 15.00 40.00
33 Ty Cobb/25 60.00 120.00

2004 Timeless Treasures HOF Materials Pants Signature
STATED PRINT RUN 25 SERIAL #'d SETS
1 Al Kaline 30.00 80.00
12 Fergie Jenkins 15.00 40.00
24 Luis Aparicio 12.50 30.00
28 Phil Rizzuto 20.00 50.00

2004 Timeless Treasures HOF Materials Combos Bat-Jersey
PRINT RUNS B/WN 1-50 COPIES PER
PRIME PRINT RUNS B/WN 1-5 COPIES PER
NO PRIME PRICING DUE TO SCARCITY
1 Al Kaline/25 20.00 50.00
2 Babe Ruth/25 150.00 300.00
4 Bobby Doerr/25 8.00 20.00
5 Brooks Robinson/50 10.00 25.00
6 Carl Yastrzemski/50 15.00 40.00
7 Carlton Fisk/50 10.00 25.00
8 Dave Winfield/50 8.00 20.00
10 Eddie Murray/50 15.00 40.00
13 Frank Robinson/50 10.00 25.00
18 Joe Morgan/50 8.00 20.00
21 Kirby Puckett/50 15.00 40.00
22 Lou Brock/50 10.00 25.00
23 Lou Gehrig/25 100.00 200.00
24 Luis Aparicio/25 8.00 20.00
25 Mel Ott/25 40.00 80.00
27 Pee Wee Reese/50 10.00 25.00
28 Phil Rizzuto/50 10.00 25.00
29 Red Schoendienst/25 10.00 25.00
30 Roberto Clemente/50 75.00 150.00
32 Paul Molitor/50 8.00 20.00
35 Willie McCovey/50 8.00 20.00
36 Willie Stargell/50 10.00 25.00

2004 Timeless Treasures HOF Materials Combos Bat-Jersey Signature
PRINT RUNS B/WN 1-25 COPIES PER
NO PRICING ON QTY OF 10 OR LESS
PRIME PRINT RUNS B/WN 1-5 COPIES PER
NO PRIME PRICING DUE TO SCARCITY
RANDOM INSERTS IN PACKS
4 Bobby Doerr/25 15.00 40.00
5 Brooks Robinson/25 30.00 60.00
11 Ernie Banks/25 60.00 120.00
13 Frank Robinson/25 30.00 60.00
18 Joe Morgan/25 20.00 50.00
22 Lou Brock/25 30.00 60.00
24 Luis Aparicio/25 30.00 60.00
29 Red Schoendienst/25 20.00 50.00
32 Paul Molitor/25 20.00 50.00

2004 Timeless Treasures HOF Materials Combos Bat-Pants
STATED PRINT RUN 25 SERIAL #'d SETS
1 Al Kaline/25 20.00 50.00
2 Babe Ruth/25 250.00 400.00
12 F.Jenkins Fld Glv-Pants/25 10.00 25.00
23 Lou Gehrig/25 150.00 250.00
24 Luis Aparicio/25 8.00 20.00
25 Mel Ott/25 40.00 80.00
31 Roy Campanella/25 30.00 60.00
33 Ty Cobb/25 150.00 250.00

2004 Timeless Treasures HOF Materials Combos Bat-Pants Signature
STATED PRINT RUN 25 SERIAL #'d SETS
1 Al Kaline/25 50.00 120.00
12 F.Jenkins Fld Glv-Pants/25 20.00 50.00
24 Luis Aparicio/25 15.00 40.00

2004 Timeless Treasures HOF Materials Combos Jersey-Pants
PRINT RUNS B/WN 10-25 COPIES PER
NO PRICING ON QTY OF 10 OR LESS
PRIME PRINT RUNS B/WN 1-5 COPIES PER
NO PRIME PRICING DUE TO SCARCITY
RANDOM INSERTS IN PACKS
2 Babe Ruth/25 300.00 500.00
23 Lou Gehrig/25 175.00 300.00
24 Luis Aparicio/25 8.00 20.00

2004 Timeless Treasures HOF Materials Combos Jersey-Pants Signature
PRINT RUNS B/WN 5-25 COPIES PER
PRIME PRINT RUNS B/WN 1-5 COPIES PER
NO PRIME PRICING DUE TO SCARCITY
RANDOM INSERTS IN PACKS
24 Luis Aparicio/25 15.00 40.00

2004 Timeless Treasures Home Away Gamers
PRINT RUNS B/WN 5-100 COPIES PER
NO PRICING ON QTY OF 10 OR LESS
PRIME PRINT RUNS B/WN 3-5 COPIES PER
NO PRIME PRICING DUE TO SCARCITY
1 Babe Ruth Jsy-Jsy/25 500.00 800.00
3 Wade Boggs Jsy-Jsy/50 10.00 25.00
4 Tony Gwynn Jsy-Jsy/50 15.00 40.00
5 Steve Carlton Jsy-Jsy/50 8.00 20.00
7 Ryne Sandberg Jsy-Jsy/50 10.00 25.00
8 Rod Carew Jsy-Jsy/50 10.00 25.00
9 R.Henderson Jsy-Jsy/50 15.00 40.00
11 Ted Williams Jsy-Jsy/100 20.00 50.00
12 Ozzie Smith Jsy-Jsy/50 8.00 20.00
13 Mike Schmidt Jsy-Jsy/50 15.00 40.00
14 Harmon Killebrew Jsy-Jsy/50 15.00 40.00
15 George Brett Jsy-Jsy/100 8.00 20.00
16 Don Mattingly Jsy-Jsy/50 10.00 25.00
17 Dale Murphy Jsy-Jsy/50 10.00 25.00
18 Cal Ripken Jsy-Jsy/100 30.00 60.00
19 Lou Gehrig Jsy-Jsy/50 175.00 300.00
20 Nolan Ryan Jsy-Jsy/100 20.00 50.00

2004 Timeless Treasures Home Away Gamers Signature
PRINT RUNS B/WN 1-25 COPIES PER
NO PRICING ON QTY OF 10 OR LESS
5 Steve Carlton Jsy-Jsy/25 20.00 50.00
13 Mike Schmidt Jsy-Jsy/20 40.00 100.00
14 H.Killebrew Jsy-Jsy/25 30.00 80.00
16 Don Mattingly Jsy-Jsy/25 100.00 200.00
17 Dale Murphy Jsy-Jsy/25 30.00 60.00

2004 Timeless Treasures Home Away Gamers Combos
PRINT RUNS B/WN 5-100 COPIES PER
NO PRICING ON QTY OF 8 OR LESS
PRIME PRINT RUNS B/WN 3-10 COPIES PER
NO PRIME PRICING DUE TO SCARCITY
1 Babe Ruth/25 700.00 1000.00
3 Wade Boggs/50 12.50 30.00
4 Tony Gwynn/50 30.00 60.00
5 Steve Carlton/50 12.50 30.00
6 Stan Musial/25 40.00 80.00
7 Ryne Sandberg/50 12.50 30.00
8 Rod Carew/50 12.50 30.00
9 Rickey Henderson/50 12.00 30.00
11 Ted Williams/100 75.00 150.00
12 Ozzie Smith/50 20.00 50.00
13 Mike Schmidt/50 30.00 60.00
14 Harmon Killebrew/25 30.00 60.00
15 George Brett/100 12.50 30.00
16 Don Mattingly/50 10.00 25.00
17 Dale Murphy/50 12.50 30.00
18 Cal Ripken/100 40.00 80.00
19 Lou Gehrig/25 350.00 600.00
20 Nolan Ryan/100 15.00 40.00

2004 Timeless Treasures Home Run Materials
RANDOM INSERTS IN PACKS
PRINT RUNS B/WN 12-100 COPIES PER
NO PRICING ON QTY OF 12 OR LESS
1 Roger Maris Bat/61 15.00 40.00
3 H.Killebrew HR 570 Bat/75 10.00 25.00
4 H.Killebrew HR 565 Bat/75 10.00 25.00
5 Jose Canseco Bat/96 6.00 15.00
6 Alex Rodriguez Bat/100 6.00 15.00
7 Sammy Sosa Jsy/100 6.00 15.00
8 Rafael Palmeiro Jsy/25 8.00 20.00
9 Ivan Rodriguez Jsy/25 8.00 20.00

2004 Timeless Treasures Home Run Materials Signature
PRINT RUNS B/WN 9-19 COPIES PER
NO PRICING ON QTY OF 12 OR LESS
3 H.Killebrew HR 570 Bat/19 50.00 100.00
4 H.Killebrew HR 565 Bat/19 50.00 100.00

2004 Timeless Treasures Material Ink Bat
RANDOM INSERTS IN PACKS
PRINT RUNS B/WN 1-50 COPIES PER
NO PRICING ON QTY OF 10 OR LESS
1 Adam Dunn/25 10.00 25.00
2 Alan Trammell/25 15.00 40.00
4 Andre Dawson/25 15.00 40.00
5 Bo Jackson/25 50.00 100.00
7 Dale Murphy/25 20.00 50.00
12 Don Mattingly/50 20.00 50.00
20 Mark Prior/25 15.00 40.00
25 Paul O'Neill/25 30.00 60.00
29 Ron Santo/50 15.00 40.00
30 Ryne Sandberg/25 15.00 40.00
32 Tony Gwynn/25 50.00 100.00
34 Will Clark/25 20.00 50.00

2004 Timeless Treasures Material Ink Jersey
PRINT RUNS B/WN 10-100 COPIES PER
NO PRICING ON QTY OF 10 OR LESS
*PRIME p/r 25: .75X TO 2X BASIC p/r 100
*PRIME p/r 25: .6X TO 1.5X BASIC p/r 50
PRIME PRINT RUNS B/WN 1-25 COPIES PER
NO PRIME PRICING ON QTY OF 10 OR LESS
1 Adam Dunn/25 10.00 25.00
2 Alan Trammell/100 10.00 25.00
4 Andre Dawson/100 10.00 25.00
5 Bo Jackson/25 30.00 60.00
7 Dale Murphy/50 15.00 40.00
8 Darryl Strawberry/100 10.00 25.00
9 Dave Parker/25 15.00 40.00
11 Doc Gooden/100 10.00 25.00
12 Don Mattingly/50 50.00 100.00
13 Dontrelle Willis/25 20.00 50.00
15 Ivan Rodriguez/25 40.00 80.00
16 Joe Carter/25 15.00 40.00
17 Jose Canseco/25 20.00 50.00
18 Kerry Wood/15 60.00 120.00
20 Mark Prior/50 10.00 25.00
21 Mark Teixeira/25 20.00 50.00
22 Marty Marion/25 12.50 30.00
26 Rocco Baldelli/25 15.00 40.00
30 Ryne Sandberg/50 40.00 80.00
31 Ernie Banks/50 30.00 60.00
33 Vladimir Guerrero/25 20.00 50.00
34 Will Clark/50 15.00 40.00

2004 Timeless Treasures Material Ink Jersey Number
*NUMBER p/r 100: .4X TO 1X BASIC p/r 100
*NUMBER p/r 50: .4X TO 1X BASIC p/r 50
*NUMBER p/r 25: .5X TO 1.2X BASIC p/r 50
*NUMBER p/r 25: .4X TO 1X BASIC p/r 25
PRINT RUNS B/WN 1-100 COPIES PER
NO PRICING ON QTY OF 10 OR LESS
10 Deion Sanders/24 40.00 80.00
19 Mark Grace/25 10.00 25.00

2004 Timeless Treasures Material Ink Combos
PRINT RUNS B/WN 1-50 COPIES PER
NO PRICING ON QTY OF 10 OR LESS
PRIME PRINT RUNS B/WN 1-10 COPIES PER
NO PRIME PRICING DUE TO SCARCITY
1 Adam Dunn Bat-Jsy/25 30.00 60.00
2 Alan Trammell Bat-Jsy/25 20.00 50.00
4 Andre Dawson Bat-Jsy/25 20.00 50.00
5 Bo Jackson Bat-Jsy/25 60.00 120.00
7 Dale Murphy Bat-Jsy/25 30.00 60.00
12 Don Mattingly Bat-Jsy/25 100.00 200.00
17 Jose Canseco Bat-Jsy/25 30.00 60.00
30 Ryne Sandberg Bat-Jsy/25 75.00 150.00
32 Tony Gwynn Bat-Jsy/25 60.00 120.00
34 Will Clark Bat-Jsy/50 12.50 30.00

2004 Timeless Treasures Milestone Materials
PRINT RUNS B/WN 16-100 COPIES PER
*NBR p/r 35-36: .5X TO 1.2X BASIC p/r 80-82
*NBR p/r 24: .6X TO 1.5X BASIC p/r 100
NUMBER PRINT RUNS B/WN 9-36 PER
NO NUMBER PRICING ON QTY 9 OR LESS
*PRIME p/r 25: 1X TO 2.5X BASIC p/r 80-100
PRIME PRINT RUN 25 SERIAL #'d SETS
2 Roger Maris Pants/61 20.00 50.00
3 R.Henderson A's Jsy/80 6.00 15.00
4 Gaylord Perry Jsy/82 4.00 10.00
6 R.Henderson Padres Jsy/100 6.00 15.00

2004 Timeless Treasures Milestone Materials Signature
PRINT RUNS B/WN 5-82 COPIES PER
NO PRICING ON QTY OF 8 OR LESS
*NBR p/r 82: .4X TO 1X BASIC p/r 82
NUMBER PRINT RUNS B/WN 5-82 PER
NO NUMBER PRICING ON QTY 5 OR LESS
*PRIME p/r 19: .75X TO 2X BASIC p/r 82
PRIME PRINT RUNS B/WN 5-19 COPIES PER
NO PRIME PRICING ON QTY OF 5 OR LESS
4 Gaylord Perry Jsy/82 10.00 25.00

2004 Timeless Treasures Rookie Year Materials
PRINT RUNS B/WN 5-100 COPIES PER
NO PRICING ON QTY OF 5 OR LESS
PRIME PRINT RUNS B/WN 5-10 COPIES PER
NO PRIME PRICING DUE TO SCARCITY
1 Stan Musial Jsy/19 20.00 50.00
2 Yogi Berra Stripe Jsy/19 20.00 50.00
3 Yogi Berra Grey Jsy/47 10.00 25.00
4 Whitey Ford Jsy/50 10.00 25.00
5 Catfish Hunter Jsy/65 6.00 15.00
6 Johnny Bench Bat/68 6.00 15.00
7 Mike Schmidt Bat/72 8.00 20.00
8 Gary Carter Jsy/74 4.00 10.00
9 Robin Yount Jsy/74 6.00 15.00
11 Cal Ripken Bat/81 10.00 25.00
12 Kirby Puckett Bat/84 6.00 15.00
13 Roger Clemens Jsy/84 8.00 20.00
15 Gary Sheffield Jsy/89 4.00 10.00
16 Juan Gonzalez Jsy/89 4.00 10.00
17 Randy Johnson Jsy/89 6.00 15.00
18 Ivan Rodriguez Jsy/91 6.00 15.00
20 Pedro Martinez Jsy/92 6.00 15.00
21 Mike Piazza Jsy/93 6.00 15.00
22 Hideo Nomo Jsy/95 6.00 15.00
23 Hideo Nomo Pants/95 6.00 15.00
24 Alex Rodriguez Jsy/95 6.00 15.00
26 Scott Rolen Jsy/96 6.00 15.00
27 Andruw Jones Jsy/96 6.00 15.00
28 Nomar Garciaparra Jsy/97 6.00 15.00
29 Vladimir Guerrero Jsy/97 6.00 15.00
31 Alfonso Soriano Jsy/100 4.00 10.00
32 Albert Pujols White Jsy/100 12.00 30.00
33 Albert Pujols Grey Jsy/100 12.00 30.00
34 Albert Pujols Bat/100 12.00 30.00
36 Mark Prior Blue Jsy/100 6.00 15.00
37 Mark Prior Grey Jsy/100 6.00 15.00
38 Dontrelle Willis Jsy/35 10.00 25.00

2004 Timeless Treasures Rookie Year Materials Number
*NBR p/r 42-51: .5X TO 1.2X BASIC p/r 89-92
*NBR p/r 27-35: .6X TO 1.5X BASIC p/r 93-100
*NBR p/r 27-35: .5X TO 1.2X BASIC p/r 65
*NBR p/r 27-35: .4X TO 1X BASIC p/r 35
*NBR p/r 21-25: .75X TO 2X BASIC p/r 84-100
*NBR p/r 16-19: .75X TO 2X BASIC p/r 74-96
*NBR p/r 16-19: .6X TO 1.5X BASIC p/r 50
PRINT RUNS B/WN 3-51 COPIES PER
NO PRICING ON QTY OF 11 OR LESS
10 Fred Lynn Jsy/19 8.00 20.00
25 Garret Anderson Jsy/16 8.00 20.00

2004 Timeless Treasures Rookie Year Materials Signature
PRINT RUNS B/WN 1-97 COPIES PER
NO PRICING ON QTY OF 11 OR LESS
*PRIME p/r 35: .5X TO 1.2X BASIC p/r 35
*PRIME p/r 25: .75X TO 2X BASIC p/r 95-97
*PRIME p/r 22: .5X TO 1.2X BASIC p/r 22
*PRIME p/r 16: .5X TO 1.2X BASIC p/r 19
PRIME PRINT RUNS B/WN 1-35 COPIES PER
NO PRIME PRICING ON QTY OF 11 OR LESS
3 Yogi Berra Grey Jsy/19 50.00 120.00
4 Whitey Ford Jsy/19 30.00 60.00
8 Gary Carter Jsy/19 20.00 50.00
10 Fred Lynn Jsy/75 8.00 20.00
14 Lenny Dykstra Fld Glv/85 10.00 25.00
16 Juan Gonzalez Jsy/19 40.00 80.00
25 Garret Anderson Jsy/95 10.00 25.00
30 Shannon Stewart Jsy/97 8.00 20.00
36 Mark Prior Blue Jsy/22 8.00 20.00
37 Mark Prior Grey Jsy/22 8.00 20.00
38 Dontrelle Willis Jsy/35 8.00 20.00
39 Rocco Baldelli Jsy/19 8.00 20.00

2004 Timeless Treasures Rookie Year Materials Signature Number
*NBR p/r 35: .4X TO 1X BASIC p/r 35
*NBR p/r 22: .4X TO 1X BASIC p/r 22
*NBR p/r 16-19: .75X TO 2X BASIC p/r 75-95
*NBR p/r 16-19: .4X TO 1X BASIC p/r 19

PRINT RUNS B/WN 1-35 COPIES PER
NO PRICING ON QTY OF 11 OR LESS
26 Scott Rolen Jsy/17 30.00 60.00

2004 Timeless Treasures Rookie Year Materials Combos

PRINT RUNS B/WN 5-35 COPIES PER
NO PRICING ON QTY OF 8 OR LESS
*PRIME: .5X TO 1.2X BASIC
PRIME PRINT RUNS B/WN 1-35 COPIES PER
NO PRIME PRICING ON QTY OF 5 OR LESS
RANDOM INSERTS IN PACKS
22 Hideo Nomo Jsy-Pants/16 15.00 40.00
36 Mark Prior Jsy-Jsy/22 12.50 30.00
38 Dontrelle Willis Jsy-Jsy/35 10.00 25.00

2004 Timeless Treasures Rookie Year Materials Combos Signature

PRINT RUNS B/WN 1-35 COPIES PER
NO PRICING ON QTY OF 8 OR LESS
*PRIME: .5X TO 1.2X BASIC
PRIME PRINT RUNS B/WN 1-35 COPIES PER
NO PRIME PRICING ON QTY OF 5 OR LESS
36 Mark Prior Jsy-Jsy/22 10.00 25.00
38 Dontrelle Willis Jsy-Jsy/35 10.00 25.00

2004 Timeless Treasures Rookie Year Materials Dual

STATED PRINT RUN 25 SERIAL #'d SETS
PRIME PRINT RUN 10 SERIAL #'d SETS
NO PRIME PRICING DUE TO SCARCITY
RANDOM INSERTS IN PACKS
40 Clemens Jsy 30.00 60.00
Nomar Jsy
41 Pedro Jsy/Piazza Jsy 20.00 50.00
42 Piazza Jsy/Nomo Jsy 20.00 50.00
43 Pedro Jsy/Nomo Jsy 12.50 30.00
44 Berra Jsy/Ford Jsy 40.00 80.00
45 Schmidt Bat/Rolen Jsy 30.00 60.00
47 J.Gonz Jsy/I.Rod Jsy 12.50 30.00

2004 Timeless Treasures Statistical Champions

PRINT RUNS B/WN 3-100 COPIES PER
NO PRICING ON QTY OF 9 OR LESS
*NBR p/r 38-51: .4X TO 1X BASIC p/r 68
*NBR p/r 38-51: .3X TO .8X BASIC p/r 19-25
*NBR p/r 26-34: .6X TO 1.5X BASIC p/r 86-100
*NBR p/r 20-25: .75X TO 2X BASIC p/r 88-100
*NBR p/r 20-25: .4X TO 1X BASIC p/r 25
*NBR p/r 21: .3X TO .8X BASIC p/r 19
*NBR p/r 17-19: .5X TO 1.2X BASIC p/r 25
NUMBER PRINT RUNS B/WN 1-51 PER
NO NUMBER PRICES ON QTY 9 OR LESS
PRIME PRINT RUNS B/WN 5-10 COPIES PER
NO PRIME PRICING DUE TO SCARCITY
2 Stan Musial 43 BA Jsy/19 12.00 30.00
3 Ralph Kiner Bat/49 3.00 8.00
4 Stan Musial 57 BA Jsy/57 8.00 20.00
5 Ted Williams Jsy/25 25.00 60.00
6 Warren Spahn Jsy/25 4.00 10.00
7 Eddie Mathews Jsy/19 8.00 20.00
8 Roger Maris 61 HR Bat/61 10.00 25.00
9 Roger Maris 61 HR Pants/61 10.00 25.00
10 Roger Maris 61 RBI Bat/61 10.00 25.00
11 R.Maris 61 RBI Pants/61 10.00 25.00
12 Roberto Clemente Jsy/19 40.00 100.00
13 Frank Robinson Bat/66 3.00 8.00
14 Bob Gibson 68 ERA Jsy/68 3.00 8.00
15 Bob Gibson 68 K Jsy/68 3.00 8.00
16 Tom Seaver Jsy/19 5.00 12.00
18 Harmon Killebrew Pants/71 5.00 12.00
19 Mike Schmidt Jsy/74 8.00 20.00
20 Reggie Jackson Jsy/19 5.00 12.00
22 Rod Carew Hat/78 2.50 6.00
23 Jim Rice 78 HR Jsy/78 2.50 6.00
24 Jim Rice 78 RBI Jsy/78 2.50 6.00
25 Reggie Jackson Hat/80 2.50 6.00
26 Dale Murphy 82 RBI Jsy/82 4.00 10.00
27 Steve Carlton Jsy/83 2.50 6.00
28 Dale Murphy 85 HR Jsy/85 4.00 10.00
29 Wade Boggs 86 BA Jsy/86 2.50 6.00
30 Wade Boggs 87 BA Jsy/87 2.50 6.00
31 Will Clark Jsy/88 2.50 6.00
32 Nolan Ryan 89 K Jsy/89 12.00 30.00
33 Nolan Ryan 90 K Jsy/90 12.00 30.00
34 Nolan Ryan 90 K Pants/90 12.00 30.00
35 Ryne Sandberg Jsy/90 8.00 20.00
36 Roger Clemens 90 K Jsy/90 5.00 12.00
37 George Brett Jsy/90 8.00 20.00
38 R.Clemens 92 ERA Jsy/100 5.00 12.00
39 R.Clemens 96 K Jsy/100 5.00 12.00
40 Tony Gwynn Jsy/25 6.00 15.00
41 P.Martinez Expos Jsy/25 4.00 10.00
42 Greg Maddux Jsy/100 5.00 12.00
43 Juan Gonzalez Pants/25 2.50 6.00
44 Manny Ramirez Bat/25 6.00 15.00
45 N.G'parra 99 BA Jsy/100 2.50 6.00
47 N.G'parra 00 BA Jsy/100 2.50 6.00
48 Todd Helton 00 BA Jsy/25 4.00 10.00
49 Todd Helton 00 RBI Jsy/25 4.00 10.00
50 Troy Glaus Jsy/25 2.50 6.00
51 Randy Johnson 00 K Jsy/25 6.00 15.00
52 Tom Glavine Jsy/25 4.00 10.00
53 Sammy Sosa 00 HR Jsy/100 4.00 10.00
54 A.Rodriguez 01 HR Bat/100 5.00 12.00
55 Curt Schilling Jsy/25 4.00 10.00
56 Pedro Martinez 99 K Jsy/25 4.00 10.00
57 A.Rodriguez 01 HR Jsy/100 5.00 12.00
58 Mark Mulder Jsy/25 2.50 6.00
59 S.Sosa 01 RBI Jsy/100 4.00 10.00
60 Manny Ramirez Jsy/25 6.00 15.00
61 Lance Berkman Jsy/25 4.00 10.00
62 Randy Johnson 02 W Jsy/25 6.00 15.00
63 A.Rodriguez 02 HR Jsy/100 5.00 12.00
64 A.Rodriguez 02 RBI Jsy/100 5.00 12.00
65 A.Rodriguez 02 HR Bat/100 5.00 12.00
66 A.Rodriguez 02 RBI Bat/100 5.00 12.00
67 Pedro Martinez 02 K Jsy/25 4.00 10.00
68 P.Martinez 02 ERA Jsy/25 4.00 10.00
69 Sammy Sosa 02 HR Jsy/100 4.00 10.00
70 Jim Thome Jsy/25 4.00 10.00
71 A.Rodriguez 03 HR Bat/100 5.00 12.00
72 Albert Pujols Bat/100 5.00 12.00
73 A.Rodriguez 03 HR Jsy/100 5.00 12.00
74 Albert Pujols Jsy/100 5.00 12.00

2004 Timeless Treasures Statistical Champions Signature

PRINT RUNS B/WN 1-88 COPIES PER
NO PRICING ON QTY OF 10 OR LESS
*NBR p/r 47: .3X TO .8X BASIC p/r 20
*NBR p/r 32-34: .4X TO 1X BASIC p/r 19-25
*NBR p/r 22: 1.25X TO 3X BASIC p/r 88
*NBR p/r 20-25: .4X TO 1X BASIC p/r 20-25
*NBR p/r 19: .4X TO 1X BASIC p/r 19
*NBR p/r 17-19: .5X TO 1.2X BASIC p/r 20-25
NUMBER PRINT RUNS B/WN 1-47 PER
NO NUMBER PRICING ON QTY 14 OR LESS
PRIME PRINT RUNS B/WN 1-10 COPIES PER
NO PRIME PRICING DUE TO SCARCITY
3 Ralph Kiner Bat/49 10.00 25.00
6 Warren Spahn Jsy/25 40.00 80.00
13 Frank Robinson Bat/66 15.00 40.00
14 Bob Gibson 68 ERA Jsy/25 20.00 50.00
15 Bob Gibson 68 K Jsy/25 20.00 50.00
17 Harmon Killebrew Jsy/71 30.00 60.00
18 Harmon Killebrew Pants/71 30.00 60.00
19 Mike Schmidt Jsy/25 60.00 120.00
20 Reggie Jackson Jsy/25 40.00 80.00
21 Phil Niekro Jsy/50 15.00 40.00
22 Rod Carew Hat/25 20.00 50.00
23 Jim Rice 78 HR Jsy/78 10.00 25.00
24 Jim Rice 78 RBI Jsy/78 10.00 25.00
25 Reggie Jackson Hat/25 40.00 80.00
26 Dale Murphy 82 RBI Jsy/25 20.00 50.00
27 Steve Carlton Jsy/25 15.00 40.00
28 Dale Murphy 85 HR Jsy/25 20.00 50.00
29 Wade Boggs 86 BA Jsy/25 20.00 50.00
30 Wade Boggs 87 BA Jsy/25 20.00 50.00
31 Will Clark Jsy/88 12.50 30.00
32 Nolan Ryan 89 K Jsy/25 75.00 150.00
33 Nolan Ryan 90 K Jsy/25 75.00 150.00
34 Nolan Ryan 90 K Pants/25 75.00 150.00
35 Ryne Sandberg Jsy/25 30.00 60.00
40 Tony Gwynn Jsy/25 50.00 100.00
43 Juan Gonzalez Pants/19 20.00 50.00
50 Troy Glaus Jsy/25 20.00 50.00
52 Tom Glavine Jsy/20 20.00 50.00
53 S.Sosa 00 HR Jsy/25 30.00 60.00
55 Curt Schilling Jsy/25 30.00 60.00
58 Mark Mulder Jsy/25 15.00 40.00
59 S.Sosa 01 RBI Jsy/25 30.00 60.00
61 Lance Berkman Jsy/20 20.00 50.00
69 S.Sosa 02 HR Jsy/25 30.00 60.00

2004 Timeless Treasures World Series Materials

PRINT RUNS B/WN 2-100 COPIES PER
NO PRICING ON QTY OF 8 OR LESS
*PRIME p/r 19-20: 1.25X TO 3X p/r 87-100
PRIME PRINT RUNS B/WN 1-20 COPIES PER
NO PRIME PRICING ON QTY OF 1
RANDOM INSERTS IN PACKS
1 Frank Robinson Bat/61 6.00 15.00
2 Ozzie Smith Jsy/87 8.00 20.00
3 Rickey Henderson Bat/93 6.00 15.00
4 Tom Glavine Jsy/96 6.00 15.00
5 Roger Clemens Jsy/100 8.00 20.00

2004 Timeless Treasures World Series Materials Signature

1-11 PRINT RUNS B/WN 2-19 COPIES PER
CARD 14 PRINT RUN 5 SERIAL #'d COPIES
NO CARD 14 PRICING DUE TO SCARCITY
PRIME PRINT RUNS B/WN 9-10 COPIES PER
NO PRIME PRICING DUE TO SCARCITY
1 Frank Robinson Bat/19 30.00 60.00
4 Tom Glavine Jsy/19 30.00 60.00

2005 Timeless Treasures

COMMON ACTIVE .60 1.50
COMMON RETIRED .60 1.50
COMMON RC .60 1.50
STATED PRINT RUN 799 SERIAL #'d SETS
1 David Ortiz 1.50 4.00
2 Derek Jeter 4.00 10.00
3 Edgar Renteria .60 1.50
4 Paul Molitor 1.50 4.00
5 Jeff Bagwell 1.00 2.50
6 Melvin Mora .60 1.50
7 Bobby Crosby .60 1.50
8 Cal Ripken 5.00 12.00
9 Hank Blalock .60 1.50
10 Hideo Nomo Rays 1.50 4.00
11 Gary Sheffield .60 1.50
12 Alfonso Soriano 1.00 2.50
13 Carl Crawford 1.00 2.50
14 Paul Konerko 1.00 2.50
15 Jim Edmonds 1.00 2.50
16 Garret Anderson .60 1.50
17 Lance Berkman 1.00 2.50
18 Javy Lopez .60 1.50
19 Tony Gwynn 2.00 5.00
20 Mark Mulder .60 1.50
21 Sammy Sosa 1.50 4.00
22 Roger Clemens Yanks 2.00 5.00
23 Mark Teixeira 1.00 2.50
24 Miguel Cabrera 1.50 4.00
25 Jim Thome 1.00 2.50
26 Mike Piazza Dgr 1.50 4.00
27 Vladimir Guerrero 1.00 2.50
28 Austin Kearns .60 1.50
29 Rod Carew 1.00 2.50
30 Ken Griffey Jr. 3.00 8.00
31 Mike Piazza Mets 1.50 4.00
32 David Wright 1.25 3.00
33 Jason Varitek 1.50 4.00
34 Kerry Wood .60 1.50
35 Frank Thomas 1.50 4.00
36 Mark Prior 1.00 2.50
37 Mike Mussina O's 1.00 2.50
38 Curt Schilling Phils 1.00 2.50
39 Greg Maddux Cubs 2.00 5.00
40 Miguel Tejada 1.00 2.50
41 Tom Seaver 1.00 2.50
42 Mariano Rivera 2.00 5.00
43 Jason Giambi .60 1.50
44 Roy Oswalt 1.00 2.50
45 Pedro Martinez 1.00 2.50
46 Jeff Niemann RC 1.50 4.00
47 Tom Glavine 1.00 2.50
48 Torii Hunter .60 1.50
49 Scott Rolen 1.00 2.50
50 Curt Schilling Sox 1.00 2.50
51 Randy Johnson 1.50 4.00
52 C.C. Sabathia 1.00 2.50
53 Rafael Palmeiro O's 1.00 2.50
54 Jake Peavy .60 1.50
55 Hideki Matsui 2.50 6.00
56 Ichiro Suzuki 2.00 5.00
57 Johan Santana 1.00 2.50
58 Todd Helton 1.00 2.50
59 Justin Verlander RC 6.00 15.00
60 Kazuo Matsui .60 1.50
61 Rafael Palmeiro Rgr 1.00 2.50
62 Sean Casey .60 1.50
63 Nolan Ryan 5.00 12.00
64 Magglio Ordonez 1.00 2.50
65 Craig Biggio 1.00 2.50
66 Vernon Wells .60 1.50
67 Manny Ramirez 1.50 4.00
68 Aramis Ramirez .60 1.50
69 Omar Vizquel 1.00 2.50
70 Eric Gagne .60 1.50
71 Troy Glaus .60 1.50
72 Carlton Fisk 1.00 2.50
73 Victor Martinez 1.00 2.50
74 Adrian Beltre 1.50 4.00
75 Barry Zito 1.00 2.50
76 Josh Beckett .60 1.50
77 Michael Young .60 1.50
78 Eric Chavez .60 1.50
79 Hideo Nomo Sox 1.50 4.00
80 Andruw Jones .60 1.50
81 Ivan Rodriguez 1.00 2.50
82 Don Mattingly 3.00 8.00
83 Larry Walker 1.00 2.50
84 Phil Humber RC 1.50 4.00
85 Juan Gonzalez .60 1.50
86 Tim Hudson 1.00 2.50
87 Alex Rodriguez 2.00 5.00
88 Greg Maddux Braves 2.00 5.00
89 J.D. Drew .60 1.50
90 Shawn Green .60 1.50
91 Roger Clemens Astros 2.00 5.00
92 Nomar Garciaparra 1.00 2.50
93 Andy Pettitte 1.00 2.50
94 Khalil Greene .60 1.50
95 Mike Schmidt 2.50 6.00
96 Carlos Beltran 1.00 2.50
97 Mike Mussina Yanks 1.00 2.50
98 Ben Sheets .60 1.50
99 Chipper Jones 1.50 4.00
100 Albert Pujols 2.00 5.00

2005 Timeless Treasures Bronze

*BRONZE: .6X TO 1.5X BASIC ACTIVE
*BRONZE: .6X TO 1.5X BASIC RETIRED
*BRONZE: .6X TO 1.5X BASIC RC's
STATED PRINT RUN 100 SERIAL #'d SETS

2005 Timeless Treasures Gold

*GOLD: 2X TO 5X BASIC ACTIVE
*GOLD: 2X TO 5X BASIC RETIRED
STATED PRINT RUN 25 SERIAL #'d SETS
NO RC YR PRICING DUE TO SCARCITY

2005 Timeless Treasures Silver

*SILVER: 1.25X TO 3X BASIC ACTIVE
*SILVER: 1.25X TO 3X BASIC RETIRED
*SILVER: 1X TO 2.5X BASIC RC's
STATED PRINT RUN 50 SERIAL #'d SETS

2005 Timeless Treasures HOF Silver

STATED PRINT RUN 500 SERIAL #'d SETS
*GOLD: 1.5X TO 4X BASIC
GOLD PRINT RUN 25 SERIAL #'d SETS
PLATINUM PRINT RUN 1 SERIAL #'d SET
NO PLATINUM PRICING DUE TO SCARCITY
RANDOM INSERTS IN PACKS
1 Pee Wee Reese 1.25 3.00
2 Red Schoendienst 1.25 3.00
3 Harmon Killebrew 2.00 5.00
4 Hack Wilson 1.25 3.00
5 Brooks Robinson 1.25 3.00
6 Stan Musial 3.00 8.00
7 Al Simmons 1.25 3.00
8 Carl Yastrzemski 2.50 6.00
9 Ted Williams 4.00 10.00
10 Phil Rizzuto 1.25 3.00
11 Luis Aparicio 1.25 3.00
12 Bobby Doerr 1.25 3.00
13 Bob Lemon 1.25 3.00
14 Ernie Banks 2.00 5.00
15 Ralph Kiner 1.25 3.00
16 Whitey Ford 1.25 3.00
17 Duke Snider 1.25 3.00
18 Willie McCovey 1.25 3.00
19 Bob Feller 1.25 3.00
20 Mike Schmidt 3.00 8.00
21 Roberto Clemente 5.00 12.00
22 Jim Palmer 1.25 3.00
23 Enos Slaughter 1.25 3.00
24 Willie Mays 4.00 10.00
25 Willie Stargell 1.25 3.00
26 Frank Robinson 1.25 3.00
27 Carl Hubbell 1.25 3.00
28 Reggie Jackson 1.25 3.00
29 Warren Spahn 1.25 3.00
30 Orlando Cepeda 1.25 3.00
31 Hoyt Wilhelm 1.25 3.00
32 Sandy Koufax 4.00 10.00
33 Hal Newhouser 1.25 3.00
34 Nolan Ryan 6.00 15.00
35 George Brett 4.00 10.00
36 Bill Dickey .75 2.00
37 Catfish Hunter 1.25 3.00
38 Frankie Frisch 1.25 3.00
39 Nellie Fox 1.25 3.00
40 Lou Boudreau 1.25 3.00
41 Hank Greenberg 2.00 5.00
42 Burleigh Grimes 1.25 3.00
43 Johnny Bench 2.00 5.00
44 Hank Aaron 4.00 10.00
45 Joe Cronin .75 2.00
46 Fergie Jenkins 1.25 3.00
47 Luke Appling 1.25 3.00
48 Yogi Berra 2.00 5.00
49 Early Wynn 1.25 3.00
50 Al Kaline 2.00 5.00

2005 Timeless Treasures Signature Bronze

OVERALL AU-GU'S ONE PER PACK
PRINT RUNS B/WN 10-100 COPIES PER
NO PRICING ON QTY OF 10
3 Edgar Renteria/50 8.00 20.00
4 Paul Molitor/100 6.00 15.00
7 Bobby Crosby/25 10.00 25.00
8 Cal Ripken/25 60.00 150.00
9 Hank Blalock/50 8.00 20.00
11 Gary Sheffield/50 12.50 30.00
12 Alfonso Soriano/50 8.00 20.00
14 Paul Konerko/50 12.50 30.00
15 Jim Edmonds/50 12.50 30.00
16 Garret Anderson/50 8.00 20.00
19 Tony Gwynn/100 20.00 50.00
20 Mark Mulder/100 10.00 25.00
23 Mark Teixeira/50 12.50 30.00
24 Miguel Cabrera/50 20.00 50.00
28 Austin Kearns/50 5.00 12.00
29 Rod Carew/100 10.00 25.00
32 David Wright/25 40.00 80.00
34 Kerry Wood/50 8.00 20.00
36 Mark Prior/100 10.00 25.00
41 Tom Seaver/100 25.00 60.00
44 Roy Oswalt/25 10.00 25.00
46 Jeff Niemann/100 6.00 15.00
48 Torii Hunter/50 8.00 20.00
49 Scott Rolen/50 12.50 30.00
52 C.C. Sabathia/25 10.00 25.00
53 Rafael Palmeiro O's/25 30.00 60.00
57 Johan Santana/50 10.00 25.00
59 Justin Verlander/100 30.00 80.00
61 Rafael Palmeiro Rgr/25 30.00 60.00
62 Sean Casey/25 10.00 25.00
63 Nolan Ryan/100 30.00 80.00
64 Magglio Ordonez/50 8.00 20.00
65 Craig Biggio/50 12.50 30.00
66 Vernon Wells/25 10.00 25.00
67 Manny Ramirez/25 30.00 60.00
69 Omar Vizquel/50 20.00 50.00
72 Carlton Fisk/100 10.00 25.00
73 Victor Martinez/50 8.00 20.00
74 Adrian Beltre/50 8.00 20.00
75 Barry Zito/50 8.00 20.00
76 Josh Beckett/25 15.00 40.00
77 Michael Young/50 8.00 20.00
78 Eric Chavez/50 8.00 20.00
82 Don Mattingly/100 30.00 60.00
84 Phil Humber/100 8.00 20.00
85 Juan Gonzalez/50 8.00 20.00
86 Tim Hudson Braves/50 12.50 30.00
90 Shawn Green/25 15.00 40.00
95 Mike Schmidt/100 20.00 50.00
98 Ben Sheets/25 6.00 15.00
99 Chipper Jones/25 50.00 100.00

2005 Timeless Treasures Signature Gold

*GOLD p/r 25: .6X TO 1.5X BRZ p/r 100
OVERALL AU-GU'S ONE PER PACK
PRINT RUNS B/WN 3-25 COPIES PER
NO PRICING ON QTY OF 10 OR LESS
NO RC YR PRICING ON QTY OF 25

2005 Timeless Treasures Signature Silver

*SILV p/r 50: .5X TO 1.2X BRZ p/r 100
*SILV p/r 50: .5X TO 1.2X BRZ RC YR p/r 100
*SILV p/r 25: .5X TO 1.2X BRZ p/r 50
OVERALL AU-GU'S ONE PER PACK
PRINT RUNS B/WN 5-50 COPIES PER
NO PRICING ON QTY OF 10 OR LESS

2005 Timeless Treasures Award Materials Number

*NBR p/r 20-29: .6X TO 1.5X YR p/r 72-99
*NBR p/r 16-19: .75X TO 2X YR p/r 72-99
*NBR p/r 16-19: .5X TO 1.2X YR p/r 20
OVERALL AU-GU'S ONE PER PACK
PRINT RUNS B/WN 1-29 COPIES PER
NO PRICING ON QTY OF 12 OR LESS

2005 Timeless Treasures Award Materials Year

OVERALL AU-GU'S ONE PER PACK
PRINT RUNS B/WN 1-99 COPIES PER
NO PRICING ON QTY OF 5 OR LESS
1 Lou Boudreau Jsy/48 8.00 20.00
2 Roger Maris Pants/61 15.00 40.00
6 Johnny Bench Jsy/72 6.00 15.00
9 Jim Palmer Pants/76 4.00 10.00
10 Rod Carew Jsy/77 6.00 15.00
12 Mike Schmidt Jsy/81 8.00 20.00
13 Robin Yount Jsy/89 6.00 15.00
14 Dale Murphy Jsy/83 6.00 15.00
15 Roger Clemens Jsy/86 6.00 15.00
16 Cal Ripken Jsy/91 12.50 30.00
17 Tom Glavine Jsy/91 4.00 10.00
18 Frank Thomas Jsy/94 4.00 10.00
19 Jeff Bagwell Pants/94 4.00 10.00
20 Randy Johnson Jsy/95 4.00 10.00
21 Pedro Martinez Jsy/97 4.00 10.00
22 Ivan Rodriguez Jsy/99 4.00 10.00
23 Jason Giambi Jsy/20 5.00 12.00
25 Miguel Tejada Jsy/20 5.00 12.00

2005 Timeless Treasures Award Materials Signature Year

PRINT RUNS B/WN 1-25 COPIES PER
NO PRICING ON QTY OF 5 OR LESS
SIG NBR PRINT RUN B/WN 1-5 COPIES PER
NO SIG NBR PRICING DUE TO SCARCITY
SIG PRIME PRINT B/WN 1-5 COPIES PER
NO SIG PRIME PRICING DUE TO SCARCITY
OVERALL AU-GU'S ONE PER PACK
6 Johnny Bench Jsy/25 30.00 60.00
9 Jim Palmer Pants/25 12.50 30.00
10 Rod Carew Jsy/25 20.00 50.00
12 Mike Schmidt Jsy/25 20.00 50.00
14 Dale Murphy Jsy/25 20.00 50.00

2005 Timeless Treasures Game Day Materials

OVERALL AU-GU'S ONE PER PACK
PRINT RUNS B/WN 5-100 COPIES PER
NO PRICING ON QTY OF 10 OR LESS
1 Rod Carew Hat/25 10.00 25.00
2 Kirby Puckett Bat/100 6.00 15.00
5 Nellie Fox Bat/25 12.50 30.00
6 Vladimir Guerrero Fld Glv/25 6.00 15.00
7 Tony Gwynn Jsy/100 6.00 15.00
8 Rickey Henderson Bat/100 6.00 15.00
9 David Ortiz Hat/100 4.00 10.00
10 Carlos Beltran Jsy/50 4.00 10.00

2005 Timeless Treasures Game Day Materials Signatures

OVERALL AU-GU'S ONE PER PACK
PRINT RUNS B/WN 3-25 COPIES PER
NO PRICING ON QTY OF 10 OR LESS
7 Tony Gwynn Jsy/25 30.00 60.00

2005 Timeless Treasures Gamers NY

OVERALL AU-GU'S ONE PER PACK
STATED PRINT RUN 25 SERIAL #'d SETS
1 Jim Thorpe Jsy-Jsy/25 175.00 300.00
2 Willie Mays Jsy-Pants/25 50.00 100.00
3 Nolan Ryan Bat-Jsy/25 40.00 80.00

2005 Timeless Treasures Gamers NY Signatures

OVERALL AU-GU'S ONE PER PACK
STATED PRINT RUN 25 SERIAL #'d SETS
2 Willie Mays Jsy-Pants/25 150.00 300.00
3 Nolan Ryan Bat-Jsy/25 125.00 200.00

2005 Timeless Treasures HOF Materials Bat

*BAT p/r 50: .5X TO 1.2X JSY p/r 100
*BAT p/r 50: .4X TO 1X JSY p/r 50
*BAT p/r 50: .3X TO .8X JSY p/r 25
*BAT p/r 25: .6X TO 1.5X JSY p/r 100
*BAT p/r 25: .5X TO 1.2X JSY p/r 50
OVERALL AU-GU'S ONE PER PACK
PRINT RUNS B/WN 5-50 COPIES PER
NO PRICING ON QTY OF 5
1 Pee Wee Reese/25 10.00 25.00
4 Hack Wilson/50 15.00 40.00
9 Ted Williams/50 20.00 50.00
11 Luis Aparicio/25 6.00 15.00
12 Bobby Doerr/25 6.00 15.00
15 Ralph Kiner/25 10.00 25.00
21 Roberto Clemente/50 40.00 80.00
26 Frank Robinson/50 5.00 12.00
30 Orlando Cepeda/50 5.00 12.00
39 Nellie Fox/50 10.00 25.00
50 Al Kaline/50 8.00 20.00

2005 Timeless Treasures HOF Materials Combos

*COMBO p/r 25: .75X TO 2X JSY p/r 100
*COMBO p/r 25: .6X TO 1.5X JSY p/r 50
*COMBO p/r 25: .5X TO 1.2X JSY p/r 25
PRINT RUNS B/WN 1-25 COPIES PER
NO PRICING ON QTY OF 10 OR LESS
PRIME PRINT RUNS B/WN 1-5 COPIES PER
NO PRIME PRICING DUE TO SCARCITY
OVERALL AU-GU'S ONE PER PACK
9 Ted Williams Bat-Jsy/25 25.00 60.00
24 Willie Mays Bat-Jsy/25 50.00 100.00

2005 Timeless Treasures HOF Materials Jersey

PRINT RUNS B/WN 1-100 COPIES PER
NO PRICING ON QTY OF 5 OR LESS
PRIME PRINT RUN B/WN 1-5 COPIES PER
NO PRIME PRICING DUE TO SCARCITY
OVERALL AU-GU'S ONE PER PACK
3 Harmon Killebrew/100 6.00 15.00
5 Brooks Robinson/50 8.00 20.00
6 Stan Musial/100 12.50 30.00
8 Carl Yastrzemski/100 8.00 20.00
9 Ted Williams/100 15.00 40.00
14 Ernie Banks/100 6.00 15.00
16 Whitey Ford/100 6.00 15.00
17 Duke Snider/25 10.00 25.00
18 Willie McCovey/25 10.00 25.00
20 Mike Schmidt/50 10.00 25.00
22 Jim Palmer/25 6.00 15.00
23 Enos Slaughter/50 8.00 20.00
24 Willie Mays/100 10.00 25.00
25 Willie Stargell/50 8.00 20.00
28 Reggie Jackson/25 10.00 25.00
29 Warren Spahn/25 10.00 25.00
31 Hoyt Wilhelm/50 5.00 12.00
32 Sandy Koufax/25 20.00 50.00
33 Hal Newhouser/50 5.00 12.00
34 Nolan Ryan/50 12.50 30.00
35 George Brett/50 10.00 25.00
37 Catfish Hunter/25 10.00 25.00
38 Frankie Frisch Jkt/50 10.00 25.00
40 Lou Boudreau/25 10.00 25.00
43 Johnny Bench/50 8.00 20.00
44 Hank Aaron/100 15.00 40.00
45 Joe Cronin/50 8.00 20.00
49 Early Wynn/50 8.00 20.00

2005 Timeless Treasures HOF Materials Jersey Number

*NBR p/r 44: .5X TO 1.2X JSY p/r 100
*NBR p/r 44: .3X TO .8X JSY p/r 25
*NBR p/r 20-34: .6X TO 1.5X JSY p/r 100
*NBR p/r 20-34: .5X TO 1.2X JSY p/r 50
*NBR p/r 20-34: .4X TO 1X JSY p/r 25
*NBR p/r 16: .75X TO 2X JSY p/r 100
*NBR p/r 16: .6X TO 1.5X JSY p/r 50
OVERALL AU-GU'S ONE PER PACK
PRINT RUNS B/WN 1-44 COPIES PER
NO PRICING ON QTY OF 14 OR LESS
32 Sandy Koufax/32 75.00 150.00

2005 Timeless Treasures HOF Materials Pants

*PANTS p/r 50: .5X TO 1.2X JSY p/r 100
*PANTS p/r 50: .4X TO 1X JSY p/r 50
*PANTS p/r 50: .3X TO .8X JSY p/r 25
*PANTS p/r 25: .4X TO 1X JSY p/r 25
OVERALL AU-GU'S ONE PER PACK
PRINT RUNS B/WN 1-50 COPIES PER
NO PRICING ON QTY OF 11 OR LESS
12 Bobby Doerr/50 5.00 12.00
19 Bob Feller/25 10.00 25.00
30 Orlando Cepeda/50 5.00 12.00
42 Burleigh Grimes/50 30.00 60.00
46 Fergie Jenkins/50 5.00 12.00

2005 Timeless Treasures HOF Materials Signature Bat

*BAT p/r 25: .4X TO 1X JSY p/r 25
OVERALL AU-GU'S ONE PER PACK
PRINT RUNS B/WN 1-25 COPIES PER
NO PRICING ON QTY OF 5 OR LESS
11 Luis Aparicio/25 12.50 30.00
12 Bobby Doerr/25 12.50 30.00
15 Ralph Kiner/25 20.00 50.00
24 Willie Mays/25 150.00 250.00
26 Frank Robinson/25 12.50 30.00
30 Orlando Cepeda/25 12.50 30.00
50 Al Kaline/25 30.00 80.00

2005 Timeless Treasures HOF Materials Signature Combos

*COMBO p/r 25: .5X TO 1.2X JSY p/r 25
PRINT RUNS B/WN 1-25 COPIES PER
NO PRICING ON QTY OF 10 OR LESS
PRIME PRINT RUNS B/WN 1-5 COPIES PER
NO PRIME PRICING DUE TO SCARCITY
OVERALL AU-GU'S ONE PER PACK
6 Stan Musial Bat-Jsy/25 60.00 120.00
12 Bobby Doerr Bat-Pants/25 15.00 40.00
24 Willie Mays Bat-Jsy/25 175.00 300.00
30 O.Cepeda Bat-Pants/25 15.00 40.00

2005 Timeless Treasures HOF Materials Signature Jersey

PRINT RUNS B/WN 1-25 COPIES PER
NO PRICING ON QTY OF 5 OR LESS
PRIME PRINT RUN B/WN 1-5 COPIES PER
NO PRIME PRICING DUE TO SCARCITY
OVERALL AU-GU'S ONE PER PACK
3 Harmon Killebrew/25 40.00 80.00
5 Brooks Robinson/25 30.00 60.00
6 Stan Musial/25 40.00 80.00
17 Duke Snider/25 20.00 50.00
18 Willie McCovey/25 25.00 60.00
20 Mike Schmidt/25 25.00 60.00
22 Jim Palmer/25 12.50 30.00
24 Willie Mays/25 150.00 250.00
34 Nolan Ryan/25 60.00 120.00
43 Johnny Bench/25 20.00 50.00

2005 Timeless Treasures HOF Materials Signature Jersey Number

*NBR p/r 44: .3X TO .8X JSY p/r 25
*NBR p/r 20-34: .4X TO 1X JSY p/r 25
OVERALL AU-GU'S ONE PER PACK
PRINT RUNS B/WN 1-44 COPIES PER
NO PRICING ON QTY OF 11 OR LESS
16 Whitey Ford/16 30.00 60.00
24 Willie Mays/24 150.00 250.00

2005 Timeless Treasures HOF Materials Signature Pants

*PANTS p/r 25: .4X TO 1X JSY p/r 25
OVERALL AU-GU'S ONE PER PACK
PRINT RUNS B/WN 1-50 COPIES PER
NO PRICING ON QTY OF 11 OR LESS
12 Bobby Doerr/50 10.00 25.00
19 Bob Feller/25 20.00 50.00
24 Willie Mays/25 150.00 250.00
30 Orlando Cepeda/25 12.50 30.00
46 Fergie Jenkins/25 12.50 30.00

2005 Timeless Treasures Home Road Gamers Duos

PRINT RUNS B/WN 1-100 COPIES PER
NO PRICING ON QTY OF 5 OR LESS
PRIME PRINT RUNS B/WN 1-10 COPIES PER
NO PRIME PRICING DUE TO SCARCITY
OVERALL AU-GU'S ONE PER PACK
3 Babe Ruth Jsy-Jsy/25 300.00 500.00
4 Paul Molitor Jsy-Pants/100 5.00 12.00
7 Ivan Rodriguez Jsy-Jsy/100 5.00 12.00
9 Ted Williams Jsy-Jsy/25 50.00 100.00
10 Andre Dawson Jsy-Jsy/25 8.00 20.00
11 Darryl Strawberry Jsy-Jsy/25 8.00 20.00
14 Ernie Banks Jsy-Jsy/25 15.00 40.00
15 Jim Edmonds Jsy-Jsy/25 6.00 15.00
16 Bo Jackson Jsy-Jsy/25 12.50 30.00
17 Mark Grace Jsy-Jsy/100 8.00 20.00
18 Albert Pujols Jsy-Jsy/100 10.00 25.00
19 Tony Gwynn Jsy-Jsy/100 8.00 20.00
20 Cal Ripken Jsy-Jsy/100 10.00 25.00
21 Chipper Jones Jsy-Jsy/50 6.00 15.00
23 Don Mattingly Jsy-Jsy/100 10.00 25.00
24 Willie Mays Jsy-Jsy/25 50.00 100.00
25 Tony Oliva Jsy-Jsy/50 6.00 15.00
28 Reggie Jackson Jsy-Jsy/100 8.00 20.00
29 Rod Carew Jsy-Jsy/100 8.00 20.00
30 Harmon Killebrew Jsy-Jsy/25 12.50 30.00
32 N.Ryan Astros Jsy-Jsy/100 12.50 30.00
33 Eddie Murray Jsy-Pants/100 8.00 20.00
35 R.Henderson Jsy-Jsy/100 8.00 20.00
36 Jim Rice Jsy-Jsy/50 6.00 15.00
37 Hoyt Wilhelm Jsy-Jsy/50 6.00 15.00
38 Curt Schilling Jsy-Jsy/100 5.00 12.00
42 Greg Maddux Jsy-Jsy/100 8.00 20.00
43 Dennis Eckersley Jsy-Jsy/50 6.00 15.00
44 W.McCovey Jsy-Pants/100 8.00 20.00
45 Willie Stargell Jsy-Jsy/50 10.00 25.00
46 Mike Mussina Jsy-Pants/50 10.00 25.00
47 Gary Carter Jsy-Jsy/50 10.00 25.00
48 Dale Murphy Jsy-Jsy/50 10.00 25.00
49 Mike Piazza Jsy-Jsy/50 6.00 15.00
50 Jim Palmer Jsy-Pants/100 5.00 12.00

2005 Timeless Treasures Home Road Gamers Trios

*TRIO p/r 100: .6X TO 1.5X DUO p/r 100
*TRIO p/r 50: .75X TO 2X DUO p/r 100
*TRIO p/r 50: .6X TO 1.5X DUO p/r 50
*TRIO p/r 25: .75X TO 2X DUO p/r 50
*TRIO p/r 25: .6X TO 1.5X DUO p/r 25
PRINT RUNS B/WN 1-100 COPIES PER
NO PRICING ON QTY OF 10 OR LESS
PRIME PRINT RUNS B/WN 1-10 COPIES PER
NO PRIME PRICING DUE TO SCARCITY
OVERALL AU-GU'S ONE PER PACK
3 Babe Ruth Bat-Jsy-Jsy/25 150.00 300.00
9 Ted Williams Bat-Jsy-Jsy/25 75.00 150.00
24 Willie Mays Bat-Jsy-Jsy/25 60.00 120.00

2005 Timeless Treasures Home Road Gamers Signature Duos

OVERALL AU-GU'S ONE PER PACK
PRINT RUNS B/WN 1-25 COPIES PER
NO PRICING ON QTY OF 10 OR LESS
4 Paul Molitor Jsy-Pants/25 15.00 40.00
11 Darryl Strawberry Jsy-Jsy/25 15.00 40.00
17 Mark Grace Jsy-Jsy/25 30.00 60.00
19 Tony Gwynn Jsy-Jsy/25 40.00 80.00
23 Don Mattingly Jsy-Jsy/25 25.00 60.00
25 Tony Oliva Jsy-Jsy/25 15.00 40.00
29 Rod Carew Jsy-Jsy/25 30.00 60.00
30 Harmon Killebrew Jsy-Jsy/25 50.00 100.00
36 Jim Rice Jsy-Jsy/25 15.00 40.00
43 Dennis Eckersley Jsy-Jsy/25 15.00 40.00
44 W.McCovey Jsy-Pants/25 30.00 60.00
47 Gary Carter Jsy-Jsy/25 15.00 40.00
48 Dale Murphy Jsy-Jsy/25 30.00 60.00
50 Jim Palmer Jsy-Pants/25 15.00 40.00

2005 Timeless Treasures Home Road Gamers Signature Trios

*SIG TRIOS: .5X TO 1.2X SIG DUOS
PRINT RUNS B/WN 1-25 COPIES PER
NO PRICING ON QTY OF 10 OR LESS
PRIME PRINT RUN B/WN 1-5 COPIES PER
NO PRIME PRICING DUE TO SCARCITY
OVERALL AU-GU'S ONE PER PACK

2005 Timeless Treasures Home Run Materials

OVERALL AU-GU'S ONE PER PACK
PRINT RUNS B/WN 1-100 COPIES PER
NO PRICING ON QTY OF 10 OR LESS
1 Ernie Banks Bat/60 8.00 20.00
2 Roger Maris Bat/61 15.00 40.00
4 Johnny Bench Pants/71 6.00 15.00
5 Harmon Killebrew Bat/75 6.00 15.00
6 Jose Canseco Bat/25 10.00 25.00
8 Sammy Sosa Jsy/100 4.00 10.00
9 Jim Thome Jsy/50 5.00 12.00
10 Rafael Palmeiro Jsy/50 5.00 12.00

2005 Timeless Treasures Home Run Materials Signature

OVERALL AU-GU'S ONE PER PACK
PRINT RUNS B/WN 1-25 COPIES PER
NO PRICING ON QTY OF 10 OR LESS
1 Ernie Banks Bat/25 40.00 80.00
4 Johnny Bench Pants/25 40.00 80.00
5 Harmon Killebrew Bat/25 50.00 100.00

2005 Timeless Treasures Material Ink Combos

*COMBO p/r 25: .6X TO 1.5X JSY p/r 50
*COMBO p/r 25: .5X TO 1.2X JSY p/r 25
PRINT RUNS B/WN 1-25 COPIES PER
NO PRICING ON QTY OF 10 OR LESS
PRIME PRINT RUNS B/WN 1-5 COPIES PER
NO PRIME PRICING DUE TO SCARCITY
OVERALL AU-GU'S ONE PER PACK
37 Miguel Cabrera Bat-Jsy/25 40.00 80.00

2005 Timeless Treasures Material Ink Jersey

PRINT RUNS B/WN 1-50 COPIES PER
NO PRICING ON QTY OF 10 OR LESS
2 Fred Lynn/50 10.00 25.00
3 Dale Murphy/50 15.00 40.00
4 Paul Molitor/50 10.00 25.00
5 Alan Trammell/50 10.00 25.00
8 Gary Carter/50 10.00 25.00
10 Andre Dawson/50 10.00 25.00
11 Luis Aparicio/50 10.00 25.00
14 Darryl Strawberry/50 10.00 25.00
18 Kirk Gibson/50 10.00 25.00
20 Don Sutton/25 12.50 30.00
23 Don Mattingly Jkt/25 40.00 80.00
24 Tony Perez/50 10.00 25.00
27 Carlton Fisk/25 20.00 50.00
29 Fred McGriff/25 20.00 50.00
30 John Kruk/25 40.00 80.00
32 Dwight Evans/50 10.00 25.00
33 Gary Sheffield/25 10.00 25.00
34 Bo Jackson/25 50.00 100.00
36 Gaylord Perry/50 10.00 25.00
39 Dave Parker/25 12.50 30.00
42 Harmon Killebrew/50 30.00 60.00
43 Dennis Eckersley/25 12.50 30.00
44 Willie McCovey/25 20.00 50.00
46 Luis Tiant/50 10.00 25.00
48 Mark Grace/25 20.00 50.00

2005 Timeless Treasures Material Ink Jersey Number

*NBR p/r 36-44: .4X TO 1X JSY p/r 50
*NBR p/r 36-44: .3X TO .8X JSY p/r 25
*NBR p/r 20-29: .5X TO 1.2X JSY p/r 50
*NBR p/r 20-29: .4X TO 1X JSY p/r 25
*NBR p/r 15-19: .6X TO 1.5X JSY p/r 50
*NBR p/r 15-19: .5X TO 1.2X JSY p/r 25
OVERALL AU-GU'S ONE PER PACK
PRINT RUNS B/WN 1-44 COPIES PER
NO PRICING ON QTY OF 11 OR LESS
22 Mark Prior/22 15.00 40.00
28 Jim Edmonds/15 12.50 30.00
40 Mark Teixeira/23 10.00 25.00

2005 Timeless Treasures Milestone Materials Number

*NBR p/r 21-31: .4X TO 1X JSY p/r 25
*NBR p/r 19: .5X TO 1.2X JSY p/r 25
OVERALL AU-GU'S ONE PER PACK
PRINT RUNS B/WN 1-31 COPIES PER
NO PRICING ON QTY OF 12 OR LESS

2005 Timeless Treasures Milestone Materials Year

PRINT RUNS B/WN 10-25 COPIES PER
NO PRICING ON QTY OF 10
PRIME PRINT RUNS B/WN 1-10 COPIES PER
NO PRIME PRICING DUE TO SCARCITY
OVERALL AU-GU'S ONE PER PACK
1 Roger Maris Pants/25 20.00 50.00
2 Nolan Ryan Jsy/25 15.00 40.00
5 Steve Garvey Jsy/25 6.00 15.00
6 Wade Boggs Jsy/25 10.00 25.00
7 Tony Gwynn Jsy/25 10.00 25.00
8 Sammy Sosa Jsy/25 6.00 15.00
9 Randy Johnson Jsy/25 6.00 15.00
10 Greg Maddux Jsy/25 10.00 25.00

2005 Timeless Treasures Milestone Materials Signature Year

PRINT RUNS B/WN 1-25 COPIES PER
NO PRICING ON QTY OF 10 OR LESS
NBR PRINT RUNS B/WN 1-10 COPIES PER
NO NBR PRICING DUE TO SCARCITY
PRIME PRINT RUNS B/WN 1-10 COPIES PER
NO PRIME PRICING DUE TO SCARCITY
OVERALL AU-GU'S ONE PER PACK

2 Nolan Ryan Jsy/25 60.00 120.00
5 Steve Garvey Jsy/25 12.50 30.00
7 Tony Gwynn Jsy/25 20.00 50.00

2005 Timeless Treasures No-Hitters

OVERALL AU-GU'S ONE PER PACK
PRINT RUNS B/WN 3-25 COPIES PER
NO PRICING ON QTY OF 10 OR LESS
7 D.Eckersley 20.00 50.00
B.Blyleven/25
8 J.Marichal 20.00 50.00
G.Perry/25
9 J.Palmer 30.00 60.00
B.Gibson/25

2005 Timeless Treasures Rookie Year Materials Number

*NBR p/r 41-44: .5X TO 1.2X YR p/r 100
*NBR p/r 41-44: .3X TO .8X YR p/r 25
*NBR p/r 20-34: .6X TO 1.5X YR p/r 100
*NBR p/r 20-34: .4X TO 1X YR p/r 25
*NBR p/r 15-19: .75X TO 2X YR p/r 100
*NBR p/r 15-19: .5X TO 1.2X YR p/r 25
OVERALL AU-GU'S ONE PER PACK
PRINT RUNS B/WN 1-44 COPIES PER
NO PRICING ON QTY OF 11 OR LESS
5 Whitey Ford Jsy/16 12.50 30.00
8 Jim Palmer Hat/22 6.00 15.00
16 Kirk Gibson Hat/23 6.00 15.00
31 Garret Anderson Jsy/16 8.00 20.00

2005 Timeless Treasures Rookie Year Materials Year

PRINT RUNS B/WN 1-100 COPIES PER
NO PRICING ON QTY OF 5 OR LESS
PRIME PRINT RUN 5 SERIAL #'d SETS
NO PRIME PRICING DUE TO SCARCITY
OVERALL AU-GU'S ONE PER PACK
1 Rod Carew Jsy/100 6.00 15.00
4 Duke Snider Jsy/100 6.00 15.00
6 Juan Marichal Jsy/100 4.00 10.00
11 Gary Carter Jsy/100 4.00 10.00
12 Robin Yount Jsy/100 6.00 15.00
13 Keith Hernandez Jsy/25 6.00 15.00
15 Ozzie Smith Jsy/25 10.00 25.00
17 Dave Righetti Jsy/25 6.00 15.00
18 Roger Clemens Jsy/100 6.00 15.00
19 Greg Maddux Jsy/25 10.00 25.00
20 David Cone Jsy/100 4.00 10.00
21 Gary Sheffield Jsy/100 3.00 8.00
22 Randy Johnson Jsy/100 4.00 10.00
23 Deion Sanders Jsy/100 6.00 15.00
24 Dwight Gooden Jsy/25 6.00 15.00
25 Ivan Rodriguez Jsy/100 4.00 10.00
26 Jeff Bagwell Pants/100 4.00 10.00
27 Pedro Martinez Jsy/100 4.00 10.00
28 Mike Piazza Jsy/100 4.00 10.00
29 Chipper Jones Jsy/100 4.00 10.00
30 Hideo Nomo Jsy/100 6.00 15.00
32 Scott Rolen Jsy/100 4.00 10.00
33 Andruw Jones Jsy/100 4.00 10.00
34 Vladimir Guerrero Jsy/100 4.00 10.00
35 Sean Casey Jsy/25 5.00 12.00
36 Paul Lo Duca Jsy/25 5.00 12.00
37 Kerry Wood Jsy/100 3.00 8.00
38 Magglio Ordonez Jsy/25 5.00 12.00
39 Vernon Wells Jsy/25 5.00 12.00
40 Mark Mulder Jsy/100 3.00 8.00
41 Lance Berkman Jsy/100 3.00 8.00
42 Alfonso Soriano Jsy/100 3.00 8.00
43 Albert Pujols Jsy/100 8.00 20.00
44 Ben Sheets Jsy/25 5.00 12.00
45 Roy Oswalt Jsy/25 5.00 12.00
46 Mark Prior Jsy/100 4.00 10.00
47 Mark Teixeira Jsy/100 4.00 10.00
48 Miguel Cabrera Jsy/100 4.00 10.00
49 Travis Hafner Jsy/25 5.00 12.00
50 Victor Martinez Jsy/25 5.00 12.00

2005 Timeless Treasures Rookie Year Materials Signature Number

*NBR p/r 20-30: .4X TO 1X YR p/r 25
*NBR p/r 15-19: .5X TO 1.2X YR p/r 25
OVERALL AU-GU'S ONE PER PACK
PRINT RUNS B/WN 1-30 COPIES PER
NO PRICING ON QTY OF 10 OR LESS

2005 Timeless Treasures Rookie Year Materials Signature Year

PRINT RUNS B/WN 1-25 COPIES PER
NO PRICING ON QTY OF 5 OR LESS
PRIME PRINT RUNS B/WN 1-5 COPIES PER
NO PRIME PRINT RUNS DUE TO SCARCITY
OVERALL AU-GU'S ONE PER PACK
1 Rod Carew Jsy/25 20.00 50.00
4 Duke Snider Jsy/25 20.00 50.00
6 Juan Marichal Jsy/25 12.50 30.00
11 Gary Carter Jsy/25 12.50 30.00
12 Robin Yount Jsy/25 40.00 80.00
13 Keith Hernandez Jsy/25 12.50 30.00
15 Ozzie Smith Jsy/25 30.00 60.00
17 Dave Righetti Jsy/25 12.50 30.00
20 David Cone Jsy/25 12.50 30.00
21 Gary Sheffield Jsy/25 20.00 50.00
24 Dwight Gooden Jsy/25 12.50 30.00
32 Scott Rolen Jsy/25 20.00 50.00
35 Sean Casey Jsy/25 12.50 30.00
36 Paul Lo Duca Jsy/25 12.50 30.00
38 Magglio Ordonez Jsy/25 12.50 30.00
39 Vernon Wells Jsy/25 12.50 30.00
40 Mark Mulder Jsy/25 12.50 30.00
42 Alfonso Soriano Jsy/25 12.50 30.00
44 Ben Sheets Jsy/25 12.50 30.00
46 Mark Prior Jsy/25 15.00 40.00
47 Mark Teixeira Jsy/25 20.00 50.00
48 Miguel Cabrera Jsy/25 30.00 60.00
49 Travis Hafner Jsy/25 12.50 30.00
50 Victor Martinez Jsy/25 12.50 30.00

2005 Timeless Treasures Salutations Signature

OVERALL AU-GU'S ONE PER PACK
PRINT RUNS B/WN 1-24 COPIES PER
NO PRICING ON QTY OF 10 OR LESS
1 Al Kaline/24 40.00 100.00
3 Bob Gibson/24 30.00 60.00
5 Dale Murphy/24 15.00 40.00
6 Don Mattingly/24 40.00 80.00
7 Duke Snider/24 30.00 60.00
9 Harmon Killebrew/24 30.00 60.00
10 Jim Palmer/24 20.00 50.00
11 Johnny Bench/24 40.00 80.00
12 Maury Wills/24 20.00 50.00
13 Dennis Eckersley/24 20.00 50.00
19 Steve Carlton/24 20.00 50.00
20 Tony Gwynn/24 40.00 80.00
21 Whitey Ford/16 40.00 80.00
24 Rod Carew/24 30.00 60.00
25 Paul Molitor/24 20.00 50.00
26 Will Clark/24 30.00 60.00

2005 Timeless Treasures Statistical Champions Materials Number

*NBR p/r 38-47: .5X TO 1.2X YR p/r 100
*NBR p/r 38-47: .3X TO .8X YR p/r 25
*NBR p/r 20-35: .6X TO 1.5X YR p/r 100
*NBR p/r 20-35: .4X TO 1X YR p/r 25
*NBR p/r 17-19: .75X TO 2X YR p/r 100
OVERALL AU-GU'S ONE PER PACK
PRINT RUNS B/WN 1-47 COPIES PER
NO PRICING ON QTY OF 11 OR LESS
32 Sandy Koufax Jsy/32 75.00 150.00

2005 Timeless Treasures Statistical Champions Materials Year

PRINT RUNS B/WN 1-100 COPIES PER
NO PRICING ON QTY OF 5 OR LESS
PRIME PRINT RUNS B/WN 1-5 COPIES PER
NO PRIME PRICING DUE TO SCARCITY
OVERALL AU-GU'S ONE PER PACK
1 Nolan Ryan Rgr Jsy/100 10.00 25.00
2 Lee Smith Jsy/25 6.00 15.00
3 Harmon Killebrew Jsy/100 6.00 15.00
4 Kerry Wood Jsy/100 3.00 8.00
5 Albert Pujols Jsy/100 8.00 20.00
6 C.Schill D'backs Jsy/100 4.00 10.00
7 Joe Cronin Pants/100 6.00 15.00
8 Cal Ripken Jsy/100 12.50 30.00
9 Barry Zito Jsy/100 3.00 8.00
10 Miguel Tejada Jsy/100 3.00 8.00
11 Edgar Martinez Jsy/25 6.00 15.00
14 Andre Dawson Jsy/25 6.00 15.00
17 Todd Helton Jsy/100 4.00 10.00
19 Tony Gwynn Jsy/100 6.00 15.00
20 Mark Mulder Jsy/100 3.00 8.00
21 Roger Clemens Jsy/100 6.00 15.00
22 Will Clark Jsy/25 10.00 25.00
23 Don Mattingly Jsy/100 8.00 20.00
24 Manny Ramirez Jsy/25 6.00 15.00
25 Billy Williams Jsy/100 4.00 10.00
26 Wade Boggs Jsy/100 6.00 15.00
27 Kevin Brown Jsy/25 5.00 12.00
28 George Brett Jsy/100 8.00 20.00
29 Adrian Beltre Jsy/25 5.00 12.00
30 Lance Berkman Jsy/100 3.00 8.00
31 Sammy Sosa Jsy/100 4.00 10.00
32 Sandy Koufax Jsy/25 75.00 150.00
33 Jose Canseco Jsy/25 10.00 25.00
34 Kirby Puckett Jsy/100 6.00 15.00
35 Rickey Henderson Jsy/100 6.00 15.00
36 Juan Gonzalez Jsy/100 3.00 8.00
38 Curt Schilling Sox Jsy/100 4.00 10.00
39 Don Sutton Jsy/100 4.00 10.00
40 Johan Santana Jsy/100 4.00 10.00
41 Nolan Ryan Astros Jsy/100 10.00 25.00
42 Mariano Rivera Jsy/25 6.00 15.00
43 Lou Brock Jsy/100 6.00 15.00
44 Roy Oswalt Jsy/25 5.00 12.00
45 Dale Murphy Jsy/100 6.00 15.00

2005 Timeless Treasures Statistical Champions Materials Signature Number

*NBR p/r 20-34: .5X TO 1.2X p/r YR p/r 50
*NBR p/r 20-34: .4X TO 1X p/r YR p/r 25
*NBR p/r 19: .6X TO 1.5X p/r YR p/r 50
*NBR p/r 19: .5X TO 1.2X p/r YR p/r 25
OVERALL AU-GU'S ONE PER PACK
PRINT RUNS B/WN 1-34 COPIES PER
NO PRICING ON QTY OF 11 OR LESS

2005 Timeless Treasures Statistical Champions Materials Signature Year

PRINT RUNS B/WN 1-50 COPIES PER
NO PRICING ON QTY OF 5 OR LESS
PRIME PRINT RUNS B/WN 1-5 COPIES PER
NO PRIME PRICING DUE TO SCARCITY
OVERALL AU-GU'S ONE PER PACK
1 Nolan Ryan Rgr Jsy/50 50.00 100.00
3 Harmon Killebrew Jsy/50 30.00 60.00
4 Kerry Wood Jsy/25 20.00 50.00
8 Cal Ripken Jsy/25 125.00 200.00
9 Barry Zito Jsy/25 12.50 30.00
11 Edgar Martinez Jsy/25 30.00 60.00
14 Andre Dawson Jsy/25 12.50 30.00
19 Tony Gwynn Jsy/50 20.00 50.00
20 Mark Mulder Jsy/25 12.50 30.00
22 Will Clark Jsy/25 20.00 50.00
23 Don Mattingly Jsy/50 30.00 60.00
26 Wade Boggs Jsy/50 25.00 60.00
29 Adrian Beltre Jsy/25 12.50 30.00
33 Jose Canseco Jsy/25 30.00 80.00
36 Juan Gonzalez Jsy/25 12.50 30.00
39 Don Sutton Jsy/25 12.50 30.00
40 Johan Santana Jsy/25 20.00 50.00
41 Nolan Ryan Astros Jsy/50 50.00 100.00
43 Lou Brock Jsy/50 15.00 40.00
45 Dale Murphy Jsy/50 15.00 40.00

2005 Timeless Treasures World Series Materials

OVERALL AU-GU'S ONE PER PACK
PRINT RUNS B/WN 1-100 COPIES PER
NO PRICING ON QTY OF 10 OR LESS
1 Frank Robinson Bat/100 4.00 10.00
3 Carl Yastrzemski Bat/100 8.00 20.00
4 Jack Morris Jsy/50 5.00 12.00
5 Wade Boggs Bat/100 6.00 15.00
8 Andruw Jones Jsy/100 4.00 10.00
10 Darryl Strawberry Jsy/25 12.50 30.00

2005 Timeless Treasures World Series Materials Signature

PRINT RUNS B/WN 1-25 COPIES PER
NO PRICING ON QTY OF 10 OR LESS
PRIME PRINT RUNS B/WN 1-10 COPIES PER
NO PRIME PRICING DUE TO SCARCITY
OVERALL AU-GU'S ONE PER PACK
1 Frank Robinson Bat/25 20.00 50.00
4 Jack Morris Jsy/25 12.50 30.00
5 Wade Boggs Bat/25 20.00 50.00
10 Darryl Strawberry Jsy/25 12.50 30.00

2019 Timeless Treasures

RANDOM INSERTS IN PACKS
*GOLD/199: 1.2X TO 3X
*BLUE/99: 1.5X TO 4X
*RED/50: 2X TO 5X
*HOLO SLVR/25: 3X TO 8X
1 Pete Alonso RC 2.00 5.00
2 Eloy Jimenez .60 1.50
3 Fernando Tatis Jr. 2.00 5.00
4 Cole Tucker .25 .60
5 Kyle Tucker .40 1.00
6 Yusei Kikuchi .25 .60
7 Chris Paddack .30 .75
8 Nathaniel Lowe .75 2.00
9 Bryce Harper .40 1.00
10 Aaron Judge .60 1.50
11 Kris Bryant .30 .75
12 Shohei Ohtani .40 1.00
13 Michael Chavis .25 .60
14 Carter Kieboom .25 .60
15 Didi Gregorius .20 .50
16 Justin Turner .25 .60
17 Austin Riley .75 2.00
18 Michael Conforto .20 .50
19 Vladimir Guerrero Jr. 2.50 6.00
20 Trey Mancini .20 .50

2020 Timeless Treasures

RANDOM INSERTS IN PACKS
1 Shogo Akiyama RC .40 1.00
2 Yordan Alvarez RC 2.50 6.00
3 Bo Bichette RC 3.00 8.00
4 Aristides Aquino RC .60 1.50
5 Gavin Lux RC 1.25 3.00
6 Yoshitomo Tsutsugo RC .60 1.50
7 Brendan McKay RC .40 1.00
8 Luis Robert RC 4.00 10.00
9 A.J. Puk RC .40 1.00
10 Kyle Lewis RC 4.00 10.00
11 Logan Allen RC .25 .60
12 Zac Gallen RC .60 1.50
13 Isan Diaz RC .40 1.00
14 Bobby Bradley RC .25 .60
15 Adbert Alzolay RC .30 .75
16 Walker Buehler .30 .75
17 Trevor Story .25 .60
18 Freddie Freeman .30 .75
19 Starling Marte .20 .50
20 Jack Flaherty .25 .60

2020 Timeless Treasures Signatures

RANDOM INSERTS IN PACKS
PRINT RUNS B/WN 5-99 COPIES PER
NO PRICING QTY 15 OR LESS
EXCHANGE DEADLINE 3/18/2022
1 Shogo Akiyama/49 6.00 15.00
2 Yordan Alvarez/50 40.00 100.00
3 Bo Bichette/30 30.00 80.00
4 Aristides Aquino/60 8.00 20.00
6 Yoshitomo Tsutsugo/99 8.00 20.00
8 Luis Robert EXCH/99 75.00 200.00
9 A.J. Puk/99 5.00 12.00
10 Kyle Lewis/99 25.00 60.00
11 Logan Allen/96 3.00 8.00
12 Zac Gallen/49 10.00 25.00
13 Isan Diaz/59 5.00 12.00
14 Bobby Bradley/96 3.00 8.00
15 Adbert Alzolay/99 4.00 10.00

1947 Tip Top

The cards in this 163-card set measure approximately 2 1/4" by 3". The 1947 Tip Top Bread issue contains unnumbered cards with black and white player photos. The set is of interest to baseball historians in that it contains cards of many players not appearing in any other card sets. The cards were issued locally for the eleven following teams: Red Sox (1-15), White Sox (16-30), Tigers (31-45), Yankees (46-60), Browns (61-75), Braves (76-90), Dodgers (91-104), Cubs (105-119), Giants (120-134), Pirates (135-148), and Cardinals (149-163). Players of the Red Sox, Tigers, White Sox, Braves, and the Cubs are scarcer than those of the other teams; players from these tougher teams are marked by SP below to indicate their scarcity. The catalog designation is D323. These unnumbered cards are listed in alphabetical order within teams (with teams also alphabetized within league) for convenience. It was thought that a card for the Giants Eugene Thompson was to be issued but it does not exist.

COMPLETE SET (163) 5000.00 10000.00
COMMON CARD (1-163) 12.50 25.00
COMMON SP PLAYER 50.00 80.00
1 Leon Culberson SP 50.00 80.00
2 Dom DiMaggio SP 90.00 150.00
3 Joe Dobson SP 50.00 80.00
4 Bob Doerr SP 175.00 300.00
5 Dave(Boo) Ferris SP 50.00 80.00
6 Mickey Harris SP 50.00 80.00
7 Frank Hayes SP 50.00 80.00
8 Cecil Hughson SP 50.00 80.00
9 Earl Johnson SP 50.00 80.00
10 Roy Partee SP 50.00 80.00
11 Johnny Pesky SP 60.00 100.00
12 Rip Russell SP 50.00 80.00
13 Hal Wagner SP 50.00 80.00
14 Rudy York SP 60.00 100.00
15 Bill Zuber SP 50.00 80.00
16 Floyd Baker SP 50.00 80.00
17 Earl Caldwell SP 50.00 80.00
18 Loyd Christopher SP 50.00 80.00
19 George Dickey SP 50.00 80.00
20 Ralph Hodgin SP 50.00 80.00
21 Bob Kennedy SP 50.00 80.00
22 Joe Kuhel SP 50.00 80.00
23 Thornton Lee SP 50.00 80.00
24 Ed Lopat SP 90.00 150.00
25 Cass Michaels SP 50.00 80.00
26 John Rigney SP 50.00 80.00
27 Mike Tresh SP 50.00 80.00
28 Thurman Tucker SP 50.00 80.00
29 Jack Wallasca SP 50.00 80.00
30 Taft Wright SP 50.00 80.00
31 Walter(Hoot)Evers SP 50.00 80.00
32 John Gorsica SP 50.00 80.00
33 Fred Hutchinson SP 60.00 100.00
34 George Kell SP 500.00
35 Eddie Lake SP 50.00 80.00
36 Ed Mayo SP 50.00 80.00
37 Arthur Mills SP 50.00 80.00
38 Pat Mullin SP 50.00 80.00
39 James Outlaw SP 50.00 80.00
40 Frank Overmire SP 50.00 80.00
41 Bob Swift SP 50.00 80.00
42 Birdie Tebbetts SP 50.00 80.00
43 Dizzy Trout SP 60.00 100.00
44 Virgil Trucks SP 60.00 100.00
45 Dick Wakefield SP 50.00 80.00
46 Yogi Berra/(Listed as Larry on card) 500.00
47 Floyd(Bill) Bevans 15.00 30.00
48 Bobby Brown 20.00 40.00
49 Thomas Byrne 15.00 30.00
50 Frank Crosetti 25.00 50.00
51 Tommy Henrich 25.00 50.00
52 Charlie Keller 25.00 50.00
53 Johnny Lindell 15.00 30.00
54 Joe Page 20.00 40.00
55 Mel Queen 15.00 30.00
56 Allie Reynolds 25.00 50.00
57 Phil Rizzuto 100.00 200.00
58 Aaron Robinson 15.00 30.00
59 George Stirnweiss 15.00 30.00
60 Charles Wensloff 15.00 30.00
61 John Berardino 25.00 50.00
62 Clifford Fannin 15.00 30.00
63 Dennis Galehouse 15.00 30.00
64 Jeff Heath 15.00 30.00
65 Walter Judnich 15.00 30.00
66 Jack Kramer 15.00 30.00
67 Paul Lehner 15.00 30.00
68 Les Moss 15.00 30.00
69 Bob Muncrief 15.00 30.00
70 Nelson Potter 15.00 30.00
71 Fred Sanford 15.00 30.00
72 Joe Schultz 15.00 30.00
73 Vern Stephens 20.00 40.00
74 Jerry Witte 15.00 30.00
75 Al Zarilla 15.00 30.00
76 Charles Barrett SP 50.00 80.00
77 Hank Camelli SP 50.00 80.00
78 Dick Culler SP 50.00 80.00
79 Nanny Fernandez SP 50.00 80.00
80 Si Johnson SP 50.00 80.00
81 Danny Litwhiler SP 50.00 80.00
82 Phil Masi SP 50.00 80.00
83 Carvel Rowell SP 50.00 80.00
84 Connie Ryan SP 50.00 80.00
85 John Sain SP 70.00 120.00
86 Ray Sanders SP 50.00 80.00
87 Sibby Sisti SP 50.00 80.00
88 Billy Southworth SP MG 60.00 100.00
89 Warren Spahn SP 600.00
90 Ed Wright SP 50.00 80.00
91 Bob Bragan 20.00 40.00
92 Ralph Branca 20.00 40.00
93 Hugh Casey 15.00 30.00
94 Bruce Edwards 15.00 30.00
95 Hal Gregg 15.00 30.00
96 Joe Hatten 15.00 30.00
97 Gene Hermanski 15.00 30.00
98 John Jorgensen 15.00 30.00
99 Harry Lavagetto 20.00 40.00
100 Vic Lombardi 15.00 30.00
101 Frank Melton 15.00 30.00
102 Ed Miksis 15.00 30.00
103 Marv Rackley 15.00 30.00
104 Ed Stevens 15.00 30.00
105 Phil Cavarretta SP 70.00 120.00
106 Bob Chipman SP 50.00 80.00
107 Stan Hack SP 60.00 100.00
108 Don Johnson SP 50.00 80.00
109 Emil Kush SP 50.00 80.00
110 Bill Lee SP 60.00 100.00
111 Mickey Livingston SP 50.00 80.00
112 Harry Lowrey SP 50.00 80.00
113 Clyde McCullough SP 50.00 80.00
114 Andy Pafko SP 60.00 100.00
115 Marv Rickert SP 50.00 80.00
116 John Schmitz SP 50.00 80.00
117 Bobby Sturgeon SP 50.00 80.00
118 Ed Waitkus SP 60.00 100.00
119 Henry Wyse SP 50.00 80.00
120 Bill Ayers 15.00 30.00
121 Buddy Blattner 15.00 30.00
122 Mike Budnick 15.00 30.00
123 Sid Gordon 15.00 30.00
124 Clint Hartung 15.00 30.00
125 Monte Kennedy 15.00 30.00
126 Dave Koslo 15.00 30.00
127 Whitey Lockman 20.00 40.00
128 Jack Lohrke 15.00 30.00
129 Ernie Lombardi 100.00
130 Willard Marshall 15.00 30.00
131 John Mize 75.00 150.00
132 Ken Trinkle 15.00 30.00
133 Bill Voiselle 15.00 30.00
134 Mickey Witek 15.00 30.00
135 Eddie Basinski 15.00 30.00
136 Ernie Bonham 15.00 30.00
137 Billy Cox 20.00 40.00
138 Elbie Fletcher 15.00 30.00
139 Frank Gustine 15.00 30.00
140 Kirby Higbe 15.00 30.00
141 Leroy Jarvis 15.00 30.00
142 Ralph Kiner 75.00 150.00
143 Fred Ostermueller 15.00 30.00
144 Preacher Roe 25.00 50.00
145 Jim Russell 15.00 30.00
146 Rip Sewell 15.00 30.00
147 Nick Strincevich 15.00 30.00
148 Honus Wagner CO 75.00 150.00
149 Alpha Brazle 15.00 30.00
150 Ken Burkhart 15.00 30.00
151 Bernard Creger 15.00 30.00
152 Joffre Cross 15.00 30.00
153 Chuck Diering 15.00 30.00
154 Ervin Dusak 15.00 30.00
155 Joe Garagiola 100.00
156 Tony Kaufmann 15.00 30.00
157 Whitey Kurowski 15.00 30.00
158 Marty Marion 25.00 50.00
159 George Munger 15.00 30.00
160 Del Rice 15.00 30.00
161 Dick Sisler 20.00 40.00
162 Enos Slaughter 75.00 150.00
163 Ted Wilks 15.00 30.00

1952 Tip Top

This set of 48 bread end-labels was issued by Tip Top in 1952. The labels measure 2 3/4" by 2 1/2". An album distributed with the labels names 47 ball players and has one blank slot with advertising. A second pose of Rizzuto -- which appears "cropped" from the first photo -- suggests either a last minute substitution for another player, or simply his popularity in the market area. These labels are unnumbered so we have sequenced them in alphabetical order. The catalog designation is D290-1.

COMPLETE SET (48) 7500.00 15000.00
1 Hank Bauer 250.00 500.00
2 Yogi Berra 600.00 1200.00
3 Ralph Branca 250.00 500.00
4 Lou Brissie 150.00 300.00
5 Roy Campanella 800.00 1600.00
6 Phil Cavarretta 250.00 500.00
7 Murray Dickson 150.00 300.00
8 Ferris Fain 150.00 300.00
9 Carl Furillo 300.00 600.00
10 Ned Garver 150.00 300.00
11 Sid Gordon 250.00 500.00
12 Johnny Groth 150.00 300.00
13 Granny Hamner 150.00 300.00
14 Jim Hearn 150.00 300.00
15 Gene Hermanski 150.00 300.00
16 Gil Hodges 500.00 1000.00
17 Larry Jansen 200.00 400.00
18 Eddie Joost 150.00 300.00
19 George Kell 400.00 800.00
20 Dutch Leonard 150.00 300.00
21 Whitey Lockman 150.00 300.00
22 Eddie Lopat 250.00 500.00
23 Sal Maglie 250.00 500.00
24 Mickey Mantle 2500.00 5000.00
25 Gil McDougald 250.00 500.00
26 Dale Mitchell 200.00 400.00
27 Don Mueller 150.00 300.00
28 Andy Pafko 150.00 300.00
29 Bob Porterfield 150.00 300.00
30 Ken Raffensberger 150.00 300.00
31 Allie Reynolds 250.00 500.00
32 Phil Rizzuto (large) 300.00 600.00
33 Phil Rizzuto (small) 300.00 600.00
34 Robin Roberts 500.00 1000.00
35 Saul Rogovin 150.00 300.00
36 Ray Scarborough 150.00 300.00
37 Red Schoendienst 300.00 600.00
38 Dick Sisler 150.00 300.00
39 Enos Slaughter 400.00 800.00
40 Duke Snider 600.00 1200.00
41 Warren Spahn 500.00 1000.00
42 Vern Stephens 150.00 300.00
43 Earl Torgeson 150.00 300.00
44 Mickey Vernon 200.00 400.00
45 Eddie Waitkus 150.00 300.00
46 Wes Westrum 150.00 300.00
47 Eddie Yost 150.00 300.00
48 Al Zarilla 150.00 300.00
XX Album

1887 Tobin Lithographs

This 11 card set measures 3" by 4 1/2" and were issued in either black and white or color. The color cards have "56" listed in the lower left hand corner with and advertisement in the upper right corner. The card features a player drawing along with an humourus statement. The player's team identification is in the upper left corner. The backs come with or without advertising. We have listed these cards in alphabetical order with the description afterwards.

COMPLETE SET 1000.00 2000.00
1 Ed Andrews 300.00 600.00
Go it Old Boy
2 Cap Anson 600.00 1200.00
Oh, Come Off
3 Dan Brouthers 500.00 1000.00
Watch me soak it
4 Charlie Ferguson 300.00 600.00
Not onto it
5 Jack Glasscock 300.00 600.00
Struck by a cyclone
6 Paul Hines 300.00 600.00
An Anxious Moment
7 Tim Keefe 500.00 1000.00
Where'l you have it
8 Mike King Kelly 600.00 1200.00
The Flower of our Flock
Identified as our own Kelly
9 Mike King Kelly/15,000 in his pocket 600.001200.00
Black and White
Measures approximately 2 1/2 by 4
Does not have 56 in corner
10 Jim McCormick 300.00 600.00
A slide for Hoome
11 Mickey Welch 500.00 1000.00
Aint it a daisy

1913 Tom Barker Game WG6

These cards were distributed as part of a baseball game produced in 1913 as indicated by the patent date on the backs of the cards. The cards each measure approximately 2 7/16" by 3 7/16" and have rounded corners. The card fronts show a sepia photo of the player, his name, his team, and the game outcome associated with that particular card. The card backs are all the same, each showing an ornate red and white design with "Tom Barker Baseball Card Game" at the bottom under a drawing of a lefthanded batter all surrounded by a thick white outer border. Since the cards are unnumbered, they are listed below in alphabetical order. The last nine cards in the set feature action photos oriented horizontally.

COMPLETE SET 3000.00 6000.00
COMMON ACTION CARD 7.50 15.00
1 Grover Alexander 250.00 400.00
2 Frank Baker 50.00 100.00
3 Chief Bender 30.00 50.00
4 Bob Bescher 15.00 25.00
5 Joe Birmingham 15.00 25.00
6 Roger Bresnahan 35.00 60.00
7 Nixey Callahan 15.00 25.00
8 Bill Carrigan 15.00 25.00
9 Frank Chance 35.00 60.00
10 Hal Chase 18.00 30.00
11 Fred Clarke 30.00 50.00
12 Ty Cobb 250.00 400.00
13 Sam Crawford 35.00 60.00
14 Jake Daubert 15.00 25.00
15 Red Dooin 15.00 25.00
16 Johnny Evers 35.00 60.00
17 Vean Gregg 15.00 25.00
18 Clark Griffith MG 30.00 50.00
19 Dick Hoblitzel 15.00 25.00
20 Miller Huggins 30.00 50.00
21 Joe Jackson 700.00 1200.00
22 Hugh Jennings MG 30.00 50.00
23 Walter Johnson 90.00 150.00
24 Ed Konetchy 15.00 25.00
25 Nap Lajoie 50.00 80.00
26 Connie Mack MG 35.00 60.00
27 Rube Marquard 30.00 50.00
28 Christy Mathewson 90.00 150.00
29 John McGraw MG 35.00 60.00
30 Chief Meyers 15.00 25.00
31 Clyde Milan 15.00 25.00
32 Marty O'Toole 15.00 25.00
33 Nap Rucker 15.00 25.00
34 Tris Speaker 50.00 80.00
35 George Stallings MG 15.00 25.00
36 Bill Sweeney 15.00 25.00
37 Joe Tinker 35.00 60.00
38 Honus Wagner 250.00 400.00
39 Ed Walsh 35.00 60.00
40 Zack Wheat 30.00 50.00
41 Ivy Wingo 15.00 25.00
42 Joe Wood 30.00 50.00
43 Cy Young 90.00 150.00
A1 Batter Swinging, Looking Forward
A2 Batter Swinging, Looking Back
A3 Runner Sliding, Fielder at Bag
A4 Runner Sliding, Umpire Behind
A5 Runner Sliding, Hugging Base
A6 Sliding Play at Plate, Umpire Left
A7 Sliding Play at Plate, Umpire Right
A8 Play at Plate, Runner Standing
A9 Runner Looking Backwards

1994 Tombstone Pizza

Produced by Michael Schlechter Associates for Pinnacle and sponsored by Tombstone Pizza, this 30-card standard-size set showcases 15 of the hottest players from the National (1-15) and American (16-30) Leagues. The promotion ran from May 15 to July 4, 1994, or while supplies lasted. One card was packaged in each Tombstone pizza. Collectors could obtain the complete set by sending in five proofs-of-purchase and 1.00 for shipping and handling. Like most MSA sets, the team logos have been airbrushed away. The cards are arranged alphabetically within each league.

COMPLETE SET (30) 6.00 15.00
1 Jeff Bagwell .30 .75
2 Jay Bell .02 .10
3 Barry Bonds .50 1.25
4 Bobby Bonilla .07 .20
5 Andres Galarraga .15 .40
6 Mark Grace .10 .30
7 Marquis Grissom .02 .10
8 Tony Gwynn .60 1.50
9 Bryan Harvey .02 .10
10 Gregg Jefferies .02 .10
11 David Justice .15 .40
12 John Kruk .07 .20
13 Barry Larkin .15 .40
14 Greg Maddux .75 2.00
15 Mike Piazza .75 2.00
16 Jim Abbott .07 .20
17 Albert Belle .07 .20
18 Cecil Fielder .07 .20
19 Juan Gonzalez .15 .40
20 Mike Greenwell .02 .10
21 Ken Griffey Jr. .75 2.00
22 Jack McDowell .02 .10
23 Jeff Montgomery .02 .10
24 John Olerud .07 .20
25 Kirby Puckett .40 1.00
26 Cal Ripken 1.25 3.00
27 Tim Salmon .15 .40
28 Ruben Sierra .07 .20
29 Frank Thomas .30 .75
30 Robin Yount .30 .75

1995 Tombstone Pizza

This 30-card standard-size set features 15 of the hottest players each from the National and the American Leagues. One card was packaged in each Tombstone Pizza. Six thousand classic player cards, autographed by Johnny Bench, George Brett or Bob Gibson, were randomly packed. Collectors who pulled one of these autograph cards could receive an 8 1/2" by 11" certificate of authenticity through a mail-in offer. Also collectors could obtain the complete set by sending in five proofs-of-purchase. The limit was two sets per family or address, and the offer expired December 31, 1995, or while supplies lasted. The cards are numbered on the back "X of 30."

COMPLETE SET (30) 6.00 15.00
1 Frank Thomas .30 .75
2 David Cone .10 .30
3 Bob Hamelin .02 .10
4 Jeff Bagwell .30 .75
5 Greg Maddux .75 2.00
6 Raul Mondesi .10 .30
7 Chili Davis .07 .20
8 Cecil Fielder .07 .20
9 Ken Griffey Jr. .75 2.00
10 Jimmy Key .07 .20
11 Kenny Lofton .10 .30
12 Paul Molitor .30 .75
13 Kirby Puckett .40 1.00
14 Cal Ripken 1.25 3.00
15 Ivan Rodriguez .30 .75
16 Kevin Seitzer .02 .10
17 Ruben Sierra .07 .20
18 Mo Vaughn .07 .20
19 Moises Alou .07 .20
20 Barry Bonds .60 1.50
21 Jeff Conine .02 .10
22 Lenny Dykstra .02 .10
23 Andres Galarraga .20 .50
24 Tony Gwynn .60 1.50
25 Barry Larkin .20 .50
26 Fred McGriff .10 .30
27 Orlando Merced .02 .10
28 Bret Saberhagen .07 .20
29 Ozzie Smith .30 .75
30 Sammy Sosa .40 1.00
AU1 Johnny Bench AU 12.50 30.00
AU2 George Brett AU 20.00 50.00
AU3 Bob Gibson AU 8.00 20.00

1948 Topps Magic Photos

The 1948 Topps Magic Photos set contains 252 small (approximately 7/8" by 1 7/16") individual cards featuring sport and non-sport subjects. They were issued in 19 lettered series with cards numbered within each series. The fronts were developed, much like a photograph, from a "blank" appearance by using moisture and sunlight. Due to varying degrees of photographic sensitivity, the clarity of these cards ranges from fully developed to poorly developed. This set contains Topps' first baseball cards. A premium album holding 126-cards was also issued. The set is sometimes confused with Topps' 1956 Hocus-Focus set, although the cards in this set are slightly smaller than those in the Hocus-Focus set. The checklist below is presented by series. Poorly developed cards are considered in lesser condition and hence have lesser value. The catalog designation for this set is R714-27. Each type of card subject has a letter prefix as follows: Boxing Champions (A), All-American Basketball (B), All-American Football (C), Wrestling Champions (D), Track and Field Champions (E), Stars of Stage and Screen (F), American Dogs (G), General Sports (H), Movie Stars (J), Baseball Hall of Fame (K), Aviation Pioneers (L), Famous Landmarks (M), American Inventors (N), American Military Leaders (O), American Explorers (P), Basketball Thrills (Q), Football Thrills (R), Figures of the Wild West (S), and General Sports (T).

COMPLETE SET (252) 3000.00 5000.00
K1 Lou Boudreau 30.00 60.00
K2 Cleveland Indians 20.00 40.00
K3 Bob Elliott 7.50 15.00
K4 Cleveland Indians 4-3 7.50 15.00
K5 Cleveland Indians 4-1 10.00 20.00
K6 Babe Ruth 714 300.00 500.00
K7 Tris Speaker 793 40.00 80.00
K8 Rogers Hornsby 60.00 120.00
K9 Connie Mack 60.00 120.00
K10 Christy Mathewson 90.00 150.00
K11 Hans Wagner 90.00 150.00
K12 Grover Alexander 60.00 120.00
K13 Ty Cobb 175.00 350.00
K14 Lou Gehrig 175.00 350.00
K15 Walter Johnson 100.00 200.00
K16 Cy Young 90.00 150.00
K17 George Sisler 257 40.00 80.00
K18 Tinker and Evers 40.00 80.00
K19 Third Base& 10.00 20.00

1951 Topps Blue Backs

The cards in this 52-card set measure approximately 2" by 2 5/8". The 1951 Topps series of blue-backed baseball cards could be used to play a baseball game by shuffling the cards and drawing them from a pile. These cards (packaged two adjoined in a penny pack) were marketed with a piece of caramel candy, which often melted or was squashed in such a way as to damage the card and wrapper (despite the fact that a paper shield was inserted between candy and card). Blue Backs are more difficult to obtain than the similarly styled Red Backs. The set is denoted on the cards as "Set B" and the Red Back set is correspondingly Set A. The only notable Rookie Card in the set is Billy Pierce.

COMPLETE SET (52) 1000.00 2500.00
WRAPPER (1-CENT) 150.00 200.00
1 Eddie Yost 30.00 80.00
2 Hank Majeski 15.00 40.00
3 Richie Ashburn 100.00 250.00
4 Del Ennis 15.00 40.00
5 Johnny Pesky 15.00 40.00
6 Red Schoendienst 60.00 150.00
7 Gerry Staley RC 15.00 40.00
8 Dick Sisler 15.00 40.00
9 Johnny Sain 30.00 80.00
10 Joe Page 30.00 80.00
11 Johnny Groth 15.00 40.00
12 Sam Jethroe 20.00 50.00
13 Mickey Vernon 15.00 40.00
14 George Munger 15.00 40.00
15 Eddie Joost 15.00 40.00
16 Murry Dickson 15.00 40.00
17 Roy Smalley 15.00 40.00
18 Ned Garver 15.00 40.00
19 Phil Masi 15.00 40.00
20 Ralph Branca 30.00 80.00
21 Billy Johnson 15.00 40.00
22 Bob Kuzava 15.00 40.00
23 Dizzy Trout 20.00 50.00
24 Sherman Lollar 15.00 40.00
25 Sam Mele 15.00 40.00
26 Chico Carrasquel RC 20.00 50.00
27 Andy Pafko 15.00 40.00
28 Harry Brecheen 15.00 40.00
29 Granville Hamner 15.00 40.00
30 Enos Slaughter 60.00 150.00
31 Lou Brissie 15.00 40.00
32 Bob Elliott 20.00 50.00
33 Don Lenhardt RC 15.00 40.00
34 Earl Torgeson 15.00 40.00
35 Tommy Byrne RC 15.00 40.00
36 Cliff Fannin 15.00 40.00
37 Bobby Doerr 60.00 150.00
38 Irv Noren 15.00 40.00
39 Ed Lopat 30.00 80.00

40 Vic Wertz	15.00	40.00
41 Johnny Schmitz	15.00	40.00
42 Bruce Edwards	15.00	40.00
43 Willie Jones	15.00	40.00
44 Johnny Wyrostek	15.00	40.00
45 Billy Pierce RC	30.00	80.00
46 Gerry Priddy	15.00	40.00
47 Herman Wehmeier	15.00	40.00
48 Billy Cox	20.00	50.00
49 Hank Sauer	20.00	50.00
50 Johnny Mize	60.00	150.00
51 Eddie Waitkus	20.00	50.00
52 Sam Chapman	30.00	80.00

1951 Topps Red Backs

The cards in this 52-card set measure approximately 2" by 2 5/8". The 1951 Topps Red Back set is identical in style to the Blue Back set of the same year. The cards have rounded corners and were designed to be used as a baseball game. Zernial, number 36, is listed with either the White Sox or Athletics, and Holmes, number 52, with either the Braves or Hartford. The set is denoted on the cards as "Set A" and the Blue Back set is correspondingly Set B. The cards were packaged as two connected cards along with a piece of caramel in a penny pack. There were 120 penny packs in a box. The most notable Rookie Card in the set is Monte Irvin.

COMPLETE SET (54)	500.00	1200.00
WRAPPER (1-CENT)	4.00	5.00
1 Yogi Berra	100.00	250.00
2 Sid Gordon	5.00	12.00
3 Ferris Fain	5.00	12.00
4 Vern Stephens	15.00	40.00
5 Phil Rizzuto	25.00	60.00
6 Allie Reynolds	20.00	50.00
7 Howie Pollet	5.00	12.00
8 Early Wynn	30.00	80.00
9 Roy Sievers	5.00	12.00
10 Mel Parnell	5.00	12.00
11 Gene Hermanski	5.00	12.00
12 Jim Hegan	10.00	25.00
13 Dale Mitchell	5.00	12.00
14 Wayne Terwilliger	5.00	12.00
15 Ralph Kiner	20.00	50.00
16 Preacher Roe	12.00	30.00
17 Gus Bell RC	8.00	20.00
18 Jerry Coleman	10.00	25.00
19 Dick Kokos	6.00	15.00
20 Dom DiMaggio	20.00	50.00
21 Larry Jansen	5.00	12.00
22 Bob Feller	60.00	150.00
23 Ray Boone RC	5.00	12.00
24 Hank Bauer	12.00	30.00
25 Cliff Chambers	5.00	12.00
26 Luke Easter RC	5.00	12.00
27 Wally Westlake	5.00	12.00
28 Elmer Valo	5.00	12.00
29 Bob Kennedy RC	5.00	12.00
30 Warren Spahn	40.00	100.00
31 Gil Hodges	25.00	60.00
32 Henry Thompson	6.00	15.00
33 William Werle	5.00	12.00
34 Grady Hatton	5.00	12.00
35 Al Rosen	12.00	30.00
36A Gus Zernial Chic	12.00	30.00
36B Gus Zernial Phila	6.00	15.00
37 Wes Westrum RC	5.00	12.00
38 Duke Snider	30.00	80.00
39 Ted Kluszewski	20.00	50.00
40 Mike Garcia	8.00	20.00
41 Whitey Lockman	6.00	15.00
42 Ray Scarborough	5.00	12.00
43 Maurice McDermott	10.00	25.00
44 Sid Hudson	8.00	20.00
45 Andy Seminick	5.00	12.00
46 Billy Goodman	10.00	25.00
47 Tommy Glaviano RC	5.00	12.00
48 Eddie Stanky	5.00	12.00
49 Al Zarilla	5.00	12.00
50 Monte Irvin RC	40.00	100.00
51 Eddie Robinson	5.00	12.00
52A T.Holmes Boston	12.00	30.00
52B T.Holmes Hartford	8.00	20.00

1951 Topps Connie Mack's All-Stars

The cards in this 11-card set measure approximately 2 1/16" by 5 1/4". The series of die-cut cards which comprise the set entitled Connie Mack All-Stars was one of Topps' most distinctive and fragile card designs. Printed on thin cardboard, these elegant cards were protected in the wrapper by panels of accompanying Red Backs, but once removed were easily damaged (after all, they were intended to be folded and used as toy figures). Cards without tops have a value less than one-half of that listed below. The cards are unnumbered and are listed below in alphabetical order.

COMPLETE SET (11)	3000.00	6000.00
WRAPPER (5-CENT)	300.00	350.00
CARDS PRICED IN EX CONDITION		
1 Grover C. Alexander	250.00	500.00
2 Mickey Cochrane	150.00	300.00
3 Eddie Collins	150.00	300.00
4 Jimmy Collins	150.00	300.00
5 Lou Gehrig	1000.00	1500.00
6 Walter Johnson	400.00	800.00
7 Connie Mack	250.00	500.00
8 Christy Mathewson	400.00	800.00
9 Babe Ruth	1500.00	2000.00
10 Tris Speaker	200.00	400.00
11 Honus Wagner	300.00	600.00

1951 Topps Major League All-Stars

The cards in this 11-card set measure approximately 2 1/16" by 5 1/4". The 1951 Topps Current All-Star series is probably the rarest of all legitimate, nationally issued, post war baseball issues. The set price listed below does not include the prices for the cards of Konstanty, Roberts and Stanky, which likely never were released to the public in gum packs. These three cards (SP in the checklist below) were probably obtained directly from the company and exist in extremely limited numbers. As with the Connie Mack set, cards without the die-cut background are worth half of the value listed below. The cards are unnumbered and are listed below in alphabetical order. These cards were issued in two card packs (one being a Current AS the other being a Topps Team card).

COMP.SET w/o SP's (8)	2000.00	4000.00
WRAPPER (5-CENT)	400.00	500.00
1 Yogi Berra	1000.00	1500.00
2 Larry Doby	250.00	400.00
3 Walt Dropo	150.00	250.00
4 Hoot Evers	150.00	250.00
5 George Kell	350.00	600.00
6 Ralph Kiner	450.00	750.00
7 Jim Konstanty SP	7500.00	12500.00
8 Bob Lemon	350.00	600.00
9 Phil Rizzuto	500.00	800.00
10 Robin Roberts SP	9000.00	15000.00
11 Eddie Stanky SP	7500.00	12500.00

1951 Topps Teams

The cards in this nine-card set measure approximately 2 1/16" by 5 1/4". These unnumbered team cards issued by Topps in 1951 carry black and white photographs framed by a yellow border. These cards were issued in the same five-cent wrapper as the Connie Mack and Current All Stars. They have been assigned reference numbers in the checklist alphabetically by team city and name. They are found with or without "1950" printed in the name panel before the team name. Although the dated variations are slightly more difficult to find, there is usually no difference in value.

COMPLETE SET (9)	1500.00	3000.00
1 Boston Red Sox	250.00	500.00
2 Brooklyn Dodgers	250.00	500.00
3 Chicago White Sox	150.00	300.00
4 Cincinnati Reds	150.00	300.00
5 New York Giants	200.00	400.00
6 Philadelphia Athletics	150.00	300.00
7 Philadelphia Phillies	150.00	300.00
8 St. Louis Cardinals	250.00	500.00
9 Washington Senators	150.00	300.00

1952 Topps

The cards in this 407-card set measure approximately 2 5/8" by 3 3/4". The 1952 Topps set is Topps' first truly major set. Card numbers 1 to 80 were issued with red or black backs, both of which are less plentiful than card numbers 81 to 250. In fact, the first series is considered the most difficult with respect to finding perfect condition cards. Card number 48 (Joe Page) and number 49 (Johnny Sain) can be found with each other's write-up on their back. However, many dealers today believe that all cards numbered 1-250 were produced in the same quantities. Card numbers 251 to 310 are somewhat scarce and numbers 311 to 407 are quite scarce. Cards 281-300 were single printed compared to the other cards in the next to last series. Cards 311-313 were double printed on the last high number printing sheet. The key card in the set is Mickey Mantle, number 311, which was Mickey's first of many Topps cards. A minor variation on cards from 311 through 313 is that they exist with the stitching on the number circle in the back pointing right or left. There seems to be no print run difference between the two versions. Card number 307, Frank Campos, can be found in a scarce version with with one red star and one black star next to the words "Topps Baseball" on the back. In the early 1980's, Topps issued a standard-size reprint set of the 52 Topps set. These cards were issued only as a factory set. Five people portrayed in the regular set: Billy Loes (number 20), Dom DiMaggio (number 22), Saul Rogovin (number 159), Solly Hemus (number 196) and Tommy Holmes (number 289) are not in the reprint set. Although rarely seen, salesman sample panels of three cards containing the fronts of regular cards with ad information on the back do exist.

COMP.MASTER SET (487)	100000.00	250000.00
COMPLETE SET (407)	75000.00	200000.00
COMMON CARD (1-80)	35.00	60.00
COMMON CARD (81-250)	20.00	40.00
COMMON CARD (251-310)	30.00	50.00
COMMON CARD (311-407)	150.00	250.00
WRAPPER (1-CENT)	200.00	250.00
WRAPPER (5-CENT)	75.00	100.00
1 Andy Pafko	2000.00	5000.00
1A Andy Pafko Black	1250.00	3000.00
2 Pete Runnels RC	100.00	250.00
2A Pete Runnels Black RC	100.00	250.00
3 Hank Thompson	30.00	70.00
3A Hank Thompson Black	30.00	70.00
4 Don Lenhardt	60.00	150.00
4A Don Lenhardt Black	50.00	120.00
5 c	50.00	120.00
5A Larry Jansen Black	50.00	120.00
6 Grady Hatton	25.00	60.00
6A Grady Hatton Black	25.00	60.00
7 Wayne Terwilliger	25.00	60.00
7A Wayne Terwilliger Black	25.00	60.00
8 Fred Marsh RC	40.00	100.00
8A Fred Marsh Black RC	40.00	100.00
9 Robert Hogue RC	25.00	60.00
9A Robert Hogue Black RC	25.00	60.00
10 Al Rosen	30.00	80.00
10A Al Rosen Black	30.00	80.00
11 Phil Rizzuto	150.00	400.00
11A Phil Rizzuto Black	150.00	400.00
12 Monty Basgall RC	25.00	60.00
12A Monty Basgall Black RC	25.00	60.00
13 Johnny Wyrostek	40.00	100.00
13A Johnny Wyrostek Black	40.00	100.00
14 Bob Elliott	30.00	80.00
14A Bob Elliott Black	30.00	80.00
15 Johnny Pesky	30.00	80.00
15A Johnny Pesky Black	30.00	80.00
16 Gene Hermanski	25.00	60.00
16A Gene Hermanski Black	25.00	60.00
17 Jim Hegan	30.00	80.00
17A Jim Hegan Black	30.00	80.00
18 Merrill Combs RC	25.00	60.00
18A Merrill Combs Black RC	25.00	60.00
19 Johnny Bucha RC	25.00	60.00
19A Johnny Bucha Black RC	25.00	60.00
20 Billy Loes SP RC	60.00	150.00
20A Billy Loes Black RC	60.00	150.00
21 Ferris Fain	30.00	80.00
21A Ferris Fain Black	30.00	80.00
22 Dom DiMaggio	50.00	125.00
22A Dom DiMaggio Black	40.00	100.00
23 Billy Goodman	30.00	80.00
23A Billy Goodman Black	30.00	80.00
24 Luke Easter	30.00	80.00
24A Luke Easter Black	30.00	80.00
25 Johnny Groth	50.00	120.00
25A Johnny Groth Black	50.00	120.00
26 Monte Irvin	75.00	200.00
26A Monte Irvin Black	75.00	200.00
27 Sam Jethroe	30.00	70.00
27A Sam Jethroe Black	30.00	70.00
28 Jerry Priddy	40.00	100.00
28A Jerry Priddy Black	40.00	100.00
29 Ted Kluszewski	50.00	125.00
29A Ted Kluszewski Black	50.00	125.00
30 Mel Parnell	30.00	70.00
30A Mel Parnell Black	30.00	70.00
31 Gus Zernial Baseballs	30.00	80.00
31A Gus Zernial Black	30.00	80.00
Posed with six baseballs		
32 Eddie Robinson	25.00	60.00
32A Eddie Robinson Black	25.00	60.00
33 Warren Spahn	125.00	300.00
33A Warren Spahn Black	125.00	300.00
34 Elmer Valo	40.00	100.00
34A Elmer Valo Black	40.00	100.00
35 Hank Sauer	60.00	150.00
35A Hank Sauer Black	60.00	150.00
36 Gil Hodges	150.00	400.00
36A Gil Hodges Black	150.00	400.00
37 Duke Snider	150.00	400.00
37A Duke Snider Black	150.00	400.00
38 Wally Westlake	25.00	60.00
38A Wally Westlake Black	25.00	60.00
39 Dizzy Trout	30.00	70.00
39A Dizzy Trout Black	30.00	70.00
40 Irv Noren	30.00	70.00
40A Irv Noren Black	30.00	70.00
41 Bob Wellman RC	25.00	60.00
41A Bob Wellman Black RC	25.00	60.00
42 Lou Kretlow RC	25.00	60.00
42A Lou Kretlow Black RC	25.00	60.00
43 Ray Scarborough	25.00	60.00
43A Ray Scarborough Black	25.00	60.00
44 Con Dempsey RC	25.00	60.00
44A Con Dempsey Black RC	25.00	60.00
45 Eddie Joost	25.00	60.00
45A Eddie Joost Black	25.00	60.00
46 Gordon Goldsberry RC	25.00	60.00
46A Gordon Goldsberry Black RC	25.00	60.00
47 Willie Jones	30.00	70.00
47A Willie Jones Black	30.00	70.00
48A Joe Page ERR BLA	150.00	400.00
48B Joe Page COR BLA	50.00	125.00
48C Joe Page COR Red	50.00	125.00
49A John Sain ERR BLA	150.00	400.00
49B John Sain COR BLA	50.00	125.00
49C Joe Page COR Red	50.00	120.00
50 Marv Rickert RC	25.00	60.00
50A Marv Rickert Black RC	25.00	60.00
51 Jim Russell	25.00	60.00
51A Jim Russell Black	25.00	60.00
52 Don Mueller	30.00	70.00
52A Don Mueller Black	30.00	70.00
53 Chris Van Cuyk RC	30.00	80.00
53A Chris Van Cuyk Black RC	30.00	80.00
54 Leo Kiely RC	40.00	100.00
54A Leo Kiely Black RC	25.00	60.00
55 Ray Boone	30.00	80.00
55A Ray Boone Black	30.00	80.00
56 Tommy Glaviano	25.00	60.00
56A Tommy Glaviano Black	25.00	60.00
57 Ed Lopat	40.00	100.00
57A Ed Lopat Black	40.00	100.00
58 Bob Mahoney RC	25.00	60.00
58A Bob Mahoney Black RC	25.00	60.00
59 Robin Roberts	75.00	200.00
59A Robin Roberts Black	75.00	200.00
60 Sid Hudson	25.00	60.00
60A Sid Hudson Black	25.00	60.00
61 Tookie Gilbert	40.00	100.00
61A Tookie Gilbert Black	40.00	100.00
62 Chuck Stobbs RC	25.00	60.00
62A Chuck Stobbs Black RC	25.00	60.00
63 Howie Pollet	50.00	120.00
63A Howie Pollet Black	50.00	120.00
64 Roy Sievers	30.00	70.00
64A Roy Sievers Black	30.00	70.00
65 Enos Slaughter	75.00	200.00
65A Enos Slaughter Black	75.00	200.00
66 Preacher Roe	40.00	100.00
66A Preacher Roe Black	40.00	100.00
67 Allie Reynolds	50.00	125.00
67A Allie Reynolds Black	50.00	125.00
68 Cliff Chambers	25.00	60.00
68A Cliff Chambers Black	25.00	60.00
69 Virgil Stallcup	25.00	60.00
69A Virgil Stallcup Black	25.00	60.00
70 Al Zarilla	25.00	60.00
70A Al Zarilla Black	25.00	60.00
71 Tom Upton RC	25.00	60.00
71A Tom Upton Black RC	25.00	60.00
72 Karl Olson RC	25.00	60.00
72A Karl Olson Black RC	25.00	60.00
73 Bill Werle	25.00	60.00
73A Bill Werle Black	25.00	60.00
74 Andy Hansen RC	25.00	60.00
74A Andy Hansen Black RC	25.00	60.00
75 Wes Westrum	30.00	70.00
75A Wes Westrum Black	30.00	70.00
76 Eddie Stanky	50.00	120.00
76A Eddie Stanky Black	30.00	70.00
77 Bob Kennedy	30.00	70.00
77A Bob Kennedy Black	30.00	70.00
78 Ellis Kinder	40.00	100.00
78A Ellis Kinder Black	40.00	100.00
79 Gerry Staley	25.00	60.00
79A Gerry Staley Black	25.00	60.00
80 Herman Wehmeier	30.00	80.00
80A Herman Wehmeier Black	30.00	80.00
81 Vernon Law	40.00	100.00
82 Duane Pillette	20.00	50.00
83 Billy Johnson	20.00	50.00
84 Vern Stephens	30.00	80.00
85 Bob Kuzava	30.00	80.00
86 Ted Gray	20.00	50.00
87 Dale Coogan	20.00	50.00
88 Bob Feller	200.00	500.00
89 Johnny Lipon	20.00	50.00
90 Mickey Grasso	20.00	50.00
91 Red Schoendienst	60.00	150.00
92 Dale Mitchell	25.00	60.00
93 Al Sima RC	25.00	60.00
94 Sam Mele	20.00	50.00
95 Ken Holcombe	25.00	60.00
96 Willard Marshall	20.00	50.00
97 Earl Torgeson	25.00	60.00
98 Billy Pierce	30.00	80.00
99 Gene Woodling	25.00	60.00
100 Del Rice	30.00	80.00
101 Max Lanier	30.00	80.00
102 Bill Kennedy	20.00	50.00
103 Cliff Mapes	20.00	50.00
104 Don Kolloway	30.00	80.00
105 Johnny Pramesa	20.00	50.00
106 Mickey Vernon	25.00	60.00
107 Connie Ryan	20.00	50.00
108 Jim Konstanty	25.00	60.00
109 Ted Wilks	20.00	50.00
110 Dutch Leonard	20.00	50.00
111 Peanuts Lowrey	20.00	50.00
112 Hank Majeski	20.00	50.00
113 Dick Sisler	20.00	50.00
114 Willard Ramsdell	20.00	50.00
115 George Munger	20.00	50.00
116 Carl Scheib	25.00	60.00
117 Sherm Lollar	30.00	80.00
118 Ken Raffensberger	20.00	50.00
119 Mickey McDermott	20.00	50.00
120 Bob Chakales RC	25.00	60.00
121 Gus Niarhos	20.00	50.00
122 Jackie Jensen	60.00	150.00
123 Eddie Yost	20.00	50.00
124 Monte Kennedy	20.00	50.00
125 Bill Rigney	20.00	50.00
126 Fred Hutchinson	20.00	50.00
127 Paul Minner RC	20.00	50.00
128 Don Bollweg RC	20.00	50.00
129 Johnny Mize	75.00	200.00
130 Sheldon Jones	25.00	60.00
131 Morrie Martin RC	20.00	50.00
132 Clyde Kluttz RC	20.00	50.00
133 Al Widmar	20.00	50.00
134 Joe Tipton	20.00	50.00
135 Dixie Howell	20.00	50.00
136 Johnny Schmitz	20.00	50.00
137 Roy McMillan RC	20.00	50.00
138 Bill MacDonald	20.00	50.00
139 Ken Wood	20.00	50.00
140 Johnny Antonelli	25.00	60.00
141 Clint Hartung	20.00	50.00
142 Harry Perkowski RC	20.00	50.00
143 Les Moss	20.00	50.00
144 Ed Blake RC	20.00	50.00
145 Joe Haynes	20.00	50.00
146 Frank House RC	20.00	50.00
147 Bob Young RC	20.00	50.00
148 Johnny Klippstein	20.00	50.00
149 Dick Kryhoski	20.00	50.00
150 Ted Beard	20.00	50.00
151 Wally Post RC	20.00	50.00
152 Al Evans	30.00	80.00
153 Bob Rush	20.00	50.00
154 Joe Muir RC	20.00	50.00
155 Frank Overmire	20.00	50.00
156 Frank Hiller RC	20.00	50.00
157 Bob Usher	20.00	50.00
158 Eddie Waitkus	20.00	50.00
159 Saul Rogovin RC	20.00	50.00
160 Owen Friend	20.00	50.00
161 Bud Byerly RC	20.00	50.00
162 Del Crandall	20.00	50.00
163 Stan Rojek	20.00	50.00
164 Walt Dubiel	20.00	50.00
165 Eddie Kazak	20.00	50.00
166 Paul LaPalme RC	20.00	50.00
167 Bill Howerton	20.00	50.00
168 Charlie Silvera RC	25.00	60.00
169 Howie Judson	20.00	50.00
170 Gus Bell	20.00	50.00
171 Ed Erautt RC	20.00	50.00
172 Eddie Miksis	30.00	80.00
173 Roy Smalley	20.00	50.00
174 Clarence Marshall RC	25.00	60.00
175 Billy Martin RC	200.00	500.00
176 Hank Edwards	20.00	50.00
177 Bill Wight	20.00	50.00
178 Cass Michaels	20.00	50.00
179 Frank Smith RC	20.00	50.00
180 Charlie Maxwell RC	20.00	50.00
181 Bob Swift	20.00	50.00
182 Billy Hitchcock	20.00	50.00
183 Erv Dusak	20.00	50.00
184 Bob Ramazzotti	20.00	50.00
185 Bill Nicholson	20.00	50.00
186 Walt Masterson	20.00	50.00
187 Bob Miller	20.00	50.00
188 Clarence Podbielan RC	20.00	50.00
189 Pete Reiser	25.00	60.00
190 Don Johnson RC	20.00	50.00
191 Yogi Berra	300.00	800.00
192 Myron Ginsberg RC	30.00	80.00
193 Harry Simpson RC	20.00	50.00
194 Joe Hatten	25.00	60.00
195 Minnie Minoso RC	100.00	250.00
196 Solly Hemus RC	25.00	60.00
197 George Strickland RC	20.00	50.00
198 Phil Haugstad RC	20.00	50.00
199 George Zuverink RC	20.00	50.00
200 Ralph Houk RC	50.00	120.00
201 Alex Kellner	20.00	50.00
202 Joe Collins RC	40.00	100.00
203 Curt Simmons	40.00	100.00
204 Ron Northey	20.00	50.00
205 Clyde King	25.00	60.00
206 Joe Ostrowski RC	30.00	80.00
207 Mickey Harris	20.00	50.00
208 Marlin Stuart RC	25.00	60.00
209 Howie Fox	20.00	50.00
210 Dick Fowler	20.00	50.00
211 Ray Coleman	20.00	50.00
212 Ned Garver	20.00	50.00
213 Nippy Jones	20.00	50.00
214 Johnny Hopp	20.00	50.00
215 Hank Bauer	60.00	150.00
216 Richie Ashburn	100.00	250.00
217 Snuffy Stirnweiss	20.00	50.00
218 Clyde McCullough	25.00	60.00
219 Bobby Shantz	30.00	80.00
220 Joe Presko RC	20.00	50.00
221 Granny Hamner	40.00	100.00
222 Hoot Evers	20.00	50.00
223 Del Ennis	30.00	80.00
224 Bruce Edwards	20.00	50.00
225 Frank Baumholtz	20.00	50.00
226 Dave Philley	20.00	50.00
227 Joe Garagiola	40.00	100.00
228 Al Brazle	20.00	50.00
229 Gene Bearden UER	20.00	50.00
230 Matt Batts	40.00	100.00
231 Sam Zoldak	20.00	50.00
232 Billy Cox	40.00	100.00
233 Bob Friend RC	40.00	100.00
234 Steve Souchock RC	20.00	50.00
235 Walt Dropo	25.00	60.00
236 Ed Fitzgerald	20.00	50.00
237 Jerry Coleman	30.00	80.00
238 Art Houtteman	20.00	50.00
239 Rocky Bridges RC	20.00	50.00
240 Jack Phillips RC	20.00	50.00
241 Tommy Byrne	25.00	60.00
242 Tom Poholsky RC	20.00	50.00
243 Larry Doby	100.00	250.00
244 Vic Wertz	30.00	80.00
245 Sherry Robertson	20.00	50.00
246 George Kell	75.00	200.00
247 Randy Gumpert	25.00	60.00
248 Frank Shea	20.00	50.00
249 Bobby Adams	20.00	50.00
250 Carl Erskine	75.00	200.00
251 Chico Carrasquel	20.00	50.00
252 Vern Bickford	20.00	50.00
253 Johnny Berardino	30.00	80.00
254 Joe Dobson	20.00	50.00
255 Clyde Vollmer	20.00	50.00
256 Pete Suder	20.00	50.00
257 Bobby Avila	60.00	150.00
258 Steve Gromek	40.00	100.00
259 Bob Addis RC	20.00	50.00
260 Pete Castiglione	20.00	50.00
261 Willie Mays	2500.00	6000.00
262 Virgil Trucks	30.00	80.00
263 Harry Brecheen	25.00	60.00
264 Roy Hartsfield	20.00	50.00
265 Chuck Diering	30.00	80.00
266 Murry Dickson	20.00	50.00
267 Sid Gordon	25.00	60.00
268 Bob Lemon	100.00	250.00
269 Willard Nixon	30.00	80.00
270 Lou Brissie	20.00	50.00
271 Jim Delsing	30.00	80.00
272 Mike Garcia	30.00	80.00
273 Erv Palica	60.00	150.00
274 Ralph Branca	100.00	250.00
275 Pat Mullin	20.00	50.00
276 Jim Wilson RC	40.00	100.00
277 Early Wynn	150.00	400.00
278 Allie Clark	30.00	80.00
279 Eddie Stewart	20.00	50.00
280 Cloyd Boyer	30.00	80.00
281 Tommy Brown SP	30.00	80.00
282 Birdie Tebbetts SP	30.00	80.00
283 Phil Masi SP	25.00	60.00
284 Hank Arft SP	30.00	80.00
285 Cliff Fannin SP	40.00	100.00
286 Joe DeMaestri SP RC	30.00	80.00
287 Steve Bilko SP	30.00	80.00
288 Chet Nichols SP RC	40.00	100.00
289 Tommy Holmes SP	40.00	100.00
290 Joe Astroth SP	25.00	60.00
291 Gil Coan SP	25.00	60.00
292 Floyd Baker SP	40.00	100.00
293 Sibby Sisti SP	25.00	60.00
294 Walker Cooper SP	25.00	60.00
295 Phil Cavarretta SP	100.00	250.00
296 Red Rolfe MG SP	60.00	150.00
297 Andy Seminick SP	25.00	60.00
298 Bob Ross SP RC	25.00	60.00
299 Ray Murray SP RC	30.00	80.00
300 Barney McCosky SP	30.00	80.00
301 Bob Porterfield	20.00	50.00
302 Max Surkont RC	40.00	100.00
303 Harry Dorish	20.00	50.00
304 Sam Dente	30.00	80.00
305 Paul Richards MG	25.00	60.00
306 Lou Sleater RC	25.00	60.00
307 Frank Campos RC	20.00	50.00
Two red stars on back in copyright line		
307A Frank Campos Star		
307B Frank Campos RC		
Partial top left border on front		
308 Luis Aloma	20.00	50.00
309 Jim Busby	25.00	60.00
310 George Metkovich	40.00	100.00
311 Mickey Mantle DP	75000.00	200000.00
311B Mickey Mantle DP	75000.00	200000.00
312 Jackie Robinson	12000.00	30000.00
312B Jackie Robinson Stitch	12000.00	30000.00
313 Bobby Thomson DP	150.00	400.00
313B Bobby Thomson Stitch	150.00	400.00
314 Roy Campanella	1250.00	3000.00
315 Leo Durocher MG	250.00	600.00
316 Dave Williams RC	125.00	300.00
317 Conrado Marrero	125.00	300.00
318 Harold Gregg RC	125.00	300.00
319 Rube Walker RC	250.00	600.00
320 John Rutherford RC	125.00	300.00
321 Joe Black RC	200.00	500.00
322 Randy Jackson RC	125.00	300.00
323 Bubba Church	150.00	400.00
324 Warren Hacker	125.00	300.00
325 Bill Serena	250.00	600.00
326 George Shuba RC	300.00	800.00
327 Al Wilson RC	125.00	300.00
328 Bob Borkowski RC	125.00	300.00
329 Ike Delock RC	250.00	600.00
330 Turk Lown RC	125.00	300.00
331 Tom Morgan RC	250.00	600.00
332 Tony Bartirome RC	1250.00	3000.00
333 Pee Wee Reese	750.00	2000.00
334 Wilmer Mizell RC	250.00	600.00
335 Ted Lepcio RC	250.00	600.00
336 Dave Koslo	100.00	250.00
337 Jim Hearn	250.00	600.00
338 Sal Yvars RC	125.00	300.00
339 Russ Meyer	125.00	300.00
340 Bob Hooper	250.00	600.00
341 Hal Jeffcoat	200.00	500.00
342 Clem Labine RC	250.00	600.00
343 Dick Gernert RC	200.00	500.00
344 Ewell Blackwell	125.00	300.00
345 Sammy White RC	100.00	250.00
346 George Spencer RC	200.00	500.00
347 Joe Adcock	250.00	600.00
348 Robert Kelly RC	100.00	250.00
349 Bob Cain	125.00	300.00
350 Cal Abrams	200.00	50.00
351 Alvin Dark	125.00	300.00
352 Karl Drews	125.00	300.00
353 Bobby Del Greco RC	125.00	300.00
354 Fred Hatfield RC	125.00	300.00
355 Bobby Morgan	300.00	800.00
356 Toby Atwell RC	125.00	300.00
357 Smoky Burgess	300.00	800.00
358 John Kucab RC	200.00	500.00
359 Dee Fondy RC	250.00	600.00
360 George Crowe RC	125.00	300.00
361 Bill Posedel CO	100.00	250.00
362 Ken Heintzelman	125.00	300.00
363 Dick Rozek RC	125.00	300.00
364 Clyde Sukeforth CO RC	125.00	300.00
365 Cookie Lavagetto CO	200.00	500.00
366 Dave Madison RC	100.00	250.00
367 Ben Thorpe RC	200.00	500.00
368 Ed Wright RC	200.00	500.00
369 Dick Groat RC	250.00	600.00
370 Billy Hoeft RC	250.00	600.00
371 Bobby Hofman	100.00	250.00
372 Gil McDougald RC	200.00	500.00
373 Jim Turner CO RC	150.00	400.00
374 Al Benton RC	250.00	600.00
375 John Merson RC	200.00	500.00
376 Faye Throneberry RC	100.00	250.00
377 Chuck Dressen MG	250.00	600.00
378 Leroy Fusselman RC	300.00	800.00
379 Joe Rossi RC	100.00	250.00
380 Clem Koshorek RC	100.00	250.00
381 Milton Stock CO RC	200.00	500.00
382 Sam Jones RC	300.00	800.00
383 Del Wilber RC	100.00	250.00
384 Frank Crosetti CO	200.00	500.00
385 Herman Franks CO RC	250.00	600.00
386 Ed Yuhas RC	125.00	300.00
387 Billy Meyer MG	250.00	600.00
388 Bob Chipman	100.00	250.00
389 Ben Wade RC	125.00	300.00
390 Rocky Nelson RC	125.00	300.00
391 Ben Chapman CO UER	100.00	250.00
392 Hoyt Wilhelm RC	600.00	1500.00
393 Ebba St.Claire RC	125.00	300.00
394 Billy Herman CO	250.00	600.00
395 Jake Pitler CO	300.00	800.00
396 Dick Williams RC	400.00	1000.00
397 Forrest Main RC	250.00	600.00
398 Hal Rice	100.00	250.00
399 Jim Fridley RC	100.00	250.00
400 Bill Dickey CO	600.00	1500.00
401 Bob Schultz RC	125.00	300.00
402 Earl Harrist RC	125.00	300.00
403 Bill Miller RC	125.00	300.00
404 Dick Brodowski RC	125.00	300.00
405 Eddie Pellagrini	300.00	800.00
406 Joe Nuxhall RC	600.00	1500.00
407 Eddie Mathews RC	8000.00	20000.00

1953 Topps

The cards in this 274-card set measure 2 5/8" by 3 3/4". Card number 69, Dick Brodowksi, features the first known drawing of a player during a night game. Although the last card is numbered 280, there are only 274 cards in the set since numbers 253, 261, 267, 268, 271, and 275 were never issued. The 1953 Topps series contains line drawings of players in full color. The name and team panel at the card base is easily damaged, making it very difficult to complete a mint set. The high number series, 221 to 280, was produced in shorter supply late in the year and hence is more difficult to complete than the lower numbers. The key cards in the set are Mickey Mantle (82) and Willie Mays (244). The key Rookie Cards in this set are Roy Face, Jim Gilliam, and Johnny Podres, all from the last series. There are a number of double-printed cards (actually not double but 50 percent more of each of these numbers were printed compared to the other cards in the series) indicated by DP in the checklist below. There were five players (10 Smoky Burgess, 44 Ellis Kinder, 61 Early Wynn, 72 Fred Hutchinson, and 81 Joe Black) held out of the first run of 1-85 (but printed in with numbers 86-165), who are each marked by SP in the checklist below. In addition, there are five numbers which were printed with the more plentiful series 166-220; these cards (94, 107, 131, 145, and 156) are also indicated by DP in the checklist below. All these aforementioned cards from 86 through 165 and the five short prints come with the biographical information on the back in either white or black lettering. These seem to be printed in equal quantities and no price differential is given for either variety. The cards were issued in one-card penny packs or six-card nickel packs. The nickel packs were issued 24 to a box. There were some three-card advertising panels produced by Topps; the players include Johnny Mize/Clem Koshorek/Toby Atwell; Jim Hearn/Johnny Groth/Sherman Lollar and Mickey Mantle/Johnny Wyrostek/

COMPLETE SET (274)	20000.00	50000.00
COMMON CARD (1-165)	12.00	30.00
COMMON DP (1-165)	6.00	15.00
COMMON CARD (166-220)	10.00	25.00
COMMON CARD (221-280)	40.00	100.00
NOT ISSUED (253/261/267)		
NOT ISSUED (268/271/275)		
WRAP.(1-CENT, DATED)	150.00	250.00
WRAP.(1-CENT,NO DATE)	250.00	300.00
WRAP.(5-CENT, DATED)	300.00	400.00
WRAP.(5-CENT,NO DATE)	275.00	350.00
1 Jackie Robinson DP	2000.00	5000.00
2 Luke Easter DP	15.00	40.00
3 George Crowe	40.00	100.00
4 Ben Wade	20.00	50.00
5 Joe Dobson	20.00	50.00
6 Sam Jones	20.00	50.00
7 Bob Borkowski DP	15.00	40.00
8 Clem Koshorek DP	15.00	40.00
9 Joe Collins	50.00	120.00
10 Smoky Burgess SP	40.00	100.00
11 Sal Yvars	20.00	50.00
12 Howie Judson DP	12.00	30.00
13 Conrado Marrero DP	15.00	40.00
14 Clem Labine DP	30.00	80.00
15 Bobo Newsom DP RC	15.00	40.00
16 Peanuts Lowrey DP	12.00	30.00
17 Billy Hitchcock	20.00	50.00
18 Ted Lepcio DP	12.00	30.00
19 Mel Parnell DP	20.00	50.00
20 Hank Thompson	20.00	50.00
21 Billy Johnson	20.00	50.00
22 Howie Fox	20.00	50.00
23 Toby Atwell DP	15.00	40.00
24 Ferris Fain	20.00	50.00
25 Ray Boone	20.00	50.00
26 Dale Mitchell DP	20.00	50.00
27 Roy Campanella DP	150.00	400.00
28 Eddie Pellagrini	15.00	40.00
29 Hal Jeffcoat	15.00	40.00
30 Willard Nixon	20.00	50.00
31 Ewell Blackwell	20.00	50.00
32 Clyde Vollmer	12.00	30.00
33 Bob Kennedy DP	12.00	30.00
34 George Shuba	20.00	50.00
35 Irv Noren DP	25.00	60.00
36 Johnny Groth DP	15.00	40.00
37 Eddie Mathews DP	200.00	500.00
38 Jim Hearn DP	15.00	40.00
39 Eddie Miksis	15.00	40.00
40 John Lipon	15.00	40.00
41 Enos Slaughter	50.00	120.00
42 Gus Zernial DP	12.00	30.00
43 Gil McDougald	40.00	100.00
44 Ellis Kinder SP	25.00	60.00
45 Grady Hatton DP	12.00	30.00
46 Johnny Klippstein DP	15.00	40.00
47 Bubba Church DP	12.00	30.00
48 Bob Del Greco DP	12.00	30.00
49 Faye Throneberry DP	15.00	40.00
50 Chuck Dressen MG DP	20.00	50.00
51 Frank Campos DP	15.00	40.00
52 Ted Gray DP	12.00	30.00
53 Sherm Lollar DP	20.00	50.00
54 Bob Feller DP	100.00	250.00
55 Maurice McDermott DP	15.00	40.00
56 Gerry Staley DP	20.00	50.00
57 Carl Scheib	12.00	30.00
58 George Metkovich	15.00	40.00
59 Karl Drews DP	15.00	40.00
60 Cloyd Boyer DP	15.00	40.00
61 Early Wynn SP	50.00	120.00
62 Monte Irvin DP	100.00	250.00
63 Gus Niarhos DP	12.00	30.00
64 Dave Philley	25.00	60.00
65 Earl Harrist	25.00	60.00
66 Minnie Minoso	60.00	150.00
67 Roy Sievers DP	12.00	30.00
68 Del Rice	15.00	40.00
69 Dick Brodowski	20.00	50.00
70 Ed Yuhas	20.00	50.00
71 Tony Bartirome	15.00	40.00
72 Fred Hutchinson SP	25.00	60.00
73 Eddie Robinson	12.00	30.00
74 Joe Rossi	20.00	50.00
75 Mike Garcia	15.00	40.00
76 Pee Wee Reese	150.00	400.00
77 Johnny Mize DP	50.00	120.00
78 Red Schoendienst	50.00	120.00
79 Johnny Wyrostek	20.00	50.00
80 Jim Hegan	15.00	40.00
81 Joe Black SP	40.00	100.00
82 Mickey Mantle	8000.00	20000.00
83 Howie Pollet	15.00	40.00
84 Bob Hooper DP	12.00	30.00
85 Bobby Morgan DP	20.00	50.00
86 Billy Martin	125.00	300.00
87 Ed Lopat	40.00	100.00
88 Willie Jones DP	25.00	60.00
89 Chuck Stobbs DP	12.00	30.00
90 Hank Edwards DP	12.00	30.00
91 Ebba St.Claire DP	15.00	40.00
92 Paul Minner DP	15.00	40.00
93 Hal Rice DP	25.00	60.00
94 Bill Kennedy DP	12.00	30.00
95 Willard Marshall DP	15.00	40.00
96 Virgil Trucks	20.00	50.00
97 Don Kolloway DP	12.00	30.00
98 Cal Abrams DP	20.00	50.00
99 Dave Madison	15.00	40.00
100 Bill Miller	25.00	60.00
101 Ted Wilks	20.00	50.00
102 Connie Ryan DP	15.00	40.00
103 Joe Astroth DP	15.00	40.00
104 Yogi Berra	200.00	500.00
105 Joe Nuxhall DP	60.00	150.00
106 Johnny Antonelli	25.00	60.00
107 Danny O'Connell DP	12.00	30.00
108 Bob Porterfield DP	12.00	30.00
109 Alvin Dark	40.00	100.00
110 Herman Wehmeier DP	12.00	30.00
111 Hank Sauer DP	20.00	50.00
112 Ned Garver DP	12.00	30.00
113 Jerry Priddy	25.00	60.00
114 Phil Rizzuto	150.00	400.00
115 George Spencer	20.00	50.00
116 Frank Smith DP	20.00	50.00
117 Sid Gordon DP	12.00	30.00
118 Gus Bell DP	15.00	40.00
119 Johnny Sain SP	40.00	100.00
120 Davey Williams	20.00	50.00
121 Walt Dropo	20.00	50.00
122 Elmer Valo	20.00	50.00
123 Tommy Byrne DP	12.00	30.00
124 Sibby Sisti DP	15.00	40.00
125 Dick Williams DP	30.00	80.00
126 Bill Connelly DP RC	15.00	40.00
127 Clint Courtney DP RC	15.00	40.00
128 Wilmer Mizell DP	20.00	50.00
Inconsistent design, logo on front with black birds		
129 Keith Thomas RC	12.00	30.00
130 Turk Lown DP	15.00	40.00
131 Harry Byrd DP RC	15.00	40.00
132 Tom Morgan	30.00	80.00
133 Gil Coan	15.00	40.00
134 Rube Walker	25.00	60.00
135 Al Rosen DP	25.00	60.00
136 Ken Heintzelman DP	20.00	50.00
137 John Rutherford DP	15.00	40.00

138 George Kell 40.00 100.00
139 Sammy White 20.00 50.00
140 Tommy Glaviano 15.00 40.00
141 Allie Reynolds DP 40.00 100.00
142 Vic Wertz 15.00 40.00
143 Billy Pierce 30.00 80.00
144 Bob Schultz DP 15.00 40.00
145 Harry Dorish DP 12.00 30.00
146 Granny Hamner 25.00 60.00
147 Warren Spahn 125.00 300.00
148 Mickey Grasso 15.00 40.00
149 Dom DiMaggio DP 40.00 100.00
150 Harry Simpson DP 12.00 30.00
151 Hoyt Wilhelm 50.00 120.00
152 Bob Adams DP 25.00 60.00
153 Andy Seminick DP 15.00 40.00
154 Dick Groat 50.00 120.00
155 Dutch Leonard 15.00 40.00
156 Jim Rivera DP RC 20.00 50.00
157 Bob Addis DP 25.00 60.00
158 Johnny Logan RC 30.00 80.00
159 Wayne Terwilliger DP 15.00 40.00
160 Bob Young 15.00 40.00
161 Vern Bickford DP 20.00 50.00
162 Ted Kluszewski 40.00 100.00
163 Fred Hatfield DP 12.00 30.00
164 Frank Shea DP 20.00 50.00
165 Billy Hoeft 20.00 50.00
166 Billy Hunter RC 20.00 50.00
167 Art Schult RC 25.00 60.00
168 Willard Schmidt RC 15.00 40.00
169 Dizzy Trout 15.00 40.00
170 Bill Werle 15.00 40.00
171 Bill Glynn RC 12.00 30.00
172 Rip Repulski RC 20.00 50.00
173 Preston Ward 12.00 30.00
174 Billy Loes 15.00 40.00
175 Ron Kline RC 20.00 50.00
176 Don Hoak RC 15.00 40.00
177 Jim Dyck RC 15.00 40.00
178 Jim Waugh RC 12.00 30.00
179 Gene Hermanski 20.00 50.00
180 Virgil Stallcup 25.00 60.00
181 Al Zarilla 12.00 30.00
182 Bobby Hofman 15.00 40.00
183 Stu Miller RC 15.00 40.00
184 Hal Brown RC 15.00 40.00
185 Jim Pendleton RC 12.00 30.00
186 Charlie Bishop RC 15.00 40.00
187 Jim Fridley 12.00 30.00
188 Andy Carey RC 40.00 100.00
189 Ray Jablonski RC 15.00 40.00
190 Dixie Walker CO 15.00 40.00
191 Ralph Kiner 60.00 150.00
192 Wally Westlake 12.00 30.00
193 Mike Clark RC 12.00 30.00
194 Eddie Kazak 15.00 40.00
195 Ed McGhee RC 12.00 30.00
196 Bob Keegan RC 12.00 30.00
197 Del Crandall 25.00 60.00
198 Forrest Main 12.00 30.00
199 Marion Fricano RC 12.00 25.00
200 Gordon Goldsberry 15.00 40.00
201 Paul LaPalme 15.00 40.00
202 Carl Sawatski RC 15.00 40.00
203 Cliff Fannin 25.00 60.00
204 Dick Bokelman RC 12.00 30.00
205 Vern Benson RC 12.00 30.00
206 Ed Bailey RC 20.00 50.00
207 Whitey Ford 150.00 400.00
208 Jim Wilson 12.00 30.00
209 Jim Greengrass RC 15.00 40.00
210 Bob Cerv RC 30.00 80.00
211 J.W. Porter RC 12.00 30.00
212 Jack Dittmer RC 15.00 40.00
213 Ray Scarborough 25.00 60.00
214 Bill Bruton RC 12.00 30.00
215 Gene Conley RC 20.00 50.00
216 Jim Hughes RC 15.00 40.00
217 Murray Wall RC 20.00 50.00
218 Les Fusselman 20.00 50.00
219 Pete Runnels UER 20.00 50.00
Photo actually
Don Johnson
220 Satchel Paige UER 1500.00 4000.00
221 Bob Milliken RC 30.00 80.00
222 Vic Janowicz DP RC 30.00 80.00
223 Johnny O'Brien DP RC 20.00 50.00
224 Lou Sleater DP 30.00 80.00
225 Bobby Shantz 50.00 120.00
226 Ed Erautt 25.00 60.00
227 Morrie Martin 25.00 60.00
228 Hal Newhouser 125.00 300.00
229 Rocky Krsnich RC 40.00 100.00
230 Johnny Lindell DP 25.00 60.00
231 Solly Hemus DP 25.00 60.00
232 Dick Kokos 40.00 100.00
233 Al Aber RC 30.00 80.00
234 Ray Murray DP 20.00 50.00
235 John Hetki DP RC 20.00 50.00
236 Harry Perkowski DP 30.00 80.00
237 Bud Podbielan DP 25.00 60.00
238 Cal Hogue DP RC 30.00 80.00
239 Jim Delsing 25.00 60.00
240 Fred Marsh 30.00 80.00
241 Al Sima DP 20.00 50.00
242 Charlie Silvera 40.00 100.00
243 Carlos Bernier DP RC 25.00 60.00
244 Willie Mays 5000.00 12000.00
245 Bill Norman CO 40.00 100.00
246 Roy Face RC DP RC 50.00 120.00
247 Mike Sandlock DP RC 20.00 50.00
248 Gene Stephens DP RC 25.00 60.00
249 Eddie O'Brien RC 30.00 80.00
250 Bob Wilson RC 60.00 150.00
251 Sid Hudson 75.00 200.00
252 Hank Foiles RC 40.00 100.00
254 Preacher Roe DP 50.00 120.00
255 Dixie Howell 50.00 120.00
256 Les Peden RC 50.00 120.00
257 Bob Boyd RC 50.00 120.00
258 Jim Gilliam RC 200.00 500.00
259 Roy McMillan DP 30.00 80.00
260 Sam Calderone RC 40.00 100.00
262 Bob Oldis RC 30.00 80.00
263 Johnny Podres RC 150.00 400.00
264 Gene Woodling DP 30.00 80.00
265 Jackie Jensen 40.00 100.00
266 Bob Cain 30.00 80.00
269 Duane Pillette 40.00 100.00
270 Vern Stephens 40.00 100.00
272 Bill Antonello RC 30.00 80.00
273 Harvey Haddix RC 125.00 300.00
274 John Riddle CO 60.00 150.00
276 Ken Raffensberger 60.00 150.00
277 Don Lund RC 50.00 120.00
278 Willie Miranda RC 75.00 200.00
279 Joe Coleman DP 25.00 60.00
280 Milt Bolling RC 150.00 400.00

1954 Topps

The cards in this 250-card set measure approximately 2 5/8" by 3 3/4". Each of the cards in the 1954 Topps set contains a large "head" shot of the player in color plus a smaller full-length photo in black and white set against a color background. The cards were issued in one-card penny packs or five-card nickel packs. Fifteen-card cello packs have also been seen. The penny packs came 120 to a box while the nickel packs came 24 to a box. The nickel boxes had a drawing of Ted Williams along with his name printed on the box to indicate that Williams was part of this product. This set contains the Rookie Cards of Hank Aaron, Ernie Banks, and Al Kaline and two separate cards of Ted Williams (number 1 and number 250). Conspicuous by his absence is Mickey Mantle who apparently was the exclusive property of Bowman during 1954 (and 1955). The first two issues of Sports Illustrated magazine contained "card" inserts on regular paper stock. The first issue showed actual cards in the set in color, while the second issue showed some created cards of New York Yankees players in black and white, including Mickey Mantle. There was also a Canadian printing of the first 50 cards. These cards can be easily discerned as they have "grey" backs rather than the white backs of the American printed cards. To celebrate this set as the first Topps set to feature Ted Williams, his visage is also featured on the five cent box. The Canadian cards came four cards to a pack and 36 packs to a box and cost five cents when issued.

COMPLETE SET (250) 10000.00 25000.00
COMMON (1-50/76-250) 8.00 20.00
COMMON CARD (51-75) 10.00 25.00
WRAP.(1-CENT, DATED) 150.00 200.00
WRAP.(1-CENT, UNDAT) 100.00 150.00
WRAP.(5-CENT, DATED) 250.00 300.00
WRAP.(5-CENT, UNDAT) 200.00 250.00
1 Ted Williams 1000.00 2500.00
2 Gus Zernial 8.00 20.00
3 Monte Irvin 30.00 80.00
4 Hank Sauer 12.00 30.00
5 Ed Lopat 12.00 30.00
6 Pete Runnels 12.00 30.00
7 Ted Kluszewski 15.00 40.00
8 Bob Young 10.00 25.00
9 Harvey Haddix 12.00 30.00
10 Jackie Robinson 1000.00 2500.00
11 Paul Leslie Smith RC 8.00 20.00
12 Del Crandall 12.00 30.00
13 Billy Martin 40.00 100.00
14 Preacher Roe UER 12.00 30.00
15 Al Rosen 15.00 40.00
16 Vic Janowicz 10.00 25.00
17 Phil Rizzuto 40.00 100.00
18 Walt Dropo 12.00 30.00
19 Johnny Lipon 10.00 25.00
20 Warren Spahn 50.00 120.00
21 Bobby Shantz 10.00 25.00
22 Jim Greengrass 8.00 20.00
23 Luke Easter 15.00 40.00
24 Granny Hamner 12.00 30.00
25 Harvey Kuenn RC 15.00 40.00
26 Ray Jablonski 10.00 25.00
27 Ferris Fain 10.00 25.00
28 Paul Minner 8.00 20.00
29 Jim Hegan 8.00 20.00
30 Eddie Mathews 50.00 120.00
31 Johnny Klippstein 10.00 25.00
32 Duke Snider 50.00 120.00
33 Johnny Schmitz 8.00 20.00
34 Jim Rivera 10.00 25.00
35 Junior Gilliam 20.00 50.00
36 Hoyt Wilhelm 25.00 60.00
37 Whitey Ford 60.00 150.00
38 Eddie Stanky MG 10.00 25.00
39 Sherm Lollar 8.00 20.00
40 Mel Parnell 8.00 20.00
41 Willie Jones 10.00 25.00
42 Don Mueller 8.00 20.00
43 Dick Groat 10.00 25.00
44 Ned Garver 10.00 25.00
45 Richie Ashburn 30.00 80.00
46 Ken Raffensberger 10.00 25.00
47 Ellis Kinder 8.00 20.00
48 Billy Hunter 12.00 30.00
49 Ray Murray 8.00 20.00
50 Yogi Berra 150.00 400.00
51 Johnny Lindell 10.00 25.00
52 Vic Power RC 15.00 40.00
53 Jack Dittmer 12.00 30.00
54 Vern Stephens 15.00 40.00
55 Phil Cavarretta MG 15.00 40.00
56 Willie Miranda 10.00 25.00
57 Luis Aloma 12.00 30.00
58 Bob Wilson 12.00 30.00
59 Gene Conley 12.00 30.00
60 Frank Baumholtz 12.00 30.00
61 Bob Cain 12.00 30.00
62 Eddie Robinson 20.00 50.00
63 Johnny Pesky 30.00 80.00
64 Hank Thompson 15.00 40.00
65 Bob Swift CO 10.00 25.00
66 Ted Lepcio 10.00 25.00
67 Jim Willis RC 10.00 25.00
68 Sam Calderone 15.00 40.00
69 Bud Podbielan 10.00 25.00
70 Larry Doby 100.00 250.00
71 Frank Smith 10.00 25.00
72 Preston Ward 15.00 40.00
73 Wayne Terwilliger 12.00 30.00
74 Bill Taylor RC 10.00 25.00
75 Fred Haney MG RC 20.00 50.00
76 Bob Scheffing CO 12.00 30.00
77 Ray Boone 10.00 25.00
78 Ted Kazanski RC 8.00 20.00
79 Andy Pafko 12.00 30.00
80 Jackie Jensen 15.00 40.00
81 Dave Hoskins RC 10.00 25.00
82 Milt Bolling 12.00 30.00
83 Joe Collins 15.00 40.00
84 Dick Cole RC 10.00 25.00
85 Bob Turley RC 20.00 50.00
86 Billy Herman CO 20.00 50.00
87 Roy Face 12.00 30.00
88 Matt Batts 12.00 30.00
89 Howie Pollet 8.00 20.00
90 Willie Mays 1000.00 2500.00
91 Bob Oldis 10.00 25.00
92 Wally Westlake 12.00 30.00
93 Sid Hudson 8.00 20.00
94 Ernie Banks RC 2500.00 6000.00
95 Hal Rice 12.00 30.00
96 Charlie Silvera 15.00 40.00
97 Jerald Hal Lane RC 8.00 20.00
98 Joe Black 40.00 100.00
99 Bobby Hofman 8.00 20.00
100 Bob Keegan 12.00 30.00
101 Gene Woodling 25.00 60.00
102 Gil Hodges 60.00 150.00
103 Jim Lemon RC 12.00 30.00
104 Mike Sandlock 10.00 25.00
105 Andy Carey 15.00 40.00
106 Dick Kokos 12.00 30.00
107 Duane Pillette 12.00 30.00
108 Thornton Kipper RC 12.00 30.00
109 Bill Bruton 12.00 30.00
110 Harry Dorish 12.00 30.00
111 Jim Delsing 12.00 30.00
112 Bill Renna RC 8.00 20.00
113 Bob Boyd 8.00 20.00
114 Dean Stone RC 10.00 25.00
115 Rip Repulski 15.00 40.00
116 Steve Bilko 12.00 30.00
117 Solly Hemus 8.00 20.00
118 Carl Scheib 8.00 20.00
119 Johnny Antonelli 15.00 40.00
120 Roy McMillan 8.00 20.00
121 Clem Labine 12.00 30.00
122 Johnny Logan 10.00 25.00
123 Bobby Adams 15.00 40.00
124 Marion Fricano 10.00 25.00
125 Harry Perkowski 10.00 25.00
126 Ben Wade 25.00 60.00
127 Steve O'Neill MG 12.00 30.00
128 Hank Aaron RC 5000.00 12000.00
129 Forrest Jacobs RC 8.00 20.00
130 Hank Bauer 25.00 60.00
131 Reno Bertoia RC 10.00 25.00
132 Tommy Lasorda RC 200.00 500.00
133 Del Baker CO 10.00 25.00
134 Cal Hogue 12.00 30.00
135 Joe Presko 10.00 25.00
136 Connie Ryan 12.00 30.00
137 Wally Moon RC 25.00 60.00
138 Bob Borkowski 12.00 30.00
139 J.O'Brien/E.O'Brien 40.00 100.00
140 Tom Wright 8.00 20.00
141 Joey Jay RC 15.00 40.00
142 Tom Poholsky 12.00 30.00
143 Rollie Hemsley CO 10.00 25.00
144 Bill Werle 10.00 25.00
145 Elmer Valo 12.00 30.00
146 Don Johnson 10.00 25.00
147 Johnny Riddle CO 12.00 30.00
148 Bob Trice RC 12.00 30.00
149 Al Robertson 8.00 20.00
150 Dick Kryhoski 12.00 30.00
151 Alex Grammas RC 10.00 25.00
152 Michael Blyzka RC 12.00 30.00
153 Al Walker 15.00 40.00
154 Mike Fornieles RC 12.00 30.00
155 Bob Kennedy 8.00 20.00
156 Joe Coleman 12.00 30.00
157 Don Lenhardt 15.00 40.00
158 Peanuts Lowrey 12.00 30.00
159 Dave Philley 12.00 30.00
160 Ralph Kress CO 15.00 40.00
161 John Hetki 8.00 20.00
162 Herman Wehmeier 12.00 30.00
163 Frank House 8.00 20.00
164 Stu Miller 10.00 25.00
165 Jim Pendleton 12.00 30.00
166 Johnny Podres 25.00 60.00
167 Don Lund 8.00 20.00
168 Morrie Martin 15.00 40.00
169 Jim Hughes 12.00 30.00
170 Dusty Rhodes RC 12.00 30.00
171 Leo Kiely 10.00 25.00
172 Harold Brown RC 8.00 20.00
173 Jack Harshman RC 8.00 20.00
174 Tom Qualters RC 15.00 40.00
175 Frank Leja RC 20.00 50.00
176 Robert Keely CO 12.00 30.00
177 Bob Milliken 10.00 25.00
178 Bill Glynn UER 12.00 30.00
179 Gair Allie RC 10.00 25.00
180 Wes Westrum 8.00 20.00
181 Mel Roach RC 10.00 25.00
182 Chuck Harmon RC 12.00 30.00
183 Earle Combs CO 15.00 40.00
184 Ed Bailey 10.00 25.00
185 Chuck Stobbs 8.00 20.00
186 Karl Olson 12.00 30.00
187 Heinie Manush CO 15.00 40.00
188 Dave Jolly RC 15.00 40.00
189 Bob Ross 12.00 30.00
190 Ray Herbert RC 12.00 30.00
191 Dick Schofield RC 12.00 30.00
192 Ellis Deal CO 10.00 25.00
193 Johnny Hopp CO 12.00 30.00
194 Bill Sarni RC 12.00 30.00
195 Billy Consolo RC 8.00 20.00
196 Stan Jok RC 12.00 30.00
197 Lynwood Rowe CO 12.00 30.00
198 Carl Sawatski 10.00 25.00
199 Glenn Rocky Nelson 8.00 20.00
200 Larry Jansen 12.00 30.00
201 Al Kaline RC 1000.00 2500.00
202 Bob Purkey RC 10.00 25.00
203 Harry Brecheen CO 10.00 25.00
204 Angel Scull RC 10.00 25.00
205 Johnny Sain 20.00 50.00
206 Ray Crone RC 10.00 25.00
207 Tom Oliver CO RC 8.00 20.00
208 Grady Hatton 12.00 30.00
209 Chuck Thompson RC 12.00 30.00
210 Bob Buhl RC 12.00 30.00
211 Don Hoak 20.00 50.00
212 Bob Micelotta RC 8.00 20.00
213 Johnny Fitzpatrick CO RC 12.00 30.00
214 Arnie Portocarrero RC 12.00 30.00
215 Ed McGhee 12.00 30.00
216 Al Sima 8.00 20.00
217 Paul Schreiber CO RC 10.00 25.00
218 Fred Marsh 12.00 30.00
219 Chuck Kress RC 10.00 25.00
220 Ruben Gomez RC 12.00 30.00
221 Dick Brodowski 15.00 40.00
222 Bill Wilson RC 12.00 30.00
223 Joe Haynes CO 10.00 25.00
224 Dick Weik RC 8.00 20.00
225 Don Liddle RC 10.00 25.00
226 Jehosie Heard RC 12.00 30.00
227 Buster Mills CO RC 20.00 50.00
228 Gene Hermanski 12.00 30.00
229 Bob Talbot RC 8.00 20.00
230 Bob Kuzava 15.00 40.00
231 Roy Smalley 8.00 20.00
232 Lou Limmer RC 12.00 30.00
233 Augie Galan CO 10.00 25.00
234 Jerry Lynch RC 10.00 25.00
235 Vern Law 15.00 40.00
236 Paul Penson RC 20.00 50.00
237 Mike Ryba CO RC 12.00 30.00
238 Al Aber 8.00 20.00
239 Bill Skowron RC 30.00 80.00
240 Sam Mele 12.00 30.00
241 Robert Miller RC 12.00 30.00
242 Curt Roberts RC 8.00 20.00
243 Ray Blades CO RC 10.00 25.00
244 Leroy Wheat RC 10.00 25.00
245 Roy Sievers 12.00 30.00
246 Howie Fox 10.00 25.00
247 Ed Mayo CO 10.00 25.00
248 Al Smith RC 12.00 30.00
249 Wilmer Mizell 12.00 30.00
250 Ted Williams 1000.00 2500.00

1955 Topps

The cards in this 206-card set measure approximately 2 5/8" by 3 3/4". Both the large "head" shot and the smaller full-length photos used on each card of the 1955 Topps set are in color. The card fronts were designed horizontally for the first time in Topps' history. The first card features Dusty Rhodes, hitting star and MVP in the New York Giants' 1954 World Series sweep over the Cleveland Indians. A "high" series, 161 to 210, is more difficult to find than cards 1 to 160. Numbers 175, 186, 203, and 209 were never issued. To fill in for the four cards not issued in the high number series, Topps double printed four players, those appearing on cards 170, 172, 184, and 188. Cards were issued in one-card penny packs or six-card nickel packs (which came 36 packs to a box) and 15-card cello packs (rarely seen). Although rarely seen, there exist salesman sample panels of three cards containing the fronts of regular cards with ad information for the 1955 Topps regular and the 1955 Topps Doubleheaders on the back. One panel depicts (from top to bottom) Danny Schell, Jake Thies, and Howie Pollet. Another Panel consists of Jackie Robinson, Bill Taylor and Curt Roberts. The key Rookie Cards in this set are Ken Boyer, Roberto Clemente, Harmon Killebrew, and Sandy Koufax. The Frank Sullivan card has a very noticable print dot which appears on some of the cards but not all of the cards. We are not listing that card as a variation at this point, but we will continue to monitor information about that card.

COMPLETE SET (206) 8000.00 20000.00
COMMON CARD (1-150) 6.00 12.00
COMMON CARD (151-160) 10.00 20.00
COMMON CARD (161-210) 15.00 30.00
NOT ISSUED (175/186/203/209)
WRAP.(1-CENT, DATED) 100.00 150.00
WRAP.(1-CENT, UNDAT) 40.00 50.00
WRAP.(5-CENT, DATED) 100.00 150.00
WRAP.(5-CENT, UNDAT) 75.00 100.00
1 Dusty Rhodes 25.00 60.00
2 Ted Williams 400.00 1000.00
3 Art Fowler RC 8.00 20.00
4 Al Kaline 150.00 400.00
5 Jim Gilliam 40.00 100.00
6 Stan Hack MG RC 12.50 30.00
7 Jim Hegan 25.00 60.00
8 Harold Smith RC 6.00 15.00
9 Robert Miller 6.00 15.00
10 Bob Keegan 6.00 15.00
11 Ferris Fain 7.50 20.00
12 Vernon Jake Thies RC 6.00 15.00
13 Fred Marsh 6.00 15.00
14 Jim Finigan RC 6.00 15.00
15 Jim Pendleton 6.00 15.00
16 Roy Sievers 8.00 20.00
17 Bobby Hofman 6.00 15.00
18 Russ Kemmerer RC 6.00 15.00
19 Billy Herman CO 8.00 20.00
20 Andy Carey 7.50 20.00
21 Alex Grammas 6.00 15.00
22 Bill Skowron 20.00 50.00
23 Jack Parks RC 15.00 40.00
24 Hal Newhouser 40.00 100.00
25 Johnny Podres 25.00 60.00
26 Dick Groat 30.00 80.00
27 Billy Gardner RC 7.50 20.00
28 Ernie Banks 200.00 500.00
29 Herman Wehmeier 6.00 15.00
30 Vic Power 7.50 20.00
31 Warren Spahn 75.00 200.00
32 Warren McGhee 6.00 15.00
33 Tom Qualters 15.00 40.00
34 Wayne Terwilliger 10.00 25.00
35 Dave Jolly 6.00 15.00
36 Leo Kiely 15.00 40.00
37 Joe Cunningham RC 8.00 20.00
38 Bob Turley 12.00 30.00
39 Bill Glynn 6.00 15.00
40 Don Hoak 8.00 20.00
41 Chuck Stobbs 10.00 25.00
42 John Windy McCall RC 12.00 30.00
43 Harvey Haddix 15.00 40.00
44 Harold Valentine RC 6.00 15.00
45 Hank Sauer 8.00 20.00
46 Ted Kazanski 6.00 15.00
47 Hank Aaron 750.00 2000.00
48 Bob Kennedy 8.00 20.00
49 J.W. Porter 6.00 15.00
50 Jackie Robinson 400.00 1000.00
51 Jim Hughes 15.00 40.00
52 Bill Tremel RC 6.00 15.00
53 Bill Taylor 6.00 15.00
54 Lou Limmer 6.00 15.00
55 Rip Repulski 6.00 15.00
56 Ray Jablonski 6.00 15.00
57 Billy O'Dell RC 6.00 15.00
58 Jim Rivera 10.00 25.00
59 Gair Allie 12.00 30.00
60 Dean Stone 8.00 20.00
61 Forrest Jacobs 6.00 15.00
62 Thornton Kipper 6.00 15.00
63 Joe Collins 20.00 50.00
64 Gus Triandos RC 12.00 30.00
65 Ray Boone 8.00 20.00
66 Ron Jackson RC 20.00 50.00
67 Wally Moon 7.50 20.00
68 Jim Davis RC 6.00 15.00
69 Ed Bailey 8.00 20.00
70 Al Rosen 15.00 40.00
71 Ruben Gomez 6.00 15.00
72 Karl Olson 20.00 50.00
73 Jack Shepard RC 6.00 15.00
74 Bob Borkowski 10.00 25.00
75 Sandy Amoros RC 25.00 60.00
76 Howie Pollet 6.00 15.00
77 Arnie Portocarrero 6.00 15.00
78 Gordon Jones RC 6.00 15.00
79 Clyde Danny Schell RC 6.00 15.00
80 Bob Grim RC 20.00 50.00
81 Gene Conley 7.50 20.00
82 Chuck Harmon 6.00 15.00
83 Tom Brewer RC 6.00 15.00
84 Camilo Pascual RC 15.00 40.00
85 Don Mossi RC 12.50 30.00
86 Bill Wilson 10.00 25.00
87 Frank House 6.00 15.00
88 Bob Skinner RC 12.00 30.00
89 Joe Frazier RC 7.50 20.00
90 Karl Spooner RC 8.00 20.00
91 Milt Bolling 12.00 30.00
92 Don Zimmer RC 40.00 100.00
93 Steve Bilko 6.00 15.00
94 Reno Bertoia 12.00 30.00
95 Preston Ward 12.00 30.00
96 Chuck Bishop 10.00 25.00
97 Carlos Paula RC 6.00 15.00
98 John Riddle CO 6.00 15.00
99 Frank Leja 6.00 15.00
100 Monte Irvin 40.00 100.00
101 Johnny Gray RC 6.00 15.00
102 Wally Westlake 10.00 25.00
103 Chuck White RC 6.00 15.00
104 Jack Harshman 12.00 30.00
105 Chuck Diering 6.00 15.00
106 Frank Sullivan RC 15.00 40.00
107 Curt Roberts 10.00 25.00
108 Rube Walker 15.00 40.00
109 Ed Lopat 15.00 40.00
110 Gus Zernial 10.00 25.00
111 Bob Milliken 7.50 20.00
112 Nelson King RC 6.00 15.00
113 Harry Brecheen CO 7.50 20.00
114 Louis Ortiz RC 6.00 15.00
115 Ellis Kinder 10.00 25.00
116 Tom Hurd RC 6.00 15.00
117 Mel Roach 10.00 25.00
118 Bob Purkey 12.00 30.00
119 Bob Lennon RC 6.00 15.00
120 Ted Kluszewski 20.00 50.00
121 Bill Renna 10.00 25.00
122 Carl Sawatski 6.00 15.00
123 Sandy Koufax RC 2500.00 6000.00
124 Harmon Killebrew RC 300.00 800.00
125 Ken Boyer RC 40.00 100.00
126 Dick Hall RC 6.00 15.00
127 Dale Long RC 7.50 20.00
128 Ted Lepcio 6.00 15.00
129 Elvin Tappe 7.50 20.00
130 Mayo Smith MG RC 10.00 25.00
131 Grady Hatton 10.00 25.00
132 Bob Trice 6.00 15.00
133 Dave Hoskins 6.00 15.00
134 Joey Jay 7.50 20.00
135 Johnny O'Brien 7.50 20.00
136 Veston (Bunky) Stewart RC 6.00 15.00
137 Harry Elliott RC 6.00 15.00
138 Ray Herbert 15.00 40.00
139 Steve Kraly RC 6.00 15.00
140 Mel Parnell 8.00 20.00
141 Tom Wright 10.00 25.00
142 Jerry Lynch 10.00 25.00
143 John Schofield 7.50 20.00
144 Joe Amalfitano RC 6.00 15.00
145 Elmer Valo 6.00 15.00
146 Dick Donovan RC 10.00 25.00
147 Hugh Pepper RC 6.00 15.00
148 Hal Brown 10.00 25.00
149 Ray Crone 10.00 25.00
150 Mike Higgins MG 6.00 15.00
151 Ralph Kress CO 10.00 25.00
152 Harry Agganis RC 50.00 120.00
153 Bud Podbielan 12.50 30.00
154 Willie Miranda 15.00 40.00
155 Eddie Mathews 60.00 150.00
156 Joe Black 40.00 100.00
157 Robert Miller 12.00 30.00
158 Tommy Carroll RC 12.50 30.00
159 Johnny Schmitz 10.00 25.00
160 Ray Narleski RC 10.00 25.00
161 Chuck Tanner RC 20.00 50.00
162 Joe Coleman 15.00 40.00
163 Faye Throneberry 15.00 40.00
164 Roberto Clemente RC 2500.00 5000.00
165 Don Johnson 15.00 40.00
166 Hank Bauer 40.00 100.00
167 Tom Casagrande RC 15.00 40.00
168 Duane Pillette 15.00 40.00
169 Bob Oldis 20.00 50.00
170 Jim Pearce DP RC 7.50 20.00
171 Dick Brodowski 15.00 40.00
172 Frank Baumholtz DP 7.50 20.00
173 Bob Kline RC 15.00 40.00
174 Rudy Minarcin RC 15.00 40.00
176 Norm Zauchin RC 15.00 40.00
177 Al Robertson 15.00 40.00
178 Bobby Adams 15.00 40.00
179 Jim Bolger RC 25.00 60.00
180 Clem Labine 30.00 80.00
181 Roy McMillan 20.00 50.00
182 Humberto Robinson RC 15.00 40.00
183 Anthony Jacobs RC 15.00 40.00
184 Harry Perkowski DP 15.00 40.00
185 Don Ferrarese RC 15.00 40.00
187 Gil Hodges 60.00 150.00
188 Charlie Silvera DP 8.00 20.00
189 Phil Rizzuto 100.00 250.00
190 Gene Woodling 25.00 60.00
191 Eddie Stanky MG 20.00 50.00
192 Jim Delsing 20.00 50.00
193 Johnny Sain 30.00 80.00
194 Willie Mays 500.00 1200.00
195 Ed Roebuck RC 40.00 100.00
196 Gale Wade RC 15.00 40.00
197 Al Smith 30.00 80.00
198 Yogi Berra 250.00 600.00
199 Bert Hamric RC 20.00 50.00
200 Jackie Jensen 30.00 80.00
201 Sherman Lollar 20.00 50.00
202 Jim Owens RC 30.00 80.00
204 Frank Smith 15.00 40.00
205 Gene Freese RC 60.00 150.00
206 Pete Daley RC 50.00 120.00
207 Billy Consolo 30.00 80.00
208 Ray Moore RC 30.00 80.00
210 Duke Snider 250.00 600.00

1955 Topps Double Heade

The cards in this 66-card set measure approximately 2 1/16" by 4 7/8". Borrowing a design from the T201 Mecca series, Topps issued a 132-player "Double Header" set in a separate wrapper in 1955. Each player is numbered in the biographical section on the reverse. When open, with perforated flap up, one player is revealed; when the flap is lowered, or closed, the player design on top incorporates a portion of the inside player artwork. When the cards are placed side by side, a continuous ballpark background is formed. Some cards have been found without perforations, and all players pictured appear in the low series of the 1955 regular issue. The cards were issued in one-card penny packs which came 120 packs to a box with a piece of bubble gum.

COMPLETE SET (66) 1250.00 3000.00
WRAPPER (5-CENT) 150.00 200.00
1 A. Rosen 30.00 50.00
C. Diering
3 M.Irvin 35.00 60.00
R.Kemmerer
5 Ted Kazanski and 25.00 40.00
6 Gordon Jones
7 Bill Taylor and 25.00 40.00
8 Billy O'Dell
9 J.W. Porter and 25.00 40.00
10 Thornton Kipper
11 Curt Roberts and 25.00 40.00
12 Arnie Portocarrero
13 Wally Westlake and 30.00 50.00
14 Frank House
15 Rube Walker and 30.00 50.00
16 Lou Limmer
17 Dean Stone and 25.00 40.00
18 Charlie White
19 Karl Spooner and 30.00 50.00
20 Jim Hughes
21 B.Skowron 35.00 60.00
F.Sullivan
23 Jack Shepard and 25.00 40.00
24 Stan Hack MG
25 J.Robinson 150.00 250.00
D.Hoak
27 Dusty Rhodes and 30.00 50.00
28 Jim Davis
29 Vic Power and 25.00 40.00
30 Ed Bailey
31 H.Pollet 125.00 200.00
E.Banks
33 Jim Pendleton and 25.00 40.00
34 Gene Conley
35 Karl Olson and 25.00 40.00
36 Andy Carey
37 W. Moon 30.00 50.00
J. Cunningham
39 Freddie Marsh and/40 Vernon Thies 25.00 40.00
41 E.Lopat 35.00 60.00
H.Haddix
43 Leo Kiely and 25.00 40.00
44 Chuck Stobbs
45 A.Kaline 125.00 200.00
H.Valentine
47 Forrest Jacobs and 25.00 40.00
48 Johnny Gray
49 Ron Jackson and 25.00 40.00
50 Jim Finigan
51 Ray Jablonski and 25.00 40.00
52 Bob Keegan
53 B.Herman 50.00 80.00
S.Amoros
55 Chuck Harmon and 25.00 40.00
56 Bob Skinner
57 Dick Hall and 25,00 40.00
58 Bob Grim
59 Billy Glynn and 30.00 50.00
60 Bob Miller
61 Billy Gardner and 25.00 40.00
62 John Hetki
63 B. Borkowski 25.00 40.00
B. Turley
65 Joe Collins and 25.00 40.00
66 Jack Harshman
67 Jim Hegan and 25.00 40.00
68 Jack Parks
69 T.Williams 250.00 500.00
M.Smith
71 Gair Allie and 25.00 40.00
72 Grady Hatton
73 Jerry Lynch and 25.00 40.00
74 Harry Brecheen CO
75 Tom Wright and 25.00 40.00
76 Vernon Stewart
77 Dave Hoskins and 25.00 40.00
78 Warren McGhee
79 Roy Sievers and 30.00 50.00
80 Art Fowler
81 Danny Schell and 25.00 40.00
82 Gus Triandos
83 Joe Frazier and 25.00 40.00
84 Don Mossi
85 Elmer Valo and 25.00 40.00
86 Hector Brown
87 Bob Kennedy and 30.00 50.00
88 Windy McCall
89 Ruben Gomez and 25.00 40.00
90 Jim Rivera
91 Louis Ortiz and 25.00 40.00
92 Milt Bolling
93 Carl Sawatski and 25.00 40.00
94 El Tappe
95 Dave Jolly and 25.00 40.00
96 Bobby Hofman
97 P.Ward 35.00 60.00
D.Zimmer
99 B. Renna 30.00 50.00
D. Groat
101 Bill Wilson and 25.00 40.00
102 Bill Tremel
103 H. Sauer 30.00 50.00
C. Pascual
105 H.Aaron 300.00 500.00
R.Herbert
107 Alex Grammas and 25.00 40.00
108 Tom Qualters
109 H.Newhouser 35.00 60.00
C.Bishop
111 H.Killebrew 100.00 250.00
J.Podres
113 Ray Boone and 25.00 40.00
114 Bob Purkey
115 Dale Long and 30.00 50.00
116 Ferris Fain
117 Steve Bilko and 25.00 40.00
118 Bob Milliken
119 Mel Parnell and 30.00 50.00
120 Tom Hurd
121 T.Kluszewski 50.00 80.00
J.Owens
123 Gus Zernial and 25.00 40.00
124 Bob Trice
125 Rip Repulski and 25.00 40.00
126 Ted Lepcio
127 W.Spahn 90.00 150.00
T.Brewer
129 J.Gilliam 50.00 80.00
E.Kinder
131 Herm Wehmeier and 25.00 40.00
132 Wayne Terwilliger

1955 Topps Test Stamps

These test issues stamps "are full-size versions of regular first series cards, but with blank, gummed backs and perforated edges." These stamps are listed in alphabetical order with their corresponding card number listed immediately after their name. Since these "stamps" show up very infrequently in the hobby -- any additions to this checklist are appreciated.

COMPLETE SET 3000.00 6000.00
1 Ray Boone 400.00 800.00
Card number 65
2 Joe Cunningham 400.00 800.00
Card number 37
3 Jim Davis 400.00 800.00
Card number 68
4 Ruben Gomez 400.00 800.00
Card number 71
5 Alex Grammas 400.00 800.00
Card number 21
6 Stan Hack MG 500.00 1000.00
Card number 6
7 Harvey Haddix 400.00 800.00
Card number 43
8 Bobby Hofman 400.00 800.00
Card number 17
9 Ray Jablonski 400.00 800.00
Card number 56
10 Dave Jolly 400.00 800.00
Card number 35
11 Don Mossi 600.00 1200.00
Card number 85
12 Jim Pendleton 400.00 800.00
Card number 15
13 Howie Pollet 400.00 800.00
Card number 76
14 Jack Shepard 400.00 800.00
Card number 73
15 Bob Skinner 500.00 1000.00
Card number 88
16 Bill Skowron 750.00 1500.00
Card number 22
17 Karl Spooner 500.00 1000.00
Card number 90
18 Bill Tremel 400.00 800.00
Card number 52
19 Corky Valentine 400.00 800.00
Card number 44
20 Rube Walker 500.00 1000.00
Card number 108
21 Charlie White 400.00 800.00
Card number 103

1956 Topps

The cards in this 340-card set measure approximately 2 5/8" by 3 3/4". Following up with another horizontally oriented card in 1956, Topps improved the format by layering the color "head" shot onto an actual action sequence involving the player. Cards 1 to 180 come with either white or gray backs: in the 1 to 100 sequence gray backs are less common and in the 101 to 180 sequence white backs are less common. The team cards, used for the first time in a regular set by

Topps, are found dated 1955, or undated, with the team name appearing on either side. The dated team cards in the first series were not printed on the gray stock. The two unnumbered checklist cards are highly prized (must be unmarked to qualify as excellent or mint). The complete set price below does not include the unnumbered checklist cards or any of the variations. The set was issued in one-card penny packs or six-card nickel packs. The six card nickel packs came 24 to a box with 24 boxes in a case while the once cent packs came 120 to a box. Both types of packs included a piece of bubble gum. Promotional three card strips were issued for this set. Among those strips were one featuring Johnny O'Brien/Harvey Haddix and Frank House. The key Rookie Cards in this set are Walt Alston, Luis Aparicio, and Roger Craig. There are ten double-printed cards in the first series as evidenced by the discovery of an uncut sheet of 110 cards (10 by 11); these DP's are listed below.

COMPLETE SET (340) 5000.00 12000.00
COMMON CARD (1-100) 5.00 10.00
COMMON CARD (101-180) 6.00 12.00
COMMON CARD (261-340) 6.00 12.00
COMMON CARD (181-260) 7.50 15.00
WRAP.(1-CENT) 200.00 250.00
WRAP.(1-CENT, REPEAT) 75.00 100.00
WRAPPER (5-CENT) 150.00 200.00
*1-100 GRAY BACK: .5X TO 1.2X
*101-180 WHITE BACK: .5X TO 1.2X
1 Will Harridge PRES 75.00 200.00
2 Warren Giles PRES DP 15.00 40.00
3 Elmer Valo 7.50 20.00
4 Carlos Paula 8.00 20.00
5 Ted Williams 300.00 500.00
6 Ray Boone 15.00 40.00
7 Ron Negray RC 5.00 12.00
8 Walter Alston MG RC 25.00 60.00
9 Ruben Gomez DP 5.00 12.00
10 Warren Spahn 40.00 100.00
11A Chicago Cubs TC Center 15.00 40.00
11B Chicago Cubs TC D'55 50.00 120.00
11C Chicago Cubs TC Left 15.00 40.00
12 Andy Carey 7.50 20.00
13 Roy Face 7.50 20.00
14 Ken Boyer DP 12.00 30.00
15 Ernie Banks DP 75.00 200.00
16 Hector Lopez RC 8.00 20.00
17 Gene Conley 8.00 20.00
18 Dick Donovan 5.00 12.00
19 Chuck Diering DP 5.00 12.00
20 Al Kaline 50.00 120.00
21 Joe Collins DP 7.50 20.00
22 Jim Finigan 5.00 12.00
23 Fred Marsh 5.00 12.00
24 Dick Groat 10.00 25.00
25 Ted Kluszewski 20.00 50.00
26 Grady Hatton 5.00 12.00
27 Nelson Burbrink DP RC 5.00 12.00
28 Bobby Hofman 5.00 12.00
29 Jack Harshman 5.00 12.00
30 Jackie Robinson DP 300.00 600.00
31 Hank Aaron UER DP 150.00 400.00
32 Frank House 5.00 12.00
33 Roberto Clemente 750.00 2000.00
34 Tom Brewer DP 5.00 12.00
35 Al Rosen 12.00 30.00
36 Rudy Minarcin 7.50 20.00
37 Alex Grammas 10.00 25.00
38 Bob Kennedy 7.50 20.00
39 Don Mossi 7.50 20.00
40 Bob Turley 7.50 20.00
41 Hank Sauer 7.50 20.00
42 Sandy Amoros 20.00 50.00
43 Ray Moore 5.00 12.00
44 Windy McCall 5.00 12.00
45 Gus Zernial 7.50 20.00
46 Gene Freese DP 5.00 12.00
47 Art Fowler 5.00 12.00
48 Jim Hegan 12.00 30.00
49 Pedro Ramos RC 8.00 20.00
50 Dusty Rhodes DP 7.50 20.00
51 Ernie Oravetz RC 5.00 12.00
52 Bob Grim DP 7.50 20.00
53 Arnie Portocarrero 5.00 12.00
54 Bob Keegan 5.00 12.00
55 Wally Moon 7.50 20.00
56 Dale Long 7.50 20.00
57 Duke Maas RC 5.00 12.00
58 Ed Roebuck 15.00 40.00
59 Jose Santiago RC 5.00 12.00
60 Mayo Smith MG DP 5.00 12.00
61 Bill Skowron 20.00 50.00
62 Hal Smith 7.50 20.00
63 Roger Craig RC 25.00 60.00
64 Luis Arroyo RC 5.00 12.00
65 Johnny O'Brien 7.50 -20.00
66 Bob Speake DP RC 5.00 12.00
67 Vic Power 7.50 20.00-
68 Chuck Stobbs 5.00 12.00
69 Chuck Tanner 7.50 20.00
70 Jim Rivera 5.00 12.00
71 Frank Sullivan 5.00 12.00
72A Philadelphia Phillies TC Center 15.00 40.00
72B Philadelphia Phillies TC D'55 50.00 120.00
72C Philadelphia Phillies TC Left DP 15.00 40.00
73 Wayne Terwilliger 5.00 12.00
74 Jim King RC 5.00 12.00
75 Roy Sievers DP 7.50 20.00
76 Ray Crone 5.00 12.00
77 Harvey Haddix 10.00 25.00
78 Herman Wehmeier 5.00 12.00
79 Sandy Koufax 200.00 400.00
80 Gus Triandos DP 5.00 12.00
81 Wally Westlake 5.00 12.00
82 Bill Renna DP 5.00 12.00
83 Karl Spooner 7.50 20.00
84 Babe Birrer RC 5.00 12.00
85A Cleveland Indians TC Center 15.00 40.00
85B Cleveland Indians TC D'55 50.00 120.00
85C Cleveland Indians TC Left 15.00 40.00
86 Ray Jablonski DP 5.00 12.00
87 Dean Stone 5.00 12.00
88 Johnny Kucks RC 7.50 20.00
89 Norm Zauchin 5.00 12.00
90A Cincinnati Redlegs TC Center 15.00 40.00
90B Cincinnati Reds TC D'55 50.00 120.00
90C Cincinnati Reds TC Left 15.00 40.00
91 Gail Harris RC 5.00 12.00
92 Bob Red Wilson 5.00 12.00
93 George Susce 5.00 12.00
94 Ron Kline UER 5.00 12.00
Facimile auto is J.Robert Klein
95A Milwaukee Braves TC Center 20.00 50.00
95B Milwaukee Braves TC D'55 50.00 120.00
95C Milwaukee Braves TC Left 20.00 50.00
96 Bill Tremel 5.00 12.00
97 Jerry Lynch 7.50 20.00
98 Camilo Pascual 7.50 20.00
99 Don Zimmer 15.00 40.00
100A Baltimore Orioles TC Center 20.00 50.00
100B Baltimore Orioles TC D'55 50.00 120.00
100C Baltimore Orioles TC Left 20.00 50.00
101 Roy Campanella 75.00 200.00
102 Jim Davis 6.00 15.00
103 Willie Miranda 6.00 15.00-
104 Bob Lennon 6.00 15.00
105 Al Smith 6.00 15.00
106 Joe Astroth 6.00 15.00
107 Eddie Mathews 40.00 100.00
108 Laurin Pepper 6.00 15.00
109 Enos Slaughter 20.00 50.00
110 Yogi Berra 125.00 300.00
111 Boston Red Sox TC 20.00 50.00
112 Dee Fondy 6.00 15.00
113 Phil Rizzuto 50.00 120.00
114 Jim Owens 7.50 20.00
115 Jackie Jensen 7.50 20.00
116 Eddie O'Brien 6.00 15.00
117 Virgil Trucks 7.50 20.00
118 Nellie Fox 20.00 50.00
119 Larry Jackson RC 8.00 20.00
120 Richie Ashburn 30.00 80.00
121 Pittsburgh Pirates TC 20.00 50.00
122 Willard Nixon 6.00 15.00
123 Roy McMillan 7.50 20.00
124 Don Kaiser 6.00 15.00
125 Minnie Minoso 20.00 50.00
126 Jim Brady RC 6.00 15.00
127 Willie Jones 7.50 20.00
128 Eddie Yost 7.50 20.00
129 Jake Martin RC 6.00 15.00
130 Willie Mays 200.00 500.00
131 Bob Roselli RC 6.00 15.00
132 Bobby Avila 6.00 15.00
133 Ray Narleski 6.00 15.00
134 St. Louis Cardinals TC 20.00 50.00
135 Mickey Mantle 1250.00 2500.00
136 Johnny Logan 7.50 20.00
137 Al Silvera RC 6.00 15.00
138 Johnny Antonelli 7.50 20.00
139 Tommy Carroll 7.50 20.00
140 Herb Score RC 20.00 50.00
141 Joe Frazier 6.00 15.00
142 Gene Baker 6.00 15.00
143 Jim Piersall 8.00 20.00
144 Leroy Powell RC 6.00 15.00
145 Gil Hodges 30.00 80.00
146 Washington Nationals TC 20.00 50.00
147 Earl Torgeson 6.00 15.00
148 Alvin Dark 12.00 30.00
149 Dixie Howell 6.00 15.00
150 Duke Snider 75.00 200.00
151 Spook Jacobs 7.50 20.00
152 Billy Hoeft 7.50 20.00
153 Frank Thomas 10.00 25.00
154 Dave Pope 6.00 15.00
155 Harvey Kuenn 7.50 20.00
156 Wes Westrum 7.50 20.00
157 Dick Brodowski 6.00 15.00
158 Wally Post 7.50 20.00
159 Clint Courtney 6.00 15.00
160 Billy Pierce 7.50 20.00
161 Joe DeMaestri 6.00 15.00
162 Dave Gus Bell 7.50 20.00
163 Gene Woodling 7.50 20.00
164 Harmon Killebrew 60.00 150.00
165 Red Schoendienst 25.00 60.00
166 Brooklyn Dodgers TC 50.00 120.00
167 Harry Dorish 6.00 15.00
168 Sammy White 6.00 15.00
169 Bob Nelson RC 6.00 15.00
170 Bill Virdon 7.50 20.00
171 Jim Wilson 6.00 15.00
172 Frank Torre RC 7.50 20.00
173 Johnny Podres 20.00 50.00
174 Glen Gorbous RC 6.00 15.00
175 Del Crandall 7.50 20.00
176 Alex Kellner 6.00 15.00
177 Hank Bauer 15.00 40.00
178 Joe Black 7.50 20.00
179 Harry Chiti 6.00 15.00
180 Robin Roberts 30.00 80.00
181 Billy Martin 40.00 100.00
182 Paul Minner 8.00 20.00
183 Stan Lopata 10.00 25.00
184 Don Bessent RC 12.00 30.00
185 Bill Bruton 10.00 25.00
186 Ron Jackson 7.50 20.00
187 Early Wynn 40.00 100.00
188 Chicago White Sox TC 30.00 80.00
189 Ned Garver 7.50 20.00
190 Carl Furillo 25.00 60.00
191 Frank Lary 10.00 25.00
192 Smoky Burgess 12.00 30.00
193 Wilmer Mizell 10.00 25.00
194 Monte Irvin 40.00 100.00
195 George Kell 25.00 60.00
196 Tom Poholsky 7.50 20.00
197 Granny Hamner 7.50 20.00
198 Ed Fitzgerald 7.50 20.00
199 Hank Thompson 10.00 25.00
200 Bob Feller 75.00 200.00
201 Rip Repulski 7.50 20.00
202 Jim Hearn 12.00 30.00
203 Bill Tuttle 12.00 30.00
204 Art Swanson RC 7.50 20.00
205 Whitey Lockman 10.00 25.00
206 Erv Palica 10.00 25.00
207 Jim Small RC 7.50 20.00
208 Elston Howard 25.00 60.00
209 Max Surkont 12.00 30.00
210 Mike Garcia 10.00 25.00
211 Murry Dickson 12.00 30.00
212 Johnny Temple 7.50 20.00
213 Detroit Tigers 30.00 80.00
214 Bob Rush 7.50 20.00
215 Tommy Byrne 12.00 30.00
216 Jerry Schoonmaker RC 7.50 20.00
217 Billy Klaus 10.00 25.00
218 Joe Nuxhall UER 10.00 25.00
219 Lew Burdette 12.00 30.00
220 Del Ennis 10.00 25.00
221 Bob Friend 15.00 40.00
222 Dave Philley 7.50 20.00
223 Randy Jackson 7.50 20.00
224 Bud Podbielan 7.50 20.00
225 Gil McDougald 20.00 50.00
226 New York Giants 25.00 60.00
227 Russ Meyer 7.50 20.00
228 Mickey Vernon 10.00 25.00
229 Harry Brecheen CO 10.00 25.00
230 Chico Carrasquel 10.00 25.00
231 Bob Hale RC 7.50 20.00
232 Toby Atwell 7.50 20.00
233 Carl Erskine 25.00 60.00
234 Pete Runnels 12.00 30.00
235 Don Newcombe 50.00 120.00
236 Kansas City Athletics 20.00 50.00
237 Jose Valdivielso RC 7.50 20.00
238 Walt Dropo 10.00 25.00
239 Harry Simpson 12.00 30.00
240 Whitey Ford 75.00 200.00
241 Don Mueller UER 10.00 25.00
242 Hershell Freeman 15.00 40.00
243 Sherm Lollar 10.00 25.00
244 Bob Buhl 15.00 40.00
245 Billy Goodman 10.00 25.00
246 Tom Gorman 7.50 20.00
247 Bill Sarni 7.50 20.00
248 Bob Porterfield 7.50 20.00
249 Johnny Klippstein 12.00 30.00
250 Larry Doby 50.00 120.00
251 New York Yankees TC UER 75.00 200.00
252 Vern Law 10.00 25.00
253 Irv Noren 18.00 40.00
254 George Crowe 8.00 20.00
255 Bob Lemon 25.00 60.00
256 Tom Hurd 7.50 20.00
257 Bobby Thomson 18.00 40.00
258 Art Ditmar 10.00 25.00
259 Sam Jones 10.00 25.00
260 Pee Wee Reese 100.00 250.00
261 Bobby Shantz 12.00 30.00
262 Howie Pollet 6.00 15.00
263 Bob Miller 6.00 15.00
264 Ray Monzant RC 12.00 30.00
265 Sandy Consuegra 6.00 15.00
266 Don Ferrarese 6.00 15.00
267 Bob Nieman 6.00 15.00
268 Dale Mitchell 7.50 20.00
269 Jack Meyer RC 8.00 20.00
270 Billy Loes 12.00 30.00
271 Foster Castleman RC 6.00 15.00
272 Danny O'Connell 6.00 15.00
273 Walker Cooper 6.00 15.00
274 Frank Baumholtz 6.00 15.00
275 Jim Greengrass 6.00 15.00
276 George Zuverink 6.00 15.00
277 Daryl Spencer 6.00 15.00
278 Chet Nichols 10.00 25.00
279 Johnny Groth 6.00 15.00
280 Jim Gilliam 25.00 60.00
281 Art Houtteman 6.00 15.00
282 Warren Hacker 10.00 25.00
283 Hal Smith RC UER 10.00 25.00
Wrong Facsimile Autograph, belongs to Hal W. Smith
284 Ike Delock 6.00 15.00
285 Eddie Miksis 6.00 15.00
286 Bill Wight 6.00 15.00
287 Bobby Adams 6.00 15.00
288 Bob Cerv 20.00 50.00
289 Hal Jeffcoat 6.00 15.00
290 Curt Simmons 10.00 25.00
291 Frank Kellert RC 6.00 15.00
292 Luis Aparicio RC 100.00 250.00
293 Stu Miller 15.00 40.00
294 Ernie Johnson 7.50 20.00
295 Clem Labine 12.00 30.00
296 Andy Seminick 6.00 15.00
297 Bob Skinner 12.00 30.00
298 Johnny Schmitz 10.00 25.00
299 Charlie Neal 25.00 60.00
300 Vic Wertz 12.00 30.00
301 Marv Grissom 6.00 15.00
302 Eddie Robinson 6.00 15.00
303 Jim Dyck 6.00 15.00
304 Frank Malzone 8.00 20.00
305 Brooks Lawrence 10.00 25.00
306 Curt Roberts 10.00 25.00
307 Hoyt Wilhelm 25.00 60.00
308 Chuck Harmon 6.00 15.00
309 Don Blasingame RC 10.00 25.00
310 Steve Gromek 6.00 15.00
311 Hal Naragon 6.00 15.00
312 Andy Pafko 7.50 20.00
313 Gene Stephens 6.00 15.00
314 Hobie Landrith 6.00 15.00
315 Milt Bolling 6.00 15.00
316 Jerry Coleman 10.00 25.00
317 Al Aber 6.00 15.00
318 Fred Hatfield 6.00 15.00
319 Jack Crimian RC 6.00 15.00
320 Joe Adcock 7.50 20.00
321 Jim Konstanty 7.50 20.00
322 Karl Olson 6.00 15.00
323 Willard Schmidt 6.00 15.00
324 Rocky Bridges 7.50 20.00
325 Don Liddle 6.00 15.00
326 Connie Johnson RC 6.00 15.00
327 Bob Wiesler RC 6.00 15.00
328 Preston Ward 6.00 15.00
329 Lou Berberet RC 6.00 15.00
330 Jim Busby 12.00 30.00
331 Dick Hall 10.00 25.00
332 Don Larsen 50.00 120.00
333 Rube Walker 12.00 30.00
334 Bob Miller 7.50 20.00
335 Don Hoak 8.00 20.00
336 Ellis Kinder 10.00 25.00
337 Bobby Morgan 12.00 30.00
338 Jim Delsing 6.00 15.00
339 Rance Pless RC 6.00 15.00
340 Mickey McDermott 30.00 80.00
CL1 Checklist 1/3 150.00 400.00
CL2 Checklist 2/4 150.00 400.00

1956 Topps Hocus Focus

The 1956 Topps Hocus Focus set is very similar in size and design to the 1948 Topps Magic Photos set. It contains at least 96 small (approximately 7/8" by 1 5/8") individual cards featuring a variety of sports and non-sport subjects. They were printed with both a series card number (by subject matter) on the back as well as a card number reflecting the entire set. The fronts were developed, much like a photograph, from a blank appearance by using moisture and sunlight. Due to varying degrees of photographic sensitivity, the clarity of these cards ranges from fully developed to poorly developed. A premium album holding 126-cards was also issued leading to the theory that there are actually 126 different cards. A few High Series (#97-126) cards have been discovered and cataloged below although a full 126-card checklist is yet unknown. The cards do reference the set name "Hocus Focus" on the backs unlike the 1948 Magic Photos. Finally, a slightly smaller version (roughly 7/8" by 1 7/16") of some of the cards has also been found, but a full checklist is not known.

5 Ted Williams 5 750.00 1500.00
8 Spook Jacobs 60 100.00 200.00
13 Jackie Robinson 13 600.00 1200.00
26 Harvey Haddix 26 125.00 250.00
30 Hank Sauer 30 125.00 250.00
31 Ray Boone 31 100.00 200.00
42 Hal Smith 100.00 200.00
43 Dick Groat 125.00 250.00
44 Ed Lopat 150.00 300.00
49 Gus Zernial 100.00 200.00
51 Mayo Smith MG 100.00 200.00
67 Jim Rivera 100.00 200.00
69 Al Rosen 150.00 300.00
79 Ted Kluszewski 200.00 400.00
84 Johnny Schmitz 100.00 200.00
86 Dusty Rhodes 86 125.00 250.00
87 Warren Spahn 87 400.00 800.00
103 Wally Moon 150.00 300.00
109 Ed Mathews 109 500.00 1000.00
117 Babe Ruth 1500.00 3000.00
118 Mel Parnell 125.00 250.00
122 Karl Spooner 100.00 200.00

1956 Topps Pins

This set of 60 full-color pins was Topps first and only baseball player pin set. Each pin measures 1 3/16" in diameter. Although the set was advertised to contain 90 pins, only 60 were issued. The checklist below lists the players in alphabetical order within team, e.g., Baltimore Orioles (1-4), Chicago Cubs (5-7), Cleveland Indians (8-11), Kansas City A's (12-15), Milwaukee Braves (16-19), Philadelphia Phillies (20-22), Boston Red Sox (23-26), New York Yankees (27-31), Chicago White Sox (32-35), Detroit Tigers (36-38), New York Giants (39-41), Pittsburgh Pirates (42-44), St. Louis Cardinals (45-48), Brooklyn Dodgers (49-53), Cincinnati Redlegs (54-57) and Washington Senators (58-60). Chuck Diering, Hector Lopez and Chuck Stobbs (noted below with SP) are more difficult to obtain than other pins in the set. The "packs" were issued as five cent packs with a piece of bubble gum which came 24 to a box. The box featured a photo of Ted Williams on the front.

COMPLETE SET (60) 2500.00 5000.00
PIN BOX (5-CENT) 150.00 200.00
1 Chuck Diering SP 250.00 500.00
2 Willie Miranda 15.00 30.00
3 Hal Smith 15.00 30.00
4 Gus Triandos 20.00 40.00
5 Ernie Banks 75.00 150.00
6 Hank Sauer 20.00 40.00
7 Bill Tremel 15.00 30.00
8 Jim Hegan 15.00 30.00
9 Don Mossi 20.00 40.00
10 Al Rosen 30.00 60.00
11 Al Smith 15.00 30.00
12 Jim Finigan 15.00 30.00
13 Hector Lopez SP 200.00 400.00
14 Vic Power 15.00 30.00
15 Gus Zernial 20.00 40.00
16 Hank Aaron 125.00 250.00
17 Gene Conley 15.00 30.00
18 Eddie Mathews 75.00 150.00
19 Warren Spahn 75.00 150.00
20 Ron Negray 15.00 30.00
21 Mayo Smith MG 15.00 30.00
22 Herman Wehmeier 15.00 30.00
23 Grady Hatton 15.00 30.00
24 Jackie Jensen 30.00 60.00
25 Frank Sullivan 15.00 30.00
26 Ted Williams 150.00 300.00
27 Yogi Berra 100.00 200.00
28 Joe Collins 20.00 40.00
29 Phil Rizzuto 50.00 100.00
30 Bill Skowron 50.00 100.00
31 Bob Turley 30.00 60.00
32 Dick Donovan 15.00 30.00
33 Jack Harshman 15.00 30.00
34 Bob Kennedy 15.00 30.00
35 Jim Rivera 15.00 30.00
36 Ray Boone 20.00 40.00
37 Frank House 15.00 30.00
38 Al Kaline 75.00 150.00
39 Ruben Gomez 15.00 30.00
40 Bobby Hofman 15.00 30.00
41 Willie Mays 125.00 250.00
42 Dick Groat 30.00 60.00
43 Dale Long 20.00 40.00
44 Johnny O'Brien 15.00 30.00
45 Luis Arroyo 15.00 30.00
46 Ken Boyer 30.00 60.00
47 Harvey Haddix 20.00 40.00
48 Wally Moon 20.00 40.00
49 Sandy Amoros 20.00 40.00
50 Gil Hodges 50.00 100.00
51 Jackie Robinson 125.00 250.00
52 Duke Snider 100.00 200.00
53 Karl Spooner 20.00 40.00
54 Joe Black 25.00 50.00
55 Art Fowler 15.00 30.00
56 Ted Kluszewski 30.00 60.00
57 Roy McMillan 15.00 30.00
58 Carlos Paula 15.00 30.00
59 Roy Sievers 15.00 30.00
60 Chuck Stobbs SP 200.00 400.00

1957 Topps

The cards in this 407-card set measure 2 1/2" by 3 1/2". In 1957, Topps returned to the vertical obverse, adopted what we now call the standard card size, and used a large, uncluttered color photo for the first time since 1952. Cards in the series 265 to 352 and the unnumbered checklist cards are scarcer than other cards in the set. However within this scarce series (265-352) there are 22 cards which were printed in double the quantity of the other cards in the series; these 22 double prints are indicated by DP in the checklist below. The first star combination cards, cards 400 and 407, are quite popular with collectors. They feature the big stars of the previous season's World Series teams, the Dodgers (Furillo, Hodges, Campanella, and Snider) and Yankees (Berra and Mantle). The complete set price below does not include the unnumbered checklist cards. Confirmed packaging includes one-cent penny packs and six-card nickel packs. Cello packs are definately known to exist and some collectors remember buying rack packs of 57's as well. The key Rookie Cards in this set are Jim Bunning, Rocky Colavito, Don Drysdale, Whitey Herzog, Tony Kubek, Bill Mazeroski, Bobby Richardson, Brooks Robinson, and Frank Robinson.

COMPLETE SET (407) 5000.00 12000.00
COMMON CARD (1-88) 5.00 10.00
COMMON CARD (89-176) 4.00 8.00
COMMON CARD (177-264) 4.00 8.00
COMMON CARD (265-352) 10.00 20.00
COMMON CARD (353-407) 4.00 8.00
COMMON DP (265-352) 6.00 12.00
WRAPPER (1-CENT) 250.00 300.00
WRAPPER (5-CENT) 150.00 200.00
1 Ted Williams 200.00 500.00
2 Yogi Berra 60.00 150.00
3 Dale Long 8.00 20.00
4 Johnny Logan 8.00 20.00
5 Sal Maglie 10.00 25.00
6 Hector Lopez 6.00 15.00
7 Luis Aparicio 20.00 50.00
8 Don Mossi 6.00 15.00
9 Johnny Temple 8.00 20.00
10 Willie Mays 250.00 600.00
11 George Zuverink 4.00 10.00
12 Dick Groat 10.00 25.00
13 Wally Burnette RC 4.00 10.00
14 Bob Nieman 10.00 25.00
15 Robin Roberts 20.00 50.00
16 Walt Moryn 4.00 10.00
17 Billy Gardner 4.00 10.00
18 Don Drysdale RC 150.00 400.00
19 Bob Wilson 4.00 10.00
20 Hank Aaron UER 250.00 600.00
21 Frank Sullivan 4.00 10.00
22 Jerry Snyder UER 4.00 10.00
23 Sherm Lollar 6.00 15.00
24 Bill Mazeroski RC 60.00 150.00
25 Whitey Ford 60.00 150.00
26 Bob Boyd 4.00 10.00
27 Ted Kazanski 4.00 10.00
28 Gene Conley 6.00 15.00
29 Whitey Herzog RC 12.00 30.00
30 Pee Wee Reese 50.00 120.00
31 Ron Northey 4.00 10.00
32 Hershell Freeman 4.00 10.00
33 Jim Small 4.00 10.00
34 Tom Sturdivant RC 6.00 15.00
35 Frank Robinson RC 400.00 1000.00
36 Bob Grim 4.00 10.00
37 Frank Torre 6.00 15.00
38 Nellie Fox 25.00 60.00
39 Al Worthington RC 4.00 10.00
40 Early Wynn 10.00 25.00
41 Hal W. Smith 4.00 10.00
42 Dee Fondy 4.00 10.00
43 Connie Johnson 4.00 10.00
44 Joe DeMaestri 4.00 10.00
45 Carl Furillo 20.00 50.00
46 Robert J. Miller 4.00 10.00
47 Don Blasingame 4.00 10.00
48 Bill Bruton 6.00 15.00
49 Daryl Spencer 4.00 10.00
50 Herb Score 12.00 30.00
51 Clint Courtney 4.00 10.00
52 Lee Walls 4.00 10.00
53 Clem Labine 8.00 20.00
54 Elmer Valo 4.00 10.00
55 Ernie Banks 100.00 250.00
56 Dave Sisler RC 4.00 10.00
57 Jim Lemon 8.00 20.00
58 Ruben Gomez 4.00 10.00
59 Dick Williams 6.00 15.00
60 Billy Hoeft 6.00 15.00
61 Dusty Rhodes 6.00 15.00
62 Billy Martin 30.00 80.00
63 Ike Delock 4.00 10.00
64 Pete Runnels 6.00 15.00
65 Wally Moon 6.00 15.00
66 Brooks Lawrence 4.00 10.00
67 Chico Carrasquel 4.00 10.00
68 Ray Crone 4.00 10.00
69 Roy McMillan 6.00 15.00
70 Richie Ashburn 25.00 60.00
71 Murry Dickson 4.00 10.00
72 Bill Tuttle 4.00 10.00
73 George Crowe 4.00 10.00
74 Vito Valentinetti RC 4.00 10.00
75 Jimmy Piersall 6.00 15.00
76 Roberto Clemente 200.00 500.00
77 Paul Foytack RC 4.00 10.00
78 Vic Wertz 6.00 15.00
79 Lindy McDaniel RC 10.00 25.00
80 Gil Hodges 30.00 80.00
81 Herman Wehmeier 4.00 10.00
82 Elston Howard 15.00 40.00
83 Lou Skizas RC 4.00 10.00
84 Moe Drabowsky RC 6.00 15.00
85 Larry Doby 30.00 80.00
86 Bill Sarni 4.00 10.00
87 Tom Gorman 4.00 10.00
88 Harvey Kuenn 6.00 15.00
89 Roy Sievers 6.00 15.00
90 Warren Spahn 40.00 •100.00
91 Mack Burk RC 3.00 8.00
92 Mickey Vernon 6.00 15.00
93 Hal Jeffcoat 3.00 8.00
94 Bobby Del Greco 3.00 8.00
95 Mickey Mantle 600.00 1200.00
96 Hank Aguirre RC 3.00 8.00
97 New York Yankees TC 30.00 80.00
98 Alvin Dark 6.00 15.00
99 Bob Keegan 3.00 8.00
100 W.Giles/W.Harridge 6.00 15.00
101 Chuck Stobbs 3.00 8.00
102 Ray Boone 6.00 15.00
103 Joe Nuxhall 6.00 15.00
104 Hank Foiles 3.00 8.00
105 Johnny Antonelli 6.00 15.00
106 Ray Moore 3.00 8.00
107 Jim Rivera 3.00 8.00
108 Tommy Byrne 6.00 15.00
109 Hank Thompson 3.00 8.00
110 Bill Virdon 6.00 15.00
111 Hal R. Smith 3.00 8.00
112 Tom Brewer 3.00 8.00
113 Wilmer Mizell 6.00 15.00
114 Milwaukee Braves TC 12.00 30.00
115 Jim Gilliam 20.00 50.00
116 Mike Fornieles 3.00 8.00
117 Joe Adcock 8.00 20.00
118 Bob Porterfield 3.00 8.00
119 Stan Lopata 3.00 8.00
120 Bob Lemon 15.00 40.00
121 Clete Boyer RC 12.00 30.00
122 Ken Boyer 15.00 40.00
123 Steve Ridzik 3.00 8.00
124 Dave Philley 3.00 8.00
125 Al Kaline 50.00 120.00
126 Bob Wiesler 3.00 8.00
127 Bob Buhl 6.00 15.00
128 Ed Bailey 6.00 15.00
129 Saul Rogovin 3.00 8.00
130 Don Newcombe 12.00 30.00
131 Milt Bolling 3.00 8.00
132 Art Ditmar 6.00 15.00
133 Del Crandall 6.00 15.00
134 Don Kaiser 3.00 8.00
135 Bill Skowron 15.00 40.00
136 Jim Hegan 8.00 20.00
137 Bob Rush 3.00 8.00
138 Minnie Minoso 10.00 25.00
139 Lou Kretlow 3.00 8.00
140 Frank Thomas 6.00 15.00
141 Al Aber 3.00 8.00
142 Charley Thompson 3.00 8.00
143 Andy Pafko 8.00 20.00
144 Ray Narleski 3.00 8.00
145 Al Smith 3.00 8.00
146 Don Ferrarese 3.00 8.00
147 Al Walker 3.00 8.00
148 Don Mueller 6.00 15.00
149 Bob Kennedy 6.00 15.00
150 Bob Friend 6.00 15.00
151 Willie Miranda 3.00 8.00
152 Jack Harshman 3.00 8.00
153 Karl Olson 3.00 8.00
154 Red Schoendienst 12.00 30.00
155 Jim Brosnan 6.00 15.00
156 Gus Triandos 6.00 15.00
157 Wally Post 6.00 15.00
158 Curt Simmons 6.00 15.00
159 Solly Drake RC 3.00 8.00
160 Billy Pierce 6.00 15.00
161 Pittsburgh Pirates TC 6.00 15.00
162 Jack Meyer 3.00 8.00
163 Sammy White 3.00 8.00
164 Tommy Carroll 3.00 8.00
165 Ted Kluszewski 60.00 150.00
166 Roy Face 6.00 15.00
167 Vic Power 6.00 15.00
168 Frank Lary 6.00 15.00
169 Herb Plews RC 3.00 8.00
170 Duke Snider 50.00 120.00
171 Boston Red Sox TC 6.00 15.00
172 Gene Woodling 6.00 15.00
173 Roger Craig 6.00 15.00
174 Willie Jones 3.00 8.00
175 Don Larsen 15.00 40.00
176A Gene Bakep ERR 150.00 400.00
176B Gene Baker COR 6.00 15.00
177 Eddie Yost 6.00 15.00
178 Don Bessent 3.00 8.00
179 Ernie Oravetz 3.00 8.00
180 Gus Bell 12.00 30.00
181 Dick Donovan 3.00 8.00
182 Hobie Landrith 3.00 8.00
183 Chicago Cubs TC 6.00 15.00
184 Tito Francona RC 3.00 8.00
185 Johnny Kucks 6.00 15.00
186 Jim King 6.00 15.00
187 Virgil Trucks 8.00 20.00
188 Felix Mantilla RC 6.00 15.00
189 Willard Nixon 3.00 8.00
190 Randy Jackson 3.00 8.00
191 Joe Margoneri RC 3.00 8.00
192 Jerry Coleman 6.00 15.00
193 Del Rice 3.00 8.00
194 Hal Brown 3.00 8.00
195 Bobby Avila 3.00 8.00
196 Larry Jackson 6.00 15.00
197 Hank Sauer 6.00 15.00
198 Detroit Tigers TC 6.00 15.00
199 Vern Law 6.00 15.00
200 Gil McDougald 10.00 25.00
201 Sandy Amoros 6.00 15.00
202 Dick Gernert 3.00 8.00
203 Hoyt Wilhelm 15.00 40.00
204 Kansas City Athletics TC 6.00 15.00
205 Charlie Maxwell 6.00 15.00
206 Willard Schmidt 3.00 8.00
207 Gordon Billy Hunter 3.00 8.00
208 Lou Burdette 6.00 15.00
209 Bob Skinner 6.00 15.00
210 Roy Campanella 40.00 100.00
211 Camilo Pascual 6.00 15.00
212 Rocky Colavito RC 40.00 100.00
213 Les Moss 3.00 8.00
214 Philadelphia Phillies TC 6.00 15.00
215 Enos Slaughter 20.00 50.00
216 Marv Grissom 3.00 8.00
217 Gene Stephens 3.00 8.00
218 Ray Jablonski 3.00 8.00
219 Tom Acker RC 3.00 8.00
220 Jackie Jensen 8.00 20.00
221 Dixie Howell 3.00 8.00
222 Alex Grammas 3.00 8.00
223 Frank House 3.00 8.00
224 Marv Blaylock 3.00 8.00
225 Harry Simpson 3.00 8.00
226 Preston Ward 3.00 8.00
227 Gerry Staley 3.00 8.00
228 Smoky Burgess UER 6.00 15.00
229 George Susce 3.00 8.00
230 George Kell 12.00 30.00
231 Solly Hemus 3.00 8.00
232 Whitey Lockman 6.00 15.00
233 Art Fowler 3.00 8.00
234 Dick Cole 3.00 8.00
235 Tom Poholsky 3.00 8.00
236 Joe Ginsberg 3.00 8.00
237 Foster Castleman 3.00 8.00
238 Eddie Robinson 3.00 8.00
239 Tom Morgan 3.00 8.00
240 Hank Bauer 20.00 50.00
241 Joe Lonnett RC 3.00 8.00
242 Charlie Neal 6.00 15.00
243 St. Louis Cardinals TC 12.00 30.00
244 Billy Loes 6.00 15.00
245 Rip Repulski 3.00 8.00
246 Jose Valdivielso 3.00 8.00
247 Turk Lown 3.00 8.00
248 Jim Finigan 3.00 8.00
249 Dave Pope 3.00 8.00
250 Eddie Mathews 40.00 100.00
251 Baltimore Orioles TC 6.00 15.00
252 Carl Erskine 12.00 30.00
253 Gus Zernial 6.00 15.00
254 Ron Negray 3.00 8.00
255 Charlie Silvera 6.00 15.00
256 Ron Kline 3.00 8.00
257 Walt Dropo 3.00 8.00
258 Steve Gromek 3.00 8.00
259 Eddie O'Brien 3.00 8.00
260 Del Ennis 6.00 15.00
261 Bob Chakales 3.00 8.00
262 Bobby Thomson 6.00 15.00
263 George Strickland 3.00 8.00
264 Bob Turley 6.00 15.00
265 Harvey Haddix DP 5.00 12.00
266 Ken Kuhn DP RC 5.00 12.00
267 Danny Kravitz RC 8.00 20.00
268 Jack Collum 8.00 20.00
269 Bob Cerv 12.00 30.00
270 Washington Senators TC 20.00 50.00
271 Danny O'Connell DP 5.00- 12.00
272 Bobby Shantz 20.00 50.00
273 Jim Davis 8.00 20.00
274 Don Hoak 6.00 15.00
275 Cleveland Indians TC UER 25.00 60.00
276 Jim Pyburn RC 8.00 20.00
277 Johnny Podres DP 25.00 60.00
278 Fred Hatfield DP 5.00 12.00
279 Bob Thurman RC 8.00 20.00
280 Alex Kellner 8.00 20.00
281 Gail Harris 8.00 20.00
282 Jack Dittmer DP 5.00 12.00
283 Wes Covington DP RC 5.00 12.00
284 Don Zimmer 20.00 50.00
285 Ned Garver 8.00 20.00
286 Bobby Richardson RC 50.00 120.00
287 Sam Jones 8.00 20.00
288 Ted Lepcio 8.00 20.00
289 Jim Bolger DP 5.00 12.00
290 Andy Carey DP 15.00 40.00
291 Windy McCall 8.00 20.00
292 Billy Klaus 8.00 20.00
293 Ted Abernathy RC 8.00 20.00
294 Rocky Bridges DP 5.00 12.00
295 Joe Collins DP 15.00 40.00
296 Johnny Klippstein 8.00 20.00
297 Jack Crimian 8.00 20.00
298 Irv Noren DP 5.00 12.00
299 Chuck Harmon 8.00 20.00
300 Mike Garcia 12.00 30.00
301 Sammy Esposito DP RC 8.00 20.00
302 Sandy Koufax DP 250.00 600.00
303 Billy Goodman 12.00 30.00
304 Joe Cunningham 12.00 30.00
305 Chico Fernandez 8.00 20.00
306 Darrell Johnson DP RC 5.00 12.00
307 Jack D. Phillips DP 5.00 12.00
308 Dick Hall 8.00 20.00
309 Jim Busby DP 5.00 12.00
310 Max Surkont DP 5.00 12.00
311 Al Pilarcik DP RC 5.00 12.00
312 Tony Kubek DP RC 50.00 120.00
313 Mel Parnell 6.00 15.00
314 Ed Bouchee DP RC 5.00 12.00
315 Lou Berberet DP 5.00 12.00
316 Billy O'Dell 8.00 20.00
317 New York Giants TC 30.00 80.00
318 Mickey McDermott 8.00 20.00
319 Gino Cimoli RC 8.00 20.00
320 Neil Chrisley RC 8.00 20.00
321 John Red Murff RC 12.00 30.00
322 Cincinnati Reds TC 30.00 80.00
323 Wes Westrum 12.00 30.00
324 Brooklyn Dodgers TC 40.00 100.00

325 Frank Bolling 15.00 40.00
326 Pedro Ramos 8.00 20.00
327 Jim Pendleton 8.00 20.00
328 Brooks Robinson RC 500.00 1200.00
329 Chicago White Sox TC 25.00 60.00
330 Jim Wilson 8.00 20.00
331 Ray Katt 8.00 20.00
332 Bob Bowman RC 8.00 20.00
333 Ernie Johnson 20.00 50.00
334 Jerry Schoonmaker 8.00 20.00
335 Granny Hamner 8.00 20.00
336 Haywood Sullivan RC 12.00 30.00
337 Rene Valdes RC 10.00 25.00
338 Jim Bunning RC 100.00 250.00
339 Bob Speake 8.00 20.00
340 Bill Wight 8.00 20.00
341 Don Gross RC 8.00 20.00
342 Gene Mauch 12.00 30.00
343 Taylor Phillips RC 6.00 15.00
344 Paul LaPalme 8.00 20.00
345 Paul Smith 8.00 20.00
346 Dick Littlefield 8.00 20.00
347 Hal Naragon 8.00 20.00
348 Jim Hearn 8.00 20.00
349 Nellie King 8.00 20.00
350 Eddie Miksis 8.00 20.00
351 Dave Hillman RC 8.00 20.00
352 Ellis Kinder 8.00 20.00
353 Cal Neeman RC 3.00 8.00
354 Rip Coleman RC 3.00 8.00
355 Frank Malzone 6.00 15.00
356 Faye Throneberry 3.00 8.00
357 Earl Torgeson 3.00 8.00
358 Jerry Lynch 6.00 15.00
359 Tom Cheney RC 3.00 8.00
360 Johnny Groth 3.00 8.00
361 Curt Barclay RC 3.00 8.00
362 Roman Mejias RC 6.00 15.00
363 Eddie Kasko RC 3.00 8.00
364 Cal McLish RC 6.00 15.00
365 Ozzie Virgil RC 3.00 8.00
366 Ken Lehman 3.00 8.00
367 Ed Fitzgerald 3.00 8.00
368 Bob Purkey 3.00 8.00
369 Milt Graff RC 3.00 8.00
370 Warren Hacker 3.00 8.00
371 Bob Lennon 3.00 8.00
372 Norm Zauchin 3.00 8.00
373 Pete Whisenant RC 3.00 8.00
374 Don Cardwell RC 3.00 8.00
375 Jim Landis RC 6.00 15.00
376 Don Elston RC 3.00 8.00
377 Andre Rodgers RC 3.00 8.00
378 Elmer Singleton 3.00 8.00
379 Don Lee RC 3.00 8.00
380 Walker Cooper 3.00 8.00
381 Dean Stone 3.00 8.00
382 Jim Brideweser 3.00 8.00
383 Juan Pizarro RC 3.00 8.00
384 Bobby G. Smith RC 3.00 8.00
385 Art Houtteman 3.00 8.00
386 Lyle Luttrell RC 3.00 8.00
387 Jack Sanford RC 6.00 15.00
388 Pete Daley 3.00 8.00
389 Dave Jolly 3.00 8.00
390 Reno Bertoia 3.00 8.00
391 Ralph Terry RC 6.00 15.00
392 Chuck Tanner 8.00 20.00
393 Raul Sanchez RC 3.00 8.00
394 Luis Arroyo 6.00 15.00
395 Bubba Phillips 3.00 8.00
396 Casey Wise RC 3.00 8.00
397 Roy Smalley 3.00 8.00
398 Al Cicotte RC 6.00 15.00
399 Billy Consolo 3.00 8.00
400 Fur/Hodges/Campy/Snider 60.00 150.00
401 Earl Battey RC 6.00 15.00
402 Jim Pisoni RC 3.00 8.00
403 Dick Hyde RC 3.00 8.00
404 Harry Anderson RC 3.00 8.00
405 Duke Maas 3.00 8.00
406 Bob Hale 3.00 8.00
407 Y.Berra/M.Mantle 250.00 600.00
CC1 Contest May 4 40.00 100.00
CC2 Contest May 25 40.00 100.00
CC3 Contest June 22 50.00 120.00
CC4 Contest July 19 50.00 120.00
NNO Checklist 1/2 Bazooka 100.00 250.00
NNO Checklist 1/2 Blony 100.00 250.00
NNO Checklist 2/3 Bazooka 150.00 400.00
NNO Checklist 2/3 Blony 150.00 400.00
NNO Checklist 3/4 Bazooka 400.00 800.00
NNO Checklist 3/4 Blony 300.00 600.00
NNO Checklist 4/5 Bazooka 500.00 1000.00
NNO Checklist 4/5 Blony 400.00 800.00
NNO Lucky Penny Charm 40.00 100.00

1958 Topps

This is a 494-card standard-size set. Card number 145, which was supposedly to be Ed Bouchee, was not issued. The 1958 Topps set contains the first Sport Magazine All-Star Selection series (475-495) and expanded use of combination cards. For the first time team cards carried series checklists on back (Milwaukee, Detroit, Baltimore, and Cincinnati are also found with players listed alphabetically). In the first series some cards were issued with yellow name (YN) or team (YT) lettering, as opposed to the common white lettering. They are explicity noted below. Cards were issued in one-card penny packs or six-card nickel packs. In the last series, All-Star cards of Stan Musial and Mickey Mantle were triple printed; the cards they replaced (443, 446, 450, and 462) on the printing sheet were hence printed in shorter supply than other cards in the last series and are marked with an SP in the list below. The All-Star card of Musial marked his first appearance on a Topps card. Technically the New York Giants team card (19) is an error as the Giants had already moved to San Francisco. The key Rookie Cards in this set are Orlando Cepeda, Curt Flood, Roger Maris, and Vada Pinson. These cards were issued in varying formats, including one cent packs which were issued 120 to a box.

COMP. MASTER SET (534) 6000.00 15000.00
COMPLETE SET (494) 4000.00 10000.00
COMMON CARD (1-110) 6.00 12.00
COMMON CARD (111-495) 4.00 8.00
WRAPPER (1-CENT) 75.00 100.00
WRAPPER (5-CENT) 100.00 125.00
1 Ted Williams 200.00 400.00
2A Bob Lemon 12.00 30.00
2B Bob Lemon YT 25.00 60.00
3 Alex Kellner 5.00 12.00
4 Hank Foiles 5.00 12.00
5 Willie Mays 125.00 300.00
6 George Zuverink 5.00 12.00
7 Dale Long 6.00 15.00
8A Eddie Kasko 5.00 12.00
8B Eddie Kasko YN 15.00 40.00
9 Hank Bauer 20.00 50.00
10 Lou Burdette 8.00 20.00
11A Jim Rivera 5.00 12.00
11B Jim Rivera YT 15.00 40.00
12 George Crowe 5.00 12.00
13A Billy Hoeft 5.00 12.00
13B Billy Hoeft YN 15.00 40.00
14 Rip Repulski 5.00 12.00
15 Jim Lemon 6.00 15.00
16 Charlie Neal 6.00 15.00
17 Felix Mantilla 5.00 12.00
18 Frank Sullivan 5.00 12.00
19 San Francisco Giants TC 15.00 40.00
20A Gil McDougald 8.00 20.00
20B Gil McDougald YN 25.00 60.00
21 Curt Barclay 5.00 12.00
22 Hal Naragon 5.00 12.00
23A Bill Tuttle 5.00 12.00
23B Bill Tuttle YN 15.00 40.00
24A Hobie Landrith 5.00 12.00
24B Hobie Landrith YN 20.00 50.00
25 Don Drysdale 40.00 100.00
26 Ron Jackson 5.00 12.00
27 Bud Freeman 5.00 12.00
28 Jim Busby 5.00 12.00
29 Ted Lepcio 5.00 12.00
30A Hank Aaron 125.00 300.00
30B Hank Aaron YN 250.00 500.00
31 Tex Clevenger RC 5.00 12.00
32A J.W. Porter 5.00 12.00
32B J.W. Porter YN 15.00 40.00
33A Cal Neeman 5.00 12.00
33B Cal Neeman YT 15.00 40.00
34 Bob Thurman 5.00 12.00
35A Don Mossi 6.00 15.00
35B Don Mossi YT 15.00 40.00
36 Ted Kazanski 5.00 12.00
37 Mike McCormick UER RC 6.00 15.00
38 Dick Gernert 5.00 12.00
39 Bob Martyn RC 5.00 12.00
40 George Kell 10.00 25.00
41 Dave Hillman 5.00 12.00
42 John Roseboro RC 30.00 80.00
43 Sal Maglie 6.00 15.00
44 Washington Senators TC 8.00 20.00
45 Dick Groat 6.00 15.00
46A Lou Sleater 5.00 12.00
46B Lou Sleater YN 15.00 40.00
47 Roger Maris RC 400.00 1000.00
48 Chuck Harmon 5.00 12.00
49 Smoky Burgess 6.00 15.00
50A Billy Pierce 6.00 15.00
50B Billy Pierce YT 15.00 40.00
51 Del Rice 5.00 12.00
52A Roberto Clemente 125.00 300.00
52B Roberto Clemente YT 250.00 500.00
53A Morrie Martin 5.00 12.00
53B Morrie Martin YN 15.00 40.00
54 Norm Siebern RC 8.00 20.00
55 Chico Carrasquel 5.00 12.00
56 Bill Fischer RC 5.00 12.00
57A Tim Thompson 5.00 12.00
57B Tim Thompson YN 15.00 40.00
58A Art Schult 5.00 12.00
58B Art Schult YT 15.00 40.00
59 Dave Sisler 5.00 12.00
60A Del Ennis 6.00 15.00
60B Del Ennis YN 15.00 40.00
61A Darrell Johnson 5.00 12.00
61B Darrell Johnson YN 15.00 40.00
62 Joe DeMaestri 5.00 12.00
63 Joe Nuxhall 6.00 15.00
64 Joe Lonnett 5.00 12.00
65A Von McDaniel RC 5.00 12.00
65B Von McDaniel YN 15.00 40.00
66 Lee Walls 5.00 12.00
67 Joe Ginsberg 5.00 12.00
68 Daryl Spencer 5.00 12.00
69 Wally Burnette 5.00 12.00
70A Al Kaline 40.00 100.00
70B Al Kaline YN 100.00 250.00
71 Los Angeles Dodgers TC 25.00 60.00
72 Bud Byerly UER 5.00 12.00
73 Pete Daley 5.00 12.00
74 Roy Face 6.00 15.00
75 Gus Bell 6.00 15.00
76A Dick Farrell RC 5.00 12.00
76B Dick Farrell YT 15.00 40.00
77A Don Zimmer 6.00 15.00
77B Don Zimmer YT 15.00 40.00
78A Ernie Johnson 6.00 15.00
78B Ernie Johnson YN 15.00 40.00
79A Dick Williams 6.00 15.00
79B Dick Williams YT 15.00 40.00
80 Dick Drott RC 5.00 12.00
81A Steve Boros RC 5.00 12.00
81B Steve Boros YT 15.00 40.00
82 Ron Kline 5.00 12.00
83 Bob Hazle RC 5.00 12.00
84 Billy O'Dell 5.00 12.00
85A Luis Aparicio 12.00 30.00
85B Luis Aparicio YT 30.00 80.00
86 Valmy Thomas RC 5.00 12.00
87 Johnny Kucks 5.00 12.00
88 Duke Snider 25.00 60.00
89 Billy Klaus 5.00 12.00
90 Robin Roberts 15.00 40.00
91 Chuck Tanner 6.00 15.00
92A Clint Courtney 5.00 12.00
92B Clint Courtney YN 15.00 40.00
93 Sandy Amoros 6.00 15.00
94 Bob Skinner 6.00 15.00
95 Frank Bolling 5.00 12.00
96 Joe Durham RC 5.00 12.00
97A Larry Jackson 5.00 12.00
97B Larry Jackson YN 15.00 40.00
98A Billy Hunter 5.00 12.00
98B Billy Hunter YN 15.00 40.00
99 Bobby Adams 5.00 12.00
100A Early Wynn 12.00 30.00
100B Early Wynn YT 30.00 80.00
101A Bobby Richardson 12.00 30.00
101B B.Richardson YN 25.00 60.00
102 George Strickland 5.00 12.00
103 Jerry Lynch 6.00 15.00
104 Jim Pendleton 5.00 12.00
105 Billy Gardner 5.00 12.00
106 Dick Schofield 6.00 15.00
107 Ossie Virgil 5.00 12.00
108A Jim Landis 5.00 12.00
108B Jim Landis YT 15.00 40.00
109 Herb Plews 5.00 12.00
110 Johnny Logan 6.00 15.00
111 Stu Miller 4.00 10.00
112 Gus Zernial 4.00 10.00
113 Jerry Walker RC 3.00 8.00
114 Irv Noren 4.00 10.00
115 Jim Bunning 12.00 30.00
116 Dave Philley 3.00 8.00
117 Frank Torre 4.00 10.00
118 Harvey Haddix 4.00 10.00
119 Harry Chiti 3.00 8.00
120 Johnny Podres 10.00 25.00
121 Eddie Miksis 3.00 8.00
122 Walt Moryn 3.00 8.00
123 Dick Tomanek RC 3.00 8.00
124 Bobby Usher 3.00 8.00
125 Alvin Dark 4.00 10.00
126 Stan Palys RC 3.00 8.00
127 Tom Sturdivant 8.00 20.00
128 Willie Kirkland RC 3.00 8.00
129 Jim Derrington RC 3.00 8.00
130 Jackie Jensen 4.00 10.00
131 Bob Henrich RC 3.00 8.00
132 Vern Law 4.00 10.00
133 Russ Nixon RC 3.00 8.00
134 Philadelphia Phillies TC 6.00 15.00
135 Mike MoeDrabowsky 4.00 10.00
136 Jim Finigan 3.00 8.00
137 Russ Kemmerer 3.00 8.00
138 Earl Torgeson 3.00 8.00
139 George Brunet RC 3.00 8.00
140 Wes Covington 4.00 10.00
141 Ken Lehman 3.00 8.00
142 Enos Slaughter 20.00 50.00
143 Billy Muffett RC 3.00 8.00
144 Bobby Morgan 3.00 8.00
146 Dick Gray RC 3.00 8.00
147 Don McMahon RC 4.00 10.00
148 Billy Consolo 3.00 8.00
149 Tom Acker 3.00 8.00
150 Mickey Mantle 500.00 1000.00
151 Buddy Pritchard RC 3.00 8.00
152 Johnny Antonelli 4.00 10.00
153 Les Moss 3.00 8.00
154 Harry Byrd 3.00 8.00
155 Hector Lopez 4.00 10.00
156 Dick Hyde 3.00 8.00
157 Dee Fondy 3.00 8.00
158 Cleveland Indians TC 6.00 15.00
159 Taylor Phillips 3.00 8.00
160 Don Hoak 4.00 10.00
161 Don Larsen 20.00 50.00
162 Gil Hodges 20.00 50.00
163 Jim Wilson 3.00 8.00
164 Bob Taylor RC 3.00 8.00
165 Bob Nieman 3.00 8.00
166 Danny O'Connell 3.00 8.00
167 Frank Baumann RC 3.00 8.00
168 Joe Cunningham 3.00 8.00
169 Ralph Terry 4.00 10.00
170 Vic Wertz 4.00 10.00
171 Harry Anderson 3.00 8.00
172 Don Gross 3.00 8.00
173 Eddie Yost 4.00 10.00
174 Kansas City Athletics TC 6.00 15.00
175 Marv Throneberry RC 6.00 15.00
176 Bob Buhl 4.00 10.00
177 Al Smith 3.00 8.00
178 Ted Kluszewski 10.00 25.00
179 Willie Miranda 3.00 8.00
180 Lindy McDaniel 8.00 20.00
181 Willie Jones 3.00 8.00
182 Joe Caffie RC 3.00 8.00
183 Dave Jolly 3.00 8.00
184 Elvin Tappe 3.00 8.00
185 Ray Boone 4.00 10.00
186 Jack Meyer 3.00 8.00
187 Sandy Koufax 125.00 300.00
188 Milt Bolling UER 3.00 8.00
189 George Susce 3.00 8.00
190 Red Schoendienst 15.00 40.00
191 Art Ceccarelli RC 3.00 8.00
192 Milt Graff 3.00 8.00
193 Jerry Lumpe RC 4.00 10.00
194 Roger Craig 4.00 10.00
195 Whitey Lockman 4.00 10.00
196 Mike Garcia 4.00 10.00
197 Haywood Sullivan 4.00 10.00
198 Bill Virdon 4.00 10.00
199 Don Blasingame 3.00 8.00
200 Bob Keegan 3.00 8.00
201 Jim Bolger 3.00 8.00
202 Woody Held RC 3.00 8.00
203 Al Walker 3.00 8.00
204 Leo Kiely 3.00 8.00
205 Johnny Temple 4.00 10.00
206 Bob Shaw RC 3.00 8.00
207 Solly Hemus 3.00 8.00
208 Cal McLish 3.00 8.00
209 Bob Anderson RC 3.00 8.00
210 Wally Moon 4.00 10.00
211 Pete Burnside RC 3.00 8.00
212 Bubba Phillips 3.00 8.00
213 Red Wilson 3.00 8.00
214 Willard Schmidt 3.00 8.00
215 Jim Gilliam 6.00 15.00
216 St. Louis Cardinals TC 6.00 15.00
217 Jack Harshman 3.00 8.00
218 Dick Rand RC 3.00 8.00
219 Camilo Pascual 4.00 10.00
220 Tom Brewer 3.00 8.00
221 Jerry Kindall RC 3.00 8.00
222 Bud Daley RC 3.00 8.00
223 Andy Pafko 4.00 10.00
224 Bob Grim 4.00 10.00
225 Billy Goodman 4.00 10.00
226 Bob Smith RC 3.00 8.00
227 Gene Stephens 3.00 8.00
228 Duke Maas 3.00 8.00
229 Frank Zupo RC 3.00 8.00
230 Richie Ashburn 25.00 60.00
231 Lloyd Merritt RC 3.00 8.00
232 Reno Bertoia 3.00 8.00
233 Mickey Vernon 4.00 10.00
234 Carl Sawatski 3.00 8.00
235 Tom Gorman 3.00 8.00
236 Ed Fitzgerald 3.00 8.00
237 Bill Wight 3.00 8.00
238 Bill Mazeroski 25.00 60.00
239 Chuck Stobbs 3.00 8.00
240 Bill Skowron 15.00 40.00
241 Dick Littlefield 3.00 8.00
242 Johnny Klippstein 3.00 8.00
243 Larry Raines RC 3.00 8.00
244 Don Demeter RC 3.00 8.00
245 Frank Lary 4.00 10.00
246 New York Yankees TC 30.00 80.00
247 Casey Wise 3.00 8.00
248 Herman Wehmeier 3.00 8.00
249 Ray Moore 3.00 8.00
250 Roy Sievers 4.00 10.00
251 Warren Hacker 3.00 8.00
252 Bob Trowbridge RC 3.00 8.00
253 Don Mueller 4.00 10.00
254 Alex Grammas 3.00 8.00
255 Bob Turley 4.00 10.00
256 Chicago White Sox TC 6.00 15.00
257 Hal Smith 3.00 8.00
258 Carl Erskine 6.00 15.00
259 Al Pilarcik 3.00 8.00
260 Frank Malzone 4.00 10.00
261 Turk Lown 3.00 8.00
262 Johnny Groth 3.00 8.00
263 Eddie Bressoud RC 4.00 10.00
264 Jack Sanford 3.00 8.00
265 Pete Runnels 3.00 8.00
266 Connie Johnson 3.00 8.00
267 Sherm Lollar 4.00 10.00
268 Granny Hamner 3.00 8.00
269 Paul Smith 3.00 8.00
270 Warren Spahn 30.00 80.00
271 Billy Martin 15.00 40.00
272 Ray Crone 3.00 8.00
273 Hal Smith 3.00 8.00
274 Rocky Bridges 3.00 8.00
275 Elston Howard 15.00 40.00
276 Bobby Avila 3.00 8.00
277 Virgil Trucks 4.00 10.00
278 Mack Burk 3.00 8.00
279 Bob Boyd 3.00 8.00
280 Jim Piersall 4.00 10.00
281 Sammy Taylor RC 3.00 8.00
282 Paul Foytack 3.00 8.00
283 Ray Shearer RC 3.00 8.00
284 Ray Katt 3.00 8.00
285 Frank Robinson 40.00 100.00
286 Gino Cimoli 3.00 8.00
287 Sam Jones 4.00 10.00
288 Harmon Killebrew 50.00 120.00
289 B.Shantz/L.Burdette 4.00 10.00
290 Dick Donovan 3.00 8.00
291 Don Landrum RC 3.00 8.00
292 Ned Garver 3.00 8.00
293 Gene Freese 3.00 8.00
294 Hal Jeffcoat 3.00 8.00
295 Minnie Minoso 10.00 25.00
296 Ryne Duren RC 15.00 40.00
297 Don Buddin RC 3.00 8.00
298 Jim Hearn 3.00 8.00
299 Harry Simpson 3.00 8.00
300 W.Harridge/W.Giles 6.00 15.00
301 Randy Jackson 3.00 8.00
302 Mike Baxes RC 3.00 8.00
303 Neil Chrisley 3.00 8.00
304 H.Kuenn/A.Kaline 10.00 25.00
305 Clem Labine 4.00 10.00
306 Whammy Douglas RC 3.00 8.00
307 Brooks Robinson 100.00 250.00
308 Paul Giel 4.00 10.00
309 Gail Harris 3.00 8.00
310 Ernie Banks 50.00 120.00
311 Bob Purkey 3.00 8.00
312 Boston Red Sox TC 6.00 15.00
313 Bob Rush 3.00 8.00
314 D.Snider/W.Alston 15.00 40.00
315 Bob Friend 4.00 10.00
316 Tito Francona 4.00 10.00
317 Albie Pearson RC 4.00 10.00
318 Frank House 3.00 8.00
319 Lou Skizas 3.00 8.00
320 Whitey Ford 50.00 120.00
321 T.Kluszewski/T.Williams 25.00 60.00
322 Harding Peterson RC 4.00 10.00
323 Elmer Valo 3.00 8.00
324 Hoyt Wilhelm 10.00 25.00
325 Joe Adcock 4.00 10.00
326 Bob Miller 3.00 8.00
327 Chicago Cubs TC 6.00 15.00
328 Ike Delock 3.00 8.00
329 Bob Cerv 4.00 10.00
330 Ed Bailey 4.00 10.00
331 Pedro Ramos 3.00 8.00
332 Jim King 3.00 8.00
333 Andy Carey 4.00 10.00
334 B.Friend/B.Pierce 4.00 10.00
335 Ruben Gomez 3.00 8.00
336 Bert Hamric 3.00 8.00
337 Hank Aguirre 3.00 8.00
338 Walt Dropo 4.00 10.00
339 Fred Hatfield 3.00 8.00
340 Don Newcombe 15.00 40.00
341 Pittsburgh Pirates TC 6.00 15.00
342 Jim Brosnan 4.00 10.00
343 Orlando Cepeda RC 100.00 250.00
344 Bob Porterfield 3.00 8.00
345 Jim Hegan 4.00 10.00
346 Steve Bilko 3.00 8.00
347 Don Rudolph RC 3.00 8.00
348 Chico Fernandez 3.00 8.00
349 Murry Dickson 3.00 8.00
350 Ken Boyer 10.00 25.00
351 Cran/Math/Aaron/Adcock 30.00 80.00
352 Herb Score 6.00 15.00
353 Stan Lopata 3.00 8.00
354 Art Ditmar 4.00 10.00
355 Bill Bruton 4.00 10.00
356 Bob Malkmus RC 3.00 8.00
357 Danny McDevitt RC 3.00 8.00
358 Gene Baker 3.00 8.00
359 Billy Loes 4.00 10.00
360 Roy McMillan 4.00 10.00
361 Mike Fornieles 3.00 8.00
362 Ray Jablonski 3.00 8.00
363 Don Elston 3.00 8.00
364 Earl Battey 3.00 8.00
365 Tom Morgan 3.00 8.00
366 Gene Green RC 3.00 8.00
367 Jack Urban RC 3.00 8.00
368 Rocky Colavito 25.00 60.00
369 Ralph Lumenti RC 3.00 8.00
370 Yogi Berra 60.00 150.00
371 Marty Keough RC 3.00 8.00
372 Don Cardwell 3.00 8.00
373 Joe Pignatano RC 3.00 8.00
374 Brooks Lawrence 3.00 8.00
375 Pee Wee Reese 30.00 80.00
376 Charley Rabe RC 3.00 8.00
377A Milwaukee Braves TC Alpha 6.00 15.00
377B Milwaukee Braves TC Num 40.00 100.00
378 Hank Sauer 4.00 10.00
379 Ray Herbert 3.00 8.00
380 Charlie Maxwell 4.00 10.00
381 Hal Brown 3.00 8.00
382 Al Cicotte 3.00 8.00
383 Lou Berberet 3.00 8.00
384 John Goryl RC 3.00 8.00
385 Wilmer Mizell 4.00 10.00
386 Bailey/Tebbets/F.Rob 15.00 40.00
387 Wally Post 4.00 10.00
388 Billy Moran RC 3.00 8.00
389 Bill Taylor 3.00 8.00
390 Del Crandall 4.00 10.00
391 Dave Melton RC 3.00 8.00
392 Bennie Daniels RC 3.00 8.00
393 Tony Kubek 12.00 30.00
394 Jim Grant RC 3.00 8.00
395 Willard Nixon 3.00 8.00
396 Dutch Dotterer RC 3.00 8.00
397A Detroit Tigers TC Alpha 6.00 15.00
397B Detroit Tigers TC Num 40.00 100.00
398 Gene Woodling 4.00 10.00
399 Marv Grissom 3.00 8.00
400 Nellie Fox 12.00 30.00
401 Don Bessent 3.00 8.00
402 Bobby Gene Smith 3.00 8.00
403 Steve Korcheck RC 3.00 8.00
404 Curt Simmons 8.00 20.00
405 Ken Aspromonte RC 3.00 8.00
406 Vic Power 4.00 10.00
407 Carlton Willey RC 4.00 10.00
408A Baltimore Orioles TC Alpha 6.00 15.00
408B Baltimore Orioles TC Num 40.00 100.00
409 Frank Thomas 4.00 10.00
410 Murray Wall 3.00 8.00
411 Tony Taylor RC 4.00 10.00
412 Gerry Staley 3.00 8.00
413 Jim Davenport RC 3.00 8.00
414 Sammy White 3.00 8.00
415 Bob Bowman 3.00 8.00
416 Foster Castleman 3.00 8.00
417 Carl Furillo 6.00 15.00
418 M.Mantle/H.Aaron 125.00 300.00
419 Bobby Shantz 4.00 10.00
420 Vada Pinson RC 25.00 60.00
421 Dixie Howell 3.00 8.00
422 Norm Zauchin 3.00 8.00
423 Phil Clark RC 3.00 8.00
424 Larry Doby UER 20.00 50.00
425 Sammy Esposito 3.00 8.00
426 Johnny O'Brien 4.00 10.00
427 Al Worthington 3.00 8.00
428A Cincinnati Reds TC Alpha 6.00 15.00
428B Cincinnati Reds TC Num 40.00 100.00
429 Gus Triandos 4.00 10.00
430 Bobby Thomson 4.00 10.00
431 Gene Conley 4.00 10.00
432 John Powers RC 3.00 8.00
433A Pancho Herrera COR RC 4.00 10.00
433B Pancho Herrer ERR 2500.00 5000.00
433C Pancho Herre ERR
433D Pancho Herr ERR
434 Harvey Kuenn 4.00 10.00
435 Ed Roebuck 4.00 10.00
436 W.Mays/D.Snider 30.00 80.00
437 Bob Speake 3.00 8.00
438 Whitey Herzog 4.00 10.00
439 Ray Narleski 3.00 8.00
440 Eddie Mathews 25.00 60.00
441 Jim Marshall RC 4.00 10.00
442 Phil Paine RC 3.00 8.00
443 Billy Harrell SP RC 8.00 20.00
444 Danny Kravitz 3.00 8.00
445 Bob Smith RC 3.00 8.00
446 Carroll Hardy SP RC 8.00 20.00
447 Ray Monzant 3.00 8.00
448 Charlie Lau RC 4.00 10.00
449 Gene Fodge RC 3.00 8.00
450 Preston Ward SP 8.00 20.00
451 Joe Taylor RC 3.00 8.00
452 Roman Mejias 3.00 8.00
453 Tom Qualters 3.00 8.00
454 Harry Hanebrink RC 3.00 8.00
455 Hal Griggs RC 3.00 8.00
456 Dick Brown RC 3.00 8.00
457 Milt Pappas RC 4.00 10.00
458 Julio Becquer RC 3.00 8.00
459 Ron Blackburn RC 3.00 8.00
460 Chuck Essegian RC 3.00 8.00
461 Ed Mayer RC 3.00 8.00
462 Gary Geiger SP RC 8.00 20.00
463 Vito Valentinetti 3.00 8.00
464 Curt Flood RC 25.00 60.00
465 Arnie Portocarrero 3.00 8.00
466 Pete Whisenant 3.00 8.00
467 Glen Hobbie RC 3.00 8.00
468 Bob Schmidt RC 3.00 8.00
469 Don Ferrarese 3.00 8.00
470 R.C. Stevens RC 3.00 8.00
471 Lenny Green RC 3.00 8.00
472 Joey Jay 4.00 10.00
473 Bill Renna 3.00 8.00
474 Roman Semproch RC 3.00 8.00
475 F.Haney/C.Stengel AS 15.00 40.00
476 Stan Musial AS TP 40.00 100.00
477 Bill Skowron AS 4.00 10.00
478 Johnny Temple AS UER 3.00 8.00
479 Nellie Fox AS 6.00 15.00
480 Eddie Mathews AS 15.00 40.00
481 Frank Malzone AS 3.00 8.00
482 Ernie Banks AS 25.00 60.00
483 Luis Aparicio AS 10.00 25.00
484 Frank Robinson AS 25.00 60.00
485 Ted Williams AS 50.00 120.00
486 Willie Mays AS 40.00 100.00
487 Mickey Mantle AS TP 75.00 200.00
488 Hank Aaron AS 30.00 80.00
489 Jackie Jensen AS 4.00 10.00
490 Ed Bailey AS 3.00 8.00
491 Sherm Lollar AS 3.00 8.00
492 Bob Friend AS 10.00 25.00
493 Bob Turley AS 4.00 10.00
494 Warren Spahn AS 10.00 25.00
495 Herb Score AS 6.00 15.00
NNO Contest Cards 15.00 40.00
NNO Felt Emblem Insert

1959 Topps

The cards in this 572-card set measure 2 1/2" by 3 1/2". The 1959 Topps set contains bust pictures of the players in a colored circle. Card numbers 551 to 572 are Sporting News All-Star Selections. High numbers 507 to 572 have the card number in a black background on the reverse rather than a green background as in the lower numbers. The high numbers are more difficult to obtain. Several cards in the 300s exist with or without an extra traded or option line on the back of the card. Cards 199 to 286 exist with either white or gray backs. There is no price differential for either colored back. Cards 461 to 470 contain "Highlights" while cards 116 to 146 give an alphabetically ordered listing of "Rookie Prospects." These Rookie Prospects (RP) were Topps' first organized inclusion of untested "Rookie" cards. Card 440 features Lew Burdette erroneously posing as a left-handed pitcher. Cards were issued in one-card penny packs or six-card nickel packs. There were some three-card advertising panels produced by Topps; the players included are from the first series. Panels which had Ted Kluszewski's card back on the back included Don McMahon/Red Wilson/Bob Boyd; Joe Pignatano/Sam Jones/Jack Urban also with Kluszewski's card back on back. Strips with Nellie Fox on the back included Billy Hunter/Chuck Stobbs/Carl Sawatski; Vito Valentinetti/Ken Lehman/Ed Bouchee; Mel Roach/Brooks Lawrence/Warren Spahn. Other panels include Harvey Kuenn/Alex Grammas/Bob Cerv; and Bob Cerv/Jim Bolger/Mickey Mantle. When separated, these advertising cards are distinguished by the non-standard card back, i.e., part of an advertisement for the 1959 Topps set instead of the typical statistics and biographical information about the player pictured. The key Rookie Cards in this set are Felipe Alou, Sparky Anderson (called George on the card), Norm Cash, Bob Gibson, and Bill White.

COMPLETE SET (572) 3000.00 8000.00
COMMON CARD (1-110) 3.00 6.00
COMMON CARD (111-506) 2.00 4.00
COMMON CARD (507-572) 7.50 15.00
WRAPPER (1-CENT) 100.00 125.00
WRAPPER (5-CENT) 75.00 100.00
1 Ford Frick COMM 40.00 100.00
2 Eddie Yost 4.00 10.00
3 Don McMahon 4.00 10.00
4 Albie Pearson 4.00 10.00
5 Dick Donovan 4.00 10.00
6 Alex Grammas 3.00 8.00
7 Al Pilarcik 3.00 8.00
8 Philadelphia Phillies CL 40.00 80.00
9 Paul Giel 4.00 10.00
10 Mickey Mantle 300.00 800.00
11 Billy Hunter 4.00 10.00
12 Vern Law 4.00 10.00
13 Dick Gernert 3.00 8.00
14 Pete Whisenant 3.00 8.00
15 Dick Drott 3.00 8.00
16 Joe Pignatano 3.00 8.00
17 Thomas/Murtaugh/Klusz 4.00 10.00
18 Jack Urban 3.00 8.00
19 Eddie Bressoud 3.00 8.00
20 Duke Snider 25.00 60.00
21 Connie Johnson 3.00 8.00
22 Al Smith 4.00 10.00
23 Murry Dickson 4.00 10.00
24 Red Wilson 3.00 8.00
25 Don Hoak 4.00 10.00
26 Chuck Stobbs 3.00 8.00
27 Andy Pafko 4.00 10.00
28 Al Worthington 3.00 8.00
29 Jim Bolger 3.00 8.00
30 Nellie Fox 15.00 40.00
31 Ken Lehman 3.00 8.00
32 Don Buddin 3.00 8.00
33 Ed Fitzgerald 3.00 8.00
34 Al Kaline/C.Maxwell 12.00 30.00
35 Ted Kluszewski 10.00 25.00
36 Hank Aguirre 3.00 8.00
37 Gene Green 3.00 8.00
38 Morrie Martin 3.00 8.00
39 Ed Bouchee 3.00 8.00
40A Warren Spahn ERR 40.00 80.00
40B Warren Spahn ERR 60.00 150.00
40C Warren Spahn COR 30.00 80.00
41 Bob Martyn 3.00 8.00
42 Murray Wall 3.00 8.00
43 Steve Bilko 3.00 8.00
44 Vito Valentinetti 3.00 8.00
45 Andy Carey 4.00 10.00
46 Bill R. Henry 3.00 8.00
47 Jim Finigan 3.00 8.00
48 Baltimore Orioles CL 12.00 30.00
49 Bill Hall RC 3.00 8.00
50 Willie Mays 60.00 150.00
51 Rip Coleman 3.00 8.00
52 Coot Veal RC 3.00 8.00
53 Stan Williams RC 4.00 10.00
54 Mel Roach 3.00 8.00
55 Tom Brewer 3.00 8.00
56 Carl Sawatski 3.00 8.00
57 Al Cicotte 3.00 8.00
58 Eddie Miksis 3.00 8.00
59 Irv Noren 4.00 10.00
60 Bob Turley 4.00 10.00
61 Dick Brown 3.00 8.00
62 Tony Taylor 4.00 10.00
63 Jim Hearn 3.00 8.00
64 Joe DeMaestri 3.00 8.00
65 Frank Torre 4.00 10.00
66 Joe Ginsberg 3.00 8.00
67 Brooks Lawrence 3.00 8.00
68 Dick Schofield 4.00 10.00
69 San Francisco Giants CL 12.00 30.00
70 Harvey Kuenn 4.00 10.00
71 Don Bessent 3.00 8.00
72 Bill Renna 3.00 8.00
73 Ron Jackson 4.00 10.00
74 Lemon/Lavagetto/Sievers 4.00 10.00
75 Sam Jones 4.00 10.00
76 Bobby Richardson 12.00 30.00
77 John Goryl 3.00 8.00
78 Pedro Ramos 3.00 8.00
79 Harry Chiti 3.00 8.00
80 Minnie Minoso 6.00 15.00
81 Hal Jeffcoat 3.00 8.00
82 Bob Boyd 3.00 8.00
83 Bob Smith 3.00 8.00
84 Reno Bertoia 3.00 8.00
85 Harry Anderson 3.00 8.00
86 Bob Keegan 4.00 10.00
87 Danny O'Connell 3.00 8.00
88 Herb Score 6.00 15.00
89 Billy Gardner 3.00 8.00
90 Bill Skowron 6.00 15.00
91 Herb Moford RC 3.00 8.00
92 Dave Philley 3.00 8.00
93 Julio Becquer 3.00 8.00
94 Chicago White Sox CL 20.00 50.00
95 Carl Willey 3.00 8.00
96 Lou Berberet 3.00 8.00
97 Jerry Lynch 4.00 10.00
98 Arnie Portocarrero 3.00 8.00
99 Ted Kazanski 3.00 8.00
100 Bob Cerv 4.00 10.00
101 Alex Kellner 3.00 8.00
102 Felipe Alou RC 15.00 40.00
103 Billy Goodman 4.00 10.00
104 Del Rice 4.00 10.00
105 Lee Walls 3.00 8.00
106 Hal Woodeshick RC 3.00 8.00
107 Norm Larker RC 4.00 10.00
108 Zack Monroe RC 4.00 10.00
109 Bob Schmidt 3.00 8.00
110 George Witt RC 4.00 10.00
111 Cincinnati Redlegs CL 7.50 20.00
112 Billy Consolo 2.00 5.00
113 Taylor Phillips 2.00 5.00
114 Earl Battey 4.00 10.00
115 Mickey Vernon 4.00 10.00
116 Bob Allison RS RC 6.00 15.00
117 John Blanchard RS RC 6.00 15.00
118 John Buzhardt RS RC 2.50 6.00
119 Johnny Callison RS RC 6.00 15.00
120 Chuck Coles RS RC 2.50 6.00
121 Bob Conley RS RC 2.50 6.00
122 Bennie Daniels RS 2.50 6.00
123 Don Dillard RS RC 2.50 6.00
124 Dan Dobbek RS RC 2.50 6.00
125 Ron Fairly RS RC 6.00 15.00
126 Eddie Haas RS RC 2.50 6.00
127 Kent Hadley RS RC 2.50 6.00
128 Bob Hartman RS RC 2.50 6.00
129 Frank Herrera RS 2.50 6.00
130 Lou Jackson RS RC 2.50 6.00
131 Deron Johnson RS RC 6.00 15.00
132 Don Lee RS 2.50 6.00
133 Bob Lillis RS RC 2.50 6.00
134 Jim McDaniel RS RC 2.50 6.00
135 Gene Oliver RS RC 2.50 6.00
136 Jim O'Toole RS RC 2.50 6.00
137 Dick Ricketts RS RC 2.50 6.00
138 John Romano RS RC 2.50 6.00
139 Ed Sadowski RS RC 2.50 6.00
140 Charlie Secrest RS RC 2.50 6.00
141 Joe Shipley RS RC 2.50 6.00
142 Dick Stigman RS RC 2.50 6.00
143 Willie Tasby RS RC 2.50 6.00
144 Jerry Walker RS 2.50 6.00
145 Dom Zanni RS RC 2.50 6.00
146 Jerry Zimmerman RS RC 2.50 6.00
147 Long/Banks/Moryn 15.00 40.00
148 Mike McCormick 4.00 10.00
149 Jim Bunning 12.00 30.00
150 Stan Musial 40.00 100.00
151 Bob Malkmus 2.00 5.00
152 Johnny Klippstein 2.00 5.00
153 Jim Marshall 2.00 5.00
154 Ray Herbert 2.00 5.00
155 Enos Slaughter 10.00 25.00
156 B.Pierce/R.Roberts 6.00 15.00
157 Felix Mantilla 2.00 5.00
158 Walt Dropo 2.00 5.00
159 Bob Shaw 4.00 10.00
160 Dick Groat 4.00 10.00
161 Frank Baumann 2.00 5.00
162 Bobby G. Smith 2.00 5.00
163 Sandy Koufax 125.00 300.00
164 Johnny Groth 2.00 5.00
165 Bill Bruton 2.00 5.00
166 Minoso/Colavito/Doby 15.00 40.00
167 Duke Maas 2.00 5.00
168 Carroll Hardy 2.00 5.00
169 Ted Abernathy 2.00 5.00

170 Gene Woodling	4.00	10.00
171 Willard Schmidt	2.00	5.00
172 Kansas City Athletics CL	7.50	20.00
173 Bill Monbouquette RC	4.00	10.00
174 Jim Pendleton	2.00	5.00
175 Dick Farrell	4.00	10.00
176 Preston Ward	2.00	5.00
177 John Briggs RC	2.00	5.00
178 Ruben Amaro RC	6.00	15.00
179 Don Rudolph	2.00	5.00
180 Yogi Berra	50.00	120.00
181 Bob Porterfield	2.00	5.00
182 Milt Graff	2.00	5.00
183 Stu Miller	4.00	10.00
184 Harvey Haddix	4.00	10.00
185 Jim Busby	2.00	5.00
186 Mudcat Grant	4.00	10.00
187 Bubba Phillips	4.00	10.00
188 Juan Pizarro	2.00	5.00
189 Neil Chrisley	2.00	5.00
190 Bill Virdon	4.00	10.00
191 Russ Kemmerer	2.00	5.00
192 Charlie Beamon RC	2.00	5.00
193 Sammy Taylor	2.00	5.00
194 Jim Brosnan	4.00	10.00
195 Rip Repulski	2.00	5.00
196 Billy Moran	2.00	5.00
197 Ray Semproch	2.00	5.00
198 Jim Davenport	4.00	10.00
199 Leo Kiely	2.00	5.00
200 W.Giles NL PRES	4.00	10.00
201 Tom Acker	2.00	5.00
202 Roger Maris	50.00	120.00
203 Ossie Virgil	2.00	5.00
204 Casey Wise	2.00	5.00
205 Don Larsen	4.00	10.00
206 Carl Furillo	6.00	15.00
207 George Strickland	2.00	5.00
208 Willie Jones	2.00	5.00
209 Lenny Green	2.00	5.00
210 Ed Bailey	2.00	5.00
211 Bob Blaylock RC	2.00	5.00
212 H.Aaron/E.Mathews	30.00	80.00
213 Jim Rivera	4.00	10.00
214 Marcelino Solis RC	2.00	5.00
215 Jim Lemon	4.00	10.00
216 Andre Rodgers	2.00	5.00
217 Carl Erskine	6.00	15.00
218 Roman Mejias	2.00	5.00
219 George Zuverink	2.00	5.00
220 Frank Malzone	4.00	10.00
221 Bob Bowman	2.00	5.00
222 Bobby Shantz	4.00	10.00
223 St. Louis Cardinals CL	8.00	20.00
224 Claude Osteen RC	4.00	10.00
225 Johnny Logan	4.00	10.00
226 Art Ceccarelli	2.00	5.00
227 Hal W. Smith	2.00	5.00
228 Don Gross	2.00	5.00
229 Vic Power	4.00	10.00
230 Bill Fischer	2.00	5.00
231 Ellis Burton RC	2.00	5.00
232 Eddie Kasko	2.00	5.00
233 Paul Foytack	2.00	5.00
234 Chuck Tanner	4.00	10.00
235 Valmy Thomas	2.00	5.00
236 Ted Bowsfield RC	2.00	5.00
237 McDougald/Turley/B.Rich	6.00	15.00
238 Gene Baker	2.00	5.00
239 Bob Trowbridge	2.00	5.00
240 Hank Bauer	6.00	15.00
241 Billy Muffett	2.00	5.00
242 Ron Samford RC	2.00	5.00
243 Marv Grissom	2.00	5.00
244 Dick Gray	2.00	5.00
245 Ned Garver	2.00	5.00
246 J.W. Porter	2.00	5.00
247 Don Ferrarese	2.00	5.00
248 Boston Red Sox CL	8.00	20.00
249 Bobby Adams	2.00	5.00
250 Billy O'Dell	2.00	5.00
251 Clete Boyer	6.00	15.00
252 Ray Boone	4.00	10.00
253 Seth Morehead RC	2.00	5.00
254 Zeke Bella RC	2.00	5.00
255 Del Ennis	4.00	10.00
256 Jerry Davie RC	2.00	5.00
257 Leon Wagner RC	4.00	10.00
258 Fred Kipp RC	2.00	5.00
259 Jim Pisoni	2.00	5.00
260 Early Wynn UER	10.00	25.00
261 Gene Stephens	2.00	5.00
262 Podres/Labine/Drysdale	6.00	15.00
263 Bud Daley	2.00	5.00
264 Chico Carrasquel	2.00	5.00
265 Ron Kline	2.00	5.00
266 Woody Held	2.00	5.00
267 John Romonosky RC	2.00	5.00
268 Tito Francona	4.00	10.00
269 Jack Meyer	2.00	5.00
270 Gil Hodges	15.00	40.00
271 Orlando Pena RC	2.00	5.00
272 Jerry Lumpe	2.00	5.00
273 Joey Jay	4.00	10.00
274 Jerry Kindall	4.00	10.00
275 Jack Sanford	4.00	10.00
276 Pete Daley	2.00	5.00
277 Turk Lown	4.00	10.00
278 Chuck Essegian	2.00	5.00
279 Ernie Johnson	2.00	5.00
280 Frank Bolling	2.00	5.00
281 Walt Craddock RC	2.00	5.00
282 R.C. Stevens	2.00	5.00
283 Russ Heman RC	2.00	5.00
284 Steve Korcheck	2.00	5.00
285 Joe Cunningham	2.00	5.00
286 Dean Stone	2.00	5.00
287 Don Zimmer	6.00	15.00
288 Dutch Dotterer	2.00	5.00
289 Johnny Kucks	4.00	10.00
290 Wes Covington	2.00	5.00
291 P.Ramos/C.Pascual	2.00	5.00
292 Dick Williams	4.00	10.00
293 Ray Moore	2.00	5.00
294 Hank Foiles	2.00	5.00
295 Billy Martin	15.00	40.00
296 Ernie Broglio RC	2.00	5.00
297 Jackie Brandt RC	2.00	5.00
298 Tex Clevenger	2.00	5.00
299 Billy Klaus	2.00	5.00
300 Richie Ashburn	15.00	40.00
301 Earl Averill Jr. RC	2.00	5.00
302 Don Mossi	4.00	10.00
303 Marty Keough	2.00	5.00
304 Chicago Cubs CL	8.00	20.00
305 Curt Raydon RC	2.00	5.00
306 Jim Gilliam	4.00	10.00
307 Curt Barclay	2.00	5.00
308 Norm Siebern	2.00	5.00
309 Sal Maglie	4.00	10.00
310 Luis Aparicio	12.00	30.00
311 Norm Zauchin	2.00	5.00
312 Don Newcombe	4.00	10.00
313 Frank House	2.00	5.00
314 Don Cardwell	2.00	5.00
315 Joe Adcock	4.00	10.00
316A Ralph Lumenti UER	2.00	5.00
316B Ralph Lumenti UER	50.00	120.00
317 R.Ashburn/W.Mays	20.00	50.00
318 Rocky Bridges	2.00	5.00
319 Dave Hillman	2.00	5.00
320 Bob Skinner	4.00	10.00
321A Bob Giallombardo RC	4.00	10.00
321B Bob Giallombardo ERR	50.00	120.00
322A Harry Hanebrink TR	4.00	10.00
322B H.Hanebrink ERR	50.00	120.00
323 Frank Sullivan	2.00	5.00
324 Don Demeter	2.00	5.00
325 Ken Boyer	6.00	15.00
326 Marv Throneberry	4.00	10.00
327 Gary Bell RC	2.00	5.00
328 Lou Skizas	2.00	5.00
329 Detroit Tigers CL	8.00	20.00
330 Gus Triandos	4.00	10.00
331 Steve Boros	2.00	5.00
332 Ray Monzant	2.00	5.00
333 Harry Simpson	2.00	5.00
334 Glen Hobbie	2.00	5.00
335 Johnny Temple	4.00	10.00
336A Billy Loes TR	4.00	10.00
336B Billy Loes ERR	50.00	120.00
337 George Crowe	2.00	5.00
338 Sparky Anderson RC	25.00	60.00
339 Roy Face	4.00	10.00
340 Roy Sievers	4.00	10.00
341 Tom Qualters	2.00	5.00
342 Ray Jablonski	2.00	5.00
343 Billy Hoeft	2.00	5.00
344 Russ Nixon	2.00	5.00
345 Gil McDougald	6.00	15.00
346 D.Sisler/T.Brewer	2.00	5.00
347 Bob Buhl	2.00	5.00
348 Ted Lepcio	2.00	5.00
349 Hoyt Wilhelm	8.00	20.00
350 Ernie Banks	40.00	100.00
351 Earl Torgeson	2.00	5.00
352 Robin Roberts	12.00	30.00
353 Curt Flood	4.00	10.00
354 Pete Burnside	2.00	5.00
355 Jimmy Piersall	4.00	10.00
356 Bob Mabe RC	2.00	5.00
357 Dick Stuart RC	4.00	10.00
358 Ralph Terry	4.00	10.00
359 Bill White RC	10.00	25.00
360 Al Kaline	25.00	60.00
361 Willard Nixon	2.00	5.00
362A Dolan Nichols RC	2.00	5.00
362B Dolan Nichols ERR	50.00	120.00
363 Bobby Avila	2.00	5.00
364 Danny McDevitt	2.00	5.00
365 Gus Bell	4.00	10.00
366 Humberto Robinson	2.00	5.00
367 Cal Neeman	2.00	5.00
368 Don Mueller	4.00	10.00
369 Dick Tomanek	2.00	5.00
370 Pete Runnels	4.00	10.00
371 Dick Brodowski	2.00	5.00
372 Jim Hegan	4.00	10.00
373 Herb Plews	2.00	5.00
374 Art Ditmar	4.00	10.00
375 Bob Nieman	2.00	5.00
376 Hal Naragon	2.00	5.00
377 John Antonelli	4.00	10.00
378 Gail Harris	2.00	5.00
379 Bob Miller	2.00	5.00
380 Hank Aaron	75.00	200.00
381 Mike Baxes	2.00	5.00
382 Curt Simmons	4.00	10.00
383 D.Larsen/C.Stengel	6.00	15.00
384 Dave Sisler	2.00	5.00
385 Sherm Lollar	4.00	10.00
386 Jim Delsing	2.00	5.00
387 Don Drysdale	15.00	40.00
388 Bob Will RC	2.00	5.00
389 Joe Nuxhall	4.00	10.00
390 Orlando Cepeda	12.00	30.00
391 Milt Pappas	4.00	10.00
392 Whitey Herzog	4.00	10.00
393 Frank Lary	4.00	10.00
394 Randy Jackson	2.00	5.00
395 Elston Howard	10.00	25.00
396 Bob Rush	2.00	5.00
397 Washington Senators CL	8.00	20.00
398 Wally Post	4.00	10.00
399 Larry Jackson	2.00	5.00
400 Jackie Jensen	4.00	10.00
401 Ron Blackburn	2.00	5.00
402 Hector Lopez	4.00	10.00
403 Clem Labine	4.00	10.00
404 Hank Sauer	4.00	10.00
405 Roy McMillan	4.00	10.00
406 Solly Drake	2.00	5.00
407 Moe Drabowsky	4.00	10.00
408 N.Fox/L.Aparicio	20.00	50.00
409 Gus Zernial	4.00	10.00
410 Billy Pierce	4.00	10.00
411 Whitey Lockman	4.00	10.00
412 Stan Lopata	2.00	5.00
413 Camilo Pascual UER	4.00	10.00
414 Dale Long	4.00	10.00
415 Bill Mazeroski	10.00	25.00
416 Haywood Sullivan	4.00	10.00
417 Virgil Trucks	4.00	10.00
418 Gino Cimoli	2.00	5.00
419 Milwaukee Braves CL	8.00	20.00
420 Rocky Colavito	15.00	40.00
421 Herman Wehmeier	2.00	5.00
422 Hobie Landrith	2.00	5.00
423 Bob Grim	4.00	10.00
424 Ken Aspromonte	2.00	5.00
425 Del Crandall	4.00	10.00
426 Gerry Staley	4.00	10.00
427 Charlie Neal	4.00	10.00
428 Kline/Friend/Law/Face	2.00	5.00
429 Bobby Thomson	4.00	10.00
430 Whitey Ford	30.00	80.00
431 Whammy Douglas	2.00	5.00
432 Smoky Burgess	4.00	10.00
433 Billy Harrell	2.00	5.00
434 Hal Griggs	2.00	5.00
435 Frank Robinson	40.00	100.00
436 Granny Hamner	2.00	5.00
437 Ike Delock	2.00	5.00
438 Sammy Esposito	2.00	5.00
439 Brooks Robinson	40.00	100.00
440 Lew Burdette UER	4.00	10.00
441 John Roseboro	4.00	10.00
442 Ray Narleski	2.00	5.00
443 Daryl Spencer	2.00	5.00
444 Ron Hansen RC	4.00	10.00
445 Cal McLish	2.00	5.00
446 Rocky Nelson	2.00	5.00
447 Bob Anderson	2.00	5.00
448 Vada Pinson UER	10.00	25.00
449 Tom Gorman	2.00	5.00
450 Eddie Mathews	25.00	60.00
451 Jimmy Constable RC	2.00	5.00
452 Chico Fernandez	2.00	5.00
453 Les Moss	2.00	5.00
454 Phil Clark	2.00	5.00
455 Larry Doby	15.00	40.00
456 Jerry Casale RC	2.00	5.00
457 Los Angeles Dodgers CL	15.00	40.00
458 Gordon Jones	2.00	5.00
459 Bill Tuttle	2.00	5.00
460 Bob Friend	4.00	10.00
461 Mickey Mantle BT	50.00	120.00
462 Rocky Colavito BT	6.00	15.00
463 Al Kaline BT	15.00	40.00
464 Willie Mays BT	25.00	60.00
465 Roy Sievers BT	4.00	10.00
466 Billy Pierce BT	4.00	10.00
467 Hank Aaron BT	20.00	50.00
468 Duke Snider BT	10.00	25.00
469 Ernie Banks BT	20.00	50.00
470 Stan Musial BT	20.00	50.00
471 Tom Sturdivant	2.00	5.00
472 Gene Freese	2.00	5.00
473 Mike Fornieles	2.00	5.00
474 Moe Thacker RC	2.00	5.00
475 Jack Harshman	2.00	5.00
476 Cleveland Indians CL	8.00	20.00
477 Barry Latman RC	2.00	5.00
478 Roberto Clemente UER	125.00	300.00
479 Lindy McDaniel	4.00	10.00
480 Red Schoendienst	10.00	25.00
481 Charlie Maxwell	4.00	10.00
482 Russ Meyer	2.00	5.00
483 Clint Courtney	2.00	5.00
484 Willie Kirkland	2.00	5.00
485 Ryne Duren	4.00	10.00
486 Sammy White	2.00	5.00
487 Hal Brown	2.00	5.00
488 Walt Moryn	2.00	5.00
489 John Powers	2.00	5.00
490 Frank Thomas	4.00	10.00
491 Don Blasingame	2.00	5.00
492 Gene Conley	4.00	10.00
493 Jim Landis	4.00	10.00
494 Don Pavletich RC	2.00	5.00
495 Johnny Podres	8.00	20.00
496 Wayne Terwilliger UER	2.00	5.00
497 Hal R. Smith	2.00	5.00
498 Dick Hyde	2.00	5.00
499 Johnny O'Brien	4.00	10.00
500 Vic Wertz	4.00	10.00
501 Bob Tiefenauer RC	2.00	5.00
502 Alvin Dark	4.00	10.00
503 Jim Owens	2.00	5.00
504 Ossie Alvarez RC	2.00	5.00
505 Tony Kubek	10.00	25.00
506 Bob Purkey	2.00	5.00
507 Bob Hale	7.50	20.00
508 Art Fowler	7.50	20.00
509 Norm Cash RC	30.00	80.00
510 New York Yankees CL	50.00	120.00
511 George Susce	7.50	20.00
512 George Altman RC	7.50	20.00
513 Tommy Carroll	7.50	20.00
514 Bob Gibson RC	500.00	1200.00
515 Harmon Killebrew	40.00	100.00
516 Mike Garcia	10.00	25.00
517 Joe Koppe RC	7.50	20.00
518 Mike Cueller UER RC	15.00	40.00
Sic, Cuellar		
519 Runnels/Gernert/Malzone	10.00	25.00
520 Don Elston	7.50	20.00
521 Gary Geiger	7.50	20.00
522 Gene Snyder RC	7.50	20.00
523 Harry Bright RC	7.50	20.00
524 Larry Osborne RC	7.50	20.00
525 Jim Coates RC	10.00	25.00
526 Bob Speake	7.50	20.00
527 Solly Hemus	7.50	20.00
528 Pittsburgh Pirates CL	50.00	120.00
529 George Bamberger RC	10.00	25.00
530 Wally Moon	10.00	25.00
531 Ray Webster RC	7.50	20.00
532 Mark Freeman RC	7.50	20.00
533 Darrell Johnson	10.00	25.00
534 Faye Throneberry	7.50	20.00
535 Ruben Gomez	7.50	20.00
536 Danny Kravitz	7.50	20.00
537 Rudolph Arias RC	7.50	20.00
538 Chick King	7.50	20.00
539 Gary Blaylock RC	7.50	20.00
540 Willie Miranda	7.50	20.00
541 Bob Thurman	7.50	20.00
542 Jim Perry RC	12.00	30.00
543 Skinner/Virdon/Clemente	25.00	60.00
544 Lee Tate RC	7.50	20.00
545 Tom Morgan	7.50	20.00
546 Al Schroll	7.50	20.00
547 Jim Baxes RC	7.50	20.00
548 Elmer Singleton	7.50	20.00
549 Howie Nunn RC	7.50	20.00
550 R.Campanella Courage	60.00	150.00
551 Fred Haney AS MG	7.50	20.00
552 Casey Stengel AS MG	15.00	30.00
553 Orlando Cepeda AS	15.00	30.00
554 Bill Skowron AS	10.00	25.00
555 Bill Mazeroski AS	15.00	40.00
556 Nellie Fox AS	20.00	50.00
557 Ken Boyer AS	15.00	40.00
558 Frank Malzone AS	7.50	20.00
559 Ernie Banks AS	25.00	60.00
560 Luis Aparicio AS	25.00	60.00
561 Hank Aaron AS	40.00	100.00
562 Al Kaline AS	20.00	50.00
563 Willie Mays AS	40.00	100.00
564 Mickey Mantle AS	125.00	300.00
565 Wes Covington AS	10.00	25.00
566 Roy Sievers AS	7.50	20.00
567 Del Crandall AS	7.50	20.00
568 Gus Triandos AS	7.50	20.00
569 Bob Friend AS	7.50	20.00
570 Bob Turley AS	8.00	20.00
571 Warren Spahn AS	30.00	80.00
572 Billy Pierce AS	25.00	60.00

1959 Topps Venezuelan

This set is a parallel version of the first 196 cards of the regular 1959 Topps set and is similar in design. The difference is found in the words "Impreso en Venezuela por Benco Co." printed on the bottom of the card back. The cards were issued for the Venezuelan market.

COMPLETED SET (196)	6000.00	12000.00
1 Ford Frick COMM	150.00	300.00
2 Eddie Yost	15.00	30.00
3 Don McMahon	15.00	30.00
4 Albie Pearson	15.00	30.00
5 Dick Donovan	15.00	30.00
6 Alex Grammas	15.00	30.00
7 Al Pilarcik	15.00	30.00
8 Phillies Team CL	200.00	400.00
9 Paul Giel	15.00	30.00
10 Mickey Mantle	2000.00	4000.00
11 Billy Hunter	15.00	30.00
12 Vern Law	15.00	30.00
13 Dick Gernert	15.00	30.00
14 Pete Whisenant	15.00	30.00
15 Dick Drott	15.00	30.00
16 Joe Pignatano	15.00	30.00
17 Danny's Stars	20.00	40.00
Frank Thomas		
Danny Murtaugh MG		
Te		
18 Jack Urban	15.00	30.00
19 Eddie Bressoud	15.00	30.00
20 Duke Snider	200.00	400.00
21 Connie Johnson	15.00	30.00
22 Al Smith	15.00	30.00
23 Murry Dickson	15.00	30.00
24 Red Wilson	15.00	30.00
25 Don Hoak	15.00	30.00
26 Chuck Stobbs	15.00	30.00
27 Andy Pafko	15.00	30.00
28 Al Worthington	15.00	30.00
29 Jim Bolger	15.00	30.00
30 Nellie Fox	30.00	60.00
31 Ken Lehman	15.00	30.00
32 Don Buddin	15.00	30.00
33 Ed Fitzgerald	15.00	30.00
34 Al Kaline	50.00	100.00
Charley Maxwell		
35 Ted Kluszewski	60.00	120.00
36 Hank Aguirre	15.00	30.00
37 Gene Green	15.00	30.00
38 Morrie Martin	15.00	30.00
39 Ed Bouchee	15.00	30.00
40 Warren Spahn	150.00	300.00
41 Bob Martyn	15.00	30.00
42 Murray Wall	15.00	30.00
43 Steve Bilko	15.00	30.00
44 Vito Valentinetti	15.00	30.00
45 Andy Carey	15.00	30.00
46 Bill R. Henry	15.00	30.00
47 Jim Finigan	15.00	30.00
48 Orioles Team CL	60.00	120.00
49 Bill Hall	15.00	30.00
50 Willie Mays	500.00	1000.00
51 Rip Coleman	15.00	30.00
52 Coot Veal	15.00	30.00
53 Stan Williams	15.00	30.00
54 Mel Roach	15.00	30.00
55 Tom Brewer	15.00	30.00
56 Carl Sawatski	15.00	30.00
57 Al Cicotte	15.00	30.00
58 Eddie Miksis	15.00	30.00
59 Irv Noren	15.00	30.00
60 Bob Turley	20.00	40.00
61 Dick Brown	15.00	30.00
62 Tony Taylor	15.00	30.00
63 Jim Hearn	15.00	30.00
64 Joe DeMaestri	15.00	30.00
65 Frank Torre	15.00	30.00
66 Joe Ginsberg	15.00	30.00
67 Brooks Lawrence	15.00	30.00
68 Dick Schofield	15.00	30.00
69 Giants Team CL	60.00	120.00
70 Harvey Kuenn	20.00	40.00
71 Don Bessent	15.00	30.00
72 Bill Renna	15.00	30.00
73 Ron Jackson	15.00	30.00
74 Directing Power	15.00	30.00
Jim Lemon		
Cookie Lavagetto MG		
R		
75 Sam Jones	15.00	30.00
76 Bobby Richardson	75.00	150.00
77 John Goryl	15.00	30.00
78 Pedro Ramos	15.00	30.00
79 Harry Chiti	15.00	30.00
80 Minnie Minoso	30.00	60.00
81 Hal Jeffcoat	15.00	30.00
82 Bob Boyd	15.00	30.00
83 Bob Smith	15.00	30.00
84 Reno Bertoia	15.00	30.00
85 Harry Anderson	15.00	30.00
86 Bob Keegan	15.00	30.00
87 Danny O'Connell	15.00	30.00
88 Herb Score	30.00	60.00
89 Billy Gardner	15.00	30.00
90 Bill Skowron	50.00	100.00
91 Herb Moford	15.00	30.00
92 Dave Philley	15.00	30.00
93 Julio Becquer	15.00	30.00
94 White Sox Team CL	40.00	80.00
95 Carl Willey	15.00	30.00
96 Lou Berberet	15.00	30.00
97 Jerry Lynch	15.00	30.00
98 Arnie Portocarrero	15.00	30.00
99 Ted Kazanski	15.00	30.00
100 Bob Cerv	15.00	30.00
101 Alex Kellner	15.00	30.00
102 Felipe Alou	100.00	200.00
103 Billy Goodman	15.00	30.00
104 Del Rice	15.00	30.00
105 Lee Walls	15.00	30.00
106 Hal Woodeshick	15.00	30.00
107 Norm Larker	15.00	30.00
108 Zack Monroe	15.00	30.00
109 Bob Schmidt	15.00	30.00
110 George Witt	15.00	30.00
111 Redlegs Team CL	30.00	60.00
112 Billy consolo	15.00	30.00
113 Taylor Phillips	15.00	30.00
114 Earl Battey	15.00	30.00
115 Mickey Vernon	20.00	40.00
116 Bob Allison RP	25.00	50.00
117 John Blanchard RP	15.00	30.00
118 John Buzhardt RP	15.00	30.00
119 John Callison RP	30.00	60.00
120 Chuck Coles RP	15.00	30.00
121 Bob Conley RP	15.00	30.00
122 Bennie Daniels RP	15.00	30.00
123 Don Dillard RP	15.00	30.00
124 Dan Dobbek RP	15.00	30.00
125 Ron Fairly RP	25.00	50.00
126 Eddie Haas RP	15.00	30.00
127 Kent Hadley RP	15.00	30.00
128 Bob Hartman RP	15.00	30.00
129 Frank Herrera RP	15.00	30.00
130 Lou Jackson RP	15.00	30.00
131 Deron Johnson RP	15.00	30.00
132 Don Lee RP	15.00	30.00
133 Bob Lillis RP	15.00	30.00
134 Jim McDaniel RP	15.00	30.00
135 Gene Oliver RP	15.00	30.00
136 Jim O'Toole RP	15.00	30.00
137 Dick Ricketts RP	15.00	30.00
138 John Romano RP	15.00	30.00
139 Ed Sadowski RP	15.00	30.00
140 Charlie Secrest RP	15.00	30.00
141 Joe Shipley RP	15.00	30.00
142 Dick Stigman RP	15.00	30.00
143 Willie Tasby RP	15.00	30.00
144 Jerry Walker RP	15.00	30.00
145 Dom Zanni RP	15.00	30.00
146 Jerry Zimmerman RP	15.00	30.00
147 Dale Long	75.00	150.00
Ernie Banks		
Walt Moryn		
148 Mike McCormick	20.00	40.00
149 Jim Bunning	60.00	120.00
150 Stan Musial	400.00	800.00
151 Bob Malkmus	15.00	30.00
152 Johnny Klippstein	15.00	30.00
153 Jim Marshall	15.00	30.00
154 Ray Herbert	15.00	30.00
155 Enos Slaughter	60.00	120.00
156 Billy Pierce	30.00	60.00
Robin Roberts		
157 Felix Mantilla	15.00	30.00
158 Walt Dropo	15.00	30.00
159 Bob Shaw	15.00	30.00
160 Dick Groat	20.00	40.00
161 Frank Baumann	15.00	30.00
162 Bobby G. Smith	15.00	30.00
163 Sandy Koufax	500.00	1000.00
164 Johnny Groth	15.00	30.00
165 Bill Burton	15.00	30.00
166 Destruction Crew	75.00	150.00
Minnie Minoso		
Rocky Colavito(Mi		
167 Duke Maas	15.00	30.00
168 Carroll Hardy	15.00	30.00
169 Ted Abernathy	15.00	30.00
170 Gene Woodling	15.00	30.00
171 Willard Schmidt	15.00	30.00
172 Athletics Team CL	30.00	60.00
173 Bill Monbouquette	15.00	30.00
174 Jim Pendleton	15.00	30.00
175 Dick Farrell	15.00	30.00
176 Preston Ward	15.00	30.00
177 John Briggs	15.00	30.00
178 Ruben Amaro	15.00	30.00
179 Don Rudolph	15.00	30.00
180 Yogi Berra	250.00	500.00
181 Bob Porterfield	15.00	30.00
182 Milt Graff	15.00	30.00
183 Stu Miller	15.00	30.00
184 Harvey Haddix	15.00	30.00
185 Jim Busby	15.00	30.00
186 Mudcat Grant	15.00	30.00
187 Bubba Phillips	15.00	30.00
188 Juan Pizarro	15.00	30.00
189 Neil Chrisley	15.00	30.00
190 Bill Virdon	15.00	30.00
191 Russ Kemmerer	15.00	30.00
192 Charlie Beamon	15.00	30.00
193 Sammy Taylor	15.00	30.00
194 Jim Brosnan	15.00	30.00
195 Rip Reuplski	15.00	30.00
196 Billy Moran	15.00	30.00

1960 Topps

The cards in this 572-card set measure 2 1/2" by 3 1/2". The 1960 Topps set is the first Topps standard size issue to use a horizontally oriented front. World Series cards appeared for the first time (385 to 391), and there is a Rookie Prospect (RP) series (117-148), the most famous of which is Carl Yastrzemski, and a Sport Magazine All-Star Selection (AS) series (553-572). There are 16 manager cards listed alphabetically from 212 through 227. The 1959 Topps All-Rookie team is featured on cards 316-325. This was the first time the Topps All-Rookie team was ever selected and the only time that all of the cards were placed together in a subset. The coaching staff of each team was also afforded their own card in a 16-card subset (455-470). There is no price differential for either color back. The high series (507-572) were printed on a more limited basis than the rest of the set. The team cards have series checklists on the reverse. Cards were issued in one-card penny packs, six-card nickel packs (which came 24 to a box), 10 cent cello packs (which came 36 packs to a box) and 36-card rack packs which cost 29 cents . Three card ad-sheets have been seen. One such sheet features Wayne Terwilliger, Kent Hadley and Faye Throneberry on the front with Gene Woodling and an Ad on the back. Another sheet featured Hank Foiles/Hobie Landrith and Hal Smith on the front. The key Rookie Cards in this set are Jim Kaat, Willie McCovey and Carl Yastrzemski. Recently, a Kent Hadley was discovered with a Kansas City A's logo on the front, while this card was rumoured to exist for years, this is the first known spotting of the card. According the published reports at the time, seven copies of the Hadley card, along with the Gino Cimoli and the Faye Throneberry cards were produced. Each series of this set had different card backs. Cards numbered 1-110 had cream colored white back, cards numbered 111-198 had grey backs, cards numbered 119-286 had cream colored white backs, cards numbered 287-

COMPLETE SET (572)	3000.00	8000.00
COMMON CARD (1-440)	1.50	4.00
COMMON CARD (441-506)	3.00	8.00
COMMON CARD (507-572)	6.00	15.00
WRAPPER (1-CENT)	500.00	1000.00
WRAP. (1-CENT REPEAT)	250.00	500.00
WRAPPER (5-CENT)	15.00	40.00
1 Early Wynn	20.00	50.00
2 Roman Mejias	1.50	4.00
3 Joe Adcock	2.50	6.00
4 Bob Purkey	1.50	4.00
5 Wally Moon	2.50	6.00
6 Lou Berberet	1.50	4.00
7 W.Mays/B.Rigney	12.00	30.00
8 Bud Daley	1.50	4.00
9 Faye Throneberry	1.50	4.00
9A Faye Throneberry		
10 Ernie Banks	40.00	100.00
11 Norm Siebern	1.50	4.00
12 Milt Pappas	2.50	6.00
13 Wally Post	2.50	6.00
14 Jim Grant	2.50	6.00
15 Pete Runnels	2.50	6.00
16 Ernie Broglio	2.50	6.00
17 Johnny Callison	2.50	6.00
18 Los Angeles Dodgers CL	20.00	50.00
19 Felix Mantilla	1.50	4.00
20 Roy Face	2.50	6.00
21 Dutch Dotterer	1.50	4.00
22 Rocky Bridges	1.50	4.00
23 Eddie Fisher RC	1.50	4.00
24 Dick Gray	1.50	4.00
25 Roy Sievers	2.50	6.00
26 Wayne Terwilliger	1.50	4.00
27 Dick Drott	1.50	4.00
28 Brooks Robinson	30.00	80.00
29 Clem Labine	2.50	6.00
30 Tito Francona	1.50	4.00
31 Sammy Esposito	1.50	4.00
32 J.O'Toole/V.Pinson	1.50	4.00
33 Tom Morgan	1.50	4.00
34 Sparky Anderson	6.00	15.00
35 Whitey Ford	30.00	80.00
36 Russ Nixon	1.50	4.00
37 Bill Bruton	1.50	4.00
38 Jerry Casale	1.50	4.00
39 Earl Averill Jr.	1.50	4.00
40 Joe Cunningham	1.50	4.00
41 Barry Latman	1.50	4.00
42 Hobie Landrith	1.50	4.00
43 Washington Senators CL	4.00	10.00
44 Bobby Locke RC	1.50	4.00
45 Roy McMillan	2.50	6.00
46 Jack Fisher RC	1.50	4.00
47 Don Zimmer	2.50	6.00
48 Hal W. Smith	1.50	4.00
49 Curt Raydon	1.50	4.00
50 Al Kaline	25.00	60.00
51 Jim Coates	2.50	6.00
52 Dave Philley	1.50	4.00
53 Jackie Brandt	1.50	4.00
54 Mike Fornieles	1.50	4.00
55 Bill Mazeroski	25.00	60.00
56 Steve Korcheck	1.50	4.00
57 T.Lown/G.Staley	1.50	4.00
58 Gino Cimoli	1.50	4.00
58A Gino Cimoli Cards		
59 Juan Pizarro	1.50	4.00
60 Gus Triandos	2.50	6.00
61 Eddie Kasko	1.50	4.00
62 Roger Craig	2.50	6.00
63 George Strickland	1.50	4.00
64 Jack Meyer	1.50	4.00
65 Elston Howard	2.50	6.00
66 Bob Trowbridge	1.50	4.00
67 Jose Pagan RC	1.50	4.00
68 Dave Hillman	1.50	4.00
69 Billy Goodman	2.50	6.00
70 Lew Burdette UER	2.50	6.00
71 Marty Keough	1.50	4.00
72 Detroit Tigers CL	10.00	25.00
73 Bob Gibson	60.00	150.00
74 Walt Moryn	1.50	4.00
75 Vic Power	2.50	6.00
76 Bill Fischer	1.50	4.00
77 Hank Foiles	1.50	4.00
78 Bob Grim	1.50	4.00
79 Walt Dropo	1.50	4.00
80 Johnny Antonelli	2.50	6.00
81 Russ Snyder RC	1.50	4.00
82 Ruben Gomez	1.50	4.00
83 Tony Kubek	8.00	20.00
84 Hal R. Smith	1.50	4.00
85 Frank Lary	2.50	6.00
86 Dick Gernert	1.50	4.00
87 John Romonosky	1.50	4.00
88 John Roseboro	2.50	6.00
89 Hal Brown	1.50	4.00
90 Bobby Avila	1.50	4.00
91 Bennie Daniels	1.50	4.00
92 Whitey Herzog	2.50	6.00
93 Art Schult	1.50	4.00
94 Leo Kiely	1.50	4.00
95 Frank Thomas	2.50	6.00
96 Ralph Terry	2.50	6.00
97 Ted Lepcio	1.50	4.00
98 Gordon Jones	1.50	4.00
99 Lenny Green	1.50	4.00
100 Nellie Fox	15.00	40.00
101 Bob Miller RC	1.50	4.00
102 Kent Hadley	1.50	4.00
102A Kent Hadley A's		
103 Dick Farrell	2.50	6.00
104 Dick Schofield	2.50	6.00
105 Larry Sherry RC	2.50	6.00
106 Billy Gardner	1.50	4.00
107 Carlton Willey	1.50	4.00
108 Pete Daley	1.50	4.00
109 Clete Boyer	6.00	15.00
110 Cal McLish	1.50	4.00
111 Vic Wertz	2.50	6.00
112 Jack Harshman	1.50	4.00
113 Bob Skinner	1.50	4.00
114 Ken Aspromonte	1.50	4.00
115 R.Face/H.Wilhelm	2.50	6.00
116 Jim Rivera	1.50	4.00
117 Tom Borland RS	1.50	4.00
118 Bob Bruce RS RC	1.50	4.00
119 Chico Cardenas RS RC	2.50	6.00
120 Duke Carmel RS RC	1.50	4.00
121 Camilo Carreon RS RC	1.50	4.00
122 Don Dillard RS	1.50	4.00
123 Dan Dobbek RS	1.50	4.00
124 Jim Donohue RS RC	1.50	4.00
125 Dick Ellsworth RS RC	2.50	6.00
126 Chuck Estrada RS RC	1.50	4.00
127 Ron Hansen RS	2.50	6.00
128 Bill Harris RS RC	1.50	4.00
129 Bob Hartman RS	1.50	4.00
130 Frank Herrera RS	1.50	4.00
131 Ed Hobaugh RS RC	1.50	4.00
132 Frank Howard RS RC	15.00	40.00
133 Julian Javier RS RC	2.50	6.00
134 Deron Johnson RS	2.50	6.00
135 Ken Johnson RS RC	1.50	4.00
136 Jim Kaat RS RC	40.00	100.00
137 Lou Klimchock RS RC	1.50	4.00
138 Art Mahaffey RS RC	2.50	6.00
139 Carl Mathias RS RC	1.50	4.00
140 Julio Navarro RS RC	1.50	4.00
141 Jim Proctor RS RC	1.50	4.00
142 Bill Short RS RC	1.50	4.00
143 Al Spangler RS RC	1.50	4.00
144 Al Stieglitz RS RC	1.50	4.00
145 Jim Umbricht RS RC	1.50	4.00
146 Ted Wieand RS RC	1.50	4.00
147 Bob Will RS	1.50	4.00
148 C.Yastrzemski RS RC	250.00	600.00
149 Bob Nieman	1.50	4.00
150 Billy Pierce	2.50	6.00
151 San Francisco Giants CL	4.00	10.00
152 Gail Harris	1.50	4.00
153 Bobby Thomson	6.00	15.00
154 Jim Davenport	2.50	6.00
155 Charlie Neal	2.50	6.00
156 Art Ceccarelli	1.50	4.00
157 Rocky Nelson	2.50	6.00
158 Wes Covington	2.50	6.00
159 Jim Piersall	2.50	6.00
160 M.Mantle/K.Boyer	40.00	100.00
161 Ray Narleski	1.50	4.00
162 Sammy Taylor	1.50	4.00
163 Hector Lopez	2.50	6.00
164 Cincinnati Reds CL	4.00	10.00
165 Jack Sanford	2.50	6.00
166 Chuck Essegian	1.50	4.00
167 Valmy Thomas	1.50	4.00
168 Alex Grammas	1.50	4.00
169 Jake Striker RC	1.50	4.00
170 Del Crandall	2.50	6.00
171 Johnny Groth	1.50	4.00
172 Willie Kirkland	1.50	4.00
173 Billy Martin	10.00	25.00
174 Cleveland Indians CL	4.00	10.00
175 Pedro Ramos	1.50	4.00
176 Vada Pinson	2.50	6.00
177 Johnny Kucks	1.50	4.00
178 Woody Held	1.50	4.00
179 Rip Coleman	1.50	4.00
180 Harry Simpson	1.50	4.00
181 Billy Loes	2.50	6.00
182 Glen Hobbie	1.50	4.00
183 Eli Grba RC	1.50	4.00
184 Gary Geiger	1.50	4.00
185 Jim Owens	1.50	4.00
186 Dave Sisler	1.50	4.00
187 Jay Hook RC	1.50	4.00
188 Dick Williams	2.50	6.00
189 Don McMahon	1.50	4.00

190 Gene Woodling 2.50 6.00
191 Johnny Klippstein 1.50 4.00
192 Danny O'Connell 1.50 4.00
193 Dick Hyde 1.50 4.00
194 Bobby Gene Smith 1.50 4.00
195 Lindy McDaniel 2.50 6.00
196 Andy Carey 2.50 6.00
197 Ron Kline 1.50 4.00
198 Jerry Lynch 2.50 6.00
199 Dick Donovan 2.50 6.00
200 Willie Mays 75.00 200.00
201 Larry Osborne 1.50 4.00
202 Fred Kipp 1.50 4.00
203 Sammy White 1.50 4.00
204 Ryne Duren 2.50 6.00
205 Johnny Logan 2.50 6.00
206 Claude Osteen 2.50 6.00
207 Bob Boyd 1.50 4.00
208 Chicago White Sox CL 4.00 10.00
209 Ron Blackburn 1.50 4.00
210 Harmon Killebrew 30.00 80.00
211 Taylor Phillips 1.50 4.00
212 Walter Alston MG 4.00 10.00
213 Chuck Dressen MG 2.50 6.00
214 Jimmy Dykes MG 2.50 6.00
215 Bob Elliott MG 2.50 6.00
216 Joe Gordon MG 2.50 6.00
217 Charlie Grimm MG 2.50 6.00
218 Solly Hemus MG 1.50 4.00
219 Fred Hutchinson MG 2.50 6.00
220 Billy Jurges MG 1.50 4.00
221 Cookie Lavagetto MG 1.50 4.00
222 Al Lopez MG 4.00 10.00
223 Danny Murtaugh MG 2.50 6.00
224 Paul Richards MG 2.50 6.00
225 Bill Rigney MG 1.50 4.00
226 Eddie Sawyer MG 1.50 4.00
227 Casey Stengel MG 15.00 40.00
228 Ernie Johnson 2.50 6.00
229 Joe M. Morgan RC 1.50 4.00
230 Burdette/Spahn/Buhl 4.00 10.00
231 Hal Naragon 1.50 4.00
232 Jim Busby 1.50 4.00
233 Don Elston 1.50 4.00
234 Don Demeter 1.50 4.00
235 Gus Bell 2.50 6.00
236 Dick Ricketts 1.50 4.00
237 Elmer Valo 1.50 4.00
238 Danny Kravitz 1.50 4.00
239 Joe Shipley 1.50 4.00
240 Luis Aparicio 12.00 30.00
241 Albie Pearson 2.50 6.00
242 St. Louis Cardinals CL 4.00 10.00
243 Bubba Phillips 1.50 4.00
244 Hal Griggs 1.50 4.00
245 Eddie Yost 2.50 6.00
246 Lee Maye RC 2.50 6.00
247 Gil McDougald 4.00 10.00
248 Del Rice 1.50 4.00
249 Earl Wilson RC 2.50 6.00
250 Stan Musial 60.00 150.00
251 Bob Malkmus 1.50 4.00
252 Ray Herbert 1.50 4.00
253 Eddie Bressoud 1.50 4.00
254 Arnie Portocarrero 1.50 4.00
255 Jim Gilliam 6.00 15.00
256 Dick Brown 1.50 4.00
257 Gordy Coleman RC 1.50 4.00
258 Dick Groat 2.50 6.00
259 George Altman 1.50 4.00
260 R.Colavito/T.Francona 6.00 15.00
261 Pete Burnside 1.50 4.00
262 Hank Bauer 2.50 6.00
263 Darrell Johnson 1.50 4.00
264 Robin Roberts 12.00 30.00
265 Rip Repulski 1.50 4.00
266 Joey Jay 2.50 6.00
267 Jim Marshall 1.50 4.00
268 Al Worthington 1.50 4.00
269 Gene Green 1.50 4.00
270 Bob Turley 2.50 6.00
271 Julio Becquer 1.50 4.00
272 Fred Green RC 2.50 6.00
273 Neil Chrisley 1.50 4.00
274 Tom Acker 1.50 4.00
275 Curt Flood 8.00 20.00
276 Ken McBride RC 1.50 4.00
277 Harry Bright 1.50 4.00
278 Stan Williams 2.50 6.00
279 Chuck Tanner 2.50 6.00
280 Frank Sullivan 1.50 4.00
281 Ray Boone 2.50 6.00
282 Joe Nuxhall 2.50 6.00
283 Johnny Blanchard 2.50 6.00
284 Don Gross 1.50 4.00
285 Harry Anderson 1.50 4.00
286 Ray Semproch 1.50 4.00
287 Felipe Alou 2.50 6.00
288 Bob Mabe 1.50 4.00
289 Willie Jones 1.50 4.00
290 Jerry Lumpe 1.50 4.00
291 Bob Keegan 1.50 4.00
292 J.Pignatano/J.Roseboro 2.50 6.00
293 Gene Conley 2.50 6.00
294 Tony Taylor 2.50 6.00
295 Gil Hodges 12.00 30.00
296 Nelson Chittum RC 1.50 4.00
297 Reno Bertoia 1.50 4.00
298 George Witt 1.50 4.00
299 Earl Torgeson 1.50 4.00
300 Hank Aaron 100.00 250.00
301 Jerry Davie 1.50 4.00
302 Philadelphia Phillies CL 4.00 10.00
303 Billy O'Dell 1.50 4.00
304 Joe Ginsberg 1.50 4.00
305 Richie Ashburn 12.00 30.00
306 Frank Baumann 1.50 4.00
307 Gene Oliver 1.50 4.00
308 Dick Hall 1.50 4.00
309 Bob Hale 1.50 4.00
310 Frank Malzone 2.50 6.00
311 Raul Sanchez 1.50 4.00
312 Charley Lau 2.50 6.00
313 Turk Lown 1.50 4.00
314 Chico Fernandez 1.50 4.00
315 Bobby Shantz 4.00 10.00
316 W.McCovey ASR RC 100.00 250.00
317 Pumpsie Green ASR RC 2.50 6.00
318 Jim Baxes ASR 2.50 6.00
319 Joe Koppe ASR 2.50 6.00
320 Bob Allison ASR 2.50 6.00
321 Ron Fairly ASR 2.50 6.00
322 Willie Tasby ASR 2.50 6.00
323 John Romano ASR 2.50 6.00
324 Jim Perry ASR 2.50 6.00
325 Jim O'Toole ASR 2.50 6.00
326 Roberto Clemente 125.00 300.00
327 Ray Sadecki RC 1.50 4.00
328 Earl Battey 1.50 4.00
329 Zack Monroe 1.50 4.00
330 Harvey Kuenn 2.50 6.00
331 Henry Mason RC 1.50 4.00
332 New York Yankees CL 20.00 50.00
333 Danny McDevitt 1.50 4.00
334 Ted Abernathy 1.50 4.00
335 Red Schoendienst 10.00 25.00
336 Ike Delock 1.50 4.00
337 Cal Neeman 1.50 4.00
338 Ray Monzant 1.50 4.00
339 Harry Chiti 1.50 4.00
340 Harvey Haddix 2.50 6.00
341 Carroll Hardy 1.50 4.00
342 Casey Wise 1.50 4.00
343 Sandy Koufax 100.00 250.00
344 Clint Courtney 1.50 4.00
345 Don Newcombe 2.50 6.00
346 J.C. Martin UER RC 2.50 6.00
347 Ed Bouchee 1.50 4.00
348 Barry Shetrone RC 1.50 4.00
349 Moe Drabowsky 2.50 6.00
350 Mickey Mantle 500.00 1000.00
351 Don Nottebart RC 1.50 4.00
352 Bell/F.Robinson/Lynch 4.00 10.00
353 Don Larsen 10.00 25.00
354 Bob Lillis 1.50 4.00
355 Bill White 2.50 6.00
356 Joe Amalfitano 1.50 4.00
357 Al Schroll 1.50 4.00
358 Joe DeMaestri 1.50 4.00
359 Buddy Gilbert RC 1.50 4.00
360 Herb Score 2.50 6.00
361 Bob Oldis 2.50 6.00
362 Russ Kemmerer 1.50 4.00
363 Gene Stephens 1.50 4.00
364 Paul Foytack 1.50 4.00
365 Minnie Minoso 10.00 25.00
366 Dallas Green RC 4.00 10.00
367 Bill Tuttle 1.50 4.00
368 Daryl Spencer 1.50 4.00
369 Billy Hoeft 1.50 4.00
370 Bill Skowron 4.00 10.00
371 Bud Byerly 1.50 4.00
372 Frank House 1.50 4.00
373 Don Hoak 2.50 6.00
374 Bob Buhl 2.50 6.00
375 Dale Long 4.00 10.00
376 John Briggs 1.50 4.00
377 Roger Maris 50.00 100.00
378 Stu Miller 2.50 6.00
379 Red Wilson 1.50 4.00
380 Bob Shaw 1.50 4.00
381 Milwaukee Braves CL 4.00 10.00
382 Ted Bowsfield 1.50 4.00
383 Leon Wagner 1.50 4.00
384 Don Cardwell 1.50 4.00
385 Charlie Neal WS1 3.00 8.00
386 Charlie Neal WS2 3.00 8.00
387 Carl Furillo WS3 3.00 8.00
388 Gil Hodges WS4 5.00 12.00
389 L.Aparicio WS5 w/M.Wills 4.00 10.00
390 Scrambling After Ball WS6 3.00 8.00
391 Champs Celebrate WS 3.00 8.00
392 Tex Clevenger 1.50 4.00
393 Smoky Burgess 2.50 6.00
394 Norm Larker 2.50 6.00
395 Hoyt Wilhelm 8.00 20.00
396 Steve Bilko 1.50 4.00
397 Don Blasingame 1.50 4.00
398 Mike Cuellar 2.50 6.00
399 Pappas/Fisher/Walker 2.50 6.00
400 Rocky Colavito 8.00 20.00
401 Bob Duliba RC 1.50 4.00
402 Dick Stuart 6.00 15.00
403 Ed Sadowski 1.50 4.00
404 Bob Rush 1.50 4.00
405 Bobby Richardson 10.00 25.00
406 Billy Klaus 1.50 4.00
407 Gary Peters UER RC 2.50 6.00
408 Carl Furillo 4.00 10.00
409 Ron Samford 1.50 4.00
410 Sam Jones 2.50 6.00
411 Ed Bailey 1.50 4.00
412 Bob Anderson 1.50 4.00
413 Kansas City Athletics CL 4.00 10.00
414 Don Williams RC 1.50 4.00
415 Bob Cerv 1.50 4.00
416 Humberto Robinson 1.50 4.00
417 Chuck Cottier RC 1.50 4.00
418 Don Mossi 2.50 6.00
419 George Crowe 1.50 4.00
420 Eddie Mathews 20.00 50.00
421 Duke Maas 1.50 4.00
422 John Powers 1.50 4.00
423 Ed Fitzgerald 1.50 4.00
424 Pete Whisenant 1.50 4.00
425 Johnny Podres 2.50 6.00
426 Ron Jackson 1.50 4.00
427 Al Grunwald RC 1.50 4.00
428 Al Smith 1.50 4.00
429 Nellie Fox/H.Kuenn 4.00 10.00
430 Art Ditmar 1.50 4.00
431 Andre Rodgers 1.50 4.00
432 Chuck Stobbs 1.50 4.00
433 Irv Noren 1.50 4.00
434 Brooks Lawrence 2.50 6.00
435 Gene Freese 1.50 4.00
436 Marv Throneberry 2.50 6.00
437 Bob Friend 2.50 6.00
438 Jim Coker RC 1.50 4.00
439 Tom Brewer 1.50 4.00
440 Jim Lemon 2.50 6.00
441 Gary Bell 4.00 10.00
442 Joe Pignatano 3.00 8.00
443 Charlie Maxwell 3.00 8.00
444 Jerry Kindall 3.00 8.00
445 Warren Spahn 30.00 80.00
446 Ellis Burton 3.00 8.00
447 Ray Moore 3.00 8.00
448 Jim Gentile RC 8.00 20.00
449 Jim Brosnan 3.00 8.00
450 Orlando Cepeda 30.00 80.00
451 Curt Simmons 3.00 8.00
452 Ray Webster 3.00 8.00
453 Vern Law 10.00 25.00
454 Hal Woodeshick 3.00 8.00
455 Baltimore Coaches 3.00 8.00
456 Red Sox Coaches 4.00 10.00
457 Cubs Coaches 3.00 8.00
458 White Sox Coaches 3.00 8.00
459 Reds Coaches 3.00 8.00
460 Indians Coaches 6.00 15.00
461 Tigers Coaches 4.00 10.00
462 Athletics Coaches 3.00 8.00
463 Dodgers Coaches 3.00 8.00
464 Braves Coaches 3.00 8.00
465 Yankees Coaches 10.00 25.00
466 Phillies Coaches 3.00 8.00
467 Pirates Coaches 3.00 8.00
468 Cardinals Coaches 3.00 8.00
469 Giants Coaches 3.00 8.00
470 Senators Coaches 3.00 8.00
471 Ned Garver 3.00 8.00
472 Alvin Dark 3.00 8.00
473 Al Cicotte 3.00 8.00
474 Haywood Sullivan 3.00 8.00
475 Don Drysdale 25.00 60.00
476 Lou Johnson RC 3.00 8.00
477 Don Ferrarese 3.00 8.00
478 Frank Torre 3.00 8.00
479 Georges Maranda RC 3.00 8.00
480 Yogi Berra 60.00 150.00
481 Wes Stock RC 3.00 8.00
482 Frank Bolling 3.00 8.00
483 Camilo Pascual 3.00 8.00
484 Pittsburgh Pirates CL 15.00 40.00
485 Ken Boyer 6.00 15.00
486 Bobby Del Greco 3.00 8.00
487 Tom Sturdivant 3.00 8.00
488 Norm Cash 10.00 25.00
489 Steve Ridzik 3.00 8.00
490 Frank Robinson 25.00 60.00
491 Mel Roach 3.00 8.00
492 Larry Jackson 3.00 8.00
493 Duke Snider 30.00 80.00
494 Baltimore Orioles CL 10.00 25.00
495 Sherm Lollar 3.00 8.00
496 Bill Virdon 4.00 10.00
497 John Tsitouris 3.00 8.00
498 Al Pilarcik 3.00 8.00
499 Johnny James RC 4.00 10.00
500 Johnny Temple 3.00 8.00
501 Bob Schmidt 3.00 8.00
502 Jim Bunning 20.00 50.00
503 Don Lee 3.00 8.00
504 Seth Morehead 3.00 8.00
505 Ted Kluszewski 10.00 25.00
506 Lee Walls 3.00 8.00
507 Dick Stigman 6.00 15.00
508 Billy Consolo 6.00 15.00
509 Tommy Davis RC 20.00 50.00
510 Gerry Staley 6.00 15.00
511 Ken Walters RC 6.00 15.00
512 Joe Gibbon RC 6.00 15.00
513 Chicago Cubs CL 12.50 30.00
514 Steve Barber RC 6.00 15.00
515 Stan Lopata 6.00 15.00
516 Marty Kutyna RC 6.00 15.00
517 Charlie James RC 10.00 25.00
518 Tony Gonzalez RC 6.00 15.00
519 Ed Roebuck 6.00 15.00
520 Don Buddin 6.00 15.00
521 Mike Lee RC 6.00 15.00
522 Ken Hunt RC 12.50 30.00
523 Clay Dalrymple RC 6.00 15.00
524 Bill Henry 6.00 15.00
525 Marv Breeding RC 6.00 15.00
526 Paul Giel 10.00 25.00
527 Jose Valdivielso 10.00 25.00
528 Ben Johnson RC 6.00 15.00
529 Norm Sherry RC 8.00 20.00
530 Mike McCormick 6.00 15.00
531 Sandy Amoros 10.00 25.00
532 Mike Garcia 8.00 20.00
533 Lu Clinton RC 6.00 15.00
534 Ken MacKenzie RC 6.00 15.00
535 Whitey Lockman 6.00 15.00
536 Wynn Hawkins RC 6.00 15.00
537 Boston Red Sox CL 12.50 30.00
538 Frank Barnes RC 6.00 15.00
539 Gene Baker 6.00 15.00
540 Jerry Walker 6.00 15.00
541 Tony Curry RC 6.00 15.00
542 Ken Hamlin RC 6.00 15.00
543 Elio Chacon RC 6.00 15.00
544 Bill Monbouquette 8.00 20.00
545 Carl Sawatski 6.00 15.00
546 Hank Aguirre 6.00 15.00
547 Bob Aspromonte RC 8.00 20.00
548 Don Mincher RC 6.00 15.00
549 John Buzhardt 6.00 15.00
550 Jim Landis 6.00 15.00
551 Ed Rakow RC 6.00 15.00
552 Walt Bond RC 6.00 15.00
553 Bill Skowron AS 8.00 20.00
554 Willie McCovey AS 30.00 80.00
555 Nellie Fox AS 10.00 25.00
556 Charlie Neal AS 6.00 15.00
557 Frank Malzone AS 6.00 15.00
558 Eddie Mathews AS 15.00 40.00
559 Luis Aparicio AS 12.50 30.00
560 Ernie Banks AS 30.00 80.00
561 Al Kaline AS 20.00 50.00
562 Joe Cunningham AS 6.00 15.00
563 Mickey Mantle AS 125.00 300.00
564 Willie Mays AS 50.00 120.00
565 Roger Maris AS 50.00 100.00
566 Hank Aaron AS 40.00 100.00
567 Sherm Lollar AS 6.00 15.00
568 Del Crandall AS 6.00 15.00
569 Camilo Pascual AS 6.00 15.00
570 Don Drysdale AS 25.00 60.00
571 Billy Pierce AS 6.00 15.00
572 Johnny Antonelli AS 12.50 30.00
NNO Iron-On Team Transfer

1960 Topps Tattoos

In 1960 this tattoo set was issued separately by both Topps and O-Pee-Chee. The Topps boxes had 120 one cent packs in it while the O-Pee-Chee boxes had 240 one cent packs in them. They are actually the reverses (inside surfaces) of the wrappers in which the (one cent) product "Tattoo Bubble Gum" was packaged. The dimensions given (1 9/16" by 3 1/2") are for the entire wrapper. The wrapper lists instructions on how to apply the tattoo. The "tattoos" were to be applied by moistening the skin and then pressing the tattoo to the moistened spot. The tattoos are unnumbered and are colored. There are 96 tattoos in the set: 55 players, 16 team logos, 15 action shots and ten autographed balls. In the checklist below the player tattoos are numbered 1-55 in alphabetical order, the team tattoos (56-71) are numbered in alphabetical team order (within league), the action photos (72-86) are numbered in alphabetical order by title and the facsimile autographed ball tattoos (87-96) are numbered in alphabetical order according to the autographing player.

COMPLETE SET (96) 2000.00 4000.00
COMMON TATTOO 3.00 8.00
COMMON TEAM (56-71) 2.00 5.00
COMMON ACTION (72-86) 1.00 2.50
COMMON BALL (87-96) 1.00 2.50
WRAPPER 4.00 10.00
1 Hank Aaron 125.00 250.00
2 Bob Allison 8.00 20.00
3 Johnny Antonelli 8.00 20.00
4 Richie Ashburn 30.00 60.00
5 Ernie Banks 50.00 100.00
6 Yogi Berra 100.00 200.00
7 Lew Burdette 8.00 20.00
8 Orlando Cepeda 20.00 50.00
9 Rocky Colavito 20.00 50.00
10 Joe Cunningham 8.00 20.00
11 Bud Daley 6.00 15.00
12 Don Drysdale 40.00 80.00
13 Ryne Duren 10.00 25.00
14 Roy Face 10.00 25.00
15 Whitey Ford 40.00 80.00
16 Nellie Fox 30.00 60.00
17 Tito Francona 6.00 15.00
18 Gene Freese 6.00 15.00
19 Jim Gilliam 12.50 30.00
20 Dick Groat 10.00 25.00
21 Ray Herbert 6.00 15.00
22 Glen Hobbie 6.00 15.00
23 Jackie Jensen 12.50 30.00
24 Sam Jones 6.00 15.00
25 Al Kaline 50.00 100.00
26 Harmon Killebrew 40.00 80.00
27 Harvey Kuenn 12.50 30.00
28 Frank Lary 8.00 20.00
29 Vern Law 10.00 25.00
30 Frank Malzone 8.00 20.00
31 Mickey Mantle 400.00 800.00
32 Roger Maris 50.00 100.00
33 Eddie Mathews 40.00 80.00
34 Willie Mays 150.00 300.00
35 Cal McLish 6.00 15.00
36 Wally Moon 8.00 20.00
37 Walt Moryn 6.00 15.00
38 Don Mossi 8.00 20.00
39 Stan Musial 75.00 150.00
40 Charlie Neal 8.00 20.00
41 Don Newcombe 10.00 25.00
42 Milt Pappas 8.00 20.00
43 Camilo Pascual 8.00 20.00
44 Billy Pierce 8.00 20.00
45 Robin Roberts 30.00 60.00
46 Frank Robinson 40.00 80.00
47 Pete Runnels 8.00 20.00
48 Herb Score 10.00 25.00
49 Warren Spahn 40.00 80.00
50 Johnny Temple 8.00 20.00
51 Gus Triandos 8.00 20.00
52 Jerry Walker 6.00 15.00
53 Bill White 12.50 30.00
54 Gene Woodling 8.00 20.00
55 Early Wynn 30.00 60.00
56 Chicago Cubs 4.00 10.00
57 Cincinnati Reds 4.00 10.00
58 Los Angeles Dodgers 6.00 15.00
59 Milwaukee Braves 4.00 10.00
60 Philadelphia Phillies 4.00 10.00
61 Pittsburgh Pirates 4.00 10.00
62 St. Louis Cardinals 4.00 10.00
63 San Francisco Giants 4.00 10.00
64 Baltimore Orioles 4.00 10.00
65 Boston Red Sox 6.00 15.00
66 Chicago White Sox 4.00 10.00
67 Cleveland Indians 4.00 10.00
68 Detroit Tigers 4.00 10.00
69 Kansas City Athletics 4.00 10.00
70 New York Yankees 8.00 20.00
71 Washington Senators 4.00 10.00
72 Circus Catch 2.00 5.00
73 Double Play 2.00 5.00
74 Grand Slam Homer 2.00 5.00
75 Great Catch 2.00 5.00
76 Left Hand Batter 2.00 5.00
77 Left Hand Pitcher 2.00 5.00
78 Out at First 2.00 5.00
79 Out at Home 2.00 5.00
80 Right Hand Batter 2.00 5.00
81 Right Hand Pitcher 2.00 5.00
82 Right Hand Pitcher/(Different pose) 2.00 5.00
83 Run Down 2.00 5.00
84 Stolen Base 2.00 5.00
85 The Final Word 2.00 5.00
86 Twisting Foul 2.00 5.00
87 Richie Ashburn/(Autographed ball) 6.00 15.00
88 Rocky Colavito/(Autographed ball) 6.00 15.00
89 Roy Face/(Autographed ball) 2.00 5.00
90 Jackie Jensen/(Autographed ball) 3.00 8.00
91 Harmon Killebrew/(Autographed ball) 8.00 20.00
92 Mickey Mantle/(Autographed ball) 200.00 400.00
93 Willie Mays/(Autographed ball) 40.00 80.00
94 Stan Musial/(Autographed ball) 20.00 50.00
95 Billy Pierce/(Autographed ball) 2.50 6.00
96 Jerry Walker/(Autographed ball) 2.00 5.00

1960 Topps Venezuelan

This set is a parallel version of the first 196 cards of the regular 1960 Topps set and are similar in design. The cards were issued for the Venezuelan market. Although the cards were printed in the United States, they are faded compared to the American issued cards.

COMPLETE SET (196) 5000.00 10000.00
1 Early Wynn 100.00 200.00
2 Roman Mejias 12.50 30.00
3 Joe Adcock 15.00 40.00
4 Bob Purkey 12.50 30.00
5 Wally Moon 12.50 30.00
6 Lou Berberet 12.50 30.00
7 Willie Mays 75.00 150.00
Bill Rigney MG
8 Bud Daley 12.50 30.00
9 Faye Throneberry 12.50 30.00
10 Ernie Banks 150.00 300.00
11 Norm Siebern 12.50 30.00
12 Milt Pappas 15.00 40.00
13 Wally Post 12.50 30.00
14 Jim Grant 12.50 30.00
15 Pete Runnels 12.50 30.00
16 Ernie Broglio 12.50 30.00
17 Johnny Callison 12.50 30.00
18 Dodgers Team CL 125.00 250.00
19 Felix Mantilla 12.50 30.00
20 Roy Face 15.00 40.00
21 Dutch Dotterer 12.50 30.00
22 Rocky Bridges 12.50 30.00
23 Eddie Fisher 12.50 30.00
24 Dick Gray 12.50 30.00
25 Roy Sievers 15.00 40.00
26 Wayne Terwilliger 12.50 30.00
27 Dick Drott 12.50 30.00
28 Brooks Robinson 150.00 300.00
29 Clem Labine 12.50 30.00
30 Tito Francona 12.50 30.00
31 Sammy Esposito 12.50 30.00
32 Jim O'Toole 12.50 30.00
Vada Pinson
33 Tom Morgan 12.50 30.00
34 Sparky Anderson 50.00 100.00
35 Whitey Ford 150.00 300.00
36 Russ Nixon 12.50 30.00
37 Bill Bruton 12.50 30.00
38 Jerry Casale 12.50 30.00
39 Earl Averill 12.50 30.00
40 Joe Cunningham 15.00 40.00
41 Barry Latman 12.50 30.00
42 Hobie Landrith 12.50 30.00
43 Senators Team CL 20.00 50.00
44 Bobby Locke 12.50 30.00
45 Roy McMillan 12.50 30.00
46 Jerry Fisher 12.50 30.00
47 Don Zimmer 12.50 30.00
48 Hal W. Smith 12.50 30.00
49 Curt Raydon 12.50 30.00
50 Al Kaline 150.00 300.00
51 Jim Coates 12.50 30.00
52 Dave Philley 12.50 30.00
53 Jackie Brandt 12.50 30.00
54 Mike Fornieles 12.50 30.00
55 Bill Mazeroski 50.00 100.00
56 Steve Korcheck 12.50 30.00
57 Win Savers 12.50 30.00
Turk Lown
Gerry Straley
58 Gino Cimoli 12.50 30.00
59 Juan Pizarro 12.50 30.00
60 Gus Triandos 12.50 30.00
61 Eddie Kasko 12.50 30.00
62 Roger Craig 12.50 30.00
63 George Strickland 12.50 30.00
64 Jack Meyer 12.50 30.00
65 Elston Howard 20.00 50.00
66 Bob Trowbridge 12.50 30.00
67 Jose Pagan 12.50 30.00
68 Dave Hillman 12.50 30.00
69 Billy Goodman 12.50 30.00
70 Lew Burdette 15.00 40.00
71 Marty Keough 12.50 30.00
72 Tigers Team CL 60.00 120.00
73 Bob Gibson 150.00 300.00
74 Walt Moryn 12.50 30.00
75 Vic Power 12.50 30.00
76 Bill Fischer 12.50 30.00
77 Hank Foiles 12.50 30.00
78 Bob Grim 12.50 30.00
79 Walt Dropo 12.50 30.00
80 Johnny Antonelli 12.50 30.00
81 Russ Snyder 12.50 30.00
82 Ruben Gomez 12.50 30.00
83 Tony Kubek 15.00 40.00
84 Hal R. Smith 12.50 30.00
85 Frank Lary 12.50 30.00
86 Dick Gernert 12.50 30.00
87 John Romonosky 12.50 30.00
88 John Roseboro 12.50 30.00
89 Hal Brown 12.50 30.00
90 Bobby Avila 12.50 30.00
91 Bennie Daniels 12.50 30.00
92 Whitey Herzog 12.50 30.00
93 Art Schult 12.50 30.00
94 Leo Kiely 12.50 30.00
95 Frank Thomas 12.50 30.00
96 Ralph Terry 12.50 30.00
97 Ted Lepcio 12.50 30.00
98 Gordon Jones 12.50 30.00
99 Lenny Green 12.50 30.00
100 Nellie Fox 50.00 100.00
101 Bob Miller 12.50 30.00
102 Kent Hadley 12.50 30.00
103 Dick Farrell 12.50 30.00
104 Dick Schofield 12.50 30.00
105 Larry Sherry 12.50 30.00
106 Billy Gardner 12.50 30.00
107 Carlton Willey 12.50 30.00
108 Pete Daley 12.50 30.00
109 Clete Boyer 12.50 30.00
110 Cal McLish 12.50 30.00
111 Vic Wertz 12.50 30.00
112 Jack Harshman 12.50 30.00
113 Bob Skinner 12.50 30.00
114 Ken Aspromonte 12.50 30.00
115 Roy Face 15.00 40.00
Hoyt Wilhelm
116 Jim Rivera 12.50 30.00
117 Tom Borland RP 12.50 30.00
118 Bob Bruce RP 12.50 30.00
119 Chico Cardenas RP 12.50 30.00
120 Duke Carmel RP 12.50 30.00
121 Camilo Carreon RP 12.50 30.00
122 Don Dillard Rp 12.50 30.00
123 Dan Dobbek RP 12.50 30.00
124 Jim Donohue RP 12.50 30.00
125 Dick Ellsworth RP 12.50 30.00
126 Chuck Estrada RP 12.50 30.00
127 Ron Hansen RP 12.50 30.00
128 Bill Harris RP 12.50 30.00
129 Bob Hartman RP 12.50 30.00
130 Frank Herrera RP 12.50 30.00
131 Ed Hobaugh RP 12.50 30.00
132 Frank Howard RP 60.00 120.00
133 Julian Javier RP 12.50 30.00
134 Deron Johnson RP 12.50 30.00
135 Ken Johnson RP 12.50 30.00
136 Jim Kaat RP 125.00 250.00
137 Lou Klimchock RP 12.50 30.00
138 Art Mahaffey RP 12.50 30.00
139 Carl Mathias RP 12.50 30.00
140 Julio Navarro RP 12.50 30.00
141 Jim Proctor RP 12.50 30.00
142 Bill Short RP 12.50 30.00
143 Al Spangler RP 12.50 30.00
144 Al Stieglitz RP 12.50 30.00
145 Jim Umbricht RP 12.50 30.00
146 Ted Wieand RP 12.50 30.00
147 Bob Will RP 12.50 30.00
148 Carl Yastrzemski RP 500.00 1000.00
149 Bob Nieman 12.50 30.00
150 Billy Pierce 15.00 40.00
151 Giants Team CL 20.00 50.00
152 Gail Harris 12.50 30.00
153 Bobby Thomson 15.00 40.00
154 Jim Davenport 12.50 30.00
155 Charlie Neal 12.50 30.00
156 Art Ceccarelli 12.50 30.00
157 Rocky Nelson 12.50 30.00
158 Wes Covington 12.50 30.00
159 Jim Piersall 15.00 40.00
160 Mickey Mantle 500.00 1000.00
Ken Boyer
161 Ray Narleski 12.50 30.00
162 Sammy Taylor 12.50 30.00
163 Hector Lopez 12.50 30.00
164 Reds Team CL 20.00 50.00
165 Jack Sanford 12.50 30.00
166 Chuck Essegian 12.50 30.00
167 Valmy Thomas 12.50 30.00
168 Alex Grammas 12.50 30.00
169 Jake Striker 12.50 30.00
170 Del Crandall 12.50 30.00
171 Johnny Groth 12.50 30.00
172 Willie Kirkland 12.50 30.00
173 Billy Martin 50.00 100.00
174 Indians Team CL 20.00 50.00
175 Pedro Ramos 12.50 30.00
176 Vada Pinson 15.00 40.00
177 Johnny Kucks 12.50 30.00
178 Woody Held 12.50 30.00
179 Rip Coleman 12.50 30.00
180 Harry Simpson 12.50 30.00
181 Billy Loes 12.50 30.00
182 Glen Hobbie 12.50 30.00
183 Eli Grba 12.50 30.00
184 Gary Geiger 12.50 30.00
185 Jim Owens 12.50 30.00
186 Dave Sisler 12.50 30.00
187 Jay Hook 12.50 30.00
188 Dick Williams 12.50 30.00
189 Don McMahon 12.50 30.00
190 Gene Woodling 12.50 30.00
191 Johnny Klippstein 12.50 30.00
192 Danny O'Connell 12.50 30.00
193 Dick Hyde 12.50 30.00
194 Bobby Gene Smith 12.50 30.00
195 Lindy McDaniel 12.50 30.00
196 Andy Carey 12.50 30.00

1961 Topps

The cards in this 587-card set measure 2 1/2" by 3 1/2". In 1961, Topps returned to the vertical obverse format. Introduced for the first time were "League Leaders" (41-50) and separate, numbered checklist cards. Two number 463s exist: the Braves team card carrying that number was meant to be number 426. There are three versions of the second series checklist card number 98; the variations are distinguished by the color of the "CHECKLIST" headline on the front of the card, the color of the printing of the card number on the bottom of the reverse, and the presence of the copyright notice running vertically on the card back. There are two groups of managers (131-139/219-226) as well as separate subsets of World Series cards (306-313), Baseball Thrills (401-410), MVP's of the 1950's (AL 471-478/NL 479-486) and Sporting News All-Stars (566-589). The usual last series scarcity (523-589) exists. Some collectors believe that 61 high numbers are the toughest of all the Topps hi series numbers. The set actually totals 587 cards since numbers 587 and 588 were never issued. These card advertising promos have been seen: Dan Dobbek/Russ Nixon/60 NL Pitching Leaders on the front along with an ad and Roger Maris on the back.Other strips feature Jack Kralick/Dick Stigman/Joe Christopher; Ed Roebuck/Bob Schmidt/Zoilo Versalles; Lindy (McDaniel) Shows Larry (Jackson)/John Blanchard/Johnny Kucks. Cards were issued in one-card penny packs, five-card nickel packs, 10 cent cello packs (which came 36 to a box) and 36-card rack packs which cost 29 cents. The one card packs came 120 to a box. The key Rookie Cards in this set are Juan Marichal, Ron Santo and Billy Williams.

COMPLETE SET (587) 3000.00 8000.00
COMMON CARD (1-370) 1.25 3.00
COMMON CARD (371-446) 1.50 4.00
COMMON CARD (447-522) 3.00 8.00
COMMON CARD (523-589) 12.50 30.00
NOT ISSUED (587/588)
WRAPPER (1-CENT) 100.00 200.00
WRAP.(1-CENT, REPEAT) 50.00 100.00
WRAPPER (5-CENT) 15.00 40.00
1 Dick Groat 12.00 30.00
2 Roger Maris 60.00 150.00
3 John Buzhardt 1.25 3.00
4 Lenny Green 1.25 3.00
5 John Romano 1.25 3.00
6 Ed Roebuck 1.25 3.00
7 Chicago White Sox TC 3.00 8.00
8 Dick Williams UER 2.50 6.00
Blurb states career high in RBI, however his career high in RBI was in 1959
9 Bob Purkey 1.25 3.00
10 Brooks Robinson 15.00 40.00
11 Curt Simmons 2.50 6.00
12 Moe Thacker 1.25 3.00
13 Chuck Cottier 1.25 3.00
14 Don Mossi 2.50 6.00
15 Willie Kirkland 1.25 3.00
16 Billy Muffett 1.25 3.00
17 Checklist 1 4.00 10.00
18 Jim Grant 2.50 6.00
19 Clete Boyer 3.00 8.00
20 Robin Roberts 10.00 25.00
21 Zoilo Versalles UER RC 3.00 8.00
22 Clem Labine 2.50 6.00
23 Don Demeter 1.25 3.00
24 Ken Johnson 2.50 6.00
25 Pinson/Bell/F.Robinson 3.00 8.00
26 Wes Stock 1.25 3.00
27 Jerry Kindall 1.25 3.00
28 Hector Lopez 2.50 6.00
29 Don Nottebart 1.25 3.00
30 Nellie Fox 10.00 25.00
31 Bob Schmidt 1.25 3.00
32 Ray Sadecki 1.25 3.00
33 Gary Geiger 1.25 3.00
34 Wynn Hawkins 1.25 3.00
35 Ron Santo RC 50.00 120.00
36 Jack Kralick RC 1.25 3.00
37 Charley Maxwell 2.50 6.00
38 Bob Lillis 1.25 3.00
39 Leo Posada RC 1.25 3.00
40 Bob Turley 2.50 6.00
41 Groat/Mays/Clemente LL 10.00 25.00
42 Runnels/Minoso/Skow LL 3.00 8.00
43 Banks/Aaron/Mathews LL 10.00 25.00
44 Mante/Maris/Colavito LL 25.00 60.00
45 McCormick/Drysdale LL 3.00 8.00
46 Baumann/Bunning/Dit LL 3.00 8.00
47 Broglio/Spahn/Burdette LL 3.00 8.00
48 Estrada/Perry/Daley LL 3.00 8.00
49 Drysdale/Koufax LL 8.00 20.00
50 Bunning/Ramos/Wynn LL 3.00 8.00
51 Detroit Tigers TC 3.00 8.00
52 George Crowe 1.25 3.00
53 Russ Nixon 1.25 3.00
54 Earl Francis RC 1.25 3.00
55 Jim Davenport 2.50 6.00
56 Russ Kemmerer 1.25 3.00
57 Marv Throneberry 2.50 6.00
58 Joe Schaffernoth RC 1.25 3.00
59 Jim Woods 1.25 3.00
60 Woody Held 1.25 3.00
61 Ron Piche RC 1.25 3.00
62 Al Pilarcik 1.25 3.00
63 Jim Kaat 3.00 8.00
64 Alex Grammas 1.25 3.00
65 Ted Kluszewski 3.00 8.00
66 Bill Henry 1.25 3.00
67 Ossie Virgil 1.25 3.00
68 Deron Johnson 2.50 6.00
69 Earl Wilson 2.50 6.00
70 Bill Virdon 2.50 6.00
71 Jerry Adair 1.25 3.00
72 Stu Miller 2.50 6.00
73 Al Spangler 1.25 3.00
74 Joe Pignatano 1.25 3.00
75 L.McDaniel/L.Jackson 2.50 6.00
76 Harry Anderson 1.25 3.00
77 Dick Stigman 1.25 3.00
78 Lee Walls 2.50 6.00
79 Joe Ginsberg 1.25 3.00
80 Harmon Killebrew 20.00 50.00
81 Tracy Stallard RC 1.25 3.00
82 Joe Christopher RC 1.25 3.00
83 Bob Bruce 1.25 3.00
84 Lee Maye 1.25 3.00
85 Jerry Walker 1.25 3.00
86 Los Angeles Dodgers TC 3.00 8.00
87 Joe Amalfitano 1.25 3.00
88 Richie Ashburn 6.00 15.00
89 Billy Martin 10.00 25.00
90 Gerry Staley 1.25 3.00
91 Walt Moryn 1.25 3.00
92 Hal Naragon 1.25 3.00
93 Tony Gonzalez 1.25 3.00
94 Johnny Kucks 1.25 3.00
95 Norm Cash 3.00 8.00
96 Billy O'Dell 1.25 3.00
97 Jerry Lynch 2.50 6.00
98A Checklist 2 Red 4.00 10.00
98B Checklist 2 Yellow B/W 4.00 10.00
98C Checklist 2 Yellow W/B 4.00 10.00
99 Don Buddin UER 1.25 3.00
100 Harvey Haddix 2.50 6.00
101 Bubba Phillips 1.25 3.00
102 Gene Stephens 1.25 3.00

103 Ruben Amaro 1.25 3.00
104 John Blanchard 3.00 8.00
105 Carl Willey 1.25 3.00
106 Whitey Herzog 1.25 3.00
107 Seth Morehead 1.25 3.00
108 Dan Dobbek 1.25 3.00
109 Johnny Podres 3.00 8.00
110 Vada Pinson 3.00 8.00
111 Jack Meyer 1.25 3.00
112 Chico Fernandez 1.25 3.00
113 Mike Fornieles 1.25 3.00
114 Hobie Landrith 1.25 3.00
115 Johnny Antonelli 2.50 6.00
116 Joe DeMaestri 1.25 3.00
117 Dale Long 2.50 6.00
118 Chris Cannizzaro RC 1.25 3.00
119 Siebern/Bauer/Lumpe 2.50 6.00
120 Eddie Mathews 20.00 50.00
121 Eli Grba 2.50 6.00
122 Chicago Cubs TC 3.00 8.00
123 Billy Gardner 1.25 3.00
124 J.C. Martin 1.25 3.00
125 Steve Barber 1.25 3.00
126 Dick Stuart 2.50 6.00
127 Ron Kline 1.25 3.00
128 Rip Repulski 1.25 3.00
129 Ed Hobaugh 1.25 3.00
130 Norm Larker 1.25 3.00
131 Paul Richards MG 2.50 6.00
132 Al Lopez MG 3.00 8.00
133 Ralph Houk MG 2.50 6.00
134 Mickey Vernon MG 2.50 6.00
135 Fred Hutchinson MG 2.50 6.00
136 Walter Alston MG 3.00 8.00
137 Chuck Dressen MG 2.50 6.00
138 Danny Murtaugh MG 2.50 6.00
139 Solly Hemus MG 2.50 6.00
140 Gus Triandos 2.50 6.00
141 Billy Williams RC 50.00 120.00
142 Luis Arroyo 2.50 6.00
143 Russ Snyder 1.25 3.00
144 Jim Coker 1.25 3.00
145 Bob Buhl 2.50 6.00
146 Marty Keough 1.25 3.00
147 Ed Rakow 1.25 3.00
148 Julian Javier 2.50 6.00
149 Bob Oldis 1.25 3.00
150 Willie Mays 40.00 100.00
151 Jim Donohue 1.25 3.00
152 Earl Torgeson 1.25 3.00
153 Don Lee 1.25 3.00
154 Bobby Del Greco 1.25 3.00
155 Johnny Temple 2.50 6.00
156 Ken Hunt 2.50 6.00
157 Cal McLish 1.25 3.00
158 Pete Daley 1.25 3.00
159 Baltimore Orioles TC 3.00 8.00
160 Whitey Ford UER 20.00 50.00
161 Sherman Jones UER RC 1.25 3.00
162 Jay Hook 1.25 3.00
163 Ed Sadowski 1.25 3.00
164 Felix Mantilla 1.25 3.00
165 Gino Cimoli 1.25 3.00
166 Danny Kravitz 1.25 3.00
167 San Francisco Giants TC 3.00 8.00
168 Tommy Davis 3.00 8.00
169 Don Elston 1.25 3.00
170 Al Smith 1.25 3.00
171 Paul Foytack 1.25 3.00
172 Don Dillard 1.25 3.00
173 Malzone/Wertz/Jensen 2.50 6.00
174 Ray Semproch 1.25 3.00
175 Gene Freese 1.25 3.00
176 Ken Aspromonte 1.25 3.00
177 Don Larsen 2.50 6.00
178 Bob Nieman 1.25 3.00
179 Joe Koppe 1.25 3.00
180 Bobby Richardson 8.00 20.00
181 Fred Green 1.25 3.00
182 Dave Nicholson RC 1.25 3.00
183 Andre Rodgers 1.25 3.00
184 Steve Bilko 2.50 6.00
185 Herb Score 2.50 6.00
186 Elmer Valo 2.50 6.00
187 Billy Klaus 1.25 3.00
188 Jim Marshall 1.25 3.00
189A Checklist 3 Copyright 263 4.00 10.00
189B Checklist 3 Copyright 264 4.00 10.00
190 Stan Williams 2.50 6.00
191 Mike de la Hoz RC 1.25 3.00
192 Dick Brown 1.25 3.00
193 Gene Conley 2.50 6.00
194 Gordy Coleman 2.50 6.00
195 Jerry Casale 1.25 3.00
196 Ed Bouchee 1.25 3.00
197 Dick Hall 1.25 3.00
198 Carl Sawatski 1.25 3.00
199 Bob Boyd 1.25 3.00
200 Warren Spahn 15.00 40.00
201 Pete Whisenant 1.25 3.00
202 Al Neiger RC 1.25 3.00
203 Eddie Bressoud 1.25 3.00
204 Bob Skinner 2.50 6.00
205 Billy Pierce 2.50 6.00
206 Gene Green 1.25 3.00
207 S.Koufax/J.Podres 15.00 40.00
208 Larry Osborne 1.25 3.00
209 Ken McBride 1.25 3.00
210 Pete Runnels 2.50 6.00
211 Bob Gibson 40.00 100.00
212 Haywood Sullivan 2.50 6.00
213 Bill Stafford RC 1.25 3.00
214 Danny Murphy RC 2.50 6.00
215 Gus Bell 2.50 6.00
216 Ted Bowsfield 1.25 3.00
217 Mel Roach 1.25 3.00
218 Hal Brown 1.25 3.00
219 Gene Mauch MG 2.50 6.00
220 Alvin Dark MG 2.50 6.00
221 Mike Higgins MG 2.50 6.00
222 Jimmy Dykes MG 2.50 6.00
223 Bob Scheffing MG 1.25 3.00
224 Joe Gordon MG 2.50 6.00
225 Bill Rigney MG 2.50 6.00
226 Cookie Lavagetto MG 2.50 6.00
227 Juan Pizarro 1.25 3.00
228 New York Yankees TC 20.00 50.00
229 Rudy Hernandez RC 1.25 3.00
230 Don Hoak 2.50 6.00
231 Dick Drott 1.25 3.00
232 Bill White 2.50 6.00
233 Joey Jay 2.50 6.00
234 Ted Lepcio 1.25 3.00
235 Camilo Pascual 2.50 6.00
236 Don Gile RC 1.25 3.00
237 Billy Loes 2.50 6.00
238 Jim Gilliam 2.50 6.00
239 Dave Sisler 1.25 3.00
240 Ron Hansen 1.25 3.00
241 Al Cicotte 1.25 3.00
242 Hal Smith 1.25 3.00
243 Frank Lary 2.50 6.00
244 Chico Cardenas 2.50 6.00
245 Joe Adcock 2.50 6.00
246 Bob Davis RC 1.25 3.00
247 Billy Goodman 2.50 6.00
248 Ed Keegan RC 1.25 3.00
249 Cincinnati Reds TC 3.00 8.00
250 V.Law/R.Face 2.50 6.00
251 Bill Bruton 1.25 3.00
252 Bill Short 1.25 3.00
253 Sammy Taylor 1.25 3.00
254 Ted Sadowski RC 2.50 6.00
255 Vic Power 2.50 6.00
256 Billy Hoeft 1.25 3.00
257 Carroll Hardy 1.25 3.00
258 Jack Sanford 2.50 6.00
259 John Schaive RC 1.25 3.00
260 Don Drysdale 20.00 50.00
261 Charlie Lau 2.50 6.00
262 Tony Curry 1.25 3.00
263 Ken Hamlin 1.25 3.00
264 Glen Hobbie 1.25 3.00
265 Tony Kubek 5.00 12.00
266 Lindy McDaniel 2.50 6.00
267 Norm Siebern 1.25 3.00
268 Ike Delock 1.25 3.00
269 Harry Chiti 1.25 3.00
270 Bob Friend 2.50 6.00
271 Jim Landis 1.25 3.00
272 Tom Morgan 1.25 3.00
273A Checklist 4 Copyright 336 6.00 15.00
273B Checklist 4 Copyright 339 4.00 10.00
274 Gary Bell 1.25 3.00
275 Gene Woodling 2.50 6.00
276 Ray Rippelmeyer RC 1.25 3.00
277 Hank Foiles 1.25 3.00
278 Don McMahon 1.25 3.00
279 Jose Pagan 1.25 3.00
280 Frank Howard 3.00 8.00
281 Frank Sullivan 1.25 3.00
282 Faye Throneberry 1.25 3.00
283 Bob Anderson 1.25 3.00
284 Dick Gernert 1.25 3.00
285 Sherm Lollar 2.50 6.00
286 George Witt 1.25 3.00
287 Carl Yastrzemski 75.00 200.00
288 Albie Pearson 2.50 6.00
289 Ray Moore 1.25 3.00
290 Stan Musial 50.00 120.00
291 Tex Clevenger 1.25 3.00
292 Jim Baumer RC 1.25 3.00
293 Tom Sturdivant 1.25 3.00
294 Don Blasingame 1.25 3.00
295 Milt Pappas 2.50 6.00
296 Wes Covington 2.50 6.00
297 Kansas City Athletics TC 3.00 8.00
298 Jim Golden RC 1.25 3.00
299 Clay Dalrymple 1.25 3.00
300 Mickey Mantle 300.00 600.00
301 Chet Nichols 1.25 3.00
302 Al Heist RC 1.25 3.00
303 Gary Peters 1.25 3.00
304 Rocky Nelson 1.25 3.00
305 Mike McCormick 2.50 6.00
306 Bill Virdon WS1 4.00 10.00
307 Mickey Mantle WS2 40.00 100.00
308 Bobby Richardson WS3 5.00 12.00
309 Gino Cimoli WS4 4.00 10.00
310 Roy Face WS5 4.00 10.00
311 Whitey Ford WS6 6.00 15.00
312 Bill Mazeroski WS7 20.00 50.00
313 Pirates Celebrate WS 6.00 15.00
314 Bob Miller 1.25 3.00
315 Earl Battey 2.50 6.00
316 Bobby Gene Smith 1.25 3.00
317 Jim Brewer RC 1.25 3.00
318 Danny O'Connell 1.25 3.00
319 Valmy Thomas 1.25 3.00
320 Lou Burdette 2.50 6.00
321 Marv Breeding 1.25 3.00
322 Bill Kunkel RC 2.50 6.00
323 Sammy Esposito 1.25 3.00
324 Hank Aguirre 1.25 3.00
325 Wally Moon 2.50 6.00
326 Dave Hillman 1.25 3.00
327 Matty Alou RC 8.00 20.00
328 Jim O'Toole 2.50 6.00
329 Julio Becquer 1.25 3.00
330 Rocky Colavito 8.00 20.00
331 Ned Garver 1.25 3.00
332 Dutch Dotterer UER 1.25 3.00
333 Fritz Brickell RC 1.25 3.00
334 Walt Bond 1.25 3.00
335 Frank Bolling 1.25 3.00
336 Don Mincher 2.50 6.00
337 Wynn/Lopez/Score 3.00 8.00
338 Don Landrum 1.25 3.00
339 Gene Baker 1.25 3.00
340 Vic Wertz 2.50 6.00
341 Jim Owens 1.25 3.00
342 Clint Courtney 1.25 3.00
343 Earl Robinson RC 1.25 3.00
344 Sandy Koufax 50.00 100.00
345 Jimmy Piersall 3.00 8.00
346 Howie Nunn 1.25 3.00
347 St. Louis Cardinals TC 3.00 8.00
348 Steve Boros 1.25 3.00
349 Danny McDevitt 1.25 3.00
350 Ernie Banks 20.00 50.00
351 Jim King 1.25 3.00
352 Bob Shaw 1.25 3.00
353 Howie Bedell RC 1.25 3.00
354 Billy Harrell 2.50 6.00
355 Bob Allison 3.00 8.00
356 Ryne Duren 1.25 3.00
357 Daryl Spencer 1.25 3.00
358 Earl Averill Jr. 2.50 6.00
359 Dallas Green 1.25 3.00
360 Frank Robinson 20.00 50.00
361A Checklist 5 No Ad on Back 6.00 15.00
361B Checklist 5 Ad on Back 6.00 15.00
362 Frank Funk RC 1.25 3.00
363 John Roseboro 2.50 6.00
364 Moe Drabowsky 2.50 6.00
365 Jerry Lumpe 1.25 3.00
366 Eddie Fisher 1.25 3.00
367 Jim Rivera 1.25 3.00
368 Bennie Daniels 1.25 3.00
369 Dave Philley 1.25 3.00
370 Roy Face 2.50 6.00
371 Bill Skowron SP 12.00 30.00
372 Bob Hendley RC 1.50 4.00
373 Boston Red Sox TC 3.00 8.00
374 Paul Giel 1.50 4.00
375 Ken Boyer 5.00 12.00
376 Mike Roarke RC 2.50 6.00
377 Ruben Gomez 1.50 4.00
378 Wally Post 2.50 6.00
379 Bobby Shantz 1.50 4.00
380 Minnie Minoso 3.00 8.00
381 Dave Wickersham RC 1.50 4.00
382 Frank Thomas 2.50 6.00
383 McCormick/Sanford/O'Dell 2.50 6.00
384 Chuck Essegian 1.50 4.00
385 Jim Perry 2.50 6.00
386 Joe Hicks 1.50 4.00
387 Duke Maas 1.50 4.00
388 Roberto Clemente 75.00 200.00
389 Ralph Terry 2.50 6.00
390 Del Crandall 3.00 8.00
391 Winston Brown RC 1.50 4.00
392 Reno Bertoia 1.50 4.00
393 D.Cardwell/G.Hobbie 1.50 4.00
394 Ken Walters 1.50 4.00
395 Chuck Estrada 2.50 6.00
396 Bob Aspromonte 2.50 6.00
397 Hal Woodeshick 1.50 4.00
398 Hank Bauer 2.50 6.00
399 Cliff Cook RC 1.50 4.00
400 Vernon Law 40.00 100.00
401 Babe Ruth 60th HR 40.00 100.00
402 Don Larsen Perfect SP 10.00 25.00
403 26 Inning Tie/Oeschger/Cadore 3.00 8.00
404 Rogers Hornsby .424 5.00 12.00
405 Lou Gehrig Streak 25.00 60.00
406 Mickey Mantle 565 HR 40.00 100.00
407 Jack Chesbro Wins 41 3.00 8.00
408 Christy Mathewson K's SP 8.00 20.00
409 Walter Johnson Shutout 8.00 20.00
410 Harvey Haddix 12 Perfect 3.00 8.00
411 Tony Taylor 2.50 6.00
412 Larry Sherry 2.50 6.00
413 Eddie Yost 2.50 6.00
414 Dick Donovan 2.50 6.00
415 Hank Aaron 75.00 200.00
416 Dick Howser RC 3.00 8.00
417 Juan Marichal SP RC 150.00 400.00
418 Ed Bailey 2.50 6.00
419 Tom Borland 1.50 4.00
420 Ernie Broglio 2.50 6.00
421 Ty Cline SP RC 8.00 20.00
422 Bud Daley 1.50 4.00
423 Charlie Neal SP 8.00 20.00
424 Turk Lown 1.50 4.00
425 Yogi Berra 40.00 100.00
426 Milwaukee Braves TC UER 5.00 12.00
427 Dick Ellsworth 2.50 6.00
428 Ray Barker SP RC 8.00 20.00
429 Al Kaline 15.00 40.00
430 Bill Mazeroski SP 10.00 25.00
431 Chuck Stobbs 1.50 4.00
432 Coot Veal 2.50 6.00
433 Art Mahaffey 1.50 4.00
434 Tom Brewer 1.50 4.00
435 Orlando Cepeda UER 12.00 30.00
436 Jim Maloney SP RC 8.00 20.00
437A Checklist 6 440 Louis 6.00 15.00
437B Checklist 6 440 Luis 6.00 15.00
438 Curt Flood 3.00 8.00
439 Phil Regan RC 2.50 6.00
440 Luis Aparicio 8.00 20.00
441 Dick Bertell RC 1.50 4.00
442 Gordon Jones 1.50 4.00
443 Duke Snider 20.00 50.00
444 Joe Nuxhall 2.50 6.00
445 Frank Malzone 2.50 6.00
446 Bob Taylor 1.50 4.00
447 Harry Bright 3.00 8.00
448 Del Rice 6.00 15.00
449 Bob Bolin RC 3.00 8.00
450 Jim Lemon 3.00 8.00
451 Spencer/White/Broglio 3.00 8.00
452 Bob Allen RC 3.00 8.00
453 Dick Schofield 3.00 8.00
454 Pumpsie Green 3.00 8.00
455 Early Wynn 6.00 15.00
456 Hal Bevan 3.00 8.00
457 Johnny James 3.00 8.00
458 Willie Tasby 3.00 8.00
459 Terry Fox RC 4.00 10.00
460 Gil Hodges 10.00 25.00
461 Smoky Burgess 6.00 15.00
462 Lou Klimchock 3.00 8.00
463 Jack Fisher See 426 3.00 8.00
464 Lee Thomas RC 4.00 10.00
465 Roy McMillan 6.00 15.00
466 Ron Moeller RC 3.00 8.00
467 Cleveland Indians TC 5.00 12.00
468 John Callison 4.00 10.00
469 Ralph Lumenti 3.00 8.00
470 Roy Sievers 4.00 10.00
471 Phil Rizzuto MVP 12.00 30.00
472 Yogi Berra MVP 25.00 60.00
473 Bob Shantz MVP 3.00 8.00
474 Al Rosen MVP 4.00 10.00
475 Mickey Mantle MVP 100.00 250.00
476 Jackie Jensen MVP 4.00 10.00
477 Nellie Fox MVP 6.00 15.00
478 Roger Maris MVP 25.00 60.00
479 Jim Konstanty MVP 3.00 8.00
480 Roy Campanella MVP 15.00 40.00
481 Hank Sauer MVP 3.00 8.00
482 Willie Mays MVP 25.00 60.00
483 Don Newcombe MVP 5.00 12.00
484 Hank Aaron MVP 25.00 60.00
485 Ernie Banks MVP 20.00 50.00
486 Dick Groat MVP 4.00 10.00
487 Gene Oliver 3.00 8.00
488 Joe McClain RC 4.00 10.00
489 Walt Dropo 3.00 8.00
490 Jim Bunning 10.00 25.00
491 Philadelphia Phillies TC 5.00 12.00
492A R.Fairly White 4.00 10.00
492B R.Fairly Green 8.00 20.00
493 Don Zimmer UER 5.00 12.00
494 Tom Cheney 4.00 10.00
495 Elston Howard 10.00 25.00
496 Ken MacKenzie 3.00 8.00
497 Willie Jones 3.00 8.00
498 Ray Herbert 3.00 8.00
499 Chuck Schilling RC 3.00 8.00
500 Harvey Kuenn 6.00 15.00
501 John DeMerit RC 3.00 8.00
502 Choo Choo Coleman RC 4.00 10.00
503 Tito Francona 3.00 8.00
504 Billy Consolo 3.00 8.00
505 Red Schoendienst 8.00 20.00
506 Willie Davis RC 8.00 20.00
507 Pete Burnside 3.00 8.00
508 Rocky Bridges 3.00 8.00
509 Camilo Carreon 3.00 8.00
510 Art Ditmar 3.00 8.00
511 Joe M. Morgan 3.00 8.00
512 Bob Will 3.00 8.00
513 Jim Brosnan 3.00 8.00
514 Jake Wood RC 3.00 8.00
515 Jackie Brandt 3.00 8.00
516A Checklist 7 6.00 15.00
(C on front partially covers Braves cap)
516B Checklist 7 6.00 15.00
(C on front fully above Braves cap)
517 Willie McCovey 20.00 50.00
518 Andy Carey 3.00 8.00
519 Jim Pagliaroni RC 3.00 8.00
520 Joe Cunningham 3.00 8.00
521 N.Sherry/L.Sherry 3.00 8.00
522 Dick Farrell UER 6.00 15.00
523 Joe Gibbon 15.00 40.00
524 Johnny Logan 12.00 30.00
525 Ron Perranoski RC 30.00 60.00
526 R.C. Stevens 12.50 30.00
527 Gene Leek RC 12.50 30.00
528 Pedro Ramos 12.50 30.00
529 Bob Roselli 12.50 30.00
530 Bob Malkmus 12.50 30.00
531 Jim Coates 20.00 50.00
532 Bob Hale 12.50 30.00
533 Jack Curtis RC 12.50 30.00
534 Eddie Kasko 15.00 40.00
535 Larry Jackson 12.50 30.00
536 Bill Tuttle 12.50 30.00
537 Bobby Locke 12.50 30.00
538 Chuck Hiller RC 12.50 30.00
539 Johnny Klippstein 12.50 30.00
540 Jackie Jensen 15.00 40.00
541 Roland Sheldon RC 20.00 50.00
542 Minnesota Twins TC 30.00 60.00
543 Roger Craig 15.00 40.00
544 George Thomas RC 12.50 30.00
545 Hoyt Wilhelm 30.00 60.00
546 Marty Kutyna 10.00 25.00
547 Leon Wagner 12.50 30.00
548 Ted Wills 12.50 30.00
549 Hal R. Smith 12.50 30.00
550 Frank Baumann 12.50 30.00
551 George Altman 15.00 40.00
552 Jim Archer RC 12.50 30.00
553 Bill Fischer 12.50 30.00
554 Pittsburgh Pirates TC 40.00 80.00
555 Sam Jones 12.50 30.00
556 Ken R. Hunt RC 12.50 30.00
557 Jose Valdivielso 12.50 30.00
558 Don Ferrarese 12.50 30.00
559 Jim Gentile 30.00 80.00
560 Barry Latman 15.00 40.00
561 Charley James 12.50 30.00
562 Bill Monbouquette 12.50 30.00
563 Bob Cerv 40.00 100.00
564 Don Cardwell 12.50 30.00
565 Felipe Alou 15.00 40.00
566 Paul Richards AS MG 12.50 30.00
567 Danny Murtaugh AS MG 12.50 30.00
568 Bill Skowron AS 15.00 40.00
569 Frank Herrera AS 15.00 40.00
570 Nellie Fox AS 30.00 60.00
571 Bill Mazeroski AS 30.00 60.00
572 Brooks Robinson AS 25.00 60.00
573 Ken Boyer AS 15.00 40.00
574 Luis Aparicio AS 30.00 60.00
575 Ernie Banks AS 40.00 80.00
576 Roger Maris AS 50.00 120.00
577 Hank Aaron AS 50.00 120.00
578 Mickey Mantle AS 150.00 400.00
579 Willie Mays AS 50.00 120.00
580 Al Kaline AS 30.00 80.00
581 Frank Robinson AS 25.00 60.00
582 Earl Battey AS 12.50 30.00
583 Del Crandall AS 12.50 30.00
584 Jim Perry AS 12.50 30.00
585 Bob Friend AS 12.50 30.00
586 Whitey Ford AS 25.00 60.00
589 Warren Spahn AS 30.00 80.00

1961 Topps Magic Rub-Offs

COMPLETE SET (36) 150.00 300.00
COMMON RUB-OFF (1-18) .75 2.00
COMMON PLAYER (19-36) 2.00 5.00
1 Detroit Tigers 2.00 5.00
2 New York Yankees 2.50 6.00
3 Minnesota Twins 1.25 3.00
4 Washington Senators 1.25 3.00
5 Boston Red Sox 2.00 5.00
6 Los Angeles Angels 1.25 3.00
7 Kansas City A's 1.25 3.00
8 Baltimore Orioles 1.25 3.00
9 Chicago White Sox 1.25 3.00
10 Cleveland Indians 1.25 3.00
11 Pittsburgh Pirates 1.25 3.00
12 San Francisco Giants 1.25 3.00
13 Los Angeles Dodgers 2.50 6.00
14 Philadelphia Phillies 1.25 3.00
15 Cincinnati Redlegs 1.25 3.00
16 St. Louis Cardinals 1.25 3.00
17 Chicago Cubs 1.25 3.00
18 Milwaukee Braves 1.25 3.00
19 John Romano 4.00 10.00
20 Ray Moore 4.00 10.00
21 Ernie Banks 20.00 50.00
22 Charlie Maxwell 4.00 10.00
23 Yogi Berra 20.00 50.00
24 Henry Dutch Dotterer 4.00 10.00
25 Jim Brosnan 4.00 10.00
26 Billy Martin 8.00 20.00
27 Jackie Brandt 4.00 10.00
28 Duke Mass/(sic, Maas) 5.00 12.00
29 Pete Runnels 5.00 12.00
30 Joe Gordon MG 5.00 12.00
31 Sam Jones 4.00 10.00
32 Walt Moryn 4.00 10.00
33 Harvey Haddix 5.00 12.00
34 Frank Howard 6.00 15.00
35 Turk Lown 4.00 10.00
36 Frank Herrera 4.00 10.00

1961 Topps Stamps

COMPLETE SET (207) 300.00 600.00
1 George Altman .75 2.00
2 Bob Anderson .75 2.00
brown
3 Richie Ashburn 2.00 5.00
4 Ernie Banks 3.00 8.00
5 Ed Bouchee .75 2.00
6 Jim Brewer .75 2.00
7 Dick Ellsworth .75 2.00
8 Don Elston .75 2.00
9 Ron Santo 2.00 5.00
10 Sammy Taylor .75 2.00
11 Bob Will .75 2.00
12 Billy Williams 2.00 5.00
13 Ed Bailey .75 2.00
14 Gus Bell .75 2.00
15 Jim Brosnan .75 2.00
brown
16 Chico Cardenas .75 2.00
17 Gene Freese .75 2.00
18 Eddie Kasko .75 2.00
19 Jerry Lynch .75 2.00
20 Billy Martin 2.00 5.00
21 Jim O'Toole .75 2.00
22 Vada Pinson 1.25 3.00
23 Wally Post .75 2.00
brown
24 Frank Robinson 3.00 8.00
25 Tommy Davis 1.25 3.00
26 Don Drysdale 2.00 5.00
27 Frank Howard 1.25 3.00
Brown
28 Norm Larker .75 2.00
29 Wally Moon .75 2.00
brown
30 Charlie Neal .75 2.00
31 Johnny Podres 1.25 3.00
32 Ed Roebuck .75 2.00
33 Johnny Roseboro .75 2.00
34 Larry Sherry .75 2.00
35 Duke Snider 3.00 8.00
36 Stan Williams .75 2.00
37 Hank Aaron 10.00 25.00
38 Joe Adcock .75 2.00
39 Bill Bruton .75 2.00
40 Bob Buhl .75 2.00
41 Wes Covington .75 2.00
brown
42 Del Crandall .75 2.00
43 Joey Jay .75 2.00
44 Felix Mantilla .75 2.00
45 Eddie Mathews 3.00 8.00
46 Roy McMillan .75 2.00
47 Warren Spahn 3.00 8.00
48 Carlton Willey .75 2.00
brown
49 John Buzhardt .75 2.00
50 Johnny Callison .75 2.00
51 Tony Curry .75 2.00
52 Clay Dalrymple .75 2.00
brown
53 Bobby Del Greco .75 2.00
brown
54 Dick Farrell .75 2.00
brown
55 Tony Gonzalez .75 2.00
56 Pancho Herrera .75 2.00
57 Art Mahaffey .75 2.00
58 Robin Roberts 1.25 3.00
59 Tony Taylor .75 2.00
60 Lee Walls .75 2.00
61 Smoky Burgess .75 2.00
62 Roy Face (brown) .75 2.00
63 Bob Friend .75 2.00
64 Dick Groat 1.25 3.00
65 Don Hoak .75 2.00
66 Vern Law .75 2.00
67 Bill Mazeroski 1.25 3.00
68 Rocky Nelson .75 2.00
69 Bob Skinner .75 2.00
70 Hal Smith .75 2.00
71 Dick Stuart .75 2.00
72 Bill Virdon .75 2.00
73 Don Blasingame .75 2.00
74 Eddie Bressoud .75 2.00
brown
75 Orlando Cepeda 1.25 3.00
76 Jim Davenport .75 2.00
77 Harvey Kuenn 1.25 3.00
Brown
78 Hobie Landrith .75 2.00
79 Juan Marichal 2.00 5.00
80 Willie Mays 10.00 25.00
81 Mike McCormick .75 2.00
82 Willie McCovey 3.00 8.00
83 Billy O'Dell .75 2.00
84 Jack Sanford .75 2.00
85 Ken Boyer 1.25 3.00
86 Curt Flood 1.25 3.00
87 Alex Grammas .75 2.00
brown
88 Larry Jackson .75 2.00
89 Julian Javier .75 2.00
90 Ron Kline .75 2.00
brown
91 Lindy McDaniel .75 2.00
92 Stan Musial 6.00 15.00
93 Curt Simmons .75 2.00
brown
94 Hal Smith .75 2.00
95 Daryl Spencer .75 2.00
96 Bill White .75 2.00
brown
97 Steve Barber .75 2.00
98 Jackie Brandt .75 2.00
brown
99 Marv Breeding .75 2.00
100 Chuck Estrada .75 2.00
101 Jim Gentile .75 2.00
102 Ron Hansen .75 2.00
103 Milt Pappas .75 2.00
104 Brooks Robinson 3.00 8.00
105 Gene Stephens .75 2.00
106 Gus Triandos .75 2.00
107 Hoyt Wilhelm 1.25 3.00
108 Tom Brewer .75 2.00
109 Gene Conley .75 2.00
brown
110 Ike Delock .75 2.00
brown
111 Gary Geiger .75 2.00
112 Jackie Jensen 1.25 3.00
113 Frank Malzone .75 2.00
114 Bill Monbouquette .75 2.00
115 Russ Nixon .75 2.00
116 Pete Runnels .75 2.00
117 Willie Tasby .75 2.00
118 Vic Wertz .75 2.00
brown
119 Carl Yastrzemski 6.00 15.00
120 Luis Aparicio 1.25 3.00
121 Russ Kemmerer .75 2.00
brown
122 Jim Landis .75 2.00
123 Sherman Lollar .75 2.00
124 J.C. Martin .75 2.00
125 Minnie Minoso 1.25 3.00
126 Billy Pierce .75 2.00
127 Bob Shaw .75 2.00
128 Roy Sievers .75 2.00
129 Al Smith .75 2.00
130 Gerry Staley .75 2.00
brown
131 Early Wynn 1.25 3.00
132 Johnny Antonelli .75 2.00
brown
133 Ken Aspromonte .75 2.00
134 Tito Francona .75 2.00
135 Jim Grant .75 2.00
136 Woody Held .75 2.00
137 Barry Latman .75 2.00
138 Jim Perry .75 2.00
139 Jimmy Piersall 1.25 3.00
140 Bubba Phillips .75 2.00
141 Vic Power .75 2.00
142 John Romano .75 2.00
143 Johnny Temple .75 2.00
144 Hank Aguirre .75 2.00
brown
145 Frank Bolling .75 2.00
146 Steve Boros .75 2.00
brown
147 Jim Bunning 1.25 3.00
148 Norm Cash 1.25 3.00
149 Harry Chiti .75 2.00
150 Chico Fernandez .75 2.00
151 Dick Gernert .75 2.00
152A Al Kaline (green) 3.00 8.00
152B Al Kaline (brown) 3.00 8.00
153 Frank Lary .75 2.00
154 Charlie Maxwell .75 2.00
155 Dave Sisler .75 2.00
156 Hank Bauer .75 2.00
157 Bob Boyd (brown) .75 2.00
158 Andy Carey .75 2.00
159 Bud Daley .75 2.00
160 Dick Hall .75 2.00
161 J.C. Hartman .75 2.00
162 Ray Herbert .75 2.00
163 Whitey Herzog 1.25 3.00
164 Jerry Lumpe .75 2.00
brown
165 Norm Siebern .75 2.00
166 Marv Throneberry .75 2.00
167 Bill Tuttle .75 2.00
168 Dick Williams .75 2.00
169 Jerry Casale .75 2.00
brown
170 Bob Cerv .75 2.00
171 Ned Garver .75 2.00
172 Ken Hunt .75 2.00
173 Ted Kluszewski 2.00 5.00
174 Ed Sadowski .75 2.00
brown
175 Eddie Yost .75 2.00
176 Bob Allison .75 2.00
177 Earl Battey .75 2.00
brown
178 Reno Bertoia .75 2.00
179 Billy Gardner .75 2.00
180 Jim Kaat 1.25 3.00
181 Harmon Killebrew 3.00 8.00
182 Jim Lemon .75 2.00
183 Camilo Pascual .75 2.00
184 Pedro Ramos .75 2.00
185 Chuck Stobbs .75 2.00
186 Zoilo Versalles .75 2.00
187 Pete Whisenant .75 2.00
188 Luis Arroyo .75 2.00
brown
189 Yogi Berra 5.00 12.00
190 John Blanchard .75 2.00
191 Clete Boyer .75 2.00
192 Art Ditmar .75 2.00
193 Whitey Ford 5.00 12.00
194 Elston Howard 2.00 5.00
195 Tony Kubek 2.00 5.00
196 Mickey Mantle 50.00 100.00
197 Roger Maris 10.00 25.00
198 Bobby Shantz .75 2.00
199 Bill Stafford .75 2.00
200 Bob Turley .75 2.00
201 Bud Daley .75 2.00
brown
202 Dick Donovan .75 2.00
203 Bobby Klaus .75 2.00
204 Johnny Klippstein .75 2.00
205 Dale Long .75 2.00
206 Ray Semproch .75 2.00
207 Gene Woodling .75 2.00
XX Stamp Album 8.00 20.00

1961 Topps Dice Game

This 18-card standard-size set may never have been issued by Topps; it is considered a very obscure "test" issue and is quite scarce. The cards are printed completely in black and white on white card stock. There is no reference to Topps anywhere on the front or back of the card. The card back lays out the batter's outcome depending on the type of pitch thrown and the sum of two dice rolled. The cards are unnumbered and hence they are ordered below and assigned numbers alphabetically.

1 Earl Battey 500.00 1000.00
2 Del Crandall 500.00 1000.00
3 Jim Davenport 500.00 1000.00
4 Don Drysdale 3000.00 6000.00
5 Dick Groat 600.00 1200.00
6 Al Kaline 3000.00 6000.00
7 Tony Kubek 750.00 1500.00
8 Mickey Mantle 50000.00 100000.00
9 Willie Mays 20000.00 40000.00
10 Bill Mazeroski 1000.00 2000.00
11 Stan Musial 20000.00 40000.00
12 Camilo Pascual 500.00 1000.00
13 Bobby Richardson 750.00 1500.00
14 Brooks Robinson 3000.00 6000.00
15 Frank Robinson 3000.00 6000.00
16 Norm Siebern 500.00 1000.00
17 Leon Wagner 500.00 1000.00
18 Bill White 600.00 1200.00

1962 Topps

The cards in this 598-card set measure 2 1/2" by 3 1/2". The 1962 Topps set contains a mini-series spotlighting Babe Ruth (135-144). Other subsets in the set include League Leaders (51-60), World Series cards (232-237), In Action cards (311-319), NL All Stars (390-399), AL All Stars (466-475), and Rookie Prospects (591-598). The All-Star selections were again provided by Sport Magazine, as in 1958 and 1960. The second series had two distinct printings which are distinguishable by numerous color and pose variations. Those cards with a distinctive "green tint" are valued at a slight premium as they are basically the result of a flawed printing process occurring early in the second series run. Card number 139 exists as A: Babe Ruth Special card, B: Hal Reniff with arms over head, or C: Hal Reniff in the same pose as card number 159. In addition, two poses exist for these cards: 129, 132, 134, 147, 174, 176, and 190. The high number series, 523 to 598, is somewhat more difficult to obtain than other cards in the set. Within the last series (523-598) there are 43 cards which were printed in lesser quantities; these are marked SP in the checklist below. In particular, the Rookie Parade subset (591-598) of this last series is even more difficult. This was the first year Topps produced multi-player Rookie Cards. The set price listed does not include the pose variations (see checklist below for individual values). A three card ad sheet has been seen. The players on the front include AL HR leaders, Barney Schultz and Carl Sawatski, while the back features an ad and a Roger Maris card. Cards were issued in one-card penny packs as well as five-card nickel packs. The five card packs came 24 to a box. The key Rookie Cards in this set are Lou Brock, Tim McCarver, Gaylord Perry, and Bob Uecker.

COMP. MASTER SET (689) 5000.00 12000.00
COMPLETE SET (598) 4000.00 10000.00
COMMON CARD (1-370) 2.00 5.00
COMMON CARD (371-446) 2.50 6.00
COMMON CARD (447-522) 5.00 12.00
COMMON CARD (523-598) 8.00 20.00
WRAPPER (1-CENT) 50.00 100.00
WRAPPER (5-CENT) 12.50 30.00
1 Roger Maris 100.00 250.00
2 Jim Brosnan 2.00 5.00
3 Pete Runnels 2.00 5.00
4 John DeMerit 3.00 8.00
5 Sandy Koufax UER 75.00 200.00
6 Marv Breeding 2.00 5.00
7 Frank Thomas 4.00 10.00
8 Ray Herbert 2.00 5.00
9 Jim Davenport 3.00 8.00
10 Roberto Clemente 125.00 300.00
11 Tom Morgan 2.00 5.00
12 Harry Craft MG 3.00 8.00
13 Dick Howser 3.00 8.00
14 Bill White 3.00 8.00
15 Dick Donovan 2.00 5.00
16 Darrell Johnson 2.00 5.00
17 Johnny Callison 3.00 8.00
18 M.Mantle/W.Mays 60.00 150.00
19 Ray Washburn RC 2.00 5.00
20 Rocky Colavito 6.00 15.00
21 Jim Kaat 3.00 8.00
22A Checklist 1 ERR 5.00 12.00

Card	Low	High
22B Checklist 1 COR	5.00	12.00
23 Norm Larker	2.00	5.00
24 Detroit Tigers TC	4.00	10.00
25 Ernie Banks	50.00	120.00
26 Chris Cannizzaro	3.00	8.00
27 Chuck Cottier	2.00	5.00
28 Minnie Minoso	4.00	10.00
29 Casey Stengel MG	10.00	25.00
30 Eddie Mathews	25.00	60.00
31 Tom Tresh RC	12.00	30.00
32 John Roseboro	3.00	8.00
33 Don Larsen	3.00	8.00
34 Johnny Temple	3.00	8.00
35 Don Schwall RC	4.00	10.00
36 Don Leppert RC	2.00	5.00
37 Latman/Stigman/Perry	2.00	5.00
38 Gene Stephens	2.00	5.00
39 Joe Koppe	2.00	5.00
40 Orlando Cepeda	10.00	25.00
41 Cliff Cook	2.00	5.00
42 Jim King	2.00	5.00
43 Los Angeles Dodgers TC	4.00	10.00
44 Don Taussig RC	2.00	5.00
45 Brooks Robinson	20.00	50.00
46 Jack Baldschun RC	2.00	5.00
47 Bob Will	2.00	5.00
48 Ralph Terry	3.00	8.00
49 Hal Jones RC	2.00	5.00
50 Stan Musial	30.00	80.00
51 Cash/Kaline/Howard LL	3.00	8.00
52 Clemente/Pins/Boyer LL	10.00	25.00
53 Maris/Mantle/Kill LL	30.00	80.00
54 Cepeda/Mays/F.Rob LL	8.00	20.00
55 Donovan/Staff/Mossi LL	3.00	8.00
56 Spahn/O'Toole/Simm LL	3.00	8.00
57 Ford/Lary/Bunning LL	3.00	8.00
58 Spahn/Jay/O'Toole LL	3.00	8.00
59 Pascual/Ford/Bunning LL	3.00	8.00
60 Koufax/Will/Drysdale LL	8.00	20.00
61 St. Louis Cardinals TC	4.00	10.00
62 Steve Boros	2.00	5.00
63 Tony Cloninger RC	3.00	8.00
64 Russ Snyder	2.00	5.00
65 Bobby Richardson	4.00	10.00
66 Cuno Barragan RC	2.00	5.00
67 Harvey Haddix	3.00	8.00
68 Ken Hunt	2.00	5.00
69 Phil Ortega RC	2.00	5.00
70 Harmon Killebrew	15.00	40.00
71 Dick LeMay RC	2.00	5.00
72 Boros/Scheffing/Wood	2.00	5.00
73 Nellie Fox	8.00	20.00
74 Bob Lillis	3.00	8.00
75 Milt Pappas	3.00	8.00
76 Howie Bedell	2.00	5.00
77 Tony Taylor	3.00	8.00
78 Gene Green	2.00	5.00
79 Ed Hobaugh	2.00	5.00
80 Vada Pinson	3.00	8.00
81 Jim Pagliaroni	2.00	5.00
82 Deron Johnson	3.00	8.00
83 Larry Jackson	2.00	5.00
84 Lenny Green	2.00	5.00
85 Gil Hodges	15.00	40.00
86 Donn Clendenon RC	3.00	8.00
87 Mike Roarke	2.00	5.00
88 Ralph Houk MG	3.00	8.00
89 Barney Schultz RC	2.00	5.00
90 Jimmy Piersall	3.00	8.00
91 J.C. Martin	2.00	5.00
92 Sam Jones	2.00	5.00
93 John Blanchard	3.00	8.00
94 Jay Hook	3.00	8.00
95 Don Hoak	3.00	8.00
96 Eli Grba	2.00	5.00
97 Tito Francona	2.00	5.00
98 Checklist 2	5.00	12.00
99 Boog Powell RC	15.00	40.00
100 Warren Spahn	15.00	40.00
101 Carroll Hardy	2.00	5.00
102 Al Schroll	2.00	5.00
103 Don Blasingame	2.00	5.00
104 Ted Savage RC	2.00	5.00
105 Don Mossi	3.00	8.00
106 Carl Sawatski	2.00	5.00
107 Mike McCormick	3.00	8.00
108 Willie Davis	3.00	8.00
109 Bob Shaw	2.00	5.00
110 Bill Skowron	3.00	8.00
110A Bill Skowron Green Tint	3.00	8.00
111 Dallas Green	3.00	8.00
111A Dallas Green Green Tint	3.00	8.00
112 Hank Foiles	2.00	5.00
112A Hank Foiles Green Tint	2.00	5.00
113 Chicago White Sox TC	4.00	10.00
113A Chicago White Sox TC Green Tint	4.00	10.00
114 Howie Koplitz RC	2.00	5.00
114A Howie Koplitz Green Tint	2.00	5.00
115 Bob Skinner	3.00	8.00
115A Bob Skinner Green Tint	3.00	8.00
116 Herb Score	3.00	8.00
116A Herb Score Green Tint	3.00	8.00
117 Gary Geiger	3.00	8.00
117A Gary Geiger Green Tint	3.00	8.00
118 Julian Javier	3.00	8.00
118A Julian Javier Green Tint	3.00	8.00
119 Danny Murphy	2.00	5.00
119A Danny Murphy Green Tint	2.00	5.00
120 Bob Purkey	2.00	5.00
120A Bob Purkey Green Tint	2.00	5.00
121 Billy Hitchcock	2.00	5.00
121A Billy Hitchcock Green Tint	2.00	5.00
122 Norm Bass RC	2.00	5.00
122A Norm Bass Green Tint	2.00	5.00
123 Mike de la Hoz	2.00	5.00
123A Mike de la Hoz Green Tint	2.00	5.00
124 Bill Pleis RC	2.00	5.00
124A Bill Pleis Green Tint	2.00	5.00
125 Gene Woodling	3.00	8.00
125A Gene Woodling Green Tint	3.00	8.00
126 Al Cicotte	2.00	5.00
126A Al Cicotte Green Tint	2.00	5.00
127 Siebern/Bauer/Lumpe	2.00	5.00
127A Siebern/Bauer/Lumpe Green Tint	2.00	5.00
128 Art Fowler	2.00	5.00
128A Art Fowler Green Tint	2.00	5.00
129A Lee Walls Facing Right	2.00	5.00
129B Lee Walls Face Lft Grn	12.50	30.00
130 Frank Bolling	2.00	5.00
130A Frank Bolling Green Tint	2.00	5.00
131 Pete Richert RC	2.00	5.00
131A Pete Richert Green Tint	2.00	5.00
132A Los Angeles Angels TC w/o inset	4.00	10.00
132B Los Angeles Angels TC w/inset	12.50	30.00
133 Felipe Alou	3.00	8.00
133A Felipe Alou Green Tint	3.00	8.00
134A Billy Hoeft Blue Sky	2.00	5.00
134B Billy Hoeft Green Sky	12.50	30.00
135 Babe as a Boy	8.00	20.00
135A Babe as a Boy Green	8.00	20.00
136 Babe Joins Yanks	8.00	20.00
136A Babe Joins Yanks Green	8.00	20.00
137 Babe with Mgr. Huggins	10.00	25.00
137A Babe with Mgr. Huggins Green	10.00	25.00
138 The Famous Slugger	8.00	20.00
138A The Famous Slugger Green	8.00	20.00
139A1 Babe Hits 60 (Pole)	12.50	30.00
139A2 Babe Hits 60 (No Pole)	12.50	30.00
139B Hal Reniff Portrait	6.00	15.00
139C Hal Reniff Pitching	30.00	60.00
140 Gehrig and Ruth	20.00	50.00
140A Gehrig and Ruth Green	20.00	50.00
141 Twilight Years	12.00	30.00
141A Twilight Years Green	12.00	30.00
142 Coaching the Dodgers	8.00	20.00
142A Coaching the Dodgers Green	8.00	20.00
143 Greatest Sports Hero	8.00	20.00
143A Greatest Sports Hero Green	8.00	20.00
144 Farewell Speech	8.00	20.00
144A Farewell Speech Green	8.00	20.00
145 Barry Latman	2.00	5.00
145A Barry Latman Green Tint	2.00	5.00
146 Don Demeter	2.00	5.00
146A Don Demeter Green Tint	2.00	5.00
147A Bill Kunkel Portrait	2.00	5.00
147B Bill Kunkel Pitching	12.50	30.00
148 Wally Post	2.00	5.00
148A Wally Post Green Tint	2.00	5.00
149 Bob Duliba	2.00	5.00
149A Bob Duliba Green Tint	2.00	5.00
150 Al Kaline	20.00	50.00
150A Al Kaline Green Tint	20.00	50.00
151 Johnny Klippstein	2.00	5.00
151A Johnny Klippstei Green Tint	2.00	5.00
152 Mickey Vernon MG	3.00	8.00
152A Mickey Vernon MG Green Tint	3.00	8.00
153 Pumpsie Green	2.50	6.00
153A Pumpsie Green Green Tint	2.50	6.00
154 Lee Thomas	2.50	6.00
154A Lee Thomas Green Tint	2.50	6.00
155 Stu Miller	2.50	6.00
155A Stu Miller Green Tint	2.50	6.00
156 Merritt Ranew RC	2.00	5.00
156A Merritt Ranew Green Tint	2.00	5.00
157 Wes Covington	3.00	8.00
157A Wes Covington Green Tint	3.00	8.00
158 Milwaukee Braves TC	4.00	10.00
158A Milwaukee Braves TC Green Tint	6.00	15.00
159 Hal Reniff RC	3.00	8.00
160 Dick Stuart	3.00	8.00
160A Dick Stuart Green Tint	3.00	8.00
161 Frank Baumann	2.00	5.00
161A Frank Baumann Green Tint	2.00	5.00
162 Sammy Drake RC	2.00	5.00
162A Sammy Drake Green Tint	2.00	5.00
163 B.Gardner/C.Boyer	3.00	8.00
163A B.Gardner/C.Boyer Green Tint	3.00	8.00
164 Hal Naragon	2.00	5.00
164A Hal Naragon Green Tint	2.00	5.00
165 Jackie Brandt	2.00	5.00
165A Jackie Brandt Green Tint	2.00	5.00
166 Don Lee	2.00	5.00
166A Don Lee Green Tint	2.00	5.00
167 Tim McCarver RC	15.00	40.00
167A Tim McCarver Green Tint	12.50	30.00
168 Leo Posada	2.00	5.00
168A Leo Posada Green Tint	2.00	5.00
169 Bob Cerv	4.00	10.00
169A Bob Cerv Green Tint	4.00	10.00
170 Ron Santo	12.00	30.00
170A Ron Santo Green Tint	12.00	30.00
171 Dave Sisler	2.00	5.00
171A Dave Sisler Green Tint	2.00	5.00
172 Fred Hutchinson MG	3.00	8.00
172A Fred Hutchinson MG Green Tint	3.00	8.00
173 Chico Fernandez	2.00	5.00
173A Chico Fernandez Green Tint	2.00	5.00
174A Carl Willey w/o Cap	2.00	5.00
174B Carl Willey w/Cap	12.50	30.00
175 Frank Howard	4.00	10.00
175A Frank Howard Green Tint	4.00	10.00
176A Eddie Yost Portrait	2.00	5.00
176B Eddie Yost Batting	12.50	30.00
177 Bobby Shantz	3.00	8.00
177A Bobby Shantz Green Tint	3.00	8.00
178 Camilo Carreon	2.00	5.00
178A Camilo Carreon Green Tint	2.00	5.00
179 Tom Sturdivant	2.00	5.00
179A Tom Sturdivant Green Tint	2.00	5.00
180 Bob Allison	4.00	10.00
180A Bob Allison Green Tint	4.00	10.00
181 Paul Brown RC	2.00	5.00
181A Paul Brown Green Tint	2.00	5.00
182 Bob Nieman	2.00	5.00
182A Bob Nieman Green Tint	2.00	5.00
183 Roger Craig	3.00	8.00
183A Roger Craig Green Tint	3.00	8.00
184 Haywood Sullivan	3.00	8.00
184A Haywood Sullivan Green Tint	3.00	8.00
185 Roland Sheldon	4.00	10.00
185A Roland Sheldon Green Tint	4.00	10.00
186 Mack Jones RC	2.00	5.00
186A Mack Jones Green Tint	2.00	5.00
187 Gene Conley	2.00	5.00
187A Gene Conley Green Tint	2.00	5.00
188 Chuck Hiller	2.00	5.00
188A Chuck Hiller Green Tint	2.00	5.00
189 Dick Hall	2.00	5.00
189A Dick Hall Green Tint	2.00	5.00
190A Wally Moon Portrait	3.00	8.00
190B Wally Moon Batting	12.50	30.00
191 Jim Brewer	2.00	5.00
191A Jim Brewer Green Tint	2.00	5.00
192A Checklist 3 w/o Comma	5.00	12.00
192B Checklist 3 w/Comma	6.00	15.00
193 Eddie Kasko	2.00	5.00
193A Eddie Kasko Green Tint	2.00	5.00
194 Dean Chance RC	3.00	8.00
194A Dean Chance Green Tint	3.00	8.00
195 Joe Cunningham	2.00	5.00
195A Joe Cunningham Green Tint	2.00	5.00
196 Terry Fox	2.00	5.00
196A Terry Fox Green Tint	2.00	5.00
197 Daryl Spencer	2.00	5.00
198 Johnny Keane MG	2.00	5.00
199 Gaylord Perry RC	50.00	120.00
200 Mickey Mantle	400.00	800.00
201 Ike Delock	2.00	5.00
202 Carl Warwick RC	2.00	5.00
203 Jack Fisher	2.00	5.00
204 Johnny Weekly RC	2.00	5.00
205 Gene Freese	2.00	5.00
206 Washington Senators TC	4.00	10.00
207 Pete Burnside	2.00	5.00
208 Billy Martin	8.00	20.00
209 Jim Fregosi RC	6.00	15.00
210 Roy Face	3.00	8.00
211 F.Bolling/R.McMillan	2.00	5.00
212 Jim Owens	2.00	5.00
213 Richie Ashburn	8.00	20.00
214 Dom Zanni	2.00	5.00
215 Woody Held	2.00	5.00
216 Ron Kline	2.00	5.00
217 Walter Alston MG	4.00	10.00
218 Joe Torre RC	40.00	100.00
219 Al Downing RC	3.00	8.00
220 Roy Sievers	3.00	8.00
221 Bill Short	2.00	5.00
222 Jerry Zimmerman	2.00	5.00
223 Alex Grammas	2.00	5.00
224 Don Rudolph	2.00	5.00
225 Frank Malzone	3.00	8.00
226 San Francisco Giants TC	4.00	10.00
227 Bob Tiefenauer	2.00	5.00
228 Dale Long	4.00	10.00
229 Jesus McFarlane RC	2.00	5.00
230 Camilo Pascual	3.00	8.00
231 Ernie Bowman RC	2.00	5.00
232 Ellie Howard WS1	4.00	10.00
233 Joey Jay WS2	4.00	10.00
234 Roger Maris WS3	15.00	40.00
235 Whitey Ford WS4	6.00	15.00
236 Yanks Crush Reds WS5	4.00	10.00
237 Yanks Celebrate WS	4.00	10.00
238 Norm Sherry	2.00	5.00
239 Cecil Butler RC	2.00	5.00
240 George Altman	2.00	5.00
241 Johnny Kucks	2.00	5.00
242 Mel McGaha MG RC	2.00	5.00
243 Robin Roberts	6.00	15.00
244 Don Gile	2.00	5.00
245 Ron Hansen	2.00	5.00
246 Art Ditmar	2.00	5.00
247 Joe Pignatano	2.00	5.00
248 Bob Aspromonte	3.00	8.00
249 Ed Keegan	2.00	5.00
250 Norm Cash	4.00	10.00
251 New York Yankees TC	20.00	50.00
252 Earl Francis	2.00	5.00
253 Harry Chiti CO	2.00	5.00
254 Gordon Windhorn RC	2.00	5.00
255 Juan Pizarro	2.00	5.00
256 Elio Chacon	3.00	8.00
257 Jack Spring RC	2.00	5.00
258 Marty Keough	2.00	5.00
259 Lou Klimchock	2.00	5.00
260 Billy Pierce	3.00	8.00
261 George Alusik RC	2.00	5.00
262 Bob Schmidt	2.00	5.00
263 Purkey/Turner/Jay	2.00	5.00
264 Dick Ellsworth	3.00	8.00
265 Joe Adcock	3.00	8.00
266 John Anderson RC	2.00	5.00
267 Dan Dobbek	2.00	5.00
268 Ken McBride	2.00	5.00
269 Bob Oldis	2.00	5.00
270 Dick Groat	3.00	8.00
271 Ray Rippelmeyer	2.00	5.00
272 Earl Robinson	2.00	5.00
273 Gary Bell	2.00	5.00
274 Sammy Taylor	2.00	5.00
275 Norm Siebern	2.00	5.00
276 Hal Kolstad RC	2.00	5.00
277 Checklist 4	6.00	15.00
278 Ken Johnson	3.00	8.00
279 Hobie Landrith UER	3.00	8.00
280 Johnny Podres	3.00	8.00
281 Jake Gibbs RC	4.00	10.00
282 Dave Hillman	2.00	5.00
283 Charlie Smith RC	2.00	5.00
284 Ruben Amaro	2.00	5.00
285 Curt Simmons	3.00	8.00
286 Al Lopez MG	4.00	10.00
287 George Witt	2.00	5.00
288 Billy Williams	40.00	100.00
289 Mike Krsnich RC	2.00	5.00
290 Jim Gentile	3.00	8.00
291 Hal Stowe RC	2.00	5.00
292 Jerry Kindall	2.00	5.00
293 Bob Miller	3.00	8.00
294 Philadelphia Phillies TC	4.00	10.00
295 Vern Law	3.00	8.00
296 Ken Hamlin	2.00	5.00
297 Ron Perranoski	3.00	8.00
298 Bill Tuttle	2.00	5.00
299 Don Wert RC	2.00	5.00
300 Willie Mays	100.00	250.00
301 Galen Cisco RC	2.00	5.00
302 Johnny Edwards RC	2.00	5.00
303 Frank Torre	3.00	8.00
304 Dick Farrell	3.00	8.00
305 Jerry Lumpe	2.00	5.00
306 L.McDaniel/L.Jackson	2.00	5.00
307 Jim Grant	3.00	8.00
308 Neil Chrisley	3.00	8.00
309 Moe Morhardt RC	2.00	5.00
310 Whitey Ford	20.00	50.00
311 Tony Kubek IA	3.00	8.00
312 Warren Spahn IA	6.00	15.00
313 Roger Maris IA	40.00	80.00
314 Rocky Colavito IA	3.00	8.00
315 Whitey Ford IA	6.00	15.00
316 Harmon Killebrew IA	6.00	15.00
317 Stan Musial IA	8.00	20.00
318 Mickey Mantle IA	40.00	100.00
319 Mike McCormick IA	2.00	5.00
320 Hank Aaron	60.00	150.00
321 Lee Stange RC	2.00	5.00
322 Alvin Dark MG	3.00	8.00
323 Don Landrum	2.00	5.00
324 Joe McClain	2.00	5.00
325 Luis Aparicio	10.00	25.00
326 Tom Parsons RC	2.00	5.00
327 Ozzie Virgil	2.00	5.00
328 Ken Walters	2.00	5.00
329 Bob Bolin	2.00	5.00
330 John Romano	2.00	5.00
331 Moe Drabowsky	3.00	8.00
332 Don Buddin	2.00	5.00
333 Frank Cipriani RC	2.00	5.00
334 Boston Red Sox TC	4.00	10.00
335 Bill Bruton	2.00	5.00
336 Billy Muffett	2.00	5.00
337 Jim Marshall	3.00	8.00
338 Billy Gardner	2.00	5.00
339 Jose Valdivielso	2.00	5.00
340 Don Drysdale	15.00	40.00
341 Mike Hershberger RC	2.00	5.00
342 Ed Rakow	2.00	5.00
343 Albie Pearson	3.00	8.00
344 Ed Bauta RC	2.00	5.00
345 Chuck Schilling	2.00	5.00
346 Jack Kralick	2.00	5.00
347 Chuck Hinton RC	2.00	5.00
348 Larry Burright RC	3.00	8.00
349 Paul Foytack	2.00	5.00
350 Frank Robinson	30.00	80.00
351 J.Torre/D.Crandall	3.00	8.00
352 Frank Sullivan	2.00	5.00
353 Bill Mazeroski	6.00	15.00
354 Roman Mejias	3.00	8.00
355 Steve Barber	2.00	5.00
356 Tom Haller RC	2.00	5.00
357 Jerry Walker	2.00	5.00
358 Tommy Davis	3.00	8.00
359 Bobby Locke	2.00	5.00
360 Yogi Berra	40.00	80.00
361 Bob Hendley	2.00	5.00
362 Ty Cline	2.00	5.00
363 Bob Roselli	2.00	5.00
364 Ken Hunt	2.00	5.00
365 Charlie Neal	3.00	8.00
366 Phil Regan	3.00	8.00
367 Checklist 5	6.00	15.00
368 Bob Tillman RC	2.00	5.00
369 Ted Bowsfield	2.00	5.00
370 Ken Boyer	4.00	10.00
371 Earl Battey	2.50	6.00
372 Jack Curtis	2.50	6.00
373 Al Heist	2.50	6.00
374 Gene Mauch MG	4.00	10.00
375 Ron Fairly	4.00	10.00
376 Bud Daley	3.00	8.00
377 John Orsino RC	2.50	6.00
378 Bennie Daniels	2.50	6.00
379 Chuck Essegian	2.50	6.00
380 Lou Burdette	4.00	10.00
381 Chico Cardenas	4.00	10.00
382 Dick Williams	3.00	8.00
383 Ray Sadecki	2.50	6.00
384 Kansas City Athletics TC	4.00	10.00
385 Early Wynn	8.00	20.00
386 Don Mincher	3.00	8.00
387 Lou Brock RC	200.00	500.00
388 Ryne Duren	3.00	8.00
389 Smoky Burgess	4.00	10.00
390 Orlando Cepeda AS	4.00	10.00
391 Bill Mazeroski AS	4.00	10.00
392 Ken Boyer AS UER	3.00	8.00
393 Roy McMillan AS	2.50	6.00
394 Hank Aaron AS	25.00	60.00
395 Willie Mays AS	20.00	50.00
396 Frank Robinson AS	10.00	25.00
397 John Roseboro AS	2.50	6.00
398 Don Drysdale AS	6.00	15.00
399 Warren Spahn AS	8.00	20.00
400 Elston Howard	4.00	10.00
401 O.Cepeda/R.Maris	15.00	40.00
402 Gino Cimoli	2.50	6.00
403 Chet Nichols	2.50	6.00
404 Tim Harkness RC	3.00	8.00
405 Jim Perry	3.00	8.00
406 Bob Taylor	2.50	6.00
407 Hank Aguirre	2.50	6.00
408 Gus Bell	3.00	8.00
409 Pittsburgh Pirates TC	4.00	10.00
410 Al Smith	2.50	6.00
411 Danny O'Connell	2.50	6.00
412 Charlie James	2.50	6.00
413 Matty Alou	4.00	10.00
414 Joe Gaines RC	2.50	6.00
415 Bill Virdon	4.00	10.00
416 Bob Scheffing MG	2.50	6.00
417 Joe Azcue RC	2.50	6.00
418 Andy Carey	2.50	6.00
419 Bob Bruce	3.00	8.00
420 Gus Triandos	3.00	8.00
421 Ken MacKenzie	3.00	8.00
422 Steve Bilko	2.50	6.00
423 R.Face/H.Wilhelm	4.00	10.00
424 Al McBean RC	2.50	6.00
425 Carl Yastrzemski	40.00	100.00
426 Bob Farley RC	2.50	6.00
427 Jake Wood	2.50	6.00
428 Joe Hicks	2.50	6.00
429 Billy O'Dell	2.50	6.00
430 Tony Kubek	6.00	15.00
431 Bob Buck Rodgers RC	3.00	8.00
432 Jim Pendleton	2.50	6.00
433 Jim Archer	2.50	6.00
434 Clay Dalrymple	2.50	6.00
435 Larry Sherry	3.00	8.00
436 Felix Mantilla	3.00	8.00
437 Ray Moore	2.50	6.00
438 Dick Brown	2.50	6.00
439 Jerry Buchek RC	2.50	6.00
440 Joey Jay	2.50	6.00
441 Checklist 6	6.00	15.00
442 Wes Stock	2.50	6.00
443 Del Crandall	3.00	8.00
444 Ted Wills	2.50	6.00
445 Vic Power	3.00	8.00
446 Don Elston	2.50	6.00
447 Willie Kirkland	5.00	12.00
448 Joe Gibbon	5.00	12.00
449 Jerry Adair	5.00	12.00
450 Jim O'Toole	6.00	15.00
451 Jose Tartabull RC	6.00	15.00
452 Earl Averill Jr.	5.00	12.00
453 Cal McLish	5.00	12.00
454 Floyd Robinson RC	5.00	12.00
455 Luis Arroyo	6.00	15.00
456 Joe Amalfitano	6.00	15.00
457 Lou Clinton	5.00	12.00
458A Bob Buhl Emblem	6.00	15.00
458B Bob Buhl No Emblem	20.00	50.00
459 Ed Bailey	5.00	12.00
460 Jim Bunning	8.00	20.00
461 Ken Hubbs RC	10.00	25.00
462A Willie Tasby Emblem	5.00	12.00
462B Willie Tasby No Emblem	20.00	50.00
463 Hank Bauer MG	6.00	15.00
464 Al Jackson RC	6.00	15.00
465 Cincinnati Reds TC	8.00	20.00
466 Norm Cash AS	6.00	15.00
467 Chuck Schilling AS	5.00	12.00
468 Brooks Robinson AS	12.00	30.00
469 Luis Aparicio AS	6.00	15.00
470 Al Kaline AS	20.00	50.00
471 Mickey Mantle AS	100.00	250.00
472 Rocky Colavito AS	6.00	15.00
473 Elston Howard AS	6.00	15.00
474 Frank Lary AS	5.00	12.00
475 Whitey Ford AS	8.00	20.00
476 Baltimore Orioles TC	8.00	20.00
477 Andre Rodgers	5.00	12.00
478 Don Zimmer	8.00	20.00
479 Joel Horlen RC	5.00	12.00
480 Harvey Kuenn	6.00	15.00
481 Vic Wertz	6.00	15.00
482 Sam Mele MG	5.00	12.00
483 Don McMahon	5.00	12.00
484 Dick Schofield	5.00	12.00
485 Pedro Ramos	5.00	12.00
486 Jim Gilliam	6.00	15.00
487 Jerry Lynch	5.00	12.00
488 Hal Brown	5.00	12.00
489 Julio Gotay RC	5.00	12.00
490 Clete Boyer UER	6.00	15.00
491 Leon Wagner	5.00	12.00
492 Hal W. Smith	6.00	15.00
493 Danny McDevitt	5.00	12.00
494 Sammy White	5.00	12.00
495 Don Cardwell	5.00	12.00
496 Wayne Causey RC	5.00	12.00
497 Ed Bouchee	6.00	15.00
498 Jim Donohue	5.00	12.00
499 Zoilo Versalles	6.00	15.00
500 Duke Snider	20.00	50.00
501 Claude Osteen	6.00	15.00
502 Hector Lopez	6.00	15.00
503 Danny Murtaugh MG	6.00	15.00
504 Eddie Bressoud	5.00	12.00
505 Juan Marichal	15.00	40.00
506 Charlie Maxwell	6.00	15.00
507 Ernie Broglio	6.00	15.00
508 Gordy Coleman	6.00	15.00
509 Dave Giusti RC	6.00	15.00
510 Jim Lemon	5.00	12.00
511 Bubba Phillips	5.00	12.00
512 Mike Fornieles	5.00	12.00
513 Whitey Herzog	6.00	15.00
514 Sherm Lollar	6.00	15.00
515 Stan Williams	6.00	15.00
516A Checklist 7 White	6.00	15.00
516B Checklist 7 Yellow	6.00	15.00
517 Dave Wickersham	5.00	12.00
518 Lee Maye	5.00	12.00
519 Bob Johnson RC	5.00	12.00
520 Bob Friend	6.00	15.00
521 Jacke Davis UER RC	5.00	12.00
522 Lindy McDaniel	6.00	15.00
523 Russ Nixon SP	12.50	30.00
524 Howie Nunn SP	12.50	30.00
525 George Thomas	8.00	20.00
526 Hal Woodeshick SP	12.50	30.00
527 Dick McAuliffe RC	12.50	30.00
528 Turk Lown	8.00	20.00
529 John Schaive SP	12.50	30.00
530 Bob Gibson SP	100.00	250.00
531 Bobby G. Smith	8.00	20.00
532 Dick Stigman	8.00	20.00
533 Charley Lau SP	12.50	30.00
534 Tony Gonzalez SP	12.50	30.00
535 Ed Roebuck	8.00	20.00
536 Dick Gernert	8.00	20.00
537 Cleveland Indians TC	20.00	50.00
538 Jack Sanford	8.00	20.00
539 Billy Moran	8.00	20.00
540 Jim Landis	12.50	30.00
541 Don Nottebart SP	12.50	30.00
542 Dave Philley	8.00	20.00
543 Bob Allen SP	12.50	30.00
544 Willie McCovey SP	100.00	250.00
545 Hoyt Wilhelm SP	20.00	50.00
546 Moe Thacker SP	12.50	30.00
547 Don Ferrarese	8.00	20.00
548 Bobby Del Greco	8.00	20.00
549 Bill Rigney MG SP	12.50	30.00
550 Art Mahaffey SP	12.50	30.00
551 Harry Bright	8.00	20.00
552 Chicago Cubs TC	20.00	50.00
553 Jim Coates	12.50	30.00
554 Bubba Morton SP RC	12.50	30.00
555 John Buzhardt SP	12.50	30.00
556 Al Spangler	8.00	20.00
557 Bob Anderson SP	12.50	30.00
558 John Goryl	8.00	20.00
559 Mike Higgins MG	8.00	20.00
560 Chuck Estrada SP	12.50	30.00
561 Gene Oliver SP	12.50	30.00
562 Bill Henry	8.00	20.00
563 Ken Aspromonte	8.00	20.00
564 Bob Grim	8.00	20.00
565 Jose Pagan	8.00	20.00
566 Marty Kutyna SP	12.50	30.00
567 Tracy Stallard SP	12.50	30.00
568 Jim Golden	8.00	20.00
569 Ed Sadowski SP	12.50	30.00
570 Bill Stafford SP	12.50	30.00
571 Billy Klaus SP	12.50	30.00
572 Bob G. Miller SP	12.50	30.00
573 Johnny Logan	8.00	20.00
574 Dean Stone	8.00	20.00
575 Red Schoendienst SP	20.00	50.00
576 Russ Kemmerer SP	12.50	30.00
577 Dave Nicholson SP	12.50	30.00
578 Jim Duffalo RC	8.00	20.00
579 Jim Schaffer SP RC	12.50	30.00
580 Bill Monbouquette	8.00	20.00
581 Mel Roach	8.00	20.00
582 Ron Piche	8.00	20.00
583 Larry Osborne	8.00	20.00
584 Minnesota Twins TC SP	30.00	60.00
585 Glen Hobbie SP	12.50	30.00
586 Sammy Esposito SP	12.50	30.00
587 Frank Funk SP	12.50	30.00
588 Birdie Tebbetts MG	8.00	20.00
589 Bob Turley	12.50	30.00
590 Curt Flood	12.50	30.00
591 Sam McDowell SP RC	50.00	120.00
592 Jim Bouton SP RC	30.00	80.00
593 Rookie Pitchers SP	20.00	50.00
594 Bob Uecker SP RC	125.00	300.00
595 Rookie Infielders SP	20.00	50.00
596 Joe Pepitone SP RC	50.00	120.00
597 Rookie Infield SP	20.00	50.00
598 Rookie Outfielders SP	40.00	80.00

1962 Topps Bucks

Card	Low	High
COMPLETE SET (96)	600.00	1200.00
WRAPPER (1-CENT)	20.00	50.00
1 Hank Aaron	30.00	60.00
2 Joe Adcock	2.50	6.00
3 George Altman	2.00	5.00
4 Jim Archer	2.00	5.00
5 Richie Ashburn	10.00	25.00
6 Ernie Banks	15.00	40.00
7 Earl Battey	2.00	5.00
8 Gus Bell	2.00	5.00
9 Yogi Berra	15.00	40.00
10 Ken Boyer	3.00	8.00
11 Jackie Brandt	2.00	5.00
12 Jim Bunning	10.00	25.00
13 Lew Burdette	2.50	6.00
14 Don Cardwell	2.00	5.00
15 Norm Cash	3.00	8.00
16 Orlando Cepeda	8.00	20.00
17 Roberto Clemente	100.00	200.00
18 Rocky Colavito	6.00	15.00
19 Chuck Cottier	2.00	5.00
20 Roger Craig	2.50	6.00
21 Bennie Daniels	2.00	5.00
22 Don Demeter	2.00	5.00
23 Don Drysdale	12.50	30.00
24 Chuck Estrada	2.00	5.00
25 Dick Farrell	2.00	5.00
26 Whitey Ford	15.00	40.00
27 Nellie Fox	10.00	25.00
28 Tito Francona	2.00	5.00
29 Bob Friend	2.00	5.00
30 Jim Gentile	2.50	6.00
31 Dick Gernert	2.00	5.00
32 Lenny Green	2.00	5.00
33 Dick Groat	2.50	6.00
34 Woodie Held	2.00	5.00
35 Don Hoak	2.00	5.00
36 Gil Hodges	10.00	25.00
37 Elston Howard	6.00	15.00
38 Frank Howard	3.00	8.00
39 Dick Howser	2.50	6.00
40 Ken Hunt	2.00	5.00
41 Larry Jackson	2.00	5.00
42 Joey Jay	2.00	5.00
43 Al Kaline	15.00	40.00
44 Harmon Killebrew	10.00	25.00
45 Sandy Koufax	40.00	80.00
46 Harvey Kuenn	2.50	6.00
47 Jim Landis	2.00	5.00
48 Norm Larker	2.00	5.00
49 Frank Lary	2.00	5.00
50 Jerry Lumpe	2.00	5.00
51 Art Mahaffey	2.00	5.00
52 Frank Malzone	2.00	5.00
53 Felix Mantilla	2.00	5.00
54 Mickey Mantle	100.00	200.00
55 Roger Maris	20.00	50.00
56 Eddie Mathews	10.00	25.00
57 Willie Mays	30.00	60.00
58 Ken McBride	2.00	5.00
59 Mike McCormick	2.00	5.00
60 Stu Miller	2.00	5.00
61 Minnie Minoso	3.00	8.00
62 Wally Moon	2.50	6.00
63 Stan Musial	30.00	60.00
64 Danny O'Connell	2.00	5.00
65 Jim O'Toole	2.00	5.00
66 Camilo Pascual	2.00	5.00
67 Jim Perry	2.50	6.00
68 Jimmy Piersall	2.50	6.00
69 Vada Pinson	3.00	8.00
70 Juan Pizarro	2.00	5.00
71 Johnny Podres	2.50	6.00
72 Vic Power	2.00	5.00
73 Bob Purkey	2.00	5.00
74 Pedro Ramos	2.00	5.00
75 Brooks Robinson	15.00	40.00
76 Floyd Robinson	2.00	5.00
77 Frank Robinson	15.00	40.00
78 John Romano	2.00	5.00
79 Pete Runnels	2.00	5.00
80 Don Schwall	2.00	5.00
81 Bobby Shantz	2.00	5.00
82 Norm Siebern	2.00	5.00
83 Roy Sievers	2.00	5.00
84 Hal Smith	2.00	5.00
85 Warren Spahn	10.00	25.00
86 Dick Stuart	2.50	6.00
87 Tony Taylor	2.00	5.00
88 Lee Thomas	2.50	6.00
89 Gus Triandos	2.00	5.00
90 Leon Wagner	2.00	5.00
91 Jerry Walker	2.00	5.00
92 Bill White	3.00	8.00
93 Billy Williams	10.00	25.00
94 Gene Woodling	2.50	6.00
95 Early Wynn	10.00	25.00
96 Carl Yastrzemski	15.00	40.00

1962 Topps Stamps

Card	Low	High
COMPLETE SET (201)	200.00	400.00
1 Baltimore Emblem	.40	1.00
2 Jerry Adair	.40	1.00
3 Jackie Brandt	.40	1.00
4 Chuck Estrada	.40	1.00
5 Jim Gentile	.60	1.50
6 Ron Hansen	.40	1.00
7 Milt Pappas	.60	1.50
8 Brooks Robinson	3.00	8.00
9 Gus Triandos	.60	1.50
10 Hoyt Wilhelm	1.00	2.50
11 Boston Emblem	.40	1.00
12 Mike Fornieles	.40	1.00
13 Gary Geiger	.40	1.00
14 Frank Malzone	.60	1.50
15 Bill Monbouquette	.40	1.00
16 Russ Nixon	.40	1.00
17 Pete Runnels	.60	1.50
18 Chuck Schilling	.40	1.00
19 Don Schwall	.40	1.00
20 Carl Yastrzemski	5.00	12.00
21 Chicago Emblem	.40	1.00
22 Luis Aparicio	1.00	2.50
23 Camilo Carreon	.40	1.00
24 Nellie Fox	1.50	4.00
25 Ray Herbert	.40	1.00
26 Jim Landis	.40	1.00
27 J.C. Martin	.40	1.00
28 Juan Pizzaro	.40	1.00
29 Floyd Robinson	.40	1.00
30 Early Wynn	1.00	2.50
31 Cleveland Emblem	.40	1.00
32 Ty Cline	.40	1.00
33 Dick Donovan	.40	1.00
34 Tito Francona	.40	1.00
35 Woody Held	.40	1.00
36 Barry Latman	.40	1.00
37 Jim Perry	.60	1.50
38 Bubba Phillips	.40	1.00
39 Vic Power	.40	1.00
40 Johnny Romano	.40	1.00
41 Detroit Emblem	.40	1.00
42 Steve Boros	.40	1.00
43 Bill Bruton	.40	1.00
44 Jim Bunning	1.00	2.50
45 Norm Cash	1.00	2.50
46 Rocky Colavito	1.00	2.50
47 Al Kaline	3.00	8.00
48 Frank Lary	.60	1.50
49 Don Mossi	.60	1.50
50 Jake Wood	.40	1.00
51 Kansas City Emblem	.40	1.00
52 Jim Archer	.40	1.00
53 Dick Howser	1.00	2.50
54 Jerry Lumpe	.40	1.00
55 Leo Posada	.40	1.00
56 Bob Shaw	.40	1.00
57 Norm Siebern	.40	1.00
59 Gene Stephens	.40	1.00
60 Haywood Sullivan	.40	1.00
61 Jerry Walker	.40	1.00
62 Los Angeles Emblem	.40	1.00
63 Steve Bilko	.40	1.00
64 Ted Bowsfield	.40	1.00
65 Ken Hunt	.40	1.00
66 Ken McBride	.40	1.00
67 Albie Pearson	.40	1.00
68 Bob Rodgers	.60	1.50
69 George Thomas	.40	1.00
70 Lee Thomas	.60	1.50
71 Leon Wagner	.40	1.00
72 Minnesota Emblem	.40	1.00
73 Bob Allison	.60	1.50
74 Earl Battey	.40	1.00
75 Lenny Green	.40	1.00
76 Harmon Killebrew	2.50	6.00
77 Jack Kralick	.40	1.00
78 Camilo Pascual	.60	1.50
79 Pedro Ramos	.40	1.00
80 Bill Tuttle	.40	1.00
81 Zoilo Versailles	.40	1.00
82 New York Emblem	.60	1.50
83 Yogi Berra	5.00	12.00
84 Clete Boyer	1.00	2.50
85 Whitey Ford	4.00	10.00
86 Elston Howard	1.50	4.00
87 Tony Kubek	1.00	2.50
88 Mickey Mantle	30.00	60.00
89 Roger Maris	8.00	20.00
90 Bobby Richardson	1.00	2.50
91 Bill Skowron	1.00	2.50
92 Washington Emblem	.40	1.00
93 Chuck Cottier	.40	1.00
94 Pete Daley	.40	1.00
95 Bennie Daniels	.40	1.00
96 Chuck Hinton	.40	1.00
97 Bob Johnson	.40	1.00
98 Joe McClain	.40	1.00
99 Danny O'Connell	.40	1.00
100 Jimmy Piersall	1.00	2.50
101 Gene Woodling	.60	1.50
102 Chicago Emblem	.40	1.00
103 George Altman	.40	1.00
104 Ernie Banks	3.00	8.00
105 Dick Bertell	.40	1.00
106 Don Cardwell	.40	1.00
107 Dick Ellsworth	.40	1.00
108 Glen Hobbie	.40	1.00
109 Ron Santo	1.00	2.50
110 Barney Schultz	.40	1.00
111 Billy Williams	1.00	2.50
112 Cincinnati Emblem	.40	1.00
113 Gordon Coleman	.40	1.00
114 Johnny Edwards	.40	1.00
115 Gene Freese	.40	1.00
116 Joey Jay	.40	1.00
117 Eddie Kasko	.40	1.00
118 Jim O'Toole	.40	1.00
119 Vada Pinson	1.00	2.50
120 Bob Purkey	.40	1.00
121 Frank Robinson	3.00	8.00

Card	Low	High
122 Houston Emblem	.40	1.00
123 Joe Amalfitano	.40	1.00
124 Bob Aspromonte	.40	1.00
125 Dick Farrell	.40	1.00
126 Al Heist	.40	1.00
127 Sam Jones	.40	1.00
128 Bobby Shantz	.60	1.50
129 Hal W. Smith	.40	1.00
130 Al Spangler	.40	1.00
131 Bob Tiefenauer	.40	1.00
132 Los Angeles Emblem	.40	1.00
133 Don Drysdale	2.50	6.00
134 Ron Fairly	.60	1.50
135 Frank Howard	1.00	2.50
136 Sandy Koufax	6.00	15.00
137 Wally Moon	.60	1.50
138 Johnny Podres	1.00	2.50
139 John Roseboro	.40	1.00
140 Duke Snider	4.00	10.00
141 Daryl Spencer	.40	1.00
142 Milwaukee Emblem	.40	1.00
143 Hank Aaron	6.00	15.00
144 Joe Adcock	.60	1.50
145 Frank Bolling	.40	1.00
146 Lou Burdette	1.00	2.50
147 Del Crandall	.40	1.00
148 Eddie Mathews	2.50	6.00
149 Roy McMillan	.40	1.00
150 Warren Spahn	3.00	8.00
151 Joe Torre	2.00	5.00
152 New York Emblem	.60	1.50
153 Gus Bell	.60	1.50
154 Roger Craig	1.00	2.50
155 Gil Hodges	2.50	6.00
156 Jay Hook	.60	1.50
157 Hobie Landrith	.60	1.50
158 Felix Mantilla	.60	1.50
159 Bob L. Miller	.60	1.50
160 Lee Walls	.60	1.50
161 Don Zimmer	1.00	2.50
162 Philadelphia Emblem	.40	1.00
163 Ruben Amaro	.40	1.00
164 Jack Baldschun	.40	1.00
165 Johnny Callison UER Name spelled Callizon	.60	1.50
166 Clay Dalrymple	.40	1.00
167 Don Demeter	.40	1.00
168 Tony Gonzalez	.40	1.00
169 Roy Sievers Phils, see also 58	1.00	2.50
170 Tony Taylor	.60	1.50
171 Art Mahaffey	.40	1.00
172 Pittsburgh Emblem	.40	1.00
173 Smoky Burgess	.60	1.50
174 Roberto Clemente	15.00	40.00
175 Roy Face	1.00	2.50
176 Bob Friend	.60	1.50
177 Dick Groat	1.00	2.50
178 Don Hoak	.40	1.00
179 Bill Mazeroski	1.50	4.00
180 Dick Stuart	.60	1.50
181 Bill Virdon	1.00	2.50
182 St. Louis Emblem	.40	1.00
183 Ken Boyer	1.00	2.50
184 Larry Jackson	.40	1.00
185 Julian Javier	.40	1.00
186 Tim McCarver	1.50	4.00
187 Lindy McDaniel	.40	1.00
188 Minnie Minoso	1.00	2.50
189 Stan Musial	6.00	15.00
190 Ray Sadecki	.40	1.00
191 Bill White	1.00	2.50
192 San Francisco Emblem	.40	1.00
193 Felipe Alou	1.00	2.50
194 Ed Bailey	.40	1.00
195 Orlando Cepeda	1.00	2.50
196 Jim Davenport	.40	1.00
197 Harvey Kuenn	1.00	2.50
198 Juan Marichal	1.50	4.00
199 Willie Mays	8.00	20.00
200 Mike McCormick	.60	1.50
201 Stu Miller	.40	1.00
NNO Stamp Album	8.00	20.00

1962 Topps Venezuelan

These 198 cards are parallel to the first 198 cards of the regular 1962 Topps set. They were issued for the Venezuelan market and are printed in Spanish. Also note this is not quite an exact parallel as cards numbered 197 and 198 were not printed but were replaced by Elio Chacon and Luis Aparicio as cards numbered 199 and 200. Both Chacon and Aparicio were natives of Venezuela.

Card	Low	High
COMPLETE SET (198)	3000.00	6000.00
1 Roger Maris	600.00	1200.00
2 Jim Brosnan	6.00	15.00
3 Pete Runnels	6.00	15.00
4 John DeMerit	6.00	15.00
5 Sandy Koufax	300.00	600.00
6 Marv Breeding	6.00	15.00
7 Frank Thomas	6.00	15.00
8 Ray Herbert	6.00	15.00
9 Jim Davenport	6.00	15.00
10 Roberto Clemente	400.00	800.00
11 Tom Morgan	6.00	15.00
12 Harry Craft MG	6.00	15.00
13 Dick Howser	6.00	15.00
14 Bill White	8.00	20.00
15 Dick Donovan	6.00	15.00
16 Darrell Johnson	6.00	15.00
17 John Callison	6.00	15.00
18 M.Mantle W.Mays	300.00	600.00
19 Ray Washburn	6.00	15.00
20 Rocky Colavito	30.00	60.00
21 Jim Kaat	15.00	40.00
22 Checklist 1	12.50	30.00
23 Norm Larker	6.00	15.00
24 Tigers Team	10.00	25.00
25 Ernie Banks	75.00	150.00
26 Chris Cannizzaro	6.00	15.00
27 Chuck Cottier	6.00	15.00
28 Minnie Minoso	10.00	25.00
29 Casey Stengel MG	30.00	60.00
30 Eddie Mathews	40.00	80.00
31 Tom Tresh RC	20.00	50.00
32 John Roseboro	6.00	15.00
33 Don Larsen	8.00	20.00
34 Johnny Temple	6.00	15.00
35 Don Schwall	6.00	15.00
36 Don Leppert	6.00	15.00
37 Tribe Hill Trio Barry Latman Dick Stigman Jim P	6.00	15.00
38 Gene Stephens	6.00	15.00
39 Joe Koppe	6.00	15.00
40 Orlando Cepeda	20.00	50.00
41 Cliff Cook	6.00	15.00
42 Jim King	6.00	15.00
43 Los Angeles Dodgers Team Card	10.00	25.00
44 Don Taussig	6.00	15.00
45 Brooks Robinson	75.00	150.00
46 Jack Baldschun	6.00	15.00
47 Bob Will	6.00	15.00
48 Ralph Terry	6.00	15.00
49 Hal Jones	6.00	15.00
50 Stan Musial	150.00	300.00
51 Cash Pier Kaline How LL	8.00	20.00
52 Clemente Boyer Moon LL	15.00	40.00
53 Maris Mantle Kill LL	150.00	300.00
54 Cepeda Mays F.Rob LL	20.00	50.00
55 AL ERA Leaders Dick Donovan Bill Stafford Don M	8.00	20.00
56 Spahn O'Toole Simm LL	8.00	20.00
57 Ford Lary Barb Bunn LL	8.00	20.00
58 Spahn Jay O'Toole LL	8.00	20.00
59 Pasc Ford Bunn Pizz LL	8.00	20.00
60 Koufax Drys O'Toole LL	12.50	30.00
61 Cardinals Team	10.00	25.00
62 Steve Boros	6.00	15.00
63 Tony Cloninger RC	6.00	15.00
64 Russ Snyder	6.00	15.00
65 Bobby Richardson	12.50	30.00
66 Cuno Barragan	6.00	15.00
67 Harvey Haddix	6.00	15.00
68 Ken Hunt	6.00	15.00
69 Phil Ortega	6.00	15.00
70 Harmon Killebrew	40.00	80.00
71 Dick LeMay	6.00	15.00
72 Bob's Pupils Steve Boros Bob Scheffing MG Jake	6.00	15.00
73 Nellie Fox	12.50	30.00
74 Bob Lillis	6.00	15.00
75 Milt Pappas	8.00	20.00
76 Howie Bedell	6.00	15.00
77 Tony Taylor	6.00	15.00
78 Gene Green	6.00	15.00
79 Ed Hobaugh	6.00	15.00
80 Vada Pinson	8.00	20.00
81 Jim Pagliaroni	6.00	15.00
82 Deron Johnson	6.00	15.00
83 Larry Jackson	6.00	15.00
84 Lenny Green	6.00	15.00
85 Gil Hodges	20.00	50.00
86 Donn Clendenon RC	8.00	20.00
87 Mike Roarke	6.00	15.00
88 Ralph Houk MG/(Berra in background)	6.00	15.00
89 Barney Schultz	6.00	15.00
90 Jim Piersall	8.00	20.00
91 J.C. Martin	6.00	15.00
92 Sam Jones	6.00	15.00
93 John Blanchard	8.00	20.00
94 Jay Hook	6.00	15.00
95 Don Hoak	6.00	15.00
96 Eli Grba	6.00	15.00
97 Tito Francona	6.00	15.00
98 Checklist 2	12.50	30.00
99 Boog Powell RC	50.00	100.00
100 Warren Spahn	50.00	100.00
101 Carroll Hardy	6.00	15.00
102 Al Schroll	6.00	15.00
103 Don Blasingame	6.00	15.00
104 Ted Savage	6.00	15.00
105 Don Mossi	6.00	15.00
106 Carl Sawatski	6.00	15.00
107 Mike McCormick	6.00	15.00
108 Willie Davis	6.00	15.00
109 Bob Shaw	6.00	15.00
110 Bill Skowron	10.00	25.00
111 Dallas Green	6.00	15.00
112 Hank Foiles	6.00	15.00
113 Chicago White Sox Team Card	10.00	25.00
114 Howie Koplitz	6.00	15.00
115 Bob Skinner	6.00	15.00
116 Herb Score	8.00	20.00
117 Gary Geiger	6.00	15.00
118 Julian Javier	6.00	15.00
119 Danny Murphy	6.00	15.00
120 Bob Purkey	6.00	15.00
121 Billy Hitchcock MG	6.00	15.00
122 Norm Bass	6.00	15.00
123 Mike de la Hoz	6.00	15.00
124 Bill Pleis	6.00	15.00
125 Gene Woodling	6.00	15.00
126 Al Cicotte	6.00	15.00
127 Pride of A's Norm Siebern Hank Bauer MG Jerry L	6.00	15.00
128 Art Fowler	6.00	15.00
129 Lee Walls	6.00	15.00
130 Frank Bolling	6.00	15.00
131 Pete Richert	6.00	15.00
132 Angels Team	10.00	25.00
133 Felipe Alou	8.00	20.00
134 Billy Hoeft	6.00	15.00
135 Babe Ruth Special 1 Babe as a Boy	30.00	60.00
136 Babe Ruth Special 2 Babe Joins Yanks	30.00	60.00
137 Babe Ruth Special 3 With Miller Huggins	30.00	60.00
138 Babe Ruth Special 4 Famous Slugger	30.00	60.00
139 Babe Ruth Story: 5	40.00	80.00
140 Babe Ruth Lou Gehrig	30.00	60.00
141 Babe Ruth Special 7 Twilight Years	30.00	60.00
142 Babe Ruth Special 8 Coaching Dodgers	30.00	60.00
143 Babe Ruth Special 9 Greatest Sports Hero	30.00	60.00
144 Babe Ruth Special 10 Farewell Speech	30.00	60.00
145 Barry Latman	6.00	15.00
146 Don Demeter	6.00	15.00
147 Bill Kunkel	6.00	15.00
148 Wally Post	6.00	15.00
149 Bob Duliba	6.00	15.00
150 Al Kaline	75.00	150.00
151 Johnny Klippstein	6.00	15.00
152 Mickey Vernon MG	6.00	15.00
153 Pumpsie Green	6.00	15.00
154 Lee Thomas	6.00	15.00
155 Stu Miller	6.00	15.00
156 Merritt Ranew	6.00	15.00
157 Wes Covington	8.00	20.00
158 Braves Team	10.00	25.00
159 Hal Reniff RC	6.00	15.00
160 Dick Stuart	6.00	15.00
161 Frank Baumann	6.00	15.00
162 Sammy Drake	6.00	15.00
163 Billy Gardner Cletis Boyer	6.00	15.00
164 Hal Naragon	6.00	15.00
165 Jackie Brandt	6.00	15.00
166 Don Lee	6.00	15.00
167 Tim McCarver RC	50.00	100.00
168 Leo Posada	6.00	15.00
169 Bob Cerv	6.00	15.00
170 Ron Santo	20.00	50.00
171 Dave Sisler	6.00	15.00
172 Fred Hutchinson MG	6.00	15.00
173 Chico Fernandez	6.00	15.00
174 Carl Willey	6.00	15.00
175 Frank Howard	8.00	20.00
176 Eddie Yost	6.00	15.00
177 Bobby Shantz	6.00	15.00
178 Camilo Carreon	6.00	15.00
179 Tom Sturdivant	6.00	15.00
180 Bob Allison	6.00	15.00
181 Paul Brown	6.00	15.00
182 Bob Nieman	6.00	15.00
183 Roger Craig	10.00	25.00
184 Haywood Sullivan	6.00	15.00
185 Roland Sheldon	6.00	15.00
186 Mack Jones	6.00	15.00
187 Gene Conley	6.00	15.00
188 Chuck Hiller	6.00	15.00
189 Dick Hall	6.00	15.00
190 Wally Moon	6.00	15.00
191 Jim Brewer	6.00	15.00
192 Checklist 3	12.50	30.00
193 Eddie Kasko	6.00	15.00
194 Dean Chance RC	6.00	15.00
195 Joe Cunningham	8.00	20.00
196 Terry Fox	6.00	15.00
199 Elio Chacon	15.00	40.00
200 Luis Aparicio	40.00	80.00

1963 Topps

The cards in this 576-card set measure 2 1/2" by 3 1/2". The sharp color photographs of the 1963 set are a vivid contrast to the drab pictures of 1962. In addition to the "League Leaders" series (1-10) and World Series cards (142-148), the seventh and last series of cards (523-576) contains seven rookie cards (each depicting four players). Cards were issued, among other ways, in one-card penny packs and five-card nickel packs. There were some three-card advertising panels produced by Topps; the players included are from the first series; one panel shows Hoyt Wilhelm, Don Lock, and Bob Duliba on the front with a Stan Musial ad/endorsement on one of the backs. Key Rookie Cards in this set are Bill Freehan, Tony Oliva, Pete Rose, Willie Stargell and Rusty Staub.

Card	Low	High
COMPLETE SET (576)	4000.00	10000.00
COMMON CARD (1-196)	1.50	4.00
COMMON CARD (197-283)	2.00	5.00
COMMON CARD (284-370)	2.00	5.00
COMMON CARD (371-446)	2.00	5.00
COMMON CARD (447-522)	10.00	25.00
COMMON CARD (523-576)	6.00	15.00
WRAPPER (1-CENT)	15.00	40.00
WRAPPER (5-CENT)	12.50	30.00
1 F.Rob/Musial/Aaron LL	10.00	25.00
2 Runnels/Mantle/Rob LL	20.00	50.00
3 Mays/Aaron/Rob/Cep/Banks LL	20.00	50.00
4 Kill/Cash/Colav/Maris LL	10.00	25.00
5 Koufax/Gibson/Drysdale LL	10.00	25.00
6 Aguirre/Roberts/Ford LL	4.00	10.00
7 Drysdale/Sanf/Purk LL	4.00	10.00
8 Terry/Donovan/Bunning LL	3.00	8.00
9 Drysdale/Koufax/Gibson LL	12.50	30.00
10 Pascual/Bunning/Kaat LL	3.00	8.00
11 Lee Walls	1.50	4.00
12 Steve Barber	1.50	4.00
13 Philadelphia Phillies TC	3.00	8.00
14 Pedro Ramos	1.50	4.00
15 Ken Hubbs UER NPO	4.00	10.00
16 Al Smith	1.50	4.00
17 Ryne Duren	3.00	8.00
18 Burg/Stu/Clemente/Skin	20.00	50.00
19 Pete Burnside	1.50	4.00
20 Tony Kubek	8.00	20.00
21 Marty Keough	1.50	4.00
22 Curt Simmons	3.00	8.00
23 Ed Lopat MG	3.00	8.00
24 Bob Bruce	1.50	4.00
25 Al Kaline	40.00	100.00
26 Ray Moore	1.50	4.00
27 Choo Choo Coleman	3.00	8.00
28 Mike Fornieles	1.50	4.00
29A Rookie Stars 1962	4.00	10.00
29B Rookie Stars 1963	1.50	4.00
30 Harvey Kuenn	3.00	8.00
31 Cal Koonce RC	1.50	4.00
32 Tony Gonzalez	1.50	4.00
33 Bo Belinsky	3.00	8.00
34 Dick Schofield	1.50	4.00
35 John Buzhardt	1.50	4.00
36 Jerry Kindall	1.50	4.00
37 Jerry Lynch	1.50	4.00
38 Bud Daley	3.00	8.00
39 Los Angeles Angels TC	3.00	8.00
40 Vic Power	3.00	8.00
41 Charley Lau	3.00	8.00
42 Stan Williams	3.00	8.00
43 C.Stengel/G.Woodling	3.00	8.00
44 Terry Fox	1.50	4.00
45 Bob Aspromonte	1.50	4.00
46 Tommie Aaron RC	3.00	8.00
47 Don Lock RC	1.50	4.00
48 Birdie Tebbetts MG	3.00	8.00
49 Dal Maxvill RC	3.00	8.00
50 Billy Pierce	3.00	8.00
51 George Alusik	1.50	4.00
52 Chuck Schilling	1.50	4.00
53 Joe Moeller RC	3.00	8.00
54A Dave DeBusschere 62	6.00	15.00
54B Dave DeBusschere 63 RC	3.00	8.00
55 Bill Virdon	3.00	8.00
56 Dennis Bennett RC	1.50	4.00
57 Billy Moran	1.50	4.00
58 Bob Will	1.50	4.00
59 Craig Anderson	1.50	4.00
60 Elston Howard	3.00	8.00
61 Ernie Bowman	1.50	4.00
62 Bob Hendley	1.50	4.00
63 Cincinnati Reds TC	3.00	8.00
64 Dick McAuliffe	3.00	8.00
65 Jackie Brandt	1.50	4.00
66 Mike Joyce RC	1.50	4.00
67 Ed Charles	1.50	4.00
68 G.Hodges/D.Snider	10.00	25.00
69 Bud Zipfel RC	1.50	4.00
70 Jim O'Toole	3.00	8.00
71 Bobby Wine RC	3.00	8.00
72 Johnny Romano	1.50	4.00
73 Bobby Bragan MG RC	3.00	8.00
74 Denny Lemaster RC	1.50	4.00
75 Bob Allison	3.00	8.00
76 Earl Wilson	3.00	8.00
77 Al Spangler	1.50	4.00
78 Marv Throneberry	3.00	8.00
79 Checklist 1	5.00	12.00
80 Jim Gilliam	3.00	8.00
81 Jim Schaffer	1.50	4.00
82 Ed Rakow	1.50	4.00
83 Charley James	1.50	4.00
84 Ron Kline	1.50	4.00
85 Tom Haller	3.00	8.00
86 Charley Maxwell	3.00	8.00
87 Bob Veale	3.00	8.00
88 Ron Hansen	1.50	4.00
89 Dick Stigman	1.50	4.00
90 Gordy Coleman	3.00	8.00
91 Dallas Green	3.00	8.00
92 Hector Lopez	3.00	8.00
93 Galen Cisco	1.50	4.00
94 Bob Schmidt	1.50	4.00
95 Larry Jackson	1.50	4.00
96 Lou Clinton	1.50	4.00
97 Bob Duliba	1.50	4.00
98 George Thomas	1.50	4.00
99 Jim Umbricht	1.50	4.00
100 Joe Cunningham	1.50	4.00
101 Joe Gibbon	1.50	4.00
102A Checklist 2 Red Yellow	5.00	12.00
102B Checklist 2 White Red	5.00	12.00
103 Chuck Essegian	1.50	4.00
104 Lew Krausse RC	1.50	4.00
105 Ron Fairly	3.00	8.00
106 Bobby Bolin	1.50	4.00
107 Jim Hickman	3.00	8.00
108 Hoyt Wilhelm	4.00	10.00
109 Lee Maye	1.50	4.00
110 Rich Rollins	3.00	8.00
111 Al Jackson	1.50	4.00
112 Dick Brown	1.50	4.00
113 Don Landrum UER	1.50	4.00
114 Dan Osinski RC	1.50	4.00
115 Carl Yastrzemski	40.00	100.00
116 Jim Brosnan	3.00	8.00
117 Jacke Davis	1.50	4.00
118 Sherm Lollar	1.50	4.00
119 Bob Lillis	1.50	4.00
120 Roger Maris	40.00	100.00
121 Jim Hannan RC	1.50	4.00
122 Julio Gotay	1.50	4.00
123 Frank Howard	3.00	8.00
124 Dick Howser	3.00	8.00
125 Robin Roberts	8.00	20.00
126 Bob Uecker	25.00	60.00
127 Bill Tuttle	1.50	4.00
128 Matty Alou	3.00	8.00
129 Gary Bell	1.50	4.00
130 Dick Groat	3.00	8.00
131 Washington Senators TC	3.00	8.00
132 Jack Hamilton	1.50	4.00
133 Gene Freese	1.50	4.00
134 Bob Scheffing MG	1.50	4.00
135 Richie Ashburn	12.00	30.00
136 Ike Delock	1.50	4.00
137 Mack Jones	1.50	4.00
138 W.Mays/S.Musial	25.00	60.00
139 Earl Averill Jr.	1.50	4.00
140 Frank Lary	3.00	8.00
141 Manny Mota RC	3.00	8.00
142 Whitey Ford WS1	8.00	20.00
143 Jack Sanford WS2	3.00	8.00
144 Roger Maris WS3	10.00	25.00
145 Chuck Hiller WS4	3.00	8.00
146 Tom Tresh WS5	3.00	8.00
147 Billy Pierce WS6	3.00	8.00
148 Ralph Terry WS7	3.00	8.00
149 Marv Breeding	1.50	4.00
150 Johnny Podres	3.00	8.00
151 Pittsburgh Pirates TC	3.00	8.00
152 Ron Nischwitz	1.50	4.00
153 Hal Smith	1.50	4.00
154 Walter Alston MG	3.00	8.00
155 Bill Stafford	1.50	4.00
156 Roy McMillan	3.00	8.00
157 Diego Segui RC	3.00	8.00
158 Tommy Harper RC	3.00	8.00
159 Jim Pagliaroni	1.50	4.00
160 Juan Pizarro	1.50	4.00
161 Frank Torre	3.00	8.00
162 Minnesota Twins TC	3.00	8.00
163 Don Larsen	3.00	8.00
164 Bubba Morton	1.50	4.00
165 Jim Kaat	3.00	8.00
166 Johnny Keane MG	1.50	4.00
167 Jim Fregosi	3.00	8.00
168 Russ Nixon	1.50	4.00
169 Gaylord Perry	10.00	25.00
170 Joe Adcock	3.00	8.00
171 Steve Hamilton RC	1.50	4.00
172 Gene Oliver	1.50	4.00
173 Tresh/Mantle/Richardson	50.00	120.00
174 Larry Burright	1.50	4.00
175 Bob Buhl	3.00	8.00
176 Jim King	1.50	4.00
177 Bubba Phillips	1.50	4.00
178 Johnny Edwards	1.50	4.00
179 Ron Piche	1.50	4.00
180 Bill Skowron	3.00	8.00
181 Sammy Esposito	1.50	4.00
182 Albie Pearson	3.00	8.00
183 Joe Pepitone	3.00	8.00
184 Vern Law	3.00	8.00
185 Chuck Hiller	1.50	4.00
186 Jerry Zimmerman	1.50	4.00
187 Willie Kirkland	1.50	4.00
188 Eddie Bressoud	1.50	4.00
189 Dave Giusti	3.00	8.00
190 Minnie Minoso	3.00	8.00
191 Checklist 3	5.00	12.00
192 Clay Dalrymple	1.50	4.00
193 Andre Rodgers	1.50	4.00
194 Joe Nuxhall	3.00	8.00
195 Manny Jimenez	1.50	4.00
196 Doug Camilli	1.50	4.00
197 Roger Craig	3.00	8.00
198 Lenny Green	2.00	5.00
199 Joe Amalfitano	2.00	5.00
200 Mickey Mantle	300.00	600.00
201 Cecil Butler	2.00	5.00
202 Boston Red Sox TC	3.00	8.00
203 Chico Cardenas	3.00	8.00
204 Don Nottebart	2.00	5.00
205 Luis Aparicio	6.00	15.00
206 Ray Washburn	2.00	5.00
207 Ken Hunt	2.00	5.00
208 Rookie Stars	2.00	5.00
209 Hobie Landrith	2.00	5.00
210 Sandy Koufax	75.00	200.00
211 Fred Whitfield RC	2.00	5.00
212 Glen Hobbie	2.00	5.00
213 Billy Hitchcock MG	2.00	5.00
214 Orlando Pena	2.00	5.00
215 Bob Skinner	3.00	8.00
216 Gene Conley	3.00	8.00
217 Joe Christopher	2.00	5.00
218 Lary/Mossi/Bunning	3.00	8.00
219 Chuck Cottier	2.00	5.00
220 Camilo Pascual	3.00	8.00
221 Cookie Rojas RC	3.00	8.00
222 Chicago Cubs TC	3.00	8.00
223 Eddie Fisher	2.00	5.00
224 Mike Roarke	2.00	5.00
225 Joey Jay	2.00	5.00
226 Julian Javier	3.00	8.00
227 Jim Grant	3.00	8.00
228 Tony Oliva RC	40.00	100.00
229 Willie Davis	3.00	8.00
230 Pete Runnels	3.00	8.00
231 Eli Grba UER	2.00	5.00
232 Frank Malzone	3.00	8.00
233 Casey Stengel MG	8.00	20.00
234 Dave Nicholson	2.00	5.00
235 Billy O'Dell	2.00	5.00
236 Bill Bryan RC	2.00	5.00
237 Jim Coates	3.00	8.00
238 Lou Johnson	2.00	5.00
239 Harvey Haddix	3.00	8.00
240 Rocky Colavito	6.00	15.00
241 Billy Smith RC	2.00	5.00
242 E.Banks/H.Aaron	50.00	120.00
243 Don Leppert	2.00	5.00
244 John Tsitouris	2.00	5.00
245 Gil Hodges	8.00	20.00
246 Lee Stange	2.00	5.00
247 New York Yankees TC	25.00	60.00
248 Tito Francona	2.00	5.00
249 Leo Burke RC	2.00	5.00
250 Stan Musial	40.00	100.00
251 Jack Lamabe	2.00	5.00
252 Ron Santo	12.00	30.00
253 Rookie Stars	2.00	5.00
254 Mike Hershberger	2.00	5.00
255 Bob Shaw	2.00	5.00
256 Jerry Lumpe	2.00	5.00
257 Hank Aguirre	2.00	5.00
258 Alvin Dark MG	3.00	8.00
259 Johnny Logan	3.00	8.00
260 Jim Gentile	3.00	8.00
261 Bob Miller	2.00	5.00
262 Ellis Burton	2.00	5.00
263 Dave Stenhouse	2.00	5.00
264 Phil Linz	2.00	5.00
265 Vada Pinson	3.00	8.00
266 Bob Allen	2.00	5.00
267 Carl Sawatski	2.00	5.00
268 Don Demeter	2.00	5.00
269 Don Mincher	2.00	5.00
270 Felipe Alou	3.00	8.00
271 Dean Stone	2.00	5.00
272 Danny Murphy	2.00	5.00
273 Sammy Taylor	2.00	5.00
274 Checklist 4	5.00	12.00
275 Eddie Mathews	25.00	60.00
276 Barry Shetrone	2.00	5.00
277 Dick Farrell	2.00	5.00
278 Chico Fernandez	2.00	5.00
279 Wally Moon	3.00	8.00
280 Bob Buck Rodgers	2.00	5.00
281 Tom Sturdivant	2.00	5.00
282 Bobby Del Greco	2.00	5.00
283 Roy Sievers	3.00	8.00
284 Dave Sisler	2.00	5.00
285 Dick Stuart	3.00	8.00
286 Stu Miller	3.00	8.00
287 Dick Bertell	2.00	5.00
288 Chicago White Sox TC	4.00	10.00
289 Hal Brown	2.00	5.00
290 Bill White	3.00	8.00
291 Don Rudolph	2.00	5.00
292 Pumpsie Green	3.00	8.00
293 Bill Pleis	2.00	5.00
294 Bill Rigney MG	2.00	5.00
295 Ed Roebuck	2.00	5.00
296 Doc Edwards	2.00	5.00
297 Jim Golden	2.00	5.00
298 Don Dillard	2.00	5.00
299 Rookie Stars	3.00	8.00
300 Willie Mays	75.00	200.00
301 Bill Fischer	2.00	5.00
302 Whitey Herzog	3.00	8.00
303 Earl Francis	2.00	5.00
304 Harry Bright	2.00	5.00
305 Don Hoak	2.00	5.00
306 E.Battey/E.Howard	4.00	10.00
307 Chet Nichols	2.00	5.00
308 Camilo Carreon	2.00	5.00
309 Jim Brewer	2.00	5.00
310 Tommy Davis	3.00	8.00
311 Joe McClain	2.00	5.00
312 Houston Colts TC	10.00	25.00
313 Ernie Broglio	2.00	5.00
314 John Goryl	2.00	5.00
315 Ralph Terry	3.00	8.00
316 Norm Sherry	3.00	8.00
317 Sam McDowell	3.00	8.00
318 Gene Mauch MG	3.00	8.00
319 Joe Gaines	2.00	5.00
320 Warren Spahn	30.00	80.00
321 Gino Cimoli	2.00	5.00
322 Bob Turley	3.00	8.00
323 Bill Mazeroski	20.00	50.00
324 Vic Davalillo RC	3.00	8.00
325 Jack Sanford	2.00	5.00
326 Hank Foiles	2.00	5.00
327 Paul Foytack	2.00	5.00
328 Dick Williams	3.00	8.00
329 Lindy McDaniel	3.00	8.00
330 Chuck Hinton	2.00	5.00
331 Stafford/Pierce	3.00	8.00
332 Joel Horlen	3.00	8.00
333 Carl Warwick	2.00	5.00
334 Wynn Hawkins	2.00	5.00
335 Leon Wagner	2.00	5.00
336 Ed Bauta	2.00	5.00
337 Los Angeles Dodgers TC	10.00	25.00
338 Russ Kemmerer	2.00	5.00
339 Ted Bowsfield	2.00	5.00
340 Yogi Berra P CO	50.00	120.00
341 Jack Baldschun	2.00	5.00
342 Gene Woodling	3.00	8.00
343 Johnny Pesky MG	3.00	8.00
344 Don Schwall	2.00	5.00
345 Brooks Robinson	25.00	60.00
346 Billy Hoeft	2.00	5.00
347 Joe Torre	8.00	20.00
348 Vic Wertz	3.00	8.00
349 Zoilo Versalles	3.00	8.00
350 Bob Purkey	2.00	5.00
351 Al Luplow	2.00	5.00
352 Ken Johnson	2.00	5.00
353 Billy Williams	25.00	60.00
354 Dom Zanni	2.00	5.00
355 Dean Chance	3.00	8.00
356 John Schaive	2.00	5.00
357 George Altman	2.00	5.00
358 Milt Pappas	3.00	8.00
359 Haywood Sullivan	3.00	8.00
360 Don Drysdale	20.00	50.00
361 Clete Boyer	4.00	10.00
362 Checklist 5	5.00	12.00
363 Dick Radatz	3.00	8.00
364 Howie Goss	2.00	5.00
365 Jim Bunning	8.00	20.00
366 Tony Taylor	3.00	8.00
367 Tony Cloninger	2.00	5.00
368 Ed Bailey	2.00	5.00
369 Jim Lemon	2.00	5.00
370 Dick Donovan	2.00	5.00
371 Rod Kanehl	3.00	8.00
372 Don Lee	2.00	5.00
373 Jim Campbell RC	2.00	5.00
374 Claude Osteen	3.00	8.00
375 Ken Boyer	6.00	15.00
376 John Wyatt RC	2.00	5.00
377 Baltimore Orioles TC	4.00	10.00
378 Bill Henry	2.00	5.00
379 Bob Anderson	2.00	5.00
380 Ernie Banks UER	50.00	100.00
381 Frank Baumann	2.00	5.00
382 Ralph Houk MG	4.00	10.00
383 Pete Richert	2.00	5.00
384 Bob Tillman	2.00	5.00
385 Art Mahaffey	2.00	5.00
386 Rookie Stars	2.00	5.00
387 Al McBean	2.00	5.00
388 Jim Davenport	3.00	8.00
389 Frank Sullivan	2.00	5.00
390 Hank Aaron	75.00	200.00
391 Bill Dailey RC	2.00	5.00
392 Romano/Francona	2.00	5.00
393 Ken MacKenzie	3.00	8.00
394 Tim McCarver	6.00	15.00
395 Don McMahon	2.00	5.00
396 Joe Koppe	2.00	5.00
397 Kansas City Athletics TC	4.00	10.00
398 Boog Powell	15.00	40.00
399 Dick Ellsworth	2.00	5.00
400 Frank Robinson	40.00	100.00
401 Jim Bouton	15.00	40.00
402 Mickey Vernon MG	3.00	8.00
403 Ron Perranoski	3.00	8.00
404 Bob Oldis	2.00	5.00
405 Floyd Robinson	2.00	5.00
406 Howie Koplitz	2.00	5.00
407 Rookie Stars	3.00	8.00
408 Billy Gardner	2.00	5.00
409 Roy Face	3.00	8.00
410 Earl Battey	2.00	5.00
411 Jim Constable	2.00	5.00
412 Podres/Drysdale/Koufax	30.00	80.00
413 Jerry Walker	2.00	5.00
414 Ty Cline	2.00	5.00
415 Bob Gibson	60.00	150.00
416 Alex Grammas	2.00	5.00
417 San Francisco Giants TC	4.00	10.00
418 John Orsino	2.00	5.00
419 Tracy Stallard	2.00	5.00
420 Bobby Richardson	6.00	15.00
421 Tom Morgan	2.00	5.00
422 Fred Hutchinson MG	3.00	8.00
423 Ed Hobaugh	2.00	5.00
424 Charlie Smith	2.00	5.00
425 Smoky Burgess	3.00	8.00
426 Barry Latman	2.00	5.00
427 Bernie Allen	2.00	5.00
428 Carl Boles RC	2.00	5.00
429 Lou Burdette	3.00	8.00
430 Norm Siebern	2.00	5.00
431A Checklist 6 White Red	5.00	12.00
431B Checklist 6 Black Orange	12.50	30.00
432 Roman Mejias	2.00	5.00
433 Denis Menke	2.00	5.00
434 John Callison	3.00	8.00
435 Woody Held	2.00	5.00
436 Tim Harkness	3.00	8.00
437 Bill Bruton	2.00	5.00
438 Wes Stock	2.00	5.00
439 Don Zimmer	3.00	8.00
440 Juan Marichal	25.00	60.00
441 Lee Thomas	3.00	8.00
442 J.C. Hartman RC	2.00	5.00
443 Jimmy Piersall	3.00	8.00
444 Jim Maloney	3.00	8.00
445 Norm Cash	4.00	10.00
446 Whitey Ford	20.00	50.00
447 Felix Mantilla	10.00	25.00
448 Jack Kralick	10.00	25.00
449 Jose Tartabull	10.00	25.00
450 Bob Friend	12.50	30.00
451 Cleveland Indians TC	15.00	40.00
452 Barney Schultz	10.00	25.00
453 Jake Wood	10.00	25.00
454A Art Fowler White	10.00	25.00
454B Art Fowler Orange	12.50	30.00
455 Ruben Amaro	10.00	25.00
456 Jim Coker	10.00	25.00
457 Tex Clevenger	10.00	25.00
458 Al Lopez MG	12.50	30.00
459 Dick LeMay	10.00	25.00
460 Del Crandall	12.50	30.00
461 Norm Bass	10.00	25.00
462 Wally Post	10.00	25.00
463 Joe Schaffernoth	10.00	25.00
464 Ken Aspromonte	10.00	25.00
465 Chuck Estrada	10.00	25.00
466 Bill Freehan SP RC	20.00	50.00
467 Phil Ortega	10.00	25.00
468 Carroll Hardy	12.50	30.00
469 Jay Hook	12.50	30.00
470 Tom Tresh SP	30.00	60.00
471 Ken Retzer	10.00	25.00
472 Lou Brock	75.00	200.00
473 New York Mets TC	50.00	100.00
474 Jack Fisher	10.00	25.00
475 Gus Triandos	12.50	30.00
476 Frank Funk	10.00	25.00
477 Donn Clendenon	12.50	30.00
478 Paul Brown	10.00	25.00
479 Ed Brinkman RC	10.00	25.00
480 Bill Monbouquette	10.00	25.00
481 Bob Taylor	10.00	25.00
482 Felix Torres	10.00	25.00
483 Jim Owens UER	10.00	25.00
484 Dale Long SP	12.50	30.00
485 Jim Landis	10.00	25.00
486 Ray Sadecki	10.00	25.00
487 John Roseboro	12.50	30.00
488 Jerry Adair	10.00	25.00
489 Paul Toth RC	10.00	25.00

490 Willie McCovey 40.00 100.00
491 Harry Craft MG 10.00 25.00
492 Dave Wickersham 10.00 25.00
493 Walt Bond 10.00 25.00
494 Phil Regan 10.00 25.00
495 Frank Thomas SP 12.50 30.00
496 Rookie Stars 40.00 100.00
497 Bennie Daniels 10.00 25.00
498 Eddie Kasko 10.00 25.00
499 J.C. Martin 10.00 25.00
500 Harmon Killebrew SP 40.00 100.00
501 Joe Azcue 10.00 25.00
502 Daryl Spencer 10.00 25.00
503 Milwaukee Braves TC 15.00 40.00
504 Bob Johnson 10.00 25.00
505 Curt Flood 15.00 40.00
506 Gene Green 10.00 25.00
507 Roland Sheldon 12.50 30.00
508 Ted Savage 10.00 25.00
509A Checklist 7 Centered 12.50 30.00
509B Checklist 7 Right 12.50 30.00
510 Ken McBride 10.00 25.00
511 Charlie Neal 12.50 30.00
512 Cal McLish 10.00 25.00
513 Gary Geiger 10.00 25.00
514 Larry Osborne 10.00 25.00
515 Don Elston 10.00 25.00
516 Purnell Goldy RC 10.00 25.00
517 Hal Woodeshick 10.00 25.00
518 Don Blasingame 10.00 25.00
519 Claude Raymond RC 10.00 25.00
520 Orlando Cepeda 15.00 40.00
521 Dan Pfister 10.00 25.00
522 Rookie Stars 12.50 30.00
523 Bill Kunkel 6.00 15.00
524 St. Louis Cardinals TC 12.50 30.00
525 Nellie Fox 15.00 40.00
526 Dick Hall 6.00 15.00
527 Ed Sadowski 6.00 15.00
528 Carl Willey 6.00 15.00
529 Wes Covington 6.00 15.00
530 Don Mossi 8.00 20.00
531 Sam Mele MG 6.00 15.00
532 Steve Boros 6.00 15.00
533 Bobby Shantz 8.00 20.00
534 Ken Walters 6.00 15.00
535 Jim Perry 8.00 20.00
536 Norm Larker 6.00 15.00
537 Pete Rose RC 800.00 1500.00
538 George Brunet 6.00 15.00
539 Wayne Causey 6.00 15.00
540 Roberto Clemente 200.00 500.00
541 Ron Moeller 6.00 15.00
542 Lou Klimchock 6.00 15.00
543 Russ Snyder 6.00 15.00
544 Rusty Staub RC 30.00 80.00
545 Jose Pagan 6.00 15.00
546 Hal Reniff 8.00 20.00
547 Gus Bell 6.00 15.00
548 Tom Satriano RC 6.00 15.00
549 Rookie Stars 6.00 15.00
550 Duke Snider 20.00 50.00
551 Billy Klaus 6.00 15.00
552 Detroit Tigers TC 10.00 25.00
553 Willie Stargell RC 200.00 500.00
554 Hank Fischer RC 6.00 15.00
555 John Blanchard 8.00 20.00
556 Al Worthington 6.00 15.00
557 Cuno Barragan 6.00 15.00
558 Ron Hunt RC 8.00 20.00
559 Danny Murtaugh MG 6.00 15.00
560 Ray Herbert 6.00 15.00
561 Mike De La Hoz 6.00 15.00
562 Dave McNally RC 15.00 40.00
563 Mike McCormick 6.00 15.00
564 George Banks RC 6.00 15.00
565 Larry Sherry 6.00 15.00
566 Cliff Cook 6.00 15.00
567 Jim Duffalo 6.00 15.00
568 Bob Sadowski 6.00 15.00
569 Luis Arroyo 8.00 20.00
570 Frank Bolling 6.00 15.00
571 Johnny Klippstein 6.00 15.00
572 Jack Spring 6.00 15.00
573 Coot Veal 6.00 15.00
574 Hal Kolstad 6.00 15.00
575 Don Cardwell 6.00 15.00
576 Johnny Temple 12.50 30.00

1963 Topps Peel-Offs

COMPLETE SET (46) 300.00 600.00
1 Hank Aaron 15.00 40.00
2 Luis Aparicio 5.00 12.00
3 Richie Ashburn 6.00 15.00
4 Bob Aspromonte 1.50 4.00
5 Ernie Banks 8.00 20.00
6 Ken Boyer 2.50 6.00
7 Jim Bunning 60.00 120.00
8 Johnny Callison 1.50 4.00
9 Roberto Clemente 30.00 60.00
10 Orlando Cepeda 5.00 12.00
11 Rocky Colavito 4.00 10.00
12 Tommy Davis 2.00 5.00
13 Dick Donovan 1.50 4.00
14 Don Drysdale 6.00 15.00
15 Dick Farrell 1.50 4.00
16 Jim Gentile 2.00 5.00
17 Ray Herbert 1.50 4.00
18 Chuck Hinton 1.50 4.00
19 Ken Hubbs 2.50 6.00
20 Al Jackson 1.50 4.00
21 Al Kaline 8.00 20.00
22 Harmon Killebrew 5.00 12.00
23 Sandy Koufax 12.50 30.00
24 Jerry Lumpe 1.50 4.00
25 Art Mahaffey 1.50 4.00
26 Mickey Mantle 50.00 100.00
27 Willie Mays 20.00 50.00
28 Bill Mazeroski 4.00 10.00
29 Bill Monbouquette 1.50 4.00
30 Stan Musial 12.50 30.00
31 Camilo Pascual 1.50 4.00
32 Bob Purkey 1.50 4.00
33 Bobby Richardson 2.50 6.00
34 Brooks Robinson 8.00 20.00
35 Floyd Robinson 1.50 4.00
36 Frank Robinson 8.00 20.00
37 Bob Rodgers 1.50 4.00
38 Johnny Romano 1.50 4.00
39 Jack Sanford 1.50 4.00
40 Norm Siebern 1.50 4.00
41 Warren Spahn 5.00 12.00
42 Dave Stenhouse 1.50 4.00
43 Ralph Terry 1.50 4.00
44 Lee Thomas 2.00 5.00
45 Bill White 2.00 5.00
46 Carl Yastrzemski 10.00 25.00

1964 Topps

The cards in this 587-card set measure 2 1/2" by 3 1/2". Players in the 1964 Topps baseball series were easy to sort by team due to the giant block lettering found at the top of each card. The name and position of the player are found underneath the picture, and the card is numbered in a ball design on the orange-colored back. The usual last series scarcity holds for this set (523 to 587). Subsets within this set include League Leaders (1-12) and World Series cards (136-140). Among other vehicles, cards were issued in one-card penny packs as well as five-card nickel packs. There were some three-card advertising panels produced by Topps; the players included are from the first series; Panels with Mickey Mantle card backs include Walt Alston/Bill Henry/Vada Pinson; Carl Willey/White Sox Rookies/Bob Friend; and Jimmie Hall/Ernie Broglio/A.L. ERA Leaders on the front with a Mickey Mantle card back on one of the backs. The key Rookie Cards in this set are Richie Allen, Tony Conigliaro, Tommy John, Tony LaRussa, Phil Niekro and Lou Piniella.

COMPLETE SET (587) 2500.00 6000.00
COMMON CARD (1-196) 1.25 3.00
COMMON CARD (197-370) 1.50 4.00
COMMON CARD (371-522) 3.00 8.00
COMMON CARD (523-587) 6.00 15.00
WRAPPER (1-CENT) 50.00 100.00
WRAP (1-CENT, REPEAT) 60.00 120.00
WRAPPER (5-CENT) 12.50 30.00
WRAPPER (5-CENT, COIN) 15.00 40.00
1 Koufax/Ellis/Friend LL 12.50 30.00
2 Peters/Pizarro/Pascual LL 3.00 8.00
3 Koufax/Marichal/Spahn LL 8.00 20.00
4 Ford/Pascual/Bouton LL 3.00 8.00
5 Koufax/Malon/Drysdale LL 6.00 15.00
6 Pascual/Bunning/Stigman LL 3.00 8.00
7 Clemente/Groat/Aaron LL 12.00 30.00
8 Yaz/Kaline/Rollins LL 10.00 25.00
9 Aaron/McCov/Mays/Cep LL 20.00 50.00
10 Killebrew/Stuart/Allison LL 3.00 8.00
11 Aaron/Boyer/White LL 10.00 25.00
12 Stuart/Kaline/Killebrew LL 3.00 8.00
13 Hoyt Wilhelm 8.00 20.00
14 D.Nen RC/N.Willhite RC 1.25 3.00
15 Zoilo Versalles 2.50 6.00
16 John Boozer 1.25 3.00
17 Willie Kirkland 1.25 3.00
18 Billy O'Dell 1.25 3.00
19 Don Wert 1.25 3.00
20 Bob Friend 2.50 6.00
21 Yogi Berra MG 30.00 80.00
22 Jerry Adair 1.25 3.00
23 Chris Zachary RC 1.25 3.00
24 Carl Sawatski 1.25 3.00
25 Bill Monbouquette 1.25 3.00
26 Gino Cimoli 1.25 3.00
27 New York Mets TC 3.00 8.00
28 Claude Osteen 2.50 6.00
29 Lou Brock 30.00 80.00
30 Ron Perranoski 2.50 6.00
31 Dave Nicholson 1.25 3.00
32 Dean Chance 2.50 6.00
33 S.Ellis/M.Queen 2.50 6.00
34 Jim Perry 2.50 6.00
35 Eddie Mathews 20.00 30.00
36 Hal Reniff 1.25 3.00
37 Smoky Burgess 2.50 6.00
38 Jim Wynn RC 12.00 30.00
39 Hank Aguirre 1.25 3.00
40 Dick Groat 2.50 6.00
41 W.McCovey/L.Wagner 3.00 8.00
42 Moe Drabowsky 2.50 6.00
43 Roy Sievers 2.50 6.00
44 Duke Carmel 1.25 3.00
45 Milt Pappas 2.50 6.00
46 Ed Brinkman 1.25 3.00
47 J.Alou RC/R.Herbel 2.50 6.00
48 Bob Perry RC 1.25 3.00
49 Bill Henry 1.25 3.00
50 Mickey Mantle 250.00 600.00
51 Pete Richert 1.25 3.00
52 Chuck Hinton 1.25 3.00
53 Denis Menke 1.25 3.00
54 Sam Mele MG 1.25 3.00
55 Ernie Banks 40.00 100.00
56 Hal Brown 1.25 3.00
57 Tim Harkness 2.50 6.00
58 Don Demeter 2.50 6.00
59 Ernie Broglio 2.50 6.00
60 Frank Malzone 2.50 6.00
61 B.Rodgers/E.Sadowski 2.50 6.00
62 Ted Savage 1.25 3.00
63 John Orsino 1.25 3.00
64 Ted Abernathy 1.25 3.00
65 Felipe Alou 2.50 6.00
66 Eddie Fisher 1.25 3.00
67 Detroit Tigers TC 2.50 6.00
68 Willie Davis 2.50 6.00
69 Clete Boyer 2.50 6.00
70 Joe Torre 3.00 8.00
71 Jack Spring 1.25 3.00
72 Chico Cardenas 2.50 6.00
73 Jimmie Hall RC 3.00 8.00
74 B.Priddy RC/T.Butters 1.25 3.00
75 Wayne Causey 1.25 3.00
76 Checklist 1 4.00 10.00
77 Jerry Walker 1.25 3.00
78 Merritt Ranew 1.25 3.00
79 Bob Heffner RC 1.25 3.00
80 Vada Pinson 3.00 8.00
81 N.Fox/H.Killebrew 5.00 12.00
82 Jim Davenport 2.50 6.00
83 Gus Triandos 2.50 6.00
84 Carl Willey 1.25 3.00
85 Pete Ward 1.25 3.00
86 Al Downing 2.50 6.00
87 St. Louis Cardinals TC 2.50 6.00
88 John Roseboro 2.50 6.00
89 Boog Powell 2.50 6.00
90 Earl Battey 1.25 3.00
91 Bob Bailey 2.50 6.00
92 Steve Ridzik 1.25 3.00
93 Gary Geiger 1.25 3.00
94 J.Britton RC/L.Maxie RC 1.25 3.00
95 George Altman 1.25 3.00
96 Bob Buhl 2.50 6.00
97 Jim Fregosi 2.50 6.00
98 Bill Bruton 1.25 3.00
99 Al Stanek RC 1.25 3.00
100 Elston Howard 2.50 6.00
101 Walt Alston MG 3.00 8.00
102 Checklist 2 4.00 10.00
103 Curt Flood 2.50 6.00
104 Art Mahaffey 2.50 6.00
105 Woody Held 1.25 3.00
106 Joe Nuxhall 2.50 6.00
107 B.Howard RC/F.Kruetzer RC 1.25 3.00
108 John Wyatt 1.25 3.00
109 Rusty Staub 2.50 6.00
110 Albie Pearson 2.50 6.00
111 Don Elston 1.25 3.00
112 Bob Tillman 1.25 3.00
113 Grover Powell RC 2.50 6.00
114 Don Lock 1.25 3.00
115 Frank Bolling 1.25 3.00
116 J.Ward RC/T.Oliva 10.00 25.00
117 Earl Francis 1.25 3.00
118 John Blanchard 2.50 6.00
119 Gary Kolb RC 1.25 3.00
120 Don Drysdale 15.00 40.00
121 Pete Runnels 2.50 6.00
122 Don McMahon 1.25 3.00
123 Jose Pagan 1.25 3.00
124 Orlando Pena 1.25 3.00
125 Pete Rose UER 300.00 800.00
126 Russ Snyder 1.25 3.00
127 A.Gatewood RC/D.Simpson 1.25 3.00
128 Mickey Lolich RC 15.00 40.00
129 Amado Samuel 1.25 3.00
130 Gary Peters 2.50 6.00
131 Steve Boros 1.25 3.00
132 Milwaukee Braves TC 2.50 6.00
133 Jim Grant 2.50 6.00
134 Don Zimmer 2.50 6.00
135 Johnny Callison 2.50 6.00
136 Sandy Koufax WS1 8.00 20.00
137 Willie Davis WS2 3.00 8.00
138 Ron Fairly WS3 3.00 8.00
139 Frank Howard WS4 3.00 8.00
140 Dodgers Celebrate WS 3.00 8.00
141 Danny Murtaugh MG 2.50 6.00
142 John Bateman 1.25 3.00
143 Bubba Phillips 1.25 3.00
144 Al Worthington 1.25 3.00
145 Norm Siebern 1.25 3.00
146 T.John RC/B.Chance RC 25.00 60.00
147 Ray Sadecki 1.25 3.00
148 J.C. Martin 1.25 3.00
149 Paul Foytack 1.25 3.00
150 Willie Mays 60.00 150.00
151 Kansas City Athletics TC 2.50 6.00
152 Denny Lemaster 1.25 3.00
153 Dick Williams 2.50 6.00
154 Dick Tracewski RC 2.50 6.00
155 Duke Snider 15.00 40.00
156 Bill Dailey 1.25 3.00
157 Gene Mauch MG 2.50 6.00
158 Ken Johnson 1.25 3.00
159 Charlie Dees RC 1.25 3.00
160 Ken Boyer 2.50 6.00
161 Dave McNally 2.50 6.00
162 D.Sisler/V.Pinson 2.50 6.00
163 Donn Clendenon 2.50 6.00
164 Bud Daley 1.25 3.00
165 Jerry Lumpe 1.25 3.00
166 Marty Keough 1.25 3.00
167 M.Brumley RC/L.Piniella RC 15.00 40.00
168 Al Weis 1.25 3.00
169 Del Crandall 2.50 6.00
170 Dick Radatz 2.50 6.00
171 Ty Cline 1.25 3.00
172 Cleveland Indians TC 2.50 6.00
173 Ryne Duren 2.50 6.00
174 Doc Edwards 1.25 3.00
175 Billy Williams 10.00 25.00
176 Tracy Stallard 1.25 3.00
177 Harmon Killebrew 12.00 30.00
178 Hank Bauer MG 2.50 6.00
179 Carl Warwick 1.25 3.00
180 Tommy Davis 2.50 6.00
181 Dave Wickersham 1.25 3.00
182 C.Yastrzemski/C.Schilling 6.00 15.00
183 Ron Taylor 1.25 3.00
184 Al Luplow 1.25 3.00
185 Jim O'Toole 2.50 6.00
186 Roman Mejias 1.25 3.00
187 Ed Roebuck 1.25 3.00
188 Checklist 3 4.00 10.00
189 Bob Hendley 1.25 3.00
190 Bobby Richardson 3.00 8.00
191 Clay Dalrymple 1.25 3.00
192 J.Boccabella RC/B.Cowan RC 2.50 6.00
193 Jerry Lynch 1.25 3.00
194 John Goryl 1.25 3.00
195 Floyd Robinson 1.25 3.00
196 Jim Gentile 1.25 3.00
197 Frank Lary 2.50 6.00
198 Len Gabrielson 1.50 4.00
199 Joe Azcue 1.50 4.00
200 Sandy Koufax 40.00 100.00
201 S.Bowens RC/W.Bunker RC 2.50 6.00
202 Galen Cisco 2.50 6.00
203 John Kennedy RC 2.50 6.00
204 Matty Alou 2.50 6.00
205 Nellie Fox 5.00 12.00
206 Steve Hamilton 2.50 6.00
207 Fred Hutchinson MG 2.50 6.00
208 Wes Covington 2.50 6.00
209 Bob Allen 1.50 4.00
210 Carl Yastrzemski 20.00 50.00
211 Jim Coker 1.50 4.00
212 Pete Lovrich 1.50 4.00
213 Los Angeles Angels TC 2.50 6.00
214 Ken McMullen 2.50 6.00
215 Ray Herbert 1.50 4.00
216 Mike de la Hoz 1.50 4.00
217 Jim King 1.50 4.00
218 Hank Fischer 1.50 4.00
219 A.Downing/J.Bouton 2.50 6.00
220 Dick Ellsworth 2.50 6.00
221 Bob Saverine 1.50 4.00
222 Billy Pierce 2.50 6.00
223 George Banks 1.50 4.00
224 Tommie Sisk 1.50 4.00
225 Roger Maris 40.00 100.00
226 J.Grote RC/L.Yellen RC 2.50 6.00
227 Barry Latman 1.50 4.00
228 Felix Mantilla 1.50 4.00
229 Charley Lau 2.50 6.00
230 Brooks Robinson 15.00 40.00
231 Dick Calmus RC 1.50 4.00
232 Al Lopez MG 3.00 8.00
233 Hal Smith 1.50 4.00
234 Gary Bell 1.50 4.00
235 Ron Hunt 1.50 4.00
236 Bill Faul 1.50 4.00
237 Chicago Cubs TC 2.50 6.00
238 Roy McMillan 2.50 6.00
239 Herm Starrette RC 1.50 4.00
240 Bill White 2.50 6.00
241 Jim Owens 1.50 4.00
242 Harvey Kuenn 2.50 6.00
243 R.Allen RC/J.Hernstein 12.50 30.00
244 Tony LaRussa RC 15.00 40.00
245 Dick Stigman 1.50 4.00
246 Manny Mota 2.50 6.00
247 Dave DeBusschere 2.50 6.00
248 Johnny Pesky MG 2.50 6.00
249 Doug Camilli 1.50 4.00
250 Al Kaline 15.00 40.00
251 Choo Choo Coleman 2.50 6.00
252 Ken Aspromonte 1.50 4.00
253 Wally Post 2.50 6.00
254 Don Hoak 2.50 6.00
255 Lee Thomas 2.50 6.00
256 Johnny Weekly 1.50 4.00
257 San Francisco Giants TC 2.50 6.00
258 Garry Roggenburk 1.50 4.00
259 Harry Bright 1.50 4.00
260 Frank Robinson 25.00 60.00
261 Jim Hannan 1.50 4.00
262 M.Shannon RC/H.Fanok 3.00 8.00
263 Chuck Estrada 1.50 4.00
264 Jim Landis 1.50 4.00
265 Jim Bunning 5.00 12.00
266 Gene Freese 1.50 4.00
267 Wilbur Wood RC 2.50 6.00
268 D.Murtaugh/B.Virdon 2.50 6.00
269 Ellis Burton 1.50 4.00
270 Rich Rollins 2.50 6.00
271 Bob Sadowski RC 1.50 4.00
272 Jake Wood 1.50 4.00
273 Mel Nelson 1.50 4.00
274 Checklist 4 4.00 10.00
275 John Tsitouris 1.50 4.00
276 Jose Tartabull 2.50 6.00
277 Ken Retzer 1.50 4.00
278 Bobby Shantz 2.50 6.00
279 Joe Koppe 1.50 4.00
280 Juan Marichal 12.00 30.00
281 J.Gibbs/T.Metcalf RC 2.50 6.00
282 Bob Bruce 1.50 4.00
283 Tom McCraw RC 1.50 4.00
284 Dick Schofield 1.50 4.00
285 Robin Roberts 6.00 15.00
286 Don Landrum 1.50 4.00
287 T.Conig.RC/B.Spans.RC 25.00 60.00
288 Al Moran 1.50 4.00
289 Frank Funk 1.50 4.00
290 Bob Allison 2.50 6.00
291 Phil Ortega 1.50 4.00
292 Mike Roarke 1.50 4.00
293 Philadelphia Phillies TC 2.50 6.00
294 Ken L. Hunt 1.50 4.00
295 Roger Craig 2.50 6.00
296 Ed Kirkpatrick 1.50 4.00
297 Ken MacKenzie 2.50 6.00
298 Harry Craft MG 1.50 4.00
299 Bill Stafford 1.50 4.00
300 Hank Aaron 60.00 150.00
301 Larry Brown RC 1.50 4.00
302 Dan Pfister 1.50 4.00
303 Jim Campbell 1.50 4.00
304 Bob Johnson 1.50 4.00
305 Jack Lamabe 1.50 4.00
306 Willie Mays/O.Cepeda 15.00 40.00
307 Joe Gibbon 1.50 4.00
308 Gene Stephens 1.50 4.00
309 Paul Toth 1.50 4.00
310 Jim Gilliam 2.50 6.00
311 Tom W. Brown RC 2.50 6.00
312 F.Fisher RC/F.Gladding RC 1.50 4.00
313 Chuck Hiller 1.50 4.00
314 Jerry Buchek 1.50 4.00
315 Bo Belinsky 2.50 6.00
316 Gene Oliver 1.50 4.00
317 Al Smith 1.50 4.00
318 Minnesota Twins TC 2.50 6.00
319 Paul Brown 1.50 4.00
320 Rocky Colavito 5.00 12.00
321 Bob Lillis 1.50 4.00
322 George Brunet 1.50 4.00
323 John Buzhardt 1.50 4.00
324 Casey Stengel MG 6.00 15.00
325 Hector Lopez 2.50 6.00
326 Ron Brand RC 1.50 4.00
327 Don Blasingame 1.50 4.00
328 Bob Shaw 1.50 4.00
329 Russ Nixon 1.50 4.00
330 Tommy Harper 2.50 6.00
331 Maris/Cash/Mantle/Kaline 60.00 150.00
332 Ray Washburn 1.50 4.00
333 Billy Moran 1.50 4.00
334 Lew Krausse 1.50 4.00
335 Don Mossi 2.50 6.00
336 Andre Rodgers 1.50 4.00
337 A.Ferrara RC/J.Torborg RC 2.50 6.00
338 Jack Kralick 1.50 4.00
339 Walt Bond 1.50 4.00
340 Joe Cunningham 1.50 4.00
341 Jim Roland 1.50 4.00
342 Willie Stargell 30.00 80.00
343 Washington Senators TC 2.50 6.00
344 Phil Linz 2.50 6.00
345 Frank Thomas 3.00 8.00
346 Joey Jay 1.50 4.00
347 Bobby Wine 2.50 6.00
348 Ed Lopat MG 2.50 6.00
349 Art Fowler 1.50 4.00
350 Willie McCovey 12.00 30.00
351 Dan Schneider 1.50 4.00
352 Eddie Bressoud 1.50 4.00
353 Wally Moon 2.50 6.00
354 Dave Giusti 1.50 4.00
355 Vic Power 2.50 6.00
356 B.McCool RC/C.Ruiz 2.50 6.00
357 Charley James 1.50 4.00
358 Ron Kline 1.50 4.00
359 Jim Schaffer 1.50 4.00
360 Joe Pepitone 5.00 12.00
361 Jay Hook 1.50 4.00
362 Checklist 5 4.00 10.00
363 Dick McAuliffe 2.50 6.00
364 Joe Gaines 1.50 4.00
365 Cal McLish 2.50 6.00
366 Nelson Mathews 1.50 4.00
367 Fred Whitfield 1.50 4.00
368 F.Ackley RC/D.Buford RC 2.50 6.00
369 Jerry Zimmerman 1.50 4.00
370 Hal Woodeshick 1.50 4.00
371 Frank Howard 3.00 8.00
372 Howie Koplitz 3.00 8.00
373 Pittsburgh Pirates TC 5.00 12.00
374 Bobby Bolin 3.00 8.00
375 Ron Santo 4.00 10.00
376 Dave Morehead 3.00 8.00
377 Bob Skinner 3.00 8.00
378 W.Woodward RC/J.Smith 4.00 10.00
379 Tony Gonzalez 3.00 8.00
380 Whitey Ford 15.00 40.00
381 Bob Taylor 3.00 8.00
382 Wes Stock 3.00 8.00
383 Bill Rigney MG 3.00 8.00
384 Ron Hansen 3.00 8.00
385 Curt Simmons 4.00 10.00
386 Lenny Green 3.00 8.00
387 Terry Fox 3.00 8.00
388 J.O'Donoghue RC/G.Williams 4.00 10.00
389 Jim Umbricht 4.00 10.00
390 Orlando Cepeda 10.00 25.00
391 Sam McDowell 4.00 10.00
392 Jim Pagliaroni 3.00 8.00
393 C.Stengel/E.Kranepool 6.00 15.00
394 Bob Miller 3.00 8.00
395 Tom Tresh 4.00 10.00
396 Dennis Bennett 3.00 8.00
397 Chuck Cottier 3.00 8.00
398 B.Haas/D.Smith 4.00 10.00
399 Jackie Brandt 3.00 8.00
400 Warren Spahn 15.00 40.00
401 Charlie Maxwell 3.00 8.00
402 Tom Sturdivant 3.00 8.00
403 Cincinnati Reds TC 5.00 12.00
404 Tony Martinez 3.00 8.00
405 Ken McBride 3.00 8.00
406 Al Spangler 3.00 8.00
407 Bill Freehan 4.00 10.00
408 J.Stewart RC/F.Burdette RC 3.00 8.00
409 Bill Fischer 3.00 8.00
410 Dick Stuart 4.00 10.00
411 Lee Walls 3.00 8.00
412 Ray Culp 4.00 10.00
413 Johnny Keane MG 3.00 8.00
414 Jack Sanford 3.00 8.00
415 Tony Kubek 10.00 25.00
416 Lee Maye 3.00 8.00
417 Don Cardwell 3.00 8.00
418 D.Knowles RC/B.Narum RC 4.00 10.00
419 Ken Harrelson RC 6.00 15.00
420 Jim Maloney 4.00 10.00
421 Camilo Carreon 3.00 8.00
422 Jack Fisher 3.00 8.00
423 H.Aaron/W.Mays 40.00 100.00
424 Dick Bertell 3.00 8.00
425 Norm Cash 4.00 10.00
426 Bob Rodgers 3.00 8.00
427 Don Rudolph 3.00 8.00
428 A.Skeen RC/P.Smith RC 3.00 8.00
429 Tim McCarver 4.00 10.00
430 Juan Pizarro 3.00 8.00
431 George Alusik 3.00 8.00
432 Ruben Amaro 4.00 10.00
433 New York Yankees TC 15.00 40.00
434 Don Nottebart 3.00 8.00
435 Vic Davalillo 3.00 8.00
436 Charlie Neal 4.00 10.00
437 Ed Bailey 3.00 8.00
438 Checklist 6 6.00 15.00
439 Harvey Haddix 4.00 10.00
440 Roberto Clemente UER 125.00 300.00
441 Bob Duliba 3.00 8.00
442 Pumpsie Green 4.00 10.00
443 Chuck Dressen MG 4.00 10.00
444 Larry Jackson 3.00 8.00
445 Bill Skowron 4.00 10.00
446 Julian Javier 6.00 15.00
447 Ted Bowsfield 3.00 8.00
448 Cookie Rojas 4.00 10.00
449 Deron Johnson 4.00 10.00
450 Steve Barber 3.00 8.00
451 Joe Amalfitano 3.00 8.00
452 G.Garrido RC/J.Hart RC 4.00 10.00
453 Frank Baumann 3.00 8.00
454 Tommie Aaron 4.00 10.00
455 Bernie Allen 3.00 8.00
456 W.Parker RC/J.Werhas RC 4.00 10.00
457 Jesse Gonder 3.00 8.00
458 Ralph Terry 4.00 10.00
459 P.Charton RC/D.Jones RC 3.00 8.00
460 Bob Gibson 30.00 80.00
461 George Thomas 3.00 8.00
462 Birdie Tebbetts MG 3.00 8.00
463 Don Leppert 3.00 8.00
464 Dallas Green 6.00 15.00
465 Mike Hershberger 3.00 8.00
466 D.Green RC/A.Monteagudo RC 4.00 10.00
467 Bob Aspromonte 3.00 8.00
468 Gaylord Perry 15.00 40.00
469 F.Norman RC/S.Slaughter RC 4.00 10.00
470 Jim Bouton 5.00 12.00
471 Gates Brown RC 4.00 10.00
472 Vern Law 4.00 10.00
473 Baltimore Orioles TC 5.00 12.00
474 Larry Sherry 4.00 10.00
475 Ed Charles 3.00 8.00
476 R.Carty RC/D.Kelley RC 6.00 15.00
477 Mike Joyce 3.00 8.00
478 Dick Howser 4.00 10.00
479 D.Bakenhaster RC/J.Lewis RC 3.00 8.00
480 Bob Purkey 3.00 8.00
481 Chuck Schilling 3.00 8.00
482 J.Briggs RC/D.Cater RC 4.00 10.00
483 Fred Valentine RC 3.00 8.00
484 Bill Pleis 3.00 8.00
485 Tom Haller 3.00 8.00
486 Bob Kennedy MG 3.00 8.00
487 Mike McCormick 3.00 8.00
488 P.Mikkelsen RC/B.Meyer RC 6.00 15.00
489 Julio Navarro 3.00 8.00
490 Ron Fairly 4.00 10.00
491 Ed Rakow 3.00 8.00
492 J.Beauchamp RC/M.White RC 3.00 8.00
493 Don Lee 3.00 8.00
494 Al Jackson 3.00 8.00
495 Bill Virdon 4.00 10.00
496 Chicago White Sox TC 5.00 12.00
497 Jeoff Long RC 3.00 8.00
498 Dave Stenhouse 3.00 8.00
499 C.Slamon RC/G.Seyfried RC 3.00 8.00
500 Camilo Pascual 4.00 10.00
501 Bob Veale 4.00 10.00
502 B.Knoop RC/B.Lee RC 3.00 8.00
503 Earl Wilson 3.00 8.00
504 Claude Raymond 3.00 8.00
505 Stan Williams 3.00 8.00
506 Bobby Bragan MG 3.00 8.00
507 Johnny Edwards 3.00 8.00
508 Diego Segui 3.00 8.00
509 G.Alley RC/O.McFarlane RC 4.00 10.00
510 Lindy McDaniel 4.00 10.00
511 Lou Jackson 4.00 10.00
512 W.Horton RC/J.Sparma RC 6.00 15.00
513 Don Larsen 4.00 10.00
514 Jim Hickman 4.00 10.00
515 Johnny Romano 3.00 8.00
516 J.Arrigo RC/D.Siebler RC 3.00 8.00
517A Checklist 7 ERR 10.00 25.00
517B Checklist 7 COR 6.00 15.00
518 Carl Bouldin 3.00 8.00
519 Charlie Smith 3.00 8.00
520 Jack Baldschun 4.00 10.00
521 Tom Satriano 3.00 8.00
522 Bob Tiefenauer 3.00 8.00
523 Lou Burdette UER 8.00 20.00
524 J.Dickson RC/B.Klaus RC 6.00 15.00
525 Al McBean 6.00 15.00
526 Lou Clinton 6.00 15.00
527 Larry Bearnarth 6.00 15.00
528 D.Duncan RC/T.Reynolds RC 8.00 20.00
529 Alvin Dark MG 8.00 20.00
530 Leon Wagner 6.00 15.00
531 Los Angeles Dodgers TC 10.00 25.00
532 B.Bloomfield RC/J.Nossek RC 6.00 15.00
533 Johnny Klippstein 6.00 15.00
534 Gus Bell 6.00 15.00
535 Phil Regan 6.00 15.00
536 L.Elliot/J.Stephenson RC 6.00 15.00
537 Dan Osinski 6.00 15.00
538 Minnie Minoso 8.00 20.00
539 Roy Face 8.00 20.00
540 Luis Aparicio 15.00 40.00
541 P.Roof/P.Niekro RC 75.00 200.00
542 Don Mincher 6.00 15.00
543 Bob Uecker 20.00 50.00
544 S.Hertz RC/J.Hoerner RC 6.00 15.00
545 Max Alvis 6.00 15.00
546 Joe Christopher 6.00 15.00
547 Gil Hodges MG 6.00 15.00
548 W.Schurr RC/P.Speckenbach RC 8.00 20.00
549 Joe Moeller 6.00 15.00
550 Ken Hubbs MEM 15.00 40.00
551 Billy Hoeft 6.00 15.00
552 T.Kelley RC/S.Siebert RC 6.00 15.00
553 Jim Brewer 6.00 15.00
554 Hank Foiles 6.00 15.00
555 Lee Stange 6.00 15.00
556 S.Dillon RC/R.Locke RC 6.00 15.00
557 Leo Burke 6.00 15.00
558 Don Schwall 6.00 15.00
559 Dick Phillips 6.00 15.00
560 Dick Farrell 6.00 15.00
561 D.Bennett RC/R.Wise RC 8.00 20.00
562 Pedro Ramos 6.00 15.00
563 Dal Maxvill 8.00 20.00
564 J.McCabe RC/J.McNertney RC 8.00 20.00
565 Stu Miller 6.00 15.00
566 Ed Kranepool 8.00 20.00
567 Jim Kaat 8.00 20.00
568 P.Gagliano RC/C.Peterson RC 6.00 15.00
569 Fred Newman 6.00 15.00
570 Bill Mazeroski 20.00 50.00
571 Gene Conley 6.00 15.00
572 D.Gray RC/D.Egan 6.00 15.00
573 Jim Duffalo 6.00 15.00
574 Manny Jimenez 6.00 15.00
575 Tony Cloninger 6.00 15.00
576 J.Hinsley RC/B.Wakefield RC 6.00 15.00
577 Gordy Coleman 6.00 15.00
578 Glen Hobbie 6.00 15.00
579 Boston Red Sox TC 10.00 25.00
580 Johnny Podres 8.00 20.00
581 P.Gonzalez/A.Moore RC 8.00 20.00
582 Rod Kanehl 8.00 20.00
583 Tito Francona 6.00 15.00
584 Joel Horlen 6.00 15.00
585 Tony Taylor 8.00 20.00
586 Jimmy Piersall 8.00 20.00
587 Bennie Daniels 8.00 20.00

1964 Topps Coins

COMPLETE SET (167) 500.00 1000.00
1 Don Zimmer 2.50 6.00
2 Jim Wynn 2.00 5.00
3 Johnny Orsino 1.50 4.00
4 Jim Bouton 2.00 5.00
5 Dick Groat 2.00 5.00
6 Leon Wagner 1.50 4.00
7 Frank Malzone 1.50 4.00
8 Steve Barber 1.50 4.00
9 Johnny Romano 1.50 4.00
10 Tom Tresh 2.50 6.00
11 Felipe Alou 2.00 5.00
12 Dick Stuart 2.00 5.00
13 Claude Osteen 1.50 4.00
14 Juan Pizarro 1.50 4.00
15 Donn Clendenon 1.50 4.00
16 Jimmie Hall 1.50 4.00
17 Al Jackson 1.50 4.00
18 Brooks Robinson 10.00 25.00
19 Bob Allison 2.00 5.00
20 Ed Roebuck 1.50 4.00
21 Pete Ward 1.50 4.00
22 Willie McCovey 4.00 10.00
23 Elston Howard 4.00 10.00
24 Diego Segui 1.50 4.00
25 Ken Boyer 2.50 6.00
26 Carl Yastrzemski 10.00 25.00
27 Bill Mazeroski 4.00 10.00
28 Jerry Lumpe 1.50 4.00
29 Woody Held 1.50 4.00
30 Dick Radatz 1.50 4.00
31 Luis Aparicio 2.50 6.00
32 Dave Nicholson 1.50 4.00
33 Eddie Mathews 10.00 25.00
34 Don Drysdale 8.00 20.00
35 Ray Culp 1.50 4.00
36 Juan Marichal 4.00 10.00
37 Frank Robinson 10.00 25.00
38 Chuck Hinton 1.50 4.00
39 Floyd Robinson 1.50 4.00
40 Tommy Harper 2.00 5.00
41 Ron Hansen 1.50 4.00
42 Ernie Banks 10.00 25.00
43 Jesse Gonder 1.50 4.00
44 Billy Williams 2.50 6.00
45 Vada Pinson 2.00 5.00
46 Rocky Colavito 5.00 12.00
47 Bill Monbouquette 1.50 4.00
48 Max Alvis 1.50 4.00
49 Norm Siebern 1.50 4.00
50 Johnny Callison 2.00 5.00
51 Rich Rollins 1.50 4.00
52 Ken McBride 1.50 4.00
53 Don Lock 1.50 4.00
54 Ron Fairly 1.50 4.00
55 Roberto Clemente 40.00 80.00
56 Dick Ellsworth 1.50 4.00
57 Tommy Davis 2.00 5.00
58 Tony Gonzalez 1.50 4.00
59 Bob Gibson 8.00 20.00
60 Jim Maloney 2.00 5.00
61 Frank Howard 2.00 5.00
62 Jim Pagliaroni 1.50 4.00
63 Orlando Cepeda 2.50 6.00
64 Ron Perranoski 1.50 4.00
65 Curt Flood 2.50 6.00
66 Alvin McBean 1.50 4.00
67 Dean Chance 1.50 4.00
68 Ron Santo 2.50 6.00
69 Jack Baldschun 1.50 4.00
70 Milt Pappas 2.00 5.00
71 Gary Peters 1.50 4.00
72 Bobby Richardson 2.50 6.00
73 Lee Thomas 1.50 4.00
74 Hank Aguirre 1.50 4.00
75 Carlton Willey 1.50 4.00
76 Camilo Pascual 2.00 5.00
77 Bob Friend 2.00 5.00
78 Bill White 2.00 5.00
79 Norm Cash 2.50 6.00
80 Willie Mays 30.00 60.00
81 Leon Carmel 1.50 4.00
82 Pete Rose 40.00 80.00
83 Hank Aaron 15.00 40.00
84 Bob Aspromonte 1.50 4.00
85 Jim O'Toole 1.50 4.00
86 Vic Davalillo 2.00 5.00
87 Bill Freehan 2.00 5.00
88 Warren Spahn 4.00 10.00
89 Ken Hunt 1.50 4.00
90 Denis Menke 1.50 4.00
91 Dick Farrell 1.50 4.00
92 Jim Hickman 2.00 5.00
93 Jim Bunning 2.50 6.00
94 Bob Hendley 1.50 4.00
95 Ernie Broglio 1.50 4.00
96 Rusty Staub 2.00 5.00
97 Lou Brock 4.00 10.00
98 Jim Fregosi 2.00 5.00
99 Jim Grant 1.50 4.00
100 Al Kaline 8.00 20.00
101 Earl Battey 2.00 5.00
102 Wayne Causey 1.50 4.00
103 Chuck Schilling 1.50 4.00
104 Boog Powell 2.50 6.00
105 Dave Wickersham 1.50 4.00
106 Sandy Koufax 10.00 25.00
107 John Bateman 2.00 5.00
108 Ed Brinkman 1.50 4.00
109 Al Downing 1.50 4.00
110 Joe Azcue 1.50 4.00
111 Albie Pearson 1.50 4.00
112 Harmon Killebrew 8.00 20.00
113 Tony Taylor 2.00 5.00
114 Larry Jackson 1.50 4.00
115 Billy O'Dell 2.00 5.00
116 Don Demeter 1.50 4.00
117 Ed Charles 1.50 4.00
118 Joe Torre 4.00 10.00
119 Don Nottebart 1.50 4.00

120 Mickey Mantle 50.00 100.00
121 Joe Pepitone AS 2.00 5.00
122 Dick Stuart AS 2.00 5.00
123 Bobby Richardson AS 2.50 6.00
124 Jerry Lumpe AS 1.50 4.00
125 Brooks Robinson AS 8.00 20.00
126 Frank Malzone AS 1.50 4.00
127 Luis Aparicio AS 2.50 6.00
128 Jim Fregosi AS 2.00 5.00
129 Al Kaline AS 6.00 15.00
130 Leon Wagner AS 1.50 4.00
131A Mickey Mantle AS Bat R 20.00 50.00
131B Mickey Mantle AS Bat L 20.00 50.00
132 Albie Pearson AS 1.50 4.00
133 Harmon Killebrew AS 6.00 15.00
134 Carl Yastrzemski AS 10.00 25.00
135 Elston Howard AS 2.50 6.00
136 Earl Battey AS 1.50 4.00
137 Camilo Pascual AS 1.50 4.00
138 Jim Bouton AS 2.00 5.00
139 Whitey Ford AS 8.00 20.00
140 Gary Peters AS 1.50 4.00
141 Bill White AS 2.00 5.00
142 Orlando Cepeda AS 2.50 6.00
143 Bill Mazeroski AS 4.00 10.00
144 Tony Taylor AS 1.50 4.00
145 Ken Boyer AS 2.50 6.00
146 Ron Santo AS 2.50 6.00
147 Dick Groat AS 2.00 5.00
148 Roy McMillan AS 1.50 4.00
149 Hank Aaron AS 10.00 25.00
150 Roberto Clemente AS 12.50 30.00
151 Willie Mays AS 12.50 30.00
152 Vada Pinson AS 2.00 5.00
153 Tommy Davis AS 2.00 5.00
154 Frank Robinson AS 8.00 20.00
155 Joe Torre AS 4.00 10.00
156 Tim McCarver AS 2.00 5.00
157 Juan Marichal AS 4.00 10.00
158 Jim Maloney AS 2.00 5.00
159 Sandy Koufax AS 10.00 25.00
160 Warren Spahn AS 4.00 10.00
161A Wayne Causey AS NL 6.00 15.00
161B Wayne Causey AS/American League 2.00 5.00
162A Chuck Hinton AS NL 8.00 20.00
162B Chuck Hinton AS/American League 2.00 5.00
163 Bob Aspromonte AS 1.50 4.00
164 Ron Hunt AS 1.50 4.00

1964 Topps Giants

The cards in this 60-card set measure approximately 3 1/8" by 5 1/4". The 1964 Topps Giants are postcard size cards containing color player photographs. They are numbered on the backs, which also contain biographical information presented in a newspaper format. These "giant size" cards were distributed in both cellophane and waxed gum packs apart from the Topps regular issue of 1964. The gum packs contain three cards. The Cards 3, 28, 42, 45, 47, 51 and 60 are more difficult to find and are indicated by SP in the checklist below.

COMPLETE SET (60) 250.00 600.00
COMMON CARD (1-60) .60 1.50
COMMON SP'S 4.00 10.00
WRAPPER (5-CENT) 15.00 40.00
1 Gary Peters .75 2.00
2 Ken Johnson .60 1.50
3 Sandy Koufax SP 60.00 150.00
4 Bob Bailey .60 1.50
5 Milt Pappas .75 2.00
6 Ron Hunt .60 1.50
7 Whitey Ford 12.00 30.00
8 Roy McMillan .60 1.50
9 Rocky Colavito 2.00 5.00
10 Jim Bunning 1.25 3.00
11 Roberto Clemente 25.00 60.00
12 Al Kaline 8.00 20.00
13 Nellie Fox 5.00 12.00
14 Tony Gonzalez .60 1.50
15 Jim Gentile .75 2.00
16 Dean Chance .75 2.00
17 Dick Ellsworth .75 2.00
18 Jim Fregosi .75 2.00
19 Dick Groat .75 2.00
20 Chuck Hinton .60 1.50
21 Elston Howard .75 2.00
22 Dick Farrell .60 1.50
23 Albie Pearson .60 1.50
24 Frank Howard .75 2.00
25 Mickey Mantle 60.00 150.00
26 Joe Torre 2.00 5.00
27 Eddie Brinkman .60 1.50
28 Bob Friend SP 8.00 20.00
29 Frank Robinson 10.00 25.00
30 Bill Freehan .75 2.00
31 Warren Spahn 6.00 15.00
32 Camilo Pascual .75 2.00
33 Pete Ward .60 1.50
34 Jim Maloney .75 2.00
35 Dave Wickersham .60 1.50
36 Johnny Callison .75 2.00
37 Juan Marichal 1.25 3.00
38 Harmon Killebrew 6.00 15.00
39 Luis Aparicio 1.25 3.00
40 Dick Radatz .60 1.50
41 Bob Gibson 12.00 30.00
42 Dick Stuart SP 5.00 12.00
43 Tommy Davis .75 2.00
44 Tony Oliva 1.25 3.00
45 Wayne Causey SP 6.00 15.00
46 Max Alvis .60 1.50
47 Galen Cisco SP 10.00 25.00
48 Carl Yastrzemski 8.00 20.00
49 Hank Aaron 40.00 100.00
50 Brooks Robinson 8.00 20.00
51 Willie Mays SP 60.00 120.00
52 Billy Williams 1.25 3.00
53 Juan Pizarro .60 1.50
54 Leon Wagner .60 1.50
55 Orlando Cepeda 1.25 3.00
56 Vada Pinson .75 2.00
57 Ken Boyer 1.25 3.00
58 Ron Santo 1.25 3.00
59 John Romano .60 1.50
60 Bill Skowron SP 12.00 30.00

1964 Topps Rookie All-Star Banquet

This 35-card set was actually the dinner program for the 1964 annual Topps Rookie All-Star Banquet and was housed in its own special presentation box. The first seven cards featured black and white photos of sport and media people and measured approximately 3" by 5 1/4". Cards 8-13 depicted the previous years' Rookie All-Star Teams each with black-and-white head shots of 10 players of that year on a light blue background. Cards 14-34A each displayed 3" by 3 1/4" black-and-white photos of one of the 1964 rookies being honored at the banquet or a photo of the PR Director for the team with a write-up of that team's rookie player.

COMPLETE SET (35) 600.00 1200.00
1 Title Card 8.00 20.00
2 T. David 40.00 80.00
J. Torborg
Santo
Williams
3 Aparicio 40.00 80.00
Bowens
Tresh
Gonzalez
Bruce
Bond
Wh
4 H. Greenberg HOF 40.00 80.00
F. Frisch HOF
T. Cohane
D. Gro
5 J. Robinson HOF 75.00 150.00
J. McDermott
J. McKenney AL DIR#
6 Sy Berger 40.00 100.00
G. MacDonald
H. Feimister
T. Wright
7 Joe Garagiola TRIB 30.00 60.00
8 1959 Rookie All-Star Team 50.00 100.00
McCovey
Green
Koppe/
9 1960 Rookie All-Star Team 40.00 80.00
Gentile
Javier
Hansen
10 1961 Rookie All-Star Team 50.00 100.00
Martin
Wood
Howser
S
11 1962 Rookie All-Star Team 20.00 50.00
Whitfield
Allen
Tresh
12 1963 Rookie All-Star Team 250.00 500.00
Rose
Staub
Weis
Ward
13 64 Rookie AS Title Card 15.00 40.00
14 Ed Uhas DIR 15.00 40.00
15 Bob Chance 40.00 80.00
16 Garry Schumacher DIR 15.00 40.00
17 Hal Lanier 20.00 50.00
18 Larry Shenk DIR 15.00 40.00
19 Richie Allen 100.00 200.00
20 Jim Schaaf DIR 15.00 40.00
21 Bert Campaneris 60.00 120.00
22 Ernie Johnson DIR 15.00 40.00
23 Rico Carty 60.00 120.00
24 Bill Crowley DIR 15.00 40.00
25 Tony Conigliaro 100.00 200.00
26 Tom Mee DIR 15.00 40.00
27 Tony Oliva 125.00 250.00
28 Burt Hawkins DIR 15.00 40.00
29 Mike Brumley 40.00 80.00
30 Hank Zureick DIR 15.00 40.00
31 Billy McCool 40.00 80.00
32 Rob Brown DIR 15.00 40.00
33 Wally Bunker 40.00 80.00
34 Minor League POY Title Card 15.00 40.00
34A Luis Tiant 60.00 120.00

1964 Topps Stand-Up

In 1964 Topps produced a die-cut "Stand-Up" card design for the first time since their Connie Mack and Current All Stars of 1951. These cards were issued in both one cent and five cent packs. The cards have full-length, color player photos set against a green and yellow background. Of the 77 cards in the set, 22 were single printed and these are marked in the checklist below with an SP. These unnumbered cards are standard-size (2 1/2" by 3 1/2"), blank backed, and have been numbered here for reference in alphabetical order of players. Interestingly there were four different wrapper designs used for this set. All the design variations are valued at the same price.

COMPLETE SET (77) 2500.00 4000.00
COMMON CARD (1-77) 4.00 10.00
COMMON CARD SP 15.00 40.00
WRAPPER (1-CENT) 75.00 150.00
WRAPPER (5-CENT) 175.00 350.00
1 Hank Aaron 75.00 200.00
2 Hank Aguirre 5.00 12.00
3 George Altman 8.00 20.00
4 Max Alvis 5.00 12.00
5 Bob Aspromonte 5.00 12.00
6 Jack Baldschun SP 20.00 50.00
7 Ernie Banks 50.00 100.00
8 Steve Barber 5.00 12.00
9 Earl Battey 5.00 12.00
10 Ken Boyer 10.00 25.00
11 Ernie Broglio 5.00 12.00
12 John Callison 5.00 12.00
13 Norm Cash SP 40.00 80.00
14 Wayne Causey 5.00 12.00
15 Orlando Cepeda 10.00 25.00
16 Ed Charles 8.00 20.00
17 Roberto Clemente 125.00 250.00
18 Donn Clendenon SP 20.00 50.00
19 Rocky Colavito 15.00 40.00
20 Ray Culp SP 30.00 60.00
21 Tommy Davis 8.00 20.00
22 Don Drysdale SP 75.00 150.00
23 Dick Ellsworth 5.00 12.00
24 Dick Farrell 5.00 12.00
25 Jim Fregosi 8.00 20.00
26 Bob Friend 5.00 12.00
27 Jim Gentile 8.00 20.00
28 Jesse Gonder SP 20.00 50.00
29 Tony Gonzalez SP 20.00 50.00
30 Dick Groat 10.00 25.00
31 Woody Held 5.00 12.00
32 Chuck Hinton 5.00 12.00
33 Elston Howard 10.00 25.00
34 Frank Howard SP 40.00 80.00
35 Ron Hunt 8.00 20.00
36 Al Jackson 5.00 12.00
37 Ken Johnson 5.00 12.00
38 Al Kaline 50.00 100.00
39 Harmon Killebrew 50.00 100.00
40 Sandy Koufax 100.00 200.00
41 Don Lock SP 20.00 50.00
42 Jerry Lumpe SP 20.00 50.00
43 Jim Maloney 8.00 20.00
44 Frank Malzone 5.00 12.00
45 Mickey Mantle 300.00 600.00
46 Juan Marichal SP 60.00 120.00
47 Eddie Mathews SP 75.00 150.00
48 Willie Mays 100.00 250.00
49 Bill Mazeroski 15.00 40.00
50 Ken McBride 5.00 12.00
51 Willie McCovey SP 60.00 120.00
52 Claude Osteen 8.00 20.00
53 Jim O'Toole 5.00 12.00
54 Camilo Pascual 8.00 20.00
55 Albie Pearson SP 30.00 60.00
56 Gary Peters 5.00 12.00
57 Vada Pinson 8.00 20.00
58 Juan Pizarro 5.00 12.00
59 Boog Powell 10.00 25.00
60 Bobby Richardson 10.00 25.00
61 Brooks Robinson 50.00 100.00
62 Floyd Robinson 5.00 12.00
63 Frank Robinson 50.00 100.00
64 Ed Roebuck SP 20.00 50.00
65 Rich Rollins 5.00 12.00
66 John Romano 5.00 12.00
67 Ron Santo SP 40.00 80.00
68 Norm Siebern 5.00 12.00
69 Warren Spahn SP 75.00 150.00
70 Dick Stuart SP 30.00 60.00
71 Lee Thomas 5.00 12.00
72 Joe Torre 10.00 25.00
73 Pete Ward 5.00 12.00
74 Bill White SP 30.00 60.00
75 Billy Williams SP 60.00 120.00
76 Hal Woodeshick SP 20.00 50.00
77 Carl Yastrzemski SP 250.00 500.00

1964 Topps Tattoos Inserts

COMPLETE SET (75) 600.00 1200.00
COMMON TATOO (1-20) 1.50 4.00
COMMON TATOO (21-75) 3.00 8.00
8 Detroit Tigers 2.00 5.00
11 Los Angeles Dodgers 5.00 12.00
14 New York Mets 2.00 5.00
15 New York Yankees 5.00 12.00
21 Hank Aaron 60.00 120.00
22 Max Alvis 3.00 8.00
23 Hank Aguirre 3.00 8.00
24 Ernie Banks 30.00 60.00
25 Steve Barber 3.00 8.00
26 Ken Boyer 5.00 12.00
27 John Callison 3.00 8.00
28 Norm Cash 4.00 10.00
29 Wayne Causey 3.00 8.00
30 Orlando Cepeda 8.00 20.00
31 Rocky Colavito 8.00 20.00
32 Ray Culp 3.00 8.00
33 Vic Davalillo 3.00 8.00
34 Moe Drabowsky 3.00 8.00
35 Dick Ellsworth 3.00 8.00
36 Curt Flood 5.00 12.00
37 Bill Freehan 4.00 10.00
38 Jim Fregosi 4.00 10.00
39 Bob Friend 3.00 8.00
40 Dick Groat 5.00 12.00
41 Woody Held 3.00 8.00
42 Frank Howard 5.00 12.00
43 Al Jackson 3.00 8.00
44 Larry Jackson 3.00 8.00
45 Ken Johnson 3.00 8.00
46 Al Kaline 30.00 60.00
47 Harmon Killebrew 15.00 40.00
48 Sandy Koufax 60.00 120.00
49 Don Lock 3.00 8.00
50 Frank Malzone 4.00 10.00
51 Mickey Mantle 150.00 300.00
52 Eddie Mathews 20.00 50.00
53 Willie Mays 60.00 120.00
54 Bill Mazeroski 6.00 15.00
55 Ken McBride 3.00 8.00
56 Bill Monbouquette 3.00 8.00
57 Dave Nicholson 3.00 8.00
58 Claude Osteen 3.00 8.00
59 Milt Pappas 4.00 10.00
60 Camilo Pascual 3.00 8.00
61 Albie Pearson 3.00 8.00
62 Ron Perranoski 3.00 8.00
63 Gary Peters 3.00 8.00
64 Boog Powell 5.00 12.00
65 Frank Robinson 20.00 50.00
66 Johnny Romano 3.00 8.00
67 Norm Siebern 3.00 8.00
68 Warren Spahn 20.00 50.00
69 Dick Stuart 4.00 10.00
70 Lee Thomas 3.00 8.00
71 Joe Torre 6.00 15.00
72 Pete Ward 3.00 8.00
73 Carlton Willey 3.00 8.00
74 Billy Williams 15.00 40.00
75 Carl Yastrzemski 30.00 60.00

1964 Topps Venezuelan

This set is a parallel version of the first 370 cards in the regular 1964 Topps set and is similar in design. The major difference is the black margin featured on the card back. The cards were issued for the Venezuelan market.

COMPLETE SET (370) 3500.00 7000.00
1 Sandy Koufax 60.00 120.00
Dick Ellsworth
Bob Friend LL
2 Gary Peters 10.00 25.00
Juan Pizarro
Camilo Pascual LL
3 Sandy Koufax 50.00 100.00
Juan Marichal
Warren Spahn
Jim Maloney LL
4 Whitey Ford 20.00 50.00
Camilo Pascual
Jim Bouton LL
5 Sandy Koufax 40.00 80.00
Jim Maloney
Don Drysdale LL
6 Camilo Pascual 10.00 25.00
Jim Bunning
Dick Stigman LL
7 Tommy Davis 50.00 100.00
Bob Clemente
Dick Groat
Hank Aaron LL
8 Carl Yastrzemski 30.00 60.00
Al Kaline
Rich Rollins LL
9 Hank Aaron 75.00 150.00
Willie McCovey
Willie Mays
Orlando Cepeda LL
10 Harmon Killebrew/Dick Stuart 20.00 50.00
Bob Allison LL
11 Hank Aaron 30.00 60.00
Ken Boyer
Bill White LL
12 Dick Stuart 20.00 50.00
Al Kaline
Harmon Killebrew LL
13 Hoyt Wilhelm 20.00 50.00
14 Dick Nen 8.00 20.00
Nick Willhite
15 Zoilo Versalles 8.00 20.00
16 John Boozer 8.00 20.00
17 Willie Kirkland 8.00 20.00
18 Billy O'Dell 8.00 20.00
19 Don Wert 8.00 20.00
20 Bob Friend 8.00 20.00
21 Yogi Berra MG 75.00 150.00
22 Jerry Adair 8.00 20.00
23 Chris Zachary 8.00 20.00
24 Carl Sawatski 8.00 20.00
25 Bill Monbouquette 8.00 20.00
26 Gino Cimoli 8.00 20.00
27 New York Mets 12.50 30.00
Team Card
28 Claude Osteen 8.00 20.00
29 Lou Brock 75.00 150.00
30 Ron Perranoski 8.00 20.00
31 Dave Nicholson 8.00 20.00
32 Dean Chance 8.00 20.00
33 Sammy Ellis 8.00 20.00
Mel Queen
34 Jim Perry 8.00 20.00
35 Eddie Mathews 40.00 80.00
36 Hal Reniff 8.00 20.00
37 Smoky Burgess 8.00 20.00
38 Jim Wynn RC 12.50 30.00
39 Hank Aguirre 8.00 20.00
40 Dick Groat 8.00 20.00
41 Willie McCovey 12.50 30.00
Leon Wagner
42 Moe Drabowsky 8.00 20.00
43 Roy Sievers 8.00 20.00
44 Duke Carmel 8.00 20.00
45 Milt Pappas 8.00 20.00
46 Ed Brinkman 8.00 20.00
47 Jesus Alou 8.00 20.00
Ron Herbel
48 Bob Perry 8.00 20.00
49 Bill Henry 8.00 20.00
50 Mickey Mantle 750.00 1500.00
51 Pete Richert 8.00 20.00
52 Chuck Hinton 8.00 20.00
53 Denis Menke 8.00 20.00
54 Sam Mele MG 8.00 20.00
55 Ernie Banks 75.00 150.00
56 Hal Brown 8.00 20.00
57 Tim Harkness 8.00 20.00
58 Don Demeter 8.00 20.00
59 Ernie Broglio 8.00 20.00
60 Frank Malzone 8.00 20.00
61 Bob Rodgers 8.00 20.00
Ed Sadowski
62 Ted Savage 8.00 20.00
63 John Orsino 8.00 20.00
64 Ted Abernathy 8.00 20.00
65 Felipe Alou 12.50 30.00
66 Eddie Fisher 8.00 20.00
67 Tigers Team 12.50 30.00
68 Willie Davis 8.00 20.00
69 Clete Boyer 10.00 25.00
70 Joe Torre 15.00 40.00
71 Jack Spring 8.00 20.00
72 Chico Cardenas 8.00 20.00
73 Jimmie Hall 8.00 20.00
74 Bob Priddy 8.00 20.00
Tom Butters
75 Wayne Causey 8.00 20.00
76 Checklist 1 15.00 40.00
77 Jerry Walker 8.00 20.00
78 Merritt Ranew 8.00 20.00
79 Bob Heffner 8.00 20.00
80 Vada Pinson 10.00 25.00
81 Nellie Fox 20.00 50.00
Harmon Killebrew
82 Jim Davenport 8.00 20.00
83 Gus Triandos 8.00 20.00
84 Carl Willey 8.00 20.00
85 Pete Ward 8.00 20.00
86 Al Downing 10.00 25.00
87 St. Louis Cardinals 12.50 30.00
Team Card
88 John Roseboro 8.00 20.00
89 Boog Powell 12.50 30.00
90 Earl Battey 8.00 20.00
91 Bob Bailey 8.00 20.00
92 Steve Ridzik 8.00 20.00
93 Gary Geiger 8.00 20.00
94 Jim Britton 8.00 20.00
Larry Maxie
95 George Altman 8.00 20.00
96 Bob Buhl 8.00 20.00
97 Jim Fregosi 8.00 20.00
98 Bill Bruton 8.00 20.00
99 Al Stanek 8.00 20.00
100 Elston Howard 12.50 30.00
101 Walt Alston MG 12.50 30.00
102 Checklist 2 15.00 40.00
103 Curt Flood 10.00 25.00
104 Art Mahaffey 8.00 20.00
105 Woody Held 8.00 20.00
106 Joe Nuxhall 8.00 20.00
107 Bruce Howard 8.00 20.00
Frank Kreutzer
108 John Wyatt 8.00 20.00
109 Rusty Staub 12.50 30.00
110 Albie Pearson 8.00 20.00
111 Don Elston 8.00 20.00
112 Bob Tillman 8.00 20.00
113 Grover Powell 8.00 20.00
114 Don Lock 8.00 20.00
115 Frank Bolling 8.00 20.00
116 Jay Ward 30.00 60.00
Tony Oliva
117 Earl Francis 8.00 20.00
118 John Blanchard 8.00 20.00
119 Gary Kolb 8.00 20.00
120 Don Drysdale 50.00 100.00
121 Pete Runnels 8.00 20.00
122 Don McMahon 8.00 20.00
123 Jose Pagan 8.00 20.00
124 Orlando Pena 8.00 20.00
125 Pete Rose 500.00 1000.00
126 Russ Snyder 8.00 20.00
127 Aubrey Gatewood 8.00 20.00
Dick Simpson
128 Mickey Lolich RC 50.00 100.00
129 Amado Samuel 8.00 20.00
130 Gary Peters 8.00 20.00
131 Steve Boros 8.00 20.00
132 Braves Team 12.50 30.00
133 Jim Grant 8.00 20.00
134 Don Zimmer 8.00 20.00
135 Johnny Callison 8.00 20.00
136 Sandy Koufax WS 40.00 80.00
Strikes out 15
137 Tommy Davis WS 10.00 25.00
138 Ron Fairly WS 10.00 25.00
139 Frank Howard WS 10.00 25.00
140 World Series Summary 10.00 25.00
Dodgers celebrate
141 Danny Murtaugh MG 8.00 20.00
142 John Bateman 8.00 20.00
143 Bubba Phillips 8.00 20.00
144 Al Worthington 8.00 20.00
145 Norm Siebern 8.00 20.00
146 Tommy John 75.00 150.00
Bob Chance
147 Ray Sadecki 8.00 20.00
148 J.C. Martin 8.00 20.00
149 Paul Foytack 8.00 20.00
150 Willie Mays 250.00 500.00
151 Athletics Team 12.50 30.00
152 Denny Lemaster 8.00 20.00
153 Dick Williams 10.00 25.00
154 Dick Tracewski 8.00 20.00
155 Duke Snider 75.00 150.00
156 Bill Dailey 8.00 20.00
157 Gene Mauch MG 8.00 20.00
158 Ken Johnson 8.00 20.00
159 Charlie Dees 8.00 20.00
160 Ken Boyer 12.50 30.00
161 Dave McNally 8.00 20.00
162 Dick Sisler CO 8.00 20.00
Vada Pinson
163 Donn Clendenon 8.00 20.00
164 Bud Daley 8.00 20.00
165 Jerry Lumpe 8.00 20.00
166 Marty Keough 8.00 20.00
167 Mike Brumley 75.00 150.00
Lou Piniella
168 Al Weis 8.00 20.00
169 Del Crandall 8.00 20.00
170 Dick Radatz 8.00 20.00
171 Ty Cline 8.00 20.00
172 Indians Team 12.50 30.00
173 Ryne Duren 8.00 20.00
174 Doc Edwards 8.00 20.00
175 Billy Williams 40.00 80.00
176 Tracy Stallard 8.00 20.00
177 Harmon Killebrew 50.00 100.00
178 Hank Bauer MG 8.00 20.00
179 Carl Warwick 8.00 20.00
180 Tommy Davis 10.00 25.00
181 Dave Wickersham 8.00 20.00
182 Carl Yastrzemski 40.00 80.00
Chuck Schilling
183 Ron Taylor 8.00 20.00
184 Al Luplow 8.00 20.00
185 Jim O'Toole 8.00 20.00
186 Roman Mejias 8.00 20.00
187 Ed Roebuck 8.00 20.00
188 Checklist 3 15.00 40.00
189 Bob Hendley 8.00 20.00
190 Bobby Richardson 15.00 40.00
191 Clay Dalrymple 8.00 20.00
192 John Boccabella 8.00 20.00
Billy Cowan
193 Jerry Lynch 8.00 20.00
194 John Goryl 8.00 20.00
195 Floyd Robinson 10.00 25.00
196 Jim Gentile 8.00 20.00
197 Frank Lary 8.00 20.00
198 Len Gabrielson 8.00 20.00
199 Joe Azcue 8.00 20.00
200 Sandy Koufax 250.00 500.00
201 Sam Bowens 8.00 20.00
Wally Bunker
202 Galen Cisco 8.00 20.00
203 John Kennedy 8.00 20.00
204 Matty Alou 10.00 25.00
205 Nellie Fox 20.00 50.00
206 Steve Hamilton 8.00 20.00
207 Fred Hutchinson MG 8.00 20.00
208 Wes Covington 8.00 20.00
209 Bob Allen 8.00 20.00
210 Carl Yastrzemski 75.00 150.00
211 Jim Coker 8.00 20.00
212 Pete Lovrich 8.00 20.00
213 Angels Team 12.50 30.00
214 Ken McMullen 8.00 20.00
215 Ray Herbert 8.00 20.00
216 Mike de la Hoz 8.00 20.00
217 Jim King 8.00 20.00
218 Hank Fischer 8.00 20.00
219 Al Downing 8.00 20.00
Jim Bouton
220 Dick Ellsworth 8.00 20.00
221 Bob Saverine 8.00 20.00
222 Billy Pierce 10.00 25.00
223 George Banks 8.00 20.00
224 Tommie Sisk 8.00 20.00
225 Roger Maris 125.00 250.00
226 Jerry Grote 10.00 25.00
Larry Yellen
227 Barry Latman 8.00 20.00
228 Felix Mantilla 8.00 20.00
229 Charley Lau 8.00 20.00
230 Brooks Robinson 75.00 150.00
231 Dick Calmus 8.00 20.00
232 Al Lopez MG 12.50 30.00
233 Hal Smith 8.00 20.00
234 Gary Bell 8.00 20.00
235 Ron Hunt 8.00 20.00
236 Bill Faul 8.00 20.00
237 Cubs Team 12.50 30.00
238 Roy McMillan 8.00 20.00
239 Herm Starrette 8.00 20.00
240 Bill White 10.00 25.00
241 Jim Owens 8.00 20.00
242 Harvey Kuenn 8.00 20.00
243 Richie Allen 75.00 150.00
John Herrnstein
244 Tony LaRussa 75.00 150.00
245 Dick Stigman 8.00 20.00
246 Manny Mota 10.00 25.00
247 Dave DeBusschere 12.50 30.00
248 Johnny Pesky MG 8.00 20.00
249 Doug Camilli 8.00 20.00
250 Al Kaline 100.00 200.00
251 Choo Choo Coleman 8.00 20.00
252 Ken Aspromonte 8.00 20.00
253 Wally Post 8.00 20.00
254 Don Hoak 8.00 20.00
255 Lee Thomas 8.00 20.00
256 Johnny Weekly 8.00 20.00
257 San Francisco Giants 12.50 30.00
Team Card
258 Garry Roggenburk 8.00 20.00
259 Harry Bright 8.00 20.00
260 Frank Robinson 75.00 150.00
261 Jim Hannan 8.00 20.00
262 Mike Shannon 15.00 40.00
Harry Fanok
263 Chuck Estrada 8.00 20.00
264 Jim Landis 8.00 20.00
265 Jim Bunning 40.00 80.00
266 Gene Freese 8.00 20.00
267 Wilbur Wood RC 12.50 30.00
268 Danny Murtaugh 8.00 20.00
Bill Virdon MG
269 Ellis Burton 8.00 20.00
270 Rich Rollins 8.00 20.00
271 Bob Sadowski 8.00 20.00
272 Jake Wood 8.00 20.00
273 Mel Nelson 8.00 20.00
274 Checklist 4 15.00 40.00
275 John Tsitouris 8.00 20.00
276 Jose Tartabull 8.00 20.00
277 Ken Retzer 8.00 20.00
278 Bobby Shantz 8.00 20.00
279 Joe Koppe UER 8.00 20.00
Glove on wrong hand
280 Juan Marichal 40.00 80.00
281 Jake Gibbs 8.00 20.00
Tom Metcalf
282 Bob Bruce 8.00 20.00
283 Tom McCraw 8.00 20.00
284 Dick Schofield 8.00 20.00
285 Robin Roberts 40.00 80.00
286 Don Landrum 8.00 20.00
287 Tony Conigliaro 125.00 250.00
Bill Spanswick
288 Al Moran 8.00 20.00
289 Frank Funk 8.00 20.00
290 Bob Allison 8.00 20.00
291 Phil Ortega 8.00 20.00
292 Mike Roarke 8.00 20.00
293 Phillies Team 12.50 30.00
294 Ken L. Hunt 8.00 20.00
295 Roger Craig 8.00 20.00
296 Ed Kirkpatrick 8.00 20.00
297 Ken MacKenzie 8.00 20.00
298 Harry Craft MG 8.00 20.00
299 Bill Stafford 8.00 20.00
300 Hank Aaron 200.00 400.00
301 Larry Brown 8.00 20.00
302 Dan Pfister 8.00 20.00
303 Jim Campbell 8.00 20.00
304 Bob Johnson 8.00 20.00
305 Jack Lamabe 8.00 20.00
306 Willie Mays 75.00 150.00
Orlando Cepeda
307 Joe Gibbon 8.00 20.00
308 Gene Stephens 8.00 20.00
309 Paul Toth 8.00 20.00
310 Jim Gilliam 10.00 25.00
311 Tom Brown 8.00 20.00
312 Fritz Fisher 8.00 20.00
Fred Gladding
313 Chuck Hiller 8.00 20.00
314 Jerry Buchek 8.00 20.00
315 Bo Belinsky 10.00 25.00
316 Gene Oliver 8.00 20.00
317 Al Smith 8.00 20.00
318 Minnesota Twins 12.50 30.00
Team Card
319 Paul Brown 8.00 20.00
320 Rocky Colavito 40.00 80.00
321 Bob Lillis 8.00 20.00
322 George Brunet 8.00 20.00
323 John Buzhardt 8.00 20.00
324 Casey Stengel MG 40.00 80.00
325 Hector Lopez 8.00 20.00
326 Ron Brand 8.00 20.00
327 Don Blasingame 8.00 20.00
328 Bob Shaw 8.00 20.00
329 Russ Nixon 8.00 20.00
330 Tommy Harper 8.00 20.00
331 Roger Maris 500.00 1000.00
Norm Cash
Mickey Mantle
Al Kaline
332 Ray Washburn 8.00 20.00
333 Billy Moran 8.00 20.00
334 Lew Krausse 8.00 20.00
335 Don Mossi 8.00 20.00
336 Andre Rodgers 8.00 20.00
337 Al Ferrara 8.00 20.00
Jeff Torborg
338 Jack Kralick 8.00 20.00
339 Walt Bond 8.00 20.00
340 Joe Cunningham 10.00 25.00
341 Jim Roland 8.00 20.00
342 Willie Stargell 75.00 150.00
343 Senators Team 12.50 30.00
344 Phil Linz 8.00 20.00
345 Frank Thomas 8.00 20.00
346 Joey Jay 8.00 20.00
347 Bobby Wine 8.00 20.00
348 Ed Lopat MG 8.00 20.00
349 Art Fowler 8.00 20.00
350 Willie McCovey 50.00 100.00
351 Dan Schneider 8.00 20.00
352 Eddie Bressoud 8.00 20.00
353 Wally Moon 8.00 20.00
354 Dave Giusti 8.00 20.00
355 Vic Power 8.00 20.00
356 Bill McCool 8.00 20.00
Chico Ruiz
357 Charley James 8.00 20.00
358 Ron Kline 8.00 20.00
359 Jim Schaffer 8.00 20.00
360 Joe Pepitone 8.00 20.00
361 Jay Hook 8.00 20.00
362 Checklist 5 15.00 40.00
363 Dick McAuliffe 8.00 20.00
364 Joe Gaines 8.00 20.00
365 Cal McLish 8.00 20.00
366 Nelson Mathews 8.00 20.00
367 Fred Whitfield 8.00 20.00
368 Fritz Ackley 8.00 20.00
Don Buford
369 Jerry Zimmerman 8.00 20.00
370 Hal Woodeshick 10.00 25.00

1965 Topps

The cards in this 598-card set measure 2 1/2" by 3 1/2". The cards comprising the 1965 Topps set have team names located within a distinctive pennant design below the picture. The cards have blue borders on the reverse and were issued by series. Within this last series (523-598) there are 44 cards that were printed in lesser quantities than the other cards in that series; these shorter-printed cards are marked by SP in the checklist below. Featured subsets within this set include League Leaders (1-12) and World Series cards (132-139). This was the last year Topps issued one-card penny packs. Card were also issued in five-card nickel packs. The key Rookie Cards in this set are Steve Carlton, Jim "Catfish" Hunter, Joe Morgan, Mansori Murakami and Tony Perez.

COMPLETE SET (598) 2500.00 6000.00
COMMON CARD (1-196) .75 2.00
COMMON CARD (197-283) 1.00 2.50
COMMON CARD (284-370) 1.50 4.00
COMMON CARD (371-598) 3.00 8.00
WRAPPER (1-CENT) 60.00 120.00
WRAPPER (5-CENT) 50.00 100.00
1 Oliva/Howard/Brooks LL 8.00 20.00
2 Clemente/Aaron/Carty LL 20.00 50.00
3 Killebrew/Mantle/Powell LL 25.00 60.00
4 Mays/B.Will/Cepeda LL 10.00 25.00
5 Brooks/Kill/Mantle LL 25.00 60.00
6 Boyer/Mays Santo LL 8.00 20.00
7 D.Chance/J.Horlen LL 2.00 5.00
8 S.Koufax/D.Drysdale LL 8.00 20.00
9 Chance/Peters/Wick LL 2.00 5.00
10 Jackson/Sad/Marichal LL 2.00 5.00
11 Downing/Chance/Pascual LL 2.00 5.00
12 Veale/Drysdale/Gibson LL 4.00 10.00
13 Pedro Ramos 1.50 4.00
14 Len Gabrielson .75 2.00
15 Robin Roberts 8.00 20.00
16 Joe Morgan RC DP 125.00 300.00
17 Johnny Romano .75 2.00
18 Bill McCool .75 2.00
19 Gates Brown 1.50 4.00
20 Jim Bunning 4.00 10.00
21 Don Blasingame .75 2.00
22 Charlie Smith .75 2.00
23 Bob Tiefenauer .75 2.00
24 Minnesota Twins TC 2.50 6.00

25 Al McBean .75 2.00
26 Bobby Knoop .75 2.00
27 Dick Bertell .75 2.00
28 Barney Schultz .75 2.00
29 Felix Mantilla .75 2.00
30 Jim Bouton 2.50 6.00
31 Mike White .75 2.00
32 Herman Franks MG .75 2.00
33 Jackie Brandt .75 2.00
34 Cal Koonce .75 2.00
35 Ed Charles .75 2.00
36 Bobby Wine .75 2.00
37 Fred Gladding .75 2.00
38 Jim King .75 2.00
39 Gerry Arrigo .75 2.00
40 Frank Howard 2.50 6.00
41 B.Howard/M.Staehle RC .75 2.00
42 Earl Wilson 1.50 4.00
43 Mike Shannon 1.50 4.00
44 Wade Blasingame RC .75 2.00
45 Roy McMillan 1.50 4.00
46 Bob Lee .75 2.00
47 Tommy Harper 1.50 4.00
48 Claude Raymond 1.50 4.00
49 C.Blefary RC/J.Miller 1.50 4.00
50 Juan Marichal 10.00 25.00
51 Bill Bryan .75 2.00
52 Ed Roebuck .75 2.00
53 Dick McAuliffe 1.50 4.00
54 Joe Gibbon .75 2.00
55 Tony Conigliaro 6.00 15.00
56 Ron Kline .75 2.00
57 St. Louis Cardinals TC 2.50 6.00
58 Fred Talbot RC .75 2.00
59 Nate Oliver .75 2.00
60 Jim O'Toole 1.50 4.00
61 Chris Cannizzaro .75 2.00
62 Jim Kaat UER DP 6.00 15.00
63 Ty Cline .75 2.00
64 Lou Burdette 1.50 4.00
65 Tony Kubek 4.00 10.00
66 Bill Rigney MG .75 2.00
67 Harvey Haddix 1.50 4.00
68 Del Crandall 1.50 4.00
69 Bill Virdon 1.50 4.00
70 Bill Skowron 2.50 6.00
71 John O'Donoghue .75 2.00
72 Tony Gonzalez .75 2.00
73 Dennis Ribant RC .75 2.00
74 R.Petrocelli RC/J.Steph RC 4.00 10.00
75 Deron Johnson 1.50 4.00
76 Sam McDowell 2.50 6.00
77 Doug Camilli .75 2.00
78 Dal Maxvill .75 2.00
79A Checklist 1 Cannizzaro 4.00 10.00
79B Checklist 1 C.Cannizzaro 4.00 10.00
80 Turk Farrell .75 2.00
81 Don Buford 1.50 4.00
82 S.Alomar RC/J.Braun RC 2.50 6.00
83 George Thomas .75 2.00
84 Ron Herbel .75 2.00
85 Willie Smith RC .75 2.00
86 Buster Narum .75 2.00
87 Nelson Mathews .75 2.00
88 Jack Lamabe .75 2.00
89 Mike Hershberger .75 2.00
90 Rich Rollins 1.50 4.00
91 Chicago Cubs TC 2.50 6.00
92 Dick Howser 1.50 4.00
93 Jack Fisher .75 2.00
94 Charlie Lau 1.50 4.00
95 Bill Mazeroski DP 10.00 25.00
96 Sonny Siebert 1.50 4.00
97 Pedro Gonzalez .75 2.00
98 Bob Miller .75 2.00
99 Gil Hodges MG 2.50 6.00
100 Ken Boyer 4.00 10.00
101 Fred Newman .75 2.00
102 Steve Boros .75 2.00
103 Harvey Kuenn 1.50 4.00
104 Checklist 2 4.00 10.00
105 Chico Salmon .75 2.00
106 Gene Oliver .75 2.00
107 P.Corrales RC/C.Shockley RC 1.50 4.00
108 Don Mincher .75 2.00
109 Walt Bond .75 2.00
110 Ron Santo 2.50 6.00
111 Lee Thomas 1.50 4.00
112 Derrell Griffith RC .75 2.00
113 Steve Barber .75 2.00
114 Jim Hickman 1.50 4.00
115 Bobby Richardson 4.00 10.00
116 D.Dowling RC/B.Tolan RC 1.50 4.00
117 Wes Stock .75 2.00
118 Hal Lanier RC 1.50 4.00
119 John Kennedy .75 2.00
120 Frank Robinson 30.00 80.00
121 Gene Alley 1.50 4.00
122 Bill Pleis .75 2.00
123 Frank Thomas 1.50 4.00
124 Tom Satriano .75 2.00
125 Juan Pizarro .75 2.00
126 Los Angeles Dodgers TC 2.50 6.00
127 Frank Lary .75 2.00
128 Vic Davalillo .75 2.00
129 Bennie Daniels .75 2.00
130 Al Kaline 30.00 80.00
131 Johnny Keane MG .75 2.00
132 Cards Take Opener WS1 4.00 10.00
133 Mel Stottlemyre WS2 2.50 6.00
134 Mickey Mantle WS3 40.00 100.00
135 Ken Boyer WS4 4.00 10.00
136 Tim McCarver WS5 2.50 6.00
137 Jim Bouton WS6 2.50 6.00
138 Bob Gibson WS7 5.00 12.00
139 Cards Celebrate WS 2.50 6.00
140 Dean Chance 1.50 4.00
141 Charlie James .75 2.00
142 Bill Monbouquette .75 2.00
143 J.Gelnar RC/J.May RC .75 2.00
144 Ed Kranepool 1.50 4.00
145 Luis Tiant RC 20.00 50.00
146 Ron Hansen .75 2.00
147 Dennis Bennett .75 2.00
148 Willie Kirkland .75 2.00
149 Wayne Schurr .75 2.00
150 Brooks Robinson 20.00 50.00
151 Kansas City Athletics TC 2.50 6.00
152 Phil Ortega .75 2.00
153 Norm Cash 10.00 25.00
154 Bob Humphreys RC .75 2.00
155 Roger Maris 40.00 100.00
156 Bob Sadowski .75 2.00
157 Zoilo Versalles 1.50 4.00
158 Dick Sisler .75 2.00
159 Jim Duffalo .75 2.00
160 Roberto Clemente UER 75.00 200.00
161 Frank Baumann .75 2.00
162 Russ Nixon .75 2.00
163 Johnny Briggs .75 2.00
164 Al Spangler .75 2.00
165 Dick Ellsworth .75 2.00
166 G.Culver RC/T.Agee RC 1.50 4.00
167 Bill Wakefield .75 2.00
168 Dick Green .75 2.00
169 Dave Vineyard RC .75 2.00
170 Hank Aaron 75.00 200.00
171 Jim Roland .75 2.00
172 Jimmy Piersall 2.50 6.00
173 Detroit Tigers TC 2.50 6.00
174 Joey Jay .75 2.00
175 Bob Aspromonte .75 2.00
176 Willie McCovey 20.00 50.00
177 Pete Mikkelsen .75 2.00
178 Dalton Jones .75 2.00
179 Hal Woodeshick .75 2.00
180 Bob Allison 1.50 4.00
181 D.Loun RC/J.McCabe .75 2.00
182 Mike de la Hoz .75 2.00
183 Dave Nicholson .75 2.00
184 John Boozer .75 2.00
185 Max Alvis .75 2.00
186 Billy Cowan .75 2.00
187 Casey Stengel MG 10.00 25.00
188 Sam Bowens .75 2.00
189 Checklist 3 4.00 10.00
190 Bill White 2.50 6.00
191 Phil Regan 1.50 4.00
192 Jim Coker .75 2.00
193 Gaylord Perry 8.00 20.00
194 B.Kelso RC/R.Reichardt RC .75 2.00
195 Bob Veale 1.50 4.00
196 Ron Fairly 1.50 4.00
197 Diego Segui 1.00 2.50
198 Smoky Burgess 1.50 4.00
199 Bob Heffner 1.00 2.50
200 Joe Torre 2.50 6.00
201 S.Valdespino RC/C.Tovar RC 1.50 4.00
202 Leo Burke 1.00 2.50
203 Dallas Green 1.50 4.00
204 Russ Snyder 1.00 2.50
205 Warren Spahn 10.00 25.00
206 Willie Horton 1.50 4.00
207 Pete Rose 100.00 250.00
208 Tommy John 2.50 6.00
209 Pittsburgh Pirates TC 2.50 6.00
210 Jim Fregosi 1.50 4.00
211 Steve Ridzik 1.00 2.50
212 Ron Brand 1.00 2.50
213 Jim Davenport 1.00 2.50
214 Bob Purkey 1.00 2.50
215 Pete Ward 1.00 2.50
216 Al Worthington 1.00 2.50
217 Walter Alston MG 2.50 6.00
218 Dick Schofield 1.00 2.50
219 Bob Meyer 1.00 2.50
220 Billy Williams 25.00 60.00
221 John Tsitouris 1.00 2.50
222 Bob Tillman 1.00 2.50
223 Dan Osinski 1.00 2.50
224 Bob Chance 1.00 2.50
225 Bo Belinsky 1.50 4.00
226 E.Jimenez RC/J.Gibbs 2.50 6.00
227 Bobby Klaus 1.00 2.50
228 Jack Sanford 1.00 2.50
229 Lou Clinton 1.00 2.50
230 Ray Sadecki 1.00 2.50
231 Jerry Adair 1.00 2.50
232 Steve Blass RC 1.50 4.00
233 Don Zimmer 1.50 4.00
234 Chicago White Sox TC 2.50 6.00
235 Chuck Hinton 1.00 2.50
236 Denny McLain RC 25.00 60.00
237 Bernie Allen 1.00 2.50
238 Joe Moeller 1.00 2.50
239 Doc Edwards 1.00 2.50
240 Bob Bruce 1.00 2.50
241 Mack Jones 1.00 2.50
242 George Brunet 1.00 2.50
243 T.Davidson RC/T.Helms RC 1.50 4.00
244 Lindy McDaniel 1.50 4.00
245 Joe Pepitone 2.50 6.00
246 Tom Butters 1.50 4.00
247 Wally Moon 1.50 4.00
248 Gus Triandos 1.50 4.00
249 Dave McNally 1.50 4.00
250 Willie Mays 75.00 200.00
251 Billy Herman MG 1.50 4.00
252 Pete Richert 1.00 2.50
253 Danny Cater 1.00 2.50
254 Roland Sheldon 1.00 2.50
255 Camilo Pascual 1.50 4.00
256 Tito Francona 1.00 2.50
257 Jim Wynn 1.50 4.00
258 Larry Bearnarth 1.00 2.50
259 J.Northrup RC/R.Oyler RC 2.50 6.00
260 Don Drysdale 20.00 50.00
261 Duke Carmel 1.00 2.50
262 Bud Daley 1.00 2.50
263 Marty Keough 1.00 2.50
264 Bob Buhl 1.50 4.00
265 Jim Pagliaroni 1.00 2.50
266 Bert Campaneris RC 10.00 25.00
267 Washington Senators TC 2.50 6.00
268 Ken McBride 1.00 2.50
269 Frank Bolling 1.00 2.50
270 Milt Pappas 1.00 2.50
271 Don Wert 1.50 4.00
272 Chuck Schilling 1.00 2.50
273 Checklist 4 4.00 10.00
274 Lum Harris MG RC 1.00 2.50
275 Dick Groat 2.50 6.00
276 Hoyt Wilhelm 10.00 25.00
277 Johnny Lewis 1.00 2.50
278 Ken Retzer 1.00 2.50
279 Dick Tracewski 1.00 2.50
280 Dick Stuart 1.50 4.00
281 Bill Stafford 1.00 2.50
282 D.Est RC/M.Murakami RC 25.00 60.00
283 Fred Whitfield 1.00 2.50
284 Nick Willhite 1.50 4.00
285 Ron Hunt 1.50 4.00
286 J.Dickson/A.Monteagudo 1.50 4.00
287 Gary Kolb 1.50 4.00
288 Jack Hamilton 1.50 4.00
289 Gordy Coleman 2.50 6.00
290 Wally Bunker 2.50 6.00
291 Jerry Lynch 1.50 4.00
292 Larry Yellen 1.50 4.00
293 Los Angeles Angels TC 2.50 6.00
294 Tim McCarver 4.00 10.00
295 Dick Radatz 2.50 6.00
296 Tony Taylor 2.50 6.00
297 Dave DeBusschere 4.00 10.00
298 Jim Stewart 1.50 4.00
299 Jerry Zimmerman 1.50 4.00
300 Sandy Koufax 75.00 200.00
301 Birdie Tebbetts MG 2.50 6.00
302 Al Stanek 1.50 4.00
303 John Orsino 1.50 4.00
304 Dave Stenhouse 1.50 4.00
305 Rico Carty 2.50 6.00
306 Bubba Phillips 1.50 4.00
307 Barry Latman 1.50 4.00
308 C.Jones RC/T.Parsons 2.50 6.00
309 Steve Hamilton 2.50 6.00
310 Johnny Callison 2.50 6.00
311 Orlando Pena 1.50 4.00
312 Joe Nuxhall 1.50 4.00
313 Jim Schaffer 1.50 4.00
314 Sterling Slaughter 1.50 4.00
315 Frank Malzone 2.50 6.00
316 Cincinnati Reds TC 2.50 6.00
317 Don McMahon 1.50 4.00
318 Matty Alou 2.50 6.00
319 Ken McMullen 1.50 4.00
320 Bob Gibson 25.00 60.00
321 Rusty Staub 4.00 10.00
322 Rick Wise 2.50 6.00
323 Hank Bauer MG 2.50 6.00
324 Bobby Locke 1.50 4.00
325 Donn Clendenon 2.50 6.00
326 Dwight Siebler 1.50 4.00
327 Denis Menke 1.50 4.00
328 Eddie Fisher 1.50 4.00
329 Hawk Taylor 1.50 4.00
330 Whitey Ford 20.00 50.00
331 A.Ferrara/J.Purdin RC 2.50 6.00
332 Ted Abernathy 1.50 4.00
333 Tom Reynolds 1.50 4.00
334 Vic Roznovsky RC 1.50 4.00
335 Mickey Lolich 8.00 20.00
336 Woody Held 1.50 4.00
337 Mike Cuellar 2.50 6.00
338 Philadelphia Phillies TC 2.50 6.00
339 Ryne Duren 2.50 6.00
340 Tony Oliva 20.00 50.00
341 Bob Bolin 1.50 4.00
342 Bob Rodgers 2.50 6.00
343 Mike McCormick 2.50 6.00
344 Wes Parker 2.50 6.00
345 Floyd Robinson 1.50 4.00
346 Bobby Bragan MG 1.50 4.00
347 Roy Face 2.50 6.00
348 George Banks 1.50 4.00
349 Larry Miller RC 1.50 4.00
350 Mickey Mantle 400.00 800.00
351 Jim Perry 2.50 6.00
352 Alex Johnson RC 2.50 6.00
353 Jerry Lumpe 1.50 4.00
354 B.Ott RC/J.Warner RC 1.50 4.00
355 Vada Pinson 4.00 10.00
356 Bill Spanswick 1.50 4.00
357 Carl Warwick 1.50 4.00
358 Albie Pearson 2.50 6.00
359 Ken Johnson 1.50 4.00
360 Orlando Cepeda 6.00 15.00
361 Checklist 5 5.00 12.00
362 Don Schwall 1.50 4.00
363 Bob Johnson 1.50 4.00
364 Galen Cisco 1.50 4.00
365 Jim Gentile 2.50 6.00
366 Dan Schneider 1.50 4.00
367 Leon Wagner 1.50 4.00
368 K.Berry RC/J.Gibson RC 2.50 6.00
369 Phil Linz 2.50 6.00
370 Herman Thomas Davis 2.50 6.00
371 Frank Kreutzer 3.00 8.00
372 Clay Dalrymple 3.00 8.00
373 Curt Simmons 3.00 8.00
374 J.Cardenal RC/D.Simpson 3.00 8.00
375 Dave Wickersham 3.00 8.00
376 Jim Landis 3.00 8.00
377 Willie Stargell 25.00 60.00
378 Chuck Estrada 3.00 8.00
379 San Francisco Giants TC 3.00 8.00
380 Rocky Colavito 10.00 25.00
381 Al Jackson 3.00 8.00
382 J.C. Martin 3.00 8.00
383 Felipe Alou 6.00 15.00
384 Johnny Klippstein 3.00 8.00
385 Carl Yastrzemski 30.00 80.00
386 P.Jaeckel RC/F.Norman 3.00 8.00
387 Johnny Podres 6.00 15.00
388 John Blanchard 6.00 15.00
389 Don Larsen 6.00 15.00
390 Bill Freehan 6.00 15.00
391 Mel McGaha MG 3.00 8.00
392 Bob Friend 6.00 15.00
393 Ed Kirkpatrick 3.00 8.00
394 Jim Hannan 3.00 8.00
395 Jim Ray Hart 3.00 8.00
396 Frank Bertaina RC 3.00 8.00
397 Jerry Buchek 3.00 8.00
398 D.Neville RC/A.Shamsky RC 6.00 15.00
399 Ray Herbert 3.00 8.00
400 Harmon Killebrew 30.00 80.00
401 Carl Willey 3.00 8.00
402 Joe Amalfitano 3.00 8.00
403 Boston Red Sox TC 3.00 8.00
404 Stan Williams 3.00 8.00
405 John Roseboro 8.00 20.00
406 Ralph Terry 6.00 15.00
407 Lee Maye 3.00 8.00
408 Larry Sherry 3.00 8.00
409 J.Beauchamp RC/L.Dierker RC 6.00 15.00
410 Luis Aparicio 10.00 25.00
411 Roger Craig 6.00 15.00
412 Bob Bailey 3.00 8.00
413 Hal Reniff 3.00 8.00
414 Al Lopez MG 6.00 15.00
415 Curt Flood 8.00 20.00
416 Jim Brewer 3.00 8.00
417 Ed Brinkman 3.00 8.00
418 Johnny Edwards 3.00 8.00
419 Ruben Amaro 3.00 8.00
420 Larry Jackson 3.00 8.00
421 G.Dotter RC/J.Ward 3.00 8.00
422 Aubrey Gatewood 3.00 8.00
423 Jesse Gonder 3.00 8.00
424 Gary Bell 3.00 8.00
425 Wayne Causey 3.00 8.00
426 Milwaukee Braves TC 3.00 8.00
427 Bob Saverine 3.00 8.00
428 Bob Shaw 3.00 8.00
429 Don Demeter 3.00 8.00
430 Gary Peters 3.00 8.00
431 N.Briles RC/W.Spiezio RC 6.00 15.00
432 Jim Grant 6.00 15.00
433 John Bateman 3.00 8.00
434 Dave Morehead 3.00 8.00
435 Willie Davis 6.00 15.00
436 Don Elston 3.00 8.00
437 Chico Cardenas 6.00 15.00
438 Harry Walker MG 3.00 8.00
439 Moe Drabowsky 6.00 15.00
440 Tom Tresh 6.00 15.00
441 Denny Lemaster 3.00 8.00
442 Vic Power 3.00 8.00
443 Checklist 6 5.00 12.00
444 Bob Hendley 3.00 8.00
445 Don Lock 3.00 8.00
446 Art Mahaffey 3.00 8.00
447 Julian Javier 6.00 15.00
448 Lee Stange 3.00 8.00
449 J.Hinsley/G.Kroll RC 6.00 15.00
450 Elston Howard 6.00 15.00
451 Jim Owens 3.00 8.00
452 Gary Geiger 3.00 8.00
453 W.Crawford RC/J.Werhas 6.00 15.00
454 Ed Rakow 3.00 8.00
455 Norm Siebern 3.00 8.00
456 Bill Henry 3.00 8.00
457 Bob Kennedy MG 6.00 15.00
458 John Buzhardt 3.00 8.00
459 Frank Kostro 3.00 8.00
460 Richie Allen 15.00 40.00
461 C.Carroll RC/P.Niekro 40.00 100.00
462 Lew Krausse UER 3.00 8.00
463 Manny Mota 6.00 15.00
464 Ron Piche 3.00 8.00
465 Tom Haller 6.00 15.00
466 P.Craig RC/D.Nen 3.00 8.00
467 Ray Washburn 3.00 8.00
468 Larry Brown 3.00 8.00
469 Don Nottebart 3.00 8.00
470 Yogi Berra P/CO 30.00 80.00
471 Billy Hoeft 3.00 8.00
472 Don Pavletich 3.00 8.00
473 P.Blair RC/D.Johnson RC 6.00 15.00
474 Cookie Rojas 6.00 15.00
475 Clete Boyer 6.00 15.00
476 Billy O'Dell 3.00 8.00
477 Steve Carlton RC 125.00 300.00
478 Wilbur Wood 6.00 15.00
479 Ken Harrelson 6.00 15.00
480 Joel Horlen 3.00 8.00
481 Cleveland Indians TC 4.00 10.00
482 Bob Priddy 3.00 8.00
483 George Smith RC 3.00 8.00
484 Ron Perranoski 8.00 20.00
485 Nellie Fox P 6.00 15.00
CO
486 T.Egan/P.Rogan RC 3.00 8.00
487 Woody Woodward 6.00 15.00
488 Ted Wills 3.00 8.00
489 Gene Mauch MG 6.00 15.00
490 Earl Battey 3.00 8.00
491 Tracy Stallard 3.00 8.00
492 Gene Freese 3.00 8.00
493 B.Roman RC/B.Brubaker RC 3.00 8.00
494 Jay Ritchie RC 3.00 8.00
495 Joe Christopher 3.00 8.00
496 Joe Cunningham 3.00 8.00
497 K.Henderson RC/J.Hiatt RC 6.00 15.00
498 Gene Stephens 3.00 8.00
499 Stu Miller 6.00 15.00
500 Eddie Mathews 25.00 60.00
501 R.Gagliano RC/J.Rittwage RC 3.00 8.00
502 Don Cardwell 3.00 8.00
503 Phil Gagliano 3.00 8.00
504 Jerry Grote 6.00 15.00
505 Ray Culp 3.00 8.00
506 Sam Mele MG 3.00 8.00
507 Sammy Ellis 3.00 8.00
508 Checklist 7 5.00 12.00
509 B.Guindon RC/G.Vezendy RC 3.00 8.00
510 Ernie Banks 40.00 100.00
511 Ron Locke 3.00 8.00
512 Cap Peterson 3.00 8.00
513 New York Yankees TC 15.00 40.00
514 Joe Azcue 3.00 8.00
515 Vern Law 6.00 15.00
516 Al Weis 3.00 8.00
517 P.Schaal RC/J.Warner 6.00 15.00
518 Ken Rowe 3.00 8.00
519 Bob Uecker UER 20.00 50.00
520 Tony Cloninger 3.00 8.00
521 D.Bennett/M.Steevens RC 3.00 8.00
522 Hank Aguirre 3.00 8.00
523 Mike Brumley SP 5.00 12.00
524 Dave Giusti SP 5.00 12.00
525 Eddie Bressoud 3.00 8.00
526 J.Odom/J.Hunter SP RC 75.00 200.00
527 Jeff Torborg SP 5.00 12.00
528 George Altman 3.00 8.00
529 Jerry Fosnow SP RC 5.00 12.00
530 Jim Maloney 6.00 15.00
531 Chuck Hiller 3.00 8.00
532 Hector Lopez 6.00 15.00
533 R.Swob/T.McGraw SP RC 20.00 50.00
534 John Herrnstein 3.00 8.00
535 Jack Kralick SP 5.00 12.00
536 Andre Rodgers SP 5.00 12.00
537 Lopez/Roof/May RC 3.00 8.00
538 Chuck Dressen MG SP 5.00 12.00
539 Herm Starrette 3.00 8.00
540 Lou Brock SP 50.00 120.00
541 G.Bollo RC/B.Locker RC 3.00 8.00
542 Lou Klimchock 3.00 8.00
543 Ed Connolly SP RC 5.00 12.00
544 Howie Reed RC 3.00 8.00
545 Jesus Alou SP 10.00 25.00
546 Davis/Hed/Bark/Weav RC 3.00 8.00
547 Jake Wood SP 5.00 12.00
548 Dick Stigman 3.00 8.00
549 R.Pena RC/G.Beckert RC 8.00 20.00
550 Mel Stottlemyre SP RC 20.00 50.00
551 New York Mets TC SP 12.50 30.00
552 Julio Gotay 3.00 8.00
553 Coombs/Ratliff/McClure RC 3.00 8.00
554 Chico Ruiz SP 5.00 12.00
555 Jack Baldschun SP 5.00 12.00
556 R.Schoendienst SP 10.00 25.00
557 Jose Santiago RC 3.00 8.00
558 Tommie Sisk 3.00 8.00
559 Ed Bailey SP 5.00 12.00
560 Boog Powell SP 8.00 20.00
561 Dab/Kek/Valle/Lefebvre RC 6.00 15.00
562 Billy Moran 3.00 8.00
563 Julio Navarro 3.00 8.00
564 Mel Nelson 3.00 8.00
565 Ernie Broglio SP 5.00 12.00
566 Blanco/Moschitto/Lopez RC 5.00 12.00
567 Tommie Aaron 3.00 8.00
568 Ron Taylor SP 5.00 12.00
569 Gino Cimoli SP 5.00 12.00
570 Claude Osteen SP 6.00 15.00
571 Ossie Virgil SP 6.00 15.00
572 Baltimore Orioles TC SP 10.00 25.00
573 Jim Lonborg SP RC 10.00 25.00
574 Roy Sievers 6.00 15.00
575 Jose Pagan 3.00 8.00
576 Terry Fox SP 5.00 12.00
577 Knowles/Busch/Schein RC 5.00 12.00
578 Camilo Carreon SP 5.00 12.00
579 Dick Smith SP 5.00 12.00
580 Jimmie Hall SP 5.00 12.00
581 Tony Perez SP RC 60.00 150.00
582 Bob Schmidt SP 5.00 12.00
583 Wes Covington SP 5.00 12.00
584 Harry Bright 6.00 15.00
585 Hank Fischer 3.00 8.00
586 Tom McCraw SP UER 5.00 12.00
Name is spelled McGraw on the back
587 Joe Sparma 3.00 8.00
588 Lenny Green 3.00 8.00
589 F.Linzy RC/B.Schroder RC 5.00 12.00
590 John Wyatt 3.00 8.00
591 Bob Skinner SP 5.00 12.00
592 Frank Bork SP RC 5.00 12.00
593 J.Sullivan RC/J.Moore RC SP 5.00 12.00
594 Joe Gaines 3.00 8.00
595 Don Lee 3.00 8.00
596 Don Landrum SP 5.00 12.00
597 Nossek/Sevcik/Reese RC 3.00 8.00
598 Al Downing SP 10.00 25.00

1965 Topps Embossed

COMPLETE SET (72) 150.00 400.00
1 Carl Yastrzemski 4.00 10.00
2 Ron Fairly .75 2.00
3 Max Alvis .75 2.00
4 Jim Ray Hart .75 2.00
5 Bill Skowron 1.25 3.00
6 Ed Kranepool .75 2.00
7 Tim McCarver 1.25 3.00
8 Sandy Koufax 8.00 20.00
9 Donn Clendenon .75 2.00
10 John Romano .75 2.00
11 Mickey Mantle 50.00 120.00
12 Joe Torre 2.00 5.00
13 Al Kaline 4.00 10.00
14 Al McBean .75 2.00
15 Don Drysdale 2.00 5.00
16 Brooks Robinson 4.00 10.00
17 Jim Bunning 1.25 3.00
18 Gary Peters .75 2.00
19 Roberto Clemente 40.00 100.00
20 Milt Pappas .75 2.00
21 Wayne Causey .75 2.00
22 Frank Robinson 2.00 5.00
23 Bill Mazeroski 2.00 5.00
24 Diego Segui .75 2.00
25 Jim Bouton 1.25 3.00
26 Eddie Mathews 2.50 6.00
27 Willie Mays 10.00 25.00
28 Ron Santo 1.25 3.00
29 Boog Powell 1.25 3.00
30 Ken McBride .75 2.00
31 Leon Wagner .75 2.00
32 Johnny Callison .75 2.00
33 Zoilo Versalles .75 2.00
34 Jack Baldschun .75 2.00
35 Ron Hunt .75 2.00
36 Richie Allen 2.00 5.00
37 Frank Malzone .75 2.00
38 Bob Allison .75 2.00
39 Jim Fregosi 1.25 3.00
40 Billy Williams 1.25 3.00
41 Bill Freehan 1.25 3.00
42 Vada Pinson 1.25 3.00
43 Bill White 1.25 3.00
44 Roy McMillan .75 2.00
45 Orlando Cepeda 1.25 3.00
46 Rocky Colavito 2.00 5.00
47 Ken Boyer 1.25 3.00
48 Dick Radatz .75 2.00
49 Tommy Davis .75 2.00
50 Walt Bond .75 2.00
51 John Orsino .75 2.00
52 Joe Christopher .75 2.00
53 Al Spangler .75 2.00
54 Jim King .75 2.00
55 Mickey Lolich 1.25 3.00
56 Harmon Killebrew 2.50 6.00
57 Bob Shaw .75 2.00
58 Ernie Banks 4.00 10.00
59 Hank Aaron 15.00 40.00
60 Chuck Hinton .75 2.00
61 Bob Aspromonte .75 2.00
62 Lee Maye .75 2.00
63 Joe Cunningham .75 2.00
64 Pete Ward .75 2.00
65 Bobby Richardson 1.25 3.00
66 Dean Chance .75 2.00
67 Dick Ellsworth .75 2.00
68 Jim Maloney .75 2.00
69 Bob Gibson 2.00 5.00
70 Earl Battey .75 2.00
71 Tony Kubek 1.25 3.00
72 Jack Kralick .75 2.00

1965 Topps Transfers Inserts

COMPLETE SET (72) 200.00 400.00
1 Bob Allison 1.00 2.50
2 Max Alvis 1.00 2.50
3 Luis Aparicio 2.50 6.00
4 Walt Bond 1.00 2.50
5 Jim Bouton 1.50 4.00
6 Jim Bunning 2.50 6.00
7 Rico Carty 1.50 4.00
8 Wayne Causey 1.00 2.50
9 Orlando Cepeda 2.50 6.00
10 Dean Chance 1.00 2.50
11 Tony Conigliaro 1.50 4.00
12 Bill Freehan 1.50 4.00
13 Jim Fregosi 1.50 4.00
14 Bob Gibson 4.00 10.00
15 Dick Groat 1.50 4.00
16 Tom Haller 1.00 2.50
17 Larry Jackson 1.00 2.50
18 Bobby Knoop 1.00 2.50
19 Jim Maloney 1.50 4.00
20 Juan Marichal 2.50 6.00
21 Lee Maye 1.00 2.50
22 Jim O'Toole 1.00 2.50
23 Camilo Pascual 1.00 2.50
24 Vada Pinson 1.50 4.00
25 Juan Pizarro 1.00 2.50
26 Bobby Richardson 2.50 6.00
27 Bob Rodgers 1.00 2.50
28 John Roseboro 1.00 2.50
29 Dick Stuart 1.50 4.00
30 Luis Tiant 1.50 4.00
31 Joe Torre 2.50 6.00
32 Bob Veale SP 5.00 12.00
33 Leon Wagner 1.00 2.50
34 Dave Wickersham 1.00 2.50
35 Billy Williams 2.50 6.00
36 Carl Yastrzemski SP 20.00 50.00
37 Hank Aaron 15.00 40.00
38 Richie Allen 4.00 10.00
39 Bob Aspromonte 1.00 2.50
40 Ken Boyer 2.50 6.00
41 Johnny Callison 1.50 4.00
42 Dean Chance 1.00 2.50
43 Joe Christopher 1.00 2.50
44 Roberto Clemente 30.00 60.00
45 Rocky Colavito 4.00 10.00
46 Tommy Davis 1.50 4.00
47 Don Drysdale 4.00 10.00
48 Chuck Hinton 1.00 2.50
49 Elston Howard 2.50 6.00
50 Ron Hunt 1.00 2.50
51 Al Kaline 8.00 20.00
52 Harmon Killebrew 5.00 12.00
53 Jim King 1.00 2.50
54 Ron Kline 1.00 2.50
55 Sandy Koufax 15.00 40.00
56 Ed Kranepool 1.00 2.50
57 Mickey Mantle 60.00 120.00
58 Willie Mays 15.00 40.00
59 Bill Mazeroski 4.00 10.00
60 Tony Oliva 2.50 6.00
61 Milt Pappas 1.00 2.50
62 Gary Peters 1.00 2.50
63 Boog Powell 2.50 6.00
64 Dick Radatz 1.00 2.50
65 Brooks Robinson 8.00 20.00
66 Frank Robinson 4.00 10.00
67 Ron Santo 2.50 6.00
68 Diego Segui 1.00 2.50
69 Bill Skowron 1.50 4.00
70 Al Spangler 1.00 2.50
71 Pete Ward 1.00 2.50
72 Bill White 1.50 4.00

1966 Topps

The cards in this 598-card set measure 2 1/2" by 3 1/2". There are the same number of cards as in the 1965 set. Once again, the seventh series cards (523 to 598) are considered more difficult to obtain than the cards of any other series in the set. Within this last series there are 43 cards that were printed in lesser quantities than the other cards in that series; these shorter-printed cards are marked by SP in the checklist below. Among other ways, cards were issued in five-card nickel wax packs, 12-card dime cello packs which came 36 packs to a box and 12 boxes to a case. These cards were also issued in 36-card rack packs which cost 29 cents. These rack packs were issued 48 to a case. The only featured subset within this set is League Leaders (215-226). Noteworthy Rookie Cards in the set include Jim Palmer (126), Ferguson Jenkins (254), and Don Sutton (288). Jim Palmer is described in the bio (on his card back) as a left-hander.

COMPLETE SET (598) 2500.00 6000.00
COMMON CARD (1-109) .60 1.50
COMMON CARD (110-283) .75 2.00
COMMON CARD (284-370) 1.25 3.00
COMMON CARD (371-446) 2.00 5.00
COMMON CARD (447-522) 4.00 10.00
COMMON CARD (523-598) 6.00 15.00
COMMON SP (523-598) 12.50 30.00
WRAPPER (5-CENT) 10.00 25.00
1 Willie Mays 100.00 250.00
2 Ted Abernathy .60 1.50
3 Sam Mele MG .60 1.50
4 Ray Culp .60 1.50
5 Jim Fregosi .75 2.00
6 Chuck Schilling .60 1.50
7 Tracy Stallard .60 1.50
8 Floyd Robinson .60 1.50
9 Clete Boyer .75 2.00
10 Tony Cloninger .60 1.50
11 B.Alyea RC/P.Craig .60 1.50
12 John Tsitouris .60 1.50
13 Lou Johnson .75 2.00
14 Norm Siebern .60 1.50
15 Vern Law .75 2.00
16 Larry Brown .60 1.50
17 John Stephenson .60 1.50
18 Roland Sheldon .60 1.50
19 San Francisco Giants TC 2.00 5.00
20 Willie Horton .75 2.00
21 Don Nottebart .60 1.50
22 Joe Nossek .60 1.50
23 Jack Sanford .60 1.50
24 Don Kessinger RC 1.50 4.00
25 Pete Ward .60 1.50
26 Ray Sadecki .60 1.50
27 D.Knowles/A.Etchebarren RC .60 1.50
28 Phil Niekro 8.00 20.00
29 Mike Brumley .60 1.50
30 Pete Rose UER DP 50.00 120.00
31 Jack Cullen .75 2.00
32 Adolfo Phillips RC .60 1.50
33 Jim Pagliaroni .60 1.50
34 Checklist 1 3.00 8.00
35 Ron Swoboda 1.50 4.00
36 Jim Hunter UER DP 8.00 20.00
37 Billy Herman MG .75 2.00
38 Ron Nischwitz .60 1.50
39 Ken Henderson .60 1.50
40 Jim Grant .60 1.50
41 Don LeJohn RC .60 1.50
42 Aubrey Gatewood .60 1.50
43A D.Landrum Dark Button .75 2.00
43B D.Landrum Airbrush Button 8.00 20.00
43C D.Landrum No Button .75 2.00
44 B.Davis/T.Kelley .60 1.50
45 Jim Gentile .75 2.00
46 Howie Koplitz .60 1.50
47 J.C. Martin .60 1.50
48 Paul Blair .75 2.00
49 Woody Woodward .75 2.00
50 Mickey Mantle DP 250.00 600.00
51 Gordon Richardson RC .60 1.50
52 W.Covington/J.Callison 1.50 4.00
53 Bob Duliba .60 1.50
54 Jose Pagan .60 1.50
55 Ken Harrelson .75 2.00
56 Sandy Valdespino .60 1.50
57 Jim Lefebvre .75 2.00
58 Dave Wickersham .60 1.50
59 Cincinnati Reds TC 2.00 5.00
60 Curt Flood 1.50 4.00
61 Bob Bolin .60 1.50
62A Merritt Ranew Sold Line .75 2.00
62B Merritt Ranew NTR 12.50 30.00
63 Jim Stewart .60 1.50
64 Bob Bruce .60 1.50
65 Leon Wagner .60 1.50
66 Al Weis .60 1.50
67 C.Jones/D.Selma RC 1.50 4.00
68 Hal Reniff .60 1.50
69 Ken Hamlin .60 1.50
70 Carl Yastrzemski 25.00 60.00
71 Frank Carpin RC .60 1.50
72 Tony Perez 30.00 80.00
73 Jerry Zimmerman .60 1.50
74 Don Mossi .75 2.00
75 Tommy Davis .75 2.00
76 Red Schoendienst MG 1.50 4.00
77 John Orsino .60 1.50
78 Frank Linzy .60 1.50
79 Joe Pepitone 1.50 4.00
80 Richie Allen 2.50 6.00
81 Ray Oyler .60 1.50
82 Bob Hendley .60 1.50
83 Albie Pearson .75 2.00
84 J.Beauchamp/D.Kelley .60 1.50
85 Eddie Fisher .60 1.50
86 John Bateman .60 1.50
87 Dan Napoleon .60 1.50
88 Fred Whitfield .60 1.50
89 Ted Davidson .60 1.50
90 Luis Aparicio 3.00 8.00
91A Bob Uecker TR 4.00 10.00
91B Bob Uecker NTR 15.00 40.00
92 New York Yankees TC 6.00 15.00
93 Jim Lonborg DP .75 2.00
94 Matty Alou .75 2.00
95 Pete Richert .60 1.50
96 Felipe Alou 1.50 4.00
97 Jim Merritt RC .60 1.50
98 Don Demeter .60 1.50
99 W.Stargell/D.Clendenon 2.50 6.00
100 Sandy Koufax 50.00 100.00
101A Checklist 2 Spahn ERR 6.00 15.00
101B Checklist 2 Henry COR 4.00 10.00
102 Ed Kirkpatrick .60 1.50
103A Dick Groat TR .75 2.00
103B Dick Groat NTR 15.00 40.00
104A Alex Johnson TR .75 2.00
104B Alex Johnson NTR 12.50 30.00
105 Milt Pappas .75 2.00
106 Rusty Staub 1.50 4.00
107 L.Stahl RC/R.Tompkins RC .60 1.50
108 Bobby Klaus .60 1.50
109 Ralph Terry .75 2.00
110 Ernie Banks 40.00 100.00
111 Gary Peters .75 2.00
112 Manny Mota 1.50 4.00
113 Hank Aguirre .75 2.00

114 Jim Gosger .75 2.00
115 Bill Henry .75 2.00
116 Walter Alston MG 2.50 6.00
117 Jake Gibbs .75 2.00
118 Mike McCormick .75 2.00
119 Art Shamsky .75 2.00
120 Harmon Killebrew 12.00 30.00
121 Ray Herbert .75 2.00
122 Joe Gaines .75 2.00
123 F.Bork/J.May .75 2.00
124 Tug McGraw 1.50 4.00
125 Lou Brock 25.00 60.00
126 Jim Palmer UER RC 50.00 120.00
127 Ken Berry .75 2.00
128 Jim Landis .75 2.00
129 Jack Kralick .75 2.00
130 Joe Torre 2.50 6.00
131 California Angels TC 2.00 5.00
132 Orlando Cepeda 3.00 8.00
133 Don McMahon .75 2.00
134 Wes Parker 1.50 4.00
135 Dave Morehead .75 2.00
136 Woody Held .75 2.00
137 Pat Corrales .75 2.00
138 Roger Repoz RC .75 2.00
139 B.Browne RC/D.Young RC .75 2.00
140 Jim Maloney 1.50 4.00
141 Tom McCraw .75 2.00
142 Don Dennis RC .75 2.00
143 Jose Tartabull 1.50 4.00
144 Don Schwall .75 2.00
145 Bill Freehan 1.50 4.00
146 George Altman .75 2.00
147 Lum Harris MG .75 2.00
148 Bob Johnson .75 2.00
149 Dick Nen .75 2.00
150 Rocky Colavito 3.00 8.00
151 Gary Wagner RC .75 2.00
152 Frank Malzone 1.50 4.00
153 Rico Carty 1.50 4.00
154 Chuck Hiller .75 2.00
155 Marcelino Lopez .75 2.00
156 D.Schofield/H.Lanier .75 2.00
157 Rene Lachemann .75 2.00
158 Jim Brewer .75 2.00
159 Chico Ruiz .75 2.00
160 Whitey Ford 20.00 50.00
161 Jerry Lumpe .75 2.00
162 Lee Maye .75 2.00
163 Tito Francona .75 2.00
164 T.Agee/M.Staehle 1.50 4.00
165 Don Lock .75 2.00
166 Chris Krug RC .75 2.00
167 Boog Powell 2.50 6.00
168 Dan Osinski .75 2.00
169 Duke Sims RC .75 2.00
170 Cookie Rojas 1.50 4.00
171 Nick Willhite .75 2.00
172 New York Mets TC 2.00 5.00
173 Al Spangler .75 2.00
174 Ron Taylor .75 2.00
175 Bert Campaneris 1.50 4.00
176 Jim Davenport .75 2.00
177 Hector Lopez .75 2.00
178 Bob Tillman .75 2.00
179 D.Aust RC/B.Tolan 1.50 4.00
180 Vada Pinson 1.50 4.00
181 Al Worthington .75 2.00
182 Jerry Lynch .75 2.00
183A Checklist 3 Large Print 3.00 8.00
183B Checklist 3 Small Print 3.00 8.00
184 Denis Menke .75 2.00
185 Bob Buhl 1.50 4.00
186 Ruben Amaro .75 2.00
187 Chuck Dressen MG 1.50 4.00
188 Al Luplow .75 2.00
189 John Roseboro 1.50 4.00
190 Jimmie Hall .75 2.00
191 Darrell Sutherland RC .75 2.00
192 Vic Power 1.50 4.00
193 Dave McNally 1.50 4.00
194 Washington Senators TC 2.00 5.00
195 Joe Morgan 30.00 80.00
196 Don Pavletich .75 2.00
197 Sonny Siebert .75 2.00
198 Mickey Stanley RC 2.50 6.00
199 Skowron/Romano/Robinson 1.50 4.00
200 Eddie Mathews 6.00 15.00
201 Jim Dickson .75 2.00
202 Clay Dalrymple .75 2.00
203 Jose Santiago .75 2.00
204 Chicago Cubs TC 2.00 5.00
205 Tom Tresh 1.50 4.00
206 Al Jackson .75 2.00
207 Frank Quilici RC .75 2.00
208 Bob Miller .75 2.00
209 F.Fisher/J.Hiller RC 1.50 4.00
210 Bill Mazeroski 10.00 25.00
211 Frank Kreutzer .75 2.00
212 Ed Kranepool 1.50 4.00
213 Fred Newman .75 2.00
214 Tommy Harper 1.50 4.00
215 Clemente/Aaron/Mays LL 30.00 80.00
216 Oliva/Yaz/Davalillo LL 2.00 5.00
217 Mays/McCovey/B.Will LL 10.00 25.00
218 Conigliaro/Cash/Horton LL 2.00 5.00
219 Johnson/F.Rob/Mays LL 10.00 25.00
220 Colavito/Horton/Oliva LL 2.00 5.00
221 Koufax/Marichal/Law LL 5.00 12.00
222 McDowell/Fisher/Siebert LL 2.00 5.00
223 Koufax/Cloni/Drysdale LL 8.00 20.00
224 Grant/Stottlemyre/Kaat LL 2.00 5.00
225 Koufax/Veale/Gibson LL 12.00 30.00
226 McDowell/Lolich/McLain LL 2.00 5.00
227 Russ Nixon .75 2.00
228 Larry Dierker 1.50 4.00
229 Hank Bauer MG 1.50 4.00
230 Johnny Callison 1.50 4.00
231 Floyd Weaver .75 2.00
232 Glenn Beckert 1.50 4.00
233 Dom Zanni .75 2.00
234 R.Beck RC/R.White RC 3.00 8.00
235 Don Cardwell .75 2.00
236 Mike Hershberger .75 2.00
237 Billy O'Dell .75 2.00
238 Los Angeles Dodgers TC 2.00 5.00
239 Orlando Pena .75 2.00
240 Earl Battey .75 2.00
241 Dennis Ribant .75 2.00
242 Jesus Alou .75 2.00
243 Nelson Briles 1.50 4.00
244 C.Harrison RC/S.Jackson .75 2.00
245 John Buzhardt .75 2.00
246 Ed Bailey .75 2.00
247 Carl Warwick .75 2.00
248 Pete Mikkelsen .75 2.00
249 Bill Rigney MG .75 2.00
250 Sammy Ellis .75 2.00
251 Ed Brinkman .75 2.00
252 Denny Lemaster .75 2.00
253 Don Wert .75 2.00
254 Fergie Jenkins RC 50.00 120.00
255 Willie Stargell 15.00 40.00
256 Lew Krausse .75 2.00
257 Jeff Torborg 1.50 4.00
258 Dave Giusti .75 2.00
259 Boston Red Sox TC 2.00 5.00
260 Bob Shaw .75 2.00
261 Ron Hansen .75 2.00
262 Jack Hamilton .75 2.00
263 Tom Egan .75 2.00
264 A.Kosco RC/T.Uhlaender RC .75 2.00
265 Stu Miller 1.50 4.00
266 Pedro Gonzalez UER .75 2.00
267 Joe Sparma .75 2.00
268 John Blanchard .75 2.00
269 Don Heffner MG .75 2.00
270 Claude Osteen 1.50 4.00
271 Hal Lanier .75 2.00
272 Jack Baldschun .75 2.00
273 B.Aspromonte/R.Staub 1.50 4.00
274 Buster Narum .75 2.00
275 Tim McCarver 1.50 4.00
276 Jim Bouton 1.50 4.00
277 George Thomas .75 2.00
278 Cal Koonce .75 2.00
279A Checklist 4 Black Cap 3.00 8.00
279B Checklist 4 Red Cap 3.00 8.00
280 Bobby Knoop .75 2.00
281 Bruce Howard .75 2.00
282 Johnny Lewis .75 2.00
283 Jim Perry 1.50 4.00
284 Bobby Wine 1.25 3.00
285 Luis Tiant 2.00 5.00
286 Gary Geiger 1.25 3.00
287 Jack Aker RC 1.25 3.00
288 D.Sutton RC/B.Singer RC 50.00 120.00
289 Larry Sherry 1.25 3.00
290 Ron Santo 2.00 5.00
291 Moe Drabowsky 2.00 5.00
292 Jim Coker 1.25 3.00
293 Mike Shannon 2.00 5.00
294 Steve Ridzik 1.25 3.00
295 Jim Ray Hart 2.00 5.00
296 Johnny Keane MG 2.00 5.00
297 Jim Owens 1.25 3.00
298 Rico Petrocelli 2.00 5.00
299 Lew Burdette 2.00 5.00
300 Bob Clemente 75.00 200.00
301 Greg Bollo 1.25 3.00
302 Ernie Bowman 1.25 3.00
303 Cleveland Indians TC 2.00 5.00
304 John Herrnstein 1.25 3.00
305 Camilo Pascual 2.00 5.00
306 Ty Cline 1.25 3.00
307 Clay Carroll 2.00 5.00
308 Tom Haller 2.00 5.00
309 Diego Segui 1.25 3.00
310 Frank Robinson 20.00 50.00
311 T.Helms/D.Simpson 2.00 5.00
312 Bob Saverine 1.25 3.00
313 Chris Zachary 1.25 3.00
314 Hector Valle 1.25 3.00
315 Norm Cash 2.00 5.00
316 Jack Fisher 1.25 3.00
317 Dalton Jones 1.25 3.00
318 Harry Walker MG 1.25 3.00
319 Gene Freese 1.25 3.00
320 Bob Gibson 20.00 50.00
321 Rick Reichardt 1.25 3.00
322 Bill Faul 1.25 3.00
323 Ray Barker 1.25 3.00
324 John Boozer UER 1.25 3.00
1965 Record is incorrect
325 Vic Davalillo 1.25 3.00
326 Atlanta Braves TC 2.00 5.00
327 Bernie Allen 1.25 3.00
328 Jerry Grote 2.00 5.00
329 Pete Charton 1.25 3.00
330 Ron Fairly 2.00 5.00
331 Ron Herbel 1.25 3.00
332 Bill Bryan 1.25 3.00
333 J.Coleman RC/J.French RC 1.25 3.00
334 Marty Keough 1.25 3.00
335 Juan Pizarro 1.25 3.00
336 Gene Alley 2.00 5.00
337 Fred Gladding 1.25 3.00
338 Dal Maxvill 1.25 3.00
339 Del Crandall 2.00 5.00
340 Dean Chance 2.00 5.00
341 Wes Westrum MG 2.00 5.00
342 Bob Humphreys 1.25 3.00
343 Joe Christopher 1.25 3.00
344 Steve Blass 2.00 5.00
345 Bob Allison 2.00 5.00
346 Mike de la Hoz 1.25 3.00
347 Phil Regan 2.00 5.00
348 Baltimore Orioles TC 3.00 8.00
349 Cap Peterson 1.25 3.00
350 Mel Stottlemyre 3.00 8.00
351 Fred Valentine 1.25 3.00
352 Bob Aspromonte 1.25 3.00
353 Al McBean 1.25 3.00
354 Smoky Burgess 2.00 5.00
355 Wade Blasingame 1.25 3.00
356 O.Johnson RC/K.Sanders RC 1.25 3.00
357 Gerry Arrigo 1.25 3.00
358 Charlie Smith 1.25 3.00
359 Johnny Briggs 1.25 3.00
360 Ron Hunt 1.25 3.00
361 Tom Satriano 1.25 3.00
362 Gates Brown 2.00 5.00
363 Checklist 5 4.00 10.00
364 Nate Oliver 1.25 3.00
365 Roger Maris UER 50.00 120.00
366 Wayne Causey 1.25 3.00
367 Mel Nelson 1.25 3.00
368 Charlie Lau 2.00 5.00
369 Jim King 1.25 3.00
370 Chico Cardenas 1.25 3.00
371 Lee Stange 2.00 5.00
372 Harvey Kuenn 3.00 8.00
373 J.Hiatt/D.Estelle 3.00 8.00
374 Bob Locker 3.00 8.00
375 Donn Clendenon 3.00 8.00
376 Paul Schaal 2.00 5.00
377 Turk Farrell 2.00 5.00
378 Dick Tracewski 2.00 5.00
379 St. Louis Cardinals TC 4.00 10.00
380 Tony Conigliaro 4.00 10.00
381 Hank Fischer 2.00 5.00
382 Phil Roof 2.00 5.00
383 Jackie Brandt 2.00 5.00
384 Al Downing 3.00 8.00
385 Ken Boyer 4.00 10.00
386 Gil Hodges MG 3.00 8.00
387 Howie Reed 2.00 5.00
388 Don Mincher 2.00 5.00
389 Jim O'Toole 3.00 8.00
390 Brooks Robinson 20.00 50.00
391 Chuck Hinton 2.00 5.00
392 B.Hands RC/R.Hundley RC 3.00 8.00
393 George Brunet 2.00 5.00
394 Ron Brand 2.00 5.00
395 Len Gabrielson 2.00 5.00
396 Jerry Stephenson 2.00 5.00
397 Bill White 3.00 8.00
398 Danny Cater 2.00 5.00
399 Ray Washburn 2.00 5.00
400 Zoilo Versalles 3.00 8.00
401 Ken McMullen 2.00 5.00
402 Jim Hickman 2.00 5.00
403 Fred Talbot 2.00 5.00
404 Pittsburgh Pirates TC 4.00 10.00
405 Elston Howard 3.00 8.00
406 Joey Jay 2.00 5.00
407 John Kennedy 2.00 5.00
408 Lee Thomas 3.00 8.00
409 Billy Hoeft 2.00 5.00
410 Al Kaline 15.00 40.00
411 Gene Mauch MG 2.00 5.00
412 Sam Bowens 2.00 5.00
413 Johnny Romano 2.00 5.00
414 Dan Coombs 2.00 5.00
415 Max Alvis 2.00 5.00
416 Phil Ortega 2.00 5.00
417 J.McGlothlin RC/E.Sukla RC 2.00 5.00
418 Phil Gagliano 2.00 5.00
419 Mike Ryan 2.00 5.00
420 Juan Marichal 12.00 30.00
421 Roy McMillan 3.00 8.00
422 Ed Charles 2.00 5.00
423 Ernie Broglio 2.00 5.00
424 L.May RC/D.Osteen RC 4.00 10.00
425 Bob Veale 3.00 8.00
426 Chicago White Sox TC 4.00 10.00
427 John Miller 2.00 5.00
428 Sandy Alomar 2.00 5.00
429 Bill Monbouquette 2.00 5.00
430 Don Drysdale 12.00 30.00
431 Walt Bond 2.00 5.00
432 Bob Heffner 2.00 5.00
433 Alvin Dark MG 3.00 8.00
434 Willie Kirkland 2.00 5.00
435 Jim Bunning 6.00 15.00
436 Julian Javier 3.00 8.00
437 Al Stanek 2.00 5.00
438 Willie Smith 2.00 5.00
439 Pedro Ramos 2.00 5.00
440 Deron Johnson 3.00 8.00
441 Tommie Sisk 2.00 5.00
442 E.Barnowski RC/E.Watt RC 2.00 5.00
443 Bill Wakefield 2.00 5.00
444 Checklist 6 4.00 10.00
445 Jim Kaat 4.00 10.00
446 Mack Jones 2.00 5.00
447 D.Ellsw UER Hubbs 6.00 15.00
448 Eddie Stanky MG 4.00 10.00
449 Joe Moeller 4.00 10.00
450 Tony Oliva 6.00 15.00
451 Barry Latman 4.00 10.00
452 Joe Azcue 4.00 10.00
453 Ron Kline 4.00 10.00
454 Jerry Buchek 4.00 10.00
455 Mickey Lolich 6.00 15.00
456 D.Brandon RC/J.Foy RC 4.00 10.00
457 Joe Gibbon 4.00 10.00
458 Manny Jiminez 4.00 10.00
459 Bill McCool 4.00 10.00
460 Curt Blefary 4.00 10.00
461 Roy Face 6.00 15.00
462 Bob Rodgers 4.00 10.00
463 Philadelphia Phillies TC 6.00 15.00
464 Larry Bearnarth 4.00 10.00
465 Don Buford 4.00 10.00
466 Ken Johnson 4.00 10.00
467 Vic Roznovsky 4.00 10.00
468 Johnny Podres 6.00 15.00
469 B.Murcer RC/D.Womack RC 15.00 40.00
470 Sam McDowell 6.00 15.00
471 Bob Skinner 4.00 10.00
472 Terry Fox 4.00 10.00
473 Rich Rollins 4.00 10.00
474 Dick Schofield 4.00 10.00
475 Dick Radatz 4.00 10.00
476 Bobby Bragan MG 4.00 10.00
477 Steve Barber 4.00 10.00
478 Tony Gonzalez 4.00 10.00
479 Jim Hannan 4.00 10.00
480 Dick Stuart 4.00 10.00
481 Bob Lee 4.00 10.00
482 J.Boccabella/D.Dowling 4.00 10.00
483 Joe Nuxhall 4.00 10.00
484 Wes Covington 4.00 10.00
485 Bob Bailey 4.00 10.00
486 Tommy John 6.00 15.00
487 Al Ferrara 4.00 10.00
488 George Banks 4.00 10.00
489 Curt Simmons 4.00 10.00
490 Bobby Richardson 10.00 25.00
491 Dennis Bennett 4.00 10.00
492 Kansas City Athletics TC 6.00 15.00
493 Johnny Klippstein 4.00 10.00
494 Gordy Coleman 4.00 10.00
495 Dick McAuliffe 6.00 15.00
496 Lindy McDaniel 4.00 10.00
497 Chris Cannizzaro 4.00 10.00
498 L.Walker RC/W.Fryman RC 4.00 10.00
499 Wally Bunker 4.00 10.00
500 Hank Aaron 60.00 150.00
501 John O'Donoghue 4.00 10.00
502 Lenny Green UER 4.00 10.00
503 Steve Hamilton 6.00 15.00
504 Grady Hatton MG 4.00 10.00
505 Jose Cardenal 4.00 10.00
506 Bo Belinsky 6.00 15.00
507 Johnny Edwards 4.00 10.00
508 Steve Hargan RC 6.00 15.00
509 Jake Wood 4.00 10.00
510 Hoyt Wilhelm 10.00 25.00
511 B.Barton RC/T.Fuentes RC 4.00 10.00
512 Dick Stigman 4.00 10.00
513 Camilo Carreon 4.00 10.00
514 Hal Woodeshick 4.00 10.00
515 Frank Howard 6.00 15.00
516 Eddie Bressoud 4.00 10.00
517A Checklist 7 White Sox 6.00 15.00
517B Checklist 7 W.Sox 6.00 15.00
518 H.Hippauf RC/A.Umbach RC 4.00 10.00
519 Bob Friend 6.00 15.00
520 Jim Wynn 6.00 15.00
521 John Wyatt 4.00 10.00
522 Phil Linz 4.00 10.00
523 Bob Sadowski 4.00 10.00
524 O.Brown RC/D.Mason RC SP 20.00 50.00
525 Gary Bell SP 12.50 30.00
526 Minnesota Twins TC SP 50.00 100.00
527 Julio Navarro 6.00 15.00
528 Jesse Gonder SP 12.50 30.00
529 Elia/Higgins/Voss RC 6.00 15.00
530 Robin Roberts 20.00 50.00
531 Joe Cunningham 6.00 15.00
532 A.Monteagudo SP 12.50 30.00
533 Jerry Adair SP 12.50 30.00
534 D.Eilers RC/R.Gardner RC 6.00 15.00
535 Willie Davis SP 15.00 40.00
536 Dick Egan 6.00 15.00
537 Herman Franks MG 6.00 15.00
538 Bob Allen SP 12.50 30.00
539 B.Heath RC/C.Sembera RC 10.00 25.00
540 Denny McLain SP 40.00 100.00
541 Gene Oliver SP 12.50 30.00
542 George Smith 6.00 15.00
543 Roger Craig SP 12.50 30.00
544 Hoerner/Kernek/Williams RC SP 12.50 30.00
545 Dick Green SP 12.50 30.00
546 Dwight Siebler 10.00 25.00
547 Horace Clarke SP RC 75.00 200.00
548 Gary Kroll SP 12.50 30.00
549 A.Closter RC/C.Cox RC 6.00 15.00
550 Willie McCovey SP 50.00 100.00
551 Bob Purkey SP 12.50 30.00
552 B.Tebbetts MG SP 12.50 30.00
553 P.Garrett RC/J.Warner 6.00 15.00
554 Jim Northrup SP 12.50 30.00
555 Ron Perranoski SP 12.50 30.00
556 Mel Queen SP 12.50 30.00
557 Felix Mantilla SP 12.50 30.00
558 Grilli/Magrini/Scott RC 8.00 20.00
559 Roberto Pena SP 12.50 30.00
560 Joel Horlen 6.00 15.00
561 Choo Choo Coleman SP 50.00 120.00
562 Russ Snyder 10.00 25.00
563 P.Cimino RC/C.Tovar RC 6.00 15.00
564 Bob Chance SP 12.50 30.00
565 Jimmy Piersall SP 15.00 40.00
566 Mike Cuellar SP 12.50 30.00
567 Dick Howser SP 15.00 40.00
568 P.Lindblad RC/R.Stone RC 6.00 15.00
569 Orlando McFarlane SP 12.50 30.00
570 Art Mahaffey SP 12.50 30.00
571 Dave Roberts SP 12.50 30.00
572 Bob Priddy 6.00 15.00
573 Derrell Griffith 6.00 15.00
574 B.Hepler RC/B.Murphy RC 6.00 15.00
575 Earl Wilson 6.00 15.00
576 Dave Nicholson SP 12.50 30.00
577 Jack Lamabe SP 12.50 30.00
578 Chi Chi Olivo SP RC 12.50 30.00
579 Bertaina/Brabender/Johnson RC 8.00 20.00
580 Billy Williams SP 30.00 60.00
581 Tony Martinez 6.00 15.00
582 Garry Roggenburk 6.00 15.00
583 Tigers TC SP UER 60.00 120.00
584 F.Fernandez RC/F.Peterson RC 6.00 15.00
585 Tony Taylor 10.00 25.00
586 Claude Raymond SP 12.50 30.00
587 Dick Bertell 6.00 15.00
588 C.Dobson RC/K.Suarez RC 6.00 15.00
589 Lou Klimchock SP 12.50 30.00
590 Bill Skowron SP 15.00 40.00
591 B.Shirley RC/G.Jackson RC SP 150.00 400.00
592 Andre Rodgers 6.00 15.00
593 Doug Camilli SP 12.50 30.00
594 Chico Salmon 6.00 15.00
595 Larry Jackson 6.00 15.00
596 N.Colbert RC/G.Sims RC SP 12.50 30.00
597 John Sullivan 6.00 15.00
598 Gaylord Perry SP 60.00 150.00

1966 Topps Rub-Offs

COMPLETE SET (120) 200.00 400.00
COMMON RUB-OFF (1-120) .60 1.50
COMMON PEN. (101-120) .40 1.00
1 Hank Aaron 10.00 25.00
2 Jerry Adair .60 1.50
3 Richie Allen .75 2.00
4 Jesus Alou .60 1.50
5 Max Alvis .60 1.50
6 Bob Aspromonte .60 1.50
7 Ernie Banks 4.00 10.00
8 Earl Battey .60 1.50
9 Curt Blefary .60 1.50
10 Ken Boyer 1.25 3.00
11 Bob Bruce .60 1.50
12 Jim Bunning 1.25 3.00
13 Johnny Callison .75 2.00
14 Bert Campaneris .75 2.00
15 Jose Cardenal .60 1.50
16 Dean Chance .60 1.50
17 Ed Charles .60 1.50
18 Roberto Clemente 30.00 60.00
19 Tony Cloninger .60 1.50
20 Rocky Colavito 2.00 5.00
21 Tony Conigliaro .75 2.00
22 Vic Davalillo .60 1.50
23 Willie Davis .75 2.00
24 Don Drysdale 2.00 5.00
25 Sammy Ellis .60 1.50
26 Dick Ellsworth .60 1.50
27 Ron Fairly .75 2.00
28 Dick Farrell .60 1.50
29 Eddie Fisher .60 1.50
30 Jack Fisher .60 1.50
31 Curt Flood .75 2.00
32 Whitey Ford 2.00 5.00
33 Bill Freehan .75 2.00
34 Jim Fregosi .75 2.00
35 Bob Gibson 2.00 5.00
36 Jim Grant .60 1.50
37 Jimmie Hall .60 1.50
38 Ken Harrelson .75 2.00
39 Jim Ray Hart .60 1.50
40 Joel Horlen .60 1.50
41 Willie Horton .75 2.00
42 Frank Howard .75 2.00
43 Deron Johnson .60 1.50
44 Al Kaline 4.00 10.00
45 Harmon Killebrew 3.00 8.00
46 Bobby Knoop .60 1.50
47 Sandy Koufax 8.00 20.00
48 Ed Kranepool .60 1.50
49 Gary Kroll .60 1.50
50 Don Landrum .60 1.50
51 Vern Law .75 2.00
52 Johnny Lewis .60 1.50
53 Don Lock .60 1.50
54 Mickey Lolich .75 2.00
55 Jim Maloney .75 2.00
56 Felix Mantilla .60 1.50
57 Mickey Mantle 30.00 60.00
58 Juan Marichal 2.00 5.00
59 Eddie Mathews 3.00 8.00
60 Willie Mays 10.00 25.00
61 Bill Mazeroski 2.00 5.00
62 Dick McAuliffe .60 1.50
63 Tim McCarver .75 2.00
64 Willie McCovey 2.00 5.00
65 Sam McDowell .75 2.00
66 Ken McMullen .60 1.50
67 Denis Menke .60 1.50
68 Bill Monbouquette .60 1.50
69 Joe Morgan 2.00 5.00
70 Fred Newman .60 1.50
71 John O'Donoghue .60 1.50
72 Tony Oliva 1.25 3.00
73 Johnny Orsino .60 1.50
74 Phil Ortega .60 1.50
75 Milt Pappas .75 2.00
76 Dick Radatz .75 2.00
77 Bobby Richardson 1.25 3.00
78 Pete Richert .60 1.50
79 Brooks Robinson 4.00 10.00
80 Floyd Robinson .60 1.50
81 Frank Robinson 2.00 5.00
82 Cookie Rojas .60 1.50
83 Pete Rose 12.50 30.00
84 John Roseboro .75 2.00
85 Ron Santo 1.25 3.00
86 Bill Skowron .75 2.00
87 Willie Stargell 2.00 5.00
88 Mel Stottlemyre .75 2.00
89 Dick Stuart .60 1.50
90 Ron Swoboda .75 2.00
91 Fred Talbot .60 1.50
92 Ralph Terry .75 2.00
93 Joe Torre 2.00 5.00
94 Tom Tresh 1.25 3.00
95 Bob Veale .60 1.50
96 Pete Ward .60 1.50
97 Bill White .75 2.00
98 Billy Williams 1.25 3.00
99 Jim Wynn .75 2.00
100 Carl Yastrzemski 5.00 12.00
101 Baltimore Orioles .40 1.00
102 Boston Red Sox 1.00 2.50
103 California Angels .40 1.00
104 Chicago Cubs .40 1.00
105 Chicago White Sox .40 1.00
106 Cincinnati Reds .40 1.00
107 Cleveland Indians .40 1.00
108 Detroit Tigers 1.00 2.50
109 Houston Astros .40 1.00
110 Kansas City Athletics .40 1.00
111 Los Angeles Dodgers 1.00 2.50
112 Atlanta Braves .40 1.00
113 Minnesota Twins .40 1.00
114 New York Mets 1.00 2.50
115 New York Yankees 1.50 4.00
116 Philadelphia Phillies .40 1.00
117 Pittsburgh Pirates .40 1.00
118 San Francisco Giants .40 1.00
119 St. Louis Cardinals .40 1.00
120 Washington Senators 1.00 2.50

1966 Topps Venezuelan

This set is a parallel version of the first 370 cards of the regular 1966 Topps set and is similar in design. The cards were issued for the Venezuelan market. The backs of these cards are noticably darker than their American counterparts.

COMPLETE SET (370) 4000.00 8000.00
1 Willie Mays 500.00 1000.00
2 Ted Abernathy 6.00 15.00
3 Sam Mele MG 6.00 15.00
4 Ray Culp 6.00 15.00
5 Jim Fregosi 6.00 15.00
6 Chuck Schilling 6.00 15.00
7 Tracy Stallard 6.00 15.00
8 Floyd Robinson 6.00 15.00
9 Clete Boyer 8.00 20.00
10 Tony Cloninger 6.00 15.00
11 Brant Alyea 6.00 15.00
Pete Craig
12 John Tsitouris 6.00 15.00
13 Lou Johnson 6.00 15.00
14 Norm Siebern 6.00 15.00
15 Vern Law 6.00 15.00
16 Larry Brown 6.00 15.00
17 John Stephenson 6.00 15.00
18 Roland Sheldon 6.00 15.00
19 San Francisco Giants 10.00 25.00
Team Card
20 Willie Horton 8.00 20.00
21 Don Nottebart 6.00 15.00
22 Joe Nossek 6.00 15.00
23 Jack Sanford 6.00 15.00
24 Don Kessinger 8.00 20.00
25 Pete Ward 6.00 15.00
26 Ray Sadecki 6.00 15.00
27 Darold Knowles 6.00 15.00
Andy Etchebarren
28 Phil Niekro 60.00 120.00
29 Mike Brumley 6.00 15.00
30 Pete Rose 150.00 300.00
31 Jack Cullen 6.00 15.00
32 Dollo Phillips 6.00 15.00
33 Jim Pagliaroni 6.00 15.00
34 Checklist 1 12.50 30.00
35 Ron Swoboda 6.00 15.00
36 Jim Hunter UER
(Stats say 1963 and 1964, should b 60.00 120.00
37 Billy Herman MG 8.00 20.00
38 Ron Nischwitz 6.00 15.00
39 Ken Henderson 6.00 15.00
40 Jim Grant 6.00 15.00
41 Don LeJohn 6.00 15.00
42 Aubrey Gatewood 6.00 15.00
43 Don Landrum 6.00 15.00
44 Bill Davis 6.00 15.00
Tom Kelley
45 Jim Gentile 6.00 15.00
46 Howie Koplitz 6.00 15.00
47 J.C. Martin 6.00 15.00
48 Paul Blair 6.00 15.00
49 Woody Woodward 6.00 15.00
50 Mickey Mantle 750.00 1500.00
51 Gordon Richardson 6.00 15.00
52 Wes Covington 6.00 15.00
Johnny Callison
53 Bob Duliba 6.00 15.00
54 Jose Pagan 6.00 15.00
55 Ken Harrelson 8.00 20.00
56 Sandy Valdespino 6.00 15.00
57 Jim Lefebvre 6.00 15.00
58 Dave Wickersham 6.00 15.00
59 Reds Team 10.00 25.00
60 Curt Flood 8.00 20.00
61 Bob Bolin 6.00 15.00
62 Merritt Ranew 6.00 15.00
63 Jim Stewart 6.00 15.00
64 Bob Bruce 6.00 15.00
65 Leon Wagner 6.00 15.00
66 Al Weis 6.00 15.00
67 Cleon Jones 6.00 15.00
Dick Selma
68 Hal Reniff 6.00 15.00
69 Ken Hamlin 6.00 15.00
70 Carl Yastrzemski 75.00 150.00
71 Frank Carpin 6.00 15.00
72 Tony Perez 75.00 150.00
73 Jerry Zimmerman 6.00 15.00
74 Don Mossi 6.00 15.00
75 Tommy Davis 8.00 20.00
76 Red Schoendienst MG 8.00 20.00
77 John Orsino 6.00 15.00
78 Frank Linzy 6.00 15.00
79 Joe Pepitone 6.00 15.00
80 Richie Allen 12.50 30.00
81 Ray Oyler 6.00 15.00
82 Bob Hendley 6.00 15.00
83 Albie Pearson 6.00 15.00
84 Jim Beauchamp 6.00 15.00
Dick Kelley
85 Eddie Fisher 6.00 15.00
86 John Bateman 6.00 15.00
87 Dan Napoleon 6.00 15.00
88 Fred Whitfield 6.00 15.00
89 Ted Davidson 6.00 15.00
90 Luis Aparicio 20.00 50.00
91 Bob Uecker 30.00 60.00
92 Yankees Team 40.00 80.00
93 Jim Lonborg 6.00 15.00
94 Matty Alou 8.00 20.00
95 Pete Richert 6.00 15.00
96 Felipe Alou 8.00 20.00
97 Jim Merritt 6.00 15.00
98 Don Demeter 6.00 15.00
99 Willie Stargell 12.50 30.00
Donn Clendenon
100 Sandy Koufax 2500.00 5000.00
101 Checklist 2 15.00 40.00
102 Ed Kirkpatrick 6.00 15.00
103 Dick Groat 6.00 15.00
104 Alex Johnson 6.00 15.00
105 Milt Pappas 8.00 20.00
106 Rusty Staub 8.00 20.00
107 Larry Stahl 6.00 15.00
Ron Tompkins
108 Bobby Klaus 6.00 15.00
109 Ralph Terry 6.00 15.00
110 Ernie Banks 100.00 200.00
111 Gary Peters 6.00 15.00
112 Manny Mota 8.00 20.00
113 Hank Aguirre 6.00 15.00
114 Jim Gosger 6.00 15.00
115 Bill Henry 6.00 15.00
116 Walt Alston MG 8.00 20.00
117 Jake Gibbs 6.00 15.00
118 Mike McCormick 6.00 15.00
119 Art Shamsky 6.00 15.00
120 Harmon Killebrew 50.00 100.00
121 Ray Herbert 6.00 15.00
122 Joe Gaines 6.00 15.00
123 Frank Bork 6.00 15.00
Jerry May
124 Tug McGraw 8.00 20.00
125 Lou Brock 60.00 120.00
126 Jim Palmer UER/(Described as a lefthander on card back) 300.00 600.00
127 Ken Berry 6.00 15.00
128 Jim Landis 6.00 15.00
129 Jack Kralick 6.00 15.00
130 Joe Torre 12.50 30.00
131 Angels Team 10.00 25.00
132 Orlando Cepeda 30.00 60.00
133 Don McMahon 6.00 15.00
134 Wes Parker 6.00 15.00
135 Dave Morehead 6.00 15.00
136 Woody Held 6.00 15.00
137 Pat Corrales 6.00 15.00
138 Roger Repoz 6.00 15.00
139 Byron Browne 6.00 15.00
Don Young
140 Jim Maloney 6.00 15.00
141 Tom McCraw 6.00 15.00
142 Don Dennis 6.00 15.00
143 Jose Tartabull 6.00 15.00
144 Don Schwall 6.00 15.00
145 Bill Freehan 8.00 20.00
146 George Altman 6.00 15.00
147 Lum Harris MG 6.00 15.00
148 Bob Johnson 6.00 15.00
149 Dick Nen 6.00 15.00
150 Rocky Colavito 12.50 30.00
151 Gary Wagner 6.00 15.00
152 Frank Malzone 6.00 15.00
153 Rico Carty 8.00 20.00
154 Chuck Hiller 6.00 15.00
155 Marcelino Lopez 6.00 15.00
156 Dick Schofield 6.00 15.00
Hal Lanier
157 Rene Lachemann 6.00 15.00
158 Jim Brewer 6.00 15.00
159 Chico Ruiz 6.00 15.00
160 Whitey Ford 75.00 150.00
161 Jerry Lumpe 6.00 15.00
162 Lee Maye 6.00 15.00
163 Tito Francona 6.00 15.00
164 Tommie Agee 6.00 15.00
Marv Staehle
165 Don Lock 6.00 15.00
166 Chris Krug 6.00 15.00
167 Boog Powell 12.50 30.00
168 Dan Osinski 6.00 15.00
169 Duke Sims 6.00 15.00
170 Cookie Rojas 6.00 15.00
171 Nick Willhite 6.00 15.00
172 Mets Team 10.00 25.00
173 Al Spangler 6.00 15.00
174 Ron Taylor 6.00 15.00
175 Bert Campaneris 8.00 20.00
176 Jim Davenport 6.00 15.00
177 Hector Lopez 6.00 15.00
178 Bob Tillman 6.00 15.00
179 Dennis Aust 6.00 15.00
Bob Tolan
180 Vada Pinson 8.00 20.00
181 Al Worthington 6.00 15.00
182 Jerry Lynch 6.00 15.00
183 Checklist 3 12.50 30.00
184 Denis Menke 6.00 15.00
185 Bob Buhl 6.00 15.00
186 Ruben Amaro 6.00 15.00
187 Chuck Dressen MG 6.00 15.00
188 Al Luplow 6.00 15.00
189 John Roseboro 6.00 15.00
190 Jimmie Hall 6.00 15.00
191 Darrell Sutherland 6.00 15.00
192 Vic Power 6.00 15.00
193 Dave McNally 6.00 15.00
194 Senators Team 6.00 15.00
195 Joe Morgan 50.00 100.00
196 Don Pavletich 6.00 15.00
197 Sonny Siebert 6.00 15.00
198 Mickey Stanley 6.00 15.00
199 Chisox Clubbers 6.00 15.00
200 Eddie Mathews 50.00 100.00
201 Jim Dickson 6.00 15.00
202 Clay Dalrymple 6.00 15.00
203 Jose Santiago 6.00 15.00
204 Cubs Team 10.00 25.00
205 Tom Tresh 8.00 20.00
206 Al Jackson 6.00 15.00
207 Frank Quilici 6.00 15.00
208 Bob Miller 6.00 15.00
209 Fritz Fisher 6.00 15.00
John Hiller
210 Bill Mazeroski 40.00 80.00
211 Frank Kreutzer 6.00 15.00
212 Ed Kranepool 6.00 15.00
213 Fred Newman 6.00 15.00
214 Tommy Harper 6.00 15.00
215 NL Batting Leaders 150.00 300.00
Bob Clemente
216 AL Batting Leaders 12.50 30.00
Tony Oliva
Carl Yastrzemski/
217 Willie Mays 60.00 120.00
Willie McCovey
Billy Williams LL
218 AL Home Run Leaders 10.00 25.00
Tony Conigliaro
Norm Cash
W
219 NL RBI Leaders 15.00 40.00
Deron Johnson
Frank Robinson
Wil
220 AL RBI Leaders 10.00 25.00
Rocky Colavito
Willie Horton
Ton
221 NL ERA Leaders 30.00 60.00
Sandy Koufax
Juan Marichal
Vern
222 AL ERA Leaders 10.00 25.00
Sam McDowell
Eddie Fisher
Sonny
223 NL Pitching Leaders 30.00 60.00
Sandy Koufax
Tony Cloninger#
224 AL Pitching Leaders 10.00 25.00
Jim Grant
Mel Stottlemyre
J
225 NL Strikeout Leaders 30.00 60.00
Sandy Koufax
Bob Veale
Bob
226 AL Strikeout Leaders 10.00 25.00

Card	Low	High
Sam McDowell		
Mickey Lolich#		
227 Russ Nixon	6.00	15.00
228 Larry Dierker	6.00	15.00
229 Hank Bauer MG	6.00	15.00
230 Johnny Callison	6.00	15.00
231 Floyd Weaver	6.00	15.00
232 Glenn Beckert	6.00	15.00
233 Dom Zanni	6.00	15.00
234 Rich Beck	10.00	25.00
Roy White		
235 Don Cardwell	6.00	15.00
236 Mike Hershberger	6.00	15.00
237 Billy O'Dell	6.00	15.00
238 Dodgers Team	10.00	25.00
239 Orlando Pena	6.00	15.00
240 Earl Battey	6.00	15.00
241 Dennis Ribant	6.00	15.00
242 Jesus Alou	6.00	15.00
243 Nelson Briles	6.00	15.00
244 Chuck Harrison	6.00	15.00
Sonny Jackson		
245 John Buzhardt	6.00	15.00
246 Ed Bailey	6.00	15.00
247 Carl Warwick	6.00	15.00
248 Pete Mikkelsen	6.00	15.00
249 Bill Rigney MG	6.00	15.00
250 Sammy Ellis	6.00	15.00
251 Ed Brinkman	6.00	15.00
252 Denny Lemaster	6.00	15.00
253 Don Wert	6.00	15.00
254 Fergie Jenkins	250.00	500.00
Bill Sorrell		
255 Willie Stargell	60.00	120.00
256 Lew Krausse	6.00	15.00
257 Jeff Torborg	6.00	15.00
258 Dave Giusti	6.00	15.00
259 Boston Red Sox	10.00	25.00
Team Card		
260 Bob Shaw	6.00	15.00
261 Ron Hansen	6.00	15.00
262 Jack Hamilton	6.00	15.00
263 Tom Egan	6.00	15.00
264 Andy Kosco	6.00	15.00
Ted Uhlaender		
265 Stu Miller	6.00	15.00
266 Pedro Gonzalez UER	6.00	15.00
Misspelled Gonzales on card ba		
267 Joe Sparma	6.00	15.00
268 John Blanchard	6.00	15.00
269 Don Heffner MG	6.00	15.00
270 Claude Osteen	6.00	15.00
271 Hal Lanier	6.00	15.00
272 Jack Bladschun	6.00	15.00
273 Bob Aspromonte	6.00	15.00
Rusty Staub		
274 Buster Narum	6.00	15.00
275 Tim McCarver	10.00	25.00
276 Jim Bouton	8.00	20.00
277 George Thomas	6.00	15.00
278 Cal Koonce	6.00	15.00
279 Checklist 4	10.00	25.00
280 Bobby Knoop	6.00	15.00
281 Bruce Howard	6.00	15.00
282 Johnny Lewis	6.00	15.00
283 Jim Perry	8.00	20.00
284 Bobby Wine	6.00	15.00
285 Luis Tiant	10.00	25.00
286 Gary Geiger	6.00	15.00
287 Jack Aker	6.00	15.00
288 Bill Singer	125.00	250.00
Don Sutton		
289 Larry Sherry	6.00	15.00
290 Ron Santo	12.50	30.00
291 Moe Drabowsky	6.00	15.00
292 Jim Coker	6.00	15.00
293 Mike Shannon	6.00	15.00
294 Steve Ridzik	6.00	15.00
295 Jim Ray Hart	6.00	15.00
296 Johnny Keane MG	6.00	15.00
297 Jim Owens	6.00	15.00
298 Rico Petrocelli	6.00	15.00
299 Lou Burdette	8.00	20.00
300 Roberto Clemente	500.00	1000.00
301 Greg Bollo	6.00	15.00
302 Ernie Bowman	6.00	15.00
303 Cleveland Indians	10.00	25.00
Team Card		
304 John Herrnstein	6.00	15.00
305 Camilo Pascual	6.00	15.00
306 Ty Cline	6.00	15.00
307 Clay Carroll	6.00	15.00
308 Tom Haller	6.00	15.00
309 Diego Segui	6.00	15.00
310 Frank Robinson	100.00	200.00
311 Tommy Helms	6.00	15.00
Dick Simpson		
312 Bob Saverine	6.00	15.00
313 Chris Zachary	6.00	15.00
314 Hector Valle	6.00	15.00
315 Norm Cash	10.00	25.00
316 Jack Fisher	6.00	15.00
317 Dalton Jones	6.00	15.00
318 Harry Walker MG	6.00	15.00
319 Gene Freese	6.00	15.00
320 Bob Gibson	75.00	150.00
321 Rick Reichardt	6.00	15.00
322 Bill Faul	6.00	15.00
323 Ray Barker	6.00	15.00
324 John Boozer	6.00	15.00
325 Vic Davlillo	6.00	15.00
326 Braves Team	10.00	25.00
327 Bernie Allen	6.00	15.00
328 Jerry Grote	6.00	15.00
329 Pete Charton	6.00	15.00
330 Ron Fairly	8.00	20.00
331 Ron Herbel	6.00	15.00
332 Bill Bryan	6.00	15.00
333 Joe Coleman	6.00	15.00
Jim French		
334 Marty Keough	6.00	15.00
335 Juan Pizarro	6.00	15.00
336 Gene Alley	6.00	15.00
337 Fred Gladding	6.00	15.00
338 Dal Maxvill	6.00	15.00
339 Del Crandall	6.00	15.00
340 Dean Chance	6.00	15.00
341 Wes Westrum MG	6.00	15.00
342 Bob Humphreys	6.00	15.00
343 Joe Christopher	6.00	15.00
344 Steve Blass	6.00	15.00
345 Bob Allison	6.00	15.00
346 Mike de la Hoz	6.00	15.00
347 Phil Regan	6.00	15.00
348 Orioles Team	12.50	30.00
349 Cap Peterson	6.00	15.00
350 Mel Stottlemyre	8.00	20.00
351 Fred Valentine	6.00	15.00
352 Bob Aspromonte	6.00	15.00
353 Al McBean	6.00	15.00
354 Smoky Burgess	6.00	15.00
355 Wade Blasingame	6.00	15.00
356 Owen Johnson	6.00	15.00
Ken Sanders		
357 Gerry Arrigo	6.00	15.00
358 Charlie Smith	6.00	15.00
359 Johnny Briggs	6.00	15.00
360 Ron Hunt	6.00	15.00
361 Tom Satriano	6.00	15.00
362 Gates Brown	6.00	15.00
363 Checklist 5	12.50	30.00
364 Nate Oliver	6.00	15.00
365 Roger Maris	100.00	200.00
366 Wayne Causey	6.00	15.00
367 Mel Nelson	6.00	15.00
368 Charlie Lau	6.00	15.00
369 Jim King	6.00	15.00
370 Chico Cardenas	6.00	15.00

1967 Topps

The cards in this 609-card set measure 2 1/2" by 3 1/2". The 1967 Topps series is considered by some collectors to be one of the company's finest accomplishments in baseball card production. Excellent color photographs are combined with easy-to-read backs. Cards 458 to 533 are slightly harder to find than numbers 1 to 457, and the inevitable high series (534 to 609) exists. Each checklist card features a small circular picture of a popular player included in that series. Printing discrepancies resulted in some high series cards being in shorter supply. The checklist below identifies (by DP) 22 double-printed high numbers; of the 76 cards in the last series, 54 cards were short printed and the other 22 cards are much more plentiful. Featured subsets within this set include World Series cards (151-155) and League Leaders (233-244). A limited number of "proof" Roger Maris cards were produced. These cards are blank backed and Maris is listed as a New York Yankee on it. Some Bob Bolin cards: (number 252) have a white smear in between his names. Another tough variation that has been recently discovered involves card number 58 Paul Schaal. The tough version has a green bat above his name. The key Rookie Cards in the set are high number cards of Rod Carew and Tom Seaver. Confirmed methods of selling these cards include five-card nickel wax packs. Although rarely seen, there exists a salesman's sample panel of three cards that pictures Earl Battey, Manny Mota, and Gene Brabender with ad information on the back about the "new" Topps cards.

Card	Low	High
COMPLETE SET (609)	3000.00	8000.00
COMMON CARD (1-109)	.60	1.50
COMMON CARD (110-283)	.75	2.00
COMMON CARD (284-370)	1.00	2.50
COMMON CARD (371-457)	1.50	4.00
COMMON CARD (458-533)	2.50	6.00
COMMON CARD (534-609)	6.00	15.00
COMMON DP (534-609)	3.00	8.00
WRAPPER (5-CENT)	10.00	25.00
1 Robinson/Bauer/Robinson DP	15.00	40.00
2 Jack Hamilton	.60	1.50
3 Duke Sims	.60	1.50
4 Hal Lanier	.60	1.50
5 Whitey Ford UER	20.00	50.00
6 Dick Simpson	.60	1.50
7 Don McMahon	.60	1.50
8 Chuck Harrison	.60	1.50
9 Ron Hansen	.60	1.50
10 Matty Alou	1.50	4.00
11 Barry Moore RC	.60	1.50
12 J.Campanis RC/B.Singer	1.50	4.00
13 Joe Sparma	.60	1.50
14 Phil Linz	1.50	4.00
15 Earl Battey	.60	1.50
16 Bill Hands	.60	1.50
17 Jim Gosger	.60	1.50
18 Gene Oliver	.60	1.50
19 Jim McGlothlin	.60	1.50
20 Orlando Cepeda	12.00	30.00
21 Dave Bristol MG RC	.60	1.50
22 Gene Brabender	.60	1.50
23 Larry Elliot	.60	1.50
24 Bob Allen	.60	1.50
25 Elston Howard	1.50	4.00
26A Bob Priddy NTR	12.50	30.00
26B Bob Priddy TR	1.50	4.00
27 Bob Saverine	.60	1.50
28 Barry Latman	.60	1.50
29 Tom McCraw	.60	1.50
30 Al Kaline DP	12.00	30.00
31 Jim Brewer	.60	1.50
32 Bob Bailey	1.50	4.00
33 S.Bando RC/R.Schwartz RC	2.50	6.00
34 Pete Cimino	.60	1.50
35 Rico Carty	1.50	4.00
36 Bob Tillman	.60	1.50
37 Rick Wise	1.50	4.00
38 Bob Johnson	.60	1.50
39 Curt Simmons	1.50	4.00
40 Rick Reichardt	.60	1.50
41 Joe Hoerner	.60	1.50
42 New York Mets TC	4.00	10.00
43 Chico Salmon	.60	1.50
44 Joe Nuxhall	1.50	4.00
45 Roger Maris	25.00	60.00
45A R.Maris Yanks/Blank Back	900.00	1500.00
46 Lindy McDaniel	1.50	4.00
47 Ken McMullen	.60	1.50
48 Bill Freehan	1.50	4.00
49 Roy Face	1.50	4.00
50 Tony Oliva	2.50	6.00
51 D.Adlesh RC/W.Bales RC	.60	1.50
52 Dennis Higgins	.60	1.50
53 Clay Dalrymple	.60	1.50
54 Dick Green	.60	1.50
55 Don Drysdale	15.00	40.00
56 Jose Tartabull	1.50	4.00
57 Pat Jarvis RC	1.50	4.00
58A Paul Schaal	8.00	20.00
Green Bat		
58B P.Schaal Normal Bat	.60	1.50
59 Ralph Terry	1.50	4.00
60 Luis Aparicio	8.00	20.00
61 Gordy Coleman	.60	1.50
62 Frank Robinson CL1	3.00	8.00
63 L.Brock/C.Flood	3.00	8.00
64 Fred Valentine	.60	1.50
65 Tom Haller	1.50	4.00
66 Manny Mota	1.50	4.00
67 Ken Berry	.60	1.50
68 Bob Buhl	1.50	4.00
69 Vic Davalillo	.60	1.50
70 Ron Santo	15.00	40.00
71 Camilo Pascual	1.50	4.00
72 G.Korince ERR RC/T.Matchick RC	.60	1.50
73 Rusty Staub	2.50	6.00
74 Wes Stock	.60	1.50
75 George Scott	1.50	4.00
76 Jim Barbieri RC	.60	1.50
77 Dooley Womack	1.50	4.00
78 Pat Corrales	.60	1.50
79 Bubba Morton	.60	1.50
80 Jim Maloney	1.50	4.00
81 Eddie Stanky MG	1.50	4.00
82 Steve Barber	.60	1.50
83 Ollie Brown	.60	1.50
84 Tommie Sisk	.60	1.50
85 Johnny Callison	1.50	4.00
86A Mike McCormick NTR	12.50	30.00
86B Mike McCormick TR	1.50	4.00
87 George Altman	.60	1.50
88 Mickey Lolich	1.50	4.00
89 Felix Millan RC	1.50	4.00
90 Jim Nash RC	.60	1.50
91 Johnny Lewis	.60	1.50
92 Ray Washburn	.60	1.50
93 S.Bahnsen RC/B.Murcer	1.50	4.00
94 Ron Fairly	1.50	4.00
95 Sonny Siebert	.60	1.50
96 Art Shamsky	.60	1.50
97 Mike Cuellar	1.50	4.00
98 Rich Rollins	.60	1.50
99 Lee Stange	.60	1.50
100 Frank Robinson DP	15.00	40.00
101 Ken Johnson	.60	1.50
102 Philadelphia Phillies TC	1.50	4.00
103A Mickey Mantle CL2 DP D.Mc	12.00	30.00
103B Mickey Mantle CL2 DP D Mc		
104 Minnie Rojas RC	.60	1.50
105 Ken Boyer	2.50	6.00
106 Randy Hundley	1.50	4.00
107 Joel Horlen	.60	1.50
108 Alex Johnson	1.50	4.00
109 R.Colavito/L.Wagner	2.50	6.00
110 Jack Aker	1.50	4.00
111 John Kennedy	.75	2.00
112 Dave Wickersham	.75	2.00
113 Dave Nicholson	.75	2.00
114 Jack Baldschun	.75	2.00
115 Paul Casanova RC	.75	2.00
116 Herman Franks MG	.75	2.00
117 Darrell Brandon	.75	2.00
118 Bernie Allen	.75	2.00
119 Wade Blasingame	.75	2.00
120 Floyd Robinson	.75	2.00
121 Eddie Bressoud	.75	2.00
122 George Brunet	.75	2.00
123 J.Price RC/L.Walker	1.50	4.00
124 Jim Stewart	.75	2.00
125 Moe Drabowsky	1.50	4.00
126 Tony Taylor	.75	2.00
127 John O'Donoghue	.75	2.00
128A Ed Spiezio	.75	2.00
128B Ed Spiezio		
Partial last name on front		
129 Phil Roof	.75	2.00
130 Phil Regan	1.50	4.00
131 New York Yankees TC	8.00	20.00
132 Ozzie Virgil	.75	2.00
133 Ron Kline	.75	2.00
134 Gates Brown	2.50	6.00
135 Deron Johnson	1.50	4.00
136 Carroll Sembera	.75	2.00
137 Rookie Stars	.75	2.00
Ron Clark RC		
Jim Ollum RC		
138 Dick Kelley	.75	2.00
139 Dalton Jones	1.50	4.00
140 Willie Stargell	12.00	30.00
141 John Miller	.75	2.00
142 Jackie Brandt	.75	2.00
143 P.Ward/D.Buford	.75	2.00
144 Bill Hepler	.75	2.00
145 Larry Brown	.75	2.00
146 Steve Carlton	30.00	80.00
147 Tom Egan	.75	2.00
148 Adolfo Phillips	.75	2.00
149 Joe Moeller	.75	2.00
150 Mickey Mantle	200.00	500.00
151 Moe Drabowsky WS1	2.00	5.00
152 Jim Palmer WS2	3.00	8.00
153 Paul Blair WS3	2.00	5.00
154 Robinson/McNally WS4	2.00	5.00
155 Orioles Celebrate WS	2.00	5.00
156 Ron Herbel	.75	2.00
157 Danny Cater	.75	2.00
158 Jimmie Coker	.75	2.00
159 Bruce Howard	.75	2.00
160 Willie Davis	1.50	4.00
161 Dick Williams MG	1.50	4.00
162 Billy O'Dell	.75	2.00
163 Vic Roznovsky	.75	2.00
164 Dwight Siebler UER	.75	2.00
165 Cleon Jones	1.50	4.00
166 Eddie Mathews	10.00	25.00
167 J.Coleman RC/T.Cullen RC	.75	2.00
168 Ray Culp	.75	2.00
169 Horace Clarke	1.50	4.00
170 Dick McAuliffe	1.50	4.00
171 Cal Koonce	.75	2.00
172 Bill Heath	.75	2.00
173 St. Louis Cardinals TC	1.50	4.00
174 Dick Radatz	1.50	4.00
175 Bobby Knoop	.75	2.00
176 Sammy Ellis	.75	2.00
177 Tito Fuentes	.60	1.50
178 John Buzhardt	.75	2.00
179 C.Vaughan RC/C.Epshaw RC	1.50	4.00
180 Curt Blefary	.75	2.00
181 Terry Fox	.75	2.00
182 Ed Charles	.75	2.00
183 Jim Pagliaroni	.75	2.00
184 George Thomas	.75	2.00
185 Ken Holtzman RC	1.50	4.00
186 E.Kranepool/R.Swoboda	1.50	4.00
187 Pedro Ramos	.75	2.00
188 Ken Harrelson	1.50	4.00
189 Chuck Hinton	.75	2.00
190 Turk Farrell	.75	2.00
191A W.Mays CL3 214 Tom	4.00	10.00
191B W.Mays CL3 214 Dick	5.00	12.00
192 Fred Gladding	.75	2.00
193 Jose Cardenal	1.50	4.00
194 Bob Allison	1.50	4.00
195 Al Jackson	.75	2.00
196 Johnny Romano	.75	2.00
197 Ron Perranoski	1.50	4.00
198 Chuck Hiller	.75	2.00
199 Billy Hitchcock MG	.75	2.00
200 Willie Mays UER	50.00	120.00
201 Hal Reniff	1.50	4.00
202 Johnny Edwards	.75	2.00
203 Al McBean	.75	2.00
204 M.Epstein RC/T.Phoebus RC	2.50	6.00
205 Dick Groat	1.50	4.00
206 Dennis Bennett	.75	2.00
207 John Orsino	.75	2.00
208 Jack Lamabe	.75	2.00
209 Joe Nossek	.75	2.00
210 Bob Gibson	15.00	40.00
211 Minnesota Twins TC	1.50	4.00
212 Chris Zachary	.75	2.00
213 Jay Johnstone RC	1.50	4.00
214 Tom Kelley	.75	2.00
215 Ernie Banks	40.00	100.00
216 A.Kaline/N.Cash	8.00	20.00
217 Rob Gardner	.75	2.00
218 Wes Parker	1.50	4.00
219 Clay Carroll	1.50	4.00
220 Jim Ray Hart	1.50	4.00
221 Woody Fryman	1.50	4.00
222 D.Osteen/L.May	1.50	4.00
223 Mike Ryan	1.50	4.00
224 Walt Bond	.75	2.00
225 Mel Stottlemyre	2.50	6.00
226 Julian Javier	1.50	4.00
227 Paul Lindblad	.75	2.00
228 Gil Hodges MG	2.50	6.00
229 Larry Jackson	.75	2.00
230 Boog Powell	2.50	6.00
231 John Bateman	.75	2.00
232 Don Buford	.75	2.00
233 Peters/Horlen/Hargan LL	1.50	4.00
234 Koufax/Cuellar/Marichal LL	10.00	25.00
235 Kaat/McLain/Wilson LL	2.50	6.00
236 Koufax/Mari/Gibs/Perry LL	15.00	40.00
237 McDowell/Kaat/Wilson LL	2.50	6.00
238 Koufax/Bunning/Veale LL	8.00	20.00
239 F.Rob/Oliva/Kaline LL	4.00	10.00
240 Alou/Alou/Carty LL	2.50	6.00
241 F.Rob/Killebrew/Powell LL	4.00	10.00
242 Aaron/Clemente/Allen LL	20.00	50.00
243 F.Rob/Killebrew/Powell LL	4.00	10.00
244 Aaron/Allen/Mays LL	12.00	30.00
245 Curt Flood	2.50	6.00
246 Jim Perry	1.50	4.00
247 Jerry Lumpe	.75	2.00
248 Gene Mauch MG	1.50	4.00
249 Nick Willhite	.75	2.00
250 Hank Aaron UER	50.00	120.00
251 Woody Held	.75	2.00
252 Bob Bolin	.75	2.00
253 B.Davis/G.Gil RC	.75	2.00
254 Milt Pappas	1.50	4.00
255 Frank Howard	1.50	4.00
256 Bob Hendley	.75	2.00
257 Charlie Smith	.75	2.00
258 Lee Maye	.75	2.00
259 Don Dennis	.75	2.00
260 Jim Lefebvre	1.50	4.00
261 John Wyatt	.75	2.00
262 Kansas City Athletics TC	1.50	4.00
263 Hank Aguirre	.75	2.00
264 Ron Swoboda	1.50	4.00
265 Lou Burdette	1.50	4.00
266 W.Stargell/D.Clendenon	1.50	4.00
267 Don Schwall	.75	2.00
268 Johnny Briggs	.75	2.00
269 Don Nottebart	.75	2.00
270 Zoilo Versalles	.75	2.00
271 Eddie Watt	.75	2.00
272 B.Connors RC/D.Dowling	1.50	4.00
273 Dick Lines RC	.75	2.00
274 Bob Aspromonte	.75	2.00
275 Fred Whitfield	.75	2.00
276 Bruce Brubaker	.75	2.00
277 Steve Whitaker RC	2.50	6.00
278 Jim Kaat CL4	3.00	8.00
279 Frank Linzy	.75	2.00
280 Tony Conigliaro	3.00	8.00
281 Bob Rodgers	.75	2.00
282 John Odom	.75	2.00
283 Gene Alley	1.50	4.00
284 Johnny Podres	1.50	4.00
285 Lou Brock	15.00	40.00
286 Wayne Causey	1.00	2.50
287 G.Goosen RC/B.Shirley	1.00	2.50
288 Denny Lemaster	1.00	2.50
289 Tom Tresh	2.00	5.00
290 Bill White	2.00	5.00
291 Jim Hannan	1.00	2.50
292 Don Pavletich	1.00	2.50
293 Ed Kirkpatrick	1.00	2.50
294 Walter Alston MG	3.00	8.00
295 Sam McDowell	2.00	5.00
296 Glenn Beckert	2.00	5.00
297 Dave Morehead	2.00	5.00
298 Ron Davis RC	1.00	2.50
299 Norm Siebern	1.00	2.50
300 Jim Kaat	2.00	5.00
301 Jesse Gonder	1.00	2.50
302 Baltimore Orioles TC	3.00	8.00
303 Gil Blanco	1.00	2.50
304 Phil Gagliano	1.00	2.50
305 Earl Wilson	2.00	5.00
306 Bud Harrelson RC	2.00	5.00
307 Jim Beauchamp	1.00	2.50
308 Al Downing	2.00	5.00
309 J.Callison/R.Allen	2.00	5.00
310 Gary Peters	1.00	2.50
311 Ed Brinkman	1.00	2.50
312 Don Mincher	1.00	2.50
313 Bob Lee	1.00	2.50
314 M.Andrews RC/R.Smith RC	3.00	8.00
315 Billy Williams	15.00	40.00
316 Jack Kralick	1.00	2.50
317 Cesar Tovar	1.00	2.50
318 Dave Giusti	1.00	2.50
319 Paul Blair	2.00	5.00
320 Gaylord Perry	6.00	15.00
321 Mayo Smith MG	1.00	2.50
322 Jose Pagan	1.00	2.50
323 Mike Hershberger	1.00	2.50
324 Hal Woodeshick	1.00	2.50
325 Chico Cardenas	2.00	5.00
326 Bob Uecker	10.00	25.00
327 California Angels TC	3.00	8.00
328 Clete Boyer UER	2.00	5.00
329 Charlie Lau	2.00	5.00
330 Claude Osteen	2.00	5.00
331 Joe Foy	2.00	5.00
332 Jesus Alou	1.00	2.50
333 Fergie Jenkins	15.00	40.00
334 H.Killebrew/B.Allison	4.00	10.00
335 Bob Veale	2.00	5.00
336 Joe Azcue	1.00	2.50
337 Joe Morgan	15.00	40.00
338 Bob Locker	1.00	2.50
339 Chico Ruiz	1.00	2.50
340 Joe Pepitone	3.00	8.00
341 D.Dietz RC/B.Sorrell	1.00	2.50
342 Hank Fischer	1.00	2.50
343 Tom Satriano	1.00	2.50
344 Ossie Chavarria RC	1.00	2.50
345 Stu Miller	2.00	5.00
346 Jim Hickman	1.00	2.50
347 Grady Hatton MG	1.00	2.50
348 Tug McGraw	2.00	5.00
349 Bob Chance	1.00	2.50
350 Joe Torre	10.00	25.00
351 Vern Law	2.00	5.00
352 Ray Oyler	1.00	2.50
353 Bill McCool	1.00	2.50
354 Chicago Cubs TC	3.00	8.00
355 Carl Yastrzemski	30.00	80.00
356 Larry Jaster RC	1.00	2.50
357 Bill Skowron	2.00	5.00
358 Ruben Amaro	1.00	2.50
359 Dick Ellsworth	1.00	2.50
360 Leon Wagner	1.00	2.50
361 Roberto Clemente CL5	8.00	20.00
362 Darold Knowles	1.00	2.50
363 Davey Johnson	2.00	5.00
364 Claude Raymond	1.00	2.50
365 John Roseboro	2.00	5.00
366 Andy Kosco	1.00	2.50
367 B.Kelso/D.Wallace RC	1.00	2.50
368 Jack Hiatt	1.00	2.50
369 Jim Hunter	15.00	40.00
370 Tommy Davis	2.00	5.00
371 Jim Lonborg	3.00	8.00
372 Mike de la Hoz	1.50	4.00
373 D.Josephson RC/F.Klages RC DP	1.50	4.00
374A Mel Queen ERR	8.00	20.00
374B Mel Queen COR DP	1.50	4.00
375 Jake Gibbs	3.00	8.00
376 Don Lock DP	1.50	4.00
377 Luis Tiant	3.00	8.00
378 Detroit Tigers TC UER	3.00	8.00
379 Jerry May DP	1.50	4.00
380 Dean Chance DP	1.50	4.00
381 Dick Schofield DP	1.50	4.00
382 Dave McNally	3.00	8.00
383 Ken Henderson DP	1.50	4.00
384 J.Cosman RC/D.Hughes RC	1.50	4.00
385 Jim Fregosi	3.00	8.00
386 Dick Selma DP	1.50	4.00
387 Cap Peterson DP	1.50	4.00
388 Arnold Earley DP	1.50	4.00
389 Alvin Dark MG DP	3.00	8.00
390 Jim Wynn DP	3.00	8.00
391 Wilbur Wood DP	3.00	8.00
392 Tommy Harper DP	3.00	8.00
393 Jim Bouton DP	3.00	8.00
394 Jake Wood DP	1.50	4.00
395 Chris Short RC	3.00	8.00
396 D.Menke/T.Cloninger	1.50	4.00
397 Willie Smith DP	1.50	4.00
398 Jeff Torborg	3.00	8.00
399 Al Worthington DP	1.50	4.00
400 Bob Clemente DP	60.00	120.00
401 Jim Coates	1.50	4.00
402A G.Jackson/B.Wilson Stat Line	8.00	20.00
402B G.Jackson/B.Wilson RC DP	3.00	8.00
403 Dick Nen	1.50	4.00
404 Nelson Briles	3.00	8.00
405 Russ Snyder	1.50	4.00
406 Lee Elia DP	1.50	4.00
407 Cincinnati Reds TC	3.00	8.00
408 Jim Northrup DP	3.00	8.00
409 Ray Sadecki	1.50	4.00
410 Lou Johnson DP	1.50	4.00
411 Dick Howser DP	1.50	4.00
412 N.Miller RC/D.Rader RC	3.00	8.00
413 Jerry Grote	1.50	4.00
414 Casey Cox	1.50	4.00
415 Sonny Jackson	1.50	4.00
416 Roger Repoz	1.50	4.00
417A Bob Bruce ERR	12.50	30.00
417B Bob Bruce COR DP	1.50	4.00
418 Sam Mele MG	1.50	4.00
419 Don Kessinger DP	3.00	8.00
420 Denny McLain	5.00	12.00
421 Dal Maxvill DP	1.50	4.00
422 Hoyt Wilhelm	6.00	15.00
423 W.Mays/W.McCovey DP	25.00	60.00
424 Pedro Gonzalez	1.50	4.00
425 Pete Mikkelsen	1.50	4.00
426 Lou Clinton	1.50	4.00
427A Ruben Gomez ERR	8.00	20.00
427B Ruben Gomez COR DP	1.50	4.00
428 T.Hutton RC/G.Michael RC DP	3.00	8.00
429 Garry Roggenburk DP	1.50	4.00
430 Pete Rose	60.00	150.00
431 Ted Uhlaender	1.50	4.00
432 Jimmie Hall DP	1.50	4.00
433 Al Luplow DP	1.50	4.00
434 Eddie Fisher DP	1.50	4.00
435 Mack Jones DP	1.50	4.00
436 Pete Ward	1.50	4.00
437 Washington Senators TC	3.00	8.00
438 Chuck Dobson	1.50	4.00
439 Byron Browne	1.50	4.00
440 Steve Hargan	1.50	4.00
441 Jim Davenport	1.50	4.00
442 B.Robinson RC/J.Verbanic RC DP	3.00	8.00
443 Tito Francona DP	1.50	4.00
444 George Smith	1.50	4.00
445 Don Sutton	10.00	25.00
446 Russ Nixon DP	1.50	4.00
447A Bo Belinsky ERR DP	1.50	4.00
447B Bo Belinsky COR	3.00	8.00
448 Harry Walker MG DP	1.50	4.00
449 Orlando Pena	1.50	4.00
450 Richie Allen	3.00	8.00
451 Fred Newman DP	1.50	4.00
452 Ed Kranepool	3.00	8.00
453 Aurelio Monteagudo DP	1.50	4.00
454A J.Marichal CL6 No Ear DP	5.00	12.00
454B Juan Marichal CL6 w/Ear DP	5.00	12.00
455 Tommie Agee	3.00	8.00
456 Phil Niekro UER	12.00	30.00
457 Andy Etchebarren DP	3.00	8.00
458 Lee Thomas	2.50	6.00
459 D.Bosman RC/P.Craig	2.50	6.00
460 Harmon Killebrew	15.00	40.00
461 Bob Miller	5.00	12.00
462 Bob Barton	2.50	6.00
463 S.McDowell/S.Siebert	5.00	12.00
464 Dan Coombs	2.50	6.00
465 Willie Horton	5.00	12.00
466 Bobby Wine	8.00	20.00
467 Jim O'Toole	2.50	6.00
468 Ralph Houk MG	2.50	6.00
469 Len Gabrielson	2.50	6.00
470 Bob Shaw	2.50	6.00
471 Rene Lachemann	2.50	6.00
472 J.Gelnar/G.Spriggs RC	2.50	6.00
473 Jose Santiago	2.50	6.00
474 Bob Tolan	4.00	10.00
475 Jim Palmer	20.00	50.00
476 Tony Perez SP	30.00	60.00
477 Atlanta Braves TC	6.00	15.00
478 Bob Humphreys	2.50	6.00
479 Gary Bell	2.50	6.00
480 Willie McCovey	15.00	40.00
481 Leo Durocher MG	8.00	20.00
482 Bill Monbouquette	2.50	6.00
483 Jim Landis	2.50	6.00
484 Jerry Adair	2.50	6.00
485 Tim McCarver	10.00	25.00
486 R.Reese RC/B.Whitby RC	2.50	6.00
487 Tommie Reynolds	2.50	6.00
488 Gerry Arrigo	2.50	6.00
489 Doug Clemens RC	2.50	6.00
490 Tony Cloninger	2.50	6.00
491 Sam Bowens	2.50	6.00
492 Pittsburgh Pirates TC	6.00	15.00
493 Phil Ortega	2.50	6.00
494 Bill Rigney MG	2.50	6.00
495 Fritz Peterson	2.50	6.00
496 Orlando McFarlane	2.50	6.00
497 Ron Campbell RC	2.50	6.00
498 Larry Dierker	5.00	12.00
499 G.Culver/J.Vidal RC	2.50	6.00
500 Juan Marichal	15.00	40.00
501 Jerry Zimmerman	2.50	6.00
502 Derrell Griffith	2.50	6.00
503 Los Angeles Dodgers TC	8.00	20.00
504 Orlando Martinez RC	2.50	6.00
505 Tommy Helms	5.00	12.00
506 Smoky Burgess	2.50	6.00
507 E.Barnowski/L.Haney RC	2.50	6.00
508 Dick Hall	2.50	6.00
509 Jim King	2.50	6.00
510 Bill Mazeroski	8.00	20.00
511 Don Wert	2.50	6.00
512 Red Schoendienst MG	10.00	25.00
513 Marcelino Lopez	2.50	6.00
514 John Werhas	2.50	6.00
515 Bert Campaneris	5.00	12.00
516 San Francisco Giants TC	6.00	15.00
517 Fred Talbot	5.00	12.00
518 Denis Menke	2.50	6.00
519 Ted Davidson	2.50	6.00
520 Max Alvis	2.50	6.00
521 B.Powell/C.Blefary	5.00	12.00
522 John Stephenson	2.50	6.00
523 Jim Merritt	2.50	6.00
524 Felix Mantilla	2.50	6.00
525 Ron Hunt	2.50	6.00
526 P.Dobson RC/G.Korince RC	2.50	6.00
527 Dennis Ribant	2.50	6.00
528 Rico Petrocelli	8.00	20.00
529 Gary Wagner	2.50	6.00
530 Felipe Alou	5.00	12.00
531 B.Robinson CL7 DP	6.00	15.00
532 Jim Hicks RC	2.50	6.00
533 Jack Fisher	2.50	6.00
534 Hank Bauer MG DP	3.00	8.00
535 Donn Clendenon	10.00	25.00
536 J.Niekro RC/P.Popovich RC	40.00	100.00
537 Chuck Estrada DP	3.00	8.00
538 J.C. Martin	6.00	15.00
539 Dick Egan DP	3.00	8.00
540 Norm Cash	25.00	60.00
541 Joe Gibbon	6.00	15.00
542 R.Monday RC/T.Pierce RC DP	10.00	25.00
543 Dan Schneider	6.00	15.00
544 Cleveland Indians TC	12.50	30.00
545 Jim Grant	15.00	40.00
546 Woody Woodward	10.00	25.00
547 R.Gibson RC/B.Rohr RC DP	3.00	8.00
548 Tony Gonzalez DP	3.00	8.00
549 Jack Sanford	6.00	15.00
550 Vada Pinson DP	4.00	10.00
551 Doug Camilli DP	3.00	8.00
552 Ted Savage	15.00	40.00
553 M.Hegan RC/T.Tillotson	15.00	40.00
554 Andre Rodgers DP	3.00	8.00
555 Don Cardwell	12.00	30.00
556 Al Weis DP	3.00	8.00
557 Al Ferrara	10.00	25.00
558 M.Belanger RC/B.Dillman RC	60.00	150.00
559 Dick Tracewski DP	3.00	8.00
560 Jim Bunning	40.00	100.00
561 Sandy Alomar	15.00	40.00
562 Steve Blass DP	3.00	8.00
563 Joe Adcock	15.00	40.00
564 A.Harris RC/A.Pointer RC DP	3.00	8.00
565 Lew Krausse	10.00	25.00
566 Gary Geiger DP	5.00	12.00
567 Steve Hamilton	15.00	40.00
568 John Sullivan	15.00	40.00
569 Rod Carew RC DP	300.00	800.00
570 Maury Wills	40.00	80.00
571 Larry Sherry	10.00	25.00
572 Don Demeter	10.00	25.00
573 Chicago White Sox TC	12.50	30.00
574 Jerry Buchek	10.00	25.00
575 Dave Boswell RC	6.00	15.00
576 R.Hernandez RC/N.Gigon RC	15.00	40.00
577 Bill Short	6.00	15.00
578 John Boccabella	6.00	15.00
579 Bill Henry	6.00	15.00
580 Rocky Colavito	75.00	150.00
581 Tom Seaver RC	750.00	2000.00
582 Jim Owens DP	3.00	8.00
583 Ray Barker	15.00	40.00
584 Jimmy Piersall	15.00	40.00
585 Wally Bunker	10.00	25.00
586 Manny Jimenez	6.00	15.00
587 D.Shaw RC/G.Sutherland RC	15.00	40.00
588 Johnny Klippstein DP	3.00	8.00
589 Dave Ricketts DP	3.00	8.00
590 Pete Richert	6.00	15.00
591 Ty Cline	10.00	25.00
592 J.Shellenback RC/R.Willis RC	40.00	100.00
593 Wes Westrum MG	20.00	50.00
594 Dan Osinski	15.00	40.00
595 Cookie Rojas	10.00	25.00
596 Galen Cisco DP	3.00	8.00
597 Ted Abernathy	6.00	15.00
598 W.Williams RC/E.Stroud RC	10.00	25.00
599 Bob Duliba DP	3.00	8.00
600 Brooks Robinson	200.00	400.00
601 Bill Bryan DP	3.00	8.00
602 Juan Pizarro	15.00	40.00
603 T.Talton RC/R.Webster RC	10.00	25.00
604 Boston Red Sox TC	60.00	150.00
605 Mike Shannon	50.00	120.00
606 Ron Taylor	10.00	25.00
607 Mickey Stanley	20.00	50.00
608 R.Nye RC/J.Upham RC DP	3.00	8.00
609 Tommy John	50.00	120.00

1967 Topps Posters Inserts

Card	Low	High
COMPLETE SET (32)	50.00	100.00
1 Boog Powell	1.00	2.50
2 Bert Campaneris	.75	2.00
3 Brooks Robinson	1.50	4.00
4 Tommie Agee	.50	1.25
5 Carl Yastrzemski	2.00	5.00
6 Mickey Mantle	12.00	30.00
7 Frank Howard	.75	2.00
8 Sam McDowell	.75	2.00
9 Orlando Cepeda	1.25	3.00
10 Chico Cardenas	.50	1.25
11 Roberto Clemente	4.00	10.00
12 Willie Mays	3.00	8.00
13 Cleon Jones	.50	1.25
14 Johnny Callison	.75	2.00
15 Hank Aaron	2.50	6.00
16 Don Drysdale	1.25	3.00
17 Bobby Knoop	.50	1.25
18 Tony Oliva	1.00	2.50
19 Frank Robinson	1.25	3.00
20 Denny McLain	1.00	2.50
21 Al Kaline	1.50	4.00
22 Joe Pepitone	.75	2.00
23 Harmon Killebrew	1.50	4.00
24 Leon Wagner	.50	1.25
25 Joe Morgan	1.25	3.00
26 Ron Santo	1.00	2.50
27 Joe Torre	1.00	2.50
28 Juan Marichal	1.00	2.50
29 Matty Alou	.50	1.25
30 Felipe Alou	.75	2.00
31 Ron Hunt	.50	1.25
32 Willie McCovey	1.25	3.00

1967 Topps Test Foil

This 24-card set of all-stars is know only in proof form and was intended to be pressed onto a pin-back button issue which never materialized. The set measures approximately 2 3/8" square and features a color player head photo in a 2 1/4" white circle on a silver foil background with the player's name and position printed in black across the neck. The word "Japan" is printed in tiny black letters at the top-left which meant that word was intended to be folded under the button's rim. The backs are blank. The cards are unnumbered and checklisted below in alphabetical order.

Card	Low	High
COMPLETE SET (23)	3000.00	6000.00
1 Hank Aaron	350.00	700.00
2 Johnny Callison	100.00	200.00

Card	Low	High
3 Bert Campaneris	125.00	250.00
4 Leo Cardenas	100.00	200.00
5 Orlando Cepeda	200.00	400.00
6 Roberto Clemente	500.00	1000.00
7 Frank Howard	125.00	250.00
8 Cleon Jones	100.00	200.00
9 Bobby Knoop	100.00	200.00
10 Sandy Koufax	350.00	700.00
11 Mickey Mantle	600.00	1200.00
12 Juan Marichal	200.00	400.00
13 Willie Mays	350.00	700.00
14 Sam McDowell	100.00	200.00
15 Denny McLain	125.00	250.00
16 Joe Morgan	200.00	400.00
17 Tony Oliva	125.00	250.00
18 Boog Powell	125.00	250.00
19 Brooks Robinson	200.00	400.00
20 Frank Robinson	200.00	400.00
21 John Romano	100.00	200.00
22 Ron Santo	150.00	300.00
23 Joe Torre	150.00	300.00
24 Carl Yastrzemski	200.00	400.00

1967 Topps Venezuelan

This set features color player photos in a white border on the fronts. The horizontal backs carry player information. The cards are printed in Spanish and were Issued for the Venezuelan market. Cards from 139 through 188 feature retired players while the rest of the set features active players. The cards which feature the same photos as the 67 Topps cards seemed trimmed. However, by checking the back -- any collector should have confidence in what they are buying. The first 138 cards in this set feature players who were then playing in the Venezuelan Winter league. Those first 138 cards have red backs. Cards numbered 139 through 188 have green backs. The rest of the set (189-338) have a light blue back. Both Bobby Cox and Dave Concepcion have cards in this set which significantly predate their Topps Rookie Cards.

Card	Low	High
COMPLETE SET	7500.00	15000.00
COMMON CARD (1-138)	12.50	30.00
COMMON CARD (139-188)	15.00	40.00
COMMON CARD (189-338)	2.00	5.00
1 Regino Otero	12.50	30.00
2 Alejandro Carrasquel	12.50	30.00
3 Pompeyo Davalillo	12.50	30.00
4 Gonzalo Marquez	12.50	30.00
5 Cookie Rojas	15.00	40.00
6 Teodoro Obregon	12.50	30.00
7 Paul Schall	15.00	40.00
8 Juan Francia	12.50	30.00
9 Luis Tiant	20.00	50.00
10 Jose Tartabull	12.50	30.00
10A Jose Tartabull	12.50	30.00
11 Vic Davalillo	12.50	30.00
12 Cesar Tovar	12.50	30.00
13 Ron Klimkowski	12.50	30.00
14 Diego Segui	12.50	30.00
15 Luis Penalver	12.50	30.00
16 Urbano Lugo	12.50	30.00
17 Aurelio Monteagudo	12.50	30.00
18 Richard Underwood	12.50	30.00
19 Nelson Castellanos	12.50	30.00
20 Manuel Mendible	12.50	30.00
21 Fidel Garcia	12.50	30.00
22 Luis Cordoba	12.50	30.00
23 Jesus Padron	12.50	30.00
24 Lorenzo Fernandez	12.50	30.00
25 Leopoldo Tovar	12.50	30.00
26 Carlos Loreto	12.50	30.00
27 Ossie Blanco	12.50	30.00
28 Syd O'Brien	12.50	30.00
29 Cesar Gutierrez	12.50	30.00
30 Luis Garcia	12.50	30.00
31 Fred Klages	12.50	30.00
32 Isasis Chavez	12.50	30.00
33 Walt Williams	12.50	30.00
34 Jim Hicks	12.50	30.00
35 Gustavo Sposito	12.50	30.00
36 Cisco Carlos	12.50	30.00
37 Jim Mooring	12.50	30.00
38 Alonso Olivares	12.50	30.00
39 Gracilliano Parra	12.50	30.00
40 Merritt Ranew	12.50	30.00
41 Everest Contramaestre	12.50	30.00
42 Orlando Reyes	12.50	30.00
43 Edicto Arteaga	12.50	30.00
44 Francisco Diaz	12.50	30.00
45 Victor Diaz	12.50	30.00
46 Ramon Diaz	12.50	30.00
46A Francisco Diaz Blue Back	12.50	30.00
47 Luis Aparicio	40.00	80.00
48 Reynaldo Cordeiro CO	12.50	30.00
49 Luis Aparicio	40.00	80.00
50 Ramon Webster	12.50	30.00
51 Remigio Hermoso	12.50	30.00
52 Mike de la Hoz	12.50	30.00
53 Enzo Hernandez	12.50	30.00
54 Ed Watt	12.50	30.00
55 Angel Bravo	12.50	30.00
56 Merv Rettenmund	12.50	30.00
57 Jose Herrera	12.50	30.00
58 Tom Fisher	12.50	30.00
59 Jim Weaver	12.50	30.00
60 Juan Quintana	12.50	30.00
60A Frank Fernandez Blue Back	12.50	30.00
61 Hector Urbano	12.50	30.00
62A Hector Brito Blue Back	12.50	30.00
63 Jesus Romero	12.50	30.00
64 Carlos Moreno	12.50	30.00
65 Nestor Mendible	12.50	30.00
66 Armando Ortiz	12.50	30.00
67 Graciano Ravelo	12.50	30.00
68 Paul Knechtges	12.50	30.00
69 Marcelino Lopez	12.50	30.00
70 Wilfredo Calvino	12.50	30.00
71 Jesus Avila	12.50	30.00
72 Carlos Pascual	12.50	30.00
73 Bob Burda	12.50	30.00
73A Bob Burda	12.50	30.00
74 Elio Chacon	12.50	30.00
75 Jacinto Hernandez	12.50	30.00
76 Jose Tovar	12.50	30.00
77 Bill Whitby	12.50	30.00
78 Enrique Izquierdo	12.50	30.00
79 Sandy Valdespino	12.50	30.00
80 John Lewis	12.50	30.00
81 Hector Martinez	12.50	30.00
82 Rene Paredes	12.50	30.00
83 Danny Morris	12.50	30.00
84 Pedro Ramos	12.50	30.00
85 Jose Ramon Lopez	12.50	30.00
86 Jesus Rizales	12.50	30.00
87 Winston Acosta	12.50	30.00
88 Pablo Bello	12.50	30.00
89 Dave Concepcion	50.00	100.00
90 Manuel Garcia	12.50	30.00
91 Anibal Longa	12.50	30.00
92 Franscico Moscoso	12.50	30.00
93 Mel McGaha MG	12.50	30.00
94 Aquiles Gomez	12.50	30.00
95 Alfonso Carrasquel UER Card numbered 115	12.50	30.00
95A Alfonso Carrasquel Blue Back	12.50	30.00
96 Tom Murray	12.50	30.00
97 Gus Gil	12.50	30.00
98 Damaso Blanco	12.50	30.00
99 Alberto Cambero	12.50	30.00
100 Don Bryant	12.50	30.00
101 George Culver	12.50	30.00
102 Teolindo Acosta	12.50	30.00
103 Aaron Pointer	12.50	30.00
104 Ed Kirkpatrick	12.50	30.00
106 Mike Daniel	12.50	30.00
108 Juan Quiroz	12.50	30.00
109 Juan Campos	12.50	30.00
110 Freddy Rivero	12.50	30.00
111 Dick Lemay	12.50	30.00
112 Raul Ortega	12.50	30.00
113 Bruno Estaba	12.50	30.00
114 Evangelista Nunez	12.50	30.00
115 Roberto Munoz	12.50	30.00
116 Tony Castanos	12.50	30.00
117 Domingo Barboza	12.50	30.00
118 Lucio Celis	12.50	30.00
119 Carlos Santeliz	12.50	30.00
120 Bart Shirley	12.50	30.00
121 Nuedo Morales	12.50	30.00
122 Bobby Cox	50.00	100.00
123 Cruz Amaya Blue Back	12.50	30.00
124 Jim Campanis	12.50	30.00
125 Dave Roberts	12.50	30.00
126 Jerry Crider	12.50	30.00
127 Domingo Carrasquel	12.50	30.00
128 Leo Marentette	12.50	30.00
129 Frank Kreutzer	12.50	30.00
130 Jim Dickson	12.50	30.00
131 Bob Oliver	12.50	30.00
132 Pablo Torrealba	12.50	30.00
133 Pablo Torrealba	12.50	30.00
134 Iran Paz	12.50	30.00
135 Eliecer Bueno	12.50	30.00
136 Claudio Urdaneta	12.50	30.00
137 Faustino Zabala	12.50	30.00
138 Dario Chirinos	12.50	30.00
139 Walter Johnson	150.00	300.00
140 Bill Dickey	75.00	150.00
141 Lou Gehrig	300.00	600.00
142 Rogers Hornsby	150.00	300.00
143 Honus Wagner	200.00	400.00
144 Pie Traynor	75.00	150.00
145 Joe DiMaggio	300.00	600.00
146 Ty Cobb	300.00	600.00
147 Babe Ruth	400.00	800.00
148 Ted Williams	300.00	600.00
149 Mel Ott	75.00	150.00
150 Cy Young	150.00	300.00
151 Christy Mathewson	150.00	300.00
152 Warren Spahn	75.00	150.00
153 Mickey Cochrane	75.00	150.00
154 George Sisler	60.00	120.00
155 Jimmy Collins	50.00	100.00
156 Tris Speaker	125.00	250.00
157 Stan Musial	150.00	300.00
158 Luke Appling	60.00	120.00
159 Nap Lajoie	125.00	250.00
160 Bob Feller	150.00	300.00
161 Bill Terry	50.00	100.00
162 Sandy Koufax	200.00	400.00
163 Jimmy Foxx (Jimmie)	150.00	300.00
164 Joe Cronin	60.00	120.00
165 Frank Frisch	60.00	120.00
166 Paul Waner	75.00	150.00
167 Lloyd Waner	60.00	120.00
168 Lefty Grove	125.00	250.00
169 Bobby Doerr	50.00	100.00
170 Al Simmons	60.00	120.00
171 Grover Alexander	150.00	300.00
172 Carl Hubbell	150.00	300.00
173 Mordecai Brown	125.00	250.00
174 Ted Lyons	50.00	100.00
175 Johnny Vander Meer	50.00	100.00
176 Alex Carrasquel	40.00	80.00
177 Satchel Paige	250.00	500.00
178 Whitey Ford	125.00	250.00
179 Yogi Berra	125.00	250.00
180 Roy Campanella	125.00	250.00
181 Chico Carrasquel	40.00	80.00
182 Johnny Mize	60.00	120.00
183 Ted Kluszewski	40.00	80.00
Ray Herbert		
184 Jackie Robinson	300.00	600.00
185 Beto Avila	40.00	80.00
186 Phil Rizzuto	125.00	250.00
187 Minnie Minoso	50.00	100.00
188 Conrado Marrero	40.00	80.00
189 Luis Aparicio	6.00	15.00
190 Vic Davalillo	8.00	20.00
191 Cesar Tovar	8.00	20.00
192 Mickey Mantle	1500.00	3000.00
193 Carl Yastrzemski	250.00	500.00
194 Frank Robinson	75.00	150.00
195 Willie Horton	10.00	25.00
196 Gary Peters	8.00	20.00
197 Bert Campaneris	8.00	20.00
198 Norm Cash	12.50	30.00
199 Boog Powell	30.00	60.00
200 George Scott	8.00	20.00
201 Frank Howard	10.00	25.00
202 Rick Reichardt	8.00	20.00
203 Jose Cardenal	8.00	20.00
204 Rico Petrocelli	8.00	20.00
205 Lew Krausse	8.00	20.00
206 Harmon Killebrew	75.00	150.00
207 Leon Wagner	8.00	20.00
208 Joe Foy	8.00	20.00
209 Joe Pepitone	10.00	25.00
210 Al Kaline	75.00	150.00
211 Brooks Robinson	100.00	200.00
212 Bill Freehan	8.00	20.00
213 Willie Mays	400.00	800.00
214 Ed Mathews	75.00	150.00
215 Dick Green	8.00	20.00
216 Tom Tresh	8.00	20.00
217 Dean Chance	8.00	20.00
218 Paul Blair	8.00	20.00
219 Larry Brown	8.00	20.00
220 Fred Valentine	8.00	20.00
221 Al Downing	8.00	20.00
222 Earl Battey	8.00	20.00
223 Don Mincher	8.00	20.00
224 Tommie Agee	8.00	20.00
225 Jim McGlothlin	8.00	20.00
226 Zoilo Versalles	8.00	20.00
227 Curt Blefary	8.00	20.00
228 Joel Horlen	8.00	20.00
229 Stu Miller	8.00	20.00
230 Tony Oliva	12.50	30.00
231 Paul Casanova	8.00	20.00
232 Orlando Pena	8.00	20.00
233 Ron Hansen	8.00	20.00
234 Earl Wilson	8.00	20.00
235 Ken Boyer	10.00	25.00
236 Jim Kaat	12.50	30.00
237 Dalton Jones	8.00	20.00
238 Pete Ward	8.00	20.00
239 Mickey Lolich	10.00	25.00
240 Jose Santiago	8.00	20.00
241 Dick McAuliffe	8.00	20.00
242 Mel Stottlemyre	10.00	25.00
243 Camilo Pascual	8.00	20.00
244 Jim Fregosi	10.00	25.00
245 Tony Conigliaro	50.00	100.00
246 Sonny Siebert	8.00	20.00
247 Jim Perry	8.00	20.00
248 Dave McNally	8.00	20.00
249 Fred Whitfield	8.00	20.00
250 Ken Berry	8.00	20.00
251 Jim Grant	8.00	20.00
252 Hank Aguirre	8.00	20.00
253 Don Wert	8.00	20.00
254 Wally Bunker	8.00	20.00
255 Elston Howard	12.50	30.00
256 Dave Johnson	8.00	20.00
257 Hoyt Wilhelm	50.00	100.00
258 Dick Buford	8.00	20.00
259 Sam McDowell	8.00	20.00
260 Bobby Knoop	8.00	20.00
261 Denny McLain	30.00	60.00
262 Steve Hargan	8.00	20.00
263 Jim Nash	8.00	20.00
264 Jerry Adair	8.00	20.00
265 Tony Gonzalez	8.00	20.00
266 Mike Shannon	8.00	20.00
267 Bob Gibson	100.00	200.00
268 John Roseboro	8.00	20.00
269 Bob Aspromonte	8.00	20.00
270 Pete Rose	400.00	800.00
271 Rico Carty	8.00	20.00
272 Juan Pizarro	8.00	20.00
273 Jim Lonborg	8.00	20.00
274 Jim Bunning	150.00	300.00
275 Ernie Banks	100.00	200.00
276 Curt Flood	10.00	25.00
277 Mack Jones	8.00	20.00
278 Roberto Clemente	500.00	1000.00
279 Sammy Ellis	8.00	20.00
280 Willie Stargell	100.00	200.00
281 Felipe Alou	10.00	25.00
282 Ed Kranepool	8.00	20.00
283 Nelson Briles	8.00	20.00
284 Hank Aaron	400.00	800.00
285 Vada Pinson	10.00	25.00
286 Jim LeFebvre	8.00	20.00
287 Hal Lanier	8.00	20.00
288 Ron Swoboda	8.00	20.00
289 Mike McCormick	8.00	20.00
290 Lou Johnson	8.00	20.00
291 Orlando Cepeda	30.00	60.00
292 Rusty Staub	12.50	30.00
293 Manny Mota	10.00	25.00
294 Tommy Harper	8.00	20.00
295 Don Drysdale	75.00	150.00
296 Mel Queen	8.00	20.00
297 Red Schoendienst	40.00	80.00
298 Matty Alou	10.00	25.00
299 Johnny Callison	8.00	20.00
300 Jual Marichal	75.00	150.00
301 Al McBean	8.00	20.00
302 Claude Osteen	8.00	20.00
303 Willie McCovey	100.00	200.00
304 Jim Owens	8.00	20.00
305 Chico Ruiz	8.00	20.00
306 Fergie Jenkins	75.00	150.00
307 Lou Brock	100.00	200.00
308 Joe Morgan	75.00	150.00
309 Ron Santo	12.50	30.00
310 Chico Cardenas	8.00	20.00
311 Richie Allen	10.00	25.00
312 Gaylord Perry	75.00	150.00
313 Bill Mazeroski	40.00	80.00
314 Tony Taylor	8.00	20.00
315 Tommy Helms	8.00	20.00
316 Jim Wynn	10.00	25.00
317 Don Sutton	75.00	150.00
318 Mike Cueller	10.00	25.00
319 Willie Davis	8.00	20.00
320 Julian Javier	8.00	20.00
321 Maury Wills	10.00	25.00
322 Gene Alley	8.00	20.00
323 Ray Sadecki	8.00	20.00
324 Joe Torre	12.50	30.00
325 Jim Maloney	8.00	20.00
326 Jim Davenport	8.00	20.00
327 Tony Perez	60.00	120.00
328 Roger Maris	150.00	300.00
329 Chris Short	8.00	20.00
330 Jesus Alou	8.00	20.00
331 Deron Johnson	8.00	20.00
332 Tommy Davis	10.00	25.00
333 Bob Veale	8.00	20.00
334 Bill McCool	8.00	20.00
335 Jim Hart	8.00	20.00
336 Roy Face	10.00	25.00
337 Billy Williams	50.00	100.00
338 Dick Groat	10.00	25.00

1967 Topps Who Am I

These are just the "baseball" players issued by Topps in this set which features famous people. The front features a drawing of the person along with their name and claim to fame on the top. The back asks some questions about the person. We are just cataloguing the baseball players here. Cards with the player's name unscratched are worth 3x the listed prices.

Card	Low	High
COMPLETE SET (44)	250.00	500.00
1 George Washington		
2 Andrew Jackson		
3 James Monroe		
4 Joan of Arc		
5 Nero		
6 Franklin D. Roosevelt		
7 Henry VIII		
8 William Shakespeare		
9 Clara Barton		
10 Napoleon Bonaparte		
11 Harry Truman		
12 Babe Ruth	50.00	120.00
13 Thomas Jefferson		
14 Dolley Madison		
15 Julius Caesar		
16 Robert Louis Stevenson		
17 Woodrow Wilson		
18 Stonewall Jackson		
19 Charles de Gaulle		
20 John Quincy Adams		
21 Christopher Columbus		
22 Mickey Mantle	75.00	150.00
23 Albert Einstein		
24 Benjamin Franklin		
25 Abraham Lincoln		
26 Leif Ericsson		
27 Adm. Richard Byrd		
28 Capt. Kidd		
29 Thomas Edison		
30 Ulysses S. Grant		
31 Queen Elizabeth II		
32 Alexander Graham Bell		
33 Willie Mays	75.00	200.00
34 Theodore Roosevelt		
35 Genghis Khan		
36 Daniel Boone		
37 Winston Churchill		
38 Paul Revere		
39 Florence Nightingale		
40 Dwight Eisenhower		
41 Sandy Koufax	50.00	100.00
42 Jacqueline Kennedy		
43 Lady Bird Johnson		
44 Lyndon Johnson		

1968 Topps

The cards in this 598-card set measure 2 1/2" by 3 1/2". The 1968 Topps set includes Sporting News All-Star Selections as card numbers 361 to 380. Other subsets in the set include League Leaders (1-12) and World Series cards (151-158). The front of each checklist card features a picture of a popular player inside a circle. Higher numbers 458 to 598 are slightly more difficult to obtain. The first series looks different from the other series, as it has a lighter, wider mesh background on the card front. The later series all had a much darker, finer mesh pattern. Among other fashions, cards were issued in five-card nickel packs. Those five cent packs were issued 24 packs to a box. Thirty-six card rack packs with an SRP of 29 cents were also issued. The key Rookie Cards in the set are Johnny Bench and Nolan Ryan. Lastly, some cards were also issued along with the "Win-A-Card" board game from Milton Bradley that included cards from the 1965 Topps Hot Rods and 1967 Topps football card sets. This version of these cards is somewhat difficult to distinguish, but are often found with a slight touch of the 1967 football set white border on the front top or bottom edge as well as a brighter yellow card back instead of the darker yellow or gold color. The known cards from this product include card numbers 16, 20, 34, 45, 108, and 149.

Card	Low	High
COMPLETE SET (608)	2500.00	6000.00
COMMON CARD (1-457)	.75	2.00
COMMON CARD (458-598)	1.50	4.00
WRAPPER (5-CENT)	10.00	25.00
1 Clemente/Gonz/Alou LL	10.00	25.00
2 Yaz/F.Rob/Kaline LL	6.00	15.00
3 Cep/Clemente/Aaron LL	15.00	40.00
4 Yaz/Killebrew/F.Rob LL	6.00	15.00
5 Aaron/Santo/McCovey LL	8.00	20.00
6 Yaz/Killebrew/Howard LL	3.00	8.00
7 Niekro/Bunning/Short LL	1.50	4.00
8 Horlen/Peters/Siebert LL	1.50	4.00
9 McCor/Jenkins/Bunning LL	1.50	4.00
10A Lonb/Wils/Chance LL ERR	1.50	4.00
10B Lonb/Wils/Chance LL COR	1.50	4.00
11 Bunning/Jenkins/Perry LL	2.50	6.00
12 Lonborg/McDow/Chance LL	1.50	4.00
13 Chuck Hartenstein RC	.75	2.00
14 Jerry McNertney	.75	2.00
15 Ron Hunt	.75	2.00
16 L.Piniella/R.Scheinblum	2.50	6.00
17 Dick Hall	.75	2.00
18 Mike Hershberger	.75	2.00
19 Juan Pizarro	.75	2.00
20 Brooks Robinson	12.00	30.00
21 Ron Davis	.75	2.00
22 Pat Dobson	1.50	4.00
23 Chico Cardenas	1.50	4.00
24 Bobby Locke	.75	2.00
25 Julian Javier	1.50	4.00
26 Darrell Brandon	.75	2.00
27 Gil Hodges MG	8.00	20.00
28 Ted Uhlaender	.75	2.00
29 Joe Verbanic	.75	2.00
30 Joe Torre	2.50	6.00
31 Ed Stroud	.75	2.00
32 Joe Gibbon	.75	2.00
33 Pete Ward	.75	2.00
34 Al Ferrara	.75	2.00
35 Steve Hargan	.75	2.00
36 B.Moose RC/B.Robertson RC	1.50	4.00
37 Billy Williams	10.00	25.00
38 Tony Pierce	.75	2.00
39 Cookie Rojas	.75	2.00
40 Denny McLain	10.00	25.00
41 Julio Gotay	.75	2.00
42 Larry Haney	.75	2.00
43 Gary Bell	.75	2.00
44 Frank Kostro	.75	2.00
45 Tom Seaver	60.00	150.00
46 Dave Ricketts	.75	2.00
47 Ralph Houk MG	1.50	4.00
48 Ted Davidson	.75	2.00
49A E.Brinkman White	.75	2.00
49B E.Brinkman Yellow Tm	20.00	50.00
50 Willie Mays	60.00	150.00
51 Bob Locker	.75	2.00
52 Hawk Taylor	.75	2.00
53 Gene Alley	1.50	4.00
54 Stan Williams	.75	2.00
55 Felipe Alou	1.50	4.00
56 D.Leonhard RC/D.May RC	.75	2.00
57 Dan Schneider	.75	2.00
58 Eddie Mathews	10.00	25.00
59 Don Lock	.75	2.00
60 Ken Holtzman	1.50	4.00
61 Reggie Smith	1.50	4.00
62 Chuck Dobson	.75	2.00
63 Dick Kenworthy RC	.75	2.00
64 Jim Merritt	.75	2.00
65 John Roseboro	1.50	4.00
66A Casey Cox White	.75	2.00
66B C.Cox Yellow Tm	50.00	100.00
67 Checklist 1/Kaat	2.50	6.00
68 Ron Willis	.75	2.00
69 Tom Tresh	1.50	4.00
70 Bob Veale	1.50	4.00
71 Vern Fuller RC	.75	2.00
72 Tommy John	2.50	6.00
73 Jim Ray Hart	1.50	4.00
74 Milt Pappas	1.50	4.00
75 Don Mincher	.75	2.00
76 J.Britton/R.Reed RC	1.50	4.00
77 Don Wilson RC	1.50	4.00
78 Jim Northrup	2.50	6.00
79 Ted Kubiak RC	.75	2.00
80 Rod Carew	20.00	50.00
81 Larry Jackson	.75	2.00
82 Sam Bowens	.75	2.00
83 John Stephenson	.75	2.00
84 Bob Tolan	.75	2.00
85 Gaylord Perry	6.00	15.00
86 Willie Stargell	15.00	40.00
87 Dick Williams MG	1.50	4.00
88 Phil Regan	1.50	4.00
89 Jake Gibbs	1.50	4.00
90 Vada Pinson	1.50	4.00
91 Jim Ollom	.75	2.00
92 Ed Kranepool	1.50	4.00
93 Tony Cloninger	.75	2.00
94 Lee Maye	.75	2.00
95 Bob Aspromonte	.75	2.00
96 F.Coggins RC/D.Nold	.75	2.00
97 Tom Phoebus	.75	2.00
98 Gary Sutherland	.75	2.00
99 Rocky Colavito	3.00	8.00
100 Bob Gibson	20.00	50.00
101 Glenn Beckert	1.50	4.00
102 Jose Cardenal	1.50	4.00
103 Don Sutton	3.00	8.00
104 Dick Dietz	.75	2.00
105 Al Downing	1.50	4.00
106 Dalton Jones	.75	2.00
107A Checklist 2/Marichal Wide	2.50	6.00
107B Checklist 2/J.Marichal Fine	2.50	6.00
108 Don Pavletich	.75	2.00
109 Bert Campaneris	1.50	4.00
110 Hank Aaron	40.00	100.00
111 Rich Reese	.75	2.00
112 Woody Fryman	.75	2.00
113 T.Matchick/D.Patterson RC	1.50	4.00
114 Ron Swoboda	1.50	4.00
115 Sam McDowell	1.50	4.00
116 Ken McMullen	.75	2.00
117 Larry Jaster	.75	2.00
118 Mark Belanger	1.50	4.00
119 Ted Savage	.75	2.00
120 Mel Stottlemyre	1.50	4.00
121 Jimmie Hall	.75	2.00
122 Gene Mauch MG	1.50	4.00
123 Jose Santiago	.75	2.00
124 Nate Oliver	.75	2.00
125 Joel Horlen	.75	2.00
126 Bobby Etheridge RC	.75	2.00
127 Paul Lindblad	.75	2.00
128 T.Dukes RC/A.Harris	.75	2.00
129 Mickey Stanley	2.50	6.00
130 Tony Perez	10.00	25.00
131 Frank Bertaina	.75	2.00
132 Bud Harrelson	1.50	4.00
133 Fred Whitfield	.75	2.00
134 Pat Jarvis	.75	2.00
135 Paul Blair	1.50	4.00
136 Randy Hundley	1.50	4.00
137 Minnesota Twins TC	1.50	4.00
138 Ruben Amaro	.75	2.00
139 Chris Short	.75	2.00
140 Tony Conigliaro	3.00	8.00
141 Dal Maxvill	.75	2.00
142 B.Bradford RC/B.Voss	.75	2.00
143 Pete Cimino	.75	2.00
144 Joe Morgan	8.00	20.00
145 Don Drysdale	20.00	50.00
146 Sal Bando	1.50	4.00
147 Frank Linzy	.75	2.00
148 Dave Bristol MG	.75	2.00
149 Bob Saverine	.75	2.00
150 Roberto Clemente	50.00	120.00
151 Lou Brock WS1	4.00	10.00
152 Carl Yastrzemski WS2	4.00	10.00
153 Nelson Briles WS3	2.00	5.00
154 Bob Gibson WS4	4.00	10.00
155 Jim Lonborg WS5	2.00	5.00
156 Rico Petrocelli WS6	2.00	5.00
157 St. Louis Wins It WS7	2.00	5.00
158 Cardinals Celebrate WS	2.00	5.00
159 Don Kessinger	1.50	4.00
160 Earl Wilson	1.50	4.00
161 Norm Miller	.75	2.00
162 H.Gilson RC/M.Torrez RC	1.50	4.00
163 Gene Brabender	.75	2.00
164 Ramon Webster	.75	2.00
165 Tony Oliva	2.50	6.00
166 Claude Raymond	.75	2.00
167 Elston Howard	2.50	6.00
168 Los Angeles Dodgers TC	1.50	4.00
169 Bob Bolin	.75	2.00
170 Jim Fregosi	1.50	4.00
171 Don Nottebart	.75	2.00
172 Walt Williams	.75	2.00
173 John Boozer	.75	2.00
174 Bob Tillman	.75	2.00
175 Maury Wills	2.50	6.00
176 Bob Allen	.75	2.00
177 N.Ryan RC/J.Koosman RC	800.00	2000.00
178 Don Wert	1.50	4.00
179 Bill Stoneman RC	.75	2.00
180 Curt Flood	2.50	6.00
181 Jerry Zimmerman	.75	2.00
182 Dave Giusti	.75	2.00
183 Bob Kennedy MG	1.50	4.00
184 Lou Johnson	.75	2.00
185 Tom Haller	.75	2.00
186 Eddie Watt	.75	2.00
187 Sonny Jackson	.75	2.00
188 Cap Peterson	.75	2.00
189 Bill Landis RC	.75	2.00
190 Bill White	1.50	4.00
191 Dan Frisella RC	.75	2.00
192A Checklist 3/Yaz Ball	3.00	8.00
192B Checklist 3/Yaz Game	3.00	8.00
193 Jack Hamilton	.75	2.00
194 Don Buford	.75	2.00
195 Joe Pepitone	1.50	4.00
196 Gary Nolan RC	1.50	4.00
197 Larry Brown	.75	2.00
198 Roy Face	1.50	4.00
199 R.Rodriguez RC/D.Osteen	.75	2.00
200 Orlando Cepeda	10.00	25.00
201 Mike Marshall RC	1.50	4.00
202 Adolfo Phillips	.75	2.00
203 Dick Kelley	.75	2.00
204 Andy Etchebarren	.75	2.00
205 Juan Marichal	3.00	8.00
206 Cal Ermer MG RC	.75	2.00
207 Carroll Sembera	.75	2.00
208 Willie Davis	1.50	4.00
209 Tim Cullen	.75	2.00
210 Gary Peters	.75	2.00
211 J.C. Martin	.75	2.00
212 Dave Morehead	.75	2.00
213 Chico Ruiz	.75	2.00
214 S.Bahnsen/F.Fernandez	1.50	4.00
215 Jim Bunning	3.00	8.00
216 Bubba Morton	.75	2.00
217 Dick Farrell	.75	2.00
218 Ken Suarez	.75	2.00
219 Rob Gardner	.75	2.00
220 Harmon Killebrew	12.00	30.00
221 Atlanta Braves TC	1.50	4.00
222 Jim Hardin RC	.75	2.00
223 Ollie Brown	.75	2.00
224 Jack Aker	.75	2.00
225 Richie Allen	2.50	6.00
226 Jimmie Price	.75	2.00
227 Joe Hoerner	.75	2.00
228 J.Billingham RC/J.Fairey RC	1.50	4.00
229 Fred Klages	.75	2.00
230 Pete Rose	50.00	120.00
231 Dave Baldwin RC	.75	2.00
232 Denis Menke	.75	2.00
233 George Scott	1.50	4.00
234 Bill Monbouquette	.75	2.00
235 Ron Santo	3.00	8.00
236 Tug McGraw	2.50	6.00
237 Alvin Dark MG	1.50	4.00
238 Tom Satriano	.75	2.00
239 Bill Henry	.75	2.00
240 Al Kaline	15.00	40.00
241 Felix Millan	.75	2.00
242 Moe Drabowsky	1.50	4.00
243 Rich Rollins	.75	2.00
244 John Donaldson RC	.75	2.00
245 Tony Gonzalez	.75	2.00
246 Fritz Peterson	1.50	4.00
247A Johnny Bench RC	150.00	400.00
247B Johnny Bench RC	150.00	400.00
248 Fred Valentine	.75	2.00
249 Bill Singer	.75	2.00
250 Carl Yastrzemski	15.00	40.00
251 Manny Sanguillen RC	2.50	6.00
252 California Angels TC	1.50	4.00
253 Dick Hughes	.75	2.00
254 Cleon Jones	1.50	4.00
255 Dean Chance	1.50	4.00
256 Norm Cash	8.00	20.00
257 Phil Niekro	8.00	20.00
258 J.Arcia RC/B.Schlesinger	.75	2.00
259 Ken Boyer	2.50	6.00
260 Jim Wynn	1.50	4.00
261 Dave Duncan	1.50	4.00
262 Rick Wise	1.50	4.00
263 Horace Clarke	1.50	4.00
264 Ted Abernathy	.75	2.00
265 Tommy Davis	1.50	4.00
266 Paul Popovich	.75	2.00
267 Herman Franks MG	.75	2.00
268 Bob Humphreys	.75	2.00
269 Bob Tiefenauer	.75	2.00
270 Matty Alou	1.50	4.00
271 Bobby Knoop	.75	2.00
272 Ray Culp	.75	2.00
273 Dave Johnson	1.50	4.00
274 Mike Cuellar	1.50	4.00
275 Tim McCarver	2.50	6.00
276 Jim Roland	.75	2.00
277 Jerry Buchek	.75	2.00
278 Checklist 4/Cepeda	2.50	6.00
279 Bill Hands	.75	2.00
280 Mickey Mantle	250.00	600.00
281 Jim Campanis	.75	2.00
282 Rick Monday	1.50	4.00
283 Mel Queen	.75	2.00
284 Johnny Briggs	.75	2.00
285 Dick McAuliffe	2.50	6.00
286 Cecil Upshaw	.75	2.00
287 M.Abarbanel RC/C.Carlos RC	.75	2.00
288 Dave Wickersham	.75	2.00
289 Woody Held	.75	2.00
290 Willie McCovey	20.00	50.00
291 Dick Lines	.75	2.00
292 Art Shamsky	.75	2.00
293 Bruce Howard	.75	2.00
294 Red Schoendienst MG	6.00	15.00
295 Sonny Siebert	.75	2.00
296 Byron Browne	.75	2.00
297 Russ Gibson	.75	2.00
298 Jim Brewer	.75	2.00
299 Gene Michael	1.50	4.00
300 Rusty Staub	1.50	4.00
301 G.Mitterwald RC/R.Renick RC	.75	2.00
302 Gerry Arrigo	.75	2.00
303 Dick Green	1.50	4.00
304 Sandy Valdespino	.75	2.00
305 Minnie Rojas	.75	2.00
306 Mike Ryan	.75	2.00
307 John Hiller	1.50	4.00
308 Pittsburgh Pirates TC	1.50	4.00
309 Ken Henderson	.75	2.00
310 Luis Aparicio	6.00	15.00
311 Jack Lamabe	.75	2.00
312 Curt Blefary	.75	2.00
313 Al Weis	.75	2.00
314 B.Rohr/G.Spriggs	.75	2.00
315 Zoilo Versalles	.75	2.00
316 Steve Barber	.75	2.00
317 Ron Brand	.75	2.00
318 Chico Salmon	.75	2.00
319 George Culver	.75	2.00
320 Frank Howard	1.50	4.00
321 Leo Durocher MG	2.50	6.00
322 Dave Boswell	.75	2.00
323 Deron Johnson	1.50	4.00
324 Jim Nash	.75	2.00
325 Manny Mota	1.50	4.00
326 Dennis Ribant	.75	2.00
327 Tony Taylor	1.50	4.00
328 C.Vinson RC/J.Weaver RC	.75	2.00
329 Duane Josephson	.75	2.00
330 Roger Maris	25.00	60.00
331 Dan Osinski	.75	2.00
332 Doug Rader	1.50	4.00
333 Ron Herbel	.75	2.00
334 Baltimore Orioles TC	1.50	4.00
335 Bob Allison	1.50	4.00
336 John Purdin	.75	2.00
337 Bill Robinson	1.50	4.00
338 Bob Johnson	.75	2.00
339 Rich Nye	.75	2.00
340 Max Alvis	.75	2.00
341 Jim Lemon MG	.75	2.00
342 Ken Johnson	.75	2.00
343 Jim Gosger	.75	2.00
344 Donn Clendenon	1.50	4.00
345 Bob Hendley	.75	2.00
346 Jerry Adair	.75	2.00
347 George Brunet	.75	2.00
348 L.Colton RC/D.Thoenen RC	.75	2.00
349 Ed Spiezio	1.50	4.00
350 Hoyt Wilhelm	5.00	12.00
351 Bob Barton	.75	2.00
352 Jackie Hernandez RC	.75	2.00
353 Mack Jones	.75	2.00
354 Pete Richert	.75	2.00
355 Ernie Banks	30.00	80.00
356A Checklist 5/Holtzman Center	2.50	6.00
356B Checklist 5/Holtzman Right	2.50	6.00
357 Len Gabrielson	.75	2.00
358 Mike Epstein	.75	2.00
359 Joe Moeller	.75	2.00
360 Willie Horton	2.50	6.00
361 Harmon Killebrew AS	8.00	20.00
362 Orlando Cepeda AS	2.50	6.00
363 Rod Carew AS	3.00	8.00
364 Joe Morgan AS	3.00	8.00
365 Brooks Robinson AS	3.00	8.00
366 Ron Santo AS	2.50	6.00
367 Jim Fregosi AS	1.50	4.00
368 Gene Alley AS	1.50	4.00
369 Carl Yastrzemski AS	10.00	25.00
370 Hank Aaron AS	20.00	50.00
371 Tony Oliva AS	2.50	6.00
372 Lou Brock AS	6.00	15.00
373 Frank Robinson AS	3.00	8.00
374 Roberto Clemente AS	30.00	80.00
375 Bill Freehan AS	1.50	4.00
376 Tim McCarver AS	1.50	4.00
377 Joel Horlen AS	1.50	4.00
378 Bob Gibson AS	3.00	8.00
379 Gary Peters AS	1.50	4.00
380 Ken Holtzman AS	1.50	4.00
381 Boog Powell AS	1.50	4.00
382 Ramon Hernandez	.75	2.00
383 Steve Whitaker	.75	2.00
384 B.Henry/H.McRae RC	2.50	6.00
385 Jim Hunter	8.00	20.00
386 Greg Goossen	.75	2.00
387 Joe Foy	.75	2.00

388 Ray Washburn .75 2.00
389 Jay Johnstone 1.50 4.00
390 Bill Mazeroski 6.00 15.00
391 Bob Priddy .75 2.00
392 Grady Hatton MG .75 2.00
393 Jim Perry 1.50 4.00
394 Tommie Aaron 2.50 6.00
395 Camilo Pascual 1.50 4.00
396 Bobby Wine .75 2.00
397 Vic Davalillo .75 2.00
398 Jim Grant .75 2.00
399 Ray Oyler 1.50 4.00
400A Mike McCormick YT 1.50 4.00
400B M.McCormick White Tm 400.00 800.00
401 Mets Team 1.50 4.00
402 Mike Hegan 1.50 4.00
403 John Buzhardt .75 2.00
404 Floyd Robinson .75 2.00
405 Tommy Helms 1.50 4.00
406 Dick Ellsworth .75 2.00
407 Gary Kolb .75 2.00
408 Steve Carlton 20.00 50.00
409 F.Peters RC/R.Stone .75 2.00
410 Ferguson Jenkins 4.00 10.00
411 Ron Hansen .75 2.00
412 Clay Carroll 1.50 4.00
413 Tom McCraw .75 2.00
414 Mickey Lolich 3.00 8.00
415 Johnny Callison 1.50 4.00
416 Bill Rigney MG .75 2.00
417 Willie Crawford .75 2.00
418 Eddie Fisher .75 2.00
419 Jack Hiatt .75 2.00
420 Cesar Tovar .75 2.00
421 Ron Taylor .75 2.00
422 Rene Lachemann .75 2.00
423 Fred Gladding .75 2.00
424 Chicago White Sox TC 1.50 4.00
425 Jim Maloney 1.50 4.00
426 Hank Allen .75 2.00
427 Dick Calmus .75 2.00
428 Vic Roznovsky .75 2.00
429 Tommie Sisk .75 2.00
430 Rico Petrocelli 1.50 4.00
431 Dooley Womack .75 2.00
432 B.Davis/J.Vidal .75 2.00
433 Bob Rodgers .75 2.00
434 Ricardo Joseph RC .75 2.00
435 Ron Perranoski 1.50 4.00
436 Hal Lanier .75 2.00
437 Don Cardwell .75 2.00
438 Lee Thomas 1.50 4.00
439 Lum Harris MG .75 2.00
440 Claude Osteen 1.50 4.00
441 Alex Johnson 1.50 4.00
442 Dick Bosman .75 2.00
443 Joe Azcue .75 2.00
444 Jack Fisher .75 2.00
445 Mike Shannon 1.50 4.00
446 Ron Kline .75 2.00
447 G.Korince/F.Lasher RC 1.50 4.00
448 Gary Wagner .75 2.00
449 Gene Oliver .75 2.00
450 Jim Kaat 2.50 6.00
451 Al Spangler .75 2.00
452 Jesus Alou .75 2.00
453 Sammy Ellis .75 2.00
454A Checklist 6/F.Rob Complete 3.00 8.00
454B Checklist 6/F.Rob Partial 3.00 8.00
455 Rico Carty 1.50 4.00
456 John O'Donoghue .75 2.00
457 Jim Lefebvre 1.50 4.00
458 Lew Krausse 2.50 6.00
459 Dick Simpson 1.50 4.00
460 Jim Lonborg 2.50 6.00
461 Chuck Hiller 1.50 4.00
462 Barry Moore 1.50 4.00
463 Jim Schaffer 1.50 4.00
464 Don McMahon 1.50 4.00
465 Tommie Agee 4.00 10.00
466 Bill Dillman 1.50 4.00
467 Dick Howser 4.00 10.00
468 Larry Sherry 1.50 4.00
469 Ty Cline 1.50 4.00
470 Bill Freehan 4.00 10.00
471 Orlando Pena 1.50 4.00
472 Walter Alston MG 2.50 6.00
473 Al Worthington 1.50 4.00
474 Paul Schaal 1.50 4.00
475 Joe Niekro 2.50 6.00
476 Woody Woodward 1.50 4.00
477 Philadelphia Phillies TC 3.00 8.00
478 Dave McNally 2.50 6.00
479 Phil Gagliano 2.50 6.00
480 Oliva/Chico/Clemente 25.00 60.00
481 John Wyatt 1.50 4.00
482 Jose Pagan 1.50 4.00
483 Darold Knowles 1.50 4.00
484 Phil Roof 1.50 4.00
485 Ken Berry 2.50 6.00
486 Cal Koonce 1.50 4.00
487 Lee May 4.00 10.00
488 Dick Tracewski 2.50 6.00
489 Wally Bunker 1.50 4.00
490 Kill/Mays/Mantle 150.00 400.00
491 Denny Lemaster 1.50 4.00
492 Jeff Torborg 2.50 6.00
493 Jim McGlothlin 1.50 4.00
494 Ray Sadecki 1.50 4.00
495 Leon Wagner 1.50 4.00
496 Steve Hamilton 2.50 6.00
497 St. Louis Cardinals TC 3.00 8.00
498 Bill Bryan 2.50 6.00
499 Steve Blass 2.50 6.00
500 Frank Robinson 12.50 30.00
501 John Odom 2.50 6.00
502 Mike Andrews 1.50 4.00
503 Al Jackson 2.50 6.00
504 Russ Snyder 1.50 4.00
505 Joe Sparma 4.00 10.00
506 Clarence Jones RC 1.50 4.00
507 Wade Blasingame 1.50 4.00
508 Duke Sims 1.50 4.00
509 Dennis Higgins 1.50 4.00
510 Ron Fairly 4.00 10.00
511 Bill Kelso 1.50 4.00
512 Grant Jackson 1.50 4.00
513 Hank Bauer MG 2.50 6.00
514 Al McBean 1.50 4.00
515 Russ Nixon 1.50 4.00
516 Pete Mikkelsen 1.50 4.00
517 Diego Segui 2.50 6.00
518A Checklist 7/Boyer ERR 5.00 12.00
518B Checklist 7/Boyer COR 5.00 12.00
519 Jerry Stephenson 1.50 4.00
520 Lou Brock 15.00 40.00
521 Don Shaw 1.50 4.00
522 Wayne Causey 1.50 4.00
523 John Tsitouris 1.50 4.00
524 Andy Kosco 2.50 6.00
525 Jim Davenport 1.50 4.00
526 Bill Denehy 1.50 4.00
527 Tito Francona 1.50 4.00
528 Detroit Tigers TC 30.00 60.00
529 Bruce Von Hoff RC 1.50 4.00
530 B.Robinson/F.Robinson 15.00 40.00
531 Chuck Hinton 1.50 4.00
532 Luis Tiant 5.00 12.00
533 Wes Parker 2.50 6.00
534 Bob Miller 2.50 6.00
535 Danny Cater 2.50 6.00
536 Bill Short 1.50 4.00
537 Norm Siebern 2.50 6.00
538 Manny Jimenez 2.50 6.00
539 J.Ray RC/M.Ferraro RC 1.50 4.00
540 Nelson Briles 2.50 6.00
541 Sandy Alomar 2.50 6.00
542 John Boccabella 1.50 4.00
543 Bob Lee 1.50 4.00
544 Mayo Smith MG 5.00 12.00
545 Lindy McDaniel 2.50 6.00
546 Roy White 2.50 6.00
547 Dan Coombs 1.50 4.00
548 Bernie Allen 1.50 4.00
549 C.Motton RC/R.Nelson RC 1.50 4.00
550 Clete Boyer 2.50 6.00
551 Darrell Sutherland 1.50 4.00
552 Ed Kirkpatrick 1.50 4.00
553 Hank Aguirre 1.50 4.00
554 Oakland Athletics TC 4.00 10.00
555 Jose Tartabull 2.50 6.00
556 Dick Selma 1.50 4.00
557 Frank Quilici 2.50 6.00
558 Johnny Edwards 1.50 4.00
559 C.Taylor RC/L.Walker 1.50 4.00
560 Paul Casanova 1.50 4.00
561 Lee Elia 1.50 4.00
562 Jim Bouton 8.00 20.00
563 Ed Charles 1.50 4.00
564 Eddie Stanky MG 2.50 6.00
565 Larry Dierker 2.50 6.00
566 Ken Harrelson 2.50 6.00
567 Clay Dalrymple 1.50 4.00
568 Willie Smith 1.50 4.00
569 I.Murrell RC/L.Rohr RC 1.50 4.00
570 Rick Reichardt 1.50 4.00
571 Tony LaRussa 5.00 12.00
572 Don Bosch RC 1.50 4.00
573 Joe Coleman 1.50 4.00
574 Cincinnati Reds TC 4.00 10.00
575 Jim Palmer 20.00 50.00
576 Dave Adlesh 1.50 4.00
577 Fred Talbot 1.50 4.00
578 Orlando Martinez 1.50 4.00
579 L.Hisle RC/M.Lum RC 4.00 10.00
580 Bob Bailey 1.50 4.00
581 Garry Roggenburk 1.50 4.00
582 Jerry Grote 4.00 10.00
583 Gates Brown 4.00 10.00
584 Larry Shepard MG RC 1.50 4.00
585 Wilbur Wood 2.50 6.00
586 Jim Pagliaroni 2.50 6.00
587 Roger Repoz 1.50 4.00
588 Dick Schofield 1.50 4.00
589 R.Clark/M.Ogier RC 1.50 4.00
590 Tommy Harper 2.50 6.00
591 Dick Nen 1.50 4.00
592 John Bateman 1.50 4.00
593 Lee Stange 1.50 4.00
594 Phil Linz 2.50 6.00
595 Phil Ortega 1.50 4.00
596 Charlie Smith 1.50 4.00
597 Bill McCool 1.50 4.00
598 Jerry May 2.50 6.00

1968 Topps Game

COMPLETE SET (33) 125.00 300.00
COMP.FACT SET (33) 125.00 300.00
1 Matty Alou 1.00 2.50
2 Mickey Mantle 50.00 120.00
3 Carl Yastrzemski 10.00 25.00
4 Hank Aaron 15.00 40.00
5 Harmon Killebrew 8.00 20.00
6 Roberto Clemente 25.00 60.00
7 Frank Robinson 12.00 30.00
8 Willie Mays 20.00 50.00
9 Brooks Robinson 8.00 20.00
10 Tommy Davis .75 2.00
11 Bill Freehan 1.00 2.50
12 Claude Osteen .75 2.00
13 Gary Peters .75 2.00
14 Jim Lonborg .75 2.00
15 Steve Hargan .75 2.00
16 Dean Chance .75 2.00
17 Mike McCormick .75 2.00
18 Tim McCarver 1.00 2.50
19 Ron Santo 1.25 3.00
20 Tony Gonzalez .75 2.00
21 Frank Howard 1.00 2.50
22 George Scott .75 2.00
23 Richie Allen 1.25 3.00
24 Jim Wynn 1.00 2.50
25 Gene Alley .75 2.00
26 Rick Monday .75 2.00
27 Al Kaline 6.00 15.00
28 Rusty Staub 1.00 2.50
29 Rod Carew 6.00 15.00
30 Pete Rose 20.00 50.00
31 Joe Torre 1.25 3.00
32 Orlando Cepeda 1.25 3.00
33 Jim Fregosi 1.00 2.50

1968 Topps Milton Bradley

These cards were included in a 1968 Milton Bradley Win-A-Card game. These cards, which are variations of some singles from the first two series, feature an "yellow" back rather than an orange back. These cards, along with some 1967 Topps Football cards and Topps Hot Rod cards were all part of the game. The key card in this set is a Nolan Ryan "Rookie".

COMPLETE SET (77) 400.00 800.00
7 Phil Niekro 1.50 4.00
Jim Bunning
Chris Short LL
8 AL ERA Leaders 1.50 4.00
Joel Horlen
Gary Peters
Sonny Siebert
10 AL Pitching Leaders 1.50 4.00
Jim Lonborg ERR/(Misspelled Lonberg
on card back)
Earl Wilson
Dean Chance
13 Chuck Hartenstein .75 2.00
16 Lou Piniella 1.50 4.00
Richie Scheinblum
17 Dick Hall .75 2.00
18 Mike Hershberger .75 2.00
19 Juan Pizarro .75 2.00
20 Brooks Robinson 10.00 25.00
24 Bobby Locke .75 2.00
26 Darrell Brandon .75 2.00
34 Al Ferrara .75 2.00
36 Bob Moose 1.00 2.50
Bob Robertson
38 Tony Pierce .75 2.00
43 Gary Bell .75 2.00
44 Frank Kostro .75 2.00
45 Tom Seaver 20.00 50.00
48 Ted Davidson .75 2.00
49 Eddie Brinkman .75 2.00
Team Name Yellow
53 Gene Alley .75 2.00
57 Dan Schneider .75 2.00
58 Eddie Mathews 6.00 15.00
60 Ken Holtzman 1.00 2.50
61 Reggie Smith 1.00 2.50
62 Chuck Dobson .75 2.00
64 Jim Merritt .75 2.00
66 Casey Cox .75 2.00
Team Name Yellow
68 Ron Willis .75 2.00
72 Tommy John 1.25 3.00
74 Milt Pappas 1.00 2.50
77 Don Wilson .75 2.00
78 Jim Northrup 1.25 3.00
80 Rod Carew 30.00 60.00
81 Larry Jackson .75 2.00
85 Gaylord Perry 3.00 8.00
89 Jake Gibbs 1.00 2.50
94 Lee Maye .75 2.00
98 Gary Sutherland .75 2.00
99 Rocky Colavito 3.00 8.00
100 Bob Gibson 10.00 25.00
105 Al Downing 1.00 2.50
106 Dalton Jones .75 2.00
107 Juan Marichal CL 2.50 6.00
107 Checklist 2 Juan Marichal
(Tan Wide Mesh) 2.50 6.00
108 Don Pavletich .75 2.00
110 Hank Aaron 30.00 60.00
112 Woody Fryman .75 2.00
113 Tom Matchick 1.00 2.50
Daryl Patterson
117 Larry Jaster .75 2.00
118 Mark Belanger .75 2.00
119 Ted Savage .75 2.00
120 Mel Stottlemyre 1.00 2.50
121 Jimmie Hall .75 2.00
124 Nate Oliver .75 2.00
127 Paul Lindblad .75 2.00
128 Tom Dukes .75 2.00
Alonzo Harris
129 Mickey Stanley 1.00 2.50
136 Randy Hundley .75 2.00
139 Chris Short .75 2.00
143 Pete Cimino .75 2.00
146 Sal Bando 1.00 2.50
149 Bob Saverine .75 2.00
155 Jim Lonborg WS 2.00 5.00
156 Rico Petrocelli WS 2.00 5.00
165 Tony Oliva 1.50 4.00
168 Dodgers Team 1.50 4.00
172 Walt Williams .75 2.00
175 Maury Wills 1.50 4.00
176 Bob Allen .75 2.00
177 Jerry Koosman 250.00 500.00
Nolan Ryan
179 Bill Stoneman .75 2.00
180 Curt Flood 1.25 3.00
185 Tom Haller .75 2.00
189 Bill Landis .75 2.00
191 Dan Frisella .75 2.00
193 Jack Hamilton .75 2.00
195 Joe Pepitone 1.25 3.00

1968 Topps 3-D

The cards in this 12-card set measure 2 1/4" by 3 1/2". Topps' experiment with "3-D" cards came two years before Kellogg's inaugural set. These cards are considered to be quite rare. This was a "test set" sold in a plain white wrapper with a sticker attached as a design, a device used by Topps for limited marketing. The cards employ a sharp foreground picture set against an indistinct background, covered by a layer of plastic to produce the "3-D" effect. The checklist below is ordered alphabetically. Test 3D cards of Sam McDowell and Brooks Robinson and were issued before this 12 card set was released. Those cards measures 2 1/4" by 3 1/4" and has the team name on the top but with no player identification. In addition, test cards of Tommy Davis, Rick Monday and John O'Donoghue were issued and recently discovered without either team identification or player identification.

COMPLETE SET (12) 6000.00 12000.00
WRAPPER (10-CENTS) 500.00 1000.00
1 Roberto Clemente 2500.00 5000.00
2 Willie Davis 500.00 1000.00
3 Ron Fairly 300.00 600.00
4 Curt Flood 500.00 1000.00
5 Jim Lonborg 500.00 1000.00
6 Jim Maloney 500.00 1000.00
7 Tony Perez 750.00 1500.00
8 Boog Powell 600.00 1200.00
9 Bill Robinson 300.00 600.00
10 Rusty Staub 500.00 1000.00
11 Mel Stottlemyre 500.00 1000.00
12 Ron Swoboda 300.00 600.00

1968 Topps Action Stickers

This test issue is a set of 16 long stickers which is perforated and can be divided into three stickers. The middle sticker features a large sticker depicting only one player, whereas the top and bottom stickers feature three smaller stickers. These stickers are attractive and colorful. These cane packed 12 packs to a box with 24 boxes in a case.

COMPLETE SET (48) 2000.00 4000.00
COMMON INDIV. PANEL 6.00 15.00
COMMON TRIPLE PANEL 12.50 30.00
WRAPPER (10-CENT) 200.00 400.00
1A Horlen 6.00 15.00
Cepeda
Mazeroski
1B Carl Yastrzemski 125.00 250.00
1C Stottlemyre 15.00 40.00
Kaline
Osteen
2A Pete Ward 6.00 15.00
Mike McCormick
Ron Swoboda
2B Harmon Killebrew 60.00 120.00
2C Scott 12.50 30.00
Phoebus
Drysdale
3A Maloney 15.00 40.00
Pepitone
Aaron
3B Frank Robinson 75.00 150.00
3C Casanova 15.00 40.00
Reichardt
Seaver
4A F. Robin 12.50 30.00
Lefebvre
Chance
4B Ron Santo 15.00 40.00
4C Johnny Callison 6.00 15.00
Jim Lonborg
Bob Aspromonte
5A Bert Campaneris 6.00 15.00
Ron Santo
Al Downing
5B Willie Mays 150.00 300.00
5C Rose 75.00 150.00
Kranepool
Horton
6A Yaz 40.00 80.00
Alvis
W. Williams
6B Al Kaline 100.00 200.00
6C Banks 40.00 80.00
McCarver
Staub
7A McCovey 15.00 40.00
Monday
Hargan
7B Mickey Mantle 400.00 800.00
7C Carew 20.00 50.00
Gonzalez
B. Williams
8A Boyer 12.50 30.00
Mincher
Bunning
8B Joel Horlen 15.00 40.00
8C Tony Conigliaro 6.00 15.00
Ken McMullen
Mike Cuellar
9A Killebrew 12.50 30.00
Fregosi
Wilson
9B Orlando Cepeda 400.00 800.00
9C Clemente 125.00 250.00
Mays
Short
10A Mantle 100.00 200.00
Hunter
Pinson
10B Hank Aaron 150.00 300.00
10C Peters 12.50 30.00
Gibson
Harrelson
11A Tony Oliva 6.00 15.00
Bob Veale
Bill Freehan
11B Don Drysdale 60.00 120.00
11C Frank Howard 75.00 150.00
Fergie Jenkins
Jim Wynn
12A Joe Torre 6.00 15.00
Dick Allen
Jim McGlothlin
12B Roberto Clemente 200.00 400.00
12C B.Robinson 20.00 50.00
Perez
McDow
13A F.Robinson 15.00 40.00
Lefeb
Chance
13B Carl Yastrzemski 125.00 250.00
13C Phoebus 12.50 30.00
Scott
Drysdale
14A Horlen 6.00 15.00
Cepeda
Mazeroski
14B Harmon Killebrew 60.00 120.00
14C Casan 15.00 40.00
Reichardt
Seaver
15A Pete Ward 6.00 15.00
Mike McCormick
Ron Swoboda
15B Frank Robinson 100.00 200.00
15C Johnny Callison 6.00 15.00
Jim Lonborg
Bob Aspromonte
16A Maloney 15.00 40.00
Pepitone
Aaron
16B Ron Santo 15.00 40.00
16C Stottle 15.00 40.00
Kaline
Osteen

1968 Topps Giant Stand Ups

This test issue is quite scarce. The set features a color portrait photo of the player on a distinctive black background on heavy card stock. Each card measures 3 1/16" by 5 1/4" and is blank backed. The cards are numbered on the front in the lower left corner. Cards are found both with and without the stand up die cut.

COMPLETE SET (24) 25000.00 50000.00
1 Pete Rose 3000.00 6000.00
2 Gary Peters 300.00 600.00
3 Frank Robinson 600.00 1200.00
4 Jim Lonborg 300.00 600.00
5 Ron Swoboda 300.00 600.00
6 Harmon Killebrew 600.00 1200.00
7 Roberto Clemente 4000.00 8000.00
8 Mickey Mantle 6000.00 12000.00
9 Jim Fregosi 300.00 600.00
10 Al Kaline 600.00 1200.00
11 Don Drysdale 600.00 1200.00
12 Dean Chance 300.00 600.00
13 Orlando Cepeda 400.00 800.00
14 Tim McCarver 400.00 800.00
15 Frank Howard 400.00 800.00
16 Max Alvis 300.00 600.00
17 Rusty Staub 400.00 800.00
18 Richie Allen 400.00 800.00
19 Willie Mays 4000.00 8000.00
20 Hank Aaron 4000.00 8000.00
21 Carl Yastrzemski 2500.00 5000.00
22 Ron Santo 400.00 800.00
23 Jim Hunter 600.00 1200.00
24 Jim Wynn 300.00 600.00

1968 Topps Plaks

These brown plastic "busts," measure roughly 1" by 2". One Checklist per pack was included with these plaks, which were issued three to a 10 cent pack (which came 12 to a box), which measured 2'1/8" by 4". The set is sequenced and therefore checklisted in alphabetical order within each league. Recent research appears to indicate that the following five plaks were never issued: Gary Peters, Frank Robinson, Hank Aaron, Don Drysdale and Willie Mays. We will keep searching to see if in fact these plaks were produced and if they were not, we will in the near future delete them from our checklist.

COMPLETE SET (26) 4000.00 8000.00
*WRAPPER (10-CENT)
1 Max Alvis 40.00 80.00
2 Dean Chance 50.00 100.00
3 Jim Fregosi 50.00 100.00
4 Frank Howard 75.00 150.00
5 Jim Hunter 100.00 200.00
6 Al Kaline 200.00 400.00
7 Harmon Killebrew 125.00 250.00
8 Jim Lonborg 50.00 100.00
9 Mickey Mantle 750.00 1500.00
10 Gary Peters 40.00 80.00
11 Frank Robinson 125.00 250.00
12 Carl Yastrzemski 150.00 300.00
13 Hank Aaron 400.00 800.00
14 Richie Allen 75.00 150.00
15 Orlando Cepeda 100.00 200.00
16 Roberto Clemente 500.00 1000.00
17 Tommy Davis 50.00 100.00
18 Don Drysdale 125.00 250.00
19 Willie Mays 400.00 800.00
20 Tim McCarver 75.00 150.00
21 Pete Rose 400.00 800.00
22 Ron Santo 75.00 150.00
23 Rusty Staub 50.00 100.00
24 Jim Wynn 50.00 100.00
NNO Checklist Card 1-12 40.00 80.00
NNO Checklist Card 13-24 40.00 80.00

1968 Topps Plaks Checklists

These two cards, which measure 2 /18" by 4", were inserted one per 1968 Topps Plak pack. Each checklist card featured all the players each league that were available in the packs.

COMPLETE SET 750.00 1500.00
1 Max Alvis 400.00 800.00
Dean Chance
Jim Fregosi
Frank Howard#
2 Hank Aaron 400.00 800.00
Richie Allen
Orlando Cepeda
Roberto

1968 Topps Posters

This 1968 color poster set is not an "insert" but was issued separately with a piece of gum and in its own wrapper. Each poster cost five cents and Mickey Mantle was the featured player on the box. The posters are numbered at the lower left and the player's name and team appear in a large star. The poster was folded six times to fit into the package, so fold lines are a factor in grading. Each poster measures 9 3/4" by 18 1/8".

COMPLETE SET (24) 150.00 300.00
WRAPPER (5-CENT) 12.50 30.00
1 Dean Chance 1.00 2.50
2 Max Alvis 1.00 2.50
3 Frank Howard 1.50 4.00
4 Jim Fregosi 1.00 2.50
5 Jim Hunter 4.00 10.00
6 Roberto Clemente 30.00 60.00
7 Don Drysdale 4.00 10.00
8 Jim Wynn 1.00 2.50
9 Al Kaline 6.00 15.00
10 Harmon Killebrew 5.00 12.00
11 Jim Lonborg 1.00 2.50
12 Orlando Cepeda 2.50 6.00
13 Gary Peters 1.00 2.50
14 Hank Aaron 8.00 20.00
15 Richie Allen 1.50 4.00
16 Carl Yastrzemski 6.00 15.00
17 Ron Swoboda 1.00 2.50
18 Mickey Mantle 40.00 80.00
19 Tim McCarver 1.50 4.00
20 Willie Mays 8.00 20.00
21 Ron Santo 1.50 4.00
22 Rusty Staub 1.50 4.00
23 Pete Rose 15.00 40.00
24 Frank Robinson 6.00 15.00

1968 Topps Venezuelan

This set is a parallel version of the first 370 cards of the regular 1968 Topps set and is similar in design. A major difference is that the Venezuelan cards are printed on a gray stock and have an orange background compared to the American Topps. There is also the "Hecho en Venezuela - C. A. Litoven" printed in faint white type at the bottom on the back of the card. However, not all of the cards have that expression printed on the bottom. Among the notable cards which do not is the Tom Seaver (number 45) card.

COMPLETE SET (376) 3500.00 7000.00
1 NL Batting Leaders 75.00 150.00
Bob Clemente
Tony Gonzalez
2 AL Batting Leaders 40.00 80.00
Carl Yastrzemski
Frank Robins
3 NL RBI Leaders 50.00 100.00
Orlando Cepeda
Bob Clemente
Hank
4 AL RBI Leaders 30.00 60.00
Carl Yastrzemski
Harmon Killebrew
5 NL Home Run Leaders 15.00 40.00
Hank Aaron
John Wynn
Ron Sa
6 AL Home Run Leaders 15.00 40.00
Carl Yastrzemski
Harmon Kill
7 NL ERA Leaders 8.00 20.00
Phil Neikro
Jim Bunning
Chris Sh
8 AL ERA Leaders 8.00 20.00
Joel Horlen
Gary Peters
Sonny Si
9 NL Pitching Leaders 8.00 20.00
Mike McCormick
Ferguson Jenk
10 AL Pitching Leaders 8.00 20.00
Jim Lonborg ERR/(Misspelled
11 NL Strikeout Leaders 10.00 25.00
Jim Bunning
Ferguson Jenkin
12 AL Strikeout Leaders 10.00 25.00
Jim Lonborg UER/(Misspelled
13 Chuck Hartenstein 5.00 12.00
14 Jerry McNertney 5.00 12.00
15 Ron Hunt 5.00 12.00
16 Lou Piniella 8.00 20.00
Richie Scheinblum
17 Dick Hall 5.00 12.00
18 Mike Hershberger 5.00 12.00
19 Juan Pizarro 5.00 12.00
20 Brooks Robinson 75.00 150.00
21 Ron Davis 5.00 12.00
22 Pat Dobson 5.00 12.00
23 Chico Cardenas 5.00 12.00
24 Bobby Locke 5.00 12.00
25 Julian Javier 5.00 12.00
26 Darrell Brandon 5.00 12.00
27 Gil Hodges MG 20.00 50.00
28 Ted Uhlaender 5.00 12.00
29 Joe Verbanic 5.00 12.00
30 Joe Torre 10.00 25.00
31 Ed Stroud 5.00 12.00
32 Joe Gibbon 5.00 12.00
33 Pete Ward 5.00 12.00
34 Al Ferrara 5.00 12.00
35 Steve Hargan 5.00 12.00
36 Bob Moose 5.00 12.00
Bob Robertson
37 Billy Williams 30.00 60.00
38 Tony Pierce 5.00 12.00
39 Cookie Rojas 5.00 12.00
40 Denny McLain 30.00 60.00
41 Julio Gotay 5.00 12.00
42 Larry Haney 5.00 12.00
43 Gary Bell 5.00 12.00
44 Frank Kostro 5.00 12.00
45 Tom Seaver 150.00 300.00
46 Dave Ricketts 5.00 12.00
47 Ralph Houk MG 5.00 12.00
48 Ted Davidson 5.00 12.00
49 Eddie Brinkman 5.00 12.00
50 Willie Mays 200.00 400.00
51 Bob Locker 5.00 12.00
52 Hawk Taylor 5.00 12.00
53 Gene Alley 5.00 12.00
54 Stan Williams 5.00 12.00
55 Felipe Alou 8.00 20.00
56 Dave Leonhard 5.00 12.00
Dave May
57 Dan Schneider 5.00 12.00
58 Eddie Mathews 50.00 100.00
59 Don Lock 5.00 12.00
60 Ken Holtzman 5.00 12.00
61 Reggie Smith 6.00 15.00
62 Chuck Dobson 5.00 12.00
63 Dick Kenworthy 5.00 12.00
64 Jim Merritt 5.00 12.00
65 John Roseboro 5.00 12.00
66 Casey Cox 5.00 12.00
67 Checklist 1 10.00 25.00
Jim Kaat
68 Ron Willis 5.00 12.00
69 Tom Tresh 6.00 15.00
70 Bob Veale 5.00 12.00
71 Vern Fuller 5.00 12.00
72 Tommy John 10.00 25.00
73 Jim Ray Hart 5.00 12.00
74 Milt Pappas 5.00 12.00
75 Don Wilson 5.00 12.00
76 Jim Britton 5.00 12.00
Ron Reed
77 Don Wilson 5.00 12.00
78 Jim Northrup 5.00 12.00
79 Ted Kubiak 5.00 12.00
80 Rod Carew 150.00 300.00
81 Larry Jackson 5.00 12.00
83 John Stephenson 5.00 12.00
83 Sam Bowens 5.00 12.00
84 Bob Tolan 5.00 12.00
85 Gaylord Perry 20.00 50.00
86 Willie Stargell 20.00 50.00
87 Dick Williams MG 6.00 15.00
88 Phil Regan 5.00 12.00
89 Jake Gibbs 5.00 12.00
90 Vada Pinson 10.00 25.00
91 Jim Ollom 5.00 12.00
92 Ed Kranepool 6.00 15.00
93 Tony Cloninger 5.00 12.00
94 Lee Maye 5.00 12.00
95 Bob Aspromonte 5.00 12.00
96 Frank Coggins 5.00 12.00
Dick Nold
97 Tom Phoebus 5.00 12.00
98 Gary Sutherland 5.00 12.00
99 Rocky Colavito 20.00 50.00
100 Bob Gibson 75.00 150.00
101 Glenn Beckert 5.00 12.00
102 Jose Cardenal 5.00 12.00
103 Don Sutton 15.00 40.00
104 Dick Dietz 5.00 12.00
105 Al Downing 5.00 12.00
106 Dalton Jones 5.00 12.00
107 Checklist 2 10.00 25.00
Juan Marichal
108 Don Pavletich 5.00 12.00
109 Bert Campaneris 6.00 15.00
110 Hank Aaron 200.00 400.00
111 Rich Reese 5.00 12.00
112 Woody Fryman 5.00 12.00
113 Tom Matchick 5.00 12.00
Daryl Patterson
114 Ron Swoboda 6.00 15.00
115 Sam McDowell 5.00 12.00
116 Ken McMullen 5.00 12.00
117 Larry Jaster 5.00 12.00
118 Mark Belanger 5.00 12.00
119 Ted Savage 5.00 12.00
120 Mel Stottlemyre 6.00 15.00
121 Jimmie Hall 5.00 12.00
122 Gene Mauch MG 5.00 12.00
123 Jose Santiago 5.00 12.00
124 Nate Oliver 5.00 12.00
125 Joel Horlen 5.00 12.00
126 Bobby Etheridge 5.00 12.00
127 Paul Lindblad 5.00 12.00
128 Tom Dukes 5.00 12.00
Alonzo Harris
129 Mickey Stanley 5.00 12.00
130 Tony Perez 20.00 50.00
131 Frank Bertaina 5.00 12.00
132 Bud Harrelson 5.00 12.00
133 Fred Whitfield 5.00 12.00
134 Pat Jarvis 5.00 12.00
135 Paul Blair 5.00 12.00
136 Randy Hundley 5.00 12.00
137 Twins Team 8.00 20.00
138 Ruben Amaro 5.00 12.00
139 Chris Short 5.00 12.00
140 Tony Conigliaro 20.00 50.00
141 Dal Maxvill 5.00 12.00
142 Buddy Bradford 5.00 12.00
Bill Voss
143 Pete Cimino 5.00 12.00
144 Joe Morgan 40.00 80.00
145 Don Drysdale 40.00 80.00
146 Sal Bando 5.00 12.00
147 Frank Linzy 5.00 12.00
148 Dave Bristol MG 5.00 12.00
149 Bob Saverine 5.00 12.00
150 Roberto Clemente 250.00 500.00
151 Lou Brock WS 30.00 60.00
152 Carl Yastrzemski WS 30.00 60.00
153 Nellie Briles WS 10.00 25.00
154 Bob Gibson WS 20.00 50.00
155 Jim Lonborg WS 10.00 25.00
156 Rico Petrocelli WS 10.00 25.00
157 World Series Game 7 10.00 25.00
St. Louis wins it
158 World Series Summary 10.00 25.00
Cardinals celebrate
159 Don Kessinger 5.00 12.00
160 Earl Wilson 5.00 12.00
161 Norm Miller 5.00 12.00
162 Hal Gibson 5.00 12.00
Mike Torrez
163 Gene Brabender 5.00 12.00
164 Ramon Webster 5.00 12.00
165 Tony Oliva 10.00 25.00
166 Claude Raymond 5.00 12.00
167 Elston Howard 10.00 25.00
168 Dodgers Team 10.00 25.00
169 Bob Bolin 5.00 12.00
170 Jim Fregosi 6.00 15.00
171 Don Nottebart 5.00 12.00
172 Walt Williams 5.00 12.00
173 John Boozer 5.00 12.00
174 Bob Tillman 5.00 12.00
175 Maury Wills 10.00 25.00
176 Bob Allen 5.00 12.00
177 Jerry Koosman 4000.00 8000.00
Nolan Ryan
178 Don Wert 5.00 12.00
179 Bill Stoneman 5.00 12.00
180 Curt Flood 8.00 20.00
181 Jerry Zimmerman 5.00 12.00
182 Dave Giusti 5.00 12.00
183 Bob Kennedy MG 5.00 12.00
184 Lou Johnson 5.00 12.00
185 Tom Haller 5.00 12.00
186 Eddie Watt 5.00 12.00
187 Sonny Jackson 5.00 12.00
188 Cap Peterson 5.00 12.00
189 Bill Landis 5.00 12.00
190 Bill White 10.00 25.00
191 Dan Frisella 5.00 12.00
192 Checklist 3 20.00 50.00
Carl Yastrzemski/(Special Baseball P
193 Jack Hamilton 5.00 12.00
194 Don Buford 5.00 12.00
195 Joe Pepitone 5.00 12.00
196 Gary Nolan 5.00 12.00
197 Larry Brown 5.00 12.00
198 Roy Face 6.00 15.00
199 Roberto Rodriguez 5.00 12.00
Darrell IOsteen
200 Orlando Cepeda 15.00 40.00
201 Mike Marshall 6.00 15.00
202 Adolfo Phillips 5.00 12.00
203 Dick Kelley 5.00 12.00
204 Andy Etchebarren 5.00 12.00
205 Juan Marichal 20.00 50.00
206 Cal Ermer MG 5.00 12.00
207 Carroll Sembera 5.00 12.00
208 Willie Davis 5.00 12.00
209 Tim Cullen 5.00 12.00
210 Gary Peters 5.00 12.00

211 J.C. Martin 5.00 12.00
212 Dave Morehead 5.00 12.00
213 Chico Ruiz 5.00 12.00
214 Stan Bahnsen 5.00 12.00
Frank Fernandez
215 Jim Bunning 20.00 50.00
216 Bubba Morton 5.00 12.00
217 Dick Farrell 5.00 12.00
218 Ken Suarez 5.00 12.00
219 Rob Gardner 5.00 12.00
220 Harmon Killebrew 50.00 100.00
221 Braves Team 8.00 20.00
222 Jim Hardin 5.00 12.00
223 Ollie Brown 5.00 12.00
224 Jack Aker 5.00 12.00
225 Richie Allen 15.00 40.00
226 Jimmie Price 5.00 12.00
227 Joe Hoerner 5.00 12.00
228 Jack Billingham 5.00 12.00
Jim Fairey
229 Fred Klages 5.00 12.00
230 Pete Rose 150.00 300.00
231 Dave Baldwin 5.00 12.00
232 Denis Menke 5.00 12.00
233 George Scott 5.00 12.00
234 Bill Monbouquette 5.00 12.00
235 Ron Santo 15.00 40.00
236 Tug McGraw 8.00 20.00
237 Alvin Dark MG 6.00 15.00
238 Tom Satriano 5.00 12.00
239 Bill Henry 5.00 12.00
240 Al Kaline 100.00 200.00
241 Felix Millan 5.00 12.00
242 Moe Drabowsky 5.00 12.00
243 Rich Rollins 5.00 12.00
244 John Donaldson 5.00 12.00
245 Tony Gonzalez 5.00 12.00
246 Fritz Peterson 5.00 12.00
247 Johnny Bench 400.00 800.00
Ron Tompkins
248 Fred Valentine 5.00 12.00
249 Bill Singer 5.00 12.00
250 Carl Yastrzemski 75.00 150.00
251 Manny Sanguillen 10.00 25.00
252 Angels Team 8.00 20.00
253 Dick Hughes 5.00 12.00
254 Cleon Jones 5.00 12.00
255 Dean Chance 5.00 12.00
256 Norm Cash 15.00 40.00
257 Phil Niekro 20.00 50.00
258 Jose Arcia 5.00 12.00
Bill Schlesinger
259 Ken Boyer 8.00 20.00
260 Jim Wynn 5.00 12.00
261 Dave Duncan 5.00 12.00
262 Rick Wise 5.00 12.00
263 Horace Clarke 5.00 12.00
264 Ted Abernathy 5.00 12.00
265 Tommy Davis 5.00 12.00
266 Paul Popovich 5.00 12.00
267 Herman Franks MG 5.00 12.00
268 Bob Humphreys 5.00 12.00
269 Bob Tiefenauer 5.00 12.00
270 Matty Alou 6.00 15.00
271 Bobby Knoop 5.00 12.00
272 Ray Culp 5.00 12.00
273 Dave Johnson 8.00 20.00
274 Mike Cuellar 6.00 15.00
275 Tim McCarver 10.00 25.00
276 Jim Roland 5.00 12.00
277 Jerry Buchek 5.00 12.00
278 Checklist 4 10.00 25.00
Orlando Cepeda
279 Bill Hands 5.00 12.00
280 Mickey Mantle 750.00 1500.00
281 Jim Campanis 5.00 12.00
282 Rick Monday 5.00 12.00
283 Mel Queen 5.00 12.00
284 Johnny Briggs 5.00 12.00
285 Dick McAuliffe 5.00 12.00
286 Cecil Upshaw 5.00 12.00
287 Mickey Abarbanel 5.00 12.00
Cisco Carlos
288 Dave Wickersham 5.00 12.00
289 Woody Held 5.00 12.00
290 Willie McCovey 40.00 80.00
291 Dick Lines 5.00 12.00
292 Art Shamsky 5.00 12.00
293 Bruce Howard 5.00 12.00
294 Red Schoendienst MG 10.00 25.00
295 Sonny Siebert 5.00 12.00
296 Byron Browne 5.00 12.00
297 Russ Gibson 5.00 12.00
298 Jim Brewer 5.00 12.00
299 Gene Michael 5.00 12.00
300 Rusty Staub 8.00 20.00
301 George Mitterwald 5.00 12.00
Rick Renick
302 Gerry Arrigo 5.00 12.00
303 Dick Green 5.00 12.00
304 Sandy Valdespino 5.00 12.00
305 Minnie Rojas 5.00 12.00
306 Mike Ryan 5.00 12.00
307 John Hiller 5.00 12.00
308 Pirates Team 8.00 20.00
309 Ken Henderson 5.00 12.00
310 Luis Aparicio 20.00 50.00
311 Jack Lamabe 5.00 12.00
312 Curt Blefary 5.00 12.00
313 Al Weis 5.00 12.00
314 Bill Rohr 5.00 12.00
George Spriggs
315 Zoilo Versalles 5.00 12.00
316 Steve Barber 5.00 12.00
317 Ron Brand 5.00 12.00
318 Chico Salmon 5.00 12.00
319 George Culver 5.00 12.00
320 Frank Howard 6.00 15.00
321 Leo Durocher MG 10.00 25.00
322 Dave Boswell 5.00 12.00
323 Deron Johnson 5.00 12.00
324 Jim Nash 5.00 12.00
325 Manny Mota 6.00 15.00
326 Dennis Ribant 5.00 12.00
327 Tony Taylor 5.00 12.00
328 Chuck Vinson 5.00 12.00
Jim Weaver
329 Duane Josephson 5.00 12.00
330 Roger Maris 125.00 250.00
331 Dan Osinski 5.00 12.00
332 Doug Rader 5.00 12.00
333 Ron Herbel 5.00 12.00
334 Orioles Team 8.00 20.00
335 Bob Allison 5.00 12.00
336 John Purdin 5.00 12.00
337 Bill Robinson 5.00 12.00
338 Bob Johnson 5.00 12.00
339 Rich Nye 5.00 12.00
340 Max Alvis 5.00 12.00
341 Jim Lemon MG 5.00 12.00
342 Ken Johnson 5.00 12.00
343 Jim Gosger 5.00 12.00
344 Donn Clendenon 5.00 12.00
345 Bob Hendley 5.00 12.00
346 Jerry Adair 5.00 12.00
347 George Brunet 5.00 12.00
348 Larry Colton 5.00 12.00
Dick Thoenen
349 Ed Spiezio 5.00 12.00
350 Hoyt Wilhelm 15.00 40.00
351 Bob Barton 5.00 12.00
352 Jackie Hernandez 5.00 12.00
353 Mack Jones 5.00 12.00
354 Pete Richert 5.00 12.00
355 Ernie Banks 75.00 150.00
356 Checklist 5 10.00 25.00
Ken Holtzman/(Head centered within c
357 Len Gabrielson 5.00 12.00
358 Mike Epstein 5.00 12.00
359 Joe Moeller 5.00 12.00
360 Willie Horton 8.00 20.00
361 Harmon Killebrew AS 15.00 40.00
362 Orlando Cepeda AS 10.00 25.00
363 Rod Carew AS 15.00 40.00
364 Joe Morgan AS 15.00 40.00
365 Brooks Robinson AS 15.00 40.00
366 Ron Santo AS 8.00 20.00
367 Jim Fregosi AS 5.00 12.00
368 Gene Alley AS 5.00 12.00
369 Carl Yastrzemski AS 30.00 60.00
370 Hank Aaron AS 60.00 120.00

1969 Topps

The cards in this 664-card set measure 2 1/2" by 3 1/2". The 1969 Topps set includes Sporting News All-Star Selections as card numbers 416 to 435. Other popular subsets within this set include League Leaders (1-12) and World Series cards (162-169). The fifth series contains several variations; the more difficult variety consists of cards with the player's first name, last name, and/or position in white letters instead of lettering in some other color. These are designated in the checklist below by WL (white letters). Each checklist card features a different popular player's picture inside a circle on the front of the checklist card. Two different team identifications of Clay Dalrymple and Donn Clendenon exist, as indicated in the checklist. The key Rookie Cards in this set are Rollie Fingers, Reggie Jackson, and Graig Nettles. This was the last year that Topps issued multi-player special star cards, ending a 13-year tradition, which they had begun in 1957. There were cropping differences in checklist cards 57, 214, and 412, due to their each being printed with two different series. The differences are difficult to explain and have not been greatly sought by collectors; hence they are not listed explicitly in the list below. The All-Star cards 426-435, when turned over and placed together, form a puzzle back of Pete Rose. This would turn out to be the final year that Topps issued cards in five-card nickel wax packs. Cards were also issued in thirty-six card rack packs which were sold for 29 cents.

COMP. MASTER SET (695) 2500.00 6000.00
COMPLETE SET (664) 1500.00 4000.00
COMMON (1-218/328-512) .60 1.50
COMMON CARD (219-327) 1.00 2.50
COMMON CARD (513-588) .75 2.00
COMMON CARD (589-664) 1.25 3.00
WRAPPER (5-CENT) 8.00 20.00
1 Yaz/Cater/Oliva LL 10.00 25.00
2 Rose/Alou/Alou LL 3.00 8.00
3 Harrelson/Howard/North LL 1.50 4.00
4 McCovey/Santo/B.Will LL 2.50 6.00
5 Howard/Horton/Harrelson LL 1.50 4.00
6 McCovey/Allen/Banks LL 2.50 6.00
7 Tiant/McDow/McNally LL 1.50 4.00
8 Gibson/Bolin/Veale LL 2.50 6.00
9 McLain/McNal/Tiant/Stott LL 1.50 4.00
10 Marichal/Gibson/Jenkins LL 3.00 8.00
11 McDowell/McLain/Tiant LL 1.50 4.00
12 Gibson/Jenkins/Singer LL 1.50 4.00
13 Mickey Stanley 1.00 2.50
14 Al McBean .60 1.50
15 Boog Powell 1.50 4.00
16 C.Gutierrez RC/R.Robertson RC .60 1.50
17 Mike Marshall 1.00 2.50
18 Dick Schofield .60 1.50
19 Ken Suarez .60 1.50
20 Ernie Banks 20.00 50.00
21 Jose Santiago .60 1.50
22 Jesus Alou 1.00 2.50
23 Lew Krausse .60 1.50
24 Walt Alston MG 1.50 4.00
25 Roy White 1.00 2.50
26 Clay Carroll 1.00 2.50
27 Bernie Allen .60 1.50
28 Mike Ryan .60 1.50
29 Dave Morehead .60 1.50
30 Bob Allison 1.00 2.50
31 G.Gentry RC/A.Otis RC 1.00 2.50
32 Sammy Ellis .60 1.50
33 Wayne Causey .60 1.50
34 Gary Peters .60 1.50
35 Joe Morgan 15.00 40.00
36 Luke Walker .60 1.50
37 Curt Motton .60 1.50
38 Zoilo Versalles 1.00 2.50
39 Dick Hughes .60 1.50
40 Mayo Smith MG .60 1.50
41 Bob Barton .60 1.50
42 Tommy Harper 1.00 2.50
43 Joe Niekro 1.00 2.50
44 Danny Cater .60 1.50
45 Maury Wills 1.00 2.50
46 Fritz Peterson 1.00 2.50
47A P.Popovich Thick Airbrush 1.00 2.50
47B P.Popovich Light Airbrush 1.00 2.50
47C P.Popovich C on Helmet 10.00 25.00
48 Brant Alyea .60 1.50
49A S.Jones/E.Rodriguez ERR 10.00 25.00
49B S.Jones RC/E.Rodriguez RC .60 1.50
50 Roberto Clemente UER 60.00 150.00
51 Woody Fryman 1.00 2.50
52 Mike Andrews .60 1.50
53 Sonny Jackson .60 1.50
54 Cisco Carlos .60 1.50
55 Jerry Grote 1.00 2.50
56 Rich Reese .60 1.50
57 Checklist 1/McLain 2.50 6.00
58 Fred Gladding .60 1.50
59 Jay Johnstone 1.00 2.50
60 Nelson Briles 1.00 2.50
61 Jimmie Hall .60 1.50
62 Chico Salmon .60 1.50
63 Jim Hickman 1.00 2.50
64 Bill Monbouquette .60 1.50
65 Willie Davis 1.00 2.50
66 M.Adamson RC/M.Rettenmund RC .60 1.50
67 Bill Stoneman 1.00 2.50
68 Dave Duncan 1.00 2.50
69 Steve Hamilton 1.00 2.50
70 Tommy Helms 1.00 2.50
71 Steve Whitaker 1.00 2.50
72 Ron Taylor .60 1.50
73 Johnny Briggs .60 1.50
74 Preston Gomez MG 1.00 2.50
75 Luis Aparicio 2.50 6.00
76 Norm Miller .60 1.50
77A R.Perranoski No LA 1.00 2.50
77B R.Perranoski LA Cap 10.00 25.00
78 Tom Satriano .60 1.50
79 Milt Pappas 1.00 2.50
80 Norm Cash 1.00 2.50
81 Mel Queen .60 1.50
82 R.Hebner RC/A.Oliver RC 3.00 8.00
83 Mike Ferraro 1.00 2.50
84 Bob Humphreys .60 1.50
85 Lou Brock 15.00 40.00
86 Pete Richert .60 1.50
87 Horace Clarke 1.00 2.50
88 Rich Nye .60 1.50
89 Russ Gibson .60 1.50
90 Jerry Koosman 1.00 2.50
91 Alvin Dark MG 1.00 2.50
92 Jack Billingham 1.00 2.50
93 Joe Foy 1.00 2.50
94 Hank Aguirre .60 1.50
95 Johnny Bench 60.00 150.00
96 Denny Lemaster .60 1.50
97 Buddy Bradford .60 1.50
98 Dave Giusti .60 1.50
99A D.Morris RC/G.Nettles RC 6.00 15.00
99B D.Morris/G.Nettles ERR 6.00 15.00
100 Hank Aaron 60.00 150.00
101 Daryl Patterson .60 1.50
102 Jim Davenport .60 1.50
103 Roger Repoz .60 1.50
104 Steve Blass .60 1.50
105 Rick Monday 1.00 2.50
106 Jim Hannan .60 1.50
107A Checklist 2/Gibson ERR 2.50 6.00
107B Checklist 2/Gibson COR 3.00 8.00
108 Tony Taylor 1.00 2.50
109 Jim Lonborg 1.00 2.50
110 Mike Shannon 1.00 2.50
111 John Morris RC .60 1.50
112 J.C. Martin 1.00 2.50
113 Dave May .60 1.50
114 A.Closter/J.Cumberland RC 1.00 2.50
115 Bill Hands .60 1.50
116 Chuck Harrison .60 1.50
117 Jim Fairey 1.00 2.50
118 Stan Williams .60 1.50
119 Doug Rader 1.00 2.50
120 Pete Rose 25.00 60.00
121 Joe Grzenda RC .60 1.50
122 Ron Fairly 1.00 2.50
123 Wilbur Wood 1.00 2.50
124 Hank Bauer MG 1.00 2.50
125 Ray Sadecki .60 1.50
126 Dick Tracewski .60 1.50
127 Kevin Collins 1.00 2.50
128 Tommie Aaron 1.00 2.50
129 Bill McCool .60 1.50
130 Carl Yastrzemski 20.00 50.00
131 Chris Cannizzaro .60 1.50
132 Dave Baldwin .60 1.50
133 Johnny Callison 1.00 2.50
134 Jim Weaver .60 1.50
135 Tommy Davis 1.00 2.50
136 S.Huntz RC/M.Torrez .60 1.50
137 Wally Bunker .60 1.50
138 John Bateman .60 1.50
139 Andy Kosco .60 1.50
140 Jim Lefebvre 1.00 2.50
141 Bill Dillman .60 1.50
142 Woody Woodward .60 1.50
143 Joe Nossek .60 1.50
144 Bob Hendley 1.00 2.50
145 Max Alvis .60 1.50
146 Jim Perry 1.00 2.50
147 Leo Durocher MG 1.50 4.00
148 Lee Stange .60 1.50
149 Ollie Brown 1.00 2.50
150 Denny McLain 1.50 4.00
151A C.Dalrymple Portrait .60 1.50
151B C.Dalrymple Catch 6.00 15.00
152 Tommie Sisk .60 1.50
153 Ed Brinkman .60 1.50
154 Jim Britton .60 1.50
155 Pete Ward .60 1.50
156 H.Gilson/L.McFadden RC .60 1.50
157 Bob Rodgers 1.00 2.50
158 Joe Gibbon .60 1.50
159 Jerry Adair .60 1.50
160 Vada Pinson 1.00 2.50
161 John Purdin .60 1.50
162 Bob Gibson WS1 3.00 8.00
163 Willie Horton WS2 2.50 6.00
164 T.McCarv w/Maris WS3 5.00 12.00
165 Lou Brock WS4 3.00 8.00
166 Al Kaline WS5 3.00 8.00
167 Jim Northrup WS6 2.50 6.00
168 M.Lolich/B.Gibson WS7 3.00 8.00
169 Tigers Celebrate WS 2.50 6.00
170 Frank Howard 1.00 2.50
171 Glenn Beckert 1.00 2.50
172 Jerry Stephenson .60 1.50
173 B.Christian RC/G.Nyman RC .60 1.50
174 Grant Jackson .60 1.50
175 Jim Bunning 2.50 6.00
176 Joe Azcue .60 1.50
177 Ron Reed .60 1.50
178 Ray Oyler 1.00 2.50
179 Don Pavletich .60 1.50
180 Willie Horton 1.00 2.50
181 Mel Nelson .60 1.50
182 Bill Rigney MG .60 1.50
183 Don Shaw 1.00 2.50
184 Roberto Pena .60 1.50
185 Tom Phoebus .60 1.50
186 Johnny Edwards .60 1.50
187 Leon Wagner .60 1.50
188 Rick Wise 1.00 2.50
189 J.Lahoud RC/J.Thibodeau RC .60 1.50
190 Willie Mays 75.00 200.00
191 Lindy McDaniel 1.00 2.50
192 Jose Pagan .60 1.50
193 Don Cardwell 1.00 2.50
194 Ted Uhlaender .60 1.50
195 John Odom .60 1.50
196 Lum Harris MG .60 1.50
197 Dick Selma .60 1.50
198 Willie Smith .60 1.50
199 Jim French .60 1.50
200 Bob Gibson 25.00 60.00
201 Russ Snyder .60 1.50
202 Don Wilson 1.00 2.50
203 Dave Johnson 1.00 2.50
204 Jack Hiatt .60 1.50
205 Rick Reichardt .60 1.50
206 L.Hisle/B.Lersch RC 1.00 2.50
207 Roy Face 1.00 2.50
208A D.Clendenon Houston 1.00 2.50
208B D.Clendenon Expos 6.00 15.00
209 Larry Haney UER .60 1.50
210 Felix Millan .60 1.50
211 Galen Cisco .60 1.50
212 Tom Tresh 1.00 2.50
213 Gerry Arrigo .60 1.50
214 Checklist 3 2.50 6.00
215 Rico Petrocelli 1.00 2.50
216 Don Sutton 2.50 6.00
217 John Donaldson .60 1.50
218 John Roseboro 1.00 2.50
219 Freddie Patek RC 1.50 4.00
220 Sam McDowell 1.50 4.00
221 Art Shamsky 1.50 4.00
222 Duane Josephson 1.00 2.50
223 Tom Dukes 1.50 4.00
224 B.Harrelson RC/S.Kealey RC 1.00 2.50
225 Don Kessinger 1.50 4.00
226 Bruce Howard 1.00 2.50
227 Frank Johnson RC 1.00 2.50
228 Dave Leonhard 1.00 2.50
229 Don Lock 1.00 2.50
230 Rusty Staub UER 1.50 4.00
231 Pat Dobson 1.50 4.00
232 Dave Ricketts 1.00 2.50
233 Steve Barber 1.50 4.00
234 Dave Bristol MG 1.00 2.50
235 Jim Hunter 4.00 10.00
236 Manny Mota 1.50 4.00
237 Bobby Cox RC 40.00 100.00
238 Ken Johnson 1.00 2.50
239 Bob Taylor 1.50 4.00
240 Ken Harrelson 1.50 4.00
241 Jim Brewer 1.00 2.50
242 Frank Kostro 1.00 2.50
243 Ron Kline 1.00 2.50
244 R.Fosse RC/G.Woodson RC 1.50 4.00
245 Ed Charles 1.50 4.00
246 Joe Coleman 1.00 2.50
247 Gene Oliver 1.00 2.50
248 Bob Priddy 1.00 2.50
249 Ed Spiezio 1.50 4.00
250 Frank Robinson 25.00 60.00
251 Ron Herbel 1.00 2.50
252 Chuck Cottier 1.00 2.50
253 Jerry Johnson RC 1.00 2.50
254 Joe Schultz MG RC 1.50 4.00
255 Steve Carlton 15.00 40.00
256 Gates Brown 1.50 4.00
257 Jim Ray 1.00 2.50
258 Jackie Hernandez 1.50 4.00
259 Bill Short 1.00 2.50
260 Reggie Jackson RC 250.00 600.00
261 Bob Johnson 1.00 2.50
262 Mike Kekich 1.50 4.00
263 Jerry May 1.00 2.50
264 Bill Landis 1.00 2.50
265 Chico Cardenas 1.50 4.00
266 T.Hutton/A.Foster RC 1.50 4.00
267 Vicente Romo RC 1.00 2.50
268 Al Spangler 1.00 2.50
269 Al Weis 1.50 4.00
270 Mickey Lolich 1.50 4.00
271 Larry Stahl 1.50 4.00
272 Ed Stroud 1.00 2.50
273 Ron Willis 1.00 2.50
274 Clyde King MG 1.00 2.50
275 Vic Davalillo 1.00 2.50
276 Gary Wagner 1.00 2.50
277 Elrod Hendricks RC 1.00 2.50
278 Gary Geiger UER 1.00 2.50
279 Roger Nelson 1.50 4.00
280 Alex Johnson 1.50 4.00
281 Ted Kubiak 1.00 2.50
282 Pat Jarvis 1.00 2.50
283 Sandy Alomar 1.50 4.00
284 J.Robertson RC/M.Wegener RC 1.50 4.00
285 Don Mincher 1.50 4.00
286 Dock Ellis RC 1.50 4.00
287 Jose Tartabull 1.50 4.00
288 Ken Holtzman 1.50 4.00
289 Bart Shirley 1.00 2.50
290 Jim Kaat 1.50 4.00
291 Vern Fuller 1.00 2.50
292 Al Downing 1.50 4.00
293 Dick Dietz 1.00 2.50
294 Jim Lemon MG 1.00 2.50
295 Tony Perez 12.00 30.00
296 Andy Messersmith RC 1.50 4.00
297 Deron Johnson 1.00 2.50
298 Dave Nicholson 1.50 4.00
299 Mark Belanger 1.50 4.00
300 Felipe Alou 1.50 4.00
301 Darrell Brandon 1.50 4.00
302 Jim Pagliaroni 1.00 2.50
303 Cal Koonce 1.50 4.00
304 B.Davis/C.Gaston RC 2.50 6.00
305 Dick McAuliffe 1.50 4.00
306 Jim Grant 1.50 4.00
307 Gary Kolb 1.00 2.50
308 Wade Blasingame 1.00 2.50
309 Walt Williams 1.00 2.50
310 Tom Haller 1.00 2.50
311 Sparky Lyle RC 4.00 10.00
312 Lee Elia 1.00 2.50
313 Bill Robinson 1.50 4.00
314 Checklist 4/Drysdale 2.50 6.00
315 Eddie Fisher 1.00 2.50
316 Hal Lanier 1.00 2.50
317 Bruce Look RC 1.00 2.50
318 Jack Fisher 1.00 2.50
319 Ken McMullen UER 1.00 2.50
320 Dal Maxvill 1.00 2.50
321 Jim McAndrew RC 1.50 4.00
322 Jose Vidal 1.50 4.00
323 Larry Miller 1.00 2.50
324 L.Cain RC/D.Campbell RC 1.50 4.00
325 Jose Cardenal 1.50 4.00
326 Gary Sutherland 1.50 4.00
327 Willie Crawford 1.00 2.50
328 Joel Horlen .60 1.50
329 Rick Joseph .60 1.50
330 Tony Conigliaro 1.50 4.00
331 G.Garrido/T.House RC 1.00 2.50
332 Fred Talbot .60 1.50
333 Ivan Murrell .60 1.50
334 Phil Roof .60 1.50
335 Bill Mazeroski 2.50 6.00
336 Jim Roland .60 1.50
337 Marty Martinez RC .60 1.50
338 Del Unser RC .60 1.50
339 S.Mingori RC/J.Pena RC .60 1.50
340 Dave McNally 1.00 2.50
341 Dave Adlesh .60 1.50
342 Bubba Morton .60 1.50
343 Dan Frisella .60 1.50
344 Tom Matchick .60 1.50
345 Frank Linzy .60 1.50
346 Wayne Comer RC .60 1.50
347 Randy Hundley 1.00 2.50
348 Steve Hargan .60 1.50
349 Dick Williams MG 1.00 2.50
350 Richie Allen 1.50 4.00
351 Carroll Sembera .60 1.50
352 Paul Schaal 1.00 2.50
353 Jeff Torborg 1.00 2.50
354 Nate Oliver .60 1.50
355 Phil Niekro 10.00 25.00
356 Frank Quilici .60 1.50
357 Carl Taylor .60 1.50
358 G.Lauzerique RC/R.Rodriguez .60 1.50
359 Dick Kelley .60 1.50
360 Jim Wynn 1.00 2.50
361 Gary Holman RC .60 1.50
362 Jim Maloney 1.00 2.50
363 Russ Nixon .60 1.50
364 Tommie Agee 1.50 4.00
365 Jim Fregosi 1.00 2.50
366 Bo Belinsky 1.00 2.50
367 Lou Johnson 1.00 2.50
368 Vic Roznovsky .60 1.50
369 Bob Skinner MG 1.00 2.50
370 Juan Marichal 3.00 8.00
371 Sal Bando 1.00 2.50
372 Adolfo Phillips .60 1.50
373 Fred Lasher .60 1.50
374 Bob Tillman .60 1.50
375 Harmon Killebrew 25.00 60.00
376 M.Fiore RC/J.Rooker RC .60 1.50
377 Gary Bell 1.00 2.50
378 Jose Herrera RC .60 1.50
379 Ken Boyer 1.00 2.50
380 Stan Bahnsen 1.00 2.50
381 Ed Kranepool 1.00 2.50
382 Pat Corrales 1.00 2.50
383 Casey Cox .60 1.50
384 Larry Shepard MG .60 1.50
385 Orlando Cepeda 2.50 6.00
386 Jim McGlothlin .60 1.50
387 Bobby Klaus .60 1.50
388 Tom McCraw .60 1.50
389 Dan Coombs .60 1.50
390 Bill Freehan 1.00 2.50
391 Ray Culp .60 1.50
392 Bob Burda RC .60 1.50
393 Gene Brabender 1.00 2.50
394 L.Piniella/M.Staehle 2.50 6.00
395 Chris Short .60 1.50
396 Jim Campanis .60 1.50
397 Chuck Dobson .60 1.50
398 Tito Francona .60 1.50
399 Bob Bailey 1.00 2.50
400 Don Drysdale 10.00 25.00
401 Jake Gibbs 1.00 2.50
402 Ken Boswell RC 1.00 2.50
403 Bob Miller .60 1.50
404 V.LaRose RC/G.Ross RC 1.00 2.50
405 Lee May 1.00 2.50
406 Phil Ortega .60 1.50
407 Tom Egan .60 1.50
408 Nate Colbert .60 1.50
409 Bob Moose .60 1.50
410 Al Kaline 10.00 25.00
411 Larry Dierker 1.00 2.50
412 Checklist 5/Mantle DP 12.00 30.00
413 Roland Sheldon 1.00 2.50
414 Duke Sims .60 1.50
415 Ray Washburn .60 1.50
416 Willie McCovey AS 3.00 8.00
417 Ken Harrelson AS 1.25 3.00
418 Tommy Helms AS 1.25 3.00
419 Rod Carew AS 4.00 10.00
420 Ron Santo AS 1.50 4.00
421 Brooks Robinson AS 3.00 8.00
422 Don Kessinger AS 1.25 3.00
423 Bert Campaneris AS 1.50 4.00
424 Pete Rose AS 10.00 25.00
425 Carl Yastrzemski AS 10.00 25.00
426 Curt Flood AS 1.50 4.00
427 Tony Oliva AS 1.50 4.00
428 Lou Brock AS 2.50 6.00
429 Willie Horton AS 1.25 3.00
430 Johnny Bench AS 20.00 50.00
431 Bill Freehan AS 1.50 4.00
432 Bob Gibson AS 6.00 15.00
433 Denny McLain AS 1.25 3.00
434 Jerry Koosman AS 1.25 3.00
435 Sam McDowell AS 1.00 2.50
436 Gene Alley 1.00 2.50
437 Luis Alcaraz RC .60 1.50
438 Gary Waslewski RC .60 1.50
439 E.Herrmann RC/D.Lazar RC .60 1.50
440A Willie McCovey 6.00 15.00
440B Willie McCovey WL 50.00 100.00
441A Dennis Higgins .60 1.50
441B Dennis Higgins WL 10.00 25.00
442 Ty Cline .60 1.50
443 Don Wert .60 1.50
444A Joe Moeller .60 1.50
444B Joe Moeller WL 10.00 25.00
445 Bobby Knoop .60 1.50
446 Claude Raymond .60 1.50
447A Ralph Houk MG 1.00 2.50
447B Ralph Houk MG WL 10.00 25.00
448 Bob Tolan 1.00 2.50
449 Paul Lindblad .60 1.50
450 Billy Williams 12.00 30.00
451A Rich Rollins 1.00 2.50
451B Rich Rollins WL 10.00 25.00
452A Al Ferrara .60 1.50
452B Al Ferrara WL 10.00 25.00
453 Mike Cuellar 1.00 2.50
454A L.Colton/D.Money RC 1.00 2.50
454B L.Colton/D.Money WL 10.00 25.00
455 Sonny Siebert .60 1.50
456 Bud Harrelson 1.00 2.50
457 Dalton Jones .60 1.50
458 Curt Blefary .60 1.50
459 Dave Boswell .60 1.50
460 Joe Torre 1.50 4.00
461A Mike Epstein .60 1.50
461B Mike Epstein WL 10.00 25.00
462 R.Schoendienst MG 1.00 2.50
463 Dennis Ribant .60 1.50
464A Dave Marshall RC .60 1.50
464B Dave Marshall WL 10.00 25.00
465 Tommy John 1.50 4.00
466 John Boccabella 1.00 2.50
467 Tommie Reynolds .60 1.50
468A B.Dal Canton RC/B.Robertson .60 1.50
468B B.Dal Canton/B.Robertson WL 10.00 25.00
469 Chico Ruiz .60 1.50
470A Mel Stottlemyre 1.00 2.50
470B Mel Stottlemyre WL 12.50 30.00
471A Ted Savage .60 1.50
471B Ted Savage WL 10.00 25.00
472 Jim Price .60 1.50
473A Jose Arcia .60 1.50
473B Jose Arcia WL 10.00 25.00
474 Tom Murphy RC .60 1.50
475 Tim McCarver 1.50 4.00
476A K.Brett RC/G.Moses 1.00 2.50
476B K.Brett/G.Moses WL 12.50 30.00
477 Jeff James RC .60 1.50
478 Don Buford .60 1.50
479 Richie Scheinblum .60 1.50
480 Tom Seaver 30.00 80.00
481 Bill Melton RC 1.00 2.50
482A Jim Gosger .60 1.50
482B Jim Gosger WL 10.00 25.00
483 Ted Abernathy .60 1.50
484 Joe Gordon MG 1.00 2.50
485A Gaylord Perry 4.00 10.00
485B Gaylord Perry WL 40.00 80.00
486A Paul Casanova .60 1.50
486B Paul Casanova WL 10.00 25.00
487 Denis Menke .60 1.50
488 Joe Sparma .60 1.50
489 Clete Boyer 1.00 2.50
490 Matty Alou 1.00 2.50
491A J.Crider RC/G.Mitterwald .60 1.50
491B J.Crider/G.Mitterwald WL 10.00 25.00
492 Tony Cloninger .60 1.50
493A Wes Parker 1.00 2.50
493B Wes Parker WL 10.00 25.00
494 Ken Berry .60 1.50
495 Bert Campaneris 1.00 2.50
496 Larry Jaster .60 1.50
497 Julian Javier 1.00 2.50
498 Juan Pizarro 1.00 2.50
499 D.Bryant RC/S.Shea RC .60 1.50
500A Mickey Mantle UER 150.00 400.00
500B Mickey Mantle UER WL 1000.00 2000.00
501A Tony Gonzalez 1.00 2.50
501B Tony Gonzalez WL 10.00 25.00
502 Minnie Rojas .60 1.50
503 Larry Brown .60 1.50
504 Checklist 6/B.Robinson 3.00 8.00
505A Bobby Bolin .60 1.50
505B Bobby Bolin WL 10.00 25.00
506 Paul Blair 1.00 2.50
507 Cookie Rojas 1.00 2.50
508 Moe Drabowsky 1.00 2.50
509 Manny Sanguillen 1.00 2.50
510 Rod Carew 15.00 40.00
511A Diego Segui 1.00 2.50
511B Diego Segui WL 10.00 25.00
512 Cleon Jones 1.00 2.50
513 Camilo Pascual 1.25 3.00
514 Mike Lum .75 2.00
515 Dick Green .75 2.00
516 Earl Weaver MG RC 8.00 20.00
517 Mike McCormick 1.25 3.00
518 Fred Whitfield .75 2.00
519 J.Kenney RC/L.Boehmer RC .75 2.00
520 Bob Veale 1.25 3.00
521 George Thomas .75 2.00
522 Joe Hoerner .75 2.00
523 Bob Chance .75 2.00
524 J.Laboy RC/F.Wicker RC 1.25 3.00
525 Earl Wilson 1.25 3.00
526 Hector Torres RC .75 2.00
527 Al Lopez MG 2.00 5.00
528 Claude Osteen 1.25 3.00
529 Ed Kirkpatrick 1.25 3.00
530 Cesar Tovar .75 2.00
531 Dick Farrell .75 2.00
532 Phoeb/Hard/McNally/Cuellar 1.25 3.00
533 Nolan Ryan 250.00 600.00
534 Jerry McNertney 1.25 3.00
535 Phil Regan 1.25 3.00
536 D.Breeden RC/D.Roberts RC .75 2.00
537 Mike Paul RC .75 2.00
538 Charlie Smith .75 2.00
539 T.Williams/M.Epstein 5.00 12.00
540 Curt Flood 1.25 3.00
541 Joe Verbanic .75 2.00
542 Bob Aspromonte .75 2.00
543 Fred Newman .75 2.00
544 M.Kilkenny RC/R.Woods RC .75 2.00
545 Willie Stargell 12.00 30.00
546 Jim Nash .75 2.00
547 Billy Martin MG 2.00 5.00
548 Bob Locker .75 2.00
549 Ron Brand .75 2.00
550 Brooks Robinson 12.50 30.00
551 Wayne Granger RC .75 2.00
552 T.Sizemore RC/B.Sudakis RC 1.25 3.00
553 Ron Davis .75 2.00
554 Frank Bertaina .75 2.00
555 Jim Ray Hart 1.25 3.00
556 Bando/Campaneris/Cater 1.25 3.00
557 Frank Fernandez .75 2.00
558 Tom Burgmeier RC 1.25 3.00
559 J.Hague RC/J.Hicks .75 2.00
560 Luis Tiant 1.25 3.00
561 Ron Clark .75 2.00
562 Bob Watson RC 3.00 8.00
563 Marty Pattin RC 1.25 3.00
564 Gil Hodges MG 4.00 10.00
565 Hoyt Wilhelm 3.00 8.00
566 Ron Hansen .75 2.00
567 E.Jimenez/J.Shellenback .75 2.00
568 Cecil Upshaw .75 2.00
569 Billy Harris .60 1.50
570 Ron Santo 3.00 8.00
571 Cap Peterson .75 2.00
572 W.McCovey/J.Marichal 6.00 15.00
573 Jim Palmer 20.00 50.00
574 George Scott 1.25 3.00
575 Bill Singer 1.25 3.00
576 R.Stone/B.Wilson .75 2.00
577 Mike Hegan 1.25 3.00
578 Don Bosch .75 2.00
579 Dave Nelson RC .75 2.00
580 Jim Northrup 1.25 3.00
581 Gary Nolan 1.25 3.00
582A Checklist 7/Oliva White 2.50 6.00
582B Checklist 7/Oliva Red 3.00 8.00
583 Clyde Wright RC .75 2.00
584 Don Mason .75 2.00
585 Ron Swoboda 1.25 3.00
586 Tim Cullen .75 2.00
587 Joe Rudi RC 3.00 8.00
588 Bill White 1.25 3.00
589 Joe Pepitone 2.00 5.00
590 Rico Carty 2.00 5.00
591 Mike Hedlund 1.25 3.00
592 R.Robles RC/A.Santorini RC 2.00 5.00
593 Don Nottebart 1.25 3.00
594 Dooley Womack 1.25 3.00
595 Lee Maye 1.25 3.00
596 Chuck Hartenstein 1.25 3.00
597 Rollie Fingers RC 40.00 100.00
598 Ruben Amaro 1.25 3.00
599 John Boozer 1.25 3.00
600 Tony Oliva 3.00 8.00
601 Tug McGraw 3.00 8.00
602 Distaso/Young/Qualls RC 2.00 5.00
603 Joe Keough RC 1.25 3.00
604 Bobby Etheridge 1.25 3.00
605 Dick Ellsworth 1.25 3.00
606 Gene Mauch MG 2.00 5.00
607 Dick Bosman 1.25 3.00
608 Dick Simpson 1.25 3.00
609 Phil Gagliano 1.25 3.00
610 Jim Hardin 1.25 3.00
611 Didier/Hriniak/Niebauer RC 2.00 5.00
612 Jack Aker 2.00 5.00
613 Jim Beauchamp 1.25 3.00
614 T.Griffin RC/S.Guinn RC 1.25 3.00
615 Len Gabrielson 1.25 3.00
616 Don McMahon 1.25 3.00
617 Jesse Gonder 1.25 3.00
618 Ramon Webster 1.25 3.00
619 Butler/Kelly/Rios RC 2.00 5.00
620 Dean Chance 2.00 5.00
621 Bill Voss 1.25 3.00
622 Dan Osinski 1.25 3.00
623 Hank Allen 1.25 3.00
624 Chaney/Dyer/Harmon RC 2.00 5.00
625 Mack Jones UER 2.00 5.00
626 Gene Michael 2.00 5.00
627 George Stone RC 1.25 3.00
628 Conigliaro/O'Brien/Wenz RC 2.00 5.00
629 Jack Hamilton 1.25 3.00
630 Bobby Bonds RC 15.00 40.00
631 John Kennedy 2.00 5.00
632 Jon Warden RC 1.25 3.00
633 Harry Walker MG 1.25 3.00
634 Andy Etchebarren 1.25 3.00
635 George Culver 1.25 3.00
636 Woody Held 1.25 3.00
637 DaVanon/Reberger/Kirby RC 2.00 5.00
638 Ed Sprague RC 1.25 3.00
639 Barry Moore 1.25 3.00
640 Ferguson Jenkins 8.00 20.00
641 Darwin/Miller/Dean RC 2.00 5.00
642 John Hiller 1.25 3.00
643 Billy Cowan 1.25 3.00

644 Chuck Hinton 1.25 3.00
645 George Brunet 1.25 3.00
646 D.McGinn RC/C.Morton RC 2.00 5.00
647 Dave Wickersham 1.25 3.00
648 Bobby Wine 2.00 5.00
649 Al Jackson 1.25 3.00
650 Ted Williams MG 8.00 20.00
651 Gus Gil 2.00 5.00
652 Eddie Watt 1.25 3.00
653 Aurelio Rodriguez UER RC 2.00 5.00
654 May/Secrist/Morales RC 2.00 5.00
655 Mike Hershberger 1.25 3.00
656 Dan Schneider 1.25 3.00
657 Bobby Murcer 3.00 8.00
658 Hall/Burbach/Miles RC 1.25 3.00
659 Johnny Podres 2.00 5.00
660 Reggie Smith 2.00 5.00
661 Jim Merritt 1.25 3.00
662 Drago/Spriggs/Oliver RC 2.00 5.00
663 Dick Radatz 2.00 5.00
664 Ron Hunt 2.00 5.00

1969 Topps Decals

COMPLETE SET (48) 250.00 500.00
1 Hank Aaron 20.00 50.00
2 Richie Allen 3.00 8.00
3 Felipe Alou 2.00 5.00
4 Matty Alou 2.00 5.00
5 Luis Aparicio 3.00 8.00
6 Roberto Clemente 30.00 60.00
7 Donn Clendenon 1.50 4.00
8 Tommy Davis 2.00 5.00
9 Don Drysdale 4.00 10.00
10 Joe Foy 1.50 4.00
11 Jim Fregosi 2.00 5.00
12 Bob Gibson 4.00 10.00
13 Tony Gonzalez 1.50 4.00
14 Tom Haller 1.50 4.00
15 Ken Harrelson 2.00 5.00
16 Tommy Helms 1.50 4.00
17 Willie Horton 2.00 5.00
18 Frank Howard 2.00 5.00
19 Reggie Jackson 20.00 50.00
20 Ferguson Jenkins 3.00 8.00
21 Harmon Killebrew 6.00 15.00
22 Jerry Koosman 2.00 5.00
23 Mickey Mantle 50.00 100.00
24 Willie Mays 10.00 25.00
25 Tim McCarver 2.00 5.00
26 Willie McCovey 4.00 10.00
27 Sam McDowell 2.00 5.00
28 Denny McLain 2.00 5.00
29 Dave McNally 2.00 5.00
30 Don Mincher 1.50 4.00
31 Rick Monday 2.00 5.00
32 Tony Oliva 3.00 8.00
33 Camilo Pascual 1.50 4.00
34 Rick Reichardt 1.50 4.00
35 Frank Robinson 4.00 10.00
36 Pete Rose 20.00 50.00
37 Ron Santo 3.00 8.00
38 Tom Seaver 12.50 30.00
39 Dick Selma 1.50 4.00
40 Chris Short 1.50 4.00
41 Rusty Staub 3.00 8.00
42 Mel Stottlemyre 2.00 5.00
43 Luis Tiant 2.00 5.00
44 Pete Ward 1.50 4.00
45 Hoyt Wilhelm 3.00 8.00
46 Maury Wills 3.00 8.00
47 Jim Wynn 2.00 5.00
48 Carl Yastrzemski 8.00 20.00

1969 Topps Deckle Edge

COMPLETE SET (35) 50.00 100.00
1 Brooks Robinson 2.50 6.00
2 Boog Powell 1.25 3.00
3 Ken Harrelson .60 1.50
4 Carl Yastrzemski 3.00 8.00
5 Jim Fregosi .75 2.00
6 Luis Aparicio 1.25 3.00
7 Luis Tiant .75 2.00
8 Denny McLain 1.25 3.00
9 Willie Horton .75 2.00
10 Bill Freehan .75 2.00
11A Hoyt Wilhelm 3.00 8.00
11B Jim Wynn 6.00 15.00
12 Rod Carew 1.50 4.00
13 Mel Stottlemyre .75 2.00
14 Rick Monday .60 1.50
15 Tommy Davis .75 2.00
16 Frank Howard .75 2.00
17 Felipe Alou .75 2.00
18 Don Kessinger .60 1.50
19 Ron Santo 1.25 3.00
20 Tommy Helms .60 1.50
21 Pete Rose 5.00 12.00
22A Rusty Staub .75 2.00
22B Joe Foy 10.00 25.00
23 Tom Haller .60 1.50
24 Maury Wills 1.25 3.00
25 Jerry Koosman .75 2.00
26 Richie Allen 1.50 4.00
27 Roberto Clemente 8.00 20.00
28 Curt Flood 1.25 3.00
29 Bob Gibson 1.50 4.00
30 Al Ferrara .60 1.50
31 Willie McCovey 1.50 4.00
32 Juan Marichal 1.25 3.00
33 Willie Mays 5.00 12.00

1969 Topps Four-in-One

This was a test issue consisting of 25 sticker cards (blank back). Each card measures 2 1/2" by 3 1/2" and features four mini-stickers. These unnumbered stickers are ordered in the checklist below alphabetically by the upper left player's name on each card. Each mini-card featured is from the 1969 Topps second series. Five of the cards were double printed (technically 50 percent more were printed) compared to the others in the set; these are marked below by DP.

COMPLETE SET (25) 1500.00 3000.00
1 Adair 200.00 400.00
Wilson
Mays
Morris
2 Gilson/McFad/Bubker/Gibbon/Cardwell 20.00 50.00
3 Clend/Woodw/TAaron/Britton 20.00 50.00
4 Tdavis/Pavl/WSG4/Pinson 40.00 80.00
5 Fairly 20.00 50.00
Wise
Alvis
Beckert
6 French 20.00 50.00
Selma
Callison
Harris
7 Gibson/WSG3?Reichardt/Haney 75.00 150.00
8 Kosco 30.00 60.00
Reed
Bunning
Brown
9 Lefebvre 20.00 50.00
Purdin
Dillman
Roseboro
10 Milan/Hands/McDan/Harrison 20.00 50.00
11 Nelson 30.00 60.00
Johnson
Hiatt
Sisk
12 Odom 30.00 60.00
Durocher
Wood
Dalrymple
13 Oyler 20.00 50.00
Bauer
Collins
Snyder
14 Jperry/WSG7/Arrigo/RSRook 30.00 60.00
15 Rader 20.00 50.00
McCool
Pena
WSG2
16 Rodgers 30.00 60.00
Horton
Face
Brink
17 Sadecki/Bald/Martin/May 20.00 50.00
18 Shannon 30.00 60.00
WSG1
Pagan
Phoebus
19 Stange/Sutton/Uhlae/Rose 450.00 900.00
20 Weaver/Trace/Gtzenda/Howard 20.00 50.00
21 WSRook/McLain/Jackson/Axcue 30.00 60.00
22 Williams/Edwards/Fairey/PhilRook 20.00 50.00
23 WSCele/Wagner/Bateman/Smith 20.00 50.00
24 YankRook/Canni/WSG5/Hendley 20.00 50.00
25 Yaz/Petro/Nossek/CardsRook 400.00 800.00

1969 Topps Bowie Kuhn

This one-card standard-size set was issued soon after Bowie Kuhn's elevation to Baseball Commissioner. The front features a superimposed photo of Kuhn in regal wear sitting on a base. The horizontal back features vital statistics as well as a brief biography.

1 Bowie Kuhn 20.00 50.00

1969 Topps Super

The cards in this 66-card set measure approximately 2 1/4" by 3 1/4". This beautiful Topps set was released independently of the regular baseball series of 1969. It is referred to as "Super Baseball" on the back of the card, a title which was also used for the postcard-size cards issued in 1970 and 1971. Complete sheets, and cards with square corners cut from these sheets, are sometimes encountered. The set numbering is in alphabetical order by teams within league. Cards from the far right of each row are usually found with a white line on the right edge. Although rarely seen, this set was issued in three-card cello packs. The set features Reggie Jackson in his Rookie Card year.

COMPLETE SET (66) 3000.00 5000.00
1 Dave McNally 8.00 20.00
2 Frank Robinson 100.00 200.00
3 Brooks Robinson 100.00 200.00
4 Ken Harrelson 10.00 25.00
5 Carl Yastrzemski 125.00 250.00
6 Ray Culp 8.00 20.00
7 Jim Fregosi 10.00 25.00
8 Rick Reichardt 8.00 20.00
9 Vic Davalillo 8.00 20.00
10 Luis Aparicio 40.00 80.00
11 Pete Ward 8.00 20.00
12 Joel Horlen 8.00 20.00
13 Luis Tiant 10.00 25.00
14 Sam McDowell 8.00 20.00
15 Jose Cardenal 8.00 20.00
16 Willie Horton 10.00 25.00
17 Denny McLain 12.50 30.00
18 Bill Freehan 10.00 25.00
19 Harmon Killebrew 75.00 150.00
20 Tony Oliva 15.00 40.00
21 Dean Chance 8.00 20.00
22 Joe Foy 8.00 20.00
23 Roger Nelson 8.00 20.00
24 Mickey Mantle 500.00 1000.00
25 Mel Stottlemyre 10.00 25.00
26 Roy White 10.00 25.00
27 Rick Monday 8.00 20.00
28 Reggie Jackson 250.00 500.00
29 Bert Campaneris 10.00 25.00
30 Frank Howard 12.50 30.00
31 Camilo Pascual 8.00 20.00
32 Tommy Davis 10.00 25.00
33 Don Mincher 8.00 20.00
34 Hank Aaron 250.00 500.00
35 Felipe Alou 12.50 30.00
36 Joe Torre 20.00 50.00
37 Ferguson Jenkins 40.00 80.00
38 Ron Santo 15.00 40.00
39 Billy Williams 40.00 80.00
40 Tommy Helms 8.00 20.00
41 Pete Rose 200.00 400.00
42 Joe Morgan 60.00 120.00
43 Jim Wynn 8.00 20.00
44 Curt Blefary 8.00 20.00
45 Willie Davis 8.00 20.00
46 Don Drysdale 50.00 100.00
47 Tom Haller 8.00 20.00
48 Rusty Staub 12.50 30.00
49 Maury Wills 15.00 40.00
50 Cleon Jones 8.00 20.00
51 Jerry Koosman 12.50 30.00
52 Tom Seaver 200.00 400.00
53 Richie Allen 12.50 30.00
54 Chris Short 8.00 20.00
55 Cookie Rojas 8.00 20.00
56 Matty Alou 8.00 20.00
57 Steve Blass 8.00 20.00
58 Roberto Clemente 300.00 600.00
59 Curt Flood 12.50 30.00
60 Bob Gibson 75.00 150.00
61 Tim McCarver 15.00 40.00
62 Dick Selma 8.00 20.00
63 Ollie Brown 8.00 20.00
64 Juan Marichal 50.00 100.00
65 Willie Mays 250.00 500.00
66 Willie McCovey 50.00 100.00

1969 Topps Stamps

The 1969 Topps set of baseball player stamps contains 240 individual stamps and 24 separate albums, 10 stamps and one album per major league team. The stamps were issued in strips of 12 and have gummed backs. Each stamp measures 1" by 1 7/16". The eight-page albums are bright orange and have an autograph feature on the back cover. The stamps are numbered here alphabetically within each team and the teams are listed in alphabetical order within league, e.g., Atlanta Braves NL (1-10), Chicago Cubs (11-20), Cincinnati Reds (21-30), Houston Astros (31-40), Los Angeles Dodgers (41-50), Montreal Expos (51-60), New York Mets (61-70), Philadelphia Phillies (71-80), Pittsburgh Pirates (81-90), San Diego Padres (91-100), San Francisco Giants (101-110), St. Louis Cardinals (111-120), Baltimore Orioles AL (121-130), Boston Red Sox (131-140), California Angels (141-150), Chicago White Sox (151-160), Cleveland Indians (161-170), Detroit Tigers (171-180), Kansas City Royals (181-190), Minnesota Twins (191-200), New York Yankees (201-210), Oakland A's (211-220), Seattle Pilots (221-230) and Washington Senators (231-240). Stamps still in the original uncut sheets are valued at twice the listed prices below. These stamps were issued in five-cent wax packs which came 24 packs to a box.

COMPLETE SET (240) 125.00 250.00
WRAPPER (5-CENT)
1 Hank Aaron 5.00 12.00
2 Felipe Alou .30 .75
3 Clete Boyer .20 .50
4 Tito Francona .10 .25
5 Sonny Jackson .10 .25
6 Pat Jarvis .10 .25
7 Felix Millan .10 .25
8 Milt Pappas .20 .50
9 Ron Reed .10 .25
10 Joe Torre .60 1.50
11 Ernie Banks 1.50 4.00
12 Glenn Beckert .10 .25
13 Bill Hands .10 .25
14 Randy Hundley .10 .25
15 Ferguson Jenkins 1.00 2.50
16 Don Kessinger .20 .50
17 Adolfo Phillips .10 .25
18 Phil Regan .10 .25
19 Ron Santo .60 1.50
20 Billy Williams 1.00 2.50
21 Ted Abernathy .10 .25
22 Gerry Arrigo .10 .25
23 Johnny Bench 2.00 5.00
24 Tommy Helms .10 .25
25 Alex Johnson .10 .25
26 Jim Maloney .20 .50
27 Lee May .20 .50
28 Tony Perez 1.00 2.50
29 Pete Rose 6.00 15.00
30 Bobby Tolan .10 .25
31 Bob Aspromonte .10 .25
32 Larry Dierker .10 .25
33 Johnny Edwards .10 .25
34 Denny Lemaster .10 .25
35 Denis Menke .10 .25
36 Joe Morgan 1.25 3.00
37 Doug Rader .10 .25
38 Rusty Staub .40 1.00
39 Don Wilson .10 .25
40 Jim Wynn .20 .50
41 Willie Davis .20 .50
42 Don Drysdale 1.00 2.50
43 Ron Fairly .10 .25
44 Len Gabrielson .10 .25
45 Tom Haller .10 .25
46 Jim LeFebvre .10 .25
47 Claude Osteen .20 .50
48 Paul Popovich .10 .25
49 Bill Singer .10 .25
50 Don Sutton 1.00 2.50
51 Jesus Alou .10 .25
52 Bob Bailey .10 .25
53 John Bateman .10 .25
54 Donn Clendenon .10 .25
55 Jim Grant .10 .25
56 Larry Jaster .10 .25
57 Mack Jones .10 .25
58 Manny Mota .20 .50
59 Gary Sutherland .10 .25
60 Maury Wills .40 1.00
61 Tommie Agee .20 .50
62 Ed Charles .10 .25
63 Jerry Grote .10 .25
64 Bud Harrelson .10 .25
65 Cleon Jones .10 .25
66 Jerry Koosman .20 .50
67 Ed Kranepool .20 .50
68 Tom Seaver 3.00 8.00
69 Art Shamsky .10 .25
70 Ron Swoboda .10 .25
71 Richie Allen .40 1.00
72 John Briggs .10 .25
73 Johnny Callison .20 .50
74 Clay Dalrymple .10 .25
75 Woodie Fryman .10 .25
76 Don Lock .10 .25
77 Cookie Rojas .20 .50
78 Chris Short .10 .25
79 Tony Taylor .10 .25
80 Rick Wise .10 .25
81 Gene Alley .10 .25
82 Matty Alou .20 .50
83 Steve Blass .10 .25
84 Jim Bunning 1.00 2.50
85 Roberto Clemente 8.00 20.00
86 Ron Kline .10 .25
87 Jerry May .10 .25
88 Bill Mazeroski 1.00 2.50
89 Willie Stargell 1.25 3.00
90 Bob Veale .10 .25
91 Jose Arcia .10 .25
92 Ollie Brown .10 .25
93 Al Ferrara .10 .25
94 Tony Gonzalez .10 .25
95 Dave Giusti .10 .25
96 Alvin McBean .10 .25
97 Roberto Pena .10 .25
98 Dick Selma .10 .25
99 Larry Stahl .10 .25
100 Zoilo Versalles .10 .25
101 Bobby Bolin .10 .25
102 Jim Davenport .10 .25
103 Dick Dietz .10 .25
104 Jim Ray Hart .10 .25
105 Ron Hunt .10 .25
106 Hal Lanier .10 .25
107 Juan Marichal 1.25 3.00
108 Willie Mays 4.00 10.00
109 Willie McCovey 1.25 3.00
110 Gaylord Perry 1.00 2.50
111 Nelson Briles .10 .25
112 Lou Brock 1.50 4.00
113 Orlando Cepeda 1.00 2.50
114 Curt Flood .40 1.00
115 Bob Gibson 1.25 3.00
116 Julian Javier .10 .25
117 Dal Maxvill .10 .25
118 Tim McCarver .40 1.00
119 Vada Pinson .30 .75
120 Mike Shannon .20 .50
121 Mark Belanger .20 .50
122 Curt Blefary .10 .25
123 Don Buford .10 .25
124 Jim Hardin .10 .25
125 Dave Johnson .30 .75
126 Dave McNally .20 .50
127 Tom Phoebus .10 .25
128 Boog Powell .40 1.00
129 Brooks Robinson 1.50 4.00
130 Frank Robinson 1.50 4.00
131 Mike Andrews .10 .25
132 Ray Culp .10 .25
133 Russ Gibson .10 .25
134 Ken Harrelson .30 .75
135 Jim Lonborg .20 .50
136 Rico Petrocelli .20 .50
137 Jose Santiago .10 .25
138 George Scott .20 .50
139 Reggie Smith .30 .75
140 Carl Yastrzemski 2.00 5.00
141 George Brunet .10 .25
142 Vic Davalillo .10 .25
143 Eddie Fisher .10 .25
144 Jim Fregosi .20 .50
145 Bobby Knoop .10 .25
146 Jim McGlothlin .10 .25
147 Rick Reichardt .10 .25
148 Roger Repoz .10 .25
149 Bob Rodgers .10 .25
150 Tom Satriano .10 .25
151 Sandy Alomar .10 .25
152 Luis Aparicio 1.00 2.50
153 Ken Berry .10 .25
154 Joel Horlen .10 .25
155 Tommy John .60 1.50
156 Duane Josephson .10 .25
157 Gary Peters .10 .25
158 Leon Wagner .10 .25
159 Pete Ward .10 .25
160 Wilbur Wood .10 .25
161 Max Alvis .10 .25
162 Joe Azcue .10 .25
163 Larry Brown .10 .25
164 Jose Cardenal .10 .25
165 Lee Maye .10 .25
166 Sam McDowell .20 .50
167 Sonny Siebert .10 .25
168 Duke Sims .10 .25
169 Luis Tiant .40 1.00
170 Stan Williams .10 .25
171 Norm Cash .40 1.00
172 Bill Freehan .20 .50
173 Willie Horton .20 .50
174 Al Kaline 1.50 4.00
175 Mickey Lolich .30 .75
176 Dick McAuliffe .10 .25
177 Denny McLain .40 1.00
178 Jim Northrup .20 .50
179 Mickey Stanley .10 .25
180 Don Wert .10 .25
181 Jerry Adair .10 .25
182 Wally Bunker .10 .25
183 Moe Drabowsky .10 .25
184 Joe Foy .10 .25
185 Jackie Hernandez .10 .25
186 Roger Nelson .10 .25
187 Bob Oliver .10 .25
188 Paul Schaal .10 .25
189 Steve Whitaker .10 .25
190 Hoyt Wilhelm 1.00 2.50
191 Bob Allison .20 .50
192 Rod Carew 1.50 4.00
193 Dean Chance .10 .25
194 Jim Kaat .40 1.00
195 Harmon Killebrew 1.25 3.00
196 Tony Oliva .60 1.50
197 Ron Perranoski .10 .25
198 Johnny Roseboro .10 .25
199 Cesar Tovar .10 .25
200 Ted Uhlaender .10 .25
201 Stan Bahnsen .10 .25
202 Horace Clarke .10 .25
203 Jake Gibbs .10 .25
204 Andy Kosco .10 .25
205 Mickey Mantle 15.00 40.00
206 Joe Pepitone .20 .50
207 Bill Robinson .10 .25
208 Mel Stottlemyre .20 .50
209 Tom Tresh .20 .50
210 Roy White .20 .50
211 Sal Bando .20 .50
212 Bert Campaneris .20 .50
213 Danny Cater .10 .25
214 Dave Duncan .10 .25
215 Dick Green .10 .25
216 Jim Hunter 1.00 2.50
217 Lew Krausse .10 .25
218 Rick Monday .20 .50
219 Jim Nash .10 .25
220 John Odom .10 .25
221 Jack Aker .10 .25
222 Steve Barber .10 .25
223 Gary Bell .10 .25
224 Tommy Davis .20 .50
225 Tommy Harper .10 .25
226 Jerry McNertney .10 .25
227 Don Mincher .10 .25
228 Ray Oyler .10 .25
229 Rich Rollins .10 .25
230 Chico Salmon .10 .25
231 Bernie Allen .10 .25
232 Ed Brinkman .10 .25
233 Paul Casanova .10 .25
234 Joe Coleman .10 .25
235 Mike Epstein .10 .25
236 Jim Hannan .10 .25
237 Dennis Higgins .10 .25
238 Frank Howard .40 1.00
239 Ken McMullen .10 .25
240 Camilo Pascual .10 .25

1969 Topps Stamp Albums

The 1969 Topps stamp set of baseball player stamps was intended to be mounted in 24 separate team albums, 10 stamps for that team's players going into that team's album. The eight-page albums are bright orange and have an autograph feature on the back cover. The albums measure approximately 2 1/2" by 3 1/2".

COMPLETE SET (24) 12.50 30.00
COMMON TEAM (1-24) .60 1.50
23 Seattle Pilots 1.00 2.50

1969 Topps Team Posters

This set was issued as a separate set by Topps, but was apparently not widely distributed. It was folded many times to fit the packaging and hence is typically found with relatively heavy fold creases. Each team poster measures approximately 12" by 20". These posters are in full color with a blank back. Each team features nine or ten individual players; a complete list is listed in the checklist below. Each player photo is accompanied by a facsimile autograph. The posters are numbered in the bottom left corner. The unopened wax packs cost 10 cents in 1969.

COMPLETE SET (24) 600.00 1200.00
WRAPPER (10-CENT)
1 Detroit Tigers 15.00 40.00
2 Atlanta Braves 30.00 60.00
3 Boston Red Sox 30.00 60.00
4 Chicago Cubs 20.00 50.00
5 Baltimore Orioles 30.00 60.00
6 Houston Astros 12.50 30.00
7 Kansas City Royals 10.00 25.00
8 Philadelphia Phillies 10.00 25.00
9 Seattle Pilots 15.00 40.00
10 Montreal Expos 10.00 25.00
11 Chicago White Sox 10.00 25.00
12 San Diego Padres 10.00 25.00
13 Cleveland Indians 10.00 25.00
14 San Francisco Giants 20.00 50.00
15 Minnesota Twins 12.50 30.00
16 Pittsburgh Pirates 60.00 120.00
17 California Angels 10.00 25.00
18 St. Louis Cardinals 15.00 40.00
19 New York Yankees 100.00 200.00
20 Cincinnati Reds 50.00 100.00
21 Oakland A's 50.00 100.00
22 Los Angeles Dodgers 12.50 30.00
23 Washington Senators 10.00 25.00
24 New York Mets 50.00 100.00

1970 Topps

The cards in this 720-card set measure 2 1/2" by 3 1/2". The Topps set for 1970 has color photos surrounded by white frame lines and gray borders. The backs have a blue biographical section and a yellow record section. All-Star selections are featured on cards 450 to 469. Other topical subsets within this set include League Leaders (61-72), Playoffs cards (195-202), and World Series cards (305-310). There are graduations of scarcity, terminating in the high series (634-720), which are outlined in the value summary. Cards were issued in ten-card dime packs as well as thirty-three card cello packs which sold for a quarter and were encased in a small Topps box, and in 54-card rack packs which sold for 39 cents. The key Rookie Card in this set is Thurman Munson.

COMPLETE SET (720) 1250.00 3000.00
COMMON CARD (1-132) .30 .75
COMMON CARD (133-372) .40 1.00
COMMON CARD (373-459) .60 1.50
COMMON CARD (460-546) .75 2.00
COMMON CARD (547-633) 1.50 4.00
COMMON CARD (634-720) 4.00 10.00
WRAPPER (10-CENT) 8.00 20.00
1 New York Mets TC 12.50 30.00
2 Diego Segui .40 1.00
3 Darrel Chaney .30 .75
4 Tom Egan .30 .75
5 Wes Parker .40 1.00
6 Grant Jackson .30 .75
7 G.Boyd RC/R.Nagelson RC .30 .75
8 Jose Martinez RC .30 .75
9 Checklist 1 5.00 12.00
10 Carl Yastrzemski 8.00 20.00
11 Nate Colbert .30 .75
12 John Hiller .30 .75
13 Jack Hiatt .30 .75
14 Hank Allen .30 .75
15 Larry Dierker .30 .75
16 Charlie Metro MG RC .30 .75
17 Hoyt Wilhelm 1.50 4.00
18 Carlos May .40 1.00
19 John Boccabella .30 .75
20 Dave McNally .40 1.00
21 V.Blue RC/G.Tenace RC 1.50 4.00
22 Ray Washburn .30 .75
23 Bill Robinson .40 1.00
24 Dick Selma .30 .75
25 Cesar Tovar .30 .75
26 Tug McGraw .75 2.00
27 Chuck Hinton .30 .75
28 Billy Wilson .30 .75
29 Sandy Alomar .40 1.00
30 Matty Alou .40 1.00
31 Marty Pattin .40 1.00
32 Harry Walker MG .30 .75
33 Don Wert .30 .75
34 Willie Crawford .30 .75
35 Joel Horlen .30 .75
36 D.Breeden/B.Carbo RC .40 1.00
37 Dick Drago .30 .75
38 Mack Jones .30 .75
39 Mike Nagy RC .30 .75
40 Rich Allen .75 2.00
41 George Lauzerique .30 .75
42 Tito Fuentes .30 .75
43 Jack Aker .30 .75
44 Roberto Pena .30 .75
45 Dave Johnson .40 1.00
46 Ken Rudolph RC .30 .75
47 Bob Miller .30 .75
48 Gil Garrido .30 .75
49 Tim Cullen .30 .75
50 Tommie Agee .40 1.00
51 Bob Christian .30 .75
52 Bruce Dal Canton .30 .75
53 John Kennedy .30 .75
54 Jeff Torborg .40 1.00
55 John Odom .30 .75
56 J.Lis RC/S.Reid RC .30 .75
57 Pat Kelly .30 .75
58 Dave Marshall .30 .75
59 Dick Ellsworth .30 .75
60 Jim Wynn .40 1.00
61 Rose/Clemente/Jones LL 5.00 12.00
62 Carew/Smith/Oliva LL .75 2.00
63 McCovey/Santo/Perez LL .75 2.00
64 Kill/Powell/Jackson LL 1.50 4.00
65 McCovey/Aaron/May LL 5.00 12.00
66 Kill/Howard/Jackson LL 1.50 4.00
67 Marichal/Carlton/Gibson LL 1.50 4.00
68 Bosman/Palmer/Cuellar LL .60 1.50
69 Seav/Niek/Jenk/Mari LL 1.50 4.00
70 McLain/Cuellar/Boswell LL .40 1.00
71 Jenkins/Gibson/Singer LL .75 2.00
72 McDowell/Lolich/Mess LL .40 1.00
73 Wayne Granger .30 .75
74 G.Washburn RC/W.Wolf .30 .75
75 Jim Kaat .40 1.00
76 Carl Taylor UER .30 .75
Collecting is spelled incorrectly in the cartoon
77 Frank Linzy .30 .75
78 Joe Lahoud .30 .75
79 Clay Kirby .30 .75
80 Don Kessinger .40 1.00
81 Dave May .30 .75
82 Frank Fernandez .30 .75
83 Don Cardwell .30 .75
84 Paul Casanova .30 .75
85 Max Alvis .30 .75
86 Lum Harris MG .30 .75
87 Steve Renko RC .30 .75
88 M.Fuentes RC/D.Baney RC .40 1.00
89 Juan Rios .30 .75
90 Tim McCarver .40 1.00
91 Rich Morales .30 .75
92 George Culver .30 .75
93 Rick Renick .30 .75
94 Freddie Patek .40 1.00
95 Earl Wilson .40 1.00
96 L.Lee RC/J.Reuss RC .60 1.50
97 Joe Moeller .30 .75
98 Gates Brown .40 1.00
99 Bobby Pfeil RC .30 .75
100 Mel Stottlemyre .40 1.00
101 Bobby Floyd .30 .75
102 Joe Rudi .40 1.00
103 Frank Reberger .30 .75
104 Gerry Moses .30 .75
105 Tony Gonzalez .30 .75
106 Darold Knowles .30 .75
107 Bobby Etheridge .30 .75
108 Tom Burgmeier .30 .75
109 G.Jestadt RC/C.Morton .30 .75
110 Bob Moose .30 .75
111 Mike Hegan .40 1.00
112 Dave Nelson .30 .75
113 Jim Ray .30 .75
114 Gene Michael .40 1.00
115 Alex Johnson .40 1.00
116 Sparky Lyle .40 1.00
117 Don Young .30 .75
118 George Mitterwald .30 .75
119 Chuck Taylor RC .30 .75
120 Sal Bando .40 1.00
121 F.Beene RC/T.Crowley RC .30 .75
122 George Stone .30 .75
123 Don Gutteridge MG RC .30 .75
124 Larry Jaster .30 .75
125 Deron Johnson .30 .75
126 Marty Martinez .30 .75
127 Joe Coleman .30 .75
128A Checklist 2 R Perranoski 2.50 6.00
128B Checklist 2 R. Perranoski 2.50 6.00
129 Jimmie Price .30 .75
130 Ollie Brown .30 .75
131 R.Lamb RC/B.Stinson RC .30 .75
132 Jim McGlothlin .30 .75
133 Clay Carroll .40 1.00
134 Danny Walton RC .40 1.00
135 Dick Dietz .40 1.00
136 Steve Hargan .40 1.00
137 Art Shamsky .40 1.00
138 Joe Foy .40 1.00
139 Rich Nye .40 1.00
140 Reggie Jackson 20.00 50.00
141 D.Cash RC/J.Jeter RC .60 1.50
142 Fritz Peterson .40 1.00
143 Phil Gagliano .40 1.00
144 Ray Culp .40 1.00
145 Rico Carty .60 1.50
146 Danny Murphy .40 1.00
147 Angel Hermoso RC .40 1.00
148 Earl Weaver MG 1.25 3.00
149 Billy Champion RC .40 1.00
150 Harmon Killebrew 3.00 8.00
151 Dave Roberts .40 1.00
152 Ike Brown RC .40 1.00
153 Gary Gentry .40 1.00
154 J.Miles/J.Dukes RC .40 1.00
155 Denis Menke .40 1.00
156 Eddie Fisher .40 1.00
157 Manny Mota .60 1.50
158 Jerry McNertney .60 1.50
159 Tommy Helms .60 1.50
160 Phil Niekro 2.00 5.00
161 Richie Scheinblum .40 1.00
162 Jerry Johnson .40 1.00
163 Syd O'Brien .40 1.00
164 Ty Cline .40 1.00
165 Ed Kirkpatrick .40 1.00
166 Al Oliver 1.25 3.00
167 Bill Burbach .40 1.00
168 Dave Watkins RC .40 1.00
169 Tom Hall .40 1.00
170 Billy Williams 2.00 5.00
171 Jim Nash .40 1.00
172 G.Hill RC/R.Garr RC .60 1.50
173 Jim Hicks .40 1.00
174 Ted Sizemore .60 1.50
175 Dick Bosman .40 1.00
176 Jim Ray Hart .60 1.50
177 Jim Northrup .60 1.50
178 Denny Lemaster .40 1.00
179 Ivan Murrell .40 1.00
180 Tommy John .60 1.50
181 Sparky Anderson MG 2.00 5.00
182 Dick Hall .40 1.00
183 Jerry Grote .60 1.50
184 Ray Fosse .40 1.00
185 Don Mincher .60 1.50
186 Rick Joseph .40 1.00
187 Mike Hedlund .40 1.00
188 Manny Sanguillen .60 1.50
189 Thurman Munson RC 75.00 200.00
190 Joe Torre 1.25 3.00
191 Vicente Romo .40 1.00
192 Jim Qualls .40 1.00
193 Mike Wegener .40 1.00
194 Chuck Manuel RC 1.00 2.50
195 Tom Seaver NLCS1 10.00 25.00
196 Ken Boswell NLCS2 .75 2.00
197 Nolan Ryan NLCS3 12.50 30.00
198 Mets Celebrate w/Ryan 6.00 15.00
199 Mike Cuellar ALCS1 .75 2.00
200 Boog Powell ALCS2 1.25 3.00
201 B.Powell/A.Etch ALCS3 .75 2.00
202 Orioles Celebrate ALCS .75 2.00
203 Rudy May .40 1.00
204 Len Gabrielson .40 1.00
205 Bert Campaneris .60 1.50
206 Clete Boyer .60 1.50
207 N.McRae RC/B.Reed RC .40 1.00
208 Fred Gladding .40 1.00
209 Ken Suarez .40 1.00
210 Juan Marichal 2.00 5.00
211 Ted Williams MG UER 15.00 40.00
212 Al Santorini .40 1.00
213 Andy Etchebarren .40 1.00
214 Ken Boswell .40 1.00
215 Reggie Smith .60 1.50
216 Chuck Hartenstein .40 1.00
217 Ron Hansen .40 1.00
218 Ron Stone .40 1.00
219 Jerry Kenney .40 1.00
220 Steve Carlton 10.00 25.00
221 Ron Brand .40 1.00
222 Jim Rooker .40 1.00
223 Nate Oliver .40 1.00
224 Steve Barber .60 1.50
225 Lee May .60 1.50
226 Ron Perranoski .40 1.00
227 J.Mayberry RC/B.Watkins RC .60 1.50
228 Aurelio Rodriguez .40 1.00
229 Rich Robertson .40 1.00
230 Brooks Robinson 8.00 20.00
231 Luis Tiant .60 1.50
232 Bob Didier .40 1.00
233 Lew Krausse .40 1.00
234 Tommy Dean .40 1.00
235 Mike Epstein .40 1.00
236 Bob Veale .40 1.00
237 Russ Gibson .40 1.00
238 Jose Laboy .40 1.00
239 Ken Berry .40 1.00
240 Ferguson Jenkins 2.00 5.00
241 A.Fitzmorris RC/S.Northey RC .40 1.00
242 Walter Alston MG 1.25 3.00
243 Joe Sparma .40 1.00
244A Checklist 3 Red Bat 2.50 6.00
244B Checklist 3 Brown Bat 2.50 6.00
245 Leo Cardenas .40 1.00
246 Jim McAndrew .40 1.00
247 Lou Klimchock .40 1.00
248 Jesus Alou .40 1.00
249 Bob Locker .40 1.00
250 Willie McCovey UER 4.00 10.00
251 Dick Schofield .40 1.00
252 Lowell Palmer RC .40 1.00
253 Ron Woods .40 1.00
254 Camilo Pascual .40 1.00
255 Jim Spencer RC .40 1.00
256 Vic Davalillo .40 1.00
257 Dennis Higgins .40 1.00
258 Paul Popovich .40 1.00
259 Tommie Reynolds .40 1.00
260 Claude Osteen .40 1.00
261 Curt Motton .40 1.00
262 J.Morales RC/J.Williams RC .40 1.00
263 Duane Josephson .40 1.00
264 Rich Hebner .40 1.00

1970 Topps

265 Randy Hundley .40 1.00
266 Wally Bunker .40 1.00
267 H.Hill RC/P.Ratliff .40 1.00
268 Claude Raymond .40 1.00
269 Cesar Gutierrez .40 1.00
270 Chris Short .40 1.00
271 Greg Goossen .60 1.50
272 Hector Torres .40 1.00
273 Ralph Houk MG .60 1.50
274 Gerry Arrigo .40 1.00
275 Duke Sims .40 1.00
276 Ron Hunt .40 1.00
277 Paul Doyle RC .40 1.00
278 Tommie Aaron .40 1.00
279 Bill Lee RC .60 1.50
280 Donn Clendenon .60 1.50
281 Casey Cox .40 1.00
282 Steve Huntz .40 1.00
283 Angel Bravo RC .40 1.00
284 Jack Baldschun .40 1.00
285 Paul Blair .60 1.50
286 J.Jenkins RC/B.Buckner RC 8.00 20.00
287 Fred Talbot .40 1.00
288 Larry Hisle .60 1.50
289 Gene Brabender .40 1.00
290 Rod Carew 10.00 25.00
291 Leo Durocher MG 1.25 3.00
292 Eddie Leon RC .40 1.00
293 Bob Bailey .60 1.50
294 Jose Azcue .40 1.00
295 Cecil Upshaw .40 1.00
296 Woody Woodward .40 1.00
297 Curt Blefary .40 1.00
298 Ken Henderson .40 1.00
299 Buddy Bradford .40 1.00
300 Tom Seaver 12.00 30.00
301 Chico Salmon .40 1.00
302 Jeff James .40 1.00
303 Brant Alyea .40 1.00
304 Bill Russell RC 2.00 5.00
305 Don Buford WS1 1.50 4.00
306 Donn Clendenon WS2 1.50 4.00
307 Tommie Agee WS3 1.50 4.00
308 J.C. Martin WS4 1.50 4.00
309 Jerry Koosman WS5 1.50 4.00
310 Mets Celebrate WS 2.00 5.00
311 Dick Green .40 1.00
312 Mike Torrez .40 1.00
313 Mayo Smith MG .40 1.00
314 Bill McCool .40 1.00
315 Luis Aparicio 6.00 15.00
316 Skip Guinn .40 1.00
317 B.Conigliaro/L.Alvarado RC .60 1.50
318 Willie Smith .40 1.00
319 Clay Dalrymple .40 1.00
320 Jim Maloney .60 1.50
321 Lou Piniella .60 1.50
322 Luke Walker .40 1.00
323 Wayne Comer .40 1.00
324 Tony Taylor .60 1.50
325 Dave Boswell .40 1.00
326 Bill Voss .40 1.00
327 Hal King RC .40 1.00
328 George Brunet .40 1.00
329 Chris Cannizzaro .40 1.00
330 Lou Brock 12.00 30.00
331 Chuck Dobson .40 1.00
332 Bobby Wine .40 1.00
333 Bobby Murcer .60 1.50
334 Phil Regan .40 1.00
335 Bill Freehan .60 1.50
336 Del Unser .40 1.00
337 Mike McCormick .60 1.50
338 Paul Schaal .40 1.00
339 Johnny Edwards .40 1.00
340 Tony Conigliaro 1.25 3.00
341 Bill Sudakis .40 1.00
342 Wilbur Wood .60 1.50
343A Checklist 4 Red Bat 2.50 6.00
343B Checklist 4 Brown Bat 2.50 6.00
344 Marcelino Lopez .40 1.00
345 Al Ferrara .40 1.00
346 Red Schoendienst MG .60 1.50
347 Russ Snyder .40 1.00
348 M.Jorgensen RC/J.Hudson RC .60 1.50
349 Steve Hamilton .40 1.00
350 Roberto Clemente 30.00 80.00
351 Tom Murphy .40 1.00
352 Bob Barton .40 1.00
353 Stan Williams .40 1.00
354 Amos Otis .60 1.50
355 Doug Rader .40 1.00
356 Fred Lasher .40 1.00
357 Bob Burda .40 1.00
358 Pedro Borbon RC .60 1.50
359 Phil Roof .40 1.00
360 Curt Flood .60 1.50
361 Ray Jarvis .40 1.00
362 Joe Hague .40 1.00
363 Tom Shopay RC .40 1.00
364 Dan McGinn .40 1.00
365 Zoilo Versalles .40 1.00
366 Barry Moore .40 1.00
367 Mike Lum .40 1.00
368 Ed Herrmann .40 1.00
369 Alan Foster .40 1.00
370 Tommy Harper .60 1.50
371 Rod Gaspar RC .40 1.00
372 Dave Giusti .40 1.00
373 Roy White .75 2.00
374 Tommie Sisk .60 1.50
375 Johnny Callison .75 2.00
376 Lefty Phillips MG RC .60 1.50
377 Bill Butler .60 1.50
378 Jim Davenport .60 1.50
379 Tom Tischinski RC .60 1.50
380 Tony Perez 2.50 6.00
381 B.Brooks RC/M.Olivo RC .60 1.50
382 Jack DiLauro RC .60 1.50
383 Mickey Stanley .75 2.00
384 Gary Neibauer .60 1.50
385 George Scott .75 2.00
386 Bill Dillman .60 1.50
387 Baltimore Orioles TC 1.25 3.00
388 Byron Browne .60 1.50
389 Jim Shellenback .60 1.50
390 Willie Davis .75 2.00
391 Larry Brown .60 1.50
392 Walt Hriniak .75 2.00
393 John Gelnar .60 1.50
394 Gil Hodges MG 1.50 4.00
395 Walt Williams .60 1.50
396 Steve Blass .75 2.00
397 Roger Repoz .60 1.50
398 Bill Stoneman .60 1.50
399 New York Yankees TC 1.25 3.00
400 Denny McLain 1.50 4.00
401 J.Harrell RC/B.Williams RC .60 1.50
402 Ellie Rodriguez .60 1.50
403 Jim Bunning 5.00 12.00
404 Rich Reese .60 1.50
405 Bill Hands .60 1.50
406 Mike Andrews .60 1.50
407 Bob Watson .75 2.00
408 Paul Lindblad .60 1.50
409 Bob Tolan .60 1.50
410 Boog Powell 1.50 4.00
411 Los Angeles Dodgers TC 1.25 3.00
412 Larry Burchart .60 1.50
413 Sonny Jackson .60 1.50
414 Paul Edmondson RC .60 1.50
415 Julian Javier .75 2.00
416 Joe Verbanic .60 1.50
417 John Bateman .60 1.50
418 John Donaldson .60 1.50
419 Ron Taylor .60 1.50
420 Ken McMullen .75 2.00
421 Pat Dobson .75 2.00
422 Kansas City Royals TC 1.25 3.00
423 Jerry May .60 1.50
424 Mike Kilkenny .60 1.50
425 Bobby Bonds 2.50 6.00
426 Bill Rigney MG .60 1.50
427 Fred Norman .60 1.50
428 Don Buford .60 1.50
429 R.Bobb RC/J.Cosman .60 1.50
430 Andy Messersmith .75 2.00
431 Ron Swoboda .75 2.00
432A Checklist 5 Yellow Ltr 2.50 6.00
432B Checklist 5 White Ltr 2.50 6.00
433 Ron Bryant RC .60 1.50
434 Felipe Alou .75 2.00
435 Nelson Briles .75 2.00
436 Philadelphia Phillies TC 1.25 3.00
437 Danny Cater .60 1.50
438 Pat Jarvis .60 1.50
439 Lee Maye .60 1.50
440 Bill Mazeroski 2.50 6.00
441 John O'Donoghue .60 1.50
442 Gene Mauch MG .75 2.00
443 Al Jackson .60 1.50
444 B.Farmer RC/J.Matias RC .60 1.50
445 Vada Pinson .75 2.00
446 Billy Grabarkewitz RC .60 1.50
447 Lee Stange .60 1.50
448 Houston Astros TC 1.25 3.00
449 Jim Palmer 10.00 25.00
450 Willie McCovey AS 10.00 25.00
451 Boog Powell AS 1.50 4.00
452 Felix Millan AS .75 2.00
453 Rod Carew AS 2.50 6.00
454 Ron Santo AS 1.50 4.00
455 Brooks Robinson AS 2.50 6.00
456 Don Kessinger AS .75 2.00
457 Rico Petrocelli AS 1.50 4.00
458 Pete Rose AS 12.00 30.00
459 Reggie Jackson AS 8.00 20.00
460 Matty Alou AS 1.25 3.00
461 Carl Yastrzemski AS 8.00 20.00
462 Hank Aaron AS 20.00 50.00
463 Frank Robinson AS 10.00 25.00
464 Johnny Bench AS 15.00 40.00
465 Bill Freehan AS 1.25 3.00
466 Juan Marichal AS 2.00 5.00
467 Denny McLain AS 1.25 3.00
468 Jerry Koosman AS 1.25 3.00
469 Sam McDowell AS 1.25 3.00
470 Willie Stargell 10.00 25.00
471 Chris Zachary .75 2.00
472 Atlanta Braves TC 1.50 4.00
473 Don Bryant .75 2.00
474 Dick Kelley .75 2.00
475 Dick McAuliffe 1.25 3.00
476 Don Shaw .75 2.00
477 A.Severinsen RC/R.Freed RC .75 2.00
478 Bobby Heise RC .75 2.00
479 Dick Woodson RC .75 2.00
480 Glenn Beckert 1.25 3.00
481 Jose Tartabull .75 2.00
482 Tom Hilgendorf RC .75 2.00
483 Gail Hopkins RC .75 2.00
484 Gary Nolan 1.25 3.00
485 Jay Johnstone 1.25 3.00
486 Terry Harmon .75 2.00
487 Cisco Carlos .75 2.00
488 J.C. Martin .75 2.00
489 Eddie Kasko MG .75 2.00
490 Bill Singer 1.25 3.00
491 Graig Nettles 2.00 5.00
492 K.Lampard RC/S.Spinks RC .75 2.00
493 Lindy McDaniel 1.25 3.00
494 Larry Stahl .75 2.00
495 Dave Morehead .75 2.00
496 Steve Whitaker .75 2.00
497 Eddie Watt .75 2.00
498 Al Weis .75 2.00
499 Skip Lockwood 1.25 3.00
500 Hank Aaron 25.00 60.00
501 Chicago White Sox TC 1.50 4.00
502 Rollie Fingers 15.00 40.00
503 Dal Maxvill .75 2.00
504 Don Pavletich .75 2.00
505 Ken Holtzman 1.25 3.00
506 Ed Stroud .75 2.00
507 Pat Corrales .75 2.00
508 Joe Niekro 1.25 3.00
509 Montreal Expos TC 1.50 4.00
510 Tony Oliva 2.00 5.00
511 Joe Hoerner .75 2.00
512 Billy Harris .75 2.00
513 Preston Gomez MG .75 2.00
514 Steve Hovley RC .75 2.00
515 Don Wilson 1.25 3.00
516 J.Ellis RC/J.Lyttle RC .75 2.00
517 Joe Gibbon .75 2.00
518 Bill Melton .75 2.00
519 Don McMahon .75 2.00
520 Willie Horton 1.25 3.00
521 Cal Koonce .75 2.00
522 California Angels TC 1.50 4.00
523 Jose Pena .75 2.00
524 Alvin Dark MG 1.25 3.00
525 Jerry Adair .75 2.00
526 Ron Herbel .75 2.00
527 Don Bosch .75 2.00
528 Elrod Hendricks .75 2.00
529 Bob Aspromonte .75 2.00
530 Bob Gibson 10.00 25.00
531 Ron Clark .75 2.00
532 Danny Murtaugh MG 1.25 3.00
533 Buzz Stephen RC .75 2.00
534 Minnesota Twins TC 1.50 4.00
535 Andy Kosco .75 2.00
536 Mike Kekich .75 2.00
537 Joe Morgan 12.00 30.00
538 Bob Humphreys .75 2.00
539 D.Doyle RC/L.Bowa RC 3.00 8.00
540 Gary Peters .75 2.00
541 Bill Heath .75 2.00
542A Checklist 6 Brown Bat 2.50 6.00
542B Checklist 6 Gray Bat 2.50 6.00
543 Clyde Wright .75 2.00
544 Cincinnati Reds TC 1.50 4.00
545 Ken Harrelson 1.25 3.00
546 Ron Reed .75 2.00
547 Rick Monday 2.50 6.00
548 Howie Reed 1.50 4.00
549 St. Louis Cardinals TC 2.50 6.00
550 Frank Howard 2.50 6.00
551 Dock Ellis 2.50 6.00
552 O'Riley/Paepke/Rico RC 1.50 4.00
553 Jim Lefebvre 2.50 6.00
554 Tom Timmermann RC 1.50 4.00
555 Orlando Cepeda 5.00 12.00
556 Dave Bristol MG 2.50 6.00
557 Ed Kranepool 2.50 6.00
558 Vern Fuller 1.50 4.00
559 Tommy Davis 2.50 6.00
560 Gaylord Perry 6.00 15.00
561 Tom McCraw 1.50 4.00
562 Ted Abernathy 1.50 4.00
563 Boston Red Sox TC 2.50 6.00
564 Johnny Briggs 1.50 4.00
565 Jim Hunter 12.00 30.00
566 Gene Alley 2.50 6.00
567 Bob Oliver 1.50 4.00
568 Stan Bahnsen 2.50 6.00
569 Cookie Rojas 2.50 6.00
570 Jim Fregosi 2.50 6.00
571 Jim Brewer 1.50 4.00
572 Frank Quilici 1.50 4.00
573 Corkins/Robles/Slocum RC 1.50 4.00
574 Bobby Bolin 2.50 6.00
575 Cleon Jones 2.50 6.00
576 Milt Pappas 2.50 6.00
577 Bernie Allen 1.50 4.00
578 Tom Griffin 1.50 4.00
579 Detroit Tigers TC 2.50 6.00
580 Pete Rose 30.00 60.00
581 Tom Satriano 1.50 4.00
582 Mike Paul 1.50 4.00
583 Hal Lanier 1.50 4.00
584 Al Downing 2.50 6.00
585 Rusty Staub 3.00 8.00
586 Rickey Clark RC 1.50 4.00
587 Jose Arcia 1.50 4.00
588A Checklist 7 Adolfo 3.00 8.00
588B Checklist 7 Adolpho 2.50 6.00
589 Joe Keough 1.50 4.00
590 Mike Cuellar 2.50 6.00
591 Mike Ryan UER 1.50 4.00
592 Daryl Patterson 1.50 4.00
593 Chicago Cubs TC 3.00 8.00
594 Jake Gibbs 1.50 4.00
595 Maury Wills 5.00 12.00
596 Mike Hershberger 2.50 6.00
597 Sonny Siebert 1.50 4.00
598 Joe Pepitone 2.50 6.00
599 Stelmaszek/Martin/Such RC 1.50 4.00
600 Willie Mays 50.00 120.00
601 Pete Richert 1.50 4.00
602 Ted Savage 1.50 4.00
603 Ray Oyler 1.50 4.00
604 Clarence Gaston 2.50 6.00
605 Rick Wise 2.50 6.00
606 Chico Ruiz 1.50 4.00
607 Gary Waslewski 1.50 4.00
608 Pittsburgh Pirates TC 2.50 6.00
609 Buck Martinez RC 2.50 6.00
610 Jerry Koosman 3.00 8.00
611 Norm Cash 2.50 6.00
612 Jim Hickman 2.50 6.00
613 Dave Baldwin 2.50 6.00
614 Mike Shannon 2.50 6.00
615 Mark Belanger 2.50 6.00
616 Jim Merritt 1.50 4.00
617 Jim French 1.50 4.00
618 Billy Wynne RC 1.50 4.00
619 Norm Miller 1.50 4.00
620 Jim Perry 2.50 6.00
621 McQueen/Evans/Kester RC 6.00 15.00
622 Don Sutton 5.00 12.00
623 Horace Clarke 2.50 6.00
624 Clyde King MG 1.50 4.00
625 Dean Chance 1.50 4.00
626 Dave Ricketts 1.50 4.00
627 Gary Wagner 1.50 4.00
628 Wayne Garrett RC 1.50 4.00
629 Merv Rettenmund 1.50 4.00
630 Ernie Banks 25.00 60.00
631 Oakland Athletics TC 2.50 6.00
632 Gary Sutherland 1.50 4.00
633 Roger Nelson 1.50 4.00
634 Bud Harrelson 6.00 15.00
635 Bob Allison 6.00 15.00
636 Jim Stewart 4.00 10.00
637 Cleveland Indians TC 5.00 12.00
638 Frank Bertaina 4.00 10.00
639 Dave Campbell 6.00 15.00
640 Al Kaline 25.00 60.00
641 Al McBean 4.00 10.00
642 Garrett/Lund/Tatum RC 4.00 10.00
643 Jose Pagan 4.00 10.00
644 Gerry Nyman 4.00 10.00
645 Don Money 6.00 15.00
646 Jim Britton 4.00 10.00
647 Tom Matchick 4.00 10.00
648 Larry Haney 4.00 10.00
649 Jimmie Hall 4.00 10.00
650 Sam McDowell 6.00 15.00
651 Jim Gosger 4.00 10.00
652 Rich Rollins 6.00 15.00
653 Moe Drabowsky 4.00 10.00
654 Gamble/Day/Mangual RC 8.00 20.00
655 John Roseboro 6.00 15.00
656 Jim Hardin 4.00 10.00
657 San Diego Padres TC 5.00 12.00
658 Ken Tatum RC 4.00 10.00
659 Pete Ward 4.00 10.00
660 Johnny Bench 60.00 150.00
661 Jerry Robertson 4.00 10.00
662 Frank Lucchesi MG RC 4.00 10.00
663 Tito Francona 4.00 10.00
664 Bob Robertson 4.00 10.00
665 Jim Lonborg 6.00 15.00
666 Adolpho Phillips 4.00 10.00
667 Bob Meyer 6.00 15.00
668 Bob Tillman 4.00 10.00
669 Johnson/Lazar/Scott RC 4.00 10.00
670 Ron Santo 10.00 25.00
671 Jim Campanis 4.00 10.00
672 Leon McFadden 4.00 10.00
673 Ted Uhlaender 4.00 10.00
674 Dave Leonhard 4.00 10.00
675 Jose Cardenal 6.00 15.00
676 Washington Senators TC 5.00 12.00
677 Woodie Fryman 4.00 10.00
678 Dave Duncan 6.00 15.00
679 Ray Sadecki 4.00 10.00
680 Rico Petrocelli 6.00 15.00
681 Bob Garibaldi RC 4.00 10.00
682 Dalton Jones 4.00 10.00
683 Geishart/McRae/Simpson RC 6.00 15.00
684 Jack Fisher 4.00 10.00
685 Tom Haller 4.00 10.00
686 Jackie Hernandez 4.00 10.00
687 Bob Priddy 4.00 10.00
688 Ted Kubiak 6.00 15.00
689 Frank Tepedino RC 6.00 15.00
690 Ron Fairly 6.00 15.00
691 Joe Grzenda 4.00 10.00
692 Duffy Dyer 4.00 10.00
693 Bob Johnson 4.00 10.00
694 Gary Ross 4.00 10.00
695 Bobby Knoop 4.00 10.00
696 San Francisco Giants TC 5.00 12.00
697 Jim Hannan 4.00 10.00
698 Tom Tresh 6.00 15.00
699 Hank Aguirre 4.00 10.00
700 Frank Robinson 25.00 60.00
701 Jack Billingham 4.00 10.00
702 Johnson/Klimkowski/Zepp RC 4.00 10.00
703 Lou Marone RC 4.00 10.00
704 Frank Baker RC 4.00 10.00
705 Tony Cloninger UER 4.00 10.00
706 John McNamara MG RC 4.00 10.00
707 Kevin Collins 4.00 10.00
708 Jose Santiago 4.00 10.00
709 Mike Fiore 4.00 10.00
710 Felix Millan 4.00 10.00
711 Ed Brinkman 4.00 10.00
712 Nolan Ryan 100.00 250.00
713 Seattle Pilots TC 10.00 25.00
714 Al Spangler 4.00 10.00
715 Mickey Lolich 6.00 15.00
716 Campisi/Cleveland/Guzman RC 6.00 15.00
717 Tom Phoebus 4.00 10.00
718 Ed Spiezio 4.00 10.00
719 Jim Roland 4.00 10.00
720 Rick Reichardt 6.00 15.00

1970 Topps Booklets

COMPLETE SET (24) 15.00 40.00
COMMON CARD (1-16) .40 1.00
COMMON CARD (17-24) .40 1.00
1 Mike Cuellar .40 1.00
2 Rico Petrocelli .40 1.00
3 Jay Johnstone .40 1.00
4 Walt Williams .40 1.00
5 Vada Pinson .40 1.00
6 Bill Freehan .40 1.00
7 Wally Bunker .40 1.00
8 Tony Oliva .60 1.50
9 Bobby Murcer .40 1.00
10 Reggie Jackson 2.50 6.00
11 Tommy Harper .40 1.00
12 Mike Epstein .40 1.00
13 Orlando Cepeda .60 1.50
14 Ernie Banks 1.50 4.00
15 Pete Rose 2.50 6.00
16 Denis Menke .40 1.00
17 Bill Singer .40 1.00
18 Rusty Staub .60 1.50
19 Cleon Jones .40 1.00
20 Deron Johnson .40 1.00
21 Bob Moose .40 1.00
22 Bob Gibson 1.00 2.50
23 Al Ferrara .40 1.00
24 Willie Mays 3.00 8.00

1970 Topps Candy Lid

This 24-card set features color player portraits printed on the bottom of candy lids and measures approximately 1 7/8" in diameter. The lids are unnumbered and checklisted below in alphabetical order.

COMPLETE SET (24) 1400.00 2800.00
1 Hank Aaron 250.00 500.00
2 Rich Allen 175.00 350.00
3 Luis Aparicio 60.00 120.00
4 Johnny Bench 250.00 500.00
5 Ollie Brown 30.00 60.00
6 Willie Davis 30.00 60.00
7 Jim Fregosi 30.00 60.00
8 Mike Hegan 30.00 60.00
9 Frank Howard 40.00 80.00
10 Reggie Jackson 175.00 350.00
11 Fergie Jenkins 75.00 150.00
12 Harmon Killebrew 225.00 450.00
13 Bill Mazeroski 75.00 150.00
14 Juan Marichal 75.00 150.00
15 Tim McCarver 40.00 80.00
16 Sam McDowell 30.00 60.00
17 Denny McLain 30.00 60.00
18 Lou Piniella 30.00 60.00
19 Frank Robinson 100.00 200.00
20 Tom Seaver 200.00 400.00
21 Rusty Staub 30.00 60.00
22 Mel Stottlemyre 30.00 60.00
23 Jim Wynn 30.00 60.00
24 Carl Yastrzemski 225.00 450.00

1970 Topps Cloth Stickers

These stickers measure the standard size, and so far all found seem to be all from the 2nd series in 1970. These cards were intended to be pasted on jackets. Obviously this checklist is far from complete so any further information is greatly appreciated.

216 Chuck Hartenstein 250.00 500.00
226 Ron Perranoski 250.00 500.00
238 Coco Laboy 250.00 500.00
257 Dennis Higgins 250.00 500.00

1970 Topps Posters Inserts

COMPLETE SET (24) 30.00 60.00
1 Joe Horlen .60 1.50
2 Phil Niekro .75 2.00
3 Willie Davis .60 1.50
4 Lou Brock 2.00 5.00
5 Ron Santo 1.25 3.00
6 Ken Harrelson .60 1.50
7 Willie McCovey 2.00 5.00
8 Rick Wise .60 1.50
9 Andy Messersmith .60 1.50
10 Ron Fairly .60 1.50
11 Johnny Bench 4.00 10.00
12 Frank Robinson 2.00 5.00
13 Tommie Agee .60 1.50
14 Roy White .60 1.50
15 Larry Dierker .60 1.50
16 Rod Carew 2.00 5.00
17 Don Mincher .60 1.50
18 Ollie Brown .60 1.50
19 Ed Kirkpatrick .60 1.50
20 Reggie Smith .75 2.00
21 Roberto Clemente 8.00 20.00
22 Frank Howard .75 2.00
23 Bert Campaneris .75 2.00
24 Denny McLain .75 2.00

1970 Topps Scratchoffs

COMPLETE SET (24) 20.00 50.00
COMMON CARD (1-24) .40 1.00
1 Hank Aaron 3.00 8.00
2 Rich Allen .60 1.50
3 Luis Aparicio 1.00 2.50
4 Sal Bando .60 1.50
5 Glenn Beckert .40 1.00
6 Dick Bosman .40 1.00
7 Nate Colbert .40 1.00
8 Mike Hegan .40 1.00
9 Mack Jones .40 1.00
10 Al Kaline 2.00 5.00
11 Harmon Killebrew 2.00 5.00
12 Juan Marichal 1.00 2.50
13 Tim McCarver .60 1.50
14 Sam McDowell .60 1.50
15 Claude Osteen .40 1.00
16 Tony Perez 1.00 2.50
17 Lou Piniella .60 1.50
18 Boog Powell 1.00 2.50
19 Tom Seaver 2.00 5.00
20 Jim Spencer .40 1.00
21 Willie Stargell 1.50 4.00
22 Mel Stottlemyre .60 1.50
23 Jim Wynn .60 1.50
24 Carl Yastrzemski 2.50 6.00

1970 Topps Super

The cards in this 42-card set measure approximately 3 1/8" by 5 1/4". The 1970 Topps Super set was a separate Topps issue printed on heavy stock and marketed in its own wrapper with gum. The blue and yellow backs are identical to the respective player's backs in the 1970 Topps regular issue. Cards 38, Boog Powell, is the key card of the set; other short print run cards are listed in the checklist with SP. The obverse pictures are borderless and contain a facsimile autograph. The set was issued in three-card wax packs which came 24 packs to a box and 24 boxes to a case.

COMPLETE SET (42) 125.00 250.00
COMMON CARD (1-42) .75 2.00
WRAPPER (10-CENT)
COMMON SP 1.50 4.00
1 Claude Osteen SP 1.50 4.00
2 Sal Bando SP 1.50 4.00
3 Luis Aparicio SP 2.00 5.00
4 Harmon Killebrew 2.00 5.00
5 Tom Seaver SP 10.00 25.00
6 Larry Dierker 1.00 2.50
7 Bill Freehan 1.00 2.50
8 Johnny Bench 6.00 15.00
9 Tommy Harper .75 2.00
10 Sam McDowell .75 2.00
11 Lou Brock 2.00 5.00
12 Roberto Clemente 12.50 30.00
13 Willie McCovey 2.00 5.00
14 Rico Petrocelli .75 2.00
15 Phil Niekro 1.50 4.00
16 Frank Howard 1.00 2.50
17 Denny McLain 1.00 2.50
18 Willie Mays 8.00 20.00
19 Willie Stargell 2.00 5.00
20 Joel Horlen .75 2.00
21 Ron Santo 1.25 3.00
22 Dick Bosman .75 2.00
23 Tim McCarver 1.25 3.00
24 Hank Aaron 8.00 20.00
25 Andy Messersmith .75 2.00
26 Tony Oliva 1.25 3.00
27 Mel Stottlemyre 1.00 2.50
28 Reggie Jackson 6.00 15.00
29 Carl Yastrzemski 10.00 25.00
30 Jim Fregosi 1.00 2.50
31 Vada Pinson 1.00 2.50
32 Lou Piniella 1.25 3.00
33 Bob Gibson 2.00 5.00
34 Pete Rose 8.00 20.00
35 Jim Wynn 1.00 2.50
36 Ollie Brown SP 2.50 6.00
37 Frank Robinson SP 8.00 20.00
38 Boog Powell SP 20.00 50.00
39 Willie Davis SP 1.50 4.00
40 Billy Williams SP 4.00 10.00
41 Rusty Staub 1.25 3.00
42 Tommie Agee 1.00 2.50

1971 Topps

The cards in this 752-card set measure 2 1/2" by 3 1/2". The 1971 Topps set is a challenge to complete in strict mint condition because the black obverse border is easily scratched and damaged. An unusual feature of this set is that the player is also pictured in black and white on the back of the card. Featured subsets within this set include League Leaders (61-72), Playoffs cards (195-202), and World Series cards (327-332). Cards 524-643 and the last series (644-752) are somewhat scarce. The last series was printed in two sheets of 132. On the printing sheets 44 cards were printed in 50 percent greater quantity than the other 66 cards. These 66 (slightly) shorter-printed numbers are identified in the checklist below by SP. The key Rookie Cards in this set are the multi-player Rookie Card of Dusty Baker and Don Baylor and the individual cards of Bert Blyleven, Dave Concepcion, Steve Garvey, and Ted Simmons. The Jim Northrup and Jim Nash cards have been seen with our without printing "blotches" on the card. There is still debate on whether those two cards are just printing issues or legitimate variations. Among the ways these cards were issued were in 54-card rack packs which retailed for 39 cents.

COMPLETE SET (752) 1500.00 4000.00
COMMON CARD (1-393) .60 1.50
COMMON CARD (394-523) 1.00 2.50
COMMON CARD (524-643) 1.50 4.00
COMMON CARD (644-752) 3.00 8.00
COMMON SP (644-752) 5.00 12.00
WRAPPER (10-CENT) 6.00 15.00
1 Baltimore Orioles TC 8.00 20.00
2 Dock Ellis .60 1.50
3 Dick McAuliffe .75 2.00
4 Vic Davalillo .60 1.50
5 Thurman Munson 60.00 120.00
6 Ed Spiezio .60 1.50
7 Jim Holt RC .60 1.50
8 Mike McQueen 1.50
9 George Scott .75 2.00
10 Claude Osteen .75 2.00
11 Elliott Maddox RC .60 1.50
12 Johnny Callison .75 2.00
13 C.Brinkman RC/D.Moloney RC .60 1.50
14 Dave Concepcion RC 25.00 60.00
15 Andy Messersmith .75 2.00
16 Ken Singleton RC 1.50 4.00
17 Billy Sorrell .60 1.50
18 Norm Miller .60 1.50
19 Skip Pitlock RC .60 1.50
20 Reggie Jackson 30.00 80.00
21 Dan McGinn .60 1.50
22 Phil Roof .60 1.50
23 Oscar Gamble .60 1.50
24 Rich Hand RC .60 1.50
25 Clarence Gaston .75 2.00
26 Bert Blyleven RC 40.00 100.00
27 F.Cambria RC/G.Clines RC .60 1.50
28 Ron Klimkowski .60 1.50
29 Don Buford .60 1.50
30 Phil Niekro 8.00 20.00
31 Eddie Kasko MG .60 1.50
32 Jerry DaVanon .60 1.50
33 Del Unser .60 1.50
34 Sandy Vance RC .60 1.50
35 Lou Piniella .75 2.00
36 Dean Chance .75 2.00
37 Rich McKinney RC .60 1.50
38 Jim Colborn RC .60 1.50
39 L.LaGrow RC/G.Lamont RC .75 2.00
40 Lee May .75 2.00
41 Rick Austin RC .60 1.50
42 Boots Day .60 1.50
43 Steve Kealey .60 1.50
44 Johnny Edwards .60 1.50
45 Jim Hunter 6.00 15.00
46 Dave Campbell .75 2.00
47 Johnny Jeter .60 1.50
48 Dave Baldwin .60 1.50
49 Don Money .60 1.50
50 Willie McCovey 15.00 40.00
51 Steve Kline RC .60 1.50
52 O.Brown RC/E.Williams RC .60 1.50
53 Paul Blair .75 2.00
54 Checklist 1 4.00 10.00
55 Steve Carlton 20.00 50.00
56 Duane Josephson .60 1.50
57 Von Joshua RC .60 1.50
58 Bill Lee .75 2.00
59 Gene Mauch MG .75 2.00
60 Dick Bosman .60 1.50
61 Johnson/Yaz/Oliva LL 1.50 4.00
62 Carty/Torre/Sang LL .75 2.00
63 Howard/Conig/Powell LL 1.50 4.00
64 Bench/Perez/B.Will LL 2.50 6.00
65 Howard/Killebrew/Yaz LL 1.50 4.00
66 Bench/B.Will/Perez LL 2.50 6.00
67 Segui/Palmer/Wright LL 1.50 4.00
68 Seaver/Simp/Walk LL 1.50 4.00
69 Cuellar/McNally/Perry LL .75 2.00
70 Gibson/Perry/Jenkins LL 2.50 6.00
71 McDowell/Lolich/John LL .75 2.00
72 Seaver/Gibson/Jenkins LL 2.50 6.00
73 George Brunet .60 1.50
74 P.Hamm RC/J.Nettles RC .60 1.50
75 Gary Nolan .75 2.00
76 Ted Savage .60 1.50
77 Mike Compton RC .60 1.50
78 Jim Spencer .60 1.50
79 Wade Blasingame .60 1.50
80 Bill Melton .60 1.50
81 Felix Millan .60 1.50
82 Casey Cox .60 1.50
83 T.Foli RC/R.Bobb .75 2.00
84 Marcel Lachemann RC .60 1.50
85 Billy Grabarkewitz .60 1.50
86 Mike Kilkenny .60 1.50
87 Jack Heidemann RC .60 1.50
88 Hal King .60 1.50
89 Ken Brett .60 1.50
90 Joe Pepitone .75 2.00
91 Bob Lemon MG .75 2.00
92 Fred Wenz .60 1.50
93 N.McRae/D.Riddleberger .60 1.50
94 Don Hahn RC .60 1.50
95 Luis Tiant .75 2.00
96 Joe Hague .60 1.50
97 Floyd Wicker .60 1.50
98 Joe Decker RC .60 1.50
99 Mark Belanger .75 2.00
100 Pete Rose 25.00 60.00
101 Les Cain .60 1.50
102 K.Forsch RC/L.Howard RC .75 2.00
103 Rich Severson RC .60 1.50
104 Dan Frisella .60 1.50
105 Tony Conigliaro .75 2.00
106 Tom Dukes .60 1.50
107 Roy Foster RC .60 1.50
108 John Cumberland .60 1.50
109 Steve Hovley .60 1.50
110 Bill Mazeroski 10.00 25.00
111 L.Colson RC/B.Mitchell RC .60 1.50
112 Manny Mota .75 2.00
113 Jerry Crider .60 1.50
114 Billy Conigliaro .75 2.00
115 Donn Clendenon .75 2.00
116 Ken Sanders .60 1.50
117 Ted Simmons RC 60.00 150.00
118 Cookie Rojas .75 2.00
119 Frank Lucchesi MG .60 1.50
120 Willie Horton .75 2.00
121 J.Dunegan/R.Skidmore RC .60 1.50
122 Eddie Watt .60 1.50
123A Checklist 2 Right 4.00 10.00
123B Checklist 2 Centered 4.00 10.00
124 Don Gullett RC .75 2.00
125 Ray Fosse .60 1.50
126 Danny Coombs .60 1.50
127 Danny Thompson RC .75 2.00
128 Frank Johnson .60 1.50
129 Aurelio Monteagudo .60 1.50
130 Denis Menke .60 1.50
131 Curt Blefary .60 1.50
132 Jose Laboy .60 1.50
133 Mickey Lolich .75 2.00
134 Jose Arcia .60 1.50
135 Rick Monday .75 2.00
136 Duffy Dyer .60 1.50
137 Marcelino Lopez .60 1.50
138 J.Lis/W.Montanez RC .75 2.00
139 Paul Casanova .60 1.50
140 Gaylord Perry 2.50 6.00
141 Frank Quilici .60 1.50
142 Mack Jones .60 1.50
143 Steve Blass .75 2.00
144 Jackie Hernandez .60 1.50
145 Bill Singer .75 2.00
146 Ralph Houk MG .75 2.00
147 Bob Priddy .60 1.50
148 John Mayberry .75 2.00
149 Mike Hershberger .60 1.50
150 Sam McDowell .75 2.00
151 Tommy Davis .75 2.00
152 L.Allen RC/W.Llenas RC .60 1.50
153 Gary Ross .60 1.50
154 Cesar Gutierrez .60 1.50
155 Ken Henderson .60 1.50
156 Bart Johnson .60 1.50
157 Bob Bailey .75 2.00
158 Jerry Reuss .75 2.00
159 Jarvis Tatum .60 1.50
160 Tom Seaver 15.00 40.00
161 Coin Checklist 4.00 10.00
162 Jack Billingham .60 1.50
163 Buck Martinez .75 2.00
164 F.Duffy RC/M.Wilcox RC .75 2.00
165 Cesar Tovar .60 1.50
166 Joe Hoerner .60 1.50
167 Tom Grieve RC .75 2.00
168 Bruce Dal Canton .60 1.50
169 Ed Herrmann .60 1.50
170 Mike Cuellar .75 2.00
171 Bobby Wine .60 1.50
172 Duke Sims .60 1.50
173 Gil Garrido .60 1.50
174 Dave LaRoche RC .60 1.50
175 Jim Hickman .60 1.50
176 B.Montgomery RC/D.Griffin RC .75 2.00
177 Hal McRae .75 2.00
178 Dave Duncan .75 2.00
179 Mike Corkins .60 1.50
180 Al Kaline UER 20.00 50.00
181 Hal Lanier .60 1.50
182 Al Downing .75 2.00
183 Gil Hodges MG 1.50 4.00
184 Stan Bahnsen .60 1.50
185 Julian Javier .60 1.50
186 Bob Spence RC .60 1.50
187 Ted Abernathy .60 1.50
188 B.Valentine RC/M.Strahler RC 6.00 15.00
189 George Mitterwald .60 1.50
190 Bob Tolan .60 1.50
191 Mike Andrews .60 1.50
192 Billy Wilson .60 1.50
193 Bob Grich RC 1.50 4.00
194 Mike Lum .60 1.50
195 Boog Powell ALCS .75 2.00
196 Dave McNally ALCS .75 2.00
197 Jim Palmer ALCS 1.50 4.00
198 Orioles Celebrate ALCS .75 2.00
199 Ty Cline NLCS .75 2.00
200 Bobby Tolan NLCS .75 2.00
201 Ty Cline NLCS .75 2.00
202 Reds Celebrate NLCS .75 2.00
203 Larry Gura RC .75 2.00
204 B.Smith RC/G.Kopacz RC .60 1.50
205 Gerry Moses .60 1.50
206 Checklist 3 4.00 10.00
207 Alan Foster .60 1.50
208 Billy Martin MG 1.50 4.00
209 Steve Renko .60 1.50
210 Rod Carew 12.00 30.00
211 Phil Hennigan RC .60 1.50

212 Rich Hebner .75 2.00
213 Frank Baker RC .60 1.50
214 Al Ferrara .60 1.50
215 Diego Segui .60 1.50
216 R.Cleveland/L.Melendez RC .60 1.50
217 Ed Stroud .60 1.50
218 Tony Cloninger .60 1.50
219 Elrod Hendricks .60 1.50
220 Ron Santo 1.50 4.00
221 Dave Morehead .60 1.50
222 Bob Watson .75 2.00
223 Cecil Upshaw .60 1.50
224 Alan Gallagher RC .60 1.50
225 Gary Peters .60 1.50
226 Bill Russell .75 2.00
227 Floyd Weaver .60 1.50
228 Wayne Garrett .60 1.50
229 Jim Hannan .60 1.50
230 Willie Stargell 20.00 50.00
231 V.Colbert RC/J.Lowenstein RC .75 2.00
232 John Strohmayer RC .60 1.50
233 Larry Bowa .75 2.00
234 Jim Lyttle .60 1.50
235 Nate Colbert .60 1.50
236 Bob Humphreys .60 1.50
237 Cesar Cedeno RC .75 2.00
238 Chuck Dobson .60 1.50
239 Red Schoendienst MG .75 2.00
240 Clyde Wright .60 1.50
241 Dave Nelson .60 1.50
242 Jim Ray .60 1.50
243 Carlos May .60 1.50
244 Bob Tillman .60 1.50
245 Jim Kaat .75 2.00
246 Tony Taylor .60 1.50
247 J.Cram RC/P.Splittorff RC .75 2.00
248 Hoyt Wilhelm 2.50 6.00
249 Chico Salmon .60 1.50
250 Johnny Bench 25.00 60.00
251 Frank Reberger .60 1.50
252 Eddie Leon .60 1.50
253 Bill Sudakis .60 1.50
254 Cal Koonce .60 1.50
255 Bob Robertson .75 2.00
256 Tony Gonzalez .60 1.50
257 Nelson Briles .75 2.00
258 Dick Green .60 1.50
259 Dave Marshall .60 1.50
260 Tommy Harper .75 2.00
261 Darold Knowles .60 1.50
262 J.Williams/D.Robinson RC .60 1.50
263 John Ellis .60 1.50
264 Joe Morgan 15.00 40.00
265 Jim Northrup .75 2.00
266 Bill Stoneman .60 1.50
267 Rich Morales .60 1.50
268 Philadelphia Phillies TC 1.50 4.00
269 Gail Hopkins .60 1.50
270 Rico Carty .75 2.00
271 Bill Zepp .60 1.50
272 Tommy Helms .75 2.00
273 Pete Richert .60 1.50
274 Ron Slocum .60 1.50
275 Vada Pinson .75 2.00
276 M.Davison RC/G.Foster RC 20.00 50.00
277 Gary Waslewski .60 1.50
278 Jerry Grote .75 2.00
279 Lefty Phillips MG .60 1.50
280 Ferguson Jenkins 2.50 6.00
281 Danny Walton .60 1.50
282 Jose Pagan .60 1.50
283 Dick Such .60 1.50
284 Jim Gosger .60 1.50
285 Sal Bando .75 2.00
286 Jerry McNertney .60 1.50
287 Mike Fiore .60 1.50
288 Joe Moeller .60 1.50
289 Chicago White Sox TC 1.50 4.00
290 Tony Oliva 1.50 4.00
291 George Culver .60 1.50
292 Jay Johnstone .75 2.00
293 Pat Corrales .75 2.00
294 Steve Dunning RC .60 1.50
295 Bobby Bonds 1.50 4.00
296 Tom Timmermann .60 1.50
297 Johnny Briggs .60 1.50
298 Jim Nelson RC .60 1.50
299 Ed Kirkpatrick .60 1.50
300 Brooks Robinson 20.00 50.00
301 Earl Wilson .60 1.50
302 Phil Gagliano .60 1.50
303 Lindy McDaniel .75 2.00
304 Ron Brand .60 1.50
305 Reggie Smith .75 2.00
306 Jim Nash .60 1.50
307 Don Wert .60 1.50
308 St. Louis Cardinals TC 1.50 4.00
309 Dick Ellsworth .60 1.50
310 Tommie Agee .75 2.00
311 Lee Stange .60 1.50
312 Harry Walker MG .60 1.50
313 Tom Hall .60 1.50
314 Jeff Torborg .75 2.00
315 Ron Fairly .75 2.00
316 Fred Scherman RC .60 1.50
317 J.Driscoll RC/A.Mangual .60 1.50
318 Rudy May .60 1.50
319 Ty Cline .60 1.50
320 Dave McNally .75 2.00
321 Tom Matchick .60 1.50
322 Jim Beauchamp .60 1.50
323 Billy Champion .60 1.50
324 Graig Nettles .75 2.00
325 Juan Marichal 12.00 30.00
326 Richie Scheinblum .60 1.50
327 Boog Powell WS .75 2.00
328 Don Buford WS .75 2.00
329 Frank Robinson WS 1.50 4.00
330 Reds Stay Alive WS .75 2.00
331 Brooks Robinson WS 2.50 6.00
332 Orioles Celebrate WS .75 2.00
333 Clay Kirby .60 1.50
334 Roberto Pena .60 1.50
335 Jerry Koosman .75 2.00
336 Detroit Tigers TC 1.50 4.00
337 Jesus Alou .60 1.50
338 Gene Tenace .75 2.00
339 Wayne Simpson .60 1.50
340 Rico Petrocelli .75 2.00
341 Steve Garvey RC 40.00 100.00
342 Frank Tepedino .75 2.00
343 E.Acosta RC/M.May RC .75 2.00
344 Ellie Rodriguez .60 1.50
345 Joel Horlen .60 1.50
346 Lum Harris MG .60 1.50
347 Ted Uhlaender .60 1.50
348 Fred Norman .60 1.50
349 Rich Reese .60 1.50
350 Billy Williams 2.50 6.00
351 Jim Shellenback .60 1.50
352 Denny Doyle .60 1.50
353 Carl Taylor .60 1.50
354 Don McMahon .60 1.50
355 Bud Harrelson 1.50 4.00
Nolan Ryan in photo
356 Bob Locker .60 1.50
357 Cincinnati Reds TC 1.50 4.00
358 Danny Cater .60 1.50
359 Ron Reed .60 1.50
360 Jim Fregosi .75 2.00
361 Don Sutton 8.00 20.00
362 M.Adamson/R.Freed .60 1.50
363 Mike Nagy .60 1.50
364 Tommy Dean .60 1.50
365 Bob Johnson .60 1.50
366 Ron Stone .60 1.50
367 Dalton Jones .60 1.50
368 Bob Veale .75 2.00
369 Checklist 4 4.00 10.00
370 Joe Torre 1.50 4.00
371 Jack Hiatt .60 1.50
372 Lew Krausse .60 1.50
373 Tom McCraw .60 1.50
374 Clete Boyer .75 2.00
375 Steve Hargan .60 1.50
376 C.Mashore RC/E.McAnally RC .60 1.50
377 Greg Garrett .60 1.50
378 Tito Fuentes .60 1.50
379 Wayne Granger .60 1.50
380 Ted Williams MG 10.00 25.00
381 Fred Gladding .60 1.50
382 Jake Gibbs .60 1.50
383 Rod Gaspar .60 1.50
384 Rollie Fingers 20.00 50.00
385 Maury Wills 1.50 4.00
386 Boston Red Sox TC .75 2.00
387 Ron Herbel .60 1.50
388 Al Oliver 1.50 4.00
389 Ed Brinkman .60 1.50
390 Glenn Beckert .75 2.00
391 S.Brye RC/C.Nash RC .75 2.00
392 Grant Jackson .60 1.50
393 Merv Rettenmund .75 2.00
394 Clay Carroll 1.00 2.50
395 Roy White 1.50 4.00
396 Dick Schofield 1.00 2.50
397 Alvin Dark MG 1.50 4.00
398 Howie Reed 1.00 2.50
399 Jim French 1.00 2.50
400 Hank Aaron 60.00 150.00
401 Tom Murphy 1.00 2.50
402 Los Angeles Dodgers TC 2.50 6.00
403 Joe Coleman 1.00 2.50
404 B.Harris RC/R.Metzger RC 1.00 2.50
405 Leo Cardenas 1.00 2.50
406 Ray Sadecki 1.00 2.50
407 Joe Rudi 1.50 4.00
408 Rafael Robles 1.00 2.50
409 Don Pavletich 1.00 2.50
410 Ken Holtzman 1.50 4.00
411 George Spriggs 1.00 2.50
412 Jerry Johnson 1.00 2.50
413 Pat Kelly 1.00 2.50
414 Woodie Fryman 1.00 2.50
415 Mike Hegan 1.00 2.50
416 Gene Alley 1.00 2.50
417 Dick Hall 1.00 2.50
418 Adolfo Phillips 1.00 2.50
419 Ron Hansen 1.00 2.50
420 Jim Merritt 1.00 2.50
421 John Stephenson 1.00 2.50
422 Frank Bertaina 1.00 2.50
423 D.Saunders/T.Marting RC 1.00 2.50
424 Roberto Rodriquez 1.00 2.50
425 Doug Rader 1.00 2.50
426 Chris Cannizzaro 1.00 2.50
427 Bernie Allen 1.00 2.50
428 Jim McAndrew 1.00 2.50
429 Chuck Hinton 1.00 2.50
430 Wes Parker 1.50 4.00
431 Tom Burgmeier 1.00 2.50
432 Bob Didier 1.00 2.50
433 Skip Lockwood 1.00 2.50
434 Gary Sutherland 1.00 2.50
435 Jose Cardenal 1.50 4.00
436 Wilbur Wood 1.50 4.00
437 Danny Murtaugh MG 1.50 4.00
438 Mike McCormick 1.50 4.00
439 G.Luzinski RC/S.Reid 8.00 20.00
440 Bert Campaneris 1.50 4.00
441 Milt Pappas 1.50 4.00
442 California Angels TC 1.50 4.00
443 Rich Robertson 1.00 2.50
444 Jimmie Price 1.00 2.50
445 Art Shamsky 1.00 2.50
446 Bobby Bolin 1.00 2.50
447 Cesar Geronimo RC 1.50 4.00
448 Dave Roberts 1.00 2.50
449 Brant Alyea 1.00 2.50
450 Bob Gibson 20.00 50.00
451 Joe Keough 1.00 2.50
452 John Boccabella 1.00 2.50
453 Terry Crowley 1.00 2.50
454 Mike Paul 1.00 2.50
455 Don Kessinger 1.50 4.00
456 Bob Meyer 1.00 2.50
457 Willie Smith 1.00 2.50
458 R.Lolich RC/D.Lemonds RC 1.00 2.50
459 Jim Lefebvre 1.00 2.50
460 Fritz Peterson 1.00 2.50
461 Jim Ray Hart 1.00 2.50
462 Washington Senators TC 2.50 6.00
463 Tom Kelley 1.00 2.50
464 Aurelio Rodriguez 1.00 2.50
465 Tim McCarver 2.50 6.00
466 Ken Berry 1.00 2.50
467 Al Santorini 1.00 2.50
468 Frank Fernandez 1.00 2.50
469 Bob Aspromonte 1.00 2.50
470 Bob Oliver 1.00 2.50
471 Tom Griffin 1.00 2.50
472 Ken Rudolph 1.00 2.50
473 Gary Wagner 1.00 2.50
474 Jim Fairey 1.00 2.50
475 Ron Perranoski 1.00 2.50
476 Dal Maxvill 1.00 2.50
477 Earl Weaver MG 2.50 6.00
478 Bernie Carbo 1.00 2.50
479 Dennis Higgins 1.00 2.50
480 Manny Sanguillen 1.50 4.00
481 Daryl Patterson 1.00 2.50
482 San Diego Padres TC 2.50 6.00
483 Gene Michael 1.00 2.50
484 Don Wilson 1.00 2.50
485 Ken McMullen 1.00 2.50
486 Steve Huntz 1.00 2.50
487 Paul Schaal 1.00 2.50
488 Jerry Stephenson 1.00 2.50
489 Luis Alvarado 1.00 2.50
490 Deron Johnson 1.00 2.50
491 Jim Hardin 1.00 2.50
492 Ken Boswell 1.00 2.50
493 Dave May 1.00 2.50
494 R.Garr/R.Kester 1.50 4.00
495 Felipe Alou 1.50 4.00
496 Woody Woodward 1.00 2.50
497 Horacio Pina RC 1.00 2.50
498 John Kennedy 1.00 2.50
499 Checklist 5 4.00 10.00
500 Jim Perry 1.50 4.00
501 Andy Etchebarren 1.00 2.50
502 Chicago Cubs TC 2.50 6.00
503 Gates Brown 1.50 4.00
504 Ken Wright RC 1.00 2.50
505 Ollie Brown 1.00 2.50
506 Bobby Knoop 1.00 2.50
507 George Stone 1.00 2.50
508 Roger Repoz 1.00 2.50
509 Jim Grant 1.00 2.50
510 Ken Harrelson 1.50 4.00
511 Chris Short w/Rose 1.50 4.00
512 D.Mills RC/M.Garman RC 1.00 2.50
513 Nolan Ryan 60.00 150.00
514 Ron Woods 1.00 2.50
515 Carl Morton 1.00 2.50
516 Ted Kubiak 1.00 2.50
517 Charlie Fox MG RC 1.00 2.50
518 Joe Grzenda 1.00 2.50
519 Willie Crawford 1.00 2.50
520 Tommy John 2.50 6.00
521 Leron Lee 1.00 2.50
522 Minnesota Twins TC 2.50 6.00
523 John Odom 1.00 2.50
524 Mickey Stanley 2.50 6.00
525 Ernie Banks 40.00 100.00
526 Ray Jarvis 1.50 4.00
527 Cleon Jones 2.50 6.00
528 Wally Bunker 1.50 4.00
529 Hernandez/Bucker/Perez RC 2.50 6.00
530 Carl Yastrzemski 25.00 60.00
531 Mike Torrez 1.50 4.00
532 Bill Rigney MG 1.50 4.00
533 Mike Ryan 1.50 4.00
534 Luke Walker 1.50 4.00
535 Curt Flood 2.50 6.00
536 Claude Raymond 1.50 4.00
537 Tom Egan 1.50 4.00
538 Angel Bravo 1.50 4.00
539 Larry Brown 1.50 4.00
540 Larry Dierker 2.50 6.00
541 Bob Burda 1.50 4.00
542 Bob Miller 1.50 4.00
543 New York Yankees TC 4.00 10.00
544 Vida Blue 2.50 6.00
545 Dick Dietz 1.50 4.00
546 John Matias 1.50 4.00
547 Pat Dobson 2.50 6.00
548 Don Mason 1.50 4.00
549 Jim Brewer 2.50 6.00
550 Harmon Killebrew 20.00 50.00
551 Frank Linzy 1.50 4.00
552 Buddy Bradford 1.50 4.00
553 Kevin Collins 1.50 4.00
554 Lowell Palmer 1.50 4.00
555 Walt Williams 1.50 4.00
556 Jim McGlothlin 1.50 4.00
557 Tom Satriano 1.50 4.00
558 Hector Torres 1.50 4.00
559 Cox/Gogolewski/Jones RC 1.50 4.00
560 Rusty Staub 2.50 6.00
561 Syd O'Brien 1.50 4.00
562 Dave Giusti 1.50 4.00
563 San Francisco Giants TC 3.00 8.00
564 Al Fitzmorris 1.50 4.00
565 Jim Wynn 2.50 6.00
566 Tim Cullen 1.50 4.00
567 Walt Alston MG 6.00 15.00
568 Sal Campisi 1.50 4.00
569 Ivan Murrell 1.50 4.00
570 Jim Palmer 10.00 25.00
571 Ted Sizemore 1.50 4.00
572 Jerry Kenney 1.50 4.00
573 Ed Kranepool 2.50 6.00
574 Jim Bunning 3.00 8.00
575 Bill Freehan 2.50 6.00
576 Garrett/Davis/Jestadt RC 1.50 4.00
577 Jim Lonborg 2.50 6.00
578 Ron Hunt 1.50 4.00
579 Marty Pattin 1.50 4.00
580 Tony Perez 20.00 50.00
581 Roger Nelson 1.50 4.00
582 Dave Cash 2.50 6.00
583 Ron Cook RC 1.50 4.00
584 Cleveland Indians TC 3.00 8.00
585 Willie Davis 2.50 6.00
586 Dick Woodson 1.50 4.00
587 Sonny Jackson 1.50 4.00
588 Tom Bradley RC 1.50 4.00
589 Bob Barton 1.50 4.00
590 Alex Johnson 2.50 6.00
591 Jackie Brown RC 1.50 4.00
592 Randy Hundley 2.50 6.00
593 Jack Aker 1.50 4.00
594 Chlupsa/Stinson/Hrabosky RC 2.50 6.00
595 Dave Johnson 2.50 6.00
596 Mike Jorgensen 1.50 4.00
597 Ken Suarez 1.50 4.00
598 Rick Wise 2.50 6.00
599 Norm Cash 2.50 6.00
600 Willie Mays 100.00 250.00
601 Ken Tatum 1.50 4.00
602 Marty Martinez 1.50 4.00
603 Pittsburgh Pirates TC 3.00 8.00
604 John Gelnar 1.50 4.00
605 Orlando Cepeda 6.00 15.00
606 Chuck Taylor 1.50 4.00
607 Paul Ratliff 1.50 4.00
608 Mike Wegener 1.50 4.00
609 Leo Durocher MG 3.00 8.00
610 Amos Otis 2.50 6.00
611 Tom Phoebus 1.50 4.00
612 Camilli/Ford/Mingori RC 1.50 4.00
613 Pedro Borbon 1.50 4.00
614 Billy Cowan 1.50 4.00
615 Mel Stottlemyre 2.50 6.00
616 Larry Hisle 2.50 6.00
617 Clay Dalrymple 1.50 4.00
618 Tug McGraw 2.50 6.00
619A Checklist 6 ERR w/o Copy 4.00 10.00
619B Checklist 6 COR w/Copy 2.50 6.00
620 Frank Howard 2.50 6.00
621 Ron Bryant 1.50 4.00
622 Joe Lahoud 1.50 4.00
623 Pat Jarvis 1.50 4.00
624 Oakland Athletics TC 3.00 8.00
625 Lou Brock 25.00 60.00
626 Freddie Patek 2.50 6.00
627 Steve Hamilton 1.50 4.00
628 John Bateman 1.50 4.00
629 John Hiller 2.50 6.00
630 Roberto Clemente 75.00 200.00
631 Eddie Fisher 1.50 4.00
632 Darrel Chaney 1.50 4.00
633 Brooks/Koegel/Northey RC 1.50 4.00
634 Phil Regan 1.50 4.00
635 Bobby Murcer 2.50 6.00
636 Denny Lemaster 1.50 4.00
637 Dave Bristol MG 1.50 4.00
638 Stan Williams 1.50 4.00
639 Tom Haller 1.50 4.00
640 Frank Robinson 15.00 40.00
641 New York Mets TC 6.00 15.00
642 Jim Roland 1.50 4.00
643 Rick Reichardt 1.50 4.00
644 Jim Stewart SP 5.00 12.00
645 Jim Maloney SP 6.00 15.00
646 Bobby Floyd SP 5.00 12.00
647 Juan Pizarro 3.00 8.00
648 Folkers/Martinez/Matlack SP RC 10.00 25.00
649 Sparky Lyle SP 15.00 40.00
650 Rich Allen SP 40.00 100.00
651 Jerry Robertson SP 5.00 12.00
652 Atlanta Braves TC 3.00 8.00
653 Russ Snyder SP 5.00 12.00
654 Don Shaw SP 5.00 12.00
655 Mike Epstein SP 5.00 12.00
656 Gerry Nyman SP 5.00 12.00
657 Jose Azcue 3.00 8.00
658 Paul Lindblad SP 5.00 12.00
659 Byron Browne SP 5.00 12.00
660 Ray Culp 3.00 8.00
661 Chuck Tanner MG SP 6.00 15.00
662 Mike Hedlund SP 5.00 12.00
663 Marv Staehle 3.00 8.00
664 Reynolds/Reynolds/Reynolds SP RC 5.00 12.00
665 Ron Swoboda SP 6.00 15.00
666 Gene Brabender SP 5.00 12.00
667 Pete Ward 3.00 8.00
668 Gary Neibauer 3.00 8.00
669 Ike Brown SP 5.00 12.00
670 Bill Hands 3.00 8.00
671 Bill Voss SP 5.00 12.00
672 Ed Crosby SP RC 5.00 12.00
673 Gerry Janeski SP RC 5.00 12.00
674 Montreal Expos TC 5.00 12.00
675 Dave Boswell 3.00 8.00
676 Tommie Reynolds 3.00 8.00
677 Jack DiLauro SP 5.00 12.00
678 George Thomas 3.00 8.00
679 Don O'Riley 3.00 8.00
680 Don Mincher SP 5.00 12.00
681 Bill Butler 3.00 8.00
682 Terry Harmon 3.00 8.00
683 Bill Burbach SP 5.00 12.00
684 Curt Motton 3.00 8.00
685 Moe Drabowsky 3.00 8.00
686 Chico Ruiz SP 5.00 12.00
687 Ron Taylor SP 5.00 12.00
688 S.Anderson MG SP 12.00 30.00
689 Frank Baker 3.00 8.00
690 Bob Moose 3.00 8.00
691 Bobby Heise 3.00 8.00
692 Haydel/Moret/Twitchell SP RC 5.00 12.00
693 Jose Pena SP 5.00 12.00
694 Rick Renick SP 5.00 12.00
695 Joe Niekro 5.00 12.00
696 Jerry Morales 3.00 8.00
697 Rickey Clark SP 5.00 12.00
698 Milwaukee Brewers TC SP 8.00 20.00
699 Jim Britton 3.00 8.00
700 Boog Powell SP 20.00 50.00
701 Bob Garibaldi 3.00 8.00
702 Milt Ramirez RC 3.00 8.00
703 Mike Kekich 3.00 8.00
704 J.C. Martin SP 5.00 12.00
705 Dick Selma SP 5.00 12.00
706 Joe Foy SP 5.00 12.00
707 Fred Lasher 3.00 8.00
708 Russ Nagelson SP 5.00 12.00
709 Baker/Baylor/Pac SP RC 50.00 120.00
710 Sonny Siebert 3.00 8.00
711 Larry Stahl SP 5.00 12.00
712 Jose Martinez 3.00 8.00
713 Mike Marshall SP 6.00 15.00
714 Dick Williams MG SP 6.00 15.00
715 Horace Clarke SP 6.00 15.00
716 Dave Leonhard 3.00 8.00
717 Tommie Aaron SP 5.00 12.00
718 Billy Wynne 3.00 8.00
719 Jerry May SP 5.00 12.00
720 Matty Alou 5.00 12.00
721 John Morris 3.00 8.00
722 Houston Astros TC SP 8.00 20.00
723 Vicente Romo SP 5.00 12.00
724 Tom Tischinski SP 5.00 12.00
725 Gary Gentry SP 5.00 12.00
726 Paul Popovich 3.00 8.00
727 Ray Lamb SP 5.00 12.00
728 Redmond/Lampard/Williams RC 3.00 8.00
729 Dick Billings RC 3.00 8.00
730 Jim Rooker 3.00 8.00
731 Jim Qualls SP 5.00 12.00
732 Bob Reed 3.00 8.00
733 Lee Maye SP 5.00 12.00
734 Rob Gardner SP 5.00 12.00
735 Mike Shannon SP 8.00 20.00
736 Mel Queen SP 5.00 12.00
737 Preston Gomez MG SP 5.00 12.00
738 Russ Gibson SP 5.00 12.00
739 Barry Lersch SP 5.00 12.00
740 Luis Aparicio SP 10.00 25.00
741 Skip Guinn 3.00 8.00
742 Kansas City Royals TC 5.00 12.00
743 John O'Donoghue SP 5.00 12.00
744 Chuck Manuel SP 5.00 12.00
745 Sandy Alomar SP 5.00 12.00
746 Andy Kosco 3.00 8.00
747 Severinsen/Spinks/Moore RC 3.00 8.00
748 John Purdin SP 5.00 12.00
749 Ken Szotkiewicz RC 3.00 8.00
750 Denny McLain SP 10.00 25.00
751 Al Weis SP 8.00 20.00
752 Dick Drago 5.00 12.00

1971 Topps Coins

COMPLETE SET (153) 200.00 400.00
1 Clarence Gaston 1.00 2.50
2 Dave Johnson 1.00 2.50
3 Jim Bunning 2.00 5.00
4 Jim Spencer .75 2.00
5 Felix Millan .75 2.00
6 Gerry Moses .75 2.00
7 Ferguson Jenkins 2.00 5.00
8 Felipe Alou 1.00 2.50
9 Jim McGlothlin .75 2.00
10 Dick McAuliffe .75 2.00
11 Joe Torre 2.00 5.00
12 Jim Perry 1.00 2.50
13 Bobby Bonds 1.25 3.00
14 Danny Cater .75 2.00
15 Bill Mazeroski 2.00 5.00
16 Luis Aparicio 2.00 5.00
17 Doug Rader .75 2.00
18 Vada Pinson 1.25 3.00
19 John Bateman .75 2.00
20 Lew Krausse .75 2.00
21 Billy Grabarkewitz 1.00 2.50
22 Frank Howard 1.25 3.00
23 Jerry Koosman 1.25 3.00
24 Rod Carew 2.00 5.00
25 Al Ferrara .75 2.00
26 Dave McNally 1.00 2.50
27 Jim Hickman .75 2.00
28 Sandy Alomar 1.00 2.50
29 Lee May 1.00 2.50
30 Rico Petrocelli 1.00 2.50
31 Don Money .75 2.00
32 Jim Rooker .75 2.00
33 Dick Dietz .75 2.00
34 Roy White 1.00 2.50
35 Carl Morton .75 2.00
36 Walt Williams .75 2.00
37 Phil Niekro 2.00 5.00
38 Bill Freehan 1.00 2.50
39 Julian Javier .75 2.00
40 Rick Monday 1.00 2.50
41 Don Wilson .75 2.00
42 Ray Fosse 1.00 2.50
43 Art Shamsky .75 2.00
44 Ted Savage .75 2.00
45 Claude Osteen .75 2.00
46 Ed Brinkman .75 2.00
47 Matty Alou 1.00 2.50
48 Bob Oliver .75 2.00
49 Danny Coombs .75 2.00
50 Frank Robinson 2.00 5.00
51 Randy Hundley .75 2.00
52 Cesar Tovar 1.00 2.50
53 Wayne Simpson .75 2.00
54 Bobby Murcer 1.25 3.00
55 Carl Taylor .75 2.00
56 Tommy John 1.00 2.50
57 Willie McCovey 2.00 5.00
58 Carl Yastrzemski 5.00 12.00
59 Bob Bailey .75 2.00
60 Clyde Wright .75 2.00
61 Orlando Cepeda 2.00 5.00
62 Al Kaline 4.00 10.00
63 Bob Gibson 2.00 5.00
64 Bert Campaneris .75 2.00
65 Ted Sizemore .75 2.00
66 Duke Sims .75 2.00
67 Bud Harrelson 1.25 3.00
68 Gerald McNertney .75 2.00
69 Jim Wynn 1.00 2.50
70 Dick Bosman 1.00 2.50
71 Roberto Clemente 12.50 30.00
72 Rich Reese .75 2.00
73 Gaylord Perry 2.00 5.00
74 Boog Powell 1.00 2.50
75 Billy Williams 2.00 5.00
76 Bill Melton .75 2.00
77 Nate Colbert .75 2.00
78 Reggie Smith 1.00 2.50
79 Deron Johnson .75 2.00
80 Jim Hunter 2.00 5.00
81 Bobby Tolan 1.00 2.50
82 Jim Northrup .75 2.00
83 Ron Fairly 1.00 2.50
84 Alex Johnson .75 2.00
85 Pat Jarvis .75 2.00
86 Sam McDowell 1.00 2.50
87 Lou Brock 2.00 5.00
88 Danny Walton .75 2.00
89 Denis Menke .75 2.00
90 Jim Palmer 2.00 5.00
91 Tommy Agee 1.00 2.50
92 Duane Josephson .75 2.00
93 Willie Davis 1.00 2.50
94 Mel Stottlemyre 1.00 2.50
95 Ron Santo 1.00 2.50
96 Amos Otis 1.00 2.50
97 Ken Henderson .75 2.00
98 George Scott 1.00 2.50
99 Dock Ellis 1.00 2.50
100 Harmon Killebrew 4.00 10.00
101 Pete Rose 8.00 20.00
102 Rick Reichardt .75 2.00
103 Cleon Jones .75 2.00
104 Ron Perranoski .75 2.00
105 Tony Perez 2.00 5.00
106 Mickey Lolich 1.00 2.50
107 Tim McCarver 1.00 2.50
108 Reggie Jackson 6.00 15.00
109 Chris Cannizzaro .75 2.00
110 Steve Hargan .75 2.00
111 Rusty Staub 1.00 2.50
112 Andy Messersmith 1.00 2.50
113 Rico Carty 1.00 2.50
114 Brooks Robinson 4.00 10.00
115 Steve Carlton 2.00 5.00
116 Mike Hegan .75 2.00
117 Joe Morgan 2.00 5.00
118 Thurman Munson 5.00 12.00
119 Don Kessinger .75 2.00
120 Joel Horlen .75 2.00
121 Wes Parker 1.00 2.50
122 Sonny Siebert .75 2.00
123 Willie Stargell 2.00 5.00
124 Ellie Rodriguez .75 2.00
125 Juan Marichal 2.00 5.00
126 Mike Epstein .75 2.00
127 Tom Seaver 5.00 12.00
128 Tony Oliva 1.00 2.50
129 Jim Merritt .75 2.00
130 Willie Horton 1.00 2.50
131 Rick Wise .75 2.00
132 Sal Bando 1.00 2.50
133 Ollie Brown .75 2.00
134 Ken Harrelson 1.00 2.50
135 Mack Jones .75 2.00
136 Jim Fregosi 1.00 2.50
137 Hank Aaron 8.00 20.00

1971 Topps Coins

This full-color set of 153 coins, which were inserted into packs, contains the photo of the player surrounded by a colored band, which contains the player's name, his team, his position and several stars. The backs contain the coin number, short biographical data and the line "Collect the entire set of 153 coins." The set was evidently produced in three groups of 51 as coins 1-51 have brass backs, coins 52-102 have chrome backs and coins 103-153 have blue backs. In fact it has been verified that the coins were printed in three sheets of 51 coins comprised of three rows of 17 coins. Each coin measures approximately 1 1/2" in diameter.

138 Fritz Peterson .75 2.00
139 Joe Hague .75 2.00
140 Tommy Harper .75 2.00
141 Larry Dierker .75 2.00
142 Tony Conigliaro 1.00 2.50
143 Glenn Beckert .75 2.00
144 Carlos May .75 2.00
145 Don Sutton 2.00 5.00
146 Paul Casanova .75 2.00
147 Bob Moose .75 2.00
148 Chico Cardenas .75 2.00
149 Johnny Bench 6.00 15.00
150 Mike Cuellar 1.00 2.50
151 Donn Clendenon .75 2.00
152 Lou Piniella 1.00 2.50
153 Willie Mays 10.00 25.00

1971 Topps Scratchoffs

COMPLETE SET (24) 15.00 40.00
1 Hank Aaron 3.00 8.00
2 Rich Allen .60 1.50
3 Luis Aparicio 1.50 4.00
4 Sal Bando .40 1.00
5 Glenn Beckert .40 1.00
6 Dick Bosman .40 1.00
7 Nate Colbert .40 1.00
8 Mike Hegan .40 1.00
9 Mack Jones .40 1.00
10 Al Kaline 2.00 5.00
11 Harmon Killebrew 2.00 5.00
12 Juan Marichal 1.50 4.00
13 Tim McCarver .75 2.00
14 Sam McDowell .50 1.25
15 Claude Osteen .40 1.00
16 Tony Perez 1.25 3.00
17 Lou Piniella .60 1.50
18 Boog Powell .60 1.50
19 Tom Seaver 2.50 6.00
20 Jim Spencer .40 1.00
21 Willie Stargell 2.00 5.00
22 Mel Stottlemyre .50 1.25
23 Jim Wynn .50 1.25
24 Carl Yastrzemski 2.00 5.00

1971 Topps Greatest Moments

COMPLETE SET (55) 750.00 1500.00
COMMON CARD (1-55) 8.00 20.00
COMMON DP 3.00 8.00
1 Thurman Munson DP 15.00 40.00
2 Hoyt Wilhelm 10.00 25.00
3 Rico Carty 8.00 20.00
4 Carl Morton DP 3.00 8.00
5 Sal Bando DP 4.00 10.00
6 Bert Campaneris DP 4.00 10.00
7 Jim Kaat 10.00 25.00
8 Harmon Killebrew 40.00 80.00
9 Brooks Robinson 40.00 80.00
10 Jim Perry 8.00 20.00
11 Tony Oliva 12.50 30.00
12 Vada Pinson 10.00 25.00
13 Johnny Bench 60.00 120.00
14 Tony Perez 12.50 30.00
15 Pete Rose DP 40.00 80.00
16 Jim Fregosi DP 4.00 10.00
17 Alex Johnson DP 3.00 8.00
18 Clyde Wright DP 3.00 8.00
19 Al Kaline DP 15.00 40.00
20 Denny McLain 12.50 30.00
21 Jim Northrup 8.00 20.00
22 Bill Freehan 8.00 20.00
23 Mickey Lolich 10.00 25.00
24 Bob Gibson DP 12.50 30.00
25 Tim McCarver DP 3.00 8.00
26 Orlando Cepeda DP 8.00 20.00
27 Lou Brock DP 12.50 30.00
28 Nate Colbert DP 3.00 8.00
29 Maury Wills 12.50 30.00
30 Wes Parker 8.00 20.00
31 Jim Wynn 10.00 25.00
32 Larry Dierker 10.00 25.00
33 Bill Melton 8.00 20.00
34 Joe Morgan 12.50 30.00
35 Rusty Staub 10.00 25.00
36 Ernie Banks DP 15.00 40.00
37 Billy Williams 12.50 30.00
38 Lou Piniella 10.00 25.00
39 Rico Petrocelli DP 4.00 10.00
40 Carl Yastrzemski DP 20.00 50.00
41 Willie Mays DP 50.00 100.00
42 Tommy Harper 8.00 20.00
43 Jim Bunning DP 4.00 10.00
44 Fritz Peterson 10.00 25.00
45 Roy White 10.00 25.00
46 Bobby Murcer 12.50 30.00
47 Reggie Jackson 100.00 200.00
48 Frank Howard 10.00 25.00
49 Dick Bosman 8.00 20.00
50 Sam McDowell DP 4.00 10.00
51 Luis Aparicio DP 4.00 10.00
52 Willie McCovey DP 12.50 30.00
53 Joe Pepitone 10.00 25.00
54 Jerry Grote 10.00 25.00
55 Bud Harrelson 8.00 20.00

1971 Topps Super

The cards in this 63-card set measure 3 1/8" by 5 1/4". The obverse format of the Topps Super set of 1971 is identical to that of the 1970 set, that is, a borderless color photograph with a facsimile autograph printed on it. The backs are enlargements of the respective player's cards of the 1971 regular baseball issue. There are no reported scarcities in the set. Just as in 1970, this set was issued in three-card wax packs.

COMPLETE SET (63) 125.00 250.00
WRAPPER (10-CENT)
1 Reggie Smith .75 2.00
2 Gaylord Perry 1.50 4.00
3 Ted Savage .60 1.50
4 Donn Clendenon .60 1.50
5 Boog Powell 1.00 2.50
6 Tony Perez 1.50 4.00
7 Dick Bosman .60 1.50
8 Alex Johnson .60 1.50
9 Rusty Staub 1.00 2.50
10 Mel Stottlemyre 1.00 2.50
11 Tony Oliva 1.00 2.50
12 Bill Freehan .75 2.00
13 Fritz Peterson .60 1.50
14 Wes Parker .75 2.00
15 Cesar Cedeno .75 2.00
16 Sam McDowell .75 2.00
17 Frank Howard .75 2.00
18 Dave McNally .75 2.00
19 Rico Petrocelli .75 2.00
20 Pete Rose 10.00 25.00
21 Luke Walker .60 1.50
22 Nate Colbert .60 1.50
23 Luis Aparicio 1.50 4.00
24 Jim Perry .75 2.00
25 Lou Brock 2.00 5.00
26 Roy White .75 2.00
27 Claude Osteen .60 1.50
28 Carl Morton .75 2.00
29 Rico Carty .75 2.00
30 Larry Dierker .60 1.50
31 Bert Campaneris .75 2.00
32 Johnny Bench 6.00 15.00
33 Felix Millan .60 1.50
34 Tim McCarver 1.00 2.50
35 Ron Santo 1.00 2.50
36 Tommie Agee .75 2.00
37 Roberto Clemente 12.50 30.00
38 Reggie Jackson 6.00 15.00
39 Clyde Wright .60 1.50
40 Rich Allen 1.00 2.50
41 Curt Flood .75 2.00
42 Ferguson Jenkins 1.50 4.00
43 Willie Stargell 1.50 4.00
44 Hank Aaron 20.00 50.00
45 Amos Otis .75 2.00
46 Willie McCovey 2.00 5.00
47 Bill Melton .60 1.50
48 Bob Gibson 2.00 5.00
49 Carl Yastrzemski 4.00 10.00
50 Glenn Beckert .60 1.50
51 Ray Fosse .60 1.50
52 Cito Gaston .60 1.50
53 Tom Seaver 4.00 10.00
54 Al Kaline 3.00 8.00
55 Jim Northrup .75 2.00
56 Willie Mays 8.00 20.00
57 Sal Bando .75 2.00
58 Deron Johnson .60 1.50
59 Brooks Robinson 3.00 8.00
60 Harmon Killebrew 2.00 5.00
61 Joe Torre 1.50 4.00
62 Lou Piniella 1.00 2.50
63 Tommy Harper .60 1.50

1971 Topps Tattoos

There are 16 different sheets (3 1/2" X 14 1/4") of baseball tattoos issued by Topps in 1971. Each contains two distinct sizes (1 3/4" by 2 3/8" and 1 3/16" by 1 3/4") of tattoos; those of players feature flesh-tone faces on red or yellow backgrounds; those of baseball figures, facsimile autographs (these are denoted by FAC in the checklist) and team pennants are one-half the player tattoo size. The "Baseball Tattoos" logo panel at the top of each sheet contains the sheet number; the sheet number is given (with an S prefix) in the checklist below after the name. The small baseball figures are not priced in the checklist. The complete tattoo panel prices can be figured as the sum of the individual (player, team and autograph) tattoos.

COMPLETE SET (134) 150.00 300.00
1 Sal Bando S1 .50 1.25
2 Dick Bosman S1 .40 1.00
3 Nate Colbert S1 .40 1.00
4 Cleon Jones S1 .40 1.00
5 Juan Marichal S1 2.00 5.00
6 Brooks Robinson S1 3.00 8.00
7 Brooks Robinson FAC S1 .75 2.00
8 Montreal Expos S1 .40 1.00
9 San Fran. Giants S1 .40 1.00
10 Glenn Beckert S2 .40 1.00

11 Tommy Harper S2 .40 1.00
12 Ken Henderson S2 .40 1.00
13 Carl Yastrzemski S2 3.00 8.00
14 Carl Yastrzemski FAC S2 .75 2.00
15 Boston Red Sox S2 .40 1.00
16 New York Mets S2 .40 1.00
17 Orlando Cepeda S3 .75 2.00
18 Jim Fregosi S3 .50 1.25
19 Jim Fregosi FAC S3 .40 1.00
20 Randy Hundley S3 .40 1.00
21 Reggie Jackson S3 4.00 10.00
22 Jerry Koosman S3 .60 1.50
23 Jim Palmer S3 2.00 5.00
24 Phila. Phillies S3 .40 1.00
25 New York Yankees S3 .50 1.25
26 Dick Dietz S4 .40 1.00
27 Clarence Gaston S4 .40 1.00
28 Dave Johnson S4 .60 1.50
29 Sam McDowell S4 .50 1.25
30 Sam McDowell FAC S4 .40 1.00
31 Gary Nolan S4 .40 1.00
32 Amos Otis S4 .50 1.25
33 Kansas City Royals S4 .40 1.00
34 Oakland A's S4 .40 1.00
35 Billy Grabarkewitz S5 .40 1.00
36 Al Kaline S5 3.00 8.00
37 Al Kaline FAC S5 .60 1.50
38 Lee May S5 .50 1.25
39 Tom Murphy S5 .40 1.00
40 Vada Pinson S5 .60 1.50
41 Manny Sanguillen S5 .40 1.00
42 Atlanta Braves S5 .40 1.00
43 Los Angeles Dodgers S5 .40 1.00
44 Luis Aparicio S6 2.00 5.00
45 Paul Blair S6 .40 1.00
46 Chris Cannizzaro S6 .40 1.00
47 Donn Clendenon S6 .40 1.00
48 Larry Dierker S6 .40 1.00
49 Harmon Killebrew S6 2.00 5.00
50 Harmon Killebrew FAC S6 .60 1.50
51 Chicago Cubs S6 .40 1.00
52 Cincinnati Reds S6 .40 1.00
53 Rich Allen S7 .75 2.00
54 Bert Campaneris S7 .50 1.25
55 Don Money S7 .40 1.00
56 Boog Powell S7 .75 2.00
57 Boog Powell FAC S7 .50 1.25
58 Ted Savage S7 .40 1.00
59 Rusty Staub S7 .60 1.50
60 Cleveland Indians S7 .40 1.00
61 Milwaukee Brewers S7 .40 1.00
62 Leo Cardenas S8 .40 1.00
63 Bill Hands S8 .40 1.00
64 Frank Howard S8 .60 1.50
65 Frank Howard FAC S8 .50 1.25
66 Wes Parker S8 .40 1.00
67 Reggie Smith S8 .50 1.25
68 Willie Stargell S8 2.00 5.00
69 Chicago White Sox S8 .40 1.00
70 San Diego Padres S8 .40 1.00
71 Hank Aaron S9 5.00 12.00
72 Hank Aaron FAC S9 .75 2.00
73 Tommy Agee S9 .40 1.00
74 Jim Hunter S9 2.00 5.00
75 Dick McAuliffe S9 .40 1.00
76 Tony Perez S9 1.50 4.00
77 Lou Piniella S9 .60 1.50
78 Detroit Tigers S9 .40 1.00
79 Roberto Clemente S10 8.00 20.00
80 Tony Conigliaro S10 .50 1.25
81 Fergie Jenkins S10 2.00 5.00
82 Fergie Jenkins FAC S10 .60 1.50
83 Thurman Munson S10 2.50 6.00
84 Gary Peters S10 .40 1.00
85 Joe Torre S10 .60 1.50
86 Baltimore Orioles S10 .40 1.00
87 Johnny Bench S11 3.00 8.00
88 Johnny Bench FAC S11 .60 1.50
89 Rico Carty S11 .50 1.25
90 Bill Mazeroski S11 1.50 4.00
91 Bob Oliver S11 .40 1.00
92 Rico Petrocelli S11 .50 1.25
93 Frank Robinson S11 2.50 6.00
94 Washington Senators S11 .40 1.00
95 Bill Freehan S12 .50 1.25
96 Dave McNally S12 .40 1.00
97 Felix Millan S12 .40 1.00
98 Mel Stottlemyre S12 .50 1.25
99 Bob Tolan S12 .40 1.00
100 Billy Williams S12 2.00 5.00
101 Billy Williams FAC S12 .60 1.50
102 Houston Astros S12 .40 1.00
103 Ray Culp S13 .40 1.00
104 Bud Harrelson S13 .40 1.00
105 Mickey Lolich S13 .60 1.50
106 Willie McCovey S13 2.00 5.00
107 Willie McCovey FAC S13 .60 1.50
108 Ron Santo S13 .75 2.00
109 Roy White S13 .50 1.25
110 Pittsburgh Pirates S13 .40 1.00
111 Bill Melton S14 .40 1.00
112 Jim Perry S14 .50 1.25
113 Pete Rose S14 5.00 12.00
114 Tom Seaver S14 4.00 10.00
115 Tom Seaver FAC S14 .75 2.00
116 Maury Wills S14 .60 1.50
117 Clyde Wright S14 .40 1.00
118 Minnesota Twins S14 .40 1.00
119 Rod Carew S15 3.00 8.00
120 Bob Gibson S15 3.00 8.00
121 Bob Gibson FAC S15 .60 1.50
122 Alex Johnson S15 .40 1.00
123 Don Kessinger S15 .40 1.00
124 Jim Merritt S15 .40 1.00
125 Rick Monday S15 .40 1.00
126 St. Louis Cardinals S15 .40 1.00
127 Larry Bowa S16 .50 1.25
128 Mike Cuellar S16 .50 1.25
129 Ray Fosse S16 .40 1.00
130 Willie Mays S16 6.00 15.00
131 Willie Mays FAC S16 .75 2.00
132 Carl Morton S16 .40 1.00
133 Tony Oliva S16 1.25 3.00
134 California Angels S16 .40 1.00

1972 Topps

The cards in this 787-card set measure 2 1/2" by 3 1/2". The 1972 Topps set contained the most cards ever for a Topps set to that point in time. Features appearing for the first time were "Boyhood Photos" (341-346/491-498), Awards and Trophy cards (621-626), "In Action" (distributed throughout the set), and "Traded Cards" (751-757). Other subsets included League Leaders (85-96), Playoffs cards (221-222), and World Series cards (223-230). The curved lines of the color picture are a departure from the rectangular designs of other years. There is a series of intermediate scarcity (526-656) and the usual high numbers (657-787). The backs of cards 692, 694, 696, 700, 706 and 710 form a picture back of Tom Seaver. The backs of cards 698, 702, 704, 708, 712, 714 form a picture back of Tony Oliva. As in previous years, cards were issued in a variety of ways including ten-card wax packs which cost a dime, 28-card cello packs which cost a quarter and 54-card rack packs which cost 39 cents. The 10 cents wax packs were issued 24 packs to a box while the cello packs were also issued 24 packs to a box. Rookie Cards in this set include Ron Cey and Carlton Fisk.

COMPLETE SET (787) 1250.00 3000.00
COMMON CARD (1-132) .25 .60
COMMON CARD (133-263) .40 1.00
COMMON CARD (264-394) .50 1.25
COMMON CARD (395-525) .60 1.50
COMMON CARD (526-656) 1.50 4.00
COMMON CARD (657-787) 5.00 12.00
WRAPPER (10-CENT) 6.00 15.00
1 Pittsburgh Pirates TC 3.00 8.00
2 Ray Culp .25 .60
3 Bob Tolan .25 .60
4 Checklist 1-132 2.50 6.00
5 John Bateman .25 .60
6 Fred Scherman .25 .60
7 Enzo Hernandez .25 .60
8 Ron Swoboda .50 1.25
9 Stan Williams .25 .60
10 Amos Otis .50 1.25
11 Bobby Valentine .50 1.25
12 Jose Cardenal .25 .60
13 Joe Grzenda .25 .60
14 Koegel/Anderson/Twitchell RC .25 .60
15 Walt Williams .25 .60
16 Mike Jorgensen .25 .60
17 Dave Duncan .50 1.25
18A Juan Pizarro Yellow .25 .60
18B Juan Pizarro Green 2.00 5.00
19 Billy Cowan .25 .60
20 Don Wilson .25 .60
21 Atlanta Braves TC .60 1.50
22 Rob Gardner .25 .60
23 Ted Kubiak .25 .60
24 Ted Ford .25 .60
25 Bill Singer .25 .60
26 Andy Etchebarren .25 .60
27 Bob Johnson .25 .60
28 Gebhard/Brye Haydel RC .25 .60
29A Bill Bonham Yellow RC .25 .60
29B Bill Bonham Green 2.00 5.00
30 Rico Petrocelli .50 1.25
31 Cleon Jones .50 1.25
32 Cleon Jones IA .25 .60
33 Billy Martin MG 1.50 4.00
34 Billy Martin IA 1.00 2.50
35 Jerry Johnson .25 .60
36 Jerry Johnson IA .25 .60
37 Carl Yastrzemski 10.00 25.00
38 Carl Yastrzemski IA 6.00 15.00
39 Bob Barton .25 .60
40 Bob Barton IA .25 .60
41 Tommy Davis .50 1.25
42 Tommy Davis IA .50 1.25
43 Rick Wise .50 1.25
44 Rick Wise IA .25 .60
45A Glenn Beckert Yellow .50 1.25
45B Glenn Beckert Green 2.00 5.00
46 Glenn Beckert IA .25 .60
47 John Ellis .25 .60
48 John Ellis IA .25 .60
49 Willie Mays 20.00 50.00
50 Willie Mays IA 10.00 25.00
51 Harmon Killebrew 3.00 8.00
52 Harmon Killebrew IA 1.50 4.00
53 Bud Harrelson .50 1.25
54 Bud Harrelson IA .25 .60
55 Clyde Wright .25 .60
56 Rich Chiles RC .25 .60
57 Bob Oliver .25 .60
58 Ernie McAnally .25 .60
59 Fred Stanley RC .25 .60
60 Manny Sanguillen .50 1.25
61 Hooten/Hisler/Stephenson RC .50 1.25
62 Angel Mangual .25 .60
63 Duke Sims .25 .60
64 Pete Broberg RC .25 .60
65 Cesar Cedeno .50 1.25
66 Ray Corbin RC .25 .60
67 Red Schoendienst MG 1.00 2.50
68 Jim York RC .25 .60
69 Roger Freed .25 .60
70 Mike Cuellar .50 1.25
71 California Angels TC .60 1.50
72 Bruce Kison RC .25 .60
73 Steve Huntz .25 .60
74 Cecil Upshaw .25 .60
75 Bert Campaneris .50 1.25
76 Don Carrithers RC .25 .60
77 Ron Theobald RC .25 .60
78 Steve Arlin RC .25 .60
79 C.Fisk RC/C.Cooper RC 30.00 80.00
80 Tony Perez 1.50 4.00
81 Mike Hedlund .25 .60
82 Ron Woods .25 .60
83 Dalton Jones .25 .60
84 Vince Colbert .25 .60
85 Torre/Garr/Beckert LL 1.00 2.50
86 Oliva/Murcer/Rett LL 1.00 2.50
87 Torre/Stargell/Aaron LL 5.00 12.00
88 Killebrew/F.Rob/Smith LL 1.50 4.00
89 Stargell/Aaron/May LL 4.00 10.00
90 Melton/Cash/Jackson LL 1.00 2.50
91 Seaver/Roberts/Wilson LL 1.00 2.50
92 Blue/Wood/Palmer LL 1.00 2.50
93 Jenkins/Carlton/Seaver LL 1.50 4.00
94 Lolich/Blue/Wood LL 1.00 2.50
95 Seaver/Jenkins/Stone LL 1.50 4.00
96 Lolich/Blue/Coleman LL 1.00 2.50
97 Tom Kelley .25 .60
98 Chuck Tanner MG .50 1.25
99 Ross Grimsley RC .25 .60
100 Frank Robinson 3.00 8.00
101 Grief/Richard/Busse RC 1.00 2.50
102 Lloyd Allen .25 .60
103 Checklist 133-263 2.50 6.00
104 Toby Harrah RC .50 1.25
105 Gary Gentry .25 .60
106 Milwaukee Brewers TC .60 1.50
107 Jose Cruz RC .50 1.25
108 Gary Waslewski .25 .60
109 Jerry May .25 .60
110 Ron Hunt .25 .60
111 Jim Grant .25 .60
112 Greg Luzinski .50 1.25
113 Rogelio Moret .25 .60
114 Bill Buckner .50 1.25
115 Jim Fregosi .50 1.25
116 Ed Farmer RC .25 .60
117A Cleo James Yellow RC .25 .60
117B Cleo James Green 2.00 5.00
118 Skip Lockwood .25 .60
119 Marty Perez .25 .60
120 Bill Freehan .50 1.25
121 Ed Sprague .25 .60
122 Larry Biittner RC .25 .60
123 Ed Acosta .25 .60
124 Closter/Torres/Hambright RC .25 .60
125 Dave Cash .50 1.25
126 Bart Johnson .25 .60
127 Duffy Dyer .25 .60
128 Eddie Watt .25 .60
129 Charlie Fox MG .25 .60
130 Bob Gibson 8.00 20.00
131 Jim Nettles .25 .60
132 Joe Morgan 2.50 6.00
133 Joe Keough .40 1.00
134 Carl Morton .40 1.00
135 Vada Pinson .75 2.00
136 Darrel Chaney .40 1.00
137 Dick Williams MG .75 2.00
138 Mike Kekich .40 1.00
139 Tim McCarver .75 2.00
140 Pat Dobson .75 2.00
141 Capra/Stanton/Matlack RC .75 2.00
142 Chris Chambliss RC 1.50 4.00
143 Garry Jestadt .40 1.00
144 Marty Pattin .40 1.00
145 Don Kessinger .75 2.00
146 Steve Kealey .40 1.00
147 Dave Kingman RC 6.00 15.00
148 Dick Billings .40 1.00
149 Gary Neibauer .40 1.00
150 Norm Cash .75 2.00
151 Jim Brewer .40 1.00
152 Gene Clines .40 1.00
153 Rick Auerbach RC .40 1.00
154 Ted Simmons 1.50 4.00
155 Larry Dierker .40 1.00
156 Minnesota Twins TC .75 2.00
157 Don Gullett .40 1.00
158 Jerry Kenney .40 1.00
159 John Boccabella .40 1.00
160 Andy Messersmith .75 2.00
161 Brock Davis .40 1.00
162 Bell/Porter/Reynolds RC .75 2.00
163 Tug McGraw 1.50 4.00
164 Tug McGraw IA .75 2.00
165 Chris Speier RC .75 2.00
166 Chris Speier IA .40 1.00
167 Deron Johnson .40 1.00
168 Deron Johnson IA .40 1.00
169 Vida Blue 1.50 4.00
170 Vida Blue IA .75 2.00
171 Darrell Evans 1.50 4.00
172 Darrell Evans IA .75 2.00
173 Clay Kirby .40 1.00
174 Clay Kirby IA .40 1.00
175 Tom Haller .40 1.00
176 Tom Haller IA .40 1.00
177 Paul Schaal .40 1.00
178 Paul Schaal IA .40 1.00
179 Dock Ellis .40 1.00
180 Dock Ellis IA .40 1.00
181 Ed Kranepool .75 2.00
182 Ed Kranepool IA .40 1.00
183 Bill Melton .40 1.00
184 Bill Melton IA .40 1.00
185 Ron Bryant .40 1.00
186 Ron Bryant IA .40 1.00
187 Gates Brown .40 1.00
188 Frank Lucchesi MG .40 1.00
189 Gene Tenace .75 2.00
190 Dave Giusti .40 1.00
191 Jeff Burroughs RC 1.50 4.00
192 Chicago Cubs TC .75 2.00
193 Kurt Bevacqua RC .40 1.00
194 Fred Norman .40 1.00
195 Orlando Cepeda 6.00 15.00
196 Mel Queen .40 1.00
197 Johnny Briggs .40 1.00
198 Hough/O'Brien/Strahler RC 4.00 10.00
199 Mike Fiore .40 1.00
200 Lou Brock 8.00 20.00
201 Phil Roof .40 1.00
202 Scipio Spinks .40 1.00
203 Ron Blomberg RC .40 1.00
204 Tommy Helms .40 1.00
205 Dick Drago .40 1.00
206 Dal Maxvill .40 1.00
207 Tom Egan .40 1.00
208 Milt Pappas .75 2.00
209 Joe Rudi .75 2.00
210 Denny McLain .75 2.00
211 Gary Sutherland .40 1.00
212 Grant Jackson .40 1.00
213 Parker/Kusnyer/Silverio RC .40 1.00
214 Mike McQueen .40 1.00
215 Alex Johnson .75 2.00
216 Joe Niekro .75 2.00
217 Roger Metzger .40 1.00
218 Eddie Kasko MG .40 1.00
219 Rennie Stennett RC .75 2.00
220 Jim Perry .75 2.00
221 NL Playoffs Bucs .75 2.00
222 AL Playoffs B.Robinson 1.50 4.00
223 Dave McNally WS .75 2.00
224 D.Johnson/M.Belanger WS .75 2.00
225 Manny Sanguillen WS .75 2.00
226 Roberto Clemente WS 3.00 8.00
227 Nellie Briles WS .75 2.00
228 F.Robinson/M.Sanguillen WS .75 2.00
229 Steve Blass WS .75 2.00
230 Pirates Celebrate WS .75 2.00
231 Casey Cox .40 1.00
232 Arnold/Barr/Rader RC .40 1.00
233 Jay Johnstone .75 2.00
234 Ron Taylor .40 1.00
235 Merv Rettenmund .40 1.00
236 Jim McGlothlin .40 1.00
237 New York Yankees TC .75 2.00
238 Leron Lee .40 1.00
239 Tom Timmermann .40 1.00
240 Rich Allen .75 2.00
241 Rollie Fingers 5.00 12.00
242 Don Mincher .40 1.00
243 Frank Linzy .40 1.00
244 Steve Braun RC .40 1.00
245 Tommie Agee .75 2.00
246 Tom Burgmeier .40 1.00
247 Milt May .40 1.00
248 Tom Bradley .40 1.00
249 Harry Walker MG .40 1.00
250 Boog Powell .75 2.00
251 Checklist 264-394 2.50 6.00
252 Ken Reynolds .40 1.00
253 Sandy Alomar .75 2.00
254 Boots Day .40 1.00
255 Jim Lonborg .75 2.00
256 George Foster .75 2.00
257 Foor/Hosley/Jata RC .40 1.00
258 Randy Hundley .40 1.00
259 Sparky Lyle .75 2.00
260 Ralph Garr .75 2.00
261 Steve Mingori .40 1.00
262 San Diego Padres TC .75 2.00
263 Felipe Alou .75 2.00
264 Tommy John .75 2.00
265 Wes Parker .75 2.00
266 Bobby Bolin .50 1.25
267 Dave Concepcion 1.50 4.00
268 D.Anderson RC/C.Floethe RC .50 1.25
269 Don Hahn .50 1.25
270 Jim Palmer 6.00 15.00
271 Ken Rudolph .50 1.25
272 Mickey Rivers RC .75 2.00
273 Bobby Floyd .50 1.25
274 Al Severinsen .50 1.25
275 Cesar Tovar .50 1.25
276 Gene Mauch MG .75 2.00
277 Elliott Maddox .50 1.25
278 Dennis Higgins .50 1.25
279 Larry Brown .50 1.25
280 Willie McCovey 2.50 6.00
281 Bill Parsons RC .50 1.25
282 Houston Astros TC .75 2.00
283 Darrell Brandon .50 1.25
284 Ike Brown .50 1.25
285 Gaylord Perry 2.50 6.00
286 Gene Alley .50 1.25
287 Jim Hardin .50 1.25
288 Johnny Jeter .50 1.25
289 Syd O'Brien .50 1.25
290 Sonny Siebert .50 1.25
291 Hal McRae .75 2.00
292 Hal McRae IA .50 1.25
293 Dan Frisella .50 1.25
294 Dan Frisella IA .50 1.25
295 Dick Dietz .50 1.25
296 Dick Dietz IA .50 1.25
297 Claude Osteen .75 2.00
298 Claude Osteen IA .50 1.25
299 Hank Aaron 25.00 60.00
300 Hank Aaron IA 8.00 20.00
301 George Mitterwald .50 1.25
302 George Mitterwald IA .50 1.25
303 Joe Pepitone .75 2.00
304 Joe Pepitone IA .50 1.25
305 Ken Boswell .50 1.25
306 Ken Boswell IA .50 1.25
307 Steve Renko .50 1.25
308 Steve Renko IA .50 1.25
309 Roberto Clemente 30.00 80.00
310 Roberto Clemente IA 12.00 30.00
311 Clay Carroll .50 1.25
312 Clay Carroll IA .50 1.25
313 Luis Aparicio 2.50 6.00
314 Luis Aparicio IA .75 2.00
315 Paul Splittorff .50 1.25
316 Bibby/Roque/Guzman RC .75 2.00
317 Rich Hand .50 1.25
318 Sonny Jackson .50 1.25
319 Aurelio Rodriguez .50 1.25
320 Steve Blass .75 2.00
321 Joe Lahoud .50 1.25
322 Jose Pena .50 1.25
323 Earl Weaver MG 1.50 4.00
324 Mike Ryan .50 1.25
325 Mel Stottlemyre .75 2.00
326 Pat Kelly .50 1.25
327 Steve Stone RC .75 2.00
328 Boston Red Sox TC .75 2.00
329 Roy Foster .50 1.25
330 Jim Hunter 2.50 6.00
331 Stan Swanson RC .50 1.25
332 Buck Martinez .50 1.25
333 Steve Barber .50 1.25
334 Fahey/Mason/Ragland RC .50 1.25
335 Bill Hands .50 1.25
336 Marty Martinez .50 1.25
337 Mike Kilkenny .50 1.25
338 Bob Grich .75 2.00
339 Ron Cook .50 1.25
340 Roy White .75 2.00
341 Joe Torre KP .50 1.25
342 Wilbur Wood KP .50 1.25
343 Willie Stargell KP .75 2.00
344 Dave McNally KP .50 1.25
345 Rick Wise KP .50 1.25
346 Jim Fregosi KP .50 1.25
347 Tom Seaver KP 1.50 4.00
348 Sal Bando KP .50 1.25
349 Al Fitzmorris .50 1.25
350 Frank Howard .75 2.00
351 House/Kester/Britton .75 2.00
352 Dave LaRoche .50 1.25
353 Art Shamsky .50 1.25
354 Tom Murphy .50 1.25
355 Bob Watson .75 2.00
356 Gerry Moses .50 1.25
357 Woody Fryman .50 1.25
358 Sparky Anderson MG 1.50 4.00
359 Don Pavletich .50 1.25
360 Dave Roberts .50 1.25
361 Mike Andrews .50 1.25
362 New York Mets TC .75 2.00
363 Ron Klimkowski .50 1.25
364 Johnny Callison .75 2.00
365 Dick Bosman .50 1.25
366 Jimmy Rosario RC .50 1.25
367 Ron Perranoski .50 1.25
368 Danny Thompson .50 1.25
369 Jim Lefebvre .75 2.00
370 Don Buford .50 1.25
371 Denny Lemaster .50 1.25
372 L.Clemons RC/M.Montgomery RC .50 1.25
373 John Mayberry .75 2.00
374 Jack Heidemann .50 1.25
375 Reggie Cleveland .50 1.25
376 Andy Kosco .50 1.25
377 Terry Harmon .50 1.25
378 Checklist 395-525 2.50 6.00
379 Ken Berry .50 1.25
380 Earl Williams .50 1.25
381 Chicago White Sox TC .75 2.00
382 Joe Gibbon .50 1.25
383 Brant Alyea .50 1.25
384 Dave Campbell .75 2.00
385 Mickey Stanley .75 2.00
386 Jim Colborn .50 1.25
387 Horace Clarke .75 2.00
388 Charlie Williams RC .50 1.25
389 Bill Rigney MG .50 1.25
390 Willie Davis .75 2.00
391 Ken Sanders .50 1.25
392 F.Cambria/R.Zisk RC .75 2.00
393 Curt Motton .50 1.25
394 Ken Forsch .75 2.00
395 Matty Alou .60 1.50
396 Paul Lindblad .60 1.50
397 Philadelphia Phillies TC .75 2.00
398 Larry Hisle .75 2.00
399 Milt Wilcox .75 2.00
400 Tony Oliva 1.50 4.00
401 Jim Nash .60 1.50
402 Bobby Heise .60 1.50
403 John Cumberland .60 1.50
404 Jeff Torborg .75 2.00
405 Ron Fairly .75 2.00
406 George Hendrick RC .75 2.00
407 Chuck Taylor .60 1.50
408 Jim Northrup .75 2.00
409 Frank Baker .60 1.50
410 Ferguson Jenkins 2.50 6.00
411 Bob Montgomery .60 1.50
412 Dick Kelley .60 1.50
413 D.Eddy RC/D.Lemonds .60 1.50
414 Bob Miller .60 1.50
415 Cookie Rojas .75 2.00
416 Johnny Edwards .60 1.50
417 Tom Hall .60 1.50
418 Tom Shopay .60 1.50
419 Jim Spencer .60 1.50
420 Steve Carlton 8.00 20.00
421 Ellie Rodriguez .60 1.50
422 Ray Lamb .60 1.50
423 Oscar Gamble .75 2.00
424 Bill Gogolewski .60 1.50
425 Ken Singleton .75 2.00
426 Ken Singleton IA .60 1.50
427 Tito Fuentes .60 1.50
428 Tito Fuentes IA .60 1.50
429 Bob Robertson .60 1.50
430 Bob Robertson IA .60 1.50
431 Clarence Gaston .75 2.00
432 Clarence Gaston IA .75 2.00
433 Johnny Bench 15.00 40.00
434 Johnny Bench IA 8.00 20.00
435 Reggie Jackson 12.00 30.00
436 Reggie Jackson IA 6.00 15.00
437 Maury Wills .75 2.00
438 Maury Wills IA .75 2.00
439 Billy Williams 2.50 6.00
440 Billy Williams IA 1.50 4.00
441 Thurman Munson 12.00 30.00
442 Thurman Munson IA 3.00 8.00
443 Ken Henderson .60 1.50
444 Ken Henderson IA .60 1.50
445 Tom Seaver 20.00 50.00
446 Tom Seaver IA 5.00 12.00
447 Willie Stargell 3.00 8.00
448 Willie Stargell IA 1.50 4.00
449 Bob Lemon MG .75 2.00
450 Mickey Lolich .75 2.00
451 Tony LaRussa 1.50 4.00
452 Ed Herrmann .60 1.50
453 Barry Lersch .60 1.50
454 Oakland Athletics TC .75 2.00
455 Tommy Harper .75 2.00
456 Mark Belanger .75 2.00
457 Fast/Thomas/Ivie RC .60 1.50
458 Aurelio Monteagudo .60 1.50
459 Rick Renick .60 1.50
460 Al Downing .60 1.50
461 Tim Cullen .60 1.50
462 Rickey Clark .60 1.50
463 Bernie Carbo .60 1.50
464 Jim Roland .60 1.50
465 Gil Hodges MG 1.50 4.00
466 Norm Miller .60 1.50
467 Steve Kline .60 1.50
468 Richie Scheinblum .60 1.50
469 Ron Herbel .60 1.50
470 Ray Fosse .60 1.50
471 Luke Walker .60 1.50
472 Phil Gagliano .60 1.50
473 Dan McGinn .60 1.50
474 Baylor/Harrison/Oates RC 6.00 15.00
475 Gary Nolan .75 2.00
476 Lee Richard RC .60 1.50
477 Tom Phoebus .60 1.50
478 Checklist 526-656 2.50 6.00
479 Don Shaw .60 1.50
480 Lee May .75 2.00
481 Billy Conigliaro .75 2.00
482 Joe Hoerner .60 1.50
483 Ken Suarez .60 1.50
484 Lum Harris MG .60 1.50
485 Phil Regan .75 2.00
486 John Lowenstein .60 1.50
487 Detroit Tigers TC .75 2.00
488 Mike Nagy .60 1.50
489 T.Humphrey RC/K.Lampard .60 1.50
490 Dave McNally .75 2.00
491 Lou Piniella KP .75 2.00
492 Mel Stottlemyre KP .75 2.00
493 Bob Bailey KP .75 2.00
494 Willie Horton KP .75 2.00
495 Bill Melton KP .75 2.00
496 Bud Harrelson KP .75 2.00
497 Jim Perry KP .75 2.00
498 Brooks Robinson KP 1.50 4.00
499 Vicente Romo .60 1.50
500 Joe Torre 1.50 4.00
501 Pete Hamm .60 1.50
502 Jackie Hernandez .60 1.50
503 Gary Peters .60 1.50
504 Ed Spiezio .60 1.50
505 Mike Marshall .75 2.00
506 Ley/Moyer/Tidrow RC .60 1.50
507 Fred Gladding .60 1.50
508 Elrod Hendricks .60 1.50
509 Don McMahon .60 1.50
510 Ted Williams MG 8.00 20.00
511 Tony Taylor .75 2.00
512 Paul Popovich .60 1.50
513 Lindy McDaniel .75 2.00
514 Ted Sizemore .60 1.50
515 Bert Blyleven 1.50 4.00
516 Oscar Brown .60 1.50
517 Ken Brett .60 1.50
518 Wayne Garrett .60 1.50
519 Ted Abernathy .60 1.50
520 Larry Bowa .75 2.00
521 Alan Foster .60 1.50
522 Los Angeles Dodgers TC .75 2.00
523 Chuck Dobson .60 1.50
524 E.Armbrister RC/M.Behney RC .60 1.50
525 Carlos May .75 2.00
526 Bob Bailey 2.50 6.00
527 Dave Leonhard 1.50 4.00
528 Ron Stone 1.50 4.00
529 Dave Nelson 2.50 6.00
530 Don Sutton 5.00 12.00
531 Freddie Patek 2.50 6.00
532 Fred Kendall RC 1.50 4.00
533 Ralph Houk MG 2.50 6.00
534 Jim Hickman 2.50 6.00
535 Ed Brinkman 1.50 4.00
536 Doug Rader 2.50 6.00
537 Bob Locker 1.50 4.00
538 Charlie Sands RC 1.50 4.00
539 Terry Forster RC 2.50 6.00
540 Felix Millan 1.50 4.00
541 Roger Repoz 1.50 4.00
542 Jack Billingham 1.50 4.00
543 Duane Josephson 1.50 4.00
544 Ted Martinez 1.50 4.00
545 Wayne Granger 1.50 4.00
546 Joe Hague 1.50 4.00
547 Cleveland Indians TC 3.00 8.00
548 Frank Reberger 1.50 4.00
549 Dave May 1.50 4.00
550 Brooks Robinson 8.00 20.00
551 Ollie Brown 1.50 4.00
552 Ollie Brown IA 1.50 4.00
553 Wilbur Wood 2.50 6.00
554 Wilbur Wood IA 1.50 4.00
555 Ron Santo 3.00 8.00
556 Ron Santo IA 2.50 6.00
557 John Odom 1.50 4.00
558 John Odom IA 1.50 4.00
559 Pete Rose 25.00 60.00
560 Pete Rose IA 10.00 25.00
561 Leo Cardenas 1.50 4.00
562 Leo Cardenas IA 1.50 4.00
563 Ray Sadecki 1.50 4.00
564 Ray Sadecki IA 1.50 4.00
565 Reggie Smith 2.50 6.00
566 Reggie Smith IA 1.50 4.00
567 Juan Marichal 6.00 15.00
568 Juan Marichal IA 2.50 6.00
569 Ed Kirkpatrick 1.50 4.00
570 Ed Kirkpatrick IA 1.50 4.00
571 Nate Colbert 1.50 4.00
572 Nate Colbert IA 1.50 4.00
573 Fritz Peterson 1.50 4.00
574 Fritz Peterson IA 1.50 4.00
575 Al Oliver 3.00 8.00
576 Leo Durocher MG 2.50 6.00
577 Mike Paul 2.50 6.00
578 Billy Grabarkewitz 1.50 4.00
579 Doyle Alexander RC 2.50 6.00
580 Lou Piniella 2.50 6.00
581 Wade Blasingame 1.50 4.00
582 Montreal Expos TC 3.00 8.00
583 Darold Knowles 1.50 4.00
584 Jerry McNertney 1.50 4.00
585 George Scott 2.50 6.00
586 Denis Menke 1.50 4.00
587 Billy Wilson 1.50 4.00
588 Jim Holt 1.50 4.00
589 Hal Lanier 1.50 4.00
590 Graig Nettles 3.00 8.00
591 Paul Casanova 1.50 4.00
592 Lew Krausse 1.50 4.00
593 Rich Morales 1.50 4.00
594 Jim Beauchamp 1.50 4.00
595 Nolan Ryan 50.00 120.00
596 Manny Mota 2.50 6.00
597 Jim Magnuson RC 1.50 4.00
598 Hal King 2.50 6.00
599 Billy Champion 1.50 4.00
600 Al Kaline 12.00 30.00
601 George Stone 1.50 4.00
602 Dave Bristol MG 1.50 4.00
603 Jim Ray 1.50 4.00
604A Checklist 657-787 Right Copy 5.00 12.00
604B Checklist 657-787 Left Copy 5.00 12.00
605 Nelson Briles 2.50 6.00
606 Luis Melendez 1.50 4.00
607 Frank Duffy 1.50 4.00
608 Mike Corkins 1.50 4.00
609 Tom Grieve 2.50 6.00
610 Bill Stoneman 2.50 6.00
611 Rich Reese 1.50 4.00
612 Joe Decker 1.50 4.00
613 Mike Ferraro 1.50 4.00
614 Ted Uhlaender 1.50 4.00
615 Steve Hargan 1.50 4.00
616 Joe Ferguson RC 2.50 6.00
617 Kansas City Royals TC 3.00 8.00
618 Rich Robertson 1.50 4.00
619 Rich McKinney 1.50 4.00
620 Phil Niekro 8.00 20.00
621 Commish Award 3.00 8.00
622 MVP Award 3.00 8.00
623 Cy Young Award 3.00 8.00
624 Minor Lg POY Award 3.00 8.00
625 Rookie of the Year 3.00 8.00
626 Babe Ruth Award 3.00 8.00
627 Moe Drabowsky 1.50 4.00
628 Terry Crowley 1.50 4.00
629 Paul Doyle 1.50 4.00
630 Rich Hebner 2.50 6.00
631 John Strohmayer 1.50 4.00
632 Mike Hegan 1.50 4.00
633 Jack Hiatt 1.50 4.00
634 Dick Woodson 1.50 4.00
635 Don Money 2.50 6.00
636 Bill Lee 2.50 6.00
637 Preston Gomez MG 1.50 4.00
638 Ken Wright 1.50 4.00
639 J.C. Martin 1.50 4.00
640 Joe Coleman 1.50 4.00
641 Mike Lum 1.50 4.00
642 Dennis Riddleberger RC 1.50 4.00
643 Russ Gibson 1.50 4.00
644 Bernie Allen 1.50 4.00
645 Jim Maloney 2.50 6.00
646 Chico Salmon 1.50 4.00
647 Bob Moose 1.50 4.00
648 Jim Lyttle 1.50 4.00
649 Pete Richert 1.50 4.00
650 Sal Bando 2.50 6.00
651 Cincinnati Reds TC 3.00 8.00
652 Marcelino Lopez 1.50 4.00
653 Jim Fairey 1.50 4.00
654 Horacio Pina 2.50 6.00
655 Jerry Grote 1.50 4.00
656 Rudy May 1.50 4.00
657 Bobby Wine 5.00 12.00
658 Steve Dunning 5.00 12.00
659 Bob Aspromonte 5.00 12.00
660 Paul Blair 6.00 15.00
661 Bill Virdon MG 5.00 12.00
662 Stan Bahnsen 5.00 12.00
663 Fran Healy RC 6.00 15.00
664 Bobby Knoop 5.00 12.00
665 Chris Short 5.00 12.00
666 Hector Torres 5.00 12.00
667 Ray Newman RC 5.00 12.00
668 Texas Rangers TC 12.50 30.00
669 Willie Crawford 5.00 12.00
670 Ken Holtzman 6.00 15.00
671 Donn Clendenon 6.00 15.00
672 Archie Reynolds 5.00 12.00
673 Dave Marshall 5.00 12.00
674 John Kennedy 5.00 12.00
675 Pat Jarvis 5.00 12.00
676 Danny Cater 5.00 12.00
677 Ivan Murrell 5.00 12.00
678 Steve Luebber RC 5.00 12.00
679 B.Fenwick RC/B.Stinson 5.00 12.00
680 Dave Johnson 6.00 15.00
681 Bobby Pfeil 5.00 12.00
682 Mike McCormick 6.00 15.00
683 Steve Hovley 5.00 12.00
684 Hal Breeden RC 5.00 12.00
685 Joel Horlen 5.00 12.00
686 Steve Garvey 20.00 50.00
687 Del Unser 5.00 12.00
688 St. Louis Cardinals TC 8.00 20.00
689 Eddie Fisher 5.00 12.00
690 Willie Montanez 6.00 15.00
691 Curt Blefary 5.00 12.00
692 Curt Blefary IA 5.00 12.00
693 Alan Gallagher 5.00 12.00
694 Alan Gallagher IA 5.00 12.00
695 Rod Carew 25.00 60.00
696 Rod Carew IA 12.00 30.00
697 Jerry Koosman 6.00 15.00
698 Jerry Koosman IA 6.00 15.00
699 Bobby Murcer 6.00 15.00
700 Bobby Murcer IA 6.00 15.00
701 Jose Pagan 5.00 12.00
702 Jose Pagan IA 5.00 12.00
703 Doug Griffin 5.00 12.00
704 Doug Griffin IA 5.00 12.00
705 Pat Corrales 6.00 15.00
706 Pat Corrales IA 6.00 15.00
707 Tim Foli 5.00 12.00
708 Tim Foli IA 5.00 12.00
709 Jim Kaat 6.00 15.00
710 Jim Kaat IA 6.00 15.00
711 Bobby Bonds 8.00 20.00
712 Bobby Bonds IA 6.00 15.00
713 Gene Michael 8.00 20.00
714 Gene Michael IA 6.00 15.00
715 Mike Epstein 5.00 12.00
716 Jesus Alou 5.00 12.00
717 Bruce Dal Canton 5.00 12.00
718 Del Rice MG 5.00 12.00
719 Cesar Geronimo 5.00 12.00
720 Sam McDowell 6.00 15.00
721 Eddie Leon 5.00 12.00
722 Bill Sudakis 5.00 12.00
723 Al Santorini 5.00 12.00
724 Curtis/Hinton/Scott RC 5.00 12.00
725 Dick McAuliffe 6.00 15.00
726 Dick Selma 5.00 12.00
727 Jose Laboy 5.00 12.00
728 Gail Hopkins 5.00 12.00
729 Bob Veale 6.00 15.00

Card	Low	High
730 Rick Monday	6.00	15.00
731 Baltimore Orioles TC	8.00	20.00
732 George Culver	5.00	12.00
733 Jim Ray Hart	6.00	15.00
734 Bob Burda	5.00	12.00
735 Diego Segui	5.00	12.00
736 Bill Russell	6.00	15.00
737 Len Randle RC	6.00	15.00
738 Jim Merritt	5.00	12.00
739 Don Mason	5.00	12.00
740 Rico Carty	6.00	15.00
741 Hutton/Milner/Miller RC	6.00	15.00
742 Jim Rooker	5.00	12.00
743 Cesar Gutierrez	5.00	12.00
744 Jim Slaton RC	5.00	12.00
745 Julian Javier	6.00	15.00
746 Lowell Palmer	5.00	12.00
747 Jim Stewart	5.00	12.00
748 Phil Hennigan	5.00	12.00
749 Walter Alston MG	8.00	20.00
750 Willie Horton	6.00	15.00
751 Steve Carlton TR	15.00	40.00
752 Joe Morgan TR	12.00	30.00
753 Denny McLain TR	8.00	20.00
754 Frank Robinson TR	10.00	25.00
755 Jim Fregosi TR	6.00	15.00
756 Rick Wise TR	6.00	15.00
757 Jose Cardenal TR	6.00	15.00
758 Gil Garrido	5.00	12.00
759 Chris Cannizzaro	5.00	12.00
760 Bill Mazeroski	10.00	25.00
761 Oglivie/Cey/Williams RC	20.00	50.00
762 Wayne Simpson	5.00	12.00
763 Ron Hansen	5.00	12.00
764 Dusty Baker	8.00	20.00
765 Ken McMullen	5.00	12.00
766 Steve Hamilton	5.00	12.00
767 Tom McCraw	6.00	15.00
768 Denny Doyle	5.00	12.00
769 Jack Aker	5.00	12.00
770 Jim Wynn	6.00	15.00
771 San Francisco Giants TC	8.00	20.00
772 Ken Tatum	5.00	12.00
773 Ron Brand	5.00	12.00
774 Luis Alvarado	5.00	12.00
775 Jerry Reuss	6.00	15.00
776 Bill Voss	5.00	12.00
777 Hoyt Wilhelm	8.00	20.00
778 Albury/Dempsey/Strickland RC	8.00	20.00
779 Tony Cloninger	5.00	12.00
780 Dick Green	5.00	12.00
781 Jim McAndrew	5.00	12.00
782 Larry Stahl	5.00	12.00
783 Les Cain	5.00	12.00
784 Ken Aspromonte	5.00	12.00
785 Vic Davalillo	5.00	12.00
786 Chuck Brinkman	5.00	12.00
787 Ron Reed	6.00	15.00

1972 Topps Candy Lids

A cross in design between the 1970 and the 1973 Topps Candy Lids. These lids do not have borders. Since the lids are unnumbered we have sequenced them alphabetically. Any further information on these lids are appreciated. These have been dated 1972 by Ray Fosse being listed as a member of the Cleveland Indians.

Card	Low	High
COMPLETE SET	1250.00	2500.00
1 Hank Aaron	250.00	500.00
2 Dick Allen	100.00	200.00
3 Carlton Fisk	400.00	800.00
4 Ray Fosse	50.00	100.00
5 Bob Gibson	100.00	200.00
6 Harmon Killebrew	10.00	25.00
7 Greg Luzinski	75.00	150.00
8 Thurman Munson	250.00	500.00
9 Gaylord Perry	100.00	200.00
10 Ellie Rodriguez	50.00	100.00

1972 Topps Posters

This giant (9 7/16" by 18"), full-color series of 24 paper-thin posters was issued as a separate set in 1972. The posters are individually numbered and unlike other Topps posters described in this book, are borderless. They are printed on thin paper and were folded five times to facilitate packaging. These posters were issued in one-poster, ten-cent packs which were issued 24 to a box. The box featured a photo of 1971 NL MVP Joe Torre.

Card	Low	High
COMPLETE SET (24)	400.00	800.00
WRAPPER (10-CENT)		
1 Dave McNally	3.00	8.00
2 Carl Yastrzemski	40.00	80.00
3 Bill Melton	3.00	8.00
4 Ray Fosse	3.00	8.00
5 Mickey Lolich	4.00	10.00
6 Amos Otis	4.00	10.00
7 Tony Oliva	5.00	12.00
8 Vida Blue	4.00	10.00
9 Hank Aaron	50.00	100.00
10 Fergie Jenkins	8.00	20.00
11 Pete Rose	50.00	100.00
12 Willie Davis	4.00	10.00
13 Tom Seaver	40.00	80.00
14 Rick Wise	3.00	8.00
15 Willie Stargell	12.50	40.00
16 Joe Torre	5.00	12.00
17 Willie Mays	50.00	100.00
18 Andy Messersmith	4.00	10.00
19 Wilbur Wood	4.00	10.00
20 Harmon Killebrew	12.50	40.00
21 Billy Williams	12.50	40.00
22 Bud Harrelson	3.00	8.00
23 Roberto Clemente	75.00	150.00
24 Willie McCovey	12.50	40.00

1972 Topps Cloth Test

These "test" issue cards look like 1972 Topps cards except that they are on a "cloth sticker". Each card measures 2 1/2" by 3 1/2". The "cards" in this set are all taken from the third series of the 1972 Topps regular issue. Cards are blank backed and unnumbered. They are listed below in alphabetical order.

Card	Low	High
COMPLETE SET (33)	500.00	1000.00
1 Hank Aaron	60.00	120.00
2 Luis Aparicio IA	12.50	40.00
3 Ike Brown	10.00	25.00
4 Johnny Callison	10.00	25.00
5 Checklist 264-319	10.00	25.00
6 Roberto Clemente	100.00	200.00
7 Dave Concepcion	12.50	30.00
8 Ron Cook	10.00	25.00
9 Willie Davis	10.00	25.00
10 Al Fitzmorris	10.00	25.00
11 Bobby Floyd	10.00	25.00
12 Roy Foster	10.00	25.00
13 Jim Fregosi KP	10.00	25.00
14 Danny Frisella IA	10.00	25.00
15 Woody Fryman	10.00	25.00
16 Terry Harmon	10.00	25.00
17 Frank Howard	10.00	25.00
18 Ron Klimkowski	10.00	25.00
19 Joe Lahoud	10.00	25.00
20 Jim Lefebvre	10.00	25.00
21 Elliott Maddox	10.00	25.00
22 Marty Martinez	10.00	25.00
23 Willie McCovey	40.00	80.00
24 Hal McRae	10.00	25.00
25 Syd O'Brien	10.00	25.00
26 Red Sox Team	10.00	25.00
27 Aurelio Rodriguez	10.00	25.00
28 Al Severinsen	10.00	25.00
29 Art Shamsky	10.00	25.00
30 Steve Stone	10.00	25.00
31 Stan Swanson	10.00	25.00
32 Bob Watson	10.00	25.00
33 Roy White	10.00	25.00

1972 Topps Test 53

These "test" issue cards were made to look like 1953 Topps cards as the cards show drawings rather than photos. The card number of the corresponding art from the 1953 Topps set is given in parentheses after the name of the player. For three of the cards in this set the player pictured in the art is not the same player as listed on the card; in these cases the actual player pictured is also listed parenthetically in the checklist below. Each card measures 2 1/2" by 3 1/2". Printing on the back is in blue ink on gray card stock.

Card	Low	High
COMPLETE SET (8)	600.00	1200.00
1 Satchell Paige/(53 Topps 220)	125.00	250.00
2 Jackie Robinson/(53 Topps 1)	125.00	250.00
3 Carl Furillo/(53 Topps 272) (picture actually B	60.00	120.00
4 Al Rosen/(53 Topps 187) (picture actually Jim F	60.00	120.00
5 Hal Newhouser/(53 Topps 228)	75.00	150.00
6 Clyde McCullough (53 Topps 222)/(picture actuall	40.00	80.00
7 Peanuts Lowrey/(53 Topps 16)	40.00	80.00
8 Johnny Mize/(53 Topps 77)	100.00	200.00

1973 Topps

The cards in this 660-card set measure 2 1/2" by 3 1/2". The 1973 Topps set marked the last year in which Topps marketed baseball cards in consecutive series. The last series (529-660) is more difficult to obtain. In some parts of the country, however, all five series were distributed together. Beginning in 1974, all Topps cards were printed at the same time, thus eliminating the "high number" factor. The set features team leader cards with small individual pictures of the coaching staff members and a larger picture of the manager. The "background" variations below with respect to these leader cards are subtle and are best understood after a side-by-side comparison of the two varieties. An "All-Time Leaders" series (471-478) appeared for the first time in this set. Kid Pictures appeared again for the second year in a row (341-346). Other topical subsets within the set included League Leaders (61-68), Playoffs cards (201-202), World Series cards (203-210), and Rookie Prospects (601-616). For the fourth and final time, cards were issued in ten-card dime packs which were issued 24 packs to a box, in addition, these cards were also released in 54-card rack packs which cost 39 cents upon release. The key Rookie Cards in this set are all in the Rookie Prospect series: Bob Boone, Dwight Evans, and Mike Schmidt.

Card	Low	High
COMPLETE SET (660)	600.00	1500.00
COMMON CARD (1-264)	.20	.50
COMMON CARD (265-396)	.30	.75
COMMON CARD (397-528)	.50	1.25
COMMON CARD (529-660)	1.25	3.00
WRAPPER (10-CENT, BAT)	6.00	15.00
WRAPPER (10-CENT)	6.00	15.00
1 Ruth/Aaron/Mays HR	25.00	60.00
2 Rich Hebner	.60	1.50
3 Jim Lonborg	.60	1.50
4 John Milner	.20	.50
5 Ed Brinkman	.20	.50
6 Mac Scarce RC	.20	.50
7 Texas Rangers TC	.75	2.00
8 Tom Hall	.20	.50
9 Johnny Oates	.60	1.50
10 Don Sutton	1.50	4.00
11 Chris Chambliss UER	.60	1.50
12A Don Zimmer MG w/o Ear	1.25	3.00
12B Don Zimmer MG w/Ear	.30	.75
13 George Hendrick	.60	1.50
14 Sonny Siebert	.20	.50
15 Ralph Garr	.60	1.50
16 Steve Braun	.20	.50
17 Fred Gladding	.20	.50
18 Leroy Stanton	.20	.50
19 Tim Foli	.20	.50
20 Stan Bahnsen	.20	.50
21 Randy Hundley	.60	1.50
22 Ted Abernathy	.20	.50
23 Dave Kingman	.60	1.50
24 Al Santorini	.20	.50
25 Roy White	.60	1.50
26 Pittsburgh Pirates TC	.75	2.00
27 Bill Gogolewski	.20	.50
28 Hal McRae	.60	1.50
29 Tony Taylor	.60	1.50
30 Tug McGraw	.60	1.50
31 Buddy Bell RC	1.00	2.50
32 Fred Norman	.20	.50
33 Jim Breazeale RC	.20	.50
34 Pat Dobson	.20	.50
35 Willie Davis	.60	1.50
36 Steve Barber	.20	.50
37 Bill Robinson	.60	1.50
38 Mike Epstein	.20	.50
39 Dave Roberts	.20	.50
40 Reggie Smith	.60	1.50
41 Tom Walker RC	.20	.50
42 Mike Andrews	.20	.50
43 Randy Moffitt RC	.20	.50
44 Rick Monday	.60	1.50
45 Ellie Rodriguez UER	.20	.50
46 Lindy McDaniel	.60	1.50
47 Luis Melendez	.20	.50
48 Paul Splittorff	.20	.50
49A Frank Quilici MG Solid	1.25	3.00
49B Frank Quilici MG Natural	.30	.75
50 Roberto Clemente	40.00	100.00
51 Chuck Seelbach RC	.20	.50
52 Denis Menke	.20	.50
53 Steve Dunning	.20	.50
54 Checklist 1-132	1.25	3.00
55 Jon Matlack	.60	1.50
56 Merv Rettenmund	.20	.50
57 Derrel Thomas	.20	.50
58 Mike Paul	.20	.50
59 Steve Yeager RC	.60	1.50
60 Ken Holtzman	.60	1.50
61 B.Williams/R.Carew LL	1.00	2.50
62 J.Bench/D.Allen LL	1.00	2.50
63 J.Bench/D.Allen LL	1.00	2.50
64 L.Brock/Campaneris LL	.60	1.50
65 S.Carlton/L.Tiant LL	.60	1.50
66 Carlton/Perry/Wood LL	.60	1.50
67 S.Carlton/N.Ryan LL	5.00	12.00
68 C.Carroll/S.Lyle LL	.60	1.50
69 Phil Gagliano	.20	.50
70 Milt Pappas	.60	1.50
71 Johnny Briggs	.20	.50
72 Ron Reed	.20	.50
73 Ed Herrmann	.20	.50
74 Billy Champion	.20	.50
75 Vada Pinson	.60	1.50
76 Doug Rader	.20	.50
77 Mike Torrez	.60	1.50
78 Richie Scheinblum	.20	.50
79 Jim Willoughby RC	.20	.50
80 Tony Oliva UER	1.00	2.50
81A W.Lockman MG w/Banks Solid	.60	1.50
81B W.Lockman MG w/Banks Natural	.60	1.50
82 Fritz Peterson	.20	.50
83 Leron Lee	.20	.50
84 Rollie Fingers	1.50	4.00
85 Ted Simmons	.60	1.50
86 Tom McCraw	.20	.50
87 Ken Boswell	.20	.50
88 Mickey Stanley	.60	1.50
89 Jack Billingham	.20	.50
90 Brooks Robinson	8.00	20.00
91 Los Angeles Dodgers TC	.75	2.00
92 Jerry Bell	.20	.50
93 Jesus Alou	.20	.50
94 Dick Billings	.20	.50
95 Steve Blass	.60	1.50
96 Doug Griffin	.20	.50
97 Willie Montanez	.60	1.50
98 Dick Woodson	.20	.50
99 Carl Taylor	.20	.50
100 Hank Aaron	20.00	50.00
101 Ken Henderson	.20	.50
102 Rudy May	.20	.50
103 Celerino Sanchez RC	.20	.50
104 Reggie Cleveland	.20	.50
105 Carlos May	.20	.50
106 Terry Humphrey	.20	.50
107 Phil Hennigan	.20	.50
108 Bill Russell	.60	1.50
109 Doyle Alexander	.60	1.50
110 Bob Watson	.60	1.50
111 Dave Nelson	.20	.50
112 Gary Ross	.20	.50
113 Jerry Grote	.60	1.50
114 Lynn McGlothen RC	.20	.50
115 Ron Santo	.60	1.50
116A Ralph Houk MG Solid	1.25	3.00
116B Ralph Houk MG Natural	.30	.75
117 Ramon Hernandez	.20	.50
118 John Mayberry	.60	1.50
119 Larry Bowa	.60	1.50
120 Joe Coleman	.20	.50
121 Dave Rader	.20	.50
122 Jim Strickland	.20	.50
123 Sandy Alomar	.60	1.50
124 Jim Hardin	.20	.50
125 Ron Fairly	.60	1.50
126 Jim Brewer	.20	.50
127 Milwaukee Brewers TC	.75	2.00
128 Ted Sizemore	.20	.50
129 Terry Forster	.60	1.50
130 Pete Rose	20.00	50.00
131A Eddie Kasko MG w/oEar	1.25	3.00
131B Eddie Kasko MG w/Ear	.60	1.50
132 Matty Alou	.60	1.50
133 Dave Roberts RC	.20	.50
134 Milt Wilcox	.20	.50
135 Lee May UER	.60	1.50
136A Earl Weaver MG Orange	.60	1.50
136B Earl Weaver MG Pale	1.25	3.00
137 Jim Beauchamp	.20	.50
138 Horacio Pina	.20	.50
139 Carmen Fanzone RC	.20	.50
140 Lou Piniella	1.00	2.50
141 Bruce Kison	.20	.50
142 Thurman Munson	12.00	30.00
143 John Curtis	.20	.50
144 Marty Perez	.20	.50
145 Bobby Bonds	1.00	2.50
146 Woodie Fryman	.20	.50
147 Mike Anderson	.20	.50
148 Dave Goltz	.20	.50
149 Ron Hunt	.20	.50
150 Wilbur Wood	.60	1.50
151 Wes Parker	.60	1.50
152 Dave May	.20	.50
153 Al Hrabosky	.60	1.50
154 Jeff Torborg	.60	1.50
155 Sal Bando	.60	1.50
156 Cesar Geronimo	.20	.50
157 Denny Riddleberger	.20	.50
158 Houston Astros TC	.75	2.00
159 Clarence Gaston	.60	1.50
160 Jim Palmer	2.50	6.00
161 Ted Martinez	.20	.50
162 Pete Broberg	.20	.50
163 Vic Davalillo	.20	.50
164 Monty Montgomery	.20	.50
165 Luis Aparicio	1.50	4.00
166 Terry Harmon	.20	.50
167 Steve Stone	.60	1.50
168 Jim Northrup	.60	1.50
169 Ron Schueler RC	.60	1.50
170 Harmon Killebrew	6.00	15.00
171 Bernie Carbo	.20	.50
172 Steve Kline	.20	.50
173 Hal Breeden	.20	.50
174 Goose Gossage RC	20.00	50.00
175 Frank Robinson	8.00	20.00
176 Chuck Taylor	.20	.50
177 Bill Plummer RC	.20	.50
178 Don Rose RC	.20	.50
179A Dick Williams w/Ear	1.50	4.00
179B Dick Williams w/o Ear	.60	1.50
180 Ferguson Jenkins	1.50	4.00
181 Jack Brohamer RC	.20	.50
182 Mike Caldwell RC	.60	1.50
183 Don Buford	.20	.50
184 Jerry Koosman	.60	1.50
185 Jim Wynn	.60	1.50
186 Bill Fahey	.20	.50
187 Luke Walker	.20	.50
188 Cookie Rojas	.60	1.50
189 Greg Luzinski	1.00	2.50
190 Bob Gibson	15.00	40.00
191 Detroit Tigers TC	1.00	2.50
192 Pat Jarvis	.20	.50
193 Carlton Fisk	12.00	30.00
194 Jorge Orta RC	.20	.50
195 Clay Carroll	.20	.50
196 Ken McMullen	.20	.50
197 Ed Goodson RC	.20	.50
198 Horace Clarke	.20	.50
199 Bert Blyleven	1.00	2.50
200 Billy Williams	1.50	4.00
201 George Hendrick ALCS	.60	1.50
202 George Foster NLCS	.60	1.50
203 Gene Tenace WS	.60	1.50
204 A's Two Straight WS	.60	1.50
205 Tony Perez WS	1.00	2.50
206 Gene Tenace WS	.60	1.50
207 Blue Moon Odom WS	.60	1.50
208 Johnny Bench WS	2.00	5.00
209 Bert Campaneris WS	.60	1.50
210 A's Win WS	.20	.50
211 Balor Moore	.20	.50
212 Joe Lahoud	.20	.50
213 Steve Garvey	6.00	15.00
214 Dave Hamilton RC	.20	.50
215 Dusty Baker	1.00	2.50
216 Toby Harrah	.60	1.50
217 Don Wilson	.20	.50
218 Aurelio Rodriguez	.20	.50
219 St. Louis Cardinals TC	1.00	2.50
220 Nolan Ryan	15.00	40.00
221 Fred Kendall	.20	.50
222 Rob Gardner	.20	.50
223 Bud Harrelson	.60	1.50
224 Bill Lee	.60	1.50
225 Al Oliver	.60	1.50
226 Ray Fosse	.20	.50
227 Wayne Twitchell	.20	.50
228 Bobby Darwin	.20	.50
229 Roric Harrison	.20	.50
230 Joe Morgan	8.00	20.00
231 Bill Parsons	.20	.50
232 Ken Singleton	.60	1.50
233 Ed Kirkpatrick	.20	.50
234 Bill North RC	.20	.50
235 Jim Hunter	1.50	4.00
236 Tito Fuentes	.20	.50
237A Eddie Mathews MG w/Ear	.60	1.50
237B Eddie Mathews MG w/o Ear	1.25	3.00
238 Tony Muser RC	.20	.50
239 Pete Richert	.20	.50
240 Bobby Murcer	.60	1.50
241 Dwain Anderson	.20	.50
242 George Culver	.20	.50
243 California Angels TC	1.00	2.50
244 Ed Acosta	.20	.50
245 Carl Yastrzemski	10.00	25.00
246 Ken Sanders	.20	.50
247 Del Unser	.20	.50
248 Jerry Johnson	.20	.50
249 Larry Biittner	.20	.50
250 Manny Sanguillen	.60	1.50
251 Roger Nelson	.20	.50
252A Charlie Fox MG Orange	1.50	4.00
252B Charlie Fox MG Pale	.60	1.50
253 Mark Belanger	.60	1.50
254 Bill Stoneman	.20	.50
255 Reggie Jackson	15.00	40.00
256 Chris Zachary	.20	.50
257A Yogi Berra MG Orange	1.25	3.00
257B Yogi Berra MG Pale	2.00	5.00
258 Tommy John	.60	1.50
259 Jim Holt	.20	.50
260 Gary Nolan	.60	1.50
261 Pat Kelly	.20	.50
262 Jack Aker	.20	.50
263 George Scott	.60	1.50
264 Checklist 133-264	1.25	3.00
265 Gene Michael	.60	1.50
266 Mike Lum	.30	.75
267 Lloyd Allen	.30	.75
268 Jerry Morales	.30	.75
269 Tim McCarver	.60	1.50
270 Luis Tiant	.60	1.50
271 Tom Hutton	.30	.75
272 Ed Farmer	.30	.75
273 Chris Speier	.30	.75
274 Darold Knowles	.30	.75
275 Tony Perez	1.50	4.00
276 Joe Lovitto RC	.30	.75
277 Bob Miller	.30	.75
278 Baltimore Orioles TC	.60	1.50
279 Mike Strahler	.30	.75
280 Al Kaline	10.00	25.00
281 Mike Jorgensen	.30	.75
282 Steve Hovley	.30	.75
283 Ray Sadecki	.30	.75
284 Glenn Borgmann RC	.30	.75
285 Don Kessinger	.60	1.50
286 Frank Linzy	.30	.75
287 Eddie Leon	.30	.75
288 Gary Gentry	.30	.75
289 Bob Oliver	.30	.75
290 Cesar Cedeno	.60	1.50
291 Rogelio Moret	.30	.75
292 Jose Cruz	.60	1.50
293 Bernie Allen	.30	.75
294 Steve Arlin	.30	.75
295 Bert Campaneris	.60	1.50
296 Sparky Anderson MG	1.00	2.50
297 Walt Williams	.30	.75
298 Ron Bryant	.30	.75
299 Ted Ford	.30	.75
300 Steve Carlton	6.00	15.00
301 Billy Grabarkewitz	.30	.75
302 Terry Crowley	.30	.75
303 Nelson Briles	.30	.75
304 Duke Sims	.30	.75
305 Willie Mays	40.00	100.00
306 Tom Burgmeier	.30	.75
307 Boots Day	.30	.75
308 Skip Lockwood	.30	.75
309 Paul Popovich	.30	.75
310 Dick Allen	.60	1.50
311 Joe Decker	.30	.75
312 Oscar Brown	.30	.75
313 Jim Ray	.30	.75
314 Ron Swoboda	.60	1.50
315 John Odom	.30	.75
316 San Diego Padres TC	.60	1.50
317 Danny Cater	.30	.75
318 Jim McGlothlin	.30	.75
319 Jim Spencer	.30	.75
320 Lou Brock	3.00	8.00
321 Rich Hinton	.30	.75
322 Garry Maddox RC	.60	1.50
323 Billy Martin MG	.60	1.50
324 Al Downing	.30	.75
325 Boog Powell	.60	1.50
326 Darrell Brandon	.30	.75
327 John Lowenstein	.30	.75
328 Bill Bonham	.30	.75
329 Ed Kranepool	.60	1.50
330 Rod Carew	3.00	8.00
331 Carl Morton	.30	.75
332 John Felske RC	.30	.75
333 Gene Clines	.30	.75
334 Freddie Patek	.30	.75
335 Bob Tolan	.30	.75
336 Tom Bradley	.30	.75
337 Dave Duncan	.60	1.50
338 Checklist 265-396	1.25	3.00
339 Dick Tidrow	.30	.75
340 Nate Colbert	.30	.75
341 Jim Palmer KP	1.00	2.50
342 Sam McDowell KP	.30	.75
343 Bobby Murcer KP	.30	.75
344 Jim Hunter KP	1.00	2.50
345 Chris Speier KP	.30	.75
346 Gaylord Perry KP	.60	1.50
347 Kansas City Royals TC	.60	1.50
348 Rennie Stennett	.30	.75
349 Dick McAuliffe	.30	.75
350 Tom Seaver	15.00	40.00
351 Jimmy Stewart	.30	.75
352 Don Stanhouse RC	.30	.75
353 Steve Brye	.30	.75
354 Billy Parker	.30	.75
355 Mike Marshall	.60	1.50
356 Chuck Tanner MG	1.50	4.00
357 Ross Grimsley	.30	.75
358 Jim Nettles	.30	.75
359 Cecil Upshaw	.30	.75
360 Joe Rudi UER	.60	1.50
361 Fran Healy	.30	.75
362 Eddie Watt	.30	.75
363 Jackie Hernandez	.30	.75
364 Rick Wise	.30	.75
365 Rico Petrocelli	.60	1.50
366 Brock Davis	.30	.75
367 Burt Hooton	.60	1.50
368 Bill Buckner	.60	1.50
369 Lerrin LaGrow	.30	.75
370 Willie Stargell	2.00	5.00
371 Mike Kekich	.30	.75
372 Oscar Gamble	.30	.75
373 Clyde Wright	.30	.75
374 Darrell Evans	.60	1.50
375 Larry Dierker	.60	1.50
376 Frank Duffy	.30	.75
377 Gene Mauch MG	1.50	4.00
378 Len Randle	.30	.75
379 Cy Acosta RC	.30	.75
380 Johnny Bench	10.00	25.00
381 Vicente Romo	.30	.75
382 Mike Hegan	.30	.75
383 Diego Segui	.30	.75
384 Don Baylor	1.50	4.00
385 Jim Perry	.60	1.50
386 Don Money	.30	.75
387 Jim Barr	.30	.75
388 Ben Oglivie	.60	1.50
389 New York Mets TC	1.50	4.00
390 Mickey Lolich	.60	1.50
391 Lee Lacy RC	.60	1.50
392 Dick Drago	.30	.75
393 Jose Cardenal	.30	.75
394 Sparky Lyle	.60	1.50
395 Roger Metzger	.30	.75
396 Grant Jackson	.30	.75
397 Dave Cash	.50	1.25
398 Rich Hand	.50	1.25
399 George Foster	.75	2.00
400 Gaylord Perry	2.00	5.00
401 Clyde Mashore	.50	1.25
402 Jack Hiatt	.50	1.25
403 Sonny Jackson	.50	1.25
404 Chuck Brinkman	.50	1.25
405 Cesar Tovar	.50	1.25
406 Paul Lindblad	.50	1.25
407 Felix Millan	.50	1.25
408 Jim Colborn	.50	1.25
409 Ivan Murrell	.50	1.25
410 Willie McCovey	2.50	6.00
411 Ray Corbin	.50	1.25
412 Manny Mota	.75	2.00
413 Tom Timmermann	.50	1.25
414 Ken Rudolph	.50	1.25
415 Marty Pattin	.50	1.25
416 Paul Schaal	.50	1.25
417 Scipio Spinks	.50	1.25
418 Bob Grich	.75	2.00
419 Casey Cox	.50	1.25
420 Tommie Agee	.50	1.25
421A B.Winkles MG RC Orange	.60	1.50
421B Bobby Winkles MG Pale	1.25	3.00
422 Bob Robertson	.50	1.25
423 Johnny Jeter	.50	1.25
424 Denny Doyle	.50	1.25
425 Alex Johnson	.50	1.25
426 Dave LaRoche	.50	1.25
427 Rick Auerbach	.50	1.25
428 Wayne Simpson	.50	1.25
429 Jim Fairey	.50	1.25
430 Vida Blue	.75	2.00
431 Gerry Moses	.50	1.25
432 Dan Frisella	.50	1.25
433 Willie Horton	.75	2.00
434 San Francisco Giants TC	1.25	3.00
435 Rico Carty	.75	2.00
436 Jim McAndrew	.50	1.25
437 John Kennedy	.50	1.25
438 Enzo Hernandez	.50	1.25
439 Eddie Fisher	.50	1.25
440 Glenn Beckert	.50	1.25
441 Gail Hopkins	.50	1.25
442 Dick Dietz	.50	1.25
443 Danny Thompson	.50	1.25
444 Ken Brett	.50	1.25
445 Ken Berry	.50	1.25
446 Jerry Reuss	.75	2.00
447 Joe Hague	.50	1.25
448 John Hiller	.50	1.25
449A K.Aspro MG w/Spahn Point	1.50	4.00
449B K.Aspro MG w/Spahn Round	1.50	4.00
450 Joe Torre	1.25	3.00
451 John Vukovich RC	.50	1.25
452 Paul Casanova	.50	1.25
453 Checklist 397-528	1.25	3.00
454 Tom Haller	.50	1.25
455 Bill Melton	.50	1.25
456 Dick Green	.50	1.25
457 John Strohmayer	.50	1.25
458 Jim Mason	.50	1.25
459 Jimmy Howarth RC	.50	1.25
460 Bill Freehan	.75	2.00
461 Mike Corkins	.50	1.25
462 Ron Blomberg	.50	1.25
463 Ken Tatum	.50	1.25
464 Chicago Cubs TC	1.25	3.00
465 Dave Giusti	.50	1.25
466 Jose Arcia	.50	1.25
467 Mike Ryan	.50	1.25
468 Tom Griffin	.50	1.25
469 Dan Monzon RC	.50	1.25
470 Mike Cuellar	.75	2.00
471 Ty Cobb LDR	4.00	10.00
472 Lou Gehrig LDR	6.00	15.00
473 Hank Aaron LDR	8.00	20.00
474 Babe Ruth LDR	8.00	20.00
475 Ty Cobb LDR	6.00	15.00
476 Walter Johnson LDR	1.25	3.00
477 Cy Young LDR	1.25	3.00
478 Walter Johnson LDR	1.25	3.00
479 Hal Lanier	.50	1.25
480 Juan Marichal	2.00	5.00
481 Chicago White Sox TC	1.25	3.00
482 Rick Reuschel RC	1.25	3.00
483 Dal Maxvill	.50	1.25
484 Ernie McAnally	.50	1.25
485 Norm Cash	.75	2.00
486A D.Ozark MG RC Orange	.60	1.50
486B Danny Ozark MG Pale	1.25	3.00
487 Bruce Dal Canton	.50	1.25
488 Dave Campbell	.75	2.00
489 Jeff Burroughs	.75	2.00
490 Claude Osteen	.75	2.00
491 Bob Montgomery	.50	1.25
492 Pedro Borbon	.50	1.25
493 Duffy Dyer	.50	1.25
494 Rich Morales	.50	1.25
495 Tommy Helms	.50	1.25
496 Ray Lamb	.50	1.25
497A R.Schoen MG Orange	.75	2.00
497B R.Schoen MG Pale	1.25	3.00
498 Graig Nettles	1.25	3.00
499 Bob Moose	.50	1.25
500 Oakland Athletics TC	1.25	3.00
501 Larry Gura	.50	1.25
502 Bobby Valentine	1.25	3.00
503 Phil Niekro	2.00	5.00
504 Earl Williams	.50	1.25
505 Bob Bailey	.50	1.25
506 Bart Johnson	.50	1.25
507 Darrel Chaney	.50	1.25
508 Gates Brown	.50	1.25
509 Jim Nash	.50	1.25
510 Amos Otis	.75	2.00
511 Sam McDowell	.75	2.00
512 Dalton Jones	.50	1.25
513 Dave Marshall	.50	1.25
514 Jerry Kenney	.50	1.25
515 Andy Messersmith	.75	2.00
516 Danny Walton	.50	1.25
517A Bill Virdon MG w/o Ear	.60	1.50
517B Bill Virdon MG w/Ear	1.25	3.00
518 Bob Veale	.50	1.25
519 Johnny Edwards	.50	1.25
520 Mel Stottlemyre	.75	2.00
521 Atlanta Braves TC	1.25	3.00
522 Leo Cardenas	.50	1.25
523 Wayne Granger	.50	1.25
524 Gene Tenace	.75	2.00
525 Jim Fregosi	.75	2.00
526 Ollie Brown	.50	1.25
527 Dan McGinn	.50	1.25
528 Paul Blair	.50	1.25
529 Milt May	1.25	3.00
530 Jim Kaat	2.00	5.00
531 Ron Woods	1.25	3.00
532 Steve Mingori	1.25	3.00
533 Larry Stahl	1.25	3.00
534 Dave Lemonds	1.25	3.00
535 Johnny Callison	2.00	5.00
536 Philadelphia Phillies TC	2.50	6.00
537 Bill Slayback RC	1.25	3.00
538 Jim Ray Hart	2.00	5.00
539 Tom Murphy	1.25	3.00
540 Cleon Jones	2.00	5.00
541 Bob Bolin	1.25	3.00
542 Pat Corrales	2.00	5.00
543 Alan Foster	1.25	3.00
544 Von Joshua	1.25	3.00
545 Orlando Cepeda	3.00	8.00
546 Jim York	1.25	3.00
547 Bobby Heise	1.25	3.00
548 Don Durham RC	1.25	3.00
549 Whitey Herzog MG	2.00	5.00
550 Dave Johnson	2.00	5.00
551 Mike Kilkenny	1.25	3.00
552 J.C. Martin	1.25	3.00
553 Mickey Scott	1.25	3.00
554 Dave Concepcion	2.00	5.00
555 Bill Hands	1.25	3.00
556 New York Yankees TC	3.00	8.00
557 Bernie Williams	1.25	3.00
558 Jerry May	1.25	3.00
559 Barry Lersch	1.25	3.00
560 Frank Howard	2.00	5.00
561 Jim Geddes RC	1.25	3.00
562 Wayne Garrett	1.25	3.00
563 Larry Haney	1.25	3.00
564 Mike Thompson RC	1.25	3.00
565 Jim Hickman	1.25	3.00
566 Lew Krausse	1.25	3.00
567 Bob Fenwick	1.25	3.00
568 Ray Newman	1.25	3.00
569 Walt Alston MG	3.00	8.00
570 Bill Singer	2.00	5.00
571 Rusty Torres	1.25	3.00
572 Gary Sutherland	1.25	3.00
573 Fred Beene	1.25	3.00
574 Bob Didier	1.25	3.00
575 Dock Ellis	1.25	3.00
576 Montreal Expos TC	2.50	6.00
577 Eric Soderholm RC	1.25	3.00
578 Ken Wright	1.25	3.00
579 Tom Grieve	2.00	5.00
580 Joe Pepitone	2.00	5.00
581 Steve Kealey	1.25	3.00
582 Darrell Porter	2.00	5.00
583 Bill Greif	1.25	3.00
584 Chris Arnold	1.25	3.00
585 Joe Niekro	2.00	5.00
586 Bill Sudakis	1.25	3.00
587 Rich McKinney	1.25	3.00
588 Checklist 529-660	8.00	20.00
589 Ken Forsch	1.25	3.00
590 Deron Johnson	1.25	3.00
591 Mike Hedlund	1.25	3.00
592 John Boccabella	1.25	3.00
593 Jack McKeon MG RC	1.50	4.00
594 Vic Harris RC	1.25	3.00
595 Don Gullett	2.00	5.00
596 Boston Red Sox TC	2.50	6.00
597 Mickey Rivers	2.00	5.00
598 Phil Roof	1.25	3.00
599 Ed Crosby	1.25	3.00
600 Dave McNally	2.00	5.00
601 Robles/Pena/Stelmaszek RC	2.00	5.00
602 Behney/Garcia/Rau RC	2.00	5.00
603 Hughes/McNulty/Reitz RC	2.00	5.00
604 Jefferson/O'Toole/Stampe RC	2.00	5.00
605 Cabell/Bourque/Marquez RC	2.00	5.00
606 Matthews/Pac/Roque RC	2.00	5.00
607 Frias/Busse/Guerrero RC	2.00	5.00
608 Busby/Colpaert/Medich RC	2.00	5.00
609 Blanks/Garcia/Lopes RC	2.00	5.00
610 Freeman/Hough/Webb RC	2.00	5.00
611 Coggins/Wohlford/Zisk RC	2.00	5.00
612 Lawson/Reynolds/Strom RC	2.00	5.00
613 Boone/Jutze/Ivie RC	6.00	15.00
614 Bumbry/Evans/Spikes RC	40.00	100.00
615 Mike Schmidt RC	150.00	400.00
616 Angelini/Blateric/Garman RC	2.00	5.00
617 Rich Chiles	1.25	3.00
618 Andy Etchebarren	1.25	3.00
619 Billy Wilson	1.25	3.00
620 Tommy Harper	2.00	5.00
621 Joe Ferguson	2.00	5.00
622 Larry Hisle	2.00	5.00
623 Steve Renko	1.25	3.00
624 Leo Durocher MG	2.00	5.00
625 Angel Mangual	1.25	3.00
626 Bob Barton	1.25	3.00
627 Luis Alvarado	1.25	3.00
628 Jim Slaton	1.25	3.00
629 Cleveland Indians TC	2.50	6.00
630 Denny McLain	3.00	8.00
631 Tom Matchick	1.25	3.00
632 Dick Selma	1.25	3.00
633 Ike Brown	1.25	3.00
634 Alan Closter	1.25	3.00
635 Gene Alley	2.00	5.00
636 Rickey Clark	1.25	3.00
637 Norm Miller	1.25	3.00
638 Ken Reynolds	1.25	3.00
639 Willie Crawford	1.25	3.00
640 Dick Bosman	1.25	3.00
641 Cincinnati Reds TC	2.50	6.00
642 Jose Laboy	1.25	3.00
643 Al Fitzmorris	1.25	3.00
644 Jack Heidemann	1.25	3.00
645 Bob Locker	1.25	3.00
646 Del Crandall MG	1.50	4.00
647 George Stone	1.25	3.00
648 Tom Egan	1.25	3.00
649 Rich Folkers	1.25	3.00
650 Felipe Alou	2.00	5.00
651 Don Carrithers	1.25	3.00
652 Ted Kubiak	1.25	3.00
653 Joe Hoerner	1.25	3.00

654 Minnesota Twins TC 2.50 6.00
655 Clay Kirby 1.25 3.00
656 John Ellis 1.25 3.00
657 Bob Johnson 1.25 3.00
658 Elliott Maddox 1.25 3.00
659 Jose Pagan 1.25 3.00
660 Fred Scherman 2.00 5.00

1973 Topps Blue Team Checklists

COMPLETE SET (24) 75.00 150.00
COMMON TEAM (1-24) 3.00 8.00
16 New York Mets 4.00 10.00
17 New York Yankees 4.00 10.00

1973 Topps Pin-Ups

This test issue of 24 pin-ups is quite scarce. Each pin-up measures approximately 3 7/16" by 4 5/8" and is very colorful with a thick white border. The thin-paper pin-ups contain a facsimile autograph on the front of the card. The set shares the same checklist with the 1973 Topps Comics. The set is unnumbered and hence is ordered below alphabetically. The team insignia and logos on the cards have been airbrushed away, which is contra-indicative of a Topps issue.

COMPLETE SET (24) 4000.00 8000.00
1 Hank Aaron 400.00 800.00
2 Dick Allen 100.00 200.00
3 Johnny Bench 300.00 600.00
4 Steve Carlton 300.00 600.00
5 Nate Colbert 75.00 150.00
6 Willie Davis 75.00 150.00
7 Mike Epstein 75.00 150.00
8 Reggie Jackson 400.00 800.00
9 Harmon Killebrew 200.00 400.00
10 Mickey Lolich 100.00 200.00
11 Mike Marshall 75.00 150.00
12 Lee May 75.00 150.00
13 Willie McCovey 200.00 400.00
14 Bobby Murcer 100.00 200.00
15 Gaylord Perry 200.00 400.00
16 Lou Piniella 100.00 200.00
17 Brooks Robinson 300.00 600.00
18 Nolan Ryan 600.00 1200.00
19 George Scott 75.00 150.00
20 Tom Seaver 400.00 800.00
21 Willie Stargell 200.00 400.00
22 Joe Torre 150.00 300.00
23 Billy Williams 200.00 400.00
24 Carl Yastrzemski 250.00 500.00

1973 Topps Candy Lids

One of Topps' most unusual test sets is this series of 55 color portraits of baseball players printed on the bottom of candy lids. These lids measure 1 7/8" in diameter. The product was called "Baseball Stars Bubble Gum" and consisted of a small tub of candy-coated gum kernels. The lids were issued in 10 cent containers which came 24 to a box. Issued in 1973, the lids are unnumbered and each has a small tab. Underneath the picture is a small ribbon design which contains the player's name, team and position. It is believed that this set was mainly tested on the east coast with some light testing in the midwest.

COMPLETE SET (55) 400.00 800.00
1 Hank Aaron 20.00 50.00
2 Dick Allen 2.00 5.00
3 Dusty Baker 2.00 5.00
4 Sal Bando 1.50 4.00
5 Johnny Bench 12.50 30.00
6 Bobby Bonds 2.00 5.00
7 Dick Bosman 1.50 4.00
8 Lou Brock 8.00 20.00
9 Rod Carew 8.00 20.00
10 Steve Carlton 8.00 20.00
11 Nate Colbert 1.50 4.00
12 Willie Davis 1.50 4.00
13 Larry Dierker 1.50 4.00
14 Mike Epstein 1.50 4.00
15 Carlton Fisk 12.50 40.00
16 Tim Foli 1.50 4.00
17 Ray Fosse 1.50 4.00
18 Bill Freehan 2.00 5.00
19 Bob Gibson 8.00 20.00
20 Bud Harrelson 1.50 4.00
21 Jim Hunter 5.00 12.00
22 Reggie Jackson 12.50 30.00
23 Ferguson Jenkins 5.00 12.00
24 Al Kaline 8.00 20.00
25 Harmon Killebrew 8.00 20.00
26 Clay Kirby 1.50 4.00
27 Mickey Lolich 2.00 5.00
28 Greg Luzinski 2.00 5.00
29 Willie McCovey 8.00 20.00
30 Mike Marshall 1.50 4.00
31 Lee May 1.50 4.00
32 John Mayberry 1.50 4.00
33 Willie Mays 20.00 50.00
34 Thurman Munson 5.00 12.00
35 Bobby Murcer 2.00 5.00
36 Gary Nolan 1.50 4.00
37 Amos Otis 1.50 4.00
38 Jim Palmer 8.00 20.00
39 Gaylord Perry 5.00 12.00
40 Lou Piniella 2.00 5.00
41 Brooks Robinson 8.00 20.00
42 Frank Robinson 8.00 20.00
43 Ellie Rodriguez 1.50 4.00
44 Pete Rose 20.00 50.00
45 Nolan Ryan 60.00 120.00
46 Manny Sanguillen 1.50 4.00
47 George Scott 1.50 4.00
48 Tom Seaver 12.50 30.00
49 Chris Speier 1.50 4.00
50 Willie Stargell 8.00 20.00
51 Don Sutton 5.00 12.00
52 Joe Torre 3.00 8.00
53 Billy Williams 5.00 12.00
54 Wilbur Wood 1.50 4.00
55 Carl Yastrzemski 12.50 30.00

1973 Topps Comics

This test issue of 24 comics is quite scarce. Each comic measures approximately 4 5/8" by 3 7/16" and is very colorful. The comics are subtitled "Career Highlights of ..." and feature six or seven panels of information about the particular player. The set shares the same checklist with the 1973 Topps Pin-Ups. The set is unnumbered and hence is ordered below alphabetically. The team insignia and logos on the cards have been airbrushed away, which is contra-indicative of a Topps issue.

COMPLETE SET (24) 1500.00 3000.00
1 Hank Aaron 300.00 600.00
2 Dick Allen 150.00 300.00
3 Johnny Bench 300.00 600.00
4 Steve Carlton 75.00 150.00
5 Nate Colbert 100.00 200.00
6 Willie Davis 100.00 200.00
7 Mike Epstein 125.00 250.00
8 Reggie Jackson 400.00 800.00
9 Harmon Killebrew 200.00 400.00
10 Mickey Lolich 125.00 250.00
11 Mike Marshall 100.00 200.00
12 Lee May 125.00 250.00
13 Willie McCovey 200.00 400.00
14 Bobby Murcer 125.00 250.00
15 Gaylord Perry 200.00 400.00
16 Lou Piniella 125.00 250.00
17 Brooks Robinson 250.00 500.00
18 Nolan Ryan 1000.00 2000.00
19 George Scott 100.00 200.00
20 Tom Seaver 300.00 600.00
21 Willie Stargell 200.00 400.00
22 Joe Torre 150.00 300.00
23 Billy Williams 200.00 400.00
24 Carl Yastrzemski 400.00 800.00

1974 Topps

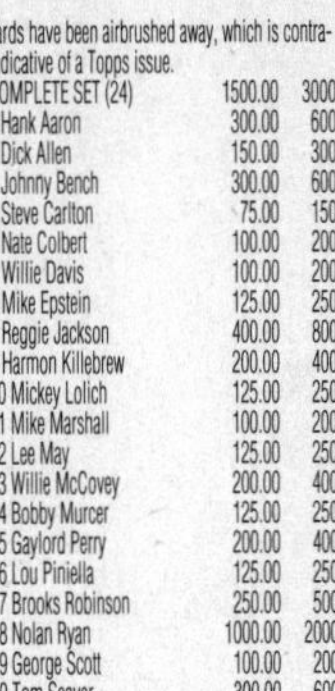

The cards in this 660-card set measure 2 1/2" by 3 1/2". This year marked the first time Topps issued all the cards of its baseball set at the same time rather than in series. Among other methods, cards were issued in eight-card fifteen-cent wax packs and 42 card rack packs. The ten cent packs were issued 36 to a box. For the first time, factory sets were issued through the JC Penny's catalog. Sales were probably disappointing for it would be several years before factory sets were issued again. Some interesting variations were created by the rumored move of the San Diego Padres to Washington. Fifteen cards (13 players, the team card, and the rookie card (599) of the Padres were printed either as "San Diego" (SD) or "Washington." The latter are the scarcer variety and are denoted in the checklist below by WAS. Each team's manager and his coaches again have a combined card with small pictures of each coach below the larger photo of the team's manager. The first six cards in the set (1-6) feature Hank Aaron and his illustrious career. Other topical subsets included in the set are League Leaders (201-208), All-Star selections (331-339), Playoffs cards (470-471), World Series cards (472-479), and Rookie Prospects (596-608). The card backs for the All-Stars (331-339) have no statistics, but form a picture puzzle of Bobby Bonds, the 1973 All-Star Game MVP. The key Rookie Cards in this set are Ken Griffey Sr., Dave Parker and Dave Winfield.

COMPLETE SET (660) 300.00 800.00
COMP.FACT.SET (660) 500.00 1200.00
WRAPPERS (10-CENTS) 4.00 10.00
1 Hank Aaron 715 15.00 40.00
2 Hank Aaron 54-57 5.00 12.00
3 Hank Aaron 58-61 5.00 12.00
4 Hank Aaron 62-65 5.00 12.00
5 Hank Aaron 66-69 5.00 12.00
6 Hank Aaron 70-73 5.00 12.00
7 Jim Hunter 1.50 4.00
8 George Theodore RC .20 .50
9 Mickey Lolich .40 1.00
10 Johnny Bench 8.00 20.00
11 Jim Bibby .20 .50
12 Dave May .20 .50
13 Tom Hilgendorf .20 .50
14 Paul Popovich .20 .50
15 Joe Torre .75 2.00
16 Baltimore Orioles TC .40 1.00
17 Doug Bird RC .20 .50
18 Gary Thomasson RC .20 .50
19 Gerry Moses .20 .50
20 Nolan Ryan 12.00 30.00
21 Bob Gallagher RC .20 .50
22 Cy Acosta .20 .50
23 Craig Robinson RC .20 .50
24 John Hiller .40 1.00
25 Ken Singleton .40 1.00
26 Bill Campbell RC .40 1.00
27 George Scott .40 1.00
28 Manny Sanguillen .40 1.00
29 Phil Niekro 1.25 3.00
30 Bobby Bonds .75 2.00
31 Preston Gomez MG .40 1.00
32A Johnny Grubb SD RC .40 1.00
32B Johnny Grubb WASH 1.50 4.00
33 Don Newhauser RC .20 .50
34 Andy Kosco .20 .50
35 Gaylord Perry 1.25 3.00
36 St. Louis Cardinals TC .40 1.00
37 Dave Sells RC .20 .50
38 Don Kessinger .40 1.00
39 Ken Suarez .20 .50
40 Jim Palmer 6.00 15.00
41 Bobby Floyd .20 .50
42 Claude Osteen .40 1.00
43 Jim Wynn .40 1.00
44 Mel Stottlemyre .40 1.00
45 Dave Johnson .40 1.00
46 Pat Kelly .20 .50
47 Dick Ruthven RC .20 .50
48 Dick Sharon RC .20 .50
49 Steve Renko .20 .50
50 Rod Carew 3.00 8.00
51 Bobby Heise .20 .50
52 Al Oliver .40 1.00
53A Fred Kendall SD .40 1.00
53B Fred Kendall WASH 1.50 4.00
54 Elias Sosa RC .20 .50
55 Frank Robinson 5.00 12.00
56 New York Mets TC .40 1.00
57 Darold Knowles .20 .50
58 Charlie Spikes .20 .50
59 Ross Grimsley .20 .50
60 Lou Brock 2.50 6.00
61 Luis Aparicio 1.25 3.00
62 Bob Locker .20 .50
63 Bill Sudakis .20 .50
64 Doug Rau .20 .50
65 Amos Otis .40 1.00
66 Sparky Lyle .40 1.00
67 Tommy Helms .20 .50
68 Grant Jackson .20 .50
69 Del Unser .20 .50
70 Dick Allen .75 2.00
71 Dan Frisella .20 .50
72 Aurelio Rodriguez .20 .50
73 Mike Marshall .75 2.00
74 Minnesota Twins TC .40 1.00
75 Jim Colborn .20 .50
76 Mickey Rivers .40 1.00
77A Rich Troedson SD RC .40 1.00
77B Rich Troedson WASH 1.50 4.00
78 Charlie Fox MG .40 1.00
79 Gene Tenace .40 1.00
80 Tom Seaver 10.00 25.00
81 Frank Duffy .20 .50
82 Dave Giusti .20 .50
83 Orlando Cepeda 1.25 3.00
84 Rick Wise .20 .50
85 Joe Morgan 3.00 8.00
86 Joe Ferguson .40 1.00
87 Fergie Jenkins 1.25 3.00
88 Freddie Patek .40 1.00
89 Jackie Brown .20 .50
90 Bobby Murcer .40 1.00
91 Ken Forsch .20 .50
92 Paul Blair .40 1.00
93 Rod Gilbreath RC .20 .50
94 Detroit Tigers TC .40 1.00
95 Steve Carlton 3.00 8.00
96 Jerry Hairston RC .20 .50
97 Bob Bailey .20 .50
98 Bert Blyleven .75 2.00
99 Del Crandall MG .40 1.00
100 Willie Stargell 2.50 6.00
101 Bobby Valentine .40 1.00
102A Bill Greif SD .40 1.00
102B Bill Greif WASH 1.50 4.00
103 Sal Bando .40 1.00
104 Ron Bryant .20 .50
105 Carlton Fisk 5.00 12.00
106 Harry Parker RC .20 .50
107 Alex Johnson .20 .50
108 Al Hrabosky .40 1.00
109 Bob Grich .40 1.00
110 Billy Williams 1.25 3.00
111 Clay Carroll .20 .50
112 Dave Lopes .75 2.00
113 Dick Drago .20 .50
114 California Angels TC .40 1.00
115 Willie Horton .40 1.00
116 Jerry Reuss .40 1.00
117 Ron Blomberg .20 .50
118 Bill Lee .40 1.00
119 Danny Ozark MG .40 1.00
120 Wilbur Wood .20 .50
121 Larry Lintz RC .20 .50
122 Jim Holt .20 .50
123 Nelson Briles .40 1.00
124 Bobby Coluccio RC .20 .50
125A Nate Colbert SD .40 1.00
125B Nate Colbert WASH 1.50 4.00
126 Checklist 1-132 1.25 3.00
127 Tom Paciorek .40 1.00
128 John Ellis .20 .50
129 Chris Speier .20 .50
130 Reggie Jackson 8.00 20.00
131 Bob Boone .75 2.00
132 Felix Millan .20 .50
133 David Clyde RC .40 1.00
134 Denis Menke .20 .50
135 Roy White .40 1.00
136 Rick Reuschel .40 1.00
137 Al Bumbry .40 1.00
138 Eddie Brinkman .20 .50
139 Aurelio Monteagudo .20 .50
140 Darrell Evans .75 2.00
141 Pat Bourque .20 .50
142 Pedro Garcia .20 .50
143 Dick Woodson .20 .50
144 Walter Alston MG 1.25 3.00
145 Dock Ellis .20 .50
146 Ron Fairly .40 1.00
147 Bart Johnson .20 .50
148A Dave Hilton SD .40 1.00
148B Dave Hilton WASH 1.50 4.00
149 Mac Scarce .20 .50
150 John Mayberry .40 1.00
151 Diego Segui .20 .50
152 Oscar Gamble .40 1.00
153 Jon Matlack .40 1.00
154 Houston Astros TC .40 1.00
155 Bert Campaneris .40 1.00
156 Randy Moffitt .20 .50
157 Vic Harris .20 .50
158 Jack Billingham .20 .50
159 Jim Ray Hart .20 .50
160 Brooks Robinson 6.00 15.00
161 Ray Burris UER RC .40 1.00
162 Bill Freehan .40 1.00
163 Ken Berry .20 .50
164 Tom House .20 .50
165 Willie Davis .40 1.00
166 Jack McKeon MG .40 1.00
167 Luis Tiant .75 2.00
168 Danny Thompson .40 1.00
169 Steve Rogers RC .75 2.00
170 Bill Melton .20 .50
171 Eduardo Rodriguez RC .20 .50
172 Gene Clines .20 .50
173A Randy Jones SD RC .75 2.00
173B Randy Jones WASH 2.00 5.00
174 Bill Robinson .40 1.00
175 Reggie Cleveland .20 .50
176 John Lowenstein .20 .50
177 Dave Roberts .20 .50
178 Garry Maddox .40 1.00
179 Yogi Berra MG 2.00 5.00
180 Ken Holtzman .40 1.00
181 Cesar Geronimo .20 .50
182 Lindy McDaniel .40 1.00
183 Johnny Oates .40 1.00
184 Texas Rangers TC .40 1.00
185 Jose Cardenal .20 .50
186 Fred Scherman .20 .50
187 Don Baylor .75 2.00
188 Rudy Meoli RC .20 .50
189 Jim Brewer .20 .50
190 Tony Oliva .75 2.00
191 Al Fitzmorris .20 .50
192 Mario Guerrero .20 .50
193 Tom Walker .20 .50
194 Darrell Porter .40 1.00
195 Carlos May .20 .50
196 Jim Fregosi .40 1.00
197A Vicente Romo SD .40 1.00
197B Vicente Romo WASH 1.50 4.00
198 Dave Cash .20 .50
199 Mike Kekich .20 .50
200 Cesar Cedeno .40 1.00
201 R.Carew/P.Rose LL 2.50 6.00
202 R.Jackson/W.Stargell LL 2.00 5.00
203 R.Jackson/W.Stargell LL 2.00 5.00
204 T.Harper/L.Brock LL .75 2.00
205 W.Wood/R.Bryant LL .40 1.00
206 J.Palmer/T.Seaver LL 2.00 5.00
207 N.Ryan/T.Seaver LL 5.00 12.00
208 J.Hiller/M.Marshall LL .40 1.00
209 Ted Sizemore .20 .50
210 Bill Singer .20 .50
211 Chicago Cubs TC .40 1.00
212 Rollie Fingers 1.25 3.00
213 Dave Rader .20 .50
214 Billy Grabarkewitz .20 .50
215 Al Kaline UER 10.00 25.00
216 Ray Sadecki .20 .50
217 Tim Foli .20 .50
218 Johnny Briggs .20 .50
219 Doug Griffin .20 .50
220 Don Sutton 1.25 3.00
221 Chuck Tanner MG .40 1.00
222 Ramon Hernandez .20 .50
223 Jeff Burroughs .75 2.00
224 Roger Metzger .20 .50
225 Paul Splittorff .20 .50
226A San Diego Padres TC SD .75 2.00
226B San Diego Padres TC WASH 3.00 8.00
227 Mike Lum .20 .50
228 Ted Kubiak .20 .50
229 Fritz Peterson .20 .50
230 Tony Perez 1.50 4.00
231 Dick Tidrow .20 .50
232 Steve Brye .20 .50
233 Jim Barr .20 .50
234 John Milner .20 .50
235 Dave McNally .40 1.00
236 Red Schoendienst MG 1.25 3.00
237 Ken Brett .20 .50
238 F.Healy w/Munson .20 .50
239 Bill Russell .40 1.00
240 Joe Coleman .20 .50
241A Glenn Beckert SD .40 1.00
241B Glenn Beckert WASH 1.50 4.00
242 Bill Gogolewski .20 .50
243 Bob Oliver .20 .50
244 Carl Morton .20 .50
245 Cleon Jones .20 .50
246 Oakland Athletics TC .75 2.00
247 Rick Miller .20 .50
248 Tom Hall .20 .50
249 George Mitterwald .20 .50
250A Willie McCovey SD 3.00 8.00
250B Willie McCovey WASH 10.00 25.00
251 Graig Nettles .75 2.00
252 Dave Parker RC 20.00 50.00
253 John Boccabella .20 .50
254 Stan Bahnsen .20 .50
255 Larry Bowa .40 1.00
256 Tom Griffin .20 .50
257 Buddy Bell .75 2.00
258 Jerry Morales .40 1.00
259 Bob Reynolds .20 .50
260 Ted Simmons .75 2.00
261 Jerry Bell .20 .50
262 Ed Kirkpatrick .20 .50
263 Checklist 133-264 1.25 3.00
264 Joe Rudi .40 1.00
265 Tug McGraw .75 2.00
266 Jim Northrup .40 1.00
267 Andy Messersmith .40 1.00
268 Tom Grieve .40 1.00
269 Bob Johnson .20 .50
270 Ron Santo .75 2.00
271 Bill Hands .20 .50
272 Paul Casanova .20 .50
273 Checklist 265-396 1.25 3.00
274 Fred Beene .20 .50
275 Ron Hunt .20 .50
276 Bobby Winkles MG .20 .50
277 Gary Nolan .40 1.00
278 Cookie Rojas .40 1.00
279 Jim Crawford RC .20 .50
280 Carl Yastrzemski 10.00 25.00
281 San Francisco Giants TC .40 1.00
282 Doyle Alexander .40 1.00
283 Mike Schmidt 25.00 60.00
284 Dave Duncan .40 1.00
285 Reggie Smith .40 1.00
286 Tony Muser .20 .50
287 Clay Kirby .20 .50
288 Gorman Thomas RC .75 2.00
289 Rick Auerbach .20 .50
290 Vida Blue .40 1.00
291 Don Hahn .20 .50
292 Chuck Seelbach .20 .50
293 Milt May .20 .50
294 Steve Foucault RC .20 .50
295 Rick Monday .40 1.00
296 Ray Corbin .20 .50
297 Hal Breeden .20 .50
298 Roric Harrison .20 .50
299 Gene Michael .20 .50
300 Pete Rose 12.00 30.00
301 Bob Montgomery .20 .50
302 Rudy May .20 .50
303 George Hendrick .40 1.00
304 Don Wilson .20 .50
305 Tito Fuentes .20 .50
306 Earl Weaver MG 1.25 3.00
307 Luis Melendez .20 .50
308 Bruce Dal Canton .20 .50
309A Dave Roberts SD .40 1.00
309B Dave Roberts WASH 2.50 6.00
310 Terry Forster .40 1.00
311 Jerry Grote .40 1.00
312 Deron Johnson .20 .50
313 Barry Lersch .20 .50
314 Milwaukee Brewers TC .40 1.00
315 Ron Cey .75 2.00
316 Jim Perry .40 1.00
317 Richie Zisk .40 1.00
318 Jim Merritt .20 .50
319 Randy Hundley .20 .50
320 Dusty Baker .75 2.00
321 Steve Braun .20 .50
322 Ernie McAnally .20 .50
323 Richie Scheinblum .20 .50
324 Steve Kline .20 .50
325 Tommy Harper .40 1.00
326 Sparky Anderson MG 1.25 3.00
327 Tom Timmermann .20 .50
328 Skip Jutze .20 .50
329 Mark Belanger .40 1.00
330 Juan Marichal 2.00 5.00
331 C.Fisk/J.Bench AS 2.00 5.00
332 D.Allen/H.Aaron AS 3.00 8.00
333 R.Carew/J.Morgan AS 1.50 4.00
334 B.Robinson/R.Santo AS .75 2.00
335 B.Campaneris/C.Speier AS .40 1.00
336 B.Murcer/P.Rose AS 2.00 5.00
337 A.Otis/C.Cedeno AS .20 .50
338 R.Jackson/B.Williams AS 2.00 5.00
339 J.Hunter/R.Wise AS 1.25 3.00
340 Thurman Munson 5.00 12.00
341 Dan Driessen RC .40 1.00
342 Jim Lonborg .40 1.00
343 Kansas City Royals TC .40 1.00
344 Mike Caldwell .20 .50
345 Bill North .20 .50
346 Ron Reed .20 .50
347 Sandy Alomar .40 1.00
348 Pete Richert .20 .50
349 John Vukovich .20 .50
350 Bob Gibson 6.00 15.00
351 Dwight Evans 1.25 3.00
352 Bill Stoneman .20 .50
353 Rich Coggins .20 .50
354 Whitey Lockman MG .40 1.00
355 Dave Nelson .20 .50
356 Jerry Koosman .40 1.00
357 Buddy Bradford .20 .50
358 Dal Maxvill .20 .50
359 Brent Strom .20 .50
360 Greg Luzinski .75 2.00
361 Don Carrithers .20 .50
362 Hal King .20 .50
363 New York Yankees TC .75 2.00
364A Cito Gaston SD .75 2.00
364B Cito Gaston WASH 3.00 8.00
365 Steve Busby .40 1.00
366 Larry Hisle .40 1.00
367 Norm Cash .75 2.00
368 Manny Mota .40 1.00
369 Paul Lindblad .20 .50
370 Bob Watson .40 1.00
371 Jim Slaton .20 .50
372 Ken Reitz .20 .50
373 John Curtis .20 .50
374 Marty Perez .20 .50
375 Earl Williams .20 .50
376 Jorge Orta .20 .50
377 Ron Woods .20 .50
378 Burt Hooton .40 1.00
379 Billy Martin MG .75 2.00
380 Bud Harrelson .40 1.00
381 Charlie Sands .20 .50
382 Bob Moose .20 .50
383 Philadelphia Phillies TC .75 2.00
384 Chris Chambliss .40 1.00
385 Don Gullett .40 1.00
386 Gary Matthews .75 2.00
387A Rich Morales SD .40 1.00
387B Rich Morales WASH 2.50 6.00
388 Phil Roof .20 .50
389 Gates Brown .40 1.00
390 Lou Piniella .75 2.00
391 Billy Champion .40 1.00
392 Dick Green .40 1.00
393 Orlando Pena .20 .50
394 Ken Henderson .20 .50
395 Doug Rader .20 .50
396 Tommy Davis .40 1.00
397 George Stone .20 .50
398 Duke Sims .20 .50
399 Mike Paul .20 .50
400 Harmon Killebrew 6.00 15.00
401 Elliott Maddox .40 1.00
402 Jim Rooker .40 1.00
403 Darrell Johnson MG .40 1.00
404 Jim Howarth .20 .50
405 Ellie Rodriguez .20 .50
406 Steve Arlin .20 .50
407 Jim Wohlford .20 .50
408 Charlie Hough .40 1.00
409 Ike Brown .20 .50
410 Pedro Borbon .40 1.00
411 Frank Baker .20 .50
412 Chuck Taylor .20 .50
413 Don Money .40 1.00
414 Checklist 397-528 1.25 3.00
415 Gary Gentry .20 .50
416 Chicago White Sox TC .40 1.00
417 Rich Folkers .20 .50
418 Walt Williams .20 .50
419 Wayne Twitchell .20 .50
420 Ray Fosse .40 1.00
421 Dan Fife RC .20 .50
422 Gonzalo Marquez .20 .50
423 Fred Stanley .20 .50
424 Jim Beauchamp .20 .50
425 Pete Broberg .20 .50
426 Rennie Stennett .20 .50
427 Bobby Bolin .20 .50
428 Gary Sutherland .20 .50
429 Dick Lange RC .20 .50
430 Matty Alou .40 1.00
431 Gene Garber RC .40 1.00
432 Chris Arnold .20 .50
433 Lerrin LaGrow .20 .50
434 Ken McMullen .20 .50
435 Dave Concepcion .75 2.00
436 Don Hood RC .20 .50
437 Jim Lyttle .20 .50
438 Ed Herrmann .20 .50
439 Norm Miller .20 .50
440 Jim Kaat .75 2.00
441 Tom Ragland .20 .50
442 Alan Foster .20 .50
443 Tom Hutton .20 .50
444 Vic Davalillo .20 .50
445 George Medich .20 .50
446 Len Randle .20 .50
447 Frank Quilici MG .40 1.00
448 Ron Hodges RC .20 .50
449 Tom McCraw .20 .50
450 Rich Hebner .40 1.00
451 Tommy John .75 2.00
452 Gene Hiser .20 .50
453 Balor Moore .20 .50
454 Kurt Bevacqua .20 .50
455 Tom Bradley .20 .50
456 Dave Winfield RC 25.00 60.00
457 Chuck Goggin RC .20 .50
458 Jim Ray .20 .50
459 Cincinnati Reds TC .75 2.00
460 Boog Powell .75 2.00
461 John Odom .20 .50
462 Luis Alvarado .20 .50
463 Pat Dobson .20 .50
464 Jose Cruz .75 2.00
465 Dick Bosman .20 .50
466 Dick Billings .20 .50
467 Winston Llenas .20 .50
468 Pepe Frias .20 .50
469 Joe Decker .20 .50
470 Reggie Jackson ALCS 2.00 5.00
471 Jon Matlack NLCS .40 1.00
472 Darold Knowles WS1 .40 1.00
473 Willie Mays WS 6.00 15.00
474 Bert Campaneris WS3 .40 1.00
475 Rusty Staub WS4 .40 1.00
476 Cleon Jones WS5 .40 1.00
477 Reggie Jackson WS6 2.00 5.00
478 Bert Campaneris WS7 .40 1.00
479 A's Celebrate WS .40 1.00
480 Willie Crawford .20 .50
481 Jerry Terrell RC .20 .50
482 Bob Didier .20 .50
483 Atlanta Braves TC .40 1.00
484 Carmen Fanzone .20 .50
485 Felipe Alou .75 2.00
486 Steve Stone .40 1.00
487 Ted Martinez .20 .50
488 Andy Etchebarren .20 .50
489 Danny Murtaugh MG .40 1.00
490 Vada Pinson .75 2.00
491 Roger Nelson .20 .50
492 Mike Rogodzinski RC .20 .50
493 Joe Hoerner .20 .50
494 Ed Goodson .20 .50
495 Dick McAuliffe .40 1.00
496 Tom Murphy .20 .50
497 Bobby Mitchell .20 .50
498 Pat Corrales .20 .50
499 Rusty Torres .20 .50
500 Lee May .40 1.00
501 Eddie Leon .20 .50
502 Dave LaRoche .20 .50
503 Eric Soderholm .20 .50
504 Joe Niekro .40 1.00
505 Bill Buckner .40 1.00
506 Ed Farmer .20 .50
507 Larry Stahl .20 .50
508 Montreal Expos TC .40 1.00
509 Jesse Jefferson .20 .50
510 Wayne Garrett .20 .50
511 Toby Harrah .40 1.00
512 Joe Lahoud .20 .50
513 Jim Campanis .20 .50
514 Paul Schaal .20 .50
515 Willie Montanez .20 .50
516 Horacio Pina .20 .50
517 Mike Hegan .20 .50
518 Derrel Thomas .20 .50
519 Bill Sharp RC .20 .50
520 Tim McCarver .75 2.00
521 Ken Aspromonte MG .40 1.00
522 J.R. Richard .75 2.00
523 Cecil Cooper .75 2.00
524 Bill Plummer .20 .50
525 Clyde Wright .20 .50
526 Frank Tepedino .40 1.00
527 Bobby Darwin .20 .50
528 Bill Bonham .20 .50
529 Horace Clarke .40 1.00
530 Mickey Stanley .40 1.00
531 Gene Mauch MG .40 1.00
532 Skip Lockwood .20 .50
533 Mike Phillips RC .20 .50
534 Eddie Watt .20 .50
535 Bob Tolan .20 .50
536 Duffy Dyer .20 .50
537 Steve Mingori .20 .50
538 Cesar Tovar .20 .50
539 Lloyd Allen .20 .50
540 Bob Robertson .20 .50
541 Cleveland Indians TC .40 1.00
542 Goose Gossage .75 2.00
543 Danny Cater .20 .50
544 Ron Schueler .20 .50
545 Billy Conigliaro .40 1.00
546 Mike Corkins .20 .50
547 Glenn Borgmann .20 .50
548 Sonny Siebert .20 .50
549 Mike Jorgensen .20 .50
550 Sam McDowell .40 1.00
551 Von Joshua .20 .50
552 Denny Doyle .20 .50
553 Jim Willoughby .20 .50
554 Tim Johnson RC .20 .50
555 Woodie Fryman .20 .50
556 Dave Campbell .40 1.00
557 Jim McGlothlin .20 .50
558 Bill Fahey .20 .50
559 Darrel Chaney .20 .50
560 Mike Cuellar .40 1.00
561 Ed Kranepool .40 1.00
562 Jack Aker .20 .50
563 Hal McRae .40 1.00
564 Mike Ryan .20 .50
565 Milt Wilcox .20 .50
566 Jackie Hernandez .20 .50
567 Boston Red Sox TC .40 1.00
568 Mike Torrez .40 1.00
569 Rick Dempsey .40 1.00
570 Ralph Garr .40 1.00
571 Rich Hand .20 .50
572 Enzo Hernandez .20 .50
573 Mike Adams RC .20 .50
574 Bill Parsons .20 .50
575 Steve Garvey 1.25 3.00
576 Scipio Spinks .20 .50
577 Mike Sadek RC .20 .50
578 Ralph Houk MG .40 1.00
579 Cecil Upshaw .20 .50
580 Jim Spencer .20 .50
581 Fred Norman .20 .50
582 Bucky Dent RC 2.00 5.00
583 Marty Pattin .20 .50
584 Ken Rudolph .20 .50
585 Merv Rettenmund .20 .50
586 Jack Brohamer .20 .50
587 Larry Christenson RC .20 .50
588 Hal Lanier .20 .50
589 Boots Day .20 .50
590 Roger Moret .20 .50
591 Sonny Jackson .20 .50
592 Ed Bane RC .20 .50
593 Steve Yeager .40 1.00
594 Leroy Stanton .20 .50
595 Steve Blass .40 1.00
596 Carl/Hold/Lit/Pole RC .20 .50
597 Chalk/Gam/Mac/Trillo RC .40 1.00
598 Ken Griffey RC 8.00 20.00
599A Dior/Freis/Ric/Shan Wash .75 2.00
599B Dior/Freis/Ric/Shan Lg 6.00 15.00
599C Dior/Freis/Ric/Shan Sm
600 Cash/Cox/Madlock/Sand RC 2.00 5.00
601 Arm/Blady/Dwng/McBride RC 1.25 3.00
602 Abb/Henn/Swan/Voss RC .40 1.00
603 Foote/Lund/Moore/Robles RC .40 1.00
604 Hugh/Knox/Thornton/White RC 2.00 5.00
605 Alb/Frail/Kob/Tanana RC 1.50 4.00
606 Fuller/Howard/Smith/Velez RC .40 1.00
607 Fost/Hein/Ros/Taveras RC .40 1.00
608A Apod/Ban/D'Acq/Wall ERR .75 2.00
608B Apod/Ban/D'Acq/Wall RC .40 1.00
609 Rico Petrocelli .40 1.00
610 Dave Kingman .75 2.00
611 Rich Stelmaszek .20 .50
612 Luke Walker .20 .50
613 Dan Monzon .20 .50
614 Adrian Devine RC .20 .50
615 Johnny Jeter UER .20 .50
616 Larry Gura .20 .50
617 Ted Ford .20 .50
618 Jim Mason .20 .50
619 Mike Anderson .20 .50
620 Al Downing .20 .50
621 Bernie Carbo .20 .50
622 Phil Gagliano .20 .50
623 Celerino Sanchez .20 .50
624 Bob Miller .20 .50
625 Ollie Brown .20 .50
626 Pittsburgh Pirates TC .40 1.00
627 Carl Taylor .20 .50
628 Ivan Murrell .20 .50
629 Rusty Staub .75 2.00
630 Tommie Agee .40 1.00
631 Steve Barber .20 .50
632 George Culver .20 .50
633 Dave Hamilton .20 .50
634 Eddie Mathews MG 1.25 3.00
635 Johnny Edwards .20 .50
636 Dave Goltz .20 .50
637 Checklist 529-660 1.25 3.00
638 Ken Sanders .20 .50
639 Joe Lovitto .20 .50
640 Milt Pappas .40 1.00
641 Chuck Brinkman .20 .50
642 Terry Harmon .20 .50
643 Los Angeles Dodgers TC .40 1.00
644 Wayne Granger .20 .50
645 Ken Boswell .20 .50
646 George Foster .75 2.00
647 Juan Beniquez RC .20 .50
648 Terry Crowley .20 .50
649 Fernando Gonzalez RC .20 .50
650 Mike Epstein .20 .50
651 Leron Lee .20 .50
652 Gail Hopkins .20 .50
653 Bob Stinson .20 .50
654A Jesus Alou NPOF 1.50 4.00
654B Jesus Alou COR .40 1.00
655 Mike Tyson RC .20 .50
656 Adrian Garrett .20 .50
657 Jim Shellenback .20 .50
658 Lee Lacy .20 .50
659 Joe Lis .20 .50
660 Larry Dierker .75 2.00

1974 Topps Traded

The cards in this 44-card set measure 2 1/2" by 3 1/2". The 1974 Topps Traded set contains 43 player cards and one unnumbered checklist card. The fronts have the word "traded" in block letters and the backs are designed in newspaper style. Card numbers are the same as in the regular set except they are followed by a "T." No known scarcities exist for this set. The cards were inserted in all packs toward the end of the production run. They were produced in large enough quantity that they are no scarcer than the regular Topps cards.

COMPLETE SET (44) 8.00 20.00
23T Craig Robinson .20 .50
42T Claude Osteen .30 .75
43T Jim Wynn .30 .75
51T Bobby Heise .20 .50
59T Ross Grimsley .20 .50
62T Bob Locker .20 .50
63T Bill Sudakis .20 .50
73T Mike Marshall .30 .75
123T Nelson Briles .30 .75
139T Aurelio Monteagudo .20 .50
151T Diego Segui .20 .50
165T Willie Davis .30 .75
175T Reggie Cleveland .20 .50
182T Lindy McDaniel .30 .75
186T Fred Scherman .20 .50
249T George Mitterwald .20 .50
262T Ed Kirkpatrick .20 .50
269T Bob Johnson .20 .50
270T Ron Santo .40 1.00
313T Barry Lersch .20 .50
319T Randy Hundley .30 .75
330T Juan Marichal .75 2.00
348T Pete Richert .20 .50
373T John Curtis .20 .50
390T Lou Piniella .40 1.00
428T Gary Sutherland .20 .50
454T Kurt Bevacqua .20 .50
458T Jim Ray .20 .50
485T Felipe Alou .40 1.00
486T Steve Stone .30 .75
496T Tom Murphy .20 .50
516T Horacio Pina .20 .50
534T Eddie Watt .20 .50
538T Cesar Tovar .20 .50
544T Ron Schueler .20 .50
579T Cecil Upshaw .20 .50
585T Merv Rettenmund .20 .50
612T Luke Walker .20 .50
616T Larry Gura .30 .75
618T Jim Mason .20 .50
630T Tommie Agee .30 .75
648T Terry Crowley .20 .50
649T Fernando Gonzalez .20 .50
NNO Traded Checklist .60 1.50

1974 Topps Team Checklists

COMPLETE SET (24) 8.00 20.00
COMMON TEAM (1-24) .40 1.00

1974 Topps Deckle Edge

The cards in this 72-card set measure 2 7/8" by 5". Returning to a format first used in 1969, Topps produced a set of black and white photo cards in 1974 bearing an unusual serrated or "deckle" border. A facsimile autograph appears on the obverse while the backs contain the card number and a "newspaper-clipping" design detailing a milestone in the player's career. This was a test set and uncut sheets are sometimes found. Card backs are either white or gray; the white back cards are slightly tougher to obtain. The wrapper is also considered collectible. Wrappers featured Reggie Jackson and Tom Seaver and come with or without the phrase "With gum".

COMPLETE SET (72) 3000.00 6000.00
WRAPPER (With Gum) 8.00 20.00
WRAPPER (Without Gum) 8.00 20.00
1 Amos Otis 10.00 25.00
2 Darrell Evans 10.00 25.00
3 Bob Gibson 75.00 150.00
4 Dave Nelson 8.00 20.00
5 Steve Carlton 125.00 250.00
6 Jim Hunter 75.00 150.00
7 Thurman Munson 100.00 200.00
8 Bob Grich 10.00 25.00
9 Tom Seaver 150.00 300.00
10 Ted Simmons 10.00 25.00
11 Bobby Valentine 10.00 25.00
12 Don Sutton 40.00 80.00
13 Wilbur Wood 8.00 20.00
14 Doug Rader 8.00 20.00
15 Chris Chambliss 8.00 20.00
16 Pete Rose 150.00 300.00
17 John Hiller 8.00 20.00
18 Burt Hooton 8.00 20.00
19 Tim Foli 8.00 20.00
20 Lou Brock 75.00 150.00
21 Ron Bryant 8.00 20.00
22 Manny Sanguillen 8.00 20.00
23 Bob Tolan 8.00 20.00
24 Greg Luzinski 10.00 25.00
25 Brooks Robinson 125.00 250.00
26 Felix Millan 8.00 20.00
27 Luis Tiant 10.00 25.00
28 Willie McCovey 75.00 150.00
29 Chris Speier 8.00 20.00
30 George Scott 8.00 20.00
31 Willie Stargell 75.00 150.00
32 Rod Carew 100.00 200.00
33 Charlie Spikes 8.00 20.00
34 Nate Colbert 8.00 20.00
35 Rich Hebner 8.00 20.00
36 Bobby Bonds 10.00 25.00
37 Buddy Bell 10.00 25.00
38 Claude Osteen 8.00 20.00
39 Dick Allen 10.00 25.00
40 Bill Russell 8.00 20.00
41 Nolan Ryan 1000.00 2000.00
42 Willie Davis 8.00 20.00
43 Carl Yastrzemski 100.00 200.00
44 Jon Matlack 8.00 20.00
45 Jim Palmer 100.00 200.00
46 Bert Campaneris 8.00 20.00
47 Bert Blyleven 10.00 25.00
48 Jeff Burroughs 8.00 20.00
49 Jim Colborn 8.00 20.00
50 Dave Johnson 10.00 25.00
51 John Mayberry 8.00 20.00
52 Don Kessinger 8.00 20.00
53 Joe Coleman 8.00 20.00
54 Tony Perez 40.00 80.00
55 Jose Cardenal 8.00 20.00
56 Paul Splittorff 8.00 20.00
57 Hank Aaron 150.00 300.00
58 Dave May 8.00 20.00
59 Fergie Jenkins 75.00 150.00
60 Ron Blomberg 8.00 20.00
61 Reggie Jackson 150.00 300.00
62 Tony Oliva 10.00 25.00
63 Bobby Murcer 10.00 25.00
64 Carlton Fisk 100.00 200.00
65 Steve Rogers 8.00 20.00
66 Frank Robinson 100.00 200.00
67 Joe Ferguson 8.00 20.00
68 Bill Melton 8.00 20.00
69 Bob Watson 8.00 20.00
70 Larry Bowa 10.00 25.00
71 Johnny Bench 125.00 250.00
72 Willie Horton 8.00 20.00

1974 Topps Puzzles

This set of 12 jigsaw puzzles was supposedly distributed by Topps in 1974 as a test issue. Each puzzle measures approximately 5" by 7 1/8" and shows a colorful picture of the player inside a white border. Puzzles contained 40 pieces. The wrapper for the puzzles is also collectible as it shows a picture of Tom Seaver. The wrapper comes two ways: either with a pre-printed price of 29 cents or 25 cents. The puzzles are blank backed and unnumbered; they are listed below alphabetically.

COMPLETE SET (12) 1000.00 2000.00
WRAPPER/25 cents 50.00 100.00
WRAPPER/29 cents 4.00 10.00
1 Hank Aaron 75.00 150.00
2 Dick Allen 30.00 60.00
3 Johnny Bench 75.00 150.00
4 Bobby Bonds 20.00 50.00
5 Bob Gibson 40.00 80.00
6 Reggie Jackson 100.00 200.00
7 Bobby Murcer 20.00 50.00
8 Jim Palmer 40.00 80.00
9 Nolan Ryan 500.00 1000.00
10 Tom Seaver 75.00 150.00
11 Willie Stargell 40.00 80.00
12 Carl Yastrzemski 60.00 120.00

1974 Topps Stamps

The 240 color portraits depicted on stamps in this 1974 Topps series have the player's name, team and position inside an oval below the picture area. Each stamp measures 1" by 1 1/2". The stamps were marketed in 12 stamp sheets, along with an album, in their own wrapper. The booklets have eight pages and measure 2 1/2" by 3 7/8". There are 24 albums, one for each team, designed to hold 10 stamps apiece. The stamps are numbered here alphabetically within each team and the teams are listed in alphabetical order within league, e.g., Atlanta Braves NL (1-10), Chicago Cubs (11-20), Cincinnati Reds (21-30), Houston Astros (31-40), Los Angeles Dodgers (41-50), Montreal Expos (51-60), New York Mets (61-70), Philadelphia Phillies (71-80), Pittsburgh Pirates (81-90), San Diego Padres (91-100), San Francisco Giants (101-110), St. Louis Cardinals (111-120), Baltimore Orioles AL (121-130), Boston Red Sox (131-140), California Angels (141-150), Chicago White Sox (151-160), Cleveland Indians (161-170), Detroit Tigers (171-180), Kansas City Royals (181-190), Milwaukee Brewers (191-200), Minnesota Twins (201-210), New York Yankees (211-220), Oakland A's (221-230) and Texas Rangers (231-240).

COMPLETE SET (240) 40.00 80.00
1 Hank Aaron 3.00 8.00
2 Dusty Baker .10 .25
3 Darrell Evans .10 .25
4 Ralph Garr .08 .15
5 Roric Harrison .08 .20
6 Dave Johnson .20 .50
7 Mike Lum .08 .20
8 Carl Morton .08 .20
9 Phil Niekro 1.00 2.50
10 Johnny Oates .08 .20
11 Glenn Beckert .08 .20
12 Jose Cardenal .08 .20
13 Vic Harris .08 .20
14 Burt Hooton .08 .20
15 Randy Hundley .08 .20
16 Don Kessinger .08 .15
17 Rick Monday .08 .15
18 Rick Reuschel .20 .50
19 Ron Santo .40 1.00
20 Billy Williams 1.00 2.50
21 Johnny Bench 2.00 5.00
22 Jack Billingham .08 .20
23 Pedro Borbon .08 .20
24 Dave Concepcion .20 .50
25 Dan Driessen .08 .15
26 Cesar Geronimo .08 .20
27 Don Gullett .08 .15
28 Joe Morgan 1.25 3.00
29 Tony Perez .60 1.50
30 Pete Rose 3.00 8.00
31 Cesar Cedeno .08 .15
32 Tommy Helms .08 .20
33 Lee May .08 .15
34 Roger Metzger .08 .20
35 Doug Rader .08 .20
36 J.R. Richard .08 .15
37 Dave Roberts .08 .20
38 Jerry Reuss .08 .15
39 Bob Watson .08 .15
40 Jim Wynn .08 .15
41 Bill Buckner .10 .25
42 Ron Cey .10 .25
43 Willie Crawford .08 .20
44 Willie Davis .08 .15
45 Joe Ferguson .08 .20
46 Davey Lopes .08 .15
47 Andy Messersmith .08 .15
48 Claude Osteen .08 .15
49 Bill Russell .08 .15
50 Don Sutton .60 1.50
51 Bob Bailey .08 .20
52 John Boccabella .08 .20
53 Ron Fairly .08 .15
54 Tim Foli .08 .20
55 Ron Hunt .08 .20
56 Mike Jorgensen .08 .20
57 Mike Marshall .08 .15
58 Steve Renko .08 .20
59 Steve Rogers .08 .15
60 Ken Singleton .10 .25
61 Wayne Garrett .08 .20
62 Jerry Grote .08 .20
63 Bud Harrelson .08 .15
64 Cleon Jones .08 .20
65 Jerry Koosman .20 .50
66 Jon Matlack .08 .15
67 Tug McGraw .20 .50
68 Felix Millan .08 .20
69 John Milner .08 .20
70 Tom Seaver 2.00 5.00
71 Bob Boone .20 .50
72 Larry Bowa .08 .15
73 Steve Carlton 2.00 5.00
74 Bill Grabarkewitz .08 .20
75 Jim Lonborg .08 .15
76 Greg Luzinski .10 .25
77 Willie Montanez .08 .20
78 Bill Robinson .08 .15
79 Wayne Twitchell .08 .20
80 Del Unser .08 .20
81 Nelson Briles .08 .15
82 Dock Ellis .08 .20
83 Dave Giusti .08 .20
84 Richie Hebner .08 .20
85 Al Oliver .10 .25
86 Dave Parker 1.00 2.50
87 Manny Sanguillen .08 .15
88 Willie Stargell 1.25 3.00
89 Rennie Stennett .08 .20
90 Richie Zisk .08 .15
91 Nate Colbert .08 .20
92 Bill Greif .08 .20
93 Johnny Grubb .08 .20
94 Randy Jones .08 .15
95 Fred Kendall .08 .20
96 Clay Kirby .08 .20
97 Willie McCovey 1.25 3.00
98 Jerry Morales .08 .20
99 Dave Roberts .08 .20
100 Dave Winfield 3.00 8.00
101 Bobby Bonds .20 .50
102 Tom Bradley .08 .20
103 Ron Bryant .08 .20
104 Tito Fuentes .08 .20
105 Ed Goodson .08 .20
106 Dave Kingman .40 1.00
107 Garry Maddox .08 .15
108 Dave Rader .08 .20
109 Elias Sosa .08 .20
110 Chris Speier .08 .15
111 Lou Brock 1.25 3.00
112 Reggie Cleveland .08 .20
113 Jose Cruz .10 .25
114 Bob Gibson 1.25 3.00
115 Tim McCarver .10 .25
116 Ted Simmons .10 .25
117 Ted Sizemore .08 .20
118 Reggie Smith .08 .15
119 Joe Torre .20 .50
120 Mike Tyson .08 .20
121 Don Baylor .20 .50
122 Mark Belanger .08 .15
123 Paul Blair .08 .20
124 Tommy Davis .08 .15
125 Bobby Grich .08 .15
126 Grant Jackson .08 .20
127 Dave McNally .08 .15
128 Jim Palmer 1.00 2.50
129 Brooks Robinson 1.50 4.00
130 Earl Williams .08 .20
131 Luis Aparicio 1.00 2.50
132 Orlando Cepeda .60 1.50
133 Carlton Fisk 1.50 4.00
134 Tommy Harper .08 .20
135 Bill Lee .08 .15
136 Rick Miller .08 .20
137 Roger Moret .08 .20
138 Luis Tiant .20 .50
139 Rick Wise .08 .20
140 Carl Yastrzemski 2.00 5.00
141 Sandy Alomar .08 .20
142 Mike Epstein .08 .20
143 Bob Oliver .08 .20
144 Vada Pinson .10 .25
145 Frank Robinson 1.50 4.00
146 Ellie Rodriguez .08 .20
147 Nolan Ryan 6.00 15.00
148 Richie Scheinblum .08 .20
149 Bill Singer .08 .20
150 Bobby Valentine .08 .15
151 Dick Allen .20 .50
152 Stan Bahnsen .08 .20
153 Terry Forster .08 .15
154 Ken Henderson .08 .20
155 Ed Herrmann .08 .20
156 Pat Kelly .08 .20
157 Carlos May .08 .20
158 Bill Melton .08 .20
159 Jorge Orta .08 .20
160 Wilbur Wood .08 .15
161 Buddy Bell .20 .50
162 Chris Chambliss .10 .25
163 Frank Duffy .08 .20
164 Dave Duncan .08 .20
165 John Ellis .08 .20
166 Oscar Gamble .08 .15
167 George Hendrick .08 .15
168 Gaylord Perry 1.00 2.50
169 Charlie Spikes .08 .20
170 Dick Tidrow .08 .20
171 Ed Brinkman .08 .20
172 Norm Cash .20 .50
173 Joe Coleman .08 .20
174 Bill Freehan .10 .25
175 John Hiller .08 .15
176 Willie Horton .08 .15
177 Al Kaline 2.00 5.00
178 Mickey Lolich .20 .50
179 Aurelio Rodriguez .08 .20
180 Mickey Stanley .08 .20
181 Steve Busby .08 .15
182 Fran Healy .08 .20
183 Ed Kirkpatrick .08 .20
184 John Mayberry .08 .15
185 Amos Otis .10 .25
186 Fred Patek .08 .20
187 Marty Pattin .08 .20
188 Lou Piniella .20 .50
189 Cookie Rojas .08 .20
190 Paul Splittorff .08 .20
191 Jerry Bell .08 .20
192 Johnny Briggs .08 .20
193 Jim Colborn .08 .20
194 Bob Collucio .08 .20
195 Pedro Garcia .08 .20
196 Dave May .08 .20
197 Don Money .08 .20
198 Darrell Porter .08 .15
199 George Scott .08 .15
200 Jim Slaton .08 .20
201 Bert Blyleven .20 .50
202 Steve Braun .08 .20
203 Rod Carew 2.00 5.00
204 Ray Corbin .08 .20
205 Bobby Darwin .08 .20
206 Joe Decker .08 .20
207 Jim Holt .08 .20
208 Harmon Killebrew 1.25 3.00
209 George Mitterwald .08 .20
210 Tony Oliva .20 .50
211 Ron Blomberg .08 .20
212 Sparky Lyle .10 .25
213 George Medich .08 .20
214 Gene Michael .08 .20
215 Thurman Munson 1.50 4.00
216 Bobby Murcer .10 .25
217 Graig Nettles .20 .50
218 Mel Stottlemyre .10 .25
219 Otto Velez .08 .20
220 Roy White .08 .15
221 Sal Bando .08 .15
222 Vida Blue .20 .50
223 Bert Campaneris .08 .15
224 Ken Holtzman .08 .15
225 Jim Hunter 1.00 2.50
226 Reggie Jackson 2.50 6.00
227 Deron Johnson .08 .20
228 Bill North .08 .20
229 Joe Rudi .08 .15
230 Gene Tenace .08 .15
231 Jim Bibby .08 .20
232 Jeff Burroughs .08 .15
233 David Clyde .08 .20
234 Jim Fregosi .10 .25
235 Toby Harrah .08 .15
236 Ferguson Jenkins 1.00 2.50
237 Alex Johnson .08 .20
238 Dave Nelson .08 .20
239 Jim Spencer .08 .20
240 Bill Sudakis .08 .20

1974 Topps Stamp Albums

The 1974 Topps stamp set of baseball player stamps was intended to be mounted in 24 separate team albums, 10 stamps for that team's players going into that team's album. The albums measure approximately 2 1/2" by 3 1/2".

COMPLETE SET (24) 200.00 400.00
COMMON TEAM (1-24) 10.00 25.00
17 New York Yankees 15.00 40.00

1975 Topps

The 1975 Topps set consists of 660 standard size cards. The design was radically different in appearance from sets of the preceding years. The most prominent change was the use of a two-color frame surrounding the picture area rather than a single, subdued color. A facsimile autograph appears on the picture, and the backs are printed in red and green on gray. Cards were released in ten-card wax packs, 18-card cello packs with a 25 cent SRP and were packaged 24 to a box and 15 boxes to a case, as well as in 42-card rack packs which cost 49 cents upon release. The cello packs were issued 24 to a box. Cards 189-212 depict the MVP's of both leagues from 1951 through 1974. The first seven cards (1-7) feature players (listed in alphabetical order) breaking records or achieving milestones during the previous season. Cards 306-313 picture league leaders in various statistical categories. Cards 459-466 depict the results of post-season action. Team cards feature a checklist back for players on that team and show a small inset photo of the manager on the front. The following players' regular issue cards are explicitly denoted as All-Stars, 1, 50, 80, 140, 170, 180, 260, 320, 350, 390, 400, 420, 440, 470, 530, 570, and 600. This set is quite popular with collectors, at least in part due to the fact that the Rookie Cards of George Brett, Gary Carter, Keith Hernandez, Fred Lynn, Jim Rice and Robin Yount are all in the set.

COMPLETE SET (660) 400.00 1000.00
WRAPPER (15-CENT) 3.00 8.00
1 Hank Aaron HL 12.00 30.00
2 Lou Brock HL 1.25 3.00
3 Bob Gibson HL 1.25 3.00
4 Al Kaline HL 6.00 15.00
5 Nolan Ryan HL 6.00 15.00
6 Mike Marshall HL .40 1.00
7 Ryan Busby/Bosman HL 3.00 8.00
8 Rogelio Moret .20 .50
9 Frank Tepedino .40 1.00
10 Willie Davis .40 1.00
11 Bill Melton .20 .50
12 David Clyde .20 .50
13 Gene Locklear RC .40 1.00
14 Milt Wilcox .20 .50
15 Jose Cardenal .40 1.00
16 Frank Tanana .75 2.00
17 Dave Concepcion .75 2.00
18 Detroit Tigers CL/Houk .75 2.00
19 Jerry Koosman .40 1.00
20 Thurman Munson 8.00 20.00
21 Rollie Fingers 1.25 3.00
22 Dave Cash .20 .50
23 Bill Russell .40 1.00
24 Al Fitzmorris .20 .50
25 Lee May .40 1.00
26 Dave McNally .40 1.00
27 Ken Reitz .20 .50
28 Tom Murphy .20 .50
29 Dave Parker 1.25 3.00
30 Bert Blyleven .75 2.00
31 Dave Rader .20 .50
32 Reggie Cleveland .20 .50
33 Dusty Baker .75 2.00
34 Steve Renko .20 .50
35 Ron Santo .40 1.00
36 Joe Lovitto .20 .50
37 Dave Freisleben .20 .50
38 Buddy Bell .75 2.00
39 Andre Thornton .40 1.00
40 Bill Singer .20 .50
41 Cesar Geronimo .40 1.00
42 Joe Coleman .20 .50
43 Cleon Jones .40 1.00
44 Pat Dobson .20 .50
45 Joe Rudi .40 1.00
46 Philadelphia Phillies CL/Ozark .75 2.00
47 Tommy John .75 2.00
48 Freddie Patek .40 1.00
49 Larry Dierker .40 1.00
50 Brooks Robinson 3.00 8.00
51 Bob Forsch RC .40 1.00
52 Darrell Porter .40 1.00
53 Dave Giusti .20 .50
54 Eric Soderholm .20 .50
55 Bobby Bonds .75 2.00
56 Rick Wise .40 1.00
57 Dave Johnson .40 1.00
58 Chuck Taylor .20 .50
59 Ken Henderson .20 .50
60 Fergie Jenkins 1.25 3.00
61 Dave Winfield 6.00 15.00
62 Fritz Peterson .20 .50
63 Steve Swisher RC .20 .50
64 Dave Chalk .20 .50
65 Don Gullett .40 1.00
66 Willie Horton .40 1.00
67 Tug McGraw .40 1.00
68 Ron Blomberg .20 .50
69 John Odom .20 .50
70 Mike Schmidt 6.00 15.00
71 Charlie Hough .40 1.00
72 Kansas City Royals CL/McKeon .75 2.00
73 J.R. Richard .40 1.00
74 Mark Belanger .40 1.00
75 Ted Simmons .75 2.00
76 Ed Sprague .20 .50
77 Richie Zisk .40 1.00
78 Ray Corbin .20 .50
79 Gary Matthews .40 1.00
80 Carlton Fisk 6.00 15.00
81 Ron Reed .20 .50
82 Pat Kelly .20 .50
83 Jim Merritt .20 .50
84 Enzo Hernandez .20 .50
85 Bill Bonham .20 .50
86 Joe Lis .20 .50
87 George Foster .75 2.00
88 Tom Egan .20 .50
89 Jim Ray .20 .50
90 Rusty Staub .75 2.00
91 Dick Green .20 .50
92 Cecil Upshaw .20 .50
93 Davey Lopes .75 2.00
94 Jim Lonborg .40 1.00
95 John Mayberry .40 1.00
96 Mike Cosgrove RC .20 .50
97 Earl Williams .20 .50
98 Rich Folkers .20 .50
99 Mike Hegan .20 .50
100 Willie Stargell 1.50 4.00
101 Montreal Expos CL/Mauch .75 2.00
102 Joe Decker .20 .50
103 Rick Miller .20 .50
104 Bill Madlock .75 2.00
105 Buzz Capra .20 .50
106 Mike Hargrove UER RC 1.25 3.00
107 Jim Barr .20 .50
108 Tom Hall .20 .50
109 George Hendrick .40 1.00
110 Wilbur Wood .20 .50
111 Wayne Garrett .20 .50
112 Larry Hardy RC .20 .50
113 Elliott Maddox .20 .50
114 Dick Lange .20 .50
115 Joe Ferguson .20 .50
116 Lerrin LaGrow .20 .50
117 Baltimore Orioles CL/Weaver 1.25 3.00
118 Mike Anderson .20 .50
119 Tommy Helms .20 .50
120 Steve Busby UER .40 1.00
121 Bill North .20 .50
122 Al Hrabosky .40 1.00
123 Johnny Briggs .20 .50
124 Jerry Reuss .40 1.00
125 Ken Singleton .40 1.00
126 Checklist 1-132 1.25 3.00
127 Glenn Borgmann .20 .50
128 Bill Lee .40 1.00
129 Rick Monday .40 1.00
130 Phil Niekro 1.25 3.00
131 Toby Harrah .40 1.00
132 Randy Moffitt .20 .50
133 Dan Driessen .40 1.00
134 Ron Hodges .20 .50
135 Charlie Spikes .20 .50
136 Jim Mason .20 .50
137 Terry Forster .40 1.00
138 Del Unser .20 .50
139 Horacio Pina .20 .50
140 Steve Garvey 1.25 3.00
141 Mickey Stanley .40 1.00
142 Bob Reynolds .20 .50
143 Cliff Johnson RC .40 1.00
144 Jim Wohlford .20 .50
145 Ken Holtzman .40 1.00
146 San Diego Padres CL/McNamara .75 2.00
147 Pedro Garcia .20 .50
148 Jim Rooker .20 .50
149 Tim Foli .20 .50
150 Bob Gibson 2.50 6.00
151 Steve Brye .20 .50
152 Mario Guerrero .20 .50
153 Rick Reuschel .40 1.00
154 Mike Lum .20 .50
155 Jim Bibby .20 .50
156 Dave Kingman .75 2.00
157 Pedro Borbon .40 1.00
158 Jerry Grote .20 .50
159 Steve Arlin .20 .50
160 Graig Nettles .75 2.00
161 Stan Bahnsen .20 .50
162 Willie Montanez .20 .50
163 Jim Brewer .20 .50
164 Mickey Rivers .40 1.00
165 Doug Rader .40 1.00
166 Woodie Fryman .20 .50
167 Rich Coggins .20 .50
168 Bill Greif .20 .50
169 Cookie Rojas .20 .50
170 Bert Campaneris .40 1.00
171 Ed Kirkpatrick .20 .50
172 Boston Red Sox CL/Johnson 1.25 3.00
173 Steve Rogers .40 1.00
174 Bake McBride .40 1.00
175 Don Money .40 1.00
176 Burt Hooton .40 1.00
177 Vic Correll RC .20 .50
178 Cesar Tovar .20 .50
179 Tom Bradley .20 .50
180 Joe Morgan 8.00 20.00
181 Fred Beene .20 .50
182 Don Hahn .20 .50
183 Mel Stottlemyre .40 1.00
184 Jorge Orta .20 .50
185 Steve Carlton 3.00 8.00
186 Willie Crawford .20 .50
187 Denny Doyle .20 .50
188 Tom Griffin .20 .50
189 Y.Berra/Campanella MVP 1.50 4.00
190 B.Shantz/H.Sauer MVP .75 2.00
191 Al Rosen/Campanella MVP .75 2.00
192 Y.Berra/W.Mays MVP 1.50 4.00
193 Y.Berra/Campanella MVP 1.25 3.00
194 M.Mantle/D.Newcombe MVP 4.00 10.00
195 M.Mantle/H.Aaron MVP 6.00 15.00
196 J.Jensen/E.Banks MVP 1.25 3.00
197 N.Fox/E.Banks MVP .75 2.00
198 R.Maris/D.Groat MVP .75 2.00
199 R.Maris/F.Robinson MVP 1.25 3.00
200 M.Mantle/M.Wills MVP 4.00 10.00
201 E.Howard/S.Koufax MVP .75 2.00
202 B.Robinson/K.Boyer MVP .40 1.00
203 Z.Versailes/W.Mays MVP .75 2.00
204 F.Robinson/B.Clemente MVP 2.50 6.00
205 C.Yastrzemski/O.Cepeda MVP .75 2.00
206 D.McLain/B.Gibson MVP .75 2.00
207 H.Killebrew/W.McCovey MVP .40 1.00
208 B.Powell/J.Bench MVP .75 2.00
209 V.Blue/J.Torre MVP .75 2.00
210 R.Allen/J.Bench MVP .75 2.00
29-Jul R.Jackson/P.Rose MVP 2.00 5.00
30-Jul J.Burroughs/S.Garvey MVP .75 2.00
31-Jul Oscar Gamble .40 1.00
1-Aug Harry Parker .20 .50
2-Aug Bobby Valentine .40 1.00
3-Aug San Francisco Giants CL/Westrum .75 2.00
4-Aug Lou Piniella .75 2.00
5-Aug Jerry Johnson .20 .50
6-Aug Ed Herrmann .20 .50
220 Don Sutton 1.25 3.00
221 Aurelio Rodriguez .20 .50
222 Dan Spillner RC .20 .50
223 Robin Yount RC 40.00 100.00
224 Ramon Hernandez .20 .50
225 Bob Grich .40 1.00
226 Bill Campbell .20 .50
227 Bob Watson .40 1.00
228 George Brett RC 75.00 200.00
229 Barry Foote .20 .50
230 Jim Hunter 1.50 4.00
231 Mike Tyson .20 .50
232 Diego Segui .20 .50
233 Billy Grabarkewitz .20 .50
234 Tom Grieve .40 1.00
235 Jack Billingham .40 1.00
236 California Angels CL/Williams .75 2.00
237 Carl Morton .40 1.00
238 Dave Duncan .40 1.00
239 George Stone .20 .50
240 Garry Maddox .40 1.00
241 Dick Tidrow .20 .50
242 Jay Johnstone .40 1.00
243 Jim Kaat .75 2.00
244 Bill Buckner .40 1.00
245 Mickey Lolich .75 2.00
246 St. Louis Cardinals CL/Schoen .75 2.00
247 Enos Cabell .20 .50
248 Randy Jones .75 2.00
249 Danny Thompson .20 .50
250 Ken Brett .20 .50
251 Fran Healy .20 .50
252 Fred Scherman .20 .50
253 Jesus Alou .20 .50
254 Mike Torrez .40 1.00
255 Dwight Evans .75 2.00
256 Billy Champion .20 .50
257 Checklist: 133-264 1.25 3.00
258 Dave LaRoche .20 .50
259 Len Randle .20 .50
260 Johnny Bench 10.00 25.00
261 Andy Hassler RC .20 .50
262 Rowland Office RC .20 .50
263 Jim Perry .40 1.00
264 John Milner .20 .50
265 Ron Bryant .20 .50
266 Sandy Alomar .40 1.00
267 Dick Ruthven .20 .50
268 Hal McRae .40 1.00
269 Doug Rau .20 .50
270 Ron Fairly .40 1.00
271 Gerry Moses .20 .50
272 Lynn McGlothen .20 .50
273 Steve Braun .20 .50
274 Vicente Romo .20 .50
275 Paul Blair .40 1.00
276 Chicago White Sox CL/Tanner .75 2.00
277 Frank Taveras .20 .50
278 Paul Lindblad .20 .50
279 Milt May .20 .50
280 Carl Yastrzemski 5.00 12.00
281 Jim Slaton .20 .50
282 Jerry Morales .20 .50
283 Steve Foucault .20 .50
284 Ken Griffey Sr. 1.50 4.00
285 Ellie Rodriguez .20 .50
286 Mike Jorgensen .20 .50
287 Roric Harrison .20 .50
288 Bruce Ellingsen RC .20 .50
289 Ken Rudolph .20 .50
290 Jon Matlack .20 .50
291 Bill Sudakis .20 .50
292 Ron Schueler .20 .50
293 Dick Sharon .20 .50
294 Geoff Zahn RC .20 .50
295 Vada Pinson .75 2.00
296 Alan Foster .20 .50
297 Craig Kusick RC .20 .50
298 Johnny Grubb .20 .50
299 Bucky Dent .75 2.00
300 Reggie Jackson 5.00 12.00
301 Dave Roberts .20 .50
302 Rick Burleson RC .40 1.00
303 Grant Jackson .20 .50
304 Pittsburgh Pirates CL/Murtaugh .75 2.00
305 Jim Colborn .20 .50
306 R.Carew/R.Garr LL .75 2.00
307 D.Allen/M.Schmidt LL 1.50 4.00
308 J.Burroughs/J.Bench LL .75 2.00
309 B.North/L.Brock LL .75 2.00
310 Hunter/Jenk/Mess/Niek LL .75 2.00
311 J.Hunter/B.Capra LL .75 2.00
312 N.Ryan/S.Carlton LL 5.00 12.00
313 T.Forster/M.Marshall LL .40 1.00
314 Buck Martinez .20 .50
315 Don Kessinger .40 1.00
316 Jackie Brown .20 .50
317 Joe Lahoud .20 .50
318 Ernie McAnally .20 .50
319 Johnny Oates .40 1.00
320 Pete Rose 12.00 30.00
321 Rudy May .20 .50
322 Ed Goodson .20 .50
323 Fred Holdsworth .20 .50
324 Ed Kranepool .40 1.00
325 Tony Oliva .75 2.00
326 Wayne Twitchell .20 .50
327 Jerry Hairston .20 .50
328 Sonny Siebert .20 .50
329 Ted Kubiak .20 .50
330 Mike Marshall .40 1.00
331 Cleveland Indians CL/Robinson .75 2.00
332 Fred Kendall .20 .50
333 Dick Drago .20 .50
334 Greg Gross RC .20 .50
335 Jim Palmer 2.50 6.00
336 Rennie Stennett .20 .50
337 Kevin Kobel .20 .50
338 Rich Stelmaszek .20 .50
339 Jim Fregosi .40 1.00
340 Paul Splittorff .20 .50
341 Hal Breeden .20 .50
342 Leroy Stanton .20 .50
343 Danny Frisella .20 .50
344 Ben Oglivie .40 1.00
345 Clay Carroll .40 1.00
346 Bobby Darwin .20 .50
347 Mike Caldwell .20 .50
348 Tony Muser .20 .50
349 Ray Sadecki .20 .50
350 Bobby Murcer .40 1.00
351 Bob Boone .75 2.00
352 Darold Knowles .20 .50
353 Luis Melendez .20 .50
354 Dick Bosman .20 .50
355 Chris Cannizzaro .20 .50
356 Rico Petrocelli .40 1.00
357 Ken Forsch UER .20 .50
358 Al Bumbry .40 1.00
359 Paul Popovich .20 .50
360 George Scott .40 1.00
361 Los Angeles Dodgers CL/Alston .75 2.00
362 Steve Hargan .20 .50
363 Carmen Fanzone .20 .50
364 Doug Bird .20 .50
365 Bob Bailey .20 .50
366 Ken Sanders .20 .50
367 Craig Robinson .20 .50
368 Vic Albury .20 .50
369 Merv Rettenmund .20 .50
370 Tom Seaver 10.00 25.00
371 Gates Brown .20 .50
372 John D'Acquisto .20 .50
373 Bill Sharp .20 .50
374 Eddie Watt .20 .50
375 Roy White .40 1.00
376 Steve Yeager .40 1.00
377 Tom Hilgendorf .20 .50
378 Derrel Thomas .20 .50
379 Bernie Carbo .20 .50
380 Sal Bando .40 1.00
381 John Curtis .20 .50
382 Don Baylor .75 2.00
383 Jim York .20 .50
384 Milwaukee Brewers CL/Crandall .75 2.00
385 Dock Ellis .20 .50
386 Checklist: 265-396 UER 1.25 3.00
387 Jim Spencer .20 .50
388 Steve Stone .40 1.00
389 Tony Solaita RC .20 .50
390 Ron Cey .75 2.00
391 Don DeMola RC .20 .50
392 Bruce Bochte RC .40 1.00
393 Gary Gentry .20 .50
394 Larvell Blanks .20 .50
395 Bud Harrelson .40 1.00
396 Fred Norman .40 1.00
397 Bill Freehan .40 1.00
398 Elias Sosa .20 .50
399 Terry Harmon .20 .50
400 Dick Allen .75 2.00
401 Mike Wallace .20 .50
402 Bob Tolan .20 .50
403 Tom Buskey RC .20 .50
404 Ted Sizemore .20 .50
405 John Montague RC .20 .50
406 Bob Gallagher .20 .50
407 Herb Washington RC .75 2.00
408 Clyde Wright UER .20 .50
409 Bob Robertson .20 .50
410 Mike Cuellar UER .40 1.00
411 George Mitterwald .20 .50
412 Bill Hands .20 .50
413 Marty Pattin .20 .50
414 Manny Mota .40 1.00
415 John Hiller .40 1.00
416 Larry Lintz .20 .50
417 Skip Lockwood .20 .50

418 Leo Foster .20 .50
419 Dave Goltz .20 .50
420 Larry Bowa .75 2.00
421 New York Mets CL/Berra 1.25 3.00
422 Brian Downing .40 1.00
423 Clay Kirby .20 .50
424 John Lowenstein .20 .50
425 Tito Fuentes .20 .50
426 George Medich .20 .50
427 Clarence Gaston .40 1.00
428 Dave Hamilton .20 .50
429 Jim Dwyer RC .20 .50
430 Luis Tiant .75 2.00
431 Rod Gilbreath .20 .50
432 Ken Berry .20 .50
433 Larry Demery RC .20 .50
434 Bob Locker .20 .50
435 Dave Nelson .20 .50
436 Ken Frailing .20 .50
437 Al Cowens RC .40 1.00
438 Don Carrithers .20 .50
439 Ed Brinkman .20 .50
440 Andy Messersmith .40 1.00
441 Bobby Heise .20 .50
442 Maximino Leon RC .20 .50
443 Minnesota Twins CL/Quilici .75 2.00
444 Gene Garber .40 1.00
445 Felix Millan .20 .50
446 Bart Johnson .20 .50
447 Terry Crowley .20 .50
448 Frank Duffy .20 .50
449 Charlie Williams .20 .50
450 Willie McCovey 2.50 6.00
451 Rick Dempsey .40 1.00
452 Angel Mangual .20 .50
453 Claude Osteen .40 1.00
454 Doug Griffin .20 .50
455 Don Wilson .20 .50
456 Bob Coluccio .20 .50
457 Mario Mendoza RC .20 .50
458 Ross Grimsley .20 .50
459 1974 AL Championships .40 1.00
460 1974 NL Championships .75 2.00
461 Reggie Jackson WS1 2.00 5.00
462 W.Alston/J.Ferguson WS2 .40 1.00
463 Rollie Fingers WS3 .75 2.00
464 A's Batter WS4 .40 1.00
465 Joe Rudi WS5 .40 1.00
466 A's Do it Again WS .75 2.00
467 Ed Halicki RC .20 .50
468 Bobby Mitchell .20 .50
469 Tom Dettore RC .20 .50
470 Jeff Burroughs .40 1.00
471 Bob Stinson .20 .50
472 Bruce Dal Canton .20 .50
473 Ken McMullen .20 .50
474 Luke Walker .20 .50
475 Darrell Evans .40 1.00
476 Ed Figueroa RC .20 .50
477 Tom Hutton .20 .50
478 Tom Burgmeier .20 .50
479 Ken Boswell .20 .50
480 Carlos May .20 .50
481 Will McEnaney RC .40 1.00
482 Tom McCraw .20 .50
483 Steve Ontiveros .20 .50
484 Glenn Beckert .40 1.00
485 Sparky Lyle .40 1.00
486 Ray Fosse .20 .50
487 Houston Astros CL/Gomez .75 2.00
488 Bill Travers RC .20 .50
489 Cecil Cooper .75 2.00
490 Reggie Smith .40 1.00
491 Doyle Alexander .40 1.00
492 Rich Hebner .40 1.00
493 Don Stanhouse .20 .50
494 Pete LaCock RC .20 .50
495 Nelson Briles .40 1.00
496 Pepe Frias .20 .50
497 Jim Nettles .20 .50
498 Al Downing .20 .50
499 Marty Perez .20 .50
500 Nolan Ryan 20.00 50.00
501 Bill Robinson .40 1.00
502 Pat Bourque .20 .50
503 Fred Stanley .20 .50
504 Buddy Bradford .20 .50
505 Chris Speier .20 .50
506 Leron Lee .20 .50
507 Tom Carroll RC .20 .50
508 Bob Hansen RC .20 .50
509 Dave Hilton .20 .50
510 Vida Blue .40 1.00
511 Texas Rangers CL/Martin .75 2.00
512 Larry Milbourne RC .20 .50
513 Dick Pole .20 .50
514 Jose Cruz .75 2.00
515 Manny Sanguillen .40 1.00
516 Don Hood .20 .50
517 Checklist: 397-528 1.25 3.00
518 Leo Cardenas .20 .50
519 Jim Todd RC .20 .50
520 Amos Otis .40 1.00
521 Dennis Blair RC .20 .50
522 Gary Sutherland .20 .50
523 Tom Paciorek .40 1.00
524 John Doherty RC .20 .50
525 Tom House .20 .50
526 Larry Hisle .40 1.00
527 Mac Scarce .20 .50
528 Eddie Leon .20 .50
529 Gary Thomasson .20 .50
530 Gaylord Perry 1.25 3.00
531 Cincinnati Reds CL/Anderson 2.00 5.00
532 Gorman Thomas .40 1.00
533 Rudy Meoli .20 .50
534 Alex Johnson .20 .50
535 Gene Tenace .40 1.00
536 Bob Moose .20 .50
537 Tommy Harper .40 1.00
538 Duffy Dyer .20 .50
539 Jesse Jefferson .20 .50
540 Lou Brock 2.50 6.00
541 Roger Metzger .20 .50
542 Pete Broberg .20 .50
543 Larry Biittner .20 .50
544 Steve Mingori .20 .50
545 Billy Williams 1.25 3.00
546 John Knox .20 .50
547 Von Joshua .20 .50
548 Charlie Sands .20 .50
549 Bill Butler .20 .50
550 Ralph Garr .40 1.00
551 Larry Christenson .20 .50
552 Jack Brohamer .20 .50
553 John Boccabella .20 .50
554 Goose Gossage .75 2.00
555 Al Oliver .40 1.00
556 Tim Johnson .20 .50
557 Larry Gura .20 .50
558 Dave Roberts .20 .50
559 Bob Montgomery .20 .50
560 Tony Perez 1.50 4.00
561 Oakland Athletics CL/Dark .75 2.00
562 Gary Nolan .40 1.00
563 Wilbur Howard .20 .50
564 Tommy Davis .40 1.00
565 Joe Torre .75 2.00
566 Ray Burris .20 .50
567 Jim Sundberg RC .75 2.00
568 Dale Murray RC .20 .50
569 Frank White .40 1.00
570 Jim Wynn .40 1.00
571 Dave Lemanczyk RC .20 .50
572 Roger Nelson .20 .50
573 Orlando Pena .20 .50
574 Tony Taylor .20 .50
575 Gene Clines .20 .50
576 Phil Roof .20 .50
577 John Morris .20 .50
578 Dave Tomlin RC .20 .50
579 Skip Pitlock .20 .50
580 Frank Robinson 2.50 6.00
581 Darrel Chaney .20 .50
582 Eduardo Rodriguez .20 .50
583 Andy Etchebarren .20 .50
584 Mike Garman .20 .50
585 Chris Chambliss .40 1.00
586 Tim McCarver .75 2.00
587 Chris Ward RC .20 .50
588 Rick Auerbach .20 .50
589 Atlanta Braves CL/King .75 2.00
590 Cesar Cedeno .40 1.00
591 Glenn Abbott .20 .50
592 Balor Moore .20 .50
593 Gene Lamont .20 .50
594 Jim Fuller .20 .50
595 Joe Niekro .40 1.00
596 Ollie Brown .20 .50
597 Winston Llenas .20 .50
598 Bruce Kison .20 .50
599 Nate Colbert .20 .50
600 Rod Carew 3.00 8.00
601 Juan Beniquez .20 .50
602 John Vukovich .20 .50
603 Lew Krausse .20 .50
604 Oscar Zamora RC .20 .50
605 John Ellis .20 .50
606 Bruce Miller RC .20 .50
607 Jim Holt .20 .50
608 Gene Michael .20 .50
609 Elrod Hendricks .20 .50
610 Ron Hunt .20 .50
611 New York Yankees CL/Virdon .75 2.00
612 Terry Hughes .20 .50
613 Bill Parsons .20 .50
614 Kuc/Mill/Ruhle/Sieb RC .40 1.00
615 Darcy/Leonard/Und/Webb RC .75 2.00
616 Jim Rice RC 20.00 50.00
617 Cubb/DeCinces/Sand/Trillo RC .75 2.00
618 East/John/McGregor/Rhoden RC .40 1.00
619 Ayala/Nyman/Smith Turner RC .40 1.00
620 Gary Carter RC 20.00 50.00
621 Denny/Eastwick/Kern/Vein RC .75 2.00
622 Fred Lynn RC 6.00 15.00
623 K.Hern RC/P.Garner RC 4.00 10.00
624 Kon/Lavelle/Otten/Sol RC .40 1.00
625 Boog Powell .75 2.00
626 Larry Haney UER .20 .50
627 Tom Walker .20 .50
628 Ron LeFlore RC .40 1.00
629 Joe Hoerner .20 .50
630 Greg Luzinski .75 2.00
631 Lee Lacy .20 .50
632 Morris Nettles RC .20 .50
633 Paul Casanova .20 .50
634 Cy Acosta .20 .50
635 Chuck Dobson .20 .50
636 Charlie Moore .20 .50
637 Ted Martinez .20 .50
638 Chicago Cubs CL/Marshall .75 2.00
639 Steve Kline .20 .50
640 Harmon Killebrew 2.50 6.00
641 Jim Northrup .40 1.00
642 Mike Phillips .20 .50
643 Brent Strom .20 .50
644 Bill Fahey .20 .50
645 Danny Cater .20 .50
646 Checklist: 529-660 1.25 3.00
647 Claudell Washington RC .75 2.00
648 Dave Pagan RC .20 .50
649 Jack Heidemann .20 .50
650 Dave May .20 .50
651 John Morlan RC .20 .50
652 Lindy McDaniel .40 1.00
653 Lee Richard UER .20 .50
654 Jerry Terrell .20 .50
655 Rico Carty .40 1.00
656 Bill Plummer .20 .50
657 Bob Oliver .20 .50
658 Vic Harris .20 .50
659 Bob Apodaca .20 .50
660 Hank Aaron 20.00 50.00

1975 Topps Mini

COMPLETE SET (660) 500.00 1200.00
*MINI VETS: .75X TO 1.5X BASIC CARDS
*MINI ROOKIES: .5X TO 1X BASIC RC

1975 Topps Team Checklist Sheet

This uncut sheet of the 24 1975 Topps team checklists measures 10 1/2" by 20 1/8". The sheet was obtained by sending 40 cents plus one wrapper to Topps. When cut, each card measures the standard size.

1 Topps Team CL Sheet 20.00 50.00

1976 Topps

The 1976 Topps set of 660 standard-size cards is known for its sharp color photographs and interesting presentation of subjects. Cards were issued in ten-card wax packs which cost 15 cents upon release, 42-card rack packs as well as cello packs and other options. Team cards feature a checklist back for players on that team and show a small inset photo of the manager on the front. A "Father and Son" series (66-70) spotlights five Major Leaguers whose fathers also made the "Big Show." Other subseries include "All Time All Stars" (341-350), "Record Breakers" from the previous season (1-6), League Leaders (191-205), Post-season cards (461-462), and Rookie Prospects (589-599). The following players' regular issue cards are explicitly denoted as All-Stars, 10, 48, 60, 140, 150, 165, 169, 240, 300, 370, 380, 395, 400, 420, 475, 500, 580, and 650. The key Rookie Cards in this set are Dennis Eckersley, Ron Guidry, and Willie Randolph. We've heard recent reports that this set was also issued in seven-card wax packs which cost a dime. Confirmation of that information would be appreciated.

COMPLETE SET (660) 250.00 600.00
1 Hank Aaron RB 10.00 25.00
2 Bobby Bonds RB .60 1.50
3 Mickey Lolich RB .30 .75
4 Dave Lopes RB .30 .75
5 Tom Seaver RB 2.00 5.00
6 Rennie Stennett RB .30 .75
7 Jim Umbarger RC .15 .40
8 Tito Fuentes .15 .40
9 Paul Lindblad .15 .40
10 Lou Brock 2.00 5.00
11 Jim Hughes .15 .40
12 Richie Zisk .30 .75
13 John Wockenfuss RC .15 .40
14 Gene Garber .30 .75
15 George Scott .30 .75
16 Bob Apodaca .15 .40
17 New York Yankees CL/Martin .60 1.50
18 Dale Murray .15 .40
19 George Brett 25.00 60.00
20 Bob Watson .30 .75
21 Dave LaRoche .15 .40
22 Bill Russell .30 .75
23 Brian Downing .15 .40
24 Cesar Geronimo .30 .75
25 Mike Torrez .30 .75
26 Andre Thornton .30 .75
27 Ed Figueroa .15 .40
28 Dusty Baker .60 1.50
29 Rick Burleson .30 .75
30 John Montefusco RC .30 .75
31 Len Randle .15 .40
32 Danny Frisella .15 .40
33 Bill North .15 .40
34 Mike Garman .15 .40
35 Tony Oliva .60 1.50
36 Frank Taveras .15 .40
37 John Hiller .30 .75
38 Garry Maddox .30 .75
39 Pete Broberg .15 .40
40 Dave Kingman .60 1.50
41 Tippy Martinez RC .30 .75
42 Barry Foote .15 .40
43 Paul Splittorff .15 .40
44 Doug Rader .30 .75
45 Boog Powell .60 1.50
46 Los Angeles Dodgers CL/Alston .60 1.50
47 Jesse Jefferson .15 .40
48 Dave Concepcion .60 1.50
49 Dave Duncan .30 .75
50 Fred Lynn 2.00 5.00
51 Ray Burris .15 .40
52 Dave Chalk .15 .40
53 Mike Beard RC .15 .40
54 Dave Rader .15 .40
55 Gaylord Perry 1.00 2.50
56 Bob Tolan .15 .40
57 Phil Garner .30 .75
58 Ron Reed .15 .40
59 Larry Hisle .30 .75
60 Jerry Reuss .30 .75
61 Ron LeFlore .30 .75
62 Johnny Oates .30 .75
63 Bobby Darwin .15 .40
64 Jerry Koosman .30 .75
65 Chris Chambliss .30 .75
66 Gus/Buddy Bell FS .30 .75
67 Bob/Ray Boone FS .30 .75
68 Joe/Joe Jr. Coleman FS .15 .40
69 Jim/Mike Hegan FS .15 .40
70 Roy/Roy Jr. Smalley FS .30 .75
71 Steve Rogers .30 .75
72 Hal McRae .30 .75
73 Baltimore Orioles CL/Weaver .60 1.50
74 Oscar Gamble .30 .75
75 Larry Dierker .30 .75
76 Willie Crawford .15 .40
77 Pedro Borbon .30 .75
78 Cecil Cooper .30 .75
79 Jerry Morales .15 .40
80 Jim Kaat .60 1.50
81 Darrell Evans .30 .75
82 Von Joshua .15 .40
83 Jim Spencer .15 .40
84 Brent Strom .15 .40
85 Mickey Rivers .30 .75
86 Mike Tyson .15 .40
87 Tom Burgmeier .15 .40
88 Duffy Dyer .15 .40
89 Vern Ruhle .15 .40
90 Sal Bando .30 .75
91 Tom Hutton .15 .40
92 Eduardo Rodriguez .15 .40
93 Mike Phillips .15 .40
94 Jim Dwyer .15 .40
95 Brooks Robinson 10.00 25.00
96 Doug Bird .15 .40
97 Wilbur Howard .15 .40
98 Dennis Eckersley RC 25.00 60.00
99 Lee Lacy .15 .40
100 Jim Hunter 1.25 3.00
101 Pete LaCock .15 .40
102 Jim Willoughby .15 .40
103 Biff Pocoroba RC .15 .40
104 Cincinnati Reds CL/Anderson 1.00 2.50
105 Gary Lavelle .15 .40
106 Tom Grieve .30 .75
107 Dave Roberts .15 .40
108 Don Kirkwood RC .15 .40
109 Larry Lintz .15 .40
110 Carlos May .15 .40
111 Danny Thompson .15 .40
112 Kent Tekulve RC .60 1.50
113 Gary Sutherland .15 .40
114 Jay Johnstone .30 .75
115 Ken Holtzman .30 .75
116 Charlie Moore .15 .40
117 Mike Jorgensen .15 .40
118 Boston Red Sox CL/Johnson .60 1.50
119 Checklist 1-132 .60 1.50
120 Rusty Staub .30 .75
121 Tony Solaita .15 .40
122 Mike Cosgrove .15 .40
123 Walt Williams .15 .40
124 Doug Rau .15 .40
125 Don Baylor .60 1.50
126 Tom Dettore .15 .40
127 Larvell Blanks .15 .40
128 Ken Griffey Sr. 1.00 2.50
129 Andy Etchebarren .15 .40
130 Luis Tiant .60 1.50
131 Bill Stein RC .15 .40
132 Don Hood .15 .40
133 Gary Matthews .30 .75
134 Mike Ivie .15 .40
135 Bake McBride .30 .75
136 Dave Goltz .15 .40
137 Bill Robinson .30 .75
138 Lerrin LaGrow .15 .40
139 Gorman Thomas .30 .75
140 Vida Blue .30 .75
141 Larry Parrish RC .60 1.50
142 Dick Drago .15 .40
143 Jerry Grote .15 .40
144 Al Fitzmorris .15 .40
145 Larry Bowa .30 .75
146 George Medich .15 .40
147 Houston Astros CL/Virdon .60 1.50
148 Stan Thomas RC .15 .40
149 Tommy Davis .30 .75
150 Steve Garvey 1.00 2.50
151 Bill Bonham .15 .40
152 Leroy Stanton .15 .40
153 Buzz Capra .15 .40
154 Bucky Dent .30 .75
155 Jack Billingham .30 .75
156 Rico Carty .30 .75
157 Mike Caldwell .15 .40
158 Ken Reitz .15 .40
159 Jerry Terrell .15 .40
160 Dave Winfield 6.00 15.00
161 Bruce Kison .15 .40
162 Jack Pierce RC .15 .40
163 Jim Slaton .15 .40
164 Pepe Mangual .15 .40
165 Gene Tenace .30 .75
166 Skip Lockwood .15 .40
167 Freddie Patek .30 .75
168 Tom Hilgendorf .15 .40
169 Graig Nettles .60 1.50
170 Rick Wise .15 .40
171 Greg Gross .15 .40
172 Texas Rangers CL/Lucchesi .60 1.50
173 Steve Swisher .15 .40
174 Charlie Hough .30 .75
175 Ken Singleton .30 .75
176 Dick Lange .15 .40
177 Marty Perez .15 .40
178 Tom Buskey .15 .40
179 George Foster .60 1.50
180 Goose Gossage .60 1.50
181 Willie Montanez .15 .40
182 Harry Rasmussen .15 .40
183 Steve Braun .15 .40
184 Bill Greif .15 .40
185 Dave Parker .60 1.50
186 Tom Walker .15 .40
187 Pedro Garcia .15 .40
188 Fred Scherman .15 .40
189 Claudell Washington .30 .75
190 Jon Matlack .15 .40
191 Madlock/Simm/Mang LL .30 .75
192 Carew/Lynn/Munson LL 1.00 2.50
193 Schmidt/King/Luz LL 1.25 3.00
194 Reggie/Scott/Mayb LL 1.25 3.00
195 Luz/Bench/Perez LL .60 1.50
196 Scott/Mayb/Lynn LL .30 .75
197 Lopes/Morgan/Brock LL .60 1.50
198 Rivers/Wash/Otis LL .30 .75
199 Seaver/Jones/Mess LL 1.00 2.50
200 Hunter/Palmer/Blue LL .60 1.50
201 Jones/Mess/Seaver LL .60 1.50
202 Palmer/Hunter/Eck LL 1.25 3.00
203 Seaver/Mont/Mess LL 1.00 2.50
204 Tanana/Blyleven/Perry LL .30 .75
205 A.Hrabosky/G.Gossage LL .30 .75
206 Manny Trillo .15 .40
207 Andy Hassler .15 .40
208 Mike Lum .15 .40
209 Alan Ashby RC .15 .40
210 Lee May .30 .75
211 Clay Carroll .30 .75
212 Pat Kelly .15 .40
213 Dave Heaverlo RC .15 .40
214 Eric Soderholm .15 .40
215 Reggie Smith .30 .75
216 Montreal Expos CL/Kuehl .60 1.50
217 Dave Freisleben .15 .40
218 John Knox .15 .40
219 Tom Murphy .15 .40
220 Manny Sanguillen .30 .75
221 Jim Todd .15 .40
222 Wayne Garrett .15 .40
223 Ollie Brown .15 .40
224 Jim York .15 .40
225 Roy White .30 .75
226 Jim Sundberg .30 .75
227 Oscar Zamora .15 .40
228 John Hale RC .15 .40
229 Jerry Remy RC .15 .40
230 Carl Yastrzemski 10.00 25.00
231 Tom House .15 .40
232 Frank Duffy .15 .40
233 Grant Jackson .15 .40
234 Mike Sadek .15 .40
235 Bert Blyleven .60 1.50
236 Kansas City Royals CL/Herzog .60 1.50
237 Dave Hamilton .15 .40
238 Larry Biittner .15 .40
239 John Curtis .15 .40
240 Pete Rose 25.00 60.00
241 Hector Torres .15 .40
242 Dan Meyer .15 .40
243 Jim Rooker .15 .40
244 Bill Sharp .15 .40
245 Felix Millan .15 .40
246 Cesar Tovar .15 .40
247 Terry Harmon .15 .40
248 Dick Tidrow .15 .40
249 Cliff Johnson .30 .75
250 Fergie Jenkins 1.00 2.50
251 Rick Monday .30 .75
252 Tim Nordbrook RC .15 .40
253 Bill Buckner .30 .75
254 Rudy Meoli .15 .40
255 Fritz Peterson .15 .40
256 Rowland Office .15 .40
257 Ross Grimsley .15 .40
258 Nyls Nyman .15 .40
259 Darrel Chaney .15 .40
260 Steve Busby .15 .40
261 Gary Thomasson .15 .40
262 Checklist 133-264 .60 1.50
263 Lyman Bostock RC .60 1.50
264 Steve Renko .15 .40
265 Willie Davis .30 .75
266 Alan Foster .15 .40
267 Aurelio Rodriguez .15 .40
268 Del Unser .15 .40
269 Rick Austin .15 .40
270 Willie Stargell 1.25 3.00
271 Jim Lonborg .30 .75
272 Rick Dempsey .30 .75
273 Joe Niekro .30 .75
274 Tommy Harper .30 .75
275 Rick Manning RC .15 .40
276 Mickey Scott .15 .40
277 Chicago Cubs CL/Marshall .60 1.50
278 Bernie Carbo .15 .40
279 Roy Howell RC .15 .40
280 Burt Hooton .30 .75
281 Dave May .15 .40
282 Dan Osborn RC .15 .40
283 Merv Rettenmund .15 .40
284 Steve Ontiveros .15 .40
285 Mike Cuellar .30 .75
286 Jim Wohlford .15 .40
287 Pete Mackanin .15 .40
288 Bill Campbell .15 .40
289 Enzo Hernandez .15 .40
290 Ted Simmons .30 .75
291 Ken Sanders .15 .40
292 Leon Roberts .15 .40
293 Bill Castro RC .15 .40
294 Ed Kirkpatrick .15 .40
295 Dave Cash .15 .40
296 Pat Dobson .15 .40
297 Roger Metzger .15 .40
298 Dick Bosman .15 .40
299 Champ Summers RC .15 .40
300 Johnny Bench 10.00 25.00
301 Jackie Brown .15 .40
302 Rick Miller .15 .40
303 Steve Foucault .15 .40
304 California Angels CL/Williams .60 1.50
305 Andy Messersmith .30 .75
306 Rod Gilbreath .15 .40
307 Al Bumbry .30 .75
308 Jim Barr .15 .40
309 Bill Melton .15 .40
310 Randy Jones .30 .75
311 Cookie Rojas .15 .40
312 Don Carrithers .15 .40
313 Dan Ford RC .15 .40
314 Ed Kranepool .15 .40
315 Al Hrabosky .30 .75
316 Robin Yount 8.00 20.00
317 John Candelaria RC .60 1.50
318 Bob Boone .60 1.50
319 Larry Gura .15 .40
320 Willie Horton .30 .75
321 Jose Cruz .60 1.50
322 Glenn Abbott .15 .40
323 Rob Sperring RC .15 .40
324 Jim Bibby .15 .40
325 Tony Perez 1.25 3.00
326 Dick Pole .15 .40
327 Dave Moates RC .15 .40
328 Carl Morton .15 .40
329 Joe Ferguson .15 .40
330 Nolan Ryan 20.00 50.00
331 San Diego Padres CL/McNamara .60 1.50
332 Charlie Williams .15 .40
333 Bob Coluccio .15 .40
334 Dennis Leonard .30 .75
335 Bob Grich .30 .75
336 Vic Albury .15 .40
337 Bud Harrelson .30 .75
338 Bob Bailey .15 .40
339 John Denny .30 .75
340 Jim Rice 12.00 30.00
341 Lou Gehrig ATG 5.00 12.00
342 Rogers Hornsby ATG 1.25 3.00
343 Pie Traynor ATG .60 1.50
344 Honus Wagner ATG 2.00 5.00
345 Babe Ruth ATG 8.00 20.00
346 Ty Cobb ATG 5.00 12.00
347 Ted Williams ATG 5.00 12.00
348 Mickey Cochrane ATG .60 1.50
349 Walter Johnson ATG 2.00 5.00
350 Lefty Grove ATG .60 1.50
351 Randy Hundley .30 .75
352 Dave Giusti .15 .40
353 Sixto Lezcano RC .30 .75
354 Ron Blomberg .15 .40
355 Steve Carlton 4.00 10.00
356 Ted Martinez .15 .40
357 Ken Forsch .15 .40
358 Buddy Bell .30 .75
359 Rick Reuschel .30 .75
360 Jeff Burroughs .30 .75
361 Detroit Tigers CL/Houk .60 1.50
362 Will McEnaney .30 .75
363 Dave Collins RC .30 .75
364 Elias Sosa .15 .40
365 Carlton Fisk 2.50 6.00
366 Bobby Valentine .30 .75
367 Bruce Miller .15 .40
368 Wilbur Wood .15 .40
369 Frank White .30 .75
370 Ron Cey .30 .75
371 Elrod Hendricks .15 .40
372 Rick Baldwin RC .15 .40
373 Johnny Briggs .15 .40
374 Dan Warthen RC .15 .40
375 Ron Fairly .30 .75
376 Rich Hebner .30 .75
377 Mike Hegan .15 .40
378 Steve Stone .30 .75
379 Ken Boswell .15 .40
380 Bobby Bonds .60 1.50
381 Denny Doyle .15 .40
382 Matt Alexander RC .15 .40
383 John Ellis .15 .40
384 Philadelphia Phillies CL/Ozark .60 1.50
385 Mickey Lolich .30 .75
386 Ed Goodson .15 .40
387 Mike Miley RC .15 .40
388 Stan Perzanowski RC .15 .40
389 Glenn Adams RC .15 .40
390 Don Gullett .30 .75
391 Jerry Hairston .15 .40
392 Checklist 265-396 .60 1.50
393 Paul Mitchell RC .15 .40
394 Fran Healy .15 .40
395 Jim Wynn .30 .75
396 Bill Lee .15 .40
397 Tim Foli .15 .40
398 Dave Tomlin .15 .40
399 Luis Melendez .15 .40
400 Rod Carew 2.50 6.00
401 Ken Brett .15 .40
402 Don Money .30 .75
403 Geoff Zahn .15 .40
404 Enos Cabell .15 .40
405 Rollie Fingers 1.00 2.50
406 Ed Herrmann .15 .40
407 Tom Underwood .15 .40
408 Charlie Spikes .15 .40
409 Dave Lemanczyk .15 .40
410 Ralph Garr .30 .75
411 Bill Singer .15 .40
412 Toby Harrah .30 .75
413 Pete Varney RC .15 .40
414 Wayne Garland .15 .40
415 Vada Pinson .60 1.50
416 Tommy John .60 1.50
417 Gene Clines .15 .40
418 Jose Morales RC .15 .40
419 Reggie Cleveland .15 .40
420 Joe Morgan 8.00 20.00
421 Oakland Athletics CL .60 1.50
422 Johnny Grubb .15 .40
423 Ed Halicki .15 .40
424 Phil Roof .15 .40
425 Rennie Stennett .15 .40
426 Bob Forsch .15 .40
427 Kurt Bevacqua .15 .40
428 Jim Crawford .15 .40
429 Fred Stanley .15 .40
430 Jose Cardenal .30 .75
431 Dick Ruthven .15 .40
432 Tom Veryzer .15 .40
433 Rick Waits RC .15 .40
434 Morris Nettles .15 .40
435 Phil Niekro 1.00 2.50
436 Bill Fahey .15 .40
437 Terry Forster .15 .40
438 Doug DeCinces .30 .75
439 Rick Rhoden .30 .75
440 John Mayberry .30 .75
441 Gary Carter 3.00 8.00
442 Hank Webb .15 .40
443 San Francisco Giants CL .60 1.50
444 Gary Nolan .30 .75
445 Rico Petrocelli .30 .75
446 Larry Haney .15 .40
447 Gene Locklear .30 .75
448 Tom Johnson .15 .40
449 Bob Robertson .15 .40
450 Jim Palmer 2.00 5.00
451 Buddy Bradford .15 .40
452 Tom Hausman RC .15 .40
453 Lou Piniella .60 1.50
454 Tom Griffin .15 .40
455 Dick Allen .60 1.50
456 Joe Coleman .15 .40
457 Ed Crosby .15 .40
458 Earl Williams .15 .40
459 Jim Brewer .15 .40
460 Cesar Cedeno .30 .75
461 NL/AL Champs .30 .75
462 1975 WS/Reds Champs .30 .75
463 Steve Hargan .15 .40
464 Ken Henderson .15 .40
465 Mike Marshall .30 .75
466 Bob Stinson .15 .40
467 Woodie Fryman .15 .40
468 Jesus Alou .15 .40
469 Rawly Eastwick .30 .75
470 Bobby Murcer .30 .75
471 Jim Burton .15 .40
472 Bob Davis RC .15 .40
473 Paul Blair .30 .75
474 Ray Corbin .15 .40
475 Joe Rudi .30 .75
476 Bob Moose .15 .40
477 Cleveland Indians CL/Robinson .60 1.50
478 Lynn McGlothen .15 .40
479 Bobby Mitchell .15 .40
480 Mike Schmidt 10.00 25.00
481 Rudy May .15 .40
482 Tim Hosley .15 .40
483 Mickey Stanley .15 .40
484 Eric Raich RC .15 .40
485 Mike Hargrove .30 .75
486 Bruce Dal Canton .15 .40
487 Leron Lee .15 .40
488 Claude Osteen .30 .75
489 Skip Jutze .15 .40
490 Frank Tanana .30 .75
491 Terry Crowley .15 .40
492 Marty Pattin .15 .40
493 Derrel Thomas .15 .40
494 Craig Swan .30 .75
495 Nate Colbert .15 .40
496 Juan Beniquez .15 .40
497 Joe McIntosh RC .15 .40
498 Glenn Borgmann .15 .40
499 Mario Guerrero .15 .40
500 Reggie Jackson 6.00 15.00
501 Billy Champion .15 .40
502 Tim McCarver .60 1.50
503 Elliott Maddox .15 .40
504 Pittsburgh Pirates CL/Murtaugh .60 1.50
505 Mark Belanger .30 .75
506 George Mitterwald .15 .40
507 Ray Bare RC .15 .40
508 Duane Kuiper RC .15 .40
509 Bill Hands .15 .40
510 Amos Otis .30 .75
511 Jamie Easterley .15 .40
512 Ellie Rodriguez .15 .40
513 Bart Johnson .15 .40
514 Dan Driessen .30 .75
515 Steve Yeager .30 .75
516 Wayne Granger .15 .40
517 John Milner .15 .40
518 Doug Flynn RC .15 .40
519 Steve Brye .15 .40
520 Willie McCovey 5.00 12.00
521 Jim Colborn .15 .40
522 Ted Sizemore .15 .40
523 Bob Montgomery .15 .40
524 Pete Falcone RC .15 .40
525 Billy Williams 1.00 2.50
526 Checklist 397-528 .60 1.50
527 Mike Anderson .15 .40
528 Dock Ellis .15 .40
529 Deron Johnson .15 .40
530 Don Sutton 1.00 2.50
531 New York Mets CL/Frazier .60 1.50
532 Milt May .15 .40
533 Lee Richard .15 .40
534 Stan Bahnsen .15 .40
535 Dave Nelson .15 .40
536 Mike Thompson .15 .40
537 Tony Muser .15 .40
538 Pat Darcy .15 .40
539 John Balaz RC .15 .40
540 Bill Freehan .30 .75
541 Steve Mingori .15 .40
542 Keith Hernandez .30 .75
543 Wayne Twitchell .15 .40
544 Pepe Frias .15 .40
545 Sparky Lyle .30 .75
546 Dave Rosello .15 .40
547 Roric Harrison .15 .40
548 Manny Mota .30 .75
549 Randy Tate RC .15 .40
550 Hank Aaron 15.00 40.00
551 Jerry DaVanon .15 .40
552 Terry Humphrey .15 .40
553 Randy Moffitt .15 .40
554 Ray Fosse .15 .40
555 Dyar Miller .15 .40
556 Minnesota Twins CL/Mauch .60 1.50
557 Dan Spillner .15 .40
558 Clarence Gaston .30 .75
559 Clyde Wright .15 .40
560 Jorge Orta .15 .40
561 Tom Carroll .15 .40
562 Adrian Garrett .15 .40
563 Larry Demery .15 .40
564 Kurt Bevacqua GUM .60 1.50
565 Tug McGraw .30 .75
566 Ken McMullen .15 .40
567 George Stone .15 .40
568 Rob Andrews RC .15 .40
569 Nelson Briles .30 .75
570 George Hendrick .30 .75
571 Don DeMola .15 .40
572 Rich Coggins .15 .40
573 Bill Travers .15 .40
574 Don Kessinger .30 .75
575 Dwight Evans .60 1.50
576 Maximino Leon .15 .40
577 Marc Hill .15 .40
578 Ted Kubiak .15 .40
579 Clay Kirby .15 .40
580 Bert Campaneris .30 .75
581 St. Louis Cardinals CL/Schoendienst.60 1.50
582 Mike Kekich .15 .40
583 Tommy Helms .15 .40
584 Stan Wall RC .15 .40
585 Joe Torre .60 1.50
586 Ron Schueler .15 .40
587 Leo Cardenas .15 .40
588 Kevin Kobel .15 .40
589 Alc/Flanagan/Pac/Torr RC .60 1.50
590 Cruz/Lemon/Valen/Whit RC .30 .75
591 Grilli/Mitch/Sosa/Throop RC .30 .75
592 Randolph/McK/Roy/Sta RC 2.00 5.00
593 And/Crosby/Litell/Metzger RC .30 .75
594 Mer/Ott/Still/White RC .30 .75
595 DeFil/Lerch/Monge/Barr RC .30 .75
596 Rey/John/LeMas/Manuel RC .30 .75
597 Aase/Kucek/LaCorte/Pazik RC .30 .75
598 Cruz/Quirk/Turner/Wallis RC .30 .75
599 Dres/Guidry/McCl/Zach RC 5.00 12.00
600 Tom Seaver 6.00 15.00
601 Ken Rudolph .15 .40
602 Doug Konieczny .15 .40
603 Jim Holt .15 .40
604 Joe Lovitto .15 .40

605 Al Downing .15 .40
606 Milwaukee Brewers CL/Grammas .60 1.50
607 Rich Hinton .15 .40
608 Vic Correll .15 .40
609 Fred Norman .15 .40
610 Greg Luzinski .60 1.50
611 Rich Folkers .15 .40
612 Joe Lahoud .15 .40
613 Tim Johnson .15 .40
614 Fernando Arroyo RC .15 .40
615 Mike Cubbage .15 .40
616 Buck Martinez .15 .40
617 Darold Knowles .15 .40
618 Jack Brohamer .15 .40
619 Bill Butler .15 .40
620 Al Oliver .30 .75
621 Tom Hall .15 .40
622 Rick Auerbach .15 .40
623 Bob Allietta RC .15 .40
624 Tony Taylor .15 .40
625 J.R. Richard .30 .75
626 Bob Sheldon .15 .40
627 Bill Plummer .15 .40
628 John D'Acquisto .15 .40
629 Sandy Alomar .30 .75
630 Chris Speier .15 .40
631 Atlanta Braves CL/Bristol .60 1.50
632 Rogelio Moret .15 .40
633 John Stearns RC .30 .75
634 Larry Christenson .15 .40
635 Jim Fregosi .30 .75
636 Joe Decker .15 .40
637 Bruce Bochte .15 .40
638 Doyle Alexander .30 .75
639 Fred Kendall .15 .40
640 Bill Madlock .60 1.50
641 Tom Paciorek .30 .75
642 Dennis Blair .15 .40
643 Checklist 529-660 .60 1.50
644 Tom Bradley .15 .40
645 Darrell Porter .30 .75
646 John Lowenstein .15 .40
647 Ramon Hernandez .15 .40
648 Al Cowens .30 .75
649 Dave Roberts .15 .40
650 Thurman Munson 10.00 25.00
651 John Odom .15 .40
652 Ed Armbrister .15 .40
653 Mike Norris RC .30 .75
654 Doug Griffin .15 .40
655 Mike Vail RC .15 .40
656 Chicago White Sox CL/Tanner .60 1.50
657 Roy Smalley RC .30 .75
658 Jerry Johnson .15 .40
659 Ben Oglivie .30 .75
660 Davey Lopes .60 1.50

1976 Topps Traded

COMPLETE SET (44) 12.50 30.00
27T Ed Figueroa .15 .40
28T Dusty Baker .60 1.50
44T Doug Rader .30 .75
58T Ron Reed .15 .40
74T Oscar Gamble .60 1.50
80T Jim Kaat .60 1.50
83T Jim Spencer .15 .40
85T Mickey Rivers .30 .75
99T Lee Lacy .15 .40
120T Rusty Staub .30 .75
127T Larvell Blanks .15 .40
146T George Medich .15 .40
158T Ken Reitz .15 .40
208T Mike Lum .15 .40
211T Clay Carroll .15 .40
231T Tom House .15 .40
250T Fergie Jenkins 1.25 3.00
259T Darrel Chaney .15 .40
292T Leon Roberts .15 .40
296T Pat Dobson .15 .40
309T Bill Melton .15 .40
338T Bob Bailey .15 .40
380T Bobby Bonds .60 1.50
383T John Ellis .15 .40
385T Mickey Lolich .30 .75
401T Ken Brett .15 .40
410T Ralph Garr .15 .40
411T Bill Singer .15 .40
428T Jim Crawford .15 .40
434T Morris Nettles .15 .40
464T Ken Henderson .15 .40
497T Joe McIntosh .15 .40
524T Pete Falcone .15 .40
527T Mike Anderson .15 .40
528T Dock Ellis .15 .40
532T Milt May .15 .40
554T Ray Fosse .15 .40
579T Clay Kirby .15 .40
583T Tommy Helms .15 .40
592T Willie Randolph 2.00 5.00
618T Jack Brohamer .15 .40
632T Rogelio Moret .15 .40
649T Dave Roberts .15 .40
NNO Traded Checklist .75 2.00

1976 Topps Team Checklist Sheet

This uncut sheet of the 24 1976 Topps team checklists measures 10" by 21". The sheet was obtained by sending 50 cents plus one wrapper to Topps. When seperated, these cards measure the standard-size.

1 Topps Team CL Sheet 50.00 100.00

1976 Topps Cloth Sticker Test

Before releasing their 1977 Cloth Sticker set, Topps experimented and produced several type cards for a 1976 Cloth Sticker set. While these standard-size cards were never released to the public, a few have made their way into the secondary market. Any more information and additions to this checklist is appreciated.

1 Bob Apodaca 20.00 50.00
2 Duffy Dyer 20.00 50.00

1976 Topps Garagiola

This one-card set was produced by Topps in honor of catcher Joe Garagiola. The front features a color portrait of the player in a thin black fame with a white border. The back displays the player's name and business address in a black cut-out bubble with the player's information and statistics printed in the background.

1 Joe Garagiola 4.00 10.00

1977 Topps

In 1977 for the fifth consecutive year, Topps produced a 660-card standard-size baseball set. Among other fashions, this set was released in 10-card wax packs as well as thirty-nine card rack packs. The player's name, team affiliation, and his position are compactly arranged over the picture area and a facsimile autograph appears on the photo. Team cards feature a checklist of that team's players in the set and a small picture of the manager on the front of the card. Appearing for the first time are the series "Brothers" (631-634) and "Turn Back the Clock" (433-437). Other subseries in the set are League Leaders (1-8), Record Breakers (231-234), Playoffs cards (276-277), World Series cards (411-413), and Rookie Prospects (472-479/487-494). The following players' regular issue cards are explicitly denoted as All-Stars, 30, 70, 100, 120, 170, 210, 240, 265, 301, 347, 400, 420, 450, 500, 521, 550, 560, and 580. The key Rookie Cards in the set are Jack Clark, Andre Dawson, Mark "The Bird" Fidrych, Dennis Martinez and Dale Murphy. Cards numbered 23 or lower, that feature Yankees and do not follow the numbering checklisted below, are not necessarily error cards. Those cards were issued in the NY area and distributed by Burger King. There was an aluminum version of the Dale Murphy rookie card number 476 produced (legally) in the early '80s; proceeds from the sales originally priced at 10.00) of this "card" went to the Huntington's Disease Foundation.

COMPLETE SET (660) 200.00 500.00
1 G.Brett/B.Madlock LL 3.00 8.00
2 G.Nettles/M.Schmidt LL 1.00 2.50
3 L.May/G.Foster LL .60 1.50
4 B.North/D.Lopes LL .30 .75
5 J.Palmer/R.Jones LL .60 1.50
6 N.Ryan/T.Seaver LL 4.00 10.00
7 M.Fidrych/J.Denny LL .30 .75
8 B.Campbell/R.Eastwick LL .30 .75
9 Doug Rader .12 .30
10 Reggie Jackson 10.00 25.00
11 Rob Dressler .12 .30
12 Larry Haney .12 .30
13 Luis Gomez RC .12 .30
14 Tommy Smith .12 .30
15 Don Gullett .30 .75
16 Bob Jones RC .12 .30
17 Steve Stone .30 .75
18 Cleveland Indians CL/Robinson .60 1.50
19 John D'Acquisto .12 .30
20 Graig Nettles .60 1.50
21 Ken Forsch .12 .30
22 Bill Freehan .30 .75
23 Dan Driessen .12 .30
24 Carl Morton .12 .30
25 Dwight Evans .60 1.50
26 Ray Sadecki .12 .30
27 Bill Buckner .30 .75
28 Woodie Fryman .12 .30
29 Bucky Dent .30 .75
30 Greg Luzinski .60 1.50
31 Jim Todd .12 .30
32 Checklist 1-132 .60 1.50
33 Wayne Garland .12 .30
34 California Angels CL/Sherry .60 1.50
35 Rennie Stennett .12 .30
36 John Ellis .12 .30
37 Steve Hargan .12 .30
38 Craig Kusick .12 .30
39 Tom Griffin .12 .30
40 Bobby Murcer .30 .75
41 Jim Kern .12 .30
42 Jose Cruz .30 .75
43 Ray Bare .12 .30
44 Bud Harrelson .30 .75
45 Rawly Eastwick .12 .30
46 Buck Martinez .12 .30
47 Lynn McGlothen .12 .30
48 Tom Paciorek .30 .75
49 Grant Jackson .12 .30
50 Ron Cey .30 .75
51 Milwaukee Brewers CL/Grammas .60 1.50
52 Ellis Valentine .12 .30
53 Paul Mitchell .12 .30
54 Sandy Alomar .30 .75
55 Jeff Burroughs .30 .75
56 Rudy May .12 .30
57 Marc Hill .12 .30
58 Chet Lemon .30 .75
59 Larry Christenson .12 .30
60 Jim Rice 1.50 4.00
61 Manny Sanguillen .30 .75
62 Eric Raich .12 .30
63 Tito Fuentes .12 .30
64 Larry Biittner .12 .30
65 Skip Lockwood .12 .30
66 Roy Smalley .30 .75
67 Joaquin Andujar RC .30 .75
68 Bruce Bochte .12 .30
69 Jim Crawford .12 .30
70 Johnny Bench 6.00 15.00
71 Dock Ellis .12 .30
72 Mike Anderson .12 .30
73 Charlie Williams .12 .30
74 Oakland Athletics CL/McKeon .60 1.50
75 Dennis Leonard .30 .75
76 Tim Foli .12 .30
77 Dyar Miller .12 .30
78 Bob Davis .12 .30
79 Don Money .30 .75
80 Andy Messersmith .30 .75
81 Juan Beniquez .12 .30
82 Jim Rooker .12 .30
83 Kevin Bell RC .12 .30
84 Ollie Brown .12 .30
85 Duane Kuiper .12 .30
86 Pat Zachry .12 .30
87 Glenn Borgmann .12 .30
88 Stan Wall .12 .30
89 Butch Hobson RC .30 .75
90 Cesar Cedeno .30 .75
91 John Verhoeven RC .12 .30
92 Dave Rosello .12 .30
93 Tom Poquette .12 .30
94 Craig Swan .12 .30
95 Keith Hernandez .30 .75
96 Lou Piniella .30 .75
97 Dave Heaverlo .12 .30
98 Milt May .12 .30
99 Tom Hausman .12 .30
100 Joe Morgan 1.50 4.00
101 Dick Bosman .12 .30
102 Jose Morales .12 .30
103 Mike Bacsik RC .12 .30
104 Omar Moreno RC .30 .75
105 Steve Yeager .30 .75
106 Mike Flanagan .30 .75
107 Bill Melton .12 .30
108 Alan Foster .12 .30
109 Jorge Orta .12 .30
110 Steve Carlton 4.00 10.00
111 Rico Petrocelli .30 .75
112 Bill Greif .12 .30
113 Toronto Blue Jays CL/Hartsfield .60 1.50
114 Bruce Dal Canton .12 .30
115 Rick Manning .12 .30
116 Joe Niekro .30 .75
117 Frank White .30 .75
118 Rick Jones RC .12 .30
119 John Stearns .12 .30
120 Rod Carew 4.00 10.00
121 Gary Nolan .12 .30
122 Ben Oglivie .30 .75
123 Fred Stanley .12 .30
124 George Mitterwald .12 .30
125 Bill Travers .12 .30
126 Rod Gilbreath .12 .30
127 Ron Fairly .30 .75
128 Tommy John .60 1.50
129 Mike Sadek .12 .30
130 Al Oliver .30 .75
131 Orlando Ramirez RC .12 .30
132 Chip Lang RC .12 .30
133 Ralph Garr .30 .75
134 San Diego Padres CL/McNamara .60 1.50
135 Mark Belanger .30 .75
136 Jerry Mumphrey RC .30 .75
137 Jeff Terpko RC .12 .30
138 Bob Stinson .12 .30
139 Fred Norman .12 .30
140 Mike Schmidt 5.00 12.00
141 Mark Littell .12 .30
142 Steve Dillard RC .12 .30
143 Ed Herrmann .12 .30
144 Bruce Sutter RC 15.00 40.00
145 Tom Veryzer .12 .30
146 Dusty Baker .60 1.50
147 Jackie Brown .12 .30
148 Fran Healy .12 .30
149 Mike Cubbage .12 .30
150 Tom Seaver 3.00 8.00
151 Johnny LeMaster .12 .30
152 Gaylord Perry 1.00 2.50
153 Ron Jackson RC .12 .30
154 Dave Giusti .12 .30
155 Joe Rudi .30 .75
156 Pete Mackanin .12 .30
157 Ken Brett .12 .30
158 Ted Kubiak .12 .30
159 Bernie Carbo .12 .30
160 Will McEnaney .12 .30
161 Garry Templeton RC .60 1.50
162 Mike Cuellar .30 .75
163 Dave Hilton .12 .30
164 Tug McGraw .30 .75
165 Jim Wynn .30 .75
166 Bill Campbell .12 .30
167 Rich Hebner .30 .75
168 Charlie Spikes .12 .30
169 Darold Knowles .12 .30
170 Thurman Munson 12.00 30.00
171 Ken Sanders .12 .30
172 John Milner .12 .30
173 Chuck Scrivener RC .12 .30
174 Nelson Briles .12 .30
175 Butch Wynegar RC .30 .75
176 Bob Robertson .12 .30
177 Bart Johnson .12 .30
178 Bombo Rivera RC .12 .30
179 Paul Hartzell RC .12 .30
180 Dave Lopes .30 .75
181 Ken McMullen .12 .30
182 Dan Spillner .12 .30
183 St.Louis Cardinals CL/V.Rapp .60 1.50
184 Bo McLaughlin RC .12 .30
185 Sixto Lezcano .12 .30
186 Doug Flynn .12 .30
187 Dick Pole .12 .30
188 Bob Tolan .12 .30
189 Rick Dempsey .30 .75
190 Ray Burris .12 .30
191 Doug Griffin .12 .30
192 Clarence Gaston .30 .75
193 Larry Gura .12 .30
194 Gary Matthews .30 .75
195 Ed Figueroa .12 .30
196 Len Randle .12 .30
197 Ed Ott .12 .30
198 Wilbur Wood .12 .30
199 Pepe Frias .12 .30
200 Frank Tanana .30 .75
201 Ed Kranepool .12 .30
202 Tom Johnson .12 .30
203 Ed Armbrister .12 .30
204 Jeff Newman RC .12 .30
205 Pete Falcone .12 .30
206 Boog Powell .60 1.50
207 Glenn Abbott .12 .30
208 Checklist 133-264 .60 1.50
209 Rob Andrews .12 .30
210 Fred Lynn .75 2.00
211 San Francisco Giants CL/Altobelli .60 1.50
212 Jim Mason .12 .30
213 Maximino Leon .12 .30
214 Darrell Porter .30 .75
215 Butch Metzger .12 .30
216 Doug DeCinces .30 .75
217 Tom Underwood .12 .30
218 John Wathan RC .30 .75
219 Joe Coleman .12 .30
220 Chris Chambliss .30 .75
221 Bob Bailey .12 .30
222 Francisco Barrios RC .12 .30
223 Earl Williams .12 .30
224 Rusty Torres .12 .30
225 Bob Apodaca .12 .30
226 Leroy Stanton .30 .75
227 Joe Sambito RC .12 .30
228 Minnesota Twins CL/Mauch .60 1.50
229 Don Kessinger .30 .75
230 Vida Blue .30 .75
231 George Brett RB 3.00 8.00
232 Minnie Minoso RB .30 .75
233 Jose Morales RB .12 .30
234 Nolan Ryan RB 5.00 12.00
235 Cecil Cooper .30 .75
236 Tom Buskey .12 .30
237 Gene Clines .12 .30
238 Tippy Martinez .12 .30
239 Bill Plummer .12 .30
240 Ron LeFlore .30 .75
241 Dave Tomlin .12 .30
242 Ken Henderson .12 .30
243 Ron Reed .12 .30
244 John Mayberry .30 .75
245 Rick Rhoden .30 .75
246 Mike Vail .12 .30
247 Chris Knapp RC .12 .30
248 Wilbur Howard .12 .30
249 Pete Redfern RC .12 .30
250 Bill Madlock .30 .75
251 Tony Muser .12 .30
252 Dale Murray .12 .30
253 John Hale .12 .30
254 Doyle Alexander .12 .30
255 George Scott .30 .75
256 Joe Hoerner .12 .30
257 Mike Miley .12 .30
258 Luis Tiant .30 .75
259 New York Mets CL/Frazier .60 1.50
260 J.R. Richard .30 .75
261 Phil Garner .30 .75
262 Al Cowens .30 .75
263 Mike Marshall .30 .75
264 Tom Hutton .12 .30
265 Mark Fidrych RC 1.25 3.00
266 Derrel Thomas .12 .30
267 Ray Fosse .12 .30
268 Rick Sawyer RC .12 .30
269 Joe Lis .12 .30
270 Dave Parker .60 1.50
271 Terry Forster .12 .30
272 Lee Lacy .12 .30
273 Eric Soderholm .12 .30
274 Don Stanhouse .12 .30
275 Mike Hargrove .30 .75
276 Chris Chambliss ALCS .60 1.50
277 Pete Rose NLCS 2.00 5.00
278 Danny Frisella .12 .30
279 Joe Wallis .12 .30
280 Jim Hunter 1.00 2.50
281 Roy Staiger .12 .30
282 Sid Monge .12 .30
283 Jerry DaVanon .12 .30
284 Mike Norris .12 .30
285 Brooks Robinson 8.00 20.00
286 Johnny Grubb .12 .30
287 Cincinnati Reds CL/Anderson .60 1.50
288 Bob Montgomery .12 .30
289 Gene Garber .30 .75
290 Amos Otis .30 .75
291 Jason Thompson RC .30 .75
292 Rogelio Moret .12 .30
293 Jack Brohamer .12 .30
294 George Medich .12 .30
295 Gary Carter 1.50 4.00
296 Don Hood .12 .30
297 Ken Reitz .12 .30
298 Charlie Hough .30 .75
299 Otto Velez .12 .30
300 Jerry Koosman .30 .75
301 Toby Harrah .30 .75
302 Mike Garman .12 .30
303 Gene Tenace .30 .75
304 Jim Hughes .12 .30
305 Mickey Rivers .30 .75
306 Rick Waits .12 .30
307 Gary Sutherland .12 .30
308 Gene Pentz RC .12 .30
309 Boston Red Sox CL/Zimmer .60 1.50
310 Larry Bowa .30 .75
311 Vern Ruhle .12 .30
312 Rob Belloir RC .12 .30
313 Paul Blair .30 .75
314 Steve Mingori .12 .30
315 Dave Chalk .12 .30
316 Steve Rogers .12 .30
317 Kurt Bevacqua .12 .30
318 Duffy Dyer .12 .30
319 Goose Gossage .60 1.50
320 Ken Griffey Sr. .60 1.50
321 Dave Goltz .12 .30
322 Bill Russell .30 .75
323 Larry Lintz .12 .30
324 John Curtis .12 .30
325 Mike Ivie .12 .30
326 Jesse Jefferson .12 .30
327 Houston Astros CL/Virdon .60 1.50
328 Tommy Boggs RC .12 .30
329 Ron Hodges .12 .30
330 George Hendrick .30 .75
331 Jim Colborn .12 .30
332 Elliott Maddox .12 .30
333 Paul Reuschel RC .12 .30
334 Bill Stein .12 .30
335 Bill Robinson .30 .75
336 Denny Doyle .12 .30
337 Ron Schueler .12 .30
338 Dave Duncan .30 .75
339 Adrian Devine .12 .30
340 Hal McRae .30 .75
341 Joe Kerrigan RC .12 .30
342 Jerry Remy .12 .30
343 Ed Halicki .12 .30
344 Brian Downing .30 .75
345 Reggie Smith .30 .75
346 Bill Singer .12 .30
347 George Foster .60 1.50
348 Brent Strom .12 .30
349 Jim Holt .12 .30
350 Larry Dierker .30 .75
351 Jim Sundberg .30 .75
352 Mike Phillips .12 .30
353 Stan Thomas .12 .30
354 Pittsburgh Pirates CL/Tanner .60 1.50
355 Lou Brock 1.50 4.00
356 Checklist 265-396 .60 1.50
357 Tim McCarver .60 1.50
358 Tom House .30 .75
359 Willie Randolph .60 1.50
360 Rick Monday .30 .75
361 Eduardo Rodriguez .12 .30
362 Tommy Davis .30 .75
363 Dave Roberts .12 .30
364 Vic Correll .12 .30
365 Mike Torrez .30 .75
366 Ted Sizemore .12 .30
367 Dave Hamilton .12 .30
368 Mike Jorgensen .12 .30
369 Terry Humphrey .12 .30
370 John Montefusco .12 .30
371 Kansas City Royals CL/Herzog .60 1.50
372 Rich Folkers .12 .30
373 Bert Campaneris .30 .75
374 Kent Tekulve .30 .75
375 Larry Hisle .30 .75
376 Nino Espinosa RC .12 .30
377 Dave McKay .12 .30
378 Jim Umbarger .12 .30
379 Larry Cox RC .12 .30
380 Lee May .30 .75
381 Bob Forsch .12 .30
382 Charlie Moore .12 .30
383 Stan Bahnsen .12 .30
384 Darrel Chaney .12 .30
385 Dave LaRoche .12 .30
386 Manny Mota .30 .75
387 New York Yankees CL/Martin 1.00 2.50
388 Terry Harmon .12 .30
389 Ken Kravec RC .12 .30
390 Dave Winfield 6.00 15.00
391 Dan Warthen .12 .30
392 Phil Roof .12 .30
393 John Lowenstein .12 .30
394 Bill Laxton RC .12 .30
395 Manny Trillo .12 .30
396 Tom Murphy .12 .30
397 Larry Herndon RC .30 .75
398 Tom Burgmeier .12 .30
399 Bruce Boisclair RC .12 .30
400 Steve Garvey 1.00 2.50
401 Mickey Scott .12 .30
402 Tommy Helms .12 .30
403 Tom Grieve .30 .75
404 Eric Rasmussen RC .12 .30
405 Claudell Washington .30 .75
406 Tim Johnson .12 .30
407 Dave Freisleben .12 .30
408 Cesar Tovar .12 .30
409 Pete Broberg .12 .30
410 Willie Montanez .12 .30
411 J.Morgan/J.Bench WS 1.00 2.50
412 Johnny Bench WS 1.00 2.50
413 Cincy Wins WS .30 .75
414 Tommy Harper .30 .75
415 Jay Johnstone .30 .75
416 Chuck Hartenstein .12 .30
417 Wayne Garrett .12 .30
418 Chicago White Sox CL/Lemon .60 1.50
419 Steve Swisher .12 .30
420 Rusty Staub .60 1.50
421 Doug Rau .12 .30
422 Freddie Patek .30 .75
423 Gary Lavelle .12 .30
424 Steve Brye .12 .30
425 Joe Torre .60 1.50
426 Dick Drago .12 .30
427 Dave Rader .12 .30
428 Texas Rangers CL/Lucchesi .60 1.50
429 Ken Boswell .12 .30
430 Fergie Jenkins 1.00 2.50
431 Dave Collins UER .30 .75
432 Buzz Capra .12 .30
433 Nate Colbert TBC .12 .30
434 Carl Yastrzemski TBC .60 1.50
435 Maury Wills TBC .30 .75
436 Bob Keegan TBC .12 .30
437 Ralph Kiner TBC .60 1.50
438 Marty Perez .12 .30
439 Gorman Thomas .30 .75
440 Jon Matlack .12 .30
441 Larvell Blanks .30 .75
442 Atlanta Braves CL/Bristol .60 1.50
443 Lamar Johnson .12 .30
444 Wayne Twitchell .12 .30
445 Ken Singleton .30 .75
446 Bill Bonham .12 .30
447 Jerry Turner .12 .30
448 Ellie Rodriguez .12 .30
449 Al Fitzmorris .12 .30
450 Pete Rose 5.00 12.00
451 Checklist 397-528 .60 1.50
452 Mike Caldwell .12 .30
453 Pedro Garcia .12 .30
454 Andy Etchebarren .12 .30
455 Rick Wise .12 .30
456 Leon Roberts .12 .30
457 Steve Luebber .12 .30
458 Leo Foster .12 .30
459 Steve Foucault .12 .30
460 Willie Stargell 1.00 2.50
461 Dick Tidrow .12 .30
462 Don Baylor .60 1.50
463 Jamie Quirk .12 .30
464 Randy Moffitt .12 .30
465 Rico Carty .30 .75
466 Fred Holdsworth .12 .30
467 Philadelphia Phillies CL/Ozark .60 1.50
468 Ramon Hernandez .12 .30
469 Pat Kelly .12 .30
470 Ted Simmons .30 .75
471 Del Unser .12 .30
472 Aase/McCl/Patt/Wehr RC .12 .30
473 Andre Dawson RC 25.00 60.00
474 Bailor/Gar/Reyn/Tav RC .30 .75
475 Batt/Camp/McGr/Sarm RC .30 .75
476 Dale Murphy RC 15.00 40.00
477 Ault/Dauer/Gonz/Mank RC .30 .75
478 Gid/Hoot/John/Lemong RC .30 .75
479 Assel/Gross/Mej/Woods RC .30 .75
480 Carl Yastrzemski 3.00 8.00
481 Roger Metzger .12 .30
482 Tony Solaita .12 .30
483 Richie Zisk .12 .30
484 Burt Hooton .30 .75
485 Roy White .30 .75
486 Ed Bane .12 .30
487 And/Glynn/Hend/Terl RC .30 .75
488 J.Clark/L.Mazzilli RC 1.25 3.00
489 Barker/Ler/Mint/Overy RC .30 .75
490 Almon/Klutts/McM/Wag RC .30 .75
491 Dennis Martinez RC 1.25 3.00
492 Armas/Kemp/Lop/Woods RC .30 .75
493 Krukow/Ott/Wheel/Will RC .30 .75
494 J.Gantner/B.Wills RC .60 1.50
495 Al Hrabosky .30 .75
496 Gary Thomasson .12 .30
497 Clay Carroll .12 .30
498 Sal Bando .30 .75
499 Pablo Torrealba .12 .30
500 Dave Kingman .60 1.50
501 Jim Bibby .12 .30
502 Randy Hundley .12 .30
503 Bill Lee .12 .30
504 Los Angeles Dodgers CL/Lasorda .60 1.50
505 Oscar Gamble .30 .75
506 Steve Grilli .12 .30
507 Mike Hegan .12 .30
508 Dave Pagan .12 .30
509 Cookie Rojas .30 .75
510 John Candelaria .12 .30
511 Bill Fahey .12 .30
512 Jack Billingham .12 .30
513 Jerry Terrell .12 .30
514 Cliff Johnson .12 .30
515 Chris Speier .12 .30
516 Bake McBride .30 .75
517 Pete Vuckovich RC .30 .75
518 Chicago Cubs CL/Franks .60 1.50
519 Don Kirkwood .12 .30
520 Garry Maddox .12 .30
521 Bob Grich .30 .75
522 Enzo Hernandez .12 .30
523 Rollie Fingers 1.00 2.50
524 Rowland Office .12 .30
525 Dennis Eckersley 4.00 10.00
526 Larry Parrish .30 .75
527 Dan Meyer .30 .75
528 Bill Castro .12 .30
529 Jim Essian RC .12 .30
530 Rick Reuschel .30 .75
531 Lyman Bostock .30 .75
532 Jim Willoughby .12 .30
533 Mickey Stanley .12 .30
534 Paul Splittorff .12 .30
535 Cesar Geronimo .12 .30
536 Vic Albury .12 .30
537 Dave Roberts .12 .30
538 Frank Taveras .12 .30
539 Mike Wallace .12 .30
540 Bob Watson .30 .75
541 John Denny .30 .75
542 Frank Duffy .12 .30
543 Ron Blomberg .12 .30
544 Gary Ross .12 .30
545 Bob Boone .30 .75
546 Baltimore Orioles CL/Weaver .60 1.50
547 Willie McCovey 1.50 4.00
548 Joel Youngblood RC .12 .30
549 Jerry Royster .12 .30
550 Randy Jones .12 .30
551 Bill North .12 .30
552 Pepe Mangual .12 .30
553 Jack Heidemann .12 .30
554 Bruce Kimm RC .12 .30
555 Dan Ford .12 .30
556 Doug Bird .12 .30
557 Jerry White .12 .30
558 Elias Sosa .12 .30
559 Alan Bannister RC .12 .30
560 Dave Concepcion .60 1.50
561 Pete LaCock .12 .30
562 Checklist 529-660 .60 1.50
563 Bruce Kison .12 .30
564 Alan Ashby .12 .30
565 Mickey Lolich .30 .75
566 Rick Miller .12 .30
567 Enos Cabell .12 .30
568 Carlos May .12 .30
569 Jim Lonborg .30 .75
570 Bobby Bonds .60 1.50
571 Darrell Evans .30 .75
572 Ross Grimsley .12 .30
573 Joe Ferguson .12 .30
574 Aurelio Rodriguez .12 .30
575 Dick Ruthven .12 .30
576 Fred Kendall .12 .30
577 Jerry Augustine RC .12 .30
578 Bob Randall RC .12 .30
579 Don Carrithers .12 .30
580 George Brett 8.00 20.00
581 Pedro Borbon .12 .30
582 Ed Kirkpatrick .12 .30
583 Paul Lindblad .12 .30
584 Ed Goodson .12 .30
585 Rick Burleson .30 .75
586 Steve Renko .12 .30
587 Rick Baldwin .12 .30
588 Dave Moates .12 .30
589 Mike Cosgrove .12 .30
590 Buddy Bell .30 .75
591 Chris Arnold .12 .30
592 Dan Briggs RC .12 .30
593 Dennis Blair .12 .30
594 Biff Pocoroba .12 .30
595 John Hiller .12 .30
596 Jerry Martin RC .12 .30
597 Seattle Mariners CL/Johnson .60 1.50
598 Sparky Lyle .30 .75
599 Mike Tyson .12 .30
600 Jim Palmer 1.50 4.00
601 Mike Lum .12 .30
602 Andy Hassler .12 .30
603 Willie Davis .30 .75
604 Jim Slaton .12 .30
605 Felix Millan .12 .30
606 Steve Braun .12 .30
607 Larry Demery .12 .30
608 Roy Howell .12 .30
609 Jim Barr .12 .30
610 Jose Cardenal .30 .75
611 Dave Lemanczyk .12 .30
612 Barry Foote .12 .30
613 Reggie Cleveland .12 .30
614 Greg Gross .12 .30
615 Phil Niekro 1.00 2.50
616 Tommy Sandt RC .12 .30
617 Bobby Darwin .12 .30
618 Pat Dobson .12 .30
619 Johnny Oates .30 .75
620 Don Sutton 1.00 2.50
621 Detroit Tigers CL/Houk .60 1.50
622 Jim Wohlford .12 .30
623 Jack Kucek .12 .30
624 Hector Cruz .12 .30
625 Ken Holtzman .30 .75
626 Al Bumbry .30 .75
627 Bob Myrick RC .12 .30
628 Mario Guerrero .12 .30
629 Bobby Valentine .30 .75
630 Bert Blyleven .60 1.50
631 Brett Brothers 2.50 6.00
632 Forsch Brothers .30 .75
633 May Brothers .30 .75
634 Reuschel Brothers UER .30 .75
635 Robin Yount 3.00 8.00
636 Santo Alcala .12 .30
637 Alex Johnson .12 .30
638 Jim Kaat .60 1.50
639 Jerry Morales .12 .30
640 Carlton Fisk 2.00 5.00
641 Dan Larson RC .12 .30
642 Willie Crawford .12 .30
643 Mike Pazik .12 .30
644 Matt Alexander .12 .30
645 Jerry Reuss .30 .75
646 Andres Mora RC .12 .30
647 Montreal Expos CL/Williams .60 1.50
648 Jim Spencer .12 .30
649 Dave Cash .12 .30
650 Nolan Ryan 12.00 30.00
651 Von Joshua .12 .30
652 Tom Walker .12 .30
653 Diego Segui .30 .75
654 Ron Pruitt RC .12 .30
655 Tony Perez 1.00 2.50
656 Ron Guidry .60 1.50
657 Mick Kelleher RC .12 .30
658 Marty Pattin .12 .30
659 Merv Rettenmund .12 .30
660 Willie Horton .60 1.50

1977 Topps Cloth Stickers

The "cards" in this 73-card set measure 2 1/2" by 3 1/2". The 1977 Cloth Stickers series was issued as a test set separately from the regular baseball series of that year. The packs of these cards contained two stickers as well as one "checklist puzzle" piece. The obverse pictures are identical to those appearing in the regular set, but the backs are completely different. There are 55 player cards and 18 unnumbered checklists, the latter bearing the title "Baseball Patches". The player cards are sequenced in alphabetical order. The checklists are puzzle pieces which, when properly arranged, form pictures of the A.L. and N.L. All-Star teams. Puzzle pieces are coded below by U (Upper), M (Middle), B (Bottom), L (left), C (Center), and R (Right). Cards marked with an SP in the checklist are in shorter supply than all others in the set. Even though we have assigned numbers 56 through 73 in our checklist for the puzzle cards, they are in fact all unnumbered. These cards came in 15 cent packs where were issued 36 packs to a box and 16 boxes to a case.

COMPLETE SET (73) 60.00 120.00
COMMON PLAYER (1-55) .10 .25
COMMON SP PLAYER (1-55) .40 1.00
COMMON PUZZLE (56-73) .08 .20
1 Alan Ashby .10 .25
2 Buddy Bell SP .50 1.25
3 Johnny Bench 1.50 4.00
4 Vida Blue .30 .75
5 Bert Blyleven .30 .75
6 Steve Braun SP .40 1.00
7 George Brett 4.00 10.00
8 Lou Brock 1.25 3.00
9 Jose Cardenal .10 .25
10 Rod Carew SP 2.50 6.00
11 Steve Carlton 1.50 4.00
12 Dave Cash .10 .25
13 Cesar Cedeno SP .50 1.25
14 Ron Cey .30 .75
15 Mark Fidrych 2.00 5.00
16 Dan Ford .10 .25
17 Wayne Garland .10 .25
18 Ralph Garr .10 .25
19 Steve Garvey 1.25 3.00
20 Mike Hargrove .30 .75
21 Jim Hunter .75 2.00
22 Reggie Jackson 1.50 4.00
23 Randy Jones .10 .25
24 Dave Kingman SP .50 1.25
25 Bill Madlock .30 .75
26 Lee May SP .50 1.25
27 John Mayberry .10 .25
28 John(Andy)Messersmith .10 .25
29 Willie Montanez .10 .25
30 John Montefusco SP .40 1.00
31 Joe Morgan .75 2.00
32 Thurman Munson .75 2.00
33 Bobby Murcer .30 .75
34 Al Oliver SP .50 1.25
35 Dave Pagan .10 .25
36 Jim Palmer SP 1.25 3.00

37 Tony Perez .75 2.00
38 Pete Rose SP 5.00 12.00
39 Joe Rudi .20 .50
40 Nolan Ryan SP 30.00 60.00
41 Mike Schmidt 4.00 10.00
42 Tom Seaver 2.00 5.00
43 Ted Simmons .30 .75
44 Bill Singer .10 .25
45 Willie Stargell 1.25 3.00
46 Rusty Staub .30 .75
47 Don Sutton .75 2.00
48 Luis Tiant .30 .75
49 Bill Travers .10 .25
50 Claudell Washington .30 .75
51 Bob Watson .30 .75
52 Dave Winfield 2.50 6.00
53 Carl Yastrzemski 1.50 4.00
54 Robin Yount 2.50 6.00
55 Richie Zisk .10 .25
56 AL Puzzle UL .08 .20
57 AL Puzzle UC .08 .20
58 AL Puzzle UR .08 .20
59 AL Puzzle ML .08 .20
60 AL Puzzle MC .08 .20
61 AL Puzzle MR .08 .20
62 AL Puzzle BL SP .08 .20
63 AL Puzzle BC SP .08 .20
64 AL Puzzle BR SP .08 .20
65 NL Puzzle UL .08 .20
66 NL Puzzle UC .08 .20
67 NL Puzzle UR .08 .20
68 NL Puzzle ML .08 .20
69 NL Puzzle MC .08 .20
70 NL Puzzle MR .08 .20
71 NL Puzzle BL .08 .20
72 NL Puzzle BC .08 .20
73 NL Puzzle BR .08 .20
CL Checklist .20 .50

1978 Topps

The cards in this 726-card set measure 2 1/2" by 3 1/2". As in previous years, this set was issued in many different ways: some of them include 14-card wax packs, 30-card supermarket packs which came 48 to a case and had an SRP of 20 cents and 39-card rack packs. The 1978 Topps set experienced an increase in number of cards from the previous five regular issue sets of 660. Card numbers 1 through 7 feature Record Breakers (RB) of the 1977 season. Other subsets within this set include League Leaders (201-208), Post-season cards (411-413), and Rookie Prospects (701-711). The key Rookie Cards in this set are the multi-player Rookie Card of Paul Molitor and Alan Trammell, Jack Morris, Eddie Murray, Lance Parrish, and Lou Whitaker. Many of the Molitor/Trammell cards are found with black printing smudges. The manager cards in the set feature a "then and now" format on the card front showing the manager as he looked during his playing days. While no scarcities exist, 66 of the cards are more abundant in supply, as they were "double printed." These 66 double-printed cards are noted in the checklist by DP. Team cards again feature a checklist of that team's players in the set on the back. Cards numbered 23 or lower, that feature Astros, Rangers, Tigers, or Yankees and do not follow the numbering checklisted below, are not necessarily error cards. They are undoubtedly Burger King cards, separate sets with their own pricing and mass distribution. The Bump Wills card has been seen with either no black mark or a major black mark on the front of the card. We will continue to investigate this card and see whether or not it should be considered a variation.

COMPLETE SET (726) 200.00 500.00
COMMON CARD (1-726) .10 .25
COMMON CARD DP .08 .20
1 Lou Brock RB 1.25 3.00
2 Sparky Lyle RB .25 .60
3 Willie McCovey RB 1.00 2.50
4 Brooks Robinson RB .50 1.25
5 Pete Rose RB 3.00 8.00
6 Nolan Ryan RB 6.00 15.00
7 Reggie Jackson RB 1.50 4.00
8 Mike Sadek .10 .25
9 Doug DeCinces .25 .60
10 Phil Niekro 1.00 2.50
11 Rick Manning .10 .25
12 Don Aase .10 .25
13 Art Howe RC .25 .60
14 Lerrin LaGrow .10 .25
15 Tony Perez DP .50 1.25
16 Roy White .25 .60
17 Mike Krukow .10 .25
18 Bob Grich .25 .60
19 Darrell Porter .25 .60
20 Pete Rose DP 5.00 12.00
21 Steve Kemp .10 .25
22 Charlie Hough .25 .60
23 Bump Wills .10 .25
24 Don Money DP .08 .20
25 Jon Matlack .10 .25
26 Rich Hebner .25 .60
27 Geoff Zahn .10 .25
28 Ed Ott .10 .25
29 Bob Lacey RC .10 .25
30 George Hendrick .25 .60
31 Glenn Abbott .10 .25
32 Garry Templeton .25 .60
33 Dave Lemanczyk .10 .25
34 Willie McCovey 1.25 3.00
35 Sparky Lyle .25 .60
36 Eddie Murray RC 25.00 60.00
37 Rick Waits .10 .25
38 Willie Montanez .10 .25
39 Floyd Bannister RC .10 .25
40 Carl Yastrzemski 4.00 10.00
41 Burt Hooton .25 .60
42 Jorge Orta .10 .25
43 Bill Atkinson RC .10 .25
44 Toby Harrah .25 .60
45 Mark Fidrych 1.00 2.50
46 Al Cowens .25 .60
47 Jack Billingham .10 .25
48 Don Baylor .50 1.25
49 Ed Kranepool .25 .60
50 Rick Reuschel .25 .60
51 Charlie Moore DP .08 .20
52 Jim Lonborg .25 .60
53 Phil Garner DP .10 .25
54 Tom Johnson .10 .25
55 Mitchell Page RC .10 .25
56 Randy Jones .10 .25
57 Dan Meyer .10 .25
58 Bob Forsch .10 .25
59 Otto Velez .10 .25
60 Thurman Munson 1.50 4.00
61 Larvell Blanks .10 .25
62 Jim Barr .10 .25
63 Don Zimmer MG .25 .60
64 Gene Pentz .10 .25
65 Ken Singleton .25 .60
66 Chicago White Sox CL .50 1.25
67 Claudell Washington .25 .60
68 Steve Foucault DP .08 .20
69 Mike Vail .10 .25
70 Goose Gossage .50 1.25
71 Terry Humphrey .10 .25
72 Andre Dawson 1.50 4.00
73 Andy Hassler .10 .25
74 Checklist 1-121 .50 1.25
75 Dick Ruthven .10 .25
76 Steve Ontiveros .10 .25
77 Ed Kirkpatrick .10 .25
78 Pablo Torrealba .10 .25
79 Darrell Johnson MG DP .08 .20
80 Ken Griffey Sr. .50 1.25
81 Pete Redfern .10 .25
82 San Francisco Giants CL .50 1.25
83 Bob Montgomery .10 .25
84 Kent Tekulve .25 .60
85 Ron Fairly .30 .75
86 Dave Tomlin .10 .25
87 John Lowenstein .10 .25
88 Mike Phillips .10 .25
89 Ken Clay RC .10 .25
90 Larry Bowa .50 1.25
91 Oscar Zamora .10 .25
92 Adrian Devine .10 .25
93 Bobby Cox DP .08 .20
94 Chuck Scrivener .10 .25
95 Jamie Quirk .10 .25
96 Baltimore Orioles CL .50 1.25
97 Stan Bahnsen .10 .25
98 Jim Essian .25 .60
99 Willie Hernandez RC .50 1.25
100 George Brett 8.00 20.00
101 Sid Monge .10 .25
102 Matt Alexander .10 .25
103 Tom Murphy .10 .25
104 Lee Lacy .10 .25
105 Reggie Cleveland .10 .25
106 Bill Plummer .10 .25
107 Ed Halicki .10 .25
108 Von Joshua .10 .25
109 Joe Torre MG .25 .60
110 Richie Zisk .10 .25
111 Mike Tyson .10 .25
112 Houston Astros CL .50 1.25
113 Don Carrithers .10 .25
114 Paul Blair .25 .60
115 Gary Nolan .10 .25
116 Tucker Ashford RC .10 .25
117 John Montague .10 .25
118 Terry Harmon .10 .25
119 Dennis Martinez 1.00 2.50
120 Gary Carter 1.00 2.50
121 Alvis Woods .10 .25
122 Dennis Eckersley 1.25 3.00
123 Manny Trillo .10 .25
124 Dave Rozema RC .10 .25
125 George Scott .25 .60
126 Paul Moskau RC .10 .25
127 Chet Lemon .25 .60
128 Bill Russell .25 .60
129 Jim Colborn .10 .25
130 Jeff Burroughs .25 .60
131 Bert Blyleven .50 1.25
132 Enos Cabell .10 .25
133 Jerry Augustine .10 .25
134 Steve Henderson RC .10 .25
135 Ron Guidry DP .50 1.25
136 Ted Sizemore .10 .25
137 Craig Kusick .10 .25
138 Larry Demery .10 .25
139 Wayne Gross .10 .25
140 Rollie Fingers 1.00 2.50
141 Ruppert Jones .10 .25
142 John Montefusco .10 .25
143 Keith Hernandez .25 .60
144 Jesse Jefferson .10 .25
145 Rick Monday .25 .60
146 Doyle Alexander .25 .60
147 Lee Mazzilli .10 .25
148 Andre Thornton .25 .60
149 Dale Murray .10 .25
150 Bobby Bonds .50 1.25
151 Milt Wilcox .10 .25
152 Ivan DeJesus RC .10 .25
153 Steve Stone .25 .60
154 Cecil Cooper DP .10 .25
155 Butch Hobson .25 .60
156 Andy Messersmith .10 .25
157 Pete LaCock DP .08 .20
158 Joaquin Andujar .25 .60
159 Lou Piniella .25 .60
160 Jim Palmer 1.25 3.00
161 Bob Boone .50 1.25
162 Paul Thormodsgard RC .10 .25
163 Bill North .10 .25
164 Bob Owchinko RC .10 .25
165 Rennie Stennett .10 .25
166 Carlos Lopez .10 .25
167 Tim Foli .10 .25
168 Reggie Smith .25 .60
169 Jerry Johnson .10 .25
170 Lou Brock 1.25 3.00
171 Pat Zachry .10 .25
172 Mike Hargrove .25 .60
173 Robin Yount UER 6.00 15.00
174 Wayne Garland .10 .25
175 Jerry Morales .10 .25
176 Milt May .10 .25
177 Gene Garber DP .10 .25
178 Dave Chalk .10 .25
179 Dick Tidrow .10 .25
180 Dave Concepcion .50 1.25
181 Ken Forsch .10 .25
182 Jim Spencer .10 .25
183 Doug Bird .10 .25
184 Checklist 122-242 .50 1.25
185 Ellis Valentine .10 .25
186 Bob Stanley DP RC .08 .20
187 Jerry Royster DP .08 .20
188 Al Bumbry .25 .60
189 Tom Lasorda MG DP 1.00 2.50
190 John Candelaria .25 .60
191 Rodney Scott RC .10 .25
192 San Diego Padres CL .50 1.25
193 Rich Chiles .10 .25
194 Derrel Thomas .10 .25
195 Larry Dierker .25 .60
196 Bob Bailor .10 .25
197 Nino Espinosa .10 .25
198 Ron Pruitt .10 .25
199 Craig Reynolds .10 .25
200 Reggie Jackson 3.00 8.00
201 D.Parker/R.Carew LL .50 1.25
202 G.Foster/J.Rice LL DP .25 .60
203 G.Foster/L.Hisle LL .25 .60
204 F.Taveras/F.Patek LL DP .10 .25
205 Carlton/Gol/Leon/Palm LL 1.00 2.50
206 P.Niekro/N.Ryan LL DP 2.50 6.00
207 J.Cand/F.Tanana LL DP .25 .60
208 R.Fingers/B.Campbell LL .50 1.25
209 Dock Ellis .10 .25
210 Jose Cardenal .10 .25
211 Earl Weaver MG DP .50 1.25
212 Mike Caldwell .10 .25
213 Alan Bannister .10 .25
214 California Angels CL .50 1.25
215 Darrell Evans .25 .60
216 Mike Paxton RC .10 .25
217 Rod Gilbreath .10 .25
218 Marty Pattin .10 .25
219 Mike Cubbage .10 .25
220 Pedro Borbon .10 .25
221 Chris Speier .10 .25
222 Jerry Martin .10 .25
223 Bruce Kison .10 .25
224 Jerry Tabb RC .10 .25
225 Don Gullett DP .10 .25
226 Joe Ferguson .10 .25
227 Al Fitzmorris .10 .25
228 Manny Mota DP .10 .25
229 Leo Foster .10 .25
230 Al Hrabosky .25 .60
231 Wayne Nordhagen RC .10 .25
232 Mickey Stanley .10 .25
233 Dick Pole .10 .25
234 Herman Franks MG .10 .25
235 Tim McCarver .25 .60
236 Terry Whitfield .10 .25
237 Rich Dauer .10 .25
238 Juan Beniquez .10 .25
239 Dyar Miller .10 .25
240 Gene Tenace .25 .60
241 Pete Vuckovich .25 .60
242 Barry Bonnell DP RC .08 .20
243 Bob McClure .10 .25
244 Montreal Expos CL DP .25 .60
245 Rick Burleson .25 .60
246 Dan Driessen .10 .25
247 Larry Christenson .10 .25
248 Frank White DP .25 .60
249 Dave Goltz DP .08 .20
250 Graig Nettles DP .25 .60
251 Don Kirkwood .10 .25
252 Steve Swisher DP .08 .20
253 Jim Kern .10 .25
254 Dave Collins .25 .60
255 Jerry Reuss .25 .60
256 Joe Altobelli MG RC .10 .25
257 Hector Cruz .10 .25
258 John Hiller .10 .25
259 Los Angeles Dodgers CL .50 1.25
260 Bert Campaneris .25 .60
261 Tim Hosley .10 .25
262 Rudy May .10 .25
263 Danny Walton .10 .25
264 Jamie Easterly .10 .25
265 Sal Bando DP .25 .60
266 Bob Shirley RC .10 .25
267 Doug Ault .10 .25
268 Gil Flores RC .10 .25
269 Wayne Twitchell .10 .25
270 Carlton Fisk 1.50 4.00
271 Randy Lerch DP .08 .20
272 Royle Stillman .10 .25
273 Fred Norman .10 .25
274 Freddie Patek .25 .60
275 Dan Ford .10 .25
276 Bill Bonham DP .08 .20
277 Bruce Boisclair .10 .25
278 Enrique Romo RC .10 .25
279 Bill Virdon MG .10 .25
280 Buddy Bell .25 .60
281 Eric Rasmussen DP .08 .20
282 New York Yankees CL 1.00 2.50
283 Omar Moreno .10 .25
284 Randy Moffitt .10 .25
285 Steve Yeager DP .25 .60
286 Ben Oglivie .25 .60
287 Kiko Garcia .10 .25
288 Dave Hamilton .10 .25
289 Checklist 243-363 .50 1.25
290 Willie Horton .25 .60
291 Gary Ross .10 .25
292 Gene Richards .10 .25
293 Mike Willis .10 .25
294 Larry Parrish .25 .60
295 Bill Lee .10 .25
296 Biff Pocoroba .10 .25
297 Warren Brusstar DP RC .08 .20
298 Tony Armas .25 .60
299 Whitey Herzog MG .25 .60
300 Joe Morgan 1.25 3.00
301 Buddy Schultz RC .10 .25
302 Chicago Cubs CL .50 1.25
303 Sam Hinds RC .10 .25
304 John Milner .10 .25
305 Rico Carty .25 .60
306 Joe Niekro .25 .60
307 Glenn Borgmann .10 .25
308 Jim Rooker .10 .25
309 Cliff Johnson .10 .25
310 Don Sutton 1.00 2.50
311 Jose Baez DP RC .08 .20
312 Greg Minton .10 .25
313 Andy Etchebarren .10 .25
314 Paul Lindblad .10 .25
315 Mark Belanger .25 .60
316 Henry Cruz DP .08 .20
317 Dave Johnson .10 .25
318 Tom Griffin .10 .25
319 Alan Ashby .10 .25
320 Fred Lynn .60 1.50
321 Santo Alcala .10 .25
322 Tom Paciorek .25 .60
323 Jim Fregosi DP .25 .60
324 Vern Rapp MG RC .10 .25
325 Bruce Sutter 1.25 3.00
326 Mike Lum DP .08 .20
327 Rick Langford DP RC .08 .20
328 Milwaukee Brewers CL .50 1.25
329 John Verhoeven .10 .25
330 Bob Watson .25 .60
331 Mark Littell .10 .25
332 Duane Kuiper .10 .25
333 Jim Todd .10 .25
334 John Stearns .10 .25
335 Bucky Dent .25 .60
336 Steve Busby .10 .25
337 Tom Grieve .25 .60
338 Dave Heaverlo .10 .25
339 Mario Guerrero .10 .25
340 Bake McBride .25 .60
341 Mike Flanagan .25 .60
342 Aurelio Rodriguez .10 .25
343 John Wathan DP .08 .20
344 Sam Ewing RC .10 .25
345 Luis Tiant .25 .60
346 Larry Biittner .10 .25
347 Terry Forster .10 .25
348 Del Unser .10 .25
349 Rick Camp DP .08 .20
350 Steve Garvey 1.00 2.50
351 Jeff Torborg .25 .60
352 Tony Scott RC .10 .25
353 Doug Bair RC .10 .25
354 Cesar Geronimo .10 .25
355 Bill Travers .10 .25
356 New York Mets CL .50 1.25
357 Tom Poquette .10 .25
358 Mark Lemongello .10 .25
359 Marc Hill .10 .25
360 Mike Schmidt 4.00 10.00
361 Chris Knapp .10 .25
362 Dave May .10 .25
363 Bob Randall .10 .25
364 Jerry Turner .10 .25
365 Ed Figueroa .10 .25
366 Larry Milbourne DP .08 .20
367 Rick Dempsey .25 .60
368 Balor Moore .10 .25
369 Tim Nordbrook .10 .25
370 Rusty Staub .50 1.25
371 Ray Burris .10 .25
372 Brian Asselstine .10 .25
373 Jim Willoughby .10 .25
374A Jose Morales .10 .25
Red stitching
374B Jose Morales
Black overprint stitching
375 Tommy John .50 1.25
376 Jim Wohlford .10 .25
377 Manny Sarmiento .10 .25
378 Bobby Winkles MG .10 .25
379 Skip Lockwood .10 .25
380 Ted Simmons .25 .60
381 Philadelphia Phillies CL .50 1.25
382 Joe Lahoud .10 .25
383 Mario Mendoza .10 .25
384 Jack Clark .50 1.25
385 Tito Fuentes .10 .25
386 Bob Gorinski RC .10 .25
387 Ken Holtzman .25 .60
388 Bill Fahey DP .08 .20
389 Julio Gonzalez RC .10 .25
390 Oscar Gamble .25 .60
391 Larry Haney .10 .25
392 Billy Almon .10 .25
393 Tippy Martinez .25 .60
394 Roy Howell DP .08 .20
395 Jim Hughes .10 .25
396 Bob Stinson DP .08 .20
397 Greg Gross .10 .25
398 Don Hood .10 .25
399 Pete Mackanin .10 .25
400 Nolan Ryan 10.00 25.00
401 Sparky Anderson MG .25 .60
402 Dave Campbell .10 .25
403 Bud Harrelson .25 .60
404 Detroit Tigers CL .50 1.25
405 Rawly Eastwick .10 .25
406 Mike Jorgensen .10 .25
407 Odell Jones RC .10 .25
408 Joe Zdeb RC .10 .25
409 Ron Schueler .10 .25
410 Bill Madlock .25 .60
411 Mickey Rivers ALCS .25 .60
412 Davey Lopes NLCS .25 .60
413 Reggie Jackson WS 1.50 4.00
414 Darold Knowles DP .08 .20
415 Ray Fosse .10 .25
416 Jack Brohamer .10 .25
417 Mike Garman DP .08 .20
418 Tony Muser .10 .25
419 Jerry Garvin RC .10 .25
420 Greg Luzinski .50 1.25
421 Junior Moore RC .10 .25
422 Steve Braun .10 .25
423 Dave Rosello .10 .25
424 Boston Red Sox CL .50 1.25
425 Steve Rogers DP .10 .25
426 Fred Kendall .10 .25
427 Mario Soto RC .25 .60
428 Joel Youngblood .10 .25
429 Mike Barlow RC .10 .25
430 Al Oliver .25 .60
431 Butch Metzger .10 .25
432 Terry Bulling RC .10 .25
433 Fernando Gonzalez .10 .25
434 Mike Norris .10 .25
435 Checklist 364-484 .50 1.25
436 Vic Harris DP .08 .20
437 Bo McLaughlin .10 .25
438 John Ellis .10 .25
439 Ken Kravec .10 .25
440 Dave Lopes .25 .60
441 Larry Gura .10 .25
442 Elliott Maddox .10 .25
443 Darrel Chaney .10 .25
444 Roy Hartsfield MG .10 .25
445 Mike Ivie .10 .25
446 Tug McGraw .25 .60
447 Leroy Stanton .10 .25
448 Bill Castro .10 .25
449 Tim Blackwell DP RC .08 .20
450 Tom Seaver 3.00 8.00
451 Minnesota Twins CL .50 1.25
452 Jerry Mumphrey .10 .25
453 Doug Flynn .10 .25
454 Dave LaRoche .10 .25
455 Bill Robinson .25 .60
456 Vern Ruhle .10 .25
457 Bob Bailey .10 .25
458 Jeff Newman .10 .25
459 Charlie Spikes .10 .25
460 Jim Hunter 1.00 2.50
461 Rob Andrews DP .08 .20
462 Rogelio Moret .10 .25
463 Kevin Bell .10 .25
464 Jerry Grote .10 .25
465 Hal McRae .25 .60
466 Dennis Blair .10 .25
467 Alvin Dark MG .25 .60
468 Warren Cromartie RC .25 .60
469 Rick Cerone .25 .60
470 J.R. Richard .25 .60
471 Roy Smalley .25 .60
472 Ron Reed .10 .25
473 Bill Buckner .25 .60
474 Jim Slaton .10 .25
475 Gary Matthews .25 .60
476 Bill Stein .10 .25
477 Doug Capilla RC .10 .25
478 Jerry Remy .10 .25
479 St. Louis Cardinals CL .50 1.25
480 Ron LeFlore .25 .60
481 Jackson Todd RC .10 .25
482 Rick Miller .10 .25
483 Ken Macha RC .10 .25
484 Jim Norris RC .10 .25
485 Chris Chambliss .25 .60
486 John Curtis .10 .25
487 Jim Tyrone .10 .25
488 Dan Spillner .10 .25
489 Rudy Meoli .10 .25
490 Amos Otis .25 .60
491 Scott McGregor .25 .60
492 Jim Sundberg .25 .60
493 Steve Renko .10 .25
494 Chuck Tanner MG .25 .60
495 Dave Cash .10 .25
496 Jim Clancy DP RC .08 .20
497 Glenn Adams .10 .25
498 Joe Sambito .10 .25
499 Seattle Mariners CL .50 1.25
500 George Foster .50 1.25
501 Dave Roberts .10 .25
502 Pat Rockett RC .10 .25
503 Ike Hampton RC .10 .25
504 Roger Freed .10 .25
505 Felix Millan .10 .25
506 Ron Blomberg .10 .25
507 Willie Crawford .10 .25
508 Johnny Oates .25 .60
509 Brent Strom .10 .25
510 Willie Stargell 1.00 2.50
511 Frank Duffy .10 .25
512 Larry Herndon .10 .25
513 Barry Foote .10 .25
514 Rob Sperring .10 .25
515 Tim Corcoran RC .10 .25
516 Gary Beare RC .10 .25
517 Andres Mora .10 .25
518 Tommy Boggs DP .08 .20
519 Brian Downing .25 .60
520 Larry Hisle .10 .25
521 Steve Staggs RC .10 .25
522 Dick Williams MG .25 .60
523 Donnie Moore RC .10 .25
524 Bernie Carbo .10 .25
525 Jerry Terrell .10 .25
526 Cincinnati Reds CL .50 1.25
527 Vic Correll .10 .25
528 Rob Picciolo RC .10 .25
529 Paul Hartzell .10 .25
530 Dave Winfield 1.50 4.00
531 Tom Underwood .10 .25
532 Skip Jutze .10 .25
533 Sandy Alomar .25 .60
534 Wilbur Howard .10 .25
535 Checklist 485-605 .50 1.25
536 Roric Harrison .10 .25
537 Bruce Bochte .10 .25
538 Johnny LeMaster .10 .25
539 Vic Davalillo DP .08 .20
540 Steve Carlton 1.50 4.00
541 Larry Cox .10 .25
542 Tim Johnson .10 .25
543 Larry Harlow DP RC .08 .20
544 Len Randle DP .08 .20
545 Bill Campbell .10 .25
546 Ted Martinez .10 .25
547 John Scott .10 .25
548 Billy Hunter MG DP .08 .20
549 Joe Kerrigan .10 .25
550 John Mayberry .25 .60
551 Atlanta Braves CL .50 1.25
552 Francisco Barrios .10 .25
553 Terry Puhl RC .25 .60
554 Joe Coleman .10 .25
555 Butch Wynegar .10 .25
556 Ed Armbrister .10 .25
557 Tony Solaita .10 .25
558 Paul Mitchell .10 .25
559 Phil Mankowski .10 .25
560 Dave Parker .50 1.25
561 Charlie Williams .10 .25
562 Glenn Burke RC .10 .25
563 Dave Rader .10 .25
564 Mick Kelleher .10 .25
565 Jerry Koosman .25 .60
566 Merv Rettenmund .10 .25
567 Dick Drago .10 .25
568 Tom Hutton .10 .25
569 Lary Sorensen RC .10 .25
570 Dave Kingman .50 1.25
571 Buck Martinez .10 .25
572 Rick Wise .10 .25
573 Luis Gomez .10 .25
574 Bob Lemon MG .50 1.25
575 Pat Dobson .10 .25
576 Sam Mejias .10 .25
577 Oakland Athletics CL .50 1.25
578 Buzz Capra .10 .25
579 Rance Mulliniks RC .10 .25
580 Rod Carew 1.50 4.00
581 Lynn McGlothen .10 .25
582 Fran Healy .10 .25
583 George Medich .10 .25
584 John Hale .10 .25
585 Woodie Fryman DP .08 .20
586 Ed Goodson .10 .25
587 John Urrea RC .10 .25
588 Jim Mason .10 .25
589 Bob Knepper RC .10 .25
590 Bobby Murcer .25 .60
591 George Zeber RC .10 .25
592 Bob Apodaca .10 .25
593 Dave Skaggs RC .10 .25
594 Dave Freisleben .10 .25
595 Sixto Lezcano .10 .25
596 Gary Wheelock .10 .25
597 Steve Dillard .10 .25
598 Eddie Solomon .10 .25
599 Gary Woods .10 .25
600 Frank Tanana .25 .60
601 Gene Mauch MG .25 .60
602 Eric Soderholm .10 .25
603 Will McEnaney .10 .25
604 Earl Williams .10 .25
605 Rick Rhoden .25 .60
606 Pittsburgh Pirates CL .50 1.25
607 Fernando Arroyo .10 .25
608 Johnny Grubb .10 .25
609 John Denny .10 .25
610 Garry Maddox .25 .60
611 Pat Scanlon RC .10 .25
612 Ken Henderson .10 .25
613 Marty Perez .10 .25
614 Joe Wallis .10 .25
615 Clay Carroll .10 .25
616 Pat Kelly .10 .25
617 Joe Nolan RC .10 .25
618 Tommy Helms .10 .25
619 Thad Bosley DP RC .08 .20
620 Willie Randolph .50 1.25
621 Craig Swan DP .08 .20
622 Champ Summers .10 .25
623 Eduardo Rodriguez .10 .25
624 Gary Alexander DP .08 .20
625 Jose Cruz .25 .60
626 Toronto Blue Jays CL DP .50 1.25
627 David Johnson .10 .25
628 Ralph Garr .25 .60
629 Don Stanhouse .10 .25
630 Ron Cey .50 1.25
631 Danny Ozark MG .10 .25
632 Rowland Office .10 .25
633 Tom Veryzer .10 .25
634 Len Barker .10 .25
635 Joe Rudi .25 .60
636 Jim Bibby .10 .25
637 Duffy Dyer .10 .25
638 Paul Splittorff .10 .25
639 Gene Clines .10 .25
640 Lee May DP .10 .25
641 Doug Rau .10 .25
642 Denny Doyle .10 .25
643 Tom House .10 .25
644 Jim Dwyer .10 .25
645 Mike Torrez .25 .60
646 Rick Auerbach DP .08 .20
647 Steve Dunning .10 .25
648 Gary Thomasson .10 .25
649 Moose Haas RC .10 .25
650 Cesar Cedeno .25 .60
651 Doug Rader .10 .25
652 Checklist 606-726 .50 1.25
653 Ron Hodges DP .08 .20
654 Pepe Frias .10 .25
655 Lyman Bostock .25 .60
656 Dave Garcia MG RC .10 .25
657 Bombo Rivera .10 .25
658 Manny Sanguillen .25 .60
659 Texas Rangers CL .50 1.25
660 Jason Thompson .25 .60
661 Grant Jackson .10 .25
662 Paul Dade RC .10 .25
663 Paul Reuschel .10 .25
664 Fred Stanley .10 .25
665 Dennis Leonard .25 .60
666 Billy Smith RC .10 .25
667 Jeff Byrd RC .10 .25
668 Dusty Baker .50 1.25
669 Pete Falcone .10 .25
670 Jim Rice 1.00 2.50
671 Gary Lavelle .10 .25
672 Don Kessinger .25 .60
673 Steve Brye .10 .25
674 Ray Knight RC 1.00 2.50
675 Jay Johnstone .25 .60
676 Bob Myrick .10 .25
677 Ed Herrmann .10 .25
678 Tom Burgmeier .10 .25
679 Wayne Garrett .10 .25
680 Vida Blue .25 .60
681 Rob Belloir .10 .25
682 Ken Brett .10 .25
683 Mike Champion .10 .25
684 Ralph Houk MG .25 .60
685 Frank Taveras .10 .25
686 Gaylord Perry 1.00 2.50
687 Julio Cruz RC .10 .25
688 George Mitterwald .10 .25
689 Cleveland Indians CL .50 1.25
690 Mickey Rivers .25 .60
691 Ross Grimsley .10 .25
692 Ken Reitz .10 .25
693 Lamar Johnson .10 .25
694 Elias Sosa .10 .25
695 Dwight Evans .50 1.25
696 Steve Mingori .10 .25
697 Roger Metzger .10 .25
698 Juan Bernhardt .10 .25
699 Jackie Brown .10 .25
700 Johnny Bench 8.00 20.00
701 Hume/Land/McC/Tay RC .25 .60
702 Nah/Pas/Sweet/Wer RC .25 .60
703 Jack Morris DP RC 10.00 25.00
704 Lou Whitaker RC 10.00 25.00
705 Berg/Milone/Hurdle/Nor RC .50 1.25
706 Cage/Cox/Put/Rev RC .25 .60
707 P.Molitor RC/A.Trammell RC 25.00 60.00
708 D.Murphy/L.Parrish RC 1.50 4.00
709 Burke/Keough/Rau/Schat RC .25 .60
710 Alston/Bos/Easler/Smith RC .50 1.25
711 Camp/Lamp/Mit/Tho DP RC .10 .25
712 Bobby Valentine .25 .60
713 Bob Davis .10 .25
714 Mike Anderson .10 .25
715 Jim Kaat .50 1.25
716 Clarence Gaston .25 .60
717 Nelson Briles .10 .25
718 Ron Jackson .10 .25
719 Randy Elliott RC .10 .25
720 Fergie Jenkins 1.00 2.50
721 Billy Martin MG .50 1.25
722 Pete Broberg .10 .25
723 John Wockenfuss .10 .25
724 Kansas City Royals CL .50 1.25
725 Kurt Bevacqua .10 .25
726 Wilbur Wood .10 .25

1978 Topps Team Checklist Sheet

As part of a mail-away offer, Topps offered all 26 team checklist cards on an uncut sheet. These cards enabled the collector to have an easy reference for which card(s) he/she needed to finish their sets. When cut from the sheet, all cards measure the standard size.

1 Team Checklist Sheet 40.00 80.00

1978 Topps Zest

This set of five standard-size cards is very similar to the 1978 Topps regular issue. Although the cards were produced by Topps, they were used in a promotion for Zest Soap. The sponsor of the set, Zest Soap, is not mentioned anywhere on the cards. The card numbers are different and the backs are written in English and Spanish. By the choice of players in this small set, Zest appears to have been targeting the Hispanic community. Each player's card number in the regular 1978 Topps set is also given. A different photo was used for Montanez, showing his head and shoulders as a New York Met rather than as an Atlanta Brave in a batting stance as shown on Willie's Topps regular card.

COMPLETE SET (5) 2.50 6.00
1 Joaquin Andujar/78T-158 .60 1.50
2 Bert Campaneris/78T-260 .75 2.00
3 Ed Figueroa/78T-365 .40 1.00
4 Willie Montanez/78T-38/(different pose)/(New Yo.60 1.50
5 Manny Mota/78T-228 .60 1.50

1979 Topps

The cards in this 726-card set measure 2 1/2" by 3 1/2". Topps continued with the same number of cards as in 1978. As in previous years, this set was released in many different formats, among them are 12-card wax packs and 39-card rack packs which cost 59 cents upon release. Those rack packs came 24 packs to a box and three boxes to a case. Various series spotlight League Leaders (1-8), "Season and Career Record Holders" (411-418), "Record Breakers" (201-206), and one "Prospects" card for each team (701-726). Team cards feature a checklist on back of that team's players in the set and a small picture of the manager on the front of the card. There are 66 cards that were double printed and these are noted in the checklist by the abbreviation DP. Bump Wills (369) was initially depicted in a Ranger uniform but with a Blue Jays affiliation; later printings correctly labeled him with Texas. The set price includes either Wills card. The key Rookie Cards in this set are Pedro Guerrero, Carney Lansford, Ozzie Smith, Bob Welch and Willie Wilson. Cards numbered 23 or lower, which feature Phillies or Yankees and do not follow the numbering checklisted below, are not necessarily error cards. They are undoubtedly Burger King cards, separate sets for each team with their own pricing and mass distribution.

COMPLETE SET (726) 200.00 500.00
COMMON CARD (1-726) .10 .25
COMMON CARD DP .08 .20
1 R.Carew/D.Parker LL 1.00 2.50
2 J.Rice/G.Foster LL .60 1.50
3 J.Rice/G.Foster LL .60 1.50
4 R.LeFlore/O.Moreno LL .30 .75
5 R.Guidry/G.Perry LL .30 .75
6 N.Ryan/J.Richard LL 2.00 5.00

7 R.Guidry/C.Swan LL .30 .75
8 R.Gossage/R.Fingers LL .60 1.50
9 Dave Campbell .10 .25
10 Lee May .30 .75
11 Marc Hill .10 .25
12 Dick Drago .10 .25
13 Paul Dade .10 .25
14 Rafael Landestoy RC .10 .25
15 Ross Grimsley .10 .25
16 Fred Stanley .10 .25
17 Donnie Moore .10 .25
18 Tony Solaita .10 .25
19 Larry Gura DP .08 .20
20 Joe Morgan DP 1.00 2.50
21 Kevin Kobel .10 .25
22 Mike Jorgensen .10 .25
23 Terry Forster .10 .25
24 Paul Molitor 10.00 25.00
25 Steve Carlton 1.25 3.00
26 Jamie Quirk .10 .25
27 Dave Goltz .10 .25
28 Steve Brye .10 .25
29 Rick Langford .10 .25
30 Dave Winfield 1.50 4.00
31 Tom House DP .08 .20
32 Jerry Mumphrey .10 .25
33 Dave Rozema .10 .25
34 Rob Andrews .10 .25
35 Ed Figueroa .10 .25
36 Alan Ashby .10 .25
37 Joe Kerrigan DP .08 .20
38 Bernie Carbo .10 .25
39 Dale Murphy 1.25 3.00
40 Dennis Eckersley 1.00 2.50
41 Minnesota Twins CL/Mauch .60 1.50
42 Ron Blomberg .10 .25
43 Wayne Twitchell .10 .25
44 Kurt Bevacqua .10 .25
45 Al Hrabosky .30 .75
46 Ron Hodges .10 .25
47 Fred Norman .10 .25
48 Merv Rettenmund .10 .25
49 Vern Ruhle .10 .25
50 Steve Garvey DP .60 1.50
51 Ray Fosse DP .08 .20
52 Randy Lerch .10 .25
53 Mick Kelleher .10 .25
54 Dell Alston DP .08 .20
55 Willie Stargell 1.00 2.50
56 John Hale .10 .25
57 Eric Rasmussen .10 .25
58 Bob Randall DP .08 .20
59 John Denny DP .10 .25
60 Mickey Rivers .30 .75
61 Bo Diaz .10 .25
62 Randy Moffitt .10 .25
63 Jack Brohamer .10 .25
64 Tom Underwood .10 .25
65 Mark Belanger .30 .75
66 Detroit Tigers CL/Moss .60 1.50
67 Jim Mason DP .08 .20
68 Joe Niekro DP .10 .25
69 Elliott Maddox .10 .25
70 John Candelaria .30 .75
71 Brian Downing .30 .75
72 Steve Mingori .10 .25
73 Ken Henderson .10 .25
74 Shane Rawley RC .10 .25
75 Steve Yeager .30 .75
76 Warren Cromartie .30 .75
77 Dan Briggs DP .08 .20
78 Elias Sosa .10 .25
79 Ted Cox .10 .25
80 Jason Thompson .30 .75
81 Roger Erickson RC .10 .25
82 New York Mets CL/Torre .60 1.50
83 Fred Kendall .10 .25
84 Greg Minton .10 .25
85 Gary Matthews .30 .75
86 Rodney Scott .10 .25
87 Pete Falcone .10 .25
88 Bob Molinaro RC .10 .25
89 Dick Tidrow .10 .25
90 Bob Boone .60 1.50
91 Terry Crowley .10 .25
92 Jim Bibby .10 .25
93 Phil Mankowski .10 .25
94 Len Barker .10 .25
95 Robin Yount 2.00 5.00
96 Cleveland Indians CL/Torborg .60 1.50
97 Sam Mejias .10 .25
98 Ray Burris .10 .25
99 John Wathan .30 .75
100 Tom Seaver DP 1.50 4.00
101 Roy Howell .10 .25
102 Mike Anderson .10 .25
103 Jim Todd .10 .25
104 Johnny Oates DP .10 .25
105 Rick Camp DP .08 .20
106 Frank Duffy .10 .25
107 Jesus Alou DP .08 .20
108 Eduardo Rodriguez .10 .25
109 Joel Youngblood .10 .25
110 Vida Blue .30 .75
111 Roger Freed .10 .25
112 Philadelphia Phillies CL/Ozark .60 1.50
113 Pete Redfern .10 .25
114 Cliff Johnson .10 .25
115 Nolan Ryan 8.00 20.00
116 Ozzie Smith RC 40.00 100.00
117 Grant Jackson .10 .25
118 Bud Harrelson .30 .75
119 Don Stanhouse .10 .25
120 Jim Sundberg .30 .75
121 Checklist 1-121 DP .30 .75
122 Mike Paxton .10 .25
123 Lou Whitaker 1.00 2.50
124 Dan Schatzeder .10 .25
125 Rick Burleson .10 .25
126 Doug Bair .10 .25
127 Thad Bosley .10 .25
128 Ted Martinez .10 .25
129 Marty Pattin DP .08 .20
130 Bob Watson DP .10 .25
131 Jim Clancy .10 .25
132 Rowland Office .10 .25
133 Bill Castro .10 .25
134 Alan Bannister .10 .25
135 Bobby Murcer .30 .75
136 Jim Kaat .30 .75
137 Larry Wolfe DP RC .08 .20
138 Mark Lee RC .10 .25
139 Luis Pujols RC .10 .25
140 Don Gullett .30 .75
141 Tom Paciorek .30 .75
142 Charlie Williams .10 .25
143 Tony Scott .10 .25
144 Sandy Alomar .10 .25
145 Rick Rhoden .10 .25
146 Duane Kuiper .10 .25
147 Dave Hamilton .10 .25
148 Bruce Boisclair .10 .25
149 Manny Sarmiento .10 .25
150 Wayne Cage .10 .25
151 John Hiller .10 .25
152 Rick Cerone .10 .25
153 Dennis Lamp .10 .25
154 Jim Gantner DP .10 .25
155 Dwight Evans .60 1.50
156 Buddy Solomon .10 .25
157 U.L. Washington UER .10 .25
158 Joe Sambito .10 .25
159 Roy White .30 .75
160 Mike Flanagan .60 1.50
161 Barry Foote .10 .25
162 Tom Johnson .10 .25
163 Glenn Burke .10 .25
164 Mickey Lolich .30 .75
165 Frank Taveras .10 .25
166 Leon Roberts .10 .25
167 Roger Metzger DP .08 .20
168 Dave Freisleben .10 .25
169 Bill Nahorodny .10 .25
170 Don Sutton 1.00 2.50
171 Gene Clines .10 .25
172 Mike Bruhert RC .10 .25
173 John Lowenstein .10 .25
174 Rick Auerbach .10 .25
175 George Hendrick .60 1.50
176 Aurelio Rodriguez .10 .25
177 Ron Reed .10 .25
178 Alvis Woods .10 .25
179 Jim Beattie DP RC .08 .20
180 Larry Hisle .10 .25
181 Mike Garman .10 .25
182 Tim Johnson .10 .25
183 Paul Splittorff .10 .25
184 Darrel Chaney .10 .25
185 Mike Torrez .30 .75
186 Eric Soderholm .10 .25
187 Mark Lemongello .10 .25
188 Pat Kelly .10 .25
189 Ed Whitson RC .10 .25
190 Ron Cey .30 .75
191 Mike Norris .10 .25
192 St. Louis Cardinals CL/Boyer .60 1.50
193 Glenn Adams .10 .25
194 Randy Jones .10 .25
195 Bill Madlock .30 .75
196 Steve Kemp DP .10 .25
197 Bob Apodaca .10 .25
198 Johnny Grubb .10 .25
199 Larry Milbourne .10 .25
200 Johnny Bench DP 2.00 5.00
201 Mike Edwards RB .10 .25
202 Ron Guidry RB .30 .75
203 J.R. Richard RB .10 .25
204 Pete Rose RB 2.00 5.00
205 John Stearns RB .10 .25
206 Sammy Stewart RB .10 .25
207 Dave Lemanczyk .10 .25
208 Clarence Gaston .10 .25
209 Reggie Cleveland .10 .25
210 Larry Bowa .30 .75
211 Dennis Martinez 1.00 2.50
212 Carney Lansford RC .60 1.50
213 Bill Travers .10 .25
214 Boston Red Sox CL/Zimmer .60 1.50
215 Willie McCovey 1.00 2.50
216 Wilbur Wood .10 .25
217 Steve Dillard .10 .25
218 Dennis Leonard .30 .75
219 Roy Smalley .30 .75
220 Cesar Geronimo .10 .25
221 Jesse Jefferson .10 .25
222 Bob Beall RC .10 .25
223 Kent Tekulve .30 .75
224 Dave Revering .10 .25
225 Goose Gossage .60 1.50
226 Ron Pruitt .10 .25
227 Steve Stone .30 .75
228 Vic Davalillo .10 .25
229 Doug Flynn .10 .25
230 Bob Forsch .10 .25
231 John Wockenfuss .10 .25
232 Jimmy Sexton RC .10 .25
233 Paul Mitchell .10 .25
234 Toby Harrah .30 .75
235 Steve Rogers .10 .25
236 Jim Dwyer .10 .25
237 Billy Smith .10 .25
238 Balor Moore .10 .25
239 Willie Horton .30 .75
240 Rick Reuschel .30 .75
241 Checklist 122-242 DP .30 .75
242 Pablo Torrealba .10 .25
243 Buck Martinez DP .08 .20
244 Pittsburgh Pirates CL/Tanner .60 1.50
245 Jeff Burroughs .10 .25
246 Darrell Jackson RC .10 .25
247 Tucker Ashford DP .08 .20
248 Pete LaCock .10 .25
249 Paul Thormodsgard .10 .25
250 Willie Randolph .30 .75
251 Jack Morris 1.00 2.50
252 Bob Stinson .10 .25
253 Rick Wise .10 .25
254 Luis Gomez .10 .25
255 Tommy John .60 1.50
256 Mike Sadek .10 .25
257 Adrian Devine .10 .25
258 Mike Phillips .10 .25
259 Cincinnati Reds CL/Anderson .60 1.50
260 Richie Zisk .10 .25
261 Mario Guerrero .10 .25
262 Nelson Briles .10 .25
263 Oscar Gamble .30 .75
264 Don Robinson RC .10 .25
265 Don Money .10 .25
266 Jim Willoughby .10 .25
267 Joe Rudi .30 .75
268 Julio Gonzalez .10 .25
269 Woodie Fryman .10 .25
270 Butch Hobson .30 .75
271 Rawly Eastwick .10 .25
272 Tim Corcoran .10 .25
273 Jerry Terrell .10 .25
274 Willie Norwood .10 .25
275 Junior Moore .10 .25
276 Jim Colborn .10 .25
277 Tom Grieve .30 .75
278 Andy Messersmith .30 .75
279 Jerry Grote DP .08 .20
280 Andre Thornton .30 .75
281 Vic Correll DP .08 .20
282 Toronto Blue Jays CL/Hartsfield .30 .75
283 Ken Kravec .10 .25
284 Johnnie LeMaster .10 .25
285 Bobby Bonds .60 1.50
286 Duffy Dyer UER .10 .25
287 Andres Mora .10 .25
288 Milt Wilcox .10 .25
289 Jose Cruz .60 1.50
290 Dave Lopes .30 .75
291 Tom Griffin .10 .25
292 Don Reynolds RC .10 .25
293 Jerry Garvin .10 .25
294 Pepe Frias .10 .25
295 Mitchell Page .10 .25
296 Preston Hanna RC .10 .25
297 Ted Sizemore .10 .25
298 Rich Gale RC .10 .25
299 Steve Ontiveros .10 .25
300 Rod Carew 1.25 3.00
301 Tom Hume .10 .25
302 Atlanta Braves CL/Cox .60 1.50
303 Lary Sorensen DP .08 .20
304 Steve Swisher .10 .25
305 Willie Montanez .10 .25
306 Floyd Bannister .10 .25
307 Larvell Blanks .10 .25
308 Bert Blyleven .60 1.50
309 Ralph Garr .30 .75
310 Thurman Munson 1.25 3.00
311 Gary Lavelle .10 .25
312 Bob Robertson .10 .25
313 Dyar Miller .10 .25
314 Larry Harlow .10 .25
315 Jon Matlack .10 .25
316 Milt May .10 .25
317 Jose Cardenal .30 .75
318 Bob Welch RC 1.00 2.50
319 Wayne Garrett .10 .25
320 Carl Yastrzemski 2.00 5.00
321 Gaylord Perry 1.00 2.50
322 Danny Goodwin RC .10 .25
323 Lynn McGlothen .10 .25
324 Mike Tyson .10 .25
325 Cecil Cooper .30 .75
326 Pedro Borbon .10 .25
327 Art Howe DP .10 .25
328 Oakland Athletics CL/McKeon .60 1.50
329 Joe Coleman .10 .25
330 George Brett 8.00 20.00
331 Mickey Mahler .10 .25
332 Gary Alexander .10 .25
333 Chet Lemon .30 .75
334 Craig Swan .10 .25
335 Chris Chambliss .30 .75
336 Bobby Thompson RC .10 .25
337 John Montague .10 .25
338 Vic Harris .10 .25
339 Ron Jackson .10 .25
340 Jim Palmer 1.00 2.50
341 Willie Upshaw RC .10 .25
342 Dave Roberts .10 .25
343 Ed Glynn .10 .25
344 Jerry Royster .10 .25
345 Tug McGraw .30 .75
346 Bill Buckner .30 .75
347 Doug Rau .10 .25
348 Andre Dawson 1.25 3.00
349 Jim Wright RC .10 .25
350 Garry Templeton .30 .75
351 Wayne Nordhagen DP .08 .20
352 Steve Renko .10 .25
353 Checklist 243-363 .60 1.50
354 Bill Bonham .10 .25
355 Lee Mazzilli .10 .25
356 San Francisco Giants CL/Altobelli .60 1.50
357 Jerry Augustine .10 .25
358 Alan Trammell 1.25 3.00
359 Dan Spillner DP .08 .20
360 Amos Otis .30 .75
361 Tom Dixon RC .10 .25
362 Mike Cubbage .10 .25
363 Craig Skok RC .10 .25
364 Gene Richards .10 .25
365 Sparky Lyle .30 .75
366 Juan Bernhardt .10 .25
367 Dave Skaggs .10 .25
368 Don Aase .10 .25
369A Bump Wills ERR 1.25 3.00
369B Bump Wills COR .75 2.00
370 Dave Kingman .60 1.50
371 Jeff Holly RC .10 .25
372 Lamar Johnson .10 .25
373 Lance Rautzhan .10 .25
374 Ed Herrmann .10 .25
375 Bill Campbell .10 .25
376 Gorman Thomas .30 .75
377 Paul Moskau .10 .25
378 Rob Picciolo DP .08 .20
379 Dale Murray .10 .25
380 John Mayberry .30 .75
381 Houston Astros CL/Virdon .60 1.50
382 Jerry Martin .10 .25
383 Phil Garner .30 .75
384 Tommy Boggs .10 .25
385 Dan Ford .10 .25
386 Francisco Barrios .10 .25
387 Gary Thomasson .10 .25
388 Jack Billingham .10 .25
389 Joe Zdeb .10 .25
390 Rollie Fingers 1.00 2.50
391 Al Oliver .30 .75
392 Doug Ault .10 .25
393 Scott McGregor .30 .75
394 Randy Stein RC .10 .25
395 Dave Cash .10 .25
396 Bill Plummer .10 .25
397 Sergio Ferrer RC .10 .25
398 Ivan DeJesus .10 .25
399 David Clyde .10 .25
400 Jim Rice .75 2.00
401 Ray Knight .30 .75
402 Paul Hartzell .10 .25
403 Tim Foli .10 .25
404 Chicago White Sox CL/Kessinger .60 1.50
405 Butch Wynegar DP .08 .20
406 Joe Wallis DP .08 .20
407 Pete Vuckovich .30 .75
408 Charlie Moore DP .08 .20
409 Willie Wilson RC .60 1.50
410 Darrell Evans .60 1.50
411 G.Sisler/T.Cobb ATL 1.00 2.50
412 H.Wilson/H.Aaron ATL 1.00 2.50
413 R.Maris/H.Aaron ATL 1.50 4.00
414 R.Hornsby/T.Cobb ATL 1.00 2.50
415 L.Brock/L.Brock ATL .60 1.50
416 J.Chesbro/C.Young ATL .30 .75
417 N.Ryan/W.Johnson ATL DP 2.00 5.00
418 D.Leonard/W.Johnson ATL DP .10 .25
419 Dick Ruthven .10 .25
420 Ken Griffey Sr. .30 .75
421 Doug DeCinces .30 .75
422 Ruppert Jones .10 .25
423 Bob Montgomery .10 .25
424 California Angels CL/Fregosi .60 1.50
425 Rick Manning .10 .25
426 Chris Speier .10 .25
427 Andy Replogle RC .10 .25
428 Bobby Valentine .30 .75
429 John Urrea DP .08 .20
430 Dave Parker .30 .75
431 Glenn Borgmann .10 .25
432 Dave Heaverlo .10 .25
433 Larry Biittner .10 .25
434 Ken Clay .10 .25
435 Gene Tenace .30 .75
436 Hector Cruz .10 .25
437 Rick Williams RC .10 .25
438 Horace Speed RC .10 .25
439 Frank White .30 .75
440 Rusty Staub .60 1.50
441 Lee Lacy .10 .25
442 Doyle Alexander .10 .25
443 Bruce Bochte .10 .25
444 Aurelio Lopez RC .10 .25
445 Steve Henderson .10 .25
446 Jim Lonborg .30 .75
447 Manny Sanguillen .30 .75
448 Moose Haas .10 .25
449 Bombo Rivera .10 .25
450 Dave Concepcion .60 1.50
451 Kansas City Royals CL/Herzog .60 1.50
452 Jerry Morales .10 .25
453 Chris Knapp .10 .25
454 Len Randle .10 .25
455 Bill Lee DP .08 .20
456 Chuck Baker RC .10 .25
457 Bruce Sutter 1.00 2.50
458 Jim Essian .10 .25
459 Sid Monge .10 .25
460 Graig Nettles .60 1.50
461 Jim Barr DP .08 .20
462 Otto Velez .10 .25
463 Steve Comer RC .10 .25
464 Joe Nolan .10 .25
465 Reggie Smith .30 .75
466 Mark Littell .10 .25
467 Don Kessinger DP .10 .25
468 Stan Bahnsen DP .08 .20
469 Lance Parrish .60 1.50
470 Garry Maddox DP .10 .25
471 Joaquin Andujar .30 .75
472 Craig Kusick .10 .25
473 Dave Roberts .10 .25
474 Dick Davis RC .10 .25
475 Dan Driessen .10 .25
476 Tom Poquette .10 .25
477 Bob Grich .30 .75
478 Juan Beniquez .10 .25
479 San Diego Padres CL/Craig .60 1.50
480 Fred Lynn .40 1.00
481 Skip Lockwood .10 .25
482 Craig Reynolds .10 .25
483 Checklist 364-484 DP .30 .75
484 Rick Waits .10 .25
485 Bucky Dent .30 .75
486 Bob Knepper .10 .25
487 Miguel Dilone .10 .25
488 Bob Owchinko .10 .25
489 Larry Cox UER .10 .25
490 Al Cowens .30 .75
491 Tippy Martinez .10 .25
492 Bob Bailor .10 .25
493 Larry Christenson .10 .25
494 Jerry White .10 .25
495 Tony Perez 1.00 2.50
496 Barry Bonnell DP .08 .20
497 Glenn Abbott .10 .25
498 Rich Chiles .10 .25
499 Texas Rangers CL/Corrales .60 1.50
500 Ron Guidry .30 .75
501 Junior Kennedy RC .10 .25
502 Steve Braun .10 .25
503 Terry Humphrey .10 .25
504 Larry McWilliams RC .10 .25
505 Ed Kranepool .10 .25
506 John D'Acquisto .10 .25
507 Tony Armas .30 .75
508 Charlie Hough .30 .75
509 Mario Mendoza UER .10 .25
510 Ted Simmons .60 1.50
511 Paul Reuschel DP .08 .20
512 Jack Clark .30 .75
513 Dave Johnson .30 .75
514 Mike Proly RC .10 .25
515 Enos Cabell .10 .25
516 Champ Summers DP .08 .20
517 Al Bumbry .30 .75
518 Jim Umbarger .10 .25
519 Ben Oglivie .30 .75
520 Gary Carter .75 2.00
521 Sam Ewing .10 .25
522 Ken Holtzman .30 .75
523 John Milner .10 .25
524 Tom Burgmeier .10 .25
525 Freddie Patek .10 .25
526 Los Angeles Dodgers CL/Lasorda .60 1.50
527 Lerrin LaGrow .10 .25
528 Wayne Gross DP .08 .20
529 Brian Asselstine .10 .25
530 Frank Tanana .30 .75
531 Fernando Gonzalez .10 .25
532 Buddy Schultz .10 .25
533 Leroy Stanton .10 .25
534 Ken Forsch .10 .25
535 Ellis Valentine .10 .25
536 Jerry Reuss .30 .75
537 Tom Veryzer .10 .25
538 Mike Ivie DP .08 .20
539 John Ellis .10 .25
540 Greg Luzinski .30 .75
541 Jim Slaton .10 .25
542 Rick Bosetti .10 .25
543 Kiko Garcia .10 .25
544 Fergie Jenkins 1.00 2.50
545 John Stearns .10 .25
546 Bill Russell .30 .75
547 Clint Hurdle .10 .25
548 Enrique Romo .10 .25
549 Bob Bailey .10 .25
550 Sal Bando .30 .75
551 Chicago Cubs CL/Franks .60 1.50
552 Jose Morales .10 .25
553 Denny Walling .10 .25
554 Matt Keough .10 .25
555 Biff Pocoroba .10 .25
556 Mike Lum .10 .25
557 Ken Brett .10 .25
558 Jay Johnstone .30 .75
559 Greg Pryor RC .10 .25
560 John Montefusco .10 .25
561 Ed Ott .10 .25
562 Dusty Baker .60 1.50
563 Roy Thomas .10 .25
564 Jerry Turner .10 .25
565 Rico Carty .30 .75
566 Nino Espinosa .10 .25
567 Richie Hebner .30 .75
568 Carlos Lopez .10 .25
569 Bob Sykes .10 .25
570 Cesar Cedeno .30 .75
571 Darrell Porter .30 .75
572 Rod Gilbreath .10 .25
573 Jim Kern .10 .25
574 Claudell Washington .30 .75
575 Luis Tiant .30 .75
576 Mike Parrott RC .10 .25
577 Milwaukee Brewers CL/Bamberger .60 1.50
578 Pete Broberg .10 .25
579 Greg Gross .10 .25
580 Ron Fairly .30 .75
581 Darold Knowles .10 .25
582 Paul Blair .30 .75
583 Julio Cruz .10 .25
584 Jim Rooker .10 .25
585 Hal McRae .60 1.50
586 Bob Horner RC .60 1.50
587 Ken Reitz .10 .25
588 Tom Murphy .10 .25
589 Terry Whitfield .10 .25
590 J.R. Richard .30 .75
591 Mike Hargrove .30 .75
592 Mike Krukow .10 .25
593 Rick Dempsey .30 .75
594 Bob Shirley .10 .25
595 Phil Niekro 1.00 2.50
596 Jim Wohlford .10 .25
597 Bob Stanley .10 .25
598 Mark Wagner .10 .25
599 Jim Spencer .10 .25
600 George Foster .30 .75
601 Dave LaRoche .10 .25
602 Checklist 485-605 .60 1.50
603 Rudy May .10 .25
604 Jeff Newman .10 .25
605 Rick Monday DP .10 .25
606 Montreal Expos CL/Williams .60 1.50
607 Omar Moreno .10 .25
608 Dave McKay .10 .25
609 Silvio Martinez RC .10 .25
610 Mike Schmidt 6.00 15.00
611 Jim Norris .10 .25
612 Rick Honeycutt RC .30 .75
613 Mike Edwards RC .30 .75
614 Willie Hernandez .30 .75
615 Ken Singleton .30 .75
616 Billy Almon .10 .25
617 Terry Puhl .10 .25
618 Jerry Remy .10 .25
619 Ken Landreaux RC .30 .75
620 Bert Campaneris .30 .75
621 Pat Zachry .10 .25
622 Dave Collins .30 .75
623 Bob McClure .10 .25
624 Larry Herndon .10 .25
625 Mark Fidrych 1.00 2.50
626 New York Yankees CL/Lemon .60 1.50
627 Gary Serum RC .10 .25
628 Del Unser .10 .25
629 Gene Garber .30 .75
630 Bake McBride .30 .75
631 Jorge Orta .10 .25
632 Don Kirkwood .10 .25
633 Rob Wilfong DP RC .08 .20
634 Paul Lindblad .10 .25
635 Don Baylor .60 1.50
636 Wayne Garland .10 .25
637 Bill Robinson .30 .75
638 Al Fitzmorris .10 .25
639 Manny Trillo .10 .25
640 Eddie Murray 4.00 10.00
641 Bobby Castillo RC .10 .25
642 Wilbur Howard DP .08 .20
643 Tom Hausman .10 .25
644 Manny Mota .30 .75
645 George Scott DP .10 .25
646 Rick Sweet .10 .25
647 Bob Lacey .10 .25
648 Lou Piniella .30 .75
649 John Curtis .10 .25
650 Pete Rose 6.00 15.00
651 Mike Caldwell .10 .25
652 Stan Papi RC .10 .25
653 Warren Brusstar DP .08 .20
654 Rick Miller .10 .25
655 Jerry Koosman .30 .75
656 Hosken Powell RC .10 .25
657 George Medich .10 .25
658 Taylor Duncan RC .10 .25
659 Seattle Mariners CL/Johnson .60 1.50
660 Ron LeFlore DP .10 .25
661 Bruce Kison .10 .25
662 Kevin Bell .10 .25
663 Mike Vail .10 .25
664 Doug Bird .10 .25
665 Lou Brock 1.00 2.50
666 Rich Dauer .10 .25
667 Don Hood .10 .25
668 Bill North .10 .25
669 Checklist 606-726 .60 1.50
670 Jim Hunter DP .60 1.50
671 Joe Ferguson DP .08 .20
672 Ed Halicki .10 .25
673 Tom Hutton .10 .25
674 Dave Tomlin .10 .25
675 Tim McCarver .60 1.50
676 Johnny Sutton RC .10 .25
677 Larry Parrish .30 .75
678 Geoff Zahn .10 .25
679 Derrel Thomas .10 .25
680 Carlton Fisk 1.25 3.00
681 John Henry Johnson RC .10 .25
682 Dave Chalk .10 .25
683 Dan Meyer DP .08 .20
684 Jamie Easterly DP .08 .20
685 Sixto Lezcano .10 .25
686 Ron Schueler DP .08 .20
687 Rennie Stennett .10 .25
688 Mike Willis .10 .25
689 Baltimore Orioles CL/Weaver .60 1.50
690 Buddy Bell DP .10 .25
691 Dock Ellis DP .08 .20
692 Mickey Stanley .10 .25
693 Dave Rader .10 .25
694 Burt Hooton .30 .75
695 Keith Hernandez .30 .75
696 Andy Hassler .10 .25
697 Dave Bergman .10 .25
698 Bill Stein .10 .25
699 Hal Dues RC .10 .25
700 Reggie Jackson DP 5.00 12.00
701 Corey/Flinn/Stewart RC .30 .75
702 Finch/Hancock/Ripley RC .30 .75
703 Anderson/Frost/Slater RC .30 .75
704 Baumgarten/Colbern/Squires RC .30 .75
705 Griffin/Norrid/Oliver RC .60 1.50
706 Stegman/Tobik/Young RC .30 .75
707 Bass/Gaudet/McGilberry RC .60 1.50
708 Bass/Romero/Yost RC .60 1.50
709 Perlozzo/Sofield/Stanfield RC .30 .75
710 Doyle/Heath/Rajisch RC .30 .75
711 Murphy/Robinson/Wirth RC .60 1.50
712 Anderson/Biercevicz/McLaughlin RC .30 .75
713 Darwin/Putnam/Sample RC .60 1.50
714 Cruz/Kelly/Whitt RC .30 .75
715 Benedict/Hubbard/Whisenton RC .60 1.50
716 Geisel/Pagel/Thompson RC .30 .75
717 LaCoss/Oester/Spilman RC .30 .75
718 Bochy/Fischlin/Pisker RC 2.00 5.00
719 Guerrero/Law/Simpson RC .60 1.50
720 Fry/Pirtle/Sanderson RC .60 1.50
721 Berenguer/Bernard/Norman RC .30 .75
722 Morrison/Smith/Wright RC .60 1.50
723 Berra/Cotes/Wiltbank RC .60 1.50
724 Bruno/Frazier/Kennedy RC .60 1.50
725 Beswick/Mura/Perkins RC .30 .75
726 Johnston/Strain/Tamargo RC .30 .75

1979 Topps Comics

This 33 card (comic) set, which measures approximately 3" by 3 1/4", is rather plentiful in spite of the fact that it was originally touted as a limited edition "test" issue. This flimsy set has never been very popular with collectors. These waxy comics are numbered and are blank backed. Each comic also features an "Inside Baseball" tip in the lower right corner.

COMPLETE SET (33) 6.00 15.00
1 Eddie Murray .50 1.25
2 Jim Rice .12 .30
3 Carl Yastrzemski .40 1.00
4 Nolan Ryan 1.50 4.00
5 Chet Lemon .08 .20
6 Andre Thornton .08 .20
7 Rusty Staub .08 .20
8 Ron LeFlore .08 .20
9 George Brett 1.25 3.00
10 Larry Hisle .08 .20
11 Rod Carew .40 1.00
12 Reggie Jackson .60 1.50
13 Ron Guidry .08 .20
14 Mitchell Page .08 .20
15 Leon Roberts .08 .20
16 Al Oliver .08 .20
17 John Mayberry .08 .20
18 Bob Horner .08 .20
19 Phil Niekro .40 1.00
20 Dave Kingman .12 .30
21 Johnny Bench .50 1.25
22 Tom Seaver .50 1.25
23 J.R. Richard .08 .20
24 Steve Garvey .12 .30
25 Reggie Smith .08 .20
26 Ross Grimsley .08 .20
27 Craig Swan .08 .20
28 Pete Rose .60 1.50
29 Dave Parker .08 .20
30 Ted Simmons .08 .20
31 Dave Winfield .40 1.00
32 Jack Clark .08 .20
33 Vida Blue .08 .20

1979 Topps Team Checklist Sheet

As part of a mail-away offer, Topps offered all 26 1979 team cards checklist cards on an uncut sheet. These cards enabled the collector to have an easy reference for which card(s) he/she needed to finish their sets. When cut from the sheet, all cards measure the standard size.

1 Team Checklist Sheet 30.00 60.00

1980 Topps

The cards in this 726-card set measure the standard size. In 1980 Topps released another set of the same size and number of cards as the previous two years. Distribution for these cards included 15-card wax packs as well as 42-card rack packs. The 15-card wax packs had an 25 cent SRP and came 36 packs to a box and 20 boxes to a case. A special experiment in 1980 was the issuance of a 28-card cello pack with a 59 cent SRP which had a three-pack of gum at the bottom so no cards would be damaged. As with those sets, Topps again produced 66 double-printed cards in the set; they are noted by DP in the checklist below. The player's name appears over the picture and his position and team are found in pennant design. Every card carries a facsimile autograph. Team cards feature a team checklist of players in the set on the back and the manager's name on the front. Cards 1-6 show Highlights (HL) of the 1979 season, cards 201-207 are League Leaders, and cards 661-686 feature American and National League rookie "Future Stars," one card for each team showing three young prospects. The key Rookie Card in this set is Rickey Henderson; other Rookie Cards included in this set are Dan Quisenberry, Dave Stieb and Rick Sutcliffe.

COMPLETE SET (726) 150.00 400.00
COMMON CARD (1-726) .10 .25
COMMON DP .08 .25
1 L.Brock/C.Yastrzemski HL 1.00 2.50
2 Willie McCovey HL .30 .75
3 Manny Mota HL .10 .25
4 Pete Rose HL 1.25 3.00
5 Garry Templeton HL .10 .25
6 Del Unser HL .10 .25
7 Mike Lum .10 .25
8 Craig Swan .10 .25
9 Steve Braun .10 .25
10 Dennis Martinez .30 .75
11 Jimmy Sexton .10 .25
12 John Curtis DP .10 .25
13 Ron Pruitt .10 .25
14 Dave Cash .30 .75
15 Bill Campbell .10 .25
16 Jerry Narron RC .10 .25
17 Bruce Sutter .60 1.50
18 Ron Jackson .10 .25
19 Balor Moore .10 .25
20 Dan Ford .10 .25
21 Manny Sarmiento .10 .25
22 Pat Putnam .10 .25
23 Derrel Thomas .10 .25
24 Jim Slaton .10 .25
25 Lee Mazzilli .30 .75
26 Marty Pattin .10 .25
27 Del Unser .10 .25
28 Bruce Kison .10 .25
29 Mark Wagner .10 .25
30 Vida Blue .30 .75
31 Jay Johnstone .30 .75
32 Julio Cruz DP .10 .25
33 Tony Scott .10 .25
34 Jeff Newman DP .10 .25
35 Luis Tiant .30 .75
36 Rusty Torres .10 .25
37 Kiko Garcia .10 .25
38 Dan Spillner DP .10 .25
39 Rowland Office .10 .25
40 Carlton Fisk 1.00 2.50
41 Texas Rangers CL/Corrales .30 .75
42 David Palmer RC .10 .25
43 Bombo Rivera .10 .25
44 Bill Fahey .10 .25
45 Frank White .30 .75
46 Rico Carty .30 .75
47 Bill Bonham DP .10 .25
48 Rick Miller .10 .25
49 Mario Guerrero .10 .25
50 J.R. Richard .30 .75
51 Joe Ferguson DP .10 .25
52 Warren Brusstar .10 .25
53 Ben Oglivie .30 .75
54 Dennis Lamp .10 .25
55 Bill Madlock .30 .75
56 Bobby Valentine .30 .75
57 Pete Vuckovich .30 .75
58 Doug Flynn .10 .25
59 Eddy Putman RC .10 .25
60 Bucky Dent .30 .75
61 Gary Serum .10 .25
62 Mike Ivie .10 .25
63 Bob Stanley .10 .25
64 Joe Nolan .10 .25
65 Al Bumbry .30 .75
66 Kansas City Royals CL/Frey .30 .75
67 Doyle Alexander .10 .25
68 Larry Harlow .10 .25
69 Rick Williams .10 .25
70 Gary Carter .60 1.50
71 John Milner DP .10 .25
72 Fred Howard DP RC .10 .25
73 Dave Collins .10 .25
74 Sid Monge .10 .25
75 Bill Russell .30 .75
76 John Stearns .10 .25
77 Dave Stieb RC .60 1.50
78 Ruppert Jones .10 .25
79 Bob Owchinko .10 .25
80 Ron LeFlore .30 .75
81 Ted Sizemore .10 .25

82 Houston Astros CL/Virdon .30 .75
83 Steve Trout RC .10 .25
84 Gary Lavelle .10 .25
85 Ted Simmons .30 .75
86 Dave Hamilton .10 .25
87 Pepe Frias .10 .25
88 Ken Landreaux .10 .25
89 Don Hood .10 .25
90 Manny Trillo .30 .75
91 Rick Dempsey .30 .75
92 Rick Rhoden .10 .25
93 Dave Roberts DP .10 .25
94 Neil Allen RC .10 .25
95 Cecil Cooper .30 .75
96 Oakland Athletics CL/Marshall .30 .75
97 Bill Lee .30 .75
98 Jerry Terrell .10 .25
99 Victor Cruz .10 .25
100 Johnny Bench 1.25 3.00
101 Aurelio Lopez .10 .25
102 Rich Dauer .10 .25
103 Bill Caudill RC .10 .25
104 Manny Mota .30 .75
105 Frank Tanana .30 .75
106 Jeff Leonard RC .60 1.50
107 Francisco Barrios .10 .25
108 Bob Horner .30 .75
109 Bill Travers .10 .25
110 Fred Lynn DP .20 .50
111 Bob Knepper .10 .25
112 Chicago White Sox CL/LaRussa .30 .75
113 Geoff Zahn .10 .25
114 Juan Beniquez .10 .25
115 Sparky Lyle .30 .75
116 Larry Cox .10 .25
117 Dock Ellis .10 .25
118 Phil Garner .30 .75
119 Sammy Stewart .10 .25
120 Greg Luzinski .30 .75
121 Checklist 1-121 .30 .75
122 Dave Rosello DP .10 .25
123 Lynn Jones RC .10 .25
124 Dave Lemanczyk .10 .25
125 Tony Perez .30 .75
126 Dave Tomlin .10 .25
127 Gary Thomasson .10 .25
128 Tom Burgmeier .10 .25
129 Craig Reynolds .10 .25
130 Amos Otis .30 .75
131 Paul Mitchell .10 .25
132 Biff Pocoroba .10 .25
133 Jerry Turner .10 .25
134 Matt Keough .10 .25
135 Bill Buckner .30 .75
136 Dick Ruthven .10 .25
137 John Castino RC .10 .25
138 Ross Baumgarten .10 .25
139 Dane Iorg RC .10 .25
140 Rich Gossage .30 .75
141 Gary Alexander .10 .25
142 Phil Huffman RC .10 .25
143 Bruce Bochte DP .10 .25
144 Steve Comer .10 .25
145 Darrell Evans .30 .75
146 Bob Welch .30 .75
147 Terry Puhl .10 .25
148 Manny Sanguillen .30 .75
149 Tom Hume .10 .25
150 Jason Thompson .10 .25
151 Tom Hausman DP .10 .25
152 John Fulgham RC .10 .25
153 Tim Blackwell .10 .25
154 Lary Sorensen .10 .25
155 Jerry Remy .10 .25
156 Tony Brizzolara RC .10 .25
157 Willie Wilson DP .20 .50
158 Rob Picciolo DP .10 .25
159 Ken Clay .10 .25
160 Eddie Murray 2.00 5.00
161 Larry Christenson .10 .25
162 Bob Randall .10 .25
163 Steve Swisher .10 .25
164 Greg Pryor .10 .25
165 Omar Moreno .10 .25
166 Glenn Abbott .10 .25
167 Jack Clark .30 .75
168 Rick Waits .10 .25
169 Luis Gomez .10 .25
170 Burt Hooton .30 .75
171 Fernando Gonzalez .10 .25
172 Ron Hodges .10 .25
173 John Henry Johnson .10 .25
174 Ray Knight .30 .75
175 Rick Reuschel .30 .75
176 Champ Summers .10 .25
177 Dave Heaverlo .10 .25
178 Tim McCarver .30 .75
179 Ron Davis RC .10 .25
180 Warren Cromartie .10 .25
181 Moose Haas .10 .25
182 Ken Reitz .10 .25
183 Jim Anderson DP .10 .25
184 Steve Renko DP .10 .25
185 Hal McRae .30 .75
186 Junior Moore .10 .25
187 Alan Ashby .10 .25
188 Terry Crowley .10 .25
189 Kevin Kobel .10 .25
190 Buddy Bell .30 .75
191 Ted Martinez .10 .25
192 Atlanta Braves CL/Cox .30 .75
193 Dave Goltz .10 .25
194 Mike Easler .10 .25
195 John Montefusco .30 .75
196 Lance Parrish .30 .75
197 Byron McLaughlin .10 .25
198 Dell Alston DP .10 .25
199 Mike LaCoss .10 .25
200 Jim Rice .30 .75
201 K.Hernandez/F.Lynn LL .30 .75
202 D.Kingman/G.Thomas LL .60 1.50
203 D.Winfield/D.Baylor LL .60 1.50
204 O.Moreno/W.Wilson LL .30 .75
205 Niekro/Niekro/Flan LL .30 .75
206 J.Richard/N.Ryan LL 2.00 5.00
207 J.Richard/R.Guidry LL .30 .75
208 Wayne Cage .10 .25
209 Von Joshua .10 .25
210 Steve Carlton .60 1.50
211 Dave Skaggs DP .10 .25
212 Dave Roberts .10 .25
213 Mike Jorgensen DP .10 .25
214 California Angels CL/Fregosi .30 .75
215 Sixto Lezcano .10 .25
216 Phil Mankowski .10 .25
217 Ed Halicki .10 .25
218 Jose Morales .10 .25
219 Steve Mingori .10 .25
220 Dave Concepcion .30 .75
221 Joe Cannon RC .10 .25
222 Ron Hassey RC .10 .25
223 Bob Sykes .10 .25
224 Willie Montanez .10 .25
225 Lou Piniella .30 .75
226 Bill Stein .10 .25
227 Len Barker .10 .25
228 Johnny Oates .30 .75
229 Jim Bibby .10 .25
230 Dave Winfield .60 1.50
231 Steve McCatty .10 .25
232 Alan Trammell .60 1.50
233 LaRue Washington RC .10 .25
234 Vern Ruhle .10 .25
235 Andre Dawson .60 1.50
236 Marc Hill .10 .25
237 Scott McGregor .30 .75
238 Rob Wilfong .10 .25
239 Don Aase .10 .25
240 Dave Kingman .30 .75
241 Checklist 122-242 .30 .75
242 Lamar Johnson .10 .25
243 Jerry Augustine .10 .25
244 St. Louis Cardinals CL/Boyer .30 .75
245 Phil Niekro .30 .75
246 Tim Foli DP .10 .25
247 Frank Riccelli .10 .25
248 Jamie Quirk .10 .25
249 Jim Clancy .10 .25
250 Jim Kaat .30 .75
251 Kip Young .10 .25
252 Ted Cox .10 .25
253 John Montague .10 .25
254 Paul Dade DP .10 .25
255 Dusty Baker DP .20 .50
256 Roger Erickson .10 .25
257 Larry Herndon .10 .25
258 Paul Moskau .10 .25
259 New York Mets CL/Torre .60 1.50
260 Al Oliver .30 .75
261 Dave Chalk .10 .25
262 Benny Ayala .10 .25
263 Dave LaRoche DP .10 .25
264 Bill Robinson .10 .25
265 Robin Yount 1.25 3.00
266 Bernie Carbo .10 .25
267 Dan Schatzeder .10 .25
268 Rafael Landestoy .10 .25
269 Dave Tobik .10 .25
270 Mike Schmidt DP 1.25 3.00
271 Dick Drago DP .10 .25
272 Ralph Garr .30 .75
273 Eduardo Rodriguez .10 .25
274 Dale Murphy 1.00 2.50
275 Jerry Koosman .30 .75
276 Tom Veryzer .10 .25
277 Rick Bosetti .10 .25
278 Jim Spencer .10 .25
279 Rob Andrews .10 .25
280 Gaylord Perry .30 .75
281 Paul Blair .30 .75
282 Seattle Mariners CL/Johnson .30 .75
283 John Ellis .10 .25
284 Larry Murray DP RC .10 .25
285 Don Baylor .30 .75
286 Darold Knowles DP .10 .25
287 John Lowenstein .10 .25
288 Dave Rozema .10 .25
289 Bruce Bochy .10 .25
290 Steve Garvey .60 1.50
291 Randy Scarberry RC .10 .25
292 Dale Berra .10 .25
293 Elias Sosa .10 .25
294 Charlie Spikes .10 .25
295 Larry Gura .30 .75
296 Dave Rader .10 .25
297 Tim Johnson .10 .25
298 Ken Holtzman .30 .75
299 Steve Henderson .10 .25
300 Ron Guidry .30 .75
301 Mike Edwards .10 .25
302 Los Angeles Dodgers CL/Lasorda .60 1.50
303 Bill Castro .10 .25
304 Butch Wynegar .10 .25
305 Randy Jones .30 .75
306 Denny Walling .10 .25
307 Rick Honeycutt .10 .25
308 Mike Hargrove .30 .75
309 Larry McWilliams .10 .25
310 Dave Parker .30 .75
311 Roger Metzger .10 .25
312 Mike Barlow .10 .25
313 Johnny Grubb .10 .25
314 Tim Stoddard RC .10 .25
315 Steve Kemp .30 .75
316 Bob Lacey .10 .25
317 Mike Anderson DP .10 .25
318 Jerry Reuss .30 .75
319 Chris Speier .10 .25
320 Dennis Eckersley .60 1.50
321 Keith Hernandez .30 .75
322 Claudell Washington .10 .25
323 Mick Kelleher .10 .25
324 Tom Underwood .10 .25
325 Dan Driessen .10 .25
326 Bo McLaughlin .10 .25
327 Ray Fosse DP .20 .50
328 Minnesota Twins CL/Mauch .30 .75
329 Bert Roberge RC .10 .25
330 Al Cowens .30 .75
331 Richie Hebner .10 .25
332 Enrique Romo .10 .25
333 Jim Norris DP .10 .25
334 Jim Beattie .10 .25
335 Willie McCovey .60 1.50
336 George Medich .10 .25
337 Carney Lansford .30 .75
338 John Wockenfuss .10 .25
339 John D'Acquisto .10 .25
340 Ken Singleton .30 .75
341 Jim Essian .10 .25
342 Odell Jones .10 .25
343 Mike Vail .10 .25
344 Randy Lerch .10 .25
345 Larry Parrish .30 .75
346 Buddy Solomon .10 .25
347 Harry Chappas RC .10 .25
348 Checklist 243-363 .30 .75
349 Jack Brohamer .10 .25
350 George Hendrick .30 .75
351 Bob Davis .10 .25
352 Dan Briggs .10 .25
353 Andy Hassler .10 .25
354 Rick Auerbach .10 .25
355 Gary Matthews .30 .75
356 San Diego Padres CL/Coleman .30 .75
357 Bob McClure .10 .25
358 Lou Whitaker .30 .75
359 Randy Moffitt .10 .25
360 Darrell Porter DP .20 .50
361 Wayne Garland .10 .25
362 Danny Goodwin .10 .25
363 Wayne Gross .10 .25
364 Ray Burris .10 .25
365 Bobby Murcer .30 .75
366 Rob Dressler .10 .25
367 Billy Smith .10 .25
368 Willie Aikens RC .30 .75
369 Jim Kern .10 .25
370 Cesar Cedeno .30 .75
371 Jack Morris .30 .75
372 Joel Youngblood .10 .25
373 Dan Petry DP RC .30 .75
374 Jim Gantner .30 .75
375 Ross Grimsley .10 .25
376 Gary Allenson RC .10 .25
377 Junior Kennedy .10 .25
378 Jerry Mumphrey .10 .25
379 Kevin Bell .10 .25
380 Garry Maddox .30 .75
381 Chicago Cubs CL/Gomez .30 .75
382 Dave Freisleben .10 .25
383 Ed Ott .10 .25
384 Joey McLaughlin RC .10 .25
385 Enos Cabell .10 .25
386 Darrell Jackson .10 .25
387A F.Stanley Yellow .75 2.00
387B F.Stanley Red Name .10 .25
388 Mike Paxton .10 .25
389 Pete LaCock .10 .25
390 Fergie Jenkins .30 .75
391 Tony Armas DP .20 .50
392 Milt Wilcox .10 .25
393 Ozzie Smith 4.00 10.00
394 Reggie Cleveland .10 .25
395 Ellis Valentine .10 .25
396 Dan Meyer .10 .25
397 Roy Thomas DP .10 .25
398 Barry Foote .10 .25
399 Mike Proly DP .10 .25
400 George Foster .30 .75
401 Pete Falcone .10 .25
402 Merv Rettenmund .10 .25
403 Pete Redfern DP .10 .25
404 Baltimore Orioles CL/Weaver .30 .75
405 Dwight Evans .60 1.50
406 Paul Molitor 1.50 4.00
407 Tony Solaita .10 .25
408 Bill North .10 .25
409 Paul Splittorff .10 .25
410 Bobby Bonds .30 .75
411 Frank LaCorte .10 .25
412 Thad Bosley .10 .25
413 Allen Ripley .10 .25
414 George Scott .30 .75
415 Bill Atkinson .10 .25
416 Tom Brookens RC .10 .25
417 Craig Chamberlain DP RC .10 .25
418 Roger Freed DP .10 .25
419 Vic Correll .10 .25
420 Butch Hobson .10 .25
421 Doug Bird .10 .25
422 Larry Milbourne .10 .25
423 Dave Frost .10 .25
424 New York Yankees CL/Howser .30 .75
425 Mark Belanger .30 .75
426 Grant Jackson .10 .25
427 Tom Hutton DP .10 .25
428 Pat Zachry .10 .25
429 Duane Kuiper .10 .25
430 Larry Hisle DP .10 .25
431 Mike Krukow .10 .25
432 Willie Norwood .10 .25
433 Rich Gale .10 .25
434 Johnnie LeMaster .10 .25
435 Don Gullett .30 .75
436 Billy Almon .10 .25
437 Joe Niekro .30 .75
438 Dave Revering .10 .25
439 Mike Phillips .10 .25
440 Don Sutton .30 .75
441 Eric Soderholm .10 .25
442 Jorge Orta .10 .25
443 Mike Parrott .10 .25
444 Alvis Woods .10 .25
445 Mark Fidrych .30 .75
446 Duffy Dyer .10 .25
447 Nino Espinosa .10 .25
448 Jim Wohlford .10 .25
449 Doug Bair .10 .25
450 George Brett 3.00 8.00
451 Cleveland Indians CL/Garcia .30 .75
452 Steve Dillard .10 .25
453 Mike Bacsik .10 .25
454 Tom Donohue RC .10 .25
455 Mike Torrez .30 .75
456 Frank Taveras .10 .25
457 Bert Blyleven .30 .75
458 Billy Sample .10 .25
459 Mickey Lolich DP .20 .50
460 Willie Randolph .30 .75
461 Dwayne Murphy .10 .25
462 Mike Sadek DP .10 .25
463 Jerry Royster .10 .25
464 John Denny .30 .75
465 Rick Monday .30 .75
466 Mike Squires .10 .25
467 Jesse Jefferson .10 .25
468 Aurelio Rodriguez .10 .25
469 Randy Niemann DP RC .10 .25
470 Bob Boone .30 .75
471 Hosken Powell DP .10 .25
472 Willie Hernandez .30 .75
473 Bump Wills .10 .25
474 Steve Busby .10 .25
475 Cesar Geronimo .30 .75
476 Bob Shirley .10 .25
477 Buck Martinez .10 .25
478 Gil Flores .10 .25
479 Montreal Expos CL/Williams .30 .75
480 Bob Watson .30 .75
481 Tom Paciorek .30 .75
482 Rickey Henderson RC 100.00 250.00
483 Bo Diaz .10 .25
484 Checklist 364-484 .30 .75
485 Mickey Rivers .30 .75
486 Mike Tyson DP .10 .25
487 Wayne Nordhagen .10 .25
488 Roy Howell .10 .25
489 Preston Hanna DP .10 .25
490 Lee May .30 .75
491 Steve Mura DP .10 .25
492 Todd Cruz RC .10 .25
493 Jerry Martin .10 .25
494 Craig Minetto RC .10 .25
495 Bake McBride .30 .75
496 Silvio Martinez .10 .25
497 Jim Mason .10 .25
498 Danny Darwin .10 .25
499 San Francisco Giants CL/Bristol .30 .75
500 Tom Seaver 1.25 3.00
501 Rennie Stennett .10 .25
502 Rich Wortham DP RC .10 .25
503 Mike Cubbage .10 .25
504 Gene Garber .10 .25
505 Bert Campaneris .30 .75
506 Tom Buskey .10 .25
507 Leon Roberts .10 .25
508 U.L. Washington .10 .25
509 Ed Glynn .10 .25
510 Ron Cey .30 .75
511 Eric Wilkins RC .10 .25
512 Jose Cardenal .10 .25
513 Tom Dixon DP .10 .25
514 Steve Ontiveros .10 .25
515 Mike Caldwell UER .10 .25
516 Hector Cruz .10 .25
517 Don Stanhouse .10 .25
518 Nelson Norman RC .10 .25
519 Steve Nicosia RC .10 .25
520 Steve Rogers .30 .75
521 Ken Brett .10 .25
522 Jim Morrison .10 .25
523 Ken Henderson .10 .25
524 Jim Wright DP .10 .25
525 Clint Hurdle .10 .25
526 Philadelphia Phillies CL/Green .30 .75
527 Doug Rau DP .10 .25
528 Adrian Devine .10 .25
529 Jim Barr .10 .25
530 Jim Sundberg DP .20 .50
531 Eric Rasmussen .10 .25
532 Willie Horton .30 .75
533 Checklist 485-605 .30 .75
534 Andre Thornton .30 .75
535 Bob Forsch .10 .25
536 Lee Lacy .10 .25
537 Alex Trevino RC .10 .25
538 Joe Strain .10 .25
539 Rudy May .10 .25
540 Pete Rose 3.00 8.00
541 Miguel Dilone .10 .25
542 Joe Coleman .10 .25
543 Pat Kelly .10 .25
544 Rick Sutcliffe RC .60 1.50
545 Jeff Burroughs .10 .25
546 Rick Langford .10 .25
547 John Wathan .10 .25
548 Dave Rajsich .10 .25
549 Larry Wolfe .10 .25
550 Ken Griffey Sr. .30 .75
551 Pittsburgh Pirates CL/Tanner .30 .75
552 Bill Nahorodny .10 .25
553 Dick Davis .10 .25
554 Art Howe .30 .75
555 Ed Figueroa .10 .25
556 Joe Rudi .30 .75
557 Mark Lee .10 .25
558 Alfredo Griffin .10 .25
559 Dale Murray .10 .25
560 Dave Lopes .30 .75
561 Eddie Whitson .10 .25
562 Joe Wallis .10 .25
563 Will McEnaney .10 .25
564 Rick Manning .10 .25
565 Dennis Leonard .10 .25
566 Bud Harrelson .30 .75
567 Skip Lockwood .10 .25
568 Gary Roenicke RC .10 .25
569 Terry Kennedy .10 .25
570 Roy Smalley .30 .75
571 Joe Sambito .10 .25
572 Jerry Morales DP .10 .25
573 Kent Tekulve .30 .75
574 Scot Thompson .10 .25
575 Ken Kravec .10 .25
576 Jim Dwyer .10 .25
577 Toronto Blue Jays CL/Mattick .30 .75
578 Scott Sanderson .10 .25
579 Charlie Moore .10 .25
580 Nolan Ryan 10.00 25.00
581 Bob Bailor .10 .25
582 Brian Doyle .10 .25
583 Bob Stinson .10 .25
584 Kurt Bevacqua .10 .25
585 Al Hrabosky .30 .75
586 Mitchell Page .10 .25
587 Garry Templeton .30 .75
588 Greg Minton .10 .25
589 Chet Lemon .30 .75
590 Jim Palmer .60 1.50
591 Rick Cerone .10 .25
592 Jon Matlack .30 .75
593 Jesus Alou .10 .25
594 Dick Tidrow .10 .25
595 Don Money .10 .25
596 Rick Matula RC .10 .25
597 Tom Poquette .10 .25
598 Fred Kendall DP .10 .25
599 Mike Norris .10 .25
600 Reggie Jackson 1.25 3.00
601 Buddy Schultz .10 .25
602 Brian Downing .30 .75
603 Jack Billingham DP .10 .25
604 Glenn Adams .10 .25
605 Terry Forster .30 .75
606 Cincinnati Reds CL/McNamara .30 .75
607 Woodie Fryman .10 .25
608 Alan Bannister .10 .25
609 Ron Reed .10 .25
610 Willie Stargell .60 1.50
611 Jerry Garvin DP .10 .25
612 Cliff Johnson .10 .25
613 Randy Stein .10 .25
614 John Hiller .10 .25
615 Doug DeCinces .30 .75
616 Gene Richards .10 .25
617 Joaquin Andujar .30 .75
618 Bob Montgomery DP .10 .25
619 Sergio Ferrer .10 .25
620 Richie Zisk .10 .25
621 Bob Grich .30 .75
622 Mario Soto .30 .75
623 Gorman Thomas .30 .75
624 Lerrin LaGrow .10 .25
625 Chris Chambliss .30 .75
626 Detroit Tigers CL/Anderson .30 .75
627 Pedro Borbon .10 .25
628 Doug Capilla .10 .25
629 Jim Todd .10 .25
630 Larry Bowa .30 .75
631 Mark Littell .10 .25
632 Barry Bonnell .10 .25
633 Bob Apodaca .10 .25
634 Glenn Borgmann DP .10 .25
635 John Candelaria .30 .75
636 Toby Harrah .30 .75
637 Joe Simpson .10 .25
638 Mark Clear RC .10 .25
639 Larry Biittner .10 .25
640 Mike Flanagan .30 .75
641 Ed Kranepool .30 .75
642 Ken Forsch DP .10 .25
643 John Mayberry .10 .25
644 Charlie Hough .30 .75
645 Rick Burleson .10 .25
646 Checklist 606-726 .30 .75
647 Milt May .10 .25
648 Roy White .30 .75
649 Tom Griffin .10 .25
650 Joe Morgan .60 1.50
651 Rollie Fingers .30 .75
652 Mario Mendoza .10 .25
653 Stan Bahnsen .10 .25
654 Bruce Boisclair DP .10 .25
655 Tug McGraw .30 .75
656 Larvell Blanks .10 .25
657 Dave Edwards RC .10 .25
658 Chris Knapp .10 .25
659 Milwaukee Brewers CL/Bamberger .30 .75
660 Rusty Staub .30 .75
661 Mark Corey .10 .25
Dave Ford RC/Wayne Krenchicki RC
662 Finch/O'Berry/Rainey RC .10 .25
663 Botting/Clark/Thon RC .30 .75
664 Colbern/Hoffman/Robinson RC .10 .25
665 Andersen/Cuellar/Wihtol RC .10 .25
666 Chris/Greene/Robbins RC .10 .25
667 Mart/Pasch/Quisenberry RC .30 .75
668 Boitano/Mueller/Sakata RC .10 .25
669 Graham/Sofield/Ward RC .30 .75
670 Brown/Gulden/Jones RC .10 .25
671 Bryant/Kingman/Morgan RC .30 .75
672 Beamon/Craig/Vasquez RC .10 .25
673 Allard/Gleaton/Mahlberg RC .10 .25
674 Edge/Kelly/Wilborn RC .10 .25
675 Benedict/Bradford/Miller RC .10 .25
676 Geisel/Macko/Pagel RC .10 .25
677 DeFreites/Pastore/Spilman RC .10 .25
678 Baldwin/Knicely/Ladd RC .10 .25
679 Beckwith/Hatcher/Patterson RC .30 .75
680 Bernazard/Miller/Tamargo RC .10 .25
681 Norman/Orosco/Scott RC .60 1.50
682 Aviles/Noles/Saucier RC .10 .25
683 Boyland/Lois/Saferight RC .10 .25
684 Frazier/Herr/O'Brien RC .30 .75
685 Flannery/Greer/Wilhelm RC .10 .25
686 Johnston/Littlejohn/Nastu RC .10 .25
687 Mike Heath DP .10 .25
688 Steve Stone .30 .75
689 Boston Red Sox CL/Zimmer .30 .75
690 Tommy John .30 .75
691 Ivan DeJesus .10 .25
692 Rawly Eastwick DP .20 .50
693 Craig Kusick .10 .25
694 Jim Rooker .10 .25
695 Reggie Smith .30 .75
696 Julio Gonzalez .10 .25
697 David Clyde .10 .25
698 Oscar Gamble .10 .25
699 Floyd Bannister .10 .25
700 Rod Carew DP .30 .75
701 Ken Oberkfell RC .10 .25
702 Ed Farmer .10 .25
703 Otto Velez .10 .25
704 Gene Tenace .30 .75
705 Freddie Patek .30 .75
706 Tippy Martinez .10 .25
707 Elliott Maddox .10 .25
708 Bob Tolan .10 .25
709 Pat Underwood RC .10 .25
710 Graig Nettles .30 .75
711 Bob Galasso RC .10 .25
712 Rodney Scott .10 .25
713 Terry Whitfield .10 .25
714 Fred Norman .10 .25
715 Sal Bando .30 .75
716 Lynn McGlothen .10 .25
717 Mickey Klutts DP .10 .25
718 Greg Gross .10 .25
719 Don Robinson .30 .75
720 Carl Yastrzemski DP .75 2.00
721 Paul Hartzell .10 .25
722 Jose Cruz .30 .75
723 Shane Rawley .10 .25
724 Jerry White .10 .25
725 Rick Wise .10 .25
726 Steve Yeager .30 .75

1980 Topps/O-Pee-Chee Retail Promotion Cards

This set features special promotional redemption cards from Mrs. Butterworth's Syrup and Kmart Stores that could be redeemed for an unopened pack of three standard Topps Baseball cards. A special "3000 or More Hits", "lifetime .300 hitters" or a "Major League Records" card came with the packs. Hunts bread did the same promotion up in Canada. The promotion was limited to certain states and to certain stores.

COMPLETE SET 8.00 20.00
1 Mrs. Butterworth's 2.00 5.00
2 Kmart 2.00 5.00
3 Squirt 2.00 5.00
4 Hunts Bread 2.00 5.00

1980 Topps Super

This 60-card set, measuring 4 7/8" by 6 7/8", consists primarily of star players. A player photo comprises the entire front with a facsimile signature at the lower portion of the photo. The backs contain a large Topps logo and the player's name. The cards were issued with either white or gray backs. The white backs have thicker card stock than the gray. White back cards were issued in three-card cellophane packs and gray back cards were issued through various promotional means. The prices below reflect those of the gray back. There are a number of cards that were Triple Printed. They are indicated by below (TP).

COMPLETE SET (60) 6.00 15.00
COMMON PLAYER (1-60) .05 .10
COMMON TP .13 .25
*WHITE BACKS: 2X GRAY BACKS
1 Willie Stargell .30 .75
2 Mike Schmidt TP .40 1.00
3 Johnny Bench .40 1.00
4 Jim Palmer .30 .75
5 Jim Rice .08 .25
6 Reggie Jackson TP .40 1.00
7 Ron Guidry .08 .25
8 Lee Mazzilli .02 .10
9 Don Baylor .20 .50
10 Fred Lynn .08 .25
11 Ken Singleton .08 .25
12 Rod Carew TP .30 .75
13 Steve Garvey TP .20 .50
14 George Brett TP .60 1.50
15 Tom Seaver .40 1.00
16 Dave Kingman .08 .25
17 Dave Parker TP .08 .25
18 Dave Winfield .30 .75
19 Pete Rose .30 .75
20 Nolan Ryan 1.25 3.00
21 Graig Nettles .08 .25
22 Carl Yastrzemski .30 .75
23 Tommy John .20 .50
24 George Foster .08 .25
25 J.R. Richard .02 .10
26 Keith Hernandez .08 .25
27 Bob Horner .02 .10
28 Eddie Murray .75 2.00
29 Steve Kemp .02 .10
30 Gorman Thomas .02 .10
31 Sixto Lezcano .02 .10
32 Bruce Sutter .40 1.00
33 Cecil Cooper .08 .25
34 Larry Bowa .08 .25
35 Al Oliver .20 .50
36 Ted Simmons .08 .25
37 Garry Templeton .02 .10
38 Jerry Koosman .08 .25
39 Darrell Porter .02 .10
40 Roy Smalley .02 .10
41 Craig Swan .02 .10
42 Jason Thompson .02 .10
43 Andre Thornton .02 .10
44 Rick Manning .02 .10
45 Kent Tekulve .02 .10
46 Phil Niekro .30 .75
47 Buddy Bell .08 .25
48 Randy Jones .02 .10
49 Brian Downing .02 .10
50 Amos Otis .02 .10
51 Rick Bosetti .02 .10
52 Gary Carter .40 1.00
53 Larry Parrish .08 .25
54 Jack Clark .08 .25
55 Bruce Bochte .02 .10
56 Cesar Cedeno .02 .10
57 Chet Lemon .02 .10
58 Dave Revering .02 .10
59 Vida Blue .08 .25
60 Dave Lopes .08 .25

1980 Topps Team Checklist Sheet

As part of a mail-away offer, Topps offered all 26 1980 team checklist cards on an uncut sheet. These cards enabled the collector to have an easy reference for which card(s) he/she needed to finish their sets. When cut from the sheet, all cards measure the standard size.

1 Team Checklist Sheet 20.00 50.00

1981 Topps

The cards in this 726-card set measure the standard size. This set was issued primarily in 15-card wax packs and 50-card rack packs. League Leaders (1-8), Record Breakers (201-208), and Post-season cards (401-404) are the topical subsets. The team cards are all grouped together (661-686) and feature team checklist backs and a very small photo of the team's manager in the upper right corner of the obverse. The obverses carry the player's position and team in a baseball cap design, and the company name is printed in a small baseball. The backs are red and gray. The 66 double-printed cards are noted in the checklist by DP. Notable Rookie Cards in the set include Harold Baines, Kirk Gibson, Tim Raines, Jeff Reardon, and Fernando Valenzuela. During 1981, a promotion existed where collectors could order complete set in sheet form from Topps for $24.

COMPLETE SET (726) 25.00 60.00
COMMON CARD (1-726) .05 .15
COMMON CARD DP .05 .15
1 G.Brett/B.Buckner LL 1.25 3.00
2 Reggie/Ogliv/Schmidt LL .60 1.50
3 C.Cooper/M.Schmidt LL .60 1.50
4 R.Henderson/LeFlore LL 1.25 3.00
5 S.Stone/S.Carlton LL .15 .40
6 Len Barker/S.Carlton LL .15 .40
7 R.May/D.Sutton LL .15 .40
8 Quis/Fingers/Hume LL .15 .40
9 Pete LaCock DP .05 .15
10 Mike Flanagan .05 .15
11 Jim Wohlford DP .05 .15
12 Mark Clear .05 .15
13 Joe Charboneau RC .60 1.50
14 John Tudor RC .60 1.50
15 Larry Parrish .05 .15
16 Ron Davis .05 .15
17 Cliff Johnson .05 .15
18 Glenn Adams .05 .15
19 Jim Clancy .05 .15
20 Jeff Burroughs .15 .40
21 Ron Oester .05 .15
22 Danny Darwin .05 .15
23 Alex Trevino .05 .15
24 Don Stanhouse .05 .15
25 Sixto Lezcano .05 .15
26 U.L. Washington .05 .15
27 Champ Summers DP .05 .15
28 Enrique Romo .05 .15
29 Gene Tenace .15 .40
30 Jack Clark .15 .40
31 Checklist 1-121 DP .08 .25
32 Ken Oberkfell .05 .15
33 Rick Honeycutt .05 .15
34 Aurelio Rodriguez .05 .15
35 Mitchell Page .05 .15
36 Ed Farmer .05 .15
37 Gary Roenicke .05 .15
38 Win Remmerswaal RC .05 .15
39 Tom Veryzer .05 .15
40 Tug McGraw .15 .40
41 Babcock/Butcher/Gleaton RC .08 .25
42 Jerry White DP .05 .15
43 Jose Morales .05 .15
44 Larry McWilliams .05 .15
45 Enos Cabell .05 .15
46 Rick Bosetti .05 .15
47 Ken Brett .05 .15
48 Dave Skaggs .05 .15
49 Bob Shirley .05 .15
50 Dave Lopes .15 .40
51 Bill Robinson DP .05 .15
52 Hector Cruz .05 .15
53 Kevin Saucier .05 .15
54 Ivan DeJesus .05 .15
55 Mike Norris .05 .15
56 Buck Martinez .05 .15
57 Dave Roberts .05 .15
58 Joel Youngblood .05 .15
59 Dan Petry .05 .15
60 Willie Randolph .15 .40
61 Butch Wynegar .05 .15
62 Joe Pettini RC .05 .15
63 Steve Renko DP .05 .15
64 Brian Asselstine .05 .15
65 Scott McGregor .05 .15
66 Castillo/Ireland/M.Jones RC .08 .25
67 Ken Kravec .05 .15
68 Matt Alexander DP .05 .15
69 Ed Halicki .05 .15
70 Al Oliver DP .08 .25
71 Hal Dues .05 .15
72 Barry Evans DP RC .05 .15
73 Doug Bair .05 .15
74 Mike Hargrove .05 .15
75 Reggie Smith .15 .40
76 Mario Mendoza .05 .15
77 Mike Barlow .05 .15
78 Steve Dillard .05 .15
79 Bruce Robbins .05 .15
80 Rusty Staub .15 .40
81 Dave Stapleton RC .05 .15
82 Heep/Knicely/Sprowl RC .08 .25
83 Mike Proly .05 .15
84 Johnnie LeMaster .05 .15
85 Mike Caldwell .05 .15
86 Wayne Gross .05 .15
87 Rick Camp .05 .15
88 Joe Lefebvre RC .05 .15
89 Darrell Jackson .05 .15
90 Bake McBride .15 .40
91 Tim Stoddard DP .05 .15
92 Mike Easler .05 .15
93 Ed Glynn DP .05 .15
94 Harry Spilman DP .05 .15
95 Jim Sundberg .15 .40
96 Beard/Camacho/Dempsey RC .08 .25
97 Chris Speier .05 .15
98 Clint Hurdle .05 .15
99 Eric Wilkins .05 .15
100 Rod Carew .30 .75
101 Benny Ayala .05 .15
102 Dave Tobik .05 .15
103 Jerry Martin .05 .15
104 Terry Forster .15 .40
105 Jose Cruz .15 .40
106 Don Money .05 .15
107 Rich Wortham .05 .15
108 Bruce Benedict .05 .15
109 Mike Scott .15 .40
110 Carl Yastrzemski 1.00 2.50
111 Greg Minton .05 .15
112 Kuntz/Mullins/Sutherland RC .08 .25
113 Mike Phillips .05 .15
114 Tom Underwood .05 .15

115 Roy Smalley .15 .40
116 Joe Simpson .05 .15
117 Pete Falcone .05 .15
118 Kurt Bevacqua .05 .15
119 Tippy Martinez .05 .15
120 Larry Bowa .15 .40
121 Larry Harlow .05 .15
122 John Denny .05 .15
123 Al Cowens .05 .15
124 Jerry Garvin .05 .15
125 Andre Dawson .30 .75
126 Charlie Leibrandt RC .30 .75
127 Rudy Law .05 .15
128 Gary Allenson DP .05 .15
129 Art Howe .05 .15
130 Larry Gura .05 .15
131 Keith Moreland RC .05 .15
132 Tommy Boggs .05 .15
133 Jeff Cox RC .05 .15
134 Steve Mura .05 .15
135 Gorman Thomas .15 .40
136 Doug Capilla .05 .15
137 Hosken Powell .05 .15
138 Rich Dotson DP RC .05 .15
139 Oscar Gamble .05 .15
140 Bob Forsch .05 .15
141 Miguel Dilone .05 .15
142 Jackson Todd .05 .15
143 Dan Meyer .05 .15
144 Allen Ripley .05 .15
145 Mickey Rivers .05 .15
146 Bobby Castillo .05 .15
147 Dale Berra .05 .15
148 Randy Niemann .05 .15
149 Joe Nolan .05 .15
150 Mark Fidrych .15 .40
151 Claudell Washington .05 .15
152 John Urrea .05 .15
153 Tom Poquette .05 .15
154 Rick Langford .05 .15
155 Chris Chambliss .15 .40
156 Bob McClure .05 .15
157 John Wathan .05 .15
158 Fergie Jenkins .15 .40
159 Brian Doyle .05 .15
160 Garry Maddox .05 .15
161 Dan Graham .05 .15
162 Doug Corbett RC .05 .15
163 Bill Almon .05 .15
164 LaMarr Hoyt RC .30 .75
165 Tony Scott .05 .15
166 Floyd Bannister .05 .15
167 Terry Whitfield .05 .15
168 Don Robinson DP .05 .15
169 John Mayberry .05 .15
170 Ross Grimsley .05 .15
171 Gene Richards .05 .15
172 Gary Woods .05 .15
173 Bump Wills .05 .15
174 Doug Rau .05 .15
175 Dave Collins .05 .15
176 Mike Krukow .05 .15
177 Rick Peters RC .05 .15
178 Jim Essian DP .05 .15
179 Rudy May .05 .15
180 Pete Rose 2.00 5.00
181 Elias Sosa .05 .15
182 Bob Grich .15 .40
183 Dick Davis DP .05 .15
184 Jim Dwyer .05 .15
185 Dennis Leonard .05 .15
186 Wayne Nordhagen .05 .15
187 Mike Parrott .05 .15
188 Doug DeCinces .05 .15
189 Craig Swan .05 .15
190 Cesar Cedeno .15 .40
191 Rick Sutcliffe .15 .40
192 Harper/Miller/Ramirez RC .08 .25
193 Pete Vuckovich .05 .15
194 Rod Scurry RC .05 .15
195 Rich Murray RC .05 .15
196 Duffy Dyer .05 .15
197 Jim Kern .05 .15
198 Jerry Dybzinski RC .05 .15
199 Chuck Rainey .05 .15
200 George Foster .15 .40
201 Johnny Bench RB .30 .75
202 Steve Carlton RB .15 .40
203 Bill Gullickson RB .05 .15
204 R.LeFlore/R.Scott RB .15 .40
205 Pete Rose RB .60 1.50
206 Mike Schmidt RB .60 1.50
207 Ozzie Smith RB .75 2.00
208 Willie Wilson RB .05 .15
209 Dickie Thon DP .05 .15
210 Jim Palmer .30 .75
211 Derrel Thomas .05 .15
212 Steve Nicosia .05 .15
213 Al Holland RC .05 .15
214 Botting/Dorsey/J.Harris RC .08 .25
215 Larry Hisle .05 .15
216 John Henry Johnson .05 .15
217 Rich Hebner .05 .15
218 Paul Splittorff .05 .15
219 Ken Landreaux .05 .15
220 Tom Seaver .60 1.50
221 Bob Davis .05 .15
222 Jorge Orta .05 .15
223 Roy Lee Jackson RC .05 .15
224 Pat Zachry .05 .15
225 Ruppert Jones .05 .15
226 Manny Sanguillen DP .08 .25
227 Fred Martinez RC .05 .15
228 Tom Paciorek .05 .15
229 Rollie Fingers .15 .40
230 George Hendrick .15 .40
231 Joe Beckwith .05 .15
232 Mickey Klutts .05 .15
233 Skip Lockwood .05 .15
234 Lou Whitaker .30 .75
235 Scott Sanderson .05 .15
236 Mike Ivie .05 .15
237 Charlie Moore .05 .15
238 Willie Hernandez .05 .15
239 Rick Miller DP .05 .15
240 Nolan Ryan 3.00 8.00
241 Checklist 122-242 DP .08 .25
242 Chet Lemon .15 .40
243 Sal Butera RC .05 .15
244 Landrum/Olmsted/Rincon RC .08 .25
245 Ed Figueroa .05 .15
246 Ed Ott DP .05 .15
247 Glenn Hubbard DP .05 .15
248 Joey McLaughlin .05 .15
249 Larry Cox .05 .15
250 Ron Guidry .15 .40
251 Tom Brookens .05 .15
252 Victor Cruz .05 .15
253 Dave Bergman .05 .15
254 Ozzie Smith 2.00 5.00
255 Mark Littell .05 .15
256 Bombo Rivera .05 .15
257 Rennie Stennett .05 .15
258 Joe Price RC .05 .15
259 M.Wilson/H.Brooks RC 2.00 5.00
260 Ron Cey .15 .40
261 Rickey Henderson 4.00 10.00
262 Sammy Stewart .05 .15
263 Brian Downing .15 .40
264 Jim Norris .05 .15
265 John Candelaria .15 .40
266 Tom Herr .05 .15
267 Stan Bahnsen .05 .15
268 Jerry Royster .05 .15
269 Ken Forsch .05 .15
270 Greg Luzinski .15 .40
271 Bill Castro .05 .15
272 Bruce Kimm .05 .15
273 Stan Papi .05 .15
274 Craig Chamberlain .05 .15
275 Dwight Evans .30 .75
276 Dan Spillner .05 .15
277 Alfredo Griffin .05 .15
278 Rick Sofield .05 .15
279 Bob Knepper .05 .15
280 Ken Griffey .15 .40
281 Fred Stanley .05 .15
282 Anderson/Biercevicz/Craig RC .08 .25
283 Billy Sample .05 .15
284 Brian Kingman .05 .15
285 Jerry Turner .05 .15
286 Dave Frost .05 .15
287 Lenn Sakata .05 .15
288 Bob Clark .05 .15
289 Mickey Hatcher .05 .15
290 Bob Boone DP .08 .25
291 Aurelio Lopez .05 .15
292 Mike Squires .05 .15
293 Charlie Lea RC .05 .15
294 Mike Tyson DP .05 .15
295 Hal McRae .15 .40
296 Bill Nahorodny DP .05 .15
297 Bob Bailor .05 .15
298 Buddy Solomon .05 .15
299 Elliott Maddox .05 .15
300 Paul Molitor .60 1.50
301 Matt Keough .05 .15
302 F.Valenzuela/M.Scioscia RC 10.00 25.00
303 Johnny Oates .15 .40
304 John Castino .05 .15
305 Ken Clay .05 .15
306 Juan Beniquez DP .05 .15
307 Gene Garber .05 .15
308 Rick Manning .05 .15
309 Luis Salazar RC .30 .75
310 Vida Blue DP .08 .25
311 Freddie Patek .05 .15
312 Rick Rhoden .05 .15
313 Luis Pujols .05 .15
314 Rich Dauer .05 .15
315 Kirk Gibson RC 3.00 8.00
316 Craig Minetto .05 .15
317 Lonnie Smith .15 .40
318 Steve Yeager .15 .40
319 Rowland Office .05 .15
320 Tom Burgmeier .05 .15
321 Leon Durham RC .30 .75
322 Neil Allen .05 .15
323 Jim Morrison DP .05 .15
324 Mike Willis .05 .15
325 Ray Knight .15 .40
326 Biff Pocoroba .05 .15
327 Moose Haas .05 .15
328 Engle/Johnston/G.Ward .08 .25
329 Joaquin Andujar .15 .40
330 Frank White .15 .40
331 Dennis Lamp .05 .15
332 Lee Lacy DP .05 .15
333 Sid Monge .05 .15
334 Dane Iorg .05 .15
335 Rick Cerone .05 .15
336 Eddie Whitson .05 .15
337 Lynn Jones .05 .15
338 Checklist 243-363 .15 .40
339 John Ellis .05 .15
340 Bruce Kison .05 .15
341 Dwayne Murphy .05 .15
342 Eric Rasmussen DP .05 .15
343 Frank Taveras .05 .15
344 Byron McLaughlin .05 .15
345 Warren Cromartie .05 .15
346 Larry Christenson DP .05 .15
347 Harold Baines RC 1.25 3.00
348 Bob Sykes .05 .15
349 Glenn Hoffman RC .05 .15
350 J.R. Richard .15 .40
351 Otto Velez .05 .15
352 Dick Tidrow DP .05 .15
353 Terry Kennedy .05 .15
354 Mario Soto .15 .40
355 Bob Horner .15 .40
356 Stablein/Stimac/Tellmann RC .08 .25
357 Jim Slaton .05 .15
358 Mark Wagner .05 .15
359 Tom Hausman .05 .15
360 Willie Wilson .15 .40
361 Joe Strain .05 .15
362 Bo Diaz .05 .15
363 Geoff Zahn .05 .15
364 Mike Davis RC .08 .25
365 Graig Nettles DP .08 .25
366 Mike Ramsey RC .08 .25
367 Dennis Martinez .15 .40
368 Leon Roberts .05 .15
369 Frank Tanana .15 .40
370 Dave Winfield .30 .75
371 Charlie Hough .15 .40
372 Jay Johnstone .05 .15
373 Pat Underwood .05 .15
374 Tommy Hutton .05 .15
375 Dave Concepcion .15 .40
376 Ron Reed .05 .15
377 Jerry Morales .05 .15
378 Dave Rader .05 .15
379 Lary Sorensen .05 .15
380 Willie Stargell .30 .75
381 Lezcano/Macko/Martz RC .08 .25
382 Paul Mirabella RC .05 .15
383 Eric Soderholm DP .05 .15
384 Mike Sadek .05 .15
385 Joe Sambito .05 .15
386 Dave Edwards .05 .15
387 Phil Niekro .15 .40
388 Andre Thornton .15 .40
389 Marty Pattin .05 .15
390 Cesar Geronimo .05 .15
391 Dave Lemanczyk DP .05 .15
392 Lance Parrish .15 .40
393 Broderick Perkins .05 .15
394 Woodie Fryman .05 .15
395 Scot Thompson .05 .15
396 Bill Campbell .05 .15
397 Julio Cruz .05 .15
398 Ross Baumgarten .05 .15
399 Boddicker/Corey/Rayford RC .30 .75
400 Reggie Jackson .60 1.50
401 George Brett ALCS 1.00 2.50
402 NL Champs .05 .15
403 Larry Bowa WS .30 .75
404 Tug McGraw WS .30 .75
405 Nino Espinosa .05 .15
406 Dickie Noles .05 .15
407 Ernie Whitt .05 .15
408 Fernando Arroyo .05 .15
409 Larry Herndon .05 .15
410 Bert Campaneris .15 .40
411 Terry Puhl .05 .15
412 Britt Burns RC .05 .15
413 Tony Bernazard .05 .15
414 John Pacella DP RC .05 .15
415 Ben Oglivie .15 .40
416 Gary Alexander .05 .15
417 Dan Schatzeder .05 .15
418 Bobby Brown .05 .15
419 Tom Hume .05 .15
420 Keith Hernandez .15 .40
421 Bob Stanley .05 .15
422 Dan Ford .05 .15
423 Shane Rawley .05 .15
424 Lollar/Robinson/Werth RC .08 .25
425 Al Bumbry .05 .15
426 Warren Brusstar .05 .15
427 John D'Acquisto .05 .15
428 John Stearns .05 .15
429 Mick Kelleher .05 .15
430 Jim Bibby .05 .15
431 Dave Roberts .05 .15
432 Len Barker .15 .40
433 Rance Mulliniks .05 .15
434 Roger Erickson .05 .15
435 Jim Spencer .05 .15
436 Gary Lucas RC .05 .15
437 Mike Heath DP .05 .15
438 John Montefusco .05 .15
439 Denny Walling .05 .15
440 Jerry Reuss .05 .15
441 Ken Reitz .05 .15
442 Ron Pruitt .05 .15
443 Jim Beattie DP .05 .15
444 Garth Iorg .05 .15
445 Ellis Valentine .05 .15
446 Checklist 364-484 .15 .40
447 Junior Kennedy DP .05 .15
448 Tim Corcoran .05 .15
449 Paul Mitchell .05 .15
450 Dave Kingman DP .08 .25
451 Bando/Brennan/Wihtol RC .08 .25
452 Renie Martin .05 .15
453 Rob Wilfong DP .05 .15
454 Andy Hassler .05 .15
455 Rick Burleson .05 .15
456 Jeff Reardon RC .60 1.50
457 Mike Lum .05 .15
458 Randy Jones .05 .15
459 Greg Gross .05 .15
460 Rich Gossage .15 .40
461 Dave McKay .05 .15
462 Jack Brohamer .05 .15
463 Milt May .05 .15
464 Adrian Devine .05 .15
465 Bill Russell .15 .40
466 Bob Molinaro .05 .15
467 Dave Stieb .15 .40
468 John Wockenfuss .05 .15
469 Jeff Leonard .15 .40
470 Manny Trillo .05 .15
471 Mike Vail .05 .15
472 Dyar Miller DP .05 .15
473 Jose Cardenal .05 .15
474 Mike LaCoss .05 .15
475 Buddy Bell .15 .40
476 Jerry Koosman .15 .40
477 Luis Gomez .05 .15
478 Juan Eichelberger RC .05 .15
479 Tim Raines RC 1.50 4.00
480 Carlton Fisk .30 .75
481 Bob Lacey DP .05 .15
482 Jim Gantner .05 .15
483 Mike Griffin RC .05 .15
484 Max Venable DP RC .05 .15
485 Garry Templeton .15 .40
486 Marc Hill .05 .15
487 Dewey Robinson .05 .15
488 Damaso Garcia RC .05 .15
489 John Littlefield RC .05 .15
490 Eddie Murray 1.00 2.50
491 Gordy Pladson RC .05 .15
492 Barry Foote .05 .15
493 Dan Quisenberry .15 .40
494 Bob Walk RC .30 .75
495 Dusty Baker .15 .40
496 Paul Dade .05 .15
497 Fred Norman .05 .15
498 Pat Putnam .05 .15
499 Frank Pastore .05 .15
500 Jim Rice .15 .40
501 Tim Foli DP .05 .15
502 Bourjos/Hargesheimer/Rowland RC .08 .25
503 Steve McCatty .05 .15
504 Dale Murphy .30 .75
505 Jason Thompson .05 .15
506 Phil Huffman .05 .15
507 Jamie Quirk .05 .15
508 Rob Dressler .05 .15
509 Pete Mackanin .05 .15
510 Lee Mazzilli .15 .40
511 Wayne Garland .05 .15
512 Gary Thomasson .05 .15
513 Frank LaCorte .05 .15
514 George Riley RC .05 .15
515 Robin Yount 1.00 2.50
516 Doug Bird .05 .15
517 Richie Zisk .05 .15
518 Grant Jackson .05 .15
519 John Tamargo DP .05 .15
520 Steve Stone .05 .15
521 Sam Mejias .05 .15
522 Mike Colbern .05 .15
523 John Fulgham .05 .15
524 Willie Aikens .05 .15
525 Mike Torrez .05 .15
526 Bystrom/Loviglio/Wright RC .08 .25
527 Danny Goodwin .05 .15
528 Gary Matthews .15 .40
529 Dave LaRoche .05 .15
530 Steve Garvey .30 .75
531 John Curtis .05 .15
532 Bill Stein .05 .15
533 Jesus Figueroa RC .05 .15
534 Dave Smith RC .30 .75
535 Omar Moreno .05 .15
536 Bob Owchinko DP .05 .15
537 Ron Hodges .05 .15
538 Tom Griffin .05 .15
539 Rodney Scott .05 .15
540 Mike Schmidt DP .75 2.00
541 Steve Swisher .05 .15
542 Larry Bradford DP .05 .15
543 Terry Crowley .05 .15
544 Rich Gale .05 .15
545 Johnny Grubb .05 .15
546 Paul Moskau .05 .15
547 Mario Guerrero .05 .15
548 Dave Goltz .05 .15
549 Jerry Remy .05 .15
550 Tommy John .15 .40
551 Law/Pena/Perez RC .30 .75
552 Steve Trout .05 .15
553 Tim Blackwell .05 .15
554 Bert Blyleven .15 .40
555 Cecil Cooper .15 .40
556 Jerry Mumphrey .05 .15
557 Chris Knapp .05 .15
558 Barry Bonnell .05 .15
559 Willie Montanez .05 .15
560 Joe Morgan .30 .75
561 Dennis Littlejohn .05 .15
562 Checklist 485-605 .15 .40
563 Jim Kaat .15 .40
564 Ron Hassey DP .05 .15
565 Burt Hooton .05 .15
566 Del Unser .05 .15
567 Mark Bomback RC .05 .15
568 Dave Revering .05 .15
569 Al Williams DP RC .05 .15
570 Ken Singleton .15 .40
571 Todd Cruz .05 .15
572 Jack Morris .30 .75
573 Phil Garner .15 .40
574 Bill Caudill .05 .15
575 Tony Perez .30 .75
576 Reggie Cleveland .05 .15
577 Leal/Milner/Schrom RC .08 .25
578 Bill Gullickson RC .30 .75
579 Tim Flannery .05 .15
580 Don Baylor .15 .40
581 Roy Howell .05 .15
582 Gaylord Perry .15 .40
583 Larry Milbourne .05 .15
584 Randy Lerch .05 .15
585 Amos Otis .15 .40
586 Silvio Martinez .05 .15
587 Jeff Newman .05 .15
588 Gary Lavelle .05 .15
589 Lamar Johnson .05 .15
590 Bruce Sutter .30 .75
591 John Lowenstein .05 .15
592 Steve Comer .05 .15
593 Steve Kemp .05 .15
594 Preston Hanna DP .05 .15
595 Butch Hobson .05 .15
596 Jerry Augustine .05 .15
597 Rafael Landestoy .05 .15
598 George Vukovich DP RC .05 .15
599 Dennis Kinney RC .05 .15
600 Johnny Bench .60 1.50
601 Don Aase .05 .15
602 Bobby Murcer .15 .40
603 John Verhoeven .05 .15
604 Rob Picciolo .05 .15
605 Don Sutton .15 .40
606 Berenyi/Combe/Householder DP RC .08 .25
607 David Palmer .05 .15
608 Greg Pryor .05 .15
609 Lynn McGlothen .05 .15
610 Darrell Porter .05 .15
611 Rick Matula DP .05 .15
612 Duane Kuiper .05 .15
613 Jim Anderson .05 .15
614 Dave Rozema .05 .15
615 Rick Dempsey .05 .15
616 Rick Wise .05 .15
617 Craig Reynolds .05 .15
618 John Milner .05 .15
619 Steve Henderson .05 .15
620 Dennis Eckersley .30 .75
621 Tom Donohue .05 .15
622 Randy Moffitt .05 .15
623 Sal Bando .15 .40
624 Bob Welch .15 .40
625 Bill Buckner .15 .40
626 Steffen/Ujdur/Weaver RC .08 .25
627 Luis Tiant .15 .40
628 Vic Correll .05 .15
629 Tony Armas .15 .40
630 Steve Carlton .30 .75
631 Ron Jackson .05 .15
632 Alan Bannister .05 .15
633 Bill Lee .15 .40
634 Doug Flynn .05 .15
635 Bobby Bonds .15 .40
636 Al Hrabosky .15 .40
637 Jerry Narron .05 .15
638 Checklist 606-726 .15 .40
639 Carney Lansford .15 .40
640 Dave Parker .15 .40
641 Mark Belanger .05 .15
642 Vern Ruhle .05 .15
643 Lloyd Moseby RC .30 .75
644 Ramon Aviles DP .05 .15
645 Rick Reuschel .05 .15
646 Marvis Foley RC .05 .15
647 Dick Drago .05 .15
648 Darrell Evans .15 .40
649 Manny Sarmiento .05 .15
650 Bucky Dent .15 .40
651 Pedro Guerrero .15 .40
652 John Montague .05 .15
653 Bill Fahey .05 .15
654 Ray Burris .05 .15
655 Dan Driessen .05 .15
656 Jon Matlack .05 .15
657 Mike Cubbage DP .05 .15
658 Milt Wilcox .05 .15
659 Flinn/Romero/Yost .30 .75
660 Gary Carter .30 .75
661 Orioles Team CL .15 .40
Earl Weaver MG
662 Red Sox Team CL .15 .40
Ralph Houk MG
663 Angels Team CL .15 .40
Jim Fregosi MG
664 White Sox Team .15 .40
Mgr./Tony LaRussa/(Checklist back
665 Indians Team CL .15 .40
Dave Garcia MG
666 Tigers Team .15 .40
Mgr./Sparky Anderson/(Checklist back
667 Royals Team CL .15 .40
Jim Frey MG
668 Brewers Team CL .15 .40
Bob Rodgers MG
669 Twins Team CL. .15 .40
John Goryl MG
670 Yankees Team CL .15 .40
Gene Michael MG
671 A's Team CL .30 .75
Billy Martin MG
672 Mariners Team CL .15 .40
Maury Wills MG
673 Rangers Team CL .15 .40
Don Zimmer MG
674 Blue Jays Team .15 .40
Mgr./Bobby Mattick/(Checklist bac
675 Braves Team CL .15 .40
Bobby Cox MG
676 Cubs Team CL .15 .40
Joe Amalfitano MG
677 Reds Team CL .15 .40
John McNamara MG
678 Astros Team CL .15 .40
Bill Virdon MG
679 Dodgers Team CL .30 .75
Tom Lasorda MG
680 Expos Team CL .15 .40
Dick Williams MG
681 Mets Team CL .30 .75
Joe Torre MG
682 Phillies Team CL .15 .40
Dallas Green MG
683 Pirates Team CL .15 .40
Chuck Tanner MG
684 Cardinals Team .15 .40
Mgr./Whitey Herzog/(Checklist bac
685 Padres Team CL .15 .40
Frank Howard MG
686 Giants Team CL .15 .40
Dave Bristol MG
687 Jeff Jones RC .05 .15
688 Kiko Garcia .05 .15
689 Bruce Hurst RC .30 .75
690 Bob Watson .05 .15
691 Dick Ruthven .05 .15
692 Lenny Randle .05 .15
693 Steve Howe RC .08 .25
694 Bud Harrelson DP .08 .25
695 Kent Tekulve .05 .15
696 Alan Ashby .05 .15
697 Rick Waits .05 .15
698 Mike Jorgensen .05 .15
699 Glenn Abbott .05 .15
700 George Brett 1.50 4.00
701 Joe Rudi .05 .15
702 George Medich .05 .15
703 Alvis Woods .05 .15
704 Bill Travers DP .05 .15
705 Ted Simmons .05 .15
706 Dave Ford .05 .15
707 Dave Cash .05 .15
708 Doyle Alexander .05 .15
709 Alan Trammell DP .20 .50
710 Ron LeFlore DP .08 .25
711 Joe Ferguson .05 .15
712 Bill Bonham .05 .15
713 Bill North .05 .15
714 Pete Redfern .05 .15
715 Bill Madlock .15 .40
716 Glenn Borgmann .05 .15
717 Jim Barr DP .05 .15
718 Larry Biittner .05 .15
719 Sparky Lyle .15 .40
720 Fred Lynn .15 .40
721 Toby Harrah .15 .40
722 Joe Niekro .05 .15
723 Bruce Bochte .05 .15
724 Lou Piniella .15 .40
725 Steve Rogers .15 .40
726 Rick Monday .15 .40

1981 Topps Traded

For the first time since 1976, Topps issued a 132-card factory boxed "traded" set in 1981, issued exclusively through hobby dealers. This set was sequentially numbered, alphabetically, from 727 to 858 and carries the same design as the regular issue 1981 Topps set. There are no key Rookie Cards in this set although Hubie Brooks, Tim Raines, Jeff Reardon, and Fernando Valenzuela are depicted in their rookie year for cards. The key extended Rookie Card in the set is Danny Ainge. According to reports at the time, dealers were required to order a minimum of two cases, which cost them $4.50 per set.

COMP.FACT.SET (132) 12.50 30.00
727 Danny Ainge XRC 2.00 5.00
728 Doyle Alexander .08 .25
729 Gary Alexander .08 .25
730 Bill Almon .08 .25
731 Joaquin Andujar .40 1.00
732 Bob Bailor .08 .25
733 Juan Beniquez .08 .25
734 Dave Bergman .08 .25
735 Tony Bernazard .08 .25
736 Larry Biittner .08 .25
737 Doug Bird .08 .25
738 Bert Blyleven .40 1.00
739 Mark Bomback .08 .25
740 Bobby Bonds .40 1.00
741 Rick Bosetti .08 .25
742 Hubie Brooks .75 2.00
743 Rick Burleson .08 .25
744 Ray Burris .08 .25
745 Jeff Burroughs .40 1.00
746 Enos Cabell .08 .25
747 Ken Clay .08 .25
748 Mark Clear .08 .25
749 Larry Cox .08 .25
750 Hector Cruz .08 .25
751 Victor Cruz .08 .25
752 Mike Cubbage .08 .25
753 Dick Davis .08 .25
754 Brian Doyle .08 .25
755 Dick Drago .08 .25
756 Leon Durham .40 1.00
757 Jim Dwyer .08 .25
758 Dave Edwards .08 .25
759 Jim Essian .08 .25
760 Bill Fahey .08 .25
761 Rollie Fingers .40 1.00
762 Carlton Fisk .75 2.00
763 Barry Foote .08 .25
764 Ken Forsch .08 .25
765 Kiko Garcia .08 .25
766 Cesar Geronimo .08 .25
767 Gary Gray XRC .08 .25
768 Mickey Hatcher .08 .25
769 Steve Henderson .08 .25
770 Marc Hill .08 .25
771 Butch Hobson .08 .25
772 Rick Honeycutt .08 .25
773 Roy Howell .08 .25
774 Mike Ivie .08 .25
775 Roy Lee Jackson .08 .25
776 Cliff Johnson .08 .25
777 Randy Jones .40 1.00
778 Ruppert Jones .08 .25
779 Mick Kelleher .08 .25
780 Terry Kennedy .08 .25
781 Dave Kingman .40 1.00
782 Bob Knepper .08 .25
783 Ken Kravec .08 .25
784 Bob Lacey .08 .25
785 Dennis Lamp .08 .25
786 Rafael Landestoy .08 .25
787 Ken Landreaux .08 .25
788 Carney Lansford .40 1.00
789 Dave LaRoche .08 .25
790 Joe Lefebvre .08 .25
791 Ron LeFlore .40 1.00
792 Randy Lerch .08 .25
793 Sixto Lezcano .08 .25
794 John Littlefield .08 .25
795 Mike Lum .08 .25
796 Greg Luzinski .40 1.00
797 Fred Lynn .40 1.00
798 Jerry Martin .08 .25
799 Buck Martinez .08 .25
800 Gary Matthews .40 1.00
801 Mario Mendoza .08 .25
802 Larry Milbourne .08 .25
803 Rick Miller .08 .25
804 John Montefusco .08 .25
805 Jerry Morales .08 .25
806 Jose Morales .08 .25
807 Joe Morgan .75 2.00
808 Jerry Mumphrey .08 .25
809 Gene Nelson XRC .08 .25
810 Ed Ott .08 .25
811 Bob Owchinko .08 .25
812 Gaylord Perry .40 1.00
813 Mike Phillips .08 .25
814 Darrell Porter .08 .25
815 Mike Proly .08 .25
816 Tim Raines 2.00 5.00
817 Lenny Randle .08 .25
818 Doug Rau .08 .25
819 Jeff Reardon .75 2.00
820 Ken Reitz .08 .25
821 Steve Renko .08 .25
822 Rick Reuschel .40 1.00
823 Dave Revering .08 .25
824 Dave Roberts .08 .25
825 Leon Roberts .08 .25
826 Joe Rudi .08 .25
827 Kevin Saucier .08 .25
828 Tony Scott .08 .25
829 Bob Shirley .08 .25
830 Ted Simmons .40 1.00
831 Lary Sorensen .08 .25
832 Jim Spencer .08 .25
833 Harry Spilman .08 .25
834 Fred Stanley .08 .25
835 Rusty Staub .40 1.00
836 Bill Stein .08 .25
837 Joe Strain .08 .25
838 Bruce Sutter .75 2.00
839 Don Sutton .40 1.00
840 Steve Swisher .08 .25
841 Frank Tanana .40 1.00
842 Gene Tenace .40 1.00
843 Jason Thompson .08 .25
844 Dickie Thon .08 .25
845 Bill Travers .08 .25
846 Tom Underwood .08 .25
847 John Urrea .08 .25
848 Mike Vail .08 .25
849 Ellis Valentine .08 .25
850 Fernando Valenzuela 12.00 30.00
851 Pete Vuckovich .08 .25
852 Mark Wagner .08 .25
853 Bob Walk .40 1.00
854 Claudell Washington .08 .25
855 Dave Winfield .75 2.00
856 Geoff Zahn .08 .25
857 Richie Zisk .08 .25
858 Checklist 727-858 .08 .25

1981 Topps Scratchoffs

The cards in this 108-card set measure 1 13/16" by 3 1/4" in a three-card panel measuring 3 1/4" by 5 1/4". The 1981 Topps Scratch-Offs were issued in their own wrapper with bubble gum. The title "Scratch-Off" refers to the black dots of each card which, when rubbed or scraped with a hard edge, reveal a baseball game. While there are only 108 possible individual cards in the set, there are 144 possible panels combinations. The N.L. players appear with green backgrounds and A.L. players with red backgrounds. The numbering of the cards in the set is according to league with American Leaguers (1-54) and National Leaguers (55-108). Some cards are found without dots. An intact panel is worth 20 percent more than the sum of its individual cards. Each card back contained a "wrapper offer" whereby collectors could send a check or money order and one Topps Scratchoffs wrapper and recieve either a "Ball Strike Indicator" ($.90 + one wrapper), a "Topps Super Sports Card Locker" ($6.50) or a "Baseball Hat" ($8.00 + one wrapper). Some cards can be found with different offers on the card backs. Those cards have been noted below.

COMPLETE SET (108) 4.00 10.00
1 George Brett .40 1.00
2 Cecil Cooper .05 .15
3 Reggie Jackson .25 .60
4 Al Oliver .05 .15
5 Fred Lynn .05 .15
6 Tony Armas .02 .10
7 Ben Oglivie .02 .10
8 Tony Perez .20 .50
9 Eddie Murray .25 .60
10 Robin Yount .20 .50
11 Steve Kemp .02 .10
12 Joe Charboneau .02 .10
13 Jim Rice .08 .25
14 Lance Parrish .05 .15
15 John Mayberry .02 .10
16 Richie Zisk .02 .10
17 Ken Singleton .02 .10
18 Rod Carew .20 .50
19 Rick Manning .02 .10
20 Willie Wilson .02 .10
21 Buddy Bell .05 .15
22 Dave Revering .02 .10
23 Tom Paciorek .02 .10
24 Champ Summers .02 .10
25 Carney Lansford .05 .15
26 Lamar Johnson .02 .10
27 Willie Aikens .02 .10
28 Rick Cerone .02 .10
29 Al Bumbry .02 .10
30 Bruce Bochte .02 .10
31 Mickey Rivers .02 .10
32 Mike Hargrove .05 .15
33 John Castino .02 .10
34 Chet Lemon .02 .10
35 Paul Molitor .20 .50
36 Willie Randolph .05 .15
37a Rick Burleson BSI .02 .10
37b Rick Burleson Hat .02 .10
38a Alan Trammell BSI .15 .40
38b Alan Trammell Locker .15 .40
39a Rickey Henderson Hat .40 1.00
39b Rickey Henderson Locker .40 1.00
40a Dan Meyer BSI .02 .10
40b Dan Meyer Hat .02 .10
41a Ken Landreaux BSI .02 .10
41b Ken Landreaux Locker .02 .10
42a Damaso Garcia Hat .02 .10
42b Damaso Garcia Locker .02 .10
43a Roy Smalley BSI .02 .10
43b Roy Smalley Hat .02 .10
44a Otto Velez BSI .02 .10
44b Otto Velez Locker .02 .10
45a Sixto Lezcano Hat .02 .10
45b Sixto Lezcano Locker .02 .10
46a Toby Harrah BSI .05 .15
46b Toby Harrah Hat .05 .15
47a Frank White BSI .05 .15
47b Frank White Locker .05 .15
48a Dave Stapleton Locker .02 .10
48b Dave Stapleton Hat .02 .10
49a Steve Stone BSI .02 .10
49b Steve Stone Hat .02 .10
50a Jim Palmer BSI .20 .50
50b Jim Palmer Locker .20 .50
51a Larry Gura Hat .02 .10
51b Larry Gura Locker .02 .10
52a Tommy John BSI .08 .25
52b Tommy John Hat .08 .25
53a Mike Norris BSI .02 .10
53b Mike Norris Locker .02 .10
54a Ed Farmer Hat .02 .10
54b Ed Farmer Locker .02 .10
55 Bill Buckner .05 .15

56 Steve Garvey .08 .25
57 Reggie Smith .05 .15
58 Bake McBride .02 .10
59 Dave Parker .05 .15
60 Mike Schmidt .30 .75
61 Bob Horner .02 .10
62 Pete Rose .30 .75
63 Ted Simmons .05 .15
64 Johnny Bench .20 .50
65 George Foster .05 .15
66 Gary Carter .20 .50
67 Keith Hernandez .05 .15
68 Ozzie Smith .30 .75
69 Dave Kingman .05 .15
70 Jack Clark .05 .15
71 Dusty Baker .05 .15
72 Dale Murphy .15 .40
73 Ron Cey .05 .15
74 Greg Luzinski .05 .15
75 Lee Mazzilli .02 .10
76 Gary Matthews .02 .10
77 Cesar Cedeno .02 .10
78 Warren Cromartie .02 .10
79 Steve Henderson .02 .10
80 Ellis Valentine .02 .10
81 Mike Easler .02 .10
82 Garry Templeton .02 .10
83 Jose Cruz .05 .15
84 Dave Collins .02 .10
85 George Hendrick .02 .10
86 Gene Richards .02 .10
87 Terry Whitfield .02 .10
88 Terry Puhl .02 .10
89 Larry Parrish .02 .10
90 Andre Dawson .15 .40
91a Ken Griffey Hat .05 .15
91b Ken Griffey BSI .05 .15
92a Dave Lopes BSI .05 .15
92b Dave Lopes Locker .05 .15
93a Doug Flynn Hat .02 .10
93b Doug Flynn Locker .02 .10
94a Ivan DeJesus BSI .02 .10
94b Ivan DeJesus Hat .02 .10
95a Dave Concepcion BSI .05 .15
95b Dave Concepcion Locker .05 .15
96a John Stearns Hat .02 .10
96b John Stearns Locker .02 .10
97a Jerry Mumphrey BSI .02 .10
97b Jerry Mumphrey Hat .02 .10
98a Jerry Martin Locker .02 .10
98b Jerry Martin BSI .02 .10
99a Art Howe Locker .02 .10
99b Art Howe Hat .02 .10
100a Omar Moreno Hat .02 .10
100b Omar Moreno BSI .02 .10
101a Ken Reitz Locker .02 .10
101b Ken Reitz BSI .02 .10
102a Phil Garner Hat .05 .15
102b Phil Garner Locker .05 .15
103a Jerry Reuss Hat .05 .15
103b Jerry Reuss BSI .05 .15
104a Steve Carlton BSI .15 .40
104b Steve Carlton Locker .15 .40
105a Jim Bibby Hat .02 .10
105b Jim Bibby Locker .02 .10
106a Steve Rogers Hat .02 .10
106b Steve Rogers BSI .02 .10
107a Tom Seaver Locker .20 .50
107b Tom Seaver BSI .20 .50
108a Vida Blue Hat .05 .15
108b Vida Blue Locker .05 .15

1981 Topps Stickers

Made for Topps by Panini, an Italian company, these 262 stickers measure 1 15/16" by 2 9/16" and are numbered on both front and back. The set was the first of the Topps/O-Pee-Chee/Panini genre of sticker sets. The fronts feature white-bordered color player action shots. The backs carry the player's name and position. Team affiliations are not shown. An album onto which the stickers could be affixed was available at retail stores. The first 32 stickers depict 1980 major league pitching and batting leaders. Stickers 33-240 are arranged by teams as follows: Baltimore Orioles (33-40), Boston Red Sox (41-48), California Angels (49-56), Chicago White Sox (57-64), Cleveland Indians (65-72), Detroit Tigers (73-80), Kansas City Royals (81-88), Milwaukee Brewers (91-98), Minnesota Twins (99-106), New York Yankees (107-114), Oakland A's (115-122), Seattle Mariners (123-130), Texas Rangers (130-136), Toronto Blue Jays (137-143), Atlanta Braves (144-150), Chicago Cubs (151-158), Cincinnati Reds (159-166), Houston Astros (167-174), Los Angeles Dodgers (175-182), Montreal Expos (183-190), New York Mets (191-198), Philadelphia Phillies (199-208), Pittsburgh Pirates (209-216), St. Louis Cardinals (217-224), San Diego Padres (225-232) and San Francisco Giants (233-240). Stickers 241-262 have color photos of "All-Star" players printed on silver (AL) or gold (NL) foil.

COMPLETE SET (262) 10.00 25.00
COMMON PLAYER (1-240) .02 .05
COMMON FOIL (241-262) .04 .10
1-Jan Steve Stone .01 .05
2-Jan Tommy John .05 .15
Mike Norris
3-Jan Rudy May .01 .05
4-Jan Mike Norris .01 .05
5-Jan Len Barker .01 .05
6-Jan Mike Norris .01 .05
7-Jan Dan Quisenberry .05 .15
8-Jan Rich Gossage .08 .25
9-Jan George Brett 1.00 2.50
10-Jan Cecil Cooper .05 .15
11-Jan Reggie Jackson .15 .40
Ben Oglivie
12-Jan Gorman Thomas .01 .05
13-Jan Cecil Cooper .05 .15
14-Jan George Brett .50 1.25
Ben Oglivie
15-Jan Rickey Henderson 1.00 2.50
16-Jan Willie Wilson .05 .15
17-Jan Bill Buckner .05 .15
18-Jan Keith Hernandez .05 .15
19-Jan Mike Schmidt .60 1.50
20-Jan Bob Horner .01 .05
21-Jan Mike Schmidt .60 1.50
22-Jan George Hendrick .01 .05
23 Ron LeFlore .05 .15
24 Omar Moreno .01 .05
25 Steve Carlton .25 .60
26 Joe Niekro .05 .15
27 Don Sutton .15 .40
28 Steve Carlton .25 .60
29 Steve Carlton .25 .60
30 Nolan Ryan 1.25 3.00
31 Rollie Fingers .05 .15
Tom Hume
32 Bruce Sutter .15 .40
33 Ken Singleton .01 .05
34 Eddie Murray .75 2.00
35 Al Bumbry .01 .05
36 Rich Dauer .01 .05
37 Scott McGregor .01 .05
38 Rick Dempsey .05 .15
39 Jim Palmer .15 .40
40 Steve Stone .01 .05
41 Jim Rice .08 .25
42 Fred Lynn .05 .15
43 Carney Lansford .05 .15
44 Tony Perez .15 .40
45 Carl Yastrzemski .25 .60
46 Carlton Fisk .30 .75
47 Dave Stapleton .01 .05
48 Dennis Eckersley .15 .40
49 Rod Carew .25 .60
50 Brian Downing .05 .15
51 Don Baylor .08 .25
52 Rick Burleson .01 .05
53 Bobby Grich .05 .15
54 Butch Hobson .01 .05
55 Andy Hassler .01 .05
56 Frank Tanana .05 .15
57 Chet Lemon .01 .05
58 Lamar Johnson .01 .05
59 Wayne Nordhagen .01 .05
60 Jim Morrison .01 .05
61 Bob Molinaro .01 .05
62 Rich Dotson .01 .05
63 Britt Burns .01 .05
64 Ed Farmer .01 .05
65 Toby Harrah .05 .15
66 Joe Charboneau .15 .40
67 Miguel Dilone .01 .05
68 Mike Hargrove .05 .15
69 Rick Manning .01 .05
70 Andre Thornton .05 .15
71 Ron Hassey .01 .05
72 Len Barker .01 .05
73 Lance Parrish .05 .15
74 Steve Kemp .01 .05
75 Alan Trammell .30 .75
76 Champ Summers .01 .05
77 Rick Peters .01 .05
78 Kirk Gibson .50 1.25
79 Johnny Wockenfuss .01 .05
80 Jack Morris .08 .25
81 Willie Wilson .05 .15
82 George Brett 1.00 2.50
83 Frank White .05 .15
84 Willie Aikens .01 .05
85 Clint Hurdle .05 .15
86 Hal McRae .05 .15
87 Dennis Leonard .01 .05
88 Larry Gura .01 .05
89 Kansas City Royals .01 .05
AL Pennant Winner
90 Kansas City Royals .01 .05
AL Pennant Winner
91 Paul Molitor .60 1.50
92 Ben Oglivie .05 .15
93 Cecil Cooper .05 .15
94 Ted Simmons .05 .15
95 Robin Yount .30 .75
96 Gorman Thomas .01 .05
97 Mike Caldwell .01 .05
98 Moose Haas .01 .05
99 John Castino .01 .05
100 Roy Smalley .01 .05
101 Ken Landreaux .01 .05
102 Butch Wynegar .01 .05
103 Ron Jackson .01 .05
104 Jerry Koosman .05 .15
105 Roger Erickson .01 .05
106 Doug Corbett .01 .05
107 Reggie Jackson .30 .75
108 Willie Randolph .05 .15
109 Rick Cerone .01 .05
110 Bucky Dent .05 .15
111 Dave Winfield .30 .75
112 Ron Guidry .05 .15
113 Rich Gossage .08 .25
114 Tommy John .08 .25
115 Rickey Henderson 1.00 2.50
116 Tony Armas .01 .05
117 Dave Revering .01 .05
118 Wayne Gross .01 .05
119 Dwayne Murphy .01 .05
120 Jeff Newman .01 .05
121 Rick Langford .01 .05
122 Mike Norris .01 .05
123 Bruce Bochte .01 .05
124 Tom Paciorek .05 .15
125 Dan Meyer .01 .05
126 Julio Cruz .01 .05
127 Richie Zisk .01 .05
128 Floyd Bannister .01 .05
129 Shane Rawley .01 .05
130 Buddy Bell .05 .15
131 Al Oliver .05 .15
132 Mickey Rivers .05 .15
133 Jim Sundberg .05 .15
134 Bump Wills .01 .05
135 Jon Matlack .01 .05
136 Danny Darwin .05 .15
137 Damaso Garcia .01 .05
138 Otto Velez .01 .05
139 John Mayberry .01 .05
140 Alfredo Griffin .01 .05
141 Alvis Woods .01 .05
142 Dave Stieb .05 .15
143 Jim Clancy .01 .05
144 Gary Matthews .05 .15
145 Bob Horner .05 .15
146 Dale Murphy .15 .40
147 Chris Chambliss .05 .15
148 Phil Niekro .15 .40
149 Glenn Hubbard .01 .05
150 Rick Camp .01 .05
151 Dave Kingman .08 .25
152 Bill Caudill .01 .05
153 Bill Buckner .05 .15
154 Barry Foote .01 .05
155 Mike Tyson .01 .05
156 Ivan DeJesus .01 .05
157 Rick Reuschel .05 .15
158 Ken Reitz .01 .05
159 George Foster .05 .15
160 Johnny Bench .30 .75
161 Dave Concepcion .05 .15
162 Dave Collins .01 .05
163 Ken Griffey .05 .15
164 Dan Driessen .01 .05
165 Tom Seaver .30 .75
166 Tom Hume .01 .05
167 Cesar Cedeno .05 .15
168 Rafael Landestoy .01 .05
169 Jose Cruz .05 .15
170 Art Howe .01 .05
171 Terry Puhl .01 .05
172 Joe Sambito .01 .05
173 Nolan Ryan 1.25 3.00
174 Joe Niekro .05 .15
175 Dave Lopes .05 .15
176 Steve Garvey .15 .40
177 Ron Cey .05 .15
178 Reggie Smith .05 .15
179 Bill Russell .05 .15
180 Burt Hooton .01 .05
181 Jerry Reuss .05 .15
182 Dusty Baker .05 .15
183 Larry Parrish .01 .05
184 Gary Carter .15 .40
185 Rodney Scott .01 .05
186 Ellis Valentine .01 .05
187 Andre Dawson .30 .75
188 Warren Cromartie .01 .05
189 Chris Speier .01 .05
190 Steve Rogers .01 .05
191 Lee Mazzilli .01 .05
192 Doug Flynn .01 .05
193 Steve Henderson .01 .05
194 John Stearns .01 .05
195 Joel Youngblood .01 .05
196 Frank Taveras .01 .05
197 Pat Zachry .01 .05
198 Neil Allen .01 .05
199 Mike Schmidt .60 1.50
200 Pete Rose .50 1.25
201 Larry Bowa .05 .15
202 Bake McBride .01 .05
203 Bob Boone .05 .15
204 Garry Maddox .01 .05
205 Tug McGraw .05 .15
206 Steve Carlton .15 .40
207 Philadelphia Phillies .01 .05
NL Pennant Winner/World Champions
208 Philadelphia Phillies .01 .05
NL Pennant Winner/World Champions
209 Phil Garner .05 .15
210 Dave Parker .05 .15
211 Omar Moreno .01 .05
212 Mike Easler .01 .05
213 Bill Madlock .05 .15
214 Ed Ott .01 .05
215 Willie Stargell .15 .40
216 Jim Bibby .01 .05
217 Garry Templeton .01 .05
218 Sixto Lezcano .01 .05
219 Keith Hernandez .05 .15
220 George Hendrick .01 .05
221 Bruce Sutter .15 .40
222 Ken Oberkfell .01 .05
223 Tony Scott .01 .05
224 Darrell Porter .05 .15
225 Gene Richards .01 .05
226 Broderick Perkins .01 .05
227 Jerry Mumphrey .01 .05
228 Luis Salazar .01 .05
229 Jerry Turner .01 .05
230 Ozzie Smith 1.00 2.50
231 John Curtis .01 .05
232 Rick Wise .01 .05
233 Terry Whitfield .01 .05
234 Jack Clark .05 .15
235 Darrell Evans .05 .15
236 Larry Herndon .01 .05
237 Milt May .01 .05
238 Greg Minton .01 .05
239 Vida Blue .05 .15
240 Eddie Whitson .01 .05
241 Cecil Cooper FOIL .08 .25
242 Willie Randolph FOIL .05 .15
243 George Brett FOIL 1.25 3.00
244 Robin Yount FOIL .40 1.00
245 Reggie Jackson FOIL .40 1.00
246 Al Oliver FOIL .08 .25
247 Willie Wilson FOIL .08 .25
248 Rick Cerone FOIL .02 .10
249 Steve Stone FOIL .02 .10
250 Tommy John FOIL .08 .25
251 Rich Gossage FOIL .08 .25
252 Steve Garvey FOIL .08 .25
253 Phil Garner FOIL .05 .15
254 Mike Schmidt FOIL .75 2.00
255 Garry Templeton FOIL .02 .10
256 George Hendrick FOIL .02 .10
257 Dave Parker FOIL .08 .25
258 Cesar Cedeno FOIL .08 .25
259 Gary Carter FOIL .15 .40
260 Jim Bibby FOIL .02 .10
261 Steve Carlton FOIL .30 .75
262 Tug McGraw FOIL .08 .25
NNO Album .40 1.00

1981 Topps Super Home Team

The cards in this 102-card set measure 4 7/8" by 6 7/8". In 1981 Topps issued an attractive series of photos of players from eleven AL and NL teams. The Phillies, Red Sox and Reds each were marketed in twelve-player subsets. Eighteen-player subsets were issued for the following areas: Chicago (nine White Sox and nine Cubs); New York (twelve Yankees and six Mets); Los Angeles (twelve Dodgers and six Angels); and Texas (six Rangers and six Astros). The cards of each subset contain a subset checklist on the reverse. Team sets could be obtained via a mail offer printed on the wrapper. These cards are often sold by the team or team pair. The checklist below is organized alphabetically by team(s); Boston (1-12), Chicago (13-30), Cincinnati (31-42), Los Angeles (43-60), New York (61-78), Philadelphia (79-90) and Texas (91-102).

COMPLETE SET (102) 12.50 30.00
1 Tom Burgmeier .02 .10
2 Dennis Eckersley .40 1.00
3 Dwight Evans .20 .50
4 Carlton Fisk .40 1.00
5 Glenn Hoffman .02 .10
6 Carney Lansford .08 .25
7 Tony Perez .40 1.00
8 Jim Rice .20 .50
9 Bob Stanley .02 .10
10 Dave Stapleton .02 .10
11 Frank Tanana .08 .25
12 Carl Yastrzemski .50 1.25
13 Britt Burns .08 .25
14 Rich Dotson .08 .25
15 Ed Farmer .02 .10
16 Lamar Johnson .02 .10
17 Ron LeFlore .02 .10
18 Chet Lemon .02 .10
19 Bob Molinaro .02 .10
20 Jim Morrison .02 .10
21 Wayne Nordhagen .02 .10
22 Tim Blackwell .02 .10
23 Bill Buckner .08 .25
24 Ivan DeJesus .02 .10
25 Leon Durham .08 .25
26 Dave Kingman .20 .50
27 Mike Krukow .02 .10
28 Ken Reitz .02 .10
29 Rick Reuschel .08 .25
30 Mike Tyson .02 .10
31 Johnny Bench .60 1.50
32 Dave Collins .02 .10
33 Dave Concepcion .08 .25
34 Dan Driessen .02 .10
35 George Foster .08 .25
36 Ken Griffey .08 .25
37 Tom Hume .02 .10
38 Ray Knight .02 .10
39 Joe Nolan .02 .10
40 Ron Oester .02 .10
41 Tom Seaver .60 1.50
42 Mario Soto .02 .10
43 Dusty Baker .08 .25
44 Ron Cey .08 .25
45 Steve Garvey .20 .50
46 Burt Hooton .02 .10
47 Steve Howe .02 .10
48 Davey Lopes .08 .25
49 Rick Monday .08 .25
50 Jerry Reuss .08 .25
51 Bill Russell .08 .25
52 Reggie Smith .08 .25
53 Bob Welch .08 .25
54 Steve Yeager .02 .10
55 Don Baylor .20 .50
56 Rick Burleson .02 .10
57 Rod Carew .40 1.00
58 Bobby Grich .08 .25
59 Butch Hobson .02 .10
60 Fred Lynn .08 .25
61 Rick Cerone .02 .10
62 Bucky Dent .08 .25
63 Rich Gossage .20 .50
64 Ron Guidry .08 .25
65 Reggie Jackson .50 1.25
66 Tommy John .20 .50
67 Ruppert Jones .02 .10
68 Rudy May .02 .10
69 Graig Nettles .20 .50
70 Willie Randolph .08 .25
71 Bob Watson .20 .50
72 Dave Winfield .60 1.50
73 Neil Allen .02 .10
74 Doug Flynn .02 .10
75 Lee Mazzilli .02 .10
76 Rusty Staub .08 .25
77 Frank Taveras .02 .10
78 Alex Trevino .02 .10
79 Bob Boone .08 .25
80 Larry Bowa .08 .25
81 Steve Carlton .40 1.00
82 Greg Luzinski .08 .25
83 Garry Maddox .02 .10
84 Bake McBride .02 .10
85 Tug McGraw .08 .25
86 Pete Rose .50 1.25
87 Dick Ruthven .02 .10
88 Mike Schmidt .50 1.25
89 Manny Trillo .02 .10
90 Del Unser .02 .10
91 Buddy Bell .08 .25
92 Jon Matlack .02 .10
93 Al Oliver .08 .25
94 Mickey Rivers .08 .25
95 Jim Sundberg .08 .25
96 Bump Wills .02 .10
97 Cesar Cedeno .08 .25
98 Jose Cruz .08 .25
99 Art Howe .02 .10
100 Terry Puhl .02 .10
101 Nolan Ryan 1.25 3.00
102 Don Sutton .40 1.00

1981 Topps Super National

The cards in this 15-card set measure 4 7/8" by 6 7/8". In a format similar to the Home Team series of 1981 and the Super Star Photo set of 1980, these cards feature excellent photos of the top stars of 1981. The pictures of players appearing in both the regional Home Team and National sets are identical, but Brett, Cooper, Palmer, Parker and Simmons are unique to the latter and are indicated in the checklist below with an asterisk. The backs of the cards contain the player's name, team and position and a single copyright line.

COMPLETE SET (15) 1.50 4.00
1 Buddy Bell .07 .20
2 Johnny Bench .20 .50
3 George Brett .40 1.00
4 Rod Carew .20 .50
5 Cecil Cooper .02 .10
6 Steve Garvey .10 .30
7 Rich Gossage .07 .20
8 Reggie Jackson .20 .50
9 Jim Palmer .20 .50
10 Dave Parker .07 .20
11 Jim Rice .07 .20
12 Pete Rose .30 .75
13 Mike Schmidt .30 .75
14 Tom Seaver .20 .50
15 Ted Simmons .07 .20

1981 Topps Team Checklist Sheet

As part of a mail-away offer, Topps offered all 26 1981 team checklist cards on an uncut sheet. These cards enabled the collector to have an easy reference for which card(s) he/she needed to finish their sets. When cut form the sheet, all cards measure the standard size.

1 Team Checklist Sheet 15.00 40.00

1982 Topps

The cards in this 792-card set measure the standard size. Cards were primarily distributed in 15-card wax packs and 51-card rack packs. The 1982 baseball series was the first of the largest sets Topps issued at one printing. The 66-card increase from the previous year's total eliminated the "double print" practice, that had occurred in every regular issue since 1978. Cards 1-6 depict Highlights of the strike-shortened 1981 season, cards 161-168 picture League Leaders, and there are subsets of AL (547-557) and NL (337-347) All-Stars (AS). The abbreviation "IA" in the checklist is given for the 40 "In Action" cards introduced in this set. The team cards are actually Team Leader (TL) cards picturing the batting average and ERA leader for that team with a checklist back. All 26 of these cards were available from Topps on a perforated sheet through an offer on wax pack wrappers. Notable Rookie Cards include Brett Butler, Chili Davis, Cal Ripken Jr., Lee Smith, and Dave Stewart. Be careful when purchasing blank-back Cal Ripken Jr. Rookie Cards. Those cards are extremely likely to be counterfeit.

COMPLETE SET (792) 30.00 80.00
1 Steve Carlton HL .10 .30
2 Ron Davis HL .05 .15
3 Tim Raines HL .10 .30
4 Pete Rose HL .25 .60
5 Nolan Ryan HL 1.25 3.00
6 Fernando Valenzuela HL .25 .60
7 Scott Sanderson .05 .15
8 Rich Dauer .05 .15
9 Ron Guidry .10 .30
10 Ron Guidry IA .05 .15
11 Gary Alexander .05 .15
12 Moose Haas .05 .15
13 Lamar Johnson .05 .15
14 Steve Howe .05 .15
15 Ellis Valentine .05 .15
16 Steve Comer .05 .15
17 Darrell Evans .10 .30
18 Fernando Arroyo .05 .15
19 Ernie Whitt .05 .15
20 Garry Maddox .05 .15
21 Cal Ripken RC 20.00 50.00
22 Jim Beattie .05 .15
23 Willie Hernandez .05 .15
24 Dave Frost .05 .15
25 Jerry Remy .05 .15
26 Jorge Orta .05 .15
27 Tom Herr .05 .15
28 John Urrea .05 .15
29 Dwayne Murphy .05 .15
30 Tom Seaver .50 1.25
31 Tom Seaver IA .10 .30
32 Gene Garber .05 .15
33 Jerry Morales .05 .15
34 Joe Sambito .05 .15
35 Willie Aikens .05 .15
36 Al Oliver .25 .60
Doc Medich TL
37 Dan Graham .05 .15
38 Charlie Lea .05 .15
39 Lou Whitaker .10 .30
40 Dave Parker .10 .30
41 Dave Parker IA .05 .15
42 Rick Sofield .05 .15
43 Mike Cubbage .05 .15
44 Britt Burns .05 .15
45 Rick Cerone .05 .15
46 Jerry Augustine .05 .15
47 Jeff Leonard .05 .15
48 Bobby Castillo .05 .15
49 Alvis Woods .05 .15
50 Buddy Bell .10 .30
51 Howell/Lezcano/Waller RC .30 .75
52 Larry Andersen .05 .15
53 Greg Gross .05 .15
54 Ron Hassey .05 .15
55 Rick Burleson .05 .15
56 Mark Littell .05 .15
57 Craig Reynolds .05 .15
58 John D'Acquisto .05 .15
59 Rich Gedman .30 .75
60 Tony Armas .10 .30
61 Tommy Boggs .05 .15
62 Mike Tyson .05 .15
63 Mario Soto .10 .30
64 Lynn Jones .05 .15
65 Terry Kennedy .05 .15
66 A.Howe/N.Ryan TL .75 2.00
67 Rich Gale .05 .15
68 Roy Howell .05 .15
69 Al Williams .05 .15
70 Tim Raines .25 .60
71 Roy Lee Jackson .05 .15
72 Rick Auerbach .05 .15
73 Buddy Solomon .05 .15
74 Bob Clark .05 .15
75 Tommy John .10 .30
76 Greg Pryor .05 .15
77 Miguel Dilone .05 .15
78 George Medich .05 .15
79 Bob Bailor .05 .15
80 Jim Palmer .10 .30
81 Jim Palmer IA .05 .15
82 Bob Welch .10 .30
83 Balboni/McGaf/Rob RC .30 .75
84 Rennie Stennett .05 .15
85 Lynn McGlothen .05 .15
86 Dane Iorg .05 .15
87 Matt Keough .05 .15
88 Biff Pocoroba .05 .15
89 Steve Henderson .05 .15
90 Nolan Ryan 2.50 6.00
91 Carney Lansford .10 .30
92 Brad Havens .05 .15
93 Larry Hisle .05 .15
94 Andy Hassler .05 .15
95 Ozzie Smith 1.00 2.50
96 George Brett .50 1.25
Larry Gura TL
97 Paul Moskau .05 .15
98 Terry Bulling .05 .15
99 Barry Bonnell .05 .15
100 Mike Schmidt 1.25 3.00
101 Mike Schmidt IA .50 1.25
102 Dan Briggs .05 .15
103 Bob Lacey .05 .15
104 Rance Mulliniks .05 .15
105 Kirk Gibson .50 1.25
106 Enrique Romo .05 .15
107 Wayne Krenchicki .05 .15
108 Bob Sykes .05 .15
109 Dave Revering .05 .15
110 Carlton Fisk .25 .60
111 Carlton Fisk IA .10 .30
112 Billy Sample .05 .15
113 Steve McCatty .05 .15
114 Ken Landreaux .05 .15
115 Gaylord Perry .10 .30
116 Jim Wohlford .05 .15
117 Rawly Eastwick .10 .30
118 Francona/Mills/Smith RC 2.00 5.00
119 Joe Pittman .05 .15
120 Gary Lucas .05 .15
121 Ed Lynch .05 .15
122 Jamie Easterly UER .05 .15
Photo actually/Reggie Cleveland
123 Danny Goodwin .05 .15
124 Reid Nichols .05 .15
125 Danny Ainge .10 .30
126 Claudell Washington .25 .60
Rick Mahler TL
127 Lonnie Smith .05 .15
128 Frank Pastore .05 .15
129 Checklist 1-132 .10 .30
130 Julio Cruz .05 .15
131 Stan Bahnsen .05 .15
132 Lee May .05 .15
133 Pat Underwood .05 .15
134 Dan Ford .05 .15
135 Andy Rincon .05 .15
136 Lenn Sakata .05 .15
137 George Cappuzzello .05 .15
138 Tony Pena .10 .30
139 Jeff Jones .05 .15
140 Ron LeFlore .10 .30
141 Bando/Brennan/Hayes RC .30 .75
142 Dave LaRoche .05 .15
143 Mookie Wilson .10 .30
144 Fred Breining .05 .15
145 Bob Horner .10 .30
146 Mike Griffin .05 .15
147 Denny Walling .05 .15
148 Mickey Klutts .05 .15
149 Pat Putnam .05 .15
150 Ted Simmons .10 .30
151 Dave Edwards .05 .15
152 Ramon Aviles .05 .15
153 Roger Erickson .05 .15
154 Dennis Werth .05 .15
155 Otto Velez .05 .15
156 Rickey Henderson .50 1.25
Steve McCatty TL
157 Steve Crawford .05 .15
158 Brian Downing .10 .30
159 Larry Biittner .05 .15
160 Luis Tiant .10 .30
161 Bill Madlock/Carney Lansford LL .10 .30
162 Mike Schmidt .50 1.25
Tony Armas/Dwight Evans/Bobby Grich/Eddie Murray LL
163 Mike Schmidt .50 1.25
Eddie Murray LL
164 Tim Raines .50 1.25
Rickey Henderson LL
165 Seav/Martinez/Morris LL .10 .30
166 Strikeout Leaders/Fernando
Valenzuela/Len Barker .10 .30
167 N.Ryan/S.McCatty LL .75 2.00
168 Bruce Sutter .10 .30
Rollie Fingers LL
169 Charlie Leibrandt .05 .15
170 Jim Bibby .05 .15
171 Brenly/Davis/Tufts RC .60 1.50
172 Bill Gullickson .05 .15
173 Jamie Quirk .05 .15
174 Dave Ford .05 .15
175 Jerry Mumphrey .05 .15
176 Dewey Robinson .05 .15
177 John Ellis .05 .15
178 Dyar Miller .05 .15
179 Steve Garvey .10 .30
180 Steve Garvey IA .05 .15
181 Silvio Martinez .05 .15
182 Larry Herndon .05 .15
183 Mike Proly .05 .15
184 Mick Kelleher .05 .15
185 Phil Niekro .10 .30
186 Keith Hernandez .10 .30
Bob Forsch TL
187 Jeff Newman .05 .15
188 Randy Martz .05 .15
189 Glenn Hoffman .05 .15
190 J.R. Richard .10 .30
191 Tim Wallach RC .60 1.50
192 Broderick Perkins .05 .15
193 Darrell Jackson .05 .15
194 Mike Vail .05 .15
195 Paul Molitor .10 .30
196 Willie Upshaw .30 .75
197 Shane Rawley .05 .15
198 Chris Speier .05 .15
199 Don Aase .05 .15
200 George Brett 1.25 3.00
201 George Brett IA .60 1.50
202 Rick Manning .05 .15
203 Barfield/Miln/Wells RC .60 1.50
204 Gary Roenicke .05 .15
205 Neil Allen .05 .15
206 Tony Bernazard .05 .15
207 Rod Scurry .05 .15
208 Bobby Murcer .10 .30
209 Gary Lavelle .05 .15
210 Keith Hernandez .10 .30
211 Dan Petry .05 .15
212 Mario Mendoza .05 .15
213 Dave Stewart RC 1.00 2.50
214 Brian Asselstine .05 .15
215 Mike Krukow .05 .15
216 Chet Lemon .25 .60
Dennis Lamp TL
217 Bo McLaughlin .05 .15
218 Dave Roberts .05 .15
219 John Curtis .05 .15
220 Manny Trillo .05 .15
221 Jim Slaton .05 .15
222 Butch Wynegar .05 .15
223 Lloyd Moseby .05 .15
224 Bruce Bochte .05 .15
225 Mike Torrez .05 .15
226 Checklist 133-264 .25 .60
227 Ray Burris .05 .15
228 Sam Mejias .05 .15
229 Geoff Zahn .05 .15
230 Willie Wilson .10 .30
231 Davis/Dernier/Virgil RC .30 .75
232 Terry Crowley .05 .15
233 Duane Kuiper .05 .15
234 Ron Hodges .05 .15
235 Mike Easler .05 .15
236 John Martin RC .08 .25
237 Rusty Kuntz .05 .15
238 Kevin Saucier .05 .15
239 Jon Matlack .05 .15
240 Bucky Dent .10 .30
241 Bucky Dent IA .05 .15
242 Milt May .05 .15
243 Bob Owchinko .05 .15
244 Rufino Linares .05 .15
245 Ken Reitz .05 .15
246 Hubie Brooks .25 .60
Mike Scott TL
247 Pedro Guerrero .10 .30
248 Frank LaCorte .05 .15
249 Tim Flannery .05 .15
250 Tug McGraw .10 .30
251 Fred Lynn .10 .30
252 Fred Lynn IA .05 .15
253 Chuck Baker .05 .15
254 Jorge Bell RC .60 1.50
George Bell
255 Tony Perez .25 .60
256 Tony Perez IA .10 .30
257 Larry Harlow .05 .15
258 Bo Diaz .05 .15
259 Rodney Scott .05 .15
260 Bruce Sutter .25 .60
261 Bailey/Castillo/Rucker RC .05 .15
262 Doug Bair .05 .15
263 Victor Cruz .05 .15
264 Dan Quisenberry .05 .15
265 Al Bumbry .05 .15
266 Rick Leach .05 .15
267 Kurt Bevacqua .05 .15
268 Rickey Keeton .05 .15
269 Jim Essian .05 .15
270 Rusty Staub .10 .30
271 Larry Bradford .05 .15
272 Bump Wills .05 .15
273 Doug Bird .05 .15
274 Bob Ojeda RC .30 .75
275 Bob Watson .05 .15
276 Rod Carew .25 .60
Ken Forsch TL
277 Terry Puhl .05 .15
278 John Littlefield .05 .15
279 Bill Russell .10 .30
280 Ben Oglivie .10 .30
281 John Verhoeven .05 .15
282 Ken Macha .05 .15
283 Brian Allard .05 .15
284 Bobby Grich .10 .30
285 Sparky Lyle .10 .30
286 Bill Fahey .05 .15
287 Alan Bannister .05 .15
288 Garry Templeton .10 .30
289 Bob Stanley .05 .15
290 Ken Singleton .10 .30
291 Law/Long/Ray RC .10 .30
292 David Palmer .05 .15
293 Rob Picciolo .05 .15
294 Mike LaCoss .05 .15
295 Jason Thompson .05 .15
296 Bob Walk .05 .15
297 Clint Hurdle .05 .15
298 Danny Darwin .05 .15
299 Steve Trout .05 .15
300 Reggie Jackson .25 .60
301 Reggie Jackson IA .10 .30
302 Doug Flynn .05 .15
303 Bill Caudill .05 .15
304 Johnnie LeMaster .05 .15
305 Don Sutton .10 .30
306 Don Sutton IA .05 .15
307 Randy Bass .30 .75
308 Charlie Moore .05 .15
309 Pete Redfern .05 .15
310 Mike Hargrove .05 .15
311 Dusty Baker .10 .30
Burt Hooton TL
312 Lenny Randle .05 .15
313 John Harris .05 .15
314 Buck Martinez .05 .15

315 Burt Hooton .05 .15
316 Steve Braun .05 .15
317 Dick Ruthven .05 .15
318 Mike Heath .05 .15
319 Dave Rozema .05 .15
320 Chris Chambliss .10 .30
321 Chris Chambliss IA .05 .15
322 Garry Hancock .05 .15
323 Bill Lee .10 .30
324 Steve Dillard .05 .15
325 Jose Cruz .10 .30
326 Pete Falcone .05 .15
327 Joe Nolan .05 .15
328 Ed Farmer .05 .15
329 U.L. Washington .05 .15
330 Rick Wise .05 .15
331 Benny Ayala .05 .15
332 Don Robinson .05 .15
333 DiPino/Edwards/Porter RC .05 .15
334 Aurelio Rodriguez .05 .15
335 Jim Sundberg .10 .30
336 Tom Paciorek .25 .60
Glenn Abbott TL
337 Pete Rose AS .25 .60
338 Dave Lopes AS .05 .15
339 Mike Schmidt AS .50 1.25
340 Dave Concepcion AS .05 .15
341 Andre Dawson AS .05 .15
342A George Foster AS w/Auto .10 .30
342B George Foster AS w/o Auto .50 1.25
343 Dave Parker AS .05 .15
344 Gary Carter AS .05 .15
345 Fernando Valenzuela AS .25 .60
346 Tom Seaver AS ERR .10 .30
't ed'
346B Tom Seaver AS COR .10 .30
347 Bruce Sutter AS .10 .30
348 Derrel Thomas .05 .15
349 George Frazier .05 .15
350 Thad Bosley .05 .15
351 Brown/Comb/House RC .05 .15
352 Dick Davis .05 .15
353 Jack O'Connor .05 .15
354 Roberto Ramos .05 .15
355 Dwight Evans .25 .60
356 Denny Lewallyn .05 .15
357 Butch Hobson .05 .15
358 Mike Parrott .05 .15
359 Jim Dwyer .05 .15
360 Len Barker .05 .15
361 Rafael Landestoy .05 .15
362 Jim Wright UER .05 .15
Wrong Jim Wright/pictured
363 Bob Molinaro .05 .15
364 Doyle Alexander .05 .15
365 Bill Madlock .10 .30
366 Luis Salazar .25 .60
Juan Eichelberger TL
367 Jim Kaat .10 .30
368 Alex Trevino .05 .15
369 Champ Summers .05 .15
370 Mike Norris .05 .15
371 Jerry Don Gleaton .05 .15
372 Luis Gomez .05 .15
373 Gene Nelson .05 .15
374 Tim Blackwell .05 .15
375 Dusty Baker .10 .30
376 Chris Welsh .05 .15
377 Kiko Garcia .05 .15
378 Mike Caldwell .05 .15
379 Rob Wilfong .05 .15
380 Dave Stieb .10 .30
381 Bruce Hurst .05 .15
Dave Schmidt RC/Julio Valdez RC
382 Joe Simpson .05 .15
383A Pascual Perez ERR 15.00 40.00
383B Pascual Perez COR .10 .30
384 Keith Moreland .05 .15
385 Ken Forsch .05 .15
386 Jerry White .05 .15
387 Tom Veryzer .05 .15
388 Joe Rudi .10 .30
389 George Vukovich .05 .15
390 Eddie Murray .50 1.25
391 Dave Tobik .05 .15
392 Rick Bosetti .05 .15
393 Al Hrabosky .05 .15
394 Checklist 265-396 .25 .60
395 Omar Moreno .05 .15
396 John Castino .25 .60
Fernando Arroyo TL
397 Ken Brett .05 .15
398 Mike Squires .05 .15
399 Pat Zachry .05 .15
400 Johnny Bench .50 1.25
401 Johnny Bench IA .25 .60
402 Bill Stein .05 .15
403 Jim Tracy .10 .30
404 Dickie Thon .05 .15
405 Rick Reuschel .10 .30
406 Al Holland .05 .15
407 Danny Boone .05 .15
408 Ed Romero .05 .15
409 Don Cooper .05 .15
410 Ron Cey .10 .30
411 Ron Cey IA .05 .15
412 Luis Leal .05 .15
413 Dan Meyer .05 .15
414 Elias Sosa .05 .15
415 Don Baylor .10 .30
416 Marty Bystrom .05 .15
417 Pat Kelly .05 .15
418 Butcher/John/Schmidt RC .05 .15
419 Steve Stone .05 .15
420 George Hendrick .10 .30
421 Mark Clear .05 .15
422 Cliff Johnson .05 .15
423 Stan Papi .05 .15
424 Bruce Benedict .05 .15
425 John Candelaria .05 .15
426 Eddie Murray .25 .60
Sammy Stewart
427 Ron Oester .05 .15
428 LaMarr Hoyt .05 .15
429 John Wathan .05 .15
430 Vida Blue .10 .30
431 Vida Blue IA .05 .15
432 Mike Scott .10 .30
433 Alan Ashby .05 .15
434 Joe Lefebvre .05 .15
435 Robin Yount .75 2.00
436 Joe Strain .05 .15
437 Juan Berenguer .05 .15
438 Pete Mackanin .05 .15
439 Dave Righetti RC 1.00 2.50
440 Jeff Burroughs .05 .15
441 Heep/Smith/Sprowl RC .05 .15
442 Bruce Kison .05 .15
443 Mark Wagner .05 .15
444 Terry Forster .10 .30
445 Larry Parrish .05 .15
446 Wayne Garland .05 .15
447 Darrell Porter .05 .15
448 Darrell Porter IA .05 .15
449 Luis Aguayo .05 .15
450 Jack Morris .10 .30
451 Ed Miller .05 .15
452 Lee Smith RC 1.25 3.00
453 Art Howe .05 .15
454 Rick Langford .05 .15
455 Tom Burgmeier .05 .15
456 Bill Buckner .10 .30
Randy Martz TL
457 Tim Stoddard .05 .15
458 Willie Montanez .05 .15
459 Bruce Berenyi .05 .15
460 Jack Clark .10 .30
461 Rich Dotson .05 .15
462 Dave Chalk .05 .15
463 Jim Kern .05 .15
464 Juan Bonilla RC .08 .25
465 Lee Mazzilli .10 .30
466 Randy Lerch .05 .15
467 Mickey Hatcher .05 .15
468 Floyd Bannister .05 .15
469 Ed Ott .05 .15
470 John Mayberry .05 .15
471 Hammaker/Jones/Motley RC .05 .15
472 Oscar Gamble .05 .15
473 Mike Stanton .05 .15
474 Ken Oberkfell .05 .15
475 Alan Trammell .10 .30
476 Brian Kingman .05 .15
477 Steve Yeager .10 .30
478 Ray Searage .05 .15
479 Rowland Office .05 .15
480 Steve Carlton .25 .60
481 Steve Carlton IA .10 .30
482 Glenn Hubbard .05 .15
483 Gary Woods .05 .15
484 Ivan DeJesus .05 .15
485 Kent Tekulve .05 .15
486 Jerry Mumphrey .10 .30
Tommy John TL
487 Bob McClure .05 .15
488 Ron Jackson .05 .15
489 Rick Dempsey .05 .15
490 Dennis Eckersley .25 .60
491 Checklist 397-528 .25 .60
492 Joe Price .05 .15
493 Chet Lemon .10 .30
494 Hubie Brooks .05 .15
495 Dennis Leonard .05 .15
496 Johnny Grubb .05 .15
497 Jim Anderson .05 .15
498 Dave Bergman .05 .15
499 Paul Mirabella .05 .15
500 Rod Carew .25 .60
501 Rod Carew IA .10 .30
502 Steve Bedrosian RC UER .60 1.50
Photo actually Larry Owen/Brett Butler RC/Larry Owen
503 Julio Gonzalez .05 .15
504 Rick Peters .05 .15
505 Graig Nettles .10 .30
506 Graig Nettles IA .05 .15
507 Terry Harper .05 .15
508 Jody Davis RC .05 .15
509 Harry Spilman .05 .15
510 Fernando Valenzuela .50 1.25
511 Ruppert Jones .05 .15
512 Jerry Dybzinski .05 .15
513 Rick Rhoden .05 .15
514 Joe Ferguson .05 .15
515 Larry Bowa .10 .30
516 Larry Bowa IA .05 .15
517 Mark Brouhard .05 .15
518 Garth Iorg .05 .15
519 Glenn Adams .05 .15
520 Mike Flanagan .05 .15
521 Bill Almon .05 .15
522 Chuck Rainey .05 .15
523 Gary Gray .05 .15
524 Tom Hausman .05 .15
525 Ray Knight .10 .30
526 Warren Cromartie .25 .60
Bill Gullickson TL
527 John Henry Johnson .05 .15
528 Matt Alexander .05 .15
529 Allen Ripley .05 .15
530 Dickie Noles .05 .15
531 Bordi/Budaska/Moore RC .05 .15
532 Toby Harrah .10 .30
533 Joaquin Andujar .10 .30
534 Dave McKay .05 .15
535 Lance Parrish .10 .30
536 Rafael Ramirez .05 .15
537 Doug Capilla .05 .15
538 Lou Piniella .10 .30
539 Vern Ruhle .05 .15
540 Andre Dawson .10 .30
541 Barry Evans .05 .15
542 Ned Yost .05 .15
543 Bill Robinson .05 .15
544 Larry Christenson .05 .15
545 Reggie Smith .10 .30
546 Reggie Smith IA .05 .15
547 Rod Carew AS .10 .30
548 Willie Randolph AS .05 .15
549 George Brett AS .60 1.50
550 Bucky Dent AS .05 .15
551 Reggie Jackson AS .10 .30
552 Ken Singleton AS .05 .15
553 Dave Winfield AS .05 .15
554 Carlton Fisk AS .10 .30
555 Scott McGregor AS .05 .15
556 Jack Morris AS .05 .15
557 Rich Gossage AS .05 .15
558 John Tudor .10 .30
559 Mike Hargrove .10 .30
Bert Blyleven TL
560 Doug Corbett .05 .15
561 Brum/DeLeon/Roof RC .05 .15
562 Mike O'Berry .05 .15
563 Ross Baumgarten .05 .15
564 Doug DeCinces .05 .15
565 Jackson Todd .05 .15
566 Mike Jorgensen .05 .15
567 Bob Babcock .05 .15
568 Joe Pettini .05 .15
569 Willie Randolph .10 .30
570 Willie Randolph IA .05 .15
571 Glenn Abbott .05 .15
572 Juan Beniquez .05 .15
573 Rick Waits .05 .15
574 Mike Ramsey .05 .15
575 Al Cowens .05 .15
576 Milt May .25 .60
Vida Blue TL
577 Rick Monday .10 .30
578 Shooty Babitt .05 .15
579 Rick Mahler .05 .15
580 Bobby Bonds .10 .30
581 Ron Reed .05 .15
582 Luis Pujols .05 .15
583 Tippy Martinez .05 .15
584 Hosken Powell .05 .15
585 Rollie Fingers .10 .30
586 Rollie Fingers IA .05 .15
587 Tim Lollar .05 .15
588 Dale Berra .05 .15
589 Dave Stapleton .05 .15
590 Al Oliver .10 .30
591 Al Oliver IA .05 .15
592 Craig Swan .05 .15
593 Billy Smith .05 .15
594 Renie Martin .05 .15
595 Dave Collins .05 .15
596 Damaso Garcia .05 .15
597 Wayne Nordhagen .05 .15
598 Bob Galasso .05 .15
599 Lovig/Patt/Suth RC .05 .15
600 Dave Winfield .10 .30
601 Sid Monge .05 .15
602 Freddie Patek .05 .15
603 Rich Hebner .05 .15
604 Orlando Sanchez .05 .15
605 Steve Rogers .10 .30
606 John Mayberry .10 .30
Dave Stieb TL
607 Leon Durham .05 .15
608 Jerry Royster .05 .15
609 Rick Sutcliffe .10 .30
610 Rickey Henderson 1.50 4.00
611 Joe Niekro .05 .15
612 Gary Ward .05 .15
613 Jim Gantner .05 .15
614 Juan Eichelberger .05 .15
615 Bob Boone .10 .30
616 Bob Boone IA .05 .15
617 Scott McGregor .05 .15
618 Tim Foli .05 .15
619 Bill Campbell .05 .15
620 Ken Griffey .10 .30
621 Ken Griffey IA .05 .15
622 Dennis Lamp .05 .15
623 Gardenhire/Leach/Leary RC .30 .75
624 Fergie Jenkins .10 .30
625 Hal McRae .10 .30
626 Randy Jones .05 .15
627 Enos Cabell .05 .15
628 Bill Travers .05 .15
629 John Wockenfuss .05 .15
630 Joe Charboneau .10 .30
631 Gene Tenace .10 .30
632 Bryan Clark RC .08 .25
633 Mitchell Page .05 .15
634 Checklist 529-660 .25 .60
635 Ron Davis .05 .15
636 Pete Rose .50 1.25
Steve Carlton TL
637 Rick Camp .05 .15
638 John Milner .05 .15
639 Ken Kravec .05 .15
640 Cesar Cedeno .10 .30
641 Steve Mura .05 .15
642 Mike Scioscia .10 .30
643 Pete Vuckovich .05 .15
644 John Castino .05 .15
645 Frank White .10 .30
646 Frank White IA .05 .15
647 Warren Brusstar .05 .15
648 Jose Morales .05 .15
649 Ken Clay .05 .15
650 Carl Yastrzemski .75 2.00
651 Carl Yastrzemski IA .50 1.25
652 Steve Nicosia .05 .15
653 Brunansky/Sanch/Scon RC .60 1.50
654 Jim Morrison .05 .15
655 Joel Youngblood .05 .15
656 Eddie Whitson .05 .15
657 Tom Poquette .05 .15
658 Tito Landrum .05 .15
659 Fred Martinez .05 .15
660 Dave Concepcion .10 .30
661 Dave Concepcion IA .05 .15
662 Luis Salazar .05 .15
663 Hector Cruz .05 .15
664 Dan Spillner .05 .15
665 Jim Clancy .05 .15
666 Steve Kemp .25 .60
Dan Petry TL
667 Jeff Reardon .10 .30
668 Dale Murphy .25 .60
669 Larry Milbourne .05 .15
670 Steve Kemp .05 .15
671 Mike Davis .05 .15
672 Bob Knepper .05 .15
673 Keith Drumwright .05 .15
674 Dave Goltz .05 .15
675 Cecil Cooper .10 .30
676 Sal Butera .05 .15
677 Alfredo Griffin .05 .15
678 Tom Paciorek .05 .15
679 Sammy Stewart .05 .15
680 Gary Matthews .10 .30
681 Marshall/Roen/Sax RC .60 1.50
682 Jesse Jefferson .05 .15
683 Phil Garner .10 .30
684 Harold Baines .10 .30
685 Bert Blyleven .10 .30
686 Gary Allenson .05 .15
687 Greg Minton .05 .15
688 Leon Roberts .05 .15
689 Lary Sorensen .05 .15
690 Dave Kingman .10 .30
691 Dan Schatzeder .05 .15
692 Wayne Gross .05 .15
693 Cesar Geronimo .05 .15
694 Dave Wehrmeister .05 .15
695 Warren Cromartie .05 .15
696 Bill Madlock .25 .60
Eddie Solomon TL
697 John Montefusco .05 .15
698 Tony Scott .05 .15
699 Dick Tidrow .05 .15
700 George Foster .10 .30
701 George Foster IA .05 .15
702 Steve Renko .05 .15
703 Cecil Cooper .25 .60
Pete Vuckovich TL
704 Mickey Rivers .05 .15
705 Mickey Rivers IA .05 .15
706 Barry Foote .05 .15
707 Mark Bomback .05 .15
708 Gene Richards .05 .15
709 Don Money .05 .15
710 Jerry Reuss .05 .15
711 Edler/Henderson/Walton RC .30 .75
712 Dennis Martinez .10 .30
713 Del Unser .05 .15
714 Jerry Koosman .10 .30
715 Willie Stargell .25 .60
716 Willie Stargell IA .10 .30
717 Rick Miller .05 .15
718 Charlie Hough .10 .30
719 Jerry Narron .05 .15
720 Greg Luzinski .10 .30
721 Greg Luzinski IA .05 .15
722 Jerry Martin .05 .15
723 Junior Kennedy .05 .15
724 Dave Rosello .05 .15
725 Amos Otis .10 .30
726 Amos Otis IA .05 .15
727 Sixto Lezcano .05 .15
728 Aurelio Lopez .05 .15
729 Jim Spencer .05 .15
730 Gary Carter .10 .30
731 Armstrong/Gwosdz/Kuhaulua RC .05 .15
732 Mike Lum .05 .15
733 Larry McWilliams .05 .15
734 Mike Ivie .05 .15
735 Rudy May .05 .15
736 Jerry Turner .05 .15
737 Reggie Cleveland .05 .15
738 Dave Engle .05 .15
739 Joey McLaughlin .05 .15
740 Dave Lopes .10 .30
741 Dave Lopes IA .05 .15
742 Dick Drago .05 .15
743 John Stearns .05 .15
744 Mike Witt .30 .75
745 Bake McBride .10 .30
746 Andre Thornton .05 .15
747 John Lowenstein .05 .15
748 Marc Hill .05 .15
749 Bob Shirley .05 .15
750 Jim Rice .10 .30
751 Rick Honeycutt .05 .15
752 Lee Lacy .05 .15
753 Tom Brookens .05 .15
754 Joe Morgan .10 .30
755 Joe Morgan IA .10 .30
756 Ken Griffey .10 .30
Tom Seaver TL
757 Tom Underwood .05 .15
758 Claudell Washington .05 .15
759 Paul Splittorff .05 .15
760 Bill Buckner .10 .30
761 Dave Smith .05 .15
762 Mike Phillips .05 .15
763 Tom Hume .05 .15
764 Steve Swisher .05 .15
765 Gorman Thomas .10 .30
766 Faedo/Hrbek/Laudner RC .60 1.50
767 Roy Smalley .05 .15
768 Jerry Garvin .05 .15
769 Richie Zisk .05 .15
770 Rich Gossage .10 .30
771 Rich Gossage IA .05 .15
772 Bert Campaneris .10 .30
773 John Denny .05 .15
774 Jay Johnstone .05 .15
775 Bob Forsch .05 .15
776 Mark Belanger .05 .15
777 Tom Griffin .05 .15
778 Kevin Hickey RC .08 .25
779 Grant Jackson .05 .15
780 Pete Rose 1.50 4.00
781 Pete Rose IA .50 1.25
782 Frank Taveras .05 .15
783 Greg Harris RC .08 .25
784 Milt Wilcox .05 .15
785 Dan Driessen .05 .15
786 Carney Lansford .25 .60
Mike Torrez TL
787 Fred Stanley .05 .15
788 Woodie Fryman .05 .15
789 Checklist 661-792 .25 .60
790 Larry Gura .05 .15
791 Bobby Brown .05 .15
792 Frank Tanana .10 .30

1982 Topps Blackless

During the 1982 Topps production, a whole sheet of cards were issued without the black ink. This caused the cards to have no facsimile autographs on the card front along with other processes missing. This affected mainly the A, B and C sheets.

COMPLETE SET (396) 1500.00 2500.00
8 Rich Dauer 2.00 5.00
9 Ron Guidry 3.00 8.00
10 Ron Guidry IA 2.50 6.00
11 Gary Alexander 2.00 5.00
12 Moose Haas 2.00 5.00
13 Lamar Johnson 2.00 5.00
14 Steve Howe 2.00 5.00
17 Darrell Evans 2.50 6.00
18 Fernando Arroyo 2.00 5.00
20 Garry Maddox 2.00 5.00
24 Dave Frost 2.00 5.00
26 Jorge Orta 2.00 5.00
28 John Urrea 2.00 5.00
31 Tom Seaver IA 7.50 15.00
35 Willie Aikens 2.00 5.00
37 Dan Graham 2.00 5.00
38 Charlie Lea 2.00 5.00
39 Lou Whitaker 3.00 8.00
40 Dave Parker 3.00 8.00
42 Rick Sofield 2.00 5.00
48 Bobby Castillo 2.00 5.00
49 Alvis Woods 2.00 5.00
50 Buddy Bell 2.50 6.00
52 Larry Andersen 2.00 5.00
54 Ron Hassey 2.00 5.00
55 Rick Burleson 2.00 5.00
60 Tony Armas 2.00 5.00
64 Lynn Jones 2.00 5.00
65 Terry Kennedy 2.00 5.00
67 Rich Gale 2.00 5.00
68 Roy Howell 2.00 5.00
70 Tim Raines 4.00 10.00
71 Roy Lee Jackson 2.00 5.00
72 Rick Auerbach 2.00 5.00
73 Buddy Solomon 2.00 5.00
74 Bob Clark 2.00 5.00
77 Miguel Dilone 2.00 5.00
78 Doc Medich 2.00 5.00
80 Jim Palmer 10.00 20.00
81 Jim Palmer IA 7.50 15.00
84 Rennie Stennett 2.00 5.00
87 Matt Keough 2.00 5.00
88 Biff Pocoroba 2.00 5.00
89 Steve Henderson 2.00 5.00
90 Nolan Ryan 25.00 50.00
91 Carney Lansford 2.50 6.00
92 Brad Havens 2.00 5.00
94 Andy Hassler 2.00 5.00
95 Ozzie Smith 12.50 30.00
98 Terry Bulling 2.00 5.00
99 Barry Bonnell 2.00 5.00
100 Mike Schmidt 20.00 40.00
101 Mike Schmidt IA 10.00 20.00
105 Kirk Gibson 4.00 10.00
107 Wayne Krenchicki 2.00 5.00
109 Dave Revering 2.00 5.00
110 Carlton Fisk 7.50 15.00
111 Carlton Fisk IA 4.00 10.00
112 Billy Sample 2.00 5.00
113 Steve McCatty 2.00 5.00
114 Ken Landreaux 2.00 5.00
115 Gaylord Perry 7.50 15.00
116 Jim Wohlford 2.00 5.00
117 Rawly Eastwick 2.00 5.00
119 Joe Pittman 2.00 5.00
120 Gary Lucas 2.00 5.00
122 Jamie Easterly 2.00 5.00
123 Danny Goodwin 2.00 5.00
125 Danny Ainge 4.00 10.00
127 Lonnie Smith 2.00 5.00
128 Frank Pastore 2.00 5.00
130 Julio Cruz 2.00 5.00
131 Stan Bahnsen 2.00 5.00
132 Lee May 2.50 6.00
134 Dan Ford 2.00 5.00
135 Andy Rincon 2.00 5.00
136 Lenn Sakata 2.00 5.00
137 George Cappuzzello 2.00 5.00
138 Tony Pena 2.50 6.00
140 Ron LeFlore 2.00 5.00
143 Mookie Wilson 2.50 6.00
147 Denny Walling 2.00 5.00
150 Ted Simmons 2.50 6.00
155 Otto Velez 2.00 5.00
157 Steve Crawford 2.00 5.00
158 Brian Downing 2.50 6.00
159 Larry Biittner 2.00 5.00
160 Luis Tiant 3.00 8.00
170 Jim Bibby 2.00 5.00
172 Bill Gullickson 2.00 5.00
173 Jamie Quirk 2.00 5.00
174 Dave Ford 2.00 5.00
175 Jerry Mumphrey 2.00 5.00
177 John Ellis 2.00 5.00
178 Dyar Miller 2.00 5.00
179 Steve Garvey 4.00 10.00
181 Silvio Martinez 2.00 5.00
183 Mike Proly 2.00 5.00
185 Phil Niekro 7.50 15.00
189 Glenn Hoffman 2.00 5.00
190 J.R. Richard 2.50 6.00
192 Broderick Perkins 2.00 5.00
198 Chris Speier 2.00 5.00
200 George Brett 20.00 40.00
201 George Brett IA 12.50 25.00
204 Gary Roenicke 2.00 5.00
209 Gary Lavelle 2.00 5.00
210 Keith Hernandez 3.00 8.00
211 Dan Petry 2.00 5.00
212 Mario Mendoza 2.00 5.00
215 Mike Krukow 2.00 5.00
220 Manny Trillo 2.00 5.00
221 Jim Slaton 2.00 5.00
222 Butch Wynegar 2.00 5.00
223 Lloyd Moseby 2.00 5.00
224 Bruce Bochte 2.00 5.00
225 Mike Torrez 2.00 5.00
228 Sam Mejias 2.00 5.00
230 Willie Wilson 2.50 6.00
232 Terry Crowley 2.00 5.00
233 Duane Kuiper 2.00 5.00
234 Ron Hodges 2.00 5.00
235 Mike Easler 2.00 5.00
237 Rusty Kuntz 2.00 5.00
238 Kevin Saucier 2.00 5.00
239 Jon Matlack 2.00 5.00
240 Bucky Dent 2.50 6.00
241 Bucky Dent IA 2.50 6.00
245 Ken Reitz 2.00 5.00
247 Pedro Guerrero 2.50 6.00
251 Fred Lynn 2.50 6.00
255 Tony Perez 7.50 15.00
256 Tony Perez IA 4.00 10.00
257 Larry Harlow 2.00 5.00
258 Bo Diaz 2.00 5.00
259 Rodney Scott 2.00 5.00
260 Bruce Sutter 6.00 15.00
262 Doug Bair 2.00 5.00
264 Dan Quisenberry 2.00 5.00
265 Al Bumbry 2.00 5.00
267 Kurt Bevacqua 2.00 5.00
270 Rusty Staub 2.50 6.00
272 Bump Wills 2.00 5.00
275 Bob Watson 2.50 6.00
278 John Littlefield 2.00 5.00
280 Ben Oglivie 2.00 5.00
281 John Verhoeven 2.00 5.00
282 Ken Macha 2.00 5.00
283 Brian Allard 2.00 5.00
285 Sparky Lyle 2.50 6.00
287 Alan Bannister 2.00 5.00
288 Garry Templeton 2.50 6.00
289 Bob Stanley 2.00 5.00
290 Ken Singleton 2.50 6.00
297 Clint Hurdle 2.50 6.00
299 Steve Trout 2.00 5.00
300 Reggie Jackson 12.50 30.00
302 Doug Flynn 2.00 5.00
305 Don Sutton 7.50 15.00
307 Randy Bass 2.00 5.00
308 Charlie Moore 2.00 5.00
310 Mike Hargrove 2.50 6.00
312 Lenny Randle 2.00 5.00
315 Burt Hooton 2.00 5.00
317 Dick Ruthven 2.00 5.00
323 Bill Lee 2.00 5.00
324 Steve Dillard 2.00 5.00
325 Jose Cruz 2.50 6.00
328 Ed Farmer 2.00 5.00
329 U.L. Washington 2.00 5.00
330 Rick Wise 2.00 5.00
332 Don Robinson 2.00 5.00
334 Aurelio Rodriguez 2.00 5.00
335 Jim Sundberg 2.00 5.00
339 Mike Schmidt AS 7.50 15.00
340 Dave Concepcion AS 2.50 6.00
342 George Foster AS 2.00 5.00
343 Dave Parker AS 2.00 5.00
344 Gary Carter AS 7.50 15.00
345 Fernando Valenzuela AS 2.50 6.00
349 George Frazier 2.00 5.00
352 Dick Davis 2.00 5.00
354 Roberto Ramos 2.00 5.00
355 Dwight Evans 4.00 10.00
357 Butch Hobson 2.00 5.00
359 Jim Dwyer 2.00 5.00
360 Len Barker 2.00 5.00
363 Bob Molinaro 2.00 5.00
365 Bill Madlock 3.00 8.00
370 Mike Norris 2.00 5.00
380 Dave Stieb 2.00 5.00
382 Joe Simpson 2.00 5.00
385 Ken Forsch 2.00 5.00
387 Tom Veryzer 2.00 5.00
388 Joe Rudi 2.00 5.00
390 Eddie Murray 10.00 20.00
397 Ken Brett 2.00 5.00
398 Mike Squires 2.00 5.00
399 Pat Zachry 2.00 5.00
400 Johnny Bench 12.50 25.00
406 Al Holland 2.00 5.00
409 Don Cooper 2.00 5.00
412 Luis Leal 2.00 5.00
413 Dan Meyer 2.00 5.00
415 Don Baylor 3.00 8.00
417 Pat Kelly 2.00 5.00
419 Steve Stone 2.50 6.00
420 George Hendrick 2.00 5.00
421 Mark Clear 2.00 5.00
422 Cliff Johnson 2.00 5.00
423 Stan Papi 2.00 5.00
424 Bruce Benedict 2.00 5.00
425 John Candelaria 2.00 5.00
430 Vida Blue 2.50 6.00
440 Jeff Burroughs 2.00 5.00
442 Bruce Kison 3.00 8.00
443 Mark Wagner 2.00 5.00
445 Larry Parrish 2.00 5.00
446 Wayne Garland 2.00 5.00
448 Darrell Porter IA 2.00 5.00
450 Jack Morris 4.00 10.00
451 Ed Miller 2.00 5.00
459 Bruce Berenyi 2.00 5.00
460 Jack Clark 3.00 8.00
461 Rich Dotson 2.00 5.00
462 Dave Chalk 2.00 5.00
463 Jim Kern 2.00 5.00
464 Juan Bonilla 2.00 5.00
465 Lee Mazzilli 2.00 5.00
467 Mickey Hatcher 2.00 5.00
468 Floyd Bannister 2.00 5.00
472 Oscar Gamble 2.00 5.00
475 Alan Trammell 3.00 8.00
477 Steve Yeager 2.00 5.00
480 Steve Carlton 12.50 25.00
481 Steve Carlton IA 10.00 20.00
484 Ivan DeJesus 2.00 5.00
490 Dennis Eckersley 7.50 15.00
492 Joe Price 2.00 5.00
493 Chet Lemon 2.00 5.00
494 Hubie Brooks 2.00 5.00
495 Dennis Leonard 2.00 5.00
496 Johnny Grubb 2.00 5.00
498 Dave Bergman 2.00 5.00
499 Paul Mirabella 2.00 5.00
500 Rod Carew 12.50 25.00
501 Rod Carew IA 10.00 20.00
503 Julio Gonzalez 2.00 5.00
507 Terry Harper 2.00 5.00
510 Fernando Valenzuela 4.00 10.00
511 Ruppert Jones 2.00 5.00
512 Jerry Dybzinski 2.00 5.00
515 Larry Bowa 2.50 6.00
518 Garth Iorg 2.00 5.00
519 Glenn Adams 2.00 5.00
520 Mike Flanagan 2.00 5.00
521 Bill Almon 2.00 5.00
523 Gary Gray 2.00 5.00
524 Tom Hausman 2.00 5.00
532 Toby Harrah 2.00 5.00
534 Dave McKay 2.00 5.00
536 Rafael Ramirez 2.00 5.00
540 Andre Dawson 4.00 10.00
541 Barry Evans 2.00 5.00
542 Ned Yost 2.50 6.00
543 Bill Robinson 2.00 5.00
547 Rod Carew AS 7.50 15.00
548 Willie Randolph AS 3.00 8.00
549 George Brett AS 12.50 25.00
550 Bucky Dent AS 2.00 5.00
551 Reggie Jackson AS 10.00 20.00
552 Ken Singleton AS 2.00 5.00
553 Dave Winfield AS 7.50 15.00
554 Carlton Fisk AS 7.50 15.00
555 Scott McGregor AS 2.00 5.00
556 Jack Morris AS 2.50 6.00
557 Rich Gossage AS 2.50 6.00
560 Doug Corbett 2.00 5.00
563 Ross Baumgarten 2.00 5.00
564 Doug DeCinces 2.50 6.00
565 Jackson Todd 2.00 5.00
567 Bob Babcock 2.00 5.00
568 Joe Pettini 2.00 5.00
569 Willie Randolph 3.00 8.00
573 Rick Waits 2.00 5.00
574 Mike Ramsey 2.00 5.00
575 Al Cowens 2.00 5.00
579 Rick Mahler 2.00 5.00
580 Bobby Bonds 2.50 6.00
581 Ron Reed 2.00 5.00
582 Luis Pujols 2.00 5.00
585 Rollie Fingers 7.50 15.00
588 Dale Berra 2.00 5.00
590 Al Oliver 2.50 6.00
594 Renie Martin 2.00 5.00
600 Dave Winfield 10.00 20.00
601 Sid Monge 2.00 5.00
602 Freddie Patek 2.00 5.00
603 Richie Hebner 2.00 5.00
608 Jerry Royster 2.00 5.00
610 Rickey Henderson 30.00 60.00
611 Joe Niekro 2.50 6.00
612 Gary Ward 2.00 5.00
613 Jim Gantner 2.00 5.00
615 Bob Boone 2.50 6.00
616 Bob Boone IA 2.50 6.00
622 Dennis Lamp 2.00 5.00
624 Fergie Jenkins 7.50 15.00
625 Hal McRae 2.50 6.00
626 Randy Jones 2.00 5.00
627 Enos Cabell 2.00 5.00
629 Johnny Wockenfuss 2.00 5.00
630 Joe Charboneau 2.50 6.00
632 Bryan Clark 2.00 5.00
635 Ron Davis 2.00 5.00
637 Rick Camp 2.00 5.00
640 Cesar Cedeno 2.50 6.00
645 Frank White 2.50 6.00
646 Frank White IA 2.00 5.00
648 Jose Morales 2.00 5.00
649 Ken Clay 2.00 5.00
654 Jim Morrison 2.00 5.00
655 Joel Youngblood 2.00 5.00
656 Eddie Whitson 2.00 5.00
661 Dave Concepcion IA 2.50 6.00
663 Hector Cruz 2.00 5.00
664 Dan Spillner 2.00 5.00
665 Jim Clancy 2.00 5.00
668 Dale Murphy 4.00 10.00
669 Larry Milbourne 2.00 5.00
670 Steve Kemp 2.00 5.00
672 Bob Knepper 2.00 5.00
675 Cecil Cooper 2.50 6.00
677 Alfredo Griffin 2.00 5.00
678 Tom Paciorek 2.00 5.00
684 Harold Baines 3.00 8.00
685 Bert Blyleven 4.00 10.00
686 Gary Allenson 2.00 5.00
690 Dave Kingman 2.50 6.00
691 Dan Schatzeder 2.00 5.00
694 Dave Wehrmeister 2.00 5.00
695 Warren Cromartie 2.00 5.00
700 George Foster 2.50 6.00
702 Steve Renko 2.00 5.00
704 Mickey Rivers 2.00 5.00
705 Mickey Rivers IA 2.50 6.00
706 Barry Foote 2.00 5.00
707 Mark Bomback 2.00 5.00
708 Gene Richards 2.00 5.00
710 Jerry Reuss 2.00 5.00
713 Del Unser 2.50 6.00
715 Willie Stargell 7.50 15.00
716 Willie Stargell IA 7.50 15.00
718 Charlie Hough 2.50 6.00
720 Greg Luzinski 2.50 6.00
721 Greg Luzinski IA 2.50 6.00
722 Jerry Martin 2.00 5.00
724 Dave Rosello 2.00 5.00
725 Amos Otis 2.00 5.00
730 Gary Carter 10.00 20.00
735 Rudy May 2.00 5.00
737 Reggie Cleveland 2.00 5.00
738 Dave Engle 2.00 5.00
739 Joey McLaughlin 2.00 5.00
740 Davey Lopes 2.50 6.00
741 Davey Lopes IA 2.50 6.00
742 Dick Drago 2.00 5.00
743 John Stearns 2.00 5.00
745 Bake McBride 2.00 5.00
747 John Lowenstein 2.00 5.00
748 Marc Hill 2.00 5.00
751 Rick Honeycutt 2.00 5.00
753 Tom Brookens 2.00 5.00
754 Joe Morgan 7.50 15.00
757 Tom Underwood 2.00 5.00
760 Bill Buckner 2.50 6.00
761 Dave Smith 2.00 5.00
764 Steve Swisher 2.00 5.00
765 Gorman Thomas 2.00 5.00
767 Roy Smalley 2.00 5.00
768 Jerry Garvin 2.00 5.00
769 Richie Zisk 2.00 5.00
771 Rich Gossage IA 2.50 6.00
775 Bob Forsch 2.00 5.00
776 Mark Belanger 2.00 5.00
777 Tom Griffin 2.00 5.00

778 Kevin Hickey 2.00 5.00
780 Pete Rose 20.00 40.00
781 Pete Rose IA 12.50 30.00
782 Frank Taveras 2.00 5.00
784 Milt Wilcox 2.00 5.00
788 Woodie Fryman 2.00 5.00
790 Larry Gura 2.00 5.00
792 Frank Tanana 2.00 5.00

1982 Topps Sticker Variations

This 48-card (skip-numbered) set is actually a slightly different version of the 1982 Topps stickers. They are the same size (1 15/16" by 2 9/16") and are easily confused. They were produced for insertion into the regular packs of cards that year. They are distinguishable from the "other" sticker set by the fact that on their backs these say the Topps sticker album is "Coming Soon." There are no foils in this set. All of the stickers in this set depict a single player. Colored borders surround the posed color player photos on the fronts, blue for the NL and red for the AL. The player's name and position appear on the back. The stickers are numbered on the front and back. Choice of players for this small set appears to have been systematic, i.e., taking every fourth player between number 17 and number 109 and every fifth player between number 151 and number 251.

COMPLETE SET (48) 1.50 4.00
17 Chris Chambliss .02 .10
21 Bruce Benedict .01 .05
25 Leon Durham .01 .05
29 Bill Buckner .02 .10
33 Dave Collins .01 .05
37 Dave Concepcion .02 .10
41 Nolan Ryan .75 2.00
45 Bob Knepper .01 .05
49 Ken Landreaux .01 .05
53 Burt Hooton .01 .05
57 Andre Dawson .10 .30
61 Gary Carter .15 .40
65 Joel Youngblood .01 .05
69 Ellis Valentine .01 .05
73 Garry Maddox .01 .05
77 Bob Boone .02 .10
81 Omar Moreno .01 .05
85 Willie Stargell .10 .30
89 Ken Oberkfell .01 .05
93 Darrell Porter .01 .05
97 Juan Eichelberger .01 .05
101 Luis Salazar .01 .05
105 Enos Cabell .01 .05
109 Larry Herndon .01 .05
143 Scott McGregor .01 .05
148 Mike Flanagan .02 .10
151 Mike Torrez .01 .05
156 Carney Lansford .02 .10
161 Fred Lynn .02 .10
166 Rich Dotson .01 .05
171 Tony Bernazard .01 .05
176 Bo Diaz .01 .05
181 Alan Trammell .08 .25
186 Milt Wilcox .01 .05
191 Dennis Leonard .01 .05
196 Willie Aikens .01 .05
201 Ted Simmons .02 .10
206 Hosken Powell .01 .05
211 Roger Erickson .01 .05
215 Graig Nettles .02 .10
216 Reggie Jackson .20 .50
221 Rickey Henderson .40 1.00
226 Cliff Johnson .01 .05
231 Jeff Burroughs .01 .05
236 Tom Paciorek .01 .05
241 Pat Putnam .01 .05
246 Lloyd Moseby .01 .05
251 Barry Bonnell .01 .05

1982 Topps Team Checklist Sheet

As part of a mail-away offer, Topps offered all 26 1982 team checklist cards on an uncut sheet. These cards enabled the collector to have an easy reference for which card(s) he/she needed to finish their sets. When cut from the sheet, all cards measure the standard-size.

1 Team Checklist Sheet 15.00 40.00

1982 Topps Traded

The cards in this 132-card set measure the standard size. These sets were shipped to hobby dealers in 100-ct cases. The 1982 Topps Traded or extended series is distinguished by a "T" printed after the number (located on the reverse). This was the first time Topps began a tradition of newly numbering (and alphabetizing) their traded series from 1T to 132T. All 131 player photos used in the set are completely new. Of this total, 112 individuals are seen in the uniform of their new team, 11 youngsters have been elevated to single card status from multi-player "Future Stars" cards, and eight more are entirely new to the 1982 Topps lineup. The backs are almost completely red in color with black print. There are no key Rookie Cards in this set. Although the Cal Ripken card is this set's most valuable card, it is not his Rookie Card since he had already been included in the 1982 regular set, albeit on a multi-player card.

COMP.FACT.SET (132) 75.00 150.00
1T Doyle Alexander .20 .50
2T Jesse Barfield 1.25 3.00
3T Ross Baumgarten .20 .50
4T Steve Bedrosian .60 1.50
5T Mark Belanger .20 .50
6T Kurt Bevacqua .20 .50
7T Tim Blackwell .20 .50
8T Vida Blue .40 1.00
9T Bob Boone .40 1.00
10T Larry Bowa .40 1.00
11T Dan Briggs .20 .50
12T Bobby Brown .20 .50
13T Tom Brunansky 1.25 3.00
14T Jeff Burroughs .20 .50
15T Enos Cabell .20 .50
16T Bill Campbell .20 .50
17T Bobby Castillo .20 .50
18T Bill Caudill .20 .50
19T Cesar Cedeno .40 1.00
20T Dave Collins .20 .50
21T Doug Corbett .20 .50
22T Al Cowens .20 .50
23T Chili Davis 1.25 3.00
24T Dick Davis .20 .50
25T Ron Davis .20 .50
26T Doug DeCinces .20 .50
27T Ivan DeJesus .20 .50
28T Bob Dernier .20 .50
29T Bo Diaz .20 .50
30T Roger Erickson .20 .50
31T Jim Essian .20 .50
32T Ed Farmer .20 .50
33T Doug Flynn .20 .50
34T Tim Foli .20 .50
35T Dan Ford .20 .50
36T George Foster .40 1.00
37T Dave Frost .20 .50
38T Rich Gale .20 .50
39T Ron Gardenhire .60 1.50
40T Ken Griffey .40 1.00
41T Greg Harris .20 .50
42T Von Hayes .60 1.50
43T Larry Herndon .20 .50
44T Kent Hrbek 1.25 3.00
45T Mike Ivie .20 .50
46T Grant Jackson .20 .50
47T Reggie Jackson .75 2.00
48T Ron Jackson .20 .50
49T Fergie Jenkins .40 1.00
50T Lamar Johnson .20 .50
51T Randy Johnson XRC .20 .50
52T Jay Johnstone .20 .50
53T Mick Kelleher .20 .50
54T Steve Kemp .20 .50
55T Junior Kennedy .20 .50
56T Jim Kern .20 .50
57T Ray Knight .40 1.00
58T Wayne Krenchicki .20 .50
59T Mike Krukow .20 .50
60T Duane Kuiper .20 .50
61T Mike LaCoss .20 .50
62T Chet Lemon .40 1.00
63T Sixto Lezcano .20 .50
64T Dave Lopes .40 1.00
65T Jerry Martin .20 .50
66T Renie Martin .20 .50
67T John Mayberry .20 .50
68T Lee Mazzilli .40 1.00
69T Bake McBride .40 1.00
70T Dan Meyer .20 .50
71T Larry Milbourne .20 .50
72T Eddie Milner .20 .50
73T Sid Monge .20 .50
74T John Montefusco .20 .50
75T Jose Morales .20 .50
76T Keith Moreland .20 .50
77T Jim Morrison .20 .50
78T Rance Mulliniks .20 .50
79T Steve Mura .20 .50
80T Gene Nelson .20 .50
81T Joe Nolan .20 .50
82T Dickie Noles .20 .50
83T Al Oliver .40 1.00
84T Jorge Orta .20 .50
85T Tom Paciorek .20 .50
86T Larry Parrish .20 .50
87T Jack Perconte .20 .50
88T Gaylord Perry .40 1.00
89T Rob Picciolo .20 .50
90T Joe Pittman .20 .50
91T Hosken Powell .20 .50
92T Mike Proly .20 .50
93T Greg Pryor .20 .50
94T Charlie Puleo .20 .50
95T Shane Rawley .20 .50
96T Johnny Ray .60 1.50
97T Dave Revering .20 .50
98T Cal Ripken 100.00 250.00
99T Allen Ripley .20 .50
100T Bill Robinson .20 .50
101T Aurelio Rodriguez .20 .50
102T Joe Rudi .40 1.00
103T Steve Sax 1.25 3.00
104T Dan Schatzeder .20 .50
105T Bob Shirley .20 .50
106T Eric Show XRC .60 1.50
107T Roy Smalley .20 .50
108T Lonnie Smith .20 .50
109T Ozzie Smith 8.00 20.00
110T Reggie Smith .40 1.00
111T Lary Sorensen .20 .50
112T Elias Sosa .20 .50
113T Mike Stanton .20 .50
114T Steve Stroughter .20 .50
115T Champ Summers .20 .50
116T Rick Sutcliffe .40 1.00
117T Frank Tanana .40 1.00
118T Frank Taveras .20 .50
119T Garry Templeton .40 1.00
120T Alex Trevino .20 .50
121T Jerry Turner .20 .50
122T Ed VandeBerg .20 .50
123T Tom Veryzer .20 .50
124T Ron Washington XRC .40 1.00
125T Bob Watson .20 .50
126T Dennis Werth .20 .50
127T Eddie Whitson .20 .50
128T Rob Wilfong .20 .50
129T Bump Wills .20 .50
130T Gary Woods .20 .50
131T Butch Wynegar .20 .50
132T Checklist: 1-132 .20 .50

1982 Topps Stickers

Made for Topps and O-Pee-Chee by Panini, an Italian company, these 260 stickers measure 1 15/16" by 2 9/16" and are numbered on both front and back. The fronts feature color player photos with color borders, blue for the NL and red for the AL. The backs carry the player's name and position and a bilingual ad for O-Pee-Chee. Team affiliations are not shown. The stickers were issued both as inserts in the regular 1982 issue and in individual gumless packs. An album onto which the stickers could be affixed was available at retail stores. The album and the sticker numbering are organized as follows: League Leaders (1-16), Atlanta Braves (17-24), Chicago Cubs (25-32), Cincinnati Reds (33-40), Houston Astros (41-48), Los Angeles Dodgers (49-56), Montreal Expos (57-65), New York Mets (66-72), Philadelphia Phillies (73-80), Pittsburgh Pirates (81-88), St. Louis Cardinals (89-96), San Diego Padres (97-104), San Francisco Giants (105-112), Highlights (113-120), NL Foil All-Stars (121-130), AL Foil All-Stars (131-140), Baltimore Orioles (141-148), Boston Red Sox (149-156), California Angels (157-164), Chicago White Sox (165-172) Cleveland Indians (173-180), Detroit Tigers (181-188), Kansas City Royals (189-196), Milwaukee Brewers (197-204), Minnesota Twins (205-212), New York Yankees (213-221), Oakland A's (222-228), Seattle Mariners (229-236), Texas Rangers (237-244), Toronto Blue Jays (245-252) and postseason games (253-260).

COMPLETE SET (260) 8.00 20.00
COMMON PLAYER (1-120) .02 .05
COMMON FOIL (121-140) .04 .10
*TOPPS AND OPC: SAME VALUE
1 Bill Madlock LL .02 .10
2 Carney Lansford LL .02 .10
3 Mike Schmidt LL .25 .60
4 AL HR:Tony Armas .08 .25
Bobby Grich/Dwight Evans/Eddie
5 Mike Schmidt LL .25 .60
6 Eddie Murray LL .25 .60
7 Tim Raines LL .05 .15
8 Rickey Henderson LL .25 .60
9 Tom Seaver LL .15 .40
10 AL Wins Leaders .01 .05
Steve McCatty/Dennis Martinez/P
11 Fernando Valenzuela LL .05 .15
12 Len Barker LL .01 .05
13 Nolan Ryan LL .60 1.50
14 Steve McCatty LL .01 .05
15 Bruce Sutter LL .02 .10
16 Rollie Fingers LL .05 .15
17 Chris Chambliss .01 .05
18 Bob Horner .02 .10
19 Dale Murphy .15 .40
20 Phil Niekro .08 .25
21 Bruce Benedict .01 .05
22 Claudell Washington .01 .05
23 Glenn Hubbard .01 .05
24 Rick Camp .01 .05
25 Leon Durham .01 .05
26 Ken Reitz .01 .05
27 Dick Tidrow .01 .05
28 Tim Blackwell .01 .05
29 Bill Buckner .02 .10
30 Steve Henderson .01 .05
31 Mike Krukow .01 .05
32 Ivan DeJesus .01 .05
33 Dave Collins .01 .05
34 Ron Oester .01 .05
35 Johnny Bench .30 .75
36 Tom Seaver .30 .75
37 Dave Concepcion .02 .10
38 Tom Hume .01 .05
39 Ray Knight .01 .05
40 George Foster .02 .10
41 Nolan Ryan 1.25 3.00
42 Terry Puhl .01 .05
43 Art Howe .01 .05
44 Jose Cruz .02 .10
45 Bob Knepper .01 .05
46 Craig Reynolds .01 .05
47 Cesar Cedeno .02 .10
48 Alan Ashby .01 .05
49 Ken Landreaux .01 .05
50 Fernando Valenzuela .15 .40
51 Ron Cey .02 .10
52 Dusty Baker .02 .10
53 Burt Hooton .01 .05
54 Steve Garvey .05 .15
55 Pedro Guerrero .02 .10
56 Jerry Reuss .02 .10
57 Andre Dawson .25 .60
58 Chris Speier .01 .05
59 Steve Rogers .01 .05
60 Warren Cromartie .01 .05
61 Gary Carter .20 .50
62 Tim Raines .15 .40
63 Scott Sanderson .01 .05
64 Larry Parrish .01 .05
65 Joel Youngblood .01 .05
66 Neil Allen .01 .05
67 Lee Mazzilli .01 .05
68 Hubie Brooks .02 .10
69 Ellis Valentine .01 .05
70 Doug Flynn .01 .05
71 Pat Zachry .01 .05
72 Dave Kingman .02 .10
73 Garry Maddox .01 .05
74 Mike Schmidt .50 1.25
75 Steve Carlton .25 .60
76 Manny Trillo .01 .05
77 Bob Boone .02 .10
78 Pete Rose .50 1.25
79 Gary Matthews .02 .10
80 Larry Bowa .02 .10
81 Omar Moreno .01 .05
82 Rick Rhoden .01 .05
83 Bill Madlock .02 .10
84 Mike Easler .01 .05
85 Willie Stargell .15 .40
86 Jim Bibby .01 .05
87 Dave Parker .02 .10
88 Tim Foli .01 .05
89 Ken Oberkfell .01 .05
90 Bob Forsch .01 .05
91 George Hendrick .01 .05
92 Keith Hernandez .02 .10
93 Darrell Porter .01 .05
94 Bruce Sutter .20 .50
95 Sixto Lezcano .01 .05
96 Garry Templeton .01 .05
97 Juan Eichelberger .01 .05
98 Broderick Perkins .01 .05
99 Ruppert Jones .01 .05
100 Terry Kennedy .01 .05
101 Luis Salazar .01 .05
102 Gary Lucas .01 .05
103 Gene Richards .01 .05
104 Ozzie Smith .75 2.00
105 Enos Cabell .01 .05
106 Jack Clark .02 .10
107 Greg Minton .01 .05
108 Johnnie LeMaster .01 .05
109 Larry Herndon .01 .05
110 Milt May .01 .05
111 Vida Blue .02 .10
112 Darrell Evans .02 .10
113 Len Barker HL .01 .05
114 Julio Cruz HL .01 .05
115 Billy Martin MG HL .02 .10
116 Tim Raines HL .05 .15
117 Pete Rose HL .25 .60
118 Bill Stein HL .01 .05
119 Fern.Valenzuela HL .05 .15
120 Carl Yastrzemski HL .08 .25
121 Pete Rose FOIL .60 1.50
122 Manny Trillo FOIL .02 .10
123 Mike Schmidt FOIL .60 1.50
124 Dave Concepcion FOIL .07 .20
125 Andre Dawson FOIL .30 .75
126 George Foster FOIL .07 .20
127 Dave Parker FOIL .10 .30
128 Gary Carter FOIL .15 .40
129 Steve Carlton FOIL .30 .75
130 Bruce Sutter FOIL .20 .50
131 Rod Carew FOIL .30 .75
132 Jerry Remy FOIL .02 .10
133 George Brett FOIL 1.00 2.50
134 Rick Burleson FOIL .02 .10
135 Dwight Evans FOIL .07 .20
136 Ken Singleton FOIL .02 .10
137 Dave Winfield FOIL .30 .75
138 Carlton Fisk FOIL .30 .75
139 Jack Morris FOIL .10 .30
140 Rich Gossage FOIL .10 .30
141 Al Bumbry .02 .10
142 Doug DeCinces .01 .05
143 Scott McGregor .01 .05
144 Ken Singleton .01 .05
145 Eddie Murray .60 1.50
146 Jim Palmer .15 .40
147 Rich Dauer .01 .05
148 Mike Flanagan .02 .10
149 Jerry Remy .01 .05
150 Jim Rice .02 .10
151 Mike Torrez .01 .05
152 Tony Perez .15 .40
153 Dwight Evans .02 .10
154 Mark Clear .01 .05
155 Carl Yastrzemski .25 .60
156 Carney Lansford .02 .10
157 Rick Burleson .01 .05
158 Don Baylor .05 .15
159 Ken Forsch .01 .05
160 Rod Carew .25 .60
161 Fred Lynn .02 .10
162 Bob Grich .02 .10
163 Dan Ford .01 .05
164 Butch Hobson .01 .05
165 Greg Luzinski .02 .10
166 Rich Dotson .01 .05
167 Billy Almon .01 .05
168 Chet Lemon .01 .05
169 Steve Trout .01 .05
170 Carlton Fisk .25 .60
171 Tony Bernazard .01 .05
172 Ron LeFlore .02 .10
173 Bert Blyleven .05 .15
174 Andre Thornton .01 .05
175 Jorge Orta .01 .05
176 Bo Diaz .01 .05
177 Toby Harrah .02 .10
178 Len Barker .01 .05
179 Rick Manning .01 .05
180 Mike Hargrove .02 .10
181 Alan Trammell .15 .40
182 Al Cowens .01 .05
183 Jack Morris .02 .10
184 Kirk Gibson .08 .25
185 Steve Kemp .01 .05
186 Milt Wilcox .01 .05
187 Lou Whitaker .08 .25
188 Lance Parrish .05 .15
189 Willie Wilson .01 .05
190 George Brett .75 2.00
191 Dennis Leonard .01 .05
192 John Wathan .01 .05
193 Frank White .02 .10
194 Amos Otis .02 .10
195 Larry Gura .01 .05
196 Willie Aikens .01 .05
197 Ben Oglivie .02 .10
198 Rollie Fingers .15 .40
199 Cecil Cooper .02 .10
200 Paul Molitor .30 .75
201 Ted Simmons .02 .10
202 Pete Vuckovich .01 .05
203 Robin Yount .25 .60
204 Gorman Thomas .02 .10
205 Rob Wilfong .01 .05
206 Hosken Powell .01 .05
207 Roy Smalley .01 .05
208 Butch Wynegar .01 .05
209 John Castino .01 .05
210 Doug Corbett .01 .05
211 Roger Erickson .01 .05
212 Mickey Hatcher .01 .05
213 Dave Winfield .25 .60
214 Tommy John .05 .15
215 Graig Nettles .02 .10
216 Reggie Jackson .30 .75
217 Rich Gossage .05 .15
218 Rick Cerone .01 .05
219 Willie Randolph .02 .10
220 Jerry Mumphrey .01 .05
221 Rickey Henderson .50 1.25
222 Mike Norris .01 .05
223 Jim Spencer .01 .05
224 Tony Armas .01 .05
225 Matt Keough .01 .05
226 Cliff Johnson .01 .05
227 Dwayne Murphy .01 .05
228 Steve McCatty .01 .05
229 Richie Zisk .01 .05
230 Lenny Randle .01 .05
231 Jeff Burroughs .01 .05
232 Bruce Bochte .01 .05
233 Gary Gray .01 .05
234 Floyd Bannister .01 .05
235 Julio Cruz .01 .05
236 Tom Paciorek .02 .10
237 Danny Darwin .01 .05
238 Buddy Bell .05 .15
239 Al Oliver .05 .15
240 Jim Sundberg .02 .10
241 Pat Putnam .01 .05
242 Steve Comer .01 .05
243 Mickey Rivers .01 .05
244 Bump Wills .01 .05
245 Damaso Garcia .01 .05
246 Lloyd Moseby .01 .05
247 Ernie Whitt .01 .05
248 John Mayberry .01 .05
249 Otto Velez .01 .05
250 Dave Stieb .02 .10
251 Barry Bonnell .01 .05
252 Alfredo Griffin .01 .05
253 Gary Carter PLAY .02 .10
254 1981 AL Playoffs/(Action at plate) .01 .05
255 Dodgers Team .02 .10
World Champions/(Left half photo)
256 Dodgers Team .02 .10
World Champions/(Right half photo)
257 Fernando Valenzuela WS .05 .15
258 Steve Garvey WS .05 .15
259 Jerry Reuss WS .02 .10
Steve Yeager
260 Pedro Guerrero WS .02 .10
NNO Album .40 1.00

1983 Topps

The cards in this 792-card set measure the standard size. Cards were primarily issued in 15-card wax packs and 51-card rack packs. The wax packs had 15 cards in each pack with an 30 cent SRP and were packed 36 packs to a box and 20 boxes to a case. Each player card front features a large action shot with a small cameo portrait at bottom right. There are special series for AL and NL All Stars (386-407), League Leaders (701-708), and Record Breakers (1-6). In addition, there are 34 "Super Veteran" (SV) cards and six numbered checklist cards. The Super Veteran cards are oriented horizontally and show two pictures of the featured player, a recent picture and a picture showing the player as a rookie. The team cards are actually Team Leader (TL) cards picturing the batting and pitching leader for that team with a checklist back. Notable Rookie Cards include Wade Boggs, Tony Gwynn and Ryne Sandberg. In each wax pack a game card was included which included prizes all the way up to a trip and tickets to the World Series. Card prizes possible from these cards included the 1983 Topps League Leaders sheet as well as with enough run accumulation, ordering of a part of the 1983 Topps Mail-Away glossy set. The factory sets were available in JC Penney's Christmas Catalog for $15.99.

COMPLETE SET (792) 30.00 80.00
1 Tony Armas RB .10 .30
2 Rickey Henderson RB .50 1.25
3 Greg Minton RB .05 .15
4 Lance Parrish RB .05 .15
5 Manny Trillo RB .05 .15
6 John Wathan RB .05 .15
7 Gene Richards .05 .15
8 Steve Balboni .05 .15
9 Joey McLaughlin .05 .15
10 Gorman Thomas .10 .30
11 Billy Gardner MG .05 .15
12 Paul Mirabella .05 .15
13 Larry Herndon .05 .15
14 Frank LaCorte .05 .15
15 Ron Cey .10 .30
16 George Vukovich .05 .15
17 Kent Tekulve .05 .15
18 Kent Tekulve SV .05 .15
19 Oscar Gamble .05 .15
20 Carlton Fisk .25 .60
21 Orioles TL .25 .60
Murray/Palmer
22 Randy Martz .05 .15
23 Mike Heath .05 .15
24 Steve Mura .05 .15
25 Hal McRae .10 .30
26 Jerry Royster .05 .15
27 Doug Corbett .05 .15
28 Bruce Bochte .05 .15
29 Randy Jones .05 .15
30 Jim Rice .10 .30
31 Bill Gullickson .05 .15
32 Dave Bergman .05 .15
33 Jack O'Connor .05 .15
34 Paul Householder .05 .15
35 Rollie Fingers .10 .30
36 Rollie Fingers SV .05 .15
37 Darrell Johnson MG .05 .15
38 Tim Flannery .05 .15
39 Terry Puhl .05 .15
40 Fernando Valenzuela .10 .30
41 Jerry Turner .05 .15
42 Dale Murray .05 .15
43 Bob Dernier .05 .15
44 Don Robinson .05 .15
45 John Mayberry .05 .15
46 Richard Dotson .05 .15
47 Dave McKay .05 .15
48 Lary Sorensen .05 .15
49 Willie McGee RC 1.00 2.50
50 Bob Horner UER .10 .30
51 Cubs TL .05 .15
F.Jenkins
52 Onix Concepcion .05 .15
53 Mike Witt .05 .15
54 Jim Maler .05 .15
55 Mookie Wilson .10 .30
56 Chuck Rainey .05 .15
57 Tim Blackwell .05 .15
58 Al Holland .05 .15
59 Benny Ayala .05 .15
60 Johnny Bench .50 1.25
61 Johnny Bench SV .25 .60
62 Bob McClure .05 .15
63 Rick Monday .10 .30
64 Bill Stein .05 .15
65 Jack Morris .10 .30
66 Bob Lillis MG .05 .15
67 Sal Butera .05 .15
68 Eric Show RC .30 .75
69 Lee Lacy .05 .15
70 Steve Carlton .25 .60
71 Steve Carlton SV .10 .30
72 Tom Paciorek .05 .15
73 Allen Ripley .05 .15
74 Julio Gonzalez .05 .15
75 Amos Otis .10 .30
76 Rick Mahler .05 .15
77 Hosken Powell .05 .15
78 Bill Caudill .05 .15
79 Mick Kelleher .05 .15
80 George Foster .10 .30
81 J.Mumphrey .10 .30
D.Righetti TL
82 Bruce Hurst .05 .15
83 Ryne Sandberg RC 12.00 30.00
84 Milt May .05 .15
85 Ken Singleton .10 .30
86 Tom Hume .05 .15
87 Joe Rudi .10 .30
88 Jim Gantner .05 .15
89 Leon Roberts .05 .15
90 Jerry Reuss .05 .15
91 Larry Milbourne .05 .15
92 Mike LaCoss .05 .15
93 John Castino .05 .15
94 Dave Edwards .05 .15
95 Alan Trammell .10 .30
96 Dick Howser MG .05 .15
97 Ross Baumgarten .05 .15
98 Vance Law .05 .15
99 Dickie Noles .05 .15
100 Pete Rose 1.50 4.00
101 Pete Rose SV .50 1.25
102 Dave Beard .05 .15
103 Darrell Porter .05 .15
104 Bob Walk .05 .15
105 Don Baylor .10 .30
106 Gene Nelson .05 .15
107 Mike Jorgensen .05 .15
108 Glenn Hoffman .05 .15
109 Luis Leal .05 .15
110 Ken Griffey .10 .30
111 Montreal Expos TL .10 .30
BA: Al Oliver/ERA: Steve Roger
112 Bob Shirley .05 .15
113 Ron Roenicke .05 .15
114 Jim Slaton .05 .15
115 Chili Davis .10 .30
116 Dave Schmidt .05 .15
117 Alan Knicely .05 .15
118 Chris Welsh .05 .15
119 Tom Brookens .05 .15
120 Len Barker .05 .15
121 Mickey Hatcher .05 .15
122 Jimmy Smith .05 .15
123 George Frazier .05 .15
124 Marc Hill .05 .15
125 Leon Durham .05 .15
126 Joe Torre MG .10 .30
127 Preston Hanna .05 .15
128 Mike Ramsey .05 .15
129 Checklist: 1-132 .10 .30
130 Dave Stieb .10 .30
131 Ed Ott .05 .15
132 Todd Cruz .05 .15
133 Jim Barr .05 .15
134 Hubie Brooks .05 .15
135 Dwight Evans .25 .60
136 Willie Aikens .05 .15
137 Woodie Fryman .05 .15
138 Rick Dempsey .05 .15
139 Bruce Berenyi .05 .15
140 Willie Randolph .10 .30
141 Indians TL .10 .30
BA: Toby Harrah/ERA: Rick Sutcliffe/
142 Mike Caldwell .05 .15
143 Joe Pettini .05 .15
144 Mark Wagner .05 .15
145 Don Sutton .10 .30
146 Don Sutton SV .05 .15
147 Rick Leach .05 .15
148 Dave Roberts .05 .15
149 Johnny Ray .05 .15
150 Bruce Sutter .25 .60
151 Bruce Sutter SV .10 .30
152 Jay Johnstone .05 .15
153 Jerry Koosman .10 .30
154 Johnnie LeMaster .05 .15
155 Dan Quisenberry .05 .15
156 Billy Martin MG .25 .60
157 Steve Bedrosian .05 .15
158 Rob Wilfong .05 .15
159 Mike Stanton .05 .15
160 Dave Kingman .10 .30
161 Dave Kingman SV .05 .15
162 Mark Clear .05 .15
163 Cal Ripken 4.00 10.00
164 David Palmer .05 .15
165 Dan Driessen .05 .15
166 John Pacella .05 .15
167 Mark Brouhard .05 .15
168 Juan Eichelberger .05 .15
169 Doug Flynn .05 .15
170 Steve Howe .05 .15
171 Giants TL .10 .30
Joe Morgan
172 Vern Ruhle .05 .15
173 Jim Morrison .05 .15
174 Jerry Ujdur .05 .15
175 Bo Diaz .05 .15
176 Dave Righetti .10 .30
177 Harold Baines .10 .30
178 Luis Tiant .10 .30
179 Luis Tiant SV .05 .15
180 Rickey Henderson 1.00 2.50
181 Terry Felton .05 .15
182 Mike Fischlin .05 .15
183 Ed VandeBerg .05 .15
184 Bob Clark .05 .15
185 Tim Lollar .05 .15
186 Whitey Herzog MG .10 .30
187 Terry Leach .05 .15
188 Rick Miller .05 .15
189 Dan Schatzeder .05 .15
190 Cecil Cooper .10 .30
191 Joe Price .05 .15
192 Floyd Rayford .05 .15
193 Harry Spilman .05 .15
194 Cesar Geronimo .05 .15
195 Bob Stoddard .05 .15
196 Bill Fahey .05 .15
197 Jim Eisenreich RC .30 .75
198 Kiko Garcia .05 .15
199 Marty Bystrom .05 .15
200 Rod Carew .25 .60
201 Rod Carew SV .10 .30
202 Blue Jays TL .10 .30
BA: Damaso Garcia/ERA: Dave Stieb/
203 Mike Morgan .05 .15
204 Junior Kennedy .05 .15
205 Dave Parker .10 .30
206 Ken Oberkfell .05 .15
207 Rick Camp .05 .15
208 Dan Meyer .05 .15
209 Mike Moore RC .30 .75
210 Jack Clark .10 .30
211 John Denny .05 .15
212 John Stearns .05 .15
213 Tom Burgmeier .05 .15
214 Jerry White .05 .15
215 Mario Soto .10 .30
216 Tony LaRussa MG .10 .30
217 Tim Stoddard .05 .15
218 Roy Howell .05 .15
219 Mike Armstrong .05 .15
220 Dusty Baker .10 .30
221 Joe Niekro .05 .15
222 Damaso Garcia .05 .15
223 John Montefusco .05 .15
224 Mickey Rivers .05 .15
225 Enos Cabell .05 .15
226 Enrique Romo .05 .15
227 Chris Bando .05 .15
228 Joaquin Andujar .10 .30
229 Phillies TL .05 .15
S.Carlton
230 Fergie Jenkins .10 .30
231 Fergie Jenkins SV .05 .15
232 Tom Brunansky .10 .30
233 Wayne Gross .05 .15
234 Larry Andersen .05 .15
235 Claudell Washington .05 .15
236 Steve Renko .05 .15
237 Dan Norman .05 .15
238 Bud Black RC .30 .75
239 Dave Stapleton .05 .15
240 Rich Gossage .10 .30
241 Rich Gossage SV .05 .15
242 Joe Nolan .05 .15
243 Duane Walker RC .05 .15
244 Dwight Bernard .05 .15
245 Steve Sax .10 .30
246 George Bamberger MG .05 .15
247 Dave Smith .05 .15
248 Bake McBride .10 .30
249 Checklist: 133-264 .10 .30
250 Bill Buckner .10 .30
251 Alan Wiggins .05 .15
252 Luis Aguayo .05 .15
253 Larry McWilliams .05 .15
254 Rick Cerone .05 .15
255 Gene Garber .05 .15
256 Gene Garber SV .05 .15
257 Jesse Barfield .10 .30
258 Manny Castillo .05 .15
259 Jeff Jones .05 .15
260 Steve Kemp .05 .15
261 Tigers TL .10 .30
BA: Larry Herndon/ERA: Dan Petry/(Che
262 Ron Jackson .05 .15
263 Renie Martin .05 .15
264 Jamie Quirk .05 .15
265 Joel Youngblood .05 .15
266 Paul Boris .05 .15
267 Terry Francona .10 .30
268 Storm Davis RC .30 .75
269 Ron Oester .05 .15
270 Dennis Eckersley .25 .60
271 Ed Romero .05 .15
272 Frank Tanana .10 .30
273 Mark Belanger .05 .15
274 Terry Kennedy .05 .15
275 Ray Knight .10 .30
276 Gene Mauch MG .05 .15
277 Rance Mulliniks .05 .15
278 Kevin Hickey .05 .15
279 Greg Gross .05 .15
280 Bert Blyleven .10 .30
281 Andre Robertson .05 .15
282 R.Smith w .50 1.25
Sandberg
283 Reggie Smith SV .05 .15
284 Jeff Lahti .05 .15
285 Lance Parrish .10 .30
286 Rick Langford .05 .15
287 Bobby Brown .05 .15
288 Joe Cowley .05 .15
289 Jerry Dybzinski .05 .15
290 Jeff Reardon .10 .30

291 Bill Madlock .10 .30
John Candelaria TL
292 Craig Swan .05 .15
293 Glenn Gulliver .05 .15
294 Dave Engle .05 .15
295 Jerry Remy .05 .15
296 Greg Harris .05 .15
297 Ned Yost .05 .15
298 Floyd Chiffer .05 .15
299 George Wright RC .30 .75
300 Mike Schmidt 1.25 3.00
301 Mike Schmidt SV .50 1.25
302 Ernie Whitt .05 .15
303 Miguel Dilone .05 .15
304 Dave Rucker .05 .15
305 Larry Bowa .10 .30
306 Tom Lasorda MG .25 .60
307 Lou Piniella .10 .30
308 Jesus Vega .05 .15
309 Jeff Leonard .05 .15
310 Greg Luzinski .10 .30
311 Glenn Brummer .05 .15
312 Brian Kingman .05 .15
313 Gary Gray .05 .15
314 Ken Dayley .05 .15
315 Rick Burleson .05 .15
316 Paul Splittorff .05 .15
317 Gary Rajsich .05 .15
318 John Tudor .10 .30
319 Lenn Sakata .05 .15
320 Steve Rogers .10 .30
321 Brewers TL .50 1.25
Robin Yount
322 Dave Van Gorder .05 .15
323 Luis DeLeon .05 .15
324 Mike Marshall .05 .15
325 Von Hayes .05 .15
326 Garth Iorg .05 .15
327 Bobby Castillo .05 .15
328 Craig Reynolds .05 .15
329 Randy Niemann .05 .15
330 Buddy Bell .10 .30
331 Mike Krukow .05 .15
332 Glenn Wilson .30 .75
333 Dave LaRoche .05 .15
334 Dave LaRoche SV .05 .15
335 Steve Henderson .05 .15
336 Rene Lachemann MG .05 .15
337 Tito Landrum .05 .15
338 Bob Owchinko .05 .15
339 Terry Harper .05 .15
340 Larry Gura .05 .15
341 Doug DeCinces .05 .15
342 Atlee Hammaker .05 .15
343 Bob Bailor .05 .15
344 Roger LaFrancois .05 .15
345 Jim Clancy .05 .15
346 Joe Pittman .05 .15
347 Sammy Stewart .05 .15
348 Alan Bannister .05 .15
349 Checklist: 265-396 .10 .30
350 Robin Yount .75 2.00
351 Reds TL .10 .30
BA: Cesar Cedeno/ERA: Mario Soto/(Check
352 Mike Scioscia .10 .30
353 Steve Comer .05 .15
354 Randy Johnson RC .05 .15
355 Jim Bibby .05 .15
356 Gary Woods .05 .15
357 Len Matuszek .05 .15
358 Jerry Garvin .05 .15
359 Dave Collins .05 .15
360 Nolan Ryan 2.50 6.00
361 Nolan Ryan SV 1.25 3.00
362 Bill Almon .05 .15
363 John Stuper .05 .15
364 Brett Butler .10 .30
365 Dave Lopes .10 .30
366 Dick Williams MG .05 .15
367 Bud Anderson .05 .15
368 Richie Zisk .05 .15
369 Jesse Orosco .05 .15
370 Gary Carter .10 .30
371 Mike Richardt .05 .15
372 Terry Crowley .05 .15
373 Kevin Saucier .05 .15
374 Wayne Krenchicki .05 .15
375 Pete Vuckovich .05 .15
376 Ken Landreaux .05 .15
377 Lee May .05 .15
378 Lee May SV .05 .15
379 Guy Sularz .05 .15
380 Ron Davis .05 .15
381 Red Sox TL .10 .30
BA: Jim Rice/ERA: Bob Stanley/(Check
382 Bob Knepper .05 .15
383 Ozzie Virgil .05 .15
384 Dave Dravecky RC .60 1.50
385 Mike Easler .05 .15
386 Rod Carew AS .10 .30
387 Bob Grich AS .05 .15
388 George Brett AS .60 1.50
389 Robin Yount AS .50 1.25
390 Reggie Jackson AS .10 .30
391 Rickey Henderson AS .50 1.25
392 Fred Lynn AS .05 .15
393 Carlton Fisk AS .10 .30
394 Pete Vuckovich AS .05 .15
395 Larry Gura AS .05 .15
396 Dan Quisenberry AS .05 .15
397 Pete Rose AS .25 .60
398 Manny Trillo AS .05 .15
399 Mike Schmidt AS .50 1.25
400 Dave Concepcion AS .05 .15
401 Dale Murphy AS .10 .30
402 Andre Dawson AS .05 .15
403 Tim Raines AS .05 .15
404 Gary Carter AS .05 .15
405 Steve Rogers AS .05 .15
406 Steve Carlton AS .05 .15
407 Bruce Sutter AS .10 .30
408 Rudy May .05 .15
409 Marvis Foley .05 .15
410 Phil Niekro .10 .30
411 Phil Niekro SV .05 .15
412 Rangers TL .10 .30
BA: Buddy Bell/ERA: Charlie Hough/(C
413 Matt Keough .05 .15
414 Julio Cruz .05 .15
415 Bob Forsch .05 .15
416 Joe Ferguson .05 .15
417 Tom Hausman .05 .15
418 Greg Pryor .05 .15
419 Steve Crawford .05 .15
420 Al Oliver .10 .30
421 Al Oliver SV .05 .15
422 George Cappuzzello .05 .15
423 Tom Lawless .05 .15
424 Jerry Augustine .05 .15
425 Pedro Guerrero .10 .30
426 Earl Weaver MG .10 .30
427 Roy Lee Jackson .05 .15
428 Champ Summers .05 .15
429 Eddie Whitson .05 .15
430 Kirk Gibson .10 .30
431 Gary Gaetti RC .60 1.50
432 Porfirio Altamirano .05 .15
433 Dale Berra .05 .15
434 Dennis Lamp .05 .15
435 Tony Armas .10 .30
436 Bill Campbell .05 .15
437 Rick Sweet .05 .15
438 Dave LaPoint .05 .15
439 Rafael Ramirez .05 .15
440 Ron Guidry .10 .30
441 Astros TL .10 .30
BA: Ray Knight/ERA: Joe Niekro/(Check
442 Brian Downing .10 .30
443 Don Hood .05 .15
444 Wally Backman .05 .15
445 Mike Flanagan .05 .15
446 Reid Nichols .05 .15
447 Bryn Smith .05 .15
448 Darrell Evans .10 .30
449 Eddie Milner .05 .15
450 Ted Simmons .10 .30
451 Ted Simmons SV .05 .15
452 Lloyd Moseby .05 .15
453 Lamar Johnson .05 .15
454 Bob Welch .10 .30
455 Sixto Lezcano .05 .15
456 Lee Elia MG .05 .15
457 Milt Wilcox .05 .15
458 Ron Washington RC .10 .25
459 Ed Farmer .05 .15
460 Roy Smalley .05 .15
461 Steve Trout .05 .15
462 Steve Nicosia .05 .15
463 Gaylord Perry .10 .30
464 Gaylord Perry SV .05 .15
465 Lonnie Smith .05 .15
466 Tom Underwood .05 .15
467 Rufino Linares .05 .15
468 Dave Goltz .05 .15
469 Ron Gardenhire .05 .15
470 Greg Minton .05 .15
471 Kansas City Royals TL .10 .30
BA: Willie Wilson/ERA: Vid
472 Gary Allenson .05 .15
473 John Lowenstein .05 .15
474 Ray Burris .05 .15
475 Cesar Cedeno .10 .30
476 Rob Picciolo .05 .15
477 Tom Niedenfuer .05 .15
478 Phil Garner .10 .30
479 Charlie Hough .05 .15
480 Toby Harrah .05 .15
481 Scot Thompson .05 .15
482 Tony Gwynn RC 20.00 50.00
483 Lynn Jones .05 .15
484 Dick Ruthven .05 .15
485 Omar Moreno .05 .15
486 Clyde King MG .05 .15
487 Jerry Hairston .05 .15
488 Alfredo Griffin .05 .15
489 Tom Herr .05 .15
490 Jim Palmer .10 .30
491 Jim Palmer SV .05 .15
492 Paul Serna .05 .15
493 Steve McCatty .05 .15
494 Bob Brenly .05 .15
495 Warren Cromartie .05 .15
496 Tom Veryzer .05 .15
497 Rick Sutcliffe .10 .30
498 Wade Boggs RC 12.00 30.00
499 Jeff Little .05 .15
500 Reggie Jackson .25 .60
501 Reggie Jackson SV .10 .30
502 Braves TL .25 .60
Murphy/Niekro
503 Moose Haas .05 .15
504 Don Werner .05 .15
505 Garry Templeton .10 .30
506 Jim Gott RC .30 .75
507 Tony Scott .05 .15
508 Tom Filer .05 .15
509 Lou Whitaker .10 .30
510 Tug McGraw .10 .30
511 Tug McGraw SV .05 .15
512 Doyle Alexander .05 .15
513 Fred Stanley .05 .15
514 Rudy Law .05 .15
515 Gene Tenace .10 .30
516 Bill Virdon MG .05 .15
517 Gary Ward .05 .15
518 Bill Laskey .05 .15
519 Terry Bulling .05 .15
520 Fred Lynn .10 .30
521 Bruce Benedict .05 .15
522 Pat Zachry .05 .15
523 Carney Lansford .10 .30
524 Tom Brennan .05 .15
525 Frank White .10 .30
526 Checklist: 397-528 .10 .30
527 Larry Biittner .05 .15
528 Jamie Easterly .05 .15
529 Tim Laudner .05 .15
530 Eddie Murray .50 1.25
531 A's TL .50 1.25
Rickey Henderson
532 Dave Stewart .10 .30
533 Luis Salazar .05 .15
534 John Butcher .05 .15
535 Manny Trillo .05 .15
536 John Wockenfuss .05 .15
537 Rod Scurry .05 .15
538 Danny Heep .05 .15
539 Roger Erickson .05 .15
540 Ozzie Smith .75 2.00
541 Britt Burns .05 .15
542 Jody Davis .05 .15
543 Alan Fowlkes .05 .15
544 Larry Whisenton .05 .15
545 Floyd Bannister .05 .15
546 Dave Garcia MG .05 .15
547 Geoff Zahn .05 .15
548 Brian Giles .05 .15
549 Charlie Puleo .05 .15
550 Carl Yastrzemski .75 2.00
551 Carl Yastrzemski SV .50 1.25
552 Tim Wallach .10 .30
553 Dennis Martinez .10 .30
554 Mike Vail .05 .15
555 Steve Yeager .10 .30
556 Willie Upshaw .05 .15
557 Rick Honeycutt .05 .15
558 Dickie Thon .05 .15
559 Pete Redfern .05 .15
560 Ron LeFlore .10 .30
561 Cardinals TL .10 .30
BA: Lonnie Smith/ERA: Joaquin Anduj
562 Dave Rozema .05 .15
563 Juan Bonilla .05 .15
564 Sid Monge .05 .15
565 Bucky Dent .10 .30
566 Manny Sarmiento .05 .15
567 Joe Simpson .05 .15
568 Willie Hernandez .05 .15
569 Jack Perconte .05 .15
570 Vida Blue .10 .30
571 Mickey Klutts .05 .15
572 Bob Watson .10 .30
573 Andy Hassler .05 .15
574 Glenn Adams .05 .15
575 Neil Allen .05 .15
576 Frank Robinson MG .25 .60
577 Luis Aponte .05 .15
578 David Green RC .30 .75
579 Rich Dauer .05 .15
580 Tom Seaver .50 1.25
581 Tom Seaver SV .10 .30
582 Marshall Edwards .05 .15
583 Terry Forster .10 .30
584 Dave Hostetler RC .05 .15
585 Jose Cruz .10 .30
586 Frank Viola RC 1.00 2.50
587 Ivan DeJesus .05 .15
588 Pat Underwood .05 .15
589 Alvis Woods .05 .15
590 Tony Pena .05 .15
591 White Sox TL .10 .30
BA: Greg Luzinski/ERA: LaMarr Hoyt/
592 Shane Rawley .05 .15
593 Broderick Perkins .05 .15
594 Eric Rasmussen .05 .15
595 Tim Raines .10 .30
596 Randy Johnson .05 .15
597 Mike Proly .05 .15
598 Dwayne Murphy .05 .15
599 Don Aase .05 .15
600 George Brett 1.25 3.00
601 Ed Lynch .05 .15
602 Rich Gedman .05 .15
603 Joe Morgan .10 .30
604 Joe Morgan SV .05 .15
605 Gary Roenicke .05 .15
606 Bobby Cox MG .05 .15
607 Charlie Leibrandt .05 .15
608 Don Money .05 .15
609 Danny Darwin .05 .15
610 Steve Garvey .10 .30
611 Bert Roberge .05 .15
612 Steve Swisher .05 .15
613 Mike Ivie .05 .15
614 Ed Glynn .05 .15
615 Garry Maddox .05 .15
616 Bill Nahorodny .05 .15
617 Butch Wynegar .05 .15
618 LaMarr Hoyt .05 .15
619 Keith Moreland .05 .15
620 Mike Norris .05 .15
621 New York Mets TL .10 .30
BA: Mookie Wilson/ERA: Craig Sw
622 Dave Edler .05 .15
623 Luis Sanchez .05 .15
624 Glenn Hubbard .05 .15
625 Ken Forsch .05 .15
626 Jerry Martin .05 .15
627 Doug Bair .05 .15
628 Julio Valdez .05 .15
629 Charlie Lea .05 .15
630 Paul Molitor .10 .30
631 Tippy Martinez .05 .15
632 Alex Trevino .05 .15
633 Vicente Romo .05 .15
634 Max Venable .05 .15
635 Graig Nettles .10 .30
636 Graig Nettles SV .05 .15
637 Pat Corrales MG .05 .15
638 Dan Petry .05 .15
639 Art Howe .05 .15
640 Andre Thornton .05 .15
641 Billy Sample .05 .15
642 Checklist: 529-660 .10 .30
643 Bump Wills .05 .15
644 Joe Lefebvre .05 .15
645 Bill Madlock .10 .30
646 Jim Essian .05 .15
647 Bobby Mitchell .05 .15
648 Jeff Burroughs .05 .15
649 Tommy Boggs .05 .15
650 George Hendrick .05 .15
651 Angels TL .10 .30
Rod Carew
652 Butch Hobson .05 .15
653 Ellis Valentine .05 .15
654 Bob Ojeda .05 .15
655 Al Bumbry .05 .15
656 Dave Frost .05 .15
657 Mike Gates .05 .15
658 Frank Pastore .05 .15
659 Charlie Moore .05 .15
660 Mike Hargrove .05 .15
661 Bill Russell .10 .30
662 Joe Sambito .05 .15
663 Tom O'Malley .05 .15
664 Bob Molinaro .05 .15
665 Jim Sundberg .10 .30
666 Sparky Anderson MG .10 .30
667 Dick Davis .05 .15
668 Larry Christenson .05 .15
669 Mike Squires .05 .15
670 Jerry Mumphrey .05 .15
671 Lenny Faedo .05 .15
672 Jim Kaat .10 .30
673 Jim Kaat SV .05 .15
674 Kurt Bevacqua .05 .15
675 Jim Beattie .05 .15
676 Biff Pocoroba .05 .15
677 Dave Revering .05 .15
678 Juan Beniquez .05 .15
679 Mike Scott .10 .30
680 Andre Dawson .10 .30
681 Dodgers Leaders .10 .30
BA: Pedro Guerrero/ERA: Fernando
682 Bob Stanley .05 .15
683 Dan Ford .05 .15
684 Rafael Landestoy .05 .15
685 Lee Mazzilli .10 .30
686 Randy Lerch .05 .15
687 U.L. Washington .05 .15
688 Jim Wohlford .05 .15
689 Ron Hassey .05 .15
690 Kent Hrbek .10 .30
691 Dave Tobik .05 .15
692 Denny Walling .05 .15
693 Sparky Lyle .10 .30
694 Sparky Lyle SV .05 .15
695 Ruppert Jones .05 .15
696 Chuck Tanner MG .05 .15
697 Barry Foote .05 .15
698 Tony Bernazard .05 .15
699 Lee Smith .25 .60
700 Keith Hernandez .10 .30
701 Willie Wilson .10 .30
Al Oliver LL
702 Reggie .10 .30
Thomas/Kingman LL
703 RBI Leaders .25 .60
AL: Hal McRae/NL: Dale Murphy/NL: A
704 R.Henderson .50 1.25
T.Raines LL
705 L.Hoyt .10 .30
S.Carlton LL
706 F.Bannister .10 .30
Carlton LL
707 Rick Sutcliffe .10 .30
Steve Rogers LL
708 Leading Firemen .10 .30
AL: Dan Quisenberry/NL: Bruce Su
709 Jimmy Sexton .05 .15
710 Willie Wilson .10 .30
711 Mariners TL .10 .30
BA: Bruce Bochte/ERA: Jim Beattie/(
712 Bruce Kison .05 .15
713 Ron Hodges .05 .15
714 Wayne Nordhagen .05 .15
715 Tony Perez .25 .60
716 Tony Perez SV .10 .30
717 Scott Sanderson .05 .15
718 Jim Dwyer .05 .15
719 Rich Gale .05 .15
720 Dave Concepcion .10 .30
721 John Martin .05 .15
722 Jorge Orta .05 .15
723 Randy Moffitt .05 .15
724 Johnny Grubb .05 .15
725 Dan Spillner .05 .15
726 Harvey Kuenn MG .05 .15
727 Chet Lemon .10 .30
728 Ron Reed .05 .15
729 Jerry Morales .05 .15
730 Jason Thompson .05 .15
731 Al Williams .05 .15
732 Dave Henderson .05 .15
733 Buck Martinez .05 .15
734 Steve Braun .05 .15
735 Tommy John .10 .30
736 Tommy John SV .05 .15
737 Mitchell Page .05 .15
738 Tim Foli .05 .15
739 Rick Ownbey .05 .15
740 Rusty Staub .10 .30
741 Rusty Staub SV .05 .15
742 Padres TL .10 .30
BA: Terry Kennedy/ERA: Tim Lollar/(Ch
743 Mike Torrez .05 .15
744 Brad Mills .05 .15
745 Scott McGregor .05 .15
746 John Wathan .05 .15
747 Fred Breining .05 .15
748 Derrel Thomas .05 .15
749 Jon Matlack .05 .15
750 Ben Oglivie .10 .30
751 Brad Havens .05 .15
752 Luis Pujols .05 .15
753 Elias Sosa .05 .15
754 Bill Robinson .05 .15
755 John Candelaria .05 .15
756 Russ Nixon MG .05 .15
757 Rick Manning .05 .15
758 Aurelio Rodriguez .05 .15
759 Doug Bird .05 .15
760 Dale Murphy .25 .60
761 Gary Lucas .05 .15
762 Cliff Johnson .05 .15
763 Al Cowens .05 .15
764 Pete Falcone .05 .15
765 Bob Boone .10 .30
766 Barry Bonnell .05 .15
767 Duane Kuiper .05 .15
768 Chris Speier .05 .15
769 Checklist: 661-792 .10 .30
770 Dave Winfield .10 .30
771 Twins TL .10 .30
BA: Kent Hrbek/ERA: Bobby Castillo/(Ch
772 Jim Kern .05 .15
773 Larry Hisle .05 .15
774 Alan Ashby .05 .15
775 Burt Hooton .05 .15
776 Larry Parrish .05 .15
777 John Curtis .05 .15
778 Rich Hebner .05 .15
779 Rick Waits .05 .15
780 Gary Matthews .10 .30
781 Rick Rhoden .05 .15
782 Bobby Murcer .10 .30
783 Bobby Murcer SV .05 .15
784 Jeff Newman .05 .15
785 Dennis Leonard .05 .15
786 Ralph Houk MG .05 .15
787 Dick Tidrow .05 .15
788 Dane Iorg .05 .15
789 Bryan Clark .05 .15
790 Bob Grich .10 .30
791 Gary Lavelle .05 .15
792 Chris Chambliss .10 .30
XX Game Insert Card .02 .10

1983 Topps Glossy Send-Ins

COMPLETE SET (40) 6.00 15.00
1 Carl Yastrzemski .40 1.25
2 Mookie Wilson .07 .20
3 Andre Thornton .02 .10
4 Keith Hernandez .07 .20
5 Robin Yount .40 1.25
6 Terry Kennedy .02 .10
7 Dave Winfield .40 1.25
8 Mike Schmidt .60 1.50
9 Buddy Bell .07 .20
10 Fernando Valenzuela .10 .30
11 Rich Gossage .07 .20
12 Bob Horner .02 .10
13 Toby Harrah .02 .10
14 Pete Rose .60 1.50
15 Cecil Cooper .07 .20
16 Dale Murphy .20 .50
17 Carlton Fisk .40 1.25
18 Ray Knight .02 .10
19 Jim Palmer .30 1.00
20 Gary Carter .12 1.00
21 Richie Zisk .02 .10
22 Dusty Baker .07 .20
23 Willie Wilson .02 .10
24 Bill Buckner .07 .20
25 Dave Stieb .02 .10
26 Bill Madlock .02 .10
27 Lance Parrish .07 .20
28 Nolan Ryan 2.00 5.00
29 Rod Carew .40 1.00
30 Al Oliver .07 .20
31 George Brett 1.00 2.50
32 Jack Clark .02 .10
33 Rickey Henderson .75 2.00
34 Dave Concepcion .07 .20
35 Kent Hrbek .07 .20
36 Steve Carlton .30 1.00
37 Eddie Murray .50 1.25
38 Ruppert Jones .02 .10
39 Reggie Jackson .40 1.25
40 Bruce Sutter .30 .75

1983 Topps Traded

For the third year in a row, Topps issued a 132-card standard-size Traded (or extended) set featuring some of the year's top rookies and players who had changed teams during the year. The cards were available through hobby dealers only in factory set form and were printed in Ireland by the Topps affiliate in that country. The set is numbered alphabetically by player. The Darryl Strawberry card number 108 can be found with either one or two asterisks (in the lower left corner of the reverse). There is no difference in value for either version. The key (extended) Rookie Cards in this set include Julio Franco, Tony Phillips and Darryl Strawberry.

COMP.FACT.SET (132) 15.00 40.00
1T Neil Allen .08 .25
2T Bill Almon .08 .25
3T Joe Altobelli MG .08 .25
4T Tony Armas .40 1.00
5T Doug Bair .08 .25
6T Steve Baker .08 .25
7T Floyd Bannister .08 .25
8T Don Baylor .40 1.00
9T Tony Bernazard .08 .25
10T Larry Biittner .08 .25
11T Dann Bilardello .08 .25
12T Doug Bird .08 .25
13T Steve Boros MG .08 .25
14T Greg Brock .08 .25
15T Mike C. Brown .08 .25
16T Tom Burgmeier .08 .25
17T Randy Bush .08 .25
18T Bert Campaneris .40 1.00
19T Ron Cey .40 1.00
20T Chris Codiroli .08 .25
21T Dave Collins .08 .25
22T Terry Crowley .08 .25
23T Julio Cruz .08 .25
24T Mike Davis .08 .25
25T Frank DiPino .08 .25
26T Bill Doran XRC .40 1.00
27T Jerry Dybzinski .08 .25
28T Jamie Easterly .08 .25
29T Juan Eichelberger .08 .25
30T Jim Essian .08 .25
31T Pete Falcone .08 .25
32T Mike Ferraro MG .08 .25
33T Terry Forster .40 1.00
34T Julio Franco XRC 3.00 8.00
35T Rich Gale .08 .25
36T Kiko Garcia .08 .25
37T Steve Garvey .40 1.00
38T Johnny Grubb .08 .25
39T Mel Hall XRC .40 1.00
40T Von Hayes .08 .25
41T Danny Heep .08 .25
42T Steve Henderson .08 .25
43T Keith Hernandez .40 1.00
44T Leo Hernandez .08 .25
45T Willie Hernandez .40 1.00
46T Al Holland .08 .25
47T Frank Howard MG .40 1.00
48T Bobby Johnson .08 .25
49T Cliff Johnson .08 .25
50T Odell Jones .08 .25
51T Mike Jorgensen .08 .25
52T Bob Kearney .08 .25
53T Steve Kemp .08 .25
54T Matt Keough .08 .25
55T Ron Kittle XRC .75 2.00
56T Mickey Klutts .08 .25
57T Alan Knicely .08 .25
58T Mike Krukow .08 .25
59T Rafael Landestoy .08 .25
60T Carney Lansford .40 1.00
61T Joe Lefebvre .08 .25
62T Bryan Little .08 .25
63T Aurelio Lopez .08 .25
64T Mike Madden .08 .25
65T Rick Manning .08 .25
66T Billy Martin MG .75 2.00
67T Lee Mazzilli .40 1.00
68T Andy McGaffigan .08 .25
69T Craig McMurtry .08 .25
70T John McNamara MG .08 .25
71T Orlando Mercado .08 .25
72T Larry Milbourne .08 .25
73T Randy Moffitt .08 .25
74T Sid Monge .08 .25
75T Jose Morales .08 .25
76T Omar Moreno .08 .25
77T Joe Morgan .40 1.00
78T Mike Morgan .08 .25
79T Dale Murray .08 .25
80T Jeff Newman .08 .25
81T Pete O'Brien XRC .40 1.00
82T Jorge Orta .08 .25
83T Alejandro Pena XRC .75 2.00
84T Pascual Perez .08 .25
85T Tony Perez .75 2.00
86T Broderick Perkins .08 .25
87T Tony Phillips XRC .75 2.00
88T Charlie Puleo .08 .25
89T Pat Putnam .08 .25
90T Jamie Quirk .08 .25
91T Doug Rader MG .08 .25
92T Chuck Rainey .08 .25
93T Bobby Ramos .08 .25
94T Gary Redus XRC .40 1.00
95T Steve Renko .08 .25
96T Leon Roberts .08 .25
97T Aurelio Rodriguez .08 .25
98T Dick Ruthven .08 .25
99T Daryl Sconiers .08 .25
100T Mike Scott .40 1.00
101T Tom Seaver .75 2.00
102T John Shelby .08 .25
103T Bob Shirley .08 .25
104T Joe Simpson .08 .25
105T Doug Sisk .08 .25
106T Mike Smithson .08 .25
107T Elias Sosa .08 .25
108T Darryl Strawberry XRC 20.00 50.00
109T Tom Tellmann .08 .25
110T Gene Tenace .40 1.00
111T Gorman Thomas .40 1.00
112T Dick Tidrow .08 .25
113T Dave Tobik .08 .25
114T Wayne Tolleson .08 .25
115T Mike Torrez .08 .25
116T Manny Trillo .08 .25
117T Steve Trout .08 .25
118T Lee Tunnell .08 .25
119T Mike Vail .08 .25
120T Ellis Valentine .08 .25
121T Tom Veryzer .08 .25
122T George Vukovich .08 .25
123T Rick Waits .08 .25
124T Greg Walker .40 1.00
125T Chris Welsh .08 .25
126T Len Whitehouse .08 .25
127T Eddie Whitson .08 .25
128T Jim Wohlford .08 .25
129T Matt Young XRC .40 1.00
130T Joel Youngblood .08 .25
131T Pat Zachry .08 .25
132T Checklist 1T-132T .08 .25

1983 Topps Foldouts

The cards in this 85-card (five folders with 17 photos in each folder) set measure 3 1/2" by 5 5/16". The 1983 Fold-Outs were an innovation by Topps featuring five sets of 17 postcard-size photos each. Each of the five sets had a theme of career leaders in a particular category. The five catagories -- batting leaders, home run leaders, stolen base leaders, pitching leaders and relief aces -- featured the 17 top active players in their respective categories. If a player were a leader in more than one category, he is pictured in more than one of the five sets. These foldout booklets are typically sold intact and are priced below at one price per complete panel. Each picture contains a facsimile autograph as well. The quality of the photos is very good. In the checklist below the leaders are listed in order of their career standing as shown on each foldout.

COMPLETE SET (5) 2.00 5.00
1 Career Wins .50 1.25
Gaylord Perry& 307/Steve Carlton/Ji
2 Home Run Leaders .60 1.50
Reggie Jackson& 464/Carl Yastrz
3 Batting Leaders .60 1.50
Rod Carew .331/George Brett/Bi
4 Relief Aces .40 1.00
Rollie Fingers& 301/Bruce Sutter/R.
5 Steals Leaders .40 1.00
Joe Morgan& 663/Cesar Cedeno/Ron

1983 Topps Leader Sheet

The cards in this 8-player sheet measure 2 1/2" by 3 1/2". The full sheet is 7 1/2" by 10 1/2". The full sheet is typically kept intact as it has not been perforated. The sheet is blank backed and features the league statistical leaders from the previous season. The cards are unnumbered and are listed below in left to right order of appearance on the sheet.

1 Willie Wilson .75 2.00
Reggie Jackson/Gorman Thomas/Al O

1983 Topps Stickers

Made for Topps and O-Pee-Chee by Panini, an Italian company, these 330 stickers measure approximately 1 15/16" by 2 9/16" and are numbered on both front and back. The fronts feature white-bordered color player photos framed with a colored and a black line. The colored line is red for AL players and blue for NL players. The backs carry player names and a bilingual ad for the O-Pee-Chee sticker album. The album, onto which the stickers could be affixed, was available at retail stores. The album and the sticker numbering are organized as follows: Home Run Kings (1-14), AL Pitching and Batting Leaders (15-22), Baltimore Orioles (23-30), Boston Red Sox (31-38), California Angels (39-46), Chicago White Sox (47-54), Cleveland Indians (55-62), Detroit Tigers (63-70), Kansas City Royals (71-78), Milwaukee Brewers (79-86), Minnesota Twins (87-94), New York Yankees (95-102), Oakland A's (103-110), Seattle Mariners (111-118), Texas Rangers (119-126), Toronto Blue Jays (127-134), 1982 Record Breakers (135-146), 1982 Championship Series (147-158), AL and NL All-Stars (159-178), 1982 World Series (179-190), 1982 Record Breakers (191-202), NL Pitching and Batting Leaders (203-210), Atlanta Braves (211-218), Chicago Cubs (219-226), Cincinnati Reds (227-234), Houston Astros (235-242), Los Angeles Dodgers (243-250), Montreal Expos (251-258), New York Mets (259-266), Philadelphia Phillies (267-274), Pittsburgh Pirates (275-282), St. Louis Cardinals (283-290), San Diego Padres (291-298), San Francisco Giants (299-306), and Stars of the Future (307-330). Wade Boggs and Ryne Sandberg are featured during their Rookie Card year.

COMPLETE SET (330) 6.00 15.00
COMMON PLAYER (1-330) .02 .05
COMMON FOILS .04 .10
*OPC: .75X TO 2X TOPPS STICKERS
1 Hank Aaron FOIL .50 1.25
2 Babe Ruth FOIL 1.25 3.00
3 Willie Mays FOIL .60 1.50
4 Frank Robinson FOIL .08 .25
5 Reggie Jackson .20 .50
6 Carl Yastrzemski .15 .40
7 Johnny Bench .20 .50
8 Tony Perez .08 .25
9 Lee May .02 .10
10 Mike Schmidt .25 .60
11 Dave Kingman .02 .10
12 Reggie Smith .02 .10
13 Graig Nettles .02 .10
14 Rusty Staub .02 .10
15 Willie Wilson .01 .05
16 LaMarr Hoyt .01 .05
17 Reggie Jackson and .05 .15
Gorman Thomas
18 Floyd Bannister .01 .05
19 Hal McRae .01 .05
20 Rick Sutcliffe .01 .05
21 Rickey Henderson .20 .50
22 Dan Quisenberry .01 .05
23 Jim Palmer FOIL .15 .40
24 John Lowenstein .01 .05
25 Mike Flanagan .02 .10
26 Cal Ripken 1.50 4.00
27 Rich Dauer .01 .05
28 Ken Singleton .02 .10
29 Eddie Murray .20 .50
30 Rick Dempsey .02 .10
31 Carl Yastrzemski FOIL .25 .60
32 Carney Lansford .02 .10
33 Jerry Remy .01 .05
34 Dennis Eckersley .20 .50
35 Dave Stapleton .01 .05
36 Mark Clear .01 .05
37 Jim Rice .02 .10
38 Dwight Evans .02 .10
39 Rod Carew .15 .40
40 Don Baylor .02 .10
41 Reggie Jackson FOIL .30 .75
42 Geoff Zahn .01 .05
43 Bobby Grich .02 .10
44 Fred Lynn .02 .10
45 Bob Boone .02 .10
46 Doug DeCinces .01 .05
47 Tom Paciorek .01 .05
48 Britt Burns .01 .05
49 Tony Bernazard .01 .05
50 Steve Kemp .01 .05
51 Greg Luzinski FOIL .05 .15
52 Harold Baines .05 .15
53 LaMarr Hoyt .01 .05
54 Carlton Fisk .20 .50
55 Andre Thornton FOIL .02 .10
56 Mike Hargrove .02 .10
57 Len Barker .01 .05
58 Toby Harrah .01 .05
59 Dan Spillner .01 .05
60 Rick Manning .01 .05
61 Rick Sutcliffe .01 .05
62 Ron Hassey .01 .05
63 Lance Parrish FOIL .05 .15
64 John Wockenfuss .01 .05
65 Lou Whitaker .05 .15
66 Alan Trammell .05 .15
67 Kirk Gibson .05 .15
68 Larry Herndon .01 .05
69 Jack Morris .02 .10
70 Dan Petry .01 .05
71 Frank White .02 .10
72 Amos Otis .02 .10
73 Willie Wilson FOIL .02 .10
74 Dan Quisenberry .01 .05
75 Hal McRae .02 .10
76 George Brett .60 1.50
77 Larry Gura .01 .05
78 John Wathan .01 .05
79 Rollie Fingers .20 .50
80 Cecil Cooper .02 .10
81 Robin Yount FOIL .20 .50
82 Ben Oglivie .01 .05
83 Paul Molitor .15 .40
84 Gorman Thomas .01 .05
85 Ted Simmons .02 .10
86 Pete Vuckovich .01 .05

87 Gary Gaetti .08 .25
88 Kent Hrbek FOIL .08 .25
89 John Castino .01 .05
90 Tom Brunansky .01 .05
91 Bobby Mitchell .01 .05
92 Gary Ward .01 .05
93 Tim Laudner .01 .05
94 Ron Davis .01 .05
95 Willie Randolph .02 .10
96 Roy Smalley .01 .05
97 Jerry Mumphrey .01 .05
98 Ken Griffey .02 .10
99 Dave Winfield FOIL .20 .50
100 Rich Gossage .08 .25
101 Butch Wynegar .01 .05
102 Ron Guidry .02 .10
103 Rickey Henderson FOIL .30 .75
104 Mike Heath .01 .05
105 Dave Lopes .02 .10
106 Rick Langford .01 .05
107 Dwayne Murphy .01 .05
108 Tony Armas .01 .05
109 Matt Keough .01 .05
110 Danny Meyer .01 .05
111 Bruce Bochte .01 .05
112 Julio Cruz .01 .05
113 Floyd Bannister .01 .05
114 Gaylord Perry FOIL .15 .40
115 Al Cowens .01 .05
116 Richie Zisk .01 .05
117 Jim Essian .01 .05
118 Bill Caudill .01 .05
119 Buddy Bell FOIL .05 .15
120 Larry Parrish .01 .05
121 Danny Darwin .01 .05
122 Bucky Dent .02 .10
123 Johnny Grubb .01 .05
124 George Wright .01 .05
125 Charlie Hough .02 .10
126 Jim Sundberg .01 .05
127 Dave Stieb FOIL .02 .10
128 Willie Upshaw .01 .05
129 Alfredo Griffin .01 .05
130 Lloyd Moseby .01 .05
131 Ernie Whitt .01 .05
132 Jim Clancy .01 .05
133 Barry Bonnell .01 .05
134 Damaso Garcia .01 .05
135 Jim Kaat RB .02 .10
136 Jim Kaat RB .02 .10
137 Greg Minton RB .01 .05
138 Greg Minton RB .01 .05
139 Paul Molitor RB .05 .15
140 Paul Molitor RB .05 .15
141 Manny Trillo RB .01 .05
142 Manny Trillo RB .01 .05
143 Joel Youngblood RB .01 .05
144 Joel Youngblood RB .01 .05
145 Robin Yount RB .05 .15
146 Robin Yount RB .05 .15
147 Willie McGee LCS .02 .10
148 Darrell Porter LCS .01 .05
149 Darrell Porter LCS .01 .05
150 Robin Yount LCS .05 .15
151 Bruce Benedict LCS .01 .05
152 Bruce Benedict LCS .01 .05
153 George Hendrick LCS .01 .05
154 Bruce Benedict LCS .01 .05
155 Doug DeCinces LCS .01 .05
156 Paul Molitor LCS .05 .15
157 Charlie Moore LCS .01 .05
158 Fred Lynn LCS .02 .10
159 Rickey Henderson .20 .50
160 Dale Murphy .05 .15
161 Willie Wilson .01 .05
162 Jack Clark .01 .05
163 Reggie Jackson .20 .50
164 Andre Dawson .08 .25
165 Dan Quisenberry .01 .05
166 Bruce Sutter .15 .40
167 Robin Yount .08 .25
168 Ozzie Smith .30 .75
169 Frank White .02 .10
170 Phil Garner .02 .10
171 Doug DeCinces .01 .05
172 Mike Schmidt .25 .60
173 Cecil Cooper .02 .10
174 Al Oliver .02 .10
175 Jim Palmer .08 .25
176 Steve Carlton .15 .40
177 Carlton Fisk .20 .50
178 Gary Carter .20 .50
179 Joaquin Andujar WS .01 .05
180 Ozzie Smith WS .08 .25
181 Cecil Cooper WS .02 .10
182 Darrell Porter WS .01 .05
183 Darrell Porter WS .01 .05
184 Mike Caldwell WS .01 .05
185 Mike Caldwell WS .01 .05
186 Ozzie Smith WS .08 .25
187 Bruce Sutter WS .08 .25
188 Keith Hernandez WS .02 .10
189 Dane Iorg WS .01 .05
190 Dane Iorg WS .01 .05
191 Tony Armas RB .01 .05
192 Tony Armas RB .01 .05
193 Lance Parrish RB .02 .10
194 Lance Parrish RB .02 .10
195 John Wathan RB .01 .05
196 John Wathan RB .01 .05
197 Rickey Henderson RB .08 .25
198 Rickey Henderson RB .08 .25
199 Rickey Henderson RB .08 .25
200 Rickey Henderson RB .08 .25
201 Rickey Henderson RB .08 .25
202 Rickey Henderson RB .08 .25
203 Steve Carlton .15 .40
204 Steve Carlton .15 .40
205 Al Oliver .02 .10
206 Dale Murphy and Al Oliver .05 .15
207 Dave Kingman .02 .10
208 Steve Rogers .01 .05
209 Bruce Sutter .15 .40
210 Tim Raines .05 .15
211 Dale Murphy FOIL .08 .25
212 Chris Chambliss .02 .10
213 Gene Garber .01 .05
214 Bob Horner .01 .05
215 Glenn Hubbard .01 .05
216 Claudell Washington .01 .05
217 Bruce Benedict .01 .05
218 Phil Niekro .20 .50
219 Leon Durham FOIL .02 .10
220 Jay Johnstone .01 .05
221 Larry Bowa .02 .10
222 Keith Moreland .01 .05
223 Bill Buckner .02 .10
224 Fergie Jenkins .20 .50
225 Dick Tidrow .01 .05
226 Jody Davis .01 .05
227 Dave Concepcion .02 .10
228 Dan Driessen .01 .05
229 Johnny Bench .20 .50
230 Ron Oester .01 .05
231 Cesar Cedeno .02 .10
232 Alex Trevino .01 .05
233 Tom Seaver .20 .50
234 Mario Soto .01 .05
235 Nolan Ryan FOIL 1.25 3.00
236 Art Howe .01 .05
237 Phil Garner .02 .10
238 Ray Knight .01 .05
239 Terry Puhl .01 .05
240 Joe Niekro .02 .10
241 Alan Ashby .01 .05
242 Jose Cruz .02 .10
243 Steve Garvey .05 .15
244 Ron Cey .02 .10
245 Dusty Baker .02 .10
246 Ken Landreaux .01 .05
247 Jerry Reuss .02 .10
248 Pedro Guerrero .02 .10
249 Bill Russell .02 .10
250 Fern.Valenzuela FOIL .07 .20
251 Al Oliver FOIL .07 .20
252 Andre Dawson .08 .25
253 Tim Raines .08 .25
254 Jeff Reardon .02 .10
255 Gary Carter .20 .50
256 Steve Rogers .01 .05
257 Tim Wallach .02 .10
258 Chris Speier .01 .05
259 Dave Kingman .05 .15
260 Bob Bailor .01 .05
261 Hubie Brooks .01 .05
262 Craig Swan .01 .05
263 George Foster .02 .10
264 John Stearns .01 .05
265 Neil Allen .01 .05
266 Mookie Wilson FOIL .05 .15
267 Steve Carlton FOIL .25 .60
268 Manny Trillo .01 .05
269 Gary Matthews .01 .05
270 Mike Schmidt .25 .60
271 Ivan DeJesus .01 .05
272 Pete Rose .30 .75
273 Bo Diaz .01 .05
274 Sid Monge .01 .05
275 Bill Madlock FOIL .07 .20
276 Jason Thompson .01 .05
277 Don Robinson .01 .05
278 Omar Moreno .01 .05
279 Dale Berra .01 .05
280 Dave Parker .02 .10
281 Tony Pena .01 .05
282 John Candelaria .01 .05
283 Lonnie Smith .01 .05
284 Bruce Sutter FOIL .20 .50
285 George Hendrick .01 .05
286 Tom Herr .01 .05
287 Ken Oberkfell .01 .05
288 Ozzie Smith .30 .75
289 Bob Forsch .01 .05
290 Keith Hernandez .02 .10
291 Garry Templeton .01 .05
292 Broderick Perkins .01 .05
293 Terry Kennedy FOIL .02 .10
294 Gene Richards .01 .05
295 Ruppert Jones .01 .05
296 Tim Lollar .01 .05
297 John Montefusco .01 .05
298 Sixto Lezcano .01 .05
299 Greg Minton .01 .05
300 Jack Clark FOIL .05 .15
301 Milt May .01 .05
302 Reggie Smith .02 .10
303 Joe Morgan .20 .50
304 John LeMaster .01 .05
305 Darrell Evans .02 .10
306 Al Holland .01 .05
307 Jesse Barfield .02 .10
308 Wade Boggs 1.50 4.00
309 Tom Brunansky .01 .05
310 Storm Davis .01 .05
311 Von Hayes .01 .05
312 Dave Hostetler .01 .05
313 Kent Hrbek .02 .10
314 Tim Laudner .01 .05
315 Cal Ripken 2.50 6.00
316 Andre Robertson .01 .05
317 Ed VandeBerg .01 .05
318 Glenn Wilson .01 .05
319 Chili Davis .08 .25
320 Bob Dernier .01 .05
321 Terry Francona .05 .15
322 Brian Giles .01 .05
323 David Green .01 .05
324 Atlee Hammaker .01 .05
325 Bill Laskey .01 .05
326 Willie McGee .40 1.00
327 Johnny Ray .01 .05
328 Ryne Sandberg 3.00 8.00
329 Steve Sax .02 .10
330 Eric Show .01 .05
NNO Album .40 1.00

1983 Topps Sticker Boxes

COMPLETE SET (8) 4.00 10.00
1 Fernando Valenzuela .30 .75
2 Gary Carter .60 1.50
3 Mike Schmidt .75 2.00
4 Reggie Jackson .75 2.00
5 Jim Palmer .60 1.50
6 Rollie Fingers .30 .75
7 Pete Rose .75 2.00
8 Rickey Henderson .75 2.00

1983 Topps Gaylord Perry

This six-card, standard-size, set depicts Gaylord Perry during various parts of his career. These cards have the looks of Topps cards and were produced by Topps but have no Topps logo on either the front or the back of the card.

COMPLETE SET (6) 6.00 15.00
COMMON PLAYER (1-6) 1.20 3.00

1983 Topps 1952 Reprint

This 402 card standard-size set feature reprinted versions of the cards in the 52 Topps set. These sets were issued in complete form only available from Topps. Five players did not agree to be in this set, that is why the set only contains 402 cards. The five cards not in this set are Billy Loes (number 20), Dom DiMaggio (number 22), Saul Rogovin (number 159), Solly Hemus (number 196) and Tommy Holmes (number 289).

COMPLETE SET (402) 75.00 150.00
COMP.FACTORY SET (402) 100.00 200.00
1 Andy Pafko 1.00 2.50
2 Pete Runnels .40 1.00
3 Hank Thompson .40 1.00
4 Don Lenhardt .20 .50
5 Larry Jansen .40 1.00
6 Grady Hatton .20 .50
7 Wayne Terwilliger .75 2.00
8 Fred Marsh .20 .50
9 Robert Hogue .20 .50
10 Al Rosen .75 2.00
11 Phil Rizzuto 5.00 10.00
12 Monty Basgall .20 .50
13 Johnny Wyrostek .20 .50
14 Bob Elliott .40 1.00
15 Johnny Pesky 1.00 2.50
16 Gene Hermanski .20 .50
17 Jim Hegan .40 1.00
18 Merrill Combs .20 .50
19 Johnny Bucha .20 .50
21 Ferris Fain .40 1.00
23 Billy Goodman .40 1.00
24 Luke Easter .40 1.00
25 Johnny Groth .20 .50
26 Monte Irvin 2.50 6.00
27 Sam Jethroe .40 1.00
28 Jerry Priddy .20 .50
29 Ted Kluszewski 2.50 6.00
30 Mel Parnell .40 1.00
31 Gus Zernial 1.00 2.50
32 Eddie Robinson .40 1.00
33 Warren Spahn 5.00 10.00
34 Elmer Valo .20 .50
35 Hank Sauer .75 2.00
36 Gil Hodges 5.00 10.00
37 Duke Snider 7.50 15.00
38 Wally Westlake .20 .50
39 Dizzy Trout .40 1.00
40 Irv Noren .40 1.00
41 Bob Wellman .20 .50
42 Lou Kretlow .20 .50
43 Ray Scarborough .20 .50
44 Con Dempsey .20 .50
45 Eddie Joost .20 .50
46 Gordon Goldsberry .20 .50
47 Willie Jones .20 .50
48 Joe Page .75 2.00
49 Johnny Sain .75 2.00
50 Marv Rickert .20 .50
51 Jim Russell .20 .50
52 Don Mueller .40 1.00
53 Chris Van Cuyk .20 .50
54 Leo Kiely .20 .50
55 Ray Boone .40 1.00
56 Tommy Glaviano .20 .50
57 Ed Lopat 1.00 2.50
58 Bob Mahoney .20 .50
59 Robin Roberts 5.00 10.00
60 Sid Hudson .20 .50
61 Tookie Gilbert .20 .50
62 Chuck Stobbs .20 .50
63 Howie Pollet .20 .50
64 Roy Sievers .40 1.00
65 Enos Slaughter 5.00 10.00
66 Preacher Roe 1.00 2.50
67 Allie Reynolds 1.00 2.50
68 Cliff Chambers .20 .50
69 Virgil Stallcup .20 .50
70 Al Zarilla .20 .50
71 Tom Upton .20 .50
72 Karl Olson .20 .50
73 Bill Werle .20 .50
74 Andy Hansen .20 .50
75 Wes Westrum .40 1.00
76 Eddie Stanky .40 1.00
77 Bob Kennedy .40 1.00
78 Ellis Kinder .20 .50
79 Gerry Staley .20 .50
80 Herman Wehmeier .20 .50
81 Vernon Law .40 1.00
82 Duane Pillette .20 .50
83 Billy Johnson .20 .50
84 Vern Stephens .40 1.00
85 Bob Kuzava .40 1.00
86 Ted Gray .20 .50
87 Dale Coogan .20 .50
88 Bob Feller 7.50 15.00
89 Johnny Lipon .20 .50
90 Mickey Grasso .20 .50
91 Red Schoendienst 2.50 6.00
92 Dale Mitchell .40 1.00
93 Al Sima .20 .50
94 Sam Mele .20 .50
95 Ken Holcombe .20 .50
96 Willard Marshall .20 .50
97 Earl Torgeson .20 .50
98 Billy Pierce .40 1.00
99 Gene Woodling .75 2.00
100 Del Rice .20 .50
101 Max Lanier .20 .50
102 Bill Kennedy .20 .50
103 Cliff Mapes .20 .50
104 Don Kolloway .20 .50
105 Johnny Pramesa .20 .50
106 Mickey Vernon .75 2.00
107 Connie Ryan .20 .50
108 Jim Konstanty .75 2.00
109 Ted Wilks .20 .50
110 Dutch Leonard .20 .50
111 Peanuts Lowrey .20 .50
112 Hank Majeski .20 .50
113 Dick Sisler .40 1.00
114 Willard Ramsdell .20 .50
115 George Munger .20 .50
116 Carl Scheib .20 .50
117 Sherm Lollar .40 1.00
118 Ken Raffensberger .20 .50
119 Mickey McDermott .20 .50
120 Bob Chakales .20 .50
121 Gus Niarhos .20 .50
122 Jackie Jensen 2.00 5.00
123 Eddie Yost .40 1.00
124 Monte Kennedy .20 .50
125 Bill Rigney .20 .50
126 Fred Hutchinson .40 1.00
127 Paul Minner .20 .50
128 Don Bollweg .20 .50
129 Johnny Mize 2.50 6.00
130 Sheldon Jones .20 .50
131 Morrie Martin .20 .50
132 Clyde Kluttz .20 .50
133 Al Widmar .20 .50
134 Joe Tipton .20 .50
135 Dixie Howell .20 .50
136 Johnny Schmitz .20 .50
137 Roy McMillan .40 1.00
138 Bill MacDonald .20 .50
139 Ken Wood .20 .50
140 Johnny Antonelli .40 1.00
141 Clint Hartung .20 .50
142 Harry Perkowski .20 .50
143 Les Moss .20 .50
144 Ed Blake .20 .50
145 Joe Haynes .20 .50
146 Frank House .20 .50
147 Bob Young .20 .50
148 Johnny Klippstein .20 .50
149 Dick Kryhoski .20 .50
150 Ted Beard .20 .50
151 Wally Post .40 1.00
152 Al Evans .20 .50
153 Bob Rush .20 .50
154 Joe Muir .20 .50
155 Frank Overmire .20 .50
156 Frank Hiller .20 .50
157 Bob Usher .20 .50
158 Eddie Waitkus .20 .50
160 Owen Friend .20 .50
161 Bud Byerly .20 .50
162 Del Crandall .40 1.00
163 Stan Rojek .20 .50
164 Walt Dubiel .20 .50
165 Eddie Kazak .20 .50
166 Paul LaPalme .20 .50
167 Bill Howerton .20 .50
168 Charlie Silvera .40 1.00
169 Howie Judson .20 .50
170 Gus Bell .40 1.00
171 Ed Erautt .20 .50
172 Eddie Miksis .20 .50
173 Roy Smalley .20 .50
174 Clarence Marshall .20 .50
175 Billy Martin 4.00 10.00
176 Hank Edwards .20 .50
177 Bill Wight .20 .50
178 Cass Michaels .20 .50
179 Frank Smith .20 .50
180 Charlie Maxwell .40 1.00
181 Bob Swift .20 .50
182 Billy Hitchcock .20 .50
183 Erv Dusak .20 .50
184 Bob Ramazzotti .20 .50
185 Bill Nicholson .40 1.00
186 Walt Masterson .20 .50
187 Bob Miller .20 .50
188 Clarence Podbielan .20 .50
189 Pete Reiser .75 2.00
190 Don Johnson .20 .50
191 Yogi Berra 6.00 15.00
192 Myron Ginsberg .20 .50
193 Harry Simpson .40 1.00
194 Joe Hatten .20 .50
195 Minnie Minoso 2.50 6.00
197 George Strickland .20 .50
198 Phil Haugstad .20 .50
199 George Zuverink .20 .50
200 Ralph Houk 1.00 2.50
201 Alex Kellner .20 .50
202 Joe Collins .75 2.00
203 Curt Simmons .75 2.00
204 Ron Northey .20 .50
205 Clyde King .40 1.00
206 Joe Ostrowski .40 1.00
207 Mickey Harris .20 .50
208 Marlin Stuart .20 .50
209 Howie Fox .20 .50
210 Dick Fowler .20 .50
211 Ray Coleman .20 .50
212 Ned Garver .20 .50
213 Nippy Jones .20 .50
214 Johnny Hopp .40 1.00
215 Hank Bauer 1.00 2.50
216 Richie Ashburn 4.00 10.00
217 Snuffy Stirnweiss .40 1.00
218 Clyde McCullough .20 .50
219 Bobby Shantz .75 2.00
220 Joe Presko .20 .50
221 Granny Hamner .20 .50
222 Hoot Evers .20 .50
223 Del Ennis .40 1.00
224 Bruce Edwards .20 .50
225 Frank Baumholtz .20 .50
226 Dave Philley .20 .50
227 Joe Garagiola 2.00 5.00
228 Al Brazle .20 .50
229 Gene Bearden UER Misspelled Beardon .20 .50
230 Matt Batts .20 .50
231 Sam Zoldak .20 .50
232 Billy Cox .20 .50
233 Bob Friend .75 2.00
234 Steve Souchock .20 .50
235 Walt Dropo .20 .50
236 Ed Fitzgerald .20 .50
237 Jerry Coleman .75 2.00
238 Art Houtteman .20 .50
239 Rocky Bridges .20 .50
240 Jack Phillips .20 .50
241 Tommy Byrne .20 .50
242 Tom Poholsky .20 .50
243 Larry Doby 2.00 5.00
244 Vic Wertz .40 1.00
245 Sherry Robertson .20 .50
246 George Kell 2.50 6.00
247 Randy Gumpert .20 .50
248 Frank Shea .20 .50
249 Bobby Adams .20 .50
250 Carl Erskine 1.00 2.50
251 Chico Carrasquel .20 .50
252 Vern Bickford .20 .50
253 Johnny Berardino .40 1.00
254 Joe Dobson .20 .50
255 Clyde Vollmer .20 .50
256 Pete Suder .20 .50
257 Bobby Avila .40 1.00
258 Steve Gromek .20 .50
259 Bob Addis .20 .50
260 Pete Castiglione .20 .50
261 Willie Mays 10.00 25.00
262 Virgil Trucks .40 1.00
263 Harry Brecheen .40 1.00
264 Roy Hartsfield .20 .50
265 Chuck Diering .20 .50
266 Murry Dickson .40 1.00
267 Sid Gordon .20 .50
268 Bob Lemon 2.50 6.00
269 Willard Nixon .20 .50
270 Lou Brissie .20 .50
271 Jim Delsing .20 .50
272 Mike Garcia .40 1.00
273 Erv Palica .20 .50
274 Ralph Branca 1.00 2.50
275 Pat Mullin .20 .50
276 Jim Wilson .20 .50
277 Early Wynn 2.50 6.00
278 Allie Clark .20 .50
279 Eddie Stewart .20 .50
280 Cloyd Boyer .40 1.00
281 Tommy Brown .20 .50
282 Birdie Tebbetts .40 1.00
283 Phil Masi .20 .50
284 Hank Arft .20 .50
285 Cliff Fannin .20 .50
286 Joe DeMaestri .20 .50
287 Steve Bilko .20 .50
288 Chet Nichols .20 .50
290 Joe Astroth .20 .50
291 Gil Coan .20 .50
292 Floyd Baker .20 .50
293 Sibby Sisti .20 .50
294 Walker Cooper .20 .50
295 Phil Cavarretta .40 1.00
296 Red Rolfe MG .40 1.00
297 Andy Seminick .40 1.00
298 Bob Ross .20 .50
299 Ray Murray .20 .50
300 Barney McCosky .20 .50
301 Bob Porterfield .20 .50
302 Max Surkont .20 .50
303 Harry Dorish .20 .50
304 Sam Dente .20 .50
305 Paul Richards MG .40 1.00
306 Lou Sleater .20 .50
307 Frank Campos .20 .50
308 Luis Aloma .20 .50
309 Jim Busby .20 .50
310 George Metkovich .40 1.00
311 Mickey Mantle 25.00 50.00
312 Jackie Robinson 12.50 25.00
313 Bobby Thomson 2.00 5.00
314 Roy Campanella 5.00 10.00
315 Leo Durocher MG 2.50 6.00
316 Dave Williams .40 1.00
317 Conrado Marrero .40 1.00
318 Harold Gregg .20 .50
319 Al Walker .20 .50
320 John Rutherford .40 1.00
321 Joe Black 2.00 5.00
322 Randy Jackson .20 .50
323 Bubba Church .20 .50
324 Warren Hacker .20 .50
325 Bill Serena .20 .50
326 George Shuba .75 2.00
327 Al Wilson .20 .50
328 Bob Borkowski .20 .50
329 Ike Delock .20 .50
330 Turk Lown .20 .50
331 Tom Morgan .20 .50
332 Tony Bartirome .20 .50
333 Pee Wee Reese 4.00 10.00
334 Wilmer Mizell .40 1.00
335 Ted Lepcio .20 .50
336 Dave Koslo .20 .50
337 Jim Hearn .20 .50
338 Sal Yvars .20 .50
339 Russ Meyer .20 .50
340 Bob Hooper .20 .50
341 Hal Jeffcoat .20 .50
342 Clem Labine 2.00 5.00
343 Dick Gernert .20 .50
344 Ewell Blackwell .75 2.00
345 Sammy White .20 .50
346 George Spencer .20 .50
347 Joe Adcock .75 2.00
348 Robert Kelly .20 .50
349 Bob Cain .20 .50
350 Cal Abrams .20 .50
351 Alvin Dark .75 2.00
352 Karl Drews .20 .50
353 Bobby Del Greco .20 .50
354 Fred Hatfield .20 .50
355 Bobby Morgan .20 .50
356 Toby Atwell .20 .50
357 Smoky Burgess .75 2.00
358 John Kucab .20 .50
359 Dee Fondy .20 .50
360 George Crowe .40 1.00
361 William Posedel CO .20 .50
362 Ken Heintzelman .20 .50
363 Dick Rozek .20 .50
364 Clyde Sukeforth CO .20 .50
365 Cookie Lavagetto CO .40 1.00
366 Dave Madison .20 .50
367 Ben Thorpe .20 .50
368 Ed Wright .20 .50
369 Dick Groat 2.00 5.00
370 Billy Hoeft .40 1.00
371 Bobby Hofman .20 .50
372 Gil McDougald 2.00 5.00
373 Jim Turner CO .75 2.00
374 John Benton .20 .50
375 John Merson .20 .50
376 Faye Throneberry .20 .50
377 Chuck Dressen MG .40 1.00
378 Leroy Fusselman .20 .50
379 Joe Rossi .20 .50
380 Clem Koshorek .20 .50
381 Milton Stock CO .20 .50
382 Sam Jones .75 2.00
383 Del Wilber .20 .50
384 Frank Crosetti CO 2.00 5.00
385 Herman Franks CO .20 .50
386 Ed Yuhas .20 .50
387 Billy Meyer MG .20 .50
388 Bob Chipman .20 .50
389 Ben Wade .20 .50
390 Rocky Nelson .20 .50
391 Ben Chapman UER CO Photo actually/Sam Chapman .20 .50
392 Hoyt Wilhelm 2.50 6.00
393 Ebba St.Claire .20 .50
394 Billy Herman CO 2.00 5.00
395 Jake Pitler CO .20 .50
396 Dick Williams 2.00 5.00
397 Forrest Main .20 .50
398 Hal Rice .20 .50
399 Jim Fridley .20 .50
400 Bill Dickey CO 2.50 6.00
401 Bob Schultz .20 .50
402 Earl Harrist .20 .50
403 Bill Miller .20 .50
404 Dick Brodowski .20 .50
405 Eddie Pellagrini .20 .50
406 Joe Nuxhall .75 2.00
407 Eddie Mathews 4.00 10.00

1983-91 Topps Traded Bronze Premiums

Dealers who ordered Topps Traded cases received these bronze replica cards as bonuses. These cards which measure approximately 1 1/4" by 1 3/4" started off by featuring current players but later switched to retired stars. We have sequenced this set by year of release.

COMPLETE SET (9) 100.00 200.00
1 Steve Carlton 12.50 30.00
2 Darryl Strawberry 6.00 15.00
3 Pete Rose 6.00 15.00
4 Mickey Mantle 20.00 50.00
5 Willie Mays 10.00 25.00
6 Duke Snider 6.00 15.00
7 Hank Aaron 8.00 20.00
8 Jackie Robinson 8.00 20.00
9 Brooks Robinson 8.00 20.00

1984 Topps

The cards in this 792-card set measure the standard size. Cards were primarily distributed in 15-card wax packs and 54-card rack packs. For the second year in a row, Topps utilized a dual picture on the front of the card. A portrait is shown in a square insert and an action shot is featured in the main photo. Card numbers 1-6 feature 1983 Highlights (HL), cards 131-138 depict League Leaders, card numbers 386-407 feature All-Stars, and card numbers 701-718 feature active Major League career leaders in various statistical categories. Each team leader (TL) card features the team's leading hitter and pitcher pictured on the front with a team checklist back. There are six numerical checklist cards in the set. The player cards feature team logos in the upper right corner of the reverse. The key Rookie Cards in this set are Don Mattingly and Darryl Strawberry. Topps tested a special send-in offer in Michigan and a few other states whereby collectors could obtain direct from Topps ten cards of their choice. Needless to say most people ordered the key (most valuable) players necessitating the printing of a special sheet to keep up with the demand. The special sheet had five cards of Darryl Strawberry, three cards of Don Mattingly, etc. The test was apparently a failure in Topps' eyes as they have never tried it again.

COMPLETE SET (792) 20.00 50.00
1 Steve Carlton HL .08 .25
2 Rickey Henderson HL .25 .60
3 Dan Quisenberry HL Sets save record .05 .15
4 N.Ryan Carlton/Perry HL .40 1.00
5 Dave Righetti& Bob Forsch&/and Mike Warren HL/(.08 .25
6 J.Bench G.Perry/C.Yaz HL .15 .40
7 Gary Lucas .05 .15
8 Don Mattingly RC 12.00 30.00
9 Jim Gott .05 .15
10 Robin Yount .40 1.00
11 Minnesota Twins TL Kent Hrbek/Ken Schrom/(Check .08 .25
12 Billy Sample .05 .15
13 Scott Holman .05 .15
14 Tom Brookens .05 .15
15 Burt Hooton .05 .15
16 Omar Moreno .05 .15
17 John Denny .05 .15
18 Dale Berra .05 .15
19 Ray Fontenot .05 .15
20 Greg Luzinski .08 .25
21 Joe Altobelli MG .05 .15
22 Bryan Clark .05 .15
23 Keith Moreland .05 .15
24 John Martin .05 .15
25 Glenn Hubbard .05 .15
26 Bud Black .05 .15
27 Daryl Sconiers .05 .15
28 Frank Viola .15 .40
29 Danny Heep .05 .15
30 Wade Boggs .60 1.50
31 Andy McGaffigan .05 .15
32 Bobby Ramos .05 .15
33 Tom Burgmeier .05 .15
34 Eddie Milner .05 .15
35 Don Sutton .08 .25
36 Denny Walling .05 .15
37 Texas Rangers TL Buddy Bell/Rick Honeycutt/(Che .08 .25
38 Luis DeLeon .05 .15
39 Garth Iorg .05 .15
40 Dusty Baker .08 .25
41 Tony Bernazard .05 .15
42 Johnny Grubb .05 .15
43 Ron Reed .05 .15
44 Jim Morrison .05 .15
45 Jerry Mumphrey .05 .15
46 Ray Smith .05 .15
47 Rudy Law .05 .15
48 Julio Franco .08 .25
49 John Stuper .05 .15
50 Chris Chambliss .08 .25
51 Jim Frey MG .05 .15
52 Paul Splittorff .05 .15
53 Juan Beniquez .05 .15
54 Jesse Orosco .05 .15
55 Dave Concepcion .08 .25
56 Gary Allenson .05 .15
57 Dan Schatzeder .05 .15
58 Max Venable .05 .15
59 Sammy Stewart .05 .15
60 Paul Molitor .08 .25
61 Chris Codiroli .05 .15
62 Dave Hostetler .05 .15
63 Ed VandeBerg .05 .15
64 Mike Scioscia .08 .25
65 Kirk Gibson .25 .60
66 Astros TL Nolan Ryan .40 1.00
67 Gary Ward .05 .15
68 Luis Salazar .05 .15
69 Rod Scurry .05 .15
70 Gary Matthews .08 .25
71 Leo Hernandez .05 .15
72 Mike Squires .05 .15
73 Jody Davis .05 .15
74 Jerry Martin .05 .15
75 Bob Forsch .05 .15
76 Alfredo Griffin .05 .15
77 Brett Butler .08 .25
78 Mike Torrez .05 .15
79 Rob Wilfong .05 .15
80 Steve Rogers .08 .25
81 Billy Martin MG .15 .40
82 Doug Bird .05 .15
83 Richie Zisk .05 .15
84 Lenny Faedo .05 .15
85 Atlee Hammaker .05 .15
86 John Shelby .05 .15
87 Frank Pastore .05 .15
88 Rob Picciolo .05 .15
89 Mike Smithson .05 .15
90 Pedro Guerrero .08 .25
91 Dan Spillner .05 .15
92 Lloyd Moseby .05 .15
93 Bob Knepper .05 .15
94 Mario Ramirez .05 .15
95 Aurelio Lopez .08 .25
96 Kansas City Royals TL Hal McRae/Larry Gura/(Che .08 .25
97 LaMarr Hoyt .05 .15
98 Steve Nicosia .05 .15
99 Craig Lefferts RC .05 .15
100 Reggie Jackson .15 .40
101 Porfirio Altamirano .05 .15
102 Ken Oberkfell .05 .15
103 Dwayne Murphy .05 .15
104 Ken Dayley .05 .15
105 Tony Armas .08 .25
106 Tim Stoddard .05 .15
107 Ned Yost .05 .15
108 Randy Moffitt .05 .15
109 Brad Wellman .05 .15
110 Ron Guidry .08 .25
111 Bill Virdon MG .05 .15
112 Tom Niedenfuer .05 .15
113 Kelly Paris .05 .15
114 Checklist 1-132 .08 .25
115 Andre Thornton .05 .15
116 George Bjorkman .05 .15
117 Tom Veryzer .05 .15
118 Charlie Hough .08 .25
119 John Wockenfuss .05 .15
120 Keith Hernandez .08 .25
121 Pat Sheridan .05 .15
122 Cecilio Guante .05 .15
123 Butch Wynegar .05 .15
124 Damaso Garcia .05 .15
125 Britt Burns .05 .15
126 Braves TL Dale Murphy .15 .40
127 Mike Madden .05 .15
128 Rick Manning .05 .15
129 Bill Laskey .05 .15
130 Ozzie Smith .40 1.00
131 W.Boggs B.Madlock LL .25 .60
132 Mike Schmidt J.Rice LL .25 .60
133 D.Murphy Coop/Rice LL .15 .40
134 T.Raines R.Henderson LL .25 .60
135 John Denny LaMarr Hoyt LL .25 .60
136 S.Carlton J.Morris LL .08 .25
137 A.Hammaker R.Honeycutt LL .08 .25
138 Al Holland Dan Quisenberry LL .08 .25
139 Bert Campaneris .08 .25
140 Storm Davis .05 .15

Card	Low	High
141 Pat Corrales MG	.05	.15
142 Rich Gale	.05	.15
143 Jose Morales	.05	.15
144 Brian Harper RC	.15	.40
145 Gary Lavelle	.05	.15
146 Ed Romero	.05	.15
147 Dan Petry	.08	.25
148 Joe Lefebvre	.05	.15
149 Jon Matlack	.05	.15
150 Dale Murphy	.15	.40
151 Steve Trout	.05	.15
152 Glenn Brummer	.05	.15
153 Dick Tidrow	.05	.15
154 Dave Henderson	.08	.25
155 Frank White	.08	.25
156 A's TL	.25	.60
Rickey Henderson		
157 Gary Gaetti	.15	.40
158 John Curtis	.05	.15
159 Darryl Cias	.05	.15
160 Mario Soto	.08	.25
161 Junior Ortiz	.05	.15
162 Bob Ojeda	.05	.15
163 Lorenzo Gray	.05	.15
164 Scott Sanderson	.05	.15
165 Ken Singleton	.08	.25
166 Jamie Nelson	.05	.15
167 Marshall Edwards	.05	.15
168 Juan Bonilla	.05	.15
169 Larry Parrish	.05	.15
170 Jerry Reuss	.05	.15
171 Frank Robinson MG	.15	.40
172 Frank DiPino	.05	.15
173 Marvell Wynne	.15	.40
174 Juan Berenguer	.05	.15
175 Graig Nettles	.08	.25
176 Lee Smith	.08	.25
177 Jerry Hairston	.05	.15
178 Bill Krueger RC	.05	.15
179 Buck Martinez	.05	.15
180 Manny Trillo	.05	.15
181 Roy Thomas	.05	.15
182 Darryl Strawberry RC	1.25	3.00
183 Al Williams	.05	.15
184 Mike O'Berry	.05	.15
185 Sixto Lezcano	.05	.15
186 Cardinal TL	.08	.25
Lonnie Smith/John Stuper/(Checklist		
187 Luis Aponte	.05	.15
188 Bryan Little	.05	.15
189 Tim Conroy	.05	.15
190 Ben Oglivie	.08	.25
191 Mike Boddicker	.05	.15
192 Nick Esasky	.05	.15
193 Darrell Brown	.05	.15
194 Domingo Ramos	.05	.15
195 Jack Morris	.08	.25
196 Don Slaught	.08	.25
197 Garry Hancock	.05	.15
198 Bill Doran RC*	.15	.40
199 Willie Hernandez	.05	.15
200 Andre Dawson	.08	.25
201 Bruce Kison	.05	.15
202 Bobby Cox MG	.08	.25
203 Matt Keough	.05	.15
204 Bobby Meacham	.05	.15
205 Greg Minton	.05	.15
206 Andy Van Slyke RC	.60	1.50
207 Donnie Moore	.05	.15
208 Jose Oquendo RC	.15	.40
209 Manny Sarmiento	.05	.15
210 Joe Morgan	.08	.25
211 Rick Sweet	.05	.15
212 Broderick Perkins	.05	.15
213 Bruce Hurst	.05	.15
214 Paul Householder	.05	.15
215 Tippy Martinez	.05	.15
216 White Sox TL	.08	.25
C.Fisk		
217 Alan Ashby	.05	.15
218 Rick Waits	.05	.15
219 Joe Simpson	.05	.15
220 Fernando Valenzuela	.08	.25
221 Cliff Johnson	.05	.15
222 Rick Honeycutt	.05	.15
223 Wayne Krenchicki	.05	.15
224 Sid Monge	.05	.15
225 Lee Mazzilli	.08	.25
226 Juan Eichelberger	.05	.15
227 Steve Braun	.05	.15
228 John Rabb	.05	.15
229 Paul Owens MG	.05	.15
230 Rickey Henderson	.40	1.00
231 Gary Woods	.05	.15
232 Tim Wallach	.05	.15
233 Checklist 133-264	.08	.25
234 Rafael Ramirez	.05	.15
235 Matt Young RC	.15	.40
236 Ellis Valentine	.05	.15
237 John Castino	.05	.15
238 Reid Nichols	.05	.15
239 Jay Howell	.05	.15
240 Eddie Murray	.25	.60
241 Bill Almon	.05	.15
242 Alex Trevino	.05	.15
243 Pete Ladd	.05	.15
244 Candy Maldonado	.05	.15
245 Rick Sutcliffe	.08	.25
246 Mets TL	.08	.25
Tom Seaver		
247 Onix Concepcion	.05	.15
248 Bill Dawley	.05	.15
249 Jay Johnstone	.05	.15
250 Bill Madlock	.08	.25
251 Tony Gwynn	1.00	2.50
252 Larry Christenson	.05	.15
253 Jim Wohlford	.05	.15
254 Shane Rawley	.05	.15
255 Bruce Benedict	.05	.15
256 Dave Geisel	.05	.15
257 Julio Cruz	.05	.15
258 Luis Sanchez	.05	.15
259 Sparky Anderson MG	.08	.25
260 Scott McGregor	.05	.15
261 Bobby Brown	.05	.15
262 Tom Candiotti RC	.30	.75
263 Jack Fimple	.05	.15
264 Doug Frobel RC	.05	.15
265 Donnie Hill	.05	.15
266 Steve Lubratich	.05	.15
267 Carmelo Martinez	.05	.15
268 Jack O'Connor	.05	.15
269 Aurelio Rodriguez	.05	.15
270 Jeff Russell RC	.15	.40
271 Moose Haas	.05	.15
272 Rick Dempsey	.05	.15
273 Charlie Puleo	.05	.15
274 Rick Monday	.08	.25
275 Len Matuszek	.05	.15
276 Angels TL	.08	.25
Rod Carew		
277 Eddie Whitson	.05	.15
278 George Bell	.08	.25
279 Ivan DeJesus	.05	.15
280 Floyd Bannister	.05	.15
281 Larry Milbourne	.05	.15
282 Jim Barr	.05	.15
283 Larry Biittner	.05	.15
284 Howard Bailey	.05	.15
285 Darrell Porter	.05	.15
286 Lary Sorensen	.05	.15
287 Warren Cromartie	.05	.15
288 Jim Beattie	.05	.15
289 Randy Johnson	.05	.15
290 Dave Dravecky	.05	.15
291 Chuck Tanner MG	.05	.15
292 Tony Scott	.05	.15
293 Ed Lynch	.05	.15
294 U.L. Washington	.05	.15
295 Mike Flanagan	.05	.15
296 Jeff Newman	.05	.15
297 Bruce Berenyi	.05	.15
298 Jim Gantner	.05	.15
299 John Butcher	.05	.15
300 Pete Rose	.75	2.00
301 Frank LaCorte	.05	.15
302 Barry Bonnell	.05	.15
303 Marty Castillo	.05	.15
304 Warren Brusstar	.05	.15
305 Roy Smalley	.05	.15
306 Dodgers TL	.08	.25
Pedro Guerrero/Bob Welch/(Checklist		
307 Bobby Mitchell	.05	.15
308 Ron Hassey	.05	.15
309 Tony Phillips RC	.30	.75
310 Willie McGee	.08	.25
311 Jerry Koosman	.08	.25
312 Jorge Orta	.05	.15
313 Mike Jorgensen	.05	.15
314 Orlando Mercado	.05	.15
315 Bob Grich	.08	.25
316 Mark Bradley	.05	.15
317 Greg Pryor	.05	.15
318 Bill Gullickson	.05	.15
319 Al Bumbry	.05	.15
320 Bob Stanley	.05	.15
321 Harvey Kuenn MG	.05	.15
322 Ken Schrom	.05	.15
323 Alan Knicely	.05	.15
324 Alejandro Pena RC*	.30	.75
325 Darrell Evans	.08	.25
326 Bob Kearney	.05	.15
327 Ruppert Jones	.05	.15
328 Vern Ruhle	.05	.15
329 Pat Tabler	.05	.15
330 John Candelaria	.05	.15
331 Bucky Dent	.08	.25
332 Kevin Gross RC	.15	.40
333 Larry Herndon	.08	.25
334 Chuck Rainey	.05	.15
335 Don Baylor	.08	.25
336 Seattle Mariners TL	.08	.25
Pat Putnam/Matt Young/(Chec		
337 Kevin Hagen	.05	.15
338 Mike Warren	.05	.15
339 Roy Lee Jackson	.05	.15
340 Hal McRae	.08	.25
341 Dave Tobik	.05	.15
342 Tim Foli	.05	.15
343 Mark Davis	.05	.15
344 Rick Miller	.05	.15
345 Kent Hrbek	.08	.25
346 Kurt Bevacqua	.05	.15
347 Allan Ramirez	.05	.15
348 Toby Harrah	.08	.25
349 Bob L. Gibson RC	.05	.15
350 George Foster	.08	.25
351 Russ Nixon MG	.05	.15
352 Dave Stewart	.08	.25
353 Jim Anderson	.05	.15
354 Jeff Burroughs	.05	.15
355 Jason Thompson	.05	.15
356 Glenn Abbott	.05	.15
357 Ron Cey	.08	.25
358 Bob Dernier	.05	.15
359 Jim Acker	.05	.15
360 Willie Randolph	.08	.25
361 Dave Smith	.05	.15
362 David Green	.05	.15
363 Tim Laudner	.05	.15
364 Scott Fletcher	.05	.15
365 Steve Bedrosian	.05	.15
366 Padres TL	.08	.25
Terry Kennedy/Dave Dravecky/(Checklis		
367 Jamie Easterly	.05	.15
368 Hubie Brooks	.05	.15
369 Steve McCatty	.05	.15
370 Tim Raines	.08	.25
371 Dave Gumpert	.05	.15
372 Gary Roenicke	.05	.15
373 Bill Scherrer	.05	.15
374 Don Money	.05	.15
375 Dennis Leonard	.05	.15
376 Dave Anderson RC	.05	.15
377 Danny Darwin	.05	.15
378 Bob Brenly	.05	.15
379 Checklist 265-396	.08	.25
380 Steve Garvey	.08	.25
381 Ralph Houk MG	.05	.15
382 Chris Nyman	.05	.15
383 Terry Puhl	.05	.15
384 Lee Tunnell	.05	.15
385 Tony Perez	.15	.40
386 George Hendrick AS	.05	.15
387 Johnny Ray AS	.05	.15
388 Mike Schmidt AS	.25	.60
389 Ozzie Smith AS	.25	.60
390 Tim Raines AS	.05	.15
391 Dale Murphy AS	.08	.25
392 Andre Dawson AS	.05	.15
393 Gary Carter AS	.05	.15
394 Steve Rogers AS	.05	.15
395 Steve Carlton AS	.08	.25
396 Jesse Orosco AS	.05	.15
397 Eddie Murray AS	.15	.40
398 Lou Whitaker AS	.05	.15
399 George Brett AS	.25	.60
400 Cal Ripken AS	.75	2.00
401 Jim Rice AS	.05	.15
402 Dave Winfield AS	.05	.15
403 Lloyd Moseby AS	.05	.15
404 Ted Simmons AS	.05	.15
405 LaMarr Hoyt AS	.05	.15
406 Ron Guidry AS	.05	.15
407 Dan Quisenberry AS	.05	.15
408 Lou Piniella	.08	.25
409 Juan Agosto	.05	.15
410 Claudell Washington	.05	.15
411 Houston Jimenez	.05	.15
412 Doug Rader MG	.05	.15
413 Spike Owen RC	.15	.40
414 Mitchell Page	.05	.15
415 Tommy John	.08	.25
416 Dane Iorg	.05	.15
417 Mike Armstrong	.05	.15
418 Ron Hodges	.05	.15
419 John Henry Johnson	.05	.15
420 Cecil Cooper	.08	.25
421 Charlie Lea	.05	.15
422 Jose Cruz	.08	.25
423 Mike Morgan	.05	.15
424 Dann Bilardello	.05	.15
425 Steve Howe	.05	.15
426 Orioles TL	.60	1.50
Cal Ripken		
427 Rick Leach	.05	.15
428 Fred Breining	.05	.15
429 Randy Bush	.05	.15
430 Rusty Staub	.08	.25
431 Chris Bando	.05	.15
432 Charles Hudson	.05	.15
433 Rich Hebner	.05	.15
434 Harold Baines	.08	.25
435 Neil Allen	.05	.15
436 Rick Peters	.05	.15
437 Mike Proly	.05	.15
438 Biff Pocoroba	.05	.15
439 Bob Stoddard	.05	.15
440 Steve Kemp	.05	.15
441 Bob Lillis MG	.05	.15
442 Byron McLaughlin	.05	.15
443 Benny Ayala	.05	.15
444 Steve Renko	.05	.15
445 Jerry Remy	.05	.15
446 Luis Pujols	.05	.15
447 Tom Brunansky	.05	.15
448 Ben Hayes	.05	.15
449 Joe Pettini	.05	.15
450 Gary Carter	.08	.25
451 Bob Jones	.05	.15
452 Chuck Porter	.05	.15
453 Willie Upshaw	.05	.15
454 Joe Beckwith	.05	.15
455 Terry Kennedy	.05	.15
456 Cubs TL	.05	.15
F.Jenkins		
457 Dave Rozema	.05	.15
458 Kiko Garcia	.05	.15
459 Kevin Hickey	.05	.15
460 Dave Winfield	.08	.25
461 Jim Maler	.05	.15
462 Lee Lacy	.05	.15
463 Dave Engle	.05	.15
464 Jeff A. Jones	.05	.15
465 Mookie Wilson	.08	.25
466 Gene Garber	.05	.15
467 Mike Ramsey	.05	.15
468 Geoff Zahn	.05	.15
469 Tom O'Malley	.05	.15
470 Nolan Ryan	1.25	3.00
471 Dick Howser MG	.05	.15
472 Mike G. Brown RC	.05	.15
473 Jim Dwyer	.05	.15
474 Greg Bargar	.05	.15
475 Gary Redus RC*	.15	.40
476 Tom Tellmann	.05	.15
477 Rafael Landestoy	.05	.15
478 Alan Bannister	.05	.15
479 Frank Tanana	.08	.25
480 Ron Kittle	.05	.15
481 Mark Thurmond	.05	.15
482 Enos Cabell	.05	.15
483 Fergie Jenkins	.08	.25
484 Ozzie Virgil	.05	.15
485 Rick Rhoden	.05	.15
486 D.Baylor	.08	.25
R.Guidry TL		
487 Ricky Adams	.05	.15
488 Jesse Barfield	.08	.25
489 Dave Von Ohlen	.05	.15
490 Cal Ripken	1.50	4.00
491 Bobby Castillo	.05	.15
492 Tucker Ashford	.05	.15
493 Mike Norris	.05	.15
494 Chili Davis	.08	.25
495 Rollie Fingers	.08	.25
496 Terry Francona	.08	.25
497 Bud Anderson	.05	.15
498 Rich Gedman	.05	.15
499 Mike Witt	.05	.15
500 George Brett	.60	1.50
501 Steve Henderson	.05	.15
502 Joe Torre MG	.08	.25
503 Elias Sosa	.05	.15
504 Mickey Rivers	.05	.15
505 Pete Vuckovich	.05	.15
506 Ernie Whitt	.05	.15
507 Mike LaCoss	.05	.15
508 Mel Hall	.08	.25
509 Brad Havens	.05	.15
510 Alan Trammell	.08	.25
511 Marty Bystrom	.05	.15
512 Oscar Gamble	.05	.15
513 Dave Beard	.05	.15
514 Floyd Rayford	.05	.15
515 Gorman Thomas	.08	.25
516 Montreal Expos TL	.08	.25
Al Oliver/Charlie Lea/(Checkl		
517 John Moses	.05	.15
518 Greg Walker	.15	.40
519 Ron Davis	.05	.15
520 Bob Boone	.08	.25
521 Pete Falcone	.05	.15
522 Dave Bergman	.05	.15
523 Glenn Hoffman	.05	.15
524 Carlos Diaz	.05	.15
525 Willie Wilson	.08	.25
526 Ron Oester	.05	.15
527 Checklist 397-528	.08	.25
528 Mark Brouhard	.05	.15
529 Keith Atherton	.05	.15
530 Dan Ford	.05	.15
531 Steve Boros MG	.05	.15
532 Eric Show	.05	.15
533 Ken Landreaux	.05	.15
534 Pete O'Brien RC*	.15	.40
535 Bo Diaz	.05	.15
536 Doug Bair	.05	.15
537 Johnny Ray	.05	.15
538 Kevin Bass	.05	.15
539 George Frazier	.05	.15
540 George Hendrick	.08	.25
541 Dennis Lamp	.05	.15
542 Duane Kuiper	.05	.15
543 Craig McMurtry	.05	.15
544 Cesar Geronimo	.05	.15
545 Bill Buckner	.08	.25
546 Indians TL	.08	.25
Mike Hargrove/Lary Sorensen/(Checkli		
547 Mike Moore	.05	.15
548 Ron Jackson	.05	.15
549 Walt Terrell	.05	.15
550 Jim Rice	.08	.25
551 Scott Ullger	.05	.15
552 Ray Burris	.05	.15
553 Joe Nolan	.05	.15
554 Ted Power	.05	.15
555 Greg Brock	.05	.15
556 Joey McLaughlin	.05	.15
557 Wayne Tolleson	.05	.15
558 Mike Davis	.05	.15
559 Mike Scott	.08	.25
560 Carlton Fisk	.15	.40
561 Whitey Herzog MG	.08	.25
562 Manny Castillo	.05	.15
563 Glenn Wilson	.08	.25
564 Al Holland	.05	.15
565 Leon Durham	.05	.15
566 Jim Bibby	.05	.15
567 Mike Heath	.05	.15
568 Pete Filson	.05	.15
569 Bake McBride	.08	.25
570 Dan Quisenberry	.05	.15
571 Bruce Bochy	.05	.15
572 Jerry Royster	.05	.15
573 Dave Kingman	.08	.25
574 Brian Downing	.08	.25
575 Jim Clancy	.05	.15
576 Giants TL	.08	.25
Jeff Leonard/Atlee Hammaker/(Checklis		
577 Mark Clear	.05	.15
578 Lenn Sakata	.05	.15
579 Bob James	.05	.15
580 Lonnie Smith	.05	.15
581 Jose DeLeon RC	.15	.40
582 Bob McClure	.05	.15
583 Derrel Thomas	.05	.15
584 Dave Schmidt	.05	.15
585 Dan Driessen	.05	.15
586 Joe Niekro	.05	.15
587 Von Hayes	.05	.15
588 Milt Wilcox	.05	.15
589 Mike Easler	.05	.15
590 Dave Stieb	.08	.25
591 Tony LaRussa MG	.08	.25
592 Andre Robertson	.05	.15
593 Jeff Lahti	.05	.15
594 Gene Richards	.05	.15
595 Jeff Reardon	.08	.25
596 Ryne Sandberg	1.00	2.50
597 Rick Camp	.05	.15
598 Rusty Kuntz	.05	.15
599 Doug Sisk	.05	.15
600 Rod Carew	.15	.40
601 John Tudor	.08	.25
602 John Wathan	.05	.15
603 Renie Martin	.05	.15
604 John Lowenstein	.05	.15
605 Mike Caldwell	.05	.15
606 Blue Jays TL	.08	.25
Lloyd Moseby/Dave Stieb/(Checklist		
607 Tom Hume	.05	.15
608 Bobby Johnson	.05	.15
609 Dan Meyer	.05	.15
610 Steve Sax	.05	.15
611 Chet Lemon	.08	.25
612 Harry Spilman	.05	.15
613 Greg Gross	.05	.15
614 Len Barker	.05	.15
615 Garry Templeton	.08	.25
616 Don Robinson	.05	.15
617 Rick Cerone	.05	.15
618 Dickie Noles	.05	.15
619 Jerry Dybzinski	.05	.15
620 Al Oliver	.08	.25
621 Frank Howard MG	.08	.25
622 Al Cowens	.05	.15
623 Ron Washington	.05	.15
624 Terry Harper	.05	.15
625 Larry Gura	.05	.15
626 Bob Clark	.05	.15
627 Dave LaPoint	.05	.15
628 Ed Jurak	.05	.15
629 Rick Langford	.05	.15
630 Ted Simmons	.08	.25
631 Dennis Martinez	.08	.25
632 Tom Foley	.05	.15
633 Mike Krukow	.05	.15
634 Mike Marshall	.05	.15
635 Dave Righetti	.08	.25
636 Pat Putnam	.05	.15
637 Phillies TL	.08	.25
Gary Matthews/John Denny/(Checklist		
638 George Vukovich	.05	.15
639 Rick Lysander	.05	.15
640 Lance Parrish	.15	.40
641 Mike Richardt	.05	.15
642 Tom Underwood	.05	.15
643 Mike C. Brown	.05	.15
644 Tim Lollar	.05	.15
645 Tony Pena	.05	.15
646 Checklist 529-660	.08	.25
647 Ron Roenicke	.05	.15
648 Len Whitehouse	.05	.15
649 Tom Herr	.05	.15
650 Phil Niekro	.08	.25
651 John McNamara MG	.05	.15
652 Rudy May	.05	.15
653 Dave Stapleton	.05	.15
654 Bob Bailor	.05	.15
655 Amos Otis	.08	.25
656 Bryn Smith	.05	.15
657 Thad Bosley	.05	.15
658 Jerry Augustine	.05	.15
659 Duane Walker	.05	.15
660 Ray Knight	.08	.25
661 Steve Yeager	.08	.25
662 Tom Brennan	.05	.15
663 Johnnie LeMaster	.05	.15
664 Dave Stegman	.05	.15
665 Buddy Bell	.08	.25
666 Tigers TL	.08	.25
Morris/Whitak		
667 Vance Law	.05	.15
668 Larry McWilliams	.05	.15
669 Dave Lopes	.08	.25
670 Rich Gossage	.08	.25
671 Jamie Quirk	.05	.15
672 Ricky Nelson	.05	.15
673 Mike Walters	.05	.15
674 Tim Flannery	.05	.15
675 Pascual Perez	.05	.15
676 Brian Giles	.05	.15
677 Doyle Alexander	.05	.15
678 Chris Speier	.05	.15
679 Art Howe	.05	.15
680 Fred Lynn	.08	.25
681 Tom Lasorda MG	.15	.40
682 Dan Morogiello	.05	.15
683 Marty Barrett RC	.15	.40
684 Bob Shirley	.05	.15
685 Willie Aikens	.05	.15
686 Joe Price	.05	.15
687 Roy Howell	.05	.15
688 George Wright	.05	.15
689 Mike Fischlin	.05	.15
690 Jack Clark	.08	.25
691 Steve Lake	.05	.15
692 Dickie Thon	.05	.15
693 Alan Wiggins	.05	.15
694 Mike Stanton	.05	.15
695 Lou Whitaker	.08	.25
696 Pirates TL	.08	.25
Bill Madlock/Rick Rhoden/(Checklist		
697 Dale Murray	.05	.15
698 Marc Hill	.05	.15
699 Dave Rucker	.05	.15
700 Mike Schmidt	.60	1.50
701 Madlock	.25	.60
Rose/Parker LL		
702 Rose	.25	.60
Staub/Perez LL		
703 Schmidt	.25	.60
Perez/Kingm LL		
704 Tony Perez	.08	.25
Rusty Staub/Al Oliver LL		
705 Morgan	.15	.40
Cedeno/Bowa LL		
706 S.Carlton	.08	.25
Jenk/Seaver LL		
707 N.Ryan	.60	1.50
Seaver/Carlton LL		
708 Seaver	.08	.25
Carlton/Rog LL		
709 NL Active Save	.08	.25
Bruce Sutter/Tug McGraw/Gene Gar		
710 Carew	.15	.40
Brett/Cooper LL		
711 Carew	.08	.25
Camp/Reggie LL		
712 Reggie	.08	.25
Nettles/Luz LL		
713 Reggie	.08	.25
Simmons/Nett LL		
714 AL Active Steals	.08	.25
Bert Campaneris/Dave Lopes/Oma		
715 Palmer	.08	.25
Sutton/John LL		
716 AL Active Strikeout	.15	.40
Don Sutton/Bert Blyleven/Je		
717 Jim Palmer	.08	.25
Fingers LL		
718 Fingers	.08	.25
Goose/Quis LL		
719 Andy Hassler	.05	.15
720 Dwight Evans	.15	.40
721 Del Crandall MG	.05	.15
722 Bob Welch	.08	.25
723 Rich Dauer	.05	.15
724 Eric Rasmussen	.05	.15
725 Cesar Cedeno	.08	.25
726 Brewers TL	.08	.25
Ted Simmons/Moose Haas/(Checklist on		
727 Joel Youngblood	.05	.15
728 Tug McGraw	.08	.25
729 Gene Tenace	.08	.25
730 Bruce Sutter	.15	.40
731 Lynn Jones	.05	.15
732 Terry Crowley	.05	.15
733 Dave Collins	.05	.15
734 Odell Jones	.05	.15
735 Rick Burleson	.05	.15
736 Dick Ruthven	.05	.15
737 Jim Essian	.05	.15
738 Bill Schroeder	.05	.15
739 Bob Watson	.05	.15
740 Tom Seaver	.25	.60
741 Wayne Gross	.05	.15
742 Dick Williams MG	.05	.15
743 Don Hood	.05	.15
744 Jamie Allen	.05	.15
745 Dennis Eckersley	.15	.40
746 Mickey Hatcher	.05	.15
747 Pat Zachry	.05	.15
748 Jeff Leonard	.05	.15
749 Doug Flynn	.05	.15
750 Jim Palmer	.08	.25
751 Charlie Moore	.05	.15
752 Phil Garner	.08	.25
753 Doug Gwosdz	.05	.15
754 Kent Tekulve	.05	.15
755 Garry Maddox	.05	.15
756 Reds TL	.08	.25
Ron Oester/Mario Soto/(Checklist on bac		
757 Larry Bowa	.08	.25
758 Bill Stein	.05	.15
759 Richard Dotson	.05	.15
760 Bob Horner	.08	.25
761 John Montefusco	.05	.15
762 Rance Mulliniks	.05	.15
763 Craig Swan	.05	.15
764 Mike Hargrove	.05	.15
765 Ken Forsch	.05	.15
766 Mike Vail	.05	.15
767 Carney Lansford	.08	.25
768 Champ Summers	.05	.15
769 Bill Caudill	.05	.15
770 Ken Griffey	.08	.25
771 Billy Gardner MG	.05	.15
772 Jim Slaton	.05	.15
773 Todd Cruz	.05	.15
774 Tom Gorman	.05	.15
775 Dave Parker	.08	.25
776 Craig Reynolds	.05	.15
777 Tom Paciorek	.05	.15
778 Andy Hawkins	.05	.15
779 Jim Sundberg	.08	.25
780 Steve Carlton	.15	.40
781 Checklist 661-792	.08	.25
782 Steve Balboni	.05	.15
783 Luis Leal	.05	.15
784 Leon Roberts	.05	.15
785 Joaquin Andujar	.08	.25
786 Red Sox TL	.15	.40
Boggs/Ojeda		
787 Bill Campbell	.05	.15
788 Milt May	.05	.15
789 Bert Blyleven	.08	.25
790 Doug DeCinces	.05	.15
791 Terry Forster	.08	.25
792 Bill Russell	.08	.25

1984 Topps Tiffany

COMP.FACT.SET (792)	200.00	400.00

*STARS: 3X TO 8X BASIC CARDS
*ROOKIES: 2.5X TO 6X BASIC CARDS
DISTRIBUTED ONLY IN FACTORY SET FORM
FACTORY SET PRICE IS FOR SEALED SETS

1984 Topps Glossy All-Stars

Card	Low	High
COMPLETE SET (22)	2.00	5.00
1 Harvey Kuenn MG	.01	.05
2 Rod Carew	.20	.50
3 Manny Trillo	.01	.05
4 George Brett	.40	1.00
5 Robin Yount	.20	.50
6 Jim Rice	.02	.10
7 Fred Lynn	.02	.10
8 Dave Winfield	.20	.50
9 Ted Simmons	.02	.10
10 Dave Stieb	.01	.05
11 Carl Yastrzemski CAPT	.20	.50
12 Whitey Herzog MG	.01	.05
13 Al Oliver	.02	.10
14 Steve Sax	.02	.10
15 Mike Schmidt	.30	.75
16 Ozzie Smith	.40	1.00
17 Tim Raines	.05	.15
18 Andre Dawson	.08	.25
19 Dale Murphy	.08	.25
20 Gary Carter	.15	.40
21 Mario Soto	.01	.05
22 Johnny Bench CAPT	.20	.50

1984 Topps Glossy Send-Ins

Card	Low	High
COMPLETE SET (40)	5.00	12.00
1 Pete Rose	.50	1.25
2 Lance Parrish	.07	.20
3 Steve Rogers	.02	.10
4 Eddie Murray	.40	1.00
5 Johnny Ray	.02	.10
6 Rickey Henderson	.75	2.00
7 Atlee Hammaker	.02	.10
8 Wade Boggs	.60	1.50
9 Gary Carter	.50	1.25
10 Jack Morris	.07	.20
11 Darrell Evans	.07	.20
12 George Brett	1.00	2.50
13 Bob Horner	.02	.10
14 Ron Guidry	.07	.20
15 Nolan Ryan	2.00	5.00
16 Dave Winfield	.40	1.00
17 Ozzie Smith	.75	2.00
18 Ted Simmons	.07	.20
19 Bill Madlock	.02	.10
20 Tony Armas	.02	.10
21 Al Oliver	.07	.20
22 Jim Rice	.07	.20
23 George Hendrick	.02	.10
24 Dave Stieb	.02	.10
25 Pedro Guerrero	.02	.10
26 Rod Carew	.40	1.00
27 Steve Carlton	.40	1.00
28 Dave Righetti	.07	.20
29 Darryl Strawberry	.20	.50
30 Lou Whitaker	.07	.20
31 Dale Murphy	.10	.30
32 LaMarr Hoyt	.02	.10
33 Jesse Orosco	.07	.20
34 Cecil Cooper	.07	.20
35 Andre Dawson	.20	.50
36 Robin Yount	.50	1.25
37 Tim Raines	.10	.30
38 Dan Quisenberry	.02	.10
39 Mike Schmidt	.75	2.00
40 Carlton Fisk	.60	1.50

1984 Topps Traded

In what was now standard procedure, Topps issued its standard-size Traded (or extended) set for the fourth year in a row. Several of 1984's top rookies not contained in the regular set are pictured in the Traded set. Extended Rookie Cards in this set include Dwight Gooden, Jimmy Key, Mark Langston, Jose Rijo, and Bret Saberhagen. Again this year, the Topps affiliate in Ireland printed the cards, and the cards were available through hobby channels only in factory set form. The set numbering is in alphabetical order by player's name. The 132-card sets were shipped to dealers in 100-ct set cases. A few cards have been seen with a "grey" logo for Topps, these cards draw a significant multiplier of the regular Topps Traded cards, but are not yet known in sufficient quantity to price in our checklist.

Card	Low	High
COMP.FACT.SET (132)	12.50	30.00
1T Willie Aikens	.15	.40
2T Luis Aponte	.15	.40
3T Mike Armstrong	.15	.40
4T Bob Bailor	.15	.40
5T Dusty Baker	.25	.60
6T Steve Balboni	.15	.40
7T Alan Bannister	.15	.40
8T Dave Beard	.15	.40
9T Joe Beckwith	.15	.40
10T Bruce Berenyi	.15	.40
11T Dave Bergman	.15	.40
12T Tony Bernazard	.15	.40
13T Yogi Berra MG	.60	1.50
14T Barry Bonnell	.15	.40
15T Phil Bradley	.40	1.00
16T Fred Breining	.15	.40
17T Bill Buckner	.25	.60
18T Ray Burris	.15	.40
19T John Butcher	.15	.40
20T Brett Butler	.25	.60
21T Enos Cabell	.15	.40
22T Bill Campbell	.15	.40
23T Bill Caudill	.15	.40
24T Bob Clark	.15	.40
25T Bryan Clark	.15	.40
26T Jaime Cocanower	.15	.40
27T Ron Darling XRC*	.75	2.00
28T Alvin Davis XRC	.40	1.00
29T Ken Dayley	.15	.40
30T Jeff Dedmon	.15	.40
31T Bob Dernier	.15	.40
32T Carlos Diaz	.15	.40
33T Mike Easler	.15	.40
34T Dennis Eckersley	.40	1.00
35T Jim Essian	.15	.40
36T Darrell Evans	.25	.60
37T Mike Fitzgerald	.15	.40
38T Tim Foli	.15	.40
39T George Frazier	.15	.40
40T Rich Gale	.15	.40
41T Barbaro Garbey	.15	.40
42T Dwight Gooden XRC	15.00	40.00
43T Rich Gossage	.25	.60
44T Wayne Gross	.15	.40
45T Mark Gubicza XRC	.40	1.00
46T Jackie Gutierrez	.15	.40
47T Mel Hall	.25	.60
48T Toby Harrah	.25	.60
49T Ron Hassey	.15	.40
50T Rich Hebner	.15	.40
51T Willie Hernandez	.15	.40
52T Ricky Horton	.15	.40
53T Art Howe	.15	.40
54T Dane Iorg	.15	.40
55T Brook Jacoby	.40	1.00
56T Mike Jeffcoat XRC	.20	.50
57T Dave Johnson MG	.15	.40
58T Lynn Jones	.15	.40
59T Ruppert Jones	.15	.40
60T Mike Jorgensen	.15	.40
61T Bob Kearney	.15	.40
62T Jimmy Key XRC	.75	2.00
63T Dave Kingman	.25	.60
64T Jerry Koosman	.25	.60
65T Wayne Krenchicki	.15	.40
66T Rusty Kuntz	.15	.40
67T Rene Lachemann MG	.15	.40
68T Frank LaCorte	.15	.40
69T Dennis Lamp	.15	.40
70T Mark Langston XRC	.75	2.00
71T Rick Leach	.15	.40
72T Craig Lefferts	.20	.50
73T Gary Lucas	.15	.40
74T Jerry Martin	.15	.40
75T Carmelo Martinez	.15	.40
76T Mike Mason XRC	.20	.50
77T Gary Matthews	.25	.60
78T Andy McGaffigan	.15	.40
79T Larry Milbourne	.15	.40
80T Sid Monge	.15	.40
81T Jackie Moore MG	.15	.40
82T Joe Morgan	.25	.60
83T Graig Nettles	.25	.60
84T Phil Niekro	.25	.60
85T Ken Oberkfell	.15	.40
86T Mike O'Berry	.15	.40
87T Al Oliver	.25	.60
88T Jorge Orta	.15	.40
89T Amos Otis	.25	.60
90T Dave Parker	.25	.60
91T Tony Perez	.40	1.00
92T Gerald Perry	.40	1.00
93T Gary Pettis	.15	.40
94T Rob Picciolo	.15	.40
95T Vern Rapp MG	.15	.40
96T Floyd Rayford	.15	.40
97T Randy Ready XRC	.40	1.00
98T Ron Reed	.15	.40
99T Gene Richards	.15	.40
100T Jose Rijo XRC	.75	2.00
101T Jeff D. Robinson	.15	.40

102T Ron Romanick .15 .40
103T Pete Rose 2.00 5.00
104T Bret Saberhagen XRC 1.50 4.00
105T Juan Samuel XRC* .75 2.00
106T Scott Sanderson .15 .40
107T Dick Schofield XRC* .40 1.00
108T Tom Seaver .60 1.50
109T Jim Slaton .15 .40
110T Mike Smithson .15 .40
111T Lary Sorensen .15 .40
112T Tim Stoddard .15 .40
113T Champ Summers .15 .40
114T Jim Sundberg .25 .60
115T Rick Sutcliffe .25 .60
116T Craig Swan .15 .40
117T Tim Teufel XRC* .40 1.00
118T Derrel Thomas .15 .40
119T Gorman Thomas .25 .60
120T Alex Trevino .15 .40
121T Manny Trillo .15 .40
122T John Tudor .25 .60
123T Tom Underwood .15 .40
124T Mike Vail .15 .40
125T Tom Waddell .15 .40
126T Gary Ward .15 .40
127T Curt Wilkerson .15 .40
128T Frank Williams .15 .40
129T Glenn Wilson .25 .60
130T John Wockenfuss .15 .40
131T Ned Yost .15 .40
132T Checklist 1T-132T .15 .40

1984 Topps Traded Tiffany

COMP.FACT.SET (132) 30.00 80.00
*STARS: .6X TO 1.5X BASIC CARDS
*ROOKIES: 1X TO 2.5X BASIC CARDS
DISTRIBUTED ONLY IN FACTORY SET FORM
FACTORY SET PRICE IS FOR SEALED SETS

1984 Topps Cereal

The cards in this 33-card set measure the standard size. The cards are numbered both on the front and the back. The 1984 Topps Cereal Series is exactly the same as the Ralston-Purina issue of this year except for a Topps logo and the words "Cereal Series" on the tops of the fronts of the cards in place of the Ralston checkerboard background. The checkerboard background is absent from the reverse, and a Topps logo is on the reverse of the cereal cards. These cards were distributed in unmarked boxes of Ralston-Purina cereal with a pack of four cards (three players and a checklist) being inside random cereal boxes. The back of the checklist details an offer to obtain any twelve cards direct from the issuer for only 1.50.

COMPLETE SET (34) 5.00 12.00
1 Eddie Murray .60 1.50
2 Ozzie Smith .75 2.00
3 Ted Simmons .07 .20
4 Pete Rose .50 1.25
5 Greg Luzinski .07 .20
6 Andre Dawson .20 .50
7 Dave Winfield .40 1.00
8 Tom Seaver .40 1.00
9 Jim Rice .07 .20
10 Fernando Valenzuela .07 .20
11 Wade Boggs .60 1.50
12 Dale Murphy .15 .40
13 George Brett .75 2.00
14 Nolan Ryan 1.50 4.00
15 Rickey Henderson .60 1.50
16 Steve Carlton .40 1.00
17 Rod Carew .30 .75
18 Steve Garvey .07 .20
19 Reggie Jackson .40 1.00
20 Dave Concepcion .07 .20
21 Robin Yount .40 1.00
22 Mike Schmidt .60 1.50
23 Jim Palmer .40 1.00
24 Bruce Sutter .30 .75
25 Dan Quisenberry .02 .10
26 Bill Madlock .02 .10
27 Cecil Cooper .07 .20
28 Gary Carter .30 .75
29 Fred Lynn .07 .20
30 Pedro Guerrero .07 .20
31 Ron Guidry .07 .20
32 Keith Hernandez .07 .20
33 Carlton Fisk .40 1.00
NNO Checklist Card .02 .10

1984 Topps Gallery of Champions

These 12 "mini" cards were issued in set form only. These "Cards" measure approximately 1 1/4" by 1 3/4" and have the same design as the regular Topps cards from that year. In 1984 and 1985 no aluminum sets were issued. We have sequenced this set in alphabetical order. These cards were issued in bronze and silver versions. We have priced the bronze version. The silver versions are valued at approximately 2.5 times the values listed below.

COMPLETE SET (12) 200.00 400.00
1 George Brett 24.00 60.00
2 Rod Carew 10.00 25.00
3 Steve Carlton 10.00 25.00
4 Rollie Fingers 4.00 10.00
5 Steve Garvey 10.00 25.00
6 Reggie Jackson 25.00 60.00
7 Joe Morgan 6.00 15.00
8 Jim Palmer 6.00 15.00
9 Pete Rose 15.00 40.00
10 Nolan Ryan 60.00 150.00
11 Mike Schmidt 20.00 50.00
12 Tom Seaver 15.00 40.00

1984 Topps Stickers

Made in Italy for Topps and O-Pee-Chee by Panini, these 386 stickers measure approximately 1 15/16" by 2 9/16" and are numbered on both front and back. The fronts feature white-bordered color player photos. The horizontal back carries the player's name and a bilingual ad for O-Pee-Chee in red lettering. The stickers were also issued boxes of seven strips of five stickers each. An album onto which the stickers could be affixed was available at retail stores. The album and the sticker numbering are organized as follows: 1983 Highlights (1-10), 1983 Championship Series (11-18), World Series (19-26), Atlanta Braves (27-38), Chicago Cubs (39-50), Cincinnati Reds (51-62), Houston Astros (63-74), Los Angeles Dodgers (75-86), Montreal Expos (87-98), 1983 Stat Leaders (99-102), New York Mets (103-114), Philadelphia Phillies (115-126), Pittsburgh Pirates (127-138), St. Louis Cardinals (139-150), San Diego Padres (151-162), San Francisco Giants (163-174), 1983 Stat Leaders (175-178), Foil All-Stars (179-198), 1983 Stat Leaders (199-202), Baltimore Orioles (203-214), Boston Red Sox (215-226), California Angels (227-238), Chicago White Sox (239-250), Cleveland Indians (251-262), Detroit Tigers (263-274), Kansas City Royals (275-286), 1983 Stat Leaders (287-290), Milwaukee Brewers (291-302), Minnesota Twins (303-314), New York Yankees (315-326), Oakland A's (327-338), Seattle Mariners (339-350), Texas Rangers (351-362), Toronto Blue Jays (363-374), and Stars of the Future (375-386). There were stickers issued which corresponded with Don Mattingly and Darryl Strawberry Rookie Year for cards.

COMPLETE SET (386) 6.00 15.00
COMMON PLAYER (1-178) .02 .05
COMMON FOIL (179-198) .04 .10
*OPC: .4X TO 1X TOPPS
1 Steve Carlton/(Top half) .05 .15
2 Steve Carlton/(Bottom half) .05 .15
3 Rickey Henderson/(Top half) .05 .15
4 Rickey Henderson/(Bottom half) .05 .15
5 Fred Lynn/(Top half) .02 .10
6 Fred Lynn/(Bottom half) .02 .10
7 Greg Luzinski/(Top half) .02 .10
8 Greg Luzinski/(Bottom half) .02 .10
9 Dan Quisenberry/(Top half) .01 .05
10 Dan Quisenberry/(Bottom half) .01 .05
11 LaMarr Hoyt LCS .01 .05
12 Mike Flanagan LCS .01 .05
13 Mike Boddicker LCS .01 .05
14 Tito Landrum LCS .01 .05
15 Steve Carlton LCS .05 .15
16 Fern.Valenzuela LCS .02 .10
17 Charlie Hudson LCS .01 .05
18 Gary Matthews LCS .01 .05
19 John Denny WS .01 .05
20 John Lowenstein WS .01 .05
21 Jim Palmer WS .05 .15
22 Benny Ayala WS .01 .05
23 Rick Dempsey WS .01 .05
24 Cal Ripken WS .50 1.25
25 Sammy Stewart WS .01 .05
26 Eddie Murray WS .05 .15
27 Dale Murphy .08 .25
28 Chris Chambliss .01 .05
29 Glenn Hubbard .01 .05
30 Bob Horner .01 .05
31 Phil Niekro .20 .50
32 Claudell Washington .01 .05
33 Rafael Ramirez (135) .01 .05
34 Bruce Benedict (82) .01 .05
35 Gene Garber (59) .01 .05
36 Pascual Perez (347) .01 .05
37 Jerry Royster (281) .01 .05
38 Steve Bedrosian(283) .01 .05
39 Keith Moreland .01 .05
40 Leon Durham .01 .05
41 Ron Cey .02 .10
42 Bill Buckner .02 .10
43 Jody Davis .01 .05
44 Lee Smith .08 .25
45 Ryne Sandberg (70) .50 1.25
46 Larry Bowa (301) .02 .10
47 Chuck Rainey (247) .01 .05
48 Fergie Jenkins (170) .08 .25
49 Dick Ruthven (333) .01 .05
50 Jay Johnstone (298) .01 .05
51 Mario Soto .01 .05
52 Gary Redus .01 .05
53 Ron Oester .01 .05
54 Cesar Cedeno .02 .10
55 Dan Driessen .01 .05
56 Dave Concepcion .02 .10
57 Dann Bilardello(147) .01 .05
58 Joe Price (98) .01 .05
59 Tom Hume (35) .01 .05
60 Eddie Milner (84) .01 .05
61 Paul Householder/(226) .01 .05
62 Bill Scherrer (269) .01 .05
63 Phil Garner .02 .10
64 Dickie Thon .01 .05
65 Jose Cruz .02 .10
66 Nolan Ryan 1.00 2.50
67 Terry Puhl .01 .05
68 Ray Knight .02 .10
69 Joe Niekro (312) .02 .10
70 Jerry Mumphrey (45) .01 .05
71 Bill Dawley (314) .01 .05
72 Alan Ashby (162) .01 .05
73 Denny Walling (81) .01 .05
74 Frank DiPino (360) .01 .05
75 Pedro Guerrero .02 .10
76 Ken Landreaux .01 .05
77 Bill Russell .02 .10
78 Steve Sax .02 .10
79 Fernando Valenzuela .02 .10
80 Dusty Baker .02 .10
81 Jerry Reuss (73) .01 .05
82 Alejandro Pena (34) .01 .05
83 Rick Monday .01 .05
84 Rick Honeycutt (60) .01 .05
85 Mike Marshall (245) .01 .05
86 Steve Yeager (284) .01 .05
87 Al Oliver .02 .10
88 Steve Rogers .01 .05
89 Jeff Reardon .02 .10
90 Gary Carter .20 .50
91 Tim Raines .08 .25
92 Andre Dawson .08 .25
93 Manny Trillo (137) .01 .05
94 Tim Wallach (348) .02 .10
95 Chris Speier (172) .01 .05
96 Bill Gullickson(134) .01 .05
97 Doug Flynn (271) .01 .05
98 Charlie Lea (58) .01 .05
99 Bill Madlock/(102B/288B) .02 .10
100 Wade Boggs/(200B/287B) .25 .60
101 Mike Schmidt (176) .25 .60
102A Jim Rice (287A/177) .02 .10
102B Reggie Jackson/(99/288B) .20 .50
103 Hubie Brooks .01 .05
104 Jesse Orosco .01 .05
105 George Foster .02 .10
106 Tom Seaver .20 .50
107 Keith Hernandez .02 .10
108 Mookie Wilson .02 .10
109 Bob Bailor (122) .01 .05
110 Walt Terrell (209) .01 .05
111 Brian Giles (126) .01 .05
112 Jose Oquendo (372) .01 .05
113 Mike Torrez (258) .01 .05
114 Junior Ortiz (371) .01 .05
115 Pete Rose .30 .75
116 Joe Morgan .20 .50
117 Mike Schmidt .25 .60
118 Gary Matthews .01 .05
119 Steve Carlton .20 .50
120 Bo Diaz .01 .05
121 Ivan DeJesus (210) .01 .05
122 John Denny (109) .01 .05
123 Garry Maddox (335) .01 .05
124 Von Hayes (224) .01 .05
125 Al Holland (158) .01 .05
126 Tony Perez (111) .15 .40
127 John Candelaria .01 .05
128 Jason Thompson .01 .05
129 Tony Pena .01 .05
130 Dave Parker .02 .10
131 Bill Madlock .01 .05
132 Kent Tekulve .02 .10
133 Larry McWilliams/(146) .01 .05
134 Johnny Ray (96) .01 .05
135 Marvell Wynne (33) .01 .05
136 Dale Berra (299) .01 .05
137 Mike Easler (93) .01 .05
138 Lee Lacy (233) .01 .05
139 George Hendrick .01 .05
140 Lonnie Smith .01 .05
141 Willie McGee .05 .15
142 Tom Herr .02 .10
143 Darrell Porter .01 .05
144 Ozzie Smith .20 .50
145 Bruce Sutter (221) .15 .40
146 Dave LaPoint (133) .01 .05
147 Neil Allen (57) .01 .05
148 Ken Oberkfell (238) .01 .05
149 David Green (324) .01 .05
150 Andy Van Slyke (235) .08 .25
151 Garry Templeton .01 .05
152 Juan Bonilla .01 .05
153 Alan Wiggins .01 .05
154 Terry Kennedy .01 .05
155 Dave Dravecky .02 .10
156 Steve Garvey .05 .15
157 Bobby Brown (361) .01 .05
158 Ruppert Jones (125) .01 .05
159 Luis Salazar (214) .01 .05
160 Tony Gwynn (212) 1.00 2.50
161 Gary Lucas (211) .01 .05
162 Eric Show (72) .01 .05
163 Darrell Evans .02 .10
164 Gary Lavelle .01 .05
165 Atlee Hammaker .01 .05
166 Jeff Leonard .01 .05
167 Jack Clark .02 .10
168 Johnny LeMaster .01 .05
169 Duane Kuiper (260) .01 .05
170 Tom O'Malley (48) .01 .05
171 Chili Davis (311) .02 .10
172 Bill Laskey (95) .01 .05
173 Joel Youngblood(300) .01 .05
174 Bob Brenly (225) .01 .05
175 Atlee Hammaker(202) .01 .05
176 Rick Honeycutt (101) .01 .05
177 John Denny/(102A/287A) .01 .05
178 LaMarr Hoyt/(200A/288A) .01 .05
179 Tim Raines FOIL .05 .15
180 Dale Murphy FOIL .15 .40
181 Andre Dawson FOIL .15 .40
182 Steve Rogers FOIL .02 .10
183 Gary Carter FOIL .08 .25
184 Steve Carlton FOIL .15 .40
185 George Hendrick FOIL .02 .10
186 Johnny Ray FOIL .02 .10
187 Ozzie Smith FOIL .15 .40
188 Mike Schmidt FOIL .30 .75
189 Jim Rice FOIL .02 .10
190 Dave Winfield FOIL .15 .40
191 Lloyd Moseby FOIL .02 .10
192 LaMarr Hoyt FOIL .02 .10
193 Ted Simmons FOIL .05 .15
194 Ron Guidry FOIL .05 .15
195 Eddie Murray FOIL .15 .40
196 Lou Whitaker FOIL .05 .15
197 Cal Ripken FOIL 1.25 3.00
198 George Brett FOIL .50 1.25
199 Dale Murphy (290) .05 .15
200A Cecil Cooper/(288A/178) .02 .10
200B Jim Rice (287B/100) .02 .10
201 Tim Raines (289) .05 .15
202 Rickey Henderson/(175) .15 .40
203 Eddie Murray .15 .40
204 Cal Ripken 1.00 2.50
205 Gary Roenicke .01 .05
206 Ken Singleton .01 .05
207 Scott McGregor .01 .05
208 Tippy Martinez .01 .05
209 John Lowenstein(110) .01 .05
210 Mike Flanagan (121) .01 .05
211 Jim Palmer (161) .08 .25
212 Dan Ford (160) .01 .05
213 Rick Dempsey (234) .01 .05
214 Rich Dauer (159) .01 .05
215 Jerry Remy .01 .05
216 Wade Boggs .25 .60
217 Jim Rice .02 .10
218 Tony Armas .01 .05
219 Dwight Evans .02 .10
220 Bob Stanley (370) .01 .05
221 Dave Stapleton (145) .01 .05
222 Rich Gedman .01 .05
223 Glenn Hoffman (272) .01 .05
224 Dennis Eckersley/(124) .05 .15
225 John Tudor (174) .01 .05
226 Bruce Hurst (61) .01 .05
227 Rod Carew .15 .40
228 Bobby Grich .02 .10
229 Doug DeCinces .01 .05
230 Fred Lynn .02 .10
231 Reggie Jackson .20 .50
232 Tommy John .02 .10
233 Luis Sanchez (138) .01 .05
234 Bob Boone (213) .02 .10
235 Bruce Kison (150) .01 .05
236 Brian Downing (262) .01 .05
237 Ken Forsch (246) .01 .05
238 Rick Burleson (148) .01 .05
239 Dennis Lamp .01 .05
240 LaMarr Hoyt .01 .05
241 Richard Dotson .01 .05
242 Harold Baines .05 .15
243 Carlton Fisk .08 .25
244 Greg Luzinski .02 .10
245 Rudy Law (85) .01 .05
246 Tom Paciorek (237) .01 .05
247 Floyd Bannister(47) .01 .05
248 Julio Cruz (369) .01 .05
249 Vance Law (358) .01 .05
250 Scott Fletcher(270) .01 .05
251 Toby Harrah .02 .10
252 Pat Tabler .01 .05
253 Gorman Thomas .01 .05
254 Rick Sutcliffe .02 .10
255 Andre Thornton .01 .05
256 Bake McBride .01 .05
257 Alan Bannister(313) .01 .05
258 Jamie Easterly(113) .01 .05
259 Lary Sorensen (285) .01 .05
260 Mike Hargrove (169) .02 .10
261 Bert Blyleven (346) .02 .10
262 Ron Hassey (236) .01 .05
263 Jack Morris .02 .10
264 Larry Herndon .01 .05
265 Lance Parrish .02 .10
266 Alan Trammell .08 .25
267 Lou Whitaker .02 .10
268 Aurelio Lopez .01 .05
269 Dan Petry (62) .01 .05
270 Glenn Wilson (250) .01 .05
271 Chet Lemon (97) .01 .05
272 Kirk Gibson (223) .05 .15
273 Enos Cabell (338) .01 .05
274 John Wockenfuss(321) .01 .05
275 George Brett .40 1.00
276 Willie Aikens .01 .05
277 Frank White .02 .10
278 Hal McRae .02 .10
279 Dan Quisenberry .01 .05
280 Willie Wilson .01 .05
281 Paul Splittorff(281) .01 .05
282 U.L. Washington(322) .01 .05
283 Bud Black (38) .01 .05
284 John Wathan (86) .01 .05
285 Larry Gura (259) .01 .05
286 Pat Sheridan (323) .01 .05
287A Rusty Staub/(102A/177) .02 .10
287B Dave Righetti/(100/200B) .01 .05
288A Bob Forsch/(178/200A) .01 .05
288B Mike Warren/(99/102B) .01 .05
289 Al Holland (201) .01 .05
290 Dan Quisenberry(199) .01 .05
291 Cecil Cooper .02 .10
292 Moose Haas .01 .05
293 Ted Simmons .02 .10
294 Paul Molitor .08 .25
295 Robin Yount .08 .25
296 Ben Oglivie .01 .05
297 Tom Tellman (325) .01 .05
298 Jim Gantner (50) .02 .10
299 Rick Manning (136) .01 .05
300 Don Sutton (173) .08 .25
301 Charlie Moore (46) .01 .05
302 Jim Slaton (337) .01 .05
303 Gary Ward .01 .05
304 Tom Brunansky .02 .10
305 Kent Hrbek .02 .10
306 Gary Gaetti .05 .15
307 John Castino .01 .05
308 Ken Schrom .01 .05
309 Ron Davis (334) .01 .05
310 Lenny Faedo (336) .01 .05
311 Darrell Brown (171) .01 .05
312 Frank Viola (69) .05 .15
313 Dave Engle (257) .01 .05
314 Randy Bush (71) .01 .05
315 Dave Righetti .01 .05
316 Rich Gossage .02 .10
317 Ken Griffey .02 .10
318 Ron Guidry .02 .10
319 Dave Winfield .08 .25
320 Don Baylor .02 .10
321 Butch Wynegar (274) .01 .05
322 Omar Moreno (282) .01 .05
323 Andre Robertson(286) .01 .05
324 Willie Randolph(149) .02 .10
325 Don Mattingly (297) 2.50 6.00
326 Graig Nettles .02 .10
327 Rickey Henderson .15 .40
328 Carney Lansford .02 .10
329 Jeff Burroughs .01 .05
330 Chris Codiroli .01 .05
331 Dave Lopes .02 .10
332 Dwayne Murphy .01 .05
333 Wayne Gross (49) .01 .05
334 Bill Almon (309) .01 .05
335 Tom Underwood (123) .01 .05
336 Dave Beard (310) .01 .05
337 Mike Heath (302) .01 .05
338 Mike Davis (273) .01 .05
339 Pat Putnam .01 .05
340 Tony Bernazard .01 .05
341 Steve Henderson .01 .05
342 Richie Zisk .01 .05
343 Dave Henderson .02 .10
344 Al Cowens .01 .05
345 Bill Caudill (359) .01 .05
346 Jim Beattie (261) .01 .05
347 Rick Nelson (36) .01 .05
348 Roy Thomas (94) .01 .05
349 Spike Owen (362) .02 .10
350 Jamie Allen (373) .01 .05
351 Buddy Bell .02 .10
352 Billy Sample .01 .05
353 George Wright .01 .05
354 Larry Parrish .01 .05
355 Jim Sundberg .02 .10
356 Charlie Hough .02 .10
357 Pete O'Brien .01 .05
358 Wayne Tolleson(249) .01 .05
359 Danny Darwin (345) .01 .05
360 Dave Stewart (74) .02 .10
361 Mickey Rivers (157) .01 .05
362 Bucky Dent (349) .02 .10
363 Willie Upshaw .01 .05
364 Damaso Garcia .01 .05
365 Lloyd Moseby .01 .05
366 Cliff Johnson .01 .05
367 Jim Clancy .01 .05
368 Dave Stieb .01 .05
369 Alfredo Griffin(248) .01 .05
370 Barry Bonnell (222) .01 .05
371 Luis Leal (114) .01 .05
372 Jesse Barfield(112) .01 .05
373 Ernie Whitt (350) .01 .05
374 Rance Mulliniks(326) .01 .05
375 Mike Boddicker .01 .05
376 Greg Brock .01 .05
377 Bill Doran .02 .10
378 Nick Esasky .01 .05
379 Julio Franco .08 .25
380 Mel Hall .01 .05
381 Bob Kearney .01 .05
382 Ron Kittle .01 .05
383 Carmelo Martinez .01 .05
384 Craig McMurtry .01 .05
385 Darryl Strawberry .50 1.25
386 Matt Young .01 .05
NNO Album .40 1.00

1984 Topps Sticker Boxes

COMPLETE SET (12) 4.00 10.00
1 Al Oliver .30 .75
Lou Whitaker
2 Ken Oberkfell .08 .25
Ted Simmons
3 Alan Wiggins .20 .50
Hal McRae
4 Tim Raines .30 .75
Lloyd Moseby
5 Lonnie Smith .08 .25
Willie Wilson
6 Keith Hernandez .50 1.25
Robin Yount
7 Johnny Ray .75 2.00
Wade Boggs
8 Willie McGee .30 .75
Ken Singleton
9 Ray Knight .30 .75
Alan Trammell
11 George Hendrick .50 1.25
Rod Carew
12 Bill Madlock .50 1.25
Eddie Murray
13 Jose Cruz 3.00 8.00
Cal Ripken

1984 Topps Rub Downs

The cards in this 112-player (32 different sheets) set measure 2 3/8" by 3 5/16". The Topps Rub Downs set was actually similar to earlier Topps tatoo or decal-type offerings. The full color photo could be transfered from the rub down to another surface by rubbing a coin over the paper backing. Distributed in packages of two rub down sheets, some contained two or three player action poses, others head shots and various pieces of player equipment. Players from all teams were included in the set. Although the sheets are unnumbered, they are numbered here in alphabetical order based on each card first being placed in alphabetical order.

COMPLETE SET 3.00 8.00
1 Tony Armas .02 .10
Harold Baines/Lonnie Smith
2 Don Baylor .02 .10
George Hendrick/Ron Kittle/Johnnie L
3 Buddy Bell .07 .20
Ray Knight/Lloyd Moseby
4 Bruce Benedict .02 .10
Atlee Hammaker/Frank White
5 Wade Boggs .30 .75
Rick Dempsey/Keith Hernandez
6 George Brett .60 1.50
Andre Dawson/Paul Molitor/Alan Wig
7 Tom Brunansky .30 .75
Pedro Guerrero/Darryl Strawberry
8 Bill Buckner .07 .20
Rich Gossage/Dave Stieb/Rick Sutcl
9 Rod Carew .30 .75
Carlton Fisk/Johnny Ray/Matt Young
10 Steve Carlton .15 .40
Bob Horner/Dan Quisenberry
11 Gary Carter .07 .20
Phil Garner/Ron Guidry
12 Ron Cey .07 .20
Steve Kemp/Greg Luzinski/Kent Tekulve
13 Chris Chambliss .15 .40
Dwight Evans/Julio Franco
14 Jack Clark .10 .30
Damaso Garcia/Hal McRae/Lance Parris
15 Dave Concepcion .10 .30
Cecil Cooper/Fred Lynn/Jesse Or
16 Jose Cruz .10 .30
Gary Matthews/Jack Morris/Jim Rice
17 Ron Davis .25 .60
Kent Hrbek/Tom Seaver
18 John Denny .07 .20
Carney Lansford/Mario Soto/Lou Whita
19 Leon Durham .02 .10
Dave Lopes/Steve Sax
20 George Foster .10 .30
Gary Gaetti/Bobby Grich/Gary Redu
21 Steve Garvey .07 .20
Jerry Remy/Bill Russell/George Wri
22 Moose Haas .02 .10
Bruce Sutter/Dickie Thon/Andre Thorn
23 Toby Harrah .30 .75
Pat Putnam/Tim Raines/Mike Schmidt
24 Rickey Henderson .50 1.25
Dave Righetti/Pete Rose
25 Steve Henderson .10 .30
Bill Madlock/Alan Trammell
26 LaMarr Hoyt .75 2.00
Larry Parrish/Nolan Ryan
27 Reggie Jackson .15 .40
Eric Show/Jason Thompson
28 Tommy John .40 1.00
Terry Kennedy/Eddie Murray/Ozzie Smi
29 Jeff Leonard .15 .40
Dale Murphy/Ken Singleton/Dave Win
30 Craig McMurtry 1.00 2.50
Cal Ripken/Steve Rogers/Willie U
31 Ben Oglivie .10 .30
Jim Palmer/Darrell Porter
32 Tony Pena .15 .40
Fernando Valenzuela/Robin Yount

1984 Topps Super

The cards in this 30-card set measure 4 7/8" by 6 7/8". The 1984 Topps Supers feature enlargements from the 1984 regular set. The cards differ from the corresponding cards of the regular set in size and number only. As one would expect, only those considered stars and superstars appear in this set.

COMPLETE SET (30) 4.00 10.00
1 Cal Ripken 1.50 4.00
2 Dale Murphy .30 .75
3 LaMarr Hoyt .02 .10
4 John Denny .02 .10
5 Jim Rice .08 .25
6 Mike Schmidt .50 1.25
7 Wade Boggs .60 1.50
8 Bill Madlock .02 .10
9 Dan Quisenberry .02 .10
10 Al Holland .02 .10
11 Ron Kittle .02 .10
12 Darryl Strawberry .30 1.00
13 George Brett .60 1.50
14 Bill Buckner .08 .25
15 Carlton Fisk .40 1.00
16 Steve Carlton .40 1.00
17 Ron Guidry .08 .25
18 Gary Carter .40 1.00
19 Rickey Henderson .60 1.50
20 Andre Dawson .20 .50
21 Reggie Jackson .40 1.00
22 Steve Garvey .08 .25
23 Fred Lynn .08 .25
24 Pedro Guerrero .08 .25
25 Eddie Murray .50 1.25
26 Keith Hernandez .08 .25
27 Dave Winfield .40 1.00
28 Nolan Ryan 1.25 3.00
29 Robin Yount .40 1.00
30 Fernando Valenzuela .08 .25

1984-91 Topps Pewter Bonuses

During the eight year period that Topps issued their Gallery of Champions set, various other metal cards were issued as well. During that period, Topps issued Pewter cards as a premium. From 1984 to 1987 these Pewters were issued as a bonus for ordering "Tiffany" cases. From 1988-91, these Pewters were issued as bonuses for Gallery of Champion cases. The cards are sequenced in year order. A different Jose Canseco card was issued in 1987 and 1989.

COMPLETE SET (8) 300.00 800.00
1 Tom Seaver '84 125.00 300.00
2 Dwight Gooden '85 20.00 50.00
3 Don Mattingly '86 40.00 80.00
4 Jose Canseco '87 20.00 50.00
5 Mark McGwire '88 40.00 80.00
6 Jose Canseco '89 12.50 30.00
7 Nolan Ryan '90 75.00 200.00
8 Rickey Henderson '91 20.00 50.00

1985 Topps

The 1985 Topps set contains 792 standard-size full-color cards. Cards were primarily distributed in 15-card wax packs, 51-card rack packs and factory (usually available through retail catalogs) sets. The wax packs were issued with an 35 cent SRP and were packaged 36 packs to a box and 20 boxes to a case. Manager cards feature the team checklist on the reverse. Full color card fronts feature both the Topps and team logos along with the team name, player's name, and his position. The first ten cards (1-10) are Record Breakers, cards 131-143 are Father and Sons, and cards 701 to 722 portray All-Star selections. Cards 271-282 represent "First Draft Picks" still active in professional baseball and cards 389-404 feature selected members of the 1984 U.S. Olympic Baseball Team. Rookie Cards include Roger Clemens, Eric Davis, Shawon Dunston, Dwight Gooden, Orel Hershiser, Jimmy Key, Mark Langston, Mark McGwire, Terry Pendleton, Kirby Puckett and Bret Saberhagen.

COMPLETE SET (792) 20.00 50.00
COMP.FACT.SET (792) 90.00 150.00
1 Carlton Fisk RB .08 .25
2 Steve Garvey RB .05 .15
3 Dwight Gooden RB .25 .60
4 Cliff Johnson RB .05 .15
5 Joe Morgan RB .05 .15
6 Pete Rose RB .15 .40
7 Nolan Ryan RB .60 1.50
8 Juan Samuel RB .05 .15
9 Bruce Sutter RB .05 .15
10 Don Sutton RB .05 .15
11 Ralph Houk MG .05 .15
12 Dave Lopes .08 .25
13 Tim Lollar .05 .15
14 Chris Bando .05 .15
15 Jerry Koosman .08 .25
16 Bobby Meacham .05 .15
17 Mike Scott .08 .25
18 Mickey Hatcher .05 .15
19 George Frazier .05 .15
20 Chet Lemon .08 .25
21 Lee Tunnell .05 .15
22 Duane Kuiper .05 .15
23 Bret Saberhagen RC .40 1.00
24 Jesse Barfield .08 .25
25 Steve Bedrosian .05 .15
26 Roy Smalley .05 .15
27 Bruce Berenyi .05 .15
28 Dann Bilardello .05 .15
29 Odell Jones .05 .15
30 Cal Ripken 1.00 2.50
31 Terry Whitfield .05 .15
32 Chuck Porter .05 .15
33 Tito Landrum .05 .15
34 Ed Nunez .05 .15
35 Graig Nettles .08 .25
36 Fred Breining .05 .15
37 Reid Nichols .05 .15
38 Jackie Moore MG .05 .15
39 John Wockenfuss .05 .15
40 Phil Niekro .08 .25
41 Mike Fischlin .05 .15
42 Luis Sanchez .05 .15
43 Andre David .05 .15
44 Dickie Thon .05 .15
45 Greg Minton .05 .15
46 Gary Woods .05 .15
47 Dave Rozema .05 .15
48 Tony Fernandez .08 .25
49 Butch Davis .05 .15
50 John Candelaria .05 .15
51 Bob Watson .05 .15
52 Jerry Dybzinski .05 .15
53 Tom Gorman .05 .15
54 Cesar Cedeno .08 .25
55 Frank Tanana .08 .25
56 Jim Dwyer .05 .15
57 Pat Zachry .05 .15
58 Orlando Mercado .05 .15
59 Rick Waits .05 .15
60 George Hendrick .08 .25
61 Curt Kaufman .05 .15
62 Mike Ramsey .05 .15
63 Steve McCatty .05 .15
64 Mark Bailey .05 .15
65 Bill Buckner .08 .25
66 Dick Williams MG .05 .15
67 Rafael Santana .05 .15
68 Von Hayes .05 .15
69 Jim Winn .05 .15
70 Don Baylor .08 .25
71 Tim Laudner .05 .15
72 Rick Sutcliffe .08 .25
73 Rusty Kuntz .05 .15
74 Mike Krukow .05 .15
75 Willie Upshaw .05 .15
76 Alan Bannister .05 .15
77 Joe Deckwith .05 .15
78 Scott Fletcher .05 .15
79 Rick Mahler .05 .15
80 Keith Hernandez .08 .25
81 Lenn Sakata .05 .15
82 Joe Price .05 .15
83 Charlie Moore .05 .15
84 Spike Owen .05 .15
85 Mike Marshall .05 .15
86 Don Aase .05 .15
87 David Green .05 .15
88 Bryn Smith .05 .15
89 Jackie Gutierrez .05 .15
90 Rich Gossage .08 .25
91 Jeff Burroughs .05 .15
92 Paul Owens MG .05 .15
93 Don Schulze .05 .15
94 Toby Harrah .08 .25
95 Jose Cruz .08 .25
96 Johnny Ray .05 .15
97 Pete Filson .05 .15
98 Steve Lake .05 .15
99 Milt Wilcox .05 .15
100 George Brett .60 1.50
101 Jim Acker .05 .15
102 Tommy Dunbar .05 .15
103 Randy Lerch .05 .15
104 Mike Fitzgerald .05 .15
105 Ron Kittle .05 .15
106 Pascual Perez .05 .15
107 Tom Foley .05 .15
108 Darnell Coles .05 .15
109 Gary Roenicke .05 .15
110 Alejandro Pena .05 .15
111 Doug DeCinces .05 .15
112 Tom Tellmann .05 .15
113 Tom Herr .05 .15
114 Bob James .05 .15
115 Rickey Henderson .30 .75
116 Dennis Boyd .05 .15
117 Greg Gross .05 .15
118 Eric Show .05 .15
119 Pat Corrales MG .05 .15
120 Steve Kemp .05 .15
121 Checklist: 1-132 .05 .15
122 Tom Brunansky .05 .15
123 Dave Smith .05 .15
124 Rich Hebner .05 .15
125 Kent Tekulve .05 .15
126 Ruppert Jones .05 .15
127 Mark Gubicza RC* .15 .40
128 Ernie Whitt .05 .15
129 Gene Garber .05 .15
130 Al Oliver .08 .25
131 Buddy .08 .25
Gus Bell FS
132 Yogi .25 .60
Dale Berra FS
133 Bob .05 .15
Ray Boone FS
134 Terry .08 .25
Tito Francona FS
135 Terry .05 .15
Bob Kennedy FS
136 Jeff .05 .15
Bill Kunkel FS
137 Vance .08 .25
Vern Law FS
138 Dick .05 .15
Dick Schofield FS
139 Joel .05 .15
Bob Skinner FS
140 Roy .05 .15
Roy Smalley FS
141 Mike .05 .15
Dave Stenhouse FS
142 Steve .05 .15
Dizzy Trout FS
143 Ozzie .05 .15
Ossie Virgil FS
144 Ron Gardenhire .05 .15

145 Alvin Davis RC* .15 .40
146 Gary Redus .05 .15
147 Bill Swaggerty .05 .15
148 Steve Yeager .08 .25
149 Dickie Noles .05 .15
150 Jim Rice .08 .25
151 Moose Haas .05 .15
152 Steve Braun .05 .15
153 Frank LaCorte .05 .15
154 Angel Salazar .05 .15
155 Yogi Berra MG/TC .25 .60
156 Craig Reynolds .05 .15
157 Tug McGraw .08 .25
158 Pat Tabler .08 .25
159 Carlos Diaz .05 .15
160 Lance Parrish .08 .25
161 Ken Schrom .05 .15
162 Benny Distefano .05 .15
163 Dennis Eckersley .15 .40
164 Jorge Orta .05 .15
165 Dusty Baker .08 .25
166 Keith Atherton .05 .15
167 Rufino Linares .05 .15
168 Garth Iorg .05 .15
169 Dan Spillner .05 .15
170 George Foster .08 .25
171 Bill Stein .05 .15
172 Jack Perconte .05 .15
173 Mike Young .05 .15
174 Rick Honeycutt .05 .15
175 Dave Parker .08 .25
176 Bill Schroeder .05 .15
177 Dave Von Ohlen .05 .15
178 Miguel Dilone .05 .15
179 Tommy John .08 .25
180 Dave Winfield .08 .25
181 Roger Clemens RC 10.00 25.00
182 Tim Flannery .05 .15
183 Larry McWilliams .05 .15
184 Carmen Castillo .05 .15
185 Al Holland .05 .15
186 Bob Lillis MG .05 .15
187 Mike Walters .05 .15
188 Greg Pryor .05 .15
189 Warren Brusstar .05 .15
190 Rusty Staub .08 .25
191 Steve Nicosia .05 .15
192 Howard Johnson .08 .25
193 Jimmy Key RC .30 .75
194 Dave Stegman .05 .15
195 Glenn Hubbard .05 .15
196 Pete O'Brien .05 .15
197 Mike Warren .05 .15
198 Eddie Milner .05 .15
199 Dennis Martinez .08 .25
200 Reggie Jackson .15 .40
201 Burt Hooton .05 .15
202 Gorman Thomas .08 .25
203 Bob McClure .05 .15
204 Art Howe .05 .15
205 Steve Rogers .05 .15
206 Phil Garner .08 .25
207 Mark Clear .05 .15
208 Champ Summers .05 .15
209 Bill Campbell .05 .15
210 Gary Matthews .08 .25
211 Clay Christiansen .05 .15
212 George Vukovich .05 .15
213 Billy Gardner MG .05 .15
214 John Tudor .08 .25
215 Bob Brenly .05 .15
216 Jerry Don Gleaton .05 .15
217 Leon Roberts .05 .15
218 Doyle Alexander .05 .15
219 Gerald Perry .05 .15
220 Fred Lynn .08 .25
221 Ron Reed .05 .15
222 Hubie Brooks .05 .15
223 Tom Hume .05 .15
224 Al Cowens .05 .15
225 Mike Boddicker .05 .15
226 Juan Beniquez .05 .15
227 Danny Darwin .05 .15
228 Dion James .05 .15
229 Dave LaPoint .05 .15
230 Gary Carter .08 .25
231 Dwayne Murphy .05 .15
232 Dave Beard .05 .15
233 Ed Jurak .05 .15
234 Jerry Narron .05 .15
235 Garry Maddox .05 .15
236 Mark Thurmond .05 .15
237 Julio Franco .08 .25
238 Jose Rijo RC .30 .75
239 Tim Teufel .05 .15
240 Dave Stieb .08 .25
241 Jim Frey MG .05 .15
242 Greg Harris .05 .15
243 Barbaro Garbey .05 .15
244 Mike Jones .05 .15
245 Chili Davis .08 .25
246 Mike Norris .05 .15
247 Wayne Tolleson .05 .15
248 Terry Forster .08 .25
249 Harold Baines .08 .25
250 Jesse Orosco .05 .15
251 Brad Gulden .05 .15
252 Dan Ford .05 .15
253 Sid Bream RC .15 .40
254 Pete Vuckovich .05 .15
255 Lonnie Smith .05 .15
256 Mike Stanton .05 .15
257 Bryan Little .05 .15
258 Mike C. Brown .05 .15
259 Gary Allenson .05 .15
260 Dave Righetti .08 .25
261 Checklist: 133-264 .05 .15
262 Greg Booker .05 .15
263 Mel Hall .05 .15
264 Joe Sambito .05 .15
265 Juan Samuel .05 .15
266 Frank Viola .08 .25
267 Henry Cotto RC .05 .15
268 Chuck Tanner MG .05 .15
269 Doug Baker .05 .15
270 Dan Quisenberry .05 .15
271 Tim Foli FDP .05 .15
272 Jeff Burroughs FDP .05 .15
273 Bill Almon FDP .05 .15
274 Floyd Bannister FDP .05 .15
275 Harold Baines FDP .05 .15
276 Bob Horner FDP .05 .15
277 Al Chambers FDP .05 .15
278 Darryl Strawberry FDP .15 .40
279 Mike Moore FDP .05 .15
280 Shawon Dunston FDP RC .30 .75
281 Tim Belcher FDP RC .15 .40
282 Shawn Abner FDP RC .05 .15
283 Fran Mullins .05 .15
284 Marty Bystrom .05 .15
285 Dan Driessen .05 .15
286 Rudy Law .05 .15
287 Walt Terrell .05 .15
288 Jeff Kunkel .05 .15
289 Tom Underwood .05 .15
290 Cecil Cooper .08 .25
291 Bob Welch .08 .25
292 Brad Komminsk .05 .15
293 Curt Young .05 .15
294 Tom Nieto .05 .15
295 Joe Niekro .05 .15
296 Ricky Nelson .05 .15
297 Gary Lucas .05 .15
298 Marty Barrett .05 .15
299 Andy Hawkins .05 .15
300 Rod Carew .15 .40
301 John Montefusco .05 .15
302 Tim Corcoran .05 .15
303 Mike Jeffcoat .05 .15
304 Gary Gaetti .08 .25
305 Dale Berra .05 .15
306 Rick Reuschel .08 .25
307 Sparky Anderson MG .08 .25
308 John Wathan .05 .15
309 Mike Witt .05 .15
310 Manny Trillo .05 .15
311 Jim Gott .05 .15
312 Marc Hill .05 .15
313 Dave Schmidt .05 .15
314 Ron Oester .05 .15
315 Doug Sisk .05 .15
316 John Lowenstein .05 .15
317 Jack Lazorko .05 .15
318 Ted Simmons .08 .25
319 Jeff Jones .05 .15
320 Dale Murphy .15 .40
321 Ricky Horton .05 .15
322 Dave Stapleton .05 .15
323 Andy McGaffigan .05 .15
324 Bruce Bochy .05 .15
325 John Denny .05 .15
326 Kevin Bass .05 .15
327 Brook Jacoby .05 .15
328 Bob Shirley .05 .15
329 Ron Washington .05 .15
330 Leon Durham .05 .15
331 Bill Laskey .05 .15
332 Brian Harper .05 .15
333 Willie Hernandez .05 .15
334 Dick Howser MG .05 .15
335 Bruce Benedict .05 .15
336 Rance Mulliniks .05 .15
337 Billy Sample .05 .15
338 Britt Burns .05 .15
339 Danny Heep .05 .15
340 Robin Yount .40 1.00
341 Floyd Rayford .05 .15
342 Ted Power .05 .15
343 Bill Russell .08 .25
344 Dave Henderson .05 .15
345 Charlie Lea .05 .15
346 Terry Pendleton RC .30 .75
347 Rick Langford .05 .15
348 Bob Boone .08 .25
349 Domingo Ramos .05 .15
350 Wade Boggs .25 .60
351 Juan Agosto .05 .15
352 Joe Morgan .08 .25
353 Julio Solano .05 .15
354 Andre Robertson .05 .15
355 Bert Blyleven .08 .25
356 Dave Meier .05 .15
357 Rich Bordi .05 .15
358 Tony Pena .05 .15
359 Pat Sheridan .05 .15
360 Steve Carlton .08 .25
361 Alfredo Griffin .05 .15
362 Craig McMurtry .05 .15
363 Ron Hodges .05 .15
364 Richard Dotson .05 .15
365 Danny Ozark MG .05 .15
366 Todd Cruz .05 .15
367 Keefe Cato .05 .15
368 Dave Bergman .05 .15
369 R.J. Reynolds .05 .15
370 Bruce Sutter .08 .25
371 Mickey Rivers .05 .15
372 Roy Howell .05 .15
373 Mike Moore .05 .15
374 Brian Downing .08 .25
375 Jeff Reardon .08 .25
376 Jeff Newman .05 .15
377 Checklist: 265-396 .05 .15
378 Alan Wiggins .05 .15
379 Charles Hudson .05 .15
380 Ken Griffey .08 .25
381 Roy Smith .05 .15
382 Denny Walling .05 .15
383 Rick Lysander .05 .15
384 Jody Davis .05 .15
385 Jose DeLeon .05 .15
386 Dan Gladden RC .15 .40
387 Buddy Biancalana .05 .15
388 Bert Roberge .05 .15
389 Rod Dedeaux OLY CO RC .08 .25
390 Sid Akins OLY RC .05 .15
391 Flavio Alfaro OLY RC .05 .15
392 Don August OLY RC .05 .15
393 Scott Bankhead OLY RC .05 .15
394 Bob Caffrey OLY RC .05 .15
395 Mike Dunne OLY RC .05 .15
396 Gary Green OLY RC .05 .15
397 John Hoover OLY RC .05 .15
398 Shane Mack OLY RC .15 .40
399 John Marzano OLY RC .05 .15
400 Oddibe McDowell OLY RC .15 .40
401 Mark McGwire OLY RC 15.00 40.00
402 Pat Pacillo OLY RC .05 .15
403 Cory Snyder OLY RC .30 .75
404 Billy Swift OLY RC .15 .40
405 Tom Veryzer .05 .15
406 Len Whitehouse .05 .15
407 Bobby Ramos .05 .15
408 Sid Monge .05 .15
409 Brad Wellman .05 .15
410 Bob Horner .08 .25
411 Bobby Cox MG .08 .25
412 Bud Black .05 .15
413 Vance Law .05 .15
414 Gary Ward .05 .15
415 Ron Darling UER .08 .25
416 Wayne Gross .05 .15
417 John Franco RC .30 .75
418 Ken Landreaux .05 .15
419 Mike Caldwell .05 .15
420 Andre Dawson .08 .25
421 Dave Rucker .05 .15
422 Carney Lansford .08 .25
423 Barry Bonnell .05 .15
424 Al Nipper .05 .15
425 Mike Hargrove .05 .15
426 Vern Ruhle .05 .15
427 Mario Ramirez .05 .15
428 Larry Andersen .05 .15
429 Rick Cerone .05 .15
430 Ron Davis .05 .15
431 U.L. Washington .05 .15
432 Thad Bosley .05 .15
433 Jim Morrison .05 .15
434 Gene Richards .05 .15
435 Dan Petry .05 .15
436 Willie Aikens .05 .15
437 Al Jones .05 .15
438 Joe Torre MG .08 .25
439 Junior Ortiz .05 .15
440 Fernando Valenzuela .08 .25
441 Duane Walker .05 .15
442 Ken Forsch .05 .15
443 George Wright .05 .15
444 Tony Phillips .05 .15
445 Tippy Martinez .05 .15
446 Jim Sundberg .08 .25
447 Jeff Lahti .05 .15
448 Derrel Thomas .05 .15
449 Phil Bradley .15 .40
450 Steve Garvey .08 .25
451 Bruce Hurst .05 .15
452 John Castino .05 .15
453 Tom Waddell .05 .15
454 Glenn Wilson .05 .15
455 Bob Knepper .05 .15
456 Tim Foli .05 .15
457 Cecilio Guante .05 .15
458 Randy Johnson .05 .15
459 Charlie Leibrandt .05 .15
460 Ryne Sandberg .50 1.25
461 Marty Castillo .05 .15
462 Gary Lavelle .05 .15
463 Dave Collins .05 .15
464 Mike Mason RC .05 .15
465 Bob Grich .08 .25
466 Tony LaRussa MG .08 .25
467 Ed Lynch .05 .15
468 Wayne Krenchicki .05 .15
469 Sammy Stewart .05 .15
470 Steve Sax .05 .15
471 Pete Ladd .05 .15
472 Jim Essian .05 .15
473 Tim Wallach .05 .15
474 Kurt Kepshire .05 .15
475 Andre Thornton .05 .15
476 Jeff Stone RC .05 .15
477 Bob Ojeda .05 .15
478 Kurt Bevacqua .05 .15
479 Mike Madden .05 .15
480 Lou Whitaker .08 .25
481 Dale Murray .05 .15
482 Harry Spilman .05 .15
483 Mike Smithson .05 .15
484 Larry Bowa .08 .25
485 Matt Young .05 .15
486 Steve Balboni .05 .15
487 Frank Williams .05 .15
488 Joel Skinner .05 .15
489 Bryan Clark .05 .15
490 Jason Thompson .05 .15
491 Rick Camp .05 .15
492 Dave Johnson MG .05 .15
493 Orel Hershiser RC .75 2.00
494 Rich Dauer .05 .15
495 Mario Soto .08 .25
496 Donnie Scott .05 .15
497 Gary Pettis UER .05 .15
498 Ed Romero .05 .15
499 Danny Cox .05 .15
500 Mike Schmidt .60 1.50
501 Dan Schatzeder .05 .15
502 Rick Miller .05 .15
503 Tim Conroy .05 .15
504 Jerry Willard .05 .15
505 Jim Beattie .05 .15
506 Franklin Stubbs .05 .15
507 Ray Fontenot .05 .15
508 John Shelby .05 .15
509 Milt May .05 .15
510 Kent Hrbek .08 .25
511 Lee Smith .08 .25
512 Tom Brookens .05 .15
513 Lynn Jones .05 .15
514 Jeff Cornell .05 .15
515 Dave Concepcion .08 .25
516 Roy Lee Jackson .05 .15
517 Jerry Martin .05 .15
518 Chris Chambliss .08 .25
519 Doug Rader MG .05 .15
520 LaMarr Hoyt .05 .15
521 Rick Dempsey .05 .15
522 Paul Molitor .08 .25
523 Candy Maldonado .05 .15
524 Rob Wilfong .05 .15
525 Darrell Porter .05 .15
526 David Palmer .05 .15
527 Checklist: 397-528 .05 .15
528 Bill Krueger .05 .15
529 Rich Gedman .05 .15
530 Dave Dravecky .05 .15
531 Joe Lefebvre .05 .15
532 Frank DiPino .05 .15
533 Tony Bernazard .05 .15
534 Brian Dayett .05 .15
535 Pat Putnam .05 .15
536 Kirby Puckett RC 12.00 30.00
537 Don Robinson .05 .15
538 Keith Moreland .05 .15
539 Aurelio Lopez .05 .15
540 Claudell Washington .05 .15
541 Mark Davis .05 .15
542 Don Slaught .05 .15
543 Mike Squires .05 .15
544 Bruce Kison .05 .15
545 Lloyd Moseby .05 .15
546 Brent Gaff .05 .15
547 Pete Rose MG/TC .15 .40
548 Larry Parrish .05 .15
549 Mike Scioscia .08 .25
550 Scott McGregor .05 .15
551 Andy Van Slyke .15 .40
552 Chris Codiroli .05 .15
553 Bob Clark .05 .15
554 Doug Flynn .05 .15
555 Bob Stanley .05 .15
556 Sixto Lezcano .05 .15
557 Len Barker .05 .15
558 Carmelo Martinez .05 .15
559 Jay Howell .05 .15
560 Bill Madlock .08 .25
561 Darryl Motley .05 .15
562 Houston Jimenez .05 .15
563 Dick Ruthven .05 .15
564 Alan Ashby .05 .15
565 Kirk Gibson .08 .25
566 Ed VandeBerg .05 .15
567 Joel Youngblood .05 .15
568 Cliff Johnson .05 .15
569 Ken Oberkfell .05 .15
570 Darryl Strawberry .25 .60
571 Charlie Hough .08 .25
572 Tom Paciorek .05 .15
573 Jay Tibbs .05 .15
574 Joe Altobelli MG .05 .15
575 Pedro Guerrero .08 .25
576 Jaime Cocanower .05 .15
577 Chris Speier .05 .15
578 Terry Francona .08 .25
579 Ron Romanick .05 .15
580 Dwight Evans .15 .40
581 Mark Wagner .05 .15
582 Ken Phelps .05 .15
583 Bobby Brown .05 .15
584 Kevin Gross .05 .15
585 Butch Wynegar .05 .15
586 Bill Scherrer .05 .15
587 Doug Frobel .05 .15
588 Bobby Castillo .05 .15
589 Bob Dernier .05 .15
590 Ray Knight .08 .25
591 Larry Herndon .05 .15
592 Jeff D. Robinson .05 .15
593 Rick Leach .05 .15
594 Curt Wilkerson .05 .15
595 Larry Gura .05 .15
596 Jerry Hairston .05 .15
597 Brad Lesley .05 .15
598 Jose Oquendo .05 .15
599 Storm Davis .05 .15
600 Pete Rose .60 1.50
601 Tom Lasorda MG .15 .40
602 Jeff Dedmon .05 .15
603 Rick Manning .05 .15
604 Daryl Sconiers .05 .15
605 Ozzie Smith .40 1.00
606 Rich Gale .05 .15
607 Bill Almon .05 .15
608 Craig Lefferts .05 .15
609 Broderick Perkins .05 .15
610 Jack Morris .08 .25
611 Ozzie Virgil .05 .15
612 Mike Armstrong .05 .15
613 Terry Puhl .05 .15
614 Al Williams .05 .15
615 Marvell Wynne .05 .15
616 Scott Sanderson .05 .15
617 Willie Wilson .08 .25
618 Pete Falcone .05 .15
619 Jeff Leonard .05 .15
620 Dwight Gooden RC .75 2.00
621 Marvis Foley .05 .15
622 Luis Leal .05 .15
623 Greg Walker .05 .15
624 Benny Ayala .05 .15
625 Mark Langston RC .30 .75
626 German Rivera .05 .15
627 Eric Davis RC .75 2.00
628 Rene Lachemann MG .05 .15
629 Dick Schofield .05 .15
630 Tim Raines .08 .25
631 Bob Forsch .05 .15
632 Bruce Bochte .05 .15
633 Glenn Hoffman .05 .15
634 Bill Dawley .05 .15
635 Terry Kennedy .05 .15
636 Shane Rawley .05 .15
637 Brett Butler .08 .25
638 Mike Pagliarulo .08 .25
639 Ed Hodge .05 .15
640 Steve Henderson .05 .15
641 Rod Scurry .05 .15
642 Dave Owen .05 .15
643 Johnny Grubb .05 .15
644 Mark Huismann .05 .15
645 Damaso Garcia .05 .15
646 Scot Thompson .05 .15
647 Rafael Ramirez .05 .15
648 Bob Jones .05 .15
649 Sid Fernandez .08 .25
650 Greg Luzinski .08 .25
651 Jeff Russell .05 .15
652 Joe Nolan .05 .15
653 Mark Brouhard .05 .15
654 Dave Anderson .05 .15
655 Joaquin Andujar .08 .25
656 Chuck Cottier MG .05 .15
657 Jim Slaton .05 .15
658 Mike Stenhouse .05 .15
659 Checklist: 529-660 .05 .15
660 Tony Gwynn .50 1.25
661 Steve Crawford .05 .15
662 Mike Heath .05 .15
663 Luis Aguayo .05 .15
664 Steve Farr RC .15 .40
665 Don Mattingly 1.00 2.50
666 Mike LaCoss .05 .15
667 Dave Engle .05 .15
668 Steve Trout .05 .15
669 Lee Lacy .05 .15
670 Tom Seaver .15 .40
671 Dane Iorg .05 .15
672 Juan Berenguer .05 .15
673 Buck Martinez .05 .15
674 Atlee Hammaker .05 .15
675 Tony Perez .15 .40
676 Albert Hall .05 .15
677 Wally Backman .05 .15
678 Joey McLaughlin .05 .15
679 Bob Kearney .05 .15
680 Jerry Reuss .05 .15
681 Ben Oglivie .08 .25
682 Doug Corbett .05 .15
683 Whitey Herzog MG .08 .25
684 Bill Doran .05 .15
685 Bill Caudill .05 .15
686 Mike Easler .05 .15
687 Bill Gullickson .05 .15
688 Len Matuszek .05 .15
689 Luis DeLeon .05 .15
690 Alan Trammell .08 .25
691 Dennis Rasmussen .05 .15
692 Randy Bush .05 .15
693 Tim Stoddard .05 .15
694 Joe Carter .25 .60
695 Rick Rhoden .05 .15
696 John Rabb .05 .15
697 Onix Concepcion .05 .15
698 George Bell .08 .25
699 Donnie Moore .05 .15
700 Eddie Murray .25 .60
701 Eddie Murray AS .15 .40
702 Damaso Garcia AS .05 .15
703 George Brett AS .25 .60
704 Cal Ripken AS .60 1.50
705 Dave Winfield AS .05 .15
706 Rickey Henderson AS .15 .40
707 Tony Armas AS .05 .15
708 Lance Parrish AS .05 .15
709 Mike Boddicker AS .05 .15
710 Frank Viola AS .05 .15
711 Dan Quisenberry AS .05 .15
712 Keith Hernandez AS .05 .15
713 Ryne Sandberg AS .25 .60
714 Mike Schmidt AS .25 .60
715 Ozzie Smith AS .25 .60
716 Dale Murphy AS .08 .25
717 Tony Gwynn AS .40 1.00
718 Jeff Leonard AS .05 .15
719 Gary Carter AS .05 .15
720 Rick Sutcliffe AS .05 .15
721 Bob Knepper AS .05 .15
722 Bruce Sutter AS .05 .15
723 Dave Stewart .08 .25
724 Oscar Gamble .05 .15
725 Floyd Bannister .05 .15
726 Al Bumbry .05 .15
727 Frank Pastore .05 .15
728 Bob Bailor .05 .15
729 Don Sutton .08 .25
730 Dave Kingman .08 .25
731 Neil Allen .05 .15
732 John McNamara MG .05 .15
733 Tony Scott .05 .15
734 John Henry Johnson .05 .15
735 Garry Templeton .05 .15
736 Jerry Mumphrey .05 .15
737 Bo Diaz .05 .15
738 Omar Moreno .05 .15
739 Ernie Camacho .05 .15
740 Jack Clark .08 .25
741 John Butcher .05 .15
742 Ron Hassey .05 .15
743 Frank White .08 .25
744 Doug Bair .05 .15
745 Buddy Bell .08 .25
746 Jim Clancy .05 .15
747 Alex Trevino .05 .15
748 Lee Mazzilli .08 .25
749 Julio Cruz .05 .15
750 Rollie Fingers .08 .25
751 Kelvin Chapman .05 .15
752 Bob Owchinko .05 .15
753 Greg Brock .05 .15
754 Larry Milbourne .05 .15
755 Ken Singleton .08 .25
756 Rob Picciolo .05 .15
757 Willie McGee .08 .25
758 Ray Burris .05 .15
759 Jim Fanning MG .05 .15
760 Nolan Ryan 1.25 3.00
761 Jerry Remy .05 .15
762 Eddie Whitson .05 .15
763 Kiko Garcia .05 .15
764 Jamie Easterly .05 .15
765 Willie Randolph .08 .25
766 Paul Mirabella .05 .15
767 Darrell Brown .05 .15
768 Ron Cey .08 .25
769 Joe Cowley .05 .15
770 Carlton Fisk .15 .40
771 Geoff Zahn .05 .15
772 Johnnie LeMaster .05 .15
773 Hal McRae .08 .25
774 Dennis Lamp .05 .15
775 Mookie Wilson .08 .25
776 Jerry Royster .05 .15
777 Ned Yost .05 .15
778 Mike Davis .05 .15
779 Nick Esasky .05 .15
780 Mike Flanagan .05 .15
781 Jim Gantner .05 .15
782 Tom Niedenfuer .05 .15
783 Mike Jorgensen .08 .25
784 Checklist: 661-792 .05 .15
785 Tony Armas .08 .25
786 Enos Cabell .05 .15
787 Jim Wohlford .05 .15
788 Steve Comer .05 .15
789 Luis Salazar .05 .15
790 Ron Guidry .08 .25
791 Ivan DeJesus .05 .15
792 Darrell Evans .08 .25

1985 Topps Tiffany

COMP.FACT.SET (792) 300.00 500.00
*STARS: 3X TO 8X BASIC CARDS
*ROOKIES: 2.5X TO 6X BASIC CARDS
DISTRIBUTED ONLY IN FACTORY SET FORM
FACTORY SET PRICE IS FOR SEALED SETS

1985 Topps Glossy All-Stars

COMPLETE SET (22) 2.00 5.00
1 Paul Owens MG .01 .05
2 Steve Garvey .05 .15
3 Ryne Sandberg .40 1.00
4 Mike Schmidt .30 .75
5 Ozzie Smith .40 1.00
6 Tony Gwynn .50 1.25
7 Dale Murphy .07 .20
8 Darryl Strawberry .02 .10
9 Gary Carter .20 .50
10 Charlie Lea .01 .05
11 Willie McCovey CAPT .02 .10
12 Joe Altobelli MG .01 .05
13 Rod Carew .20 .50
14 Lou Whitaker .02 .10
15 George Brett .40 1.00
16 Cal Ripken .75 2.00
17 Dave Winfield .20 .50
18 Chet Lemon .01 .05
19 Reggie Jackson .20 .50
20 Lance Parrish .01 .05
21 Dave Stieb .01 .05
22 Hank Greenberg CAPT .02 .10

1985 Topps Glossy Send-Ins

COMPLETE SET (40) 4.00 10.00
1 Dale Murphy .10 .30
2 Jesse Orosco .07 .20
3 Bob Brenly .02 .10
4 Mike Boddicker .02 .10
5 Dave Kingman .07 .20
6 Jim Rice .07 .20
7 Frank Viola .07 .20
8 Alvin Davis .02 .10
9 Rick Sutcliffe .02 .10
10 Pete Rose .50 1.25
11 Leon Durham .02 .10
12 Joaquin Andujar .02 .10
13 Keith Hernandez .07 .20
14 Dave Winfield .30 .75
15 Reggie Jackson .30 .75
16 Alan Trammell .10 .30
17 Bert Blyleven .07 .20
18 Tony Armas .02 .10
19 Rich Gossage .07 .20
20 Jose Cruz .07 .20
21 Ryne Sandberg .75 2.00
22 Bruce Sutter .30 .75
23 Mike Schmidt .50 1.25
24 Cal Ripken 2.00 5.00
25 Dan Petry .02 .10
26 Jack Morris .07 .20
27 Don Mattingly 1.00 2.50
28 Eddie Murray .40 1.00
29 Tony Gwynn 1.00 2.50
30 Charlie Lea .02 .10
31 Juan Samuel .02 .10
32 Phil Niekro .30 .75
33 Alejandro Pena .02 .10
34 Harold Baines .07 .20
35 Dan Quisenberry .02 .10
36 Gary Carter .30 .75
37 Mario Soto .02 .10
38 Dwight Gooden .20 .50
39 Tom Brunansky .02 .10
40 Dave Stieb .02 .10

1985 Topps Traded

In its now standard procedure, Topps issued its standard-size Traded (or extended) set for the fifth year in a row. In addition to the typical factory set hobby distribution, Topps tested the limited issuance of these Traded cards in wax packs. Card design is identical to the regular-issue 1985 Topps set except for whiter card stock and T-suffixed numbering on back. The set numbering is in alphabetical order by player's name. The key extended Rookie Cards in this set include Vince Coleman, Ozzie Guillen, and Mickey Tettleton.

COMP.FACT.SET (132) 3.00 8.00
1T Don Aase .05 .15
2T Bill Almon .05 .15
3T Benny Ayala .05 .15
4T Dusty Baker .15 .40
5T George Bamberger MG .05 .15
6T Dale Berra .05 .15
7T Rich Bordi .05 .15
8T Daryl Boston XRC* .08 .25
9T Hubie Brooks .05 .15
10T Chris Brown XRC .08 .25
11T Tom Browning XRC* .20 .50
12T Al Bumbry .05 .15
13T Ray Burris .05 .15
14T Jeff Burroughs .05 .15
15T Bill Campbell .05 .15
16T Don Carman .05 .15
17T Gary Carter .15 .40
18T Bobby Castillo .05 .15
19T Bill Caudill .05 .15
20T Rick Cerone .05 .15
21T Bryan Clark .05 .15
22T Jack Clark .15 .40
23T Pat Clements .05 .15
24T Vince Coleman XRC .40 1.00
25T Dave Collins .05 .15
26T Danny Darwin .05 .15
27T Jim Davenport MG .05 .15
28T Jerry Davis .05 .15
29T Brian Dayett .05 .15
30T Ivan DeJesus .05 .15
31T Ken Dixon .05 .15
32T Mariano Duncan XRC .20 .50
33T John Felske MG .05 .15
34T Mike Fitzgerald .05 .15
35T Ray Fontenot .05 .15
36T Greg Gagne XRC* .20 .50
37T Oscar Gamble .05 .15
38T Scott Garrelts .05 .15
39T Bob L. Gibson .05 .15
40T Jim Gott .05 .15
41T David Green .05 .15
42T Alfredo Griffin .05 .15
43T Ozzie Guillen XRC 2.00 5.00
44T Eddie Haas MG .05 .15
45T Terry Harper .05 .15
46T Toby Harrah .15 .40
47T Greg Harris .05 .15
48T Ron Hassey .05 .15
49T Rickey Henderson 1.00 2.50
50T Steve Henderson .05 .15
51T George Hendrick .15 .40
52T Joe Hesketh .05 .15
53T Teddy Higuera XRC .20 .50
54T Donnie Hill .05 .15
55T Al Holland .05 .15
56T Burt Hooton .05 .15
57T Jay Howell .05 .15
58T Ken Howell .05 .15
59T LaMarr Hoyt .05 .15
60T Tim Hulett XRC* .08 .25
61T Bob James .05 .15
62T Steve Jeltz XRC .08 .25
63T Cliff Johnson .05 .15
64T Howard Johnson .15 .40
65T Ruppert Jones .05 .15
66T Steve Kemp .05 .15
67T Bruce Kison .05 .15
68T Alan Knicely .05 .15
69T Mike LaCoss .05 .15
70T Lee Lacy .05 .15
71T Dave LaPoint .05 .15
72T Gary Lavelle .05 .15
73T Vance Law .05 .15
74T Johnnie LeMaster .05 .15
75T Sixto Lezcano .05 .15
76T Tim Lollar .05 .15
77T Fred Lynn .15 .40
78T Billy Martin MG .30 .75
79T Ron Mathis .05 .15
80T Len Matuszek .05 .15
81T Gene Mauch MG .05 .15
82T Oddibe McDowell .20 .50
83T Roger McDowell XRC .20 .50
84T John McNamara MG .05 .15
85T Donnie Moore .05 .15
86T Gene Nelson .05 .15
87T Steve Nicosia .05 .15
88T Al Oliver .15 .40
89T Joe Orsulak XRC .20 .50
90T Rob Picciolo .05 .15
91T Chris Pittaro .05 .15
92T Jim Presley .20 .50
93T Rick Reuschel .15 .40
94T Bert Roberge .05 .15
95T Bob Rodgers MG .05 .15
96T Jerry Royster .05 .15
97T Dave Rozema .05 .15
98T Dave Rucker .05 .15
99T Vern Ruhle .05 .15
100T Paul Runge XRC .08 .25
101T Mark Salas .05 .15
102T Luis Salazar .05 .15
103T Joe Sambito .05 .15
104T Rick Schu .05 .15
105T Donnie Scott .05 .15
106T Larry Sheets XRC .08 .25
107T Don Slaught .05 .15
108T Roy Smalley .05 .15
109T Lonnie Smith .05 .15
110T Nate Snell UER(Headings on back for a batter) .05 .15
111T Chris Speier .05 .15
112T Mike Stenhouse .05 .15
113T Tim Stoddard .05 .15
114T Jim Sundberg .15 .40
115T Bruce Sutter .15 .40
116T Don Sutton .15 .40
117T Kent Tekulve .05 .15
118T Tom Tellmann .05 .15
119T Walt Terrell .05 .15
120T Mickey Tettleton XRC .20 .50
121T Derrel Thomas .05 .15
122T Rich Thompson .05 .15
123T Alex Trevino .05 .15
124T John Tudor .15 .40
125T Jose Uribe .05 .15
126T Bobby Valentine MG .15 .40
127T Dave Von Ohlen .05 .15
128T U.L. Washington .05 .15
129T Earl Weaver MG .15 .40
130T Eddie Whitson .05 .15
131T Herm Winningham .05 .15
132T Checklist 1-132 .05 .15

1985 Topps Traded Tiffany

COMP.FACT.SET (132) 20.00 50.00
*STARS: 1.5X TO 4X BASIC CARDS
*ROOKIES: 1.5X TO 4X BASIC CARDS
DISTRIBUTED ONLY IN FACTORY SET FORM
FACTORY SET PRICE IS FOR SEALED SETS

1985 Topps 3-D

This innovative 30-card set was issued in packs of one. These large cards are very difficult to store (due to the 3-D effect) as they are not really stackable and are crumpled if placed in an album using plastic sheets. The cards are blank-backed except for two covered adhesive strips and measure approximately 4 1/4" by 5 7/8". Cards are numbered on the front and feature a prominent team logo on the front as well.

COMPLETE SET (30) 5.00 12.00
1 Mike Schmidt .40 1.00
2 Eddie Murray .40 1.00
3 Dale Murphy .10 .30
4 George Brett .75 2.00
5 Pete Rose .40 1.00
6 Jim Rice .07 .20
7 Ryne Sandberg .60 1.50
8 Don Mattingly .75 2.00
9 Darryl Strawberry .07 .20
10 Rickey Henderson .30 .75
11 Keith Hernandez .07 .20
12 Dave Kingman .02 .10

13 Tony Gwynn .75 2.00
14 Reggie Jackson .30 .75
15 Gary Carter .30 .75
16 Cal Ripken 1.50 4.00
17 Tim Raines .07 .20
18 Dave Winfield .30 .75
19 Dwight Gooden .20 .50
20 Dave Stieb .02 .10
21 Fernando Valenzuela .07 .20
22 Mark Langston .02 .10
23 Bruce Sutter .30 .75
24 Dan Quisenberry .02 .10
25 Steve Carlton .30 .75
26 Mike Boddicker .02 .10
27 Rich Gossage .07 .20
28 Jack Morris .07 .20
29 Rick Sutcliffe .02 .10
30 Tom Seaver .30 1.00

1985 Topps Gallery of Champions

This would be the second year that Topps issued a 12-card set featuring baseball stars. These "cards" were made of either silver or bronze and measure approximately 1 1/4" by 1 3/4". Since the cards are replicas of the 1985 Topps cards and would be skip-numbered, we have sequenced these cards in alphabetical order. This would be the last year that no aluminum cards were produced. The silver cards are valued at 2.5X the bronze versions.

COMPLETE SET (12) 175.00 350.00
1 Tony Armas 4.00 10.00
2 Alvin Davis 4.00 10.00
3 Dwight Gooden 12.50 30.00
4 Tony Gwynn 25.00 60.00
5 Willie Hernandez 4.00 10.00
6 Don Mattingly 25.00 60.00
7 Dale Murphy 15.00 40.00
8 Dan Quisenberry 4.00 10.00
9 Ryne Sandberg 25.00 60.00
10 Mike Schmidt 15.00 40.00
11 Rick Sutcliffe 5.00 12.00
12 Bruce Sutter 8.00 20.00

1985 Topps Rose

This set of 120 different standard-size cards is dedicated to Pete Rose. The set was sold in a red and white box and distributed by Renata Galasso, Inc. The checklist below gives the distinguishing features of each of the cards. Many of the backs feature a question and answer back. Since many of the pictures are similar, the back question is frequently excerpted below. The first three cards feature traditional statistical backs and the last 30 cards (91-120) feature backs that form a puzzle which, when completely assembled, shows in color all of Pete's Topps baseball cards up through 1985. In the set there are several cards which picture paintings of Pete at various stages of his career by artist Ron Lewis.

COMP. FACT SET (120) 10.00 25.00
COMMON PLAYER (1-120) .10 .25
1 Pete Rose .20 .50
Statistics '60s; Lewis painting
5 Pete Rose .08 .25
Pete Rose Jr./hit number 3631
56 Pete Rose .08 .25
Tyler Rose/with horse
68 Pete Rose .08 .25
Ray Fosse/collision
69 Pete Rose .08 .25
Ray Fosse/Pete got hurt in collision
70 Pete Rose .08 .25
Bud Harrelson/fight; Lewis painting
83 Pete Rose .08 .25
Pete Rose Jr./Hugs
87 Pete Rose .08 .25
Babe Ruth
88 Pete Rose .08 .25
Talking on Phone
AU1 Pete Rose
Card number 1 autographed

1985 Topps Stickers

Made in Italy for Topps and O-Pee-Chee by Panini, these 376 stickers measure approximately 2 1/8" by 3" and are numbered on both front and back. Some stickers are player cutouts. The fronts feature white-bordered color player photos. The horizontal backs carry a bilingual ad for O-Pee-Chee in blue lettering. An album onto which the stickers could be affixed was available at retail stores. The album and the sticker numbering are organized as follows: 1984 Record Breakers (1-8), 1984 Championship Series (9-14), 1984 World Series (15-21), Atlanta Braves (22-33), Chicago Cubs (34-45), Cincinnati Reds (46-57), Houston Astros (58-69), Los Angeles Dodgers (70-81), Montreal Expos (82-93), 1984 Stat Leaders (94-97), New York Mets (98-109), Philadelphia Phillies (110-121), Pittsburgh Pirates (122-133), St. Louis Cardinals (134-145), San Diego Padres (146-157), San Francisco Giants (158-169), 1984 Stat Leaders (170-173), Foil All-Stars (174-191), 1984 Stat Leaders (192-195), Baltimore Orioles (196-207), Boston Red Sox (208-219), California Angels (220-231), Chicago White Sox (232-243), Cleveland Indians (244-255), Detroit Tigers (256-267), Kansas City Royals (268-279), 1984 Stat Leaders (280-283), Milwaukee Brewers (284-295), Minnesota Twins (296-307), New York Yankees (308-319), Oakland A's (320-331), Seattle Mariners (332-343), Texas Rangers (344-355), Toronto Blue Jays (356-367) and Future Stars (368-376). For those stickers featuring more than one player, the other numbers on that sticker are given below in parentheses. Kirby Puckett, Mark Langston and Dwight Gooden are featured in their Rookie Card year.

COMPLETE SET (376) 6.00 15.00
COMMON PLAYER (1-376) .02 .05
COMMON FOIL .04 .10
*OPC: .4X TO 1X TOPPS STICKERS
1 Steve Garvey FOIL/(Top half) .05 .15
2 Steve Garvey FOIL/(Bottom half) .05 .15
3 Dwight Gooden/(Top half) .20 .50
4 Dwight Gooden/(Bottom half) .20 .50
5 Joe Morgan/(Top half) .02 .10
6 Joe Morgan/(Bottom half) .02 .10
7 Don Sutton/(Top half) .02 .10
8 Don Sutton/(Bottom half) .02 .10
9 AL Championships/(Jack Morris) .02 .10
10 AL Championships/(Milt Wilcox) .01 .05
11 AL Championships/(Kirk Gibson) .02 .10
12 AL Championships/(Gary Matthews) .01 .05
13 NL Championships
(Steve Garvey swings) .02 .10
14 NL Championships/(Steve Garvey) .02 .10
15 World Series/(Jack Morris) .02 .10
16 World Series/(Kurt Bevacqua) .01 .05
17 World Series/(Milt Wilcox) .01 .05
18 World Series/(Alan Trammell .02 .10
ready to throw)
19 World Series/(Kirk Gibson) .02 .10
20 World Series/(Alan Trammell) .02 .10
21 World Series/(Chet Lemon back) .01 .05
22 Dale Murphy .05 .15
23 Steve Bedrosian .01 .05
24 Bob Horner .01 .05
25 Claudell Washington .01 .05
26 Rick Mahler (212) .01 .05
27 Rafael Ramirez (213) .01 .05
28 Craig McMurtry (214) .01 .05
29 Chris Chambliss(215) .02 .10
30 Alex Trevino (216) .01 .05
31 Bruce Benedict (217) .01 .05
32 Ken Oberkfell (218) .01 .05
33 Glenn Hubbard (219) .01 .05
34 Ryne Sandberg .50 1.25
35 Rick Sutcliffe .01 .05
36 Leon Durham .01 .05
37 Jody Davis .01 .05
38 Bob Dernier (224) .01 .05
39 Keith Moreland(225) .01 .05
40 Scott Sanderson(226) .01 .05
41 Lee Smith (227) .08 .25
42 Ron Cey (228) .02 .10
43 Steve Trout (229) .01 .05
44 Gary Matthews(230) .01 .05
45 Larry Bowa (231) .02 .10
46 Mario Soto .01 .05
47 Dave Parker .02 .10
48 Dave Concepcion .02 .10
49 Gary Redus .01 .05
50 Ted Power (236) .01 .05
51 Nick Esasky (237) .01 .05
52 Duane Walker (238) .01 .05
53 Eddie Milner (239) .01 .05
54 Ron Oester (240) .01 .05
55 Cesar Cedeno (241) .02 .10
56 Joe Price (242) .01 .05
57 Pete Rose (243) .30 .75
58 Nolan Ryan 1.00 2.50
59 Jose Cruz .02 .10
60 Jerry Mumphrey .01 .05
61 Enos Cabell .01 .05
62 Bob Knepper (248) .01 .05
63 Dickie Thon (249) .01 .05
64 Phil Garner (250) .02 .10
65 Craig Reynolds (251) .01 .05
66 Frank DiPino (252) .01 .05
67 Terry Puhl (253) .01 .05
68 Bill Doran (254) .01 .05
69 Joe Niekro (255) .01 .05
70 Pedro Guerrero .02 .10
71 Fernando Valenzuela .02 .10
72 Mike Marshall .01 .05
73 Alejandro Pena .01 .05
74 Orel Hershiser(260) .30 .75
75 Ken Landreaux (261) .01 .05
76 Bill Russell (262) .02 .10
77 Steve Sax (263) .02 .10
78 Rick Honeycutt(264) .01 .05
79 Mike Scioscia (265) .02 .10
80 Tom Niedenfuer(266) .01 .05
81 Candy Maldonado(267) .01 .05
82 Tim Raines .02 .10
83 Gary Carter .05 .15
84 Charlie Lea .01 .05
85 Jeff Reardon .02 .10
86 Andre Dawson (272) .05 .15
87 Tim Wallach (273) .02 .10
88 Terry Francona (274) .02 .10
89 Steve Rogers (275) .01 .05
90 Bryn Smith (276) .01 .05
91 Bill Gullickson(277) .01 .05
92 Dan Driessen (278) .01 .05
93 Doug Flynn (279) .01 .05
94 Mike Schmidt/(170/192/280) .25 .60
95 Tony Armas/(171/193/281) .01 .05
96 Dale Murphy/(172/194/282) .05 .15
97 Rick Sutcliffe/(173/195/283) .01 .05
98 Keith Hernandez .02 .10
99 George Foster .02 .10
100 Darryl Strawberry .02 .10
101 Jesse Orosco .01 .05
102 Mookie Wilson (288) .02 .10
103 Doug Sisk (289) .01 .05
104 Hubie Brooks (290) .01 .05
105 Ron Darling (291) .02 .10
106 Wally Backman (292) .01 .05
107 Dwight Gooden (293) .30 .75
108 Mike Fitzgerald(294) .01 .05
109 Walt Terrell (295) .01 .05
110 Ozzie Virgil .01 .05
111 Mike Schmidt .25 .60
112 Steve Carlton .15 .40
113 Al Holland .01 .05
114 Juan Samuel (300) .01 .05
115 Von Hayes (301) .01 .05
116 Jeff Stone (302) .01 .05
117 Jerry Koosman (303) .02 .10
118 Al Oliver (304) .02 .10
119 John Denny (305) .01 .05
120 Charles Hudson (306) .01 .05
121 Garry Maddox (307) .01 .05
122 Bill Madlock .02 .10
123 John Candelaria .01 .05
124 Tony Pena .01 .05
125 Jason Thompson .01 .05
126 Lee Lacy (312) .01 .05
127 Rick Rhoden (313) .01 .05
128 Doug Frobel (314) .01 .05
129 Kent Tekulve (315) .01 .05
130 Johnny Ray (316) .01 .05
131 Marvell Wynne (317) .01 .05
132 Larry McWilliams(318) .01 .05
133 Dale Berra (319) .01 .05
134 George Hendrick .01 .05
135 Bruce Sutter .02 .10
136 Joaquin Andujar .01 .05
137 Ozzie Smith .15 .40
138 Andy Van Slyke (324) .05 .15
139 Lonnie Smith (325) .01 .05
140 Darrell Porter (326) .01 .05
141 Willie McGee (327) .02 .10
142 Tom Herr (328) .02 .10
143 Dave LaPoint (329) .01 .05
144 Neil Allen (330) .01 .05
145 David Green (331) .01 .05
146 Tony Gwynn .75 2.00
147 Rich Gossage .02 .10
148 Terry Kennedy .01 .05
149 Steve Garvey .05 .15
150 Alan Wiggins (336) .01 .05
151 Garry Templeton(337) .01 .05
152 Ed Whitson (338) .01 .05
153 Tim Lollar (339) .01 .05
154 Dave Dravecky (340) .02 .10
155 Graig Nettles (341) .02 .10
156 Eric Show (342) .01 .05
157 Carmelo Martinez(343) .01 .05
158 Bob Brenly .01 .05
159 Gary Lavelle .01 .05
160 Jack Clark .02 .10
161 Jeff Leonard .01 .05
162 Chili Davis (348) .02 .10
163 Mike Krukow (349) .01 .05
164 Johnnie LeMaster(350) .01 .05
165 Atlee Hammaker (351) .01 .05
166 Dan Gladden (352) .01 .05
167 Greg Minton (353) .01 .05
168 Joel Youngblood(354) .01 .05
169 Frank Williams (355) .01 .05
170 Tony Gwynn/(94/192/280) .60 1.50
171 Don Mattingly/(95/193/281) .75 2.00
172 Bruce Sutter/(96/194/282) .02 .10
173 Dan Quisenberry/(97/195/283) .01 .05
174 Tony Gwynn FOIL 1.00 2.50
175 Ryne Sandberg FOIL .60 1.50
176 Steve Garvey FOIL .08 .25
177 Dale Murphy FOIL .08 .25
178 Mike Schmidt FOIL
179 Dar.Strawberry FOIL .20 .50
180 Gary Carter FOIL .08 .25
181 Ozzie Smith FOIL .25 .60
182 Charlie Lea FOIL .02 .10
183 Lou Whitaker FOIL .05 .15
184 Rod Carew FOIL .25 .60
185 Cal Ripken FOIL 1.25 3.00
186 Dave Winfield FOIL .20 .50
187 Reggie Jackson FOIL .30 .75
188 George Brett FOIL .50 1.25
189 Lance Parrish FOIL .05 .15
190 Chet Lemon FOIL .02 .10
191 Dave Stieb FOIL .02 .10
192 Gary Carter/(94/170/280) .02 .10
193 Mike Schmidt/(95/171/281) .25 .60
194 Tony Armas/(96/172/282) .01 .05
195 Mike Witt/(97/173/283) .01 .05
196 Eddie Murray .15 .40
197 Cal Ripken 1.00 2.50
198 Scott McGregor .01 .05
199 Rick Dempsey .01 .05
200 Tippy Martinez (360) .01 .05
201 Ken Singleton (361) .01 .05
202 Mike Boddicker (362) .01 .05
203 Rich Dauer (363) .01 .05
204 John Shelby (364) .01 .05
205 Al Bumbry (365) .01 .05
206 John Lowenstein(366) .01 .05
207 Mike Flanagan (367) .01 .05
208 Jim Rice .02 .10
209 Tony Armas .01 .05
210 Wade Boggs .20 .50
211 Bruce Hurst .01 .05
212 Dwight Evans (26) .02 .10
213 Mike Easler (27) .01 .05
214 Bill Buckner (28) .02 .10
215 Bob Stanley (29) .01 .05
216 Jackie Gutierrez(30) .01 .05
217 Rich Gedman (31) .01 .05
218 Jerry Remy (32) .01 .05
219 Marty Barrett (33) .01 .05
220 Reggie Jackson .20 .50
221 Geoff Zahn .01 .05
222 Doug DeCinces .01 .05
223 Rod Carew .15 .40
224 Brian Downing (38) .02 .10
225 Fred Lynn (39) .02 .10
226 Gary Pettis (40) .01 .05
227 Mike Witt (41) .01 .05
228 Bob Boone (42) .02 .10
229 Tommy John (43) .05 .15
230 Bobby Grich (44) .02 .10
231 Ron Romanick (45) .01 .05
232 Ron Kittle .01 .05
233 Richard Dotson .01 .05
234 Harold Baines .02 .10
235 Tom Seaver .20 .50
236 Greg Walker (50) .01 .05
237 Roy Smalley (51) .01 .05
238 Greg Luzinski (52) .02 .10
239 Julio Cruz (53) .01 .05
240 Scott Fletcher (54) .01 .05
241 Rudy Law (55) .01 .05
242 Vance Law (56) .01 .05
243 Carlton Fisk (57) .08 .25
244 Andre Thornton .01 .05
245 Julio Franco .02 .10
246 Brett Butler .02 .10
247 Bert Blyleven .02 .10
248 Mike Hargrove (62) .01 .05
249 George Vukovich(63) .01 .05
250 Pat Tabler (64) .01 .05
251 Brook Jacoby (65) .01 .05
252 Tony Bernazard (66) .01 .05
253 Ernie Camacho (67) .01 .05
254 Mel Hall (68) .01 .05
255 Carmen Castillo (69) .01 .05
256 Jack Morris .02 .10
257 Willie Hernandez .02 .10
258 Alan Trammell .05 .15
259 Lance Parrish .02 .10
260 Chet Lemon (74) .01 .05
261 Lou Whitaker (75) .05 .15
262 Howard Johnson (76) .02 .10
263 Barbaro Garbey (77) .01 .05
264 Dan Petry (78) .01 .05
265 Aurelio Lopez (79) .01 .05
266 Larry Herndon (80) .01 .05
267 Kirk Gibson (81) .02 .10
268 George Brett .30 .75
269 Dan Quisenberry .01 .05
270 Hal McRae .02 .10
271 Steve Balboni .01 .05
272 Pat Sheridan (86) .01 .05
273 Jorge Orta (87) .01 .05
274 Frank White (88) .02 .10
275 Bud Black (89) .01 .05
276 Darryl Motley (90) .01 .05
277 Willie Wilson (91) .02 .10
278 Larry Gura (92) .01 .05
279 Don Slaught (93) .01 .05
280 Dwight Gooden/(94/170/192) .60 1.50
281 Mark Langston/(95/171/193) .08 .25
282 Tim Raines/(96/172/194) .02 .10
283 Rickey Henderson/(97/173/195/283) .08 .25
284 Robin Yount .08 .25
285 Rollie Fingers .08 .25
286 Jim Sundberg .01 .05
287 Cecil Cooper .02 .10
288 Jamie Cocanower(102) .01 .05
289 Mike Caldwell (103) .01 .05
290 Don Sutton (104) .08 .25
291 Rick Manning (105) .01 .05
292 Ben Oglivie (106) .01 .05
293 Moose Haas (107) .01 .05
294 Ted Simmons (108) .02 .10
295 Jim Gantner (109) .01 .05
296 Kent Hrbek .02 .10
297 Ron Davis .01 .05
298 Dave Engle .01 .05
299 Tom Brunansky .01 .05
300 Frank Viola (114) .02 .10
301 Mike Smithson (115) .01 .05
302 Gary Gaetti (116) .02 .10
303 Tim Teufel (117) .01 .05
304 Mickey Hatcher(118) .01 .05
305 John Butcher (119) .01 .05
306 Darrell Brown (120) .01 .05
307 Kirby Puckett (121) 2.50 6.00
308 Dave Winfield .08 .25
309 Phil Niekro .08 .25
310 Don Mattingly .75 2.00
311 Don Baylor .02 .10
312 Willie Randolph(126) .02 .10
313 Ron Guidry (127) .02 .10
314 Dave Righetti (128) .02 .10
315 Bobby Meacham (129) .01 .05
316 Butch Wynegar (130) .01 .05
317 Mike Pagliarulo(131) .01 .05
318 Joe Cowley (132) .01 .05
319 John Montefusco(133) .01 .05
320 Dave Kingman .02 .10
321 Rickey Henderson .20 .50
322 Bill Caudill .01 .05
323 Dwayne Murphy .01 .05
324 Steve McCatty (138) .01 .05
325 Joe Morgan (139) .08 .25
326 Mike Heath (140) .01 .05
327 Chris Codiroli (141) .01 .05
328 Ray Burris (142) .01 .05
329 Tony Phillips (143) .02 .10
330 Carney Lansford(144) .02 .10
331 Bruce Bochte (145) .01 .05
332 Alvin Davis .02 .10
333 Al Cowens .01 .05
334 Jim Beattie .01 .05
335 Bob Kearney .01 .05
336 Ed VandeBerg (150) .01 .05
337 Mark Langston (151) .08 .25
338 Dave Henderson (152) .02 .10
339 Spike Owen (153) .01 .05
340 Matt Young (154) .01 .05
341 Jack Perconte (155) .01 .05
342 Barry Bonnell (156) .01 .05
343 Mike Stanton (157) .01 .05
344 Pete O'Brien .01 .05
345 Charlie Hough .02 .10
346 Larry Parrish .01 .05
347 Buddy Bell .02 .10
348 Frank Tanana (162) .01 .05
349 Curt Wilkerson (163) .01 .05
350 Jeff Kunkel (164) .01 .05
351 Billy Sample (165) .01 .05
352 Danny Darwin (166) .01 .05
353 Gary Ward (167) .01 .05
354 Mike Mason (168) .01 .05
355 Mickey Rivers (169) .01 .05
356 Dave Stieb .01 .05
357 Damaso Garcia .01 .05
358 Willie Upshaw .01 .05
359 Lloyd Moseby .01 .05
360 George Bell (200) .02 .10
361 Luis Leal (201) .01 .05
362 Jesse Barfield (202) .01 .05
363 Dave Collins (203) .01 .05
364 Roy Lee Jackson(204) .01 .05
365 Doyle Alexander(205) .01 .05
366 Alfredo Griffin(206) .01 .05
367 Cliff Johnson (207) .01 .05
368 Alvin Davis .02 .10
369 Juan Samuel .01 .05
370 Brook Jacoby .01 .05
371 Mark Langston and .08 .25
Dwight Gooden
372 Mike Fitzgerald .01 .05
373 Jackie Gutierrez .01 .05
374 Dan Gladden .01 .05
375 Carmelo Martinez .01 .05
376 Kirby Puckett 2.50 6.00
NNO Album .40 1.00

1985 Topps/OPC Minis

This test issue looks exactly like the 1985 Topps standard-size counterparts, but measures a slightly smaller 2 3/8" by 3 9/32" and are printed on white OPC-like card stock. These cards were produced in extremely limited quantities and probably were supposed to be destroyed. Only one of the six 132-card sheets were produced in this fashion, thus none of the key Rookie Cards exist in mini form. It is estimated that 100 or less of each card exists. Approximately 2/3 of the cards were printed with the complete backs while the others are blank backed. Values for the blank back cards are from the same value to 1.5 times the prices listed below. Card numbering matches the 1985 Topps issues; therefore we have listed the cards in skip numbered fashion below.

COMPLETE SET (132) 1000.00 2000.00
12 Davey Lopes 8.00 20.00
15 Jerry Koosman 8.00 20.00
17 Mike Scott 8.00 20.00
25 Steve Bedrosian 4.00 10.00
44 Dickie Thon 4.00 10.00
65 Bill Buckner 8.00 20.00
68 Von Hayes 4.00 10.00
72 Rick Sutcliffe 8.00 20.00
75 Willie Upshaw 4.00 10.00
82 Joe Price 4.00 10.00
88 Bryn Smith 4.00 10.00
91 Jeff Burroughs 8.00 20.00
95 Jose Cruz 8.00 20.00
96 Johnny Ray 4.00 10.00
109 Gary Roenicke 4.00 10.00
113 Tom Herr 4.00 10.00
114 Bob James 4.00 10.00
117 Greg Gross 4.00 10.00
120 Steve Kemp 4.00 10.00
121 Checklist 4.00 10.00
128 Ernie Whitt 4.00 10.00
148 Steve Yeager 4.00 10.00
150 Jim Rice 15.00 40.00
151 Moose Haas 4.00 10.00
154 Argel Salazar 4.00 10.00
156 Craig Reynolds 4.00 10.00
160 Lance Parrish 8.00 20.00
165 Dusty Baker 15.00 40.00
170 George Foster 8.00 20.00
178 Miguel Dilone 4.00 10.00
185 Al Holland 4.00 10.00
190 Rusty Staub 8.00 20.00
198 Eddie Milner 4.00 10.00
201 Burt Hooton 4.00 10.00
205 Steve Rogers 4.00 10.00
209 Bill Campbell 4.00 10.00
210 Gary Matthews 4.00 10.00
218 Doyle Alexander 4.00 10.00
222 Hubie Brooks 4.00 10.00
223 Tom Hume 4.00 10.00
225 Mike Boddicker 4.00 10.00
229 Dave LaPoint 4.00 10.00
230 Gary Carter 40.00 80.00
235 Garry Maddox 4.00 10.00
236 Mark Thurmond 4.00 10.00
237 Julio Franco 25.00 60.00
239 Tim Teufel 4.00 10.00
248 Terry Forster 4.00 10.00
250 Jesse Orosco 8.00 20.00
251 Brad Gulden 4.00 10.00
255 Lonnie Smith 4.00 10.00
261 Checklist 4.00 10.00
263 Mel Hall 4.00 10.00
266 Frank Viola 8.00 20.00
287 Walt Terrell 4.00 10.00
306 Rick Reuschel 8.00 20.00
310 Manny Trillo 4.00 10.00
324 Dave Schmidt 4.00 10.00
325 John Denny 4.00 10.00
330 Leon Durham 4.00 10.00
333 Willie Hernandez 4.00 10.00
340 Robin Yount 40.00 80.00
343 Bill Russell 4.00 10.00
345 Charlie Lea 4.00 10.00
352 Joe Morgan 40.00 100.00
355 Bert Blyleven 15.00 40.00
358 Tony Pena 4.00 10.00
360 Steve Carlton 50.00 120.00
362 Craig McMurtry 4.00 10.00
375 Jeff Reardon 8.00 20.00
379 Charles Hudson 4.00 10.00
415 Ron Darling 4.00 10.00
445 Tippy Martinez 4.00 10.00
446 Jim Sundberg 4.00 10.00
450 Steve Garvey 15.00 40.00
452 John Castino 4.00 10.00
464 Mike Mason 4.00 10.00
470 Steve Sax 4.00 10.00
485 Matt Young 4.00 10.00
487 Frank Williams 4.00 10.00
489 Bryan Clark 4.00 10.00
491 Rick Camp 4.00 10.00
495 Mario Soto 4.00 10.00
500 Mike Schmidt 75.00 200.00
501 Dan Schatzeder 4.00 10.00
504 Jerry Willard 4.00 10.00
511 Lee Smith 15.00 40.00
515 Dave Concepcion 8.00 20.00
520 LaMarr Hoyt 4.00 10.00
526 Dave Palmer 4.00 10.00
530 Dave Dravecky 8.00 20.00
538 Keith Moreland 4.00 10.00
545 Lloyd Moseby 4.00 10.00
551 Andy Van Slyke 4.00 10.00
554 Doug Flynn 4.00 10.00
556 Sixto Lezcano 4.00 10.00
560 Bill Madlock 8.00 20.00
563 Dick Ruthven 4.00 10.00
566 Ed Vande Berg 4.00 10.00
568 Cliff Johnson 4.00 10.00
569 Ken Oberkfell 4.00 10.00
575 Pedro Guerrero 8.00 20.00
580 Dwight Evans 15.00 40.00
589 Bob Dernier 4.00 10.00
592 Jeff D. Robinson 4.00 10.00
603 Rick Manning 4.00 10.00
608 Craig Lefferts 4.00 10.00
610 Jack Morris 15.00 40.00
613 Terry Puhl 4.00 10.00
615 Marvell Wynne 4.00 10.00
619 Jeffrey Leonard 4.00 10.00
625 Mark Langston 15.00 40.00
630 Tim Raines 15.00 40.00
634 Bill Dawley 4.00 10.00
670 Tom Seaver 75.00 200.00
673 Buck Martinez 4.00 10.00
674 Atlee Hammaker 4.00 10.00
685 Bill Caudill 4.00 10.00
700 Eddie Murray 100.00 250.00
725 Floyd Bannister 4.00 10.00
729 Don Sutton 40.00 80.00
731 Neil Allen 4.00 10.00
736 Jerry Mumphrey 4.00 10.00
748 Lee Mazzilli 4.00 10.00
753 Greg Brock 4.00 10.00
755 Ken Singleton 4.00 10.00
757 Willie McGee 15.00 40.00
760 Nolan Ryan 200.00 400.00
762 Eddie Whitson 4.00 10.00
775 Mookie Wilson 8.00 20.00
780 Mike Flanagan 4.00 10.00
782 Tom Neidenfuer 4.00 10.00

1985 Topps Rub Downs

The cards in this 112 player (32 different sheets) set measure 2 3/8" by 3 5/16". The full color photo could be transfered from the rub down to another surface by rubbing a coin over the paper backing. Distributed in packages of two rub down sheets, some contained two or three player action poses, others head shots and various pieces of player equipment. Players from all teams were included in the set. Although the sheets are unnumbered, they are numbered here in alphabetical order based on each card first being placed in alphabetical order.

COMPLETE SET (32) 6.00 15.00
1 Tony Armas .02 .10
Harold Baines/Lonnie Smith
2 Don Baylor .02 .10
George Hendrick/Ron Kittle/Johnnie L
3 Buddy Bell .75 2.00
Tony Gwynn/Lloyd Moseby
4 Bruce Benedict .02 .10
Atlee Hammaker/Frank White
5 Mike Boddicker .40 1.00
Rod Carew/Carlton Fisk/Johnny Ra
6 Wade Boggs .30 .75
Rick Dempsey/Keith Hernandez
7 George Brett .60 1.50
Andre Dawson/Paul Molitor/Alan Wig
8 Tom Brunansky .10 .30
Pedro Guerrero/Darryl Strawberry
9 Bill Buckner .75 2.00
Tim Raines/Ryne Sandberg/Mike Schm
10 Steve Carlton .15 .40
Bob Horner/Dan Quisenberry
11 Gary Carter .15 .40
Phil Garner/Ron Guidry
12 Jack Clark .07 .20
Damaso Garcia/Hal McRae/Lance Parris
13 Dave Concepcion .07 .20
Cecil Cooper/Fred Lynn/Jesse Or
14 Jose Cruz .10 .30
Jack Morris/Jim Rice/Rick Sutcliffe
15 Alvin Davis .07 .20
Steve Kemp/Greg Luzinski/Kent Tekul
16 Ron Davis .02 .10
Kent Hrbek/Juan Samuel
17 John Denny .02 .10
Carney Lansford/Mario Soto/Lou Whita
18 Leon Durham .02 .10
Willie Hernandez/Steve Sax
19 Dwight Evans .40 1.00
Julio Franco/Dwight Gooden
20 George Foster .07 .20
Gary Gaetti/Bobby Grich/Gary Redu
21 Steve Garvey .10 .30
Jerry Remy/Bill Russell/George Wri
22 Kirk Gibson 1.00 2.50
Rich Gossage/Don Mattingly/Dave Sti
23 Moose Haas .02 .10
Bruce Sutter/Dickie Thon/Andre Thorn
24 Rickey Henderson .60 1.50
Dave Righetti/Pete Rose
25 Steve Henderson .10 .30
Bill Madlock/Alan Trammell
26 LaMarr Hoyt 1.00 2.50
Larry Parrish/Nolan Ryan
27 Reggie Jackson .15 .40
Eric Show/Jason Thompson
28 Terry Kennedy .60 1.50
Eddie Murray/Tom Seaver/Ozzie Smi
29 Mark Langston .15 .40
Ben Oglivie/Darrell Porter
30 Jeff Leonard .15 .40
Gary Matthews/Dale Murphy/Dave Win
31 Craig McMurtry .75 2.00
Cal Ripken/Steve Rogers/Willie U
32 Tony Pena .15 .40
Fernando Valenzuela/Robin Yount

1985 Topps Super

This 60-card set was issued in packs of three. These large cards measure 4 7/8" by 6 7/8". The fronts of the cards are merely a blow-up of the Topps regular issue. In fact, the cards differ from the corresponding cards of the regular set in size and number only. As one would expect, only those considered stars and superstars appear in this set. Backs are green with maroon printing. A checklist for the set is contained on the back of the wrapper. The back of the wrapper also gives details of Topps' offer to send your "missing" cards.

COMPLETE SET (60) 4.00 10.00
1 Ryne Sandberg .60 1.50
2 Willie Hernandez .02 .10
3 Rick Sutcliffe .07 .20
4 Don Mattingly .60 1.50
5 Tony Gwynn .60 1.50
6 Alvin Davis .02 .10
7 Dwight Gooden .15 .40
8 Dan Quisenberry .02 .10
9 Bruce Sutter .30 .75
10 Tony Armas .02 .10
11 Dale Murphy .15 .40
12 Mike Schmidt .30 .75
13 Gary Carter .25 .60
14 Rickey Henderson .40 1.00
15 Tim Raines .07 .20
16 Mike Boddicker .02 .10
17 Alejandro Pena .02 .10
18 Eddie Murray .30 .75
19 Gary Matthews .02 .10
20 Mark Langston .02 .10
21 Mario Soto .02 .10
22 Dave Stieb .02 .10
23 Nolan Ryan 1.25 3.00
24 Steve Carlton .30 .75
25 Alan Trammell .15 .40
26 Steve Garvey .15 .40
27 Kirk Gibson .07 .20
28 Juan Samuel .02 .10
29 Reggie Jackson .30 .75
30 Darryl Strawberry .07 .20
31 Tom Seaver .30 .75
32 Pete Rose .30 .75
33 Dwight Evans .07 .20
34 Jose Cruz .07 .20
35 Bert Blyleven .07 .20
36 Keith Hernandez .07 .20
37 Robin Yount .30 .75
38 Joaquin Andujar .02 .10
39 Lloyd Moseby .02 .10
40 Chili Davis .07 .20
41 Kent Hrbek .07 .20
42 Dave Parker .07 .20
43 Jack Morris .07 .20
44 Pedro Guerrero .07 .20
45 Mike Witt .02 .10
46 George Brett .60 1.50
47 Ozzie Smith .60 1.50
48 Cal Ripken 1.25 3.00
49 Rich Gossage .07 .20
50 Jim Rice .07 .20
51 Harold Baines .15 .40
52 Fernando Valenzuela .07 .20
53 Buddy Bell .02 .10
54 Jesse Orosco .07 .20
55 Lance Parrish .02 .10
56 Jason Thompson .02 .10
57 Tom Brunansky .02 .10
58 Dave Righetti .02 .10
59 Dave Kingman .07 .20
60 Dave Winfield .30 .75

1986 Topps

This set consists of 792 standard-size cards. Cards were primarily distributed in 15-card wax packs, 48-card rack packs and factory sets. This was also the first year Topps offered a factory set to hobby dealers. Standard card fronts feature a black and white split border framing a color photo with team name on top and player name on bottom. Subsets include Pete Rose tribute (1-7), Record Breakers (201-207), Turn Back the Clock (401-405), All-Stars (701-722) and Team Leaders (seeded throughout the set). Manager cards feature the team checklist on the reverse. There are two uncorrected errors involving misnumbered cards; see card numbers 51, 57, 141, and 171 in the checklist below. The key Rookie Cards in this set are Darren Daulton, Len Dykstra, Cecil Fielder, and Mickey Tettleton.

COMPLETE SET (792) 10.00 25.00
COMP.X-MAS.SET (792) 60.00 120.00
1 Pete Rose .75 2.00
2 Rose Special: '63-'66 .08 .25
3 Rose Special: '67-'70 .08 .25
4 Rose Special: '71-'74 .08 .25
5 Rose Special: '75-'78 .08 .25
6 Rose Special: '79-'82 .08 .25
7 Rose Special: '83-'85 .08 .25
8 Dwayne Murphy .02 .10
9 Roy Smith .02 .10
10 Tony Gwynn .25 .60
11 Bob Ojeda .02 .10
12 Jose Uribe .02 .10
13 Bob Kearney .02 .10
14 Julio Cruz .02 .10
15 Eddie Whitson .02 .10
16 Rick Schu .02 .10
17 Mike Stenhouse .02 .10
18 Brent Gaff .02 .10
19 Rich Hebner .02 .10
20 Lou Whitaker .05 .15
21 George Bamberger MG .02 .10
22 Duane Walker .02 .10
23 Manuel Lee RC* .02 .10
24 Len Barker .02 .10
25 Willie Wilson .05 .15
26 Frank DiPino .02 .10
27 Ray Knight .05 .15
28 Eric Davis .15 .40
29 Tony Phillips .02 .10
30 Eddie Murray .15 .40
31 Jamie Easterly .02 .10
32 Steve Yeager .05 .15
33 Jeff Lahti .02 .10
34 Ken Phelps .02 .10
35 Jeff Reardon .05 .15
36 Tigers Leaders .05 .15
Lance Parrish
37 Mark Thurmond .02 .10
38 Glenn Hoffman .02 .10
39 Dave Rucker .02 .10
40 Ken Griffey .05 .15
41 Brad Wellman .02 .10
42 Geoff Zahn .02 .10
43 Dave Engle .02 .10
44 Lance McCullers .02 .10
45 Damaso Garcia .02 .10
46 Billy Hatcher .05 .15
47 Juan Berenguer .02 .10
48 Bill Almon .02 .10
49 Rick Manning .02 .10
50 Dan Quisenberry .02 .10
51 Bobby Meacham MG ERR
(Checklist back)/(Number of ca .02 .10

52 Chris Welsh .02 .10
53 Len Dykstra RC .30 .75
54 John Franco .05 .15
55 Fred Lynn .05 .15
56 Tom Niedenfuer .02 .10
57 Bill Doran/(See also 51) .02 .10
58 Bill Krueger .02 .10
59 Andre Thornton .02 .10
60 Dwight Evans .08 .25
61 Karl Best .02 .10
62 Bob Boone .05 .15
63 Ron Roenicke .02 .10
64 Floyd Bannister .02 .10
65 Dan Driessen .02 .10
66 Cardinals Leaders .02 .10
Bob Forsch
67 Carmelo Martinez .02 .10
68 Ed Lynch .02 .10
69 Luis Aguayo .02 .10
70 Dave Winfield .05 .15
71 Ken Schrom .02 .10
72 Shawon Dunston .05 .15
73 Randy O'Neal .02 .10
74 Rance Mulliniks .02 .10
75 Jose DeLeon .02 .10
76 Dion James .02 .10
77 Charlie Leibrandt .02 .10
78 Bruce Benedict .02 .10
79 Dave Schmidt .02 .10
80 Darryl Strawberry .08 .25
81 Gene Mauch MG .02 .10
82 Tippy Martinez .02 .10
83 Phil Garner .05 .15
84 Curt Young .02 .10
85 Tony Perez w .05 .15
E.Davis
86 Tom Waddell .02 .10
87 Candy Maldonado .02 .10
88 Tom Nieto .02 .10
89 Randy St.Claire .02 .10
90 Garry Templeton .05 .15
91 Steve Crawford .02 .10
92 Al Cowens .02 .10
93 Scot Thompson .02 .10
94 Rich Bordi .02 .10
95 Ozzie Virgil .02 .10
96 Blue Jays Leaders .02 .10
Jim Clancy
97 Gary Gaetti .05 .15
98 Dick Ruthven .02 .10
99 Buddy Biancalana .02 .10
100 Nolan Ryan .75 2.00
101 Dave Bergman .02 .10
102 Joe Orsulak RC* .08 .25
103 Luis Salazar .02 .10
104 Sid Fernandez .02 .10
105 Gary Ward .02 .10
106 Ray Burris .02 .10
107 Rafael Ramirez .02 .10
108 Ted Power .02 .10
109 Len Matuszek .02 .10
110 Scott McGregor .02 .10
111 Roger Craig MG .05 .15
112 Bill Campbell .02 .10
113 U.L. Washington .02 .10
114 Mike C. Brown .02 .10
115 Jay Howell .02 .10
116 Brook Jacoby .02 .10
117 Bruce Kison .02 .10
118 Jerry Royster .02 .10
119 Barry Bonnell .02 .10
120 Steve Carlton .05 .15
121 Nelson Simmons .02 .10
122 Pete Filson .02 .10
123 Greg Walker .02 .10
124 Luis Sanchez .02 .10
125 Dave Lopes .05 .15
126 Mets Leaders .02 .10
Mookie Wilson
127 Jack Howell .02 .10
128 John Wathan .02 .10
129 Jeff Dedmon .02 .10
130 Alan Trammell .05 .15
131 Checklist: 1-132 .05 .15
132 Razor Shines .02 .10
133 Andy McGaffigan .02 .10
134 Carney Lansford .05 .15
135 Joe Niekro .02 .10
136 Mike Hargrove .02 .10
137 Charlie Moore .02 .10
138 Mark Davis .02 .10
139 Daryl Boston .02 .10
140 John Candelaria .02 .10
141 Chuck Cottier MG .02 .10
See also 171
142 Bob Jones .02 .10
143 Dave Van Gorder .02 .10
144 Doug Sisk .02 .10
145 Pedro Guerrero .05 .15
146 Jack Perconte .02 .10
147 Larry Sheets .02 .10
148 Mike Heath .02 .10
149 Brett Butler .05 .15
150 Joaquin Andujar .05 .15
151 Dave Stapleton .02 .10
152 Mike Morgan .02 .10
153 Ricky Adams .02 .10
154 Bert Roberge .02 .10
155 Bob Grich .05 .15
156 White Sox Leaders .02 .10
Richard Dotson
157 Ron Hassey .02 .10
158 Derrel Thomas .02 .10
159 Orel Hershiser UER .15 .40
160 Chet Lemon .05 .15
161 Lee Tunnell .02 .10
162 Greg Gagne .02 .10
163 Pete Ladd .02 .10
164 Steve Balboni .02 .10
165 Mike Davis .02 .10
166 Dickie Thon .02 .10
167 Zane Smith .02 .10
168 Jeff Burroughs .02 .10
169 George Wright .02 .10
170 Gary Carter .05 .15
171 Bob Rodgers MG ERR
(Checklist back)/(Number of c .02 .10
172 Jerry Reed .02 .10
173 Wayne Gross .02 .10
174 Brian Snyder .02 .10
175 Steve Sax .02 .10
176 Jay Tibbs .02 .10
177 Joel Youngblood .02 .10
178 Ivan DeJesus .02 .10
179 Stu Cliburn .02 .10
180 Don Mattingly .50 1.25
181 Al Nipper .02 .10
182 Bobby Brown .02 .10
183 Larry Andersen .02 .10
184 Tim Laudner .02 .10
185 Rollie Fingers .05 .15
186 Astros Leaders .02 .10
Jose Cruz
187 Scott Fletcher .02 .10
188 Bob Dernier .02 .10
189 Mike Mason .02 .10
190 George Hendrick .05 .15
191 Wally Backman .02 .10
192 Milt Wilcox .02 .10
193 Daryl Sconiers .02 .10
194 Craig McMurtry .02 .10
195 Dave Concepcion .05 .15
196 Doyle Alexander .02 .10
197 Enos Cabell .02 .10
198 Ken Dixon .02 .10
199 Dick Howser MG .02 .10
200 Mike Schmidt .40 1.00
201 Vince Coleman RB .05 .15
Most stolen bases&/season& rook
202 Dwight Gooden RB .08 .25
203 Keith Hernandez RB .02 .10
204 Phil Niekro RB .05 .15
Oldest shutout pitcher
205 Tony Perez RB .05 .15
Oldest grand slammer
206 Pete Rose RB .15 .40
207 Fernando Valenzuela RB .02 .10
Most cons. innings&/start
208 Ramon Romero .02 .10
209 Randy Ready .02 .10
210 Calvin Schiraldi .02 .10
211 Ed Wojna .02 .10
212 Chris Speier .02 .10
213 Bob Shirley .02 .10
214 Randy Bush .02 .10
215 Frank White .05 .15
216 A's Leaders .02 .10
Dwayne Murphy
217 Bill Scherrer .02 .10
218 Randy Hunt .02 .10
219 Dennis Lamp .02 .10
220 Bob Horner .05 .15
221 Dave Henderson .02 .10
222 Craig Gerber .02 .10
223 Atlee Hammaker .02 .10
224 Cesar Cedeno .05 .15
225 Ron Darling .05 .15
226 Lee Lacy .02 .10
227 Al Jones .02 .10
228 Tom Lawless .02 .10
229 Bill Gullickson .02 .10
230 Terry Kennedy .02 .10
231 Jim Frey MG .02 .10
232 Rick Rhoden .02 .10
233 Steve Lyons .02 .10
234 Doug Corbett .02 .10
235 Butch Wynegar .02 .10
236 Frank Eufemia .02 .10
237 Ted Simmons .05 .15
238 Larry Parrish .02 .10
239 Joel Skinner .02 .10
240 Tommy John .05 .15
241 Tony Fernandez .02 .10
242 Rich Thompson .02 .10
243 Johnny Grubb .02 .10
244 Craig Lefferts .02 .10
245 Jim Sundberg .05 .15
246 Steve Carlton TL .02 .10
247 Terry Harper .02 .10
248 Spike Owen .02 .10
249 Rob Deer .02 .10
250 Dwight Gooden .15 .40
251 Rich Dauer .02 .10
252 Bobby Castillo .02 .10
253 Dann Bilardello .02 .10
254 Ozzie Guillen RC .60 1.50
255 Tony Armas .05 .15
256 Kurt Kepshire .02 .10
257 Doug DeCinces .02 .10
258 Tim Burke .02 .10
259 Dan Pasqua .02 .10
260 Tony Pena .02 .10
261 Bobby Valentine MG .05 .15
262 Mario Ramirez .02 .10
263 Checklist: 133-264 .05 .15
264 Darren Daulton RC .20 .50
265 Ron Davis .02 .10
266 Keith Moreland .02 .10
267 Paul Molitor .05 .15
268 Mike Scott .05 .15
269 Dane Iorg .02 .10
270 Jack Morris .05 .15
271 Dave Collins .02 .10
272 Tim Tolman .02 .10
273 Jerry Willard .02 .10
274 Ron Gardenhire .02 .10
275 Charlie Hough .05 .15
276 Yankees Leaders .05 .15
Willie Randolph
277 Jaime Cocanower .02 .10
278 Sixto Lezcano .02 .10
279 Al Pardo .02 .10
280 Tim Raines .05 .15
281 Steve Mura .02 .10
282 Jerry Mumphrey .02 .10
283 Mike Fischlin .02 .10
284 Brian Dayett .02 .10
285 Buddy Bell .05 .15
286 Luis DeLeon .02 .10
287 John Christensen .02 .10
288 Don Aase .02 .10
289 Johnnie LeMaster .02 .10
290 Carlton Fisk .08 .25
291 Tom Lasorda MG .08 .25
292 Chuck Porter .02 .10
293 Chris Chambliss .05 .15
294 Danny Cox .02 .10
295 Kirk Gibson .05 .15
296 Geno Petralli .02 .10
297 Tim Lollar .02 .10
298 Craig Reynolds .02 .10
299 Bryn Smith .02 .10
300 George Brett .40 1.00
301 Dennis Rasmussen .02 .10
302 Greg Gross .02 .10
303 Curt Wardle .02 .10
304 Mike Gallego RC .02 .10
305 Phil Bradley .02 .10
306 Padres Leaders .02 .10
Terry Kennedy
307 Dave Sax .02 .10
308 Ray Fontenot .02 .10
309 John Shelby .02 .10
310 Greg Minton .02 .10
311 Dick Schofield .02 .10
312 Tom Filer .02 .10
313 Joe DeSa .02 .10
314 Frank Pastore .02 .10
315 Mookie Wilson .05 .15
316 Sammy Khalifa .02 .10
317 Ed Romero .02 .10
318 Terry Whitfield .02 .10
319 Rick Camp .02 .10
320 Jim Rice .05 .15
321 Earl Weaver MG .05 .15
322 Bob Forsch .02 .10
323 Jerry Davis .02 .10
324 Dan Schatzeder .02 .10
325 Juan Beniquez .02 .10
326 Kent Tekulve .02 .10
327 Mike Pagliarulo .02 .10
328 Pete O'Brien .02 .10
329 Kirby Puckett .40 1.00
330 Rick Sutcliffe .05 .15
331 Alan Ashby .02 .10
332 Darryl Motley .02 .10
333 Tom Henke .05 .15
334 Ken Oberkfell .02 .10
335 Don Sutton .05 .15
336 Indians Leaders .05 .15
Andre Thornton
337 Darnell Coles .02 .10
338 Jorge Bell .05 .15
339 Bruce Berenyi .02 .10
340 Cal Ripken .60 1.50
341 Frank Williams .02 .10
342 Gary Redus .02 .10
343 Carlos Diaz .02 .10
344 Jim Wohlford .02 .10
345 Donnie Moore .02 .10
346 Bryan Little .02 .10
347 Teddy Higuera RC* .08 .25
348 Cliff Johnson .02 .10
349 Mark Clear .02 .10
350 Jack Clark .05 .15
351 Chuck Tanner MG .02 .10
352 Harry Spilman .02 .10
353 Keith Atherton .02 .10
354 Tony Bernazard .02 .10
355 Lee Smith .05 .15
356 Mickey Hatcher .02 .10
357 Ed VandeBerg .02 .10
358 Rick Dempsey .02 .10
359 Mike LaCoss .02 .10
360 Lloyd Moseby .02 .10
361 Shane Rawley .02 .10
362 Tom Paciorek .02 .10
363 Terry Forster .05 .15
364 Reid Nichols .02 .10
365 Mike Flanagan .02 .10
366 Reds Leaders .05 .15
Dave Concepcion
367 Aurelio Lopez .02 .10
368 Greg Brock .02 .10
369 Al Holland .02 .10
370 Vince Coleman RC .20 .50
371 Bill Stein .02 .10
372 Ben Oglivie .05 .15
373 Urbano Lugo .02 .10
374 Terry Francona .05 .15
375 Rich Gedman .02 .10
376 Bill Dawley .02 .10
377 Joe Carter .05 .15
378 Bruce Bochte .02 .10
379 Bobby Meacham .02 .10
380 LaMarr Hoyt .02 .10
381 Ray Miller MG .02 .10
382 Ivan Calderon RC* .08 .25
383 Chris Brown RC .02 .10
384 Steve Trout .02 .10
385 Cecil Cooper .05 .15
386 Cecil Fielder RC .40 1.00
387 Steve Kemp .02 .10
388 Dickie Noles .02 .10
389 Glenn Davis .02 .10
390 Tom Seaver .08 .25
391 Julio Franco .05 .15
392 John Russell .02 .10
393 Chris Pittaro .02 .10
394 Checklist: 265-396 .05 .15
395 Scott Garrelts .02 .10
396 Red Sox Leaders .08 .25
Dwight Evans
397 Steve Buechele RC .08 .25
398 Earnie Riles .02 .10
399 Bill Swift .02 .10
400 Rod Carew .08 .25
401 Fernando Valenzuela TBC '81 .02 .10
402 Tom Seaver TBC .05 .15
403 Willie Mays TBC .15 .40
404 Frank Robinson TBC .05 .15
405 Roger Maris TBC .15 .40
406 Scott Sanderson .02 .10
407 Sal Butera .02 .10
408 Dave Smith .02 .10
409 Paul Runge RC .02 .10
410 Dave Kingman .05 .15
411 Sparky Anderson MG .05 .15
412 Jim Clancy .02 .10
413 Tim Flannery .02 .10
414 Tom Gorman .02 .10
415 Hal McRae .05 .15
416 Dennis Martinez .05 .15
417 R.J. Reynolds .02 .10
418 Alan Knicely .02 .10
419 Frank Wills .02 .10
420 Von Hayes .02 .10
421 David Palmer .02 .10
422 Mike Jorgensen .02 .10
423 Dan Spillner .02 .10
424 Rick Miller .02 .10
425 Larry McWilliams .02 .10
426 Brewers Leaders .02 .10
Charlie Moore
427 Joe Cowley .02 .10
428 Max Venable .02 .10
429 Greg Booker .02 .10
430 Kent Hrbek .05 .15
431 George Frazier .02 .10
432 Mark Bailey .02 .10
433 Chris Codiroli .02 .10
434 Curt Wilkerson .02 .10
435 Bill Caudill .02 .10
436 Doug Flynn .02 .10
437 Rick Mahler .02 .10
438 Clint Hurdle .02 .10
439 Rick Honeycutt .02 .10
440 Alvin Davis .02 .10
441 Whitey Herzog MG .08 .25
442 Ron Robinson .02 .10
443 Bill Buckner .05 .15
444 Alex Trevino .02 .10
445 Bert Blyleven .05 .15
446 Lenn Sakata .02 .10
447 Jerry Don Gleaton .02 .10
448 Herm Winningham .02 .10
449 Rod Scurry .02 .10
450 Graig Nettles .05 .15
451 Mark Brown .02 .10
452 Bob Clark .02 .10
453 Steve Jeltz .02 .10
454 Burt Hooton .02 .10
455 Willie Randolph .05 .15
456 Braves Leaders .08 .25
Dale Murphy
457 Mickey Tettleton RC .08 .25
458 Kevin Bass .02 .10
459 Luis Leal .02 .10
460 Leon Durham .02 .10
461 Walt Terrell .02 .10
462 Domingo Ramos .02 .10
463 Jim Gott .02 .10
464 Ruppert Jones .02 .10
465 Jesse Orosco .02 .10
466 Tom Foley .02 .10
467 Bob James .02 .10
468 Mike Scioscia .05 .15
469 Storm Davis .02 .10
470 Bill Madlock .05 .15
471 Bobby Cox MG .05 .15
472 Joe Hesketh .02 .10
473 Mark Brouhard .02 .10
474 John Tudor .05 .15
475 Juan Samuel .02 .10
476 Ron Mathis .02 .10
477 Mike Easler .02 .10
478 Andy Hawkins .02 .10
479 Bob Melvin .02 .10
480 Oddibe McDowell .02 .10
481 Scott Bradley .02 .10
482 Rick Lysander .02 .10
483 George Vukovich .02 .10
484 Donnie Hill .02 .10
485 Gary Matthews .05 .15
486 Angels Leaders .02 .10
Bobby Grich
487 Bret Saberhagen .05 .15
488 Lou Thornton .02 .10
489 Jim Winn .02 .10
490 Jeff Leonard .02 .10
491 Pascual Perez .02 .10
492 Kelvin Chapman .02 .10
493 Gene Nelson .02 .10
494 Gary Roenicke .02 .10
495 Mark Langston .05 .15
496 Jay Johnstone .02 .10
497 John Stuper .02 .10
498 Tito Landrum .02 .10
499 Bob L. Gibson .02 .10
500 Rickey Henderson .15 .40
501 Dave Johnson MG .02 .10
502 Glen Cook .02 .10
503 Mike Fitzgerald .02 .10
504 Denny Walling .02 .10
505 Jerry Koosman .05 .15
506 Bill Russell .05 .15
507 Steve Ontiveros RC .02 .10
508 Alan Wiggins .02 .10
509 Ernie Camacho .02 .10
510 Wade Boggs .08 .25
511 Ed Nunez .02 .10
512 Thad Bosley .02 .10
513 Ron Washington .02 .10
514 Mike Jones .02 .10
515 Darrell Evans .05 .15
516 Giants Leaders .02 .10
Greg Minton
517 Milt Thompson RC .08 .25
518 Buck Martinez .02 .10
519 Danny Darwin .02 .10
520 Keith Hernandez .05 .15
521 Nate Snell .02 .10
522 Bob Bailor .02 .10
523 Joe Price .02 .10
524 Darrell Miller .02 .10
525 Marvell Wynne .02 .10
526 Charlie Lea .02 .10
527 Checklist: 397-528 .05 .15
528 Terry Pendleton .05 .15
529 Marc Sullivan .02 .10
530 Rich Gossage .05 .15
531 Tony LaRussa MG .05 .15
532 Don Carman .02 .10
533 Billy Sample .02 .10
534 Jeff Calhoun .02 .10
535 Toby Harrah .05 .15
536 Jose Rijo .05 .15
537 Mark Salas .02 .10
538 Dennis Eckersley .08 .25
539 Glenn Hubbard .02 .10
540 Dan Petry .02 .10
541 Jorge Orta .02 .10
542 Don Schulze .02 .10
543 Jerry Narron .02 .10
544 Eddie Milner .02 .10
545 Jimmy Key .05 .15
546 Mariners Leaders .02 .10
Dave Henderson
547 Roger McDowell RC* .08 .25
548 Mike Young .02 .10
549 Bob Welch .05 .15
550 Tom Herr .02 .10
551 Dave LaPoint .02 .10
552 Marc Hill .02 .10
553 Jim Morrison .02 .10
554 Paul Householder .02 .10
555 Hubie Brooks .02 .10
556 John Denny .02 .10
557 Gerald Perry .02 .10
558 Tim Stoddard .02 .10
559 Tommy Dunbar .02 .10
560 Dave Righetti .05 .15
561 Bob Lillis MG .02 .10
562 Joe Beckwith .02 .10
563 Alejandro Sanchez .02 .10
564 Warren Brusstar .02 .10
565 Tom Brunansky .02 .10
566 Alfredo Griffin .02 .10
567 Jeff Barkley .02 .10
568 Donnie Scott .02 .10
569 Jim Acker .02 .10
570 Rusty Staub .05 .15
571 Mike Jeffcoat .02 .10
572 Paul Zuvella .02 .10
573 Tom Hume .02 .10
574 Ron Kittle .02 .10
575 Mike Boddicker .02 .10
576 Andre Dawson TL .02 .10
577 Jerry Reuss .02 .10
578 Lee Mazzilli .05 .15
579 Jim Slaton .02 .10
580 Willie McGee .05 .15
581 Bruce Hurst .02 .10
582 Jim Gantner .02 .10
583 Al Bumbry .02 .10
584 Brian Fisher RC .02 .10
585 Garry Maddox .02 .10
586 Greg Harris .02 .10
587 Rafael Santana .02 .10
588 Steve Lake .02 .10
589 Sid Bream .02 .10
590 Bob Knepper .02 .10
591 Jackie Moore MG .02 .10
592 Frank Tanana .05 .15
593 Jesse Barfield .05 .15
594 Chris Bando .02 .10
595 Dave Parker .05 .15
596 Onix Concepcion .02 .10
597 Sammy Stewart .02 .10
598 Jim Presley .02 .10
599 Rick Aguilera RC .08 .25
600 Dale Murphy .08 .25
601 Gary Lucas .02 .10
602 Mariano Duncan RC .08 .25
603 Bill Laskey .02 .10
604 Gary Pettis .02 .10
605 Dennis Boyd .02 .10
606 Royals Leaders .05 .15
Hal McRae
607 Ken Dayley .02 .10
608 Bruce Bochy .02 .10
609 Barbaro Garbey .02 .10
610 Ron Guidry .05 .15
611 Gary Woods .02 .10
612 Richard Dotson .02 .10
613 Roy Smalley .02 .10
614 Rick Waits .02 .10
615 Johnny Ray .02 .10
616 Glenn Brummer .02 .10
617 Lonnie Smith .02 .10
618 Jim Pankovits .02 .10
619 Danny Heep .02 .10
620 Bruce Sutter .05 .15
621 John Felske MG .02 .10
622 Gary Lavelle .02 .10
623 Floyd Rayford .02 .10
624 Steve McCatty .02 .10
625 Bob Brenly .02 .10
626 Roy Thomas .02 .10
627 Ron Oester .02 .10
628 Kirk McCaskill RC .08 .25
629 Mitch Webster .02 .10
630 Fernando Valenzuela .05 .15
631 Steve Braun .02 .10
632 Dave Von Ohlen .02 .10
633 Jackie Gutierrez .02 .10
634 Roy Lee Jackson .02 .10
635 Jason Thompson .02 .10
636 Lee Smith TL .02 .10
637 Rudy Law .02 .10
638 John Butcher .02 .10
639 Bo Diaz .02 .10
640 Jose Cruz .05 .15
641 Wayne Tolleson .02 .10
642 Ray Searage .02 .10
643 Tom Brookens .02 .10
644 Mark Gubicza .02 .10
645 Dusty Baker .05 .15
646 Mike Moore .02 .10
647 Mel Hall .02 .10
648 Steve Bedrosian .02 .10
649 Ronn Reynolds .02 .10
650 Dave Stieb .05 .15
651 Billy Martin MG .08 .25
TC
652 Tom Browning .02 .10
653 Jim Dwyer .02 .10
654 Ken Howell .02 .10
655 Manny Trillo .02 .10
656 Brian Harper .02 .10
657 Juan Agosto .02 .10
658 Rob Wilfong .02 .10
659 Checklist: 529-660 .05 .15
660 Steve Garvey .05 .15
661 Roger Clemens 1.50 4.00
662 Bill Schroeder .02 .10
663 Neil Allen .02 .10
664 Tim Corcoran .02 .10
665 Alejandro Pena .02 .10
666 Rangers Leaders .05 .15
Charlie Hough
667 Tim Teufel .02 .10
668 Cecilio Guante .02 .10
669 Ron Cey .05 .15
670 Willie Hernandez .02 .10
671 Lynn Jones .02 .10
672 Rob Picciolo .02 .10
673 Ernie Whitt .02 .10
674 Pat Tabler .02 .10
675 Claudell Washington .02 .10
676 Matt Young .02 .10
677 Nick Esasky .02 .10
678 Dan Gladden .02 .10
679 Britt Burns .02 .10
680 George Foster .05 .15
681 Dick Williams MG .02 .10
682 Junior Ortiz .02 .10
683 Andy Van Slyke .08 .25
684 Bob McClure .02 .10
685 Tim Wallach .02 .10
686 Jeff Stone .02 .10
687 Mike Trujillo .02 .10
688 Larry Herndon .02 .10
689 Dave Stewart .05 .15
690 Ryne Sandberg .30 .75
691 Mike Madden .02 .10
692 Dale Berra .02 .10
693 Tom Tellmann .02 .10
694 Garth Iorg .02 .10
695 Mike Smithson .02 .10
696 Dodgers Leaders .05 .15
Bill Russell
697 Bud Black .02 .10
698 Brad Komminsk .02 .10
699 Pat Corrales MG .02 .10
700 Reggie Jackson .08 .25
701 Keith Hernandez AS .02 .10
702 Tom Herr AS .02 .10
703 Tim Wallach AS .02 .10
704 Ozzie Smith AS .15 .40
705 Dale Murphy AS .05 .15
706 Pedro Guerrero AS .02 .10
707 Willie McGee AS .02 .10
708 Gary Carter AS .02 .10
709 Dwight Gooden AS .08 .25
710 John Tudor AS .02 .10
711 Jeff Reardon AS .02 .10
712 Don Mattingly AS .25 .60
713 Damaso Garcia AS .02 .10
714 George Brett AS .15 .40
715 Cal Ripken AS .15 .40
716 Rickey Henderson AS .08 .25
717 Dave Winfield AS .02 .10
718 George Bell AS .02 .10
719 Carlton Fisk AS .05 .15
720 Bret Saberhagen AS .02 .10
721 Ron Guidry AS .02 .10
722 Dan Quisenberry AS .02 .10
723 Marty Bystrom .02 .10
724 Tim Hulett .02 .10
725 Mario Soto .05 .15
726 Orioles Leaders .05 .15
Rick Dempsey
727 David Green .02 .10
728 Mike Marshall .02 .10
729 Jim Beattie .02 .10
730 Ozzie Smith .25 .60
731 Don Robinson .02 .10
732 Floyd Youmans .02 .10
733 Ron Romanick .02 .10
734 Marty Barrett .02 .10
735 Dave Dravecky .02 .10
736 Glenn Wilson .02 .10
737 Pete Vuckovich .02 .10
738 Andre Robertson .02 .10
739 Dave Rozema .02 .10
740 Lance Parrish .05 .15
741 Pete Rose MG .15 .40
TC
742 Frank Viola .05 .15
743 Pat Sheridan .02 .10
744 Lary Sorensen .02 .10
745 Willie Upshaw .02 .10
746 Denny Gonzalez .02 .10
747 Rick Cerone .02 .10
748 Steve Henderson .02 .10
749 Ed Jurak .02 .10
750 Gorman Thomas .05 .15
751 Howard Johnson .05 .15
752 Mike Krukow .02 .10
753 Dan Ford .02 .10
754 Pat Clements .02 .10
755 Harold Baines .05 .15
756 Pirates Leaders .02 .10
Rick Rhoden
757 Darrell Porter .02 .10
758 Dave Anderson .02 .10
759 Moose Haas .02 .10
760 Andre Dawson .05 .15
761 Don Slaught .02 .10
762 Eric Show .02 .10
763 Terry Puhl .02 .10
764 Kevin Gross .02 .10
765 Don Baylor .05 .15
766 Rick Langford .02 .10
767 Jody Davis .02 .10
768 Vern Ruhle .02 .10
769 Harold Reynolds RC .30 .75
770 Vida Blue .05 .15
771 John McNamara MG .02 .10
772 Brian Downing .05 .15
773 Greg Pryor .02 .10
774 Terry Leach .02 .10
775 Al Oliver .05 .15
776 Gene Garber .02 .10
777 Wayne Krenchicki .02 .10
778 Jerry Hairston .02 .10
779 Rick Reuschel .05 .15
780 Robin Yount .25 .60
781 Joe Nolan .02 .10
782 Ken Landreaux .02 .10
783 Ricky Horton .02 .10
784 Alan Bannister .02 .10
785 Bob Stanley .02 .10
786 Twins Leaders .02 .10
Mickey Hatcher
787 Vance Law .02 .10
788 Marty Castillo .02 .10
789 Kurt Bevacqua .02 .10
790 Phil Niekro .05 .15
791 Checklist: 661-792 .05 .15
792 Charles Hudson .02 .10

1986 Topps Tiffany

COMP.FACT.SET (792) 100.00 200.00
*STARS: 5X TO 12X BASIC CARDS
*ROOKIES: 5X TO 12X BASIC CARDS
DISTRIBUTED ONLY IN FACTORY SET FORM
FACTORY SET PRICE IS FOR SEALED SETS

1986 Topps Glossy All-Stars

COMPLETE SET (22) 2.00 5.00
1 Sparky Anderson MG .01 .05
2 Eddie Murray .20 .50
3 Lou Whitaker .02 .10
4 George Brett .40 1.00
5 Cal Ripken .75 2.00
6 Jim Rice .02 .10
7 Rickey Henderson .20 .50
8 Dave Winfield .20 .50
9 Carlton Fisk .15 .40
10 Jack Morris .02 .10
11 AL Team Photo .01 .05
12 Dick Williams MG .01 .05
13 Steve Garvey .02 .10
14 Tom Herr .01 .05
15 Graig Nettles .02 .10
16 Ozzie Smith .40 1.00
17 Tony Gwynn .40 1.00
18 Dale Murphy .07 .20
19 Darryl Strawberry .02 .10
20 Terry Kennedy .01 .05
21 LaMarr Hoyt .01 .05
22 NL Team Photo .01 .05

1986 Topps Glossy Send-Ins

COMPLETE SET (60) 5.00 12.00
1 Oddibe McDowell .02 .10
2 Reggie Jackson .30 .75
3 Fernando Valenzuela .07 .20
4 Jack Clark .02 .10
5 Rickey Henderson .40 1.25
6 Steve Balboni .02 .10
7 Keith Hernandez .07 .20
8 Lance Parrish .07 .20
9 Willie McGee .07 .20
10 Chris Brown .02 .10
11 Darryl Strawberry .07 .20
12 Ron Guidry .07 .20
13 Dave Parker .07 .20
14 Cal Ripken 1.50 4.00
15 Tim Raines .07 .20
16 Rod Carew .30 .75
17 Mike Schmidt .40 1.00
18 George Brett .75 2.00
19 Joe Hesketh .02 .10
20 Dan Pasqua .02 .10
21 Vince Coleman .07 .20
22 Tom Seaver .30 .75
23 Gary Carter .30 .75
24 Orel Hershiser .07 .20
25 Pedro Guerrero .02 .10
26 Wade Boggs .30 .75
27 Bret Saberhagen .07 .20
28 Carlton Fisk .30 .75
29 Kirk Gibson .07 .20
30 Brian Fisher .02 .10
31 Don Mattingly .75 2.00
32 Tom Herr .02 .10
33 Eddie Murray .30 .75
34 Ryne Sandberg .60 1.50
35 Dan Quisenberry .02 .10
36 Jim Rice .07 .20
37 Dale Murphy .10 .30
38 Steve Garvey .07 .20
39 Roger McDowell .02 .10
40 Earnie Riles .02 .10
41 Dwight Gooden .07 .20
42 Dave Winfield .30 .75
43 Dave Stieb .02 .10
44 Bob Horner .02 .10
45 Nolan Ryan 1.50 4.00
46 Ozzie Smith .75 2.00
47 George Bell .02 .10
48 Gorman Thomas .02 .10
49 Tom Browning .02 .10
50 Larry Sheets .02 .10
51 Pete Rose .40 1.00
52 Brett Butler .07 .20
53 John Tudor .02 .10
54 Phil Bradley .02 .10
55 Jeff Reardon .07 .20
56 Rich Gossage .07 .20
57 Tony Gwynn .75 2.00
58 Ozzie Guillen .20 .50
59 Glenn Davis .02 .10
60 Darrell Evans .02 .10

1986 Topps Wax Box Cards

COMPLETE SET (16) 3.00 8.00
A George Bell .07 .20
B Wade Boggs .40 1.00
C George Brett .75 2.00
D Vince Coleman .15 .40
E Carlton Fisk .40 1.00
F Dwight Gooden .15 .40
G Pedro Guerrero .15 .40
H Ron Guidry .15 .40
I Reggie Jackson .40 1.00
J Don Mattingly .75 2.00
K Oddibe McDowell .07 .20
L Willie McGee .15 .40
M Dale Murphy .30 .75
N Pete Rose .50 1.25
O Bret Saberhagen .15 .40
P Fernando Valenzuela .15 .40

1986 Topps Traded

This 132-card standard-size Traded set was distributed in factory set form, which were packed 100 to a case, in a red and white box through hobby dealers. The cards are identical in style to regular-issue 1986 Topps cards except for whiter stock and t-suffixed numbering. The key extended Rookie Cards in this set are Barry Bonds, Bobby Bonilla, Jose Canseco, Will Clark, Andres Galarraga, Bo Jackson, Wally Joyner, John Kruk, and Kevin Mitchell.

Card		
COMP.FACT.SET (132)	12.50	30.00
1T Andy Allanson XRC	.02	.10
2T Neil Allen	.02	.10
3T Joaquin Andujar	.05	.15
4T Paul Assenmacher	.15	.40
5T Scott Bailes	.02	.10
6T Don Baylor	.05	.15
7T Steve Bedrosian	.02	.10
8T Juan Beniquez	.02	.10
9T Juan Berenguer	.02	.10
10T Mike Bielecki	.02	.10
11T Barry Bonds XRC	10.00	25.00
12T Bobby Bonilla XRC	.30	.75
13T Juan Bonilla	.02	.10
14T Rich Bordi	.02	.10
15T Steve Boros MG	.02	.10
16T Rick Burleson	.02	.10
17T Bill Campbell	.02	.10
18T Tom Candiotti	.02	.10
19T John Cangelosi	.02	.10
20T Jose Canseco XRC	6.00	15.00
21T Carmen Castillo	.02	.10
22T Rick Cerone	.02	.10
23T John Cerutti	.02	.10
24T Will Clark XRC	5.00	12.00
25T Mark Clear	.02	.10
26T Darnell Coles	.02	.10
27T Dave Collins	.02	.10
28T Tim Conroy	.02	.10
29T Joe Cowley	.02	.10
30T Joel Davis	.02	.10
31T Rob Deer	.02	.10
32T John Denny	.02	.10
33T Mike Easler	.02	.10
34T Mark Eichhorn	.02	.10
35T Steve Farr	.02	.10
36T Scott Fletcher	.02	.10
37T Terry Forster	.05	.15
38T Terry Francona	.05	.15
39T Jim Fregosi MG	.02	.10
40T Andres Galarraga XRC	.40	1.00
41T Ken Griffey	.05	.15
42T Bill Gullickson	.02	.10
43T Jose Guzman XRC	.02	.10
44T Moose Haas	.02	.10
45T Billy Hatcher	.02	.10
46T Mike Heath	.02	.10
47T Tom Hume	.02	.10
48T Pete Incaviglia XRC	.15	.40
49T Dane Iorg	.02	.10
50T Bo Jackson XRC	10.00	25.00
51T Wally Joyner XRC	.30	.75
52T Charlie Kerfeld	.02	.10
53T Eric King	.02	.10
54T Bob Kipper	.02	.10
55T Wayne Krenchicki	.02	.10
56T John Kruk XRC	.40	1.00
57T Mike LaCoss	.02	.10
58T Pete Ladd	.02	.10
59T Mike Laga	.02	.10
60T Hal Lanier MG	.02	.10
61T Dave LaPoint	.02	.10
62T Rudy Law	.02	.10
63T Rick Leach	.02	.10
64T Tim Leary	.02	.10
65T Dennis Leonard	.02	.10
66T Jim Leyland MG XRC	.20	.50
67T Steve Lyons	.02	.10
68T Mickey Mahler	.02	.10
69T Candy Maldonado	.02	.10
70T Roger Mason XRC	.02	.10
71T Bob McClure	.02	.10
72T Andy McGaffigan	.02	.10
73T Gene Michael MG	.02	.10
74T Kevin Mitchell XRC	.30	.75
75T Omar Moreno	.02	.10
76T Jerry Mumphrey	.02	.10
77T Phil Niekro	.05	.15
78T Randy Niemann	.02	.10
79T Juan Nieves	.02	.10
80T Otis Nixon XRC	.30	.75
81T Bob Ojeda	.02	.10
82T Jose Oquendo	.02	.10
83T Tom Paciorek	.02	.10
84T David Palmer	.02	.10
85T Frank Pastore	.02	.10
86T Lou Piniella MG	.05	.15
87T Dan Plesac	.15	.40
88T Darrell Porter	.02	.10
89T Rey Quinones	.02	.10
90T Gary Redus	.02	.10
91T Bip Roberts XRC	.15	.40
92T Billy Jo Robidoux XRC	.02	.10
93T Jeff D. Robinson	.02	.10
94T Gary Roenicke	.02	.10
95T Ed Romero	.02	.10
96T Angel Salazar	.02	.10
97T Joe Sambito	.02	.10
98T Billy Sample	.02	.10
99T Dave Schmidt	.02	.10
100T Ken Schrom	.02	.10
101T Tom Seaver	.08	.25
102T Ted Simmons	.05	.15
103T Sammy Stewart	.02	.10
104T Kurt Stillwell	.02	.10
105T Franklin Stubbs	.02	.10
106T Dale Sveum	.02	.10
107T Chuck Tanner MG	.02	.10
108T Danny Tartabull	.05	.15
109T Tim Teufel	.02	.10
110T Bob Tewksbury XRC	.15	.40
111T Andres Thomas	.02	.10
112T Milt Thompson	.15	.40
113T Robby Thompson XRC	.15	.40
114T Jay Tibbs	.02	.10
115T Wayne Tolleson	.02	.10
116T Alex Trevino	.02	.10
117T Manny Trillo	.02	.10
118T Ed VandeBerg	.02	.10
119T Ozzie Virgil	.02	.10
120T Bob Walk	.02	.10
121T Gene Walter	.02	.10
122T Claudell Washington	.02	.10
123T Bill Wegman XRC	.02	.10
124T Dick Williams MG	.02	.10
125T Mitch Williams XRC	.15	.40
126T Bobby Witt XRC	.15	.40
127T Todd Worrell XRC	.15	.40
128T George Wright	.02	.10
129T Ricky Wright	.02	.10
130T Steve Yeager	.05	.15
131T Paul Zuvella	.02	.10
132T Checklist 1T-132T	.02	.10

1986 Topps Traded Tiffany

Card		
COMP.FACT.SET (132)	200.00	400.00
*STARS: 5X TO 12X BASIC CARDS		
*ROOKIES: 4X TO 10X BASIC CARDS		
DISTRIBUTED ONLY IN FACTORY SET FORM		
FACTORY SET PRICE IS FOR SEALED SETS		
OPENED SETS SELL FOR 50-60% OF SEALED		

1986 Topps 3-D

This set consists of 30 plastic-sculpted "cards" each measuring 4 3/8" by 6". Each card was individually wrapped in a red paper wrapper. The card back is blank except for two adhesive strips which could used for mounting the card. Cards are numbered on the front in the lower right corner above the name.

Card		
COMPLETE SET (30)	10.00	25.00
1 Bert Blyleven	.08	.25
2 Gary Carter	.40	1.25
3 Wade Boggs	1.00	2.50
4 Dwight Gooden	.20	.50
5 George Brett	2.00	5.00
6 Rich Gossage	.20	.50
7 Darrell Evans	.08	.25
8 Pedro Guerrero	.08	.25
9 Ron Guidry	.20	.50
10 Keith Hernandez	.30	.75
11 Rickey Henderson	1.00	2.50
12 Orel Hershiser	.30	.75
13 Reggie Jackson	.60	1.50
14 Willie McGee	.30	.75
15 Don Mattingly	2.00	5.00
16 Dale Murphy	.40	1.00
17 Jack Morris	.20	.50
18 Dave Parker	.20	.50
19 Eddie Murray	.60	1.50
20 Jeff Reardon	.08	.25
21 Dan Quisenberry	.08	.25
22 Pete Rose	.60	1.50
23 Jim Rice	.30	.75
24 Mike Schmidt	.60	1.50
25 Bret Saberhagen	.20	.50
26 Darryl Strawberry	.20	.50
27 Dave Stieb	.08	.25
28 John Tudor	.08	.25
29 Dave Winfield	.60	1.50
30 Fernando Valenzuela	.20	.50

1986 Topps Gallery of Champions

This 12 card set features various 1985 league leaders or award winners. For the second straight year, these replica cards were issued in either aluminum, bronze or silver. The cards measure approximately 1 1/4" by 1 3/4" and we have sequenced the set in alphabetical order. The bronze cards are valued at 2X to 4X the aluminum cards while the silvers have a value between 5X and 10X of the aluminums.

Card		
COMPLETE SET (12)	10.00	25.00
1 Wade Boggs	4.00	10.00
2 Vince Coleman	1.00	2.50
3 Darrell Evans	1.00	2.50
4 Dwight Gooden	2.00	5.00
5 Ozzie Guillen	1.00	2.50
6 Don Mattingly	5.00	12.00
7 Willie McGee	1.50	4.00
8 Dale Murphy	3.00	8.00
9 Dan Quisenberry	1.00	2.50
10 Jeff Reardon	1.00	2.50
11 Pete Rose	4.00	10.00
12 Bret Saberhagen	1.00	2.50

1986 Topps Mini Leaders

The 1986 Topps Mini set of Major League Leaders features 66 cards of leaders of the various statistical categories for the 1985 season. The cards are numbered on the back and measure approximately 2 1/8" by 2 15/16". They are very similar in design to the Team Leader "Dean" cards in the 1986 Topps regular issue. The order of the set numbering is alphabetical by player's name as well as alphabetical by team city name within league.

Card		
COMPLETE SET (66)	1.50	4.00
1 Eddie Murray	.20	.50
2 Cal Ripken	.75	2.00
3 Wade Boggs	.20	.50
4 Dennis Boyd	.01	.05
5 Dwight Evans	.02	.10
6 Bruce Hurst	.01	.05
7 Gary Pettis	.01	.05
8 Harold Baines	.05	.15
9 Floyd Bannister	.01	.05
10 Britt Burns	.01	.05
11 Carlton Fisk	.20	.50
12 Brett Butler	.02	.10
13 Darrell Evans	.02	.10
14 Jack Morris	.02	.10
15 Lance Parrish	.01	.05
16 Walt Terrell	.01	.05
17 Steve Balboni	.01	.05
18 George Brett	.40	1.00
19 Charlie Leibrandt	.01	.05
20 Bret Saberhagen	.02	.10
21 Lonnie Smith	.01	.05
22 Willie Wilson	.01	.05
23 Bert Blyleven	.02	.10
24 Mike Smithson	.01	.05
25 Frank Viola	.02	.10
26 Ron Guidry	.02	.10
27 Rickey Henderson	.30	.75
28 Don Mattingly	.40	1.00
29 Dave Winfield	.15	.40
30 Mike Moore	.01	.05
31 Gorman Thomas	.01	.05
32 Toby Harrah	.01	.05
33 Charlie Hough	.01	.05
34 Doyle Alexander	.01	.05
35 Jimmy Key	.02	.10
36 Dave Stieb	.01	.05
37 Dale Murphy	.07	.20
38 Keith Moreland	.01	.05
39 Ryne Sandberg	.30	.75
40 Tom Browning	.01	.05
41 Dave Parker	.02	.10
42 Mario Soto	.01	.05
43 Nolan Ryan	.75	2.00
44 Pedro Guerrero	.01	.05
45 Orel Hershiser	.05	.15
46 Mike Scioscia	.02	.10
47 Fernando Valenzuela	.02	.10
48 Bob Welch	.01	.05
49 Tim Raines	.02	.10
50 Gary Carter	.20	.50
51 Sid Fernandez	.01	.05
52 Dwight Gooden	.02	.10
53 Keith Hernandez	.02	.10
54 Juan Samuel	.01	.05
55 Mike Schmidt	.20	.50
56 Glenn Wilson	.01	.05
57 Rick Reuschel	.01	.05
58 Joaquin Andujar	.01	.05
59 Jack Clark	.01	.05
60 Vince Coleman	.02	.10
61 Danny Cox	.01	.05
62 Tom Herr	.01	.05
63 Willie McGee	.02	.10
64 John Tudor	.01	.05
65 Tony Gwynn	.40	1.00
66 Checklist Card	.01	.05

1986 Topps Stickers

Made in Italy for O-Pee-Chee by Panini, these 315 stickers measure approximately 2 1/8" by 3" and are numbered on both front and back. The fronts feature white-bordered color player photos. The horizontal backs carry a bilingual ad for O-Pee-Chee. An album onto which the stickers could be affixed was available at retail stores. The album and the sticker numbering are organized as follows: 1985 Highlights (1-10), 1985 Championship Series (11-16), 1985 World Series (17-23), Houston Astros (24-33), Atlanta Braves (34-43), St. Louis Cardinals (44-53), Chicago Cubs (54-63), Los Angeles Dodgers (64-73), Montreal Expos (74-83), San Francisco Giants (84-93), New York Mets (94-103), San Diego Padres (104-113), Philadelphia Phillies (114-123), Pittsburgh Pirates (124-133), Cincinnati Reds (134-143), 1985 NL Stat Leaders (144, 145), Foil All-Stars (146-163), 1985 AL Stat Leaders (164, 165), Oakland A's (166-175), California Angels (176-185), Toronto Blue Jays (186-195), Milwaukee Brewers (196-205), Cleveland Indians (206-215), Seattle Mariners (216-225), Baltimore Orioles (226-235), Texas Rangers (236-245), Boston Red Sox (246-255), Kansas City Royals (256-265), Detroit Tigers (266-275), Minnesota Twins (276-285), Chicago White Sox (286-295), New York Yankees (296-305), and Future Stars (306-315). For those stickers featuring more than one player, the other numbers on that sticker are given below in parentheses. The Topps stickers contain offers on the back to obtain either a trip for four to Spring Training of the team of your choice or a complete set of Topps baseball cards directly from Topps.

Card		
COMPLETE SET (315)	6.00	15.00
COMMON PLAYER (1-315)	.02	.05
COMMON FOIL PLAYER	.04	.10
*OPC: .4X TO 1X TOPPS STICKERS		
1 Pete Rose FOIL/(Top half)	.25	.60
2 Pete Rose FOIL/(Bottom half)	.25	.60
3 George Brett (175)	.30	.75
4 Rod Carew (178)	.15	.40
5 Vince Coleman (179)	.05	.15
6 Dwight Gooden (180)	.08	.25
7 Phil Niekro (181)	.08	.25
8 Tony Perez (182)	.08	.25
9 Nolan Ryan (183)	.75	2.00
10 Tom Seaver (184)	.20	.50
11 NL Championship (Ozzie Smith batting)	.05	.15
12 NL Championship/(Bill Madlock)	.02	.10
13 NL Championship (Cardinals celebrate)	.02	.10
14 AL Championship/(Al Oliver swings)	.02	.10
15 AL Championship/(Jim Sundberg)	.01	.05
16 AL Championship (George Brett swings)	.30	.75
17 World Series/(Bret Saberhagen)	.02	.10
18 World Series/(Dane Iorg swings)	.01	.05
19 World Series/(Tito Landrum)	.01	.05
20 World Series/(John Tudor)	.01	.05
21 World Series/(Buddy Biancalana)	.01	.05
22 World Series/(Darryl Motley)	.01	.05
23 World Series/(George Brett and Frank White)	.08	.25
24 Nolan Ryan	.75	2.00
25 Bill Doran	.01	.05
26 Jose Cruz (185)	.02	.10
27 Mike Scott (188)	.01	.05
28 Kevin Bass (189)	.01	.05
29 Glenn Davis (190)	.02	.10
30 Mark Bailey (191)	.01	.05
31 Dave Smith (192)	.01	.05
32 Phil Garner (193)	.02	.10
33 Dickie Thon (194)	.01	.05
34 Bob Horner	.01	.05
35 Dale Murphy	.05	.15
36 Glenn Hubbard (195)	.01	.05
37 Bruce Sutter (198)	.02	.10
38 Ken Oberkfell (199)	.01	.05
39 Claudell Washington/(200)	.01	.05
40 Steve Bedrosian (201)	.01	.05
41 Terry Harper (202)	.01	.05
42 Rafael Ramirez (203)	.01	.05
43 Rick Mahler (204)	.01	.05
44 Joaquin Andujar	.01	.05
45 Willie McGee	.05	.15
46 Ozzie Smith (205)	.15	.40
47 Vince Coleman (208)	.05	.15
48 Danny Cox (209)	.01	.05
49 Tom Herr (210)	.01	.05
50 Jack Clark (211)	.02	.10
51 Andy Van Slyke (212)	.02	.10
52 John Tudor (213)	.01	.05
53 Terry Pendleton(214)	.05	.15
54 Keith Moreland	.01	.05
55 Ryne Sandberg	.25	.60
56 Lee Smith (215)	.05	.15
57 Steve Trout (218)	.01	.05
58 Jody Davis (219)	.01	.05
59 Gary Matthews (220)	.01	.05
60 Leon Durham (221)	.01	.05
61 Rick Sutcliffe (222)	.01	.05
62 Dennis Eckersley/(223)	.05	.15
63 Bob Dernier (224)	.01	.05
64 Fernando Valenzuela	.02	.10
65 Pedro Guerrero	.01	.05
66 Jerry Reuss (225)	.01	.05
67 Greg Brock (228)	.01	.05
68 Mike Scioscia (229)	.01	.05
69 Ken Howell (230)	.01	.05
70 Bill Madlock (231)	.02	.10
71 Mike Marshall (232)	.01	.05
72 Steve Sax (233)	.01	.05
73 Orel Hershiser (234)	.05	.15
74 Andre Dawson	.08	.25
75 Tim Raines	.02	.10
76 Jeff Reardon (235)	.02	.10
77 Hubie Brooks (238)	.01	.05
78 Bill Gullickson(239)	.01	.05
79 Bryn Smith (240)	.01	.05
80 Terry Francona (241)	.02	.10
81 Vance Law (242)	.01	.05
82 Tim Wallach (243)	.01	.05
83 He.Winningham (244)	.01	.05
84 Jeff Leonard	.01	.05
85 Chris Brown	.01	.05
86 Scott Garrelts (245)	.01	.05
87 Jose Uribe (248)	.01	.05
88 Manny Trillo (249)	.01	.05
89 Dan Driessen (250)	.01	.05
90 Dan Gladden (251)	.01	.05
91 Mark Davis (252)	.01	.05
92 Bob Brenly (253)	.01	.05
93 Mike Krukow (254)	.01	.05
94 Dwight Gooden	.08	.25
95 Darryl Strawberry	.05	.15
96 Gary Carter (255)	.02	.10
97 Wally Backman (258)	.01	.05
98 Ron Darling (259)	.01	.05
99 Keith Hernandez(260)	.02	.10
100 George Foster (261)	.02	.10
101 Howard Johnson (262)	.02	.10
102 Rafael Santana (263)	.01	.05
103 Roger McDowell (264)	.02	.10
104 Steve Garvey	.05	.15
105 Tony Gwynn	.40	1.00
106 Graig Nettles (265)	.02	.10
107 Rich Gossage (268)	.02	.10
108 Andy Hawkins (269)	.01	.05
109 Carmelo Martinez/(270)	.01	.05
110 Garry Templeton(271)	.01	.05
111 Terry Kennedy (272)	.01	.05
112 Tim Flannery (273)	.01	.05
113 LaMarr Hoyt (274)	.01	.05
114 Mike Schmidt	.25	.60
115 Ozzie Virgil	.01	.05
116 Steve Carlton (275)	.15	.40
117 Garry Maddox (278)	.01	.05
118 Glenn Wilson (279)	.01	.05
119 Kevin Gross (280)	.01	.05
120 Von Hayes (281)	.01	.05
121 Juan Samuel (282)	.01	.05
122 Rick Schu (283)	.01	.05
123 Shane Rawley (284)	.01	.05
124 Johnny Ray	.01	.05
125 Tony Pena	.01	.05
126 Rick Reuschel (285)	.01	.05
127 Sammy Khalifa (288)	.01	.05
128 Marvell Wynne (289)	.01	.05
129 Jason Thompson (290)	.01	.05
130 Rick Rhoden (291)	.01	.05
131 Bill Almon (292)	.01	.05
132 Joe Orsulak (293)	.01	.05
133 Jim Morrison (294)	.01	.05
134 Pete Rose	.30	.75
135 Dave Parker	.02	.10
136 Mario Soto (295)	.01	.05
137 Dave Concepcion(298)	.02	.10
138 Ron Oester (299)	.01	.05
139 Buddy Bell (300)	.02	.10
140 Ted Power (301)	.01	.05
141 Tom Browning (302)	.01	.05
142 John Franco (303)	.05	.15
143 Tony Perez (304)	.05	.15
144 Willie McGee (305)	.02	.10
145 Dale Murphy (306)	.05	.15
146 Tony Gwynn FOIL	.60	1.50
147 Tom Herr FOIL	.02	.10
148 Steve Garvey FOIL	.08	.25
149 Dale Murphy FOIL	.07	.20
150 Darryl Strawberry FOIL	.08	.25
151 Graig Nettles FOIL	.07	.20
152 Terry Kennedy FOIL	.02	.10
153 Ozzie Smith FOIL	.25	.60
154 LaMarr Hoyt FOIL	.02	.10
155 Rickey Henderson FOIL	.15	.40
156 Lou Whitaker FOIL	.05	.15
157 George Brett FOIL	.50	1.25
158 Eddie Murray FOIL	.20	.50
159 Cal Ripken FOIL	1.25	3.00
160 Dave Winfield FOIL	.15	.40
161 Jim Rice FOIL	.05	.15
162 Carlton Fisk FOIL	.15	.40
163 Jack Morris FOIL	.05	.15
164 Wade Boggs (307)	.08	.25
165 Darrell Evans (308)	.02	.10
166 Mike Davis	.01	.05
167 Dave Kingman	.02	.10
168 Alfredo Griffin(309)	.01	.05
169 Carney Lansford(310)	.02	.10
170 Bruce Bochte (311)	.01	.05
171 Dwayne Murphy (312)	.01	.05
172 Dave Collins (313)	.01	.05
173 Chris Codiroli (314)	.01	.05
174 Mike Heath (315)	.01	.05
175 Jay Howell (3)	.01	.05
176 Rod Carew	.15	.40
177 Reggie Jackson	.20	.50
178 Doug DeCinces (4)	.01	.05
179 Bob Boone (5)	.02	.10
180 Ron Romanick (6)	.01	.05
181 Bob Grich (7)	.02	.10
182 Donnie Moore (8)	.01	.05
183 Brian Downing (9)	.01	.05
184 Ruppert Jones (10)	.01	.05
185 Juan Beniquez (26)	.01	.05
186 Dave Stieb	.01	.05
187 George Bell	.01	.05
188 Willie Upshaw (27)	.01	.05
189 Tom Henke (28)	.02	.10
190 Damaso Garcia (29)	.01	.05
191 Jimmy Key (30)	.05	.15
192 Jesse Barfield (31)	.01	.05
193 Dennis Lamp (32)	.01	.05
194 Tony Fernandez (33)	.01	.05
195 Lloyd Moseby (36)	.01	.05
196 Cecil Cooper	.02	.10
197 Robin Yount	.05	.15
198 Rollie Fingers (37)	.05	.15
199 Ted Simmons (38)	.02	.10
200 Ben Oglivie (39)	.01	.05
201 Moose Haas (40)	.01	.05
202 Jim Gantner (41)	.01	.05
203 Paul Molitor (42)	.05	.15
204 Charlie Moore (43)	.01	.05
205 Danny Darwin (46)	.01	.05
206 Brett Butler	.02	.10
207 Brook Jacoby	.01	.05
208 Andre Thornton (47)	.01	.05
209 Tom Waddell (48)	.01	.05
210 Tony Bernazard (49)	.01	.05
211 Julio Franco (50)	.02	.10
212 Pat Tabler (51)	.01	.05
213 Joe Carter (52)	.08	.25
214 George Vukovich (53)	.01	.05
215 Rich Thompson (56)	.01	.05
216 Gorman Thomas	.01	.05
217 Phil Bradley	.01	.05
218 Alvin Davis (57)	.01	.05
219 Jim Presley (58)	.01	.05
220 Matt Young (59)	.01	.05
221 Mike Moore (60)	.01	.05
222 Dave Henderson (61)	.01	.05
223 Ed Nunez (62)	.01	.05
224 Spike Owen (63)	.01	.05
225 Mark Langston (66)	.01	.05
226 Cal Ripken	.75	2.00
227 Eddie Murray	.08	.25
228 Fred Lynn (67)	.02	.10
229 Lee Lacy (68)	.01	.05
230 Scott McGregor (69)	.01	.05
231 Storm Davis (70)	.01	.05
232 Rick Dempsey (71)	.02	.10
233 Mike Boddicker (72)	.01	.05
234 Mike Young (73)	.01	.05
235 Sammy Stewart (76)	.01	.05
236 Pete O'Brien	.01	.05
237 Oddibe McDowell	.01	.05
238 Toby Harrah (77)	.01	.05
239 Gary Ward (78)	.01	.05
240 Larry Parrish (79)	.01	.05
241 Charlie Hough (80)	.02	.10
242 Burt Hooton (81)	.01	.05
243 Don Slaught (82)	.01	.05
244 Curt Wilkerson (83)	.01	.05
245 Greg Harris (86)	.01	.05
246 Jim Rice	.02	.10
247 Wade Boggs	.08	.25
248 Rich Gedman (87)	.01	.05
249 Dennis Boyd (88)	.01	.05
250 Marty Barrett (89)	.01	.05
251 Dwight Evans (90)	.02	.10
252 Bill Buckner (91)	.02	.10
253 Bob Stanley (92)	.01	.05
254 Tony Armas (93)	.01	.05
255 Mike Easler (96)	.01	.05
256 George Brett	.30	.75
257 Dan Quisenberry	.01	.05
258 Willie Wilson (97)	.01	.05
259 Jim Sundberg (98)	.01	.05
260 Bret Saberhagen (99)	.02	.10
261 Bud Black (100)	.01	.05
262 Charlie Leibrandt(101)	.01	.05
263 Frank White (102)	.02	.10
264 Lonnie Smith (103)	.01	.05
265 Steve Balboni (106)	.01	.05
266 Kirk Gibson	.02	.10
267 Alan Trammell	.05	.15
268 Jack Morris (107)	.02	.10
269 Darrell Evans (108)	.02	.10
270 Dan Petry (109)	.01	.05
271 Larry Herndon (110)	.01	.05
272 Lou Whitaker (111)	.02	.10
273 Lance Parrish (112)	.02	.10
274 Chet Lemon (113)	.01	.05
275 Willie Hernandez(116)	.01	.05
276 Tom Brunansky	.01	.05
277 Kent Hrbek	.02	.10
278 Mark Salas (117)	.01	.05
279 Bert Blyleven (118)	.02	.10
280 Tim Teufel (119)	.01	.05
281 Ron Davis (120)	.01	.05
282 Mike Smithson (121)	.01	.05
283 Gary Gaetti (122)	.02	.10
284 Frank Viola (123)	.02	.10
285 Kirby Puckett (126)	.60	1.50
286 Carlton Fisk	.08	.25
287 Tom Seaver	.20	.50
288 Harold Baines (127)	.02	.10
289 Ron Kittle (128)	.01	.05
290 Bob James (129)	.01	.05
291 Rudy Law (130)	.01	.05
292 Britt Burns (131)	.01	.05
293 Greg Walker (132)	.01	.05
294 Ozzie Guillen (133)	.05	.15
295 Tim Hulett (136)	.01	.05
296 Don Mattingly	.60	1.50
297 Rickey Henderson	.08	.25
298 Dave Winfield (137)	.08	.25
299 Butch Wynegar (138)	.01	.05
300 Don Baylor (139)	.02	.10
301 Eddie Whitson (140)	.01	.05
302 Ron Guidry (141)	.02	.10
303 Dave Righetti (142)	.01	.05
304 Bobby Meacham (143)	.01	.05
305 Willie Randolph(144)	.02	.10
306 Vince Coleman (145)	.05	.15
307 Oddibe McDowell(164)	.01	.05
308 Larry Sheets (165)	.01	.05
309 Ozzie Guillen (168)	.05	.15
310 Ernie Riles (169)	.01	.05
311 Chris Brown (170)	.01	.05
312 Brian Fisher and Roger McDowell (171)	.01	.05
313 Tom Browning (172)	.01	.05
314 Glenn Davis (173)	.01	.05
315 Mark Salas (174)	.01	.05
NNO Album	.40	1.00

1986 Topps Super

This 60-card set actually consists of giant-sized versions of the Topps regular issue of some of the most popular players. The cards measure 4 7/8" by 6 7/8". Cards are very similar to the Topps regular issue; two exceptions are that on the back they are numbered differently and an additional line of type is printed at the bottom of the back noting an accomplishment of that player at the end of the 1985 season.

Card		
COMPLETE SET (60)	8.00	20.00
1 Don Mattingly	.75	2.00
2 Willie McGee	.07	.20
3 Bret Saberhagen	.07	.20
4 Dwight Gooden	.07	.20
5 Dan Quisenberry	.02	.10
6 Jeff Reardon	.02	.10
7 Ozzie Guillen	.20	.50
8 Vince Coleman	.07	.20
9 Harold Baines	.10	.30
10 Jorge Bell	.02	.10
11 Bert Blyleven	.07	.20
12 Wade Boggs	.40	1.00
13 Phil Bradley	.02	.10
14 George Brett	.75	2.00
15 Hubie Brooks	.02	.10
16 Tom Browning	.02	.10
17 Bill Buckner	.02	.10
18 Brett Butler	.07	.20
19 Gary Carter	.30	.75
20 Cecil Cooper	.02	.10
21 Darrell Evans	.02	.10
22 Dwight Evans	.07	.20
23 Carlton Fisk	.20	.50
24 Steve Garvey	.10	.30
25 Kirk Gibson	.07	.20
26 Rich Gossage	.07	.20
27 Pedro Guerrero	.02	.10
28 Ron Guidry	.07	.20
29 Tony Gwynn	.75	2.00
30 Rickey Henderson	.40	1.25
31 Keith Hernandez	.07	.20
32 Tom Herr	.02	.10
33 Orel Hershiser	.10	.30
34 Jay Howell	.02	.10
35 Reggie Jackson	.30	.75
36 Bob James	.02	.10
37 Charlie Leibrandt	.02	.10
38 Jack Morris	.07	.20
39 Dale Murphy	.10	.30
40 Eddie Murray	.30	.75
41 Dave Parker	.07	.20
42 Tim Raines	.07	.20
43 Jim Rice	.07	.20
44 Dave Righetti	.02	.10
45 Cal Ripken	1.50	4.00
46 Pete Rose	.40	1.00
47 Nolan Ryan	1.50	4.00
48 Ryne Sandberg	.75	2.00
49 Mike Schmidt	.30	.75
50 Tom Seaver	.30	.75
51 Bryn Smith	.02	.10
52 Lee Smith	.10	.30
53 Ozzie Smith	.75	2.00
54 Dave Stieb	.02	.10
55 Darryl Strawberry	.07	.20
56 Gorman Thomas	.02	.10
57 John Tudor	.02	.10
58 Fernando Valenzuela	.07	.20
59 Willie Wilson	.02	.10
60 Dave Winfield	.30	.75

1986 Topps Tattoos

This set of 24 different tattoo sheets was distributed one sheet (with gum) per pack as a separate issue by Topps (and also by O-Pee-Chee). Each tattoo sheet measures approximately 3 7/16" by 14 1/4" whereas the individual player tattoos are approximately 1 13/16" by 2 3/8". The wrapper advertises 18 tattoos in the pack, which includes eight small (half-size) generic action shots. The players have their names and team names reverse printed beneath their transfers. The 1986 Topps (or O-Pee-Chee) copyright mark is shown at the bottom right. The checklist below lists only the individual player tattoos; they are listed in order of appearance top to bottom on the sheet. Each tattoo sheet is numbered at the top "X of 24."

Card		
COMPLETE SET (24)	3.00	8.00
*O-PEE-CHEE: SAME VALUE		
1 Sheet 1	.15	.40
Dickie Thon/Charlie Leibrandt/Dave Winf		
2 Sheet 2	.15	.40
Dale Murphy/Brian Fisher/Bret Saberhage		
3 Sheet 3	.10	.30
Steve Carlton/Dan Quisenberry/Bob James		
4 Sheet 4	.75	2.00
Johnny Ray/Darrell Evans/Mike Davis/Le		
5 Sheet 5	.10	.30
Jesse Orosco/Rick Dempsey/John Candelar		
6 Sheet 6	.40	1.00
Ron Kittle/Pete Rose/Sammy Khalifa/Bru		
7 Sheet 7	.75	2.00
Larry Sheets/John Franco/Graig Nettles#		
8 Sheet 8	.30	.75
Phil Niekro/Ryne Sandberg/Mike Krukow/		
9 Sheet 9	.15	.40
Chris Codiroli/Glenn Wilson/Rick Rhoden		
10 Sheet 10	.15	.40
Chet Lemon/Mike Smithson/Ron Darling/		
11 Sheet 11	.07	.20
Rick Mahler/Dave Righetti/Jay Howell/		
12 Sheet 12	.02	.10
Keith Moreland/Alvin Davis/Doug DeCinc		
13 Sheet 13	.60	1.50
Charles Hudson/Dwight Evans/Kirby Puck		
14 Sheet 14	.07	.20
LaMarr Hoyt/Brian Downing/Ron Guidry/		
15 Sheet 15	.15	.40
Tito Landrum/Hal McRae/Joe Carter/Jef		
16 Sheet 16	.30	.75
Scott Garrelts/Dennis Boyd/Donnie Moor		
17 Sheet 17	.30	.75
Claudell Washington/Rich Gedman/Reggie		
18 Sheet 18	.07	.20
Ron Davis/Glenn Davis/Chris Brown/Bur		
19 Sheet 19	.07	.20
Jack Clark/Toby Harrah/Larry Parrish/		
20 Sheet 20	.30	.75
21 Sheet 21	.02	.10
Steve Balboni/Rick Sutcliffe/Charlie L		
22 Sheet 22	.15	.40
Lance Parrish/Tom Herr/Bryn Smith/Kir		
23 Sheet 23	.15	.40
Dave Stieb/Willie McGee/Bob Grich/Pau		
24 Sheet 24	1.25	3.00
Tony Gwynn/Rickey Henderson/Damaso Gar		

1987 Topps

This set consists of 792 standard-size cards. Cards were primarily issued in 17-card wax packs, 50-card rack packs and factory sets. Card fronts feature wood grain borders encasing a color photo (reminiscent of Topps' classic 1962 baseball set). Subsets include Record Breakers (1-7), Turn Back the Clock (311-315), All-Star selections (595-616) and Team Leaders (scattered throughout the set). The manager cards contain a team checklist on back. The key Rookie Cards in this set are Barry Bonds, Bobby Bonilla, Will Clark, Bo Jackson, Wally Joyner, John Kruk, Barry Larkin, Rafael Palmiero, Ruben Sierra, and Devon White.

Card		
COMPLETE SET (792)	10.00	25.00
COMP.FACT SET (792)	15.00	40.00
COMP.HOBBY SET (792)	15.00	40.00
COMP.X-MAS.SET (792)	15.00	40.00
1 Roger Clemens RB	.40	1.00
2 Jim Deshaies RB	.01	.05
Most cons. K's&/start of game		
3 Dwight Evans RB	.05	.15
Earliest home run&/season		
4 Davey Lopes RB	.01	.05
Most steals& season&/40-year-old		
5 Dave Righetti RB	.01	.05
Most saves& season		
6 Ruben Sierra RB	.08	.25
7 Todd Worrell RB	.01	.05
Most saves&/season& rookie		
8 Terry Pendleton	.02	.10
9 Jay Tibbs	.01	.05
10 Cecil Cooper	.02	.10
11 Indians Team/(Mound conference)	.01	.05
12 Jeff Sellers	.01	.05
13 Nick Esasky	.01	.05
14 Dave Stewart	.02	.10
15 Claudell Washington	.01	.05
16 Pat Clements	.01	.05
17 Pete O'Brien	.01	.05
18 Dick Howser MG	.01	.05
19 Matt Young	.01	.05
20 Gary Carter	.02	.10
21 Mark Davis	.01	.05
22 Doug DeCinces	.01	.05
23 Lee Smith	.02	.10
24 Tony Walker	.01	.05
25 Bert Blyleven	.02	.10
26 Greg Brock	.01	.05
27 Joe Cowley	.01	.05
28 Rick Dempsey	.01	.05
29 Jimmy Key	.02	.10
30 Tim Raines	.02	.10
31 Braves Team/(Glenn Hubbard and Rafael Ramirez)	.01	.05
32 Tim Leary	.01	.05
33 Andy Van Slyke	.05	.15
34 Jose Rijo	.02	.10
35 Sid Bream	.01	.05
36 Eric King	.01	.05
37 Marvell Wynne	.01	.05
38 Dennis Leonard	.01	.05
39 Marty Barrett	.01	.05
40 Dave Righetti	.02	.10
41 Bo Diaz	.01	.05
42 Gary Redus	.01	.05
43 Gene Michael MG	.01	.05
44 Greg Harris	.01	.05
45 Jim Presley	.01	.05
46 Dan Gladden	.01	.05
47 Dennis Powell	.01	.05
48 Wally Backman	.01	.05
49 Terry Harper	.01	.05
50 Dave Smith	.01	.05
51 Mel Hall	.01	.05
52 Keith Atherton	.01	.05
53 Ruppert Jones	.01	.05
54 Bill Dawley	.01	.05
55 Tim Wallach	.01	.05
56 Brewers Team/(Mound conference)	.02	.10
57 Scott Nielsen	.01	.05
58 Thad Bosley	.01	.05
59 Ken Dayley	.01	.05
60 Tony Pena	.01	.05
61 Bobby Thigpen RC	.08	.25
62 Bobby Meacham	.01	.05
63 Fred Toliver	.01	.05
64 Harry Spilman	.01	.05
65 Tom Browning	.01	.05
66 Marc Sullivan	.01	.05
67 Bill Swift	.01	.05
68 Tony LaRussa MG	.02	.10
69 Lonnie Smith	.01	.05
70 Charlie Hough	.02	.10
71 Mike Aldrete	.01	.05
72 Walt Terrell	.01	.05
73 Dave Anderson	.01	.05
74 Dan Pasqua	.01	.05
75 Ron Darling	.02	.10
76 Rafael Ramirez	.01	.05

77 Bryan Oelkers .01 .05
78 Tom Foley .01 .05
79 Juan Nieves .01 .05
80 Wally Joyner RC .15 .40
81 Padres Team/(Andy Hawkins and Terry Kennedy) .01 .05
82 Rob Murphy .01 .05
83 Mike Davis .01 .05
84 Steve Lake .01 .05
85 Kevin Bass .01 .05
86 Nate Snell .01 .05
87 Mark Salas .01 .05
88 Ed Wojna .01 .05
89 Ozzie Guillen .05 .15
90 Dave Stieb .02 .10
91 Harold Reynolds .02 .10
92A Urbano Lugo ERR (no trademark) .05 .15
92B Urbano Lugo COR .01 .05
93 Jim Leyland MG TC RC * .08 .25
94 Calvin Schiraldi .01 .05
95 Oddibe McDowell .01 .05
96 Frank Williams .01 .05
97 Glenn Wilson .01 .05
98 Bill Scherrer .01 .05
99 Darryl Motley/(Now with Braves on card front) .01 .05
100 Steve Garvey .02 .10
101 Carl Willis RC .02 .10
102 Paul Zuvella .01 .05
103 Rick Aguilera .01 .05
104 Billy Sample .01 .05
105 Floyd Youmans .01 .05
106 Blue Jays Team/(George Bell and Jesse Barfield) .01 .05
107 John Butcher .01 .05
108 Jim Gantner UER/(Brewers logo reversed) .01 .05
109 R.J. Reynolds .01 .05
110 John Tudor .02 .10
111 Alfredo Griffin .01 .05
112 Alan Ashby .01 .05
113 Neil Allen .01 .05
114 Billy Beane .02 .10
115 Donnie Moore .01 .05
116 Bill Russell .02 .10
117 Jim Beattie .01 .05
118 Bobby Valentine MG .02 .10
119 Ron Robinson .01 .05
120 Eddie Murray .08 .25
121 Kevin Romine RC .01 .05
122 Jim Clancy .01 .05
123 John Kruk RC .20 .50
124 Ray Fontenot .01 .05
125 Bob Brenly .01 .05
126 Mike Loynd RC .02 .10
127 Vance Law .01 .05
128 Checklist 1-132 .01 .05
129 Rick Cerone .01 .05
130 Dwight Gooden .05 .15
131 Pirates Team/(Sid Bream and Tony Pena) .01 .05
132 Paul Assenmacher .08 .25
133 Jose Oquendo .01 .05
134 Rich Yett .01 .05
135 Mike Easler .01 .05
136 Ron Romanick .01 .05
137 Jerry Willard .01 .05
138 Roy Lee Jackson .01 .05
139 Devon White RC .15 .40
140 Bret Saberhagen .02 .10
141 Herm Winningham .01 .05
142 Rick Sutcliffe .02 .10
143 Steve Boros MG .01 .05
144 Mike Scioscia .02 .10
145 Charlie Kerfeld .01 .05
146 Tracy Jones .01 .05
147 Randy Niemann .01 .05
148 Dave Collins .01 .05
149 Ray Searage .01 .05
150 Wade Boggs .05 .15
151 Mike LaCoss .01 .05
152 Toby Harrah .02 .10
153 Duane Ward RC * .08 .25
154 Tom O'Malley .01 .05
155 Eddie Whitson .01 .05
156 Mariners Team/(Mound conference).01 .05
157 Danny Darwin .01 .05
158 Tim Teufel .01 .05
159 Ed Olwine .01 .05
160 Julio Franco .02 .10
161 Steve Ontiveros .01 .05
162 Mike LaValliere RC * .08 .25
163 Kevin Gross .01 .05
164 Sammy Khalifa .01 .05
165 Jeff Reardon .02 .10
166 Bob Boone .02 .10
167 Jim Deshaies RC * .02 .10
168 Lou Piniella MG .02 .10
169 Ron Washington .01 .05
170 Bo Jackson RC 3.00 8.00
171 Chuck Cary .01 .05
172 Ron Oester .01 .05
173 Alex Trevino .01 .05
174 Henry Cotto .01 .05
175 Bob Stanley .01 .05
176 Steve Buechele .01 .05
177 Keith Moreland .01 .05
178 Cecil Fielder .02 .10
179 Bill Wegman .01 .05
180 Chris Brown .01 .05
181 Cardinals Team/(Mound conference).01 .05
182 Lee Lacy .01 .05
183 Andy Hawkins .01 .05
184 Bobby Bonilla RC .15 .40
185 Roger McDowell .01 .05
186 Bruce Benedict .01 .05
187 Mark Huismann .01 .05
188 Tony Phillips .01 .05
189 Joe Hesketh .01 .05
190 Jim Sundberg .02 .10
191 Charles Hudson .01 .05
192 Cory Snyder .01 .05
193 Roger Craig MG .02 .10
194 Kirk McCaskill .01 .05
195 Mike Pagliarulo .01 .05
196 Randy O'Neal UER/(Wrong ML career.01 .05
W-L totals)
197 Mark Bailey .01 .05
198 Lee Mazzilli .02 .10
199 Mariano Duncan .01 .05
200 Pete Rose .25 .60
201 John Cangelosi .01 .05
202 Ricky Wright .01 .05
203 Mike Kingery RC .02 .10
204 Sammy Stewart .01 .05
205 Graig Nettles .02 .10
206 Twins Team/(Frank Viola and Tim Laudner) .01 .05
207 George Frazier .01 .05
208 John Shelby .01 .05
209 Rick Schu .01 .05
210 Lloyd Moseby .01 .05
211 John Morris .01 .05
212 Mike Fitzgerald .01 .05
213 Randy Myers RC .15 .40
214 Omar Moreno .01 .05
215 Mark Langston .01 .05
216 B.J. Surhoff RC .15 .40
217 Chris Codiroli .01 .05
218 Sparky Anderson MG .02 .10
219 Cecilio Guante .01 .05
220 Joe Carter .02 .10
221 Vern Ruhle .01 .05
222 Denny Walling .01 .05
223 Charlie Leibrandt .01 .05
224 Wayne Tolleson .01 .05
225 Mike Smithson .01 .05
226 Max Venable .01 .05
227 Jamie Moyer RC .20 .50
228 Curt Wilkerson .01 .05
229 Mike Birkbeck .02 .10
230 Don Baylor .02 .10
231 Giants Team/(Bob Brenly and Jim Gott) .01 .05
232 Reggie Williams .01 .05
233 Russ Morman .01 .05
234 Pat Sheridan .01 .05
235 Alvin Davis .01 .05
236 Tommy John .02 .10
237 Jim Morrison .01 .05
238 Bill Krueger .01 .05
239 Juan Espino .01 .05
240 Steve Balboni .01 .05
241 Danny Heep .01 .05
242 Rick Mahler .01 .05
243 Whitey Herzog MG .02 .10
244 Dickie Noles .01 .05
245 Willie Upshaw .01 .05
246 Jim Dwyer .01 .05
247 Jeff Reed .01 .05
248 Gene Walter .01 .05
249 Jim Pankovits .01 .05
250 Teddy Higuera .01 .05
251 Rob Wilfong .01 .05
252 Dennis Martinez .02 .10
253 Eddie Milner .01 .05
254 Bob Tewksbury RC * .08 .25
255 Juan Samuel .01 .05
256 Royals TL George Brett .05 .15
257 Bob Forsch .01 .05
258 Steve Yeager .02 .10
259 Mike Greenwell RC .08 .25
260 Vida Blue .02 .10
261 Ruben Sierra RC .20 .50
262 Jim Winn .01 .05
263 Stan Javier .01 .05
264 Checklist 133-264 .01 .05
265 Darrell Evans .02 .10
266 Jeff Hamilton .01 .05
267 Howard Johnson .02 .10
268 Pat Corrales MG .01 .05
269 Cliff Speck .01 .05
270 Jody Davis .01 .05
271 Mike G. Brown .01 .05
272 Andres Galarraga .02 .10
273 Gene Nelson .01 .05
274 Jeff Hearron UER/(Duplicate 1986 .01 .05
stat line on ba
275 LaMarr Hoyt .01 .05
276 Jackie Gutierrez .01 .05
277 Juan Agosto .01 .05
278 Gary Pettis .01 .05
279 Dan Plesac .01 .05
280 Jeff Leonard .01 .05
281 Reds TL Rose .08 .25
282 Jeff Calhoun .01 .05
283 Doug Drabek RC .15 .40
284 John Moses .01 .05
285 Dennis Boyd .01 .05
286 Mike Woodard .01 .05
287 Dave Von Ohlen .01 .05
288 Tito Landrum .01 .05
289 Bob Kipper .01 .05
290 Leon Durham .01 .05
291 Mitch Williams RC * .08 .25
292 Franklin Stubbs .01 .05
293 Bob Rodgers MG/(Checklist back&.01 .05
inconsistent des
294 Steve Jeltz .01 .05
295 Len Dykstra .02 .10
296 Andres Thomas .01 .05
297 Don Schulze .01 .05
298 Larry Herndon .01 .05
299 Joel Davis .01 .05
300 Reggie Jackson .05 .15
301 Luis Aquino UER/(No trademark never corrected) .01 .05
302 Bill Schroeder .01 .05
303 Juan Berenguer .01 .05
304 Phil Garner .02 .10
305 John Franco .02 .10
306 Red Sox TL Seaver .02 .10
307 Lee Guetterman .01 .05
308 Don Slaught .01 .05
309 Mike Young .01 .05
310 Frank Viola .02 .10
311 Rickey Henderson TBC .05 .15
312 Reggie Jackson TBC .02 .10
313 Roberto Clemente TBC .08 .25
314 Carl Yastrzemski TBC .08 .25
315 Maury Wills TBC '62 .02 .10
316 Brian Fisher .01 .05
317 Clint Hurdle .01 .05
318 Jim Fregosi MG .01 .05
319 Greg Swindell RC .08 .25
320 Barry Bonds RC 6.00 15.00
321 Mike Laga .01 .05
322 Chris Bando .01 .05
323 Al Newman RC .01 .05
324 David Palmer .01 .05
325 Garry Templeton .02 .10
326 Mark Gubicza .01 .05
327 Dale Sveum .01 .05
328 Bob Welch .02 .10
329 Ron Roenicke .01 .05
330 Mike Scott .02 .10
331 Mets TL Carter/Straw .02 .10
332 Joe Price .01 .05
333 Ken Phelps .01 .05
334 Ed Correa .01 .05
335 Candy Maldonado .01 .05
336 Allan Anderson RC .01 .05
337 Darrell Miller .01 .05
338 Tim Conroy .01 .05
339 Donnie Hill .01 .05
340 Roger Clemens .60 1.50
341 Mike C. Brown .01 .05
342 Bob James .01 .05
343 Hal Lanier MG .01 .05
344A Joe Niekro/(Copyright inside righthand border) .01 .05
344B Joe Niekro/(Copyright outside righthand border) .01 .05
345 Andre Dawson .02 .10
346 Shawon Dunston .01 .05
347 Mickey Brantley .01 .05
348 Carmelo Martinez .01 .05
349 Storm Davis .01 .05
350 Keith Hernandez .02 .10
351 Gene Garber .01 .05
352 Mike Felder .01 .05
353 Ernie Camacho .01 .05
354 Jamie Quirk .01 .05
355 Don Carman .01 .05
356 White Sox Team/(Mound conference).01 .05
357 Steve Fireovid .01 .05
358 Sal Butera .01 .05
359 Doug Corbett .01 .05
360 Pedro Guerrero .02 .10
361 Mark Thurmond .01 .05
362 Luis Quinones .01 .05
363 Jose Guzman .01 .05
364 Randy Bush .01 .05
365 Rick Rhoden .01 .05
366 Mark McGwire 2.00 5.00
367 Jeff Lahti .01 .05
368 John McNamara MG .01 .05
369 Brian Dayett .01 .05
370 Fred Lynn .02 .10
371 Mark Eichhorn .01 .05
372 Jerry Mumphrey .01 .05
373 Jeff Dedmon .01 .05
374 Glenn Hoffman .01 .05
375 Ron Guidry .02 .10
376 Scott Bradley .01 .05
377 John Henry Johnson .01 .05
378 Rafael Santana .01 .05
379 John Russell .01 .05
380 Rich Gossage .02 .10
381 Expos Team/(Mound conference) .01 .05
382 Rudy Law .01 .05
383 Ron Davis .01 .05
384 Johnny Grubb .01 .05
385 Orel Hershiser .05 .15
386 Dickie Thon .01 .05
387 T.R. Bryden .01 .05
388 Geno Petralli .01 .05
389 Jeff D. Robinson .01 .05
390 Gary Matthews .02 .10
391 Jay Howell .01 .05
392 Checklist 265-396 .01 .05
393 Pete Rose MG TC .05 .15
394 Mike Bielecki .01 .05
395 Damaso Garcia .01 .05
396 Tim Lollar .01 .05
397 Greg Walker .01 .05
398 Brad Havens .01 .05
399 Curt Ford .01 .05
400 George Brett .25 .60
401 Billy Joe Robidoux .01 .05
402 Mike Trujillo .01 .05
403 Jerry Royster .01 .05
404 Doug Sisk .01 .05
405 Brook Jacoby .01 .05
406 Yankees TL Hend/Matt .20 .50
407 Jim Acker .01 .05
408 John Mizerock .01 .05
409 Milt Thompson .01 .05
410 Fernando Valenzuela .02 .10
411 Darnell Coles .01 .05
412 Eric Davis .05 .15
413 Moose Haas .01 .05
414 Joe Orsulak .01 .05
415 Bobby Witt RC .08 .25
416 Tom Nieto .01 .05
417 Pat Perry .01 .05
418 Dick Williams MG .01 .05
419 Mark Portugal RC * .08 .25
420 Will Clark RC .40 1.00
421 Jose DeLeon .01 .05
422 Jack Howell .01 .05
423 Jaime Cocanower .01 .05
424 Chris Speier .01 .05
425 Tom Seaver .05 .15
426 Floyd Rayford .01 .05
427 Edwin Nunez .01 .05
428 Bruce Bochy .01 .05
429 Tim Pyznarski .01 .05
430 Mike Schmidt .20 .50
431 Dodgers Team/(Mound conference).01 .05
432 Jim Slaton .01 .05
433 Ed Hearn RC .01 .05
434 Mike Fischlin .01 .05
435 Bruce Sutter .02 .10
436 Andy Allanson RC .01 .05
437 Ted Power .01 .05
438 Kelly Downs RC .02 .10
439 Karl Best .01 .05
440 Willie McGee .02 .10
441 Dave Leiper .01 .05
442 Mitch Webster .01 .05
443 John Felske MG .01 .05
444 Jeff Russell .01 .05
445 Dave Lopes .02 .10
446 Chuck Finley RC .15 .40
447 Bill Almon .01 .05
448 Chris Bosio RC .08 .25
449 Pat Dodson .02 .10
450 Kirby Puckett .20 .50
451 Joe Sambito .01 .05
452 Dave Henderson .01 .05
453 Scott Terry RC .02 .10
454 Luis Salazar .01 .05
455 Mike Boddicker .01 .05
456 A's Team/(Mound conference) .01 .05
457 Len Matuszek .01 .05
458 Kelly Gruber .01 .05
459 Dennis Eckersley .05 .15
460 Darryl Strawberry .02 .10
461 Craig McMurtry .01 .05
462 Scott Fletcher .01 .05
463 Tom Candiotti .01 .05
464 Butch Wynegar .01 .05
465 Todd Worrell .01 .05
466 Kal Daniels .01 .05
467 Randy St.Claire .01 .05
468 George Bamberger MG .01 .05
469 Mike Diaz .01 .05
470 Dave Dravecky .01 .05
471 Ronn Reynolds .01 .05
472 Bill Doran .01 .05
473 Steve Farr .01 .05
474 Jerry Narron .01 .05
475 Scott Garrelts .01 .05
476 Danny Tartabull .01 .05
477 Ken Howell .01 .05
478 Tim Laudner .01 .05
479 Bob Sebra .01 .05
480 Jim Rice .02 .10
481 Phillies Team/(Glenn Wilson& Juan Samuel& and/V .01 .05
482 Daryl Boston .01 .05
483 Dwight Lowry .01 .05
484 Jim Traber .01 .05
485 Tony Fernandez .01 .05
486 Otis Nixon .01 .05
487 Dave Gumpert .01 .05
488 Ray Knight .02 .10
489 Bill Gullickson .01 .05
490 Dale Murphy .05 .15
491 Ron Karkovice RC .08 .25
492 Mike Heath .01 .05
493 Tom Lasorda MG .05 .15
494 Barry Jones .01 .05
495 Gorman Thomas .02 .10
496 Bruce Bochte .01 .05
497 Dale Mohorcic .01 .05
498 Bob Kearney .01 .05
499 Bruce Ruffin RC .02 .10
500 Don Mattingly .25 .60
501 Craig Lefferts .01 .05
502 Dick Schofield .01 .05
503 Larry Andersen .01 .05
504 Mickey Hatcher .01 .05
505 Bryn Smith .01 .05
506 Orioles Team/(Mound conference) .01 .05
507 Dave L. Stapleton .01 .05
508 Scott Bankhead .01 .05
509 Enos Cabell .01 .05
510 Tom Henke .01 .05
511 Steve Lyons .01 .05
512 Dave Magadan RC .08 .25
513 Carmen Castillo .01 .05
514 Orlando Mercado .01 .05
515 Willie Hernandez .01 .05
516 Ted Simmons .02 .10
517 Mario Soto .02 .10
518 Gene Mauch MG .01 .05
519 Curt Young .01 .05
520 Jack Clark .02 .10
521 Rick Reuschel .02 .10
522 Checklist 397-528 .01 .05
523 Earnie Riles .01 .05
524 Bob Shirley .01 .05
525 Phil Bradley .01 .05
526 Roger Mason .01 .05
527 Jim Wohlford .01 .05
528 Ken Dixon .01 .05
529 Alvaro Espinoza RC .02 .10
530 Tony Gwynn .10 .30
531 Astros TL Y.Berra .02 .10
532 Jeff Stone .01 .05
533 Angel Salazar .01 .05
534 Scott Sanderson .01 .05
535 Tony Armas .02 .10
536 Terry Mulholland RC .08 .25
537 Rance Mulliniks .01 .05
538 Tom Niedenfuer .01 .05
539 Reid Nichols .01 .05
540 Terry Kennedy .01 .05
541 Rafael Belliard RC .08 .25
542 Ricky Horton .01 .05
543 Dave Johnson MG .01 .05
544 Zane Smith .01 .05
545 Buddy Bell .02 .10
546 Mike Morgan .01 .05
547 Rob Deer .01 .05
548 Bill Mooneyham .01 .05
549 Bob Melvin .01 .05
550 Pete Incaviglia RC * .08 .25
551 Frank Wills .01 .05
552 Larry Sheets .01 .05
553 Mike Maddux RC .01 .05
554 Buddy Biancalana .01 .05
555 Dennis Rasmussen .01 .05
556 Angels Team/(Rene Lachemann CO&.01 .05
Mike Witt& and/
557 John Cerutti .01 .05
558 Greg Gagne .01 .05
559 Lance McCullers .01 .05
560 Glenn Davis .01 .05
561 Rey Quinones .01 .05
562 Bryan Clutterbuck .01 .05
563 John Stefero .01 .05
564 Larry McWilliams .01 .05
565 Dusty Baker .02 .10
566 Tim Hulett .01 .05
567 Greg Mathews .01 .05
568 Earl Weaver MG .02 .10
569 Wade Rowdon .01 .05
570 Sid Fernandez .01 .05
571 Ozzie Virgil .01 .05
572 Pete Ladd .01 .05
573 Hal McRae .02 .10
574 Manny Lee .01 .05
575 Pat Tabler .01 .05
576 Frank Pastore .01 .05
577 Dann Bilardello .01 .05
578 Billy Hatcher .01 .05
579 Rick Burleson .01 .05
580 Mike Krukow .01 .05
581 Cubs Team/(Ron Cey and Steve Trout) .01 .05
582 Bruce Berenyi .01 .05
583 Junior Ortiz .01 .05
584 Ron Kittle .01 .05
585 Scott Bailes .01 .05
586 Ben Oglivie .02 .10
587 Eric Plunk .01 .05
588 Wallace Johnson .01 .05
589 Steve Crawford .01 .05
590 Vince Coleman .01 .05
591 Spike Owen .01 .05
592 Chris Welsh .01 .05
593 Chuck Tanner MG .01 .05
594 Rick Anderson .01 .05
595 Keith Hernandez AS .01 .05
596 Steve Sax AS .01 .05
597 Mike Schmidt AS .08 .25
598 Ozzie Smith AS .08 .25
599 Tony Gwynn AS .05 .15
600 Dave Parker AS .01 .05
601 Darryl Strawberry AS .01 .05
602 Gary Carter AS .01 .05
603A Dwight Gooden AS NoTM .02 .10
603B Dwight Gooden AS TM .02 .10
604 Fernando Valenzuela AS .01 .05
605 Todd Worrell AS .01 .05
606 Don Mattingly AS .10 .30
606A Don Mattingly AS NoTM .40 1.00
607 Tony Bernazard AS .01 .05
608 Wade Boggs AS .02 .10
609 Cal Ripken AS .08 .25
610 Jim Rice AS .01 .05
611 Kirby Puckett AS .08 .25
612 George Bell AS .01 .05
613 Lance Parrish AS UER (Pitcher heading on back) .01 .05
614 Roger Clemens AS .40 1.00
615 Teddy Higuera AS .01 .05
616 Dave Righetti AS .01 .05
617 Al Nipper .01 .05
618 Tom Kelly MG .01 .05
619 Jerry Reed .01 .05
620 Jose Canseco .40 1.00
621 Danny Cox .01 .05
622 Glenn Braggs RC .02 .10
623 Kurt Stillwell .01 .05
624 Tim Burke .01 .05
625 Mookie Wilson .02 .10
626 Joel Skinner .01 .05
627 Ken Oberkfell .01 .05
628 Bob Walk .01 .05
629 Larry Parrish .01 .05
630 John Candelaria .01 .05
631 Tigers Team/(Mound conference) .01 .05
632 Rob Woodward .01 .05
633 Jose Uribe .01 .05
634 Rafael Palmeiro RC .60 1.50
635 Ken Schrom .01 .05
636 Darren Daulton .02 .10
637 Bip Roberts RC .08 .25
638 Rich Bordi .01 .05
639 Gerald Perry .01 .05
640 Mark Clear .01 .05
641 Domingo Ramos .01 .05
642 Al Pulido .01 .05
643 Ron Shepherd .01 .05
644 John Denny .01 .05
645 Dwight Evans .05 .15
646 Mike Mason .01 .05
647 Tom Lawless .01 .05
648 Barry Larkin RC 1.00 2.50
649 Mickey Tettleton .01 .05
650 Hubie Brooks .01 .05
651 Benny Distefano .01 .05
652 Terry Forster .02 .10
653 Kevin Mitchell RC * .15 .40
654 Checklist 529-660 .02 .10
655 Jesse Barfield .02 .10
656 Rangers Team/(Bobby Valentine MG.01 .05
and Ricky Wrigh
657 Tom Waddell .01 .05
658 Robby Thompson RC * .08 .25
659 Aurelio Lopez .01 .05
660 Bob Horner .02 .10
661 Lou Whitaker .02 .10
662 Frank DiPino .01 .05
663 Cliff Johnson .01 .05
664 Mike Marshall .01 .05
665 Rod Scurry .01 .05
666 Von Hayes .01 .05
667 Ron Hassey .01 .05
668 Juan Bonilla .01 .05
669 Bud Black .01 .05
670 Jose Cruz .02 .10
671A Ray Soff ERR/(No D* before copyright line) .01 .05
671B Ray Soff COR/(D* before copyright line) .01 .05
672 Chili Davis .02 .10
673 Don Sutton .02 .10
674 Bill Campbell .01 .05
675 Ed Romero .01 .05
676 Charlie Moore .01 .05
677 Bob Grich .02 .10
678 Carney Lansford .02 .10
679 Kent Hrbek .02 .10
680 Ryne Sandberg .15 .40
681 George Bell .02 .10
682 Jerry Reuss .01 .05
683 Gary Roenicke .01 .05
684 Kent Tekulve .01 .05
685 Jerry Hairston .01 .05
686 Doyle Alexander .01 .05
687 Alan Trammell .02 .10
688 Juan Beniquez .01 .05
689 Darrell Porter .01 .05
690 Dane Iorg .01 .05
691 Dave Parker .02 .10
692 Frank White .02 .10
693 Terry Puhl .01 .05
694 Phil Niekro .02 .10
695 Chico Walker .01 .05
696 Gary Lucas .01 .05
697 Ed Lynch .01 .05
698 Ernie Whitt .01 .05
699 Ken Landreaux .01 .05
700 Dave Bergman .01 .05
701 Willie Randolph .02 .10
702 Greg Gross .01 .05
703 Dave Schmidt .01 .05
704 Jesse Orosco .01 .05
705 Bruce Hurst .01 .05
706 Rick Manning .01 .05
707 Bob McClure .01 .05
708 Scott McGregor .01 .05
709 Dave Kingman .02 .10
710 Gary Gaetti .02 .10
711 Ken Griffey .02 .10
712 Don Robinson .01 .05
713 Tom Brookens .01 .05
714 Dan Quisenberry .01 .05
715 Bob Dernier .01 .05
716 Rick Leach .01 .05
717 Ed VandeBerg .01 .05
718 Steve Carlton .02 .10
719 Tom Hume .01 .05
720 Richard Dotson .01 .05
721 Tom Herr .01 .05
722 Bob Knepper .01 .05
723 Brett Butler .02 .10
724 Greg Minton .01 .05
725 George Hendrick .02 .10
726 Frank Tanana .02 .10
727 Mike Moore .01 .05
728 Tippy Martinez .01 .05
729 Tom Paciorek .01 .05
730 Eric Show .01 .05
731 Dave Concepcion .02 .10
732 Manny Trillo .01 .05
733 Bill Caudill .01 .05
734 Bill Madlock .02 .10
735 Rickey Henderson .08 .25
736 Steve Bedrosian .01 .05
737 Floyd Bannister .01 .05
738 Jorge Orta .01 .05
739 Chet Lemon .02 .10
740 Rich Gedman .01 .05
741 Paul Molitor .02 .10
742 Andy McGaffigan .01 .05
743 Dwayne Murphy .01 .05
744 Roy Smalley .01 .05
745 Glenn Hubbard .01 .05
746 Bob Ojeda .01 .05
747 Johnny Ray .01 .05
748 Mike Flanagan .01 .05
749 Ozzie Smith .15 .40
750 Steve Trout .01 .05
751 Garth Iorg .01 .05
752 Dan Petry .01 .05
753 Rick Honeycutt .01 .05
754 Dave LaPoint .01 .05
755 Luis Aguayo .01 .05
756 Carlton Fisk .05 .15
757 Nolan Ryan .40 1.00
758 Tony Bernazard .01 .05
759 Joel Youngblood .01 .05
760 Mike Witt .01 .05
761 Greg Pryor .01 .05
762 Gary Ward .01 .05
763 Tim Flannery .01 .05
764 Bill Buckner .02 .10
765 Kirk Gibson .02 .10
766 Don Aase .01 .05
767 Ron Cey .02 .10
768 Dennis Lamp .01 .05
769 Steve Sax .01 .05
770 Dave Winfield .02 .10
771 Shane Rawley .01 .05
772 Harold Baines .02 .10
773 Robin Yount .15 .40
774 Wayne Krenchicki .01 .05
775 Joaquin Andujar .02 .10
776 Tom Brunansky .01 .05
777 Chris Chambliss .02 .10
778 Jack Morris .02 .10
779 Craig Reynolds .01 .05
780 Andre Thornton .01 .05
781 Atlee Hammaker .01 .05
782 Brian Downing .02 .10
783 Willie Wilson .02 .10
784 Cal Ripken .30 .75
785 Terry Francona .02 .10
786 Jimy Williams MG .01 .05
787 Alejandro Pena .01 .05
788 Tim Stoddard .01 .05
789 Dan Schatzeder .01 .05
790 Julio Cruz .01 .05
791 Lance Parrish UER/(No trademark&.02 .10
never corrected
792 Checklist 661-792 .01 .05

1987 Topps Tiffany

COMP.FACT.SET (792) 40.00 80.00
*STARS: 2.5X TO 6X BASIC CARDS
*ROOKIES: 2.5X TO 6X BASIC CARDS
DISTRIBUTED ONLY IN FACTORY SET FORM
FACTORY SET PRICE IS FOR SEALED SETS

1987 Topps Glossy All-Stars

COMPLETE SET (22) 2.00 5.00
1 Whitey Herzog MG .02 .10
2 Keith Hernandez .02 .10
3 Ryne Sandberg .40 1.00
4 Mike Schmidt .20 .50
5 Ozzie Smith .40 1.00
6 Tony Gwynn .40 1.00
7 Dale Murphy .07 .20
8 Darryl Strawberry .02 .10
9 Gary Carter .20 .50
10 Dwight Gooden .05 .15
11 Fernando Valenzuela .02 .10
12 Dick Howser MG .01 .05
13 Wally Joyner .02 .10
14 Lou Whitaker .02 .10
15 Wade Boggs .20 .50
16 Cal Ripken .75 2.00
17 Dave Winfield .20 .50
18 Rickey Henderson .25 .60
19 Kirby Puckett .30 .75
20 Lance Parrish .02 .10
21 Roger Clemens .40 1.00
22 Teddy Higuera .01 .05

1987 Topps Glossy Send-Ins

COMPLETE SET (60) 10.00 25.00
DISTRIBUTED VIA MAIL EXCH.PROGRAM
1 Don Mattingly .75 2.00
2 Tony Gwynn .40 1.00
3 Gary Gaetti .10 .30
4 Glenn Davis .07 .20
5 Roger Clemens 1.25 3.00
6 Dale Murphy .20 .50
7 Lou Whitaker .10 .30
8 Roger McDowell .07 .20
9 Cory Snyder .07 .20
10 Todd Worrell .10 .30
11 Gary Carter .10 .30
12 Eddie Murray .30 .75
13 Bob Knepper .07 .20
14 Harold Baines .10 .30
15 Jeff Reardon .10 .30
16 Joe Carter .10 .30
17 Dave Parker .10 .30
18 Wade Boggs .20 .50
19 Danny Tartabull .07 .20
20 Jim Deshaies .07 .20
21 Rickey Henderson .30 .75
22 Rob Deer .07 .20
23 Ozzie Smith .50 1.25
24 Dave Righetti .10 .30
25 Kent Hrbek .10 .30
26 Keith Hernandez .10 .30
27 Don Baylor .10 .30
28 Mike Schmidt .60 1.50
29 Pete Incaviglia .10 .30
30 Barry Bonds 5.00 12.00
31 George Brett .75 2.00
32 Darryl Strawberry .10 .30
33 Mike Witt .07 .20
34 Kevin Bass .07 .20
35 Jesse Barfield .07 .20
36 Bob Ojeda .07 .20
37 Cal Ripken 1.00 2.50
38 Vince Coleman .07 .20
39 Wally Joyner .20 .50
40 Robby Thompson .10 .30
41 Pete Rose .75 2.00
42 Jim Rice .10 .30
43 Tony Bernazard .07 .20
44 Eric Davis .20 .50
45 George Bell .07 .20
46 Hubie Brooks .07 .20
47 Jack Morris .10 .30
48 Tim Raines .10 .30
49 Mark Eichhorn .07 .20
50 Kevin Mitchell .10 .30
51 Dwight Gooden .20 .50
52 Doug DeCinces .07 .20
53 Fernando Valenzuela .10 .30
54 Reggie Jackson .20 .50
55 Johnny Ray .07 .20
56 Mike Pagliarulo .07 .20
57 Kirby Puckett .40 1.00
58 Lance Parrish .10 .30
59 Jose Canseco .60 1.50
60 Greg Mathews .07 .20

1987 Topps Rookies

COMPLETE SET (22) 5.00 12.00
ONE PER RETAIL JUMBO PACK
1 Andy Allanson .08 .25
2 John Cangelosi .08 .25
3 Jose Canseco .75 2.00
4 Will Clark 1.00 2.50
5 Mark Eichhorn .08 .25
6 Pete Incaviglia .20 .50
7 Wally Joyner .30 .75
8 Eric King .08 .25
9 Dave Magadan .20 .50
10 John Morris .08 .25
11 Juan Nieves .08 .25
12 Rafael Palmeiro 2.00 5.00
13 Billy Joe Robidoux .08 .25
14 Bruce Ruffin .08 .25
15 Ruben Sierra .40 1.00
16 Cory Snyder .08 .25
17 Kurt Stillwell .08 .25
18 Dale Sveum .08 .25
19 Danny Tartabull .08 .25
20 Andres Thomas .08 .25
21 Robby Thompson .20 .50
22 Todd Worrell .20 .50

1987 Topps Wax Box Cards

COMPLETE SET (8) 1.25 3.00
A Don Baylor .08 .25
B Steve Carlton .30 .75
C Ron Cey .08 .25
D Cecil Cooper .02 .10
E Rickey Henderson .30 .75
F Jim Rice .08 .25
G Don Sutton .30 .75
H Dave Winfield .30 .75

1987 Topps Traded

This 132-card standard-size Traded set was distributed exclusively in factory set form in a special green and white box through hobby dealers. The card fronts are identical in style to the Topps regular issue except for whiter stock and t-suffixed numbering on back. The cards are ordered alphabetically by player's last name. The key extended Rookie Cards in this set are Ellis Burks, David Cone, Greg Maddux, Fred McGriff and Matt Williams.

COMP.FACT.SET (132) 5.00 12.00
1T Bill Almon .01 .05
2T Scott Bankhead .01 .05
3T Eric Bell .02 .10
4T Juan Beniquez .01 .05
5T Juan Berenguer .01 .05
6T Greg Booker .01 .05
7T Thad Bosley .01 .05
8T Larry Bowa MG .02 .10
9T Greg Brock .01 .05
10T Bob Brower .01 .05
11T Jerry Browne .02 .10
12T Ralph Bryant .01 .05
13T DeWayne Buice .01 .05
14T Ellis Burks XRC .20 .50
15T Ivan Calderon .01 .05
16T Jeff Calhoun .01 .05
17T Casey Candaele .01 .05
18T John Cangelosi .01 .05
19T Steve Carlton .02 .10
20T Juan Castillo .02 .10
21T Rick Cerone .01 .05
22T Ron Cey .02 .10
23T John Christensen .01 .05
24T David Cone XRC .30 .75
25T Chuck Crim .01 .05
26T Storm Davis .01 .05
27T Andre Dawson .02 .10
28T Rick Dempsey .01 .05
29T Doug Drabek .20 .50
30T Mike Dunne .01 .05
31T Dennis Eckersley .05 .15
32T Lee Elia MG .01 .05
33T Brian Fisher .01 .05
34T Terry Francona .02 .10
35T Willie Fraser .02 .10
36T Billy Gardner MG .01 .05
37T Ken Gerhart .01 .05
38T Dan Gladden .01 .05
39T Jim Gott .01 .05
40T Cecilio Guante .01 .05
41T Albert Hall .01 .05
42T Terry Harper .01 .05
43T Mickey Hatcher .01 .05
44T Brad Havens .01 .05
45T Neal Heaton .01 .05
46T Mike Henneman XRC .08 .25
47T Donnie Hill .01 .05
48T Guy Hoffman .01 .05
49T Brian Holton .01 .05
50T Charles Hudson .01 .05
51T Danny Jackson .01 .05
52T Reggie Jackson .05 .15
53T Chris James XRC .02 .10
54T Dion James .01 .05
55T Stan Jefferson .01 .05
56T Joe Johnson .01 .05
57T Terry Kennedy .01 .05
58T Mike Kingery .02 .10
59T Ray Knight .02 .10
60T Gene Larkin XRC .08 .25
61T Mike LaValliere .08 .25
62T Jack Lazorko .01 .05
63T Terry Leach .01 .05
64T Tim Leary .01 .05
65T Jim Lindeman .02 .10
66T Steve Lombardozzi .01 .05
67T Bill Long .01 .05
68T Barry Lyons .01 .05
69T Shane Mack .01 .05
70T Greg Maddux XRC 6.00 15.00
71T Bill Madlock .02 .10
72T Joe Magrane XRC .02 .10
73T Dave Martinez XRC .08 .25
74T Fred McGriff .25 .60
75T Mark McLemore .02 .10
76T Kevin McReynolds .01 .05
77T Dave Meads .01 .05
78T Eddie Milner .01 .05
79T Greg Minton .01 .05
80T John Mitchell XRC .02 .10
81T Kevin Mitchell .05 .15
82T Charlie Moore .01 .05
83T Jeff Musselman .01 .05
84T Gene Nelson .01 .05
85T Graig Nettles .02 .10
86T Al Newman .01 .05
87T Reid Nichols .01 .05
88T Tom Niedenfuer .01 .05
89T Joe Niekro .01 .05
90T Tom Nieto .01 .05
91T Matt Nokes XRC .08 .25
92T Dickie Noles .01 .05
93T Pat Pacillo .01 .05
94T Lance Parrish .02 .10
95T Tony Pena .01 .05
96T Luis Polonia XRC .08 .25
97T Randy Ready .01 .05
98T Jeff Reardon .02 .10
99T Gary Redus .01 .05
100T Jeff Reed .01 .05
101T Rick Rhoden .01 .05
102T Cal Ripken Sr. MG .01 .05
103T Wally Ritchie .01 .05
104T Jeff M. Robinson .01 .05
105T Gary Roenicke .01 .05
106T Jerry Royster .01 .05
107T Mark Salas .01 .05
108T Luis Salazar .01 .05
109T Benito Santiago .02 .10
110T Dave Schmidt .01 .05
111T Kevin Seitzer XRC .08 .25
112T John Shelby .01 .05
113T Steve Shields .01 .05
114T John Smiley XRC .08 .25
115T Chris Speier .01 .05
116T Mike Stanley XRC .08 .25
117T Terry Steinbach XRC .20 .50
118T Les Straker .01 .05
119T Jim Sundberg .02 .10
120T Danny Tartabull .01 .05
121T Tom Trebelhorn MG .01 .05
122T Dave Valle XRC .02 .10
123T Ed VandeBerg .01 .05
124T Andy Van Slyke .05 .15
125T Gary Ward .01 .05
126T Alan Wiggins .01 .05
127T Bill Wilkinson .01 .05
128T Frank Williams .01 .05
129T Matt Williams XRC .40 1.00
130T Jim Winn .01 .05
131T Matt Young .01 .05
132T Checklist 1T-132T .01 .05

1987 Topps Traded Tiffany

COMP.FACT.SET (132) 15.00 40.00
*STARS: 1.5X TO 4X BASIC CARDS
*ROOKIES: 2X TO 5X BASIC CARDS
DISTRIBUTED ONLY IN FACTORY SET FORM
FACTORY SET PRICE IS FOR SEALED SETS

1987 Topps Gallery of Champions

These 12 cards, issued in complete set form only, are "metal" versions of regular Topps cards. These 12 players were either 1986 award winners or league leaders. These cards measure approximately 1 14" by 1 3/4" and were issued in aluminum, silver and bronze versions. We have priced the aluminum versions with the bronze valued at 2X to 4X the aluminums and the silvers are 5X to 10X the values listed below. The set is sequenced in alphabetical order.

COMPLETE SET (12) 15.00 40.00
1 Jesse Barfield 1.00 2.50
2 Wade Boggs 2.50 6.00
3 Jose Canseco 2.50 6.00
4 Joe Carter 1.50 4.00
5 Roger Clemens 3.00 8.00
6 Tony Gwynn 3.00 8.00
7 Don Mattingly 3.00 8.00
8 Tim Raines 1.00 2.50
9 Dave Righetti 1.00 2.50
10 Mike Schmidt 2.50 6.00
11 Mike Scott 1.00 2.50
12 Todd Worrell 1.00 2.50

1987 Topps Mini Leaders

The 1987 Topps Mini set of Major League Leaders features 77 cards of leaders of the various statistical categories for the 1986 season. The cards are numbered on the back and measure approximately 2 5/32" by 3". The card backs are printed in orange and brown on white card stock. They are very similar in design to the Team Leader cards in the 1987 Topps regular issue. The cards were distributed as a separate issue in wax packs of seven for 30 cents. Eleven of the cards were double printed and are hence more plentiful; they are marked DP in the checklist below. The order of the set is alphabetical by player's name within team; the teams themselves are ordered alphabetically by city name within each league.

COMPLETE SET (77) 2.00 5.00
COMMON PLAYER (1-77) .02 .05
COMMON DP .02 .05
1 Bob Horner DP .01 .05
2 Dale Murphy .07 .20
3 Lee Smith .05 .15
4 Eric Davis .05 .15
5 John Franco .02 .10
6 Dave Parker .02 .10
7 Kevin Bass .01 .05
8 Glenn Davis DP .01 .05
9 Bill Doran DP .01 .05
10 Bob Knepper DP .01 .05
11 Mike Scott .01 .05
12 Dave Smith .01 .05
13 Mariano Duncan .01 .05
14 Orel Hershiser .02 .10
15 Steve Sax DP .01 .05
16 Fernando Valenzuela .02 .10
17 Tim Raines .02 .10
18 Jeff Reardon .02 .10
19 Floyd Youmans .01 .05
20 Gary Carter DP .15 .40
21 Ron Darling .01 .05
22 Sid Fernandez .01 .05
23 Dwight Gooden .02 .10
24 Keith Hernandez .02 .10
25 Bob Ojeda .01 .05
26 Darryl Strawberry .02 .10
27 Steve Bedrosian .01 .05
28 Von Hayes DP .01 .05
29 Juan Samuel .01 .05
30 Mike Schmidt .20 .50
31 Rick Rhoden .01 .05
32 Vince Coleman .01 .05
33 Danny Cox .01 .05
34 Todd Worrell .02 .10
35 Tony Gwynn .30 .75
36 Mike Krukow .01 .05
37 Candy Maldonado .01 .05
38 Don Aase .01 .05
39 Eddie Murray .15 .40
40 Cal Ripken .60 1.50
41 Wade Boggs .15 .40
42 Roger Clemens .30 .75
43 Bruce Hurst .01 .05
44 Jim Rice .02 .10
45 Wally Joyner .05 .15
46 Donnie Moore .01 .05
47 Gary Pettis .01 .05
48 Mike Witt .01 .05
49 John Cangelosi .01 .05
50 Tom Candiotti .02 .10
51 Joe Carter .05 .15
52 Pat Tabler .01 .05
53 Kirk Gibson DP .02 .10
54 Willie Hernandez .01 .05
55 Jack Morris .02 .10
56 Alan Trammell DP .05 .15
57 George Brett .30 .75
58 Willie Wilson .02 .10
59 Rob Deer .01 .05
60 Teddy Higuera .01 .05
61 Bert Blyleven DP .01 .05
62 Gary Gaetti DP .02 .10
63 Kirby Puckett .20 .50
64 Rickey Henderson .20 .50
65 Don Mattingly .30 .75
66 Dennis Rasmussen .01 .05
67 Dave Righetti .01 .05
68 Jose Canseco .30 .75
69 Dave Kingman .02 .10
70 Phil Bradley .01 .05
71 Mark Langston .01 .05
72 Pete O'Brien .01 .05
73 Jesse Barfield .01 .05
74 George Bell .01 .05
75 Tony Fernandez .02 .10
76 Tom Henke .01 .05
77 Checklist Card .01 .05

1987 Topps Stickers

Made in Italy for Topps and O-Pee-Chee by Panini, these 313 stickers measure approximately 2 1/8" by 3" and are numbered on both front and back. The fronts feature white-bordered color player photos. The horizontal backs carry a bilingual ad for O-Pee-Chee. The Topps stickers contain offers on the back to obtain either a trip for four to Spring Training of the team of your choice or a complete set of Topps baseball cards directly from Topps. An album onto which the stickers could be affixed was available at retail stores. The album and the sticker numbering are organized as follows: 1986 Highlights (1-12), 1986 Championship Series (13-18), 1986 World Series (19-25), Houston Astros (26-35), Atlanta Braves (36-45), St. Louis Cardinals (46-55), Chicago Cubs (56-65), Los Angeles Dodgers (66-75), Montreal Expos (76-85), San Francisco Giants (86-95), New York Mets (96-105), San Diego Padres (106-115), Philadelphia Phillies (116-125), Pittsburgh Pirates (126-135), Cincinnati Reds (136-145), Foil All-Stars (146-163), Oakland A's (164-173), California Angels (174-183), Toronto Blue Jays (184-193), Milwaukee Brewers (194-203), Cleveland Indians (204-213), Seattle Mariners (214-223), Baltimore Orioles (224-233), Texas Rangers (234-243), Boston Red Sox (244-253), Kansas City Royals (254-263), Detroit Tigers (264-273), Minnesota Twins (274-283), Chicago White Sox (284-293), New York Yankees (294-303), and Future Stars (304-313). For those stickers featuring more than one player, the other numbers on that sticker are given below in parentheses. There was a variation of this set that was test-marketed by Topps. Its stickers had card backings (precursors of the Super Stars sticker backs) rather than the paper backing Topps had been using in previous years. Apparently the test was successful as both Topps and O-Pee-Chee switched to the home-printed, stiffer-backed stickers the following year.Will Clark and Barry Bonds are featured on stickers during their Rookie Card Year

COMPLETE SET (313) 6.00 15.00
COMMON PLAYER (1-145) .02 .05
COMMON FOIL (146-163) .04 .10
*OPC: .4X TO 1X TOPPS STICKERS
1 Jim Deshaies (172) .01 .05
2 Roger Clemens (175)/(Top half) .05 .15
3 Roger Clemens (176)/(Bottom half) .05 .15
4 Dwight Evans (177) .02 .10
5 Dwight Gooden (178)/(Top half) .05 .15
6 Dwight Gooden (180)/(Bottom half) .05 .15
7 Dave Lopes (181) .02 .10
8 Dave Righetti (182)/(Top half) .01 .05
9 Dave Righetti (183)/(Bottom half) .01 .05
10 Ruben Sierra (185) .08 .25
11 Todd Worrell (186)/(Top half) .02 .10
12 Todd Worrell (187)/(Bottom half) .02 .10
13 Len Dykstra LCS .05 .15
14 Gary Carter LCS .02 .10
15 Mike Scott LCS .01 .05
16 Gary Pettis LCS .01 .05
17 Jim Rice LCS .02 .10
18 Marty Barrett LCS .01 .05
19 Bruce Hurst WS .01 .05
20 Dwight Evans WS .02 .10
21 Len Dykstra WS .05 .15
22 Gary Carter WS .02 .10
23 Dave Henderson WS .01 .05
24 Ray Knight WS .01 .05
25 Mets Celebrate WS .02 .10
26 Glenn Davis .01 .05
27 Nolan Ryan (188) .75 2.00
28 Charlie Kerfeld(189) .01 .05
29 Jose Cruz (190) .02 .10
30 Phil Garner (191) .02 .10
31 Bill Doran (192) .01 .05
32 Bob Knepper (195) .01 .05
33 Denny Walling (196) .01 .05
34 Kevin Bass (197) .01 .05
35 Mike Scott .01 .05
36 Dale Murphy .08 .25
37 Paul Assenmacher/(198) .05 .15
38 Ken Oberkfell (200) .01 .05
39 Andres Thomas (201) .01 .05
40 Gene Garber (202) .01 .05
41 Bob Horner .01 .05
42 Rafael Ramirez (203) .01 .05
43 Rick Mahler (204) .01 .05
44 Omar Moreno (205) .01 .05
45 Dave Palmer (206) .01 .05
46 Ozzie Smith .15 .40
47 Bob Forsch (207) .01 .05
48 Willie McGee (209) .02 .10
49 Tom Herr (210) .01 .05
50 Vince Coleman (211) .01 .05
51 Andy Van Slyke (212) .02 .10
52 Jack Clark (215) .02 .10
53 John Tudor (216) .01 .05
54 Terry Pendleton(217) .02 .10
55 Todd Worrell .02 .10
56 Lee Smith .05 .15
57 Leon Durham (218) .01 .05
58 Jerry Mumphrey (219) .01 .05
59 Shawon Dunston (220) .01 .05
60 Scott Sanderson(221) .01 .05
61 Ryne Sandberg .20 .50
62 Gary Matthews (222) .01 .05
63 Dennis Eckersley/(225) .08 .25
64 Jody Davis (226) .01 .05
65 Keith Moreland (227) .01 .05
66 Mike Marshall (228) .01 .05
67 Bill Madlock (229) .02 .10
68 Greg Brock (230) .01 .05
69 Pedro Guerrero (231) .01 .05
70 Steve Sax .01 .05
71 Rick Honeycutt (232) .01 .05
72 Franklin Stubbs(235) .01 .05
73 Mike Scioscia (236) .01 .05
74 Mariano Duncan (237) .01 .05
75 Fernando Valenzuela .02 .10
76 Hubie Brooks .01 .05
77 Andre Dawson (238) .08 .25
78 Tim Burke (240) .01 .05
79 Floyd Youmans (241) .01 .05
80 Tim Wallach (242) .01 .05
81 Jeff Reardon (243) .02 .10
82 Mitch Webster (244) .01 .05
83 Bryn Smith (245) .01 .05
84 Andres Galarraga/(246) .20 .50
85 Tim Raines .02 :10
86 Chris Brown .01 .05
87 Bob Brenly (247) .01 .05
88 Will Clark (249) .60 1.50
89 Scott Garrelts (250) .01 .05
90 Jeffrey Leonard(251) .01 .05
91 Robby Thompson (252) .02 .10
92 Mike Krukow (255) .01 .05
93 Danny Gladden (256) .01 .05
94 Candy Maldonado(257) .01 .05
95 Chili Davis .05 .15
96 Dwight Gooden .05 .15
97 Sid Fernandez (258) .01 .05
98 Len Dykstra (259) .05 .15
99 Bob Ojeda (260) .01 .05
100 Wally Backman (261) .01 .05
101 Gary Carter .05 .15
102 Keith Hernandez(262) .02 .10
103 Darryl Strawberry/(265) .05 .15
104 Roger McDowell (266) .01 .05
105 Ron Darling (267) .01 .05
106 Tony Gwynn .30 .75
107 Dave Dravecky (268) .02 .10
108 Terry Kennedy (269) .01 .05
109 Rich Gossage (270) .02 .10
110 Garry Templeton(271) .01 .05
111 Lance McCullers(272) .01 .05
112 Eric Show (275) .01 .05
113 John Kruk (276) .20 .50
114 Tim Flannery (277) .01 .05
115 Steve Garvey .05 .15
116 Mike Schmidt .25 .60
117 Glenn Wilson (278) .01 .05
118 Kent Tekulve (280) .01 .05
119 Gary Redus (281) .01 .05
120 Shane Rawley (282) .01 .05
121 Von Hayes .01 .05
122 Don Carman (283) .01 .05
123 Bruce Ruffin (285) .01 .05
124 Steve Bedrosian(286) .01 .05
125 Juan Samuel (287) .01 .05
126 Sid Bream (288) .01 .05
127 Cecilio Guante (289) .01 .05
128 Rick Reuschel (290) .01 .05
129 Tony Pena (291) .01 .05
130 Rick Rhoden .01 .05
131 Barry Bonds (292) 2.50 6.00
132 Joe Orsulak (295) .01 .05
133 Jim Morrison (296) .01 .05
134 R.J. Reynolds (297) .01 .05
135 Johnny Ray .01 .05
136 Eric Davis .05 .15
137 Tom Browning (298) .01 .05
138 John Franco (300) .02 .10
139 Pete Rose (301) .30 .75
140 Bill Gullickson(302) .01 .05
141 Ron Oester (303) .01 .05
142 Bo Diaz (304) .01 .05
143 Buddy Bell (305) .02 .10
144 Eddie Milner (306) .01 .05
145 Dave Parker .02 .10
146 Kirby Puckett FOIL .40 1.00
147 Rickey Henderson FOIL .15 .40
148 Wade Boggs FOIL .15 .40
149 Lance Parrish FOIL .05 .15
150 Wally Joyner FOIL .30 .75
151 Cal Ripken FOIL 1.25 3.00
152 Dave Winfield FOIL .15 .40
153 Lou Whitaker FOIL .05 .15
154 Roger Clemens FOIL .25 .60
155 Tony Gwynn FOIL .50 1.25
156 Ryne Sandberg FOIL .30 .75
157 Keith Hernandez FOIL .05 .15
158 Gary Carter FOIL .08 .25
159 Darryl Strawberry FOIL .07 .20
160 Mike Schmidt FOIL .40 1.00
161 Dale Murphy FOIL .08 .25
162 Ozzie Smith FOIL .25 .60
163 Dwight Gooden FOIL .08 .25
164 Jose Canseco .40 1.00
165 Curt Young (307) .01 .05
166 Alfredo Griffin(308) .01 .05
167 Dave Stewart (309) .02 .10
168 Mike Davis (310) .01 .05
169 Bruce Bochte (311) .01 .05
170 Dwayne Murphy (312) .01 .05
171 Carney Lansford(313) .02 .10
172 Joaquin Andujar (1) .01 .05
173 Dave Kingman .02 .10
174 Wally Joyner .20 .50
175 Gary Pettis (2) .01 .05
176 Dick Schofield (3) .01 .05
177 Donnie Moore (4) .01 .05
178 Brian Downing (5) .01 .05
179 Mike Witt .01 .05
180 Bob Boone (6) .02 .10
181 Kirk McCaskill (7) .01 .05
182 Doug DeCinces (8) .01 .05
183 Don Sutton (9) .08 .25
184 Jesse Barfield .01 .05
185 Tom Henke (10) .01 .05
186 Willie Upshaw (11) .01 .05
187 Mark Eichhorn (12) .01 .05
188 Damaso Garcia (27) .01 .05
189 Jim Clancy (28) .01 .05
190 Lloyd Moseby (29) .01 .05
191 Tony Fernandez (30) .01 .05
192 Jimmy Key (31) .05 .15
193 George Bell .01 .05
194 Rob Deer .01 .05
195 Mark Clear (32) .01 .05
196 Robin Yount (33) .08 .25
197 Jim Gantner (34) .01 .05
198 Cecil Cooper (35) .02 .10
199 Teddy Higuera .01 .05
200 Paul Molitor (38) .08 .25
201 Dan Plesac (39) .01 .05
202 Billy Joe Robidoux/(40) .01 .05
203 Earnie Riles (42) .01 .05
204 Ken Schrom (43) .01 .05
205 Pat Tabler (44) .01 .05
206 Mel Hall (45) .01 .05
207 Tony Bernazard (47) .01 .05
208 Joe Carter .08 .25
209 Ernie Camacho (48) .01 .05
210 Julio Franco (49) .02 .10
211 Tom Candiotti (50) .01 .05
212 Brook Jacoby (51) .01 .05
213 Cory Snyder .01 .05
214 Jim Presley .01 .05
215 Mike Moore (52) .01 .05
216 Harold Reynolds (53) .02 .10
217 Scott Bradley (54) .01 .05
218 Matt Young (57) .01 .05
219 Mark Langston (58) .02 .10
220 Alvin Davis (59) .01 .05
221 Phil Bradley (60) .01 .05
222 Ken Phelps (62) .01 .05
223 Danny Tartabull .01 .05
224 Eddie Murray .08 .25
225 Rick Dempsey (63) .01 .05
226 Fred Lynn (64) .02 .10
227 Mike Boddicker (65) .01 .05
228 Don Aase (66) .01 .05
229 Larry Sheets (67) .01 .05
230 Storm Davis (68) .01 .05
231 Lee Lacy (69) .01 .05
232 Jim Traber (71) .01 .05
233 Cal Ripken .75 2.00
234 Larry Parrish .01 .05
235 Gary Ward (72) .01 .05
236 Pete Incaviglia (73) .02 .10
237 Scott Fletcher (74) .01 .05
238 Greg Harris (77) .01 .05
239 Pete O'Brien .01 .05
240 Charlie Hough (78) .01 .05
241 Don Slaught (79) .01 .05
242 Steve Buechele (80) .01 .05
243 Oddibe McDowell (81) .01 .05
244 Roger Clemens (82) .15 .40
245 Bob Stanley (83) .01 .05
246 Tom Seaver (84) .20 .50
247 Rich Gedman (87) .01 .05
248 Jim Rice .02 .10
249 Dennis Boyd (88) .01 .05
250 Bill Buckner (89) .02 .10
251 Dwight Evans (90) .02 .10
252 Don Baylor (91) .02 .10
253 Wade Boggs .08 .25
254 George Brett .30 .75
255 Steve Farr (92) .01 .05
256 Jim Sundberg (93) .01 .05
257 Dan Quisenberry (94) .01 .05
258 Charlie Leibrandt(97) .01 .05
259 Angel Salazar (98) .01 .05
260 Frank White (99) .02 .10
261 Willie Wilson (100) .02 .10
262 Lonnie Smith (102) .01 .05
263 Steve Balboni .01 .05
264 Darrell Evans .02 .10
265 Johnny Grubb (103) .01 .05
266 Jack Morris (104) .02 .10
267 Lou Whitaker (105) .02 .10
268 Chet Lemon (107) .01 .05
269 Lance Parrish (108) .02 .10
270 Alan Trammell (109) .05 .15
271 Darnell Coles (110) .01 .05
272 Willie Hernandez/(111) .01 .05
273 Kirk Gibson .02 .10
274 Kirby Puckett .25 .60
275 Mike Smithson (112) .01 .05
276 Mickey Hatcher (113) .01 .05
277 Frank Viola (114) .01 .05
278 Bert Blyleven (117) .02 .10
279 Gary Gaetti .02 .10
280 Tom Brunansky (118) .01 .05
281 Kent Hrbek (119) .02 .10
282 Roy Smalley (120) .01 .05
283 Greg Gagne (122) .01 .05
284 Harold Baines .02 .10
285 Ron Hassey (123) .01 .05
286 Floyd Bannister(124) .01 .05
287 Ozzie Guillen (125) .01 .05
288 Carlton Fisk (126) .08 .25
289 Tim Hulett (127) .01 .05
290 Joe Cowley (128) .01 .05
291 Greg Walker (129) .01 .05
292 Neil Allen (131) .01 .05
293 John Cangelosi .01 .05
294 Don Mattingly .40 1.00
295 Mike Easler (132) .01 .05
296 Rickey Henderson(133) .08 .25
297 Dan Pasqua (134) .01 .05
298 Dave Winfield (137) .08 .25
299 Dave Righetti " .01 .05
300 Mike Pagliarulo(138) .01 .05
301 Ron Guidry (139) .02 .10
302 Willie Randolph(140) .02 .10
303 Dennis Rasmussen/(141) .01 .05
304 Jose Canseco (142) .40 1.00
305 Andres Thomas (143) .01 .05
306 Danny Tartabull(144) .01 .05
307 Robby Thompson (165) .02 .10
308 Pete Incaviglia(166) .02 .10
309 Dale Sveum (167) .01 .05
310 Todd Worrell (168) .02 .10
311 Andy Allanson (169) .01 .05
312 Bruce Ruffin (170) .01 .05
313 Wally Joyner (171) .20 .50
NNO Album .40 1.00

1988 Topps

This set consists of 792 standard-size cards. The cards were primarily issued in 15-card wax packs, 42-card rack packs and factory sets. Card fronts feature white borders encasing a color photo with team name running across the top and player name diagonally across the bottom. Subsets include Record Breakers (1-7), All-Stars (386-407), Turn Back the Clock (661-665), and Team Leaders (scattered throughout the set). The manager cards contain a team checklist on back. The key Rookie Cards in this set are Ellis Burks, Ken Caminiti, Tom Glavine, and Matt Williams.

COMPLETE SET (792) 8.00 20.00
COMP.FACT SET (792) 8.00 20.00
COMP.X-MAS.SET (792) 15.00 40.00
1 Vince Coleman RB .01 .05
2 Don Mattingly RB .10 .30
3 Mark McGwire RB .30 .75
3A Mark McGwire RB .30 .75
4 Eddie Murray RB .05 .15
Switch Home Runs,/Two Straight Games/No caption on front
4A Eddie Murray RB .20 .50
5 Phil Niekro .02 .10
Joe Niekro RB
6 Nolan Ryan RB .15 .40
7 Benito Santiago RB .01 .05
8 Kevin Elster .01 .05
9 Andy Hawkins .01 .05
10 Ryne Sandberg .15 .40
11 Mike Young .01 .05
12 Bill Schroeder .01 .05
13 Andres Thomas .01 .05
14 Sparky Anderson MG .02 .10
15 Chili Davis .02 .10
16 Kirk McCaskill .01 .05
17 Ron Oester .01 .05
18A Al Leiter ERR .20 .50
18B A.Leiter RC COR .20 .50
19 Mark Davidson .01 .05
20 Kevin Gross .01 .05
21 Wade Boggs .02 .10
Spike Owen TL
22 Greg Swindell .01 .05
23 Ken Landreaux .01 .05
24 Jim Deshaies .01 .05
25 Andres Galarraga .02 .10
26 Mitch Williams .01 .05
27 R.J. Reynolds .01 .05
28 Jose Nunez .01 .05
29 Angel Salazar .01 .05
30 Sid Fernandez .01 .05
31 Bruce Bochy .01 .05
32 Mike Morgan .01 .05
33 Rob Deer .01 .05
34 Ricky Horton .01 .05
35 Harold Baines .02 .10
36 Jamie Moyer .02 .10
37 Ed Romero .01 .05
38 Jeff Calhoun .01 .05
39 Gerald Perry .01 .05
40 Orel Hershiser .02 .10
41 Bob Melvin .01 .05
42 Bill Landrum .01 .05
43 Dick Schofield .01 .05
44 Lou Piniella MG .02 .10
45 Kent Hrbek .02 .10
46 Darnell Coles .01 .05
47 Joaquin Andujar .02 .10
48 Alan Ashby .01 .05
49 Dave Clark .01 .05
50 Hubie Brooks .01 .05
51 E.Murray/C.Ripken TL .15 .40
52 Don Robinson .01 .05
53 Curt Wilkerson .01 .05
54 Jim Clancy .01 .05
55 Phil Bradley .01 .05
56 Ed Hearn .01 .05
57 Tim Crews RC .08 .25
58 Dave Magadan .01 .05
59 Danny Cox .01 .05
60 Rickey Henderson .07 .20
61 Mark Knudson .01 .05
62 Jeff Hamilton .01 .05
63 Jimmy Jones .01 .05
64 Ken Caminiti RC .75 2.00
65 Leon Durham .01 .05
66 Shane Rawley .01 .05
67 Ken Oberkfell .01 .05
68 Dave Dravecky .01 .05
69 Mike Hart .01 .05
70 Roger Clemens .40 1.00
71 Gary Pettis .01 .05
72 Dennis Eckersley .05 .15
73 Randy Bush .01 .05
74 Tom Lasorda MG .05 .15
75 Joe Carter .02 .10
76 Dennis Martinez .02 .10
77 Tom O'Malley .01 .05
78 Dan Petry .01 .05
79 Ernie Whitt .01 .05
80 Mark Langston .01 .05
81 Ron Robinson .01 .05
John Franco TL
82 Darrel Akerfelds RC .01 .05
83 Jose Oquendo .01 .05
84 Cecilio Guante .01 .05
85 Howard Johnson .02 .10
86 Ron Karkovice .01 .05
87 Mike Mason .01 .05
88 Earnie Riles .01 .05
89 Gary Thurman RC .01 .05
90 Dale Murphy .05 .15
91 Joey Cora RC .08 .25
92 Len Matuszek .01 .05
93 Bob Sebra .01 .05
94 Chuck Jackson .01 .05
95 Lance Parrish .02 .10
96 Todd Benzinger RC .08 .25
97 Scott Garrelts .01 .05
98 Rene Gonzales RC .02 .10
99 Chuck Finley .02 .10
100 Jack Clark .02 .10
101 Allan Anderson .01 .05
102 Barry Larkin .05 .15
103 Curt Young .01 .05
104 Dick Williams MG .01 .05
105 Jesse Orosco .01 .05
106 Jim Walewander .01 .05
107 Scott Bailes .01 .05
108 Steve Lyons .01 .05
109 Joel Skinner .01 .05
110 Teddy Higuera .01 .05
111 Hubie Brooks .01 .05
Vance Law TL
112 Les Lancaster .01 .05
113 Kelly Gruber .01 .05
114 Jeff Russell .01 .05
115 Johnny Ray .01 .05
116 Jerry Don Gleaton .01 .05
117 James Steels .01 .05
118 Bob Welch .02 .10
119 Robbie Wine .01 .05
120 Kirby Puckett .07 .20
121 Checklist 1-132 .01 .05
122 Tony Bernazard .01 .05
123 Tom Candiotti .01 .05
124 Ray Knight .02 .10
125 Bruce Hurst .01 .05
126 Steve Jeltz .01 .05
127 Jim Gott .01 .05
128 Johnny Grubb .01 .05
129 Greg Minton .01 .05
130 Buddy Bell .02 .10
131 Don Schulze .01 .05
132 Donnie Hill .01 .05
133 Greg Mathews .01 .05
134 Chuck Tanner MG .01 .05
135 Dennis Rasmussen .01 .05
136 Brian Dayett .01 .05
137 Chris Bosio .01 .05
138 Mitch Webster .01 .05
139 Jerry Browne .01 .05
140 Jesse Barfield .02 .10
141 George Brett .07 .20
Bret Saberhagen TL
142 Andy Van Slyke .05 .15
143 Mickey Tettleton .01 .05
144 Don Gordon .01 .05
145 Bill Madlock .02 .10
146 Donell Nixon .01 .05
147 Bill Buckner .02 .10
148 Carmelo Martinez .01 .05
149 Ken Howell .01 .05
150 Eric Davis .02 .10
151 Bob Knepper .01 .05
152 Jody Reed RC .08 .25
153 John Habyan .01 .05
154 Jeff Stone .01 .05
155 Bruce Sutter .02 .10
156 Gary Matthews .02 .10
157 Atlee Hammaker .01 .05
158 Tim Hulett .01 .05
159 Brad Arnsberg .01 .05
160 Willie McGee .02 .10
161 Bryn Smith .01 .05
162 Mark McLemore .01 .05
163 Dale Mohorcic .01 .05
164 Dave Johnson MG .01 .05
165 Robin Yount .10 .30
166 Rick Rodriquez .01 .05
167 Rance Mulliniks .01 .05
168 Barry Jones .01 .05
169 Ross Jones .01 .05
170 Rich Gossage .02 .10
171 Shawon Dunston .01 .05
Manny Trillo TL
172 Lloyd McClendon RC .08 .25
173 Eric Plunk .01 .05
174 Phil Garner .02 .10
175 Kevin Bass .01 .05
176 Jeff Reed .01 .05
177 Frank Tanana .02 .10
178 Dwayne Henry .01 .05
179 Charlie Puleo .01 .05
180 Terry Kennedy .01 .05
181 David Cone .02 .10
182 Ken Phelps .01 .05
183 Tom Lawless .01 .05
184 Ivan Calderon .01 .05
185 Rick Rhoden .01 .05
186 Rafael Palmeiro .15 .40
187 Steve Kiefer .01 .05
188 John Russell .01 .05
189 Wes Gardner .01 .05
190 Candy Maldonado .01 .05
191 John Cerutti .01 .05
192 Devon White .02 .10
193 Brian Fisher .01 .05
194 Tom Kelly MG .01 .05
195 Dan Quisenberry .01 .05
196 Dave Engle .01 .05
197 Lance McCullers .01 .05
198 Franklin Stubbs .01 .05
199 Dave Meads .01 .05
200 Wade Boggs .05 .15
201 Bobby Valentine MG .01 .05
Pete O'Brien/Pete Incaviglia/Steve Buechele TL
202 Glenn Hoffman .01 .05
203 Fred Toliver .01 .05
204 Paul O'Neill .05 .15
205 Nelson Liriano RC .01 .05
206 Domingo Ramos .01 .05
207 John Mitchell RC .02 .10
208 Steve Lake .01 .05
209 Richard Dotson .01 .05
210 Willie Randolph .02 .10
211 Frank DiPino .01 .05
212 Greg Brock .01 .05
213 Albert Hall .01 .05
214 Dave Schmidt .01 .05
215 Von Hayes .01 .05
216 Jerry Reuss .01 .05

217 Harry Spilman .01 .05
218 Dan Schatzeder .01 .05
219 Mike Stanley .01 .05
220 Tom Henke .01 .05
221 Rafael Belliard .01 .05
222 Steve Farr .01 .05
223 Stan Jefferson .01 .05
224 Tom Trebelhorn MG .01 .05
225 Mike Scioscia .02 .10
226 Dave Lopes .02 .10
227 Ed Correa .01 .05
228 Wallace Johnson .01 .05
229 Jeff Musselman .01 .05
230 Pat Tabler .01 .05
231 B.Bonds/B.Bonilla .40 1.00
232 Bob James .01 .05
233 Rafael Santana .01 .05
234 Ken Dayley .01 .05
235 Gary Ward .01 .05
236 Ted Power .01 .05
237 Mike Heath .01 .05
238 Luis Polonia RC .08 .25
239 Roy Smalley .01 .05
240 Lee Smith .02 .10
241 Damaso Garcia .01 .05
242 Tom Niedenfuer .01 .05
243 Mark Ryal .01 .05
244 Jeff D. Robinson .01 .05
245 Rich Gedman .01 .05
246 Mike Campbell RC .01 .05
247 Thad Bosley .01 .05
248 Storm Davis .01 .05
249 Mike Marshall .01 .05
250 Nolan Ryan .40 1.00
251 Tom Foley .01 .05
252 Bob Brower .01 .05
253 Checklist 133-264 .01 .05
254 Lee Elia MG .01 .05
255 Mookie Wilson .02 .10
256 Ken Schrom .01 .05
257 Jerry Royster .01 .05
258 Ed Nunez .01 .05
259 Ron Kittle .01 .05
260 Vince Coleman .01 .05
261 Giants TL .01 .05
Five players
262 Drew Hall .01 .05
263 Glenn Braggs .01 .05
264 Les Straker .01 .05
265 Bo Diaz .01 .05
266 Paul Assenmacher .01 .05
267 Billy Bean RC .02 .10
268 Bruce Ruffin .01 .05
269 Ellis Burks RC .15 .40
270 Mike Witt .01 .05
271 Ken Gerhart .01 .05
272 Steve Ontiveros .01 .05
273 Garth Iorg .01 .05
274 Junior Ortiz .01 .05
275 Kevin Seitzer .01 .05
276 Luis Salazar .01 .05
277 Alejandro Pena .01 .05
278 Jose Cruz .02 .10
279 Randy St.Claire .01 .05
280 Pete Incaviglia .01 .05
281 Jerry Hairston .01 .05
282 Pat Perry .01 .05
283 Phil Lombardi .01 .05
284 Larry Bowa MG .02 .10
285 Jim Presley .01 .05
286 Chuck Crim .01 .05
287 Manny Trillo .01 .05
288 Pat Pacillo .01 .05
289 Dave Bergman .01 .05
290 Tony Fernandez .01 .05
291 Billy Hatcher .01 .05
Kevin Bass TL
292 Carney Lansford .02 .10
293 Doug Jones RC .08 .25
294 Al Pedrique .01 .05
295 Bert Blyleven .02 .10
296 Floyd Rayford .01 .05
297 Zane Smith .01 .05
298 Milt Thompson .01 .05
299 Steve Crawford .01 .05
300 Don Mattingly .25 .60
301 Bud Black .01 .05
302 Jose Uribe .01 .05
303 Eric Show .01 .05
304 George Hendrick .02 .10
305 Steve Sax .01 .05
306 Billy Hatcher .01 .05
307 Mike Trujillo .01 .05
308 Lee Mazzilli .02 .10
309 Bill Long .01 .05
310 Tom Herr .01 .05
311 Scott Sanderson .01 .05
312 Joey Meyer .01 .05
313 Bob McClure .01 .05
314 Jimy Williams MG .01 .05
315 Dave Parker .02 .10
316 Jose Rijo .02 .10
317 Tom Nieto .01 .05
318 Mel Hall .01 .05
319 Mike Loynd .01 .05
320 Alan Trammell .02 .10
321 Harold Baines .02 .10
Carlton Fisk TL
322 Vicente Palacios RC .01 .05
323 Rick Leach .01 .05
324 Danny Jackson .01 .05
325 Glenn Hubbard .01 .05
326 Al Nipper .01 .05
327 Larry Sheets .01 .05
328 Greg Cadaret .01 .05
329 Chris Speier .01 .05
330 Eddie Whitson .01 .05
331 Brian Downing .02 .10
332 Jerry Reed .01 .05
333 Wally Backman .01 .05
334 Dave LaPoint .01 .05
335 Claudell Washington .01 .05
336 Ed Lynch .01 .05
337 Jim Gantner .01 .05
338 Brian Holton UER .01 .05
1987 ERA .389,should be 3.89
339 Kurt Stillwell .01 .05
340 Jack Morris .02 .10
341 Carmen Castillo .01 .05
342 Larry Andersen .01 .05
343 Greg Gagne .01 .05
344 Tony LaRussa MG .02 .10
345 Scott Fletcher .01 .05
346 Vance Law .01 .05
347 Joe Johnson .01 .05
348 Jim Eisenreich .01 .05
349 Bob Walk .01 .05
350 Will Clark .07 .20
351 Red Schoendienst CO .02 .10
Tony Pena TL
352 Bill Ripken RC .01 .05
353 Ed Olwine .01 .05
354 Marc Sullivan .01 .05
355 Roger McDowell .01 .05
356 Luis Aguayo .01 .05
357 Floyd Bannister .01 .05
358 Rey Quinones .01 .05
359 Tim Stoddard .01 .05
360 Tony Gwynn .10 .30
361 Greg Maddux .40 1.00
362 Juan Castillo .01 .05
363 Willie Fraser .01 .05
364 Nick Esasky .01 .05
365 Floyd Youmans .01 .05
366 Chet Lemon .02 .10
367 Tim Leary .01 .05
368 Gerald Young .01 .05
369 Greg Harris .01 .05
370 Jose Canseco .20 .50
371 Joe Hesketh .01 .05
372 Matt Williams RC .30 .75
373 Checklist 265-396 .01 .05
374 Doc Edwards MG .01 .05
375 Tom Brunansky .01 .05
376 Bill Wilkinson .01 .05
377 Sam Horn RC .02 .10
378 Todd Frohwirth .01 .05
379 Rafael Ramirez .01 .05
380 Joe Magrane RC .02 .10
381 Wally Joyner .02 .10
Jack Howell TL
382 Keith A. Miller RC .08 .25
383 Eric Bell .01 .05
384 Neil Allen .01 .05
385 Carlton Fisk .05 .15
386 Don Mattingly AS .10 .30
387 Willie Randolph AS .01 .05
388 Wade Boggs AS .02 .10
389 Alan Trammell AS .01 .05
390 George Bell AS .01 .05
391 Kirby Puckett AS .05 .15
392 Dave Winfield AS .01 .05
393 Matt Nokes AS .01 .05
394 Roger Clemens AS .20 .50
395 Jimmy Key AS .01 .05
396 Tom Henke AS .01 .05
397 Jack Clark AS .01 .05
398 Juan Samuel AS .01 .05
399 Tim Wallach AS .01 .05
400 Ozzie Smith AS .07 .20
401 Andre Dawson AS .01 .05
402 Tony Gwynn AS .05 .15
403 Tim Raines AS .01 .05
404 Benny Santiago AS .01 .05
405 Dwight Gooden AS .01 .05
406 Shane Rawley AS .01 .05
407 Steve Bedrosian AS .01 .05
408 Dion James .01 .05
409 Joel McKeon .01 .05
410 Tony Pena .01 .05
411 Wayne Tolleson .01 .05
412 Randy Myers .02 .10
413 John Christensen .01 .05
414 John McNamara MG .01 .05
415 Don Carman .01 .05
416 Keith Moreland .01 .05
417 Mark Ciardi .01 .05
418 Joel Youngblood .01 .05
419 Scott McGregor .01 .05
420 Wally Joyner .02 .10
421 Ed VandeBerg .01 .05
422 Dave Concepcion .02 .10
423 John Smiley RC .08 .25
424 Dwayne Murphy .01 .05
425 Jeff Reardon .02 .10
426 Randy Ready .01 .05
427 Paul Kilgus .01 .05
428 John Shelby .01 .05
429 Alan Trammell .02 .10
Kirk Gibson TL
430 Glenn Davis .01 .05
431 Casey Candaele .01 .05
432 Mike Moore .01 .05
433 Bill Pecota RC .01 .05
434 Rick Aguilera .01 .05
435 Mike Pagliarulo .01 .05
436 Mike Bielecki .01 .05
437 Fred Manrique .01 .05
438 Rob Ducey RC .01 .05
439 Dave Martinez .01 .05
440 Steve Bedrosian .01 .05
441 Rick Manning .01 .05
442 Tom Bolton .01 .05
443 Ken Griffey .02 .10
444 Cal Ripken Sr. MG UER .01 .05
two copyrights
445 Mike Krukow .01 .05
446 Doug DeCinces .01 .05
Now with Cardinals/on card front
447 Jeff Montgomery RC .08 .25
448 Mike Davis .01 .05
449 Jeff M. Robinson .01 .05
450 Barry Bonds .75 2.00
451 Keith Atherton .01 .05
452 Willie Wilson .02 .10
453 Dennis Powell .01 .05
454 Marvell Wynne .01 .05
455 Shawn Hillegas RC .01 .05
456 Dave Anderson .01 .05
457 Terry Leach .01 .05
458 Ron Hassey .01 .05
459 Dave Winfield .02 .10
Willie Randolph TL
460 Ozzie Smith .10 .30
461 Danny Darwin .01 .05
462 Don Slaught .01 .05
463 Fred McGriff .07 .20
464 Jay Tibbs .01 .05
465 Paul Molitor .02 .10
466 Jerry Mumphrey .02 .10
467 Don Aase .01 .05
468 Darren Daulton .02 .10
469 Jeff Dedmon .01 .05
470 Dwight Evans .05 .15
471 Donnie Moore .01 .05
472 Robby Thompson .01 .05
473 Joe Niekro .01 .05
474 Tom Brookens .01 .05
475 Pete Rose MG .20 .50
476 Dave Stewart .02 .10
477 Jamie Quirk .01 .05
478 Sid Bream .01 .05
479 Brett Butler .02 .10
480 Dwight Gooden .02 .10
481 Mariano Duncan .01 .05
482 Mark Davis .01 .05
483 Rod Booker .01 .05
484 Pat Clements .01 .05
485 Harold Reynolds .02 .10
486 Pat Keedy .01 .05
487 Jim Pankovits .01 .05
488 Andy McGaffigan .01 .05
489 Pedro Guerrero .01 .05
Fernando Valenzuela TL
490 Larry Parrish .01 .05
491 B.J. Surhoff .02 .10
492 Doyle Alexander .01 .05
493 Mike Greenwell .01 .05
494 Wally Ritchie .01 .05
495 Eddie Murray .07 .20
496 Guy Hoffman .01 .05
497 Kevin Mitchell .02 .10
498 Bob Boone .02 .10
499 Eric King .01 .05
500 Andre Dawson .02 .10
501 Tim Birtsas .01 .05
502 Dan Gladden .01 .05
503 Junior Noboa .01 .05
504 Bob Rodgers MG .01 .05
505 Willie Upshaw .01 .05
506 John Cangelosi .01 .05
507 Mark Gubicza .01 .05
508 Tim Teufel .01 .05
509 Bill Dawley .01 .05
510 Dave Winfield .02 .10
511 Joel Davis .01 .05
512 Alex Trevino .01 .05
513 Tim Flannery .01 .05
514 Pat Sheridan .01 .05
515 Juan Nieves .01 .05
516 Jim Sundberg .02 .10
517 Ron Robinson .01 .05
518 Greg Gross .01 .05
519 Harold Reynolds .01 .05
Phil Bradley TL
520 Dave Smith .01 .05
521 Jim Dwyer .01 .05
522 Bob Patterson .01 .05
523 Gary Roenicke .01 .05
524 Gary Lucas .01 .05
525 Marty Barrett .01 .05
526 Juan Berenguer .01 .05
527 Steve Henderson .01 .05
528A Checklist 397-528 .05 .15
ERR 455 S. Carlton
528B Checklist 397-528 .02 .10
COR 455 S. Hillegas
529 Tim Burke .01 .05
530 Gary Carter .02 .10
531 Rich Yett .01 .05
532 Mike Kingery .01 .05
533 John Farrell RC .02 .10
534 John Wathan MG .01 .05
535 Ron Guidry .02 .10
536 John Morris .01 .05
537 Steve Buechele .01 .05
538 Bill Wegman .01 .05
539 Mike LaValliere .01 .05
540 Bret Saberhagen .02 .10
541 Juan Beniquez .01 .05
542 Paul Noce .01 .05
543 Kent Tekulve .01 .05
544 Jim Traber .01 .05
545 Don Baylor .02 .10
546 John Candelaria .01 .05
547 Felix Fermin .01 .05
548 Shane Mack .01 .05
549 Albert Hall .02 .10
Dale Murphy/Ken Griffey/Dion James TL
550 Pedro Guerrero .02 .10
551 Terry Steinbach .02 .10
552 Mark Thurmond .01 .05
553 Tracy Jones .01 .05
554 Mike Smithson .01 .05
555 Brook Jacoby .01 .05
556 Stan Clarke .01 .05
557 Craig Reynolds .01 .05
558 Bob Ojeda .01 .05
559 Ken Williams RC .01 .05
560 Tim Wallach .01 .05
561 Rick Cerone .01 .05
562 Jim Lindeman .01 .05
563 Jose Guzman .01 .05
564 Frank Lucchesi MG .01 .05
565 Lloyd Moseby .01 .05
566 Charlie O'Brien RC .01 .05
567 Mike Diaz .01 .05
568 Chris Brown .01 .05
569 Charlie Leibrandt .01 .05
570 Jeffrey Leonard .01 .05
571 Mark Williamson .01 .05
572 Chris James .01 .05
573 Bob Stanley .01 .05
574 Graig Nettles .02 .10
575 Don Sutton .02 .10
576 Tommy Hinzo .01 .05
577 Tom Browning .01 .05
578 Gary Gaetti .02 .10
579 Gary Carter .01 .05
Kevin McReynolds TL
580 Mark McGwire .60 1.50
581 Tito Landrum .01 .05
582 Mike Henneman RC .08 .25
583 Dave Valle .01 .05
584 Steve Trout .01 .05
585 Ozzie Guillen .02 .10
586 Bob Forsch .01 .05
587 Terry Puhl .01 .05
588 Jeff Parrett .01 .05
589 Geno Petralli .01 .05
590 George Bell .02 .10
591 Doug Drabek .01 .05
592 Dale Sveum .01 .05
593 Bob Tewksbury .01 .05
594 Bobby Valentine MG .02 .10
595 Frank White .02 .10
596 John Kruk .02 .10
597 Gene Garber .01 .05
598 Lee Lacy .01 .05
599 Calvin Schiraldi .01 .05
600 Mike Schmidt .20 .50
601 Jack Lazorko .01 .05
602 Mike Aldrete .01 .05
603 Rob Murphy .01 .05
604 Chris Bando .01 .05
605 Kirk Gibson .07 .20
606 Moose Haas .01 .05
607 Mickey Hatcher .01 .05
608 Charlie Kerfeld .01 .05
609 Gary Gaetti .02 .10
Kent Hrbek TL
610 Keith Hernandez .02 .10
611 Tommy John .02 .10
612 Curt Ford .01 .05
613 Bobby Thigpen .01 .05
614 Herm Winningham .01 .05
615 Jody Davis .01 .05
616 Jay Aldrich .01 .05
617 Oddibe McDowell .01 .05
618 Cecil Fielder .02 .10
619 Mike Dunne .01 .05
Inconsistent design,/black name on front
620 Cory Snyder .01 .05
621 Gene Nelson .01 .05
622 Kal Daniels .01 .05
623 Mike Flanagan .01 .05
624 Jim Leyland MG .02 .10
625 Frank Viola .02 .10
626 Glenn Wilson .01 .05
627 Joe Boever .01 .05
628 Dave Henderson .01 .05
629 Kelly Downs .01 .05
630 Darrell Evans .02 .10
631 Jack Howell .01 .05
632 Steve Shields .01 .05
633 Barry Lyons .01 .05
634 Jose DeLeon .01 .05
635 Terry Pendleton .02 .10
636 Charles Hudson .01 .05
637 Jay Bell RC .15 .40
638 Steve Balboni .01 .05
639 Glenn Braggs .01 .05
Tony Muser CO TL
640 Garry Templeton .02 .10
Inconsistent design,/green border
641 Rick Honeycutt .01 .05
642 Bob Dernier .01 .05
643 Rocky Childress .01 .05
644 Terry McGriff .01 .05
645 Matt Nokes RC .08 .25
646 Checklist 529-660 .01 .05
647 Pascual Perez .01 .05
648 Al Newman .01 .05
649 DeWayne Buice .01 .05
650 Cal Ripken .30 .75
651 Mike Jackson RC .08 .25
652 Bruce Benedict .01 .05
653 Jeff Sellers .01 .05
654 Roger Craig MG .02 .10
655 Len Dykstra .02 .10
656 Lee Guetterman .01 .05
657 Gary Redus .01 .05
658 Tim Conroy .01 .05
Inconsistent design,/name in white
659 Bobby Meacham .01 .05
660 Rick Reuschel .02 .10
661 Nolan Ryan TBC '83 .20 .50
662 Jim Rice TBC .01 .05
663 Ron Blomberg TBC .01 .05
664 Bob Gibson TBC '68 .08 .25
665 Stan Musial TBC '63 .07 .20
666 Mario Soto .02 .10
667 Luis Quinones .01 .05
668 Walt Terrell .01 .05
669 Lance Parrish .01 .05
Mike Ryan CO TL
670 Dan Plesac .01 .05
671 Tim Laudner .01 .05
672 John Davis RC .01 .05
673 Tony Phillips .01 .05
674 Mike Fitzgerald .01 .05
675 Jim Rice .02 .10
676 Ken Dixon .01 .05
677 Eddie Milner .01 .05
678 Jim Acker .01 .05
679 Darrell Miller .01 .05
680 Charlie Hough .02 .10
681 Bobby Bonilla .02 .10
682 Jimmy Key .02 .10
683 Julio Franco .02 .10
684 Hal Lanier MG .01 .05
685 Ron Darling .02 .10
686 Terry Francona .02 .10
687 Mickey Brantley .01 .05
688 Jim Winn .01 .05
689 Tom Pagnozzi RC .02 .10
690 Jay Howell .01 .05
691 Dan Pasqua .01 .05
692 Mike Birkbeck .01 .05
693 Benito Santiago .02 .10
694 Eric Nolte .01 .05
695 Shawon Dunston .02 .10
696 Duane Ward .01 .05
697 Steve Lombardozzi .01 .05
698 Brad Havens .01 .05
699 Benito Santiago .02 .10
Tony Gwynn TL
700 George Brett .20 .50
701 Sammy Stewart .01 .05
702 Mike Gallego .01 .05
703 Bob Brenly .01 .05
704 Dennis Boyd .01 .05
705 Juan Samuel .01 .05
706 Rick Mahler .01 .05
707 Fred Lynn .02 .10
708 Gus Polidor .01 .05
709 George Frazier .01 .05
710 Darryl Strawberry .02 .10
711 Bill Gullickson .01 .05
712 John Moses .01 .05
713 Willie Hernandez .01 .05
714 Jim Fregosi MG .01 .05
715 Todd Worrell .01 .05
716 Lenn Sakata .01 .05
717 Jay Baller .01 .05
718 Mike Felder .01 .05
719 Denny Walling .01 .05
720 Tim Raines .02 .10
721 Pete O'Brien .01 .05
722 Manny Lee .01 .05
723 Bob Kipper .01 .05
724 Danny Tartabull .01 .05
725 Mike Boddicker .01 .05
726 Alfredo Griffin .01 .05
727 Greg Booker .01 .05
728 Andy Allanson .01 .05
729 George Bell .02 .10
Fred McGriff TL
730 John Franco .02 .10
731 Rick Schu .01 .05
732 David Palmer .01 .05
733 Spike Owen .01 .05
734 Craig Lefferts .01 .05
735 Kevin McReynolds .01 .05
736 Matt Young .01 .05
737 Butch Wynegar .01 .05
738 Scott Bankhead .01 .05
739 Daryl Boston .01 .05
740 Rick Sutcliffe .02 .10
741 Mike Easler .01 .05
742 Mark Clear .01 .05
743 Larry Herndon .01 .05
744 Whitey Herzog MG .02 .10
745 Bill Doran .01 .05
746 Gene Larkin RC .08 .25
747 Bobby Witt .01 .05
748 Reid Nichols .01 .05
749 Mark Eichhorn .01 .05
750 Bo Jackson .07 .20
751 Jim Morrison .01 .05
752 Mark Grant .01 .05
753 Danny Heep .01 .05
754 Mike LaCoss .01 .05
755 Ozzie Virgil .01 .05
756 Mike Maddux .01 .05
757 John Marzano .01 .05
758 Eddie Williams RC .02 .10
759 McGwire/Canseco TL UER .40 1.00
760 Mike Scott .01 .05
761 Tony Armas .02 .10
762 Scott Bradley .01 .05
763 Doug Sisk .01 .05
764 Greg Walker .01 .05
765 Neal Heaton .01 .05
766 Henry Cotto .01 .05
767 Jose Lind RC .08 .25
768 Dickie Noles .01 .05
Now with Tigers/on card front
769 Cecil Cooper .02 .10
770 Lou Whitaker .02 .10
771 Ruben Sierra .02 .10
772 Sal Butera .01 .05
773 Frank Williams .01 .05
774 Gene Mauch MG .02 .10
775 Dave Stieb .02 .10
776 Checklist 661-792 .01 .05
777 Lonnie Smith .01 .05
778A Keith Comstock ERR .75 2.00
778B Keith Comstock COR .01 .05
Blue Padres
779 Tom Glavine RC 1.25 3.00
780 Fernando Valenzuela .02 .10
781 Keith Hughes RC .01 .05
782 Jeff Ballard RC .01 .05
783 Ron Roenicke .01 .05
784 Joe Sambito .01 .05
785 Alvin Davis .01 .05
786 Joe Price .01 .05
Inconsistent design,/orange team name
787 Bill Almon .01 .05
788 Ray Searage .01 .05
789 Joe Carter .01 .05
Cory Snyder TL
790 Dave Righetti .02 .10
791 Ted Simmons .02 .10
792 John Tudor .02 .10

1988 Topps Tiffany

COMP.FACT.SET (792) 30.00 80.00
*STARS: 4X TO 10X BASIC CARDS
*ROOKIES: 3X TO 8X BASIC CARDS
DISTRIBUTED ONLY IN FACTORY SET FORM
FACTORY SET PRICE IS FOR SEALED SETS

1988 Topps Glossy All-Stars

COMPLETE SET (22) 1.50 4.00
1 John McNamara MG .01 .05
2 Don Mattingly .40 1.00
3 Willie Randolph .02 .10
4 Wade Boggs .20 .50
5 Cal Ripken .75 2.00
6 George Bell .01 .05
7 Rickey Henderson .30 .75
8 Dave Winfield .15 .40
9 Terry Kennedy .01 .05
10 Bret Saberhagen .01 .05
11 Jim Hunter CAPT .08 .25
12 Dave Johnson MG .01 .05
13 Jack Clark .02 .10
14 Ryne Sandberg .40 1.00
15 Mike Schmidt .20 .50
16 Ozzie Smith .40 1.00
17 Eric Davis .02 .10
18 Andre Dawson .07 .20
19 Darryl Strawberry .02 .10
20 Gary Carter .15 .40
21 Mike Scott .01 .05
22 Billy Williams CAPT .08 .25

1988 Topps Glossy Send-Ins

COMPLETE SET (60) 4.00 10.00
1 Andre Dawson .15 .40
2 Jesse Barfield .02 .10
3 Mike Schmidt .40 1.00
4 Ruben Sierra .07 .20
5 Mike Scott .02 .10
6 Cal Ripken 1.50 4.00
7 Gary Carter .30 .75
8 Kent Hrbek .07 .20
9 Kevin Seitzer .02 .10
10 Mike Henneman .07 .20
11 Don Mattingly .75 2.00
12 Tim Raines .07 .20
13 Roger Clemens .75 2.00
14 Ryne Sandberg .60 1.50
15 Tony Fernandez .07 .20
16 Eric Davis .07 .20
17 Jack Morris .07 .20
18 Tim Wallach .02 .10
19 Mike Dunne .02 .10
20 Mike Greenwell .02 .10
21 Dwight Evans .07 .20
22 Darryl Strawberry .07 .20
23 Cory Snyder .02 .10
24 Pedro Guerrero .02 .10
25 Rickey Henderson .40 1.25
26 Dale Murphy .15 .40
27 Kirby Puckett .40 1.00
28 Steve Bedrosian .02 .10
29 Devon White .07 .20
30 Benito Santiago .07 .20
31 George Bell .02 .10
32 Keith Hernandez .07 .20
33 Dave Stewart .07 .20
34 Dave Parker .07 .20
35 Tom Henke .02 .10
36 Willie McGee .07 .20
37 Alan Trammell .10 .30
38 Tony Gwynn .75 2.00
39 Mark McGwire .75 2.00
40 Joe Magrane .02 .10
41 Jack Clark .07 .20
42 Willie Randolph .07 .20
43 Juan Samuel .02 .10
44 Joe Carter .10 .30
45 Shane Rawley .02 .10
46 Dave Winfield .20 .50
47 Ozzie Smith .75 2.00
48 Wally Joyner .07 .20
49 B.J. Surhoff .07 .20
50 Ellis Burks .30 .75
51 Wade Boggs .30 .75
52 Howard Johnson .02 .10
53 George Brett .75 2.00
54 Dwight Gooden .07 .20
55 Jose Canseco .40 1.00
56 Lee Smith .07 .20
57 Paul Molitor .30 .75
58 Andres Galarraga .15 .40
59 Matt Nokes .02 .10
60 Casey Candaele .02 .10

1988 Topps Rookies

COMPLETE SET (22) 10.00 25.00
ONE PER RETAIL JUMBO PACK
1 Bill Ripken .08 .25
2 Ellis Burks .40 1.00
3 Mike Greenwell .08 .25
4 DeWayne Buice .08 .25
5 Devon White .20 .50
6 Fred Manrique .08 .25
7 Mike Henneman .20 .50
8 Matt Nokes .08 .25
9 Kevin Seitzer .20 .50
10 B.J. Surhoff .20 .50
11 Casey Candaele .08 .25
12 Randy Myers .30 .75
13 Mark McGwire 6.00 15.00
14 Luis Polonia .08 .25
15 Terry Steinbach .20 .50
16 Mike Dunne .08 .25
17 Al Pedrique .08 .25
18 Benito Santiago .20 .50
19 Kelly Downs .08 .25
20 Joe Magrane .08 .25
21 Jerry Browne .08 .25
22 Jeff Musselman .08 .25

1988 Topps Wax Box Cards

COMPLETE SET (16) 2.00 5.00
A Don Baylor .07 .20
B Steve Bedrosian .02 .10
C Juan Beniquez .02 .10
D Bob Boone .07 .20
E Darrell Evans .07 .20
F Tony Gwynn .50 1.25
G John Kruk .07 .20
H Marvell Wynne .02 .10
I Joe Carter .15 .40
J Eric Davis .07 .20
K Howard Johnson .02 .10
L Darryl Strawberry .07 .20
M Rickey Henderson .40 1.00
N Nolan Ryan 1.00 2.50
O Mike Schmidt .30 .75
P Kent Tekulve .02 .10

1988 Topps Traded

This standard-size 132-card Traded set was distributed exclusively in factory set form in blue and white taped boxes through hobby dealers. The cards are identical in style to the Topps regular issue except for whiter stock and t-suffixed numbering on back. Cards are ordered alphabetically by player's last name. This set generated additional interest upon release due to the inclusion of members of the 1988 U.S. Olympic baseball team. These Olympians are indicated in the checklist below by OLY. The key extended Rookie Cards in this set are Jim Abbott, Roberto Alomar, Brady Anderson, Andy Benes, Jay Buhner, Ron Gant, Mark Grace, Tino Martinez, Charles Nagy, Robin Ventura and Walt Weiss.

COMP.FACT.SET (132) 3.00 8.00
1T Jim Abbott OLY XRC .75 2.00
2T Juan Agosto .02 .10
3T Luis Alicea XRC .20 .50
4T Roberto Alomar XRC .75 2.00
5T Brady Anderson XRC .30 .75
6T Jack Armstrong XRC .20 .50
7T Don August .02 .10
8T Floyd Bannister .02 .10
9T Bret Barberie OLY XRC .08 .25
10T Jose Bautista XRC .08 .25
11T Don Baylor .07 .20
12T Tim Belcher .02 .10
13T Buddy Bell .07 .20
14T Andy Benes OLY XRC .30 .75
15T Damon Berryhill XRC* .20 .50
16T Bud Black .02 .10
17T Pat Borders XRC .20 .50
18T Phil Bradley .02 .10
19T Jeff Branson XRC OLY .20 .50
20T Tom Brunansky .02 .10
21T Jay Buhner XRC .40 1.00
22T Brett Butler .07 .20
23T Jim Campanis OLY XRC .02 .10
24T Sil Campusano .02 .10
25T John Candelaria .02 .10
26T Jose Cecena .02 .10
27T Rick Cerone .02 .10
28T Jack Clark .07 .20
29T Kevin Coffman .02 .10
30T Pat Combs OLY XRC .08 .25
31T Henry Cotto .02 .10
32T Chili Davis .07 .20
33T Mike Davis .02 .10
34T Jose DeLeon .02 .10
35T Richard Dotson .02 .10
36T Cecil Espy XRC .02 .10
37T Tom Filer .02 .10
38T Mike Fiore OLY .02 .10
39T Ron Gant XRC .30 .75
40T Kirk Gibson .20 .50
41T Rich Gossage .07 .20
42T Mark Grace XRC .75 2.00
43T Alfredo Griffin .02 .10
44T Ty Griffin OLY .02 .10
45T Bryan Harvey XRC .20 .50
46T Ron Hassey .02 .10
47T Ray Hayward .02 .10
48T Dave Henderson .02 .10
49T Tom Herr .02 .10
50T Bob Horner .07 .20
51T Ricky Horton .02 .10
52T Jay Howell .02 .10
53T Glenn Hubbard .02 .10
54T Jeff Innis .02 .10
55T Danny Jackson .02 .10
56T Darrin Jackson XRC .08 .25
57T Roberto Kelly XRC .20 .50
58T Ron Kittle .02 .10
59T Ray Knight .07 .20
60T Vance Law .02 .10
61T Jeffrey Leonard .02 .10
62T Mike Macfarlane XRC .20 .50
63T Scotti Madison .02 .10
64T Kirt Manwaring .02 .10
65T Mark Marquess OLY CO .02 .10
66T Tino Martinez OLY XRC 1.25 3.00
67T Billy Masse OLY XRC .08 .25
68T Jack McDowell XRC .30 .75
69T Jack McKeon MG .07 .20
70T Larry McWilliams .02 .10
71T Mickey Morandini OLY XRC .20 .50
72T Keith Moreland .02 .10
73T Mike Morgan .02 .10
74T Charles Nagy OLY XRC .20 .50
75T Al Nipper .02 .10
76T Russ Nixon MG .02 .10
77T Jesse Orosco .02 .10
78T Joe Orsulak .02 .10
79T Dave Palmer .02 .10
80T Mark Parent XRC .02 .10
81T Dave Parker .07 .20
82T Dan Pasqua .02 .10
83T Melido Perez XRC .20 .50
84T Steve Peters .02 .10
85T Dan Petry .02 .10
86T Gary Pettis .02 .10
87T Jeff Pico .02 .10
88T Jim Poole OLY XRC .08 .25
89T Ted Power .02 .10
90T Rafael Ramirez .02 .10
91T Dennis Rasmussen .02 .10
92T Jose Rijo .07 .20
93T Ernie Riles .02 .10
94T Luis Rivera .02 .10
95T Doug Robbins OLY XRC .08 .25
96T Frank Robinson MG .10 .30
97T Cookie Rojas MG .02 .10
98T Chris Sabo XRC .30 .75
99T Mark Salas .02 .10
100T Luis Salazar .02 .10
101T Rafael Santana .02 .10
102T Nelson Santovenia .02 .10
103T Mackey Sasser XRC .20 .50
104T Calvin Schiraldi .02 .10
105T Mike Schooler .02 .10
106T Scott Servais OLY XRC .20 .50
107T Dave Silvestri OLY XRC .08 .25
108T Don Slaught .02 .10
109T Joe Slusarski OLY XRC .08 .25
110T Lee Smith .07 .20
111T Pete Smith XRC .08 .25
112T Jim Snyder MG .02 .10
113T Ed Sprague OLY XRC .20 .50
114T Pete Stanicek RC .02 .10
115T Kurt Stillwell .02 .10
116T Todd Stottlemyre XRC .20 .50
117T Bill Swift .02 .10
118T Pat Tabler .02 .10
119T Scott Terry .02 .10
120T Mickey Tettleton .02 .10
121T Dickie Thon .02 .10

122T Jeff Treadway XRC .20 .50
123T Willie Upshaw .02 .10
124T Robin Ventura OLY XRC .60 1.50
125T Ron Washington .02 .10
126T Walt Weiss XRC .30 .75
127T Bob Welch .07 .20
128T David Wells XRC .60 1.50
129T Glenn Wilson .02 .10
130T Ted Wood OLY XRC .08 .25
131T Don Zimmer MG .07 .20
132T Checklist 1T-132T .02 .10

1988 Topps Traded Tiffany

COMP.FACT.SET (132) 15.00 40.00
*STARS: 1.5X TO 4X BASIC CARDS
*ROOKIES: 2.5X TO 6X BASIC CARDS
DISTRIBUTED ONLY IN FACTORY SET FORM
FACTORY SET PRICE IS FOR SEALED SETS
66T Tino Martinez OLY 4.00 10.00

1988 Topps Big

This set of 264 cards was issued as three separately distributed series of 88 cards each. Cards were distributed in wax packs with seven cards for a suggested retail of 40 cents. These cards are very reminiscent in style of the 1956 Topps card set. The cards measure approximately 2 5/8" by 3 3/4" and are oriented horizontally.

COMPLETE SET (264) 8.00 20.00
1 Paul Molitor .40 1.00
2 Milt Thompson .01 .05
3 Billy Hatcher .01 .05
4 Mike Witt .01 .05
5 Vince Coleman .01 .05
6 Dwight Evans .02 .10
7 Tim Wallach .01 .05
8 Alan Trammell .05 .15
9 Will Clark .40 1.00
10 Jeff Reardon .02 .10
11 Dwight Gooden .02 .10
12 Benito Santiago .02 .10
13 Jose Canseco .50 1.25
14 Dale Murphy .20 .50
15 George Bell .01 .05
16 Ryne Sandberg .60 1.50
17 Brook Jacoby .01 .05
18 Fernando Valenzuela .02 .10
19 Scott Fletcher .01 .05
20 Eric Davis .02 .10
21 Willie Wilson .01 .05
22 B.J. Surhoff .02 .10
23 Steve Bedrosian .01 .05
24 Dave Winfield .30 .75
25 Bobby Bonilla .02 .10
26 Larry Sheets .01 .05
27 Ozzie Guillen .05 .15
28 Checklist 1-88 .01 .05
29 Nolan Ryan 2.00 5.00
30 Bob Boone .02 .10
31 Tom Herr .01 .05
32 Wade Boggs .40 1.00
33 Neal Heaton .01 .05
34 Doyle Alexander .01 .05
35 Candy Maldonado .01 .05
36 Kirby Puckett .75 2.00
37 Gary Carter .40 1.00
38 Lance McCullers .01 .05
39A Terry Steinbach/(Topps logo in black).05 .15
39B Terry Steinbach/(Topps logo in white).05 .15
40 Gerald Perry .01 .05
41 Tom Henke .01 .05
42 Leon Durham .01 .05
43 Cory Snyder .01 .05
44 Dale Sveum .01 .05
45 Lance Parrish .01 .05
46 Steve Sax .01 .05
47 Charlie Hough .02 .10
48 Kal Daniels .01 .05
49 Bo Jackson .08 .25
50 Ron Guidry .02 .10
51 Bill Doran .01 .05
52 Wally Joyner .05 .15
53 Terry Pendleton .02 .10
54 Marty Barrett .01 .05
55 Andres Galarraga .20 .50
56 Larry Herndon .01 .05
57 Kevin Mitchell .02 .10
58 Greg Gagne .01 .05
59 Keith Hernandez .02 .10
60 John Kruk .02 .10
61 Mike LaValliere .01 .05
62 Cal Ripken 2.00 5.00
63 Ivan Calderon .01 .05
64 Alvin Davis .01 .05
65 Luis Polonia .01 .05
66 Robin Yount .20 .50
67 Juan Samuel .01 .05
68 Andres Thomas .01 .05
69 Jeff Musselman .01 .05
70 Jerry Mumphrey .01 .05
71 Joe Carter .08 .25
72 Mike Scioscia .02 .10
73 Pete Incaviglia .01 .05
74 Barry Larkin .40 1.00
75 Frank White .02 .10
76 Willie Randolph .02 .10
77 Kevin Bass .01 .05
78 Brian Downing .01 .05
79 Willie McGee .02 .10
80 Ellis Burks .30 .75
81 Hubie Brooks .01 .05
82 Darrell Evans .02 .10
83 Robby Thompson .01 .05
84 Kent Hrbek .02 .10
85 Ron Darling .01 .05
86 Stan Jefferson .01 .05
87 Teddy Higuera .01 .05
88 Mike Schmidt .30 .75
89 Barry Bonds .75 2.00
90 Jim Presley .01 .05
91 Orel Hershiser .02 .10
92 Jesse Barfield .01 .05
93 Tom Candiotti .01 .05
94 Bret Saberhagen .02 .10
95 Jose Uribe .01 .05
96 Tom Browning .01 .05
97 Johnny Ray .01 .05
98 Mike Morgan .01 .05
99 Lou Whitaker .02 .10
100 Jim Sundberg .01 .05
101 Roger McDowell .01 .05
102 Randy Ready .01 .05
103 Mike Gallego .01 .05
104 Steve Buechele .01 .05
105 Greg Walker .01 .05
106 Jose Lind .01 .05
107 Steve Trout .01 .05
108 Rick Rhoden .01 .05
109 Jim Pankovits .01 .05
110 Ken Griffey Sr. .02 .10
111 Danny Cox .01 .05
112 Franklin Stubbs .01 .05
113 Lloyd Moseby .01 .05
114 Mel Hall .01 .05
115 Kevin Seitzer .02 .10
116 Tim Raines .02 .10
117 Juan Castillo .01 .05
118 Roger Clemens 1.00 2.50
119 Mike Aldrete .01 .05
120 Mario Soto .01 .05
121 Jack Howell .01 .05
122 Rick Schu .01 .05
123 Jeff D. Robinson .01 .05
124 Doug Drabek .02 .10
125 Henry Cotto .01 .05
126 Checklist 89-176 .01 .05
127 Gary Gaetti .02 .10
128 Rick Sutcliffe .02 .10
129 Howard Johnson .01 .05
130 Chris Brown .01 .05
131 Dave Henderson .01 .05
132 Curt Wilkerson .01 .05
133 Mike Marshall .01 .05
134 Kelly Gruber .01 .05
135 Julio Franco .02 .10
136 Kurt Stillwell .01 .05
137 Donnie Hill .01 .05
138 Mike Pagliarulo .01 .05
139 Von Hayes .01 .05
140 Mike Scott .01 .05
141 Bob Kipper .01 .05
142 Harold Reynolds .02 .10
143 Bob Brenly .01 .05
144 Dave Concepcion .02 .10
145 Devon White .02 .10
146 Jeff Stone .01 .05
147 Chet Lemon .01 .05
148 Ozzie Virgil .01 .05
149 Todd Worrell .02 .10
150 Mitch Webster .01 .05
151 Rob Deer .01 .05
152 Rich Gedman .01 .05
153 Andre Dawson .20 .50
154 Mike Davis .01 .05
155 Nelson Liriano .01 .05
156 Greg Swindell .01 .05
157 George Brett .60 1.50
158 Kevin McReynolds .01 .05
159 Brian Fisher .01 .05
160 Mike Kingery .01 .05
161 Tony Gwynn 1.00 2.50
162 Don Baylor .02 .10
163 Jerry Browne .01 .05
164 Dan Pasqua .01 .05
165 Rickey Henderson .60 1.50
166 Brett Butler .02 .10
167 Nick Esasky .01 .05
168 Kirk McCaskill .01 .05
169 Fred Lynn .01 .05
170 Jack Morris .02 .10
171 Pedro Guerrero .01 .05
172 Dave Stieb .01 .05
173 Pat Tabler .01 .05
174 Floyd Bannister .01 .05
175 Rafael Belliard .01 .05
176 Mark Langston .01 .05
177 Greg Mathews .01 .05
178 Claudell Washington .01 .05
179 Mark McGwire 1.00 2.50
180 Bert Blyleven .02 .10
181 Jim Rice .02 .10
182 Mookie Wilson .02 .10
183 Willie Fraser .01 .05
184 Andy Van Slyke .02 .10
185 Matt Nokes .01 .05
186 Eddie Whitson .01 .05
187 Tony Fernandez .02 .10
188 Rick Reuschel .02 .10
189 Ken Phelps .01 .05
190 Juan Nieves .01 .05
191 Kirk Gibson .08 .25
192 Glenn Davis .01 .05
193 Zane Smith .01 .05
194 Jose DeLeon .01 .05
195 Gary Ward .01 .05
196 Pascual Perez .01 .05
197 Carlton Fisk .30 .75
198 Oddibe McDowell .01 .05
199 Mark Gubicza .01 .05
200 Glenn Hubbard .01 .05
201 Frank Viola .01 .05
202 Jody Reed .02 .10
203 Len Dykstra .02 .10
204 Dick Schofield .01 .05
205 Sid Bream .01 .05
206 Willie Hernandez .01 .05
207 Keith Moreland .01 .05
208 Mark Eichhorn .01 .05
209 Rene Gonzales .01 .05
210 Dave Valle .01 .05
211 Tom Brunansky .01 .05
212 Charles Hudson .01 .05
213 John Farrell .01 .05
214 Jeff Treadway .01 .05
215 Eddie Murray .40 1.00
216 Checklist 177-264 .01 .05
217 Greg Brock .01 .05
218 John Shelby .01 .05
219 Craig Reynolds .01 .05
220 Dion James .01 .05
221 Carney Lansford .02 .10
222 Juan Berenguer .01 .05
223 Luis Rivera .01 .05
224 Harold Baines .05 .15
225 Shawon Dunston .01 .05
226 Luis Aguayo .01 .05
227 Pete O'Brien .01 .05
228 Ozzie Smith .60 1.50
229 Don Mattingly 1.00 2.50
230 Danny Tartabull .01 .05
231 Andy Allanson .01 .05
232 John Franco .02 .10
233 Mike Greenwell .01 .05
234 Bob Ojeda .01 .05
235 Chili Davis .05 .15
236 Mike Dunne .01 .05
237 Jim Morrison .01 .05
238 Carmelo Martinez .01 .05
239 Ernie Whitt .01 .05
240 Scott Garrelts .01 .05
241 Mike Moore .01 .05
242 Dave Parker .02 .10
243 Tim Laudner .01 .05
244 Bill Wegman .01 .05
245 Bob Horner .01 .05
246 Rafael Santana .01 .05
247 Alfredo Griffin .01 .05
248 Mark Bailey .01 .05
249 Ron Gant .20 .50
250 Bryn Smith .01 .05
251 Lance Johnson .02 .10
252 Sam Horn .01 .05
253 Darryl Strawberry .02 .10
254 Chuck Finley .05 .15
255 Darnell Coles .01 .05
256 Mike Henneman .02 .10
257 Andy Hawkins .01 .05
258 Jim Clancy .01 .05
259 Atlee Hammaker .01 .05
260 Glenn Wilson .01 .05
261 Larry McWilliams .01 .05
262 Jack Clark .02 .10
263 Walt Weiss .02 .10
264 Gene Larkin .02 .10

1988 Topps Cloth

This 120-card set was actually an "Experimental Issue" produced by Topps and was discarded even though it appeared in the collectors market in a limited way. The set features a color player head photo printed on a thin gauze fabric which supposedly expanded into a sponge when submerged in water. The backs are blank. The cards are unnumbered and checklisted below in alphabetical order.

COMPLETE SET (120) 2000.00 4000.00
1 Rick Aguilera 10.00 25.00
2 Andy Allanson 6.00 15.00
3 Tony Armas 6.00 15.00
4 Keith Atherton 6.00 15.00
5 Steve Balboni 6.00 15.00
6 Billy Bean 10.00 25.00
7 Steve Bedrosian AS 10.00 25.00
8 George Bell AS 10.00 25.00
9 Bruce Benedict 6.00 15.00
10 Dave Bergman 6.00 15.00
11 Mike Bielicki 6.00 15.00
12 Tim Birtsas 6.00 15.00
13 Bruce Bochy 6.00 15.00
14 Wade Boggs AS 30.00 60.00
15 Rod Booker 6.00 15.00
16 Dennis Boyd 6.00 15.00
17 Tom Browning 6.00 15.00
18 Carmen Castillo 6.00 15.00
19 Rick Cerone 6.00 15.00
20 Jack Clark AS 10.00 25.00
21 Mark Clear 6.00 15.00
22 Roger Clemens AS 20.00 50.00
23 Pat Clements 6.00 15.00
24 Keith Comstock 6.00 15.00
25 Cecil Cooper 10.00 25.00
26 Joey Cora 6.00 15.00
27 Ed Correa 6.00 15.00
28 Mark Davidson 6.00 15.00
29 Mark Davis 6.00 15.00
30 Jeff Dedmon 6.00 15.00
31 Jim Dwyer 6.00 15.00
32 Doc Edwards 6.00 15.00
33 John Farrell 6.00 15.00
34 Mike Felder 6.00 15.00
35 Curt Ford 6.00 15.00
36 Bob Forsch 6.00 15.00
37 Damaso Garcia 6.00 15.00
38 Tom Glavine 90.00 150.00
39 Mark Grant 6.00 15.00
40 Tony Gwynn AS 30.00 60.00
41 Drew Hall 6.00 15.00
42 Jeff Hamilton 6.00 15.00
43 Mike Hart 6.00 15.00
44 Andy Hawkins 6.00 15.00
45 Ed Hearn 6.00 15.00
46 Tom Henke AS 10.00 25.00
47 Whitey Herzog MG 10.00 25.00
48 Shawn Hillegas 6.00 15.00
49 Kent Hrbek 20.00 50.00
Gary Gaetti
50 Charles Hudson 6.00 15.00
51 Dave Johnson 10.00 25.00
52 Ron Karkovice 6.00 15.00
53 Pat Keedy 6.00 15.00
54 Jimmy Key AS 10.00 25.00
55 Steve Kiefer 6.00 15.00
56 Bob Kipper 6.00 15.00
57 Les Lancaster 6.00 15.00
58 Ken Landreaux 6.00 15.00
59 Craig Lefferts 6.00 15.00
60 Jim Leyland MG 10.00 25.00
61 Jose Lind 6.00 15.00
62 Gary Lucas 6.00 15.00
63 Frank Lucchesi MG 6.00 15.00
64 Barry Lyons 6.00 15.00
65 John Marzano 6.00 15.00
66 Greg Matthews 6.00 15.00
67 Don Mattingly AS 90.00 150.00
68 Len Matuszek 6.00 15.00
69 Kurt McCaskill 6.00 15.00
70 Terry McGriff 6.00 15.00
71 Mark McGwire 200.00 400.00
Jose Canseco
72 Joey Meyer 6.00 15.00
73 John Mitchell 6.00 15.00
74 Jeff Montgomery 6.00 15.00
75 John Morris 6.00 15.00
76 John Moses 6.00 15.00
77 Dale Murphy TL 150.00 300.00
78 Tom Nieto 6.00 15.00
79 Matt Nokes 6.00 15.00
80 Charlie O'Brien 6.00 15.00
81 Ed Olwine 6.00 15.00
82 Paul O'Neill 30.00 60.00
83 Steve Ontiveros 6.00 15.00
84 Pat Pacillo 6.00 15.00
85 Tom Pagnozzi 6.00 15.00
86 Jim Pankovits 6.00 15.00
87 Bill Pecota 6.00 15.00
88 Geno Petralli 6.00 15.00
89 Eric Plunk 6.00 15.00
90 Gus Polidor 6.00 15.00
91 Dennis Powell 6.00 15.00
92 Terry Puhl 6.00 15.00
93 Charlie Puleo 6.00 15.00
94 Shane Rawley AS 6.00 15.00
95 Rick Rodriquez 6.00 15.00
96 Ron Roenicke 6.00 15.00
97 Pete Rose MG 50.00 100.00
98 Lenn Sakata 6.00 15.00
99 Joe Sambito 6.00 15.00
100 Juan Samuel AS 6.00 15.00
101 Rafael Santana 6.00 15.00
102 Dan Schatzeder 6.00 15.00
103 Pat Sheridan 6.00 15.00
104 Steve Shields 6.00 15.00
105 Nelson Simmons 6.00 15.00
106 Doug Sisk 6.00 15.00
107 Joel Skinner 6.00 15.00
108 Ozzie Smith AS 100.00 200.00
109 Chris Speier 6.00 15.00
110 Jim Sundberg 6.00 15.00
111 Don Sutton 20.00 50.00
112 Chuck Tanner MG 6.00 15.00
113 Mickey Tettleton 6.00 15.00
114 Tim Teufel 6.00 15.00
115 Gary Thurman 6.00 15.00
116 Alex Trevino 6.00 15.00
117 Mike Trujillo 6.00 15.00
118 Tim Wallach AS 6.00 15.00
119 Frank Williams 6.00 15.00
120 Dave Winfield AS 20.00 50.00
121 Butch Wynegar 6.00 15.00

1988 Topps Gallery of Champions

This set marked the fifth consecutive season that Topps issued metal versions of some leading players. The players pictured in this set were either league leaders or award winners. The cards measure approximately 1 1/4" by 1 3/4" and were produced in aluminum, bronze and silver versions. We have priced the aluminum versions and the bronze values are 2X to 4X the aluminum values while the silver cards are valued between 5X and 10X the aluminum cards. We have sequenced this set in alphabetical order.

COMPLETE SET (12) 15.00 40.00
1 Steve Bedrosian 1.00 2.50
2 George Bell 1.00 2.50
3 Wade Boggs 3.00 8.00
4 Jack Clark 1.00 2.50
5 Roger Clemens 6.00 15.00
6 Andre Dawson 2.00 5.00
7 Tony Gwynn 5.00 12.00
8 Mark Langston 1.00 2.50
9 Mark McGwire 6.00 15.00
10 Dave Righetti 1.00 2.50
11 Nolan Ryan 10.00 25.00
12 Benito Santiago 1.50 4.00

1988 Topps Mattingly World of Baseball

This one-card Special World of Baseball Edition set features a color portrait of Don Mattingly with white borders. The back displays player information and career statistics.

1 Don Mattingly 20.00 50.00

1988 Topps Mini Leaders

The 1988 Topps Mini set of Major League Leaders features 77 cards of leaders of the various statistical categories for the 1987 season. The cards are numbered on the back and measure approximately 2 1/8" by 3". The set numbering is alphabetical by player within team and the teams themselves are in alphabetical order as well. The card backs are printed in blue, red, and yellow on white card stock. The cards were distributed as a separate issue in wax packs.

COMPLETE SET (77) 2.00 5.00
1 Wade Boggs .15 .40
2 Roger Clemens .40 1.00
3 Dwight Evans .02 .10
4 DeWayne Buice .01 .05
5 Brian Downing .01 .05
6 Wally Joyner .02 .10
7 Ivan Calderon .01 .05
8 Carlton Fisk .15 .40
9 Gary Redus .01 .05
10 Darrell Evans .02 .10
11 Jack Morris .02 .10
12 Alan Trammell .05 .15
13 Lou Whitaker .02 .10
14 Bret Saberhagen .02 .10
15 Kevin Seitzer .01 .05
16 Danny Tartabull .01 .05
17 Willie Wilson .01 .05
18 Teddy Higuera .01 .05
19 Paul Molitor .20 .50
20 Dan Plesac .01 .05
21 Robin Yount .15 .40
22 Kent Hrbek .02 .10
23 Kirby Puckett .25 .60
24 Jeff Reardon .02 .10
25 Frank Viola .01 .05
26 Rickey Henderson .30 .75
27 Don Mattingly .40 1.00
28 Willie Randolph .02 .10
29 Dave Righetti .01 .05
30 Jose Canseco .20 .50
31 Mark McGwire .40 1.00
32 Dave Stewart .02 .10
33 Phil Bradley .01 .05
34 Mark Langston .01 .05
35 Harold Reynolds .02 .10
36 Charlie Hough .02 .10
37 George Bell .01 .05
38 Tom Henke .01 .05
39 Jimmy Key .01 .05
40 Dion James .01 .05
41 Dale Murphy .07 .20
42 Zane Smith .01 .05
43 Andre Dawson .07 .20
44 Lee Smith .02 .10
45 Rick Sutcliffe .02 .10
46 Eric Davis .02 .10
47 John Franco .02 .10
48 Dave Parker .02 .10
49 Billy Hatcher .01 .05
50 Nolan Ryan .75 2.00
51 Mike Scott .01 .05
52 Pedro Guerrero .01 .05
53 Orel Hershiser .02 .10
54 Fernando Valenzuela .02 .10
55 Bob Welch .01 .05
56 Andres Galarraga .07 .20
57 Tim Raines .02 .10
58 Tim Wallach .01 .05
59 Len Dykstra .02 .10
60 Dwight Gooden .02 .10
61 Howard Johnson .01 .05
62 Roger McDowell .01 .05
63 Darryl Strawberry .02 .10
64 Steve Bedrosian .01 .05
65 Shane Rawley .01 .05
66 Juan Samuel .01 .05
67 Mike Schmidt .20 .50
68 Mike Dunne .01 .05
69 Jack Clark .02 .10
70 Vince Coleman .01 .05
71 Willie McGee .02 .10
72 Ozzie Smith .30 .75
73 Todd Worrell .02 .10
74 Tony Gwynn .40 1.00
75 John Kruk .02 .10
76 Rick Reuschel .01 .05
77 Checklist Card .01 .05

1988 Topps Stickers

Printed in Canada, these 313 stickers measure approximately 2 1/8" by 3" and are numbered on their fronts. The sticker backs are actually cards (1988 O-Pee-Chee Super Stars) and are considered a separate set. The stickers feature yellow- and red-bordered color player photos. An album onto which the stickers could be affixed was available at retail stores. The album and the sticker numbering are organized as follows: 1987 Highlights (1-12), 1987 Championship Series (13-18), 1987 World Series (19-25), Houston Astros (26-35), Atlanta Braves (36-45), St. Louis Cardinals (46-55), Chicago Cubs (56-65), Los Angeles Dodgers (66-75), Montreal Expos (76-85), San Francisco Giants (86-95), New York Mets (96-105), San Diego Padres (106-115), Philadelphia Phillies (116-125), Pittsburgh Pirates (126-135), Cincinnati Reds (136-145), Foil All-Stars (146-163), Oakland A's (164-173), California Angels (174-183), Toronto Blue Jays (184-193), Milwaukee Brewers (194-203), Cleveland Indians (204-213), Seattle Mariners (214-223), Baltimore Orioles (224-233), Texas Rangers (234-243), Boston Red Sox (244-253), Kansas City Royals (254-263), Detroit Tigers (264-273), Minnesota Twins (274-283), Chicago White Sox (284-293), New York Yankees (294-303) and Future Stars (304-313). For those stickers featuring more than one player, the other numbers on that sticker are given below in parentheses. Although the prices listed below are for the stickers only, there are instances where having an especially desirable sticker card back (attached to that sticker) will increase the values listed below.

COMPLETE SET (313) 6.00 15.00
COMMON PLAYER (1-145) .02 .05
COMMON FOIL (146-163) .04 .10
*OPC: .4X TO 1X TOPPS STICKERS
1 Mark McGwire (263) 1.50 4.00
2 Benny Santiago (304) .01 .05
3 Don Mattingly (187) .40 1.00
4 Vince Coleman (223) .01 .05
5 Bob Boone (272) .02 .10
6 Steve Bedrosian(278) .01 .05
7 Nolan Ryan (276) .75 2.00
8 Darrell Evans (306) .02 .10
9 Mike Schmidt (255) .25 .60
10 Don Baylor (256) .02 .10
11 Eddie Murray (145) .20 .50
12 Juan Beniquez (237) .01 .05
13 John Tudor .01 .05
14 Jeff Reardon .02 .10
15 Tom Brunansky .01 .05
16 Jeffrey Leonard .01 .05
17 Gary Gaetti .02 .10
18 Jose Oquendo .01 .05
19 Dan Gladden .01 .05
20 Bert Blyleven .02 .10
21 John Tudor .01 .05
22 Tom Lawless .01 .05
23 Curt Ford .01 .05
24 Kent Hrbek .02 .10
25 Frank Viola .01 .05
26 Dave Smith (216) .01 .05
27 Jim Deshaies (240) .01 .05
28 Billy Hatcher (171) .01 .05
29 Kevin Bass (196) .01 .05
30 Mike Scott .01 .05
31 Denny Walling (224) .01 .05
32 Alan Ashby (185) .01 .05
33 Ken Caminiti (292) .30 .75
34 Bill Doran (245) .01 .05
35 Glenn Davis .01 .05
36 Ozzie Virgil .01 .05
37 Ken Oberkfell (260) .01 .05
38 Ken Griffey (183) .02 .10
39 Albert Hall (287) .01 .05
40 Zane Smith (310) .01 .05
41 Andres Thomas (207) .01 .05
42 Dion James (178) .01 .05
43 Jim Acker (249) .01 .05
44 Tom Glavine (226) .75 2.00
45 Dale Murphy .08 .25
46 Jack Clark .02 .10
47 Vince Coleman (269) .01 .05
48 Ricky Horton (221) .01 .05
49 Terry Pendleton(303) .02 .10
50 Tom Herr (271) .01 .05
51 Joe Magrane (265) .01 .05
52 Tony Pena (211) .01 .05
53 Ozzie Smith (298) .15 .40
54 Todd Worrell (169) .02 .10
55 Willie McGee .02 .10
56 Andre Dawson .08 .25
57 Ryne Sandberg (225) .20 .50
58 Keith Moreland (291) .01 .05
59 Greg Maddux (198) 1.25 3.00
60 Jody Davis (290) .01 .05
61 Rick Sutcliffe .01 .05
62 Jamie Moyer (295) .01 .05
63 Leon Durham (172) .01 .05
64 Lee Smith (313) .02 .10
65 Shawon Dunston (250) .01 .05
66 Franklin Stubbs(257) .01 .05
67 Mike Scioscia (235) .01 .05
68 Orel Hershiser (177) .02 .10
69 Mike Marshall (289) .01 .05
70 Fernando Valenzuela .02 .10
71 Mickey Hatcher (281) .01 .05
72 Matt Young (166) .01 .05
73 Bob Welch (236) .01 .05
74 Steve Sax (170) .01 .05
75 Pedro Guerrero .01 .05
76 Tim Raines .02 .10
77 Casey Candaele (252) .01 .05
78 Mike Fitzgerald(248) .01 .05
79 Andres Galarraga/(301) .08 .25
80 Neal Heaton (212) .01 .05
81 Hubie Brooks (296) .01 .05
82 Floyd Youmans (258) .01 .05
83 Herm Winningham(201) .01 .05
84 Denny Martinez (307) .02 .10
85 Tim Wallach .01 .05
86 Jeffrey Leonard .01 .05
87 Will Clark (251) .15 .40
88 Kevin Mitchell (288) .02 .10
89 Mike Aldrete (267) .01 .05
90 Scott Garrelts (191) .01 .05
91 Jose Uribe (231) .01 .05
92 Bob Brenly (246) .01 .05
93 Robby Thompson (189) .01 .05
94 Don Robinson (217) .01 .05
95 Candy Maldonado .01 .05
96 Darryl Strawberry .02 .10
97 Keith Hernandez(192) .02 .10
98 Ron Darling (220) .01 .05
99 Howard Johnson (218) .01 .05
100 Roger McDowell (190) .01 .05
101 Dwight Gooden .02 .10
102 Kevin McReynolds/(165) .01 .05
103 Sid Fernandez (275) .01 .05
104 Dave Magadan (241) .01 .05
105 Gary Carter (167) .05 .15
106 Carmelo Martinez/(302) .01 .05
107 Eddie Whitson (205) .01 .05
108 Tim Flannery (180) .01 .05
109 Stan Jefferson (266) .01 .05
110 John Kruk .02 .10
111 Chris Brown (168) .01 .05
112 Benito Santiago (215) .01 .05
113 Garry Templeton(270) .01 .05
114 Lance McCullers(186) .01 .05
115 Tony Gwynn .30 .75
116 Steve Bedrosian .01 .05
117 Von Hayes (247) .01 .05
118 Kevin Gross (279) .01 .05
119 Bruce Ruffin (238) .01 .05
120 Juan Samuel (184) .01 .05
121 Shane Rawley (182) .01 .05
122 Chris James (222) .01 .05
123 Lance Parrish (199) .01 .05
124 Glenn Wilson (181) .01 .05
125 Mike Schmidt .25 .60
126 Andy Van Slyke .02 .10
127 Jose Lind (297) .01 .05
128 Al Pedrique (176) .01 .05
129 Bobby Bonilla (277) .02 .10
130 Sid Bream (175) .01 .05
131 Mike LaValliere(230) .01 .05
132 Mike Dunne (197) .01 .05
133 Jeff D. Robinson (232) .01 .05
134 Doug Drabek (195) .02 .10
135 Barry Bonds .30 .75
136 Dave Parker .02 .10
137 Nick Esasky (208) .01 .05
138 Buddy Bell (280) .02 .10
139 Kal Daniels (239) .01 .05
140 Barry Larkin (285) .20 .50
141 Eric Davis .02 .10
142 John Franco (227) .02 .10
143 Bo Diaz (229) .01 .05
144 Ron Oester (261) .01 .05
145 Dennis Rasmussen(11) .01 .05
146 Eric Davis FOIL .05 .15
147 Ryne Sandberg FOIL .30 .75
148 Andre Dawson FOIL .08 .25
149 Mike Schmidt FOIL .40 1.00
150 Jack Clark FOIL .07 .20
151 Dar.Strawberry FOIL .07 .20
152 Gary Carter FOIL .08 .25
153 Ozzie Smith FOIL .25 .60
154 Mike Scott FOIL .02 .10
155 Rickey Henderson FOIL .15 .40
156 Don Mattingly FOIL .60 1.50
157 Wade Boggs FOIL .15 .40
158 George Bell FOIL .02 .10
159 Dave Winfield FOIL .15 .40
160 Cal Ripken FOIL 1.25 3.00
161 Terry Kennedy FOIL .02 .10
162 Willie Randolph FOIL .05 .15
163 Bret Saberhagen FOIL .02 .10
164 Mark McGwire 1.50 4.00
165 Tony Phillips (102) .01 .05
166 Jay Howell (72) .01 .05
167 Carney Lansford(105) .02 .10
168 Dave Stewart (111) .02 .10
169 Alfredo Griffin (54) .01 .05
170 Dennis Eckersley(74) .02 .10
171 Mike Davis (28) .01 .05
172 Luis Polonia (63) .01 .05
173 Jose Canseco .30 .75
174 Mike Witt .01 .05
175 Jack Howell (130) .01 .05
176 Greg Minton (128) .01 .05
177 Dick Schofield (68) .01 .05
178 Gary Pettis (42) .01 .05
179 Wally Joyner .05 .15
180 DeWayne Buice (108) .01 .05
181 Brian Downing (124) .01 .05
182 Bob Boone (121) .02 .10
183 Devon White (38) .02 .10
184 Jim Clancy (120) .01 .05
185 Willie Upshaw (32) .01 .05
186 Tom Henke (114) .01 .05
187 Ernie Whitt (3) .01 .05
188 George Bell .01 .05
189 Lloyd Moseby (93) .01 .05
190 Jimmy Key (100) .02 .10
191 Dave Stieb (90) .01 .05
192 Jesse Barfield (97) .01 .05
193 Tony Fernandez .01 .05
194 Paul Molitor .08 .25
195 Jim Gantner (134) .01 .05
196 Teddy Higuera (29) .01 .05
197 Glenn Braggs (132) .01 .05
198 Rob Deer (59) .01 .05
199 Dale Sveum (123) .01 .05
200 Bill Wegman (308) .01 .05
201 Robin Yount (83) .08 .25
202 B.J. Surhoff .02 .10
203 Dan Plesac .01 .05
204 Pat Tabler .01 .05
205 Mel Hall (107) .01 .05
206 Scott Bailes (305) .01 .05
207 Julio Franco (41) .01 .05
208 Cory Snyder (137) .01 .05
209 Chris Bando (312) .01 .05
210 Greg Swindell (311) .01 .05
211 Brook Jacoby (52) .01 .05
212 Brett Butler (80) .02 .10
213 Joe Carter .08 .25
214 Mark Langston .01 .05
215 Rey Quinones (112) .01 .05
216 Ed Nunez (16) .01 .05
217 Jim Presley (94) .01 .05
218 Phil Bradley (99) .01 .05
219 Alvin Davis .01 .05
220 Dave Valle (98) .01 .05
221 Harold Reynolds (48) .02 .10
222 Scott Bradley (122) .01 .05
223 Gary Matthews (4) .01 .05
224 Eric Bell (31) .01 .05
225 Terry Kennedy (57) .01 .05
226 Dave Schmidt (44) .01 .05
227 Billy Ripken (142) .01 .05
228 Cal Ripken .75 2.00
229 Ray Knight (143) .01 .05
230 Larry Sheets (131) .01 .05
231 Mike Boddicker (91) .01 .05
232 Tom Niedenfuer (133) .01 .05
233 Eddie Murray .20 .50
234 Ruben Sierra .02 .10
235 Steve Buechele (67) .01 .05
236 Charlie Hough (73) .02 .10
237 Oddibe McDowell (12) .01 .05
238 Mike Stanley (119) .01 .05
239 Pete Incaviglia(139) .01 .05
240 Pete O'Brien (27) .01 .05
241 Scott Fletcher (104) .01 .05
242 Dale Mohorcic (300) .01 .05
243 Larry Parrish .01 .05
244 Wade Boggs .08 .25
245 Dwight Evans (34) .02 .10
246 Sam Horn (92) .01 .05
247 Jim Rice (117) .02 .10
248 Marty Barrett (78) .01 .05
249 Mike Greenwell (43) .01 .05
250 Ellis Burks (65) .20 .50
251 Roger Clemens (87) .30 .75
252 Rich Gedman (77) .01 .05
253 Bruce Hurst .01 .05
254 Bret Saberhagen .02 .10
255 Frank White (9) .02 .10
256 Dan Quisenberry (10) .01 .05
257 Danny Tartabull (66) .01 .05
258 Bo Jackson (82) .08 .25
259 George Brett .30 .75
260 Charlie Leibrandt(37) .01 .05
261 Kevin Seitzer (144) .02 .10
262 Mark Gubicza (282) .01 .05
263 Willie Wilson (1) .01 .05
264 Frank Tanana (286) .01 .05
265 Darrell Evans (51) .02 .10
266 Bill Madlock (109) .02 .10
267 Kirk Gibson (89) .02 .10
268 Jack Morris .02 .10
269 Matt Nokes (47) .01 .05
270 Lou Whitaker (113) .02 .10
271 Eric King (50) .01 .05
272 Jim Morrison (5) .01 .05
273 Alan Trammell .05 .15
274 Kent Hrbek .02 .10
275 Tom Brunansky (103) .01 .05
276 Bert Blyleven (7) .02 .10
277 Gary Gaetti (129) .02 .10
278 Tim Laudner (6) .01 .05
279 Gene Larkin (118) .01 .05
280 Jeff Reardon (138) .02 .10
281 Danny Gladden (71) .01 .05
282 Frank Viola (262) .01 .05
283 Kirby Puckett .25 .60
284 Ozzie Guillen .01 .05
285 Ivan Calderon (140) .01 .05
286 Donnie Hill (264) .01 .05
287 Ken Williams (39) .01 .05
288 Jim Winn (88) .01 .05
289 Bob James (69) .01 .05
290 Carlton Fisk (60) .08 .25
291 Richard Dotson (58) .01 .05
292 Greg Walker (33) .01 .05
293 Harold Baines .02 .10
294 Willie Randolph .02 .10
295 Mike Pagliarulo (62) .01 .05
296 Ron Guidry (81) .01 .05
297 Rickey Henderson(127) .08 .25
298 Rick Rhoden (53) .01 .05
299 Don Mattingly .40 1.00
300 Dave Righetti (242) .01 .05

Card	Low	High
301 Clau.Washington (79)	.01	.05
302 Dave Winfield (106)	.08	.25
303 Gary Ward (49)	.01	.05
304 Al Pedrique (2)	.01	.05
305 Casey Candaele (206)	.01	.05
306 Kevin Seitzer (8)	.02	.10
307 Mike Dunne (84)	.01	.05
308 Jeff Musselman (200)	.01	.05
309 Mark McGwire	1.50	4.00
310 Ellis Burks (40)	.20	.50
311 Matt Nokes (210)	.01	.05
312 Mike Greenwell (209)	.01	.05
313 Devon White (64)	.02	.10
NNO Album	.40	1.00

1988 Topps/O-Pee-Chee Sticker Backs

Card	Low	High
COMPLETE SET (67)	2.50	6.00
1 Jack Clark	.02	.10
2 Andres Galarraga	.08	.25
3 Keith Hernandez	.02	.10
4 Tom Herr	.01	.05
5 Juan Samuel	.01	.05
6 Ryne Sandberg	.20	.50
7 Terry Pendleton	.02	.10
8 Mike Schmidt	.20	.50
9 Tim Wallach	.01	.05
10 Hubie Brooks	.01	.05
11 Shawon Dunston	.01	.05
12 Ozzie Smith	.15	.40
13 Andre Dawson	.08	.25
14 Eric Davis	.02	.10
15 Pedro Guerrero	.01	.05
16 Tony Gwynn	.30	.75
17 Jeffrey Leonard	.01	.05
18 Dale Murphy	.08	.25
19 Dave Parker	.02	.10
20 Tim Raines	.02	.10
21 Darryl Strawberry	.01	.05
22 Gary Carter	.15	.40
23 Jody Davis	.01	.05
24 Ozzie Virgil	.01	.05
25 Dwight Gooden	.02	.10
26 Mike Scott	.01	.05
27 Rick Sutcliffe	.01	.05
28 Sid Fernandez	.01	.05
29 Neal Heaton	.01	.05
30 Fernando Valenzuela	.02	.10
31 Steve Bedrosian	.01	.05
32 John Franco	.02	.10
33 Lee Smith	.02	.10
34 Wally Joyner	.05	.15
35 Don Mattingly	.30	.75
36 Mark McGwire	.40	1.00
37 Willie Randolph	.02	.10
38 Lou Whitaker	.02	.10
39 Frank White	.02	.10
40 Wade Boggs	.10	.30
41 George Brett	.30	.75
42 Paul Molitor	.08	.25
43 Tony Fernandez	.01	.05
44 Cal Ripken	.60	1.50
45 Alan Trammell	.05	.15
46 Jesse Barfield	.01	.05
47 George Bell	.01	.05
48 Jose Canseco	.15	.40
49 Joe Carter	.08	.25
50 Dwight Evans	.02	.10
51 Rickey Henderson	.15	.40
52 Kirby Puckett	.20	.50
53 Cory Snyder	.01	.05
54 Dave Winfield	.08	.25
55 Terry Kennedy	.01	.05
56 Matt Nokes	.01	.05
57 B.J. Surhoff	.02	.10
58 Roger Clemens	.30	.75
59 Jack Morris	.02	.10
60 Bret Saberhagen	.02	.10
61 Ron Guidry	.01	.05
62 Bruce Hurst	.01	.05
63 Mark Langston	.01	.05
64 Tom Henke	.01	.05
65 Dan Plesac	.01	.05
66 Dave Righetti	.01	.05
67 Checklist	.01	.05

1988 Topps Revco League Leaders

Topps produced this 33-card boxed standard-size set for Revco stores subtitled "League Leaders". The cards feature a high-gloss, full-color photo of the player inside a white border. The card backs are printed in red and black on white card stock. The statistics provided on the card backs cover only two lines, last season and Major League totals.

Card	Low	High
COMP. FACT SET (33)	2.00	5.00
1 Tony Gwynn	.40	1.00
2 Andre Dawson	.07	.20
3 Vince Coleman	.01	.05
4 Jack Clark	.02	.10
5 Tim Raines	.02	.10
6 Tim Wallach	.01	.05
7 Juan Samuel	.01	.05
8 Nolan Ryan	.75	2.00
9 Rick Sutcliffe	.01	.05
10 Kent Tekulve	.01	.05
11 Steve Bedrosian	.01	.05
12 Orel Hershiser	.02	.10
13 Rick Reuschel	.01	.05
14 Fernando Valenzuela	.02	.10
15 Bob Welch	.01	.05
16 Wade Boggs	.15	.40
17 Mark McGwire	.40	1.00
18 George Bell	.01	.05
19 Harold Reynolds	.02	.10
20 Paul Molitor	.15	.40
21 Kirby Puckett	.20	.50
22 Kevin Seitzer	.02	.10
23 Brian Downing	.01	.05
24 Dwight Evans	.02	.10
25 Willie Wilson	.01	.05
26 Danny Tartabull	.01	.05
27 Jimmy Key	.02	.10
28 Roger Clemens	.40	1.00
29 Dave Stewart	.02	.10
30 Mark Eichhorn	.01	.05
31 Tom Henke	.01	.05
32 Charlie Hough	.02	.10
33 Mark Langston	.01	.05

1988 Topps Rite-Aid Team MVP's

Topps produced this 33-card boxed standard-size set for Rite Aid Drug and Discount Stores subtitled "Team MVP's". The Rite Aid logo is at the top of every obverse. The cards feature a high-gloss, full-color photo of the player inside a red, white, and blue border. The card backs are printed in blue and black on white card stock. The checklist for the set is found on the back panel of the small collector box. The statistics provided on the card backs cover only two lines, last season and Major League totals.

Card	Low	High
COMPLETE SET (33)	1.50	4.00
1 Dale Murphy	.07	.20
2 Andre Dawson	.07	.20
3 Eric Davis	.02	.10
4 Mike Scott	.01	.05
5 Pedro Guerrero	.01	.05
6 Tim Raines	.02	.10
7 Darryl Strawberry	.02	.10
8 Mike Schmidt	.20	.50
9 Mike Dunne	.01	.05
10 Jack Clark	.02	.10
11 Tony Gwynn	.40	1.00
12 Will Clark	.07	.20
13 Cal Ripken	.75	2.00
14 Wade Boggs	.20	.50
15 Wally Joyner	.02	.10
16 Harold Baines	.02	.10
17 Joe Carter	.02	.10
18 Alan Trammell	.05	.15
19 Kevin Seitzer	.02	.10
20 Paul Molitor	.20	.50
21 Kirby Puckett	.20	.50
22 Don Mattingly	.40	1.00
23 Mark McGwire	.40	1.00
24 Alvin Davis	.01	.05
25 Ruben Sierra	.02	.10
26 George Bell	.01	.05
27 Jack Morris	.02	.10
28 Jeff Reardon	.02	.10
29 John Tudor	.01	.05
30 Rick Reuschel	.02	.10
31 Gary Gaetti	.02	.10
32 Jeffrey Leonard	.01	.05
33 Frank Viola	.01	.05

1988 Topps UK Minis

The 1988 Topps UK (United Kingdom) Mini set of "American Baseball" features 88 cards. The cards measure approximately 2 1/8" by 3". The card backs are printed in blue, red, and yellow on white card stock. The cards were distributed as a separate issue in packs. A custom black and yellow small set box was also available for holding a complete set; the box has a complete checklist on the back panel. The set player numbering is according to alphabetical order.

Card	Low	High
COMPLETE SET (88)	2.00	5.00
COMP.FACT SET (88)		
*TIFFANY: 4X BASIC CARDS		
1 Harold Baines	.02	.10
2 Steve Bedrosian	.01	.05
3 George Bell	.01	.05
4 Wade Boggs	.15	.40
5 Barry Bonds	.30	.75
6 Bob Boone	.02	.10
7 George Brett	.30	.75
8 Hubie Brooks	.01	.05
9 Ivan Calderon	.01	.05
10 Jose Canseco	.20	.50
11 Gary Carter	.15	.40
12 Joe Carter	.02	.10
13 Jack Clark	.02	.10
14 Will Clark	.15	.40
15 Roger Clemens	.40	1.00
16 Vince Coleman	.01	.05
17 Alvin Davis	.01	.05
18 Eric Davis	.02	.10
19 Glenn Davis	.01	.05
20 Andre Dawson	.05	.15
21 Mike Dunne	.01	.05
22 Dwight Evans	.02	.10
23 Tony Fernandez	.02	.10
24 John Franco	.02	.10
25 Gary Gaetti	.02	.10
26 Kirk Gibson	.02	.10
27 Dwight Gooden	.02	.10
28 Pedro Guerrero	.01	.05
29 Tony Gwynn	.40	1.00
30 Billy Hatcher	.01	.05
31 Rickey Henderson	.30	.75
32 Tom Henke	.01	.05
33 Keith Hernandez	.02	.10
34 Orel Hershiser	.02	.10
35 Teddy Higuera	.01	.05
36 Charlie Hough	.02	.10
37 Kent Hrbek	.02	.10
38 Brook Jacoby	.01	.05
39 Dion James	.01	.05
40 Wally Joyner	.02	.10
41 John Kruk	.02	.10
42 Mark Langston	.01	.05
43 Jeffrey Leonard	.01	.05
44 Candy Maldonado	.01	.05
45 Don Mattingly	.40	1.00
46 Willie McGee	.02	.10
47 Mark McGwire	.40	1.00
48 Kevin Mitchell	.02	.10
49 Paul Molitor	.15	.40
50 Jack Morris	.02	.10
51 Lloyd Moseby	.01	.05
52 Dale Murphy	.07	.20
53 Eddie Murray	.20	.50
54 Matt Nokes	.01	.05
55 Dave Parker	.02	.10
56 Larry Parrish	.01	.05
57 Kirby Puckett	.20	.50
58 Tim Raines	.02	.10
59 Willie Randolph	.02	.10
60 Harold Reynolds	.02	.10
61 Cal Ripken	.75	2.00
62 Nolan Ryan	.75	2.00
63 Bret Saberhagen	.02	.10
64 Juan Samuel	.01	.05
65 Ryne Sandberg	.30	.75
66 Benito Santiago	.02	.10
67 Mike Schmidt	.20	.50
68 Mike Scott	.01	.05
69 Kevin Seitzer	.01	.05
70 Larry Sheets	.01	.05
71 Ruben Sierra	.02	.10
72 Ozzie Smith	.30	.75
73 Zane Smith	.01	.05
74 Cory Snyder	.01	.05
75 Dave Stewart	.02	.10
76 Darryl Strawberry	.02	.10
77 Rick Sutcliffe	.01	.05
78 Danny Tartabull	.01	.05
79 Alan Trammell	.05	.15
80 Fernando Valenzuela	.02	.10
81 Andy Van Slyke	.02	.10
82 Frank Viola	.01	.05
83 Greg Walker	.01	.05
84 Tim Wallach	.01	.05
85 Dave Winfield	.15	.40
86 Mike Witt	.01	.05
87 Robin Yount	.15	.40
88 Checklist Card	.01	.05

1989 Topps

This set consists of 792 standard-size cards. Cards were primarily issued in 15-card wax packs, 42-card rack packs and factory sets. Subsets in the set include Record Breakers (1-7), Turn Back the Clock (661-665), All-Star selections (386-407) and First Draft Picks, Future Stars and Team Leaders (all scattered throughout the set). The manager cards contain a team checklist on back. The key Rookie Cards in this set are Jim Abbott, Sandy Alomar Jr., Brady Anderson, Steve Avery, Andy Benes, Dante Bichette, Craig Biggio, Randy Johnson, Ramon Martinez, Gary Sheffield, John Smoltz, and Robin Ventura.

Card	Low	High
COMPLETE SET (792)	8.00	20.00
COMP.FACT SET (792)	10.00	25.00
COMP.X-MAS.SET (792)	10.00	25.00
FS SUBSET VARIATIONS EXIST		
FS PHOTOS ARE PLACED HIGHER/LOWER		
1 George Bell RB	.01	.05
Slams 3 HR on/Opening Day		
2 Wade Boggs RB	.02	.10
3 Gary Carter RB	.01	.05
Sets Record for/Career Putouts		
4 Andre Dawson RB	.01	.05
Logs Double Figures/in HR and SB		
5 Orel Hershiser RB	.01	.05
Pitches 59/Scoreless Innings		
6 Doug Jones RB UER	.01	.05
Earns His 15th/Straight Save//Photo actually Chris Codiroli		
7 Kevin McReynolds RB	.01	.05
Steals 21 Without/Being Caught		
8 Dave Eiland	.01	.05
9 Tim Teufel	.01	.05
10 Andre Dawson	.02	.10
11 Bruce Sutter	.02	.10
12 Dale Sveum	.01	.05
13 Doug Sisk	.01	.05
14 Tom Kelly MG	.01	.05
15 Robby Thompson	.01	.05
16 Ron Robinson	.01	.05
17 Brian Downing	.02	.10
18 Rick Rhoden	.01	.05
19 Greg Gagne	.01	.05
20 Steve Bedrosian	.01	.05
21 Greg Walker TL	.01	.05
22 Tim Crews	.01	.05
23 Mike Fitzgerald	.01	.05
24 Larry Andersen	.01	.05
25 Frank White	.02	.10
26 Dale Mohorcic	.01	.05
27A Orestes Destrade	.02	.10
F* next to copyright RC		
27B Orestes Destrade	.02	.10
E*F* next to/copyright VAR		
28 Mike Moore	.01	.05
29 Kelly Gruber	.01	.05
30 Dwight Gooden	.02	.10
31 Terry Francona	.02	.10
32 Dennis Rasmussen	.01	.05
33 B.J. Surhoff	.02	.10
34 Ken Williams	.01	.05
35 John Tudor UER	.02	.10
With Red Sox in '84,should be Pirates		
36 Mitch Webster	.01	.05
37 Bob Stanley	.01	.05
38 Paul Runge	.01	.05
39 Mike Maddux	.01	.05
40 Steve Sax	.01	.05
41 Terry Mulholland	.01	.05
42 Jim Eppard	.01	.05
43 Guillermo Hernandez	.01	.05
44 Jim Snyder MG	.01	.05
45 Kal Daniels	.01	.05
46 Mark Portugal	.01	.05
47 Carney Lansford	.02	.10
48 Tim Burke	.01	.05
49 Craig Biggio RC	1.25	3.00
50 George Bell	.02	.10
51 Mark McLemore TL	.01	.05
52 Bob Brenly	.01	.05
53 Ruben Sierra	.02	.10
54 Steve Trout	.01	.05
55 Julio Franco	.02	.10
56 Pat Tabler	.01	.05
57 Alejandro Pena	.01	.05
58 Lee Mazzilli	.02	.10
59 Mark Davis	.01	.05
60 Tom Brunansky	.01	.05
61 Neil Allen	.01	.05
62 Alfredo Griffin	.01	.05
63 Mark Clear	.01	.05
64 Alex Trevino	.01	.05
65 Rick Reuschel	.02	.10
66 Manny Trillo	.01	.05
67 Dave Palmer	.01	.05
68 Darrell Miller	.01	.05
69 Jeff Ballard	.01	.05
70 Mark McGwire	.40	1.00
71 Mike Boddicker	.01	.05
72 John Moses	.01	.05
73 Pascual Perez	.01	.05
74 Nick Leyva MG	.01	.05
75 Tom Henke	.01	.05
76 Terry Blocker	.01	.05
77 Doyle Alexander	.01	.05
78 Jim Sundberg	.02	.10
79 Scott Bankhead	.01	.05
80 Cory Snyder	.01	.05
81 Tim Raines TL	.01	.05
82 Dave Leiper	.01	.05
83 Jeff Blauser	.01	.05
84 Bill Bene FDP	.01	.05
85 Kevin McReynolds	.01	.05
86 Al Nipper	.01	.05
87 Larry Owen	.01	.05
88 Darryl Hamilton RC	.08	.25
89 Dave LaPoint	.01	.05
90 Vince Coleman UER	.01	.05
Wrong birth year		
91 Floyd Youmans	.01	.05
92 Jeff Kunkel	.01	.05
93 Ken Howell	.01	.05
94 Chris Speier	.01	.05
95 Gerald Young	.01	.05
96 Rick Cerone	.01	.05
97 Greg Mathews	.01	.05
98 Larry Sheets	.01	.05
99 Sherman Corbett RC	.01	.05
100 Mike Schmidt	.20	.50
101 Les Straker	.01	.05
102 Mike Gallego	.01	.05
103 Tim Birtsas	.01	.05
104 Dallas Green MG	.01	.05
105 Ron Darling	.02	.10
106 Willie Upshaw	.01	.05
107 Jose DeLeon	.01	.05
108 Fred Manrique	.01	.05
109 Hipolito Pena	.01	.05
110 Paul Molitor	.02	.10
111 Eric Davis TL	.01	.05
112 Jim Presley	.01	.05
113 Lloyd Moseby	.01	.05
114 Bob Kipper	.01	.05
115 Jody Davis	.01	.05
116 Jeff Montgomery	.01	.05
117 Dave Anderson	.01	.05
118 Checklist 1-132	.01	.05
119 Terry Puhl	.01	.05
120 Frank Viola	.02	.10
121 Garry Templeton	.02	.10
122 Lance Johnson	.01	.05
123 Spike Owen	.01	.05
124 Jim Traber	.01	.05
125 Mike Krukow	.01	.05
126 Sid Bream	.01	.05
127 Walt Terrell	.01	.05
128 Milt Thompson	.01	.05
129 Terry Clark	.01	.05
130 Gerald Perry	.01	.05
131 Dave Otto	.01	.05
132 Curt Ford	.01	.05
133 Bill Long	.01	.05
134 Don Zimmer MG	.02	.10
135 Jose Rijo	.02	.10
136 Joey Meyer	.01	.05
137 Geno Petralli	.01	.05
138 Wallace Johnson	.01	.05
139 Mike Flanagan	.01	.05
140 Shawon Dunston	.01	.05
141 Brook Jacoby TL	.01	.05
142 Mike Diaz	.01	.05
143 Mike Campbell	.01	.05
144 Jay Bell	.02	.10
145 Dave Stewart	.02	.10
146 Gary Pettis	.01	.05
147 DeWayne Buice	.01	.05
148 Bill Pecota	.01	.05
149 Doug Dascenzo	.01	.05
150 Fernando Valenzuela	.02	.10
151 Terry McGriff	.01	.05
152 Mark Thurmond	.01	.05
153 Jim Pankovits	.01	.05
154 Don Carman	.01	.05
155 Marty Barrett	.01	.05
156 Dave Gallagher	.01	.05
157 Tom Glavine	.08	.25
158 Mike Aldrete	.01	.05
159 Pat Clements	.01	.05
160 Jeffrey Leonard	.01	.05
161 Gregg Olson RC FDP UER	.08	.25
Born Scribner, NE,/should be Omaha, NE		
162 John Davis	.01	.05
163 Bob Forsch	.01	.05
164 Hal Lanier MG	.01	.05
165 Mike Dunne	.01	.05
166 Doug Jennings RC	.01	.05
167 Steve Searcy FS	.01	.05
168 Willie Wilson	.02	.10
169 Mike Jackson	.01	.05
170 Tony Fernandez	.01	.05
171 Andres Thomas TL	.01	.05
172 Frank Williams	.01	.05
173 Mel Hall	.01	.05
174 Todd Burns	.01	.05
175 John Shelby	.01	.05
176 Jeff Parrett	.01	.05
177 Monty Fariss FDP	.01	.05
178 Mark Grant	.01	.05
179 Ozzie Virgil	.01	.05
180 Mike Scott	.02	.10
181 Craig Worthington	.01	.05
182 Bob McClure	.01	.05
183 Oddibe McDowell	.01	.05
184 John Costello RC	.01	.05
185 Claudell Washington	.01	.05
186 Pat Perry	.01	.05
187 Darren Daulton	.02	.10
188 Dennis Lamp	.01	.05
189 Kevin Mitchell	.02	.10
190 Mike Witt	.01	.05
191 Sil Campusano	.01	.05
192 Paul Mirabella	.01	.05
193 Sparky Anderson MG	.02	.10
UER 553 Salazer		
194 Greg W. Harris RC	.02	.10
195 Ozzie Guillen	.02	.10
196 Denny Walling	.01	.05
197 Neal Heaton	.01	.05
198 Danny Heep	.01	.05
199 Mike Schooler RC	.02	.10
200 George Brett	.25	.60
201 Kelly Gruber TL	.01	.05
202 Brad Moore	.01	.05
203 Rob Ducey	.01	.05
204 Brad Havens	.01	.05
205 Dwight Evans	.05	.15
206 Roberto Alomar	.08	.25
207 Terry Leach	.01	.05
208 Tom Pagnozzi	.01	.05
209 Jeff Bittiger	.01	.05
210 Dale Murphy	.05	.15
211 Mike Pagliarulo	.01	.05
212 Scott Sanderson	.01	.05
213 Rene Gonzales	.01	.05
214 Charlie O'Brien	.01	.05
215 Kevin Gross	.01	.05
216 Jack Howell	.01	.05
217 Joe Price	.01	.05
218 Mike LaValliere	.01	.05
219 Jim Clancy	.01	.05
220 Gary Gaetti	.02	.10
221 Cecil Espy	.01	.05
222 Mark Lewis FDP RC	.08	.25
223 Jay Buhner	.02	.10
224 Tony LaRussa MG	.02	.10
225 Ramon Martinez RC	.08	.25
226 Bill Doran	.01	.05
227 John Farrell	.01	.05
228 Nelson Santovenia	.01	.05
229 Jimmy Key	.02	.10
230 Ozzie Smith	.15	.40
231 Roberto Alomar TL	.08	.25
Gary Carter at plate		
232 Ricky Horton	.01	.05
233 Gregg Jefferies FS	.01	.05
234 Tom Browning	.01	.05
235 John Kruk	.02	.10
236 Charles Hudson	.01	.05
237 Glenn Hubbard	.01	.05
238 Eric King	.01	.05
239 Tim Laudner	.01	.05
240 Greg Maddux	.20	.50
241 Brett Butler	.02	.10
242 Ed VandeBerg	.01	.05
243 Bob Boone	.02	.10
244 Jim Acker	.01	.05
245 Jim Rice	.02	.10
246 Rey Quinones	.01	.05
247 Shawn Hillegas	.01	.05
248 Tony Phillips	.01	.05
249 Tim Leary	.01	.05
250 Cal Ripken	.30	.75
251 John Dopson	.01	.05
252 Billy Hatcher	.01	.05
253 Jose Alvarez RC	.02	.10
254 Tom Lasorda MG	.05	.15
255 Ron Guidry	.02	.10
256 Benny Santiago	.02	.10
257 Rick Aguilera	.01	.05
258 Checklist 133-264	.01	.05
259 Larry McWilliams	.01	.05
260 Dave Winfield	.02	.10
261 Tom Brunansky	.01	.05
Luis Alicea TL		
262 Jeff Pico	.01	.05
263 Mike Felder	.01	.05
264 Rob Dibble RC	.15	.40
265 Kent Hrbek	.02	.10
266 Luis Aquino	.01	.05
267 Jeff M. Robinson	.01	.05
268 Keith Miller RC	.08	.25
269 Tom Bolton	.01	.05
270 Wally Joyner	.02	.10
271 Jay Tibbs	.01	.05
272 Ron Hassey	.01	.05
273 Jose Lind	.01	.05
274 Mark Eichhorn	.01	.05
275 Danny Tartabull UER	.01	.05
Born San Juan, PR/should be Miami, FL		
276 Paul Kilgus	.01	.05
277 Mike Davis	.01	.05
278 Andy McGaffigan	.01	.05
279 Scott Bradley	.01	.05
280 Bob Knepper	.01	.05
281 Gary Redus	.01	.05
282 Cris Carpenter RC	.02	.10
283 Andy Allanson	.01	.05
284 Jim Leyland MG	.02	.10
285 John Candelaria	.01	.05
286 Darrin Jackson	.02	.10
287 Juan Nieves	.01	.05
288 Pat Sheridan	.01	.05
289 Ernie Whitt	.01	.05
290 John Franco	.02	.10
291 Darryl Strawberry	.01	.05
Keith Hernandez/Kevin McReynolds TL		
292 Jim Corsi	.01	.05
293 Glenn Wilson	.01	.05
294 Juan Berenguer	.01	.05
295 Scott Fletcher	.01	.05
296 Ron Gant	.02	.10
297 Oswald Peraza RC	.01	.05
298 Chris James	.01	.05
299 Steve Ellsworth	.01	.05
300 Darryl Strawberry	.02	.10
301 Charlie Leibrandt	.01	.05
302 Gary Ward	.01	.05
303 Felix Fermin	.01	.05
304 Joel Youngblood	.01	.05
305 Dave Smith	.01	.05
306 Tracy Woodson	.01	.05
307 Lance McCullers	.01	.05
308 Ron Karkovice	.01	.05
309 Mario Diaz	.01	.05
310 Rafael Palmeiro	.08	.25
311 Chris Bosio	.01	.05
312 Tom Lawless	.01	.05
313 Dennis Martinez	.02	.10
314 Bobby Valentine MG	.02	.10
315 Greg Swindell	.01	.05
316 Walt Weiss	.01	.05
317 Jack Armstrong RC	.08	.25
318 Gene Larkin	.01	.05
319 Greg Booker	.01	.05
320 Lou Whitaker	.02	.10
321 Jody Reed TL	.01	.05
322 John Smiley	.01	.05
323 Gary Thurman	.01	.05
324 Bob Milacki	.01	.05
325 Jesse Barfield	.02	.10
326 Dennis Boyd	.01	.05
327 Mark Lemke RC	.15	.40
328 Rick Honeycutt	.01	.05
329 Bob Melvin	.01	.05
330 Eric Davis	.02	.10
331 Curt Wilkerson	.01	.05
332 Tony Armas	.02	.10
333 Bob Ojeda	.01	.05
334 Steve Lyons	.01	.05
335 Dave Righetti	.02	.10
336 Steve Balboni	.01	.05
337 Calvin Schiraldi	.01	.05
338 Jim Adduci	.01	.05
339 Scott Bailes	.01	.05
340 Kirk Gibson	.02	.10
341 Jim Deshaies	.01	.05
342 Tom Brookens	.01	.05
343 Gary Sheffield FS RC	.60	1.50
344 Tom Trebelhorn MG	.01	.05
345 Charlie Hough	.02	.10
346 Rex Hudler	.01	.05
347 John Cerutti	.01	.05
348 Ed Hearn	.01	.05
349 Ron Jones	.02	.10
350 Andy Van Slyke	.05	.15
351 Bob Melvin	.01	.05
Bill Fahey CO TL		
352 Rick Schu	.01	.05
353 Marvell Wynne	.01	.05
354 Larry Parrish	.01	.05
355 Mark Langston	.01	.05
356 Kevin Elster	.01	.05
357 Jerry Reuss	.01	.05
358 Ricky Jordan RC	.08	.25
359 Tommy John	.02	.10
360 Ryne Sandberg	.15	.40
361 Kelly Downs	.01	.05
362 Jack Lazorko	.01	.05
363 Rich Yett	.01	.05
364 Rob Deer	.01	.05
365 Mike Henneman	.01	.05
366 Herm Winningham	.01	.05
367 Johnny Paredes	.01	.05
368 Brian Holton	.01	.05
369 Ken Caminiti	.05	.15
370 Dennis Eckersley	.05	.15
371 Manny Lee	.01	.05
372 Craig Lefferts	.01	.05
373 Tracy Jones	.01	.05
374 John Wathan MG	.01	.05
375 Terry Pendleton	.02	.10
376 Steve Lombardozzi	.01	.05
377 Mike Smithson	.01	.05
378 Checklist 265-396	.01	.05
379 Tim Flannery	.01	.05
380 Rickey Henderson	.08	.25
381 Larry Sheets TL	.01	.05
382 John Smoltz RC	.60	1.50
383 Howard Johnson	.02	.10
384 Mark Salas	.01	.05
385 Von Hayes	.01	.05
386 Andres Galarraga AS	.01	.05
387 Ryne Sandberg AS	.08	.25
388 Bobby Bonilla AS	.01	.05
389 Ozzie Smith AS	.08	.25
390 Darryl Strawberry AS	.01	.05
391 Andre Dawson AS	.01	.05
392 Andy Van Slyke AS	.02	.10
393 Gary Carter AS	.01	.05
394 Orel Hershiser AS	.01	.05
395 Danny Jackson AS	.01	.05
396 Kirk Gibson AS	.02	.10
397 Don Mattingly AS	.10	.30
398 Julio Franco AS	.01	.05
399 Wade Boggs AS	.02	.10
400 Alan Trammell AS	.01	.05
401 Jose Canseco AS	.05	.15
402 Mike Greenwell AS	.01	.05
403 Kirby Puckett AS	.05	.15
404 Bob Boone AS	.01	.05
405 Roger Clemens AS	.20	.50
406 Frank Viola AS	.01	.05
407 Dave Winfield AS	.01	.05
408 Greg Walker	.01	.05
409 Ken Dayley	.01	.05
410 Jack Clark	.02	.10
411 Mitch Williams	.01	.05
412 Barry Lyons	.01	.05
413 Mike Kingery	.01	.05
414 Jim Fregosi MG	.01	.05
415 Rich Gossage	.02	.10
416 Fred Lynn	.02	.10
417 Mike LaCoss	.01	.05
418 Bob Dernier	.01	.05
419 Tom Filer	.01	.05
420 Joe Carter	.02	.10
421 Kirk McCaskill	.01	.05
422 Bo Diaz	.01	.05
423 Brian Fisher	.01	.05
424 Luis Polonia UER	.01	.05
Wrong birthdate		
425 Jay Howell	.01	.05
426 Dan Gladden	.01	.05
427 Eric Show	.01	.05
428 Craig Reynolds	.01	.05
429 Greg Gagne TL	.01	.05
430 Mark Gubicza	.01	.05
431 Luis Rivera	.01	.05
432 Chad Kreuter RC	.08	.25
433 Albert Hall	.01	.05
434 Ken Patterson	.01	.05
435 Len Dykstra	.02	.10
436 Bobby Meacham	.01	.05
437 Andy Benes FDP RC	.15	.40
438 Greg Gross	.01	.05
439 Frank DiPino	.01	.05
440 Bobby Bonilla	.02	.10
441 Jerry Reed	.01	.05
442 Jose Oquendo	.01	.05
443 Rod Nichols	.01	.05
444 Moose Stubing MG	.01	.05
445 Matt Nokes	.01	.05
446 Rob Murphy	.01	.05
447 Donell Nixon	.01	.05
448 Eric Plunk	.01	.05
449 Carmelo Martinez	.01	.05
450 Roger Clemens	.40	1.00
451 Mark Davidson	.01	.05
452 Israel Sanchez	.01	.05
453 Tom Prince	.01	.05
454 Paul Assenmacher	.01	.05
455 Johnny Ray	.01	.05
456 Tim Belcher	.01	.05
457 Mackey Sasser	.01	.05
458 Donn Pall	.01	.05
459 Dave Valle TL	.01	.05
460 Dave Stieb	.02	.10
461 Buddy Bell	.02	.10
462 Jose Guzman	.01	.05
463 Steve Lake	.01	.05
464 Bryn Smith	.01	.05
465 Mark Grace	.08	.25
466 Chuck Crim	.01	.05
467 Jim Walewander	.01	.05
468 Henry Cotto	.01	.05
469 Jose Bautista RC	.02	.10
470 Lance Parrish	.02	.10
471 Steve Curry	.01	.05
472 Brian Harper	.01	.05
473 Don Robinson	.01	.05
474 Bob Rodgers MG	.01	.05
475 Dave Parker	.02	.10
476 Jon Perlman	.01	.05
477 Dick Schofield	.01	.05
478 Doug Drabek	.01	.05
479 Mike Macfarlane RC	.08	.25
480 Keith Hernandez	.02	.10
481 Chris Brown	.01	.05
482 Steve Peters	.01	.05
483 Mickey Hatcher	.01	.05
484 Steve Shields	.01	.05
485 Hubie Brooks	.01	.05
486 Jack McDowell	.02	.10
487 Scott Lusader	.01	.05
488 Kevin Coffman	.01	.05
Now with Cubs		
489 Mike Schmidt TL	.05	.15
490 Chris Sabo RC	.15	.40
491 Mike Birkbeck	.01	.05
492 Alan Ashby	.01	.05
493 Todd Benzinger	.01	.05
494 Shane Rawley	.01	.05
495 Candy Maldonado	.01	.05
496 Dwayne Henry	.01	.05
497 Pete Stanicek	.01	.05
498 Dave Valle	.01	.05
499 Don Heinkel	.01	.05
500 Jose Canseco	.08	.25
501 Vance Law	.01	.05
502 Duane Ward	.01	.05
503 Al Newman	.01	.05
504 Bob Walk	.01	.05
505 Pete Rose MG	.20	.50
506 Kirt Manwaring	.01	.05
507 Steve Farr	.01	.05
508 Wally Backman	.01	.05
509 Bud Black	.01	.05
510 Bob Horner	.02	.10
511 Richard Dotson	.01	.05
512 Donnie Hill	.01	.05
513 Jesse Orosco	.01	.05
514 Chet Lemon	.02	.10
515 Barry Larkin	.05	.15
516 Eddie Whitson	.01	.05
517 Greg Brock	.01	.05
518 Bruce Ruffin	.01	.05
519 Willie Randolph TL	.01	.05
520 Rick Sutcliffe	.02	.10
521 Mickey Tettleton	.01	.05
522 Randy Kramer	.01	.05
523 Andres Thomas	.01	.05
524 Checklist 397-528	.01	.05
525 Chili Davis	.02	.10
526 Wes Gardner	.01	.05
527 Dave Henderson	.01	.05
528 Luis Medina	.01	.05
Lower left front/has white triangle		
529 Tom Foley	.01	.05
530 Nolan Ryan	.40	1.00
531 Dave Hengel	.01	.05
532 Jerry Browne	.01	.05
533 Andy Hawkins	.01	.05
534 Doc Edwards MG	.01	.05
535 Todd Worrell UER	.01	.05
4 wins in '88,/should be 5		
536 Joel Skinner	.01	.05
537 Pete Smith	.01	.05
538 Juan Castillo	.01	.05
539 Barry Jones	.01	.05
540 Bo Jackson	.08	.25
541 Cecil Fielder	.02	.10
542 Todd Frohwirth	.01	.05
543 Damon Berryhill	.01	.05
544 Jeff Sellers	.01	.05
545 Mookie Wilson	.02	.10
546 Mark Williamson	.01	.05
547 Mark McLemore	.01	.05
548 Bobby Witt	.01	.05
549 Jamie Moyer TL	.01	.05
550 Orel Hershiser	.02	.10
551 Randy Ready	.01	.05
552 Greg Cadaret	.01	.05
553 Luis Salazar	.01	.05
554 Nick Esasky	.01	.05
555 Bert Blyleven	.02	.10
556 Bruce Fields	.01	.05
557 Keith A. Miller	.01	.05
558 Dan Pasqua	.01	.05
559 Juan Agosto	.01	.05
560 Tim Raines	.02	.10
561 Luis Aguayo	.01	.05
562 Danny Cox	.01	.05
563 Bill Schroeder	.01	.05
564 Russ Nixon MG	.01	.05
565 Jeff Russell	.01	.05
566 Al Pedrique	.01	.05

567 David Wells UER .02 .10
Complete Pitching/Recor
568 Mickey Brantley .01 .05
569 German Jimenez .01 .05
570 Tony Gwynn UER .10 .30
571 Billy Ripken .01 .05
572 Atlee Hammaker .01 .05
573 Jim Abbott FDP RC .40 1.00
574 Dave Clark .01 .05
575 Juan Samuel .01 .05
576 Greg Minton .01 .05
577 Randy Bush .01 .05
578 John Morris .01 .05
579 Glenn Davis TL .01 .05
580 Harold Reynolds .02 .10
581 Gene Nelson .01 .05
582 Mike Marshall .01 .05
583 Paul Gibson .01 .05
584 Randy Velarde UER .01 .05
Signed 1935,/should be 1985
585 Harold Baines .02 .10
586 Joe Boever .01 .05
587 Mike Stanley .01 .05
588 Luis Alicea RC .08 .25
589 Dave Meads .01 .05
590 Andres Galarraga .02 .10
591 Jeff Musselman .01 .05
592 John Cangelosi .01 .05
593 Drew Hall .01 .05
594 Jimy Williams MG .01 .05
595 Teddy Higuera .01 .05
596 Kurt Stillwell .01 .05
597 Terry Taylor RC .02 .10
598 Ken Gerhart .01 .05
599 Tom Candiotti .01 .05
600 Wade Boggs .05 .15
601 Dave Dravecky .01 .05
602 Devon White .02 .10
603 Frank Tanana .02 .10
604 Paul O'Neill .05 .15
605A Bob Welch ERR 4.00 10.00
605B Bob Welch COR .02 .10
606 Rick Dempsey .01 .05
607 Willie Ansley FDP RC .02 .10
608 Phil Bradley .01 .05
609 Frank Tanana .01 .05
Alan Trammell/Mike Heath TL
610 Randy Myers .02 .10
611 Don Slaught .01 .05
612 Dan Quisenberry .01 .05
613 Gary Varsho .01 .05
614 Joe Hesketh .01 .05
615 Robin Yount .15 .40
616 Steve Rosenberg .01 .05
617 Mark Parent RC .01 .05
618 Rance Mulliniks .01 .05
619 Checklist 529-660 .01 .05
620 Barry Bonds .60 1.50
621 Rick Mahler .01 .05
622 Stan Javier .01 .05
623 Fred Toliver .01 .05
624 Jack McKeon MG .02 .10
625 Eddie Murray .08 .25
626 Jeff Reed .01 .05
627 Greg A. Harris .01 .05
628 Matt Williams .08 .25
629 Pete O'Brien .01 .05
630 Mike Greenwell .01 .05
631 Dave Bergman .01 .05
632 Bryan Harvey RC .08 .25
633 Daryl Boston .01 .05
634 Marvin Freeman .01 .05
635 Willie Randolph .02 .10
636 Bill Wilkinson .01 .05
637 Carmen Castillo .01 .05
638 Floyd Bannister .01 .05
639 Walt Weiss TL .01 .05
640 Willie McGee .02 .10
641 Curt Young .01 .05
642 Angel Salazar .01 .05
643 Louie Meadows RC .01 .05
644 Lloyd McClendon .01 .05
645 Jack Morris .02 .10
646 Kevin Bass .01 .05
647 Randy Johnson RC 1.00 2.50
648 Sandy Alomar FS RC .15 .40
649 Stu Cliburn .01 .05
650 Kirby Puckett .08 .25
651 Tom Niedenfuer .01 .05
652 Rich Gedman .01 .05
653 Tommy Barrett .01 .05
654 Whitey Herzog MG .02 .10
655 Dave Magadan .01 .05
656 Ivan Calderon .01 .05
657 Joe Magrane .01 .05
658 R.J. Reynolds .01 .05
659 Al Leiter .08 .25
660 Will Clark .05 .15
661 Dwight Gooden TBC 84 .01 .05
662 Lou Brock TBC79 .02 .10
663 Hank Aaron TBC74 .08 .25
664 Gil Hodges TBC 69 .02 .10
665B Tony Oliva TBC 64 .02 .10
COR fabricated/card
666 Randy St.Claire .01 .05
667 Dwayne Murphy .01 .05
668 Mike Bielecki .01 .05
669 Orel Hershiser .02 .10
Mike Scioscia TL
670 Kevin Seitzer .01 .05
671 Jim Gantner .01 .05
672 Allan Anderson .01 .05
673 Don Baylor .02 .10
674 Otis Nixon .01 .05
675 Bruce Hurst .01 .05
676 Ernie Riles .01 .05
677 Dave Schmidt .01 .05
678 Dion James .01 .05
679 Willie Fraser .01 .05
680 Gary Carter .02 .10
681 Jeff D. Robinson .01 .05
682 Rick Leach .01 .05
683 Jose Cecena .01 .05
684 Dave Johnson MG .01 .05
685 Jeff Treadway .01 .05
686 Scott Terry .01 .05
687 Alvin Davis .01 .05
688 Zane Smith .01 .05
689A Stan Jefferson 4.00 10.00
689B Stan Jefferson .01 .05
Violet triangle on/front bottom left
690 Doug Jones .01 .05
691 Roberto Kelly UER .01 .05
982
692 Steve Ontiveros .01 .05
693 Pat Borders RC .08 .25
694 Les Lancaster .01 .05
695 Carlton Fisk .05 .15
696 Don August .01 .05
697A Franklin Stubbs ERR 4.00 10.00
697B Franklin Stubbs .01 .05
Team name on front/in gray
698 Keith Atherton .01 .05
699 Al Pedrique TL .01 .05
Tony Gwynn sliding
700 Don Mattingly .25 .60
701 Storm Davis .01 .05
702 Jamie Quirk .01 .05
703 Scott Garrelts .01 .05
704 Carlos Quintana RC .02 .10
705 Terry Kennedy .01 .05
706 Pete Incaviglia .01 .05
707 Steve Jeltz .01 .05
708 Chuck Finley .02 .10
709 Tom Herr .01 .05
710 David Cone .02 .10
711 Candy Sierra .01 .05
712 Bill Swift .01 .05
713 Ty Griffin FDP .01 .05
714 Joe Morgan MG .02 .10
715 Tony Pena .01 .05
716 Wayne Tolleson .01 .05
717 Jamie Moyer .02 .10
718 Glenn Braggs .01 .05
719 Danny Darwin .01 .05
720 Tim Wallach .01 .05
721 Ron Tingley .01 .05
722 Todd Stottlemyre .01 .05
723 Rafael Belliard .01 .05
724 Jerry Don Gleaton .01 .05
725 Terry Steinbach .02 .10
726 Dickie Thon .01 .05
727 Joe Orsulak .01 .05
728 Charlie Puleo .01 .05
729 Steve Buechele TL .01 .05
Inconsistent design,/team name on front/surrounded by black,/should be white
730 Danny Jackson .01 .05
731 Mike Young .01 .05
732 Steve Buechele .01 .05
733 Randy Bockus .01 .05
734 Jody Reed .01 .05
735 Roger McDowell .01 .05
736 Jeff Hamilton .01 .05
737 Norm Charlton RC .08 .25
738 Darnell Coles .01 .05
739 Brook Jacoby .01 .05
740 Dan Plesac .01 .05
741 Ken Phelps .01 .05
742 Mike Harkey FS RC .02 .10
743 Mike Heath .01 .05
744 Roger Craig MG .02 .10
745 Fred McGriff .05 .15
746 German Gonzalez UER .01 .05
Wrong birthdate
747 Wil Tejada .01 .05
748 Jimmy Jones .01 .05
749 Rafael Ramirez .01 .05
750 Bret Saberhagen .02 .10
751 Ken Oberkfell .01 .05
752 Jim Gott .01 .05
753 Jose Uribe .01 .05
754 Bob Brower .01 .05
755 Mike Scioscia .02 .10
756 Scott Medvin .01 .05
757 Brady Anderson RC .15 .40
758 Gene Walter .01 .05
759 Rob Deer TL .01 .05
760 Lee Smith .02 .10
761 Dante Bichette RC .15 .40
762 Bobby Thigpen .01 .05
763 Dave Martinez .01 .05
764 Robin Ventura FDP RC .30 .75
765 Glenn Davis .01 .05
766 Cecilio Guante .01 .05
767 Mike Capel .01 .05
768 Bill Wegman .01 .05
769 Junior Ortiz .01 .05
770 Alan Trammell .02 .10
771 Ron Kittle .01 .05
772 Ron Oester .01 .05
773 Keith Moreland .01 .05
774 Frank Robinson MG .05 .15
775 Jeff Reardon .02 .10
776 Nelson Liriano .01 .05
777 Ted Power .01 .05
778 Bruce Benedict .01 .05
779 Craig McMurtry .01 .05
780 Pedro Guerrero .02 .10
781 Greg Briley .02 .10
782 Checklist 661-792 .01 .05
783 Trevor Wilson RC .02 .10
784 Steve Avery FDP RC .08 .25
785 Ellis Burks .02 .10
786 Melido Perez .01 .05
787 Dave West RC .02 .10
788 Mike Morgan .01 .05
789 Bo Jackson TL .08 .25
790 Sid Fernandez .01 .05
791 Jim Lindeman .01 .05
792 Rafael Santana .01 .05

1989 Topps Tiffany

COMP.FACT.SET (792) 60.00 150.00
*STARS: 5X TO 12X BASIC CARDS
*ROOKIES: 5X TO 12X BASIC CARDS
DISTRIBUTED ONLY IN FACTORY SET FORM
FACTORY SET PRICE IS FOR SEALED SETS

1989 Topps Batting Leaders

COMPLETE SET (22) 30.00 60.00
1 Wade Boggs 3.00 8.00
2 Tony Gwynn 6.00 15.00
3 Don Mattingly 6.00 15.00
4 Kirby Puckett 5.00 12.00
5 George Brett 6.00 15.00
6 Pedro Guerrero .20 .50
7 Tim Raines .40 1.00
8 Keith Hernandez .40 1.00
9 Jim Rice .40 1.00
10 Paul Molitor 2.50 6.00
11 Eddie Murray 2.50 6.00
12 Willie McGee .40 1.00
13 Dave Parker .40 1.00
14 Julio Franco .40 1.00
15 Rickey Henderson 4.00 10.00
16 Kent Hrbek .40 1.00
17 Willie Wilson .20 .50
18 Johnny Ray .20 .50
19 Pat Tabler .20 .50
20 Carney Lansford .20 .50
21 Robin Yount 2.50 6.00
22 Alan Trammell .60 1.50

1989 Topps Glossy All-Stars

COMPLETE SET (22) 1.25 3.00
1 Tom Kelly MG .01 .05
2 Mark McGwire .30 .75
3 Paul Molitor .15 .40
4 Wade Boggs .10 .30
5 Cal Ripken .60 1.50
6 Jose Canseco .08 .25
7 Rickey Henderson .25 .60
8 Dave Winfield .15 .40
9 Terry Steinbach .01 .05
10 Frank Viola .01 .05
11 Bobby Doerr CAPT .08 .25
12 Whitey Herzog MG .01 .05
13 Will Clark .07 .20
14 Ryne Sandberg .20 .50
15 Bobby Bonilla .02 .10
16 Ozzie Smith .20 .50
17 Vince Coleman .01 .05
18 Andre Dawson .07 .20
19 Darryl Strawberry .02 .10
20 Gary Carter .15 .40
21 Dwight Gooden .02 .10
22 Willie Stargell CAPT .08 .25

1989 Topps Glossy Send-Ins

COMPLETE SET (60) 8.00 20.00
1 Kirby Puckett .40 1.00
2 Eric Davis .07 .20
3 Joe Carter .07 .20
4 Andy Van Slyke .02 .10
5 Wade Boggs .25 .60
6 David Cone .07 .20
7 Kent Hrbek .07 .20
8 Darryl Strawberry .07 .20
9 Jay Buhner .07 .20
10 Ron Gant .07 .20
11 Will Clark .15 .40
12 Jose Canseco .30 .75
13 Juan Samuel .02 .10
14 George Brett .60 1.50
15 Benito Santiago .07 .20
16 Dennis Eckersley .25 .60
17 Gary Carter .25 .60
18 Frank Viola .02 .10
19 Roberto Alomar .60 1.50
20 Paul Gibson .02 .10
21 Dave Winfield .25 .60
22 Howard Johnson .02 .10
23 Roger Clemens .60 1.50
24 Bobby Bonilla .07 .20
25 Alan Trammell .10 .30
26 Kevin McReynolds .02 .10
27 George Bell .02 .10
28 Bruce Hurst .02 .10
29 Mark Grace .30 .75
30 Tim Belcher .02 .10
31 Mike Greenwell .02 .10
32 Glenn Davis .02 .10
33 Gary Gaetti .07 .20
34 Ryne Sandberg .60 1.50
35 Rickey Henderson .30 1.00
36 Dwight Evans .07 .20
37 Dwight Gooden .07 .20
38 Robin Yount .25 .60
39 Damon Berryhill .02 .10
40 Chris Sabo .02 .10
41 Mark McGwire .60 1.50
42 Ozzie Smith .60 1.50
43 Paul Molitor .25 .60
44 Andres Galarraga .15 .40
45 Dave Stewart .07 .20
46 Tom Browning .02 .10
47 Cal Ripken 1.25 3.00
48 Orel Hershiser .07 .20
49 Dave Gallagher .02 .10
50 Walt Weiss .02 .10
51 Don Mattingly .60 1.50
52 Tony Fernandez .02 .10
53 Tim Raines .07 .20
54 Jeff Reardon .07 .20
55 Kirk Gibson .07 .20
56 Jack Clark .02 .10
57 Danny Jackson .02 .10
58 Tony Gwynn .60 1.50
59 Cecil Espy .02 .10
60 Jody Reed .02 .10

1989 Topps Rookies

COMPLETE SET (22) 5.00 12.00
1 Roberto Alomar 1.00 2.50
2 Brady Anderson .30 .75
3 Tim Belcher .08 .25
4 Damon Berryhill .08 .25
5 Jay Buhner .40 1.00
6 Kevin Elster .08 .25
7 Cecil Espy .08 .25
8 Dave Gallagher .08 .25
9 Ron Gant .40 1.00
10 Paul Gibson .08 .25
11 Mark Grace .75 2.00
12 Darrin Jackson .08 .25
13 Gregg Jefferies .20 .50
14 Ricky Jordan .08 .25
15 Al Leiter .40 1.00
16 Melido Perez .08 .25
17 Chris Sabo .08 .25
18 Nelson Santovenia .08 .25
19 Mackey Sasser .08 .25
20 Gary Sheffield 1.25 3.00
21 Walt Weiss .08 .25
22 David Wells .75 2.00

1989 Topps Wax Box Cards

COMPLETE SET (16) 3.00 8.00
A George Brett .40 1.00
B Bill Buckner .07 .20
C Darrell Evans .07 .20
D Rich Gossage .07 .20
E Greg Gross .02 .10
F Rickey Henderson .30 .75
G Keith Hernandez .07 .20
H Tom Lasorda MG .15 .40
I Jim Rice .07 .20
J Cal Ripken .75 2.00
K Nolan Ryan .75 2.00
L Mike Schmidt .30 .75
M Bruce Sutter .20 .50
N Don Sutton .20 .50
O Kent Tekulve .02 .10
P Dave Winfield .30 .75

1989 Topps Traded

The 1989 Topps Traded set contains 132 standard-size cards. The cards were distributed exclusively in factory set form in red and white taped boxes through hobby dealers. The cards are identical to the 1989 Topps regular issue cards except for whiter stock and t-suffixed numbering on back. Rookie Cards in this set include Ken Griffey Jr., Kenny Rogers, Deion Sanders and Omar Vizquel.

COMP.FACT.SET (132) 4.00 10.00
1T Don Aase .01 .05
2T Jim Abbott .20 .50
3T Kent Anderson .01 .05
4T Keith Atherton .01 .05
5T Wally Backman .01 .05
6T Steve Balboni .01 .05
7T Jesse Barfield .02 .10
8T Steve Bedrosian .01 .05
9T Todd Benzinger .01 .05
10T Geronimo Berroa .01 .05
11T Bert Blyleven .02 .10
12T Bob Boone .02 .10
13T Phil Bradley .01 .05
14T Jeff Brantley RC .08 .25
15T Kevin Brown .08 .25
16T Jerry Browne .01 .05
17T Chuck Cary .01 .05
18T Carmen Castillo .01 .05
19T Jim Clancy .01 .05
20T Jack Clark .02 .10
21T Bryan Clutterbuck .01 .05
22T Jody Davis .01 .05
23T Mike Devereaux .01 .05
24T Frank DiPino .01 .05
25T Benny Distefano .01 .05
26T John Dopson .01 .05
27T Len Dykstra .02 .10
28T Jim Eisenreich .01 .05
29T Nick Esasky .01 .05
30T Alvaro Espinoza .01 .05
31T Darrell Evans UER .02 .10
32T Junior Felix RC .02 .10
33T Felix Fermin .01 .05
34T Julio Franco .02 .10
35T Terry Francona .02 .10
36T Cito Gaston MG .01 .05
37T Bob Geren UER RC .01 .05
38T Tom Gordon RC .20 .50
39T Tommy Gregg .01 .05
40T Ken Griffey Sr. .02 .10
41T Ken Griffey Jr. RC 10.00 25.00
42T Kevin Gross .01 .05
43T Lee Guetterman .01 .05
44T Mel Hall .01 .05
45T Erik Hanson RC .08 .25
46T Gene Harris RC .02 .10
47T Andy Hawkins .01 .05
48T Rickey Henderson .08 .25
49T Tom Herr .01 .05
50T Ken Hill RC .08 .25
51T Brian Holman RC .02 .10
52T Brian Holton .01 .05
53T Art Howe MG .01 .05
54T Ken Howell .01 .05
55T Bruce Hurst .01 .05
56T Chris James .01 .05
57T Randy Johnson .75 2.00
58T Jimmy Jones .01 .05
59T Terry Kennedy .01 .05
60T Paul Kilgus .01 .05
61T Eric King .01 .05
62T Ron Kittle .01 .05
63T John Kruk .02 .10
64T Randy Kutcher .01 .05
65T Steve Lake .01 .05
66T Mark Langston .01 .05
67T Dave LaPoint .01 .05
68T Rick Leach .01 .05
69T Terry Leach .01 .05
70T Jim Lefebvre MG .01 .05
71T Al Leiter .08 .25
72T Jeffrey Leonard .01 .05
73T Derek Lilliquist RC .02 .10
74T Rick Mahler .01 .05
75T Tom McCarthy .01 .05
76T Lloyd McClendon .01 .05
77T Lance McCullers .01 .05
78T Oddibe McDowell .01 .05
79T Roger McDowell .01 .05
80T Larry McWilliams .01 .05
81T Randy Milligan .01 .05
82T Mike Moore .01 .05
83T Keith Moreland .01 .05
84T Mike Morgan .01 .05
85T Jamie Moyer .02 .10
86T Rob Murphy .01 .05
87T Eddie Murray .08 .25
88T Pete O'Brien .01 .05
89T Gregg Olson .08 .25
90T Steve Ontiveros .01 .05
91T Jesse Orosco .01 .05
92T Spike Owen .01 .05
93T Rafael Palmeiro .08 .25
94T Clay Parker .01 .05
95T Jeff Parrett .01 .05
96T Lance Parrish .02 .10
97T Dennis Powell .01 .05
98T Rey Quinones .01 .05
99T Doug Rader MG .01 .05
100T Willie Randolph .02 .10
101T Shane Rawley .01 .05
102T Randy Ready .01 .05
103T Bip Roberts .01 .05
104T Kenny Rogers RC .75 2.00
105T Ed Romero .01 .05
106T Nolan Ryan .60 1.50
107T Luis Salazar .01 .05
108T Juan Samuel .01 .05
109T Alex Sanchez RC .01 .05
110T Deion Sanders RC .60 1.50
111T Steve Sax .01 .05
112T Rick Schu .01 .05
113T Dwight Smith RC .08 .25
114T Lonnie Smith .01 .05
115T Billy Spiers RC .08 .25
116T Kent Tekulve .01 .05
117T Walt Terrell .01 .05
118T Milt Thompson .01 .05
119T Dickie Thon .01 .05
120T Jeff Torborg MG .01 .05
121T Jeff Treadway .01 .05
122T Omar Vizquel RC .40 1.00
123T Jerome Walton RC .08 .25
124T Gary Ward .01 .05
125T Claudell Washington .01 .05
126T Curt Wilkerson .01 .05
127T Eddie Williams .01 .05
128T Frank Williams .01 .05
129T Ken Williams .01 .05
130T Mitch Williams .01 .05
131T Steve Wilson RC .02 .10
132T Checklist 1T-132T .01 .05

1989 Topps Traded Tiffany

COMP.FACT.SET (132) 60.00 120.00
*STARS: 4X TO 10X BASIC CARDS
*ROOKIES: 4X TO 10X BASIC CARDS
DISTRIBUTED ONLY IN FACTORY SET FORM
FACTORY SET PRICE IS FOR SEALED SETS

1989 Topps Ames 20/20 Club

The 1989 (Topps) Ames 20/20 Club set contains 33 standard-size glossy cards. The fronts resemble plaques with gold and silver trim. The vertically oriented backs show career stats. The cards were distributed at Ames department stores as a boxed set. The set was produced by Topps for Ames; the Topps logo is also on the front of each card. The set includes active major leaguers who have had seasons of at least 20 home runs and 20 stolen bases. The backs include lifetime batting records with home run and stolen base totals for their 20/20 years highlighted. The subject list for the set is printed on the back panel of the set's custom box. These numbered cards are ordered alphabetically by player's name.

COMPLETE SET (33) 2.00 5.00
1 Jesse Barfield .01 .05
2 Kevin Bass .01 .05
3 Don Baylor .02 .10
4 George Bell .01 .05
5 Barry Bonds .30 .75
6 Phil Bradley .01 .05
7 Ellis Burks .05 .15
8 Jose Canseco .10 .30
9 Joe Carter .02 .10
10 Kal Daniels .01 .05
11 Eric Davis .02 .10
12 Mike Davis .01 .05
13 Andre Dawson .07 .20
14 Kirk Gibson .02 .10
15 Pedro Guerrero .01 .05
16 Rickey Henderson .25 .60
17 Bo Jackson .07 .20
18 Howard Johnson .01 .05
19 Jeffrey Leonard .01 .05
20 Kevin McReynolds .01 .05
21 Dale Murphy .07 .20
22 Dwayne Murphy .01 .05
23 Dave Parker .02 .10
24 Kirby Puckett .20 .50
25 Juan Samuel .01 .05
26 Ryne Sandberg .20 .50
27 Mike Schmidt .20 .50
28 Darryl Strawberry .02 .10
29 Alan Trammell .05 .15
30 Andy Van Slyke .01 .05
31 Devon White .02 .10
32 Dave Winfield .15 .40
33 Robin Yount .15 .40

1989 Topps Award Winners

This commemorative sheet measures 8 3/4" by 8 1/8" and features the MVP, Cy Young and Rookie of the Year award winners from the AL and the NL. If the cards were cut they would measure the standard size. Fronts feature glossy color player photos with different color inner and outer borders. The player's name and the award he received is listed in a color stripe at the bottom of the card. The backs are blank and unnumbered. The players are checklisted below in alphabetical order. This sheet was included in a blister pack with a complete set of 1990 Topps Stickers.

COMPLETE SET (6) .75 2.00
1 Mark Davis .02 .10
2 Kevin Mitchell .05 .15
3 Gregg Olson .05 .15
4 Bret Saberhagen .20 .50
5 Jerome Walton .02 .10
6 Robin Yount .75 2.00

1989 Topps Baseball Talk/LJN

The BB Talk Soundcards include action photos of players, complete player statistics, exclusive specially recorded baseball programs and player autographs. These cards were produced by LJN Toys. The fronts of the cards feature oversized replicas of Topps cards. Card numbers 41, 82, 123 and 164 were issued only with the record player. They might well be tougher to acquire now.

COMPLETE SET (164) 100.00 250.00
1 1975 World Series 1.00 2.50
Game 6
2 1986 World Series .75 2.00
Game 6
3 1986 A.L. Championship .75 2.00
Game 5
4 1956 World Series .75 2.00
Game 5
5 1986 N.L. Championship .75 2.00
Game 6
6 1969 World Series .75 2.00
Game 5
7 1984 World Series .75 2.00
Game 5
8 1988 World Series 1.00 2.50
Game 1
9 Reggie Jackson 1.50 4.00
10 Brooks Robinson 1.00 2.50
11 Billy Williams 1.00 2.50
12 Bobby Thomson .75 2.00
13 Harmon Killebrew 1.00 2.50
14 Johnny Bench 1.50 4.00
15 Tom Seaver 2.00 5.00
16 Willie Stargell 1.00 2.50
17 Ernie Banks 1.50 4.00
18 Gaylord Perry 1.00 2.50
19 Bill Mazeroski 1.00 2.50
20 Babe Ruth 8.00 20.00
21 Lou Gehrig 5.00 12.00
22 Ty Cobb 3.00 8.00
23 Bob Gibson 1.00 2.50
24 Al Kaline 1.00 2.50
25 Rod Carew 1.00 2.50
26 Lou Brock 1.00 2.50
27 Stan Musial 2.00 5.00
28 Joe L. Morgan 1.00 2.50
29 Willie McCovey 1.00 2.50
30 Duke Snider 1.00 2.50
31 Whitey Ford 1.00 2.50
32 Eddie Mathews 1.00 2.50
33 Carl Yastrzemski 1.00 2.50
34 Pete Rose 2.00 5.00
35 Hank Aaron 3.00 8.00
36 Ralph Kiner 1.00 2.50
37 Steve Carlton 1.00 2.50
38 Roberto Clemente 4.00 10.00
39 Don Drysdale 1.00 2.50
40 Robin Roberts 1.00 2.50
41 Hank Aaron 3.00 8.00
42 Dave Winfield 1.50 4.00
43 Alan Trammell .75 2.00
44 Darryl Strawberry .60 1.50
45 Ozzie Smith 3.00 8.00
46 Kirby Puckett 3.00 8.00
47 Will Clark 1.50 4.00
48 Keith Hernandez .60 1.50
49 Wally Joyner .60 1.50
50 Mike Scott .40 1.00
51 Eric Davis .60 1.50
52 George Brett 4.00 10.00
53 George Bell .40 1.00
54 Tommy Lasorda MG 1.00 2.50
55 Rickey Henderson 2.00 5.00
56 Robin Yount 2.00 5.00
57 Wade Boggs 2.00 5.00
58 Roger Clemens 4.00 10.00
59 Alvin Davis .40 1.00
60 Jose Canseco 1.50 4.00
61 Fernando Valenzuela .60 1.50
62 Tony Gwynn 4.00 10.00
63 Dwight Gooden .60 1.50
64 Mark McGwire 5.00 12.00
65 Jack Clark .40 1.00
66 Dale Murphy 1.00 2.50
67 Kirk Gibson .60 1.50
68 Jack Morris .60 1.50
69 Ryne Sandberg 3.00 8.00
70 Nolan Ryan 8.00 20.00
71 John Tudor .40 1.00
72 Mike Schmidt 1.50 4.00
73 Dave Righetti .40 1.00
74 Pedro Guerrero .40 1.00
75 Rick Sutcliffe .40 1.00
76 Gary Carter 1.50 4.00
77 Cal Ripken 8.00 20.00
78 Andre Dawson 1.00 2.50
79 Andy Van Slyke .40 1.00
80 Tim Raines .60 1.50
81 Frank Viola .40 1.00
82 Don Mattingly 4.00 10.00
83 Rick Reuschel .40 1.00
84 Willie McGee .60 1.50
85 Mark Langston .40 1.00
86 Ron Darling .40 1.00
87 Gregg Jefferies .40 1.00
88 Harold Baines .60 1.50
89 Eddie Murray 2.00 5.00
90 Barry Larkin 1.00 2.50
91 Gary Gaetti .60 1.50
92 Bret Saberhagen .60 1.50
93 Roger McDowell .40 1.00
94 Joe Magrane .40 1.00
95 Juan Samuel .40 1.00
96 Bert Blyleven .60 1.50
97 Kal Daniels .40 1.00
98 Kevin Bass .40 1.00
99 Glenn Davis .40 1.00
100 Steve Sax .40 1.00
101 Rich Gossage .60 1.50
102 Roger Craig MG .40 1.00
103 Carney Lansford .40 1.00
104 Joe Carter .60 1.50
105 Bruce Sutter .60 1.50
106 Barry Bonds 1.25 3.00
107 Danny Jackson .40 1.00
108 Mike Flanagan .40 1.00
109 Dwight Evans .60 1.50
110 Ron Guidry .60 1.50
111 Bruce Hurst .40 1.00
112 Jim Rice .60 1.50
113 Oddibe McDowell .40 1.00
114 Bobby Bonilla .60 1.50
115 Bob Welch .40 1.00
116 Dave Parker .60 1.50
117 Tim Wallach .40 1.00
118 Tom Henke .40 1.00
119 Mike Greenwell .40 1.00
120 Kevin Seitzer .40 1.00
121 Randy Myers .60 1.50
122 Andres Galarraga .75 2.00
123 Orel Hershiser 1.00 2.50
124 Cory Snyder .40 1.00
125 Mike Witt .40 1.00
126 Mike LaValliere .40 1.00
127 Pete Incaviglia .40 1.00
128 Dennis Eckersley 1.25 3.00
129 Jimmy Key .60 1.50
130 John Franco .60 1.50
131 Dan Plesac .40 1.00
132 Tony LaRussa MG .60 1.50
133 Hubie Brooks .40 1.00
134 Chili Davis .60 1.50
135 Bob Boone .60 1.50
136 Jeff Reardon .60 1.50
137 Candy Maldonado .40 1.00
138 Mike Marshall .40 1.00
139 Tommy John .60 1.50
140 Chris Sabo .40 1.00
141 Vince Coleman .40 1.00
142 Frank White .60 1.50
143 Harold Reynolds .60 1.50
144 Lee Smith .60 1.50
145 John Kruk .60 1.50
146 Tony Fernandez .60 1.50
147 Steve Bedrosian .40 1.00
148 Benito Santiago .60 1.50
149 Ozzie Guillen .75 2.00
150 Gerald Perry .40 1.00
151 Carlton Fisk 2.00 5.00
152 Tom Brunansky .40 1.00
153 Paul Molitor 1.25 3.00
154 Todd Worrell .40 1.00
155 Brett Butler .60 1.50
156 Sparky Anderson MG .75 2.00
157 Kent Hrbek .60 1.50
158 Frank Tanana .40 1.00
159 Kevin Mitchell .40 1.00
160 Charlie Hough .60 1.50
161 Doug Jones .40 1.00
162 Lou Whitaker .60 1.50
163 Fred Lynn .40 1.00
164 Checklist .40 1.00

1989 Topps Big

The 1989 Topps Big Baseball set contains 330 glossy cards measuring approximately 2 1/2" by 3 3/4". The fronts feature mug shots superimposed on action photos. The horizontally oriented backs have color cartoons and statistics for the player's previous season and total career. Team members for the United States Olympic team were also included in this set. The set was released in three series of 110 cards. The cards were distributed in seven-card packs marked with the series number.

COMPLETE SET (330) 10.00 25.00
1 Orel Hershiser .02 .10
2 Harold Reynolds .02 .10
3 Jody Davis .01 .05
4 Greg Walker .01 .05
5 Barry Bonds .60 1.50
6 Bret Saberhagen .02 .10
7 Johnny Ray .01 .05
8 Mike Fiore .01 .05
9 Juan Castillo .01 .05
10 Todd Burns .01 .05
11 Carmelo Martinez .01 .05
12 Geno Petralli .01 .05
13 Mel Hall .01 .05
14 Tom Browning .01 .05
15 Fred McGriff .20 .50
16 Kevin Elster .01 .05
17 Tim Leary .01 .05
18 Jim Rice .02 .10
19 Bret Barberie .01 .05
20 Jay Buhner .07 .20
21 Atlee Hammaker .01 .05
22 Lou Whitaker .02 .10
23 Paul Runge .01 .05
24 Carlton Fisk .20 .50
25 Jose Lind .01 .05
26 Mark Gubicza .01 .05
27 Billy Ripken .01 .05
28 Mike Pagliarulo .01 .05
29 Jim Deshaies .01 .05
30 Mark McLemore .01 .05
31 Scott Terry .01 .05
32 Franklin Stubbs .01 .05
33 Don August .01 .05
34 Mark McGwire .75 2.00
35 Eric Show .01 .05
36 Cecil Espy .01 .05
37 Ron Tingley .01 .05
38 Mickey Brantley .01 .05
39 Paul O'Neill .05 .15
40 Ed Sprague .05 .15
41 Len Dykstra .02 .10
42 Roger Clemens .75 2.00
43 Ron Gant .02 .10
44 Dan Pasqua .01 .05
45 Jeff D. Robinson .01 .05
46 George Brett .75 2.00
47 Bryn Smith .01 .05
48 Mike Marshall .01 .05
49 Doug Robbins .01 .05
50 Don Mattingly .75 2.00

51 Mike Scott .01 .05
52 Steve Jeltz .01 .05
53 Dick Schofield .01 .05
54 Tom Brunansky .01 .05
55 Gary Sheffield 1.25 3.00
56 Dave Valle .01 .05
57 Carney Lansford .02 .10
58 Tony Gwynn .75 2.00
59 Checklist 1-110 .01 .05
60 Damon Berryhill .01 .05
61 Jack Morris .02 .10
62 Brett Butler .02 .10
63 Mickey Hatcher .01 .05
64 Bruce Sutter .20 .50
65 Robin Ventura .40 1.00
66 Junior Ortiz .01 .05
67 Pat Tabler .01 .05
68 Greg Swindell .01 .05
69 Jeff Branson .01 .05
70 Manny Lee .01 .05
71 Dave Magadan .01 .05
72 Rich Gedman .01 .05
73 Tim Raines .02 .10
74 Mike Maddux .01 .05
75 Jim Presley .01 .05
76 Chuck Finley .02 .10
77 Jose Oquendo .01 .05
78 Rob Deer .01 .05
79 Jay Howell .01 .05
80 Terry Steinbach .01 .05
81 Ed Whitson .01 .05
82 Ruben Sierra .02 .10
83 Bruce Benedict .01 .05
84 Fred Manrique .01 .05
85 John Smiley .01 .05
86 Mike Macfarlane .01 .05
87 Rene Gonzales .01 .05
88 Charles Hudson .01 .05
89 Glenn Davis .01 .05
90 Les Straker .01 .05
91 Carmen Castillo .01 .05
92 Tracy Woodson .01 .05
93 Tino Martinez .40 1.00
94 Herm Winningham .01 .05
95 Kelly Gruber .01 .05
96 Terry Leach .01 .05
97 Jody Reed .01 .05
98 Nelson Santovenia .01 .05
99 Tony Armas .01 .05
100 Greg Brock .01 .05
101 Dave Stewart .02 .10
102 Roberto Alomar .60 1.50
103 Jim Sundberg .01 .05
104 Albert Hall .01 .05
105 Steve Lyons .02 .10
106 Sid Bream .01 .05
107 Danny Tartabull .01 .05
108 Rick Dempsey .01 .05
109 Rich Renteria .01 .05
110 Ozzie Smith .60 1.50
111 Steve Sax .01 .05
112 Kelly Downs .01 .05
113 Larry Sheets .01 .05
114 Andy Benes .07 .20
115 Pete O'Brien .01 .05
116 Kevin McReynolds .01 .05
117 Juan Berenguer .01 .05
118 Billy Hatcher .01 .05
119 Rick Cerone .01 .05
120 Andre Dawson .07 .20
121 Storm Davis .01 .05
122 Devon White .01 .05
123 Alan Trammell .05 .15
124 Vince Coleman .01 .05
125 Al Leiter .07 .20
126 Dale Sveum .01 .05
127 Pete Incaviglia .01 .05
128 Dave Stieb .01 .05
129 Kevin Mitchell .01 .05
130 Dave Schmidt .01 .05
131 Gary Redus .01 .05
132 Ron Robinson .01 .05
133 Darnell Coles .01 .05
134 Benito Santiago .02 .10
135 John Farrell .01 .05
136 Willie Wilson .01 .05
137 Steve Bedrosian .01 .05
138 Don Slaught .01 .05
139 Darryl Strawberry .02 .10
140 Frank Viola .01 .05
141 Dave Silvestri .01 .05
142 Carlos Quintana .01 .05
143 Vance Law .01 .05
144 Dave Parker .02 .10
145 Tim Belcher .01 .05
146 Will Clark .40 1.00
147 Mark Williamson .01 .05
148 Ozzie Guillen .05 .15
149 Kirk McCaskill .01 .05
150 Pat Sheridan .01 .05
151 Terry Pendleton .02 .10
152 Roberto Kelly .01 .05
153 Joey Meyer .01 .05
154 Mark Grant .01 .05
155 Joe Carter .07 .20
156 Steve Buechele .01 .05
157 Tony Fernandez .02 .10
158 Jeff Reed .01 .05
159 Bobby Bonilla .02 .10
160 Henry Cotto .01 .05
161 Kurt Stillwell .01 .05
162 Mickey Morandini .01 .05
163 Robby Thompson .01 .05
164 Rick Schu .01 .05
165 Stan Jefferson .01 .05
166 Ron Darling .01 .05
167 Kirby Puckett .50 1.25
168 Bill Doran .01 .05
169 Dennis Lamp .01 .05
170 Ty Griffin .01 .05
171 Ron Hassey .01 .05
172 Dale Murphy .20 .50
173 Andres Galarraga .07 .20
174 Tim Flannery .01 .05
175 Cory Snyder .01 .05
176 Checklist 111-220 .01 .05
177 Tommy Barrett .01 .05
178 Dan Petry .01 .05
179 Billy Masse .01 .05
180 Terry Kennedy .01 .05
181 Joe Orsulak .01 .05
182 Doyle Alexander .01 .05
183 Willie McGee .02 .10
184 Jim Gantner .01 .05
185 Keith Hernandez .02 .10
186 Greg Gagne .01 .05
187 Kevin Bass .01 .05
188 Mark Eichhorn .01 .05
189 Mark Grace .40 1.00
190 Jose Canseco .20 .50
191 Bobby Witt .01 .05
192 Rafael Santana .01 .05
193 Dwight Evans .02 .10
194 Greg Booker .01 .05
195 Brook Jacoby .02 .05
196 Rafael Belliard .01 .05
197 Candy Maldonado .01 .05
198 Mickey Tettleton .02 .10
199 Barry Larkin .30 .75
200 Frank White .02 .10
201 Wally Joyner .02 .10
202 Chet Lemon .01 .05
203 Joe Magrane .01 .05
204 Glenn Braggs .01 .05
205 Scott Fletcher .01 .05
206 Gary Ward .01 .05
207 Nelson Liriano .01 .05
208 Howard Johnson .01 .05
209 Kent Hrbek .02 .10
210 Ken Caminiti .07 .20
211 Mike Greenwell .01 .05
212 Ryne Sandberg .60 1.50
213 Joe Slusarski .01 .05
214 Donell Nixon .01 .05
215 Tim Wallach .01 .05
216 John Kruk .02 .10
217 Charles Nagy .05 .15
218 Alvin Davis .01 .05
219 Oswald Peraza .01 .05
220 Mike Schmidt .30 .75
221 Spike Owen .01 .05
222 Mike Smithson .01 .05
223 Dion James .01 .05
224 Ernie Whitt .01 .05
225 Mike Davis .01 .05
226 Gene Larkin .02 .10
227 Pat Combs .01 .05
228 Jack Howell .01 .05
229 Ron Oester .01 .05
230 Paul Gibson .01 .05
231 Mookie Wilson .02 .10
232 Glenn Hubbard .01 .05
233 Shawon Dunston .01 .05
234 Otis Nixon .01 .05
235 Melido Perez .01 .05
236 Jerry Browne .01 .05
237 Rick Rhoden .01 .05
238 Bo Jackson .08 .25
239 Randy Velarde .01 .05
240 Jack Clark .01 .05
241 Wade Boggs .30 .75
242 Lonnie Smith .01 .05
243 Mike Flanagan .01 .05
244 Willie Randolph .02 .10
245 Oddibe McDowell .01 .05
246 Ricky Jordan .01 .05
247 Greg Briley .01 .05
248 Rex Hudler .02 .10
249 Robin Yount .20 .50
250 Lance Parrish .02 .10
251 Chris Sabo .01 .05
252 Mike Henneman .01 .05
253 Gregg Jefferies .01 .05
254 Curt Young .01 .05
255 Andy Van Slyke .01 .05
256 Rod Booker .01 .05
257 Rafael Palmeiro .30 .75
258 Jose Uribe .01 .05
259 Ellis Burks .20 .50
260 John Smoltz .20 .50
261 Tom Foley .01 .05
262 Lloyd Moseby .01 .05
263 Jim Poole .01 .05
264 Gary Gaetti .02 .10
265 Bob Dernier .01 .05
266 Harold Baines .05 .15
267 Tom Candiotti .01 .05
268 Rafael Ramirez .01 .05
269 Bob Boone .02 .10
270 Buddy Bell .02 .10
271 Rickey Henderson .40 1.25
272 Willie Fraser .01 .05
273 Eric Davis .02 .10
274 Jeff M. Robinson .01 .05
275 Damaso Garcia .01 .05
276 Sid Fernandez .01 .05
277 Stan Javier .01 .05
278 Marty Barrett .01 .05
279 Gerald Perry .01 .05
280 Rob Ducey .01 .05
281 Mike Scioscia .02 .10
282 Randy Bush .01 .05
283 Tom Herr .01 .05
284 Glenn Wilson .01 .05
285 Pedro Guerrero .01 .05
286 Cal Ripken 1.50 4.00
287 Randy Johnson 1.50 4.00
288 Julio Franco .02 .10
289 Ivan Calderon .01 .05
290 Rich Yett .01 .05
291 Scott Servais .01 .05
292 Bill Pecota .01 .05
293 Ken Phelps .01 .05
294 Chili Davis .02 .10
295 Manny Trillo .01 .05
296 Mike Boddicker .01 .05
297 Geronimo Berroa .01 .05
298 Todd Stottlemyre .02 .10
299 Kirk Gibson .02 .10
300 Wally Backman .01 .05
301 Hubie Brooks .01 .05
302 Von Hayes .01 .05
303 Matt Nokes .01 .05
304 Dwight Gooden .02 .10
305 Walt Weiss .01 .05
306 Mike LaValliere .01 .05
307 Cris Carpenter .01 .05
308 Ted Wood .01 .05
309 Jeff Russell .01 .05
310 Dave Gallagher .01 .05
311 Andy Allanson .01 .05
312 Craig Reynolds .01 .05
313 Kevin Seitzer .01 .05
314 Dave Winfield .25 .60
315 Andy McGaffigan .01 .05
316 Nick Esasky .01 .05
317 Jeff Blauser .01 .05
318 George Bell .01 .05
319 Eddie Murray .30 .75
320 Mark Davidson .01 .05
321 Juan Samuel .01 .05
322 Jim Abbott .07 .20
323 Kal Daniels .01 .05
324 Mike Brumley .01 .05
325 Gary Carter .20 .50
326 Dave Henderson .01 .05
327 Checklist 221-330 .01 .05
328 Garry Templeton .01 .05
329 Pat Perry .01 .05
330 Paul Molitor .30 .75

1989 Topps Cap'n Crunch

The 1989 Topps Cap'n Crunch set contains 22 standard-size cards. The fronts have red, white and blue borders surrounding "mugshot" photos. The backs are horizontally oriented and show lifetime stats. The team logos have been airbrushed out. Two cards were included (in a cellophane wrapper with a piece of gum) in each specially marked Cap'n Crunch cereal box. The set was not available as a complete set as part of any mail-in offer.

COMPLETE SET (22) 8.00 20.00
1 Jose Canseco .40 1.00
2 Kirk Gibson .15 .40
3 Orel Hershiser .15 .40
4 Frank Viola .07 .20
5 Tony Gwynn .75 2.00
6 Cal Ripken 1.50 4.00
7 Darryl Strawberry .15 .40
8 Don Mattingly .75 2.00
9 George Brett .75 2.00
10 Andre Dawson .30 .75
11 Dale Murphy .30 .75
12 Alan Trammell .25 .60
13 Eric Davis .15 .40
14 Jack Clark .07 .20
15 Eddie Murray .40 1.00
16 Mike Schmidt .40 1.00
17 Dwight Gooden .15 .40
18 Roger Clemens .75 2.00
19 Will Clark .30 .75
20 Kirby Puckett .50 1.25
21 Robin Yount .40 1.00
22 Mark McGwire .75 2.00

1989 Topps Doubleheaders All-Stars

The 1989 Topps Doubleheaders were a novel idea from Topps to capitalize on the interest in rookie cards. The one side of the plastic holder shows a small color photo of the rookie card while the other side shows a photo of the current year Topps card. The holders measure 2" by 2 1/8". The set contains 24 holders, eight starting players, two starting pitchers, one reliever, and one DH from each league. They are unnumbered. Apparently the twelve from each league are considered by Topps as the "best" at each position.

COMPLETE SET (24) 8.00 20.00
1 Don Mattingly 1.50 4.00
2 Julio Franco .20 .50
3 Wade Boggs .75 2.00
4 Alan Trammell .30 .75
5 Jose Canseco .60 1.50
6 Mike Greenwell .08 .25
7 Kirby Puckett 1.00 2.50
8 Carlton Fisk .50 1.25
9 Roger Clemens 1.50 4.00
10 Frank Viola .08 .25
11 Dennis Eckersley .60 1.50
12 Mark McGwire 1.50 4.00
13 Will Clark .40 1.00
14 Ryne Sandberg 1.50 4.00
15 Bobby Bonilla .20 .50
16 Ozzie Smith 1.50 4.00
17 Andre Dawson .40 1.00
18 Darryl Strawberry .20 .50
19 Andy Van Slyke .08 .25
20 Alan Ashby .08 .25
21 Orel Hershiser .20 .50
22 Danny Jackson .08 .25
23 John Franco .20 .50
24 Kirk Gibson .20 .50

1989 Topps Doubleheaders Mets/Yankees Test

This set of 24 Doubleheaders, which was test marketed by Topps, and is extremely tough to find, features the New York Mets (1-13) and the New York Yankees (14-24). Each item is a clear plastic stand-up holder containing two mini-reproductions of the player's cards. On one side is the 1989 Topps card, and on the reverse is a reproduction of the rookie card.

COMPLETE SET (24) 200.00 400.00
1 Darryl Strawberry 6.00 15.00
2 Gregg Jefferies 4.00 10.00
3 Kevin McReynolds 4.00 10.00
4 Gary Carter 15.00 40.00
5 Dwight Gooden 6.00 15.00
6 David Cone 10.00 25.00
7 Ron Darling 6.00 15.00
8 Keith Hernandez 6.00 15.00
9 Randy Myers 6.00 15.00
10 Howard Johnson 6.00 15.00
11 Tim Teufel 4.00 10.00
12 Len Dykstra 6.00 15.00
13 Mookie Wilson 6.00 15.00
14 Don Mattingly 40.00 100.00
15 Dave Winfield 15.00 40.00
16 Rickey Henderson 40.00 80.00
17 Claudell Washington 4.00 10.00
18 Dave Righetti 6.00 15.00
19 Steve Sax 4.00 10.00
20 Mike Pagliarulo 4.00 10.00
21 Rafael Santana 4.00 10.00
22 Richard Dotson 4.00 10.00
23 Rick Rhoden 4.00 10.00
24 Ken Phelps 4.00 10.00

1989 Topps Gallery of Champions

These 12 mini "cards" were produced by Topps and sold in complete set form only. The players selected for this set were either award winners or were league leaders. These approximately 1 1/4" by 1 3/4" cards were printed using either aluminum, bronze or silver. We have priced the aluminum versions of these cards. The bronze versions have a value of between 2X to 4X the aluminums while the silvers have a value between 5X to 10X the aluminum cards. We have sequenced this set in alphabetical order.

COMPLETE SET (12) 40.00 100.00
1 Wade Boggs 8.00 20.00
2 Jose Canseco 7.50 15.00
3 Will Clark 8.00 20.00
4 Dennis Eckersley 6.00 15.00
5 John Franco 3.00 8.00
6 Kirk Gibson 3.00 8.00
7 Tony Gwynn 10.00 25.00
8 Orel Hershiser 3.00 8.00
9 Chris Sabo 2.00 5.00
10 Darryl Strawberry 3.00 8.00
11 Frank Viola 2.00 5.00
12 Walt Weiss 2.00 5.00

1989 Topps Heads Up Test

This very limited distribution set features baseball superstars. A large photo of the player's head is featured. These "faces" were released one per pack and the player's name and team are noted on the back.

COMPLETE SET (24) 1500.00 3000.00
1 Tony Gwynn 125.00 300.00
2 Will Clark 50.00 120.00
3 Dwight Gooden 25.00 60.00
4 Ricky Jordan 15.00 40.00
5 Ken Griffey Jr. 300.00 800.00
6 Darryl Strawberry 25.00 60.00
7 Frank Viola 15.00 40.00
8 Bo Jackson 25.00 60.00
9 Ryne Sandberg 100.00 250.00
10 Gregg Jefferies 25.00 60.00
11 Wade Boggs 60.00 150.00
12 Ellis Burks 25.00 60.00
13 Gary Sheffield 125.00 300.00
14 Mark McGwire 200.00 400.00
15 Mark Grace 75.00 200.00
16 Jim Abbott 25.00 60.00
17 Ozzie Smith 75.00 200.00
18 Jose Canseco 60.00 150.00
19 Don Mattingly 125.00 300.00
20 Kirby Puckett 75.00 200.00
21 Eric Davis 25.00 60.00
22 Mike Greenwell 15.00 40.00
23 Dale Murphy 40.00 100.00
24 Mike Schmidt 100.00 200.00

1989 Topps Hills Team MVP's

The 1989 Topps Hills Team MVP's set contains 33 glossy standard-size cards. The fronts and backs are yellow, red, white and navy. The horizontally oriented backs are green. The cards were distributed through Hills stores as a boxed set. The set was printed in Ireland. These numbered cards are ordered alphabetically by player's name.

COMPLETE SET (33) 2.00 5.00
1 Harold Baines .02 .10
2 Wade Boggs .15 .40
3 George Brett .30 .75
4 Tom Brunansky .01 .05
5 Jose Canseco .10 .30
6 Joe Carter .05 .15
7 Will Clark .15 .40
8 Roger Clemens .30 .75
9 David Cone .05 .15
10 Glenn Davis .01 .05
11 Andre Dawson .07 .20
12 Dennis Eckersley .15 .40
13 Andres Galarraga .07 .20
14 Kirk Gibson .02 .10
15 Mike Greenwell .01 .05
16 Tony Gwynn .30 .75
17 Orel Hershiser .02 .10
18 Danny Jackson .01 .05
19 Mark Langston .01 .05
20 Fred McGriff .15 .40
21 Dale Murphy .07 .20
22 Eddie Murray .15 .40
23 Kirby Puckett .20 .50
24 Johnny Ray .01 .05
25 Juan Samuel .01 .05
26 Ruben Sierra .02 .10
27 Dave Stewart .02 .10
28 Darryl Strawberry .02 .10
29 Alan Trammell .05 .15
30 Andy Van Slyke .01 .05
31 Frank Viola .01 .05
32 Dave Winfield .15 .40
33 Robin Yount .15 .40

1989 Topps Mini Leaders

The 1989 Topps Mini League Leaders set contains 77 cards measuring approximately 2 1/8" by 3". The fronts have color photos with large white borders. The backs are yellow and feature 1988 and career stats. The cards were distributed in seven-card cello packs. These numbered cards are ordered alphabetically by player within team and the teams themselves are ordered alphabetically.

COMPLETE SET (77) 3.00 8.00
1 Dale Murphy .07 .20
2 Gerald Perry .01 .05
3 Andre Dawson .07 .20
4 Greg Maddux .50 1.25
5 Rafael Palmeiro .15 .40
6 Tom Browning .01 .05
7 Kal Daniels .01 .05
8 Eric Davis .02 .10
9 John Franco .02 .10
10 Danny Jackson .01 .05
11 Barry Larkin .10 .30
12 Jose Rijo .01 .05
13 Chris Sabo .01 .05
14 Nolan Ryan .75 2.00
15 Mike Scott .01 .05
16 Gerald Young .01 .05
17 Kirk Gibson .02 .10
18 Orel Hershiser .02 .10
19 Steve Sax .01 .05
20 John Tudor .01 .05
21 Hubie Brooks .01 .05
22 Andres Galarraga .07 .20
23 Otis Nixon .01 .05
24 David Cone .05 .15
25 Sid Fernandez .01 .05
26 Dwight Gooden .02 .10
27 Kevin McReynolds .01 .05
28 Darryl Strawberry .02 .10
29 Juan Samuel .01 .05
30 Bobby Bonilla .01 .05
31 Sid Bream .01 .05
32 Jim Gott .01 .05
33 Andy Van Slyke .01 .05
34 Vince Coleman .01 .05
35 Jose DeLeon .01 .05
36 Joe Magrane .01 .05
37 Ozzie Smith .30 .75
38 Todd Worrell .01 .05
39 Tony Gwynn .40 1.00
40 Brett Butler .02 .10
41 Will Clark .15 .40
42 Rick Reuschel .01 .05
43 Checklist Card .01 .05
44 Eddie Murray .20 .50
45 Wade Boggs .15 .40
46 Roger Clemens .40 1.00
47 Dwight Evans .02 .10
48 Mike Greenwell .01 .05
49 Bruce Hurst .01 .05
50 Johnny Ray .01 .05
51 Doug Jones .01 .05
52 Greg Swindell .01 .05
53 Gary Pettis .01 .05
54 George Brett .40 1.00
55 Mark Gubicza .01 .05
56 Willie Wilson .01 .05
57 Teddy Higuera .01 .05
58 Paul Molitor .15 .40
59 Robin Yount .15 .40
60 Allan Anderson .01 .05
61 Gary Gaetti .02 .10
62 Kirby Puckett .25 .60
63 Jeff Reardon .02 .10
64 Frank Viola .01 .05
65 Jack Clark .01 .05
66 Rickey Henderson .25 .60
67 Dave Winfield .15 .40
68 Jose Canseco .15 .40
69 Dennis Eckersley .15 .40
70 Mark McGwire .40 1.00
71 Dave Stewart .02 .10
72 Alvin Davis .01 .05
73 Mark Langston .01 .05
74 Harold Reynolds .02 .10
75 George Bell .01 .05
76 Tony Fernandez .02 .10
77 Fred McGriff .15 .40

1989 Topps Stickers

Printed in Canada, these 326 stickers measure approximately 2 1/8" by 3" and feature white-bordered color player photos. The borders are highlighted by colored lines and baseball icons. The stickers are numbered at the lower right. The sticker backs are actually cards (1989 O-Pee-Chee Super Stars) and are considered a separate set. An album onto which the stickers could be affixed was available at retail stores. The album and the sticker numbering are organized as follows: 1988 Highlights (1-12), Houston Astros (13-23), Atlanta Braves (24-34), St. Louis Cardinals (35-45), Chicago Cubs (46-56), Los Angeles Dodgers (57-67), Montreal Expos (68-78), San Francisco Giants (79-89), New York Mets (90-100), San Diego Padres (101-111), Philadelphia Phillies (112-122), Pittsburgh Pirates (123-133), Cincinnati Reds (134-144), Foil All-Stars (145-162), Oakland A's (163-173), California Angels (174-184), Toronto Blue Jays (185-195), Milwaukee Brewers (196-206), Cleveland Indians (207-217), Seattle Mariners (218-228), Baltimore Orioles (229-239), Texas Rangers (240-250), Boston Red Sox (251-261), Kansas City Royals (262-272), Detroit Tigers (273-283), Minnesota Twins (284-294), Chicago White Sox (295-305), New York Yankees (306-316) and Future Stars (317-326). For those stickers featuring more than one player, the other numbers on that sticker are given below in parentheses. Although the prices listed below are for the stickers only, there are instances where having an especially desirable sticker card back (attached to that sticker) will increase the values listed below.

COMPLETE SET (326) 6.00 15.00
COMMON PLAYER (1-326) .02 .05
*OPC: .4X TO 1X TOPPS STICKERS
1 George Bell .01 .05
2 Gary Carter .05 .15
3 Doug Jones .01 .05
4 John Franco .02 .10
5 Andre Dawson .08 .25
6 Pat Tabler .01 .05
7 Tom Browning .01 .05
8 Jeff Reardon .02 .10
9 Wade Boggs .08 .25
10 Kevin McReynolds .01 .05
11 Jose Canseco .08 .25
12 Orel Hershiser .02 .10
13 Dave Smith .01 .05
14 Kevin Bass .01 .05
15 Mike Scott .01 .05
16 Bill Doran .01 .05
17 Rafael Ramirez .01 .05
18 Buddy Bell .02 .10
19 Billy Hatcher .01 .05
20 Nolan Ryan .75 2.00
21 Glenn Davis .01 .05
22 Bob Knepper .01 .05
23 Gerald Young .01 .05
24 Dion James .01 .05
25 Bruce Sutter .01 .05
26 Andres Thomas .01 .05
27 Zane Smith .01 .05
28 Ozzie Virgil .01 .05
29 Rick Mahler .01 .05
30 Albert Hall .01 .05
31 Pete Smith .01 .05
32 Dale Murphy .08 .25
33 Gerald Perry .01 .05
34 Ron Gant .02 .10
35 Bob Horner .01 .05
36 Willie McGee .02 .10
37 Luis Alicea .01 .05
38 Tony Pena .01 .05
39 Todd Worrell .02 .10
40 Pedro Guerrero .01 .05
41 Tom Brunansky .01 .05
42 Terry Pendleton .02 .10
43 Vince Coleman .01 .05
44 Ozzie Smith .20 .50
45 Jose Oquendo .01 .05
46 Vance Law .01 .05
47 Rafael Palmeiro .08 .25
48 Greg Maddux 1.00 2.50
49 Shawon Dunston .01 .05
50 Mark Grace .15 .40
51 Damon Berryhill .01 .05
52 Rick Sutcliffe .01 .05
53 Jamie Moyer .01 .05
54 Andre Dawson .08 .25
55 Ryne Sandberg .20 .50
56 Calvin Schiraldi .01 .05
57 Steve Sax .01 .05
58 Mike Scioscia .01 .05
59 Alfredo Griffin .01 .05
60 Fernando Valenzuela .02 .10
61 Jay Howell .01 .05
62 Tim Leary .01 .05
63 John Shelby .01 .05
64 John Tudor .01 .05
65 Orel Hershiser .02 .10
66 Kirk Gibson .02 .10
67 Mike Marshall .01 .05
68 Luis Rivera .01 .05
69 Tim Burke .01 .05
70 Tim Wallach .01 .05
71 Pascual Perez .01 .05
72 Hubie Brooks .01 .05
73 Jeff Parrett .01 .05
74 Denny Martinez .02 .10
75 Andy McGaffigan .01 .05
76 Andres Galarraga .08 .25
77 Tim Raines .02 .10
78 Nelson Santovenia .01 .05
79 Rick Reuschel .01 .05
80 Mike Aldrete .01 .05
81 Kelly Downs .01 .05
82 Jose Uribe .01 .05
83 Mike Krukow .01 .05
84 Kevin Mitchell .02 .10
85 Brett Butler .02 .10
86 Don Robinson .01 .05
87 Robby Thompson .01 .05
88 Will Clark .08 .25
89 Candy Maldonado .01 .05
90 Len Dykstra .02 .10
91 Howard Johnson .01 .05
92 Roger McDowell .01 .05
93 Keith Hernandez .02 .10
94 Gary Carter .05 .15
95 Kevin McReynolds .01 .05
96 Dave Cone .08 .25
(David)
97 Randy Myers .02 .10
98 Darryl Strawberry .02 .10
99 Dwight Gooden .02 .10
100 Ron Darling .01 .05
101 Benito Santiago .01 .05
102 John Kruk .02 .10
103 Chris Brown .01 .05
104 Roberto Alomar .40 1.00
105 Keith Moreland .01 .05
106 Randy Ready .01 .05
107 Marvell Wynne .01 .05
108 Lance McCullers .01 .05
109 Tony Gwynn .30 .75
110 Mark Davis .01 .05
111 Andy Hawkins .01 .05
112 Steve Bedrosian .01 .05
113 Phil Bradley .01 .05
114 Steve Jeltz .01 .05
115 Von Hayes .01 .05
116 Kevin Gross .01 .05
117 Juan Samuel .01 .05
118 Shane Rawley .01 .05
119 Chris James .01 .05
120 Mike Schmidt .25 .60
121 Don Carman .01 .05
122 Bruce Ruffin .01 .05
123 Bob Walk .01 .05
124 John Smiley .01 .05
125 Sid Bream .01 .05
126 Jose Lind .01 .05
127 Barry Bonds .25 .60
128 Mike LaValliere .01 .05
129 Jeff D. Robinson .01 .05
130 Mike Dunne .01 .05
131 Bobby Bonilla .02 .10
132 Andy Van Slyke .02 .10
133 Rafael Belliard .01 .05
134 Nick Esasky .01 .05
135 Bo Diaz .01 .05
136 John Franco .02 .10
137 Barry Larkin .08 .25
138 Eric Davis .02 .10
139 Jeff Treadway .01 .05
140 Jose Rijo .01 .05
141 Tom Browning .01 .05
142 Chris Sabo .01 .05
143 Danny Jackson .01 .05
144 Kal Daniels .01 .05
145 Rickey Henderson AS .08 .25
146 Paul Molitor AS .08 .25
147 Wade Boggs AS .08 .25
148 Jose Canseco AS .02 .10
149 Dave Winfield AS .02 .10
150 Cal Ripken AS .40 1.00
151 Mark McGwire AS .08 .25
152 Terry Steinbach AS .02 .10
153 Frank Viola AS .01 .05
154 Vince Coleman AS .01 .05
155 Ryne Sandberg AS .08 .25
156 Andre Dawson AS .02 .10
157 Darryl Strawberry AS .02 .10
158 Bobby Bonilla AS .02 .10
159 Will Clark AS .02 .10
160 Gary Carter AS .05 .15
161 Ozzie Smith AS .08 .25
162 Dwight Gooden AS .02 .10
163 Dave Stewart .02 .10
164 Dave Henderson .01 .05
165 Terry Steinbach .02 .10
166 Bob Welch .01 .05
167 Dennis Eckersley .05 .15
168 Walt Weiss .01 .05
169 Dave Parker .02 .10
170 Carney Lansford .02 .10
171 Jose Canseco .08 .25
172 Mark McGwire 1.50 4.00
173 Ron Hassey .01 .05
174 Dick Schofield .01 .05
175 Bob Boone .02 .10
176 Mike Witt .01 .05
177 Chili Davis .02 .10
178 Brian Downing .01 .05
179 Devon White .02 .10
180 Bryan Harvey .01 .05
181 Jack Howell .01 .05
182 Johnny Ray .01 .05
183 Wally Joyner .02 .10
184 Kirk McCaskill .01 .05
185 Fred McGriff .20 .50
186 Jimmy Key .02 .10
187 Kelly Gruber .01 .05
188 Lloyd Moseby .01 .05
189 Tony Fernandez .01 .05
190 Mike Flanagan .01 .05
191 Pat Borders .01 .05
192 Rance Mulliniks .01 .05
193 George Bell .01 .05
194 Dave Stieb .01 .05
195 Tom Henke .01 .05
196 Glenn Braggs .01 .05
197 Dan Plesac .01 .05
198 Teddy Higuera .01 .05
199 Jeffrey Leonard .01 .05
200 B.J. Surhoff .02 .10
201 Greg Brock .01 .05
202 Rob Deer .01 .05
203 Jim Gantner .01 .05
204 Paul Molitor .08 .25
205 Robin Yount .08 .25
206 Dale Sveum .01 .05
207 Andy Allanson .01 .05
208 Julio Franco .01 .05
209 Bud Black .01 .05
210 Cory Snyder .01 .05
211 Tom Candiotti .01 .05
212 Brook Jacoby .01 .05
213 Greg Swindell .01 .05
214 John Farrell .01 .05
215 Doug Jones .01 .05
216 Joe Carter .05 .15
217 Scott Bailes .01 .05
218 Henry Cotto .01 .05
219 Mickey Brantley .01 .05
220 Mike Moore .01 .05
221 Mark Langston .02 .10
222 Steve Balboni .01 .05
223 Jim Presley .01 .05
224 Rey Quinones .01 .05
225 Scott Bradley .01 .05
226 Harold Reynolds .01 .05
227 Alvin Davis .01 .05
228 Bill Swift .01 .05
229 Jose Bautista .01 .05
230 Jeff Ballard .01 .05
231 Mickey Tettleton .02 .10
232 Pete Stanicek .01 .05
233 Jim Traber .01 .05
234 Rene Gonzales .01 .05
235 Terry Kennedy .01 .05
236 Tom Niedenfuer .01 .05
237 Cal Ripken .75 2.00
238 Eddie Murray .08 .25
239 Larry Sheets .01 .05
240 Cecil Espy .01 .05
241 Jose Guzman .01 .05
242 Ruben Sierra .01 .05
243 Jeff Russell .01 .05
244 Mike Stanley .01 .05
245 Charlie Hough .02 .10
246 Scott Fletcher .01 .05
247 Mitch Williams .01 .05
248 Pete O'Brien .01 .05
249 Pete Incaviglia .01 .05
250 Steve Buechele .01 .05
251 Lee Smith .02 .10
252 Dwight Evans .02 .10
253 Rich Gedman .01 .05
254 Ellis Burks .05 .15
255 Mike Greenwell .01 .05
256 Jim Rice .02 .10
257 Marty Barrett .01 .05
258 Bob Stanley .01 .05
259 Roger Clemens .20 .50
260 Wade Boggs .08 .25
261 Mike Boddicker .01 .05
262 Frank White .02 .10
263 Bret Saberhagen .02 .10
264 Kevin Seitzer .01 .05
265 Bo Jackson .05 .15
266 Kurt Stillwell .01 .05
267 Danny Tartabull .01 .05
268 Willie Wilson .01 .05
269 Floyd Bannister .01 .05
270 George Brett .30 .75
271 Mark Gubicza .01 .05
272 Steve Farr .01 .05
273 Mike Henneman .01 .05
274 Doyle Alexander .01 .05
275 Frank Tanana .01 .05
276 Luis Salazar .01 .05

277 Jack Morris .02 .10
278 Tom Brookens .01 .05
279 Gary Pettis .01 .05
280 Matt Nokes .01 .05
281 Alan Trammell .05 .15
282 Lou Whitaker .02 .10
283 Chet Lemon .01 .05
284 Jeff Reardon .02 .10
285 Bert Blyleven .02 .10
286 Danny Gladden .01 .05
287 Kent Hrbek .02 .10
288 Greg Gagne .01 .05
289 Gary Gaetti .02 .10
290 Tim Laudner .01 .05
291 Juan Berenguer .01 .05
292 Frank Viola .01 .05
293 Kirby Puckett .20 .50
294 Gene Larkin .01 .05
295 Dave Gallagher .01 .05
296 Melido Perez .01 .05
297 Ivan Calderon .01 .05
298 Steve Lyons .01 .05
299 Carlton Fisk .08 .25
300 Fred Manrique .01 .05
301 Dan Pasqua .01 .05
302 Jack McDowell .02 .10
303 Ozzie Guillen .01 .05
304 Harold Baines .02 .10
305 Bobby Thigpen .01 .05
306 John Candelaria .01 .05
307 Dave Righetti .01 .05
308 Jack Clark .01 .05
309 Willie Randolph .02 .10
310 Tommy John .02 .10
311 Mike Pagliarulo .01 .05
312 Rickey Henderson .08 .25
313 Rafael Santana .01 .05
314 Don Mattingly .40 1.00
315 Dave Winfield .08 .25
316 Richard Dotson .01 .05
317 Tim Belcher .01 .05
318 Damon Berryhill .01 .05
319 Jay Buhner .15 .40
320 Cecil Espy .01 .05
321 Dave Gallagher .01 .05
322 Ron Gant .02 .10
323 Paul Gibson .01 .05
324 Mark Grace .15 .40
325 Chris Sabo ROY .01 .05
326 Walt Weiss ROY .01 .05
NNO Album .40 1.00

1989 Topps/O-Pee-Chee Sticker Backs

COMPLETE SET (67) 2.50 6.00
1 George Brett .25 .60
2 Don Mattingly .30 .75
3 Mark McGwire .40 1.00
4 Julio Franco .01 .05
5 Harold Reynolds .01 .05
6 Lou Whitaker .02 .10
7 Wade Boggs .10 .30
8 Gary Gaetti .02 .10
9 Paul Molitor .15 .40
10 Tony Fernandez .01 .05
11 Cal Ripken .60 1.50
12 Alan Trammell .05 .15
13 Jose Canseco .15 .40
14 Joe Carter .02 .10
15 Dwight Evans .02 .10
16 Mike Greenwell .01 .05
17 Dave Henderson .01 .05
18 Rickey Henderson .15 .40
19 Kirby Puckett .20 .50
20 Dave Winfield .20 .50
21 Robin Yount .15 .40
22 Bob Boone .02 .10
23 Carlton Fisk .15 .40
24 Geno Petralli .01 .05
25 Roger Clemens .30 .75
26 Mark Gubicza .01 .05
27 Dave Stewart .02 .10
28 Teddy Higuera .01 .05
29 Bruce Hurst .01 .05
30 Frank Viola .01 .05
31 Dennis Eckersley .15 .40
32 Doug Jones .01 .05
33 Jeff Reardon .02 .10
34 Will Clark .08 .25
35 Glenn Davis .01 .05
36 Andres Galarraga .08 .25
37 Juan Samuel .01 .05
38 Ryne Sandberg .15 .40
39 Steve Sax .01 .05
40 Bobby Bonilla .02 .10
41 Howard Johnson .01 .05
42 Vance Law .01 .05
43 Shawon Dunston .01 .05
44 Barry Larkin .08 .25
45 Ozzie Smith .15 .40
46 Barry Bonds .30 .75
47 Eric Davis .02 .10
48 Andre Dawson .05 .15
49 Kirk Gibson .02 .10
50 Tony Gwynn .25 .60
51 Kevin McReynolds .01 .05
52 Rafael Palmeiro .15 .40
53 Darryl Strawberry .01 .05
54 Andy Van Slyke .02 .10
55 Gary Carter .20 .50
56 Mike LaValliere .01 .05
57 Benito Santiago .01 .05
58 Dave Cone .08 .25
(David)
59 Dwight Gooden .02 .10
60 Orel Hershiser .02 .10
61 Tom Browning .01 .05
62 Danny Jackson .01 .05
63 Bob Knepper .01 .05
64 Mark Davis .01 .05
65 John Franco .01 .05
66 Randy Myers .02 .10
67 Checklist .01 .05

1989 Topps Ritz Mattingly

This set is actually a sheet of cards all featuring the career of Don Mattingly. The set was produced by Topps for Nabisco (Ritz Crackers) and was available via a send-in offer involving two proofs of purchase of boxes of Ritz Crackers. The uncut sheet is approximately 14" by 10 5/8". Included on the sheet are eight standard sized cards surrounding one large (5 1/8" by 7") card. In each case the Yankee logo has been airbrushed off the card.

COMPLETE SET (9) 2.50 6.00
COMMON PLAYER (1-9) .40 1.00

1989 Topps UK Minis

The 1989 Topps UK Minis baseball set contains 88 cards measuring approximately 2 1/8" by 3". The fronts are red, white and blue. The backs are yellow and red, and feature 1988 and career stats. The cards were distributed in five-card poly packs. The card set numbering is in alphabetical order by player's name.

COMPLETE SET (88) 5.00 12.00
1 Brady Anderson .10 .30
2 Harold Baines .07 .20
3 George Bell .02 .10
4 Wade Boggs .30 .75
5 Barry Bonds .50 1.25
6 Bobby Bonilla .07 .20
7 George Brett .60 1.50
8 Hubie Brooks .02 .10
9 Tom Brunansky .02 .10
10 Jay Buhner .10 .30
11 Brett Butler .07 .20
12 Jose Canseco .20 .50
13 Joe Carter .07 .20
14 Jack Clark .02 .10
15 Will Clark .15 .40
16 Roger Clemens .60 1.50
17 David Cone .15 .40
18 Alvin Davis .02 .10
19 Eric Davis .07 .20
20 Glenn Davis .02 .10
21 Andre Dawson .15 .40
22 Bill Doran .02 .10
23 Dennis Eckersley .25 .60
24 Dwight Evans .07 .20
25 Tony Fernandez .10 .30
26 Carlton Fisk .20 .50
27 John Franco .07 .20
28 Andres Galarraga .15 .40
29 Ron Gant .07 .20
30 Kirk Gibson .07 .20
31 Dwight Gooden .07 .20
32 Mike Greenwell .02 .10
33 Mark Gubicza .02 .10
34 Pedro Guerrero .02 .10
35 Ozzie Guillen .10 .30
36 Tony Gwynn .60 1.50
37 Rickey Henderson .30 .75
38 Orel Hershiser .07 .20
39 Teddy Higuera .02 .10
40 Charlie Hough .07 .20
41 Kent Hrbek .07 .20
42 Bruce Hurst .02 .10
43 Bo Jackson .20 .50
44 Gregg Jefferies .02 .10
45 Ricky Jordan .02 .10
46 Wally Joyner .07 .20
47 Mark Langston .02 .10
48 Mike Marshall .02 .10
49 Don Mattingly .60 1.50
50 Fred McGriff .15 .40
51 Mark McGwire .60 1.50
52 Kevin McReynolds .02 .10
53 Paul Molitor .25 .60
54 Jack Morris .07 .20
55 Dale Murphy .15 .40
56 Eddie Murray .30 .75
57 Pete O'Brien .02 .10
58 Rafael Palmeiro .15 .40
59 Gerald Perry .02 .10
60 Kirby Puckett .60 1.50
61 Tim Raines .07 .20
62 Johnny Ray .02 .10
63 Rick Reuschel .02 .10
64 Cal Ripken 1.25 3.00
65 Chris Sabo .02 .10
66 Juan Samuel .02 .10
67 Ryne Sandberg .60 1.50
68 Benito Santiago .07 .20
69 Steve Sax .02 .10
70 Mike Schmidt .40 1.00
71 Ruben Sierra .07 .20
72 Ozzie Smith .60 1.50
73 Cory Snyder .02 .10
74 Dave Stewart .07 .20
75 Darryl Strawberry .07 .20
76 Greg Swindell .02 .10
77 Alan Trammell .10 .30
78 Fernando Valenzuela .07 .20
79 Andy Van Slyke .02 .10
80 Frank Viola .02 .10
81 Claudell Washington .02 .10
82 Walt Weiss .02 .10
83 Lou Whitaker .07 .20
84 Dave Winfield .20 .50
85 Mike Witt .02 .10
86 Gerald Young .02 .10
87 Robin Yount .25 .60
88 Checklist Card .02 .10

1989-90 Topps Senior League

The 1989-90 Topps Senior League baseball set was issued second among the three sets commemorating the first Senior league season. This set was issued in set form in its own box containing all 132 standard-size cards.

COMPLETE SET (132) 2.00 5.00
1 George Foster .05 .15
2 Dwight Lowry .01 .05
3 Bob Jones .01 .05
4 Clete Boyer MG .02 .10
5 Rafael Landestoy .01 .05
6 Bob Shirley .01 .05
7 Ivan Murrell .01 .05
8 Jerry White .01 .05
9 Steve Henderson .01 .05
10 Marty Castillo .01 .05
11 Bruce Kison .01 .05
12 George Hendrick .02 .10
13 Bernie Carbo .01 .05
14 Jerry Martin .01 .05
15 Al Hrabosky .02 .10
16 Luis Gomez .01 .05
17 Dick Drago .01 .05
18 Bobby Ramos .01 .05
19 Joe Pittman .01 .05
20 Ike Blessitt .01 .05
21 Bill Travers .01 .05
22 Dick Williams MG .02 .10
23 Randy Lerch .01 .05
24 Tom Spencer .01 .05
25 Graig Nettles .05 .15
26 Jim Gideon .01 .05
27 Al Bumbry .01 .05
28 Tom Murphy .01 .05
29 Rodney Scott .01 .05
30 Alan Bannister .01 .05
31 John D'Acquisto .01 .05
32 Bert Campaneris .02 .10
33 Bill Lee .02 .10
34 Jerry Grote .02 .10
35 Ken Reitz .01 .05
36 Al Oliver .02 .10
37 Tim Stoddard .01 .05
38 Lenny Randle .01 .05
39 Rick Manning .01 .05
40 Bobby Bonds .08 .25
41 Rick Wise .01 .05
42 Sal Butera .01 .05
43 Ed Figueroa .01 .05
44 Ron Washington .01 .05
45 Elias Sosa .01 .05
46 Dan Driessen .01 .05
47 Wayne Nordhagen .02 .05
48 Vida Blue .02 .10
49 Butch Hobson .01 .05
50 Randy Bass .01 .05
51 Paul Mirabella .01 .05
52 Steve Kemp .01 .05
53 Kim Allen .01 .05
54 Stan Cliburn .01 .05
55 Derrel Thomas .01 .05
56 Pete Falcone .01 .05
57 Willie Aikens .01 .05
58 Toby Harrah .02 .10
59 Bob Tolan .01 .05
60 Rick Waits .01 .05
61 Jim Morrison .01 .05
62 Mike Kekich .01 .05
63 Gene Richards .01 .05
64 Dave Cash .01 .05
65 Rollie Fingers .20 .50
66 Butch Benton .01 .05
67 Tim Ireland .01 .05
68 Rick Lysander .01 .05
69 Cesar Cedeno .02 .10
70 Ozzie Virgil .01 .05
71 Johnny Grubb .05 .15
72 Lee Lacy .01 .05
73 Milt Wilcox .01 .05
74 Ron Pruitt .01 .05
75 Wayne Krenchicki .01 .05
76 Earl Weaver MG .20 .50
77 Pedro Borbon .01 .05
78 Jose Cruz .02 .10
79 Randy Niemann .01 .05
80 Mike Easler .01 .05
81 Amos Otis .02 .10
82 Mickey Mahler .01 .05
83 Orlando Gonzalez .01 .05
84 Doug Simunic .01 .05
85 Felix Millan .01 .05
86 Garth Iorg .01 .05
87 Pete Broberg .01 .05
88 Roy Howell .01 .05
89 Dave LaRoche .01 .05
90 Jerry Manuel .01 .05
91 Tony Scott .01 .05
92 Larvell Blanks .01 .05
93 Joaquin Andujar .02 .10
94 Tito Landrum .01 .05
95 Joe Sambito .01 .05
96 Pat Dobson .01 .05
97 Dan Meyer .01 .05
98 Clint Hurdle .02 .10
99 Pete LaCock .01 .05
100 Curt Flood .05 .15
101 Dave Kingman .08 .25
102 Jon Matlack .01 .05
103 Larry Harlow .01 .05
104 Rick Peterson .01 .05
105 Joe Hicks .01 .05
106 Bill Campbell .01 .05
107 Tom Paciorek .01 .05
108 Ray Burris .01 .05
109 Ken Landreaux .01 .05
110 Steve McCatty .01 .05
111 Ron LeFlore .02 .10
112 Joe Decker .01 .05
113 Leon Roberts .01 .05
114 Doug Corbett .01 .05
115 Mickey Rivers .02 .10
116 Dock Ellis .01 .05
117 Ron Jackson .01 .05
118 Bob Molinaro .01 .05
119 Fergie Jenkins .20 .50
120 U.L. Washington .01 .05
121 Roy Thomas .01 .05
122 Hal McRae .02 .10
123 Juan Eichelberger .01 .05
124 Gary Rajsich .01 .05
125 Dennis Leonard .01 .05
126 Walt Williams .01 .05
127 Rennie Stennett .01 .05
128 Jim Bibby .01 .05
129 Dyar Miller .01 .05
130 Luis Pujols .01 .05
131 Juan Beniquez .01 .05
132 Checklist Card .01 .05

1990 Topps

The 1990 Topps set contains 792 standard-size cards. Cards were issued primarily in wax packs, rack packs and hobby and retail Christmas factory sets. Card fronts feature various colored borders with the player's name at the bottom and team name at top. Subsets include All-Stars (385-407), Turn Back the Clock (661-665) and Draft Picks (scattered throughout the set). The key Rookie Cards in this set are Juan Gonzalez, Marquis Grissom, Sammy Sosa, Frank Thomas, Larry Walker and Bernie Williams. The Frank Thomas card (#414A) was printed without his name on the front, as well as portions of the black borders being omitted, creating a scarce variation. Several additional cards in the set were subsequently discovered missing portions of the black borders or missing some of the black printing in the backgrounds of the photos that occurred in the same printing that created the Thomas error. These cards are rarely seen and the Thomas card, for a newer issue, has experienced unprecedented growth as far as value. Be careful when purchasing the Frank Thomas NNOF version as counterfeits have been produced. A very few cards of President George Bush made their ways into packs. While these cards were supposed to have never been issued, a few collectors did receive these cards when opening packs.

COMPLETE SET (792) 8.00 20.00
COMP.FACT.SET (792) 10.00 25.00
COMP.X-MAS.SET (792) 15.00 40.00
BEWARE COUNTERFEIT THOMAS NNOF
1 Nolan Ryan .40 1.00
2 Nolan Ryan Mets .20 .50
3 Nolan Ryan Angels .20 .50
4 Nolan Ryan Astros .20 .50
5 N.Ryan Rangers UER .20 .50
Says Texas Stadium/rather than/Arlington Stadium
6 Vince Coleman RB .01 .05
7 Rickey Henderson RB .05 .15
8 Cal Ripken RB .08 .25
9 Eric Plunk .01 .05
10 Barry Larkin .05 .15
11 Paul Gibson .01 .05
12 Joe Girardi .05 .15
13 Mark Williamson .01 .05
14 Mike Fetters RC .08 .25
15 Teddy Higuera .01 .05
16 Kent Anderson .01 .05
17 Kelly Downs .01 .05
18 Carlos Quintana .01 .05
19 Al Newman .01 .05
20 Mark Gubicza .01 .05
21 Jeff Torborg MG .01 .05
22 Bruce Ruffin .01 .05
23 Randy Velarde .01 .05
24 Joe Hesketh .01 .05
25 Willie Randolph .02 .10
26 Don Slaught .01 .05
27 Rick Leach .01 .05
28 Duane Ward .01 .05
29 John Cangelosi .01 .05
30 David Cone .02 .10
31 Henry Cotto .01 .05
32 John Farrell .01 .05
33 Greg Walker .01 .05
34 Tony Fossas RC .01 .05
35 Benito Santiago .02 .10
36 John Costello .01 .05
37 Domingo Ramos .01 .05
38 Wes Gardner .01 .05
39 Curt Ford .01 .05
40 Jay Howell .01 .05
41 Matt Williams .02 .10
42 Jeff M. Robinson .01 .05
43 Dante Bichette .02 .10
44 Roger Salkeld FDP RC .02 .10
45 Dave Parker UER .02 .10
46 Rob Dibble .02 .10
47 Brian Harper .01 .05
48 Zane Smith .01 .05
49 Tom Lawless .01 .05
50 Glenn Davis .01 .05
51 Doug Rader MG .01 .05
52 Jack Daugherty RC .01 .05
53 Mike LaCoss .01 .05
54 Joel Skinner .01 .05
55 Darrell Evans UER .02 .10
HR total should be/414, not 424
56 Franklin Stubbs .01 .05
57 Greg Vaughn .01 .05
58 Keith Miller .01 .05
59 Ted Power .01 .05
60 George Brett .25 .60
61 Deion Sanders .08 .25
62 Ramon Martinez .01 .05
63 Mike Pagliarulo .01 .05
64 Danny Darwin .01 .05
65 Devon White .02 .10
66 Greg Litton .01 .05
67 Scott Sanderson .01 .05
68 Dave Henderson .01 .05
69 Todd Frohwirth .01 .05
70 Mike Greenwell .01 .05
71 Allan Anderson .01 .05
72 Jeff Huson RC .02 .10
73 Bob Milacki .01 .05
74 Jeff Jackson FDP RC .02 .10
75 Doug Jones .01 .05
76 Dave Valle .01 .05
77 Dave Bergman .01 .05
78 Mike Flanagan .01 .05
79 Ron Kittle .01 .05
80 Jeff Russell .01 .05
81 Bob Rodgers MG .01 .05
82 Scott Terry .01 .05
83 Hensley Meulens .01 .05
84 Ray Searage .01 .05
85 Juan Samuel .01 .05
86 Paul Kilgus .01 .05
87 Rick Luecken RC .01 .05
88 Glenn Braggs .01 .05
89 Clint Zavaras RC .01 .05
90 Jack Clark .02 .10
91 Steve Frey RC .01 .05
92 Mike Stanley .01 .05
93 Shawn Hillegas .01 .05
94 Herm Winningham .01 .05
95 Todd Worrell .01 .05
96 Jody Reed .01 .05
97 Curt Schilling .40 1.00
98 Jose Gonzalez .01 .05
99 Rich Monteleone .01 .05
100 Will Clark .05 .15
101 Shane Rawley .01 .05
102 Stan Javier .01 .05
103 Marvin Freeman .01 .05
104 Bob Knepper .01 .05
105 Randy Myers .02 .10
106 Charlie O'Brien .01 .05
107 Fred Lynn .01 .05
108 Rod Nichols .01 .05
109 Roberto Kelly .01 .05
110 Tommy Helms MG .01 .05
111 Ed Whited RC .01 .05
112 Glenn Wilson .01 .05
113 Manny Lee .01 .05
114 Mike Bielecki .01 .05
115 Tony Pena .01 .05
116 Floyd Bannister .01 .05
117 Mike Sharperson .01 .05
118 Erik Hanson .01 .05
119 Billy Hatcher .01 .05
120 John Franco .02 .10
121 Robin Ventura .08 .25
122 Shawn Abner .01 .05
123 Rich Gedman .01 .05
124 Dave Dravecky .02 .10
125 Kent Hrbek .02 .10
126 Randy Kramer .01 .05
127 Mike Devereaux .01 .05
128 Checklist 1 .01 .05
129 Ron Jones .01 .05
130 Bert Blyleven .02 .10
131 Matt Nokes .01 .05
132 Lance Blankenship .01 .05
133 Ricky Horton .01 .05
134 Earl Cunningham FDP RC .02 .10
135 Dave Magadan .01 .05
136 Kevin Brown .02 .10
137 Marty Pevey RC .01 .05
138 Al Leiter .08 .25
139 Greg Brock .01 .05
140 Andre Dawson .02 .10
141B John Hart MG RC .01 .05
142 Jeff Wetherby RC .01 .05
143 Rafael Belliard .01 .05
144 Bud Black .01 .05
145 Terry Steinbach .01 .05
146 Rob Richie RC .01 .05
147 Chuck Finley .02 .10
148 Edgar Martinez .05 .15
149 Steve Farr .01 .05
150 Kirk Gibson .02 .10
151 Rick Mahler .01 .05
152 Lonnie Smith .01 .05
153 Randy Milligan .01 .05
154 Mike Maddux .01 .05
155 Ellis Burks .05 .15
156 Ken Patterson .01 .05
157 Craig Biggio .08 .25
158 Craig Lefferts .01 .05
159 Mike Felder .01 .05
160 Dave Righetti .01 .05
161 Harold Reynolds .02 .10
162 Todd Zeile .02 .10
163 Phil Bradley .01 .05
164 Jeff Juden FDP RC .02 .10
165 Walt Weiss .01 .05
166 Bobby Witt .01 .05
167 Kevin Appier .02 .10
168 Jose Lind .01 .05
169 Richard Dotson .01 .05
170 George Bell .01 .05
171 Russ Nixon MG .01 .05
172 Tom Lampkin .01 .05
173 Tim Belcher .01 .05
174 Jeff Kunkel .01 .05
175 Mike Moore .01 .05
176 Luis Quinones .01 .05
177 Mike Henneman .01 .05
178 Chris James .01 .05
179 Brian Holton .01 .05
180 Tim Raines .02 .10
181 Juan Agosto .01 .05
182 Mookie Wilson .02 .10
183 Steve Lake .01 .05
184 Danny Cox .01 .05
185 Ruben Sierra .02 .10
186 Dave LaPoint .01 .05
187 Rick Wrona .01 .05
188 Mike Smithson .01 .05
189 Dick Schofield .01 .05
190 Rick Reuschel .01 .05
191 Pat Borders .01 .05
192 Don August .01 .05
193 Andy Benes .02 .10
194 Glenallen Hill .01 .05
195 Tim Burke .01 .05
196 Gerald Young .01 .05
197 Doug Drabek .01 .05
198 Mike Marshall .01 .05
199 Sergio Valdez RC .01 .05
200 Don Mattingly .25 .60
201 Cito Gaston MG .01 .05
202 Mike Macfarlane .01 .05
203 Mike Roesler RC .01 .05
204 Bob Dernier .01 .05
205 Mark Davis .01 .05
206 Nick Esasky .01 .05
207 Bob Ojeda .01 .05
208 Brook Jacoby .01 .05
209 Greg Mathews .01 .05
210 Ryne Sandberg .15 .40
211 John Cerutti .01 .05
212 Joe Orsulak .01 .05
213 Scott Bankhead .01 .05
214 Terry Francona .02 .10
215 Kirk McCaskill .01 .05
216 Ricky Jordan .01 .05
217 Don Robinson .01 .05
218 Wally Backman .01 .05
219 Donn Pall .01 .05
220 Barry Bonds .40 1.00
221 Gary Mielke RC .01 .05
222 Kurt Stillwell UER .01 .05
Graduate misspelled/as gradute
223 Tommy Gregg .01 .05
224 Delino DeShields RC .08 .25
225 Jim Deshaies .01 .05
226 Mickey Hatcher .01 .05
227B Kevin Tapani RC .08 .25
228 Dave Martinez .01 .05
229 David Wells .02 .10
230 Keith Hernandez .02 .10
231 Jack McKeon MG .01 .05
232 Darnell Coles .01 .05
233 Ken Hill .02 .10
234 Mariano Duncan .01 .05
235 Jeff Reardon .02 .10
236 Hal Morris .01 .05
237 Kevin Ritz RC .01 .05
238 Felix Jose .01 .05
239 Eric Show .01 .05
240 Mark Grace .05 .15
241 Mike Krukow .01 .05
242 Fred Manrique .01 .05
243 Barry Jones .01 .05
244 Bill Schroeder .01 .05
245 Roger Clemens .40 1.00
246 Jim Eisenreich .01 .05
247 Jerry Reed .01 .05
248 Dave Anderson .01 .05
249 Mike Texas Smith RC .01 .05
250 Jose Canseco .05 .15
251 Jeff Blauser .01 .05
252 Otis Nixon .01 .05
253 Mark Portugal .01 .05
254 Francisco Cabrera .01 .05
255 Bobby Thigpen .01 .05
256 Marvell Wynne .01 .05
257 Jose DeLeon .01 .05
258 Barry Lyons .01 .05
259 Lance McCullers .01 .05
260 Eric Davis .02 .10
261 Whitey Herzog MG .02 .10
262 Checklist 2 .01 .05
263 Mel Stottlemyre Jr. .01 .05
264 Bryan Clutterbuck .01 .05
265 Pete O'Brien .01 .05
266 German Gonzalez .01 .05
267 Mark Davidson .01 .05
268 Rob Murphy .01 .05
269 Dickie Thon .01 .05
270 Dave Stewart .02 .10
271 Chet Lemon .01 .05
272 Bryan Harvey .01 .05
273 Bobby Bonilla .02 .10
274 Mauro Gozzo RC .01 .05
275 Mickey Tettleton .01 .05
276 Gary Thurman .01 .05
277 Lenny Harris .01 .05
278 Pascual Perez .01 .05
279 Steve Buechele .01 .05
280 Lou Whitaker .02 .10
281 Kevin Bass .01 .05
282 Derek Lilliquist .01 .05
283 Joey Belle .08 .25
284 Mark Gardner RC .02 .10
285 Willie McGee .02 .10
286 Lee Guetterman .01 .05
287 Vance Law .01 .05
288 Greg Briley .01 .05
289 Norm Charlton .01 .05
290 Robin Yount .15 .40
291 Dave Johnson MG .02 .10
292 Jim Gott .01 .05
293 Mike Gallego .01 .05
294 Craig McMurtry .01 .05
295 Fred McGriff .08 .25
296 Jeff Ballard .01 .05
297 Tommy Herr .01 .05
298 Dan Gladden .01 .05
299 Adam Peterson .01 .05
300 Bo Jackson .08 .25
301 Don Aase .01 .05
302B Marcus Lawton RC .01 .05
303 Rick Cerone .01 .05
304 Marty Clary .01 .05
305 Eddie Murray .08 .25
306 Tom Niedenfuer .01 .05
307 Bip Roberts .01 .05
308 Jose Guzman .01 .05
309 Eric Yelding RC .01 .05
310 Steve Bedrosian .01 .05
311 Dwight Smith .01 .05
312 Dan Quisenberry .01 .05
313 Gus Polidor .01 .05
314 Donald Harris FDP RC .01 .05
315 Bruce Hurst .01 .05
316 Carney Lansford .02 .10
317 Mark Guthrie RC .01 .05
318 Wallace Johnson .01 .05
319 Dion James .01 .05
320 Dave Stieb .02 .10
321 Joe Morgan MG .01 .05
322 Junior Ortiz .01 .05
323 Willie Wilson .01 .05
324 Pete Harnisch .01 .05
325 Robby Thompson .01 .05
326 Tom McCarthy .01 .05
327 Ken Williams .01 .05
328 Curt Young .01 .05
329 Oddibe McDowell .01 .05
330 Ron Darling .01 .05
331 Juan Gonzalez RC .40 1.00
332 Paul O'Neill .05 .15
333 Bill Wegman .01 .05
334 Johnny Ray .01 .05
335 Andy Hawkins .01 .05
336 Ken Griffey Jr. .40 1.00
337 Lloyd McClendon .01 .05
338 Dennis Lamp .01 .05
339 Dave Clark .01 .05
340 Fernando Valenzuela .02 .10
341 Tom Foley .01 .05
342 Alex Trevino .01 .05
343 Frank Tanana .01 .05
344 George Canale RC .01 .05
345 Harold Baines .02 .10
346 Jim Presley .01 .05
347 Junior Felix .01 .05
348 Gary Wayne .01 .05
349 Steve Finley .02 .10
350 Bret Saberhagen .02 .10
351 Roger Craig MG .01 .05
352 Bryn Smith .01 .05
353 Sandy Alomar Jr. .02 .10
Not listed as Jr./on card front
354 Stan Belinda RC .02 .10
355 Marty Barrett .01 .05
356 Randy Ready .01 .05
357 Dave West .01 .05
358 Andres Thomas .01 .05
359 Jimmy Jones .01 .05
360 Paul Molitor .02 .10
361 Randy McCament RC .01 .05
362 Damon Berryhill .01 .05
363 Dan Petry .01 .05
364 Rolando Roomes .01 .05
365 Ozzie Guillen .02 .10
366 Mike Heath .01 .05
367 Mike Morgan .01 .05
368 Bill Doran .01 .05
369 Todd Burns .01 .05
370 Tim Wallach .01 .05
371 Jimmy Key .02 .10
372 Terry Kennedy .01 .05
373 Alvin Davis .01 .05
374 Steve Cummings RC .01 .05
375 Dwight Evans .05 .15
376 Checklist 3 UER .01 .05
Higuera misalphabet-/ized in Brewer list
377 Mickey Weston RC .01 .05
378 Luis Salazar .01 .05
379 Steve Rosenberg .01 .05
380 Dave Winfield .02 .10
381 Frank Robinson MG .05 .15
382 Jeff Musselman .01 .05
383B John Morris .01 .05
384 Pat Combs .01 .05
385B Fred McGriff AS .02 .10
386B Julio Franco AS .01 .05
387 Wade Boggs AS .02 .10
388 Cal Ripken AS .15 .40
389 Robin Yount AS .08 .25
390 Ruben Sierra AS .01 .05
391 Kirby Puckett AS .05 .15
392B Carlton Fisk AS .02 .10
393 Bret Saberhagen AS .01 .05
394 Jeff Ballard AS .01 .05
395B Jeff Russell AS .01 .05
396 Bart Giamatti MEM .08 .25
397 Will Clark AS .01 .05
398 Ryne Sandberg AS .08 .25
399 Howard Johnson AS .01 .05
400 Ozzie Smith AS .08 .25
401 Kevin Mitchell AS .01 .05
402 Eric Davis AS .01 .05
403 Tony Gwynn AS .05 .15
404B Craig Biggio AS .08 .25
405 Mike Scott AS .01 .05
406B Joe Magrane AS .01 .05
407 Mark Davis AS .01 .05
408 Trevor Wilson .01 .05
409 Tom Brunansky .01 .05
410 Joe Boever .01 .05
411 Ken Phelps .01 .05
412 Jamie Moyer .02 .10
413 Brian DuBois RC .01 .05
414A F.Thomas ERR NNOF 2500.00 5000.00
414B Frank Thomas RC 1.50 4.00
415 Shawon Dunston .01 .05
416 Dave Wayne Johnson RC .01 .05
417 Jim Gantner .01 .05
418 Tom Browning .01 .05
419 Beau Allred RC .01 .05
420 Carlton Fisk .05 .15
421 Greg Minton .01 .05
422 Pat Sheridan .01 .05
423 Fred Toliver .01 .05
424 Jerry Reuss .01 .05
425 Bill Landrum .01 .05
426 Jeff Hamilton UER .01 .05
427 Carmen Castillo .01 .05
428 Steve Davis RC .01 .05
429 Tom Kelly MG .01 .05
430 Pete Incaviglia .01 .05
431 Randy Johnson .20 .50
432 Damaso Garcia .01 .05
433 Steve Olin RC .08 .25
434 Mark Carreon .01 .05
435 Kevin Seitzer .01 .05
436 Mel Hall .01 .05
437 Les Lancaster .01 .05
438 Greg Myers .01 .05
439 Jeff Parrett .01 .05
440 Alan Trammell .02 .10
441 Bob Kipper .01 .05
442 Jerry Browne .01 .05
443 Cris Carpenter .01 .05
444 Kyle Abbott FDP RC .01 .05
445 Danny Jackson .01 .05
446 Dan Pasqua .01 .05
447 Atlee Hammaker .01 .05
448 Greg Gagne .01 .05
449 Dennis Rasmussen .01 .05
450 Rickey Henderson .08 .25
451 Mark Lemke .01 .05
452 Luis DeLosSantos .01 .05
453 Jody Davis .01 .05
454 Jeff King .01 .05
455 Jeffrey Leonard .01 .05
456 Chris Gwynn .01 .05
457 Gregg Jefferies .02 .10
458 Bob McClure .01 .05
459 Jim Lefebvre MG .01 .05
460 Mike Scott .01 .05
461 Carlos Martinez .01 .05
462 Denny Walling .01 .05
463 Drew Hall .01 .05
464 Jerome Walton .01 .05
465 Kevin Gross .01 .05
466 Rance Mulliniks .01 .05
467 Juan Nieves .01 .05
468 Bill Ripken .01 .05
469 John Kruk .02 .10
470 Frank Viola .01 .05
471 Mike Brumley .01 .05
472 Jose Uribe .01 .05
473 Joe Price .01 .05
474 Rich Thompson .01 .05
475 Bob Welch .01 .05
476 Brad Komminsk .01 .05

477 Willie Fraser .01 .05
478 Mike LaValliere .01 .05
479 Frank White .02 .10
480 Sid Fernandez .01 .05
481 Garry Templeton .01 .05
482 Steve Carter .01 .05
483 Alejandro Pena .01 .05
484 Mike Fitzgerald .01 .05
485 John Candelaria .01 .05
486 Jeff Treadway .01 .05
487 Steve Searcy .01 .05
488 Ken Oberkfell .01 .05
489 Nick Leyva MG .01 .05
490 Dan Plesac .01 .05
491 Dave Cochrane RC .01 .05
492 Ron Oester .01 .05
493 Jason Grimsley RC .02 .10
494 Terry Puhl .01 .05
495 Lee Smith .02 .10
496 Cecil Espy UER .01 .05
'88 stats have 3/SB's, should be 33
497 Dave Schmidt .01 .05
498 Rick Schu .01 .05
499 Bill Long .01 .05
500 Kevin Mitchell .01 .05
501 Matt Young .01 .05
502 Mitch Webster .01 .05
503 Randy St.Claire .01 .05
504 Tom O'Malley .01 .05
505 Kelly Gruber .01 .05
506 Tom Glavine .05 .15
507 Gary Redus .01 .05
508 Terry Leach .01 .05
509 Tom Pagnozzi .01 .05
510 Dwight Gooden .02 .10
511 Clay Parker .01 .05
512 Gary Pettis .01 .05
513 Mark Eichhorn .01 .05
514 Andy Allanson .01 .05
515 Len Dykstra .02 .10
516 Tim Leary .01 .05
517 Roberto Alomar .05 .15
518 Bill Krueger .01 .05
519 Bucky Dent MG .01 .05
520 Mitch Williams .01 .05
521 Craig Worthington .01 .05
522 Mike Dunne .01 .05
523 Jay Bell .02 .10
524 Daryl Boston .01 .05
525 Wally Joyner .02 .10
526 Checklist 4 .01 .05
527 Ron Hassey .01 .05
528 Kevin Wickander UER .01 .05
Monthly scoreboard/strikeout total was 2.2,/that was his innings/pitched total
529 Greg A. Harris .01 .05
530 Mark Langston .01 .05
531 Ken Caminiti .02 .10
532 Cecilio Guante .01 .05
533 Tim Jones .01 .05
534 Louie Meadows .01 .05
535 John Smoltz .08 .25
536 Bob Geren .01 .05
537 Mark Grant .01 .05
538 Bill Spiers UER .01 .05
Photo actually/George Canale
539 Neal Heaton .01 .05
540 Danny Tartabull .01 .05
541 Pat Perry .01 .05
542 Darren Daulton .02 .10
543 Nelson Liriano .01 .05
544 Dennis Boyd .01 .05
545 Kevin McReynolds .01 .05
546 Kevin Hickey .01 .05
547 Jack Howell .01 .05
548 Pat Clements .01 .05
549 Don Zimmer MG .01 .05
550 Julio Franco .02 .10
551 Tim Crews .01 .05
552 Mike Miss. Smith RC .01 .05
553 Scott Scudder UER .01 .05
Cedar Rap1ds
554 Jay Buhner .02 .10
555 Jack Morris .02 .10
556 Gene Larkin .01 .05
557 Jeff Innis RC .01 .05
558 Rafael Ramirez .01 .05
559 Andy McGaffigan .01 .05
560 Steve Sax .01 .05
561 Ken Dayley .01 .05
562 Chad Kreuter .01 .05
563 Alex Sanchez .01 .05
564 Tyler Houston FDP RC .08 .25
565 Scott Fletcher .01 .05
566 Mark Knudson .01 .05
567 Ron Gant .02 .10
568 John Smiley .01 .05
569 Ivan Calderon .01 .05
570 Cal Ripken .30 .75
571 Brett Butler .02 .10
572 Greg W. Harris .01 .05
573 Danny Heep .01 .05
574 Bill Swift .01 .05
575 Lance Parrish .01 .05
576 Mike Dyer RC .01 .05
577 Charlie Hayes .01 .05
578 Joe Magrane .01 .05
579 Art Howe MG .01 .05
580 Joe Carter .02 .10
581 Ken Griffey Sr. .02 .10
582 Rick Honeycutt .01 .05
583 Bruce Benedict .01 .05
584 Phil Stephenson .01 .05
585 Kal Daniels .01 .05
586 Edwin Nunez .01 .05
587 Lance Johnson .01 .05
588 Rick Rhoden .01 .05
589 Mike Aldrete .01 .05
590 Ozzie Smith .15 .40
591 Todd Stottlemyre .02 .10
592 R.J. Reynolds .01 .05
593 Scott Bradley .01 .05
594 Luis Sojo RC .01 .05
595 Greg Swindell .01 .05
596 Jose DeJesus .01 .05
597 Chris Bosio .01 .05
598 Brady Anderson .02 .10
599 Frank Williams .01 .05
600 Darryl Strawberry .02 .10
601 Luis Rivera .01 .05
602 Scott Garrelts .01 .05
603 Tony Armas .01 .05
604 Ron Robinson .01 .05
605 Mike Scioscia .01 .05
606 Storm Davis .01 .05
607 Steve Jeltz .01 .05
608 Eric Anthony RC .02 .10
609 Sparky Anderson MG .02 .10
610 Pedro Guerrero .01 .05
611 Walt Terrell .01 .05
612 Dave Gallagher .01 .05
613 Jeff Pico .01 .05
614 Nelson Santovenia .01 .05
615 Rob Deer .01 .05
616 Brian Holman .01 .05
617 Geronimo Berroa .01 .05
618 Ed Whitson .01 .05
619 Rob Ducey .01 .05
620 Tony Castillo .01 .05
621 Melido Perez .01 .05
622 Sid Bream .01 .05
623 Jim Corsi .01 .05
624B Darrin Jackson .01 .05
625 Roger McDowell .01 .05
626 Bob Melvin .01 .05
627 Jose Rijo .01 .05
628 Candy Maldonado .01 .05
629 Eric Hetzel .01 .05
630 Gary Gaetti .02 .10
631 John Wetteland .08 .25
632 Scott Lusader .01 .05
633 Dennis Cook .01 .05
634 Luis Polonia .01 .05
635 Brian Downing .01 .05
636 Jesse Orosco .01 .05
637 Craig Reynolds .01 .05
638 Jeff Montgomery .02 .10
639 Tony LaRussa MG .02 .10
640 Rick Sutcliffe .02 .10
641 Doug Strange RC .01 .05
642 Jack Armstrong .01 .05
643 Alfredo Griffin .01 .05
644 Paul Assenmacher .01 .05
645 Jose Oquendo .01 .05
646 Checklist 5 .01 .05
647 Rex Hudler .01 .05
648 Jim Clancy .01 .05
649 Dan Murphy RC .02 .10
650 Mike Witt .01 .05
651 Rafael Santana .01 .05
652 Mike Boddicker .01 .05
653 John Moses .01 .05
654 Paul Coleman FDP RC .02 .10
655 Gregg Olson .02 .10
656 Mackey Sasser .01 .05
657 Terry Mulholland .01 .05
658 Donell Nixon .01 .05
659 Greg Cadaret .01 .05
660 Vince Coleman .01 .05
661 Dick Howser TBC'85 .01 .05
UER Seaver's 300th/on 7/11/85, should/be 8/4/85
662 Mike Schmidt TBC'80 .08 .25
663 Fred Lynn TBC'75 .01 .05
664 Johnny Bench TBC'70 .05 .15
665 Sandy Koufax TBC'65 .20 .50
666 Brian Fisher .01 .05
667 Curt Wilkerson .01 .05
668 Joe Oliver .01 .05
669 Tom Lasorda MG .08 .25
670 Dennis Eckersley .02 .10
671 Bob Boone .02 .10
672 Roy Smith .01 .05
673 Joey Meyer .01 .05
674 Spike Owen .01 .05
675 Jim Abbott .05 .15
676 Randy Kutcher .01 .05
677 Jay Tibbs .01 .05
678 Kirt Manwaring UER .01 .05
'88 Phoenix stats/repeated
679 Gary Ward .01 .05
680 Howard Johnson .01 .05
681 Mike Schooler .01 .05
682 Dann Bilardello .01 .05
683 Kenny Rogers .02 .10
684 Julio Machado RC .01 .05
685 Tony Fernandez .01 .05
686 Carmelo Martinez .01 .05
687 Tim Birtsas .01 .05
688 Milt Thompson .01 .05
689 Rich Yett .01 .05
690 Mark McGwire .25 .60
691 Chuck Cary .01 .05
692 Sammy Sosa RC .75 2.00
693 Calvin Schiraldi .01 .05
694 Mike Stanton RC .08 .25
695 Tom Henke .01 .05
696 B.J. Surhoff .02 .10
697 Mike Davis .01 .05
698 Omar Vizquel .08 .25
699 Jim Leyland MG .01 .05
700 Kirby Puckett .08 .25
701 Bernie Williams RC .60 1.50
702 Tony Phillips .01 .05
703 Jeff Brantley .01 .05
704 Chip Hale RC .01 .05
705 Claudell Washington .01 .05
706 Geno Petralli .01 .05
707 Luis Aquino .01 .05
708 Larry Sheets .01 .05
709 Juan Berenguer .01 .05
710 Von Hayes .01 .05
711 Rick Aguilera .02 .10
712 Todd Benzinger .01 .05
713 Tim Drummond RC .01 .05
714 Marquis Grissom RC .15 .40
715 Greg Maddux .15 .40
716 Steve Balboni .01 .05
717 Ron Karkovice .01 .05
718 Gary Sheffield .08 .25
719 Wally Whitehurst .01 .05
720 Andres Galarraga .02 .10
721 Lee Mazzilli .01 .05
722 Felix Fermin .01 .05
723 Jeff D. Robinson .01 .05
724 Juan Bell .01 .05
725 Terry Pendleton .02 .10
726 Gene Nelson .01 .05
727 Pat Tabler .01 .05
728B Jim Acker .01 .05
729 Bobby Valentine MG .01 .05
730 Tony Gwynn .10 .30
731 Don Carman .01 .05
732 Ernest Riles .01 .05
733 John Dopson .01 .05
734 Kevin Elster .01 .05
735 Charlie Hough .02 .10
736 Rick Dempsey .01 .05
737 Chris Sabo .01 .05
738 Gene Harris .01 .05
739 Dale Sveum .01 .05
740 Jesse Barfield .01 .05
741 Steve Wilson .01 .05
742 Ernie Whitt .01 .05
743 Tom Candiotti .01 .05
744 Kelly Mann RC .01 .05
745 Hubie Brooks .01 .05
746 Dave Smith .01 .05
747 Randy Bush .01 .05
748 Doyle Alexander .01 .05
749 Mark Parent UER .01 .05
'87 BA .80,/should be .080
750 Dale Murphy .05 .15
751 Steve Lyons .01 .05
752 Tom Gordon .02 .10
753 Chris Speier .01 .05
754 Bob Walk .01 .05
755 Rafael Palmeiro .05 .15
756 Ken Howell .01 .05
757 Larry Walker RC .40 1.00
758 Mark Thurmond .01 .05
759 Tom Trebelhorn MG .01 .05
760 Wade Boggs .05 .15
761 Mike Jackson .01 .05
762 Doug Dascenzo .01 .05
763 Dennis Martinez .02 .10
764 Tim Teufel .01 .05
765 Chili Davis .02 .10
766 Brian Meyer .01 .05
767 Tracy Jones .01 .05
768 Chuck Crim .01 .05
769 Greg Hibbard RC .02 .10
770 Cory Snyder .01 .05
771 Pete Smith .01 .05
772 Jeff Reed .01 .05
773 Dave Leiper .01 .05
774 Ben McDonald RC .08 .25
775 Andy Van Slyke .05 .15
776 Charlie Leibrandt .01 .05
777 Tim Laudner .01 .05
778 Mike Jeffcoat .01 .05
779 Lloyd Moseby .01 .05
780 Orel Hershiser .02 .10
781 Mario Diaz .01 .05
782 Jose Alvarez .01 .05
783 Checklist 6 .01 .05
784 Scott Bailes .01 .05
785 Jim Rice .02 .10
786 Eric King .01 .05
787 Rene Gonzales .01 .05
788 Frank DiPino .01 .05
789 John Wathan MG .01 .05
790 Gary Carter .02 .10
791 Alvaro Espinoza .01 .05
792 Gerald Perry .01 .05
USA1 George Bush PRES
USA1 George Bush PRES GLOSSY

1990 Topps Tiffany

COMP.FACT.SET (792) 100.00 200.00
*STARS: 6X TO 15X BASIC CARDS
*ROOKIES: 4X TO 10X BASIC CARDS
DISTRIBUTED ONLY IN FACTORY SET FORM
STATED PRINT RUN 15,000 SETS
FACTORY SET PRICE IS FOR SEALED SETS
414 Frank Thomas FDP 30.00 80.00

1990 Topps Batting Leaders

COMPLETE SET (22) 12.50 30.00
1 Wade Boggs 4.00 10.00
2 Tony Gwynn 8.00 20.00
3 Kirby Puckett 6.00 15.00
4 Don Mattingly 8.00 20.00
5 George Brett 8.00 20.00
6 Pedro Guerrero .40 1.00
7 Tim Raines .40 1.00
8 Paul Molitor 3.00 8.00
9 Jim Rice .40 1.00
10 Keith Hernandez .40 1.00
11 Julio Franco .40 1.00
12 Carney Lansford .40 1.00
13 Dave Parker .40 1.00
14 Willie McGee .40 1.00
15 Robin Yount 3.00 8.00
16 Tony Fernandez .40 1.00
17 Eddie Murray 3.00 8.00
18 Johnny Ray .40 1.00
19 Lonnie Smith .40 1.00
20 Phil Bradley .40 1.00
21 Rickey Henderson 5.00 12.00
22-Jan Kent Hrbek .40 1.00

1990 Topps Glossy All-Stars

COMPLETE SET (22) 1.25 3.00
1-Jan Tom Lasorda MG .07 .20
2-Jan Will Clark .07 .20
3-Jan Ryne Sandberg .20 .50
4-Jan Howard Johnson .01 .05
5-Jan Ozzie Smith .25 .60
6-Jan Kevin Mitchell .01 .05
7-Jan Eric Davis .02 .10
8-Jan Tony Gwynn .30 .75
9-Jan Benito Santiago .02 .10
10-Jan Rick Reuschel .01 .05
11-Jan Don Drysdale CAPT .08 .25
12-Jan Tony LaRussa MG .01 .05
13-Jan Mark McGwire .30 .75
14-Jan Julio Franco .02 .10
15 Wade Boggs .15 .40
16 Cal Ripken .60 1.50
17-Jan Bo Jackson .08 .25
18-Jan Kirby Puckett .15 .40
19-Jan Ruben Sierra .02 .10
20-Jan Terry Steinbach .01 .05
21-Jan Dave Stewart .02 .10
22-Jan Carl Yastrzemski CAPT .10 .30

1990 Topps Glossy Send-Ins

COMPLETE SET (60) 5.00 12.00
1-Jan Ryne Sandberg .60 1.50
2-Jan Nolan Ryan 2.00 5.00
3-Jan Glenn Davis .02 .10
4-Jan Dave Stewart .07 .20
5-Jan Barry Larkin .15 .40
6-Jan Carney Lansford .07 .20
7-Jan Darryl Strawberry .07 .20
8-Jan Steve Sax .02 .10
9-Jan Carlos Martinez .02 .10
10-Jan Gary Sheffield .30 .75
11-Jan Don Mattingly 1.00 2.50
12-Jan Mark Grace .40 1.00
13-Jan Bret Saberhagen .07 .20
14 Mike Scott .02 .10
15 Robin Yount .20 .50
16 Ozzie Smith .60 1.50
17 Jeff Ballard .02 .10
18 Rick Reuschel .02 .10
19 Greg Briley .02 .10
20 Ken Griffey Jr. 1.25 3.00
21 Kevin Mitchell .02 .10
22 Wade Boggs .30 .75
23 Dwight Gooden .07 .20
24 George Bell .02 .10
25 Eric Davis .07 .20
26 Ruben Sierra .07 .20
27 Roberto Alomar .30 .75
28 Gary Gaetti .07 .20
29-Jan Gregg Olson .02 .10
30-Jan Tom Gordon .10 .30
31-Jan Jose Canseco .30 .75
1-Feb Pedro Guerrero .02 .10
2-Feb Joe Carter .07 .20
3-Feb Mike Scioscia .07 .20
4-Feb Julio Franco .07 .20
5-Feb Joe Magrane .02 .10
6-Feb Rickey Henderson .40 1.00
7-Feb Tim Raines .07 .20
8-Feb Jerome Walton .02 .10
9-Feb Bob Geren .02 .10
10-Feb Andre Dawson .15 .40
11-Feb Mark McGwire 1.00 2.50
12-Feb Howard Johnson .02 .10
13-Feb Bo Jackson .20 .50
14-Feb Shawon Dunston .02 .10
15-Feb Carlton Fisk .20 .50
16-Feb Mitch Williams .02 .10
17-Feb Kirby Puckett .40 1.00
18-Feb Craig Worthington .02 .10
19-Feb Jim Abbott .20 .50
20-Feb Cal Ripken 2.00 5.00
21-Feb Will Clark .15 .40
22-Feb Dennis Eckersley .20 .50
23-Feb Craig Biggio .10 .30
24-Feb Fred McGriff .15 .40
25-Feb Tony Gwynn .75 2.00
26-Feb Mickey Tettleton .07 .20
27-Feb Mark Davis .02 .10
28-Feb Omar Vizquel .15 .40
29-Feb Gregg Jefferies .02 .10

1990 Topps Rookies

COMPLETE SET (33) 10.00 25.00
ONE PER RETAIL JUMBO PACK
1-Jan Jim Abbott .30 .75
2-Jan Albert Belle .40 1.00
3-Jan Andy Benes .20 .50
4-Jan Greg Briley .08 .25
5-Jan Kevin Brown .20 .50
6 Mark Carreon .08 .25
7 Mike Devereaux .08 .25
8 Junior Felix .08 .25
9 Bob Geren .08 .25
10 Tom Gordon .20 .50
11 Ken Griffey Jr. 2.50 6.00
12 Pete Harnisch .08 .25
13 Greg W. Harris .08 .25
14 Greg Hibbard .08 .25
15 Ken Hill .08 .25
16 Gregg Jefferies .08 .25
17 Jeff King .08 .25
18 Derek Lilliquist .08 .25
19 Carlos Martinez .08 .25
20 Ramon Martinez .08 .25
21 Bob Milacki .08 .25
22 Gregg Olson .08 .25
23 Donn Pall .08 .25
24 Kenny Rogers .20 .50
25 Gary Sheffield .40 1.00
26 Dwight Smith .08 .25
27 Billy Spiers .08 .25
28 Omar Vizquel .40 1.00
29 Jerome Walton .08 .25
30 Dave West .08 .25
31 John Wetteland .20 .50
32 Steve Wilson .08 .25
33 Craig Worthington .08 .25

1990 Topps Wax Box Cards

COMPLETE SET (16) 3.00 8.00
A Wade Boggs .20 .50
B George Brett .40 1.00
C Andre Dawson .15 .40
D Darrell Evans .07 .20
E Dwight Gooden .07 .20
F Rickey Henderson .30 .75
G Tom Lasorda MG .10 .30
H Fred Lynn .02 .10
I Mark McGwire .50 1.25
J Dave Parker .07 .20
K Jeff Reardon .07 .20
L Rick Reuschel .02 .10
M Jim Rice .07 .20
N Cal Ripken 1.00 2.50
O Nolan Ryan 1.00 2.50
P Ryne Sandberg .20 .50

1990 Topps Traded

The 1990 Topps Traded Set was the tenth consecutive year Topps issued a 132-card standard-size set at the end of the year. For the first time, Topps not only issued the set in factory set form but also distributed (on a significant basis) the set via seven-card wax packs. Unlike the factory set cards (which feature the whiter paper stock typical of the previous years Traded sets), the wax pack cards feature gray paper stock. Gray and white stock cards are equally valued. This set was arranged alphabetically by player and includes a mix of traded players and rookies for whom Topps did not include a card in the regular set. The key Rookie Cards in this set are Travis Fryman, Todd Hundley and Dave Justice.

COMPLETE SET (132) 1.25 3.00
COMP.FACT.SET (132) 1.25 3.00
1T Darrel Akerfelds .01 .05
2T Sandy Alomar Jr. .02 .10
3T Brad Arnsberg .01 .05
4T Steve Avery .01 .05
5T Wally Backman .01 .05
6T Carlos Baerga RC .08 .25
7T Kevin Bass .01 .05
8T Willie Blair RC .02 .10
9T Mike Blowers RC .08 .25
10T Shawn Boskie RC .02 .10
11T Daryl Boston .01 .05
12T Dennis Boyd .01 .05
13T Glenn Braggs .01 .05
14T Hubie Brooks .01 .05
15T Tom Brunansky .01 .05
16T John Burkett .01 .05
17T Casey Candaele .01 .05
18T John Candelaria .01 .05
19T Gary Carter .02 .10
20T Joe Carter .02 .10
21T Rick Cerone .01 .05
22T Scott Coolbaugh RC .01 .05
23T Bobby Cox MG .02 .10
24T Mark Davis .01 .05
25T Storm Davis .01 .05
26T Edgar Diaz RC .01 .05
27T Wayne Edwards RC .01 .05
28T Mark Eichhorn .01 .05
29T Scott Erickson RC .08 .25
30T Nick Esasky .01 .05
31T Cecil Fielder .02 .10
32T John Franco .02 .10
33T Travis Fryman RC .15 .40
34T Bill Gullickson .01 .05
35T Darryl Hamilton .01 .05
36T Mike Harkey .01 .05
37T Bud Harrelson MG .01 .05
38T Billy Hatcher .01 .05
39T Keith Hernandez .02 .10
40T Joe Hesketh .01 .05
41T Dave Hollins RC .08 .25
42T Sam Horn .01 .05
43T Steve Howard RC .01 .05
44T Todd Hundley RC .08 .25
45T Jeff Huson .01 .05
46T Chris James .01 .05
47T Stan Javier .01 .05
48T David Justice RC .20 .50
49T Jeff Kaiser .01 .05
50T Dana Kiecker RC .01 .05
51T Joe Klink RC .01 .05
52T Brent Knackert RC .02 .10
53T Brad Komminsk .01 .05
54T Mark Langston .01 .05
55T Tim Layana RC .01 .05
56T Rick Leach .01 .05
57T Terry Leach .01 .05
58T Tim Leary .01 .05
59T Craig Lefferts .01 .05
60T Charlie Leibrandt .01 .05
61T Jim Leyritz RC .08 .25
62T Fred Lynn .01 .05
63T Kevin Maas RC .08 .25
64T Shane Mack .01 .05
65T Candy Maldonado .01 .05
66T Fred Manrique .01 .05
67T Mike Marshall .01 .05
68T Carmelo Martinez .01 .05
69T John Marzano .01 .05
70T Ben McDonald .01 .05
71T Jack McDowell .01 .05
72T John McNamara MG .01 .05
73T Orlando Mercado .01 .05
74T Stump Merrill MG RC .01 .05
75T Alan Mills RC .02 .10
76T Hal Morris .01 .05
77T Lloyd Moseby .01 .05
78T Randy Myers .02 .10
79T Tim Naehring RC .02 .10
80T Junior Noboa .01 .05
81T Matt Nokes .01 .05
82T Pete O'Brien .01 .05
83T John Olerud RC .20 .50
84T Greg Olson (C) RC .02 .10
85T Junior Ortiz .01 .05
86T Dave Parker .02 .10
87T Rick Parker RC .01 .05
88T Bob Patterson .01 .05
89T Alejandro Pena .01 .05
90T Tony Pena .01 .05
91T Pascual Perez .01 .05
92T Gerald Perry .01 .05
93T Dan Petry .01 .05
94T Gary Pettis .01 .05
95T Tony Phillips .01 .05
96T Lou Piniella MG .02 .10
97T Luis Polonia .01 .05
98T Jim Presley .01 .05
99T Scott Radinsky RC .02 .10
100T Willie Randolph .02 .10
101T Jeff Reardon .02 .10
102T Greg Riddoch MG RC .01 .05
103T Jeff Robinson .01 .05
104T Ron Robinson .01 .05
105T Kevin Romine .01 .05
106T Scott Ruskin RC .01 .05
107T John Russell .01 .05
108T Bill Sampen RC .01 .05
109T Juan Samuel .01 .05
110T Scott Sanderson .01 .05
111T Jack Savage .01 .05
112T Dave Schmidt .01 .05
113T Red Schoendienst MG .08 .25
114T Terry Shumpert RC .01 .05
115T Matt Sinatro .01 .05
116T Don Slaught .01 .05
117T Bryn Smith .01 .05
118T Lee Smith .02 .10
119T Paul Sorrento RC .08 .25
120T Franklin Stubbs UER ('84 says '99 and has the sa .01 .05
121T Russ Swan RC .02 .10
122T Bob Tewksbury .01 .05
123T Wayne Tolleson .01 .05
124T John Tudor .01 .05
125T Randy Veres .01 .05
126T Hector Villanueva RC .02 .10
127T Mitch Webster .01 .05
128T Ernie Whitt .01 .05
129T Frank Wills .01 .05
130T Dave Winfield .02 .10
131T Matt Young .01 .05
132T Checklist 1T-132T .01 .05

1990 Topps Traded Tiffany

COMP.FACT.SET (132) 15.00 40.00
*STARS: 6X TO 15X BASIC CARDS
*ROOKIES: 6X TO 15X BASIC CARDS
DISTRIBUTED ONLY IN FACTORY SET FORM
STATED PRINT RUN 15,000 SETS
FACTORY SET PRICE IS FOR SEALED SETS

1990 Topps Ames All-Stars

The 1990 Topps Ames All-Stars set was issued by Topps for the Ames department stores for the second straight year. This standard-size set featured 33 of the leading hitters active in major league baseball.

COMPLETE SET (33) 2.00 5.00
1 Dave Winfield .15 .40
2 George Brett .30 .75
3 Jim Rice .02 .10
4 Dwight Evans .02 .10
5 Robin Yount .15 .40
6 Dave Parker .02 .10
7 Eddie Murray .15 .40
8 Keith Hernandez .02 .10
9 Andre Dawson .07 .20
10 Fred Lynn .01 .05
11 Dale Murphy .07 .20
12 Jack Clark .02 .10
13 Rickey Henderson .30 .75
14 Paul Molitor .15 .40
15 Cal Ripken .75 2.00
16 Wade Boggs .20 .50
17 Tim Raines .02 .10
18 Don Mattingly .40 1.00
19 Kent Hrbek .02 .10
20 Kirk Gibson .02 .10
21 Julio Franco .02 .10
22 George Bell .01 .05
23 Darryl Strawberry .02 .10
24 Kirby Puckett .20 .50
25 Juan Samuel .01 .05
26 Alvin Davis .01 .05
27 Joe Carter .02 .10
28 Eric Davis .02 .10
29 Jose Canseco .10 .30
30 Wally Joyner .01 .05
31 Will Clark .07 .20
32 Ruben Sierra .02 .10
33 Danny Tartabull .01 .05

1990 Topps Big

The 1990 Topps Big set contains 330 cards each measuring a slightly over-sized 2 5/8" by 3 3/4". In 1989 Topps had issued two oversize sets (Bigs and Bowmans), but in 1990 only the Topps Big were issued by Topps as an oversize set. The set was issued in three series of 110 cards. Some dealers believe the third series was distributed in far less quantity than the first two series. An early card of slugger Sammy Sosa was included in this set.

COMPLETE SET (330) 10.00 25.00
1 Dwight Evans .20 .50
2 Kirby Puckett .30 .75
3 Kevin Gross .07 .20
4 Ron Hassey .07 .20
5 Lloyd McClendon .07 .20
6 Bo Jackson .30 .75
7 Lonnie Smith .07 .20
8 Alvaro Espinoza .07 .20
9 Roberto Alomar .20 .50
10 Glenn Braggs .07 .20
11 David Cone .10 .30
12 Claudell Washington .07 .20
13 Pedro Guerrero .07 .20
14 Todd Benzinger .07 .20
15 Jeff Russell .07 .20
16 Terry Kennedy .07 .20
17 Kelly Gruber .07 .20
18 Alfredo Griffin .07 .20
19 Mark Grace .20 .50
20 Dave Winfield .10 .30
21 Bret Saberhagen .10 .30
22 Roger Clemens .75 2.00
23 Bob Walk .07 .20
24 Dave Magadan .07 .20
25 Spike Owen .07 .20
26 Jody Davis .07 .20
27 Kent Hrbek .10 .30
28 Mark McGwire .75 2.00
29 Eddie Murray .30 .75
30 Paul O'Neill .20 .50
31 Jose DeLeon .07 .20
32 Steve Lyons .07 .20
33 Dan Plesac .07 .20
34 Jack Howell .07 .20
35 Greg Briley .07 .20
36 Andy Hawkins .07 .20
37 Cecil Espy .07 .20
38 Rick Sutcliffe .10 .30
39 Jack Clark .10 .30
40 Dale Murphy .20 .50
41 Mike Henneman .07 .20
42 Rick Honeycutt .07 .20
43 Willie Randolph .10 .30
44 Marty Barrett .07 .20
45 Willie Wilson .07 .20
46 Wallace Johnson .07 .20
47 Greg Brock .07 .20
48 Tom Browning .07 .20
49 Gerald Young .07 .20
50 Dennis Eckersley .10 .30
51 Scott Garrelts .07 .20
52 Gary Redus .07 .20
53 Al Newman .07 .20
54 Daryl Boston .07 .20
55 Ron Oester .07 .20
56 Danny Tartabull .07 .20
57 Gregg Jefferies .10 .30
58 Tom Foley .07 .20
59 Robin Yount .50 1.25
60 Pat Borders .07 .20
61 Mike Greenwell .07 .20
62 Shawon Dunston .07 .20
63 Steve Buechele .07 .20
64 Dave Stewart .10 .30
65 Jose Oquendo .07 .20
66 Ron Gant .10 .30
67 Mike Scioscia .07 .20
68 Randy Velarde .07 .20
69 Von Hayes .07 .20
70 Tim Wallach .07 .20
71 Eric Show .07 .20
72 Eric Davis .10 .30
73 Mike Gallego .07 .20
74 Rob Deer .07 .20
75 Ryne Sandberg .50 1.25
76 Kevin Seitzer .07 .20
77 Wade Boggs .20 .50
78 Greg Gagne .07 .20
79 John Smiley .07 .20
80 Ivan Calderon .07 .20
81 Pete Incaviglia .07 .20
82 Orel Hershiser .10 .30
83 Carney Lansford .10 .30
84 Mike Fitzgerald .07 .20
85 Don Mattingly .75 2.00
86 Chet Lemon .07 .20
87 Rolando Roomes .07 .20
88 Billy Spiers .07 .20
89 Pat Tabler .07 .20
90 Danny Heep .07 .20
91 Andre Dawson .10 .30
92 Randy Bush .07 .20
93 Tony Gwynn .40 1.00
94 Tom Brunansky .07 .20
95 Johnny Ray .07 .20
96 Matt Williams .10 .30
97 Barry Lyons .07 .20
98 Jeff Hamilton .07 .20
99 Tom Glavine .20 .50
100 Ken Griffey Sr. .10 .30
101 Tom Henke .07 .20
102 Dave Righetti .07 .20
103 Paul Molitor .10 .30
104 Mike LaValliere .07 .20
105 Frank White .10 .30
106 Bob Welch .07 .20
107 Ellis Burks .20 .50
108 Andres Galarraga .10 .30
109 Mitch Williams .07 .20
110 Checklist 1-110 .07 .20
111 Craig Biggio .30 .75
112 Dave Stieb .10 .30
113 Ron Darling .07 .20
114 Bert Blyleven .10 .30
115 Dickie Thon .07 .20
116 Carlos Martinez .07 .20
117 Jeff King .07 .20
118 Terry Steinbach .07 .20
119 Frank Tanana .07 .20
120 Mark Lemke .07 .20
121 Chris Sabo .07 .20
122 Glenn Davis .07 .20
123 Mel Hall .07 .20
124 Jim Gantner .07 .20
125 Benito Santiago .10 .30
126 Milt Thompson .07 .20
127 Rafael Palmeiro .20 .50
128 Barry Bonds .75 2.00
129 Mike Bielecki .07 .20
130 Lou Whitaker .10 .30
131 Bob Ojeda .07 .20
132 Dion James .07 .20
133 Dennis Martinez .10 .30
134 Fred McGriff .30 .75
135 Terry Pendleton .10 .30
136 Pat Combs .07 .20
137 Kevin Mitchell .07 .20
138 Marquis Grissom .30 .75
139 Chris Bosio .07 .20
140 Omar Vizquel .30 .75
141 Steve Sax .07 .20
142 Nelson Liriano .07 .20
143 Kevin Elster .07 .20
144 Dan Pasqua .07 .20
145 Dave Smith .07 .20
146 Craig Worthington .07 .20
147 Dan Gladden .07 .20
148 Oddibe McDowell .07 .20
149 Bip Roberts .07 .20
150 Randy Ready .07 .20
151 Dwight Smith .07 .20
152 Eddie Whitson .07 .20
153 George Bell .07 .20
154 Tim Raines .10 .30
155 Sid Fernandez .07 .20
156 Henry Cotto .07 .20
157 Harold Baines .10 .30
158 Willie McGee .10 .30
159 Bill Doran .07 .20
160 Steve Balboni .07 .20
161 Pete Smith .07 .20
162 Frank Viola .07 .20
163 Gary Sheffield .30 .75
164 Bill Landrum .07 .20
165 Tony Fernandez .07 .20
166 Mike Heath .07 .20
167 Jody Reed .07 .20
168 Wally Joyner .10 .30
169 Robby Thompson .07 .20
170 Ken Caminiti .10 .30
171 Nolan Ryan 1.25 3.00
172 Ricky Jordan .07 .20
173 Lance Blankenship .07 .20

174 Dwight Gooden .10 .30
175 Ruben Sierra .10 .30
176 Carlton Fisk .20 .50
177 Garry Templeton .07 .20
178 Mike Devereaux .07 .20
179 Mookie Wilson .10 .30
180 Jeff Blauser .07 .20
181 Scott Bradley .07 .20
182 Luis Salazar .07 .20
183 Rafael Ramirez .07 .20
184 Vince Coleman .07 .20
185 Doug Drabek .07 .20
186 Darryl Strawberry .10 .30
187 Tim Burke .07 .20
188 Jesse Barfield .07 .20
189 Barry Larkin .20 .50
190 Alan Trammell .10 .30
191 Steve Lake .07 .20
192 Derek Lilliquist .07 .20
193 Don Robinson .07 .20
194 Kevin McReynolds .07 .20
195 Melido Perez .07 .20
196 Jose Lind .07 .20
197 Eric Anthony .07 .20
198 B.J. Surhoff .10 .30
199 John Olerud .40 1.00
200 Mike Moore .07 .20
201 Mark Gubicza .07 .20
202 Phil Bradley .07 .20
203 Ozzie Smith .50 1.25
204 Greg Maddux .50 1.25
205 Julio Franco .10 .30
206 Tom Herr .07 .20
207 Scott Fletcher .07 .20
208 Bobby Bonilla .10 .30
209 Bob Geren .07 .20
210 Junior Felix .07 .20
211 Dick Schofield .07 .20
212 Jim Deshaies .07 .20
213 Jose Uribe .07 .20
214 John Kruk .10 .30
215 Ozzie Guillen .10 .30
216 Howard Johnson .07 .20
217 Andy Van Slyke .20 .50
218 Tim Laudner .07 .20
219 Manny Lee .07 .20
220 Checklist 111-220 .07 .20
221 Cory Snyder .07 .20
222 Billy Hatcher .07 .20
223 Bud Black .07 .20
224 Will Clark .20 .50
225 Kevin Tapani .30 .75
226 Mike Pagliarulo .07 .20
227 Dave Parker .10 .30
228 Ben McDonald .07 .20
229 Carlos Baerga .10 .30
230 Roger McDowell .07 .20
231 Delino DeShields .30 .75
232 Mark Langston .07 .20
233 Wally Backman .07 .20
234 Jim Eisenreich .07 .20
235 Mike Schooler .07 .20
236 Kevin Bass .07 .20
237 John Farrell .07 .20
238 Kal Daniels .07 .20
239 Tony Phillips .07 .20
240 Todd Stottlemyre .10 .30
241 Greg Olson .07 .20
242 Charlie Hough .10 .30
243 Mariano Duncan .07 .20
244 Bill Ripken .07 .20
245 Joe Carter .10 .30
246 Tim Belcher .07 .20
247 Roberto Kelly .07 .20
248 Candy Maldonado .07 .20
249 Mike Scott .07 .20
250 Ken Griffey Jr. 1.50 4.00
251 Nick Esasky .07 .20
252 Tom Gordon .10 .30
253 John Tudor .07 .20
254 Gary Gaetti .10 .30
255 Neal Heaton .07 .20
256 Jerry Browne .07 .20
257 Jose Rijo .07 .20
258 Mike Boddicker .07 .20
259 Brett Butler .10 .30
260 Andy Benes .10 .30
261 Kevin Brown .10 .30
262 Hubie Brooks .07 .20
263 Randy Milligan .07 .20
264 John Franco .10 .30
265 Sandy Alomar Jr. .10 .30
266 Dave Valle .07 .20
267 Jerome Walton .07 .20
268 Bob Boone .10 .30
269 Ken Howell .07 .20
270 Jose Canseco .20 .50
271 Joe Magrane .07 .20
272 Brian DuBois .07 .20
273 Carlos Quintana .07 .20
274 Lance Johnson .07 .20
275 Steve Bedrosian .07 .20
276 Brook Jacoby .07 .20
277 Fred Lynn UER .07 .20
278 Jeff Ballard .07 .20
279 Otis Nixon .07 .20
280 Chili Davis .10 .30
281 Joe Oliver .07 .20
282 Brian Holman .07 .20
283 Juan Samuel .07 .20
284 Rick Aguilera .10 .30
285 Jeff Reardon .10 .30
286 Sammy Sosa 1.50 4.00
287 Carmelo Martinez .07 .20
288 Greg Swindell .07 .20
289 Erik Hanson .07 .20
290 Tony Pena .07 .20
291 Pascual Perez .07 .20
292 Rickey Henderson .30 .75
293 Kurt Stillwell .07 .20
294 Todd Zeile .10 .30
295 Bobby Thigpen .07 .20
296 Larry Walker .60 1.50
297 Rob Murphy .07 .20
298 Mitch Webster .07 .20
299 Devon White .10 .30
300 Len Dykstra .10 .30
301 Keith Hernandez .10 .30
302 Gene Larkin .07 .20
303 Jeffrey Leonard .07 .20
304 Jim Presley .07 .20
305 Lloyd Moseby .07 .20
306 John Smoltz .30 .75
307 Sam Horn .07 .20
308 Greg Litton .07 .20
309 Dave Henderson .07 .20
310 Mark McLemore .07 .20
311 Gary Pettis .07 .20
312 Mark Davis .07 .20
313 Cecil Fielder .10 .30
314 Jack Armstrong .07 .20
315 Alvin Davis .07 .20
316 Doug Jones .07 .20
317 Eric Yelding .07 .20
318 Joe Orsulak .07 .20
319 Chuck Finley .10 .30
320 Glenn Wilson .07 .20
321 Harold Reynolds .10 .30
322 Teddy Higuera .07 .20
323 Lance Parrish .07 .20
324 Bruce Hurst .07 .20
325 Dave West .07 .20
326 Kirk Gibson .10 .30
327 Cal Ripken 1.00 2.50
328 Rick Reuschel .07 .20
329 Jim Abbott .20 .50
330 Checklist 221-330 .07 .20

1990 Topps Debut '89

The 1990 Topps Major League Debut Set is a 152-card, standard-size set arranged in alphabetical order by player's name. Each card front features the date of the player's first major league appearance. Strangely enough, even though the set commemorates the 1989 Major League debuts, the set was not issued until-the 1990 season had almost begun. Key cards in this set include Joey (Albert) Belle, Juan Gonzalez, Ken Griffey, Jr., David Justice, Deion Sanders and Sammy Sosa (pictured as a member of the Texas Rangers). These sets were issued 50 to a case.

COMP.FACT.SET (152) 6.00 15.00
1 Jim Abbott .20 .50
2 Beau Allred .05 .15
3 Wilson Alvarez .08 .25
4 Kent Anderson .05 .15
5 Eric Anthony .05 .15
6 Kevin Appier .08 .25
7 Larry Arndt .05 .15
8 John Barfield .05 .15
9 Billy Bates .05 .15
10 Kevin Batiste .05 .15
11 Blaine Beatty .05 .15
12 Stan Belinda .05 .15
13 Juan Bell .05 .15
14 Albert Belle .30 .75
15 Andy Benes .08 .25
16 Mike Benjamin .05 .15
17 Geronimo Berroa .05 .15
18 Mike Blowers .08 .25
19 Brian Brady .05 .15
20 Francisco Cabrera .05 .15
21 George Canale .05 .15
22 Jose Cano .05 .15
23 Steve Carter .05 .15
24 Pat Combs .05 .15
25 Scott Coolbaugh .05 .15
26 Steve Cummings .05 .15
27 Pete Dalena .05 .15
28 Jeff Datz .05 .15
29 Bobby Davidson .05 .15
30 Drew Denson .05 .15
31 Gary DiSarcina .08 .25
32 Brian DuBois .05 .15
33 Mike Dyer .05 .15
34 Wayne Edwards .05 .15
35 Junior Felix .05 .15
36 Mike Fetters .05 .15
37 Steve Finley .08 .25
38 Darrin Fletcher .08 .25
39 LaVel Freeman .05 .15
40 Steve Frey .05 .15
41 Mark Gardner .05 .15
42 Joe Girardi .08 .25
43 Juan Gonzalez 1.00 2.50
44 Goose Gozzo .05 .15
45 Tommy Greene .05 .15
46 Ken Griffey Jr. 2.50 6.00
47 Jason Grimsley .05 .15
48 Marquis Grissom .30 .75
49 Mark Guthrie .05 .15
50 Chip Hale .05 .15
51 Jack Hardy .05 .15
52 Gene Harris .05 .15
53 Mike Hartley .05 .15
54 Scott Hemond .05 .15
55 Xavier Hernandez .05 .15
56 Eric Hetzel .05 .15
57 Greg Hibbard .05 .15
58 Mark Higgins .05 .15
59 Glenallen Hill .05 .15
60 Chris Hoiles .08 .25
61 Shawn Holman .05 .15
62 Dann Howitt .05 .15
63 Mike Huff .05 .15
64 Terry Jorgensen .05 .15
65 David Justice .40 1.00
66 Jeff King .05 .15
67 Matt Kinzer .05 .15
68 Joe Kraemer .05 .15
69 Marcus Lawton .05 .15
70 Derek Lilliquist .05 .15
71 Scott Little .05 .15
72 Greg Litton .05 .15
73 Rick Luecken .05 .15
74 Julio Machado .05 .15
75 Tom Magrann .05 .15
76 Kelly Mann .05 .15
77 Randy McCament .05 .15
78 Ben McDonald .05 .15
79 Chuck McElroy .05 .15
80 Jeff McKnight .05 .15
81 Kent Mercker .05 .15
82 Matt Merullo .05 .15
83 Hensley Meulens .05 .15
84 Kevin Mmahat .05 .15
85 Mike Munoz .05 .15
86 Dan Murphy .05 .15
87 Jaime Navarro .05 .15
88 Randy Nosek .05 .15
89 John Olerud .40 1.00
90 Steve Olin .08 .25
91 Joe Oliver .05 .15
92 Francisco Oliveras .05 .15
93 Gregg Olson .08 .25
94 John Orton .05 .15
95 Dean Palmer .20 .50
96 Ramon Pena .05 .15
97 Jeff Peterek .05 .15
98 Marty Pevey .05 .15
99 Rusty Richards .05 .15
100 Jeff Richardson .05 .15
101 Rob Richie .05 .15
102 Kevin Ritz .05 .15
103 Rosario Rodriguez .05 .15
104 Mike Roesler .05 .15
105 Kenny Rogers .08 .25
106 Bobby Rose .05 .15
107 Alex Sanchez .05 .15
108 Deion Sanders .30 .75
109 Jeff Schaefer .05 .15
110 Jeff Schulz .05 .15
111 Mike Schwabe .05 .15
112 Dick Scott .05 .15
113 Scott Scudder .05 .15
114 Rudy Seanez .05 .15
115 Joe Skalski .05 .15
116 Dwight Smith .05 .15
117 Greg Smith .05 .15
118 Mike Smith .05 .15
119 Paul Sorrento .08 .25
120 Sammy Sosa 1.50 4.00
121 Billy Spiers .05 .15
122 Mike Stanton .05 .15
123 Phil Stephenson .05 .15
124 Doug Strange .05 .15
125 Russ Swan .05 .15
126 Kevin Tapani .08 .25
127 Stu Tate .05 .15
128 Greg Vaughn .05 .15
129 Robin Ventura .30 .75
130 Randy Veres .05 .15
131 Jose Vizcaino .08 .25
132 Omar Vizquel .30 .75
133 Larry Walker 1.00 2.50
134 Jerome Walton .05 .15
135 Gary Wayne .05 .15
136 Lenny Webster .05 .15
137 Mickey Weston .05 .15
138 Jeff Wetherby .05 .15
139 John Wetteland .20 .50
140 Ed Whited .05 .15
141 Wally Whitehurst .05 .15
142 Kevin Wickander .05 .15
143 Dean Wilkins .05 .15
144 Dana Williams .05 .15
145 Paul Wilmet .05 .15
146 Craig Wilson .05 .15
147 Matt Winters .05 .15
148 Eric Yelding .05 .15
149 Clint Zavaras .05 .15
150 Todd Zeile .20 .50
151 Checklist Card .05 .15
152 Checklist Card .05 .15

1990 Topps Doubleheaders

The 1990 Topps Double Headers set consists of 72 collectibles. Each Double Header consists of a clear plastic holder that contains a mini-reproduction of the player's 1990 card on one side and a mini-reproduction of his rookie card on the other side. The Double Headers were packaged in a paper pouch to conceal the player's identity prior to purchase. Three different checklists (A, B, and C) are printed on the outside of the packs, with the players listed in alphabetical order, and the double headers are checklisted below in alphabetcal order.

COMPLETE SET (72) 10.00 25.00
1 Jim Abbott .20 .50
2 Jeff Ballard .08 .25
3 George Bell .08 .25
4 Wade Boggs .75 2.00
5 Barry Bonds 1.25 3.00
6 Bobby Bonilla .08 .25
7 Ellis Burks .20 .50
8 Jose Canseco .50 1.25
9 Joe Carter .20 .50
10 Will Clark .60 1.50
11 Roger Clemens 1.50 4.00
12 Vince Coleman .08 .25
13 Alvin Davis .08 .25
14 Eric Davis .20 .50
15 Glenn Davis .08 .25
16 Mark Davis .08 .25
17 Andre Dawson .40 1.00
18 Shawon Dunston .08 .25
19 Dennis Eckersley .60 1.50
20 Sid Fernandez .08 .25
21 Tony Fernandez .20 .50
22 Chuck Finley .08 .25
23 Carlton Fisk .60 1.50
24 Julio Franco .20 .50
25 Gary Gaetti .20 .50
26 Doc Gooden .20 .50
27 Mark Grace .40 1.00
28 Mike Greenwell .08 .25
29 Ken Griffey Jr. 2.00 5.00
30 Pedro Guerrero .08 .25
31 Tony Gwynn 1.50 4.00
32 Von Hayes .08 .25
33 Rickey Henderson 1.25 3.00
34 Orel Hershiser .20 .50
35 Bo Jackson .40 1.00
36 Gregg Jefferies .08 .25
37 Howard Johnson .08 .25
38 Ricky Jordan .08 .25
39 Carney Lansford .08 .25
40 Barry Larkin .60 1.50
41 Greg Maddux 2.00 5.00
42 Joe Magrane .08 .25
43 Don Mattingly 1.50 4.00
44 Fred McGriff .40 1.00
45 Mark McGwire 1.50 4.00
46 Kevin McReynolds .08 .25
47 Kevin Mitchell .08 .25
48 Gregg Olson .08 .25
49 Kirby Puckett 1.00 2.50
50 Rock Raines .20 .50
51 Harold Reynolds .20 .50
52 Cal Ripken 3.00 8.00
53 Nolan Ryan 3.00 8.00
54 Bret Saberhagen .08 .25
55 Ryne Sandberg 1.25 3.00
56 Benny Santiago .20 .50
57 Steve Sax .08 .25
58 Mike Scioscia .20 .50
59 Mike Scott .08 .25
60 Ruben Sierra .20 .50
61 Lonnie Smith .08 .25
62 Ozzie Smith 1.25 3.00
63 Dave Stewart .08 .25
64 Darryl Strawberry .20 .50
65 Greg Swindell .08 .25
66 Alan Trammell .30 .75
67 Frank Viola .08 .25
68 Tim Wallach .08 .25
69 Jerome Walton .08 .25
70 Lou Whitaker .20 .50
71 Mitch Williams .08 .25
72 Robin Yount .75 2.00

1990 Topps Gallery of Champions

This would be the seventh out of eight consecutive seasons that Topps issued small "metal" versions of some leading players from their regular issue set. These 12 cards, issued in complete set form only, feature league leaders and award winners. The cards measure approximately 1 1/4" by 1 3/4" and were produced in aluminum, bronze and silver versions. We have valued the aluminum cards, the bronze cards are valued at 2X to 5X the values of the aluminum versions while the silvers are 7X to 15X the aluminums. We have sequenced this set in alphabetical order.

COMPLETE SET (12) 10.00 25.00
1 Mark Davis 1.00 2.50
2 Jose DeLeon 1.00 2.50
3 Tony Gwynn 6.00 15.00
4 Fred McGriff 2.50 6.00
5 Kevin Mitchell 1.00 2.50
6 Gregg Olson 1.00 2.50
7 Kirby Puckett 4.00 10.00
8 Jeff Russell 1.00 2.50
9 Nolan Ryan 10.00 25.00
10 Bret Saberhagen 1.00 2.50
11 Jerome Walton 1.00 2.50
12 Robin Yount 3.00 8.00

1990 Topps Heads Up

Though this collectible item made a limited appearance in 1989, the 1990 Topps set features 24 different Heads-Up pin-ups. Each item is a die-cut pin-up of a baseball star printed on thick white board, with a suction cup attached to the back. The die-cuts follow the contours of the player's hat and head, and they can be attached to any flat surface. The player's name and number appear on the back. The pin-ups are listed below according to the checklist prifted on the back of each wrapper.

COMPLETE SET (24) 4.00 10.00
1 Tony Gwynn .60 1.50
2 Will Clark .20 .50
3 Doc Gooden .07 .20
4 Dennis Eckersley .25 .60
5 Ken Griffey Jr. .75 2.00
6 Craig Biggio .10 .30
7 Bret Saberhagen .02 .10
8 Bo Jackson .20 .50
9 Ryne Sandberg .30 .75
10 Gregg Olson .02 .10
11 John Franco .07 .20
12 Rafael Palmeiro .25 .60
13 Gary Sheffield .30 .75
14 Mark McGwire .60 1.50
15 Kevin Mitchell .02 .10
16 Jim Abbott .07 .20
17 Harold Reynolds .07 .20
18 Jose Canseco .20 .50
19 Don Mattingly .60 1.50
20 Kirby Puckett .25 .60
21 Tom Gordon .10 .30
22 Craig Worthington .02 .10
23 Dwight Smith .02 .10
24 Jerome Walton .02 .10

1990 Topps Hills Hit Men

The 1990 Topps Hit Men set is a standard-size 33-card set arranged in order of slugging percentage. The set was produced by Topps for Hills Department stores. Each card in the set has a glossy-coated front.

COMPLETE SET (33) 2.00 5.00
1 Eric Davis .02 .10
2 Will Clark .15 .40
3 Don Mattingly .40 1.00
4 Darryl Strawberry .02 .10
5 Kevin Mitchell .01 .05
6 Pedro Guerrero .01 .05
7 Jose Canseco .15 .40
8 Jim Rice .02 .10
9 Danny Tartabull .01 .05
10 George Brett .40 1.00
11 Kent Hrbek .02 .10
12 George Bell .01 .05
13 Eddie Murray .15 .40
14 Fred Lynn .01 .05
15 Andre Dawson .08 .25
16 Dale Murphy .08 .25
17 Dave Winfield .15 .40
18 Jack Clark .02 .10
19 Wade Boggs .20 .50
20 Ruben Sierra .02 .10
21 Dave Parker .02 .10
22 Glenn Davis .01 .05
23 Dwight Evans .02 .10
24 Jesse Barfield .01 .05
25 Kirk Gibson .02 .10
26 Alvin Davis .01 .05
27 Kirby Puckett .20 .50
28 Joe Carter .02 .10
29 Carlton Fisk .15 .40
30 Harold Baines .05 .15
31 Andres Galarraga .08 .25
32 Cal Ripken .75 2.00
33 Howard Johnson .01 .05

1990 Topps Mini Leaders

The 1990 Topps League Leader Minis is an 88-card set with cards measuring approximately 2 1/8" by 3". The set features players who finished 1989 in the top five in any major hitting or pitching category. This set marked the fifth year that Topps issued their Mini set. The card numbering is alphabetical by player within team and the teams themselves are ordered alphabetically.

COMPLETE SET (88) 3.00 8.00
1 Jeff Ballard .01 .05
2 Phil Bradley .01 .05
3 Wade Boggs .30 .75
4 Roger Clemens .60 1.50
5 Nick Esasky .01 .05
6 Jody Reed .01 .05
7 Bert Blyleven .02 .10
8 Chuck Finley .02 .10
9 Kirk McCaskill .01 .05
10 Devon White .01 .05
11 Ivan Calderon .01 .05
12 Bobby Thigpen .01 .05
13 Joe Carter .02 .10
14 Gary Pettis .01 .05
15 Tom Gordon .02 .10
16 Bo Jackson .15 .40
17 Bret Saberhagen .02 .10
18 Kevin Seitzer .01 .05
19 Chris Bosio .01 .05
20 Paul Molitor .30 .75
21 Dan Plesac .01 .05
22 Robin Yount .20 .50
23 Kirby Puckett .25 .60
24 Don Mattingly .60 1.50
25 Steve Sax .01 .05
26 Storm Davis .01 .05
27 Dennis Eckersley .20 .50
28 Rickey Henderson .30 .75
29 Carney Lansford .01 .05
30 Mark McGwire .60 1.50
31 Mike Moore .01 .05
32 Dave Stewart .02 .10
33 Alvin Davis .01 .05
34 Harold Reynolds .02 .10
35 Mike Schooler .01 .05
36 Cecil Espy .01 .05
37 Julio Franco .02 .10
38 Jeff Russell .01 .05
39 Nolan Ryan 1.25 3.00
40 Ruben Sierra .02 .10
41 George Bell .01 .05
42 Tony Fernandez .02 .10
43 Fred McGriff .08 .25
44 Dave Stieb .01 .05
45 Checklist Card .01 .05
46 Lonnie Smith .01 .05
47 John Smoltz .08 .25
48 Mike Bielecki .01 .05
49 Mark Grace .30 .75
50 Greg Maddux .60 1.50
51 Ryne Sandberg .40 1.00
52 Mitch Williams .01 .05
53 Eric Davis .02 .10
54 John Franco .02 .10
55 Glenn Davis .01 .05
56 Mike Scott .01 .05
57 Tim Belcher .01 .05
58 Orel Hershiser .02 .10
59 Jay Howell .01 .05
60 Eddie Murray .30 .75
61 Tim Burke .01 .05
62 Mark Langston .01 .05
63 Tim Raines .02 .10
64 Tim Wallach .01 .05
65 David Cone .08 .25
66 Sid Fernandez .01 .05
67 Howard Johnson .01 .05
68 Juan Samuel .01 .05
69 Von Hayes .01 .05
70 Barry Bonds .60 1.50
71 Bobby Bonilla .02 .10
72 Andy Van Slyke .01 .05
73 Vince Coleman .01 .05
74 Jose DeLeon .01 .05
75 Pedro Guerrero .01 .05
76 Joe Magrane .01 .05
77 Roberto Alomar .30 .75
78 Jack Clark .02 .10
79 Mark Davis .01 .05
80 Tony Gwynn .60 1.50
81 Bruce Hurst .01 .05
82 Eddie Whitson .01 .05
83 Brett Butler .02 .10
84 Will Clark .08 .25
85 Scott Garrelts .01 .05
86 Kevin Mitchell .01 .05
87 Rick Reuschel .01 .05
88 Robby Thompson .01 .05

1990 Topps Mylar Stickers Test

These six standard-size stickers represent Topps attempt to change their sticker format from the smaller size used throughout the 1980's to a larger item. The test, obviously, did not work as these were never issued as a full set. These stickers are in the same design as the regular 1990 Topps set. As the stickers are unnumbered we have sequenced them in alphabetical order.

COMPLETE SET (6) 30.00 80.00
1 Joe Carter 8.00 20.00
2 Shane Mack 4.00 10.00
3 Alan Mills 4.00 10.00
4 Alejandro Pena 4.00 10.00
5 Gerald Perry 4.00 10.00
6 Dave Winfield 15.00 40.00

1990 Topps Sticker Backs

COMPLETE SET (67) 6.00 15.00
1 Will Clark .08 .25
2 Glenn Davis .01 .05
3 Pedro Guerrero .01 .05
4 Roberto Alomar .20 .50
5 Gregg Jefferies .01 .05
6 Ryne Sandberg .25 .60
7 Bobby Bonilla .01 .05
8 Howard Johnson .01 .05
9 Tim Wallach .01 .05
10 Shawon Dunston .01 .05
11 Barry Larkin .08 .25
12 Ozzie Smith .30 .75
13 Eric Davis .02 .10
14 Andre Dawson .08 .25
15 Tony Gwynn .50 1.25
16 Von Hayes .01 .05
17 Kevin Mitchell .01 .05
18 Rock Raines .02 .10
19 Lonnie Smith .01 .05
20 Darryl Strawberry .01 .05
21 Jerome Walton .01 .05
22 Craig Biggio .20 .50
23 Benny Santiago .01 .05
24 Mike Scioscia .02 .10
25 Doc Gooden .02 .10
26 Rick Reuschel .01 .05
27 Mike Scott .01 .05
28 Sid Fernandez .01 .05
29 Mark Langston .01 .05
30 Joe Magrane .01 .05
31 Mark Davis .01 .05
32 Jay Howell .01 .05
33 Mitch Williams .01 .05
34 Don Mattingly .60 1.50
35 Fred McGriff .08 .25
36 Mark McGwire .75 2.00
37 Julio Franco .01 .05
38 Steve Sax .01 .05
39 Lou Whitaker .02 .10
40 Wade Boggs .20 .50
41 Gary Gaetti .02 .10
42 Carney Lansford .02 .10
43 Tony Fernandez .01 .05
44 Cal Ripken 1.25 3.00
45 Alan Trammell .05 .15
46 George Bell .01 .05
47 Jose Canseco .20 .50
48 Joe Carter .02 .10
49 Ken Griffey Jr. 1.00 2.50
50 Rickey Henderson .30 .75
51 Bo Jackson .08 .25
52 Kirby Puckett .30 .75
53 Ruben Sierra .01 .05
54 Robin Yount .20 .50
55 Carlton Fisk .15 .40
56 Terry Steinbach .01 .05
57 Mickey Tettleton .02 .10
58 Nolan Ryan 1.25 3.00
59 Bret Saberhagen .02 .10
60 Dave Stewart .02 .10
61 Jeff Ballard .01 .05
62 Chuck Finley .02 .10
63 Greg Swindell .01 .05
64 Dennis Eckersley .15 .40
65 Gregg Olson .01 .05
66 Jeff Russell .01 .05
67 Checklist .01 .05

1990 Topps TV All-Stars

This All-Star team set contains 66 cards measuring the standard size. The fronts feature posed or action color player photos with a high gloss. In block lettering, the words "All-Star" are printed vertically in blue on the left side of the card. The player's name appears in a red plaque below the picture, and white borders round out the card face. The backs are printed in black lettering and have a red and white background. Inside a decal design, biographical information and career bests are superimposed on a blue, pink, and white background. These cards were offered only on television as a complete set for sale through an 800 number.

COMP.FACT. SET (66) 12.50 30.00
1 Mark McGwire 2.50 6.00
2 Julio Franco .40 1.00
3 Ozzie Guillen .75 2.00
4 Carney Lansford .40 1.00
5 Bo Jackson 1.00 2.50
6 Kirby Puckett 1.50 4.00
7 Ruben Sierra .40 1.00
8 Carlton Fisk 1.25 3.00
9 Nolan Ryan 5.00 12.00
10 Rickey Henderson 2.00 5.00
11 Jose Canseco 1.25 3.00
12 Mark Davis .20 .50
13 Dennis Eckersley 1.25 3.00
14 Chuck Finley .40 1.00
15 Bret Saberhagen .40 1.00
16 Dave Stewart .40 1.00
17 Don Mattingly 2.50 6.00
18 Steve Sax .20 .50
19 Cal Ripken 5.00 12.00
20 Wade Boggs 1.25 3.00
21 George Bell .20 .50
22 Mike Greenwell .20 .50
23 Robin Yount 1.25 3.00
24 Mickey Tettleton .40 1.00
25 Roger Clemens 2.50 6.00
26 Fred McGriff 1.00 2.50
27 Jeff Ballard .20 .50
28 Dwight Evans .40 1.00
29 Paul Molitor 1.25 3.00
30 Gregg Olson .20 .50
31 Dan Plesac .20 .50
32 Greg Swindell .20 .50
33 Tony LaRussa MG .40 1.00
Cito Gaston MG
34 Will Clark 1.25 3.00
35 Roberto Alomar 1.00 2.50
36 Barry Larkin 1.00 2.50
37 Ken Caminiti 1.00 2.50
38 Eric Davis .40 1.00
39 Tony Gwynn 2.50 6.00
40 Kevin Mitchell .20 .50
41 Craig Biggio 1.00 2.50
42 Mike Scott .20 .50
43 Joe Carter .40 1.00
44 Jack Clark .40 1.00
45 Glenn Davis .20 .50
46 Orel Hershiser .40 1.00
47 Jay Howell .20 .50
48 Bruce Hurst .20 .50
49 Dave Smith .20 .50
50 Pedro Guerrero .20 .50
51 Ryne Sandberg 2.50 6.00
52 Ozzie Smith 2.50 6.00
53 Howard Johnson .20 .50
54 Von Hayes .20 .50
55 Tim Raines .40 1.00
56 Darryl Strawberry .40 1.00
57 Mike LaValliere .20 .50
58 Dwight Gooden .40 1.00
59 Bobby Bonilla .20 .50
60 Tim Burke .20 .50
61 Sid Fernandez .20 .50
62 Andres Galarraga 1.00 2.50
63 Mark Grace 1.00 2.50
64 Joe Magrane .20 .50
65 Mitch Williams .20 .50
66 Roger Craig MG and .20 .50
Don Zimmer MG

1990-93 Topps Magazine

These cards were inserted either four or eight cards per issue of Topps magazine. The cards were all issued in perforated form and when separated measured the standard size. The backs are unnumbered with a "TM" prefix. Some cards were issued in every Topps magazine from its inagural issue through the magazine's final issue.

COMPLETE SET (112) 10.00 25.00
1 Dave Staton .02 .10
2 Dan Peltier .02 .10
3 Ken Griffey Jr. .75 2.00
4 Ruben Sierra .07 .20
5 Bret Saberhagen .07 .20
6 Jerome Walton .02 .10
7 Kevin Mitchell .02 .10
8 Mike Scott .02 .10
9 Bo Jackson .15 .40
10 Nolan Ryan 1.25 3.00
11 Will Clark .15 .40
12 Robin Yount .30 .75
13 Joe Morgan .30 .75
14 Jim Palmer .30 .75
15 Ben McDonald .02 .10
16 John Olerud .10 .30
17 Don Mattingly .60 1.50
18 E.Davis .10 .30
B.Larkin/C.Sabo
19 Jim Abbott .10 .30
20 Sandy Alomar .10 .30
21 Jose Canseco .20 .50
22 Delino DeShields .15 .40
23 Wade Boggs .30 .75
24 Kirby Puckett .25 .60
25 Ryne Sandberg .40 1.00
26 Roger Clemens .60 1.50
27 Ken Griffey Jr. .40 1.00
Sr.
28 Cecil Fielder .07 .20
29 Steve Avery .02 .10
30 Rickey Henderson .40 1.00
31 Kevin Maas .02 .10
32 Len Dykstra .07 .20
33 Darryl Strawberry .02 .10
34 Mark McGwire .60 1.50
35 Matt Williams .10 .30
36 David Justice .15 .40
37 Cincinnati Reds .07 .20
38 Todd Van Poppel .02 .10
39 Jose Offerman .02 .10
40 Alex Fernandez .02 .10
41 Carlton Fisk .30 .75
42 Barry Bonds .50 1.25
43 Bobby Bonilla .02 .10
44 Bob Welch .02 .10
45 Mo Vaughn .07 .20
46 Tino Martinez .10 .30
47 D.J. Dozier .02 .10
48 Frank Thomas .30 .75
49 Cal Ripken 1.25 3.00
50 Dave Winfield .30 .75
51 Dwight Gooden .07 .20
52 Bo Jackson .15 .40
53 Kirk Dressendorfer .02 .10
54 Gary Scott .02 .10
55 Steve Decker .02 .10
56 Ray Lankford .15 .40
57 Ozzie Smith .50 1.25
58 Joe Carter .07 .20
59 Dave Henderson .02 .10
60 Tony Gwynn .60 1.50
61 Jeff Bagwell .40 1.00
62 Scott Erickson .02 .10
63 Pat Kelly .02 .10
64 Orlando Merced .02 .10
65 Andre Dawson .15 .40
66 Reggie Sanders .02 .10
67 Phil Plantier .02 .10
68 Paul Molitor .30 .75
69 Terry Pendleton .07 .20
70 Julio Franco .02 .10
71 Lee Smith .07 .20
72 Minnesota Twins .07 .20
73 Royce Clayton .02 .10
74 Tom Glavine .15 .40
75 Roger Salkeld .02 .10
76 Robin Ventura .15 .40
77 John Goodman .15 .40
As Babe Ruth
78 Jack Morris .07 .20
79 Brien Taylor .02 .10
80 Howard Johnson .02 .10
81 Barry Larkin .15 .40
82 Deion Sanders .15 .40
83 Mike Mussina .20 .50
84 Juan Gonzalez .30 .75
85 Roberto Alomar .15 .40
86 Fred McGriff .10 .30
87 Doug Drabek .02 .10
88 George Brett .30 .75
89 Otis Nixon .07 .20
90 Brady Anderson .15 .40
91 Gary Sheffield .25 .60
92 Dave Fleming .02 .10
93 Jeff Reardon .07 .20
94 Mark McGwire .60 1.50
95 Larry Walker .20 .50
96 John Kruk .07 .20
97 Carlos Baerga .02 .10

98 Pat Listach .02 .10
99 Toronto Blue Jays .10 .30
100 Eric Karros .07 .20
101 Bret Boone .15 .40
102 Al Martin .02 .10
103 Wil Cordero .02 .10
104 Tim Salmon .15 .40
105 Danny Tartabull .02 .10
106 J.T. Snow .07 .20
107 Mike Piazza .75 2.00
108 Frank Viola .02 .10
109 Nolan Ryan 1.25 3.00
Mets
110 Nolan Ryan 1.25 3.00
Angels
111 Nolan Ryan 1.25 3.00
Astros
112 Nolan Ryan 1.25 3.00
Rangers

1991 Topps

This set marks Topps tenth consecutive year of issuing a 792-card standard-size set. Cards were primarily issued in wax packs, rack packs and factory sets. The fronts feature a full color player photo with a white border. Topps also commemorated their fortieth anniversary by including a "Topps 40" logo on the front and back of each card. Virtually all of the cards have been discovered without the 40th logo on the back. Subsets include Record Breakers (2-8) and All-Stars (386-407). In addition, First Draft Picks and Future Stars subset cards are scattered throughout the set. The key Rookie Cards include Chipper Jones and Brian McRae. As a special promotion Topps inserted (randomly) into their wax packs one of every previous card they ever issued.

COMPLETE SET (792) 8.00 20.00
COMP.FACT.SET (792) 10.00 25.00
SUBSET CARDS HALF VALUE OF BASE CARDS
1 Nolan Ryan .60 1.50
2 George Brett RB .10 .30
3 Carlton Fisk RB .02 .10
4 Kevin Maas RB .01 .05
5 Cal Ripken RB .15 .40
6 Nolan Ryan RB .20 .50
7 Ryne Sandberg RB .08 .25
8 Bobby Thigpen RB .01 .05
9 Darrin Fletcher .01 .05
10 Gregg Olson .01 .05
11 Roberto Kelly .01 .05
12 Paul Assenmacher .01 .05
13 Mariano Duncan .01 .05
14 Dennis Lamp .01 .05
15 Von Hayes .01 .05
16 Mike Heath .01 .05
17 Jeff Brantley .01 .05
18 Nelson Liriano .01 .05
19 Jeff D. Robinson .01 .05
20 Pedro Guerrero .02 .10
21 Joe Morgan MG .01 .05
22 Storm Davis .01 .05
23 Jim Gantner .01 .05
24 Dave Martinez .01 .05
25 Tim Belcher .01 .05
26 Luis Sojo UER .01 .05
Born in Barquisimento,/not Caracas
27 Bobby Witt .01 .05
28 Alvaro Espinoza .01 .05
29 Bob Walk .01 .05
30 Gregg Jefferies .01 .05
31 Colby Ward RC .01 .05
32 Mike Simms RC .01 .05
33 Barry Jones .01 .05
34 Atlee Hammaker .01 .05
35 Greg Maddux .15 .40
36 Donnie Hill .01 .05
37 Tom Bolton .01 .05
38 Scott Bradley .01 .05
39 Jim Neidlinger RC .01 .05
40 Kevin Mitchell .01 .05
41 Ken Dayley .01 .05
42 Chris Hoiles .01 .05
43 Roger McDowell .01 .05
44 Mike Felder .01 .05
45 Chris Sabo .01 .05
46 Tim Drummond .01 .05
47 Brook Jacoby .01 .05
48 Dennis Boyd .01 .05
49A Pat Borders ERR .08 .25
40 steals at/Kinston in '86
49B Pat Borders COR .01 .05
0 steals at/Kinston in '86
50 Bob Welch .01 .05
51 Art Howe MG .01 .05
52 Francisco Oliveras .01 .05
53 Mike Sharperson UER .01 .05
Born in 1961, not 1960
54 Gary Mielke .01 .05
55 Jeffrey Leonard .01 .05
56 Jeff Parrett .01 .05
57 Jack Howell .01 .05
58 Mel Stottlemyre Jr. .01 .05
59 Eric Yelding .01 .05
60 Frank Viola .02 .10
61 Stan Javier .01 .05
62 Lee Guetterman .01 .05
63 Milt Thompson .01 .05
64 Tom Herr .01 .05
65 Bruce Hurst .01 .05
66 Terry Kennedy .01 .05
67 Rick Honeycutt .01 .05
68 Gary Sheffield .02 .10
69 Steve Wilson .01 .05
70 Ellis Burks .02 .10
71 Jim Acker .01 .05
72 Junior Ortiz .01 .05
73 Craig Worthington .01 .05
74 Shane Andrews RC .08 .25
75 Jack Morris .02 .10
76 Jerry Browne .01 .05
77 Drew Hall .01 .05
78 Geno Petralli .01 .05
79 Frank Thomas .08 .25
80A Fernando Valenzuela .15 .40
ERR 104 earned runs/in '90 tied for/league lead
80B Fernando Valenzuela .02 .10
COR 104 earned runs/in '90 led league, 20/CG's in 1986 now/italicized
81 Cito Gaston MG .01 .05
82 Tom Glavine .05 .15
83 Daryl Boston .01 .05
84 Bob McClure .01 .05
85 Jesse Barfield .01 .05
86 Les Lancaster .01 .05
87 Tracy Jones .01 .05
88 Bob Tewksbury .01 .05
89 Darren Daulton .02 .10
90 Danny Tartabull .01 .05
91 Greg Colbrunn RC .08 .25
92 Danny Jackson .01 .05
93 Ivan Calderon .01 .05
94 John Dopson .01 .05
95 Paul Molitor .02 .10
96 Trevor Wilson .01 .05
97A Brady Anderson ERR .15 .40
September, 2 RBI and/3 hits, should be 3/RBI and 14 hits
97B Brady Anderson COR .02 .10
98 Sergio Valdez .01 .05
99 Chris Gwynn .01 .05
100 Don Mattingly COR .25 .60
100A Don Mattingly ERR .75 2.00
101 Rob Ducey .01 .05
102 Gene Larkin .01 .05
103 Tim Costo RC .01 .05
104 Don Robinson .01 .05
105 Kevin McReynolds .01 .05
106 Ed Nunez .01 .05
107 Luis Polonia .01 .05
108 Matt Young .01 .05
109 Greg Riddoch MG .01 .05
110 Tom Henke .01 .05
111 Andres Thomas .01 .05
112 Frank DiPino .01 .05
113 Carl Everett RC .20 .50
114 Lance Dickson RC .02 .10
115 Hubie Brooks .01 .05
116 Mark Davis .01 .05
117 Dion James .01 .05
118 Tom Edens RC .01 .05
119 Carl Nichols .01 .05
120 Joe Carter .02 .10
121 Eric King .01 .05
122 Paul O'Neill .05 .15
123 Greg A. Harris .01 .05
124 Randy Bush .01 .05
125 Steve Bedrosian .01 .05
126 Bernard Gilkey .01 .05
127 Joe Price .01 .05
128 Travis Fryman .02 .10
Front has SS/back has SS-3B
129 Mark Eichhorn .01 .05
130 Ozzie Smith .15 .40
131A Checklist 1 ERR .08 .25
727 Phil Bradley
131B Checklist 1 COR .01 .05
717 Phil Bradley
132 Jamie Quirk .01 .05
133 Greg Briley .01 .05
134 Kevin Elster .01 .05
135 Jerome Walton .01 .05
136 Dave Schmidt .01 .05
137 Randy Ready .01 .05
138 Jamie Moyer .02 .10
139 Jeff Treadway .01 .05
140 Fred McGriff .05 .15
141 Nick Leyva MG .01 .05
142 Curt Wilkerson .01 .05
143 John Smiley .01 .05
144 Dave Henderson .01 .05
145 Lou Whitaker .02 .10
146 Dan Plesac .01 .05
147 Carlos Baerga .01 .05
148 Rey Palacios .01 .05
149 Al Osuna UER RC .02 .10
150 Cal Ripken .30 .75
151 Tom Browning .01 .05
152 Mickey Hatcher .01 .05
153 Bryan Harvey .01 .05
154 Jay Buhner .02 .10
155A Dwight Evans ERR .20 .50
Led league with/162 games in '82
155B Dwight Evans COR .05 .15
Tied for lead with/162 games in '82
156 Carlos Martinez .01 .05
157 John Smoltz .05 .15
158 Jose Uribe .01 .05
159 Joe Boever .01 .05
160 Vince Coleman UER .01 .05
Wrong birth year,/born 9/22/60
161 Tim Leary .01 .05
162 Ozzie Canseco .01 .05
163 Dave Johnson .01 .05
164 Edgar Diaz .01 .05
165 Sandy Alomar Jr. .01 .05
166 Harold Baines .02 .10
167A Randy Tomlin ERR .08 .25
Harriburg
167B Randy Tomlin COR RC .02 .10
168 John Olerud .02 .10
169 Luis Aquino .01 .05
170 Carlton Fisk .05 .15
171 Tony LaRussa MG .02 .10
172 Pete Incaviglia .01 .05
173 Jason Grimsley .01 .05
174 Ken Caminiti .01 .05
175 Jack Armstrong .01 .05
176 John Orton .01 .05
177 Reggie Harris .01 .05
178 Dave Valle .01 .05
179 Pete Harnisch .01 .05
180 Tony Gwynn .10 .30
181 Duane Ward .01 .05
182 Junior Noboa .01 .05
183 Clay Parker .01 .05
184 Gary Green .01 .05
185 Joe Magrane .01 .05
186 Rod Booker .01 .05
187 Greg Cadaret .01 .05
188 Damon Berryhill .01 .05
189 Daryl Irvine RC .01 .05
190 Matt Williams .02 .10
191 Willie Blair .01 .05
192 Rob Deer .01 .05
193 Felix Fermin .01 .05
194 Xavier Hernandez .01 .05
195 Wally Joyner .02 .10
196 Jim Vatcher RC .01 .05
197 Chris Nabholz .01 .05
198 R.J. Reynolds .01 .05
199 Mike Hartley .01 .05
200 Darryl Strawberry .02 .10
201 Tom Kelly MG .01 .05
202 Jim Leyritz .01 .05
203 Gene Harris .01 .05
204 Herm Winningham .01 .05
205 Mike Perez RC .02 .10
206 Carlos Quintana .01 .05
207 Gary Wayne .01 .05
208 Willie Wilson .01 .05
209 Ken Howell .01 .05
210 Lance Parrish .02 .10
211 Brian Barnes RC .01 .05
212 Steve Finley .02 .10
213 Frank Wills .01 .05
214 Joe Girardi .01 .05
215 Dave Smith .01 .05
216 Greg Gagne .01 .05
217 Chris Bosio .01 .05
218 Rick Parker .01 .05
219 Jack McDowell .01 .05
220 Tim Wallach .01 .05
221 Don Slaught .01 .05
222 Brian McRae RC .08 .25
223 Allan Anderson .01 .05
224 Juan Gonzalez .08 .25
225 Randy Johnson .10 .30
226 Alfredo Griffin .01 .05
227 Steve Avery UER .01 .05
Pitched 13 games for/Durham in 1989, not 2
228 Rex Hudler .01 .05
229 Rance Mulliniks .01 .05
230 Sid Fernandez .01 .05
231 Doug Rader MG .01 .05
232 Jose DeJesus .01 .05
233 Al Leiter .02 .10
234 Scott Erickson .01 .05
235 Dave Parker .02 .10
236A Frank Tanana ERR .08 .25
Tied for lead with/269 K's in '75
236B Frank Tanana COR .01 .05
Led league with/269 K's in '75
237 Rick Cerone .01 .05
238 Mike Dunne .01 .05
239 Darren Lewis .01 .05
240 Mike Scott .01 .05
241 Dave Clark UER .01 .05
Career totals 19 HR/and 5 3B, should/be 22 and 3
242 Mike LaCoss .01 .05
243 Lance Johnson .01 .05
244 Mike Jeffcoat .01 .05
245 Kal Daniels .01 .05
246 Kevin Wickander .01 .05
247 Jody Reed .01 .05
248 Tom Gordon .01 .05
249 Bob Melvin .01 .05
250 Dennis Eckersley .02 .10
251 Mark Lemke .01 .05
252 Mel Rojas .01 .05
253 Garry Templeton .01 .05
254 Shawn Boskie .01 .05
255 Brian Downing .01 .05
256 Greg Hibbard .01 .05
257 Tom O'Malley .01 .05
258 Chris Hammond .01 .05
259 Hensley Meulens .01 .05
260 Harold Reynolds .02 .10
261 Bud Harrelson MG .01 .05
262 Tim Jones .01 .05
263 Checklist 2 .01 .05
264 Dave Hollins .01 .05
265 Mark Gubicza .01 .05
266 Carmelo Castillo .01 .05
267 Mark Knudson .01 .05
268 Tom Brookens .01 .05
269 Joe Hesketh .01 .05
270 Mark McGwire COR .30 .75
270A Mark McGwire ERR .75 2.00
271 Omar Olivares RC .02 .10
272 Jeff King .01 .05
273 Johnny Ray .01 .05
274 Ken Williams .01 .05
275 Alan Trammell .02 .10
276 Bill Swift .01 .05
277 Scott Coolbaugh .01 .05
278 Alex Fernandez UER .01 .05
No '90 White Sox stats
279A Jose Gonzalez ERR .08 .25
Photo actually/Billy Bean
279B Jose Gonzalez COR .01 .05
280 Bret Saberhagen .02 .10
281 Larry Sheets .01 .05
282 Don Carman .01 .05
283 Marquis Grissom .02 .10
284 Billy Spiers .01 .05
285 Jim Abbott .05 .15
286 Ken Oberkfell .01 .05
287 Mark Grant .01 .05
288 Derrick May .01 .05
289 Tim Birtsas .01 .05
290 Steve Sax .01 .05
291 John Wathan MG .01 .05
292 Bud Black .01 .05
293 Jay Bell .02 .10
294 Mike Moore .01 .05
295 Rafael Palmeiro .05 .15
296 Mark Williamson .01 .05
297 Manny Lee .01 .05
298 Omar Vizquel .05 .15
299 Scott Radinsky .01 .05
300 Kirby Puckett .08 .25
301 Steve Farr .01 .05
302 Tim Teufel .01 .05
303 Mike Boddicker .01 .05
304 Kevin Reimer .01 .05
305 Mike Scioscia .01 .05
306A Lonnie Smith ERR .15 .40
136 games in '90
306B Lonnie Smith COR .01 .05
135 games in '90
307 Andy Benes .01 .05
308 Tom Pagnozzi .01 .05
309 Norm Charlton .01 .05
310 Gary Carter .02 .10
311 Jeff Pico .01 .05
312 Charlie Hayes .01 .05
313 Ron Robinson .01 .05
314 Gary Pettis .01 .05
315 Roberto Alomar .05 .15
316 Gene Nelson .01 .05
317 Mike Fitzgerald .01 .05
318 Rick Aguilera .02 .10
319 Jeff McKnight .01 .05
320 Tony Fernandez .01 .05
321 Bob Rodgers MG .01 .05
322 Terry Shumpert .01 .05
323 Cory Snyder .01 .05
324A Ron Kittle ERR .15 .40
Set another/standard ...
324B Ron Kittle COR .01 .05
Tied another/standard ...
325 Brett Butler .02 .10
326 Ken Patterson .01 .05
327 Ron Hassey .01 .05
328 Walt Terrell .01 .05
329 Dave Justice UER .02 .10
Drafted third round/on card, should say/fourth pick
330 Dwight Gooden .02 .10
331 Eric Anthony .01 .05
332 Kenny Rogers .02 .10
333 Chipper Jones RC 6.00 15.00
334 Todd Benzinger .01 .05
335 Mitch Williams .01 .05
336 Matt Nokes .01 .05
337A Keith Comstock ERR .08 .25
Cubs logo on front
337B Keith Comstock COR .01 .05
Mariners logo on front
338 Luis Rivera .01 .05
339 Larry Walker .08 .25
340 Ramon Martinez .01 .05
341 John Moses .01 .05
342 Mickey Morandini .01 .05
343 Jose Oquendo .01 .05
344 Jeff Russell .01 .05
345 Len Dykstra .02 .10
346 Jesse Orosco .01 .05
347 Greg Vaughn .01 .05
348 Todd Stottlemyre .01 .05
349 Dave Gallagher .01 .05
350 Glenn Davis .01 .05
351 Joe Torre MG .02 .10
352 Frank White .02 .10
353 Tony Castillo .01 .05
354 Sid Bream .01 .05
355 Chili Davis .02 .10
356 Mike Marshall .01 .05
357 Jack Savage .01 .05
358 Mark Parent .01 .05
359 Chuck Cary .01 .05
360 Tim Raines .02 .10
361 Scott Garrelts .01 .05
362 Hector Villenueva .01 .05
363 Rick Mahler .01 .05
364 Dan Pasqua .01 .05
365 Mike Schooler .01 .05
366A Checklist 3 ERR .08 .25
19 Carl Nichols
366B Checklist 3 COR .01 .05
119 Carl Nichols
367 Dave Walsh RC .01 .05
368 Felix Jose .01 .05
369 Steve Searcy .01 .05
370 Kelly Gruber .01 .05
371 Jeff Montgomery .01 .05
372 Spike Owen .01 .05
373 Darrin Jackson .01 .05
374 Larry Casian RC .01 .05
375 Tony Pena .01 .05
376 Mike Harkey .01 .05
377 Rene Gonzales .01 .05
378A Wilson Alvarez ERR .08 .25
'89 Port Charlotte/and '90 Birmingham/stat lines omitted
378B Wilson Alvarez COR .01 .05
Text still says 143/K's in 1988, /whereas stats say 134
379 Randy Velarde .01 .05
380 Willie McGee .02 .10
381 Jim Leyland MG .01 .05
382 Mackey Sasser .01 .05
383 Pete Smith .01 .05
384 Gerald Perry .01 .05
385 Mickey Tettleton .01 .05
386 Cecil Fielder AS .01 .05
387 Julio Franco AS .01 .05
388 Kelly Gruber AS .01 .05
389 Alan Trammell AS .02 .10
390 Jose Canseco AS .02 .10
391 Rickey Henderson AS .05 .15
392 Ken Griffey Jr. AS .20 .50
393 Carlton Fisk AS .02 .10
394 Bob Welch AS .01 .05
395 Chuck Finley AS .01 .05
396 Bobby Thigpen AS .01 .05
397 Eddie Murray AS .05 .15
398 Ryne Sandberg AS .08 .25
399 Matt Williams AS .01 .05
400 Barry Larkin AS .02 .10
401 Barry Bonds AS .20 .50
402 Darryl Strawbery AS .01 .05
403 Bobby Bonilla AS .01 .05
404 Mike Scioscia AS .01 .05
405 Doug Drabek AS .01 .05
406 Frank Viola AS .01 .05
407 John Franco AS .01 .05
408 Earnest Riles .01 .05
409 Mike Stanley .01 .05
410 Dave Righetti .02 .10
411 Lance Blankenship .01 .05
412 Dave Bergman .01 .05
413 Terry Mulholland .01 .05
414 Sammy Sosa .08 .25
415 Rick Sutcliffe .02 .10
416 Randy Milligan .01 .05
417 Bill Krueger .01 .05
418 Nick Esasky .01 .05
419 Jeff Reed .01 .05
420 Bobby Thigpen .01 .05
421 Alex Cole .01 .05
422 Rick Reuschel .01 .05
423 Rafael Ramirez UER .01 .05
Born 1959, not 1958
424 Calvin Schiraldi .01 .05
425 Andy Van Slyke .05 .15
426 Joe Grahe RC .02 .10
427 Rick Dempsey .01 .05
428 John Barfield .01 .05
429 Stump Merrill MG .01 .05
430 Gary Gaetti .02 .10
431 Paul Gibson .01 .05
432 Delino DeShields .02 .10
433 Pat Tabler .01 .05
434 Julio Machado .01 .05
435 Kevin Maas .01 .05
436 Scott Bankhead .01 .05
437 Doug Dascenzo .01 .05
438 Vicente Palacios .01 .05
439 Dickie Thon .01 .05
440 George Bell .01 .05
441 Zane Smith .01 .05
442 Charlie O'Brien .01 .05
443 Jeff Innis .01 .05
444 Glenn Braggs .01 .05
445 Greg Swindell .01 .05
446 Craig Grebeck .01 .05
447 John Burkett .01 .05
448 Craig Lefferts .01 .05
449 Juan Berenguer .01 .05
450 Wade Boggs .05 .15
451 Neal Heaton .01 .05
452 Bill Schroeder .01 .05
453 Lenny Harris .01 .05
454A Kevin Appier ERR .15 .40
'90 Omaha stat/line omitted
454B Kevin Appier COR .02 .10
455 Walt Weiss .01 .05
456 Charlie Leibrandt .01 .05
457 Todd Hundley .01 .05
458 Brian Holman .01 .05
459 Tom Trebelhorn MG UER .01 .05
Pitching and batting/columns switched
460 Dave Stieb .01 .05
461 Robin Ventura .02 .10
462 Steve Frey .01 .05
463 Dwight Smith .01 .05
464 Steve Buechele .01 .05
465 Ken Griffey Sr. .02 .10
466 Charles Nagy .01 .05
467 Dennis Cook .01 .05
468 Tim Hulett .01 .05
469 Chet Lemon .01 .05
470 Howard Johnson .01 .05
471 Mike Lieberthal RC .15 .40
472 Kirt Manwaring .01 .05
473 Curt Young .01 .05
474 Phil Plantier RC .02 .10
475 Ted Higuera .01 .05
476 Glenn Wilson .01 .05
477 Mike Fetters .01 .05
478 Kurt Stillwell .01 .05
479 Bob Patterson UER .01 .05
Has a decimal point/between 7 and 9
480 Dave Magadan .01 .05
481 Eddie Whitson .01 .05
482 Tino Martinez .08 .25
483 Mike Aldrete .01 .05
484 Dave LaPoint .01 .05
485 Terry Pendleton .02 .10
486 Tommy Greene .01 .05
487 Rafael Belliard .01 .05
488 Jeff Manto .01 .05
489 Bobby Valentine MG .01 .05
490 Kirk Gibson .02 .10
491 Kurt Miller RC .01 .05
492 Ernie Whitt .01 .05
493 Jose Rijo .01 .05
494 Chris James .01 .05
495 Charlie Hough .02 .10
496 Marty Barrett .01 .05
497 Ben McDonald .01 .05
498 Mark Salas .01 .05
499 Melido Perez .01 .05
500 Will Clark .05 .15
501 Mike Bielecki .01 .05
502 Carney Lansford .02 .10
503 Roy Smith .01 .05
504 Julio Valera .01 .05
505 Chuck Finley .02 .10
506 Darnell Coles .01 .05
507 Steve Jeltz .01 .05
508 Mike York RC .01 .05
509 Glenallen Hill .01 .05
510 John Franco .02 .10
511 Steve Balboni .01 .05
512 Jose Mesa .01 .05
513 Jerald Clark .01 .05
514 Mike Stanton .01 .05
515 Alvin Davis .01 .05
516 Karl Rhodes .01 .05
517 Joe Oliver .01 .05
518 Cris Carpenter .01 .05
519 Sparky Anderson MG .02 .10
520 Mark Grace .05 .15
521 Joe Orsulak .01 .05
522 Stan Belinda .01 .05
523 Rodney McCray RC .01 .05
524 Darrel Akerfelds .01 .05
525 Willie Randolph .02 .10
526A Moises Alou ERR .15 .40
37 runs in 2 games/for '90 Pirates
526B Moises Alou COR .02 .10
0 runs in 2 games/for '90 Pirates
527A Checklist 4 ERR .08 .25
105 Keith Miller/719 Kevin McReynolds
527B Checklist 4 COR .01 .05
105 Kevin McReynolds/719 Keith Miller
528 Dennis Martinez .02 .10
529 Marc Newfield RC .02 .10
530 Roger Clemens .30 .75
531 Dave Rohde .01 .05
532 Kirk McCaskill .01 .05
533 Oddibe McDowell .01 .05
534 Mike Jackson .01 .05
535 Ruben Sierra UER .02 .10
Back reads 100 Runs/amd 100 RBI's
536 Mike Witt .01 .05
537 Jose Lind .01 .05
538 Bip Roberts .01 .05
539 Scott Terry .01 .05
540 George Brett .25 .60
541 Domingo Ramos .01 .05
542 Rob Murphy .01 .05
543 Junior Felix .01 .05
544 Alejandro Pena .01 .05
545 Dale Murphy .05 .15
546 Jeff Ballard .01 .05
547 Mike Pagliarulo .01 .05
548 Jaime Navarro .01 .05
549 John McNamara MG .01 .05
550 Eric Davis .02 .10
551 Bob Kipper .01 .05
552 Jeff Hamilton .01 .05
553 Joe Klink .01 .05
554 Brian Harper .01 .05
555 Turner Ward RC .02 .10
556 Gary Ward .01 .05
557 Wally Whitehurst .01 .05
558 Otis Nixon .01 .05
559 Adam Peterson .01 .05
560 Greg Smith .01 .05
561 Tim McIntosh .01 .05
562 Jeff Kunkel .01 .05
563 Brent Knackert .01 .05
564 Dante Bichette .02 .10
565 Craig Biggio .05 .15
566 Craig Wilson RC .01 .05
567 Dwayne Henry .01 .05
568 Ron Karkovice .01 .05
569 Curt Schilling .08 .25
570 Barry Bonds .40 1.00
571 Pat Combs .01 .05
572 Dave Anderson .01 .05
573 Rich Rodriguez UER RC .01 .05
574 John Marzano .01 .05
575 Robin Yount .15 .40
576 Jeff Kaiser .01 .05
577 Bill Doran .01 .05
578 Dave West .01 .05
579 Roger Craig MG .01 .05
580 Dave Stewart .02 .10
581 Luis Quinones .01 .05
582 Marty Clary .01 .05
583 Tony Phillips .01 .05
584 Kevin Brown .02 .10
585 Pete O'Brien .01 .05
586 Fred Lynn .01 .05
587 Jose Offerman UER .01 .05
Text says he signed/7/24/86, but bio/says 1988
588A Mark Whiten .01 .05
588B M.Whiten FTC UER 60.00 150.00
589 Scott Ruskin .01 .05
590 Eddie Murray .08 .25
591 Ken Hill .01 .05
592 B.J. Surhoff .02 .10
593A Mike Walker ERR .08 .25
'90 Canton-Akron/stat line omitted
593B Mike Walker COR .01 .05
594 Rich Garces RC .02 .10
595 Bill Landrum .01 .05
596 Ronnie Walden RC .02 .10
597 Jerry Don Gleaton .01 .05
598 Sam Horn .01 .05
599A Greg Myers ERR .08 .25
'90 Syracuse/stat line omitted
599B Greg Myers COR .01 .05
600 Bo Jackson .08 .25
601 Bob Ojeda .01 .05
602 Casey Candaele .01 .05
603A Wes Chamberlain ERR .15 .40
603B Wes Chamberlain COR RC .02 .10
604 Billy Hatcher .01 .05
605 Jeff Reardon .02 .10
606 Jim Gott .01 .05
607 Edgar Martinez .05 .15
608 Todd Burns .01 .05
609 Jeff Torborg MG .01 .05
610 Andres Galarraga .02 .10
611 Dave Eiland .01 .05
612 Steve Lyons .01 .05
613 Eric Show .01 .05
614 Luis Salazar .01 .05
615 Bert Blyleven .02 .10
616 Todd Zeile .01 .05
617 Bill Wegman .01 .05
618 Sil Campusano .01 .05
619 David Wells .02 .10
620 Ozzie Guillen .02 .10
621 Ted Power .01 .05
622 Jack Daugherty .01 .05
623 Jeff Blauser .01 .05
624 Tom Candiotti .01 .05
625 Terry Steinbach .01 .05
626 Gerald Young .01 .05
627 Tim Layana .01 .05
628 Greg Litton .01 .05
629 Wes Gardner .01 .05
630 Dave Winfield .02 .10
631 Mike Morgan .01 .05
632 Lloyd Moseby .01 .05
633 Kevin Tapani .01 .05
634 Henry Cotto .01 .05
635 Andy Hawkins .01 .05
636 Geronimo Pena .01 .05
637 Bruce Ruffin .01 .05
638 Mike Macfarlane .01 .05
639 Frank Robinson MG .05 .15
640 Andre Dawson .02 .10
641 Mike Henneman .01 .05
642 Hal Morris .01 .05
643 Jim Presley .01 .05
644 Chuck Crim .01 .05
645 Juan Samuel .01 .05
646 Andujar Cedeno .01 .05
647 Mark Portugal .01 .05
648 Lee Stevens .01 .05
649 Bill Sampen .01 .05
650 Jack Clark .02 .10
651 Alan Mills .01 .05
652 Kevin Romine .01 .05
653 Anthony Telford RC .01 .05
654 Paul Sorrento .01 .05
655 Erik Hanson .01 .05
656A Checklist 5 ERR .08 .25
348 Vicente Palacios/381 Jose Lind/537 Mike LaValliere/665 Jim Leyland
656B Checklist 5 ERR .08 .25
433 Vicente Palacios/Palacios should be 438/537 Jose Lind/665 Mike LaValliere/381 Jim Leyland
656C Checklist 5 COR .01 .05
438 Vicente Palacios/537 Jose Lind/665 Mike LaValliere/381 Jim Leyland
657 Mike Kingery .01 .05
658 Scott Aldred .01 .05
659 Oscar Azocar .01 .05
660 Lee Smith .02 .10
661 Steve Lake .01 .05
662 Ron Dibble .02 .10
663 Greg Brock .01 .05
664 John Farrell .01 .05
665 Mike LaValliere .01 .05
666 Danny Darwin .01 .05
667 Kent Anderson .01 .05
668 Bill Long .01 .05
669 Lou Piniella MG .02 .10
670 Rickey Henderson .08 .25
671 Andy McGaffigan .01 .05
672 Shane Mack .01 .05
673 Greg Olson UER .01 .05
6 RBI in '88 at Tidewater/and 2 RBI in '87,/should be 48 and 15
674A Kevin Gross ERR .08 .25
89 BB with Phillies/in '88 tied for/league lead
674B Kevin Gross COR .01 .05
89 BB with Phillies/in '88 led league
675 Tom Brunansky .01 .05
676 Scott Chiamparino .01 .05
677 Billy Ripken .01 .05
678 Mark Davidson .01 .05
679 Bill Bathe .01 .05
680 David Cone .02 .10
681 Jeff Schaefer .01 .05
682 Ray Lankford .02 .10
683 Derek Lilliquist .01 .05
684 Milt Cuyler .01 .05
685 Doug Drabek .01 .05
686 Mike Gallego .01 .05
687A John Cerutti ERR .08 .25
4.46 ERA in '90
687B John Cerutti COR .01 .05
4.76 ERA in '90
688 Rosario Rodriguez RC .01 .05
689 John Kruk .02 .10
690 Orel Hershiser .02 .10
691 Mike Blowers .01 .05
692A Efrain Valdez ERR .08 .25
692B Efrain Valdez COR RC .01 .05
693 Francisco Cabrera .01 .05
694 Randy Veres .01 .05
695 Kevin Seitzer .01 .05
696 Steve Olin .01 .05
697 Shawn Abner .01 .05
698 Mark Guthrie .01 .05
699 Jim Lefebvre MG .01 .05
700 Jose Canseco .05 .15
701 Pascual Perez .01 .05
702 Tim Naehring .01 .05
703 Juan Agosto .01 .05
704 Devon White .02 .10
705 Robby Thompson .01 .05
706A Brad Arnsberg ERR .08 .25
68.2 IP in '90
706B Brad Arnsberg COR .01 .05
62.2 IP in '90
707 Jim Eisenreich .01 .05
708 John Mitchell .01 .05
709 Matt Sinatro .01 .05
710 Kent Hrbek .02 .10
711 Jose DeLeon .01 .05
712 Ricky Jordan .01 .05
713 Scott Scudder .01 .05
714 Marvell Wynne .01 .05
715 Tim Burke .01 .05
716 Bob Geren .01 .05
717 Phil Bradley .01 .05
718 Steve Crawford .01 .05
719 Keith Miller .01 .05
720 Cecil Fielder .02 .10
721 Mark Lee RC .01 .05
722 Wally Backman .01 .05
723 Candy Maldonado .01 .05
724 David Segui .01 .05
725 Ron Gant .02 .10
726 Phil Stephenson .01 .05
727 Mookie Wilson .02 .10
728 Scott Sanderson .01 .05
729 Don Zimmer MG .02 .10
730 Barry Larkin .05 .15
731 Jeff Gray RC .01 .05
732 Franklin Stubbs .01 .05
733 Kelly Downs .01 .05
734 John Russell .01 .05
735 Ron Darling .01 .05
736 Dick Schofield .01 .05
737 Tim Crews .01 .05
738 Mel Hall .01 .05
739 Russ Swan .01 .05
740 Ryne Sandberg .15 .40
741 Jimmy Key .02 .10
742 Tommy Gregg .01 .05
743 Bryn Smith .01 .05
744 Nelson Santovenia .01 .05
745 Doug Jones .01 .05
746 John Shelby .01 .05
747 Tony Fossas .01 .05
748 Al Newman .01 .05
749 Greg W. Harris .01 .05
750 Bobby Bonilla .02 .10
751 Wayne Edwards .01 .05
752 Kevin Bass .01 .05
753 Paul Marak UER RC .01 .05
754 Bill Pecota .01 .05
755 Mark Langston .01 .05
756 Jeff Huson .01 .05

757 Mark Gardner .01 .05
758 Mike Devereaux .01 .05
759 Bobby Cox MG .01 .05
760 Benny Santiago .02 .10
761 Larry Andersen .01 .05
762 Mitch Webster .01 .05
763 Dana Kiecker .01 .05
764 Mark Carreon .01 .05
765 Shawon Dunston .01 .05
766 Jeff Robinson .01 .05
767 Dan Wilson RC .08 .25
768 Don Pall .01 .05
769 Tim Sherrill .01 .05
770 Jay Howell .01 .05
771 Gary Redus UER .01 .05
Born in Tanner,/should say Athens
772 Kent Mercker UER .01 .05
Born in Indianapolis,/should say Dublin, Ohio
773 Tom Foley .01 .05
774 Dennis Rasmussen .01 .05
775 Julio Franco .02 .10
776 Brent Mayne .01 .05
777 John Candelaria .01 .05
778 Dan Gladden .01 .05
779 Carmelo Martinez .01 .05
780A Randy Myers ERR .15 .40
15 career losses
780B Randy Myers COR .01 .05
19 career losses
781 Darryl Hamilton .01 .05
782 Jim Deshaies .01 .05
783 Joel Skinner .01 .05
784 Willie Fraser .01 .05
785 Scott Fletcher .01 .05
786 Eric Plunk .01 .05
787 Checklist 6 .01 .05
788 Bob Milacki .01 .05
789 Tom Lasorda MG .08 .25
790 Ken Griffey Jr. .40 1.00
791 Mike Benjamin .01 .05
792 Mike Greenwell .01 .05

1991 Topps Desert Shield

COMMON CARD (1-792) 2.50 6.00
DIST.TO ARMED FORCES IN SAUDI ARABIA
333 Chipper Jones 300.00 800.00

1991 Topps Micro

This 792 card set parallels the regular Topps issue. The cards are significantly smaller (slightly larger than a postage stamp) than the regular Topps cards and are valued at a percentage of the regular 1991 Topps cards.

COMPLETE FACT.SET (792) 8.00 20.00
*STARS: .4X to 1X BASIC CARDS

1991 Topps Tiffany

COMP.FACT.SET (792) 100.00 200.00
*STARS: 12.5X TO 30X BASIC CARDS
*ROOKIES: 6X TO 15X BASIC CARDS
DISTRIBUTED ONLY IN FACTORY SET FORM
FACTORY SET PRICE IS FOR SEALED SETS

1991 Topps Rookies

COMPLETE SET (33) 8.00 20.00
1 Sandy Alomar .20 .50
2 Kevin Appier .20 .50
3 Steve Avery .08 .25
4 Carlos Baerga .20 .50
5 John Burkett .08 .25
6 Alex Cole .08 .25
7 Pat Combs .08 .25
8 Delino DeShields .20 .50
9 Travis Fryman .20 .50
10 Marquis Grissom .40 1.00
11 Mike Harkey .08 .25
12 Glenallen Hill .08 .25
13 Jeff Huson .08 .25
14 Felix Jose .08 .25
15 Dave Justice .60 1.50
16 Jim Leyritz .08 .25
17 Kevin Maas .08 .25
18 Ben McDonald .08 .25
19 Kent Mercker .08 .25
20 Hal Morris .08 .25
21 Chris Nabholz .08 .25
22 Tim Naehring .08 .25
23 Jose Offerman .08 .25
24 John Olerud .75 2.00
25 Scott Radinsky .08 .25
26 Scott Ruskin .08 .25
27 Kevin Tapani .08 .25
28 Frank Thomas 3.00 8.00
29 Randy Tomlin .08 .25
30 Greg Vaughn .20 .50
31 Robin Ventura .40 1.00
32 Larry Walker .60 1.50
33 Todd Zeile .20 .50

1991 Topps Wax Box Cards

COMPLETE SET (16) 2.50 6.00
A Bert Blyleven .07 .20
B George Brett .40 1.00
C Brett Butler .02 .10
D Andre Dawson .20 .50
E Dwight Evans .07 .20
F Carlton Fisk .25 .60
G Alfredo Griffin .02 .10
H Rickey Henderson .25 .60
I Willie McGee .07 .20
J Dale Murphy .20 .50
K Eddie Murray .25 .60
L Dave Parker .07 .20
M Jeff Reardon .07 .20
N Nolan Ryan 1.00 2.50
O Juan Samuel .02 .10
P Robin Yount .25 .60

1991 Topps Traded

The 1991 Topps Traded set contains 132 standard-size cards. The cards were issued primarily in factory set form through hobby dealers but were also made available on a limited basis in wax packs. The cards in the wax packs (gray backs) and collated factory sets (white backs) are from different card stock. Both versions are valued equally. The card design is identical to the regular issue 1991 Topps cards except for the whiter stock (for factory set cards) and T-suffixed numbering. The set is numbered in alphabetical order. The set includes a Team U.S.A. subset, featuring 25 of America's top collegiate players. The key Rookie Cards in this set are Jeff Bagwell, Jason Giambi, Luis Gonzalez, Charles Johnson and Ivan Rodriguez.

COMPLETE SET (132) 4.00 10.00
COMP.FACT.SET (132) 4.00 10.00
1T Juan Agosto .01 .05
2T Roberto Alomar .05 .15
3T Wally Backman .01 .05
4T Jeff Bagwell RC .60 1.50
5T Skeeter Barnes .01 .05
6T Steve Bedrosian .01 .05
7T Derek Bell .02 .10
8T George Bell .01 .05
9T Rafael Belliard .01 .05
10T Dante Bichette .02 .10
11T Bud Black .01 .05
12T Mike Boddicker .01 .05
13T Sid Bream .01 .05
14T Hubie Brooks .01 .05
15T Brett Butler .02 .10
16T Ivan Calderon .01 .05
17T John Candelaria .01 .05
18T Tom Candiotti .01 .05
19T Gary Carter .02 .10
20T Joe Carter .02 .10
21T Rick Cerone .01 .05
22T Jack Clark .02 .10
23T Vince Coleman .01 .05
24T Scott Coolbaugh .01 .05
25T Danny Cox .01 .05
26T Danny Darwin .01 .05
27T Chili Davis .02 .10
28T Glenn Davis .01 .05
29T Steve Decker RC .01 .05
30T Rob Deer .01 .05
31T Rich DeLucia RC .01 .05
32T John Dettmer USA RC .08 .25
33T Brian Downing .01 .05
34T Darren Dreifort USA RC .08 .25
35T Kirk Dressendorfer RC .01 .05
36T Jim Essian MG .01 .05
37T Dwight Evans .05 .15
38T Steve Farr .01 .05
39T Jeff Fassero RC .08 .25
40T Junior Felix .01 .05
41T Tony Fernandez .01 .05
42T Steve Finley .02 .10
43T Jim Fregosi MG .01 .05
44T Gary Gaetti .02 .10
45T Jason Giambi USA RC 3.00 8.00
46T Kirk Gibson .02 .10
47T Leo Gomez .01 .05
48T Luis Gonzalez RC .20 .50
49T Jeff Granger USA RC .08 .25
50T Todd Greene USA RC .20 .50
51T Jeffrey Hammonds USA RC .20 .50
52T Mike Hargrove MG .01 .05
53T Pete Harnisch .01 .05
54T Rick Helling USA RC .20 .50
55T Glenallen Hill .01 .05
56T Charlie Hough .02 .10
57T Pete Incaviglia .01 .05
58T Bo Jackson .08 .25
59T Danny Jackson .01 .05
60T Reggie Jefferson .01 .05
61T Charles Johnson USA RC .30 .75
62T Jeff Johnson RC .01 .05
63T Todd Johnson USA RC .08 .25
64T Barry Jones .01 .05
65T Chris Jones RC .02 .10
66T Scott Kamieniecki RC .02 .10
67T Pat Kelly RC .02 .10
68T Darryl Kile .02 .10
69T Chuck Knoblauch .02 .10
70T Bill Krueger .01 .05
71T Scott Leius .01 .05
72T Donnie Leshnock USA RC .08 .25
73T Mark Lewis .01 .05
74T Candy Maldonado .01 .05
75T Jason McDonald USA RC .08 .25
76T Willie McGee .02 .10
77T Fred McGriff .05 .15
78T Billy McMillon USA RC .08 .25
79T Hal McRae MG .02 .10
80T Dan Melendez USA RC .08 .25
81T Orlando Merced RC .02 .10
82T Jack Morris .02 .10
83T Phil Nevin USA RC .30 .75
84T Otis Nixon .01 .05
85T Johnny Oates MG .01 .05
86T Bob Ojeda .01 .05
87T Mike Pagliarulo .01 .05
88T Dean Palmer .02 .10
89T Dave Parker .02 .10
90T Terry Pendleton .02 .10
91T Tony Phillips (P) USA RC .08 .25
92T Doug Piatt RC .01 .05
93T Ron Polk USA CO .08 .25
94T Tim Raines .02 .10
95T Willie Randolph .02 .10
96T Dave Righetti .02 .10
97T Ernie Riles .01 .05
98T Chris Roberts USA RC .08 .25
99T Jeff D. Robinson .01 .05
100T Jeff M. Robinson .01 .05
101T Ivan Rodriguez RC 1.25 3.00
102T Steve Rodriguez USA RC .08 .25
103T Tom Runnells MG .01 .05
104T Scott Sanderson .01 .05
105T Bob Scanlan RC .01 .05
106T Pete Schourek RC .02 .10
107T Gary Scott RC .01 .05
108T Paul Shuey USA RC .20 .50
109T Doug Simons RC .01 .05
110T Dave Smith .01 .05
111T Cory Snyder .01 .05
112T Luis Sojo .01 .05
113T Kennie Steenstra USA RC .08 .25
114T Darryl Strawberry .02 .10
115T Franklin Stubbs .01 .05
116T Todd Taylor USA RC .08 .25
117T Wade Taylor RC .01 .05
118T Garry Templeton .01 .05
119T Mickey Tettleton .01 .05
120T Tim Teufel .01 .05
121T Mike Timlin RC .08 .25
122T David Tuttle USA RC .08 .25
123T Mo Vaughn .02 .10
124T Jeff Ware USA RC .08 .25
125T Devon White .02 .10
126T Mark Whiten .01 .05
127T Mitch Williams .01 .05
128T Craig Wilson USA RC .08 .25
129T Willie Wilson .01 .05
130T Chris Wimmer USA RC .08 .25
131T Ivan Zweig USA RC .08 .25
132T Checklist 1T-132T .01 .05

1991 Topps Traded Tiffany

COMP.FACT.SET (132) 75.00 150.00
*STARS: 12.5X TO 30X BASIC CARDS
*ROOKIES: 10X TO 25X BASIC CARDS
*USA ROOKIES: 6X TO 15X BASIC CARDS
DISTRIBUTED ONLY IN FACTORY SET FORM
FACTORY SET PRICE IS FOR SEALED SETS

1991 Topps Cracker Jack I

This 36-card set is the first of two 36-card series produced by Topps for Cracker Jack, and the cards were inserted inside specially marked packages of Cracker Jack. These cards were the "toy surprise" inside. The cards measure approximately one-fourth standard-size (1 1/4" by 1 3/4") and are frequently referenced as micro-cards. The micro-cards have color player photos with different color borders but are otherwise identical to the corresponding cards in the Topps regular issue. Standard-size cards featuring four micro-cards each were seen at trade shows but were not inserted inside the product. These were apparently test runs or uncut sheets. Although each mini-card is numbered on the back, the numbering of the four cards on any standard-size card is not consecutive.

COMPLETE SET (36) 6.00 15.00
1 Nolan Ryan 1.00 2.50
2 Paul Molitor .20 .50
3 Tim Raines .07 .20
4 Frank Viola .02 .10
5 Sandy Alomar Jr. .07 .20
6 Ryne Sandberg .40 1.00
7 Don Mattingly .50 1.25
8 Pedro Guerrero .02 .10
9 Jose Rijo .07 .20
10 Jose Canseco .20 .50
11 Dave Parker .07 .20
12 Doug Drabek .02 .10
13 Cal Ripken 1.00 2.50
14 Dave Justice .15 .40
15 George Brett .40 1.00
16 Eric Davis .07 .20
17 Mark Langston .02 .10
18 Rickey Henderson .40 1.00
19 Barry Bonds .50 1.25
20 Kevin Maas .02 .10
21 Len Dykstra .07 .20
22 Roger Clemens .50 1.25
23 Robin Yount .20 .50
24 Mark Grace .15 .40
25 Bo Jackson .15 .40
26 Tony Gwynn .50 1.25
27 Mark McGwire .50 1.25
28 Dwight Gooden .07 .20
29 Wade Boggs .20 .50
30 Kevin Mitchell .02 .10
31 Cecil Fielder .07 .20
32 Bobby Thigpen .02 .10
33 Benito Santiago .07 .20
34 Kirby Puckett .25 .60
35 Will Clark .15 .40
36 Ken Griffey Jr. .60 1.50

1991 Topps Cracker Jack II

This 36-card set is the second of two different 36-card series produced by Topps for Cracker Jack, and the cards were inserted inside specially marked packages of Cracker Jack. These cards were the "toy surprise" inside. The cards measure approximately one-fourth standard-size (1 1/4" by 1 3/4") and are frequently referenced as micro-cards. The micro-cards have color player photos with different color borders but are otherwise identical to the corresponding cards in the Topps regular issue. Standard-size cards featuring four micro-cards each were seen at trade shows but were not inserted inside the product. These were apparently test runs or uncut sheets. Although each mini-card is numbered on the back, the numbering of the four cards on any standard-size card is not consecutive.

COMPLETE SET (36) 2.50 6.00
1 Eddie Murray .20 .50
2 Carlton Fisk .20 .50
3 Eric Anthony .02 .10
4 Kelly Gruber .02 .10
5 Von Hayes .02 .10
6 Ben McDonald .02 .10
7 Andre Dawson .15 .40
8 Ellis Burks .07 .20
9 Matt Williams .10 .30
10 Dave Stewart .07 .20
11 Barry Larkin .15 .40
12 Chuck Finley .07 .20
13 Shane Andrews .02 .10
14 Bret Saberhagen .07 .20
15 Bobby Bonilla .02 .10
16 Roberto Kelly .02 .10
17 Orel Hershiser .07 .20
18 Ruben Sierra .07 .20
19 Ron Gant .07 .20
20 Frank Thomas .20 .50
21 Tim Wallach .02 .10
22 Gregg Olson .02 .10
23 Shawon Dunston .02 .10
24 Kent Hrbek .07 .20
25 Ramon Martinez .02 .10
26 Alan Trammell .10 .30
27 Ozzie Smith .30 .75
28 Bob Welch .02 .10
29 Chris Sabo .02 .10
30 Steve Sax .02 .10
31 Bip Roberts .02 .10
32 Dave Stieb .02 .10
33 Howard Johnson .02 .10
34 Mike Greenwell .02 .10
35 Delino DeShields .02 .10
36 Alex Fernandez .02 .10

1991 Topps Debut '90

The 1991 Topps Major League Debut Set contains 171 standard-size cards. Although the checklist card is arranged chronologically in order of first major league appearance in 1990, the player cards are arranged alphabetically by the player's last name. Carlos Baerga and Frank Thomas are among the more prominent players featured in this set.

COMP.FACT SET (171) 8.00 20.00
DISTRIBUTED ONLY IN FACTORY SET FORM
1 Paul Abbott .05 .15
2 Steve Adkins .05 .15
3 Scott Aldred .05 .15
4 Gerald Alexander .05 .15
5 Moises Alou .30 .75
6 Steve Avery .05 .15
7 Oscar Azocar .05 .15
8 Carlos Baerga .05 .15
9 Kevin Baez .05 .15
10 Jeff Baldwin .05 .15
11 Brian Barnes .05 .15
12 Kevin Bearse .05 .15
13 Kevin Belcher .05 .15
14 Mike Bell .05 .15
15 Sean Berry .30 .75
16 Joe Bitker .05 .15
17 Willie Blair .05 .15
18 Brian Bohanon .05 .15
19 Mike Bordick .30 .75
20 Shawn Boskie .05 .15
21 Rod Brewer .05 .15
22 Kevin D. Brown .05 .15
23 Dave Burba .30 .75
24 Jim Campbell .05 .15
25 Ozzie Canseco .05 .15
26 Chuck Carr .05 .15
27 Larry Casian .05 .15
28 Andujar Cedeno .05 .15
29 Wes Chamberlain .05 .15
30 Scott Chiamparino .05 .15
31 Steve Chitren .05 .15
32 Pete Coachman .05 .15
33 Alex Cole .05 .15
34 Jeff Conine .30 .75
35 Scott Cooper .05 .15
36 Milt Cuyler .05 .15
37 Steve Decker .05 .15
38 Rich DeLucia .05 .15
39 Delino DeShields .30 .75
40 Mark Dewey .05 .15
41 Carlos Diaz .05 .15
42 Lance Dickson .05 .15
43 Narciso Elvira .05 .15
44 Luis Encarnacion .05 .15
45 Scott Erickson .05 .15
46 Paul Faries .05 .15
47 Howard Farmer .05 .15
48 Alex Fernandez .05 .15
49 Travis Fryman .30 .75
50 Rich Garces .05 .15
51 Carlos Garcia .05 .15
52 Mike Gardiner .05 .15
53 Bernard Gilkey .05 .15
54 Tom Gilles .05 .15
55 Jerry Goff .05 .15
56 Leo Gomez .05 .15
57 Luis Gonzalez 1.25 3.00
58 Joe Grahe .05 .15
59 Craig Grebeck .05 .15
60 Kip Gross .05 .15
61 Eric Gunderson .05 .15
62 Chris Hammond .05 .15
63 Dave Hansen .05 .15
64 Reggie Harris .05 .15
65 Bill Haselman .05 .15
66 Randy Hennis .05 .15
67 Carlos Hernandez .05 .15
68 Howard Hilton .05 .15
69 Dave Hollins .05 .15
70 Darren Holmes .30 .75
71 John Hoover .05 .15
72 Steve Howard .05 .15
73 Thomas Howard .05 .15
74 Todd Hundley .05 .15
75 Daryl Irvine .05 .15
76 Chris Jelic .05 .15
77 Dana Kiecker .05 .15
78 Brent Knackert .05 .15
79 Jimmy Kremers .05 .15
80 Jerry Kutzler .05 .15
81 Ray Lankford .30 .75
82 Tim Layana .05 .15
83 Terry Lee .05 .15
84 Mark Leiter .05 .15
85 Scott Leius .05 .15
86 Mark Leonard .05 .15
87 Darren Lewis .05 .15
88 Scott Lewis .05 .15
89 Jim Leyritz .05 .15
90 Dave Liddell .05 .15
91 Luis Lopez .05 .15
92 Kevin Maas .05 .15
93 Bob MacDonald .05 .15
94 Carlos Maldonado .05 .15
95 Chuck Malone .05 .15
96 Ramon Manon .05 .15
97 Jeff Manto .05 .15
98 Paul Marak .05 .15
99 Tino Martinez 1.25 3.00
100 Derrick May .05 .15
101 Brent Mayne .05 .15
102 Paul McClellan .05 .15
103 Rodney McCray .05 .15
104 Tim McIntosh .05 .15
105 Brian McRae .30 .75
106 Jose Melendez .05 .15
107 Orlando Merced .05 .15
108 Alan Mills .05 .15
109 Gino Minutelli .05 .15
110 Mickey Morandini .05 .15
111 Pedro Munoz .05 .15
112 Chris Nabholz .05 .15
113 Tim Naehring .05 .15
114 Charles Nagy .05 .15
115 Jim Neidlinger .05 .15
116 Rafael Novoa .05 .15
117 Jose Offerman .05 .15
118 Omar Olivares .30 .75
119 Javier Ortiz .05 .15
120 Al Osuna .05 .15
121 Rick Parker .05 .15
122 Dave Pavlas .05 .15
123 Geronimo Pena .05 .15
124 Mike Perez .05 .15
125 Phil Plantier .05 .15
126 Jim Poole .05 .15
127 Tom Quinlan .05 .15
128 Scott Radinsky .05 .15
129 Darren Reed .05 .15
130 Karl Rhodes .05 .15
131 Jeff Richardson .05 .15
132 Rich Rodriguez .05 .15
133 Dave Rohde .05 .15
134 Mel Rojas .05 .15
135 Vic Rosario .05 .15
136 Rich Rowland .05 .15
137 Scott Ruskin .05 .15
138 Bill Sampen .05 .15
139 Andres Santana .05 .15
140 David Segui .05 .15
141 Jeff Shaw .05 .15
142 Tim Sherrill .05 .15
143 Terry Shumpert .05 .15
144 Mike Simms .05 .15
145 Daryl Smith .05 .15
146 Luis Sojo .05 .15
147 Steve Springer .05 .15
148 Ray Stephens .05 .15
149 Lee Stevens .05 .15
150 Mel Stottlemyre Jr. .05 .15
151 Glenn Sutko .05 .15
152 Anthony Telford .05 .15
153 Frank Thomas 2.00 5.00
154 Randy Tomlin .05 .15
155 Brian Traxler .05 .15
156 Efrain Valdez .05 .15
157 Rafael Valdez .05 .15
158 Julio Valera .05 .15
159 Jim Vatcher .05 .15
160 Hector Villanueva .05 .15
161 Hector Wagner .05 .15
162 Dave Walsh .05 .15
163 Steve Wapnick .05 .15
164 Colby Ward .05 .15
165 Turner Ward .30 .75
166 Terry Wells .05 .15
167 Mark Whiten .05 .15
168 Mike York .05 .15
169 Cliff Young .05 .15
170 Checklist Card .05 .15
171 Checklist Card .05 .15

1991 Topps East Coast National

This four-card, standard-size set was included in the paid admission for the 1991 East Coast National Show (August 15-18). Each card is a reproduction of the player's first Topps card: Aaron, ('54 Topps) Mantle, ('52 Topps) Musial, ('58 Topps) and Robinson ('57 Topps). In blue print on white, the backs indicate that these cards are reprints. The cards are unnumbered and checklisted below in alphabetical order.

COMPLETE SET (4) 8.00 20.00
1 Hank Aaron 2.50 6.00
2 Mickey Mantle 4.00 10.00
3 Stan Musial 2.00 5.00
4 Frank Robinson 1.25 3.00

1991 Topps Gallery of Champions

In what would be the final season for this issue. Topps issued these 12 cards to honor award winners and league leaders. These "metal" cards measure approximately 1 1/4" by 1 3/4" and were made in aluminum, silver and bronze. We have valued the aluminum versions. The bronze cards are worth 2X to 3X the aluminums while the silvers are worth 4X to 6X the aluminum versions. This set, just as all the other Topps Gallery sets, were issued in complete set form only. We have sequenced this set in alphabetical order.

COMPLETE SET (12) 30.00 60.00
1 Sandy Alomar 3.00 8.00
2 Barry Bonds 15.00 40.00
3 George Brett 15.00 40.00
4 Doug Drabek 2.00 5.00
5 Cecil Fielder 3.00 8.00
6 John Franco 3.00 8.00
7 Rickey Henderson 12.50 30.00
8 Dave Justice 6.00 15.00
9 Willie McGee 3.00 8.00
10 Ryne Sandberg 12.50 30.00
11 Bobby Thigpen 2.00 5.00
12 Bob Welch 2.00 5.00

1991 Topps Glossy All-Stars

COMPLETE SET (22) 4.00 10.00
1 Tony LaRussa MG .07 .20
2 Mark McGwire .60 1.50
3 Steve Sax .02 .10
4 Wade Boggs .20 .50
5 Cal Ripken Jr 1.25 3.00
6 Rickey Henderson .30 .75
7 Ken Griffey, Jr. .75 2.00
8 Jose Canseco .20 .50
9 Sandy Alomar, Jr. .07 .20
10 Bob Welch .02 .10
11 Al Lopez CAPT .20 .50
12 Roger Craig MG .02 .10
13 Will Clark .20 .50
14 Ryne Sandberg .30 .75
15 Chris Sabo .02 .10
16 Ozzie Smith .40 1.00
17 Kevin Mitchell .02 .10
18 Len Dykstra .07 .20
19 Andre Dawson .20 .50
20 Mike Scoscia .07 .20
21 Jack Armstrong .02 .10
22 Juan Marichal CAPT .20 .50

1991 Topps Ruth

This 11-card set was produced by Topps to commemorate the NBC made-for-television movie about Ruth that aired Sunday, October 6, 1991.

COMPLETE SET (11) 4.00 10.00
1 Babe Ruth-Sunday .40 1.00
October 6th NBC
2 Babe Ruth .40 1.00
Stephen Lang as/Babe Ruth
3 Babe Ruth .40 1.00
Bruce Weitz as/Miller Huggins
4 Babe Ruth .40 1.00
Lisa Zane as/Claire Ruth
5 Babe Ruth .40 1.00
Donald Moffat as/Jacob Ruppert
6 Babe Ruth .40 1.00
Neil McDonough as/Lou Gehrig
7 Babe Ruth .75 2.00
Pete Rose/as Ty Cobb
8 Babe Ruth .60 1.50
Rod Carew/Baseball Consultant
9 Babe Ruth .40 1.00
Ruth and Mgr. Huggins
10 Babe Ruth .40 1.00
Ruth in Action
11 Babe Ruth .40 1.00
Babe Calls His Shot

1991 Topps Stand-Ups

These stand-ups were not widely distributed and therefore appear to be a test issue. The stand-ups are packaged in a wrapper that has a checklist on the back. Each stand-up is actually a 2" by 2 1/2" plastic semi-transparent green container filled with sweet-tart type candy. The National League players came in green, the American league players came in red. There are also clear plastic variations for all players which are much tougher.

COMPLETE SET (36) 100.00 200.00
1 Jim Abbott .40 1.00
2 Sandy Alomar Jr. .75 2.00
3 Wade Boggs 2.00 5.00
4 Barry Bonds 4.00 10.00
5 Bobby Bonilla .40 1.00
6 George Brett 4.00 10.00
7 Jose Canseco 2.00 5.00
8 Will Clark 1.50 4.00
9 Roger Clemens 5.00 12.00
10 Eric Davis .75 2.00
11 Andre Dawson 1.50 4.00
12 Len Dykstra .75 2.00
13 Cecil Fielder .75 2.00
14 Carlton Fisk 2.00 5.00
15 Dwight Gooden .75 2.00
16 Mark Grace 1.50 4.00
17 Ken Griffey Jr. 6.00 15.00
18 Tony Gwynn 5.00 12.00
19 Rickey Henderson 3.00 8.00
20 Bo Jackson 1.50 4.00
21 Dave Justice 1.50 4.00
22 Kevin Maas .40 1.00
23 Ramon Martinez .75 2.00
24 Don Mattingly 5.00 12.00
25 Ben McDonald .75 2.00
26 Mark McGwire 6.00 15.00
27 Kevin Mitchell .40 1.00
28 Cal Ripken 10.00 25.00
29 Nolan Ryan 10.00 25.00
30 Ryne Sandberg 3.00 8.00
31 Ozzie Smith 3.00 8.00
32 Dave Stewart .40 1.00
33 Darryl Strawberry .75 2.00
34 Frank Viola .40 1.00
35 Matt Williams 1.25 3.00
36 Robin Yount 2.00 5.00

1991 Topps Triple Headers

These balls feature the players' photo and fascimile autographs. Three players per team are featured. A piece of candy was included in each pack. We have sequenced this set in alphabetical order by league. There are reports that the Chicago Cub and St. Louis Cardinal balls were issued less frequently than other teams. They are noted as SP's below.

COMPLETE SET (26) 60.00 120.00
A1 Ben McDonald 6.00 15.00
Cal Ripken/Gregg Olson
A2 Wade Boggs 3.00 8.00
Mike Greenwell/Roger Clemens
A3 Chuck Finley 1.50 4.00
Dave Winfield/Wally Joyner
A4 Carlton Fisk 6.00 15.00
Robin Ventura/Frank Thomas
A5 Sandy Alomar .75 2.00
Alex Cole/Mark Lewis
A6 Cecil Fielder 1.50 4.00
Tony Phillips/Alan Trammell
A7 George Brett 3.00 8.00
Danny Tartabull/Bret Saberhagen
A8 Paul Molitor 2.50 6.00
Robin Yount/Greg Vaughn
A9 Scott Erickson 3.00 8.00
Kirby Puckett/Kent Hrbek
A10 Don Mattingly 3.00 8.00
Steve Sax/Willie Randolph
A11 Jose Canseco 2.50 6.00
Dave Henderson/Rickey Henderson
A12 Ken Griffey Jr. 8.00 20.00
Harold Reynolds/Ken Griffey Sr.
A13 Julio Franco 6.00 15.00
Nolan Ryan/Juan Gonzalez
A14 Roberto Alomar 1.50 4.00
Kelly Gruber/Joe Carter
N1 Ron Gant 1.50 4.00
Tom Glavine/David Justice
N2 Chicago Cubs 10.00 25.00
Ryne Sandberg/George Bell/Andre Dawson
N3 Eric Davis .75 2.00
Barry Larkin/Chris Sabo
N4 Jeff Bagwell 15.00 40.00
Craig Biggio/Ken Caminiti
N5 Ramon Martinez 1.50 4.00
Eddie Murray/Darryl Strawberry
N6 Delino DeShields .75 2.00
Dennis Martinez/Ivan Calderon
N7 Vince Coleman .75 2.00
Dwight Gooden/Howard Johnson
N8 Len Dykstra 1.50 4.00
John Kruk/Dale Murphy
N9 Barry Bonds .75 2.00
Bobby Bonilla/Andy Van Slyke
N10 Fred McGriff 2.50 6.00
Tony Gwynn/Benito Santiago
N11 Will Clark 2.50 6.00
Kevin Mitchell/Matt Williams
N12 Pedro Guerrero SP 6.00 15.00
Ozzie Smith/Todd Zeile

1991-94 Topps Golden Spikes

From 1991 through 1994, Topps produced a special card for the Golden Spikes award winner that was given away to attendees of the annual United States Baseball Federation luncheon. The USBF sponsors the Golden Spikes award, given to the top amateur baseball player. The unnumbered card backs indicate the player's name, year of award and luncheon date. The card fronts vary -- the 1991 and 1992 cards use slightly altered Topps Major League Debut designs, the 1993 and 1994 cards use slightly altered Topps Traded USA designs.

COMPLETE SET (4) 100.00 200.00
1 Alex Fernandez/1991 ML Debut 15.00 40.00
2 Mike Kelly/1992 ML Debut 8.00 20.00
3 Phil Nevin 1993 USA 20.00 50.00
4 Darren Dreifort/1994 USA 15.00 40.00

1992 Topps Pre-Production Sheet

COMPLETE SET (9) 2.00 5.00
3 Shawon Dunston .20 .50
16 Mike Heath .20 .50
18 Todd Frohwirth .20 .50
20 Bip Roberts .20 .50
131 Rob Dibble .40 1.00
174 Otis Nixon .20 .50
273 Denny Martinez .40 1.00
325 Brett Butler .40 1.00
798 Tom Lasorda MG .75 2.00

1992 Topps Gold Pre-Production Sheet

COMPLETE SET (9) 10.00 25.00
1 Nolan Ryan 4.00 10.00
15 Denny Martinez .60 1.50
20 Bip Roberts .40 1.00
40 Cal Ripken 4.00 10.00
Gehrig
261 Tom Lasorda MG 1.00 2.50
370 Shawon Dunston .40 1.00
512 Mike Heath .40 1.00
655 Brett Butler .60 1.50
757 Rob Dibble .40 1.00

1992 Topps

The 1992 Topps set contains 792 standard-size cards. Cards were distributed in plastic wrap packs, jumbo packs, rack packs and factory sets. The fronts have either posed or action color player photos on a white card face. Different color stripes frame the pictures, and the player's name and team name appear in two short color stripes respectively at the bottom. Special subsets included are Record Breakers (2-5), Prospects (58, 126, 179, 473, 551, 591, 618, 656, 676), and All-Stars (386-407). The key Rookie Cards in this set are Shawn Green and Manny Ramirez.

COMPLETE SET (792) 12.00 30.00
COMP.FACT.SET (802) 12.00 30.00
COMP.HOLIDAY SET (811) 15.00 40.00
1 Nolan Ryan .40 1.00
2 Rickey Henderson RB .05 .15
Most career SB's/Some cards have print/marks that show 1.991/on the front
3 Jeff Reardon RB .01 .05
4 Nolan Ryan RB .20 .50
5 Dave Winfield RB .01 .05
6 Brien Taylor RC .08 .25
7 Jim Olander .01 .05
8 Bryan Hickerson RC .02 .10
9 Jon Farrell RC .02 .10
10 Wade Boggs .05 .15
11 Jack McDowell .01 .05
12 Luis Gonzalez .02 .10
13 Mike Scioscia .01 .05
14 Wes Chamberlain .01 .05
15 Dennis Martinez .02 .10
16 Jeff Montgomery .01 .05
17 Randy Milligan .01 .05
18 Greg Cadaret .01 .05
19 Jamie Quirk .01 .05
20 Bip Roberts .01 .05
21 Buck Rodgers MG .01 .05
22 Bill Wegman .01 .05
23 Chuck Knoblauch .02 .10
24 Randy Myers .01 .05
25 Ron Gant .02 .10
26 Mike Bielecki .01 .05
27 Juan Gonzalez .05 .15
28 Mike Schooler .01 .05
29 Mickey Tettleton .01 .05
30 John Kruk .02 .10
31 Bryn Smith .01 .05
32 Chris Nabholz .01 .05
33 Carlos Baerga .01 .05
34 Jeff Juden .01 .05
35 Dave Righetti .02 .10
36 Scott Ruffcorn RC .02 .10
37 Luis Polonia .01 .05
38 Tom Candiotti .01 .05
39 Greg Olson .01 .05
40 Cal Ripken .75 2.00
41 Craig Lefferts .01 .05
42 Mike Macfarlane .01 .05
43 Jose Lind .01 .05
44 Rick Aguilera .02 .10
45 Gary Carter .02 .10
46 Steve Farr .01 .05
47 Rex Hudler .01 .05
48 Scott Scudder .01 .05

49 Damon Berryhill .01 .05
50 Ken Griffey Jr. .20 .50
51 Tom Runnells MG .01 .05
52 Juan Bell .01 .05
53 Tommy Gregg .01 .05
54 David Wells .02 .10
55 Rafael Palmeiro .05 .15
56 Charlie O'Brien .01 .05
57 Donn Pall .01 .05
58 Brad Ausmus RC .60 1.50
59 Mo Vaughn .02 .10
60 Tony Fernandez .01 .05
61 Paul O'Neill .05 .15
62 Gene Nelson .01 .05
63 Randy Ready .01 .05
64 Bob Kipper .01 .05
65 Willie McGee .02 .10
66 Scott Stahoviak RC .02 .10
67 Luis Salazar .01 .05
68 Marvin Freeman .01 .05
69 Kenny Lofton .05 .15
70 Gary Gaetti .02 .10
71 Erik Hanson .01 .05
72 Eddie Zosky .01 .05
73 Brian Barnes .01 .05
74 Scott Leius .01 .05
75 Bret Saberhagen .02 .10
76 Mike Gallego .01 .05
77 Jack Armstrong .01 .05
78 Ivan Rodriguez .08 .25
79 Jesse Orosco .01 .05
80 David Justice .02 .10
81 Ced Landrum .01 .05
82 Doug Simons .01 .05
83 Tommy Greene .01 .05
84 Leo Gomez .01 .05
85 Jose DeLeon .01 .05
86 Steve Finley .02 .10
87 Bob MacDonald .01 .05
88 Darrin Jackson .01 .05
89 Neal Heaton .01 .05
90 Robin Yount .15 .40
91 Jeff Reed .01 .05
92 Lenny Harris .01 .05
93 Reggie Jefferson .01 .05
94 Sammy Sosa .08 .25
95 Scott Bailes .01 .05
96 Tom McKinnon RC .02 .10
97 Luis Rivera .01 .05
98 Mike Harkey .01 .05
99 Jeff Treadway .01 .05
100 Jose Canseco .05 .15
101 Omar Vizquel .05 .15
102 Scott Kamieniecki .01 .05
103 Ricky Jordan .01 .05
104 Jeff Ballard .01 .05
105 Felix Jose .01 .05
106 Mike Boddicker .01 .05
107 Dan Pasqua .01 .05
108 Mike Timlin .01 .05
109 Roger Craig MG .01 .05
110 Ryne Sandberg .15 .40
111 Mark Carreon .01 .05
112 Oscar Azocar .01 .05
113 Mike Greenwell .01 .05
114 Mark Portugal .01 .05
115 Terry Pendleton .02 .10
116 Willie Randolph .02 .10
117 Scott Terry .01 .05
118 Chili Davis .02 .10
119 Mark Gardner .01 .05
120 Alan Trammell .02 .10
121 Derek Bell .02 .10
122 Gary Varsho .01 .05
123 Bob Ojeda .01 .05
124 Shawn Livsey RC .02 .10
125 Chris Hoiles .01 .05
126 Klesko/Jaha/Brogna/Staton .08 .25
127 Carlos Quintana .01 .05
128 Kurt Stillwell .01 .05
129 Melido Perez .01 .05
130 Alvin Davis .01 .05
131 Checklist 1-132 .01 .05
132 Eric Show .01 .05
133 Rance Mulliniks .01 .05
134 Darryl Kile .02 .10
135 Von Hayes .01 .05
136 Bill Doran .01 .05
137 Jeff D. Robinson .01 .05
138 Monty Fariss .01 .05
139 Jeff Innis .01 .05
140 Mark Grace UER .05 .15
Home Calie., should/be Calif.
141 Jim Leyland MG UER .02 .10
No closed parenthesis/after East in 1991
142 Todd Van Poppel .01 .05
143 Paul Gibson .01 .05
144 Bill Swift .01 .05
145 Danny Tartabull .01 .05
146 Al Newman .01 .05
147 Cris Carpenter .01 .05
148 Anthony Young .01 .05
149 Brian Bohanon .01 .05
150 Roger Clemens UER .20 .50
151 Jeff Hamilton .01 .05
152 Charlie Leibrandt .01 .05
153 Ron Karkovice .01 .05
154 Hensley Meulens .01 .05
155 Scott Bankhead .01 .05
156 Manny Ramirez RC 2.00 5.00
157 Keith Miller .01 .05
158 Todd Frohwirth .01 .05
159 Darrin Fletcher .01 .05
160 Bobby Bonilla .02 .10
161 Casey Candaele .01 .05
162 Paul Faries .01 .05
163 Dana Kiecker .01 .05
164 Shane Mack .01 .05
165 Mark Langston .01 .05
166 Geronimo Pena .01 .05
167 Andy Allanson .01 .05
168 Dwight Smith .01 .05
169 Chuck Crim .01 .05
170 Alex Cole .01 .05
171 Bill Plummer MG .01 .05
172 Juan Berenguer .01 .05
173 Brian Downing .01 .05
174 Steve Frey .01 .05
175 Orel Hershiser .02 .10
176 Ramon Garcia .01 .05
177 Dan Gladden .01 .05
178 Jim Acker .01 .05
179 DeJard/Bern/Moreno/Stank .01 .05
180 Kevin Mitchell .01 .05
181 Hector Villanueva .01 .05
182 Jeff Reardon .02 .10
183 Brent Mayne .01 .05
184 Jimmy Jones .01 .05
185 Benito Santiago .02 .10
186 Cliff Floyd RC .30 .75
187 Ernie Riles .01 .05
188 Jose Guzman .01 .05
189 Junior Felix .01 .05
190 Glenn Davis .01 .05
191 Charlie Hough .02 .10
192 Dave Fleming .01 .05
193 Omar Olivares .01 .05
194 Eric Karros .02 .10
195 David Cone .02 .10
196 Frank Castillo .01 .05
197 Glenn Braggs .01 .05
198 Scott Aldred .01 .05
199 Jeff Blauser .01 .05
200 Len Dykstra .02 .10
201 Buck Showalter MG RC .08 .25
202 Rick Honeycutt .01 .05
203 Greg Myers .01 .05
204 Trevor Wilson .01 .05
205 Jay Howell .01 .05
206 Luis Sojo .01 .05
207 Jack Clark .02 .10
208 Julio Machado .01 .05
209 Lloyd McClendon .01 .05
210 Ozzie Guillen .02 .10
211 Jeremy Hernandez RC .02 .10
212 Randy Velarde .01 .05
213 Les Lancaster .01 .05
214 Andy Mota .01 .05
215 Rich Gossage .02 .10
216 Brent Gates RC .02 .10
217 Brian Harper .01 .05
218 Mike Flanagan .01 .05
219 Jerry Browne .01 .05
220 Jose Rijo .01 .05
221 Skeeter Barnes .01 .05
222 Jaime Navarro .01 .05
223 Mel Hall .01 .05
224 Bret Barberie .01 .05
225 Roberto Alomar .05 .15
226 Pete Smith .01 .05
227 Daryl Boston .01 .05
228 Eddie Whitson .01 .05
229 Shawn Boskie .01 .05
230 Dick Schofield .01 .05
231 Brian Drahman .01 .05
232 John Smiley .01 .05
233 Mitch Webster .01 .05
234 Terry Steinbach .01 .05
235 Jack Morris .02 .10
236 Bill Pecota .01 .05
237 Jose Hernandez RC .08 .25
238 Greg Litton .01 .05
239 Brian Holman .01 .05
240 Andres Galarraga .02 .10
241 Gerald Young .01 .05
242 Mike Mussina .08 .25
243 Alvaro Espinoza .01 .05
244 Darren Daulton .02 .10
245 John Smoltz .05 .15
246 Jason Pruitt RC .02 .10
247 Chuck Finley .02 .10
248 Jim Gantner .01 .05
249 Tony Fossas .01 .05
250 Ken Griffey Sr. .02 .10
251 Kevin Elster .01 .05
252 Dennis Rasmussen .01 .05
253 Terry Kennedy .01 .05
254 Ryan Bowen .01 .05
255 Robin Ventura .02 .10
256 Mike Aldrete .01 .05
257 Jeff Russell .01 .05
258 Jim Lindeman .01 .05
259 Ron Darling .01 .05
260 Devon White .02 .10
261 Tom Lasorda MG .02 .10
262 Terry Lee .01 .05
263 Bob Patterson .01 .05
264 Checklist 133-264 .01 .05
265 Teddy Higuera .01 .05
266 Roberto Kelly .01 .05
267 Steve Bedrosian .01 .05
268 Brady Anderson .02 .10
269 Ruben Amaro .01 .05
270 Tony Gwynn .10 .30
271 Tracy Jones .01 .05
272 Jerry Don Gleaton .01 .05
273 Craig Grebeck .01 .05
274 Bob Scanlan .01 .05
275 Todd Zeile .01 .05
276 Shawn Green RC .40 1.00
277 Scott Chiamparino .01 .05
278 Darryl Hamilton .01 .05
279 Jim Clancy .01 .05
280 Carlos Martinez .01 .05
281 Kevin Appier .02 .10
282 John Wehner .01 .05
283 Reggie Sanders .02 .10
284 Gene Larkin .01 .05
285 Bob Welch .01 .05
286 Gilberto Reyes .01 .05
287 Pete Schourek .01 .05
288 Andujar Cedeno .01 .05
289 Mike Morgan .01 .05
290 Bo Jackson .08 .25
291 Phil Garner MG .02 .10
292 Ray Lankford .02 .10
293 Mike Henneman .01 .05
294 Dave Valle .01 .05
295 Alonzo Powell .01 .05
296 Tom Brunansky .01 .05
297 Kevin Brown .02 .10
298 Kelly Gruber .01 .05
299 Charles Nagy .01 .05
300 Don Mattingly .25 .60
301 Kirk McCaskill .01 .05
302 Joey Cora .01 .05
303 Dan Plesac .01 .05
304 Joe Oliver .01 .05
305 Tom Glavine .05 .15
306 Al Shirley RC .02 .10
307 Bruce Ruffin .01 .05
308 Craig Shipley .01 .05
309 Dave Martinez .01 .05
310 Jose Mesa .01 .05
311 Henry Cotto .01 .05
312 Mike LaValliere .01 .05
313 Kevin Tapani .01 .05
314 Jeff Huson .01 .05
315 Juan Samuel .01 .05
316 Curt Schilling .05 .15
317 Mike Bordick .01 .05
318 Steve Howe .01 .05
319 Tony Phillips .01 .05
320 George Bell .01 .05
321 Lou Piniella MG .02 .10
322 Tim Burke .01 .05
323 Milt Thompson .01 .05
324 Danny Darwin .01 .05
325 Joe Orsulak .01 .05
326 Eric King .01 .05
327 Jay Buhner .02 .10
328 Joel Johnston .01 .05
329 Franklin Stubbs .01 .05
330 Will Clark .05 .15
331 Steve Lake .01 .05
332 Chris Jones .01 .05
333 Pat Tabler .01 .05
334 Kevin Gross .01 .05
335 Dave Henderson .01 .05
336 Greg Anthony RC .02 .10
337 Alejandro Pena .01 .05
338 Shawn Abner .01 .05
339 Tom Browning .01 .05
340 Otis Nixon .01 .05
341 Bob Geren .01 .05
342 Tim Spehr .01 .05
343 John Vander Wal .01 .05
344 Jack Daugherty .01 .05
345 Zane Smith .01 .05
346 Rheal Cormier .01 .05
347 Kent Hrbek .02 .10
348 Rick Wilkins .01 .05
349 Steve Lyons .01 .05
350 Gregg Olson .01 .05
351 Greg Riddoch MG .01 .05
352 Ed Nunez .01 .05
353 Braulio Castillo .01 .05
354 Dave Bergman .01 .05
355 Warren Newson .01 .05
356 Luis Quinones .01 .05
357 Mike Witt .01 .05
358 Ted Wood .01 .05
359 Mike Moore .01 .05
360 Lance Parrish .02 .10
361 Barry Jones .01 .05
362 Javier Ortiz .01 .05
363 John Candelaria .01 .05
364 Glenallen Hill .01 .05
365 Duane Ward .01 .05
366 Checklist 265-396 .01 .05
367 Rafael Belliard .01 .05
368 Bill Krueger .01 .05
369 Steve Whitaker RC .02 .10
370 Shawon Dunston .01 .05
371 Dante Bichette .02 .10
372 Kip Gross .01 .05
373 Don Robinson .01 .05
374 Bernie Williams .05 .15
375 Bert Blyleven .02 .10
376 Chris Donnels .01 .05
377 Bob Zupcic RC .02 .10
378 Joel Skinner .01 .05
379 Steve Chitren .01 .05
380 Barry Bonds .40 1.00
381 Sparky Anderson MG .02 .10
382 Sid Fernandez .01 .05
383 Dave Hollins .01 .05
384 Mark Lee .01 .05
385 Tim Wallach .01 .05
386 Will Clark AS .02 .10
387 Ryne Sandberg AS .08 .25
388 Howard Johnson AS .01 .05
389 Barry Larkin AS .02 .10
390 Barry Bonds AS .20 .50
391 Ron Gant AS .01 .05
392 Bobby Bonilla AS .01 .05
393 Craig Biggio AS .02 .10
394 Dennis Martinez AS .01 .05
395 Tom Glavine AS .02 .10
396 Lee Smith AS .01 .05
397 Cecil Fielder AS .01 .05
398 Julio Franco AS .01 .05
399 Wade Boggs AS .02 .10
400 Cal Ripken AS .15 .40
401 Jose Canseco AS .05 .15
402 Joe Carter AS .01 .05
403 Ruben Sierra AS .01 .05
404 Matt Nokes AS .01 .05
405 Roger Clemens AS .08 .25
406 Jim Abbott AS .02 .10
407 Bryan Harvey AS .01 .05
408 Bob Milacki .01 .05
409 Geno Petralli .01 .05
410 Dave Stewart .02 .10
411 Mike Jackson .01 .05
412 Luis Aquino .01 .05
413 Tim Teufel .01 .05
414 Jeff Ware .01 .05
415 Jim Deshaies .01 .05
416 Ellis Burks .02 .10
417 Allan Anderson .01 .05
418 Alfredo Griffin .01 .05
419 Wally Whitehurst .01 .05
420 Sandy Alomar Jr. .01 .05
421 Juan Agosto .01 .05
422 Sam Horn .01 .05
423 Jeff Fassero .01 .05
424 Paul McClellan .01 .05
425 Cecil Fielder .02 .10
426 Tim Raines .02 .10
427 Eddie Taubensee RC .08 .25
428 Dennis Boyd .01 .05
429 Tony LaRussa MG .02 .10
430 Steve Sax .01 .05
431 Tom Gordon .01 .05
432 Billy Hatcher .01 .05
433 Cal Eldred .01 .05
434 Wally Backman .01 .05
435 Mark Eichhorn .01 .05
436 Mookie Wilson .02 .10
437 Scott Servais .01 .05
438 Mike Maddux .01 .05
439 Chico Walker .01 .05
440 Doug Drabek .01 .05
441 Rob Deer .01 .05
442 Dave West .01 .05
443 Spike Owen .01 .05
444 Tyrone Hill RC .02 .10
445 Matt Williams .02 .10
446 Mark Lewis .01 .05
447 David Segui .01 .05
448 Tom Pagnozzi .01 .05
449 Jeff Johnson .01 .05
450 Mark McGwire .25 .60
451 Tom Henke .01 .05
452 Wilson Alvarez .01 .05
453 Gary Redus .01 .05
454 Darren Holmes .01 .05
455 Pete O'Brien .01 .05
456 Pat Combs .01 .05
457 Hubie Brooks .01 .05
458 Frank Tanana .01 .05
459 Tom Kelly MG .01 .05
460 Andre Dawson .02 .10
461 Doug Jones .01 .05
462 Rich Rodriguez .01 .05
463 Mike Simms .01 .05
464 Mike Jeffcoat .01 .05
465 Barry Larkin .05 .15
466 Stan Belinda .01 .05
467 Lonnie Smith .01 .05
468 Greg Harris .01 .05
469 Jim Eisenreich .01 .05
470 Pedro Guerrero .02 .10
471 Jose DeJesus .01 .05
472 Rich Rowland RC .02 .10
473 Bolick/Paquette/Red/Russo .01 .05
474 Mike Rossiter RC .02 .10
475 Robby Thompson .01 .05
476 Randy Bush .01 .05
477 Greg Hibbard .01 .05
478 Dale Sveum .01 .05
479 Chito Martinez .01 .05
480 Scott Sanderson .01 .05
481 Tino Martinez .05 .15
482 Jimmy Key .02 .10
483 Terry Shumpert .01 .05
484 Mike Hartley .01 .05
485 Chris Sabo .01 .05
486 Bob Walk .01 .05
487 John Cerutti .01 .05
488 Scott Cooper .01 .05
489 Bobby Cox MG .02 .10
490 Julio Franco .02 .10
491 Jeff Brantley .01 .05
492 Mike Devereaux .01 .05
493 Jose Offerman .01 .05
494 Gary Thurman .01 .05
495 Carney Lansford .02 .10
496 Joe Grahe .01 .05
497 Andy Ashby .01 .05
498 Gerald Perry .01 .05
499 Dave Otto .01 .05
500 Vince Coleman .01 .05
501 Rob Mallicoat .01 .05
502 Greg Briley .01 .05
503 Pascual Perez .01 .05
504 Aaron Sele RC .08 .25
505 Bobby Thigpen .01 .05
506 Todd Benzinger .01 .05
507 Candy Maldonado .01 .05
508 Bill Gullickson .01 .05
509 Doug Dascenzo .01 .05
510 Frank Viola .02 .10
511 Kenny Rogers .02 .10
512 Mike Heath .01 .05
513 Kevin Bass .01 .05
514 Kim Batiste .01 .05
515 Delino DeShields .01 .05
516 Ed Sprague .01 .05
517 Jim Gott .01 .05
518 Jose Melendez .01 .05
519 Hal McRae MG .02 .10
520 Jeff Bagwell .08 .25
521 Joe Hesketh .01 .05
522 Milt Cuyler .01 .05
523 Shawn Hillegas .01 .05
524 Don Slaught .01 .05
525 Randy Johnson .08 .25
526 Doug Piatt .01 .05
527 Checklist 397-528 .01 .05
528 Steve Foster .01 .05
529 Joe Girardi .01 .05
530 Jim Abbott .05 .15
531 Larry Walker .05 .15
532 Mike Huff .01 .05
533 Mackey Sasser .01 .05
534 Benji Gil RC .08 .25
535 Dave Stieb .01 .05
536 Willie Wilson .01 .05
537 Mark Leiter .01 .05
538 Jose Uribe .01 .05
539 Thomas Howard .01 .05
540 Ben McDonald .01 .05
541 Jose Tolentino .01 .05
542 Keith Mitchell .01 .05
543 Jerome Walton .01 .05
544 Cliff Brantley .01 .05
545 Andy Van Slyke .05 .15
546 Paul Sorrento .01 .05
547 Herm Winningham .01 .05
548 Mark Guthrie .01 .05
549 Joe Torre MG .02 .10
550 Darryl Strawberry .02 .10
551 Chipper Jones .08 .25
552 Dave Gallagher .01 .05
553 Edgar Martinez .05 .15
554 Donald Harris .01 .05
555 Frank Thomas .08 .25
556 Storm Davis .01 .05
557 Dickie Thon .01 .05
558 Scott Garrelts .01 .05
559 Steve Olin .01 .05
560 Rickey Henderson .08 .25
561 Jose Vizcaino .01 .05
562 Wade Taylor .01 .05
563 Pat Borders .01 .05
564 Jimmy Gonzalez RC .02 .10
565 Lee Smith .02 .10
566 Bill Sampen .01 .05
567 Dean Palmer .02 .10
568 Bryan Harvey .01 .05
569 Tony Pena .01 .05
570 Lou Whitaker .02 .10
571 Randy Tomlin .01 .05
572 Greg Vaughn .01 .05
573 Kelly Downs .01 .05
574 Steve Avery UER .01 .05
Should be 13 games/for Durham in 1989
575 Kirby Puckett .08 .25
576 Heathcliff Slocumb .01 .05
577 Kevin Seitzer .01 .05
578 Lee Guetterman .01 .05
579 Johnny Oates MG .01 .05
580 Greg Maddux .15 .40
581 Stan Javier .01 .05
582 Vicente Palacios .01 .05
583 Mel Rojas .01 .05
584 Wayne Rosenthal RC .02 .10
585 Lenny Webster .01 .05
586 Rod Nichols .01 .05
587 Mickey Morandini .01 .05
588 Russ Swan .01 .05
589 Mariano Duncan .01 .05
590 Howard Johnson .01 .05
591 Burnitz/Brum/Coc/Dozier .02 .10
592 Denny Neagle .02 .10
593 Steve Decker .01 .05
594 Brian Barber RC .02 .10
595 Bruce Hurst .01 .05
596 Kent Mercker .01 .05
597 Mike Magnante RC .02 .10
598 Jody Reed .01 .05
599 Steve Searcy .01 .05
600 Paul Molitor .02 .10
601 Dave Smith .01 .05
602 Mike Fetters .01 .05
603 Luis Mercedes .01 .05
604 Chris Gwynn .01 .05
605 Scott Erickson .01 .05
606 Brook Jacoby .01 .05
607 Todd Stottlemyre .01 .05
608 Scott Bradley .01 .05
609 Mike Hargrove MG .02 .10
610 Eric Davis .02 .10
611 Brian Hunter .01 .05
612 Pat Kelly .01 .05
613 Pedro Munoz .01 .05
614 Al Osuna .01 .05
615 Matt Merullo .01 .05
616 Larry Andersen .01 .05
617 Junior Ortiz .01 .05
618 Hern/Hosey/McNeely/Pelt .01 .05
619 Danny Jackson .01 .05
620 George Brett .25 .60
621 Dan Gakeler .01 .05
622 Steve Buechele .01 .05
623 Bob Tewksbury .01 .05
624 Shawn Estes RC .08 .25
625 Kevin McReynolds .01 .05
626 Chris Haney .01 .05
627 Mike Sharperson .01 .05
628 Mark Williamson .01 .05
629 Wally Joyner .02 .10
630 Carlton Fisk .05 .15
631 Armando Reynoso RC .08 .25
632 Felix Fermin .01 .05
633 Mitch Williams .01 .05
634 Manuel Lee .01 .05
635 Harold Baines .02 .10
636 Greg Harris .01 .05
637 Orlando Merced .01 .05
638 Chris Bosio .01 .05
639 Wayne Housie .01 .05
640 Xavier Hernandez .01 .05
641 David Howard .01 .05
642 Tim Crews .01 .05
643 Rick Cerone .01 .05
644 Terry Leach .01 .05
645 Deion Sanders .05 .15
646 Craig Wilson .01 .05
647 Marquis Grissom .02 .10
648 Scott Fletcher .01 .05
649 Norm Charlton .01 .05
650 Jesse Barfield .01 .05
651 Joe Slusarski .01 .05
652 Bobby Rose .01 .05
653 Dennis Lamp .01 .05
654 Allen Watson RC .02 .10
655 Brett Butler .02 .10
656 Pem/H.Rod/Tinsley/G.Will .02 .10
657 Dave Johnson .01 .05
658 Checklist 529-660 .01 .05
659 Brian McRae .01 .05
660 Fred McGriff .05 .15
661 Bill Landrum .01 .05
662 Juan Guzman .01 .05
663 Greg Gagne .01 .05
664 Ken Hill .01 .05
665 Dave Haas .01 .05
666 Tom Foley .01 .05
667 Roberto Hernandez .01 .05
668 Dwayne Henry .01 .05
669 Jim Fregosi MG .01 .05
670 Harold Reynolds .02 .10
671 Mark Whiten .01 .05
672 Eric Plunk .01 .05
673 Todd Hundley .01 .05
674 Mo Sanford .01 .05
675 Bobby Witt .01 .05
676 Mil/Mahomes/Wendell/Salk .08 .25
677 John Marzano .01 .05
678 Joe Klink .01 .05
679 Pete Incaviglia .01 .05
680 Dale Murphy .05 .15
681 Rene Gonzales .01 .05
682 Andy Benes .01 .05
683 Jim Poole .01 .05
684 Trever Miller RC .02 .10
685 Scott Livingstone .01 .05
686 Rich DeLucia .01 .05
687 Harvey Pulliam .01 .05
688 Tim Belcher .01 .05
689 Mark Lemke .01 .05
690 John Franco .02 .10
691 Walt Weiss .01 .05
692 Scott Ruskin .01 .05
693 Jeff King .01 .05
694 Mike Gardiner .01 .05
695 Gary Sheffield .02 .10
696 Joe Boever .01 .05
697 Mike Felder .01 .05
698 John Habyan .01 .05
699 Cito Gaston MG .01 .05
700 Ruben Sierra .02 .10
701 Scott Radinsky .01 .05
702 Lee Stevens .01 .05
703 Mark Wohlers .01 .05
704 Curt Young .01 .05
705 Dwight Evans .05 .15
706 Rob Murphy .01 .05
707 Gregg Jefferies .01 .05
708 Tom Bolton .01 .05
709 Chris James .01 .05
710 Kevin Maas .01 .05
711 Ricky Bones .01 .05
712 Curt Wilkerson .01 .05
713 Roger McDowell .01 .05
714 Pokey Reese RC .08 .25
715 Craig Biggio .05 .15
716 Kirk Dressendorfer .01 .05
717 Ken Dayley .01 .05
718 B.J. Surhoff .02 .10
719 Terry Mulholland .01 .05
720 Kirk Gibson .02 .10
721 Mike Pagliarulo .01 .05
722 Walt Terrell .01 .05
723 Jose Oquendo .01 .05
724 Kevin Morton .01 .05
725 Dwight Gooden .02 .10
726 Kirt Manwaring .01 .05
727 Chuck McElroy .01 .05
728 Dave Burba .01 .05
729 Art Howe MG .01 .05
730 Ramon Martinez .01 .05
731 Donnie Hill .01 .05
732 Nelson Santovenia .01 .05
733 Bob Melvin .01 .05
734 Scott Hatteberg RC .08 .25
735 Greg Swindell .01 .05
736 Lance Johnson .01 .05
737 Kevin Reimer .01 .05
738 Dennis Eckersley .02 .10
739 Rob Ducey .01 .05
740 Ken Caminiti .02 .10
741 Mark Gubicza .01 .05
742 Bill Spiers .01 .05
743 Darren Lewis .01 .05
744 Chris Hammond .01 .05
745 Dave Magadan .01 .05
746 Bernard Gilkey .01 .05
747 Willie Banks .01 .05
748 Matt Nokes .01 .05
749 Jerald Clark .01 .05
750 Travis Fryman .02 .10
751 Steve Wilson .01 .05
752 Billy Ripken .01 .05
753 Paul Assenmacher .01 .05
754 Charlie Hayes .01 .05
755 Alex Fernandez .01 .05
756 Gary Pettis .01 .05
757 Rob Dibble .02 .10
758 Tim Naehring .01 .05
759 Jeff Torborg MG .01 .05
760 Ozzie Smith .15 .40
761 Mike Fitzgerald .01 .05
762 John Burkett .01 .05
763 Kyle Abbott .01 .05
764 Tyler Green RC .02 .10
765 Pete Harnisch .01 .05
766 Mark Davis .01 .05
767 Kal Daniels .01 .05
768 Jim Thome .08 .25
769 Jack Howell .01 .05
770 Sid Bream .01 .05
771 Arthur Rhodes .01 .05
772 Garry Templeton UER .01 .05
Stat heading in for pitchers
773 Hal Morris .01 .05
774 Bud Black .01 .05
775 Ivan Calderon .01 .05
776 Doug Henry RC .02 .10
777 John Olerud .02 .10
778 Tim Leary .01 .05
779 Jay Bell .02 .10
780 Eddie Murray .08 .25
781 Paul Abbott .01 .05
782 Phil Plantier .01 .05
783 Joe Magrane .01 .05
784 Ken Patterson .01 .05
785 Albert Belle .02 .10
786 Royce Clayton .01 .05
787 Checklist 661-792 .01 .05
788 Mike Stanton .01 .05
789 Bobby Valentine MG .01 .05
790 Joe Carter .02 .10
791 Danny Cox .01 .05
792 Dave Winfield .02 .10

1992 Topps Gold

COMPLETE SET (792) 30.00 80.00
COMP.FACT.SET (793) 30.00 80.00
*STARS: 6X TO 15X BASIC CARDS
*ROOKIES: 4X TO 10X BASIC CARDS
RANDOM INSERTS IN PACKS
TEN PER BASIC FACTORY SET
131 Terry Mathews .30 .75
264 Rod Beck .30 .75
366 Tony Perezchica .30 .75
527 Terry McDaniel .30 .75
658 John Ramos .30 .75
787 Brian Williams .30 .75
793 Brien Taylor AU/12000 5.00 12.00

1992 Topps Gold Winners

COMPLETE SET (792) 15.00 40.00
*STARS: 1.25X TO 3X BASIC CARDS
*ROOKIES: 1.25X TO 3X BASIC CARDS
REDEEMED WITH WINNING GAME CARDS
131 Terry Mathews .05 .15
264 Rod Beck .05 .15
366 Tony Perezchica .05 .15
527 Terry McDaniel .05 .15
658 John Ramos .05 .15
787 Brian Williams .05 .15

1992 Topps Micro

This 804 card parallel set was issued in factory set form only. The set is an exact replica of the regular issue 1992 Topps set (not including the Traded set).The cards, however, measure considerably smaller (1" by 1 3/8") than the regular cards. The set also includes 12 special gold foil parallel mini cards which are listed below. Please refer to the multipliers provided for values on the other singles.

COMPLETE FACT.SET (802) 12.50 30.00
COMMON GOLD INSERT .04 .10
*STARS: .4X TO 1X BASIC CARDS
G1 Nolan Ryan RB 1.00 2.50
G2 Rickey Henderson RB .20 .50
G10 Wade Boggs Gold .20 .50
G50 Ken Griffey Jr. 1.25 3.00
G100 Jose Canseco .20 .50
G270 Tony Gwynn .50 1.25
G300 Don Mattingly .50 1.25
G380 Barry Bonds .20 .50
G397 Cecil Fielder AS .02 .10
G403 Ruben Sierra AS .02 .10
G460 Andre Dawson .15 .40
G725 Dwight Gooden .07 .20

1992 Topps Traded

The 1992 Topps Traded set comprises 132 standard-size cards. The set was distributed exclusively in factory set form through hobby dealers. As in past editions, the set focuses on promising rookies, new managers, and players who changed teams. The set also includes a Team U.S.A. subset, featuring 25 of America's top college players and the Team U.S.A. coach. Card design is identical to the regular issue 1992 Topps cards except for the T-suffixed numbering. The cards are arranged in alphabetical order by player's last name. The key Rookie Cards in this set are Nomar Garciaparra, Brian Jordan and Jason Varitek.

COMP.FACT.SET (132) 10.00 25.00
1T Willie Adams USA RC .08 .25
2T Jeff Alkire USA RC .08 .25
3T Felipe Alou MG .07 .20
4T Moises Alou .07 .20
5T Ruben Amaro .02 .10
6T Jack Armstrong .02 .10
7T Scott Bankhead .02 .10
8T Tim Belcher .02 .10
9T George Bell .02 .10
10T Freddie Benavides .02 .10
11T Todd Benzinger .02 .10
12T Joe Boever .02 .10
13T Ricky Bones .02 .10
14T Bobby Bonilla .07 .20
15T Hubie Brooks .02 .10
16T Jerry Browne .02 .10
17T Jim Bullinger .02 .10
18T Dave Burba .02 .10
19T Kevin Campbell .02 .10
20T Tom Candiotti .02 .10
21T Mark Carreon .02 .10
22T Gary Carter .07 .20
23T Archi Cianfrocco RC .02 .10
24T Phil Clark .02 .10
25T Chad Curtis RC .15 .40
26T Eric Davis .07 .20
27T Tim Davis USA RC .08 .25
28T Gary DiSarcina .02 .10
29T Darren Dreifort USA .02 .10
30T Mariano Duncan .02 .10
31T Mike Fitzgerald .02 .10
32T John Flaherty RC .02 .10
33T Darrin Fletcher .02 .10
34T Scott Fletcher .02 .10
35T Ron Fraser USA CO RC .08 .25
36T Andres Galarraga .07 .20
37T Dave Gallagher .02 .10
38T Mike Gallego .02 .10
39T Nomar Garciaparra USA RC 5.00 12.00
40T Jason Giambi USA .40 1.00
41T Danny Gladden .02 .10
42T Rene Gonzales .02 .10
43T Jeff Granger USA .02 .10
44T Rick Greene USA RC .08 .25
45T Jeffrey Hammonds USA .07 .20
46T Charlie Hayes .02 .10
47T Von Hayes .02 .10
48T Rick Helling USA .02 .10
49T Butch Henry RC .02 .10
50T Carlos Hernandez .02 .10
51T Ken Hill .02 .10
52T Butch Hobson .02 .10
53T Vince Horsman .02 .10
54T Pete Incaviglia .02 .10
55T Gregg Jefferies .02 .10
56T Charles Johnson USA .07 .20
57T Doug Jones .02 .10
58T Brian Jordan RC .30 .75
59T Wally Joyner .07 .20
60T Daron Kirkreit USA RC .08 .25
61T Bill Krueger .02 .10
62T Gene Lamont MG .02 .10
63T Jim Lefebvre MG .02 .10
64T Danny Leon .02 .10
65T Pat Listach RC .15 .40
66T Kenny Lofton .10 .30
67T Dave Martinez .02 .10
68T Derrick May .02 .10
69T Kirk McCaskill .02 .10
70T Chad McConnell USA RC .08 .25
71T Kevin McReynolds .02 .10

72T Rusty Meacham .02 .10
73T Keith Miller .02 .10
74T Kevin Mitchell .02 .10
75T Jason Moler USA RC .08 .25
76T Mike Morgan .02 .10
77T Jack Morris .07 .20
78T Calvin Murray USA RC .30 .75
79T Eddie Murray .20 .50
80T Randy Myers .02 .10
81T Denny Neagle .07 .20
82T Phil Nevin USA .07 .20
83T Dave Nilsson .02 .10
84T Junior Ortiz .02 .10
85T Donovan Osborne .02 .10
86T Bill Pecota .02 .10
87T Melido Perez .02 .10
88T Mike Perez .02 .10
89T Hipolito Pichardo RC .02 .10
90T Willie Randolph .07 .20
91T Darren Reed .02 .10
92T Bip Roberts .02 .10
93T Chris Roberts USA .02 .10
94T Steve Rodriguez USA .02 .10
95T Bruce Ruffin .02 .10
96T Scott Ruskin .02 .10
97T Bret Saberhagen .07 .20
98T Rey Sanchez RC .15 .40
99T Steve Sax .02 .10
100T Curt Schilling .10 .30
101T Dick Schofield .02 .10
102T Gary Scott .02 .10
103T Kevin Seitzer .02 .10
104T Frank Seminara RC .02 .10
105T Gary Sheffield .07 .20
106T John Smiley .02 .10
107T Cory Snyder .02 .10
108T Paul Sorrento .02 .10
109T Sammy Sosa Cubs .60 1.50
110T Matt Stairs RC .20 .50
111T Andy Stankiewicz .02 .10
112T Kurt Stillwell .02 .10
113T Rick Sutcliffe .07 .20
114T Bill Swift .02 .10
115T Jeff Tackett .02 .10
116T Danny Tartabull .02 .10
117T Eddie Taubensee .07 .20
118T Dickie Thon .02 .10
119T Michael Tucker USA RC .30 .75
120T Scooter Tucker .02 .10
121T Marc Valdes USA RC .08 .25
122T Julio Valera .02 .10
123T Jason Varitek USA RC 5.00 12.00
124T Ron Villone USA RC .08 .25
125T Frank Viola .07 .20
126T B.J.Wallace USA RC .08 .25
127T Dan Walters .02 .10
128T Craig Wilson USA .02 .10
129T Chris Wimmer USA .02 .10
130T Dave Winfield .07 .20
131T Herm Winningham .02 .10
132T Checklist 1T-132T .02 .10

1992 Topps Traded Gold

COMP.FACT.SET (132) 15.00 40.00
*GOLD STARS: 1.5X TO 4X BASIC CARDS
*GOLD RC's: .75X TO 2X BASIC CARDS
GOLD SOLD ONLY IN FACTORY SET FORM

1992 Topps Cashen

This one-card set was given away at the 1992 New York Sports Commission Luncheon and honors New York Mets General Manager Frank Cashen who was selected as Sportsman of the Year by the Commission.

1 Frank Cashen

1992 Topps Dairy Queen Team USA

This 33-card standard size set was produced by Topps for Dairy Queen. The set was available in four-card packs with the purchase of a regular-sized sundae in a Team USA helmet during June and July 1992. The set features 16 Team USA players from the 1984 and 1988 teams who are now major league stars as well as 15 1992 Team USA prospects. Completing the set is a 1988 Gold Medal team celebration card and the 1992 Head Coach Ron Fraser.

COMPLETE SET (33) 10.00 25.00
1 Mark McGwire 2.50 6.00
2 Will Clark 1.00 2.50
3 John Marzano .08 .25
4 Barry Larkin 1.00 2.50
5 Bobby Witt .08 .25
6 Scott Bankhead .08 .25
7 B.J. Surhoff .30 .75
8 Shane Mack .08 .25
9 Jim Abbott .20 .50
10 Ben McDonald .08 .25
11 Robin Ventura .40 1.00
12 Charles Nagy .08 .25
13 Andy Benes .08 .25
14 Joe Slusarski .08 .25
15 Ed Sprague .08 .25
16 Bret Barberie .08 .25
17 Team USA Strikes Gold .20 .50
18 Jeff Granger .08 .25
19 John Dettmer .08 .25
20 Todd Greene .08 .25
21 Jeffrey Hammonds .08 .25
22 Dan Melendez .08 .25
23 Kennie Steenstra .08 .25
24 Todd Johnson .08 .25
25 Chris Roberts .08 .25
26 Steve Rodriguez .08 .25
27 Charles Johnson .20 .50
28 Chris Wimmer .08 .25
29 Tony Phillips P .08 .25
30 Craig Wilson .08 .25
31 Jason Giambi 4.00 10.00
32 Paul Shuey .08 .25
33 Ron Fraser CO .08 .25

1992 Topps Debut '91

The 1991 Topps Debut '91 set contains 194 standard-size cards. The fronts feature a mix of either posed or action glossy color player photos, framed with two color border stripes on a white card face. Future MVP's Jeff Bagwell, Ivan Rodriguez and Mo Vaughn along with Vinny Castilla and Mike Mussina are among the featured players in the set.

COMP.FACT.SET (194) 6.00 15.00
1 Kyle Abbott .08 .25
2 Dana Allison .08 .25
3 Rich Amaral .08 .25
4 Ruben Amaro .08 .25
5 Andy Ashby .08 .25
6 Jim Austin .08 .25
7 Jeff Bagwell .75 2.00
8 Jeff Banister .40 1.00
9 Willie Banks .08 .25
10 Bret Barberie .08 .25
11 Kim Batiste .08 .25
12 Chris Beasley .08 .25
13 Rod Beck .20 .50
14 Derek Bell .20 .50
15 Esteban Beltre .08 .25
16 Freddie Benavides .08 .25
17 Ricky Bones .08 .25
18 Denis Boucher .08 .25
19 Ryan Bowen .08 .25
20 Cliff Brantley .08 .25
21 John Briscoe .08 .25
22 Scott Brosius .75 2.00
23 Terry Bross .08 .25
24 Jarvis Brown .08 .25
25 Scott Bullett .08 .25
26 Kevin Campbell .08 .25
27 Amalio Carreno .08 .25
28 Matlas Carrillo .08 .25
29 Jeff Carter .08 .25
30 Vinny Castilla 1.25 3.00
31 Braulio Castillo .08 .25
32 Frank Castillo .08 .25
33 Darrin Chapin .08 .25
34 Mike Christopher .08 .25
35 Mark Clark .20 .50
36 Royce Clayton .08 .25
37 Stu Cole .08 .25
38 Gary Cooper .08 .25
39 Archie Corbin .08 .25
40 Rheal Cormier .08 .25
41 Chris Cron .08 .25
42 Mike Dalton .08 .25
43 Mark Davis .08 .25
44 Francisco de la Rosa .08 .25
45 Chris Donnels .08 .25
46 Brian Drahman .08 .25
47 Tom Drees .08 .25
48 Kirk Dressendorfer .08 .25
49 Bruce Egloff .08 .25
50 Cal Eldred .08 .25
51 Jose Escobar .08 .25
52 Tony Eusebio .20 .50
53 Hector Fajardo .08 .25
54 Monty Fariss .08 .25
55 Jeff Fassero .08 .25
56 Dave Fleming .08 .25
57 Kevin Flora .08 .25
58 Steve Foster .08 .25
59 Dan Gakeler .08 .25
60 Ramon Garcia .08 .25
61 Chris Gardner .08 .25
62 Jeff Gardner .08 .25
63 Chris George .08 .25
64 Ray Giannelli .08 .25
65 Tom Goodwin .08 .25
66 Mark Grater .08 .25
67 Johnny Guzman .08 .25
68 Juan Guzman .08 .25
69 Dave Haas .08 .25
70 Chris Haney .08 .25
71 Shawn Hare .08 .25
72 Donald Harris .08 .25
73 Doug Henry .08 .25
74 Pat Hentgen .08 .25
75 Gil Heredia .20 .50
76 Jeremy Hernandez .08 .25
77 Jose Hernandez .20 .50
78 Roberto Hernandez .08 .25
79 Bryan Hickerson .08 .25
80 Milt Hill .08 .25
81 Vince Horsman .08 .25
82 Wayne Housie .08 .25
83 Chris Howard .08 .25
84 David Howard .08 .25
85 Mike Humphreys .08 .25
86 Brian Hunter .08 .25
87 Jim Hunter .08 .25
88 Mike Ignasiak .08 .25
89 Reggie Jefferson .08 .25
90 Jeff Johnson .08 .25
91 Joel Johnston .08 .25
92 Calvin Jones .08 .25
93 Chris Jones .08 .25
94 Stacy Jones .08 .25
95 Jeff Juden .08 .25
96 Scott Kamieniecki .08 .25
97 Eric Karros .20 .50
98 Pat Kelly .08 .25
99 John Kiely .08 .25
100 Darryl Kile .20 .50
101 Wayne Kirby .08 .25
102 Garland Kiser .08 .25
103 Chuck Knoblauch .20 .50
104 Randy Knorr .08 .25
105 Tom Kramer .08 .25
106 Ced Landrum .08 .25
107 Patrick Lennon .08 .25
108 Jim Lewis .08 .25
109 Mark Lewis .08 .25
110 Doug Lindsey .08 .25
111 Scott Livingstone .08 .25
112 Kenny Lofton .40 1.00
113 Ever Magallanes .08 .25
114 Mike Magnante .08 .25
115 Barry Manuel .08 .25
116 Josias Manzanillo .08 .25
117 Chito Martinez .08 .25
118 Terry Mathews .08 .25
119 Rob Maurer .08 .25
120 Tim Mauser .08 .25
121 Terry McDaniel .08 .25
122 Rusty Meacham .08 .25
123 Luis Mercedes .08 .25
124 Paul Miller .08 .25
125 Keith Mitchell .08 .25
126 Bobby Moore .08 .25
127 Kevin Morton .08 .25
128 Andy Mota .08 .25
129 Jose Mota .08 .25
130 Mike Mussina .75 2.00
131 Jeff Mutis .08 .25
132 Denny Neagle .20 .50
133 Warren Newson .08 .25
134 Jim Olander .08 .25
135 Erik Pappas .08 .25
136 Jorge Pedre .08 .25
137 Yorkis Perez .08 .25
138 Mark Petkovsek .08 .25
139 Doug Piatt .08 .25
140 Jeff Plympton .08 .25
141 Harvey Pulliam .08 .25
142 John Ramos .08 .25
143 Mike Remlinger .08 .25
144 Laddie Renfroe .08 .25
145 Armando Reynoso .20 .50
146 Arthur Rhodes .08 .25
147 Pat Rice .08 .25
148 Nikco Riesgo .08 .25
149 Carlos Rodriguez .08 .25
150 Ivan Rodriguez .75 2.00
151 Wayne Rosenthal .08 .25
152 Rico Rossy .08 .25
153 Stan Royer .08 .25
154 Rey Sanchez .20 .50
155 Reggie Sanders .20 .50
156 Mo Sanford .08 .25
157 Bob Scanlan .08 .25
158 Pete Schourek .08 .25
159 Gary Scott .08 .25
160 Tim Scott .08 .25
161 Tony Scruggs .08 .25
162 Scott Servais .08 .25
163 Doug Simons .08 .25
164 Heathcliff Slocumb .08 .25
165 Joe Slusarski .08 .25
166 Tim Spehr .08 .25
167 Ed Sprague .08 .25
168 Jeff Tackett .08 .25
169 Eddie Taubensee .20 .50
170 Wade Taylor .08 .25
171 Jim Thome .75 2.00
172 Mike Timlin .08 .25
173 Jose Tolentino .08 .25
174 John Vander Wal .08 .25
175 Todd Van Poppel .08 .25
176 Mo Vaughn .20 .50
177 Dave Wainhouse .08 .25
178 Don Wakamatsu .08 .25
179 Bruce Walton .08 .25
180 Kevin Ward .08 .25
181 Dave Weathers .08 .25
182 Eric Wedge .08 .25
183 John Wehner .08 .25
184 Rick Wilkins .08 .25
185 Bernie Williams .40 1.00
186 Brian Williams .08 .25
187 Ron Witmeyer .08 .25
188 Mark Wohlers .08 .25
189 Ted Wood .08 .25
190 Anthony Young .08 .25
191 Eddie Zosky .08 .25
192 Bob Zupcic .08 .25
193 Checklist 1 .08 .25
194 Checklist 2 .08 .25

1992 Topps Kids

This 132-card standard size set was packaged in seven-card wax packs with a stick of bubble gum. The set numbering is arranged by teams in alphabetical order within division.

COMPLETE SET (132) 6.00 15.00
1 Ryne Sandberg .20 .50
2 Andre Dawson .07 .20
3 George Bell .01 .05
4 Mark Grace .05 .15
5 Shawon Dunston .01 .05
6 Tim Wallach .01 .05
7 Ivan Calderon .01 .05
8 Marquis Grissom .01 .05
9 Delino DeShields .02 .10
10 Dennis Martinez .02 .10
11 Dwight Gooden .02 .10
12 Howard Johnson .01 .05
13 John Franco .02 .10
14 Gregg Jefferies .01 .05
15 Kevin McReynolds .01 .05
16 David Cone .02 .10
17 Len Dykstra .02 .10
18 John Kruk .02 .10
19 Von Hayes .01 .05
20 Mitch Williams .01 .05
21 Barry Bonds .30 .75
22 Bobby Bonilla .02 .10
23 Andy Van Slyke .01 .05
24 Doug Drabek .01 .05
25 Ozzie Smith .30 .75
26 Pedro Guerrero .01 .05
27 Todd Zeile .02 .10
28 Lee Smith .02 .10
29 Felix Jose .01 .05
30 Jose DeLeon .01 .05
31 David Justice .07 .20
32 Ron Gant .02 .10
33 Terry Pendleton .01 .05
34 Tom Glavine .07 .20
35 Otis Nixon .01 .05
36 Steve Avery .01 .05
37 Barry Larkin .07 .20
38 Eric Davis .02 .10
39 Chris Sabo .01 .05
40 Rob Dibble .01 .05
41 Paul O'Neill .02 .10
42 Jose Rijo .01 .05
43 Craig Biggio .07 .20
44 Jeff Bagwell .30 .75
45 Ken Caminiti .07 .20
46 Steve Finley .05 .15
47 Darryl Strawberry .02 .10
48 Ramon Martinez .01 .05
49 Brett Butler .02 .10
50 Eddie Murray .20 .50
51 Kal Daniels .01 .05
52 Orel Hershiser .02 .10
53 Tony Gwynn .40 1.00
54 Benito Santiago .02 .10
55 Fred McGriff .05 .15
56 Bip Roberts .01 .05
57 Tony Fernandez .01 .05
58 Will Clark .07 .20
59 Kevin Mitchell .02 .10
60 Matt Williams .05 .15
61 Willie McGee .02 .10
62 Dave Righetti .01 .05
63 Cal Ripken .75 2.00
64 Ben McDonald .01 .05
65 Glenn Davis .01 .05
66 Gregg Olson .01 .05
67 Roger Clemens .40 1.00
68 Wade Boggs .20 .50
69 Mike Greenwell .01 .05
70 Ellis Burks .02 .10
71 Sandy Alomar Jr. .02 .10
72 Greg Swindell .01 .05
73 Albert Belle .02 .10
74 Mark Whiten .01 .05
75 Alan Trammell .05 .15
76 Cecil Fielder .02 .10
77 Lou Whitaker .02 .10
78 Travis Fryman .02 .10
79 Tony Phillips .01 .05
80 Robin Yount .20 .50
81 Paul Molitor .20 .50
82 B.J. Surhoff .02 .10
83 Greg Vaughn .02 .10
84 Don Mattingly .40 1.00
85 Steve Sax .01 .05
86 Kevin Maas .01 .05
87 Mel Hall .01 .05
88 Roberto Kelly .01 .05
89 Joe Carter .02 .10
90 Roberto Alomar .07 .20
91 Dave Stieb .01 .05
92 Kelly Gruber .01 .05
93 Tom Henke .01 .05
94 Chuck Finley .02 .10
95 Wally Joyner .01 .05
96 Dave Winfield .20 .50
97 Jim Abbott .02 .10
98 Mark Langston .01 .05
99 Frank Thomas .20 .50
100 Ozzie Guillen .05 .15
101 Bobby Thigpen .01 .05
102 Robin Ventura .07 .20
103 Bo Jackson .07 .20
104 Tim Raines .02 .10
105 George Brett .30 .75
106 Danny Tartabull .01 .05
107 Bret Saberhagen .02 .10
108 Brian McRae .02 .10
109 Kirby Puckett .20 .50
110 Scott Erickson .02 .10
111 Kent Hrbek .02 .10
112 Chuck Knoblauch .05 .15
113 Chili Davis .02 .10
114 Rick Aguilera .02 .10
115 Jose Canseco .15 .40
116 Dave Henderson .01 .05
117 Dave Stewart .02 .10
118 Rickey Henderson .30 .75
119 Dennis Eckersley .15 .40
120 Harold Baines .02 .10
121 Mark McGwire .40 1.00
122 Ken Griffey Jr. .50 1.25
123 Harold Reynolds .02 .10
124 Erik Hanson .01 .05
125 Edgar Martinez .05 .15
126 Randy Johnson .30 .75
127 Nolan Ryan .75 2.00
128 Ruben Sierra .02 .10
129 Julio Franco .02 .10
130 Rafael Palmeiro .15 .40
131 Juan Gonzalez .15 .40
132 Checklist Card .01 .05

1992 Topps McDonald's

This 44-card standard-size set was produced by Topps for McDonald's and distributed in the New York, New Jersey, and Connecticut areas. The set was subtitled "McDonald's Baseball's Best". For 99 cents with the purchase of an Extra Value Meal or 1.79 with any other food purchase, the collector received a five-card cello pack. The top card of each pack was always one of eleven different rookies (34-44) randomly packed with four other non-rookie cards.

COMPLETE SET (44) 6.00 15.00
1 Cecil Fielder .07 .20
2 Benny Santiago .07 .20
3 Rickey Henderson .50 1.25
4 Roberto Alomar .15 .40
5 Ryne Sandberg .60 1.50
6 George Brett .75 2.00
7 Terry Pendleton .02 .10
8 Ken Griffey Jr. 1.00 2.50
9 Bobby Bonilla .02 .10
10 Roger Clemens .75 2.00
11 Ozzie Smith .60 1.50
12 Barry Bonds .75 2.00
13 Cal Ripken 1.50 4.00
14 Ron Gant .07 .20
15 Carlton Fisk .30 .75
16 Steve Avery .02 .10
17 Robin Yount .30 .75
18 Will Clark .15 .40
19 Kirby Puckett .40 1.00
20 Jim Abbott .07 .20
21 Barry Larkin .10 .30
22 Jose Canseco .20 .50
23 Howard Johnson .02 .10
24 Nolan Ryan 1.50 4.00
25 Frank Thomas .40 1.00
26 Danny Tartabull .02 .10
27 Julio Franco .07 .20
28 David Justice .15 .40
29 Joe Carter .07 .20
30 Dale Murphy .15 .40
31 Andre Dawson .15 .40
32 Dwight Gooden .07 .20
33 Bo Jackson .15 .40
34 Jeff Bagwell .60 1.50
35 Chuck Knoblauch .10 .30
36 Derek Bell .02 .10
37 Jim Thome .40 1.00
38 Royce Clayton .02 .10
39 Ryan Klesko .20 .50
40 Chito Martinez .02 .10
41 Ivan Rodriguez .60 1.50
42 Todd Hundley .07 .20
43 Eric Karros .15 .40
44 Todd Van Poppel .02 .10

1993 Topps Pre-Production

COMPLETE SET (9) 3.00 8.00
1 Robin Yount .40 1.00
2 Barry Bonds .60 1.50
11 Eric Karros .20 .50
32 Don Mattingly .75 2.00
100 Mark McGwire 1.00 2.50
150 Frank Thomas .40 1.00
179 Ken Griffey Jr. 1.00 2.50
225 Matt Williams
230 Carlton Fisk .40 1.00
250 Chuck Knoblauch .08 .25
397 George Brett

1993 Topps Pre-Production Sheet

COMPLETE SET (9) 2.50 6.00
1 Roberto Alomar .30 .75
2 Bobby Bonilla .07 .20
3 Gary Carter .40 1.00
4 Andre Dawson .30 .75
5 Dave Fleming .07 .20
6 Ken Griffey Jr. 1.50 4.00
7 Pete Incaviglia .07 .20
8 Spike Owen .07 .20
9 Larry Walker .30 .75

1993 Topps

The 1993 Topps baseball set consists of two series, respectively, of 396 and 429 standard-size cards. A Topps Gold card was inserted in every 15-card pack. In addition, hobby and retail factory sets were produced. The fronts feature color action player photos with white borders. The player's name appears in a stripe at the bottom of the picture, and this stripe and two short diagonal stripes at the bottom corners of the picture are team color-coded. The backs are colorful and carry a color head shot, biography, complete statistical information, with a career highlight if space permitted. Cards 401-411 comprise an All-Star subset. Rookie Cards in this set include Jim Edmonds, Derek Jeter and Jason Kendall.

COMPLETE SET (825) 20.00 50.00
COMP.HOBBY.SET (847) 20.00 50.00
COMP.RETAIL.SET (838) 20.00 50.00
COMPLETE SERIES 1 (396) 10.00 25.00
COMPLETE SERIES 2 (429) 10.00 25.00
1 Robin Yount .30 .75
2 Barry Bonds .60 1.50
3 Ryne Sandberg .30 .75
4 Roger Clemens .40 1.00
5 Tony Gwynn .25 .60
6 Jeff Tackett .02 .10
7 Pete Incaviglia .02 .10
8 Mark Wohlers .02 .10
9 Kent Hrbek .07 .20
10 Will Clark .10 .30
11 Eric Karros .07 .20
12 Lee Smith .07 .20
13 Esteban Beltre .02 .10
14 Greg Briley .02 .10
15 Marquis Grissom .07 .20
16 Dan Plesac .02 .10
17 Dave Hollins .02 .10
18 Terry Steinbach .02 .10
19 Ed Nunez .02 .10
20 Tim Salmon .10 .30
21 Luis Salazar .02 .10
22 Jim Eisenreich .02 .10
23 Todd Stottlemyre .02 .10
24 Tim Naehring .02 .10
25 John Franco .07 .20
26 Skeeter Barnes .02 .10
27 Carlos Garcia .02 .10
28 Joe Orsulak .02 .10
29 Dwayne Henry .02 .10
30 Fred McGriff .10 .30
31 Derek Lilliquist .02 .10
32 Don Mattingly .50 1.25
33 B.J. Wallace .02 .10
34 Juan Gonzalez .07 .20
35 John Smoltz .10 .30
36 Scott Servais .02 .10
37 Lenny Webster .02 .10
38 Chris James .02 .10
39 Roger McDowell .02 .10
40 Ozzie Smith .30 .75
41 Alex Fernandez .02 .10
42 Spike Owen .02 .10
43 Ruben Amaro .02 .10
44 Kevin Seitzer .02 .10
45 Dave Fleming .02 .10
46 Eric Fox .02 .10
47 Bob Scanlan .02 .10
48 Bert Blyleven .07 .20
49 Brian McRae .02 .10
50 Roberto Alomar .10 .30
51 Mo Vaughn .07 .20
52 Bobby Bonilla .07 .20
53 Frank Tanana .02 .10
54 Mike LaValliere .02 .10
55 Mark McLemore .02 .10
56 Chad Mottola RC .02 .10
57 Norm Charlton .02 .10
58 Jose Melendez .02 .10
59 Carlos Martinez .02 .10
60 Roberto Kelly .02 .10
61 Gene Larkin .02 .10
62 Rafael Belliard .02 .10
63 Al Osuna .02 .10
64 Scott Chiamparino .02 .10
65 Brett Butler .07 .20
66 John Burkett .02 .10
67 Felix Jose .02 .10
68 Omar Vizquel .10 .30
69 John Vander Wal .02 .10
70 Roberto Hernandez .02 .10
71 Ricky Bones .02 .10
72 Jeff Grotewold .02 .10
73 Mike Moore .02 .10
74 Steve Buechele .02 .10
75 Juan Guzman .02 .10
76 Kevin Appier .07 .20
77 Junior Felix .02 .10
78 Greg W. Harris .02 .10
79 Dick Schofield .02 .10
80 Cecil Fielder .07 .20
81 Lloyd McClendon .02 .10
82 David Segui .02 .10
83 Reggie Sanders .07 .20
84 Kurt Stillwell .02 .10
85 Sandy Alomar Jr. .02 .10
86 John Habyan .02 .10
87 Kevin Reimer .02 .10
88 Mike Stanton .02 .10
89 Eric Anthony .02 .10
90 Scott Erickson .02 .10
91 Craig Colbert .02 .10
92 Tom Pagnozzi .02 .10
93 Pedro Astacio .02 .10
94 Lance Johnson .02 .10
95 Larry Walker .07 .20
96 Russ Swan .02 .10
97 Scott Fletcher .02 .10
98 Derek Jeter RC 15.00 40.00
99 Mike Williams .02 .10
100 Mark McGwire .50 1.25
101 Jim Bullinger .02 .10
102 Brian Hunter .02 .10
103 Jody Reed .02 .10
104 Mike Butcher .02 .10
105 Gregg Jefferies .02 .10
106 Howard Johnson .02 .10
107 John Kiely .02 .10
108 Jose Lind .02 .10
109 Sam Horn .02 .10
110 Barry Larkin .10 .30
111 Bruce Hurst .02 .10
112 Brian Barnes .02 .10
113 Thomas Howard .02 .10
114 Mel Hall .02 .10
115 Robby Thompson .02 .10
116 Mark Lemke .02 .10
117 Eddie Taubensee .02 .10
118 David Hulse RC .02 .10
119 Pedro Munoz .02 .10
120 Ramon Martinez .02 .10
121 Todd Worrell .02 .10
122 Joey Cora .02 .10
123 Moises Alou .07 .20
124 Franklin Stubbs .02 .10
125 Pete O'Brien .02 .10
126 Bob Ayrault .02 .10
127 Carney Lansford .07 .20
128 Kal Daniels .02 .10
129 Joe Grahe .02 .10
130 Jeff Montgomery .02 .10
131 Dave Winfield .07 .20
132 Preston Wilson RC .30 .75
133 Steve Wilson .02 .10
134 Lee Guetterman .02 .10
135 Mickey Tettleton .02 .10
136 Jeff King .02 .10
137 Alan Mills .02 .10
138 Joe Oliver .02 .10
139 Gary Gaetti .07 .20
140 Gary Sheffield .07 .20
141 Dennis Cook .02 .10
142 Charlie Hayes .02 .10
143 Jeff Huson .02 .10
144 Kent Mercker .02 .10
145 Eric Young .02 .10
146 Scott Leius .02 .10
147 Bryan Hickerson .02 .10
148 Steve Finley .07 .20
149 Rheal Cormier .02 .10
150 Frank Thomas UER .20 .50
Categories leading/league are italicized/but not printed in red
151 Archi Cianfrocco .02 .10
152 Rich DeLucia .02 .10
153 Greg Vaughn .02 .10
154 Wes Chamberlain .02 .10
155 Dennis Eckersley .07 .20
156 Sammy Sosa .20 .50
157 Gary DiSarcina .02 .10
158 Kevin Koslofski .02 .10
159 Doug Linton .02 .10
160 Lou Whitaker .07 .20
161 Chad McConnell .02 .10
162 Joe Hesketh .02 .10
163 Tim Wakefield .20 .50
164 Leo Gomez .02 .10
165 Jose Rijo .02 .10
166 Tim Scott .02 .10
167 Steve Olin UER .02 .10
Born 10/4/65/should say 10/10/65
168 Kevin Maas .02 .10
169 Kenny Rogers .07 .20
170 David Justice .07 .20
171 Doug Jones .02 .10
172 Jeff Reboulet .02 .10
173 Andres Galarraga .07 .20
174 Randy Velarde .02 .10
175 Kirk McCaskill .02 .10
176 Darren Lewis .02 .10
177 Lenny Harris .02 .10
178 Jeff Fassero .02 .10
179 Ken Griffey Jr. .40 1.00
180 Darren Daulton .07 .20
181 John Jaha .02 .10
182 Ron Darling .02 .10
183 Greg Maddux .30 .75
184 Damion Easley .02 .10
185 Jack Morris .07 .20
186 Mike Magnante .02 .10
187 John Dopson .02 .10
188 Sid Fernandez .02 .10
189 Tony Phillips .02 .10
190 Doug Drabek .02 .10
191 Sean Lowe RC .02 .10
192 Bob Milacki .02 .10
193 Steve Foster .02 .10
194 Jerald Clark .02 .10
195 Pete Harnisch .02 .10
196 Pat Kelly .02 .10
197 Jeff Frye .02 .10
198 Alejandro Pena .02 .10
199 Junior Ortiz .02 .10
200 Kirby Puckett .20 .50
201 Jose Uribe .02 .10
202 Mike Scioscia .02 .10
203 Bernard Gilkey .02 .10
204 Dan Pasqua .02 .10
205 Gary Carter .07 .20
206 Henry Cotto .02 .10
207 Paul Molitor .07 .20
208 Mike Hartley .02 .10
209 Jeff Parrett .02 .10
210 Mark Langston .02 .10
211 Doug Dascenzo .02 .10
212 Rick Reed .02 .10
213 Candy Maldonado .02 .10
214 Danny Darwin .02 .10
215 Pat Howell .02 .10
216 Mark Leiter .02 .10
217 Kevin Mitchell .02 .10
218 Ben McDonald .02 .10
219 Bip Roberts .02 .10
220 Benny Santiago .07 .20
221 Carlos Baerga .02 .10
222 Bernie Williams .10 .30
223 Roger Pavlik .02 .10
224 Sid Bream .02 .10
225 Matt Williams .07 .20
226 Willie Banks .02 .10
227 Jeff Bagwell .10 .30
228 Tom Goodwin .02 .10
229 Mike Perez .02 .10
230 Carlton Fisk .10 .30
231 John Wetteland .07 .20
232 Tino Martinez .10 .30
233 Rick Greene .02 .10
234 Tim McIntosh .02 .10
235 Mitch Williams .02 .10
236 Kevin Campbell .02 .10
237 Jose Vizcaino .02 .10
238 Chris Donnels .02 .10
239 Mike Boddicker .02 .10
240 John Olerud .07 .20
241 Mike Gardiner .02 .10
242 Charlie O'Brien .02 .10
243 Rob Deer .02 .10
244 Denny Neagle .07 .20
245 Chris Sabo .02 .10
246 Gregg Olson .02 .10
247 Frank Seminara UER .02 .10
Acquired 12/3/98
248 Scott Scudder .02 .10
249 Tim Burke .02 .10
250 Chuck Knoblauch .07 .20
251 Mike Bielecki .02 .10
252 Xavier Hernandez .02 .10
253 Jose Guzman .02 .10
254 Cory Snyder .02 .10
255 Orel Hershiser .07 .20
256 Wil Cordero .02 .10
257 Luis Alicea .02 .10
258 Mike Schooler .02 .10
259 Craig Grebeck .02 .10
260 Duane Ward .02 .10
261 Bill Wegman .02 .10
262 Mickey Morandini .02 .10
263 Vince Horsman .02 .10
264 Paul Sorrento .02 .10
265 Andre Dawson .07 .20
266 Rene Gonzales .02 .10
267 Keith Miller .02 .10
268 Derek Bell .02 .10
269 Todd Steverson RC .02 .10
270 Frank Viola .07 .20
271 Wally Whitehurst .02 .10
272 Kurt Knudsen .02 .10
273 Dan Walters .02 .10
274 Rick Sutcliffe .07 .20
275 Andy Van Slyke .10 .30
276 Paul O'Neill .10 .30
277 Mark Whiten .02 .10
278 Chris Nabholz .02 .10
279 Todd Burns .02 .10
280 Tom Glavine .10 .30
281 Butch Henry .02 .10
282 Shane Mack .02 .10
283 Mike Jackson .02 .10
284 Henry Rodriguez .02 .10
285 Bob Tewksbury .02 .10
286 Ron Karkovice .02 .10
287 Mike Gallego .02 .10
288 Dave Cochrane .02 .10
289 Jesse Orosco .02 .10
290 Dave Stewart .07 .20
291 Tommy Greene .02 .10
292 Rey Sanchez .02 .10
293 Rob Ducey .02 .10
294 Brent Mayne .02 .10
295 Dave Stieb .02 .10
296 Luis Rivera .02 .10
297 Jeff Innis .02 .10
298 Scott Livingstone .02 .10
299 Bob Patterson .02 .10
300 Cal Ripken .60 1.50
301 Cesar Hernandez .02 .10
302 Randy Myers .02 .10
303 Brook Jacoby .02 .10
304 Melido Perez .02 .10
305 Rafael Palmeiro .10 .30
306 Damon Berryhill .02 .10

307 Dan Serafini RC .02 .10
308 Darryl Kile .07 .20
309 J.T. Bruett .02 .10
310 Dave Righetti .07 .20
311 Jay Howell .02 .10
312 Geronimo Pena .02 .10
313 Greg Hibbard .02 .10
314 Mark Gardner .02 .10
315 Edgar Martinez .10 .30
316 Dave Nilsson .02 .10
317 Kyle Abbott .02 .10
318 Willie Wilson .02 .10
319 Paul Assenmacher .02 .10
320 Tim Fortugno .02 .10
321 Rusty Meacham .02 .10
322 Pat Borders .02 .10
323 Mike Greenwell .02 .10
324 Willie Randolph .07 .20
325 Bill Gullickson .02 .10
326 Gary Varsho .02 .10
327 Tim Hulett .02 .10
328 Scott Ruskin .02 .10
329 Mike Maddux .02 .10
330 Danny Tartabull .02 .10
331 Kenny Lofton .07 .20
332 Geno Petralli .02 .10
333 Otis Nixon .02 .10
334 Jason Kendall RC .40 1.00
335 Mark Portugal .02 .10
336 Mike Pagliarulo .02 .10
337 Kirt Manwaring .02 .10
338 Bob Ojeda .02 .10
339 Mark Clark .02 .10
340 John Kruk .07 .20
341 Mel Rojas .02 .10
342 Erik Hanson .02 .10
343 Doug Henry .02 .10
344 Jack McDowell .02 .10
345 Harold Baines .07 .20
346 Chuck McElroy .02 .10
347 Luis Sojo .02 .10
348 Andy Stankiewicz .02 .10
349 Hipolito Pichardo .02 .10
350 Joe Carter .07 .20
351 Ellis Burks .07 .20
352 Pete Schourek .02 .10
353 Buddy Groom .02 .10
354 Jay Bell .07 .20
355 Brady Anderson .07 .20
356 Freddie Benavides .02 .10
357 Phil Stephenson .02 .10
358 Kevin Wickander .02 .10
359 Mike Stanley .02 .10
360 Ivan Rodriguez .10 .30
361 Scott Bankhead .02 .10
362 Luis Gonzalez .07 .20
363 John Smiley .02 .10
364 Trevor Wilson .02 .10
365 Tom Candiotti .02 .10
366 Craig Wilson .02 .10
367 Steve Sax .02 .10
368 Delino DeShields .02 .10
369 Jaime Navarro .02 .10
370 Dave Valle .02 .10
371 Mariano Duncan .02 .10
372 Rod Nichols .02 .10
373 Mike Morgan .02 .10
374 Julio Valera .02 .10
375 Wally Joyner .07 .20
376 Tom Henke .02 .10
377 Herm Winningham .02 .10
378 Orlando Merced .02 .10
379 Mike Munoz .02 .10
380 Todd Hundley .02 .10
381 Mike Flanagan .02 .10
382 Tim Belcher .02 .10
383 Jerry Browne .02 .10
384 Mike Benjamin .02 .10
385 Jim Leyritz .02 .10
386 Ray Lankford .07 .20
387 Devon White .07 .20
388 Jeremy Hernandez .02 .10
389 Brian Harper .02 .10
390 Wade Boggs .10 .30
391 Derrick May .02 .10
392 Travis Fryman .07 .20
393 Ron Gant .07 .20
394 Checklist 1-132 .02 .10
395 CL 133-264 UER .02 .10
Eckersley
396 Checklist 265-396 .02 .10
397 George Brett .50 1.25
398 Bobby Witt .02 .10
399 Daryl Boston .02 .10
400 Bo Jackson .20 .50
401 Fred McGriff .10 .30
Frank Thomas AS
402 Ryne Sandberg .20 .50
Carlos Baerga AS
403 Gary Sheffield .07 .20
Edgar Martinez AS
404 Barry Larkin .07 .20
Travis Fryman AS
405 Andy Van Slyke .25 .60
Ken Griffey Jr. AS
406 Larry Walker .10 .30
Kirby Puckett AS
407 Barry Bonds .30 .75
Joe Carter AS
408 Darren Daulton .07 .20
Brian Harper AS
409 Greg Maddux .20 .50
Roger Clemens AS
410 Tom Glavine .07 .20
Dave Fleming AS
411 Lee Smith .07 .20
Dennis Eckersley AS
412 Jamie McAndrew .02 .10
413 Pete Smith .02 .10
414 Juan Guerrero .02 .10
415 Todd Frohwirth .02 .10
416 Randy Tomlin .02 .10
417 B.J. Surhoff .07 .20
418 Jim Gott .02 .10
419 Mark Thompson RC .02 .10
420 Kevin Tapani .02 .10
421 Curt Schilling .07 .20
422 J.T. Snow RC .20 .50
423 Ryan Klesko .07 .20
424 John Valentin .02 .10
425 Joe Girardi .02 .10
426 Nigel Wilson .02 .10
427 Bob MacDonald .02 .10
428 Todd Zeile .02 .10
429 Milt Cuyler .02 .10
430 Eddie Murray .20 .50
431 Rich Amaral .02 .10
432 Pete Young .02 .10
433 Tom Schmidt RC .02 .10
434 Jack Armstrong .02 .10
435 Willie McGee .07 .20
436 Greg W. Harris .02 .10
437 Chris Hammond .02 .10
438 Ritchie Moody RC .02 .10
439 Bryan Harvey .02 .10
440 Ruben Sierra .07 .20
441 Don Lemon .02 .10
Todd Pridy RC
442 Kevin McReynolds .02 .10
443 Terry Leach .02 .10
444 David Nied .02 .10
445 Dale Murphy .10 .30
446 Luis Mercedes .02 .10
447 Keith Shepherd RC .02 .10
448 Ken Caminiti .07 .20
449 Jim Austin .02 .10
450 Darryl Strawberry .07 .20
451 Quinton McCracken RC .08 .25
452 Bob Wickman .02 .10
453 Victor Cole .02 .10
454 John Johnstone RC .02 .10
455 Chili Davis .07 .20
456 Scott Taylor .02 .10
457 Tracy Woodson .02 .10
458 David Wells .07 .20
459 Derek Wallace RC .02 .10
460 Randy Johnson .20 .50
461 Steve Reed RC .02 .10
462 Felix Fermin .02 .10
463 Scott Aldred .02 .10
464 Greg Colbrunn .02 .10
465 Tony Fernandez .02 .10
466 Mike Felder .02 .10
467 Lee Stevens .02 .10
468 Matt Whiteside RC .02 .10
469 Dave Hansen .02 .10
470 Rob Dibble .07 .20
471 Dave Gallagher .02 .10
472 Chris Gwynn .02 .10
473 Dave Henderson .02 .10
474 Ozzie Guillen .07 .20
475 Jeff Reardon .07 .20
476 Will Scalzitti RC .02 .10
477 Jimmy Jones .02 .10
478 Greg Cadaret .02 .10
479 Todd Pratt RC .02 .10
480 Pat Listach .02 .10
481 Ryan Luzinski RC .02 .10
482 Darren Reed .02 .10
483 Brian Griffiths RC .02 .10
484 John Wehner .02 .10
485 Glenn Davis .02 .10
486 Eric Wedge RC .02 .10
487 Jesse Hollins .02 .10
488 Manuel Lee .02 .10
489 Scott Fredrickson RC .02 .10
490 Omar Olivares .02 .10
491 Shawn Hare .02 .10
492 Tom Lampkin .02 .10
493 Jeff Nelson .02 .10
494 L.Lucca RC/E.Perez .02 .10
495 Ken Hill .02 .10
496 Reggie Jefferson .02 .10
497 Willie Brown RC .02 .10
498 Bud Black .02 .10
499 Chuck Crim .02 .10
500 Jose Canseco .10 .30
501 Johnny Oates MG .07 .20
Bobby Cox MG
502 Butch Hobson MG .02 .10
Jim Lefebvre MG
503 Buck Rodgers MG .07 .20
Tony Perez MG
504 Gene Lamont MG .07 .20
Don Baylor MG
505 Mike Hargrove MG .07 .20
Rene Lachemann MG
506 Sparky Anderson MG .07 .20
Art Howe MG
507 Hal McRae MG .07 .20
Tom Lasorda MG
508 Phil Garner MG .07 .20
Felipe Alou MG
509 Tom Kelly MG .02 .10
Jeff Torborg MG
510 Buck Showalter MG .07 .20
Jim Fregosi MG
511 Tony LaRussa MG .07 .20
Jim Leyland MG
512 Lou Piniella MG .07 .20
Joe Torre MG
513 Kevin Kennedy MG .02 .10
Jim Riggleman MG
514 Cito Gaston MG .07 .20
Dusty Baker MG
515 Greg Swindell .02 .10
516 Alex Arias .02 .10
517 Bill Pecota .02 .10
518 Benji Grigsby RC .02 .10
519 David Howard .02 .10
520 Charlie Hough .07 .20
521 Kevin Flora .02 .10
522 Shane Reynolds .02 .10
523 Doug Bochtler RC .02 .10
524 Chris Hoiles .02 .10
525 Scott Sanderson .02 .10
526 Mike Sharperson .02 .10
527 Mike Fetters .02 .10
528 Paul Quantrill .02 .10
529 Chipper Jones .20 .50
530 Sterling Hitchcock RC .08 .25
531 Joe Millette .02 .10
532 Tom Brunansky .02 .10
533 Frank Castillo .02 .10
534 Randy Knorr .02 .10
535 Jose Oquendo .02 .10
536 Dave Haas .02 .10
537 Jason Hutchins RC .02 .10
538 Jimmy Baron RC .02 .10
539 Kerry Woodson .02 .10
540 Ivan Calderon .02 .10
541 Denis Boucher .02 .10
542 Royce Clayton .02 .10
543 Reggie Williams .02 .10
544 Steve Decker .02 .10
545 Dean Palmer .07 .20
546 Hal Morris .02 .10
547 Ryan Thompson .02 .10
548 Lance Blankenship .02 .10
549 Hensley Meulens .02 .10
550 Scott Radinsky .02 .10
551 Eric Young .02 .10
552 Jeff Blauser .02 .10
553 Andujar Cedeno .02 .10
554 Arthur Rhodes .02 .10
555 Terry Mulholland .02 .10
556 Darryl Hamilton .02 .10
557 Pedro Martinez .40 1.00
558 Ryan Whitman RC .02 .10
559 Jamie Arnold RC .02 .10
560 Zane Smith .02 .10
561 Matt Nokes .02 .10
562 Bob Zupcic .02 .10
563 Shawn Boskie .02 .10
564 Mike Timlin .02 .10
565 Jerald Clark .02 .10
566 Rod Brewer .02 .10
567 Mark Carreon .02 .10
568 Andy Benes .02 .10
569 Shawn Barton RC .02 .10
570 Tim Wallach .02 .10
571 Dave Mlicki .02 .10
572 Trevor Hoffman .20 .50
573 John Patterson .02 .10
574 De Shawn Warren RC .02 .10
575 Monty Fariss .02 .10
576 Cliff Floyd .07 .20
577 Tim Costo .02 .10
578 Dave Magadan .02 .10
579 Jason Bates RC .02 .10
580 Walt Weiss .02 .10
581 Chris Haney .02 .10
582 Shawn Abner .02 .10
583 Marvin Freeman .02 .10
584 Casey Candaele .02 .10
585 Ricky Jordan .02 .10
586 Jeff Tabaka RC .02 .10
587 Manny Alexander .02 .10
588 Mike Trombley .02 .10
589 Carlos Hernandez .02 .10
590 Cal Eldred .02 .10
591 Alex Cole .02 .10
592 Phil Plantier .02 .10
593 Brett Merriman RC .02 .10
594 Jerry Nielsen .02 .10
595 Shawon Dunston .02 .10
596 Jimmy Key .07 .20
597 Gerald Perry .02 .10
598 Rico Brogna .02 .10
599 Clemente Nunez .02 .10
600 Bret Saberhagen .07 .20
601 Craig Shipley .02 .10
602 Henry Mercedes .02 .10
603 Jim Thome .10 .30
604 Rod Beck .02 .10
605 Chuck Finley .07 .20
606 Jayhawk Owens RC .02 .10
607 Dan Smith .02 .10
608 Bill Doran .02 .10
609 Lance Parrish .07 .20
610 Dennis Martinez .07 .20
611 Tom Gordon .02 .10
612 Byron Mathews RC .02 .10
613 Joel Adamson RC .02 .10
614 Brian Williams .02 .10
615 Steve Avery .02 .10
616 Midre Cummings RC .02 .10
617 Craig Lefferts .02 .10
618 Tony Pena .02 .10
619 Billy Spiers .02 .10
620 Todd Benzinger .02 .10
621 Greg Boyd RC .02 .10
622 Ben Rivera .02 .10
623 Al Martin .02 .10
624 Sam Militello UER .02 .10
Profile says drafted/in 1988, bio says/drafted in 1990
625 Rick Aguilera .02 .10
626 Dan Gladden .02 .10
627 Andres Berumen RC .02 .10
628 Kelly Gruber .02 .10
629 Cris Carpenter .02 .10
630 Mark Grace .10 .30
631 Jeff Brantley .02 .10
632 Chris Widger RC .08 .25
633 Three Russians .02 .10
634 Mo Sanford .02 .10
635 Albert Belle .07 .20
636 Tim Teufel .02 .10
637 Greg Myers .02 .10
638 Brian Bohanon .02 .10
639 Mike Bordick .02 .10
640 Dwight Gooden .07 .20
641 P.Leahy/G.Baugh RC .02 .10
642 Milt Hill .02 .10
643 Luis Aquino .02 .10
644 Dante Bichette .07 .20
645 Bobby Thigpen .02 .10
646 Rich Scheid RC .02 .10
647 Brian Sackinsky RC .02 .10
648 Ryan Hawblitzel .02 .10
649 Tom Marsh .02 .10
650 Terry Pendleton .07 .20
651 Rafael Bournigal .02 .10
652 Dave West .02 .10
653 Steve Hosey .02 .10
654 Gerald Williams .02 .10
655 Scott Cooper .02 .10
656 Gary Scott .02 .10
657 Mike Harkey .02 .10
658 J.Burnitz/S.Walker RC .07 .20
659 Ed Sprague .02 .10
660 Alan Trammell .07 .20
661 Garvin Alston RC .02 .10
662 Donovan Osborne .02 .10
663 Jeff Gardner .02 .10
664 Calvin Jones .02 .10
665 Darrin Fletcher .02 .10
666 Glenallen Hill .02 .10
667 Jim Rosenbohm RC .02 .10
668 Scott Lewis .02 .10
669 Kip Yaughn RC .02 .10
670 Julio Franco .07 .20
671 Dave Martinez .02 .10
672 Kevin Bass .02 .10
673 Todd Van Poppel .02 .10
674 Mark Gubicza .02 .10
675 Tim Raines .07 .20
676 Rudy Seanez .02 .10
677 Charlie Leibrandt .02 .10
678 Randy Milligan .02 .10
679 Kim Batiste .02 .10
680 Craig Biggio .10 .30
681 Darren Holmes .02 .10
682 John Candelaria .02 .10
683 Eddie Christian RC .02 .10
684 Pat Mahomes .02 .10
685 Bob Walk .02 .10
686 Russ Springer .02 .10
687 Tony Sheffield RC .02 .10
688 Dwight Smith .02 .10
689 Eddie Zosky .02 .10
690 Bien Figueroa .02 .10
691 Jim Tatum RC .02 .10
692 Chad Kreuter .02 .10
693 Rich Rodriguez .02 .10
694 Shane Turner .02 .10
695 Kent Bottenfield .02 .10
696 Jose Mesa .02 .10
697 Darrell Whitmore RC .02 .10
698 Ted Wood .02 .10
699 Chad Curtis .02 .10
700 Nolan Ryan .75 2.00
701 M.Piazza/C.Delgado 1.50 4.00
702 Tim Pugh RC .02 .10
703 Jeff Kent .20 .50
704 J.Goodrich/D.Figueroa RC .02 .10
705 Bob Welch .02 .10
706 Sherard Clinkscales RC .02 .10
707 Donn Pall .02 .10
708 Greg Olson .02 .10
709 Jeff Juden .02 .10
710 Mike Mussina .10 .30
711 Scott Chiamparino .02 .10
712 Stan Javier .02 .10
713 John Doherty .02 .10
714 Kevin Gross .02 .10
715 Greg Gagne .02 .10
716 Steve Cooke .02 .10
717 Steve Farr .02 .10
718 Jay Buhner .07 .20
719 Butch Henry .02 .10
720 David Cone .07 .20
721 Rick Wilkins .02 .10
722 Chuck Carr .02 .10
723 Kenny Felder RC .02 .10
724 Guillermo Velasquez .02 .10
725 Billy Hatcher .02 .10
726 Mike Veneziale RC .02 .10
727 Jonathan Hurst .02 .10
728 Steve Frey .02 .10
729 Mark Leonard .02 .10
730 Charles Nagy .02 .10
731 Donald Harris .02 .10
732 Travis Buckley RC .02 .10
733 Tom Browning .02 .10
734 Anthony Young .02 .10
735 Steve Shifflett .02 .10
736 Jeff Russell .02 .10
737 Wilson Alvarez .02 .10
738 Lance Painter RC .02 .10
739 Dave Weathers .02 .10
740 Len Dykstra .07 .20
741 Mike Devereaux .02 .10
742 R.Arocha RC/A.Embree .08 .25
743 Dave Landaker RC .02 .10
744 Chris George .02 .10
745 Eric Davis .07 .20
746 Lamar Rogers RC .02 .10
747 Carl Willis .02 .10
748 Stan Belinda .02 .10
749 Scott Kamieniecki .02 .10
750 Rickey Henderson .20 .50
751 Eric Hillman .02 .10
752 Pat Hentgen .02 .10
753 Jim Corsi .02 .10
754 Brian Jordan .07 .20
755 Bill Swift .02 .10
756 Mike Henneman .02 .10
757 Harold Reynolds .07 .20
758 Sean Berry .02 .10
759 Charlie Hayes .02 .10
760 Luis Polonia .02 .10
761 Darrin Jackson .02 .10
762 Mark Lewis .02 .10
763 Rob Maurer .02 .10
764 Willie Greene .02 .10
765 Vince Coleman .02 .10
766 Todd Revenig .02 .10
767 Rich Ireland RC .02 .10
768 Mike Macfarlane .02 .10
769 Francisco Cabrera .02 .10
770 Robin Ventura .07 .20
771 Kevin Ritz .02 .10
772 Chito Martinez .02 .10
773 Cliff Brantley .02 .10
774 Curt Leskanic RC .08 .25
775 Chris Bosio .02 .10
776 Jose Offerman .02 .10
777 Mark Guthrie .02 .10
778 Don Slaught .02 .10
779 Rich Monteleone .02 .10
780 Jim Abbott .10 .30
781 Jack Clark .07 .20
782 R.Mendoza/D.Roman RC .02 .10
783 Heathcliff Slocumb .02 .10
784 Jeff Branson .02 .10
785 Kevin Brown .07 .20
786 K.Ryan/Gandarillas RC .07 .20
787 Mike Matthews RC .07 .20
788 Mackey Sasser .02 .10
789 Jeff Conine UER .07 .20
No inclusion of 1990/RBI stats in career total
790 George Bell .02 .10
791 Pat Rapp .02 .10
792 Joe Boever .02 .10
793 Jim Poole .02 .10
794 Andy Ashby .02 .10
795 Deion Sanders .10 .30
796 Scott Brosius .07 .20
797 Brad Pennington .02 .10
798 Greg Blosser .02 .10
799 Jim Edmonds RC .75 2.00
800 Shawn Jeter .02 .10
801 Jesse Levis .02 .10
802 Phil Clark UER .02 .10
Word a is missing in/sentence beginning/with In 1992...
803 Ed Pierce RC .02 .10
804 Jose Valentin RC .08 .25
805 Terry Jorgensen .02 .10
806 Mark Hutton .02 .10
807 Troy Neel .02 .10
808 Bret Boone .07 .20
809 Cris Colon .02 .10
810 Domingo Martinez RC .02 .10
811 Javier Lopez .10 .30
812 Matt Walbeck RC .02 .10
813 Dan Wilson .07 .20
814 Scooter Tucker .02 .10
815 Billy Ashley .02 .10
816 Tim Laker RC .02 .10
817 Bobby Jones .07 .20
818 Brad Brink .02 .10
819 William Pennyfeather .02 .10
820 Stan Royer .02 .10
821 Doug Brocail .02 .10
822 Kevin Rogers .02 .10
823 Checklist 397-540 .02 .10
824 Checklist 541-691 .02 .10
825 Checklist 692-825 .02 .10

1993 Topps Gold

*STARS: 1X TO 2.5X BASIC CARDS
*ROOKIES: 1.25X TO 3X BASIC CARDS
GOLD CARDS 1 PER WAX PACK
GOLD CARDS 3 PER RACK PACK
GOLD CARDS 5 PER JUMBO PACK
GOLD CARDS 10 PER FACTORY SET
98 Derek Jeter 60.00 150.00
394 Bernardo Brito .08 .25
395 Jim McNamara .08 .25
396 Rich Sauveur .08 .25
823 Keith Brown .08 .25
824 Russ McGinnis .08 .25
825 Mike Walker UER .08 .25

1993 Topps Inaugural Marlins

COMP.FACT.SET (825) 75.00 150.00
*STARS: 2.5X TO 6X BASIC CARDS
*ROOKIES: 2.5X TO 6X BASIC CARDS
DISTRIBUTED IN FACTORY SET FORM ONLY
NO MORE THAN 10,000 SETS PRODUCED

1993 Topps Inaugural Rockies

COMP.FACT.SET (825) 75.00 150.00
*STARS: 2.5X TO 6X BASIC CARDS
*ROOKIES: 2.5X TO 6X BASIC CARDS
DISTRIBUTED IN FACTORY SET FORM ONLY
NO MORE THAN 10,000 SETS PRODUCED

1993 Topps Micro

COMPLETE SET (825) 15.00 40.00
COMMON PRISM INSERT .04 .10
*MICRO: .25X TO .6X BASIC CARDS
98 Derek Jeter 20.00 50.00
P1 Robin Yount .20 .50
P20 Tim Salmon .15 .40
P32 Don Mattingly .50 1.25
P50 Roberto Alomar .15 .40
P150 Frank Thomas .40 1.00
P155 Dennis Eckersley .07 .20
P179 Ken Griffey Jr. 1.25 3.00
P200 Kirby Puckett .40 1.00
P397 George Brett .40 1.00
P426 Nigel Wilson .02 .10
P444 David Nied .02 .10
P700 Nolan Ryan 1.00 2.50

1993 Topps Black Gold

COMPLETE SET (44) 6.00 15.00
COMP.SERIES 1 (22) 2.50 6.00
COMP.SERIES 2 (22) 4.00 10.00
STATED ODDS 1:72 H/R, 1:12 J, 1:24 RACK
STATED ODDS 1:35 34CT JUM, 1:37 18CT JUM
THREE PER FACTORY SET
1 Barry Bonds 1.00 2.50
2 Will Clark .20 .50
3 Darren Daulton .10 .30
4 Andre Dawson .10 .30
5 Delino DeShields .05 .15
6 Tom Glavine .20 .50
7 Marquis Grissom .10 .30
8 Tony Gwynn .40 1.00
9 Eric Karros .10 .30
10 Ray Lankford .10 .30
11 Barry Larkin .20 .50
12 Greg Maddux .50 1.25
13 Fred McGriff .20 .50
14 Joe Oliver .05 .15
15 Terry Pendleton .10 .30
16 Bip Roberts .05 .15
17 Ryne Sandberg .50 1.25
18 Gary Sheffield .10 .30
19 Lee Smith .10 .30
20 Ozzie Smith .50 1.25
21 Andy Van Slyke .20 .50
22 Larry Walker .10 .30
23 Roberto Alomar .20 .50
24 Brady Anderson .10 .30
25 Carlos Baerga .05 .15
26 Joe Carter .10 .30
27 Roger Clemens .60 1.50
28 Mike Devereaux .05 .15
29 Dennis Eckersley .10 .30
30 Cecil Fielder .10 .30
31 Travis Fryman .10 .30
32 Juan Gonzalez .10 .30
33 Ken Griffey Jr. .60 1.50
34 Brian Harper .05 .15
35 Pat Listach .05 .15
36 Kenny Lofton .10 .30
37 Edgar Martinez .20 .50
38 Jack McDowell .05 .15
39 Mark McGwire .75 2.00
40 Kirby Puckett .30 .75
41 Mickey Tettleton .05 .15
42 Frank Thomas .30 .75
43 Robin Ventura .10 .30
44 Dave Winfield .10 .30
A1 Winner A 1-11 EXCH 2.50 6.00
A2 Winner A 1-11 Prize .60 1.50
B1 Winner B 12-22 EXCH 2.50 6.00
B2 Winner B 12-22 Prize .60 1.50
C1 Winner C 23-33 EXCH 2.50 6.00
UER Cards 1-11 Pictured
C2 Winner C 23-33 Prize .60 1.50
D1 Winner D 34-44 EXCH 2.50 6.00
UER Cards 12-22 Pictured
D2 Winner D 34-44 Prize .60 1.50
AB1 Winner AB 1-22 EXCH 3.00 8.00
AB2 Winner AB 1-22 Prize .75 2.00
CD1 Winner CD 23-44 EXCH 3.00 8.00
CD2 Winner CD 23-44 Prize .75 2.00
ABCD1 Winner ABCD 1-44 EXCH 8.00 20.00
ABCD2 Winner ABCD 1-44 Prize 2.00 5.00

1993 Topps Traded

This 132-card standard-size set focuses on promising rookies, new managers, free agents, and players who changed teams. The set also includes 22 members of Team USA. The set has the same design on the front as the regular 1993 Topps issue. The backs are also the same design and carry a head shot, biography, stats, and career highlights. Rookie Cards in this set include Todd Helton.

COMP.FACT.SET (132) 10.00 25.00
1T Barry Bonds .60 1.50
2T Rich Renteria .02 .10
3T Aaron Sele .02 .10
4T Carlton Loewer USA RC .08 .25
5T Erik Pappas .02 .10
6T Greg McMichael RC .08 .25
7T Freddie Benavides .02 .10
8T Kirk Gibson .07 .20
9T Tony Fernandez .02 .10
10T Jay Gainer RC .08 .25
11T Orestes Destrade .02 .10
12T A.J. Hinch USA RC .20 .50
13T Bobby Munoz .02 .10
14T Tom Henke .02 .10
15T Rob Butler .02 .10
16T Gary Wayne .02 .10
17T David McCarty .02 .10
18T Walt Weiss .02 .10
19T Todd Helton USA RC 2.50 6.00
20T Mark Whiten .02 .10
21T Ricky Gutierrez .02 .10
22T Dustin Hermanson USA RC .40 1.00
23T Sherman Obando RC .08 .25
24T Mike Piazza 1.25 3.00
25T Jeff Russell .02 .10
26T Jason Bere .02 .10
27T Jack Voigt RC .08 .25
28T Chris Bosio .02 .10
29T Phil Hiatt .02 .10
30T Matt Beaumont USA RC .08 .25
31T Andres Galarraga .07 .20
32T Greg Swindell .02 .10
33T Vinny Castilla .20 .50
34T Pat Clougherty RC USA .08 .25
35T Greg Briley .02 .10
36T Dallas Green MG .02 .10
Davey Johnson MG
37T Tyler Green .02 .10
38T Craig Paquette .02 .10
39T Danny Sheaffer RC .08 .25
40T Jim Converse RC .08 .25
41T Terry Harvey USA RC .08 .25
42T Phil Plantier .02 .10
43T Doug Saunders RC .08 .25
44T Benny Santiago .07 .20
45T Dante Powell USA RC .08 .25
46T Jeff Parrett .02 .10
47T Wade Boggs .10 .30
48T Paul Molitor .07 .20
49T Turk Wendell .02 .10
50T David Wells .07 .20
51T Gary Sheffield .07 .20
52T Kevin Young .07 .20
53T Nelson Liriano .02 .10
54T Greg Maddux .30 .75
55T Derek Bell .02 .10
56T Matt Turner RC .08 .25
57T Charlie Nelson USA RC .08 .25
58T Mike Hampton .07 .20
59T Troy O'Leary RC .20 .50
60T Benji Gil .02 .10
61T Mitch Lyden RC .08 .25
62T J.T.Snow .10 .30
63T Damon Buford .02 .10
64T Gene Harris .02 .10
65T Randy Myers .02 .10
66T Felix Jose .02 .10
67T Todd Dunn USA RC .08 .25
68T Jimmy Key .07 .20
69T Pedro Castellano .02 .10
70T Mark Merila USA RC .08 .25
71T Rich Rodriguez .02 .10
72T Matt Mieske .02 .10
73T Pete Incaviglia .02 .10
74T Carl Everett .07 .20
75T Jim Abbott .10 .30
76T Luis Aquino .02 .10
77T Rene Arocha .07 .20
78T Jon Shave .02 .10
79T Todd Walker USA RC .40 1.00
80T Jack Armstrong .02 .10
81T Jeff Richardson .02 .10
82T Blas Minor .02 .10
83T Dave Winfield .07 .20
84T Paul O'Neill .10 .30
85T Steve Reich USA RC .08 .25
86T Chris Hammond .02 .10
87T Hilly Hathaway RC .08 .25
88T Fred McGriff .10 .30
89T Dave Telgheder RC .08 .25
90T Richie Lewis RC .08 .25
91T Brent Gates .02 .10
92T Andre Dawson .07 .20
93T Andy Barkett USA RC .08 .25
94T Doug Drabek .02 .10
95T Joe Klink .02 .10
96T Willie Blair .02 .10
97T Danny Graves USA RC .20 .50
98T Pat Meares RC .20 .50
99T Mike Lansing RC .20 .50
100T Marcos Armas RC .08 .25
101T Darren Grass USA RC .08 .25
102T Chris Jones .02 .10
103T Ken Ryan RC .08 .25
104T Ellis Burks .07 .20
105T Roberto Kelly .02 .10
106T Dave Magadan .02 .10
107T Paul Wilson USA RC .20 .50
108T Rob Natal .02 .10
109T Paul Wagner .02 .10
110T Jeromy Burnitz .07 .20
111T Monty Fariss .02 .10
112T Kevin Mitchell .02 .10
113T Scott Pose RC .08 .25
114T Dave Stewart .07 .20
115T Russ Johnson USA RC .08 .25
116T Armando Reynoso .02 .10
117T Geronimo Berroa .02 .10
118T Woody Williams RC .40 1.00
119T Tim Bogar RC .08 .25
120T Bob Scafa USA RC .08 .25
121T Henry Cotto .02 .10
122T Gregg Jefferies .02 .10
123T Norm Charlton .02 .10
124T Bret Wagner USA RC .08 .25
125T David Cone .07 .20
126T Daryl Boston .02 .10
127T Tim Wallach .02 .10
128T Mike Martin USA RC .08 .25
129T John Cummings RC .08 .25
130T Ryan Bowen .02 .10
131T John Powell USA RC .08 .25
132T Checklist 1-132 .02 .10

1993 Topps Commanders of the Hill

This 30-card standard-size set issued by Topps features pitchers of the American and National Leagues. The cards were available for an additional 25 cents per pack with the purchase of a fountain coke at military installation snack bars and food courts only, through the PX/BX. Each pack contained five cards.

COMPLETE SET (30) 4.00 10.00
1 Dennis Eckersley .20 .50
2 Mike Mussina .20 .50
3 Roger Clemens .75 2.00
4 Jim Abbott .07 .20
5 Jack McDowell .02 .10
6 Charles Nagy .02 .10
7 Bill Gullickson .02 .10
8 Kevin Appier .02 .10
9 Bill Wegman .02 .10
10 John Smiley .02 .10
11 Melido Perez .02 .10
12 Dave Stewart .07 .20
13 Dave Fleming .02 .10
14 Kevin Brown .10 .30
15 Juan Guzman .02 .10
16 Randy Johnson .40 1.00
17 Greg Maddux 1.00 2.50
18 Tom Glavine .20 .50
19 Greg Maddux 1.00 2.50
20 Jose Rijo .02 .10
21 Pete Harnisch .02 .10
22 Tom Candiotti .02 .10
23 Denny Martinez .07 .20
24 Sid Fernandez .02 .10
25 Curt Schilling .30 .75
26 Doug Drabek .02 .10
27 Bob Tewksbury .02 .10
28 Andy Benes .02 .10
29 Bill Swift .02 .10
30 John Smoltz .15 .40

1993 Topps Full Shots

Issued as one-card inserts in retail re-packs containing a pack each of 1993 Topps Series I and II, and in specially marked jumbo boxes of 1993 Bowman, these 21 cards measure approximately 3 1/2" by 5" and feature on their fronts white-bordered color player action photos. In contrast to many of the oversized cards offered by other baseball card manufacturers, Full Shots were unique cards rather than enlarged versions of existing cards.

COMPLETE SET (21) 15.00 40.00
1 Frank Thomas .75 2.00
2 Ken Griffey Jr. 2.00 5.00
3 Barry Bonds 1.25 3.00
4 Juan Gonzalez .60 1.50
5 Roberto Alomar .60 1.50
6 Mike Piazza 2.00 5.00
7 Tony Gwynn 1.50 4.00
8 Jeff Bagwell .75 2.00
9 Tim Salmon .60 1.50
10 John Olerud .30 .75
11 Cal Ripken 3.00 8.00
12 David McCarty .20 .50
13 Darren Daulton .30 .75
14 Carlos Baerga .20 .50
15 Roger Clemens 1.50 4.00
16 John Kruk .30 .75
17 Barry Larkin .60 1.50
18 Gary Sheffield 1.00 2.50
19 Tom Glavine .75 2.00
20 Andres Galarraga .60 1.50
21 Fred McGriff .60 1.50

1993 Topps Magazine Jumbo Rookie Cards

This set was inserted in the last four issues of Topps Magazine. When removed from the magazine the cards measure 5" by 7". The players featured autographed 100 of these cards: 50 for subscriber copies and 50 for newstand issues. The cards are all reprinted version of

earlier Topps cards. The original Rookie Card year is noted after the player's name
COMPLETE SET (4) 2.00 5.00
1 Dennis Eckersley/1976 .20 .50
2 Dave Winfield/1974 .40 1.00
3 George Brett/1975 .60 1.50
4 Nolan Ryan/1968 1.25 3.00

1993 Topps Nikon House

This one-card set commemorates the opening day of the Celebrating Baseball photographic show at Nikon House Photo Gallery on April 13, 1993. The front features a photo of a baseball player batting inside a baseball park. The back displays information about the photo gallery and the Baseball photo show.
1 Batter in Major League Park 1.25 3.00

1993 Topps Postcards

This three-card set is a promotional issue produced by Topps and features a preview of the cards in the 1993 regular Topps set as well as Topps Stadium Club Series II and Series III. Each card displays three different card fronts from the same set. The backs have a postcard format. The cards are unnumbered.
COMPLETE SET (3) 4.00 10.00
1 Topps regular issue 1.50 4.00
Ryne Sandberg/Robin Ventura
2 Topps Stadium Club 1.25 3.00
Walt Weiss/Alex
3 Topps Stadium Club 1.25 3.00
Benny Santiago/Walt Weiss

1994 Topps Pre-Production

COMPLETE SET (9) 3.00 8.00
2 Barry Bonds .50 1.25
6 Jeff Tackett .08 .25
34 Juan Gonzalez .50 1.25
225 Matt Williams .30 .75
294 Carlos Quintana .08 .25
331 Kenny Lofton .20 .50
390 Wade Boggs .40 1.00
397 George Brett .60 1.50
700 Nolan Ryan 1.25 3.00
horizontal
700 Nolan Ryan 1.25 3.00
vertical

1994 Topps

These 792 standard-size cards were issued in two series of 396. Two types of factory sets were also issued. One features the 792 basic cards, ten Topps Gold, three Black Gold and three Finest Pre-Production cards for a total of 808. The other factory set (Bakers Dozen) includes the 792 basic cards, ten Topps Gold, three Black Gold, nine 1995 Topps Pre-Production cards and a sample pack of three special Topps cards for a total of 817. The standard cards feature glossy color player photos with white borders on the fronts. The player's name is in white cursive lettering at the bottom left, with the team name and player's position printed on a team color-coded bar. There is an inner multicolored border along the left side that extends obliquely across the bottom. The horizontal backs carry an action shot of the player with biography, statistics and highlights. Subsets include Draft Picks (201-210/739-762), All-Stars (384-394) and Stat Twins (601-609). Rookie Cards include Billy Wagner.
COMPLETE SET (792) 15.00 40.00
COMP.FACT.SET (808) 20.00 50.00
COMP.BAKER SET (817) 20.00 50.00
COMPLETE SERIES 1 (396) 8.00 20.00
COMPLETE SERIES 2 (396) 8.00 20.00
1 Mike Piazza .40 1.00
2 Bernie Williams .10 .30
3 Kevin Rogers .02 .10
4 Paul Carey .02 .10
5 Ozzie Guillen .07 .20
6 Derrick May .02 .10
7 Jose Mesa .02 .10
8 Todd Hundley .02 .10
9 Chris Haney .02 .10
10 John Olerud .07 .20
11 Andujar Cedeno .02 .10
12 John Smiley .02 .10
13 Phil Plantier .02 .10
14 Willie Banks .02 .10
15 Jay Bell .07 .20
16 Doug Henry .02 .10
17 Lance Blankenship .02 .10
18 Greg W. Harris .02 .10
19 Scott Livingstone .02 .10
20 Bryan Harvey .02 .10
21 Wil Cordero .02 .10
22 Roger Pavlik .02 .10
23 Mark Lemke .02 .10
24 Jeff Nelson .02 .10
25 Todd Zeile .02 .10
26 Billy Hatcher .02 .10
27 Joe Magrane .02 .10
28 Tony Longmire .02 .10
29 Omar Daal .02 .10
30 Kirt Manwaring .02 .10
31 Melido Perez .02 .10
32 Tim Hulett .02 .10
33 Jeff Schwarz .02 .10
34 Nolan Ryan .75 2.00
35 Jose Guzman .02 .10
36 Felix Fermin .02 .10
37 Jeff Innis .02 .10
38 Brett Mayne .02 .10
39 Huck Flener RC .02 .10
40 Jeff Bagwell .10 .30
41 Kevin Wickander .02 .10
42 Ricky Gutierrez .02 .10
43 Pat Mahomes .02 .10
44 Jeff King .02 .10
45 Cal Eldred .02 .10
46 Craig Paquette .02 .10
47 Richie Lewis .02 .10
48 Tony Phillips .02 .10
49 Armando Reynoso .02 .10
50 Moises Alou .07 .20
51 Manuel Lee .02 .10
52 Otis Nixon .02 .10
53 Billy Ashley .02 .10
54 Mark Whiten .02 .10
55 Jeff Russell .02 .10
56 Chad Curtis .02 .10
57 Kevin Stocker .02 .10
58 Mike Jackson .02 .10
59 Matt Nokes .02 .10
60 Chris Bosio .02 .10
61 Damon Buford .02 .10
62 Tim Belcher .02 .10
63 Glenallen Hill .02 .10
64 Bill Wertz .02 .10
65 Eddie Murray .20 .50
66 Tom Gordon .02 .10
67 Alex Gonzalez .02 .10
68 Eddie Taubensee .02 .10
69 Jacob Brumfield .02 .10
70 Andy Benes .02 .10
71 Rich Becker .02 .10
72 Steve Cooke .02 .10
73 Billy Spiers .02 .10
74 Scott Brosius .07 .20
75 Alan Trammell .07 .20
76 Luis Aquino .02 .10
77 Jerald Clark .02 .10
78 Mel Rojas .02 .10
79 Craig McClure RC .02 .10
80 Jose Canseco .10 .30
81 Greg McMichael .02 .10
82 Brian Turang RC .02 .10
83 Tom Urbani .02 .10
84 Garret Anderson .20 .50
85 Tony Pena .02 .10
86 Ricky Jordan .02 .10
87 Jim Gott .02 .10
88 Pat Kelly .02 .10
89 Bud Black .02 .10
90 Robin Ventura .07 .20
91 Rick Sutcliffe .07 .20
92 Jose Bautista .02 .10
93 Bob Ojeda .02 .10
94 Phil Hiatt .02 .10
95 Tim Pugh .02 .10
96 Randy Knorr .02 .10
97 Todd Jones .02 .10
98 Ryan Thompson .02 .10
99 Tim Mauser .02 .10
100 Kirby Puckett .20 .50
101 Mark Dewey .02 .10
102 B.J. Surhoff .07 .20
103 Sterling Hitchcock .02 .10
104 Alex Arias .02 .10
105 David Wells .07 .20
106 Daryl Boston .02 .10
107 Mike Stanton .02 .10
108 Gary Redus .02 .10
109 Delino DeShields .02 .10
110 Lee Smith .07 .20
111 Greg Litton .02 .10
112 Frankie Rodriguez .02 .10
113 Russ Springer .02 .10
114 Mitch Williams .02 .10
115 Eric Karros .07 .20
116 Jeff Brantley .02 .10
117 Jack Voigt .02 .10
118 Jason Bere .02 .10
119 Kevin Roberson .02 .10
120 Jimmy Key .07 .20
121 Reggie Jefferson .02 .10
122 Jeromy Burnitz .07 .20
123 Billy Brewer .02 .10
124 Willie Canate .02 .10
125 Greg Swindell .02 .10
126 Hal Morris .02 .10
127 Brad Ausmus .10 .30
128 George Tsamis .02 .10
129 Denny Neagle .07 .20
130 Pat Listach .02 .10
131 Steve Karsay .02 .10
132 Bret Barberie .02 .10
133 Mark Leiter .02 .10
134 Greg Colbrunn .02 .10
135 David Nied .02 .10
136 Dean Palmer .07 .20
137 Steve Avery .02 .10
138 Bill Haselman .02 .10
139 Tripp Cromer .02 .10
140 Frank Viola .07 .20
141 Rene Gonzales .02 .10
142 Curt Schilling .07 .20
143 Tim Wallach .02 .10
144 Bobby Munoz .02 .10
145 Brady Anderson .07 .20
146 Rod Beck .02 .10
147 Mike LaValliere .02 .10
148 Greg Hibbard .02 .10
149 Kenny Lofton .07 .20
150 Dwight Gooden .07 .20
151 Greg Gagne .02 .10
152 Ray McDavid .02 .10
153 Chris Donnels .02 .10
154 Dan Wilson .02 .10
155 Todd Stottlemyre .02 .10
156 David McCarty .02 .10
157 Paul Wagner .02 .10
158 Derek Jeter UER 1.25 3.00
159 Mike Fetters .02 .10
160 Scott Lydy .02 .10
161 Darrell Whitmore .02 .10
162 Bob MacDonald .02 .10
163 Vinny Castilla .07 .20
164 Denis Boucher .02 .10
165 Ivan Rodriguez .10 .30
166 Ron Gant .07 .20
167 Tim Davis .02 .10
168 Steve Dixon .02 .10
169 Scott Fletcher .02 .10
170 Terry Mulholland .02 .10
171 Greg Myers .02 .10
172 Brett Butler .07 .20
173 Bob Wickman .02 .10
174 Dave Martinez .02 .10
175 Fernando Valenzuela .07 .20
176 Craig Grebeck .02 .10
177 Shawn Boskie .02 .10
178 Albie Lopez .02 .10
179 Butch Huskey .02 .10
180 George Brett .50 1.25
181 Juan Guzman .02 .10
182 Eric Anthony .02 .10
183 Rob Dibble .07 .20
184 Craig Shipley .02 .10
185 Kevin Tapani .02 .10
186 Marcus Moore .02 .10
187 Graeme Lloyd .02 .10
188 Mike Bordick .02 .10
189 Chris Hammond .02 .10
190 Cecil Fielder .07 .20
191 Curt Leskanic .02 .10
192 Lou Frazier .02 .10
193 Steve Dreyer RC .02 .10
194 Javier Lopez .07 .20
195 Edgar Martinez .10 .30
196 Allen Watson .02 .10
197 John Flaherty .02 .10
198 Kurt Stillwell .02 .10
199 Danny Jackson .02 .10
200 Cal Ripken .60 1.50
201 Mike Bell RC .02 .10
202 Alan Benes RC .08 .25
203 Matt Farner RC .02 .10
204 Jeff Granger .02 .10
205 Brooks Kieschnick RC .02 .10
206 Jeremy Lee RC .02 .10
207 Charles Peterson RC .02 .10
208 Andy Rice RC .02 .10
209 Billy Wagner RC .60 1.50
210 Kelly Wunsch RC .08 .25
211 Tom Candiotti .02 .10
212 Domingo Jean .02 .10
213 John Burkett .02 .10
214 George Bell .02 .10
215 Dan Plesac .02 .10
216 Manny Ramirez .20 .50
217 Mike Maddux .02 .10
218 Kevin McReynolds .02 .10
219 Pat Borders .02 .10
220 Doug Drabek .02 .10
221 Larry Luebbers RC .02 .10
222 Trevor Hoffman .10 .30
223 Pat Meares .02 .10
224 Danny Miceli .02 .10
225 Greg Vaughn .02 .10
226 Scott Hemond .02 .10
227 Pat Rapp .02 .10
228 Kirk Gibson .07 .20
229 Lance Painter .02 .10
230 Larry Walker .07 .20
231 Benji Gil .02 .10
232 Mark Wohlers .02 .10
233 Rich Amaral .02 .10
234 Eric Pappas .02 .10
235 Scott Cooper .02 .10
236 Mike Butcher .02 .10
237 Pride RC .20 .50
Green/Sweeney RC
238 Kim Batiste .02 .10
239 Paul Assenmacher .02 .10
240 Will Clark .10 .30
241 Jose Offerman .02 .10
242 Todd Frohwirth .02 .10
243 Tim Raines .07 .20
244 Rick Wilkins .02 .10
245 Bret Saberhagen .07 .20
246 Thomas Howard .02 .10
247 Stan Belinda .02 .10
248 Rickey Henderson .20 .50
249 Brian Williams .02 .10
250 Barry Larkin .10 .30
251 Jose Valentin .02 .10
252 Lenny Webster .02 .10
253 Blas Minor .02 .10
254 Tim Teufel .02 .10
255 Bobby Witt .02 .10
256 Walt Weiss .02 .10
257 Chad Kreuter .02 .10
258 Roberto Mejia .02 .10
259 Cliff Floyd .07 .20
260 Julio Franco .07 .20
261 Rafael Belliard .02 .10
262 Marc Newfield .02 .10
263 Gerald Perry .02 .10
264 Ken Ryan .02 .10
265 Chili Davis .07 .20
266 Dave West .02 .10
267 Royce Clayton .02 .10
268 Pedro Martinez .20 .50
269 Mark Hutton .02 .10
270 Frank Thomas .20 .50
271 Brad Pennington .02 .10
272 Mike Harkey .02 .10
273 Sandy Alomar Jr. .02 .10
274 Dave Gallagher .02 .10
275 Wally Joyner .07 .20
276 Ricky Trlicek .02 .10
277 Al Osuna .02 .10
278 Pokey Reese .02 .10
279 Kevin Higgins .02 .10
280 Rick Aguilera .02 .10
281 Orlando Merced .02 .10
282 Mike Mohler .02 .10
283 John Jaha .02 .10
284 Robb Nen .07 .20
285 Travis Fryman .07 .20
286 Mark Thompson .02 .10
287 Mike Lansing .02 .10
288 Craig Lefferts .02 .10
289 Damon Berryhill .02 .10
290 Randy Johnson .20 .50
291 Jeff Reed .02 .10
292 Danny Darwin .02 .10
293 J.T.Snow .07 .20
294 Tyler Green .02 .10
295 Chris Hoiles .02 .10
296 Roger McDowell .02 .10
297 Spike Owen .02 .10
298 Salomon Torres .02 .10
299 Wilson Alvarez .02 .10
300 Ryne Sandberg .30 .75
301 Derek Lilliquist .02 .10
302 Howard Johnson .02 .10
303 Greg Cadaret .02 .10
304 Pat Hentgen .02 .10
305 Craig Biggio .10 .30
306 Scott Service .02 .10
307 Melvin Nieves .02 .10
308 Mike Trombley .02 .10
309 Carlos Garcia .02 .10
310 Robin Yount .30 .75
311 Marcos Armas .02 .10
312 Rich Rodriguez .02 .10
313 Justin Thompson .02 .10
314 Danny Sheaffer .02 .10
315 Ken Hill .02 .10
316 Terrell Wade RC .02 .10
317 Cris Carpenter .02 .10
318 Jeff Blauser .02 .10
319 Ted Power .02 .10
320 Ozzie Smith .30 .75
321 John Dopson .02 .10
322 Chris Turner .02 .10
323 Pete Incaviglia .02 .10
324 Alan Mills .02 .10
325 Jody Reed .02 .10
326 Rich Monteleone .02 .10
327 Mark Carreon .02 .10
328 Donn Pall .02 .10
329 Matt Walbeck .02 .10
330 Charley Nagy .02 .10
331 Jeff McKnight .02 .10
332 Jose Lind .02 .10
333 Mike Timlin .02 .10
334 Doug Jones .02 .10
335 Kevin Mitchell .02 .10
336 Luis Lopez .02 .10
337 Shane Mack .02 .10
338 Randy Tomlin .02 .10
339 Matt Mieske .02 .10
340 Mark McGwire .50 1.25
341 Nigel Wilson .02 .10
342 Danny Gladden .02 .10
343 Mo Sanford .02 .10
344 Sean Berry .02 .10
345 Kevin Brown .07 .20
346 Greg Olson .02 .10
347 Dave Magadan .02 .10
348 Rene Arocha .02 .10
349 Carlos Quintana .02 .10
350 Jim Abbott .10 .30
351 Gary DiSarcina .02 .10
352 Ben Rivera .02 .10
353 Carlos Hernandez .02 .10
354 Darren Lewis .02 .10
355 Harold Reynolds .07 .20
356 Scott Ruffcorn .02 .10
357 Mark Gubicza .02 .10
358 Paul Sorrento .02 .10
359 Anthony Young .02 .10
360 Mark Grace .10 .30
361 Rob Butler .02 .10
362 Kevin Dass .02 .10
363 Eric Helfand .02 .10
364 Derek Bell .02 .10
365 Scott Erickson .02 .10
366 Al Martin .02 .10
367 Ricky Bones .02 .10
368 Jeff Branson .02 .10
369 J.Giambi .20 .50
D.Bell RC
370 Benito Santiago .07 .20
371 John Doherty .02 .10
372 Joe Girardi .02 .10
373 Tim Scott .02 .10
374 Marvin Freeman .02 .10
375 Deion Sanders .10 .30
376 Roger Salkeld .02 .10
377 Bernard Gilkey .02 .10
378 Tony Fossas .02 .10
379 Mark McLemore UER .02 .10
380 Darren Daulton .07 .20
381 Chuck Finley .07 .20
382 Mitch Webster .02 .10
383 Gerald Williams .02 .10
384 F.Thomas .10 .30
F.McGriff AS
385 R.Alomar .07 .20
R.Thompson AS
386 W.Boggs .07 .20
M.Williams AS
387 C.Ripken .20 .50
J.Blauser AS
388 K.Griffey .25 .60
L.Dykstra AS
389 J.Gonzalez .07 .20
D.Justice AS
390 A.Belle .30 .75
B.Bonds AS
391 M.Stanley .20 .50
M.Piazza AS
392 J.McDowell .10 .30
G.Maddux AS
393 J.Key .07 .20
T.Glavine AS
394 J.Montgomery .02 .10
R.Myers AS
395 Checklist 1-198 .02 .10
396 Checklist 199-396 .02 .10
397 Tim Salmon .10 .30
398 Todd Benzinger .02 .10
399 Frank Castillo .02 .10
400 Ken Griffey Jr. .40 1.00
401 John Kruk .07 .20
402 Dave Telgheder .02 .10
403 Gary Gaetti .07 .20
404 Jim Edmonds .20 .50
405 Don Slaught .02 .10
406 Jose Oquendo .02 .10
407 Bruce Ruffin .02 .10
408 Phil Clark .02 .10
409 Joe Klink .02 .10
410 Lou Whitaker .07 .20
411 Kevin Seitzer .02 .10
412 Darrin Fletcher .02 .10
413 Kenny Rogers .07 .20
414 Bill Pecota .02 .10
415 Dave Fleming .02 .10
416 Luis Alicea .02 .10
417 Paul Quantrill .02 .10
418 Damion Easley .02 .10
419 Wes Chamberlain .02 .10
420 Harold Baines .07 .20
421 Scott Radinsky .02 .10
422 Rey Sanchez .02 .10
423 Junior Ortiz .02 .10
424 Jeff Kent .10 .30
425 Brian McRae .02 .10
426 Ed Sprague .02 .10
427 Tom Edens .02 .10
428 Willie Greene .02 .10
429 Bryan Hickerson .02 .10
430 Dave Winfield .07 .20
431 Pedro Astacio .02 .10
432 Mike Gallego .02 .10
433 Dave Burba .02 .10
434 Bob Walk .02 .10
435 Darryl Hamilton .02 .10
436 Vince Horsman .02 .10
437 Bob Natal .02 .10
438 Mike Henneman .02 .10
439 Willie Blair .02 .10
440 Dennis Martinez .07 .20
441 Dan Peltier .02 .10
442 Tony Tarasco .02 .10
443 John Cummings .02 .10
444 Geronimo Pena .02 .10
445 Aaron Sele .02 .10
446 Stan Javier .02 .10
447 Mike Williams .02 .10
448 D.J. Boston RC .02 .10
449 Jim Poole .02 .10
450 Carlos Baerga .02 .10
451 Bob Scanlan .02 .10
452 Lance Johnson .02 .10
453 Eric Hillman .02 .10
454 Keith Miller .02 .10
455 Dave Stewart .07 .20
456 Pete Harnisch .02 .10
457 Roberto Kelly .02 .10
458 Tim Worrell .02 .10
459 Pedro Munoz .02 .10
460 Orel Hershiser .07 .20
461 Randy Velarde .02 .10
462 Trevor Wilson .02 .10
463 Jerry Goff .02 .10
464 Bill Wegman .02 .10
465 Dennis Eckersley .07 .20
466 Jeff Conine .07 .20
467 Joe Boever .02 .10
468 Dante Bichette .07 .20
469 Jeff Shaw .02 .10
470 Rafael Palmeiro .10 .30
471 Phil Leftwich RC .02 .10
472 Jay Buhner .07 .20
473 Bob Tewksbury .02 .10
474 Tim Naehring .02 .10
475 Tom Glavine .10 .30
476 Dave Hollins .02 .10
477 Arthur Rhodes .02 .10
478 Joey Cora .02 .10
479 Mike Morgan .02 .10
480 Albert Belle .07 .20
481 John Franco .07 .20
482 Hipolito Pichardo .02 .10
483 Duane Ward .02 .10
484 Luis Gonzalez .07 .20
485 Joe Oliver .02 .10
486 Wally Whitehurst .02 .10
487 Mike Benjamin .02 .10
488 Eric Davis .07 .20
489 Scott Kamieniecki .02 .10
490 Kent Hrbek .07 .20
491 John Hope RC .02 .10
492 Jesse Orosco .02 .10
493 Troy Neel .02 .10
494 Ryan Bowen .02 .10
495 Mickey Tettleton .02 .10
496 Chris Jones .02 .10
497 John Wetteland .07 .20
498 David Hulse .02 .10
499 Greg Maddux .30 .75
500 Bo Jackson .20 .50
501 Donovan Osborne .02 .10
502 Mike Greenwell .02 .10
503 Steve Frey .02 .10
504 Jim Eisenreich .02 .10
505 Robby Thompson .02 .10
506 Leo Gomez .02 .10
507 Dave Staton .02 .10
508 Wayne Kirby .02 .10
509 Tim Bogar .02 .10
510 David Cone .07 .20
511 Devon White .07 .20
512 Xavier Hernandez .02 .10
513 Tim Costo .02 .10
514 Gene Harris .02 .10
515 Jack McDowell .02 .10
516 Kevin Gross .02 .10
517 Scott Leius .02 .10
518 Lloyd McClendon .02 .10
519 Alex Diaz RC .02 .10
520 Wade Boggs .10 .30
521 Bob Welch .02 .10
522 Henry Cotto .02 .10
523 Mike Moore .02 .10
524 Tim Laker .02 .10
525 Andres Galarraga .07 .20
526 Jamie Moyer .07 .20
527 J.Hardtke RC .02 .10
C.Sexton RC
528 Sid Bream .02 .10
529 Erik Hanson .02 .10
530 Ray Lankford .07 .20
531 Rob Deer .02 .10
532 Rod Correia .02 .10
533 Roger Mason .02 .10
534 Mike Devereaux .02 .10
535 Jeff Montgomery .02 .10
536 Dwight Smith .02 .10
537 Jeremy Hernandez .02 .10
538 Ellis Burks .07 .20
539 Bobby Jones .02 .10
540 Paul Molitor .07 .20
541 Jeff Juden .02 .10
542 Chris Sabo .02 .10
543 Larry Casian .02 .10
544 Jeff Gardner .02 .10
545 Ramon Martinez .02 .10
546 Paul O'Neill .10 .30
547 Steve Hosey .02 .10
548 Dave Nilsson .02 .10
549 Ron Darling .02 .10
550 Matt Williams .07 .20
551 Jack Armstrong .02 .10
552 Bill Krueger .02 .10
553 Freddie Benavides .02 .10
554 Jeff Fassero .02 .10
555 Chuck Knoblauch .07 .20
556 Guillermo Velasquez .02 .10
557 Joel Johnston .02 .10
558 Tom Lampkin .02 .10
559 Todd Van Poppel .02 .10
560 Gary Sheffield .07 .20
561 Skeeter Barnes .02 .10
562 Darren Holmes .02 .10
563 John Vander Wal .02 .10
564 Mike Ignasiak .02 .10
565 Fred McGriff .10 .30
566 Luis Polonia .02 .10
567 Mike Perez .02 .10
568 John Valentin .02 .10
569 Mike Felder .02 .10
570 Tommy Greene .02 .10
571 David Segui .02 .10
572 Roberto Hernandez .02 .10
573 Steve Wilson .02 .10
574 Willie McGee .07 .20
575 Randy Myers .02 .10
576 Darrin Jackson .02 .10
577 Eric Plunk .02 .10
578 Mike Macfarlane .02 .10
579 Doug Brocail .02 .10
580 Steve Finley .07 .20
581 John Roper .02 .10
582 Danny Cox .02 .10
583 Chip Hale .02 .10
584 Scott Bullett .02 .10
585 Kevin Reimer .02 .10
586 Brent Gates .02 .10
587 Matt Turner .02 .10
588 Rich Rowland .02 .10
589 Kent Bottenfield .02 .10
590 Marquis Grissom .07 .20
591 Doug Strange .02 .10
592 Jay Howell .02 .10
593 Omar Vizquel .10 .30
594 Rheal Cormier .02 .10
595 Andre Dawson .07 .20
596 Hilly Hathaway .02 .10
597 Todd Pratt .02 .10
598 Mike Mussina .10 .30
599 Alex Fernandez .02 .10
600 Don Mattingly .50 1.25
601 Frank Thomas MOG .10 .30
602 Ryne Sandberg MOG .20 .50
603 Wade Boggs MOG .07 .20
604 Cal Ripken MOG .30 .75
605 Barry Bonds MOG .30 .75
606 Ken Griffey Jr. MOG .25 .60
607 Kirby Puckett MOG .10 .30
608 Darren Daulton MOG .02 .10
609 Paul Molitor MOG .02 .10
610 Terry Steinbach .02 .10
611 Todd Worrell .02 .10
612 Jim Thome .10 .30
613 Chuck McElroy .02 .10
614 John Habyan .02 .10
615 Sid Fernandez .02 .10
616 Jermaine Allensworth RC .02 .10
617 Steve Bedrosian .02 .10
618 Rob Ducey .02 .10
619 Tom Browning .02 .10
620 Tony Gwynn .25 .60
621 Carl Willis .02 .10
622 Kevin Young .02 .10
623 Rafael Novoa .02 .10
624 Jerry Browne .02 .10
625 Charlie Hough .07 .20
626 Chris Gomez .02 .10
627 Steve Reed .02 .10
628 Kirk Rueter .02 .10
629 Matt Whiteside .02 .10
630 David Justice .07 .20
631 Brad Holman .02 .10
632 Brian Jordan .07 .20
633 Scott Bankhead .02 .10
634 Torey Lovullo .02 .10
635 Len Dykstra .07 .20
636 Ben McDonald .02 .10
637 Steve Howe .02 .10
638 Jose Vizcaino .02 .10
639 Bill Swift .02 .10
640 Darryl Strawberry .07 .20
641 Steve Farr .02 .10
642 Tom Kramer .02 .10
643 Joe Orsulak .02 .10
644 Tom Henke .02 .10
645 Joe Carter .07 .20
646 Ken Caminiti .07 .20
647 Reggie Sanders .07 .20
648 Andy Ashby .02 .10
649 Derek Parks .02 .10
650 Andy Van Slyke .10 .30
651 Juan Bell .02 .10
652 Roger Smithberg .02 .10
653 Chuck Carr .02 .10
654 Bill Gullickson .02 .10
655 Charlie Hayes .02 .10
656 Chris Nabholz .02 .10
657 Karl Rhodes .02 .10
658 Pete Smith .02 .10
659 Bret Boone .07 .20
660 Gregg Jefferies .02 .10
661 Bob Zupcic .02 .10
662 Steve Sax .02 .10
663 Mariano Duncan .02 .10
664 Jeff Tackett .02 .10
665 Mark Langston .02 .10
666 Steve Buechele .02 .10
667 Candy Maldonado .02 .10
668 Woody Williams .07 .20
669 Tim Wakefield .10 .30
670 Danny Tartabull .02 .10
671 Charlie O'Brien .02 .10
672 Felix Jose .02 .10
673 Bobby Ayala .02 .10
674 Scott Servais .02 .10
675 Roberto Alomar .10 .30
676 Pedro A.Martinez RC .02 .10
677 Eddie Guardado .07 .20
678 Mark Lewis .02 .10
679 Jaime Navarro .02 .10
680 Ruben Sierrra .07 .20
681 Rick Renteria .02 .10
682 Storm Davis .02 .10
683 Cory Snyder .02 .10
684 Ron Karkovice .02 .10
685 Juan Gonzalez .07 .20
686 Carlos Delgado .10 .30
687 John Smoltz .10 .30
688 Brian Dorsett .02 .10
689 Omar Olivares .02 .10
690 Mo Vaughn .07 .20
691 Joe Grahe .02 .10
692 Mickey Morandini .02 .10
693 Tino Martinez .10 .30
694 Brian Barnes .02 .10
695 Mike Stanley .02 .10
696 Mark Clark .02 .10
697 Dave Hansen .02 .10
698 Willie Wilson .02 .10
699 Pete Schourek .02 .10
700 Barry Bonds .60 1.50
701 Kevin Appier .07 .20
702 Tony Fernandez .02 .10
703 Darryl Kile .07 .20
704 Archi Cianfrocco .02 .10
705 Jose Rijo .02 .10
706 Brian Harper .02 .10
707 Zane Smith .02 .10
708 Dave Henderson .02 .10
709 Angel Miranda UER .02 .10
710 Orestes Destrade .02 .10
711 Greg Gohr .02 .10
712 Eric Young .02 .10
713 Bullinger .02 .10
Will/Wat/Welch
714 Tim Spehr .02 .10
715 Hank Aaron 715 HR .20 .50
716 Nate Minchey .02 .10
717 Mike Blowers .02 .10
718 Kent Mercker .02 .10
719 Tom Pagnozzi .02 .10
720 Roger Clemens .40 1.00
721 Eduardo Perez .02 .10
722 Milt Thompson .02 .10
723 Gregg Olson .02 .10
724 Kirk McCaskill .02 .10
725 Sammy Sosa .20 .50
726 Alvaro Espinoza .02 .10
727 Henry Rodriguez .02 .10
728 Jim Leyritz .02 .10
729 Steve Scarsone .02 .10
730 Bobby Bonilla .07 .20
731 Chris Gwynn .02 .10
732 Al Leiter .07 .20
733 Bip Roberts .02 .10
734 Mark Portugal .02 .10
735 Terry Pendleton .07 .20
736 Dave Valle .02 .10
737 Paul Kilgus .02 .10
738 Greg A. Harris .02 .10
739 Jon Ratliff RC .02 .10
740 Kirk Presley RC .02 .10
741 Josue Estrada RC .02 .10
742 Wayne Gomes RC .02 .10
743 Pat Watkins RC .02 .10
744 Jamey Wright RC .08 .25
745 Jay Powell RC .02 .10
746 Ryan McGuire RC .02 .10
747 Marc Barcelo RC .02 .10
748 Sloan Smith RC .02 .10
749 John Wasdin RC .02 .10
750 Marc Valdes .02 .10
751 Dan Ehler RC .02 .10
752 Andre King RC .02 .10
753 Greg Keagle RC .02 .10
754 Jason Myers RC .02 .10
755 Dax Winslett RC .02 .10
756 Casey Whitten RC .02 .10
757 Tony Fuduric RC .02 .10
758 Greg Norton RC .08 .25
759 Jeff D'Amico RC .02 .10
760 Ryan Hancock RC .02 .10
761 David Cooper RC .02 .10
762 Kevin Orie RC .02 .10
763 J.O'Donoghue .02 .10
M.Oquist
764 C.Bailey RC .02 .10
S.Hatteberg
765 M.Holzemer .02 .10
P.Swingle RC
766 J.Baldwin .02 .10
R.Bolton
767 J.Tavarez RC .08 .25
J.DiPoto
768 D.Bautista .02 .10
S.Bergman
769 B.Hamelin .02 .10
J.Vitiello
770 M.Kiefer .02 .10
T.O'Leary
771 D.Hocking .02 .10
O.Munoz RC
772 Russ Davis .02 .10
B.Taylor
773 K.Abbott .08 .25
M.Jimenez
774 K.King RC .02 .10
Plantenberg RC
775 J.Shave .02 .10
D.Wilson
776 D.Cedeno .02 .10
P.Spoljaric
777 C.Jones .20 .50
R.Klesko
778 S.Trachsel .02 .10
T.Wendell
779 J.Spradlin RC .02 .10
J.Ruffin
780 J.Bates .02 .10
J.Burke
781 C.Everett .07 .20
D.Weathers
782 J.Mouton .02 .10
G.Mota
783 R.Mondesi .07 .20
B.Van Ryn
784 R.White .07 .20
G.White
785 B.Pulsipher .07 .20
B.Fordyce
786 K.Foster RC .02 .10
G.Schall
787 Rich Aude RC .02 .10

M.Cummings
788 B.Barber .02 .10
R.Batchelor
789 B.Johnson RC .02 .10
S.Sanders
790 J.Phillips .02 .10
R.Faneyte
791 Checklist 3 .02 .10
792 Checklist 4 .02 .10

1994 Topps Gold

*STARS: 1.5X TO 4X BASIC CARDS
*ROOKIES: 1.25X TO 3X BASIC CARDS
ONE PER PACK OR MINIPACK
TWO PER FOURTH PACK OR MINI JUMBO
395 Bill Brennan .15 .40
396 Jeff Bronkey .15 .40
791 Mike Cook .15 .40
792 Dan Pasqua .15 .40

1994 Topps Spanish

*STARS: 3X to 6X BASIC CARDS
L1 Felipe Alou .30 .75
L2 Ruben Amaro .08 .25
L3 Luis Aparicio .40 1.00
L4 Rod Carew .40 1.00
L5 Chico Carrasquel .20 .50
L6 Orlando Cepeda .40 1.00
L7 Juan Marichal .40 1.00
L8 Minnie Minoso .30 .75
L9 Cookie Rojas .08 .25
L10 Luis Tiant .20 .50

1994 Topps Black Gold

COMPLETE SET (44) 10.00 25.00
COMPLETE SERIES 1 (22) 6.00 15.00
COMPLETE SERIES 2 (22) 4.00 10.00
STAT.ODDS 1:72H/R,1:18J,1:24RAC,1:36CEL
THREE PER FACTORY SET
1 Roberto Alomar .25 .60
2 Carlos Baerga .07 .20
3 Albert Belle .15 .40
4 Joe Carter .15 .40
5 Cecil Fielder .15 .40
6 Travis Fryman .15 .40
7 Juan Gonzalez .15 .40
8 Ken Griffey Jr. .75 2.00
9 Chris Hoiles .07 .20
10 Randy Johnson .40 1.00
11 Kenny Lofton .15 .40
12 Jack McDowell .07 .20
13 Paul Molitor .15 .40
14 Jeff Montgomery .07 .20
15 John Olerud .15 .40
16 Rafael Palmeiro .25 .60
17 Kirby Puckett .40 1.00
18 Cal Ripken 1.25 3.00
19 Tim Salmon .25 .60
20 Mike Stanley .07 .20
21 Frank Thomas .40 1.00
22 Robin Ventura .15 .40
23 Jeff Bagwell .25 .60
24 Jay Bell .15 .40
25 Craig Biggio .25 .60
26 Jeff Blauser .07 .20
27 Barry Bonds 1.25 3.00
28 Darren Daulton .15 .40
29 Len Dykstra .15 .40
30 Andres Galarraga .15 .40
31 Ron Gant .15 .40
32 Tom Glavine .25 .60
33 Mark Grace .25 .60
34 Marquis Grissom .15 .40
35 Gregg Jefferies .07 .20
36 David Justice .15 .40
37 John Kruk .15 .40
38 Greg Maddux .60 1.50
39 Fred McGriff .25 .60
40 Randy Myers .07 .20
41 Mike Piazza .75 2.00
42 Sammy Sosa .40 1.00
43 Robby Thompson .07 .20
44 Matt Williams .15 .40
A Winner A 1-11 Expired .07 .20
B Winner B 12-22 .07 .20
C Winner C 23-33 .07 .20
D Winner D 34-44 .07 .20
AB Winner AB 1-22 10.00 25.00
CD Winner CD 23-44 10.00 25.00
ABCD Win.ABCD 1-44 75.00 150.00

1994 Topps Traded

This set consists of 132 standard-size cards featuring traded players in their new uniforms, rookies and draft choices. Factory sets consisted of 140 cards including a set of eight Topps Finest cards. Card fronts feature a player photo with the player's name, team and position at the bottom. The horizontal backs have a player photo to the left with complete career statisics and highlights. Rookie Cards include Rusty Greer, Ben Grieve, Paul Konerko Terrence Long and Chan Ho Park.

COMP.FACT.SET (140) 15.00 40.00
1T Paul Wilson .02 .10
2T Bill Taylor RC .40 1.00
3T Dan Wilson .02 .10
4T Mark Smith .02 .10
5T Toby Borland RC .08 .25
6T Dave Clark .02 .10
7T Dennis Martinez .07 .20
8T Dave Gallagher .02 .10
9T Josias Manzanillo .02 .10
10T Brian Anderson RC .40 1.00
11T Damon Berryhill .02 .10
12T Alex Cole .02 .10
13T Jacob Shumate RC .08 .25
14T Oddibe McDowell .02 .10
15T Willie Banks .02 .10
16T Jerry Browne .02 .10
17T Donnie Elliott .02 .10
18T Ellis Burks .07 .20
19T Chuck McElroy .02 .10
20T Luis Polonia .02 .10
21T Brian Harper .02 .10
22T Mark Portugal .02 .10
23T Dave Henderson .02 .10
24T Mark Acre RC .08 .25
25T Julio Franco .07 .20
26T Darren Hall RC .08 .25
27T Eric Anthony .02 .10
28T Sid Fernandez .02 .10
29T Rusty Greer RC .60 1.50
30T Riccardo Ingram RC .08 .25
31T Gabe White .02 .10
32T Tim Belcher .02 .10
33T Terrence Long RC .40 1.00
34T Mark Dalesandro RC .08 .25
35T Mike Kelly .02 .10
36T Jack Morris .07 .20
37T Jeff Brantley .02 .10
38T Larry Barnes RC .08 .25
39T Brian R. Hunter .02 .10
40T Otis Nixon .02 .10
41T Bret Wagner .02 .10
42T P.Martinez .20 .50
D.Deshields TR
43T Heathcliff Slocumb .02 .10
44T Ben Grieve RC .40 1.00
45T John Hudek RC .08 .25
46T Shawon Dunston .02 .10
47T Greg Colbrunn .02 .10
48T Joey Hamilton .02 .10
49T Marvin Freeman .02 .10
50T Terry Mulholland .02 .10
51T Keith Mitchell .02 .10
52T Dwight Smith .02 .10
53T Shawn Boskie .02 .10
54T Kevin Witt RC .40 1.00
55T Ron Gant .07 .20
56T Jason Schmidt RC 4.00 10.00
57T Jody Reed .02 .10
58T Rick Helling .02 .10
59T John Powell .02 .10
60T Eddie Murray .20 .50
61T Joe Hall RC .08 .25
62T Jorge Fabregas .02 .10
63T Mike Mordecai RC .08 .25
64T Ed Vosberg .02 .10
65T Rickey Henderson .20 .50
66T Tim Grieve RC .08 .25
67T Jon Lieber .07 .20
68T Chris Howard .02 .10
69T Matt Walbeck .02 .10
70T Chan Ho Park RC .60 1.50
71T Bryan Eversgerd RC .08 .25
72T John Dettmer .02 .10
73T Erik Hanson .02 .10
74T Mike Thurman RC .08 .25
75T Bobby Ayala .02 .10
76T Rafael Palmeiro .10 .30
77T Bret Boone .07 .20
78T Paul Shuey .02 .10
79T Kevin Foster RC .08 .25
80T Dave Magadan .02 .10
81T Bip Roberts .02 .10
82T Howard Johnson .02 .10
83T Xavier Hernandez .02 .10
84T Ross Powell RC .08 .25
85T Doug Million RC .08 .25
86T Geronimo Berroa .02 .10
87T Mark Farris RC .08 .25
88T Butch Henry .02 .10
89T Junior Felix .02 .10
90T Bo Jackson .20 .50
91T Hector Carrasco .02 .10
92T Charlie O'Brien .02 .10
93T Omar Vizquel .10 .30
94T David Segui .02 .10
95T Dustin Hermanson .02 .10
96T Gar Finnvold RC .08 .25
97T Dave Stevens .02 .10
98T Corey Pointer RC .08 .25
99T Felix Fermin .02 .10
100T Lee Smith .07 .20
101T Reid Ryan RC .40 1.00
102T Bobby Munoz .02 .10
103T D.Sanders .10 .30
R.Kelly TR
104T Turner Ward .02 .10
105T W.VanLandingham RC .08 .25
106T Vince Coleman .02 .10
107T Stan Javier .02 .10
108T Darrin Jackson .02 .10
109T C.J.Nitkowski RC .08 .25
110T Anthony Young .02 .10
111T Kurt Miller .02 .10
112T Paul Konerko RC 6.00 15.00
113T Walt Weiss .02 .10
114T Daryl Boston .02 .10
115T Will Clark .10 .30
116T Matt Smith RC .08 .25
117T Mark Leiter .02 .10
118T Gregg Olson .02 .10
119T Tony Pena .02 .10
120T Jose Vizcaino .02 .10
121T Rick White RC .08 .25
122T Rich Rowland .02 .10
123T Jeff Reboulet .02 .10
124T Greg Hibbard .02 .10
125T Chris Sabo .02 .10
126T Doug Jones .02 .10
127T Tony Fernandez .02 .10
128T Carlos Reyes RC .08 .25
129T Kevin L.Brown RC .40 1.00
130T Ryne Sandberg HL .50 1.25
131T Ryne Sandberg HL .50 1.25
132T Checklist 1-132 .02 .10

1994 Topps Traded Finest Inserts

COMPLETE SET (8) 2.00 5.00
ONE SET PER TRADED FACTORY SET
1 Greg Maddux .30 .75
2 Mike Piazza .40 1.00
3 Matt Williams .07 .20
4 Raul Mondesi .07 .20
5 Ken Griffey Jr. .40 1.00
6 Kenny Lofton .07 .20
7 Frank Thomas .20 .50
8 Manny Ramirez .20 .50

1994 Topps Porcelain Promo

700 Nolan Ryan 12.50 30.00

1995 Topps Pre-Production

COMPLETE SET (9) 1.50 4.00
*SPECTRALITE: 3X BASIC CARDS
PP1 Larry Walker .40 1.00
PP2 Mike Piazza .40 1.00
PP3 Greg Vaughn .15 .40
PP4 Sandy Alomar .15 .40
PP5 Travis Fryman .15 .40
PP6 Ken Griffey Jr. .75 2.00
PP7 Mike Devereaux .15 .40
PP8 Roberto Hernandez .15 .40
PP9 Alex Fernandez .15 .40

1995 Topps

These 660 standard-size cards feature color action player photos with white borders on the fronts. This set was released in two series. The first series contained 396 cards while the second series had 264 cards. Cards were distributed in 11-card packs (SRP $1.29), jumbo packs and factory sets. One "Own The Game" instant winner card has been inserted in every 120 packs. Rookie cards in this set include Rey Ordonez. Due to the 1994 baseball strike, it was publicly announced that production for this set was the lowest print run since 1966.

COMPLETE SET (660) 25.00 60.00
COMP.HOBBY SET (677) 30.00 80.00
COMP.RETAIL SET (677) 30.00 80.00
COMPLETE SERIES 1 (396) 15.00 40.00
COMPLETE SERIES 2 (264) 15.00 40.00
1 Frank Thomas .30 .75
2 Mickey Morandini .05 .15
3 Babe Ruth 100th B-Day .75 2.00
4 Scott Cooper .05 .15
5 David Cone .10 .30
6 Jacob Shumate .05 .15
7 Trevor Hoffman .10 .30
8 Shane Mack .05 .15
9 Delino DeShields .05 .15
10 Matt Williams .10 .30
11 Sammy Sosa .30 .75
12 Gary DiSarcina .05 .15
13 Kenny Rogers .10 .30
14 Jose Vizcaino .05 .15
15 Lou Whitaker .10 .30
16 Ron Darling .05 .15
17 Dave Nilsson .05 .15
18 Chris Hammond .05 .15
19 Sid Bream .05 .15
20 Denny Martinez .10 .30
21 Orlando Merced .05 .15
22 John Wetteland .10 .30
23 Mike Devereaux .05 .15
24 Rene Arocha .05 .15
25 Jay Buhner .10 .30
26 Darren Holmes .05 .15
27 Hal Morris .05 .15
28 Brian Buchanan RC .05 .15
29 Keith Miller .05 .15
30 Paul Molitor .10 .30
31 Dave West .05 .15
32 Tony Tarasco .05 .15
33 Scott Sanders .05 .15
34 Eddie Zambrano .05 .15
35 Ricky Bones .05 .15
36 John Valentin .05 .15
37 Kevin Tapani .05 .15
38 Tim Wallach .05 .15
39 Darren Lewis .05 .15
40 Travis Fryman .10 .30
41 Mark Leiter .05 .15
42 Jose Bautista .05 .15
43 Pete Smith .05 .15
44 Bret Barberie .05 .15
45 Dennis Eckersley .10 .30
46 Ken Hill .05 .15
47 Chad Ogea .05 .15
48 Pete Harnisch .05 .15
49 James Baldwin .05 .15
50 Mike Mussina .20 .50
51 Al Martin .05 .15
52 Mark Thompson .05 .15
53 Matt Smith .05 .15
54 Joey Hamilton .05 .15
55 Edgar Martinez .20 .50
56 John Smiley .05 .15
57 Rey Sanchez .05 .15
58 Mike Timlin .05 .15
59 Ricky Bottalico .05 .15
60 Jim Abbott .20 .50
61 Mike Kelly .05 .15
62 Brian Jordan .10 .30
63 Ken Ryan .05 .15
64 Matt Mieske .05 .15
65 Rick Aguilera .05 .15
66 Ismael Valdes .05 .15
67 Royce Clayton .05 .15
68 Junior Felix .05 .15
69 Harold Reynolds .10 .30
70 Juan Gonzalez .10 .30
71 Kelly Stinnett .05 .15
72 Carlos Reyes .05 .15
73 Dave Weathers .05 .15
74 Mel Rojas .05 .15
75 Doug Drabek .05 .15
76 Charles Nagy .05 .15
77 Tim Raines .10 .30
78 Midre Cummings .05 .15
79 Ray Brown RC .05 .15
80 Rafael Palmeiro .20 .50
81 Charlie Hayes .05 .15
82 Ray Lankford .10 .30
83 Tim Davis .05 .15
84 C.J. Nitkowski .05 .15
85 Andy Ashby .05 .15
86 Gerald Williams .05 .15
87 Terry Shumpert .05 .15
88 Heathcliff Slocumb .05 .15
89 Domingo Cedeno .05 .15
90 Mark Grace .20 .50
91 Brad Woodall RC .05 .15
92 Gar Finnvold .05 .15
93 Jaime Navarro .05 .15
94 Carlos Hernandez .05 .15
95 Mark Langston .05 .15
96 Chuck Carr .05 .15
97 Mike Gardiner .05 .15
98 Dave McCarty .05 .15
99 Cris Carpenter .05 .15
100 Barry Bonds .75 2.00
101 David Segui .05 .15
102 Scott Brosius .10 .30
103 Mariano Duncan .05 .15
104 Kenny Lofton .10 .30
105 Ken Caminiti .10 .30
106 Darrin Jackson .05 .15
107 Jim Poole .05 .15
108 Wil Cordero .05 .15
109 Danny Miceli .05 .15
110 Walt Weiss .05 .15
111 Tom Pagnozzi .05 .15
112 Terrence Long .05 .15
113 Bret Boone .10 .30
114 Daryl Boston .05 .15
115 Wally Joyner .10 .30
116 Rob Butler .05 .15
117 Rafael Belliard .05 .15
118 Luis Lopez .05 .15
119 Tony Fossas .05 .15
120 Len Dykstra .10 .30
121 Mike Morgan .05 .15
122 Denny Hocking .05 .15
123 Kevin Gross .05 .15
124 Todd Benzinger .05 .15
125 John Doherty .05 .15
126 Eduardo Perez .05 .15
127 Dan Smith .05 .15
128 Joe Orsulak .05 .15
129 Brent Gates .05 .15
130 Jeff Conine .10 .30
131 Doug Henry .05 .15
132 Paul Sorrento .05 .15
133 Mike Hampton .10 .30
134 Tim Spehr .05 .15
135 Julio Franco .10 .30
136 Mike Dyer .05 .15
137 Chris Sabo .05 .15
138 Rheal Cormier .05 .15
139 Paul Konerko .40 1.00
140 Dante Bichette .10 .30
141 Chuck McElroy .05 .15
142 Mike Stanley .05 .15
143 Bob Hamelin .05 .15
144 Tommy Greene .05 .15
145 John Smoltz .20 .50
146 Ed Sprague .05 .15
147 Ray McDavid .05 .15
148 Otis Nixon .05 .15
149 Turk Wendell .05 .15
150 Chris James .05 .15
151 Derek Parks .05 .15
152 Jose Offerman .05 .15
153 Tony Clark .05 .15
154 Chad Curtis .05 .15
155 Mark Portugal .05 .15
156 Bill Pulsipher .05 .15
157 Troy Neel .05 .15
158 Dave Winfield .10 .30
159 Bill Wegman .05 .15
160 Benito Santiago .10 .30
161 Jose Mesa .05 .15
162 Luis Gonzalez .10 .30
163 Alex Fernandez .05 .15
164 Freddie Benavides .05 .15
165 Ben McDonald .05 .15
166 Blas Minor .05 .15
167 Bret Wagner .05 .15
168 Mac Suzuki .05 .15
169 Roberto Mejia .05 .15
170 Wade Boggs .20 .50
171 Pokey Reese .05 .15
172 Hipolito Pichardo .05 .15
173 Kim Batiste .05 .15
174 Darren Hall .05 .15
175 Tom Glavine .20 .50
176 Phil Plantier .05 .15
177 Chris Howard .05 .15
178 Karl Rhodes .05 .15
179 LaTroy Hawkins .05 .15
180 Raul Mondesi .10 .30
181 Jeff Reed .05 .15
182 Milt Cuyler .05 .15
183 Jim Edmonds .20 .50
184 Hector Fajardo .05 .15
185 Jeff Kent .10 .30
186 Wilson Alvarez .05 .15
187 Geronimo Berroa .05 .15
188 Billy Spiers .05 .15
189 Derek Lilliquist .05 .15
190 Craig Biggio .20 .50
191 Roberto Hernandez .05 .15
192 Bob Natal .05 .15
193 Bobby Ayala .05 .15
194 Travis Miller RC .05 .15
195 Bob Tewksbury .05 .15
196 Rondell White .10 .30
197 Steve Cooke .05 .15
198 Jeff Branson .05 .15
199 Derek Jeter .75 2.00
200 Tim Salmon .20 .50
201 Steve Frey .05 .15
202 Kent Mercker .05 .15
203 Randy Johnson .30 .75
204 Todd Worrell .05 .15
205 Mo Vaughn .10 .30
206 Howard Johnson .05 .15
207 John Wasdin .05 .15
208 Eddie Williams .05 .15
209 Tim Belcher .05 .15
210 Jeff Montgomery .05 .15
211 Kirt Manwaring .05 .15
212 Ben Grieve .05 .15
213 Pat Hentgen .05 .15
214 Shawon Dunston .05 .15
215 Mike Greenwell .05 .15
216 Alex Diaz .05 .15
217 Pat Mahomes .05 .15
218 Dave Hansen .05 .15
219 Kevin Rogers .05 .15
220 Cecil Fielder .10 .30
221 Andrew Lorraine .05 .15
222 Jack Armstrong .05 .15
223 Todd Hundley .05 .15
224 Mark Acre .05 .15
225 Darrell Whitmore .05 .15
226 Randy Milligan .05 .15
227 Wayne Kirby .05 .15
228 Darryl Kile .10 .30
229 Bob Zupcic .05 .15
230 Jay Bell .10 .30
231 Dustin Hermanson .05 .15
232 Harold Baines .10 .30
233 Alan Benes .05 .15
234 Felix Fermin .05 .15
235 Ellis Burks .10 .30
236 Jeff Brantley .05 .15
237 Karim Garcia RC .05 .15
238 Matt Nokes .05 .15
239 Ben Rivera .05 .15
240 Joe Carter .10 .30
241 Jeff Granger .05 .15
242 Terry Pendleton .10 .30
243 Melvin Nieves .05 .15
244 Frankie Rodriguez .05 .15
245 Darryl Hamilton .05 .15
246 Brooks Kieschnick .05 .15
247 Todd Hollandsworth .05 .15
248 Joe Rosselli .05 .15
249 Bill Gullickson .05 .15
250 Chuck Knoblauch .10 .30
251 Kurt Miller .05 .15
252 Bobby Jones .05 .15
253 Lance Blankenship .05 .15
254 Matt Whiteside .05 .15
255 Darrin Fletcher .05 .15
256 Eric Plunk .05 .15
257 Shane Reynolds .05 .15
258 Norberto Martin .05 .15
259 Mike Thurman .05 .15
260 Andy Van Slyke .20 .50
261 Dwight Smith .05 .15
262 Allen Watson .05 .15
263 Dan Wilson .05 .15
264 Brent Mayne .05 .15
265 Bip Roberts .05 .15
266 Sterling Hitchcock .05 .15
267 Alex Gonzalez .05 .15
268 Greg Harris .05 .15
269 Ricky Jordan .05 .15
270 Johnny Ruffin .05 .15
271 Mike Stanton .05 .15
272 Rich Rowland .05 .15
273 Steve Trachsel .05 .15
274 Pedro Munoz .05 .15
275 Ramon Martinez .05 .15
276 Dave Henderson .05 .15
277 Chris Gomez .05 .15
278 Joe Grahe .05 .15
279 Rusty Greer .10 .30
280 John Franco .10 .30
281 Mike Bordick .05 .15
282 Jeff D'Amico .05 .15
283 Dave Magadan .05 .15
284 Tony Pena .05 .15
285 Greg Swindell .05 .15
286 Doug Million .05 .15
287 Gabe White .05 .15
288 Trey Beamon .05 .15
289 Arthur Rhodes .05 .15
290 Juan Guzman .05 .15
291 Jose Oquendo .05 .15
292 Willie Blair .05 .15
293 Eddie Taubensee .05 .15
294 Steve Howe .05 .15
295 Greg Maddux .50 1.25
296 Mike Macfarlane .05 .15
297 Curt Schilling .10 .30
298 Phil Clark .05 .15
299 Woody Williams .05 .15
300 Jose Canseco .20 .50
301 Aaron Sele .05 .15
302 Carl Willis .05 .15
303 Steve Buechele .05 .15
304 Dave Burba .05 .15
305 Orel Hershiser .10 .30
306 Damion Easley .05 .15
307 Mike Henneman .05 .15
308 Josias Manzanillo .05 .15
309 Kevin Seitzer .05 .15
310 Ruben Sierra .10 .30
311 Bryan Harvey .05 .15
312 Jim Thome .20 .50
313 Ramon Castro RC .15 .40
314 Lance Johnson .05 .15
315 Marquis Grissom .10 .30
316 Eddie Priest RC .05 .15
317 Paul Wagner .05 .15
318 Jamie Moyer .10 .30
319 Todd Zeile .05 .15
320 Chris Bosio .05 .15
321 Steve Reed .05 .15
322 Erik Hanson .05 .15
323 Luis Polonia .05 .15
324 Ryan Klesko .10 .30
325 Kevin Appier .10 .30
326 Jim Eisenreich .05 .15
327 Randy Knorr .05 .15
328 Craig Shipley .05 .15
329 Tim Naehring .05 .15
330 Randy Myers .05 .15
331 Alex Cole .05 .15
332 Jim Gott .05 .15
333 Mike Jackson .05 .15
334 John Flaherty .05 .15
335 Chili Davis .10 .30
336 Benji Gil .05 .15
337 Jason Jacome .05 .15
338 Stan Javier .05 .15
339 Mike Fetters .05 .15
340 Rich Renteria .05 .15
341 Kevin Witt .05 .15
342 Scott Servais .05 .15
343 Craig Grebeck .05 .15
344 Kirk Rueter .05 .15
345 Don Slaught .05 .15
346 Armando Benitez .05 .15
347 Ozzie Smith .50 1.25
348 Mike Blowers .05 .15
349 Armando Reynoso .05 .15
350 Barry Larkin .20 .50
351 Mike Williams .05 .15
352 Scott Kamieniecki .05 .15
353 Gary Gaetti .10 .30
354 Todd Stottlemyre .05 .15
355 Fred McGriff .20 .50
356 Tim Mauser .05 .15
357 Chris Gwynn .05 .15
358 Frank Castillo .05 .15
359 Jeff Reboulet .05 .15
360 Roger Clemens .60 1.50
361 Mark Carreon .05 .15
362 Chad Kreuter .05 .15
363 Mark Farris .05 .15
364 Bob Welch .05 .15
365 Dean Palmer .10 .30
366 Jeromy Burnitz .10 .30
367 B.J. Surhoff .10 .30
368 Mike Butcher .05 .15
369 B.Buckles RC .05 .15
B.Clontz
370 Eddie Murray .30 .75
371 Orlando Miller .05 .15
372 Ron Karkovice .05 .15
373 Richie Lewis .05 .15
374 Lenny Webster .05 .15
375 Jeff Tackett .05 .15
376 Tom Urbani .05 .15
377 Tino Martinez .20 .50
378 Mark Dewey .05 .15
379 Charles O'Brien .05 .15
380 Terry Mulholland .05 .15
381 Thomas Howard .05 .15
382 Chris Haney .05 .15
383 Billy Hatcher .05 .15
384 F.Thomas .20 .50
J.Bagwell AS
385 B.Boone .10 .30
C.Baerga AS
386 M.Williams .10 .30
W.Boggs AS
387 C.Ripken .30 .75
W.Cordero AS
388 K.Griffey Jr. .50 1.25
B.Bonds AS
389 T.Gwynn .10 .30
A.Belle AS
390 D.Bichette .20 .50
K.Puckett AS
391 M.Piazza .30 .75
M.Stanley AS
392 G.Maddux .30 .75
D.Cone AS
393 D.Jackson .05 .15
J.Key AS
394 J.Franco .05 .15
L.Smith AS
395 Checklist 1-198 .05 .15
396 Checklist 199-396 .05 .15
397 Ken Griffey Jr. .60 1.50
398 Rick Heiserman RC .05 .15
399 Don Mattingly .75 2.00
400 Henry Rodriguez .05 .15
401 Lenny Harris .05 .15
402 Ryan Thompson .05 .15
403 Darren Oliver .05 .15
404 Omar Vizquel .20 .50
405 Jeff Bagwell .20 .50
406 Doug Webb RC .05 .15
407 Todd Van Poppel .05 .15
408 Leo Gomez .05 .15
409 Mark Whiten .05 .15
410 Pedro A.Martinez .05 .15
411 Reggie Sanders .10 .30
412 Kevin Foster .05 .15
413 Danny Tartabull .05 .15
414 Jeff Blauser .05 .15
415 Mike Magnante .05 .15
416 Tom Candiotti .05 .15
417 Rod Beck .05 .15
418 Jody Reed .05 .15
419 Vince Coleman .05 .15
420 Danny Jackson .05 .15
421 Ryan Nye RC .05 .15
422 Larry Walker .10 .30
423 Russ Johnson DP .05 .15
424 Pat Borders .05 .15
425 Lee Smith .10 .30
426 Paul O'Neill .20 .50
427 Devon White .10 .30
428 Jim Bullinger .05 .15
429 Rob Welch RC .05 .15
430 Steve Avery .05 .15
431 Tony Gwynn .40 1.00
432 Pat Meares .05 .15
433 Bill Swift .05 .15
434 David Wells .10 .30
435 John Briscoe .05 .15
436 Roger Pavlik .05 .15
437 Jayson Peterson RC .05 .15
438 Roberto Alomar .20 .50
439 Billy Brewer .05 .15
440 Gary Sheffield .10 .30
441 Lou Frazier .05 .15
442 Terry Steinbach .05 .15
443 Jay Payton RC .30 .75
444 Jason Bere .05 .15
445 Denny Neagle .10 .30
446 Andres Galarraga .10 .30
447 Hector Carrasco .05 .15
448 Bill Risley .05 .15
449 Andy Benes .05 .15
450 Jim Leyritz .05 .15
451 Jose Oliva .05 .15
452 Greg Vaughn .05 .15
453 Rich Monteleone .05 .15
454 Tony Eusebio .05 .15
455 Chuck Finley .10 .30
456 Kevin Brown .10 .30
457 Joe Boever .05 .15
458 Bobby Munoz .05 .15
459 Bret Saberhagen .10 .30
460 Kurt Abbott .05 .15
461 Bobby Witt .05 .15
462 Cliff Floyd .10 .30
463 Mark Clark .05 .15
464 Andujar Cedeno .05 .15
465 Marvin Freeman .05 .15
466 Mike Piazza .50 1.25
467 Willie Greene .05 .15
468 Pat Kelly .05 .15
469 Carlos Delgado .10 .30
470 Willie Banks .05 .15
471 Matt Walbeck .05 .15
472 Mark McGwire .75 2.00
473 McKay Christensen RC .05 .15
474 Alan Trammell .10 .30
475 Tom Gordon .05 .15
476 Greg Colbrunn .05 .15
477 Darren Daulton .10 .30
478 Albie Lopez .05 .15
479 Robin Ventura .10 .30
480 Eddie Perez RC .15 .40
481 Bryan Eversgerd .05 .15
482 Dave Fleming .05 .15
483 Scott Livingstone .05 .15
484 Pete Schourek .05 .15
485 Bernie Williams .20 .50
486 Mark Lemke .05 .15
487 Eric Karros .10 .30
488 Scott Ruffcorn .05 .15
489 Billy Ashley .05 .15
490 Rico Brogna .05 .15
491 John Burkett .05 .15
492 Cade Gaspar RC .05 .15
493 Jorge Fabregas .05 .15
494 Greg Gagne .05 .15
495 Doug Jones .05 .15
496 Troy O'Leary .05 .15
497 Pat Rapp .05 .15
498 Butch Henry .05 .15
499 John Olerud .10 .30
500 John Hudek .05 .15
501 Jeff King .05 .15
502 Bobby Bonilla .10 .30
503 Albert Belle .10 .30
504 Rick Wilkins .05 .15
505 John Jaha .05 .15
506 Nigel Wilson .05 .15
507 Sid Fernandez .05 .15
508 Deion Sanders .20 .50
509 Gil Heredia .05 .15
510 Scott Elarton RC .15 .40
511 Melido Perez .05 .15
512 Greg McMichael .05 .15
513 Rusty Meacham .05 .15
514 Shawn Green .10 .30
515 Carlos Garcia .05 .15
516 Dave Stevens .05 .15
517 Eric Young .05 .15
518 Omar Daal .05 .15
519 Kirk Gibson .10 .30
520 Spike Owen .05 .15
521 Jacob Cruz RC .10 .30
522 Sandy Alomar Jr. .05 .15
523 Steve Bedrosian .05 .15
524 Ricky Gutierrez .05 .15
525 Dave Veres .05 .15
526 Gregg Jefferies .05 .15
527 Jose Valentin .05 .15
528 Robb Nen .10 .30
529 Jose Rijo .05 .15
530 Sean Berry .05 .15
531 Mike Gallego .05 .15
532 Roberto Kelly .05 .15
533 Kevin Stocker .05 .15
534 Kirby Puckett .30 .75
535 Chipper Jones .30 .75
536 Russ Davis .05 .15
537 Jon Lieber .05 .15
538 Trey Moore RC .05 .15
539 Joe Girardi .05 .15
540 Miguel Cairo RC .05 .15
541 Tony Phillips .05 .15
542 Brian Anderson .05 .15
543 Ivan Rodriguez .20 .50
544 Jeff Cirillo .05 .15
545 Joey Cora .05 .15
546 Chris Hoiles .05 .15
547 Bernard Gilkey .05 .15
548 Mike Lansing .05 .15
549 Jimmy Key .10 .30
550 Mark Wohlers .05 .15
551 Chris Clemons RC .05 .15
552 Vinny Castilla .10 .30
553 Mark Guthrie .05 .15
554 Mike Lieberthal .10 .30
555 Tommy Davis RC .05 .15
556 Robby Thompson .05 .15
557 Danny Bautista .05 .15
558 Will Clark .20 .50
559 Rickey Henderson .30 .75
560 Todd Jones .05 .15
561 Jack McDowell .05 .15
562 Carlos Rodriguez .05 .15
563 Mark Eichhorn .05 .15
564 Jeff Nelson .05 .15
565 Eric Anthony .05 .15
566 Randy Velarde .05 .15
567 Javier Lopez .10 .30
568 Kevin Mitchell .05 .15
569 Steve Karsay .05 .15
570 Brian Meadows RC .05 .15
571 Rey Ordonez RC .30 .75
572 John Kruk .10 .30
573 Scott Leius .05 .15
574 John Patterson .05 .15
575 Kevin Brown .10 .30
576 Mike Moore .05 .15
577 Manny Ramirez .20 .50
578 Jose Lind .05 .15
579 Derrick May .05 .15
580 Cal Eldred .05 .15
581 A.Boone RC .30 .75

D.Bell
582 J.T. Snow .10 .30
583 Luis Sojo .05 .15
584 Moises Alou .10 .30
585 Dave Clark .05 .15
586 Dave Hollins .05 .15
587 Nomar Garciaparra .75 2.00
588 Cal Ripken 1.00 2.50
589 Pedro Astacio .05 .15
590 J.R. Phillips .05 .15
591 Jeff Frye .05 .15
592 Bo Jackson .30 .75
593 Steve Ontiveros .05 .15
594 David Nied .05 .15
595 Brad Ausmus .10 .30
596 Carlos Baerga .05 .15
597 James Mouton .05 .15
598 Ozzie Guillen .10 .30
599 Johnny Damon .30 .75
600 Yorkis Perez .05 .15
601 Rich Rodriguez .05 .15
602 Mark McLemore .05 .15
603 Jeff Fassero .05 .15
604 John Roper .05 .15
605 Mark Johnson RC .15 .40
606 Wes Chamberlain .05 .15
607 Felix Jose .05 .15
608 Tony Longmire .05 .15
609 Duane Ward .05 .15
610 Brett Butler .10 .30
611 William VanLandingham .05 .15
612 Mickey Tettleton .05 .15
613 Brady Anderson .10 .30
614 Reggie Jefferson .05 .15
615 Mike Kingery .05 .15
616 Derek Bell .05 .15
617 Scott Erickson .05 .15
618 Bob Wickman .05 .15
619 Phil Leftwich .05 .15
620 David Justice .10 .30
621 Paul Wilson .05 .15
622 Pedro Martinez .20 .50
623 Terry Mathews .05 .15
624 Brian McRae .05 .15
625 Bruce Ruffin .05 .15
626 Steve Finley .10 .30
627 Ron Gant .10 .30
628 Rafael Bournigal .05 .15
629 Darryl Strawberry .10 .30
630 Luis Alicea .05 .15
631 Mark Smith .05 .15
632 C.Bailey .05 .15
S.Hatteberg
633 Todd Greene .10 .30
634 Rod Bolton .05 .15
635 Herbert Perry .05 .15
636 Sean Bergman .05 .15
637 J.Randa .10 .30
J.Vitiello
638 Jose Mercedes .05 .15
639 Marty Cordova .05 .15
640 R.Rivera .10 .30
A.Pettitte
641 W.Adams .05 .15
S.Spiezio
642 Eddy Diaz RC .05 .15
643 Jon Shave .05 .15
644 Paul Spoljaric .05 .15
645 Damon Hollins .05 .15
646 Doug Glanville .05 .15
647 Tim Belk .05 .15
648 Rod Pedraza .05 .15
649 Marc Valdes .05 .15
650 Rick Huisman .05 .15
651 Ron Coomer RC .05 .15
652 Carlos Perez RC .15 .40
653 Jason Isringhausen .10 .30
654 Kevin Jordan .05 .15
655 Esteban Loaiza .05 .15
656 John Frascatore .05 .15
657 Bryce Florie .05 .15
658 Keith Williams .05 .15
659 Checklist .05 .15
660 Checklist .05 .15

1995 Topps Cyberstats

COMPLETE SET (396) 12.00 30.00
COMPLETE SERIES 1 (198) 5.00 12.00
COMPLETE SERIES 2 (198) 8.00 20.00
*STARS: 1X TO 2.5X BASIC CARDS
ONE PER PACK/THREE PER JUMBO

1995 Topps Cyber Season in Review

COMPLETE SET (7) 4.00 10.00
1 Barry Bonds 1.50 4.00
2 Jose Canseco .75 2.00
3 Juan Gonzalez .60 1.50
4 Fred McGriff .40 1.00
5 Carlos Baerga .20 .50
6 Ryan Klesko .40 1.00
7 Kenny Lofton .30 .75

1995 Topps Finest Inserts

COMPLETE SET (15) 25.00 60.00
SER.2 ODDS 1:36 HOB/RET, 1:20 JUM
1 Jeff Bagwell 1.25 3.00
2 Albert Belle .75 2.00
3 Ken Griffey Jr. 4.00 10.00
4 Frank Thomas 2.00 5.00
5 Matt Williams .75 2.00
6 Dante Bichette .75 2.00
7 Barry Bonds 5.00 12.00
8 Moises Alou .75 2.00
9 Andres Galarraga .75 2.00
10 Kenny Lofton .75 2.00
11 Rafael Palmeiro 1.25 3.00
12 Tony Gwynn 2.50 6.00
13 Kirby Puckett 2.00 5.00
14 Jose Canseco 1.25 3.00
15 Jeff Conine .75 2.00

1995 Topps League Leaders

COMPLETE SET (50) 20.00 50.00
COMPLETE SERIES 1 (25) 8.00 20.00
COMPLETE SERIES 2 (25) 12.50 30.00
STATED ODDS 1:6 RETAIL, 1:3 JUMBO
LL1 Albert Belle .25 .60
LL2 Kevin Mitchell .10 .30
LL3 Wade Boggs .40 1.00
LL4 Tony Gwynn .75 2.00
LL5 Moises Alou .25 .60
LL6 Andres Galarraga .25 .60
LL7 Matt Williams .25 .60
LL8 Barry Bonds 1.50 4.00
LL9 Frank Thomas .60 1.50
LL10 Jose Canseco .40 1.00
LL11 Jeff Bagwell .40 1.00
LL12 Kirby Puckett .60 1.50
LL13 Julio Franco .25 .60
LL14 Albert Belle .25 .60
LL15 Fred McGriff .40 1.00
LL16 Kenny Lofton .25 .60
LL17 Otis Nixon .10 .30
LL18 Brady Anderson .25 .60
LL19 Deion Sanders .40 1.00
LL20 Chuck Carr .10 .30
LL21 Pat Hentgen .10 .30
LL22 Andy Benes .10 .30
LL23 Roger Clemens 1.25 3.00
LL24 Greg Maddux 1.00 2.50
LL25 Pedro Martinez .10 .30
LL26 Paul O'Neill .40 1.00
LL27 Jeff Bagwell .40 1.00
LL28 Frank Thomas .60 1.50
LL29 Hal Morris .10 .30
LL30 Kenny Lofton .25 .60
LL31 Ken Griffey Jr. 1.25 3.00
LL32 Jeff Bagwell .40 1.00
LL33 Albert Belle .25 .60
LL34 Fred McGriff .40 1.00
LL35 Cecil Fielder .25 .60
LL36 Matt Williams .25 .60
LL37 Joe Carter .25 .60
LL38 Dante Bichette .25 .60
LL39 Frank Thomas .60 1.50
LL40 Mike Piazza 1.00 2.50
LL41 Craig Biggio .40 1.00
LL42 Vince Coleman .10 .30
LL43 Marquis Grissom .25 .60
LL44 Chuck Knoblauch .25 .60
LL45 Darren Lewis .10 .30
LL46 Randy Johnson .60 1.50
LL47 Jose Rijo .10 .30
LL48 Chuck Finley .25 .60
LL49 Bret Saberhagen .25 .60
LL50 Kevin Appier .25 .60

1995 Topps Opening Day

This 10 card standard size set was inserted into all retail factory sets. The borderless fronts feature the player's photo set against a prismatic star background and the player's name on the bottom. In the lower right, the player's opening day highlight is mentioned and there is an "Opening Day" verbiage and logo in the upper right. The horizontal back has a player photo, description of the player's opening day as well as a line score for the player.

COMPLETE SET (10) 10.00 25.00
1 Kevin Appier .20 .50
2 Dante Bichette .40 1.00
3 Ken Griffey Jr. 8.00 20.00
4 Todd Hundley .40 1.00
5 John Jaha .20 .50
6 Fred McGriff .60 1.50
7 Raul Mondesi .40 1.00
8 Manny Ramirez 2.50 6.00
9 Danny Tartabull .20 .50
10 Devon White .40 1.00

1995 Topps Traded

This set contains 165 standard-size cards and was sold in 11-card packs for $1.29. The set features rookies, draft picks and players who had been traded. The fronts contain a photo with a white border. The backs have a player picture in a scoreboard and his statistics and information. Subsets featured are: At the Break (1T-10T) and All-Stars (156T-164T). Rookie Cards in this set include Michael Barrett, Carlos Beltran, Ben Davis, Hideo Nomo and Richie Sexson.

COMPLETE SET (165) 15.00 40.00
1T Frank Thomas AB .25 .60
2T Ken Griffey Jr. AB .50 1.25
3T Barry Bonds AB .50 1.25
4T Albert Belle AB .15 .40
5T Cal Ripken AB .60 1.50
6T Mike Piazza AB .40 1.00
7T Tony Gwynn AB .25 .60
8T Jeff Bagwell AB .15 .40
9T Mo Vaughn AB .07 .20
10T Matt Williams AB .07 .20
11T Ray Durham .15 .40
12T J.LeBron RC UER Beltran 1.50 4.00
13T Shawn Green .15 .40
14T Kevin Gross .07 .20
15T Jon Nunnally .07 .20
16T Brian Maxcy RC .08 .25
17T Mark Kiefer .07 .20
18T C.Beltran RC UER LeBron 4.00 10.00
19T Michael Mimbs RC .08 .25
20T Larry Walker .15 .40
21T Chad Curtis .07 .20
22T Jeff Barry .07 .20
23T Joe Oliver .07 .20
24T Tomas Perez RC .08 .25
25T Michael Barrett RC .40 1.00
26T Brian McRae .07 .20
27T Derek Bell .07 .20
28T Ray Durham .15 .40
29T Todd Williams .07 .20
30T Ryan Jaroncyk RC .08 .25
31T Todd Steverson .07 .20
32T Mike Devereaux .07 .20
33T Rheal Cormier .07 .20
34T Benny Santiago .15 .40
35T Bob Higginson RC .40 1.00
36T Jack McDowell .07 .20
37T Mike MacFarlane .07 .20
38T Tony McKnight RC .08 .25
39T Brian L.Hunter .07 .20
40T Hideo Nomo RC 1.50 4.00
41T Brett Butler .15 .40
42T Donovan Osborne .07 .20
43T Scott Karl .07 .20
44T Tony Phillips .07 .20
45T Marty Cordova .07 .20
46T Dave Mlicki .07 .20
47T Bronson Arroyo RC 2.50 6.00
48T John Burkett .07 .20
49T J.D.Smart RC .08 .25
50T Mickey Tettleton .07 .20
51T Todd Stottlemyre .07 .20
52T Mike Perez .07 .20
53T Terry Mulholland .07 .20
54T Edgardo Alfonzo .07 .20
55T Zane Smith .07 .20
56T Jacob Brumfield .07 .20
57T Andujar Cedeno .07 .20
58T Jose Parra .07 .20
59T Manny Alexander .07 .20
60T Tony Tarasco .07 .20
61T Orel Hershiser .15 .40
62T Tim Scott .07 .20
63T Felix Rodriguez RC .08 .25
64T Ken Hill .07 .20
65T Marquis Grissom .15 .40
66T Lee Smith .15 .40
67T Jason Bates .07 .20
68T Felipe Lira .07 .20
69T Alex Hernandez RC .08 .25
70T Tony Fernandez .07 .20
71T Scott Radinsky .07 .20
72T Jose Canseco .25 .60
73T Mark Grudzielanek RC .40 1.00
74T Ben Davis RC .08 .25
75T Jim Abbott .25 .60
76T Roger Bailey .07 .20
77T Gregg Jefferies .07 .20
78T Erik Hanson .07 .20
79T Brad Radke RC .40 1.00
80T Jaime Navarro .07 .20
81T John Wetteland .15 .40
82T Chad Fonville RC .08 .25
83T John Mabry .07 .20
84T Glenallen Hill .07 .20
85T Ken Caminiti .15 .40
86T Tom Goodwin .07 .20
87T Darren Bragg .07 .20
88T Robbie Bell RC .08 .25
89T Jeff Russell .07 .20
90T Dave Gallagher .07 .20
91T Steve Finley .15 .40
92T Vaughn Eshelman .07 .20
93T Kevin Jarvis .07 .20
94T Mark Gubicza .07 .20
95T Tim Wakefield .15 .40
96T Bob Tewksbury .07 .20
97T Sid Roberson RC .08 .25
98T Tom Henke .07 .20
99T Michael Tucker .07 .20
100T Jason Bates .07 .20
101T Otis Nixon .07 .20
102T Mark Whiten .07 .20
103T Dilson Torres RC .08 .25
104T Melvin Bunch RC .08 .25
105T Terry Pendleton .15 .40
106T Corey Jenkins RC .08 .25
107T Glenn Dishman RC .08 .25
108T Reggie Taylor RC .08 .25
109T Curtis Goodwin .07 .20
110T David Cone .15 .40
111T Antonio Osuna .07 .20
112T Paul Shuey .07 .20
113T Doug Jones .07 .20
114T Mark McLemore .07 .20
115T Kevin Ritz .07 .20
116T John Kruk .15 .40
117T Trevor Wilson .07 .20
118T Jerald Clark .07 .20
119T Julian Tavarez .07 .20
120T Tim Pugh .07 .20
121T Todd Zeile .07 .20
122T R.Sexson 1.50 4.00
B.Schneider RC
123T Bobby Witt .07 .20
124T Hideo Nomo ROY .60 1.50
125T Joey Cora .07 .20
126T Jim Scharrer RC .08 .25
127T Paul Quantrill .07 .20
128T Chipper Jones ROY .25 .60
129T Kenny James RC .08 .25
130T Mariano Rivera 4.00 10.00
131T Tyler Green .07 .20
132T Brad Clontz .07 .20
133T Jon Nunnally .07 .20
134T Dave Magadan .07 .20
135T Al Leiter .15 .40
136T Bret Barberie .07 .20
137T Bill Swift .07 .20
138T Scott Cooper .07 .20
139T Roberto Kelly .07 .20
140T Charlie Hayes .07 .20
141T Pete Harnisch .07 .20
142T Rich Amaral .07 .20
143T Rudy Seanez .07 .20
144T Pat Listach .07 .20
145T Quilvio Veras .07 .20
146T Jose Olmeda RC .08 .25
147T Roberto Petagine .07 .20
148T Kevin Brown .15 .40
149T Phil Plantier .07 .20
150T Carlos Perez .15 .40
151T Pat Borders .07 .20
152T Tyler Green .07 .20
153T Stan Belinda .07 .20
154T Dave Stewart .15 .40
155T Andre Dawson .15 .40
156T F.Thomas .25 .60
F.McGriff AS
157T C.Baerga .15 .40
C.Biggio AS
158T W.Boggs .15 .40
M.Williams AS
159T C.Ripken .40 1.00
O.Smith AS
160T K.Griffey .50 1.25
T.Gwynn AS
161T A.Belle .50 1.25
B.Bonds AS
162T K.Puckett .25 .60
L.Dykstra AS
163T I.Rodriguez .40 1.00
M.Piazza AS
164T H.Nomo .60 1.50
R.Johnson AS
165T Checklist .07 .20

1995 Topps Traded Proofs

NNO Shawn Green 4.00 10.00

1995 Topps Traded Power Boosters

COMPLETE SET (10) 30.00 80.00
STATED ODDS 1:36
1 Frank Thomas 4.00 10.00
2 Ken Griffey Jr. 8.00 20.00
3 Barry Bonds 8.00 20.00
4 Albert Belle 2.50 6.00
5 Cal Ripken 10.00 25.00
6 Mike Piazza 6.00 15.00
7 Tony Gwynn 4.00 10.00
8 Jeff Bagwell 2.50 6.00
9 Mo Vaughn 1.25 3.00
10 Matt Williams 1.25 3.00

1995 Topps Legends of the '60s Medallions

These 12 bronze medallions feature some of the best players of the 60's, duplicating the regular issue Topps cards from various years. This was a special offering for Topps Stadium Club members. One medallion was issued each month; the issue price was $39.95 per card.

COMPLETE SET (12) 75.00 150.00
1 Willie Mays/1964 10.00 25.00
2 Hank Aaron/1965 10.00 25.00
3 Bob Gibson/1964 8.00 20.00
4 Don Drysdale/1965 8.00 20.00
5 Frank Robinson/1962 8.00 20.00
6 Carl Yastrzemski/1966 8.00 20.00
7 Willie McCovey/1961 8.00 20.00
8 Roberto Clemente/1969 10.00 25.00
9 Juan Marichal/1966 8.00 20.00
10 Brooks Robinson/1969 8.00 20.00
11 Harmon Killebrew/1968 8.00 20.00
12 Billy Williams/1967 8.00 20.00

1996 Topps Pre-Production

PP1 Cal Ripken Jr. 1.25 3.00
PP2 Thomas Howard .15 .40
PP3 Rafael Bournigal .15 .40
PP4 Ron Gant .15 .40
PP5 Chipper Jones .40 1.00
PP6 Frank Thomas .40 1.00
PP7 Barry Bonds .60 1.50
PP8 Fred McGriff .25 .60
PP9 Hideo Nomo .40 1.00

1996 Topps

This set consists of 440 standard-size cards. These cards were issued in 12-card foil packs with a suggested retail price of $1.29. The fronts feature full-color photos surrounded by a white background. Information on the backs includes a player photo, season and career stats and text. First series subsets include Star Power (1-6, 8-12), Draft Picks (13-26), AAA Stars (101-104), and Future Stars (210-219). A special Mickey Mantle card was issued as card number 7 (his uniform number) and became the last card to be issued as card number 7 in the Topps brand set. Rookie Cards in this set include Sean Casey, Geoff Jenkins and Daryle Ward.

COMPLETE SET (440) 15.00 40.00
COMP.HOBBY SET (449) 15.00 40.00
COMP.CEREAL SET (444) 20.00 50.00
COMPLETE SERIES 1 (220) 8.00 20.00
COMPLETE SERIES 2 (220) 8.00 20.00
COMMON CARD (1-440) .07 .20
COMMON RC .08 .25
SUBSET CARDS HALF VALUE OF BASE CARDS
ONE LAST DAY MANTLE PER HOBBY SET
1 Tony Gwynn STP .10 .30
2 Mike Piazza STP .20 .50
3 Greg Maddux STP .20 .50
4 Jeff Bagwell STP .07 .20
5 Larry Walker STP .07 .20
6 Barry Larkin STP .07 .20
7 Mickey Mantle 1.50 4.00
8 Tom Glavine STP .07 .20
9 Craig Biggio STP .07 .20
10 Barry Bonds STP .30 .75
11 Heathcliff Slocumb STP .07 .20
12 Matt Williams STP .07 .20
13 Todd Helton .40 1.00
14 Mark Redman .08 .25
15 Michael Barrett .08 .25
16 Ben Davis .08 .25
17 Juan LeBron .08 .25
18 Tony McKnight .08 .25
19 Ryan Jaroncyk .08 .25
20 Corey Jenkins .08 .25
21 Jim Scharrer .08 .25
22 Mark Bellhorn RC .40 1.00
23 Jarrod Washburn RC .30 .75
24 Geoff Jenkins RC .30 .75
25 Sean Casey RC 1.50 4.00
26 Brett Tomko RC .15 .40
27 Tony Fernandez .07 .20
28 Rich Becker .07 .20
29 Andujar Cedeno .07 .20
30 Paul Molitor .07 .20
31 Brent Gates .07 .20
32 Glenallen Hill .07 .20
33 Mike Macfarlane .07 .20
34 Manny Alexander .07 .20
35 Todd Zeile .07 .20
36 Joe Girardi .07 .20
37 Tony Tarasco .07 .20
38 Tim Belcher .07 .20
39 Tom Goodwin .07 .20
40 Orel Hershiser .07 .20
41 Tripp Cromer .07 .20
42 Sean Bergman .07 .20
43 Troy Percival .07 .20
44 Kevin Stocker .07 .20
45 Albert Belle .07 .20
46 Tony Eusebio .07 .20
47 Sid Roberson .07 .20
48 Todd Hollandsworth .07 .20
49 Mark Wohlers .07 .20
50 Kirby Puckett .20 .50
51 Darren Holmes .07 .20
52 Ron Karkovice .07 .20
53 Al Martin .07 .20
54 Pat Rapp .07 .20
55 Mark Grace .10 .30
56 Greg Gagne .07 .20
57 Stan Javier .07 .20
58 Scott Sanders .07 .20
59 J.T. Snow .07 .20
60 David Justice .07 .20
61 Royce Clayton .07 .20
62 Kevin Foster .07 .20
63 Tim Naehring .07 .20
64 Orlando Miller .07 .20
65 Mike Mussina .10 .30
66 Jim Eisenreich .07 .20
67 Felix Fermin .07 .20
68 Bernie Williams .10 .30
69 Robb Nen .07 .20
70 Ron Gant .07 .20
71 Felipe Lira .07 .20
72 Jacob Brumfield .07 .20
73 John Mabry .07 .20
74 Mark Carreon .07 .20
75 Carlos Baerga .07 .20
76 Jim Dougherty .07 .20
77 Ryan Thompson .07 .20
78 Scott Leius .07 .20
79 Roger Pavlik .07 .20
80 Gary Sheffield .07 .20
81 Julian Tavarez .07 .20
82 Andy Ashby .07 .20
83 Mark Lemke .07 .20
84 Omar Vizquel .10 .30
85 Darren Daulton .07 .20
86 Mike Lansing .07 .20
87 Rusty Greer .07 .20
88 Dave Stevens .07 .20
89 Jose Offerman .07 .20
90 Tom Henke .07 .20
91 Troy O'Leary .07 .20
92 Michael Tucker .07 .20
93 Marvin Freeman .07 .20
94 Alex Diaz .07 .20
95 John Wetteland .07 .20
96 Cal Ripken 2131 .75 2.00
97 Mike Mimbs .07 .20
98 Bobby Higginson .07 .20
99 Edgardo Alfonzo .07 .20
100 Frank Thomas .20 .50
101 Bob Abreu .20 .50
102 B.Givens .08 .25
T.J.Mathews
103 C.Pritchett .08 .25
T.Hubbard
104 E.Owens .08 .25
B.Huskey
105 Doug Drabek .07 .20
106 Tomas Perez .07 .20
107 Mark Leiter .07 .20
108 Joe Oliver .07 .20
109 Tony Castillo .07 .20
110 Checklist (1-110) .07 .20
111 Kevin Seitzer .07 .20
112 Pete Schourek .07 .20
113 Sean Berry .07 .20
114 Todd Stottlemyre .07 .20
115 Joe Carter .07 .20
116 Jeff King .07 .20
117 Dan Wilson .07 .20
118 Kurt Abbott .07 .20
119 Lyle Mouton .07 .20
120 Jose Rijo .07 .20
121 Curtis Goodwin .07 .20
122 Jose Valentin .07 .20
123 Ellis Burks .07 .20
124 David Cone .07 .20
125 Eddie Murray .20 .50
126 Brian Jordan .07 .20
127 Darrin Fletcher .07 .20
128 Curt Schilling .07 .20
129 Ozzie Guillen .07 .20
130 Kenny Rogers .07 .20
131 Tom Pagnozzi .07 .20
132 Garret Anderson .07 .20
133 Bobby Jones .07 .20
134 Chris Gomez .07 .20
135 Mike Stanley .07 .20
136 Hideo Nomo .20 .50
137 Jon Nunnally .07 .20
138 Tim Wakefield .07 .20
139 Steve Finley .07 .20
140 Ivan Rodriguez .10 .30
141 Quilvio Veras .07 .20
142 Mike Fetters .07 .20
143 Mike Greenwell .07 .20
144 Bill Pulsipher .07 .20
145 Mark McGwire .50 1.25
146 Frank Castillo .07 .20
147 Greg Vaughn .07 .20
148 Pat Hentgen .07 .20
149 Walt Weiss .07 .20
150 Randy Johnson .20 .50
151 David Segui .07 .20
152 Benji Gil .07 .20
153 Tom Candiotti .07 .20
154 Geronimo Berroa .07 .20
155 John Franco .07 .20
156 Jay Bell .07 .20
157 Mark Gubicza .07 .20
158 Hal Morris .07 .20
159 Wilson Alvarez .07 .20
160 Derek Bell .07 .20
161 Ricky Bottalico .07 .20
162 Bret Boone .07 .20
163 Brad Radke .07 .20
164 John Valentin .07 .20
165 Steve Avery .07 .20
166 Mark McLemore .07 .20
167 Danny Jackson .07 .20
168 Tino Martinez .10 .30
169 Shane Reynolds .07 .20
170 Terry Pendleton .07 .20
171 Jim Edmonds .07 .20
172 Esteban Loaiza .07 .20
173 Ray Durham .07 .20
174 Carlos Perez .07 .20
175 Raul Mondesi .07 .20
176 Steve Ontiveros .07 .20
177 Chipper Jones .20 .50
178 Otis Nixon .07 .20
179 John Burkett .07 .20
180 Gregg Jefferies .07 .20
181 Denny Martinez .07 .20
182 Ken Caminiti .07 .20
183 Doug Jones .07 .20
184 Brian McRae .07 .20
185 Don Mattingly .50 1.25
186 Mel Rojas .07 .20
187 Marty Cordova .07 .20
188 Vinny Castilla .07 .20
189 John Smoltz .10 .30
190 Travis Fryman .07 .20
191 Chris Hoiles .07 .20
192 Chuck Finley .07 .20
193 Ryan Klesko .07 .20
194 Alex Fernandez .07 .20
195 Dante Bichette .07 .20
196 Eric Karros .07 .20
197 Roger Clemens .40 1.00
198 Randy Myers .07 .20
199 Tony Phillips .07 .20
200 Cal Ripken .60 1.50
201 Rod Beck .07 .20
202 Chad Curtis .07 .20
203 Jack McDowell .07 .20
204 Gary Gaetti .07 .20
205 Ken Griffey Jr. .40 1.00
206 Ramon Martinez .07 .20
207 Jeff Kent .07 .20
208 Brad Ausmus .07 .20
209 Devon White .07 .20
210 Jason Giambi .07 .20
211 Nomar Garciaparra .30 .75
212 Billy Wagner .07 .20
213 Todd Greene .07 .20
214 Paul Wilson .07 .20
215 Johnny Damon .10 .30
216 Alan Benes .07 .20
217 Karim Garcia .07 .20
218 Dustin Hermanson .07 .20
219 Derek Jeter .50 1.25
220 Checklist (111-220) .07 .20
221 Kirby Puckett STP .10 .30
222 Cal Ripken STP .30 .75
223 Albert Belle STP .07 .20
224 Randy Johnson STP .10 .30
225 Wade Boggs STP .07 .20
226 Carlos Baerga STP .07 .20
227 Ivan Rodriguez STP .07 .20
228 Mike Mussina STP .07 .20
229 Frank Thomas STP .10 .30
230 Ken Griffey Jr. STP .25 .60
231 Jose Mesa STP .07 .20
232 Matt Morris RC .60 1.50
233 Craig Wilson RC .30 .75
234 Alvie Shepherd RC .08 .25
235 Randy Winn RC .30 .75
236 David Yocum RC .08 .25
237 Jason Brester RC .08 .25
238 Shane Monahan RC .08 .25
239 Brian McNichol RC .08 .25
240 Reggie Taylor .08 .25
241 Garrett Long .08 .25
242 Jonathan Johnson .08 .25
243 Jeff Liefer RC .08 .25
244 Brian Powell .08 .25
245 Brian Buchanan RC .08 .25
246 Mike Piazza .30 .75
247 Edgar Martinez .10 .30
248 Chuck Knoblauch .07 .20
249 Andres Galarraga .07 .20
250 Tony Gwynn .25 .60
251 Lee Smith .07 .20
252 Sammy Sosa .20 .50
253 Jim Thome .10 .30
254 Frank Rodriguez .07 .20
255 Charlie Hayes .07 .20
256 Bernard Gilkey .07 .20
257 John Smiley .07 .20
258 Brady Anderson .07 .20
259 Rico Brogna .07 .20
260 Kirt Manwaring .07 .20
261 Len Dykstra .07 .20
262 Tom Glavine .10 .30
263 Vince Coleman .07 .20
264 John Olerud .07 .20
265 Orlando Merced .07 .20
266 Kent Mercker .07 .20
267 Terry Steinbach .07 .20
268 Brian L. Hunter .07 .20
269 Jeff Fassero .07 .20
270 Jay Buhner .07 .20
271 Jeff Brantley .07 .20
272 Tim Raines .07 .20
273 Jimmy Key .07 .20
274 Mo Vaughn .07 .20
275 Andre Dawson .07 .20
276 Jose Mesa .07 .20
277 Brett Butler .07 .20
278 Luis Gonzalez .07 .20
279 Steve Sparks .07 .20
280 Chili Davis .07 .20
281 Carl Everett .07 .20
282 Jeff Cirillo .07 .20
283 Thomas Howard .07 .20
284 Paul O'Neill .10 .30
285 Pat Meares .07 .20
286 Mickey Tettleton .07 .20
287 Rey Sanchez .07 .20
288 Bip Roberts .07 .20
289 Roberto Alomar .10 .30
290 Ruben Sierra .07 .20
291 John Flaherty .07 .20
292 Bret Saberhagen .07 .20
293 Barry Larkin .10 .30
294 Sandy Alomar Jr. .07 .20
295 Ed Sprague .07 .20
296 Gary DiSarcina .07 .20
297 Marquis Grissom .07 .20
298 John Frascatore .07 .20
299 Will Clark .10 .30
300 Barry Bonds .60 1.50
301 Ozzie Smith .30 .75
302 Dave Nilsson .07 .20
303 Pedro Martinez .10 .30
304 Joey Cora .07 .20
305 Rick Aguilera .07 .20
306 Craig Biggio .10 .30
307 Jose Vizcaino .07 .20
308 Jeff Montgomery .07 .20
309 Moises Alou .07 .20
310 Robin Ventura .07 .20
311 David Wells .07 .20
312 Delino DeShields .07 .20
313 Trevor Hoffman .07 .20
314 Andy Benes .07 .20
315 Deion Sanders .10 .30
316 Jim Bullinger .07 .20
317 John Jaha .07 .20
318 Greg Maddux .30 .75
319 Tim Salmon .10 .30
320 Ben McDonald .07 .20
321 Sandy Martinez .07 .20
322 Dan Miceli .07 .20
323 Wade Boggs .10 .30
324 Ismael Valdes .07 .20
325 Juan Gonzalez .07 .20
326 Charles Nagy .07 .20
327 Ray Lankford .07 .20
328 Mark Portugal .07 .20
329 Bobby Bonilla .07 .20
330 Reggie Sanders .07 .20
331 Jamie Brewington RC .08 .25
332 Aaron Sele .07 .20
333 Pete Harnisch .07 .20
334 Cliff Floyd .07 .20
335 Cal Eldred .07 .20
336 Jason Bates .07 .20
337 Tony Clark .07 .20
338 Jose Herrera .07 .20
339 Alex Ochoa .07 .20
340 Mark Loretta .07 .20
341 Donne Wall .07 .20
342 Jason Kendall .07 .20
343 Shannon Stewart .07 .20
344 Brooks Kieschnick .07 .20
345 Chris Snopek .07 .20
346 Ruben Rivera .07 .20
347 Jeff Suppan .07 .20
348 Phil Nevin .07 .20
349 John Wasdin .07 .20
350 Jay Payton .07 .20
351 Tim Crabtree .07 .20
352 Rick Krivda .07 .20
353 Bob Wolcott .07 .20
354 Jimmy Haynes .07 .20
355 Herb Perry .07 .20
356 Ryne Sandberg .30 .75
357 Harold Baines .07 .20
358 Chad Ogea .07 .20
359 Lee Tinsley .07 .20
360 Matt Williams .07 .20
361 Randy Velarde .07 .20
362 Jose Canseco .10 .30
363 Larry Walker .07 .20
364 Kevin Appier .07 .20
365 Darryl Hamilton .07 .20
366 Jose Lima .07 .20
367 Javy Lopez .07 .20
368 Dennis Eckersley .07 .20
369 Jason Isringhausen .07 .20
370 Mickey Morandini .07 .20
371 Scott Cooper .07 .20
372 Jim Abbott .10 .30
373 Paul Sorrento .07 .20
374 Chris Hammond .07 .20
375 Lance Johnson .07 .20
376 Kevin Brown .07 .20
377 Luis Alicea .07 .20
378 Andy Pettitte .10 .30
379 Dean Palmer .07 .20
380 Jeff Bagwell .10 .30
381 Jaime Navarro .07 .20
382 Rondell White .07 .20
383 Erik Hanson .07 .20
384 Pedro Munoz .07 .20
385 Heathcliff Slocumb .07 .20
386 Wally Joyner .07 .20
387 Bob Tewksbury .07 .20
388 David Bell .07 .20
389 Fred McGriff .10 .30
390 Mike Henneman .07 .20
391 Robby Thompson .07 .20
392 Norm Charlton .07 .20
393 Cecil Fielder .07 .20
394 Benito Santiago .07 .20
395 Rafael Palmeiro .10 .30
396 Ricky Bones .07 .20
397 Rickey Henderson .20 .50
398 C.J. Nitkowski .07 .20
399 Shawon Dunston .07 .20
400 Manny Ramirez .10 .30
401 Bill Swift .07 .20
402 Chad Fonville .07 .20
403 Joey Hamilton .07 .20
404 Alex Gonzalez .07 .20
405 Roberto Hernandez .07 .20
406 Jeff Blauser .07 .20
407 LaTroy Hawkins .07 .20
408 Greg Colbrunn .07 .20
409 Todd Hundley .07 .20
410 Glenn Dishman .07 .20
411 Joe Vitiello .07 .20
412 Todd Worrell .07 .20
413 Wil Cordero .07 .20
414 Ken Hill .07 .20
415 Carlos Garcia .07 .20
416 Bryan Rekar .07 .20
417 Shawn Green .07 .20
418 Tyler Green .07 .20
419 Mike Blowers .07 .20
420 Kenny Lofton .07 .20
421 Denny Neagle .07 .20
422 Jeff Conine .07 .20
423 Mark Langston .07 .20
424 Ron Wright RC .30 .75
D.Lee
425 D.Ward RC .40 1.00
R.Sexson
426 Adam Riggs RC .08 .25
427 N.Perez .08 .25
E.Wilson
428 Bartolo Colon .20 .50
429 Marty Janzen RC .08 .25
430 Rich Hunter RC .08 .25
431 Dave Coggin RC .08 .25
432 R.Ibanez RC .60 1.50
P.Konerko
433 Marc Kroon .07 .20

434 S.Rolen .20 .50
S.Spiezio
435 V.Guerrero 1.00 2.50
A.Jones
436 Shane Spencer RC .15 .40
437 A.French .08 .25
D.Stovall RC
438 Michael Coleman RC .08 .25
Jacob Cruz/Richard Hidalgo/Charles Peterson
439 Jermaine Dye .07 .20
440 Checklist .07 .20
F7 Mickey Mantle Last Day 2.00 5.00
NNO Derek Jeter Tri-Card 20.00 50.00
NNO Mickey Mantle 1.25 3.00
Tribute Card, promotes the Mantle F

1996 Topps Classic Confrontations

COMPLETE SET (15) 2.50 6.00
ONE PER SPECIAL SER.1 RETAIL PACK
CC1 Ken Griffey Jr. .30 .75
CC2 Cal Ripken .50 1.25
CC3 Edgar Martinez .08 .25
CC4 Kirby Puckett .15 .40
CC5 Frank Thomas .15 .40
CC6 Barry Bonds .50 1.25
CC7 Reggie Sanders .05 .15
CC8 Andres Galarraga .05 .15
CC9 Tony Gwynn .20 .50
CC10 Mike Piazza .25 .60
CC11 Randy Johnson .15 .40
CC12 Mike Mussina .08 .25
CC13 Roger Clemens .30 .75
CC14 Tom Glavine .08 .25
CC15 Greg Maddux .25 .60

1996 Topps Mantle

COMPLETE SET (19) 20.00 50.00
COMMON MANTLE 2.50 6.00
SER.1 ODDS 1:9 HOB, 1:6 RET, 1:2 JUM
FOUR PER CEREAL FACT.SET
CARDS 15-19 SHORTPRINTED BY 20%
ONE CASE PER SER.2 HOB/JUM/VEND CASE
FINEST SER.2 ODDS 1:18 RET, 1:12 ANCO
REF.SER.2 ODDS 1:96 HOB, 1:144 RET
RDMP.SER.2 ODDS 1:72 ANCO, 1:108 RET

1996 Topps Mantle Finest

COMPLETE SET (19) 30.00 60.00
COMMON MANTLE (1-14) 3.00 8.00
COMMON MANTLE SP (15-19) 4.00 10.00
SER.2 STATED ODDS 1:18 RET, 1:12 ANCO
CARDS 15-19 SHORTPRINTED BY 20%
1 Mickey Mantle 1951 Bowman 6.00 15.00
2 Mickey Mantle 1952 Topps 6.00 15.00
3 Mickey Mantle 1953 Topps 3.00 8.00

1996 Topps Masters of the Game

COMPLETE SET (20) 12.50 30.00
SER.1 STATED ODDS 1:18 HOBBY
TWO PER HOBBY FACTORY SET
1 Dennis Eckersley .40 1.00
2 Denny Martinez .40 1.00
3 Eddie Murray 1.00 2.50
4 Paul Molitor .40 1.00
5 Ozzie Smith 1.50 4.00
6 Rickey Henderson 1.00 2.50
7 Tim Raines .40 1.00
8 Lee Smith .40 1.00
9 Cal Ripken 3.00 8.00
10 Chili Davis .40 1.00
11 Wade Boggs .60 1.50
12 Tony Gwynn 1.25 3.00
13 Don Mattingly 2.50 6.00
14 Bret Saberhagen .40 1.00
15 Kirby Puckett 1.00 2.50
16 Joe Carter .40 1.00
17 Roger Clemens 2.00 5.00
18 Barry Bonds 3.00 8.00
19 Greg Maddux 1.50 4.00
20 Frank Thomas 1.00 2.50

1996 Topps Mystery Finest

COMPLETE SET (26) 60.00 120.00
SER.1 STATED ODDS 1:36 HOB/RET, 1:8 JUM
*REF: 1.25X TO 3X BASIC MYSTERY FINEST
REF.SER.1 ODDS 1:216 HOB/RET, 1:36 JUM
M1 Hideo Nomo 2.00 5.00
M2 Greg Maddux 3.00 8.00
M3 Randy Johnson 2.00 5.00
M4 Chipper Jones 2.00 5.00
M5 Marty Cordova .75 2.00
M6 Garret Anderson .75 2.00
M7 Cal Ripken 6.00 15.00
M8 Kirby Puckett 2.00 5.00
M9 Tony Gwynn 2.50 6.00
M10 Manny Ramirez 1.25 3.00
M11 Jim Edmonds .75 2.00
M12 Mike Piazza 3.00 8.00
M13 Barry Bonds 6.00 15.00
M14 Raul Mondesi .75 2.00
M15 Sammy Sosa 2.00 5.00
M16 Ken Griffey Jr. 4.00 10.00
M17 Albert Belle .75 2.00
M18 Dante Bichette .75 2.00
M19 Mo Vaughn .75 2.00
M20 Jeff Bagwell 1.25 3.00
M21 Frank Thomas 2.00 5.00
M22 Hideo Nomo 2.00 5.00
M23 Cal Ripken 6.00 15.00
M24 Mike Piazza 3.00 8.00
M25 Ken Griffey Jr. 4.00 10.00
M26 Frank Thomas 2.00 5.00

1996 Topps Power Boosters

COMPLETE SET (25) 75.00 150.00
COMP.STAR POW.SET (11) 25.00 50.00
COMMON STAR POW. (1-6/8-12) .75 2.00
STR.PWR.SER.1 ODDS 1:36 RETAIL
COMP.DRAFT PICKS SET (14) 1.25 3.00
COMMON DRAFT PICK (13-26) .75 2.00
DP SER.1 STATED ODDS 1:36 HOBBY
CARD #7 DOES NOT EXIST
1 Tony Gwynn 2.50 6.00
2 Mike Piazza 3.00 8.00
3 Greg Maddux 3.00 8.00
4 Jeff Bagwell 1.25 3.00
5 Larry Walker .75 2.00
6 Barry Larkin 1.25 3.00
8 Tom Glavine 1.25 3.00
9 Craig Biggio 1.25 3.00
10 Barry Bonds 6.00 15.00
11 Heathcliff Slocumb .75 2.00
12 Matt Williams .75 2.00
13 Todd Helton 3.00 8.00
14 Mark Redman .75 2.00
15 Michael Barrett .75 2.00
16 Ben Davis .75 2.00
17 Juan LeBron .75 2.00
18 Tony McKnight .75 2.00
19 Ryan Jaroncyk .75 2.00
20 Corey Jenkins .75 2.00
21 Jim Scharrer .75 2.00
22 Mark Bellhorn 4.00 10.00
23 Jarrod Washburn 3.00 8.00
24 Geoff Jenkins 3.00 8.00
25 Sean Casey 6.00 15.00
26 Brett Tomko 2.00 5.00

1996 Topps Profiles

COMPLETE SET (40) 15.00 40.00
COMPLETE SERIES 1 (20) 12.50 30.00
COMPLETE SERIES 2 (20) 4.00 10.00
STAT.ODDS 1:12 HOB/RET,1:6 JUM,1:8 ANCO
1 SER.1 AND 2 SER.2 PER HOB.FACT.SET
AL1 Roberto Alomar .30 .75
AL2 Carlos Baerga .20 .50
AL3 Albert Belle .20 .50
AL4 Cecil Fielder .20 .50
AL5 Ken Griffey Jr. 1.00 2.50
AL6 Randy Johnson .50 1.25
AL7 Paul O'Neill .30 .75
AL8 Cal Ripken 1.50 4.00
AL9 Frank Thomas .50 1.25
AL10 Mo Vaughn .20 .50
AL11 Jay Buhner .20 .50
AL12 Marty Cordova .20 .50
AL13 Jim Edmonds .20 .50
AL14 Juan Gonzalez .20 .50
AL15 Kenny Lofton .20 .50
AL16 Edgar Martinez .30 .75
AL17 Don Mattingly 1.25 3.00
AL18 Mark McGwire 1.25 3.00
AL19 Rafael Palmeiro .30 .75
AL20 Tim Salmon .30 .75
NL1 Jeff Bagwell .30 .75
NL2 Derek Bell .20 .50
NL3 Barry Bonds 1.50 4.00
NL4 Greg Maddux .75 2.00
NL5 Fred McGriff .30 .75
NL6 Raul Mondesi .20 .50
NL7 Mike Piazza .75 2.00
NL8 Reggie Sanders .20 .50
NL9 Sammy Sosa .50 1.25
NL10 Larry Walker .20 .50
NL11 Dante Bichette .20 .50
NL12 Andres Galarraga .20 .50
NL13 Ron Gant .20 .50
NL14 Tom Glavine .30 .75
NL15 Chipper Jones .50 1.25
NL16 David Justice .20 .50
NL17 Barry Larkin .30 .75
NL18 Hideo Nomo .50 1.25
NL19 Gary Sheffield .20 .50
NL20 Matt Williams .20 .50

1996 Topps Road Warriors

COMPLETE SET (20) 5.00 12.00
ONE PER SPECIAL SER.2 RETAIL PACK
RW1 Derek Bell .15 .40
RW2 Albert Belle .15 .40
RW3 Craig Biggio .25 .60
RW4 Barry Bonds 1.25 3.00
RW5 Jay Buhner .15 .40
RW6 Jim Edmonds .15 .40
RW7 Gary Gaetti .15 .40
RW8 Ron Gant .15 .40
RW9 Edgar Martinez .25 .60
RW10 Tino Martinez .25 .60
RW11 Mark McGwire 1.00 2.50
RW12 Mike Piazza .60 1.50
RW13 Manny Ramirez .25 .60
RW14 Tim Salmon .25 .60
RW15 Reggie Sanders .15 .40
RW16 Frank Thomas .40 1.00
RW17 John Valentin .15 .40
RW18 Mo Vaughn .15 .40
RW19 Robin Ventura .15 .40
RW20 Matt Williams .15 .40

1996 Topps Wrecking Crew

COMPLETE SET (15) 25.00 60.00
SER.2 STATED ODDS 1:18 HOBBY
ONE PER HOBBY FACTORY SET
WC1 Jeff Bagwell 1.25 3.00
WC2 Albert Belle .75 2.00
WC3 Barry Bonds 6.00 15.00
WC4 Jose Canseco 1.25 3.00
WC5 Joe Carter .75 2.00
WC6 Cecil Fielder .75 2.00
WC7 Ron Gant .75 2.00
WC8 Juan Gonzalez .75 2.00
WC9 Ken Griffey Jr 4.00 10.00
WC10 Fred McGriff 1.25 3.00
WC11 Mark McGwire 5.00 12.00
WC12 Mike Piazza 3.00 8.00
WC13 Frank Thomas 2.00 5.00
WC14 Mo Vaughn .75 2.00
WC15 Matt Williams .75 2.00

1996 Topps Bronze League Leaders

This six-card set features color action player images on a background of silver rays, sealed to a bed of solid bronze, and silk-screened with the player's league leading 1995 stats plus career numbers. Only 2,000 of this set was produced.

COMPLETE SET (6) 40.00 100.00
1 Barry Larkin 6.00 15.00
2 Greg Maddux 10.00 25.00
3 Hideo Nomo 8.00 20.00
4 Mo Vaughn 4.00 10.00
5 Randy Johnson 8.00 20.00
6 Marty Cordova 4.00 10.00

1996 Topps Mantle Ceramic

This eight-card set features reprints of the original Mickey Mantle cards issued from 1951 through 1969 and are printed on a ceramic card stock. The fronts look the same as the original cards, while the backs state that they were manufactured by R and N China Co. under license from the Topps Company and have a 1996 copyright date. Only 1000 of each card was reproduced and are sequentially numbered. These cards honor Yankee great Mickey Mantle, who passed away in August 1995 after a gallant battle against cancer. The cards are checklisted below according to the year they were originally produced.

COMPLETE SET (8) 100.00 200.00
COMMON CARD (1-8) 10.00 25.00
1 Mickey Mantle/1951 Bowman 12.50 30.00
2 Mickey Mantle/1952 Topps 16.00 40.00

1996-97 Topps Members Only 55

This 55-card set features color player photos of Topps' selection of 50 (numbers 1-50) top American and National League players. The set includes five Finest Cards (numbers 51-55) which represent Topps' selection of the top rookies from 1997. The backs carry information about the player. Each card displays the "Member Only" gold foil stamp.

COMPLETE SET (55) 8.00 20.00
1 Brady Anderson .07 .20
2 Carlos Baerga .02 .10
3 Jeff Bagwell .30 .75
4 Albert Belle .07 .20
5 Dante Bichette .07 .20
6 Craig Biggio .15 .40
7 Wade Boggs .30 .75
8 Barry Bonds .50 1.25
9 Jay Buhner .07 .20
10 Ellis Burks .07 .20
11 Ken Caminiti .15 .40
12 Jose Canseco .20 .50
13 Joe Carter .07 .20
14 Roger Clemens .60 1.50
15 Jeff Conine .02 .10
16 Andres Galarraga .15 .40
17 Ron Gant .02 .10
18 Juan Gonzalez .15 .40
19 Mark Grace .10 .30
20 Ken Griffey Jr. .75 2.00
21 Tony Gwynn .60 1.50
22 Pat Hentgen .07 .20
23 Todd Hollandsworth .02 .10
24 Todd Hundley .07 .20
25 Derek Jeter 1.25 3.00
26 Randy Johnson .30 .75
27 Chipper Jones .60 1.50
28 Ryan Klesko .07 .20
29 Chuck Knoblauch .10 .30
30 Barry Larkin .15 .40
31 Kenny Lofton .07 .20
32 Greg Maddux .75 2.00
33 Mark McGwire .60 1.50
34 Paul Molitor .20 .50
35 Raul Mondesi .07 .20
36 Hideo Nomo .30 .75
37 Rafael Palmeiro .20 .50
38 Mike Piazza .75 2.00
39 Manny Ramirez .30 .75
40 Cal Ripken 1.25 3.00
41 Ivan Rodriguez .30 .75
42 Tim Salmon .10 .30
43 Gary Sheffield .25 .60
44 John Smoltz .15 .40
45 Sammy Sosa .40 1.00
46 Frank Thomas .30 .75
47 Jim Thome .30 .75
48 Mo Vaughn .07 .20
49 Bernie Williams .15 .40
50 Matt Williams .10 .30
51 Darin Erstad .40 1.00
52 Vladimir Guerrero .60 1.50
53 Andruw Jones .40 1.00
54 Scott Rolen .30 .75
55 Todd Walker .02 .10

1996 Topps Team Topps

Parallel cards from nine selected team sets were issued by Topps in 1996 and distributed in team set form to commemorate their superior performances in 1995. The team sets were issued with the "Big Topps cards" in special packaging for retail stores. Each team set carried an SRP of $4.99. Please note, alphabetical prefixes have been added to the card numbers below for easier checklisting purposes. The actual cards do not carry these prefixes. The Cubs, Orioles, Rangers, White Sox and Yankees cards carry a "Team Topps" logo on each card front. The four other teams carry logos on the card fronts as follows: Braves - "World Champions", Dodgers - "35 Seasons", Indians - "1995 American League Champions" and Mariners - "1995 AL West Champions". It's interesting to note that a parallel version of star first basemen Sean Casey's Rookie Card was included within the Indians team set.

COMPLETE SET (150) 40.00 100.00
B3 Greg Maddux STAR 1.25 3.00
B8 Tom Glavine STAR .50 1.25
B12 Jim Scharrer .08 .25
B49 Mark Wohlers .08 .25
B60 David Justice .40 1.00
B83 Mark Lemke .08 .25
B165 Steve Avery .08 .25
B177 Chipper Jones 1.25 3.00
B189 John Smoltz .30 .75
B193 Ryan Klesko .20 .50
B262 Tom Glavine .50 1.25
B266 Kent Mercker .08 .25
B297 Marquis Grissom .08 .25
B318 Greg Maddux 1.25 3.00
B367 Javy Lopez .40 1.00
B389 Fred McGriff .30 .75
B406 Jeff Blauser .08 .25
C35 Todd Zeile .08 .25
C55 Mark Grace .40 1.00
C62 Kevin Foster .08 .25
C146 Frank Castillo .08 .25
C184 Brian McRae .08 .25
C198 Randy Myers .08 .25
C239 Brian McNichol .08 .25
C252 Sammy Sosa .60 1.50
C278 Luis Gonzalez .40 1.00
C287 Rey Sanchez .08 .25
C316 Jim Bullinger .08 .25
C344 Brooks Kieschnick .08 .25
C356 Ryne Sandberg .50 1.25
C381 Jaime Navarro .08 .25
C399 Shawon Dunston .08 .25
D2 Mike Piazza UER 1.25 3.00
D48 Todd Hollandsworth .08 .25
D89 Jose Offerman .08 .25
D136 Hideo Nomo .50 1.25
D153 Tom Candiotti .08 .25
D175 Raul Mondesi .20 .50
D196 Eric Karros .20 .50
D206 Ramon Martinez .08 .25
D217 Karim Garcia .08 .25
D236 David Yocum .08 .25
D246 Mike Piazza STAR UER 1.25 3.00
D277 Brett Butler .20 .50
D312 Delino DeShields .20 .50
D324 Ismael Valdes .08 .25
D402 Chad Fonville .08 .25
D412 Todd Worrell .08 .25
I25 Sean Casey 1.25 3.00
I40 Orel Hershiser .20 .50
I45 Albert Belle .20 .50
I75 Carlos Baerga .08 .25
I81 Julian Tavarez .08 .25
I84 Omar Vizquel .40 1.00
I125 Eddie Murray .50 1.25
I181 Denny Martinez .20 .50
I223 Albert Belle STAR .20 .50
I226 Carlos Baerga STAR .08 .25
I231 Jose Mesa STAR .20 .50
I253 Jim Thome .40 1.00
I276 Jose Mesa .20 .50
I294 Sandy Alomar Jr. .20 .50
I326 Charles Nagy .08 .25
I355 Herb Perry .08 .25
I358 Chad Ogea .08 .25
I373 Paul Sorrento .08 .25
I400 Manny Ramirez .50 1.25
I414 Ken Hill .08 .25
I420 Kenny Lofton .20 .50
M38 Tim Belcher .08 .25
M67 Felix Fermin .08 .25
M94 Alex Diaz .08 .25
M117 Dan Wilson .08 .25
M150 Randy Johnson .50 1.25
M168 Tino Martinez .20 .50
M205 Ken Griffey Jr. 1.25 3.00
M224 Randy Johnson STAR .50 1.25
M230 Ken Griffey Jr. STAR 1.25 3.00
M238 Shane Monahan .08 .25
M247 Edgar Martinez .30 .75
M263 Vince Coleman .08 .25
M270 Jay Buhner .20 .50
M304 Joey Cora .08 .25
M314 Andy Benes .08 .25
M353 Bob Wolcott .08 .25
M392 Norm Charlton .08 .25
M419 Mike Blowers .08 .25
O34 Manny Alexander .08 .25
O65 Mike Mussina STAR UER .40 1.00
O96 Cal Ripken 2131 2.00 5.00
O121 Curtis Goodwin .08 .25
O183 Doug Jones .08 .25
O191 Chris Hoiles .08 .25
O200 Cal Ripken 2.00 5.00
O222 Cal Ripken STAR 2.00 5.00
O228 Mike Mussina UER .40 1.00
O234 Alvie Shepherd .08 .25
O258 Brady Anderson .20 .50
O320 Ben McDonald .08 .25
O329 Bobby Bonilla .08 .25
O352 Rick Krivda .08 .25
O354 Jimmy Haynes .08 .25
O357 Harold Baines .20 .50
O376 Kevin Brown .30 .75
O395 Rafael Palmeiro .50 1.25
R79 Roger Pavlik .08 .25
R87 Rusty Greer .20 .50
R130 Kenny Rogers .08 .25
R140 Ivan Rodriguez .50 1.25
R152 Benji Gil .08 .25
R166 Mark McLemore .08 .25
R178 Otis Nixon .08 .25
R227 Ivan Rodriguez STAR .50 1.25
R242 Jonathan Johnson .08 .25
R286 Mickey Tettleton .08 .25
R299 Will Clark .40 1.00
R325 Juan Gonzalez .50 1.25
R379 Dean Palmer .08 .25
R387 Bob Tewksbury .08 .25
W52 Ron Karkovice .08 .25
W100 Frank Thomas .60 1.50
W119 Lyle Mouton .08 .25
W129 Ozzie Guillen .08 .25
W159 Wilson Alvarez .08 .25
W173 Ray Durham .20 .50
W194 Alex Fernandez .08 .25
W229 Frank Thomas STAR .60 1.50
W243 Jeff Lifer .08 .25
W272 Tim Raines .20 .50
W310 Robin Ventura .40 1.00
W345 Chris Snopek .08 .25
W375 Lance Johnson .08 .25
W405 Roberto Hernandez .08 .25
Y7 Mickey Mantle 4.00 10.00
Y27 Tony Fernandez .20 .50
Y68 Bernie Williams .40 1.00
Y95 John Wetteland .20 .50
Y124 David Cone .30 .75
Y135 Mike Stanley .08 .25
Y185 Don Mattingly 1.00 2.50
Y203 Jack McDowell .08 .25
Y219 Derek Jeter 12.00 30.00
Y225 Wade Boggs STAR .50 1.25
Y245 Brian Buchanan .08 .25
Y273 Jimmy Key .20 .50
Y284 Paul O'Neill .40 1.00
Y290 Ruben Sierra .20 .50
Y323 Wade Boggs .50 1.25
Y346 Ruben Rivera .08 .25
Y361 Randy Velarde .08 .25
Y378 Andy Pettitte .30 .75

1996 Topps Team Topps Big

COMPLETE SET (9) 8.00 20.00
1 Albert Belle .20 .50
2 Juan Gonzalez .40 1.00
3 Ken Griffey Jr. 1.25 3.00
4 Derek Jeter 20.00 50.00
5 Greg Maddux 1.25 3.00
6 Hideo Nomo .50 1.25
7 Cal Ripken 2.00 5.00
8 Ryne Sandberg .50 1.25
9 Frank Thomas .50 1.25

1996 Topps 22K Mantle

This standard-size was issued by Topps seemingly as part of a series of cards honoring retired greats. The cards are exact replicas of already issued cards and it is believed that there might be more cards so any additions to this checklist is appreciated. The back has serial numbering and mentions that Topps copywrited this card in 1996

1 Mickey Mantle 8.00 20.00

1996 Topps R and N China Ripken

1 Cal Ripken Jr./1982 Topps Traded
2 Cal Ripken Jr./1983 Topps
3 Cal Ripken Jr./1984 Topps
4 Cal Ripken Jr./1992 Topps
5 Cal Ripken Jr./1996 Topps
6 Cal Ripken Jr./1992 Topps
7 Cal Ripken Jr./1995 Topps
8 Cal Ripken Jr./1996 Topps #96
9 Cal Ripken Jr./1996 Topps #200

1997 Topps

This 495-card set was primarily distributed in first and second series 11-card packs with a suggested retail price of $1.29. In addition, eight-card retail packs, 40-card jumbo packs and 504-card factory sets (containing the complete 495-card set plus a random selection of eight insert cards and one hermetically sealed Willie Mays or Mickey Mantle Reprint insert) were made available. The card fronts feature a color action player photo with a gloss coating and a spot matte finish on the outside border with gold foil stamping. The backs carry another player photo, player information and statistics. The set includes the following subsets: Season Highlights (100-104, 462-466), Prospects (200-207, 487-494), the first ever expansion team cards of the Arizona Diamondbacks (249-251,468-469 and the Tampa Bay Devil Rays (252-253, 470-472) and Draft Picks (269-274, 477-483). Card 42 is a special Jackie Robinson tribute card commemorating the 50th anniversary of his contribution to baseball history and numbered for his Dodgers uniform number. Card number 7 does not exist because it was retired in honor of Mickey Mantle. Card number 84 does not exist because Mike Fetters' card was incorrectly numbered 61. Card number 277 does not exist because Chipper Jones' card was incorrectly numbered 276. Rookie Cards include Kris Benson and Eric Chavez. The Derek Jeter autograph card found at the end of our checklist was seeded one every 576 second series packs.

COMPLETE SET (495) 30.00 80.00
COMPLETE SERIES 1 (276) 15.00 40.00
COMPLETE SERIES 2 (220) 20.00 40.00
SUBSET CARDS HALF VALUE OF BASE CARDS
CARDS 7, 84 AND 277 DON'T EXIST
ELSTER AND FETTERS NUMBERED 61
CL 276 AND C.JONES NUMBERED 276
1 Barry Bonds .60 1.50
2 Tom Pagnozzi .07 .20
3 Terrell Wade .07 .20
4 Jose Valentin .07 .20
5 Mark Clark .07 .20
6 Brady Anderson .07 .20
8 Wade Boggs .10 .30
9 Scott Stahoviak .07 .20
10 Andres Galarraga .07 .20
11 Steve Avery .07 .20
12 Rusty Greer .07 .20
13 Derek Jeter .50 1.25
14 Ricky Bottalico .07 .20
15 Andy Ashby .07 .20
16 Paul Shuey .07 .20
17 F.P. Santangelo .07 .20
18 Royce Clayton .07 .20
19 Mike Mohler .07 .20
20 Mike Piazza .30 .75
21 Jaime Navarro .07 .20
22 Billy Wagner .07 .20
23 Mike Timlin .07 .20
24 Garret Anderson .07 .20
25 Ben McDonald .07 .20
26 Mel Rojas .07 .20
27 John Burkett .07 .20
28 Jeff King .07 .20
29 Reggie Jefferson .07 .20
30 Kevin Appier .07 .20
31 Felipe Lira .07 .20
32 Kevin Tapani .07 .20
33 Mark Portugal .07 .20
34 Carlos Garcia .07 .20
35 Joey Cora .07 .20
36 David Segui .07 .20
37 Mark Grace .10 .30
38 Erik Hanson .07 .20
39 Jeff D'Amico .07 .20
40 Jay Buhner .07 .20
41 B.J. Surhoff .07 .20
42 Jackie Robinson TRIB .20 .50
43 Roger Pavlik .07 .20
44 Hal Morris .07 .20
45 Mariano Duncan .07 .20
46 Harold Baines .07 .20
47 Jorge Fabregas .07 .20
48 Jose Herrera .07 .20
49 Jeff Cirillo .07 .20
50 Tom Glavine .10 .30
51 Pedro Astacio .07 .20
52 Mark Gardner .07 .20
53 Arthur Rhodes .07 .20
54 Troy O'Leary .07 .20
55 Bip Roberts .07 .20
56 Mike Lieberthal .07 .20
57 Shane Andrews .07 .20
58 Scott Karl .07 .20
59 Gary DiSarcina .07 .20
60 Andy Pettitte .10 .30
61 Kevin Elster .07 .20
61B Mike Fetters UER .07 .20
62 Mark McGwire .50 1.25
63 Dan Wilson .07 .20
64 Mickey Morandini .07 .20
65 Chuck Knoblauch .07 .20
66 Tim Wakefield .07 .20
67 Raul Mondesi .07 .20
68 Todd Jones .07 .20
69 Albert Belle .07 .20
70 Trevor Hoffman .07 .20
71 Eric Young .07 .20
72 Robert Perez .07 .20
73 Butch Huskey .07 .20
74 Brian McRae .07 .20
75 Jim Edmonds .07 .20
76 Mike Henneman .07 .20
77 Frank Rodriguez .07 .20
78 Danny Tartabull .07 .20
79 Robb Nen .07 .20
80 Reggie Sanders .07 .20
81 Ron Karkovice .07 .20
82 Benito Santiago .07 .20
83 Mike Lansing .07 .20
85 Craig Biggio .10 .30
86 Mike Bordick .07 .20
87 Ray Lankford .07 .20
88 Charles Nagy .07 .20
89 Paul Wilson .07 .20
90 John Wetteland .07 .20
91 Tom Candiotti .07 .20
92 Carlos Delgado .07 .20
93 Derek Bell .07 .20
94 Mark Lemke .07 .20
95 Edgar Martinez .10 .30
96 Rickey Henderson .20 .50
97 Greg Myers .07 .20
98 Jim Leyritz .07 .20
99 Mark Johnson .07 .20
100 Dwight Gooden HL .07 .20
101 Al Leiter HL .07 .20
102 John Mabry HL .07 .20
103 Alex Ochoa HL .07 .20
104 Mike Piazza HL .20 .50
105 Jim Thome .10 .30
106 Ricky Otero .07 .20
107 Jamey Wright .07 .20
108 Frank Thomas .20 .50
109 Jody Reed .07 .20
110 Orel Hershiser .07 .20
111 Terry Steinbach .07 .20
112 Mark Loretta .07 .20
113 Turk Wendell .07 .20
114 Marvin Benard .07 .20
115 Kevin Brown .07 .20
116 Robert Person .07 .20
117 Joey Hamilton .07 .20
118 Francisco Cordova .07 .20
119 John Smiley .07 .20
120 Travis Fryman .07 .20
121 Jimmy Key .07 .20
122 Tom Goodwin .07 .20
123 Mike Greenwell .07 .20
124 Juan Gonzalez .07 .20
125 Pete Harnisch .07 .20
126 Roger Cedeno .07 .20
127 Ron Gant .07 .20
128 Mark Langston .07 .20
129 Tim Crabtree .07 .20
130 Greg Maddux .30 .75
131 William VanLandingham .07 .20
132 Wally Joyner .07 .20
133 Randy Myers .07 .20
134 John Valentin .07 .20
135 Bret Boone .07 .20
136 Bruce Ruffin .07 .20
137 Chris Snopek .07 .20
138 Paul Molitor .07 .20
139 Mark McLemore .07 .20
140 Rafael Palmeiro .10 .30
141 Herb Perry .07 .20
142 Luis Gonzalez .07 .20
143 Doug Drabek .07 .20
144 Ken Ryan .07 .20
145 Todd Hundley .07 .20
146 Ellis Burks .07 .20
147 Ozzie Guillen .07 .20
148 Rich Becker .07 .20
149 Sterling Hitchcock .07 .20
150 Bernie Williams .10 .30
151 Mike Stanley .07 .20
152 Roberto Alomar .10 .30
153 Jose Mesa .07 .20
154 Steve Trachsel .07 .20
155 Alex Gonzalez .07 .20
156 Troy Percival .07 .20
157 John Smoltz .10 .30
158 Pedro Martinez .10 .30
159 Jeff Conine .07 .20
160 Bernard Gilkey .07 .20
161 Jim Eisenreich .07 .20
162 Mickey Tettleton .07 .20
163 Justin Thompson .07 .20
164 Jose Offerman .07 .20
165 Tony Phillips .07 .20
166 Ismael Valdes .07 .20
167 Ryne Sandberg .30 .75
168 Matt Mieske .07 .20
169 Geronimo Berroa .07 .20
170 Otis Nixon .07 .20
171 John Mabry .07 .20
172 Shawon Dunston .07 .20
173 Omar Vizquel .10 .30
174 Chris Hoiles .07 .20
175 Dwight Gooden .07 .20
176 Wilson Alvarez .07 .20
177 Todd Hollandsworth .07 .20
178 Roger Salkeld .07 .20
179 Rey Sanchez .07 .20
180 Rey Ordonez .07 .20
181 Denny Martinez .07 .20
182 Ramon Martinez .07 .20
183 Dave Nilsson .07 .20
184 Marquis Grissom .07 .20
185 Randy Velarde .07 .20
186 Ron Coomer .07 .20
187 Tino Martinez .10 .30
188 Jeff Brantley .07 .20
189 Steve Finley .07 .20
190 Andy Benes .07 .20
191 Terry Adams .07 .20
192 Mike Blowers .07 .20
193 Russ Davis .07 .20
194 Darryl Hamilton .07 .20
195 Jason Kendall .07 .20
196 Johnny Damon .10 .30
197 Dave Martinez .07 .20
198 Mike Macfarlane .07 .20
199 Norm Charlton .07 .20
200 Damian Moss .08 .25
201 Jenkins .07 .20
Ibanez/Cameron
202 Sean Casey .10 .30
203 J.Hansen .07 .20
H.Bush/F.Crespo
204 K.Orie .07 .20
G.Alvarez/A.Boone
205 B.Davis .07 .20
K.Brown/B.Estalella
206 Bubba Trammell RC .15 .40
207 Jarrod Washburn .07 .20
208 Brian Hunter .07 .20
209 Jason Giambi .07 .20
210 Henry Rodriguez .07 .20
211 Edgar Renteria .07 .20
212 Edgardo Alfonzo .07 .20
213 Fernando Vina .07 .20
214 Shawn Green .07 .20
215 Ray Durham .07 .20
216 Joe Randa .07 .20
217 Armando Reynoso .07 .20
218 Eric Davis .07 .20
219 Bob Tewksbury .07 .20
220 Jacob Cruz .07 .20
221 Glenallen Hill .07 .20
222 Gary Gaetti .07 .20
223 Donne Wall .07 .20
224 Brad Clontz .07 .20
225 Marty Janzen .07 .20
226 Todd Worrell .07 .20
227 John Franco .07 .20
228 David Wells .07 .20
229 Gregg Jefferies .07 .20
230 Tim Naehring .07 .20
231 Thomas Howard .07 .20
232 Roberto Hernandez .07 .20
233 Kevin Ritz .07 .20
234 Julian Tavarez .07 .20
235 Ken Hill .07 .20
236 Greg Gagne .07 .20
237 Bobby Chouinard .07 .20
238 Joe Carter .07 .20
239 Jermaine Dye .07 .20
240 Antonio Osuna .07 .20
241 Julio Franco .07 .20
242 Mike Grace .07 .20
243 Aaron Sele .07 .20
244 David Justice .07 .20
245 Sandy Alomar Jr. .07 .20
246 Jose Canseco .10 .30
247 Paul O'Neill .10 .30
248 Sean Berry .07 .20
249 N.Bierbrodt .08 .25
K.Sweeney RC
250 Vladimir Nunez RC .08 .25
251 R.Hartman .08 .25
D.Hayman RC
252 A.Sanchez .15 .40
M.Quatraro RC
253 Ronni Seberino RC .08 .25
254 Rex Hudler .07 .20
255 Orlando Miller .07 .20
256 Mariano Rivera .20 .50
257 Brad Radke .07 .20
258 Bobby Higginson .07 .20
259 Jay Bell .07 .20
260 Mark Grudzielanek .07 .20
261 Lance Johnson .07 .20
262 Ken Caminiti .07 .20
263 J.T. Snow .07 .20
264 Gary Sheffield .07 .20
265 Darrin Fletcher .07 .20
266 Eric Owens .07 .20
267 Luis Castillo .07 .20
268 Scott Rolen .10 .30
269 T.Noel .08 .25
J.Oliver RC
270 Robert Stratton RC .15 .40
271 Gil Meche RC .40 1.00
272 E.Milton RC .15 .40
D.Brown RC
273 Chris Reitsma RC .15 .40
274 J.Marquis .30 .75
A.J.Zapp RC
275 Checklist .07 .20
276 Checklist .07 .20
277 Chipper Jones UER276 .20 .50
278 Orlando Merced .07 .20
279 Ariel Prieto .07 .20
280 Al Leiter .07 .20
281 Pat Meares .07 .20
282 Darryl Strawberry .07 .20
283 Jamie Moyer .07 .20
284 Scott Servais .07 .20
285 Delino DeShields .07 .20
286 Danny Graves .07 .20
287 Gerald Williams .07 .20
288 Todd Greene .07 .20
289 Rico Brogna .07 .20

1997 Topps

290 Derrick Gibson .07 .20
291 Joe Girardi .07 .20
292 Darren Lewis .07 .20
293 Nomar Garciaparra .30 .75
294 Greg Colbrunn .07 .20
295 Jeff Bagwell .10 .30
296 Brent Gates .07 .20
297 Jose Vizcaino .07 .20
298 Alex Ochoa .07 .20
299 Sid Fernandez .07 .20
300 Ken Griffey Jr. .40 1.00
301 Chris Gomez .07 .20
302 Wendell Magee .07 .20
303 Darren Oliver .07 .20
304 Mel Nieves .07 .20
305 Sammy Sosa .20 .50
306 George Arias .07 .20
307 Jack McDowell .07 .20
308 Stan Javier .07 .20
309 Kimera Bartee .07 .20
310 James Baldwin .07 .20
311 Rocky Coppinger .07 .20
312 Keith Lockhart .07 .20
313 C.J. Nitkowski .07 .20
314 Allen Watson .07 .20
315 Darryl Kile .07 .20
316 Amaury Telemaco .07 .20
317 Jason Isringhausen .07 .20
318 Manny Ramirez .10 .30
319 Terry Pendleton .07 .20
320 Tim Salmon .10 .30
321 Eric Karros .07 .20
322 Mark Whiten .07 .20
323 Rick Krivda .07 .20
324 Brett Butler .07 .20
325 Randy Johnson .20 .50
326 Eddie Taubensee .07 .20
327 Mark Leiter .07 .20
328 Kevin Gross .07 .20
329 Ernie Young .07 .20
330 Pat Hentgen .07 .20
331 Rondell White .07 .20
332 Bobby Witt .07 .20
333 Eddie Murray .20 .50
334 Tim Raines .07 .20
335 Jeff Fassero .07 .20
336 Chuck Finley .07 .20
337 Willie Adams .07 .20
338 Chan Ho Park .07 .20
339 Jay Powell .07 .20
340 Ivan Rodriguez .10 .30
341 Jermaine Allensworth .07 .20
342 Jay Payton .07 .20
343 T.J. Mathews .07 .20
344 Tony Batista .07 .20
345 Ed Sprague .07 .20
346 Jeff Kent .07 .20
347 Scott Erickson .07 .20
348 Jeff Suppan .07 .20
349 Pete Schourek .07 .20
350 Kenny Lofton .07 .20
351 Alan Benes .07 .20
352 Fred McGriff .10 .30
353 Charlie O'Brien .07 .20
354 Darren Bragg .07 .20
355 Alex Fernandez .07 .20
356 Al Martin .07 .20
357 Bob Wells .07 .20
358 Chad Mottola .07 .20
359 Devon White .07 .20
360 David Cone .07 .20
361 Bobby Jones .07 .20
362 Scott Sanders .07 .20
363 Karim Garcia .07 .20
364 Kirt Manwaring .07 .20
365 Chili Davis .07 .20
366 Mike Hampton .07 .20
367 Chad Ogea .07 .20
368 Curt Schilling .07 .20
369 Phil Nevin .07 .20
370 Roger Clemens .40 1.00
371 Willie Greene .07 .20
372 Kenny Rogers .07 .20
373 Jose Rijo .07 .20
374 Bobby Bonilla .07 .20
375 Mike Mussina .10 .30
376 Curtis Pride .07 .20
377 Todd Walker .07 .20
378 Jason Bere .07 .20
379 Heathcliff Slocumb .07 .20
380 Dante Bichette .07 .20
381 Carlos Baerga .07 .20
382 Livan Hernandez .07 .20
383 Jason Schmidt .07 .20
384 Kevin Stocker .07 .20
385 Matt Williams .07 .20
386 Bartolo Colon .07 .20
387 Will Clark .10 .30
388 Dennis Eckersley .07 .20
389 Brooks Kieschnick .07 .20
390 Ryan Klesko .07 .20
391 Mark Carreon .07 .20
392 Tim Worrell .07 .20
393 Dean Palmer .07 .20
394 Wil Cordero .07 .20
395 Javy Lopez .07 .20
396 Rich Aurilia .07 .20
397 Greg Vaughn .07 .20
398 Vinny Castilla .07 .20
399 Jeff Montgomery .07 .20
400 Cal Ripken .60 1.50
401 Walt Weiss .07 .20
402 Brad Ausmus .07 .20
403 Ruben Rivera .07 .20
404 Mark Wohlers .07 .20
405 Rick Aguilera .07 .20
406 Tony Clark .07 .20
407 Lyle Mouton .07 .20
408 Bill Pulsipher .07 .20
409 Jose Rosado .07 .20
410 Tony Gwynn .25 .60
411 Cecil Fielder .07 .20
412 John Flaherty .07 .20
413 Lenny Dykstra .07 .20
414 Ugueth Urbina .07 .20
415 Brian Jordan .07 .20
416 Bob Abreu .10 .30
417 Craig Paquette .07 .20
418 Sandy Martinez .07 .20
419 Jeff Blauser .07 .20
420 Barry Larkin .10 .30
421 Kevin Seitzer .07 .20
422 Tim Belcher .07 .20
423 Paul Sorrento .07 .20
424 Cal Eldred .07 .20
425 Robin Ventura .07 .20
426 John Olerud .07 .20
427 Bob Wolcott .07 .20
428 Matt Lawton .07 .20
429 Rod Beck .07 .20
430 Shane Reynolds .07 .20
431 Mike James .07 .20
432 Steve Wojciechowski .07 .20
433 Vladimir Guerrero .20 .50
434 Dustin Hermanson .07 .20
435 Marty Cordova .07 .20
436 Marc Newfield .07 .20
437 Todd Stottlemyre .07 .20
438 Jeffrey Hammonds .07 .20
439 Dave Stevens .07 .20
440 Hideo Nomo .20 .50
441 Mark Thompson .07 .20
442 Mark Lewis .07 .20
443 Quinton McCracken .07 .20
444 Cliff Floyd .07 .20
445 Denny Neagle .07 .20
446 John Jaha .07 .20
447 Mike Sweeney .07 .20
448 John Wasdin .07 .20
449 Chad Curtis .07 .20
450 Mo Vaughn .07 .20
451 Donovan Osborne .07 .20
452 Ruben Sierra .07 .20
453 Michael Tucker .07 .20
454 Kurt Abbott .07 .20
455 Andruw Jones UER .10 .30
456 Shannon Stewart .07 .20
457 Scott Brosius .07 .20
458 Juan Guzman .07 .20
459 Ron Villone .07 .20
460 Moises Alou .07 .20
461 Larry Walker .07 .20
462 Eddie Murray SH .10 .30
463 Paul Molitor SH .07 .20
464 Hideo Nomo SH .07 .20
465 Barry Bonds SH .30 .75
466 Todd Hundley SH .07 .20
467 Rheal Cormier .07 .20
468 J.Sandoval .08 .25
J.Conti RC
469 R.Barajas .60 1.50
J.Rexrode RC
470 Jared Sandberg RC .08 .25
471 P.Wilder .08 .25
C.Gunner RC
472 M.DeCelle .08 .25
M.McCain RC
473 Todd Zeile .07 .20
474 Neifi Perez .07 .20
475 Jeromy Burnitz .07 .20
476 Trey Beamon .07 .20
477 J.Patterson .30 .75
B.Looper RC
478 Jake Westbrook RC .20 .50
479 E.Chavez .75 2.00
A.Eaton RC
480 P.Tucci .08 .25
J.Lawrence RC
481 K.Benson .20 .50
B.Koch RC
482 J.Nicholson .08 .25
A.Prater RC
483 M.Kotsay .30 .75
M.Johnson RC
484 Armando Benitez .07 .20
485 Mike Matheny .07 .20
486 Jeff Reed .07 .20
487 M.Bellhorn .07 .20
R.Johnson/E.Wilson
488 R.Hidalgo .07 .20
B.Grieve
489 Konerko .10 .30
D.Lee/Wright
490 Bill Mueller RC .50 1.25
491 J.Abbott .07 .20
S.Monahan/E.Velazquez
492 Jimmy Anderson RC .08 .25
493 Carl Pavano .07 .20
494 Nelson Figueroa RC .08 .25
495 Checklist (277-400) .07 .20
496 Checklist (401-496) .07 .20
NNO Derek Jeter AU 125.00 250.00

1997 Topps All-Stars

COMPLETE SET (22) 10.00 25.00
SER.1 STATED ODDS 1:18 HOB/RET, 1:6 JUM
AS1 Ivan Rodriguez .40 1.00
AS2 Todd Hundley .25 .60
AS3 Frank Thomas .60 1.50
AS4 Andres Galarraga .25 .60
AS5 Chuck Knoblauch .25 .60
AS6 Eric Young .25 .60
AS7 Jim Thome .40 1.00
AS8 Chipper Jones .60 1.50
AS9 Cal Ripken 2.00 5.00
AS10 Barry Larkin .40 1.00
AS11 Albert Belle .25 .60
AS12 Barry Bonds 2.00 5.00
AS13 Ken Griffey Jr. 1.25 3.00
AS14 Ellis Burks .25 .60
AS15 Juan Gonzalez .25 .60
AS16 Gary Sheffield .25 .60
AS17 Andy Pettitte .40 1.00
AS18 Tom Glavine .40 1.00
AS19 Pat Hentgen .25 .60
AS20 John Smoltz .40 1.00
AS21 Roberto Hernandez .25 .60
AS22 Mark Wohlers .25 .60

1997 Topps Awesome Impact

COMPLETE SET (20) 40.00 100.00
SER.2 STATED ODDS 1:18 RETAIL
AI1 Jaime Bluma 1.25 3.00
AI2 Tony Clark 1.25 3.00
AI3 Jermaine Dye 1.25 3.00
AI4 Nomar Garciaparra 5.00 12.00
AI5 Vladimir Guerrero 3.00 8.00
AI6 Todd Hollandsworth 1.25 3.00
AI7 Derek Jeter 8.00 20.00
AI8 Andruw Jones 2.00 5.00
AI9 Chipper Jones 3.00 8.00
AI10 Jason Kendall 1.25 3.00
AI11 Brooks Kieschnick 1.25 3.00
AI12 Alex Ochoa 1.25 3.00
AI13 Rey Ordonez 1.25 3.00
AI14 Neifi Perez 1.25 3.00
AI15 Edgar Renteria 1.25 3.00
AI16 Mariano Rivera 3.00 8.00
AI17 Ruben Rivera 1.25 3.00
AI18 Scott Rolen 2.00 5.00
AI19 Billy Wagner 1.25 3.00
AI20 Todd Walker 1.25 3.00

1997 Topps Hobby Masters

COMPLETE SET (20) 30.00 80.00
COMPLETE SERIES 1 (10) 15.00 40.00
COMPLETE SERIES 2 (10) 15.00 40.00
STATED ODDS 1:36 HOBBY
HM1 Ken Griffey Jr. 3.00 8.00
HM2 Cal Ripken 5.00 12.00
HM3 Greg Maddux 2.50 6.00
HM4 Albert Belle .60 1.50
HM5 Tony Gwynn 2.00 5.00
HM6 Jeff Bagwell 1.00 2.50
HM7 Randy Johnson 1.50 4.00
HM8 Raul Mondesi .60 1.50
HM9 Juan Gonzalez .60 1.50
HM10 Kenny Lofton .60 1.50
HM11 Frank Thomas 1.50 4.00
HM12 Mike Piazza 2.50 6.00
HM13 Chipper Jones 1.50 4.00
HM14 Brady Anderson .60 1.50
HM15 Ken Caminiti .60 1.50
HM16 Barry Bonds 5.00 12.00
HM17 Mo Vaughn .60 1.50
HM18 Derek Jeter 4.00 10.00
HM19 Sammy Sosa 1.50 4.00
HM20 Andres Galarraga .60 1.50

1997 Topps Inter-League Finest

COMPLETE SET (14) 25.00 60.00
SER.1 ODDS 1:36 HOB/RET,1:10 JUM
*REF.: 1X TO 2.5X BASIC INTER-LG
REF.SER.1 ODDS 1:216 HOB/RET, 1:56 JUM
ILM1 M.McGwire 4.00 10.00
B.Bonds
ILM2 M.Piazza 2.50 6.00
T.Salmon
ILM3 K.Griffey Jr. 3.00 8.00
D.Bichette
ILM4 J.Gonzalez 2.00 5.00
T.Gwynn
ILM5 S.Sosa 1.50 4.00
F.Thomas
ILM6 A.Belle .60 1.50
B.Larkin
ILM7 J.Damon .60 1.50
B.Jordan
ILM8 P.Molitor .60 1.50
J.King
ILM9 J.Bagwell 1.00 2.50
J.Jaha
ILM10 B.Williams 1.00 2.50
T.Hundley
ILM11 J.Carter .60 1.50
H.Rodriguez
ILM12 C.Ripken 5.00 12.00
G.Jefferies
ILM13 C.Jones 1.50 4.00
M.Vaughn
ILM14 T.Fryman .60 1.50
G.Sheffield

1997 Topps Mantle

COMPLETE SET (16) 40.00 100.00
COMMON MANTLE (21-36) 3.00 8.00
SER.1 ODDS 1:12 HOB/RET,1:3 JUM
COMMON FINEST (21-36) 3.00 8.00
FINEST SER.2 1:24 HOB/RET, 1:6 JUM
COMMON REF. (21-36) 12.50 30.00
REF.SER.2 1:216 HOB/RET,1:60 JUM

1997 Topps Mays

COMPLETE SET (27) 30.00 60.00
COMMON MAYS (3-27) 1.50 4.00
SER.1 ODDS 1:8 HOB/RET, 1:2 JUM
COMMON FINEST (1-27) 1.50 4.00
*'51-'52 FINEST: .4X TO 1X LISTED CARDS
FINEST SER.2 1:20 HOB/RET,1:4 JUM
COMMON REF. (1-27) 4.00 10.00
*'51-'52 REF: 1X TO 2.5X BASIC MAYS
REF.SER.2 1:180 HOB/RET,1:48 JUM
1 1951 Bowman 3.00 8.00
2 1952 Topps 2.50 6.00
J261 Willie Mays 1952 Jumbo 3.00 8.00

1997 Topps Mays Autographs

COMMON CARD (1953-1958) 100.00 200.00
COMMON CARD (1960-1973) 78.00 150.00
SER.1 ODDS 1:2400 H/R, 1:625 JUM
MAYS SIGNED APPX. 65 OF EACH CARD
NO AU'S: 54B-56T-59T-62T-67T-68T-71T
1 Willie Mays 1951 Bowman 100.00 200.00
2 Willie Mays 1952 Topps 100.00 200.00

1997 Topps Season's Best

COMPLETE SET (25) 10.00 25.00
SER.2 STATED ODDS 1:6 HOB/RET, 1:1 JUM
SB1 Tony Gwynn 1.00 2.50
SB2 Frank Thomas .75 2.00
SB3 Ellis Burks .30 .75
SB4 Paul Molitor .30 .75
SB5 Chuck Knoblauch .30 .75
SB6 Mark McGwire 2.00 5.00
SB7 Brady Anderson .30 .75
SB8 Ken Griffey Jr. 1.50 4.00
SB9 Albert Belle .30 .75
SB10 Andres Galarraga .30 .75
SB11 Andres Galarraga .30 .75
SB12 Albert Belle .30 .75
SB13 Juan Gonzalez .30 .75
SB14 Mo Vaughn .30 .75
SB15 Rafael Palmeiro .50 1.25
SB16 John Smoltz .50 1.25
SB17 Andy Pettitte .50 1.25
SB18 Pat Hentgen .30 .75
SB19 Mike Mussina .50 1.25
SB20 Andy Benes .30 .75
SB21 Kenny Lofton .30 .75
SB22 Tom Goodwin .30 .75
SB23 Otis Nixon .30 .75
SB24 Eric Young .30 .75
SB25 Lance Johnson .30 .75

1997 Topps Sweet Strokes

COMPLETE SET (15) 15.00 40.00
SER.1 STATED ODDS 1:12 RETAIL
SS1 Roberto Alomar .60 1.50
SS2 Jeff Bagwell .60 1.50
SS3 Albert Belle .40 1.00
SS4 Barry Bonds 3.00 8.00
SS5 Mark Grace .60 1.50
SS6 Ken Griffey Jr. 2.00 5.00
SS7 Tony Gwynn 1.25 3.00
SS8 Chipper Jones 1.00 2.50
SS9 Edgar Martinez .60 1.50
SS10 Mark McGwire 2.50 6.00
SS11 Rafael Palmeiro .60 1.50
SS12 Mike Piazza 1.50 4.00
SS13 Gary Sheffield .40 1.00
SS14 Frank Thomas 1.00 2.50
SS15 Mo Vaughn .40 1.00

1997 Topps Team Timber

COMPLETE SET (16) 15.00 40.00
SER.2 STATED ODDS 1:36 HOB/RET, 1:8 JUM
TT1 Ken Griffey Jr. 2.00 5.00
TT2 Ken Caminiti .40 1.00
TT3 Bernie Williams .60 1.50
TT4 Jeff Bagwell .60 1.50
TT5 Frank Thomas 1.00 2.50
TT6 Andres Galarraga .40 1.00
TT7 Barry Bonds 3.00 8.00
TT8 Rafael Palmeiro .60 1.50
TT9 Brady Anderson .40 1.00
TT10 Juan Gonzalez .40 1.00
TT11 Mo Vaughn .40 1.00
TT12 Mark McGwire 2.50 6.00
TT13 Gary Sheffield .40 1.00
TT14 Albert Belle .40 1.00
TT15 Chipper Jones 1.00 2.50
TT16 Mike Piazza 1.50 4.00

1997 Topps 22K Gold

This one-card set is an embossed 22 karat gold foil replica of the 1997 Topps regular Ken Griffey Jr. card. Only a limited number of this set were produced and are serially numbered. Each card is packed in a protective display holder.

1 Ken Griffey Jr. 15.00 40.00

1998 Topps Pre-Production

COMPLETE SET (6) 3.00 8.00
PP1 Carlos Baerga .08 .25
PP2 Jeff Bagwell .40 1.00
PP3 Marquis Grissom .15 .40
PP4 Derek Jeter 1.50 4.00
PP5 Randy Johnson .40 1.00
PP6 Mike Piazza 1.25 3.00

1998 Topps

This 503-card set was distributed in two separate series: 282 cards in first series and 221 cards in second series. 11-card packs carried a suggested retail price of $1.29. Cards were also distributed in Home Team Advantage jumbo packs and hobby, retail and Christmas factory sets. Card fronts feature color action player photos printed on 16 pt. stock with player information and career statistics on the back. Card number 7 was permanently retired in 1996 to honor Mickey Mantle. Series one contains the following subsets: Draft Picks (245-249), Prospects (250-259), Season Highlights (265-269), Interleague (270-274) Checklists (275-276) and World Series (277-283). Series two contains Season Highlights (474-478), Interleague (479-483), Prospects (484-495/498-501) and Checklists (502-503). Rookie Cards of note include Ryan Anderson, Michael Cuddyer, Jack Cust and Troy Glaus. This set also features Topps long-awaited first regular-issue Alex Rodriguez card (504). The superstar shortstop was left out of all Topps sets for the first four years of his career due to a problem between Topps and Rodriguez's agent Scott Boras. Finally, as part of an agreement with the Baseball Hall of Fame, Topps produced commemorative admission tickets featuring Roberto Clemente memorabilia from the Hall in the form of a Topps card. These were the standard admission tickets for the shrine, and were also included one per case in 1998 Topps series two baseball.

COMPLETE SET (503) 25.00 60.00
COMP.HOBBY SET (511) 30.00 80.00
COMP.RETAIL SET (511) 30.00 80.00
COMPLETE SERIES 1 (282) 12.50 30.00
COMPLETE SERIES 2 (221) 12.50 30.00
CARD NUMBER 7 DOES NOT EXIST
1 Tony Gwynn .25 .60
2 Larry Walker .07 .20
3 Billy Wagner .07 .20
4 Denny Neagle .07 .20
5 Vladimir Guerrero .20 .50
6 Kevin Brown .10 .30
8 Mariano Rivera .20 .50
9 Tony Clark .07 .20
10 Deion Sanders .10 .30
11 Francisco Cordova .07 .20
12 Matt Williams .07 .20
13 Carlos Baerga .07 .20
14 Mo Vaughn .07 .20
15 Bobby Witt .07 .20
16 Matt Stairs .07 .20
17 Chan Ho Park .07 .20
18 Mike Bordick .07 .20
19 Michael Tucker .07 .20
20 Frank Thomas .20 .50
21 Roberto Clemente .40 1.00
22 Dmitri Young .07 .20
23 Steve Trachsel .07 .20
24 Jeff Kent .07 .20
25 Scott Rolen .10 .30
26 John Thomson .07 .20
27 Joe Vitiello .07 .20
28 Eddie Guardado .07 .20
29 Charlie Hayes .07 .20
30 Juan Gonzalez .07 .20
31 Garret Anderson .07 .20
32 John Jaha .07 .20
33 Omar Vizquel .10 .30
34 Brian Hunter .07 .20
35 Jeff Bagwell .10 .30
36 Mark Lemke .07 .20
37 Doug Glanville .07 .20
38 Dan Wilson .07 .20
39 Steve Cooke .07 .20
40 Chili Davis .07 .20
41 Mike Cameron .07 .20
42 F.P. Santangelo .07 .20
43 Brad Ausmus .07 .20
44 Gary DiSarcina .07 .20
45 Pat Hentgen .07 .20
46 Wilton Guerrero .07 .20
47 Devon White .07 .20
48 Danny Patterson .07 .20
49 Pat Meares .07 .20
50 Rafael Palmeiro .10 .30
51 Mark Gardner .07 .20
52 Jeff Blauser .07 .20
53 Dave Hollins .07 .20
54 Carlos Garcia .07 .20
55 Ben McDonald .07 .20
56 John Mabry .07 .20
57 Trevor Hoffman .07 .20
58 Tony Fernandez .07 .20
59 Rich Loiselle RC .07 .20
60 Mark Leiter .07 .20
61 Pat Kelly .07 .20
62 John Flaherty .07 .20
63 Roger Bailey .07 .20
64 Tom Gordon .07 .20
65 Ryan Klesko .07 .20
66 Darryl Hamilton .07 .20
67 Jim Eisenreich .07 .20
68 Butch Huskey .07 .20
69 Mark Grudzielanek .07 .20
70 Marquis Grissom .07 .20
71 Mark McLemore .07 .20
72 Gary Gaetti .07 .20
73 Greg Gagne .07 .20
74 Lyle Mouton .07 .20
75 Jim Edmonds .07 .20
76 Shawn Green .07 .20
77 Greg Vaughn .07 .20
78 Terry Adams .07 .20
79 Kevin Polcovich .07 .20
80 Troy O'Leary .07 .20
81 Jeff Shaw .07 .20
82 Rich Becker .07 .20
83 David Wells .07 .20
84 Steve Karsay .07 .20
85 Charles Nagy .07 .20
86 B.J. Surhoff .07 .20
87 Jamey Wright .07 .20
88 James Baldwin .07 .20
89 Edgardo Alfonzo .07 .20
90 Jay Buhner .07 .20
91 Brady Anderson .07 .20
92 Scott Servais .07 .20
93 Edgar Renteria .07 .20
94 Mike Lieberthal .07 .20
95 Rick Aguilera .07 .20
96 Walt Weiss .07 .20
97 Deivi Cruz .07 .20
98 Kurt Abbott .07 .20
99 Henry Rodriguez .07 .20
100 Mike Piazza .30 .75
101 Bill Taylor .07 .20
102 Todd Zeile .07 .20
103 Rey Ordonez .07 .20
104 Willie Greene .07 .20
105 Tony Womack .07 .20
106 Mike Sweeney .07 .20
107 Jeffrey Hammonds .07 .20
108 Kevin Orie .07 .20
109 Alex Gonzalez .07 .20
110 Jose Canseco .10 .30
111 Paul Sorrento .07 .20
112 Joey Hamilton .07 .20
113 Brad Radke .07 .20
114 Steve Avery .07 .20
115 Esteban Loaiza .07 .20
116 Stan Javier .07 .20
117 Chris Gomez .07 .20
118 Royce Clayton .07 .20
119 Orlando Merced .07 .20
120 Kevin Appier .07 .20
121 Mel Nieves .07 .20
122 Joe Girardi .07 .20
123 Rico Brogna .07 .20
124 Kent Mercker .07 .20
125 Manny Ramirez .10 .30
126 Jeromy Burnitz .07 .20
127 Kevin Foster .07 .20
128 Matt Morris .07 .20
129 Jason Dickson .07 .20
130 Tom Glavine .10 .30
131 Wally Joyner .07 .20
132 Rick Reed .07 .20
133 Todd Jones .07 .20
134 Dave Martinez .07 .20
135 Sandy Alomar Jr. .07 .20
136 Mike Lansing .07 .20
137 Sean Berry .07 .20
138 Doug Jones .07 .20
139 Todd Stottlemyre .07 .20
140 Jay Bell .07 .20
141 Jaime Navarro .07 .20
142 Chris Hoiles .07 .20
143 Joey Cora .07 .20
144 Scott Spiezio .07 .20
145 Joe Carter .07 .20
146 Jose Guillen .07 .20
147 Damion Easley .07 .20
148 Lee Stevens .07 .20
149 Alex Fernandez .07 .20
150 Randy Johnson .20 .50
151 J.T. Snow .07 .20
152 Chuck Finley .07 .20
153 Bernard Gilkey .07 .20
154 David Segui .07 .20
155 Dante Bichette .07 .20
156 Kevin Stocker .07 .20
157 Carl Everett .07 .20
158 Jose Valentin .07 .20
159 Pokey Reese .07 .20
160 Derek Jeter .50 1.25
161 Roger Pavlik .07 .20
162 Mark Wohlers .07 .20
163 Ricky Bottalico .07 .20
164 Ozzie Guillen .07 .20
165 Mike Mussina .10 .30
166 Gary Sheffield .07 .20
167 Hideo Nomo .20 .50
168 Mark Grace .10 .30
169 Aaron Sele .07 .20
170 Darryl Kile .07 .20
171 Shawn Estes .07 .20
172 Vinny Castilla .07 .20
173 Ron Coomer .07 .20
174 Jose Rosado .07 .20
175 Kenny Lofton .07 .20
176 Jason Giambi .07 .20
177 Hal Morris .07 .20
178 Darren Bragg .07 .20
179 Orel Hershiser .07 .20
180 Ray Lankford .07 .20
181 Hideki Irabu .07 .20
182 Kevin Young .07 .20
183 Javy Lopez .07 .20
184 Jeff Montgomery .07 .20
185 Mike Holtz .07 .20
186 George Williams .07 .20
187 Cal Eldred .07 .20
188 Tom Candiotti .07 .20
189 Glenallen Hill .07 .20
190 Brian Giles .07 .20
191 Dave Mlicki .07 .20
192 Garrett Stephenson .07 .20
193 Jeff Frye .07 .20
194 Joe Oliver .07 .20
195 Bob Hamelin .07 .20
196 Luis Sojo .07 .20
197 LaTroy Hawkins .07 .20
198 Kevin Elster .07 .20
199 Jeff Reed .07 .20
200 Dennis Eckersley .07 .20
201 Bill Mueller .07 .20
202 Russ Davis .07 .20
203 Armando Benitez .07 .20
204 Quilvio Veras .07 .20
205 Tim Naehring .07 .20
206 Quinton McCracken .07 .20
207 Raul Casanova .07 .20
208 Matt Lawton .07 .20
209 Luis Alicea .07 .20
210 Luis Gonzalez .07 .20
211 Allen Watson .07 .20
212 Gerald Williams .07 .20
213 David Bell .07 .20
214 Todd Hollandsworth .07 .20
215 Wade Boggs .10 .30
216 Jose Mesa .07 .20
217 Jamie Moyer .07 .20
218 Darren Daulton .07 .20
219 Mickey Morandini .07 .20
220 Rusty Greer .07 .20
221 Jim Bullinger .07 .20
222 Jose Offerman .07 .20
223 Matt Karchner .07 .20
224 Woody Williams .07 .20
225 Mark Loretta .07 .20
226 Mike Hampton .07 .20
227 Willie Adams .07 .20
228 Scott Hatteberg .07 .20
229 Rich Amaral .07 .20
230 Terry Steinbach .07 .20
231 Glendon Rusch .07 .20
232 Bret Boone .07 .20
233 Robert Person .07 .20
234 Jose Hernandez .07 .20
235 Doug Drabek .07 .20
236 Jason McDonald .07 .20
237 Chris Widger .07 .20
238 Tom Martin .07 .20
239 Dave Burba .07 .20
240 Pete Rose Jr. .07 .20
241 Bobby Ayala .07 .20
242 Tim Wakefield .07 .20
243 Dennis Springer .07 .20
244 Tim Belcher .07 .20
245 J.Garland .10 .30
G.Goetz
246 L.Berkman .10 .30
G.Davis
247 V.Wells .10 .30
A.Akin
248 A.Kennedy .07 .20
J.Romano
249 J.Dellaero .07 .20
T.Cameron
250 J.Sandberg .07 .20
A.Sanchez
251 P.Ortega .07 .20
J.Manias
252 Mike Stoner RC .07 .20
253 J.Patterson .07 .20
L.Rodriguez
254 R.Minor RC .10 .30
A.Beltre
255 B.Grieve .07 .20
D.Brown
256 Wood .10 .30
Pavano/Meche
257 D.Ortiz 1.00 2.50
Sexson/Ward
258 J.Encarn .07 .20
Winn/Vessel
259 Bens .07 .20
T.Smith RC/C.Dunc RC
260 Warren Morris RC .07 .20
261 R.Hernandez .07 .20
B.Davis/E.Marrero
262 E.Chavez .10 .30
R.Branyan
263 Ryan Jackson RC .07 .20
264 B.Fuentes RC .60 1.50
Clement/Halladay
265 Randy Johnson SH .10 .30
266 Kevin Brown SH .07 .20
267 R.Rincon .07 .20
F.Cordova SH
268 Nomar Garciaparra SH .20 .50
269 Tino Martinez SH .07 .20
270 Chuck Knoblauch IL .07 .20
271 Pedro Martinez IL .10 .30
272 Denny Neagle IL .07 .20
273 Juan Gonzalez IL .07 .20
274 Andres Galarraga IL .07 .20
275 Checklist (1-195) .07 .20
276 Checklist (196-283 .07 .20
inserts)
277 Moises Alou WS .07 .20
278 Sandy Alomar Jr. WS .07 .20
279 Gary Sheffield WS .07 .20
280 Matt Williams WS .07 .20
281 Livan Hernandez WS .07 .20
282 Chad Ogea WS .07 .20
283 Marlins Champs .07 .20
284 Tino Martinez .10 .30
285 Roberto Alomar .10 .30
286 Jeff King .07 .20
287 Brian Jordan .07 .20
288 Darin Erstad .07 .20
289 Ken Caminiti .07 .20
290 Jim Thome .10 .30
291 Paul Molitor .07 .20
292 Ivan Rodriguez .10 .30
293 Bernie Williams .10 .30
294 Todd Hundley .07 .20
295 Andres Galarraga .07 .20
296 Greg Maddux .30 .75
297 Edgar Martinez .10 .30
298 Ron Gant .07 .20
299 Derek Bell .07 .20
300 Roger Clemens .40 1.00
301 Rondell White .07 .20
302 Barry Larkin .10 .30
303 Robin Ventura .07 .20
304 Jason Kendall .07 .20
305 Chipper Jones .20 .50
306 John Franco .07 .20
307 Sammy Sosa .20 .50
308 Troy Percival .07 .20
309 Chuck Knoblauch .07 .20
310 Ellis Burks .07 .20
311 Al Martin .07 .20
312 Tim Salmon .10 .30
313 Moises Alou .07 .20
314 Lance Johnson .07 .20
315 Justin Thompson .07 .20
316 Will Clark .10 .30
317 Barry Bonds .60 1.50
318 Craig Biggio .10 .30
319 John Smoltz .10 .30
320 Cal Ripken .60 1.50
321 Ken Griffey Jr. .40 1.00
322 Paul O'Neill .10 .30
323 Todd Helton .10 .30
324 John Olerud .07 .20
325 Mark McGwire .50 1.25
326 Jose Cruz Jr. .07 .20
327 Jeff Cirillo .07 .20
328 Dean Palmer .07 .20
329 John Wetteland .07 .20
330 Steve Finley .07 .20
331 Albert Belle .07 .20
332 Curt Schilling .07 .20
333 Raul Mondesi .07 .20
334 Andruw Jones .10 .30
335 Nomar Garciaparra .30 .75
336 David Justice .07 .20
337 Andy Pettitte .10 .30
338 Pedro Martinez .10 .30
339 Travis Miller .07 .20
340 Chris Stynes .07 .20
341 Gregg Jefferies .07 .20
342 Jeff Fassero .07 .20
343 Craig Counsell .07 .20
344 Wilson Alvarez .07 .20
345 Bip Roberts .07 .20
346 Kelvim Escobar .07 .20
347 Mark Bellhorn .07 .20
348 Cory Lidle RC .60 1.50
349 Fred McGriff .10 .30
350 Chuck Carr .07 .20
351 Bob Abreu .07 .20
352 Juan Guzman .07 .20
353 Fernando Vina .07 .20
354 Andy Benes .07 .20
355 Dave Nilsson .07 .20
356 Bobby Bonilla .07 .20
357 Ismael Valdes .07 .20
358 Carlos Perez .07 .20
359 Kirk Rueter .07 .20
360 Bartolo Colon .07 .20
361 Mel Rojas .07 .20
362 Johnny Damon .10 .30
363 Geronimo Berroa .07 .20
364 Reggie Sanders .07 .20
365 Jermaine Allensworth .07 .20
366 Orlando Cabrera .07 .20
367 Jorge Fabregas .07 .20
368 Scott Stahoviak .07 .20
369 Ken Cloude .07 .20
370 Donovan Osborne .07 .20
371 Roger Cedeno .07 .20
372 Neifi Perez .07 .20
373 Chris Holt .07 .20
374 Cecil Fielder .07 .20
375 Marty Cordova .07 .20
376 Tom Goodwin .07 .20
377 Jeff Suppan .07 .20
378 Jeff Brantley .07 .20
379 Mark Langston .07 .20
380 Shane Reynolds .07 .20
381 Mike Fetters .07 .20
382 Todd Greene .07 .20
383 Ray Durham .07 .20
384 Carlos Delgado .07 .20
385 Jeff D'Amico .07 .20
386 Brian McRae .07 .20
387 Alan Benes .07 .20

388 Heathcliff Slocumb .07 .20
389 Eric Young .07 .20
390 Travis Fryman .07 .20
391 David Cone .07 .20
392 Otis Nixon .07 .20
393 Jeremi Gonzalez .07 .20
394 Jeff Juden .07 .20
395 Jose Vizcaino .07 .20
396 Ugueth Urbina .07 .20
397 Ramon Martinez .07 .20
398 Robb Nen .07 .20
399 Harold Baines .07 .20
400 Delino DeShields .07 .20
401 John Burkett .07 .20
402 Sterling Hitchcock .07 .20
403 Mark Clark .07 .20
404 Terrell Wade .07 .20
405 Scott Brosius .07 .20
406 Chad Curtis .07 .20
407 Brian Johnson .07 .20
408 Roberto Kelly .07 .20
409 Dave Dellucci RC .15 .40
410 Michael Tucker .07 .20
411 Mark Kotsay .07 .20
412 Mark Lewis .07 .20
413 Ryan McGuire .07 .20
414 Shawon Dunston .07 .20
415 Brad Rigby .07 .20
416 Scott Erickson .07 .20
417 Bobby Jones .07 .20
418 Darren Oliver .07 .20
419 John Smiley .07 .20
420 T.J. Mathews .07 .20
421 Dustin Hermanson .07 .20
422 Mike Timlin .07 .20
423 Willie Blair .07 .20
424 Manny Alexander .07 .20
425 Bob Tewksbury .07 .20
426 Pete Schourek .07 .20
427 Reggie Jefferson .07 .20
428 Ed Sprague .07 .20
429 Jeff Conine .07 .20
430 Roberto Hernandez .07 .20
431 Tom Pagnozzi .07 .20
432 Jaret Wright .07 .20
433 Livan Hernandez .07 .20
434 Andy Ashby .07 .20
435 Todd Dunn .07 .20
436 Bobby Higginson .07 .20
437 Rod Beck .07 .20
438 Jim Leyritz .07 .20
439 Matt Williams .07 .20
440 Brett Tomko .07 .20
441 Joe Randa .07 .20
442 Chris Carpenter .07 .20
443 Dennis Reyes .07 .20
444 Al Leiter .07 .20
445 Jason Schmidt .07 .20
446 Ken Hill .07 .20
447 Shannon Stewart .07 .20
448 Enrique Wilson .07 .20
449 Fernando Tatis .07 .20
450 Jimmy Key .07 .20
451 Darrin Fletcher .07 .20
452 John Valentin .07 .20
453 Kevin Tapani .07 .20
454 Eric Karros .07 .20
455 Jay Bell .07 .20
456 Walt Weiss .07 .20
457 Devon White .07 .20
458 Carl Pavano .07 .20
459 Mike Lansing .07 .20
460 John Flaherty .07 .20
461 Richard Hidalgo .07 .20
462 Quinton McCracken .07 .20
463 Karim Garcia .07 .20
464 Miguel Cairo .07 .20
465 Edwin Diaz .07 .20
466 Bobby Smith .07 .20
467 Yamil Benitez .07 .20
468 Rich Butler .07 .20
469 Ben Ford RC .07 .20
470 Bubba Trammell .07 .20
471 Brent Brede .07 .20
472 Brooks Kieschnick .07 .20
473 Carlos Castillo .07 .20
474 Brad Radke SH .07 .20
475 Roger Clemens SH .20 .50
476 Curt Schilling SH .07 .20
477 John Olerud SH .07 .20
478 Mark McGwire SH .25 .60
479 M.Piazza .25 .60
K.Griffey Jr. IL
480 J.Bagwell .10 .30
F.Thomas IL
481 C.Jones .10 .30
N.Garciaparra IL
482 L.Walker .07 .20
J.Gonzalez IL
483 G.Sheffield .07 .20
T.Martinez IL
484 D.Gib .07 .20
M.Colem/Hutchins
485 B.Rose .07 .20
Looper/Politte
486 E.Milton .07 .20
Marquis/C.Lee
487 Robert Fick RC .10 .30
488 A.Ramirez .10 .30
A.Gonz/Casey
489 D.Bridges .07 .20
T.Drew RC
490 D.McDonald .07 .20
N.Ndungidi RC
491 Ryan Anderson RC .07 .20
492 Troy Glaus RC .50 1.25
493 J.Werth .07 .20
D.Reichert RC
494 Michael Cuddyer RC .30 .75
495 Jack Cust RC .20 .50
496 Brian Anderson .07 .20
497 Tony Saunders .07 .20
498 J.Sandoval .07 .20
V.Nunez
499 B.Penny .10 .30
N.Bierbrodt
500 D.Carr .07 .20
L.Cruz RC
501 C.Bowers .07 .20
M.McCain
502 Checklist .07 .20
503 Checklist .07 .20
504 Alex Rodriguez .75 2.00

1998 Topps Minted in Cooperstown

*STARS: 5X TO 12X BASIC CARDS
*ROOKIES: 6X TO 15X BASIC CARDS
STATED ODDS: 1:8
CARD NUMBER 7 DOES NOT EXIST

1998 Topps Inaugural Devil Rays

COMP.FACT.SET (503) 40.00 100.00
*STARS: 1.5X TO 4X BASIC CARDS
*ROOKIES: 2.5X TO 6X BASIC CARDS
DISTRIBUTED ONLY IN FACT.SET FORM

1998 Topps Inaugural Diamondbacks

COMP.FACT.SET (503) 60.00 120.00
*STARS: 1.5X TO 4X BASIC CARDS
*ROOKIES: 2.5X TO 6X BASIC CARDS
DISTRIBUTED ONLY IN FACT.SET FORM

1998 Topps Baby Boomers

COMPLETE SET (15) 5.00 12.00
SER.1 STATED ODDS 1:36 RETAIL
BB1 Derek Jeter 2.50 6.00
BB2 Scott Rolen .60 1.50
BB3 Nomar Garciaparra .60 1.50
BB4 Jose Cruz Jr. .40 1.00
BB5 Darin Erstad .40 1.00
BB6 Todd Helton .60 1.50
BB7 Tony Clark .40 1.00
BB8 Jose Guillen .40 1.00
BB9 Andruw Jones .40 1.00
BB10 Vladimir Guerrero .60 1.50
BB11 Mark Kotsay .40 1.00
BB12 Todd Greene .40 1.00
BB13 Andy Pettitte .60 1.50
BB14 Justin Thompson .40 1.00
BB15 Alan Benes .40 1.00

1998 Topps Clemente

COMPLETE SET (19) 30.00 60.00
COMPLETE SERIES 1 (10) 12.50 30.00
COMPLETE SERIES 2 (9) 12.50 30.00
COMMON CARD (2-19) 1.50 4.00
STATED ODDS 1:18
ODD NUMBERS IN 1ST SERIES PACKS
EVEN NUMBERS IN 2ND SERIES PACKS
1 Roberto Clemente 1955 3.00 8.00

1998 Topps Clemente Memorabilia Madness

COMMON CARD (1-46) 100.00 200.00
SER.1 ODDS 1:3708 HOBBY, 1:1020 HTA
SER.1 WILD CARD ODDS 1:72
NNO Wild Card .40 1.00

1998 Topps Clemente Sealed

*SEALED: .4X TO 1X BASIC CLEMENTE
ONE PER HOBBY FACTORY SET

1998 Topps Clemente Tins

COMMON TIN (1-4) 2.00 5.00

1998 Topps Clemente Tribute

COMPLETE SET (5) 3.00 8.00
COMMON CARD (RC1-RC5) .75 2.00
SER.1 STATED ODDS 1:12

1998 Topps Clout Nine

COMPLETE SET (9) 10.00 25.00
SER.2 STATED ODDS 1:72
C1 Edgar Martinez 1.25 3.00
C2 Mike Piazza 2.00 5.00
C3 Frank Thomas 2.00 5.00
C4 Craig Biggio 1.25 3.00
C5 Vinny Castilla .75 2.00
C6 Jeff Blauser .75 2.00
C7 Barry Bonds 3.00 8.00
C8 Ken Griffey Jr. 4.00 10.00
C9 Larry Walker 1.25 3.00

1998 Topps Etch-A-Sketch

COMPLETE SET (9) 12.50 30.00
SER.1 STATED ODDS 1:36
ES1 Albert Belle .50 1.25
ES2 Barry Bonds 4.00 10.00
ES3 Ken Griffey Jr. 2.50 6.00
ES4 Greg Maddux 2.00 5.00
ES5 Hideo Nomo 1.25 3.00
ES6 Mike Piazza 2.00 5.00
ES7 Cal Ripken 4.00 10.00
ES8 Frank Thomas 1.25 3.00
ES9 Mo Vaughn .50 1.25

1998 Topps Flashback

COMPLETE SET (10) 12.00 30.00
SER.1 STATED ODDS 1:72
FB1 Barry Bonds 2.50 6.00
FB2 Ken Griffey Jr. 3.00 8.00
FB3 Paul Molitor 1.50 4.00
FB4 Randy Johnson 1.50 4.00
FB5 Cal Ripken 5.00 12.00
FB6 Tony Gwynn 1.50 4.00
FB7 Kenny Lofton .60 1.50
FB8 Gary Sheffield .60 1.50
FB9 Deion Sanders 1.00 2.50
FB10 Brady Anderson .60 1.50

1998 Topps Focal Points

COMPLETE SET (15) 30.00 80.00
SER.2 STATED ODDS 1:36 HOBBY
FP1 Juan Gonzalez .75 2.00
FP2 Nomar Garciaparra 3.00 8.00
FP3 Jose Cruz Jr. .75 2.00
FP4 Cal Ripken 6.00 15.00
FP5 Ken Griffey Jr. 4.00 10.00
FP6 Ivan Rodriguez 1.25 3.00
FP7 Larry Walker .75 2.00
FP8 Barry Bonds 6.00 15.00
FP9 Roger Clemens 4.00 10.00
FP10 Frank Thomas 2.00 5.00
FP11 Chuck Knoblauch .75 2.00
FP12 Mike Piazza 3.00 8.00
FP13 Greg Maddux 3.00 8.00
FP14 Vladimir Guerrero 2.00 5.00
FP15 Andruw Jones 1.25 3.00

1998 Topps HallBound

COMPLETE SET (15) 20.00 50.00
SER.1 STATED ODDS 1:36 HOBBY
HB1 Paul Molitor .75 2.00
HB2 Tony Gwynn 2.50 6.00
HB3 Wade Boggs 1.25 3.00
HB4 Roger Clemens 4.00 10.00
HB5 Dennis Eckersley .75 2.00
HB6 Cal Ripken 6.00 15.00
HB7 Greg Maddux 3.00 8.00
HB8 Rickey Henderson 1.25 3.00
HB9 Ken Griffey Jr. 4.00 10.00
HB10 Frank Thomas 2.00 5.00
HB11 Mark McGwire 5.00 12.00
HB12 Barry Bonds 6.00 15.00
HB13 Mike Piazza 3.00 8.00
HB14 Juan Gonzalez .75 2.00
HB15 Randy Johnson 2.00 5.00

1998 Topps Milestones

COMPLETE SET (10) 20.00 50.00
SER.2 STATED ODDS 1:36 RETAIL
MS1 Barry Bonds 5.00 12.00
MS2 Roger Clemens 3.00 8.00
MS3 Dennis Eckersley .60 1.50
MS4 Juan Gonzalez .60 1.50
MS5 Ken Griffey Jr. 3.00 8.00
MS6 Tony Gwynn 2.00 5.00
MS7 Greg Maddux 2.50 6.00
MS8 Mark McGwire 4.00 10.00
MS9 Cal Ripken 5.00 12.00
MS10 Frank Thomas 1.50 4.00

1998 Topps Mystery Finest

COMPLETE SET (20) 30.00 80.00
SER.1 STATED ODDS 1:36
*REFRACTOR: 1X TO 2.5X BASIC MYS.FIN.
REFRACTOR SER.1 STATED ODDS: 1:144
ILM1 Chipper Jones 2.00 5.00
ILM2 Cal Ripken 6.00 15.00
ILM3 Greg Maddux 3.00 8.00
ILM4 Rafael Palmeiro 1.25 3.00
ILM5 Todd Hundley .75 2.00
ILM6 Derek Jeter 5.00 12.00
ILM7 John Olerud .75 2.00
ILM8 Tino Martinez 1.25 3.00
ILM9 Larry Walker .75 2.00
ILM10 Ken Griffey Jr. 4.00 10.00
ILM11 Andres Galarraga .75 2.00
ILM12 Randy Johnson 2.00 5.00
ILM13 Mike Piazza 3.00 8.00
ILM14 Jim Edmonds .75 2.00
ILM15 Eric Karros .75 2.00
ILM16 Tim Salmon 1.25 3.00
ILM17 Sammy Sosa 2.00 5.00
ILM18 Frank Thomas 2.00 5.00
ILM19 Mark Grace 1.25 3.00
ILM20 Albert Belle .75 2.00

1998 Topps Mystery Finest Bordered

COMPLETE SET (20) 30.00 60.00
SER.2 STATED ODDS 1:36
*BORDERED REF: .75X TO 2X BORDERED
BORDERED REF.SER.2 ODDS 1:108
*BORDERLESS: .6X TO 1.5X BORDERED
BORDERLESS SER.2 ODDS 1:72
*BORDERLESS REF: 1.25X TO 3X BORDERED
BORDERLESS REF.SER.2 ODDS 1:288
M1 Nomar Garciaparra 3.00 8.00
M2 Chipper Jones 2.00 5.00
M3 Scott Rolen 1.25 3.00
M4 Albert Belle .75 2.00
M5 Mo Vaughn .75 2.00
M6 Jose Cruz Jr. .75 2.00
M7 Mark McGwire 5.00 12.00
M8 Derek Jeter 5.00 12.00
M9 Tony Gwynn 2.50 6.00
M10 Frank Thomas 2.00 5.00
M11 Tino Martinez 1.25 3.00
M12 Greg Maddux 3.00 8.00
M13 Juan Gonzalez .75 2.00
M14 Larry Walker .75 2.00
M15 Mike Piazza 3.00 8.00
M16 Cal Ripken 6.00 15.00
M17 Jeff Bagwell 1.25 3.00
M18 Andruw Jones 1.25 3.00
M19 Barry Bonds 6.00 15.00
M20 Ken Griffey Jr. 4.00 10.00

1998 Topps Rookie Class

COMPLETE SET (10) 2.50 6.00
SER.2 STATED ODDS 1:12
R1 Travis Lee .30 .75
R2 Richard Hidalgo .30 .75
R3 Todd Helton .50 1.25
R4 Paul Konerko .30 .75
R5 Mark Kotsay .30 .75
R6 Derrek Lee .30 .75
R7 Eli Marrero .30 .75
R8 Fernando Tatis .30 .75
R9 Juan Encarnacion .30 .75
R10 Ben Grieve .30 .75

1998 Topps Fruit Roll-Ups

This eight-card set measures approximately 1 1/2" by 2" and were found on boxes of specially marked 38-pack Betty Crocker Fruit Roll-ups. The fronts of these perforated cards feature color action player photos with a thin red border. The backs are blank. The cards are unnumbered and checklisted below in alphabetical order.

COMPLETE SET (8) 8.00 20.00
1 Tony Gwynn 1.00 2.50
2 Derek Jeter 2.00 5.00
3 Kenny Lofton .20 .50
4 Mark McGwire 1.00 2.50
5 Mike Piazza 1.25 3.00
6 Cal Ripken 2.00 5.00
7 Ivan Rodriguez .50 1.25
8 Frank Thomas .50 1.25

1999 Topps Pre-Production

COMPLETE SET (6) 4.00 10.00
PP1 Roger Clemens 1.00 2.50
PP2 Sammy Sosa .60 1.50
PP3 Derek Jeter 2.00 5.00
PP4 Walt Weiss .08 .25
PP5 Darin Erstad .40 1.00
PP6 Jason Kendall .30 .75

1999 Topps

The 1999 Topps set consisted of 462 standard-size cards. Each 11 card pack carried a suggested retail price of $1.29 per pack. Cards were also distributed in 40-card Home Team advantage jumbo packs, hobby, retail and Christmas factory sets. The Mark McGwire number 220 card was issued in 70 different varieties to honor his record setting season. The Sammy Sosa number 461 card was issued in 66 different varieties to honor his 1998 season. Basic sets are considered complete with any one of the 70 McGwire and 66 Sosa variations. A.J. Burnett, Pat Burrell, and Alex Escobar are the most notable Rookie Cards in the set. Card number 7 was not issued as Topps continues to honor the memory of Mickey Mantle. The Christmas factory set contains one Nolan Ryan finest reprint card as an added bonus, while the hobby and retail factory sets just contained the regular sets in a factory box.

COMPLETE SET (462) 25.00 60.00
COMP.HOBBY SET (462) 25.00 60.00
COMP.X-MAS SET (463) 25.00 60.00
COMPLETE SERIES 1 (241) 12.50 30.00
COMPLETE SERIES 2 (221) 12.50 30.00
COMP.MAC HR SET (70) 100.00 200.00
CARD 220 AVAIL.IN 70 VARIATIONS
COMP.SOSA HR SET (66) 60.00 120.00
CARD 461 AVAILABLE IN 66 VARIATIONS
CARD NUMBER 7 DOES NOT EXIST
SER.1 SET INCLUDES 1 CARD 220 VARIATION
SER.2 SET INCLUDES 1 CARD 461 VARIATION
1 Roger Clemens .40 1.00
2 Andres Galarraga .07 .20
3 Scott Brosius .07 .20
4 John Flaherty .07 .20
5 Jim Leyritz .07 .20
6 Ray Durham .07 .20
8 Jose Vizcaino .07 .20
9 Will Clark .10 .30
10 David Wells .07 .20
11 Jose Guillen .07 .20
12 Scott Hatteberg .07 .20
13 Edgardo Alfonzo .07 .20
14 Mike Bordick .07 .20
15 Manny Ramirez .10 .30
16 Greg Maddux .30 .75
17 David Segui .07 .20
18 Darryl Strawberry .07 .20
19 Brad Radke .07 .20
20 Kerry Wood .07 .20
21 Matt Anderson .07 .20
22 Derrek Lee .10 .30
23 Mickey Morandini .07 .20
24 Paul Konerko .07 .20
25 Travis Lee .07 .20
26 Ken Hill .07 .20
27 Kenny Rogers .07 .20
28 Paul Sorrento .07 .20
29 Quilvio Veras .07 .20
30 Todd Walker .07 .20
31 Ryan Jackson .07 .20
32 John Olerud .07 .20
33 Doug Glanville .07 .20
34 Nolan Ryan .75 2.00
35 Ray Lankford .07 .20
36 Mark Loretta .07 .20
37 Jason Dickson .07 .20
38 Sean Bergman .07 .20
39 Quinton McCracken .07 .20
40 Bartolo Colon .07 .20
41 Brady Anderson .07 .20
42 Chris Stynes .07 .20
43 Jorge Posada .10 .30
44 Justin Thompson .07 .20
45 Johnny Damon .10 .30
46 Armando Benitez .07 .20
47 Brant Brown .07 .20
48 Charlie Hayes .07 .20
49 Darren Dreifort .07 .20
50 Juan Gonzalez .07 .20
51 Chuck Knoblauch .07 .20
52 Todd Helton .10 .30
53 Rick Reed .07 .20
54 Chris Gomez .07 .20
55 Gary Sheffield .07 .20
56 Rod Beck .07 .20
57 Rey Sanchez .07 .20
58 Garret Anderson .07 .20
59 Jimmy Haynes .07 .20
60 Steve Woodard .07 .20
61 Rondell White .07 .20
62 Vladimir Guerrero .20 .50
63 Eric Karros .07 .20
64 Russ Davis .07 .20
65 Mo Vaughn .07 .20
66 Sammy Sosa .20 .50
67 Troy Percival .07 .20
68 Kenny Lofton .07 .20
69 Bill Taylor .07 .20
70 Mark McGwire .50 1.25
71 Roger Cedeno .07 .20
72 Javy Lopez .07 .20
73 Damion Easley .07 .20
74 Andy Pettitte .10 .30
75 Tony Gwynn .25 .60
76 Ricardo Rincon .07 .20
77 F.P. Santangelo .07 .20
78 Jay Bell .07 .20
79 Scott Servais .07 .20
80 Jose Canseco .10 .30
81 Roberto Hernandez .07 .20
82 Todd Dunwoody .07 .20
83 John Wetteland .07 .20
84 Mike Caruso .07 .20
85 Derek Jeter .50 1.25
86 Aaron Sele .07 .20
87 Jose Lima .07 .20
88 Ryan Christenson .07 .20
89 Jeff Cirillo .07 .20
90 Jose Hernandez .07 .20
91 Mark Kotsay .07 .20
92 Darren Bragg .07 .20
93 Albert Belle .07 .20
94 Matt Lawton .07 .20
95 Pedro Martinez .10 .30
96 Greg Vaughn .07 .20
97 Neifi Perez .07 .20
98 Gerald Williams .07 .20
99 Derek Bell .07 .20
100 Ken Griffey Jr. .40 1.00
101 David Cone .07 .20
102 Brian Johnson .07 .20
103 Dean Palmer .07 .20
104 Javier Valentin .07 .20
105 Trevor Hoffman .07 .20
106 Butch Huskey .07 .20
107 Dave Martinez .07 .20
108 Billy Wagner .07 .20
109 Shawn Green .07 .20
110 Ben Grieve .07 .20
111 Tom Goodwin .07 .20
112 Jaret Wright .07 .20
113 Aramis Ramirez .07 .20
114 Dmitri Young .07 .20
115 Hideki Irabu .07 .20
116 Roberto Kelly .07 .20
117 Jeff Fassero .07 .20
118 Mark Clark .07 .20
119 Jason McDonald .07 .20
120 Matt Williams .07 .20
121 Dave Burba .07 .20
122 Bret Saberhagen .07 .20
123 Deivi Cruz .07 .20
124 Chad Curtis .07 .20
125 Scott Rolen .10 .30
126 Lee Stevens .07 .20
127 J.T. Snow .07 .20
128 Rusty Greer .07 .20
129 Brian Meadows .07 .20
130 Jim Edmonds .07 .20
131 Ron Gant .07 .20
132 A.J. Hinch .07 .20
133 Shannon Stewart .07 .20
134 Brad Fullmer .07 .20
135 Cal Eldred .07 .20
136 Matt Walbeck .07 .20
137 Carl Everett .07 .20
138 Walt Weiss .07 .20
139 Fred McGriff .10 .30
140 Darin Erstad .07 .20
141 Dave Nilsson .07 .20
142 Eric Young .07 .20
143 Dan Wilson .07 .20
144 Jeff Reed .07 .20
145 Brett Tomko .07 .20
146 Terry Steinbach .07 .20
147 Seth Greisinger .07 .20
148 Pat Meares .07 .20
149 Livan Hernandez .07 .20
150 Jeff Bagwell .10 .30
151 Bob Wickman .07 .20
152 Omar Vizquel .10 .30
153 Eric Davis .07 .20
154 Larry Sutton .07 .20
155 Magglio Ordonez .07 .20
156 Eric Milton .07 .20
157 Darren Lewis .07 .20
158 Rick Aguilera .07 .20
159 Mike Lieberthal .07 .20
160 Robb Nen .07 .20
161 Brian Giles .07 .20
162 Jeff Brantley .07 .20
163 Gary DiSarcina .07 .20
164 John Valentin .07 .20
165 David Dellucci .07 .20
166 Chan Ho Park .07 .20
167 Masato Yoshii .07 .20
168 Jason Schmidt .07 .20
169 LaTroy Hawkins .07 .20
170 Bret Boone .07 .20
171 Jerry DiPoto .07 .20
172 Mariano Rivera .20 .50
173 Mike Cameron .07 .20
174 Scott Erickson .07 .20
175 Charles Johnson .07 .20
176 Bobby Jones .07 .20
177 Francisco Cordova .07 .20
178 Todd Jones .07 .20
179 Jeff Montgomery .07 .20
180 Mike Mussina .10 .30
181 Bob Abreu .07 .20
182 Ismael Valdes .07 .20
183 Andy Fox .07 .20
184 Woody Williams .07 .20
185 Denny Neagle .07 .20
186 Jose Valentin .07 .20
187 Darrin Fletcher .07 .20
188 Gabe Alvarez .07 .20
189 Eddie Taubensee .07 .20
190 Edgar Martinez .10 .30
191 Jason Kendall .07 .20
192 Darryl Kile .07 .20
193 Jeff King .07 .20
194 Rey Ordonez .07 .20
195 Andruw Jones .10 .30
196 Tony Fernandez .07 .20
197 Jamey Wright .07 .20
198 B.J. Surhoff .07 .20
199 Vinny Castilla .07 .20
200 David Wells HL .07 .20
201 Mark McGwire HL .25 .60
202 Sammy Sosa HL .10 .30
203 Roger Clemens HL .20 .50
204 Kerry Wood HL .07 .20
205 L.Berkman .15 .40
G.Kapler
206 Alex Escobar RC .15 .40
207 Peter Bergeron RC .08 .25
208 M.Barrett .08 .25
B.Davis/R.Fick
209 P.Cline .08 .25
R.Hernandez/J.Werth
210 R.Anderson .08 .25
Chen/Enochs
211 B.Penny .08 .25
Dotel/Lincoln
212 Chuck Abbott RC .08 .25
213 C.Jones .08 .25
J.Urban RC
214 T.Torcato .08 .25
A.McDowell RC
215 J.Tyner .08 .25
J.McKinley RC
216 M.Burch .08 .25
S.Etherton RC
217 R.Elder .08 .25
M.Tucker RC
218 J.M.Gold .08 .25
R.Mills RC
219 A.Brown .08 .25
C.Freeman RC
220A Mark McGwire HR 1 8.00 20.00
220B Mark McGwire HR 2 3.00 8.00
220C Mark McGwire HR 3 3.00 8.00
220D Mark McGwire HR 4 3.00 8.00
220E Mark McGwire HR 5 3.00 8.00
220F Mark McGwire HR 6 3.00 8.00
220G Mark McGwire HR 7 3.00 8.00
220H Mark McGwire HR 8 3.00 8.00
220I Mark McGwire HR 9 3.00 8.00
220J Mark McGwire HR 10 3.00 8.00
220K Mark McGwire HR 11 3.00 8.00
220L Mark McGwire HR 12 3.00 8.00
220M Mark McGwire HR 13 3.00 8.00
220N Mark McGwire HR 14 3.00 8.00
220O Mark McGwire HR 15 3.00 8.00
220P Mark McGwire HR 16 3.00 8.00
220Q Mark McGwire HR 17 3.00 8.00
220R Mark McGwire HR 18 3.00 8.00
220S Mark McGwire HR 19 3.00 8.00
220T Mark McGwire HR 20 3.00 8.00
220U Mark McGwire HR 21 3.00 8.00
220V Mark McGwire HR 22 3.00 8.00
220W Mark McGwire HR 23 3.00 8.00
220X Mark McGwire HR 24 3.00 8.00
220Y Mark McGwire HR 25 3.00 8.00
220Z Mark McGwire HR 26 3.00 8.00
220AA Mark McGwire HR 27 3.00 8.00
220AB Mark McGwire HR 28 3.00 8.00
220AC Mark McGwire HR 29 3.00 8.00
220AD Mark McGwire HR 30 3.00 8.00
220AE Mark McGwire HR 31 3.00 8.00
220AF Mark McGwire HR 32 3.00 8.00
220AG Mark McGwire HR 33 3.00 8.00
220AH Mark McGwire HR 34 3.00 8.00
220AI Mark McGwire HR 35 3.00 8.00
220AJ Mark McGwire HR 36 3.00 8.00
220AK Mark McGwire HR 37 3.00 8.00
220AL Mark McGwire HR 38 3.00 8.00
220AM Mark McGwire HR 39 3.00 8.00
220AN Mark McGwire HR 40 3.00 8.00
220AO Mark McGwire HR 41 3.00 8.00
220AP Mark McGwire HR 42 3.00 8.00
220AQ Mark McGwire HR 43 3.00 8.00
220AR Mark McGwire HR 44 3.00 8.00
220AS Mark McGwire HR 45 3.00 8.00
220AT Mark McGwire HR 46 3.00 8.00
220AU Mark McGwire HR 47 3.00 8.00
220AV Mark McGwire HR 48 3.00 8.00
220AW Mark McGwire HR 49 3.00 8.00
220AX Mark McGwire HR 50 3.00 8.00
220AY Mark McGwire HR 51 3.00 8.00
220AZ Mark McGwire HR 52 3.00 8.00
220BB Mark McGwire HR 53 3.00 8.00
220CC Mark McGwire HR 54 3.00 8.00
220DD Mark McGwire HR 55 3.00 8.00
220EE Mark McGwire HR 56 3.00 8.00
220FF Mark McGwire HR 57 3.00 8.00
220GG Mark McGwire HR 58 3.00 8.00
220HH Mark McGwire HR 59 3.00 8.00
220II Mark McGwire HR 60 3.00 8.00
220JJ Mark McGwire HR 61 6.00 15.00
220KK Mark McGwire HR 62 8.00 20.00
220LL Mark McGwire HR 63 3.00 8.00
220MM Mark McGwire HR 64 3.00 8.00
220NN Mark McGwire HR 65 3.00 8.00
220OO Mark McGwire HR 66 3.00 8.00
220PP Mark McGwire HR 67 3.00 8.00
220QQ Mark McGwire HR 68 3.00 8.00
220RR Mark McGwire HR 69 3.00 8.00
220SS Mark McGwire HR 70 10.00 25.00
221 Larry Walker LL .07 .20
222 Bernie Williams LL .07 .20
223 Mark McGwire LL .25 .60
224 Ken Griffey Jr. LL .25 .60
225 Sammy Sosa LL .10 .30
226 Juan Gonzalez LL .07 .20
227 Dante Bichette LL .07 .20
228 Alex Rodriguez LL .20 .50
229 Sammy Sosa LL .10 .30
230 Derek Jeter LL .25 .60
231 Greg Maddux LL .20 .50
232 Roger Clemens LL .20 .50
233 Ricky Ledee WS .07 .20
234 Chuck Knoblauch WS .07 .20
235 Bernie Williams WS .07 .20
236 Tino Martinez WS .07 .20
237 Orlando Hernandez WS .07 .20
238 Scott Brosius WS .07 .20
239 Andy Pettitte WS .07 .20
240 Mariano Rivera WS .10 .30
241 Checklist 1 .07 .20
242 Checklist 2 .07 .20
243 Tom Glavine .10 .30
244 Andy Benes .07 .20
245 Sandy Alomar Jr. .07 .20
246 Wilton Guerrero .07 .20
247 Alex Gonzalez .07 .20
248 Roberto Alomar .10 .30
249 Ruben Rivera .07 .20
250 Eric Chavez .07 .20
251 Ellis Burks .07 .20
252 Richie Sexson .07 .20
253 Steve Finley .07 .20
254 Dwight Gooden .07 .20
255 Dustin Hermanson .07 .20
256 Kirk Rueter .07 .20
257 Steve Trachsel .07 .20
258 Gregg Jefferies .07 .20
259 Matt Stairs .07 .20
260 Shane Reynolds .07 .20
261 Gregg Olson .07 .20
262 Kevin Tapani .07 .20
263 Matt Morris .07 .20
264 Carl Pavano .07 .20
265 Nomar Garciaparra .30 .75
266 Kevin Young .07 .20
267 Rick Helling .07 .20
268 Matt Franco .07 .20
269 Brian McRae .07 .20
270 Cal Ripken .60 1.50
271 Jeff Abbott .07 .20
272 Tony Batista .07 .20
273 Bill Simas .07 .20
274 Brian Hunter .07 .20
275 John Franco .07 .20
276 Devon White .07 .20
277 Rickey Henderson .20 .50
278 Chuck Finley .07 .20
279 Mike Blowers .07 .20
280 Mark Grace .10 .30
281 Randy Winn .07 .20
282 Bobby Bonilla .07 .20
283 David Justice .07 .20
284 Shane Monahan .07 .20
285 Kevin Brown .10 .30
286 Todd Zeile .07 .20
287 Al Martin .07 .20
288 Troy O'Leary .07 .20
289 Darryl Hamilton .07 .20
290 Tino Martinez .10 .30
291 David Ortiz .20 .50
292 Tony Clark .07 .20
293 Ryan Minor .07 .20
294 Mark Leiter .07 .20
295 Wally Joyner .07 .20
296 Cliff Floyd .07 .20
297 Shawn Estes .07 .20
298 Pat Hentgen .07 .20
299 Scott Elarton .07 .20
300 Alex Rodriguez .30 .75
301 Ozzie Guillen .07 .20
302 Hideo Nomo .20 .50
303 Ryan McGuire .07 .20
304 Brad Ausmus .07 .20
305 Alex Gonzalez .07 .20
306 Brian Jordan .07 .20
307 John Jaha .07 .20
308 Mark Grudzielanek .07 .20
309 Juan Guzman .07 .20
310 Tony Womack .07 .20
311 Dennis Reyes .07 .20
312 Marty Cordova .07 .20
313 Ramiro Mendoza .07 .20
314 Robin Ventura .07 .20
315 Rafael Palmeiro .10 .30
316 Ramon Martinez .07 .20
317 Pedro Astacio .07 .20
318 Dave Hollins .07 .20
319 Tom Candiotti .07 .20
320 Al Leiter .07 .20
321 Rico Brogna .07 .20
322 Reggie Jefferson .07 .20
323 Bernard Gilkey .07 .20
324 Jason Giambi .07 .20
325 Craig Biggio .10 .30
326 Troy Glaus .10 .30
327 Delino DeShields .07 .20
328 Fernando Vina .07 .20
329 John Smoltz .10 .30
330 Jeff Kent .07 .20
331 Roy Halladay .20 .50
332 Andy Ashby .07 .20
333 Tim Wakefield .07 .20
334 Roger Clemens .40 1.00
335 Bernie Williams .10 .30
336 Desi Relaford .07 .20
337 John Burkett .07 .20
338 Mike Hampton .07 .20
339 Royce Clayton .07 .20
340 Mike Piazza .30 .75
341 Jeremi Gonzalez .07 .20
342 Mike Lansing .07 .20
343 Jamie Moyer .07 .20
344 Ron Coomer .07 .20
345 Barry Larkin .10 .30
346 Fernando Tatis .07 .20
347 Chili Davis .07 .20
348 Bobby Higginson .07 .20
349 Hal Morris .07 .20
350 Larry Walker .07 .20
351 Carlos Guillen .07 .20
352 Miguel Tejada .07 .20
353 Travis Fryman .07 .20
354 Jarrod Washburn .07 .20
355 Chipper Jones .20 .50
356 Todd Stottlemyre .07 .20
357 Henry Rodriguez .07 .20
358 Eli Marrero .07 .20
359 Alan Benes .07 .20
360 Tim Salmon .10 .30
361 Luis Gonzalez .07 .20
362 Scott Spiezio .07 .20
363 Chris Carpenter .07 .20
364 Bobby Howry .07 .20
365 Raul Mondesi .07 .20
366 Ugueth Urbina .07 .20
367 Tom Evans .07 .20
368 Kerry Ligtenberg RC .08 .25
369 Adrian Beltre .07 .20
370 Ryan Klesko .07 .20
371 Wilson Alvarez .07 .20
372 John Thomson .07 .20
373 Tony Saunders .07 .20
374 Dave Mlicki .07 .20
375 Ken Caminiti .07 .20
376 Jay Buhner .07 .20
377 Bill Mueller .07 .20
378 Jeff Blauser .07 .20
379 Edgar Renteria .07 .20
380 Jim Thome .10 .30
381 Joey Hamilton .07 .20
382 Calvin Pickering .07 .20
383 Marquis Grissom .07 .20
384 Omar Daal .07 .20
385 Curt Schilling .07 .20
386 Jose Cruz Jr. .07 .20
387 Chris Widger .07 .20
388 Pete Harnisch .07 .20
389 Charles Nagy .07 .20
390 Tom Gordon .07 .20
391 Bobby Smith .07 .20
392 Derrick Gibson .07 .20
393 Jeff Conine .07 .20

394 Carlos Perez .07 .20
395 Barry Bonds .60 1.50
396 Mark McLemore .07 .20
397 Juan Encarnacion .07 .20
398 Wade Boggs .10 .30
399 Ivan Rodriguez .10 .30
400 Moises Alou .07 .20
401 Jeromy Burnitz .07 .20
402 Sean Casey .07 .20
403 Jose Offerman .07 .20
404 Joe Fontenot .07 .20
405 Kevin Millwood .07 .20
406 Lance Johnson .07 .20
407 Richard Hidalgo .07 .20
408 Mike Jackson .07 .20
409 Brian Anderson .07 .20
410 Jeff Shaw .07 .20
411 Preston Wilson .07 .20
412 Todd Hundley .07 .20
413 Jim Parque .07 .20
414 Justin Baughman .07 .20
415 Dante Bichette .07 .20
416 Paul O'Neill .10 .30
417 Miguel Cairo .07 .20
418 Randy Johnson .20 .50
419 Jesus Sanchez .07 .20
420 Carlos Delgado .07 .20
421 Ricky Ledee .07 .20
422 Orlando Hernandez .07 .20
423 Frank Thomas .20 .50
424 Pokey Reese .07 .20
425 C.Lee .15 .40
M.Lowell
426 M.Cuddyer .08 .25
DeRosa/Hairston
427 M.Anderson .15 .40
Belliard/Cabrera
428 M.Bowie .08 .25
P.Norton RC/Wolf
429 J.Cressend RC .15 .40
Rocker
430 R.Mateo .08 .25
M.Zywica RC
431 J.LaRue .08 .25
LeCroy/Meluskey
432 Gabe Kapler .15 .40
433 A.Kennedy .08 .25
M.Lopez RC
434 Jose Fernandez RC .08 .25
C.Truby
435 Doug Mientkiewicz RC .20 .50
436 R.Brown RC .08 .25
V.Wells
437 A.J. Burnett RC .30 .75
438 M.Belisle .08 .25
M.Roney RC
439 A.Kearns .60 1.50
C.George RC
440 N.Cornejo .08 .25
N.Bump RC
441 B.Lidge .60 1.50
M.Nannini RC
442 M.Holliday 1.50 4.00
J.Winchester RC
443 A.Everett .20 .50
C.Ambres RC
444 P.Burrell .60 1.50
E.Valent RC
445 Roger Clemens SK .20 .50
446 Kerry Wood SK .07 .20
447 Curt Schilling SK .07 .20
448 Randy Johnson SK .10 .30
449 Pedro Martinez SK .10 .30
450 Bagwell .20 .50
Galar/McGwire AT
451 Olerud .07 .20
Thome/Martinez AT
452 ARod .25 .60
Nomar/Jeter AT
453 Castilla .10 .30
Jones/Rolen AT
454 Sosa .25 .60
Griffey/Gonzalez AT
455 Bonds .30 .75
Ramirez/Walker AT
456 Thomas .20 .50
Salmon/Justice AT
457 Lee .07 .20
Helton/Grieve AT
458 Guerrero .07 .20
Vaughn/B.Will AT
459 Piazza .20 .50
IRod/Kendall AT
460 Clemens .20 .50
Wood/Maddux AT
461A Sammy Sosa HR 1 3.00 8.00
461B Sammy Sosa HR 2 1.25 3.00
461C Sammy Sosa HR 3 1.25 3.00
461D Sammy Sosa HR 4 1.25 3.00
461E Sammy Sosa HR 5 1.25 3.00
461F Sammy Sosa HR 6 1.25 3.00
461G Sammy Sosa HR 7 1.25 3.00
461H Sammy Sosa HR 8 1.25 3.00
461I Sammy Sosa HR 9 1.25 3.00
461J Sammy Sosa HR 10 1.25 3.00
461K Sammy Sosa HR 11 1.25 3.00
461L Sammy Sosa HR 12 1.25 3.00
461M Sammy Sosa HR 13 1.25 3.00
461N Sammy Sosa HR 14 1.25 3.00
461O Sammy Sosa HR 15 1.25 3.00
461P Sammy Sosa HR 16 1.25 3.00
461Q Sammy Sosa HR 17 1.25 3.00
461R Sammy Sosa HR 18 1.25 3.00
461S Sammy Sosa HR 19 1.25 3.00
461T Sammy Sosa HR 20 1.25 3.00
461U Sammy Sosa HR 21 1.25 3.00
461V Sammy Sosa HR 22 1.25 3.00
461W Sammy Sosa HR 23 1.25 3.00
461X Sammy Sosa HR 24 1.25 3.00
461Y Sammy Sosa HR 25 1.25 3.00
461Z Sammy Sosa HR 26 1.25 3.00
461AA Sammy Sosa HR 27 1.25 3.00
461AB Sammy Sosa HR 28 1.25 3.00
461AC Sammy Sosa HR 29 1.25 3.00
461AD Sammy Sosa HR 30 1.25 3.00
461AE Sammy Sosa HR 31 1.25 3.00
461AF Sammy Sosa HR 32 1.25 3.00
461AG Sammy Sosa HR 33 1.25 3.00
461AH Sammy Sosa HR 34 1.25 3.00
461AI Sammy Sosa HR 35 1.25 3.00
461AJ Sammy Sosa HR 36 1.25 3.00
461AK Sammy Sosa HR 37 1.25 3.00
461AL Sammy Sosa HR 38 1.25 3.00
461AM Sammy Sosa HR 39 1.25 3.00
461AN Sammy Sosa HR 40 1.25 3.00
461AO Sammy Sosa HR 41 1.25 3.00
461AP Sammy Sosa HR 42 1.25 3.00
461AR Sammy Sosa HR 43 1.25 3.00
461AS Sammy Sosa HR 44 1.25 3.00
461AT Sammy Sosa HR 45 1.25 3.00
461AU Sammy Sosa HR 46 1.25 3.00
461AV Sammy Sosa HR 47 1.25 3.00
461AW Sammy Sosa HR 48 1.25 3.00
461AX Sammy Sosa HR 49 1.25 3.00
461AY Sammy Sosa HR 50 1.25 3.00
461AZ Sammy Sosa HR 51 1.25 3.00
461BB Sammy Sosa HR 52 1.25 3.00
461CC Sammy Sosa HR 53 1.25 3.00
461DD Sammy Sosa HR 54 1.25 3.00
461EE Sammy Sosa HR 55 1.25 3.00
461FF Sammy Sosa HR 56 1.25 3.00
461GG Sammy Sosa HR 57 1.25 3.00
461HH Sammy Sosa HR 58 1.25 3.00
461II Sammy Sosa HR 59 1.25 3.00
461JJ Sammy Sosa HR 60 1.25 3.00
461KK Sammy Sosa HR 61 3.00 8.00
461LL Sammy Sosa HR 62 4.00 10.00
461MM Sammy Sosa HR 63 1.50 4.00
461NN Sammy Sosa HR 64 1.50 4.00
46100 Sammy Sosa HR 65 1.50 4.00
461PP Sammy Sosa HR 66 10.00 25.00
462 Checklist .07 .20
463 Checklist .07 .20

1999 Topps MVP Promotion

*STARS: 30X TO 80X BASIC CARDS
*ROOKIES: 12X TO 30X BASIC CARDS
SER.1 ODDS 1:515 HOB, 1:142 HTA
SER.2 ODDS 1:504 HOB, 1:139 HTA, 1:504 RET
STATED PRINT RUN 100 SETS
MVP PARALLELS ARE UNNUMBERED
EXCHANGE DEADLINE: 12/31/99
PRIZE CARDS MAILED OUT ON 2/15/00
35 Ray Lankford W 6.00 15.00
52 Todd Helton W 10.00 25.00
70 Mark McGwire W 40.00 100.00
96 Greg Vaughn W 6.00 15.00
101 David Cone W 6.00 15.00
125 Scott Rolen W 10.00 25.00
127 J.T. Snow W 6.00 15.00
139 Fred McGriff W 10.00 25.00
159 Mike Lieberthal W 6.00 15.00
198 B.J. Surhoff W 6.00 15.00
248 Roberto Alomar W 10.00 25.00
265 Nomar Garciaparra W 25.00 60.00
290 Tino Martinez W 10.00 25.00
292 Tony Clark W 6.00 15.00
300 Alex Rodriguez W 25.00 60.00
315 Rafael Palmeiro W 10.00 25.00
340 Mike Piazza W 25.00 60.00
346 Fernando Tatis W 6.00 15.00
350 Larry Walker W 6.00 15.00
352 Miguel Tejada W 6.00 15.00
355 Chipper Jones W 15.00 40.00
360 Tim Salmon W 10.00 25.00
365 Raul Mondesi W 6.00 15.00
416 Paul O'Neill W 10.00 25.00
418 Randy Johnson W 15.00 40.00

1999 Topps MVP Promotion Exchange

COMP.FACT.SET (25) 20.00 50.00
ONE SET VIA MAIL PER '99 MVP WINNER
MVP1 Raul Mondesi .60 1.50
MVP2 Tim Salmon 1.00 2.50
MVP3 Fernando Tatis .60 1.50
MVP4 Larry Walker .60 1.50
MVP5 Fred McGriff 1.00 2.50
MVP6 Nomar Garciaparra 2.50 6.00
MVP7 Rafael Palmeiro 1.00 2.50
MVP8 Randy Johnson 1.50 4.00
MVP9 Mike Lieberthal .60 1.50
MVP10 B.J. Surhoff .60 1.50
MVP11 Todd Helton 1.00 2.50
MVP12 Tino Martinez 1.00 2.50
MVP13 Scott Rolen 1.00 2.50
MVP14 Mike Piazza 2.50 6.00
MVP15 David Cone .60 1.50
MVP16 Tony Clark .60 1.50
MVP17 Roberto Alomar 1.00 2.50
MVP18 Miguel Tejada .60 1.50
MVP19 Alex Rodriguez 2.50 6.00
MVP20 J.T. Snow .60 1.50
MVP21 Ray Lankford .60 1.50
MVP22 Greg Vaughn .60 1.50
MVP23 Paul O'Neill 1.00 2.50
MVP24 Chipper Jones 1.50 4.00
MVP25 Mark McGwire 4.00 10.00

1999 Topps Oversize

COMPLETE SERIES 1 (8) 6.00 15.00
COMPLETE SERIES 2 (8) 6.00 15.00
ONE PER HTA OR HOBBY BOX

1999 Topps All-Matrix

COMPLETE SET (30) 12.00 30.00
SER.2 ODDS 1:18 HOB/RET, 1:5 HTA
AM1 Mark McGwire 2.00 5.00
AM2 Sammy Sosa 1.25 3.00
AM3 Ken Griffey Jr. 2.50 6.00
AM4 Greg Vaughn .50 1.25
AM5 Albert Belle .50 1.25
AM6 Vinny Castilla .50 1.25
AM7 Jose Canseco .75 2.00
AM8 Juan Gonzalez .50 1.25
AM9 Manny Ramirez 1.25 3.00
AM10 Andres Galarraga .75 2.00
AM11 Rafael Palmeiro .75 2.00
AM12 Alex Rodriguez 1.50 4.00
AM13 Mo Vaughn .50 1.25
AM14 Eric Chavez .50 1.25
AM15 Gabe Kapler .50 1.25
AM16 Calvin Pickering .50 1.25
AM17 Ruben Mateo .50 1.25
AM18 Roy Halladay .75 2.00
AM19 Jeremy Giambi .50 1.25
AM20 Alex Gonzalez .50 1.25
AM21 Ron Belliard .50 1.25
AM22 Marlon Anderson .50 1.25
AM23 Carlos Lee .50 1.25
AM24 Kerry Wood .50 1.25
AM25 Roger Clemens 1.50 4.00
AM26 Curt Schilling .50 1.25
AM27 Kevin Brown .50 1.25
AM28 Randy Johnson 1.25 3.00
AM29 Pedro Martinez .75 2.00
AM30 Orlando Hernandez .50 1.25

1999 Topps All-Topps Mystery Finest

COMPLETE SET (33) 20.00 50.00
SER.2 ODDS 1:36 HOB/RET, 1:8 HTA
*REFRACTORS: 1X TO 2.5X BASIC ATMF
SER.2 REF.ODDS 1:144 HOB/RET, 1:32 HTA
M1 Jeff Bagwell .60 1.50
M2 Andres Galarraga .60 1.50
M3 Mark McGwire 1.50 4.00
M4 John Olerud .40 1.00
M5 Jim Thome .60 1.50
M6 Tino Martinez .40 1.00
M7 Alex Rodriguez 1.25 3.00
M8 Nomar Garciaparra .60 1.50
M9 Derek Jeter 2.50 6.00
M10 Vinny Castilla .40 1.00
M11 Chipper Jones 1.00 2.50
M12 Scott Rolen .60 1.50
M13 Sammy Sosa 1.00 2.50
M14 Ken Griffey Jr. 2.00 5.00
M15 Juan Gonzalez .40 1.00
M16 Barry Bonds 1.50 4.00
M17 Manny Ramirez 1.00 2.50
M18 Larry Walker .60 1.50
M19 Frank Thomas 1.00 2.50
M20 Tim Salmon .40 1.00
M21 Dave Justice .40 1.00
M22 Travis Lee .40 1.00
M23 Todd Helton .60 1.50
M24 Ben Grieve .40 1.00
M25 Vladimir Guerrero .60 1.50
M26 Greg Vaughn .40 1.00
M27 Bernie Williams .60 1.50
M28 Mike Piazza 1.00 2.50
M29 Ivan Rodriguez .60 1.50
M30 Jason Kendall .40 1.00
M31 Roger Clemens 1.25 3.00
M32 Kerry Wood .40 1.00
M33 Greg Maddux 1.25 3.00

1999 Topps Autographs

SER.1 ODDS 1:532 HOB, 1:146 HTA
SER.2 ODDS 1:501 HOB, 1:138 HTA
A1 Roger Clemens 25.00 60.00
A2 Chipper Jones 25.00 60.00
A3 Scott Rolen 8.00 20.00
A4 Alex Rodriguez 20.00 50.00
A5 Andres Galarraga 8.00 20.00
A6 Rondell White 6.00 15.00
A7 Ben Grieve 4.00 10.00
A8 Troy Glaus 6.00 15.00
A9 Moises Alou 6.00 15.00
A10 Barry Bonds 75.00 200.00
A11 Vladimir Guerrero 12.00 30.00
A12 Andruw Jones 8.00 20.00
A13 Darin Erstad 6.00 15.00
A14 Shawn Green 8.00 20.00
A15 Eric Chavez 4.00 10.00
A16 Pat Burrell 4.00 10.00

1999 Topps Hall of Fame Collection

COMPLETE SET (10) 8.00 20.00
SER.1 ODDS 1:12 HOB/RET, 1:3 HTA
HOF1 Mike Schmidt 1.50 4.00
HOF2 Brooks Robinson .75 2.00
HOF3 Stan Musial 1.25 3.00
HOF4 Willie McCovey .75 2.00
HOF5 Eddie Mathews .75 2.00
HOF6 Reggie Jackson .75 2.00
HOF7 Ernie Banks .75 2.00
HOF8 Whitey Ford .75 2.00
HOF9 Bob Feller .75 2.00
HOF10 Yogi Berra .75 2.00

1999 Topps Lords of the Diamond

COMPLETE SET (15) 10.00 25.00
SER.1 ODDS 1:18 HOB/RET, 1:5 HTA
LD1 Ken Griffey Jr. 2.00 5.00
LD2 Chipper Jones 1.00 2.50
LD3 Sammy Sosa 1.00 2.50
LD4 Frank Thomas 1.00 2.50
LD5 Mark McGwire 1.50 4.00
LD6 Jeff Bagwell .60 1.50
LD7 Alex Rodriguez 1.25 3.00
LD8 Juan Gonzalez .40 1.00
LD9 Barry Bonds 1.50 4.00
LD10 Nomar Garciaparra .60 1.50
LD11 Darin Erstad .40 1.00
LD12 Tony Gwynn 1.00 2.50
LD13 Andres Galarraga .60 1.50
LD14 Mike Piazza 1.00 2.50
LD15 Greg Maddux 1.25 3.00

1999 Topps New Breed

COMPLETE SET (15) 10.00 25.00
SER.1 ODDS 1:18 HOB/RET, 1:5 HTA
NB1 Darin Erstad .30 .75
NB2 Brad Fullmer .30 .75
NB3 Kerry Wood .30 .75
NB4 Nomar Garciaparra 1.25 3.00
NB5 Travis Lee .30 .75
NB6 Scott Rolen .50 1.25
NB7 Todd Helton .50 1.25
NB8 Vladimir Guerrero .75 2.00
NB9 Derek Jeter 2.00 5.00
NB10 Alex Rodriguez 1.25 3.00
NB11 Ben Grieve .30 .75
NB12 Andruw Jones .50 1.25
NB13 Paul Konerko .30 .75
NB14 Aramis Ramirez .30 .75
NB15 Adrian Beltre .30 .75

1999 Topps Picture Perfect

COMPLETE SET (10) 6.00 15.00
SER.1 ODDS 1:8 HOB/RET, 1:2 HTA
P1 Ken Griffey Jr. .75 2.00
P2 Kerry Wood .15 .40
P3 Pedro Martinez .25 .60
P4 Mark McGwire 1.00 2.50
P5 Greg Maddux .60 1.50
P6 Sammy Sosa .40 1.00
P7 Greg Vaughn .15 .40
P8 Juan Gonzalez .15 .40
P9 Jeff Bagwell .25 .60
P10 Derek Jeter 1.00 2.50

1999 Topps Power Brokers

COMPLETE SET (20) 60.00 120.00
SER.1 ODDS 1:36 HOB/RET, 1:8 HTA
*REFRACTORS: 1X TO 2.5X BASIC BROKERS
SER.1 REF.ODDS 1:144 HOB/RET, 1:32 HTA
PB1 Mark McGwire 5.00 12.00
PB2 Andres Galarraga .75 2.00
PB3 Ken Griffey Jr. 4.00 10.00
PB4 Sammy Sosa 2.00 5.00
PB5 Juan Gonzalez .75 2.00
PB6 Alex Rodriguez 3.00 8.00
PB7 Frank Thomas 2.00 5.00
PB8 Jeff Bagwell 1.25 3.00
PB9 Vinny Castilla .75 2.00
PB10 Mike Piazza 3.00 8.00
PB11 Greg Vaughn .75 2.00
PB12 Barry Bonds 6.00 15.00
PB13 Mo Vaughn .75 2.00
PB14 Jim Thome 1.25 3.00
PB15 Larry Walker .75 2.00
PB16 Chipper Jones 2.00 5.00
PB17 Nomar Garciaparra 3.00 8.00
PD10 Manny Ramirez 1.25 3.00
PB19 Roger Clemens 4.00 10.00
PB20 Kerry Wood .75 2.00

1999 Topps Record Numbers

COMPLETE SET (10) 6.00 15.00
SER.2 ODDS 1:8 HOB/RET, 1:2 HTA
RN1 Mark McGwire 1.00 2.50
RN2 Mike Piazza .60 1.50
RN3 Curt Schilling .15 .40
RN4 Ken Griffey Jr. .75 2.00
RN5 Sammy Sosa .40 1.00
RN6 Nomar Garciaparra .60 1.50
RN7 Kerry Wood .15 .40
RN8 Roger Clemens .75 2.00
RN9 Cal Ripken 1.25 3.00
RN10 Mark McGwire 1.00 2.50

1999 Topps Record Numbers Gold

RANDOM INSERTS IN ALL SER.2 PACKS
PRINT RUNS B/WN 20-2632 COPIES PER
NO PRICING ON QTY OF 30 OR LESS
RN1 Mark McGwire/70 50.00 100.00
RN2 Mike Piazza/362 6.00 15.00
RN3 Curt Schilling/319 3.00 8.00
RN4 Ken Griffey Jr./350 10.00 25.00
RN5 Sammy Sosa/20
RN6 Nomar Garciaparra/30
RN7 Kerry Wood/20
RN8 Roger Clemens/20
RN9 Cal Ripken/2632 6.00 15.00
RN10 Mark McGwire/162 15.00 40.00

1999 Topps Ryan

COMPLETE SET (27) 30.00 80.00
COMPLETE SERIES 1 (14) 15.00 40.00
COMPLETE SERIES 2 (13) 15.00 40.00
COMMON CARD (1-27) 2.00 5.00
STATED ODDS 1:18 HOB/RET, 1:5 HTA
ODD NUMBERS DISTRIBUTED IN SER.1
EVEN NUMBERS DISTRIBUTED IN SER.2
1 Nolan Ryan 1968 4.00 10.00

1999 Topps Ryan Autographs

COMMON CARD (1-13) 125.00 200.00
COMMON CARD (14-27) 100.00 200.00
SER.1 ODDS 1:4260 HOB, 1:1172 HTA
SER.2 ODDS 1:5007 HOB
1 Nolan Ryan 1968 300.00 500.00

1999 Topps Traded

This set contains 121 cards and was distributed as factory boxed sets only. The fronts feature color action player photo. The backs carry player information. Rookie Cards include Sean Burroughs, Josh Hamilton, Corey Patterson and Alfonso Soriano.

COMP.FACT.SET (122) 15.00 40.00
COMPLETE SET (121) 12.50 30.00
DISTRIBUTED ONLY IN FACTORY SET FORM
FACT.SET PRICE IS FOR SEALED SET W/AUTO
T1 Seth Etherton .07 .20
T2 Mark Harriger RC .08 .25
T3 Matt Wise RC .08 .25
T4 Carlos Eduardo Hernandez RC .15 .40
T5 Julio Lugo RC .30 .75
T6 Mike Nannini .07 .20
T7 Justin Bowles RC .08 .25
T8 Mark Mulder RC .60 1.50
T9 Roberto Vaz RC .08 .25
T10 Felipe Lopez RC .60 1.50
T11 Matt Belisle .20 .50
T12 Micah Bowie .07 .20
T13 Ruben Quevedo RC .08 .25
T14 Jose Garcia RC .08 .25
T15 David Kelton RC .08 .25
T16 Phil Norton .07 .20
T17 Corey Patterson RC .40 1.00
T18 Ron Walker RC .08 .25
T19 Paul Hoover RC .08 .25
T20 Ryan Rupe RC .08 .25
T21 J.D. Closser RC .15 .40
T22 Rob Ryan RC .08 .25
T23 Steve Colyer RC .08 .25
T24 Bubba Crosby RC .25 .60
T25 Luke Prokopec RC .08 .25
T26 Matt Blank RC .08 .25
T27 Josh McKinley .07 .20
T28 Nate Bump .07 .20
T29 Giuseppe Chiaramonte RC .08 .25
T30 Arturo McDowell .07 .20
T31 Tony Torcato .07 .20
T32 Dave Roberts RC .25 .60
T33 C.C. Sabathia RC 4.00 10.00
T34 Sean Spencer RC .08 .25
T35 Chip Ambres .07 .20
T36 A.J. Burnett .40 1.00
T37 Mo Bruce RC .08 .25
T38 Jason Tyner .07 .20
T39 Mamon Tucker .07 .20
T40 Sean Burroughs RC .25 .60
T41 Kevin Eberwein RC .08 .25
T42 Junior Herndon RC .08 .25
T43 Bryan Wolff RC .08 .25
T44 Pat Burrell .50 1.25
T45 Eric Valent .07 .20
T46 Carlos Pena RC .20 .50
T47 Mike Zywica .07 .20
T48 Adam Everett .10 .30
T49 Juan Pena RC .15 .40
T50 Adam Dunn RC 1.50 4.00
T51 Austin Kearns .50 1.25
T52 Jacobo Sequea RC .08 .25
T53 Choo Freeman .07 .20
T54 Jeff Winchester .07 .20
T55 Matt Burch .07 .20
T56 Chris George .07 .20
T57 Scott Mullen RC .08 .25
T58 Kit Pellow .07 .20
T59 Mark Quinn RC .08 .25
T60 Nate Cornejo .08 .25
T61 Ryan Mills .07 .20
T62 Kevin Beirne RC .08 .25
T63 Kip Wells RC .15 .40
T64 Juan Rivera RC .40 1.00
T65 Alfonso Soriano RC 2.00 5.00
T66 Josh Hamilton RC 3.00 8.00
T67 Josh Girdley RC .08 .25
T68 Kyle Snyder RC .08 .25
T69 Mike Paradis RC .08 .25
T70 Jason Jennings RC .25 .60
T71 David Walling RC .08 .25
T72 Omar Ortiz RC .08 .25
T73 Jay Gehrke RC .15 .40
T74 Casey Burns RC .15 .40
T75 Carl Crawford RC 1.50 4.00
T76 Reggie Sanders .07 .20
T77 Will Clark .10 .30
T78 David Wells .07 .20
T79 Paul Konerko .07 .20
T80 Armando Benitez .07 .20
T81 Brant Brown .07 .20
T82 Mo Vaughn .07 .20
T83 Jose Canseco .10 .30
T84 Albert Belle .07 .20
T85 Dean Palmer .07 .20
T86 Greg Vaughn .07 .20
T87 Mark Clark .07 .20
T88 Pat Meares .07 .20
T89 Eric Davis .07 .20
T90 Brian Giles .07 .20
T91 Jeff Brantley .07 .20
T92 Bret Boone .07 .20
T93 Ron Gant .07 .20
T94 Mike Cameron .07 .20
T95 Charles Johnson .07 .20
T96 Denny Neagle .07 .20
T97 Brian Hunter .07 .20
T98 Jose Hernandez .07 .20
T99 Rick Aguilera .07 .20
T100 Tony Batista .07 .20
T101 Roger Cedeno .07 .20
T102 Creighton Gubanich RC .08 .25
T103 Tim Belcher .07 .20
T104 Bruce Aven .07 .20
T105 Brian Daubach RC .15 .40
T106 Ed Sprague .07 .20
T107 Michael Tucker .07 .20
T108 Homer Bush .07 .20
T109 Armando Reynoso .07 .20
T110 Brook Fordyce .07 .20
T111 Matt Mantei .07 .20
T112 Dave Mlicki .07 .20
T113 Kenny Rogers .07 .20
T114 Livan Hernandez .07 .20
T115 Butch Huskey .07 .20
T116 David Segui .07 .20
T117 Darryl Hamilton .07 .20
T118 Terry Mulholland .07 .20
T119 Randy Velarde .07 .20
T120 Bill Taylor .07 .20
T121 Kevin Appier .07 .20

1999 Topps Traded Autographs

COMPLETE SET (75) 400.00 800.00
ONE AUTO PER FACTORY SET
T1 Seth Etherton 2.00 5.00
T2 Mark Harriger 3.00 8.00
T3 Matt Wise 3.00 8.00
T4 Carlos Eduardo Hernandez 3.00 8.00
T5 Julio Lugo 3.00 8.00
T6 Mike Nannini 2.00 5.00
T7 Justin Bowles 3.00 8.00
T8 Mark Mulder 4.00 10.00
T9 Roberto Vaz 2.00 5.00
T10 Felipe Lopez 3.00 8.00
T11 Matt Belisle 2.00 5.00
T12 Micah Bowie 2.00 5.00
T13 Ruben Quevedo 2.00 5.00
T14 Jose Garcia 3.00 8.00
T15 David Kelton 2.00 5.00
T16 Phil Norton 3.00 8.00
T17 Corey Patterson 2.00 5.00
T18 Ron Walker 2.00 5.00
T19 Paul Hoover 3.00 8.00
T20 Ryan Rupe 2.00 5.00
T21 J.D. Closser 3.00 8.00
T22 Rob Ryan 2.00 5.00
T23 Steve Colyer 2.00 5.00
T24 Bubba Crosby 3.00 8.00
T25 Luke Prokopec 2.00 5.00
T26 Matt Blank 3.00 8.00
T27 Josh McKinley 2.00 5.00
T28 Nate Bump 3.00 8.00
T29 Giuseppe Chiaramonte 2.00 5.00
T30 Arturo McDowell 2.00 5.00
T31 Tony Torcato 2.00 5.00
T32 Dave Roberts 4.00 10.00
T33 C.C. Sabathia 30.00 80.00
T34 Sean Spencer 2.00 5.00
T35 Chip Ambres 2.00 5.00
T36 A.J. Burnett 6.00 15.00
T37 Mo Bruce 2.00 5.00
T38 Jason Tyner 2.00 5.00
T39 Mamon Tucker 2.00 5.00
T40 Sean Burroughs 6.00 15.00
T41 Kevin Eberwein 2.00 5.00
T42 Junior Herndon 2.00 5.00
T43 Bryan Wolff 3.00 8.00
T44 Pat Burrell 6.00 15.00
T45 Eric Valent 3.00 8.00
T46 Carlos Pena 10.00 25.00
T47 Mike Zywica 3.00 8.00
T48 Adam Everett 6.00 15.00
T49 Juan Pena 3.00 8.00
T50 Adam Dunn 10.00 25.00
T51 Austin Kearns 4.00 10.00
T52 Jacobo Sequea 2.00 5.00
T53 Choo Freeman 3.00 8.00
T54 Jeff Winchester 2.00 5.00
T55 Matt Burch 3.00 8.00
T56 Chris George 2.00 5.00
T57 Scott Mullen 2.00 5.00
T58 Kit Pellow 2.00 5.00
T59 Mark Quinn 2.00 5.00
T60 Nate Cornejo 2.00 5.00
T61 Ryan Mills 2.00 5.00
T62 Kevin Beirne 3.00 8.00
T63 Kip Wells 3.00 8.00
T64 Juan Rivera 4.00 10.00
T65 Alfonso Soriano 15.00 40.00
T66 Josh Hamilton 20.00 50.00
T67 Josh Girdley 2.00 5.00
T68 Kyle Snyder 2.00 5.00
T69 Mike Paradis 2.00 5.00
T70 Jason Jennings 6.00 15.00
T71 David Walling 2.00 5.00
T72 Omar Ortiz 3.00 8.00
T73 Jay Gehrke 3.00 8.00
T74 Casey Burns 3.00 8.00
T75 Carl Crawford 4.00 10.00

2000 Topps Pre-Production

COMPLETE SET (3) .75 2.00
PP1 Brady Anderson .40 1.00
PP2 Jason Kendall .40 1.00
PP3 Ryan Klesko .40 1.00

2000 Topps

COMPLETE SET (478) 20.00 50.00
COMP.HOBBY SET (478) 15.00 40.00
COMPLETE SERIES 1 (239) 10.00 25.00
COMPLETE SERIES 2 (240) 10.00 25.00
COMMON CARD (1-6/8-479) .07 .20
COMMON RC .15 .40
MCGWIRE MM SET (5) 3.00 8.00
MCGWIRE MM (236A-236E) 1.00 2.50
AARON MM SET (5) 3.00 8.00
AARON MM (237A-237E) 1.00 2.50
RIPKEN MM SET (5) 6.00 15.00
RIPKEN MM (238A-238E) 2.00 5.00
BOGGS MM SET (5) .75 2.00
BOGGS MM (239A-239E) .30 .75
GWYNN MM SET (5) 1.50 4.00
GWYNN MM (240A-240E) .50 1.25
GRIFFEY MM SET (5) 2.50 6.00
GRIFFEY MM (475A-475E) .75 2.00
BONDS MM SET (5) 3.00 8.00
BONDS MM (476A-476E) 1.00 2.50
SOSA MM SET (5) 1.50 4.00
SOSA MM (477A-477E) .50 1.25
JETER MM SET (5) 4.00 10.00
JETER MM (478A-478E) 1.25 3.00
A.ROD MM SET (5) 2.50 6.00
A.ROD MM (479A-479E) .75 2.00
CARD NUMBER 7 DOES NOT EXIST
SER.1 HAS ONLY 1 VERSION OF 236-240
SER.2 HAS ONLY 1 VERSION OF 475-479
MCGWIRE '85 ODDS 1:36 HOB/RET, 1:8 HTA
1 Mark McGwire .30 .75
2 Tony Gwynn .20 .50
3 Wade Boggs .12 .30
4 Cal Ripken .60 1.50
5 Matt Williams .07 .20
6 Jay Buhner .07 .20
8 Jeff Conine .07 .20
9 Todd Greene .07 .20
10 Mike Lieberthal .07 .20
11 Steve Avery .07 .20
12 Bret Saberhagen .07 .20
13 Magglio Ordonez .12 .30
14 Brad Radke .07 .20
15 Derek Jeter .50 1.25
16 Javy Lopez .07 .20
17 Russ Davis .07 .20
18 Armando Benitez .07 .20
19 B.J. Surhoff .07 .20
20 Darryl Kile .07 .20
21 Mark Lewis .07 .20
22 Mike Williams .07 .20
23 Mark McLemore .07 .20
24 Sterling Hitchcock .07 .20
25 Darin Erstad .07 .20
26 Ricky Gutierrez .07 .20
27 John Jaha .07 .20
28 Homer Bush .07 .20
29 Darrin Fletcher .07 .20
30 Mark Grace .12 .30
31 Fred McGriff .12 .30
32 Omar Daal .07 .20
33 Eric Karros .07 .20
34 Orlando Cabrera .07 .20
35 J.T. Snow .07 .20
36 Luis Castillo .07 .20
37 Rey Ordonez .07 .20
38 Bob Abreu .07 .20
39 Warren Morris .07 .20
40 Juan Gonzalez .07 .20
41 Mike Lansing .07 .20
42 Chili Davis .07 .20
43 Dean Palmer .07 .20
44 Hank Aaron .40 1.00
45 Jeff Bagwell .12 .30
46 Jose Valentin .07 .20
47 Shannon Stewart .07 .20
48 Kent Bottenfield .07 .20
49 Jeff Shaw .07 .20
50 Sammy Sosa .20 .50
51 Randy Johnson .20 .50
52 Benny Agbayani .07 .20
53 Dante Bichette .07 .20
54 Pete Harnisch .07 .20
55 Frank Thomas .20 .50
56 Jorge Posada .12 .30
57 Todd Walker .07 .20
58 Juan Encarnacion .07 .20
59 Mike Sweeney .07 .20
60 Pedro Martinez .12 .30
61 Lee Stevens .07 .20
62 Brian Giles .07 .20
63 Chad Ogea .07 .20
64 Ivan Rodriguez .12 .30
65 Roger Cedeno .07 .20
66 David Justice .07 .20
67 Steve Trachsel .07 .20
68 Eli Marrero .07 .20
69 Dave Nilsson .07 .20
70 Ken Caminiti .07 .20
71 Tim Raines .12 .30
72 Brian Jordan .07 .20
73 Jeff Blauser .07 .20
74 Bernard Gilkey .07 .20
75 John Flaherty .07 .20
76 Brent Mayne .07 .20
77 Jose Vidro .07 .20
78 David Bell .07 .20
79 Bruce Aven .07 .20
80 John Olerud .07 .20
81 Pokey Reese .07 .20
82 Woody Williams .07 .20
83 Ed Sprague .07 .20
84 Joe Girardi .12 .30
85 Barry Larkin .12 .30
86 Mike Caruso .07 .20
87 Bobby Higginson .07 .20
88 Roberto Kelly .07 .20
89 Edgar Martinez .12 .30
90 Mark Kotsay .07 .20
91 Paul Sorrento .07 .20
92 Fric Young .07 .20
93 Carlos Delgado .07 .20
94 Troy Glaus .07 .20
95 Ben Grieve .07 .20
96 Jose Lima .07 .20
97 Garret Anderson .07 .20
98 Luis Gonzalez .07 .20
99 Carl Pavano .07 .20
100 Alex Rodriguez .25 .60
101 Preston Wilson .07 .20
102 Ron Gant .07 .20
103 Brady Anderson .07 .20
104 Rickey Henderson .20 .50
105 Gary Sheffield .07 .20
106 Mickey Morandini .07 .20
107 Jim Edmonds .07 .20
108 Kris Benson .07 .20
109 Adrian Beltre .20 .50
110 Alex Fernandez .07 .20
111 Dan Wilson .07 .20
112 Mark Clark .07 .20
113 Greg Vaughn .07 .20
114 Neifi Perez .07 .20
115 Paul O'Neill .12 .30
116 Jermaine Dye .07 .20
117 Todd Jones .07 .20
118 Terry Steinbach .07 .20
119 Greg Norton .07 .20
120 Curt Schilling .12 .30
121 Todd Zeile .07 .20
122 Edgardo Alfonzo .07 .20
123 Ryan McGuire .07 .20
124 Rich Aurilia .07 .20
125 John Smoltz .20 .50
126 Bob Wickman .07 .20
127 Richard Hidalgo .07 .20
128 Chuck Finley .07 .20
129 Billy Wagner .07 .20
130 Todd Hundley .07 .20
131 Dwight Gooden .07 .20
132 Russ Ortiz .07 .20
133 Mike Lowell .07 .20
134 Reggie Sanders .07 .20
135 John Valentin .07 .20
136 Brad Ausmus .07 .20
137 Chad Kreuter .07 .20
138 David Cone .07 .20
139 Brook Fordyce .07 .20
140 Roberto Alomar .12 .30
141 Charles Nagy .07 .20
142 Brian Hunter .07 .20
143 Mike Mussina .12 .30
144 Robin Ventura .07 .20
145 Kevin Brown .07 .20
146 Pat Hentgen .07 .20
147 Ryan Klesko .07 .20
148 Derek Bell .07 .20
149 Andy Sheets .07 .20
150 Larry Walker .12 .30
151 Scott Williamson .07 .20
152 Jose Offerman .07 .20
153 Doug Mientkiewicz .07 .20
154 John Snyder RC .15 .40
155 Sandy Alomar Jr. .07 .20
156 Joe Nathan .07 .20
157 Lance Johnson .07 .20
158 Odalis Perez .07 .20
159 Hideo Nomo .20 .50
160 Steve Finley .07 .20
161 Dave Martinez .07 .20
162 Matt Walbeck .07 .20
163 Bill Spiers .07 .20
164 Fernando Tatis .07 .20
165 Kenny Lofton .07 .20
166 Paul Byrd .07 .20
167 Aaron Sele .07 .20
168 Eddie Taubensee .07 .20
169 Reggie Jefferson .07 .20
170 Roger Clemens .25 .60
171 Francisco Cordova .07 .20

172 Mike Bordick .07 .20
173 Wally Joyner .07 .20
174 Marvin Benard .07 .20
175 Jason Kendall .07 .20
176 Mike Stanley .07 .20
177 Chad Allen .07 .20
178 Carlos Beltran .12 .30
179 Deivi Cruz .07 .20
180 Chipper Jones .20 .50
181 Vladimir Guerrero .12 .30
182 Dave Burba .07 .20
183 Tom Goodwin .07 .20
184 Brian Daubach .07 .20
185 Jay Bell .07 .20
186 Roy Halladay .12 .30
187 Miguel Tejada .12 .30
188 Armando Rios .07 .20
189 Fernando Vina .07 .20
190 Eric Davis .07 .20
191 Henry Rodriguez .07 .20
192 Joe McEwing .07 .20
193 Jeff Kent .07 .20
194 Mike Jackson .07 .20
195 Mike Morgan .07 .20
196 Jeff Montgomery .07 .20
197 Jeff Zimmerman .07 .20
198 Tony Fernandez .07 .20
199 Jason Giambi .07 .20
200 Jose Canseco .12 .30
201 Alex Gonzalez .07 .20
202 J.Cust .07 .20
M.Colangelo/D.Brown
203 A.Soriano .20 .50
F.Lopez/P.Ozuna
204 Durazo .07 .20
Burrell/Johnson
205 J.Sneed RC .15 .40
K.Wells/M.Blank
206 J.Kalinowski .15 .40
M.Tejera/C.Mears
207 L.Berkman .12 .30
C.Patterson/R.Brown
208 K.Pellow .07 .20
K.Barker/R.Branyan
209 B.Garbe .15 .40
L.Bigbie
210 B.Bradley .15 .40
E.Munson
211 J.Girdley .07 .20
K.Snyder
212 C.Caple .15 .40
J.Jennings
213 B.Myers .50 1.25
R.Christianson
214 J.Stumm .15 .40
R.Purvis RC
215 D.Walling .07 .20
M.Paradis
216 O.Ortiz .07 .20
J.Gehrke
217 David Cone HL .07 .20
218 Jose Jimenez HL .07 .20
219 Chris Singleton HL .07 .20
220 Fernando Tatis HL .07 .20
221 Todd Helton HL .12 .30
222 Kevin Millwood DIV .07 .20
223 Todd Pratt DIV .07 .20
224 Orlando Hernandez DIV .07 .20
225 Pedro Martinez DIV .12 .30
226 Tom Glavine LCS .12 .30
227 Bernie Williams LCS .12 .30
228 Mariano Rivera WS .25 .60
229 Tony Gwynn 20CB .20 .50
230 Wade Boggs 20CB .12 .30
231 Lance Johnson CB .07 .20
232 Mark McGwire 20CB .30 .75
233 Rickey Henderson 20CB .20 .50
234 Rickey Henderson 20CB .20 .50
235 Roger Clemens 20CB .25 .60
236A M.McGwire MM 1st HR .75 2.00
236B M.McGwire MM 1987 ROY .75 2.00
236C M.McGwire MM 62nd HR .75 2.00
236D M.McGwire MM 70th HR .75 2.00
236E M.McGwire MM 500th HR .75 2.00
237A H.Aaron MM 1st Career HR 1.00 2.50
237B H.Aaron MM 1957 MVP 1.00 2.50
237C H.Aaron MM 3000th Hit 1.00 2.50
237D H.Aaron MM 715th HR 1.00 2.50
237E H.Aaron MM 755th HR 1.00 2.50
238A C.Ripken MM 1982 ROY 1.50 4.00
238B C.Ripken MM 1991 MVP 1.50 4.00
238C C.Ripken MM 2131 Game 1.50 4.00
238D C.Ripken MM Streak Ends 1.50 4.00
238E C.Ripken MM 400th HR 1.50 4.00
239A W.Boggs MM 1983 Batting .30 .75
239B W.Boggs MM 1988 Batting .30 .75
239C W.Boggs MM 2000th Hit .30 .75
239D W.Boggs MM 1996 Champs .30 .75
239E W.Boggs MM 3000th Hit .30 .75
240A T.Gwynn MM 1984 Batting .50 1.25
240B T.Gwynn MM 1984 NLCS .50 1.25
240C T.Gwynn MM 1995 Batting .50 1.25
240D T.Gwynn MM 1998 NLCS .50 1.25
240E T.Gwynn MM 3000th Hit .50 1.25
241 Tom Glavine .12 .30
242 David Wells .07 .20
243 Kevin Appier .07 .20
244 Troy Percival .07 .20
245 Ray Lankford .07 .20
246 Marquis Grissom .07 .20
247 Randy Winn .07 .20
248 Miguel Batista .07 .20
249 Darren Dreifort .07 .20
250 Barry Bonds .30 .75
251 Harold Baines .12 .30
252 Cliff Floyd .07 .20
253 Freddy Garcia .07 .20
254 Kenny Rogers .07 .20
255 Ben Davis .07 .20
256 Charles Johnson .07 .20
257 Bubba Trammell .07 .20
258 Desi Relaford .07 .20
259 Al Martin .07 .20
260 Andy Pettitte .12 .30
261 Carlos Lee .07 .20
262 Matt Lawton .07 .20
263 Andy Fox .07 .20
264 Chan Ho Park .12 .30
265 Billy Koch .07 .20
266 Dave Roberts .12 .30
267 Carl Everett .07 .20
268 Orel Hershiser .07 .20
269 Trot Nixon .07 .20
270 Rusty Greer .07 .20
271 Will Clark .12 .30
272 Quilvio Veras .07 .20
273 Rico Brogna .07 .20
274 Devon White .07 .20
275 Tim Hudson .12 .30
276 Mike Hampton .07 .20
277 Miguel Cairo .07 .20
278 Darren Oliver .07 .20
279 Jeff Cirillo .07 .20
280 Al Leiter .07 .20
281 Shane Andrews .07 .20
282 Carlos Febles .07 .20
283 Pedro Astacio .07 .20
284 Juan Guzman .07 .20
285 Orlando Hernandez .07 .20
286 Paul Konerko .07 .20
287 Tony Clark .07 .20
288 Aaron Boone .07 .20
289 Ismael Valdes .07 .20
290 Moises Alou .07 .20
291 Kevin Tapani .07 .20
292 John Franco .07 .20
293 Todd Zeile .07 .20
294 Jason Schmidt .07 .20
295 Johnny Damon .12 .30
296 Scott Brosius .07 .20
297 Travis Fryman .07 .20
298 Jose Vizcaino .07 .20
299 Eric Chavez .07 .20
300 Mike Piazza .20 .50
301 Matt Clement .07 .20
302 Cristian Guzman .07 .20
303 C.J. Nitkowski .07 .20
304 Michael Tucker .07 .20
305 Brett Tomko .07 .20
306 Mike Lansing .07 .20
307 Eric Owens .07 .20
308 Livan Hernandez .07 .20
309 Rondell White .07 .20
310 Todd Stottlemyre .07 .20
311 Chris Carpenter .12 .30
312 Ken Hill .07 .20
313 Mark Loretta .07 .20
314 John Rocker .07 .20
315 Richie Sexson .07 .20
316 Ruben Mateo .07 .20
317 Joe Randa .07 .20
318 Mike Sirotka .07 .20
319 Jose Rosado .07 .20
320 Matt Mantei .07 .20
321 Kevin Millwood .07 .20
322 Gary Disarcina .07 .20
323 Dustin Hermanson .07 .20
324 Mike Stanton .07 .20
325 Kirk Rueter .07 .20
326 Damian Miller RC .15 .40
327 Doug Glanville .07 .20
328 Scott Rolen .12 .30
329 Ray Durham .07 .20
330 Butch Huskey .07 .20
331 Mariano Rivera .25 .60
332 Darren Lewis .07 .20
333 Mike Timlin .07 .20
334 Mark Grudzielanek .07 .20
335 Mike Cameron .07 .20
336 Kelvim Escobar .07 .20
337 Bret Boone .07 .20
338 Mo Vaughn .07 .20
339 Craig Biggio .12 .30
340 Michael Barrett .07 .20
341 Marlon Anderson .07 .20
342 Bobby Jones .07 .20
343 John Halama .07 .20
344 Todd Ritchie .07 .20
345 Chuck Knoblauch .07 .20
346 Rick Reed .07 .20
347 Kelly Stinnett .07 .20
348 Tim Salmon .07 .20
349 A.J. Hinch .07 .20
350 Jose Cruz Jr. .07 .20
351 Roberto Hernandez .07 .20
352 Edgar Renteria .07 .20
353 Jose Hernandez .07 .20
354 Brad Fullmer .07 .20
355 Trevor Hoffman .12 .30
356 Troy O'Leary .07 .20
357 Justin Thompson .07 .20
358 Kevin Young .07 .20
359 Hideki Irabu .07 .20
360 Jim Thome .12 .30
361 Steve Karsay .07 .20
362 Octavio Dotel .07 .20
363 Omar Vizquel .12 .30
364 Raul Mondesi .07 .20
365 Shane Reynolds .07 .20
366 Bartolo Colon .07 .20
367 Chris Widger .07 .20
368 Gabe Kapler .07 .20
369 Bill Simas .07 .20
370 Tino Martinez .07 .20
371 John Thomson .07 .20
372 Delino Deshields .07 .20
373 Carlos Perez .07 .20
374 Eddie Perez .07 .20
375 Jeromy Burnitz .07 .20
376 Jimmy Haynes .07 .20
377 Travis Lee .07 .20
378 Darryl Hamilton .07 .20
379 Jamie Moyer .07 .20
380 Alex Gonzalez .07 .20
381 John Wetteland .07 .20
382 Vinny Castilla .07 .20
383 Jeff Suppan .07 .20
384 Jim Leyritz .07 .20
385 Robb Nen .07 .20
386 Wilson Alvarez .07 .20
387 Andres Galarraga .12 .30
388 Mike Remlinger .07 .20
389 Geoff Jenkins .07 .20
390 Matt Stairs .07 .20
391 Bill Mueller .07 .20
392 Mike Lowell .07 .20
393 Andy Ashby .07 .20
394 Ruben Rivera .07 .20
395 Todd Helton .12 .30
396 Bernie Williams .12 .30
397 Royce Clayton .07 .20
398 Manny Ramirez .20 .50
399 Kerry Wood .07 .20
400 Ken Griffey Jr. .40 1.00
401 Enrique Wilson .07 .20
402 Joey Hamilton .07 .20
403 Shawn Estes .07 .20
404 Ugueth Urbina .07 .20
405 Albert Belle .07 .20
406 Rick Helling .07 .20
407 Steve Parris .07 .20
408 Eric Milton .07 .20
409 Dave Mlicki .07 .20
410 Shawn Green .07 .20
411 Jaret Wright .07 .20
412 Tony Womack .07 .20
413 Vernon Wells .07 .20
414 Ron Belliard .07 .20
415 Ellis Burks .07 .20
416 Scott Erickson .07 .20
417 Rafael Palmeiro .12 .30
418 Damion Easley .07 .20
419 Jamey Wright .07 .20
420 Corey Koskie .07 .20
421 Bobby Howry .07 .20
422 Ricky Ledee .07 .20
423 Dmitri Young .07 .20
424 Sidney Ponson .07 .20
425 Greg Maddux .25 .60
426 Jose Guillen .07 .20
427 Jon Lieber .07 .20
428 Andy Benes .07 .20
429 Randy Velarde .07 .20
430 Sean Casey .07 .20
431 Torii Hunter .07 .20
432 Ryan Rupe .07 .20
433 David Segui .07 .20
434 Todd Pratt .07 .20
435 Nomar Garciaparra .12 .30
436 Denny Neagle .07 .20
437 Ron Coomer .07 .20
438 Chris Singleton .07 .20
439 Tony Batista .07 .20
440 Andruw Jones .07 .20
441 A.Huff .07 .20
S.Burroughs/A.Piatt
442 Furcal .12 .30
Dawkins/Dellaero
443 M.Lamb RC .15 .40
J.Crede/W.Veras
444 J.Zuleta .15 .40
J.Toca/D.Stenson
445 G.Maddox Jr. .15 .40
G.Matthews Jr./T.Raines Jr.
446 M.Mulder .12 .30
C.Sabathia/M.Riley
447 S.Downs .15 .40
C.George/M.Belisle
448 D.Mirabelli .12 .30
B.Petrick/J.Werth
449 J.Hamilton .50 1.25
C.Meyers
450 B.Christensen .15 .40
R.Stahl
451 B.Zito 1.25 3.00
B.Sheets RC
452 K.Ainsworth .15 .40
T.Howington
453 R.Asadoorian .15 .40
V.Faison
454 K.Reed .15 .40
J.Heaverlo
455 M.MacDougal .25 .60
B.Baker
456 Mark McGwire SH .30 .75
457 Cal Ripken SH .60 1.50
458 Wade Boggs SH .12 .30
459 Tony Gwynn SH .20 .50
460 Jesse Orosco SH .07 .20
461 L.Walker .12 .30
N.Garciaparra LL
462 K.Griffey Jr. .40 1.00
M.McGwire LL
463 M.Ramirez .30 .75
M.McGwire LL
464 P.Martinez .20 .50
R.Johnson LL
465 P.Martinez .20 .50
R.Johnson LL
466 D.Jeter .50 1.25
L.Gonzalez LL
467 L.Walker .20 .50
M.Ramirez LL
468 Tony Gwynn 20CB .20 .50
469 Mark McGwire 20CB .30 .75
470 Frank Thomas 20CB .20 .50
471 Harold Baines 20CB .12 .30
472 Roger Clemens 20CB .25 .60
473 John Franco 20CB .07 .20
474 John Franco 20CB .07 .20
475A K.Griffey Jr. MM 350th HR 1.00 2.50
475B K.Griffey Jr. MM 1997 MVP 1.00 2.50
475C K.Griffey Jr. MM HR Dad 1.00 2.50
475D K.Griffey Jr. MM 1992 AS MVP 1.00 2.50
475E K.Griffey Jr. MM 50 HR 1997 1.00 2.50
476A B.Bonds MM 400HR/400SB .75 2.00
476B B.Bonds MM 40HR/40SB .75 2.00
476C B.Bonds MM 1993 MVP .75 2.00
476D B.Bonds MM 1990 MVP .75 2.00
476E B.Bonds MM 1992 MVP .75 2.00
477A S.Sosa MM 20 HR June .50 1.25
477B S.Sosa MM 66 HR 1998 .50 1.25
477C S.Sosa MM 60 HR 1999 .50 1.25
477D S.Sosa MM 1998 MVP .50 1.25
477E S.Sosa MM HR's 61/62 .50 1.25
478A D.Jeter MM 1996 ROY 1.25 3.00
478B D.Jeter MM Wins 1999 WS 1.25 3.00
478C D.Jeter MM Wins 1998 WS 1.25 3.00
478D D.Jeter MM Wins 1996 WS 1.25 3.00
478E D.Jeter MM 17 GM Hit Streak 1.25 3.00
479A A.Rodriguez MM 40HR/40SB .60 1.50
479B A.Rodriguez MM 100th HR .60 1.50
479C A.Rodriguez MM 1996 POY .60 1.50
479D A.Rodriguez MM Wins 1 Million .60 1.50
479E A.Rodriguez MM
1996 Batting Leader .60 1.50
NNO M.McGwire 85 Reprint 1.00 2.50

2000 Topps 20th Century Best Sequential

SER.1 STATED ODDS 1:869 HOBBY, 1:239 HTA
SER.2 STATED ODDS 1:362 HOBBY, 1:100 HTA
PRINT RUNS B/WN 117-3316 COPIES PER
CB1 T.Gwynn AVG/339 10.00 25.00
CB2 W.Boggs 2B/578 6.00 15.00
CB3 L.Johnson 3B/117 6.00 15.00
CB4 M.McGwire HR/522 15.00 40.00
CB5 R.Henderson SB/1334 6.00 15.00
CB6 R.Henderson RUN/2103 6.00 15.00
CB7 R.Clemens WIN/247 12.00 30.00
CB8 Tony Gwynn HIT/3067 6.00 15.00
CB9 Mark McGwire SLG/587 15.00 40.00
CB10 Frank Thomas OBP/440 10.00 25.00
CB11 Harold Baines RBI/1583 4.00 10.00
CB12 Roger Clemens K's/3316 8.00 20.00
CB13 John Franco ERA/264 4.00 10.00
CB14 John Franco SV/416 4.00 10.00

2000 Topps Home Team Advantage

COMP.FACT.SET (479) 40.00 80.00
*HTA: .75X TO 2X BASIC CARDS
DISTRIBUTED ONLY IN HTA FACTORY SETS

2000 Topps MVP Promotion

SER.1 ODDS 1:510 HOB/RET, 1:140 HTA
SER.2 ODDS 1:378 HOB/RET, 1:104 HTA
STATED PRINT RUN 100 SETS
EXCHANGE DEADLINE 12/31/00
CARD NUMBERS 7 AND 44 DO NOT EXIST
MVP PARALLELS ARE UNNUMBERED
1 Mark McGwire 20.00 50.00
2 Tony Gwynn 12.00 30.00
3 Wade Boggs 8.00 20.00
4 Cal Ripken 40.00 100.00
5 Matt Williams 5.00 12.00
6 Jay Buhner 5.00 12.00
8 Jeff Conine 5.00 12.00
9 Todd Greene 5.00 12.00
10 Mike Lieberthal 5.00 12.00
11 Steve Avery 5.00 12.00
12 Bret Saberhagen 5.00 12.00
13 Magglio Ordonez W 8.00 20.00
14 Brad Radke 5.00 12.00
15 Derek Jeter W 30.00 80.00
16 Javy Lopez 5.00 12.00
17 Russ Davis 5.00 12.00
18 Armando Benitez 5.00 12.00
19 B.J. Surhoff 5.00 12.00
20 Darryl Kile 5.00 12.00
21 Mark Lewis 5.00 12.00
22 Mike Williams 5.00 12.00
23 Mark McLemore 5.00 12.00
24 Sterling Hitchcock 5.00 12.00
25 Darin Erstad 5.00 12.00
26 Ricky Gutierrez 5.00 12.00
27 John Jaha 5.00 12.00
28 Homer Bush 5.00 12.00
29 Darrin Fletcher 5.00 12.00
30 Mark Grace 8.00 20.00
31 Fred McGriff 8.00 20.00
32 Omar Daal 5.00 12.00
33 Eric Karros 5.00 12.00
34 Orlando Cabrera 5.00 12.00
35 J.T. Snow 5.00 12.00
36 Luis Castillo 5.00 12.00
37 Rey Ordonez 5.00 12.00
38 Bob Abreu 5.00 12.00
39 Warren Morris 5.00 12.00
40 Juan Gonzalez 5.00 12.00
41 Mike Lansing 5.00 12.00
42 Chili Davis 5.00 12.00
43 Dean Palmer 5.00 12.00
45 Jeff Bagwell W 8.00 20.00
46 Jose Valentin 5.00 12.00
47 Shannon Stewart 5.00 12.00
48 Kent Bottenfield 5.00 12.00
49 Jeff Shaw 5.00 12.00
50 Sammy Sosa W 12.00 30.00
51 Randy Johnson 12.00 30.00
52 Benny Agbayani 5.00 12.00
53 Dante Bichette W 5.00 12.00
54 Pete Harnisch 5.00 12.00
55 Frank Thomas W 12.00 30.00
56 Jorge Posada 8.00 20.00
57 Todd Walker 5.00 12.00
58 Juan Encarnacion 5.00 12.00
59 Mike Sweeney 5.00 12.00
60 Pedro Martinez W 8.00 20.00
61 Lee Stevens 5.00 12.00
62 Brian Giles 5.00 12.00
63 Chad Ogea 5.00 12.00
64 Ivan Rodriguez 8.00 20.00
65 Roger Cedeno 5.00 12.00
66 David Justice 5.00 12.00
67 Steve Trachsel 5.00 12.00
68 Eli Marrero 5.00 12.00
69 Dave Nilsson 5.00 12.00
70 Ken Caminiti 5.00 12.00
71 Tim Raines 8.00 20.00
72 Brian Jordan W 5.00 12.00
73 Jeff Blauser 5.00 12.00
74 Bernard Gilkey 5.00 12.00
75 John Flaherty 5.00 12.00
76 Brent Mayne 5.00 12.00
77 Jose Vidro 5.00 12.00
78 David Bell 5.00 12.00
79 Bruce Aven 5.00 12.00
80 John Olerud 5.00 12.00
81 Juan Guzman 5.00 12.00
82 Woody Williams 5.00 12.00
83 Ed Sprague 5.00 12.00
84 Joe Girardi 8.00 20.00
85 Barry Larkin 8.00 20.00
86 Mike Caruso 5.00 12.00
87 Bobby Higginson W 5.00 12.00
88 Roberto Kelly 5.00 12.00
89 Edgar Martinez 8.00 20.00
90 Mark Kotsay W 5.00 12.00
91 Paul Sorrento 5.00 12.00
92 Eric Young 5.00 12.00
93 Carlos Delgado W 5.00 12.00
94 Troy Glaus 5.00 12.00
95 Ben Grieve 5.00 12.00
96 Jose Lima 5.00 12.00
97 Garret Anderson 5.00 12.00
98 Luis Gonzalez 5.00 12.00
99 Carl Pavano 5.00 12.00
100 Alex Rodriguez 15.00 40.00
101 Preston Wilson 5.00 12.00
102 Ron Gant 5.00 12.00
103 Brady Anderson 5.00 12.00
104 Rickey Henderson 12.00 30.00
105 Gary Sheffield 5.00 12.00
106 Mickey Morandini 5.00 12.00
107 Jim Edmonds W 5.00 12.00
108 Kris Benson 5.00 12.00
109 Adrian Beltre W 12.00 30.00
110 Alex Fernandez 5.00 12.00
111 Dan Wilson 5.00 12.00
112 Mark Clark 5.00 12.00
113 Greg Vaughn 5.00 12.00
114 Neifi Perez 5.00 12.00
115 Paul O'Neill 8.00 20.00
116 Jermaine Dye W 5.00 12.00
117 Todd Jones 5.00 12.00
118 Terry Steinbach 5.00 12.00
119 Greg Norton 5.00 12.00
120 Curt Schilling 8.00 20.00
121 Todd Zeile 5.00 12.00
122 Edgardo Alfonzo 5.00 12.00
123 Ryan McGuire 5.00 12.00
124 Rich Aurilia 5.00 12.00
125 John Smoltz 12.00 30.00
126 Bob Wickman 5.00 12.00
127 Billy Wagner 5.00 12.00
128 Chuck Finley 5.00 12.00
129 Billy Wagner 5.00 12.00
130 Todd Hundley 5.00 12.00
131 Dwight Gooden 5.00 12.00
132 Russ Ortiz 5.00 12.00
133 Mike Lowell 5.00 12.00
134 Reggie Sanders 5.00 12.00
135 John Valentin 5.00 12.00
136 Brad Ausmus 5.00 12.00
137 Chad Kreuter 5.00 12.00
138 David Cone 5.00 12.00
139 Brook Fordyce 5.00 12.00
140 Roberto Alomar 8.00 20.00
141 Charles Nagy 5.00 12.00
142 Brian Hunter 5.00 12.00
143 Mike Mussina 8.00 20.00
144 Robin Ventura 5.00 12.00
145 Kevin Brown 5.00 12.00
146 Pat Hentgen 5.00 12.00
147 Ryan Klesko 5.00 12.00
148 Derek Bell W 5.00 12.00
149 Andy Sheets 5.00 12.00
150 Larry Walker 8.00 20.00
151 Scott Williamson 5.00 12.00
152 Jose Offerman 5.00 12.00
153 Doug Mientkiewicz 5.00 12.00
154 John Snyder 5.00 12.00
155 Sandy Alomar Jr. 5.00 12.00
156 Joe Nathan 5.00 12.00
157 Lance Johnson 5.00 12.00
158 Odalis Perez 5.00 12.00
159 Hideo Nomo 12.00 30.00
160 Steve Finley 5.00 12.00
161 Dave Martinez 5.00 12.00
162 Matt Walbeck 5.00 12.00
163 Bill Spiers 5.00 12.00
164 Fernando Tatis 5.00 12.00
165 Kenny Lofton W 5.00 12.00
166 Paul Byrd 5.00 12.00
167 Aaron Sele 5.00 12.00
168 Eddie Taubensee 5.00 12.00
169 Reggie Jefferson 5.00 12.00
170 Roger Clemens 15.00 40.00
171 Francisco Cordova 5.00 12.00
172 Mike Bordick 5.00 12.00
173 Wally Joyner 5.00 12.00
174 Marvin Benard 5.00 12.00
175 Jason Kendall 5.00 12.00
176 Mike Stanley 5.00 12.00
177 Chad Allen 5.00 12.00
178 Carlos Beltran 8.00 20.00
179 Deivi Cruz 5.00 12.00
180 Chipper Jones W 12.00 30.00
181 Vladimir Guerrero 8.00 20.00
182 Dave Burba 5.00 12.00
183 Tom Goodwin 5.00 12.00
184 Brian Daubach 5.00 12.00
185 Jay Bell 5.00 12.00
186 Roy Halladay 8.00 20.00
187 Miguel Tejada 8.00 20.00
188 Armando Rios 5.00 12.00
189 Fernando Vina 5.00 12.00
190 Eric Davis 5.00 12.00
191 Henry Rodriguez 5.00 12.00
192 Joe McEwing 5.00 12.00
193 Jeff Kent 5.00 12.00
194 Mike Jackson 5.00 12.00
195 Mike Morgan 5.00 12.00
196 Jeff Montgomery 5.00 12.00
197 Jeff Zimmerman 5.00 12.00
198 Tony Fernandez 5.00 12.00
199 Jason Giambi W 5.00 12.00
200 Jose Canseco 8.00 20.00
201 Alex Gonzalez 5.00 12.00
241 Tom Glavine 8.00 20.00
242 David Wells 5.00 12.00
243 Kevin Appier 5.00 12.00
244 Troy Percival 5.00 12.00
245 Ray Lankford 5.00 12.00
246 Marquis Grissom 5.00 12.00
247 Randy Winn 5.00 12.00
248 Miguel Batista 5.00 12.00
249 Darren Dreifort 5.00 12.00
250 Barry Bonds W 20.00 50.00
251 Harold Baines 8.00 20.00
252 Cliff Floyd 5.00 12.00
253 Freddy Garcia 5.00 12.00
254 Kenny Rogers 5.00 12.00
255 Ben Davis 5.00 12.00
256 Charles Johnson 5.00 12.00
257 Bubba Trammell 5.00 12.00
258 Desi Relaford 5.00 12.00
259 Al Martin 5.00 12.00
260 Andy Pettitte 8.00 20.00
261 Carlos Lee 5.00 12.00
262 Matt Lawton 5.00 12.00
263 Andy Fox 5.00 12.00
264 Chan Ho Park 8.00 20.00
265 Billy Koch 5.00 12.00
266 Dave Roberts 8.00 20.00
267 Carl Everett 5.00 12.00
268 Orel Hershiser 5.00 12.00
269 Trot Nixon 5.00 12.00
270 Rusty Greer 5.00 12.00
271 Will Clark W 8.00 20.00
272 Quilvio Veras 5.00 12.00
273 Rico Brogna 5.00 12.00
274 Devon White 5.00 12.00
275 Tim Hudson 8.00 20.00
276 Mike Hampton 5.00 12.00
277 Miguel Cairo 5.00 12.00
278 Darren Oliver 5.00 12.00
279 Jeff Cirillo 5.00 12.00
280 Al Leiter 5.00 12.00
281 Shane Andrews 5.00 12.00
282 Carlos Febles 5.00 12.00
283 Pedro Astacio 5.00 12.00
284 Juan Guzman 5.00 12.00
285 Orlando Hernandez 5.00 12.00
286 Paul Konerko 5.00 12.00
287 Tony Clark 5.00 12.00
288 Aaron Boone 5.00 12.00
289 Ismael Valdes 5.00 12.00
290 Moises Alou 5.00 12.00
291 Kevin Tapani 5.00 12.00
292 John Franco 5.00 12.00
293 Todd Zeile 5.00 12.00
294 Jason Schmidt 5.00 12.00
295 Johnny Damon 8.00 20.00
296 Scott Brosius 5.00 12.00
297 Travis Fryman 5.00 12.00
298 Jose Vizcaino 5.00 12.00
299 Eric Chavez 5.00 12.00
300 Mike Piazza 12.00 30.00
301 Matt Clement 5.00 12.00
302 Cristian Guzman 5.00 12.00
303 C.J. Nitkowski 5.00 12.00
304 Michael Tucker 5.00 12.00
305 Brett Tomko 5.00 12.00
306 Mike Lansing 5.00 12.00
307 Eric Owens 5.00 12.00
308 Livan Hernandez 5.00 12.00
309 Rondell White 5.00 12.00
310 Todd Stottlemyre 5.00 12.00
311 Chris Carpenter 8.00 20.00
312 Ken Hill 5.00 12.00
313 Mark Loretta 5.00 12.00
314 John Rocker 5.00 12.00
315 Richie Sexson 5.00 12.00
316 Ruben Mateo 5.00 12.00
317 Joe Randa 5.00 12.00
318 Mike Sirotka 5.00 12.00
319 Jose Rosado 5.00 12.00
320 Matt Mantei 5.00 12.00
321 Kevin Millwood 5.00 12.00
322 Gary Disarcina 5.00 12.00
323 Dustin Hermanson 5.00 12.00
324 Mike Stanton 5.00 12.00
325 Kirk Rueter 5.00 12.00
326 Damian Miller 5.00 12.00
327 Doug Glanville 5.00 12.00
328 Scott Rolen 8.00 20.00
329 Ray Durham 5.00 12.00
330 Butch Huskey 5.00 12.00
331 Mariano Rivera 15.00 40.00
332 Darren Lewis 5.00 12.00
333 Mike Timlin 5.00 12.00
334 Mark Grudzielanek 5.00 12.00
335 Mike Cameron 5.00 12.00
336 Kelvim Escobar 5.00 12.00
337 Bret Boone 5.00 12.00
338 Mo Vaughn 5.00 12.00
339 Craig Biggio 8.00 20.00
340 Michael Barrett 5.00 12.00
341 Marlon Anderson 5.00 12.00
342 Bobby Jones 5.00 12.00
343 John Halama 5.00 12.00
344 Todd Ritchie 5.00 12.00
345 Chuck Knoblauch 5.00 12.00
346 Rick Reed 5.00 12.00
347 Kelly Stinnett 5.00 12.00
348 Tim Salmon 5.00 12.00
349 A.J. Hinch 5.00 12.00
350 Jose Cruz Jr. W 5.00 12.00
351 Roberto Hernandez 5.00 12.00
352 Edgar Renteria 5.00 12.00
353 Jose Hernandez 5.00 12.00
354 Brad Fullmer 5.00 12.00
355 Trevor Hoffman 8.00 20.00
356 Troy O'Leary 5.00 12.00
357 Justin Thompson 5.00 12.00
358 Kevin Young 5.00 12.00
359 Hideki Irabu 5.00 12.00
360 Jim Thome 8.00 20.00
361 Steve Karsay 5.00 12.00
362 Octavio Dotel 5.00 12.00
363 Omar Vizquel 8.00 20.00
364 Raul Mondesi 5.00 12.00
365 Shane Reynolds 5.00 12.00
366 Bartolo Colon 5.00 12.00
367 Chris Widger 5.00 12.00
368 Gabe Kapler 5.00 12.00
369 Bill Simas 5.00 12.00
370 Tino Martinez 5.00 12.00
371 John Thomson 5.00 12.00
372 Delino Deshields 5.00 12.00
373 Carlos Perez 5.00 12.00
374 Eddie Perez 5.00 12.00
375 Jeromy Burnitz 5.00 12.00
376 Jimmy Haynes 5.00 12.00
377 Travis Lee 5.00 12.00
378 Darryl Hamilton 5.00 12.00
379 Jamie Moyer 5.00 12.00
380 Alex Gonzalez 5.00 12.00
381 John Wetteland 5.00 12.00
382 Vinny Castilla 5.00 12.00
383 Jeff Suppan 5.00 12.00
384 Jim Leyritz 5.00 12.00
385 Robb Nen 5.00 12.00
386 Wilson Alvarez 5.00 12.00
387 Andres Galarraga 8.00 20.00
388 Mike Remlinger 5.00 12.00
389 Geoff Jenkins 5.00 12.00
390 Matt Stairs 5.00 12.00
391 Bill Mueller 5.00 12.00
392 Mike Lowell 5.00 12.00
393 Andy Ashby 5.00 12.00
394 Ruben Rivera 5.00 12.00
395 Todd Helton W 8.00 20.00
396 Bernie Williams 8.00 20.00
397 Royce Clayton 5.00 12.00
398 Manny Ramirez W 12.00 30.00
399 Kerry Wood 5.00 12.00
400 Ken Griffey Jr. 25.00 60.00
401 Enrique Wilson 5.00 12.00
402 Joey Hamilton 5.00 12.00
403 Shawn Estes W 5.00 12.00
404 Ugueth Urbina 5.00 12.00
405 Albert Belle 5.00 12.00
406 Rick Helling 5.00 12.00
407 Steve Parris 5.00 12.00
408 Eric Milton 5.00 12.00
409 Dave Mlicki 5.00 12.00
410 Shawn Green 5.00 12.00
411 Jaret Wright 5.00 12.00
412 Tony Womack 5.00 12.00
413 Vernon Wells 5.00 12.00
414 Ron Belliard 5.00 12.00
415 Ellis Burks 5.00 12.00
416 Scott Erickson 5.00 12.00
417 Rafael Palmeiro 8.00 20.00
418 Damion Easley 5.00 12.00
419 Jamey Wright 5.00 12.00
420 Corey Koskie 5.00 12.00
421 Bobby Howry 5.00 12.00
422 Ricky Ledee 5.00 12.00
423 Dmitri Young 5.00 12.00
424 Sidney Ponson 5.00 12.00
425 Greg Maddux 15.00 40.00
426 Jose Guillen 5.00 12.00
427 Jon Lieber W 5.00 12.00
428 Andy Benes 5.00 12.00
429 Randy Velarde 5.00 12.00
430 Sean Casey 5.00 12.00
431 Torii Hunter 5.00 12.00
432 Ryan Rupe 5.00 12.00
433 David Segui 5.00 12.00
434 Todd Pratt 5.00 12.00
435 Nomar Garciaparra 8.00 20.00
436 Denny Neagle 5.00 12.00
437 Ron Coomer 5.00 12.00
438 Chris Singleton 5.00 12.00
439 Tony Batista 5.00 12.00
440 Andruw Jones 5.00 12.00

2000 Topps MVP Promotion Exchange

COMPLETE SET (25) 15.00 40.00
ONE SET VIA MAIL PER '00 MVP WINNER
MVP1 Pedro Martinez 1.00 2.50
MVP2 Jim Edmonds .60 1.50
MVP3 Derek Bell .60 1.50
MVP4 Jermaine Dye .60 1.50
MVP5 Jose Cruz Jr. .60 1.50
MVP6 Todd Helton 1.00 2.50
MVP7 Brian Jordan .60 1.50
MVP8 Shawn Estes .60 1.50
MVP9 Dante Bichette .60 1.50
MVP10 Carlos Delgado .60 1.50
MVP11 Bobby Higginson .60 1.50
MVP12 Mark Kotsay .60 1.50
MVP13 Magglio Ordonez 1.00 2.50
MVP14 Jon Lieber .60 1.50
MVP15 Frank Thomas 1.50 4.00
MVP16 Manny Ramirez 1.50 4.00
MVP17 Sammy Sosa 1.50 4.00
MVP18 Will Clark 1.00 2.50
MVP19 Jeff Bagwell 1.00 2.50
MVP20 Derek Jeter 4.00 10.00
MVP21 Adrian Beltre 1.50 4.00
MVP22 Kenny Lofton .60 1.50
MVP23 Barry Bonds 2.50 6.00
MVP24 Jason Giambi .60 1.50
MVP25 Chipper Jones 1.50 4.00

2000 Topps Oversize

COMPLETE SERIES 1 (8) 4.00 10.00
COMPLETE SERIES 2 (8) 4.00 10.00
ONE PER HOBBY AND HTA BOX
A1 Mark McGwire .75 2.00
A2 Hank Aaron 1.00 2.50
A3 Derek Jeter 1.25 3.00
A4 Sammy Sosa .50 1.25
A5 Alex Rodriguez .60 1.50
A6 Chipper Jones .50 1.25
A7 Cal Ripken 1.50 4.00
A8 Pedro Martinez .30 .75
B1 Barry Bonds .75 2.00
B2 Orlando Hernandez .20 .50
B3 Mike Piazza .50 1.25
B4 Manny Ramirez .50 1.25
B5 Ken Griffey Jr. 1.00 2.50
B6 Rafael Palmeiro .30 .75
B7 Greg Maddux .60 1.50
B8 Nomar Garciaparra .30 .75

2000 Topps 21st Century

COMPLETE SET (10) 4.00 10.00
SER.1 STATED ODDS 1:18 HOB/RET, 1:5 HTA
C1 Ben Grieve .15 .40
C2 Alex Gonzalez .15 .40
C3 Derek Jeter 1.00 2.50
C4 Sean Casey .15 .40
C5 Nomar Garciaparra .25 .60
C6 Alex Rodriguez .50 1.25
C7 Scott Rolen .25 .60
C8 Andruw Jones .15 .40
C9 Vladimir Guerrero .25 .60
C10 Todd Helton .25 .60

2000 Topps Aaron

COMPLETE SET (23) 30.00 60.00
COMPLETE SERIES 1 (12) 12.50 30.00
COMPLETE SERIES 2 (11) 12.50 30.00
STATED ODDS 1:18 HOB/RET, 1:5 HTA
EVEN YEAR CARDS DISTRIBUTED IN SER.1
ODD YEAR CARDS DISTRIBUTED IN SER.2
1 Hank Aaron 1954 2.00 5.00

2000 Topps Aaron Autographs

COMMON CARD (2-23) 200.00 400.00
SER.1 ODDS 1:4361 HOB/RET, 1:1199 HTA
SER.2 ODDS 1:3672 HOB/RET, 1:1007 HTA
EVEN YEAR CARDS DISTRIBUTED IN SER.1
ODD YEAR CARDS DISTRIBUTED IN SER.2

SER.1 EXCHANGE DEADLINE: 05/31/00
1 Hank Aaron 1954 300.00 500.00

2000 Topps Aaron Chrome

COMPLETE SET (23) 40.00 80.00
COMPLETE SERIES 1 (11) 15.00 40.00
COMPLETE SERIES 2 (12) 15.00 40.00
COMMON CARD (1-23) 2.00 5.00
STATED ODDS 1:72 HOB/RET, 1:16 HTA
*CHROME REF: 1X TO 2.5X CHROME
CH.REF.ODDS 1:288 HOB/RET, 1:76 HTA
ODD YEAR CARDS DISTRIBUTED IN SER.1
EVEN YEAR CARDS DISTRIBUTED IN SER.2
1 Hank Aaron 1954 3.00 8.00

2000 Topps All-Star Rookie Team

COMPLETE SET (10) 6.00 15.00
SER.2 STATED ODDS 1:36 HOB/RET, 1:8 HTA
RT1 Mark McGwire 1.25 3.00
RT2 Chuck Knoblauch .30 .75
RT3 Chipper Jones .75 2.00
RT4 Cal Ripken 2.50 6.00
RT5 Manny Ramirez .75 2.00
RT6 Jose Canseco .50 1.25
RT7 Ken Griffey Jr. 1.50 4.00
RT8 Mike Piazza .75 2.00
RT9 Dwight Gooden .30 .75
RT10 Billy Wagner .30 .75

2000 Topps All-Topps

COMPLETE SET (20) 6.00 15.00
COMPLETE N.L.TEAM (10) 3.00 8.00
COMPLETE A.L.TEAM (10) 3.00 8.00
N.L. CARDS DISTRIBUTED IN SERIES 1
A.L. CARDS DISTRIBUTED IN SERIES 2
STATED ODDS 1:12 HOB/RET, 1:3 HTA
AT1 Greg Maddux .50 1.25
AT2 Mike Piazza .40 1.00
AT3 Mark McGwire .60 1.50
AT4 Craig Biggio .25 .60
AT5 Chipper Jones .40 1.00
AT6 Barry Larkin .25 .60
AT7 Barry Bonds .60 1.50
AT8 Andruw Jones .15 .40
AT9 Sammy Sosa .40 1.00
AT10 Larry Walker .25 .60
AT11 Pedro Martinez .25 .60
AT12 Ivan Rodriguez .25 .60
AT13 Rafael Palmeiro .25 .60
AT14 Roberto Alomar .25 .60
AT15 Cal Ripken 1.25 3.00
AT16 Derek Jeter 1.00 2.50
AT17 Albert Belle .15 .40
AT18 Ken Griffey Jr. .75 2.00
AT19 Manny Ramirez .40 1.00
AT20 Jose Canseco .25 .60

2000 Topps Autographs

SER.1 GROUP A 1:7589 H/R, 1:2087 HTA
SER.2 GROUP A 1:5840 H/R, 1:1607 HTA
SER.1 GROUP B 1:4553 H/R, 1:1252 HTA
SER.2 GROUP B 1:2337 H/R, 1:643 HTA
SER.1 GROUP C 1:1518 H/R, 1:417 HTA
SER.2 GROUP C 1:1169 H/R, 1:321 HTA
SER.1 GROUP D 1:911 H/R, 1:250 HTA
SER.2 GROUP D 1:701 H/R, 1:193 HTA
SER.1 GROUP E 1:1138 H/R, 1:313 HTA
SER.2 GROUP E 1:1754 H/R, 1:482 HTA
TA1 Alex Rodriguez A 50.00 100.00
TA2 Tony Gwynn A 30.00 80.00
TA3 Vinny Castilla B 10.00 25.00
TA4 Sean Casey B 10.00 25.00
TA5 Shawn Green C 15.00 40.00
TA6 Rey Ordonez C 6.00 15.00
TA7 Matt Lawton C 6.00 15.00
TA8 Tony Womack C 6.00 15.00
TA9 Gabe Kapler D 10.00 25.00
TA10 Pat Burrell D 10.00 25.00
TA11 Preston Wilson D 10.00 25.00
TA12 Troy Glaus D 6.00 15.00
TA13 Carlos Beltran D 10.00 25.00
TA14 Josh Girdley E 6.00 15.00
TA15 B.J. Garbe E 6.00 15.00
TA16 Derek Jeter A 100.00 250.00
TA17 Cal Ripken A 60.00 150.00
TA18 Ivan Rodriguez B 15.00 40.00
TA19 Rafael Palmeiro B 30.00 60.00
TA20 Vladimir Guerrero B 6.00 15.00
TA21 Raul Mondesi C 6.00 15.00
TA22 Scott Rolen C 6.00 15.00
TA23 Billy Wagner C 6.00 15.00
TA24 Fernando Tatis C 6.00 15.00
TA25 Ruben Mateo D 6.00 15.00
TA26 Carlos Febles D 6.00 15.00
TA27 Mike Sweeney D 10.00 25.00
TA28 Alex Gonzalez D 6.00 15.00
TA29 Miguel Tejada D 6.00 15.00
TA30 Josh Hamilton 10.00 40.00

2000 Topps Combos

COMPLETE SET (10) 12.50 30.00
SER.2 STATED ODDS 1:18 HOB/RET, 1:5 HTA
TC1 Tribe-unal 1.00 2.50
TC2 Batter Baffler's 1.25 3.00
TC3 Torre's Terrors 2.50 6.00
TC4 All-Star Backstops 1.00 2.50
TC5 Three of a Kind 2.50 6.00
TC6 Home Run Kings 1.50 4.00
TC7 Strikeout Kings 1.00 2.50
TC8 Executive Producers 2.00 5.00
TC9 MVP's 1.00 2.50
TC10 3000 Hit Brigade 3.00 8.00

2000 Topps Hands of Gold

COMPLETE SET (7) 5.00 12.00
SER.1 STATED ODDS 1:18 HOB/RET, 1:5 HTA
HG1 Barry Bonds 1.50 4.00
HG2 Ivan Rodriguez .60 1.50
HG3 Ken Griffey Jr. 2.00 5.00
HG4 Roberto Alomar .60 1.50
HG5 Tony Gwynn 1.00 2.50
HG6 Omar Vizquel .60 1.50
HG7 Greg Maddux 1.25 3.00

2000 Topps Own the Game

COMPLETE SET (30) 20.00 50.00
SER.2 STATED ODDS 1:12 HOB/RET, 1:3 HTA
OTG1 Derek Jeter 2.50 6.00
OTG2 B.J. Surhoff .40 1.00
OTG3 Luis Gonzalez .40 1.00
OTG4 Manny Ramirez 1.00 2.50
OTG5 Rafael Palmeiro .60 1.50
OTG6 Mark McGwire 1.50 4.00
OTG7 Mark McGwire 1.50 4.00
OTG8 Sammy Sosa 1.00 2.50
OTG9 Ken Griffey Jr. 2.00 5.00
OTG10 Larry Walker .60 1.50
OTG11 Nomar Garciaparra .60 1.50
OTG12 Derek Jeter 2.50 6.00
OTG13 Larry Walker .60 1.50
OTG14 Mark McGwire 1.50 4.00
OTG15 Manny Ramirez 1.00 2.50
OTG16 Pedro Martinez .60 1.50
OTG17 Randy Johnson 1.00 2.50
OTG18 Kevin Millwood .40 1.00
OTG19 Randy Johnson 1.00 2.50
OTG20 Pedro Martinez .60 1.50
OTG21 Kevin Brown .40 1.00
OTG22 Chipper Jones 1.00 2.50
OTG23 Ivan Rodriguez .60 1.50
OTG24 Mariano Rivera 1.25 3.00
OTG25 Scott Williamson .40 1.00
OTG26 Carlos Beltran .60 1.50
OTG27 Randy Johnson 1.00 2.50
OTG28 Pedro Martinez .60 1.50
OTG29 Sammy Sosa 1.00 2.50
OTG30 Manny Ramirez 1.00 2.50

2000 Topps Perennial All-Stars

COMPLETE SET (10) 6.00 15.00
SER.1 STATED ODDS 1:18 HOB/RET, 1:5 HTA
PA1 Ken Griffey Jr. 1.00 2.50
PA2 Derek Jeter 1.25 3.00
PA3 Sammy Sosa .50 1.25
PA4 Cal Ripken 1.50 4.00
PA5 Mike Piazza .50 1.25
PA6 Nomar Garciaparra .30 .75
PA7 Jeff Bagwell .30 .75
PA8 Barry Bonds .75 2.00
PA9 Alex Rodriguez .60 1.50
PA10 Mark McGwire .75 2.00

2000 Topps Power Players

COMPLETE SET (20) 5.00 12.00
SER.1 STATED ODDS 1:8 HOB/RET, 1:2 HTA
P1 Juan Gonzalez .15 .40
P2 Ken Griffey Jr. .75 2.00
P3 Mark McGwire .60 1.50
P4 Nomar Garciaparra .25 .60
P5 Barry Bonds .60 1.50
P6 Mo Vaughn .15 .40
P7 Larry Walker .25 .60
P8 Alex Rodriguez .50 1.25
P9 Jose Canseco .25 .60
P10 Jeff Bagwell .25 .60
P11 Manny Ramirez .40 1.00
P12 Albert Belle .15 .40
P13 Frank Thomas .40 1.00
P14 Mike Piazza .40 1.00
P15 Chipper Jones .40 1.00
P16 Sammy Sosa .40 1.00
P17 Vladimir Guerrero .25 .60
P18 Scott Rolen .25 .60
P19 Raul Mondesi .15 .40
P20 Derek Jeter 1.00 2.50

2000 Topps Stadium Autograph Relics

SER.1 STATED ODDS 1:165 HTA
SER.2 STATED ODDS 1:135 HTA
SR1 Don Mattingly 60.00 150.00
SR2 Carl Yastrzemski 50.00 120.00
SR3 Ernie Banks 50.00 120.00
SR4 Johnny Bench 60.00 150.00
SR5 Willie Mays 150.00 400.00
SR6 Mike Schmidt 40.00 80.00
SR7 Lou Brock 50.00 120.00
SR8 Al Kaline 40.00 100.00
SR9 Paul Molitor 25.00 60.00
SR10 Eddie Mathews 25.00 60.00

2000 Topps Limited

COMP.FACT.SET (619) 40.00 80.00
COMPLETE SET (478) 30.00 60.00
*STARS: 1.5X TO 4X BASIC CARDS
*YNG.STARS: 1.5X TO 4X BASIC CARDS
*ROOKIES: 1.5X TO 4X BASIC CARDS
*MAGIC MOMENTS: .75X TO 2X BASIC MM
MCGWIRE MM (236A-236E) 4.00 10.00
AARON MM (237A-237E) 3.00 8.00
RIPKEN MM (238A-238E) 5.00 12.00
BOGGS MM (239A-239E) 1.00 2.50
GWYNN MM (240A-240E) 2.50 6.00
GRIFFEY MM (475A-475E) 2.50 6.00
BONDS MM (476A-476E) 4.00 10.00
SOSA MM (477A-477E) 2.50 6.00
JETER MM (478A-478E) 5.00 12.00
A.ROD MM (479A-479E) 3.00 8.00
STATED PRINT RUN 4000 FACTORY SETS
MM PRINT RUN 800 OF EACH CARD
CARD NUMBER 7 DOES NOT EXIST

2000 Topps Limited 21st Century

COMPLETE SET (10) 6.00 15.00
*LIMITED: 1X TO 2.5X TOPPS 21ST CENT.
ONE SET PER FACTORY SET

2000 Topps Limited Aaron

COMPLETE SET (23) 30.00 60.00
*LIMITED: 3X TO .8X TOPPS AARON
ONE SET PER FACTORY SET
1 Hank Aaron 1954 3.00 8.00

2000 Topps Limited All-Star Rookie Team

COMPLETE SET (10) 10.00 25.00
*LIMITED: .5X TO 1.2X TOPPS AS ROOK.
ONE SET PER FACTORY SET

2000 Topps Limited All-Topps

COMPLETE SET (20) 15.00 40.00
*LIMITED: 1X TO 2.5X TOPPS ALL-TOPPS
ONE SET PER FACTORY SET

2000 Topps Limited Combos

COMPLETE SET (10) 12.50 30.00
*LIMITED: .5X TO 1.2X TOPPS COMBOS
ONE SET PER FACTORY SET

2000 Topps Limited Hands of Gold

COMPLETE SET (7) 6.00 15.00
*LIMITED: .5X TO 1.2X TOPPS HANDS
ONE SET PER FACTORY SET

2000 Topps Limited Own the Game

COMPLETE SET (30) 25.00 60.00
*LIMITED: .5X TO 1.2X TOPPS OTG
ONE SET PER FACTORY SET

2000 Topps Limited Perennial All-Stars

COMPLETE SET (10) 12.50 30.00
*LIMITED: 1X TO 2.5X TOPPS PER.AS
ONE SET PER FACTORY SET

2000 Topps Limited Power Players

COMPLETE SET (20) 12.50 30.00
*LIMITED: 1X TO 2.5X TOPPS POWER
ONE SET PER FACTORY SET

2000 Topps Traded

COMP.FACT.SET (136) 50.00 100.00
COMPLETE SET (135) 40.00 80.00
COMMON CARD (T1-T135) .12 .30
COMMON RC .12 .30
FACT.SET PRICE IS FOR SEALED SETS
T1 Mike MacDougal .20 .50
T2 Andy Tracy RC .12 .30
T3 Brandon Phillips RC .50 1.25
T4 Brandon Inge RC .75 2.00
T5 Robbie Morrison RC .12 .30
T6 Josh Pressley RC .12 .30
T7 Todd Moser RC .12 .30
T8 Rob Purvis .12 .30
T9 Chance Caple .12 .30
T10 Ben Sheets .30 .75
T11 Russ Jacobson RC .12 .30
T12 Brian Cole RC .12 .30
T13 Brad Baker .12 .30
T14 Alex Cintron RC .12 .30
T15 Lyle Overbay RC .20 .50
T16 Mike Edwards RC .12 .30
T17 Sean McGowan RC .12 .30
T18 Jose Molina .12 .30
T19 Marcos Castillo RC .12 .30
T20 Josue Espada RC .12 .30
T21 Alex Gordon RC .12 .30
T22 Rob Pugmire RC .12 .30
T23 Jason Stumm .12 .30
T24 Ty Howington .12 .30
T25 Brett Myers .40 1.00
T26 Maicer Izturis RC .20 .50
T27 John McDonald .12 .30
T28 Wilfredo Rodriguez RC .12 .30
T29 Carlos Zambrano RC .75 2.00
T30 Alejandro Diaz RC .12 .30
T31 Geraldo Guzman RC .12 .30
T32 J.R. House RC .12 .30
T33 Elvin Nina RC .12 .30
T34 Juan Pierre RC .60 1.50
T35 Ben Johnson RC .12 .30
T36 Jeff Bailey RC .12 .30
T37 Miguel Olivo RC .20 .50
T38 Francisco Rodriguez RC .75 2.00
T39 Tony Pena Jr. RC .12 .30
T40 Miguel Cabrera RC 75.00 200.00
T41 Asdrubal Oropeza RC .12 .30
T42 Junior Zamora RC .12 .30
T43 Jovanny Cedeno RC .12 .30
T44 John Sneed .12 .30
T45 Josh Kalinowski .12 .30
T46 Mike Young RC 1.25 3.00
T47 Rico Washington RC .12 .30
T48 Chad Durbin RC .12 .30
T49 Junior Brignac RC .12 .30
T50 Carlos Hernandez RC .12 .30
T51 Cesar Izturis RC .12 .30
T52 Oscar Salazar RC .12 .30
T53 Pat Strange RC .12 .30
T54 Rick Asadoorian .12 .30
T55 Keith Reed .12 .30
T56 Leo Estrella RC .12 .30
T57 Wascar Serrano RC .12 .30
T58 Richard Gomez RC .12 .30
T59 Ramon Santiago RC .12 .30
T60 Jovanny Sosa RC .12 .30
T61 Aaron Rowand RC .60 1.50
T62 Junior Guerrero RC .12 .30
T63 Luis Terrero RC .12 .30
T64 Brian Sanches RC .12 .30
T65 Scott Sobkowiak RC .12 .30
T66 Gary Majewski RC .12 .30
T67 Barry Zito 1.00 2.50
T68 Ryan Christianson .12 .30
T69 Cristian Guerrero RC .12 .30
T70 Tomas De La Rosa RC .12 .30
T71 Andrew Beinbrink RC .12 .30
T72 Ryan Knox RC .12 .30
T73 Alex Graman RC .12 .30
T74 Juan Guzman RC .12 .30
T75 Ruben Salazar RC .12 .30
T76 Luis Matos RC .12 .30
T77 Tony Mota RC .12 .30
T78 Doug Davis .12 .30
T79 Ben Christensen .12 .30
T80 Mike Lamb .12 .30
T81 Adrian Gonzalez RC 3.00 8.00
T82 Mike Stodolka RC .12 .30
T83 Adam Johnson RC .12 .30
T84 Matt Wheatland RC .12 .30
T85 Corey Smith RC .12 .30
T86 Rocco Baldelli RC .30 .75
T87 Keith Bucktrot RC .12 .30
T88 Adam Wainwright RC 1.25 3.00
T89 Scott Thorman RC .20 .50
T90 Tripper Johnson RC .12 .30
T91 Jim Edmonds Cards .12 .30
T92 Masato Yoshii .12 .30
T93 Adam Kennedy .12 .30
T94 Darryl Kile .12 .30
T95 Mark McLemore .12 .30
T96 Ricky Gutierrez .12 .30
T97 Juan Gonzalez .12 .30
T98 Melvin Mora .12 .30
T99 Dante Bichette .12 .30
T100 Lee Stevens .12 .30
T101 Roger Cedeno .12 .30
T102 John Olerud .12 .30
T103 Eric Young .12 .30
T104 Mickey Morandini .12 .30
T105 Travis Lee .12 .30
T106 Greg Vaughn .12 .30
T107 Todd Zeile .12 .30
T108 Chuck Finley .12 .30
T109 Ismael Valdes .12 .30
T110 Reggie Sanders .12 .30
T111 Pat Hentgen .12 .30
T112 Ryan Klesko .12 .30
T113 Derek Bell .12 .30
T114 Hideo Nomo .30 .75
T115 Aaron Sele .12 .30
T116 Fernando Vina .12 .30
T117 Wally Joyner .12 .30
T118 Brian Hunter .12 .30
T119 Joe Girardi .20 .50
T120 Omar Daal .12 .30
T121 Brook Fordyce .12 .30
T122 Jose Valentin .12 .30
T123 Curt Schilling .20 .50
T124 B.J. Surhoff .12 .30
T125 Henry Rodriguez .12 .30
T126 Mike Bordick .12 .30
T127 David Justice .12 .30
T128 Charles Johnson .12 .30
T129 Will Clark .20 .50
T130 Dwight Gooden .12 .30
T131 David Segui .12 .30
T132 Denny Neagle .12 .30
T133 Jose Canseco .20 .50
T134 Bruce Chen .12 .30
T135 Jason Bere .12 .30

2000 Topps Traded Autographs

ONE PER FACTORY SET
TTA1 Mike MacDougal 3.00 8.00
TTA2 Andy Tracy 2.00 5.00
TTA3 Brandon Phillips 15.00 40.00
TTA4 Brandon Inge 12.50 30.00
TTA5 Robbie Morrison 2.00 5.00
TTA6 Josh Pressley 2.00 5.00
TTA7 Todd Moser 2.00 5.00
TTA8 Rob Purvis 3.00 8.00
TTA9 Chance Caple 2.00 5.00
TTA10 Ben Sheets 6.00 15.00
TTA11 Russ Jacobson 2.00 5.00
TTA12 Brian Cole 6.00 15.00
TTA13 Brad Baker 2.00 5.00
TTA14 Alex Cintron 3.00 8.00
TTA15 Lyle Overbay 10.00 25.00
TTA16 Mike Edwards 2.00 5.00
TTA17 Sean McGowan 2.00 5.00
TTA18 Jose Molina 5.00 12.00
TTA19 Marcos Castillo 2.00 5.00
TTA20 Josue Espada 2.00 5.00
TTA21 Alex Gordon 2.00 5.00
TTA22 Rob Pugmire 2.00 5.00
TTA23 Jason Stumm 2.00 5.00
TTA24 Ty Howington 2.00 5.00
TTA25 Brett Myers 10.00 25.00
TTA26 Maicer Izturis 6.00 15.00
TTA27 John McDonald 2.00 5.00
TTA28 Wilfredo Rodriguez 2.00 5.00
TTA29 Carlos Zambrano 5.00 12.00
TTA30 Alejandro Diaz 2.00 5.00
TTA31 Geraldo Guzman 2.00 5.00
TTA32 J.R. House 2.00 5.00
TTA33 Elvin Nina 2.00 5.00
TTA34 Juan Pierre 4.00 10.00
TTA35 Ben Johnson 10.00 25.00
TTA36 Jeff Bailey 2.00 5.00
TTA37 Miguel Olivo 5.00 12.00
TTA38 Francisco Rodriguez 15.00 40.00
TTA39 Tony Pena Jr. 2.00 5.00
TTA40 Miguel Cabrera 750.00 2000.00
TTA41 Asdrubal Oropeza 2.00 5.00
TTA42 Junior Zamora 2.00 5.00
TTA43 Jovanny Cedeno 2.00 5.00
TTA44 John Sneed 2.00 5.00
TTA45 Josh Kalinowski 3.00 8.00
TTA46 Mike Young 15.00 40.00
TTA47 Rico Washington 2.00 5.00
TTA48 Chad Durbin 2.00 5.00
TTA49 Junior Brignac 2.00 5.00
TTA50 Carlos Hernandez 3.00 8.00
TTA51 Cesar Izturis 6.00 15.00
TTA52 Oscar Salazar 2.00 5.00
TTA53 Pat Strange 2.00 5.00
TTA54 Rick Asadoorian 3.00 8.00
TTA55 Keith Reed 2.00 5.00
TTA56 Leo Estrella 2.00 5.00
TTA57 Wascar Serrano 2.00 5.00
TTA58 Richard Gomez 2.00 5.00
TTA59 Ramon Santiago 2.00 5.00
TTA60 Jovanny Sosa 2.00 5.00
TTA61 Aaron Rowand 8.00 20.00
TTA62 Junior Guerrero 2.00 5.00
TTA63 Luis Terrero 3.00 8.00
TTA64 Brian Sanches 2.00 5.00
TTA65 Scott Sobkowiak 2.00 5.00
TTA66 Gary Majewski 2.00 5.00
TTA67 Barry Zito 8.00 20.00
TTA68 Ryan Christianson 2.00 5.00
TTA69 Cristian Guerrero 2.00 5.00
TTA70 Tomas De La Rosa 2.00 5.00
TTA71 Andrew Beinbrink 3.00 8.00
TTA72 Ryan Knox 2.00 5.00
TTA73 Alex Graman 2.00 5.00
TTA74 Juan Guzman 2.00 5.00
TTA75 Ruben Salazar 2.00 5.00
TTA76 Luis Matos 2.00 5.00
TTA77 Tony Mota 2.00 5.00
TTA78 Doug Davis 6.00 15.00
TTA79 Ben Christensen 2.00 5.00
TTA80 Mike Lamb 6.00 15.00

2001 Topps Press Release Jumbos

COMPLETE SET (8) 10.00 25.00
1 Title Card .40 1.00
2 Topps Checklist .40 1.00
3 Hank Aaron 1.60 4.00
4 Johnny Bench 1.20 3.00
5 B.Gibson .80 2.00
P.Martinez
6 Mark McGwire 2.00 5.00
7 Nolan Ryan 3.20 8.00
8 Mike Schmidt 1.20 3.00

2001 Topps

COMPLETE SET (790) 40.00 80.00
COMP.FACT.BLUE SET (795) 50.00 100.00
COMPLETE SERIES 1 (405) 20.00 40.00
COMPLETE SERIES 2 (385) 20.00 40.00
COMMON CARD (1-6/8-791) .07 .20
COMMON (352-376/727-751) .08 .25
CARD NO.7 DOES NOT EXIST
HISTORY SER.1 ODDS 1:911 H/R, 1:202 HTA
HISTORY SER.2 ODDS 1:686 H/R, 1:152 HTA
BO/DEION BAT SER.2 ODDS 1:30167 H/R
BO/DEION BAT SER.2 ODDS 1:6753 HTA
MANTLE VINTAGE SER.1 ODDS 1:27370 H/R
MANTLE VINTAGE SER.1 ODDS 1:6112 HTA
MANTLE VINTAGE SER.2 ODDS 1:21377 H/R
MANTLE VINTAGE SER.2 ODDS 1:4772 HTA
THOMSON/BRANCA SER.1 ODDS 1:7299 H/R
THOMSON/BRANCA SER.1 ODDS 1:1625 HTA
VINTAGE STARS SER.1 ODDS 1:4363 H/R
VINTAGE STARS SER.1 ODDS 1:970 HTA
VINTAGE STARS SER.2 ODDS 1:3656 H/R
VINTAGE STARS SER.2 ODDS 1:812 HTA
1 Cal Ripken .60 1.50
2 Chipper Jones .20 .50
3 Roger Cedeno .07 .20
4 Garret Anderson .07 .20
5 Robin Ventura .07 .20
6 Daryle Ward .07 .20
8 Craig Paquette .07 .20
9 Phil Nevin .07 .20
10 Jermaine Dye .07 .20
11 Chris Singleton .07 .20
12 Mike Stanton .07 .20
13 Brian Hunter .07 .20
14 Mike Redmond .07 .20
15 Jim Thome .10 .30
16 Brian Jordan .07 .20
17 Joe Girardi .07 .20
18 Steve Woodard .07 .20
19 Dustin Hermanson .07 .20
20 Shawn Green .07 .20
21 Todd Stottlemyre .07 .20
22 Dan Wilson .07 .20
23 Todd Pratt .07 .20
24 Derek Lowe .07 .20
25 Juan Gonzalez .07 .20
26 Clay Bellinger .07 .20
27 Jeff Fassero .07 .20
28 Pat Meares .07 .20
29 Eddie Taubensee .07 .20
30 Paul O'Neill .10 .30
31 Jeffrey Hammonds .07 .20
32 Pokey Reese .07 .20
33 Mike Mussina .10 .30
34 Rico Brogna .07 .20
35 Jay Buhner .07 .20
36 Steve Cox .07 .20
37 Quilvio Veras .07 .20
38 Marquis Grissom .07 .20
39 Shigetoshi Hasegawa .07 .20
40 Shane Reynolds .07 .20
41 Adam Piatt .07 .20
42 Luis Polonia .07 .20
43 Brook Fordyce .07 .20
44 Preston Wilson .07 .20
45 Ellis Burks .07 .20
46 Armando Rios .07 .20
47 Chuck Finley .07 .20
48 Dan Plesac .07 .20
49 Shannon Stewart .07 .20
50 Mark McGwire .50 1.25
51 Mark Loretta .07 .20
52 Gerald Williams .07 .20
53 Eric Young .07 .20
54 Peter Bergeron .07 .20
55 Dave Hansen .07 .20
56 Arthur Rhodes .07 .20
57 Bobby Jones .07 .20
58 Matt Clement .07 .20
59 Mike Benjamin .07 .20
60 Pedro Martinez .10 .30
61 Jose Canseco .10 .30
62 Matt Anderson .07 .20
63 Torii Hunter .07 .20
64 Carlos Lee .07 .20
65 David Cone .07 .20
66 Rey Sanchez .07 .20
67 Eric Chavez .07 .20
68 Rick Helling .07 .20
69 Manny Alexander .07 .20
70 John Franco .07 .20
71 Mike Bordick .07 .20
72 Andres Galarraga .07 .20
73 Jose Cruz Jr. .07 .20
74 Mike Matheny .07 .20
75 Randy Johnson .20 .50
76 Richie Sexson .07 .20
77 Vladimir Nunez .07 .20
78 Harold Baines .07 .20
79 Aaron Boone .07 .20
80 Darin Erstad .07 .20
81 Alex Gonzalez .07 .20
82 Gil Heredia .07 .20
83 Shane Andrews .07 .20
84 Todd Hundley .07 .20
85 Bill Mueller .07 .20
86 Mark McLemore .07 .20
87 Scott Spiezio .07 .20
88 Kevin McGlinchy .07 .20
89 Bubba Trammell .07 .20
90 Manny Ramirez .10 .30
91 Mike Lamb .07 .20
92 Scott Karl .07 .20
93 Brian Buchanan .07 .20
94 Chris Turner .07 .20
95 Mike Sweeney .07 .20
96 John Wetteland .07 .20
97 Rob Bell .07 .20
98 Pat Rapp .07 .20
99 John Burkett .07 .20
100 Derek Jeter .50 1.25
101 J.D. Drew .07 .20
102 Jose Offerman .07 .20
103 Rick Reed .07 .20
104 Will Clark .10 .30
105 Rickey Henderson .20 .50
106 Dave Berg .07 .20
107 Kirk Rueter .07 .20
108 Lee Stevens .07 .20
109 Jay Bell .07 .20
110 Fred McGriff .10 .30
111 Julio Zuleta .07 .20
112 Brian Anderson .07 .20
113 Orlando Cabrera .07 .20
114 Alex Fernandez .07 .20
115 Derek Bell .07 .20
116 Eric Owens .07 .20
117 Brian Bohanon .07 .20
118 Dennys Reyes .07 .20
119 Mike Stanley .07 .20
120 Jorge Posada .10 .30
121 Rich Becker .07 .20
122 Paul Konerko .07 .20
123 Mike Remlinger .07 .20
124 Travis Lee .07 .20
125 Ken Caminitj .07 .20
126 Kevin Barker .07 .20
127 Paul Quantrill .07 .20
128 Ozzie Guillen .07 .20
129 Kevin Tapani .07 .20
130 Mark Johnson .07 .20
131 Randy Wolf .07 .20
132 Michael Tucker .07 .20
133 Darren Lewis .07 .20
134 Joe Randa .07 .20
135 Jeff Cirillo .07 .20
136 David Ortiz .20 .50
137 Herb Perry .07 .20
138 Jeff Nelson .07 .20
139 Chris Stynes .07 .20
140 Johnny Damon .10 .30
141 Jeff Reboulet .07 .20
142 Jason Schmidt .07 .20
143 Charles Johnson .07 .20
144 Pat Burrell .07 .20
145 Gary Sheffield .07 .20
146 Tom Glavine .10 .30
147 Jason Isringhausen .07 .20
148 Chris Carpenter .07 .20
149 Jeff Suppan .07 .20
150 Ivan Rodriguez .10 .30
151 Luis Sojo .07 .20
152 Ron Villone .07 .20
153 Mike Sirotka .07 .20
154 Chuck Knoblauch .07 .20
155 Jason Kendall .07 .20
156 Dennis Cook .07 .20
157 Bobby Estalella .07 .20
158 Jose Guillen .07 .20
159 Thomas Howard .07 .20
160 Carlos Delgado .07 .20
161 Benji Gil .07 .20
162 Tim Bogar .07 .20
163 Kevin Elster .07 .20
164 Einar Diaz .07 .20
165 Andy Benes .07 .20
166 Adrian Beltre .07 .20
167 David Bell .07 .20
168 Turk Wendell .07 .20
169 Pete Harnisch .07 .20
170 Roger Clemens .40 1.00
171 Scott Williamson .07 .20
172 Kevin Jordan .07 .20
173 Brad Penny .07 .20
174 John Flaherty .07 .20
175 Troy Glaus .07 .20
176 Kevin Appier .07 .20
177 Walt Weiss .07 .20
178 Tyler Houston .07 .20
179 Michael Barrett .07 .20
180 Mike Hampton .07 .20
181 Francisco Cordova .07 .20
182 Mike Jackson .07 .20
183 David Segui .07 .20
184 Carlos Febles .07 .20
185 Roy Halladay .07 .20
186 Seth Etherton .07 .20
187 Charlie Hayes .07 .20
188 Fernando Tatis .07 .20
189 Steve Trachsel .07 .20
190 Livan Hernandez .07 .20
191 Joe Oliver .07 .20
192 Stan Javier .07 .20
193 B.J. Surhoff .07 .20
194 Rob Ducey .07 .20
195 Barry Larkin .10 .30
196 Danny Patterson .07 .20
197 Bobby Howry .07 .20
198 Dmitri Young .07 .20
199 Brian Hunter .07 .20
200 Alex Rodriguez .25 .60
201 Hideo Nomo .20 .50
202 Luis Alicea .07 .20
203 Warren Morris .07 .20
204 Antonio Alfonseca .07 .20
205 Edgardo Alfonzo .07 .20
206 Mark Grudzielanek .07 .20
207 Fernando Vina .07 .20
208 Willie Greene .07 .20
209 Homer Bush .07 .20
210 Jason Giambi .07 .20
211 Mike Morgan .07 .20
212 Steve Karsay .07 .20
213 Matt Lawton .07 .20
214 Wendell Magee Jr. .07 .20
215 Rusty Greer .07 .20
216 Keith Lockhart .07 .20
217 Billy Koch .07 .20
218 Todd Hollandsworth .07 .20
219 Raul Ibanez .07 .20
220 Tony Gwynn .25 .60
221 Carl Everett .07 .20
222 Hector Carrasco .07 .20
223 Jose Valentin .07 .20
224 Deivi Cruz .07 .20
225 Bret Boone .07 .20
226 Kurt Abbott .07 .20
227 Melvin Mora .07 .20
228 Danny Graves .07 .20
229 Jose Jimenez .07 .20
230 James Baldwin .07 .20
231 C.J. Nitkowski .07 .20
232 Jeff Zimmerman .07 .20
233 Mike Lowell .07 .20
234 Hideki Irabu .07 .20
235 Greg Vaughn .07 .20
236 Omar Daal .07 .20
237 Darren Dreifort .07 .20
238 Gil Meche .07 .20
239 Damian Jackson .07 .20
240 Frank Thomas .20 .50
241 Travis Miller .07 .20
242 Jeff Frye .07 .20
243 Dave Magadan .07 .20
244 Luis Castillo .07 .20
245 Bartolo Colon .07 .20
246 Steve Kline .07 .20
247 Shawon Dunston .07 .20
248 Rick Aguilera .07 .20
249 Omar Olivares .07 .20
250 Craig Biggio .10 .30
251 Scott Schoeneweis .07 .20
252 Dave Veres .07 .20
253 Ramon Martinez .07 .20
254 Jose Vidro .07 .20
255 Todd Helton .10 .30
256 Greg Norton .07 .20
257 Jacque Jones .07 .20
258 Jason Grimsley .07 .20
259 Dan Reichert .07 .20
260 Robb Nen .07 .20
261 Mark Clark .07 .20
262 Scott Hatteberg .07 .20
263 Doug Brocail .07 .20
264 Mark Johnson .07 .20
265 Eric Davis .07 .20
266 Terry Shumpert .07 .20
267 Kevin Millar .07 .20
268 Ismael Valdes .07 .20
269 Richard Hidalgo .07 .20
270 Randy Velarde .07 .20
271 Bengie Molina .07 .20
272 Tony Womack .07 .20
273 Enrique Wilson .07 .20
274 Jeff Brantley .07 .20
275 Rick Ankiel .07 .20
276 Terry Mulholland .07 .20
277 Ron Belliard .07 .20
278 Terrence Long .07 .20
279 Alberto Castillo .07 .20
280 Royce Clayton .07 .20
281 Joe McEwing .07 .20
282 Jason McDonald .07 .20
283 Ricky Bottalico .07 .20
284 Keith Foulke .07 .20
285 Brad Radke .07 .20
286 Gabe Kapler .07 .20
287 Pedro Astacio .07 .20
288 Armando Reynoso .07 .20
289 Darryl Kile .07 .20
290 Reggie Sanders .07 .20
291 Esteban Yan .07 .20
292 Joe Nathan .07 .20
293 Jay Payton .07 .20
294 Francisco Cordero .07 .20
295 Gregg Jefferies .07 .20
296 LaTroy Hawkins .07 .20
297 Jeff Tam RC .15 .40
298 Jacob Cruz .07 .20
299 Chris Holt .07 .20
300 Vladimir Guerrero .20 .50
301 Marvin Benard .07 .20
302 Alex Ramirez .07 .20
303 Mike Williams .07 .20
304 Sean Bergman .07 .20
305 Juan Encarnacion .07 .20
306 Russ Davis .07 .20
307 Hanley Frias .07 .20
308 Ramon Hernandez .07 .20
309 Matt Walbeck .07 .20
310 Bill Spiers .07 .20
311 Bob Wickman .07 .20
312 Sandy Alomar Jr. .07 .20
313 Eddie Guardado .07 .20
314 Shane Halter .07 .20
315 Geoff Jenkins .07 .20
316 Brian Meadows .07 .20
317 Damian Miller .07 .20
318 Darrin Fletcher .07 .20
319 Rafael Furcal .07 .20
320 Mark Grace .10 .30
321 Mark Mulder .07 .20
322 Joe Torre MG .10 .30
323 Bobby Cox MG .07 .20
324 Mike Scioscia MG .07 .20
325 Mike Hargrove MG .07 .20
326 Jimy Williams MG .07 .20
327 Jerry Manuel MG .07 .20
328 Buck Showalter MG .07 .20
329 Charlie Manuel MG .07 .20
330 Don Baylor MG .07 .20
331 Phil Garner MG .07 .20
332 Jack McKeon MG .07 .20
333 Tony Muser MG .07 .20
334 Buddy Bell MG .07 .20
335 Tom Kelly MG .07 .20
336 John Boles MG .07 .20
337 Art Howe MG .07 .20
338 Larry Dierker MG .07 .20
339 Lou Piniella MG .07 .20
340 Davey Johnson MG .07 .20
341 Larry Rothschild MG .07 .20
342 Davey Lopes MG .07 .20
343 Johnny Oates MG .07 .20
344 Felipe Alou MG .07 .20
345 Jim Fregosi MG .07 .20
346 Bobby Valentine MG .07 .20
347 Terry Francona MG .07 .20
348 Gene Lamont MG .07 .20
349 Tony LaRussa MG .07 .20
350 Bruce Bochy MG .07 .20
351 Dusty Baker MG .07 .20
352 A.Gonzalez .60 1.50
A.Johnson
353 M.Wheatland .08 .25

B.Digby
354 T.Johnson .08 .25
S.Thorman
355 P.Dumatrait .20 .50
A.Wainwright
356 David Parrish RC .08 .25
357 M.Folsom RC .15 .40
R.Baldelli
358 Dominic Rich RC .08 .25
359 M.Stodolka .08 .25
S.Burnett
360 D.Thompson .08 .25
C.Smith
361 D.Borrell RC .08 .25
J.Bourgeois RC
362 Josh Hamilton .20 .50
363 B.Zito .20 .50
C.Sabathia
364 Ben Sheets .20 .50
365 Howington .08 .25
Kalinowski/Girdley
366 Hee Seop Choi RC .20 .50
367 Bradley .15 .40
Ainsworth/Tsao
368 Glendenning .08 .25
Kelly/Silvestre
369 J.R. House .08 .25
370 Rafael Soriano RC .15 .40
371 T.Hafner RC 1.50 4.00
B.Jacobsen
372 Conti .08 .25
Wakeland/Cole
373 Seabol .30 .75
Huff/Crede
374 Everett .08 .25
Ortiz/Ginter
375 Hernandez .08 .25
Guzman/Eaton
376 Kielty .15 .40
Bradley/J.Rivera
377 Mark McGwire GM .25 .60
378 Don Larsen GM .07 .20
379 Bobby Thomson GM .07 .20
380 Bill Mazeroski GM .07 .20
381 Reggie Jackson GM .10 .30
382 Kirk Gibson GM .07 .20
383 Roger Maris GM .10 .30
384 Cal Ripken GM .30 .75
385 Hank Aaron GM .20 .50
386 Joe Carter GM .07 .20
387 Cal Ripken SH .60 1.50
388 Randy Johnson SH .10 .30
389 Ken Griffey Jr. SH .40 1.00
390 Troy Glaus SH .07 .20
391 Kazuhiro Sasaki SH .07 .20
392 S.Sosa .10 .30
T.Glaus LL
393 T.Helton .07 .20
E.Martinez LL
394 T.Helton .20 .50
N.Garicaparra LL
395 B.Bonds .30 .75
J.Giambi LL
396 T.Helton .07 .20
M.Ramirez LL
397 T.Helton .07 .20
D.Erstad LL
398 K.Brown .10 .30
P.Martinez LL
399 R.Johnson .10 .30
P.Martinez LL
400 Will Clark HL .10 .30
401 New York Mets HL .20 .50
402 New York Yankees HL .30 .75
403 Seattle Mariners HL .07 .20
404 Mike Hampton HL .07 .20
405 New York Yankees HL .40 1.00
406 New York Yankees Champs .75 2.00
407 Jeff Bagwell .10 .30
408 Brant Brown .07 .20
409 Brad Fullmer .07 .20
410 Dean Palmer .07 .20
411 Greg Zaun .07 .20
412 Jose Vizcaino .07 .20
413 Jeff Abbott .07 .20
414 Travis Fryman .07 .20
415 Mike Cameron .07 .20
416 Matt Mantei .07 .20
417 Alan Benes .07 .20
418 Mickey Morandini .07 .20
419 Troy Percival .07 .20
420 Eddie Perez .07 .20
421 Vernon Wells .07 .20
422 Ricky Gutierrez .07 .20
423 Carlos Hernandez .07 .20
424 Chan Ho Park .07 .20
425 Armando Benitez .07 .20
426 Sidney Ponson .07 .20
427 Adrian Brown .07 .20
428 Ruben Mateo .07 .20
429 Alex Ochoa .07 .20
430 Jose Rosado .07 .20
431 Masato Yoshii .07 .20
432 Corey Koskie .07 .20
433 Andy Pettitte .10 .30
434 Brian Daubach .07 .20
435 Sterling Hitchcock .07 .20
436 Timo Perez .07 .20
437 Shawn Estes .07 .20
438 Tony Armas Jr. .07 .20
439 Danny Bautista .07 .20
440 Randy Winn .07 .20
441 Wilson Alvarez .07 .20
442 Rondell White .07 .20
443 Jeromy Burnitz .07 .20
444 Kelvim Escobar .07 .20
445 Paul Bako .07 .20
446 Javier Vazquez .07 .20
447 Eric Gagne .07 .20
448 Kenny Lofton .07 .20
449 Mark Kotsay .07 .20
450 Jamie Moyer .07 .20
451 Delino DeShields .07 .20
452 Rey Ordonez .07 .20
453 Russ Ortiz .07 .20
454 Dave Burba .07 .20
455 Eric Karros .07 .20
456 Felix Martinez .07 .20
457 Tony Batista .07 .20
458 Bobby Higginson .07 .20
459 Jeff D'Amico .07 .20
460 Shane Spencer .07 .20
461 Brent Mayne .07 .20
462 Glendon Rusch .07 .20
463 Chris Gomez .07 .20
464 Jeff Shaw .07 .20
465 Damon Buford .07 .20
466 Mike DiFelice .07 .20
467 Jimmy Haynes .07 .20
468 Billy Wagner .07 .20
469 A.J. Hinch .07 .20
470 Gary DiSarcina .07 .20
471 Tom Lampkin .07 .20
472 Adam Eaton .07 .20
473 Brian Giles .07 .20
474 John Thomson .07 .20
475 Cal Eldred .07 .20
476 Ramiro Mendoza .07 .20
477 Scott Sullivan .07 .20
478 Scott Rolen .10 .30
479 Todd Ritchie .07 .20
480 Pablo Ozuna .07 .20
481 Carl Pavano .07 .20
482 Matt Morris .07 .20
483 Matt Stairs .07 .20
484 Tim Belcher .07 .20
485 Lance Berkman .07 .20
486 Brian Meadows .07 .20
487 Bob Abreu .07 .20
488 John VanderWal .07 .20
489 Donnie Sadler .07 .20
490 Damion Easley .07 .20
491 David Justice .07 .20
492 Ray Durham .07 .20
493 Todd Zeile .07 .20
494 Desi Relaford .07 .20
495 Cliff Floyd .07 .20
496 Scott Downs .07 .20
497 Barry Bonds .50 1.25
498 Jeff D'Amico .07 .20
499 Octavio Dotel .07 .20
500 Kent Mercker .07 .20
501 Craig Grebeck .07 .20
502 Roberto Hernandez .07 .20
503 Matt Williams .07 .20
504 Bruce Aven .07 .20
505 Brett Tomko .07 .20
506 Kris Benson .07 .20
507 Neifi Perez .07 .20
508 Alfonso Soriano .10 .30
509 Keith Osik .07 .20
510 Matt Franco .07 .20
511 Steve Finley .07 .20
512 Olmedo Saenz .07 .20
513 Esteban Loaiza .07 .20
514 Adam Kennedy .07 .20
515 Scott Elarton .07 .20
516 Moises Alou .07 .20
517 Bryan Rekar .07 .20
518 Darryl Hamilton .07 .20
519 Osvaldo Fernandez .07 .20
520 Kip Wells .07 .20
521 Bernie Williams .10 .30
522 Mike Darr .07 .20
523 Marlon Anderson .07 .20
524 Derrek Lee .10 .30
525 Ugueth Urbina .07 .20
526 Vinny Castilla .07 .20
527 David Wells .07 .20
528 Jason Marquis .07 .20
529 Orlando Palmeiro .07 .20
530 Carlos Perez .07 .20
531 J.T. Snow .07 .20
532 Al Leiter .07 .20
533 Jimmy Anderson .07 .20
534 Brett Laxton .07 .20
535 Butch Huskey .07 .20
536 Orlando Hernandez .07 .20
537 Magglio Ordonez .07 .20
538 Willie Blair .07 .20
539 Kevin Sefcik .07 .20
540 Chad Curtis .07 .20
541 John Halama .07 .20
542 Andy Fox .07 .20
543 Juan Guzman .07 .20
544 Frank Menechino RC .07 .20
545 Raul Mondesi .07 .20
546 Tim Salmon .10 .30
547 Ryan Rupe .07 .20
548 Jeff Reed .07 .20
549 Mike Mordecai .07 .20
550 Jeff Kent .07 .20
551 Wiki Gonzalez .07 .20
552 Kenny Rogers .07 .20
553 Kevin Young .07 .20
554 Brian Johnson .07 .20
555 Tom Goodwin .07 .20
556 Tony Clark .07 .20
557 Mac Suzuki .07 .20
558 Brian Moehler .07 .20
559 Jim Parque .07 .20
560 Mariano Rivera .20 .50
561 Trot Nixon .07 .20
562 Mike Mussina .10 .30
563 Nelson Figueroa .07 .20
564 Alex Gonzalez .07 .20
565 Benny Agbayani .07 .20
566 Ed Sprague .07 .20
567 Scott Erickson .07 .20
568 Abraham Nunez .07 .20
569 Jerry DiPoto .07 .20
570 Sean Casey .07 .20
571 Wilton Veras .07 .20
572 Joe Mays .07 .20
573 Bill Simas .07 .20
574 Doug Glanville .07 .20
575 Scott Sauerbeck .07 .20
576 Ben Davis .07 .20
577 Jesus Sanchez .07 .20
578 Ricardo Rincon .07 .20
579 John Olerud .07 .20
580 Curt Schilling .07 .20
581 Alex Cora .07 .20
582 Pat Hentgen .07 .20
583 Javy Lopez .07 .20
584 Ben Grieve .07 .20
585 Frank Castillo .07 .20
586 Kevin Stocker .07 .20
587 Mark Sweeney .07 .20
588 Ray Lankford .07 .20
589 Turner Ward .07 .20
590 Felipe Crespo .07 .20
591 Omar Vizquel .10 .30
592 Mike Lieberthal .07 .20
593 Ken Griffey Jr. .40 1.00
594 Troy O'Leary .07 .20
595 Dave Mlicki .07 .20
596 Manny Ramirez Sox .10 .30
597 Mike Lansing .07 .20
598 Rich Aurilia .07 .20
599 Russell Branyan .07 .20
600 Russ Johnson .07 .20
601 Greg Colbrunn .07 .20
602 Andruw Jones .10 .30
603 Henry Blanco .07 .20
604 Jarrod Washburn .07 .20
605 Tony Eusebio .07 .20
606 Aaron Sele .07 .20
607 Charles Nagy .07 .20
608 Ryan Klesko .07 .20
609 Dante Bichette .07 .20
610 Bill Haselman .07 .20
611 Jerry Spradlin .07 .20
612 Alex Rodriguez .25 .60
613 Jose Silva .07 .20
614 Darren Oliver .07 .20
615 Pat Mahomes .07 .20
616 Roberto Alomar .10 .30
617 Edgar Renteria .07 .20
618 Jon Lieber .07 .20
619 John Rocker .07 .20
620 Miguel Tejada .07 .20
621 Mo Vaughn .07 .20
622 Jose Lima .07 .20
623 Kerry Wood .07 .20
624 Mike Timlin .07 .20
625 Wil Cordero .07 .20
626 Albert Belle .07 .20
627 Bobby Jones .07 .20
628 Doug Mirabelli .07 .20
629 Jason Tyner .07 .20
630 Andy Ashby .07 .20
631 Jose Hernandez .07 .20
632 Devon White .07 .20
633 Ruben Rivera .07 .20
634 Steve Parris .07 .20
635 David McCarty .07 .20
636 Jose Canseco .10 .30
637 Todd Walker .07 .20
638 Stan Spencer .07 .20
639 Wayne Gomes .07 .20
640 Freddy Garcia .07 .20
641 Jeremy Giambi .07 .20
642 Luis Lopez .07 .20
643 John Smoltz .10 .30
644 Kelly Stinnett .07 .20
645 Kevin Brown .07 .20
646 Wilton Guerrero .07 .20
647 Al Martin .07 .20
648 Woody Williams .07 .20
649 Brian Rose .07 .20
650 Rafael Palmeiro .10 .30
651 Pete Schourek .07 .20
652 Kevin Jarvis .07 .20
653 Mark Redman .07 .20
654 Ricky Ledee .07 .20
655 Larry Walker .07 .20
656 Paul Byrd .07 .20
657 Jason Bere .07 .20
658 Rick White .07 .20
659 Calvin Murray .07 .20
660 Greg Maddux .30 .75
661 Ron Gant .07 .20
662 Eli Marrero .07 .20
663 Graeme Lloyd .07 .20
664 Trevor Hoffman .07 .20
665 Nomar Garciaparra .30 .75
666 Glenallen Hill .07 .20
667 Matt LeCroy .07 .20
668 Justin Thompson .07 .20
669 Brady Anderson .07 .20
670 Miguel Batista .07 .20
671 Erubiel Durazo .07 .20
672 Kevin Millwood .07 .20
673 Mitch Meluskey .07 .20
674 Luis Gonzalez .07 .20
675 Edgar Martinez .10 .30
676 Robert Person .07 .20
677 Benito Santiago .07 .20
678 Todd Jones .07 .20
679 Tino Martinez .10 .30
680 Carlos Beltran .07 .20
681 Gabe White .07 .20
682 Bret Saberhagen .07 .20
683 Jeff Conine .07 .20
684 Jaret Wright .07 .20
685 Bernard Gilkey .07 .20
686 Garrett Stephenson .07 .20
687 Jamey Wright .07 .20
688 Sammy Sosa .20 .50
689 John Jaha .07 .20
690 Ramon Martinez .07 .20
691 Robert Fick .07 .20
692 Eric Milton .07 .20
693 Denny Neagle .07 .20
694 Ron Coomer .07 .20
695 John Valentin .07 .20
696 Placido Polanco .07 .20
697 Tim Hudson .07 .20
698 Marty Cordova .07 .20
699 Chad Kreuter .07 .20
700 Frank Catalanotto .07 .20
701 Tim Wakefield .07 .20
702 Jim Edmonds .07 .20
703 Michael Tucker .07 .20
704 Cristian Guzman .07 .20
705 Joey Hamilton .07 .20
706 Mike Piazza .30 .75
707 Dave Martinez .07 .20
708 Mike Hampton .07 .20
709 Bobby Bonilla .07 .20
710 Juan Pierre .07 .20
711 John Parrish .07 .20
712 Kory DeHaan .07 .20
713 Brian Tollberg .07 .20
714 Chris Truby .07 .20
715 Emil Brown .07 .20
716 Ryan Dempster .07 .20
717 Rich Garces .07 .20
718 Mike Myers .07 .20
719 Luis Ordaz .07 .20
720 Kazuhiro Sasaki .07 .20
721 Mark Quinn .07 .20
722 Ramon Ortiz .07 .20
723 Kerry Ligtenberg .07 .20
724 Rolando Arrojo .07 .20
725 Tsuyoshi Shinjo RC .20 .50
726 Ichiro Suzuki RC 30.00 80.00
727 Oswalt .30 .75
Strange/Rauch
728 Jake Peavy RC UER .75 2.00
729 S.Smyth RC .08 .25
Bynum/Haynes
730 Cuddyer .08 .25
Lawrence/Freeman
731 C.Pena .08 .25
Barnes/Wise
732 Dawkins/Almonte/Lopez .08 .25
733 Escobar .08 .25
Valent/Wilkerson
734 Hall .08 .25
Barajas/Goldbach
735 Romano .15 .40
Giles/Ozuna
736 D.Brown .08 .25
Cust/V.Wells
737 L.Montanez RC .08 .25
D.Espinosa
738 J.Wayne RC .08 .25
A.Pluta RC
739 J.Axelson RC .08 .25
C.Cali RC
740 S.Boyd RC .08 .25
C.Morris RC
741 T.Arko RC .08 .25
D.Moylan RC
742 L.Cotto RC .08 .25
L.Escobar
743 B.Mims RC .08 .25
B.Williams RC
744 C.Russ RC .08 .25
B.Edwards
745 J.Torres .08 .25
B.Diggins
746 Edwin Encarnacion RC 1.50 4.00
747 B.Bass RC .08 .25
O.Ayala RC
748 M.Matthews RC .08 .25
J.Kaanoi
749 S.McFarland RC .08 .25
A.Sterrett RC
750 D.Krynzel .60 1.50
G.Sizemore
751 K.Bucktrot .08 .25
D.Sardinha
752 Anaheim Angels TC .07 .20
753 Arizona Diamondbacks TC .07 .20
754 Atlanta Braves TC .07 .20
755 Baltimore Orioles TC .07 .20
756 Boston Red Sox TC .07 .20
757 Chicago Cubs TC .07 .20
758 Chicago White Sox TC .07 .20
759 Cincinnati Reds TC .07 .20
760 Cleveland Indians TC .07 .20
761 Colorado Rockies TC .07 .20
762 Detroit Tigers TC .07 .20
763 Florida Marlins TC .07 .20
764 Houston Astros TC .07 .20
765 Kansas City Royals TC .07 .20
766 Los Angeles Dodgers TC .07 .20
767 Milwaukee Brewers TC .07 .20
768 Minnesota Twins TC .07 .20
769 Montreal Expos TC .07 .20
770 New York Mets TC .07 .20
771 New York Yankees TC .40 1.00
772 Oakland Athletics TC .07 .20
773 Philadelphia Phillies TC .07 .20
774 Pittsburgh Pirates TC .07 .20
775 San Diego Padres TC .07 .20
776 San Francisco Giants TC .07 .20
777 Seattle Mariners TC .07 .20
778 St. Louis Cardinals TC .07 .20
779 Tampa Bay Devil Rays TC .07 .20
780 Texas Rangers TC .07 .20
781 Toronto Blue Jays TC .07 .20
782 Bucky Dent GM .07 .20
783 Jackie Robinson GM .20 .50
784 Roberto Clemente GM .25 .60
785 Nolan Ryan GM .30 .75
786 Kerry Wood GM .07 .20
787 Rickey Henderson GM .07 .20
788 Lou Brock GM .10 .30
789 David Wells GM .07 .20
790 Andruw Jones GM .07 .20
791 Carlton Fisk GM .07 .20
TK B.Jackson/D.Sanders Bat 30.00 60.00
NNO B.Thomson/R.Branca AU 30.00 60.00

2001 Topps Employee

*STARS: 6X TO 15X BASIC CARDS
CARD NO.7 DOES NOT EXIST
726 Ichiro Suzuki 75.00 200.00

2001 Topps Gold

COMPLETE SET (790) 60.00 120.00
*STARS: 10X TO 25X BASIC CARDS
*PROSPECTS 352-376/725/751: 4X TO 10X
*ROOKIES 352-376/725-751: 4X TO 10X
SER.1 STATED ODDS 1:17 H/R, 1:4 HTA
SER.2 STATED ODDS 1:14 H/R, 1:3 HTA
STATED PRINT RUN 2001 SERIAL #'d SETS
CARD NO.7 DOES NOT EXIST
726 Ichiro Suzuki 750.00 2000.00

2001 Topps Home Team Advantage

COMP.HTA GOLD SET (790) 60.00 120.00
*HTA: .75X TO 2X BASIC CARDS
DISTRIBUTED IN FACT.SET FORM ONLY
CARD NO.7 DOES NOT EXIST

2001 Topps Limited

COMP.FACT.SET (790) 60.00 150.00
*STARS: 1.5X TO 4X BASIC CARDS
*ROOKIES: 1.5X TO 4X BASIC CARDS
DISTRIBUTED ONLY IN FACTORY SET FORM
STATED PRINT RUN 3805 SETS
FIVE ARCH.RSV.FUTURE REPRINTS PER SET
SEE TOPPS ARCH.RSV.FOR INSERT PRICING

2001 Topps A Look Ahead

COMPLETE SET (10) 12.50 30.00
SER.1 STATED ODDS 1:25 H/R, 1:5 HTA
LA1 Vladimir Guerrero 1.00 2.50
LA2 Derek Jeter 2.50 6.00
LA3 Todd Helton .60 1.50
LA4 Alex Rodriguez 1.25 3.00
LA5 Ken Griffey Jr. 2.00 5.00
LA6 Nomar Garciaparra 1.50 4.00
LA7 Chipper Jones 1.00 2.50
LA8 Ivan Rodriguez .60 1.50
LA9 Pedro Martinez .60 1.50
LA10 Rick Ankiel .40 1.00

2001 Topps A Tradition Continues

COMPLETE SET (30) 50.00 100.00
SER.1 STATED ODDS 1:17 H/R, 1:5 HTA
TRC1 Chipper Jones 1.25 3.00
TRC2 Cal Ripken 4.00 10.00
TRC3 Mike Piazza 2.00 5.00
TRC4 Ken Griffey Jr. 2.50 6.00
TRC5 Randy Johnson 1.25 3.00
TRC6 Derek Jeter 3.00 8.00
TRC7 Scott Rolen .75 2.00
TRC8 Nomar Garciaparra 2.00 5.00
TRC9 Roberto Alomar .75 2.00
TRC10 Greg Maddux 2.00 5.00
TRC11 Ivan Rodriguez .75 2.00
TRC12 Jeff Bagwell .75 2.00
TRC13 Alex Rodriguez 1.50 4.00
TRC14 Pedro Martinez .75 2.00
TRC15 Sammy Sosa 1.25 3.00
TRC16 Jim Edmonds .50 1.25
TRC17 Mo Vaughn .50 1.25
TRC18 Barry Bonds 3.00 8.00
TRC19 Larry Walker .50 1.25
TRC20 Mark McGwire 3.00 8.00
TRC21 Vladimir Guerrero 1.25 3.00
TRC22 Andruw Jones .75 2.00
TRC23 Todd Helton .75 2.00
TRC24 Kevin Brown .50 1.25
TRC25 Tony Gwynn 1.50 4.00
TRC26 Manny Ramirez .75 2.00
TRC27 Roger Clemens 2.50 6.00
TRC28 Frank Thomas 1.25 3.00
TRC29 Shawn Green .50 1.25
TRC30 Jim Thome .75 2.00

2001 Topps Base Hit Autograph Relics

SER.2 STATED ODDS 1:1462 H/R, 1:325 HTA
BH1 Mike Scioscia 40.00 80.00
BH2 Larry Dierker 20.00 50.00
BH3 Art Howe 40.00 80.00
BH4 Jim Fregosi 20.00 50.00
BH5 Bobby Cox 50.00 100.00
BH6 Davey Lopes 20.00 50.00
BH7 Tony LaRussa 40.00 80.00
BH8 Don Baylor 40.00 100.00
BH9 Larry Rothschild 20.00 50.00
BH10 Buck Showalter 20.00 50.00
BH11 Davey Johnson 20.00 50.00
BH12 Felipe Alou 40.00 80.00
BH13 Charlie Manuel 30.00 60.00
BH14 Lou Piniella 40.00 80.00
BH15 John Boles 20.00 50.00
BH16 Bobby Valentine 40.00 80.00
BH17 Mike Hargrove 40.00 80.00
BH18 Bruce Bochy 20.00 50.00
BH19 Terry Francona 60.00 120.00
BH20 Gene Lamont 20.00 50.00
BH21 Johnny Oates 50.00 100.00
BH22 Jimy Williams 20.00 50.00
BH23 Jack McKeon 40.00 80.00
BH24 Buddy Bell 40.00 80.00
BH25 Tony Muser 20.00 50.00
BH26 Phil Garner 40.00 80.00
BH27 Tom Kelly 20.00 50.00
BH28 Jerry Manuel 20.00 50.00

2001 Topps Before There Was Topps

COMPLETE SET (10) 15.00 40.00
SER.2 STATED ODDS 1:25 H/R, 1:5 HTA
BT1 Lou Gehrig 2.50 6.00
BT2 Babe Ruth 4.00 10.00
BT3 Cy Young 1.25 3.00
BT4 Walter Johnson 1.25 3.00
BT5 Ty Cobb 2.00 5.00
BT6 Rogers Hornsby 1.25 3.00
BT7 Honus Wagner 1.25 3.00
BT8 Christy Mathewson 1.25 3.00
BT9 Grover Alexander 1.25 3.00
BT10 Joe DiMaggio 2.50 6.00

2001 Topps Combos

COMPLETE SET (20) 12.50 30.00
COMPLETE SERIES 1 (10) 6.00 15.00
COMPLETE SERIES 2 (10) 6.00 15.00
SER.1 AND SER.2 ODDS 1:12 H/R, 1:4 HTA
TC1 Decades of Excellence 2.00 5.00
TC2 Power Corner .60 1.50
TC3 Glove Birds 1.50 4.00
TC4 Mound Marksmen .60 1.50
TC5 Tools of Success .60 1.50
TC6 Shortstop Supremacy .75 2.00
TC7 Big Red Machine .75 2.00
TC8 Latin Heat .60 1.50
TC9 Home Run Royalty 1.00 2.50
TC10 New York State of Mind 1.25 3.00
TC11 Dodger Blue 1.25 3.00
TC12 60 Home Run Club 1.50 4.00
TC13 Heroes of Fenway 1.25 3.00
TC14 Mound Masters 1.00 2.50
TC15 Sweetness 1.25 3.00
TC16 Ironmen 2.00 5.00
TC17 Southpaw Greatness 2.00 5.00
TC18 Best There is Was .75 2.00
TC19 All in the Family 1.50 4.00
TC20 Barrier Breakers .60 1.50

2001 Topps Golden Anniversary

COMPLETE SET (50) 40.00 80.00
SER.1 STATED ODDS 1:10 H/R, 1:1 HTA
GA1 Hank Aaron 2.00 5.00
GA2 Ernie Banks 1.00 2.50
GA3 Mike Schmidt 2.00 5.00
GA4 Willie Mays 2.00 5.00
GA5 Johnny Bench 1.00 2.50
GA6 Tom Seaver .60 1.50
GA7 Frank Robinson .60 1.50
GA8 Sandy Koufax 3.00 8.00
GA9 Bob Gibson .60 1.50
GA10 Ted Williams 2.00 5.00
GA11 Cal Ripken 3.00 8.00
GA12 Tony Gwynn 1.25 3.00
GA13 Mark McGwire 2.50 6.00
GA14 Ken Griffey Jr. 2.00 5.00
GA15 Greg Maddux 1.50 4.00
GA16 Roger Clemens 2.00 5.00
GA17 Barry Bonds 2.50 6.00
GA18 Rickey Henderson 1.00 2.50
GA19 Mike Piazza 1.50 4.00
GA20 Jose Canseco .60 1.50
GA21 Derek Jeter 2.50 6.00
GA22 Nomar Garciaparra 1.50 4.00
GA23 Alex Rodriguez 1.25 3.00
GA24 Sammy Sosa 1.00 2.50
GA25 Ivan Rodriguez .60 1.50
GA26 Vladimir Guerrero 1.00 2.50
GA27 Chipper Jones 1.00 2.50
GA28 Jeff Bagwell .60 1.50
GA29 Pedro Martinez .60 1.50
GA30 Randy Johnson 1.00 2.50
GA31 Pat Burrell .40 1.00
GA32 Josh Hamilton .75 2.00
GA33 Ryan Anderson .40 1.00
GA34 Corey Patterson .40 1.00
GA35 Eric Munson .40 1.00
GA36 Sean Burroughs .40 1.00
GA37 C.C. Sabathia .40 1.00
GA38 Chin-Feng Chen .40 1.00
GA39 Barry Zito .60 1.50
GA40 Adrian Gonzalez 2.50 6.00
GA41 Mark McGwire 2.50 6.00
GA42 Nomar Garciaparra 1.50 4.00
GA43 Todd Helton .60 1.50
GA44 Matt Williams .40 1.00
GA45 Troy Glaus .40 1.00
GA46 Geoff Jenkins .40 1.00
GA47 Frank Thomas 1.00 2.50
GA48 Mo Vaughn .40 1.00
GA49 Barry Larkin .60 1.50
GA50 J.D. Drew .40 1.00

2001 Topps Golden Anniversary Autographs

SER.1 GROUP A 1:22866 H/R, 1:5056 HTA
SER.1 GROUP B 1:3054 H/R, 1:678 HTA
SER.2 GROUP B 1:11781 H/R, 1:2612 HTA
SER.1 GROUP C 1:1431 H/R, 1:318 HTA
SER.2 GROUP C 1:4236 H/R, 1:942 HTA
SER.1 GROUP D 1:18339H/R,1:4,095HTA
SER.2 GROUP D 1:981 H/R, 1:218 HTA
SER.1 GROUP E 1:13737 H/R,1:3,056HTA
SER.2 GROUP E 1:14157 H/R, 1:3139 HTA
SER.1 GROUP F 1:11015 H/R, 1:2438 HTA
SER.2 GROUP F 1:3532 H/R, 1:785 HTA
SER.1 GROUP G 1:625 H/R, 1:139 HTA
SER.2 GROUP G 1:3532 H/R, 1:785 HTA
SER.2 GROUP H 1:2,037 H/R, 1:452 HTA
SER.2 GROUP I 1:481 H/R, 1:107 HTA
SER.1 OVERALL 1:346 H/R, 1:77 HTA
SER.2 OVERALL 1:216 H/R, 1:48 HTA
SER.1 EXCH.DEADLINE 11/30/01
SER.2 EXCH.DEADLINE 04/30/03
SER.2 GROUP J 1:10583 H/R, 1:2355 HTA
GAAAG Adrian Gonzalez G1-I2 4.00 10.00
GAAAH Aaron Herr I2 5.00 12.00
GAAAJ Adam Johnson G1-I2 4.00 10.00
GAAAO Augie Ojeda B2 10.00 25.00
GAAAP Andy Pafko C1 8.00 20.00
GAABB Barry Bonds B2 125.00 300.00
GAABE Brian Esposito I2 4.00 10.00
GAABG Bob Gibson C2 20.00 50.00
GAABK Bobby Kielty I2 6.00 15.00
GAABO Ben Oglivie D2 4.00 10.00
GAABR Brooks Robinson B1 30.00 80.00
GAABT Brian Tollberg I2 4.00 10.00
GAACC Chris Clapinski I2 6.00 15.00
GAACD Chad Durbin I2 6.00 15.00
GAACE Carl Erskine D2 4.00 10.00
GAACJ Chipper Jones B1 60.00 120.00
GAACL Colby Lewis I2 6.00 15.00
GAACR Chris Richard I2 6.00 15.00
GAACS Carlos Silva I2 12.00 30.00
GAACY Carl Yastrzemski C2 40.00 100.00
GAADA Dick Allen C1 10.00 25.00
GAADA Denny Abreu I2 4.00 10.00
GAADG Dick Groat D2 6.00 15.00
GAADT Derek Thompson I2 6.00 15.00
GAAEB Ernie Banks B1 100.00 250.00
GAAEB Eric Byrnes I2 10.00 25.00
GAAEF Eddy Furniss I2 4.00 10.00
GAAEM Eric Munson G2 4.00 10.00
GAAER Erasmo Ramirez I2 4.00 10.00
GAAGB George Bell D2 5.00 12.00
GAAGG Geraldo Guzman I2 4.00 10.00
GAAGM Gary Matthews D2 6.00 15.00
GAAGS Grady Sizemore I2 4.00 10.00
GAAGT Garry Templeton C1 4.00 10.00
GAAHA Hank Aaron B1 200.00 400.00
GAAJB Johnny Bench C2 50.00 100.00
GAAJC Jorge Cantu I2 6.00 15.00
GAAJL John Lackey I2 8.00 20.00
GAAJM Jason Marquis G1 4.00 10.00
GAAJR Joe Rudi C1 6.00 15.00
GAAJR Juan Rincon I2 6.00 15.00
GAAJS Juan Salas I2 4.00 10.00
GAAJV Jose Vidro F1 4.00 10.00
GAAJW Justin Wayne H2 4.00 10.00
GAAKG Kevin Gregg B2 8.00 20.00
GAAKH Ken Holtzman D2 6.00 15.00
GAAKT Kent Tekulve D2 8.00 20.00
GAALB Lou Brock B1 6.00 15.00
GAALM Luis Montanez H2 4.00 10.00
GAALR Luis Rivas I2 4.00 10.00
GAAMB Milton Bradley G2 6.00 15.00
GAAMC Mike Cuellar C1 8.00 20.00
GAAMG Mike Glendenning I2 4.00 10.00
GAAML Matt Lawton F2 5.00 12.00
GAAML Mike Lamb G1 4.00 10.00
GAAMM Mike Mussina 12.00 30.00
GAAMO Magglio Ordonez B1 12.00 30.00
GAAMS Mike Schmidt B1 60.00 120.00
GAAMS Mike Sweeney F2 4.00 10.00
GAAMS Mike Stodolka I2 4.00 10.00
GAAMW Matt Wheatland G1 4.00 10.00
GAAMW Michael Wenner I2 4.00 10.00
GAANG Nick Green I2 4.00 10.00
GAANJ Neil Jenkins I2 8.00 20.00
GAANR Nolan Ryan A2 175.00 350.00
GAAPB Pat Burrell G1 6.00 15.00
GAAPM Phil Merrell I2 4.00 10.00
GAARA Rick Ankiel D1 6.00 15.00
GAARB Rocco Baldelli G1-I2 4.00 10.00
GAARC Rod Carew B1 12.00 30.00
GAARF Rafael Furcal G1 6.00 15.00
GAARJ Reggie Jackson A2 125.00 200.00
GAARS Ron Swoboda C1 6.00 15.00
GAASH Scott Heard G1 4.00 10.00
GAASK Sandy Koufax A1 400.00 800.00
GAASM Stan Musial A2 175.00 300.00
GAASR Scott Rolen F2 5.00 12.00
GAAST Scott Thorman I2 4.00 10.00
GAATA Tony Alvarez I2 8.00 20.00
GAATH Todd Helton B2 4.00 10.00
GAATJ Tripper Johnson I2 4.00 10.00
GAATS Tom Seaver A2 75.00 200.00
GAAVL Vernon Law C1 4.00 10.00
GAAWD Willie Davis D2 10.00 25.00
GAAWF Whitey Ford C2 40.00 80.00
GAAWH Willie Hernandez C1 4.00 10.00
GAAWM Willie Mays A1 350.00 450.00
GAAWW Wilbur Wood D2 6.00 15.00
GAAYB Yogi Berra B1 50.00 120.00
GAAYH Yamid Haad I2 6.00 15.00
GAAYT Yorvit Torrealba I2 10.00 25.00
GAACCS Corey Smith I2 4.00 10.00
GAAGHB George Brett A2 125.00 250.00
GAAJDD J.D. Drew E2 5.00 12.00
GAAMAB Mike Bynum I2 4.00 10.00
GAAMFL Mike Lockwood I2 4.00 10.00
GAAMJS Mike Stodolka G1 4.00 10.00
GAAMJW Matt Wheatland I2 6.00 15.00
GAATDLR Tomas De la Rosa I2 6.00 15.00

2001 Topps Hit Parade Bat Relics

SER.2 STATED ODDS 1:2607 RETAIL
HP1 Reggie Jackson 12.50 30.00
HP2 Dave Winfield 12.50 30.00
HP3 Eddie Murray 12.50 30.00
HP4 Rickey Henderson 12.50 30.00
HP5 Robin Yount 12.50 30.00
HP6 Carl Yastrzemski 12.50 30.00

2001 Topps King of Kings Relics

SER.1 STATED ODDS 1:2056 H/R, 1:457 HTA
SER.2 GROUP A 1:7205 H/R, 1:1,605 HTA
SER.2 GROUP B 1:2391 H/R, 1:531 HTA
SER.1 KKGE ODDS 1:8903 HTA
SER.2 KKLE2 ODDS 1:7615 HTA
KKR1 Hank Aaron Jsy 10.00 25.00
KKR2 Nolan Ryan Jsy 15.00 40.00
KKR3 Rickey Henderson Jsy 10.00 25.00
KKR4 Mark McGwire Jsy B 10.00 25.00
KKR5 Bob Gibson Jsy A 10.00 25.00
KKR6 Nolan Ryan Jsy B 10.00 25.00
KKGE Aaron/Ryan/Henderson 175.00 300.00
KKLE2 McGwire/Gib/Ryan 300.00 500.00

2001 Topps Noteworthy

COMPLETE SET (50) 20.00 50.00
SER.2 STATED ODDS 1:8 H/R, 1:1 HTA
TN1 Mark McGwire 1.50 4.00
TN2 Derek Jeter 1.50 4.00
TN3 Sammy Sosa .60 1.50
TN4 Todd Helton .40 1.00
TN5 Alex Rodriguez .75 2.00
TN6 Chipper Jones .60 1.50
TN7 Barry Bonds 1.50 4.00
TN8 Ken Griffey Jr. 1.25 3.00
TN9 Nomar Garciaparra 1.00 2.50
TN10 Frank Thomas .60 1.50
TN11 Randy Johnson .60 1.50
TN12 Cal Ripken 2.00 5.00
TN13 Mike Piazza 1.00 2.50
TN14 Ivan Rodriguez .40 1.00
TN15 Jeff Bagwell .40 1.00
TN16 Vladimir Guerrero .60 1.50
TN17 Greg Maddux 1.00 2.50
TN18 Tony Gwynn .75 2.00
TN19 Larry Walker .40 1.00
TN20 Juan Gonzalez .40 1.00
TN21 Scott Rolen .40 1.00
TN22 Jason Giambi .40 1.00
TN23 Jeff Kent .40 1.00
TN24 Pat Burrell .40 1.00
TN25 Pedro Martinez .40 1.00
TN26 Willie Mays 1.50 4.00
TN27 Whitey Ford .40 1.00
TN28 Jackie Robinson .60 1.50
TN29 Ted Williams 1.50 4.00
TN30 Babe Ruth 3.00 8.00
TN31 Warren Spahn .40 1.00
TN32 Nolan Ryan 2.50 6.00
TN33 Yogi Berra .60 1.50
TN34 Mike Schmidt 1.50 4.00
TN35 Steve Carlton .40 1.00
TN36 Brooks Robinson .40 1.00
TN37 Bob Gibson .40 1.00
TN38 Reggie Jackson .40 1.00
TN39 Johnny Bench .60 1.50
TN40 Ernie Banks .60 1.50
TN41 Eddie Mathews .60 1.50
TN42 Don Mattingly 1.50 4.00

TN43 Duke Snider .40 1.00
TN44 Hank Aaron 1.50 4.00
TN45 Roberto Clemente 2.00 5.00
TN46 Harmon Killebrew .60 1.50
TN47 Frank Robinson .40 1.00
TN48 Stan Musial 1.25 3.00
TN49 Lou Brock .40 1.00
TN50 Joe Morgan .40 1.00

2001 Topps Originals Relics

SER.1 STATED ODDS 1:1172 H/R, 1:260 HTA
SER.2 STATED ODDS 1:1023 H/R, 1:227 HTA
1 Roberto Clemente 55 Jsy 50.00 120.00
2 Carl Yastrzemski 60 Jsy 15.00 40.00
3 Mike Schmidt 73 Jsy 10.00 25.00
4 Wade Boggs 83 Jsy 6.00 15.00
5 Chipper Jones 91 Jsy 10.00 25.00
6 Willie Mays 52 Jkt 15.00 40.00
7 Lou Brock 62 Jsy 10.00 25.00
8 Dave Parker 74 Jsy 6.00 15.00
9 Barry Bonds 86 Jsy 6.00 15.00
10 Alex Rodriguez 98 Jsy 10.00 25.00

2001 Topps Team Topps Legends Autographs

BOW.BEST GROUP A ODDS 1:404
BOW.BEST GROUP B ODDS 1:87
BOW.HERITAGE GROUP 1 ODDS 1:1570
BOW.HERITAGE GROUP 2 ODDS 1:1556
BOW.HERITAGE GROUP 3 ODDS 1:1937
BOW.HERITAGE GROUP 4 ODDS 1:1453
BOW.HERITAGE GROUP 5 ODDS 1:1899
TOPPS TRD.GROUP A ODDS 1:1567
TOPPS TRD.GROUP B ODDS 1:1881
TOPPS TRD.GROUP C ODDS 1:626
TOPPS TRD.GROUP D ODDS 1:TBD
TOPPS TRD.OVERALL ODDS 1:361
TOPPS AMERICAN PIE ODDS 1:211
TOPPS GALLERY ODDS 1:286
AP SUFFIX ON AMERICAN PIE DISTRIBUTION
TOPPS AMER.PIE EXCH.DEADLINE 11/01/03
TOPPS GALLERY EXCH.DEADLINE 06/30/03
02 TOPPS EXCH.DEADLINE 12/01/03
TT1F Willie Mays 73 125.00 250.00
TT1R Willie Mays 52 125.00 200.00
TT3F Stan Musial 63 40.00 80.00
TT3R Stan Musial 58 AS 40.00 80.00
TT6F Whitey Ford 67 20.00 50.00
TT6R Whitey Ford 53 15.00 40.00
TT7R Nolan Ryan 68 75.00 200.00
TT8F Carl Yastrzemski 83 40.00 80.00
TT8R Carl Yastrzemski 60 25.00 60.00
TT9R Brooks Robinson 57 25.00 60.00
TT10F Frank Robinson 75 12.00 30.00
TT10R Frank Robinson 57 20.00 50.00
TT11R Tom Seaver 67 30.00 80.00
TT11F Tom Seaver 87 30.00 80.00
TT12R Duke Snider 52 8.00 20.00
TT13F Warren Spahn 65 12.50 30.00
TT13R Warren Spahn 52 15.00 40.00
TT14F Johnny Bench 83 30.00 60.00
TT14R Johnny Bench 68 40.00 80.00
TT15R Reggie Jackson 69 40.00 80.00
TT16R Al Kaline 54 12.00 30.00
TT18F Bob Gibson 75 15.00 40.00
TT18R Bob Gibson 59 12.00 30.00
TT19R Mike Schmidt 73 25.00 60.00
TT20R Harmon Killebrew 55 40.00 80.00
TT21R Bob Feller 52 10.00 25.00
TT23F Gil McDougald 60 6.00 15.00
TT23R Gil McDougald 52 6.00 15.00
TT25F Luis Tiant 83 6.00 15.00
TT25R Luis Tiant 65 6.00 15.00
TT27F Andy Pafko 59 8.00 20.00
TT27R Andy Pafko 52 8.00 20.00
TT28F Herb Score 62 6.00 15.00
TT28R Herb Score 56 6.00 15.00
TT29F Bill Skowron 67 8.00 20.00
TT29R Bill Skowron 54 6.00 15.00
TT31F Clete Boyer 71 6.00 15.00
TT31R Clete Boyer 57 8.00 20.00
TT33F Vida Blue 87 6.00 15.00
TT33R Vida Blue 70 6.00 15.00
TT34R Don Larsen 56 8.00 20.00
TT35F Joe Pepitone 73 8.00 20.00
TT35R Joe Pepitone 62 6.00 15.00
TT36F Enos Slaughter 59 10.00 25.00
TT36R Enos Slaughter 52 15.00 40.00
TT37F Tug McGraw 85 12.50 30.00
TT37R Tug McGraw 65 12.50 30.00
TT38R Fergie Jenkins 66 8.00 20.00
TT40R Gaylord Perry 62 10.00 25.00
TT43F Bobby Thomson 60 8.00 20.00
TT43R Bobby Thomson 52 10.00 25.00
TT46F Robin Roberts 66 10.00 25.00
TT46R Robin Roberts 52 6.00 15.00
TT47F Frank Howard 73 6.00 15.00
TT47R Frank Howard 60 10.00 25.00
TT48F Bobby Richardson 66 6.00 15.00
TT48R Bobby Richardson 57 6.00 15.00
TT49R Tony Kubek 57 40.00 80.00
TT50F Mickey Lolich 80 6.00 15.00
TT50R Mickey Lolich 64 6.00 15.00
TT51RF Ralph Branca 52 6.00 15.00
TTGC Gary Carter 75 25.00 60.00
TTGG Rich Gossage 73 6.00 15.00
TTGN Graig Nettles 69 6.00 15.00
TTJB Jim Bunning 65 10.00 25.00
TTJM Joe Morgan 65 15.00 40.00
TTJP Jim Palmer 66 10.00 25.00
TTJS Johnny Sain 52 6.00 15.00
TTLA Luis Aparicio 56 10.00 25.00
TTLB Lou Brock 62 15.00 40.00
TTPB Paul Blair 65 6.00 15.00
TTRY Robin Yount 75 40.00 80.00
TTVL Vern Law 52 6.00 15.00

2001 Topps Through the Years Reprints

COMPLETE SET (50) 20.00 50.00
SER.1 STATED ODDS 1:8 H/R, 1:1 HTA
1 Yogi Berra '57 1.25 3.00
2 Roy Campanella '56 1.25 3.00
3 Willie Mays '53 2.00 5.00
4 Andy Pafko '52 1.25 3.00
5 Jackie Robinson '52 1.25 3.00
6 Stan Musial '59 1.50 4.00
7 Duke Snider '56 1.25 3.00
8 Warren Spahn '56 1.25 3.00
9 Ted Williams '54 3.00 8.00
10 Eddie Mathews '55 1.25 3.00
11 Willie McCovey '60 1.25 3.00
12 Frank Robinson '69 1.25 3.00
13 Ernie Banks '66 1.25 3.00
14 Hank Aaron '65 2.00 5.00
15 Sandy Koufax '61 2.50 6.00
16 Bob Gibson '68 1.25 3.00
17 Harmon Killebrew '67 1.25 3.00
18 Whitey Ford '64 1.25 3.00
19 Roberto Clemente '63 3.00 8.00
20 Juan Marichal '62 1.25 3.00
21 Johnny Bench '70 1.25 3.00
22 Willie Stargell '73 1.25 3.00
23 Joe Morgan '74 1.25 3.00
24 Carl Yastrzemski '71 1.50 4.00
25 Reggie Jackson '76 1.25 3.00
26 Tom Seaver '78 1.25 3.00
27 Steve Carlton '77 1.25 3.00
28 Jim Palmer 79' 1.25 3.00
29 Rod Carew '72 1.25 3.00
30 George Brett '75 3.00 8.00
31 Roger Clemens '85 2.50 6.00
32 Don Mattingly '84 3.00 8.00
33 Ryne Sandberg '89 2.00 5.00
34 Mike Schmidt '81 2.00 5.00
35 Cal Ripken '82 4.00 10.00
36 Tony Gwynn '83 1.50 4.00
37 Ozzie Smith '87 2.00 5.00
38 Wade Boggs '88 1.25 3.00
39 Nolan Ryan '80 2.50 6.00
40 Robin Yount '86 1.25 3.00
41 Mark McGwire '99 2.50 6.00
42 Ken Griffey Jr. '92 2.00 5.00
43 Sammy Sosa '90 1.25 3.00
44 Alex Rodriguez '98 1.25 3.00
45 Barry Bonds '94 2.50 6.00
46 Mike Piazza '95 1.50 4.00
47 Chipper Jones '91 1.25 3.00
48 Greg Maddux '96 1.50 4.00
49 Nomar Garciaparra '97 1.50 4.00
50 Derek Jeter '93 3.00 8.00

2001 Topps What Could Have Been

COMPLETE SET (10) 10.00 25.00
SER.2 STATED ODDS 1:25 H/R, 1:5 HTA
WCB1 Josh Gibson 2.00 5.00
WCB2 Satchel Paige 1.25 3.00
WCB3 Buck Leonard .75 2.00
WCB4 James Bell 1.25 3.00
WCB5 Rube Foster 1.25 3.00
WCB6 Martin DiHigo .75 2.00
WCB7 William Johnson .75 2.00
WCB8 Mule Suttles .75 2.00
WCB9 Ray Dandridge .75 2.00
WCB10 John Lloyd .75 2.00

2001 Topps Traded

COMPLETE SET (265) 60.00 150.00
COMMON CARD (1-99/145-265) .15 .40
COMMON REPRINT (100-144) .40 1.00
REPRINTS ARE NOT SP'S!
T1 Sandy Alomar Jr. .15 .40
T2 Kevin Appier .20 .50
T3 Brad Ausmus .20 .50
T4 Derek Bell .15 .40
T5 Bret Boone .20 .50
T6 Rico Brogna .15 .40
T7 Ellis Burks .20 .50
T8 Ken Caminiti .20 .50
T9 Roger Cedeno .15 .40
T10 Royce Clayton .15 .40
T11 Enrique Wilson .15 .40
T12 Rheal Cormier .15 .40
T13 Eric Davis .20 .50
T14 Shawon Dunston .15 .40
T15 Andres Galarraga .20 .50
T16 Tom Gordon .15 .40
T17 Mark Grace .30 .75
T18 Jeffrey Hammonds .15 .40
T19 Dustin Hermanson .15 .40
T20 Quinton McCracken .15 .40
T21 Todd Hundley .15 .40
T22 Charles Johnson .20 .50
T23 Marquis Grissom .20 .50
T24 Jose Mesa .15 .40
T25 Brian Boehringer .15 .40
T26 John Rocker .20 .50
T27 Jeff Frye .15 .40
T28 Reggie Sanders .20 .50
T29 David Segui .15 .40
T30 Mike Sirotka .15 .40
T31 Fernando Tatis .15 .40
T32 Steve Trachsel .15 .40
T33 Ismael Valdes .15 .40
T34 Randy Velarde .15 .40
T35 Ryan Kohlmeier .15 .40
T36 Mike Bordick .20 .50
T37 Kent Bottenfield .15 .40
T38 Pat Rapp .15 .40
T39 Jeff Nelson .15 .40
T40 Ricky Bottalico .15 .40
T41 Luke Prokopec .15 .40
T42 Hideo Nomo .50 1.25
T43 Bill Mueller .20 .50
T44 Roberto Kelly .15 .40
T45 Chris Holt .15 .40
T46 Mike Jackson .15 .40
T47 Devon White .20 .50
T48 Gerald Williams .15 .40
T49 Eddie Taubensee .15 .40
T50 Brian Hunter .15 .40
T51 Nelson Cruz .15 .40
T52 Jeff Fassero .15 .40
T53 Bubba Trammell .15 .40
T54 Bo Porter .15 .40
T55 Greg Norton .15 .40
T56 Benito Santiago .20 .50
T57 Ruben Rivera .15 .40
T58 Dee Brown .15 .40
T59 Jose Canseco .30 .75
T60 Chris Michalak .15 .40
T61 Tim Worrell .15 .40
T62 Matt Clement .20 .50
T63 Bill Pulsipher .15 .40
T64 Troy Brohawn RC .15 .40
T65 Mark Kotsay .20 .50
T66 Jimmy Rollins .20 .50
T67 Shea Hillenbrand .20 .50
T68 Ted Lilly .15 .40
T69 Jermaine Dye .20 .50
T70 Jerry Hairston Jr. .15 .40
T71 John Mabry .15 .40
T72 Kurt Abbott .15 .40
T73 Eric Owens .15 .40
T74 Jeff Brantley .15 .40
T75 Roy Oswalt .50 1.25
T76 Doug Mientkiewicz .20 .50
T77 Rickey Henderson .50 1.25
T78 Jason Grimsley .15 .40
T79 Christian Parker RC .15 .40
T80 Donne Wall .15 .40
T81 Alex Arias .15 .40
T82 Willis Roberts .15 .40
T83 Ryan Minor .15 .40
T84 Jason LaRue .15 .40
T85 Ruben Sierra .20 .50
T86 Johnny Damon .30 .75
T87 Juan Gonzalez .20 .50
T88 C.C. Sabathia .20 .50
T89 Tony Batista .15 .40
T90 Jay Witasick .15 .40
T91 Brent Abernathy .15 .40
T92 Paul LoDuca .20 .50
T93 Wes Helms .15 .40
T94 Mark Wohlers .15 .40
T95 Rob Bell .15 .40
T96 Tim Redding .15 .40
T97 Bud Smith RC .15 .40
T98 Adam Dunn .30 .75
T99 I.Suzuki 75.00 200.00
A.Pujols ROY
T100 Carlton Fisk 81 .50 1.25
T101 Tim Raines 81 .40 1.00
T102 Juan Marichal 74 .40 1.00
T103 Dave Winfield 81 .40 1.00
T104 Reggie Jackson 82 .50 1.25
T105 Cal Ripken 82 2.50 6.00
T106 Ozzie Smith 82 1.25 3.00
T107 Tom Seaver 83 .50 1.25
T108 Lou Piniella 74 .40 1.00
T109 Dwight Gooden 84 .40 1.00
T110 Bret Saberhagen 84 .40 1.00
T111 Gary Carter 85 .40 1.00
T112 Jack Clark 85 .40 1.00
T113 Rickey Henderson 85 .75 2.00
T114 Barry Bonds 86 2.00 5.00
T115 Bobby Bonilla 86 .40 1.00
T116 Jose Canseco 86 .50 1.25
T117 Will Clark 86 .50 1.25
T118 Andres Galarraga 86 .40 1.00
T119 Bo Jackson 86 .75 2.00
T120 Wally Joyner 86 .40 1.00
T121 Ellis Burks 87 .40 1.00
T122 David Cone 87 .40 1.00
T123 Greg Maddux 87 1.25 3.00
T124 Willie Randolph 76 .40 1.00
T125 Dennis Eckersley 87 .40 1.00
T126 Matt Williams 87 .40 1.00
T127 Joe Morgan 81 .40 1.00
T128 Fred McGriff 87 .50 1.25
T129 Roberto Alomar 88 .50 1.25
T130 Lee Smith 88 .40 1.00
T131 David Wells 88 .40 1.00
T132 Ken Griffey Jr. 89 1.50 4.00
T133 Deion Sanders 89 .50 1.25
T134 Nolan Ryan 89 1.50 4.00
T135 David Justice 90 .40 1.00
T136 Joe Carter 91 .40 1.00
T137 Jack Morris 92 .40 1.00
T138 Mike Piazza 93 1.25 3.00
T139 Barry Bonds 93 2.00 5.00
T140 Terrence Long 94 .40 1.00
T141 Ben Grieve 94 .40 1.00
T142 Richie Sexson 95 .40 1.00
T143 Sean Burroughs 99 .40 1.00
T144 Alfonso Soriano 99 .50 1.25
T145 Bob Boone MG .20 .50
T146 Larry Bowa MG .20 .50
T147 Bob Brenly MG .15 .40
T148 Buck Martinez MG .15 .40
T149 Lloyd McClendon MG .15 .40
T150 Jim Tracy MG .15 .40
T151 Jared Abruzzo RC .15 .40
T152 Kurt Ainsworth .15 .40
T153 Willie Bloomquist .20 .50
T154 Ben Broussard .15 .40
T155 Bobby Bradley .15 .40
T156 Mike Bynum .15 .40
T157 A.J. Hinch .15 .40
T158 Ryan Christianson .15 .40
T159 Carlos Silva .15 .40
T160 Joe Crede .50 1.25
T161 Jack Cust .15 .40
T162 Ben Diggins .15 .40
T163 Phil Dumatrait .15 .40
T164 Alex Escobar .15 .40
T165 Miguel Olivo .15 .40
T166 Chris George .15 .40
T167 Marcus Giles .20 .50
T168 Keith Ginter .15 .40
T169 Josh Girdley .15 .40
T170 Tony Alvarez .15 .40
T171 Scott Seabol .15 .40
T172 Josh Hamilton .30 .75
T173 Jason Hart .15 .40
T174 Israel Alcantara .15 .40
T175 Jake Peavy .40 1.00
T176 Stubby Clapp RC .15 .40
T177 D'Angelo Jimenez .15 .40
T178 Nick Johnson .20 .50
T179 Ben Johnson .20 .50
T180 Larry Bigbie .15 .40
T181 Allen Levrault .15 .40
T182 Felipe Lopez .20 .50
T183 Sean Burnett .15 .40
T184 Nick Neugebauer .15 .40
T185 Austin Kearns .20 .50
T186 Corey Patterson .15 .40
T187 Carlos Pena .15 .40
T188 Ricardo Rodriguez RC .15 .40
T189 Juan Rivera .15 .40
T190 Grant Roberts .15 .40
T191 Adam Pettyjohn RC .15 .40
T192 Jared Sandberg .15 .40
T193 Xavier Nady .15 .40
T194 Dane Sardinha .15 .40
T195 Shawn Sonnier .15 .40
T196 Rafael Soriano .15 .40
T197 Brian Specht RC .15 .40
T198 Aaron Myette .15 .40
T199 Juan Uribe RC .20 .50
T200 Jayson Werth .15 .40
T201 Brad Wilkerson .15 .40
T202 Horacio Estrada .15 .40
T203 Joel Pineiro .20 .50
T204 Matt LeCroy .15 .40
T205 Michael Coleman .15 .40
T206 Ben Sheets .30 .75
T207 Eric Byrnes .15 .40
T208 Sean Burroughs .15 .40
T209 Ken Harvey .15 .40
T210 Travis Hafner 1.50 4.00
T211 Erick Almonte .15 .40
T212 Jason Belcher RC .15 .40
T213 Wilson Betemit RC .60 1.50
T214 Hank Blalock RC 1.00 2.50
T215 Danny Borrell .15 .40
T216 John Buck RC .20 .50
T217 Freddie Bynum RC .15 .40
T218 Noel Devarez RC .15 .40
T219 Juan Diaz RC .15 .40
T220 Felix Diaz RC .15 .40
T221 Josh Fogg RC .15 .40
T222 Matt Ford RC .15 .40
T223 Scott Heard .15 .40
T224 Ben Hendrickson RC .15 .40
T225 Cody Ross RC .60 1.50
T226 Adrian Hernandez RC .15 .40
T227 Alfredo Amezaga RC .15 .40
T228 Bob Keppel RC .15 .40
T229 Ryan Madson RC .30 .75
T230 Octavio Martinez RC .15 .40
T231 Hee Seop Choi .20 .50
T232 Thomas Mitchell .15 .40
T233 Luis Montanez .15 .40
T234 Andy Morales RC .15 .40
T235 Justin Morneau RC 3.00 8.00
T236 Toe Nash RC .15 .40
T237 Valentino Pascucci RC .15 .40
T238 Roy Smith RC .15 .40
T239 Antonio Perez RC .20 .50
T240 Chad Petty RC .15 .40
T241 Steve Smyth .15 .40
T242 Jose Reyes RC 3.00 8.00
T243 Eric Reynolds RC .15 .40
T244 Dominic Rich .15 .40
T245 Jason Richardson RC .15 .40
T246 Ed Rogers RC .15 .40
T247 Albert Pujols RC 125.00 300.00
T248 Esix Snead RC .15 .40
T249 Luis Torres RC .15 .40
T250 Matt White RC .15 .40
T251 Blake Williams .15 .40
T252 Chris Russ .15 .40
T253 Joe Kennedy RC .20 .50
T254 Jeff Randazzo RC .15 .40
T255 Beau Hale RC .15 .40
T256 Brad Hennessey RC .50 1.25
T257 Jake Gautreau RC .15 .40
T258 Jeff Mathis RC .20 .50
T259 Aaron Heilman RC .20 .50
T260 Bronson Sardinha RC .15 .40
T261 Irvin Guzman RC 1.50 4.00
T262 Gabe Gross RC .20 .50
T263 J.D. Martin RC .15 .40
T264 Chris Smith RC .15 .40
T265 Kenny Baugh RC .15 .40

2001 Topps Traded Gold

*STARS: 4X TO 10X BASIC CARDS
*REPRINTS: 1.5X TO 4X BASIC
*ROOKIES: 1X TO 2.5X BASIC
STATED ODDS 1:3
STATED PRINT RUN 2001 SERIAL #'d SETS
T247 Albert Pujols 750.00 2000.00

2001 Topps Traded Autographs

STATED ODDS 1:626
TTAJD Johnny Damon 10.00 25.00
TTAMM Mike Mussina 8.00 20.00

2001 Topps Traded Dual Jersey Relics

STATED ODDS 1:376
TTRBG Ben Grieve 6.00 15.00
TTRDH Dustin Hermanson 6.00 15.00
TTRFT Fernando Tatis 6.00 15.00
TTRMR Manny Ramirez 8.00 20.00

2001 Topps Traded Farewell Dual Bat Relic

STATED ODDS 1:4693
FRRG C.Ripken/T.Gwynn 25.00 60.00

2001 Topps Traded Hall of Fame Bat Relic

STATED ODDS 1:2796
HFRPW K.Puckett/D.Winfield 10.00 25.00

2001 Topps Traded Relics

STATED ODDS 1:29
AG Andres Galarraga Bat 4.00 10.00
BB1 Bobby Bonilla Bat 4.00 10.00
BB2 Bret Boone Jsy 4.00 10.00
BM Bill Mueller Jsy 6.00 15.00
CJ Charles Johnson Jsy 4.00 10.00
DB Derek Bell Bat 4.00 10.00
DN Denny Neagle Jsy 4.00 10.00
DW David Wells Jsy 4.00 10.00
ED Eric Davis Bat 4.00 10.00
EW Enrique Wilson Bat 4.00 10.00
FM Fred McGriff Bat 6.00 15.00
GW Gerald Williams Bat 4.00 10.00
HR Hideo Nomo Jsy 10.00 25.00
JC Jose Canseco Bat 6.00 15.00
JD Jermaine Dye Bat SP 4.00 10.00
JD1 Johnny Damon Bat 6.00 15.00
JD2 Johnny Damon Jsy 6.00 15.00
JG Juan Gonzalez Bat 4.00 10.00
JH Jeffrey Hammonds Jsy 4.00 10.00
KC Ken Caminiti Bat 4.00 10.00
KS Kelly Stinnett Bat SP 4.00 10.00
MG1 Mark Grace Bat 6.00 15.00
MG2 Marquis Grissom Bat 4.00 10.00
MH Mike Hampton Jsy 4.00 10.00
MS Matt Stairs Jsy 4.00 10.00
NP Neifi Perez Bat 4.00 10.00
RB Rico Brogna Jsy 4.00 10.00
RG Ron Gant Bat 4.00 10.00
ROC Roger Cedeno Jsy 4.00 10.00
RS Ruben Sierra Bat 4.00 10.00
RSC Royce Clayton Bat 4.00 10.00
SA Sandy Alomar Jr. Bat 4.00 10.00
TH Todd Hundley Jsy 4.00 10.00
TR Tim Raines Jsy 4.00 10.00

2001 Topps Traded Rookie Relics

STATED ODDS 1:91
TRRAB Angel Berroa Jsy 4.00 10.00
TRRAP Albert Pujols Bat SP 50.00 120.00
TRRBO Bill Ortega Jsy 3.00 8.00
TRRER Ed Rogers Bat SP 4.00 10.00
TRRHC Humberto Cota Jsy 3.00 8.00
TRRJL Jason Lane Jsy 3.00 8.00
TRRJS Jae Seo Jsy 3.00 8.00
TRRJS Jamal Strong Jsy 3.00 8.00
TRRJV Jose Valverde Jsy 3.00 8.00
TRRJY Jason Young Jsy 3.00 8.00
TRRNC Nate Cornejo Jsy 3.00 8.00
TRRNN Nick Neugebauer Jsy 3.00 8.00
TRRPF Pedro Feliz Jsy SP 3.00 8.00
TRRRS Richard Stahl Jsy 3.00 8.00
TRRSB Sean Burroughs Jsy 3.00 8.00
TRRTS Tsuyoshi Shinjo Bat SP 4.00 10.00
TRRWB Wilson Betemit Bat 4.00 10.00
TRRWR Wilkin Ruan Jsy 3.00 8.00

2001 Topps Traded Who Would Have Thought

COMPLETE SET (20) 12.00 30.00
STATED ODDS 1:8
WWHT1 Nolan Ryan 2.50 6.00
WWHT2 Ozzie Smith 1.50 4.00
WWHT3 Tom Seaver .60 1.50
WWHT4 Steve Carlton .60 1.50
WWHT5 Reggie Jackson .60 1.50
WWHT6 Frank Robinson .60 1.50
WWHT7 Keith Hernandez .60 1.50
WWHT8 Andre Dawson .60 1.50
WWHT9 Lou Brock .60 1.50
WWHT10 Dennis Eckersley .60 1.50
WWHT11 Dave Winfield .60 1.50
WWHT12 Rod Carew .60 1.50
WWHT13 Willie Randolph .60 1.50
WWHT14 Dwight Gooden .60 1.50
WWHT15 Carlton Fisk .60 1.50
WWHT16 Dale Murphy .60 1.50
WWHT17 Paul Molitor .60 1.50
WWHT18 Gary Carter .60 1.50
WWHT19 Wade Boggs .60 1.50
WWHT20 Willie Mays 2.00 5.00

2002 Topps Promos

COMPLETE SET (3) 1.50 3.00
P1 Sammy Sosa .50 1.25
P2 Jason Giambi .40 1.00
P3 Curt Schilling .50 1.25

2002 Topps

COMPLETE SET (718) 25.00 60.00
COMP.FACT.BROWN SET (723) 40.00 80.00
COMP.FACT.GREEN SET (723) 40.00 80.00
COMPLETE SERIES 1 (364) 12.50 30.00
COMPLETE SERIES 2 (354) 12.50 30.00
COMMON CARD (1-6/8-719) .07 .20
COMMON (307-331/671-695) .20 .50
COMMON CARD (332-364) .20 .50
CARD NUMBER 7 DOES NOT EXIST
CARD 365 AVAIL. IN 73 VARIATIONS
SER.1 SET INCLUDES 1 CARD 365 VARIATION
BUYBACK SER.1 ODDS 1:616 HOB
BUYBACK SER.1 ODDS 1:169 HTA, 1:484 RET
BUYBACK SER.2 ODDS 1:431 HOB
BUYBACK SER.2 ODDS 1:113 HTA, 1:331 RET
1 Pedro Martinez .10 .30
2 Mike Stanton .07 .20
3 Brad Penny .07 .20
4 Mike Matheny .07 .20
5 Johnny Damon .10 .30
6 Bret Boone .07 .20
8 Chris Truby .07 .20
9 B.J. Surhoff .07 .20
10 Mike Hampton .07 .20
11 Juan Pierre .07 .20
12 Mark Buehrle .07 .20
13 Bob Abreu .07 .20
14 David Cone .07 .20
15 Aaron Sele .07 .20
16 Fernando Tatis .07 .20
17 Bobby Jones .07 .20
18 Rick Helling .07 .20
19 Dmitri Young .07 .20
20 Mike Mussina .10 .30
21 Mike Sweeney .07 .20
22 Cristian Guzman .07 .20
23 Ryan Kohlmeier .07 .20
24 Adam Kennedy .07 .20
25 Larry Walker .07 .20
26 Eric Davis .07 .20
27 Jason Tyner .07 .20
28 Eric Young .07 .20
29 Jason Marquis .07 .20
30 Luis Gonzalez .07 .20
31 Kevin Tapani .07 .20
32 Orlando Cabrera .07 .20
33 Marty Cordova .07 .20
34 Brad Ausmus .07 .20
35 Livan Hernandez .07 .20
36 Alex Gonzalez .07 .20
37 Edgar Renteria .07 .20
38 Bengie Molina .07 .20
39 Frank Menechino .07 .20
40 Rafael Palmeiro .10 .30
41 Brad Fullmer .07 .20
42 Julio Zuleta .07 .20
43 Darren Dreifort .07 .20
44 Trot Nixon .07 .20
45 Trevor Hoffman .07 .20
46 Vladimir Nunez .07 .20
47 Mark Kotsay .07 .20
48 Kenny Rogers .07 .20
49 Ben Petrick .07 .20
50 Jeff Bagwell .10 .30
51 Juan Encarnacion .07 .20
52 Ramiro Mendoza .07 .20
53 Brian Meadows .07 .20
54 Chad Curtis .07 .20
55 Aramis Ramirez .07 .20
56 Mark McLemore .07 .20
57 Dante Bichette .07 .20
58 Scott Schoeneweis .07 .20
59 Jose Cruz Jr. .07 .20
60 Roger Clemens .40 1.00
61 Jose Guillen .07 .20
62 Darren Oliver .07 .20
63 Chris Reitsma .07 .20
64 Jeff Abbott .07 .20
65 Robin Ventura .07 .20
66 Denny Neagle .07 .20
67 Al Martin .07 .20
68 Benito Santiago .07 .20
69 Roy Oswalt .07 .20
70 Juan Gonzalez .07 .20
71 Garret Anderson .07 .20
72 Bobby Bonilla .07 .20
73 Danny Bautista .07 .20
74 J.T. Snow .07 .20
75 Derek Jeter .50 1.25
76 John Olerud .07 .20
77 Kevin Appier .07 .20
78 Phil Nevin .07 .20
79 Sean Casey .07 .20
80 Troy Glaus .07 .20
81 Joe Randa .07 .20
82 Jose Valentin .07 .20
83 Ricky Bottalico .07 .20
84 Todd Zeile .07 .20
85 Barry Larkin .10 .30
86 Bob Wickman .07 .20
87 Jeff Shaw .07 .20
88 Greg Vaughn .07 .20
89 Fernando Vina .07 .20
90 Mark Mulder .07 .20
91 Paul Bako .07 .20
92 Aaron Boone .07 .20
93 Esteban Loaiza .07 .20
94 Richie Sexson .07 .20
95 Alfonso Soriano .07 .20
96 Tony Womack .07 .20
97 Paul Shuey .07 .20
98 Melvin Mora .07 .20
99 Tony Gwynn .25 .60
100 Vladimir Guerrero .20 .50
101 Keith Osik .07 .20
102 Bud Smith .07 .20
103 Scott Williamson .07 .20
104 Daryle Ward .07 .20
105 Doug Mientkiewicz .07 .20
106 Stan Javier .07 .20
107 Russ Ortiz .07 .20
108 Wade Miller .07 .20
109 Luke Prokopec .07 .20
110 Andruw Jones .10 .30
111 Ron Coomer .07 .20
112 Dan Wilson .07 .20
113 Luis Castillo .07 .20
114 Derek Bell .07 .20
115 Gary Sheffield .07 .20
116 Ruben Rivera .07 .20
117 Paul O'Neill .10 .30
118 Craig Paquette .07 .20
119 Kelvin Escobar .07 .20
120 Brad Radke .07 .20
121 Jorge Fabregas .07 .20
122 Randy Winn .07 .20
123 Tom Goodwin .07 .20
124 Jaret Wright .07 .20
125 Manny Ramirez .10 .30
126 Al Leiter .07 .20
127 Ben Davis .07 .20
128 Frank Catalanotto .07 .20
129 Jose Cabrera .07 .20
130 Magglio Ordonez .07 .20
131 Jose Macias .07 .20
132 Ted Lilly .07 .20
133 Chris Holt .07 .20
134 Eric Milton .07 .20
135 Shannon Stewart .07 .20
136 Omar Olivares .07 .20
137 David Segui .07 .20
138 Jeff Nelson .07 .20
139 Matt Williams .07 .20
140 Ellis Burks .07 .20
141 Jason Bere .07 .20
142 Jimmy Haynes .07 .20
143 Ramon Hernandez .07 .20
144 Craig Counsell .07 .20
145 John Smoltz .10 .30
146 Homer Bush .07 .20
147 Quilvio Veras .07 .20
148 Esteban Yan .07 .20
149 Ramon Ortiz .07 .20
150 Carlos Delgado .07 .20
151 Lee Stevens .07 .20
152 Wil Cordero .07 .20
153 Mike Bordick .07 .20
154 John Flaherty .07 .20
155 Omar Daal .07 .20
156 Todd Ritchie .07 .20
157 Carl Everett .07 .20
158 Scott Sullivan .07 .20
159 Deivi Cruz .07 .20
160 Albert Pujols .40 1.00
161 Royce Clayton .07 .20
162 Jeff Suppan .07 .20
163 C.C. Sabathia .07 .20
164 Jimmy Rollins .07 .20
165 Rickey Henderson .20 .50
166 Rey Ordonez .07 .20
167 Shawn Estes .07 .20
168 Reggie Sanders .07 .20
169 Jon Lieber .07 .20
170 Armando Benitez .07 .20
171 Mike Remlinger .07 .20
172 Billy Wagner .07 .20
173 Troy Percival .07 .20
174 Devon White .07 .20
175 Ivan Rodriguez .10 .30
176 Dustin Hermanson .07 .20
177 Brian Anderson .07 .20
178 Graeme Lloyd .07 .20
179 Russell Branyan .07 .20
180 Bobby Higginson .07 .20
181 Alex Gonzalez .07 .20
182 John Franco .07 .20
183 Sidney Ponson .07 .20
184 Jose Mesa .07 .20
185 Todd Hollandsworth .07 .20
186 Kevin Young .07 .20
187 Tim Wakefield .07 .20
188 Craig Biggio .10 .30
189 Jason Isringhausen .07 .20
190 Mark Quinn .07 .20
191 Glendon Rusch .07 .20
192 Damian Miller .07 .20
193 Sandy Alomar Jr. .07 .20
194 Scott Brosius .07 .20
195 Dave Martinez .07 .20
196 Danny Graves .07 .20
197 Shea Hillenbrand .07 .20
198 Jimmy Anderson .07 .20
199 Travis Lee .07 .20
200 Randy Johnson .20 .50
201 Carlos Beltran .07 .20
202 Jerry Hairston .07 .20
203 Jesus Sanchez .07 .20
204 Eddie Taubensee .07 .20
205 David Wells .07 .20
206 Russ Davis .07 .20
207 Michael Barrett .07 .20
208 Marquis Grissom .07 .20
209 Byung-Hyun Kim .07 .20
210 Hideo Nomo .20 .50
211 Ryan Rupe .07 .20
212 Ricky Gutierrez .07 .20
213 Darryl Kile .07 .20
214 Rico Brogna .07 .20
215 Terrence Long .07 .20
216 Mike Jackson .07 .20
217 Jamey Wright .07 .20
218 Adrian Beltre .07 .20
219 Benny Agbayani .07 .20
220 Chuck Knoblauch .07 .20
221 Randy Wolf .07 .20
222 Andy Ashby .07 .20
223 Corey Koskie .07 .20
224 Roger Cedeno .07 .20
225 Ichiro Suzuki .40 1.00
226 Keith Foulke .07 .20
227 Ryan Minor .07 .20
228 Shawon Dunston .07 .20
229 Alex Cora .07 .20
230 Jeromy Burnitz .07 .20
231 Mark Grace .10 .30
232 Aubrey Huff .07 .20
233 Jeffrey Hammonds .07 .20
234 Olmedo Saenz .07 .20
235 Brian Jordan .07 .20
236 Jeremy Giambi .07 .20
237 Joe Girardi .07 .20
238 Eric Gagne .07 .20
239 Masato Yoshii .07 .20
240 Greg Maddux .30 .75
241 Bryan Rekar .07 .20
242 Ray Durham .07 .20
243 Torii Hunter .07 .20
244 Derrek Lee .10 .30
245 Jim Edmonds .07 .20
246 Einar Diaz .07 .20
247 Brian Bohanon .07 .20
248 Ron Belliard .07 .20
249 Mike Lowell .07 .20
250 Sammy Sosa .20 .50
251 Richard Hidalgo .07 .20
252 Bartolo Colon .07 .20
253 Jorge Posada .10 .30
254 LaTroy Hawkins .07 .20
255 Paul LoDuca .07 .20
256 Carlos Febles .07 .20
257 Nelson Cruz .07 .20
258 Edgardo Alfonzo .07 .20
259 Joey Hamilton .07 .20
260 Cliff Floyd .07 .20
261 Wes Helms .07 .20
262 Jay Bell .07 .20
263 Mike Cameron .07 .20
264 Paul Konerko .07 .20
265 Jeff Kent .07 .20
266 Robert Fick .07 .20
267 Allen Levrault .07 .20
268 Placido Polanco .07 .20
269 Marlon Anderson .07 .20
270 Mariano Rivera .20 .50
271 Chan Ho Park .07 .20
272 Jose Vizcaino .07 .20
273 Jeff D'Amico .07 .20
274 Mark Gardner .07 .20
275 Travis Fryman .07 .20
276 Darren Lewis .07 .20
277 Bruce Bochy MG .07 .20
278 Jerry Manuel MG .07 .20
279 Bob Brenly MG .07 .20
280 Don Baylor MG .07 .20
281 Davey Lopes MG .07 .20
282 Jerry Narron MG .07 .20
283 Tony Muser MG .07 .20
284 Hal McRae MG .07 .20
285 Bobby Cox MG .07 .20
286 Larry Dierker MG .07 .20
287 Phil Garner MG .07 .20
288 Joe Kerrigan MG .07 .20
289 Bobby Valentine MG .07 .20
290 Dusty Baker MG .07 .20
291 Lloyd McClendon MG .07 .20
292 Mike Scioscia MG .07 .20
293 Buck Martinez MG .07 .20
294 Larry Bowa MG .07 .20
295 Tony LaRussa MG .07 .20
296 Jeff Torborg MG .07 .20

297 Tom Kelly MG .07 .20
298 Mike Hargrove MG .07 .20
299 Art Howe MG .07 .20
300 Lou Piniella MG .07 .20
301 Charlie Manuel MG .07 .20
302 Buddy Bell MG .07 .20
303 Tony Perez MG .07 .20
304 Bob Boone MG .07 .20
305 Joe Torre MG .10 .30
306 Jim Tracy MG .07 .20
307 Jason Lane PROS .20 .50
308 Chris George PROS .20 .50
309 Hank Blalock PROS .40 1.00
310 Joe Borchard PROS .20 .50
311 Marlon Byrd PROS .20 .50
312 Raymond Cabrera PROS RC .20 .50
313 Freddy Sanchez PROS RC .75 2.00
314 Scott Wiggins PROS RC .20 .50
315 Jason Maule PROS RC .20 .50
316 Dionys Cesar PROS RC .20 .50
317 Boof Bonser PROS .20 .50
318 Juan Tolentino PROS RC .20 .50
319 Earl Snyder PROS RC .20 .50
320 Travis Wade PROS RC .20 .50
321 Napoleon Calzado PROS RC .20 .50
322 Eric Glaser PROS RC .20 .50
323 Craig Kuzmic PROS RC .20 .50
324 Nic Jackson PROS RC .20 .50
325 Mike Rivera PROS .20 .50
326 Jason Bay PROS RC 1.50 4.00
327 Chris Smith DP .20 .50
328 Jake Gautreau DP .20 .50
329 Gabe Gross DP .20 .50
330 Kenny Baugh DP .20 .50
331 J.D. Martin DP .20 .50
332 Barry Bonds HL .50 1.25
333 Rickey Henderson HL .20 .50
334 Bud Smith HL .20 .50
335 Rickey Henderson HL .20 .50
336 Barry Bonds HL .50 1.25
337 Ichiro .20 .50
Giambi/Alomar LL
338 A.Rod .15 .40
Ichiro/Boone LL
339 A.Rod .15 .40
Thome/Palmeiro LL
340 Boone .15 .40
J.Gonz/A.Rod LL
341 Garcia .20 .50
Mussina/Mays LL
342 Nomo .20 .50
Mussina/Clemens LL
343 Walker .20 .50
Helton/Alou/Berk LL
344 Sosa .30 .75
Helton/Bonds LL
345 Bonds .30 .75
Sosa/L.Gonz LL
346 Sosa .20 .50
Helton/L.Gonz LL
347 R.John .20 .50
Schilling/Burkett LL
348 R.John .20 .50
Schilling/Park LL
349 Seattle Mariners PB .20 .50
350 Oakland Athletics PB .20 .50
351 New York Yankees PB .20 .50
352 Cleveland Indians PB .20 .50
353 Arizona Diamondbacks PB .20 .50
354 Atlanta Braves PB .20 .50
355 St. Louis Cardinals PB .20 .50
356 Houston Astros PB .20 .50
357 Diamondbacks-Astros UWS .20 .50
358 Mike Piazza UWS .20 .50
359 Braves-Phillies UWS .20 .50
360 Curt Schilling UWS .20 .50
361 R.Clemens .20 .50
L.Mazzilli UWS
362 Sammy Sosa UWS .10 .30
363 Lampkin .20 .50
Ichiro/Boone UWS
364 B.Bonds .30 .75
J.Bagwell UWS
365 Barry Bonds HR 1 6.00 15.00
365 Barry Bonds HR 2 4.00 10.00
365 Barry Bonds HR 3 4.00 10.00
365 Barry Bonds HR 4 4.00 10.00
365 Barry Bonds HR 5 4.00 10.00
365 Barry Bonds HR 6 4.00 10.00
365 Barry Bonds HR 7 4.00 10.00
365 Barry Bonds HR 8 4.00 10.00
365 Barry Bonds HR 9 4.00 10.00
365 Barry Bonds HR 10 4.00 10.00
365 Barry Bonds HR 11 4.00 10.00
365 Barry Bonds HR 12 4.00 10.00
365 Barry Bonds HR 13 4.00 10.00
365 Barry Bonds HR 14 4.00 10.00
365 Barry Bonds HR 15 4.00 10.00
365 Barry Bonds HR 16 4.00 10.00
365 Barry Bonds HR 17 4.00 10.00
365 Barry Bonds HR 18 4.00 10.00
365 Barry Bonds HR 19 4.00 10.00
365 Barry Bonds HR 20 4.00 10.00
365 Barry Bonds HR 21 4.00 10.00
365 Barry Bonds HR 22 4.00 10.00
365 Barry Bonds HR 23 4.00 10.00
365 Barry Bonds HR 24 4.00 10.00
365 Barry Bonds HR 25 4.00 10.00
365 Barry Bonds HR 26 4.00 10.00
365 Barry Bonds HR 27 4.00 10.00
365 Barry Bonds HR 28 4.00 10.00
365 Barry Bonds HR 29 4.00 10.00
365 Barry Bonds HR 30 4.00 10.00
365 Barry Bonds HR 31 4.00 10.00
365 Barry Bonds HR 32 4.00 10.00
365 Barry Bonds HR 33 4.00 10.00
365 Barry Bonds HR 34 4.00 10.00
365 Barry Bonds HR 35 4.00 10.00
365 Barry Bonds HR 36 4.00 10.00
365 Barry Bonds HR 37 4.00 10.00
365 Barry Bonds HR 38 4.00 10.00
365 Barry Bonds HR 39 4.00 10.00
365 Barry Bonds HR 40 4.00 10.00
365 Barry Bonds HR 41 4.00 10.00
365 Barry Bonds HR 42 4.00 10.00
365 Barry Bonds HR 43 4.00 10.00
365 Barry Bonds HR 44 4.00 10.00
365 Barry Bonds HR 45 4.00 10.00
365 Barry Bonds HR 46 4.00 10.00
365 Barry Bonds HR 47 4.00 10.00
365 Barry Bonds HR 48 4.00 10.00
365 Barry Bonds HR 49 4.00 10.00
365 Barry Bonds HR 50 4.00 10.00
365 Barry Bonds HR 51 4.00 10.00
365 Barry Bonds HR 52 4.00 10.00
365 Barry Bonds HR 53 4.00 10.00
365 Barry Bonds HR 54 4.00 10.00
365 Barry Bonds HR 55 4.00 10.00
365 Barry Bonds HR 56 4.00 10.00
365 Barry Bonds HR 57 4.00 10.00
365 Barry Bonds HR 58 4.00 10.00
365 Barry Bonds HR 59 4.00 10.00
365 Barry Bonds HR 60 4.00 10.00
365 Barry Bonds HR 61 6.00 15.00
365 Barry Bonds HR 62 4.00 10.00
365 Barry Bonds HR 63 4.00 10.00
365 Barry Bonds HR 64 4.00 10.00
365 Barry Bonds HR 65 4.00 10.00
365 Barry Bonds HR 66 4.00 10.00
365 Barry Bonds HR 67 4.00 10.00
365 Barry Bonds HR 68 4.00 10.00
365 Barry Bonds HR 69 4.00 10.00
365 Barry Bonds HR 70 6.00 15.00
365 Barry Bonds HR 71 4.00 10.00
365 Barry Bonds HR 72 4.00 10.00
365 Barry Bonds HR 73 5.00 12.00
366 Pat Meares .07 .20
367 Mike Lieberthal .07 .20
368 Larry Bigbie .07 .20
369 Ron Gant .07 .20
370 Moises Alou .07 .20
371 Chad Kreuter .07 .20
372 Willis Roberts .07 .20
373 Toby Hall .07 .20
374 Miguel Batista .07 .20
375 John Burkett .07 .20
376 Cory Lidle .07 .20
377 Nick Neugebauer .07 .20
378 Jay Payton .07 .20
379 Steve Karsay .07 .20
380 Eric Chavez .07 .20
381 Kelly Stinnett .07 .20
382 Jarrod Washburn .07 .20
383 Rick White .07 .20
384 Jeff Conine .07 .20
385 Fred McGriff .10 .30
386 Marvin Benard .07 .20
387 Joe Crede .07 .20
388 Dennis Cook .07 .20
389 Rick Reed .07 .20
390 Tom Glavine .10 .30
391 Rondell White .07 .20
392 Matt Morris .07 .20
393 Pat Rapp .07 .20
394 Robert Person .07 .20
395 Omar Vizquel .10 .30
396 Jeff Cirillo .07 .20
397 Dave Mlicki .07 .20
398 Jose Ortiz .07 .20
399 Ryan Dempster .07 .20
400 Curt Schilling .07 .20
401 Peter Bergeron .07 .20
402 Kyle Lohse .07 .20
403 Craig Wilson .07 .20
404 David Justice .07 .20
405 Darin Erstad .07 .20
406 Jose Mercedes .07 .20
407 Carl Pavano .07 .20
408 Albie Lopez .07 .20
409 Alex Ochoa .07 .20
410 Chipper Jones .20 .50
411 Tyler Houston .07 .20
412 Dean Palmer .07 .20
413 Damian Jackson .07 .20
414 Josh Towers .07 .20
415 Rafael Furcal .07 .20
416 Mike Morgan .07 .20
417 Herb Perry .07 .20
418 Mike Sirotka .07 .20
419 Mark Wohlers .07 .20
420 Nomar Garciaparra .30 .75
421 Felipe Lopez .07 .20
422 Joe McEwing .07 .20
423 Jacque Jones .07 .20
424 Julio Franco .07 .20
425 Frank Thomas .20 .50
426 So Taguchi RC .30 .75
427 Kazuhisa Ishii RC .20 .50
428 D'Angelo Jimenez .07 .20
429 Chris Stynes .07 .20
430 Kerry Wood .07 .20
431 Chris Singleton .07 .20
432 Erubiel Durazo .07 .20
433 Matt Lawton .07 .20
434 Bill Mueller .07 .20
435 Jose Canseco .10 .30
436 Ben Grieve .07 .20
437 Terry Mulholland .07 .20
438 David Bell .07 .20
439 A.J. Pierzynski .07 .20
440 Adam Dunn .07 .20
441 Jon Garland .07 .20
442 Jeff Fassero .07 .20
443 Julio Lugo .07 .20
444 Carlos Guillen .07 .20
445 Orlando Hernandez .07 .20
446 M.Loretta UER Leskanic .07 .20
447 Scott Spiezio .07 .20
448 Kevin Millwood .07 .20
449 Jamie Moyer .07 .20
450 Todd Helton .10 .30
451 Todd Walker .07 .20
452 Jose Lima .07 .20
453 Brook Fordyce .07 .20
454 Aaron Rowand .07 .20
455 Barry Zito .07 .20
456 Eric Owens .07 .20
457 Charles Nagy .07 .20
458 Raul Ibanez .07 .20
459 Joe Mays .07 .20
460 Jim Thome .10 .30
461 Adam Eaton .07 .20
462 Felix Martinez .07 .20
463 Vernon Wells .07 .20
464 Donnie Sadler .07 .20
465 Tony Clark .07 .20
466 Jose Hernandez .07 .20
467 Ramon Martinez .07 .20
468 Rusty Greer .07 .20
469 Rod Barajas .07 .20
470 Lance Berkman .07 .20
471 Brady Anderson .07 .20
472 Pedro Astacio .07 .20
473 Shane Halter .07 .20
474 Bret Prinz .07 .20
475 Edgar Martinez .10 .30
476 Steve Trachsel .07 .20
477 Gary Matthews Jr. .07 .20
478 Ismael Valdes .07 .20
479 Juan Uribe .07 .20
480 Shawn Green .07 .20
481 Kirk Rueter .07 .20
482 Damion Easley .07 .20
483 Chris Carpenter .07 .20
484 Kris Benson .07 .20
485 Antonio Alfonseca .07 .20
486 Kyle Farnsworth .07 .20
487 Brandon Lyon .07 .20
488 Hideki Irabu .07 .20
489 David Ortiz .20 .50
490 Mike Piazza .30 .75
491 Derek Lowe .07 .20
492 Chris Gomez .07 .20
493 Mark Johnson .07 .20
494 John Rocker .07 .20
495 Eric Karros .07 .20
496 Bill Haselman .07 .20
497 Dave Veres .07 .20
498 Pete Harnisch .07 .20
499 Tomokazu Ohka .07 .20
500 Barry Bonds .50 1.25
501 David Dellucci .07 .20
502 Wendell Magee .07 .20
503 Tom Gordon .07 .20
504 Javier Vazquez .07 .20
505 Ben Sheets .07 .20
506 Wilton Guerrero .07 .20
507 John Halama .07 .20
508 Mark Redman .07 .20
509 Jack Wilson .07 .20
510 Bernie Williams .10 .30
511 Miguel Cairo .07 .20
512 Denny Hocking .07 .20
513 Tony Batista .07 .20
514 Mark Grudzielanek .07 .20
515 Jose Vidro .07 .20
516 Sterling Hitchcock .07 .20
517 Billy Koch .07 .20
518 Matt Clement .07 .20
519 Bruce Chen .07 .20
520 Roberto Alomar .10 .30
521 Orlando Palmeiro .07 .20
522 Steve Finley .07 .20
523 Danny Patterson .07 .20
524 Terry Adams .07 .20
525 Tino Martinez .10 .30
526 Tony Armas Jr. .07 .20
527 Geoff Jenkins .07 .20
528 Kerry Robinson .07 .20
529 Corey Patterson .07 .20
530 Brian Giles .07 .20
531 Jose Jimenez .07 .20
532 Joe Kennedy .07 .20
533 Armando Rios .07 .20
534 Osvaldo Fernandez .07 .20
535 Ruben Sierra .07 .20
536 Octavio Dotel .07 .20
537 Luis Sojo .07 .20
538 Brent Butler .07 .20
539 Pablo Ozuna .07 .20
540 Freddy Garcia .07 .20
541 Chad Durbin .07 .20
542 Orlando Merced .07 .20
543 Michael Tucker .07 .20
544 Roberto Hernandez .07 .20
545 Pat Burrell .07 .20
546 A.J. Burnett .07 .20
547 Bubba Trammell .07 .20
548 Scott Elarton .07 .20
549 Mike Darr .07 .20
550 Ken Griffey Jr. .40 1.00
551 Ugueth Urbina .07 .20
552 Todd Jones .07 .20
553 Delino Deshields .07 .20
554 Adam Piatt .07 .20
555 Jason Kendall .07 .20
556 Hector Ortiz .07 .20
557 Turk Wendell .07 .20
558 Rob Bell .07 .20
559 Sun Woo Kim .07 .20
560 Raul Mondesi .07 .20
561 Brent Abernathy .07 .20
562 Seth Etherton .07 .20
563 Shawn Wooten .07 .20
564 Jay Buhner .07 .20
565 Andres Galarraga .07 .20
566 Shane Reynolds .07 .20
567 Rod Beck .07 .20
568 Dee Brown .07 .20
569 Pedro Feliz .07 .20
570 Ryan Klesko .07 .20
571 John Vander Wal .07 .20
572 Nick Bierbrodt .07 .20
573 Joe Nathan .07 .20
574 James Baldwin .07 .20
575 J.D. Drew .07 .20
576 Greg Colbrunn .07 .20
577 Doug Glanville .07 .20
578 Brandon Duckworth .07 .20
579 Shawn Chacon .07 .20
580 Rich Aurilia .07 .20
581 Chuck Finley .07 .20
582 Abraham Nunez .07 .20
583 Kenny Lofton .07 .20
584 Brian Daubach .07 .20
585 Miguel Tejada .07 .20
586 Nate Cornejo .07 .20
587 Kazuhiro Sasaki .07 .20
588 Chris Richard .07 .20
589 Armando Reynoso .07 .20
590 Tim Hudson .07 .20
591 Neifi Perez .07 .20
592 Steve Cox .07 .20
593 Henry Blanco .07 .20
594 Ricky Ledee .07 .20
595 Tim Salmon .10 .30
596 Luis Rivas .07 .20
597 Jeff Zimmerman .07 .20
598 Matt Stairs .07 .20
599 Preston Wilson .07 .20
600 Mark McGwire .50 1.25
601 Timo Perez .07 .20
602 Matt Anderson .07 .20
603 Todd Hundley .07 .20
604 Rick Ankiel .07 .20
605 Tsuyoshi Shinjo .07 .20
606 Woody Williams .07 .20
607 Jason LaRue .07 .20
608 Carlos Lee .07 .20
609 Russ Johnson .07 .20
610 Scott Rolen .10 .30
611 Brent Mayne .07 .20
612 Darrin Fletcher .07 .20
613 Ray Lankford .07 .20
614 Troy O'Leary .07 .20
615 Javier Lopez .07 .20
616 Randy Velarde .07 .20
617 Vinny Castilla .07 .20
618 Milton Bradley .07 .20
619 Ruben Mateo .07 .20
620 Jason Giambi Yankees .07 .20
621 Andy Benes .07 .20
622 Joe Mauer RC 5.00 12.00
623 Andy Pettitte .10 .30
624 Jose Offerman .07 .20
625 Mo Vaughn .07 .20
626 Steve Sparks .07 .20
627 Mike Matthews .07 .20
628 Robb Nen .07 .20
629 Kip Wells .07 .20
630 Kevin Brown .07 .20
631 Arthur Rhodes .07 .20
632 Gabe Kapler .07 .20
633 Jermaine Dye .07 .20
634 Josh Beckett .07 .20
635 Pokey Reese .07 .20
636 Benji Gil .07 .20
637 Marcus Giles .07 .20
638 Julian Tavarez .07 .20
639 Jason Schmidt .07 .20
640 Alex Rodriguez .25 .60
641 Anaheim Angels TC .07 .20
642 Arizona Diamondbacks TC .10 .30
643 Atlanta Braves TC .07 .20
644 Baltimore Orioles TC .07 .20
645 Boston Red Sox TC .07 .20
646 Chicago Cubs TC .07 .20
647 Chicago White Sox TC .07 .20
648 Cincinnati Reds TC .07 .20
649 Cleveland Indians TC .07 .20
650 Colorado Rockies TC .07 .20
651 Detroit Tigers TC .07 .20
652 Florida Marlins TC .07 .20
653 Houston Astros TC .07 .20
654 Kansas City Royals TC .07 .20
655 Los Angeles Dodgers TC .07 .20
656 Milwaukee Brewers TC .07 .20
657 Minnesota Twins TC .07 .20
658 Montreal Expos TC .07 .20
659 New York Mets TC .07 .20
660 New York Yankees TC .20 .50
661 Oakland Athletics TC .07 .20
662 Philadelphia Phillies TC .07 .20
663 Pittsburgh Pirates TC .07 .20
664 San Diego Padres TC .07 .20
665 San Francisco Giants TC .07 .20
666 Seattle Mariners TC .10 .30
667 St. Louis Cardinals TC .07 .20
668 Tampa Bay Devil Rays TC .07 .20
669 Texas Rangers TC .07 .20
670 Toronto Blue Jays TC .07 .20
671 Juan Cruz PROS .20 .50
672 Kevin Cash PROS RC .20 .50
673 Jimmy Gobble PROS RC .20 .50
674 Mike Hill PROS RC .20 .50
675 Taylor Buchholz PROS RC .20 .50
676 Bill Hall PROS .20 .50
677 Brett Roneberg PROS RC .20 .50
678 Royce Huffman PROS RC .20 .50
679 Chris Tritle PROS RC .20 .50
680 Nate Espy PROS RC .20 .50
681 Nick Alvarez PROS RC .20 .50
682 Jason Botts PROS RC .20 .50
683 Ryan Gripp PROS RC .20 .50
684 Dan Phillips PROS RC .20 .50
685 Pablo Arias PROS RC .20 .50
686 John Rodriguez PROS RC .20 .50
687 Rich Harden PROS RC 1.25 3.00
688 Neal Frendling PROS RC .20 .50
689 Rich Thompson PROS RC .20 .50
690 Greg Montalbano PROS RC .20 .50
691 Len Dinardo DP RC .20 .50
692 Ryan Raburn DP RC .40 1.00
693 Josh Barfield DP RC 1.00 2.50
694 David Bacani DP RC .20 .50
695 Dan Johnson DP RC .40 1.00
696 Mike Mussina GG .07 .20
697 Ivan Rodriguez GG .10 .30
698 Doug Mientkiewicz GG .07 .20
699 Roberto Alomar GG .07 .20
700 Eric Chavez GG .07 .20
701 Omar Vizquel GG .07 .20
702 Mike Cameron GG .07 .20
703 Torii Hunter GG .07 .20
704 Ichiro Suzuki GG .20 .50
705 Greg Maddux GG .20 .50
706 Brad Ausmus GG .07 .20
707 Todd Helton GG .07 .20
708 Fernando Vina GG .07 .20
709 Scott Rolen GG .07 .20
710 Orlando Cabrera GG .07 .20
711 Andruw Jones GG .07 .20
712 Jim Edmonds GG .07 .20
713 Larry Walker GG .07 .20
714 Roger Clemens CY .20 .50
715 Randy Johnson CY .10 .30
716 Ichiro Suzuki MVP .20 .50
717 Barry Bonds MVP .30 .75
718 Ichiro Suzuki ROY .20 .50
719 Albert Pujols ROY .20 .50

2002 Topps Gold

*GOLD 1-306/366-670: 8X TO 20X BASIC
*GOLD 307-330/671-695: 1.5X TO 4X BASIC
*GOLD 426-427: 1.5X TO 4X BASIC
SER.1 ODDS 1:19 HOB, 1:5 HTA, 1:15 RET
SER.2 ODDS 1:12 HOB, 1:3 HTA, 1:9 RET
STATED PRINT RUN 2002 SERIAL #'d SETS
622 Joe Mauer 12.00 30.00

2002 Topps Home Team Advantage

COMP.FACT.SET (718) 40.00 80.00
*HTA: .75X TO 2X BASIC
*BONDS HR 70: .2X TO .5X BASIC HR 70
DISTRIBUTED IN FACT.SET FORM
HTA FACT.SET IS BLUE BOXED

2002 Topps Limited

COMP.FACT.SET (790) 60.00 150.00
*LTD STARS: 1.5X TO 4X BASIC CARDS
*307-331/426-427/622/671-695: 1.5X TO 4X
*BONDS HR: .2X TO .5X BASIC BONDS HR
DISTRIBUTED ONLY IN FACTORY SET FORM
STATED PRINT RUN 1950 SETS
622 Joe Mauer 30.00 80.00

2002 Topps '52 Reprints

COMPLETE SET (19) 20.00 50.00
COMPLETE SERIES 1 (9) 10.00 25.00
COMPLETE SERIES 2 (10) 10.00 25.00
SER.1 ODDS 1:25 HOB, 1:5 HTA, 1:16 RET
SER.2 ODDS 1:25 HOB, 1:5 HTA, 1:16 RET
52R1 Roy Campanella 2.00 5.00
52R2 Duke Snider 1.50 4.00
52R3 Carl Erskine 1.50 4.00
52R4 Andy Pafko 1.50 4.00
52R5 Johnny Mize 1.50 4.00
52R6 Billy Martin 1.50 4.00
52R7 Phil Rizzuto 2.00 5.00
52R8 Gil McDougald 1.50 4.00
52R9 Allie Reynolds 1.50 4.00
52R10 Jackie Robinson 2.00 5.00
52R11 Preacher Roe 1.50 4.00
52R12 Gil Hodges 2.00 5.00
52R13 Billy Cox 1.50 4.00
52R14 Yogi Berra 2.00 5.00
52R15 Gene Woodling 1.50 4.00
52R16 Johnny Sain 1.50 4.00
52R17 Ralph Houk 1.50 4.00
52R18 Joe Collins 1.50 4.00
52R19 Hank Bauer 1.50 4.00

2002 Topps '52 Reprints Autographs

SER.1 ODDS 1:10,268 H, 1:2826 HTA, 1:8005 R
SER.2 ODDS 1:7524 H, 1:1985 HTA, 1:5839 R
SER.1 EXCH. DEADLINE 12/01/03
APA Andy Pafko S1 100.00 175.00
CEA Carl Erskine S1 50.00 100.00
DSA Duke Snider S1 25.00 60.00
GMA Gil McDougald S1 30.00 60.00
HBA Hank Bauer S2 15.00 60.00
JBA Joe Black S1 50.00 100.00
JSA Johnny Sain S2 12.00 30.00
PRA Preacher Roe S2 12.00 30.00
PRA Phil Rizzuto S1 40.00 100.00
RHA Ralph Houk S2 50.00 100.00
YBA Yogi Berra S2 60.00 120.00

2002 Topps '52 World Series Highlights

COMPLETE SET (7) 4.00 10.00
COMPLETE SERIES 1 (3) 1.50 4.00
COMPLETE SERIES 2 (4) 2.50 6.00
SER.1 ODDS 1:25 HOB, 1:5 HTA, 1:16 RET
SER.2 ODDS 1:25 HOB, 1:5 HTA, 1:16 RET
52WS1 Dodgers Line Up 1 .75 2.00
52WS2 Billy Martin's Homer 2 .75 2.00
52WS3 Dodgers Celebrate 1 .75 2.00
52WS4 Yanks Slip Dodgers 2 .75 2.00
52WS5 Carl Erskine 1 .75 2.00
52WS6 Stengel .75 2.00
Reynolds 2
52WS7 Reynolds Relieves 2 .75 2.00

2002 Topps 5-Card Stud Aces Relics

SER.2 ODDS 1:1180 H, 1:293 HTA, 1:966 R
5AGM Greg Maddux Jsy 12.50 30.00
5AMH Mike Hampton Jsy 10.00 25.00
5AMM Mark Mulder Jsy 10.00 25.00
5APM Pedro Martinez Jsy 15.00 40.00
5ARJ Randy Johnson Jsy 15.00 40.00

2002 Topps 5-Card Stud Deuces are Wild Relics

SER.2 A ODDS 1:3078 H, 1:796 HTA, 1:2422 R
SER.2 B ODDS 1:5410 H, 1:1254 HTA, 1:4827 R
SER.2 ODDS 1:1962 H, 1:487 HTA, 1:1609 R
5DBG B.Boone/F.Garcia A 15.00 40.00
5DBK B.Bonds/J.Kent A 40.00 80.00
5DJG R.Johnson/L.Gonzalez B 15.00 40.00
5DTA J.Thome/R.Alomar B 30.00 60.00
5DWH L.Walker/T.Helton B 30.00 60.00

2002 Topps 5-Card Stud Jack of All Trades Relics

SER.2 A ODDS 1:1454 H, 1:357 HTA, 1:1211 R
SER.2B ODDS 1:18883 H,1:4943 HTA,1:14736 R
SER.2 ODDS 1:1350 H, 1:333 HTA, 1:1119
5JAJ Andruw Jones A 10.00 25.00
5JBB Barry Bonds A 10.00 25.00
5JBW Bernie Williams A 10.00 25.00
5JIR Ivan Rodriguez A 10.00 25.00
5JRO Roberto Alomar B 10.00 25.00

2002 Topps 5-Card Stud Kings of the Clubhouse Relics

SER.2 A ODDS 1:1570 H, 1:358 HTA, 1:1211 R
SER.2B ODDS 1:18883 H,1:4943 HTA,1:14736 R
SER.2 ODDS 1:1449 H, 1:334 HTA, 1:1119 R
5KEM Edgar Martinez A 6.00 15.00
5KPO Paul O'Neill B 6.00 15.00
5KRJ Randy Johnson A 6.00 15.00
5KTG Tom Glavine A 6.00 15.00
5KTH Todd Helton A 6.00 15.00

2002 Topps 5-Card Stud Three of a Kind Relics

SER.2 A ODDS 1:3078 H, 1:796 HTA, 1:2422 R
SER.2 B ODDS 1:6043 H, 1:1532 HTA, 1:4827 R
SER.2 ODDS 1:2039 H, 1:524 HTA, 1:1609 R
5TBDB Burnett/Demp/Beckett A 30.00 60.00
5TFBJ Furcal/Betemit/A.Jones B 30.00 60.00
5TLOC Lee/Ordonez/Canseco B 30.00 60.00
5TPSW Posada/Soriano/Will B 30.00 60.00
5TSPA Shinjo/Piazza/Alfonzo A 30.00 60.00

2002 Topps All-World Team

COMPLETE SET (25) 30.00 60.00
SER.2 STATED ODDS 1:12 HOB/RET, 1:4 HTA
AW1 Ichiro Suzuki 1.50 4.00
AW2 Barry Bonds 2.00 5.00
AW3 Pedro Martinez .60 1.50
AW4 Juan Gonzalez .60 1.50
AW5 Larry Walker .60 1.50
AW6 Sammy Sosa .75 2.00
AW7 Mariano Rivera .75 2.00
AW8 Vladimir Guerrero .75 2.00
AW9 Alex Rodriguez 1.00 2.50
AW10 Albert Pujols 1.50 4.00
AW11 Luis Gonzalez .60 1.50
AW12 Ken Griffey Jr. 1.50 4.00
AW13 Kazuhiro Sasaki .60 1.50
AW14 Bob Abreu .60 1.50
AW15 Todd Helton .60 1.50
AW16 Nomar Garciaparra 1.25 3.00
AW17 Miguel Tejada .60 1.50
AW18 Roger Clemens 1.50 4.00
AW19 Mike Piazza 1.25 3.00
AW20 Carlos Delgado .60 1.50
AW21 Derek Jeter 2.00 5.00
AW22 Hideo Nomo .75 2.00
AW23 Randy Johnson .75 2.00
AW24 Ivan Rodriguez .60 1.50
AW25 Chan Ho Park .60 1.50

2002 Topps Autographs

C1 MINOR STARS 10.00 25.00
SER.1 A 1:15,402 H, 1:4256 HTA, 1:12,008 R
SER.2 A 1:10,071 H, 1:2404, 1:7702 R
SER.1 B 1:49,599 H, 1:12,312 HTA, 1:46,944 R
SER.2 B 1:1867 H, 1:487 HTA, 1:1449 R
SER.1 C 1:4104 H, 1:1130 HTA, 1:3238 R
SER.2 C 1:10,071 H, 1:2646 HTA, 1:7702 R
SER.1 D 1:9853 H, 1:2714 HTA, 1:7284 R
SER.2 D 1:1885 H, 1:496 HTA, 1:1449 R
SER.1 E 1:4104 H, 1:1130 HTA, 1:3238 R
SER.2 E 1:5023 H, 1:1323 HTA, 1:3851 R
SER.1 F 1:985 H, 1:271 HTA, 1:776 R
SER.2 F 1:940 H, 1:247 HTA, 1:725 R
SER.2 G 1:3017 H, 1:794 HTA, 1:2327 R
SER.1 EXCHANGE DEADLINE 12/01/03
NO A1 PRICING DUE TO SCARCITY
TA1 Carlos Delgado B1 6.00 15.00
TA3 Miguel Tejada C1 4.00 15.00
TA4 Geoff Jenkins E1 6.00 15.00
TA6 Tim Hudson C1 6.00 15.00
TA7 Terrence Long E1 4.00 10.00
TA8 Gabe Kapler C1 10.00 25.00
TA9 Magglio Ordonez C1 6.00 15.00
TA11 Pat Burrell C1 10.00 25.00
TA13 Eric Valent F1 4.00 10.00
TA14 Xavier Nady F1 4.00 10.00
TA15 Cristian Guerrero F1 4.00 10.00
TA16 Ben Sheets F1 6.00 15.00
TA17 Corey Patterson C1 6.00 15.00
TA18 Carlos Pena F1 4.00 10.00
TA19 Alex Rodriguez D1-A2 20.00 50.00
TAAB Adrian Beltre B2 6.00 15.00
TAAE Alex Escobar F2 4.00 10.00
TABG Brian Giles B2 6.00 15.00
TABW Brad Wilkerson G2 4.00 10.00
TACF Cliff Floyd C2 4.00 10.00
TACG Cristian Guzman B2 6.00 15.00
TAJD Jermaine Dye D2 4.00 10.00
TAJH Josh Hamilton 10.00 25.00
TAJO Jose Ortiz D2 6.00 15.00
TAJR Jimmy Rollins D2 10.00 25.00
TAJW Justin Wayne D2 6.00 15.00
TAKG Keith Ginter F2 4.00 10.00
TAMS Mike Sweeney B2 12.50 30.00
TANJ Nick Johnson F2 6.00 15.00
TARF Rafael Furcal B2 6.00 15.00
TARK Ryan Klesko B2 12.50 30.00
TARO Roy Oswalt F2 4.00 10.00
TARP Rafael Palmeiro A2 15.00 40.00
TARS Richie Sexson B2 12.50 30.00
TATG Troy Glaus A2 8.00 20.00
TABGR Ben Grieve B2 8.00 20.00

2002 Topps Coaches Collection Relics

SER.2 BAT ODDS 1:404 RETAIL
SER.2 UNIFORM ODDS 1:565 RETAIL
OVERALL SER.2 ODDS 1:236 RETAIL
CCAH Art Howe Bat 10.00 25.00
CCAT Alan Trammell Bat 15.00 40.00
CCBB Bruce Bochy Bat 10.00 25.00
CCBM Buck Martinez Bat 10.00 25.00
CCBV Bobby Valentine Bat 15.00 40.00
CCBW Billy Williams Jsy 15.00 40.00
CCBBE Buddy Bell Bat 15.00 40.00
CCBBR Bob Brenly Bat 15.00 40.00
CCDB Dusty Baker Bat 15.00 40.00
CCDL Davey Lopes Bat 15.00 40.00
CCDBA Don Baylor Bat 15.00 40.00
CCEH Elrod Hendricks Bat 10.00 25.00
CCEM Eddie Murray Bat 30.00 60.00
CCFW Frank White Bat 15.00 40.00
CCHM Hal McRae Jsy 4.00 10.00
CCJT Joe Torre Jsy 6.00 15.00
CCKG Ken Griffey Sr. Jsy 4.00 10.00
CCLB Larry Bowa Bat 15.00 40.00
CCLP Lance Parrish Bat 15.00 40.00
CCMH Mike Hargrove Bat 15.00 40.00
CCMS Mike Scioscia Bat 15.00 40.00
CCMW Mookie Wilson Bat 15.00 40.00
CCPG Phil Garner Bat 15.00 40.00
CCPM Paul Molitor Bat 15.00 40.00
CCTP Tony Perez Jsy 4.00 10.00
CCWR Willie Randolph Bat 15.00 40.00

2002 Topps Draft Picks

COMPLETE SET (10) 15.00 40.00
COMP.SERIES 1 SET (5) 6.00 15.00
COMP.SERIES 2 SET (5) 10.00 25.00
1-5 DIST.IN 02 TOPPS GREEN FACTORY SET
6-10 DIST.IN 02 TOPPS BLUE FACTORY SET
1 Scott Moore 2.00 5.00
2 Val Majewski 1.50 4.00
3 Brian Slocum 1.50 4.00
4 Chris Gruler 1.50 4.00
5 Mark Schramek 1.50 4.00
6 Joe Saunders 3.00 8.00
7 Jeff Francis 3.00 8.00
8 Royce Ring 1.50 4.00
9 Greg Miller 1.50 4.00
10 Brandon Weeden 1.50 4.00

2002 Topps East Meets West

COMPLETE SET (8) 6.00 15.00
SER.1 STATED ODDS 1:24 HOB/HTA/RET
EWHI H.Irabu .75 2.00
M.Murakami
EWHN H.Nomo .75 2.00
M.Murakami
EWKS K.Sasaki .75 2.00
M.Murakami
EWMS M.Suzuki .75 2.00
M.Murakami
EWMY M.Yoshii .75 2.00
M.Murakami
EWSH S.Hasagawa .75 2.00
M.Murakami
EWTO T.Ohka .75 2.00
M.Murakami
EWTS T.Shinjo .75 2.00
M.Murakami

2002 Topps East Meets West Relics

SR1 BAT 1:12296 H,1:3380 HTA,1:9606 R
SER.1 JSY 1:3419 H, 1:939 HTA, 1:2685 R
EWRHN Hideo Nomo Jsy 20.00 50.00
EWRKS Kazuhiro Sasaki Jsy 10.00 25.00
EWRTS Tsuyoshi Shinjo Bat 10.00 25.00

2002 Topps Ebbets Field Seat Relics

SER.1 ODDS 1:9116 H, 1:2516 HTA, 1:7222 R
EFRAP Andy Pafko 75.00 150.00
EFRBC Billy Cox 200.00 300.00
EFRCF Carl Furillo 75.00 150.00
EFRDS Duke Snider 150.00 250.00
EFRGH Gil Hodges 150.00 250.00
EFRJB Joe Black 75.00 150.00
EFRJR Jackie Robinson 200.00 300.00
EFRRC Roy Campanella 200.00 300.00
EFRPWR Pee Wee Reese 200.00 300.00

2002 Topps Hall of Fame Vintage BuyBacks AutoProofs

SER.1 ODDS 1:2,341 H, 1:643 HTA, 1:1841 R
SER.2 ODDS 1:2,431 H, 1:641 HTA, 1:1866 R
SEE BECKETT.COM FOR CHECKLIST
SEEDED IN MANY 2002 TOPPS BRANDS
BW1 Billy Williams 74 AS/100 20.00 50.00
BW2 Billy Williams 76/100 20.00 50.00
EW8 Earl Weaver 83/100 6.00 15.00
JP3 Jim Palmer 82 IA/100 10.00 25.00
OC2 Orl Cepeda 82 KM/200 10.00 25.00
SA1 Sparky Anderson 85/100 15.00 40.00
SC7 Steve Carlton 84 LL V/100 10.00 25.00
SC8 Steve Carlton 85/200 10.00 25.00
BR17 B.Robinson 82 KM/200 15.00 40.00
EW10 Earl Weaver 87/100 10.00 25.00
FJ33 Fergie Jenkins 84/100 10.00 25.00
GP21 Gaylord Perry 79/100 8.00 20.00
GP26 Gaylord Perry 82/100 10.00 25.00
GP29 Gaylord Perry 83/100 6.00 15.00
GP30 Gaylord Perry 83 SV/200 10.00 25.00
RF14 Rollie Fingers 80/100 6.00 15.00
RF15 Rollie Fingers 81/300 10.00 25.00
RF16 Rollie Fingers 81 LL/100 10.00 25.00
RF18 Rollie Fingers 82/100 10.00 25.00
RF19 Rollie Fingers 82 IA/200 10.00 25.00
RF21 Rollie Fingers 82 KM/300 10.00 25.00
RF22 Rollie Fingers 83/200 6.00 15.00
RF24 Rollie Fingers 84/200 10.00 25.00
RF27 Rollie Fingers 85/300 10.00 25.00
RF28 Rollie Fingers 86/100 10.00 25.00
SC10 Steve Carlton 87/200 10.00 25.00

2002 Topps Hobby Masters

COMPLETE SET (20) 30.00 80.00
SER.1 ODDS 1:25 HOBBY, 1:5 HTA 1:16 RETAIL
HM1 Mark McGwire 3.00 8.00
HM2 Derek Jeter 3.00 8.00
HM3 Chipper Jones 1.25 3.00
HM4 Roger Clemens 2.50 6.00
HM5 Vladimir Guerrero 1.25 3.00
HM6 Ichiro Suzuki 2.50 6.00
HM7 Todd Helton 1.25 3.00
HM8 Alex Rodriguez 1.50 4.00
HM9 Albert Pujols 2.50 6.00
HM10 Sammy Sosa 1.25 3.00
HM11 Ken Griffey Jr. 2.50 6.00
HM12 Randy Johnson 1.25 3.00
HM13 Nomar Garciaparra 2.00 5.00
HM14 Ivan Rodriguez 1.25 3.00
HM15 Manny Ramirez 1.25 3.00
HM16 Barry Bonds 3.00 8.00
HM17 Mike Piazza 2.00 5.00
HM18 Pedro Martinez 1.25 3.00
HM19 Jeff Bagwell 1.25 3.00
HM20 Luis Gonzalez 1.25 3.00

2002 Topps Like Father Like Son Relics

COMMON CARD 10.00 25.00

SER.1 GROUP A ODDS 1:6259 RETAIL
SER.1 GROUP B ODDS 1:6259 RETAIL
SER.1 GROUP C ODDS 1:2235 RETAIL
SER.1 OVERALL ODDS 1:1304 RETAIL
FSAL The Alomar Family A 40.00 80.00
FSBE The Berra Family C 10.00 25.00
FSBON The Bonds Family C 12.50 30.00
FSBOO The Boone Family A 10.00 25.00
FSCR The Cruz Family B 10.00 25.00

2002 Topps Own the Game

COMPLETE SET (30) 15.00 40.00
SER.1 ODDS 1:12 HOBBY, 1:4 HTA, 1:8 RETAIL
OG1 Moises Alou .40 1.00
OG2 Roberto Alomar .60 1.50
OG3 Luis Gonzalez .40 1.00
OG4 Bret Boone .40 1.00
OG5 Barry Bonds 2.50 6.00
OG6 Jim Thome .60 1.50
OG7 Jimmy Rollins .40 1.00
OG8 Cristian Guzman .40 1.00
OG9 Lance Berkman .40 1.00
OG10 Mike Sweeney .40 1.00
OG11 Rich Aurilia .40 1.00
OG12 Ichiro Suzuki 2.00 5.00
OG13 Luis Gonzalez .40 1.00
OG14 Ichiro Suzuki 2.00 5.00
OG15 Jimmy Rollins .40 1.00
OG16 Roger Cedeno .40 1.00
OG17 Barry Bonds 2.50 6.00
OG18 Jim Thome .60 1.50
OG19 Curt Schilling .40 1.00
OG20 Roger Clemens 2.00 5.00
OG21 Curt Schilling .40 1.00
OG22 Brad Radke .40 1.00
OG23 Greg Maddux 1.50 4.00
OG24 Mark Mulder .40 1.00
OG25 Jeff Shaw .40 1.00
OG26 Mariano Rivera 1.00 2.50
OG27 Randy Johnson 1.00 2.50
OG28 Pedro Martinez .60 1.50
OG29 John Burkett .40 1.00
OG30 Tim Hudson .40 1.00

2002 Topps Prime Cuts Autograph Relics

PCAAE Alex Escobar S2 12.50 30.00
PCABB Barry Bonds S1 400.00 600.00
PCAJH Josh Hamilton 50.00 100.00
PCANJ Nick Johnson S2 15.00 40.00
PCATH Toby Hall S2 15.00 40.00
PCAWB Wilson Betemit S2 15.00 40.00
PCAXN Xavier Nady S2 10.00 25.00
PCACPE Carlos Pena S2 15.00 40.00

2002 Topps Prime Cuts Barrel Relics

PCAAD Adam Dunn 8.00 20.00
PCAAG Alexis Gomez 8.00 20.00
PCAAR Aaron Rowand 10.00 25.00
PCACP Corey Patterson 8.00 20.00
PCAJC Joe Crede 8.00 20.00
PCAMG Marcus Giles
PCARS Ruben Salazar
PCASB Sean Burroughs 8.00 20.00

2002 Topps Prime Cuts Pine Tar Relics

SER.1 ODDS 1:4420 HOBBY, 1:1214 HTA
SER.2 ODDS 1:1043 HOBBY, 1:275 HTA
STATED PRINT RUN 200 SERIAL #'d SETS
PCPAD Adam Dunn 2 5.00 12.00
PCPAE Alex Escobar 2 5.00 12.00
PCPAG Alexis Gomez 2 5.00 12.00
PCPAP Albert Pujols 1 10.00 25.00
PCPAR Aaron Rowand 2 6.00 15.00
PCPBB Barry Bonds 1 10.00 25.00
PCPCP Corey Patterson 2 5.00 12.00
PCPJC Joe Crede 2 5.00 12.00
PCPJH Josh Hamilton 8.00 25.00
PCPLG Luis Gonzalez 1 6.00 15.00
PCPMG Marcus Giles 2 5.00 12.00
PCPNJ Nick Johnson 2 5.00 12.00
PCPRS Ruben Salazar 2 5.00 12.00
PCPSB Sean Burroughs 2 5.00 12.00
PCPTG Tony Gwynn 1 6.00 15.00
PCPTH Todd Helton 1 8.00 20.00
PCPTH Toby Hall 2 5.00 12.00
PCPWB Wilson Betemit 2 5.00 12.00
PCPXN Xavier Nady 2 5.00 12.00
PCPCPE Carlos Pena 2 6.00 15.00

2002 Topps Prime Cuts Trademark Relics

SER.1 ODDS 1:8868 HOBBY, 1:2428 HTA
SER.2 ODDS 1:2087 HOBBY, 1:549 HTA
STATED PRINT RUN 100 SERIAL #'d SETS
PCTAD Adam Dunn 2 10.00 25.00
PCTAE Alex Escobar 2 10.00 25.00
PCTAG Alexis Gomez 2 10.00 25.00
PCTAP Albert Pujols 1 15.00 40.00
PCTAR Aaron Rowand 2 10.00 25.00
PCTBB Barry Bonds 1 20.00 50.00
PCTCP Corey Patterson 2 10.00 25.00
PCTJC Joe Crede 2 10.00 25.00
PCTJH Josh Hamilton 15.00 40.00
PCTLG Luis Gonzalez 1 10.00 25.00
PCTMG Marcus Giles 2 10.00 25.00
PCTNJ Nick Johnson 2 10.00 25.00
PCTRS Ruben Salazar 2 10.00 25.00
PCTSB Sean Burroughs 2 10.00 25.00
PCTTG Tony Gwynn 1 10.00 25.00
PCTTH Todd Helton 1 10.00 25.00
PCTTH Toby Hall 2 10.00 25.00
PCTWB Wilson Betemit 2 10.00 25.00
PCTXN Xavier Nady 2 10.00 25.00
PCTCPE Carlos Pena 2 10.00 25.00

2002 Topps Ring Masters

COMPLETE SET (10) 10.00 25.00
SER.1 ODDS 1:25 HOBBY, 1:5 HTA 1:16 RETAIL
RM1 Derek Jeter 2.00 5.00
RM2 Mark McGwire 2.00 5.00
RM3 Mariano Rivera .75 2.00
RM4 Gary Sheffield .60 1.50
RM5 Al Leiter .60 1.50
RM6 Chipper Jones .75 2.00
RM7 Roger Clemens 1.50 4.00
RM8 Greg Maddux 1.25 3.00
RM9 Roberto Alomar .60 1.50
RM10 Paul O'Neill .60 1.50

2002 Topps Summer School Battery Mates Relics

SER.1 ODDS 1:4401 H, 1:1210 HTA, 1:3477 R
BMLP A.Leiter/M.Piazza 6.00 15.00
BMML G.Maddux/J.Lopez 10.00 25.00

2002 Topps Summer School Heart of the Order Relics

SER.1 A 1:8,220 H, 1:2253 HTA, 1:6452 R
SER.1 B 1:8,778 H, 1:2411 HTA, 1:6862 R
SER.1 ODDS 1:4,247 H, 1:1165 HTA, 1:3325 R
HTOARB Abreu/Rolen/Burrell A 40.00 80.00
HTOKBA Kent/Bonds/Aurilia A 50.00 100.00
HTOOWM O'Neill/B.Will/Tino A 40.00 80.00
HTOTGA Thome/Gonz/Alom B 40.00 80.00

2002 Topps Summer School Hit and Run Relics

SER.1 A 1:24591 H, 1:6760 HTA, 1:19649 R
SER.1 B 1:12296 H, 1:3380 HTA, 1:9606 R
SER.1 C 1:8788 H, 1:2411 HTA, 1:6862 R
SER.1 ODDS 1:4241 H, 1:1165 HTA, 1:3325 R
HRRDE Darin Erstad Bat B 6.00 15.00
HRRJD Johnny Damon Bat A 10.00 25.00
HRRRF Rafael Furcal Jsy C 6.00 15.00

2002 Topps Summer School Turn Two Relics

SER.1 ODDS 1:4401 H, 1:1210 HTA, 1:3477 R
TTRTW A.Trammell/L.Whitaker 10.00 25.00
TTRVA O.Vizquel/R.Alomar 10.00 25.00

2002 Topps Summer School Two Bagger Relics

SER.1 A 1:4401 H, 1:1210 HTA, 1:3477 R
SER.1 B 1:24591 H, 1:6760 HTA, 1:19649 R
SER.1 ODDS 1:3733 H, 1:1026 HTA, 1:2941 R
2BSR Scott Rolen Jsy A 10.00 25.00
2BTG Tony Gwynn Bat B 10.00 25.00
2BTH Todd Helton Jsy A 10.00 25.00

2002 Topps Yankee Stadium Seat Relics

SER.2 ODDS 1:5579 H, 1:1472 HTA, 1:4313 R
YSRAR Allie Reynolds 20.00 50.00
YSRBM Billy Martin 30.00 60.00
YSRGM Gil McDougald 12.50 30.00
YSRGW Gene Woodling 10.00 25.00
YSRHB Hank Bauer 10.00 25.00
YSRJC Joe Collins 15.00 40.00
YSRJM Johnny Mize 40.00 80.00
YSRPR Phil Rizzuto 40.00 80.00
YSRYB Yogi Berra 10.00 25.00

2002 Topps Traded

COMPLETE SET (275) 150.00 300.00
COMMON CARD (T1-T110) 1.00 2.50
1-110 ODDS ONE PER PACK
COMMON CARD (T111-T275) .15 .40
REPURCHASED ODDS 1:24 H/R, 1:10 HTA
T1 Jeff Weaver 1.00 2.50
T2 Jay Powell 1.00 2.50
T3 Alex Gonzalez 1.00 2.50
T4 Jason Isringhausen 1.00 2.50
T5 Tyler Houston 1.00 2.50
T6 Ben Broussard 1.00 2.50
T7 Chuck Knoblauch 1.00 2.50
T8 Brian L. Hunter 1.00 2.50
T9 Dustan Mohr 1.00 2.50
T10 Eric Hinske 1.00 2.50
T11 Roger Cedeno 1.00 2.50
T12 Eddie Perez 1.00 2.50
T13 Jeromy Burnitz 1.00 2.50
T14 Bartolo Colon 1.00 2.50
T15 Rick Helling 1.00 2.50
T16 Dan Plesac 1.00 2.50
T17 Scott Strickland 1.00 2.50
T18 Antonio Alfonseca 1.00 2.50
T19 Ricky Gutierrez 1.00 2.50
T20 John Valentin 1.00 2.50
T21 Raul Mondesi 1.00 2.50
T22 Ben Davis 1.00 2.50
T23 Nelson Figueroa 1.00 2.50
T24 Earl Snyder 1.00 2.50
T25 Robin Ventura 1.00 2.50
T26 Jimmy Haynes 1.00 2.50
T27 Kenny Kelly 1.00 2.50
T28 Morgan Ensberg 1.00 2.50
T29 Reggie Sanders 1.00 2.50
T30 Shigetoshi Hasegawa 1.00 2.50
T31 Mike Timlin 1.00 2.50
T32 Russell Branyan 1.00 2.50
T33 Alan Embree 1.00 2.50
T34 D'Angelo Jimenez 1.00 2.50
T35 Kent Mercker 1.00 2.50
T36 Jesse Orosco 1.00 2.50
T37 Gregg Zaun 1.00 2.50
T38 Reggie Taylor 1.00 2.50
T39 Andres Galarraga 1.50 4.00
T40 Chris Truby 1.00 2.50
T41 Bruce Chen 1.00 2.50
T42 Darren Lewis 1.00 2.50
T43 Ryan Kohlmeier 1.00 2.50
T44 John McDonald 1.00 2.50
T45 Omar Daal 1.00 2.50
T46 Matt Clement 1.00 2.50
T47 Glendon Rusch 1.00 2.50
T48 Chan Ho Park 1.50 4.00
T49 Benny Agbayani 1.00 2.50
T50 Juan Gonzalez 1.00 2.50
T51 Carlos Baerga 1.00 2.50
T52 Tim Raines 1.50 4.00
T53 Kevin Appier 1.00 2.50
T54 Marty Cordova 1.00 2.50
T55 Jeff D'Amico 1.00 2.50
T56 Dmitri Young 1.00 2.50
T57 Roosevelt Brown 1.00 2.50
T58 Dustin Hermanson 1.00 2.50
T59 Jose Rijo 1.00 2.50
T60 Todd Ritchie 1.00 2.50
T61 Lee Stevens 1.00 2.50
T62 Placido Polanco 1.00 2.50
T63 Eric Young 1.00 2.50
T64 Chuck Finley 1.00 2.50
T65 Dicky Gonzalez 1.00 2.50
T66 Jose Macias 1.00 2.50
T67 Gabe Kapler 1.00 2.50
T68 Sandy Alomar Jr. 1.00 2.50
T69 Henry Blanco 1.00 2.50
T70 Julian Tavarez 1.00 2.50
T71 Paul Bako 1.00 2.50
T72 Scott Rolen 1.50 4.00
T73 Brian Jordan 1.00 2.50
T74 Rickey Henderson 2.50 6.00
T75 Kevin Mench 1.00 2.50
T76 Hideo Nomo 2.50 6.00
T77 Jeremy Giambi 1.00 2.50
T78 Brad Fullmer 1.00 2.50
T79 Carl Everett 1.00 2.50
T80 David Wells 1.00 2.50
T81 Aaron Sele 1.00 2.50
T82 Todd Hollandsworth 1.00 2.50
T83 Vicente Padilla 1.00 2.50
T84 Kenny Lofton 1.00 2.50
T85 Corky Miller 1.00 2.50
T86 Josh Fogg 1.00 2.50
T87 Cliff Floyd 1.00 2.50
T88 Craig Paquette 1.00 2.50
T89 Jay Payton 1.00 2.50
T90 Carlos Pena 1.50 4.00
T91 Juan Encarnacion 1.00 2.50
T92 Rey Sanchez 1.00 2.50
T93 Ryan Dempster 1.00 2.50
T94 Mario Encarnacion 1.00 2.50
T95 Jorge Julio 1.00 2.50
T96 John Mabry 1.00 2.50
T97 Todd Zeile 1.00 2.50
T98 Johnny Damon Sox 1.50 4.00
T99 Deivi Cruz 1.00 2.50
T100 Gary Sheffield 1.00 2.50
T101 Ted Lilly 1.00 2.50
T102 Todd Van Poppel 1.00 2.50
T103 Shawn Estes 1.00 2.50
T104 Cesar Izturis 1.00 2.50
T105 Ron Coomer 1.00 2.50
T106 Grady Little MG RC 1.00 2.50
T107 Jimy Williams MG 1.00 2.50
T108 Tony Pena MG 1.00 2.50
T109 Frank Robinson MG 1.50 4.00
T110 Ron Gardenhire MG 1.00 2.50
T111 Dennis Tankersley .15 .40
T112 Alejandro Cadena RC .15 .40
T113 Justin Reid RC .15 .40
T114 Nate Field RC .15 .40
T115 Rene Reyes RC .15 .40
T116 Nelson Castro RC .15 .40
T117 Miguel Olivo .15 .40
T118 David Espinosa .15 .40
T119 Chris Bootcheck RC .15 .40
T120 Rob Henkel RC .15 .40
T121 Steve Bechler RC .15 .40
T122 Mark Outlaw RC .15 .40
T123 Henry Pichardo RC .15 .40
T124 Michael Floyd RC .15 .40
T125 Richard Lane RC .15 .40
T126 Pete Zamora RC .15 .40
T127 Javier Colina .15 .40
T128 Greg Sain RC .15 .40
T129 Ronnie Merrill .15 .40
T130 Gavin Floyd RC .40 1.00
T131 Josh Bonifay RC .15 .40
T132 Tommy Marx RC .15 .40
T133 Gary Cates Jr. RC .15 .40
T134 Neal Cotts RC .40 1.00
T135 Angel Berroa .15 .40
T136 Elio Serrano RC .15 .40
T137 J.J. Putz RC .20 .50
T138 Ruben Gotay RC .20 .50
T139 Eddie Rogers .15 .40
T140 Wily Mo Pena .15 .40
T141 Tyler Yates RC .15 .40
T142 Colin Young RC .15 .40
T143 Chance Caple .15 .40
T144 Ben Howard RC .15 .40
T145 Ryan Bukvich RC .15 .40
T146 Cliff Bartosh RC .15 .40
T147 Brandon Claussen .15 .40
T148 Cristian Guerrero .15 .40
T149 Derrick Lewis .15 .40
T150 Eric Miller RC .15 .40
T151 Justin Huber RC .30 .75
T152 Adrian Gonzalez .15 .40
T153 Brian West RC .15 .40
T154 Chris Baker RC .15 .40
T155 Drew Henson .15 .40
T156 Scott Hairston RC .20 .50
T157 Jason Simontacchi RC .15 .40
T158 Jason Arnold RC .15 .40
T159 Brandon Phillips .15 .40
T160 Adam Roller RC .15 .40
T161 Scotty Layfield RC .15 .40
T162 Freddie Money RC .15 .40
T163 Noochie Varner RC .15 .40
T164 Terrance Hill RC .15 .40
T165 Jeremy Hill RC .15 .40
T166 Carlos Cabrera RC .15 .40
T167 Jose Morban RC .15 .40
T168 Kevin Frederick RC .15 .40
T169 Mark Teixeira .60 1.50
T170 Brian Rogers .15 .40
T171 Anastacio Martinez RC .15 .40
T172 Bobby Jenks RC .60 1.50
T173 David Gil RC .15 .40
T174 Andres Torres .15 .40
T175 James Barrett RC .15 .40
T176 Jimmy Journell .15 .40
T177 Brett Kay RC .15 .40
T178 Jason Young RC .15 .40
T179 Mark Hamilton RC .15 .40
T180 Jose Bautista RC 2.00 5.00
T181 Blake McGinley RC .15 .40
T182 Ryan Mottl RC .15 .40
T183 Jeff Austin RC .15 .40
T184 Xavier Nady .15 .40
T185 Kyle Kane RC .15 .40
T186 Travis Foley RC .15 .40
T187 Nathan Kaup RC .15 .40
T188 Eric Cyr .15 .40
T189 Josh Cisneros RC .15 .40
T190 Brad Nelson RC .15 .40
T191 Clint Weibl RC .15 .40
T192 Ron Calloway RC .15 .40
T193 Jung Bong .15 .40
T194 Rolando Viera RC .15 .40
T195 Jason Bulger RC .15 .40
T196 Chone Figgins RC .60 1.50
T197 Jimmy Alvarez RC .15 .40
T198 Joel Crump RC .15 .40
T199 Ryan Doumit RC .25 .60
T200 Demetrius Heath RC .15 .40
T201 John Ennis RC .15 .40
T202 Doug Sessions RC .15 .40
T203 Clinton Hosford RC .15 .40
T204 Chris Narveson RC .15 .40
T205 Ross Peeples RC .15 .40
T206 Alex Requena RC .15 .40
T207 Matt Erickson RC .15 .40
T208 Brian Forystek RC .15 .40
T209 Dewon Brazelton .15 .40
T210 Nathan Haynes .15 .40
T211 Jack Cust .15 .40
T212 Jesse Foppert RC .20 .50
T213 Jesus Cota RC .15 .40
T214 Juan M. Gonzalez RC .15 .40
T215 Tim Kalita RC .15 .40
T216 Manny Delcarmen RC .20 .50
T217 Jim Kavourias RC .15 .40
T218 C.J. Wilson RC .50 1.25
T219 Edwin Yan RC .15 .40
T220 Andy Van Hekken .15 .40
T221 Michael Cuddyer .15 .40
T222 Jeff Verplancke RC .15 .40
T223 Mike Wilson RC .15 .40
T224 Corwin Malone RC .15 .40
T225 Chris Snelling RC .25 .60
T226 Joe Rogers RC .15 .40
T227 Jason Bay 1.50 4.00
T228 Ezequiel Astacio RC .15 .40
T229 Joey Hammond RC .15 .40
T230 Chris Duffy RC .20 .50
T231 Mark Prior .60 1.50
T232 Hansel Izquierdo RC .15 .40
T233 Franklyn German RC .15 .40
T234 Alexis Gomez .15 .40
T235 Jorge Padilla RC .15 .40
T236 Ryan Snare RC .15 .40
T237 Deivis Santos .15 .40
T238 Taggert Bozied RC .20 .50
T239 Mike Peeples RC .15 .40
T240 Ronald Acuna RC .15 .40
T241 Koyie Hill .15 .40
T242 Garrett Guzman RC .15 .40
T243 Ryan Church RC .40 1.00
T244 Tony Fontana RC .15 .40
T245 Keto Anderson RC .15 .40
T246 Brad Bouras RC .15 .40
T247 Jason Dubois RC .20 .50
T248 Angel Guzman RC .30 .75
T249 Joel Hanrahan RC .15 .40
T250 Joe Jiannetti RC .15 .40
T251 Sean Pierce RC .15 .40
T252 Jake Mauer RC .15 .40
T253 Marshall McDougall RC .15 .40
T254 Edwin Almonte RC .15 .40
T255 Shawn Riggans RC .15 .40
T256 Steven Shell RC .15 .40
T257 Kevin Hooper RC .15 .40
T258 Michael Frick RC .15 .40
T259 Travis Chapman RC .15 .40
T260 Tim Hummel RC .15 .40
T261 Adam Morrissey RC .15 .40
T262 Dontrelle Willis RC 1.25 3.00
T263 Justin Sherrod RC .15 .40
T264 Gerald Smiley RC .15 .40
T265 Tony Miller RC .15 .40
T266 Nolan Ryan WW 1.00 2.50
T267 Reggie Jackson WW .25 .60
T268 Steve Garvey WW .15 .40
T269 Wade Boggs WW .25 .60
T270 Sammy Sosa WW .40 1.00
T271 Curt Schilling WW .15 .40
T272 Mark Grace WW .25 .60
T273 Jason Giambi WW .15 .40
T274 Ken Griffey Jr. WW .75 2.00
T275 Roberto Alomar WW .25 .60

2002 Topps Traded Gold

*GOLD 1-110: .6X TO 1.5X BASIC
*GOLD 111-275: 2.5X TO 6X BASIC
*GOLD RC'S 111-275: 1.5X TO 4X BASIC
STATED ODDS 1:3 HOBBY/RETAIL, 1:1 HTA
STATED PRINT RUN 2002 SERIAL #'D SETS

2002 Topps Traded Farewell Relic

STATED ODDS 1:590 H, 1:169 HTA, 1:595 R
FWJC Jose Canseco Bat 6.00 15.00

2002 Topps Traded Hall of Fame Relic

STATED ODDS 1:1533 H,1:439 HTA,1:1574 R
HOFOS Ozzie Smith Bat 12.50 30.00

2002 Topps Traded Signature Moves

A ODDS 1:15,292 H, 1:4288 HTA, 1:22,032 R
B ODDS 1:3846 H, 1:1105 HTA, 1:3840 R
C ODDS 1:6147 H, 1:1778 HTA, 1:6418 R
D ODDS 1:1917 H, 1:548 HTA, 1:1953 R
E ODDS 1:341 H, 1:97 HTA, 1:342 R
F ODDS 1:2247 H, 1:645 HTA, 1:2261 R
G ODDS 1:568 H, 1:162 HTA, 1:571 R
GROUP H ODDS 1:256 H/R, 1:73 HTA
I ODDS 1:1023 H, 1:293 HTA, 1:1025 R
OVERALL ODDS 1:91 HOB/RET, 1:26 HTA
AC Antoine Cameron D 4.00 10.00
AM Andy Morales H 3.00 8.00
BB Boof Bonser E 4.00 10.00
BC Brandon Claussen E 4.00 10.00
CS Chris Smith G 3.00 8.00
CU Chase Utley E 30.00 60.00
CW Corwin Malone H 3.00 8.00
DT Dennis Tankersley F 4.00 10.00
FJ Forrest Johnson E 4.00 10.00
JD Johnny Damon Sox B 8.00 20.00
JD Jeff DaVanon I 3.00 8.00
JM Jake Mauer G 6.00 15.00
JM Justin Morneau H 6.00 15.00
JP Juan Pena E 4.00 10.00
JS Juan Silvestre D 4.00 10.00
JW Justin Wayne E 4.00 10.00
KI Kazuhisa Ishii A 15.00 40.00
MC Matt Cooper E 4.00 10.00
MO Moises Alou B 6.00 15.00
MT Marcus Thames G 5.00 12.00
RA Roberto Alomar C 10.00 25.00
RH Ryan Hannaman E 4.00 10.00
RM Ramon Moreta H 4.00 10.00
TB Tony Blanco E 4.00 10.00
TL Todd Linden H 4.00 10.00
VD Victor Diaz H 4.00 10.00

2002 Topps Traded Tools of the Trade Dual Relics

A ODDS 1:3407 H, 1:972 HTA, 1:3672 R
B ODDS 1:639 H, 1:183 HTA, 1:642 R
OVERALL ODDS 1:539 H, 1:155 HTA, 1:542 R
DTRRCP Chan Ho Park Jsy-Jsy B 6.00 15.00
DTRRHN Hideo Nomo Jsy-Jsy A 15.00 40.00
DTRRMO Moises Alou Jsy-Jsy B 6.00 15.00

2002 Topps Traded Tools of the Trade Relics

BAT A 1:1203 H, 1:344 HTA, 1:1224 R
BAT B 1:1807 H, 1:517 HTA, 1:1836 R
BAT C 1:35 H/R, 1:10 HTA
OVERALL BAT RELIC 1:34 H/R, 1:10 HTA
JERSEY ODDS 1:426 H, 1:122 HTA, 1:427 R
AB Roberto Alomar Bat C 4.00 10.00
AG Andres Galarraga Bat C 3.00 8.00
BF Brad Fullmer Bat C 3.00 8.00
BJ Brian Jordan Bat C 3.00 8.00
CE Carl Everett Bat C 3.00 8.00
CK Chuck Knoblauch Bat C 3.00 8.00
CP Carlos Pena Bat A 4.00 10.00
DB David Bell Bat C 3.00 8.00
DJ Dave Justice Bat C 3.00 8.00
EY Eric Young Bat C 3.00 8.00
GS Gary Sheffield Bat C 3.00 8.00
HB Rickey Henderson Bat C 4.00 10.00
JBU Jeromy Burnitz Bat C 3.00 8.00
JCI Jeff Cirillo Bat B 3.00 8.00
JDB Johnny Damon Sox Bat C 4.00 10.00
JG Juan Gonzalez Jsy 3.00 8.00
JP Josh Phelps Jsy 3.00 8.00
JV John Vander Wal Bat C 3.00 8.00
KL Kenny Lofton Bat C 3.00 8.00
MA Moises Alou Bat C 3.00 8.00
MLB Matt Lawton Bat C 3.00 8.00
MT Michael Tucker Bat C 3.00 8.00
MVB Mo Vaughn Bat C 3.00 8.00
MVJ Mo Vaughn Jsy 3.00 8.00
PP Placido Polanco Bat A 4.00 10.00
RS Reggie Sanders Bat C 3.00 8.00
RV Robin Ventura Bat C 3.00 8.00
RW Rondell White Bat C 3.00 8.00
SI Ruben Sierra Bat C 3.00 8.00
SR Scott Rolen Bat A 10.00 25.00
TC Tony Clark Bat C 3.00 8.00
TM Tino Martinez Bat C 4.00 10.00
TR Tim Raines Bat C 3.00 8.00
TS Tsuyoshi Shinjo Bat C 3.00 8.00
VC Vinny Castilla Bat C 3.00 8.00

2003 Topps Promos

COMPLETE SET (3) 1.50 4.00
PP1 Albert Pujols .75 2.00
PP2 Josh Beckett .25 .60
PP3 Nomar Garciaparra .40 1.00

2003 Topps

COMPLETE SET (720) 30.00 60.00
COMP.FACT.BLUE SET (725) 40.00 80.00
COMP.FACT.RED SET (725) 40.00 80.00
COMPLETE SERIES 1 (366) 12.50 30.00
COMPLETE SERIES 2 (354) 12.50 30.00
COMMON CARD (1-6/8-721) .07 .20
COMMON (292-331/660-684) .20 .50
CARD 7 DOES NOT EXIST
1 Alex Rodriguez .25 .60
2 Dan Wilson .07 .20
3 Jimmy Rollins .12 .30
4 Jermaine Dye .07 .20
5 Steve Karsay .07 .20
6 Timo Perez .07 .20
8 Jose Vidro .07 .20
9 Eddie Guardado .07 .20
10 Mark Prior .12 .30
11 Curt Schilling .12 .30
12 Dennis Cook .07 .20
13 Andruw Jones .07 .20
14 David Segui .07 .20
15 Trot Nixon .07 .20
16 Kerry Wood .07 .20
17 Magglio Ordonez .12 .30
18 Jason LaRue .07 .20
19 Danys Baez .07 .20
20 Todd Helton .12 .30
21 Denny Neagle .07 .20
22 Dave Mlicki .07 .20
23 Roberto Hernandez .07 .20
24 Odalis Perez .07 .20
25 Nick Neugebauer .07 .20
26 David Ortiz .20 .50
27 Andres Galarraga .12 .30
28 Edgardo Alfonzo .07 .20
29 Chad Bradford .07 .20
30 Jason Giambi .07 .20
31 Brian Giles .07 .20
32 Deivi Cruz .07 .20
33 Robb Nen .07 .20
34 Jeff Nelson .07 .20
35 Edgar Renteria .07 .20
36 Aubrey Huff .07 .20
37 Brandon Duckworth .07 .20
38 Juan Gonzalez .07 .20
39 Sidney Ponson .07 .20
40 Eric Hinske .07 .20
41 Kevin Appier .07 .20
42 Danny Bautista .07 .20
43 Javier Lopez .07 .20
44 Jeff Conine .07 .20
45 Carlos Baerga .07 .20
46 Ugueth Urbina .07 .20
47 Mark Buehrle .12 .30
48 Aaron Boone .07 .20
49 Jason Simontacchi .07 .20
50 Sammy Sosa .20 .50
51 Jose Jimenez .07 .20
52 Bobby Higginson .07 .20
53 Luis Castillo .07 .20
54 Orlando Merced .07 .20
55 Brian Jordan .07 .20
56 Eric Young .07 .20
57 Bobby Kielty .07 .20
58 Luis Rivas .07 .20
59 Brad Wilkerson .07 .20
60 Roberto Alomar .12 .30
61 Roger Clemens .25 .60
62 Scott Hatteberg .07 .20
63 Andy Ashby .07 .20
64 Mike Williams .07 .20
65 Ron Gant .07 .20
66 Benito Santiago .07 .20
67 Bret Boone .07 .20
68 Matt Morris .07 .20
69 Troy Glaus .07 .20
70 Austin Kearns .07 .20
71 Jim Thome .12 .30
72 Rickey Henderson .20 .50
73 Luis Gonzalez .07 .20
74 Brad Fullmer .07 .20
75 Herbert Perry .07 .20
76 Randy Wolf .07 .20
77 Miguel Tejada .12 .30
78 Jimmy Anderson .07 .20
79 Ramon Martinez .07 .20
80 Ivan Rodriguez .12 .30
81 John Flaherty .07 .20
82 Shannon Stewart .07 .20
83 Orlando Palmeiro .07 .20
84 Rafael Furcal .07 .20
85 Kenny Rogers .07 .20
86 Terry Adams .07 .20
87 Mo Vaughn .07 .20
88 Jose Cruz Jr. .07 .20
89 Mike Matheny .07 .20
90 Alfonso Soriano .12 .30
91 Orlando Cabrera .07 .20
92 Jeffrey Hammonds .07 .20
93 Hideo Nomo .20 .50
94 Carlos Febles .07 .20
95 Billy Wagner .07 .20
96 Alex Gonzalez .07 .20
97 Todd Zeile .07 .20
98 Omar Vizquel .12 .30
99 Jose Rijo .07 .20
100 Ichiro Suzuki .25 .60
101 Steve Cox .07 .20
102 Hideki Irabu .07 .20
103 Roy Halladay .12 .30
104 David Eckstein .07 .20
105 Greg Maddux .25 .60
106 Jay Gibbons .07 .20
107 Travis Driskill .07 .20
108 Fred McGriff .12 .30
109 Frank Thomas .20 .50
110 Shawn Green .07 .20
111 Ruben Quevedo .07 .20
112 Jacque Jones .07 .20
113 Tomo Ohka .07 .20
114 Joe McEwing .07 .20
115 Ramiro Mendoza .07 .20
116 Mark Mulder .07 .20
117 Mike Lieberthal .07 .20
118 Jack Wilson .07 .20
119 Randall Simon .07 .20
120 Bernie Williams .12 .30
121 Marvin Benard .07 .20
122 Jamie Moyer .07 .20
123 Andy Benes .07 .20
124 Tino Martinez .07 .20
125 Esteban Yan .07 .20
126 Juan Uribe .07 .20
127 Jason Isringhausen .07 .20
128 Chris Carpenter .12 .30
129 Mike Cameron .07 .20
130 Gary Sheffield .07 .20
131 Geronimo Gil .07 .20
132 Brian Daubach .07 .20
133 Corey Patterson .07 .20
134 Aaron Rowand .07 .20
135 Chris Reitsma .07 .20
136 Bob Wickman .07 .20
137 Cesar Izturis .07 .20
138 Jason Jennings .07 .20
139 Brandon Inge .07 .20
140 Larry Walker .12 .30
141 Ramon Santiago .07 .20
142 Vladimir Nunez .07 .20
143 Jose Vizcaino .07 .20
144 Mark Quinn .07 .20
145 Michael Tucker .07 .20
146 Darren Dreifort .07 .20
147 Ben Sheets .07 .20
148 Corey Koskie .07 .20
149 Tony Armas Jr. .07 .20
150 Kazuhisa Ishii .07 .20
151 Al Leiter .07 .20
152 Steve Trachsel .07 .20
153 Mike Stanton .07 .20
154 David Justice .07 .20
155 Marlon Anderson .07 .20
156 Jason Kendall .07 .20
157 Brian Lawrence .07 .20
158 J.T. Snow .07 .20
159 Edgar Martinez .12 .30
160 Pat Burrell .07 .20
161 Kerry Robinson .07 .20
162 Greg Vaughn .07 .20
163 Carl Everett .07 .20
164 Vernon Wells .07 .20
165 Jose Mesa .07 .20
166 Troy Percival .07 .20
167 Erubiel Durazo .07 .20
168 Jason Marquis .07 .20
169 Jerry Hairston Jr. .07 .20
170 Vladimir Guerrero .12 .30
171 Byung-Hyun Kim .07 .20
172 Marcus Giles .07 .20
173 Johnny Damon .12 .30
174 Jon Lieber .07 .20
175 Terrence Long .07 .20
176 Sean Casey .07 .20
177 Adam Dunn .12 .30
178 Juan Pierre .07 .20
179 Wendell Magee .07 .20
180 Barry Zito .12 .30
181 Aramis Ramirez .07 .20
182 Pokey Reese .07 .20
183 Jeff Kent .07 .20
184 Russ Ortiz .07 .20
185 Ruben Sierra .07 .20
186 Brent Abernathy .07 .20
187 Ismael Valdes .07 .20
188 Tom Wilson .07 .20
189 Craig Counsell .07 .20
190 Mike Mussina .12 .30
191 Ramon Hernandez .07 .20
192 Adam Kennedy .07 .20
193 Tony Womack .07 .20
194 Wes Helms .07 .20
195 Tony Batista .07 .20
196 Rolando Arrojo .07 .20
197 Kyle Farnsworth .07 .20
198 Gary Bennett .07 .20
199 Scott Sullivan .07 .20
200 Albert Pujols .25 .60
201 Kirk Rueter .07 .20
202 Phil Nevin .07 .20
203 Kip Wells .07 .20
204 Ron Coomer .07 .20
205 Jeromy Burnitz .07 .20
206 Kyle Lohse .07 .20
207 Mike DeJean .07 .20
208 Paul Lo Duca .07 .20
209 Carlos Beltran .12 .30
210 Roy Oswalt .12 .30
211 Mike Lowell .07 .20
212 Robert Fick .07 .20
213 Todd Jones .07 .20
214 C.C. Sabathia .12 .30
215 Danny Graves .07 .20
216 Todd Hundley .07 .20
217 Tim Wakefield .12 .30
218 Derek Lowe .07 .20
219 Kevin Millwood .07 .20
220 Jorge Posada .12 .30
221 Bobby J. Jones .07 .20
222 Carlos Guillen .07 .20
223 Fernando Vina .07 .20
224 Ryan Rupe .07 .20
225 Kelvim Escobar .07 .20
226 Ramon Ortiz .07 .20
227 Junior Spivey .07 .20
228 Juan Cruz .07 .20
229 Melvin Mora .07 .20
230 Lance Berkman .12 .30
231 Brent Butler .07 .20
232 Shane Halter .07 .20
233 Derrek Lee .07 .20
234 Matt Lawton .07 .20
235 Chuck Knoblauch .07 .20
236 Eric Gagne .07 .20
237 Alex Sanchez .07 .20
238 Denny Hocking .07 .20
239 Eric Milton .07 .20
240 Rey Ordonez .07 .20
241 Orlando Hernandez .07 .20
242 Robert Person .07 .20
243 Sean Burroughs .07 .20
244 Jeff Cirillo .07 .20
245 Mike Lamb .07 .20
246 Jose Valentin .07 .20
247 Ellis Burks .07 .20
248 Shawn Chacon .07 .20
249 Josh Beckett .07 .20
250 Nomar Garciaparra .12 .30
251 Craig Biggio .12 .30
252 Joe Randa .07 .20
253 Mark Grudzielanek .07 .20
254 Glendon Rusch .07 .20
255 Michael Barrett .07 .20
256 Omar Daal .07 .20
257 Elmer Dessens .07 .20
258 Wade Miller .07 .20
259 Adrian Beltre .20 .50
260 Vicente Padilla .07 .20
261 Kazuhiro Sasaki .07 .20
262 Mike Scioscia MG .07 .20
263 Bobby Cox MG .07 .20
264 Mike Hargrove MG .07 .20
265 Grady Little MG RC .07 .20
266 Alex Gonzalez .07 .20
267 Jerry Manuel MG .07 .20
268 Bob Boone MG .07 .20
269 Joel Skinner MG .07 .20
270 Clint Hurdle MG .07 .20
271 Miguel Batista .07 .20
272 Bob Brenly MG .07 .20
273 Jeff Torborg MG .07 .20
274 Jimy Williams MG .07 .20
275 Tony Pena MG .07 .20
276 Jim Tracy MG .07 .20
277 Jerry Royster MG .07 .20
278 Ron Gardenhire MG .07 .20
279 Frank Robinson MG .12 .30
280 John Halama .07 .20
281 Joe Torre MG .12 .30
282 Art Howe MG .07 .20
283 Larry Bowa MG .07 .20
284 Lloyd McClendon MG .07 .20
285 Bruce Bochy MG .12 .30
286 Dusty Baker MG .07 .20
287 Lou Piniella MG .07 .20
288 Tony LaRussa MG .12 .30
289 Todd Walker .07 .20
290 Jerry Narron MG .07 .20
291 Carlos Tosca MG .07 .20
292 Chris Duncan FY RC .60 1.50
293 Franklin Gutierrez FY RC .50 1.25
294 Adam LaRoche FY .20 .50
295 Manuel Ramirez FY RC .20 .50
296 Il Kim FY RC .20 .50
297 Wayne Lydon FY RC .20 .50
298 Daryl Clark FY RC .20 .50
299 Sean Pierce FY .20 .50
300 Andy Marte FY RC .20 .50
301 Matthew Peterson FY RC .20 .50
302 Gonzalo Lopez FY RC .20 .50
303 Bernie Castro FY RC .20 .50
304 Cliff Lee FY 1.25 3.00
305 Jason Perry FY RC .20 .50

306 Jaime Bubela FY RC .20 .50
307 Alexis Rios FY .20 .50
308 Brendan Harris FY RC .20 .50
309 Ramon Nivar-Martinez FY RC .20 .50
310 Terry Tiffee FY RC .20 .50
311 Kevin Youkilis FY RC 1.25 3.00
312 Ruddy Lugo FY RC .20 .50
313 C.J. Wilson FY 1.50 4.00
314 Mike McNutt FY RC .20 .50
315 Jeff Clark FY RC .20 .50
316 Mark Malaska FY RC .20 .50
317 Doug Waechter FY RC .20 .50
318 Derell McCall FY RC .20 .50
319 Scott Tyler FY RC .20 .50
320 Craig Brazell FY RC .20 .50
321 Walter Young FY .20 .50
322 M.Byrd .20 .50
J.Padilla FS
323 C.Snelling .30 .75
S.Choo FS
324 H.Blalock .30 .75
M.Teixeira FS
325 Josh Hamilton .30 .75
326 O.Hudson .20 .50
J.Phelps FS
327 J.Cust .20 .50
R.Reyes FS
328 A.Berroa .20 .50
A.Gomez FS
329 M.Cuddyer .20 .50
M.Restovich FS
330 J.Rivera .20 .50
M.Thames FS
331 B.Puffer .20 .50
J.Bong FS
332 Mike Cameron SH .07 .20
333 Shawn Green SH .07 .20
334 Oakland A's SH .07 .20
335 Jason Giambi SH .07 .20
336 Derek Lowe SH .07 .20
337 AL Batting Average LL .20 .50
338 AL Runs Scored LL .50 1.25
339 AL Home Runs LL .25 .60
340 AL RBI's LL .25 .60
341 AL ERA LL .12 .30
342 AL Strikeouts LL .25 .60
343 NL Batting Average LL .12 .30
344 NL Runs Scored LL .25 .60
345 NL Home Runs LL .20 .50
346 NL RBI's LL .25 .60
347 NL ERA LL .25 .60
348 NL Strikeouts LL .20 .50
349 AL Division Angels .12 .30
350 AL .10 .30
NL Division Twins/Cards
351 AL .10 .30
NL Division Angels/Giants
352 NL Division Cardinals .12 .30
353 Adam Kennedy ALCS .07 .20
354 J.T. Snow WS .07 .20
355 David Bell NLCS .07 .20
356 Jason Giambi AS .07 .20
357 Alfonso Soriano AS .12 .30
358 Alex Rodriguez AS .25 .60
359 Eric Chavez AS .07 .20
360 Torii Hunter AS .07 .20
361 Bernie Williams AS .12 .30
362 Garret Anderson AS .07 .20
363 Jorge Posada AS .12 .30
364 Derek Lowe AS .07 .20
365 Barry Zito AS .12 .30
366 Manny Ramirez AS .20 .50
367 Mike Scioscia AS .07 .20
368 Francisco Rodriguez .12 .30
369 Chris Hammond .07 .20
370 Chipper Jones .20 .50
371 Chris Singleton .07 .20
372 Cliff Floyd .07 .20
373 Bobby Hill .07 .20
374 Antonio Osuna .07 .20
375 Barry Larkin .12 .30
376 Charles Nagy .07 .20
377 Denny Stark .07 .20
378 Dean Palmer .07 .20
379 Eric Owens .07 .20
380 Randy Johnson .20 .50
381 Jeff Suppan .07 .20
382 Eric Karros .07 .20
383 Luis Vizcaino .07 .20
384 Johan Santana .12 .30
385 Javier Vazquez .07 .20
386 John Thomson .07 .20
387 Nick Johnson .07 .20
388 Mark Ellis .07 .20
389 Doug Glanville .07 .20
390 Ken Griffey Jr. .40 1.00
391 Bubba Trammell .07 .20
392 Livan Hernandez .07 .20
393 Desi Relaford .07 .20
394 Eli Marrero .07 .20
395 Jared Sandberg .07 .20
396 Barry Bonds .30 .75
397 Esteban Loaiza .07 .20
398 Aaron Sele .07 .20
399 Geoff Blum .07 .20
400 Derek Jeter .50 1.25
401 Eric Byrnes .07 .20
402 Mike Timlin .07 .20
403 Mark Kotsay .07 .20
404 Rich Aurilia .07 .20
405 Joel Pineiro .07 .20
406 Chuck Finley .07 .20
407 Bengie Molina .07 .20
408 Steve Finley .07 .20
409 Julio Franco .07 .20
410 Marty Cordova .07 .20
411 Shea Hillenbrand .07 .20
412 Mark Bellhorn .07 .20
413 Jon Garland .07 .20
414 Reggie Taylor .07 .20
415 Milton Bradley .07 .20
416 Carlos Pena .12 .30
417 Andy Fox .07 .20
418 Brad Ausmus .07 .20
419 Brent Mayne .07 .20
420 Paul Quantrill .07 .20
421 Carlos Delgado .07 .20
422 Kevin Mench .07 .20
423 Joe Kennedy .07 .20
424 Mike Crudale .07 .20
425 Mark McLemore .07 .20
426 Bill Mueller .07 .20
427 Rob Mackowiak .07 .20
428 Ricky Ledee .07 .20
429 Ted Lilly .07 .20
430 Sterling Hitchcock .07 .20
431 Scott Strickland .07 .20
432 Damion Easley .07 .20
433 Torii Hunter .07 .20
434 Brad Radke .07 .20
435 Geoff Jenkins .07 .20
436 Paul Byrd .07 .20
437 Morgan Ensberg .07 .20
438 Mike Maroth .07 .20
439 Mike Hampton .07 .20
440 Adam Hyzdu .07 .20
441 Vance Wilson .07 .20
442 Todd Ritchie .07 .20
443 Tom Gordon .07 .20
444 John Burkett .07 .20
445 Rodrigo Lopez .07 .20
446 Tim Spooneybarger .07 .20
447 Quinton Mccracken .07 .20
448 Tim Salmon .07 .20
449 Jarrod Washburn .07 .20
450 Pedro Martinez .12 .30
451 Dustan Mohr .07 .20
452 Julio Lugo .07 .20
453 Scott Stewart .07 .20
454 Armando Benitez .07 .20
455 Raul Mondesi .07 .20
456 Robin Ventura .07 .20
457 Bobby Abreu .07 .20
458 Josh Fogg .07 .20
459 Ryan Klesko .07 .20
460 Tsuyoshi Shinjo .07 .20
461 Jim Edmonds .12 .30
462 Cliff Politte .07 .20
463 Chan Ho Park .12 .30
464 John Mabry .07 .20
465 Woody Williams .07 .20
466 Jason Michaels .07 .20
467 Scott Schoeneweis .07 .20
468 Brian Anderson .07 .20
469 Brett Tomko .07 .20
470 Scott Erickson .07 .20
471 Kevin Millar Sox .07 .20
472 Danny Wright .07 .20
473 Jason Schmidt .07 .20
474 Scott Williamson .07 .20
475 Einar Diaz .07 .20
476 Jay Payton .07 .20
477 Juan Acevedo .07 .20
478 Ben Grieve .07 .20
479 Raul Ibanez .12 .30
480 Richie Sexson .07 .20
481 Rick Reed .07 .20
482 Pedro Astacio .07 .20
483 Adam Piatt .07 .20
484 Bud Smith .07 .20
485 Tomas Perez .07 .20
486 Adam Eaton .07 .20
487 Rafael Palmeiro .12 .30
488 Jason Tyner .07 .20
489 Scott Rolen .12 .30
490 Randy Winn .07 .20
491 Ryan Jensen .07 .20
492 Trevor Hoffman .12 .30
493 Craig Wilson .07 .20
494 Jeremy Giambi .07 .20
495 Daryle Ward .07 .20
496 Shane Spencer .07 .20
497 Andy Pettitte .12 .30
498 John Franco .07 .20
499 Felipe Lopez .07 .20
500 Mike Piazza .20 .50
501 Cristian Guzman .07 .20
502 Jose Hernandez .07 .20
503 Octavio Dotel .07 .20
504 Brad Penny .07 .20
505 Dave Veres .07 .20
506 Ryan Dempster .07 .20
507 Joe Crede .07 .20
508 Chad Hermansen .07 .20
509 Gary Matthews Jr. .07 .20
510 Matt Franco .07 .20
511 Ben Weber .07 .20
512 Dave Berg .07 .20
513 Michael Young .07 .20
514 Frank Catalanotto .07 .20
515 Darin Erstad .07 .20
516 Matt Williams .07 .20
517 B.J. Surhoff .07 .20
518 Kerry Ligtenberg .07 .20
519 Mike Bordick .07 .20
520 Arthur Rhodes .07 .20
521 Joe Girardi .12 .30
522 D'Angelo Jimenez .07 .20
523 Paul Konerko .12 .30
524 Jose Macias .07 .20
525 Joe Mays .07 .20
526 Marquis Grissom .07 .20
527 Neifi Perez .07 .20
528 Preston Wilson .07 .20
529 Jeff Weaver .07 .20
530 Eric Chavez .07 .20
531 Placido Polanco .07 .20
532 Matt Mantei .07 .20
533 James Baldwin .07 .20
534 Toby Hall .07 .20
535 Brendan Donnelly .07 .20
536 Benji Gil .07 .20
537 Damian Moss .07 .20
538 Jorge Julio .07 .20
539 Matt Clement .07 .20
540 Brian Moehler .07 .20
541 Lee Stevens .07 .20
542 Jimmy Haynes .07 .20
543 Terry Mulholland .07 .20
544 Dave Roberts .12 .30
545 J.C. Romero .07 .20
546 Bartolo Colon .07 .20
547 Roger Cedeno .07 .20
548 Mariano Rivera .25 .60
549 Billy Koch .07 .20
550 Manny Ramirez .20 .50
551 Travis Lee .07 .20
552 Oliver Perez .07 .20
553 Tim Worrell .07 .20
554 Rafael Soriano .07 .20
555 Damian Miller .07 .20
556 John Smoltz .20 .50
557 Willis Roberts .07 .20
558 Tim Hudson .12 .30
559 Moises Alou .07 .20
560 Gary Glover .07 .20
561 Corky Miller .07 .20
562 Ben Broussard .07 .20
563 Gabe Kapler .07 .20
564 Chris Woodward .07 .20
565 Paul Wilson .07 .20
566 Todd Hollandsworth .07 .20
567 So Taguchi .07 .20
568 John Olerud .07 .20
569 Reggie Sanders .07 .20
570 Jake Peavy .07 .20
571 Kris Benson .07 .20
572 Todd Pratt .07 .20
573 Ray Durham .07 .20
574 Boomer Wells .07 .20
575 Chris Widger .07 .20
576 Shawn Wooten .07 .20
577 Tom Glavine .12 .30
578 Antonio Alfonseca .07 .20
579 Keith Foulke .07 .20
580 Shawn Estes .07 .20
581 Mark Grace .12 .30
582 Dmitri Young .07 .20
583 A.J. Burnett .07 .20
584 Richard Hidalgo .07 .20
585 Mike Sweeney .07 .20
586 Alex Cora .12 .30
587 Matt Stairs .07 .20
588 Doug Mientkiewicz .07 .20
589 Fernando Tatis .07 .20
590 David Weathers .07 .20
591 Cory Lidle .07 .20
592 Dan Plesac .07 .20
593 Jeff Bagwell .12 .30
594 Steve Sparks .07 .20
595 Sandy Alomar Jr. .07 .20
596 John Lackey .12 .30
597 Rick Helling .07 .20
598 Mark DeRosa .07 .20
599 Carlos Lee .07 .20
600 Garret Anderson .07 .20
601 Vinny Castilla .07 .20
602 Ryan Drese .07 .20
603 LaTroy Hawkins .07 .20
604 David Bell .07 .20
605 Freddy Garcia .07 .20
606 Miguel Cairo .07 .20
607 Scott Spiezio .07 .20
608 Mike Remlinger .07 .20
609 Tony Graffanino .07 .20
610 Russell Branyan .07 .20
611 Chris Magruder .07 .20
612 Jose Contreras RC .20 .50
613 Carl Pavano .07 .20
614 Kevin Brown .07 .20
615 Tyler Houston .07 .20
616 A.J. Pierzynski .07 .20
617 Tony Fiore .07 .20
618 Peter Bergeron .07 .20
619 Rondell White .07 .20
620 Brett Myers .07 .20
621 Kevin Young .07 .20
622 Kenny Lofton .07 .20
623 Ben Davis .07 .20
624 J.D. Drew .07 .20
625 Chris Gomez .07 .20
626 Karim Garcia .07 .20
627 Ricky Gutierrez .07 .20
628 Mark Redman .07 .20
629 Juan Encarnacion .07 .20
630 Anaheim Angels TC .10 .30
631 Arizona Diamondbacks TC .07 .20
632 Atlanta Braves TC .07 .20
633 Baltimore Orioles TC .07 .20
634 Boston Red Sox TC .07 .20
635 Chicago Cubs TC .07 .20
636 Chicago White Sox TC .07 .20
637 Cincinnati Reds TC .07 .20
638 Cleveland Indians TC .07 .20
639 Colorado Rockies TC .07 .20
640 Detroit Tigers TC .07 .20
641 Florida Marlins TC .07 .20
642 Houston Astros TC .07 .20
643 Kansas City Royals TC .07 .20
644 Los Angeles Dodgers TC .07 .20
645 Milwaukee Brewers TC .07 .20
646 Minnesota Twins TC .07 .20
647 Montreal Expos TC .07 .20
648 New York Mets TC .07 .20
649 New York Yankees TC .10 .30
650 Oakland Athletics TC .07 .20
651 Philadelphia Phillies TC .07 .20
652 Pittsburgh Pirates TC .07 .20
653 San Diego Padres TC .07 .20
654 San Francisco Giants TC .07 .20
655 Seattle Mariners TC .07 .20
656 St. Louis Cardinals TC .07 .20
657 Tampa Bay Devil Rays TC .07 .20
658 Texas Rangers TC .07 .20
659 Toronto Blue Jays TC .07 .20
660 Bryan Bullington DP RC .20 .50
661 Jeremy Guthrie DP .20 .50
662 Joey Gomes DP RC .20 .50
663 Evel Bastida-Martinez DP RC .20 .50
664 Brian Wright DP RC .20 .50
665 B.J. Upton DP .30 .75
666 Jeff Francis DP .20 .50
667 Drew Meyer DP .20 .50
668 Jeremy Hermida DP .30 .75
669 Khalil Greene DP .30 .75
670 Darrell Rasner DP RC .20 .50
671 Cole Hamels DP .60 1.50
672 James Loney DP .30 .75
673 Sergio Santos DP .20 .50
674 Jason Pridie DP .20 .50
675 B.Phillips .30 .75
V.Martinez
676 H.Choi .20 .50
N.Jackson
677 D.Willis .20 .50
J.Stokes
678 C.Tracy .20 .50
L.Overbay
679 J.Borchard .20 .50
C.Malone
680 J.Mauer .50 1.25
J.Morneau
681 D.Henson .20 .50
B.Claussen
682 C.Utley .30 .75
G.Floyd
683 T.Bozied .20 .50
X.Nady
684 A.Heilman .50 1.25
J.Reyes
685 Kenny Rogers AW .07 .20
686 Bengie Molina AW .07 .20
687 John Olerud AW .07 .20
688 Bret Boone AW .07 .20
689 Eric Chavez AW .07 .20
690 Alex Rodriguez AW .25 .60
691 Darin Erstad AW .07 .20
692 Ichiro Suzuki AW .25 .60
693 Torii Hunter AW .07 .20
694 Greg Maddux AW .25 .60
695 Brad Ausmus AW .07 .20
696 Todd Helton AW .12 .30
697 Fernando Vina AW .07 .20
698 Scott Rolen AW .12 .30
699 Edgar Renteria AW .07 .20
700 Andruw Jones AW .07 .20
701 Larry Walker AW .12 .30
702 Jim Edmonds AW .12 .30
703 Barry Zito AW .12 .30
704 Randy Johnson AW .20 .50
705 Miguel Tejada AW .12 .30
706 Barry Bonds AW .30 .75
707 Eric Hinske AW .07 .20
708 Jason Jennings AW .07 .20
709 Todd Helton AS .12 .30
710 Jeff Kent AS .07 .20
711 Edgar Renteria AS .07 .20
712 Scott Rolen AS .12 .30
713 Barry Bonds AS .30 .75
714 Sammy Sosa AS .20 .50
715 Vladimir Guerrero AS .12 .30
716 Mike Piazza AS .20 .50
717 Curt Schilling AS .12 .30
718 Randy Johnson AS .20 .50
719 Bobby Cox AS .07 .20
720 Anaheim Angels WS .10 .30
721 Anaheim Angels WS .20 .50

2003 Topps Black

COM 1-291/368-659/685-721 6.00 15.00
SEMIS 1-291/368-659/685-721 10.00 25.00
UNL 1-291/368-659/685-721 15.00 40.00
COM. 292-331/660-684 6.00 15.00
SEMIS 292-331/660-684 10.00 25.00
UNL 292-331/660-684 15.00 40.00
COM: 292-331/612/660-684 6.00 15.00
SEMIS 292-331/612/660-684 10.00 25.00
UNL 92-331/612/660-684 15.00 40.00
SERIES 1 STATED ODDS 1:16 HTA
SERIES 2 STATED ODDS 1:10 HTA
STATED PRINT RUN 52 SERIAL #'d SETS
CARD 7 DOES NOT EXIST
1 Alex Rodriguez 20.00 50.00
61 Roger Clemens 20.00 50.00
100 Ichiro Suzuki 20.00 50.00
105 Greg Maddux 20.00 50.00
200 Albert Pujols 20.00 50.00
292 Chris Duncan FY 20.00 50.00
304 Cliff Lee FY 40.00 100.00
311 Kevin Youkilis FY 40.00 100.00
313 C.J. Wilson FY 50.00 125.00
390 Ken Griffey Jr. 30.00 80.00
396 Barry Bonds 25.00 60.00
400 Derek Jeter 40.00 100.00
671 Cole Hamels DP 20.00 50.00
690 Alex Rodriguez AW 20.00 50.00
692 Ichiro Suzuki AW 20.00 50.00
694 Greg Maddux AW 20.00 50.00
706 Barry Bonds AW 25.00 60.00
713 Barry Bonds AS 25.00 60.00

2003 Topps Box Bottoms

A-Rod/Schill/Helt/L.Gonz 1.50 4.00
Sosa/Soriano/Ishii/Pujols 2.00 5.00
*BOX BOTTOM CARDS: 1X TO 2.5X BASIC
ONE 4-CARD SHEET PER HTA BOX
1 Alex Rodriguez 1 .60 1.50
10 Mark Prior 4 .30 .75
11 Curt Schilling 1 .30 .75
20 Todd Helton 1 .30 .75
50 Sammy Sosa 2 .50 1.25
73 Luis Gonzalez 1 .20 .50
77 Miguel Tejada 4 .30 .75
80 Ivan Rodriguez 4 .30 .75
90 Alfonso Soriano 2 .30 .75
150 Kazuhisa Ishii 2 .20 .50
160 Pat Burrell 4 .20 .50
177 Adam Dunn 3 .30 .75
180 Barry Zito 3 .30 .75
200 Albert Pujols 2 .60 1.50
230 Lance Berkman 3 .30 .75
250 Nomar Garciaparra 3 .30 .75
368 Francisco Rodriguez 5 .30 .75
370 Chipper Jones 8 .50 1.25
380 Randy Johnson 8 .50 1.25
387 Nick Johnson 7 .20 .50
390 Ken Griffey Jr. 6 1.00 2.50
396 Barry Bonds 5 .75 2.00
433 Torii Hunter 5 .20 .50
450 Pedro Martinez 6 .30 .75
489 Scott Rolen 8 .30 .75
500 Mike Piazza 6 .50 1.25
530 Eric Chavez 6 .20 .50
550 Manny Ramirez 7 .50 1.25
558 Tim Hudson 7 .30 .75
585 Mike Sweeney 8 .30 .75
593 Jeff Bagwell 5 .30 .75
600 Garret Anderson 7 .20 .50

2003 Topps Gold

*GOLD 1-291/368-659/685-721: 6X TO 15X
*GOLD: 292-331/660-684: 2.5X TO 6X
*GOLD RC's: 292-331/612/660-684: 6X TO 15X
SERIES 1 STATED ODDS 1:16 H, 1:5 HTA
SERIES 2 STATED ODDS 1:7 H, 1:2 HTA, 1:5 R
STATED PRINT RUN 2003 SERIAL #'d SETS
CARD 7 DOES NOT EXIST

2003 Topps Home Team Advantage

COMP.FACT.SET (720) 40.00 80.00
*HTA: .75X TO 2X BASIC
DISTRIBUTED IN FACTORY SET FORM
CARD 7 DOES NOT EXIST

2003 Topps Trademark Variations

SER.1 ODDS 1:8852 H, 1:2665 HTA
SER.2 ODDS 1:4487 H, 1:1277 HTA, 1:3763 R
NO PRICING DUE TO SCARCITY
SKIP-NUMBERED 45-CARD SET

2003 Topps All-Stars

COMPLETE SET (20) 12.50 30.00
SERIES 2 ODDS 1:15 HOBBY, 1:5 HTA
1 Alfonso Soriano .60 1.50
2 Barry Bonds 1.50 4.00
3 Ichiro Suzuki 1.25 3.00
4 Alex Rodriguez 1.25 3.00
5 Miguel Tejada .60 1.50
6 Nomar Garciaparra .60 1.50
7 Jason Giambi .40 1.00
8 Manny Ramirez 1.00 2.50
9 Derek Jeter 2.50 6.00
10 Garret Anderson .40 1.00
11 Barry Zito .60 1.50
12 Sammy Sosa 1.00 2.50
13 Adam Dunn .60 1.50
14 Vladimir Guerrero .60 1.50
15 Mike Piazza 1.00 2.50
16 Shawn Green .40 1.00
17 Luis Gonzalez .40 1.00
18 Todd Helton .60 1.50
19 Torii Hunter .40 1.00
20 Curt Schilling .60 1.50

2003 Topps Autographs

GROUP A1 SER.1 1:8910 H, 1:2533 HTA
GROUP B1 SER.1 1:24,710 H, 1:7037 HTA
GROUP C1 SER.1 1:11,097 H, 1:3167 HTA
GROUP D1 SER.1 1:20,144 H, 1:5758 HTA
GROUP E1 SER.1 1:11,730 H, 1:3333 HTA
GROUP F1 SER.1 1:2209 H, 1:395 HTA
GROUP G1 SER.1 1:3471 H, 1:460 HTA
GROUP A2 1:31,408 H, 1:8808 HTA, 1:26,208 R
GROUP B2 1:5188 H, 1:1460 HTA, 1:4368 R
GROUP C2 1:864 H, 1:232 HTA, 1:708 R
GROUP D2 1:790 H, 1:214 HTA, 1:647 R
SERIES 1 EXCH.DEADLINE 11/30/04
AJ Andruw Jones A1 10.00 25.00
AK1 Austin Kearns F1 4.00 10.00
AK2 Austin Kearns C2 4.00 10.00
AP Albert Pujols B2 50.00 120.00
AS Alfonso Soriano A1 30.00 60.00
BH Brad Hawpe D2 8.00 20.00
BS Ben Sheets E1 6.00 15.00
BU B.J. Upton D2 4.00 10.00
BZ Barry Zito C2 4.00 10.00
CE Clint Everts D2 4.00 10.00
CF Cliff Floyd C2 6.00 15.00
DE Darin Erstad B1 6.00 15.00
DW Dontrelle Willis D2 4.00 10.00
EC Eric Chavez A1 8.00 20.00
EH Eric Hinske C2 6.00 15.00
EM Eric Milton C1 6.00 15.00
HB Hank Blalock F1 10.00 25.00
JB Josh Beckett C2 6.00 15.00
JDM J.D. Martin G1 4.00 10.00
JL Jason Lane G1 6.00 15.00
JM Joe Mauer F1 20.00 50.00
JPH Josh Phelps C2 6.00 15.00
JV Jose Vidro C2 6.00 15.00
LB Lance Berkman A2 6.00 15.00
MB Mark Buehrle C1 6.00 15.00
MO Maggilo Ordonez B2 4.00 10.00
MP Mark Prior F1 10.00 25.00
MTE Mark Teixeira F1 6.00 15.00
MTH Marcus Thames G1 4.00 10.00
MT1 Miguel Tejada A1 6.00 15.00
MT2 Miguel Tejada C2 15.00 40.00
NN Nick Neugebauer D1 6.00 15.00
OH Orlando Hudson G1 4.00 10.00
PK Paul Konerko C2 6.00 15.00
PL1 Paul Lo Duca F1 6.00 15.00
PL2 Paul Lo Duca C2 10.00 25.00
SR Scott Rolen A1 30.00 60.00
TH Torii Hunter C2 6.00 15.00

2003 Topps Blue Backs

COMPLETE SET (40) 20.00 50.00
SERIES 1 STATED ODDS 1:12 HOB, 1:4 HTA
BB1 Albert Pujols 1.25 3.00
BB2 Ichiro Suzuki 1.25 3.00
BB3 Sammy Sosa 1.00 2.50
BB4 Kazuhisa Ishii .40 1.00
BB5 Alex Rodriguez 1.25 3.00
BB6 Derek Jeter 2.50 6.00
BB7 Vladimir Guerrero .60 1.50
BB8 Ken Griffey Jr. 2.00 5.00
BB9 Jason Giambi .40 1.00
BB10 Todd Helton .60 1.50
BB11 Mike Piazza 1.00 2.50
BB12 Nomar Garciaparra .60 1.50
BB13 Chipper Jones 1.00 2.50
BB14 Ivan Rodriguez .60 1.50
BB15 Luis Gonzalez .40 1.00
BB16 Pat Burrell .40 1.00
BB17 Mark Prior .60 1.50
BB18 Adam Dunn .60 1.50
BB19 Jeff Bagwell .60 1.50
BB20 Austin Kearns .40 1.00
BB21 Alfonso Soriano .60 1.50
BB22 Jim Thome .60 1.50
BB23 Bernie Williams .60 1.50
BB24 Pedro Martinez .60 1.50
BB25 Lance Berkman .60 1.50
BB26 Randy Johnson 1.00 2.50
BB27 Rafael Palmeiro .60 1.50
BB28 Richie Sexson .40 1.00
BB29 Troy Glaus .40 1.00
BB30 Shawn Green .40 1.00
BB31 Larry Walker .60 1.50
BB32 Eric Hinske .40 1.00
BB33 Andruw Jones .40 1.00
BB34 Barry Bonds 1.50 4.00
BB35 Curt Schilling .60 1.50
BB36 Greg Maddux 1.25 3.00
BB37 Jimmy Rollins .60 1.50
BB38 Eric Chavez .40 1.00
BB39 Scott Rolen .60 1.50
BB40 Mike Sweeney .40 1.00

2003 Topps Blue Chips Autographs

SEEDED IN VARIOUS 03-06 TOPPS BRANDS
AH Aubrey Huff 6.00 15.00
BC Bobby Crosby 6.00 15.00
BEP Brandon Phillips 4.00 10.00
BF Ben Fritz 4.00 10.00
BS Brian Slocum 4.00 10.00
CCE Clint Everts 4.00 10.00
CH Cole Hamels 15.00 40.00
CN Clint Nageotte 4.00 10.00
CT Chad Tracy 4.00 10.00
JG Jay Gibbons 4.00 10.00
JHA J.J. Hardy 4.00 10.00
JHU Justin Huber 4.00 10.00
JR Jeremy Reed 4.00 10.00
JRB Jason Bay 6.00 15.00
KH Kris Honel 4.00 10.00
MB Milton Bradley 4.00 10.00
OH Orlando Hudson 4.00 10.00
RN Ramon Nivar 4.00 10.00
VM Val Majewski 4.00 10.00
ZG Zack Greinke 20.00 50.00

2003 Topps Draft Picks

COMPLETE SET (10) 50.00 100.00
COMPLETE SERIES 1 (5) 30.00 60.00
COMPLETE SERIES 2 (5) 20.00 40.00
COMMON CARD (1-10) .75 2.00
1-5 ISSUED IN RETAIL SETS
6-10 DISTRIBUTED IN HOLIDAY SETS
1 Brandon Wood 5.00 12.00
2 Ryan Wagner .75 2.00
3 Sean Rodriguez 1.25 3.00
4 Chris Lubanski .75 2.00
5 Chad Billingsley 4.00 10.00
6 Javi Herrera .75 2.00
7 Brian McFall .75 2.00
8 Nick Markakis 6.00 15.00
9 Adam Miller 3.00 8.00
10 Daric Barton 1.25 3.00

2003 Topps Farewell to Riverfront Stadium Relics

SERIES 2 STATED ODDS 1:37 HTA
AD Adam Dunn 10.00 25.00
AK Austin Kearns 10.00 25.00
BL Barry Larkin 15.00 40.00
DC Dave Concepcion 12.00 30.00
JB Johnny Bench 15.00 40.00
JM Joe Morgan 20.00 50.00
KG Ken Griffey Jr. 20.00 50.00
PO Paul O'Neill 10.00 25.00
TP Tony Perez 15.00 40.00
TS Tom Seaver 15.00 40.00

2003 Topps First Year Player Bonus

1-5 ISSUED IN RED HOBBY SETS
6-10 ISSUED IN BLUE SEARS/JC PENNEY SETS
1 Ismael Castro .40 1.00
2 Branden Florence .40 1.00
3 Michael Garciaparra .40 1.00
4 Pete LaForest .40 1.00
5 Hanley Ramirez 3.00 8.00
6 Rajai Davis .40 1.00
7 Gary Schneidmiller .40 1.00
8 Corey Shafer .40 1.00
9 Thomari Story-Harden .40 1.00
10 Bryan Grace .40 1.00

2003 Topps Flashback

SERIES 1 STATED ODDS 1:12 HTA
AR Al Rosen .75 2.00
BM Bill Madlock .75 2.00
CY Carl Yastrzemski 3.00 8.00
DM Dale Murphy 2.00 5.00
EM Eddie Mathews 2.00 5.00
GB George Brett 4.00 10.00
HK Harmon Killebrew 2.00 5.00
JP Jim Palmer 1.25 3.00
LD Lenny Dykstra .75 2.00
MP Mike Piazza 2.00 5.00
NR Nolan Ryan 6.00 15.00
RJ Randy Johnson 2.00 5.00
RR Robin Roberts 1.25 3.00
TS Tom Seaver 1.25 3.00
WS Warren Spahn 1.25 3.00

2003 Topps Hit Parade

COMPLETE SET (30) 15.00 40.00
SERIES 2 ODDS 1:15 HOB, 1:5 HTA, 1:10 RET
1 Barry Bonds 1.50 4.00
2 Sammy Sosa 1.00 2.50
3 Rafael Palmeiro .60 1.50
4 Fred McGriff .60 1.50
5 Ken Griffey Jr. 2.00 5.00
6 Juan Gonzalez .40 1.00
7 Andres Galarraga .60 1.50
8 Jeff Bagwell .60 1.50
9 Frank Thomas 1.00 2.50
10 Matt Williams .40 1.00
11 Barry Bonds 1.50 4.00
12 Rafael Palmeiro .60 1.50
13 Fred McGriff .60 1.50
14 Andres Galarraga .60 1.50
15 Ken Griffey Jr. 2.00 5.00
16 Sammy Sosa 1.00 2.50
17 Jeff Bagwell .60 1.50
18 Juan Gonzalez .60 1.50
19 Frank Thomas 1.00 2.50
20 Matt Williams .40 1.00
21 Rickey Henderson 1.00 2.50
22 Rafael Palmeiro .60 1.50
23 Roberto Alomar .60 1.50
24 Barry Bonds 1.50 4.00
25 Mark Grace .60 1.50
26 Fred McGriff .60 1.50
27 Julio Franco .40 1.00
28 Craig Biggio .60 1.50
29 Andres Galarraga .60 1.50
30 Barry Larkin .60 1.50

2003 Topps Hobby Masters

COMPLETE SET (20) 12.50 30.00
SERIES 1 STATED ODDS 1:18 HOB, 1:6 HTA
HM1 Ichiro Suzuki 1.25 3.00
HM2 Kazuhisa Ishii .40 1.00
HM3 Derek Jeter 2.50 6.00
HM4 Sammy Sosa 1.00 2.50
HM5 Alex Rodriguez 1.25 3.00
HM6 Mike Piazza 1.00 2.50
HM7 Chipper Jones 1.00 2.50
HM8 Vladimir Guerrero .60 1.50
HM9 Nomar Garciaparra .60 1.50
HM10 Todd Helton .60 1.50
HM11 Jason Giambi .40 1.00
HM12 Ken Griffey Jr. 2.00 5.00
HM13 Albert Pujols 1.25 3.00
HM14 Ivan Rodriguez .60 1.50
HM15 Mark Prior .60 1.50
HM16 Adam Dunn .60 1.50
HM17 Randy Johnson 1.00 2.50
HM18 Barry Bonds 1.50 4.00
HM19 Alfonso Soriano .60 1.50
HM20 Pat Burrell .40 1.00

2003 Topps Own the Game

COMPLETE SET (30) 15.00 40.00
SERIES 1 STATED ODDS 1:12 HOB, 1:4 HTA
OG1 Ichiro Suzuki 1.25 3.00
OG2 Todd Helton .60 1.50
OG3 Larry Walker .60 1.50
OG4 Mike Sweeney .40 1.00
OG5 Sammy Sosa 1.00 2.50
OG6 Lance Berkman .60 1.50
OG7 Alex Rodriguez 1.25 3.00
OG8 Jim Thome .60 1.50
OG9 Shawn Green .40 1.00
OG10 Nomar Garciaparra .60 1.50
OG11 Miguel Tejada .60 1.50
OG12 Jason Giambi .40 1.00
OG13 Magglio Ordonez .60 1.50
OG14 Manny Ramirez 1.00 2.50
OG15 Alfonso Soriano .60 1.50
OG16 Johnny Damon .60 1.50
OG17 Derek Jeter 2.50 6.00
OG18 Albert Pujols 1.25 3.00
OG19 Luis Castillo .40 1.00
OG20 Barry Bonds 1.50 4.00
OG21 Garret Anderson .40 1.00
OG22 Jimmy Rollins .60 1.50
OG23 Curt Schilling .60 1.50
OG24 Barry Zito .60 1.50
OG25 Randy Johnson 1.00 2.50
OG26 Tom Glavine .60 1.50
OG27 Roger Clemens 1.25 3.00
OG28 Pedro Martinez .60 1.50
OG29 Derek Lowe .40 1.00
OG30 John Smoltz 1.00 2.50

2003 Topps Prime Cuts Relics

SER.1 ODDS 1:37,066 H, 1:5067 HTA
SER.2 ODDS 1:116,208 H,1:1480 HTA,1:4368 R
STATED PRINT RUN 50 SERIAL #'d SETS
NO PRICING DUE TO SCARCITY
AD1 Adam Dunn 1 50.00 100.00
AD2 Adam Dunn 2 50.00 100.00
AP Albert Pujols 1 60.00 120.00
AR1 Alex Rodriguez 1 50.00 100.00
AR2 Alex Rodriguez 2 50.00 100.00
AS Alfonso Soriano 2 20.00 50.00
BBO Barry Bonds 2 50.00 100.00
BW Bernie Williams 1 20.00 50.00
CD Carlos Delgado 2 30.00 60.00
EC Eric Chavez 2 30.00 60.00
EM Edgar Martinez 2 40.00 80.00
FT Frank Thomas 1 60.00 120.00
HB Hank Blalock 2 20.00 50.00
IR Ivan Rodriguez 1 50.00 100.00
JG Juan Gonzalez 1 50.00 100.00
JP Jorge Posada 2 40.00 80.00
LB Lance Berkman 1 20.00 50.00
LG Luis Gonzalez 2 20.00 50.00
MP Mark Prior 2 60.00 120.00
MP Mike Piazza 1 60.00 120.00
MV Mo Vaughn 1 50.00 100.00
NG1 Nomar Garciaparra 1 30.00 60.00
NG2 Nomar Garciaparra 2 30.00 60.00
RA1 Roberto Alomar 1 20.00 50.00
RA2 Roberto Alomar 2 20.00 50.00
RH Rickey Henderson 2 60.00 120.00
RJ Randy Johnson 2 20.00 50.00
RP Rafael Palmeiro 2 40.00 80.00
TG Tony Gwynn 2 60.00 120.00
TH Todd Helton 1 30.00 60.00
TM Tino Martinez 2 20.00 50.00

2003 Topps Prime Cuts Autograph Relics

SER.1 ODDS 1:27,661 H, 1:7917 HTA
SER2 ODDS 1:232,416H,1:8808HTA,1:28,598R
STATED PRINT RUN 50 SERIAL #'d SETS
NO PRICING DUE TO SCARCITY
AJ Andruw Jones 1 60.00 120.00
CJ Chipper Jones 1 30.00 60.00
DE Darin Erstad 1 30.00 60.00
EC Eric Chavez 1 30.00 60.00
LB Lance Berkman 2 60.00 120.00
MO Magglio Ordonez 2 60.00 120.00
MT Miguel Tejada 1 30.00 60.00
SR Scott Rolen 1 30.00 60.00

2003 Topps Prime Cuts Pine Tar Relics

SER.1 ODDS 1:9266 H, 1:1267 HTA
SER.2 ODDS 1:4288 H, 1:587 HTA, 1:928 R
STATED PRINT RUN 200 SERIAL #'d SETS
AD1 Adam Dunn 1 6.00 15.00
AD2 Adam Dunn 2 6.00 15.00
AJ Andruw Jones 1 6.00 15.00
AP1 Albert Pujols 1 30.00 60.00

Card	Low	High
AP2 Albert Pujols 2	30.00	60.00
AR1 Alex Rodriguez 1	10.00	25.00
AR2 Alex Rodriguez 2	10.00	25.00
AS1 Alfonso Soriano 1	6.00	15.00
AS2 Alfonso Soriano 2	6.00	15.00
BBO Barry Bonds 2	60.00	120.00
BW Bernie Williams 1	6.00	15.00
CD Carlos Delgado 2	6.00	15.00
CJ Chipper Jones 1	6.00	15.00
DE Darin Erstad 1	6.00	15.00
EC1 Eric Chavez 1	6.00	15.00
EC2 Eric Chavez 2	6.00	15.00
EM Edgar Martinez 2	6.00	15.00
FT Frank Thomas 1	6.00	15.00
HB Hank Blalock 2	6.00	15.00
IR Ivan Rodriguez 1	6.00	15.00
JG Juan Gonzalez 1	6.00	15.00
JP Jorge Posada 2	6.00	15.00
LB1 Lance Berkman 1	6.00	15.00
LB2 Lance Berkman 2	6.00	15.00
LG Luis Gonzalez 2	6.00	15.00
MO Magglio Ordonez 2	6.00	15.00
MP Mark Prior 2	6.00	15.00
MP Mike Piazza 1	6.00	15.00
MT Miguel Tejada 1	6.00	15.00
MV Mo Vaughn 1	6.00	15.00
NG1 Nomar Garciaparra 1	6.00	15.00
NG2 Nomar Garciaparra 2	6.00	15.00
RA1 Roberto Alomar 1	6.00	15.00
RA2 Roberto Alomar 2	6.00	15.00
RH Rickey Henderson 2	6.00	15.00
RJ Randy Johnson 2	6.00	15.00
RP1 Rafael Palmeiro 1	10.00	25.00
RP2 Rafael Palmeiro 2	10.00	25.00
SR Scott Rolen 1	6.00	15.00
TG Tony Gwynn 2	40.00	80.00
TH Todd Helton 1	6.00	15.00
TM Tino Martinez 2	6.00	15.00

2003 Topps Prime Cuts Trademark Relics

SER.1 ODDS 1:18,533 H, 1:2533 HTA
SER.2 ODDS 1:12,912 H, 1:881 HTA, 1:1857 R
STATED PRINT RUN 100 SERIAL #'d SETS

Card	Low	High
AD1 Adam Dunn 1	40.00	80.00
AD2 Adam Dunn 2	40.00	80.00
AJ Andruw Jones 1	50.00	100.00
AP1 Albert Pujols 1	75.00	150.00
AP2 Albert Pujols 2	75.00	150.00
AR1 Alex Rodriguez 1	60.00	120.00
AR2 Alex Rodriguez 2	60.00	120.00
AS1 Alfonso Soriano 1	50.00	100.00
AS2 Alfonso Soriano 2	50.00	100.00
BBO Barry Bonds 2	75.00	150.00
BW Bernie Williams 1	50.00	100.00
CD Carlos Delgado 2	40.00	80.00
CJ Chipper Jones 1	50.00	100.00
DE Darin Erstad 1	40.00	80.00
EC1 Eric Chavez 1	40.00	80.00
EC2 Eric Chavez 2	40.00	80.00
EM Edgar Martinez 2	50.00	100.00
FT Frank Thomas 1	50.00	100.00
HB Hank Blalock 2	40.00	80.00
IR Ivan Rodriguez 1	50.00	100.00
JG Juan Gonzalez 1	40.00	80.00
JP Jorge Posada 2	50.00	100.00
LB1 Lance Berkman 1	40.00	80.00
LB2 Lance Berkman 2	40.00	80.00
LG Luis Gonzalez 2	40.00	80.00
MO Magglio Ordonez 2	40.00	80.00
MP Mark Prior 2	50.00	100.00
MP Mike Piazza 1	50.00	100.00
MT Miguel Tejada 1	40.00	80.00
MV Mo Vaughn 1	40.00	80.00
NG1 Nomar Garciaparra 1	50.00	100.00
NG2 Nomar Garciaparra 2	50.00	100.00
RA1 Roberto Alomar 1	10.00	25.00
RA2 Roberto Alomar 2	10.00	25.00
RH Rickey Henderson 2	50.00	100.00
RJ Randy Johnson 2	50.00	100.00
RP1 Rafael Palmeiro 1	50.00	100.00
RP2 Rafael Palmeiro 2	50.00	100.00
SR Scott Rolen 1	20.00	50.00
TG Tony Gwynn 2	50.00	100.00
TH Todd Helton 1	50.00	100.00
TM Tino Martinez 2	50.00	100.00

2003 Topps Record Breakers

Card	Low	High
COMPLETE SET (100)	75.00	150.00
COMPLETE SERIES 1 (50)	40.00	80.00
COMPLETE SERIES 2 (50)	40.00	80.00
SERIES 1 ODDS 1:6 HOB, 1:2 HTA		
SERIES 2 ODDS 1:6 HOB, 1:2 HTA, 1:4 RET		
AG Andres Galarraga 1	.60	1.50
AR1 Alex Rodriguez 1	1.25	3.00
AR2 Alex Rodriguez 2	1.25	3.00
BB1 Barry Bonds 1	1.50	4.00
BB2 Barry Bonds 2	1.50	4.00
BF Bob Feller 2	.60	1.50
BG Bob Gibson 1	.60	1.50
CB Craig Biggio 2	.60	1.50
CD1 Carlos Delgado 1	.40	1.00
CD2 Carlos Delgado 2	.40	1.00
CF Cliff Floyd 1	.40	1.00
CJ Chipper Jones 1	1.00	2.50
CK Chuck Klein 1	.40	1.00
CS Curt Schilling 1	.60	1.50
DE Darin Erstad 2	.40	1.00
DG Dwight Gooden 2	.40	1.00
DM Don Mattingly 1	2.00	5.00
EM Edgar Martinez 2	.60	1.50
EM Eddie Mathews 1	1.00	2.50
FJ Fergie Jenkins 1	.60	1.50
FM Fred McGriff 1	.60	1.50
FR1 Frank Robinson 1	.60	1.50
FR2 Frank Robinson 2	.60	1.50
FT Frank Thomas 2	1.00	2.50
GA Garret Anderson 2	.40	1.00
GB1 George Brett 1	2.00	5.00
GB2 George Brett 2	2.00	5.00
GF1 George Foster 1	.40	1.00
GF2 George Foster 2	.40	1.00
GM Greg Maddux 2	1.25	3.00
GS Gary Sheffield 1	.40	1.00
HG Hank Greenberg 1	1.00	2.50
HK Harmon Killebrew 1	1.00	2.50
HW Hack Wilson 1	.60	1.50
IS Ichiro Suzuki 2	1.25	3.00
JB1 Jeff Bagwell 1	.60	1.50
JB2 Jeff Bagwell 2	.60	1.50
JD Johnny Damon 2	.60	1.50
JG Jason Giambi 1	.40	1.00
JK Jeff Kent 2	.40	1.00
JME Jose Mesa 2	.40	1.00
JM1 Juan Marichal 1	.60	1.50
JM2 Juan Marichal 2	.60	1.50
JO John Olerud 1	.40	1.00
JP Jim Palmer 2	.60	1.50
JR Jim Rice 2	.60	1.50
JS John Smoltz 2	1.00	2.50
JT Jim Thome 2	.60	1.50
KG1 Ken Griffey Jr. 1	2.00	5.00
KG2 Ken Griffey Jr. 2	2.00	5.00
LA Luis Aparicio 2	.60	1.50
LBR1 Lou Brock 1	.60	1.50
LBR2 Lou Brock 2	.60	1.50
LB1 Lance Berkman 1	.60	1.50
LB2 Lance Berkman 2	.60	1.50
LC Luis Castillo 1	.40	1.00
LD Lenny Dykstra 2	.40	1.00
LG1 Luis Gonzalez 1	.40	1.00
LG2 Luis Gonzalez 2	.40	1.00
LW Larry Walker 2	.60	1.50
MP Mike Piazza 1	1.00	2.50
MR Manny Ramirez 2	1.00	2.50
MS Mike Sweeney 1	.40	1.00
MSC Mike Schmidt 1	1.50	4.00
NG Nomar Garciaparra 2	.60	1.50
NR Nolan Ryan 1	3.00	8.00
PM Pedro Martinez 1	.60	1.50
PM Paul Molitor 2	1.00	2.50
PW Preston Wilson 1	.40	1.00
RA Roberto Alomar 2	.60	1.50
RC Roger Clemens 1	1.25	3.00
RCA Rod Carew 1	.60	1.50
RG Ron Guidry 1	.40	1.00
RH1 Rickey Henderson 1	1.00	2.50
RH2 Rickey Henderson 2	1.00	2.50
RJ1 Randy Johnson 1	1.00	2.50
RJ2 Randy Johnson 2	1.00	2.50
RP Rafael Palmeiro 1	.60	1.50
RS1 Richie Sexson 1	.40	1.00
RS2 Richie Sexson 2	.40	1.00
RY1 Robin Yount 1	1.00	2.50
RY2 Robin Yount 2	1.00	2.50
SG1 Shawn Green 1	.40	1.00
SG2 Shawn Green 2	.40	1.00
SS1 Sammy Sosa 1	1.00	2.50
SS2 Sammy Sosa 2	1.00	2.50
TG Troy Glaus 1	.40	1.00
TG1 Tony Gwynn 1	1.00	2.50
TG2 Tony Gwynn 2	1.00	2.50
TH1 Todd Helton 1	.60	1.50
TH2 Todd Helton 2	.60	1.50
TK Ted Kluszewski 2	.60	1.50
TR Tim Raines 2	.60	1.50
TS1 Tom Seaver 1	.60	1.50
TS2 Tom Seaver 2	.60	1.50
VG1 Vladimir Guerrero 1	.60	1.50
VG2 Vladimir Guerrero 2	.60	1.50
WB Wade Boggs 2	.60	1.50
WM Willie Mays 2	2.00	5.00
WS Willie Stargell 2	.60	1.50

2003 Topps Record Breakers Autographs

Card	Low	High
GROUP A1 SER.1 1:6941 H, 1:1178 HTA		
GROUP B1 SER.1 1:34,320 H, 1.9744 HTA		
GRP 2 SER.2 1:2218 H,1:634 HTA,1:1850 R		
CF Cliff Floyd A1	8.00	20.00
CJ Chipper Jones A1	30.00	60.00
DM Don Mattingly 2	50.00	120.00
FJ Fergie Jenkins A1	8.00	20.00
GF George Foster 2	8.00	20.00
HK Harmon Killebrew A1	20.00	50.00
JM Juan Marichal 2	8.00	20.00
LA Luis Aparicio 2	10.00	25.00
LB Lance Berkman 2	10.00	25.00
LBR Lou Brock 2	12.00	30.00
LG Luis Gonzalez B1	8.00	20.00
MS Mike Schmidt A1	25.00	60.00
RP Rafael Palmeiro A1	8.00	20.00
RS Richie Sexson A1	8.00	20.00
RY Robin Yount A1	40.00	80.00
SG Shawn Green A1	30.00	60.00
SW Mike Sweeney A1	8.00	20.00
WM Willie Mays 2	50.00	120.00

2003 Topps Record Breakers Relics

Card	Low	High
BAT B1/BAT 2/UNI B2 MINORS	4.00	10.00
BAT B1/BAT 2/UNI B2 SEMIS	6.00	15.00
BAT A1 SER.1 ODDS 1:13,528 H, 1:4872 HTA		
BAT B1 SER.1 ODDS 1:9058 H, 1:1689 HTA		
BAT C1 SER.1 ODDS 1:743 H, 1:90 HTA		
UNI A1 SER.1 ODDS 1:6178 H, 1:700 HTA		
UNI B1 SER.1 ODDS 1:355 H, 1:51 HTA		
BAT 2 SER.2 ODDS 1:191 H, 1:59 HTA		
UNI A2 SER.2 ODDS 1:5235, 1:400 HTA		
UNI B2 SER.2 ODDS 1:418, 1:176 HTA		
UNI C2 SER.2 ODDS 1:1151, 1:87 HTA		
AR1 Alex Rodriguez Uni B1	6.00	15.00
AR2 Alex Rodriguez Uni B2	6.00	15.00
CD1 Carlos Delgado Uni B1	4.00	10.00
CD2 Carlos Delgado Uni B2	4.00	10.00
CJ Chipper Jones Uni B1	6.00	15.00
DE Darin Erstad Uni A2	4.00	10.00
DG Dwight Gooden Uni B2	4.00	10.00
DM Don Mattingly Bat C1	10.00	25.00
EM Edgar Martinez Bat 2	6.00	15.00
FR1 Frank Robinson Bat C1	6.00	15.00
FR2 Frank Robinson Bat 2	6.00	15.00
FT Frank Thomas Bat 2	6.00	15.00
GB1 George Brett Bat C1	10.00	25.00
GB2 George Brett Bat 2	10.00	25.00
HG Hank Greenberg Bat B1	10.00	25.00
HW Hack Wilson Bat A1	15.00	40.00
JB Jeff Bagwell Uni B1	6.00	15.00
JR Jim Rice Uni B2	4.00	10.00
LBE Lance Berkman Bat C1	4.00	10.00
LC Luis Castillo Bat C1	4.00	10.00
LG Luis Gonzalez Bat 2	4.00	10.00
LGO Luis Gonzalez Uni B1	4.00	10.00
MP Mike Piazza Bat C1	10.00	25.00
MS Mike Sweeney Bat C1	4.00	10.00
NR Nolan Ryan Uni A1	20.00	50.00
NRA Nolan Ryan Uni C2	20.00	50.00
PM Pedro Martinez Uni B1	6.00	15.00
RH Rickey Henderson Bat C1	6.00	15.00
RHO Rogers Hornsby Bat 2	10.00	25.00
RS Richie Sexson Uni C2	4.00	10.00
RY1 Robin Yount Uni B1	10.00	25.00
RY2 Robin Yount Bat 2	10.00	25.00
SG Shawn Green Uni B1	4.00	10.00
TG Tony Gwynn 2B Bat 2	6.00	15.00
TG2 Tony Gwynn Avg Bat 2	6.00	15.00
TH1 Todd Helton Uni B1	6.00	15.00
TH2 Todd Helton Uni B2	6.00	15.00
TK Ted Kluszewski Bat 2	6.00	15.00
TR Tim Raines Bat 2	4.00	10.00
WB Wade Boggs Bat 2	6.00	15.00

2003 Topps Record Breakers Nolan Ryan

Card	Low	High
COMPLETE SET (7)	30.00	60.00
COMMON CARD (NR1-NR7)	4.00	10.00
SER.2 RB CUMULATIVE ODDS 1:2 HTA		

2003 Topps Record Breakers Nolan Ryan Autographs

Card	Low	High
COMMON CARD	125.00	200.00
SERIES 2 STATED ODDS 1:1894 HTA		

2003 Topps Red Backs

Card	Low	High
COMPLETE SET (40)	30.00	60.00
SERIES 2 ODDS 1:12 HOBBY, 1:8 RETAIL		
1 Nomar Garciaparra	.60	1.50
2 Ichiro Suzuki	1.25	3.00
3 Alex Rodriguez	1.25	3.00
4 Sammy Sosa	1.00	2.50
5 Barry Bonds	1.50	4.00
6 Vladimir Guerrero	.60	1.50
7 Derek Jeter	2.50	6.00
8 Miguel Tejada	.60	1.50
9 Alfonso Soriano	.60	1.50
10 Manny Ramirez	1.00	2.50
11 Adam Dunn	.60	1.50
12 Jason Giambi	.40	1.00
13 Mike Piazza	1.00	2.50
14 Scott Rolen	.60	1.50
15 Shawn Green	.40	1.00
16 Randy Johnson	1.00	2.50
17 Todd Helton	.60	1.50
18 Garret Anderson	.40	1.00
19 Curt Schilling	.60	1.50
20 Albert Pujols	1.25	3.00
21 Chipper Jones	1.00	2.50
22 Luis Gonzalez	.40	1.00
23 Mark Prior	.60	1.50
24 Jim Thome	.60	1.50
25 Ivan Rodriguez	.60	1.50
26 Torii Hunter	.40	1.00
27 Lance Berkman	.60	1.50
28 Troy Glaus	.40	1.00
29 Andruw Jones	.40	1.00
30 Barry Zito	.60	1.50
31 Jeff Bagwell	.60	1.50
32 Magglio Ordonez	.60	1.50
33 Pat Burrell	.40	1.00
34 Mike Sweeney	.40	1.00
35 Rafael Palmeiro	.60	1.50
36 Larry Walker	.60	1.50
37 Carlos Delgado	.40	1.00
38 Brian Giles	.40	1.00
39 Pedro Martinez	.60	1.50
40 Greg Maddux	1.25	3.00

2003 Topps Turn Back the Clock Autographs

Card	Low	High
GROUP A SER.1 ODDS 1:134 HTA		
GROUP B SER.1 ODDS 1:268 HTA		
BM Bill Madlock B	6.00	15.00
DM Dale Murphy A	10.00	25.00
JP Jim Palmer A	8.00	20.00
LD Lenny Dykstra A	8.00	20.00

2003 Topps Traded

Card	Low	High
COMPLETE SET (275)	25.00	60.00
COMMON CARD (T1-T120)	.07	.20
COMMON CARD (121-165)	.15	.40
COMMON CARD (166-275)	.15	.40
T1 Juan Pierre	.07	.20
T2 Mark Grudzielanek	.07	.20
T3 Tanyon Sturtze	.07	.20
T4 Greg Vaughn	.07	.20
T5 Greg Myers	.07	.20
T6 Randall Simon	.07	.20
T7 Todd Hundley	.07	.20
T8 Marlon Anderson	.07	.20
T9 Jeff Reboulet	.07	.20
T10 Alex Sanchez	.07	.20
T11 Mike Rivera	.07	.20
T12 Todd Walker	.07	.20
T13 Ray King	.07	.20
T14 Shawn Estes	.07	.20
T15 Gary Matthews Jr.	.07	.20
T16 Jaret Wright	.07	.20
T17 Edgardo Alfonzo	.07	.20
T18 Omar Daal	.07	.20
T19 Ryan Rupe	.07	.20
T20 Tony Clark	.07	.20
T21 Jeff Suppan	.07	.20
T22 Mike Stanton	.07	.20
T23 Ramon Martinez	.07	.20
T24 Armando Rios	.07	.20
T25 Johnny Estrada	.07	.20
T26 Joe Girardi	.12	.30
T27 Ivan Rodriguez	.12	.30
T28 Robert Fick	.07	.20
T29 Rick White	.07	.20
T30 Robert Person	.07	.20
T31 Alan Benes	.07	.20
T32 Chris Carpenter	.12	.30
T33 Chris Widger	.07	.20
T34 Travis Hafner	.07	.20
T35 Mike Venafro	.07	.20
T36 Jon Lieber	.07	.20
T37 Orlando Hernandez	.07	.20
T38 Aaron Myette	.07	.20
T39 Paul Bako	.07	.20
T40 Erubiel Durazo	.07	.20
T41 Mark Guthrie	.07	.20
T42 Steve Avery	.07	.20
T43 Damian Jackson	.07	.20
T44 Rey Ordonez	.07	.20
T45 John Flaherty	.07	.20
T46 Byung-Hyun Kim	.07	.20
T47 Tom Goodwin	.07	.20
T48 Elmer Dessens	.07	.20
T49 Al Martin	.07	.20
T50 Gene Kingsale	.07	.20
T51 Lenny Harris	.07	.20
T52 David Ortiz Sox	.20	.50
T53 Jose Lima	.07	.20
T54 Mike Difelice	.07	.20
T55 Jose Hernandez	.07	.20
T56 Todd Zeile	.07	.20
T57 Roberto Hernandez	.07	.20
T58 Albie Lopez	.07	.20
T59 Roberto Alomar	.12	.30
T60 Russ Ortiz	.07	.20
T61 Brian Daubach	.07	.20
T62 Carl Everett	.07	.20
T63 Jeromy Burnitz	.07	.20
T64 Mark Bellhorn	.07	.20
T65 Ruben Sierra	.07	.20
T66 Mike Fetters	.07	.20
T67 Armando Benitez	.07	.20
T68 Deivi Cruz	.07	.20
T69 Jose Cruz Jr.	.07	.20
T70 Jeremy Fikac	.07	.20
T71 Jeff Kent	.07	.20
T72 Andres Galarraga	.12	.30
T73 Rickey Henderson	.20	.50
T74 Royce Clayton	.07	.20
T75 Troy O'Leary	.07	.20
T76 Ron Coomer	.07	.20
T77 Greg Colbrunn	.07	.20
T78 Wes Helms	.07	.20
T79 Kevin Millwood	.07	.20
T80 Damion Easley	.07	.20
T81 Bobby Kielty	.07	.20
T82 Keith Osik	.07	.20
T83 Ramiro Mendoza	.07	.20
T84 Shea Hillenbrand	.07	.20
T05 Shannon Stewart	.07	.20
T86 Eddie Perez	.07	.20
T87 Ugueth Urbina	.07	.20
T88 Orlando Palmeiro	.07	.20
T89 Graeme Lloyd	.07	.20
T90 John Vander Wal	.07	.20
T91 Gary Bennett	.07	.20
T92 Shane Reynolds	.07	.20
T93 Steve Parris	.07	.20
T94 Julio Lugo	.07	.20
T95 John Halama	.07	.20
T96 Carlos Baerga	.07	.20
T97 Jim Parque	.07	.20
T98 Mike Williams	.07	.20
T99 Fred McGriff	.12	.30
T100 Kenny Rogers	.07	.20
T101 Matt Herges	.07	.20
T102 Jay Bell	.07	.20
T103 Esteban Yan	.07	.20
T104 Eric Owens	.07	.20
T105 Aaron Fultz	.07	.20
T106 Rey Sanchez	.07	.20
T107 Jim Thome	.12	.30
T108 Aaron Boone	.07	.20
T109 Raul Mondesi	.07	.20
T110 Kenny Lofton	.07	.20
T111 Jose Guillen	.07	.20
T112 Aramis Ramirez	.07	.20
T113 Sidney Ponson	.07	.20
T114 Scott Williamson	.07	.20
T115 Robin Ventura	.07	.20
T116 Dusty Baker MG	.07	.20
T117 Felipe Alou MG	.07	.20
T118 Buck Showalter MG	.07	.20
T119 Jack McKeon MG	.07	.20
T120 Art Howe MG	.07	.20
T121 Bobby Crosby PROS	.15	.40
T122 Adrian Gonzalez PROS	.30	.75
T123 Kevin Cash PROS	.15	.40
T124 Shin-Soo Choo PROS	.25	.60
T125 Chin-Feng Chen PROS	.15	.40
T126 Miguel Cabrera PROS	2.00	5.00
T127 Jason Young PROS	.15	.40
T128 Alex Herrera PROS	.15	.40
T129 Jason Dubois PROS	.15	.40
T130 Jeff Mathis PROS	.15	.40
T131 Casey Kotchman PROS	.15	.40
T132 Ed Rogers PROS	.15	.40
T133 Wilson Betemit PROS	.15	.40
T134 Jim Kavourias PROS	.15	.40
T135 Taylor Buchholz PROS	.15	.40
T136 Adam LaRoche PROS	.15	.40
T137 Dallas McPherson PROS	.15	.40
T138 Jesus Cota PROS	.15	.40
T139 Clint Nageotte PROS	.15	.40
T140 Boof Bonser PROS	.15	.40
T141 Walter Young PROS	.15	.40
T142 Joe Crede PROS	.15	.40
T143 Denny Bautista PROS	.15	.40
T144 Victor Diaz PROS	.15	.40
T145 Chris Narveson PROS	.15	.40
T146 Gabe Gross PROS	.15	.40
T147 Jimmy Journell PROS	.15	.40
T148 Rafael Soriano PROS	.15	.40
T149 Jerome Williams PROS	.15	.40
T150 Aaron Cook PROS	.15	.40
T151 Anastacio Martinez PROS	.15	.40
T152 Scott Hairston PROS	.15	.40
T153 John Buck PROS	.15	.40
T154 Ryan Ludwick PROS	.15	.40
T155 Chris Bootcheck PROS	.15	.40
T156 John Rheinecker PROS	.15	.40
T157 Jason Lane PROS	.15	.40
T158 Shelley Duncan PROS	.15	.40
T159 Adam Wainwright PROS	.25	.60
T160 Jason Arnold PROS	.15	.40
T161 Jonny Gomes PROS	.15	.40
T162 James Loney PROS	.25	.60
T163 Mike Fontenot PROS	.15	.40
T164 Khalil Greene PROS	.25	.60
T165 Sean Burnett PROS	.15	.40
T166 David Martinez FY RC	.15	.40
T167 Felix Pie FY RC	.25	.60
T168 Joe Valentine FY RC	.15	.40
T169 Brandon Webb FY RC	.50	1.25
T170 Matt Diaz FY RC	.25	.60
T171 Lew Ford FY RC	.15	.40
T172 Jeremy Griffiths FY RC	.15	.40
T173 Matt Hensley FY RC	.15	.40
T174 Charlie Manning FY RC	.15	.40
T175 Elizardo Ramirez FY RC	.15	.40
T176 Greg Aquino FY RC	.15	.40
T177 Felix Sanchez FY RC	.15	.40
T178 Kelly Shoppach FY RC	.25	.60
T179 Bubba Nelson FY RC	.15	.40
T180 Mike O'Keefe FY RC	.15	.40
T181 Hanley Ramirez FY RC	1.25	3.00
T182 Todd Wellemeyer FY RC	.15	.40
T183 Dustin Moseley FY RC	.15	.40
T184 Eric Crozier FY RC	.15	.40
T185 Ryan Shealy FY RC	.15	.40
T186 Jeremy Bonderman FY RC	.60	1.50
T187 T.Story-Harden FY RC	.15	.40
T188 Dusty Brown FY RC	.15	.40
T189 Rob Hammock FY RC	.15	.40
T190 Jorge Piedra FY RC	.15	.40
T191 Chris De La Cruz FY RC	.15	.40
T192 Eli Whiteside FY RC	.15	.40
T193 Jason Kubel FY RC	.50	1.25
T194 Jon Schuerholz FY RC	.15	.40
T195 Stephen Randolph FY RC	.15	.40
T196 Andy Sisco FY RC	.15	.40
T197 Sean Smith FY RC	.15	.40
T198 Jon-Mark Sprowl FY RC	.15	.40
T199 Matt Kata FY RC	.15	.40
T200 Robinson Cano FY RC	8.00	20.00
T201 Nook Logan FY RC	.15	.40
T202 Ben Francisco FY RC	.15	.40
T203 Arnie Munoz FY RC	.15	.40
T204 Ozzie Chavez FY RC	.15	.40
T205 Eric Riggs FY RC	.15	.40
T206 Beau Kemp FY RC	.15	.40
T207 Travis Wong FY RC	.15	.40
T208 Dustin Yount FY RC	.15	.40
T209 Brian McCann FY RC	1.25	3.00
T210 Wilton Reynolds FY RC	.15	.40
T211 Matt Bruback FY RC	.15	.40
T212 Andrew Brown FY RC	.15	.40
T213 Edgar Gonzalez FY RC	.15	.40
T214 Eider Torres FY RC	.15	.40
T215 Aquilino Lopez FY RC	.15	.40
T216 Bobby Basham FY RC	.15	.40
T217 Tim Olson FY RC	.15	.40
T218 Nathan Panther FY RC	.15	.40
T219 Bryan Grace FY RC	.15	.40
T220 Dusty Gomon FY RC	.15	.40
T221 Wil Ledezma FY RC	.15	.40
T222 Josh Willingham FY RC	.50	1.25
T223 David Cash FY RC	.15	.40
T224 Oscar Villarreal FY RC	.15	.40
T225 Jeff Duncan FY RC	.15	.40
T226 Kade Johnson FY RC	.15	.40
T227 Luke Steidlmayer FY RC	.15	.40
T228 Brandon Watson FY RC	.15	.40
T229 Jose Morales FY RC	.15	.40
T230 Mike Gallo FY RC	.15	.40
T231 Tyler Adamczyk FY RC	.15	.40
T232 Adam Stern FY RC	.15	.40
T233 Brennan King FY RC	.15	.40
T234 Dan Haren FY RC	.75	2.00
T235 Michel Hernandez FY RC	.15	.40
T236 Ben Fritz FY RC	.15	.40
T237 Clay Hensley FY RC	.15	.40
T238 Tyler Johnson FY RC	.15	.40
T239 Pete LaForest FY RC	.15	.40
T240 Tyler Martin FY RC	.15	.40
T241 J.D. Durbin FY RC	.15	.40
T242 Shane Victorino FY RC	.50	1.25
T243 Rajai Davis FY RC	.15	.40
T244 Ismael Castro FY RC	.15	.40
T245 Chien-Ming Wang FY RC	.60	1.50
T246 Travis Ishikawa FY RC	.40	1.00
T247 Corey Shafer FY RC	.15	.40
T248 Gary Schneidmiller FY RC	.15	.40
T249 Dave Pember FY RC	.15	.40
T250 Keith Stamler FY RC	.15	.40
T251 Tyson Graham FY RC	.15	.40
T252 Ryan Cameron FY RC	.15	.40
T253 Eric Eckenstahler FY	.15	.40
T254 Matthew Peterson FY RC	.15	.40
T255 Dustin McGowan FY RC	.15	.40
T256 Prentice Redman FY RC	.15	.40
T257 Haj Turay FY RC	.15	.40
T258 Carlos Guzman FY RC	.15	.40
T259 Matt DeMarco FY RC	.15	.40
T260 Derek Michaelis FY RC	.15	.40
T261 Brian Burgamy FY RC	.15	.40
T262 Jay Sitzman FY RC	.15	.40
T263 Chris Fallon FY RC	.15	.40
T264 Mike Adams FY RC	.25	.60
T265 Clint Barmes FY RC	.40	1.00
T266 Eric Reed FY RC	.15	.40
T267 Willie Eyre FY RC	.15	.40
T268 Carlos Duran FY RC	.15	.40
T269 Nick Trzesniak FY RC	.15	.40
T270 Ferdin Tejeda FY RC	.15	.40
T271 Michael Garciaparra FY RC	.15	.40
T272 Michael Hinckley FY RC	.15	.40
T273 Branden Florence FY RC	.15	.40
T274 Trent Oeltjen FY RC	.15	.40
T275 Mike Neu FY RC	.15	.40

2003 Topps Traded Gold

*GOLD 1-120: 3X TO 8X BASIC
*GOLD 121-165: 1.5X TO 4X BASIC
*GOLD 166-275: 1.5X TO 4X BASIC
STATED ODDS 1:2 HOB/RET, 1:1 HTA
STATED PRINT RUN 2003 SERIAL #'d SETS

2003 Topps Traded Future Phenoms Relics

Card	Low	High
GROUP A ODDS 1:2330 HOB/RET, 1:669 HTA		
GROUP B ODDS 1:505 HOB/RET, 1:144 HTA		
GROUP C ODDS 1:101 HOB/RET, 1:29 HTA		
BP Brandon Phillips Bat B	3.00	8.00
CC Chin-Feng Chen Jsy C	10.00	25.00
CDC Carl Crawford Bat C	3.00	8.00
CS Chris Snelling Bat C	3.00	8.00
HB Hank Blalock Bat C	3.00	8.00
JM Justin Morneau Bat C	3.00	8.00
JT Joe Thurston Jsy C	3.00	8.00
MB Marlon Byrd Bat C	3.00	8.00
MR Michael Restovich Bat B	3.00	8.00
MT Mark Teixeira Bat B	4.00	10.00
RB Rocco Baldelli Bat B	3.00	8.00
TAH Trey Hodges Jsy C	3.00	8.00
TH Travis Hafner Bat C	3.00	8.00
WB Wilson Betemit Bat C	3.00	8.00
WPB Willie Bloomquist Bat A	6.00	15.00

2003 Topps Traded Hall of Fame Relics

Card	Low	High
STATED ODDS 1:1009 HOB/RET, 1:289 HTA		
EM Eddie Murray Bat	10.00	25.00
GC Gary Carter Uni	6.00	15.00

2003 Topps Traded Hall of Fame Dual Relic

Card	Low	High
STATED ODDS 1:2015 HOB/RET, 1:578 HTA		
CM G.Carter Uni/E.Murray Bat	12.50	30.00

2003 Topps Traded Signature Moves Autographs

Card	Low	High
GROUP A ODDS 1:280 HOB/RET, 1:80 HTA		
GROUP B ODDS 1:114 HOB/RET, 1:33 HTA		
BC Bartolo Colon A	6.00	15.00
BU B.J. Upton B	6.00	15.00
CF Cliff Floyd A	6.00	15.00
DB David Bell A	6.00	15.00
EA Erick Almonte B	4.00	10.00
ER Elizardo Ramirez B	4.00	10.00
FP Felix Pie B	6.00	15.00
IR Robert Fick A	4.00	10.00
JB Joe Borchard B	4.00	10.00
JC Jose Cruz Jr. A	4.00	10.00
JF Jesse Foppert B	4.00	10.00
JG Joey Gomes B	4.00	10.00
JJC Jack Cust A	4.00	10.00
JL James Loney B	6.00	15.00
JR Jose Reyes B	4.00	10.00
JS Jason Stokes A	4.00	10.00
KG Khalil Greene A	10.00	25.00
MT Mark Teixeira A	4.00	10.00
VM Victor Martinez B	6.00	15.00
WY Walter Young B	4.00	10.00

2003 Topps Traded Transactions Bat Relics

Card	Low	High
GROUP A ODDS 1:168 HOB/RET, 1:48 HTA		
GROUP B ODDS 1:78 HOB/RET, 1:22 HTA		
AG Andres Galarraga A	3.00	8.00
CF Cliff Floyd B	3.00	8.00
DB David Bell B	3.00	8.00
EA Edgardo Alfonzo B	3.00	8.00
ED Erubiel Durazo B	3.00	8.00
EK Eric Karros B	3.00	8.00
FL Felipe Lopez A	3.00	8.00
FM Fred McGriff B	4.00	10.00
JC Jose Cruz Jr. B	3.00	8.00
JG Jeremy Giambi A	3.00	8.00
JK Jeff Kent B	3.00	8.00
JP Juan Pierre B	3.00	8.00
JT Jim Thome A	4.00	10.00
KL Kenny Lofton A	4.00	10.00
KM Kevin Millar Sox B	4.00	10.00
PW Preston Wilson A	3.00	8.00
RD Ray Durham A	3.00	8.00
RF Robert Fick A	3.00	8.00
RO Rey Ordonez B	3.00	8.00
RS Ruben Sierra A	3.00	8.00
RW Rondell White B	3.00	8.00
SH Tsuyoshi Shinjo B	3.00	8.00
SS Shane Spencer A	3.00	8.00
TG Tom Glavine A	4.00	10.00
TZ Todd Zeile A	3.00	8.00

2003 Topps Traded Transactions Dual Relics

Card	Low	High
STATED ODDS 1:421 HOB/RET, 1:120 HTA		
IR Ivan Rodriguez Marlins-Rgr	8.00	20.00
JT Jim Thome Phils-Indians	8.00	20.00
KM Kevin Millwood Phils-Braves	6.00	15.00

2004 Topps Pre-Production

Card	Low	High
COMPLETE SET (3)	1.25	3.00
PP1 Jason Giambi	.60	1.50
PP2 Curt Schilling	1.00	2.50
PP3 Jimmy Rollins	1.00	2.50

2004 Topps

Card	Low	High
COMP.HOBBY SET (737)	25.00	60.00
COMP.HOLIDAY SET (742)	25.00	60.00
COMP.RETAIL SET (737)	25.00	60.00
COMP.ASTROS SET (737)	25.00	60.00
COMP.CUBS SET (737)	25.00	60.00
COMP.RED SOX SET (737)	25.00	60.00
COMP.YANKEES SET (737)	25.00	60.00
COMPLETE SET (732)	20.00	50.00
COMPLETE SERIES 1 (366)	10.00	25.00
COMPLETE SERIES 2 (366)	10.00	25.00
COMMON CARD (1-6/8-732)	.07	.20
COMMON (297-326/668-687)	.20	.50
COMMON (327-331/688-692)	.20	.50
CARDS 7 AND 274 DO NOT EXIST		
SCIOSCIA AND J.CASTRO NUMBERED 267		
1 Jim Thome	.12	.30
2 Reggie Sanders	.07	.20
3 Mark Kotsay	.07	.20
4 Edgardo Alfonzo	.07	.20
5 Ben Davis	.07	.20
6 Mike Matheny	.07	.20
8 Marlon Anderson	.07	.20
9 Chan Ho Park	.12	.30
10 Ichiro Suzuki	.25	.60
11 Kevin Millwood	.07	.20
12 Bengie Molina	.07	.20
13 Tom Glavine	.12	.30
14 Junior Spivey	.07	.20
15 Marcus Giles	.07	.20
16 David Segui	.07	.20
17 Kevin Millar	.07	.20
18 Corey Patterson	.07	.20
19 Aaron Rowand	.07	.20
20 Derek Jeter	.50	1.25
21 Jason LaRue	.07	.20
22 Chris Hammond	.07	.20
23 Jay Payton	.07	.20
24 Bobby Higginson	.07	.20
25 Lance Berkman	.12	.30
26 Juan Pierre	.07	.20
27 Brent Mayne	.07	.20
28 Fred McGriff	.07	.20
29 Richie Sexson	.07	.20
30 Tim Hudson	.12	.30
31 Mike Piazza	.20	.50
32 Brad Radke	.07	.20
33 Jeff Weaver	.07	.20
34 Ramon Hernandez	.07	.20
35 David Bell	.07	.20
36 Craig Wilson	.07	.20
37 Jake Peavy	.07	.20
38 Tim Worrell	.07	.20
39 Gil Meche	.07	.20
40 Albert Pujols	.25	.60
41 Michael Young	.07	.20
42 Josh Phelps	.07	.20
43 Brendan Donnelly	.07	.20
44 Steve Finley	.07	.20
45 John Smoltz	.20	.50
46 Jay Gibbons	.07	.20
47 Trot Nixon	.07	.20
48 Carl Pavano	.07	.20
49 Frank Thomas	.20	.50
50 Mark Prior	.12	.30
51 Danny Graves	.07	.20
52 Milton Bradley UER	.07	.20
53 Jose Jimenez	.07	.20
54 Shane Halter	.07	.20
55 Mike Lowell	.07	.20
56 Geoff Blum	.07	.20
57 Michael Tucker UER	.07	.20
58 Paul Lo Duca	.07	.20
59 Vicente Padilla	.07	.20
60 Jacque Jones	.07	.20
61 Fernando Tatis	.07	.20
62 Ty Wigginton	.07	.20
63 Pedro Astacio	.07	.20
64 Andy Pettitte	.12	.30
65 Terrence Long	.07	.20
66 Cliff Floyd	.07	.20
67 Mariano Rivera	.25	.60
68 Carlos Silva	.07	.20
69 Marlon Byrd	.07	.20
70 Mark Mulder	.07	.20
71 Kerry Ligtenberg	.07	.20
72 Carlos Guillen	.07	.20
73 Fernando Vina	.07	.20
74 Lance Carter	.07	.20
75 Hank Blalock	.07	.20
76 Jimmy Rollins	.12	.30
77 Francisco Rodriguez	.12	.30
78 Javy Lopez	.07	.20
79 Jerry Hairston Jr.	.07	.20
80 Andruw Jones	.07	.20
81 Rodrigo Lopez	.07	.20
82 Johnny Damon	.12	.30
83 Hee Seop Choi	.07	.20
84 Miguel Olivo	.07	.20
85 Jon Garland	.07	.20
86 Matt Lawton	.07	.20
87 Juan Uribe	.07	.20
88 Steve Sparks	.07	.20
89 Tim Spooneybarger	.07	.20
90 Jose Vidro	.07	.20
91 Luis Rivas	.07	.20
92 Hideo Nomo	.20	.50
93 Javier Vazquez	.07	.20
94 Al Leiter	.07	.20
95 Darren Dreifort	.07	.20
96 Alex Cintron	.07	.20
97 Zach Day	.07	.20
98 Jorge Posada	.12	.30
99 John Halama	.07	.20
100 Alex Rodriguez	.25	.60
101 Orlando Palmeiro	.07	.20
102 Dave Berg	.07	.20
103 Brad Fullmer	.07	.20
104 Mike Hampton	.07	.20
105 Willis Roberts	.07	.20
106 Ramiro Mendoza	.07	.20
107 Juan Cruz	.07	.20
108 Esteban Loaiza	.07	.20
109 Russell Branyan	.07	.20
110 Todd Helton	.12	.30
111 Braden Looper	.07	.20
112 Octavio Dotel	.07	.20
113 Mike MacDougal	.07	.20
114 Cesar Izturis	.07	.20
115 Johan Santana	.12	.30
116 Jose Contreras	.07	.20
117 Placido Polanco	.07	.20
118 Jason Phillips	.07	.20
119 Adam Eaton	.07	.20
120 Vernon Wells	.07	.20
121 Ben Grieve	.07	.20
122 Randy Winn	.07	.20
123 Ismael Valdes	.07	.20
124 Eric Owens	.07	.20
125 Curt Schilling	.12	.30
126 Russ Ortiz	.07	.20
127 Mark Buehrle	.12	.30
128 Danys Baez	.07	.20
129 Dmitri Young	.07	.20
130 Kazuhisa Ishii	.07	.20
131 A.J. Pierzynski	.07	.20
132 Michael Barrett	.07	.20
133 Joe McEwing	.07	.20
134 Alex Cora	.12	.30
135 Tom Wilson	.07	.20
136 Carlos Zambrano	.12	.30
137 Brett Tomko	.07	.20
138 Shigetoshi Hasegawa	.07	.20
139 Jarrod Washburn	.07	.20
140 Greg Maddux	.25	.60
141 Craig Counsell	.07	.20
142 Reggie Taylor	.07	.20
143 Omar Vizquel	.12	.30
144 Alex Gonzalez	.07	.20
145 Billy Wagner	.07	.20
146 Brian Jordan	.07	.20
147 Wes Helms	.07	.20
148 Kyle Lohse	.07	.20
149 Timo Perez	.07	.20
150 Jason Giambi	.07	.20
151 Erubiel Durazo	.07	.20
152 Mike Lieberthal	.07	.20
153 Jason Kendall	.07	.20
154 Xavier Nady	.07	.20
155 Kirk Rueter	.07	.20

156 Mike Cameron .07 .20
157 Miguel Cairo .07 .20
158 Woody Williams .07 .20
159 Toby Hall .07 .20
160 Bernie Williams .12 .30
161 Darin Erstad .07 .20
162 Matt Mantei .07 .20
163 Geronimo Gil .07 .20
164 Bill Mueller .07 .20
165 Damian Miller .07 .20
166 Tony Graffanino .07 .20
167 Sean Casey .07 .20
168 Brandon Phillips .07 .20
169 Mike Remlinger .07 .20
170 Adam Dunn .12 .30
171 Carlos Lee .07 .20
172 Juan Encarnacion .07 .20
173 Angel Berroa .07 .20
174 Desi Relaford .07 .20
175 Paul Quantrill .07 .20
176 Ben Sheets .07 .20
177 Eddie Guardado .07 .20
178 Rocky Biddle .07 .20
179 Mike Stanton .07 .20
180 Eric Chavez .07 .20
181 Jason Michaels .07 .20
182 Terry Adams .07 .20
183 Kip Wells .07 .20
184 Brian Lawrence .07 .20
185 Bret Boone .07 .20
186 Tino Martinez .12 .30
187 Aubrey Huff .07 .20
188 Kevin Mench .07 .20
189 Tim Salmon .07 .20
190 Carlos Delgado .07 .20
191 John Lackey .12 .30
192 Oscar Villarreal .07 .20
193 Luis Matos .07 .20
194 Derek Lowe .07 .20
195 Mark Grudzielanek .07 .20
196 Tom Gordon .07 .20
197 Matt Clement .07 .20
198 Byung-Hyun Kim .07 .20
199 Brandon Inge .07 .20
200 Nomar Garciaparra .12 .30
201 Antonio Osuna .07 .20
202 Jose Mesa .07 .20
203 Bo Hart .07 .20
204 Jack Wilson .07 .20
205 Ray Durham .07 .20
206 Freddy Garcia .07 .20
207 J.D. Drew .07 .20
208 Einar Diaz .07 .20
209 Roy Halladay .12 .30
210 David Eckstein UER .07 .20
211 Jason Marquis .07 .20
212 Jorge Julio .07 .20
213 Tim Wakefield .12 .30
214 Moises Alou .07 .20
215 Bartolo Colon .07 .20
216 Jimmy Haynes .07 .20
217 Preston Wilson .07 .20
218 Luis Castillo .07 .20
219 Richard Hidalgo .07 .20
220 Manny Ramirez .20 .50
221 Mike Mussina .12 .30
222 Randy Wolf .07 .20
223 Kris Benson .07 .20
224 Ryan Klesko .07 .20
225 Rich Aurilia .07 .20
226 Kelvim Escobar .07 .20
227 Francisco Cordero .07 .20
228 Kazuhiro Sasaki .07 .20
229 Danny Bautista .07 .20
230 Rafael Furcal .07 .20
231 Travis Driskill .07 .20
232 Kyle Farnsworth .07 .20
233 Jose Valentin .07 .20
234 Felipe Lopez .07 .20
235 C.C. Sabathia .12 .30
236 Brad Penny .07 .20
237 Brad Ausmus .07 .20
238 Raul Ibanez .12 .30
239 Adrian Beltre .20 .50
240 Rocco Baldelli .07 .20
241 Orlando Hudson .07 .20
242 Dave Roberts .12 .30
243 Doug Mientkiewicz .07 .20
244 Brad Wilkerson .07 .20
245 Scott Strickland .07 .20
246 Ryan Franklin .07 .20
247 Chad Bradford .07 .20
248 Gary Bennett .07 .20
249 Jose Cruz Jr. .07 .20
250 Jeff Kent .07 .20
251 Josh Beckett .07 .20
252 Ramon Ortiz .07 .20
253 Miguel Batista .07 .20
254 Jung Bong .07 .20
255 Deivi Cruz .07 .20
256 Alex Gonzalez .07 .20
257 Shawn Chacon .07 .20
258 Runelvys Hernandez .07 .20
259 Joe Mays .07 .20
260 Eric Gagne .07 .20
261 Dustan Mohr .07 .20
262 Tomokazu Ohka .07 .20
263 Eric Byrnes .07 .20
264 Frank Catalanotto .07 .20
265 Cristian Guzman .07 .20
266 Orlando Cabrera .07 .20
267A Juan Castro .07 .20
267B Mike Scioscia MG UER 274 .07 .20
268 Bob Brenly MG .07 .20
269 Bobby Cox MG .07 .20
270 Mike Hargrove MG .07 .20
271 Grady Little MG .07 .20
272 Dusty Baker MG .07 .20
273 Jerry Manuel MG .07 .20
275 Eric Wedge MG .07 .20
276 Clint Hurdle MG .07 .20
277 Alan Trammell MG .12 .30
278 Jack McKeon MG .07 .20
279 Jimy Williams MG .07 .20
280 Tony Pena MG .07 .20
281 Jim Tracy MG .07 .20
282 Ned Yost MG .07 .20
283 Ron Gardenhire MG .07 .20
284 Frank Robinson MG .12 .30
285 Art Howe MG .07 .20
286 Joe Torre MG .12 .30
287 Ken Macha MG .07 .20
288 Larry Bowa MG .07 .20
289 Lloyd McClendon MG .07 .20
290 Bruce Bochy MG .12 .30
291 Felipe Alou MG .07 .20
292 Bob Melvin MG .07 .20
293 Tony LaRussa MG .12 .30
294 Lou Piniella MG .07 .20
295 Buck Showalter MG .07 .20
296 Carlos Tosca MG .07 .20
297 Anthony Acevedo FY RC .20 .50
298 Anthony Lerew FY RC .20 .50
299 Blake Hawksworth FY RC .20 .50
300 Brayan Pena FY RC .20 .50
301 Casey Myers FY RC .20 .50
302 Craig Ansman FY RC .20 .50
303 David Murphy FY RC .30 .75
304 Dave Crouthers FY RC .20 .50
305 Dioner Navarro FY RC .30 .75
306 Donald Levinski FY RC .20 .50
307 Jesse Roman FY RC .20 .50
308 Sung Jung FY RC .20 .50
309 Jon Knott FY RC .20 .50
310 Josh Labandeira FY RC .20 .50
311 Kenny Perez FY RC .20 .50
312 Khalid Ballouli FY RC .20 .50
313 Kyle Davies FY RC .20 .50
314 Marcus McBeth FY RC .20 .50
315 Matt Creighton FY RC .20 .50
316 Chris O'Riordan FY RC .20 .50
317 Mike Gosling FY RC .20 .50
318 Nic Ungs FY RC .20 .50
319 Omar Falcon FY RC .20 .50
320 Rodney Choy Foo FY RC .20 .50
321 Tim Frend FY RC .20 .50
322 Todd Self FY RC .20 .50
323 Tydus Meadows FY RC .20 .50
324 Yadier Molina FY RC 40.00 100.00
325 Zach Duke FY RC .30 .75
326 Zach Miner FY RC .30 .75
327 B.Castro .30 .75
K.Greene FS
328 R.Madson .20 .50
E.Ramirez FS
329 R.Harden .20 .50
B.Crosby FS
330 Z.Greinke .75 2.00
J.Gobble FS
331 B.Jenks .20 .50
C.Kotchman FS
332 Sammy Sosa HL .20 .50
333 Kevin Millwood HL .07 .20
334 Rafael Palmeiro HL .12 .30
335 Roger Clemens HL .25 .60
336 Eric Gagne HL .07 .20
337 Mueller .50 1.25
Manny/Jeter LL
338 V.Wells .25 .60
Ichiro/M.Young LL
339 A-Rod .25 .60
Thomas/Delgado LL
340 Delgado .25 .60
A-Rod/Boone LL
341 Pedro .12 .30
Hudson/Loaiza LL
342 Loaiza .12 .30
Pedro/Halladay LL
343 Pujols .25 .60
Helton/Renteria LL
344 Pujols .25 .60
Helton/Pierre LL
345 Thome .12 .30
Sexson/J.Lopez LL
346 P.Wilson .12 .30
Sheff/Thome LL
347 Schmidt .12 .30
K.Brown/Prior LL
348 Wood .12 .30
Prior/Vazquez LL
349 R.Clemens .25 .60
D.Wells ALDS
350 K.Wood .12 .30
M.Prior NLDS
351 Beckett .20 .50
Cabrera/I.Rod NLCS
352 Giambi .25 .60
Rivera/Boone ALCS
353 D.Lowe .12 .30
I.Rod AL/NLDS
354 Pedro .25 .60
Posa/Clemens ALCS
355 Juan Pierre WS .07 .20
356 Carlos Delgado AS .07 .20
357 Bret Boone AS .07 .20
358 Alex Rodriguez AS .25 .60
359 Bill Mueller AS .07 .20
360 Vernon Wells AS .07 .20
361 Garret Anderson AS .07 .20
362 Magglio Ordonez AS .12 .30
363 Jorge Posada AS .12 .30
364 Roy Halladay AS .12 .30
365 Andy Pettitte AS .12 .30
366 Frank Thomas AS .20 .50
367 Jody Gerut AS .07 .20
368 Sammy Sosa .20 .50
369 Joe Crede .07 .20
370 Gary Sheffield .07 .20
371 Coco Crisp .07 .20
372 Torii Hunter .07 .20
373 Derrek Lee .07 .20
374 Adam Everett .07 .20
375 Miguel Tejada .12 .30
376 Jeremy Affeldt .07 .20
377 Robin Ventura .07 .20
378 Scott Podsednik .07 .20
379 Matthew LeCroy .07 .20
380 Vladimir Guerrero .12 .30
381 Tike Redman .07 .20
382 Jeff Nelson .07 .20
383 Cliff Lee .12 .30
384 Bobby Abreu .07 .20
385 Josh Fogg .07 .20
386 Trevor Hoffman .12 .30
387 Jesse Foppert .07 .20
388 Edgar Martinez .12 .30
389 Edgar Renteria .07 .20
390 Chipper Jones .20 .50
391 Eric Munson .07 .20
392 Dewon Brazelton .07 .20
393 John Thomson .07 .20
394 Chris Woodward .07 .20
395 Adam LaRoche .07 .20
396 Elmer Dessens .07 .20
397 Johnny Estrada .07 .20
398 Damian Moss .07 .20
399 Gabe Kapler .07 .20
400 Dontrelle Willis .07 .20
401 Troy Glaus .07 .20
402 Raul Mondesi .07 .20
403 Shane Reynolds .07 .20
404 Kurt Ainsworth .07 .20
405 Pedro Martinez .12 .30
406 Eric Karros .07 .20
407 Billy Koch .07 .20
408 Scott Schoeneweis .07 .20
409 Paul Wilson .07 .20
410 Mike Sweeney .07 .20
411 Jason Bay .12 .30
412 Mark Redman .07 .20
413 Jason Jennings .07 .20
414 Rondell White .07 .20
415 Todd Hundley .07 .20
416 Shannon Stewart .07 .20
417 Jae Weong Seo .07 .20
418 Livan Hernandez .07 .20
419 Mark Ellis .07 .20
420 Pat Burrell .07 .20
421 Mark Loretta .07 .20
422 Robb Nen .07 .20
423 Joel Pineiro .07 .20
424 Jason Simontacchi .07 .20
425 Sterling Hitchcock .07 .20
426 Rey Ordonez .07 .20
427 Greg Myers .07 .20
428 Shane Spencer .07 .20
429 Carlos Baerga .07 .20
430 Garret Anderson .07 .20
431 Horacio Ramirez .07 .20
432 Brian Roberts .07 .20
433 Damian Jackson .07 .20
434 Doug Glanville .07 .20
435 Brian Daubach .07 .20
436 Alex Escobar .07 .20
437 Alex Sanchez .07 .20
438 Jeff Bagwell .12 .30
439 Darrell May .07 .20
440 Shawn Green .07 .20
441 Geoff Jenkins .07 .20
442 Endy Chavez .07 .20
443 Nick Johnson .07 .20
444 Jose Guillen .07 .20
445 Tomas Perez .07 .20
446 Phil Nevin .07 .20
447 Jason Schmidt .07 .20
448 Julio Mateo .07 .20
449 So Taguchi .07 .20
450 Randy Johnson .20 .50
451 Paul Byrd .07 .20
452 Chone Figgins .07 .20
453 Larry Bigbie .07 .20
454 Scott Williamson .07 .20
455 Ramon Martinez .07 .20
456 Roberto Alomar .12 .30
457 Ryan Dempster .07 .20
458 Ryan Ludwick .07 .20
459 Ramon Santiago .07 .20
460 Jeff Conine .07 .20
461 Brad Lidge .07 .20
462 Ken Harvey .07 .20
463 Guillermo Mota .07 .20
464 Rick Reed .07 .20
465 Joey Eischen .07 .20
466 Wade Miller .07 .20
467 Steve Karsay .07 .20
468 Chase Utley .12 .30
469 Matt Stairs .07 .20
470 Yorvit Torrealba .07 .20
471 Joe Kennedy .07 .20
472 Reed Johnson .07 .20
473 Victor Zambrano .07 .20
474 Jeff Davanon .07 .20
475 Luis Gonzalez .07 .20
476 Eli Marrero .07 .20
477 Ray King .07 .20
478 Jack Cust .07 .20
479 Omar Daal .07 .20
480 Todd Walker .07 .20
481 Shawn Estes .07 .20
482 Chris Reitsma .07 .20
483 Jake Westbrook .07 .20
484 Jeremy Bonderman .07 .20
485 A.J. Burnett .07 .20
486 Roy Oswalt .12 .30
487 Kevin Brown .07 .20
488 Eric Milton .07 .20
489 Claudio Vargas .07 .20
490 Roger Cedeno .07 .20
491 David Wells .07 .20
492 Scott Hatteberg .07 .20
493 Ricky Ledee .07 .20
494 Eric Young .07 .20
495 Armando Benitez .07 .20
496 Dan Haren .07 .20
497 Carl Crawford .12 .30
498 Laynce Nix .07 .20
499 Eric Hinske .07 .20
500 Ivan Rodriguez .12 .30
501 Scot Shields .07 .20
502 Brandon Webb .07 .20
503 Mark DeRosa .07 .20
504 Jhonny Peralta .07 .20
505 Adam Kennedy .07 .20
506 Tony Batista .07 .20
507 Jeff Suppan .07 .20
508 Kenny Lofton .07 .20
509 Scott Sullivan .07 .20
510 Ken Griffey Jr. .40 1.00
511 Billy Traber .07 .20
512 Larry Walker .12 .30
513 Mike Maroth .07 .20
514 Todd Hollandsworth .07 .20
515 Kirk Saarloos .07 .20
516 Carlos Beltran .12 .30
517 Juan Rivera .07 .20
518 Roger Clemens .25 .60
519 Karim Garcia .07 .20
520 Jose Reyes .12 .30
521 Brandon Duckworth .07 .20
522 Brian Giles .07 .20
523 J.T. Snow .07 .20
524 Jamie Moyer .07 .20
525 Jason Isringhausen .07 .20
526 Julio Lugo .07 .20
527 Mark Teixeira .12 .30
528 Cory Lidle .07 .20
529 Lyle Overbay .07 .20
530 Troy Percival .07 .20
531 Robby Hammock .07 .20
532 Robert Fick .07 .20
533 Jason Johnson .07 .20
534 Brandon Lyon .07 .20
535 Antonio Alfonseca .07 .20
536 Tom Goodwin .07 .20
537 Paul Konerko .12 .30
538 D'Angelo Jimenez .07 .20
539 Ben Broussard .07 .20
540 Magglio Ordonez .12 .30
541 Ellis Burks .07 .20
542 Carlos Pena .12 .30
543 Chad Fox .07 .20
544 Jeriome Robertson .07 .20
545 Travis Hafner .07 .20
546 Joe Randa .07 .20
547 Wil Cordero .07 .20
548 Brady Clark .07 .20
549 Ruben Sierra .07 .20
550 Barry Zito .12 .30
551 Brett Myers .07 .20
552 Oliver Perez .07 .20
553 Trey Hodges .07 .20
554 Benito Santiago .07 .20
555 David Ross .07 .20
556 Ramon Vazquez .07 .20
557 Joe Nathan .07 .20
558 Dan Wilson .07 .20
559 Joe Mauer .15 .40
560 Jim Edmonds .12 .30
561 Shawn Wooten .07 .20
562 Matt Kata .07 .20
563 Vinny Castilla .07 .20
564 Marty Cordova .07 .20
565 Aramis Ramirez .07 .20
566 Carl Everett .07 .20
567 Ryan Freel .07 .20
568 Jason Davis .07 .20
569 Mark Bellhorn Sox .07 .20
570 Craig Monroe .07 .20
571 Roberto Hernandez .07 .20
572 Tim Redding .07 .20
573 Kevin Appier .07 .20
574 Jeromy Burnitz .07 .20
575 Miguel Cabrera .20 .50
576 Ramon Nivar .07 .20
577 Casey Blake .07 .20
578 Aaron Boone .07 .20
579 Jermaine Dye .07 .20
580 Jerome Williams .07 .20
581 John Olerud .07 .20
582 Scott Rolen .12 .30
583 Bobby Kielty .07 .20
584 Travis Lee .07 .20
585 Jeff Cirillo .07 .20
586 Scott Spiezio .07 .20
587 Stephen Randolph .07 .20
588 Melvin Mora .07 .20
589 Mike Timlin .07 .20
590 Kerry Wood .07 .20
591 Tony Womack .07 .20
592 Jody Gerut .07 .20
593 Franklyn German .07 .20
594 Morgan Ensberg .07 .20
595 Odalis Perez .07 .20
596 Michael Cuddyer .07 .20
597 Jon Lieber .07 .20
598 Mike Williams .07 .20
599 Jose Hernandez .07 .20
600 Alfonso Soriano .12 .30
601 Marquis Grissom .07 .20
602 Matt Morris .07 .20
603 Damian Rolls .07 .20
604 Juan Gonzalez .07 .20
605 Aquilino Lopez .07 .20
606 Jose Valverde .07 .20
607 Kenny Rogers .07 .20
608 Joe Borowski .07 .20
609 Josh Bard .07 .20
610 Austin Kearns .07 .20
611 Chin-Hui Tsao .07 .20
612 Wil Ledezma .07 .20
613 Aaron Guiel .07 .20
614 LaTroy Hawkins .07 .20
615 Tony Armas Jr. .07 .20
616 Steve Trachsel .07 .20
617 Ted Lilly .07 .20
618 Todd Pratt .07 .20
619 Sean Burroughs .07 .20
620 Rafael Palmeiro .12 .30
621 Jeremi Gonzalez .07 .20
622 Quinton McCracken .07 .20
623 David Ortiz .20 .50
624 Randall Simon .07 .20
625 Wily Mo Pena .07 .20
626 Nate Cornejo .07 .20
627 Brian Anderson .07 .20
628 Corey Koskie .07 .20
629 Keith Foulke Sox .07 .20
630 Rheal Cormier .07 .20
631 Sidney Ponson .07 .20
632 Gary Matthews Jr. .07 .20
633 Herbert Perry .07 .20
634 Shea Hillenbrand .07 .20
635 Craig Biggio .12 .30
636 Barry Larkin .12 .30
637 Arthur Rhodes .07 .20
638 Anaheim Angels TC .07 .20
639 Arizona Diamondbacks TC .07 .20
640 Atlanta Braves TC .07 .20
641 Baltimore Orioles TC .07 .20
642 Boston Red Sox TC .10 .30
643 Chicago Cubs TC .07 .20
644 Chicago White Sox TC .07 .20
645 Cincinnati Reds TC .07 .20
646 Cleveland Indians TC .07 .20
647 Colorado Rockies TC .07 .20
648 Detroit Tigers TC .07 .20
649 Florida Marlins TC .07 .20
650 Houston Astros TC .07 .20
651 Kansas City Royals TC .07 .20
652 Los Angeles Dodgers TC .07 .20
653 Milwaukee Brewers TC .07 .20
654 Minnesota Twins TC .07 .20
655 Montreal Expos TC .07 .20
656 New York Mets TC .07 .20
657 New York Yankees TC .20 .50
658 Oakland Athletics TC .07 .20
659 Philadelphia Phillies TC .07 .20
660 Pittsburgh Pirates TC .07 .20
661 San Diego Padres TC .07 .20
662 San Francisco Giants TC .07 .20
663 Seattle Mariners TC .07 .20
664 St. Louis Cardinals TC .07 .20
665 Tampa Bay Devil Rays TC .07 .20
666 Texas Rangers TC .07 .20
667 Toronto Blue Jays TC .07 .20
668 Kyle Sleeth DP RC .20 .50
669 Bradley Sullivan DP RC .20 .50
670 Carlos Quentin DP RC .75 2.00
671 Conor Jackson DP RC .60 1.50
672 Jeffrey Allison DP RC .20 .50
673 Matthew Moses DP RC .30 .75
674 Tim Stauffer DP RC .30 .75
675 Estee Harris DP RC .20 .50
676 David Aardsma DP RC .20 .50
677 Omar Quintanilla DP RC .20 .50
678 Aaron Hill DP .20 .50
679 Tony Richie DP RC .20 .50
680 Lastings Milledge DP RC .30 .75
681 Brad Snyder DP RC .20 .50
682 Jason Hirsh DP RC .20 .50
683 Logan Kensing DP RC .20 .50
684 Chris Lubanski DP .20 .50
685 Ryan Harvey DP .20 .50
686 Ryan Wagner DP .20 .50
687 Rickie Weeks DP .20 .50
688 G.Sizemore .30 .75
J.Guthrie
689 E.Jackson .20 .50
G.Miller
690 J.Reed .20 .50
N.Cotts
691 A.Loewen .40 1.00
N.Markakis
692 B.Upton .30 .75
D.Young
693 A.Rodriguez .50 1.25
D.Jeter
694 I.Suzuki .25 .60
A.Pujols
695 J.Thome .30 .75
M.Schmidt
696 Mike Mussina GG .12 .30
697 Bengie Molina GG .07 .20
698 John Olerud GG .07 .20
699 Bret Boone GG .07 .20
700 Eric Chavez GG .07 .20
701 Alex Rodriguez GG .25 .60
702 Mike Cameron GG .07 .20
703 Ichiro Suzuki GG .25 .60
704 Torii Hunter GG .07 .20
705 Mike Hampton GG .07 .20
706 Mike Matheny GG .07 .20
707 Derrek Lee GG .07 .20
708 Luis Castillo GG .07 .20
709 Scott Rolen GG .12 .30
710 Edgar Renteria GG .07 .20
711 Andruw Jones GG .07 .20
712 Jose Cruz Jr. GG .07 .20
713 Jim Edmonds GG .12 .30
714 Roy Halladay CY .12 .30
715 Eric Gagne CY .07 .20
716 Alex Rodriguez MVP .25 .60
717 Angel Berroa ROY .07 .20
718 Dontrelle Willis ROY .07 .20
719 Todd Helton AS .12 .30
720 Marcus Giles AS .07 .20
721 Edgar Renteria AS .07 .20
722 Scott Rolen AS .12 .30
723 Albert Pujols AS .25 .60
724 Gary Sheffield AS .07 .20
725 Javy Lopez AS .07 .20
726 Eric Gagne AS .07 .20
727 Randy Wolf AS .07 .20
728 Bobby Cox AS .07 .20
729 Scott Podsednik AS .07 .20
730 Alex Gonzalez WS .07 .20
731 Brad Penny WS .07 .20
732 Beckett .12 .30
I.Rod/A.Gonz WS
733 Josh Beckett WS MVP .07 .20

2004 Topps Black

COM. (1-6/8-331/368-695) 6.00 15.00
SEMIS 1-296/368-667/693-695 10.00 25.00
UNL 1-296/368-667/693-695 20.00 40.00
COM. 297-326/668-687 6.00 15.00
SEMIS 297-326/668-687 10.00 25.00
UNL 297-326/668-687 15.00 40.00
COM. 327-331/688-692 6.00 15.00
SEMIS 327-331/688-692 10.00 25.00
UNL 327-331/688-692 20.00 40.00
SERIES 1 ODDS 1:13 HTA
SERIES 2 ODDS 1:12 HTA
STATED PRINT RUN 53 SERIAL #'d SETS
CARDS 7 AND 274 DO NOT EXIST
SCIOSCIA AND J.CASTRO NUMBERED 267
10 Ichiro Suzuki 20.00 50.00
20 Derek Jeter 40.00 100.00
40 Albert Pujols 20.00 50.00
100 Alex Rodriguez 20.00 50.00
140 Greg Maddux 20.00 50.00
510 Ken Griffey Jr. 30.00 80.00
518 Roger Clemens 20.00 50.00
670 Carlos Quentin DP 25.00 60.00
671 Conor Jackson DP 20.00 50.00
680 Lastings Milledge DP 10.00 25.00
693 A.Rodriguez 40.00 100.00
D.Jeter
694 I.Suzuki 20.00 50.00
A.Pujols
695 J.Thome 25.00 60.00
M.Schmidt

2004 Topps Box Bottoms

A-Rod/Piazza/Andruw/Manny 1.50 4.00
*BOX BOTTOM CARDS: 1X TO 2.5X BASIC
ONE 4-CARD SHEET PER HTA BOX

2004 Topps Gold

*GOLD 1-296/368-667/693-695: 6X TO 15X
*GOLD 297-326/668-687: 1.25X TO 3X
*GOLD 327-331/688-692: 6X TO 15X
SERIES 1 ODDS 1:11 HOB, 1:3 HTA, 1:10 RET
SERIES 2 ODDS 1:8 HOB, 1:2 HTA, 1:8 RET
STATED PRINT RUN 2004 SERIAL #'d SETS
CARDS 7 AND 274 DO NOT EXIST
SCIOSCIA AND J.CASTRO NUMBERED 267

2004 Topps All-Star Patch Relics

SER.2 ODDS 1:7698 H, 1:2208 HTA, 1:7819 R
STATED PRINT RUN 15 SETS
CARDS ARE NOT SERIAL-NUMBERED
PRINT RUN INFO PROVIDED BY TOPPS
NO PRICING DUE TO SCARCITY

2004 Topps 1st Edition

*1st.ED 1-296/332-667/693-732: 1.25X TO 3X
*1st.ED 297-326/668-687: 1.25X TO 3X
*1st.ED 327-331/688-692: 1.25X TO 3X
DISTRIBUTED IN 1ST EDITION BOXES
CARDS 7 AND 274 DO NOT EXIST
SCIOSCIA AND J.CASTRO NUMBERED 267

2004 Topps All-Star Stitches Jersey Relics

SERIES 1 ODDS 1:137 HOB/RET, 1:39 HTA
AB Aaron Boone 4.00 10.00
AJ Andruw Jones 4.00 10.00
AR Alex Rodriguez 6.00 15.00
BD Brendan Donnelly 4.00 10.00
BW Billy Wagner 4.00 10.00
CE Carl Everett 4.00 10.00
EG Eddie Guardado 4.00 10.00
EGA Eric Gagne 4.00 10.00
EL Esteban Loaiza 4.00 10.00
EM Edgar Martinez 4.00 10.00
ER Edgar Renteria 4.00 10.00
HB Hank Blalock 4.00 10.00
JL Javy Lopez 4.00 10.00
JM Jamie Moyer 4.00 10.00
JP Jorge Posada 4.00 10.00
JS Jason Schmidt 4.00 10.00
JV Jose Vidro 4.00 10.00
KF Keith Foulke 4.00 10.00
KW Kerry Wood 4.00 10.00
ML Mike Lowell 4.00 10.00
MM Mark Mulder 4.00 10.00
MMO Melvin Mora 4.00 10.00
NG Nomar Garciaparra 6.00 15.00
PL Paul Lo Duca 4.00 10.00
PW Preston Wilson 4.00 10.00
RF Rafael Furcal 4.00 10.00
RH Ramon Hernandez 4.00 10.00
RO Russ Ortiz 4.00 10.00
RW Randy Wolf 4.00 10.00
RWH Rondell White 4.00 10.00
SH Shigetoshi Hasegawa 4.00 10.00
SR Scott Rolen 4.00 10.00
TG Troy Glaus 4.00 10.00
TH Todd Helton 4.00 10.00
VW Vernon Wells 4.00 10.00
WW Woody Williams 4.00 10.00

2004 Topps All-Stars

COMPLETE SET (20) 8.00 20.00
SERIES 2 ODDS 1:16 H, 1:4 HTA
TAS1 Jason Giambi .40 1.00
TAS2 Ichiro Suzuki 1.25 3.00
TAS3 Alex Rodriguez 1.25 3.00
TAS4 Albert Pujols 1.25 3.00
TAS5 Alfonso Soriano .60 1.50
TAS6 Nomar Garciaparra .60 1.50
TAS7 Andruw Jones .40 1.00
TAS8 Carlos Delgado .40 1.00
TAS9 Gary Sheffield .40 1.00
TAS10 Jorge Posada .60 1.50
TAS11 Magglio Ordonez .60 1.50
TAS12 Kerry Wood .40 1.00
TAS13 Garret Anderson .40 1.00
TAS14 Bret Boone .40 1.00
TAS15 Hank Blalock .40 1.00
TAS16 Mike Lowell .40 1.00
TAS17 Todd Helton .60 1.50
TAS18 Vernon Wells .40 1.00
TAS19 Roger Clemens 1.25 3.00
TAS20 Scott Rolen .60 1.50

2004 Topps Autographs

SER.1 A 1:18,502 H, 1:4735 HTA, 1:18,432 R
SER.1 B 1:7362 H, 1:1911 HTA, 1:7472 R
SER.1 C 1:10,900 H, 1:2741 HTA, 1:11,059 R
SER.1 D 1:1053 H, 1:273 HTA, 1:1055 R
SER.1 E 1:6278 H, 1:1640 HTA, 1:6284 R
SER.1 F 1:1229 H, 1:318 HTA, 1:1229 R
SER.1 G 1:2340 H, 1:668 HTA, 1:1881 R
SER.1 H 1:1167 H, 1:351 HTA, 1:1229 R
SER.2 A 1:10,530 H, 1:2848 HTA, 1:9774 R
SER.2 B 1:1504 H, 1:391 HTA, 1:1422 R
SER.2 C 1:1319 H, 1:333 HTA, 1:1303 R
SER.1 EXCH.DEADLINE 11/30/05
SER.2 EXCH.DEADLINE 04/30/06
AB Aaron Boone B2 12.00 30.00
AH Aubrey Huff B2 6.00 15.00
AK Austin Kearns B1 6.00 15.00
BB Bobby Brownlie C2 10.00 25.00
BS Benito Santiago D1 10.00 25.00
BU B.J. Upton F1 6.00 15.00
CF Cliff Floyd D1 6.00 15.00
DM Dustin McGowan C2 4.00 10.00
DW Dontrelle Willis B2 4.00 10.00
EH Eric Hinske H1 4.00 10.00
ER Elizardo Ramirez H1 4.00 10.00
GA Garret Anderson B2 6.00 15.00
HB Hank Blalock D1 6.00 15.00
IR Ivan Rodriguez B2 10.00 25.00
JB Josh Beckett B1 4.00 10.00
JG Jay Gibbons A1 6.00 15.00
JP1 Josh Phelps G1 4.00 10.00
JP2 Jorge Posada B2 20.00 50.00
JV Jose Vidro F1 4.00 10.00
KG Khalil Greene H1 4.00 10.00
LB Lance Berkman A2 10.00 25.00
MC Miguel Cabrera C2 30.00 80.00
ML Mike Lowell F1 6.00 15.00
MO Magglio Ordonez F1 6.00 15.00
MP Mark Prior D1 6.00 15.00
MS Mike Sweeney D1 6.00 15.00
MT Mark Teixeira D1 6.00 15.00
PK Paul Konerko G1 6.00 15.00
PL Paul Lo Duca E1 6.00 15.00
SP Scott Podsednik B2 10.00 25.00
TH Torii Hunter C1 8.00 20.00
VM Victor Martinez D1 6.00 15.00
ZG Zack Greinke C2 4.00 10.00

2004 Topps Derby Digs Jersey Relics

SERIES 1 ODDS 1:585 H, 1:167 HTA, 1:586 R
AP Albert Pujols 10.00 25.00
BB Bret Boone 4.00 10.00
CD Carlos Delgado 4.00 10.00
GA Garret Anderson 4.00 10.00
JE Jim Edmonds 4.00 10.00
JG Jason Giambi 4.00 10.00
RS Richie Sexson 4.00 10.00

2004 Topps Draft Pick Bonus

COMPLETE SET (10) 10.00 25.00
COMP.RETAIL SET (5) 6.00 15.00
COMP.HOLIDAY SET (10) 4.00 10.00
1-5 ISSUED IN BLUE RETAIL FACT.SET
6-15 ISSUED IN GREEN HOLIDAY FACT.SET
1 Josh Johnson .50 1.25
2 Donny Lucy .50 1.25
3 Greg Golson .50 1.25
4 K.C. Herren .50 1.25
5 Jeff Marquez .50 1.25
6 Mark Rogers .75 2.00
7 Eric Hurley .50 1.25
8 Gio Gonzalez .75 2.00
9 Thomas Diamond .50 1.25
10 Matt Bush .75 2.00
11 Kyle Waldrop .50 1.25
12 Neil Walker .75 2.00
13 Mike Ferris .50 1.25
14 Ray Liotta .50 1.25
15 Philip Hughes 1.25 3.00

2004 Topps Fall Classic Covers

COMPLETE SET (99) 60.00 120.00
COMPLETE SERIES 1 (48) 30.00 60.00
COMPLETE SERIES 2 (51) 30.00 60.00
COMMON CARD 1.50 4.00
SERIES 1 ODDS 1:12 HOB/RET, 1:4 HTA
SERIES 2 ODDS 1:12 HOB/RET, 1:5 HTA
EVEN YEARS DISTRIBUTED IN SERIES 1
ODD YEARS DISTRIBUTED IN SERIES 2

2004 Topps First Year Player Bonus

COMPLETE SET (10) 8.00 20.00
COMPLETE SERIES 1 (5) 4.00 10.00
COMPLETE SERIES 2 (5) 4.00 10.00
1-5 ISSUED IN BROWN HOBBY FACT.SETS
6-10 ISSUED IN JC PENNEY FACT.SETS
1 Travis Blackley .50 1.25
2 Rudy Guillen .50 1.25
3 Ervin Santana 1.25 3.00
4 Wanell Severino .50 1.25
5 Kevin Kouzmanoff 3.00 8.00
6 Alberto Callaspo 1.25 3.00
7 Bobby Brownlie .50 1.25
8 Travis Hanson .50 1.25
9 Joaquin Arias 1.25 3.00
10 Merkin Valdez .50 1.25

2004 Topps Hit Parade

COMPLETE SET (30) 12.50 30.00
SERIES 2 ODDS 1:7 HOB, 1:2 HTA, 1:9 RET
HP1 Sammy Sosa HR 1.00 2.50
HP2 Rafael Palmeiro HR .60 1.50
HP3 Fred McGriff HR .40 1.00
HP4 Ken Griffey Jr. HR 2.00 5.00
HP5 Juan Gonzalez HR .40 1.00
HP6 Frank Thomas HR 1.00 2.50
HP7 Andres Galarraga HR .60 1.50
HP8 Jim Thome HR .60 1.50
HP9 Jeff Bagwell HR .60 1.50
HP10 Gary Sheffield HR .40 1.00
HP11 Rafael Palmeiro RBI .60 1.50
HP12 Sammy Sosa RBI 1.00 2.50
HP13 Fred McGriff RBI .40 1.00
HP14 Andres Galarraga RBI .60 1.50
HP15 Juan Gonzalez RBI .40 1.00
HP16 Frank Thomas RBI 1.00 2.50
HP17 Jeff Bagwell RBI .60 1.50
HP18 Ken Griffey Jr. RBI 2.00 5.00
HP19 Ruben Sierra RBI .40 1.00
HP20 Gary Sheffield RBI .40 1.00
HP21 Rafael Palmeiro Hits .60 1.50
HP22 Roberto Alomar Hits .60 1.50
HP22A Roberto Alomar Hits .60 1.50
White Card Number
HP23 Julio Franco Hits .40 1.00
HP24 Andres Galarraga Hits .60 1.50
HP25 Fred McGriff Hits .40 1.00
HP26 Craig Biggio Hits .60 1.50

HP27 Barry Larkin Hits .60 1.50
HP28 Steve Finley Hits .40 1.00
HP29 B.J. Surhoff Hits .40 1.00
HP30 Jeff Bagwell Hits .60 1.50

2004 Topps Hobby Masters

COMPLETE SET (20) 12.50 30.00
SERIES 1 ODDS 1:12 HOBBY, 1:4 HTA
1 Albert Pujols 1.25 3.00
2 Mark Prior .60 1.50
3 Alex Rodriguez 1.25 3.00
4 Nomar Garciaparra .60 1.50
5 Barry Bonds 1.50 4.00
6 Sammy Sosa 1.00 2.50
7 Alfonso Soriano .60 1.50
8 Ichiro Suzuki 1.25 3.00
9 Derek Jeter 2.50 6.00
10 Jim Thome .60 1.50
11 Jason Giambi .40 1.00
12 Mike Piazza 1.00 2.50
13 Barry Zito .60 1.50
14 Randy Johnson 1.00 2.50
15 Adam Dunn .60 1.50
16 Vladimir Guerrero .60 1.50
17 Gary Sheffield .40 1.00
18 Carlos Delgado .40 1.00
19 Chipper Jones 1.00 2.50
20 Dontrelle Willis .40 1.00

2004 Topps Own the Game

COMPLETE SET (30) 15.00 40.00
SERIES 1 ODDS 1:18 HOB/RET, 1:6 HTA
1 Jim Thome .60 1.50
2 Albert Pujols 1.25 3.00
3 Alex Rodriguez 1.25 3.00
4 Barry Bonds 1.50 4.00
5 Ichiro Suzuki 1.25 3.00
6 Derek Jeter 2.50 6.00
7 Nomar Garciaparra .60 1.50
8 Alfonso Soriano .60 1.50
9 Gary Sheffield .40 1.00
10 Jason Giambi .40 1.00
11 Todd Helton .60 1.50
12 Garret Anderson .40 1.00
13 Carlos Delgado .40 1.00
14 Manny Ramirez 1.00 2.50
15 Richie Sexson .40 1.00
16 Vernon Wells .40 1.00
17 Preston Wilson .40 1.00
18 Frank Thomas 1.00 2.50
19 Shawn Green .40 1.00
20 Rafael Furcal .40 1.00
21 Juan Pierre .40 1.00
22 Javy Lopez .40 1.00
23 Edgar Renteria .40 1.00
24 Mark Prior .60 1.50
25 Pedro Martinez .60 1.50
26 Kerry Wood .40 1.00
27 Curt Schilling .60 1.50
28 Roy Halladay .60 1.50
29 Eric Gagne .40 1.00
30 Brandon Webb .40 1.00

2004 Topps Presidential First Pitch Seat Relics

SERIES 2 ODDS 1:592 H, 1:169 HTA, 1:592 R
BC Bill Clinton 20.00 50.00
CC Calvin Coolidge 10.00 25.00
DE Dwight Eisenhower 10.00 25.00
FR Franklin D. Roosevelt 15.00 40.00
GB George W. Bush 15.00 40.00
GF Gerald Ford 15.00 40.00
HH Herbert Hoover 10.00 25.00
HT Harry Truman 10.00 25.00
JK John F. Kennedy 12.00 30.00
LJ Lyndon B. Johnson 10.00 25.00
RN Richard Nixon 12.00 30.00
RR Ronald Reagan 12.00 30.00
WH Warren Harding 10.00 25.00
WT William Taft 10.00 25.00
WW Woodrow Wilson 10.00 25.00
GHB George H.W. Bush 15.00 40.00

2004 Topps Presidential Pastime

COMPLETE SET (42) 50.00 100.00
SERIES 2 ODDS 1:6 HOB, 1:2 HTA, 1:6 RET
PP1 George Washington 2.00 5.00
PP2 John Adams 1.25 3.00
PP3 Thomas Jefferson 2.00 5.00
PP4 James Madison 1.25 3.00
PP5 James Monroe 1.25 3.00
PP6 John Quincy Adams 1.25 3.00
PP7 Andrew Jackson 1.25 3.00
PP8 Martin Van Buren 1.25 3.00
PP9 William Harrison 1.25 3.00
PP10 John Tyler 1.25 3.00
PP11 James Polk 1.25 3.00
PP12 Zachary Taylor 1.25 3.00
PP13 Millard Fillmore 1.25 3.00
PP14 Franklin Pierce 1.25 3.00
PP15 James Buchanan 1.25 3.00
PP16 Abraham Lincoln 2.00 5.00
PP17 Andrew Johnson 1.25 3.00
PP18 Ulysses S. Grant 1.50 4.00
PP19 Rutherford B. Hayes 1.25 3.00
PP20 James Garfield 1.25 3.00
PP21 Chester Arthur 1.25 3.00
PP22 Grover Cleveland 1.25 3.00
PP23 Benjamin Harrison 1.25 3.00
PP24 William McKinley 1.25 3.00
PP25 Theodore Roosevelt 1.50 4.00
PP26 William Taft 1.25 3.00
PP27 Woodrow Wilson 1.25 3.00
PP28 Warren Harding 1.25 3.00
PP29 Calvin Coolidge 1.25 3.00
PP30 Herbert Hoover 1.25 3.00
PP31 Franklin D. Roosevelt 1.50 4.00
PP32 Harry Truman 1.25 3.00
PP33 Dwight Eisenhower 1.25 3.00
PP34 John F. Kennedy 1.50 4.00
PP35 Lyndon B. Johnson 1.25 3.00
PP36 Richard Nixon 1.50 4.00
PP37 Gerald Ford 1.50 4.00
PP38 Jimmy Carter 1.25 3.00
PP39 Ronald Reagan 4.00 10.00
PP40 George H.W. Bush 1.50 4.00
PP41 Bill Clinton 2.00 5.00
PP42 George W. Bush 2.00 5.00

2004 Topps Team Set Prospect Bonus

COMP.ASTROS SET (5) 3.00 8.00
COMP.CUBS SET (5) 3.00 8.00
COMP.RED SOX SET (5) 3.00 8.00
COMP.YANKEES SET (5) 3.00 8.00
A1-A5 ISSUED IN ASTROS FACTORY SET
C1-C5 ISSUED IN CUBS FACTORY SET
R1-R5 ISSUED IN RED SOX FACTORY SET
Y1-Y5 ISSUED IN YANKEES FACTORY SET
A1 Brooks Conrad .75 2.00
A2 Hector Gimenez .75 2.00
A3 Kevin Davidson .75 2.00
A4 Chris Burke .75 2.00
A5 John Buck .75 2.00
C1 Bobby Brownlie .75 2.00
C2 Felix Pie .75 2.00
C3 Jon Connolly .75 2.00
C4 David Kelton .75 2.00
C5 Ricky Nolasco 1.25 3.00
R1 David Murphy 1.25 3.00
R2 Kevin Youkilis .75 2.00
R3 Juan Cedeno .75 2.00
R4 Matt Murton .75 2.00
R5 Kenny Perez .75 2.00
Y1 Rudy Guillen .75 2.00
Y2 David Parrish .75 2.00
Y3 Brad Halsey .75 2.00
Y4 Hector Made .75 2.00
Y5 Robinson Cano 2.50 6.00

2004 Topps Series Seats Relics

SERIES 2 ODDS 1:316 HOB/RET, 1:89 HTA
AK Al Kaline 10.00 25.00
BF Bob Feller 6.00 15.00
BM Bill Mazeroski 10.00 25.00
BP Boog Powell 6.00 15.00
BR Brooks Robinson 6.00 15.00
FR Frank Robinson 6.00 15.00
HK Harmon Killebrew 10.00 25.00
JP Jim Palmer 6.00 15.00
LA Luis Aparicio 6.00 15.00
LP Lou Piniella 6.00 15.00
PM Paul Molitor 6.00 15.00
RJ Reggie Jackson 6.00 15.00
RY Robin Yount 10.00 25.00
WM Willie Mays 15.00 40.00
WS Warren Spahn 10.00 25.00

2004 Topps Series Stitches Relics

SER.2 GROUP A 1:829 H, 1:236 HTA, 1:832 R
SER.2 GROUP B 1:980 H, 1:280 HTA, 1:986 R
SER.2 GROUP C 1:686 H, 1:196 HTA, 1:686 R
AS Alfonso Soriano Bat B 6.00 15.00
CJ Chipper Jones Jsy C 6.00 15.00
DG Dwight Gooden Jsy A 4.00 10.00
DJ David Justice Bat B 6.00 15.00
FR Frank Robinson Bat A 6.00 15.00
GB George Brett Bat A 15.00 40.00
GC Gary Carter Jkt C 4.00 10.00
HK Harmon Killebrew Bat A 15.00 40.00
JB Johnny Bench Bat A 10.00 25.00
JBE Josh Beckett Jsy C 4.00 10.00
JC Joe Carter Bat B 6.00 15.00
JCA Jose Canseco Bat C 10.00 25.00
KG Kirk Gibson Bat B 6.00 15.00
KP Kirby Puckett Bat B 10.00 25.00
LD Lenny Dykstra Bat A 6.00 15.00
MS Mike Schmidt Uni A 15.00 40.00
PO Paul O'Neill Bat A 6.00 15.00
RC Roger Clemens Uni C 8.00 20.00
RJ Randy Johnson Jsy A 6.00 15.00
RJA Reggie Jackson Bat B 10.00 25.00
RY Robin Yount Uni A 6.00 15.00
SG Steve Garvey Bat B 6.00 15.00
TS Tom Seaver Uni A 6.00 15.00
WM Willie Mays Bat A 15.00 40.00

2004 Topps Legends Autographs

ISSUED IN VARIOUS 03-05 TOPPS BRANDS
SER.1 ODDS 1:1399 H, 1:421 HTA, 1:1494 R
SER.2 ODDS 1:766 H, 1:216 HTA, 1:802 R
AD Andre Dawson 8.00 20.00
BC Bert Campaneris 6.00 15.00
BP Boog Powell 6.00 15.00
CE Carl Erskine 6.00 15.00
DE Dwight Evans 8.00 20.00
DJ Davey Johnson 6.00 15.00
JP Jim Piersall 6.00 15.00
JP Johnny Podres 6.00 15.00
JR Joe Rudi 6.00 15.00
NR Nolan Ryan 125.00 300.00
SA Sparky Anderson 8.00 20.00
SG Steve Garvey 6.00 15.00
WM Willie Mays 100.00 200.00

2004 Topps World Series Highlights

COMPLETE SET (30) 15.00 40.00
COMPLETE SERIES 1 (15) 8.00 20.00
COMPLETE SERIES 2 (15) 8.00 20.00
SERIES 1 ODDS 1:18 HOB/RET, 1:6 HTA
SERIES 2 ODDS 1:18 HOB/RET, 1:7 HTA
AJ Andruw Jones 2 .40 1.00
AK Al Kaline 2 1.00 2.50
BM Bill Mazeroski 1 .60 1.50
BR Brooks Robinson 1 .60 1.50
BT Bobby Thomson 2 .60 1.50
CF Carlton Fisk 1 .60 1.50
CY Carl Yastrzemski 1 1.00 2.50
DB Dusty Baker 2 .40 1.00
DJ David Justice 2 .40 1.00
DL Don Larsen 1 .40 1.00
DS Duke Snider 2 .60 1.50
FR Frank Robinson 2 .60 1.50
JB Johnny Bench 2 1.00 2.50
JC Joe Carter 2 .40 1.00
JCA Jose Canseco 2 .60 1.50
JP1 Jim Palmer 1 .60 1.50
JP2 Johnny Podres 2 .40 1.00
KG Kirk Gibson 1 .40 1.00
KP Kirby Puckett 1 1.00 2.50
LB Lou Brock 1 .60 1.50
LG Luis Gonzalez 2 .40 1.00
MS Mike Schmidt 1 1.50 4.00
OS Ozzie Smith 2 1.25 3.00
RJ Reggie Jackson 1 .60 1.50
RY Robin Yount 1 1.00 2.50
SM Stan Musial 1 1.50 4.00
TS Tom Seaver 1 .60 1.50
WF Whitey Ford 2 .60 1.50
WM1 Willie Mays 1 2.00 5.00
WM2 Willie McCovey 2 .60 1.50

2004 Topps World Series Highlights Autographs

SERIES 1 ODDS 1:74 HTA
SERIES 2 ODDS 1:69 HTA
AK Al Kaline 2 20.00 50.00
BM Bill Mazeroski 1 15.00 40.00
BR Brooks Robinson 1 15.00 40.00
BT Bobby Thomson 2 12.00 30.00
CF Carlton Fisk 1 40.00 80.00
DB Dusty Baker 2 10.00 25.00
DJ David Justice 2 15.00 40.00
DL Don Larsen 1 10.00 25.00
DS Duke Snider 2 15.00 40.00
HK Harmon Killebrew 1 20.00 50.00
JB Johnny Bench 2 30.00 80.00
JP1 Jim Palmer 1 10.00 25.00
JP2 Johnny Podres 2 10.00 25.00
KG Kirk Gibson 1 30.00 80.00
LB Lou Brock 1 15.00 40.00
MS Mike Schmidt 1 30.00 80.00
RJ Reggie Jackson 2 20.00 50.00
RY Robin Yount 1 15.00 40.00
SM Stan Musial 2 40.00 80.00
WF Whitey Ford 2 20.00 50.00

2004 Topps Traded

COMPLETE SET (220) 20.00 50.00
COMMON CARD (1-70) .07 .20
COMMON CARD (71-90) .20 .50
COMMON CARD (91-110) .20 .50
COMMON CARD (111-220) .20 .50
BONDS AVAIL VIA HTA SHOP EXCHANGE
PLATE ODDS 1:151 H, 1:1173 R, 1:327 HTA
PLATE PRINT RUN 1 SET PER COLOR
BLACK-CYAN-MAGENTA-YELLOW ISSUED
NO PLATE PRICING DUE TO SCARCITY
T1 Pokey Reese .07 .20
T2 Tony Womack .07 .20
T3 Richard Hidalgo .07 .20
T4 Juan Uribe .07 .20
T5 J.D. Drew .07 .20
T6 Alex Gonzalez .07 .20
T7 Carlos Guillen .07 .20
T8 Doug Mientkiewicz .07 .20
T9 Fernando Vina .07 .20
T10 Milton Bradley .07 .20
T11 Kelvim Escobar .07 .20
T12 Ben Grieve .07 .20
T13 Brian Jordan .07 .20
T14 A.J. Pierzynski .07 .20
T15 Billy Wagner .07 .20
T16 Terrence Long .07 .20
T17 Carlos Beltran .12 .30
T18 Carl Everett .07 .20
T19 Reggie Sanders .07 .20
T20 Javy Lopez .07 .20
T21 Jay Payton .07 .20
T22 Octavio Dotel .07 .20
T23 Eddie Guardado .07 .20
T24 Andy Pettitte .12 .30
T25 Richie Sexson .07 .20
T26 Ronnie Belliard .07 .20
T27 Michael Tucker .07 .20
T28 Brad Fullmer .07 .20
T29 Freddy Garcia .07 .20
T30 Bartolo Colon .07 .20
T31 Larry Walker Cards .12 .30
T32 Mark Kotsay .07 .20
T33 Jason Marquis .07 .20
T34 Dustan Mohr .07 .20
T35 Javier Vazquez .07 .20
T36 Nomar Garciaparra .12 .30
T37 Tino Martinez .12 .30
T38 Hee Seop Choi .07 .20
T39 Damian Miller .07 .20
T40 Jose Lima .07 .20
T41 Ty Wigginton .07 .20
T42 Raul Ibanez .12 .30
T43 Danys Baez .07 .20
T44 Tony Clark .07 .20
T45 Greg Maddux .25 .60
T46 Victor Zambrano .07 .20
T47 Orlando Cabrera Sox .07 .20
T48 Jose Cruz Jr. .07 .20
T49 Kris Benson .07 .20
T50 Alex Rodriguez .25 .60
T51 Steve Finley .07 .20
T52 Ramon Hernandez .07 .20
T53 Esteban Loaiza .07 .20
T54 Ugueth Urbina .07 .20
T55 Jeff Weaver .07 .20
T56 Flash Gordon .07 .20
T57 Jose Contreras .07 .20
T58 Paul Lo Duca .07 .20
T59 Junior Spivey .07 .20
T60 Curt Schilling .12 .30
T61 Brad Penny .07 .20
T62 Braden Looper .07 .20
T63 Miguel Cairo .07 .20
T64 Juan Encarnacion .07 .20
T65 Miguel Batista .07 .20
T66 Terry Francona MG .07 .20
T67 Lee Mazzilli MG .07 .20
T68 Al Pedrique MG .07 .20
T69 Ozzie Guillen MG .07 .20
T70 Phil Garner MG .07 .20
T71 Matt Bush DP RC .30 .75
T72 Homer Bailey DP RC .30 .75
T73 Greg Golson DP RC .20 .50
T74 Kyle Waldrop DP RC .20 .50
T75 Richie Robnett DP RC .20 .50
T76 Jay Rainville DP RC .20 .50
T77 Bill Bray DP RC .20 .50
T78 Philip Hughes DP RC .50 1.25
T79 Scott Elbert DP RC .20 .50
T80 Josh Fields DP RC .30 .75
T81 Justin Orenduff DP RC .30 .75
T82 Dan Putnam DP RC .20 .50
T83 Chris Nelson DP RC .30 .75
T84 Blake DeWitt DP RC .30 .75
T85 J.P. Howell DP RC .20 .50
T86 Huston Street DP RC .30 .75
T87 Kurt Suzuki DP RC .30 .75
T88 Erick San Pedro DP RC .20 .50
T89 Matt Tuiasosopo DP RC .50 1.25
T90 Matt Macri DP RC .30 .75
T91 Chad Tracy PROS .20 .50
T92 Scott Hairston PROS .20 .50
T93 Jonny Gomes PROS .20 .50
T94 Chin-Feng Chen PROS .20 .50
T95 Chien-Ming Wang PROS .75 2.00
T96 Dustin McGowan PROS .20 .50
T97 Chris Burke PROS .20 .50
T98 Denny Bautista PROS .20 .50
T99 Preston Larrison PROS .20 .50
T100 Kevin Youkilis PROS .20 .50
T101 John Maine PROS .20 .50
T102 Guillermo Quiroz PROS .20 .50
T103 Dave Krynzel PROS .20 .50
T104 David Kelton PROS .20 .50
T105 Edwin Encarnacion PROS .50 1.25
T106 Chad Gaudin PROS .20 .50
T107 Sergio Mitre PROS .20 .50
T108 Laynce Nix PROS .20 .50
T109 David Parrish PROS .20 .50
T110 Brandon Claussen PROS .20 .50
T111 Frank Francisco FY RC .20 .50
T112 Brian Dallimore FY RC .20 .50
T113 Jim Crowell FY RC .20 .50
T114 Andres Blanco FY RC .20 .50
T115 Eduardo Villacis FY RC .20 .50
T116 Kazuhito Tadano FY RC .20 .50
T117 Aarom Baldiris FY RC .20 .50
T118 Justin Germano FY RC .20 .50
T119 Joey Gathright FY RC .20 .50
T120 Franklyn Gracesqui FY RC .20 .50
T121 Chin-Lung Hu FY RC .20 .50
T122 Scott Olsen FY RC .20 .50
T123 Tyler Davidson FY RC .20 .50
T124 Fausto Carmona FY RC .30 .75
T125 Tim Hutting FY RC .20 .50
T126 Ryan Meaux FY RC .20 .50
T127 Jon Connolly FY RC .20 .50
T128 Hector Made FY RC .20 .50
T129 Jamie Brown FY RC .20 .50
T130 Paul McAnulty FY RC .20 .50
T131 Chris Saenz FY RC .20 .50
T132 Marland Williams FY RC .20 .50
T133 Mike Huggins FY RC .20 .50
T134 Jesse Crain FY RC .30 .75
T135 Chad Bentz FY RC .20 .50
T136 Kazuo Matsui FY RC .30 .75
T137 Paul Maholm FY RC .30 .75
T138 Brock Jacobsen FY RC .20 .50
T139 Casey Daigle FY RC .20 .50
T140 Nyjer Morgan FY RC .20 .50
T141 Tom Mastny FY RC .20 .50
T142 Kody Kirkland FY RC .20 .50
T143 Jose Capellan FY RC .20 .50
T144 Felix Hernandez FY RC 3.00 8.00
T145 Shawn Hill FY RC .20 .50
T146 Danny Gonzalez FY RC .20 .50
T147 Scott Dohmann FY RC .20 .50
T148 Tommy Murphy FY RC .20 .50
T149 Akinori Otsuka FY RC .20 .50
T150 Miguel Perez FY RC .20 .50
T151 Mike Rouse FY RC .20 .50
T152 Ramon Ramirez FY RC .20 .50
T153 Luke Hughes FY RC .50 1.25
T154 Howie Kendrick FY RC 1.00 2.50
T155 Ryan Budde FY RC .20 .50
T156 Charlie Zink FY RC .20 .50
T157 Warner Madrigal FY RC .20 .50
T158 Jason Szuminski FY RC .20 .50
T159 Chad Chop FY RC .20 .50
T160 Shingo Takatsu FY RC .20 .50
T161 Matt Lemanczyk FY RC .20 .50
T162 Wardell Starling FY RC .20 .50
T163 Nick Gorneault FY RC .20 .50
T164 Scott Proctor FY RC .20 .50
T165 Brooks Conrad FY RC .20 .50
T166 Hector Gimenez FY RC .20 .50
T167 Kevin Howard FY RC .20 .50
T168 Vince Perkins FY RC .20 .50
T169 Brock Peterson FY RC .20 .50
T170 Chris Shelton FY RC .20 .50
T171 Erick Aybar FY RC .50 1.25
T172 Paul Bacot FY RC .20 .50
T173 Matt Capps FY RC .20 .50
T174 Kory Casto FY RC .20 .50
T175 Juan Cedeno FY RC .20 .50
T176 Vito Chiaravalloti FY RC .20 .50
T177 Alec Zumwalt FY RC .20 .50
T178 J.J. Furmaniak FY RC .20 .50
T179 Lee Gwaltney FY RC .20 .50
T180 Donald Kelly FY RC .30 .75
T181 Benji DeQuin FY RC .20 .50
T182 Brant Colamarino FY RC .20 .50
T183 Juan Gutierrez FY RC .20 .50
T184 Carl Loadenthal FY RC .20 .50
T185 Ricky Nolasco FY RC .30 .75
T186 Jeff Salazar FY RC .20 .50
T187 Rob Tejeda FY RC .20 .50
T188 Alex Romero FY RC .20 .50
T189 Yoann Torrealba FY RC .20 .50
T190 Carlos Sosa FY RC .20 .50
T191 Tim Bittner FY RC .20 .50
T192 Chris Aguila FY RC .20 .50
T193 Jason Frasor FY RC .20 .50
T194 Reid Gorecki FY RC .20 .50
T195 Dustin Nippert FY RC .20 .50
T196 Javier Guzman FY RC .20 .50
T197 Harvey Garcia FY RC .20 .50
T198 Ivan Ochoa FY RC .20 .50
T199 David Wallace FY RC .20 .50
T200 Joel Zumaya FY RC .75 2.00
T201 Casey Kopitzke FY RC .20 .50
T202 Lincoln Holdzkom FY RC .20 .50
T203 Chad Santos FY RC .20 .50
T204 Brian Pilkington FY RC .20 .50
T205 Terry Jones FY RC .20 .50
T206 Jerome Gamble FY RC .20 .50
T207 Brad Eldred FY RC .20 .50
T208 David Pauley FY RC .30 .75
T209 Kevin Davidson FY RC .30 .75
T210 Damaso Espino FY RC .20 .50
T211 Tom Farmer FY RC .20 .50
T212 Michael Mooney FY RC .20 .50
T213 James Tomlin FY RC .20 .50
T214 Greg Thissen FY RC .20 .50
T215 Calvin Hayes FY RC .20 .50
T216 Fernando Cortez FY RC .20 .50
T217 Sergio Silva FY RC .20 .50
T218 Jon de Vries FY RC .20 .50
T219 Don Sutton FY RC .20 .50
T220 Leo Nunez FY RC .20 .50
T221 Barry Bonds HTA 1.50 4.00

2004 Topps Traded Gold

*GOLD 1-70: 6X TO 15X BASIC
*GOLD 71-90: 1.2X TO 3X BASIC
*GOLD 91-110: 1.2X TO 3X BASIC
*GOLD 111-220: 1.2X TO 3X BASIC
STATED ODDS 1:2 HOB/RET, 1:1 HTA
STATED PRINT RUN 2004 SERIAL #'d SETS

2004 Topps Traded Future Phenoms Relics

GROUP A ODDS 1:184 H/R, 1:53 HTA
GROUP B ODDS 1:65 H/R, 1:27 HTA
AG Adrian Gonzalez Bat A 3.00 8.00
BC Bobby Crosby Bat A 4.00 10.00
BU B.J. Upton Bat A 6.00 15.00
DN Dioner Navarro Bat B 3.00 8.00
DY Delmon Young Bat A 6.00 15.00
ED Eric Duncan Bat B 2.00 5.00
EJ Edwin Jackson Jsy B 2.00 5.00
JH J.J. Hardy Bat B 6.00 15.00
JM Justin Morneau Bat A 4.00 10.00
JW Jayson Werth Bat A 6.00 15.00
KC Kevin Cash Bat B 2.00 5.00
KM Kazuo Matsui Bat A 4.00 10.00
LM Lastings Milledge Bat B 4.00 10.00
MM Mark Malaska Jsy A 3.00 8.00
NG Nick Green Bat A 3.00 8.00
RN Ramon Nivar Bat A 3.00 8.00
VM Victor Martinez Bat A 4.00 10.00

2004 Topps Traded Hall of Fame Relics

A ODDS 1:3388 H, 1:3518 R, 1:966 HTA
B ODDS 1:1011 H, 1:1026 R, 1:289 HTA
DE Dennis Eckersley Jsy B 6.00 15.00
PM Paul Molitor Bat A 6.00 15.00

2004 Topps Traded Hall of Fame Dual Relic

ODDS 1:3388 H, 1:3518 R, 1:966 HTA
ME Molitor Bat/Eckersley Jsy 10.00 25.00

2004 Topps Traded Puzzle

COMPLETE PUZZLE (110) 25.00 50.00
COMMON PIECE (1-110) .20 .50
ONE PER PACK
1 Puzzle Piece 1 .20 .50
2 Puzzle Piece 2 .20 .50
3 Puzzle Piece 3 .20 .50
4 Puzzle Piece 4 .20 .50
5 Puzzle Piece 5 .20 .50
6 Puzzle Piece 6 .20 .50
7 Puzzle Piece 7 .20 .50
8 Puzzle Piece 8 .20 .50
9 Puzzle Piece 9 .20 .50
10 Puzzle Piece 10 .20 .50
11 Puzzle Piece 11 .20 .50
12 Puzzle Piece 12 .20 .50
13 Puzzle Piece 13 .20 .50
14 Puzzle Piece 14 .20 .50
15 Puzzle Piece 15 .20 .50
16 Puzzle Piece 16 .20 .50
17 Puzzle Piece 17 .20 .50
18 Puzzle Piece 18 .20 .50
19 Puzzle Piece 19 .20 .50
20 Puzzle Piece 20 .20 .50
21 Puzzle Piece 21 .20 .50
22 Puzzle Piece 22 .20 .50
23 Puzzle Piece 23 .20 .50
24 Puzzle Piece 24 .20 .50
25 Puzzle Piece 25 .20 .50
26 Puzzle Piece 26 .20 .50
27 Puzzle Piece 27 .20 .50
28 Puzzle Piece 28 .20 .50
29 Puzzle Piece 29 .20 .50
30 Puzzle Piece 30 .20 .50
31 Puzzle Piece 31 .20 .50
32 Puzzle Piece 32 .20 .50
33 Puzzle Piece 33 .20 .50
34 Puzzle Piece 34 .20 .50
35 Puzzle Piece 35 .20 .50
36 Puzzle Piece 36 .20 .50
37 Puzzle Piece 37 .20 .50
38 Puzzle Piece 38 .20 .50
39 Puzzle Piece 39 .20 .50
40 Puzzle Piece 40 .20 .50
41 Puzzle Piece 41 .20 .50
42 Puzzle Piece 42 .20 .50
43 Puzzle Piece 43 .20 .50
44 Puzzle Piece 44 .20 .50
45 Puzzle Piece 45 .20 .50
46 Puzzle Piece 46 .20 .50
47 Puzzle Piece 47 .20 .50
48 Puzzle Piece 48 .20 .50
49 Puzzle Piece 49 .20 .50
50 Puzzle Piece 50 .20 .50
51 Puzzle Piece 51 .20 .50
52 Puzzle Piece 52 .20 .50
53 Puzzle Piece 53 .20 .50
54 Puzzle Piece 54 .20 .50
55 Puzzle Piece 55 .20 .50
56 Puzzle Piece 56 .20 .50
57 Puzzle Piece 57 .20 .50
58 Puzzle Piece 58 .20 .50
59 Puzzle Piece 59 .20 .50
60 Puzzle Piece 60 .20 .50
61 Puzzle Piece 61 .20 .50
62 Puzzle Piece 62 .20 .50
63 Puzzle Piece 63 .20 .50
64 Puzzle Piece 64 .20 .50
65 Puzzle Piece 65 .20 .50
66 Puzzle Piece 66 .20 .50
67 Puzzle Piece 67 .20 .50
68 Puzzle Piece 68 .20 .50
69 Puzzle Piece 69 .20 .50
70 Puzzle Piece 70 .20 .50
71 Puzzle Piece 71 .20 .50
72 Puzzle Piece 72 .20 .50
73 Puzzle Piece 73 .20 .50
74 Puzzle Piece 74 .20 .50
75 Puzzle Piece 75 .20 .50
76 Puzzle Piece 76 .20 .50
77 Puzzle Piece 77 .20 .50
78 Puzzle Piece 78 .20 .50
79 Puzzle Piece 79 .20 .50
80 Puzzle Piece 80 .20 .50
81 Puzzle Piece 81 .20 .50
82 Puzzle Piece 82 .20 .50
83 Puzzle Piece 83 .20 .50
84 Puzzle Piece 84 .20 .50
85 Puzzle Piece 85 .20 .50
86 Puzzle Piece 86 .20 .50
87 Puzzle Piece 87 .20 .50
88 Puzzle Piece 88 .20 .50
89 Puzzle Piece 89 .20 .50
90 Puzzle Piece 90 .20 .50
91 Puzzle Piece 91 .20 .50
92 Puzzle Piece 92 .20 .50
93 Puzzle Piece 93 .20 .50
94 Puzzle Piece 94 .20 .50
95 Puzzle Piece 95 .20 .50
96 Puzzle Piece 96 .20 .50
97 Puzzle Piece 97 .20 .50
98 Puzzle Piece 98 .20 .50
99 Puzzle Piece 99 .20 .50
100 Puzzle Piece 100 .20 .50
101 Puzzle Piece 101 .20 .50
102 Puzzle Piece 102 .20 .50
103 Puzzle Piece 103 .20 .50
104 Puzzle Piece 104 .20 .50
105 Puzzle Piece 105 .20 .50
106 Puzzle Piece 106 .20 .50
107 Puzzle Piece 107 .20 .50
108 Puzzle Piece 108 .20 .50
109 Puzzle Piece 109 .20 .50
110 Puzzle Piece 110 .20 .50

2004 Topps Traded Signature Moves

A ODDS 1:675 H, 1:684 R, 1:193 HTA
B ODDS 1:169 H/R, 1:48 HTA
EXCHANGE DEADLINE 10/31/06
AR Alex Rodriguez A 40.00 80.00
AW Adam Wainwright B 12.50 30.00
EM Eli Marrero B 4.00 10.00
FV Fernando Vina B 4.00 10.00
JV Javier Vazquez A 6.00 15.00
MB Milton Bradley B 6.00 15.00
MK Mark Kotsay B 6.00 15.00
MN Mike Neu B 4.00 10.00

2004 Topps Traded Transactions Relics

STATED ODDS 1:106 H, 1:107 R, 1:30 HTA
AP Andy Pettitte Bat 4.00 10.00
AR Alex Rodriguez Yanks Jsy 10.00 25.00
BJ Brian Jordan Bat 3.00 8.00
CE Carl Everett Bat 3.00 8.00
GS Gary Sheffield Bat 4.00 10.00
HC Hee Seop Choi Bat 3.00 8.00
IR Ivan Rodriguez Bat 4.00 10.00
JB Jeromy Burnitz Bat 3.00 8.00
JG Juan Gonzalez Bat 3.00 8.00
JL Javy Lopez Bat 3.00 8.00
KL Kenny Lofton Bat 3.00 8.00
KM Kazuo Matsui Bat 3.00 8.00
MT Miguel Tejada Bat 3.00 8.00
RA Roberto Alomar Bat 4.00 10.00
RC Roger Clemens Bat 6.00 15.00
RLS Richie Sexson Bat 3.00 8.00
RP Rafael Palmeiro Bat 4.00 10.00
RS Reggie Sanders Bat 3.00 8.00
RW Rondell White Bat 3.00 8.00
VG Vladimir Guerrero Bat 4.00 10.00

2004 Topps Traded Transactions Dual Relics

STATED ODDS 1:562 H, 1:563 R, 1:160 HTA
AR Alex Rodriguez Rgr-Yanks 10.00 25.00
CS Curt Schilling D'backs-Sox 6.00 15.00
RP Rafael Palmeiro O's-Rgr 6.00 15.00

2004 Topps McGruff

COMPLETE SET 2.00 5.00
1 Ichiro Suzuki .40 1.00
McGruff/Bullying
2 Albert Pujols .40 1.00
McGruff/Hearing Threats
3 Nomar Garciaparra .20 .50
McGruff/Home Safety
4 Derek Jeter .75 2.00
McGruff/Internet Safety
5 Sammy Sosa .30 .75
McGruff/Solving Problems
6 Carlos Delgado .12 .30
McGruff/Volunteerism

2005 Topps Pre-Production

COMPLETE SET (3) .75 2.00
PP1 Alex Rodriguez .60 1.50
PP2 Jim Thome .30 .75
PP3 Ivan Rodriguez .30 .75

2005 Topps

COMP.HOBBY SET (737) 40.00 80.00
COMP.HOLIDAY SET (742) 40.00 80.00
COMP.CUBS SET (737) 40.00 80.00
COMP.GIANTS SET (737) 40.00 80.00
COMP.NATIONALS SET (737) 40.00 80.00
COMP.RED SOX SET (737) 40.00 80.00
COMP.TIGERS SET (737) 40.00 80.00
COMP.YANKEES SET (737) 40.00 80.00
COMPLETE SET (732) 40.00 80.00
COMPLETE SERIES 1 (366) 20.00 40.00
COMPLETE SERIES 2 (366) 20.00 40.00
COMMON CARD (1-6/8-734) .07 .20
COMMON (297-326/668-687) .20 .50
COMMON (327-331/688-692) .20 .50
COM (349-355/368/731-734) .20 .50
CARD NUMBER 7 DOES NOT EXIST
OVERALL PLATE SER.1 ODDS 1:154 HTA
OVERALL PLATE SER.2 ODDS 1:112 HTA
PLATE PRINT RUN 1 SET PER COLOR
BLACK-CYAN-MAGENTA-YELLOW ISSUED
NO PLATE PRICING DUE TO SCARCITY
1 Alex Rodriguez .25 .60
2 Placido Polanco .07 .20
3 Torii Hunter .07 .20
4 Lyle Overbay .07 .20
5 Johnny Damon .12 .30
6 Johnny Estrada .07 .20
8 Francisco Rodriguez .12 .30
9 Jason LaRue .07 .20
10 Sammy Sosa .20 .50
11 Randy Wolf .07 .20
12 Jason Bay .07 .20
13 Tom Glavine .12 .30
14 Michael Tucker .07 .20
15 Brian Giles .07 .20
16 Dan Wilson .07 .20
17 Jim Edmonds .12 .30
18 Danys Baez .07 .20
19 Roy Halladay .12 .30
20 Hank Blalock .07 .20
21 Darin Erstad .07 .20
22 Robby Hammock .07 .20
23 Mike Hampton .07 .20
24 Mark Bellhorn .07 .20
25 Jim Thome .12 .30
26 Scott Schoeneweis .07 .20
27 Jody Gerut .07 .20
28 Vinny Castilla .07 .20
29 Luis Castillo .07 .20
30 Ivan Rodriguez .12 .30
31 Craig Biggio .12 .30
32 Joe Randa .07 .20
33 Adrian Beltre .20 .50
34 Scott Podsednik .07 .20
35 Cliff Floyd .07 .20
36 Livan Hernandez .07 .20
37 Eric Byrnes .07 .20
38 Gabe Kapler .07 .20
39 Jack Wilson .07 .20
40 Gary Sheffield .07 .20
41 Chan Ho Park .12 .30
42 Carl Crawford .12 .30
43 Miguel Batista .07 .20
44 David Bell .07 .20
45 Jeff DaVanon .07 .20
46 Brandon Webb .12 .30
47 Bronson Arroyo .07 .20
48 Melvin Mora .07 .20
49 David Ortiz .20 .50
50 Andruw Jones .07 .20
51 Chone Figgins .07 .20
52 Danny Graves .07 .20
53 Preston Wilson .07 .20
54 Jeremy Bonderman .07 .20
55 Chad Fox .07 .20
56 Dan Miceli .07 .20
57 Jimmy Gobble .07 .20
58 Darren Dreifort .07 .20
59 Matt LeCroy .07 .20
60 Jose Vidro .07 .20
61 Al Leiter .07 .20
62 Javier Vazquez .07 .20
63 Erubiel Durazo .07 .20
64 Doug Glanville .07 .20
65 Scot Shields .07 .20
66 Edgardo Alfonzo .07 .20
67 Ryan Franklin .07 .20
68 Francisco Cordero .07 .20
69 Brett Myers .07 .20
70 Curt Schilling .12 .30
71 Matt Kata .07 .20
72 Mark DeRosa .07 .20
73 Rodrigo Lopez .07 .20
74 Tim Wakefield .12 .30
75 Frank Thomas .20 .50
76 Jimmy Rollins .12 .30
77 Barry Zito .12 .30
78 Hideo Nomo .20 .50
79 Brad Wilkerson .07 .20
80 Adam Dunn .12 .30
81 Billy Traber .07 .20
82 Fernando Vina .07 .20
83 Nate Robertson .07 .20
84 Brad Ausmus .07 .20
85 Mike Sweeney .07 .20
86 Kip Wells .07 .20
87 Chris Reitsma .07 .20
88 Zach Day .07 .20
89 Tony Clark .07 .20
90 Bret Boone .07 .20
91 Mark Loretta .07 .20
92 Jerome Williams .07 .20
93 Randy Winn .07 .20
94 Marlon Anderson .07 .20
95 Aubrey Huff .07 .20
96 Kevin Mench .07 .20
97 Frank Catalanotto .07 .20
98 Flash Gordon .07 .20
99 Scott Hatteberg .07 .20
100 Albert Pujols .25 .60
101 Jose .07 .20
Bengie Molina
102 Oscar Villarreal .07 .20
103 Jay Gibbons .07 .20
104 Byung-Hyun Kim .07 .20
105 Joe Borowski .07 .20
106 Mark Grudzielanek .07 .20
107 Mark Buehrle .12 .30
108 Paul Wilson .07 .20
109 Ronnie Belliard .07 .20
110 Reggie Sanders .07 .20
111 Tim Redding .07 .20
112 Brian Lawrence .07 .20
113 Darrell May .07 .20
114 Jose Hernandez .07 .20
115 Ben Sheets .07 .20
116 Johan Santana .12 .30
117 Billy Wagner .07 .20
118 Mariano Rivera .25 .60
119 Steve Trachsel .07 .20
120 Akinori Otsuka .07 .20
121 Bobby Kielty .07 .20
122 Orlando Hernandez .07 .20
123 Raul Ibanez .12 .30
124 Mike Matheny .07 .20
125 Vernon Wells .07 .20
126 Jason Isringhausen .07 .20
127 Jose Guillen .07 .20
128 Danny Bautista .07 .20
129 Marcus Giles .07 .20
130 Javy Lopez .07 .20
131 Kevin Millar .07 .20
132 Kyle Farnsworth .07 .20
133 Carl Pavano .07 .20
134 D'Angelo Jimenez .07 .20
135 Casey Blake .07 .20
136 Matt Holliday .20 .50
137 Bobby Higginson .07 .20
138 Nate Field .07 .20
139 Alex Gonzalez .07 .20

140 Jeff Kent .07 .20
141 Aaron Guiel .07 .20
142 Shawn Green .07 .20
143 Bill Hall .07 .20
144 Shannon Stewart .07 .20
145 Juan Rivera .07 .20
146 Coco Crisp .07 .20
147 Mike Mussina .12 .30
148 Eric Chavez .07 .20
149 Jon Lieber .07 .20
150 Vladimir Guerrero .12 .30
151 Alex Cintron .07 .20
152 Horacio Ramirez .07 .20
153 Sidney Ponson .07 .20
154 Trot Nixon .07 .20
155 Greg Maddux .25 .60
156 Edgar Renteria .07 .20
157 Ryan Freel .07 .20
158 Matt Lawton .07 .20
159 Shawn Chacon .07 .20
160 Josh Beckett .07 .20
161 Ken Harvey .07 .20
162 Juan Cruz .07 .20
163 Juan Encarnacion .07 .20
164 Wes Helms .07 .20
165 Brad Radke .07 .20
166 Claudio Vargas .07 .20
167 Mike Cameron .07 .20
168 Billy Koch .07 .20
169 Bobby Crosby .07 .20
170 Mike Lieberthal .07 .20
171 Rob Mackowiak .07 .20
172 Sean Burroughs .07 .20
173 J.T. Snow Jr. .07 .20
174 Paul Konerko .12 .30
175 Luis Gonzalez .07 .20
176 John Lackey .12 .30
177 Antonio Alfonseca .07 .20
178 Brian Roberts .07 .20
179 Bill Mueller .07 .20
180 Carlos Lee .07 .20
181 Corey Patterson .07 .20
182 Sean Casey .07 .20
183 Cliff Lee .12 .30
184 Jason Jennings .07 .20
185 Dmitri Young .07 .20
186 Juan Uribe .07 .20
187 Andy Pettitte .12 .30
188 Juan Gonzalez .07 .20
189 Pokey Reese .07 .20
190 Jason Phillips .07 .20
191 Rocky Biddle .07 .20
192 Lew Ford .07 .20
193 Mark Mulder .07 .20
194 Bobby Abreu .07 .20
195 Jason Kendall .07 .20
196 Terrence Long .07 .20
197 A.J. Pierzynski .07 .20
198 Eddie Guardado .07 .20
199 So Taguchi .07 .20
200 Jason Giambi .07 .20
201 Tony Batista .07 .20
202 Kyle Lohse .07 .20
203 Trevor Hoffman .12 .30
204 Tike Redman .07 .20
205 Matt Herges .07 .20
206 Gil Meche .07 .20
207 Chris Carpenter .12 .30
208 Ben Broussard .07 .20
209 Eric Young .07 .20
210 Doug Waechter .07 .20
211 Jarrod Washburn .07 .20
212 Chad Tracy .07 .20
213 John Smoltz .20 .50
214 Jorge Julio .07 .20
215 Todd Walker .07 .20
216 Shingo Takatsu .07 .20
217 Jose Acevedo .07 .20
218 David Riske .07 .20
219 Shawn Estes .07 .20
220 Lance Berkman .12 .30
221 Carlos Guillen .07 .20
222 Jeremy Affeldt .07 .20
223 Cesar Izturis .07 .20
224 Scott Sullivan .07 .20
225 Kazuo Matsui .07 .20
226 Josh Fogg .07 .20
227 Jason Schmidt .07 .20
228 Jason Marquis .07 .20
229 Scott Spiezio .07 .20
230 Miguel Tejada .12 .30
231 Bartolo Colon .07 .20
232 Jose Valverde .07 .20
233 Derrek Lee .07 .20
234 Scott Williamson .07 .20
235 Joe Crede .07 .20
236 John Thomson .07 .20
237 Mike MacDougal .07 .20
238 Eric Gagne .07 .20
239 Alex Sanchez .07 .20
240 Miguel Cabrera .20 .50
241 Luis Rivas .07 .20
242 Adam Everett .07 .20
243 Jason Johnson .07 .20
244 Travis Hafner .07 .20
245 Jose Valentin .07 .20
246 Stephen Randolph .07 .20
247 Rafael Furcal .07 .20
248 Adam Kennedy .07 .20
249 Luis Matos .07 .20
250 Mark Prior .12 .30
251 Angel Berroa .07 .20
252 Phil Nevin .07 .20
253 Oliver Perez .07 .20
254 Orlando Hudson .07 .20
255 Braden Looper .07 .20
256 Khalil Greene .07 .20
257 Tim Worrell .07 .20
258 Carlos Zambrano .12 .30
259 Odalis Perez .07 .20
260 Gerald Laird .07 .20
261 Jose Cruz Jr. .07 .20
262 Michael Barrett .07 .20
263 Michael Young UER .07 .20
264 Toby Hall .07 .20
265 Woody Williams .07 .20
266 Rich Harden .07 .20
267 Mike Scioscia MG .07 .20
268 Al Pedrique MG .07 .20
269 Bobby Cox MG .07 .20
270 Lee Mazzilli MG .07 .20
271 Terry Francona MG .12 .30
272 Dusty Baker MG .07 .20
273 Ozzie Guillen MG .07 .20
274 Dave Miley MG .07 .20
275 Eric Wedge MG .07 .20
276 Clint Hurdle MG .07 .20
277 Alan Trammell MG .12 .30
278 Jack McKeon MG .12 .30
279 Phil Garner MG .07 .20
280 Tony Pena MG .07 .20
281 Jim Tracy MG .07 .20
282 Ned Yost MG .07 .20
283 Ron Gardenhire MG .07 .20
284 Frank Robinson MG .12 .30
285 Art Howe MG .07 .20
286 Joe Torre MG .12 .30
287 Ken Macha MG .07 .20
288 Larry Bowa MG .07 .20
289 Lloyd McClendon MG .07 .20
290 Bruce Bochy MG .12 .30
291 Felipe Alou MG .07 .20
292 Bob Melvin MG .07 .20
293 Tony LaRussa MG .12 .30
294 Lou Piniella MG .07 .20
295 Buck Showalter MG .07 .20
296 John Gibbons MG .07 .20
297 Steve Doetsch FY RC .20 .50
298 Melky Cabrera FY RC .60 1.50
299 Luis Ramirez FY RC .20 .50
300 Chris Seddon FY RC .20 .50
301 Nate Schierholtz FY .20 .50
302 Ian Kinsler FY RC .40 1.00
303 Brandon Moss FY RC .75 2.00
304 Chadd Blasko FY RC .30 .75
305 Jeremy West FY RC .20 .50
306 Sean Marshall FY RC .50 1.25
307 Matt DeSalvo FY RC .20 .50
308 Ryan Sweeney FY RC .30 .75
309 Matthew Lindstrom FY RC .20 .50
310 Ryan Goleski FY RC .20 .50
311 Brett Harper FY RC .20 .50
312 Chris Roberson FY RC .20 .50
313 Andre Ethier FY RC 1.50 4.00
314 Chris Denorfia FY RC .20 .50
315 Ian Bladergroen FY RC .20 .50
316 Darren Fenster FY RC .20 .50
317 Kevin West FY RC .20 .50
318 Chaz Lytle FY RC .30 .75
319 James Jurries FY RC .20 .50
320 Matt Rogelstad FY RC .20 .50
321 Wade Robinson FY RC .20 .50
322 Jake Dittler FY .20 .50
323 Brian Stavisky FY RC .20 .50
324 Kole Strayhorn FY RC .20 .50
325 Jose Vaquedano FY RC .20 .50
326 Elvys Quezada FY RC .20 .50
327 J.Maine
V.Majewski FS .20 .50
328 R.Weeks
J.Hardy FS .20 .50
329 G.Gross
G.Quiroz FS .20 .50
330 D.Wright
C.Brazell FS .40 1.00
331 D.McPherson
J.Mathis FS .30 .75
332 Randy Johnson SH .20 .50
333 Randy Johnson SH .20 .50
334 Ichiro Suzuki SH .25 .60
335 Ken Griffey Jr. SH .40 1.00
336 Greg Maddux SH .25 .60
337 Ichiro
Mora/Guerrero LL .25 .60
338 Ichiro
Young/Guerrero LL .25 .60
339 Manny
Konerko/Ortiz LL .20 .50
340 Tejada
Ortiz/Manny LL .20 .50
341 Johan
Schill/West LL .12 .30
342 Johan
Pedro/Schill LL .12 .30
343 Helton
Loretta/Beltre LL .20 .50
344 Pierre
Loretta/Wilson LL .07 .20
345 Beltre
Dunn/Pujols LL .25 .60
346 Castilla
Rolen/Pujols LL .25 .60
347 Peavy
Johnson/Sheets LL .20 .50
348 Johnson
Sheets/Schmidt LL .20 .50
349 A.Rodriguez
R.Sierra ALDS .60 1.50
350 L.Walker
A.Pujols NLDS .60 1.50
351 C.Schilling
D.Ortiz ALDS .50 1.25
352 Curt Schilling WS2 .30 .75
353 Sox Celeb
Ortiz-Schil ALCS .50 1.25
354 Cards Celeb
Puj-Edm NLCS .60 1.50
355 Mark Bellhorn WS1 .20 .50
356 Paul Konerko AS .12 .30
357 Alfonso Soriano AS .12 .30
358 Miguel Tejada AS .12 .30
359 Melvin Mora AS .07 .20
360 Vladimir Guerrero AS .12 .30
361 Ichiro Suzuki AS .25 .60
362 Manny Ramirez AS .20 .50
363 Ivan Rodriguez AS .12 .30
364 Johan Santana AS .12 .30
365 Paul Konerko AS .12 .30
366 David Ortiz AS .20 .50
367 Bobby Crosby AS .07 .20
368 Sox Celeb
Ram-Lowe WS4 .50 1.25
369 Garret Anderson .07 .20
370 Randy Johnson .20 .50
371 Charles Thomas .07 .20
372 Rafael Palmeiro .12 .30
373 Kevin Youkilis .07 .20
374 Freddy Garcia .07 .20
375 Magglio Ordonez .12 .30
376 Aaron Harang .07 .20
377 Grady Sizemore .12 .30
378 Chin-Hui Tsao .07 .20
379 Eric Munson .07 .20
380 Juan Pierre .07 .20
381 Brad Lidge .07 .20
382 Brian Anderson .07 .20
383 Alex Cora .12 .30
384 Brady Clark .07 .20
385 Todd Helton .12 .30
386 Chad Cordero .07 .20
387 Kris Benson .07 .20
388 Brad Halsey .07 .20
389 Jermaine Dye .07 .20
390 Manny Ramirez .20 .50
391 Daryle Ward .07 .20
392 Adam Eaton .07 .20
393 Brett Tomko .07 .20
394 Bucky Jacobsen .07 .20
395 Dontrelle Willis .07 .20
396 B.J. Upton .12 .30
397 Rocco Baldelli .07 .20
398 Ted Lilly .07 .20
399 Ryan Drese .07 .20
400 Ichiro Suzuki .25 .60
401 Brendan Donnelly .07 .20
402 Brandon Lyon .07 .20
403 Nick Green .07 .20
404 Jerry Hairston Jr. .07 .20
405 Mike Lowell .07 .20
406 Kerry Wood .07 .20
407 Carl Everett .07 .20
408 Hideki Matsui .30 .75
409 Omar Vizquel .12 .30
410 Joe Kennedy .07 .20
411 Carlos Pena .12 .30
412 Armando Benitez .07 .20
413 Carlos Beltran .12 .30
414 Kevin Appier .07 .20
415 Jeff Weaver .07 .20
416 Chad Moeller .07 .20
417 Joe Mays .07 .20
418 Termel Sledge .07 .20
419 Richard Hidalgo .07 .20
420 Kenny Lofton .07 .20
421 Justin Duchscherer .07 .20
422 Eric Milton .07 .20
423 Jose Mesa .07 .20
424 Ramon Hernandez .07 .20
425 Jose Reyes .12 .30
426 Joel Pineiro .07 .20
427 Matt Morris .07 .20
428 John Halama .07 .20
429 Gary Matthews Jr. .07 .20
430 Ryan Madson .07 .20
431 Mark Kotsay .07 .20
432 Carlos Delgado .07 .20
433 Casey Kotchman .07 .20
434 Greg Aquino .07 .20
435 Eli Marrero .07 .20
436 David Newhan .07 .20
437 Mike Timlin .07 .20
438 LaTroy Hawkins .07 .20
439 Jose Contreras .07 .20
440 Ken Griffey Jr. .40 1.00
441 C.C. Sabathia .12 .30
442 Brandon Inge .07 .20
443 Pete Munro .07 .20
444 John Buck .07 .20
445 Hee Seop Choi .07 .20
446 Chris Capuano .07 .20
447 Jesse Crain .07 .20
448 Geoff Jenkins .07 .20
449 Brian Schneider .07 .20
450 Mike Piazza .20 .50
451 Jorge Posada .12 .30
452 Nick Swisher .12 .30
453 Kevin Millwood .07 .20
454 Mike Gonzalez .07 .20
455 Jake Peavy .07 .20
456 Dustin Hermanson .07 .20
457 Jeremy Reed .07 .20
458 Julian Tavarez .07 .20
459 Geoff Blum .07 .20
460 Alfonso Soriano .12 .30
461 Alexis Rios .07 .20
462 David Eckstein .07 .20
463 Shea Hillenbrand .07 .20
464 Russ Ortiz .07 .20
465 Kurt Ainsworth .07 .20
466 Orlando Cabrera .07 .20
467 Carlos Silva .07 .20
468 Ross Gload .07 .20
469 Josh Phelps .07 .20
470 Marquis Grissom .07 .20
471 Mike Maroth .07 .20
472 Guillermo Mota .07 .20
473 Chris Burke .07 .20
474 David DeJesus .07 .20
475 Jose Lima .07 .20
476 Cristian Guzman .07 .20
477 Nick Johnson .07 .20
478 Victor Zambrano .07 .20
479 Rod Barajas .07 .20
480 Damian Miller .07 .20
481 Chase Utley .12 .30
482 Todd Pratt .07 .20
483 Sean Burnett .07 .20
484 Boomer Wells .07 .20
485 Dustan Mohr .07 .20
486 Bobby Madritsch .07 .20
487 Ray King .07 .20
488 Reed Johnson .07 .20
489 R.A. Dickey .07 .20
490 Scott Kazmir .20 .50
491 Tony Womack .07 .20
492 Tomas Perez .07 .20
493 Esteban Loaiza .07 .20
494 Tomo Ohka .07 .20
495 Mike Lamb .07 .20
496 Ramon Ortiz .07 .20
497 Richie Sexson .07 .20
498 J.D. Drew .07 .20
499 David Segui .07 .20
500 Barry Bonds .30 .75
501 Aramis Ramirez .07 .20
502 Wily Mo Pena .07 .20
503 Jeromy Burnitz .07 .20
504 Craig Monroe .07 .20
505 Nomar Garciaparra .12 .30
506 Brandon Backe .07 .20
507 Marcus Thames .07 .20
508 Derek Lowe .07 .20
509 Doug Davis .07 .20
510 Joe Mauer .15 .40
511 Endy Chavez .07 .20
512 Bernie Williams .12 .30
513 Mark Redman .07 .20
514 Jason Michaels .07 .20
515 Craig Wilson .07 .20
516 Ryan Klesko .07 .20
517 Ray Durham .07 .20
518 Jose Lopez .07 .20
519 Jeff Suppan .07 .20
520 Julio Lugo .07 .20
521 Mike Wood .07 .20
522 David Bush .07 .20
523 Juan Rincon .07 .20
524 Paul Quantrill .07 .20
525 Marlon Byrd .07 .20
526 Roy Oswalt .12 .30
527 Rondell White .07 .20
528 Troy Glaus .07 .20
529 Scott Hairston .07 .20
530 Chipper Jones .20 .50
531 Daniel Cabrera .07 .20
532 Doug Mientkiewicz .07 .20
533 Glendon Rusch .07 .20
534 Jon Garland .07 .20
535 Austin Kearns .07 .20
536 Jake Westbrook .07 .20
537 Aaron Miles .07 .20
538 Omar Infante .07 .20
539 Paul Lo Duca .07 .20
540 Morgan Ensberg .07 .20
541 Tony Graffanino .07 .20
542 Milton Bradley .07 .20
543 Keith Ginter .07 .20
544 Justin Morneau .12 .30
545 Tony Armas Jr. .07 .20
546 Mike Stanton .07 .20
547 Kevin Brown .07 .20
548 Marco Scutaro .12 .30
549 Tim Hudson .12 .30
550 Pat Burrell .07 .20
551 Ty Wigginton .07 .20
552 Jeff Cirillo .07 .20
553 Jim Brower .07 .20
554 Jamie Moyer .07 .20
555 Larry Walker .12 .30
556 Dewon Brazelton .07 .20
557 Brian Jordan .07 .20
558 Josh Towers .07 .20
559 Shigetoshi Hasegawa .07 .20
560 Octavio Dotel .07 .20
561 Travis Lee .07 .20
562 Michael Cuddyer .07 .20
563 Junior Spivey .07 .20
564 Zack Greinke .25 .60
565 Roger Clemens .25 .60
566 Chris Shelton .07 .20
567 Ugueth Urbina .07 .20
568 Rafael Betancourt .07 .20
569 Willie Harris .07 .20
570 Todd Hollandsworth .07 .20
571 Keith Foulke .07 .20
572 Larry Bigbie .07 .20
573 Paul Byrd .07 .20
574 Troy Percival .07 .20
575 Pedro Martinez .12 .30
576 Matt Clement .07 .20
577 Ryan Wagner .07 .20
578 Jeff Francis .07 .20
579 Jeff Conine .07 .20
580 Wade Miller .07 .20
581 Matt Stairs .07 .20
582 Gavin Floyd .07 .20
583 Kazuhisa Ishii .07 .20
584 Victor Santos .07 .20
585 Jacque Jones .07 .20
586 Sunny Kim .07 .20
587 Dan Kolb .07 .20
588 Cory Lidle .07 .20
589 Jose Castillo .07 .20
590 Alex Gonzalez .07 .20
591 Kirk Rueter .07 .20
592 Jolbert Cabrera .07 .20
593 Erik Bedard .07 .20
594 Ben Grieve .07 .20
595 Ricky Ledee .07 .20
596 Mark Hendrickson .07 .20
597 Laynce Nix .07 .20
598 Jason Frasor .07 .20
599 Kevin Gregg .07 .20
600 Derek Jeter .50 1.25
601 Luis Terrero .07 .20
602 Jaret Wright .07 .20
603 Edwin Jackson .07 .20
604 Dave Roberts .12 .30
605 Moises Alou .07 .20
606 Aaron Rowand .07 .20
607 Kazuhito Tadano .07 .20
608 Luis A. Gonzalez .07 .20
609 A.J. Burnett .07 .20
610 Jeff Bagwell .12 .30
611 Brad Penny .07 .20
612 Craig Counsell .07 .20
613 Corey Koskie .07 .20
614 Mark Ellis .07 .20
615 Felix Rodriguez .07 .20
616 Jay Payton .07 .20
617 Hector Luna .07 .20
618 Miguel Olivo .07 .20
619 Rob Bell .07 .20
620 Scott Rolen .12 .30
621 Ricardo Rodriguez .07 .20
622 Eric Hinske .07 .20
623 Tim Salmon .07 .20
624 Adam LaRoche .07 .20
625 B.J. Ryan .07 .20
626 Roberto Alomar .12 .30
627 Steve Finley .07 .20
628 Joe Nathan .07 .20
629 Scott Linebrink .07 .20
630 Vicente Padilla .07 .20
631 Raul Mondesi .07 .20
632 Yadier Molina 6.00 15.00
633 Tino Martinez .12 .30
634 Mark Teixeira .12 .30
635 Kelvim Escobar .07 .20
636 Pedro Feliz .07 .20
637 Rich Aurilia .07 .20
638 Los Angeles Angels TC .07 .20
639 Arizona Diamondbacks TC .07 .20
640 Atlanta Braves TC .12 .30
641 Baltimore Orioles TC .07 .20
642 Boston Red Sox TC .20 .50
643 Chicago Cubs TC .12 .30
644 Chicago White Sox TC .07 .20
645 Cincinnati Reds TC .07 .20
646 Cleveland Indians TC .07 .20
647 Colorado Rockies TC .07 .20
648 Detroit Tigers TC .07 .20
649 Florida Marlins TC .07 .20
650 Houston Astros TC .07 .20
651 Kansas City Royals TC .07 .20
652 Los Angeles Dodgers TC .07 .20
653 Milwaukee Brewers TC .07 .20
654 Minnesota Twins TC .07 .20
655 Montreal Expos TC .07 .20
656 New York Mets TC .07 .20
657 New York Yankees TC .20 .50
658 Oakland Athletics TC .07 .20
659 Philadelphia Phillies TC .07 .20
660 Pittsburgh Pirates TC .07 .20
661 San Diego Padres TC .07 .20
662 San Francisco Giants TC .07 .20
663 Seattle Mariners TC .07 .20
664 St. Louis Cardinals TC .12 .30
665 Tampa Bay Devil Rays TC .07 .20
666 Texas Rangers TC .07 .20
667 Toronto Blue Jays TC .07 .20
668 Billy Butler FY RC 1.00 2.50
669 Wes Swackhamer FY RC .20 .50
670 Matt Campbell FY RC .20 .50
671 Ryan Webb FY .20 .50
672 Glen Perkins FY RC .20 .50
673 Michael Rogers FY RC .20 .50
674 Kevin Melillo FY RC .20 .50
675 Erik Cordier FY RC .20 .50
676 Landon Powell FY RC .20 .50
677 Justin Verlander FY RC 25.00 60.00
678 Eric Nielsen FY RC .20 .50
679 Alexander Smit FY RC .20 .50
680 Ryan Garko FY RC .20 .50
681 Bobby Livingston FY RC .20 .50
682 Jeff Niemann FY RC .50 1.25
683 Wladimir Balentien FY RC .30 .75
684 Chip Cannon FY RC .20 .50
685 Yorman Bazardo FY RC .20 .50
686 Mike Bourn FY RC .50 1.25
687 Andy LaRoche FY RC .20 .50
688 F.Hernandez
J.Leone .60 1.50
689 R.Howard
C.Hamels .60 1.50
690 M.Cain
M.Valdez 1.25 3.00
691 A.Marte
J.Francoeur .50 1.25
692 C.Billingsley
J.Guzman .20 .50
693 J.Hairston Jr.
S.Hairston .07 .20
694 M.Tejada
L.Berkman .12 .30
695 Kenny Rogers GG .07 .20
696 Ivan Rodriguez GG .12 .30
697 Darin Erstad GG .07 .20
698 Bret Boone GG .07 .20
699 Eric Chavez GG .07 .20
700 Derek Jeter GG .50 1.25
701 Vernon Wells GG .07 .20
702 Ichiro Suzuki GG .25 .60
703 Torii Hunter GG .07 .20
704 Greg Maddux GG .25 .60
705 Mike Matheny GG .07 .20
706 Todd Helton GG .12 .30
707 Luis Castillo GG .07 .20
708 Scott Rolen GG .12 .30
709 Cesar Izturis GG .07 .20
710 Jim Edmonds GG .12 .30
711 Andruw Jones GG .07 .20
712 Steve Finley GG .07 .20
713 Johan Santana CY .12 .30
714 Roger Clemens CY .25 .60
715 Vladimir Guerrero MVP .12 .30
716 Barry Bonds MVP .30 .75
717 Bobby Crosby ROY .07 .20
718 Jason Bay ROY .07 .20
719 Albert Pujols AS .25 .60
720 Mark Loretta AS .07 .20
721 Edgar Renteria AS .07 .20
722 Scott Rolen AS .12 .30
723 J.D. Drew AS .07 .20
724 Jim Edmonds AS .12 .30
725 Johnny Estrada AS .07 .20
726 Jason Schmidt AS .07 .20
727 Chris Carpenter AS .12 .30
728 Eric Gagne AS .07 .20
729 Jason Bay AS .07 .20
730 Bobby Cox MG AS .07 .20
731 D.Ortiz
M.Bellhorn WS1 .50 1.25
732 Curt Schilling WS2 .30 .75
733 M.Ramirez
P.Martinez WS3 .50 1.25
734 Sox Win Damon
Lowe WS4 .30 .75

2005 Topps 1st Edition

*1st ED 1-296/332-348/356-367: 1.25X TO 3X
*1st ED 369-667/693-730: 1.25X TO 3X
*1st ED 297-326/668-687: .6X TO 1.5X
*1st ED 327-331/688-692: .6X TO 1.5X
*1st ED 349-355/368/731-734: 1.25X TO 3X
ISSUED IN SER.1 & 2 1ST EDITION BOXES
CARD NUMBER 7 DOES NOT EXIST

2005 Topps Black

COMMON (1-6/8-331/369-734) 8.00 20.00
COMMON 297-326/668-687 8.00 20.00
COMMON 327-331/688-692 8.00 20.00
COMMON 731-734 8.00 20.00
SERIES 1 ODDS 1:13 HTA
SERIES 2 ODDS 1:9 HTA
STATED PRINT RUN 54 SERIAL #'d SETS
CARD NUMBER 7 DOES NOT EXIST
1 Alex Rodriguez 25.00 60.00
2 Placido Polanco 8.00 20.00
3 Torii Hunter 8.00 20.00
4 Lyle Overbay 8.00 20.00
5 Johnny Damon 12.00 30.00
6 Johnny Estrada 8.00 20.00
8 Francisco Rodriguez 12.00 30.00
9 Jason LaRue 8.00 20.00
10 Sammy Sosa 20.00 50.00
11 Randy Wolf 8.00 20.00
12 Jason Bay 8.00 20.00
13 Tom Glavine 12.00 30.00
14 Michael Tucker 8.00 20.00
15 Brian Giles 8.00 20.00
16 Dan Wilson 8.00 20.00
17 Jim Edmonds 12.00 30.00
18 Danys Baez 8.00 20.00
19 Roy Halladay 12.00 30.00
20 Hank Blalock 8.00 20.00
21 Darin Erstad 8.00 20.00
22 Robby Hammock 8.00 20.00
23 Mike Hampton 8.00 20.00
24 Mark Bellhorn 8.00 20.00
25 Jim Thome 12.00 30.00
26 Scott Schoeneweis 8.00 20.00
27 Jody Gerut 8.00 20.00
28 Vinny Castilla 8.00 20.00
29 Luis Castillo 8.00 20.00
30 Ivan Rodriguez 12.00 30.00
31 Craig Biggio 12.00 30.00
32 Joe Randa 8.00 20.00
33 Adrian Beltre 20.00 50.00
34 Scott Podsednik 8.00 20.00
35 Cliff Floyd 8.00 20.00
36 Livan Hernandez 8.00 20.00
37 Eric Byrnes 8.00 20.00
38 Gabe Kapler 8.00 20.00
39 Jack Wilson 8.00 20.00
40 Gary Sheffield 8.00 20.00
41 Chan Ho Park 12.00 30.00
42 Carl Crawford 12.00 30.00
43 Miguel Batista 8.00 20.00
44 David Bell 8.00 20.00
45 Jeff DaVanon 8.00 20.00
46 Brandon Webb 12.00 30.00
47 Bronson Arroyo 8.00 20.00
48 Melvin Mora 8.00 20.00
49 David Ortiz 20.00 50.00
50 Andruw Jones 8.00 20.00
51 Chone Figgins 8.00 20.00
52 Danny Graves 8.00 20.00
53 Preston Wilson 8.00 20.00
54 Jeremy Bonderman 8.00 20.00
55 Chad Fox 8.00 20.00
56 Dan Miceli 8.00 20.00
57 Jimmy Gobble 8.00 20.00
58 Darren Dreifort 8.00 20.00
59 Matt LeCroy 8.00 20.00
60 Jose Vidro 8.00 20.00
61 Al Leiter 8.00 20.00
62 Javier Vazquez 8.00 20.00
63 Erubiel Durazo 8.00 20.00
64 Doug Glanville 8.00 20.00
65 Scot Shields 8.00 20.00
66 Edgardo Alfonzo 8.00 20.00
67 Ryan Franklin 8.00 20.00
68 Francisco Cordero 8.00 20.00
69 Brett Myers 8.00 20.00
70 Curt Schilling 12.00 30.00
71 Matt Kata 8.00 20.00
72 Mark DeRosa 8.00 20.00
73 Rodrigo Lopez 8.00 20.00
74 Tim Wakefield 12.00 30.00
75 Frank Thomas 20.00 50.00
76 Jimmy Rollins 12.00 30.00
77 Barry Zito 12.00 30.00
78 Hideo Nomo 20.00 50.00
79 Brad Wilkerson 8.00 20.00
80 Adam Dunn 12.00 30.00
81 Billy Traber 8.00 20.00
82 Fernando Vina 8.00 20.00
83 Nate Robertson 8.00 20.00
84 Brad Ausmus 8.00 20.00
85 Mike Sweeney 8.00 20.00
86 Kip Wells 8.00 20.00
87 Chris Reitsma 8.00 20.00
88 Zach Day 8.00 20.00
89 Tony Clark 8.00 20.00
90 Bret Boone 8.00 20.00
91 Mark Loretta 8.00 20.00
92 Jerome Williams 8.00 20.00
93 Randy Winn 8.00 20.00
94 Marlon Anderson 8.00 20.00
95 Aubrey Huff 8.00 20.00
96 Kevin Mench 8.00 20.00
97 Frank Catalanotto 8.00 20.00
98 Flash Gordon 8.00 20.00
99 Scott Hatteberg 8.00 20.00
100 Albert Pujols 25.00 60.00
101 Jose
Bengie Molina 8.00 20.00
102 Oscar Villarreal 8.00 20.00
103 Jay Gibbons 8.00 20.00
104 Byung-Hyun Kim 8.00 20.00
105 Joe Borowski 8.00 20.00
106 Mark Grudzielanek 8.00 20.00
107 Mark Buehrle 12.00 30.00
108 Paul Wilson 8.00 20.00
109 Ronnie Belliard 8.00 20.00
110 Reggie Sanders 8.00 20.00
111 Tim Redding 8.00 20.00
112 Brian Lawrence 8.00 20.00
113 Darrell May 8.00 20.00
114 Jose Hernandez 8.00 20.00
115 Ben Sheets 8.00 20.00
116 Johan Santana 12.00 30.00
117 Billy Wagner 8.00 20.00
118 Mariano Rivera 25.00 60.00
119 Steve Trachsel 8.00 20.00
120 Akinori Otsuka 8.00 20.00
121 Bobby Kielty 8.00 20.00
122 Orlando Hernandez 8.00 20.00
123 Raul Ibanez 12.00 30.00
124 Mike Matheny 8.00 20.00
125 Vernon Wells 8.00 20.00
126 Jason Isringhausen 8.00 20.00
127 Jose Guillen 8.00 20.00
128 Danny Bautista 8.00 20.00
129 Marcus Giles 8.00 20.00
130 Javy Lopez 8.00 20.00
131 Kevin Millar 8.00 20.00
132 Kyle Farnsworth 8.00 20.00
133 Carl Pavano 8.00 20.00
134 D'Angelo Jimenez 8.00 20.00
135 Casey Blake 8.00 20.00
136 Matt Holliday 20.00 50.00
137 Bobby Higginson 8.00 20.00
138 Nate Field 8.00 20.00
139 Alex Gonzalez 8.00 20.00
140 Jeff Kent 8.00 20.00
141 Aaron Guiel 8.00 20.00
142 Shawn Green 8.00 20.00
143 Bill Hall 8.00 20.00
144 Shannon Stewart 8.00 20.00
145 Juan Rivera 8.00 20.00
146 Coco Crisp 8.00 20.00
147 Mike Mussina 12.00 30.00
148 Eric Chavez 8.00 20.00
149 Jon Lieber 8.00 20.00
150 Vladimir Guerrero 12.00 30.00
151 Alex Cintron 8.00 20.00
152 Horacio Ramirez 8.00 20.00
153 Sidney Ponson 8.00 20.00
154 Trot Nixon 8.00 20.00
155 Greg Maddux 25.00 60.00
156 Edgar Renteria 8.00 20.00
157 Ryan Freel 8.00 20.00
158 Matt Lawton 8.00 20.00
159 Shawn Chacon 8.00 20.00
160 Josh Beckett 8.00 20.00
161 Ken Harvey 8.00 20.00
162 Juan Cruz 8.00 20.00
163 Juan Encarnacion 8.00 20.00
164 Wes Helms 8.00 20.00
165 Brad Radke 8.00 20.00
166 Claudio Vargas 8.00 20.00
167 Mike Cameron 8.00 20.00
168 Billy Koch 8.00 20.00
169 Bobby Crosby 8.00 20.00
170 Mike Lieberthal 8.00 20.00
171 Rob Mackowiak 8.00 20.00
172 Sean Burroughs 8.00 20.00
173 J.T. Snow Jr. 8.00 20.00
174 Paul Konerko 12.00 30.00
175 Luis Gonzalez 8.00 20.00
176 John Lackey 12.00 30.00
177 Antonio Alfonseca 8.00 20.00
178 Brian Roberts 8.00 20.00
179 Bill Mueller 8.00 20.00
180 Carlos Lee 8.00 20.00
181 Corey Patterson 8.00 20.00
182 Sean Casey 8.00 20.00
183 Cliff Lee 12.00 30.00
184 Jason Jennings 8.00 20.00
185 Dmitri Young 8.00 20.00
186 Juan Uribe 8.00 20.00
187 Andy Pettitte 12.00 30.00
188 Juan Gonzalez 8.00 20.00
189 Pokey Reese 8.00 20.00
190 Jason Phillips 8.00 20.00
191 Rocky Biddle 8.00 20.00
192 Lew Ford 8.00 20.00
193 Mark Mulder 8.00 20.00
194 Bobby Abreu 8.00 20.00
195 Jason Kendall 8.00 20.00
196 Terrence Long 8.00 20.00
197 A.J. Pierzynski 8.00 20.00
198 Eddie Guardado 8.00 20.00
199 So Taguchi 8.00 20.00
200 Jason Giambi 8.00 20.00
201 Tony Batista 8.00 20.00
202 Kyle Lohse 8.00 20.00
203 Trevor Hoffman 12.00 30.00
204 Tike Redman 8.00 20.00
205 Matt Herges 8.00 20.00
206 Gil Meche 8.00 20.00
207 Chris Carpenter 12.00 30.00
208 Ben Broussard 8.00 20.00
209 Eric Young 8.00 20.00
210 Doug Waechter 8.00 20.00
211 Jarrod Washburn 8.00 20.00
212 Chad Tracy 8.00 20.00
213 John Smoltz 20.00 50.00
214 Jorge Julio 8.00 20.00
215 Todd Walker 8.00 20.00
216 Shingo Takatsu 8.00 20.00
217 Jose Acevedo 8.00 20.00
218 David Riske 8.00 20.00
219 Shawn Estes 8.00 20.00
220 Lance Berkman 12.00 30.00
221 Carlos Guillen 8.00 20.00
222 Jeremy Affeldt 8.00 20.00
223 Cesar Izturis 8.00 20.00
224 Scott Sullivan 8.00 20.00
225 Kazuo Matsui 8.00 20.00
226 Josh Fogg 8.00 20.00
227 Jason Schmidt 8.00 20.00
228 Jason Marquis 8.00 20.00
229 Scott Spiezio 8.00 20.00
230 Miguel Tejada 12.00 30.00
231 Bartolo Colon 8.00 20.00
232 Jose Valverde 8.00 20.00
233 Derrek Lee 8.00 20.00
234 Scott Williamson 8.00 20.00
235 Joe Crede 8.00 20.00
236 John Thomson 8.00 20.00
237 Mike MacDougal 8.00 20.00
238 Eric Gagne 8.00 20.00
239 Alex Sanchez 8.00 20.00
240 Miguel Cabrera 20.00 50.00
241 Luis Rivas 8.00 20.00
242 Adam Everett 8.00 20.00
243 Jason Johnson 8.00 20.00
244 Travis Hafner 8.00 20.00
245 Jose Valentin 8.00 20.00
246 Stephen Randolph 8.00 20.00
247 Rafael Furcal 8.00 20.00
248 Adam Kennedy 8.00 20.00
249 Luis Matos 8.00 20.00
250 Mark Prior 12.00 30.00

251 Angel Berroa 8.00 20.00
252 Phil Nevin 8.00 20.00
253 Oliver Perez 8.00 20.00
254 Orlando Hudson 8.00 20.00
255 Braden Looper 8.00 20.00
256 Khalil Greene 8.00 20.00
257 Tim Worrell 8.00 20.00
258 Carlos Zambrano 12.00 30.00
259 Odalis Perez 8.00 20.00
260 Gerald Laird 8.00 20.00
261 Jose Cruz Jr. 8.00 20.00
262 Michael Barrett 8.00 20.00
263 Michael Young UER 8.00 20.00
264 Toby Hall 8.00 20.00
265 Woody Williams 8.00 20.00
266 Rich Harden 8.00 20.00
267 Mike Scioscia MG 8.00 20.00
268 Al Pedrique MG 8.00 20.00
269 Bobby Cox MG 8.00 20.00
270 Lee Mazzilli MG 8.00 20.00
271 Terry Francona MG 12.00 30.00
272 Dusty Baker MG 8.00 20.00
273 Ozzie Guillen MG 8.00 20.00
274 Dave Miley MG 8.00 20.00
275 Eric Wedge MG 8.00 20.00
276 Clint Hurdle MG 8.00 20.00
277 Alan Trammell MG 12.00 30.00
278 Jack McKeon MG 8.00 20.00
279 Phil Garner MG 8.00 20.00
280 Tony Pena MG 8.00 20.00
281 Jim Tracy MG 8.00 20.00
282 Ned Yost MG 8.00 20.00
283 Ron Gardenhire MG 8.00 20.00
284 Frank Robinson MG 12.00 30.00
285 Art Howe MG 8.00 20.00
286 Joe Torre MG 12.00 30.00
287 Ken Macha MG 8.00 20.00
288 Larry Bowa MG 8.00 20.00
289 Lloyd McClendon MG 8.00 20.00
290 Bruce Bochy MG 12.00 30.00
291 Felipe Alou MG 8.00 20.00
292 Bob Melvin MG 8.00 20.00
293 Tony LaRussa MG 12.00 30.00
294 Lou Piniella MG 8.00 20.00
295 Buck Showalter MG 8.00 20.00
296 John Gibbons MG 8.00 20.00
297 Steve Doetsch FY 8.00 20.00
298 Melky Cabrera FY 25.00 60.00
299 Luis Ramirez FY 8.00 20.00
300 Chris Seddon FY 8.00 20.00
301 Nate Schierholtz FY 8.00 20.00
302 Ian Kinsler FY 40.00 100.00
303 Brandon Moss FY 30.00 80.00
304 Chadd Blasko FY 12.00 30.00
305 Jeremy West FY 8.00 20.00
306 Sean Marshall FY 20.00 50.00
307 Matt DeSalvo FY 8.00 20.00
308 Ryan Sweeney FY 12.00 30.00
309 Matthew Lindstrom FY 8.00 20.00
310 Ryan Goleski FY 8.00 20.00
311 Brett Harper FY 8.00 20.00
312 Chris Roberson FY 8.00 20.00
313 Andre Ethier FY 60.00 150.00
314 Chris Denorfia FY 8.00 20.00
315 Ian Bladergroen FY 8.00 20.00
316 Darren Fenster FY 8.00 20.00
317 Kevin West FY 8.00 20.00
318 Chaz Lytle FY 12.00 30.00
319 James Jurries FY 8.00 20.00
320 Matt Rogelstad FY 8.00 20.00
321 Wade Robinson FY 8.00 20.00
322 Jake Dittler FY 8.00 20.00
323 Brian Stavisky FY 8.00 20.00
324 Kole Strayhorn FY 8.00 20.00
325 Jose Vaquedano FY 8.00 20.00
326 Elvys Quezada FY 8.00 20.00
327 J.Maine 8.00 20.00
V.Majewski FS
328 R.Weeks 8.00 20.00
J.Hardy FS
329 G.Gross 8.00 20.00
G.Quiroz FS
330 D.Wright 15.00 40.00
C.Brazell FS
331 D.McPherson 12.00 30.00
J.Mathis FS
369 Garret Anderson 8.00 20.00
370 Randy Johnson 20.00 50.00
371 Charles Thomas 8.00 20.00
372 Rafael Palmeiro 12.00 30.00
373 Kevin Youkilis 8.00 20.00
374 Freddy Garcia 8.00 20.00
375 Magglio Ordonez 12.00 30.00
376 Aaron Harang 8.00 20.00
377 Grady Sizemore 12.00 30.00
378 Chin-Hui Tsao 8.00 20.00
379 Eric Munson 8.00 20.00
380 Juan Pierre 8.00 20.00
381 Brad Lidge 8.00 20.00
382 Brian Anderson 8.00 20.00
383 Alex Cora 12.00 30.00
384 Brady Clark 8.00 20.00
385 Todd Helton 12.00 30.00
386 Chad Cordero 8.00 20.00
387 Kris Benson 8.00 20.00
388 Brad Halsey 8.00 20.00
389 Jermaine Dye 8.00 20.00
390 Manny Ramirez 20.00 50.00
391 Daryle Ward 8.00 20.00
392 Adam Eaton 8.00 20.00
393 Brett Tomko 8.00 20.00
394 Bucky Jacobsen 8.00 20.00
395 Dontrelle Willis 8.00 20.00
396 B.J. Upton 12.00 30.00
397 Rocco Baldelli 8.00 20.00
398 Ted Lilly 8.00 20.00
399 Ryan Drese 8.00 20.00
400 Ichiro Suzuki 25.00 60.00
401 Brendan Donnelly 8.00 20.00
402 Brandon Lyon 8.00 20.00
403 Nick Green 8.00 20.00
404 Jerry Hairston Jr. 8.00 20.00
405 Mike Lowell 8.00 20.00
406 Kerry Wood 8.00 20.00
407 Carl Everett 8.00 20.00
408 Hideki Matsui 30.00 80.00
409 Omar Vizquel 12.00 30.00
410 Joe Kennedy 8.00 20.00
411 Carlos Pena 12.00 30.00
412 Armando Benitez 8.00 20.00
413 Carlos Beltran 12.00 30.00
414 Kevin Appier 8.00 20.00
415 Jeff Weaver 8.00 20.00
416 Chad Moeller 8.00 20.00
417 Joe Mays 8.00 20.00
418 Termel Sledge 8.00 20.00
419 Richard Hidalgo 8.00 20.00
420 Kenny Lofton 8.00 20.00
421 Justin Duchscherer 8.00 20.00
422 Eric Milton 8.00 20.00
423 Jose Mesa 8.00 20.00
424 Ramon Hernandez 8.00 20.00
425 Jose Reyes 12.00 30.00
426 Joel Pineiro 8.00 20.00
427 Matt Morris 8.00 20.00
428 John Halama 8.00 20.00
429 Gary Matthews Jr. 8.00 20.00
430 Ryan Madson 8.00 20.00
431 Mark Kotsay 8.00 20.00
432 Carlos Delgado 8.00 20.00
433 Casey Kotchman 8.00 20.00
434 Greg Aquino 8.00 20.00
435 Eli Marrero 8.00 20.00
436 David Newhan 8.00 20.00
437 Mike Timlin 8.00 20.00
438 LaTroy Hawkins 8.00 20.00
439 Jose Contreras 8.00 20.00
440 Ken Griffey Jr. 40.00 100.00
441 C.C. Sabathia 12.00 30.00
442 Brandon Inge 8.00 20.00
443 Pete Munro 8.00 20.00
444 John Buck 8.00 20.00
445 Hee Seop Choi 8.00 20.00
446 Chris Capuano 8.00 20.00
447 Jesse Crain 8.00 20.00
448 Geoff Jenkins 8.00 20.00
449 Brian Schneider 8.00 20.00
450 Mike Piazza 20.00 50.00
451 Jorge Posada 12.00 30.00
452 Nick Swisher 12.00 30.00
453 Kevin Millwood 8.00 20.00
454 Mike Gonzalez 8.00 20.00
455 Jake Peavy 8.00 20.00
456 Dustin Hermanson 8.00 20.00
457 Jeremy Reed 8.00 20.00
458 Julian Tavarez 8.00 20.00
459 Geoff Blum 8.00 20.00
460 Alfonso Soriano 12.00 30.00
461 Alexis Rios 8.00 20.00
462 David Eckstein 8.00 20.00
463 Shea Hillenbrand 8.00 20.00
464 Russ Ortiz 8.00 20.00
465 Kurt Ainsworth 8.00 20.00
466 Orlando Cabrera 8.00 20.00
467 Carlos Silva 8.00 20.00
468 Ross Gload 8.00 20.00
469 Josh Phelps 8.00 20.00
470 Marquis Grissom 8.00 20.00
471 Mike Maroth 8.00 20.00
472 Guillermo Mota 8.00 20.00
473 Chris Burke 8.00 20.00
474 David DeJesus 8.00 20.00
475 Jose Lima 8.00 20.00
476 Cristian Guzman 8.00 20.00
477 Nick Johnson 8.00 20.00
478 Victor Zambrano 8.00 20.00
479 Rod Barajas 8.00 20.00
480 Damian Miller 8.00 20.00
481 Chase Utley 12.00 30.00
482 Todd Pratt 8.00 20.00
483 Sean Burnett 8.00 20.00
484 Boomer Wells 8.00 20.00
485 Dustan Mohr 8.00 20.00
486 Bobby Madritsch 8.00 20.00
487 Ray King 8.00 20.00
488 Reed Johnson 8.00 20.00
489 R.A. Dickey 12.00 30.00
490 Scott Kazmir 20.00 50.00
491 Tony Womack 8.00 20.00
492 Tomas Perez 8.00 20.00
493 Esteban Loaiza 8.00 20.00
494 Tomo Ohka 8.00 20.00
495 Mike Lamb 8.00 20.00
496 Ramon Ortiz 8.00 20.00
497 Richie Sexson 8.00 20.00
498 J.D. Drew 8.00 20.00
499 David Segui 8.00 20.00
500 Barry Bonds 30.00 80.00
501 Aramis Ramirez 8.00 20.00
502 Wily Mo Pena 8.00 20.00
503 Jeromy Burnitz 8.00 20.00
504 Craig Monroe 8.00 20.00
505 Nomar Garciaparra 12.00 30.00
506 Brandon Backe 8.00 20.00
507 Marcus Thames 8.00 20.00
508 Derek Lowe 8.00 20.00
509 Doug Davis 8.00 20.00
510 Joe Mauer 15.00 40.00
511 Endy Chavez 8.00 20.00
512 Bernie Williams 12.00 30.00
513 Mark Redman 8.00 20.00
514 Jason Michaels 8.00 20.00
515 Craig Wilson 8.00 20.00
516 Ryan Klesko 8.00 20.00
517 Ray Durham 8.00 20.00
518 Jose Lopez 8.00 20.00
519 Jeff Suppan 8.00 20.00
520 Julio Lugo 8.00 20.00
521 Mike Wood 8.00 20.00
522 David Bush 8.00 20.00
523 Juan Rincon 8.00 20.00
524 Paul Quantrill 8.00 20.00
525 Marlon Byrd 8.00 20.00
526 Roy Oswalt 12.00 30.00
527 Rondell White 8.00 20.00
528 Troy Glaus 8.00 20.00
529 Scott Hairston 8.00 20.00
530 Chipper Jones 20.00 50.00
531 Daniel Cabrera 8.00 20.00
532 Doug Mientkiewicz 8.00 20.00
533 Glendon Rusch 8.00 20.00
534 Jon Garland 8.00 20.00
535 Austin Kearns 8.00 20.00
536 Jake Westbrook 8.00 20.00
537 Aaron Miles 8.00 20.00
538 Omar Infante 8.00 20.00
539 Paul Lo Duca 8.00 20.00
540 Morgan Ensberg 8.00 20.00
541 Tony Graffanino 8.00 20.00
542 Milton Bradley 8.00 20.00
543 Keith Ginter 8.00 20.00
544 Justin Morneau 12.00 30.00
545 Tony Armas Jr. 8.00 20.00
546 Mike Stanton 8.00 20.00
547 Kevin Brown 8.00 20.00
548 Marco Scutaro 12.00 30.00
549 Tim Hudson 12.00 30.00
550 Pat Burrell 8.00 20.00
551 Ty Wigginton 8.00 20.00
552 Jeff Cirillo 8.00 20.00
553 Jim Brower 8.00 20.00
554 Jamie Moyer 8.00 20.00
555 Larry Walker 12.00 30.00
556 Dewon Brazelton 8.00 20.00
557 Brian Jordan 8.00 20.00
558 Josh Towers 8.00 20.00
559 Shigetoshi Hasegawa 8.00 20.00
560 Octavio Dotel 8.00 20.00
561 Travis Lee 8.00 20.00
562 Michael Cuddyer 8.00 20.00
563 Junior Spivey 8.00 20.00
564 Zack Greinke 25.00 60.00
565 Roger Clemens 25.00 60.00
566 Chris Shelton 8.00 20.00
567 Ugueth Urbina 8.00 20.00
568 Rafael Betancourt 8.00 20.00
569 Willie Harris 8.00 20.00
570 Todd Hollandsworth 8.00 20.00
571 Keith Foulke 8.00 20.00
572 Larry Bigbie 8.00 20.00
573 Paul Byrd 8.00 20.00
574 Troy Percival 8.00 20.00
575 Pedro Martinez 12.00 30.00
576 Matt Clement 8.00 20.00
577 Ryan Wagner 8.00 20.00
578 Jeff Francis 8.00 20.00
579 Jeff Conine 8.00 20.00
580 Wade Miller 8.00 20.00
581 Matt Stairs 8.00 20.00
582 Gavin Floyd 8.00 20.00
583 Kazuhisa Ishii 8.00 20.00
584 Victor Santos 8.00 20.00
585 Jacque Jones 8.00 20.00
586 Sunny Kim 8.00 20.00
587 Dan Kolb 8.00 20.00
588 Cory Lidle 8.00 20.00
589 Jose Castillo 8.00 20.00
590 Alex Gonzalez 8.00 20.00
591 Kirk Rueter 8.00 20.00
592 Jolbert Cabrera 8.00 20.00
593 Erik Bedard 8.00 20.00
594 Ben Grieve 8.00 20.00
595 Ricky Ledee 8.00 20.00
596 Mark Hendrickson 8.00 20.00
597 Laynce Nix 8.00 20.00
598 Jason Frasor 8.00 20.00
599 Kevin Gregg 8.00 20.00
600 Derek Jeter 50.00 125.00
601 Luis Terrero 8.00 20.00
602 Jaret Wright 8.00 20.00
603 Edwin Jackson 8.00 20.00
604 Dave Roberts 12.00 30.00
605 Moises Alou 8.00 20.00
606 Aaron Rowand 8.00 20.00
607 Kazuhito Tadano 8.00 20.00
608 Luis A. Gonzalez 8.00 20.00
609 A.J. Burnett 8.00 20.00
610 Jeff Bagwell 12.00 30.00
611 Brad Penny 8.00 20.00
612 Craig Counsell 8.00 20.00
613 Corey Koskie 8.00 20.00
614 Mark Ellis 8.00 20.00
615 Felix Rodriguez 8.00 20.00
616 Jay Payton 8.00 20.00
617 Hector Luna 8.00 20.00
618 Miguel Olivo 8.00 20.00
619 Rob Bell 8.00 20.00
620 Scott Rolen 12.00 30.00
621 Ricardo Rodriguez 8.00 20.00
622 Eric Hinske 8.00 20.00
623 Tim Salmon 8.00 20.00
624 Adam LaRoche 8.00 20.00
625 B.J. Ryan 8.00 20.00
626 Roberto Alomar 12.00 30.00
627 Steve Finley 8.00 20.00
628 Joe Nathan 8.00 20.00
629 Scott Linebrink 8.00 20.00
630 Vicente Padilla 8.00 20.00
631 Raul Mondesi 8.00 20.00
633 Tino Martinez 12.00 30.00
634 Mark Teixeira 12.00 30.00
635 Kelvim Escobar 8.00 20.00
636 Pedro Feliz 8.00 20.00
637 Rich Aurilia 8.00 20.00
638 Los Angeles Angels TC 8.00 20.00
639 Arizona Diamondbacks TC 8.00 20.00
640 Atlanta Braves TC 12.00 30.00
641 Baltimore Orioles TC 8.00 20.00
642 Boston Red Sox TC 20.00 50.00
643 Chicago Cubs TC 12.00 30.00
644 Chicago White Sox TC 8.00 20.00
645 Cincinnati Reds TC 8.00 20.00
646 Cleveland Indians TC 8.00 20.00
647 Colorado Rockies TC 8.00 20.00
648 Detroit Tigers TC 8.00 20.00
649 Florida Marlins TC 8.00 20.00
650 Houston Astros TC 8.00 20.00
651 Kansas City Royals TC 8.00 20.00
652 Los Angeles Dodgers TC 8.00 20.00
653 Milwaukee Brewers TC 8.00 20.00
654 Minnesota Twins TC 8.00 20.00
655 Montreal Expos TC 8.00 20.00
656 New York Mets TC 8.00 20.00
657 New York Yankees TC 20.00 50.00
658 Oakland Athletics TC 8.00 20.00
659 Philadelphia Phillies TC 8.00 20.00
660 Pittsburgh Pirates TC 8.00 20.00
661 San Diego Padres TC 8.00 20.00
662 San Francisco Giants TC 8.00 20.00
663 Seattle Mariners TC 8.00 20.00
664 St. Louis Cardinals TC 12.00 30.00
665 Tampa Bay Devil Rays TC 8.00 20.00
666 Texas Rangers TC 8.00 20.00
667 Toronto Blue Jays TC 8.00 20.00
668 Billy Butler FY 40.00 100.00
669 Wes Swackhamer FY 8.00 20.00
670 Matt Campbell FY 8.00 20.00
671 Ryan Webb FY 8.00 20.00
672 Glen Perkins FY 8.00 20.00
673 Michael Rogers FY 8.00 20.00
674 Kevin Melillo FY 8.00 20.00
675 Erik Cordier FY 8.00 20.00
676 Landon Powell FY 8.00 20.00
677 Justin Verlander FY 250.00 600.00
678 Eric Nielsen FY 8.00 20.00
679 Alexander Smit FY 8.00 20.00
680 Ryan Garko FY 8.00 20.00
681 Bobby Livingston FY 8.00 20.00
682 Jeff Niemann FY 20.00 50.00
683 Wladimir Balentien FY 12.00 30.00
684 Chip Cannon FY 8.00 20.00
685 Yorman Bazardo FY 8.00 20.00
686 Mike Bourn FY 20.00 50.00
687 Andy LaRoche FY 8.00 20.00
688 F.Hernandez 25.00 60.00
J.Leone
689 R.Howard 25.00 60.00
C.Hamels
690 M.Cain 50.00 125.00
M.Valdez
691 A.Marte 20.00 50.00
J.Francoeur
692 C.Billingsley 8.00 20.00
J.Guzman
693 J.Hairston Jr. 8.00 20.00
S.Hairston
694 M.Tejada 12.00 30.00
L.Berkman
695 Kenny Rogers GG 8.00 20.00
696 Ivan Rodriguez GG 12.00 30.00
697 Darin Erstad GG 8.00 20.00
698 Bret Boone GG 8.00 20.00
699 Eric Chavez GG 8.00 20.00
700 Derek Jeter GG 50.00 125.00
701 Vernon Wells GG 8.00 20.00
702 Ichiro Suzuki GG 25.00 60.00
703 Torii Hunter GG 8.00 20.00
704 Greg Maddux GG 25.00 60.00
705 Mike Matheny GG 8.00 20.00
706 Todd Helton GG 12.00 30.00
707 Luis Castillo GG 8.00 20.00
708 Scott Rolen GG 12.00 30.00
709 Cesar Izturis GG 8.00 20.00
710 Jim Edmonds GG 12.00 30.00
711 Andruw Jones GG 8.00 20.00
712 Steve Finley GG 8.00 20.00
713 Johan Santana CY 12.00 30.00
714 Roger Clemens CY 25.00 60.00
715 Vladimir Guerrero MVP 12.00 30.00
716 Barry Bonds MVP 30.00 80.00
717 Bobby Crosby ROY 8.00 20.00
718 Jason Bay ROY 8.00 20.00
719 Albert Pujols AS 25.00 60.00
720 Mark Loretta AS 8.00 20.00
721 Edgar Renteria AS 8.00 20.00
722 Scott Rolen AS 12.00 30.00
723 J.D. Drew AS 8.00 20.00
724 Jim Edmonds AS 12.00 30.00
725 Johnny Estrada AS 8.00 20.00
726 Jason Schmidt AS 8.00 20.00
727 Chris Carpenter AS 12.00 30.00
728 Eric Gagne AS 8.00 20.00
729 Jason Bay AS 8.00 20.00
730 Bobby Cox MG AS 8.00 20.00
731 D.Ortiz 20.00 50.00
M.Bellhorn WS1
732 Curt Schilling WS2 12.00 30.00
733 M.Ramirez 20.00 50.00
P.Martinez WS3
734 Sox Win Damon 12.00 30.00
Lowe WS4

2005 Topps Box Bottoms

ONE 4-CARD SHEET PER HTA BOX
1 Alex Rodriguez 1 .60 1.50
10 Sammy Sosa 1 .50 1.25
20 Hank Blalock 2 .20 .50
25 Jim Thome 2 .30 .75
30 Ivan Rodriguez 3 .30 .75
40 Gary Sheffield 1 .20 .50
78 Hideo Nomo 4 .50 1.25
80 Adam Dunn 2 .30 .75
100 Albert Pujols 3 .60 1.50
120 Akinori Otsuka 4 .20 .50
150 Vladimir Guerrero 1 .30 .75
200 Jason Giambi 2 .20 .50
216 Shingo Takatsu 4 .20 .50
225 Kazuo Matsui 4 .20 .50
230 Miguel Tejada 3 .30 .75
240 Miguel Cabrera 3 .50 1.25
369 Garret Anderson 8 .20 .50
385 Todd Helton 6 .30 .75
390 Manny Ramirez 7 .50 1.25
395 Dontrelle Willis 7 .20 .50
406 Kerry Wood 5 .20 .50
431 Mark Kotsay 6 .20 .50
450 Mike Piazza 5 .50 1.25
455 Jake Peavy 8 .20 .50
460 Alfonso Soriano 6 .30 .75
500 Barry Bonds 5 .75 2.00
505 Nomar Garciaparra 7 .30 .75
510 Joe Mauer 7 .40 1.00
526 Roy Oswalt 6 .30 .75
530 Chipper Jones 5 .50 1.25
550 Pat Burrell 8 .20 .50
620 Scott Rolen 8 .30 .75

2005 Topps Gold

*GOLD 1-296/369-667/693-730: 6X TO 15X
*GOLD 297-326/668-687: 2X TO 5X
*GOLD 327-331/688-692: 2X TO 5X
*GOLD 731-734: 3X TO 8X
SERIES 1 ODDS 1:8 HOB, 1:3 HTA, 1:10 RET
SERIES 2 ODDS 1:5 HOB, 1:2 HTA, 1:6 RET
STATED PRINT RUN 2005 SERIAL #'d SETS
CARD NUMBER 7 DOES NOT EXIST

2005 Topps A-Rod Spokesman

COMPLETE SET (4) 4.00 10.00
SER.2 ODDS 1:24 HOB, 1:8 HTA, 1:24 RET
1 Alex Rodriguez 1994 1.00 2.50
2 Alex Rodriguez 1995 1.00 2.50
3 Alex Rodriguez 1996 1.00 2.50
4 Alex Rodriguez 1997 1.00 2.50

2005 Topps A-Rod Spokesman Autographs

SER.2 ODDS 1:22,279 H, 1:6749 HTA
SER.2 ODDS 1:24,439 R
PRINT RUNS B/WN 1-200 COPIES PER
NO PRICING ON QTY OF 25 OR LESS
3 Alex Rodriguez 1996/100 75.00 150.00
4 Alex Rodriguez 1997/200 25.00 60.00

2005 Topps A-Rod Spokesman Jersey Relics

SER.2 ODDS 1:3550 H, 1:1015 HTA, 1:3564 R
PRINT RUNS B/WN 1-800 COPIES PER
NO PRICING ON QTY OF 1
2 Alex Rodriguez 1995/50 30.00 60.00
3 Alex Rodriguez 1996/300 8.00 20.00
4 Alex Rodriguez 1997/800 6.00 15.00

2005 Topps All-Star Stitches Relics

SERIES 1 ODDS 1:96 H, 1:27 HTA, 1:80 R
AP Albert Pujols 8.00 20.00
AS Alfonso Soriano 4.00 10.00
BA Bobby Abreu 4.00 10.00
BL Barry Larkin 4.00 10.00
BS Ben Sheets 4.00 10.00
CB Carlos Beltran 4.00 10.00
CC Carl Crawford 4.00 10.00
CP Carl Pavano 4.00 10.00
CS C.C. Sabathia 4.00 10.00
CZ Carlos Zambrano 4.00 10.00
DK Danny Kolb 4.00 10.00
DO David Ortiz 4.00 10.00
EL Esteban Loaiza 4.00 10.00
ER Edgar Renteria 4.00 10.00
FG Tom Gordon 4.00 10.00
FR Francisco Rodriguez 4.00 10.00
GS Gary Sheffield 4.00 10.00
HB Hank Blalock 4.00 10.00
IR Ivan Rodriguez 4.00 10.00
JE Johnny Estrada 4.00 10.00
JG Jason Giambi 4.00 10.00
JK Jeff Kent 4.00 10.00
JN Joe Nathan 4.00 10.00
JT Jim Thome 4.00 10.00
JW Jack Wilson 4.00 10.00
KH Ken Harvey 4.00 10.00
LB Lance Berkman 4.00 10.00
MA Moises Alou 4.00 10.00
MC Miguel Cabrera 4.00 10.00
ML Mike Lowell 4.00 10.00
MLA Matt Lawton 4.00 10.00
MLO Mark Loretta 4.00 10.00
MM Mark Mulder 4.00 10.00
MP Mike Piazza 4.00 10.00
MR Manny Ramirez 4.00 10.00
MRI Mariano Rivera 6.00 15.00
MT Miguel Tejada 4.00 10.00
MY Michael Young 4.00 10.00
PL Paul Lo Duca 4.00 10.00
RB Ronnie Belliard 4.00 10.00
SR Scott Rolen 4.00 10.00
SS Sammy Sosa 4.00 10.00
TG Tom Glavine 4.00 10.00
TH Todd Helton 4.00 10.00
TL Ted Lilly 4.00 10.00
VG Vladimir Guerrero 4.00 10.00
VM Victor Martinez 4.00 10.00

2005 Topps All-Stars

COMPLETE SET (15) 10.00 25.00
SER.2 ODDS 1:9 HOBBY, 1:3 HTA
1 Todd Helton .60 1.50
2 Albert Pujols 1.25 3.00
3 Vladimir Guerrero .60 1.50
4 Ichiro Suzuki 1.25 3.00
5 Randy Johnson 1.00 2.50
6 Manny Ramirez 1.00 2.50
7 Sammy Sosa 1.00 2.50
8 Alfonso Soriano .60 1.50
9 Jim Thome .60 1.50
10 Barry Bonds 1.50 4.00
11 Roger Clemens 1.25 3.00
12 Mike Piazza 1.00 2.50
13 Derek Jeter 2.50 6.00
14 Alex Rodriguez 1.25 3.00
15 Carlos Beltran .60 1.50

2005 Topps Autographs

SER.1 A 1:2683 H, 1:767 HTA, 1:2238 R
SER.1 B 1:3950 H, 1:1129 HTA, 1:3300 R
SER.1 C 1:305 H, 1:87 HTA, 1:254 R
SER.1 D 1:2913 H, 1:833 HTA, 1:2432 R
SER.2 A 1:178,234H,1:51,744HTA,1:171,072R
SER.2 B 1:89,117 H, 1:22,176 HTA, 1:85,536 R
SER.2 C 1:2751 H, 1:780 HTA, 1:2715 R
SER.2 D 1:1367 H, 1:390 HTA, 1:1369 R
SER.2 E 1:2039 H, 1:586 HTA, 1:2061 R
SER.2 F 1:285 H, 1:129 HTA, 1:301 R
SER.2 GROUP A PRINT RUN 25 COPIES
SER.2 GROUP B PRINT RUN 50 COPIES
SER.2 GROUP A-B ARE NOT SERIAL #'d
PRINT RUN INFO PROVIDED BY TOPPS
SER.1 EXCH.DEADLINE 11/30/06
SER.2 EXCH.DEADLINE 04/30/07
NO GROUP A2 PRICING DUE TO SCARCITY
AR Alex Rodriguez A1 60.00 150.00
AR2 Alex Rodriguez B2/50 * 30.00 80.00
ARI Alexis Rios C1 4.00 10.00
BB Billy Butler E2 6.00 15.00
CB Carlos Beltran A1 8.00 20.00
CB2 Carlos Beltran C2 8.00 20.00
CC Carl Crawford D2 10.00 25.00
CK Casey Kotchman C1 4.00 10.00
CT Chad Tracy C1 4.00 10.00
CW Craig Wilson D2 6.00 15.00
DD David DeJesus C1 4.00 10.00
DM Dallas McPherson D1 4.00 10.00
DW David Wright C1 8.00 20.00
EC Eric Chavez A1 10.00 25.00
EC2 Eric Chavez C2 10.00 25.00
ECO Erik Cordier F2 4.00 10.00
EG Eric Gagne C2 15.00 40.00
FH Felix Hernandez D2 10.00 25.00
GP Glen Perkins F2 6.00 15.00
IR Ivan Rodriguez C2 12.00 30.00
JB Jason Bay D2 10.00 25.00
JC Jose Capellan B1 4.00 10.00
JM Justin Morneau C1 6.00 15.00
JMA John Maine C1 6.00 15.00
JS Johan Santana C2 8.00 20.00
JSM Jeff Mathis C1 4.00 10.00
LP Landon Powell F2 6.00 15.00
MB Milton Bradley D2 10.00 25.00
MC Miguel Cabrera C1 15.00 40.00
MCA Matt Campbell F2 4.00 10.00
MH Matt Holliday C1 6.00 15.00
ML Mark Loretta D2 6.00 15.00
MR Michael Rogers F2 4.00 10.00
SK Scott Kazmir C2 10.00 25.00
TH Torii Hunter A1 10.00 25.00
TS Termel Sledge E2 4.00 10.00
VW Vernon Wells A1 10.00 25.00
ZG Zack Greinke C1 5.00 12.00

2005 Topps Barry Bonds Chase to 715

COMMON CARD 15.00 40.00
SER.2 ODDS 1:2539 H, 1:722 HTA, 1:2516 R
STATED PRINT RUN 1 SERIAL #'d SET

2005 Topps Barry Bonds Home Run History

COMP.SERIES 3 (48) 20.00 50.00
COMP.06 UPDATE (26) 10.00 25.00
COMP.07 UPDATE (22) 20.00 50.00
COMMON CARD (1-754) 1.25 3.00
COMMON HR 1 15.00 40.00
COMMON HR 100/200/300/400 6.00 15.00
COMMON HR 500/600 6.00 15.00
COMMON HR 661/700 3.00 8.00
COMMON HR 755-762 2.00 5.00
05 SER.2 ODDS 1:4 H, 1:1 HTA, 1:4 R
05 UPDATE ODDS 1:4 H, 1:1 HTA, 1:4 R
06 SER.1 ODDS 1:4 HOB, 1:4 MINI, 1:4 RET
06 SER.1 ODDS 1:2 RACK
06 UPDATE ODDS 1:6 HOB,1:6 RET
07 UPDATE ODDS 1:12 HOBBY
05 SER.2 EXCH ODDS 1:178,234 HOB
05 SER.2 EXCH ODDS 1:51,744 HTA
05 SER.2 EXCH ODDS 1:171,072 RET
07 UPDATE ODDS 1:12 H,1:3 HTA,1:12 R
EXCH CARD PRINT RUN 25 COPIES
EXCH.CARD PRINT RUN INFO FROM TOPPS
NO EXCH CARD PRICING DUE TO SCARCITY
1-330 ISSUED IN 05 SERIES 2 PACKS
331-660 ISSUED IN 05 UPDATE PACKS
661-708 ISSUED IN 06 SERIES 1 PACKS
709-734 ISSUED IN 06 UPDATE PACKS
735-575 ISSUED IN 07 UPDATE PACKS
1/100/200/300/400/500/600 ARE GOLD FOIL
661/700/755/766 ARE SILVER FOIL

2005 Topps Barry Bonds MVP

SER.2 ODDS 1:2613 H, 1:743 HTA, 1:2592 R
PRINT RUNS B/WN 25-500 COPIES PER
NO PRICING ON QTY OF 25
3 Barry Bonds 1993/100 10.00 25.00
4 Barry Bonds 2001/200 8.00 20.00
5 Barry Bonds 2002/300 8.00 20.00
6 Barry Bonds 2003/400 6.00 15.00
7 Barry Bonds 2004/500 6.00 15.00

2005 Topps Barry Bonds MVP Jersey Relics

SER.2 ODDS 1:2613 H, 1:743 HTA, 1:2592 R
PRINT RUNS B/WN 25-500 COPIES PER
NO PRICING ON QTY OF 25
3 Barry Bonds 1993/100 50.00 100.00
4 Barry Bonds 2001/200 30.00 60.00
5 Barry Bonds 2002/300 20.00 50.00
6 Barry Bonds 2003/400 15.00 40.00
7 Barry Bonds 2004/500 12.50 30.00

2005 Topps Celebrity Threads Jersey Relics

SERIES 1 ODDS 1:562 H, 1:161 HTA, 1:468 R
RELICS ARE FROM CELEBRITY AS EVENT
CC Cesar Cedeno 4.00 10.00
CF Cecil Fielder 6.00 15.00
DW Dave Winfield 4.00 10.00
GG Goose Gossage 4.00 10.00
HR Harold Reynolds 4.00 10.00
MS Mike Scott 4.00 10.00
OS Ozzie Smith 8.00 20.00
RF Rollie Fingers 4.00 10.00

2005 Topps Dem Bums

COMPLETE SET (21) 20.00 50.00
SERIES 1 ODDS 1:12 H, 1:4 HTA, 1:12 R
BB Bob Borkowski 1.25 3.00
CE Carl Erskine 1.25 3.00
CF Carl Furillo 1.25 3.00
CL Clem Labine 1.25 3.00
DH Don Hoak 1.25 3.00
DN Don Newcombe 1.25 3.00
DS Duke Snider 2.00 5.00
DZ Don Zimmer 1.25 3.00
ER Ed Roebuck 1.25 3.00
GS George Shuba 1.25 3.00
JB Joe Black 1.25 3.00
JG Jim Gilliam 1.25 3.00
JH Jim Hughes 1.25 3.00
JP Johnny Podres 1.25 3.00
JR Jackie Robinson 2.00 5.00
KS Karl Spooner 1.25 3.00
RC Roy Campanella 2.00 5.00
RCR Roger Craig 1.25 3.00
RM Russ Meyer 1.25 3.00
RW Rube Walker 1.25 3.00
WA Walter Alston 2.00 5.00

2005 Topps Dem Bums Autographs

SERIES 1 ODDS 1:150 HTA
SERIES 2 ODDS 1:182 HTA
SER.2 EXCH.DEADLINE 04/30/07
CE Carl Erskine 15.00 40.00
CL Clem Labine 15.00 40.00
DN Don Newcombe 20.00 50.00
DS Duke Snider 20.00 50.00
DZ Don Zimmer 20.00 50.00
ER Ed Roebuck 20.00 50.00
JP Johnny Podres 15.00 40.00
RC Roger Craig 15.00 40.00

2005 Topps Derby Digs Jersey Relics

SER.1 ODDS 1:11,208 HOBBY, 1:3232 HTA
SER.1 ODDS 1:9630 RETAIL
STATED PRINT RUN 100 SERIAL #'d SETS
DO David Ortiz 15.00 40.00
HB Hank Blalock 10.00 25.00
JT Jim Thome 15.00 40.00
LB Lance Berkman 10.00 25.00
MT Miguel Tejada 10.00 25.00
SS Sammy Sosa 15.00 40.00

2005 Topps Factory Set Draft Picks Bonus

COMPLETE SET (5) 10.00 20.00
ONE SET PER FACTORY SET
1 Beau Jones 2.00 5.00
2 Cliff Pennington .75 2.00
3 Chris Volstad 2.00 5.00
4 Ricky Romero 1.25 3.00
5 Jay Bruce 6.00 15.00

2005 Topps Factory Set First Year Draft Bonus

COMPLETE SET (10) 15.00 30.00
ONE SET PER GREEN HOLIDAY FACT.SET
1 Nick Webber .75 2.00
2 Aaron Thompson 1.25 3.00
3 Matt Garza 1.25 3.00
4 Tyler Greene .75 2.00
5 Ryan Braun 6.00 15.00
6 C.J. Henry 1.25 3.00
7 Ryan Zimmerman 4.00 10.00
8 John Mayberry Jr. 2.00 5.00
9 Cesar Carrillo 1.25 3.00
10 Mark McCormick .75 2.00

2005 Topps Factory Set First Year Player Bonus

COMPLETE SERIES 1 (5) 6.00 15.00
1-5 ISSUED IN RED HOBBY SETS
1 Bill McCarthy .75 2.00
2 John Hudgins .75 2.00
3 Kyle Nichols .75 2.00
4 Thomas Pauly .75 2.00
5 Philip Humber 2.00 5.00

2005 Topps Factory Set Team Bonus

COMP.CUBS SET (5) 6.00 15.00
COMP.GIANTS SET (5) 6.00 15.00
COMP.NATIONALS SET (5) 6.00 15.00
COMP.RED SOX SET (5) 6.00 15.00
COMP.TIGERS SET (5) 6.00 15.00
COMP.YANKEES SET (5) 6.00 15.00
C1-C5 ISSUED IN CUBS FACTORY SET
G1-G5 ISSUED IN GIANTS FACTORY SET
N1-N5 ISSUED IN NATIONALS FACTORY SET
R1-R5 ISSUED IN RED SOX FACTORY SET
T1-T5 ISSUED IN TIGERS FACTORY SET
Y1-Y5 ISSUED IN YANKEES FACTORY SET
C1 Casey McGehee 1.25 3.00
C2 Andy Santana .75 2.00
C3 Buck Coats .75 2.00
C4 Kevin Collins .75 2.00
C5 Brandon Sing .75 2.00
G1 Pat Misch .75 2.00
G2 J.B. Thurmond .75 2.00
G3 Billy Sadler .75 2.00
G4 Jonathan Sanchez 3.00 8.00
G5 Fred Lewis 1.25 3.00
N1 Daryl Thompson .75 2.00
N2 Ender Chavez .75 2.00
N3 Ryan Church .75 2.00
N4 Brendan Harris .75 2.00
N5 Darrell Rasner .75 2.00
R1 Stefan Bailie .75 2.00
R2 Willy Mota .75 2.00
R3 Matt Van Der Bosch .75 2.00
R4 Mike Garber .75 2.00
R5 Dustin Pedroia 5.00 12.00
T1 Eulogio de la Cruz .75 2.00
T2 Humberto Sanchez 1.25 3.00
T3 Danny Zell .75 2.00
T4 Kyle Sleeth .75 2.00
T5 Curtis Granderson 1.50 4.00
Y1 T.J. Beam .75 2.00
Y2 Ben Jones .75 2.00
Y3 Robinson Cano 2.50 6.00
Y4 Steven White .75 2.00
Y5 Philip Hughes 2.00 5.00

2005 Topps Grudge Match

COMPLETE SET (10) 5.00 12.00
SERIES 1 ODDS 1:24 H, 1:8 HTA, 1:18 R
1 J.Posada .60 1.50
P.Martinez
2 M.Piazza 1.25 3.00
R.Clemens
3 M.Rivera 1.25 3.00
L.Gonzalez
4 J.Edmonds .60 1.50
C.Zambrano
5 A.Boone .60 1.50
T.Wakefield
6 M.Ramirez 1.25 3.00
R.Clemens
7 M.Tucker .40 1.00
E.Gagne
8 I.Rodriguez .60 1.50
J.Snow
9 A.Rodriguez 1.25 3.00
B.Arroyo
10 C.Miller 1.00 2.50
S.Sosa

2005 Topps Hit Parade

COMPLETE SET (30) 30.00 60.00
SER.2 ODDS 1:12 H, 1:4 HTA, 1:12 R
HR1 Barry Bonds HR 1.50 4.00
HR2 Sammy Sosa HR 1.00 2.50
HR3 Rafael Palmeiro HR .60 1.50
HR4 Ken Griffey Jr. HR 2.00 5.00
HR5 Jeff Bagwell HR .60 1.50
HR6 Frank Thomas HR 1.00 2.50

HR7 Juan Gonzalez HR .40 1.00
HR8 Jim Thome HR .60 1.50
HR9 Gary Sheffield HR .40 1.00
HR10 Manny Ramirez HR 1.00 2.50
HIT1 Rafael Palmeiro HIT .60 1.50
HIT2 Barry Bonds HIT 1.50 4.00
HIT3 Roberto Alomar HIT .60 1.50
HIT4 Craig Biggio HIT .60 1.50
HIT5 Julio Franco HIT .40 1.00
HIT6 Steve Finley HIT .40 1.00
HIT7 Jeff Bagwell HIT .60 1.50
HIT8 B.J. Surhoff HIT .40 1.00
HIT9 Marquis Grissom HIT .40 1.00
HIT10 Sammy Sosa HIT 1.00 2.50
RBI1 Barry Bonds RBI 1.50 4.00
RBI2 Rafael Palmeiro RBI .60 1.50
RBI3 Sammy Sosa RBI 1.00 2.50
RBI4 Jeff Bagwell RBI .60 1.50
RBI5 Ken Griffey Jr. RBI 2.00 5.00
RBI6 Frank Thomas RBI 1.00 2.50
RBI7 Juan Gonzalez RBI .40 1.00
RBI8 Gary Sheffield RBI .40 1.00
RBI9 Ruben Sierra RBI .40 1.00
RBI10 Manny Ramirez RBI 1.00 2.50

2005 Topps Hobby Masters

COMPLETE SET (20) 12.50 30.00
SERIES 1 ODDS 1:18 HOBBY, 1:6 HTA
1 Alex Rodriguez 1.25 3.00
2 Sammy Sosa 1.00 2.50
3 Ichiro Suzuki 1.25 3.00
4 Albert Pujols 1.25 3.00
5 Derek Jeter 2.50 6.00
6 Jim Thome .60 1.50
7 Vladimir Guerrero .60 1.50
8 Nomar Garciaparra .60 1.50
9 Mike Piazza 1.00 2.50
10 Jason Giambi .40 1.00
11 Ivan Rodriguez .60 1.50
12 Alfonso Soriano .60 1.50
13 Dontrelle Willis .40 1.00
14 Chipper Jones 1.00 2.50
15 Mark Prior .60 1.50
16 Todd Helton .60 1.50
17 Randy Johnson 1.00 2.50
18 Hank Blalock .40 1.00
19 Ken Griffey Jr. 2.00 5.00
20 Roger Clemens 1.25 3.00

2005 Topps On Deck Circle Relics

SER.2 ODDS 1:1493 H, 1:425 HTA, 1:1488 R
STATED PRINT RUN 275 SETS
CARDS ARE NOT SERIAL-NUMBERED
PRINT RUN INFO PROVIDED BY TOPPS
AP Albert Pujols 15.00 40.00
AR Alex Rodriguez 15.00 40.00
AS Alfonso Soriano 4.00 10.00
CB Carlos Beltran 4.00 10.00
HB Hank Blalock 4.00 10.00
IR Ivan Rodriguez 6.00 15.00
JT Jim Thome 6.00 15.00
SR Scott Rolen 6.00 15.00
SS Sammy Sosa 6.00 15.00
TH Todd Helton 6.00 15.00

2005 Topps Own the Game

COMPLETE SET (30) 12.50 30.00
SERIES 1 ODDS 1:12 H, 1:4 HTA, 1:12 R
1 Ichiro Suzuki 1.25 3.00
2 Todd Helton .60 1.50
3 Adrian Beltre 1.00 2.50
4 Albert Pujols 1.25 3.00
5 Adam Dunn .60 1.50
6 Jim Thome .60 1.50
7 Miguel Tejada .60 1.50
8 David Ortiz 1.00 2.50
9 Manny Ramirez 1.00 2.50
10 Scott Rolen .60 1.50
11 Gary Sheffield .40 1.00
12 Vladimir Guerrero .60 1.50
13 Jim Edmonds .60 1.50
14 Ivan Rodriguez .60 1.50
15 Lance Berkman .60 1.50
16 Michael Young .40 1.00
17 Juan Pierre .40 1.00
18 Craig Biggio .60 1.50
19 Johnny Damon .60 1.50
20 Jimmy Rollins .60 1.50
21 Scott Podsednik .40 1.00
22 Bobby Abreu .40 1.00
23 Lyle Overbay .40 1.00
24 Carl Crawford .60 1.50
25 Mark Loretta .40 1.00
26 Vinny Castilla .40 1.00
27 Curt Schilling .60 1.50
28 Johan Santana .60 1.50
29 Randy Johnson 1.00 2.50
30 Pedro Martinez .60 1.50

2005 Topps Spokesman Jersey Relic

SER.1 ODDS 1:5627 H, 1:1604 HTA, 1:4692 R
RELIC IS EVENT WORN
AR Alex Rodriguez 20.00 50.00

2005 Topps Team Topps Autographs

BOWMAN DRAFT ODDS 1:697 H
TOP.UP.ODDS 1:5374H,1:1537 HTA,1:5347R
BH Ben Hendrickson BD 4.00 10.00
JK Josh Kroeger BD 4.00 10.00
KS Kurt Suzuki TU 4.00 10.00

2005 Topps World Champions Red Sox Relics

SER.2 A ODDS 1:649 H, 1:185 HTA, 1:648 R
SER.2 B ODDS 1:311 H, 1:89 HTA, 1:310 R
BM Bill Mueller Bat A 6.00 15.00
BM2 Bill Mueller Jsy B 6.00 15.00
CS Curt Schilling Jsy B 6.00 15.00
DL Derek Lowe Jsy B 6.00 15.00
DMI Doug Mientkiewicz Bat B 6.00 15.00
DO David Ortiz Bat B 15.00 40.00
DO2 David Ortiz Jsy B 8.00 20.00
DR Dave Roberts Bat A 8.00 20.00
JD Johnny Damon Bat A 6.00 15.00
JD2 Johnny Damon Jsy B 6.00 15.00
KM Kevin Millar Bat B 12.00 30.00
KY Kevin Youkilis Bat A 4.00 10.00
MR Manny Ramirez Bat A 6.00 15.00
MR2 Manny Ramirez Home Jsy B 6.00 15.00
MR3 Manny Ramirez Road Jsy B 6.00 15.00
OC Orlando Cabrera Bat A 6.00 15.00
OC2 Orlando Cabrera Jsy B 6.00 15.00
PM Pedro Martinez Uni A 6.00 15.00
PR Pokey Reese Bat B 4.00 10.00
TN Trot Nixon Bat A 6.00 15.00

2005 Topps Update

COMPLETE SET (330) 15.00 40.00
COMP.FACT.SET (330) 25.00 40.00
COMMON CARD (1-330) .07 .20
COM (90-110/203-220) .40 1.00
COMMON (116-134) .20 .50
COM (14/66/221-310) .40 1.00
COMMON (311-330) .40 1.00
PLATE ODDS 1:2009 H, 1:582 HTA, 1:2009 R
PLATE PRINT RUN 1 SET PER COLOR
BLACK-CYAN-MAGENTA-YELLOW ISSUED
NO PLATE PRICING DUE TO SCARCITY
1 Sammy Sosa .20 .50
2 Jeff Francoeur .20 .50
3 Tony Clark .07 .20
4 Michael Tucker .07 .20
5 Mike Matheny .07 .20
6 Eric Young .07 .20
7 Jose Valentin .07 .20
8 Matt Lawton .07 .20
9 Juan Rivera .07 .20
10 Shawn Green .07 .20
11 Aaron Boone .07 .20
12 Woody Williams .07 .20
13 Brad Wilkerson .07 .20
14 Anthony Reyes RC .60 1.50
15 Russ Adams .07 .20
16 Gustavo Chacin .07 .20
17 Michael Restovich .07 .20
18 Humberto Quintero .07 .20
19 Matt Ginter .07 .20
20 Scott Podsednik .07 .20
21 Byung-Hyun Kim .07 .20
22 Orlando Hernandez .07 .20
23 Mark Grudzielanek .07 .20
24 Jody Gerut .07 .20
25 Adrian Beltre .20 .50
26 Scott Schoeneweis .07 .20
27 Marlon Anderson .07 .20
28 Jason Vargas .07 .20
29 Claudio Vargas .07 .20
30 Jason Kendall .07 .20
31 Aaron Small .07 .20
32 Juan Cruz .07 .20
33 Placido Polanco .07 .20
34 Jorge Sosa .07 .20
35 John Olerud .07 .20
36 Ryan Langerhans .07 .20
37 Randy Winn .07 .20
38 Zach Duke .07 .20
39 Garrett Atkins .07 .20
40 Al Leiter .07 .20
41 Shawn Chacon .07 .20
42 Mark DeRosa .07 .20
43 Miguel Ojeda .07 .20
44 A.J. Pierzynski .07 .20
45 Carlos Lee .07 .20
46 LaTroy Hawkins .07 .20
47 Nick Green .07 .20
48 Shawn Estes .07 .20
49 Eli Marrero .07 .20
50 Jeff Kent .07 .20
51 Joe Randa .07 .20
52 Jose Hernandez .07 .20
53 Joe Blanton .07 .20
54 Huston Street .07 .20
55 Marlon Byrd .07 .20
56 Alex Sanchez .07 .20
57 Livan Hernandez .07 .20
58 Chris Young .12 .30
59 Brad Eldred .07 .20
60 Terrence Long .07 .20
61 Phil Nevin .07 .20
62 Kyle Farnsworth .07 .20
63 Jon Lieber .07 .20
64 Antonio Alfonseca .07 .20
65 Tony Graffanino .07 .20
66 Tadahito Iguchi RC .60 1.50
67 Brad Thompson .07 .20
68 Jose Vidro .07 .20
69 Jason Phillips .07 .20
70 Carl Pavano .07 .20
71 Pokey Reese .07 .20
72 Jerome Williams .07 .20
73 Kazuhisa Ishii .07 .20
74 Zach Day .07 .20
75 Edgar Renteria .07 .20
76 Mike Myers .07 .20
77 Jeff Cirillo .07 .20
78 Endy Chavez .07 .20
79 Jose Guillen .07 .20
80 Ugueth Urbina .07 .20
81 Vinny Castilla .07 .20
82 Javier Vazquez .07 .20
83 Willy Taveras .07 .20
84 Mark Mulder .07 .20
85 Mike Hargrove MG .07 .20
86 Buddy Bell MG .07 .20
87 Charlie Manuel MG .07 .20
88 Willie Randolph MG .07 .20
89 Bob Melvin MG .07 .20
90 Chris Lambert PROS .40 1.00
91 Homer Bailey PROS .40 1.00
92 Ervin Santana PROS .40 1.00
93 Bill Bray PROS .40 1.00
94 Thomas Diamond PROS .40 1.00
95 Trevor Plouffe PROS 1.00 2.50
96 James Houser PROS .40 1.00
97 Jake Stevens PROS .40 1.00
98 Anthony Whittington PROS .40 1.00
99 Philip Hughes PROS 1.00 2.50
100 Greg Golson PROS .40 1.00
101 Paul Maholm PROS .40 1.00
102 Carlos Quentin PROS .60 1.50
103 Dan Johnson PROS .40 1.00
104 Mark Rogers PROS .40 1.00
105 Neil Walker PROS .60 1.50
106 Omar Quintanilla PROS .40 1.00
107 Blake DeWitt PROS .60 1.50
108 Taylor Tankersley PROS .40 1.00
109 David Murphy PROS .60 1.50
110 Felix Hernandez PROS 1.25 3.00
111 Craig Biggio HL .12 .30
112 Greg Maddux HL .25 .60
113 Bobby Abreu HL .07 .20
114 Alex Rodriguez HL .25 .60
115 Trevor Hoffman HL .12 .30
116 A.Pierzynski .20 .50
T.Iguchi ALDS
117 Reggie Sanders NLDS .12 .30
118 B.Molina .12 .30
E.Santana ALDS
119 Burke .20 .50
Berkman/LaR NLDS
120 Garret Anderson ALCS .12 .30
121 A.J. Pierzynski ALCS .12 .30
122 Paul Konerko ALCS .20 .50
123 Joe Crede ALCS .12 .30
124 M.Buehrle .20 .50
J.Garland ALCS
125 F.Garcia .12 .30
J.Contreras ALCS
126 Reggie Sanders NLCS .12 .30
127 Roy Oswalt NLCS .20 .50
128 Roger Clemens NLCS .40 1.00
129 Albert Pujols NLCS .40 1.00
130 Roy Oswalt NLCS .20 .50
131 J.Crede .12 .30
B.Jenks WS
132 P.Konerko .20 .50
S.Podsed WS
133 Geoff Blum WS .12 .30
134 White Sox Sweep WS .12 .30
135 ARod .25 .60
Ortiz/Manny AL HR
136 Young .25 .60
ARod/Vlad AL BA
137 Ortiz .20 .50
Teix/Manny AL RBI
138 Colon .12 .30
Garland/Lee AL W
139 Mill .12 .30
Johan/Buehrle AL ERA
140 Johan .20 .50
Randy/Lackey AL K
141 Andruw .25 .60
Lee/Pujols NL HR
142 Lee .25 .60
Pujols/Cabrera NL BA
143 Andruw .25 .60
Pujols/Burr NL RBI
144 Willis .12 .30
Carp/Oswalt NL W
145 Roger .25 .60
Andy/Willis NL ERA
146 Peavy .12 .30
Carp/Pedro NL K
147 Mark Teixeira AS .12 .30
148 Brian Roberts AS .07 .20
149 Michael Young AS .07 .20
150 Alex Rodriguez AS .25 .60
151 Johnny Damon AS .12 .30
152 Vladimir Guerrero AS .12 .30
153 Manny Ramirez AS .20 .50
154 David Ortiz AS .20 .50
155 Mariano Rivera AS .25 .60
156 Joe Nathan AS .07 .20
157 Albert Pujols AS .25 .60
158 Jeff Kent AS .07 .20
159 Felipe Lopez AS .07 .20
160 Morgan Ensberg AS .07 .20
161 Miguel Cabrera AS .20 .50
162 Ken Griffey Jr. AS .40 1.00
163 Andruw Jones AS .07 .20
164 Paul Lo Duca AS .07 .20
165 Chad Cordero AS .07 .20
166 Ken Griffey Jr. Comeback .40 1.00
167 Jason Giambi Comeback .07 .20
168 Willy Taveras ROY .07 .20
169 Huston Street ROY .07 .20
170 Chris Carpenter AS .12 .30
171 Bartolo Colon AS .07 .20
172 Bobby Cox AS MG .07 .20
173 Ozzie Guillen AS MG .07 .20
174 Andruw Jones POY .07 .20
175 Johnny Damon AS .12 .30
176 Alex Rodriguez AS .25 .60
177 David Ortiz AS .20 .50
178 Manny Ramirez AS .20 .50
179 Miguel Tejada AS .12 .30
180 Vladimir Guerrero AS .12 .30
181 Mark Teixeira AS .12 .30
182 Ivan Rodriguez AS .12 .30
183 Brian Roberts AS .07 .20
184 Mark Buehrle AS .12 .30
185 Bobby Abreu AS .07 .20
186 Carlos Beltran AS .12 .30
187 Albert Pujols AS .25 .60
188 Derrek Lee AS .07 .20
189 Jim Edmonds AS .12 .30
190 Aramis Ramirez AS .07 .20
191 Mike Piazza AS .20 .50
192 Jeff Kent AS .07 .20
193 David Eckstein AS .07 .20
194 Chris Carpenter AS .12 .30
195 Bobby Abreu HR .07 .20
196 Ivan Rodriguez HR .12 .30
197 Carlos Lee HR .07 .20
198 David Ortiz HR .20 .50
199 Hee-Seop Choi HR .07 .20
200 Andruw Jones HR .07 .20
201 Mark Teixeira HR .12 .30
202 Jason Bay HR .07 .20
203 Hanley Ramirez FUT .60 1.50
204 Shin-Soo Choo FUT .60 1.50
205 Justin Huber FUT .40 1.00
206 Nelson Cruz FUT RC 5.00 12.00
207 Edwin Encarnacion FUT 1.00 2.50
208 Miguel Montero FUT RC 1.25 3.00
209 William Bergolla FUT .40 1.00
210 Luis Montanez FUT .40 1.00
211 Francisco Liriano FUT 1.00 2.50
212 Kevin Thompson FUT .40 1.00
213 B.J. Upton FUT .60 1.50
214 Conor Jackson FUT .60 1.50
215 Delmon Young FUT 1.00 2.50
216 Andy LaRoche FUT .40 1.00
217 Ryan Garko FUT .40 1.00
218 Josh Barfield FUT .60 1.50
219 Chris B.Young FUT 1.25 3.00
220 Justin Verlander FUT 8.00 20.00
221 Drew Anderson FY RC .40 1.00
222 Luis Hernandez FY RC .40 1.00
223 Jim Burt FY RC .40 1.00
224 Mike Morse FY RC 1.25 3.00
225 Elliot Johnson FY RC .40 1.00
226 C.J. Smith FY RC .40 1.00
227 Casey McGehee FY RC .60 1.50
228 Brian Miller FY RC .40 1.00
229 Chris Vines FY RC .40 1.00
230 D.J. Houlton FY RC .40 1.00
231 Chuck Tiffany FY RC 1.00 2.50
232 Humberto Sanchez FY RC .60 1.50
233 Baltazar Lopez FY RC .40 1.00
234 Russ Martin FY RC 1.25 3.00
235 Dana Eveland FY RC .40 1.00
236 Johan Silva FY RC .40 1.00
237 Adam Harben FY RC .40 1.00
238 Brian Bannister FY RC .60 1.50
239 Adam Boeve FY RC .40 1.00
240 Thomas Oldham FY RC .40 1.00
241 Cody Haerther FY RC .40 1.00
242 Dan Santin FY RC .40 1.00
243 Daniel Haigwood FY RC .40 1.00
244 Craig Tatum FY RC .40 1.00
245 Martin Prado FY RC 2.50 6.00
246 Errol Simonitsch FY RC .40 1.00
247 Lorenzo Scott FY RC .40 1.00
248 Hayden Penn FY RC .40 1.00
249 Heath Totten FY RC .40 1.00
250 Nick Masset FY RC .40 1.00
251 Pedro Lopez FY RC .40 1.00
252 Ben Harrison FY .40 1.00
253 Mike Spidale FY RC .40 1.00
254 Jeremy Harts FY RC .40 1.00
255 Danny Zell FY RC .40 1.00
256 Kevin Collins FY RC .40 1.00
257 Tony Arnerich FY RC .40 1.00
258 Matt Albers FY RC .40 1.00
259 Ricky Barrett FY RC .40 1.00
260 Hernan Iribarren FY RC .40 1.00
261 Sean Tracey FY RC .40 1.00
262 Jerry Owens FY RC .40 1.00
263 Steve Nelson FY RC .40 1.00
264 Brandon McCarthy FY RC .60 1.50
265 David Shepard FY RC .40 1.00
266 Steven Bondurant FY RC .40 1.00
267 Billy Sadler FY RC .40 1.00
268 Ryan Feierabend FY RC .40 1.00
269 Stuart Pomeranz FY RC .40 1.00
270 Shaun Marcum FY 1.00 2.50
271 Erik Schindewolf FY RC .40 1.00
272 Stefan Bailie FY RC .40 1.00
273 Mike Esposito FY RC .40 1.00
274 Buck Coats FY RC .40 1.00
275 Andy Sides FY RC .40 1.00
276 Micah Schnurstein FY RC .40 1.00
277 Jesse Gutierrez FY RC .40 1.00
278 Jake Postlewait FY RC .40 1.00
279 Willy Mota FY RC .40 1.00
280 Ryan Speier FY RC .40 1.00
281 Frank Mata FY RC .40 1.00
282 Jair Jurrjens FY RC 2.00 5.00
283 Nick Touchstone FY RC .40 1.00
284 Matthew Kemp FY RC 2.00 5.00
285 Vinny Rottino FY RC .40 1.00
286 J.B. Thurmond FY RC .40 1.00
287 Kelvin Pichardo FY RC .40 1.00
288 Scott Mitchinson FY RC .40 1.00
289 Darwinson Salazar FY RC .40 1.00
290 George Kottaras FY RC .60 1.50
291 Kenny Durost FY RC .40 1.00
292 Jonathan Sanchez FY RC 1.50 4.00
293 Brandon Moorhead FY RC .40 1.00
294 Kennard Bibbs FY RC .40 1.00
295 David Gassner FY RC .40 1.00
296 Micah Furtado FY RC .40 1.00
297 Ismael Ramirez FY RC .40 1.00
298 Carlos Gonzalez FY RC 3.00 8.00
299 Brandon Sing FY RC .40 1.00
300 Jason Motte FY RC .60 1.50
301 Chuck James FY RC 1.00 2.50
302 Andy Santana FY RC .40 1.00
303 Manny Parra FY RC 1.00 2.50
304 Chris B.Young FY RC 1.25 3.00
305 Juan Senreiso FY RC .40 1.00
306 Franklin Morales FY RC .60 1.50
307 Jared Gothreaux FY RC .40 1.00
308 Jayce Tingler FY RC .40 1.00
309 Matt Brown FY RC .40 1.00
310 Frank Diaz FY RC .40 1.00
311 Stephen Drew DP RC 1.25 3.00
312 Jered Weaver DP RC 2.00 5.00
313 Ryan Braun DP RC 3.00 8.00
314 John Mayberry Jr. DP RC 1.00 2.50
315 Aaron Thompson DP RC .60 1.50
316 Cesar Carrillo DP RC .40 1.00
317 Jacoby Ellsbury DP RC 3.00 8.00
318 Matt Garza DP RC .60 1.50
319 Cliff Pennington DP RC .40 1.00
320 Colby Rasmus DP RC 1.00 2.50
321 Chris Volstad DP RC 1.00 2.50
322 Ricky Romero DP RC .60 1.50
323 Ryan Zimmerman DP RC 3.00 8.00
324 C.J. Henry DP RC .60 1.50
325 Jay Bruce DP RC 3.00 8.00
326 Beau Jones DP RC 1.00 2.50
327 Mark McCormick DP RC .40 1.00
328 Eli Iorg DP RC .40 1.00
329 Andrew McCutchen DP RC 5.00 12.00
330 Mike Costanzo DP RC .40 1.00

2005 Topps Update Box Bottoms

*BOX BOTTOM: 1X TO 2.5X BASIC
*BOX BOTTOM: .6X TO 1.5X BASIC RC
ONE FOUR-CARD SHEET PER HTA BOX
CL: 1/10/20/22/25/45/50/57/70/84/110
CL: 224/264/311-313

2005 Topps Update Gold

*GOLD 1-89: 3X TO 8X BASIC
*GOLD 90-110: 2X TO 5X BASIC
*GOLD 111-115/135-202: 3X TO 8X BASIC
*GOLD: 116-134: 1.5X TO 4X BASIC
*GOLD: 203-220: 2X TO 5X BASIC
*GOLD 14/66/221-310: 2X TO 5X BASIC
*GOLD 311-330: .6X TO 1.5X BASIC
STATED ODDS 1:4 H, 1:1 HTA, 1:4 R
STATED PRINT RUN 2005 SERIAL #'d SETS

2005 Topps Update All-Star Patches

STATED ODDS 1:910 H, 1:268 HTA, 1:910 R
PRINT RUNS B/WN 20-70 COPIES PER
NO PRICING ON QTY OF 25 OR LESS
AJ Andruw Jones/70 12.50 30.00
AP Albert Pujols/35 30.00 60.00
AR Alex Rodriguez/50 15.00 40.00
ARA Aramis Ramirez/60 10.00 25.00
BA Bobby Abreu/65 10.00 25.00
BC Bartolo Colon/60 10.00 25.00
BL Brad Lidge/65 10.00 25.00
BW Billy Wagner/50 10.00 25.00
CB Carlos Beltran/60 10.00 25.00
CC Chris Carpenter/70 10.00 25.00
CCO Chad Cordero/65 6.00 15.00
CL Carlos Lee/65 10.00 25.00
DE David Eckstein/65 12.50 30.00
DL Derrek Lee/65 12.50 30.00
DO David Ortiz/70 12.50 30.00
DW Dontrelle Willis/60 10.00 25.00
FL Felipe Lopez/35 8.00 20.00
GS Gary Sheffield/50 10.00 25.00
IS Ichiro Suzuki/50 20.00 50.00
JB Jason Bay/50 10.00 25.00
JD Johnny Damon/60 12.50 30.00
JE Jim Edmonds/50 10.00 25.00
JG Jon Garland/70 12.50 30.00
JI Jason Isringhausen/65 10.00 25.00
JK Jeff Kent/65 10.00 25.00
JN Joe Nathan/65 6.00 15.00
JP Jake Peavy/60 10.00 25.00
JS Johan Santana/60 12.50 30.00
JSM John Smoltz/65 12.50 30.00
KR Kenny Rogers/50 6.00 15.00
LG Luis Gonzalez/70 10.00 25.00
LH Livan Hernandez/50 10.00 25.00
MA Moises Alou/65 6.00 15.00
MB Mark Buehrle/60 10.00 25.00
MC Miguel Cabrera/70 12.50 30.00
MCL Matt Clement/70 10.00 25.00
ME Morgan Ensberg/60 10.00 25.00
MM Melvin Mora/30 12.50 30.00
MP Mike Piazza/50 15.00 40.00
MR Manny Ramirez/65 12.50 30.00
MRI Mariano Rivera/65 15.00 40.00
MT Miguel Tejada/60 10.00 25.00
MTE Mark Teixeira/60 12.50 30.00
MY Michael Young/50 10.00 25.00
PK Paul Konerko/70 10.00 25.00
RO Roy Oswalt/60 10.00 25.00
SP Scott Podsednik/65 10.00 25.00

2005 Topps Update All-Star Stitches

GROUP A ODDS 1:131 H, 1:81 HTA, 1:127 R
GROUP B ODDS 1:91 H, 1:45 HTA, 1:91 R
GROUP C ODDS 1:100 H, 1:41 HTA, 1:100 R
GROUP D ODDS 1:109 H, 1:34 HTA, 1:109 R
GROUP E ODDS 1:98 H, 1:29 HTA, 1:98 R
GROUP F ODDS 1:272 H, 1:69 HTA, 1:272 R
AJ Andruw Jones C 4.00 10.00
AP Albert Pujols E 8.00 20.00
AR Alex Rodriguez D 6.00 15.00
ARA Aramis Ramirez E 3.00 8.00
BA Bobby Abreu B 3.00 8.00
BC Bartolo Colon D 3.00 8.00
BL Brad Lidge D 3.00 8.00
BR Brian Roberts C 3.00 8.00
BW Billy Wagner C 3.00 8.00
CB Carlos Beltran D 3.00 8.00
CC Chris Carpenter E 4.00 10.00
CCO Chad Cordero D 3.00 8.00
CL Carlos Lee E 3.00 8.00
DE David Eckstein B 6.00 15.00
DL Derrek Lee F 4.00 10.00
DO David Ortiz E 4.00 10.00
DW Dontrelle Willis F 3.00 8.00
FL Felipe Lopez B 3.00 8.00
GS Gary Sheffield D 3.00 8.00
IR Ivan Rodriguez A 4.00 10.00
IS Ichiro Suzuki A 8.00 20.00
JB Jason Bay C 3.00 8.00
JD Johnny Damon B 4.00 10.00
JE Jim Edmonds A 3.00 8.00
JG Jon Garland E 4.00 10.00
JI Jason Isringhausen E 3.00 8.00
JK Jeff Kent C 3.00 8.00
JN Joe Nathan D 3.00 8.00
JP Jake Peavy D 3.00 8.00
JS Johan Santana C 4.00 10.00
JSM John Smoltz D 4.00 10.00
KR Kenny Rogers A 3.00 8.00
LC Luis Castillo B 3.00 8.00
LG Luis Gonzalez C 3.00 8.00
LH Livan Hernandez F 3.00 8.00
MA Moises Alou C 3.00 8.00
MB Mark Buehrle B 3.00 8.00
MC Miguel Cabrera E 4.00 10.00
MCL Matt Clement B 3.00 8.00
ME Morgan Ensberg B 3.00 8.00
MM Melvin Mora B 3.00 8.00
MP Mike Piazza C 4.00 10.00
MR Manny Ramirez E 4.00 10.00
MRI Mariano Rivera B 4.00 10.00
MT Miguel Tejada B 3.00 8.00
MTE Mark Teixeira C 4.00 10.00
MY Michael Young A 3.00 8.00
PK Paul Konerko A 3.00 8.00
RO Roy Oswalt A 3.00 8.00
SP Scott Podsednik A 6.00 15.00

2005 Topps Update Derby Digs Jersey Relics

STATED ODDS 1:3320 H,1:637 HTA,1:3320 R
STATED PRINT RUN 100 SERIAL #'d SETS
AJ Andruw Jones 10.00 25.00
BA Bobby Abreu 10.00 25.00
CL Carlos Lee 6.00 15.00
DO David Ortiz 10.00 25.00
IR Ivan Rodriguez 10.00 25.00
JB Jason Bay 6.00 15.00
MT Mark Teixeira 10.00 25.00

2005 Topps Update Hall of Fame Bat Relics

A ODDS 1:6406 H, 1:2012 HTA, 1:6406 R
B ODDS 1:1860 H, 1:548 HTA, 1:1860 R
RS Ryne Sandberg B 8.00 20.00
WB Wade Boggs A 6.00 15.00

2005 Topps Update Hall of Fame Dual Bat Relic

ODDS 1:13,392 H, 1:3815 HTA, 1:13,392 R
STATED PRINT RUN 200 SERIAL #'d CARDS
BS W.Boggs/R.Sandberg 12.50 30.00

2005 Topps Update Legendary Sacks Relics

STATED ODDS 1:965 H, 1:281 HTA, 1:965 R
STATED PRINT RUN 300 SERIAL #'d SETS
CARDS FEATURE CELEBRITY JSY SWATCH
AD Andre Dawson 6.00 15.00
BJ Bo Jackson 10.00 25.00
DW Dave Winfield 6.00 15.00
HR Harold Reynolds 6.00 15.00
JA Jim Abbott 6.00 15.00
LW Lou Whitaker 6.00 15.00
MF Mark Fidrych 10.00 25.00
OS Ozzie Smith 10.00 25.00
RF Rollie Fingers 6.00 15.00

2005 Topps Update Midsummer Covers Ball Relics

STATED ODDS 1:524 H, 1:512 HTA
STATED PRINT RUN 150 SERIAL #'d SETS
AP Albert Pujols 20.00 50.00
AR Alex Rodriguez 12.00 30.00
BR Brian Roberts 10.00 25.00
CB Carlos Beltran 10.00 25.00
DL Derrek Lee 15.00 40.00
DW Dontrelle Willis 10.00 25.00
IS Ichiro Suzuki 12.00 30.00
MT Miguel Tejada 10.00 25.00
RC Roger Clemens 15.00 40.00
VG Vladimir Guerrero 15.00 40.00

2005 Topps Update Signature Moves

A ODDS 1:317,088H,1:103,008HTA,1:40,176R
B ODDS 1:126,836 H,1:51,504 HTA,1:40,176 R
C ODDS 1:1220 H, 1:339 HTA, 1:1220 R
D ODDS 1:1128 H, 1:323 HTA, 1:1128 R
E ODDS 1:916 H, 1:262 HTA, 1:916 R
GROUP A PRINT RUN 15 #'d CARDS
GROUP B PRINT RUN 25 #'d CARDS
GROUP C PRINT RUN 275 #'d SETS
GROUP D PRINT RUN 475 #'d SETS
NO GROUP A-B PRICING DUE TO SCARCITY
RED ODDS 1:6676 H, 1:1908 HTA, 1:6676 R
RED FOIL PRINT RUN 25 SERIAL #'d SETS
NO RED FOIL PRICING DUE TO SCARCITY
BL Bobby Livingston D/475 6.00 15.00
BS Benito Santiago E 12.50 30.00
CJS C.J. Smith D/475 6.00 15.00
GK George Kottaras D/475 8.00 20.00
GP Glen Perkins C/275 8.00 20.00
HS Humberto Sanchez E 10.00 25.00
JP Jake Postlewait C/275 6.00 15.00
JV Justin Verlander C/275 50.00 100.00
KI Kazuhisa Ishii C/275 10.00 25.00
MA Matt Albers D/475 6.00 15.00
MM Mark Mulder C/275 10.00 25.00
RS Richie Sexson C/275 10.00 25.00
TC Travis Chick D/475 6.00 15.00
TG Troy Glaus C/275 10.00 25.00
TH Tim Hudson C/275 10.00 25.00
TW Tony Womack E 6.00 15.00

2005 Topps Update Touch Em All Base Relics

STATED ODDS 1:238 H, 1:77 HTA, 1:238 R
STATED PRINT RUN 1000 SERIAL #'d SETS
AP Albert Pujols 12.50 30.00
AR Alex Rodriguez 8.00 20.00
DL Derrek Lee 6.00 15.00
DO David Ortiz 6.00 15.00
GS Gary Sheffield 4.00 10.00
IR Ivan Rodriguez 6.00 15.00
IS Ichiro Suzuki 10.00 25.00
MR Manny Ramirez 6.00 15.00
MT Miguel Tejada 4.00 10.00
VG Vladimir Guerrero 6.00 15.00

2005 Topps Update Washington Nationals Inaugural Lineup

COMPLETE SET (10) 2.50 6.00
STATED ODDS 1:10 H, 1:4 HTA, 1:10 R
BS Brian Schneider .40 1.00
BW Brad Wilkerson .40 1.00
CG Cristian Guzman .40 1.00
JG Jose Guillen .40 1.00
JV Jose Vidro .40 1.00
LH Livan Hernandez .40 1.00
NJ Nick Johnson .40 1.00
TS Termel Sledge .40 1.00
VC Vinny Castilla .40 1.00
TEAM Team Photo .40 1.00

2005 Topps 1955 National

COMPLETE SET (4) 8.00 20.00
175 Stan Musial 6.00 15.00
186 Whitey Ford 2.50 6.00
203 Bob Feller 2.50 6.00
209 Herb Score 1.50 4.00

2005 Topps XXL Cubs

COMPLETE SET (4) 2.00 5.00
ONE 4-CARD SET PER PACK
1 Derrek Lee .40 1.00
2 Mark Prior .60 1.50
3 Nomar Garciaparra .60 1.50
4 Greg Maddux 1.25 3.00

2005 Topps XXL Red Sox

COMPLETE SET (4) 2.00 5.00
ONE 4-CARD SET PER PACK
1 David Ortiz 1.00 2.50
2 Manny Ramirez 1.00 2.50
3 Johnny Damon .60 1.50
4 Curt Schilling .60 1.50

2005 Topps XXL Yankees

COMPLETE SET (4) 4.00 10.00
ONE 4-CARD SET PER PACK
1 Alex Rodriguez 1.25 3.00
2 Derek Jeter 2.50 6.00
3 Hideki Matsui 1.50 4.00
4 Randy Johnson 1.00 2.50

2006 Topps Pre-Production

COMPLETE SET (3) .75 2.00
3-CARD SETS MAILED TO HOBBY DEALERS
PP1 Ichiro Suzuki .60 1.50
PP2 Alex Rodriguez .60 1.50
PP3 Albert Pujols .60 1.50

2006 Topps

COMP.HOBBY SET (664) 50.00 80.00
COMP.HOLIDAY SET (659) 50.00 80.00
COMP.CARDINALS SET (664) 50.00 80.00
COMP.CUBS SET (664) 50.00 80.00
COMP.PIRATES SET (664) 50.00 80.00
COMP.RED SOX SET (664) 50.00 80.00
COMP.YANKEES SET (664) 50.00 80.00
COMPLETE SET (659) 30.00 80.00
COMPLETE SERIES 1 (329) 15.00 40.00
COMPLETE SERIES 2 (330) 15.00 40.00
COMMON CARD (1-660) .07 .20
COMP.SER.1 SET EXCLUDES CARD 297
CARD 297 NOT INTENDED FOR RELEASE
CARDS 287b AND 312b ISSUED IN FACT.SET
2 TICKETS EXCH.CARD RANDOM IN PACKS
OVERALL PLATE SER.1 ODDS 1:246 HTA
OVERALL PLATE SER.2 ODDS 1:193 HTA
PLATE PRINT RUN 1 SET PER COLOR
BLACK-CYAN-MAGENTA-YELLOW ISSUED
NO PLATE PRICING DUE TO SCARCITY
1 Alex Rodriguez .25 .60
2 Jose Valentin .07 .20
3 Garrett Atkins .07 .20
4 Scott Hatteberg .07 .20
5 Carl Crawford .12 .30
6 Armando Benitez .07 .20
7 Mickey Mantle .60 1.50
8 Mike Morse .07 .20
9 Damian Miller .07 .20
10 Clint Barmes .07 .20
11 Michael Barrett .07 .20
12 Coco Crisp .07 .20
13 Tadahito Iguchi .07 .20
14 Chris Snyder .07 .20
15 Brian Roberts .07 .20
16 David Wright .15 .40
17 Victor Santos .07 .20
18 Trevor Hoffman .12 .30
19 Jeremy Reed .07 .20
20 Bobby Abreu .07 .20
21 Lance Berkman .12 .30
22 Zach Day .07 .20
23 Jonny Gomes .07 .20
24 Jason Marquis .07 .20
25 Chipper Jones .20 .50
26 Scott Hairston .07 .20
27 Ryan Dempster .07 .20
28 Brandon Inge .07 .20
29 Aaron Harang .07 .20
30 Jon Garland .07 .20
31 Pokey Reese .07 .20
32 Mike MacDougal .07 .20
33 Mike Lieberthal .07 .20
34 Cesar Izturis .07 .20
35 Brad Wilkerson .07 .20
36 Jeff Suppan .07 .20
37 Adam Everett .07 .20
38 Bengie Molina .07 .20
39 Rickie Weeks .07 .20
40 Jorge Posada .12 .30
41 Rheal Cormier .07 .20
42 Reed Johnson .07 .20
43 Laynce Nix .07 .20
44 Carl Everett .07 .20
45 Greg Maddux .25 .60
46 Jeff Francis .07 .20
47 Felipe Lopez .07 .20
48 Dan Johnson .07 .20
49 Humberto Cota .07 .20
50 Manny Ramirez .20 .50
51 Juan Uribe .07 .20
52 Jaret Wright .07 .20
53 Tomo Ohka .07 .20
54 Mike Matheny .07 .20
55 Joe Mauer .12 .30
56 Jarrod Washburn .07 .20
57 Randy Winn .07 .20
58 Pedro Feliz .07 .20
59 Kenny Rogers .07 .20
60 Rocco Baldelli .07 .20
61 Eric Hinske .07 .20
62 Damaso Marte .07 .20
63 Desi Relaford .07 .20
64 Juan Encarnacion .07 .20
65 Nomar Garciaparra .12 .30
66 Shawn Estes .07 .20
67 Brian Jordan .07 .20
68 Steve Kline .07 .20
69 Braden Looper .07 .20
70 Carlos Lee .07 .20
71 Tom Glavine .12 .30
72 Craig Biggio .12 .30
73 Steve Finley .07 .20

74 David Newhan .07 .20
75 Eric Gagne .07 .20
76 Tony Graffanino .07 .20
77 Dallas McPherson .07 .20
78 Nick Punto .07 .20
79 Mark Kotsay .07 .20
80 Kerry Wood .07 .20
81 Kyle Farnsworth .07 .20
82 Huston Street .07 .20
83 Endy Chavez .07 .20
84 So Taguchi .07 .20
85 Hank Blalock .07 .20
86 Brad Radke .07 .20
87 Chien-Ming Wang .12 .30
88 B.J. Surhoff .07 .20
89 Glendon Rusch .07 .20
90 Mark Buehrle .12 .30
91 Rafael Betancourt .07 .20
92 Lance Cormier .07 .20
93 Alex Gonzalez .07 .20
94 Matt Stairs .07 .20
95 Andy Pettitte .12 .30
96 Jesse Crain .07 .20
97 Kenny Lofton .07 .20
98 Geoff Blum .07 .20
99 Mark Redman .07 .20
100 Barry Bonds .30 .75
101 Chad Orvella .07 .20
102 Xavier Nady .07 .20
103 Junior Spivey .07 .20
104 Bernie Williams .12 .30
105 Victor Martinez .12 .30
106 Nook Logan .07 .20
107 Mark Teahen .07 .20
108 Mike Lamb .07 .20
109 Jayson Werth .12 .30
110 Mariano Rivera .25 .60
111 Erubiel Durazo .07 .20
112 Ryan Vogelsong .07 .20
113 Bobby Madritsch .07 .20
114 Travis Lee .07 .20
115 Adam Dunn .12 .30
116 David Riske .07 .20
117 Troy Percival .07 .20
118 Chad Tracy .07 .20
119 Andy Marte .07 .20
120 Edgar Renteria .07 .20
121 Jason Giambi .07 .20
122 Justin Morneau .12 .30
123 J.T. Snow .07 .20
124 Danys Baez .07 .20
125 Carlos Delgado .07 .20
126 John Buck .07 .20
127 Shannon Stewart .07 .20
128 Mike Cameron .07 .20
129 Joe McEwing .07 .20
130 Richie Sexson .07 .20
131 Rod Barajas .07 .20
132 Russ Adams .07 .20
133 J.D. Closser .07 .20
134 Ramon Ortiz .07 .20
135 Josh Beckett .07 .20
136 Ryan Freel .07 .20
137 Victor Zambrano .07 .20
138 Ronnie Belliard .07 .20
139 Jason Michaels .07 .20
140 Brian Giles .07 .20
141 Randy Wolf .07 .20
142 Robinson Cano .12 .30
143 Joe Blanton .07 .20
144 Esteban Loaiza .07 .20
145 Troy Glaus .07 .20
146 Matt Clement .07 .20
147 Geoff Jenkins .07 .20
148 John Thomson .07 .20
149 A.J. Pierzynski .07 .20
150 Pedro Martinez .12 .30
151 Roger Clemens .25 .60
152 Jack Wilson .07 .20
153 Ray King .07 .20
154 Ryan Church .07 .20
155 Paul Lo Duca .07 .20
156 Dan Wheeler .07 .20
157 Carlos Zambrano .12 .30
158 Mike Timlin .07 .20
159 Brandon Claussen .07 .20
160 Travis Hafner .07 .20
161 Chris Shelton .07 .20
162 Rafael Furcal .07 .20
163 Tom Gordon .07 .20
164 Noah Lowry .07 .20
165 Larry Walker .12 .30
166 Dave Roberts .12 .30
167 Scott Schoeneweis .07 .20
168 Julian Tavarez .07 .20
169 Jhonny Peralta .07 .20
170 Vernon Wells .07 .20
171 Jorge Cantu .07 .20
172 Todd Greene .07 .20
173 Willy Taveras .07 .20
174 Corey Patterson .07 .20
175 Ivan Rodriguez .12 .30
176 Bobby Kielty .07 .20
177 Jose Reyes .12 .30
178 Barry Zito .12 .30
179 Deivi Cruz .07 .20
180 Mark Teixeira .12 .30
181 Chone Figgins .07 .20
182 Aaron Rowand .07 .20
183 Tim Wakefield .12 .30
184 Mike Maroth .07 .20
185 Johnny Damon .12 .30
186 Vicente Padilla .07 .20
187 Ryan Klesko .07 .20
188 Gary Matthews .07 .20
189 Jose Mesa .07 .20
190 Nick Johnson .07 .20
191 Freddy Garcia .07 .20
192 Larry Bigbie .07 .20
193 Chris Ray .07 .20
194 Torii Hunter .07 .20
195 Mike Sweeney .07 .20
196 Brad Penny .07 .20
197 Jason Frasor .07 .20
198 Kevin Mench .07 .20
199 Adam Kennedy .07 .20
200 Albert Pujols .25 .60
201 Jody Gerut .07 .20
202 Luis Gonzalez .07 .20
203 Zack Greinke .20 .50
204 Miguel Cairo .07 .20
205 Jimmy Rollins .12 .30
206 Edgardo Alfonzo .07 .20
207 Billy Wagner .07 .20
208 B.J. Ryan .07 .20
209 Orlando Hudson .07 .20
210 Preston Wilson .07 .20
211 Melvin Mora .07 .20
212 Bill Mueller .07 .20
213 Javy Lopez .07 .20
214 Wilson Betemit .07 .20
215 Garret Anderson .07 .20
216 Russell Branyan .07 .20
217 Jeff Weaver .07 .20
218 Doug Mientkiewicz .07 .20
219 Mark Ellis .07 .20
220 Jason Bay .07 .20
221 Adam LaRoche .07 .20
222 C.C. Sabathia .12 .30
223 Humberto Quintero .07 .20
224 Bartolo Colon .07 .20
225 Ichiro Suzuki .25 .60
226 Brett Tomko .07 .20
227 Corey Koskie .07 .20
228 David Eckstein .07 .20
229 Cristian Guzman .07 .20
230 Jeff Kent .07 .20
231 Chris Capuano .07 .20
232 Rodrigo Lopez .07 .20
233 Jason Phillips .07 .20
234 Luis Rivas .07 .20
235 Cliff Floyd .07 .20
236 Gil Meche .07 .20
237 Adam Eaton .07 .20
238 Matt Morris .07 .20
239 Kyle Davies .07 .20
240 David Wells .07 .20
241 John Smoltz .20 .50
242 Felix Hernandez .12 .30
243 Kenny Rogers GG .07 .20
244 Mark Teixeira GG .12 .30
245 Orlando Hudson GG .07 .20
246 Derek Jeter GG .50 1.25
247 Eric Chavez GG .07 .20
248 Torii Hunter GG .07 .20
249 Vernon Wells GG .07 .20
250 Ichiro Suzuki GG .25 .60
251 Greg Maddux GG .25 .60
252 Mike Matheny GG .07 .20
253 Derrek Lee GG .07 .20
254 Luis Castillo GG .07 .20
255 Omar Vizquel GG .12 .30
256 Mike Lowell GG .07 .20
257 Andruw Jones GG .07 .20
258 Jim Edmonds GG .12 .30
259 Bobby Abreu GG .07 .20
260 Bartolo Colon CY .07 .20
261 Chris Carpenter CY .12 .30
262 Alex Rodriguez MVP .25 .60
263 Albert Pujols MVP .25 .60
264 Huston Street ROY .07 .20
265 Ryan Howard ROY .15 .40
266 Bob Melvin MG .07 .20
267 Bobby Cox MG .07 .20
268 Baltimore Orioles TC .07 .20
269 Boston Red Sox TC .12 .30
270 Chicago White Sox TC .07 .20
271 Dusty Baker MG .07 .20
272 Jerry Narron MG .07 .20
273 Cleveland Indians TC .07 .20
274 Clint Hurdle MG .07 .20
275 Detroit Tigers TC .07 .20
276 Jack McKeon MG .07 .20
277 Phil Garner MG .07 .20
278 Kansas City Royals TC .07 .20
279 Jim Tracy MG .07 .20
280 Los Angeles Angels TC .07 .20
281 Milwaukee Brewers TC .07 .20
282 Minnesota Twins TC .07 .20
283 Willie Randolph MG .07 .20
284 New York Yankees TC .12 .30
285 Oakland Athletics TC .07 .20
286 Charlie Manuel MG .07 .20
287a Pete Mackanin MG ERR .07 .20
287b Pete Mackanin MG COR .07 .20
288 Bruce Bochy MG .12 .30
289 Felipe Alou MG .07 .20
290 Seattle Mariners TC .07 .20
291 Tony LaRussa MG .12 .30
292 Tampa Bay Devil Rays TC .07 .20
293 Texas Rangers TC .07 .20
294 Toronto Blue Jays TC .07 .20
295 Frank Robinson MG .12 .30
296 Anderson Hernandez (RC) .20 .50
297A Alex Gordon (RC) Full 150.00 250.00
297B Alex Gordon Cut Out 30.00 60.00
297C Alex Gordon Blank Gold 20.00 50.00
297D Alex Gordon Blank Silver
298 Jason Botts (RC) .20 .50
299 Jeff Mathis (RC) .20 .50
300 Ryan Garko (RC) .20 .50
301 Charlton Jimerson (RC) .20 .50
302 Chris Denorfia (RC) .20 .50
303 Anthony Reyes (RC) .20 .50
304 Bryan Bullington (RC) .20 .50
305 Chuck James (RC) .20 .50
306 Danny Sandoval RC .20 .50
307 Walter Young (RC) .20 .50
308 Fausto Carmona (RC) .20 .50
309 Francisco Liriano (RC) .50 1.25
310 Hong-Chih Kuo (RC) .50 1.25
311 Joe Saunders (RC) .20 .50
312a John Koronka Cubs (RC) .20 .50
312b John Koronka Rangers (RC) .20 .50
313 Robert Andino RC .20 .50
314 Shaun Marcum (RC) .20 .50
315 Tom Gorzelanny (RC) .20 .50
316 Craig Breslow RC .20 .50
317 Chris DeMaria RC .20 .50
318 Brayan Pena (RC) .20 .50
319 Rich Hill (RC) .50 1.25
320 Rick Short (RC) .20 .50
321 C.J. Wilson (RC) .30 .75
322 Marshall McDougall (RC) .20 .50
323 Darrell Rasner (RC) .20 .50
324 Brandon Watson (RC) .20 .50
325 Paul McAnulty (RC) .20 .50
326 D.Jeter .50 1.25
A.Rodriguez TS
327 M.Tejada .12 .30
M.Mora TS
328 M.Giles .20 .50
C.Jones TS
329 M.Ramirez .20 .50
D.Ortiz TS
330 M.Barrett .25 .60
G.Maddux TS
331 Matt Holliday .20 .50
332 Orlando Cabrera .07 .20
333 Ryan Langerhans .07 .20
334 Lew Ford .07 .20
335 Mark Prior .12 .30
336 Ted Lilly .07 .20
337 Michael Young .07 .20
338 Livan Hernandez .07 .20
339 Yadier Molina .25 .60
340 Eric Chavez .07 .20
341 Miguel Batista .07 .20
342 Bruce Chen .07 .20
343 Sean Casey .07 .20
344 Doug Davis .07 .20
345 Andruw Jones .07 .20
346 Hideki Matsui .20 .50
347 Joe Randa .07 .20
348 Reggie Sanders .07 .20
349 Jason Jennings .07 .20
350 Joe Nathan .07 .20
351 Jose Lopez .07 .20
352 John Lackey .12 .30
353 Claudio Vargas .07 .20
354 Grady Sizemore .12 .30
355 Jon Papelbon (RC) 1.00 2.50
356 Luis Matos .07 .20
357 Orlando Hernandez .07 .20
358 Jamie Moyer .07 .20
359 Chase Utley .12 .30
360 Moises Alou .07 .20
361 Chad Cordero .07 .20
362 Brian McCann .07 .20
363 Jermaine Dye .07 .20
364 Ryan Madson .07 .20
365 Aramis Ramirez .07 .20
366 Matt Treanor .07 .20
367 Ray Durham .07 .20
368 Khalil Greene .07 .20
369 Mike Hampton .07 .20
370 Mike Mussina .12 .30
371 Brad Hawpe .07 .20
372 Marlon Byrd .07 .20
373 Woody Williams .07 .20
374 Victor Diaz .07 .20
375 Brady Clark .07 .20
376 Luis Gonzalez .07 .20
377 Raul Ibanez .12 .30
378 Tony Clark .07 .20
379 Shawn Chacon .07 .20
380 Marcus Giles .07 .20
381 Odalis Perez .07 .20
382 Steve Trachsel .07 .20
383 Russ Ortiz .07 .20
384 Toby Hall .07 .20
385 Bill Hall .07 .20
386 Luke Hudson .07 .20
387 Ken Griffey Jr. .40 1.00
388 Tim Hudson .12 .30
389 Brian Moehler .07 .20
390 Jake Peavy .07 .20
391 Casey Blake .07 .20
392 Sidney Ponson .07 .20
393 Brian Schneider .07 .20
394 J.J. Hardy .07 .20
395 Austin Kearns .07 .20
396 Pat Burrell .07 .20
397 Jason Vargas .07 .20
398 Ryan Howard .15 .40
399 Joe Crede .07 .20
400 Vladimir Guerrero .12 .30
401 Roy Halladay .12 .30
402 David Dellucci .07 .20
403 Brandon Webb .12 .30
404 Marlon Anderson .07 .20
405 Miguel Tejada .12 .30
406 Ryan Doumit .07 .20
407 Kevin Youkilis .07 .20
408 Jon Lieber .07 .20
409 Edwin Encarnacion .20 .50
410 Miguel Cabrera .20 .50
411 A.J. Burnett .07 .20
412 David Bell .07 .20
413 Gregg Zaun .07 .20
414 Lance Niekro .07 .20
415 Shawn Green .07 .20
416 Roberto Hernandez .07 .20
417 Jay Gibbons .07 .20
418 Johnny Estrada .07 .20
419 Omar Vizquel .12 .30
420 Gary Sheffield .07 .20
421 Brad Halsey .07 .20
422 Aaron Cook .07 .20
423 David Ortiz .20 .50
424 Tony Womack .07 .20
425 Joe Kennedy .07 .20
426 Dustin McGowan .07 .20
427 Carl Pavano .07 .20
428 Nick Green .07 .20
429 Francisco Cordero .07 .20
430 Octavio Dotel .07 .20
431 Julio Franco .07 .20
432 Brett Myers .07 .20
433 Casey Kotchman .07 .20
434 Frank Catalanotto .07 .20
435 Paul Konerko .12 .30
436 Keith Foulke .07 .20
437 Juan Rivera .07 .20
438 Todd Pratt .07 .20
439 Ben Broussard .07 .20
440 Scott Kazmir .12 .30
441 Rich Aurilia .07 .20
442 Craig Monroe .07 .20
443 Danny Kolb .07 .20
444 Curtis Granderson .15 .40
445 Jeff Francoeur .20 .50
446 Dustin Hermanson .07 .20
447 Jacque Jones .07 .20
448 Bobby Crosby .07 .20
449 Jason LaRue .07 .20
450 Derrek Lee .07 .20
451 Curt Schilling .12 .30
452 Jake Westbrook .07 .20
453 Daniel Cabrera .07 .20
454 Bobby Jenks .07 .20
455 Dontrelle Willis .07 .20
456 Brad Lidge .07 .20
457 Shea Hillenbrand .07 .20
458 Luis Castillo .07 .20
459 Mark Hendrickson .07 .20
460 Randy Johnson .20 .50
461 Placido Polanco .07 .20
462 Aaron Boone .07 .20
463 Todd Walker .07 .20
464 Nick Swisher .12 .30
465 Joel Pineiro .07 .20
466 Jay Payton .07 .20
467 Cliff Lee .12 .30
468 Johan Santana .12 .30
469 Josh Willingham .12 .30
470 Jeremy Bonderman .07 .20
471 Runelvys Hernandez .07 .20
472 Duaner Sanchez .07 .20
473 Jason Lane .07 .20
474 Trot Nixon .07 .20
475 Ramon Hernandez .07 .20
476 Mike Lowell .07 .20
477 Chan Ho Park .12 .30
478 Doug Waechter .07 .20
479 Carlos Silva .07 .20
480 Jose Contreras .07 .20
481 Vinny Castilla .07 .20
482 Chris Reitsma .07 .20
483 Jose Guillen .07 .20
484 Aaron Hill .07 .20
485 Kevin Millwood .07 .20
486 Wily Mo Pena .07 .20
487 Rich Harden .07 .20
488 Chris Carpenter .12 .30
489 Jason Bartlett .07 .20
490 Magglio Ordonez .12 .30
491 John Rodriguez .07 .20
492 Bob Wickman .07 .20
493 Eddie Guardado .07 .20
494 Kip Wells .07 .20
495 Adrian Beltre .20 .50
496 Jose Capellan (RC) .20 .50
497 Scott Podsednik .07 .20
498 Brad Thompson .07 .20
499 Aaron Heilman .07 .20
500 Derek Jeter .50 1.25
501 Emil Brown .07 .20
502 Morgan Ensberg .07 .20
503 Nate Bump .07 .20
504 Phil Nevin .07 .20
505 Jason Schmidt .07 .20
506 Michael Cuddyer .07 .20
507 John Patterson .07 .20
508 Danny Haren .07 .20
509 Freddy Sanchez .07 .20
510 J.D. Drew .07 .20
511 Dmitri Young .07 .20
512 Eric Milton .07 .20
513 Ervin Santana .07 .20
514 Mark Loretta .07 .20
515 Mark Grudzielanek .07 .20
516 Derrick Turnbow .07 .20
517 Denny Bautista .07 .20
518 Lyle Overbay .07 .20
519 Julio Lugo .07 .20
520 Carlos Beltran .12 .30
521 Jose Cruz Jr. .07 .20
522 Jason Isringhausen .07 .20
523 Bronson Arroyo .07 .20
524 Ben Sheets .07 .20
525 Zach Duke .07 .20
526 Ryan Wagner .07 .20
527 Jose Vidro .07 .20
528 Doug Mirabelli .07 .20
529 Kris Benson .07 .20
530 Carlos Guillen .07 .20
531 Juan Pierre .07 .20
532 Scot Shields .07 .20
533 Scott Hatteberg .07 .20
534 Tim Stauffer .07 .20
535 Jim Edmonds .12 .30
536 Scot Eyre .07 .20
537 Ben Johnson .07 .20
538 Mark Mulder .07 .20
539 Juan Rincon .07 .20
540 Gustavo Chacin .07 .20
541 Oliver Perez .07 .20
542 Chris Young .07 .20
543 Edinson Volquez .07 .20
544 Mark Bellhorn .07 .20
545 Kelvim Escobar .07 .20
546 Andy Sisco .07 .20
547 Derek Lowe .07 .20
548 Sean Burroughs .07 .20
549 Erik Bedard .07 .20
550 Alfonso Soriano .12 .30
551 Matt Murton .07 .20
552 Eric Byrnes .07 .20
553 Chris Duffy .07 .20
554 Kazuo Matsui .07 .20
555 Scott Rolen .12 .30
556 Rob Mackowiak .07 .20
557 Chris Burke .07 .20
558 Jeromy Burnitz .07 .20
559 Jerry Hairston Jr. .07 .20
560 Jim Thome .12 .30
561 Miguel Olivo .07 .20
562 Jose Castillo .07 .20
563 Brad Ausmus .07 .20
564 Yorvit Torrealba .07 .20
565 David DeJesus .07 .20
566 Paul Byrd .07 .20
567 Brandon Backe .07 .20
568 Aubrey Huff .07 .20
569 Mike Jacobs .07 .20
570 Todd Helton .12 .30
571 Angel Berroa .07 .20
572 Todd Jones .07 .20
573 Jeff Bagwell .12 .30
574 Darin Erstad .07 .20
575 Roy Oswalt .12 .30
576 Rondell White .07 .20
577 Alex Rios .07 .20
578 Wes Helms .07 .20
579 Javier Vazquez .07 .20
580 Frank Thomas .20 .50
581 Brian Fuentes .07 .20
582 Francisco Rodriguez .12 .30
583 Craig Counsell .07 .20
584 Jorge Sosa .07 .20
585 Mike Piazza .20 .50
586 Mike Scioscia MG .07 .20
587 Joe Torre MG .12 .30
588 Ken Macha MG .07 .20
589 John Gibbons MG .07 .20
590 Joe Maddon MG .07 .20
591 Eric Wedge MG .07 .20
592 Mike Hargrove MG .07 .20
593 Sam Perlozzo MG .07 .20
594 Buck Showalter MG .07 .20
595 Terry Francona MG .07 .20
596 Buddy Bell MG .07 .20
597 Jim Leyland MG .07 .20
598 Ron Gardenhire MG .07 .20
599 Ozzie Guillen MG .07 .20
600 Ned Yost MG .07 .20
601 Atlanta Braves TC .07 .20
602 Philadelphia Phillies TC .07 .20
603 New York Mets TC .12 .30
604 Washington Nationals TC .07 .20
605 Florida Marlins TC .07 .20
606 Houston Astros TC .07 .20
607 Chicago Cubs TC .07 .20
608 St. Louis Cardinals TC .12 .30
609 Pittsburgh Pirates TC .07 .20
610 Cincinnati Reds TC .07 .20
611 Colorado Rockies TC .07 .20
612 Los Angeles Dodgers TC .12 .30
613 San Francisco Giants TC .07 .20
614 San Diego Padres TC .07 .20
615 Arizona Diamondbacks TC .07 .20
616 Kenji Johjima RC .50 1.25
617 Ryan Zimmerman (RC) .60 1.50
618 Craig Hansen RC .50 1.25
619 Joey Devine RC .20 .50
620 Hanley Ramirez (RC) .30 .75
621 Scott Olsen (RC) .20 .50
622 Jason Bergmann RC .20 .50
623 Geovany Soto (RC) .50 1.25
624 J.J. Furmaniak (RC) .20 .50
625 Jeremy Accardo RC .20 .50
626 Mark Woodyard (RC) .20 .50
627 Matt Capps (RC) .20 .50
628 Tim Corcoran RC .20 .50
629 Ryan Jorgensen RC .20 .50
630 Ronny Paulino (RC) .20 .50
631 Dan Uggla (RC) .30 .75
632 Ian Kinsler (RC) .60 1.50
633 Josh Barfield (RC) .20 .50
634 Reggie Abercrombie (RC) .20 .50
635 Joel Zumaya (RC) .50 1.25
636 Matt Cain (RC) 1.25 3.00
637 Conor Jackson (RC) .30 .75
638 Brian Anderson (RC) .20 .50
639 Prince Fielder (RC) 1.00 2.50
640 Jeremy Hermida (RC) .20 .50
641 Justin Verlander (RC) 5.00 12.00
642 Brian Bannister (RC) .20 .50
643 Willie Eyre (RC) .20 .50
644 Ricky Nolasco (RC) .20 .50
645 Paul Maholm (RC) .20 .50
646 J.Damon .12 .30
J.Giambi
647 R.White .07 .20
L.Ford
648 O.Hernandez .07 .20
O.Hudson
649 A.Dunn .40 1.00
K.Griffey Jr.
650 P.Burrell .07 .20
M.Lieberthal
651 J.Reyes .12 .30
K.Matsui
652 H.Blalock .07 .20
M.Young
653 P.Fielder .40 1.00
R.Weeks
654 T.Lee .07 .20
R.Baldelli
655 D.Lee .07 .20
A.Ramirez
656 G.Sizemore .12 .30
A.Boone
657 Gonzalez .07 .20
Green/Hill
658 I.Rodriguez .12 .30
C.Guillen
659 A.Rodriguez .25 .60
G.Sheffield
660 E.Santana .12 .30
F.Rodriguez
RC1 Alay Soler 15.00 40.00

2006 Topps Black

COMMON CARD (1-660) 6.00 15.00
SEMISTARS 10.00 25.00
UNLISTED STARS 50.00 40.00
SERIES 1 ODDS 1:18 HTA
SERIES 2 ODDS 1:14 HTA
STATED PRINT RUN 55 SERIAL #'d SETS
CARD 297 DOES NOT EXIST

2006 Topps Box Bottoms

A.Rod/Wright/Abreu/Lee 1.50 4.00
Young/Tejada/Johan/Fielder 1.50 4.00
ONE 4-CARD SHEET PER HTA BOX
1 Alex Rodriguez .60 1.50
16 David Wright .40 1.00
20 Bobby Abreu .20 .50
25 Chipper Jones .50 1.25
50 Manny Ramirez .50 1.25
70 Carlos Lee .20 .50
90 Mark Buehrle .30 .75
100 Barry Bonds .75 2.00
115 Adam Dunn .30 .75
125 Carlos Delgado .20 .50
150 Pedro Martinez .30 .75
151 Roger Clemens .60 1.50
180 Mark Teixeira .30 .75
194 Torii Hunter .20 .50
200 Albert Pujols .60 1.50
225 Ichiro Suzuki .60 1.50
337 Michael Young .20 .50
345 Andruw Jones .20 .50
357 Orlando Hernandez .20 .50
390 Jake Peavy .20 .50
405 Miguel Tejada .30 .75
423 David Ortiz .50 1.25
450 Derrek Lee .20 .50
468 Johan Santana .30 .75
550 Alfonso Soriano .30 .75
560 Jim Thome .30 .75
570 Todd Helton .30 .75
599 Ozzie Guillen MG .20 .50
616 Kenji Johjima .50 1.25
637 Conor Jackson .30 .75
639 Prince Fielder 1.00 2.50
659 A.Rodriguez/G.Sheffield .60 1.50

2006 Topps Gold

*GOLD 1-295/326-615/646-660: 6X TO 15X
*GOLD 296-325/616-645: 2.5X TO 6X
SER.1 ODDS 1:15 HOB, 1:4 HTA, 1:26 MINI
SER.1 ODDS 1:8 RACK, 1:14 RET
SER.2 ODDS 1:11 HOB, 1:4 HTA, 1:21 MINI
SER.2 ODDS 1:6 RACK, 1:11 RET
STATED PRINT RUN 2006 SERIAL #'d SETS
CARD 297 DOES NOT EXIST

2006 Topps 2K All-Stars

SER.1 ODDS 1:18 H, 1:18 HTA, 1:18 MINI
SER.1 ODDS 1:6 RACK, 1:18 RETAIL
1-6 ISSUED IN 2K ALL-STAR GAMES
7-11 ISSUED IN SER.1 TOPPS PACKS
1 Derek Jeter 4.00 10.00
2 Andruw Jones .60 1.50
3 Miguel Cabrera 1.50 4.00
4 Derrek Lee .60 1.50
5 Mariano Rivera 2.00 5.00
6 Ivan Rodriguez 1.00 2.50
7 Vladimir Guerrero 1.00 2.50
8 Albert Pujols 2.00 5.00
9 Alex Rodriguez 2.00 5.00
10 Alfonso Soriano 1.00 2.50
11 Dontrelle Willis .60 1.50

2006 Topps Autographs

SER.1 A 1:681,120 HOBBY, 1:152,750 HTA
SER.1 A 1:220,032 RACK
SER.1 B 1:14500 H,1:2932 HTA,1:26,900 MINI
SER.1 B 1:7124 RACK, 1:11,500 RETAIL
SER.1 C 1:17400 H,1:4966 HTA, 1:28,622 MINI
SER.1 C 1:8400 RACK, 1:14,000 RET
SER.1 D 1:42,570 H, 1:11,841 HTA
SER.1 D 1:70,000 MINI, 1:20,000 RACK
SER.1 D 1:33,000 RETAIL
SER.1 E 1:3451 H, 1:980 HTA, 1:5800 MINI
SER.1 E 1:1650 RACK, 1:2900 RET
SER.1 F 1:2090 H, 1:560 HTA, 1:3480 MINI
SER.1 F 1:995 RACK, 1:1750 RETAIL
SER.1 G 1:3481 H, 1:944 HTA, 1:5800 MINI
SER.1 G 1:1660 RACK, 1:2900 RETAIL
SER.1 H 1:430 H, 1:121 HTA, 1:725 MINI
SER.1 H 1:207 RACK, 1:363 RETAIL
OVERALL SER.1 AU-GU ODDS 1:137 H/R
OVERALL SER.1 AU-GU ODDS 1:47 HTA
GROUP A PRINT RUN 10 #'d CARDS
GROUP B PRINT RUN 100 #'d SETS
GROUP C PRINT RUN 200 #'d SETS
GROUP D PRINT RUN 250 #'d CARDS
NO GROUP A PRICING DUE TO SCARCITY
B.LIVINGSTON ISSUED IN SER.2 PACKS
EXCHANGE DEADLINE 02/28/08
AG Alex Gordon H 5.00 12.00
AL Anthony Lerew H 4.00 10.00
AR Alex Rodriguez B/100 75.00 200.00
ARE Anthony Reyes H 10.00 25.00
BC Brian Cashman B/100 50.00 120.00
BL Bobby Livingston F2 4.00 10.00
BW Brad Wilkerson E 6.00 15.00
CB Craig Breslow H 4.00 10.00
CG Carlos Guillen E 12.00 30.00
CJ Chuck James G 15.00 40.00
DD Doug DeVore H 4.00 10.00
DO David Ortiz B/100 40.00 100.00
DP Dustin Pedrioa 10.00 25.00
DR Darrell Rasner H 4.00 10.00
DW Dave Winfield B/100 60.00 150.00
EC Eric Chavez C/200 10.00 25.00
FC Fausto Carmona H 4.00 10.00
FL Francisco Liriano H 4.00 10.00
GN Graig Nettles E 6.00 15.00
GS Gary Sheffield C/200 20.00 50.00
HR Horacio Ramirez F 4.00 10.00
JB Jason Botts H 4.00 10.00
JJ Josh Johnson H 6.00 15.00
JM Jeff Mathis F 4.00 10.00
LC Lance Cormier E 6.00 15.00
LH Livan Hernandez F 6.00 15.00
MB Milton Bradley C/200 15.00 40.00
MY Michael Young E 10.00 25.00
NC Nelson Cruz G 6.00 15.00
RG Ryan Garko F 6.00 15.00
RH Rich Hill H 3.00 8.00
RO Roy Oswalt F 6.00 15.00
RS Ryne Sandberg B/100 50.00 120.00
SO Scott Olsen H 4.00 10.00
TS Terrmel Sledge E 6.00 15.00
WB Wade Boggs D/250 15.00 40.00

2006 Topps Autographs Green

SER.2 A 1:160,000 HOBBY, 1:48,000 HTA
SER.2 A 1:350,000 MINI, 1:90,000 RACK
SER.2 A 1:150,000 RETAIL
SER.2 B 1:70,000 HOBBY, 1:12,000 HTA
SER.2 B 1:125,000 MINI, 1:33,000 RACK
SER.2 B 1:80,000 RETAIL
SER.2 C 1:4060 H, 1:1150 HTA, 1:6800 MINI
SER.2 C 1:1400 R, 1:1940 RACK
SER.2 D 1:4750 H, 1:1000 HTA, 1:6500 MINI
SER.2 D 1:4750 R, 1:2000 RACK
SER.2 E 1:2030 H, 1:575 HTA, 1:3390 MINI
SER.2 E 1:2025 R, 1:966 RACK
SER.2 F 1:510 H, 1:190 HTA, 1:1125 MINI
SER.2 F 1:506 R, 1:325 RACK
GROUP A PRINT RUN 50 CARDS
GROUP B PRINT RUN 120 CARDS
GROUP C PRINT RUN 250 SETS
A-C ARE NOT SERIAL-NUMBERED
A-C PRINT RUNS PROVIDED BY TOPPS
NO GROUP A PRICING DUE TO SCARCITY
EXCHANGE DEADLINE 06/30/08
AJ Andruw Jones C/250 * 20.00 50.00
BB Barry Bonds B/120 * 100.00 250.00
BC Brandon Claussen F 4.00 10.00
BM Brandon McCarthy E 6.00 15.00
BR Brian Roberts C/250 * 10.00 25.00
CB Clint Barmes E 6.00 15.00
CO Chad Orvella F 4.00 10.00
CV Claudio Vargas F 4.00 10.00
DD Doug Drabek C/250 * 6.00 15.00
DJ Dan Johnson D 6.00 15.00
DS Darryl Strawberry C/250 * 25.00 60.00
DSN Duke Snider C/250 * 15.00 40.00
GA Garrett Atkins D 6.00 15.00
GC Gary Carter C/250 * 6.00 15.00
JB Jose Bautista F 6.00 15.00
JF Jeff Francis D 6.00 15.00
JP Jonathan Papelbon F 6.00 15.00
RC Robinson Cano E 10.00 25.00
RZ Ryan Zimmerman E 8.00 20.00
SK Scott Kazmir D 4.00 10.00
WP Wily Mo Pena C/250 * 15.00 40.00

2006 Topps Barry Bonds Chase to 715

COMMON CARD 20.00 50.00
SER.1 ODDS 1:4800 HOBBY, 1:5400 HTA
SER.1 ODDS 1:10,900 MINI, 1:3076 RACK
SER.1 ODDS 1:5,300 RETAIL
STATED PRINT RUN 1 SERIAL #'d SET

2006 Topps United States Constitution

COMPLETE SET (42) 30.00 60.00
SER.2 ODDS 1:8 HOBBY, 1:2 HTA, 1:16 MINI
SER.2 ODDS 1:8 RETAIL, 1:4 RACK
AB Abraham Baldwin .75 2.00
AH Alexander Hamilton .75 2.00
BF Benjamin Franklin 1.25 3.00
CP Charles Pinckney .75 2.00
DB David Brearly .75 2.00
DC Daniel Carroll .75 2.00
DJ Daniel of St. Thomas Jenifer .75 2.00
GB Gunning Bedford Jr. .75 2.00
GC George Clymer .75 2.00
GM Gouverneur Morris .75 2.00
GR George Read .75 2.00
GW George Washington 1.25 3.00
HW Hugh Williamson .75 2.00
JB John Blair .75 2.00
JD Jonathan Dayton .75 2.00
JI Jared Ingersoll .75 2.00
JL John Langdon .75 2.00
JM James Madison .75 2.00
JR John Rutledge .75 2.00
JW James Wilson .75 2.00
NG Nicholas Gilman .75 2.00
PB Pierce Butler .75 2.00
RB Richard Bassett .75 2.00
RK Rufus King .75 2.00
RM Robert Morris .75 2.00
RS Roger Sherman .75 2.00
TF Thomas Fitzsimons .75 2.00
TM Thomas Mifflin .75 2.00
WB William Blount .75 2.00
WF William Few .75 2.00
WJ William Samuel Johnson .75 2.00
WL William Livingston .75 2.00
WP William Paterson .75 2.00
CCP Charles Cotesworth Pinckney .75 2.00
JBR Jacob Broom .75 2.00
JDI John Dickinson .75 2.00
JMC James McHenry .75 2.00
NGO Nathaniel Gorham .75 2.00
RDS Richard Dobbs Spaight .75 2.00
HDR1 Header Card 1 .75 2.00
HDR2 Header Card 2 .75 2.00
HDR3 Header Card 3 .75 2.00

2006 Topps Declaration of Independence

COMPLETE SET (56) 70.00 120.00
SER.1 ODDS 1:8 HOBBY, 1:4 HTA, 1:12 MINI
SER.1 ODDS 1:4 RACK, 1:6 RETAIL
AC Abraham Clark 1.25 3.00
AM Arthur Middleton 1.25 3.00
BF Benjamin Franklin 2.00 5.00
BG Button Gwinnett 1.25 3.00
BH Benjamin Harrison 1.25 3.00
BR Benjamin Rush 1.25 3.00
CB Carter Braxton 1.25 3.00
CC Charles Carroll 1.25 3.00
CR Caesar Rodney 1.25 3.00
EG Elbridge Gerry 1.25 3.00
ER Edward Rutledge 1.25 3.00
FH Francis Hopkinson 1.25 3.00
FL Francis Lewis 1.25 3.00
FLL Francis Lightfoot Lee 1.25 3.00
GC George Clymer 1.25 3.00
GR George Ross 1.25 3.00
GRE George Read 1.25 3.00
GT Georgе Taylor 1.25 3.00
GW George Walton 1.25 3.00
GWY George Wythe 1.25 3.00
JA John Adams 1.25 3.00
JB Josiah Bartlett 1.25 3.00
JH John Hancock 2.00 5.00
JHA John Hart 1.25 3.00
JHE Joseph Hewes 1.25 3.00
JM John Morton 1.25 3.00
JP John Penn 1.25 3.00
JS James Smith 1.25 3.00
JW James Wilson 1.25 3.00
JWI John Witherspoon 1.25 3.00
LH Lyman Hall 1.25 3.00
LM Lewis Morris 1.25 3.00
MT Matthew Thornton 1.25 3.00
OW Oliver Wolcott 1.25 3.00
PL Philip Livingston 1.25 3.00
RHL Richard Henry Lee 1.25 3.00
RM Robert Morris 1.25 3.00
RS Roger Sherman 1.25 3.00
RST Richard Stockton 1.25 3.00
RTP Robert Treat Paine 1.25 3.00
SA Samuel Adams 2.00 5.00
SC Samuel Chase 1.25 3.00
SH Stephen Hopkins 1.25 3.00
SHU Samuel Huntington 1.25 3.00
TH Thomas Heyward Jr. 1.25 3.00

TJ Thomas Jefferson 2.00 5.00
TL Thomas Lynch Jr. 1.25 3.00
TM Thomas McKean 1.25 3.00
TN Thomas Nelson Jr. 1.25 3.00
TS Thomas Stone 1.25 3.00
WE William Ellery 1.25 3.00
WF William Floyd 1.25 3.00
WH William Hooper 1.25 3.00
WP William Paca 1.25 3.00
WW William Whipple 1.25 3.00
WWI William Williams 1.25 3.00

2006 Topps Factory Set Rookie Bonus

COMP.RETAIL SET (5) 6.00 15.00
COMP.HOBBY SET (5) 6.00 15.00
COMP.HOLIDAY SET (10) 10.00 25.00
1-5 ISSUED IN RETAIL FACTORY SETS
6-10 ISSUED IN HOBBY FACTORY SETS
11-20 ISSUED IN HOLIDAY FACTORY SETS
1 Nick Markakis .75 2.00
2 Kelly Shoppach .40 1.00
3 Jordan Tata .40 1.00
4 Ruddy Lugo .40 1.00
5 Josh Wilson .40 1.00
6 Fernando Nieve .40 1.00
7 Sendy Rleal .40 1.00
8 Jason Kubel .40 1.00
9 James Loney .60 1.50
10 Fabio Castro .40 1.00
11 Jonathan Broxton .40 1.00
12 Eliezer Alfonzo .40 1.00
13 Jason Hirsh .40 1.00
14 Rajai Davis .40 1.00
15 Henry Owens .40 1.00
16 Kevin Frandsen .40 1.00
17 Matt Garza .40 1.00
18 Chris Duncan .60 1.50
19 Chris Coste 1.00 2.50
20 Jeff Karstens .40 1.00

2006 Topps Factory Set Team Bonus

COMP.CARDINALS SET (5) 6.00 15.00
COMP.CUBS SET (5) 6.00 15.00
COMP.PIRATES SET (5) 6.00 15.00
COMP.RED SOX SET (5) 10.00 25.00
COMP.YANKEES SET (5) 8.00 20.00
BRS1-5 ISSUED IN RED SOX FACTORY SET
CC1-5 ISSUED IN CUBS FACTORY SET
NYY1-5 ISSUED IN YANKEES FACTORY SET
PP1-5 ISSUED IN PIRATES FACTORY SET
SLC1-5 ISSUED IN CARDINALS FACTORY SET
BRS1 Jonathan Papelbon 2.00 5.00
BRS2 Manny Ramirez 1.00 2.50
BRS3 David Ortiz 1.00 2.50
BRS4 Josh Beckett .40 1.00
BRS5 Curt Schilling .60 1.50
CC1 Sean Marshall .40 1.00
CC2 Freddie Bynum .40 1.00
CC3 Derrek Lee .40 1.00
CC4 Juan Pierre .40 1.00
CC5 Carlos Zambrano .60 1.50
NYY1 Wil Nieves .40 1.00
NYY2 Alex Rodriguez 1.25 3.00
NYY3 Derek Jeter 2.50 6.00
NYY4 Mariano Rivera 1.25 3.00
NYY5 Randy Johnson 1.00 2.50
PP1 Matt Capps .40 1.00
PP2 Paul Maholm .40 1.00
PP3 Nate McLouth .40 1.00
PP4 John Van Benschoten .40 1.00
PP5 Jason Bay .40 1.00
SLC1 Adam Wainwright .60 1.50
SLC2 Skip Schumaker .60 1.50
SLC3 Albert Pujols 1.25 3.00
SLC4 Jim Edmonds .60 1.50
SLC5 Scott Rolen .60 1.50

2006 Topps Hit Parade

COMPLETE SET (30) 35.00 60.00
SER.2 ODDS 1:18 H, 1:6 HTA, 1:27 MINI
SER.2 ODDS 1:18 R, 1:9 RACK
HR1 Barry Bonds HR 2.50 6.00
HR2 Ken Griffey Jr HR 3.00 8.00
HR3 Jeff Bagwell HR 1.00 2.50
HR4 Gary Sheffield HR .60 1.50
HR5 Frank Thomas HR 1.50 4.00
HR6 Manny Ramirez HR 1.50 4.00
HR7 Jim Thome HR 1.00 2.50
HR8 Alex Rodriguez HR 2.00 5.00
HR9 Mike Piazza HR 1.50 4.00
HIT1 Craig Biggio HIT 1.00 2.50
HIT2 Barry Bonds HIT 2.50 6.00
HIT3 Julio Franco HIT .60 1.50
HIT4 Steve Finley HIT .60 1.50
HIT5 Gary Sheffield HIT .60 1.50
HIT6 Jeff Bagwell HIT 1.00 2.50
HIT7 Ken Griffey Jr HIT 3.00 8.00
HIT8 Omar Vizquel HIT 1.00 2.50
HIT9 Marquis Grissom HIT .60 1.50
HR10 Carlos Delgado HR .60 1.50
RBI1 Barry Bonds RBI 2.50 6.00
RBI2 Ken Griffey Jr RBI 3.00 8.00
RBI3 Jeff Bagwell RBI 1.00 2.50
RBI4 Gary Sheffield RBI .60 1.50
RBI5 Frank Thomas RBI 1.50 4.00
RBI6 Manny Ramirez RBI 1.50 4.00
RBI7 Ruben Sierra RBI .60 1.50
RBI8 Jeff Kent RBI .60 1.50
RBI9 Luis Gonzalez RBI .60 1.50
HIT10 Bernie Williams HIT 1.00 2.50
RBI10 Alex Rodriguez RBI 2.00 5.00

2006 Topps Hobby Masters

COMPLETE SET (20) 8.00 20.00
SER.1 ODDS 1:18 HOBBY, 1:6 HTA
HM1 Derrek Lee .40 1.00
HM2 Albert Pujols 1.25 3.00
HM3 Nomar Garciaparra .60 1.50
HM4 Alfonso Soriano .60 1.50
HM5 Derek Jeter 2.50 6.00
HM6 Miguel Tejada .60 1.50
HM7 Alex Rodriguez 1.25 3.00
HM8 Jim Edmonds UER .60 1.50
HM9 Mark Prior .60 1.50
HM10 Roger Clemens 1.25 3.00
HM11 Randy Johnson 1.00 2.50
HM12 Manny Ramirez 1.00 2.50
HM13 Curt Schilling .60 1.50
HM14 Vladimir Guerrero .60 1.50
HM15 Barry Bonds 1.50 4.00
HM16 Ichiro Suzuki 1.25 3.00
HM17 Pedro Martinez .60 1.50
HM18 Carlos Beltran .60 1.50
HM19 David Ortiz 1.00 2.50
HM20 Andruw Jones .40 1.00

2006 Topps Mantle Collection

COMPLETE SET (10) 60.00 120.00
SER.1 ODDS 1:36 HOB, 1:36 HTA, 1:36 MINI
SER.1 ODDS 1:12 RACK, 1:36 RETAIL
BLACK SER.1 ODDS 1:4,665 HTA
BLACK PRINT RUN 7 SERIAL #'d SETS
NO BLACK PRICING DUE TO SCARCITY
*GOLD p/r 477-977: 1.25X TO 3X BASIC
*GOLD p/r 277-377: 1.5X TO 4X BASIC
*GOLD p/r 177: 2X TO 5X BASIC
*GOLD p/r 77: 4X TO 10X BASIC
GOLD SER.1 ODDS 1:1500 HOB, 1:2332 HTA
GOLD SER.1 ODDS 1:3376 MINI, 1:970 RACK
GOLD SER.1 ODDS 1:1500 RETAIL
GOLD PRINT RUNS B/WN 77-977 PER
1996 Mickey Mantle 96 6.00 15.00
1997 Mickey Mantle 97 6.00 15.00
1998 Mickey Mantle 98 6.00 15.00
1999 Mickey Mantle 99 6.00 15.00
2000 Mickey Mantle 00 6.00 15.00
2001 Mickey Mantle 01 6.00 15.00
2002 Mickey Mantle 02 6.00 15.00
2003 Mickey Mantle 03 6.00 15.00
2004 Mickey Mantle 04 6.00 15.00
2005 Mickey Mantle 05 6.00 15.00

2006 Topps Mantle Collection Bat Relics

SER.1 ODDS 1:4540 HOBBY, 1:8552 HTA
SER.1 ODDS 1:14,000 MINI, 1:6500 RETAIL
PRINT RUNS B/WN 77-167 COPIES PER
BLACK SER.1 ODDS 1:4,665 HTA
BLACK PRINT RUN 7 SERIAL #'d SETS
NO BLACK PRICING DUE TO SCARCITY
1996 Mickey Mantle 96/77 15.00 40.00
1997 Mickey Mantle 97/87 15.00 40.00
1998 Mickey Mantle 98/97 15.00 40.00
1999 Mickey Mantle 99/107 15.00 40.00
2000 Mickey Mantle 00/117 15.00 40.00
2001 Mickey Mantle 01/127 15.00 40.00
2002 Mickey Mantle 02/137 15.00 40.00
2003 Mickey Mantle 03/147 15.00 40.00
2004 Mickey Mantle 04/157 15.00 40.00
2005 Mickey Mantle 05/167 15.00 40.00

2006 Topps Mantle Home Run History

COMPLETE SET (501) 500.00 900.00
COMP.06 SERIES 1-2 SET (1-101) 60.00 120.00
COMP.06 UPDATE (102-201) 60.00 120.00
COMP.07 SERIES 1 SET (202-301) 75.00 150.00
COMP.07 SERIES 2 SET (302-401) 125.00 250.00
COMP.07 UPDATE (402-501) 125.00 250.00
COMP.08 TOPPS (502-536) 20.00 50.00
COMMON CARD (1-201) .40 1.00
COMMON CARD (202-301) 1.00 2.50
COMMON CARD (302-536) .75 2.00
SER.1 ODDS 1:4 HOBBY, 1:1 HTA, 1:4 MINI
SER.1 ODDS 1:2 RACK, 1:4 RETAIL
SER.2 ODDS 1:4 HOBBY, 1:1 HTA, 1:8 MINI
SER.2 ODDS 1:2 RACK, 1:4 RETAIL
UPDATE ODDS 1:4 HOB,1:4 RET
07 SER.1 ODDS 1:9 H, 1:2 HTA, 1:9 K-MART
07 SER.1 ODDS 1:9 RACK, 1:9 TARGET
07 SER.1 ODDS 1:9 WAL-MART
07 SER.2 ODDS 1:9 HOBBY
07 UPDATE ODDS 1:9 HOB, 1:9 RET
08 SER.1 ODDS 1:9 HOB, 1:9 RET
CARD 1 ISSUED IN SERIES 1 PACKS
CARDS 2-101 ISSUED IN SERIES 2 PACKS
CARDS 102-201 ISSUED IN UPDATE PACKS
CARDS 202-301 ISSUED IN 07 SERIES 1
CARDS 302-401 ISSUED IN 07 SERIES 2
CARDS 402-501 ISSUED IN 07 UPDATE
CARDS 502-537 ISSUED IN 08 SERIES 1

2006 Topps Mantle Home Run History Bat Relics

COMMON CARD (R1-R536) 40.00 80.00
SER.1 ODDS 1:681,120 H, 1:102,624 HTA
SER.2 ODDS 1:6250 H, 1:16,000 HTA
SER.2 ODDS 1:21,000 MINI, 1:1575 R
UPD ODDS 1:5100 H,1:1859 HTA,1:5800 R
07 SER.1 ODDS 1:14,618 H, 1:494 HTA
07 SER.1 ODDS 1:32,000 K-MART
07 SER.1 ODDS 1:16,225 RACK
07 SER.1 ODDS 1:32,00 WAL-MART
07 SER.2 ODDS 1:12,106 HOBBY, 1:693 HTA
07 UPD. ODDS 1:5,550 HOBBY
07 UPD. ODDS 1:1,475 HTA
07 UPD. ODDS 1:5,550 RETAIL
08 SER.1 ODDS 1:29,331 H,1:1492 HTA
08 SER.1 ODDS 1:207,000 RETAIL
1 ISSUED IN SERIES 1 PACKS
2-101 ISSUED IN SERIES 2 PACKS
102-201 ISSUED IN UPDATE PACKS
202-301 ISSUED IN 07 SERIES 1 PACKS
302-401 ISSUED IN 07 SERIES 2 PACKS
402-501 ISSUED IN 07 UPDATE
502-536 ISSUED IN 08 SERIES 1
STATED PRINT RUN 7 SERIAL #'d SETS

2006 Topps Opening Day Team vs. Team

COMPLETE SET (15) 6.00 15.00
SER.2 ODDS 1:12 HOBBY, 1:3 HTA, 1:24 MINI
SER.2 ODDS 1:6 RACK, 1:12 RETAIL
AM Houston Astros vs. Marlins .60 1.50
AY Oakland Athletics vs. Yankees .60 1.50
BP Milwaukee Brewers vs. Pirates .60 1.50
DB Los Angeles Dodgers vs. Braves .60 1.50
JT Toronto Blue Jays vs. Twins .60 1.50
MA Seattle Mariners vs. Angels .60 1.50
MN New York Mets vs. Nationals .60 1.50
OD Baltimore Orioles vs. Devil Rays .60 1.50
PC Philadelphia Phillies vs. Cardinals .60 1.50
PG San Diego Padres vs. Giants .60 1.50
RC Cincinnati Reds vs. Cubs .60 1.50
RD Colorado Rockies vs. Diamondbacks .60 1.50
RR Texas Rangers vs. Red Sox .60 1.50
RT Kansas City Royals vs. Tigers .60 1.50
WI Chicago White Sox vs. Indians .60 1.50

2006 Topps Opening Day Team vs. Team Relics

SER.2 A ODDS 1:8800 H, 1:22,000 HTA
SER.2 A ODDS 1:25,000 MINI, 1:2100 R
SER.2 B ODDS 1:810 H, 1:2850 HTA
SER.2 B ODDS 1:3075 MINI, 1:1200 R
GROUP A PRINT RUN 50 SERIAL #'d SETS
NO GROUP A PRICING DUE TO SCARCITY
EXCHANGE DEADLINE 06/30/08
AY Oakland Athletics Base B 6.00 15.00
OD Baltimore Orioles Base B 6.00 15.00
RD Colorado Rockies Base B 6.00 15.00
RT Kansas City Royals Base B 10.00 25.00

2006 Topps Own the Game

COMPLETE SET (30) 20.00 50.00
SER.1 ODDS 1:12 HOB, 1:4 HTA, 1:12 MINI
SER.1 ODDS 1:6 RACK, 1:8 RETAIL
OG1 Derrek Lee .40 1.00
OG2 Michael Young .40 1.00
OG3 Albert Pujols 1.25 3.00
OG4 Roger Clemens 1.25 3.00
OG5 Andy Pettitte .60 1.50
OG6 Dontrelle Willis .40 1.00
OG7 Michael Young .40 1.00
OG8 Ichiro Suzuki 1.25 3.00
OG9 Derek Jeter 2.50 6.00
OG10 Andruw Jones .40 1.00
OG11 Alex Rodriguez 1.25 3.00
OG12 David Ortiz 1.00 2.50
OG13 David Ortiz 1.00 2.50
OG14 Manny Ramirez 1.00 2.50
OG15 Mark Teixeira .60 1.50
OG16 Albert Pujols 1.25 3.00
OG17 Alex Rodriguez 1.25 3.00
OG18 Derek Jeter 2.50 6.00
OG19 Chad Cordero .40 1.00
OG20 Francisco Rodriguez .60 1.50
OG21 Mariano Rivera 1.25 3.00
OG22 Chone Figgins .40 1.00
OG23 Jose Reyes .60 1.50
OG24 Scott Podsednik .40 1.00
OG25 Jake Peavy .40 1.00
OG26 Johan Santana .60 1.50
OG27 Pedro Martinez .60 1.50
OG28 Dontrelle Willis .40 1.00
OG29 Chris Carpenter .60 1.50
OG30 Bartolo Colon .40 1.00

2006 Topps Rookie of the Week

COMPLETE SET (25) 15.00 40.00
COMMON CARD (1-13) .50 1.25
ISSUED ONE PER WEEK VIA HTA SHOPS
1 Mickey Mantle 52 4.00 10.00
2 Barry Bonds 87 2.00 5.00
3 Roger Clemens 85 1.50 4.00
4 Ernie Banks 54 1.25 3.00
5 Nolan Ryan 68 4.00 10.00
6 Albert Pujols 01 1.50 4.00
7 Roberto Clemente 55 3.00 8.00
8 Frank Robinson 57 .75 2.00
9 Brooks Robinson 57 .75 2.00
10 Harmon Killebrew 55 1.25 3.00
11 Reggie Jackson 69 .75 2.00
12 George Brett 75 2.50 6.00
13 Ichiro Suzuki 01 1.50 4.00
14 Cal Ripken 82 4.00 10.00
15 Tom Seaver 68 .75 2.00
16 Johnny Bench 68 1.25 3.00
17 Mike Schmidt 73 2.00 5.00
18 Derek Jeter 93 3.00 8.00
19 Bob Gibson 59 .75 2.00
20 Ozzie Smith 79 1.50 4.00
21 Rickey Henderson 80 1.25 3.00
22 Tony Gwynn 83 1.25 3.00
23 Wade Boggs 83 .75 2.00
24 Ryne Sandberg 83 2.50 6.00
25 Mickey Mantle TBD 4.00 10.00

2006 Topps Stars

COMPLETE SET (15) 6.00 15.00
SER.2 ODDS 1:12 HOBBY, 1:4 HTA
AP Albert Pujols 1.00 2.50
AR Alex Rodriguez 1.00 2.50
AS Alfonso Soriano .50 1.25
BB Barry Bonds 1.25 3.00
DJ Derek Jeter 2.00 5.00
DO David Ortiz .75 2.00
HM Hideki Matsui .75 2.00
IS Ichiro Suzuki 1.00 2.50
MC Miguel Cabrera .75 2.00
MR Manny Ramirez .75 2.00
MT Miguel Tejada .50 1.25
PM Pedro Martinez .50 1.25
RC Roger Clemens 1.00 2.50
TH Todd Helton .50 1.25
VG Vladimir Guerrero .50 1.25

2006 Topps Target Factory Set Mantle Memorabilia

MMR52 Mickey Mantle 52T 20.00 50.00

2006 Topps Team Topps Autographs

ISSUED IN VARIOUS 06 TOPPS PRODUCTS
SEE '03 TOPPS BLUE CHIPS FOR ADD'L INFO
BF Bob Feller 10.00 25.00
CS Chris Snyder 4.00 10.00
DD Doug Drabek 6.00 15.00
DS Duke Snider 15.00 40.00
DZ Don Zimmer 8.00 20.00
ED Eric Davis 6.00 15.00
JF Josh Fields 6.00 15.00
JL Jim Leyritz 4.00 10.00
JP Johnny Podres 6.00 15.00
JP1 Jimmy Piersall 6.00 15.00
MC Mike Cuellar 6.00 15.00
MP Manny Parra 4.00 10.00
MR Mickey Rivers 6.00 15.00
RS Ryan Sweeney 4.00 10.00
SE Scott Elbert 4.00 10.00
TJ Tommy John 6.00 15.00

2006 Topps Trading Places

COMPLETE SET (20) 10.00 25.00
SER.2 ODDS 1:18 H, 1:4 HTA, 1:32 MINI
SER.2 ODDS 1:18 R, 1:8 RACK
AS Alfonso Soriano 1.00 2.50
BM Bill Mueller .60 1.50
BW Brad Wilkerson .60 1.50
CC Coco Crisp .60 1.50
CD Carlos Delgado .60 1.50
CP Corey Patterson .60 1.50
ER Edgar Renteria .60 1.50
FT Frank Thomas 1.50 4.00
JD Johnny Damon 1.00 2.50
JP Juan Pierre .60 1.50
JT Jim Thome 1.00 2.50
KL Kenny Lofton .60 1.50
MB Milton Bradley .60 1.50
NG Nomar Garciaparra 1.00 2.50
PW Preston Wilson .60 1.50
RF Rafael Furcal .60 1.50
RH Ramon Hernandez .60 1.50
TG Troy Glaus .60 1.50
JDN Juan Encarnacion .60 1.50
MJP Mike Piazza 1.50 4.00

2006 Topps Wal-Mart

COMPLETE SERIES 1 (18) 12.50 30.00
COMPLETE SERIES 2 (18) 50.00 100.00
THREE PER WAL-MART BLASTER BOX
S1 CARDS ISSUED IN SERIES 1 PACKS
S2 CARDS ISSUED IN SERIES 2 PACKS
WM1 Stan Musial 52 S1 2.00 5.00
WM2 Ted Williams 87 S1 2.50 6.00
WM3 Yogi Berra 54 S2 8.00 20.00
WM4 Joe Mauer 96 UPD .75 2.00
WM5 Mickey Mantle 02 S1 4.00 10.00
WM6 Mickey Mantle 57 S2 6.00 15.00
WM7 Alex Rodriguez 58 S2 5.00 12.00
WM8 Carlos Zambrano 92 UPD .75 2.00
WM9 Gary Carter 60 S2 12.50 30.00
WM10 Roy Oswalt 61 S2 10.00 25.00
WM11 Mickey Mantle 70 UPD 8.00 20.00
WM12 Randy Johnson 62 UPD 1.25 3.00
WM13 Carlos Lee 64 S1 .50 1.25
WM14 Johan Santana 65 S2 8.00 20.00
WM15 Roberto Clemente 66 S2 6.00 15.00
WM16 Carl Yastrzemski 67 S2 6.00 15.00
WM17 Chase Utley 63 UPD .75 2.00
WM18 Pedro Martinez 68 UPD .75 2.00
WM19 Jason Bay 69 UPD .50 1.25
WM20 Alex Rodriguez 59 UPD 1.50 4.00
WM21 Chipper Jones 72 S2 12.50 30.00
WM22 Ichiro Suzuki 01 S1 1.50 4.00
WM23 Bobby Abreu 94 S1 .50 1.25
WM24 Tom Seaver 95 S1 .75 2.00
WM25 Alfonso Soriano 76 S2
WM26 Andruw Jones 92 S1 .50 1.25
WM27 Hanley Ramirez 71 UPD .75 2.00
WM28 Adam Dunn 91 S1 .75 2.00
WM29 Carl Crawford 00 UPD .75 2.00
WM30 Mark Teixeira 81 S1 .75 2.00
WM31 Albert Pujols 82 S2 3.00 8.00
WM32 Cal Ripken 83 S2 5.00 12.00
WM33 Ryne Sandberg 84 S1 2.50 6.00
WM34 Don Mattingly 85 S1 2.50 6.00
WM35 Roger Clemens 86 S1 1.50 4.00
WM36 Jose Reyes 53 S2 5.00 12.00
WM37 Curt Schilling 80 UPD .75 2.00
WM38 Derrek Lee 56 S2 6.00 15.00
WM39 Miguel Cabrera 73 S2 5.00 12.00
WM40 Manny Ramirez 88 UPD 1.25 3.00
WM41 Barry Bonds 89 S1 2.00 5.00
WM42 Barry Bonds 74 S2 5.00 12.00
WM43 Jeff Francoeur 98 UPD 1.25 3.00
WM44 Livan Hernandez 75 S2 6.00 15.00
WM45 Derek Jeter 77 S2 10.00 25.00
WM46 David Ortiz 97 S1 1.25 3.00
WM47 Carlos Delgado 78 UPD .50 1.25
WM48 Ivan Rodriguez 99 S1 .75 2.00
WM49 Todd Helton 05 UPD .75 2.00
WM50 Barry Bonds 79 UPD 2.00 5.00
WM51 Miguel Tejada 55 UPD .75 2.00
WM52 Alex Rodriguez 03 S1 1.50 4.00
WM53 Vladimir Guerrero 04 S1 .75 2.00
WM54 Paul Konerko 90 UPD .75 2.00

2006 Topps Trading Places Autographs

SER.2 A ODDS 1:110,000 HOBBY
SER.2 A ODDS 1:28,000 HTA
SER.2 A ODDS 1:250,000 MINI
SER.2 A ODDS 1:160,000 RACK
SER.2 A ODDS 1:150,000 RETAIL
SER.2 B ODDS 1:18,000 H, 1:5100 HTA
SER.2 B ODDS 1:30,000 MINI, 1:17,000 R
SER.2 B ODDS 1:8700 RACK
SER.2 C ODDS 1:4280 H, 1:1175 HTA
SER.2 C ODDS 1:7200 MINI, 1:4200 R
SER.2 C ODDS 1:2040 RACK
GROUP A PRINT RUN 75 CARDS
GROUP B PRINT RUN 225 SETS
A-B ARE NOT SERIAL-NUMBERED
A-B PRINT RUNS PROVIDED BY TOPPS
BR B.J. Ryan B 15.00 40.00
BW Billy Wagner C 5.00 12.00
JE Johnny Estrada C 4.00 10.00
KJ Kenji Johjima A 20.00 50.00
ML Mike Lowell C 10.00 25.00
PL Paul LoDuca B 15.00 40.00
TS Termel Sledge C 4.00 10.00

2006 Topps Trading Places Relics

SER.2 A ODDS 1:645 HOBBY 1:115 HTA
SER.2 A ODDS 1:1355 MINI, 1:810 RETAIL
SER.2 B ODDS 1:410 HOBBY 1:120 HTA
SER.2 B ODDS 1:903 MINI, 1:500 RETAIL
AS Alfonso Soriano Bat A 3.00 8.00
BM Bill Mueller Bat A 3.00 8.00
BR B.J. Ryan Jsy B 3.00 8.00
CP Corey Patterson Bat A 3.00 8.00
ER Edgar Renteria Bat A 3.00 8.00
JD Johnny Damon Jsy B 6.00 15.00
JE Johnny Estrada Bat B 3.00 8.00
JP Juan Pierre Bat A 3.00 8.00
JT Jim Thome Bat A 6.00 15.00
KJ Kenji Johjima Bat B 6.00 15.00
KL Kenny Lofton Bat B 3.00 8.00
MB Milton Bradley Bat B 3.00 8.00
ML Mike Lowell Bat A 3.00 8.00
NG Nomar Garciaparra Bat A 4.00 10.00
PL Paul Lo Duca Bat A 3.00 8.00
PW Preston Wilson Bat A 3.00 8.00
RH Ramon Hernandez Bat B 3.00 8.00
TS Termel Sledge Bat B 3.00 8.00
BW1 Billy Wagner Jsy B 3.00 8.00
BW2 Brad Wilkerson Bat B 3.00 8.00

2006 Topps World Series Champion Relics

SER.1 A ODDS 1:23,755 H, 1:9329 HTA
SER.1 A ODDS 1:55,000 MINI, 1:27,000 R
SER.1 B ODDS 1:11,289 H, 1:2544 HTA
SER.1 B ODDS 1:24,000 MINI, 1:11,500 R
SER.1 C ODDS 1:1941 H, 1:880 HTA
SER.1 C ODDS 1:5100 MINI, 1:2500 R
SER.1 D ODDS 1:3144 H, 1:2168 HTA
SER.1 D ODDS 1:9200 MINI, 1:4700 R
SER.1 E ODDS 1:4984 H, 1:3346 HTA
SER.1 E ODDS 1:14,500 MINI, 1:7200 R
SER.1 F ODDS 1:1006 H, 1:617 HTA
SER.1 F ODDS 1:2800 MINI, 1:1430 R
SER.1 G ODDS 1:1396 H, 1:465 HTA
SER.1 G ODDS 1:3500 MINI, 1:1750 R
OVERALL SER.1 AU-GU ODDS 1:137 H/R
OVERALL SER.1 AU-GU ODDS 1:47 HTA
GROUP A PRINT RUN 100 SETS
GROUP A ARE NOT SERIAL-NUMBERED
GROUP A PRINT RUN PROVIDED BY TOPPS
AP A.J. Pierzynski Bat E 15.00 40.00
AR Aaron Rowand Bat D 10.00 25.00
BJ Bobby Jenks Glv A/100 * 250.00 350.00
CEB Carl Everett Bat F 6.00 15.00
CEU Carl Everett Uni A/100 * 6.00 15.00
FT Frank Thomas Uni F 12.50 30.00
JC Joe Crede Bat D 15.00 40.00
JD Jermaine Dye Bat C 30.00 60.00
JG Jon Garland Uni F 12.50 30.00
JU Juan Uribe Bat B 12.50 30.00
MB Mark Buehrle Glv A/100 * 150.00 250.00
PKB Paul Konerko Bat G 10.00 25.00
PKU Paul Konerko Uni G 10.00 25.00
SP Scott Podsednik Bat C 15.00 40.00
TI Tadahito Iguchi Bat C 20.00 50.00
TP Timo Perez Bat C 10.00 25.00
WH Willie Harris Bat F 4.00 10.00

2006 Topps Update

COMPLETE SET (330) 20.00 50.00
COMMON CARD (1-132) .07 .20
COMMON ROOKIE (133-170) .40 1.00
COMMON CARD (171-330) .12 .30
UNLISTED STARS 171-330 .30 .75
1-330 PLATE ODDS 1:85 HTA
PLATE PRINT RUN 1 SET PER COLOR
BLACK-CYAN-MAGENTA-YELLOW ISSUED
NO PLATE PRICING DUE TO SCARCITY
1 Austin Kearns .07 .20
2 Adam Eaton .07 .20
3 Juan Encarnacion .07 .20
4 Jarrod Washburn .07 .20
5 Alex Gonzalez .07 .20
6 Toby Hall .07 .20
7 Preston Wilson .07 .20
8 Ramon Ortiz .07 .20
9 Jason Michaels .07 .20
10 Jeff Weaver .07 .20
11 Russell Branyan .07 .20
12 Brett Tomko .07 .20
13 Doug Mientkiewicz .07 .20
14 David Wells .07 .20
15 Corey Koskie .07 .20
16 Russ Ortiz .07 .20
17 Carlos Pena .12 .30
18 Mark Hendrickson .07 .20
19 Julian Tavarez .07 .20
20 Jeff Conine .07 .20
21 Dioner Navarro .07 .20
22 Bob Wickman .07 .20
23 Felipe Lopez .07 .20
24 Eddie Guardado .07 .20
25 David Dellucci .07 .20
26 Ryan Wagner .07 .20
27 Nick Green .07 .20
28 Gary Majewski .07 .20
29 Shea Hillenbrand .07 .20
30 Jae Seo .07 .20
31 Royce Clayton .07 .20
32 Dave Riske .07 .20
33 Joey Gathright .07 .20
34 Robinson Tejada .07 .20
35 Edwin Jackson .07 .20
36 Aubrey Huff .07 .20
37 Akinori Otsuka .07 .20
38 Juan Castro .07 .20
39 Zach Day .07 .20
40 Jeremy Accardo .07 .20
41 Shawn Green .07 .20
42 Kazuo Matsui .07 .20
43 J.J. Putz .07 .20
44 David Ross .07 .20
45 Scott Williamson .07 .20
46 Joe Borchard .07 .20
47 Elmer Dessens .07 .20
48 Odalis Perez .07 .20
49 Kelly Shoppach .07 .20
50 Brandon Phillips .07 .20
51 Guillermo Mota .07 .20
52 Alex Cintron .07 .20
53 Denny Bautista .07 .20
54 Josh Bard .07 .20
55 Julio Lugo .07 .20
56 Doug Mirabelli .07 .20
57 Kip Wells .07 .20
58 Adrian Gonzalez .15 .40
59 Shawn Chacon .07 .20
60 Marcus Thames .07 .20
61 Craig Wilson .07 .20
62 Cory Sullivan .07 .20
63 Ben Broussard .07 .20
64 Todd Walker .07 .20
65 Greg Maddux .25 .60
66 Xavier Nady .07 .20
67 Oliver Perez .07 .20
68 Sean Casey .07 .20
69 Kyle Lohse .07 .20
70 Carlos Lee .07 .20
71 Rheal Cormier .07 .20
72 Ronnie Belliard .07 .20
73 Cory Lidle .07 .20
74 David Bell .07 .20
75 Wilson Betemit .07 .20
76 Danys Baez .07 .20
77 Mike Stanton .07 .20
78 Kevin Mench .07 .20
79 Sandy Alomar Jr. .07 .20
80 Cesar Izturis .07 .20
81 Jeremy Affeldt .07 .20
82 Matt Stairs .07 .20
83 Hector Luna .07 .20
84 Tony Graffanino .07 .20
85 J.P Howell .07 .20
86 Bengie Molina .07 .20
87 Maicer Izturis .07 .20
88 Marco Scutaro .12 .30
89 Daryle Ward .07 .20
90 Sal Fasano .07 .20
91 Oscar Villarreal .07 .20
92 Gabe Gross .07 .20
93 Phil Nevin .07 .20
94 Damon Hollins .07 .20
95 Juan Cruz .07 .20
96 Marlon Anderson .07 .20
97 Jason Davis .07 .20
98 Ryan Shealy .07 .20
99 Francisco Cordero .07 .20
100 Bobby Abreu .07 .20
101 Roberto Hernandez .07 .20
102 Gary Bennett .07 .20
103 Aaron Sele .07 .20
104 Nook Logan .07 .20
105 Alfredo Amezaga .07 .20
106 Chris Woodward .07 .20
107 Kevin Jarvis .07 .20
108 B.J. Upton .07 .20
109 Alan Embree .07 .20
110 Milton Bradley .07 .20
111 Pete Orr .07 .20
112 Jeff Cirillo .07 .20
113 Corey Patterson .07 .20
114 Josh Paul .07 .20
115 Fernando Rodney .07 .20
116 Jerry Hairston Jr. .07 .20
117 Scott Proctor .07 .20
118 Ambiorix Burgos .07 .20
119 Jose Bautista .20 .50
120 Livan Hernandez .07 .20
121 John McDonald .07 .20
122 Ronny Cedeno .07 .20
123 Nate Robertson .07 .20
124 Jamey Carroll .07 .20
125 Alex Escobar .07 .20
126 Endy Chavez .07 .20
127 Jorge Julio .07 .20
128 Kenny Lofton .07 .20
129 Matt Diaz .07 .20
130 Dave Bush .07 .20
131 Jose Molina .07 .20
132 Mike MacDougal .07 .20
133 Ben Zobrist (RC) 2.00 5.00
134 Shane Komine RC .60 1.50
135 Casey Janssen RC .40 1.00
136 Kevin Frandsen (RC) .40 1.00
137 John Rheinecker (RC) .40 1.00
138 Matt Kemp (RC) 1.00 2.50
139 Scott Mathieson (RC) .40 1.00
140 Jered Weaver (RC) 1.25 3.00
141 Joel Guzman (RC) .40 1.00
142 Anibal Sanchez (RC) .40 1.00
143 Melky Cabrera (RC) .60 1.50
144 Howie Kendrick (RC) .75 2.00
145 Cole Hamels (RC) 1.25 3.00
146 Willy Aybar (RC) .40 1.00
147 Jamie Shields RC 1.25 3.00
148 Kevin Thompson (RC) .40 1.00
149 Jon Lester RC 1.50 4.00
150 Stephen Drew (RC) .75 2.00
151 Andre Ethier (RC) 1.25 3.00
152 Jordan Tata RC .40 1.00
153 Mike Napoli RC .60 1.50
154 Kason Gabbard (RC) .40 1.00
155 Lastings Milledge (RC) .40 1.00
156 Erick Aybar (RC) .40 1.00
157 Fausto Carmona (RC) .40 1.00
158 Russ Martin (RC) .60 1.50
159 David Pauley (RC) .40 1.00
160 Andy Marte (RC) .40 1.00
161 Carlos Quentin (RC) .60 1.50
162 Franklin Gutierrez (RC) .40 1.00
163 Taylor Buchholz (RC) .40 1.00
164 Josh Johnson (RC) 1.00 2.50
165 Chad Billingsley (RC) .60 1.50
166 Kendry Morales (RC) 1.00 2.50
167 Adam Loewen (RC) .40 1.00
168 Yusmeiro Petit (RC) .40 1.00
169 Matt Albers (RC) .40 1.00
170 John Maine (RC) .60 1.50
171 Alex Rodriguez SH .40 1.00
172 Mike Piazza SH .30 .75
173 Cory Sullivan SH .12 .30
174 Anibal Sanchez SH .12 .30
175 Trevor Hoffman SH .20 .50
176 Barry Bonds SH .50 1.25
177 Derek Jeter SH .75 2.00
178 Jose Reyes SH .20 .50
179 Manny Ramirez SH .30 .75
180 Vladimir Guerrero SH .20 .50
181 Mariano Rivera SH .40 1.00
182 Mark Kotsay PH .12 .30
183 Derek Jeter PH .75 2.00
184 Carlos Delgado PH .12 .30
185 Frank Thomas PH .30 .75
186 Albert Pujols PH .40 1.00
187 Magglio Ordonez PH .20 .50
188 Carlos Delgado PH .12 .30
189 Kenny Rogers PH .12 .30
190 Tom Glavine PH .20 .50
191 P.Polanco .12 .30
J.Suppan PH
192 Jose Reyes PH .20 .50
193 E.Chavez .40 1.00
Y.Molina PH
194 Craig Monroe PH .12 .30
195 J.Verlander 1.00 2.50
J.Zumaya PH
196 P.LoDuca .20 .50
C.Beltran PH
197 A.Pujols .40 1.00
J.Edmonds/S.Rolen PH
198 Anthony Reyes PH .12 .30
199 Chris Carpenter PH .20 .50
200 David Eckstein PH .12 .30
201 Jered Weaver PH .40 1.00
202 D.Ortiz .30 .75
J.Dye/T.Hafner LL
203 J.Mauer .75 2.00
D.Jeter/R.Cano LL
204 D.Ortiz .30 .75
J.Morneau/R.Ibanez LL
205 Crawford/Figgins/Ichiro LL .40 1.00
206 J.Santana .20 .50
C.Wang/J.Garland LL
207 J.Santana .20 .50
R.Halladay/C.Sabathia LL
208 J.Santana .20 .50
J.Bonderman/J.Lackey LL
209 F.Rodriguez .20 .50
B.Jenks/B.Ryan LL
210 R.Howard .40 1.00
A.Pujols/A.Soriano LL
211 Sanch./Cabrera/Pujols LL .40 1.00
212 Howard/Pujols/Berk.LL .40 1.00
213 J.Reyes .20 .50
J.Pierre/H.Ramirez LL
214 D.Lowe .20 .50
B.Webb/C.Zambrano LL
215 R.Oswalt .20 .50
C.Carpenter/B.Webb LL
216 A.Harang .30 .75
J.Peavy/J.Smoltz LL
217 T.Hoffman .20 .50
B.Wagner/J.Borowski LL
218 Ichiro Suzuki AS .40 1.00
219 Derek Jeter AS .75 2.00
220 Alex Rodriguez AS .40 1.00
221 David Ortiz AS .30 .75
222 Vladimir Guerrero AS .20 .50
223 Ivan Rodriguez AS .20 .50
224 Vernon Wells AS .12 .30
225 Mark Loretta AS .12 .30
226 Kenny Rogers AS .12 .30
227 Alfonso Soriano AS .20 .50
228 Carlos Beltran AS .20 .50
229 Albert Pujols AS .40 1.00
230 Jason Bay AS .12 .30
231 Edgar Renteria AS .12 .30
232 David Wright AS .25 .60
233 Chase Utley AS .20 .50
234 Paul LoDuca AS .12 .30
235 Brad Penny AS .12 .30
236 Derrick Turnbow AS .12 .30
237 Mark Redman AS .12 .30
238 Francisco Liriano AS .30 .75
239 A.J. Pierzynski AS .12 .30
240 Grady Sizemore AS .20 .50
241 Jose Contreras AS .12 .30
242 Jermaine Dye AS .12 .30
243 Jason Schmidt AS .12 .30
244 Nomar Garciaparra AS .20 .50
245 Scott Kazmir AS .20 .50
246 Johan Santana AS .20 .50
247 Chris Capuano AS .12 .30
248 Magglio Ordonez AS .20 .50
249 Gary Matthews Jr. AS .12 .30
250 Carlos Lee AS .12 .30
251 David Eckstein AS .12 .30
252 Michael Young AS .12 .30
253 Matt Holliday AS .30 .75
254 Lance Berkman AS .20 .50
255 Scott Rolen AS .20 .50
256 Bronson Arroyo AS .20 .50
257 Barry Zito AS .20 .50
258 Brian McCann AS .20 .50
259 Jose Lopez AS .12 .30
260 Chris Carpenter AS .20 .50
261 Roy Halladay AS .20 .50
262 Jim Thome AS .20 .50
263 Dan Uggla AS .20 .50
264 Mariano Rivera AS .40 1.00
265 Roy Oswalt AS .20 .50
266 Tom Gordon AS .12 .30
267 Troy Glaus AS .12 .30
268 Bobby Jenks AS .12 .30
269 Freddy Sanchez AS .12 .30
270 Paul Konerko AS .20 .50
271 Joe Mauer AS .20 .50
272 B.J. Ryan AS .12 .30
273 Ryan Howard AS .25 .60
274 Brian Fuentes AS .12 .30
275 Miguel Cabrera AS .30 .75
276 Brandon Webb AS .20 .50
277 Mark Buehrle AS .20 .50
278 Trevor Hoffman AS .20 .50
279 Jonathan Papelbon AS .60 1.50
280 Andruw Jones AS .12 .30
281 Miguel Tejada AS .20 .50
282 Carlos Zambrano AS .20 .50
283 Ryan Howard HRD .25 .60
284 David Wright HRD .25 .60
285 Miguel Cabrera HRD .30 .75
286 David Ortiz HRD .30 .75
287 Jermaine Dye HRD .12 .30
288 Miguel Tejada HRD .20 .50
289 Lance Berkman HRD .20 .50
290 Troy Glaus HRD .12 .30
291 D.Wright .25 .60
T.Glavine TL
292 R.Howard .25 .60
T.Gordon TL

293 M.Cabrera .30 .75
D.Willis TL
294 A.Jones .30 .75
J.Smoltz TL
295 A.Soriano .20 .50
A.Soriano TL
296 A.Pujols .40 1.00
C.Carpenter TL
297 A.Dunn .20 .50
B.Arroyo TL
298 L.Berkman .20 .50
R.Oswalt TL
299 C.Capuano .60 1.50
P.Fielder TL
300 F.Sanchez .12 .30
J.Bay TL
301 C.Zambrano .20 .50
J.Pierre TL
302 A.Gonzalez .25 .60
T.Hoffman TL
303 D.Lowe .12 .30
R.Furcal TL
304 O.Vizquel .20 .50
J.Schmidt TL
305 B.Webb .20 .50
C.Tracy TL
306 M.Holliday .30 .75
G.Atkins TL
307 A.Rodriguez .40 1.00
C.Wang TL
308 C.Schilling .30 .75
D.Ortiz TL
309 R.Halladay .20 .50
V.Wells TL
310 M.Tejada .20 .50
E.Bedard TL
311 C.Crawford .20 .50
S.Kazmir TL
312 J.Bonderman .20 .50
M.Ordonez TL
313 J.Morneau .20 .50
J.Santana TL
314 J.Garland .12 .30
J.Dye TL
315 T.Hafner .20 .50
C.Sabathia TL
316 E.Brown .12 .30
M.Grudzielanek TL
317 F.Thomas .30 .75
B.Zito TL
318 J.Weaver .40 1.00
V.Guerrero TL
319 M.Young .12 .30
G.Matthews TL
320 I.Suzuki .40 1.00
J.Putz TL
321 D.Jeter .75 2.00
R.Cano CD
322 C.Carpenter .20 .50
M.Mulder CD
323 J.Schmidt .20 .50
T.Hoffman CD
324 D.Wright .25 .60
P.LoDuca CD
325 L.Berkman .20 .50
R.Oswalt CD
326 D.Jeter .75 2.00
J.Reyes CD
327 C.Floyd .25 .60
D.Wright CD
328 F.Liriano .30 .75
J.Santana CD
329 J.Drew .25 .60
S.Drew CD
330 J.Weaver .40 1.00
J.Weaver CD

2006 Topps Update 1st Edition

*1ST ED 1-132: 3X TO 8X BASIC
*1ST ED 133-170: .6X TO 1.5X BASIC RC
*1ST ED 171-330: 2X TO 5X BASIC
STATED ODDS 1:36 HOB, 1:12 HTA

2006 Topps Update Black

*BLACK 1-132: 20X TO 50X BASIC
*BLACK RC: 4X TO 10X BASIC
*BLACK 171-330: 12X TO 30X BASIC
STATED ODDS 1:7 HTA
STATED PRINT RUN 55 SER.#'d SETS

2006 Topps Update Gold

*GOLD 1-132: 2X TO 5X BASIC
*GOLD 133-170: .4X TO 1X BASIC RC
*GOLD 171-330: 1.2X TO 3X BASIC
STATED ODDS 1:4 HOB, 1:2 HTA, 1:6 RET
STATED PRINT RUN 2006 SER.#'d SETS

2006 Topps Update All Star Stitches

STATED ODDS 1:43 H,1:15 HTA,1:53 R
PATCH ODDS 1:2300 HOBBY,1:377 HTA
PATCH PRINT RUN 10 SER. #'d SETS
NO PATCH PRICING DUE TO SCARCITY
AJ Andruw Jones Jsy 5.00 12.00
AJP A.J. Pierzynski Jsy 4.00 10.00
AP Albert Pujols Jsy 12.50 30.00
AR Alex Rodriguez Jsy 6.00 15.00
AS Alfonso Soriano Jsy 5.00 12.00
BA Bronson Arroyo Jsy 5.00 12.00
BF Brian Fuentes Jsy 3.00 8.00
BJ Bobby Jenks Jsy 4.00 10.00
BM Brian McCann Jsy 6.00 15.00
BP Brad Penny Jsy 4.00 10.00
BR B.J. Ryan Jsy 4.00 10.00
BW Brandon Webb Jsy 5.00 12.00
CB Carlos Beltran Jsy 4.00 10.00
CC Chris Carpenter Jsy 5.00 12.00
CFC Chris Capuano Jsy 3.00 8.00
CL Carlos Lee Jsy 4.00 10.00
CU Chase Utley Jsy 5.00 12.00
CZ Carlos Zambrano Jsy 4.00 10.00
DE David Eckstein Jsy 6.00 15.00
DO David Ortiz Jsy 6.00 15.00
DT Derrick Turnbow Jsy 3.00 8.00
DU Dan Uggla Jsy 4.00 10.00
DW David Wright Jsy 8.00 20.00
ER Edgar Renteria Jsy 4.00 10.00
FS Freddy Sanchez Jsy 5.00 12.00
GM Gary Matthews Jr. Jsy 3.00 8.00
GS Grady Sizemore Jsy 5.00 12.00
IR Ivan Rodriguez Jsy 5.00 12.00
JB Jason Bay Jsy 6.00 15.00
JC Jose Contreras Jsy 4.00 10.00
JD Jermaine Dye Jsy 4.00 10.00
JDS Jason Schmidt Jsy 4.00 10.00
JL Jose Lopez Jsy 3.00 8.00
JM Joe Mauer Jsy 5.00 12.00
JP Jonathan Papelbon Jsy 8.00 20.00
JR Jose Reyes Jsy 3.00 8.00
JS Johan Santana Jsy 4.00 10.00
JT Jim Thome Jsy 5.00 12.00
KR Kenny Rogers Jsy 4.00 10.00
LB Lance Berkman Jsy 4.00 10.00
MAR Mark Redman Jsy 4.00 10.00
MB Mark Buehrle Jsy 4.00 10.00
MC Miguel Cabrera Jsy 5.00 12.00
MH Matt Holliday Jsy 5.00 12.00
ML Mark Loretta Jsy 4.00 10.00
MO Magglio Ordonez Jsy 4.00 10.00
MR Mariano Rivera Jsy 5.00 12.00
MT Miguel Tejada Jsy 3.00 8.00
MY Michael Young Jsy 3.00 8.00
PK Paul Konerko Jsy 4.00 10.00
PL Paul LoDuca Jsy 3.00 8.00
RC Robinson Cano Jsy 6.00 15.00
RH Roy Halladay Jsy 4.00 10.00
RJH Ryan Howard Jsy 12.50 30.00
RO Roy Oswalt Jsy 3.00 8.00
SK Scott Kazmir Jsy 4.00 10.00
SR Scott Rolen Jsy 5.00 12.00
TEG Troy Glaus Jsy 3.00 8.00
TG Tom Gordon Jsy 4.00 10.00
TH Trevor Hoffman Jsy 3.00 8.00
TMG Tom Glavine Jsy 5.00 12.00
VG Vladimir Guerrero Jsy 4.00 10.00
VW Vernon Wells Jsy 4.00 10.00

2006 Topps Update All Star Stitches Dual

STATED ODDS 1:2550 HOBBY,1:752 HTA
STATED PRINT RUN 50 SER.#'d SETS
CJ A.Jones/M.Cabrera 10.00 25.00
HS J.Santana/R.Halladay 10.00 25.00
HT J.Thome Jsy/R.Howard Jsy 20.00 50.00
MM J.Mauer/B.McCann 10.00 25.00
PW D.Wright/A.Pujols 30.00 60.00
RH M.Rivera Jsy/T.Hoffman Jsy 30.00 60.00
RO D.Ortiz/A.Rodriguez 20.00 50.00
SS I.Suzuki/A.Soriano 20.00 50.00
TG M.Tejada/V.Guerrero 10.00 25.00
WS G.Sizemore Jsy/V.Wells Jsy 12.50 30.00

2006 Topps Update Barry Bonds 715

STATED ODDS 1:36 H,1:36 HTA,1:36 R
BB Barry Bonds 1.50 4.00

2006 Topps Update Barry Bonds 715 Relics

ODDS 1:5000 H,1:1827 HTA,1:5950 R
STATED PRINT RUN 715 SER.#'d SETS
BB Barry Bonds Jsy 20.00 50.00

2006 Topps Update Box Bottoms

HTA1 Shawn Green .20 .50
HTA2 Austin Kearns .20 .50
HTA3 Brandon Phillips .20 .50
HTA4 Jered Weaver .60 1.50
HTA5 Carlos Lee .20 .50
HTA6 Bobby Abreu .20 .50
HTA7 Shea Hillenbrand .20 .50
HTA8 Cole Hamels .60 1.50
HTA9 Greg Maddux .60 1.50
HTA10 B.J. Upton .20 .50
HTA11 Aubrey Huff .20 .50
HTA12 Stephen Drew .40 1.00
HTA13 Sean Casey .20 .50
HTA14 Jeff Conine .20 .50
HTA15 Johan Santana .50 1.25
Francisco Liriano
HTA16 Melky Cabrera .30 .75

2006 Topps Update Rookie Debut

COMPLETE SET (45) 15.00 40.00
STATED ODDS 1:4 HOB, 1:4 RET
RD1 Joel Zumaya 1.00 2.50
RD2 Ian Kinsler 1.25 3.00
RD3 Kenji Johjima 1.00 2.50
RD4 Josh Barfield .40 1.00
RD5 Nick Markakis .75 2.00
RD6 Dan Uggla .60 1.50
RD7 Eric Reed .40 1.00
RD8 Carlos Martinez .40 1.00
RD9 Angel Pagan .40 1.00
RD10 Jason Childers .40 1.00
RD11 Ruddy Lugo .40 1.00
RD12 James Loney .60 1.50
RD13 Fernando Nieve .40 1.00
RD14 Reggie Abercrombie .40 1.00
RD15 Boone Logan .40 1.00
RD16 Brian Bannister .40 1.00
RD17 Ricky Nolasco .40 1.00
RD18 Willie Eyre .40 1.00
RD19 Fabio Castro .40 1.00
RD20 Jordan Tata .40 1.00
RD21 Taylor Buchholz .40 1.00
RD22 Sean Marshall .40 1.00
RD23 John Rheinecker .40 1.00
RD24 Casey Janssen .40 1.00
RD25 Russ Martin .60 1.50
RD26 Yusmeiro Petit .40 1.00
RD27 Kendry Morales 1.00 2.50
RD28 Alay Soler .40 1.00
RD29 Jered Weaver 1.25 3.00
RD30 Matt Kemp 1.00 2.50
RD31 Enrique Gonzalez .40 1.00
RD32 Lastings Milledge .40 1.00
RD33 Jamie Shields 1.25 3.00
RD34 David Pauley .40 1.00
RD35 Zach Jackson .40 1.00
RD36 Zach Minor .40 1.00
RD37 Jon Lester 1.50 4.00
RD38 Chad Billingsley .60 1.50
RD39 Scott Thorman .40 1.00
RD40 Anibal Sanchez .40 1.00
RD41 Mike Thompson .40 1.00
RD42 T.J. Beam .40 1.00
RD43 Stephen Drew .75 2.00
RD44 Joe Saunders .40 1.00
RD45 Carlos Quentin .60 1.50

2006 Topps Update Rookie Debut Autographs

A ODDS 1:10,600 H,1:4416 HTA,1:15,500 R
B ODDS 1:5600 H, 1:2163 HTA,1:7500 R
C ODDS 1:2200 H, 1:815 HTA,1:2650 R
D ODDS 1:1180 H, 1:415 HTA,1:1500 R
NO GROUP A PRICING DUE TO SCARCITY
AL Adam Loewen B 6.00 15.00
BL Bobby Livingston C 6.00 15.00
EF Emiliano Fruto C 6.00 15.00
FC Fausto Carmona C 6.00 15.00
JL Jon Lester D 8.00 20.00
JS Jeremy Sowers B 6.00 15.00
MN Mike Napoli D 12.50 30.00
MP Martin Prado D 8.00 20.00
RN Ricky Nolasco D 6.00 15.00
ST Scott Thorman C 6.00 15.00
YP Yusmeiro Petit D 6.00 15.00

2006 Topps Update Touch 'Em All Base Relics

STATED ODDS 1:610 HOBBY,1:90 HTA
AP Albert Pujols 12.50 30.00
AR Alex Rodriguez 10.00 25.00
CB Carlos Beltran 5.00 12.00
DO David Ortiz 8.00 20.00
DW David Wright 10.00 25.00
IS Ichiro Suzuki 10.00 25.00
JM Joe Mauer 6.00 15.00
MT Miguel Tejada 5.00 12.00
MY Michael Young 5.00 12.00
RH Ryan Howard 10.00 25.00

2006 Topps All-Star FanFest

1 Ichiro Suzuki 1.25 3.00
2 Roberto Clemente 2.50 6.00
3 Albert Pujols 1.25 3.00
4 Mickey Mantle 3.00 8.00
5 Alex Rodriguez 1.25 3.00

2006 Topps National 1955-56 VIP Promos

211 Mickey Mantle 55 6.00 15.00
341 Frank Robinson 56 1.25 3.00
342 Duke Snider 56 HR 1.25 3.00
343 Brooks Robinson 56 1.25 3.00
344 Mickey Mantle 56 TC 6.00 15.00

2007 Topps Pre-Production

COMPLETE SET (3) 4.00 10.00
1 David Ortiz 1.25 3.00
2 David Wright 1.00 2.50
3 Ryan Howard 1.00 2.50

2007 Topps

COMP.HOBBY SET (661) 40.00 80.00
COMP.HOLIDAY SET (661) 40.00 80.00
COMP.CARDINALS SET (661) 40.00 80.00
COMP.CUBS SET (661) 40.00 80.00
COMP.DODGERS SET (661) 40.00 80.00
COMP.RED SOX SET (661) 40.00 80.00
COMP.YANKEES SET (661) 40.00 80.00
COMP.SET w/o VAR. (661) 40.00 80.00
COMPLETE SERIES 1 (330) 15.00 40.00
COMP.SERIES 1 w/o #40 (329) 10.00 25.00
COMPLETE SERIES 2 (331) 25.00 50.00
COMMON CARD (1-330) .07 .20
COMMON RC .20 .50
SER.1 VAR. ODDS 1:3700 WAL-MART
SER.2 VAR.ODDS 1:30 HOBBY
NO SER.1 VAR.PRICING DUE TO SCARTIY
OVERALL PLATE SER.1 ODDS 1:98 HTA
OVERALL PLATE SER.2 ODDS 1:139 HTA
PLATE PRINT RUN 1 SET PER COLOR
BLACK-CYAN-MAGENTA-YELLOW ISSUED
NO PLATE PRICING DUE TO SCARCITY
1 John Lackey .12 .30
2 Nick Swisher .12 .30
3 Brad Lidge .07 .20
4 Bengie Molina .07 .20
5 Bobby Abreu .07 .20
6 Edgar Renteria .07 .20
7 Mickey Mantle .60 1.50
8 Preston Wilson .07 .20
9 Ryan Dempster .07 .20
10 C.C. Sabathia .12 .30
11 Julio Lugo .07 .20
12 J.D. Drew .07 .20
13 Miguel Batista .07 .20
14 Eliezer Alfonzo .07 .20
15a Andrew Miller RC .75 2.00
15b A.Miller Posed RC .75 2.00
16 Jason Varitek .20 .50
17 Saul Rivera .07 .20
18 Orlando Hernandez .07 .20
19 Alfredo Amezaga .07 .20
20a D.Young Face Right (RC) .30 .75
20b D.Young Face Left (RC) .30 .75
21 Chris Britton .07 .20
22 Corey Patterson .07 .20
23 Josh Bard .07 .20
24 Tom Gordon .07 .20
25 Gary Matthews .07 .20
26 Jason Jennings .07 .20
27 Joey Gathright .07 .20
28 Brandon Inge .07 .20
29 Pat Neshek .40 1.00
30 Bronson Arroyo .07 .20
31 Jay Payton .07 .20
32 Andy Pettitte .12 .30
33 Ervin Santana .07 .20
34 Paul Konerko .12 .30
35 Joel Zumaya .07 .20
36 Gregg Zaun .07 .20
37 Tony Gwynn Jr. .07 .20
38 Adam LaRoche .07 .20
39 Jim Edmonds .12 .30
40a D.Jeter w Mantle/Bush 5.00 12.00
40b Derek Jeter .50 1.25
41 Rich Hill .07 .20
42 Livan Hernandez .07 .20
43 Aubrey Huff .07 .20
44 Todd Greene .07 .20
45 Andre Ethier .12 .30
46 Jeremy Sowers .07 .20
47 Ben Broussard .07 .20
48 Darren Oliver .07 .20
49 Nook Logan .07 .20
50 Miguel Cabrera .20 .50
51 Carlos Lee .07 .20
52 Jose Castillo .07 .20
53 Mike Piazza .20 .50
54 Daniel Cabrera .07 .20
55 Cole Hamels .15 .40
56 Mark Loretta .07 .20
57 Brian Fuentes .07 .20
58 Todd Coffey .07 .20
59 Brent Clevlen .07 .20
60 John Smoltz .20 .50
61 Jason Grilli .07 .20
62 Dan Wheeler .07 .20
63 Scott Proctor .07 .20
64 Bobby Kielty .07 .20
65 Dan Uggla .07 .20
66 Lyle Overbay .07 .20
67 Geoff Jenkins .07 .20
68 Michael Barrett .07 .20
69 Casey Fossum .07 .20
70 Ivan Rodriguez .12 .30
71 Jose Lopez .07 .20
72 Jake Westbrook .07 .20
73 Moises Alou .07 .20
74 Jose Valverde .07 .20
75 Jered Weaver .12 .30
76 Lastings Milledge .12 .30
77 Austin Kearns .07 .20
78 Adam Loewen .07 .20
79 Josh Barfield .07 .20
80 Johan Santana .12 .30
81 Ian Kinsler .12 .30
82 Ian Snell .07 .20
83 Mike Lowell .07 .20
84 Elizardo Ramirez .07 .20
85 Scott Rolen .12 .30
86 Shannon Stewart .07 .20
87 Alexis Gomez .07 .20
88 Jimmy Gobble .07 .20
89 Jamey Carroll .07 .20
90 Chipper Jones .20 .50
91 Carlos Silva .07 .20
92 Joe Crede .07 .20
93 Mike Napoli .07 .20
94 Willy Taveras .07 .20
95 Rafael Furcal .07 .20
96 Phil Nevin .07 .20
97 Dave Bush .07 .20
98 Marcus Giles .07 .20
99 Joe Blanton .07 .20
100 Dontrelle Willis .07 .20
101 Scott Kazmir .12 .30
102 Jeff Kent .07 .20
103 Pedro Feliz .07 .20
104 Johnny Estrada .07 .20
105 Travis Hafner .07 .20
106 Ryan Garko .07 .20
107 Rafael Soriano .07 .20
108 Wes Helms .07 .20
109 Billy Wagner .07 .20
110 Aaron Rowand .07 .20
111 Felipe Lopez .07 .20
112 Jeff Conine .07 .20
113 Nick Markakis .15 .40
114 John Koronka .07 .20
115 B.J. Ryan .07 .20
116 Tim Wakefield .12 .30
117 David Ross .07 .20
118 Emil Brown .07 .20
119 Michael Cuddyer .07 .20
120 Jason Giambi .07 .20
121 Alex Cintron .07 .20
122 Luke Scott .07 .20
123 Chone Figgins .07 .20
124 Huston Street .07 .20
125 Carlos Delgado .07 .20
126 Daryle Ward .07 .20
127 Chris Duncan .07 .20
128 Damian Miller .07 .20
129 Aramis Ramirez .07 .20
130 Albert Pujols .25 .60
131 Chris Snyder .07 .20
132 Ray Durham .07 .20
133 Gary Sheffield .07 .20
134 Mike Jacobs .07 .20
135a Troy Tulowitzki (RC) .60 1.50
135b T.Tulowitzki Throw (RC) .60 1.50
136 Jon Rauch .07 .20
137 Jay Gibbons .07 .20
138 Adrian Gonzalez .15 .40
139 Prince Fielder .12 .30
140 Freddy Sanchez .07 .20
141 Rich Aurilia .07 .20
142 Trot Nixon .07 .20
143 Vicente Padilla .07 .20
144 Jack Wilson .07 .20
145 Jake Peavy .07 .20
146 Luke Hudson .07 .20
147 Javier Vazquez .07 .20
148 Scott Podsednik .07 .20
149 M.Ordonez .12 .30
I.Rodriguez CC
150 Todd Helton .12 .30
151 Kendry Morales .07 .20
152 Adam Everett .07 .20
153 Bob Wickman .07 .20
154 Bill Hall .07 .20
155 Jeremy Bonderman .07 .20
156 Ryan Theriot .07 .20
157 Rocco Baldelli .07 .20
158 Noah Lowry .07 .20
159 Jason Michaels .07 .20
160 Justin Verlander .20 .50
161 Eduardo Perez .07 .20
162 Chris Ray .07 .20
163 Dave Roberts .12 .30
164 Zach Duke .07 .20
165 Mark Buehrle .12 .30
166 Hank Blalock .07 .20
167 Royce Clayton .07 .20
168 Mark Teahen .07 .20
169 Todd Jones .07 .20
170 Chien-Ming Wang .12 .30
171 Nick Punto .07 .20
172 Morgan Ensberg .07 .20
173 Rob Mackowiak .07 .20
174 Frank Catalanotto .07 .20
175 Matt Murton .07 .20
176 A.Soriano .12 .30
C.Beltran CC
177 Francisco Cordero .07 .20
178 Jason Marquis .07 .20
179 Joe Nathan .07 .20
180 Roy Halladay .12 .30
181 Melvin Mora .07 .20
182 Ramon Ortiz .07 .20
183 Jose Valentin .07 .20
184 Gil Meche .07 .20
185 B.J. Upton .07 .20
186 Grady Sizemore .12 .30
187 Matt Cain .12 .30
188 Eric Byrnes .07 .20
189 Carl Crawford .12 .30
190 J.J. Putz .07 .20
191 Cla Meredith .07 .20
192 Matt Capps .07 .20
193 Rod Barajas .07 .20
194 Edwin Encarnacion .20 .50
195 James Loney .07 .20
196 Johnny Damon .12 .30
197 Freddy Garcia .07 .20
198 Mike Redmond .07 .20
199 Ryan Shealy .07 .20
200 Carlos Beltran .12 .30
201 Chuck James .07 .20
202 Mark Ellis .07 .20
203 Brad Ausmus .07 .20
204 Juan Rivera .07 .20
205 Cory Sullivan .07 .20
206 Ben Sheets .07 .20
207 Mark Mulder .07 .20
208 Carlos Quentin .07 .20
209 Jonathan Broxton .07 .20
210 Kazuo Matsui .07 .20
211 Armando Benitez .07 .20
212 Richie Sexson .07 .20
213 Josh Johnson .20 .50
214 Brian Schneider .07 .20
215 Craig Monroe .07 .20
216 Chris Duffy .07 .20
217 Chris Coste .07 .20
218 Clay Hensley .07 .20
219 Chris Gomez .07 .20
220 Hideki Matsui .20 .50
221 Robinson Tejeda .07 .20
222 Scott Hatteberg .07 .20
223 Jeff Francis .07 .20
224 Matt Thornton .07 .20
225 Robinson Cano .12 .30
226 Chicago White Sox .07 .20
227 Oakland Athletics .07 .20
228 St. Louis Cardinals .07 .20
229 New York Mets .07 .20
230 Barry Zito .12 .30
231 Baltimore Orioles .07 .20
232 Seattle Mariners .07 .20
233 Houston Astros .07 .20
234 Pittsburgh Pirates .07 .20
235 Reed Johnson .07 .20
236 Boston Red Sox .20 .50
237 Cincinnati Reds .07 .20
238 Philadelphia Phillies .07 .20
239 New York Yankees .20 .50
240 Chris Carpenter .12 .30
241 Atlanta Braves .07 .20
242 San Francisco Giants .07 .20
243 Joe Torre MG .12 .30
244 Tampa Bay Devil Rays .07 .20
245 Chad Tracy .07 .20
246 Clint Hurdle MG .07 .20
247 Mike Scioscia MG .07 .20
248 Ron Gardenhire MG .07 .20
249 Tony LaRussa MG .12 .30
250 Anibal Sanchez .07 .20
251 Charlie Manuel MG .07 .20
252 John Gibbons MG .07 .20
253 Jim Tracy MG .07 .20
254 Jerry Narron MG .07 .20
255 Brad Penny .07 .20
256 Bobby Cox MG .07 .20
257 Bob Melvin MG .07 .20
258 Mike Hargrove MG .07 .20
259 Phil Garner MG .07 .20
260 David Wright .15 .40
261 Vinny Rottino (RC) .20 .50
262 Ryan Braun RC .20 .50
263 Kevin Kouzmanoff (RC) .20 .50
264 David Murphy (RC) .20 .50
265 Jimmy Rollins .12 .30
266 Joe Maddon MG .12 .30
267 Grady Little MG .07 .20
268 Ryan Sweeney (RC) .20 .50
269 Fred Lewis (RC) .30 .75
270 Alfonso Soriano .12 .30
271a Delwyn Young (RC) .20 .50
271b D.Young Swing (RC) .20 .50
272 Jeff Salazar (RC) .20 .50
273 Miguel Montero (RC) .20 .50
274 Shawn Riggans (RC) .20 .50
275 Greg Maddux .25 .60
276 Brian Stokes (RC) .20 .50
277 Philip Humber (RC) .20 .50
278 Scott Moore (RC) .20 .50
279 Adam Lind (RC) .20 .50
280 Curt Schilling .12 .30
281 Chris Narveson (RC) .20 .50
282 Oswaldo Navarro RC .20 .50
283 Drew Anderson RC .20 .50
284 Jerry Owens (RC) .20 .50
285 Stephen Drew .07 .20
286 Joaquin Arias (RC) .20 .50
287 Jose Garcia RC .20 .50
288 Shane Youman RC .20 .50
289 Brian Burres (RC) .20 .50
290 Matt Holliday .20 .50
291 Ryan Feierabend (RC) .20 .50
292a Josh Fields (RC) .20 .50
292b J.Fields Running (RC) .20 .50
293 Glen Perkins (RC) .20 .50
294 Mike Rabelo RC .20 .50
295 Jorge Posada .12 .30
296 Ubaldo Jimenez (RC) .60 1.50
297 Brad Ausmus GG .07 .20
298 Eric Chavez GG .07 .20
299 Orlando Hudson GG .07 .20
300 Vladimir Guerrero .12 .30
301 Derek Jeter GG .50 1.25
302 Scott Rolen GG .12 .30
303 Mark Grudzielanek GG .07 .20
304 Kenny Rogers GG .07 .20
305 Frank Thomas .20 .50
306 Mike Cameron GG .07 .20
307 Torii Hunter GG .07 .20
308 Albert Pujols GG .25 .60
309 Mark Teixeira GG .12 .30
310 Jonathan Papelbon .20 .50
311 Greg Maddux GG .25 .60
312 Carlos Beltran GG .12 .30
313 Ichiro Suzuki GG .25 .60
314 Andruw Jones GG .07 .20
315 Manny Ramirez .20 .50
316 Vernon Wells GG .07 .20
317 Omar Vizquel GG .12 .30
318 Ivan Rodriguez GG .12 .30
319 Brandon Webb CY .12 .30
320 Magglio Ordonez .12 .30
321 Johan Santana CY .12 .30
322 Ryan Howard MVP .15 .40
323 Justin Morneau MVP .12 .30
324 Hanley Ramirez ROY .12 .30
325 Joe Mauer .15 .40
326 Justin Verlander ROY .20 .50
327 B.Abreu .50 1.25
D.Jeter CC
328 C.Delgado .15 .40
D.Wright CC
329 Y.Molina .25 .60
A.Pujols CC
330 Ryan Howard .15 .40
331 Kelly Johnson .07 .20
332 Chris Young .07 .20
333 Mark Kotsay .07 .20
334 A.J. Burnett .07 .20
335 Brian McCann .07 .20
336 Woody Williams .07 .20
337 Jason Isringhausen .07 .20
338 Juan Pierre .07 .20
339 Jonny Gomes .07 .20
340 Roger Clemens .25 .60
341 Akinori Iwamura RC .50 1.25
342 Bengie Molina .07 .20
343 Shin-Soo Choo .12 .30
344 Kenji Johjima .20 .50
345 Joe Borowski .07 .20
346 Shawn Green .07 .20
347 Chicago Cubs .07 .20
348 Rodrigo Lopez .07 .20
349 Brian Giles .07 .20
350 Chase Utley .12 .30
351 Mark DeRosa .07 .20
352 Carl Pavano .07 .20
353 Kyle Lohse .07 .20
354 Chris Iannetta .07 .20
355 Oliver Perez .07 .20
356 Curtis Granderson .15 .40
357 Sean Casey .07 .20
358 Jason Tyner .07 .20
359 Jon Garland .07 .20
360 David Ortiz .20 .50
361 Adam Kennedy .07 .20
362 Chris Burke .07 .20
363 Bobby Crosby .07 .20
364 Conor Jackson .07 .20
365 Tim Hudson .12 .30
366 Rickie Weeks .07 .20
367 Cristian Guzman .07 .20
368 Mark Prior .12 .30
369 Ben Zobrist .12 .30
370 Troy Glaus .07 .20
371 Kenny Lofton .07 .20
372 Shane Victorino .07 .20
373 Cliff Lee .12 .30
374 Adrian Beltre .20 .50
375 Miguel Olivo .07 .20
376 Endy Chavez .07 .20
377 Zack Segovia (RC) .20 .50
378 Ramon Hernandez .07 .20
379 Chris Young .07 .20
380 Jason Schmidt .07 .20
381 Ronny Paulino .07 .20
382 Kevin Millwood .07 .20
383 Jon Lester .12 .30
384 Alex Gonzalez .07 .20
385 Brad Hawpe .07 .20
386 Placido Polanco .07 .20
387 Nate Robertson .07 .20
388 Torii Hunter .07 .20
389 Gavin Floyd .07 .20
390 Roy Oswalt .12 .30
391 Kelvim Escobar .07 .20
392 Craig Wilson .07 .20
393 Milton Bradley .07 .20
394 Aaron Hill .07 .20
395 Matt Diaz .07 .20
396 Chris Capuano .07 .20
397 Juan Encarnacion .07 .20
398 Jacque Jones .07 .20
399 James Shields .07 .20
400 Ichiro Suzuki .25 .60
401 Matt Kemp .15 .40
402 Matt Morris .07 .20
403 Casey Blake .07 .20
404 Corey Hart .07 .20
405 Josh Willingham .12 .30
406 Ryan Madson .07 .20
407 Nick Johnson .07 .20
408 Kevin Millar .07 .20
409 Khalil Greene .07 .20
410 Tom Glavine .12 .30
411a Jason Bay .12 .30
411b Jason Bay No Sig 2.00 5.00
412 Gerald Laird .07 .20
413 Coco Crisp .07 .20
414 Brandon Phillips .07 .20
415 Aaron Cook .07 .20
416 Mark Redman .07 .20
417 Mike Maroth .07 .20
418 Boof Bonser .07 .20
419 Jorge Cantu .07 .20
420 Jeff Weaver .07 .20
421 Melky Cabrera .07 .20
422 Francisco Rodriguez .12 .30
423 Mike Lamb .07 .20
424 Dan Haren .07 .20
425 Tomo Ohka .07 .20
426 Jeff Francoeur .20 .50
427 Randy Wolf .07 .20
428 So Taguchi .07 .20
429 Carlos Zambrano .12 .30
430 Justin Morneau .12 .30
431 Luis Gonzalez .07 .20
432 Takashi Saito .07 .20
433 Brandon Morrow RC 1.00 2.50
434 Victor Martinez .12 .30
435 Felix Hernandez .12 .30
436 Ricky Nolasco .07 .20
437a Paul LoDuca .07 .20
437b Paul LoDuca No Sig 2.00 5.00
438 Chad Cordero .07 .20
439 Miguel Tejada .12 .30
440 Mark Teixeira .12 .30
441 Pat Burrell .07 .20
442 Paul Maholm .07 .20
443 Mike Cameron .07 .20
444 Josh Beckett .07 .20
445 Pablo Ozuna .07 .20
446 Jaret Wright .07 .20
447 Angel Berroa .07 .20
448 Fernando Rodney .07 .20
449 Francisco Liriano .07 .20
450 Ken Griffey Jr. .40 1.00
451 Bobby Jenks .07 .20
452 Mike Mussina .12 .30
453 Howie Kendrick .07 .20
454 Milwaukee Brewers .07 .20
455 Dan Johnson .07 .20
456 Ted Lilly .07 .20
457 Mike Hampton .07 .20
458 J.J. Hardy .07 .20
459 Jeff Suppan .07 .20
460 Jose Reyes .12 .30
461 Jae Seo .07 .20
462 Edgar Gonzalez .07 .20
463 Russell Martin .07 .20
464 Omar Vizquel .12 .30
465 Jhonny Peralta .07 .20
466 Raul Ibanez .12 .30
467 Hanley Ramirez .12 .30
468 Kerry Wood .07 .20
469 Ryan Church .07 .20
470 Gary Sheffield .07 .20
471 David Wells .07 .20
472 David Dellucci .07 .20
473 Xavier Nady .07 .20
474 Michael Young .07 .20
475 Kevin Youkilis .07 .20
476 Aaron Harang .07 .20
477 Brian Lawrence .07 .20
478 Octavio Dotel .07 .20
479 Chris Shelton .07 .20
480 Matt Garza .07 .20
481a Jim Thome .12 .30
481b Jim Thome No Sig 2.00 5.00
482 Jose Contreras .07 .20
483 Kris Benson .07 .20
484 John Maine .07 .20
485 Tadahito Iguchi .07 .20
486 Wandy Rodriguez .07 .20
487 Eric Chavez .07 .20
488 Vernon Wells .07 .20
489 Doug Davis .07 .20
490 Andruw Jones .07 .20
491 David Eckstein .07 .20
492a Michael Barrett .07 .20
492b John Buck 2.00 5.00
493 Greg Norton .07 .20
494 Orlando Hudson .07 .20
495 Wilson Betemit .07 .20
496 Ryan Klesko .07 .20
497 Fausto Carmona .07 .20
498 Jarrod Washburn .07 .20
499 Aaron Boone .07 .20
500 Pedro Martinez .12 .30
501 Mike O'Connor .07 .20
502 Brian Roberts .07 .20
503 Jeff Cirillo .07 .20
504 Brett Myers .07 .20
505 Jose Bautista .12 .30
506 Akinori Otsuka .07 .20
507 Shea Hillenbrand .07 .20
508 Ryan Langerhans .07 .20
509 Josh Fogg .07 .20
510 Alex Rodriguez .25 .60
511 Kenny Rogers .07 .20
512 Jason Kubel .07 .20
513 Jermaine Dye .07 .20
514 Mark Grudzielanek .07 .20
515 Josh Phelps .07 .20
516 Bartolo Colon .07 .20
517 Craig Biggio .12 .30
518 Esteban Loaiza .07 .20
519 Alex Rios .07 .20
520 Adam Dunn .12 .30
521 Derrick Turnbow .07 .20
522 Anthony Reyes .07 .20
523 Derrek Lee .07 .20
524 Ty Wigginton .07 .20
525 Jeremy Hermida .07 .20
526 Derek Lowe .07 .20
527 Randy Winn .07 .20
528 Paul Byrd .07 .20
529 Chris Snelling .07 .20
530 Brandon Webb .12 .30
531 Julio Franco .07 .20
532 Jose Vidro .07 .20
533 Erik Bedard .07 .20
534 Termel Sledge .07 .20
535 Jon Lieber .07 .20
536 Tom Gorzelanny .07 .20
537 Kip Wells .07 .20
538 Wily Mo Pena .07 .20
539 Eric Milton .07 .20

540 Chad Billingsley .12 .30
541 David DeJesus .07 .20
542 Omar Infante .07 .20
543 Rondell White .07 .20
544 Juan Uribe .07 .20
545 Miguel Cairo .07 .20
546 Orlando Cabrera .07 .20
547 Byung-Hyun Kim .07 .20
548 Jason Kendall .07 .20
549 Horacio Ramirez .07 .20
550 Trevor Hoffman .12 .30
551 Ronnie Belliard .07 .20
552 Chris Woodward .07 .20
553 Ramon Martinez .07 .20
554 Elizardo Ramirez .07 .20
555 Andy Marte .07 .20
556 John Patterson .07 .20
557 Scott Olsen .07 .20
558 Steve Trachsel .07 .20
559 Doug Mientkiewicz .07 .20
560 Randy Johnson .20 .50
561 Chan Ho Park .12 .30
562 Jamie Moyer .07 .20
563 Mike Gonzalez .07 .20
564 Nelson Cruz .20 .50
565 Alex Cora .12 .30
566 Ryan Freel .07 .20
567 Chris Stewart RC .20 .50
568 Carlos Guillen .07 .20
569 Jason Bartlett .07 .20
570 Mariano Rivera .25 .60
571 Norris Hopper .07 .20
572 Alex Escobar .07 .20
573 Gustavo Chacin .07 .20
574 Brandon McCarthy .07 .20
575 Seth McClung .07 .20
576 Yuniesky Betancourt .07 .20
577 Jason LaRue .07 .20
578 Dustin Pedroia .20 .50
579 Taylor Tankersley .07 .20
580 Garret Anderson .07 .20
581 Mike Sweeney .07 .20
582 Scott Thorman .07 .20
583 Joe Inglett .07 .20
584 Clint Barmes .07 .20
585 Willie Bloomquist .07 .20
586 Willy Aybar .07 .20
587 Brian Bannister .07 .20
588 Jose Guillen UER .07 .20
589 Brad Wilkerson .07 .20
590 Lance Berkman .12 .30
591 Toronto Blue Jays .07 .20
592 Florida Marlins .07 .20
593 Washington Nationals .07 .20
594 Los Angeles Angels .07 .20
595 Cleveland Indians .07 .20
596 Texas Rangers .07 .20
597 Detroit Tigers .07 .20
598 Arizona Diamondbacks .07 .20
599 Kansas City Royals .07 .20
600 Ryan Zimmerman .12 .30
601 Colorado Rockies .07 .20
602 Minnesota Twins .07 .20
603 Los Angeles Dodgers .07 .20
604 San Diego Padres .07 .20
605 Bruce Bochy MG .12 .30
606 Ron Washington MG .07 .20
607 Manny Acta MG .07 .20
608 Sam Perlozzo MG .07 .20
609 Terry Francona MG .12 .30
610 Jim Leyland MG .07 .20
611 Eric Wedge MG .07 .20
612 Ozzie Guillen MG .07 .20
613 Buddy Bell MG .07 .20
614 Bob Geren MG .07 .20
615 Lou Piniella MG .07 .20
616 Fredi Gonzalez MG .07 .20
617 Ned Yost MG .07 .20
618 Willie Randolph MG .07 .20
619 Bud Black MG .07 .20
620 Garrett Atkins .07 .20
621 Alexi Casilla RC .30 .75
622 Matt Chico (RC) .20 .50
623 Alejandro De Aza RC .30 .75
624 Jeremy Brown .07 .20
625 Josh Hamilton (RC) .60 1.50
626 Doug Slaten RC .20 .50
627 Andy Cannizaro RC .20 .50
628 Juan Salas (RC) .20 .50
629 Levale Speigner RC .20 .50
630a D.Matsuzaka English RC .75 2.00
630b D.Matsuzaka Japanese 1.50 4.00
630c Daisuke Matsuzaka No Sig 1.50 4.00
631 Elijah Dukes RC .30 .75
632 Kevin Cameron RC .20 .50
633 Juan Perez RC .20 .50
634a Alex Gordon RC .60 1.50
634b A.Gordon No Sig 2.00 5.00
635 Juan Lara RC .20 .50
636a Mike Rabelo RC .20 .50
636b Billy Butler (RC)
637 Justin Hampson (RC) .20 .50
638 Cesar Jimenez RC .20 .50
639 Joe Smith RC .20 .50
640 Kei Igawa RC .50 1.25
641 Hideki Okajima RC 1.00 2.50
642 Sean Henn (RC) .20 .50
643 Jay Marshall RC .20 .50
644 Jared Burton RC .20 .50
645 Angel Sanchez RC .20 .50
646 Devern Hansack RC .20 .50
647 Juan Morillo (RC) .20 .50
648 Hector Gimenez (RC) .20 .50
649 Brian Barden RC .20 .50
650 A.Rodriguez .25 .60
J.Giambi CC
651 J.Michaels .07 .20
T.Hafner CC
652 J.Johnson .20 .50
M.Olivo CC
653 S.Casey .07 .20
P.Polanco CC
654 I.Rodriguez .12 .30
F.Rodney CC
655 D.Uggla .12 .30
H.Ramirez CC
656 C.Beltran .12 .30
J.Reyes CC
657 A.Rodriguez .50 1.25
D.Jeter CC
658 A.Rowand .12 .30
J.Rollins CC
659 A.Berroa .07 .20
A.Blanco CC
660a Yadier Molina .25 .60
660b Yadier Molina No Sig 2.00 5.00
661 Barry Bonds 3.00 8.00

2007 Topps 1st Edition

*1st ED: 3X TO 8X BASIC
*1st ED RC: 1.25X TO 3X BASIC
SER.1 ODDS 1:36 HOBBY, 1:5 HTA
SER.2 ODDS 1:36 HOBBY, 1:5 HTA

2007 Topps Copper

COMMON CARD (1-660) 6.00 15.00
UNLISTED STARS 10.00 25.00
SER.1 ODDS 1:7 HTA
SER.2 ODDS 1:10 HTA
STATED PRINT RUN 56 SERIAL #'d SETS
7 Mickey Mantle 75.00 150.00
15 Andrew Miller 100.00 150.00
29 Pat Neshek 30.00 60.00
40 D.Jeter w Mantle/Bush 400.00 800.00
53 Mike Piazza 15.00 40.00
58 Todd Coffey 10.00 25.00
130 Albert Pujols 30.00 60.00
170 Chien-Ming Wang 30.00 60.00
236 Boston Red Sox CL 6.00 15.00
239 New York Yankees CL 10.00 25.00
260 David Wright 15.00 40.00
275 Greg Maddux 15.00 40.00
301 Derek Jeter GG 40.00 80.00
305 Frank Thomas 15.00 40.00
308 Albert Pujols GG 30.00 60.00
311 Greg Maddux GG 15.00 40.00
313 Ichiro Suzuki GG 15.00 40.00
322 Ryan Howard MVP 15.00 40.00
327 B.Abreu 20.00 50.00
D.Jeter CC
328 C.Delgado 15.00 40.00
D.Wright CC
329 Y.Molina 10.00 25.00
A.Pujols CC
330 Ryan Howard 15.00 40.00
340 Roger Clemens 20.00 50.00
341 Akinori Iwamura 15.00 40.00
360 David Ortiz 20.00 50.00
362 Chris Burke 10.00 25.00
400 Ichiro Suzuki 12.50 30.00
403 Casey Blake 15.00 40.00
413 Coco Crisp 10.00 25.00
444 Josh Beckett 10.00 25.00
450 Ken Griffey Jr. 30.00 80.00
460 Jose Reyes 10.00 25.00
475 Kevin Youkilis 10.00 25.00
510 Alex Rodriguez 20.00 50.00
625 Josh Hamilton 30.00 60.00
630 Daisuke Matsuzaka 100.00 150.00
634 Alex Gordon 15.00 40.00
641 Hideki Okajima 20.00 50.00
650 A.Rodriguez 15.00 40.00
J.Giambi CC
657 A.Rodriguez 20.00 50.00
D.Jeter CC

2007 Topps Gold

*GOLD: 6X TO 15X BASIC
*GOLD RC: 2.5X TO 6X BASIC RC
SER.1 ODDS 1:11 H, 1:3 HTA, 1:24 K-MART
SER.1 ODDS 1:6 RACK, 1:11 TARGET
SER.1 ODDS 1:24 WAL-MART
SER.2 ODDS 1:11 HOBBY, 1:2 HTA
STATED PRINT RUN 2007 SER.#'d SETS
40 D.Jeter w Mantle/Bush 125.00 250.00

2007 Topps Red Back

COMP.SERIES 1 (330) 40.00 80.00
COMP.SERIES 2 (330) 40.00 80.00
*RED: 1X TO 2.5X BASIC
*RED RC: .5X TO 1.2X BASIC RC
SER.1 ODDS 2:1 H, 10:1 HTA, 3:1 RACK
40 Jeter/Mantle/Bush 10.00 25.00

2007 Topps '52 Mantle Reprint Relic

SER.1 ODDS 1:158,700 H, 1:8721 HTA
SER.1 ODDS 1:602,600 K-MART
SER.1 ODDS 1:127,100 TARGET
SER 1 ODDS 1:602,600 WAL-MART
STATED PRINT RUN 52 SERIAL #'d SETS
NO PRICING DUE TO SCARCITY
52MM Mickey Mantle Bat 125.00 250.00

2007 Topps Alex Rodriguez Road to 500

COMMON CARD (1-75/101-425) 1.00 2.50
COMMON CARD (76-100) 12.00 30.00
COMMON CARD (401-425) 5.00 12.00
COMMON CARD (451-475) 3.00 8.00
COMMON CARD (476-499) 3.00 8.00
SER.1 ODDS 1:36 H, 1:5 HTA, 1:36 K-MART
SER.1 ODDS 1:36 RACK, 1:36 TARGET
SER.1 ODDS 1:36 WAL-MART
FINEST ODDS TWO PER AROD BOX TOPPER
HERITAGE ODDS 1:24 HOBBY/RETAIL
OPENING DAY ODDS 1:36 H, 1:36 R
MOMENTS ODDS TWO PER BOX TOPPER
CO-SIG ODDS TWO PER AROD BOX TOPPER
BOWMAN ODDS 1:6 HOBBY, 1:2 HTA
SER.2 ODDS 1:36 HOBBY, 1:5 HTA
T.CHROME ODDS TWO PER BOX TOPPER
ALLEN AND GINTER ODDS 1:24 H, 1:24 R
BOW.CHR. ODDS 1:9 HOBBY
TURKEY RED ODDS 1:24 HOBBY/RETAIL
BOW.HER ODDS TWO PER BOX TOPPER
UPDATE ODDS 1:36 H, 1:5 HTA, 1:36 R
TOPPS 52 ODDS 1:20 H, 1:20 R
CARDS 1-25 ISSUED IN SERIES 1
CARDS 26-50 ISSUED IN FINEST
CARDS 51-75 ISSUED IN HERITAGE
CARDS 76-100 ISSUED IN OPENING DAY
CARDS 101-125 ISSUED IN MOMENTS
CARDS 126-175 ISSUED IN BOWMAN
CARDS 176-200 ISSUED IN CO-SIGNERS
CARDS 201-225 ISSUED IN SERIES 2
CARDS 226-250 ISSUED IN TOP.CHROME
CARDS 251-275 ISSUED IN ALLEN GINTER
CARDS 276-300 ISSUED IN BOW.CHR.
CARDS 301-325 ISSUSED IN TUR.RED
CARDS 326-350 ISSUED IN 08 FINEST
CARDS 351-375 ISSUED IN BOW.HER.
CARDS 376-400 ISSUED IN UPDATE
CARDS 401-425 ISSUED IN BOW.BEST
CARDS 426-450 ISSUED IN BOW.DRAFT
CARDS 451-475 ISSUED IN BOW.STERL.
CARDS 476-500 ISSUED IN TOPPS 52
ARHR500 Alex Rodriguez 500HR 8.00 20.00

2007 Topps All Stars

COMPLETE SET (12) 6.00 15.00
SER.1 ODDS ONE PER RACK PACK
AS1 Alfonso Soriano .60 1.50
AS2 Paul Konerko .60 1.50
AS3 Carlos Beltran .60 1.50
AS4 Troy Glaus .40 1.00
AS5 Jason Bay .60 1.50
AS6 Vladimir Guerrero .60 1.50
AS7 Chase Utley .60 1.50
AS8 Michael Young .40 1.00
AS9 David Wright .75 2.00
AS10 Gary Matthews .40 1.00
AS11 Brad Penny .40 1.00
AS12 Roy Halladay .60 1.50

2007 Topps All Star Rookies

COMPLETE SET (10) 6.00 15.00
SER.1 ODDS ONE PER RACK PACK
ASR1 Prince Fielder .60 1.50
ASR2 Dan Uggla .40 1.00
ASR3 Ryan Zimmerman .60 1.50
ASR4 Hanley Ramirez .60 1.50
ASR5 Melky Cabrera .40 1.00
ASR6 Andre Ethier .60 1.50
ASR7 Nick Markakis .75 2.00
ASR8 Justin Verlander 1.00 2.50
ASR9 Francisco Liriano .40 1.00
ASR10 Russell Martin .40 1.00

2007 Topps DiMaggio Streak

COMPLETE SET (56) 20.00 50.00
COMMON CARD .60 1.50
SER.2 ODDS 1:9 HOBBY

2007 Topps DiMaggio Streak Before the Streak

COMPLETE SET (61) 12.50 30.00
COMMON CARD .60 1.50
SER.2 ODDS 1:9 HOBBY

2007 Topps Distinguished Service

COMPLETE SET (30) 10.00 25.00
COMP.SERIES 1 (1-20) 6.00 15.00
COMP.SERIES 2 (21-30) 5.00 12.00
SER.1 ODDS 1:12 H, 1:12 HTA, 1:12 K-MART
SER.1 ODDS 1:12 RACK, 1:12 WAL-MART
SER.2 ODDS 1:12 HOBBY, 1:2 HTA
DS1 Duke Snider .60 1.50
DS2 Yogi Berra 1.00 2.50
DS3 Bob Feller .60 1.50
DS4 Bobby Doerr .60 1.50
DS5 Monte Irvin .60 1.50
DS6 Dwight D. Eisenhower .40 1.00
DS7 George Marshall .40 1.00
DS8 Franklin D. Roosevelt .40 1.00
DS9 Harry Truman .40 1.00
DS10 Douglas MacArthur .40 1.00
DS11 Ralph Kiner .60 1.50
DS12 Hank Sauer .40 1.00
DS13 Elmer Valo .40 1.00
DS14 Sibby Sisti .40 1.00
DS15 Hoyt Wilhelm .60 1.50
DS16 James Doolittle .40 1.00
DS17 Curtis Lemay .40 1.00
DS18 Omar Bradley .40 1.00
DS19 Chester Nimitz .40 1.00
DS20 Mark Clark .40 1.00
DS21 Joe DiMaggio 2.00 5.00
DS22 Warren Spahn .60 1.50
DS23 Stan Musial 1.50 4.00
DS24 Red Schoendienst .60 1.50
DS25 Ted Williams 2.00 5.00
DS26 Winston Churchill .40 1.00
DS27 Charles de Gaulle .40 1.00
DS28 George Bush .40 1.00
DS29 John F. Kennedy 1.50 4.00
DS30 Richard Bong .40 1.00

2007 Topps Distinguished Service Autographs

SER.1 ODDS 1:20,000 H, 1:830 HTA
SER.1 ODDS 1:41,225 K-MART,1:9200 RACK
SER.1 ODDS 1:20,000 TARGET
SER.1 ODDS 1:41,225 WAL-MART
BD Bobby Doerr 15.00 40.00
BF Bob Feller 20.00 50.00
DS Duke Snider 20.00 50.00
MI Monte Irvin 30.00 60.00
RK Ralph Kiner 10.00 25.00

2007 Topps Factory Set All Star Bonus

1 Alex Rodriguez 1.25 3.00
2 David Wright .75 2.00
3 David Ortiz 1.00 2.50
4 Ichiro Suzuki 1.25 3.00
5 Ryan Howard .75 2.00

2007 Topps Factory Set Cardinals Team Bonus

1 Skip Schumaker .40 1.00
2 Josh Hancock .40 1.00
3 Tyler Johnson .40 1.00
4 Randy Keisler .40 1.00
5 Randy Flores .40 1.00

2007 Topps Factory Set Cubs Team Bonus

1 Ronny Cedeno .40 1.00
2 Cesar Izturis .40 1.00
3 Neal Cotts .40 1.00
4 Wade Miller .40 1.00
5 Michael Wuertz .40 1.00

2007 Topps Factory Set Dodgers Team Bonus

1 Chin-Hui Tsao .60 1.50
2 Olmedo Saenz .40 1.00
3 Brett Tomko .40 1.00
4 Marlon Anderson .40 1.00
5 Brady Clark .40 1.00

2007 Topps Factory Set Red Sox Team Bonus

1 Daisuke Matsuzaka 1.50 4.00
2 Eric Hinske .40 1.00
3 Brendan Donnelly .40 1.00
4 Hideki Okajima 2.00 5.00
5 J.C. Romero .40 1.00

2007 Topps Factory Set Rookie Bonus

COMPLETE SET (20) 12.50 30.00
1 Felix Pie .40 1.00
2 Rick Vanden Hurk .40 1.00
3 Jeff Baker .40 1.00
4 Don Kelly .40 1.00
5 Matt Lindstrom .40 1.00
6 Chase Wright 1.00 2.50
7 Jon Coutlangus .40 1.00
8 Lee Gardner .40 1.00
9 Gustavo Molina .40 1.00
10 Kory Casto .40 1.00
11 Daisuke Matsuzaka 1.50 4.00
12 Tim Lincecum 2.00 5.00
13 Phil Hughes 1.00 2.50
14 Ryan Braun 2.00 5.00
15 Billy Butler .60 1.50
16 Jarrod Saltalamacchia .60 1.50
17 Hideki Okajima 2.00 5.00
18 Akinori Iwamura 1.00 2.50
19a Joba Chamberlain .60 1.50
19b Joba Chamberlain Houston Astros UER .60
1.50
20 Hunter Pence 1.25 3.00

2007 Topps Factory Set Yankees Team Bonus

1 Darrell Rasner .40 1.00
2 Phil Hughes 1.00 2.50
3 Wil Nieves .40 1.00
4 Kei Igawa 1.00 2.50
5 Kevin Thompson .40 1.00

2007 Topps Flashback Fridays

COMPLETE SET (25) 6.00 15.00
ISSUED VIA HTA SHOPS
FF1 Ryan Howard .40 1.00
FF2 Derek Jeter 1.25 3.00
FF3 Ken Griffey Jr 1.00 2.50
FF4 Miguel Tejada .30 .75
FF5 David Wright .40 1.00
FF6 Alfonso Soriano .30 .75
FF7 Matt Holliday .50 1.25
FF8 Jason Bay .30 .75
FF9 Ryan Zimmerman .30 .75
FF10 Alex Rodriguez .60 1.50
FF11 Jermaine Dye .20 .50
FF12 Miguel Cabrera .50 1.25
FF13 Johan Santana .30 .75
FF14 Brandon Webb .30 .75
FF15 Ivan Rodriguez .30 .75
FF16 Ichiro Suzuki .60 1.50
FF17 Michael Young .20 .50
FF18 David Ortiz .50 1.25
FF19 Roger Clemens .60 1.50
FF20 Frank Thomas .50 1.25
FF21 Trevor Hoffman .30 .75
FF22 Gary Matthews .20 .50
FF23 Rafael Furcal .20 .50
FF24 Chipper Jones .50 1.25
FF25 Albert Pujols .60 1.50

2007 Topps Generation Now

SER.1 ODDS 1:4 H, 1:4 K-MART, 1:4 RACK
SER.1 ODDS 1:4 TARGET, 1:4 WAL-MART
SER.2 ODDS 1:4 HOBBY
UPDATE ODDS 1:4 HOB, 1:4 RET
CARDS OF SAME PLAYER EQUALLY PRICED
GN1 Ryan Howard .60 1.50
GN51 Chase Utley .50 1.25
GN85 Chien-Ming Wang .50 1.25
GN103 Mike Napoli .30 .75
GN117 Justin Morneau .50 1.25
GN147 David Wright .60 1.50
GN187 Jered Weaver .50 1.25
GN195 Andre Ethier .50 1.25
GN219 Ryan Zimmerman .50 1.25
GN279 Russell Martin .30 .75
GN283 Justin Verlander .75 2.00
GN299 Hanley Ramirez .50 1.25
GN350 Nick Markakis .60 1.50
GN360 Nick Swisher .50 1.25
GN397 Prince Fielder .50 1.25
GN425 Ian Kinsler .50 1.25
GN452 Kenji Johjima .75 2.00
GN481 Jonathan Papelbon .75 2.00
GN516 Jose Reyes .50 1.25
GN520 Curtis Granderson .60 1.50
GN551 Josh Barfield .30 .75

2007 Topps Generation Now Vintage

RANDOM INSERTS IN K-MART PACKS
1-18 ISSUED IN SER.1 PACKS
19-36 ISSUED IN SER.2 PACKS
37-54 ISSUED IN 07 UPDATE PACKS
GNV1 Ryan Howard .40 1.00
GNV2 Jeff Francoeur .50 1.25
GNV3 Nick Swisher .30 .75
GNV4 Joey Gathright .20 .50
GNV5 Jhonny Peralta .20 .50
GNV6 Willy Taveras .20 .50
GNV7 Cory Sullivan .20 .50
GNV8 Chris Young .20 .50
GNV9 Jered Weaver .30 .75
GNV10 Jonathan Papelbon .50 1.25
GNV11 Russell Martin .20 .50
GNV12 Hanley Ramirez .30 .75
GNV13 Justin Verlander .50 1.25
GNV14 Matt Cain .30 .75
GNV15 Kenji Johjima .50 1.25
GNV16 Angel Pagan .20 .50
GNV17 Brandon Phillips .20 .50
GNV18 Mark Teahen .20 .50
GNV19 Stephen Drew .20 .50
GNV20 Nick Markakis .40 1.00
GNV21 Anibal Sanchez .20 .50
GNV22 Jeremy Hermida .20 .50
GNV23 James Loney .20 .50
GNV24 Prince Fielder .30 .75
GNV25 Josh Barfield .20 .50
GNV26 Ian Kinsler .30 .75
GNV27 Ryan Zimmerman .30 .75
GNV28 David Wright .40 1.00
GNV29 Jose Reyes .30 .75
GNV30 Delmon Young .30 .75
GNV31 Zach Duke .20 .50
GNV32 Brian McCann .20 .50
GNV33 Bobby Jenks .20 .50
GNV34 Robinson Cano .30 .75
GNV35 Jose Lopez .20 .50
GNV36 Daisuke Matsuzaka .75 2.00
GNV37 Alex Rios .20 .50
GNV38 Cole Hamels .40 1.00
GNV39 Matt Kemp .40 1.00
GNV40 Dan Uggla .20 .50
GNV41 Scott Kazmir .30 .75
GNV42 J.J. Hardy .20 .50
GNV43 Hunter Pence .60 1.50
GNV44 Jason Bay .30 .75
GNV45 James Shields .20 .50
GNV46 Chase Utley .30 .75
GNV47 Justin Morneau .30 .75
GNV48 Chien-Ming Wang .30 .75
GNV49 Troy Tulowitski .60 1.50
GNV50 Joe Mauer .40 1.00
GNV51 Brandon Webb .30 .75
GNV52 Matt Holliday .50 1.25
GNV53 Grady Sizemore .30 .75
GNV54 Homer Bailey .30 .75

2007 Topps Gibson Home Run History

COMPLETE SET (110) 60.00 120.00
COMMON GIBSON .60 1.50
SER.1 ODDS 1:9 H, 1:2 HTA, 1:9 K-MART
SER.1 ODDS 1:9 RACK, 1:9 TARGET
SER.1 ODDS 1:9 WAL-MART
CARDS 1-110 ISSUED IN SERIES 1 PACKS

2007 Topps Highlights Autographs

SER.1 A 1:50,842 H, 1:2105 HTA
SER.1 A 1:101,000 K-MART,1:18,396 RACK
SER.1 A 1:50,842 TARGET
SER.1 A 1:101,000 WAL-MART
SER.2 A 1:37,162 HOBBY, 1:523 HTA
SER.1 B 1:24,150 H, 1:1034 HTA
SER.1 B 1:51,800 K-MART, 1:12,264 RACK
SER.1 B 1:25,420 TARGET
SER.1 B 1:51,800 WAL-MART
SER.2 B 1:7330 HOBBY, 1:105 HTA
SER.1 C 1:13,000 H, 1:555 HTA
SER.1 C 1:27,300 K-MART, 1:7350 RACK
SER.1 C 1:13,600 TARGET
SER.1 C 1:27,300 WAL-MART
SER.2 C 1:7330 HOBBY, 1:105 HTA
SER.1 D 1:4916 H, 1:208 HTA
SER.1 D 1:10,250 K-MART, 1:2628 RACK
SER.1 D 1:5100 TARGET, 1:10,250 WAL-MART
SER.2 D 1:12,198 HOBBY, 1:174 HTA
SER.1 E 1:2460 H, 1:52 HTA, 1:5125 K-MART
SER.1 E 1:1314 RACK, 1:2550 TARGET
SER.1 E 1:5125 WAL-MART
SER.2 E 1:1410 HOBBY, 1:20 HTA
SER.1 F 1:1256 H, 1:52 HTA, 1:2564 K-MART
SER.1 F 1:657 RACK, 1:1277 TARGET
SER.1 F 1:2564 WAL-MART
SER.1 G 1:376 H, 1:16 HTA, 1:789 K-MART
SER.1 G 1:203 RACK,1:393 TARGET
SER.1 G 1:789 WAL-MART
GROUP A1 PRINT RUN B/WN 25-50 PER
GROUP B1 PRINT RUN 100 SETS
GROUP C1 PRINT RUN 250 SETS
A1-C1 ARE NOT SERIAL-NUMBERED
A1-C1 PRINT RUNS PROVIDED BY TOPPS
NO GROUP A1 PRICING DUE TO SCARCITY
EXCH * = PARTIAL EXCHANGE
EXCHANGE DEADLINE 02/28/09
AB Aaron Boone E2 4.00 10.00
AJ Andruw Jones B2 12.00 30.00
AM Andrew Miller G 4.00 10.00
AP Albert Pujols A2 60.00 150.00
APA Angel Pagan G 4.00 10.00
AR Anthony Reyes E2 6.00 15.00
AGS A.Soriano B/100 * 8.00 20.00
AS Anibal Sanchez G 4.00 10.00
CG Curtis Granderson B2 4.00 10.00
CQ Carlos Quentin F 4.00 10.00
CW Chien-Ming Wang B/100 * 30.00 80.00
CW Craig Wilson E2 6.00 15.00
DO David Ortiz B/100 * 60.00 120.00
DO David Ortiz B2 20.00 50.00
DT Derrick Turnbow D2 6.00 15.00
DU Dan Uggla E2 4.00 10.00
DW David Wright D 10.00 25.00
DW David Wright C2 10.00 25.00
DWW Dontrelle Willis E 10.00 25.00
DWW Dontrelle Willis C2 6.00 15.00
DY Delmon Young E 4.00 10.00
EC Endy Chavez B2 10.00 25.00
EF Emiliano Fruto G 4.00 10.00
ES Ervin Santana E2 4.00 10.00
HR Hanley Ramirez G 4.00 10.00
JAS John Smoltz C/250 * 20.00 50.00
JD Johnny Damon B2 12.00 30.00
JEM Justin Morneau E 10.00 25.00
JF Josh Fields F 3.00 8.00
JG Jon Garland E2 4.00 10.00
JH John Hattig G 4.00 10.00
JL James Loney G 4.00 10.00
JM John Maine F 4.00 10.00
JS Johan Santana C/250 * 12.00 30.00
JT Jim Thome A2 25.00 60.00
JV Justin Verlander B2 15.00 40.00
JZ Joel Zumaya E2 3.00 8.00
KE Kelvim Escobar C2 6.00 15.00
KM Kevin Mench D 4.00 10.00
KM Kendry Morales B2 4.00 10.00
LM Lastings Milledge E2 4.00 10.00
MC Miguel Cabrera C/250 * 20.00 50.00
MC Melky Cabrera E2 4.00 10.00
MG Matt Garza F 4.00 10.00
MH Matt Holliday G 6.00 15.00
MN Mike Napoli G 6.00 15.00
MP Mike Piazza A/50 * 90.00 150.00
MTC Matt Cain D2 4.00 10.00
PL Paul LoDuca B2 12.00 30.00
RC Robinson Cano E2 6.00 15.00
RH Ryan Howard B/100 * 75.00 150.00
RH Ryan Howard A2 20.00 50.00
RM Russell Martin C2 10.00 25.00
RZ Ryan Zimmerman E 6.00 15.00
RZ Ryan Zimmerman C2 6.00 15.00
SC Shawn Chacon E2 4.00 10.00
SP Scott Podsednik E2 4.00 10.00
SR Shawn Riggans E2 4.00 10.00
SSC Shin-Soo Choo B2 12.00 30.00
ST Steve Trachsel A2 10.00 25.00
TG Tom Glavine B2 8.00 20.00
TH Travis Hafner D 10.00 25.00
TT Troy Tulowitzki G 6.00 15.00
VG Vladimir Guerrero A2 6.00 15.00

2007 Topps Highlights Relics

SER.1 A 1:933 H, 1:33 HTA, 1:2160 K-MART
SER.1 A 1:1070 TARGET, 1:2160 WAL-MART
SER.2 A 1:2435 HOBBY, 1:138 HTA
SER.1 B 1:726 H, 1:19 HTA, 1:1270 K-MART
SER.1 B 1:631 TARGET, 1:1270 WAL-MART
SER.2 B 1:609 HOBBY, 1:35 HTA
SER.1 C 1:2468 H, 1:87 HTA, 1:5675 K-MART
SER.1 C 1:2825 TARGET, 1:5675 WAL-MART
SER.2 C 1:1420 HOBBY, 1:80 HTA
SER.2 D 1:533 HOBBY, 1:30 HTA
SER.2 E 1:1705 HOBBY, 1:96 HTA
AB Adrian Beltre B2 3.00 8.00
AER Alex Rodriguez C2 8.00 20.00
AJ Andruw Jones E2 3.00 8.00
ALR Anthony Reyes B2 4.00 10.00
AP Albert Pujols Pants B 8.00 20.00
AP Albert Pujols B2 8.00 20.00
AP2 Albert Pujols Jsy B 8.00 20.00
AR Alex Rodriguez Jsy B 8.00 20.00
AR Aramis Ramirez D2 3.00 8.00
AR2 Alex Rodriguez Bat A 8.00 20.00
AS Alfonso Soriano Bat A 4.00 10.00
AS Alfonso Soriano A2 4.00 10.00
BM Brian McCann Bat A 3.00 8.00
CB Craig Biggio Pants A 4.00 10.00
CD Carlos Delgado Bat B 3.00 8.00
CIB Carlos Beltran Jsy B 3.00 8.00
CJ Chipper Jones B2 3.00 8.00
CQ Carlos Quentin Bat A 3.00 8.00
CS Curt Schilling Jsy A 3.00 8.00
DE David Eckstein A2 5.00 12.00
DO David Ortiz Bat B 4.00 10.00
DO David Ortiz D2 4.00 10.00
DW Dontrelle Willis Jsy B 4.00 10.00
DW David Wright D2 5.00 12.00
DW2 Dontrelle Willis Pants B 4.00 10.00
DWW Dontrelle Willis E2 4.00 10.00
ER Edgar Renteria Bat B 3.00 8.00
FT Frank Thomas Bat B 4.00 10.00
GA Garrett Atkins A2 3.00 8.00
GS Gary Sheffield Bat B 3.00 8.00
GS Grady Sizemore A2 5.00 12.00
IR Ivan Rodriguez Bat C 3.00 8.00
IS Ichiro Suzuki Bat A 6.00 15.00
JAS John Smoltz Pants A 4.00 10.00
JB Jason Bay Jsy A 3.00 8.00
JB2 Jason Bay Bat A 3.00 8.00
JD Jermaine Dye C2 3.00 8.00
JDD Johnny Damon A2 4.00 10.00
JM Justin Morneau Bat B 3.00 8.00
JPM Joe Mauer Bat A 4.00 10.00
JR Jose Reyes Jsy A 3.00 8.00
JS Johan Santana Jsy A 4.00 10.00
JT Jim Thome B2 5.00 12.00
JV Justin Verlander A2 5.00 12.00
LB Lance Berkman C2 3.00 8.00
MAR Manny Ramirez Jsy B 3.00 8.00
2-Mar Manny Ramirez Bat C 3.00 8.00
MC Matt Cain B2 3.00 8.00
MCT Mark Teixeira B2 3.00 8.00
MEC Melky Cabrera B2 4.00 10.00
MO Magglio Ordonez Bat B 4.00 10.00
MR Mariano Rivera Jsy A 4.00 10.00
MR Manny Ramirez D2 3.00 8.00
MT Miguel Tejada Bat A 3.00 8.00
MT Miguel Tejada B2 3.00 8.00
NS Nick Swisher D2 4.00 10.00
PK Paul Konerko Bat A 3.00 8.00
PK Paul Konerko B2 3.00 8.00
PM Pedro Martinez D2 3.00 8.00
RC Robinson Cano Pants A 4.00 10.00
RC Robinson Cano B2 4.00 10.00
RH Ryan Howard Bat B 6.00 15.00
RH Roy Halladay B2 3.00 8.00
RJH Ryan Howard B2 6.00 15.00
RO Roy Oswalt Jsy A 3.00 8.00
SK Scott Kazmir C2 3.00 8.00
SK Scott Kazmir Jsy B 3.00 8.00
SR Scott Rolen Jsy A 4.00 10.00
TG Tom Glavine A2 4.00 10.00
TG1 Tom Glavine Jsy A 4.00 10.00
TG2 Troy Glaus Bat B 3.00 8.00
VG Vladimir Guerrero D2 4.00 10.00
VW Vernon Wells D2 3.00 8.00
VW Vernon Wells Bat A 3.00 8.00

2007 Topps Hit Parade

SER.2 ODDS 1:9 HOBBY, 1:2 HTA
HP1 Barry Bonds 1.50 4.00
HP2 Ken Griffey Jr. 2.00 5.00
HP3 Frank Thomas 1.00 2.50
HP4 Jim Thome .60 1.50
HP5 Manny Ramirez 1.00 2.50
HP6 Alex Rodriguez 1.25 3.00
HP7 Gary Sheffield .40 1.00
HP8 Mike Piazza 1.00 2.50
HP9 Carlos Delgado .40 1.00
HP10 Chipper Jones 1.00 2.50
HP11 Barry Bonds 1.50 4.00
HP12 Ken Griffey Jr. 2.00 5.00
HP13 Frank Thomas 1.00 2.50
HP14 Manny Ramirez 1.00 2.50
HP15 Gary Sheffield .40 1.00
HP16 Jeff Kent .40 1.00
HP17 Alex Rodriguez 1.25 3.00
HP18 Luis Gonzalez .40 1.00
HP19 Jim Thome .60 1.50
HP20 Mike Piazza 1.00 2.50
HP21 Craig Biggio .60 1.50
HP22 Barry Bonds 1.50 4.00
HP23 Julio Franco .40 1.00
HP24 Steve Finley .40 1.00
HP25 Omar Vizquel .60 1.50
HP26 Ken Griffey Jr. 2.00 5.00
HP27 Gary Sheffield .40 1.00
HP28 Luis Gonzalez .40 1.00
HP29 Ivan Rodriguez .60 1.50
HP30 Bernie Williams .60 1.50

2007 Topps Hobby Masters

COMPLETE SET (20) 10.00 25.00
SER.1 ODDS 1:6 H, 1:4 HTA
HM1 David Wright .75 2.00
HM2 Albert Pujols 1.25 3.00
HM3 David Ortiz 1.00 2.50
HM4 Ryan Howard .75 2.00
HM5 Alfonso Soriano .60 1.50
HM6 Delmon Young .60 1.50
HM7 Jered Weaver .60 1.50
HM8 Derek Jeter 2.50 6.00
HM9 Freddy Sanchez .40 1.00
HM10 Alex Rodriguez 1.25 3.00
HM11 Johan Santana .60 1.50
HM12 Ichiro Suzuki 1.25 3.00
HM13 Andruw Jones .40 1.00
HM14 Vladimir Guerrero .60 1.50
HM15 Miguel Cabrera 1.00 2.50
HM16 Todd Helton .60 1.50
HM17 Manny Ramirez 1.00 2.50
HM18 Carlos Beltran .60 1.50
HM19 Justin Morneau .60 1.50
HM20 Francisco Liriano .40 1.00

2007 Topps Homerun Derby Contest

RANDOM INSERTS IN SER.2 PACKS
STATED ODDS 999 SER.#'d SETS
AB Adrian Beltre 1.50 4.00
AD Adam Dunn 1.00 2.50
AER Alex Rodriguez 2.00 5.00
AJ Andruw Jones .60 1.50
AL Adam LaRoche .60 1.50
AP Albert Pujols 2.00 5.00
AR Aramis Ramirez .60 1.50
AS Alfonso Soriano 1.00 2.50
BH Bill Hall .60 1.50
CB Carlos Beltran 1.00 2.50
CD Carlos Delgado .60 1.50
CL Carlos Lee .60 1.50
CM Craig Monroe .60 1.50
CU Chase Utley 1.00 2.50
DO David Ortiz 1.50 4.00
DU Dan Uggla .60 1.50
DW David Wright 1.25 3.00
DY Delmon Young 1.00 2.50
FT Frank Thomas 1.50 4.00
GA Garrett Atkins .60 1.50
GS Grady Sizemore 1.00 2.50
JB Jason Bay 1.00 2.50
JC Joe Crede .60 1.50
JD Jermaine Dye .60 1.50
JDD Johnny Damon 1.00 2.50
JF Jeff Francoeur 1.50 4.00
JG Jason Giambi .60 1.50
JM Justin Morneau 1.00 2.50
JT Jim Thome 1.00 2.50
KG Ken Griffey Jr 3.00 8.00
LB Lance Berkman 1.00 2.50
MC Miguel Cabrera 1.50 4.00
MH Matt Holliday 1.50 4.00
MMT Marcus Thames .60 1.50
MOT Miguel Tejada 1.00 2.50
MP Mike Piazza 1.50 4.00
MR Manny Ramirez 1.50 4.00
MT Mark Teixeira 1.00 2.50
NS Nick Swisher 1.00 2.50
PB Pat Burrell .60 1.50
PF Prince Fielder 1.00 2.50
PK Paul Konerko 1.00 2.50
RH Ryan Howard 1.25 3.00
RI Raul Ibanez .60 1.50
RS Richie Sexson .60 1.50
TG Troy Glaus .60 1.50
TH Travis Hafner .60 1.50
TKH Torii Hunter .60 1.50
VG Vladimir Guerrero 1.00 2.50
VW Vernon Wells .60 1.50

2007 Topps In the Name Letter Relics

SER.1 ODDS 1:8292 H, 1:488 HTA
STATED PRINT RUN 1 SERIAL #'d SET
NO PRICING DUE TO SCARCITY

2007 Topps Mickey Mantle Story

COMPLETE SET (57) 50.00 100.00
COMP.SERIES 1 (1-15) 8.00 20.00
COMP.SERIES 2 (16-30) 8.00 20.00
COMP.UPD.SET (31-45) 12.50 30.00
COMP.08 SER.1 SET (46-57) 6.00 15.00
COMP.08 SER.2 SET (58-67) 6.00 15.00
COMP.08 UPD SET (68-77) 6.00 15.00
COMMON MANTLE (1-77) .75 2.00
SER.1 ODDS 1:18 H, 1:18 HTA, 1:18 K-MART
SER.1 ODDS 1:18 RACK, 1:18 TARGET
SER.1 ODDS 1:18 WAL-MART
SER.2 ODDS 1:18 H, 1:3 HTA, 1:18 R
UPDATE ODDS 1:18 H, 1:3 HTA, 1:18 R
08 SER.1 ODDS 1:18 H, 1:3 HTA

08 SER.2 ODDS 1:18 H,1:3 HTA, 1:18 R
08 UPD.ODDS 1:18 HOBBY
1-15 ISSUED IN SERIES 1
16-30 ISSUED IN SERIES 2
31-45 ISSUED IN UPDATE
46-57 ISSSUED IN 08 SERIES 1
58-65 ISSUED IN 08 SERIES 2
66-77 ISSUED IN 08 UPDATE

2007 Topps Opening Day Team vs. Team

COMPLETE SET (15) 6.00 15.00
SER.2 ODDS 1:12 HOBBY, 1:3 HTA
OD1 New York Mets/St. Louis Cardinals .40 1.00
OD2 Atlanta Braves/Philadelphia Phillies .40 1.00
OD3 Florida Marlins
Washington Nationals .40 1.00
OD4 Tampa Bay Devil Rays
New York Yankees 1.00 2.50
OD5 Toronto Blue Jays/Detroit Tigers .40 1.00
OD6 Cleveland Indians
Chicago White Sox .40 1.00
OD7 Los Angeles Dodgers
Milwaukee Brewers .40 1.00
OD8 Chicago Cubs/Cincinnati Reds .60 1.50
OD9 Arizona Diamondbacks
Colorado Rockies .40 1.00
OD10 Boston Red Sox/Kansas City Royals 1.00 2.50
OD11 Oakland Athletics/Seattle Mariners .40 1.00
OD12 Baltimore Orioles/Minnesota Twigs .40 1.00
OD13 Pittsburgh Pirates/Houston Astros .40 1.00
OD14 Texas Rangers/Los Angeles Angels .40 1.00
OD15 San Diego Padres
San Francisco Giants .40 1.00

2007 Topps Own the Game

COMPLETE SET (25) 10.00 25.00
SER.1 ODDS 1:6 H, 1:2 HTA, 1:6 K-MART
SER.1 ODDS 1:6 RACK, 1:6 TARGET
SER.1 ODDS 1:6 WAL-MART
OTG1 Ryan Howard .75 2.00
OTG2 David Ortiz 1.00 2.50
OTG3 Alfonso Soriano .60 1.50
OTG4 Albert Pujols 1.25 3.00
OTG5 Lance Berkman .60 1.50
OTG6 Jermaine Dye .40 1.00
OTG7 Travis Hafner .40 1.00
OTG8 Jim Thome .60 1.50
OTG9 Carlos Beltran .60 1.50
OTG10 Adam Dunn .60 1.50
OTG11 Ryan Howard .75 2.00
OTG12 David Ortiz 1.00 2.50
OTG13 Albert Pujols 1.25 3.00
OTG14 Lance Berkman .60 1.50
OTG15 Justin Morneau .60 1.50
OTG16 Andruw Jones .40 1.00
OTG17 Jermaine Dye .40 1.00
OTG18 Travis Hafner .40 1.00
OTG19 Alex Rodriguez 1.25 3.00
OTG20 David Wright .75 2.00
OTG21 Johan Santana .60 1.50
OTG22 Chris Carpenter .60 1.50
OTG23 Brandon Webb .60 1.50
OTG24 Roy Oswalt .60 1.50
OTG25 Roy Halladay .60 1.50

2007 Topps Rookie Stars

COMPLETE SET (10) 6.00 15.00
SER.2 ODDS 1:9 HOBBY
RS1 Daisuke Matsuzaka 1.25 3.00
RS2 Kevin Kouzmanoff .30 .75
RS3 Elijah Dukes .50 1.25
RS4 Andrew Miller 1.25 3.00
RS5 Kei Igawa .75 2.00
RS6 Troy Tulowitzki 1.00 2.50
RS7 Ubaldo Jimenez 1.00 2.50
RS8 Alex Gordon 1.00 2.50
RS9 Josh Hamilton 1.00 2.50
RS10 Delmon Young .50 1.25

2007 Topps Stars

COMPLETE SET (15) 6.00 15.00
SER.2 ODDS 1:9 HOBBY
TS1 Ryan Howard .60 1.50
TS2 Alfonso Soriano .50 1.25
TS3 Todd Helton .50 1.25
TS4 Johan Santana .50 1.25
TS5 David Wright .60 1.50
TS6 Albert Pujols 1.00 2.50
TS7 Daisuke Matsuzaka 1.25 3.00
TS8 Miguel Cabrera .75 2.00
TS9 David Ortiz .75 2.00
TS10 Alex Rodriguez 1.00 2.50
TS11 Vladimir Guerrero .50 1.25
TS12 Ichiro Suzuki 1.00 2.50
TS13 Derek Jeter 2.00 5.00
TS14 Lance Berkman .50 1.25
TS15 Ryan Zimmerman .50 1.25

2007 Topps Target Factory Set Mantle Memorabilia

COMMON MANTLE MEMORABILIA 1.50 30.00
DISTRIBUTED WITH TOPPS TARGET FACT.SETS
MMR53 Mickey Mantle 53T 15.00 40.00
MMR56 Mickey Mantle 56T 15.00 40.00
MMR57 Mickey Mantle 57T 15.00 40.00

2007 Topps Target Factory Set Red Backs

1 Mickey Mantle 3.00 8.00
2 Ted Williams 2.00 5.00

2007 Topps Trading Places

COMPLETE SET (25) 6.00 15.00
SER.2 ODDS 1:9 HOBBY
TP1 Jeff Weaver .40 1.00
TP2 Frank Thomas 1.00 2.50
TP3 Mike Piazza 1.00 2.50
TP4 Alfonso Soriano .60 1.50
TP5 Freddy Garcia .40 1.00
TP6 Jason Marquis .40 1.00
TP7 Ted Lilly .40 1.00
TP8 Mark Loretta .40 1.00
TP9 Marcus Giles .40 1.00
TP10 Barry Zito .60 1.50
TP11 Andy Pettitte .60 1.50
TP12 J.D. Drew .40 1.00
TP13 Gary Matthews .40 1.00
TP14 Jay Payton .40 1.00
TP15 Aubrey Huff .40 1.00
TP16 Brian Bannister .40 1.00
TP17 Jeff Conine .40 1.00
TP18 Gary Sheffield .40 1.00
TP19 Shea Hillenbrand .40 1.00
TP20 Wes Helms .40 1.00
TP21 Frank Catalanotto .40 1.00
TP22 Adam LaRoche .40 1.00
TP23 Mike Gonzalez .40 1.00
TP24 Greg Maddux 1.25 3.00
TP25 Jason Schmidt .40 1.00

2007 Topps Trading Places Autographs

SER.2 ODDS 1:3,055 HOBBY, 1:44 HTA
AH Aubrey Huff 6.00 15.00
AL Adam LaRoche 4.00 10.00
BB Brian Bannister 5.00 12.00
FC Frank Catalanotto 4.00 10.00
FG Freddy Garcia 6.00 15.00
GS Gary Sheffield 6.00 15.00
JS Jason Schmidt 6.00 15.00
MG Mike Gonzalez 4.00 10.00
SH Shea Hillenbrand 4.00 10.00
WH Wes Helms 4.00 10.00

2007 Topps Trading Places Relics

SER.2 ODDS 1:2,435 HOBBY, 1:137 HTA
AP Andy Pettitte 5.00 12.00
AS Alfonso Soriano 5.00 12.00
BZ Barry Zito 4.00 10.00
FT Frank Thomas 5.00 12.00
GM Greg Maddux 5.00 12.00
GS Gary Sheffield 5.00 12.00
JW Jeff Weaver 4.00 10.00
MG Marcus Giles 4.00 10.00
ML Mark Loretta 4.00 10.00
MP Mike Piazza 6.00 15.00

2007 Topps Unlock the Mick

COMPLETE SET (5) 3.00 8.00
COMMON MANTLE 1.00 2.50
SER.1 ODDS 1:18 H, 1:18 HTA, 1:18 K-MART
SER.1 ODDS 1:18 RACK, 1:18 TARGET
SER.1 ODDS 1:18 WAL-MART

2007 Topps Wal-Mart

COMP.SERIES 1 (18) 15.00 40.00
STATED ODDS 1:4 WAL-MART
SER.1 ODDS 3 PER $9.99 WAL-MART BOX
SER.1 ODDS 6 PER $19.99 WAL-MART BOX
1-18 ISSUED IN SERIES 1
19-36 ISSUED IN SERIES 2
37-54 ISSUED IN UPDATE
WM1 Frank Thomas 41 PB 1.00 2.50
WM2 Mike Piazza 34 DS 1.00 2.50
WM3 Ivan Rodriguez 22 Caramel .60 1.50
WM4 David Ortiz T207 1.00 2.50
WM5 David Wright 1887 AG .75 2.00
WM6 Greg Maddux 52T 1.25 3.00
WM7 Mickey Mantle 51T 3.00 8.00
WM8 Jose Reyes 65T .60 1.50
WM9 John Smoltz T205 1.00 2.50
WM10 Jim Edmonds 56T .60 1.50
WM11 Ryan Howard 58T .75 2.00
WM12 Miguel Cabrera T206 1.00 2.50
WM13 Carlos Delgado 10 Turkey .40 1.00
WM14 Miguel Tejada 55B .60 1.50
WM15 Ichiro Suzuki 33 DeLong 1.25 3.00
WM16 Albert Pujols 49B 1.25 3.00
WM17 Derek Jeter 91 SC 2.50 6.00
WM18 Vladimir Guerrero 61 Baz .60 1.50
WM19 Lance Berkman .60 1.50
WM20 Chase Utley .60 1.50
WM21 Gary Matthews .40 1.00
WM22 Johan Santana .60 1.50
WM23 Todd Helton .60 1.50
WM24 Carlos Beltran .60 1.50
WM25 Alex Rodriguez 1.25 3.00
WM26 Cole Hamels .75 2.00
WM27 Daisuke Matsuzaka 1.50 4.00
WM28 Kei Igawa 1.00 2.50
WM29 Hanley Ramirez .60 1.50
WM30 Joe Mauer .75 2.00
WM31 Brandon Webb .60 1.50
WM32 Michael Young .40 1.00
WM33 Nick Swisher .60 1.50
WM34 Jason Bay .60 1.50
WM35 Manny Ramirez 1.00 2.50
WM36 Ryan Zimmerman .60 1.50
WM37 Grady Sizemore .60 1.50
WM38 Matt Holliday 1.00 2.50
WM39 Jimmy Rollins .60 1.50
WM40 Magglio Ordonez .60 1.50
WM41 Prince Fielder .60 1.50
WM42 Jorge Posada .60 1.50
WM43 Hideki Okajima 2.00 5.00
WM44 Dan Uggla .40 1.00
WM45 Jake Peavy .40 1.00
WM46 Carlos Lee .40 1.00
WM47 C.C. Sabathia .60 1.50
WM48 Gary Sheffield .40 1.00
WM49 Tim Lincecum 2.00 5.00
WM50 J.J. Putz .40 1.00
WM51 Justin Verlander 1.00 2.50
WM52 Akinori Iwamura 1.00 2.50
WM53 Adam LaRoche .40 1.00
WM54 Alfonso Soriano .60 1.50

2007 Topps Williams 406

COMPLETE SET (36) 12.50 30.00
COMP.SERIES 1 (18) 6.00 15.00
COMP.SERIES 2 (18) 6.00 15.00
COMMON WILLIAMS .60 1.50
SER.1 ODDS 1:4 TARGET

2007 Topps World Champion Relics

SER.1 ODDS 1:7,550 H, 1:226 HTA
SER.1 ODDS 1:14,750 K-MART
SER.1 ODDS 1:7,550 TARGET
SER.1 ODDS 1:14,750 WAL-MART
STATED PRINT RUN 100 SETS
CARDS ARE NOT SERIAL NUMBERED
PRINT RUNS PROVIDED BY TOPPS
WCR1 Jeff Weaver Jsy/100 * 15.00 40.00
WCR2 Chris Duncan Jsy/100 * 40.00 80.00
WCR3 Chris Carpenter Jsy/100 * 20.00 50.00
WCR4 Yadier Molina Jsy/100 * 60.00 120.00
WCR5 Albert Pujols Bat/100 * 75.00 150.00
WCR6 Jim Edmonds Jsy/100 * 40.00 80.00
WCR7 Ronnie Belliard Bat/100 * 40.00 80.00
WCR8 So Taguchi Bat/100 * 60.00 120.00
WCR9 Juan Encarnacion Bat/100 * 15.00 40.00
WCR10 Scott Rolen Jsy/100 * 15.00 40.00
WCR11 Anthony Reyes Jsy/100 * 40.00 80.00
WCR12 Preston Wilson Bat/100 * 50.00 100.00
WCR13 Jeff Suppan Jsy/100 * 25.00 60.00
WCR14 Adam Wainwright Jsy/100 * 40.00 80.00
WCR15 David Eckstein Bat/100 * 15.00 40.00

2007 Topps World Domination

WD1 Ryan Howard .75 2.00
WD2 Justin Morneau .60 1.50
WD3 Ivan Rodriguez .60 1.50
WD4 Albert Pujols 1.25 3.00
WD5 Jorge Cantu .40 1.00
WD6 Johan Santana .60 1.50
WD7 Ichiro Suzuki 1.25 3.00
WD8 Chien-Ming Wang .60 1.50
WD9 Mariano Rivera 1.25 3.00
WD10 Andruw Jones .40 1.00

2007 Topps Update

COMP.SET w/o SPs (330) 15.00 40.00
COMMON CARD (1-330) .12 .30
COMMON ROOKIE (1-330) .40 1.00
1-330 PLATE ODDS 1:54 HTA
PLATE PRINT RUN 1 SET PER COLOR
BLACK-CYAN-MAGENTA-YELLOW ISSUED
NO PLATE PRICING DUE TO SCARCITY
1 Tony Armas Jr. .12 .30
2 Shannon Stewart .12 .30
3 Jason Marquis .12 .30
4 Josh Wilson .12 .30
5 Steve Trachsel .12 .30
6 J.D. Drew .12 .30
7 Ronnie Belliard .12 .30
8 Trot Nixon .12 .30
9 Adam LaRoche .12 .30
10 Mark Loretta .12 .30
11 Matt Morris .12 .30
12 Marlon Anderson .12 .30
13 Jorge Julio .12 .30
14 Brady Clark .12 .30
15 David Wells .12 .30
16 Francisco Rosario .12 .30
17 Jason Ellison .12 .30
18 Adam Jones .20 .50
19 Russell Branyan .12 .30
20 Rob Bowen .12 .30
21 J.D. Durbin .12 .30
22 Jeff Salazar .12 .30
23 Tadahito Iguchi .12 .30
24 Brad Hennessey .12 .30
25 Mark Hendrickson .12 .30
26 Kameron Loe .12 .30
27 Yusmeiro Petit .12 .30
28 Olmedo Saenz .12 .30
29 Carlos Silva .12 .30
30 Kevin Frandsen .12 .30
31 Tony Pena .12 .30
32 Russ Ortiz .12 .30
33 Hong-Chih Kuo .12 .30
34 Paul McAnulty .12 .30
35 Hiram Bocachica .12 .30
36 Justin Germano .12 .30
37 Jason Simontacchi .12 .30
38 Jose Cruz .12 .30
39 Wilfredo Ledezma .12 .30
40 Chris Denorfia UER .12 .30
41 Ryan Langerhans .12 .30
42 Chris Snelling .12 .30
43 Ubaldo Jimenez .40 1.00
44 Scott Spiezio .12 .30
45 Byung-Hyun Kim .12 .30
46 Brandon Lyon .12 .30
47 Scott Hairston .12 .30
48 Chad Durbin .12 .30
49 Sammy Sosa .30 .75
50 Jason Smith .12 .30
51 Zack Greinke .30 .75
52 Armando Benitez .12 .30
53 Randy Messenger .12 .30
54 Mark Teixeira .20 .50
55 Mike Maroth .12 .30
56 Jamie Burke .12 .30
57 Carlos Marmol .20 .50
58 David Weathers .12 .30
59 Ryan Doumit .12 .30
60 Michael Barrett .12 .30
61 Shawn Chacon .12 .30
62 Mike Fontenot .12 .30
63 Cesar Izturis .12 .30
64 Cliff Floyd .12 .30
65 Angel Pagan .12 .30
66 Aaron Miles .12 .30
67 Tony Graffanino .12 .30
68 Kevin Mench .12 .30
69 Claudio Vargas .12 .30
70 Jose Capellan .12 .30
71 A.J. Pierzynski .12 .30
72 Darin Erstad .12 .30
73 Boone Logan .12 .30
74 Luis Castillo .12 .30
75 Marcus Thames .12 .30
76 Nelfi Perez .12 .30
77 Esteban German .12 .30
78 Tony Pena .12 .30
79 Adam Wainwright .20 .50
80 Reggie Sanders .12 .30
81 Kelly Shoppach .12 .30
82 Rafael Betancourt .12 .30
83 Tom Mastny .12 .30
84 Kyle Farnsworth .12 .30
85 Rick Ankiel .12 .30
86 Kevin Thompson .12 .30
87 Jeff Karstens .12 .30
88 Eric Hinske .12 .30
89 Doug Mirabelli .12 .30
90 Julian Tavarez .12 .30
91 Carlos Pena .20 .50
92 Brendan Harris .12 .30
93 Chris Sampson .12 .30
94 Al Reyes .12 .30
95 Dmitri Young .12 .30
96 Jason Bergmann .12 .30
97 Shawn Hill .12 .30
98 Greg Dobbs .12 .30
99 Carlos Ruiz .12 .30
100a Abraham Nunez .12 .30
100b Jacoby Ellsbury (RC) 6.00 15.00
101 Jayson Werth .20 .50
102 Adam Eaton .12 .30
103 Antonio Alfonseca .12 .30
104 Jorge Sosa .12 .30
105 Ramon Castro .12 .30
106 Ruben Gotay .12 .30
107 Damion Easley .12 .30
108 David Newhan .12 .30
109 Jason Wood .12 .30
110 Reggie Abercrombie .12 .30
111 Kevin Gregg .12 .30
112 Henry Owens .12 .30
113 Willie Harris .12 .30
114 Pete Orr .12 .30
115 Casey Janssen .12 .30
116 Jason Frasor .12 .30
117 Jeremy Accardo .12 .30
118 John McDonald .12 .30
119 Matt Stairs .12 .30
120 Jason Phillips .12 .30
121 Justin Duchscherer .12 .30
122 Rich Harden .12 .30
123 Jack Cust .12 .30
124 Lenny DiNardo .12 .30
125 Joe Kennedy .12 .30
126 Chad Gaudin .12 .30
127 Marco Scutaro .20 .50
128 Brad Thompson .12 .30
129 Dustin Moseley .12 .30
130 Eric Gagne .12 .30
131 Marlon Byrd .12 .30
132 Scot Shields .12 .30
133 Victor Diaz .12 .30
134 Reggie Willits .12 .30
135 Jose Molina .12 .30
136 Ramon Vazquez .12 .30
137 Erick Aybar .12 .30
138 Sean Marshall .12 .30
139 Casey Kotchman .12 .30
140 Ryan Spilborghs .12 .30
141 Cameron Maybin RC .60 1.50
142 Jeremy Guthrie .12 .30
143 Jeff Baker .12 .30
144 Edwin Jackson .12 .30
145 Macay McBride .12 .30
146 Freddie Bynum .12 .30
147 Eric Patterson .40 1.00
148 Dustin McGowan .12 .30
149 Homer Bailey (RC) .60 1.50
150 Ryan Braun (RC) 2.00 5.00
151 Tony Abreu RC 1.00 2.50
152 Tyler Clippard (RC) .60 1.50
153 Mark Reynolds RC 1.25 3.00
154 Jesse Litsch RC .60 1.50
155 Carlos Gomez RC .75 2.00
156 Matt DeSalvo (RC) .40 1.00
157 Andy LaRoche (RC) .40 1.00
158 Tim Lincecum RC 2.00 5.00
159 Jarrod Saltalamacchia (RC) .60 1.50
160 Hunter Pence (RC) 1.25 3.00
161 Brandon Wood (RC) .40 1.00
162 Phil Hughes (RC) 1.00 2.50
163 Rocky Cherry RC 1.00 2.50
164 Chase Wright RC 1.00 2.50
165 Dallas Braden RC .60 1.50
166 Felix Pie (RC) .40 1.00
167 Zach McClellan RC .40 1.00
168 Rick Vanden Hurk RC .40 1.00
169 Micah Owings (RC) .40 1.00
170 Jon Coutlangus (RC) .40 1.00
171 Andy Sonnanstine RC .40 1.00
172 Yunel Escobar (RC) .40 1.00
173 Kevin Slowey (RC) 1.00 2.50
174 Curtis Thigpen (RC) .40 1.00
175 Masumi Kuwata RC .40 1.00
176 Kurt Suzuki (RC) .40 1.00
177 Travis Buck (RC) .40 1.00
178 Matt Lindstrom (RC) .40 1.00
179 Jesus Flores RC .40 1.00
180 Joakim Soria RC .40 1.00
181 Nathan Haynes (RC) .40 1.00
182 Matt Brown (RC) .40 1.00
183 Travis Metcalf RC .60 1.50
184 Yovani Gallardo (RC) 1.00 2.50
185 Nate Schierholtz (RC) .40 1.00
186 Kyle Kendrick RC 1.00 2.50
187 Kevin Melillo (RC) .40 1.00
188 Ryan Rowland-Smith .12 .30
189 Lee Gronkiewicz RC .40 1.00
190 Eulogio De La Cruz (RC) .40 1.00
191 Brett Carroll RC .40 1.00
192 Terry Evans RC .40 1.00
193 Chase Headley (RC) .40 1.00
194 Guillermo Rodriguez RC .40 1.00
195 Marcus McBeth (RC) .40 1.00
196 Brian Wolfe (RC) .40 1.00
197 Troy Cate RC .40 1.00
198 Mike Zagurski RC .40 1.00
199 Yoel Hernandez RC .40 1.00
200 Brad Salmon RC .40 1.00
201 Alberto Arias RC .40 1.00
202 Danny Putnam (RC) .40 1.00
203 Jamie Vermilyea RC .40 1.00
204 Kyle Lohse .12 .30
205 Sammy Sosa .30 .75
206 Tom Glavine .20 .50
207 Prince Fielder .20 .50
208 Mark Buehrle .20 .50
209 Troy Tulowitzki .40 1.00
210 Daisuke Matsuzaka RC 1.50 4.00
211 Randy Johnson .30 .75
212 Justin Verlander .30 .75
213 Trevor Hoffman .20 .50
214 Alex Rodriguez .40 1.00
215 Ivan Rodriguez .20 .50
216 David Ortiz .30 .75
217 Placido Polanco .12 .30
218 Derek Jeter .75 2.00
219 Alex Rodriguez .40 1.00
220 Vladimir Guerrero .20 .50
221 Magglio Ordonez .20 .50
222 Ichiro Suzuki .40 1.00
223 Russell Martin .12 .30
224 Prince Fielder .20 .50
225 Chase Utley .20 .50
226 Jose Reyes .20 .50
227 David Wright .25 .60
228 Carlos Beltran .20 .50
229 Barry Bonds .50 1.25
230 Ken Griffey Jr. .60 1.50
231 Torii Hunter .12 .30
232 Jonathan Papelbon .30 .75
233 J.J. Putz .12 .30
234 Francisco Rodriguez .20 .50
235 C.C. Sabathia .20 .50
236 Johan Santana .20 .50
237 Justin Verlander .30 .75
238 Francisco Cordero .12 .30
239 Mike Lowell .12 .30
240 Cole Hamels .25 .60
241 Trevor Hoffman .20 .50
242 Manny Ramirez .30 .75
243 Jake Peavy .12 .30
244 Brad Penny .12 .30
245 Takashi Saito .12 .30
246 Ben Sheets .12 .30
247 Hideki Okajima .60 1.50
248 Roy Oswalt .20 .50
249 Billy Wagner .12 .30
250 Carl Crawford .20 .50
251 Chris Young .12 .30
252 Brian McCann .12 .30
253 Derrek Lee .12 .30
254 Albert Pujols .40 1.00
255 Dmitri Young .12 .30
256 Orlando Hudson .12 .30
257 J.J. Hardy .12 .30
258 Miguel Cabrera .30 .75
259 Freddy Sanchez .12 .30
260 Matt Holliday .30 .75
261 Carlos Lee .12 .30
262 Aaron Rowand .12 .30
263 Alfonso Soriano .20 .50
264 Victor Martinez .20 .50
265 Jorge Posada .20 .50
266 Justin Morneau .20 .50
267 Brian Roberts .12 .30
268 Carlos Guillen .12 .30
269 Grady Sizemore .20 .50
270 Josh Beckett .12 .30
271 Dan Haren .12 .30
272 Bobby Jenks .12 .30
273 John Lackey .20 .50
274 Gil Meche .12 .30
275 M.Fontenot/K.Greene .12 .30
276 A.Rodriguez/R.Martin .40 1.00
277 T.Tulowitzki/J.Reyes .40 1.00
278 Posada/Jeter/ARod .75 2.00
279 C.Utley/Ichiro .40 1.00
280 C.Crawford/C.Guillen .20 .50
281 C.Hamels/R.Martin .25 .60
282 J.Papelbon/J.Posada .30 .75
283 C.Crawford/V.Martinez .20 .50
284 A.Soriano/J.Hardy .20 .50
285 Justin Morneau .20 .50
286 Prince Fielder .20 .50
287 Alex Rios .12 .30
288 Vladimir Guerrero .20 .50
289 Albert Pujols .40 1.00
290 Ryan Howard .25 .60
291 Magglio Ordonez .20 .50
292 Matt Holliday .30 .75
293 Wilson Betemit .12 .30
294 Todd Wellemeyer .12 .30
295 Scott Baker .12 .30
296 Edgar Gonzalez .12 .30
297 J.P. Howell .12 .30
298 Shaun Marcum .12 .30
299 Edinson Volquez .12 .30
300 Kason Gabbard .12 .30
301 Bob Howry .12 .30
302 J.A. Happ .50 1.25
303 Scott Feldman .20 .50
304 D'Angelo Jimenez .12 .30
305 Orlando Palmeiro .12 .30
306 Paul Bako .12 .30
307 Kyle Davies .12 .30
308 Gabe Gross .12 .30
309 John Wasdin .12 .30
310 Jon Knott .12 .30
311 Josh Phelps .12 .30
312a J.Chamberlain RC .60 1.50
312b J.Chamberlain Rev.Neg 30.00 80.00
312c J.Chamberlain Hou UER
313 Octavio Dotel .12 .30
314 Craig Monroe .12 .30
315 Edward Mujica .12 .30
316 Brandon Watson .12 .30
317 Chris Schroder .12 .30
318 Scott Proctor .12 .30
319 Ty Wigginton .12 .30
320 Troy Percival .12 .30
321 Scott Linebrink .12 .30
322 David Murphy .12 .30
323 Jorge Cantu .12 .30
324 Dan Wheeler .12 .30
325 Jason Kendall .12 .30
326 Milton Bradley .12 .30
327 Justin Upton RC 1.25 3.00
328 Kenny Lofton .12 .30
329 Roger Clemens .40 1.00
330 Brian Burres .12 .30
SQ1 Poley Walnuts 10.00 25.00

2007 Topps Update 1st Edition

*1ST ED VET: 2X TO 5X BASIC
*1ST ED RC: .6X TO 1.5X BASIC RC
STATED ODDS 1:36 HOB, 1:5 HTA

2007 Topps Update Gold

*GOLD VET: 2.5X TO 6X BASIC
*GOLD RC: .75X TO 2X BASIC RC
STATED ODDS 1:4 HOB, 1:4 RET
STATED PRINT RUN 2007 SER.#'d SETS

2007 Topps Update Red Back

COMPLETE SET (330) 30.00 60.00
*RED VET: .5X TO 1.2X BASIC
*RED RC: .5X TO 1.2X BASIC RC
STATED ODDS XXX

2007 Topps Update 2007 Highlights Autographs

GROUP A ODDS 1:14,900 H, 1:252 HTA
GROUP A ODDS 1:14,900 RETAIL
GROUP B ODDS 1:925 H, 19 HTA
GROUP B ODDS 1:1,165 RETAIL
GROUP C ODDS 1:10,100 H, 1:165 HTA
GROUP C ODDS 1:9,700 RETAIL
GROUP D ODDS 1:22,000 H,1:88 HTA
GROUP D ODDS 1:18,400 RETAIL
GROUP E ODDS 1:7,200 H, 1:125 HTA
GROUP E ODDS 1:7,605 RETAIL
GROUP F ODDS 1:7,000 H, 1:123 HTA
GROUP F ODDS 1:7,352 RETAIL
GROUP G ODDS 1:5,025 H, 1:105 HTA
GROUP G ODDS 1:6,563 RETAIL
AC Asdrubal Cabrera G 12.50 30.00
AE Andre Ethier B 6.00 15.00
AG Alex Gordon B 10.00 25.00
AH Aaron Heilman B 4.00 10.00
AJ Andruw Jones A 10.00 25.00
AL Anthony Lerew B 4.00 10.00
AP Albert Pujols A 150.00 200.00
AR Alex Rodriguez A 100.00 175.00
BB Brian Bruney B 4.00 10.00
CJ Conor Jackson B 4.00 10.00
CS C.C. Sabathia B 8.00 20.00
DE Damion Easley F 4.00 10.00
DW David Wright A 15.00 40.00
FC Francisco Cordero B 4.00 10.00
GS Gary Sheffield B 6.00 15.00
JR Jimmy Rollins B 12.50 30.00
JS Jarrod Saltalamacchia B 4.00 10.00
JT Jim Thome A 30.00 60.00
MC Miguel Cairo E 4.00 10.00
PF Prince Fielder B 8.00 20.00
RB Rod Barajas C 4.00 10.00
RC Robinson Cano B 15.00 40.00
RH Ryan Howard A 40.00 80.00
RW Ron Washington D 6.00 15.00
TT Troy Tulowitzki B 4.00 10.00

2007 Topps Update All-Star Stitches

STATED ODDS 1:45 H,1:10 HTA,1:55 R
AIR Alex Rios 3.00 8.00
AP Albert Pujols 8.00 20.00
AR Alex Rodriguez 6.00 15.00
ARR Aaron Rowand 3.00 8.00
BF Brian Fuentes 3.00 8.00
BJ Bobby Jenks 3.00 8.00
BM Brian McCann 5.00 12.00
BR Brian Roberts 3.00 8.00
BS Ben Sheets 3.00 8.00
BW Brandon Webb 3.00 8.00
CB Carlos Beltran 3.00 8.00
CC Carl Crawford 3.00 8.00
CH Cole Hamels 4.00 10.00
CL Carlos Lee 3.00 8.00
CS C.C. Sabathia 5.00 12.00
CU Chase Utley 5.00 12.00
CY Chris Young 3.00 8.00
DO David Ortiz 6.00 15.00
DW David Wright 6.00 15.00
DY Dmitri Young 3.00 8.00
FC Francisco Cordero 3.00 8.00
FR Francisco Rodriguez 3.00 8.00
FS Freddy Sanchez 3.00 8.00
GM Gil Meche 3.00 8.00
GS Grady Sizemore 5.00 12.00
HO Hideki Okajima 5.00 12.00
IR Ivan Rodriguez 5.00 12.00
IS Ichiro Suzuki 10.00 25.00
JB Josh Beckett 5.00 12.00
JEP Jake Peavy 3.00 8.00
JH J.J. Hardy 3.00 8.00
JL John Lackey 3.00 8.00
JM Justin Morneau 3.00 8.00
JP J.J. Putz 3.00 8.00
JR Jose Reyes 5.00 12.00
JRP Jorge Posada 5.00 12.00
JRV Jose Valverde 3.00 8.00
JS Johan Santana 5.00 12.00
JV Justin Verlander 6.00 15.00
MH Matt Holliday 5.00 12.00
ML Mike Lowell 5.00 12.00
MR Manny Ramirez 5.00 12.00
OH Orlando Hudson 3.00 8.00
PF Prince Fielder 5.00 12.00
RH Ryan Howard 6.00 15.00
RM Russell Martin 5.00 12.00
RO Roy Oswalt 3.00 8.00
TH Torii Hunter 3.00 8.00
TS Takashi Saito 5.00 12.00
TWH Trevor Hoffman 3.00 8.00
VM Victor Martinez 3.00 8.00

2007 Topps Update Barry Bonds 756

STATED ODDS 1:36 H, 1:5 HTA, 1:36 R
HRK Barry Bonds 1.00 2.50

2007 Topps Update Barry Bonds 756 Relic

STATED ODDS 1:5,145 H,1:1,400 HTA
STATED ODDS 1:5,145 RETAIL
STATED PRINT RUN 756 SER.#'d SETS
HRKR Barry Bonds 12.00 30.00

2007 Topps Update Chrome

STATED ODDS XXX
STATED PRINT RUN 415 SER.#'d SETS
TRC1 Homer Bailey 2.50 6.00
TRC2 Ryan Braun 8.00 20.00
TRC3 Tony Abreu 4.00 10.00
TRC4 Tyler Clippard 2.50 6.00
TRC5 Mark Reynolds 5.00 12.00
TRC6 Jesse Litsch 2.50 6.00
TRC7 Carlos Gomez 3.00 8.00
TRC8 Matt DeSalvo 1.50 4.00
TRC9 Andy LaRoche 1.50 4.00
TRC10 Tim Lincecum 8.00 20.00
TRC11 Jarrod Saltalamacchia 2.50 6.00
TRC12 Hunter Pence 5.00 12.00
TRC13 Brandon Wood 1.50 4.00
TRC14 Phil Hughes 4.00 10.00
TRC15 Rocky Cherry 4.00 10.00
TRC16 Chase Wright 4.00 10.00
TRC17 Dallas Braden 2.50 6.00
TRC18 Felix Pie 1.50 4.00
TRC19 Zach McClellan 1.50 4.00
TRC20 Rick VandenHurk 1.50 4.00
TRC21 Micah Owings 1.50 4.00
TRC22 Jon Coutlangus 1.50 4.00
TRC23 Andy Sonnanstine 1.50 4.00
TRC24 Yunel Escobar 1.50 4.00
TRC25 Kevin Slowey 4.00 10.00
TRC26 Curtis Thigpen 1.50 4.00
TRC27 Masumi Kuwata 1.50 4.00
TRC28 Kurt Suzuki 1.50 4.00
TRC29 Travis Buck 1.50 4.00
TRC30 Matt Lindstrom 1.50 4.00
TRC31 Jesus Flores 1.50 4.00
TRC32 Joakim Soria 1.50 4.00
TRC33 Nathan Haynes 1.50 4.00
TRC34 Matthew Brown 1.50 4.00
TRC35 Travis Metcalf 2.50 6.00
TRC36 Yovani Gallardo 4.00 10.00
TRC37 Nate Schierholtz 1.50 4.00
TRC38 Kyle Kendrick 4.00 10.00
TRC39 Kevin Melillo 1.50 4.00
TRC40 Cameron Maybin 2.50 6.00
TRC41 Lee Gronkiewicz 1.50 4.00
TRC42 Eulogio De La Cruz 2.50 6.00
TRC43 Brett Carroll 1.50 4.00
TRC44 Terry Evans 1.50 4.00
TRC45 Chase Headley 1.50 4.00
TRC46 Guillermo Rodriguez 1.50 4.00
TRC47 Marcus McBeth 1.50 4.00
TRC48 Brian Wolfe 1.50 4.00
TRC49 Troy Cate 1.50 4.00
TRC50 Justin Upton 5.00 12.00
TRC51 Joba Chamberlain 2.50 6.00
TRC52 Brad Salmon 1.50 4.00
TRC53 Alberto Arias 1.50 4.00
TRC54 Danny Putnam 1.50 4.00
TRC55 Jamie Vermilyea 1.50 4.00

2007 Topps Update Target

COMMON CARD .75 2.00
STATED ODDS XXX

2007 Topps Update World Series Watch

COMPLETE SET (15) 8.00 20.00
STATED ODDS 1:36 H, 1:5 HTA, 1:36 R
WSW1 New York Mets .75 2.00
WSW2 Detroit Tigers .75 2.00
WSW3 Boston Red Sox 2.00 5.00
WSW4 Milwaukee Brewers .75 2.00
WSW5 Cleveland Indians .75 2.00
WSW6 Los Angeles Angels .75 2.00
WSW7 San Diego Padres .75 2.00
WSW8 Los Angeles Dodgers .75 2.00
WSW9 Philadelphia Phillies .75 2.00
WSW10 Chicago Cubs .75 2.00
WSW11 St. Louis Cardinals .75 2.00
WSW12 Arizona Diamondbacks .75 2.00
WSW13 New York Yankees 2.00 5.00
WSW14 Seattle Mariners .75 2.00
WSW15 Atlanta Braves .75 2.00

2008 Topps

COMP.HOBBY SET (660) 30.00 60.00
COMP.CUBS SET (660) 30.00 60.00
COMP.DODGERS SET (660) 30.00 60.00
COMP.METS SET (660) 30.00 60.00
COMP.RED SOX SET (660) 30.00 60.00
COMP.TIGERS SET (660) 30.00 60.00
COMP.YANKEES SET (660) 30.00 60.00
COMP.SET w/o VAR (660) 30.00 60.00
COMP.SERIES 1 (331) 12.50 30.00
COMP.SERIES 2 (330) 12.50 30.00
COMMON CARD (1-660) .12 .30
COMMON RC (1-660) .25 .60
SERIES 1 SET DOES NOT INCLUDE FS1
SERIES 1 SET DOES NOT INCLUDE #234C
SER.2 SET DOES NOT INCLUDE #661
SER.2 SET DOES NOT INCLUDE NNO CARDS
1 Alex Rodriguez .40 1.00
2 Barry Zito .20 .50
3 Jeff Suppan .12 .30
4 Rick Ankiel .12 .30
5 Scott Kazmir .20 .50
6 Felix Pie .12 .30
7 Mickey Mantle 1.00 2.50
8 Stephen Drew .12 .30
9 Randy Wolf .12 .30
10 Miguel Cabrera .30 .75
11 Yorvit Torrealba .12 .30
12 Jason Bartlett .12 .30
13 Kendry Morales .12 .30
14 Lenny DiNardo .20 .50
15 Ordon/Suzuki/Polan .40 1.00
16 Kevin Gregg .12 .30
17 Cristian Guzman .12 .30
18 J.D. Durbin .12 .30
19 Robinson Tejeda .12 .30
20 Daisuke Matsuzaka .20 .50
21 Edwin Encarnacion .30 .75
22 Ron Washington MG .12 .30
23 Chin-Lung Hu (RC) .25 .60
24 ARod/Ordon/Vlad .40 1.00
25 Kaz Matsui .12 .30
26 Manny Ramirez .30 .75
27 Bob Melvin MG .12 .30
28 Kyle Kendrick .12 .30
29 Anibal Sanchez .12 .30
30 Jimmy Rollins .20 .50
31 Ronny Paulino .12 .30
32 Howie Kendrick .12 .30
33 Joe Mauer .25 .60

34 Aaron Cook .12 .30
35 Cole Hamels .25 .60
36 Brendan Harris .12 .30
37 Jason Marquis .12 .30
38 Preston Wilson .12 .30
39 Yovanni Gallardo .12 .30
40 Miguel Tejada .20 .50
41 Rich Aurilia .12 .30
42 Corey Hart .12 .30
43 Ryan Dempster .12 .30
44 Jonathan Broxton .12 .30
45 Dontrelle Willis .12 .30
46 Zack Greinke .30 .75
47 Orlando Cabrera .20 .50
48 Zach Duke .12 .30
49 Orlando Hernandez .12 .30
50 Jake Peavy .12 .30
51 Erik Bedard .12 .30
52 Trevor Hoffman .20 .50
53 Hank Blalock .12 .30
54 Victor Martinez .20 .50
55 Chris Young .12 .30
56 Seth Smith (RC) .25 .60
57 Wladimir Balentien (RC) .25 .60
58 Holliday/Howard/Mig.Cabrera .30 .75
59 Grady Sizemore .20 .50
60 Jose Reyes .20 .50
61 ARod/Pena/Ortiz .40 1.00
62 Rich Thompson RC .40 1.00
63 Jason Michaels .12 .30
64 Mike Lowell .12 .30
65 Billy Wagner .12 .30
66 Brad Wilkerson .12 .30
67 Wes Helms .12 .30
68 Kevin Millar .12 .30
69 Bobby Cox MG .12 .30
70 Dan Uggla .12 .30
71 Jarrod Washburn .12 .30
72 Mike Piazza .30 .75
73 Mike Napoli .20 .50
74 Garrett Atkins .12 .30
75 Felix Hernandez .20 .50
76 Ivan Rodriguez .20 .50
77 Angel Guzman .12 .30
78 Radhames Liz RC .40 1.00
79 Omar Vizquel .20 .50
80 Alex Rios .12 .30
81 Ray Durham .12 .30
82 So Taguchi .12 .30
83 Mark Reynolds .12 .30
84 Brian Fuentes .12 .30
85 Jason Bay .20 .50
86 Scott Podsednik .12 .30
87 Maicer Izturis .12 .30
88 Jack Cust .12 .30
89 Josh Willingham .20 .50
90 Vladimir Guerrero .20 .50
91 Marcus Giles .12 .30
92 Ross Detwiler RC .40 1.00
93 Kenny Lofton .12 .30
94 Bud Black MG .12 .30
95 John Lackey .20 .50
96 Sam Fuld RC .75 2.00
97 Clint Sammons (RC) .25 .60
98 R.Howard/C.Utley .20 .50
99 D.Ortiz/M.Ramirez .30 .75
100 Ryan Howard .20 .50
101 Ryan Braun ROY .20 .50
102 Ross Ohlendorf RC .40 1.00
103 Jonathan Albaladejo RC .40 1.00
104 Kevin Youkilis .12 .30
105 Roger Clemens .40 1.00
106 Josh Bard .12 .30
107 Shawn Green .12 .30
108 B.J. Ryan .12 .30
109 Joe Nathan .12 .30
110 Justin Morneau .20 .50
111 Ubaldo Jimenez .12 .30
112 Jacque Jones .12 .30
113 Kevin Frandsen .12 .30
114 Mike Fontenot .12 .30
115 Johan Santana .20 .50
116 Chuck James .12 .30
117 Boof Bonser .12 .30
118 Marco Scutaro .20 .50
119 Jeremy Hermida .12 .30
120 Andruw Jones .12 .30
121 Mike Cameron .12 .30
122 Jason Varitek .30 .75
123 Terry Francona MG .20 .50
124 Bob Geren MG .12 .30
125 Tim Hudson .20 .50
126 Brandon Jones RC .60 1.50
127 Steve Pearce RC 1.25 3.00
128 Kenny Lofton .12 .30
129 Kevin Hart (RC) .25 .60
130 Justin Upton .20 .50
131 Norris Hopper .12 .30
132 Ramon Vazquez .12 .30
133 Mike Bacsik .12 .30
134 Matt Stairs .12 .30
135 Brad Penny .12 .30
136 Robinson Cano .20 .50
137 Jamey Carroll .12 .30
138 Dan Wheeler .12 .30
139 Johnny Estrada .12 .30
140 Brandon Webb .20 .50
141 Ryan Klesko .12 .30
142 Chris Duncan .12 .30
143 Willie Harris .12 .30
144 Jerry Owens .12 .30
145 Magglio Ordonez .20 .50
146 Aaron Hill .12 .30
147 Marlon Anderson .12 .30
148 Gerald Laird .12 .30
149 Luke Hochevar RC .40 1.00
150 Alfonso Soriano .20 .50
151 Adam Loewen .12 .30
152 Bronson Arroyo .12 .30
153 Luis Mendoza (RC) .25 .60
154 David Ross .12 .30
155 Carlos Zambrano .20 .50
156 Brandon McCarthy .12 .30
157 Tim Redding .12 .30
158 Jose Bautista UER .20 .50
159 Luke Scott .12 .30
160 Ben Sheets .12 .30
161 Matt Garza .12 .30
162 Andy Laroche .12 .30
163 Doug Davis .12 .30
164 Nate Schierholtz .12 .30
165 Tim Lincecum .20 .50
166 Andy Sonnanstine .12 .30
167 Jason Hirsh .12 .30
168 Phil Hughes .12 .30
169 Adam Lind .12 .30
170 Scott Rolen .20 .50
171 John Maine .12 .30
172 Chris Ray .12 .30
173 Jamie Moyer .12 .30
174 Julian Tavarez .12 .30
175 Delmon Young .20 .50
176 Troy Patton (RC) .25 .60
177 Josh Anderson (RC) .25 .60
178 Dustin Pedroia ROY .30 .75
179 Chris Young .12 .30
180 Jose Valverde .12 .30
181 Borowski/Jenks/Putz .12 .30
182 Billy Buckner (RC) .25 .60
183 Paul Byrd .12 .30
184 Tadahito Iguchi .12 .30
185 Yunel Escobar .12 .30
186 Lastings Milledge .12 .30
187 Dustin McGowan .12 .30
188 Kei Igawa .12 .30
189 Esteban German .12 .30
190 Russell Martin .12 .30
191 Orlando Hudson .12 .30
192 Jim Edmonds .20 .50
193 J.J. Hardy .12 .30
194 Chad Billingsley .20 .50
195 Todd Helton .20 .50
196 Ross Gload .12 .30
197 Melky Cabrera .12 .30
198 Shannon Stewart .12 .30
199 Adrian Beltre .30 .75
200 Manny Ramirez .30 .75
201 Matt Capps .12 .30
202 Mike Lamb .12 .30
203 Jason Tyner .12 .30
204 Rafael Furcal .12 .30
205 Gil Meche .12 .30
206 Geoff Jenkins .12 .30
207 Jeff Kent .12 .30
208 David DeJesus .12 .30
209 Andy Phillips .12 .30
210 Mark Teahen .12 .30
211 Lyle Overbay .12 .30
212 Moises Alou .12 .30
213 Michael Barrett .12 .30
214 C.J. Wilson .12 .30
215 Bobby Jenks .12 .30
216 Ryan Garko .12 .30
217 Josh Beckett .12 .30
218 Clint Hurdle MG .12 .30
219 Kevin Kouzmanoff .12 .30
220 Roy Oswalt .20 .50
221 Ian Snell .12 .30
222 Mark Grudzielanek .12 .30
223 Odalis Perez .12 .30
224 Mark Buehrle .20 .50
225 Hunter Pence .20 .50
226 Kurt Suzuki .12 .30
227 Alfredo Amezaga .12 .30
228 Geoff Blum .12 .30
229 Dustin Pedroia .30 .75
230 Roy Halladay .20 .50
231 Casey Blake .12 .30
232 Clay Buchholz (RC) .40 1.00
233 Jimmy Rollins MVP .20 .50
234a Boston Red Sox .50 1.25
234b Red Sox w/Giuliani 3.00 8.00
234c Red Sox w/Giuliani Red 30.00 60.00
235 Rich Harden .12 .30
236 Joe Koshansky (RC) .25 .60
237 Eric Wedge MG .12 .30
238 Shane Victorino .12 .30
239 Richie Sexson .12 .30
240 Jim Thome .20 .50
241 Ervin Santana .12 .30
242 Manny Acta .12 .30
243 Akinori Iwamura .12 .30
244 Adam Wainwright .20 .50
245 Dan Haren .12 .30
246 Jason Isringhausen .12 .30
247 Edgar Gonzalez .12 .30
248 Jose Contreras .12 .30
249 Chris Sampson .12 .30
250 Jonathan Papelbon .20 .50
251 Dan Johnson .12 .30
252 Dmitri Young .12 .30
253 Bronson Sardinha (RC) .25 .60
254 David Murphy .12 .30
255 Brandon Phillips .12 .30
256 A.Rodriguez MVP .40 1.00
257 A.Kearns/D.Young .12 .30
258 M.Ramirez/K.Youkilis .30 .75
259 Emilio Bonifacio RC .60 1.50
260 Chad Cordero .12 .30
261 Josh Barfield .12 .30
262 Brett Myers .12 .30
263 Nook Logan .12 .30
264 Byung-Hyun Kim .12 .30
265 Fredi Gonzalez .12 .30
266 Ryan Doumit .12 .30
267 Chris Burke .12 .30
268 Daric Barton (RC) .25 .60
269 James Loney .12 .30
270 C.C. Sabathia .20 .50
271 Chad Tracy .12 .30
272 Anthony Reyes .12 .30
273 Rafael Soriano .12 .30
274 Jermaine Dye .12 .30
275 C.C. Sabathia .20 .50
276 Brad Ausmus .12 .30
277 Aubrey Huff .12 .30
278 Xavier Nady .12 .30
279 Damion Easley .12 .30
280 Willie Randolph MG .12 .30
281 Carlos Ruiz .12 .30
282 Jon Lester .20 .50
283 Jorge Sosa .12 .30
284 Lance Broadway (RC) .25 .60
285 Tony LaRussa MG .20 .50
286 Jeff Clement (RC) .40 1.00
287 Morneau/Santana/Mauer .25 .60
288 I.Rodriguez/J.Verlander .30 .75
289 Justin Ruggiano RC .40 1.00
290 Edgar Renteria .12 .30
291 Eugenio Velez RC .25 .60
292 Mark Loretta .20 .50
293 Gavin Floyd .12 .30
294 Brian McCann .20 .50
295 Tim Wakefield .20 .50
296 Paul Konerko .20 .50
297 Jorge Posada .20 .50
298 Fielder/Howard/Dunn .20 .50
299 Cesar Izturis .12 .30
300 Chien-Ming Wang .20 .50
301 Chris Duffy .12 .30
302 Horacio Ramirez .12 .30
303 Jose Lopez .12 .30
304 Jose Vidro .12 .30
305 Carlos Delgado .12 .30
306 Scott Olsen .12 .30
307 Shawn Hill .12 .30
308 Felipe Lopez .12 .30
309 Ryan Church .12 .30
310 Kelvim Escobar .20 .50
311 Jeremy Guthrie .12 .30
312 Ramon Hernandez .12 .30
313 Kameron Loe .12 .30
314 Ian Kinsler .20 .50
315 David Weathers .12 .30
316 Scott Hatteberg .12 .30
317 Cliff Lee .20 .50
318 Ned Yost MG .12 .30
319 Joey Votto (RC) 2.00 5.00
320 Ichiro Suzuki .40 1.00
321 J.R. Towles RC .40 1.00
322 Kazmir/Santana/Bedard .20 .50
323 Valverde/Cordero/Hoffman .20 .50
324 Jake Peavy .12 .30
325 Jim Leyland MG .12 .30
326 Holliday/Chipper/Hanley .30 .75
327 Peavy/Harang/Smoltz .30 .75
328 Nyjer Morgan (RC) .25 .60
329 Lou Piniella MG .12 .30
330 Curtis Granderson .20 .50
331 Dave Roberts .20 .50
332 Grady Sizemore/Jhonny Peralta .20 .50
333 Jayson Nix (RC) .25 .60
334 Oliver Perez .12 .30
335 Eric Byrnes .12 .30
336 Jhonny Peralta .12 .30
337 Livan Hernandez .12 .30
338 Matt Diaz .12 .30
339 Troy Percival .12 .30
340 David Wright .20 .50
341 Daniel Cabrera .12 .30
342 Matt Belisle .12 .30
343 Kason Gabbard .12 .30
344 Mike Rabelo .12 .30
345 Carl Crawford .20 .50
346 Adam Everett .12 .30
347 Chris Capuano .12 .30
348 Craig Monroe .12 .30
349 Mike Mussina .20 .50
350 Mark Teixeira .20 .50
351 Bobby Crosby .12 .30
352 Miguel Batista .12 .30
353 Brendan Ryan .12 .30
354 Edwin Jackson .12 .30
355 Brian Roberts .12 .30
356 Manny Corpas .12 .30
357 Jeremy Accardo .20 .50
358 John Patterson .12 .30
359 Evan Meek RC .25 .60
360 David Ortiz .30 .75
361 Wesley Wright RC .25 .60
362 Fernando Hernandez RC .25 .60
363 Brian Barton RC .40 1.00
364 Al Reyes .12 .30
365 Derrek Lee .12 .30
366 Jeff Weaver .12 .30
367 Khalil Greene .12 .30
368 Michael Bourn .12 .30
369 Luis Castillo .12 .30
370 Adam Dunn .20 .50
371 Rickie Weeks .12 .30
372 Matt Kemp .25 .60
373 Casey Kotchman .12 .30
374 Jason Jennings .12 .30
375 Fausto Carmona .12 .30
376 Willy Taveras .12 .30
377 Jake Westbrook .12 .30
378 Ozzie Guillen .12 .30
379 Hideki Okajima .12 .30
380 Grady Sizemore .20 .50
381 Jeff Francoeur .20 .50
382 Micah Owings .12 .30
383 Jered Weaver .20 .50
384 Carlos Quentin .12 .30
385 Troy Tulowitzki .30 .75
386 Julio Lugo .12 .30
387 Sean Marshall .12 .30
388 Jorge Cantu .12 .30
389 Callix Crabbe (RC) .25 .60
390 Troy Glaus .20 .50
391 Nick Markakis .25 .60
392 Joey Gathright .12 .30
393 Michael Cuddyer .12 .30
394 Mark Ellis .12 .30
395 Lance Berkman .20 .50
396 Randy Johnson .30 .75
397 Brian Wilson .30 .75
398 Kenji Johjima .12 .30
399 Jarrod Saltalamacchia .12 .30
400 Matt Holliday .30 .75
401 Scott Hairston .12 .30
402 Taylor Buchholz .12 .30
403 Nate Robertson .12 .30
404 Cecil Cooper .12 .30
405 Travis Hafner .12 .30
406 Takashi Saito .12 .30
407 Johnny Damon .20 .50
408 Edinson Volquez .12 .30
409 Jason Giambi .12 .30
410 Alex Gordon .20 .50
411 Jason Kubel .12 .30
412 Joel Zumaya .12 .30
413 Wandy Rodriguez .12 .30
414 Andrew Miller .20 .50
415 Derek Lowe .12 .30
416 Elijah Dukes .12 .30
417 Brian Bass (RC) .25 .60
418 Dioner Navarro .12 .30
419 Bengie Molina .12 .30
420 Nick Swisher .20 .50
421 Brandon Backe .12 .30
422 Erick Aybar .12 .30
423 Mike Scioscia MG .12 .30
424 Aaron Harang .12 .30
425 Hanley Ramirez .20 .50
426 Franklin Gutierrez .12 .30
427 Carlos Guillen .12 .30
428 Jair Jurrjens .12 .30
429 Billy Butler .12 .30
430 Ryan Braun .20 .50
431 Delwyn Young .12 .30
432 Jason Kendall .12 .30
433 Carlos Silva .12 .30
434 Ron Gardenhire MG .12 .30
435 Torii Hunter .12 .30
436 Joe Blanton .12 .30
437 Brandon Wood .12 .30
438 Jay Payton .12 .30
439 Josh Hamilton .20 .50
440 Pedro Martinez .20 .50
441 Miguel Olivo .12 .30
442 Luis Gonzalez .12 .30
443 Greg Dobbs .12 .30
444 Jack Wilson .12 .30
445 Hideki Matsui .30 .75
446 Randor Bierd RC .25 .60
447 Chipper Jones/Mark Teixeira .30 .75
448 Cameron Maybin .12 .30
449 Braden Looper .12 .30
450 Prince Fielder .20 .50
451 Brian Giles .12 .30
452 Kevin Slowey .12 .30
453 Josh Fogg .12 .30
454 Mike Hampton .12 .30
455 Derek Jeter .75 2.00
456 Chone Figgins .12 .30
457 Josh Fields .12 .30
458 Brad Hawpe .12 .30
459 Mike Sweeney .12 .30
460 Chase Utley .20 .50
461 Jacoby Ellsbury .25 .60
462 Freddy Sanchez .12 .30
463 John McLaren .12 .30
464 Rocco Baldelli .12 .30
465 Huston Street .20 .50
466 Miguel Cabrera/Ivan Rodriguez .30 .75
467 Nick Blackburn RC .40 1.00
468 Gregor Blanco (RC) .25 .60
469 Brian Bocock RC .25 .60
470 Tom Gorzelanny .12 .30
471 Brian Schneider .12 .30
472 Shaun Marcum .12 .30
473 Joe Maddon .12 .30
474 Yuniesky Betancourt .12 .30
475 Adrian Gonzalez .20 .50
476 Johnny Cueto RC .60 1.50
477 Ben Broussard .12 .30
478 Geovany Soto .30 .75
479 Bobby Abreu .12 .30
480 Matt Cain .20 .50
481 Manny Parra .12 .30
482 Kazuo Fukumori RC .40 1.00
483 Mike Jacobs .12 .30
484 Todd Jones .12 .30
485 J.J. Putz .12 .30
486 Javier Vazquez .12 .30
487 Corey Patterson .12 .30
488 Mike Gonzalez .12 .30
489 Joakim Soria .12 .30
490 Albert Pujols .40 1.00
491 Cliff Floyd .12 .30
492 Harvey Garcia (RC) .25 .60
493 Steve Holm RC .25 .60
494 Paul Maholm .12 .30
495 James Shields .12 .30
496 Brad Lidge .12 .30
497 Cla Meredith .12 .30
498 Matt Chico .12 .30
499 Milton Bradley .12 .30
500 Chipper Jones .30 .75
501 Elliot Johnson (RC) .25 .60
502 Alex Cora .20 .50
503 Jeremy Bonderman .12 .30
504 Conor Jackson .12 .30
505 B.J. Upton .20 .50
506 Jay Gibbons .12 .30
507 Mark DeRosa .12 .30
508 John Danks .12 .30
509 Alex Gonzalez .12 .30
510 Justin Verlander .30 .75
511 Jeff Francis .12 .30
512 Placido Polanco .12 .30
513 Rick Vanden Hurk .12 .30
514 Tony Pena .12 .30
515 A.J. Burnett .12 .30
516 Jason Schmidt .12 .30
517 Bill Hall .12 .30
518 Ian Stewart .12 .30
519 Travis Buck .20 .50
520 Vernon Wells .12 .30
521 Jayson Werth .20 .50
522 Nate McLouth .12 .30
523 Noah Lowry .12 .30
524 Raul Ibanez .20 .50
525 Gary Matthews .12 .30
526 Juan Encarnacion .12 .30
527 Marlon Byrd .12 .30
528 Paul Lo Duca .12 .30
529 Masahide Kobayashi RC .40 1.00
530 Ryan Zimmerman .20 .50
531 Hiroki Kuroda RC .60 1.50
532 Tim Lahey RC .25 .60
533 Kyle McClellan RC .25 .60
534 Matt Tupman RC .25 .60
535 Francisco Rodriguez .20 .50
536 A.Pujols/P.Fielder .40 1.00
537 Scott Moore .12 .30
538 Alex Romero (RC) .40 1.00
539 Clete Thomas RC .40 1.00
540 John Smoltz .30 .75
541 Adam Jones .20 .50
542 Adam Kennedy .12 .30
543 Carlos Lee .12 .30
544 Chad Gaudin .20 .50
545 Chris Young .12 .30
546 Francisco Liriano .12 .30
547 Fred Lewis .12 .30
548 Garrett Olson .12 .30
549 Gregg Zaun .12 .30
550 Curt Schilling .20 .50
551 Erick Threets (RC) .25 .60
552 J.D. Drew .12 .30
553 Jo-Jo Reyes .12 .30
554 Joe Borowski .12 .30
555 Josh Beckett .12 .30
556 John Gibbons .12 .30
557 John McDonald .12 .30
558 John Russell .12 .30
559 Jonny Gomes .12 .30
560 Aramis Ramirez .12 .30
561 Matt Tolbert RC .40 1.00
562 Ronnie Belliard .12 .30
563 Ramon Troncoso RC .25 .60
564 Frank Catalanotto .12 .30
565 A.J. Pierzynski .12 .30
566 Kevin Millwood .12 .30
567 David Eckstein .12 .30
568 Jose Guillen .12 .30
569 Brad Hennessey .12 .30
570 Homer Bailey .20 .50
571 Eric Gagne .12 .30
572 Adam Eaton .12 .30
573 Tom Gordon .12 .30
574 Scott Baker .12 .30
575 Ty Wigginton .20 .50
576 Dave Bush .12 .30
577 John Buck .12 .30
578 Ricky Nolasco .12 .30
579 Jesse Litsch .20 .50
580 Ken Griffey Jr. .60 1.50
581 Kazuo Matsui .12 .30
582 Dusty Baker .12 .30
583 Nick Punto .12 .30
584 Ryan Theriot .12 .30
585 Brian Bannister .12 .30
586 Coco Crisp .12 .30
587 Chris Snyder .12 .30
588 Tony Gwynn .12 .30
589 Dave Trembley .12 .30
590 Mariano Rivera .40 1.00
591 Rico Washington (RC) .25 .60
592 Matt Morris .12 .30
593 Randy Wells RC .40 1.00
594 Mike Morse .12 .30
595 Francisco Cordero .12 .30
596 Joba Chamberlain .12 .30
597 Kyle Davies .12 .30
598 Bruce Bochy .20 .50
599 Austin Kearns .12 .30
600 Tom Glavine .20 .50
601 Felipe Paulino RC .40 1.00
602 Lyle Overbay/Vernon Wells .12 .30
603 Blake DeWitt (RC) .40 1.00
604 Wily Mo Pena .12 .30
605 Andre Ethier .20 .50
606 Jason Bergmann .12 .30
607 Ryan Spilborghs .12 .30
608 Brian Burres .12 .30
609 Ted Lilly .12 .30
610 Carlos Beltran .20 .50
611 Garret Anderson .12 .30
612 Kelly Johnson .12 .30
613 Melvin Mora .12 .30
614 Rich Hill .12 .30
615 Pat Burrell .12 .30
616 Jon Garland .12 .30
617 Asdrubal Cabrera .20 .50
618 Pat Neshek .20 .50
619 Sergio Mitre .12 .30
620 Gary Sheffield .12 .30
621 Denard Span .20 .50
622 Jorge De La Rosa .12 .30
623 Trey Hillman MG .12 .30
624 Joe Torre MG .20 .50
625 Greg Maddux .40 1.00
626 Mike Redmond .12 .30
627 Mike Pelfrey .12 .30
628 Andy Pettitte .20 .50
629 Eric Chavez .12 .30
630 Chris Carpenter .20 .50
631 Joe Girardi MG .20 .50
632 Charlie Manuel MG .12 .30
633 Adam LaRoche .12 .30
634 Kenny Rogers .12 .30
635 Michael Young .12 .30
636 Rafael Betancourt .12 .30
637 Jose Castillo .12 .30
638 Juan Pierre .12 .30
639 Juan Uribe .12 .30
640 Carlos Pena .20 .50
641 Marcus Thames .12 .30
642 Mark Kotsay .12 .30
643 Matt Murton .12 .30
644 Reggie Willits .12 .30
645 Andy Marte .12 .30
646 Rajai Davis .12 .30
647 Randy Winn .12 .30
648 Ryan Freel .12 .30
649 Joe Crede .12 .30
650 Frank Thomas .30 .75
651 Martin Prado .12 .30
652 Rod Barajas .12 .30
653 Endy Chavez .12 .30
654 Willy Aybar .12 .30
655 Aaron Rowand .12 .30
656 Darin Erstad .12 .30
657 Jeff Keppinger .12 .30
658 Kerry Wood .12 .30
659 Vicente Padilla .12 .30
660 Yadier Molina .40 1.00
661 Johan Santana NoNo 125.00 250.00
FS1 Kazuo Uzuki .75 2.00
NNO Alexei Ramirez 15.00 40.00
NNO Kosuke Fukudome 20.00 50.00
NNO Yasuhiko Yabuta 40.00 80.00

2008 Topps Black

SER.1 ODDS 1:95 HOBBY
SER.2 ODDS 1:63 HOBBY
STATED PRINT RUN 57 SER.#'d SETS
1 Alex Rodriguez 12.00 30.00
2 Barry Zito 6.00 15.00
3 Jeff Suppan 6.00 15.00
4 Rick Ankiel 6.00 15.00
5 Scott Kazmir 6.00 15.00
6 Felix Pie 6.00 15.00
7 Mickey Mantle 60.00 120.00
8 Stephen Drew 6.00 15.00
9 Randy Wolf 6.00 15.00
10 Miguel Cabrera 10.00 25.00
11 Yorvit Torrealba 6.00 15.00
12 Jason Bartlett 6.00 15.00
13 Kendry Morales 6.00 15.00
14 Lenny DiNardo 6.00 15.00
15 Ordonez/Ichiro/Polanco 12.00 30.00
16 Kevin Gregg 6.00 15.00
17 Cristian Guzman 6.00 15.00
18 J.D. Durbin 6.00 15.00
19 Robinson Tejeda 6.00 15.00
20 Daisuke Matsuzaka 6.00 15.00
21 Edwin Encarnacion 6.00 15.00
22 Ron Washington MG 6.00 15.00
23 Chin-Lung Hu 30.00 60.00
24 A.Rod/Ordonez/Vlad 12.00 30.00
25 Kaz Matsui 6.00 15.00
26 Manny Ramirez 10.00 25.00
27 Bob Melvin MG 6.00 15.00
28 Kyle Kendrick 6.00 15.00
29 Anibal Sanchez 6.00 15.00
30 Jimmy Rollins 10.00 25.00
31 Ronny Paulino 6.00 15.00
32 Howie Kendrick 6.00 15.00
33 Joe Mauer 10.00 25.00
34 Aaron Cook 6.00 15.00
35 Cole Hamels 10.00 25.00
36 Brendan Harris 6.00 15.00
37 Jason Marquis 6.00 15.00
38 Preston Wilson 6.00 15.00
39 Yovanni Gallardo 6.00 15.00
40 Miguel Tejada 6.00 15.00
41 Rich Aurilia 6.00 15.00
42 Corey Hart 6.00 15.00
43 Ryan Dempster 6.00 15.00
44 Jonathan Broxton 6.00 15.00
45 Dontrelle Willis 6.00 15.00
46 Zack Greinke 6.00 15.00
47 Orlando Cabrera 6.00 15.00
48 Zach Duke 6.00 15.00
49 Orlando Hernandez 6.00 15.00
50 Jake Peavy 10.00 25.00
51 Erik Bedard 6.00 15.00
52 Trevor Hoffman 6.00 15.00
53 Hank Blalock 6.00 15.00
54 Victor Martinez 6.00 15.00
55 Chris Young 6.00 15.00
56 Seth Smith 6.00 15.00
57 Wladimir Balentien 6.00 15.00
58 Holliday/Howard/Cabrera 10.00 25.00
59 Grady Sizemore 10.00 25.00
60 Jose Reyes 10.00 25.00
61 A.Rod/C.Pena/Ortiz 12.00 30.00
62 Rich Thompson 6.00 15.00
63 Jason Michaels 6.00 15.00
64 Mike Lowell 10.00 25.00
65 Billy Wagner 6.00 15.00
66 Brad Wilkerson 6.00 15.00
67 Wes Helms 6.00 15.00
68 Kevin Millar 6.00 15.00
69 Bobby Cox MG 6.00 15.00
70 Dan Uggla 6.00 15.00
71 Jarrod Washburn 6.00 15.00
72 Mike Piazza 20.00 50.00
73 Mike Napoli 6.00 15.00
74 Garrett Atkins 6.00 15.00
75 Felix Hernandez 10.00 25.00
76 Ivan Rodriguez 10.00 25.00
77 Angel Guzman 6.00 15.00
78 Radhames Liz 10.00 25.00
79 Omar Vizquel 6.00 15.00
80 Alex Rios 6.00 15.00
81 Ray Durham 6.00 15.00
82 So Taguchi 6.00 15.00
83 Mark Reynolds 6.00 15.00
84 Brian Fuentes 6.00 15.00
85 Jason Bay 10.00 25.00
86 Scott Podsednik 6.00 15.00
87 Maicer Izturis 6.00 15.00
88 Jack Cust 6.00 15.00
89 Josh Willingham 6.00 15.00
90 Vladimir Guerrero 10.00 25.00
91 Marcus Giles 6.00 15.00
92 Ross Detwiler 10.00 25.00
93 Kenny Lofton 6.00 15.00
94 Bud Black MG 6.00 15.00
95 John Lackey 6.00 15.00
96 Sam Fuld 6.00 15.00
97 Clint Sammons 6.00 15.00
98 R.Howard/C.Utley 12.50 30.00
99 D.Ortiz/M.Ramirez 12.50 30.00
100 Ryan Howard 12.50 30.00
101 Ryan Braun ROY 12.50 30.00
102 Ross Ohlendorf 10.00 25.00
103 Jonathan Albaladejo 6.00 15.00
104 Kevin Youkilis 10.00 25.00
105 Roger Clemens 12.00 30.00
106 Josh Bard 6.00 15.00
107 Shawn Green 6.00 15.00
108 B.J. Ryan 6.00 15.00
109 Joe Nathan 6.00 15.00
110 Justin Morneau 6.00 15.00
111 Ubaldo Jimenez 6.00 15.00
112 Jacque Jones 6.00 15.00
113 Kevin Frandsen 6.00 15.00
114 Mike Fontenot 6.00 15.00
115 Johan Santana 12.50 30.00
116 Chuck James 6.00 15.00
117 Boof Bonser 6.00 15.00
118 Marco Scutaro 6.00 15.00
119 Jeremy Hermida 6.00 15.00
120 Andruw Jones 6.00 15.00
121 Mike Cameron 6.00 15.00
122 Jason Varitek 10.00 25.00
123 Terry Francona MG 6.00 15.00
124 Bob Geren MG 6.00 15.00
125 Tim Hudson 6.00 15.00
126 Brandon Jones 6.00 15.00
127 Steve Pearce 15.00 40.00
128 Kenny Lofton 6.00 15.00
129 Kevin Hart 6.00 15.00
130 Justin Upton 10.00 25.00
131 Norris Hopper 6.00 15.00
132 Ramon Vazquez 6.00 15.00
133 Mike Bacsik 6.00 15.00
134 Matt Stairs 6.00 15.00
135 Brad Penny 6.00 15.00
136 Robinson Cano 10.00 25.00
137 Jamey Carroll 6.00 15.00
138 Dan Wheeler 6.00 15.00
139 Johnny Estrada 6.00 15.00
140 Brandon Webb 6.00 15.00
141 Ryan Klesko 6.00 15.00
142 Chris Duncan 6.00 15.00
143 Willie Harris 6.00 15.00
144 Jerry Owens 6.00 15.00
145 Magglio Ordonez 10.00 25.00
146 Aaron Hill 6.00 15.00
147 Marlon Anderson 6.00 15.00
148 Gerald Laird 6.00 15.00
149 Luke Hochevar 10.00 25.00
150 Alfonso Soriano 10.00 25.00
151 Adam Loewen 6.00 15.00
152 Bronson Arroyo 6.00 15.00
153 Luis Mendoza 6.00 15.00
154 David Ross 6.00 15.00
155 Carlos Zambrano 6.00 15.00
156 Brandon McCarthy 6.00 15.00
157 Tim Redding 6.00 15.00
158 Jose Bautista UER 6.00 15.00
Wrong photo
159 Luke Scott 6.00 15.00
160 Ben Sheets 6.00 15.00
161 Matt Garza 6.00 15.00
162 Andy Laroche 6.00 15.00
163 Doug Davis 6.00 15.00
164 Nate Schierholtz 6.00 15.00
165 Tim Lincecum 10.00 25.00
166 Andy Sonnanstine 6.00 15.00
167 Jason Hirsh 6.00 15.00
168 Phil Hughes 12.50 30.00
169 Adam Lind 6.00 15.00
170 Scott Rolen 10.00 25.00
171 John Maine 6.00 15.00
172 Chris Ray 6.00 15.00
173 Jamie Moyer 6.00 15.00
174 Julian Tavarez 6.00 15.00
175 Delmon Young 10.00 25.00
176 Troy Patton 6.00 15.00
177 Josh Anderson 6.00 15.00
178 Dustin Pedroia ROY 10.00 25.00
179 Chris Young 6.00 15.00
180 Jose Valverde 6.00 15.00
181 Joe Borowski/Bobby Jenks/J.J. Putz 6.00 15.00
182 Billy Buckner 6.00 15.00
183 Paul Byrd 6.00 15.00
184 Tadahito Iguchi 6.00 15.00
185 Yunel Escobar 6.00 15.00
186 Lastings Milledge 6.00 15.00
187 Dustin McGowan 6.00 15.00
188 Kei Igawa 6.00 15.00
189 Esteban German 6.00 15.00
190 Russell Martin 6.00 15.00
191 Orlando Hudson 6.00 15.00
192 Jim Edmonds 6.00 15.00
193 J.J. Hardy 6.00 15.00
194 Chad Billingsley 6.00 15.00
195 Todd Helton 10.00 25.00
196 Ross Gload 6.00 15.00
197 Melky Cabrera 6.00 15.00
198 Shannon Stewart 6.00 15.00
199 Adrian Beltre 6.00 15.00
200 Manny Ramirez 10.00 25.00
201 Matt Capps 6.00 15.00
202 Mike Lamb 6.00 15.00
203 Jason Tyner 6.00 15.00
204 Rafael Furcal 6.00 15.00
205 Gil Meche 6.00 15.00
206 Geoff Jenkins 6.00 15.00
207 Jeff Kent 6.00 15.00
208 David DeJesus 6.00 15.00
209 Andy Phillips 6.00 15.00
210 Mark Teahen 6.00 15.00
211 Lyle Overbay 6.00 15.00
212 Moises Alou 6.00 15.00
213 Michael Barrett 6.00 15.00
214 C.J. Wilson 6.00 15.00
215 Bobby Jenks 6.00 15.00
216 Ryan Garko 6.00 15.00
217 Josh Beckett 15.00 40.00
218 Clint Hurdle MG 6.00 15.00
219 Kevin Kouzmanoff 6.00 15.00
220 Roy Oswalt 6.00 15.00
221 Ian Snell 6.00 15.00
222 Mark Grudzielanek 6.00 15.00
223 Odalis Perez 6.00 15.00
224 Mark Buehrle 6.00 15.00
225 Hunter Pence 12.50 30.00
226 Kurt Suzuki 6.00 15.00
227 Alfredo Amezaga 6.00 15.00
228 Geoff Blum 6.00 15.00
229 Dustin Pedroia 12.50 30.00
230 Roy Halladay 6.00 15.00
231 Casey Blake 6.00 15.00
232 Clay Buchholz 30.00 60.00
233 Jimmy Rollins MVP 10.00 25.00
234 Boston Red Sox 30.00 60.00
235 Rich Harden 6.00 15.00
236 Joe Koshansky 6.00 15.00
237 Eric Wedge MG 6.00 15.00
238 Shane Victorino 6.00 15.00
239 Richie Sexson 6.00 15.00
240 Jim Thome 10.00 25.00
241 Ervin Santana 6.00 15.00
242 Manny Acta 6.00 15.00
243 Akinori Iwamura 6.00 15.00
244 Adam Wainwright 6.00 15.00
245 Dan Haren 6.00 15.00
246 Jason Isringhausen 6.00 15.00
247 Edgar Gonzalez 6.00 15.00
248 Jose Contreras 6.00 15.00
249 Chris Sampson 6.00 15.00
250 Jonathan Papelbon 12.50 30.00
251 Dan Johnson 6.00 15.00
252 Dmitri Young 6.00 15.00
253 Bronson Sardinha 6.00 15.00
254 David Murphy 6.00 15.00
255 Brandon Phillips 6.00 15.00
256 Alex Rodriguez MVP 12.00 30.00
257 Austin Kearns/Dimitri Young 6.00 15.00

258 Manny Ramirez/Kevin Youkilis 10.00 25.00
259 Emilio Bonifacio 6.00 15.00
260 Chad Cordero 6.00 15.00
261 Josh Barfield 6.00 15.00
262 Brett Myers 6.00 15.00
263 Nook Logan 6.00 15.00
264 Byung-Hyun Kim 6.00 15.00
265 Fredi Gonzalez 6.00 15.00
266 Ryan Doumit 6.00 15.00
267 Chris Burke 6.00 15.00
268 Daric Barton 6.00 15.00
269 James Loney 12.50 30.00
270 C.C. Sabathia 6.00 15.00
271 Chad Tracy 6.00 15.00
272 Anthony Reyes 6.00 15.00
273 Rafael Soriano 6.00 15.00
274 Jermaine Dye 6.00 15.00
275 C.C. Sabathia 6.00 15.00
276 Brad Ausmus 6.00 15.00
277 Aubrey Huff 6.00 15.00
278 Xavier Nady 6.00 15.00
279 Damion Easley 6.00 15.00
280 Willie Randolph MG 6.00 15.00
281 Carlos Ruiz 6.00 15.00
282 Jon Lester 10.00 25.00
283 Jorge Sosa 6.00 15.00
284 Lance Broadway 6.00 15.00
285 Tony LaRussa MG 6.00 15.00
286 Jeff Clement 6.00 15.00
287 Morneau/Santana/Mauer 12.50 30.00
288 IRod/Verlander 10.00 25.00
289 Justin Ruggiano 6.00 15.00
290 Edgar Renteria 6.00 15.00
291 Eugenio Velez 6.00 15.00
292 Mark Loretta 6.00 15.00
293 Gavin Floyd 6.00 15.00
294 Brian McCann 6.00 15.00
295 Tim Wakefield 6.00 15.00
296 Paul Konerko 6.00 15.00
297 Jorge Posada 10.00 25.00
298 Prince Fielder/Ryan Howard/Adam Dunn 10.00 25.00
299 Cesar Izturis 6.00 15.00
300 Chien-Ming Wang 12.50 30.00
301 Chris Duffy 6.00 15.00
302 Horacio Ramirez 6.00 15.00
303 Jose Lopez 6.00 15.00
304 Jose Vidro 6.00 15.00
305 Carlos Delgado 6.00 15.00
306 Scott Olsen 6.00 15.00
307 Shawn Hill 6.00 15.00
308 Felipe Lopez 6.00 15.00
309 Ryan Church 6.00 15.00
310 Kelvim Escobar 6.00 15.00
311 Jeremy Guthrie 6.00 15.00
312 Ramon Hernandez 6.00 15.00
313 Kameron Loe 6.00 15.00
314 Ian Kinsler 6.00 15.00
315 David Weathers 6.00 15.00
316 Scott Hatteberg 6.00 15.00
317 Cliff Lee 6.00 15.00
318 Ned Yost MG 6.00 15.00
319 Joey Votto 10.00 25.00
320 Ichiro Suzuki 20.00 50.00
321 J.R. Towles 10.00 25.00
322 Scott Kazmir/Johan Santana/Erik Bedard 10.00 25.00
323 Jose Valverde/Francisco Cordero/Trevor Hoffman 6.00 15.00
324 Jake Peavy 10.00 25.00
325 Jim Leyland MG 6.00 15.00
326 Matt Holliday/Chipper Jones/Hanley Ramirez 10.00 25.00
327 Jake Peavy/Aaron Harang John Smoltz 10.00 25.00
328 Nyjer Morgan 6.00 15.00
329 Lou Piniella 6.00 15.00
330 Curtis Granderson 10.00 25.00
331 Dave Roberts 6.00 15.00
332 Grady Sizemore/Jhonny Peralta 10.00 25.00
333 Jayson Nix 6.00 15.00
334 Oliver Perez 6.00 15.00
335 Erio Bynoo 6.00 15.00
336 Jhonny Peralta 6.00 15.00
337 Livan Hernandez 6.00 15.00
338 Matt Diaz 6.00 15.00
339 Troy Percival 6.00 15.00
340 David Wright 12.50 30.00
341 Daniel Cabrera 6.00 15.00
342 Matt Belisle 6.00 15.00
343 Kason Gabbard 6.00 15.00
344 Mike Rabelo 6.00 15.00
345 Carl Crawford 6.00 15.00
346 Adam Everett 6.00 15.00
347 Chris Capuano 6.00 15.00
348 Craig Monroe 6.00 15.00
349 Mike Mussina 6.00 15.00
350 Mark Teixeira 10.00 25.00
351 Bobby Crosby 6.00 15.00
352 Miguel Batista 6.00 15.00
353 Brendan Ryan 15.00 40.00
354 Edwin Jackson 6.00 15.00
355 Brian Roberts 6.00 15.00
356 Manny Corpas 6.00 15.00
357 Jeremy Accardo 6.00 15.00
358 John Patterson 6.00 15.00
359 Evan Meek 6.00 15.00
360 David Ortiz 12.50 30.00
361 Wesley Wright 10.00 25.00
362 Fernando Hernandez 6.00 15.00
363 Brian Barton 12.50 30.00
364 Al Reyes 6.00 15.00
365 Derrek Lee 6.00 15.00
366 Jeff Weaver 6.00 15.00
367 Khalil Greene 6.00 15.00
368 Michael Bourn 6.00 15.00
369 Luis Castillo 6.00 15.00
370 Adam Dunn 6.00 15.00
371 Rickie Weeks 6.00 15.00
372 Matt Kemp 6.00 15.00
373 Casey Kotchman 6.00 15.00
374 Jason Jennings 6.00 15.00
375 Fausto Carmona 6.00 15.00
376 Willy Taveras 6.00 15.00
377 Jake Westbrook 6.00 15.00
378 Ozzie Guillen 6.00 15.00
379 Hideki Okajima 10.00 25.00
380 Grady Sizemore 10.00 25.00
381 Jeff Francoeur 10.00 25.00
382 Micah Owings 10.00 25.00
383 Jered Weaver 6.00 15.00
384 Carlos Quentin 6.00 15.00
385 Troy Tulowitzki 10.00 25.00
386 Julio Lugo 6.00 15.00
387 Sean Marshall 6.00 15.00
388 Jorge Cantu 6.00 15.00
389 Callix Crabbe 6.00 15.00
390 Troy Glaus 6.00 15.00
391 Nick Markakis 10.00 25.00
392 Joey Gathright 6.00 15.00
393 Michael Cuddyer 6.00 15.00
394 Mark Ellis 6.00 15.00
395 Lance Berkman 6.00 15.00
396 Randy Johnson 10.00 25.00
397 Brian Wilson 6.00 15.00
398 Kenji Johjima 6.00 15.00
399 Jarrod Saltalamacchia 6.00 15.00
400 Matt Holliday 6.00 15.00
401 Scott Hairston 6.00 15.00
402 Taylor Buchholz 6.00 15.00
403 Nate Robertson 6.00 15.00
404 Cecil Cooper 6.00 15.00
405 Travis Hafner 6.00 15.00
406 Takashi Saito 10.00 25.00
407 Johnny Damon 6.00 15.00
408 Edinson Volquez 10.00 25.00
409 Jason Giambi 10.00 25.00
411 Jason Kubel 6.00 15.00
412 Joel Zumaya 6.00 15.00
413 Wandy Rodriguez 6.00 15.00
414 Andrew Miller 6.00 15.00
415 Derek Lowe 10.00 25.00
416 Elijah Dukes 6.00 15.00
417 Brian Bass 10.00 25.00
418 Dioner Navarro 6.00 15.00
419 Bengie Molina 6.00 15.00
420 Nick Swisher 6.00 15.00
421 Brandon Backe 6.00 15.00
422 Erick Aybar 6.00 15.00
423 Mike Scioscia 6.00 15.00
424 Aaron Harang 6.00 15.00
425 Hanley Ramirez 10.00 25.00
426 Franklin Gutierrez 6.00 15.00
427 Carlos Guillen 6.00 15.00
428 Jair Jurrjens 6.00 15.00
429 Billy Butler 6.00 15.00
430 Ryan Braun 15.00 40.00
431 Delwyn Young 6.00 15.00
432 Jason Kendall 6.00 15.00
433 Carlos Silva 6.00 15.00
434 Ron Gardenhire MG 6.00 15.00
435 Torii Hunter 6.00 15.00
436 Joe Blanton 6.00 15.00
437 Brandon Wood 6.00 15.00
438 Jay Payton 6.00 15.00
439 Josh Hamilton 30.00 60.00
440 Pedro Martinez 10.00 25.00
441 Miguel Olivo 6.00 15.00
442 Luis Gonzalez 6.00 15.00
443 Greg Dobbs 6.00 15.00
444 Jack Wilson 6.00 15.00
445 Hideki Matsui 12.50 30.00
446 Randor Bierd 6.00 15.00
447 Chipper Jones/Mark Teixeira 10.00 25.00
448 Cameron Maybin 12.50 30.00
449 Braden Looper 6.00 15.00
450 Prince Fielder 12.50 30.00
451 Brian Giles 6.00 15.00
452 Kevin Slowey 10.00 25.00
453 Josh Fogg 6.00 15.00
454 Mike Hampton 6.00 15.00
455 Derek Jeter 40.00 80.00
456 Chone Figgins 6.00 15.00
457 Josh Fields 6.00 15.00
458 Brad Hawpe 6.00 15.00
459 Mike Sweeney 6.00 15.00
460 Chase Utley 12.50 30.00
461 Jacoby Ellsbury 20.00 50.00
462 Freddy Sanchez 6.00 15.00
463 John McLaren 6.00 15.00
464 Rocco Baldelli 6.00 15.00
465 Huston Street 6.00 15.00
466 M.Cabrera/I.Rodriguez 10.00 25.00
467 Nick Blackburn 15.00 40.00
468 Gregor Blanco 6.00 15.00
469 Brian Bocock 10.00 25.00
470 Tom Gorzelanny 6.00 15.00
471 Brian Schneider 6.00 15.00
472 Shaun Marcum 6.00 15.00
473 Joe Maddon 6.00 15.00
474 Yuniesky Betancourt 6.00 15.00
475 Adrian Gonzalez 6.00 15.00
476 Johnny Cueto 12.50 30.00
477 Ben Broussard 6.00 15.00
478 Geovany Soto 15.00 40.00
479 Bobby Abreu 6.00 15.00
480 Matt Cain 6.00 15.00
481 Manny Parra 6.00 15.00
482 Kazuo Fukumori 10.00 25.00
483 Mike Jacobs 6.00 15.00
484 Todd Jones 6.00 15.00
485 J.J. Putz 6.00 15.00
486 Javier Vazquez 6.00 15.00
487 Corey Patterson 6.00 15.00
488 Mike Gonzalez 6.00 15.00
489 Joakim Soria 6.00 15.00
490 Albert Pujols 20.00 50.00
491 Cliff Floyd 6.00 15.00
492 Harvey Garcia 6.00 15.00
493 Steve Holm 6.00 15.00
494 Paul Maholm 6.00 15.00
495 James Shields 6.00 15.00
496 Brad Lidge 6.00 15.00
497 Cla Meredith 6.00 15.00
498 Matt Chico 6.00 15.00
499 Milton Bradley 6.00 15.00
500 Chipper Jones 12.50 30.00
501 Elliot Johnson 6.00 15.00
502 Alex Cora 6.00 15.00
503 Jeremy Bonderman 10.00 25.00
504 Conor Jackson 6.00 15.00
505 B.J. Upton 6.00 15.00
506 Jay Gibbons 6.00 15.00
507 Mark DeRosa 6.00 15.00
508 John Danks 6.00 15.00
509 Alex Gonzalez 6.00 15.00
510 Justin Verlander 10.00 25.00
511 Jeff Francis 6.00 15.00
512 Placido Polanco 6.00 15.00
513 Rick Vanden Hurk 6.00 15.00
514 Tony Pena 6.00 15.00
515 A.J. Burnett 6.00 15.00
516 Jason Schmidt 6.00 15.00
517 Bill Hall 6.00 15.00
518 Ian Stewart 6.00 15.00
519 Travis Buck 6.00 15.00
520 Vernon Wells 6.00 15.00
521 Jayson Werth 6.00 15.00
522 Nate McLouth 15.00 40.00
523 Noah Lowry 6.00 15.00
524 Raul Ibanez 6.00 15.00
525 Gary Matthews 6.00 15.00
526 Juan Encarnacion 6.00 15.00
527 Marlon Byrd 6.00 15.00
528 Paul Lo Duca 6.00 15.00
529 Masahide Kobayashi 10.00 25.00
530 Ryan Zimmerman 10.00 25.00
531 Hiroki Kuroda 12.50 30.00
532 Tim Lahey 6.00 15.00
533 Kyle McClellan 6.00 15.00
534 Matt Tupman 6.00 15.00
535 Francisco Rodriguez 6.00 15.00
536 Albert Pujols/Prince Fielder 12.50 30.00
537 Scott Moore 6.00 15.00
538 Alex Romero 6.00 15.00
539 Clete Thomas 6.00 15.00
540 John Smoltz 10.00 25.00
541 Adam Jones 6.00 15.00
542 Adam Kennedy 6.00 15.00
543 Carlos Lee 6.00 15.00
544 Chad Gaudin 6.00 15.00
545 Chris Young 6.00 15.00
546 Francisco Liriano 6.00 15.00
547 Fred Lewis 6.00 15.00
548 Garrett Olson 6.00 15.00
549 Gregg Zaun 6.00 15.00
550 Curt Schilling 10.00 25.00
551 Erick Threets 6.00 15.00
552 J.D. Drew 6.00 15.00
553 Jo-Jo Reyes 6.00 15.00
554 Joe Borowski 6.00 15.00
555 Josh Beckett 10.00 25.00
556 John Gibbons 6.00 15.00
557 John McDonald 6.00 15.00
558 John Russell 6.00 15.00
559 Jonny Gomes 6.00 15.00
560 Aramis Ramirez 6.00 15.00
561 Matt Tolbert 10.00 25.00
562 Ronnie Belliard 6.00 15.00
563 Ramon Troncoso 6.00 15.00
564 Frank Catalanotto 6.00 15.00
565 A.J. Pierzynski 6.00 15.00
566 Kevin Millwood 6.00 15.00
567 David Eckstein 6.00 15.00
568 Jose Guillen 6.00 15.00
569 Brad Hennessey 6.00 15.00
570 Homer Bailey 6.00 15.00
571 Eric Gagne 6.00 15.00
572 Adam Eaton 6.00 15.00
573 Tom Gordon 6.00 15.00
574 Scott Baker 6.00 15.00
575 Ty Wigginton 6.00 15.00
576 Dave Bush 6.00 15.00
577 John Buck 6.00 15.00
578 Ricky Nolasco 6.00 15.00
579 Jesse Litsch 6.00 15.00
580 Ken Griffey Jr. 25.00 60.00
581 Kazuo Matsui 6.00 15.00
582 Dusty Baker 6.00 15.00
583 Nick Punto 6.00 15.00
584 Ryan Theriot 6.00 15.00
585 Brian Bannister 10.00 25.00
586 Coco Crisp 10.00 25.00
587 Chris Snyder 6.00 15.00
588 Tony Gwynn 6.00 15.00
589 Dave Trembley 6.00 15.00
590 Mariano Rivera 12.50 30.00
591 Rico Washington 6.00 15.00
592 Matt Morris 6.00 15.00
593 Randy Wells 6.00 15.00
594 Mike Morse 6.00 15.00
595 Francisco Cordero 6.00 15.00
596 Joba Chamberlain 20.00 50.00
597 Kyle Davies 6.00 15.00
598 Bruce Bochy 6.00 15.00
599 Austin Kearns 6.00 15.00
600 Tom Glavine 10.00 25.00
601 Felipe Paulino 6.00 15.00
602 Lyle Overbay/Vernon Wells 6.00 15.00
603 Blake DeWitt 15.00 40.00
604 Wily Mo Pena 6.00 15.00
605 Andre Ethier 10.00 25.00
606 Jason Bergmann 6.00 15.00
607 Ryan Spilborghs 6.00 15.00
608 Brian Burres 6.00 15.00
609 Ted Lilly 6.00 15.00
610 Carlos Beltran 6.00 15.00
611 Garret Anderson 6.00 15.00
612 Kelly Johnson 6.00 15.00
613 Melvin Mora 6.00 15.00
614 Rich Hill 6.00 15.00
615 Pat Burrell 6.00 15.00
616 Jon Garland 6.00 15.00
617 Asdrubal Cabrera 6.00 15.00
618 Pat Neshek 6.00 15.00
619 Sergio Mitre 6.00 15.00
620 Gary Sheffield 6.00 15.00
621 Denard Span 6.00 15.00
622 Jorge De La Rosa 6.00 15.00
623 Trey Hillman MG 6.00 15.00
624 Joe Torre MG 12.50 30.00
625 Greg Maddux 15.00 40.00
626 Mike Redmond 6.00 15.00
627 Mike Pelfrey 6.00 15.00
628 Andy Pettitte 10.00 25.00
629 Eric Chavez 6.00 15.00
630 Chris Carpenter 6.00 15.00
631 Joe Girardi MG 6.00 15.00
632 Charlie Manuel MG 6.00 15.00
633 Adam LaRoche 6.00 15.00
634 Kenny Rogers 6.00 15.00
635 Michael Young 6.00 15.00
636 Rafael Betancourt 6.00 15.00
637 Jose Castillo 6.00 15.00
638 Juan Pierre 6.00 15.00
639 Juan Uribe 6.00 15.00
640 Carlos Pena 6.00 15.00
641 Marcus Thames 6.00 15.00
642 Mark Kotsay 6.00 15.00
643 Matt Murton 6.00 15.00
644 Reggie Willits 6.00 15.00
645 Andy Marte 6.00 15.00
646 Rajai Davis 6.00 15.00
647 Randy Winn 6.00 15.00
648 Ryan Freel 6.00 15.00
649 Joe Crede 6.00 15.00
650 Frank Thomas 12.50 30.00
651 Martin Prado 6.00 15.00
652 Rod Barajas 6.00 15.00
653 Endy Chavez 6.00 15.00
654 Willy Aybar 6.00 15.00
655 Aaron Rowand 6.00 15.00
656 Darin Erstad 6.00 15.00
657 Jeff Keppinger 6.00 15.00
658 Kerry Wood 6.00 15.00
659 Vicente Padilla 6.00 15.00
660 Yadier Molina 6.00 15.00

2008 Topps Gold Border

*GOLD: 3X TO 8X BASIC
*GOLD RC: 2X TO 5X BASIC RC
SER.1 ODDS 1:9 H,1:3 HTA,1:13 R
SER.2 ODDS 1:5 H,1:2 HTA,1:12 R
STATED PRINT RUN 2008 SER.#'d SETS
234b Red Sox w/Giuliani 60.00 120.00

2008 Topps Gold Foil

*GOLD FOIL: 1X TO 2.5X BASIC
*GOLD FOIL RC: .6X TO 1.5X BASIC RC
RANDOM INSERTS IN PACKS
234b Red Sox w/Giuliani 4.00 10.00

2008 Topps 1956 Reprint Relic

SER.2 ODDS 1:43,030 HOBBY
SER.2 ODDS 1:5249 HTA
STATED PRINT RUN 56 SER.#'d SETS
56MM Mickey Mantle 90.00 150.00

2008 Topps 50th Anniversary All Rookie Team

COMPLETE SET (110) 50.00 100.00
COMP.SER.1.SET (55) 20.00 50.00
COMP.SER.2.SET (55) 20.00 50.00
SER.1 ODDS 1:5 HOB, 1:5 RET
SER.2 ODDS 1:5 H,1:5 HTA,1:5 RET
AR1 Darryl Strawberry .40 1.00
AR2 Gary Sheffield .40 1.00
AR3 Dwight Gooden .40 1.00
AR4 Melky Cabrera .40 1.00
AR5 Gary Carter .60 1.50
AR6 Lou Piniella .40 1.00
AR7 Dave Justice .40 1.00
AR8 Andre Dawson .60 1.50
AR9 Mark Ellis .40 1.00
AR10 Dave Johnson .40 1.00
AR11 Jermaine Dye .40 1.00
AR12 Dan Johnson .40 1.00
AR13 Alfonso Soriano .60 1.50
AR14 Prince Fielder .60 1.50
AR15 Hanley Ramirez .60 1.50
AR16 Matt Holliday 1.00 2.50
AR17 Justin Verlander 1.00 2.50
AR18 Mark Teixeira .60 1.50
AR19 Julio Franco .40 1.00
AR20 Ivan Rodriguez .60 1.50
AR21 Jason Bay .60 1.50
AR22 Brandon Webb .60 1.50
AR23 Dontrelle Willis .40 1.00
AR24 Brad Wilkerson .40 1.00
AR25 Dan Uggla .40 1.00
AR26 Ozzie Smith 1.25 3.00
AR27 Andruw Jones .40 1.00
AR28 Garret Anderson .40 1.00
AR29 Jimmy Rollins .60 1.50
AR30 Brian McCann .60 1.50
AR31 Scott Podsednik .40 1.00
AR32 Garrett Atkins .40 1.00
AR33 Billy Wagner .40 1.00
AR34 Chipper Jones 1.00 2.50
AR35 Roger McDowell .40 1.00
AR36 Austin Kearns .40 1.00
AR37 Boog Powell .40 1.00
AR38 Ron Swoboda .40 1.00
AR39 Roy Oswalt .60 1.50
AR40 Mike Piazza 1.00 2.50
AR41 Albert Pujols 1.25 3.00
AR42 Ichiro Suzuki 1.25 3.00
AR43 C.C. Sabathia .60 1.50
AR44 Todd Helton .60 1.50
AR45 Scott Rolen .60 1.50
AR46 Derek Jeter 2.50 6.00
AR47 Shawn Green .40 1.00
AR48 Manny Ramirez 1.00 2.50
AR49 Tom Seaver UER .60 1.50
AR50 Kenny Lofton .40 1.00
AR51 Francisco Liriano .40 1.00
AR52 Ryan Zimmerman .60 1.50
AR53 Jeff Francoeur .60 1.50
AR54 Joe Mauer .75 2.00
AR55 Magglio Ordonez .60 1.50
AR56 Carlos Beltran .60 1.50
AR57 Andre Ethier .60 1.50
AR58 Brian Bannister .40 1.00
AR59 Chris Young .40 1.00
AR60 Troy Tulowitzki 1.00 2.50
AR61 Hideki Okajima .40 1.00
AR62 Delmon Young .60 1.50
AR63 Craig Wilson .40 1.00
AR64 Hunter Pence .60 1.50
AR65 Tadahito Iguchi .40 1.00
AR66 Mark Kotsay .40 1.00
AR67 Nick Markakis .75 2.00
AR68 Russ Adams .40 1.00
AR69 Russ Martin .40 1.00
AR70 James Loney .40 1.00
AR71 Ryan Braun .60 1.50
AR72 Jonny Gomes .40 1.00
AR73 Carlos Ruiz .40 1.00
AR74 Willy Taveras .40 1.00
AR75 Joe Torre .60 1.50
AR76 Jeff Kent .40 1.00
AR77 Huston Street .60 1.50
AR78 Dustin Pedroia 1.00 2.50
AR79 Gustavo Chacin .40 1.00
AR80 Adam Dunn .60 1.50
AR81 Pat Burrell .40 1.00
AR82 Rocco Baldelli .40 1.00
AR83 Chad Tracy .40 1.00
AR84 Adam LaRoche .40 1.00
AR85 Aaron Miles .40 1.00
AR86 Khalil Greene .40 1.00
AR87 Daniel Cabrera .40 1.00
AR88 Mike Gonzalez .40 1.00
AR89 Ty Wigginton .60 1.50
AR90 Angel Berroa .40 1.00
AR91 Moises Alou .40 1.00
AR92 Miguel Olivo .40 1.00
AR93 Nick Johnson .40 1.00
AR94 Eric Hinske .40 1.00
AR95 Ramon Santiago .40 1.00
AR96 Jason Jennings .40 1.00
AR97 Adam Kennedy .40 1.00
AR98 Mike Lamb .40 1.00
AR99 Rafael Furcal .40 1.00
AR100 Jay Payton .40 1.00
AR101 Bengie Molina .40 1.00
AR102 Mark Redman .40 1.00
AR103 Alex Gonzalez .40 1.00
AR104 Ray Durham .40 1.00
AR105 Miguel Cairo .40 1.00
AR106 Kerry Wood .40 1.00
AR107 Dmitri Young .40 1.00
AR108 Jose Cruz .40 1.00
AR109 Jose Guillen .40 1.00
AR110 Scott Hatteberg .40 1.00

2008 Topps 50th Anniversary All Rookie Team Gold

COMMON CARD 5.00 12.00
SEMISTARS 8.00 20.00
UNLISTED STARS 12.50 30.00
SER.1 ODDS 1:1290 H,1:1100 HTA
SER.1 ODDS 1:1290 RETAIL
SER.2 ODDS 1:740 HOB,1:505 HTA
SER.2 ODDS 1:1100 RETAIL
STATED PRINT RUN 99 SER.#'d SETS
AR1 Darryl Strawberry 5.00 12.00
AR2 Gary Sheffield 5.00 12.00
AR3 Dwight Gooden 5.00 12.00
AR4 Melky Cabrera 5.00 12.00
AR5 Gary Carter 8.00 20.00
AR6 Lou Piniella 5.00 12.00
AR7 Dave Justice 5.00 12.00
AR8 Andre Dawson 8.00 20.00
AR9 Mark Ellis 5.00 12.00
AR10 Dave Johnson 5.00 12.00
AR11 Jermaine Dye 5.00 12.00
AR12 Dan Johnson 5.00 12.00
AR13 Alfonso Soriano 8.00 20.00
AR14 Prince Fielder 8.00 20.00
AR15 Hanley Ramirez 8.00 20.00
AR16 Matt Holliday 12.00 30.00
AR17 Justin Verlander 12.00 30.00
AR18 Mark Teixeira 8.00 20.00
AR19 Julio Franco 5.00 12.00
AR20 Ivan Rodriguez 8.00 20.00
AR21 Jason Bay 8.00 20.00
AR22 Brandon Webb 8.00 20.00
AR23 Dontrelle Willis 5.00 12.00
AR24 Brad Wilkerson 5.00 12.00
AR25 Dan Uggla 5.00 12.00
AR26 Ozzie Smith 15.00 40.00
AR27 Andruw Jones 5.00 12.00
AR28 Garret Anderson 5.00 12.00
AR29 Jimmy Rollins 8.00 20.00
AR30 Brian McCann 8.00 20.00
AR31 Scott Podsednik 5.00 12.00
AR32 Garrett Atkins 5.00 12.00
AR33 Billy Wagner 5.00 12.00
AR34 Chipper Jones 12.00 30.00
AR35 Roger McDowell 5.00 12.00
AR36 Austin Kearns 5.00 12.00
AR37 Boog Powell 5.00 12.00
AR38 Ron Swoboda 5.00 12.00
AR39 Roy Oswalt 8.00 20.00
AR40 Mike Piazza 12.00 30.00
AR41 Albert Pujols 20.00 50.00
AR42 Ichiro Suzuki 15.00 40.00
AR43 C.C. Sabathia 8.00 20.00
AR44 Todd Helton 8.00 20.00
AR45 Scott Rolen 8.00 20.00
AR46 Derek Jeter 20.00 50.00
AR47 Shawn Green 5.00 12.00
AR48 Manny Ramirez 12.00 30.00
AR49 Tom Seaver 8.00 20.00
AR50 Kenny Lofton 5.00 12.00
AR51 Francisco Liriano 5.00 12.00
AR52 Ryan Zimmerman 8.00 20.00
AR53 Jeff Francoeur 8.00 20.00
AR54 Joe Mauer 10.00 25.00
AR55 Magglio Ordonez 8.00 20.00
AR56 Carlos Beltran 8.00 20.00
AR57 Andre Ethier 8.00 20.00
AR58 Brian Bannister 5.00 12.00
AR59 Chris Young 5.00 12.00
AR60 Troy Tulowitzki 12.00 30.00
AR61 Hideki Okajima 5.00 12.00
AR62 Delmon Young 8.00 20.00
AR63 Craig Wilson 15.00 40.00
AR64 Hunter Pence 8.00 20.00
AR65 Tadahito Iguchi 5.00 12.00
AR66 Mark Kotsay 5.00 12.00
AR67 Nick Markakis 10.00 25.00
AR68 Russ Adams 5.00 12.00
AR69 Russ Martin 10.00 25.00
AR70 James Loney 5.00 12.00
AR71 Ryan Braun 12.50 30.00
AR72 Jonny Gomes 5.00 12.00
AR73 Carlos Ruiz 5.00 12.00
AR74 Willy Taveras 5.00 12.00
AR75 Joe Torre 8.00 20.00
AR76 Jeff Kent 5.00 12.00
AR77 Huston Street 8.00 20.00
AR78 Dustin Pedroia 12.00 30.00
AR79 Gustavo Chacin 5.00 12.00
AR80 Adam Dunn 8.00 20.00
AR81 Pat Burrell 5.00 12.00
AR82 Rocco Baldelli 5.00 12.00
AR83 Chad Tracy 5.00 12.00
AR84 Adam LaRoche 5.00 12.00
AR85 Aaron Miles 5.00 12.00
AR86 Khalil Greene 5.00 12.00
AR87 Daniel Cabrera 5.00 12.00
AR88 Mike Gonzalez 5.00 12.00
AR89 Ty Wigginton 8.00 20.00
AR90 Angel Berroa 5.00 12.00
AR91 Moises Alou 5.00 12.00
AR92 Miguel Olivo 5.00 12.00
AR93 Nick Johnson 5.00 12.00
AR94 Eric Hinske 5.00 12.00
AR95 Ramon Santiago 5.00 12.00
AR96 Jason Jennings 5.00 12.00
AR97 Adam Kennedy 8.00 20.00
AR98 Mike Lamb 5.00 12.00
AR99 Rafael Furcal 5.00 12.00
AR100 Jay Payton 5.00 12.00
AR101 Bengie Molina 5.00 12.00
AR102 Mark Redman 5.00 12.00
AR103 Alex Gonzalez 5.00 12.00
AR104 Ray Durham 5.00 12.00
AR105 Miguel Cairo 5.00 12.00
AR106 Kerry Wood 5.00 12.00
AR107 Dmitri Young 10.00 25.00
AR108 Jose Cruz 5.00 12.00
AR109 Jose Guillen 5.00 12.00
AR110 Scott Hatteberg 5.00 12.00

2008 Topps 50th Anniversary All Rookie Team Relics

SER.1 ODDS 1:7178 H, 1:366 HTA
SER.1 ODDS 1:50,700 RETAIL
SER.2 ODDS 1:2378 H,1:290 HTA
STATED PRINT RUN 50 SER.#'d SETS
AD Adam Dunn 12.50 30.00
AD Andre Dawson 30.00 60.00
AE Andre Ethier 20.00 50.00
AJ Andruw Jones 12.50 30.00
AS Alfonso Soriano 12.50 30.00
BM Brian McCann 10.00 25.00
BW Brandon Webb 15.00 40.00
CJ Chipper Jones 15.00 40.00
CS C.C. Sabathia 12.50 30.00
DG Dwight Gooden 10.00 25.00
DJ Dave Justice 12.50 30.00
DS Darryl Strawberry 20.00 50.00
DU Dan Uggla 12.50 30.00
DW Dontrelle Willis 12.50 30.00
FL Francisco Liriano 15.00 40.00
GA Garret Anderson 10.00 25.00
GC Gary Carter 20.00 50.00
GS Gary Sheffield 30.00 60.00
HR Hanley Ramirez 10.00 25.00
IR Ivan Rodriguez 12.50 30.00
IS Ichiro Suzuki 30.00 60.00
JB Jason Bay 30.00 60.00
JM Joe Mauer 8.00 20.00
JR Jimmy Rollins 15.00 40.00
JV Justin Verlander 15.00 40.00
MH Matt Holliday 20.00 50.00
MO Magglio Ordonez 20.00 50.00
MP Mike Piazza 20.00 50.00
MT Mark Teixeira 15.00 40.00
NJ Nick Johnson 30.00 60.00
NM Nick Markakis 10.00 25.00
OS Ozzie Smith 15.00 40.00
PB Pat Burrell 12.50 30.00
PF Prince Fielder 15.00 40.00
RB Rocco Baldelli 12.50 30.00
RO Roy Oswalt 10.00 25.00
TH Todd Helton 10.00 25.00
TS Tom Seaver 12.50 30.00

2008 Topps Back to School

TB1 Miguel Cabrera 6.00 15.00
TB2 Albert Pujols 8.00 20.00
TB3 Grady Sizemore 4.00 10.00
TB4 Ken Griffey Jr 20.00 50.00
TB5 David Wright 4.00 10.00
TB6 Ichiro Suzuki 12.00 30.00
TB7 Alex Rodriguez 8.00 20.00
TB8 Chipper Jones 6.00 15.00

2008 Topps Campaign 2008

COMPLETE SET (12) 12.50 30.00
STATED ODDS 1:9 H,1:2 HTA,1:9 R
GOLD ODDS 1:5 HTA
AG Al Gore
AS Arnold Schwarzenegger
BO Barack Obama 6.00 15.00
BR Bill Richardson .60 1.50
DK Dennis Kucinich .60 1.50
FT Fred Thompson .60 1.50
HC Hillary Clinton 2.00 5.00
JB Joseph Biden 6.00 15.00
JE John Edwards 1.00 2.50
JM John McCain 2.00 5.00
MH Mike Huckabee 1.00 2.50
MR Mitt Romney 1.00 2.50
RG Rudy Giuliani 1.00 2.50
RP Ron Paul .60 1.50
SP Sarah Palin 6.00 15.00
SP Sarah Palin Pageant 10.00 25.00

2008 Topps Campaign 2008 Gold

COMPLETE SET 50.00 100.00
*GOLD: .75X TO 2X BASIC
STATED ODDS 1:5 HTA

2008 Topps Campaign 2008 Letter Patches

SER.2 ODDS 1:2642 H,1:322 HTA
STATED PRINT RUN 50 SER.#'d SETS
BO Barack Obama O 60.00 120.00
BO Barack Obama B 60.00 120.00
BO Barack Obama A 60.00 120.00
BO Barack Obama M 60.00 120.00
BO Barack Obama A 60.00 120.00
HC Hillary Clinton C 30.00 60.00
HC Hillary Clinton L 30.00 60.00
HC Hillary Clinton I 30.00 60.00
HC Hillary Clinton N 30.00 60.00
HC Hillary Clinton T 30.00 60.00
HC Hillary Clinton O 30.00 60.00
HC Hillary Clinton N 30.00 60.00
JM John McCain M 10.00 25.00
JM John McCain c 10.00 25.00
JM John McCain C 10.00 25.00
JM John McCain A 10.00 25.00
JM John McCain I 10.00 25.00
JM John McCain N 10.00 25.00

2008 Topps Commemorative Patch Relics

SER.2 ODDS 1:792 HOB,1:97 HTA
STATED PRINT RUN 100 SER.#'d SETS
AP Andy Pettitte 30.00 60.00
AR Alex Rodriguez 50.00 100.00
BA Bobby Abreu 20.00 50.00
BS Brian Schneider 10.00 25.00
BW Billy Wagner 10.00 25.00
CB Carlos Beltran 10.00 25.00
CD Carlos Delgado 10.00 25.00
CMW Chien-Ming Wang. 50.00 100.00
DJ Derek Jeter 20.00 50.00
DW David Wright 20.00 50.00
EC Endy Chavez 8.00 20.00
HM Hideki Matsui 15.00 40.00
JC Joba Chamberlain 50.00 100.00
JD Johnny Damon 30.00 60.00
JG Jason Giambi 40.00 80.00
JM John Maine 10.00 25.00
JP Jorge Posada 20.00 50.00
JR Jose Reyes 12.50 30.00
LC Luis Castillo 8.00 20.00
MA Moises Alou 8.00 20.00
MC Melky Cabrera 20.00 50.00
MM Mike Mussina 40.00 80.00
MP Mike Pelfrey 12.50 30.00
MR Mariano Rivera 20.00 50.00
OH Orlando Hernandez 8.00 20.00
OP Oliver Perez 8.00 20.00
PH Phil Hughes 20.00 50.00
PM Pedro Martinez 10.00 25.00
RC Robinson Cano 30.00 60.00
RMC Ryan Church 10.00 25.00

2008 Topps Dick Perez

WMDP1 Manny Ramirez .60 1.50
WMDP2 Cameron Maybin .25 .60
WMDP3 Ryan Howard .40 1.00
WMDP4 David Ortiz .60 1.50
WMDP5 Tim Lincecum .40 1.00
WMDP6 David Wright .40 1.00
WMDP7 Mickey Mantle 2.00 5.00
WMDP8 Joba Chamberlain .25 .60
WMDP9 Ichiro Suzuki .75 2.00
WMDP10 Prince Fielder .40 1.00
WMDP11 Jacoby Ellsbury .50 1.25
WMDP12 Jake Peavy .25 .60
WMDP13 Miguel Cabrera .60 1.50
WMDP14 Josh Beckett .25 .60
WMDP15 Jimmy Rollins .40 1.00
WMDP16 Torii Hunter .25 .60
WMDP17 Alfonso Soriano .40 1.00
WMDP18 Jose Reyes .40 1.00
WMDP19 C.C. Sabathia .40 1.00
WMDP20 Alex Rodriguez .75 2.00
WMDP21 Ryan Braun .40 1.00
WMDP22 Johan Santana .40 1.00
WMDP23 Matt Holliday .60 1.50
WMDP24 Ervin Santana .25 .60
WMDP25 Daisuke Matsuzaka .40 1.00
WMDP26 Josh Hamilton .40 1.00
WMDP27 Chipper Jones .60 1.50
WMDP28 Lance Berkman .40 1.00
WMDP29 Hanley Ramirez .40 1.00
WMDP30 Mariano Rivera .75 2.00

2008 Topps Factory Set Mickey Mantle Blue

MMR52 Mickey Mantle 52T 8.00 20.00
MMR53 Mickey Mantle 53T 8.00 20.00
MMR54 Mickey Mantle 54T 8.00 20.00

2008 Topps Factory Set Mickey Mantle Gold

MMR52 Mickey Mantle 52T 10.00 25.00
MMR53 Mickey Mantle 53T 10.00 25.00
MMR54 Mickey Mantle 54T 10.00 25.00

2008 Topps Highlights Autographs

SER.1 A ODDS 1:32,000 H,1:1463 HTA
SER.1 A ODDS 1:159,000 RETAIL
SER.2 A ODDS 1:28,927 H,1:965 HTA
SER.2 A ODDS 1:76,245 RETAIL
UPD.A ODDS 1:38,362 HOBBY
SER.1 B ODDS 1:4792 H,1:244 HTA
SER.1 B ODDS 1:33,333 RETAIL
SER.2 B ODDS 1:923 H,1:31 HTA
SER.2 B ODDS 1:2451 RETAIL
UPD.B ODDS 1:11,066 HOBBY
SER.1 C ODDS 1:958 H,1:49 HTA
SER.1 C ODDS 1:6470 RETAIL
SER.2 C ODDS 1:651 H,1:87 HTA
SER.2 C ODDS 1:6862 RETAIL
UPD.C ODDS 1:4082 HOBBY
SER.1 D ODDS 1:1425 H,1:70 HTA
SER.1 D ODDS 1:14,250 RETAIL
SER.2 D ODDS 1:15,370 H,1:181 HTA
SER.2 D ODDS 1:14,296 RETAIL
UPD.D ODDS 1:5587 HOBBY
SER.1 E ODDS 1:1075 H,1:117 HTA
SER.1 E ODDS 1:880 RETAIL
SER.2 E ODDS 1:814 H,1:27 HTA
SER.2 E ODDS 1:2144 RETAIL
UPD.E ODDS 1:6851 HOBBY
SER.1 F ODDS 1:895 H,1:23 HTA
SER.1 F ODDS 1:1370 RETAIL

SER.2 F ODDS 1:3254 H,1:108 HTA
SER.2 F ODDS 1:8578 RETAIL
UPD.F ODDS 1:1116 HOBBY
SER.1 G ODDS 1:3070 H,1:224 HTA
SER.1 G ODDS 1:4055 RETAIL
UPD.G ODDS 1:1109 HOBBY
UPD.H ODDS 1:1985 HOBBY
NO GROUP A PRICING AVAILABLE
NO GROUP A2 PRICING AVAILABLE
AC Asdrubal Cabrera C UPD 6.00 15.00
AG Armando Galarraga D UPD 4.00 10.00
AH Aaron Heilman B2 6.00 15.00
AK Austin Kearns F2 4.00 10.00
AL Adam Lind C 4.00 10.00
BB Billy Butler C UPD 10.00 25.00
BC Bobby Crosby B2 6.00 15.00
BD Blake DeWitt C UPD 12.00 30.00
BDB Brian Barton F UPD 4.00 10.00
BP Brandon Phillips B UPD 4.00 10.00
BP Brad Penny B 10.00 25.00
BR B.J. Ryan D UPD 4.00 10.00
CB Clay Buchholz C 4.00 10.00
CC Carl Crawford B 8.00 20.00
CF Chone Figgins B2 6.00 15.00
CG Carlos Gomez C UPD 4.00 10.00
CK Clayton Kershaw B UPD 40.00 80.00
CM Craig Monroe B2 6.00 15.00
CMW Chien-Ming Wang B 100.00 150.00
CP Carlos Pena C 4.00 10.00
CR Carlos Ruiz F UPD 4.00 10.00
CV Carlos Villanueva F 4.00 10.00
CV Claudio Vargas C2 4.00 10.00
CW Chase Wright E2 4.00 10.00
DB Dallas Braden C2 12.00 30.00
DB Daric Barton G 4.00 10.00
DE Darin Erstad B2 4.00 10.00
DH Dan Haren B 4.00 10.00
DM Dustin McGowan UPD 6.00 15.00
DM Dustin Moseley F 4.00 10.00
DW David Wright B 30.00 60.00
DY Delwyn Young E2 4.00 10.00
EC Eric Chavez B2 4.00 10.00
ED Eulogio De La Cruz C 4.00 10.00
ES Ervin Santana C 4.00 10.00
ES Ervin Santana E2 4.00 10.00
EV Edinson Volquez D UPD 8.00 20.00
FC Fausto Carmona E2 4.00 10.00
FC Fausto Carmona C 6.00 15.00
FL Francisco Liriano B2 6.00 15.00
FS Freddy Sanchez C 6.00 15.00
GS Gary Sheffield B 10.00 25.00
HCK Hong-Chih Kuo C2 6.00 15.00
HK Howie Kendrick D 4.00 10.00
HR Hanley Ramirez B 6.00 15.00
JA Josh Anderson E 4.00 10.00
JAB Jason Bartlett D2 4.00 10.00
JAR Jo-Jo Reyes C2 4.00 10.00
JB Jeremy Bonderman B2 6.00 15.00
JBR John Buck D 4.00 10.00
JBR Jose Reyes B 30.00 60.00
JC Joba Chamberlain B2 10.00 25.00
JEM Justin Morneau B 10.00 25.00
JF Josh Fields C 4.00 10.00
JH Josh Hamilton B UPD 30.00 60.00
JKM John Maine B2 6.00 15.00
JL John Lackey C 5.00 12.00
JLC Jorge Cantu C2 4.00 10.00
JM Jose Molina D 4.00 10.00
JP Jake Peavy B 5.00 12.00
JR Jo-Jo Reyes E UPD 4.00 10.00
JR Jimmy Rollins B 40.00 80.00
JS Jeff Salazar G UPD 4.00 10.00
JTD Jermaine Dye B 4.00 10.00
JTD Jermaine Dye B2 4.00 10.00
JV Joey Votto C UPD 20.00 50.00
JV Jason Varitek B 40.00 80.00
JW Josh Willingham B2 6.00 15.00
JZ Joel Zumaya B2 4.00 10.00
KM Kendry Morales B2 4.00 10.00
LB Lance Broadway E 4.00 10.00
LC Luis Castillo C 4.00 10.00
MB Mike Bacsik F 4.00 10.00
MC Melky Cabrera B2 10.00 25.00
ME Mark Ellis F 4.00 10.00
MG Matt Garza C 4.00 10.00
MG Matt Garza B2 4.00 10.00
MK Masa Kobayashi C UPD 6.00 15.00
MMT Marcus Thames B2 4.00 10.00
MS Max Scherzer B UPD 60.00 150.00
MW Mark Worrell H UPD 4.00 10.00
MY Michael Young B 6.00 15.00
NJM Nyjer Morgan E 4.00 10.00
NM Nick Markakis B UPD 10.00 25.00
NM Nick Markakis C 6.00 15.00
NM Nick Markakis B2 6.00 15.00
NR Nate Robertson B2 4.00 10.00
PF Prince Fielder B 15.00 40.00
PF Prince Fielder B2 30.00 60.00
PH Philip Humber D2 4.00 10.00
PJF Pedro Feliciano B2 6.00 15.00
RB Ryan Braun A UPD 60.00 120.00
RB Ryan Braun B2 20.00 50.00
RC Robinson Cano B2 12.00 30.00
RC Ramon Castro D 4.00 10.00
RH Rich Hill D 6.00 15.00
RJC Robinson Cano B 15.00 40.00
RJM Randy Messenger F 4.00 10.00
RM Russell Martin C 6.00 15.00
RM Russ Martin B2 6.00 15.00
RN Ricky Nolasco B2 4.00 10.00
RP Ronny Paulino E2 4.00 10.00
RR Ryan Roberts E2 4.00 10.00
SF Sam Fuld E 4.00 10.00
SH Steve Holm F UPD 4.00 10.00
SM Scott Moore F 4.00 10.00
SS Seth Smith G UPD 4.00 10.00
SS Seth Smith E 4.00 10.00
SV Shane Victorino B2 8.00 20.00
TG Tom Gorzelanny E2 4.00 10.00
TG Tom Gorzelanny F 4.00 10.00
TT Taylor Tankersley B2 4.00 10.00
UJ Ubaldo Jimenez F 6.00 15.00
WN Wil Nieves C 4.00 10.00
YG Yovani Gallardo C 8.00 20.00
ZG Zack Greinke C UPD 10.00 25.00
ZG Zack Greinke E2 10.00 25.00

2008 Topps Highlights Relics

SER.1 A ODDS 1:3597 H,1:183 HTA
SER.1 A ODDS 1:25,000 RETAIL
SER.2 A ODDS 1:85 H,1:11 HTA
SER.1 B ODDS 1:21,250 H,1:958 HTA
SER.1 B ODDS 1:7500 RETAIL
SER.2 B ODDS 1:108 H, 1:14 HTA
SER.1 C ODDS 1:1725 H,1:705 HTA
SER.1 C ODDS 1:3050 RETAIL
SER.2 C ODDS 1:651 H, 1:80 HTA
SER.1 D ODDS 1:244 RETAIL
SER.1 D ODDS 1:1965 H,1:33 HTA
AG Alex Gordon B2 5.00 12.00
AP Albert Pujols B2 6.00 15.00
AP Albert Pujols D 6.00 15.00
AR Aramis Ramirez B2 3.00 8.00
BP Brandon Phillips B2 3.00 8.00
BU B.J. Upton C2 3.00 8.00
BW Brandon Webb C2 3.00 8.00
CB Carlos Beltran Bat C 3.00 8.00
CC Carl Crawford D 3.00 8.00
CC Carl Crawford Pants B2 3.00 8.00
CM Cameron Maybin Bat C2 3.00 8.00
CM Cameron Maybin D 3.00 8.00
CMW Chien-Ming Wang Jsy B2 8.00 20.00
CS Curt Schilling Jsy D 4.00 10.00
CU Chase Utley Jsy B2 5.00 12.00
DL Derrek Lee B2 3.00 8.00
DO David Ortiz D 4.00 10.00
DO1 David Ortiz B2 4.00 10.00
DO2 David Ortiz B2 4.00 10.00
DU Dan Uggla Jsy B2 3.00 8.00
DW David Wright Jsy C2 5.00 12.00
DW David Wright D 5.00 12.00
DWW Dontrelle Willis D 3.00 8.00
DY Delmon Young Jsy B2 3.00 8.00
EC Eric Chavez D 3.00 8.00
HR Hanley Ramirez B2 3.00 8.00
IR Ivan Rodriguez D 5.00 12.00
IS Ichiro Suzuki D 6.00 15.00
IS Ichiro Suzuki C2 6.00 15.00
JB Jeremy Bonderman B2 3.00 8.00
JL James Loney B2 3.00 8.00
JP Jake Peavy B2 3.00 8.00
JR Jose Reyes B2 5.00 12.00
JR Jose Reyes A2 5.00 12.00
JT Jim Thome C2 3.00 8.00
JV Justin Verlander D 5.00 12.00
LB Lance Berkman C 3.00 8.00
MH Matt Holliday B 3.00 8.00
MR Manny Ramirez D 4.00 10.00
MT Miguel Tejada D 3.00 8.00
PF Prince Fielder A 4.00 10.00
PF Prince Fielder B2 4.00 10.00
RB Ryan Braun B2 6.00 15.00
RF Rafael Furcal C2 3.00 8.00
RH Ryan Howard B2 5.00 12.00
RO Roy Oswalt A2 3.00 8.00
RZ Ryan Zimmerman B2 3.00 8.00
ST Scott Thorman B2 3.00 8.00
TH Todd Helton D 3.00 8.00
VG Vladimir Guerrero 4.00 10.00
IBB A
VG Vladimir Guerrero 4.00 10.00
Silver Slugger B2

2008 Topps Historical Campaign Match-Ups

COMPLETE SET (55) 30.00 60.00
SER.2 ODDS 1:6 HOB,1:6 HTA,1:6 RET
1792 G.Washington/J.Adams 1.00 2.50
1796 J.Adams/T.Jefferson 1.00 2.50
1800 T.Jefferson/A.Burr .75 2.00
1804 T.Jefferson/C.Pinckney .75 2.00
1808 James Madison/Charles Pinckney .60 1.50
1812 James Madison/DeWitt Clinton .60 1.50
1816 James Monroe/Rufus King .60 1.50
1820 James Monroe/John Quincy Adams .60 1.50
1824 John Quincy Adams
Andrew Jackson .60 1.50
1828 Andrew Jackson
John Quincy Adams .60 1.50
1832 Andrew Jackson/Henry Clay .40 1.00
1836 Martin Van Buren
William Henry Harrison .40 1.00
1840 William Henry Harrison
Martin Van Buren .50 1.25
1844 James K. Polk/Henry Clay .40 1.00
1848 Zachary Taylor/Lewis Cass .40 1.00
1852 Franklin Pierce/Winfield Scott .40 1.00
1856 James Buchanan/John C. Fremont .50 1.25
1860 A.Lincoln/J.Breckinridge .75 2.00
1864 A.Lincoln/G.McClellan .75 2.00
1868 Ulysses S. Grant/Horatio Seymour .50 1.25
1872 Ulysses S. Grant/Horace Greeley .50 1.25
1876 Rutherford B. Hayes
Samuel J. Tilden .40 1.00
1880 James Garfield/Winfield
Scott Hancock .40 1.00
1884 Grover Cleveland/James G. Blaine .40 1.00
1888 Benjamin Harrison/Grover Cleveland .40 1.00
1892 Grover Cleveland/Benjamin Harrison .40 1.00
1896 William McKinley/William
Jennings Bryan .50 1.25
1900 William McKinley
William Jennings Bryan .40 1.00
1904 Theodore Roosevelt/Alton B. Parker .60 1.50
1908 William H. Taft
William Jennings Bryan .50 1.25
1912 Woodrow Wilson
Theodore Roosevelt .60 1.50
1916 Woodrow Wilson
Charles Evans Hughes .40 1.00
1920 Warren G. Harding/James M. Cox .40 1.00
1924 Calvin Coolidge/John W. Davis .40 1.00
1928 Herbert Hoover/Al Smith .40 1.00
1932 Franklin D. Roosevelt
Herbert Hoover .60 1.50
1936 Franklin D. Roosevelt/Alf Landon .60 1.50
1940 Franklin D. Roosevelt
Wendell Willkie .60 1.50
1944 Franklin D. Roosevelt
Thomas E. Dewey .50 1.25
1948 Harry S Truman/Thomas E. Dewey .50 1.25
1952 Dwight D. Eisenhower
Adlai Stevenson .60 1.50
1956 Dwight D. Eisenhower
Adlai Stevenson .60 1.50
1960 J.Kennedy/R.Nixon 1.25 3.00
1964 Lyndon B. Johnson/Barry Goldwater .60 1.50
1968 Richard Nixon/Hubert H. Humphrey .40 1.00
1972 Richard Nixon/George McGovern .60 1.50
1976 J.Carter/G.Ford .75 2.00
1980 R.Reagan/J.Carter 1.25 3.00
1984 R.Reagan/W.Mondale .75 2.00
1988 George Bush/Michael Dukakis .60 1.50
1992 B.Clinton/G.Bush .75 2.00
1996 B.Clinton/B.Dole .75 2.00
2000 G.Bush/A.Gore .75 2.00
2004 G.Bush/J.Kerry .75 2.00
2008D H.Clinton/B.Obama 1.50 4.00

2008 Topps K-Mart

COMPLETE SET (30) 15.00 40.00
RANDOM INSERTS IN KMART PACKS
RV1 Chin Lung Hu .75 2.00
RV2 Steve Pearce 4.00 10.00
RV3 Luke Hochevar 1.25 3.00
RV4 Joey Votto 6.00 15.00
RV5 Clay Buchholz 1.25 3.00
RV6 Emilio Bonifacio 2.00 5.00
RV7 Daric Barton .75 2.00
RV8 Eugenio Velez .75 2.00
RV9 J.R. Towles 1.25 3.00
RV10 Wladimir Balentien .75 2.00
RV11 Ross Detwiler 1.25 3.00
RV12 Troy Patton .75 2.00
RV13 Brandon Jones 2.00 5.00
RV14 Billy Buckner .75 2.00
RV15 Ross Ohlendorf 1.25 3.00
RV16 Nick Blackburn 1.25 3.00
RV17 Masahide Kobayashi 1.25 3.00
RV18 Jayson Nix .75 2.00
RV19 Blake DeWitt 1.25 3.00
RV20 Hiroki Kuroda 2.00 5.00
RV21 Matt Tolbert 1.25 3.00
RV22 Brian Bass .75 2.00
RV23 Fernando Hernandez .75 2.00
RV24 Kazuo Fukumori 1.25 3.00
RV25 Brian Barton 1.25 3.00
RV26 Clete Thomas 1.25 3.00
RV27 Rico Washington .75 2.00
RV28 Erick Threets .75 2.00
RV29 Callix Crabbe .75 2.00
RV30 Johnny Cueto 2.00 5.00

2008 Topps of the Class

RANDOM INSERTS IN PACKS
NNO David Wright .60 1.50

2008 Topps Own the Game

COMPLETE SET (25) 6.00 15.00
STATED ODDS 1:6 HOB, 1:6 RET
OTG1 Alex Rodriguez 1.00 2.50
OTG2 Prince Fielder .50 1.25
OTG3 Ryan Howard .50 1.25
OTG4 Carlos Pena .50 1.25
OTG5 Adam Dunn .50 1.25
OTG6 Matt Holliday .75 2.00
OTG7 David Ortiz .75 2.00
OTG8 Jim Thome .50 1.25
OTG9 Lance Berkman .50 1.25
OTG10 Miguel Cabrera .75 2.00
OTG11 Alex Rodriguez 1.00 2.50
OTG12 Magglio Ordonez .50 1.25
OTG13 Matt Holliday .75 2.00
OTG14 Ryan Howard .50 1.25
OTG15 Vladimir Guerrero .50 1.25
OTG16 Carlos Pena .50 1.25
OTG17 Mike Lowell .30 .75
OTG18 Miguel Cabrera .75 2.00
OTG19 Prince Fielder .50 1.25
OTG20 Carlos Lee .30 .75
OTG21 Jake Peavy .30 .75
OTG22 John Lackey .50 1.25
OTG23 Brandon Webb .50 1.25
OTG24 Brad Penny .30 .75
OTG25 Fausto Carmona .30 .75

2008 Topps Presidential Stamp Collection

SER.1 ODDS 1:1950 H, 1:1240 HTA
SER.1 ODDS 1:3300 RETAIL
SER.2 ODDS 1:1600 H,1:700 HTA
SER.2 ODDS 1:2000 RETAIL
STATED PRINT RUN 90 SER.#'d SETS
ALL VERSIONS PRICED EQUALLY
AJ1 Andrew Jackson 40.00 80.00
AJO1 Andrew Johnson 20.00 50.00
AL1 Abraham Lincoln 10.00 25.00
AL2 Abraham Lincoln 10.00 25.00
AL3 Abraham Lincoln 10.00 25.00
AL4 Abraham Lincoln 10.00 25.00
AL5 Abraham Lincoln 10.00 25.00
AL6 Abraham Lincoln 10.00 25.00
BH1 Benjamin Harrison 30.00 60.00
CAA1 Chester A. Arthur 50.00 100.00
DDE1 Dwight D. Eisenhower 40.00 80.00
FDR1 Franklin Delano Roosevelt 30.00 60.00
FP1 Franklin Pierce 30.00 60.00
GC1 Grover Cleveland 10.00 25.00
GW1 George Washington 10.00 25.00
GW2 George Washington 10.00 25.00
GW3 George Washington 10.00 25.00
GW4 George Washington 10.00 25.00
GW5 George Washington 10.00 25.00
GW6 George Washington 10.00 25.00
GW7 George Washington 10.00 25.00
GW8 George Washington 10.00 25.00
GW9 George Washington 10.00 25.00
GW10 George Washington 10.00 25.00
GW11 George Washington 10.00 25.00
GW12 George Washington 10.00 25.00
GW13 George Washington 10.00 25.00
HH1 Herbert Hoover 20.00 50.00
HST1 Harry S. Truman 30.00 60.00
JB1 James Buchanan 50.00 100.00
JFK1 John F. Kennedy 12.00 30.00
JFK2 John F. Kennedy 12.00 30.00
JG1 James Garfield 10.00 25.00
JG2 James Garfield 10.00 25.00
JKP1 James K. Polk 50.00 100.00
JM1 James Monroe 10.00 25.00
JM2 James Monroe 10.00 25.00
JMA1 James Madison 50.00 100.00
JMA2 James Madison 50.00 100.00
JQA1 John Quincy Adams 12.00 30.00
JT1 John Tyler 20.00 50.00
LBJ1 Lyndon B. Johnson 12.50 30.00
MF1 Millard Fillmore 30.00 60.00
MVB1 Martin Van Buren 30.00 60.00
RBH1 Rutherford B. Hayes 50.00 100.00
RBH2 Rutherford B. Hayes 50.00 100.00
RN1 Richard Nixon 30.00 60.00
RR1 Ronald Reagan 30.00 60.00
TJ1 Thomas Jefferson 15.00 40.00
TJ2 Thomas Jefferson 15.00 40.00
TJ3 Thomas Jefferson 15.00 40.00
TJ4 Thomas Jefferson 15.00 40.00
TR1 Teddy Roosevelt 30.00 60.00
TR2 Theodore Roosevelt 10.00 25.00
TR3 Theodore Roosevelt 10.00 25.00
USG1 Ulysses S. Grant 10.00 25.00
USG2 Ulysses S. Grant 10.00 25.00
WGH1 Warren G. Harding 50.00 100.00
WGH2 Warren G. Harding 50.00 100.00
WHH1 William Henry Harrison 30.00 60.00
WHT1 William Howard Taft 30.00 60.00
WM1 William McKinley 20.00 50.00
WW1 Woodrow Wilson 10.00 25.00
WW2 Woodrow Wilson 10.00 25.00
ZT1 Zachary Taylor 20.00 50.00

2008 Topps Red Hot Rookie Redemption

COMMON EXCH 6.00 15.00
RANDOM INSERTS IN SER.2 PACKS
EXCHANGE DEADLINE 5/30/2010
1 Jay Bruce AU 8.00 20.00
2 Justin Masterson 3.00 8.00
3 John Bowker 1.25 3.00
4 Kosuke Fukudome 4.00 10.00
5 Mike Aviles 2.00 5.00
6 Chris Davis 8.00 20.00
7 Chris Volstad 1.25 3.00
8 Jeff Samardzija 4.00 10.00
9 Brad Ziegler 6.00 15.00
10 Gio Gonzalez 2.00 5.00
11 Clayton Kershaw 40.00 100.00
12 Daniel Murphy 5.00 12.00
13 Chris Dickerson 2.00 5.00
14 Pablo Sandoval 5.00 12.00
15 Nick Evans 1.25 3.00
16 Clayton Richard 1.25 3.00
17 Evan Longoria AU 20.00 50.00
18 Taylor Teagarden 2.00 5.00
19 Collin Balester 1.25 3.00
20 Lou Montanez 1.25 3.00

2008 Topps Replica Mini Jerseys

STATED ODDS 1:412 H,1:19 HTA
STATED ODDS 1:6300 RETAIL
PRINT RUNS B/WN 379-539 COPIES PER
AIR Alex Rios/539 5.00 12.00
AP Albert Pujols 10.00 25.00
AR Alex Rodriguez/539 10.00 25.00
BW Brandon Webb 5.00 12.00
CC Carl Crawford/539 5.00 12.00
CH Cole Hamels 6.00 15.00
CMS Curt Schilling 6.00 15.00
CS C.C. Sabathia/539 5.00 12.00
CU Chase Utley 6.00 15.00
DAO David Ortiz 8.00 20.00
DO David Ortiz 8.00 20.00
DP Dustin Pedroia 10.00 25.00
DW David Wright 8.00 20.00
GS Grady Sizemore/539 6.00 15.00
HO Hideki Okajima 8.00 20.00
IS Ichiro Suzuki 10.00 25.00
JAV Jason Varitek 6.00 15.00
JB Josh Beckett 10.00 25.00
JCL Julio Lugo 6.00 15.00
JDD J.D. Drew 6.00 15.00
JE Jacoby Ellsbury 15.00 40.00
JL Jon Lester 8.00 20.00
JM Justin Morneau/539 5.00 12.00
JP Jake Peavy 6.00 15.00
JR Jose Reyes 6.00 15.00
JRP Jonathan Papelbon 8.00 20.00
JV Justin Verlander/539 6.00 15.00
KY Kevin Youkilis 6.00 15.00
MH Matt Holliday 6.00 15.00
ML Mike Lowell 10.00 25.00
MR Manny Ramirez 10.00 25.00
MT Mike Timlin 6.00 15.00
PF Prince Fielder 8.00 20.00
RH Ryan Howard/379 8.00 20.00
RM Russell Martin 5.00 12.00

2008 Topps Retail Relics

ONE PER RETAIL BLASTER BOX
*GOLD UPD/99: .5X TO 1.2X BASIC
*BLACK UPD/25: .6X TO 1.5X BASIC
AB Angel Berroa UPD 2.00 5.00
AC Asdrubal Cabrera UPD 3.00 8.00
AD Adam Dunn 3.00 8.00
AER Alex Rodriguez UPD 6.00 15.00
AH Aaron Harang 2.00 5.00
AL Adam LaRoche 2.00 5.00
AR Aramis Ramirez UPD 2.00 5.00
AR Aaron Rowand 2.00 5.00
BA Bronson Arroyo 2.00 5.00
BC Bobby Crosby 2.00 5.00
BG Brian Giles 2.00 5.00
BH Brad Hawpe 2.00 5.00
BJ Bobby Jenks 2.00 5.00
BKA Bobby Abreu 2.00 5.00
BP Brad Penny 2.00 5.00
BS Ben Sheets 2.00 5.00
BW Brandon Webb 3.00 8.00
CB Carlos Beltran 3.00 8.00
CC Coco Crisp UPD 2.00 5.00
CC Chris Capuano 2.00 5.00
CD Carlos Delgado 2.00 5.00
CDC Carl Crawford 3.00 8.00
CG Curtis Granderson UPD 3.00 8.00
CJC Chris Carpenter 3.00 8.00
CK Casey Kotchman 2.00 5.00
DE Darin Erstad 2.00 5.00
DN Dioner Navarro UPD 2.00 5.00
DP Dustin Pedroia UPD 5.00 12.00
DW David Wright UPD 3.00 8.00
EB Erik Bedard UPD 2.00 5.00
EC Eric Chavez UPD 2.00 5.00
EC Eric Chavez 2.00 5.00
EE Edwin Encarnacion 5.00 12.00
FL Fred Lewis 2.00 5.00
FR Francisco Rodriguez 3.00 8.00
GA Garrett Atkins 2.00 5.00
HB Hank Blalock 2.00 5.00
HK Hong-Chih Kuo UPD 2.00 5.00
IK Ian Kinsler UPD 3.00 8.00
IR Ivan Rodriguez 3.00 8.00
IS Ian Snell 2.00 5.00
JB Jason Bay 3.00 8.00
JD Jermaine Dye 2.00 5.00
JE Johnny Estrada UPD 2.00 5.00
JE Jim Edmonds 3.00 8.00
JF Jeff Francis UPD 2.00 5.00
JJH J.J. Hardy 3.00 8.00
JL Jon Lester UPD 3.00 8.00
JL Jon Lester 3.00 8.00
JM John Maine UPD 2.00 5.00
JP Jake Peavy 2.00 5.00
JR Justin Ruggiano UPD 3.00 8.00
JR Jimmy Rollins 3.00 8.00
JRH Rich Harden 2.00 5.00
KG Khalil Greene 2.00 5.00
KH Kevin Hart UPD 2.00 5.00
KM Kendry Morales 2.00 5.00
KW Kerry Wood UPD 2.00 5.00
KW Kerry Wood 2.00 5.00
LB Lance Berkman 3.00 8.00
LB1 Lance Broadway 2.00 5.00
LH Livan Hernandez 2.00 5.00
LM Lastings Milledge UPD 2.00 5.00
MB Mark Buehrle 3.00 8.00
MH Mike Hampton 2.00 5.00
MK Matt Kemp UPD 4.00 10.00
MM Mark Mulder UPD 2.00 5.00
MM Melvin Mora 2.00 5.00
MMM Mike Mussina 3.00 8.00
MS Mike Sweeney 2.00 5.00
MT Mark Teahen 2.00 5.00
MY Michael Young 2.00 5.00
OG Ozzie Guillen UPD 2.00 5.00
OG Ozzie Guillen 2.00 5.00
PB Pat Burrell 2.00 5.00
PM Pedro Martinez 3.00 8.00
RB Rocco Baldelli UPD 2.00 5.00
RF Rafael Furcal UPD 2.00 5.00
RF Rafael Furcal 2.00 5.00
RH Roy Halladay 3.00 8.00
RW Rickie Weeks 2.00 5.00
SC Sean Casey UPD 2.00 5.00
SK Scott Kazmir 2.00 5.00
TG Troy Glaus 3.00 8.00
TH Todd Helton UPD 3.00 8.00
TH Todd Helton 3.00 8.00
TP Tony Pena 2.00 5.00
VW Vernon Wells 2.00 5.00
ZG Zack Greinke 5.00 12.00

2008 Topps Silk Collection

SER.2 ODDS 1:300 HOB, 1:139 RET
STATED PRINT RUN 100 SER.#'d SETS
1-100 FOUND IN SERIES 2
UPD ODDS 1:246 HOBBY
STATED PRINT RUN 100 SER.#'d SETS
101-200 FOUND IN UPDATE
SC1 Alex Rodriguez 12.00 30.00
SC2 Scott Kazmir 6.00 15.00
SC3 Ivan Rodriguez 6.00 15.00
SC4 Joe Mauer 8.00 20.00
SC5 Ken Griffey Jr. 20.00 50.00
SC6 Nick Markakis 8.00 20.00
SC7 Mickey Mantle 30.00 80.00
SC8 Erik Bedard 4.00 10.00
SC9 Derrek Lee 4.00 10.00
SC10 Miguel Cabrera 10.00 25.00
SC11 Yovani Gallardo 4.00 10.00
SC12 Victor Martinez 6.00 15.00
SC13 Curtis Granderson 6.00 15.00
SC14 Chris Young 4.00 10.00
SC15 Jimmy Rollins 6.00 15.00
SC16 Dan Uggla 4.00 10.00
SC17 Felix Hernandez 6.00 15.00
SC18 Alex Rios 4.00 10.00
SC19 Jason Bay 6.00 15.00
SC20 Jose Reyes 6.00 15.00
SC21 Mike Lowell 4.00 10.00
SC22 Carl Crawford 6.00 15.00
SC23 Chipper Jones 10.00 25.00
SC24 Troy Glaus 4.00 10.00
SC25 Cole Hamels 8.00 20.00
SC26 Chris Young 4.00 10.00
SC27 Torii Hunter 4.00 10.00
SC28 Hideki Matsui 10.00 25.00
SC29 Freddy Sanchez 4.00 10.00
SC30 Josh Beckett 6.00 15.00
SC31 Mark Buehrle 4.00 10.00
SC32 Brian Bannister 4.00 10.00
SC33 Carlos Beltran 6.00 15.00
SC34 Dontrelle Willis 4.00 10.00
SC35 Vladimir Guerrero 6.00 15.00
SC36 Matt Holliday 10.00 25.00
SC37 Adam Dunn 6.00 15.00
SC38 Gary Matthews 4.00 10.00
SC39 Travis Hafner 4.00 10.00
SC40 Chase Utley 6.00 15.00
SC41 Vernon Wells 4.00 10.00
SC42 Lance Berkman 6.00 15.00
SC43 Jeff Francis 4.00 10.00
SC44 Curt Schilling 6.00 15.00
SC45 Alfonso Soriano 6.00 15.00
SC46 Jarrod Saltalamacchia 4.00 10.00
SC47 Hideki Okajima 4.00 10.00
SC48 Pedro Martinez 6.00 15.00
SC49 Jorge Posada 6.00 15.00
SC50 Justin Upton 6.00 15.00
SC51 Tom Gorzelanny 4.00 10.00
SC52 Carlos Delgado 4.00 10.00
SC53 Edgar Renteria 4.00 10.00
SC54 Chien-Ming Wang 6.00 15.00
SC55 C.C. Sabathia 6.00 15.00
SC56 B.J. Upton 6.00 15.00
SC57 Delmon Young 6.00 15.00
SC58 Tim Lincecum 6.00 15.00
SC59 Carlos Zambrano 6.00 15.00
SC60 Magglio Ordonez 6.00 15.00
SC61 Brandon Webb 6.00 15.00
SC62 Ben Sheets 4.00 10.00
SC63 Brad Penny 4.00 10.00
SC64 John Lackey 6.00 15.00
SC65 Hanley Ramirez 6.00 15.00
SC66 Gary Sheffield 4.00 10.00
SC67 Ubaldo Jimenez 4.00 10.00
SC68 Barry Zito 6.00 15.00
SC69 Daisuke Matsuzaka 6.00 15.00
SC70 Justin Morneau 6.00 15.00
SC71 Jacoby Ellsbury 8.00 20.00
SC72 John Smoltz 10.00 25.00
SC73 Chris Carpenter 6.00 15.00
SC74 Ryan Braun 6.00 15.00
SC75 Prince Fielder 6.00 15.00
SC76 Carlos Lee 4.00 10.00
SC77 Ryan Zimmerman 6.00 15.00
SC78 Troy Tulowitzki 10.00 25.00
SC79 Michael Young 4.00 10.00
SC80 Johan Santana 6.00 15.00
SC81 Hunter Pence 6.00 15.00
SC82 Adrian Gonzalez 6.00 15.00
SC83 Jake Peavy 4.00 10.00
SC84 Derek Jeter 25.00 60.00
SC85 Ichiro Suzuki 12.00 30.00
SC86 Miguel Tejada 6.00 15.00
SC87 Trevor Hoffman 6.00 15.00
SC88 Kevin Youkilis 4.00 10.00
SC89 David Wright 6.00 15.00
SC90 Albert Pujols 12.00 30.00
SC91 Todd Helton 6.00 15.00
SC92 Rich Harden 4.00 10.00
SC93 Fausto Carmona 4.00 10.00
SC94 Mark Teixeira 6.00 15.00
SC95 Justin Verlander 10.00 25.00
SC96 Tim Hudson 6.00 15.00
SC97 Jeff Francoeur 6.00 15.00
SC98 Manny Ramirez 10.00 25.00
SC99 David Ortiz 10.00 25.00
SC100 Ryan Howard 6.00 15.00
SC101 Johan Santana 6.00 15.00
SC102 Cristian Guzman 4.00 10.00
SC103 Brendan Harris 4.00 10.00
SC104 Randy Wolf 4.00 10.00
SC105 Cliff Lee 6.00 15.00
SC106 Roy Halladay 6.00 15.00
SC107 Dustin Pedroia 10.00 25.00
SC108 Chris Iannetta 4.00 10.00
SC109 Kerry Wood 4.00 10.00
SC110 Jim Edmonds 6.00 15.00
SC111 Jon Rauch 4.00 10.00
SC112 Ryan Sweeney 4.00 10.00
SC113 Ryan Ludwick 4.00 10.00
SC114 George Sherrill 4.00 10.00
SC115 Matt Garza 4.00 10.00
SC116 Nate McLouth 4.00 10.00
SC117 Eric Hinske 4.00 10.00
SC118 Adrian Gonzalez 6.00 15.00
SC119 Carlos Marmol 6.00 15.00
SC120 Jose Valverde 4.00 10.00
SC121 Shane Victorino 4.00 10.00
SC122 Brad Wilkerson 4.00 10.00
SC123 Dana Eveland 4.00 10.00
SC124 Luke Scott 4.00 10.00
SC125 Mike Cameron 4.00 10.00
SC126 Ervin Santana 4.00 10.00
SC127 Ryan Dempster 4.00 10.00
SC128 Geoff Jenkins 4.00 10.00
SC129 Billy Wagner 4.00 10.00
SC130 Pedro Feliz 4.00 10.00
SC131 Stephen Drew 4.00 10.00
SC132 Mark Hendrickson 4.00 10.00
SC133 Orlando Hudson 4.00 10.00
SC134 Pat Burrell 4.00 10.00
SC135 Russ Martin 4.00 10.00
SC136 James Loney 4.00 10.00
SC137 Justin Masterson 10.00 25.00
SC138 Matt Kemp 8.00 20.00
SC139 Hiroki Kuroda 10.00 25.00
SC140 Joe Crede 4.00 10.00
SC141 Joakim Soria 4.00 10.00
SC142 Armando Galarraga 6.00 15.00
SC143 Jason Varitek 10.00 25.00
SC144 Aaron Cook 4.00 10.00
SC145 Orlando Cabrera 4.00 10.00
SC146 Ian Kinsler 6.00 15.00
SC147 Carlos Gomez 4.00 10.00
SC148 Mike Aviles 6.00 15.00
SC149 Carlos Guillen 4.00 10.00
SC150 Erik Bedard 4.00 10.00
SC151 J.D. Drew 4.00 10.00
SC152 Marco Scutaro 4.00 10.00
SC153 James Shields 4.00 10.00
SC154 Cesar Izturis 4.00 10.00
SC155 Akinori Iwamura 4.00 10.00
SC156 Aramis Ramirez 4.00 10.00
SC157 Joe Mauer 8.00 20.00
SC158 Brad Lidge 4.00 10.00
SC159 Milton Bradley 4.00 10.00
SC160 Jay Bruce 12.00 30.00
SC161 Andrew Miller 6.00 15.00
SC162 Mark Reynolds 4.00 10.00
SC163 Johnny Damon 6.00 15.00
SC164 Michael Bourn 4.00 10.00
SC165 Andre Ethier 6.00 15.00
SC166 Carlos Pena 6.00 15.00
SC167 Joe Nathan 4.00 10.00
SC168 Cody Ross 4.00 10.00
SC169 Joba Chamberlain 6.00 15.00
SC170 Clayton Kershaw 10.00 25.00
SC171 Francisco Rodriguez 6.00 15.00
SC172 Mark DeRosa 6.00 15.00
SC173 Ben Sheets 4.00 10.00
SC174 Brian Wilson 10.00 25.00
SC175 Emil Brown 4.00 10.00
SC176 Geovany Soto 10.00 25.00
SC177 Jason Giambi 4.00 10.00
SC178 Shaun Marcum 4.00 10.00
SC179 Edinson Volquez 4.00 10.00
SC180 Max Scherzer 40.00 100.00
SC181 Kelly Johnson 4.00 10.00
SC182 Mariano Rivera 12.00 30.00
SC183 Chris Perez 6.00 15.00
SC184 Jose Guillen 4.00 10.00
SC185 Kyle Lohse 4.00 10.00
SC186 Kosuke Fukudome 12.00 30.00
SC187 Takashi Saito 4.00 10.00
SC188 Mike Mussina 6.00 15.00
SC189 J.J. Putz 4.00 10.00
SC190 Evan Longoria 20.00 50.00
SC191 Jered Weaver 6.00 15.00
SC192 Grady Sizemore 6.00 15.00
SC193 Carlos Gonzalez 10.00 25.00
SC194 Brian McCann 6.00 15.00
SC195 Jonathan Papelbon 6.00 15.00
SC196 Dioner Navarro 4.00 10.00
SC197 Bobby Abreu 4.00 10.00
SC198 Carlos Quentin 4.00 10.00
SC199 Josh Hamilton 6.00 15.00
SC200 Dan Haren 4.00 10.00

2008 Topps Stars

COMPLETE SET (25) 8.00 20.00
SER.2 ODDS 1:6 HOB, 1:6 RET
TS1 Alex Rodriguez 1.00 2.50
TS2 Magglio Ordonez .50 1.25
TS3 Justin Morneau .50 1.25
TS4 Josh Beckett .30 .75
TS5 David Wright .50 1.25
TS6 Jimmy Rollins .50 1.25
TS7 Ichiro Suzuki 1.00 2.50
TS8 Chipper Jones .75 2.00
TS9 Brandon Webb .50 1.25
TS10 Ryan Howard .50 1.25
TS11 Derek Jeter 2.00 5.00
TS12 Vladimir Guerrero .50 1.25
TS13 Manny Ramirez .75 2.00
TS14 Jake Peavy .30 .75
TS15 David Ortiz .75 2.00
TS16 Jose Reyes .50 1.25
TS17 Miguel Cabrera .75 2.00
TS18 Victor Martinez .50 1.25
TS19 C.C. Sabathia .50 1.25
TS20 Prince Fielder .50 1.25
TS21 Alfonso Soriano .50 1.25
TS22 Grady Sizemore .50 1.25
TS23 Albert Pujols 1.00 2.50
TS24 Pedro Martinez .50 1.25
TS25 Matt Holliday .75 2.00

2008 Topps Trading Card History

COMPLETE SET (75) 20.00 50.00
SER.1 ODDS 1:12 HOBBY
SER.2 ODDS 1:6 HOBBY
TCH1 Jacoby Ellsbury .75 2.00
TCH2 Joba Chamberlain .40 1.00
TCH3 Daisuke Matsuzaka .60 1.50
TCH4 Price Fielder .60 1.50
TCH5 Clay Buchholz .60 1.50
TCH6 Alex Rodriguez 1.25 3.00
TCH7 Mickey Mantle 2.50 6.00
TCH8 Ryan Braun .60 1.50
TCH9 Albert Pujols 1.25 3.00
TCH10 Joe Mauer .75 2.00
TCH11 Jose Reyes .60 1.50
TCH12 Joey Votto 3.00 8.00
TCH13 Johan Santana .60 1.50
TCH14 Hunter Pence .60 1.50
TCH15 Hideki Okajima .40 1.00
TCH16 Cameron Maybin .40 1.00
TCH17 Roger Clemens 1.25 3.00
TCH18 Tim Lincecum .60 1.50
TCH19 Mark Teixeira/Jeff Francoeur .60 1.50
TCH20 Justin Upton .60 1.50
TCH21 Alfonso Soriano .60 1.50
TCH22 Pedro Martinez .60 1.50
TCH23 Chien-Ming Wang .60 1.50
TCH24 Ichiro Suzuki 1.25 3.00
TCH25 Grady Sizemore .60 1.50
TCH26 Ryan Howard .60 1.50
TCH27 David Wright .60 1.50
TCH28 Chin-Lung Hu .40 1.00
TCH29 Jimmy Rollins .60 1.50
TCH30 Ken Griffey Jr. 2.00 5.00
TCH31 Chipper Jones 1.00 2.50
TCH32 Justin Verlander 1.00 2.50
TCH33 Manny Ramirez 1.00 2.50
TCH34 Chase Utley .60 1.50
TCH35 Ivan Rodriguez .60 1.50
TCH36 Josh Beckett .40 1.00
TCH37 Tom Glavine .60 1.50
TCH38 Vladimir Guerrero .60 1.50
TCH39 Lance Berkman .60 1.50
TCH40 Gary Sheffield .40 1.00
TCH41 Luke Hochevar .60 1.50
TCH42 David Ortiz 1.00 2.50
TCH43 Miguel Cabrera 1.00 2.50
TCH44 Andruw Jones .40 1.00
TCH45 Hideki Matsui 1.00 2.50
TCH46 C.C. Sabathia .60 1.50
TCH47 Magglio Ordonez .60 1.50
TCH48 Pedro Martinez .60 1.50
TCH49 Curtis Granderson .60 1.50
TCH50 Derek Jeter 2.50 6.00
TCH51 Victor Martinez .60 1.50
TCH52 Hanley Ramirez .60 1.50
TCH53 Jake Peavy .40 1.00
TCH54 Brandon Webb .60 1.50
TCH55 Matt Holliday 1.00 2.50
TCH56 Hiroki Kuroda 1.00 2.50
TCH57 Mike Lowell .40 1.00
TCH58 Carlos Lee .40 1.00
TCH59 Nick Markakis .75 2.00
TCH60 Carlos Beltran .60 1.50
TCH61 Francisco Rodriguez .60 1.50
TCH62 Troy Tulowitzki 1.00 2.50
TCH63 Russ Martin .40 1.00
TCH64 Justin Morneau .60 1.50
TCH65 Phil Hughes .40 1.00
TCH66 Torii Hunter .40 1.00
TCH67 Adam Dunn .60 1.50

TCH68 Raul Ibanez .60 1.50
TCH69 Robinson Cano .60 1.50
TCH70 Brad Hawpe .40 1.00
TCH71 Michael Young .40 1.00
TCH72 Jim Thome .60 1.50
TCH73 Chris Young .40 1.00
TCH74 Carlos Zambrano .60 1.50
TCH75 Felix Hernandez .60 1.50

2008 Topps World Champion Relics

STATED ODDS 1:4792 H, 1:244 HTA
STATED ODDS 1:33,333 RETAIL
STATE PRINT RUN 100 SER.#'d SETS
WCR1 Josh Beckett 20.00 50.00
WCR2 Hideki Okajima 10.00 25.00
WCR3 Curt Schilling 6.00 15.00
WCR4 Jason Varitek 15.00 40.00
WCR5 Mike Lowell 12.00 30.00
WCR6 Jacoby Ellsbury 40.00 80.00
WCR7 Dustin Pedroia 15.00 40.00
WCR8 Jonathan Papelbon 8.00 20.00
WCR9 Julio Lugo 12.00 30.00
WCR10 Manny Ramirez 12.00 30.00
WCR11 David Ortiz 10.00 25.00
WCR12 Eric Gagne 6.00 15.00
WCR13 Jon Lester 30.00 60.00
WCR14 J.D. Drew 6.00 15.00
WCR15 Kevin Youkilis 15.00 40.00

2008 Topps World Champion Relics Autographs

STATED ODDS 1:14,417 H, 1:732 HTA
STATED ODDS 1:99,000 RETAIL
PRINT RUNS B/WN 25-50 COPIES PER
NO PRICING ON MOST DUE TO SCARCITY
WCAR10 Manny Ramirez/50 100.00 200.00

2008 Topps Year in Review

COMPLETE SET (178) 50.00 100.00
COMP.SER.1.SET (60) 12.50 30.00
COMP.SER.2.SET (60) 12.50 30.00
COMP.UPD SET (58) 12.50 30.00
SER.1 ODDS 1:6 HOB, 1:6 RET
SER.2 ODDS 1:6 HOB, 1:6 RET
UPD ODDS 1:6 HOBBY
YR1 Paul Lo Duca .30 .75
YR2 Felix Hernandez .50 1.25
YR3 Ian Snell .30 .75
YR4 Carlos Beltran .50 1.25
YR5 Daisuke Matsuzaka .50 1.25
YR6 Jose Reyes .50 1.25
YR7 Alex Rodriguez 1.00 2.50
YR8 Scott Kazmir .50 1.25
YR9 Adam Everett .30 .75
YR10 J.Beckett/J.Hamilton .50 1.25
YR11 Craig Monroe .30 .75
YR12 Justin Morneau .50 1.25
YR13 Roy Halladay .50 1.25
YR14 Jeff Suppan .30 .75
YR15 Marco Scutaro .50 1.25
YR16 Ivan Rodriguez .50 1.25
YR17 Dimtri Young .30 .75
YR18 Mark Buehrle .50 1.25
YR19 Alex Rodriguez 1.00 2.50
YR20 Joe Saunders .30 .75
YR21 Russell Martin .30 .75
YR22 Manny Ramirez .75 2.00
YR23 Chase Utley .50 1.25
YR24 Travis Hafner .30 .75
YR25 Jake Peavy .30 .75
YR26 Shawn Hill .30 .75
YR27 Daisuke Matsuzaka .50 1.25
YR28 Matt Belisle .30 .75
YR29 Troy Tulowitzki .75 2.00
YR30 Andruw Jones .30 .75
YR31 Phil Hughes .30 .75
YR32 Derrek Lee .30 .75
YR33 Ichiro Suzuki 1.00 2.50
YR34 Julio Franco .30 .75
YR35 Chien-Ming Wang .50 1.25
YR36 Hideki Matsui .75 2.00
YR37 Brad Penny .30 .75
YR38 Jack Wilson .30 .75
YR39 Francisco Cordero .30 .75
YR40 Omar Vizquel .50 1.25
YR41 Tim Lincecum .50 1.25
YR42 Bartolo Colon .30 .75
YR43 Fred Lewis .30 .75
YR44 Jeff Kent .30 .75
YR45 Randy Johnson .75 2.00
YR46 Rafael Furcal .30 .75
YR47 Delmon Young .50 1.25
YR48 Andrew Miller .50 1.25
YR49 D.Ortiz/M.Lowell .75 2.00
YR50 Justin Verlander .75 2.00
YR51 C.C. Sabathia .50 1.25
YR52 Felipe Lopez .30 .75
YR53 Oliver Perez .30 .75
YR54 John Smoltz .75 2.00
YR55 Mark Reynolds .30 .75
YR56 Jeremy Accardo .50 1.25
YR57 Todd Helton .50 1.25
YR58 Adrian Beltre .75 2.00
YR59 Carlos Delgado .30 .75
YR60 Chris Young .30 .75
YR61 Roy Halladay .50 1.25
YR62 Kevin Youkilis .30 .75
YR63 Joe Blanton .30 .75
YR64 Chad Gaudin .50 1.25
YR65 Derek Lowe .30 .75
YR66 C.C. Sabathia .50 1.25
YR67 Luis Castillo .30 .75
YR68 Curt Schilling .50 1.25
YR69 Pedro Feliz .30 .75
YR70 James Shields .30 .75
YR71 Masumi Kuwata .30 .75
YR72 Raul Ibanez .50 1.25
YR73 Justin Verlander .75 2.00
YR74 Tim Lincecum .50 1.25
YR75 Hideki Matsui .75 2.00
YR76 Julio Franco .30 .75
YR77 Russell Branyan .30 .75
YR78 Chipper Jones .75 2.00
YR79 Chone Figgins .30 .75
YR80 Chris Young .30 .75
YR81 Sammy Sosa .75 2.00
YR82 Miguel Tejada .50 1.25
YR83 Wil Ledezma .30 .75
YR84 Victor Martinez .50 1.25
YR85 Dustin McGowan .30 .75
YR86 Mike Fontenot .30 .75
YR87 Mark Ellis .30 .75
YR88 Ryan Howard .50 1.25
YR89 Frank Thomas .75 2.00
YR90 Aubrey Huff .30 .75
YR91 Jake Peavy .30 .75
YR92 Dan Haren .30 .75
YR93 Damian Miller .30 .75
YR94 Billy Butler .30 .75
YR95 Dmitri Young .30 .75
YR96 Chipper Jones .75 2.00
YR97 Justin Morneau .50 1.25
YR98 Erik Bedard .30 .75
YR99 Scott Hatteberg .30 .75
YR100 Vladimir Guerrero .50 1.25
YR101 Ichiro Suzuki 1.00 2.50
YR102 Jose Reyes .50 1.25
YR103 Ryan Garko .30 .75
YR104 Jeff Francoeur .50 1.25
YR105 Joe Mauer .60 1.50
YR106 Manny Ramirez .75 2.00
YR107 Chase Utley .50 1.25
YR108 Magglio Ordonez .50 1.25
YR109 Chris Young .30 .75
YR110 B.J. Upton .50 1.25
YR111 Willie Harris .30 .75
YR112 Shelley Duncan .30 .75
YR113 Jon Lester .50 1.25
YR114 Travis Buck .50 1.25
YR115 Ryan Raburn .30 .75
YR116 Eric Byrnes .30 .75
YR117 Kenny Lofton .30 .75
YR118 Jason Isringhausen .30 .75
YR119 Todd Helton .50 1.25
YR120 Carl Crawford .50 1.25
YR121 Mark Teixeira .50 1.25
YR122 Alex Gordon .50 1.25
YR123 Jermaine Dye .30 .75
YR124 Vladimir Guerrero .50 1.25
YR125 Alex Rodriguez 1.00 2.50
YR126 Tom Glavine .50 1.25
YR127 Scott Rolen .50 1.25
YR128 Billy Wagner .30 .75
YR129 Rick Ankiel .30 .75
YR130 Jack Cust .30 .75
YR131 Mike Mussina .50 1.25
YR132 Magglio Ordonez .50 1.25
YR133 Placido Polanco .30 .75
YR134 Russell Branyan .30 .75
YR135 David Price .60 1.50
YR136 Mike Cameron .30 .75
YR137 Brandon Webb .50 1.25
YR138 Cameron Maybin .30 .75
YR139 Johan Santana .50 1.25
YR140 Bobby Jenks .30 .75
YR141 Garret Anderson .30 .75
YR142 Jarrod Saltalamacchia .30 .75
YR143 Adrian Gonzalez .50 1.25
YR144 Carlos Guillen .30 .75
YR145 Tom Shearn .30 .75
YR146 John Lackey .50 1.25
YR147 Jayson Werth .50 1.25
YR148 Aaron Harang .30 .75
YR149 Chien-Ming Wang .50 1.25
YR150 Scott Baker .30 .75
YR151 Clay Buchholz .50 1.25
YR152 Tom Glavine .50 1.25
YR153 Pedro Martinez .50 1.25
YR154 Doug Davis .30 .75
YR155 Brandon Phillips .30 .75
YR156 Jason Varitek .75 2.00
YR157 Jim Thome .50 1.25
YR158 Alex Rodriguez 1.00 2.50
YR159 Curtis Granderson .50 1.25
YR160 Scott Kazmir .50 1.25
YR161 Marlon Byrd .30 .75
YR162 David Ortiz .75 2.00
YR163 Greg Maddux 1.00 2.50
YR164 Johnny Damon .50 1.25
YR165 Carlos Lee .30 .75
YR166 Jim Thome .50 1.25
YR167 Frank Thomas .75 2.00
YR168 Greg Maddux 1.00 2.50
YR169 Matt Holliday .75 2.00
YR170 J.R. Towles .50 1.25
YR171 Lance Berkman .50 1.25
YR172 Melky Cabrera .30 .75
YR173 Vladimir Guerrero .50 1.25
YR174 Nick Markakis .60 1.50
YR175 Prince Fielder .50 1.25
YR176 Moises Alou .30 .75
YR177 Micah Owings .30 .75
YR178 Carlos Zambrano .50 1.25

2008 Topps Update

COMP.SET w/o VAR (330) 125.00 300.00
COMMON CARD (1-330) .12 .30
COMMON ROOKIE (1-330) .40 1.00
1-330 PLATE ODDS 1:457 HOBBY
PLATE PRINT RUN 1 SET PER COLOR
BLACK-CYAN-MAGENTA-YELLOW ISSUED
NO PLATE PRICING DUE TO SCARCITY
UH1A Kosuke Fukudome RC 1.25 3.00
UH1B Kosuke Fukudome VAR 15.00 40.00
UH2 Sean Casey .12 .30
UH3 Freddie Bynum .12 .30
UH4 Brent Lillibridge (RC) .40 1.00
UH5 Chipper Jones AS .30 .75
UH6 Yamid Haad .12 .30
UH7 Josh Anderson .12 .30
UH8 Jeff Mathis .12 .30
UH9 Shawn Riggans .12 .30
UH10A Evan Longoria RC 2.00 5.00
UH10B Evan Longoria VAR 10.00 25.00
UH11 Matt Holliday AS .30 .75
UH12 Trot Nixon .12 .30
UH13 Geoff Blum .12 .30
UH14 Bartolo Colon .12 .30
UH15 Kevin Cash .12 .30
UH16 Paul Janish (RC) .40 1.00
UH17 Russell Martin AS .12 .30
UH18 Andy Phillips .12 .30
UH19 Johnny Estrada .12 .30
UH20 Justin Masterson RC 1.00 2.50
UH21 Darrell Rasner .12 .30
UH22 Brian Moehler .12 .30
UH23 Cristian Guzman AS .12 .30
UH24 Tony Armas Jr. .12 .30
UH25 Lance Berkman AS .20 .50
UH26 Chris Iannetta .12 .30
UH27 Reid Brignac .20 .50
UH28 Miguel Tejada AS .20 .50
UH29 Ryan Ludwick AS .12 .30
UH30 Brendan Harris .12 .30
UH31 Marco Scutaro .20 .50
UH32 Cody Ross .12 .30
UH33 Carlos Marmol .20 .50
UH34 Nate McLouth AS .12 .30
UH35 Hanley Ramirez AS .20 .50
UH36 Xavier Nady .12 .30
UH37 Connor Robertson .12 .30
UH38 Carlos Villanueva .12 .30
UH39 Jose Molina .12 .30
UH40 Jon Rauch .12 .30
UH41 Joe Mauer AS .25 .60
UH42 Chip Ambres .12 .30
UH43 Jason Bartlett .12 .30
UH44 Ryan Sweeney .12 .30
UH45 Eric Hurley (RC) .40 1.00
UH46 Kevin Youkilis AS .12 .30
UH47 Dustin Pedroia AS .30 .75
UH48 Grant Balfour .12 .30
UH49 Ryan Ludwick .12 .30
UH50 Matt Garza .12 .30
UH51 Fernando Tatis .12 .30
UH52 Derek Jeter AS .75 2.00
UH53 Justin Duchscherer AS .12 .30
UH54 Matt Ginter .12 .30
UH55 Cesar Izturis .12 .30
UH56 Roy Halladay AS .20 .50
UH57 Ramon Castro .12 .30
UH58 Scott Kazmir AS .20 .50
UH59 Cliff Lee AS .20 .50
UH60 Jim Edmonds .20 .50
UH61 Randy Wolf .12 .30
UH62 Matt Albers .12 .30
UH63 Eric Bruntlett .12 .30
UH64 Joe Nathan AS .12 .30
UH65 Alex Rodriguez AS .40 1.00
UH66 Robinson Cancel .12 .30
UH67 Jamey Carroll .12 .30
UH68 Jonathan Papelbon AS .20 .50
UH69 Chad Moeller .12 .30
UH70 George Sherrill .12 .30
UH71 Mariano Rivera AS .40 1.00
UH72 Pete Orr .12 .30
UH73 Jonathan Albaladejo RC .60 1.50
UH74 Corey Patterson .12 .30
UH75 Matt Treanor .12 .30
UH76 Francisco Rodriguez AS .20 .50
UH77 Ervin Santana AS .12 .30
UH78 Dallas Braden .20 .50
UH79 Willie Harris .12 .30
UH80 Erik Bedard .12 .30
UH81 J.C. Romero .12 .30
UH82 Joe Saunders AS .12 .30
UH83 George Sherrill AS .12 .30
UH84 Julian Tavarez .12 .30
UH85 Chad Gaudin .20 .50
UH86 David Aardsma .12 .30
UH87 Ryan Langerhans .12 .30
UH88 Dan Haren .12 .30
Russell Martin
UH89 Joakim Soria AS .12 .30
UH90 Dan Haren .12 .30
UH91 Billy Buckner .12 .30
UH92 Eric Hinske .12 .30
UH93 Chris Coste .12 .30
UH94 Edinson Volquez .12 .30
Russell Martin
UH95 Ichiro Suzuki AS .40 1.00
UH96 Vladimir Nunez .12 .30
UH97 Sean Gallagher .12 .30
UH98 Denny Bautista .12 .30
UH99 Hanley Ramirez/David Ortiz .30 .75
UH100 Jay Bruce (RC) 1.25 3.00
UH100B Jay Bruce VAR 20.00 50.00
UH101 Dioner Navarro AS .12 .30
UH102 Matt Murton .12 .30
UH103 Chris Burke .12 .30
UH104 Omar Infante .12 .30
UH105 Dan Giese (RC) .40 1.00
UH106 C.Guillen/J.Hamilton .20 .50
UH107 Jason Varitek AS .30 .75
UH108 Shin- Soo Choo .20 .50
UH109 Alberto Callaspo .12 .30
UH110 Jose Valverde .12 .30
UH111 Brandon Boggs (RC) .60 1.50
UH112 J.Hamilton/J.Drew .20 .50
UH113 Justin Morneau AS .20 .50
UH114 Billy Traber .12 .30
UH115 Mike Lamb .12 .30
UH116 Odalis Perez .12 .30
UH117 Jed Lowrie (RC) .40 1.00
UH118 Justin Morneau/David Ortiz .30 .75
UH119 Ken Griffey Jr. HL .60 1.50
UH120 Angel Berroa .12 .30
UH121 Jacque Jones .12 .30
UH122 DeWayne Wise .12 .30
UH123 Matt Joyce RC 1.00 2.50
UH124 A.Rodriguez/E.Longoria .60 1.50
UH125 John Smoltz HL .30 .75
UH126 Morgan Ensberg .12 .30
UH127 M.Young/D.Jeter .75 2.00
UH128 LaTroy Hawkins .12 .30
UH129 Nick Adenhart (RC) .40 1.00
UH130 Mike Cameron .12 .30
UH131 Manny Ramirez HL .30 .75
UH132 Jorge De La Rosa .12 .30
UH133 Tadahito Iguchi .12 .30
UH134 Joey Devine .12 .30
UH135 Jose Arredondo RC .60 1.50
UH136 H.Ramirez/A.Pujols .40 1.00
UH137 Evan Longoria HL .60 1.50
UH138 T.J. Beam .12 .30
UH139 Jon Lieber .12 .30
UH140 Dana Eveland .12 .30
UH141 Michael Aubrey RC .60 1.50
UH142 Adrian Gonzalez/Matt Holliday .30 .75
UH143 Chipper Jones HL .30 .75
UH144 Robinson Tejeda .12 .30
UH145 Kip Wells .12 .30
UH146 Carlos Gonzalez (RC) 1.00 2.50
UH147 Josh Banks (RC) .40 1.00
UH148 David Wright AS .20 .50
UH149 Paul Hoover .12 .30
UH150 Jon Lester HL .20 .50
UH151 Darin Erstad .12 .30
UH152 Steve Trachsel .12 .30
UH153 Armando Galarraga RC .60 1.50
UH154 Grady Sizemore HRD .20 .50
UH155 Jay Bruce HL .40 1.00
UH156 Juan Rincon .12 .30
UH157 Mark Hendrickson .12 .30
UH158 Chad Durbin .12 .30
UH159 Mike Aviles RC .60 1.50
UH160 Orlando Cabrera .20 .50
UH161 Asdrubal Cabrera HL .20 .50
UH162 Eric Stults .12 .30
UH163 Miguel Cairo .12 .30
UH164 Jason LaRue .12 .30
UH165 Burke Badenhop RC .60 1.50
UH166 Ryan Braun HRD .20 .50
UH167 Justin Morneau HRD .20 .50
UH168 Ben Zobrist .20 .50
UH169 Eulogio De La Cruz .12 .30
UH170 Greg Smith (RC) .40 1.00
UH171 Brian Bixler (RC) .40 1.00
UH172 Evan Longoria HRD .60 1.50
UH173 Randy Johnson HL .30 .75
UH174 D.J. Carrasco .12 .30
UH175 Luis Vizcaino .12 .30
UH176 Brad Wilkerson .12 .30
UH177 Emmanuel Burriss RC .60 1.50
UH178 Lance Berkman HRD .20 .50
UH179 Johnny Damon HL .20 .50
UH180 Scott Rolen .20 .50
UH181 Runelvys Hernandez .12 .30
UH182 Sidney Ponson .12 .30
UH183 Greg Reynolds RC .60 1.50
UH184 Chase Utley HRD .20 .50
UH185 Joey Votto HL 1.00 2.50
UH186 Wes Littleton .12 .30
UH187 Rod Barajas .12 .30
UH188 Ray Durham .12 .30
UH189 Micah Hoffpauir RC 1.25 3.00
UH190 Manny Ramirez AS .30 .75
UH191 Ian Kinsler AS .20 .50
UH192 Craig Hansen .12 .30
UH193 Jeremy Affeldt .12 .30
UH194 Gary Bennett .12 .30
UH195 Chris Carter (RC) .60 1.50
UH196 Dan Uggla HRD .12 .30
UH197 Michael Young AS .12 .30
UH198 Andy LaRoche .12 .30
UH199 Lance Cormier .12 .30
UH200 Luke Scott .12 .30
UH201 Travis Denker RC .60 1.50
UH202 Josh Hamilton .20 .50
UH203 Joe Crede AS .12 .30
UH204 Franquelis Osoria .12 .30
UH205 Octavio Dotel .12 .30
UH206 Russell Branyan .12 .30
UH207 Alberto Gonzalez RC .60 1.50
UH208 Kerry Wood AS .12 .30
UH209 Carlos Guillen AS .12 .30
UH210 Joe Saunders .12 .30
UH211 Brett Tomko .12 .30
UH212 Guillermo Mota .12 .30
UH213 German Duran RC .60 1.50
UH214 Carlos Zambrano AS .20 .50
UH215 Josh Hamilton AS .20 .50
UH216 Jason Bay .20 .50
UH217 Willy Aybar .12 .30
UH218 Salomon Torres .12 .30
UH219 Damaso Marte .12 .30
UH220 Geoff Jenkins .12 .30
UH221 J.D. Drew AS .12 .30
UH222 Dave Borkowski .12 .30
UH223 Jeff Ridgway RC .60 1.50
UH224 Angel Pagan .12 .30
UH225 Ryan Tucker (RC) .40 1.00
UH226 Brian McCann AS .20 .50
UH227 Carlos Quentin AS .12 .30
UH228 Joe Blanton .12 .30
UH229 Adrian Gonzalez AS .20 .50
UH230 Jason Jennings .12 .30
UH231 Chris Davis RC .75 2.00
UH232 Geovany Soto AS .30 .75
UH233 Grady Sizemore AS .20 .50
UH234 Carl Pavano .12 .30
UH235 Eddie Guardado .12 .30
UH236 Chris Snelling .12 .30
UH237 Manny Ramirez .30 .75
UH238 Dan Uggla AS .12 .30
UH239 Milton Bradley AS .12 .30
UH240 Clayton Kershaw RC 75.00 200.00
UH241 Chase Utley AS .20 .50
UH242 Raul Chavez .12 .30
UH243 Joe Mather RC .60 1.50
UH244 Brandon Webb AS .20 .50
UH245 Ryan Braun .20 .50
UH246 Kelvin Jimenez .12 .30
UH247 Scott Podsednik .12 .30
UH248 Doug Mientkiewicz .12 .30
UH249 Chris Volstad (RC) .40 1.00
UH250 Pedro Feliz .12 .30
UH251 Mark Redman .12 .30
UH252 Tony Clark .12 .30
UH253 Josh Johnson .20 .50
UH254 Jose Castillo .12 .30
UH255 Brian Horwitz RC .40 1.00
UH256 Aramis Ramirez AS .12 .30
UH257 Casey Blake .12 .30
UH258 Arthur Rhodes .12 .30
UH259 Aaron Boone .20 .50
UH260 Emil Brown .12 .30
UH261 Matt Macri (RC) .40 1.00
UH262 Brian Wilson AS .30 .75
UH263 Eric Patterson .12 .30
UH264 David Ortiz .30 .75
UH265 Tony Abreu .12 .30
UH266 Rob Mackowiak .12 .30
UH267 Gregorio Petit RC .60 1.50
UH268 Alfonso Soriano AS .20 .50
UH269 Robert Andino .12 .30
UH270 Justin Duchscherer .12 .30
UH271 Brad Thompson .12 .30
UH272 Guillermo Quiroz .12 .30
UH273 Chris Perez RC .60 1.50
UH274 Albert Pujols AS .40 1.00
UH275 Rich Harden .12 .30
UH276 Corey Hart AS .12 .30
UH277 John Rheinecker .12 .30
UH278 So Taguchi .12 .30
UH279 Alex Hinshaw RC .60 1.50
UH280 Max Scherzer RC 30.00 80.00
UH281 Chris Aguila .12 .30
UH282 Carlos Marmol AS .20 .50
UH283 Alex Cintron .12 .30
UH284 Curtis Thigpen .12 .30
UH285 Kosuke Fukudome AS .40 1.00
UH286 Aaron Cook AS .12 .30
UH287 Chase Headley .12 .30
UH288 Evan Longoria AS .60 1.50
UH289 Chris Gomez .12 .30
UH290 Carlos Gomez .12 .30
UH291 Jonathan Herrera RC .60 1.50
UH292 Ryan Dempster AS .12 .30
UH293 Adam Dunn .20 .50
UH294 Mark Teixeira .20 .50
UH295 Aaron Miles .12 .30
UH296 Gabe Gross .12 .30
UH297 Cory Wade (RC) .40 1.00
UH298 Dan Haren AS .12 .30
UH299 Jolbert Cabrera .12 .30
UH300 C.C. Sabathia .20 .50
UH301 Tony Pena .12 .30
UH302 Brandon Moss .12 .30
UH303 Taylor Teagarden RC .60 1.50
UH304 Brad Lidge AS .12 .30
UH305 Ben Francisco .12 .30
UH306 Casey Kotchman .12 .30
UH307 Greg Norton .12 .30
UH308 Shelley Duncan .12 .30
UH309 John Bowker (RC) .40 1.00
UH310 Kyle Lohse .12 .30
UH311 Oscar Salazar .12 .30
UH312 Ivan Rodriguez .20 .50
UH313 Tim Lincecum AS .20 .50
UH314 Wilson Betemit .12 .30
UH315 Sean Rodriguez (RC) .40 1.00
UH316 Ben Sheets AS .12 .30
UH317 Brian Buscher .12 .30
UH318 Kyle Farnsworth .12 .30
UH319 Ruben Gotay .12 .30
UH320 Heath Bell .12 .30
UH321 Jeff Niemann (RC) .40 1.00
UH322 Edinson Volquez AS .12 .30
UH323 Jorge Velandia .12 .30
UH324 Ken Griffey Jr. .60 1.50
UH325 Clay Hensley .12 .30
UH326 Kevin Mench .12 .30
UH327 Hernan Iribarren (RC) .60 1.50
UH328 Billy Wagner AS .12 .30
UH329 Jeremy Sowers .12 .30
UH330 Johan Santana .20 .50

2008 Topps Update Black

COMMON CARD (1-330) 4.00 10.00
STATED ODDS 1:59 HOBBY
STATED PRINT RUN 57 SER.#'d SETS
UH1 Kosuke Fukudome 12.00 30.00
UH2 Sean Casey 10.00 25.00
UH3 Freddie Bynum 4.00 10.00
UH4 Brent Lillibridge 4.00 10.00
UH5 Chipper Jones AS 6.00 15.00
UH6 Yamid Haad 4.00 10.00
UH7 Josh Anderson 4.00 10.00
UH8 Jeff Mathis 4.00 10.00
UH9 Shawn Riggans 4.00 10.00
UH10 Evan Longoria 20.00 50.00
UH11 Matt Holliday AS 10.00 25.00
UH12 Trot Nixon 4.00 10.00
UH13 Geoff Blum 4.00 10.00
UH14 Bartolo Colon 4.00 10.00
UH15 Kevin Cash 4.00 10.00
UH16 Paul Janish 4.00 10.00
UH17 Russ Martin AS 15.00 40.00
UH18 Andy Phillips 4.00 10.00
UH19 Johnny Estrada 4.00 10.00
UH20 Justin Masterson 30.00 60.00
UH21 Darrell Rasner 4.00 10.00
UH22 Brian Moehler 4.00 10.00
UH23 Cristian Guzman AS 4.00 10.00
UH24 Tony Armas Jr. 4.00 10.00
UH25 Lance Berkman AS 6.00 15.00
UH26 Chris Iannetta 4.00 10.00
UH27 Reid Brignac 6.00 15.00
UH28 Miguel Tejada AS 6.00 15.00
UH29 Ryan Ludwick AS 4.00 10.00
UH30 Brendan Harris 4.00 10.00
UH31 Marco Scutaro 6.00 15.00
UH32 Cody Ross 4.00 10.00
UH33 Carlos Marmol 6.00 15.00
UH34 Nate McLouth AS 12.50 30.00
UH35 Hanley Ramirez AS 6.00 15.00
UH36 Xavier Nady 4.00 10.00
UH37 Connor Robertson 4.00 10.00
UH38 Carlos Villanueva 4.00 10.00
UH39 Jose Molina 4.00 10.00
UH40 Jon Rauch 4.00 10.00
UH41 Joe Mauer AS 8.00 20.00
UH42 Chip Ambres 4.00 10.00
UH43 Jason Bartlett 4.00 10.00
UH44 Ryan Sweeney 4.00 10.00
UH45 Eric Hurley 4.00 10.00
UH46 Kevin Youkilis AS 10.00 25.00
UH47 Dustin Pedroia AS 10.00 25.00
UH48 Grant Balfour 4.00 10.00
UH49 Ryan Ludwick 6.00 15.00
UH50 Matt Garza 4.00 10.00
UH51 Fernando Tatis 4.00 10.00
UH52 Derek Jeter AS 25.00 60.00
UH53 Justin Duchscherer AS 4.00 10.00
UH54 Matt Ginter 4.00 10.00
UH55 Cesar Izturis 4.00 10.00
UH56 Roy Halladay AS 6.00 15.00
UH57 Ramon Castro 4.00 10.00
UH58 Scott Kazmir AS 6.00 15.00
UH59 Cliff Lee AS 6.00 15.00
UH60 Jim Edmonds 6.00 15.00
UH61 Randy Wolf 4.00 10.00
UH62 Matt Albers 4.00 10.00
UH63 Eric Bruntlett 4.00 10.00
UH64 Joe Nathan AS 4.00 10.00
UH65 Alex Rodriguez AS 10.00 25.00
UH66 Robinson Cancel 4.00 10.00
UH67 Jamey Carroll 4.00 10.00
UH68 Jonathan Papelbon AS 6.00 15.00
UH69 Chad Moeller 4.00 10.00
UH70 George Sherrill 4.00 10.00
UH71 Mariano Rivera AS 12.00 30.00
UH72 Pete Orr 4.00 10.00
UH73 Jonathan Albaladejo 6.00 15.00
UH74 Corey Patterson 4.00 10.00
UH75 Matt Treanor 4.00 10.00
UH76 Francisco Rodriguez AS 6.00 15.00
UH77 Ervin Santana AS 4.00 10.00
UH78 Dallas Braden 6.00 15.00
UH79 Willie Harris 4.00 10.00
UH80 Erik Bedard 4.00 10.00
UH81 J.C. Romero 4.00 10.00
UH82 Joe Saunders AS 4.00 10.00
UH83 George Sherrill AS 4.00 10.00
UH84 Julian Tavarez 4.00 10.00
UH85 Chad Gaudin 6.00 15.00
UH86 David Aardsma 4.00 10.00
UH87 Ryan Langerhans 4.00 10.00
UH88 Dan Haren/Russ Martin 4.00 10.00
UH89 Joakim Soria AS 4.00 10.00
UH90 Dan Haren 4.00 10.00
UH91 Billy Buckner 4.00 10.00
UH92 Eric Hinske 4.00 10.00
UH93 Chris Coste 4.00 10.00
UH94 Edinson Volquez/Russ Martin 4.00 10.00
UH95 Ichiro Suzuki AS 20.00 50.00
UH96 Vladimir Nunez 4.00 10.00
UH97 Sean Gallagher 4.00 10.00
UH98 Denny Bautista 4.00 10.00
UH99 Hanley Ramirez/David Ortiz 10.00 25.00
UH100 Jay Bruce 10.00 25.00
UH101 Dioner Navarro AS 4.00 10.00
UH102 Matt Murton 4.00 10.00
UH103 Chris Burke 4.00 10.00
UH104 Omar Infante 4.00 10.00
UH105 Dan Giese 4.00 10.00
UH106 Carlos Guillen/Josh Hamilton 12.50 30.00
UH107 Jason Varitek AS 10.00 25.00
UH108 Shin- Soo Choo 6.00 15.00
UH109 Alberto Callaspo 4.00 10.00
UH110 Jose Valverde 4.00 10.00
UH111 Brandon Boggs 6.00 15.00
UH112 Josh Hamilton/J.D. Drew 12.50 30.00
UH113 Justin Morneau AS 6.00 15.00
UH114 Billy Traber 4.00 10.00
UH115 Mike Lamb 4.00 10.00
UH116 Odalis Perez 4.00 10.00
UH117 Jed Lowrie 4.00 10.00
UH118 Justin Morneau/David Ortiz 10.00 25.00
UH119 Ken Griffey Jr. HL 20.00 50.00
UH120 Angel Berroa 4.00 10.00
UH121 Jacque Jones 4.00 10.00
UH122 DeWayne Wise 4.00 10.00
UH123 Matt Joyce 10.00 25.00
UH124 Alex Rodriguez/Evan Longoria 20.00 50.00
UH125 John Smoltz HL 10.00 25.00
UH126 Morgan Ensberg 4.00 10.00
UH127 Michael Young/Derek Jeter 25.00 60.00
UH128 LaTroy Hawkins 4.00 10.00
UH129 Nick Adenhart 10.00 25.00
UH130 Mike Cameron 4.00 10.00
UH131 Manny Ramirez HL 12.50 30.00
UH132 Jorge De La Rosa 4.00 10.00
UH133 Tadahito Iguchi 4.00 10.00
UH134 Joey Devine 4.00 10.00
UH135 Jose Arredondo 6.00 15.00
UH136 Hanley Ramirez/Albert Pujols 12.00 30.00
UH137 Evan Longoria HL 15.00 40.00
UH138 T.J. Beam 4.00 10.00
UH139 Jon Lieber 4.00 10.00
UH140 Dana Eveland 4.00 10.00
UH141 Michael Aubrey 6.00 15.00
UH142 Adrian Gonzalez/Matt Holliday 10.00 25.00
UH143 Chipper Jones HL 6.00 15.00
UH144 Robinson Tejeda 4.00 10.00
UH145 Kip Wells 4.00 10.00
UH146 Carlos Gonzalez 10.00 25.00
UH147 Josh Banks 4.00 10.00
UH148 David Wright AS 12.50 30.00
UH149 Paul Hoover 4.00 10.00
UH150 Jon Lester HL 12.50 30.00
UH151 Darin Erstad 4.00 10.00
UH152 Steve Trachsel 4.00 10.00
UH153 Armando Galarraga 6.00 15.00
UH154 Grady Sizemore HRD 6.00 15.00
UH155 Jay Bruce HL 10.00 25.00
UH156 Juan Rincon 4.00 10.00
UH157 Mark Hendrickson 4.00 10.00
UH158 Chad Durbin 4.00 10.00
UH159 Mike Aviles 6.00 15.00
UH160 Orlando Cabrera 6.00 15.00
UH161 Asdrubal Cabrera HL 6.00 15.00
UH162 Eric Stults 4.00 10.00
UH163 Miguel Cairo 4.00 10.00
UH164 Jason LaRue 4.00 10.00
UH165 Burke Badenhop 6.00 15.00
UH166 Ryan Braun HRD 12.50 30.00
UH167 Justin Morneau HRD 6.00 15.00
UH168 Ben Zobrist 6.00 15.00
UH169 Eulogio De La Cruz 4.00 10.00
UH170 Greg Smith 4.00 10.00
UH171 Brian Bixler 4.00 10.00
UH172 Evan Longoria HRD 15.00 40.00
UH173 Randy Johnson HL 10.00 25.00
UH174 D.J. Carrasco 4.00 10.00
UH175 Luis Vizcaino 4.00 10.00
UH176 Brad Wilkerson 4.00 10.00
UH177 Emmanuel Burriss 6.00 15.00
UH178 Lance Berkman HRD 6.00 15.00
UH179 Johnny Damon HL 6.00 15.00
UH180 Scott Rolen 6.00 15.00
UH181 Runelvys Hernandez 4.00 10.00
UH182 Sidney Ponson 4.00 10.00
UH183 Greg Reynolds 6.00 15.00
UH184 Chase Utley HRD 6.00 15.00
UH185 Joey Votto HL 30.00 80.00
UH186 Wes Littleton 4.00 10.00
UH187 Rod Barajas 4.00 10.00
UH188 Ray Durham 4.00 10.00
UH189 Micah Hoffpauir 12.00 30.00
UH190 Manny Ramirez AS 10.00 25.00
UH191 Ian Kinsler AS 6.00 15.00
UH192 Craig Hansen 4.00 10.00
UH193 Jeremy Affeldt 4.00 10.00
UH194 Gary Bennett 4.00 10.00
UH195 Chris Carter 6.00 15.00
UH196 Dan Uggla HRD 4.00 10.00
UH197 Michael Young AS 4.00 10.00
UH198 Andy LaRoche 4.00 10.00
UH199 Lance Cormier 4.00 10.00
UH200 Luke Scott 4.00 10.00
UH201 Travis Denker 6.00 15.00
UH202 Josh Hamilton 12.50 30.00
UH203 Joe Crede AS 4.00 10.00
UH204 Franquelis Osoria 4.00 10.00
UH205 Octavio Dotel 4.00 10.00
UH206 Russell Branyan 4.00 10.00
UH207 Alberto Gonzalez 6.00 15.00
UH208 Kerry Wood AS 4.00 10.00
UH209 Carlos Guillen AS 4.00 10.00
UH210 Joe Saunders 4.00 10.00
UH211 Brett Tomko 4.00 10.00
UH212 Guillermo Mota 4.00 10.00
UH213 German Duran 6.00 15.00
UH214 Carlos Zambrano AS 6.00 15.00
UH215 Josh Hamilton AS 12.50 30.00
UH216 Jason Bay 12.50 30.00
UH217 Willy Aybar 4.00 10.00
UH218 Salomon Torres 4.00 10.00
UH219 Damaso Marte 4.00 10.00
UH220 Geoff Jenkins 4.00 10.00
UH221 J.D. Drew AS 4.00 10.00
UH222 Dave Borkowski 4.00 10.00
UH223 Jeff Ridgway 6.00 15.00
UH224 Angel Pagan 4.00 10.00
UH225 Ryan Tucker 4.00 10.00
UH226 Brian McCann AS 6.00 15.00
UH227 Carlos Quentin AS 4.00 10.00
UH228 Joe Blanton 4.00 10.00
UH229 Adrian Gonzalez AS 6.00 15.00
UH230 Jason Jennings 4.00 10.00
UH231 Chris Davis 10.00 25.00
UH232 Geovany Soto AS 10.00 25.00
UH233 Grady Sizemore AS 6.00 15.00
UH234 Carl Pavano 4.00 10.00
UH235 Eddie Guardado 4.00 10.00
UH236 Chris Snelling 4.00 10.00
UH237 Manny Ramirez 20.00 50.00
UH238 Dan Uggla AS 4.00 10.00
UH239 Milton Bradley AS 4.00 10.00
UH240 Clayton Kershaw 500.00 1200.00
UH241 Chase Utley AS 6.00 15.00
UH242 Raul Chavez 4.00 10.00
UH243 Joe Mather 6.00 15.00
UH244 Brandon Webb AS 6.00 15.00
UH245 Ryan Braun 12.50 30.00
UH246 Kelvin Jimenez 4.00 10.00
UH247 Scott Podsednik 4.00 10.00
UH248 Doug Mientkiewicz 4.00 10.00
UH249 Chris Volstad 4.00 10.00
UH250 Pedro Feliz 4.00 10.00
UH251 Mark Redman 4.00 10.00
UH252 Tony Clark 4.00 10.00
UH253 Josh Johnson 6.00 15.00
UH254 Jose Castillo 4.00 10.00
UH255 Brian Horwitz 4.00 10.00
UH256 Aramis Ramirez AS 4.00 10.00
UH257 Casey Blake 10.00 25.00
UH258 Arthur Rhodes 4.00 10.00
UH259 Aaron Boone 6.00 15.00
UH260 Emil Brown 4.00 10.00
UH261 Matt Macri 4.00 10.00
UH262 Brian Wilson AS 10.00 25.00
UH263 Eric Patterson 4.00 10.00
UH264 David Ortiz 10.00 25.00
UH265 Tony Abreu 4.00 10.00
UH266 Rob Mackowiak 4.00 10.00
UH267 Gregorio Petit 6.00 15.00
UH268 Alfonso Soriano AS 6.00 15.00
UH269 Robert Andino 4.00 10.00
UH270 Justin Duchscherer 4.00 10.00
UH271 Brad Thompson 4.00 10.00
UH272 Guillermo Quiroz 4.00 10.00
UH273 Chris Perez 6.00 15.00
UH274 Albert Pujols AS 12.50 30.00
UH275 Rich Harden 4.00 10.00
UH276 Corey Hart AS 4.00 10.00
UH277 John Rheinecker 4.00 10.00
UH278 So Taguchi 4.00 10.00
UH279 Alex Hinshaw 6.00 15.00
UH280 Max Scherzer 300.00 800.00
UH281 Chris Aguila 4.00 10.00
UH282 Carlos Marmol AS 6.00 15.00
UH283 Alex Cintron 4.00 10.00
UH284 Curtis Thigpen 4.00 10.00
UH285 Kosuke Fukudome AS 10.00 25.00
UH286 Aaron Cook AS 4.00 10.00
UH287 Chase Headley 4.00 10.00
UH288 Evan Longoria AS 15.00 40.00
UH289 Chris Gomez 4.00 10.00
UH290 Carlos Gomez 6.00 15.00
UH291 Jonathan Herrera 6.00 15.00
UH292 Ryan Dempster AS 4.00 10.00
UH293 Adam Dunn 6.00 15.00
UH294 Mark Teixeira 6.00 15.00
UH295 Aaron Miles 4.00 10.00
UH296 Gabe Gross 4.00 10.00
UH297 Cory Wade 4.00 10.00
UH298 Dan Haren AS 4.00 10.00
UH299 Jolbert Cabrera 4.00 10.00
UH300 C.C. Sabathia 6.00 15.00
UH301 Tony Pena 4.00 10.00
UH302 Brandon Moss 4.00 10.00
UH303 Taylor Teagarden 6.00 15.00
UH304 Brad Lidge AS 4.00 10.00
UH305 Ben Francisco 4.00 10.00
UH306 Casey Kotchman 4.00 10.00
UH307 Greg Norton 4.00 10.00
UH308 Shelley Duncan 4.00 10.00
UH309 John Bowker 4.00 10.00
UH310 Kyle Lohse 4.00 10.00
UH311 Oscar Salazar 4.00 10.00
UH312 Ivan Rodriguez 6.00 15.00
UH313 Tim Lincecum AS 6.00 15.00
UH314 Wilson Betemit 4.00 10.00
UH315 Sean Rodriguez 4.00 10.00
UH316 Ben Sheets AS 4.00 10.00
UH317 Brian Buscher 4.00 10.00
UH318 Kyle Farnsworth 4.00 10.00
UH319 Ruben Gotay 4.00 10.00
UH320 Heath Bell 4.00 10.00
UH321 Jeff Niemann 4.00 10.00
UH322 Edinson Volquez AS 4.00 10.00
UH323 Jorge Velandia 4.00 10.00
UH324 Ken Griffey Jr. 20.00 50.00
UH325 Clay Hensley 4.00 10.00
UH326 Kevin Mench 4.00 10.00
UH327 Hernan Iribarren 6.00 15.00

UH328 Billy Wagner AS 4.00 10.00
UH329 Jeremy Sowers 4.00 10.00
UH330 Johan Santana 6.00 15.00

2008 Topps Update Gold Border

*GLD BDR VET: 2X TO 5X BASIC
*GLD BDR RC: .6X TO 1.5X BASIC RC
STATED ODDS 1:5 HOBBY
STATED PRINT RUN 2008 SER.#'d SETS
UH240 Clayton Kershaw 200.00 500.00

2008 Topps Update Gold Foil

*GLD FOIL VET: 1.2X TO 3X BASIC
*GLD FOIL RC: .4X TO 1X BASIC RC
STATED ODDS 1:2 HOBBY
UH240 Clayton Kershaw 75.00 200.00

2008 Topps Update 1957 Mickey Mantle Reprint Relic

STATED ODDS 17,982 HOBBY
STATED PRINT RUN 57 SER.#'d SETS
MMR57 Mickey Mantle Uni/57 60.00 120.00

2008 Topps Update 2008 Presidential Picks

STATED ODDS 1:15,984 HOBBY
STATED PRINT RUN 100 SER.#'d SETS
BO Barack Obama EXCH 150.00 250.00
JM John McCain EXCH 40.00 80.00
OPBO Barack Obama Patch/100

2008 Topps Update All-Star Stitches

STATED ODDS 1:44 HOBBY
AC Aaron Cook 3.00 8.00
AER Alex Rodriguez 6.00 15.00
AG Adrian Gonzalez 3.00 8.00
AP Albert Pujols 6.00 15.00
AR Aramis Ramirez 3.00 8.00
AS Alfonso Soriano 3.00 8.00
BL Brad Lidge 5.00 12.00
BM Brian McCann 4.00 10.00
BS Ben Sheets 3.00 8.00
BTW Brandon Webb 3.00 8.00
CAG Carlos Guillen 3.00 8.00
CG Cristian Guzman 3.00 8.00
CH Corey Hart 3.00 8.00
CJ Chipper Jones 4.00 10.00
CL Cliff Lee 4.00 10.00
CM Carlos Marmol 3.00 8.00
CQ Carlos Quentin 3.00 8.00
CU Chase Utley 4.00 10.00
CZ Carlos Zambrano 4.00 10.00
DH Dan Haren 3.00 8.00
DN Dioner Navarro 4.00 10.00
DO David Ortiz 4.00 10.00
DP Dustin Pedroia 5.00 12.00
DU Dan Uggla 3.00 8.00
DW David Wright 5.00 12.00
EL Evan Longoria 12.50 30.00
ES Ervin Santana 3.00 8.00
EV Edinson Volquez 3.00 8.00
FR Francisco Rodriguez 4.00 10.00
GFS George Sherrill 3.00 8.00
GPS Geovany Soto 5.00 12.00
GS Grady Sizemore 4.00 10.00
HR Hanley Ramirez 3.00 8.00
IK Ian Kinsler 3.00 8.00
IS Ichiro Suzuki 8.00 20.00
JC Joe Crede 3.00 8.00
JCD Justin Duchscherer 4.00 10.00
JD J.D. Drew 4.00 10.00
JEM Justin Morneau 4.00 10.00
JH Josh Hamilton 8.00 20.00
JM Joe Mauer 4.00 10.00
JN Joe Nathan 3.00 8.00
JP Jonathan Papelbon 4.00 10.00
JS Joakim Soria 3.00 8.00
JV Jason Varitek 4.00 10.00
KF Kosuke Fukudome 10.00 25.00
KW Kerry Wood 3.00 8.00
KY Kevin Youkilis 3.00 8.00
LB Lance Berkman 4.00 10.00
MB Milton Bradley 3.00 8.00
MH Matt Holliday 3.00 8.00
MR Manny Ramirez 4.00 10.00
MSR Mariano Rivera 4.00 10.00
MT Miguel Tejada 3.00 8.00
MY Michael Young 3.00 8.00
NM Nate McLouth 5.00 12.00
RB Ryan Braun 4.00 10.00
RD Ryan Dempster 3.00 8.00
RH Roy Halladay 3.00 8.00
RL Ryan Ludwick 5.00 12.00
RM Russ Martin 3.00 8.00
SK Scott Kazmir 3.00 8.00
TL Tim Lincecum 12.50 30.00
WW Billy Wagner 3.00 8.00

2008 Topps Update All-Star Stitches Gold

*GOLD: .75X TO 2X BASIC
STATED ODDS 1:373 HOBBY
STATED PRINT RUN 50 SER.#'d SETS
AER Alex Rodriguez 30.00 60.00
EL Evan Longoria 20.00 50.00
IS Ichiro Suzuki 20.00 50.00
KY Kevin Youkilis 30.00 60.00

2008 Topps Update All-Star Stitches Autographs

STATED ODDS 1:6394 HOBBY
STATED PRINT RUN 25 SER.#'d SETS
CJ Chipper Jones 100.00 200.00
DP Dustin Pedroia 75.00 150.00
DU Dan Uggla 10.00 25.00
EV Edinson Volquez 30.00 60.00
HR Hanley Ramirez 30.00 60.00
JH Josh Hamilton 60.00 120.00
JV Jason Varitek 50.00 100.00
RB Ryan Braun 40.00 80.00
RM Russ Martin 20.00 50.00
TL Tim Lincecum 100.00 200.00

2008 Topps Update All-Star Stitches Dual

STATED ODDS 1:5994
STATED PRINT RUN 25 SER.#'d SETS
NO PRICING ON FEW DUE TO SCARCITY
FL K.Fukudome/I.Suzuki 40.00 80.00
HB J.Hamilton/R.Braun 30.00 60.00
LS C.Lee/B.Sheets 10.00 25.00
IV T.Lincecum/E.Volquez 12.50 30.00
RR M.Rivera/F.Rodriguez 30.00 60.00
RT H.Ramirez/M.Tejada 8.00 20.00
UU C.Utley/D.Uggla 20.00 50.00

2008 Topps Update All-Star Stitches Triple

STATED ODDS 1:5994 HOBBY
STATED PRINT RUN 25 SER.#'d SETS
NO PRICING ON FEW DUE TO SCARCITY
HFB Holliday/Fukudome/Braun 20.00 50.00
HRS Hamilton/Manny/Ichiro 30.00 60.00
KHY Kinsler/Bradley/Young 8.00 20.00
MNM Martin/Navarro/McCann 40.00 80.00
PDY Pedroia/Drew/Ortiz 20.00 50.00
PGB Pujols/Gonzalez/Berkman 30.00 60.00
RSS KRod/E.Santana/Saunders 50.00 100.00
RWJ ARod/Wright/Chipper 40.00 80.00
WLW Wood/Lidge/Wagner 20.00 50.00
ZSD Zambrano/Aramis/Dempster 50.00 100.00

2008 Topps Update Chrome

ONE PER BOX TOPPER
CHR1 Jay Bruce 6.00 15.00
CHR2 Dan Giese 2.00 5.00
CHR3 Brandon Boggs 3.00 8.00
CHR4 Jed Lowrie 2.00 5.00
CHR5 Matt Joyce 5.00 12.00
CHR6 Nick Adenhart 2.00 5.00
CHR7 Jose Arredondo 3.00 8.00
CHR8 Michael Aubrey 3.00 8.00
CHR9 Josh Banks 2.00 5.00
CHR10 Armando Galarraga 3.00 8.00
CHR11 Mike Aviles 3.00 8.00
CHR12 Burke Badenhop 3.00 8.00
CHR13 Reid Brignac 3.00 8.00
CHR14 Emmanuel Burriss 3.00 8.00
CHR15 Greg Reynolds 3.00 8.00
CHR16 Chris Volstad 2.00 5.00
CHR17 Brian Bixler 2.00 5.00
CHR18 Chris Carter 3.00 8.00
CHR19 Travis Denker 3.00 8.00
CHR20 Alberto Gonzalez 3.00 8.00
CHR21 Robinzon Diaz 2.00 5.00
CHR22 Brett Gardner 5.00 12.00
CHR23 Micah Hoffpauir 6.00 15.00
CHR24 Hernan Iribarren 3.00 8.00
CHR25 Greg Smith 2.00 5.00
CHR26 German Duran 3.00 8.00
CHR27 Kosuke Fukudome 6.00 15.00
CHR28 Ryan Tucker 2.00 5.00
CHR29 Paul Janish 2.00 5.00
CHR30 Clayton Kershaw 400.00 1000.00
CHR31 Chris Davis 4.00 10.00
CHR32 Joe Mather 3.00 8.00
CHR33 Nick Hundley 2.00 5.00
CHR34 Brian Horwitz 2.00 5.00
CHR35 Carlos Gonzalez 5.00 12.00
CHR36 Matt Macri 2.00 5.00
CHR37 Gregorio Petit 3.00 8.00
CHR38 Chris Perez 3.00 8.00
CHR39 Alex Hinshaw 3.00 8.00
CHR40 Max Scherzer 150.00 400.00
CHR41 Jonathan Van Every 2.00 5.00
CHR42 Jonathan Herrera 3.00 8.00
CHR43 Cory Wade 2.00 5.00
CHR44 Max Ramirez 2.00 5.00
CHR45 John Bowker 2.00 5.00
CHR46 Sean Rodriguez 2.00 5.00
CHR47 Jeff Niemann 2.00 5.00
CHR48 Taylor Teagarden 3.00 8.00
CHR49 Mark Worrell 2.00 5.00
CHR50 Evan Longoria 10.00 25.00
CHR51 Chris Smith 2.00 5.00
CHR52 Brent Lillibridge 2.00 5.00
CHR53 Colt Morton 3.00 8.00
CHR54 Eric Hurley 2.00 5.00
CHR55 Justin Masterson 5.00 12.00

2008 Topps Update First Couples

COMPLETE SET (41) 15.00 40.00
STATED ODDS 1:6 HOBBY
FC1 G.Washington/M.Washington .75 2.00
FC2 John Adams/Abagail Adams .60 1.50
FC3 Thomas Jefferson/Martha Jefferson.60 1.50
FC4 James Madison/Dolley Madison .40 1.00
FC5 James Monroe/Elizabeth Kotright Monroe .40 1.00
FC6 John Quincy Adams Louisa Catherine Adams .40 1.00
FC7 Andrew Jackson/Rachel Jackson .40 1.00
FC8 Martin Van Buren/Hannah Van Buren.40 1.00
FC9 William Henry Harrison Anna Harrison .40 1.00
FC10 John Tyler/Julia Tyler .40 1.00
FC11 James K. Polk /Sarah Polk .40 1.00
FC12 Zachary Taylor/Margaret Taylor .40 1.00
FC13 Millard Fillmore/Abigail Fillmore .40 1.00
FC14 Franklin Pierce/Jane M. Pierce .40 1.00
FC15 A.Lincoln/M.Lincoln .75 2.00
FC16 Andrew Johnson/Eliza Johnson .40 1.00
FC17 Ulysses S. Grant/Julia Grant .40 1.00
FC18 Rutherford B. Hayes/ Lucy Hayes .40 1.00
FC19 James A. Garfield/Lucretia Garfield.40 1.00
FC20 Chester A. Arthur/Ellen Arthur .40 1.00
FC21 Grover Cleveland/Frances Cleveland.40 1.00
FC22 Benjamin Harrison Caroline Harrison .40 1.00
FC23 William McKinley/Ida McKinley .40 1.00
FC24 Theodore Roosevelt/Edith Roosevelt.60 1.50
FC25 William H. Taft/Helen Taft .40 1.00
FC26 Woodrow Wilson/Edith Wilson .40 1.00
FC27 Warren G. Harding Florence Harding .40 1.00
FC28 Calvin Coolidge/Grace Coolidge .40 1.00
FC29 Herbert Hoover/Lou Hoover .40 1.00
FC30 Franklin D. Roosevelt Eleanor Roosevelt .60 1.50
FC31 Harry S. Truman /Bess Truman .40 1.00
FC32 Dwight D. Eisenhower Mamie Eisenhower .60 1.50
FC33 J.Kennedy/J.Kennedy 1.00 2.50
FC34 Lyndon B. Johnson Lady Bird Johnson .60 1.50
FC35 Richard M. Nixon /Pat Nixon .60 1.50
FC36 Gerald R. Ford /Betty Ford .60 1.50
FC37 Jimmy Carter /Rosalynn Carter .60 1.50
FC38 R.Reagan /N.Reagan 1.00 2.50
FC39 George Bush /Barbara Bush .60 1.50
FC40 B.Clinton /H.Clinton .75 2.00
FC41 G.Bush /L.Bush .75 2.00

2008 Topps Update Ring of Honor 1986 New York Mets

COMPLETE SET (10) 5.00 12.00
STATED ODDS 1:18 HOBBY
GOLD ODDS 1:11,743 HOBBY
GOLD PRINT RUN 25 SER.#'d SETS
NO GOLD PRICING AVAILABLE
DG Dwight Gooden .60 1.50
DJ Davey Johnson .60 1.50
DS Darryl Strawberry .60 1.50
GC Gary Carter 1.00 2.50
HJ Howard Johnson .60 1.50
JO Jesse Orosco .60 1.50
KH Keith Hernandez .60 1.50
KM Kevin Mitchell .60 1.50
RD Ron Darling .60 1.50
RK Ray Knight .60 1.50

2008 Topps Update Ring of Honor 1986 New York Mets Autographs

STATED ODDS 1:2849 HOBBY
DG Dwight Gooden 30.00 60.00
DJ Davey Johnson 10.00 25.00
DS Darryl Strawberry 15.00 40.00
GC Gary Carter 20.00 50.00
HJ Howard Johnson 12.50 30.00
JO Jesse Orosco 15.00 40.00
KH Keith Hernandez 10.00 25.00
KM Kevin Mitchell 10.00 25.00
RD Ron Darling 10.00 25.00
RK Ray Knight 12.50 30.00

2008 Topps Update Ring of Honor World Series Champions

COMPLETE SET (10) 5.00 12.00
STATED ODDS 1:18 HOBBY
GOLD ODDS 1:11,743 HOBBY
GOLD PRINT RUN 25 SER.#'d SETS
NO GOLD PRICING AVAILABLE
BS Bruce Sutter 1.00 2.50
DC David Cone COR .60 1.50
DC1 David Cone UER .60 1.50
DJ David Justice .60 1.50
DS Duke Snider 1.00 2.50
JP Johnny Podres .60 1.50
LA Luis Aparicio 1.00 2.50
MI Monte Irvin 1.00 2.50
ML Mike Lowell .60 1.50
OC Orlando Cepeda 1.00 2.50
RK Ray Knight .60 1.50
WF Whitey Ford 1.00 2.50

2008 Topps Update Ring of Honor World Series Champions Autographs

STATED ODDS 1:2569 HOBBY
BS Bruce Sutter 15.00 40.00
DC David Cone 30.00 60.00
DJ David Justice 15.00 40.00
DS Duke Snider 15.00 40.00
JP Johnny Podres 15.00 40.00
LA Luis Aparicio 15.00 40.00
MI Monte Irvin 50.00 100.00
ML Mike Lowell 20.00 50.00
OC Orlando Cepeda 30.00 60.00
WF Whitey Ford 30.00 60.00

2008 Topps Update Take Me Out To The Ballgame

STATED ODDS 1:72 HOBBY
BG 100th Anniversary .75 2.00

2008 Topps Update World Baseball Classic Preview

COMPLETE SET (25) 8.00 20.00
STATED ODDS 1:9 HOBBY
WBC1 Daisuke Matsuzaka .40 1.00
WBC2 Alexei Ramirez .75 2.00
WBC3 Derrek Lee .25 .60
WBC4 Akinori Iwamura .25 .60
WBC5 Chase Utley .40 1.00
WBC6 Jose Reyes .40 1.00
WBC7 Jake Peavy .25 .60
WBC8 Justin Huber .25 .60
WBC9 Justin Morneau .40 1.00
WBC10 Ichiro Suzuki .75 2.00
WBC11 Adrian Gonzalez .40 1.00
WBC12 Carlos Zambrano .40 1.00
WBC13 Miguel Cabrera .60 1.50
WBC14 Carlos Beltran .40 1.00
WBC15 Albert Pujols .75 2.00
WBC16 Paul Bell .25 .60
WBC17 Frank Catalanotto .25 .60
WBC18 Jason Varitek .60 1.50
WBC19 Andruw Jones .25 .60
WBC20 Johan Santana .40 1.00
WBC21 Carlos Lee .25 .60
WBC22 David Ortiz .60 1.50
WBC23 Francisco Rodriguez .40 1.00
WBC24 Chin-Lung Hu .25 .60
WBC25 Kosuke Fukudome .75 2.00

2009 Topps

COMP.HOBBY SET (660) 40.00 80.00
COMP.HOLIDAY SET (660) 40.00 80.00
COMP.ALLSTAR.SET (660) 40.00 80.00
COMP.CUBS SET (660) 40.00 80.00
COMP.METS SET (660) 40.00 80.00
COMP.RED SOX SET (660) 40.00 80.00
COMP.YANKEES SET (660) 40.00 80.00
COMP.SET w/o SP's (660) 40.00 80.00
COMP.SER.1 SET w/o SP's (330) 15.00 40.00
COMP.SER.2 SET w/o SP's (330) 15.00 40.00
COMMON CARD (1-696) .15 .40
SER.1 SP VAR ODDS 1:95 HOBBY
SER.2 SP VAR ODDS 1:82 HOBBY
COMMON RC (1-696) .30 .75
SER.1 PLATE ODDS 1:925 HOBBY
SER.2 PLATE ODDS 1:1056 HOBBY
PLATE PRINT RUN 1 SET PER COLOR
BLACK-CYAN-MAGENTA-YELLOW ISSUED
NO PLATE PRICING DUE TO SCARCITY
1a Alex Rodriguez .50 1.25
1b Babe Ruth SP 10.00 25.00
2a Omar Vizquel .25 .60
2b Pee Wee Reese SP 6.00 15.00
3 Andy Marte .15 .40
4 Chipper/Pujols/Holliday LL .50 1.25
5 John Lackey .25 .60
6 Raul Ibanez .25 .60
7 Mickey Mantle 1.25 3.00
8 Terry Francona MG .25 .60
9 Dallas McPherson .15 .40
10a Dan Uggla .15 .40
10b Rogers Hornsby SP 6.00 15.00
11 Fernando Tatis .15 .40
12 Andrew Carpenter RC .50 1.25
13 Ryan Langerhans .15 .40
14 Jon Rauch .15 .40
15 Nate McLouth .15 .40
16 Evan Longoria HL .25 .60
17 Bobby Cox MG .15 .40
18 George Sherrill .15 .40
19 Edgar Gonzalez .15 .40
20 Brad Lidge .15 .40
21 Jack Wilson .15 .40
22 E.Longoria/D.Price CC .30 .75
23 Gerald Laird .15 .40
24 Frank Thomas .40 1.00
25 Jon Lester .25 .60
26 Jason Giambi .15 .40
27 Jonathon Niese RC .50 1.25
28 Mike Lowell .15 .40
29 Jerry Hairston .15 .40
30a Ken Griffey Jr. .75 2.00
30b Jackie Robinson SP 8.00 20.00
31 Ian Stewart .15 .40
32 Daric Barton .15 .40
33 Jose Guillen .15 .40
34 Brandon Inge .15 .40
35 David Price RC .60 1.50
36 Kevin Slowey .25 .60
37 Erick Aybar .15 .40
38 Eric Wedge MG .15 .40
39 Stephen Drew .15 .40
40 Carl Crawford .25 .60
41 Mike Mussina .25 .60
42 Jeff Francoeur .25 .60
43 Mauer/Ped/Brad LL .40 1.00
44a Geoff Jenkins .15 .40
44b Barack Obama SP 6.00 15.00
45 Aubrey Huff .15 .40
46 Brad Ziegler .15 .40
47 Jose Valverde .15 .40
48 Mike Napoli .15 .40
49 Kazuo Matsui .15 .40
50 David Ortiz .40 1.00
51 Will Venable RC .30 .75
52 Marco Scutaro .25 .60
53 Jonathan Sanchez .15 .40
54 Dusty Baker MG .15 .40
55 J.J. Hardy .15 .40
56 Edwin Encarnacion .40 1.00
57 Jo-Jo Reyes .15 .40
58 Travis Snider RC .50 1.25
59 Eric Gagne .15 .40
60a Mariano Rivera .50 1.25
60b Cy Young SP 5.00 12.00
61 Lance Berkman/Carlos Lee CC .25 .60
62 Brian Barton .15 .40
63 Josh Outman RC .50 1.25
64 Miguel Montero .15 .40
65 Mike Pelfrey .15 .40
66a Dustin Pedroia .40 1.00
66b Ty Cobb SP 12.50 30.00
67 Andruw Jones .15 .40
68 Kyle Lohse .15 .40
69 Rich Aurilia .15 .40
70 Jermaine Dye .15 .40
71 Mat Gamel RC .75 2.00
72 David Dellucci .15 .40
73 Shane Victorino .15 .40
74 Trey Hillman MG .15 .40
75 Rich Harden .15 .40
76 Marcus Thames .15 .40
77 Jed Lowrie .15 .40
78 Tim Lincecum .25 .60
79 David Eckstein .15 .40
80 Brian McCann .25 .60
81 Howard/Dunn/Delgado LL .30 .75
82 Miguel Cairo .15 .40
83 Ryan Garko .15 .40
84 Rod Barajas .15 .40
85 Justin Verlander .40 1.00
86 Kila Kaaihue (RC) .50 1.25
87 Brad Hawpe .15 .40
88 Fredi Gonzalez MG .15 .40
89 Jon Lester Jason Bay HL .25 .60
90 Justin Morneau .25 .60
91 Cody Ross .15 .40
92 Luis Castillo .15 .40
93 James Parr (RC) .30 .75
94 Adam Lind .15 .40
95 Andrew Miller .25 .60
96 Dexter Fowler (RC) .50 1.25
97 Willie Harris .15 .40
98 Akinori Iwamura .15 .40
99 Juan Castro .15 .40
100 David Wright .30 .75
101 Nick Hundley .15 .40
102 Garrett Atkins .15 .40
103 Kyle Kendrick .15 .40
104 Brandon Moss .15 .40
105 Francisco Liriano .15 .40
106 Marlon Byrd .15 .40
107 Pedro Feliz .15 .40
108 Alcides Escobar RC .50 1.25
109 Tom Gorzelanny .15 .40
110 Hideki Matsui .40 1.00
111 Troy Percival .15 .40
112 Hideki Okajima .15 .40
113 Chris Young .15 .40
114 Chris Dickerson .15 .40
115a Kevin Youkilis .15 .40
115b George Sisler SP 8.00 20.00
116 Omar Infante .15 .40
117 Ron Gardenhire MG .15 .40
118 Josh Johnson .25 .60
119 Craig Counsell .15 .40
120 Mark Teixeira .25 .60
121 Greg Golson (RC) .30 .75
122 Joe Mather .15 .40
123 Casey Blake .15 .40
124 Reed Johnson .15 .40
125 Roy Oswalt .25 .60
126 Orlando Hudson .15 .40
127 M.Cabrera/Quentin/ARod LL .50 1.25
128 Johnny Cueto .25 .60
129 Angel Berroa .15 .40
130 Vladimir Guerrero .25 .60
131 Joe Torre MG .25 .60
132 Juan Pierre .15 .40
133 Brandon Jones .15 .40
134 Evan Longoria .25 .60
135 Carlos Delgado .15 .40
136 Tim Hudson .25 .60
137 Angel Salome (RC) .30 .75
138 Ubaldo Jimenez .15 .40
139 Matt Stairs HL .15 .40
140 Brandon Webb .25 .60
141 Mark Teahen .15 .40
142 Brad Penny .15 .40
143 Matt Joyce .15 .40
144 Matt Tuiasosopo (RC) .30 .75
145 Alex Gordon .25 .60
146 Glen Perkins .15 .40
147 Howard/Wright/A.Gonzalez LL .30 .75
148 Ty Wigginton .25 .60
149 Juan Uribe .15 .40
150 Kosuke Fukudome .25 .60
151 Carl Pavano .15 .40
152 Cody Ransom .15 .40
153 Lastings Milledge .15 .40
154 A.J. Pierzynski .15 .40
155 Roy Halladay .25 .60
156 Carlos Pena .25 .60
157 Brandon Webb/Dan Haren CC .25 .60
158 Ray Durham .15 .40
159 Matt Antonelli RC .50 1.25
160 Evan Longoria .25 .60
161 Brendan Harris .15 .40
162 Mike Cameron .15 .40
163 Ross Gload .15 .40
164 Bob Geren MG .15 .40
165 Matt Kemp .30 .75
166 Jeff Baker .15 .40
167 Aaron Harang .15 .40
168 Mark DeRosa .25 .60
169 Juan Miranda RC .50 1.25
170a CC Sabathia .25 .60
170b Sabathia Yanks SP 5.00 12.00
171 Jeff Bailey .15 .40
172 Yadier Molina .50 1.25
173 Manny Delcarmen .15 .40
174 James Shields .15 .40
175 Jeff Samardzija .25 .60
176 Ham/Morneau/Cabrera .40 1.00
177 Eric Hinske .15 .40
178 Frank Catalanotto .15 .40
179 Rafael Furcal .15 .40
180 Cliff Lee .25 .60
181 Jerry Manuel MG .15 .40
182 Daniel Murphy RC 1.25 3.00
183 Jason Michaels .15 .40
184 Bobby Parnell RC .50 1.25
185 Randy Johnson .40 1.00
186 Ryan Madson .15 .40
187 Jon Garland .15 .40
188 Josh Bard .15 .40
189 Jay Payton .15 .40
190 Chien-Ming Wang .25 .60
191 Shane Victorino HL .15 .40
192 Collin Balester .15 .40
193 Zack Greinke .40 1.00
194 Jeremy Guthrie .15 .40
195a Tim Lincecum .25 .60
195b Christy Mathewson SP 8.00 20.00
196 Jason Motte (RC) .50 1.25
197 Ronnie Belliard .15 .40
198 Conor Jackson .15 .40
199 Ramon Castro .15 .40
200a Chase Utley .25 .60
200b Jimmie Foxx SP 6.00 15.00
201 Jarrod Saltalamacchia Josh Hamilton CC .25 .60
202 Gaby Sanchez RC .50 1.25
203 Jair Jurrjens .15 .40
204 Andy Sonnanstine .15 .40
205a Miguel Tejada .25 .60
205b Honus Wagner SP 8.00 20.00
206 Santana/Lince/Peavy LL .25 .60
207 Joe Blanton .15 .40
208 James McDonald RC .75 2.00
209 Alfredo Amezaga .15 .40
210a Geovany Soto .25 .60
210b Roy Campanella SP 10.00 25.00
211 Ryan Rowland-Smith .15 .40
212 Denard Span .15 .40
213 Jeremy Sowers .15 .40
214 Scott Elbert (RC) .30 .75
215 Ian Kinsler .25 .60
216 Joe Maddon MG .15 .40
217 Albert Pujols .50 1.25
218 Emmanuel Burriss .15 .40
219 Shin-Soo Choo .25 .60
220 Jay Bruce .25 .60
221 C.Lee/Halladay/Matsuzaka LL .25 .60
222 Mark Sweeney .15 .40
223 Dave Roberts .25 .60
224 Max Scherzer .40 1.00
225 Aaron Cook .15 .40
226 Neal Cotts .15 .40
227 Freddy Sandoval (RC) .30 .75
228 Scott Rolen .25 .60
229 Cesar Izturis .15 .40
230 Justin Upton .25 .60
231 Xavier Nady .15 .40
232 Gabe Kapler .15 .40
233 Erik Bedard .15 .40
234 John Russell MG .15 .40
235 Chad Billingsley .25 .60
236 Kelly Johnson .15 .40
237 Aaron Cunningham RC .30 .75
238 Jorge Cantu .15 .40
239 Brandon League .15 .40
240a Ryan Braun .25 .60
240b Mel Ott SP 8.00 20.00
241 David Newhan .15 .40
242 Ricky Nolasco .15 .40
243 Chase Headley .15 .40
244 Sean Rodriguez .15 .40
245 Pat Burrell .15 .40
246 B.Upton/Crawford/Longoria HL .25 .60
247 Yuniesky Betancourt .15 .40
248 Scott Lewis (RC) .30 .75
249 Jack Hannahan .15 .40
250 Josh Hamilton .25 .60
251 Greg Smith .15 .40
252 Brandon Wood .15 .40
253 Edgar Renteria .15 .40
254 Cito Gaston MG .15 .40
255 Joe Crede .25 .60
256 Reggie Abercrombie .15 .40
257 George Kottaras (RC) .30 .75
258 Casey Kotchman .15 .40
259 Lince/Haren/Santana LL .25 .60
260 Manny Ramirez .40 1.00
261 Jose Bautista .25 .60
262 Mike Gonzalez .15 .40
263 Elijah Dukes .15 .40
264 Dave Bush .15 .40
265 Carlos Zambrano .25 .60
266 Todd Wellemeyer .15 .40
267 Michael Bowden (RC) .30 .75
268 Chris Burke .15 .40
269 Hunter Pence .25 .60
270a Grady Sizemore .25 .60
270b Tris Speaker SP 8.00 20.00
271 Cliff Lee .25 .60
272 Chan Ho Park .25 .60
273 Brian Roberts .15 .40
274 Alex Hinshaw .15 .40
275 Alex Rios .15 .40
276 Geovany Soto .25 .60
277 Asdrubal Cabrera .25 .60
278 Philadelphia Phillies HL .15 .40
279 Ryan Church .15 .40
280 Joe Saunders .15 .40
281 Tug Hulett .15 .40
282 Chris Lambert (RC) .30 .75
283 John Baker .15 .40
284 Luis Ayala .15 .40
285 Justin Duchscherer .15 .40
286 Odalis Perez .15 .40
287a Greg Maddux .50 1.25
287b Walter Johnson SP 6.00 15.00
288 Guillermo Quiroz .15 .40
289 Josh Banks .15 .40
290a Albert Pujols .50 1.25
290b Lou Gehrig SP 12.50 30.00
291 Chris Coste .15 .40
292 Francisco Cervelli RC .75 2.00
293 Brian Bixler .15 .40
294 Brandon Boggs .15 .40
295 Derrek Lee .15 .40
296 Reid Brignac .15 .40
297 Bud Black MG .15 .40
298 Jonathan Van Every .15 .40
299 Cole Hamels HL .30 .75
300 Ichiro Suzuki .50 1.25
301 Clint Barmes .15 .40
302 Brian Giles .15 .40
303 Zach Duke .15 .40
304 Jason Kubel .15 .40
305a Ivan Rodriguez .25 .60
305b Thurman Munson SP 6.00 15.00
306 Javier Vazquez .15 .40
307 A.J. Burnett/Ervin Santana Roy Halladay LL .25 .60
308 Chris Duncan .15 .40
309 Humberto Sanchez (RC) .30 .75
310 Johan Santana .25 .60
311 Kelly Shoppach .15 .40
312 Ryan Sweeney .15 .40
313 Jamey Carroll .15 .40
314 Matt Treanor .15 .40
315 Hiroki Kuroda .15 .40
316 Brian Stokes .15 .40
317 Jarrod Saltalamacchia .15 .40
318 Manny Acta MG .15 .40
319 Brian Fuentes .15 .40
320a Miguel Cabrera .40 1.00
320b Johnny Mize SP 8.00 20.00
321 S.Kazmir/D.Price CC .30 .75
322 John Buck .15 .40
323 Vicente Padilla .15 .40
324 Mark Reynolds .15 .40
325 Dustin McGowan .15 .40
326 Manny Ramirez HL .40 1.00
327 Phil Coke RC .50 1.25
328 Doug Mientkiewicz .15 .40
329 Gil Meche .15 .40
330 Daisuke Matsuzaka .25 .60
331 Luke Scott .15 .40
332 Chone Figgins .15 .40
333 Jeremy Sowers/Aaron Laffey .15 .40
334 Blake DeWitt .15 .40
335 Chris Young .15 .40
336 Jordan Schafer (RC) .50 1.25
337 Bobby Jenks .15 .40
338 Daniel Cabrera .15 .40
339 Jim Leyland MG .15 .40
340a Joe Mauer .30 .75
340b Wade Boggs SP 10.00 25.00
341 Willy Taveras .15 .40
342 Gerald Laird .15 .40
343 Ian Snell .15 .40
344 J.R. Towles .15 .40
345 Stephen Drew .15 .40
346 Mike Cameron .15 .40
347 Jason Bartlett .15 .40
348 Tony Pena .15 .40
349 Justin Masterson .15 .40
350a Dustin Pedroia .40 1.00
350b Ryne Sandberg SP 10.00 25.00
351 Chris Snyder .15 .40
352 Gregor Blanco .15 .40
353a Derek Jeter 1.00 2.50
353b Cal Ripken Jr. SP 6.00 15.00
354 Mike Aviles .15 .40
355a John Smoltz .40 1.00
355b Jim Palmer SP 5.00 12.00
356 Ervin Santana .15 .40
357 Huston Street .15 .40
358 Chad Tracy .15 .40
359 Jason Varitek .40 1.00
360 Jorge Posada .25 .60
361 Alex Rios/Vernon Wells .15 .40
362 Luke Montz RC .30 .75
363 Jhonny Peralta .15 .40
364 Kevin Millwood .15 .40
365 Mark Buehrle .25 .60
366 Alexi Casilla .15 .40
367 Bobby Abreu .15 .40
368 Trevor Hoffman .25 .60
369 Matt Harrison .15 .40
370 Victor Martinez .25 .60
371 Jeff Francis .15 .40
372 Rickie Weeks .15 .40
373 Joe Martinez RC .50 1.25
374 Kevin Kouzmanoff .15 .40
375 Carlos Quentin .15 .40
376 Rajai Davis .15 .40
377 Trevor Crowe RC .30 .75
378 Mark Hendrickson .15 .40
379 Howie Kendrick .15 .40
380 Aramis Ramirez .15 .40
381 Sharon Martis RC .50 1.25
382 Wily Mo Pena .15 .40
383 Everth Cabrera RC .50 1.25
384 Bob Melvin MG .15 .40
385 Mike Jacobs .15 .40
386 Jonathan Papelbon .25 .60
387 Adam Everett .15 .40
388 Humberto Quintero .15 .40
389 Garrett Olson .15 .40
390 Joey Votto .40 1.00
391 Dan Haren .15 .40
392 Brandon Phillips .15 .40
393 Alex Cintron .15 .40
394 Barry Zito .25 .60
395 Magglio Ordonez .25 .60
396 Alex Cora .25 .60
397 Carlos Ruiz .15 .40
398 Cameron Maybin .15 .40
399 Wandy Rodriguez .15 .40
400a Alfonso Soriano .25 .60
400b Frank Robinson SP 6.00 15.00
401 Tony La Russa MG .25 .60
402 Nick Blackburn .15 .40
403 Trevor Cahill RC .75 2.00
404 Matt Capps .15 .40
405 Todd Helton .25 .60
406 Mark Ellis .15 .40
407 Dave Trembley MG .15 .40
408 Ronny Paulino .15 .40
409 Jesse Chavez RC .30 .75
410 Lou Piniella MG .15 .40
411 Troy Tulowitzki .40 1.00
412 Taylor Teagarden .15 .40
413 Ruben Gotay .15 .40
414 Cha Seung Baek .15 .40
415a Josh Beckett .15 .40
415b Bob Gibson SP 10.00 25.00
416 Josh Whitesell RC .50 1.25
417 Jason Marquis .15 .40
418 Andy Pettitte .25 .60
419 Braden Looper .15 .40
420 Scott Baker .15 .40
421 B.J. Ryan .15 .40
422 Hank Blalock .15 .40
423 Melvin Mora .15 .40
424 Jorge Campillo .15 .40
425 Curtis Granderson .30 .75
426 Pablo Sandoval .30 .75
427 Brian Duensing RC .50 1.25
428 Jamie Moyer .15 .40
429 Mike Hampton .15 .40
430 Francisco Rodriguez .25 .60
431 Ramon Hernandez .15 .40
432 Wladimir Balentien .15 .40
433 Coco Crisp .15 .40
434 C.Guillen/M.Cabrera .40 1.00
435 Carlos Lee .15 .40
436 Ryan Theriot .15 .40
437 Austin Kearns .15 .40
438 Mark Loretta .15 .40
439 Ryan Spilborghs .15 .40
440 Fausto Carmona .15 .40
441 Andrew Bailey RC .75 2.00
442 Cliff Pennington .15 .40
443 Gavin Floyd .15 .40
444 Jody Gerut .15 .40
445 Joe Nathan .15 .40
446 Matt Holliday .40 1.00
447 Freddy Sanchez .15 .40
448 Jeff Clement .15 .40
449 Mike Fontenot .15 .40
450 Hanley Ramirez .25 .60
451 Ryan Perry RC .75 2.00

452 Orlando Cabrera .15 .40
453 Javier Valentin .15 .40
454 Carlos Silva .15 .40
455 Adam Jones .25 .60
456 Jason Kendall .15 .40
457 John Maine .15 .40
458 Jeremy Bonderman .15 .40
459 Brian Bannister .15 .40
460 Nick Markakis .30 .75
461 Mike Scioscia MG .15 .40
462 James Loney .15 .40
463 Brian Wilson .40 1.00
464 Bobby Crosby .15 .40
465 Troy Glaus .15 .40
466 Wilson Betemit .15 .40
467 Chris Volstad .15 .40
468 Derek Lowe .15 .40
469 Michael Cuddyer .15 .40
470 Lance Berkman .25 .60
471 Kerry Wood .15 .40
472 Bill Hall .15 .40
473 Jered Weaver .25 .60
474 Franklin Gutierrez .15 .40
475a Chipper Jones .40 1.00
475b Mike Schmidt SP 6.00 15.00
476a Edinson Volquez .15 .40
476b Juan Marichal SP 5.00 12.00
477 Josh Willingham .25 .60
478 Jose Molina .15 .40
479 Brad Nelson (RC) .30 .75
480 Prince Fielder .25 .60
481 Nyjer Morgan .15 .40
482 Jason Jaramillo (RC) .30 .75
483 John Lannan .15 .40
484 Chris Carpenter .25 .60
485 Aaron Rowand .15 .40
486 J.J. Putz .15 .40
487 Travis Hafner .15 .40
488 Ozzie Guillen MG .15 .40
489 Matt Guerrier .15 .40
490a Joba Chamberlain .15 .40
490b Nolan Ryan SP 8.00 20.00
491 Paul Bako .15 .40
492 Andre Ethier .25 .60
493 Ramiro Pena RC .50 1.25
494 Gary Matthews .15 .40
495a Eric Chavez .15 .40
495b Brooks Robinson SP 6.00 15.00
496 Charlie Manuel MG .15 .40
497 Clint Hurdle MG .15 .40
498 Kyle Davies .15 .40
499 Edwin Moreno (RC) .30 .75
500 Ryan Howard .30 .75
501 Jeff Suppan .15 .40
502 Yovani Gallardo .15 .40
503 Carlos Gonzalez .25 .60
504 Felix Pie .15 .40
505 Scott Olsen .15 .40
506 Paul Konerko .25 .60
507 Melky Cabrera .15 .40
508 Kenji Johjima .25 .60
509 Lou Montanez .15 .40
510 Ryan Ludwick .25 .60
511 Chad Qualls .15 .40
512 Steve Pearce .40 1.00
513 Bronson Arroyo .15 .40
514 Nick Hundley .15 .40
515a Gary Sheffield .15 .40
515b Reggie Jackson SP 10.00 25.00
516 Brian Anderson .15 .40
517 Kevin Frandsen .15 .40
518 Chris Perez .15 .40
519 Dioner Navarro .15 .40
520a Adrian Gonzalez .30 .75
520b Tony Gwynn SP 6.00 15.00
521 Dana Eveland .15 .40
522 Gio Gonzalez .25 .60
523 Brandon Morrow .15 .40
524 Andy LaRoche .15 .40
525 Jimmy Rollins .25 .60
526 Bruce Bochy MG .25 .60
527 Jason Isringhausen .15 .40
528 Nick Swisher .25 .60
529 Fernando Rodney .16 .40
530 Felix Hernandez .25 .60
531 Frank Francisco .15 .40
532 Garret Anderson .15 .40
533 Darin Erstad .15 .40
534 Skip Schumaker .15 .40
535 Ryan Doumit .15 .40
536 Khalil Greene .15 .40
537 Anthony Reyes .15 .40
538 Carlos Guillen .15 .40
539 Miguel Olivo .15 .40
540 Russell Martin .15 .40
541 Jason Bay .25 .60
542 Chris Ray .15 .40
543 Travis Ishikawa .15 .40
544 Pat Neshek .25 .60
545 Matt Garza .15 .40
546 Matt Cain .25 .60
547 Jack Cust .15 .40
548 John Danks .15 .40
549 Randy Winn .15 .40
550 Carlos Beltran .25 .60
551 Tim Redding .15 .40
552 Eric Byrnes .15 .40
553 Jeff Karstens .15 .40
554 Adam LaRoche .15 .40
555 Joe Girardi MG .25 .60
556 Brendan Ryan .15 .40
557 Jayson Werth .25 .60
558 Edgar Renteria .15 .40
559 Esteban German .15 .40
560 Adrian Beltre .40 1.00
561 Ryan Freel .15 .40
562 Cecil Cooper MG .15 .40
563 Francisco Cordero .15 .40
564 Jesus Flores .15 .40
565 Jose Lopez .15 .40
566 Dontrelle Willis .15 .40
567 Willy Aybar .15 .40
568 Greg Reynolds .15 .40
569 Ted Lilly .15 .40
570 David DeJesus .15 .40
571 Noah Lowry .15 .40
572 Michael Bourn .15 .40
573 Adam Wainwright .25 .60
574 Nate Schierholtz .15 .40
575 Clayton Kershaw .60 1.50
576 Don Wakamatsu MG .15 .40
577 Jose Contreras .15 .40
578 Adam Kennedy .15 .40
579 Rocco Baldelli .15 .40
580 Scott Kazmir .15 .40
581 David Purcey .15 .40
582 Yunel Escobar .15 .40
583 Brett Anderson RC .50 1.25
584 Ron Washington MG .15 .40
585 Alexei Ramirez .25 .60
586 Nelson Cruz .40 1.00
587 Adam Dunn .25 .60
588 Jorge De La Rosa .15 .40
589 Rickey Romero (RC) .50 1.25
590 Johnny Damon .25 .60
591 Elvis Andrus RC .75 2.00
592 Fred Lewis .15 .40
593 Kenshin Kawakami RC .50 1.25
594 Milton Bradley .15 .40
595a Vernon Wells .15 .40
595b Robin Yount SP 6.00 15.00
596 Radhames Liz .15 .40
597 Randy Wolf .15 .40
598 Micah Owings .15 .40
599 Placido Polanco .15 .40
600a Jake Peavy .15 .40
600b Greg Maddux SP 20.00 50.00
601 Ryan Howard/Jimmy Rollins .30 .75
602 Carlos Gomez .15 .40
603 Jose Reyes .25 .60
604 Gregg Zaun .15 .40
605 Rick Ankiel .15 .40
606 Nick Johnson .15 .40
607 Jarrod Washburn .15 .40
608 Cristian Guzman .15 .40
609 Juan Rivera .15 .40
610a Michael Young .15 .40
610b Paul Molitor SP 10.00 25.00
611 Jeremy Hermida .15 .40
612 Joel Pineiro .15 .40
613 Kendry Morales .15 .40
614 David Murphy .15 .40
615 Robinson Cano .25 .60
616 Koji Uehara RC .75 2.00
617 Shaun Marcum .15 .40
618 Brandon Backe .15 .40
619 Chris Carter .15 .40
620 Ryan Zimmerman .25 .60
621 Oliver Perez .15 .40
622 Kurt Suzuki .15 .40
623 Aaron Hill .15 .40
624 Ben Francisco .15 .40
625 Jim Thome .25 .60
626 Scott Hairston .15 .40
627 Billy Butler .15 .40
628 Justin Upton/Chris Young .15 .40
629 Lyle Overbay .15 .40
630 A.J. Burnett .15 .40
631 Colby Rasmus (RC) .50 1.25
632 Brett Myers .15 .40
633 David Patton RC .50 1.25
634 Chris Davis .25 .60
635 Joakim Soria .15 .40
636 Armando Galarraga .15 .40
637 Donald Veal RC .50 1.25
638 Eugenio Velez .15 .40
639 Corey Hart .15 .40
640 B.J. Upton .25 .60
641 Jesse Litsch .15 .40
642 Ken Macha MG .15 .40
643 David Freese RC 1.00 2.50
644 Alfredo Aceves RC .50 1.25
645 Paul Maholm .15 .40
646 Chris Iannetta .15 .40
647 Manny Parra .15 .40
648 J.D. Drew .15 .40
649 Luke Hochevar .15 .40
650a Cole Hamels .30 .75
650b Steve Carlton SP 10.00 25.00
651 Jake Westbrook .15 .40
652 Doug Davis .15 .40
653 Nick Evans .15 .40
654 Brian Schneider .15 .40
655 Bengie Molina .15 .40
656 Delmon Young .25 .60
657 Aaron Heilman .15 .40
658 Rick Porcello RC 1.00 2.50
659 Torii Hunter .15 .40
660a Jacoby Ellsbury .30 .75
660b Carl Yastrzemski SP 10.00 25.00

2009 Topps Gold Border

*GOLD VET: 2X TO 5X BASIC
*GOLD RC: 1X TO 2.5X BASIC RC
SER.1 ODDS 1:7 HOBBY
SER.2 ODDS 1:5 HOBBY
STATED PRINT RUN 2009 SER.#'d SETS
7 Mickey Mantle 8.00 20.00
658 Rick Porcello 5.00 12.00

2009 Topps Target

*VETS: .5X TO 1.2X BASIC TOPPS CARDS
*RC: .5X TO 1.2X BASIC TOPPS RC CARDS

2009 Topps Target Legends Gold

*GOLD: .6X TO 1.5X BASIC
RANDOM INSERTS IN TARGET PACKS

2009 Topps Wal-Mart Black Border

*VETS: .5X TO 1.2X BASIC TOPPS CARDS
*RC: .5X TO 1.2X BASIC TOPPS RC CARDS

2009 Topps 1952 Autographs

STATED ODDS 1:60,000 HOBBY
NNO Billy Crystal 100.00 175.00

2009 Topps Career Best Autographs

GROUP A1 ODDS 1:6708 HOBBY
GROUP A2 ODDS 1:3140 HOBBY
GROUP B1 ODDS 1:416 HOBBY
GROUP B2 ODDS 1:613 HOBBY
UPDATE ODDS 1:352 HOBBY
MOST GROUP A PRICING NOT AVAILABLE
AE Andre Ethier UPD 6.00 15.00
AG Armando Galarraga B1 3.00 8.00
AI Akinori Iwamura B1 5.00 12.00
AI Akinori Iwamura B2 5.00 12.00
AJ Andrew Jones UPD 5.00 12.00
AK Austin Kearns B2 3.00 8.00
AMS Andy Sonnanstine A2 3.00 8.00
AR Aramis Ramirez A1 6.00 15.00
AR Alex Rodriguez A2 75.00 150.00
ASO Alfonso Soriano A2 10.00 25.00
BD Blake DeWitt B2 3.00 8.00
BM Brandon Moss A2 3.00 8.00
BZ Ben Zobrist UPD 10.00 25.00
CD Chris Dickerson B2 3.00 8.00
CF Chone Figgins A2 3.00 8.00
CG Curtis Granderson B1 6.00 15.00
CG Carlos Gomez B2 6.00 15.00
CK Clayton Kershaw A1 20.00 50.00
CK Clayton Kershaw B2 20.00 50.00
CV Chris Volstad B2 3.00 8.00
CW C.J. Wilson B1 4.00 10.00
DM Dallas McPherson B1 3.00 8.00
DMM Dustin McGowan B1 3.00 8.00
DO David Ortiz A1 20.00 50.00
DP David Price A2 20.00 50.00
EK Eddie Kunz B1 3.00 8.00
EL Evan Longoria A2 10.00 25.00
FC Fausto Carmona B2 3.00 8.00
FH Felix Hernandez B2 12.00 30.00
FL Fred Lewis B1 3.00 8.00
GA Garrett Atkins B1 3.00 8.00
GS Greg Smith B1 3.00 8.00
GS Gary Sheffield UPD 10.00 25.00
GTS Greg Smith B2 3.00 8.00
HB Heath Bell UPD 3.00 8.00
HR Hanley Ramirez A1 12.00 30.00
IR Ivan Rodriguez UPD 12.00 30.00
JB Jay Bruce A1 20.00 50.00
JB Jeff Baker B2 3.00 8.00
JCH Joba Chamberlain A2 15.00 40.00
JD Johnny Damon A2 30.00 60.00
JG Jason Giambi UPD 15.00 40.00
JH Josh Hamilton A1 20.00 50.00
JH Josh Hamilton A2 20.00 50.00
JL Jon Lester A2 10.00 25.00
JN Jayson Nix UPD 3.00 8.00
JN Jeff Niemann A2 3.00 8.00
JS Jeff Samardzija A2 8.00 20.00
KG Kevin Gregg UPD 3.00 8.00
KK Kevin Kouzmanoff A2 6.00 15.00
LB Lance Berkman A2 10.00 25.00
LH Luke Hochevar B1 4.00 10.00
MB Milton Bradley UPD 4.00 10.00
MG Mat Gamel B1 6.00 15.00
MH Matt Holliday UPD 20.00 50.00
NM Nick Markakis A1 10.00 25.00
NM Nate McLouth UPD 12.00 30.00
OH Orlando Hudson UPD 5.00 12.00
PF Prince Fielder A1 10.00 25.00
PF Prince Fielder B2 10.00 25.00
PM Peter Moylan UPD 3.00 8.00
PN Pat Neshek B1 3.00 8.00
RC Robinson Cano B2 10.00 25.00
RH Rich Hill UPD 3.00 8.00
RH Ryan Howard A2 75.00 150.00
RI Raul Ibanez UPD 8.00 20.00
RO Roy Oswalt UPD 6.00 15.00
RO Roy Oswalt A2 10.00 25.00
RP Ronny Paulino B1 3.00 8.00
SP Steve Pearce B1 5.00 12.00
SR Sean Rodriguez B1 12.00 30.00
SV Shane Victorino B1 8.00 20.00
TS Travis Snider B1 6.00 15.00
VG Vladimir Guerrero UPD 6.00 15.00
YG Yovani Gallardo B1 6.00 15.00
YG Yovani Gallardo A2 6.00 15.00
ZG Zack Greinke B1 10.00 25.00

2009 Topps Career Best Relics

GROUP A1 ODDS 1:70 HOBBY
GROUP A2 ODDS 1:344 HOBBY
GROUP B1 ODDS 1:146 HOBBY
GROUP B2 ODDS 1:92 HOBBY
AB Angel Berroa Bat B2 2.50 6.00
AE Andre Ethier Jsy B2 3.00 8.00
AER Alex Rodriguez Bat A1 6.00 15.00
AG Alex Gordon Jsy A1 4.00 10.00
AG Alex Gordon Jsy B2 2.50 6.00
AP Albert Pujols Jsy A1 6.00 15.00
AR Aramis Ramirez Jsy B1 2.50 6.00
AR Alex Rodriguez Jsy A2 6.00 15.00
BM Brian McCann Bat A1 2.50 6.00
CB Carlos Beltran Pants B2 2.50 6.00
CG Curtis Granderson Jsy A1 3.00 8.00
CG Curtis Granderson Jsy B2 3.00 8.00
CGG Cristian Guzman Bat A1 2.50 6.00
CH Cole Hamels Jsy B2 4.00 10.00
CJ Conor Jackson Bat A1 2.50 6.00
CJ Conor Jackson Jsy B2 2.50 6.00
CM Cameron Maybin Bat B1 2.50 6.00
DM Daisuke Matsuzaka Jsy A1 4.00 10.00
DO David Ortiz Bat A1 4.00 10.00
DW David Wright Bat A1 5.00 12.00
DW David Wright Bat A2 5.00 12.00
EC Eric Chavez Bat B2 2.50 6.00
FS Freddy Sanchez Jsy A1 2.50 6.00
GA Garret Anderson Jsy A2 4.00 10.00
HO Hideki Okajima Jsy B1 3.00 8.00
IK Ian Kinsler Jsy B1 2.50 6.00
IS Ichiro Suzuki Jsy A1 10.00 25.00
JA Josh Anderson Jsy A1 3.00 8.00
JB Jeremy Bonderman Jsy A1 2.50 6.00
JB Jay Bruce Bat A2 4.00 10.00
JC Johnny Cueto Jsy A1 3.00 8.00
JC Jorge Cantu Bat A2 2.50 6.00
JD Jermaine Dye Jsy A1 2.50 6.00
JD J.D. Drew Bat A2 3.00 8.00
JE Jacoby Ellsbury Jsy A1 8.00 20.00
JH Jeremy Hermida Jsy A1 2.50 6.00
JM Justin Morneau Bat A1 2.50 6.00
JP Jonathan Papelbon Jsy B1 2.50 6.00
JR Jose Reyes Jsy A1 3.00 8.00
LG Luis Gonzalez Bat A2 2.50 6.00
MA Mike Aviles Jsy B1 2.50 6.00
MC Miguel Cabrera Bat A2 4.00 10.00
MK Matt Kemp Jsy B2 4.00 10.00
MO Magglio Ordonez Bat A2 4.00 10.00
OD Octavio Dotel Jsy B2 2.50 6.00
PF Prince Fielder Jsy A1 3.00 8.00
PF Prince Fielder Jsy A2 3.00 8.00
RB Ryan Braun Jsy B1 4.00 10.00
RC Robinson Cano Bat B2 3.00 8.00
RD Ray Durham Bat A2 2.50 6.00
RF Rafael Furcal Bat A2 3.00 8.00
RG Ryan Garko Jsy A1 2.50 6.00
RH Ryan Howard Jsy A1 5.00 12.00
RH Ryan Howard Bat B2 5.00 12.00
SK Scott Kazmir Jsy A1 2.50 6.00
VM Victor Martinez Bat A1 2.50 6.00
VM Victor Martinez Jsy B2 2.50 6.00
ARA Aramis Ramirez Jsy B2 2.50 6.00
JBE Josh Beckett Jsy B2 3.00 8.00
JCU Johnny Cueto Jsy A2 2.50 6.00
RBA Rocco Baldelli Bat B2 2.50 6.00
RBR Ryan Braun Jsy A2 4.00 10.00

2009 Topps Career Best Relics Silver

*SILVER 99: .6X TO 1.5X BASIC
STATED ODDS 1:1033 HOBBY
STATED PRINT RUN 99 SER.#'d SETS

2009 Topps Career Best Relic Autographs

SER.1 ODDS 1:2210 HOBBY
SER.2 ODDS 1:2845 HOBBY
STATED PRINT RUN 50 SER.#'d SETS
AER Alex Rodriguez Bat 100.00 200.00
AI Akinori Iwamura 8.00 20.00
AK Austin Kearns 12.50 30.00
AR Aramis Ramirez Jsy 8.00 20.00
BD Blake DeWitt 10.00 25.00
CC Carl Crawford Jsy 8.00 20.00
DP Dustin Pedroia Jsy 50.00 100.00
DW David Wright Bat 20.00 50.00
EL Evan Longoria 20.00 50.00
FC Fausto Carmona 10.00 25.00
FH Felix Hernandez 20.00 50.00
FL Fred Lewis 8.00 20.00
HR Hanley Ramirez Jsy 20.00 50.00
JC Joba Chamberlain 20.00 50.00
JH Josh Hamilton Jsy 12.50 30.00
JH Josh Hamilton 12.50 30.00
JL Jon Lester 20.00 50.00
JR Jose Reyes Jsy 30.00 60.00
NM Nick Markakis Jsy 8.00 20.00
PF Prince Fielder Jsy 15.00 40.00
RB Ryan Braun Jsy 20.00 50.00

2009 Topps Career Best Relics Dual

STATED ODDS 1:472 HOBBY
STATED PRINT RUN 99 SER.#'d SETS
BL Braun Jsy/Longoria Jsy 12.50 30.00
CP Cabrera Bat/Pujols Jsy 12.50 30.00
EP Ellsbury Jsy/Pedroia Jsy 15.00 40.00
FH Fielder Bat/Howard Jsy 6.00 15.00
GJ Tom Glavine Jsy 6.00 15.00
Randy Johnson Jsy
GO Guerrero Jsy/Ortiz Jsy 20.00 50.00
HH Hamilton Jsy/Braun Jsy 12.50 30.00
HC Howard Jsy/Cabrera Bat 6.00 15.00
HR Howard Jsy/Longoria Bat 10.00 25.00
HU Ryan Howard Jsy 10.00 25.00
Chase Utley Jsy
LC Tim Lincecum Jsy 10.00 25.00
Matt Cain Jsy
LS Longoria Jsy/Soto Jsy 8.00 20.00
MM Joe Mauer Jsy 8.00 20.00
Brian McCann Jsy
OL Magglio Ordonez Bat 6.00 15.00
Carlos Lee Bat
OP Roy Oswalt Jsy 6.00 15.00
Jake Peavy Jsy
OR Ortiz Bat/Rodriguez Bat 12.50 30.00
PB Pence Bat/Braun Jsy 12.50 30.00
PK Dustin Pedroia Jsy 8.00 20.00
Ian Kinsler Jsy
RB Alex Rios Jsy 10.00 25.00
Carlos Beltran Pants
RR Jimmy Rollins Jsy 6.00 15.00
Jose Reyes Jsy
RU Hanley Ramirez Jsy 6.00 15.00
Dan Uggla Jsy
SM Suzuki Jsy/Matsuzaka Jsy 30.00 60.00
TS Jim Thome Jsy 6.00 15.00
Gary Sheffield Bat
UU Justin Upton Bat 6.00 15.00
B.J. Upton Bat
VP Jason Varitek Bat 6.00 15.00
Jorge Posada Uni
WJ Wright Pants/Jones Jsy 10.00 25.00
WL Wright Jsy/Longoria Jsy 12.50 30.00
ZL Zimm Jsy/Longoria Jsy 8.00 20.00
OPU Ortiz Bat/Pujols Jsy 8.00 20.00
RRA Rollins Jsy/Ramirez Jsy 6.00 15.00

2009 Topps Factory Set JCPenney Bonus

COMPLETE SET (5) 3.00 8.00
JCP1 Rick Porcello 1.25 3.00
JCP2 David Price .75 2.00
JCP3 Koji Uehara 1.00 2.50
JCP4 Colby Rasmus .60 1.50
JCP5 Jordan Schafer .60 1.50

2009 Topps Factory Set Rookie Bonus

COMPLETE SET (20) 8.00 20.00
1 David Price .75 2.00
2 Rick Porcello 1.25 3.00
3 Ryan Perry 1.00 2.50
4 Brett Anderson .60 1.50
5 David Freese 1.25 3.00
6 Koji Uehara 1.00 2.50
7 Elvis Andrus 1.00 2.50
8 Trevor Cahill 1.00 2.50
9 Andrew Bailey 1.00 2.50
10 Jordan Schafer .60 1.50
11 Colby Rasmus .60 1.50
12 Kenshin Kawakami .60 1.50
13 Michael Bowden .40 1.00
14 Edwin Moreno .40 1.00
15 Ricky Romero .60 1.50
16 Tommy Hanson 1.00 2.50
17 Ramiro Pena .60 1.50
18 Freddy Sandoval .40 1.00
19 Andrew McCutchen 2.00 5.00
20 George Kottaras .40 1.00

2009 Topps Factory Set Target Ruth Chrome Gold Refractors

COMPLETE SET (3) 15.00 40.00
1 Babe Ruth 8.00 20.00
2 Babe Ruth 8.00 20.00
3 Babe Ruth 8.00 20.00

2009 Topps Legendary Letters Commemorative Patch

STATED ODDS 1:630 HOBBY
EACH LETTER SER.#'d TO 50
COMBINED PRINT RUNS LISTED BELOW
BG Bob Gibson/300 * 10.00 25.00
BR Babe Ruth/200 * 12.50 30.00
CM C.Mathewson/450 * 8.00 20.00
CMY C.Yastrzemski/550 * 8.00 20.00
CR C.Ripken Jr./300 * 12.50 30.00
CY Cy Young/250 * 12.50 30.00
GS George Sisler/300 * 4.00 10.00
HW H.Wagner/300 * 10.00 25.00
JF Jimmie Foxx/200 * 4.00 10.00
JM Johnny Mize/200 * 6.00 15.00
JR J.Robinson/400 * 8.00 20.00
LG Lou Gehrig/300 * 12.50 30.00
MM M.Mantle/300 * 8.00 20.00
MO Mel Ott/150 * 4.00 10.00
NR Nolan Ryan/200 * 12.50 30.00
PWR Pee Wee Reese/250 * 8.00 20.00
RC R.Campanella/500 * 8.00 20.00
RH R.Hornsby/350 * 4.00 10.00
TC Ty Cobb/200 * 12.50 30.00
TM T.Munson/300 * 10.00 25.00
TS Tris Speaker/350 * 5.00 12.00
WJ W.Johnson/350 * 5.00 12.00

2009 Topps Legends Chrome Target Cereal

COMPLETE SET (30) 30.00 60.00
RANDOM INSERTS IN TARGET CEREAL PACKS
GR1 Ted Williams 3.00 8.00
GR2 Bob Gibson 1.00 2.50
GR3 Babe Ruth 4.00 10.00
GR4 Roy Campanella 1.50 4.00
GR5 Ty Cobb 2.50 6.00
GR6 Cy Young 1.50 4.00
GR7 Mickey Mantle 5.00 12.00
GR8 Walter Johnson 1.50 4.00
GR9 Roberto Clemente 4.00 10.00
GR10 Jimmie Foxx 1.50 4.00
GR11 Christy Mathewson 1.50 4.00
GR12 Jackie Robinson 1.50 4.00
GR13 Ty Cobb 2.50 6.00
GR14 Honus Wagner 1.50 4.00
GR15 Lou Gehrig 3.00 8.00
GR16 Nolan Ryan 5.00 12.00
GR17 Cal Ripken Jr 5.00 12.00
GR18 Thurman Munson 1.50 4.00
GR19 Rogers Hornsby 1.00 2.50
GR20 George Sisler 1.00 2.50
LLG21 Rickey Henderson 1.50 4.00
LLG22 Ozzie Smith 2.00 5.00
LLG23 Babe Ruth 4.00 10.00
LLG24 Roger Maris 2.50 6.00
LLG25 Nolan Ryan 5.00 12.00
LLG26 Reggie Jackson 1.00 2.50
LLG27 Frank Robinson 1.00 2.50
LLG28 Ryne Sandberg 3.00 8.00
LLG29 Steve Carlton 1.00 2.50
LLG30 Johnny Bench 1.50 4.00

2009 Topps Legends Chrome Target Cereal Refractors

*REF: .5X TO 1.2X BASIC
RANDOM INSERTS IN TARGET PACKS

2009 Topps Legends Chrome Target Cereal Gold Refractors

*GOLD REF: .75X TO 2X BASIC
RANDOM INSERTS IN TARGET PACKS

2009 Topps Legends Chrome Wal-Mart Cereal

RANDOM INSERTS IN WALMART CEREAL PACKS
PR1 Ted Williams 3.00 8.00
PR2 Jackie Robinson 1.50 4.00
PR3 Babe Ruth 4.00 10.00
PR4 Honus Wagner 1.50 4.00
PR5 Lou Gehrig 3.00 8.00
PR6 Nolan Ryan 5.00 12.00
PR7 Mickey Mantle 5.00 12.00
PR8 Thurman Munson 1.50 4.00
PR9 Cal Ripken Jr. 5.00 12.00
PR10 George Sisler 1.00 2.50
PR11 Mel Ott 1.50 4.00
PR12 Bob Gibson 1.00 2.50
PR13 Jackie Robinson 1.50 4.00
PR14 Roy Campanella 1.50 4.00
PR15 Ty Cobb 2.50 6.00
PR16 Cy Young 1.50 4.00
PR17 Cal Ripken Jr 5.00 12.00
PR18 Walter Johnson 1.50 4.00
PR19 Lou Gehrig 3.00 8.00
PR20 Jimmie Foxx 1.50 4.00
PR21 Babe Ruth 4.00 10.00
PR22 Rogers Hornsby 1.00 2.50
PR23 Johnny Mize 1.00 2.50
PR24 Ty Cobb 2.50 6.00
PR25 Tris Speaker 1.00 2.50
PR26 Rickey Henderson 1.50 4.00
PR27 Ozzie Smith 2.00 5.00
PR28 Nolan Ryan 5.00 12.00
PR29 Reggie Jackson 1.00 2.50
PR30 Frank Robinson 1.00 2.50

2009 Topps Legends Chrome Wal-Mart Cereal Refractors

*REF: .5X TO 1.2X BASIC
RANDOM INSERTS IN TARGET PACKS

2009 Topps Legends Chrome Wal-Mart Cereal Gold Refractors

*GOLD REF: .75X TO 2X BASIC
RANDOM INSERTS IN TARGET PACKS

2009 Topps Legends Commemorative Patch

SERIES 1 ODDS 1:343 HOBBY
UPDATE RANDOMLY INSERTED
1-100 ISSUED IN SERIES 1
101-150 ISSUED IN UPDATE
LPR1 B.Ruth 1921 WS 8.00 20.00
LPR2 B.Ruth 1927 WS 8.00 20.00
LPR3 L.Gehrig 1928 WS 6.00 15.00
LPR4 L.Gehrig 1933 ASG 6.00 15.00
LPR5 Jimmie Foxx 1934 ASG 8.00 20.00
LPR6 Mel Ott 1934 ASG 4.00 10.00
LPR7 T.Williams 1946 ASG 6.00 15.00
LPR8 T.Williams 1949 ASG 6.00 15.00
LPR9 J.Robinson 1949 ASG 8.00 20.00
LPR10 Campy 1949 ASG 12.50 30.00
LPR11 M.Mantle 1951 WS 12.50 30.00
LPR12 M.Mantle 1952 WS 12.50 30.00
LPR13 T.Williams 1963 ASG 6.00 15.00
LPR14 Campy 1953 ASG 4.00 10.00
LPR15 T.Williams 1954 ASG 6.00 15.00
LPR16 M.Mantle 1954 ASG 6.00 15.00
LPR17 Duke Snider 1954 ASG 10.00 25.00
LPR18 Whitey Ford 1954 ASG 6.00 15.00
LPR19 J.Robinson 1955 WS 8.00 20.00
LPR20 M.Mantle 1956 WS 6.00 15.00
LPR21 Don Larsen 1956 WS 4.00 10.00
LPR22 T.Williams 1960 ASG 6.00 15.00
LPR23 E.Banks 1960 ASG 8.00 20.00
LPR24 Clemente 1961 ASG 10.00 25.00
LPR25 Clemente 1962 ASG 10.00 25.00
LPR26 Clemente 1962 ASG 10.00 25.00
LPR27 E.Banks 1962 ASG 8.00 20.00
LPR28 M.Mantle 1962 WS 12.50 30.00
LPR29 Clemente 1963 ASG 10.00 25.00
LPR30 N.Ryan 1969 WS 6.00 15.00
LPR31 Tom Seaver 1969 WS 10.00 25.00
LPR32 Clemente 1971 ASG 10.00 25.00
LPR33 T.Munson 1971 ASG 6.00 15.00
LPR34 Carl Yastrzemski 1971 ASG 10.00 25.00
LPR35 N.Ryan 1972 ASG 6.00 15.00
LPR36 Bob Gibson 1972 ASG 8.00 20.00
LPR37 Carl Yastrzemski 1972 ASG 10.00 25.00
LPR38 N.Ryan 1973 ASG 6.00 15.00
LPR39 Tom Seaver 1973 ASG 10.00 25.00
LPR40 Reggie Jackson 1973 WS 10.00 25.00
LPR41 Reggie Jackson 1977 WS 10.00 25.00
LPR42 T.Munson 1978 WS 8.00 20.00
LPR43 C.Ripken 1983 ASG 12.50 30.00
LPR44 M.Schmidt 1983 ASG 10.00 25.00
LPR45 C.Ripken 1983 WS 12.50 30.00
LPR46 N.Ryan 1985 ASG 6.00 15.00
LPR47 C.Ripken 1985 ASG 12.50 30.00
LPR48 N.Ryan 1989 ASG 6.00 15.00
LPR49 C.Ripken 1989 ASG 12.50 30.00
LPR50 C.Ripken 2001 ASG 12.50 30.00
LPR51 Cy Young 10.00 25.00
LPR52 Christy Mathewson 6.00 15.00
LPR53 Honus Wagner 6.00 15.00
LPR54 Walter Johnson 6.00 15.00
LPR55 Rogers Hornsby 10.00 25.00
LPR56 Lou Gehrig 8.00 20.00
LPR57 Babe Ruth 8.00 20.00
LPR58 Jimmie Foxx 8.00 20.00
LPR59 Jimmie Foxx 8.00 20.00
LPR60 Babe Ruth 8.00 20.00
LPR61 Lou Gehrig 6.00 15.00
LPR62 Johnny Mize 10.00 25.00
LPR63 Pee Wee Reese 6.00 15.00
LPR64 Jackie Robinson 8.00 20.00
LPR65 Johnny Mize 10.00 25.00
LPR66 Mickey Mantle 8.00 20.00
LPR67 Jackie Robinson 8.00 20.00
LPR68 Roy Campanella 12.50 30.00
LPR69 Mickey Mantle 12.50 30.00
LPR70 Brooks Robinson 6.00 15.00
LPR71 Bill Mazeroski 6.00 15.00
LPR72 Frank Robinson 10.00 25.00
LPR73 Carl Yastrzemski 10.00 25.00
LPR74 Juan Marichal 10.00 25.00
LPR75 Brooks Robinson 6.00 15.00
LPR76 Frank Robinson 10.00 25.00
LPR77 Steve Carlton 8.00 20.00
LPR78 Jim Palmer 8.00 20.00
LPR79 Frank Robinson 10.00 25.00
LPR80 Jim Palmer 8.00 20.00
LPR81 Reggie Jackson 10.00 25.00
LPR82 Thurman Munson 8.00 20.00
LPR83 Mike Schmidt 10.00 25.00
LPR84 Robin Yount 10.00 25.00
LPR85 Robin Yount 10.00 25.00
LPR86 Ryne Sandberg 10.00 25.00
LPR87 Tony Gwynn 8.00 20.00
LPR88 Mike Schmidt 10.00 25.00
LPR89 Paul Molitor 4.00 10.00
LPR90 Frank Thomas 4.00 410.00
LPR91 Chipper Jones 10.00 25.00
LPR92 John Smoltz 10.00 25.00
LPR93 Wade Boggs 10.00 25.00
LPR94 Greg Maddux 12.50 30.00
LPR95 Tony Gwynn 8.00 20.00
LPR96 Mariano Rivera 5.00 12.00
LPR97 Manny Ramirez 10.00 25.00
LPR98 Albert Pujols 6.00 15.00
LPR99 Ichiro Suzuki 12.50 30.00
LPR100 Alex Rodriguez 10.00 25.00
LPR101 Babe Ruth 8.00 20.00
LPR102 Babe Ruth 8.00 20.00
LPR103 Lou Gehrig 6.00 15.00
LPR104 Hank Greenberg 10.00 25.00
LPR105 Jimmie Foxx 8.00 20.00
LPR106 Lou Gehrig 6.00 15.00
LPR107 Stan Musial 15.00 40.00
LPR108 Hank Greenberg 10.00 25.00
LPR109 Pee Wee Reese 6.00 15.00
LPR110 Johnny Mize 10.00 25.00
LPR111 Jackie Robinson 8.00 20.00
LPR112 Roy Campanella 12.50 30.00
LPR113 Whitey Ford 6.00 15.00
LPR114 Robin Roberts 4.00 10.00
LPR115 Roy Campanella 12.50 30.00
LPR116 Johnny Mize 10.00 25.00
LPR117 Jackie Robinson 8.00 20.00
LPR118 Mickey Mantle 12.50 30.00
LPR119 Ernie Banks 8.00 20.00
LPR120 Duke Snider 10.00 25.00
LPR121 Mickey Mantle 12.50 30.00
LPR122 Brooks Robinson 6.00 15.00
LPR123 Mickey Mantle 12.50 30.00
LPR124 Whitey Ford 6.00 15.00
LPR125 Duke Snider 10.00 25.00
LPR126 Bob Gibson 8.00 20.00
LPR127 Ernie Banks 8.00 20.00
LPR128 Frank Robinson 10.00 25.00
LPR129 Jim Palmer 8.00 20.00
LPR130 Bob Gibson 8.00 20.00
LPR131 Steve Carlton 8.00 20.00
LPR132 Reggie Jackson 10.00 25.00
LPR133 Willie McCovey 10.00 25.00
LPR134 Carl Yastrzemski 10.00 25.00
LPR135 Tom Seaver 10.00 25.00
LPR136 Brooks Robinson 6.00 15.00
LPR137 Frank Robinson 10.00 25.00
LPR138 Thurman Munson 8.00 20.00
LPR139 Thurman Munson 8.00 20.00
LPR140 Carl Yastrzemski 10.00 25.00
LPR141 Nolan Ryan 6.00 15.00
LPR142 Robin Yount 10.00 25.00
LPR143 Reggie Jackson 10.00 25.00
LPR144 Cal Ripken 6.00 15.00
LPR145 Wade Boggs 10.00 25.00
LPR146 Mike Schmidt 6.00 15.00
LPR147 Ryne Sandberg 10.00 25.00
LPR148 Paul Molitor 10.00 25.00
LPR149 Cal Ripken 12.50 30.00
LPR150 Tony Gwynn 8.00 20.00

2009 Topps Legends of the Game

COMPLETE SET (75) 40.00 80.00
COMP.UPD.SET (25) 8.00 20.00
STATED ODDS 1:6 HOBBY
1-25 ISSUED IN TOPPS 1
26-50 ISSUED IN TOPPS 2
51-75 ISSUED IN UPDATE
*GOLD: 1.5X TO 4X BASIC
GOLD SER.1 ODDS 1:1975 HOBBY
GOLD SER.2 ODDS 1:1725 HOBBY
GOLD UPD.ODDS 1:950 HOBBY
GOLD PRINT RUN 99 SER.#'d SETS
*PLATINUM: 4X TO 10X BASIC
PLAT.SER.1 ODDS 1:8200 HOBBY
PLAT.SER.2 ODDS 1:6900 HOBBY
PLAT.UPD.ODDS 1:3800 HOBBY
PLATINUM PRINT RUN 25 SER.#'d SETS
LG1 Cy Young .75 2.00
LG2 Honus Wagner .75 2.00
LG3 Christy Mathewson .75 2.00
LG4 Ty Cobb 1.25 3.00
LG5 Walter Johnson .75 2.00
LG6 Tris Speaker .50 1.25
LG7 Babe Ruth 2.00 5.00
LG8 George Sisler .50 1.25
LG9 Rogers Hornsby .50 1.25
LG10 Jimmie Foxx .75 2.00
LG11 Lou Gehrig 1.50 4.00
LG12 Mel Ott .75 2.00
LG13 Jackie Robinson .75 2.00
LG14 Johnny Mize .50 1.25
LG15 Pee Wee Reese .50 1.25
LG16 Roy Campanella .75 2.00
LG17 Ted Williams 1.50 4.00
LG18 Roger Maris .75 2.00
LG19 Bob Gibson .50 1.25
LG20 Mickey Mantle 2.50 6.00
LG21 Roberto Clemente 2.00 5.00
LG22 Thurman Munson .75 2.00
LG23 Carl Yastrzemski 1.25 3.00
LG24 Nolan Ryan 2.50 6.00
LG25 Cal Ripken Jr. 2.50 6.00
LGAP Albert Pujols 1.00 2.50
LGAR Alex Rodriguez 1.00 2.50
LGBR Brooks Robinson .50 1.25
LGCJ Chipper Jones .75 2.00
LGFR Frank Robinson .50 1.25
LGFT Frank Thomas .75 2.00
LGGM Greg Maddux 1.00 2.50
LGIS Ichiro Suzuki 1.00 2.50
LGJM Juan Marichal .50 1.25
LGJP Jim Palmer .50 1.25
LGJS John Smoltz .75 2.00
LGMR Mariano Rivera 1.00 2.50
LGMS Mike Schmidt 1.25 3.00
LGPM Paul Molitor .75 2.00
LGRJ Reggie Jackson .50 1.25
LGRS Ryne Sandberg 1.50 4.00
LGRY Robin Yount .75 2.00
LGSC Steve Carlton .50 1.25
LGTG Tony Gwynn .75 2.00
LGTH Trevor Hoffman .50 1.25
LGVG Vladimir Guerrero .50 1.25
LGWB Wade Boggs .50 1.25
LGMRA Manny Ramirez .75 2.00
LGRJO Randy Johnson .75 2.00
LGTGL Tom Glavine .50 1.25
LGU01 Cy Young .75 2.00
LGU02 Honus Wagner .75 2.00
LGU03 Christy Mathewson .75 2.00
LGU04 Ty Cobb 1.25 3.00
LGU05 Tris Speaker .50 1.25
LGU06 Babe Ruth 2.00 5.00
LGU07 George Sisler .50 1.25
LGU08 Rogers Hornsby .50 1.25
LGU09 Jimmie Foxx .75 2.00
LGU10 Johnny Mize .50 1.25
LGU11 Nolan Ryan 2.50 6.00
LGU12 Juan Marichal .50 1.25
LGU13 Steve Carlton .50 1.25

LGU14 Reggie Jackson .50 1.25
LGU15 Frank Robinson .50 1.25
LGU16 Wade Boggs .50 1.25
LGU17 Paul Molitor .75 2.00
LGU18 Babe Ruth 2.00 5.00
LGU19 Nolan Ryan 2.50 6.00
LGU20 Frank Robinson .50 1.25
LGU21 Reggie Jackson .50 1.25
LGU22 Wade Boggs .50 1.25
LGU23 Rogers Hornsby .50 1.25
LGU24 Paul Molitor .75 2.00
LGU25 Johnny Mize .50 1.25

2009 Topps Legends of the Game Career Best

RANDOM INSERTS IN PACKS
BR Babe Ruth 2.50 6.00
CY Cy Young 1.00 2.50
GS George Sisler .60 1.50
HW Honus Wagner 1.00 2.50
JF Jimmie Foxx 1.00 2.50
JR Jackie Robinson 1.00 2.50
LG Lou Gehrig 2.00 5.00
MM Mickey Mantle 3.00 8.00
MO Mel Ott 1.00 2.50
RC Roy Campanella 1.00 2.50
RH Rogers Hornsby .60 1.50
TC Ty Cobb 1.50 4.00
TS Tris Speaker .60 1.50
WJ Walter Johnson 1.00 2.50
CZM Christy Mathewson 1.00 2.50

2009 Topps Legends of the Game Nickname Letter Patch

RANDOM INSERTS IN PACKS
EACH LETTER SER.#'d TO 50
COMBINED PRINT RUNS LISTED BELOW
BG Bob Gibson/250 * 10.00 25.00
BO B.Obama/800 * 10.00 25.00
BR Babe Ruth/350 * 6.00 15.00
BR Brooks Robinson/650 * 4.00 10.00
CM C.Mathewson/300 * 4.00 10.00
CMY Yastrzemski/150 * 10.00 25.00
CR C.Ripken Jr./350 * 15.00 40.00
CY Cy Young/350 * 4.00 10.00
FR Frank Robinson/400 * 6.00 15.00
GM Greg Maddux/300 * 10.00 25.00
GS George Sisler/400 * 4.00 10.00
HW H.Wagner/400 * 10.00 25.00
JB Joe Biden/650 * 6.00 15.00
JF Jimmie Foxx/400 * 4.00 10.00
JM Johnny Mize/450 * 4.00 10.00
JM Juan Marichal/700 * 4.00 10.00
JR J.Robinson/300 * 12.50 30.00
LG Lou Gehrig/450 * 12.50 30.00
MIO M.Obama/450 * 12.50 30.00
MM M.Mantle/350 * 15.00 40.00
MM2 M.Mantle/650 * 15.00 40.00
MO Mel Ott/300 * 6.00 15.00
NR Nolan Ryan/700 * 6.00 15.00
PM Paul Molitor/350 * 6.00 15.00
PWR P.Reese/300 * 6.00 15.00
RC Campanella/250 * 10.00 25.00
RCW R.Clemente/300 * 20.00 50.00
RH R.Hornsby/250 * 4.00 10.00
RJ Reggie Jackson/500 * 6.00 15.00
RM Roger Maris/700 * 10.00 25.00
TC Ty Cobb/350 * 6.00 15.00
TM T.Munson/350 * 10.00 25.00
TS Tris Speaker/450 * 4.00 10.00
TW T.Williams/650 * 12.50 30.00
WB Wade Boggs/500 * 5.00 12.00
WJ W.Johnson/400 * 8.00 20.00

2009 Topps Legends of the Game Framed Stamps

SERIES 1 ODDS 1:1555 HOBBY
SERIES 2 ODDS 1:9400 HOBBY
SERIES 1 PRINT RUN 95 SER.#'d SETS
SERIES 2 PRINT RUN 90 SER.#'d SETS
BR1 Babe Ruth 20.00 50.00
BR2 Babe Ruth 20.00 50.00
BR3 Babe Ruth 20.00 50.00
BR4 Babe Ruth 20.00 50.00
BR5 Babe Ruth 20.00 50.00
BR6 Babe Ruth 20.00 50.00
BR7 Babe Ruth 20.00 50.00
BR8 Babe Ruth 20.00 50.00
BR9 Babe Ruth 20.00 50.00
CM1 Christy Mathewson 12.50 30.00
CY1 Cy Young 12.50 30.00
GS1 George Sisler 4.00 10.00
HW1 Honus Wagner 20.00 50.00
JF1 Jimmie Foxx 12.50 30.00
JR1 Jackie Robinson 10.00 25.00
JR2 Jackie Robinson 10.00 25.00
JR3 Jackie Robinson 10.00 25.00
JR4 Jackie Robinson 10.00 25.00
JR5 Jackie Robinson 10.00 25.00
JR6 Jackie Robinson 10.00 25.00
JR7 Jackie Robinson 10.00 25.00
LG1 Lou Gehrig 30.00 60.00
LG2 Lou Gehrig 30.00 60.00
LG3 Lou Gehrig 30.00 60.00
MM1 Mickey Mantle 15.00 40.00
MM2 Mickey Mantle 15.00 40.00
RC1 Roberto Clemente 30.00 60.00
RH1 Rogers Hornsby 12.50 30.00
TC1 Ty Cobb 15.00 40.00
TS1 Tris Speaker 10.00 25.00
WJ1 Walter Johnson 15.00 40.00

2009 Topps Red Hot Rookie Redemption

COMPLETE SET (10) 15.00 40.00
COMMON EXCHANGE 6.00 15.00
STATED ODDS 1:36 HOBBY
1:10 G.BECKHAM CARDS ARE SIGNED
EXCHANGE DEADLINE 6/30/2010
RHR1 Fernando Martinez 3.00 8.00
RHR2A Gordon Beckham 2.00 5.00
RHR3 Andrew McCutchen 6.00 15.00
RHR4 Tommy Hanson 3.00 8.00
RHR5 Nolan Reimold 1.25 3.00
RHR6 Neftali Feliz 2.00 5.00
RHR7 Mat Latos 4.00 10.00
RHR8 Julio Borbon 1.25 3.00
RHR9 Jhoulys Chacin 2.00 5.00
RHR10 Chris Coghlan 3.00 8.00

2009 Topps Ring Of Honor

COMPLETE SET (100) 30.00 60.00
COMP.UPD SET (25) 6.00 15.00
STATED ODDS 1:6 HOBBY
101-125 ISSUED IN UPDATE
RH1 David Justice .40 1.00
RH2 Whitey Ford .60 1.50
RH3 Orlando Cepeda .60 1.50
RH4 Cole Hamels .75 2.00
RH5 Darryl Strawberry .40 1.00
RH6 Johnny Bench 1.00 2.50
RH7 David Ortiz 1.00 2.50
RH8 Derek Jeter 2.50 6.00
RH9 Dwight Gooden .40 1.00
RH10 Brooks Robinson .60 1.50
RH11 Ivan Rodriguez .60 1.50
RH12 David Eckstein .40 1.00
RH13 Derek Jeter 2.50 6.00
RH14 Paul Molitor 1.00 2.50
RH15 Don Zimmer .40 1.00
RH16 Jermaine Dye .40 1.00
RH17 Gary Sheffield .40 1.00
RH18 Bob Gibson .60 1.50
RH19 Pedro Martinez .60 1.50
RH20 Manny Ramirez 1.00 2.50
RH21 Johnny Podres .40 1.00
RH22 Johnny Podres .40 1.00
RH23 Mariano Rivera 1.25 3.00
RH24 Curt Schilling .60 1.50
RH25 Lou Piniella .40 1.00
RH26 Roberto Clemente 2.50 6.00
RH27 Kevin Mitchell .40 1.00
RH28 Frank Robinson .60 1.50
RH29 Francisco Rodriguez .60 1.50
RH30 Troy Glaus .40 1.00
RH31 Tony LaRussa .60 1.50
RH32 Mike Schmidt 1.50 4.00
RH33 Brad Lidge .40 1.00
RH34 Randy Johnson 1.00 2.50
RH35 Duke Snider .60 1.50
RH36 Rollie Fingers .60 1.50
RH37 Luis Gonzalez .40 1.00
RH38 Josh Beckett .40 1.00
RH39 Gary Carter .60 1.50
RH40 Bob Gibson .60 1.50
RH41 Andy Pettitte .60 1.50
RH42 Reggie Jackson .60 1.50
RH43 Jim Leyland .40 1.00
RH44 Mariano Rivera 1.25 3.00
RH45 Albert Pujols 1.25 3.00
RH46 Don Larsen .40 1.00
RH47 Roger Clemens 1.25 3.00
RH48 Tom Glavine .60 1.50
RH49 Ryan Howard .75 2.00
RH50 Reggie Jackson .60 1.50
RH51 Carlos Ruiz .40 1.00
RH52 Tyler Johnson .40 1.00
RH53 Jason Varitek 1.00 2.50
RH54 Darryl Strawberry .40 1.00
RH55 Dusty Baker .40 1.00
RH56 Dustin Pedroia 1.00 2.50
RH57 Jayson Werth .60 1.50
RH58 Garret Anderson .40 1.00
RH59 Dontrelle Willis .40 1.00
RH60 David Justice .40 1.00
RH61 Luis Aparicio .60 1.50
RH62 John Smoltz 1.00 2.50
RH63 Miguel Cabrera 1.00 2.50
RH64 Yadier Molina 1.25 3.00
RH65 Jacoby Ellsbury .75 2.00
RH66 Mark Buehrle .60 1.50
RH67 Johnny Damon .60 1.50
RH68 Brad Penny .40 1.00
RH69 Joe Torre .60 1.50
RH70 Chris Carpenter .60 1.50
RH71 Bobby Cox .40 1.00
RH72 Jonathan Papelbon .60 1.50
RH73 Joe Girardi .60 1.50
RH74 Aaron Rowand .40 1.00
RH75 Daisuke Matzusaka .60 1.50
RH76 Babe Ruth 2.50 6.00
RH77 Jackie Robinson 1.00 2.50
RH78 Chris Duncan .40 1.00
RH79 Christy Mathewson 1.00 2.50
RH80 Cy Young 1.00 2.50
RH81 Jermaine Dye .40 1.00
RH82 Honus Wagner 1.00 2.50
RH83 Chone Figgins .40 1.00
RH84 Walter Johnson 1.00 2.50
RH85 Jon Garland .40 1.00
RH86 Mel Ott 1.00 2.50
RH87 Jimmie Foxx 1.00 2.50
RH88 Hideki Okajima .40 1.00
RH89 Johnny Mize .60 1.50
RH90 Rogers Hornsby .60 1.50
RH91 Miguel Cabrera 1.00 2.50
RH92 Pee Wee Reese .60 1.50
RH93 Darin Erstad .40 1.00
RH94 Tris Speaker .60 1.50
RH95 Steve Garvey .40 1.00
RH96 Lou Gehrig 2.00 5.00
RH97 Babe Ruth 2.50 6.00
RH98 David Ortiz 1.00 2.50
RH99 Thurman Munson 1.00 2.50
RH100 Roy Campanella 1.00 2.50

2009 Topps Silk Collection

SER.1 ODDS 1:241 HOBBY
SER.2 ODDS 1:280 HOBBY
UPDATE ODDS 1:163 HOBBY
STATED PRINT RUN 50 SER.#'d SETS
1-100 ISSUED IN SERIES 1
101-200 ISSUED IN SERIES 2
201-300 ISSUED IN UPDATE
S1 David Wright 8.00 20.00
S2 Nate McLouth 4.00 10.00
S3 Brandon Jones 4.00 10.00
S4 Mike Mussina 6.00 15.00
S5 Kevin Youkilis 4.00 10.00
S6 Kyle Lohse 4.00 10.00
S7 Rich Aurilia 4.00 10.00
S8 Rich Harden 4.00 10.00
S9 Chase Headley 4.00 10.00
S10 Vladimir Guerrero 6.00 15.00
S11 Denard Span 4.00 10.00
S12 Andrew Miller 6.00 15.00
S13 Justin Upton 6.00 15.00
S14 Aaron Cook 4.00 10.00
S15 Travis Snider 6.00 15.00
S16 Scott Rolen 6.00 15.00
S17 Chad Billingsley 6.00 15.00
S18 Brandon Wood 4.00 10.00
S19 Brad Lidge 4.00 10.00
S20 Dexter Fowler 6.00 15.00
S21 Ian Kinsler 6.00 15.00
S22 Joe Crede 6.00 15.00
S23 Jay Bruce 6.00 15.00
S24 Frank Thomas 10.00 25.00
S25 Roy Halladay 6.00 15.00
S26 Justin Duchscherer 4.00 10.00
S27 Carl Crawford 6.00 15.00
S28 Jeff Francoeur 6.00 15.00
S29 Mike Napoli 4.00 10.00
S30 Ryan Braun 6.00 15.00
S31 Yuniesky Betancourt 4.00 10.00
S32 James Shields 4.00 10.00
S33 Hunter Pence 6.00 15.00
S34 Ian Stewart 4.00 10.00
S35 David Price 8.00 20.00
S36 Hideki Okajima 4.00 10.00
S37 Brad Penny 4.00 10.00
S38 Ivan Rodriguez 6.00 15.00
S39 Chris Duncan 4.00 10.00
S40 Johan Santana 6.00 15.00
S41 Joe Saunders 4.00 10.00
S42 Jose Valverde 4.00 10.00
S43 Tim Lincecum 6.00 15.00
S44 Miguel Tejada 6.00 15.00
S45 Geovany Soto 6.00 15.00
S46 Mark DeRosa 6.00 15.00
S47 Yadier Molina 12.00 30.00
S48 Collin Balester 4.00 10.00
S49 Zack Greinke 10.00 25.00
S50 Manny Ramirez 10.00 25.00
S51 Brian Giles 4.00 10.00
S52 J.J. Hardy 4.00 10.00
S53 Jarrod Saltalamacchia 4.00 10.00
S54 Aubrey Huff 4.00 10.00
S55 Carlos Zambrano 6.00 15.00
S56 Ken Griffey Jr. 20.00 50.00
S57 Daric Barton 4.00 10.00
S58 Randy Johnson 10.00 25.00
S59 Jon Garland 4.00 10.00
S60 Daisuke Matsuzaka 6.00 15.00
S61 Miguel Cabrera 10.00 25.00
S62 Orlando Hudson 4.00 10.00
S63 Johnny Cueto 6.00 15.00
S64 Omar Vizquel 6.00 15.00
S65 Derrek Lee 4.00 10.00
S66 Brad Ziegler 4.00 10.00
S67 Shane Victorino 4.00 10.00
S68 Roy Oswalt 6.00 15.00
S69 Cliff Lee 6.00 15.00
S70 Ichiro Suzuki 12.00 30.00
S71 Casey Blake 4.00 10.00
S72 Kelly Shoppach 4.00 10.00
S73 Ryan Sweeney 4.00 10.00
S74 Carlos Pena 6.00 15.00
S75 Carlos Delgado 4.00 10.00
S76 Tim Hudson 6.00 15.00
S77 Brandon Webb 6.00 15.00
S78 Adam Lind 4.00 10.00
S79 Akinori Iwamura 4.00 10.00
S80 Mariano Rivera 12.00 30.00
S81 Pat Burrell 4.00 10.00
S82 Mark Teixeira 6.00 15.00
S83 Matt Kemp 8.00 20.00
S84 Jeff Samardzija 6.00 15.00
S85 Kosuke Fukudome 6.00 15.00
S86 Aaron Harang 4.00 10.00
S87 Conor Jackson 4.00 10.00
S88 Andy Sonnanstine 4.00 10.00
S89 Joe Blanton 4.00 10.00
S90 CC Sabathia 6.00 15.00
S91 Greg Maddux 12.00 30.00
S92 Gabe Kapler 4.00 10.00
S93 Garrett Atkins 4.00 10.00
S94 Hideki Matsui 10.00 25.00
S95 Chien-Ming Wang 6.00 15.00
S96 Josh Johnson 6.00 15.00
S97 Dustin McGowan 4.00 10.00
S98 Gil Meche 4.00 10.00
S99 Justin Morneau 6.00 15.00
S100 Evan Longoria 6.00 15.00
S101 Joe Mauer 8.00 20.00
S102 Derek Jeter 25.00 60.00
S103 Jorge Posada 6.00 15.00
S104 Victor Martinez 6.00 15.00
S105 Carlos Quentin 4.00 10.00
S106 Jonathan Papelbon 6.00 15.00
S107 Brandon Phillips 4.00 10.00
S108 Alfonso Soriano 6.00 15.00
S109 Carlos Lee 4.00 10.00
S110 Joe Nathan 4.00 10.00
S111 Jeremy Bonderman 4.00 10.00
S112 Nick Markakis 8.00 20.00
S113 Troy Glaus 4.00 10.00
S114 Travis Hafner 4.00 10.00
S115 Joba Chamberlain 4.00 10.00
S116 Melky Cabrera 4.00 10.00
S117 Kenji Johjima 6.00 15.00
S118 Carlos Guillen 4.00 10.00
S119 Matt Cain 6.00 15.00
S120 Clayton Kershaw 15.00 40.00
S121 Yunel Escobar 4.00 10.00
S122 Michael Young 4.00 10.00
S123 Stephen Drew 4.00 10.00
S124 Justin Masterson 4.00 10.00
S125 Mike Aviles 4.00 10.00
S126 Josh Beckett 4.00 10.00
S127 Fausto Carmona 4.00 10.00
S128 Gavin Floyd 4.00 10.00
S129 Hanley Ramirez 6.00 15.00
S130 Adam Jones 6.00 15.00
S131 Jered Weaver 6.00 15.00
S132 Edinson Volquez 4.00 10.00
S133 Prince Fielder 6.00 15.00
S134 Adrian Gonzalez 8.00 20.00
S135 Jimmy Rollins 6.00 15.00
S136 Felix Hernandez 6.00 15.00
S137 Ryan Doumit 4.00 10.00
S138 Russell Martin 4.00 10.00
S139 Carlos Beltran 6.00 15.00
S140 Nelson Cruz 10.00 25.00
S141 Jeremy Hermida 4.00 10.00
S142 Robinson Cano 6.00 15.00
S143 Armando Galarraga 4.00 10.00
S144 Luke Hochevar 4.00 10.00
S145 Delmon Young 6.00 15.00
S146 Chris Young 4.00 10.00
S147 Dustin Pedroia 10.00 25.00
S148 Ervin Santana 4.00 10.00
S149 Jhonny Peralta 4.00 10.00
S150 Alexi Casilla 4.00 10.00
S151 Kevin Kouzmanoff 4.00 10.00
S152 Aramis Ramirez 4.00 10.00
S153 Joey Votto 10.00 25.00
S154 Barry Zito 6.00 15.00
S155 Cameron Maybin 4.00 10.00
S156 Todd Helton 6.00 15.00
S157 Curtis Granderson 8.00 20.00
S158 Jamie Moyer 4.00 10.00
S159 Wladimir Balentien 4.00 10.00
S160 John Maine 4.00 10.00
S161 Chris Carpenter 6.00 15.00
S162 Andre Ethier 6.00 15.00
S163 Yovani Gallardo 4.00 10.00
S164 Nick Hundley 4.00 10.00
S165 Brandon Morrow 4.00 10.00
S166 Jason Bay 6.00 15.00
S167 Randy Winn 4.00 10.00
S168 Willy Aybar 4.00 10.00
S169 David DeJesus 4.00 10.00
S170 Scott Kazmir 4.00 10.00
S171 Johnny Damon 6.00 15.00
S172 Carlos Gomez 4.00 10.00
S173 Jose Reyes 6.00 15.00
S174 Rick Ankiel 4.00 10.00
S175 Ryan Zimmerman 6.00 15.00
S176 Jim Thome 6.00 15.00
S177 Chris Davis 6.00 15.00
S178 Paul Maholm 4.00 10.00
S179 Manny Parra 4.00 10.00
S180 Rickie Weeks 4.00 10.00
S181 Dan Haren 4.00 10.00
S182 Magglio Ordonez 6.00 15.00
S183 Troy Tulowitzki 10.00 25.00
S184 Freddy Sanchez 4.00 10.00
S185 James Loney 4.00 10.00
S186 Michael Cuddyer 4.00 10.00
S187 Lance Berkman 6.00 15.00
S188 Chipper Jones 10.00 25.00
S189 Eric Chavez 4.00 10.00
S190 Ryan Howard 8.00 20.00
S191 Gary Sheffield 4.00 10.00
S192 Eric Byrnes 4.00 10.00
S193 Jayson Werth 6.00 15.00
S194 Adrian Beltre 10.00 25.00
S195 Fred Lewis 4.00 10.00
S196 Vernon Wells 4.00 10.00
S197 Jake Peavy 4.00 10.00
S198 Joakim Soria 4.00 10.00
S199 B.J. Upton 6.00 15.00
S200 J.D. Drew 4.00 10.00
S201 Ivan Rodriguez 6.00 15.00
S202 Felipe Lopez 4.00 10.00
S203 David Hernandez 4.00 10.00
S204 Brian Fuentes 4.00 10.00
S205 Jonathan Broxton 4.00 10.00
S206 Tommy Hanson 10.00 25.00
S207 Daniel Schlereth 4.00 10.00
S208 Gordon Beckham 12.00 30.00
S209 Sean O'Sullivan 4.00 10.00
S210 Gabe Gross 4.00 10.00
S211 Orlando Hudson 4.00 10.00
S212 Matt Murton 4.00 10.00
S213 Rich Hill 4.00 10.00
S214 J.A. Happ 6.00 15.00
S215 Kris Medlen 10.00 25.00
S216 Daniel Bard 4.00 10.00
S217 Laynce Nix 4.00 10.00
S218 Jake Fox 6.00 15.00
S219 Carl Pavano 4.00 10.00
S220 Clayton Richard 4.00 10.00
S221 Edwin Jackson 4.00 10.00
S222 Gary Sheffield 4.00 10.00
S223 Kyle Blanks 6.00 15.00
S224 Vin Mazzaro 4.00 10.00
S225 Juan Uribe 4.00 10.00
S226 David Ross 4.00 10.00
S227 Russell Branyan 4.00 10.00
S228 David Eckstein 4.00 10.00
S229 Wilkin Ramirez 4.00 10.00
S230 John Mayberry Jr. 6.00 15.00
S231 Sean West 6.00 15.00
S232 Matt Lindstrom 4.00 10.00
S233 Jermey Reed 4.00 10.00
S234 Emilio Bonifacio 4.00 10.00
S235 Gerardo Parra 6.00 15.00
S236 Joe Crede 6.00 15.00
S237 Tony Gwynn 4.00 10.00
S238 Kevin Gregg 4.00 10.00
S239 CC Sabathia 6.00 15.00
S240 Nick Green 4.00 10.00
S241 Anthony Swarzak 4.00 10.00
S242 Livan Hernandez 4.00 10.00
S243 Chris Coghlan 10.00 25.00
S244 Jeff Weaver 4.00 10.00
S245 Alfredo Figaro 4.00 10.00
S246 Aaron Poreda 4.00 10.00
S247 Delwyn Young 6.00 15.00
S248 Fernando Martinez 10.00 25.00
S249 Gaby Sanchez 6.00 15.00
S250 Derek Holland 6.00 15.00
S251 Jayson Nix 4.00 10.00
S252 Raul Ibanez 6.00 15.00
S253 Andrew McCutchen 20.00 50.00
S254 Edgar Renteria 4.00 10.00
S255 Chris Perez 4.00 10.00
S256 Maicer Izturis 4.00 10.00
S257 Mark Kotsay 4.00 10.00
S258 Jason Giambi 4.00 10.00
S259 Tyler Greene 4.00 10.00
S260 Omar Vizquel 6.00 15.00
S261 Diory Hernandez 4.00 10.00
S262 Ben Zobrist 6.00 15.00
S263 Landon Powell 4.00 10.00
S264 Ty Wigginton 6.00 15.00
S265 Randy Johnson 10.00 25.00
S266 Jordan Zimmermann 10.00 25.00
S267 Victor Martinez 6.00 15.00
S268 Andruw Jones 4.00 10.00
S269 Jason Vargas 4.00 10.00
S270 Brad Bergensen 4.00 10.00
S271 Craig Stammen 4.00 10.00
S272 Matt LaPorta 6.00 15.00
S273 Takashi Saito 4.00 10.00
S274 Kevin Millar 4.00 10.00
S275 Randy Wells 4.00 10.00
S276 Javier Vazquez 4.00 10.00
S277 Mark Teixeira 6.00 15.00
S278 Cesar Izturis 4.00 10.00
S279 Omir Santos 4.00 10.00
S280 Jeff Niemann 4.00 10.00
S281 Chris Getz 4.00 10.00
S282 Brad Penny 4.00 10.00
S283 Mark DeRosa 6.00 15.00
S284 Jon Garland 4.00 10.00
S285 Matt Holliday 10.00 25.00
S286 Casey McGehee 4.00 10.00
S287 Brett Cecil 4.00 10.00
S288 Ryan Langerhans 4.00 10.00
S289 Endy Chavez 4.00 10.00
S290 Heath Bell 4.00 10.00
S291 Scott Podsednik 4.00 10.00
S292 Scott Richmond 4.00 10.00
S293 David Huff 4.00 10.00
S294 Ramon Castro 4.00 10.00
S295 Sean Marshall 4.00 10.00
S296 Ramon Ramirez 4.00 10.00
S297 Nolan Reimold 4.00 10.00
S298 Nate McLouth 4.00 10.00
S299 Matt Palmer 4.00 10.00
S300 Ken Griffey Jr. 20.00 50.00

2009 Topps Target Legends

RANDOM INSERTS IN TARGET PACKS
LLG1 Ted Williams 2.00 5.00
LLG2 Jackie Robinson 1.00 2.50
LLG3 Babe Ruth 2.50 6.00
LLG4 Honus Wagner 1.00 2.50
LLG5 Lou Gehrig 2.00 5.00
LLG6 Nolan Ryan 3.00 8.00
LLG7 Mickey Mantle 3.00 8.00
LLG8 Thurman Munson 1.00 2.50
LLG9 Cal Ripken Jr. 3.00 8.00
LLG10 George Sisler .60 1.50
LLG11 Mel Ott 1.00 2.50
LLG12 Bob Gibson .60 1.50
LLG13 Babe Ruth 2.50 6.00
LLG14 Roy Campanella 1.00 2.50
LLG15 Ty Cobb 1.50 4.00
LLG16 Cy Young 1.25 3.00
LLG17 Mickey Mantle 3.00 8.00
LLG18 Walter Johnson 1.00 2.50
LLG19 Pee Wee Reese .60 1.50
LLG20 Jimmie Foxx 1.00 2.50
LLG21 Rickey Henderson 1.00 2.50
LLG22 Ozzie Smith 1.25 3.00
LLG23 Babe Ruth 2.50 6.00
LLG24 Roger Maris 1.00 2.50
LLG25 Nolan Ryan 3.00 8.00
LLG26 Reggie Jackson .60 1.50
LLG27 Frank Robinson .60 1.50
LLG28 Ryne Sandberg 2.00 5.00
LLG29 Steve Carlton .60 1.50
LLG30 Johnny Bench 1.00 2.50

2009 Topps Topps Town

COMPLETE SET (75) 15.00 40.00
COMP.UPD.SET (25) 5.00 12.00
RANDOM INSERTS IN PACKS
UPDATE ODDS 1:9 HOBBY
1-50 ISSUED IN TOPPS
51-75 ISSUED IN UPDATE
COMP.GOLD SET (50) 40.00 80.00
COMP.UPD.GLD.SET (25) 8.00 20.00
*GOLD: 1X TO 2.5X BASIC
GOLD RANDOMLY INSERTED
TTT1 Alex Rodriguez .60 1.50
TTT2 Roy Halladay .30 .75
TTT3 Grady Sizemore .30 .75
TTT4 Brandon Webb .30 .75
TTT5 Evan Longoria .30 .75
TTT6 Johan Santana .30 .75
TTT7 Hanley Ramirez .30 .75
TTT8 Alex Gordon .30 .75
TTT9 Ryan Howard .40 1.00
TTT10 Jake Peavy .20 .50
TTT11 Nick Markakis .40 1.00
TTT12 Justin Morneau .30 .75
TTT13 Albert Pujols .60 1.50
TTT14 CC Sabathia .30 .75
TTT15 Alfonso Soriano .30 .75
TTT16 Ichiro Suzuki .60 1.50
TTT17 Francisco Rodriguez .30 .75
TTT18 Miguel Cabrera .50 1.25
TTT19 Carlos Quentin .20 .50
TTT20 Lance Berkman .30 .75
TTT21 Chipper Jones .50 1.25
TTT22 Tim Lincecum .30 .75
TTT23 Josh Hamilton .30 .75
TTT24 Jay Bruce .30 .75
TTT25 Daisuke Matsuzaka .30 .75
TTT26 Joe Mauer .40 1.00
TTT27 David Ortiz .50 1.25
TTT28 Jimmy Rollins .30 .75
TTT29 Derek Jeter 1.25 3.00
TTT30 Ryan Braun .30 .75
TTT31 Vladimir Guerrero .30 .75
TTT32 David Wright .40 1.00
TTT33 Carlos Lee .20 .50
TTT34 Dustin Pedroia .50 1.25
TTT35 Prince Fielder .30 .75
TTT36 Ian Kinsler .30 .75
TTT37 Justin Upton .30 .75
TTT38 Kosuke Fukudome .30 .75
TTT39 Carlos Zambrano .30 .75
TTT40 Nate McLouth .20 .50
TTT41 Manny Ramirez .50 1.25
TTT42 Kevin Youkilis .20 .50
TTT43 Curtis Granderson .40 1.00
TTT44 Todd Helton .30 .75
TTT45 Alex Rios .20 .50
TTT46 Roy Oswalt .30 .75
TTT47 Carlos Beltran .30 .75
TTT48 Mark Teixeira .30 .75
TTT49 Daisuke Matsuzaka .30 .75
TTT50 Chase Utley .30 .75
TTT51 Mariano Rivera .60 1.50
TTT52 Torii Hunter .20 .50
TTT53 Felix Hernandez .30 .75
TTT54 Adam Jones .30 .75
TTT55 Vernon Wells .20 .50
TTT56 Josh Beckett .20 .50
TTT57 Joey Votto .50 1.25
TTT58 Adrian Gonzalez .40 1.00
TTT59 Justin Verlander .50 1.25
TTT60 Dan Uggla .20 .50
TTT61 Zack Greinke .50 1.25
TTT62 Russell Martin .20 .50
TTT63 Jose Reyes .30 .75
TTT64 Jorge Posada .30 .75
TTT65 Raul Ibanez .30 .75
TTT66 Chris Carpenter .30 .75
TTT67 Carl Crawford .30 .75
TTT68 Michael Young .20 .50
TTT69 Victor Martinez .30 .75
TTT70 Hunter Pence .30 .75
TTT71 Troy Tulowitzki .50 1.25
TTT72 Jacoby Ellsbury .40 1.00
TTT73 Matt Cain .30 .75
TTT74 Brian McCann .30 .75
TTT75 Alexei Ramirez .30 .75

2009 Topps Turkey Red

COMPLETE SET (150) 75.00 150.00
COMP.UPD.SET (50) 20.00 50.00
STATED ODDS 1:4 HOBBY
UPDATE ODDS 1:4 HOBBY
1-100 ISSUED IN TOPPS
101-150 ISSUED IN UPDATE
TR1 Babe Ruth 2.50 6.00
TR2 Evan Longoria .60 1.50
TR3 Jimmie Foxx 1.00 2.50
TR4 Alex Rios .40 1.00
TR5 Nick Markakis .75 2.00
TR6 Ian Kinsler .60 1.50
TR7 Andre Ethier .60 1.50
TR8 Ryan Ludwick .60 1.50
TR9 Tim Lincecum .60 1.50
TR10 Jackie Robinson 1.00 2.50
TR11 Bengie Molina .40 1.00
TR12 Jermaine Dye .40 1.00
TR13 Brian Giles .40 1.00
TR14 Chase Utley .60 1.50
TR15 David Ortiz 1.00 2.50
TR16 Joe Mauer .75 2.00
TR17 Conor Jackson .40 1.00
TR18 Jose Lopez .40 1.00
TR19 Brian McCann .60 1.50
TR20 George Sisler .60 1.50
TR21 Garret Anderson .40 1.00
TR22 Cliff Lee .60 1.50
TR23 Garrett Atkins .40 1.00
TR24 Curtis Granderson .75 2.00
TR25 Alex Rodriguez 1.25 3.00
TR26 Cristian Guzman .40 1.00
TR27 Aubrey Huff .40 1.00
TR28 Delmon Young .60 1.50
TR29 Carlos Quentin .40 1.00
TR30 Christy Mathewson 1.00 2.50
TR31 Justin Upton .60 1.50
TR32 Shane Victorino .40 1.00
TR33 Joey Votto 1.00 2.50
TR34 Kelly Johnson .40 1.00
TR35 David Wright .75 2.00
TR36 Jacoby Ellsbury .75 2.00
TR37 Kevin Kouzmanoff .40 1.00
TR38 Hunter Pence .60 1.50
TR39 Corey Hart .40 1.00
TR40 Kosuke Fukudome .60 1.50
TR41 Cole Hamels .75 2.00
TR42 Geovany Soto .60 1.50
TR43 Torii Hunter .40 1.00
TR44 Ervin Santana .40 1.00
TR45 Miguel Cabrera 1.00 2.50
TR46 Josh Johnson .60 1.50
TR47 Carlos Gomez .40 1.00
TR48 Nate McLouth .40 1.00
TR49 Ben Sheets .40 1.00
TR50 Tris Speaker .60 1.50
TR51 Josh Hamilton .60 1.50
TR52 Rich Harden .40 1.00
TR53 Francisco Rodriguez .60 1.50
TR54 Alex Gordon .60 1.50
TR55 Manny Ramirez 1.00 2.50
TR56 Carlos Zambrano .60 1.50
TR57 Brandon Webb .60 1.50
TR58 Alfonso Soriano .60 1.50
TR59 Mel Ott 1.00 2.50
TR60 Carlos Lee .40 1.00
TR61 Lou Gehrig 2.00 5.00
TR62 Adam Jones .60 1.50
TR63 Josh Beckett .40 1.00
TR64 Prince Fielder .60 1.50
TR65 Jimmy Rollins .60 1.50
TR66 Justin Morneau .60 1.50
TR67 Dan Uggla .40 1.00
TR68 Lance Berkman .60 1.50
TR69 Chipper Jones 1.00 2.50
TR70 Jon Lester .60 1.50
TR71 Albert Pujols 1.25 3.00
TR72 Ryan Braun .60 1.50
TR73 Grady Sizemore .60 1.50
TR74 Carlos Beltran .60 1.50
TR75 Hanley Ramirez .60 1.50
TR76 Jay Bruce .60 1.50
TR77 Derek Jeter 2.50 6.00
TR78 Matt Cain .60 1.50
TR79 Roy Campanella 1.00 2.50
TR80 Rogers Hornsby .60 1.50
TR81 Ryan Zimmerman .60 1.50
TR82 Dustin Pedroia 1.00 2.50
TR83 B.J. Upton .60 1.50
TR84 Jose Reyes .60 1.50
TR85 Johnny Mize .60 1.50
TR86 Magglio Ordonez .60 1.50
TR87 Ty Cobb 1.50 4.00
TR88 Michael Young .40 1.00
TR89 Todd Helton .60 1.50
TR90 Walter Johnson 1.00 2.50
TR91 Matt Kemp .75 2.00
TR92 Adrian Gonzalez .75 2.00
TR93 Pee Wee Reese .60 1.50
TR94 Ryan Doumit .40 1.00
TR95 Ryan Howard .75 2.00
TR96 Ichiro Suzuki 1.25 3.00
TR97 Cy Young 1.00 2.50
TR98 Mark Teixeira .60 1.50
TR99 Vladimir Guerrero .60 1.50
TR100 Honus Wagner 1.00 2.50
TR101 Ty Cobb 1.50 4.00
TR102 David Price .75 2.00
TR103 Jorge Posada .60 1.50
TR104 Brian Roberts .40 1.00
TR105 Tris Speaker .60 1.50
TR106 John Lackey .60 1.50
TR107 Miguel Tejada .60 1.50
TR108 Dan Haren .40 1.00
TR109 Troy Tulowitzki 1.00 2.50
TR110 Yunel Escobar .40 1.00
TR111 Koji Uehara 1.00 2.50
TR112 Vernon Wells .40 1.00
TR113 Jimmie Foxx 1.00 2.50
TR114 CC Sabathia .60 1.50
TR115 Alexei Ramirez .60 1.50
TR116 Rick Porcello 1.25 3.00
TR117 Gary Sheffield .40 1.00
TR118 Ryan Dempster .40 1.00
TR119 Shin-Soo Choo .60 1.50
TR120 Adam Dunn .60 1.50
TR121 Edinson Volquez .40 1.00
TR122 Kevin Youkilis .40 1.00
TR123 Roy Halladay .60 1.50
TR124 Justin Verlander 1.00 2.50
TR125 Max Scherzer 1.00 2.50
TR126 Jorge Cantu .40 1.00
TR127 Roy Oswalt .60 1.50
TR128 Tommy Hanson 1.00 2.50
TR129 Raul Ibanez .60 1.50
TR130 Johan Santana .60 1.50
TR131 Jermaine Dye .40 1.00
TR132 Mariano Rivera 1.25 3.00
TR133 Rogers Hornsby .60 1.50
TR134 Daisuke Matsuzaka .60 1.50
TR135 Andrew McCutchen 2.00 5.00
TR136 Jake Peavy .40 1.00
TR137 Jason Bay .60 1.50
TR138 Ken Griffey 2.00 5.00
TR139 Chris Carpenter .60 1.50
TR140 Carl Crawford .60 1.50
TR141 Victor Martinez .60 1.50
TR142 Brad Hawpe .40 1.00
TR143 Aaron Hill .40 1.00
TR144 Randy Johnson 1.00 2.50
TR145 Gordon Beckham .60 1.50
TR146 Jordan Zimmermann 1.00 2.50
TR147 Freddy Sanchez .40 1.00
TR148 Carlos Pena .60 1.50
TR149 Johnny Cueto .60 1.50
TR150 Babe Ruth 2.50 6.00

2009 Topps Wal-Mart Legends

RANDOM INSERTS IN WALMART PACKS
LLP1 Ted Williams 2.00 5.00
LLP2 Bob Gibson .60 1.50
LLP3 Babe Ruth 2.50 6.00
LLP4 Roy Campanella 1.00 2.50
LLP5 Ty Cobb 1.50 4.00
LLP6 Cy Young 1.00 2.50
LLP7 Mickey Mantle 3.00 8.00
LLP8 Walter Johnson 1.00 2.50
LLP9 Roberto Clemente 2.50 6.00
LLP10 Jimmie Foxx 1.00 2.50
LLP11 Johnny Mize .60 1.50
LLP11 Johnny Mize .60 1.50
LLP12 Jackie Robinson 1.00 2.50
LLP12 Jackie Robinson 1.00 2.50
LLP13 Babe Ruth 2.50 6.00
LLP13 Babe Ruth 2.50 6.00
LLP14 Honus Wagner 1.00 2.50
LLP14 Honus Wagner 1.00 2.50
LLP15 Lou Gehrig 2.00 5.00
LLP15 Lou Gehrig 2.00 5.00
LLP16 Nolan Ryan 3.00 8.00
LLP16 Nolan Ryan 3.00 8.00
LLP17 Mickey Mantle 3.00 8.00
LLP17 Mickey Mantle 3.00 8.00
LLP18 Thurman Munson 1.00 2.50
LLP18 Thurman Munson 1.00 2.50
LLP19 Christy Mathewson 1.00 2.50
LLP19 Christy Mathewson 1.00 2.50
LLP20 George Sisler .60 1.50
LLP20 George Sisler .60 1.50
LLP21 Babe Ruth 2.50 6.00
LLP22 Rickey Henderson 1.00 2.50
LLP23 Roger Maris 1.00 2.50
LLP24 Nolan Ryan 3.00 8.00
LLP25 Reggie Jackson .60 1.50
LLP26 Steve Carlton .60 1.50
LLP27 Tony Gwynn 1.00 2.50
LLP28 Paul Molitor 1.00 2.50
LLP29 Brooks Robinson .60 1.50
LLP30 Wade Boggs .60 1.50

2009 Topps Wal-Mart Legends Gold

*GOLD: .6X TO 1.5X BASIC
RANDOM INSERTS IN WAL MART PACKS

2009 Topps WBC Autographs

COMMON CARD 10.00 25.00
STATED ODDS 1:1418 HOBBY
STATED PRINT RUN 100 SER.#'d SETS
BM Brian McCann 10.00 25.00
CD Carlos Delgado 12.50 30.00
CG Curtis Granderson 10.00 25.00
CR Carlos Ruiz 10.00 25.00
DO David Ortiz 75.00 200.00
DP Dustin Pedroia 25.00 60.00
DW David Wright 75.00 150.00
JR Jose Reyes 10.00 25.00
RB Ryan Braun 12.00 30.00
AIR Alex Rios 10.00 25.00

2009 Topps WBC Autograph Relics

STATED ODDS 1:14,200 HOBBY

STATED PRINT RUN 50 SER.#'d SETS
CR Carlos Ruiz 15.00 40.00
JR Jose Reyes 12.50 30.00

2009 Topps WBC Stars

COMPLETE SET (25) 12.50 30.00
STATED ODDS 1:12 HOBBY
BCS1 David Wright .75 2.00
BCS2 Jin Young Kee .60 1.50
BCS3 Yulieski Gourriel 1.25 3.00
BCS4 Hiroyuki Nakajima .60 1.50
BCS5 Ichiro Suzuki 1.25 3.00
BCS6 Jose Reyes .60 1.50
BCS7 Yu Darvish 1.50 4.00
BCS8 Carlos Lee .40 1.00
BCS9 Fu-Te Ni .60 1.50
BCS10 Derek Jeter 2.50 6.00
BCS11 Adrian Gonzalez .75 2.00
BCS12 Dylan Lindsay .60 1.50
BCS13 Greg Halman .60 1.50
BCS14 Miguel Cabrera 1.00 2.50
BCS15 Chris Denorfia .40 1.00
BCS16 Aroldis Chapman 2.00 5.00
BCS17 Alex Rios .40 1.00
BCS18 Luke Hughes .40 1.00
BCS19 Gregor Blanco .40 1.00
BCS20 Bernie Williams .60 1.50
BCS21 Philippe Aumont .60 1.50
BCS22 Shuichi Murata .60 1.50
BCS23 Frederich Cepeda .60 1.50
BCS24 Dustin Pedroia 1.00 2.50
BCS25 David Ortiz 1.00 2.50

2009 Topps WBC Stars Relics

STATED ODDS 1:219 HOBBY
AC Aroldis Chapman 8.00 20.00
BW Bernie Williams 4.00 10.00
DL Dylan Lindsay 3.00 8.00
FC Frederich Cepeda 3.00 8.00
GH Greg Halman 3.00 8.00
HR Hanley Ramirez 4.00 10.00
MO Magglio Ordonez 3.00 8.00
PA Phillippe Aumont 4.00 10.00
RM Russell Martin 4.00 10.00
FTN Fu-Te Ni 4.00 10.00
JRO Jimmy Rollins 5.00 12.00
LJY Jin Young Lee 3.00 8.00

2009 Topps WBC Stamp Collection

STATED ODDS 1:9400 HOBBY
STATED PRINT RUN 90 SER.#'d SETS
WBC1 Pro Baseball 10.00 25.00
WBC2 Baseball Centennial 15.00 40.00
WBC3 Take Me Out 10.00 25.00
WBC4 USA 12.50 30.00

2009 Topps World Baseball Classic Rising Star Redemption

COMPLETE SET (10) 8.00 20.00
1 Lee Jin Young .60 1.50
2 Derek Jeter 4.00 10.00
3 Gift Ngoepe .60 1.50
4 Ubaldo Jimenez .60 1.50
5 Sidney De Jong .60 1.50
6 Yoennis Cespedes 6.00 15.00
7 Yu Darvish 12.50 30.00
8 Dae Ho Lee .60 1.50
9 Jung Keun Bong .60 1.50
10 Daisuke Matsuzaka 1.00 2.50

2009 Topps World Champion Autographs

STATED ODDS 1:20,000 HOBBY
CR Carlos Ruiz 60.00 120.00
JW Jayson Werth 60.00 120.00
SV Shane Victorino 100.00 200.00

2009 Topps World Champion Relics

STATED ODDS 1:5600 HOBBY
STATED PRINT RUN 100 SER.#'d SETS
CH Cole Hamels Jsy 30.00 60.00
CU Chase Utley Jsy 40.00 80.00
JR Jimmy Rollins Jsy 30.00 60.00
PB Pat Burrell Bat 20.00 50.00
RH Ryan Howard Jsy 50.00 100.00

2009 Topps World Champion Relics Autographs

STATED ODDS 1:11,400 HOBBY
PRINT RUNS B/WN 8-50 COPIES PER
NO HAMELS PRICING AVAILABLE
JR Jimmy Rollins Jsy 75.00 150.00
RH Ryan Howard Jsy 200.00 400.00

2009 Topps Update

COMP.SET w/o VAR (330) 20.00 50.00
COMMON CARD (1-330) .12 .30
COMMON SP VAR (1-330) 5.00 12.00
SP VAR ODDS 1:32 HOBBY
COMMON RC (1-330) .40 1.00
PRINTING PLATE ODDS 1:615 HOBBY
PLATE PRINT RUN 1 SET PER COLOR
BLACK-CYAN-MAGENTA-YELLOW ISSUED
NO PLATE PRICING DUE TO SCARCITY
UH1 Ivan Rodriguez .20 .50
UH2 Felipe Lopez .12 .30
UH3 Michael Saunders RC 1.00 2.50
UH4 David Hernandez RC .40 1.00
UH5 Brian Fuentes .12 .30
UH6 Josh Barfield .12 .30
UH7 Brayan Pena .12 .30
UH8 Lance Broadway .12 .30
UH9 Jonathan Broxton .12 .30
UH10 Tommy Hanson RC 1.00 2.50
UH11 Daniel Schlereth RC .40 1.00
UH12 Edwin Maysonet .12 .30
UH13 Scott Hairston .12 .30
UH14 Yadier Molina .40 1.00
UH15 Jacoby Ellsbury .25 .60
UH16 Brian Buscher .12 .30
UH17 D.Jeter/D.Wright .75 2.00
UH18 John Grabow .12 .30
UH19 Nelson Cruz .30 .75
UH20 Gordon Beckham RC .60 1.50
UH21 Matt Diaz .12 .30
UH22 Brett Gardner .20 .50
UH23 Sean O'Sullivan RC .40 1.00
UH24 Gabe Gross .12 .30
UH25 Orlando Hudson .12 .30
UH26 Ryan Howard .25 .60
UH27 Josh Reddick RC .60 1.50
UH28 Matt Murton .12 .30
UH29 Rich Hill .12 .30
UH30 J.A. Happ .20 .50
UH31 Adam Jones .20 .50
UH32 Kris Medlen RC 1.00 2.50
UH33 Daniel Bard RC .40 1.00
UH34 Laynce Nix .12 .30
UH35 Tom Gorzelanny .12 .30
UH36 Paul Konerko/Jermaine Dye .20 .50
UH37 Adam Kennedy .12 .30
UH38 Justin Upton .20 .50
UH39 Jake Fox .20 .50
UH40 Carl Pavano .12 .30
UH41 Xavier Paul (RC) .40 1.00
UH42 Eric Hinske .12 .30
UH43 Koyie Hill .12 .30
UH44 Seth Smith .12 .30
UH45 Brad Ausmus .12 .30
UH46 Clayton Richard .12 .30
UH47a Carlos Beltran .20 .50
UH47b D.Snider SP 6.00 15.00
UH48a Albert Pujols .40 1.00
UH48b R.Maris SP 6.00 15.00
UH49 Edwin Jackson .12 .30
UH50 Gary Sheffield .12 .30
UH51 Jesus Guzman RC .40 1.00
UH52a Kyle Blanks RC .60 1.50
UH52b Bo Jackson SP 5.00 12.00
UH53 Clete Thomas .12 .30
UH54 Vin Mazzaro RC .40 1.00
UH55 Ben Zobrist .12 .30
UH56 Wes Helms .12 .30
UH57 Juan Uribe .12 .30
UH58 Omar Quintanilla .12 .30
UH59 David Ross .12 .30
UH60 Brandon Inge .12 .30
UH61 Jamie Hoffmann RC .40 1.00
UH62 Russell Branyan .12 .30
UH63 Mark Rzepczynski RC .60 1.50
UH64 Alex Gonzalez .12 .30
UH65a Joe Mauer .25 .60
UH65b Paul Molitor SP 5.00 12.00
UH66 Jhoulys Chacin RC .60 1.50
UH67 Brandon McCarthy .12 .30
UH68 David Eckstein .12 .30
UH69 J.Girardi/D.Jeter .75 2.00
UH70 Wilkin Ramirez RC .40 1.00
UH71a Chase Utley .20 .50
UH71b Rogers Hornsby SP 5.00 12.00
UH71c R.Sandberg SP 6.00 15.00
UH72 John Mayberry Jr. (RC) .60 1.50
UH73 Sean West (RC) .60 1.50
UH74 Mitch Maier .12 .30
UH75 Matt Lindstrom .12 .30
UH76 Scott Rolen .20 .50
UH77 Jeremy Reed .12 .30
UH78 LaTroy Hawkins .12 .30
UH79 Robert Andino .12 .30
UH80 Matt Stairs .12 .30
UH81 Mark Teixeira .20 .50
UH82 David Wright .25 .60
UH83 Emilio Bonifacio .12 .30
UH84 Gerardo Parra RC .60 1.50
UH85 Joe Crede .20 .50
UH86 Carlos Pena .20 .50
UH87 Jake Peavy .12 .30
UH88 Jim Leyland/Tony La Russa .12 .30
UH89 Phil Hughes .12 .30
UH90 Orlando Cabrera .12 .30
UH91 Anderson Hernandez .12 .30
UH92 Edwin Encarnacion .30 .75
UH93 Pedro Martinez .20 .50
UH94 Jarrod Washburn .12 .30
UH95 Ryan Freel .12 .30
UH96 Tony Gwynn .12 .30
UH97 Juan Castro .12 .30
UH98a Hanley Ramirez .20 .50
UH98b Honus Wagner SP 5.00 12.00
UH99 Kevin Gregg .12 .30
UH100 CC Sabathia .20 .50
UH101 Nick Green .12 .30
UH102 Brett Hayes (RC) .40 1.00
UH103a Evan Longoria .20 .60
UH103b Wade Boggs SP 5.00 12.00
UH104 Geoff Blum .12 .30
UH105 Luis Valbuena .20 .50
UH106 Jonny Gomes .12 .30
UH107 Anthony Swarzak (RC) .40 1.00
UH108 Chris Tillman RC .60 1.50
UH109 Orlando Hudson .12 .30
UH110 Justin Masterson .12 .30
UH111 Livan Hernandez .12 .30
UH112 Kyle Farnsworth .12 .30
UH113 Francisco Rodriguez .20 .50
UH114 Chris Coghlan RC 1.00 2.50
UH115 Jeff Weaver .12 .30
UH116 Alfredo Figaro RC .40 1.00
UH117 Alex Rios .12 .30
UH118 Blake Hawksworth (RC) .40 1.00
UH119 Bud Norris RC .40 1.00
UH120 Aaron Poreda RC .40 1.00
UH121 Brandon Inge .12 .30
UH122 Youk/Wright/Jeter/Vict .75 2.00
UH123 Ryan Braun .20 .50
UH124 Delwyn Young .12 .30
UH125 Fernando Martinez RC 1.00 2.50
UH126 Matt Tolbert .12 .30
UH127 Shane Robinson RC .40 1.00
UH128 Chone Figgins .12 .30
UH129 Shane Victorino .12 .30
UH130 Randy Johnson .30 .75
UH131 Derek Jeter .75 2.00
UH132 Joe Thurston .12 .30
UH133 Graham Taylor RC .60 1.50
UH134 Derek Holland RC .60 1.50
UH135 R.Perry/R.Porcello .40 1.00
UH136 Raul Ibanez .20 .50
UH137 Ross Ohlendorf .12 .30
UH138 Ryan Church .12 .30
UH139 Brian Moehler .12 .30
UH140 Jack Wilson .12 .30
UH141 Jason Hammel .12 .30
UH142 Jorge Posada .20 .50
UH143 Matt Maloney (RC) .40 1.00
UH144 Ronny Cedeno .12 .30
UH145 Micah Hoffpauir .12 .30
UH146 Juan Cruz .12 .30
UH147 Jayson Nix .12 .30
UH148a Jason Bay .20 .50
UH148b Tris Speaker SP 5.00 12.00
UH149 Joel Hanrahan .20 .50
UH150a Raul Ibanez .20 .50
UH150b Ty Cobb SP 5.00 12.00
UH151 Jayson Werth .20 .50
UH152 Barbaro Canizares RC .40 1.00
UH153a Ichiro Suzuki .40 1.00
UH153b George Sisler SP 5.00 12.00
UH154 Gerardo Parra .20 .50
UH155 Andrew McCutchen (RC) 2.00 5.00
UH156 Heath Bell .12 .30
UH157 Josh Hamilton .20 .50
UH158 Wilson Valdez .12 .30
UH159 Chad Billingsley .20 .50
UH160 Edgar Renteria .12 .30
UH161 Andrew Bailey .30 .75
UH162 Chris Perez .12 .30
UH163 Alejandro De Aza .12 .30
UH164 Brett Tomko .12 .30
UH165 Maicer Izturis .12 .30
UH166 Mike Redmond .12 .30
UH167 Julio Borbon RC .40 1.00
UH168 Paul Phillips .12 .30
UH169 Mark Kotsay .12 .30
UH170 Jason Giambi .12 .30
UH171 Trevor Hoffman .20 .50
UH172 Tyler Greene (RC) .40 1.00
UH173 David Robertson .12 .30
UH174 Omar Vizquel .20 .50
UH175 Jody Gerut .12 .30
UH176 Diory Hernandez RC .40 1.00
UH177 Neftali Feliz RC .60 1.50
UH178 Josh Beckett .12 .30
UH179 Carl Crawford .20 .50
UH180 Mariano Rivera .40 1.00
UH181 Zach Duke .12 .30
UH182 Mark Buehrle .20 .50
UH183 Guillermo Quiroz .12 .30
UH184 Francisco Cordero .12 .30
UH185 Kevin Correia .12 .30
UH186a Zack Greinke .30 .75
UH186b Christy Mathewson SP 5.00 12.00
UH187 Ryan Franklin .20 .50
UH188 Jeff Francouer .20 .50
UH189 Michael Young
Josh Hamilton/Ian Kinsler .20 .50
UH190 Ken Griffey Jr. .60 1.50
UH191 Ben Zobrist .20 .50
UH192 Prince Fielder .20 .50
UH193 Landon Powell (RC) .40 1.00
UH194 Ty Wigginton .20 .50
UH195 P.J. Walters RC .40 1.00
UH196 Brian Fuentes .12 .30
UH197 Dan Haren .12 .30
UH198a Roy Halladay .20 .50
UH198b Cy Young SP 5.00 12.00
UH199 Mike Rivera .12 .30
UH200 Randy Johnson .30 .75
UH201 Jordan Zimmermann RC 1.00 2.50
UH202 Angel Berroa .12 .30
UH203 Ben Francisco .12 .30
UH204 Brian Barden .12 .30
UH205 Dallas Braden .12 .30
UH206 Chris Burke .12 .30
UH207 Garrett Jones .20 .50
UH208 Chad Gaudin .12 .30
UH209 Andruw Jones .12 .30
UH210 Jason Vargas .12 .30
UH211 Brad Bergesen (RC) .40 1.00
UH212 Ian Kinsler .20 .50
UH213 Josh Johnson .20 .50
UH214 Jason Grilli .12 .30
UH215 Felix Hernandez .20 .50
UH216 Mat Latos RC 1.25 3.00
UH217 Craig Stammen RC .40 1.00
UH218 Cliff Lee .20 .50
UH219 Ken Takahashi RC .60 1.50
UH220 Matt LaPorta RC .60 1.50
UH221 Adrian Gonzalez .25 .60
UH222 Ted Lilly .12 .30
UH223 Jack Hannahan .12 .30
UH224 Takashi Saito .12 .30
UH225 Gregorio Petit .12 .30
UH226 Kevin Hart .12 .30
UH227 Edwin Jackson .12 .30
UH228 Jason LaRue .12 .30
UH229 Kevin Millar .12 .30
UH230 Freddy Sanchez .12 .30
UH231 Josh Bard .12 .30
UH232a Tim Lincecum .20 .50
UH232b N.Ryan CAL SP 6.00 15.00
UH232c N.Ryan NYM SP 6.00 15.00
UH233 Ramon Santiago .12 .30
UH234 Mike Sweeney .12 .30
UH235 Joe Nathan .12 .30
UH236 Kris Benson .12 .30
UH237 Dustin Pedroia .30 .75
UH238 Kevin Cash .12 .30
UH239 George Sherrill .12 .30
UH240 Jason Marquis .12 .30
UH241 Dewayne Wise .12 .30
UH242 Randy Wells .12 .30
UH243 Jonathan Papelbon .20 .50
UH244 Johan Santana .20 .50
UH245 Mariano Rivera .40 1.00
UH246 Javier Vazquez .12 .30
UH247 Lastings Milledge .12 .30
UH248 Chan Ho Park .20 .50
UH249 Brian McCann .20 .50
UH250a Mark Teixeira .20 .50
UH250c Johnny Mize NYG SP 5.00 12.00
UH250b Johnny Mize NYY SP 5.00 12.00
UH251 Ian Snell .12 .30
UH252 Justin Verlander .30 .75
UH253a Prince Fielder .20 .50
UH253b Reggie Jackson CAL SP 5.00 12.00
UH253c Reggie Jackson OAK SP 5.00 12.00
UH254 Cesar Izturis .12 .30
UH255 Omir Santos RC .40 1.00
UH256 Tim Wakefield .20 .50
UH257 Adrian Gonzalez .25 .60
UH258 Nyjer Morgan .12 .30
UH259 Victor Martinez .20 .50
UH260a Ryan Howard .25 .60
UH260b Willie McCovey SP 5.00 12.00
UH261 Aaron Bates RC .40 1.00
UH262 Jeff Niemann .12 .30
UH263 Matt Holliday .30 .75
UH264 Adam LaRoche .12 .30
UH265 Justin Morneau .20 .50
UH266 Jonathan Broxton .12 .30
UH267 Miguel Cairo .12 .30
UH268 Chris Getz .12 .30
UH269 Cliff Floyd .12 .30
UH270 D.Ortiz/A.Rodriguez .40 1.00
UH271 Frank Catalanotto .12 .30
UH272 Carlos Pena .20 .50
UH273 Mark Lowe .12 .30
UH274 Joe Mauer .25 .60
UH275 Ryan Garko .12 .30
UH276 Brad Penny .12 .30
UH277 Orlando Hudson .20 .50
UH278 Gaby Sanchez RC .60 1.50
UH279 Ross Detwiler .12 .30
UH280 Mark DeRosa .20 .50
UH281a Kevin Youkilis .12 .30
UH281b Jimmie Foxx SP 5.00 12.00
UH282 Victor Martinez .20 .50
UH283 Freddy Sanchez .12 .30
UH284 Mark Melancon RC .40 1.00
UH285 Ryan Franklin .20 .50
UH286 Sidney Ponson .12 .30
UH287 Matt Joyce .12 .30
UH288 Jon Garland .12 .30
UH289 Nick Johnson .12 .30
UH290 Jason Michaels .12 .30
UH291 Ross Gload .12 .30
UH292 Yuniesky Betancourt .12 .30
UH293 Aaron Hill .12 .30
UH294 Josh Anderson .12 .30
UH295 Miguel Tejada .20 .50
UH296 Casey McGehee .12 .30
UH297 Brett Cecil RC .40 1.00
UH298 Jason Bartlett .12 .30
UH299 Ryan Langerhans .12 .30
UH300 Albert Pujols .40 1.00
UH301 Ryan Zimmerman .20 .50
UH302 Casey Kotchman .12 .30
UH303 Luke French (RC) .40 1.00
UH304 Nick Swisher/Johnny Damon .20 .50
UH305 Michael Young .12 .30
UH306 Endy Chavez .12 .30
UH307 Heath Bell .12 .30
UH308 Matt Cain .20 .50
UH309 Scott Podsednik .12 .30
UH310 Scott Richmond .12 .30
UH311 David Huff RC .40 1.00
UH312 Ryan Hanigan .12 .30
UH313 Jeff Baker .12 .30
UH314 Brad Hawpe .12 .30
UH315 Jerry Hairston Jr. .12 .30
UH316 H.Pence/R.Braun .20 .50
UH317 Nelson Cruz .30 .75
UH318a Carl Crawford .20 .50
UH318b Rickey Henderson SP 5.00 12.00
UH319 Ramon Castro .12 .30
UH320 Mark Schlereth/Daniel Schlereth .12 .30
UH321 Hunter Pence .12 .30
UH322 Sean Marshall .12 .30
UH323 Ramon Ramirez .12 .30
UH324 Nolan Reimold (RC) .40 1.00
UH325a Torii Hunter .12 .30
UH325b Frank Robinson SP 5.00 12.00
UH326 Nate McLouth .12 .30
UH327 Julio Lugo .12 .30
UH328 Matt Palmer .12 .30
UH329 Curtis Granderson .25 .60
UH330a Ken Griffey Jr. .60 1.50
UH330b B.Ruth Braves SP 8.00 20.00
UH330c B.Ruth Sox SP 8.00 20.00

2009 Topps Update Black

STATED ODDS 1:44 HOBBY
STATED PRINT RUN 58 SER.#'d SETS
UH1 Ivan Rodriguez 6.00 15.00
UH2 Felipe Lopez 4.00 10.00
UH3 Michael Saunders 10.00 25.00
UH4 David Hernandez 4.00 10.00
UH5 Brian Fuentes 4.00 10.00
UH6 Josh Barfield 4.00 10.00
UH7 Brayan Pena 4.00 10.00
UH8 Lance Broadway 4.00 10.00
UH9 Jonathan Broxton 4.00 10.00
UH10 Tommy Hanson 10.00 25.00
UH11 Daniel Schlereth 4.00 10.00
UH12 Edwin Maysonet 4.00 10.00
UH13 Scott Hairston 4.00 10.00
UH14 Yadier Molina 12.00 30.00
UH15 Jacoby Ellsbury 8.00 20.00
UH16 Brian Buscher 4.00 10.00
UH17 D.Jeter/D.Wright 25.00 60.00
UH18 John Grabow 4.00 10.00
UH19 Nelson Cruz 10.00 25.00
UH20 Gordon Beckham 6.00 15.00
UH21 Matt Diaz 4.00 10.00
UH22 Brett Gardner 6.00 15.00
UH23 Sean O'Sullivan 4.00 10.00
UH24 Gabe Gross 4.00 10.00
UH25 Orlando Hudson 4.00 10.00
UH26 Ryan Howard 8.00 20.00
UH27 Josh Reddick 6.00 15.00
UH28 Matt Murton 4.00 10.00
UH29 Rich Hill 4.00 10.00
UH30 J.A. Happ 6.00 15.00
UH31 Adam Jones 6.00 15.00
UH32 Kris Medlen 10.00 25.00
UH33 Daniel Bard 4.00 10.00
UH34 Laynce Nix 4.00 10.00
UH35 Tom Gorzelanny 4.00 10.00
UH36 Paul Konerko/Jermaine Dye 6.00 15.00
UH37 Adam Kennedy 4.00 10.00
UH38 Justin Upton 6.00 15.00
UH39 Jake Fox 6.00 15.00
UH40 Carl Pavano 4.00 10.00
UH41 Xavier Paul 4.00 10.00
UH42 Eric Hinske 4.00 10.00
UH43 Koyie Hill 4.00 10.00
UH44 Seth Smith 4.00 10.00
UH45 Brad Ausmus 4.00 10.00
UH46 Clayton Richard 4.00 10.00
UH47 Carlos Beltran 4.00 10.00
UH48 Albert Pujols 12.00 30.00
UH49 Edwin Jackson 4.00 10.00
UH50 Gary Sheffield 4.00 10.00
UH51 Jesus Guzman 4.00 10.00
UH52 Kyle Blanks 6.00 15.00
UH53 Clete Thomas 4.00 10.00
UH54 Vin Mazzaro 4.00 10.00
UH55 Ben Zobrist 6.00 15.00
UH56 Wes Helms 4.00 10.00
UH57 Juan Uribe 4.00 10.00
UH58 Omar Quintanilla 4.00 10.00
UH59 David Ross 4.00 10.00
UH60 Brandon Inge 4.00 10.00
UH61 Jamie Hoffmann 4.00 10.00
UH62 Russell Branyan 4.00 10.00
UH63 Mark Rzepczynski 6.00 15.00
UH64 Alex Gonzalez 4.00 10.00
UH65 Joe Mauer 8.00 20.00
UH66 Jhoulys Chacin 6.00 15.00
UH67 Brandon McCarthy 4.00 10.00
UH68 David Eckstein 4.00 10.00
UH69 J.Girardi/D.Jeter 25.00 60.00
UH70 Wilkin Ramirez 4.00 10.00
UH71 Chase Utley 6.00 15.00
UH72 John Mayberry Jr. 6.00 15.00
UH73 Sean West 6.00 15.00
UH74 Mitch Maier 4.00 10.00
UH75 Matt Lindstrom 4.00 10.00
UH76 Scott Rolen 6.00 15.00
UH77 Jeremy Reed 4.00 10.00
UH78 LaTroy Hawkins 4.00 10.00
UH79 Robert Andino 4.00 10.00
UH80 Matt Stairs 4.00 10.00
UH81 Mark Teixeira 6.00 15.00
UH82 David Wright 8.00 20.00
UH83 Emilio Bonifacio 4.00 10.00
UH84 Gerardo Parra 6.00 15.00
UH85 Joe Crede 6.00 15.00
UH86 Carlos Pena 6.00 15.00
UH87 Jake Peavy 4.00 10.00
UH88 Jim Leyland/Tony La Russa 4.00 10.00
UH89 Phil Hughes 4.00 10.00
UH90 Orlando Cabrera 4.00 10.00
UH91 Anderson Hernandez 4.00 10.00
UH92 Edwin Encarnacion 10.00 25.00
UH93 Pedro Martinez 6.00 15.00
UH94 Jarrod Washburn 4.00 10.00
UH95 Ryan Freel 4.00 10.00
UH96 Tony Gwynn 4.00 10.00
UH97 Juan Castro 4.00 10.00
UH98 Hanley Ramirez 6.00 15.00
UH99 Kevin Gregg 4.00 10.00
UH100 CC Sabathia 6.00 15.00
UH101 Nick Green 4.00 10.00
UH102 Brett Hayes 4.00 10.00
UH103 Evan Longoria 6.00 15.00
UH104 Geoff Blum 4.00 10.00
UH105 Luis Valbuena 6.00 15.00
UH106 Jonny Gomes 4.00 10.00
UH107 Anthony Swarzak 4.00 10.00
UH108 Chris Tillman 6.00 15.00
UH109 Orlando Hudson 4.00 10.00
UH110 Justin Masterson 4.00 10.00
UH111 Livan Hernandez 4.00 10.00
UH112 Kyle Farnsworth 4.00 10.00
UH113 Francisco Rodriguez 6.00 15.00
UH114 Chris Coghlan 10.00 25.00
UH115 Jeff Weaver 4.00 10.00
UH116 Alfredo Figaro 4.00 10.00
UH117 Alex Rios 4.00 10.00
UH118 Blake Hawksworth 4.00 10.00
UH119 Bud Norris 4.00 10.00
UH120 Aaron Poreda 4.00 10.00
UH121 Brandon Inge 4.00 10.00
UH122 Youk/Wrig/Jet/Vict 25.00 60.00
UH123 Ryan Braun 6.00 15.00
UH124 Delwyn Young 6.00 15.00
UH125 Fernando Martinez 10.00 25.00
UH126 Matt Tolbert 4.00 10.00
UH127 Shane Robinson 4.00 10.00
UH128 Chone Figgins 4.00 10.00
UH129 Shane Victorino 4.00 10.00
UH130 Randy Johnson 10.00 25.00
UH131 Derek Jeter 25.00 60.00
UH132 Joe Thurston 4.00 10.00
UH133 Graham Taylor 6.00 15.00
UH134 Derek Holland 6.00 15.00
UH135 R.Perry/R.Porcello 12.00 30.00
UH136 Raul Ibanez 6.00 15.00
UH137 Ross Ohlendorf 4.00 10.00
UH138 Ryan Church 4.00 10.00
UH139 Brian Moehler 4.00 10.00
UH140 Jack Wilson 4.00 10.00
UH141 Jason Hammel 4.00 10.00
UH142 Jorge Posada 6.00 15.00
UH143 Matt Maloney 4.00 10.00
UH144 Ronny Cedeno 4.00 10.00
UH145 Micah Hoffpauir 4.00 10.00
UH146 Juan Cruz 4.00 10.00
UH147 Jayson Nix 4.00 10.00
UH148 Jason Bay 6.00 15.00
UH149 Joel Hanrahan 6.00 15.00
UH150 Raul Ibanez 6.00 15.00
UH151 Jayson Werth 6.00 15.00
UH152 Barbaro Canizares 4.00 10.00
UH153 Ichiro Suzuki 12.00 30.00
UH154 Gerardo Parra 6.00 15.00
UH155 Andrew McCutchen 20.00 50.00
UH156 Heath Bell 4.00 10.00
UH157 Josh Hamilton 6.00 15.00
UH158 Wilson Valdez 4.00 10.00
UH159 Chad Billingsley 6.00 15.00
UH160 Edgar Renteria 4.00 10.00
UH161 Andrew Bailey 10.00 25.00
UH162 Chris Perez 4.00 10.00
UH163 Alejandro De Aza 4.00 10.00
UH164 Brett Tomko 4.00 10.00
UH165 Maicer Izturis 4.00 10.00
UH166 Mike Redmond 4.00 10.00
UH167 Julio Borbon 4.00 10.00
UH168 Paul Phillips 4.00 10.00
UH169 Mark Kotsay 4.00 10.00
UH170 Jason Giambi 4.00 10.00
UH171 Trevor Hoffman 6.00 15.00
UH172 Tyler Greene 4.00 10.00
UH173 David Robertson 4.00 10.00
UH174 Omar Vizquel 6.00 15.00
UH175 Jody Gerut 4.00 10.00
UH176 Diory Hernandez 4.00 10.00
UH177 Neftali Feliz 6.00 15.00
UH178 Josh Beckett 4.00 10.00
UH179 Carl Crawford 6.00 15.00
UH180 Mariano Rivera 12.00 30.00
UH181 Zach Duke 4.00 10.00
UH182 Mark Buehrle 6.00 15.00
UH183 Guillermo Quiroz 4.00 10.00
UH184 Francisco Cordero 4.00 10.00
UH185 Kevin Correia 4.00 10.00
UH186 Zack Greinke 10.00 25.00
UH187 Ryan Franklin 6.00 15.00
UH188 Jeff Francouer 6.00 15.00
UH189 Young/Hamil/Kinsler 6.00 15.00
UH190 Ken Griffey Jr. 20.00 50.00
UH191 Ben Zobrist 6.00 15.00
UH192 Prince Fielder 6.00 15.00
UH193 Landon Powell 4.00 10.00
UH194 Ty Wigginton 6.00 15.00
UH195 P.J. Walters 4.00 10.00
UH196 Brian Fuentes 4.00 10.00
UH197 Dan Haren 4.00 10.00
UH198 Roy Halladay 6.00 15.00
UH199 Mike Rivera 4.00 10.00
UH200 Randy Johnson 10.00 25.00
UH201 Jordan Zimmermann 10.00 25.00
UH202 Angel Berroa 4.00 10.00
UH203 Ben Francisco 4.00 10.00
UH204 Brian Barden 4.00 10.00
UH205 Dallas Braden 4.00 10.00
UH206 Chris Burke 4.00 10.00
UH207 Garrett Jones 6.00 15.00
UH208 Chad Gaudin 4.00 10.00
UH209 Andruw Jones 4.00 10.00
UH210 Jason Vargas 4.00 10.00
UH211 Brad Bergesen 4.00 10.00
UH212 Ian Kinsler 6.00 15.00
UH213 Josh Johnson 6.00 15.00
UH214 Jason Grilli 4.00 10.00
UH215 Felix Hernandez 6.00 15.00
UH216 Mat Latos 12.00 30.00
UH217 Craig Stammen 4.00 10.00
UH218 Cliff Lee 6.00 15.00
UH219 Ken Takahashi 6.00 15.00
UH220 Matt LaPorta 6.00 15.00
UH221 Adrian Gonzalez 8.00 20.00
UH222 Ted Lilly 4.00 10.00
UH223 Jack Hannahan 4.00 10.00
UH224 Takashi Saito 4.00 10.00
UH225 Gregorio Petit 4.00 10.00
UH226 Kevin Hart 4.00 10.00
UH227 Edwin Jackson 4.00 10.00
UH228 Jason LaRue 4.00 10.00
UH229 Kevin Millar 4.00 10.00
UH230 Freddy Sanchez 4.00 10.00
UH231 Josh Bard 4.00 10.00
UH232 Tim Lincecum 6.00 15.00
UH233 Ramon Santiago 4.00 10.00
UH234 Mike Sweeney 4.00 10.00
UH235 Joe Nathan 4.00 10.00
UH236 Kris Benson 4.00 10.00
UH237 Dustin Pedroia 10.00 25.00
UH238 Kevin Cash 4.00 10.00
UH239 George Sherrill 4.00 10.00
UH240 Jason Marquis 4.00 10.00
UH241 Dewayne Wise 4.00 10.00
UH242 Randy Wells 4.00 10.00
UH243 Jonathan Papelbon 6.00 15.00
UH244 Johan Santana 6.00 15.00
UH245 Mariano Rivera 12.00 30.00
UH246 Javier Vazquez 4.00 10.00
UH247 Lastings Milledge 4.00 10.00
UH248 Chan Ho Park 6.00 15.00
UH249 Brian McCann 6.00 15.00
UH250 Mark Teixeira 6.00 15.00
UH251 Ian Snell 4.00 10.00
UH252 Justin Verlander 10.00 25.00
UH253 Prince Fielder 6.00 15.00
UH254 Cesar Izturis 4.00 10.00
UH255 Omir Santos 4.00 10.00
UH256 Tim Wakefield 6.00 15.00
UH257 Adrian Gonzalez 8.00 20.00
UH258 Nyjer Morgan 4.00 10.00
UH259 Victor Martinez 6.00 15.00
UH260 Ryan Howard 8.00 20.00
UH261 Aaron Bates 4.00 10.00
UH262 Jeff Niemann 4.00 10.00
UH263 Matt Holliday 10.00 25.00
UH264 Adam LaRoche 4.00 10.00
UH265 Justin Morneau 6.00 15.00
UH266 Jonathan Broxton 4.00 10.00
UH267 Miguel Cairo 4.00 10.00
UH268 Chris Getz 4.00 10.00
UH269 Cliff Floyd 4.00 10.00
UH270 D.Ortiz/A.Rodriguez 12.00 30.00
UH271 Frank Catalanotto 4.00 10.00
UH272 Carlos Pena 6.00 15.00
UH273 Mark Lowe 4.00 10.00
UH274 Joe Mauer 8.00 20.00
UH275 Ryan Garko 4.00 10.00
UH276 Brad Penny 4.00 10.00
UH277 Orlando Hudson 4.00 10.00
UH278 Gaby Sanchez 6.00 15.00
UH279 Ross Detwiler 4.00 10.00
UH280 Mark DeRosa 6.00 15.00
UH281 Kevin Youkilis 6.00 15.00
UH282 Victor Martinez 6.00 15.00
UH283 Freddy Sanchez 4.00 10.00
UH284 Mark Melancon 4.00 10.00
UH285 Ryan Franklin 6.00 15.00
UH286 Sidney Ponson 4.00 10.00
UH287 Matt Joyce 4.00 10.00
UH288 Jon Garland 4.00 10.00
UH289 Nick Johnson 4.00 10.00
UH290 Jason Michaels 4.00 10.00
UH291 Ross Gload 4.00 10.00
UH292 Yuniesky Betancourt 4.00 10.00
UH293 Aaron Hill 4.00 10.00
UH294 Josh Anderson 4.00 10.00
UH295 Miguel Tejada 6.00 15.00
UH296 Casey McGehee 4.00 10.00
UH297 Brett Cecil 4.00 10.00
UH298 Jason Bartlett 4.00 10.00
UH299 Ryan Langerhans 4.00 10.00
UH300 Albert Pujols 12.00 30.00
UH301 Ryan Zimmerman 6.00 15.00
UH302 Casey Kotchman 4.00 10.00
UH303 Luke French 4.00 10.00
UH304 Nick Swisher/Johnny Damon 6.00 15.00
UH305 Michael Young 4.00 10.00
UH306 Endy Chavez 4.00 10.00
UH307 Heath Bell 4.00 10.00
UH308 Matt Cain 6.00 15.00
UH309 Scott Podsednik 4.00 10.00
UH310 Scott Richmond 4.00 10.00
UH311 David Huff 4.00 10.00
UH312 Ryan Hanigan 4.00 10.00
UH313 Jeff Baker 4.00 10.00
UH314 Brad Hawpe 4.00 10.00
UH315 Jerry Hairston Jr. 4.00 10.00
UH316 H.Pence/R.Braun 6.00 15.00
UH317 Nelson Cruz 10.00 25.00
UH318 Carl Crawford 6.00 15.00
UH319 Ramon Castro 4.00 10.00
UH320 Mark Schlereth/Daniel Schlereth 4.00 10.00
UH321 Hunter Pence 6.00 15.00
UH322 Sean Marshall 4.00 10.00
UH323 Ramon Ramirez 4.00 10.00
UH324 Nolan Reimold 4.00 10.00
UH325 Torii Hunter 4.00 10.00
UH326 Nate McLouth 4.00 10.00
UH327 Julio Lugo 4.00 10.00
UH328 Matt Palmer 4.00 10.00
UH329 Curtis Granderson 8.00 20.00
UH330 Ken Griffey Jr. 20.00 50.00

2009 Topps Update Gold Border

*GOLD VET: 2.5X TO 6X BASIC
*GOLD RC: .75X TO 2X BASIC RC
STATED ODDS 1:3 HOBBY
STATED PRINT RUN 2009 SER.#'d SETS

2009 Topps Update Target

*VETS: .5X TO 1.2X BASIC TOPPS CARDS
*RC: .5X TO 1.2X BASIC TOPSP RC CARDS

2009 Topps Update All-Star Stitches

STATED ODDS 1:58 HOBBY
AST1 Chase Utley 5.00 12.00
AST2 Nelson Cruz 3.00 8.00
AST3 Adam Jones 4.00 10.00
AST4 Justin Upton 3.00 8.00
AST5 Albert Pujols 15.00 40.00
AST6 Ben Zobrist 4.00 10.00
AST7 Joe Mauer 5.00 12.00
AST8 Yadier Molina 3.00 8.00
AST9 Mark Teixeira 5.00 12.00
AST10 David Wright 5.00 12.00
AST11 Carlos Pena 3.00 8.00
AST12 Hanley Ramirez 4.00 10.00
AST13 Adrian Gonzalez 4.00 10.00
AST14 Francisco Rodriguez 4.00 10.00
AST15 Evan Longoria 6.00 15.00
AST16 Brandon Inge 5.00 12.00
AST17 Shane Victorino 5.00 12.00
AST18 Raul Ibanez 5.00 12.00
AST19 Jason Bay 4.00 10.00
AST20 Jayson Werth 6.00 15.00
AST21 Ichiro Suzuki 10.00 25.00
AST22 Heath Bell 3.00 8.00
AST23 Andrew Bailey 3.00 8.00
AST24 Chad Billingsley 3.00 8.00
AST25 Josh Hamilton 4.00 10.00
AST26 Trevor Hoffman 3.00 8.00
AST27 Josh Beckett 4.00 10.00
AST28 Zach Duke 4.00 10.00
AST29 Mark Buehrle 3.00 8.00
AST30 Zack Greinke 5.00 12.00
AST31 Francisco Cordero 3.00 8.00
AST32 Ryan Franklin 12.50 30.00
AST33 Brian Fuentes 3.00 8.00
AST34 Dan Haren 3.00 8.00
AST35 Roy Halladay 4.00 10.00
AST36 Josh Johnson 3.00 8.00
AST37 Felix Hernandez 4.00 10.00
AST38 Ted Lilly 3.00 8.00
AST39 Edwin Jackson 4.00 10.00
AST40 Tim Lincecum 6.00 15.00
AST41 Joe Nathan 4.00 10.00
AST42 Jason Marquis 3.00 8.00
AST43 Jonathan Papelbon 3.00 8.00
AST44 Johan Santana 4.00 10.00
AST45 Mariano Rivera 4.00 10.00
AST46 Brian McCann 4.00 10.00
AST47 Justin Verlander 5.00 12.00
AST48 Prince Fielder 4.00 10.00
AST49 Tim Wakefield 3.00 8.00
AST50 Ryan Braun 4.00 10.00
AST51 Victor Martinez 3.00 8.00
AST52 Ryan Zimmerman 3.00 8.00
AST53 Orlando Hudson 3.00 8.00
AST54 Kevin Youkilis 3.00 8.00
AST55 Freddy Sanchez 3.00 8.00
AST56 Aaron Hill 4.00 10.00
AST57 Miguel Tejada 3.00 8.00
AST58 Jason Bartlett 3.00 8.00
AST59 Ryan Howard 8.00 20.00
AST60 Michael Young 3.00 8.00
AST61 Brad Hawpe 3.00 8.00
AST62 Carl Crawford 3.00 8.00
AST63 Hunter Pence 3.00 8.00
AST64 Curtis Granderson 4.00 10.00
AST65 Jonathan Broxton 3.00 8.00
AST66 Matt Cain 3.00 8.00

2009 Topps Update All-Star Stitches Gold

*GOLD: .75X TO 2X BASIC
STATED ODDS 1:616 HOBBY
STATED PRINT RUN 50 SER.#'d SETS

2009 Topps Update Career Quest Autographs

STATED ODDS 1:546 HOBBY
AM Andrew McCutchen 10.00 25.00
DH David Hernandez 3.00 8.00
DS Daniel Schlereth 3.00 8.00
GB Gordon Beckham 4.00 10.00
JZ Jordan Zimmermann 4.00 10.00
KU Koji Uehara 8.00 20.00
MG Mat Gamel 4.00 10.00
RB Reid Brignac 4.00 10.00
RP Ryan Perry 4.00 10.00
TH Tommy Hanson 5.00 12.00
VM Vin Mazzaro 4.00 10.00
RPO Rick Porcello 4.00 10.00

2009 Topps Update Chrome Rookie Refractors

ONE PER BOX TOPPER
CHR1 Michael Saunders 5.00 12.00
CHR2 David Hernandez 2.00 5.00

CHR3 Tommy Hanson 5.00 12.00
CHR4 Daniel Schlereth 2.00 5.00
CHR5 Gordon Beckham 4.00 10.00
CHR6 Sean O'Sullivan 2.00 5.00
CHR7 Josh Reddick 3.00 8.00
CHR8 Kris Medlen 5.00 12.00
CHR9 Daniel Bard 2.00 5.00
CHR10 Xavier Paul 2.00 5.00
CHR11 Jesus Guzman 2.00 5.00
CHR12 Kyle Blanks 3.00 8.00
CHR13 Vin Mazzaro 2.00 5.00
CHR14 Jamie Hoffmann 2.00 5.00
CHR15 Mark Rzepczynski 3.00 8.00
CHR16 Jhoulys Chacin 3.00 8.00
CHR17 Wilkin Ramirez 2.00 5.00
CHR18 John Mayberry Jr. 3.00 8.00
CHR19 Sean West 3.00 8.00
CHR20 Gerardo Parra 3.00 8.00
CHR21 Brett Hayes 2.00 5.00
CHR22 Anthony Swarzak 2.00 5.00
CHR23 Chris Tillman 3.00 8.00
CHR24 Chris Coghlan 5.00 12.00
CHR25 Alfredo Figaro 2.00 5.00
CHR26 Blake Hawksworth 2.00 5.00
CHR27 Bud Norris 2.00 5.00
CHR28 Aaron Poreda 2.00 5.00
CHR29 Fernando Martinez 5.00 12.00
CHR30 Shane Robinson 2.00 5.00
CHR31 Graham Taylor 3.00 8.00
CHR32 Derek Holland 3.00 8.00
CHR33 Matt Maloney 2.00 5.00
CHR34 Barbaro Canizares 2.00 5.00
CHR35 Andrew McCutchen 10.00 25.00
CHR36 Julio Borbon 2.00 5.00
CHR37 Tyler Greene 2.00 5.00
CHR38 Diory Hernandez 2.00 5.00
CHR39 Neftali Feliz 3.00 8.00
CHR40 Landon Powell 2.00 5.00
CHR41 P.J. Walters 2.00 5.00
CHR42 Jordan Zimmermann 5.00 12.00
CHR43 Brad Bergesen 2.00 5.00
CHR44 Mat Latos 6.00 15.00
CHR45 Craig Stammen 2.00 5.00
CHR46 Ken Takahashi 3.00 8.00
CHR47 Matt LaPorta 3.00 8.00
CHR48 Omir Santos 2.00 5.00
CHR49 Aaron Bates 2.00 5.00
CHR50 Gaby Sanchez 3.00 8.00
CHR51 Mark Melancon 2.00 5.00
CHR52 Brett Cecil 2.00 5.00
CHR53 Luke French 2.00 5.00
CHR54 David Huff 2.00 5.00
CHR55 Nolan Reimold 2.00 5.00

2009 Topps Update Legends of the Game Team Name Letter Patch

STATED ODDS 1:408 HOBBY
STATED PRINT RUN 50 SER.#'d SETS
BR Babe Ruth/50 * 10.00 25.00
CM Christy Mathewson/50 * 4.00 10.00
CY Cy Young/50 * 4.00 10.00
GS George Sisler/50 * 4.00 10.00
HW Honus Wagner/50 * 6.00 15.00
JF Jimmie Foxx/50 * 8.00 20.00
JM Johnny Mize/50 * 4.00 10.00
JR Jackie Robinson/50 * 6.00 15.00
LG Lou Gehrig/50 * 12.50 30.00
MM Mickey Mantle/50 * 12.50 30.00
PR Pee Wee Reese/50 * 6.00 15.00
RC Roy Campanella/50 * 10.00 25.00
RH Rogers Hornsby/50 * 12.50 30.00
TC Ty Cobb/50 * 10.00 25.00
TM Thurman Munson/50 * 10.00 25.00
TS Tris Speaker/50 * 4.00 10.00
WJ Walter Johnson/50 * 8.00 20.00
BR2 Babe Ruth/50 * 10.00 25.00

2009 Topps Update Propaganda

COMPLETE SET (30) 8.00 20.00
STATED ODDS 1:6 HOBBY
PP01 Adam Dunn .50 1.25
PP02 Adrian Gonzalez .60 1.50
PP03 Albert Pujols 1.00 2.50
PP04 Andrew McCutchen 1.50 4.00
PP05 Alfonso Soriano .50 1.25
PP06 Carlos Quentin .30 .75
PP07 Chipper Jones .75 2.00
PP08 David Wright .60 1.50
PP09 Dustin Pedroia .75 2.00
PP10 Evan Longoria .50 1.25
PP11 Grady Sizemore .50 1.25
PP12 Hanley Ramirez .50 1.25
PP13 Hunter Pence .50 1.25
PP14 Ichiro Suzuki 1.00 2.50
PP15 Andrew Bailey .75 2.00
PP16 Jay Bruce .50 1.25
PP17 Joe Mauer .60 1.50
PP18 Josh Hamilton .50 1.25
PP19 Justin Upton .50 1.25
PP20 Manny Ramirez .75 2.00
PP21 Mark Teixeira .50 1.25
PP22 Miguel Cabrera .75 2.00
PP23 Nick Markakis .60 1.50
PP24 Roy Halladay .50 1.25
PP25 Ryan Braun .50 1.25
PP26 Ryan Howard .60 1.50
PP27 Tim Lincecum .50 1.25
PP28 Todd Helton .50 1.25
PP29 Vladimir Guerrero .50 1.25
PP30 Zack Greinke .75 2.00

2009 Topps Update Stadium Stamp Collection

STATED ODDS 1:2280 HOBBY
STATED PRINT RUN 90 SER.#'d SETS
SSC1 Polo Grounds 12.50 30.00
SSC2 Forbes Field 10.00 25.00
SSC3 Wrigley Field 12.50 30.00
SSC4 Yankee Stadium 15.00 40.00
SSC5 Tiger Stadium 12.50 30.00
SSC6 Shibe Park 10.00 25.00
SSC7 Crosley Field 10.00 25.00
SSC8 Comiskey Park 10.00 25.00
SSC9 Fenway Park 12.50 30.00
SSC10 Ebbets Field 10.00 25.00

2010 Topps

COMP.HOBBY.SET (661) 40.00 80.00
COMP.ALLSTAR.SET (661) 40.00 80.00
COMP.PHILLIES SET (661) 40.00 80.00
COMP.RED SOX SET (661) 40.00 80.00
COMP.YANKEES SET (661) 40.00 80.00
COMP.SET w/o SPs (660) 30.00 60.00
COMP.SER. 1 SET w/o SPs (330) 12.50 30.00
COMP.SER. 2 SET w/o SPs (330) 12.50 30.00
COMMON CARD (1-660) .15 .40
COMMON RC (1-660) .25 .60
COMMON SP VAR (1-660) 5.00 12.00
COMMON PIE SP (1-660) 15.00 40.00
SER. 1 PRINTING PLATE ODDS 1:1417 HOBBY
SER. 2 PRINTING PLATE ODDS 1:1642 HOBBY
661B ISSUED IN FACTORY SETS
1A Prince Fielder .25 .60
1B H.Greenberg SP 6.00 15.00
2 Buster Posey RC 6.00 15.00
3 Derrek Lee .15 .40
4 Hanley/Pablo/Pujols .50 1.25
5 Texas Rangers .15 .40
6 Chicago White Sox .15 .40
7 Mickey Mantle 1.25 3.00
8 Mauer/Ichiro/Jeter 1.00 2.50
9 T.Lincecum NL CY .25 .60
10 Clayton Kershaw .60 1.50
11 Orlando Cabrera .15 .40
12 Doug Davis .15 .40
13A Melvin Mora COR .15 .40
Mora pictured on back
13B Melvin Mora ERR
Adam Jones pictured on back
14 Ted Lilly .15 .40
15 Bobby Abreu .15 .40
16 Johnny Cueto .25 .60
17 Dexter Fowler .25 .60
18 Tim Stauffer .15 .40
19 Felipe Lopez .15 .40
20A Tommy Hanson .15 .40
20B Warren Spahn SP 5.00 12.00
21 Cristian Guzman .15 .40
22 Anthony Swarzak .15 .40
23 Shane Victorino .25 .60
24 John Maine .15 .40
25 Adam Jones .25 .60
26 Zach Duke .15 .40
27 Lance Berkman/Mike Hampton .25 .60
28 Jonathan Sanchez .15 .40
29 Aubrey Huff .15 .40
30 Victor Martinez .25 .60
31 Jason Grilli .15 .40
32 Cincinnati Reds .15 .40
33 Adam Moore RC .25 .60
34 Michael Dunn RC .25 .60
35 Rick Porcello .25 .60
36 Tobi Stoner RC .40 1.00
37 Garret Anderson .15 .40
38 Houston Astros .15 .40
39 Jeff Baker .15 .40
40 Josh Johnson .25 .60
41 Los Angeles Dodgers .25 .60
42 Prince/Howard/Pujols .50 1.25
43 Marco Scutaro .25 .60
44 Howie Kendrick .15 .40
45 David Hernandez .15 .40
46 Chad Tracy .15 .40
47 Brad Penny .15 .40
48 Joey Votto .40 1.00
49 Jorge De La Rosa .15 .40
50A Zack Greinke .40 1.00
50B C.Young SP 5.00 12.00
51 Eric Young Jr .15 .40
52 Billy Butler .15 .40
53 Craig Counsell .15 .40
54 John Lackey .25 .60
55 Manny Ramirez .40 1.00
56A Andy Pettitte .25 .60
56B W.Ford SP 6.00 15.00
57 CC Sabathia .25 .60
58 Kyle Blanks .15 .40
59 Kevin Gregg .15 .40
60 David Wright .30 .75
61 Skip Schumaker .15 .40
62 Kevin Millwood .15 .40
63 Josh Bard .15 .40
64 Drew Stubbs RC .60 1.50
65A Nick Swisher .25 .60
65B N.Swisher Pie 100.00 200.00
66 Kyle Phillips RC .25 .60
67 Matt LaPorta .15 .40
68 Brandon Inge .25 .60
69 Kansas City Royals .15 .40
70 Cole Hamels .30 .75
71 Mike Hampton .15 .40
72 Milwaukee Brewers .15 .40
73 Adam Wainwright/Chris Carpenter/Jorge De La Rosa .25 .60
74 Casey Blake .15 .40
75 Adrian Gonzalez .30 .75
76 Joe Saunders .15 .40
77 Kenshin Kawakami .25 .60
78 Cesar Izturis .15 .40
79 Francisco Cordero .15 .40
80A Tim Lincecum .25 .60
80B C.Mathewson SP 6.00 15.00
81 Ryan Theriot .15 .40
82 Jason Marquis .15 .40
83 Mark Teahen .15 .40
84 Nate Robertson .15 .40
85A Ken Griffey Jr. .75 2.00
85B J.Robinson SP 6.00 15.00
86 Gil Meche .15 .40
87 Darin Erstad .15 .40
88A Jerry Hairston Jr. .15 .40
88B J.Hairston Jr. Pie 15.00 40.00
89 J.A. Happ .25 .60
90A Ian Kinsler .25 .60
90B R.Hornsby SP 6.00 15.00
91 Erik Bedard .15 .40
92 David Eckstein .15 .40
93 Joe Nathan .15 .40
94A Ivan Rodriguez .25 .60
94B C.Fisk SP 6.00 15.00
95A Carl Crawford .25 .60
95B R.Henderson SP 6.00 15.00
96 Jon Garland .15 .40
97 Luis Durango RC .25 .60
98 Cesar Ramos (RC) .25 .60
99 Garrett Jones .15 .40
100A Albert Pujols .50 1.25
100B S.Musial SP 6.00 15.00
101 Scott Baker .15 .40
102 Minnesota Twins .15 .40
103 Daniel Murphy .30 .75
104 New York Mets .25 .60
105 Madison Bumgarner RC 2.50 6.00
106 Carp/Lince/Jurrjens .25 .60
107 Scott Hairston .15 .40
108 Erick Aybar .15 .40
109 Justin Masterson .15 .40
110A Andrew McCutchen .40 1.00
110B W.Stargell SP 6.00 15.00
111 Ty Wigginton .15 .40
112 Kevin Correia .15 .40
113 Willy Taveras .15 .40
114 Chris Iannetta .15 .40
115 Gordon Beckham .15 .40
116A Carlos Gomez .15 .40
116B R.Yount SP 6.00 15.00
117 David DeJesus .15 .40
118 Brandon Morrow .15 .40
119 Wilkin Ramirez .15 .40
120A Jorge Posada .25 .60
120B J.Posada Pie 30.00 60.00
121 Brett Anderson .15 .40
122 Carlos Ruiz .15 .40
123A Jeff Samardzija .15 .40
123B Samardzija Abe SP 75.00 150.00
124 Rickie Weeks .15 .40
125A Ichiro Suzuki .50 1.25
125B G.Sisler SP 5.00 12.00
126 John Smoltz .40 1.00
127 Hank Blalock .15 .40
128 Garrett Mock .15 .40
129 Reid Gorecki (RC) .40 1.00
130A Vladimir Guerrero .25 .60
130B R.Jackson SP 5.00 12.00
131 Dustin Richardson RC .25 .60
132 Cliff Lee .25 .60
133 Freddy Sanchez .15 .40
134 Philadelphia Phillies .15 .40
135A Ryan Dempster .15 .40
135B Dempster Abe SP 75.00 150.00
136 Adam Wainwright .25 .60
137 A's/R.Henderson .40 1.00
138 Carlos Pena/Mark Teixeira/Jason Bay .25 .60
139 Frank Francisco .15 .40
140 Matt Holliday .40 1.00
141 Chone Figgins .15 .40
142 Tim Hudson .25 .60
143 Omar Vizquel .25 .60
144 Rich Harden .15 .40
145 Justin Upton .25 .60
146 Yunel Escobar .15 .40
147 Huston Street .15 .40
148 Cody Ross .15 .40
149 Jose Guillen .15 .40
150 Joe Mauer .30 .75
151 Mat Gamel .15 .40
152 Nyjer Morgan .15 .40
153 Justin Duchscherer .15 .40
154 Pedro Feliz .15 .40
155 Zack Greinke AL CY .40 1.00
156 Tony Gwynn Jr. .15 .40
157 Mike Sweeney .15 .40
158 Jeff Niemann .15 .40
159 Vernon Wells .15 .40
160 Miguel Tejada .25 .60
161 Denard Span .15 .40
162 Wade Davis (RC) .40 1.00
163 Josh Butler RC .25 .60
164 Carlos Carrasco (RC) .60 1.50
165A Brandon Phillips .15 .40
165B J.Morgan SP 5.00 12.00
166 Eric Byrnes .15 .40
167 San Diego Padres .15 .40
168 Brad Kilby RC .25 .60
169 Pittsburgh Pirates .15 .40
170 Jason Bay .25 .60
171 Felix/CC/Verland .40 1.00
172 Joe Mauer AL MVP .30 .75
173 Kendry Morales .15 .40
174 Mike Gonzalez .15 .40
175A Josh Hamilton .25 .60
175B R.Maris SP 6.00 15.00
176 Yovani Gallardo .15 .40
177 Adam Lind .25 .60
178 Kerry Wood .15 .40
179 Ryan Spilborghs .15 .40
180 Jayson Nix .15 .40
181 Nick Johnson .15 .40
182 Coco Crisp .15 .40
183 Jonathan Papelbon .25 .60
184 Jeff Francoeur .25 .60
185A Hideki Matsui .40 1.00
185B H.Matsui Pie 40.00 80.00
186 Andrew Bailey .15 .40
187 Will Venable .15 .40
188 Joe Blanton .15 .40
189 Adrian Beltre .40 1.00
190 Pablo Sandoval .25 .60
191 Mat Latos .25 .60
192 Andruw Jones .15 .40
193 Shairon Martis .15 .40
194 Neill Walker (RC) .40 1.00
195 James Shields .15 .40
196 Ian Desmond (RC) .40 1.00
197 Cleveland Indians .15 .40
198 Florida Marlins .15 .40
199 Seattle Mariners .15 .40
200A Roy Halladay .25 .60
200B W.Johnson SP 6.00 15.00
201 Detroit Tigers .15 .40
202 San Francisco Giants .15 .40
203 Zack Greinke/Felix Hernandez/Roy Halladay .40 1.00
204 Elvis Andrus/Ian Kinsler .25 .60
205 Chris Coghlan .15 .40
206 Pujols/Prince/Howard .50 1.25
207 Colby Rasmus .25 .60
208 Tim Wakefield .25 .60
209 Alexei Ramirez .25 .60
210 Josh Beckett .15 .40
211 Kelly Shoppach .15 .40
212 Magglio Ordonez .25 .60
213 Ricky Nolasco .15 .40
214 Matt Kemp .30 .75
215 Max Scherzer .40 1.00
216 Mike Cameron .15 .40
217 Gio Gonzalez .25 .60
218 Fernando Martinez .15 .40
219 Kevin Hart .15 .40
220 Randy Johnson .40 1.00
221 Russell Branyan .15 .40
222A Curtis Granderson .30 .75
Tigers
222B Granderson SP Yanks 10.00 25.00
223 Ryan Church .15 .40
224 Rod Barajas .15 .40
225A David Price .30 .75
225B D.Price Pie 12.50 30.00
226 Juan Rivera .15 .40
227 Josh Thole RC .40 1.00
228 Chris Pettit RC .25 .60
229 Daniel McCutchen RC .40 1.00
230 Jonathan Broxton .15 .40
231 Luke Scott .15 .40
232 St. Louis Cardinals .25 .60
233 Mark Teixeira/Jason Bay/Adam Lind .25 .60
234 Tampa Bay Rays .15 .40
235 Neftali Feliz .15 .40
236 Andrew Bailey AL ROY .15 .40
237 R.Braun/P.Fielder .25 .60
238 Ian Stewart .15 .40
239 Juan Uribe .15 .40
240 Ricky Romero .15 .40
241 Rocco Baldelli .15 .40
242 Bobby Jenks .15 .40
243 Asdrubal Cabrera .25 .60
244 Barry Zito .25 .60
245 Lance Berkman .25 .60
246 Leo Nunez .15 .40
247 Andre Ethier .25 .60
248 Jason Kendall .15 .40
249 Jon Niese .15 .40
250A Mark Teixeira .25 .60
250B M.Teixeira Pie 30.00 60.00
250C L.Gehrig SP 8.00 20.00
251 John Lannan .15 .40
252 Ronny Cedeno .15 .40
253 Bengie Molina .15 .40
254 Edwin Jackson .15 .40
255 Chris Davis .25 .60
256 Akinori Iwamura .15 .40
257 Bobby Crosby .15 .40
258 Edwin Encarnacion .40 1.00
259 Daniel Hudson RC .40 1.00
260 New York Yankees .40 1.00
261 Matt Carson (RC) .25 .60
262 Homer Bailey .15 .40
263 Placido Polanco .15 .40
264 Arizona Diamondbacks .15 .40
265 Los Angeles Angels .15 .40
266 Humberto Quintero .15 .40
267 Toronto Blue Jays .15 .40
268 Juan Pierre .15 .40
269 ARod/Jeter/Cano 1.00 2.50
270 Michael Brantley RC .40 1.00
271 Jermaine Dye .15 .40
272 Jair Jurrjens .15 .40
273 Pat Neshek .15 .40
274 Stephen Drew .15 .40
275 Chris Coghlan NL ROY .15 .40
276 Matt Lindstrom .15 .40
277 Jarrod Washburn .15 .40
278 Carlos Delgado .15 .40
279 Randy Wolf .15 .40
280 Mark DeRosa .15 .40
281 Braden Looper .15 .40
282 Washington Nationals .15 .40
283 Adam Kennedy .15 .40
284 Ross Ohlendorf .15 .40
285 Kurt Suzuki .15 .40
286 Javier Vazquez .15 .40
287 Jhonny Peralta .15 .40
288 Boston Red Sox .25 .60
289 Lyle Overbay .15 .40
290 Orlando Hudson .15 .40
291 Austin Kearns .15 .40
292 Tommy Manzella (RC) .25 .60
293 Brent Dlugach (RC) .25 .60
294A Adam Dunn .25 .60
294B B.Ruth SP 10.00 25.00
295 Kevin Youkilis .15 .40
296 Atlanta Braves .15 .40
297 Ben Zobrist .25 .60
298 Baltimore Orioles .15 .40
299 Gary Sheffield .15 .40
300A Chase Utley .25 .60
300B R.Sandberg SP 6.00 15.00
301 Jack Cust .15 .40
302 Kevin Youkilis/David Ortiz .40 1.00
303 Chris Snyder .15 .40
304 Adam LaRoche .15 .40
305 Juan Francisco RC .40 1.00
306A Milton Bradley .25 .60
306B M.Bradley Abe SP 60.00 120.00
307 Henry Rodriguez RC .25 .60
308 Robinzon Diaz .15 .40
309 Gerald Laird .15 .40
310 Elvis Andrus .25 .60
311 Jose Valverde .15 .40
312 Tyler Flowers RC .40 1.00
313 Jason Kubel .15 .40
314 Angel Pagan .15 .40
315 Scott Kazmir .15 .40
316 Chris Young .15 .40
317 Ryan Doumit .15 .40
318 Nate Schierholtz .15 .40
319 Ryan Franklin .15 .40
320 Brian McCann .25 .60
321 Pat Burrell .15 .40
322 Travis Buck .15 .40
323 Jim Thome .25 .60
324 Alex Rios .15 .40
325 Julio Lugo .15 .40
326A Tyler Colvin RC .40 1.00
326B Colvin Abe SP 60.00 120.00
327 A.Pujols NL MVP .50 1.25
328 Chicago Cubs .25 .60
329 Colorado Rockies .15 .40
330 Brandon Allen (RC) .25 .60
331A Ryan Braun .25 .60
331B Eddie Mathews SP 6.00 15.00
332 Brad Hawpe .15 .40
333 Ryan Ludwick .15 .40
334 Jayson Werth .25 .60
335 Jordan Norberto RC .25 .60
336 C.J. Wilson .15 .40
337 Carlos Zambrano .25 .60
338 Brett Cecil .15 .40
339 Jose Reyes .25 .60
340 John Buck .15 .40
341 Texas Rangers .15 .40
342 Melky Cabrera .15 .40
343 Brian Bruney .15 .40
344 Brett Myers .15 .40
345 Chris Volstad .15 .40
346 Taylor Teagarden .15 .40
347 Aaron Harang .15 .40
348 Jordan Zimmermann .25 .60
349 Felix Pie .15 .40
350 Prince Fielder/Ryan Braun .25 .60
351 Koji Uehara .15 .40
352 Cameron Maybin .15 .40
353A Jason Heyward RC 1.00 2.50
353B J.Heyward Pie 8.00 20.00
354A Evan Longoria .25 .60
354B Johnny Mize SP 5.00 12.00
355 James Russell RC .60 1.50
356 Los Angeles Angels .15 .40
357 Scott Downs .15 .40
358 Mark Buehrle .25 .60
359 Aramis Ramirez .15 .40
360 Justin Morneau .25 .60
361 Washington Nationals .15 .40
362 Travis Snider .15 .40
363 Joba Chamberlain .15 .40
364 Trevor Hoffman .25 .60
365 Logan Ondrusek RC .25 .60
366 Hiroki Kuroda .15 .40
367 Wandy Rodriguez .15 .40
368 Wade LeBlanc .15 .40
369a David Ortiz .40 1.00
369b Jimmie Foxx SP 6.00 15.00
370A Robinson Cano .25 .60
370B R.Cano Pie 30.00 60.00
370C R.Cano Pie 30.00 60.00
370D Mel Ott SP 6.00 15.00
371 Nick Hundley .15 .40
372 Philadelphia Phillies .15 .40
373 Clint Barmes .15 .40
374 Scott Feldman .15 .40
375 Mike Leake RC .75 2.00
376 Esmil Rogers RC .25 .60
377A Felix Hernandez .25 .60
377B Tom Seaver SP 6.00 15.00
378 George Sherrill .15 .40
379 Phil Hughes .15 .40
380 J.D. Drew .15 .40
381 Miguel Montero .15 .40
382 Kyle Davies .15 .40
383 Derek Lowe .15 .40
384 Chris Johnson RC .40 1.00
385 Torii Hunter .15 .40
386 Dan Haren .15 .40
387 Josh Fields .15 .40
388 Joel Pineiro .15 .40
389 Troy Tulowitzki .40 1.00
390 Ervin Santana .15 .40
391 Manny Parra .15 .40
392 Carlos Monasterios RC .40 1.00
393 Jason Frasor .15 .40
394 Luis Castillo .15 .40
395 Jenrry Mejia RC .40 1.00
396 Jake Westbrook .15 .40
397 Colorado Rockies .15 .40
398 Carlos Gonzalez .25 .60
399A Matt Garza .15 .40
399B M.Garza UPD Pie 12.50 30.00
400A Alex Rodriguez .50 1.25
400B A.Rodriguez Pie 75.00 150.00
400C A.Rodriguez Pie 50.00 100.00
400D Frank Robinson SP 6.00 15.00
401 Chad Billingsley .25 .60
402 J.P. Howell .15 .40
403A Jimmy Rollins .25 .60
403B Ozzie Smith SP 6.00 15.00
404 Mariano Rivera .50 1.25
405 Dustin McGowan .15 .40
406 Jeff Francis .15 .40
407 Nick Punto .15 .40
408 Detroit Tigers .15 .40
409A Kosuke Fukudome .25 .60
409B Richie Ashburn SP 10.00 25.00
410 Oakland Athletics .15 .40
411 Jack Wilson .15 .40
412 San Francisco Giants .15 .40
413 J.J. Hardy .15 .40
414 Sean West .15 .40
415 Cincinnati Reds .15 .40
416 Ruben Tejada RC .40 1.00
417 Dallas Braden .25 .60
418 Aaron Laffey .15 .40
419 David Aardsma .15 .40
420 Shin-Soo Choo .25 .60
421 Doug Fister RC .40 1.00
422A Vin Mazzaro .15 .40
422B F.Cervelli Pie 30.00 60.00
423 Brad Bergesen .15 .40
424 David Herndon RC .25 .60
425 Dontrelle Willis .15 .40
426 Mark Reynolds .15 .40
427 Brandon Webb .25 .60
428 Baltimore Orioles .15 .40
429 Seth Smith .15 .40
430 Kazuo Matsui .15 .40
431 John Raynor RC .25 .60
432 A.J. Burnett .15 .40
433 Julio Borbon .15 .40
434 Kevin Slowey .15 .40
435A Nelson Cruz .40 1.00
435B N.Cruz Pie 15.00 30.00
436 New York Mets .25 .60
437 Luke Hochevar .15 .40
438 Jason Bartlett .15 .40
439 Emilio Bonifacio .15 .40
440 Willie Harris .15 .40
441 Clete Thomas .15 .40
442 Dan Runzler RC .40 1.00
443 Jason Hammel .25 .60
444 Yuniesky Betancourt .15 .40
445 Miguel Olivo .15 .40
446 Gavin Floyd .15 .40
447 Jeremy Guthrie .15 .40
448 Joakim Soria .15 .40
449 Ryan Sweeney .15 .40
450A Omir Santos .15 .40
450B O.Santos UPD Cup SP 15.00 40.00
451 Michael Saunders .25 .60
452 Allen Craig RC .60 1.50
453 Jesse English (RC) .25 .60
454 James Loney .15 .40
455 St. Louis Cardinals .25 .60
456 Clayton Richard .15 .40
457 Kanekoa Texeira RC .25 .60
458 Todd Wellemeyer .15 .40
459 Joel Zumaya .15 .40
460 Aaron Cunningham .15 .40
461 Tyson Ross RC .25 .60
462 Alcides Escobar .25 .60
463 Carlos Marmol .25 .60
464 Francisco Liriano .15 .40
465 Chien-Ming Wang .25 .60
466 Jered Weaver .25 .60
467A Fausto Carmona .15 .40
467B M.Talbot Pie 15.00 30.00
468 Delmon Young .25 .60
469 Alex Burnett RC .25 .60
470 New York Yankees .40 1.00
471 Drew Butera (RC) .25 .60
472 Toronto Blue Jays .15 .40
473 Jason Varitek .40 1.00
474 Kyle Kendrick .15 .40
475A Johnny Damon .25 .60
475B J.Damon Pie 20.00 50.00
476A Yadier Molina .50 1.25
476B Thurman Munson SP 6.00 15.00
477 Nate McLouth .15 .40
478 Conor Jackson .15 .40
479A Chris Carpenter .25 .60
479B Dizzy Dean SP 6.00 15.00
480 Boston Red Sox .25 .60
481 Scott Rolen .25 .60
482 Mike McCoy RC .25 .60
483 Daisuke Matsuzaka .25 .60
484 Mike Fontenot .15 .40
485 Jesus Flores .15 .40
486 Raul Ibanez .25 .60
487 Dan Uggla .15 .40
488 Delwyn Young .15 .40
489A Russell Martin .15 .40
489B Roy Campanella SP 6.00 15.00
490 Michael Bourn .15 .40
491 Rafael Furcal .15 .40
492 Brian Wilson .40 1.00
493A Travis Ishikawa .15 .40
493B T.Ishikawa UPD CUP SP 12.00 30.00
494 Andrew Miller .25 .60
495 Carlos Pena .25 .60
496 Rajai Davis .15 .40
497 Edgar Renteria .15 .40
498 Sergio Santos (RC) .25 .60
499 Michael Bowden .15 .40
500 Brad Lidge .15 .40
501 Jake Peavy .15 .40
502 Jhoulys Chacin .15 .40
503 Austin Jackson RC .40 1.00
504 Jeff Mathis .15 .40
505 Andy Marte .15 .40
506 Jose Lopez .15 .40
507 Francisco Rodriguez .25 .60
508A Chris Getz .15 .40
508B C.Getz UPD Cup SP 10.00 25.00
509A Todd Helton .25 .60
509B I.Davis Pie 20.00 50.00
510 Justin Upton/Mark Reynolds .25 .60
511 Chicago Cubs .25 .60
512 Scot Shields .15 .40
513 Scott Sizemore RC .40 1.00
514 Rafael Soriano .15 .40
515 Seattle Mariners .15 .40
516 Marlon Byrd .15 .40
517 Cliff Pennington .15 .40
518 Corey Hart .15 .40
519 Alexi Casilla .15 .40
520 Randy Wells .15 .40
521 Jeremy Bonderman .15 .40
522 Jordan Schafer .15 .40
523 Phil Coke .15 .40
524 Dusty Hughes RC .25 .60
525 David Huff .15 .40
526 Carlos Guillen .15 .40
527 Brandon Wood .15 .40
528 Brian Bannister .15 .40
529 Carlos Lee .15 .40
530 Steve Pearce .40 1.00
531 Matt Cain .25 .60
532A Hunter Pence .25 .60
532B Dale Murphy SP 6.00 15.00
533 Gary Matthews Jr. .15 .40
534 Hideki Okajima .15 .40
535 Andy Sonnanstine .15 .40
536 Matt Palmer .15 .40
537 Michael Cuddyer .15 .40
538 Travis Hafner .15 .40
539 Arizona Diamondbacks .15 .40
540 Sean Rodriguez .15 .40
541 Jason Motte .15 .40
542 Heath Bell .15 .40
543 Adam Jones/Nick Markakis .30 .75
544 Kevin Kouzmanoff .15 .40
545 Fred Lewis .15 .40
546 Bud Norris .15 .40
547 Brett Gardner .25 .60
548 Minnesota Twins .15 .40
549A Derek Jeter 1.00 2.50
549B Pee Wee Reese SP 6.00 15.00
550 Freddy Garcia .15 .40
551 Everth Cabrera .15 .40
552 Chris Tillman .15 .40
553 Florida Marlins .15 .40
554 Ramon Hernandez .15 .40
555 B.J. Upton .25 .60
556 Chicago White Sox .15 .40
557 Aaron Hill .15 .40
558 Ronny Paulino .15 .40
559A Nick Markakis .30 .75
559B Eddie Murray SP 6.00 15.00
560 Ryan Rowland-Smith .15 .40
561 Ryan Zimmerman .25 .60
562 Carlos Quentin .15 .40
563 Bronson Arroyo .15 .40
564 Houston Astros .15 .40
565 Franklin Morales .15 .40
566 Maicer Izturis .15 .40
567 Mike Pelfrey .15 .40
568 Jarrod Saltalamacchia .15 .40
569A Jacoby Ellsbury .30 .75
569B Tris Speaker SP 6.00 15.00
570 Josh Willingham .25 .60
571 Brandon Lyon .15 .40
572 Clay Buchholz .15 .40
573 Johan Santana .25 .60
574 Milwaukee Brewers .15 .40
575 Ryan Perry .15 .40
576 Paul Maholm .15 .40
577 Jason Jaramillo .15 .40
578 Aaron Rowand .15 .40
579A Trevor Cahill .15 .40
579B J.Miranda Pie 15.00 40.00
580 Ian Snell .15 .40
581 Chris Dickerson .15 .40
582 Martin Prado .15 .40
583 Anibal Sanchez .15 .40
584 Matt Capps .15 .40
585 Dioner Navarro .15 .40
586 Roy Oswalt .25 .60
587 David Murphy .15 .40
588 Landon Powell .15 .40
589 Edinson Volquez .15 .40
590A Ryan Howard .30 .75
590B Ernie Banks SP 6.00 15.00
591 Fernando Rodney .15 .40
592 Brian Roberts .15 .40
593 Derek Holland .15 .40
594 Andy LaRoche .15 .40
595 Mike Lowell .15 .40
596 Brendan Ryan .15 .40
597 J.R. Towles .15 .40
598 Alberto Callaspo .15 .40
599 Jay Bruce .25 .60
600A Hanley Ramirez .25 .60
600B Honus Wagner SP 6.00 15.00
601 Blake DeWitt .15 .40
602 Kansas City Royals .15 .40
603 Gerardo Parra .15 .40
604 Atlanta Braves .15 .40
605 A.J. Pierzynski .15 .40
606 Chad Qualls .15 .40
607 Ubaldo Jimenez .15 .40
608 Pittsburgh Pirates .15 .40
609 Jeff Suppan .15 .40
610 Alex Gordon .25 .60
611 Josh Outman .15 .40
612 Lastings Milledge .15 .40
613 Eric Chavez .15 .40
614 Kelly Johnson .15 .40
615A Justin Verlander .40 1.00
615B Nolan Ryan SP 8.00 20.00
616 Franklin Gutierrez .15 .40
617 Luis Valbuena .15 .40
618 Jorge Cantu .15 .40
619 Mike Napoli .15 .40
620 Geovany Soto .25 .60
621 Aaron Cook .15 .40
622 Cleveland Indians .15 .40
623 Miguel Cabrera .40 1.00
624 Carlos Beltran .25 .60
625 Grady Sizemore .25 .60
626 Glen Perkins .15 .40
627 Jeremy Hermida .15 .40
628 Ross Detwiler .15 .40
629 Oliver Perez .15 .40
630 Ben Francisco .15 .40
631 Marc Rzepczynski .15 .40
632 Daric Barton .15 .40
633 Daniel Bard .15 .40
634 Casey Kotchman .15 .40
635 Carl Pavano .15 .40
636 Evan Longoria/B.J. Upton .25 .60
637 Babe Ruth/Lou Gehrig 1.00 2.50
638 Paul Konerko .25 .60
639 Los Angeles Dodgers .25 .60
640 Matt Diaz .15 .40
641 Chase Headley .15 .40
642 San Diego Padres .15 .40
643 Michael Young .15 .40
644 David Purcey .15 .40
645 Texas Rangers .15 .40
646 Trevor Crowe .15 .40
647 Alfonso Soriano .25 .60
648 Brian Fuentes .15 .40
649 Casey McGehee .15 .40
650A Dustin Pedroia .40 1.00
650B Ty Cobb SP 6.00 15.00
651 Mike Aviles .15 .40
652A Chipper Jones .40 1.00
652B Mickey Mantle SP 8.00 20.00
653A Nolan Reimold .15 .40
653B N.Reimold UPD Cup SP 10.00 25.00
654 Collin Balester .15 .40
655 Ryan Madson .15 .40
656 Jon Lester .25 .60
657 Chris Young .15 .40
658 Tommy Hunter .15 .40
659 Nick Blackburn .15 .40
660 Brandon McCarthy .15 .40
661A S.Strasburg MCG 10.00 25.00
661B S.Strasburg FS 5.00 12.00
661C Strasburg MCG AU/299 75.00 200.00
661D S.Strasburg UPD 4.00 10.00
661E S.Strasburg UPD SP VAR 25.00 60.00
661F S.Strasburg UPD Pie 40.00 100.00
661G B.Gibson UPD SP VAR 6.00 15.00

2010 Topps Black

SER.1 ODDS 1:96 HOBBY
SER.2 ODDS 1:112 HOBBY
STATED PRINT RUN 59 SER.#'d SETS
1 Prince Fielder 5.00 12.00
3 Derrek Lee 4.00 10.00
4 Hanley/Pablo/Pujols 10.00 25.00
5 Texas Rangers 5.00 12.00
6 Chicago White Sox 5.00 12.00
7 Mickey Mantle 25.00 60.00
8 Mauer/Ichiro/Jeter 20.00 50.00
9 T.Lincecum NL CY 5.00 12.00
10 Clayton Kershaw 12.00 30.00
11 Orlando Cabrera 5.00 12.00
12 Doug Davis 5.00 12.00

13 Melvin Mora 5.00 12.00
14 Ted Lilly 5.00 12.00
15 Bobby Abreu 5.00 12.00
16 Johnny Cueto 8.00 20.00
17 Dexter Fowler 8.00 20.00
18 Tim Stauffer 5.00 12.00
19 Felipe Lopez 5.00 12.00
20 Tommy Hanson 4.00 10.00
21 Cristian Guzman 5.00 12.00
22 Anthony Swarzak 5.00 12.00
23 Shane Victorino 6.00 15.00
24 John Maine 5.00 12.00
25 Adam Jones 6.00 15.00
26 Zach Duke 5.00 12.00
27 Lance Berkman/Mike Hampton 6.00 15.00
28 Jonathan Sanchez 5.00 12.00
29 Aubrey Huff 5.00 12.00
30 Victor Martinez 6.00 15.00
31 Jason Grilli 5.00 12.00
32 Cincinnati Reds 5.00 12.00
33 Adam Moore 5.00 12.00
34 Michael Dunn 5.00 12.00
35 Rick Porcello 5.00 12.00
36 Tobi Stoner 6.00 15.00
37 Garret Anderson 5.00 12.00
38 Houston Astros 5.00 12.00
39 Jeff Baker 5.00 12.00
40 Josh Johnson 6.00 15.00
41 Los Angeles Dodgers 6.00 15.00
42 Prince/Howard/Pujols 10.00 25.00
43 Marco Scutaro 8.00 20.00
44 Howie Kendrick 5.00 12.00
45 David Hernandez 5.00 12.00
46 Chad Tracy 5.00 12.00
47 Brad Penny 5.00 12.00
48 Joey Votto 8.00 20.00
49 Jorge De La Rosa 5.00 12.00
50 Zack Greinke 8.00 20.00
51 Eric Young Jr 5.00 12.00
52 Billy Butler 5.00 12.00
53 Craig Counsell 5.00 12.00
54 John Lackey 8.00 20.00
55 Manny Ramirez 8.00 20.00
56 Andy Pettitte 6.00 15.00
57 CC Sabathia 6.00 15.00
58 Kyle Blanks 5.00 12.00
59 Kevin Gregg 5.00 12.00
60 David Wright 6.00 15.00
61 Skip Schumaker 5.00 12.00
62 Kevin Millwood 5.00 12.00
63 Josh Bard 5.00 12.00
64 Drew Stubbs 8.00 20.00
65 Nick Swisher 6.00 15.00
66 Kyle Phillips 5.00 12.00
67 Matt LaPorta 3.00 8.00
68 Brandon Inge 6.00 15.00
69 Kansas City Royals 5.00 12.00
70 Cole Hamels 6.00 15.00
71 Mike Hampton 5.00 12.00
72 Milwaukee Brewers 5.00 12.00
73 Adam Wainwright
Chris Carpenter/Jorge De La Rosa 6.00 15.00
74 Casey Blake 5.00 12.00
75 Adrian Gonzalez 8.00 20.00
76 Joe Saunders 5.00 12.00
77 Kenshin Kawakami 6.00 15.00
78 Cesar Izturis 5.00 12.00
79 Francisco Cordero 5.00 12.00
80 Tim Lincecum 5.00 12.00
81 Ryan Theriot 5.00 12.00
82 Jason Marquis 5.00 12.00
83 Mark Teahen 5.00 12.00
84 Nate Robertson 5.00 12.00
85 Ken Griffey Jr. 15.00 40.00
86 Gil Meche 5.00 12.00
87 Darin Erstad 5.00 12.00
88 Jerry Hairston Jr. 5.00 12.00
89 J.A. Happ 6.00 15.00
90 Ian Kinsler 6.00 15.00
91 Erik Bedard 5.00 12.00
92 David Eckstein 5.00 12.00
93 Joe Nathan 5.00 12.00
94 Ivan Rodriguez 6.00 15.00
95 Carl Crawford 6.00 15.00
96 Jon Garland 5.00 12.00
97 Luis Durango 5.00 12.00
98 Cesar Ramos 5.00 12.00
99 Garrett Jones 5.00 12.00
100 Albert Pujols 10.00 25.00
101 Scott Baker 5.00 12.00
102 Minnesota Twins 5.00 12.00
103 Daniel Murphy 10.00 25.00
104 New York Mets 6.00 15.00
105 Madison Bumgarner 30.00 80.00
106 Carp/Linc/Jurrjens 5.00 12.00
107 Scott Hairston 5.00 12.00
108 Erick Aybar 5.00 12.00
109 Justin Masterson 5.00 12.00
110 Andrew McCutchen 8.00 20.00
111 Ty Wigginton 5.00 12.00
112 Kevin Correia 5.00 12.00
113 Willy Taveras 5.00 12.00
114 Chris Iannetta 5.00 12.00
115 Gordon Beckham 4.00 10.00
116 Carlos Gomez 5.00 12.00
117 David DeJesus 5.00 12.00
118 Brandon Morrow 5.00 12.00
119 Wilkin Ramirez 5.00 12.00
120 Jorge Posada 6.00 15.00
121 Brett Anderson 5.00 12.00
122 Carlos Ruiz 5.00 12.00
123 Jeff Samardzija 5.00 12.00
124 Rickie Weeks 5.00 12.00
125 Ichiro Suzuki 10.00 25.00
126 John Smoltz 8.00 20.00
127 Hank Blalock 5.00 12.00
128 Garrett Mock 5.00 12.00
129 Reid Gorecki 6.00 15.00
130 Vladimir Guerrero 5.00 12.00
131 Dustin Richardson 5.00 12.00
132 Cliff Lee 6.00 15.00
133 Freddy Sanchez 5.00 12.00
134 Philadelphia Phillies 5.00 12.00
135 Ryan Dempster 5.00 12.00
136 Adam Wainwright 6.00 15.00
137 Oakland Athletics 5.00 12.00
138 Carlos Pena/Mark Teixeira/Jason Bay 5.00 12.00
139 Frank Francisco 5.00 12.00
140 Matt Holliday 8.00 20.00
141 Chone Figgins 5.00 12.00
142 Tim Hudson 8.00 20.00
143 Omar Vizquel 6.00 15.00
144 Rich Harden 5.00 12.00
145 Justin Upton 6.00 15.00
146 Yunel Escobar 5.00 12.00
147 Hunter Pence 5.00 12.00
148 Cody Ross 5.00 12.00
149 Jose Guillen 5.00 12.00
150 Joe Mauer 6.00 15.00
151 Mat Gamel 5.00 12.00
152 Nyjer Morgan 5.00 12.00
153 Justin Duchscherer 5.00 12.00
154 Pedro Feliz 5.00 12.00
155 Zack Greinke AL CY 8.00 20.00
156 Tony Gwynn Jr. 5.00 12.00
157 Mike Sweeney 5.00 12.00
158 Jeff Niemann 5.00 12.00
159 Vernon Wells 5.00 12.00
160 Miguel Tejada 6.00 15.00
161 Denard Span 5.00 12.00
162 Wade Davis 8.00 20.00
163 Josh Butler 5.00 12.00
164 Carlos Carrasco 8.00 20.00
165 Brandon Phillips 5.00 12.00
166 Eric Byrnes 5.00 12.00
167 San Diego Padres 5.00 12.00
168 Brad Kilby 5.00 12.00
169 Pittsburgh Pirates 5.00 12.00
170 Jason Bay 6.00 15.00
171 King Felix/Sabathia/Verlander 10.00 25.00
172 Joe Mauer AL MVP 6.00 15.00
173 Kendry Morales 5.00 12.00
174 Mike Gonzalez 5.00 12.00
175 Josh Hamilton 6.00 15.00
176 Yovani Gallardo 5.00 12.00
177 Adam Lind 6.00 15.00
178 Kerry Wood 5.00 12.00
179 Ryan Spilborghs 5.00 12.00
180 Jayson Nix 5.00 12.00
181 Nick Johnson 5.00 12.00
182 Coco Crisp 5.00 12.00
183 Jonathan Papelbon 6.00 15.00
184 Jeff Francoeur 6.00 15.00
185 Hideki Matsui 8.00 20.00
186 Andrew Bailey 5.00 12.00
187 Will Venable 5.00 12.00
188 Joe Blanton 5.00 12.00
189 Adrian Beltre 12.00 30.00
190 Pablo Sandoval 6.00 15.00
191 Mat Latos 8.00 20.00
192 Andruw Jones 5.00 12.00
193 Shairon Martis 5.00 12.00
194 Neil Walker 8.00 20.00
195 James Shields 5.00 12.00
196 Ian Desmond 8.00 20.00
197 Cleveland Indians 5.00 12.00
198 Florida Marlins 5.00 12.00
199 Seattle Mariners 5.00 12.00
200 Roy Halladay 5.00 12.00
201 Detroit Tigers 5.00 12.00
202 San Francisco Giants 5.00 12.00
203 Zack Greinke/Felix
Hernandez/Roy Halladay 8.00 20.00
204 Elvis Andrus/Ian Kinsler 6.00 15.00
205 Chris Coghlan 4.00 10.00
206 Pujols/Prince/Howard 10.00 25.00
207 Colby Rasmus 5.00 12.00
208 Tim Wakefield 8.00 20.00
209 Alexei Ramirez 8.00 20.00
210 Josh Beckett 4.00 10.00
211 Kelly Shoppach 5.00 12.00
212 Magglio Ordonez 6.00 15.00
213 Ricky Nolasco 5.00 12.00
214 Matt Kemp 8.00 20.00
215 Max Scherzer 12.00 30.00
216 Mike Cameron 5.00 12.00
217 Gio Gonzalez 8.00 20.00
218 Fernando Martinez 5.00 12.00
219 Kevin Hart 5.00 12.00
220 Randy Johnson 10.00 25.00
221 Russell Branyan 5.00 12.00
222 Curtis Granderson 8.00 20.00
223 Ryan Church 5.00 12.00
224 Rod Barajas 5.00 12.00
225 David Price 6.00 15.00
226 Juan Rivera 5.00 12.00
227 Josh Thole 6.00 15.00
228 Chris Pettit 5.00 12.00
229 Daniel McCutchen 6.00 15.00
230 Jonathan Broxton 5.00 12.00
231 Luke Scott 5.00 12.00
232 St. Louis Cardinals 6.00 15.00
233 Mark Teixeira/Jason Bay/Adam Lind 5.00 12.00
234 Tampa Bay Rays 5.00 12.00
235 Neftali Feliz 4.00 10.00
236 Andrew Bailey AL ROY 5.00 12.00
237 Braun/Prince 5.00 12.00
238 Ian Stewart 5.00 12.00
239 Juan Uribe 5.00 12.00
240 Ricky Romero 5.00 12.00
241 Rocco Baldelli 5.00 12.00
242 Bobby Jenks 5.00 12.00
243 Asdrubal Cabrera 8.00 20.00
244 Barry Zito 8.00 20.00
245 Lance Berkman 6.00 15.00
246 Leo Nunez 5.00 12.00
247 Andre Ethier 5.00 12.00
248 Jason Kendall 5.00 12.00
249 Jon Niese 5.00 12.00
250 Mark Teixeira 5.00 12.00
251 John Lannan 5.00 12.00
252 Ronny Cedeno 5.00 12.00
253 Bengie Molina 5.00 12.00
254 Edwin Jackson 5.00 12.00
255 Chris Davis 8.00 20.00
256 Akinori Iwamura 5.00 12.00
257 Bobby Crosby 5.00 12.00
258 Edwin Encarnacion 12.00 30.00
259 Daniel Hudson 6.00 15.00
260 New York Yankees 8.00 20.00
261 Matt Carson 5.00 12.00
262 Homer Bailey 5.00 12.00
263 Placido Polanco 5.00 12.00
264 Arizona Diamondbacks 5.00 12.00
265 Los Angeles Angels 5.00 12.00
266 Humberto Quintero 5.00 12.00
267 Toronto Blue Jays 5.00 12.00
268 Juan Pierre 5.00 12.00
269 A.Rod/Jeter/Cano 20.00 50.00
270 Michael Brantley 8.00 20.00
271 Jermaine Dye 5.00 12.00
272 Jair Jurrjens 5.00 12.00
273 Pat Neshek 5.00 12.00
274 Stephen Drew 4.00 10.00
275 Chris Coghlan NL ROY 4.00 10.00
276 Matt Lindstrom 5.00 12.00
277 Jarrod Washburn 6.00 15.00
278 Carlos Delgado 5.00 12.00
279 Randy Wolf 5.00 12.00
280 Mark DeRosa 5.00 12.00
281 Braden Looper 5.00 12.00
282 Washington Nationals 5.00 12.00
283 Adam Kennedy 5.00 12.00
284 Ross Ohlendorf 5.00 12.00
285 Kurt Suzuki 5.00 12.00
286 Javier Vazquez 5.00 12.00
287 Jhonny Peralta 5.00 12.00
288 Boston Red Sox 6.00 15.00
289 Lyle Overbay 5.00 12.00
290 Orlando Hudson 5.00 12.00
291 Austin Kearns 5.00 12.00
292 Tommy Manzella 5.00 12.00
293 Brent Dlugach 5.00 12.00
294 Adam Dunn 8.00 20.00
295 Kevin Youkilis 4.00 10.00
296 Atlanta Braves 5.00 12.00
297 Ben Zobrist 8.00 20.00
298 Baltimore Orioles 5.00 12.00
299 Gary Sheffield 5.00 12.00
300 Chase Utley 5.00 12.00
301 Jack Cust 5.00 12.00
302 Kevin Youkilis/David Ortiz 10.00 25.00
303 Chris Snyder 5.00 12.00
304 Adam LaRoche 5.00 12.00
305 Juan Francisco 6.00 15.00
306 Milton Bradley 5.00 12.00
307 Henry Rodriguez 5.00 12.00
308 Robinzon Diaz 5.00 12.00
309 Gerald Laird 5.00 12.00
310 Elvis Andrus 6.00 15.00
311 Jose Valverde 5.00 12.00
312 Tyler Flowers 6.00 15.00
313 Jason Kubel 5.00 12.00
314 Angel Pagan 5.00 12.00
315 Scott Kazmir 5.00 12.00
316 Chris Young 5.00 12.00
317 Ryan Doumit 5.00 12.00
318 Nate Schierholtz 5.00 12.00
319 Ryan Franklin 5.00 12.00
320 Brian McCann 6.00 15.00
321 Pat Burrell 5.00 12.00
322 Travis Buck 5.00 12.00
323 Jim Thome 6.00 15.00
324 Alex Rios 4.00 10.00
325 Julio Lugo 5.00 12.00
326 Tyler Colvin 6.00 15.00
327 A.Pujols NL MVP 10.00 25.00
328 Chicago Cubs 6.00 15.00
329 Colorado Rockies 5.00 12.00
330 Brandon Allen 5.00 12.00
331 Ryan Braun 5.00 12.00
332 Brad Hawpe 5.00 12.00
333 Ryan Ludwick 5.00 12.00
334 Jayson Werth 8.00 20.00
335 Jordan Norberto 5.00 12.00
336 C.J. Wilson 5.00 12.00
337 Carlos Zambrano 6.00 15.00
338 Brett Cecil 5.00 12.00
339 Jose Reyes 6.00 15.00
340 John Buck 5.00 12.00
341 Texas Rangers 5.00 12.00
342 Melky Cabrera 5.00 12.00
343 Brian Bruney 5.00 12.00
344 Brett Myers 5.00 12.00
345 Chris Volstad 5.00 12.00
346 Taylor Teagarden 5.00 12.00
347 Aaron Harang 5.00 12.00
348 Jordan Zimmermann 8.00 20.00
349 Felix Pie 5.00 12.00
350 Prince Fielder/Ryan Braun 5.00 12.00
351 Koji Uehara 4.00 10.00
352 Cameron Maybin 4.00 10.00
353 Jason Heyward 100.00 175.00
354 Evan Longoria 5.00 12.00
355 James Russell 8.00 20.00
356 Los Angeles Angels 5.00 12.00
357 Scott Downs 5.00 12.00
358 Mark Buehrle 8.00 20.00
359 Aramis Ramirez 5.00 12.00
360 Justin Morneau 6.00 15.00
361 Washington Nationals 5.00 12.00
362 Travis Snider 5.00 12.00
363 Joba Chamberlain 4.00 10.00
364 Trevor Hoffman 8.00 20.00
365 Logan Ondrusek 5.00 12.00
366 Hiroki Kuroda 5.00 12.00
367 Wandy Rodriguez 5.00 12.00
368 Wade LeBlanc 5.00 12.00
369 David Ortiz 10.00 25.00
370 Robinson Cano 6.00 15.00
371 Nick Hundley 5.00 12.00
372 Philadelphia Phillies 5.00 12.00
373 Clint Barmes 5.00 12.00
374 Scott Feldman 5.00 12.00
375 Mike Leake 10.00 25.00
376 Esmil Rogers 5.00 12.00
377 Felix Hernandez 6.00 15.00
378 George Sherrill 5.00 12.00
379 Phil Hughes 5.00 12.00
380 J.D. Drew 5.00 12.00
381 Miguel Montero 5.00 12.00
382 Kyle Davies 5.00 12.00
383 Derek Lowe 8.00 20.00
384 Chris Johnson 8.00 20.00
385 Torii Hunter 5.00 12.00
386 Dan Haren 5.00 12.00
387 Josh Fields 5.00 12.00
388 Joel Pineiro 5.00 12.00
389 Troy Tulowitzki 10.00 25.00
390 Ervin Santana 5.00 12.00
391 Manny Parra 5.00 12.00
392 Carlos Monasterios 6.00 15.00
393 Jason Frasor 5.00 12.00
394 Luis Castillo 5.00 12.00
395 Jenrry Mejia 8.00 20.00
396 Jake Westbrook 5.00 12.00
397 Colorado Rockies 5.00 12.00
398 Carlos Gonzalez 8.00 20.00
399 Matt Garza 5.00 12.00
400 Alex Rodriguez 10.00 25.00
401 Chad Billingsley 8.00 20.00
402 J.P. Howell 5.00 12.00
403 Jimmy Rollins 6.00 15.00
404 Mariano Rivera 10.00 25.00
405 Dustin McGowan 5.00 12.00
406 Jeff Francis 5.00 12.00
407 Nick Punto 5.00 12.00
408 Detroit Tigers 5.00 12.00
409 Kosuke Fukudome 5.00 12.00
410 Oakland Athletics 5.00 12.00
411 Jack Wilson 5.00 12.00
412 San Francisco Giants 5.00 12.00
413 J.J. Hardy 5.00 12.00
414 Sean West 5.00 12.00
415 Cincinnati Reds 5.00 12.00
416 Ruben Tejada 6.00 15.00
417 Dallas Braden 6.00 15.00
418 Aaron Laffey 5.00 12.00
419 David Aardsma 5.00 12.00
420 Shin-Soo Choo 8.00 20.00
421 Doug Fister 5.00 12.00
422 Vin Mazzaro 5.00 12.00
423 Brad Bergesen 5.00 12.00
424 David Herndon 5.00 12.00
425 Dontrelle Willis 5.00 12.00
426 Mark Reynolds 5.00 12.00
427 Brandon Webb 6.00 15.00
428 Baltimore Orioles 5.00 12.00
429 Seth Smith 5.00 12.00
430 Kazuo Matsui 5.00 12.00
431 John Raynor 5.00 12.00
432 A.J. Burnett 4.00 10.00
433 Julio Borbon 5.00 12.00
434 Kevin Slowey 5.00 12.00
435 Nelson Cruz 12.00 30.00
436 New York Mets 6.00 15.00
437 Luke Hochevar 5.00 12.00
438 Jason Bartlett 5.00 12.00
439 Emilio Bonifacio 5.00 12.00
440 Willie Harris 5.00 12.00
441 Clete Thomas 5.00 12.00
442 Dan Runzler 6.00 15.00
443 Jason Hammel 8.00 20.00
444 Yuniesky Betancourt 4.00 10.00
445 Miguel Olivo 5.00 12.00
446 Gavin Floyd 5.00 12.00
447 Jeremy Guthrie 5.00 12.00
448 Joakim Soria 5.00 12.00
449 Ryan Sweeney 5.00 12.00
450 Omir Santos 5.00 12.00
451 Michael Saunders 8.00 20.00
452 Allen Craig 12.00 30.00
453 Jesse English 5.00 12.00
454 James Loney 4.00 10.00
455 St. Louis Cardinals 6.00 15.00
456 Clayton Richard 5.00 12.00
457 Kanekoa Texeira 5.00 12.00
458 Todd Wellemeyer 5.00 12.00
459 Joel Zumaya 5.00 12.00
460 Aaron Cunningham 5.00 12.00
461 Tyson Ross 5.00 12.00
462 Alcides Escobar 6.00 15.00
463 Carlos Marmol 8.00 20.00
464 Francisco Liriano 5.00 12.00
465 Chien-Ming Wang 5.00 12.00
466 Jered Weaver 8.00 20.00
467 Fausto Carmona 5.00 12.00
468 Delmon Young 6.00 15.00
469 Alex Burnett 5.00 12.00
470 New York Yankees 8.00 20.00
471 Drew Butera 5.00 12.00
472 Toronto Blue Jays 5.00 12.00
473 Jason Varitek 8.00 20.00
474 Kyle Kendrick 5.00 12.00
475 Johnny Damon 6.00 15.00
476 Yadier Molina 12.00 30.00
477 Nate McLouth 5.00 12.00
478 Conor Jackson 5.00 12.00
479 Chris Carpenter 6.00 15.00
480 Boston Red Sox 6.00 15.00
481 Scott Rolen 6.00 15.00
482 Mike McCoy 5.00 12.00
483 Daisuke Matsuzaka 5.00 12.00
484 Mike Fontenot 5.00 12.00
485 Jesus Flores 5.00 12.00
486 Raul Ibanez 6.00 15.00
487 Dan Uggla 4.00 10.00
488 Delwyn Young 5.00 12.00
489 Russell Martin 4.00 10.00
490 Michael Bourn 5.00 12.00
491 Rafael Furcal 5.00 12.00
492 Brian Wilson 12.00 30.00
493 Travis Ishikawa 5.00 12.00
494 Andrew Miller 8.00 20.00
495 Carlos Pena 6.00 15.00
496 Rajai Davis 5.00 12.00
497 Edgar Renteria 5.00 12.00
498 Sergio Santos 5.00 12.00
499 Michael Bowden 5.00 12.00
500 Brad Lidge 5.00 12.00
501 Jake Peavy 4.00 10.00
502 Jhoulys Chacin 5.00 12.00
503 Austin Jackson 5.00 12.00
504 Jeff Mathis 5.00 12.00
505 Andy Marte 5.00 12.00
506 Jose Lopez 5.00 12.00
507 Francisco Rodriguez 6.00 15.00
508 Chris Getz 5.00 12.00
509 Todd Helton 6.00 15.00
510 Justin Upton/Mark Reynolds 6.00 15.00
511 Chicago Cubs 6.00 15.00
512 Scot Shields 5.00 12.00
513 Scott Sizemore 6.00 15.00
514 Rafael Soriano 5.00 12.00
515 Seattle Mariners 5.00 12.00
516 Marlon Byrd 5.00 12.00
517 Cliff Pennington 5.00 12.00
518 Corey Hart 5.00 12.00
519 Alexi Casilla 5.00 12.00
520 Randy Wells 5.00 12.00
521 Jeremy Bonderman 5.00 12.00
522 Jordan Schafer 5.00 12.00
523 Phil Coke 5.00 12.00
524 Dusty Hughes 5.00 12.00
525 David Huff 5.00 12.00
526 Carlos Guillen 5.00 12.00
527 Brandon Wood 5.00 12.00
528 Brian Bannister 5.00 12.00
529 Carlos Lee 5.00 12.00
530 Steve Pearce 12.00 30.00
531 Matt Cain 6.00 15.00
532 Hunter Pence 6.00 15.00
533 Gary Matthews Jr. 5.00 12.00
534 Hideki Okajima 5.00 12.00
535 Andy Sonnanstine 5.00 12.00
536 Matt Palmer 5.00 12.00
537 Michael Cuddyer 5.00 12.00
538 Travis Hafner 5.00 12.00
539 Arizona Diamondbacks 5.00 12.00
540 Sean Rodriguez 5.00 12.00
541 Jason Motte 5.00 12.00
542 Heath Bell 5.00 12.00
543 Adam Jones/Nick Markakis 8.00 20.00
544 Kevin Kouzmanoff 5.00 12.00
545 Fred Lewis 5.00 12.00
546 Bud Norris 5.00 12.00
547 Brett Gardner 8.00 20.00
548 Minnesota Twins 5.00 12.00
549 Derek Jeter 20.00 50.00
550 Freddy Garcia 5.00 12.00
551 Everth Cabrera 5.00 12.00
552 Chris Tillman 5.00 12.00
553 Florida Marlins 5.00 12.00
554 Ramon Hernandez 5.00 12.00
555 B.J. Upton 6.00 15.00
556 Chicago White Sox 5.00 12.00
557 Aaron Hill 5.00 12.00
558 Ronny Paulino 5.00 12.00
559 Nick Markakis 8.00 20.00
560 Ryan Rowland-Smith 5.00 12.00
561 Ryan Zimmerman 6.00 15.00
562 Carlos Quentin 4.00 10.00
563 Bronson Arroyo 5.00 12.00
564 Houston Astros 5.00 12.00
565 Franklin Morales 5.00 12.00
566 Maicer Izturis 5.00 12.00
567 Mike Pelfrey 5.00 12.00
568 Jarrod Saltalamacchia 5.00 12.00
569 Jacoby Ellsbury 6.00 15.00
570 Josh Willingham 8.00 20.00
571 Brandon Lyon 5.00 12.00
572 Clay Buchholz 4.00 10.00
573 Johan Santana 5.00 12.00
574 Milwaukee Brewers 5.00 12.00
575 Ryan Perry 5.00 12.00
576 Paul Maholm 5.00 12.00
577 Jason Jaramillo 5.00 12.00
578 Aaron Rowand 5.00 12.00
579 Trevor Cahill 5.00 12.00
580 Ian Snell 5.00 12.00
581 Chris Dickerson 5.00 12.00
582 Martin Prado 5.00 12.00
583 Anibal Sanchez 5.00 12.00
584 Matt Capps 5.00 12.00
585 Dioner Navarro 5.00 12.00
586 Roy Oswalt 6.00 15.00
587 David Murphy 5.00 12.00
588 Landon Powell 5.00 12.00
589 Edinson Volquez 5.00 12.00
590 Ryan Howard 6.00 15.00
591 Fernando Rodney 5.00 12.00
592 Brian Roberts 5.00 12.00
593 Derek Holland 5.00 12.00
594 Andy LaRoche 5.00 12.00
595 Mike Lowell 5.00 12.00
596 Brendan Ryan 5.00 12.00
597 J.R. Towles 5.00 12.00
598 Alberto Callaspo 5.00 12.00
599 Jay Bruce 6.00 15.00
600 Hanley Ramirez 5.00 12.00
601 Blake DeWitt 5.00 12.00
602 Kansas City Royals 5.00 12.00
603 Gerardo Parra 5.00 12.00
604 Atlanta Braves 5.00 12.00
605 A.J. Pierzynski 5.00 12.00
606 Chad Qualls 5.00 12.00
607 Ubaldo Jimenez 4.00 10.00
608 Pittsburgh Pirates 6.00 15.00
609 Jeff Suppan 5.00 12.00
610 Alex Gordon 6.00 15.00
611 Josh Outman 5.00 12.00
612 Lastings Milledge 5.00 12.00
613 Eric Chavez 5.00 12.00
614 Kelly Johnson 5.00 12.00
615 Justin Verlander 10.00 25.00
616 Franklin Gutierrez 5.00 12.00
617 Luis Valbuena 5.00 12.00
618 Jorge Cantu 5.00 12.00
619 Mike Napoli 5.00 12.00
620 Geovany Soto 6.00 15.00
621 Aaron Cook 5.00 12.00
622 Cleveland Indians 5.00 12.00
623 Miguel Cabrera 10.00 25.00
624 Carlos Beltran 8.00 20.00
625 Grady Sizemore 6.00 15.00
626 Glen Perkins 5.00 12.00
627 Jeremy Hermida 5.00 12.00
628 Ross Detwiler 5.00 12.00
629 Oliver Perez 5.00 12.00
630 Ben Francisco 5.00 12.00
631 Marc Rzepczynski 5.00 12.00
632 Daric Barton 5.00 12.00
633 Daniel Bard 5.00 12.00
634 Casey Kotchman 5.00 12.00
635 Carl Pavano 5.00 12.00
636 Evan Longoria/B.J. Upton 5.00 12.00
637 Babe Ruth/Lou Gehrig 20.00 50.00
638 Paul Konerko 8.00 20.00
639 Los Angeles Dodgers 6.00 15.00
640 Matt Diaz 5.00 12.00
641 Chase Headley 5.00 12.00
642 San Diego Padres 5.00 12.00
643 Michael Young 4.00 10.00
644 David Purcey 5.00 12.00
645 Texas Rangers 5.00 12.00
646 Trevor Crowe 5.00 12.00
647 Alfonso Soriano 6.00 15.00
648 Brian Fuentes 5.00 12.00
649 Casey McGehee 5.00 12.00
650 Dustin Pedroia 8.00 20.00
651 Mike Aviles 5.00 12.00
652 Chipper Jones 8.00 20.00
653 Nolan Reimold 4.00 10.00
654 Collin Balester 5.00 12.00
655 Ryan Madson 5.00 12.00
656 Jon Lester 6.00 15.00
657 Chris Young 6.00 15.00
658 Tommy Hunter 5.00 12.00
659 Nick Blackburn 5.00 12.00
660 Brandon McCarthy 5.00 12.00

2010 Topps Copper

*COPPER VET: 4X TO 10X BASIC
*COPPER RC: 2.5X TO 6X BASIC RC
STATED ODDS 1:11 WM RETAIL
STATED PRINT RUN 399 SER.#'d SETS

2010 Topps Gold Border

*GOLD VET: 2X TO 5X BASIC
*GOLD RC: 1.2X TO 3X BASIC RC
STATED ODDS 1:6 HOBBY
STATED PRINT RUN 2010 SER.#'d SETS
1-330 ISSUED IN SERIES 1
331-660 ISSUE IN SERIES 2

2010 Topps Target

*VETS: .5X TO 1.2X BASIC TOPPS CARDS
*RC: .5X TO 1.2X BASIC TOPPS RC CARDS

2010 Topps Wal-Mart Black Border

*VETS: .5X TO 1.2X BASIC TOPPS CARDS
*RC: .5X TO 1.2X BASIC TOPPS RC CARDS

2010 Topps 2020

COMPLETE SET (20) 6.00 15.00
STATED ODDS 1:6 HOBBY
T1 Ryan Braun .50 1.25
T2 Gordon Beckham .30 .75
T3 Andre Ethier .50 1.25
T4 David Price .60 1.50
T5 Justin Upton .50 1.25
T6 Hunter Pence .50 1.25
T7 Ryan Howard .60 1.50
T8 Buster Posey 2.50 6.00
T9 Madison Bumgarner 3.00 8.00
T10 Evan Longoria .50 1.25
T11 Joe Mauer .60 1.50
T12 Chris Coghlan .30 .75
T13 Andrew McCutchen .75 2.00
T14 Ubaldo Jimenez .30 .75
T15 Pablo Sandoval .50 1.25
T16 David Wright .60 1.50
T17 Tommy Hanson .30 .75
T18 Clayton Kershaw 1.25 3.00
T19 Zack Greinke .75 2.00
T20 Matt Kemp .60 1.50

2010 Topps Blue Back

INSERTED IN WAL MART PACKS
31-45 ISSUED IN UPD WM PACKS
1 Babe Ruth 2.50 6.00
2 Stan Musial 1.50 4.00
3 George Sisler .60 1.50
4 Tim Lincecum .60 1.50
5 Ichiro Suzuki 1.25 3.00
6 Roy Halladay .60 1.50
7 Walter Johnson 1.00 2.50
8 Nolan Ryan 3.00 8.00
9 Hanley Ramirez .60 1.50
10 Derek Jeter 2.50 6.00
11 Tom Seaver .60 1.50
12 Roger Maris 1.00 2.50
13 Honus Wagner 1.00 2.50
14 Vladimir Guerrero .60 1.50
15 Mel Ott 1.00 2.50
16 Mickey Mantle 3.00 8.00
17 Cal Ripken Jr. 3.00 8.00
18 Cy Young 1.00 2.50
19 Jackie Robinson 1.00 2.50
20 Jimmie Foxx 1.00 2.50
21 Lou Gehrig 2.00 5.00
22 Rogers Hornsby .60 1.50
23 Ty Cobb 1.50 4.00
24 Dizzy Dean .60 1.50
25 Reggie Jackson .60 1.50
26 Warren Spahn .60 1.50
27 Albert Pujols 1.25 3.00
28 Chipper Jones 1.00 2.50
29 Mariano Rivera 1.25 3.00
30 David Wright .75 2.00
31 Babe Ruth 2.50 6.00
32 Jimmie Foxx 1.00 2.50
33 Rogers Hornsby .60 1.50
34 Ty Cobb 1.50 4.00
35 Dizzy Dean .60 1.50
36 Reggie Jackson .60 1.50
37 Nolan Ryan 3.00 8.00
38 Tom Seaver .60 1.50
39 Roger Maris 1.00 2.50
40 Vladimir Guerrero .60 1.50
41 Roy Campanella 1.00 2.50
42 Johnny Mize .60 1.50
43 Christy Mathewson 1.00 2.50
44 Carl Yastrzemski 1.50 4.00
45 Joe Mauer .75 2.00

2010 Topps Cards Your Mom Threw Out

COMPLETE SET (174) 40.00 100.00
SER.1 ODDS 1:3 HOBBY
SER.2 ODDS 1:3 HOBBY
UPD ODDS 1:3 HOBBY
CMT1 Mickey Mantle 52 3.00 8.00
CMT2 Jackie Robinson 1.00 2.50
CMT3 Ernie Banks 1.00 2.50
CMT4 Duke Snider .60 1.50
CMT5 Luis Aparicio .60 1.50
CMT6 Frank Robinson .60 1.50
CMT7 Orlando Cepeda .60 1.50
CMT8 Bob Gibson .60 1.50
CMT9 Carl Yastrzemski 1.50 4.00
CMT10 Roger Maris 1.00 2.50
CMT11 Mickey Mantle 3.00 8.00
CMT12 Stan Musial 1.50 4.00
CMT13 Brooks Robinson .60 1.50
CMT14 Juan Marichal .60 1.50
CMT15 Jim Palmer .60 1.50
CMT16 Willie McCovey .60 1.50
CMT17 Mickey Mantle 3.00 8.00
CMT18 Reggie Jackson .60 1.50
CMT19 Steve Carlton .60 1.50
CMT20 Thurman Munson 1.00 2.50
CMT21 Tom Seaver .60 1.50
CMT22 Johnny Bench 1.00 2.50
CMT23 Dave Winfield .60 1.50
CMT24 Robin Yount 1.00 2.50
CMT25 Mike Schmidt 1.50 4.00
CMT26 Reggie Jackson .60 1.50
CMT27 Nolan Ryan 3.00 8.00
CMT28 Ozzie Smith 1.25 3.00
CMT29 Rickey Henderson 1.00 2.50
CMT30 Eddie Murray .60 1.50
CMT31 Paul Molitor 1.00 2.50
CMT32 Ryne Sandberg 2.00 5.00
CMT33 Don Mattingly 2.00 5.00
CMT34 Dwight Gooden .40 1.00
CMT35 Tony Gwynn 1.00 2.50
CMT36 Bo Jackson 1.00 2.50
CMT37 Nolan Ryan 3.00 8.00
CMT38 Gary Sheffield .40 1.00
CMT39 Frank Thomas 1.00 2.50
CMT40 Chipper Jones 1.00 2.50
CMT41 Manny Ramirez 1.00 2.50
CMT42 Derek Jeter 2.50 6.00
CMT43 Tony Gwynn 1.00 2.50
CMT44 Mike Piazza 1.00 2.50
CMT45 Cal Ripken 3.00 8.00
CMT46 Pedro Martinez .60 1.50
CMT47 Alex Rodriguez 1.25 3.00
CMT48 Ivan Rodriguez .60 1.50
CMT49 Randy Johnson 1.00 2.50
CMT50 Ichiro Suzuki 1.25 3.00
CMT51 Albert Pujols 1.25 3.00
CMT52 Kevin Youkilis .40 1.00
CMT53 Alfonso Soriano .60 1.50
CMT54 R.Howard/C.Hamels .75 2.00
CMT55 Alex Gordon .60 1.50
CMT56 Dustin Pedroia 1.00 2.50
CMT57 Tim Lincecum .60 1.50
CMT58 Evan Longoria .60 1.50
CMT59 Phil Rizzuto .60 1.50
CMT60 Mickey Mantle 3.00 8.00
CMT61 Al Kaline 1.00 2.50
CMT62 Yogi Berra 1.00 2.50
CMT63 Ernie Banks 1.00 2.50
CMT64 Whitey Ford .60 1.50
CMT65 Duke Snider .60 1.50
CMT66 Warren Spahn .60 1.50
CMT67 Willie McCovey .60 1.50
CMT68 Brooks Robinson .60 1.50
CMT69 Roger Maris 1.00 2.50
CMT70 Harmon Killebrew 1.00 2.50
CMT71 Eddie Mathews 1.00 2.50
CMT72 Carl Yastrzemski 1.50 4.00
CMT73 Gaylord Perry .60 1.50
CMT74 Jim Bunning .60 1.50
CMT75 Rod Carew .60 1.50
CMT76 Nolan Ryan 3.00 8.00
CMT77 Johnny Bench 1.00 2.50
CMT78 Frank Robinson .60 1.50
CMT79 Juan Marichal .60 1.50
CMT80 Reggie Jackson .60 1.50
CMT81 Willie McCovey .60 1.50
CMT82 George Brett 2.00 5.00
CMT83 Dennis Eckersley .60 1.50
CMT84 Tom Seaver .60 1.50
CMT85 Eddie Murray .60 1.50
CMT86 Paul Molitor 1.00 2.50
CMT87 Joe Morgan .60 1.50
CMT88 Rickey Henderson 1.00 2.50
CMT89 Steve Carlton .60 1.50
CMT90 Tony Gwynn 1.00 2.50
CMT91 Ryne Sandberg 2.00 5.00
CMT92 Robin Yount 1.00 2.50
CMT93 Mike Schmidt 1.50 4.00
CMT94 Don Mattingly 2.00 5.00
CMT95 Darryl Strawberry .40 1.00
CMT96 Randy Johnson 1.00 2.50
CMT97 Frank Thomas 1.00 2.50
CMT98 Ken Griffey Jr. 2.00 5.00
CMT99 Cal Ripken 3.00 8.00
CMT100 Ozzie Smith 1.25 3.00
CMT101 Bo Jackson 1.00 2.50
CMT102 Babe Ruth 2.50 6.00
CMT103 Manny Ramirez 1.00 2.50
CMT104 John Smoltz 1.00 2.50
CMT105 Derek Jeter 2.50 6.00
CMT106 Alex Rodriguez 1.25 3.00
CMT107 Chipper Jones 1.00 2.50
CMT108 Mariano Rivera 1.25 3.00
CMT109 Joe Mauer .75 2.00
CMT110 Cole Hamels .75 2.00
CMT111 I.Suzuki/A.Pujols 1.25 3.00
CMT112 Andre Ethier .60 1.50
CMT113 Justin Verlander 1.00 2.50
CMT114 Derek Jeter 2.50 6.00
CMT115 Ryan Zimmerman .60 1.50
CMT116 Rick Porcello .60 1.50
CMT117 Eddie Mathews 1.00 2.50
CMT118 John Podres .40 1.00
CMT119 Tom Lasorda .60 1.50
CMT120 Harmon Killebrew 1.00 2.50
CMT121 Jackie Robinson 1.00 2.50
CMT122 Y.Berra/M.Mantle 3.00 8.00
CMT123 Roger Maris 1.00 2.50
CMT124 Lew Burdette .40 1.00
CMT125 Roger Maris 1.00 2.50
CMT126 Carl Yastrzemski 1.50 4.00
CMT127 Lou Brock .60 1.50
CMT128 Willie McCovey .60 1.50
CMT129 Willie Stargell .60 1.50
CMT130 Ernie Banks 1.00 2.50
CMT131 Robin Roberts .60 1.50
CMT132 Brooks Robinson .60 1.50
CMT133 Tom Seaver .60 1.50
CMT134 Mickey Mantle 3.00 8.00
CMT135 Nolan Ryan 3.00 8.00
CMT136 Steve Garvey .40 1.00
CMT137 Frank Robinson .60 1.50
CMT138 Luis Aparicio .60 1.50
CMT139 Nolan Ryan 3.00 8.00
CMT140 Yogi Berra 1.00 2.50
Roy Campanella
CMT141 Reggie Jackson .60 1.50
CMT142 Mark Fidrych .40 1.00
CMT143 Andre Dawson .60 1.50
CMT144 Dale Murphy 1.00 2.50
CMT145 L.Brock/C.Yastrzemski 1.50 4.00
CMT146 Ozzie Smith 1.25 3.00

CMT147 Rickey Henderson 1.00 2.50
CMT148 Wade Boggs .60 1.50
CMT149 Darryl Strawberry .40 1.00
CMT150 Dave Winfield .60 1.50
CMT151 Paul Molitor 1.00 2.50
CMT152 Barry Larkin .60 1.50
CMT153 Eddie Murray .60 1.50
CMT154 Craig Biggio .60 1.50
CMT155 Larry Walker .60 1.50
CMT156 Nolan Ryan 3.00 8.00
CMT157 Don Mattingly 2.00 5.00
CMT158 Frank Thomas 1.00 2.50
CMT159 Billy Wagner .40 1.00
CMT160 Derek Jeter 2.50 6.00
CMT161 Chipper Jones 1.00 2.50
CMT162 Derek Jeter 2.50 6.00
CMT163 Mike Piazza/Ken Griffey Jr. 2.00 5.00
CMT164 A.Rod/Nomar/Jeter 2.50 6.00
CMT165 Barry Zito .60 1.50
Ben Sheets
CMT166 Vladimir Guerrero .60 1.50
CMT167 Jason Bay .60 1.50
CMT168 Josh Hamilton .60 1.50
Carl Crawford
CMT169 J.Thome/M.Schmidt 1.50 4.00
CMT170 Ian Kinsler .60 1.50
CMT171 Ryan Zimmerman .60 1.50
CMT172 Ubaldo Jimenez .40 1.00
CMT173 Joey Votto 1.00 2.50
CMT174 David Price .75 2.00

2010 Topps Cards Your Mom Threw Out Original Back

*ORIG: .6X TO 1.5X BASIC
STATED ODDS 1:36 HOBBY

2010 Topps Commemorative Patch

1-50 ISSUED IN SERIES 1
51-100 ISSUED IN SERIES 2
101-150 ISSUED IN UPDATE
MCP1 Tris Speaker 8.00 20.00
MCP2 Babe Ruth 12.50 30.00
MCP3 Babe Ruth 12.50 30.00
MCP4 Mel Ott 4.00 10.00
MCP5 Dizzy Dean 8.00 20.00
MCP6 Jimmie Foxx 4.00 10.00
MCP7 Hank Greenberg 4.00 10.00
MCP8 Lou Gehrig 6.00 15.00
MCP9 Lou Gehrig 6.00 15.00
MCP10 Ralph Kiner 4.00 10.00
MCP11 Johnny Mize 4.00 10.00
MCP12 Robin Roberts 4.00 10.00
MCP13 Monte Irvin 4.00 10.00
MCP14 Duke Snider 5.00 12.00
MCP15 Eddie Mathews 5.00 12.00
MCP16 Mickey Mantle 8.00 20.00
MCP17 Roger Maris 6.00 15.00
MCP18 Johnny Podres 4.00 10.00
MCP19 Bob Gibson 4.00 10.00
MCP20 Juan Marichal 4.00 10.00
MCP21 Orlando Cepeda 4.00 10.00
MCP22 Al Kaline 4.00 10.00
MCP23 Frank Robinson 4.00 10.00
MCP24 Bobby Murcer 8.00 20.00
MCP25 Willie Stargell 8.00 20.00
MCP26 Johnny Bench 10.00 25.00
MCP27 Ozzie Smith 5.00 12.00
MCP28 Eddie Murray 4.00 10.00
MCP29 Gary Carter 4.00 10.00
MCP30 Dennis Eckersley 4.00 10.00
MCP31 Ryne Sandberg 4.00 10.00
MCP32 Gary Sheffield 4.00 10.00
MCP33 Frank Thomas 5.00 12.00
MCP34 Vladimir Guerrero 4.00 10.00
MCP35 Ichiro Suzuki 5.00 10.00
MCP36 Curt Schilling 4.00 10.00
MCP37 Chipper Jones 4.00 10.00
MCP38 Ryan Zimmerman 4.00 10.00
MCP39 Roy Halladay 5.00 12.00
MCP40 Grady Sizemore 4.00 10.00
MCP41 Manny Ramirez 4.00 10.00
MCP42 Tim Lincecum 10.00 25.00
MCP43 Evan Longoria 8.00 20.00
MCP44 David Wright 5.00 12.00
MCP45 Chase Utley 5.00 12.00
MCP46 Mariano Rivera 8.00 20.00
MCP47 Joe Mauer 8.00 20.00
MCP48 Albert Pujols 6.00 15.00
MCP49 Ichiro Suzuki 8.00 20.00
MCP50 Mark Teixeira 5.00 12.00
MCP51 Richie Ashburn 10.00 25.00
MCP52 Johnny Bench 10.00 25.00
MCP53 Yogi Berra 4.00 10.00
MCP54 Rod Carew 8.00 20.00
MCP55 Orlando Cepeda 4.00 10.00
MCP56 Rickey Henderson 5.00 12.00
MCP57 Bob Feller 5.00 12.00
MCP58 Rollie Fingers 5.00 12.00
MCP60 Catfish Hunter 5.00 12.00
MCP61 Monte Irvin 4.00 10.00
MCP62 Reggie Jackson 4.00 10.00
MCP63 Fergie Jenkins 4.00 10.00
MCP64 Al Kaline 4.00 10.00
MCP65 George Kell 5.00 12.00
MCP66 Harmon Killebrew 8.00 20.00
MCP67 Ralph Kiner 4.00 10.00
MCP68 Juan Marichal 4.00 10.00
MCP69 Eddie Mathews 5.00 12.00
MCP70 Bill Mazeroski 4.00 10.00
MCP71 Willie McCovey 4.00 10.00
MCP72 Joe Morgan 5.00 12.00
MCP73 Eddie Murray 4.00 10.00
MCP74 Ryne Sandberg 4.00 10.00
MCP75 Tom Seaver 8.00 20.00
MCP76 Hal Newhouser 5.00 12.00
MCP79 Tony Perez 5.00 12.00
MCP80 Phil Rizzuto 5.00 12.00
MCP81 Robin Roberts 4.00 10.00
MCP82 Brooks Robinson 4.00 10.00
MCP83 Mike Schmidt 5.00 12.00
MCP84 Red Schoendienst 5.00 12.00
MCP85 Ozzie Smith 5.00 12.00
MCP86 Warren Spahn 8.00 20.00
MCP87 Willie Stargell 8.00 20.00
MCP88 Hoyt Wilhelm 4.00 10.00
MCP89 Jimmie Foxx 4.00 10.00
MCP90 Mickey Mantle 8.00 20.00
MCP91 Jackie Robinson 4.00 10.00
MCP92 Lou Gehrig 5.00 12.00
MCP93 Babe Ruth 10.00 25.00
MCP94 Albert Pujols 6.00 15.00
MCP95 David Wright 5.00 12.00
MCP96 Mariano Rivera 10.00 25.00
MCP97 Ryan Howard 6.00 15.00
MCP98 Ryan Braun 5.00 12.00
MCP99 Joe Mauer 8.00 20.00
MCP100 CC Sabathia 5.00 12.00
MCP101 Tris Speaker 8.00 20.00
MCP102 Dizzy Dean 6.00 15.00
MCP103 Lou Gehrig 5.00 12.00
MCP104 Jimmie Foxx 4.00 10.00
MCP105 Hank Greenberg 4.00 10.00
MCP106 Bob Feller 5.00 12.00
MCP107 Mel Ott 4.00 10.00
MCP108 Johnny Mize 4.00 10.00
MCP109 Phil Rizzuto 5.00 12.00
MCP110 Enos Slaughter 5.00 12.00
MCP111 Pee Wee Reese 5.00 12.00
MCP112 Stan Musial 10.00 25.00
MCP113 Hal Newhouser 5.00 12.00
MCP114 Red Schoendienst 5.00 12.00
MCP115 Yogi Berra 6.00 15.00
MCP116 Larry Doby 6.00 15.00
MCP117 Richie Ashburn 10.00 25.00
MCP119 Johnny Podres 4.00 10.00
MCP120 Duke Snider 5.00 12.00
MCP121 Roger Maris 8.00 20.00
MCP122 Lou Brock 6.00 15.00
MCP123 Luis Aparicio 5.00 12.00
MCP124 Eddie Mathews 5.00 12.00
MCP125 Rollie Fingers 5.00 12.00
MCP126 Reggie Jackson 4.00 10.00
MCP127 Joe Morgan 5.00 12.00
MCP128 Johnny Bench 10.00 25.00
MCP129 Steve Carlton 4.00 10.00
MCP130 Barry Larkin 8.00 20.00
MCP131 Roberto Alomar 5.00 12.00
MCP132 Greg Maddux 4.00 10.00
MCP133 Derek Jeter 12.50 30.00
MCP135 Derek Jeter 10.00 25.00
MCP136 Chipper Jones 4.00 10.00
MCP137 Alex Rodriguez 5.00 12.00
MCP138 Roy Halladay 5.00 12.00
MCP139 Josh Beckett 5.00 12.00
MCP140 Hideki Matsui 12.50 30.00
MCP142 Ryan Braun 5.00 12.00
MCP143 Andre Ethier 4.00 10.00
MCP144 Justin Morneau 5.00 12.00
MCP145 Joe Mauer 8.00 20.00
MCP146 Chase Utley 5.00 12.00
MCP147 Vladimir Guerrero 4.00 10.00
MCP148 Evan Longoria 8.00 20.00
MCP149 Derek Jeter 10.00 25.00
MCP150 Albert Pujols 6.00 15.00

2010 Topps Factory Set All Star Bonus

COMPLETE SET (5) 1.25 3.00
AS1 Hideki Matsui 1.00 2.50
AS2 Kendry Morales .40 1.00
AS3 Torii Hunter .40 1.00
AS4 Scott Kazmir .40 1.00
AS5 Bobby Abreu .40 1.00

2010 Topps Factory Set Phillies Team Bonus

COMPLETE SET (5) 2.50 6.00
PHI1 Roy Halladay .60 1.50
PHI2 Ryan Howard .75 2.00
PHI3 Chase Utley .60 1.50
PHI4 Jimmy Rollins .60 1.50
PHI5 Jayson Werth .60 1.50

2010 Topps Factory Set Red Sox Team Bonus

COMPLETE SET (5) 3.00 8.00
BOS1 Dustin Pedroia 1.00 2.50
BOS2 Jacoby Ellsbury .75 2.00
BOS3 Victor Martinez .60 1.50
BOS4 John Lackey .60 1.50
BOS5 Daisuke Matsuzaka .60 1.50

2010 Topps Factory Set Retail Bonus

COMPLETE SET (5) 6.00 15.00
RS1 Ryan Howard .75 2.00
RS2 Ichiro Suzuki 1.25 3.00
RS3 Hanley Ramirez .60 1.50
RS4 Derek Jeter 2.50 6.00
RS5 Albert Pujols 1.25 3.00

2010 Topps Factory Set Target Ruth Chrome Gold Refractors

COMPLETE SET (3) 15.00 40.00
COMMON RUTH 8.00 20.00
1 Babe Ruth 8.00 20.00
2 Babe Ruth 8.00 20.00
3 Babe Ruth 8.00 20.00

2010 Topps Factory Set Wal-Mart Mantle Chrome Gold Refractors

COMPLETE SET (3) 20.00 50.00
COMMON MANTLE 10.00 25.00
1 Mickey Mantle 10.00 25.00
2 Mickey Mantle 10.00 25.00
3 Mickey Mantle 10.00 25.00

2010 Topps Factory Set Yankees Team Bonus

COMPLETE SET (5) 4.00 10.00
NYY1 Derek Jeter 2.50 6.00
NYY2 Alex Rodriguez 1.25 3.00
NYY3 Mariano Rivera 1.25 3.00
NYY4 Mark Teixeira .60 1.50
NYY5 Curtis Granderson .75 2.00

2010 Topps History of the Game

STATED ODDS 1:6 HOBBY
HOG1 Alexander Cartwright .40 1.00
Baseball Invented
HOG2 First Professional Baseball Game.40 1.00
HOG3 National League Created .40 1.00
HOG4 American League Elevated .40 1.00
to Major League Status
HOG5 First World Series Game Played .40 1.00
HOG6 Wiliam H. Taft .40 1.00
Taft Attends Opening Day
HOG7 Ruth Sold 1.25 3.00
HOG8 Baseball hits the Airwaves .40 1.00
HOG9 Gehrig Replaces Pipp 1.00 2.50
HOG10 Ruth Sets HR Mark 1.25 3.00
HOG11 Babe Ruth
BabeFirst MLB All-Star Game
HOG12 Babe Ruth
First Night Game Played
HOG13 Ruth Retires 1.25 3.00
HOG14 1st Hall of Fame Class Inducted.40 1.00
HOG15 Robinson Plays MLB 1.00 2.50
HOG16 First Televised Game .40 1.00
HOG17 Dodgers & Giants move to CA .40 1.00
HOG18 Maris HR Record .75 2.00
HOG19 Johnny Bench
First MLB Draft
HOG20 F.Robinson MVP .40 1.00
HOG21 DH rule created .40 1.00
HOG22 Ryan 7th No-Hitter 1.50 4.00
HOG23 Ripken Breaks Streak 1.50 4.00
HOG24 Interleague Play Introduced .40 1.00
HOG25 1st MLB game played in Japan .40 1.00

2010 Topps History of the World Series

COMPLETE SET (25) 8.00 20.00
STATED ODDS 1:6 HOBBY
HWS1 Christy Mathewson .75 2.00
HWS2 Walter Johnson .75 2.00
HWS3 Babe Ruth 2.00 5.00
HWS4 Rogers Hornsby .50 1.25
HWS5 Babe Ruth 2.00 5.00
HWS6 Mickey Mantle 2.50 6.00
HWS7 Mel Ott .75 2.00
HWS8 Enos Slaughter .50 1.25
HWS9 Bob Feller .50 1.25
HWS10 Whitey Ford .50 1.25
HWS11 Johnny Podres .30 .75
HWS12 Yogi Berra .75 2.00
HWS13 Yogi Berra .75 2.00
HWS14 Jim Palmer .50 1.25
HWS15 Bob Gibson .50 1.25
HWS16 Brooks Robinson .50 1.25
HWS17 Dennis Eckersley .50 1.25
HWS18 Paul Molitor .75 2.00
HWS19 Jason Varitek .75 2.00
HWS20 Edgar Renteria .30 .75
HWS21 Derek Jeter 2.00 5.00
HWS22 Alex Gonzalez .30 .75
HWS23 Cole Hamels .60 1.50
HWS24 Chase Utley .50 1.25
HWS25 New York Yankees .75 2.00

2010 Topps Legendary Lineage

STATED ODDS 1:4 HOBBY
UPDATE ODDS 1:8 HOBBY
1-30 ISSUED IN SERIES 1
31-60 ISSUED IN SERIES 2
61-75 ISSUED IN UPDATE
LL1 W.McCovey/R.Howard .60 1.50
LL2 M.Mantle/C.Jones 2.50 6.00
LL3 B.Ruth/A.Rodriguez 2.00 5.00
LL4 L.Gehrig/M.Teixeira 1.50 4.00
LL5 T.Cobb/C.Granderson 1.25 3.00
LL6 Jimmie Foxx/Manny Ramirez .75 2.00
LL7 G.Sisler/I.Suzuki 1.00 2.50
LL8 Tris Speaker/Grady Sizemore .50 1.25
LL9 Honus Wagner/Hanley Ramirez .75 2.00
LL10 Johnny Bench/Ivan Rodriguez .75 2.00
LL11 M.Schmidt/E.Longoria 1.25 3.00
LL12 O.Smith/J.Reyes 1.00 2.50
LL13 Reggie Jackson/Adam Dunn .50 1.25
LL14 Warren Spahn/Tommy Hanson .50 1.25
LL15 Duke Snider/Andre Ethier .50 1.25
LL16 S.Musial/A.Pujols 1.25 3.00
LL17 C.Ripken/D.Jeter 2.50 6.00
LL18 G.Carter/D.Wright .60 1.50
LL19 Whitey Ford/CC Sabathia .50 1.25
LL20 Frank Thomas/Prince Fielder .75 2.00
LL21 H.Greenberg/R.Braun .75 2.00
LL22 Frank Robinson/Vladimir Guerrero.50 1.25
LL23 Jackie Robinson/Matt Kemp .75 2.00
LL24 B.Gibson/T.Lincecum .50 1.25
LL25 Tom Seaver/Roy Halladay .50 1.25
LL26 D.Eckersley/M.Rivera 1.00 2.50
LL27 Tony Gwynn/Joe Mauer .75 2.00
LL28 N.Ryan/Z.Greinke 2.50 6.00
LL29 C.Yaz/K.Youkilis 1.25 3.00
LL30 Rickey Henderson/Carl Crawford .75 2.00
LL31 Joe Mauer/Johnny Bench .75 2.00
LL32 Orlando Cepeda/Pablo Sandoval .50 1.25
LL33 Carlton Fisk/Victor Martinez .50 1.25
LL34 Eddie Mathews/Chipper Jones .75 2.00
LL35 A.Kaline/M.Cabrera .75 2.00
LL36 Andre Dawson/Alfonso Soriano .50 1.25
LL37 J.Robinson/I.Suzuki 1.00 2.50
LL38 C.Ripken Jr./H.Ramirez 2.50 6.00
LL39 P.Rizzuto/D.Jeter 2.00 5.00
LL40 Harmon Killebrew/Justin Morneau.75 2.00
LL41 Jimmie Foxx/Prince Fielder .75 2.00
LL42 L.Gehrig/A.Pujols 1.50 4.00
LL43 M.Schmidt/A.Rodriguez 1.25 3.00
LL44 Bo Jackson/Justin Upton .75 2.00
LL45 B.Ruth/R.Howard 2.00 5.00
LL46 Luis Aparicio/Alexei Ramirez .50 1.25
LL47 F.Robinson/R.Braun .50 1.25
LL48 S.Musial/M.Holliday 1.25 3.00
LL49 Lou Brock/Carl Crawford .50 1.25
LL50 Tris Speaker/Jacoby Ellsbury .60 1.50
LL51 J.Marichal/T.Lincecum .50 1.25
LL52 Dale Murphy/Matt Kemp .75 2.00
LL53 N.Ryan/J.Verlander 2.50 6.00
LL54 O.Smith/E.Andrus 1.00 2.50
LL55 Rickey Henderson/B.J. Upton .75 2.00
LL56 Brooks Robinson/Ryan Zimmerman.50 1.25
LL57 Yogi Berra/Jorge Posada .75 2.00
LL58 H.Wagner/A.McCutchen .75 2.00
LL59 M.Mantle/M.Teixeira 2.50 6.00
LL60 R.Sandberg/C.Utley 1.50 4.00
LL61 D.Winfield/J.Heyward 1.25 3.00
LL62 W.Johnson/S.Strasburg 2.50 6.00
LL63 V.Martinez/C.Santana 1.00 2.50
LL64 Rod Carew/Robinson Cano .50 1.25
LL65 Bob Gibson/Ubaldo Jimenez .50 1.25
LL66 M.Cabrera/M.Stanton 2.50 6.00
LL67 H.Greenberg/I.Davis .75 2.00
LL68 Mark Teixeira/Logan Morrison .50 1.25
LL69 T.Seaver/M.Leake 1.00 2.50
LL70 E.Banks/S.Castro .75 2.00
LL71 J.Palmer/B.Matusz .75 2.00
LL72 Larry Walker/Justin Morneau .50 1.25
LL73 Steve Carlton/Jon Lester .50 1.25
LL74 J.Bench/B.Posey 2.50 6.00
LL75 Joe Nathan/Drew Storen .50 1.25
LR38 C.Ripken Jr./H.Ramirez

2010 Topps Legendary Lineage Relics

SER.1 ODDS 1:7540 HOBBY
SER.2 ODDS 1:6075 HOBBY
STATED PRINT RUN 50 SER.#'d SETS
BC L.Brock/C.Crawford 10.00 25.00
BM Y.Berra/J.Posada 25.00 60.00
CR Johnny Bench/Ivan Rodriguez 12.50 30.00
CS O.Cepeda/P.Sandoval 15.00 40.00
CW G.Carter/D.Wright 15.00 40.00
ER Eckersley/Rivera 40.00 80.00
FR J.Foxx/M.Ramirez 30.00 60.00
GB H.Greenberg/R.Braun 30.00 60.00
HU R.Henderson/B.Upton 30.00 60.00
KC A.Kaline/M.Cabrera 30.00 60.00
KM H.Killebrew/J.Morneau 10.00 25.00
MH W.McCovey/R.Howard 12.50 30.00
MJ M.Mantle/C.Jones 60.00 120.00
MJ E.Mathews/C.Jones 60.00 120.00
MK D.Murphy/M.Kemp 10.00 25.00
MP S.Musial/A.Pujols 75.00 150.00
MT M.Mantle/M.Teixeira 75.00 150.00
RB F.Robinson/R.Braun 10.00 25.00
RH B.Ruth/R.Howard 30.00 80.00
RR C.Ripken Jr/H.Ramirez 20.00 50.00
SE D.Snider/A.Ethier 12.50 30.00
SH W.Spahn/T.Hanson 60.00 120.00
SL M.Schmidt/E.Longoria 20.00 50.00
SR M.Schmidt/A.Rodriguez 30.00 60.00
SS G.Sisler/I.Suzuki 60.00 120.00
SU R.Sandberg/C.Utley 12.50 30.00
TF F.Thomas/P.Fielder 60.00 120.00
WR H.Wagner/H.Ramirez 50.00 100.00
BMA J.Bench/J.Mauer 40.00 80.00
SSI T.Speaker/G.Sizemore 20.00 50.00

2010 Topps Legends Gold Chrome Target Cereal

INSERTED IN TARGET PACKS
GC1 Babe Ruth 6.00 15.00
GC2 Honus Wagner 2.50 6.00
GC3 Ichiro Suzuki 3.00 8.00
GC4 Nolan Ryan 8.00 20.00
GC5 Jackie Robinson 2.50 6.00
GC6 Tom Seaver 1.50 4.00
GC7 Derek Jeter 6.00 15.00
GC8 George Sisler 1.50 4.00
GC9 Roger Maris 2.50 6.00
GC10 Lou Gehrig 5.00 12.00
GC11 Mickey Mantle 8.00 20.00
GC12 Willie McCovey 1.50 4.00
GC13 Ty Cobb 4.00 10.00
GC14 Warren Spahn 1.50 4.00
GC15 Albert Pujols 3.00 8.00
GC16 Lou Gehrig 5.00 12.00
GC17 Mariano Rivera 3.00 8.00
GC18 Jimmie Foxx 2.50 6.00
GC19 Babe Ruth 6.00 15.00
GC20 Honus Wagner 2.50 6.00

2010 Topps Legends Platinum Chrome Wal-Mart Cereal

INSERTED IN WAL MART PACKS
PC1 Mickey Mantle 8.00 20.00
PC2 Jackie Robinson 2.50 6.00
PC3 Ty Cobb 4.00 10.00
PC4 Warren Spahn 1.50 4.00
PC5 Albert Pujols 3.00 8.00
PC6 Lou Gehrig 5.00 12.00
PC7 Mariano Rivera 3.00 8.00
PC8 Jimmie Foxx 2.50 6.00
PC9 Cy Young 2.50 6.00
PC10 Honus Wagner 2.50 6.00
PC11 Babe Ruth 6.00 15.00
PC12 Mickey Mantle 8.00 20.00
PC13 Ichiro Suzuki 3.00 8.00
PC14 Nolan Ryan 8.00 20.00
PC15 Jackie Robinson 2.50 6.00
PC16 Tom Seaver 1.50 4.00
PC17 Derek Jeter 6.00 15.00
PC18 Ty Cobb 4.00 10.00
PC19 Roger Maris 2.50 6.00
PC20 Lou Gehrig 5.00 12.00

2010 Topps Logoman HTA

DISTRIBUTED IN HTA STORES
1 Albert Pujols .75 2.00
2 Hanley Ramirez .40 1.00
3 Mike Schmidt 1.00 2.50
4 CC Sabathia .40 1.00
5 Babe Ruth 1.50 4.00
6 George Sisler .40 1.00
7 Gordon Beckham .25 .60
8 Tris Speaker .40 1.00
9 Ryan Braun .40 1.00
10 Jackie Robinson .60 1.50
11 Stan Musial 1.00 2.50
12 Ichiro Suzuki .75 2.00
13 Manny Ramirez .60 1.50
14 Ty Cobb 1.00 2.50
15 Tommy Hanson .25 .60
16 Joe Mauer .50 1.25
17 David Ortiz .60 1.50
18 Tim Lincecum .40 1.00
19 Andrew McCutchen .60 1.50
20 Reggie Jackson .40 1.00
21 Nolan Ryan 2.00 5.00
22 Evan Longoria .40 1.00
23 Johan Santana .40 1.00
24 Mark Teixeira .40 1.00
25 Pablo Sandoval .40 1.00
26 Jimmie Foxx .60 1.50
27 Roy Halladay .40 1.00
28 Lou Gehrig 1.25 3.00
29 Alex Rodriguez .75 2.00
30 Thurman Munson .60 1.50
31 Mel Ott .60 1.50
32 Mickey Mantle 2.00 5.00
33 Johnny Mize .40 1.00
34 Rogers Hornsby .40 1.00
35 Chase Utley .40 1.00
36 Walter Johnson .60 1.50
37 Zack Greinke .60 1.50
38 Honus Wagner .60 1.50
39 Roy Campanella .60 1.50
40 Prince Fielder .40 1.00
41 Cal Ripken Jr. 2.00 5.00
42 Carl Yastrzemski 1.00 2.50
43 David Wright .50 1.25
44 Tom Seaver .40 1.00
45 Cy Young .60 1.50
46 Christy Mathewson .60 1.50
47 Justin Morneau .40 1.00
48 Ryan Howard .50 1.25
49 Rick Porcello .40 1.00
50 Nolan Reimold .25 .60

2010 Topps Manufactured Hat Logo Patch

SER.1 ODDS 1:432 HOBBY
SER.2 ODDS 1:420 HOBBY
STATED PRINT RUN 99 SER.#'d SETS
1-186 ISSUED IN SERIES 1
187-416 ISSUED IN SERIES 2
VAR.OF SAME PLAYER EQUALLY PRICED
MHR1 Babe Ruth 10.00 25.00
MHR2 Babe Ruth 10.00 25.00
MHR3 George Sisler 8.00 20.00
MHR4 George Sisler 8.00 20.00
MHR5 Honus Wagner 10.00 25.00
MHR6 Jackie Robinson 10.00 25.00
MHR7 Jimmie Foxx 8.00 20.00
MHR8 Jimmie Foxx 8.00 20.00
MHR9 Johnny Mize 5.00 12.00
MHR10 Johnny Mize 5.00 12.00
MHR11 Johnny Mize 5.00 12.00
MHR12 Lou Gehrig 8.00 20.00
MHR13 Mel Ott 10.00 25.00
MHR14 Rogers Hornsby 4.00 10.00
MHR15 Rogers Hornsby 4.00 10.00
MHR16 Roy Campanella 10.00 25.00
MHR17 Thurman Munson 10.00 25.00
MHR18 Tris Speaker 10.00 25.00
MHR19 Ty Cobb 10.00 25.00
MHR20 Ty Cobb 10.00 25.00
MHR21 Mickey Mantle 12.50 30.00
MHR22 Richie Ashburn 10.00 25.00
MHR23 Bo Jackson 8.00 20.00
MHR24 Bo Jackson 8.00 20.00
MHR25 Paul Molitor 10.00 25.00
MHR26 Paul Molitor 10.00 25.00
MHR27 Paul Molitor 10.00 25.00
MHR28 Tony Gwynn 6.00 15.00
MHR29 Tony Gwynn 6.00 15.00
MHR30 Tony Gwynn 6.00 15.00
MHR31 Al Kaline 8.00 20.00
MHR32 Andre Dawson 6.00 15.00
MHR33 Andre Dawson 6.00 15.00
MHR34 Bob Feller 6.00 15.00
MHR35 Bob Gibson 8.00 20.00
MHR36 Bobby Murcer 6.00 15.00
MHR37 Carl Erskine 10.00 25.00
MHR38 Carl Erskine 10.00 25.00
MHR39 Curt Schilling 6.00 15.00
MHR40 Curt Schilling 6.00 15.00
MHR41 Curt Schilling 6.00 15.00
MHR42 Dale Murphy 10.00 25.00
MHR43 Dale Murphy 10.00 25.00
MHR44 Dizzy Dean 6.00 15.00
MHR45 Dizzy Dean 6.00 15.00
MHR46 Duke Snider 8.00 20.00
MHR47 Duke Snider 8.00 20.00
MHR48 Duke Snider 8.00 20.00
MHR49 Dwight Gooden 6.00 15.00
MHR50 Dwight Gooden 6.00 15.00
MHR51 Eddie Mathews 10.00 25.00
MHR52 Eddie Mathews 10.00 25.00
MHR53 Eddie Murray 10.00 25.00
MHR54 Eddie Murray 10.00 25.00
MHR55 Eddie Murray 10.00 25.00
MHR56 Eddie Murray 10.00 25.00
MHR57 Fergie Jenkins 8.00 20.00
MHR58 Fergie Jenkins 8.00 20.00
MHR59 Frank Robinson 8.00 20.00
MHR60 Frank Robinson 8.00 20.00
MHR61 Frank Thomas 10.00 25.00
MHR62 Frank Thomas 10.00 25.00
MHR63 Frank Thomas 10.00 25.00
MHR64 Gary Carter 10.00 25.00
MHR65 Gary Carter 10.00 25.00
MHR66 George Kell 8.00 20.00
MHR67 Hank Greenberg 6.00 15.00
MHR68 Jim Palmer 6.00 15.00
MHR69 Jim Palmer 6.00 15.00
MHR70 Jim Palmer 6.00 15.00
MHR71 Jimmy Piersall 12.50 30.00
MHR72 Johnny Bench 10.00 25.00
MHR73 Johnny Bench 10.00 25.00
MHR74 Johnny Podres 12.50 30.00
MHR75 Johnny Podres 12.50 30.00
MHR76 Juan Marichal 8.00 20.00
MHR77 Juan Marichal 8.00 20.00
MHR78 Monte Irvin 6.00 15.00
MHR79 Nolan Ryan 20.00 50.00
MHR80 Nolan Ryan 20.00 50.00
MHR81 Nolan Ryan 20.00 50.00
MHR82 Nolan Ryan 20.00 50.00
MHR83 Orlando Cepeda 4.00 10.00
MHR84 Orlando Cepeda 4.00 10.00
MHR85 Ozzie Smith 15.00 40.00
MHR86 Ozzie Smith 15.00 40.00
MHR87 Ralph Kiner 6.00 15.00
MHR88 Reggie Jackson 15.00 40.00
MHR89 Reggie Jackson 15.00 40.00
MHR90 Reggie Jackson 15.00 40.00
MHR91 Reggie Jackson 15.00 40.00
MHR92 Reggie Jackson 15.00 40.00
MHR93 Robin Roberts 12.50 30.00
MHR94 Robin Yount 12.50 30.00
MHR95 Robin Yount 12.50 30.00
MHR96 Roger Maris 12.50 30.00
MHR97 Roger Maris 12.50 30.00
MHR98 Roger Maris 12.50 30.00
MHR99 Stan Musial 12.50 30.00
MHR100 Steve Carlton 8.00 20.00
MHR101 Steve Carlton 8.00 20.00
MHR102 Tom Seaver 8.00 20.00
MHR103 Tom Seaver 8.00 20.00
MHR104 Tony Perez 6.00 15.00
MHR105 Warren Spahn 10.00 25.00
MHR106 Warren Spahn 10.00 25.00
MHR107 Willie McCovey 6.00 15.00
MHR108 Willie McCovey 6.00 15.00
MHR109 Willie Stargell 12.50 30.00
MHR110 Rickey Henderson 12.50 30.00
MHR111 Rickey Henderson 12.50 30.00
MHR112 Rickey Henderson 12.50 30.00
MHR113 Rickey Henderson 12.50 30.00
MHR114 Carlton Fisk 8.00 20.00
MHR115 Carlton Fisk 8.00 20.00
MHR116 Dennis Eckersley 8.00 20.00
MHR117 Dennis Eckersley 8.00 20.00
MHR118 Ryne Sandberg 15.00 40.00
MHR119 Ryne Sandberg 15.00 40.00
MHR120 Lou Brock 8.00 20.00
MHR121 Carl Yastrzemski 10.00 25.00
MHR122 Ernie Banks 10.00 25.00
MHR123 Mike Schmidt 12.50 30.00
MHR124 Alex Rodriguez 12.50 30.00
MHR125 Alex Rodriguez 12.50 30.00
MHR126 Alex Rodriguez 12.50 30.00
MHR127 Kevin Youkilis 10.00 25.00
MHR128 Vladimir Guerrero 10.00 25.00
MHR129 Vladimir Guerrero 10.00 25.00
MHR130 Chipper Jones 8.00 20.00
MHR131 Dustin Pedroia 12.50 30.00
MHR132 Ian Kinsler 4.00 10.00
MHR133 Dustin Pedroia 12.50 30.00
MHR134 Ryan Howard 12.50 30.00
MHR135 Prince Fielder 8.00 20.00
MHR136 David Wright 10.00 25.00
MHR137 Carl Crawford 6.00 15.00
MHR138 Justin Upton 10.00 25.00
MHR139 Dan Haren 4.00 10.00
MHR140 Randy Johnson 10.00 25.00
MHR141 Randy Johnson 10.00 25.00
MHR142 Randy Johnson 10.00 25.00
MHR143 Randy Johnson 10.00 25.00
MHR144 Randy Johnson 10.00 25.00
MHR145 Randy Johnson 10.00 25.00
MHR146 David Ortiz 10.00 25.00
MHR147 Roy Halladay 10.00 25.00
MHR148 Tim Lincecum 20.00 50.00
MHR149 Pablo Sandoval 10.00 25.00
MHR150 Albert Pujols 30.00 60.00
MHR151 Hanley Ramirez 6.00 15.00
MHR152 Nick Markakis 8.00 20.00
MHR153 Ichiro Suzuki 20.00 50.00
MHR154 Adam Jones 4.00 10.00
MHR155 Evan Longoria 10.00 25.00
MHR156 Joe Mauer 12.50 30.00
MHR157 Matt Kemp 8.00 20.00
MHR158 Justin Verlander 12.50 30.00
MHR159 Zack Greinke 8.00 20.00
MHR160 Miguel Cabrera 8.00 20.00
MHR161 Chase Utley 12.50 30.00
MHR162 Adam Dunn 6.00 15.00
MHR163 Manny Ramirez 8.00 20.00
MHR164 Manny Ramirez 8.00 20.00
MHR165 Grady Sizemore 12.50 30.00
MHR166 Felix Hernandez 12.50 30.00
MHR167 Mark Teixeira 10.00 25.00
MHR168 Joey Votto 15.00 40.00
MHR169 Ryan Braun 12.50 30.00
MHR170 Mariano Rivera 12.50 30.00
MHR171 Tommy Hanson 6.00 15.00
MHR172 Matt Cain 6.00 15.00
MHR173 Josh Johnson 10.00 25.00
MHR174 Clayton Kershaw 4.00 10.00
MHR175 Jon Lester 10.00 25.00
MHR176 Elvis Andrus 5.00 12.00
MHR177 Dexter Fowler 5.00 12.00
MHR178 Rick Porcello 6.00 15.00
MHR179 Andrew McCutchen 8.00 20.00
MHR180 Colby Rasmus 10.00 25.00
MHR181 Chris Coghlan 4.00 10.00
MHR182 Nolan Reimold 5.00 12.00
MHR183 Buster Posey 40.00 80.00
MHR184 Koji Uehara 6.00 15.00
MHR185 Madison Bumgarner 12.50 30.00
MHR186 Neftali Feliz 6.00 15.00
MHR187 Mark Teixeira 10.00 25.00
MHR188 Vladimir Guerrero 10.00 25.00
MHR189 Joe Mauer 12.50 30.00
MHR190 Max Scherzer 4.00 10.00
MHR191 Adrian Gonzalez 4.00 10.00
MHR192 Josh Beckett 10.00 25.00
MHR193 Jose Reyes 10.00 25.00
MHR194 Ryan Braun 12.50 30.00
MHR195 Cliff Lee 4.00 10.00
MHR196 Kendry Morales 5.00 12.00
MHR197 Tim Lincecum 20.00 50.00
MHR198 Prince Fielder 8.00 20.00
MHR199 Ichiro Suzuki 20.00 50.00
MHR200 Chipper Jones 8.00 20.00
MHR201 Chase Utley 12.50 30.00
MHR202 Felix Hernandez 12.50 30.00
MHR203 Nolan Reimold 5.00 12.00
MHR204 Albert Pujols 30.00 60.00
MHR205 Torii Hunter 6.00 15.00
MHR206 Evan Longoria 12.50 30.00
MHR207 CC Sabathia 8.00 20.00
MHR208 Mariano Rivera 12.50 30.00
MHR209 B.J. Upton 6.00 15.00
MHR210 Justin Upton 10.00 25.00
MHR211 Ivan Rodriguez 6.00 15.00
MHR212 Curtis Granderson 5.00 12.00
MHR213 Josh Hamilton 8.00 20.00
MHR214 Tim Hudson 8.00 20.00
MHR215 Neftali Feliz 6.00 15.00
MHR216 Babe Ruth 10.00 25.00
MHR217 Adam Lind 4.00 10.00
MHR218 David Price 8.00 20.00
MHR219 Tommy Hanson 6.00 15.00
MHR220 Andrew McCutchen 8.00 20.00
MHR221 Adam Dunn 6.00 15.00
MHR222 Victor Martinez 5.00 12.00
MHR223 Pablo Sandoval 10.00 25.00
MHR224 Ricky Romero 5.00 12.00
MHR225 Brian McCann 4.00 10.00
MHR226 Jered Weaver 5.00 12.00
MHR227 Andrew Bailey 4.00 10.00
MHR228 Joe Saunders 4.00 10.00
MHR229 Colby Rasmus 10.00 25.00
MHR230 Nick Markakis 8.00 20.00
MHR231 Mark Reynolds 5.00 12.00
MHR232 Ryan Howard 12.50 30.00
MHR233 Stephen Drew 4.00 10.00
MHR234 David Ortiz 10.00 25.00
MHR235 Kenshin Kawakami 6.00 15.00
MHR236 Michael Young 4.00 10.00
MHR237 Jayson Werth 8.00 20.00
MHR238 John Lackey 4.00 10.00
MHR239 Dustin Pedroia 12.50 30.00
MHR240 Travis Snider 6.00 15.00
MHR241 Rajai Davis 8.00 20.00
MHR242 Edgar Renteria 4.00 10.00
MHR243 Justin Morneau 10.00 25.00
MHR244 Jimmy Rollins 8.00 20.00
MHR245 Elvis Andrus 5.00 12.00
MHR246 David Wright 10.00 25.00
MHR247 Javier Vazquez 6.00 15.00
MHR248 Jorge Posada 6.00 15.00
MHR249 Carlos Beltran 8.00 20.00
MHR250 Jonathan Broxton 4.00 10.00
MHR251 Adam Jones 8.00 20.00
MHR252 Alex Rodriguez 12.50 30.00
MHR253 Koji Uehara 5.00 12.00
MHR254 Brandon Webb 6.00 15.00
MHR255 Kevin Kouzmanoff 8.00 20.00
MHR256 Ryan Zimmerman 12.50 30.00
MHR257 Brian Roberts 5.00 12.00
MHR258 Alfonso Soriano 4.00 10.00
MHR259 Jason Varitek 8.00 20.00
MHR260 Aramis Ramirez 4.00 10.00
MHR261 Jeremy Guthrie 6.00 15.00
MHR262 Johnny Cueto 5.00 12.00
MHR263 Jacoby Ellsbury 10.00 25.00
MHR264 Carlos Quentin 4.00 10.00
MHR265 Kosuke Fukudome 6.00 15.00
MHR266 Grady Sizemore 12.50 30.00
MHR267 Troy Tulowitzki 8.00 20.00
MHR268 Alexei Ramirez 4.00 10.00
MHR269 Jeff Francis 4.00 10.00
MHR270 Jay Bruce 4.00 10.00
MHR271 Rick Porcello 6.00 15.00
MHR272 Gordon Beckham 6.00 15.00
MHR273 Justin Verlander 12.50 30.00
MHR274 Magglio Ordonez 8.00 20.00
MHR275 Miguel Cabrera 8.00 20.00
MHR276 Jake Peavy 4.00 10.00
MHR277 Ryan Ludwick 4.00 10.00
MHR278 Todd Helton 6.00 15.00
MHR279 Carlos Lee 4.00 10.00
MHR280 Mark Buehrle 6.00 15.00
MHR281 Billy Butler 6.00 15.00
MHR282 Chris Coghlan 4.00 10.00
MHR283 Brett Anderson 8.00 20.00
MHR284 Lance Berkman 4.00 10.00
MHR285 Chone Figgins 4.00 10.00
MHR286 Ubaldo Jimenez 5.00 12.00
MHR287 Jason Kubel 6.00 15.00
MHR288 Manny Ramirez 8.00 20.00
MHR289 Joe Nathan 5.00 12.00
MHR290 Jimmie Foxx 8.00 20.00
MHR291 J.J. Hardy 8.00 20.00
MHR292 Mike Cameron 4.00 10.00
MHR293 Roy Oswalt 4.00 10.00
MHR294 Carlos Delgado 5.00 12.00
MHR295 Rogers Hornsby 4.00 10.00
MHR296 Hunter Pence 4.00 10.00
MHR297 Scott Kazmir 8.00 20.00
MHR298 Tris Speaker 10.00 25.00
MHR299 Jhoulys Chacin 4.00 10.00
MHR300 Michael Cuddyer 8.00 20.00
MHR301 Zack Greinke 8.00 20.00
MHR302 Jeff Francoeur 4.00 10.00
MHR303 Matt Kemp 8.00 20.00
MHR304 Dan Haren 4.00 10.00
MHR305 Andy Pettitte 4.00 10.00
MHR306 David DeJesus 4.00 10.00
MHR307 A.J. Burnett 5.00 12.00
MHR308 Ty Cobb 10.00 25.00
MHR309 Johnny Mize 5.00 12.00
MHR310 Joakim Soria 6.00 15.00
MHR311 Chris Carpenter 6.00 15.00
MHR312 Asdrubal Cabrera 10.00 25.00
MHR313 Shane Victorino 12.50 30.00
MHR314 Andre Ethier 6.00 15.00
MHR315 Kurt Suzuki 6.00 15.00
MHR316 Honus Wagner 10.00 25.00
MHR317 Clayton Kershaw 4.00 10.00
MHR318 Zach Duke 4.00 10.00
MHR319 Shin-Soo Choo 10.00 25.00
MHR320 Matt Cain 6.00 15.00
MHR321 Russell Martin 5.00 12.00
MHR322 Joba Chamberlain 6.00 15.00
MHR323 Jason Bay 5.00 12.00
MHR324 Delmon Young 6.00 15.00
MHR325 Matt Holliday 6.00 15.00
MHR326 Scott Rolen 8.00 20.00
MHR327 Adam Wainwright 5.00 12.00
MHR328 Hanley Ramirez 6.00 15.00
MHR329 Cal Ripken Jr. 10.00 25.00
MHR330 Mickey Mantle 12.50 30.00
MHR331 Chase Headley 4.00 10.00
MHR332 Rich Harden 4.00 10.00
MHR333 Garrett Jones 5.00 12.00
MHR334 Dexter Fowler 5.00 12.00
MHR335 Ian Kinsler 4.00 10.00
MHR336 Raul Ibanez 6.00 15.00
MHR337 Roy Halladay 10.00 25.00
MHR338 Ryan Spilborghs 6.00 15.00
MHR339 Cole Hamels 10.00 25.00
MHR340 Thurman Munson 10.00 25.00
MHR341 Robinson Cano 6.00 15.00
MHR342 Matt LaPorta 5.00 12.00
MHR343 Travis Hafner 5.00 12.00
MHR344 Lou Gehrig 8.00 20.00
MHR345 Nelson Cruz 6.00 15.00
MHR346 Derrek Lee 6.00 15.00
MHR347 Juan Marichal 8.00 20.00
MHR348 Rollie Fingers 5.00 12.00
MHR349 Carl Yastrzemski 10.00 25.00
MHR350 Frank Robinson 8.00 20.00
MHR351 Joe Morgan 6.00 15.00
MHR352 Steve Carlton 8.00 20.00
MHR353 Catfish Hunter 10.00 25.00

Card	Low	High
MHR354 Willie Stargell	12.50	30.00
MHR355 Early Wynn	5.00	12.00
MHR356 Larry Doby	5.00	12.00
MHR357 Bill Mazeroski	6.00	15.00
MHR358 Carlton Fisk	8.00	20.00
MHR359 Dave Winfield	5.00	12.00
MHR360 Enos Slaughter	10.00	25.00
MHR361 Ernie Banks	10.00	25.00
MHR362 Joe Morgan	6.00	15.00
MHR363 Rollie Fingers	5.00	12.00
MHR364 Phil Rizzuto	8.00	20.00
MHR365 Bo Jackson	8.00	20.00
MHR366 Dave Winfield	5.00	12.00
MHR367 Babe Ruth	10.00	5.00
MHR368 Luis Aparicio	5.00	12.00
MHR369 Duke Snider	8.00	20.00
MHR370 Richie Ashburn	10.00	25.00
MHR371 Early Wynn	5.00	12.00
MHR372 Yogi Berra	10.00	25.00
MHR373 Lou Brock	8.00	20.00
MHR374 Roger Maris	12.50	30.00
MHR375 Orlando Cepeda	4.00	10.00
MHR376 Catfish Hunter	10.00	25.00
MHR377 Ralph Kiner	6.00	15.00
MHR378 Bob Gibson	8.00	20.00
MHR379 Robin Yount	12.50	30.00
MHR380 Harmon Killebrew	10.00	25.00
MHR381 Orlando Cepeda	4.00	10.00
MHR382 Steve Carlton	8.00	20.00
MHR383 Bob Feller	6.00	15.00
MHR384 Dennis Eckersley	8.00	20.00
MHR385 Robin Roberts	12.50	30.00
MHR386 Willie McCovey	6.00	15.00
MHR387 Hank Greenberg	5.00	12.00
MHR388 Johnny Bench	10.00	25.00
MHR389 Eddie Murray	12.50	30.00
MHR390 Red Schoendienst	5.00	12.00
MHR391 Roger Maris	12.50	30.00
MHR392 Tris Speaker	10.00	25.00
MHR393 Dale Murphy	10.00	25.00
MHR394 Forgie Jenkins	8.00	20.00
MHR395 Frank Robinson	8.00	20.00
MHR396 Willie McCovey	6.00	15.00
MHR397 George Kell	8.00	20.00
MHR398 Dave Winfield	5.00	12.00
MHR399 Ozzie Smith	15.00	40.00
MHR400 Rogers Hornsby	4.00	10.00
MHR401 Jim Palmer	6.00	15.00
MHR402 Carlton Fisk	8.00	20.00
MHR403 Duke Snider	8.00	20.00
MHR404 Gary Carter	10.00	25.00
MHR405 Luis Aparicio	5.00	12.00
MHR406 Andre Dawson	6.00	15.00
MHR407 Hal Newhouser	8.00	20.00
MHR408 Al Kaline	8.00	20.00
MHR409 Bo Jackson	8.00	20.00
MHR410 Johnny Mize	5.00	12.00
MHR411 Mike Schmidt	12.50	30.00
MHR412 Jim Bunning	6.00	15.00
MHR413 Tony Perez	6.00	15.00
MHR414 Dizzy Dean	6.00	15.00
MHR415 Frank Thomas	12.00	30.00
MHR416 Stan Musial	12.50	30.00

2010 Topps Manufactured MLB Logoman Patch

RANDOM INSERTS IN VARIOUS 2010 PRODUCTS
STATED PRINT RUN 50 SER.#'d SETS

Card	Low	High
LM1 Albert Pujols	12.00	30.00
LM2 Hanley Ramirez	6.00	15.00
LM3 Mike Schmidt	15.00	40.00
LM4 Nick Markakis	8.00	20.00
LM5 CC Sabathia	6.00	15.00
LM6 Babe Ruth	25.00	60.00
LM7 George Sisler	6.00	15.00
LM8 Gordon Beckham	4.00	10.00
LM9 Adrian Gonzalez	8.00	20.00
LM10 Ozzie Smith	12.00	30.00
LM11 Yogi Berra	10.00	25.00
LM12 Tris Speaker	6.00	15.00
LM13 Ryan Braun	6.00	15.00
LM14 Juan Marichal	6.00	15.00
LM21 Joe Mauer	8.00	20.00
LM22 David Ortiz	10.00	25.00
LM23 Tim Lincecum	6.00	15.00
LM25 Miguel Cabrera	10.00	25.00
LM27 Lou Gehrig	20.00	50.00
LM28 Stan Musial	15.00	40.00
LM29 Whitey Ford	6.00	15.00
LM30 Ty Cobb	15.00	40.00
LM31 Dustin Pedroia	10.00	25.00
LM32 Evan Longoria	6.00	15.00
LM33 Clayton Kershaw	10.00	25.00
LM35 Mark Teixeira	6.00	15.00
LM36 Frank Robinson	6.00	15.00
LM37 Johnny Bench	10.00	25.00
LM38 Ryne Sandberg	20.00	50.00
LM39 Reggie Jackson	6.00	15.00
LM40 Nolan Ryan	30.00	80.00
LM41 Steve Carlton	6.00	15.00
LM42 Johnny Podres	4.00	10.00
LM43 Jim Palmer	6.00	15.00
LM44 Jimmie Foxx	10.00	25.00
LM45 Robin Yount	10.00	25.00
LM46 Justin Upton	6.00	15.00
LM47 Alfonso Soriano	6.00	15.00
LM48 Grady Sizemore	6.00	15.00
LM49 Matt Kemp	8.00	20.00
LM50 B.J. Upton	6.00	15.00
LM52 Roy Halladay	6.00	15.00
LM54 Chipper Jones	10.00	25.00
LM55 Alex Rodriguez	12.00	30.00
LM56 Andre Dawson	6.00	15.00
LM57 Tony Gwynn	10.00	25.00
LM58 Mickey Mantle	30.00	80.00
LM59 Johnny Mize	6.00	15.00
LM61 Walter Johnson	10.00	25.00
LM62 Honus Wagner	10.00	25.00
LM63 Bob Gibson	6.00	15.00
LM64 Warren Spahn	6.00	15.00
LM65 Dizzy Dean	6.00	15.00
LM66 Roy Campanella	10.00	25.00
LM67 Cal Ripken Jr.	30.00	80.00
LM68 Carl Yastrzemski	15.00	40.00
LM69 Mel Ott	10.00	25.00
LM70 Roger Maris	10.00	25.00
LM72 Justin Verlander	10.00	25.00
LM73 Aaron Hill	4.00	10.00
LM74 Josh Beckett	4.00	10.00
LM75 Adam Wainwright	6.00	15.00
LM77 Derrek Lee	4.00	10.00
LM78 Chase Utley	6.00	15.00
LM79 Zack Greinke	10.00	25.00
LM81 Tom Seaver	6.00	15.00
LM82 Cy Young	10.00	25.00
LM83 Christy Mathewson	10.00	25.00
LM84 Thurman Munson	10.00	25.00
LM85 Eddie Mathews	10.00	25.00
LM87 Willie McCovey	6.00	15.00
LM88 Willie Stargell	6.00	15.00
LM90 Ernie Banks	10.00	25.00
LM91 Felix Hernandez	6.00	15.00
LM92 Prince Fielder	6.00	15.00
LM93 David Wright	8.00	20.00
LM94 Kevin Youkilis	4.00	10.00
LM95 Justin Morneau	6.00	15.00
LM96 Ryan Howard	8.00	20.00
LM97 Todd Helton	6.00	15.00
LM98 Rick Porcello	6.00	15.00
LM99 Nolan Reimold	4.00	10.00
LM100 Dan Haren	4.00	10.00

2010 Topps Mickey Mantle Reprint Relics

SERIES 1 ODDS 1:88,000
UPDATE ODDS 1:60,000 HOBBY
SER.1 PRINT RUN 61 SER.#'d SETS
SER.2 PRINT RUN 62 SER.#'d SETS
UPD PRINT RUN 63 SER.#'d SETS

Card	Low	High
MMR61 M.Mantle Bat/61	150.00	400.00
MMR66 M.Mantle Bat/63	90.00	150.00

2010 Topps Mickey Mouse All-Stars

Card	Low	High
COMPLETE SET (10)	20.00	50.00
COMP.FANFEST SET (5)	10.00	25.00
COMP.UPDATE SET (5)	10.00	25.00
MM1 All Star Game	2.50	6.00
MM2 American League	2.50	6.00
MM3 National League	2.50	6.00
MM4 Los Angeles Angels	2.50	6.00
MM5 Los Angeles Dodgers	2.50	6.00
MM6 Atlanta Braves	2.50	6.00
MM7 Chicago Cubs	2.50	6.00
MM8 New York Mets	2.50	6.00
MM9 New York Yankees	4.00	10.00
MM10 San Francisco Giants	2.50	6.00

2010 Topps Million Card Giveaway

Card	Low	High
COMMON CARD	1.50	4.00
RANDOM INSERTS IN VAR.TOPPS PRODUCTS		
TMC1 Roy Campanella	1.50	4.00
TMC2 Gary Carter	1.50	4.00
TMC3 Bob Gibson	1.50	4.00
TMC4 Ichiro Suzuki	1.50	4.00
TMC5 Mickey Mantle	1.50	4.00
TMC6 Mickey Mantle	1.50	4.00
TMC7 Roger Maris	1.50	4.00
TMC8 Thurman Munson	1.50	4.00
TMC9 Mike Schmidt	1.50	4.00
TMC10 Carl Yastrzemski	1.50	4.00
TMC11 Roy Campanella	1.50	4.00
TMC12 Gary Carter	1.50	4.00
TMC13 Bob Gibson	1.50	4.00
TMC14 Ichiro Suzuki	1.50	4.00
TMC15 Mickey Mantle	1.50	4.00
TMC16 Mickey Mantle	1.50	4.00
TMC17 Roger Maris	1.50	4.00
TMC18 Thurman Munson	1.50	4.00
TMC19 Mike Schmidt	1.50	4.00
TMC20 Carl Yastrzemski	1.50	4.00
TMC21 Roy Campanella	1.50	4.00
TMC22 Gary Carter	1.50	4.00
TMC23 Bob Gibson	1.50	4.00
TMC24 Ichiro Suzuki	1.50	4.00
TMC25 Mickey Mantle	1.50	4.00
TMC26 Roger Maris	1.50	4.00
TMC27 Thurman Munson	1.50	4.00
TMC28 Mike Schmidt	1.50	4.00
TMC29 Carl Yastrzemski	1.50	4.00
TMC30 Mickey Mantle	1.50	4.00

2010 Topps Peak Performance

STATED ODDS 1:4 HOBBY
UPDATE ODDS 1:8 HOBBY
1-50 ISSUED IN SERIES 1
51-100 ISSUED IN SERIES 2
101-125 ISSUED IN UPDATE

Card	Low	High
1 Albert Pujols	1.00	2.50
2 Tim Lincecum	.50	1.25
3 Honus Wagner	.75	2.00
4 Walter Johnson	.75	2.00
5 Babe Ruth	2.00	5.00
6 Steve Carlton	.50	1.25
7 Grady Sizemore	.50	1.25
8 Justin Morneau	.50	1.25
9 Bob Gibson	.50	1.25
10 Christy Mathewson	.75	2.00
11 Mel Ott	.75	2.00
12 Lou Gehrig	1.50	4.00
13 Mariano Rivera	1.00	2.50
14 Raul Ibanez	.50	1.25
15 Alex Rodriguez	1.00	2.50
16 Vladimir Guerrero	.50	1.25
17 Reggie Jackson	.50	1.25
18 Mickey Mantle	2.50	6.00
19 Tris Speaker	.50	1.25
20 Mark Teixeira	.50	1.25
21 Jimmie Foxx	.75	2.00
22 George Sisler	.50	1.25
23 Stan Musial	1.25	3.00
24 Willie Stargell	.50	1.25
25 Chase Utley	.50	1.25
26 Joe Mauer	.60	1.50
27 Tom Seaver	.50	1.25
28 Johnny Mize	.50	1.25
29 Roy Campanella	.75	2.00
30 Prince Fielder	.50	1.25
31 Manny Ramirez	.75	2.00
32 Ryan Howard	.60	1.50
33 Cy Young	.75	2.00
34 Ichiro Suzuki	1.00	2.50
35 Miguel Cabrera	.75	2.00
36 Dizzy Dean	.50	1.25
37 Hanley Ramirez	.50	1.25
38 David Ortiz	.75	2.00
39 Chipper Jones	.75	2.00
40 Alfonso Soriano	.50	1.25
41 David Wright	.60	1.50
42 Ryan Braun	.50	1.25
43 Dustin Pedroia	.75	2.00
44 Roy Halladay	.50	1.25
45 Jackie Robinson	.75	2.00
46 Rogers Hornsby	.50	1.25
47 Roger Maris	.75	2.00
48 Curt Schilling	.50	1.25
49 Evan Longoria	.50	1.25
50 Ty Cobb	1.25	3.00
51 Luis Aparicio	.50	1.25
52 Lance Berkman	.50	1.25
53 Ubaldo Jimenez	.30	.75
54 Ian Kinsler	.50	1.25
55 George Kell	.50	1.25
56 Felix Hernandez	.50	1.25
57 Max Scherzer	.75	2.00
58 Magglio Ordonez	.50	1.25
59 Derek Jeter	2.00	5.00
60 Mike Schmidt	1.25	3.00
61 Hunter Pence	.50	1.25
62 Jason Bay	.50	1.25
63 Clay Buchholz	.30	.75
64 Josh Hamilton	.50	1.25
65 Willie McCovey	.50	1.25
66 Aaron Hill	.30	.75
67 Derrek Lee	.30	.75
68 Andre Ethier	.50	1.25
69 Ryan Zimmerman	.50	1.25
70 Joe Morgan	.50	1.25
71 Carlos Lee	.30	.75
72 Chad Billingsley	.50	1.25
73 Adam Dunn	.50	1.25
74 Dan Uggla	.30	.75
75 Jermaine Dye	.30	.75
76 Monte Irvin	.50	1.25
77 Curtis Granderson	.60	1.50
78 Mark Reynolds	.30	.75
79 Matt Kemp	.60	1.50
80 Ozzie Smith	1.00	2.50
81 Brandon Phillips	.30	.75
82 Yogi Berra	.75	2.00
83 Bobby Abreu	.30	.75
84 Catfish Hunter	.50	1.25
85 Justin Upton	.50	1.25
86 Justin Verlander	.75	2.00
87 Troy Tulowitzki	.75	2.00
88 Phil Rizzuto	.50	1.25
89 B.J. Upton	.50	1.25
90 Richie Ashburn	.50	1.25
91 Matt Cain	.50	1.25
92 Joey Votto	.75	2.00
93 Robin Roberts	.50	1.25
94 Nick Markakis	.60	1.50
95 Al Kaline	.75	2.00
96 Dan Haren	.30	.75
97 Thurman Munson	.75	2.00
98 Victor Martinez	.50	1.25
99 Brian McCann	.50	1.25
100 Zack Greinke	.75	2.00
101 Stephen Strasburg	2.50	6.00
102 Vladimir Guerrero	.50	1.25
103 Hideki Matsui	.75	2.00
104 Chone Figgins	.30	.75
105 John Lackey	.50	1.25
106 Max Scherzer	.75	2.00
107 Carlos Pena	.50	1.25
108 Ubaldo Jimenez	.30	.75
109 Colby Rasmus	.50	1.25
110 Jered Weaver	.50	1.25
111 Ryan Zimmerman	.50	1.25
112 Jason Heyward	1.25	3.00
113 Carlos Santana	1.00	2.50
114 Mike Leake	1.00	2.50
115 Ike Davis	.60	1.50
116 Starlin Castro	.75	2.00
117 Mike Stanton	2.50	6.00
118 Austin Jackson	.50	1.25
119 Dustin Pedroia	.75	2.00
120 Tyler Colvin	.50	1.25
121 Brennan Boesch	.75	2.00
122 Dallas Braden	.50	1.25
123 Edwin Jackson	.30	.75
124 Daniel Nava	.30	.75
125 Roy Halladay	.50	1.25

2010 Topps Peak Performance Autographs

SER.1 A ODDS 1:19,950 HOBBY
SER.2 A ODDS 1:6800 HOBBY
UPD A ODDS 1:9310 HOBBY
SER.1 B ODDS 1:1125 HOBBY
SER.2 B ODDS 1:826 HOBBY
UPD B ODDS 1:914 HOBBY
SER.1 C ODDS 1:600 HOBBY
SER.2 C ODDS 1:526 HOBBY
UPD C ODDS 1:1775 HOBBY
SER.1 D ODDS 1:1850 HOBBY

Card	Low	High
AB Andrew Bailey B2	8.00	20.00
AC Andrew Carpenter	3.00	8.00
AD Jason Donald UPD	3.00	8.00
AE Andre Ethier UPD B	10.00	25.00
AE Andre Ethier B2	4.00	10.00
AES Alcides Escobar UPD B	5.00	12.00
AG A.Gonzalez UPD A	10.00	25.00
AH Aaron Hill B2	6.00	15.00
AL Adam Lind UPD B	3.00	8.00
AM A.McCutchen UPD B	12.00	30.00
BM Peter Moylan	3.00	8.00
BP Buster Posey B1	60.00	150.00
BPA Bobby Parnell C1	3.00	8.00
CB Clay Buchholz B2	6.00	15.00
CB Collin Balester C1	3.00	8.00
CBI Chad Billingsley C2	5.00	12.00
CC Chris Coghlan UPD B	4.00	10.00
CCR Carl Crawford UPD A	8.00	20.00
CF Chone Figgins UPD B	4.00	10.00
CGE Chris Getz C2	3.00	8.00
CGO Carlos Gomez B2	3.00	8.00
CK Clayton Kershaw C1	50.00	120.00
CM Cameron Maybin C2	3.00	8.00
CP Carlos Pena UPD B	4.00	10.00
CPE Cliff Pennington	3.00	8.00
CR Colby Rasmus UPD B	3.00	8.00
CR Carlos Ruiz C2	10.00	25.00
CV Chris Volstad C2	3.00	8.00
CY Chris Young C1	3.00	8.00
DB Daniel Bard B1	8.00	20.00
DB Dallas Braden C2	5.00	12.00
DM Daniel Murphy B2	10.00	25.00
DMC Dustin McGowan B2	3.00	8.00
DP Dustin Pedroia B2	15.00	40.00
DP Dustin Pedroia B1	15.00	40.00
DS Drew Stubbs UPD B	3.00	8.00
DS Daniel Schlereth C1	3.00	8.00
DS Denard Span B2	4.00	10.00
DS Daniel Stange	3.00	8.00
DW David Wright UPD A	15.00	40.00
EC Everth Cabrera C2	3.00	8.00
ES Ervin Santana UPD B	4.00	10.00
EV Edinson Volquez B2	3.00	8.00
FC F.Carmona UPD B	4.00	10.00
FC Fausto Carmona B2	4.00	10.00
FM Franklin Morales D1	3.00	8.00
FP Felipe Paulino	6.00	15.00
GB Gordon Beckham B1	6.00	15.00
GC Gary Carter B1	15.00	40.00
GG Gio Gonzalez C2	3.00	8.00
GK George Kell B2	12.50	30.00
GP Gerardo Parra	3.00	8.00
GP Glen Perkins	3.00	8.00
HB Heath Bell UPD C	3.00	8.00
HK Howie Kendrick B2	4.00	10.00
HR Hanley Ramirez B1	5.00	12.00
JB J.Bautista UPD C	6.00	15.00
JB Jason Bartlett B2	4.00	10.00
JB Jay Bruce C1	4.00	10.00
JC Johnny Cueto UPD B	4.00	10.00
JC Johnny Cueto C1	4.00	10.00
JD Jermaine Dye B2	6.00	15.00
JDE Joey Devine C2	3.00	8.00
JFR Jeff Francis B2	4.00	10.00
JH Joel Hanrahan	3.00	8.00
JJ Josh Johnson	6.00	15.00
JL John Lackey UPD A	6.00	15.00
JL Jon Lester B2	4.00	10.00
JLM Jason Motte C2	5.00	12.00
JM J.Masterson UPD B	4.00	10.00
JM Joe Morgan A2	20.00	50.00
JMI Jose Mijares D1	3.00	8.00
JO Josh Outman B2	3.00	8.00
JP Jhonny Peralta B2	5.00	12.00
JR Juan Rivera B2	4.00	10.00
JRE Josh Reddick C2	4.00	10.00
JS Joe Saunders B2	5.00	12.00
JSO Joakim Soria B2	3.00	8.00
JU Justin Upton UPD A	8.00	20.00
KG Kevin Gregg UPD B	4.00	10.00
KK K.Kouzmanoff UPD B	4.00	10.00
KS Kurt Suzuki	3.00	8.00
LM Lou Marson C2	3.00	8.00
MB Milton Bradley B1	4.00	10.00
MC Matt Capps UPD B	4.00	10.00
MCA Matt Cain UPD B	4.00	10.00
MG Mat Gamel C1	4.00	10.00
MN Mike Napoli B2	8.00	20.00
MS Max Scherzer UPD B	12.00	30.00
MS Max Scherzer B1	12.00	30.00
MSC Max Scherzer B2	12.00	30.00
MT Matt Tolbert	3.00	8.00
NE Nick Evans C2	3.00	8.00
NF Neftali Feliz UPD B	6.00	15.00
NM Nyjer Morgan UPD B	3.00	8.00
NS Nick Swisher B2	10.00	25.00
PF Prince Fielder UPD A	6.00	15.00
PH Phil Hughes B2	10.00	25.00
PH Phil Hughes B1	8.00	20.00
PP P.Polanco UPD B	3.00	8.00
PS P.Sandoval UPD B	8.00	20.00
RB Ryan Braun UPD A	10.00	25.00
RB Reid Brignac	3.00	8.00
RB Ryan Braun B1	20.00	50.00
RC R.Cano UPD A	10.00	25.00
RC Robinson Cano B1	12.50	30.00
RH Ryan Howard UPD A	30.00	60.00
RN Ricky Nolasco UPD B	3.00	8.00
RP Ryan Perry C1	4.00	10.00
RP Ryan Perry C2	3.00	8.00
RR R.Romero UPD C	3.00	8.00
RR Randy Ruiz B1	6.00	15.00
RW Randy Wells UPD C	3.00	8.00
SP Steve Pearce	5.00	12.00
SR Sean Rodriguez UPD B	3.00	8.00
SV Shane Victorino C1	3.00	8.00
TC Trevor Cahill UPD B	5.00	12.00
TC Trevor Cahill B2	4.00	10.00
TH T.Hanson UPD B	8.00	20.00
TH Tommy Hanson B1	10.00	25.00
TS Travis Snider B2	5.00	12.00
TT Troy Tulowitzki B1	6.00	15.00
TW Tim Wood UPD C	3.00	8.00
UJ U.Jimenez UPD B	6.00	15.00
UJ Ubaldo Jimenez B2	12.50	30.00
VW Vernon Wells UPD A	10.00	25.00
WD Wade Davis B2	5.00	12.00
WD Wade Davis B1	10.00	25.00

2010 Topps Peak Performance Autograph Relics

SERIES 1 ODDS 1:3740 HOBBY
SERIES 20DDS 1:4350 HOBBY
STATED PRINT RUN 50 SER.#'d SETS

Card	Low	High
CG Curtis Granderson	15.00	40.00
DO David Ortiz	30.00	60.00
DW David Wright	30.00	60.00
GB Gordon Beckham	75.00	150.00
HP Hunter Pence S2	12.50	30.00
HR Hanley Ramirez S2	6.00	15.00
JJ Josh Johnson	12.50	30.00
JM Justin Morneau S2	20.00	50.00
JU Justin Upton S2	15.00	40.00
MK Matt Kemp S2	12.50	30.00
PF Prince Fielder S2	12.50	30.00
PF Prince Fielder	12.50	30.00
RB Ryan Braun	20.00	50.00
RH Ryan Howard	40.00	80.00
RH Ryan Howard S2	50.00	100.00
TT Troy Tulowitzki S2	15.00	40.00

2010 Topps Peak Performance Dual Relics

STATED ODDS 1:6315 HOBBY
STATED PRINT RUN 50 SER.#'d SETS

Card	Low	High
BR G.Beckham/A.Ramirez	30.00	60.00
GY A.Gonzalez/K.Youkilis	12.00	30.00
HJ F.Hernandez/U.Jimenez	8.00	20.00
IF I.Suzuki/K.Fukudome	30.00	60.00
KE M.Kemp/A.Ethier	10.00	25.00
LB Carlos Lee/Lance Berkman	8.00	20.00
LS T.Lincecum/P.Sandoval	40.00	80.00
RTU H.Ramirez/T.Tulowitzki	30.00	60.00
SU R.Sandberg/C.Utley	20.00	50.00
UU B.Upton/J.Upton	8.00	20.00
WL D.Wright/E.Longoria	20.00	50.00

2010 Topps Peak Performance Relics

SER.1 A ODDS 1:1555 HOBBY
SER.1 B ODDS 1:71 HOBBY
SER.1 C ODDS 1:153 HOBBY
SER.2 ODDS 1:49 HOBBY

Card	Low	High
AC Asdrubal Cabrera B	3.00	8.00
AE Alcides Escobar C	3.00	8.00
AG Adrian Gonzalez S2	4.00	10.00
AH Aaron Hill S2	2.00	5.00
AH1 Aaron Hill Bat B	2.00	5.00
AH2 Aaron Hill Jsy B	2.00	5.00
AJ Adam Jones S2	3.00	8.00
AJ Adam Jones B	3.00	8.00
AK Al Kaline S2	5.00	12.00
AL Adam LaRoche A	2.00	5.00
AM Andrew McCutchen S2	5.00	12.00
AP Albert Pujols B	6.00	15.00
AP Andy Pettitte S2	3.00	8.00
AR Alexei Ramirez S2	3.00	8.00
AR Aramis Ramirez C	2.00	5.00
ARA Aramis Ramirez S2	2.00	5.00
AS Alfonso Soriano S2	3.00	8.00
BG Bob Gibson A	8.00	20.00
BM Brian McCann C	3.00	8.00
BP Buster Posey S2	10.00	25.00
BR Brad Lidge B	2.00	5.00
BRU Babe Ruth A	150.00	300.00
CC Chris Coghlan S2	2.00	5.00
CF Carlton Fisk A	8.00	20.00
CH Cole Hamels B	4.00	10.00
CJ Chipper Jones B	5.00	12.00
CJ Chipper Jones S2	5.00	12.00
CL Cliff Lee B	3.00	8.00
CR Cal Ripken Jr. B	8.00	20.00
CR Colby Rasmus S2	3.00	8.00
CS CC Sabathia S2	3.00	8.00
CU Chase Utley B	3.00	8.00
CZ Carlos Zambrano S2	3.00	8.00
DE Dennis Eckersley B	3.00	8.00
DG Dwight Gooden B	2.00	5.00
DH Dan Haren S2	2.00	5.00
DL Derrek Lee S2	2.00	5.00
DL Derrek Lee B	2.00	5.00
DM Daniel Murphy A	4.00	10.00
DO David Ortiz B	5.00	12.00
DO David Ortiz S2	5.00	12.00
DP David Price S2	4.00	10.00
DP Dustin Pedroia B	5.00	12.00
DU Dan Uggla B	2.00	5.00
DU Dan Uggla S2	2.00	5.00
DW Dave Winfield C	3.00	8.00
DW David Wright C	4.00	10.00
DY Delmon Young B	3.00	8.00
EL Evan Longoria B	3.00	8.00
FC Fausto Carmona B	2.00	5.00
FH Felix Hernandez B	3.00	8.00
FH Felix Hernandez S2	3.00	8.00
GB Gordon Beckham S2	2.00	5.00
GK George Kell S2	3.00	8.00
GS Grady Sizemore S2	3.00	8.00
GS Gary Sheffield A	2.00	5.00
GSI George Sisler A	15.00	40.00
GSI George Sisler S2	15.00	40.00
GSO Geovany Soto S2	3.00	8.00
GSO Geovany Soto C	3.00	8.00
HG Hank Greenberg B	8.00	20.00
HM Hideki Matsui B	5.00	12.00
HR Hanley Ramirez S2	3.00	8.00
HW Honus Wagner S2	40.00	100.00
HW Honus Wagner A	40.00	100.00
IK Ian Kinsler S2	3.00	8.00
IS Ichiro Suzuki S2	6.00	15.00
IS Ichiro Suzuki B	6.00	15.00
JB Jason Bulger B	2.00	5.00
JBO Jeremy Bonderman B	2.00	5.00
JC Johnny Cueto S2 EXCH	3.00	8.00
JD J.D. Drew B	2.00	5.00
JE Jacoby Ellsbury B	4.00	10.00
JG Jody Gerut B	2.00	5.00
JH Jeremy Hermida B	2.00	5.00
JH Josh Hamilton S2	3.00	8.00
JM Justin Morneau S2	3.00	8.00
JM Johnny Mize A	12.00	30.00
JMI Johnny Mize S2	3.00	8.00
JP Willie Stargell S2	3.00	8.00
JP Jonathan Papelbon B	3.00	8.00
JPO Jorge Posada B	3.00	8.00
JR Jose Reyes B	3.00	8.00
JS Joakim Soria B	2.00	5.00
JV Joey Votto S2	5.00	12.00
JV1 Joey Votto Bat B	5.00	12.00
JV2 Joey Votto Jsy B	5.00	12.00
JW Jayson Werth A	3.00	8.00
JWI Josh Willingham B	3.00	8.00
JZ Jordan Zimmermann B	3.00	8.00
KF Kosuke Fukudome B	3.00	8.00
KF Kosuke Fukudome S2	3.00	8.00
KJ Kenji Johjima B	2.00	5.00
KK Kenshin Kawakami S2	3.00	8.00
KY1 Kevin Youkilis Bat B	2.00	5.00
KY2 Kevin Youkilis Jsy C	2.00	5.00
LB Lance Berkman S2	3.00	8.00
MC Matt Cain S2	3.00	8.00
MC Matt Cain B	3.00	8.00
MCA Melky Cabrera B	2.00	5.00
MF Mike Fontenot S2	2.00	5.00
MG Matt Gamel C	2.00	5.00
MK Matt Kemp C	4.00	10.00
MM Melvin Mora B	2.00	5.00
MMA Mickey Mantle A	125.00	250.00
MO Mel Ott A	15.00	40.00
MO Mel Ott S2	15.00	40.00
MP Manny Parra C	2.00	5.00
MS Mike Schmidt A	8.00	20.00
MT Mark Teixeira S2	3.00	8.00
MY Michael Young B	2.00	5.00
NF Neftali Feliz S2	2.00	5.00
NM Nick Markakis S2	4.00	10.00
NS Nick Swisher S2	3.00	8.00
NS Nick Swisher C	3.00	8.00
OS Ozzie Smith S2	6.00	15.00
PF Prince Fielder S2	3.00	8.00
PF Prince Fielder B	3.00	8.00
PH Phil Hughes S2	2.00	5.00
PM Paul Molitor B	5.00	12.00
PS Pablo Sandoval S2 EXCH	3.00	8.00
PWR Pee Wee Reese A	12.00	30.00
PWR Pee Wee Reese S2	15.00	40.00
RA Richie Ashburn S2	15.00	40.00
RA Rick Ankiel B	2.00	5.00
RB Ryan Braun B	3.00	8.00
RC Roy Campanella S2	10.00	25.00
RCA Robinson Cano S2	3.00	8.00
RD Ryan Dempster S2	2.00	5.00
RH Ryan Howard S2	4.00	10.00
RH Rich Harden B	2.00	5.00
RHE Rickey Henderson B	10.00	25.00
RHO Ryan Howard B	4.00	10.00
RHO Rogers Hornsby S2	15.00	40.00
RP Rick Porcello S2	3.00	8.00
RR Robin Roberts S2	12.00	30.00
RT Ryan Theriot S2	2.00	5.00
RW Rickie Weeks C	2.00	5.00
SC Shin-Soo Choo B	3.00	8.00
SK1 Scott Kazmir Rays Jsy B	2.00	5.00
SK2 Scott Kazmir LAA Jsy C	2.00	5.00
TG Tony Gwynn B	5.00	12.00
TH Tim Hudson B	3.00	8.00
THA Tommy Hanson B	2.00	5.00
TL Ted Lilly S2	2.00	5.00
TM Thurman Munson S2	12.00	30.00
TM Thurman Munson A	12.00	30.00
TS Tris Speaker A	10.00	25.00
TS Tris Speaker S2	15.00	40.00
TT Troy Tulowitzki S2	5.00	12.00
TT Troy Tulowitzki B	5.00	12.00
UJ Ubaldo Jimenez S2	2.00	5.00
YB Yogi Berra S2	6.00	15.00
YG Yovani Gallardo S2	2.00	5.00
YG Yovani Gallardo B	2.00	5.00
ZG Zack Greinke S2	5.00	12.00

2010 Topps Peak Performance Relics Blue

*BLUE: .6X TO 1.5X BASIC
RANDOM INSERTS IN SER.2 PACKS
STATED PRINT RUN 99 SER.#'d SETS

Card	Low	High
CH Catfish Hunter S2	10.00	25.00

2010 Topps Red Back

INSERTED IN TARGET PACKS
31-45 ISSUED IN UPD TARGET PACKS

Card	Low	High
1 Mickey Mantle	3.00	8.00
2 Rogers Hornsby	.60	1.50
3 Warren Spahn	.60	1.50
4 Jackie Robinson	1.00	2.50
5 Ty Cobb	1.50	4.00
6 Cy Young	1.00	2.50
7 Albert Pujols	1.25	3.00
8 Mariano Rivera	1.25	3.00
9 Jimmie Foxx	1.00	2.50
10 Reggie Jackson	.60	1.50
11 Lou Gehrig	2.00	5.00
12 Dizzy Dean	.60	1.50
13 Chipper Jones	1.00	2.50
14 Cal Ripken Jr.	3.00	8.00
15 David Wright	.75	2.00
16 Babe Ruth	2.50	6.00
17 Honus Wagner	1.00	2.50
18 Ichiro Suzuki	1.25	3.00
19 Nolan Ryan	3.00	8.00
20 Stan Musial	1.50	4.00
21 Tom Seaver	.60	1.50
22 Derek Jeter	2.50	6.00
23 Roy Halladay	.60	1.50
24 Mel Ott	1.00	2.50
25 George Sisler	.60	1.50
26 Roger Maris	1.00	2.50
27 Walter Johnson	1.00	2.50
28 Vladimir Guerrero	.60	1.50
29 Tim Lincecum	.60	1.50
30 Hanley Ramirez	.60	1.50
31 Babe Ruth	2.50	6.00
32 Jimmie Foxx	1.00	2.50
33 Rogers Hornsby	.60	1.50
34 Warren Spahn	.60	1.50
35 Reggie Jackson	.60	1.50
36 Nolan Ryan	3.00	8.00
37 Tom Seaver	.60	1.50
38 George Sisler	.60	1.50
39 Roger Maris	1.00	2.50
40 Vladimir Guerrero	.60	1.50
41 Thurman Munson	1.00	2.50
42 Johnny Mize	.60	1.50
43 Pee Wee Reese	.60	1.50
44 Hank Greenberg	1.00	2.50
45 Ryan Braun	.60	1.50

2010 Topps Red Hot Rookie Redemption

Card	Low	High
COMPLETE SET (10)	15.00	40.00
STATED ODDS 1:36 HOBBY		
RHR1 Carlos Santana	2.00	5.00
RHR2 Jose Tabata	1.00	2.50
RHR3 Brennan Boesch	1.50	4.00
RHR4 Mike Stanton	15.00	40.00
RHR5 Starlin Castro	1.50	4.00
RHR6 Logan Morrison	1.00	2.50
RHR7 Dominic Brown	2.50	6.00
RHR8 Stephen Strasburg	6.00	15.00
RHR9 Mike Minor	1.00	2.50
RHR10A Brett Wallace	1.50	4.00
RHR10B Brett Wallace AU	6.00	15.00

2010 Topps Series 2 Attax Code Cards

Card	Low	High
COMPLETE SET (27)	5.00	12.00
1 Jason Bay	.50	1.25
2 Lance Berkman	.50	1.25
3 Billy Butler	.30	.75
4 Stephen Drew	.30	.75
5 Yunel Escobar	.30	.75
6 Yovani Gallardo	.30	.75
7 Zack Greinke	.75	2.00
8 Felix Hernandez	.50	1.25
9 Matt Holliday	.75	2.00
10 Torii Hunter	.30	.75
11 Josh Johnson	.50	1.25
12 Matt Kemp	.60	1.50
13 Ian Kinsler	.50	1.25
14 Derrek Lee	.30	.75
15 Jon Lester	.50	1.25
16 Tim Lincecum	.50	1.25
17 Justin Morneau	.50	1.25
18 Alexei Ramirez	.50	1.25
19 Alex Rodriguez	1.00	2.50
20 Pablo Sandoval	.50	1.25
21 Max Scherzer	.75	2.00
22 Grady Sizemore	.50	1.25
23 B.J. Upton	.50	1.25
24 Chase Utley	.50	1.25
25 Justin Verlander	.75	2.00
26 Joey Votto	.75	2.00
27 Ryan Zimmerman	.50	1.25

2010 Topps Silk Collection

SER.1 ODDS 1:373 HOBBY
SER.2 ODDS 1:431 HOBBY
UPDATE ODDS 1:412 HOBBY
STATED PRINT RUN 50 SER.#'d SETS
1-50 ISSUED IN SERIES 1
51-100 ISSUED IN SERIES 2
101-200 ISSUED IN UPDATE

Card	Low	High
S1 Prince Fielder	6.00	15.00
S3 Derrek Lee	4.00	10.00
S4 Mickey Mantle	30.00	80.00
S5 Clayton Kershaw	15.00	40.00
S6 Bobby Abreu	4.00	10.00
S7 Johnny Cueto	6.00	15.00
S8 Dexter Fowler	6.00	15.00
S9 Felipe Lopez	4.00	10.00
S10 Tommy Hanson	4.00	10.00
S11 Shane Victorino	6.00	15.00
S12 Adam Jones	6.00	15.00
S13 Victor Martinez	6.00	15.00
S14 Rick Porcello	6.00	15.00
S15 Garret Anderson	4.00	10.00
S16 Josh Johnson	6.00	15.00
S17 Marco Scutaro	6.00	15.00
S18 Howie Kendrick	4.00	10.00
S19 Joey Votto	10.00	25.00
S20 Jorge De La Rosa	4.00	10.00
S21 Zack Greinke	10.00	25.00
S23 Billy Butler	4.00	10.00
S24 John Lackey	6.00	15.00
S25 Manny Ramirez	10.00	25.00
S26 CC Sabathia	6.00	15.00
S27 David Wright	8.00	20.00
S28 Nick Swisher	6.00	15.00
S29 Matt LaPorta	4.00	10.00
S30 Brandon Inge	6.00	15.00
S31 Cole Hamels	8.00	20.00
S32 Adrian Gonzalez	8.00	20.00
S33 Joe Saunders	4.00	10.00
S34 Tim Lincecum	6.00	15.00
S35 Ken Griffey Jr.	20.00	50.00
S36 J.A. Happ	6.00	15.00
S37 Ian Kinsler	6.00	15.00
S38 Ivan Rodriguez	6.00	15.00
S39 Carl Crawford	6.00	15.00
S40 Jon Garland	4.00	10.00
S41 Albert Pujols	12.00	30.00
S43 Andrew McCutchen	10.00	25.00
S44 Gordon Beckham	4.00	10.00
S45 Jorge Posada	6.00	15.00
S46 Ichiro Suzuki	12.00	30.00
S47 Vladimir Guerrero	6.00	15.00
S48 Cliff Lee	6.00	15.00
S49 Freddy Sanchez	4.00	10.00
S50 Ryan Dempster	4.00	10.00
S51 Adam Wainwright	6.00	15.00
S52 Matt Holliday	10.00	25.00
S53 Chone Figgins	4.00	10.00
S54 Tim Hudson	6.00	15.00
S55 Rich Harden	4.00	10.00
S56 Justin Upton	6.00	15.00
S57 Joe Mauer	8.00	20.00
S58 Vernon Wells	4.00	10.00
S59 Miguel Tejada	6.00	15.00
S60 Denard Span	4.00	10.00
S61 Brandon Phillips	4.00	10.00
S62 Jason Bay	6.00	15.00
S63 Kendry Morales	4.00	10.00
S64 Josh Hamilton	6.00	15.00
S65 Yovani Gallardo	4.00	10.00
S66 Adam Lind	6.00	15.00
S67 Hideki Matsui	10.00	25.00
S68 Will Venable	4.00	10.00
S69 Joe Blanton	4.00	10.00
S70 Adrian Beltre	10.00	25.00
S71 Pablo Sandoval	6.00	15.00
S72 Roy Halladay	6.00	15.00
S73 Chris Coghlan	4.00	10.00
S74 Colby Rasmus	6.00	15.00
S75 Alexei Ramirez	6.00	15.00
S76 Josh Beckett	4.00	10.00
S77 Matt Kemp	8.00	20.00
S78 Max Scherzer	10.00	25.00
S79 Randy Johnson	10.00	25.00
S80 Curtis Granderson	8.00	20.00
S81 David Price	8.00	20.00
S82 Neftali Feliz	4.00	10.00
S83 Ricky Romero	4.00	10.00
S84 Lance Berkman	6.00	15.00
S85 Andre Ethier	6.00	15.00
S86 Mark Teixeira	6.00	15.00
S87 Edwin Jackson	4.00	10.00
S88 Akinori Iwamura	4.00	10.00
S90 Jair Jurrjens	4.00	10.00
S91 Stephen Drew	4.00	10.00
S92 Javier Vazquez	4.00	10.00
S93 Orlando Hudson	4.00	10.00
S94 Adam Dunn	6.00	15.00
S95 Kevin Youkilis	4.00	10.00
S96 Chase Utley	6.00	15.00
S98 Brian McCann	6.00	15.00
S99 Jim Thome	6.00	15.00

S100 Alex Rios 4.00 10.00
S101 Geovany Soto 6.00 15.00
S102 Joakim Soria 4.00 10.00
S103 Chad Billingsley 6.00 15.00
S104 Jacoby Ellsbury 8.00 20.00
S105 Justin Morneau 6.00 15.00
S106 Jeff Francis 4.00 10.00
S107 Francisco Rodriguez 6.00 15.00
S108 Torii Hunter 4.00 10.00
S109 A.J Burnett 4.00 10.00
S110 Chris Young 4.00 10.00
S111 Bud Norris 4.00 10.00
S112 Todd Helton 6.00 15.00
S113 Shin-Soo Choo 6.00 15.00
S114 Matt Cain 6.00 15.00
S115 Jered Weaver 6.00 15.00
S116 Jason Bartlett 4.00 10.00
S117 Chris Carpenter 6.00 15.00
S118 Kosuke Fukudome 6.00 15.00
S119 Roy Oswalt 6.00 15.00
S120 Alex Rodriguez 12.00 30.00
S121 Dan Haren 4.00 10.00
S122 Hiroki Kuroda 4.00 10.00
S123 Hunter Pence 6.00 15.00
S124 Jeremy Guthrie 4.00 10.00
S125 Grady Sizemore 6.00 15.00
S126 Mark Reynolds 4.00 10.00
S127 Johnny Damon 6.00 15.00
S128 Aaron Rowand 4.00 10.00
S129 Carlos Beltran 6.00 15.00
S130 Alfonso Soriano 6.00 15.00
S131 Nelson Cruz 10.00 25.00
S132 Edinson Volquez 4.00 10.00
S133 Jayson Werth 6.00 15.00
S134 Mariano Rivera 12.00 30.00
S135 Brandon Webb 6.00 15.00
S136 Jordan Zimmermann 6.00 15.00
S137 Michael Young 4.00 10.00
S138 Daisuke Matsuzaka 6.00 15.00
S139 Ubaldo Jimenez 4.00 10.00
S140 Evan Longoria 6.00 15.00
S141 Brad Lidge 4.00 10.00
S142 Carlos Zambrano 6.00 15.00
S143 Heath Bell 4.00 10.00
S144 Trevor Cahill 4.00 10.00
S145 Carlos Gonzalez 6.00 15.00
S146 Jose Reyes 6.00 15.00
S147 Ian Snell 4.00 10.00
S148 Manny Parra 4.00 10.00
S149 Michael Cuddyer 4.00 10.00
S150 Melky Cabrera 4.00 10.00
S151 Justin Verlander 10.00 25.00
S152 Delmon Young 6.00 15.00
S153 Kelly Johnson 4.00 10.00
S154 Derek Lowe 4.00 10.00
S155 Derek Jeter 25.00 60.00
S156 Paul Maholm 4.00 10.00
S157 Mike Napoli 4.00 10.00
S158 Aramis Ramirez 4.00 10.00
S159 Alex Gordon 6.00 15.00
S160 Jorge Cantu 4.00 10.00
S161 Brad Hawpe 4.00 10.00
S162 Troy Tulowitzki 10.00 25.00
S163 Casey Kotchman 4.00 10.00
S164 Carlos Guillen 4.00 10.00
S165 J.D. Drew 4.00 10.00
S166 Dustin Pedroia 10.00 25.00
S167 Francisco Liriano 4.00 10.00
S168 Jimmy Rollins 6.00 15.00
S169 Wade LeBlanc 4.00 10.00
S170 Miguel Cabrera 10.00 25.00
S171 Jeremy Hermida 4.00 10.00
S172 Koji Uehara 4.00 10.00
S173 Tommy Hunter 4.00 10.00
S174 Dustin McGowan 4.00 10.00
S175 Corey Hart 4.00 10.00
S176 Jake Peavy 4.00 10.00
S177 Jason Varitek 10.00 25.00
S178 Chris Dickerson 4.00 10.00
S179 Robinson Cano 6.00 15.00
S180 Michael Bourn 4.00 10.00
S181 Chris Volstad 4.00 10.00
S182 Mark Buehrle 6.00 15.00
S183 Jarrod Saltalamacchia 4.00 10.00
S184 Aaron Hill 4.00 10.00
S185 Carlos Pena 6.00 15.00
S186 Luke Hochevar 4.00 10.00
S187 Derek Holland 4.00 10.00
S188 Carlos Quentin 4.00 10.00
S189 J.J. Hardy 4.00 10.00
S190 Ryan Zimmerman 6.00 15.00
S191 Travis Snider 4.00 10.00
S192 Russell Martin 4.00 10.00
S193 Brian Roberts 4.00 10.00
S194 Ryan Ludwick 4.00 10.00
S195 Aaron Cook 4.00 10.00
S196 Jay Bruce 6.00 15.00
S197 Kevin Slowey 4.00 10.00
S198 Johan Santana 6.00 15.00
S199 Carlos Lee 4.00 10.00
S200 David Ortiz 10.00 25.00
S201 Doug Davis 4.00 10.00
S202 Coco Crisp 4.00 10.00
S203 Jason Kendall 4.00 10.00
S204 Jason Bay 6.00 15.00
S205 Jim Thome 6.00 15.00
S206 Omar Vizquel 6.00 15.00
S207 Jose Valverde 4.00 10.00
S208 Adam Kennedy 4.00 10.00
S209 Kelly Shoppach 4.00 10.00
S210 Akinori Iwamura 4.00 10.00
S211 Brad Penny 4.00 10.00
S212 Kevin Millwood 4.00 10.00
S213 Cliff Lee 6.00 15.00
S214 Andruw Jones 4.00 10.00
S215 Rod Barajas 4.00 10.00
S216 Pedro Feliz 4.00 10.00
S218 Placido Polanco 4.00 10.00
S219 Jhan Marinez 4.00 10.00
S220 Bobby Wilson 4.00 10.00
S221 Kris Medlen 6.00 15.00
S222 Aaron Heilman 4.00 10.00
S223 Shaun Marcum 4.00 10.00
S224 Alfredo Simon 4.00 10.00
S225 Matt Thornton 4.00 10.00
S226 Billy Wagner 4.00 10.00
S227 Troy Glaus 4.00 10.00
S228 Jesus Feliciano 4.00 10.00
S229 Dana Eveland 4.00 10.00
S230 Scott Olsen 4.00 10.00
S231 Corey Patterson 4.00 10.00
S232 Livan Hernandez 4.00 10.00
S233 Bill Hall 4.00 10.00
S234 Josh Reddick 4.00 10.00
S235 Xavier Nady 4.00 10.00
S236 Koyie Hill 4.00 10.00
S237 Tom Gorzelanny 4.00 10.00
S238 Kevin Frandsen 4.00 10.00
S239 Mark Kotsay 4.00 10.00
S240 Arthur Rhodes 4.00 10.00
S241 Micah Owings 4.00 10.00
S242 Shelley Duncan 4.00 10.00
S243 Mike Redmond 4.00 10.00
S244 Chris Perez 4.00 10.00
S245 Don Kelly 4.00 10.00
S246 Alex Avila 6.00 15.00
S247 Geoff Blum 4.00 10.00
S248 Mitch Maier 4.00 10.00
S249 Roy Halladay 6.00 15.00
S250 Matt Daley 4.00 10.00
S251 Vicente Padilla 4.00 10.00
S252 Kila Ka'aihue 6.00 15.00
S253 Dave Bush 4.00 10.00
S254 Jody Gerut 4.00 10.00
S255 George Kottaras 4.00 10.00
S256 LaTroy Hawkins 4.00 10.00
S257 Brendan Harris 4.00 10.00
S258 Alex Cora 6.00 15.00
S259 Randy Winn 4.00 10.00
S260 Matt Harrison 4.00 10.00
S261 Pat Burrell 4.00 10.00
S262 Mark Ellis 4.00 10.00
S263 Conor Jackson 4.00 10.00
S264 Matt Downs 4.00 10.00
S265 Jeff Clement 4.00 10.00
S266 Joel Hanrahan 6.00 15.00
S267 John Jaso 4.00 10.00
S268 John Danks 4.00 10.00
S269 Eugenio Velez 4.00 10.00
S270 Jason Vargas 4.00 10.00
S271 Rob Johnson 4.00 10.00
S272 Gabe Gross 4.00 10.00
S273 David Freese 6.00 15.00
S274 Jamie Garcia 6.00 15.00
S275 Gabe Kapler 4.00 10.00
S276 Colby Lewis 4.00 10.00
S277 Carlos Santana 12.00 30.00
S278 Cole Gillespie 4.00 10.00
S279 Jonny Venters 4.00 10.00
S280 Jeff Suppan 4.00 10.00
S281 Lance Zawadzki 4.00 10.00
S282 Mike Leake 12.00 30.00
S283 John Ely 4.00 10.00
S284 Mike Stanton 30.00 80.00
S285 Rhyne Hughes 4.00 10.00
S286 Jeanmar Gomez 6.00 15.00
S287 Brennan Boesch 10.00 25.00
S288 Austin Jackson 6.00 15.00
S289 Alex Sanabia 4.00 10.00
S290 Jason Donald 4.00 10.00
S291 Andrew Cashner 4.00 10.00
S292 Josh Bell 4.00 10.00
S293 Travis Wood 6.00 15.00
S294 Mike Stanton 12.00 30.00
S295 Jose Tabata 6.00 15.00
S296 Jake Arrieta 10.00 25.00
S297 Carlos Santana 12.00 30.00
S298 Sam Demel 4.00 10.00
S299 Felix Doubront 4.00 10.00
S300 Stephen Strasburg 12.00 30.00

2010 Topps Tales of the Game

STATED ODDS 1:6 HOBBY
TOG1 Spikes Up .75 2.00
TOG2 The Curse of the Bambino 1.25 3.00
TOG3 Ruth Calls His Shot 1.25 3.00
TOG4 Topps Dumps 1952 Cards in the River .40 1.00
TOG5 Jackie Robinson Steals Home in World Series .75 2.00
TOG6 Let's Play Two .75 2.00
TOG7 Mazeroski Hits World Series Walk-Off .60 1.50
TOG8 Maris Chases #61 .75 2.00
TOG9 Mantle HR Off Facade 1.50 4.00
TOG10 Piersall Runs Backwards for HR #100 .40 1.00
TOG11 1969 Amazin' Mets .60 1.50
TOG12 Reggie has Light Tower Power .60 1.50
TOG13 Carlton Fisk: The Wave .60 1.50
TOG14 Reggie's World Series HR Hat Trick .60 1.50
TOG15 Ozzie Smith Flips Out .60 1.50
TOG16 Bo Knows Wall Climbing .75 2.00
TOG17 Wade Boggs Who You Calling Chicken? .60 1.50
TOG18 Prince: BP HR at Age 12 .50 1.25
TOG19 Old Cal Clutch 1.50 4.00
TOG20 Jeter: The Flip 1.25 3.00
TOG21 Schilling's Bloody Sock .60 1.50
TOG22 Pesky's Pole .40 1.00
TOG23 Manny Being Manny .75 2.00
TOG24 The Great Ham-Bino .50 1.25
TOG25 Yankees Dig Up Ortiz' Jersey 1.00 2.50

2010 Topps Topps Town

RANDOM INSERTS IN PACKS
TTT1 Joe Mauer .40 1.00
TTT2 David Wright .40 1.00
TTT3 Hanley Ramirez .30 .75
TTT4 Adrian Gonzalez .40 1.00
TTT5 Evan Longoria .30 .75
TTT6 Ichiro Suzuki .60 1.50
TTT7 Josh Hamilton .30 .75
TTT8 Zack Greinke .50 1.25
TTT9 Roy Halladay .30 .75
TTT10 Tim Lincecum .30 .75
TTT11 Brian McCann .30 .75
TTT12 Miguel Tejada .30 .75
TTT13 Ryan Howard .40 1.00
TTT14 Albert Pujols .60 1.50
TTT15 Miguel Cabrera .50 1.25
TTT16 Kevin Youkilis .20 .50
TTT17 Todd Helton .30 .75
TTT18 Vladimir Guerrero .30 .75
TTT19 Justin Upton .30 .75
TTT20 Adam Jones .30 .75
TTT21 Adam Dunn .30 .75
TTT22 Andrew McCutchen .50 1.25
TTT23 CC Sabathia .30 .75
TTT24 Ryan Braun .30 .75
TTT25 Manny Ramirez .50 1.25

2010 Topps Topps Town Gold

*GOLD: .75X TO 2X BASIC
RANDOM INSERTS IN PACKS

2010 Topps Turkey Red

STATED ODDS 1:4 HOBBY
1-50 ISSUED IN SERIES 1
51-100 ISSUED IN SERIES 2
101-150 ISSUED IN UPDATE
TR1 Ryan Howard .60 1.50
TR2 Miguel Tejada .50 1.25
TR3 Nolan Ryan 2.50 6.00
TR4 Albert Pujols 1.00 2.50
TR5 Josh Beckett .30 .75
TR6 Justin Upton .50 1.25
TR7 Andre Ethier .50 1.25
TR8 Tommy Hanson .30 .75
TR9 Josh Johnson .50 1.25
TR10 Jonathan Papelbon .50 1.25
TR11 Cole Hamels .60 1.50
TR12 Manny Ramirez .75 2.00
TR13 Yovani Gallardo .30 .75
TR14 Kevin Youkilis .30 .75
TR15 Hank Greenberg .75 2.00
TR16 Ozzie Smith 1.00 2.50
TR17 Derrek Lee .30 .75
TR18 Ryan Braun .50 1.25
TR19 Cal Ripken Jr. 2.50 6.00
TR20 CC Sabathia .50 1.25
TR21 Johnny Bench .75 2.00
TR22 Tim Lincecum .50 1.25
TR23 Mike Schmidt 1.25 3.00
TR24 Clayton Kershaw 1.25 3.00
TR25 Ernie Banks .75 2.00
TR26 Dexter Fowler .50 1.25
TR27 Edwin Jackson .30 .75
TR28 Mickey Mantle 2.50 6.00
TR29 Gordon Beckham .30 .75
TR30 Victor Martinez .50 1.25
TR31 Mel Ott .75 2.00
TR32 Zack Greinke .75 2.00
TR33 Roy Halladay .50 1.25
TR34 David Wright .60 1.50
TR35 Stephen Drew .30 .75
TR36 Matt Holliday .75 2.00
TR37 Chase Utley .50 1.25
TR38 Rick Porcello .50 1.25
TR39 Vladimir Guerrero .50 1.25
TR40 Mark Teixeira .50 1.25
TR41 Evan Longoria .50 1.25
TR42 Ian Kinsler .50 1.25
TR43 Adrian Gonzalez .60 1.50
TR44 Matt Kemp .60 1.50
TR45 Ryne Sandberg 1.50 4.00
TR46 Babe Ruth 2.00 5.00
TR47 Curtis Granderson .60 1.50
TR48 Willie McCovey .50 1.25
TR49 Josh Hamilton .50 1.25
TR50 Pablo Sandoval .50 1.25
TR51 Torii Hunter .30 .75
TR52 Adam Dunn .50 1.25
TR53 Alexei Ramirez .50 1.25
TR54 Andrew McCutchen .75 2.00
TR55 Aaron Hill .30 .75
TR56 Alcides Escobar .50 1.25
TR57 Jimmie Foxx .75 2.00
TR58 Joey Votto .75 2.00
TR59 Jose Reyes .50 1.25
TR60 Al Kaline .75 2.00
TR61 Felix Hernandez .50 1.25
TR62 Troy Tulowitzki .75 2.00
TR63 Nate McLouth .30 .75
TR64 Justin Morneau .50 1.25
TR65 Prince Fielder .50 1.25
TR66 Nelson Cruz .75 2.00
TR67 Grady Sizemore .50 1.25
TR68 Hanley Ramirez .50 1.25
TR69 Brooks Robinson .50 1.25
TR70 Jackie Robinson .75 2.00
TR71 Nick Markakis .60 1.50
TR72 Roy Oswalt .50 1.25
TR73 Chad Billingsley .50 1.25
TR74 Tom Seaver .50 1.25
TR75 B.J. Upton .50 1.25
TR76 Chris Coghlan .30 .75
TR77 Luis Aparicio .50 1.25
TR78 Dan Haren .30 .75
TR79 Raul Ibanez .50 1.25
TR80 Kosuke Fukudome .50 1.25
TR81 Denard Span .30 .75
TR82 Joe Morgan .50 1.25
TR83 Yogi Berra .75 2.00
TR84 Dustin Pedroia .75 2.00
TR85 Lou Gehrig 1.50 4.00
TR86 Billy Butler .30 .75
TR87 Jake Peavy .30 .75
TR88 Eddie Mathews .75 2.00
TR89 Ubaldo Jimenez .30 .75
TR90 Johan Santana .50 1.25
TR91 Buster Posey 2.50 6.00
TR92 George Sisler .50 1.25
TR93 Ian Desmond .50 1.25
TR94 Kurt Suzuki .30 .75
TR95 Ty Cobb 1.25 3.00
TR96 Magglio Ordonez .50 1.25
TR97 Chase Headley .30 .75
TR98 Hunter Pence .50 1.25
TR99 Ryan Ludwick .30 .75
TR100 Derek Jeter 2.00 5.00
TR101 Hideki Matsui .75 2.00
TR102 Kelly Johnson .30 .75
TR103 Jason Heyward 1.25 3.00
TR104 Adam Jones .50 1.25
TR105 John Lackey .50 1.25
TR106 Roy Campanella .75 2.00
TR107 Aramis Ramirez .30 .75
TR108 Carlos Quentin .30 .75
TR109 Brandon Phillips .30 .75
TR110 Shin-Soo Choo .50 1.25
TR111 Ian Stewart .30 .75
TR112 Miguel Cabrera .75 2.00
TR113 Josh Johnson .50 1.25
TR114 Carlos Lee .30 .75
TR115 Joakim Soria .30 .75
TR116 Jonathan Broxton .30 .75
TR117 Carlos Gomez .30 .75
TR118 Joe Mauer .60 1.50
TR119 Jason Bay .50 1.25
TR120 Curtis Granderson .60 1.50
TR121 A.J. Burnett .30 .75
TR122 Ben Sheets .30 .75
TR123 Roy Halladay .50 1.25
TR124 Ryan Doumit .30 .75
TR125 Kyle Blanks .30 .75
TR126 Matt Cain .50 1.25
TR127 Ichiro Suzuki 1.00 2.50
TR128 Chris Carpenter .50 1.25
TR129 Matt Garza .30 .75
TR130 Vladimir Guerrero .50 1.25
TR131 Vernon Wells .30 .75
TR132 Ryan Zimmerman .50 1.25
TR133 Lou Brock .50 1.25
TR134 Rod Carew .50 1.25
TR135 Orlando Cepeda .50 1.25
TR136 Rogers Hornsby .50 1.25
TR137 Walter Johnson .75 2.00
TR138 Christy Mathewson .75 2.00
TR139 Johnny Mize .50 1.25
TR140 Thurman Munson .75 2.00
TR141 Pee Wee Reese .50 1.25
TR142 Tris Speaker .50 1.25
TR143 Honus Wagner .75 2.00
TR144 Cy Young .75 2.00
TR145 Robin Yount .75 2.00
TR146 Duke Snider .50 1.25
TR147 Frank Robinson .50 1.25
TR148 Stephen Strasburg 2.50 6.00
TR149 Mike Stanton 2.50 6.00
TR150 Starlin Castro .75 2.00

2010 Topps Vintage Legends Collection

COMPLETE SET (50) 15.00 40.00
COM.UPDATE SET (25) 5.00 12.00
STATED ODDS 1:4 HOBBY
26-50 ISSUED IN UPDATE
VLC1 Lou Gehrig 1.50 4.00
VLC2 Johnny Mize .50 1.25
VLC3 Reggie Jackson .50 1.25
VLC4 Tris Speaker .50 1.25
VLC5 George Sisler .50 1.25
VLC6 Willie McCovey .50 1.25
VLC7 Tom Seaver .50 1.25
VLC8 Walter Johnson .75 2.00
VLC9 Ozzie Smith 1.00 2.50
VLC10 Babe Ruth 2.00 5.00
VLC11 Christy Mathewson .75 2.00
VLC12 Jackie Robinson .75 2.00
VLC13 Eddie Murray .50 1.25
VLC14 Mel Ott .75 2.00
VLC15 Jimmie Foxx .75 2.00
VLC16 Thurman Munson .75 2.00
VLC17 Mike Schmidt 1.25 3.00
VLC18 Johnny Bench .75 2.00
VLC19 Rogers Hornsby .50 1.25
VLC20 Ty Cobb 1.25 3.00
VLC21 Nolan Ryan 2.50 6.00
VLC22 Roy Campanella .75 2.00
VLC23 Cy Young .75 2.00
VLC24 Pee Wee Reese .50 1.25
VLC25 Honus Wagner .75 2.00
VLC26 Johnny Mize .50 1.25
VLC27 Cy Young .75 2.00
VLC28 Ozzie Smith 1.00 2.50
VLC29 Nolan Ryan 2.50 6.00
VLC30 George Sisler .50 1.25
VLC31 Babe Ruth 2.00 5.00
VLC32 Reggie Jackson .50 1.25
VLC33 Christy Mathewson .75 2.00
VLC34 Mike Schmidt 1.25 3.00
VLC35 Mel Ott .75 2.00
VLC36 Ty Cobb 1.25 3.00
VLC37 Eddie Murray .50 1.25
VLC38 Lou Gehrig 1.50 4.00
VLC39 Roy Campanella .75 2.00
VLC40 Tom Seaver .50 1.25
VLC41 Honus Wagner .75 2.00
VLC42 Jackie Robinson .75 2.00
VLC43 Johnny Bench .75 2.00
VLC44 Pee Wee Reese .50 1.25
VLC45 Thurman Munson .75 2.00
VLC46 Rogers Hornsby .50 1.25
VLC47 Jimmie Foxx .75 2.00
VLC48 Willie McCovey .50 1.25
VLC49 Tris Speaker .50 1.25
VLC50 Walter Johnson .75 2.00

2010 Topps When They Were Young

STATED ODDS 1:6 HOBBY
AP Aaron Poreda .40 1.00
AR Alex Rodriguez 1.25 3.00
BR Brian Roberts .40 1.00
CM Charlie Morton 1.00 2.50
CR Cody Ross .40 1.00
CS Clint Sammons .40 1.00
DM Daniel McCutchen .60 1.50
DO David Ortiz 1.00 2.50
DW David Wright .75 2.00
GB Gordon Beckham .40 1.00
JB Jason Berken .40 1.00
JD Johnny Damon .60 1.50
JV Justin Verlander 1.00 2.50
RD Ryan Doumit .40 1.00
RM Russell Martin .40 1.00
RN Ricky Nolasco .40 1.00
SO Scott Olsen .40 1.00
YM Yadier Molina 1.25 3.00

2010 Topps World Champion Autograph Relics

STATED ODDS 1:7,500 HOBBY
STATED PRINT RUN 50 SER.#'d SETS
AR Alex Rodriguez 100.00 200.00
CS CC Sabathia 40.00 100.00
MC Melky Cabrera 30.00 60.00
MR Mariano Rivera 125.00 250.00
RC Robinson Cano 100.00 200.00

2010 Topps World Champion Autographs

STATED ODDS 1:22,600 HOBBY
STATED PRINT RUN 50 SER.#'d SETS
AR Alex Rodriguez 125.00 250.00
CS CC Sabathia 125.00 250.00
MC Melky Cabrera 20.00 50.00
MR Mariano Rivera 100.00 200.00
RC Robinson Cano 50.00 100.00

2010 Topps World Champion Relics

STATED ODDS 1:3750 HOBBY
STATED PRINT RUN 100 SER.#'d SETS
AP Andy Pettitte 20.00 50.00
AR Alex Rodriguez 30.00 60.00
BG Brett Gardner 10.00 25.00
CS CC Sabathia 20.00 50.00
EH Eric Hinske 15.00 40.00
HM Hideki Matsui 40.00 80.00
JD Johnny Damon 20.00 50.00
JG Joe Girardi 15.00 40.00
JH Jerry Hairston Jr. 30.00 60.00
JP Jorge Posada 20.00 50.00
MC Melky Cabrera 15.00 40.00
MR Mariano Rivera 25.00 60.00
MT Mark Teixeira 30.00 60.00
NS Nick Swisher 15.00 40.00
RC Robinson Cano 30.00 60.00

2010 Topps Update

COMP.SET w/o SPs (330) 50.00 120.00
COMMON CARD (1-330) .12 .30
COMMON SP VAR (1-330) 6.00 15.00
COMMON RC (1-330) .40 1.00
PRINTING PLATE ODDS 1:1550 HOBBY
US1 Vladimir Guerrero .20 .50
US2 Dayan Viciedo RC .60 1.50
US3 Sam Demel RC .40 1.00
US4 Alex Cora .20 .50
US5 Troy Glaus .12 .30
US6 Adam Ottavino RC .40 1.00
US7 Sam LeCure (RC) .40 1.00
US8 Fred Lewis .12 .30
US9 Danny Worth RC .40 1.00
US10 Hideki Matsui .30 .75
US11 Vernon Wells .12 .30
US12 Jason Michaels .12 .30
US13 Max Scherzer .30 .75
US14 Ike Davis .25 .60
US15A Ike Davis RC .75 2.00
US15B Willie McCovey VAR SP 6.00 15.00
US16 Felipe Paulino .12 .30
US17 Marlon Byrd .12 .30
US18 Omar Beltre (RC) .40 1.00
US19 Russell Branyan .12 .30
US20 Jason Bay .20 .50
US21 Roy Oswalt .20 .50
US22 Ty Wigginton .12 .30
US23 Andy Pettitte .20 .50
US24 V.Guerrero/M.Cabrera .30 .75
US25A Andrew Bailey .12 .30
US25B Philadelphia Athletics VAR SP 6.00 15.00
US26 Jesus Feliciano RC .40 1.00
US27 Koyie Hill .12 .30
US28 Bill Hall .12 .30
US29 Livan Hernandez .12 .30
US30 Roy Halladay .20 .50
US31 Corey Patterson .12 .30
US32 Doug Davis .12 .30
US33 Matt Capps .12 .30
US34 Shaun Marcum .12 .30
US35 Ryan Braun .20 .50
US36 Omar Vizquel .20 .50
US37 Alex Avila .20 .50
US38 Chris Young .12 .30
US39 Kila Ka'aihue .20 .50
US40 Evan Longoria .20 .50
US41 Anthony Slama RC .40 1.00
US42 Conor Jackson .12 .30
US43 Brennan Boesch .30 .75
US44 Scott Rolen .20 .50
US45A David Price .25 .60
US45B Steve Carlton VAR SP 6.00 15.00
US46 Colby Lewis .12 .30
US47 Jody Gerut .12 .30
US48 Geoff Blum .12 .30
US49 Bobby Wilson .12 .30
US50A Mike Stanton RC 8.00 20.00
US50B Reggie Jackson VAR SP 6.00 15.00
US51 Tom Gorzelanny .12 .30
US52 Andy Oliver RC .40 1.00
US53 Jordan Smith RC .40 1.00
US54 Akinori Iwamura .12 .30
US55 Stephen Strasburg 1.00 2.50
US56 Matt Holliday .30 .75
US57 Derek Jeter/Elvis Andrus .75 2.00
US58A Brian Wilson .30 .75
US58B New York Giants VAR SP 6.00 15.00
US59A Jeanmar Gomez RC .60 1.50
US59B J.Gomez Pie SP 10.00 25.00
US60 Miguel Tejada .20 .50
US61 Alfredo Simon .12 .30
US62 Chris Narveson .12 .30
US63 David Ortiz .30 .75
US64 Jose Valverde .12 .30
US65 Victor Martinez/Robinson Cano .20 .50
US66 Ronnie Belliard .12 .30
US67 Kyle Farnsworth .12 .30
US68 John Danks .12 .30
US69 Lance Cormier .12 .30
US70 Jonathan Broxton .12 .30
US71 Jason Giambi .12 .30
US72 Milton Bradley .12 .30
US73 Torii Hunter .12 .30
US74 Ryan Church .12 .30
US75 Jason Heyward .50 1.25
US76 Jose Tabata .20 .50
US77 John Axford RC .40 1.00
US78 Jon Link RC .40 1.00
US79 Jonny Gomes .12 .30
US80 David.Ortiz .30 .75
US81 Rich Harden .12 .30
US82 Emmanuel Burriss .12 .30
US83 Jeff Suppan .12 .30
US84 Melvin Mora .12 .30
US85A Starlin Castro RC 1.00 2.50
US85B Andre Dawson VAR SP 6.00 15.00
US86 Matt Guerrier .12 .30
US87 Trevor Plouffe (RC) 1.00 2.50
US88 Lance Berkman .20 .50
US89 Frank Herrmann RC .40 1.00
US90 Rafael Furcal .12 .30
US91 Nick Johnson .12 .30
US92 Pedro Feliciano .12 .30
US93 Jon Rauch .12 .30
US94 Reid Brignac .12 .30
US95 Jamie Moyer .12 .30
US96 John Bowker .12 .30
US97 Troy Tulowitzki/Matt Holliday .30 .75
US98 Yunel Escobar .12 .30
US99 Jose Bautista .20 .50
US100A Roy Halladay .20 .50
US100B Robin Roberts VAR SP 6.00 15.00
US101 Jake Westbrook .12 .30
US102 Chris Carter RC .60 1.50
US103 Matt Tuiasosopo .12 .30
US104 Paul Konerko .20 .50
US105 Chone Figgins .12 .30
US106 Orlando Cabrera .12 .30
US107 Matt Capps .12 .30
US108 John Buck .12 .30
US109 Luke Hughes (RC) .40 1.00
US110 Curtis Granderson .25 .60
US111 Willie Bloomquist .12 .30
US112 Chad Qualls .12 .30
US113 Brad Ziegler .12 .30
US114 Kenley Jansen RC 1.25 3.00
US115 Brad Lincoln RC .60 1.50
US116 Brandon Morrow .12 .30
US117 Martin Prado .12 .30
US118 Jose Bautista .20 .50
US119 Adam LaRoche .12 .30
US120 Brennan Boesch RC 1.00 2.50
US121 J.A. Happ .20 .50
US122 Darnell McDonald .12 .30
US123 Alberto Callaspo .12 .30
US124 Chris Young .12 .30
US125 Adam Wainwright .20 .50
US126 Elvis Andrus .20 .50
US127 Nick Swisher .20 .50
US128 Reed Johnson .12 .30
US129 Gregor Blanco .12 .30
US130 Ichiro Suzuki .40 1.00
US131 Takashi Saito .12 .30
US132 Corey Hart .12 .30
US133 Javier Vazquez .12 .30
US134 Rick Ankiel .12 .30
US135 Starlin Castro .30 .75
US136 Jarrod Saltalamacchia .12 .30
US137 Austin Kearns .12 .30
US138 Brandon League .12 .30
US139 Jorge Cantu .12 .30
US140 Josh Hamilton .20 .50
US141 Phil Hughes .12 .30
US142 Mike Cameron .12 .30
US143 Jonathan Lucroy RC 1.00 2.50
US144 Eric Patterson .12 .30
US145 Adrian Beltre .30 .75
US146 Peter Bourjos RC .60 1.50
US147 Argenis Diaz RC .60 1.50
US148 J.J. Putz .12 .30
US149A Kevin Russo RC .40 1.00
US149B B.Ruth VAR SP 10.00 25.00
US150 Hanley Ramirez .20 .50
US151 Kerry Wood .12 .30
US152 Ian Kennedy .12 .30
US153 Brian McCann .20 .50
US154 Jose Guillen .12 .30
US155 Ivan Rodriguez .20 .50
US156 Matt Thornton .12 .30
US157 Jason Marquis .12 .30
US158 CC Sabathia/Carl Crawford .20 .50
US159 Octavio Dotel .12 .30
US160 Josh Johnson .20 .50
US161 Matt Holliday .30 .75
US162 Hong-Chih Kuo .12 .30
US163 Marco Scutaro .20 .50
US164 Gaby Sanchez .12 .30
US165 Omar Infante .12 .30
US166 Jon Garland .12 .30
US167 Ramon Santiago .12 .30
US168 Wilson Ramos RC 1.00 2.50
US169 Ryan Ludwick .12 .30
US170 Carl Crawford .20 .50
US171 Cristian Guzman .12 .30
US172 Josh Donaldson RC 2.00 5.00
US173 Lorenzo Cain RC 1.00 2.50
US174 Matt Lindstrom .12 .30
US175A Drew Storen RC .60 1.50
US175B Bruce Sutter VAR SP 6.00 15.00
US176 Felipe Lopez .12 .30
US177 Chris Heisey RC .60 1.50
US178 Jim Edmonds .20 .50
US179 Juan Pierre .12 .30
US180 David Wright .25 .60
US181 J.P. Arencibia RC .75 2.00
US182 Randy Wolf .12 .30
US183 Luis Atilano RC .40 1.00
US184 Blake DeWitt .12 .30
US185A Brian Matusz RC 1.00 2.50
US185B Jim Palmer VAR SP 6.00 15.00
US186 Scott Hairston .12 .30
US187 Phil Hughes/David Price .25 .60
US188 Orlando Hudson .12 .30
US189 Derrek Lee .12 .30
US190 John Lackey .20 .50
US191 Danny Valencia RC 2.50 6.00
US192 Daniel Nava RC .40 1.00
US193 Ryan Theriot .12 .30
US194 Vernon Wells .12 .30
US195 Mark DeRosa .12 .30
US196 Aubrey Huff .12 .30
US197 Sean Marshall .12 .30
US198 Francisco Cervelli .12 .30
US199 Jhonny Peralta .12 .30
US200A Albert Pujols .40 1.00
US200B St. Louis Browns VAR SP 6.00 15.00
US201 Jeffrey Marquez RC .60 1.50
US202 Mitch Moreland RC .60 1.50
US203A Jon Jay RC .60 1.50
US203B Tony Gwynn VAR SP 6.00 15.00
US204 Carlos Silva .12 .30
US205 Ben Sheets .12 .30
US206 Garret Anderson .12 .30
US207 Jerry Hairston Jr. .12 .30
US208 Jeff Keppinger .12 .30
US209 Bengie Molina .12 .30
US210 Ubaldo Jimenez .12 .30
US211 Daniel Hudson .20 .50
US212 Mitch Talbot .12 .30
US213 Alex Gonzalez .12 .30
US214A Jason Heyward .50 1.25
US214B Dave Winfield VAR SP 6.00 15.00
US215 Albert Pujols/Ryan Braun .40 1.00
US216 John Baker .12 .30
US217 Yorvit Torrealba .12 .30
US218 Kevin Gregg .12 .30
US219 Bobby Crosby .12 .30
US220A Jon Lester .20 .50
US220B Boston Americans VAR SP 6.00 15.00
US221 Heath Bell .12 .30
US222 Ted Lilly .12 .30
US223 Henry Blanco .12 .30
US224 Scott Olsen .12 .30
US225A Josh Bell (RC) .40 1.00
US225B Brooks Robinson VAR SP 6.00 15.00
US226 Scott Podsednik .12 .30
US227 Mark Kotsay .12 .30
US228 Brandon Phillips/Martin Prado .12 .30
US229 Joe Saunders .12 .30
US230 Robinson Cano .20 .50
US231 Gabe Kapler .12 .30
US232 Jason Kendall .12 .30
US233 Brendan Harris .12 .30
US234 Matt Downs RC .40 1.00
US235 Jose Tabata RC .60 1.50
US236 Matt Daley .12 .30
US237 Jhan Marinez RC .40 1.00
US238 Mark Ellis .12 .30
US239 Gabe Gross .12 .30
US240 Adrian Gonzalez .25 .60
US241 Joey Votto .30 .75
US242 Shelley Duncan .12 .30
US243 Michael Bourn .12 .30
US244 Mike Redmond .12 .30
US245 Placido Polanco .12 .30
US246 LaTroy Hawkins .12 .30
US247 Nick Swisher .20 .50
US248 Matt Harrison .12 .30
US249 Rafael Soriano .12 .30
US250 Miguel Cabrera .30 .75
US251A Jake Arrieta RC 1.00 2.50
US251B J.Arrieta Pie SP 15.00 40.00
US252 Jim Thome .20 .50
US253 Mike Minor RC .60 1.50
US254 Chris Perez .12 .30
US255 Kevin Millwood .12 .30
US256 Mike Gonzalez .12 .30
US257 Joel Hanrahan .20 .50
US258 Dana Eveland .12 .30
US259 Yadier Molina .40 1.00
US260A Andre Ethier .20 .50
US260B Brooklyn Dodgers VAR SP 6.00 15.00
US261 Jason Vargas .12 .30
US262 Rob Johnson .12 .30
US263 Randy Winn .12 .30
US264 Vicente Padilla .12 .30
US265 Ryan Howard .25 .60
US266 Billy Wagner .12 .30
US267 Eugenio Velez .12 .30
US268 Logan Morrison RC .60 1.50
US269 Dave Bush .12 .30
US270 Vladimir Guerrero .20 .50
US271 Travis Wood (RC) .60 1.50
US272 Brian Stokes .12 .30
US273 John Jaso .12 .30
US274 S.Strasburg/I.Rodriguez 1.00 2.50
US275 Hong-Chih Kuo .12 .30
US276A Austin Jackson .20 .50
US276B Rickey Henderson VAR SP 6.00 15.00
US277 Micah Owings .12 .30
US278 Brad Penny .12 .30
US279 Hanley Ramirez .20 .50
US280 Alex Rodriguez .40 1.00
US281 Jose Valverde .12 .30
US282 Rhyne Hughes RC .40 1.00
US283 Kevin Frandsen .12 .30
US284 Josh Reddick .12 .30
US285 Jaime Garcia .20 .50
US286 Arthur Rhodes .12 .30
US287 Alex Sanabia RC .40 1.00
US288 Jonny Venters RC .40 1.00
US289 Adam Kennedy .12 .30
US290 Justin Verlander .30 .75
US291 Corey Hart .12 .30
US292 Kelly Shoppach .12 .30
US293 Pat Burrell .12 .30
US294 Aaron Heilman .12 .30
US295 Andrew Cashner RC .40 1.00
US296 Lance Zawadzki RC .40 1.00
US297 Don Kelly (RC) .40 1.00
US298 David Freese .20 .50
US299 Xavier Nady .12 .30
US300 Cliff Lee .20 .50
US301 Jeff Clement .12 .30
US302 Pedro Feliz .12 .30
US303 Brandon Phillips .12 .30
US304 Kris Medlen .20 .50
US305 Cliff Lee .20 .50
US306 Dan Haren .12 .30
US307 Carlos Santana .40 1.00
US308 Matt Thornton .12 .30

US309 Andruw Jones .12 .30
US310 Derek Jeter .75 2.00
US311 Felix Doubront RC .40 1.00
US312 Coco Crisp .12 .30
US313 Mitch Maier .12 .30
US314 Cole Gillespie RC .40 1.00
US315A Edwin Jackson .12 .30
US315B E.Jackson Pie SP 10.00 25.00
US316 Rod Barajas .12 .30
US317A Mike Leake .40 1.00
US317B B.Ruth VAR SP 8.00 20.00
US318A Domonic Brown RC 1.50 4.00
US318B Bo Jackson VAR SP 6.00 15.00
US319 Josh Tomlin RC 1.00 2.50
US320A Joe Mauer .25 .60
US320B Washington Senators VAR SP 6.00 15.00
US321 Jason Donald RC .40 1.00
US322 John Ely RC .40 1.00
US323 Ryan Kalish RC .60 1.50
US324 George Kottaras .12 .30
US325 Ian Kinsler .20 .50
US326 Miguel Cabrera .30 .75
US327 Mike Stanton 1.00 2.50
US328 Adrian Beltre .30 .75
US329 Jose Reyes/Hanley Ramriez .20 .50
US330A Carlos Santana RC 1.25 3.00
US330B Cleveland Naps VAR SP 6.00 15.00
US330C Johnny Bench VAR SP 6.00 15.00

2010 Topps Update Black

STATED ODDS 1:105 HOBBY
STATED PRINT RUN 59 SER.#'d SETS
US1 Vladimir Guerrero 8.00 20.00
US2 Dayan Viciedo 8.00 20.00
US3 Sam Demel 5.00 12.00
US4 Alex Cora 8.00 20.00
US5 Troy Glaus 5.00 12.00
US6 Adam Ottavino 5.00 12.00
US7 Sam LeCure 5.00 12.00
US8 Fred Lewis 5.00 12.00
US9 Danny Worth 5.00 12.00
US10 Hideki Matsui 10.00 25.00
US11 Vernon Wells 5.00 12.00
US12 Jason Michaels 5.00 12.00
US13 Max Scherzer 12.00 30.00
US14 Ike Davis 8.00 20.00
US15 Ike Davis 8.00 20.00
US16 Felipe Paulino 5.00 12.00
US17 Marlon Byrd 5.00 12.00
US18 Omar Beltre 5.00 12.00
US19 Russell Branyan 5.00 12.00
US20 Jason Bay 8.00 20.00
US21 Roy Oswalt 8.00 20.00
US22 Ty Wigginton 5.00 12.00
US23 Andy Pettitte 8.00 20.00
US24 V.Guerrero/M.Cabrera 10.00 25.00
US25 Andrew Bailey 5.00 12.00
US26 Jesus Feliciano 5.00 12.00
US27 Koyie Hill 5.00 12.00
US28 Bill Hall 5.00 12.00
US29 Livan Hernandez 5.00 12.00
US30 Roy Halladay 6.00 15.00
US31 Corey Patterson 5.00 12.00
US32 Doug Davis 5.00 12.00
US33 Matt Capps 5.00 12.00
US34 Shaun Marcum 5.00 12.00
US35 Ryan Braun 6.00 15.00
US36 Omar Vizquel 8.00 20.00
US37 Alex Avila 8.00 20.00
US38 Chris Young 5.00 12.00
US39 Kila Ka'aihue 8.00 20.00
US40 Evan Longoria 6.00 15.00
US41 Anthony Slama 5.00 12.00
US42 Conor Jackson 5.00 12.00
US43 Brennan Boesch 10.00 25.00
US44 Scott Rolen 8.00 20.00
US45 David Price 8.00 20.00
US46 Colby Lewis 5.00 12.00
US47 Jody Gerut 5.00 12.00
US48 Geoff Blum 5.00 12.00
US49 Bobby Wilson 5.00 12.00
US50 Mike Stanton 30.00 80.00
US51 Tom Gorzelanny 5.00 12.00
US52 Andy Oliver 5.00 12.00
US53 Jordan Smith 5.00 12.00
US54 Akinori Iwamura 5.00 12.00
US55 Stephen Strasburg 15.00 40.00
US56 Matt Holliday 10.00 25.00
US57 Derek Jeter/Elvis Andrus 25.00 60.00
US58 Brian Wilson 12.00 30.00
US59 Jeanmar Gomez 6.00 15.00
US60 Miguel Tejada 8.00 20.00
US61 Alfredo Simon 5.00 12.00
US62 Chris Narveson 5.00 12.00
US63 David Ortiz 12.00 30.00
US64 Jose Valverde 5.00 12.00
US65 Victor Martinez/Robinson Cano 6.00 15.00
US66 Ronnie Belliard 5.00 12.00
US67 Kyle Farnsworth 5.00 12.00
US68 John Danks 5.00 12.00
US69 Lance Cormier 5.00 12.00
US70 Jonathan Broxton 5.00 12.00
US71 Jason Giambi 5.00 12.00
US72 Milton Bradley 5.00 12.00
US73 Torii Hunter 5.00 12.00
US74 Ryan Church 5.00 12.00
US75 Jason Heyward 15.00 40.00
US76 Jose Tabata 6.00 15.00
US77 John Axford 5.00 12.00
US78 Jon Link 5.00 12.00
US79 Jonny Gomes 5.00 12.00
US80 David Ortiz 12.00 30.00
US81 Rich Harden 5.00 12.00
US82 Emmanuel Burriss 5.00 12.00
US83 Jeff Suppan 5.00 12.00
US84 Melvin Mora 5.00 12.00
US85 Starlin Castro 10.00 25.00
US86 Matt Guerrier 5.00 12.00
US87 Trevor Plouffe 12.00 30.00
US88 Lance Berkman 8.00 20.00
US89 Frank Herrmann 5.00 12.00
US90 Rafael Furcal 5.00 12.00
US91 Nick Johnson 5.00 12.00
US92 Pedro Feliciano 5.00 12.00
US93 Jon Rauch 5.00 12.00
US94 Reid Brignac 5.00 12.00
US95 Jamie Moyer 5.00 12.00
US96 John Bowker 5.00 12.00
US97 Troy Tulowitzki/Matt Holliday 10.00 25.00
US98 Yunel Escobar 5.00 12.00
US99 Jose Bautista 8.00 20.00
US100 Roy Halladay 6.00 15.00
US101 Jake Westbrook 5.00 12.00
US102 Chris Carter 8.00 20.00
US103 Matt Tuiasosopo 5.00 12.00
US104 Paul Konerko 8.00 20.00
US105 Chone Figgins 5.00 12.00
US106 Orlando Cabrera 5.00 12.00
US107 Matt Capps 5.00 12.00
US108 John Buck 5.00 12.00
US109 Luke Hughes 5.00 12.00
US110 Curtis Granderson 10.00 25.00
US111 Willie Bloomquist 5.00 12.00
US112 Chad Qualls 5.00 12.00
US113 Brad Ziegler 5.00 12.00
US114 Kenley Jansen 15.00 40.00
US115 Brad Lincoln 8.00 20.00
US116 Brandon Morrow 5.00 12.00
US117 Martin Prado 5.00 12.00
US118 Jose Bautista 8.00 20.00
US119 Adam LaRoche 5.00 12.00
US120 Brennan Boesch 10.00 25.00
US121 J.A. Happ 8.00 20.00
US122 Darnell McDonald 5.00 12.00
US123 Alberto Callaspo 5.00 12.00
US124 Chris Young 5.00 12.00
US125 Adam Wainwright 8.00 20.00
US126 Elvis Andrus 8.00 20.00
US127 Nick Swisher 8.00 20.00
US128 Reed Johnson 5.00 12.00
US129 Gregor Blanco 5.00 12.00
US130 Ichiro Suzuki 12.00 30.00
US131 Takashi Saito 5.00 12.00
US132 Corey Hart 5.00 12.00
US133 Javier Vazquez 5.00 12.00
US134 Rick Ankiel 5.00 12.00
US135 Starlin Castro 10.00 25.00
US136 Jarrod Saltalamacchia 5.00 12.00
US137 Austin Kearns 5.00 12.00
US138 Brandon League 5.00 12.00
US139 Jorge Cantu 5.00 12.00
US140 Josh Hamilton 6.00 15.00
US141 Phil Hughes 5.00 12.00
US142 Mike Cameron 5.00 12.00
US143 Jonathan Lucroy 12.00 30.00
US144 Eric Patterson 5.00 12.00
US145 Adrian Beltre 12.00 30.00
US146 Peter Bourjos 8.00 20.00
US147 Argenis Diaz 8.00 20.00
US148 J.J. Putz 5.00 12.00
US149 Kevin Russo 5.00 12.00
US150 Hanley Ramirez 6.00 15.00
US151 Kerry Wood 5.00 12.00
US152 Ian Kennedy 5.00 12.00
US153 Brian McCann 8.00 20.00
US154 Jose Guillen 5.00 12.00
US155 Ivan Rodriguez 8.00 20.00
US156 Matt Thornton 5.00 12.00
US157 Jason Marquis 5.00 12.00
US158 CC Sabathia/Carl Crawford 8.00 20.00
US159 Octavio Dotel 5.00 12.00
US160 Josh Johnson 6.00 15.00
US161 Matt Holliday 10.00 25.00
US162 Hong-Chih Kuo 5.00 12.00
US163 Marco Scutaro 8.00 20.00
US164 Gaby Sanchez 5.00 12.00
US165 Omar Infante 5.00 12.00
US166 Jon Garland 5.00 12.00
US167 Ramon Santiago 5.00 12.00
US168 Wilson Ramos 12.00 30.00
US169 Ryan Ludwick 5.00 12.00
US170 Carl Crawford 8.00 20.00
US171 Cristian Guzman 5.00 12.00
US172 Josh Donaldson 25.00 60.00
US173 Lorenzo Cain 12.00 30.00
US174 Matt Lindstrom 5.00 12.00
US175 Drew Storen 8.00 20.00
US176 Felipe Lopez 5.00 12.00
US177 Chris Heisey 6.00 15.00
US178 Jim Edmonds 8.00 20.00
US179 Juan Pierre 5.00 12.00
US180 David Wright 8.00 20.00
US181 J.P. Arencibia 10.00 25.00
US182 Randy Wolf 5.00 12.00
US183 Luis Atilano 5.00 12.00
US184 Blake DeWitt 5.00 12.00
US185 Brian Matusz 10.00 25.00
US186 Scott Hairston 5.00 12.00
US187 Phil Hughes/David Price 8.00 20.00
US188 Orlando Hudson 5.00 12.00
US189 Derrek Lee 5.00 12.00
US190 John Lackey 8.00 20.00
US191 Danny Valencia 25.00 60.00
US192 Daniel Nava 4.00 10.00
US193 Ryan Theriot 5.00 12.00
US194 Vernon Wells 5.00 12.00
US195 Mark DeRosa 5.00 12.00
US196 Aubrey Huff 5.00 12.00
US197 Sean Marshall 5.00 12.00
US198 Francisco Cervelli 5.00 12.00
US199 Jhonny Peralta 5.00 12.00
US200 Albert Pujols 12.00 30.00
US201 Jeffrey Marquez 8.00 20.00
US202 Mitch Moreland 6.00 15.00
US203 Jon Jay 6.00 15.00
US204 Carlos Silva 5.00 12.00
US205 Ben Sheets 5.00 12.00
US206 Garret Anderson 5.00 12.00
US207 Jerry Hairston Jr. 5.00 12.00
US208 Jeff Keppinger 5.00 12.00
US209 Bengie Molina 5.00 12.00
US210 Ubaldo Jimenez 4.00 10.00
US211 Daniel Hudson 6.00 15.00
US212 Mitch Talbot 5.00 12.00
US213 Alex Gonzalez 5.00 12.00
US214 Jason Heyward 15.00 40.00
US215 Albert Pujols/Ryan Braun 12.00 30.00
US216 John Baker 5.00 12.00
US217 Yorvit Torrealba 5.00 12.00
US218 Kevin Gregg 5.00 12.00
US219 Bobby Crosby 5.00 12.00
US220 Jon Lester 8.00 20.00
US221 Heath Bell 5.00 12.00
US222 Ted Lilly 5.00 12.00
US223 Henry Blanco 5.00 12.00
US224 Scott Olsen 5.00 12.00
US225 Josh Bell 5.00 12.00
US226 Scott Podsednik 5.00 12.00
US227 Mark Kotsay 5.00 12.00
US228 Brandon Phillips/Martin Prado 5.00 12.00
US229 Joe Saunders 5.00 12.00
US230 Robinson Cano 6.00 15.00
US231 Gabe Kapler 5.00 12.00
US232 Jason Kendall 5.00 12.00
US233 Brendan Harris 5.00 12.00
US234 Matt Downs 5.00 12.00
US235 Jose Tabata 6.00 15.00
US236 Matt Daley 5.00 12.00
US237 Jhan Marinez 5.00 12.00
US238 Mark Ellis 5.00 12.00
US239 Gabe Gross 5.00 12.00
US240 Adrian Gonzalez 10.00 25.00
US241 Joey Votto 10.00 25.00
US242 Shelley Duncan 5.00 12.00
US243 Michael Bourn 5.00 12.00
US244 Mike Redmond 5.00 12.00
US245 Placido Polanco 5.00 12.00
US246 LaTroy Hawkins 5.00 12.00
US247 Nick Swisher 8.00 20.00
US248 Matt Harrison 5.00 12.00
US249 Rafael Soriano 5.00 12.00
US250 Miguel Cabrera 10.00 25.00
US251 Jake Arrieta 12.00 30.00
US252 Jim Thome 8.00 20.00
US253 Mike Minor 6.00 15.00
US254 Chris Perez 5.00 12.00
US255 Kevin Millwood 5.00 12.00
US256 Mike Gonzalez 5.00 12.00
US257 Joel Hanrahan 8.00 20.00
US258 Dana Eveland 5.00 12.00
US259 Yadier Molina 15.00 40.00
US260 Andre Ethier 6.00 15.00
US261 Jason Vargas 5.00 12.00
US262 Rob Johnson 5.00 12.00
US263 Randy Winn 5.00 12.00
US264 Vicente Padilla 5.00 12.00
US265 Ryan Howard 8.00 20.00
US266 Billy Wagner 5.00 12.00
US267 Eugenio Velez 5.00 12.00
US268 Logan Morrison 8.00 20.00
US269 Dave Bush 5.00 12.00
US270 Vladimir Guerrero 6.00 15.00
US271 Travis Wood 6.00 15.00
US272 Brian Stokes 5.00 12.00
US273 John Jaso 5.00 12.00
US274 S.Strasburg/I.Rodriguez 15.00 40.00
US275 Hong-Chih Kuo 5.00 12.00
US276 Austin Jackson 6.00 15.00
US277 Micah Owings 5.00 12.00
US278 Brad Penny 5.00 12.00
US279 Hanley Ramirez 6.00 15.00
US280 Alex Rodriguez 12.00 30.00
US281 Jose Valverde 5.00 12.00
US282 Rhyne Hughes 5.00 12.00
US283 Kevin Frandsen 5.00 12.00
US284 Josh Reddick 5.00 12.00
US285 Jaime Garcia 8.00 20.00
US286 Arthur Rhodes 5.00 12.00
US287 Alex Sanabia 5.00 12.00
US288 Jonny Venters 5.00 12.00
US289 Adam Kennedy 5.00 12.00
US290 Justin Verlander 12.00 30.00
US291 Corey Hart 5.00 12.00
US292 Kelly Shoppach 5.00 12.00
US293 Pat Burrell 5.00 12.00
US294 Aaron Heilman 5.00 12.00
US295 Andrew Cashner 5.00 12.00
US296 Lance Zawadzki 5.00 12.00
US297 Don Kelly 5.00 12.00
US298 David Freese 8.00 20.00
US299 Xavier Nady 5.00 12.00
US300 Cliff Lee 8.00 20.00
US301 Jeff Clement 5.00 12.00
US302 Pedro Feliz 5.00 12.00
US303 Brandon Phillips 5.00 12.00
US304 Kris Medlen 8.00 20.00
US305 Cliff Lee 8.00 20.00
US306 Dan Haren 5.00 12.00
US307 Carlos Santana 12.00 30.00
US308 Matt Thornton 5.00 12.00
US309 Andruw Jones 5.00 12.00
US310 Derek Jeter 25.00 60.00
US311 Felix Doubront 5.00 12.00
US312 Coco Crisp 5.00 12.00
US313 Mitch Maier 5.00 12.00
US314 Cole Gillespie 5.00 12.00
US315 Edwin Jackson 5.00 12.00
US316 Rod Barajas 5.00 12.00
US317 Mike Leake 12.00 30.00
US318 Domonic Brown 15.00 40.00
US319 Josh Tomlin 12.00 30.00
US320 Joe Mauer 8.00 20.00
US321 Jason Donald 5.00 12.00
US322 John Ely 5.00 12.00
US323 Ryan Kalish 6.00 15.00
US324 George Kottaras 5.00 12.00
US325 Ian Kinsler 8.00 20.00
US326 Miguel Cabrera 12.00 30.00
US327 Mike Stanton 30.00 80.00
US328 Adrian Beltre 12.00 30.00
US329 Jose Reyes/Hanley Ramriez 6.00 15.00
US330 Carlos Santana 12.00 30.00

2010 Topps Update Gold

*GOLD VET: 2X TO 5X BASIC
*GOLD RC: ..6X TO 1.5X BASIC RC
STATED ODDS 1:6 HOBBY
STATED PRINT RUN 2010 SER.#'d SETS
US55 Stephen Strasburg 4.00 10.00
US274 S.Strasburg/I.Rodriguez 4.00 10.00

2010 Topps Update Target

*VETS: .5X TO 1.2X BASIC TOPPS UPD CARDS
*RC: .5X TO 1.2X BASIC TOPPS UPD RC CARDS

2010 Topps Update Wal-Mart Black Border

*VETS: .5X TO 1.2X BASIC TOPPS UPD CARDS
*RC: .5X TO 1.2X BASIC TOPPS UPD RC CARDS

2010 Topps Update All-Star Stitches

STATED ODDS 1:53 HOBBY
AB Andrew Bailey 3.00 8.00
AE Andre Ethier 3.00 8.00
AG Adrian Gonzalez 3.00 8.00
AP Andy Pettitte 5.00 12.00
AR Alex Rodriguez 5.00 12.00
AW Adam Wainwright 4.00 10.00
BM Brian McCann 4.00 10.00
BP Brandon Phillips 3.00 8.00
BW Brian Wilson 5.00 12.00
CB Clay Buchholz 3.00 8.00
CC Carl Crawford 3.00 8.00
CH Corey Hart 3.00 8.00
CL Cliff Lee 4.00 10.00
CY Chris Young 3.00 8.00
DJ Derek Jeter 10.00 25.00
DO David Ortiz 3.00 8.00
DP David Price 4.00 10.00
DW David Wright 3.00 8.00
EA Elvis Andrus 4.00 10.00
EL Evan Longoria 5.00 12.00
EM Evan Meek 3.00 8.00
FC Fausto Carmona 3.00 8.00
HB Heath Bell 4.00 10.00
HR Hanley Ramirez 3.00 8.00
IK Ian Kinsler 3.00 8.00
IS Ichiro Suzuki 10.00 25.00
JB Jose Bautista 4.00 10.00
JH Josh Hamilton 4.00 10.00
JJ Josh Johnson 3.00 8.00
JL Jon Lester 3.00 8.00
JM Joe Mauer 5.00 12.00
JR Jose Reyes 4.00 10.00
JS Joakim Soria 3.00 8.00
JV Justin Verlander 3.00 8.00
JW Jered Weaver 3.00 8.00
MB Marlon Byrd 4.00 10.00
MC Miguel Cabrera 4.00 10.00
MH Matt Holliday 4.00 10.00
MP Martin Prado 3.00 8.00
MT Matt Thornton 3.00 8.00
NF Neftali Feliz 4.00 10.00
OI Omar Infante 3.00 8.00
PH Phil Hughes 4.00 10.00
PK Paul Konerko 3.00 8.00
RB Ryan Braun 3.00 8.00
RC Robinson Cano 5.00 12.00
RF Rafael Furcal 3.00 8.00
RH Roy Halladay 5.00 12.00
RS Rafael Soriano 3.00 8.00
SR Scott Rolen 4.00 10.00
TC Trevor Cahill 3.00 8.00
TH Torii Hunter 3.00 8.00
TL Tim Lincecum 8.00 20.00
TT Troy Tulowitzki 4.00 10.00
TW Ty Wigginton 4.00 10.00
UJ Ubaldo Jimenez 3.00 8.00
VG Vladimir Guerrero 3.00 8.00
VM Victor Martinez 3.00 8.00
VW Vernon Wells 3.00 8.00
YG Yovani Gallardo 3.00 8.00
YM Yadier Molina 4.00 10.00
ABE Adrian Beltre 4.00 10.00
APU Albert Pujols 8.00 20.00
ARH Arthur Rhodes 3.00 8.00
CCA Chris Carpenter 4.00 10.00
CCS CC Sabathia 3.00 8.00
DPE Dustin Pedroia 4.00 10.00
HCK Hong-Chih Kuo 4.00 10.00
JBR Jonathan Broxton 3.00 8.00
JBU John Buck 3.00 8.00
JHE Jason Heyward 6.00 15.00
JVO Joey Votto 5.00 12.00
MBO Michael Bourn 3.00 8.00
MCA Matt Capps 3.00 8.00
RHO Ryan Howard 4.00 10.00
THU Tim Hudson 3.00 8.00

2010 Topps Update All-Star Stitches Gold

*GOLD: .6X TO 1.5X BASIC
STATED ODDS 1:1047 HOBBY
STATED PRINT RUN 50 SER.#'d SETS

2010 Topps Update Attax Code Cards

28 Jered Weaver .50 1.25
29 Hideki Matsui .75 2.00
30 Mark Reynolds .30 .75
31 Justin Upton .50 1.25
32 Jason Heyward 1.25 3.00
33 Brian McCann .50 1.25
34 Adam Jones .50 1.25
35 Nick Markakis .60 1.50
36 Kevin Youkilis .30 .75
37 Victor Martinez .50 1.25
38 John Lackey .50 1.25
39 Starlin Castro .75 2.00
40 Alfonso Soriano .50 1.25
41 Jake Peavy .30 .75
42 Paul Konerko .50 1.25
43 Carlos Santana 1.00 2.50
44 Shin-Soo Choo .50 1.25
45 Mike Leake 1.00 2.50
46 Ubaldo Jimenez .30 .75
47 Miguel Cabrera .75 2.00
48 Austin Jackson .50 1.25
49 Hanley Ramirez .50 1.25
50 Mike Stanton 2.50 6.00
51 Hunter Pence .50 1.25
52 Joakim Soria .30 .75
53 Andre Ethier .50 1.25
54 Clayton Kershaw 1.25 3.00
55 Ryan Braun .50 1.25
56 Joe Mauer .60 1.50
57 Francisco Liriano .30 .75
58 Ike Davis .60 1.50
59 David Wright .60 1.50
60 Robinson Cano .50 1.25
61 Derek Jeter 2.00 5.00
62 Kurt Suzuki .30 .75
63 Roy Halladay .50 1.25
64 Ryan Howard .60 1.50
65 Andrew McCutchen .75 2.00
66 Albert Pujols 1.00 2.50
67 Adam Wainwright .50 1.25
68 Adrian Gonzalez .60 1.50
69 Buster Posey 2.50 6.00
70 Matt Cain .50 1.25
71 Ichiro Suzuki 1.00 2.50
72 Evan Longoria .50 1.25
73 David Price .60 1.50
74 Josh Hamilton .50 1.25
75 Vernon Wells .30 .75
76 Stephen Strasburg 2.50 6.00
77 Adam Dunn .50 1.25

2010 Topps Update Chrome Rookie Refractors

CHR01 Stephen Strasburg 8.00 20.00
CHR02 Wilson Ramos 2.50 6.00
CHR03 Lance Zawadzki 1.00 2.50
CHR04 Jesus Feliciano 1.00 2.50
CHR05 Logan Morrison 1.50 4.00
CHR06 Josh Donaldson 5.00 12.00
CHR07 Travis Wood 1.50 4.00
CHR08 Cole Gillespie 1.00 2.50
CHR09 Ryan Kalish 1.50 4.00
CHR10 Domonic Brown 4.00 10.00
CHR11 Jason Donald 1.00 2.50
CHR12 Jeffrey Marquez 1.50 4.00
CHR13 Adam Ottavino 1.00 2.50
CHR14 Luke Hughes 1.00 2.50
CHR15 Jose Tabata 1.50 4.00
CHR16 Josh Bell 1.00 2.50
CHR17 Jon Link 1.00 2.50
CHR18 John Ely 1.00 2.50
CHR19 Jeanmar Gomez 1.50 4.00
CHR20 Mike Stanton 8.00 20.00
CHR21 Luis Atilano 1.00 2.50
CHR22 Chris Heisey 1.50 4.00
CHR23 Jake Arrieta 2.50 6.00
CHR24 Jonathan Lucroy 2.50 6.00
CHR25 Andrew Cashner 1.00 2.50
CHR26 Sam LeCure 1.00 2.50
CHR27 Danny Valencia 6.00 15.00
CHR28 Rhyne Hughes 1.00 2.50
CHR29 Kenley Jansen 3.00 8.00
CHR30 Ike Davis 2.00 5.00
CHR31 Lorenzo Cain 2.50 6.00
CHR32 Jonny Venters 1.00 2.50
CHR33 Andy Oliver 1.00 2.50
CHR34 Jon Jay 1.50 4.00
CHR35 Drew Storen 1.50 4.00
CHR36 Omar Beltre 1.00 2.50
CHR37 Alex Sanabia 1.00 2.50
CHR38 Jordan Smith 1.00 2.50
CHR39 Trevor Plouffe 2.50 6.00
CHR40 Starlin Castro 2.50 6.00
CHR41 Jhan Marinez 1.00 2.50
CHR42 Brad Lincoln 1.50 4.00
CHR43 Kevin Russo 1.00 2.50
CHR44 Frank Herrmann 1.00 2.50
CHR45 Brennan Boesch 2.50 6.00
CHR46 Daniel Nava 1.00 2.50
CHR47 Sam Demel 1.00 2.50
CHR48 Dayan Viciedo 1.50 4.00
CHR49 Felix Doubront 1.00 2.50
CHR50 Carlos Santana 3.00 8.00
CHR51 Josh Tomlin 2.50 6.00
CHR52 Anthony Slama 1.00 2.50
CHR53 Chris Carter 1.50 4.00
CHR54 J.P. Arencibia 2.00 5.00
CHR55 Mitch Moreland 1.50 4.00
CHR56 Peter Bourjos 1.50 4.00
CHR57 Argenis Diaz 1.50 4.00
CHR58 Mike Minor 1.50 4.00
CHR59 Brian Matusz 2.50 6.00
CHR60 Jason Heyward 4.00 10.00
CHR61 Mike Stanton 8.00 20.00
CHR62 Ike Davis 2.00 5.00
CHR63 Carlos Santana 3.00 8.00
CHR64 Austin Jackson 1.50 4.00
CHR65 Mike Leake 3.00 8.00
CHR66 Brennan Boesch 2.50 6.00
CHR67 Stephen Strasburg 8.00 20.00
CHR68 Jose Tabata 1.50 4.00
CHR69 Starlin Castro 2.50 6.00
CHR70 Danny Worth 1.00 2.50

2010 Topps Update Manufactured Bat Barrel

STATED ODDS 1:380 HOBBY
STATED PRINT RUN 99 SER.#'d SETS
BLACK ODDS 1:1960 HOBBY
BLACK PRINT RUN 25 SER.#'d SETS
PINK ODDS 1:44,000 HOBBY
PINK PRINT RUN 1 SER.#'d SET
MB1 Ryan Braun 5.00 12.00
MB2 Derek Jeter 20.00 50.00
MB3 Torii Hunter 3.00 8.00
MB4 Chase Utley 5.00 12.00
MB5 Justin Upton 5.00 12.00
MB6 David Wright 6.00 15.00
MB7 Troy Tulowitzki 8.00 20.00
MB8 Kevin Youkilis 3.00 8.00
MB9 Jose Reyes 5.00 12.00
MB10 Albert Pujols 10.00 25.00
MB11 Jimmy Rollins 5.00 12.00
MB12 Victor Martinez 5.00 12.00
MB13 Shane Victorino 5.00 12.00
MB14 Matt Holliday 8.00 20.00
MB15 Prince Fielder 5.00 12.00
MB16 Hideki Matsui 8.00 20.00
MB17 Nick Markakis 6.00 15.00
MB18 Alfonso Soriano 5.00 12.00
MB19 Shin-Soo Choo 5.00 12.00
MB20 Evan Longoria 5.00 12.00
MB21 Joey Votto 8.00 20.00
MB22 Andrew McCutchen 8.00 20.00
MB23 Mark Reynolds 3.00 8.00
MB24 Andre Ethier 5.00 12.00
MB25 Robinson Cano 5.00 12.00
MB26 Casey McGehee 3.00 8.00
MB27 Paul Konerko 5.00 12.00
MB28 Adam Lind 5.00 12.00
MB29 Dustin Pedroia 8.00 20.00
MB30 Jason Heyward 12.00 30.00
MB31 Billy Butler 3.00 8.00
MB32 Justin Morneau 5.00 12.00
MB33 Aaron Hill 3.00 8.00
MB34 Pablo Sandoval 5.00 12.00
MB35 Miguel Cabrera 8.00 20.00
MB36 Ryan Zimmerman 5.00 12.00
MB37 Hunter Pence 5.00 12.00
MB38 Adrian Gonzalez 6.00 15.00
MB39 Adam Dunn 5.00 12.00
MB40 Vladimir Guerrero 5.00 12.00
MB41 Jason Bay 5.00 12.00
MB42 Matt Kemp 6.00 15.00
MB43 Dan Uggla 3.00 8.00
MB44 Brandon Phillips 3.00 8.00
MB45 Alex Rodriguez 10.00 25.00
MB46 Manny Ramirez 8.00 20.00
MB47 Nick Swisher 5.00 12.00
MB48 Vernon Wells 3.00 8.00
MB49 Corey Hart 3.00 8.00
MB50 Joe Mauer 6.00 15.00
MB51 David Ortiz 8.00 20.00
MB52 Josh Hamilton 5.00 12.00
MB53 Kendry Morales 3.00 8.00
MB54 Colby Rasmus 5.00 12.00
MB55 Chipper Jones 8.00 20.00
MB56 Lance Berkman 5.00 12.00
MB57 James Loney 3.00 8.00
MB58 Ian Kinsler 5.00 12.00
MB59 Carl Crawford 5.00 12.00
MB60 Hanley Ramirez 5.00 12.00
MB61 Buster Posey 25.00 60.00
MB62 Ike Davis 6.00 15.00
MB63 Adam Jones 5.00 12.00
MB64 Brian McCann 5.00 12.00
MB65 Mark Teixeira 5.00 12.00
MB66 Kurt Suzuki 3.00 8.00
MB67 Mike Stanton 20.00 50.00
MB68 Jayson Werth 5.00 12.00
MB69 Nelson Cruz 8.00 20.00
MB70 Ryan Howard 6.00 15.00
MB71 Martin Prado 3.00 8.00
MB72 Michael Young 3.00 8.00
MB73 Ben Zobrist 5.00 12.00
MB74 Carlos Lee 3.00 8.00
MB75 Ichiro Suzuki 10.00 25.00
MB76 Carlos Quentin 3.00 8.00
MB77 B.J. Upton 5.00 12.00
MB78 Alex Rios 3.00 8.00
MB79 Magglio Ordonez 5.00 12.00
MB80 Jose Bautista 5.00 12.00
MB81 Garrett Jones 3.00 8.00
MB82 Carlos Pena 5.00 12.00
MB83 Jay Bruce 5.00 12.00
MB84 Austin Jackson 5.00 12.00
MB85 Chris Young 3.00 8.00
MB86 Alexei Ramirez 5.00 12.00
MB87 Carlos Gonzalez 5.00 12.00
MB88 Howie Kendrick 3.00 8.00
MB89 Ryan Ludwick 3.00 8.00
MB90 Miguel Tejada 5.00 12.00
MB91 Derrek Lee 3.00 8.00
MB92 Adrian Beltre 8.00 20.00
MB93 Gordon Beckham 3.00 8.00
MB94 Yadier Molina 10.00 25.00
MB95 Starlin Castro 8.00 20.00
MB96 Stephen Drew 3.00 8.00
MB97 Carlos Santana 10.00 25.00
MB98 Bobby Abreu 3.00 8.00
MB99 Ty Wigginton 3.00 8.00
MB100 Scott Rolen 5.00 12.00
MB101 Grady Sizemore 5.00 12.00
MB102 Miguel Montero 3.00 8.00
MB103 Todd Helton 5.00 12.00
MB104 Chris Coghlan 3.00 8.00
MB105 Curtis Granderson 6.00 15.00
MB106 Troy Glaus 3.00 8.00
MB107 Placido Polanco 3.00 8.00
MB108 Elvis Andrus 5.00 12.00
MB109 Aramis Ramirez 3.00 8.00
MB110 Jose Tabata 5.00 12.00
MB111 Ian Desmond 5.00 12.00
MB112 Craig Biggio 5.00 12.00
MB113 Bernie Williams 5.00 12.00
MB114 Frank Robinson 5.00 12.00
MB115 Babe Ruth 20.00 50.00
MB116 Jimmie Foxx 8.00 20.00
MB117 Yogi Berra 8.00 20.00
MB118 Lou Gehrig 15.00 40.00
MB119 Tris Speaker 5.00 12.00
MB120 Roy Campanella 8.00 20.00
MB121 Bobby Murcer 3.00 8.00
MB122 Jimmy Piersall 3.00 8.00
MB123 Bo Jackson 8.00 20.00
MB124 Frank Thomas 8.00 20.00
MB125 Rogers Hornsby 5.00 12.00
MB126 Lou Brock 5.00 12.00
MB127 Richie Ashburn 5.00 12.00
MB128 Steve Garvey 3.00 8.00
MB129 Larry Doby 5.00 12.00
MB130 Jackie Robinson 8.00 20.00
MB131 Andre Dawson 5.00 12.00
MB132 Tony Gwynn 8.00 20.00
MB133 Don Mattingly 15.00 40.00
MB134 Carl Yastrzemski 12.00 30.00
MB135 Hank Greenberg 8.00 20.00
MB136 Dale Murphy 8.00 20.00
MB137 Paul Molitor 8.00 20.00
MB138 Eddie Murray 5.00 12.00
MB139 Mike Piazza 8.00 20.00
MB140 Ty Cobb 12.00 30.00
MB141 Al Kaline 8.00 20.00
MB142 Joe Morgan 5.00 12.00
MB143 Willie McCovey 5.00 12.00
MB144 Bill Mazeroski 5.00 12.00
MB145 George Sisler 5.00 12.00
MB146 Carlton Fisk 5.00 12.00
MB147 Sal Bando 3.00 8.00
MB148 Rod Carew 5.00 12.00
MB149 Orlando Cepeda 5.00 12.00
MB150 Mickey Mantle 25.00 60.00
MB151 Mike Schmidt 12.00 30.00
MB152 Rickey Henderson 8.00 20.00
MB153 Monte Irvin 5.00 12.00
MB154 George Kell 5.00 12.00
MB155 Pee Wee Reese 5.00 12.00
MB156 Robin Yount 8.00 20.00
MB157 Tony Perez 5.00 12.00
MB158 Ryne Sandberg 15.00 40.00
MB159 Luis Aparicio 5.00 12.00
MB160 Honus Wagner 8.00 20.00
MB161 Roger Maris 8.00 20.00
MB162 Duke Snider 5.00 12.00
MB163 Willie Stargell 5.00 12.00
MB164 Dave Winfield 5.00 12.00
MB165 Johnny Mize 5.00 12.00
MB166 Phil Rizzuto 5.00 12.00
MB167 Johnny Bench 8.00 20.00
MB168 Ozzie Smith 10.00 25.00
MB169 Reggie Jackson 5.00 12.00
MB170 Thurman Munson 8.00 20.00
MB171 Harmon Killebrew 8.00 20.00
MB172 Eddie Mathews 8.00 20.00
MB173 Ralph Kiner 5.00 12.00
MB174 Brooks Robinson 5.00 12.00
MB175 Mel Ott 8.00 20.00

2010 Topps Update Manufactured Rookie Logo Patch

STATED ODDS 1:1125 HOBBY
STATED PRINT RUN 500 SER.#'d SETS
AJ Austin Jackson 5.00 12.00
JH Jason Heyward 8.00 20.00
SS Stephen Strasburg 12.00 30.00

2010 Topps Update More Tales of the Game

STATED ODDS 1:6 HOBBY
1 Joel Youngblood .40 1.00
2 Triple Billing .40 1.00
3 Seven Touchdowns .40 1.00
4 Eddie Mathews .75 2.00
5 Babe Ruth 1.25 3.00
6 Intracity Sweep .40 1.00
7 Mike Schmidt .75 2.00
8 Mile-High Humidor .40 1.00
9 Andre Dawson/Alex Rodriguez .60 1.50
10 Walter Johnson .75 2.00
11 Warren Spahn .60 1.50
12 There's No Tying in Baseball .40 1.00
13 Harry Truman .40 1.00
14 Stephen Strasburg 1.50 4.00
15 Roy Halladay .50 1.25

2010 Topps Update Peek Performance Autographs

GROUP A ODDS 1:2450 HOBBY
GROUP B ODDS 1:834 HOBBY
TCO Tyler Colvin A 5.00 12.00
AC Andrew Cashner B 3.00 8.00
AJ Austin Jackson A 8.00 20.00
AO Adam Ottavino B 4.00 10.00
AOL Andy Oliver B 5.00 12.00
BB Brennan Boesch B 4.00 10.00
BL Brad Lincoln A 4.00 10.00
BP Buster Posey A 50.00 100.00
CS Carlos Santana A 8.00 20.00
DST Drew Storen A 4.00 10.00
ID Ike Davis A 6.00 15.00
JCA Jason Castro B 4.00 10.00
JD Jason Donald B 3.00 8.00
JE John Ely B 3.00 8.00
JH Jason Heyward A 12.00 30.00
JT Jose Tabata A 8.00 20.00
JV Jonny Venters B 8.00 20.00
LA Luis Atilano B 3.00 8.00
ML Mike Leake A 8.00 20.00
MST Mike Stanton A 30.00 60.00
SC Starlin Castro A 10.00 25.00
SS Stephen Strasburg A 40.00 80.00

2011 Topps

COMP.FACT.HOBBY.SET (660) 30.00 60.00
COMP.ALLSTAR.SET (660) 30.00 60.00
COMP.FACT.BLUE SET (660) 30.00 60.00
COMP.FACT.HOLIDAY SET (660) 30.00 60.00
COMP.FACT.ORANGE SET (660) 30.00 60.00
COMP.FACT.RED SET (660) 30.00 60.00
COMP.SET w/o SP's (660) 30.00 60.00
COMP.SER.1 w/o SP's (330) 12.50 30.00
COMP.SER.2 w/o SP's (330) 12.50 30.00
COMMON CARD (1-660) .15 .40
COMMON RC (1-660) .25 .60
COMMON SP VAR (1-660) 6.00 15.00
SER.1 PLATE ODDS 1:1500 HOBBY
PLATE PRINT RUN 1 SET PER COLOR
BLACK-CYAN-MAGENTA-YELLOW ISSUED
NO PLATE PRICING DUE TO SCARCITY
1 Ryan Braun .25 .60
2 Jake Westbrook .15 .40
3 Jon Lester .25 .60
4 Jason Kubel .15 .40
5A Joey Votto .40 1.00
5B Lou Gehrig SP 10.00 25.00
6 Neftali Feliz .15 .40
7 Mickey Mantle 1.25 3.00
8 Julio Borbon .15 .40
9 Gil Meche .15 .40
10 Stephen Strasburg .40 1.00
11 Roy Halladay/Adam Wainwright
Ubaldo Jimenez LL .25 .60
12 Carlos Marmol .25 .60
13 Billy Wagner .15 .40
14 Randy Wolf .15 .40
15 David Wright .30 .75
16 Aramis Ramirez .15 .40
17 Mark Ellis .15 .40
18 Kevin Millwood .15 .40
19 Derek Lowe .15 .40
20 Hanley Ramirez .25 .60
21 Michael Cuddyer .15 .40
22 Barry Zito .25 .60
23 Jaime Garcia .25 .60
24 Neil Walker .25 .60
25A Carl Crawford .25 .60
25B Crawford Red Sox SP 10.00 25.00
25C Carl Yastrzemski SP 6.00 15.00
26 Neftali Feliz .15 .40
27 Ben Zobrist .25 .60
28 Carlos Carrasco .25 .60
29 Josh Hamilton .25 .60
30 Gio Gonzalez .25 .60
31 Erick Aybar .15 .40
32 Chris Johnson .15 .40
33 Max Scherzer .40 1.00
34 Rick Ankiel .15 .40
35 Shin-Soo Choo .25 .60
36 Ted Lilly .15 .40
37 Vicente Padilla .15 .40
38 Ryan Dempster .15 .40

39 Ian Kennedy .15 .40
40 Justin Upton .25 .60
41 Freddy Garcia .15 .40
42 Mariano Rivera .50 1.25
43 Brendan Ryan .15 .40
44A Martin Prado .15 .40
44B Rogers Hornsby SP 6.00 15.00
45 Hunter Pence .25 .60
46 Hong-Chih Kuo .15 .40
47 Kevin Correia .15 .40
48 Andrew Cashner .15 .40
49 Los Angeles Angels TC .15 .40
50A Alex Rodriguez .50 1.25
50B Mike Schmidt SP 8.00 20.00
51 David Eckstein .15 .40
52 Tampa Bay Rays TC .15 .40
53 Arizona Diamondbacks TC .15 .40
54 Brian Fuentes .15 .40
55 Matt Joyce .15 .40
56 Johan Santana .25 .60
57 Mark Trumbo (RC) .60 1.50
58 Edgar Renteria .15 .40
59 Gaby Sanchez .15 .40
60 Andrew McCutchen .40 1.00
61 David Price .30 .75
62 Jonathan Papelbon .25 .60
63 Edinson Volquez .15 .40
64 Yorvit Torrealba .15 .40
65 Chris Sale RC 2.00 5.00
66 R.A. Dickey .25 .60
67 Vladimir Guerrero .25 .60
68 Cleveland Indians TC .15 .40
69 Brett Gardner .25 .60
70 Kyle Drabek RC .40 1.00
71 Trevor Hoffman .25 .60
72 Jair Jurrjens .15 .40
73 James McDonald .15 .40
74 Tyler Clippard .15 .40
75 Jered Weaver .25 .60
76 Tom Gorzelanny .15 .40
77 Tim Hudson .25 .60
78 Mike Stanton .40 1.00
79 Kurt Suzuki .15 .40
80A Desmond Jennings RC .40 1.00
80B Jackie Robinson SP 8.00 20.00
81 Omar Infante .15 .40
82 Josh Johnson/Adam
Wainwright/Roy Halladay LL .25 .60
83 Greg Halman RC .40 1.00
84 Roger Bernadina .15 .40
85 Jack Wilson .15 .40
86 Carlos Silva .15 .40
87 Daniel Descalso RC .25 .60
88 Brian Bogusevic (RC) .25 .60
89 Placido Polanco .15 .40
90A Yadier Molina .50 1.25
90B Yogi Berra SP 8.00 20.00
91 Lucas May RC .25 .60
92 Chris Narveson .15 .40
93A Paul Konerko .25 .60
93B Frank Thomas SP 6.00 15.00
94 Ryan Raburn .15 .40
95 Pedro Alvarez RC .50 1.25
96 Zach Duke .15 .40
97 Carlos Gomez .15 .40
98 Bronson Arroyo .15 .40
99 Ben Revere RC .40 1.00
100A Albert Pujols .50 1.25
100B Stan Musial SP 10.00 25.00
101 Gregor Blanco .15 .40
102A CC Sabathia .25 .60
102B Christy Mathewson SP 6.00 15.00
103 Cliff Lee .25 .60
104 Ian Stewart .15 .40
105 Jonathan Lucroy .25 .60
106 Felix Pie .15 .40
107 Aubrey Huff .15 .40
108 Zack Greinke .40 1.00
109 Hamilton/Cabrera/Mauer LL .40 1.00
110 Aroldis Chapman RC .75 2.00
111 Kevin Gregg .15 .40
112 Jorge Cantu .15 .40
113 Arthur Rhodes .15 .40
114 Russell Martin .15 .40
115 Jason Varitek .40 1.00
116 Russell Branyan .15 .40
117 Brett Sinkbeil RC .25 .60
118 Howie Kendrick .15 .40
119 Jason Bay .25 .60
120 Mat Latos .25 .60
121 Brandon Inge .15 .40
122 Bobby Jenks .15 .40
123 Mike Lowell .15 .40
124 CC Sabathia/Jon Lester
David Price LL .30 .75
125 Evan Meek .15 .40
126 San Diego Padres TC .15 .40
127 Chris Volstad .15 .40
128 Manny Ramirez .40 1.00
129 Lucas Duda RC .60 1.50
130 Robinson Cano .25 .60
131 Kevin Kouzmanoff .15 .40
132 Brian Duensing .15 .40
133 Miguel Tejada .25 .60
134 Carlos Gonzalez/Joey
Votto/Omar Infante LL .40 1.00
135A Mike Stanton .40 1.00
135B Dale Murphy SP 6.00 15.00
136 Jason Marquis .15 .40
137 Xavier Nady .15 .40
138 Pujols/Gonzalez/Votto LL .50 1.25
139 Eric Young Jr. .15 .40
140 Brett Anderson .15 .40
141 Ubaldo Jimenez .15 .40
142 Johnny Cueto .25 .60
143 Jeremy Jeffress RC .25 .60
144 Lance Berkman .25 .60
145 Freddie Freeman RC 4.00 10.00
146 Roy Halladay .25 .60
147 Jon Niese .15 .40
148 Ricky Romero .15 .40
149 David Aardsma .15 .40
150A Miguel Cabrera .40 1.00
150B Hank Greenberg SP 6.00 15.00
151 Fausto Carmona .15 .40
152 Baltimore Orioles TC .15 .40
153 A.J. Pierzynski .15 .40
154 Marlon Byrd .15 .40
155 Alex Rodriguez .50 1.25
156 Josh Thole .15 .40
157 New York Mets TC .25 .60
158 Casey Blake .15 .40
159 Chris Perez .15 .40
160 Josh Tomlin .15 .40
161 Chicago White Sox TC .15 .40
162 Ronny Cedeno .15 .40
163 Carlos Pena .25 .60
164 Koji Uehara .15 .40
165 Jeremy Hellickson RC .60 1.50
166 Josh Johnson .25 .60
167 Clay Hensley .15 .40
168 Felix Hernandez .25 .60
169 Chipper Jones .40 1.00
170 David DeJesus .15 .40
171 Garrett Jones .15 .40
172 Lyle Overbay .15 .40
173 Jose Lopez .15 .40
174 Roy Oswalt .25 .60
175 Brennan Boesch .25 .60
176 Daniel Hudson .15 .40
177 Brian Matusz .15 .40
178 Heath Bell .15 .40
179 Armando Galarraga .15 .40
180 Paul Maholm .15 .40
181 Magglio Ordonez .25 .60
182 Jeremy Bonderman .15 .40
183 Stephen Strasburg .40 1.00
184 Brandon Morrow .15 .40
185 Peter Bourjos .25 .60
186 Carl Pavano .15 .40
187 Milwaukee Brewers TC .15 .40
188 Pablo Sandoval .25 .60
189 Kerry Wood .15 .40
190 Coco Crisp .15 .40
191 Jay Bruce .25 .60
192 Cincinnati Reds TC .15 .40
193 Cory Luebke RC .25 .60
194 Andres Torres .15 .40
195 Nick Markakis .30 .75
196 Jose Ceda RC .25 .60
197 Aaron Hill .15 .40
198A Buster Posey .50 1.25
198B Johnny Bench SP 8.00 20.00
199A Jimmy Rollins .25 .60
199B Ozzie Smith SP 6.00 15.00
200A Ichiro Suzuki .50 1.25
200B Ty Cobb SP 8.00 20.00
201 Mike Napoli .15 .40
202 Bautista/Konerko/Cabrera LL .40 1.00
203 Dillon Gee RC .40 1.00
204 Oakland Athletics TC .15 .40
205 Ty Wigginton .15 .40
206 Chase Headley .15 .40
207 Angel Pagan .15 .40
208 Clay Buchholz .15 .40
209A Carlos Santana .40 1.00
209B Roy Campanella SP 6.00 15.00
20B Honus Wagner SP 6.00 15.00
210 Brian Wilson .40 1.00
211 Joey Votto .40 1.00
212 Pedro Feliz .15 .40
213 Brandon Snyder (RC) .25 .60
214 Chase Utley .25 .60
215 Edwin Encarnacion .40 1.00
216 Jose Bautista .25 .60
217 Yunel Escobar .15 .40
218 Victor Martinez .25 .60
219A Carlos Ruiz .15 .40
219B Thurman Munson SP 6.00 15.00
220 Todd Helton .25 .60
221 Scott Hairston .15 .40
222 Matt Lindstrom .15 .40
223 Gregory Infante RC .25 .60
224 Milton Bradley .15 .40
225 Josh Willingham .25 .60
226 Jose Guillen .15 .40
227 Nate McLouth .15 .40
228 Scott Rolen .25 .60
229 Jonathan Sanchez .15 .40
230 Aaron Cook .15 .40
231 Mark Buehrle .25 .60
232 Jamie Moyer .15 .40
233 Ramon Hernandez .15 .40
234 Miguel Montero .15 .40
235 Felix Hernandez/Clay
Buchholz/David Price LL .30 .75
236 Nelson Cruz .40 1.00
237 Jason Vargas .15 .40
238 Pedro Ciriaco RC .40 1.00
239 Jhoulys Chacin .15 .40
240 Andre Ethier .25 .60
241 Wandy Rodriguez .15 .40
242 Brad Lidge .15 .40
243 Omar Vizquel .25 .60
244 Mike Aviles .15 .40
245 Neil Walker .25 .60
246 John Lannan .15 .40
247A Starlin Castro .25 .60
247B Ernie Banks SP 6.00 15.00
248 Wade LeBlanc .15 .40
249 Aaron Harang .15 .40
250A Carlos Gonzalez .25 .60
250B Mel Ott SP 6.00 15.00
251 Alcides Escobar .25 .60
252 Michael Saunders .25 .60
253 Jim Thome .25 .60
254 Lars Anderson RC .40 1.00
255 Torii Hunter .15 .40
256 Tyler Colvin .15 .40
257 Travis Hafner .15 .40
258 Rafael Soriano .15 .40
259 Kyle Davies .15 .40
260 Freddy Sanchez .15 .40
261 Alexei Ramirez .25 .60
262 Alex Gordon .25 .60
263 Joel Pineiro .15 .40
264 Ryan Perry .15 .40
265 John Danks .15 .40
266 Rickie Weeks .15 .40
267 Jose Contreras .15 .40
268 Jake McGee (RC) .50 1.25
269 Stephen Drew .15 .40
270 Ubaldo Jimenez .15 .40
271A Adam Dunn .25 .60
271B Babe Ruth SP 10.00 25.00
272 J.J. Hardy .15 .40
273 Derrek Lee .15 .40
274 Michael Brantley .15 .40
275 Clayton Kershaw .60 1.50
276 Miguel Olivo .15 .40
277 Trevor Hoffman .25 .60
278 Marco Scutaro .25 .60
279 Nick Swisher .25 .60
280 Andrew Bailey .15 .40
281 Kevin Slowey .15 .40
282 Buster Posey .50 1.25
283 Colorado Rockies TC .15 .40
284 Reid Brignac .15 .40
285 Hank Conger RC .40 1.00
286 Melvin Mora .15 .40
287 Scott Cousins RC .25 .60
288 Matt Capps .15 .40
289 Yuniesky Betancourt .15 .40
290 Ike Davis .15 .40
291 Juan Gutierrez .15 .40
292 Darren Ford RC .25 .60
293A Justin Morneau .25 .60
293B Harmon Killebrew SP 6.00 15.00
294 Luke Scott .15 .40
295 Jon Jay .15 .40
296 John Buck .15 .40
297 Jason Jaramillo .15 .40
298 Jeff Keppinger .15 .40
299 Chris Carpenter .25 .60
300A Roy Halladay .25 .60
300B Walter Johnson SP 6.00 15.00
301 Seth Smith .15 .40
302 Adrian Beltre .40 1.00
303 Emilio Bonifacio .15 .40
304 Jim Thome .25 .60
305 James Loney .15 .40
306 Cabrera/ARod/Bautista LL .50 1.25
307 Alex Rios .15 .40
308 Ian Desmond .15 .40
309 Chicago Cubs TC .25 .60
310 Alex Gonzalez .15 .40
311 James Shields .15 .40
312 Gaby Sanchez .15 .40
313 Chris Coghlan .15 .40
314 Ryan Kalish .25 .60
315A David Ortiz .40 1.00
315B Jimmie Foxx SP 6.00 15.00
316 Chris Young .15 .40
317 Yonder Alonso RC .40 1.00
318 Pujols/Dunn/Votto LL .50 1.25
319 Atlanta Braves TC .15 .40
320 Michael Young .15 .40
321 Jeremy Guthrie .15 .40
322 Brent Morel RC .25 .60
323 C.J. Wilson .15 .40
324 Boston Red Sox TC .25 .60
325 Jayson Werth .25 .60
326 Ozzie Martinez RC .25 .60
327 Christian Guzman .15 .40
328 David Price .30 .75
329 Brett Wallace .15 .40
330A Derek Jeter 1.00 2.50
330B Phil Rizzuto SP 6.00 15.00
331 Carlos Guillen .15 .40
332 Melky Cabrera .15 .40
333 Tom Wilhelmsen RC .25 .60
334 St. Louis Cardinals .25 .60
335 Buster Posey .50 1.25
336 Chris Heisey .15 .40
337 Jordan Walden .15 .40
338 Jason Hammel .25 .60
339 Alexi Casilla .15 .40
340 Evan Longoria .25 .60
341 Kyle Kendrick .15 .40
342 Jorge De La Rosa .15 .40
343 Mason Tobin RC .25 .60
344 Michael Kohn RC .25 .60
345 Austin Jackson .15 .40
346 Jose Bautista .25 .60
347 Darwin Barney RC .75 2.00
348 Landon Powell .15 .40
349 Drew Stubbs .15 .40
350A Francisco Liriano .15 .40
350B Gonzalez Red Sox SP 10.00 25.00
351 Jacoby Ellsbury .30 .75
352 Colby Lewis .15 .40
353 Cliff Pennington .15 .40
354 Scott Baker .15 .40
355A Justin Verlander .40 1.00
355B Bob Feller SP 6.00 15.00
356 Alfonso Soriano .25 .60
357 Mike Cameron .15 .40
358 Paul Janish .15 .40
359 Roy Halladay .25 .60
360 Ivan Rodriguez .25 .60
361 Florida Marlins .15 .40
362 Doug Fister .15 .40
363 Aaron Rowand .15 .40
364 Tim Wakefield .25 .60
365 Adam Lind .25 .60
366 Joe Nathan .15 .40
367 Hiroki Kuroda .15 .40
368 Brian Broderick RC .25 .60
369 Wilson Betemit .15 .40
370 Matt Garza .15 .40
371 Taylor Teagarden .15 .40
372 Jarrod Saltalamacchia .15 .40
373 Trever Miller .15 .40
374 Washington Nationals .15 .40
375A Matt Kemp .30 .75
375B Andre Dawson SP 6.00 15.00
376 Clayton Richard .15 .40
377 Esmil Rogers .15 .40
378 Mark Reynolds .15 .40
379 Ben Francisco .15 .40
380 Jose Reyes .25 .60
381 Michael Gonzalez .15 .40
382 Travis Snider .15 .40
383 Ryan Ludwick .15 .40
384 Nick Hundley .15 .40
385 Ichiro Suzuki .50 1.25
386 Barry Enright RC .15 .40
387 Danny Valencia .25 .60
388 Kenley Jansen .25 .60
389 Carlos Quentin .15 .40
390 Danny Valencia .25 .60
391 Phil Coke .15 .40
392 Kris Medlen .25 .60
393A Jake Arrieta .30 .75
393B Jim Palmer SP 6.00 15.00
394 Austin Jackson .15 .40
395 Tyler Flowers .15 .40
396 Adam Jones .25 .60
397 Sean Rodriguez .15 .40
398 Pittsburgh Pirates .15 .40
399 Adam Moore .15 .40
400 Troy Tulowitzki .40 1.00
401 Michael Crotta RC .25 .60
402 Jack Cust .15 .40
403 Felix Hernandez .25 .60
404 Chris Capuano .15 .40
405A Ian Kinsler .25 .60
405B Ryne Sandberg SP 6.00 15.00
406 John Lackey .25 .60
407 Jonathan Broxton .15 .40
408 Denard Span .15 .40
409 Vin Mazzaro .15 .40
410A Prince Fielder .25 .60
410B Reggie Jackson SP 6.00 15.00
411 Josh Bell .15 .40
412 Samuel Deduno RC .25 .60
413 Derek Holland .15 .40
414 Jose Molina .15 .40
415 Brian McCann .25 .60
416 Everth Cabrera .15 .40
417 Miguel Cairo .15 .40
418 Zach Britton RC .60 1.50
419 Kelly Johnson .15 .40
420 Ryan Howard .30 .75
421 Domonic Brown .30 .75
422 Juan Pierre .15 .40
423 Hideki Okajima .15 .40
424 New York Yankees .25 .60
425A Adrian Gonzalez .30 .75
425B Johnny Mize SP 6.00 15.00
426 Travis Buck .15 .40
427 Brad Emaus RC .25 .60
428 Brett Myers .15 .40
429 Skip Schumaker .15 .40
430 Trevor Crowe .15 .40
431 Marcos Mateo RC .40 1.00
432 Matt Harrison .15 .40
433 Curtis Granderson .30 .75
434 Mark DeRosa .15 .40
435A Elvis Andrus .25 .60
435B Pee Wee Reese SP 6.00 15.00
436 Trevor Cahill .15 .40
437 Jordan Schafer .15 .40
438 Ryan Theriot .15 .40
439 Ervin Santana .15 .40
440 Grady Sizemore .25 .60
441 Rafael Furcal .15 .40
442 Brad Bergesen .15 .40
443 Brian Roberts .15 .40
444 Brett Cecil .15 .40
445 Mitch Talbot .15 .40
446 Brandon Beachy RC .60 1.50
447 Toronto Blue Jays .15 .40
448 Colby Rasmus .25 .60
449 Austin Kearns .15 .40
450A Mark Teixeira .25 .60
450B Mickey Mantle SP 10.00 25.00
451 Livan Hernandez .15 .40
452 David Freese .15 .40
453 Joe Saunders .15 .40
454 Alberto Callaspo .15 .40
455 Logan Morrison .15 .40
456 Ryan Doumit .15 .40
457 Brandon Allen .15 .40
458 Javier Vazquez .15 .40
459 Frank Francisco .15 .40
460A Cole Hamels .30 .75
460B Robin Roberts SP 6.00 15.00
461 Eric Sogard RC .25 .60
462 Daric Barton .15 .40
463 Will Venable .15 .40
464 Daniel Bard .15 .40
465 Yovani Gallardo .15 .40
466 Johnny Damon .25 .60
467 Wade Davis .15 .40
468 Chone Figgins .15 .40
469 Joe Blanton .15 .40
470 Billy Butler .15 .40
471 Tim Collins RC .25 .60
472 Jason Kendall .15 .40
473 Chad Billingsley .25 .60
474 Jeff Mathis .15 .40
475 Phil Hughes .15 .40
476 Matt LaPorta .15 .40
477 Franklin Gutierrez .15 .40
478 Mike Minor .15 .40
479 Justin Duchscherer .15 .40
480A Dustin Pedroia .40 1.00
480B Roberto Alomar SP 6.00 15.00
481 Randy Wells .15 .40
482 Eric Hinske .15 .40
483 Justin Smoak RC .25 .60
484 Gerardo Parra .15 .40
485 Delmon Young .25 .60
486 Francisco Rodriguez .25 .60
487 Chris Snyder .15 .40
488 Brayan Villarreal RC .25 .60
489 Marc Rzepczynski .15 .40
490A Matt Holliday .40 1.00
490B Duke Snider SP 6.00 15.00
491 Fernando Abad RC .25 .60
492 A.J. Burnett .15 .40
493 Ryan Sweeney .15 .40
494 Drew Storen .15 .40
495 Shane Victorino .25 .60
496 Gavin Floyd .15 .40
497 Alex Avila .25 .60
498 Scott Feldman .15 .40
499 J.A. Happ .25 .60
500 Kevin Youkilis .15 .40
501 Tsuyoshi Nishioka RC .75 2.00
502 Jeff Baker .15 .40
503 Nathan Adcock RC .25 .60
504 Jhonny Peralta .15 .40
505A Tommy Hanson .15 .40
505B Greg Maddux SP 6.00 15.00
506 Aneury Rodriguez RC .25 .60
507 Huston Street .15 .40
508 Homer Bailey .15 .40
509 Michael Bourn .15 .40
510A Jason Heyward .30 .75
510B Hank Aaron SP 8.00 20.00
511 Philadelphia Phillies .15 .40
512 Octavio Dotel .15 .40
513 Adam LaRoche .15 .40
514 Kelly Shoppach .15 .40
515 Carlos Beltran .25 .60
516A Mike Leake .25 .60
516B Tom Seaver SP 6.00 15.00
517 Fred Lewis .15 .40
518 Michael Morse .15 .40
519 Corey Hart .15 .40
520 Jorge Posada .25 .60
521 Joaquin Benoit .15 .40
522 Asdrubal Cabrera .25 .60
523 Mike Nickeas (RC) .25 .60
524 Michael Martinez RC .40 1.00
525 Vernon Wells .15 .40
526 Jason Donald .15 .40
527 Kila Ka'aihue .15 .40
528 Bobby Abreu .15 .40
529 Maicer Izturis .15 .40
530A Felix Hernandez .25 .60
530B Sandy Koufax SP 10.00 25.00
531 Juan Rivera .15 .40
532 Erik Bedard .15 .40
533 Lorenzo Cain .15 .40
534 Bud Norris .15 .40
535 Rich Harden .15 .40
536 Tony Sipp .15 .40
537 Jake Peavy .15 .40
538 Jason Motte .15 .40
539 Brandon Lyon .15 .40
540 Joakim Soria .15 .40
541 John Jaso .15 .40
542 Mike Pelfrey .15 .40
543 Texas Rangers .15 .40
544 Justin Masterson .15 .40
545 Jose Tabata .15 .40
546 Pat Burrell .15 .40
547 Albert Pujols .50 1.25
548 Ryan Franklin .15 .40
549 Jayson Nix .15 .40
550 Joe Mauer .30 .75
551 Marcus Thames .15 .40
552 San Francisco Giants .15 .40
553 Kyle Lohse .15 .40
554 Cedric Hunter RC .25 .60
555 Madison Bumgarner .30 .75
556 B.J. Upton .25 .60
557 Wes Helms .15 .40
558 Carlos Zambrano .25 .60
559 Reggie Willits .15 .40
560 Chris Iannetta .15 .40
561 Luke Gregerson .15 .40
562 Gordon Beckham .15 .40
563 Josh Rodriguez RC .25 .60
564 Jeff Samardzija .15 .40
565 Mark Teahen .15 .40
566 Jordan Zimmermann .25 .60
567 Dallas Braden .15 .40
568 Kansas City Royals .15 .40
569 Cameron Maybin .15 .40
570A Matt Cain .25 .60
570B Bert Blyleven SP 6.00 15.00
571 Jeremy Affeldt .15 .40
572 Brad Hawpe .15 .40
573 Nyjer Morgan .15 .40
574 Brandon Kintzler RC .25 .60
575 Rod Barajas .15 .40
576 Jed Lowrie .15 .40
577 Mike Fontenot .15 .40
578 Willy Aybar .15 .40
579 Jeff Niemann .15 .40
580 Chris Young .15 .40
581 Fernando Rodney .15 .40
582 Kosuke Fukudome .25 .60
583 Ryan Spilborghs .15 .40
584 Jason Bartlett .15 .40
585 Dan Johnson .15 .40
586 Carlos Lee .15 .40
587 J.P. Arencibia .15 .40
588 Rajai Davis .15 .40
589 Seattle Mariners .15 .40
590A Tim Lincecum .25 .60
590B Juan Marichal SP 6.00 15.00
591 John Axford .15 .40
592 Dayan Viciedo .15 .40
593 Francisco Cordero .15 .40
594 Jose Valverde .15 .40
595 Michael Pineda RC .60 1.50
596 Anibal Sanchez .15 .40
597 Rick Porcello .25 .60
598 Jonny Gomes .15 .40
599 Travis Ishikawa .15 .40
600A Neftali Feliz .15 .40
600B John Smoltz SP 6.00 15.00
601 J.J. Putz .15 .40
602 Ivan DeJesus RC .25 .60
603 David Murphy .15 .40
604 Joe Paterson RC .40 1.00
605 Brandon Belt RC .60 1.50
606 Juan Miranda .15 .40
607 Daniel Murphy .30 .75
608 Casey McGehee .15 .40
609 Juan Francisco .15 .40
610 Josh Beckett .15 .40
611 Geovany Soto .25 .60
612 Detroit Tigers .15 .40
613 Dexter Fowler .25 .60
614 Minnesota Twins .15 .40
615 Shaun Marcum .15 .40
616 Ross Ohlendorf .15 .40
617 Joel Zumaya .15 .40
618 Josh Lueke RC .25 .60
619 Jonny Venters .15 .40
620 Luke Hochevar .15 .40
621 Omar Beltre .15 .40
622 Matt Thornton .15 .40
623 Leo Nunez .15 .40
624 Luke French .15 .40
625 Ruben Tejada .15 .40
626A Dan Haren .15 .40
626B Nolan Ryan SP 10.00 25.00
627 Kyle Blanks .15 .40
628 Blake DeWitt .15 .40
629 Ivan Nova .25 .60
630A Brandon Phillips .15 .40
630B Joe Morgan SP 6.00 15.00
631 Houston Astros .15 .40
632 Scott Kazmir .15 .40
633 Aaron Crow RC .40 1.00
634 Mitch Moreland .15 .40
635 Jason Heyward .30 .75
636 Chris Tillman .15 .40
637 Ricky Nolasco .15 .40
638 Ryan Madson .15 .40
639 Pedro Beato RC .25 .60
640A Dan Uggla .15 .40
640B Eddie Mathews SP 6.00 15.00
641 Travis Wood .15 .40
642 Jason Hammel .25 .60
643 Jaime Garcia .25 .60
644 Joel Hanrahan .25 .60
645A Adam Wainwright .25 .60
645B Bob Gibson SP 6.00 15.00
646 Los Angeles Dodgers .25 .60
647 Jeanmar Gomez .15 .40
648 Cody Ross .15 .40
649 Joba Chamberlain .15 .40
650A Josh Hamilton .25 .60
650B Frank Robinson SP 6.00 15.00
651A Kendrys Morales .15 .40
651B Eddie Murray SP 6.00 15.00
652 Edwin Jackson .15 .40
653 J.D. Drew .15 .40
654 Chris Getz .15 .40
655 Starlin Castro .25 .60
656 Raul Ibanez .25 .60
657 Nick Blackburn .15 .40
658 Mitch Maier .15 .40
659 Clint Barmes .15 .40
660A Ryan Zimmerman .25 .60
660B Brooks Robinson SP 6.00 15.00

2011 Topps Black

SER.1 ODDS 1:100 HOBBY
STATED PRINT RUN 60 SER.#'d SETS
1 Ryan Braun 6.00 15.00
2 Jake Westbrook 6.00 15.00
3 Jon Lester 6.00 15.00
4 Jason Kubel 6.00 15.00
5 Joey Votto 10.00 25.00
6 Neftali Feliz 6.00 15.00
7 Mickey Mantle 50.00 120.00
8 Julio Borbon 6.00 15.00
9 Gil Meche 6.00 15.00
10 Stephen Strasburg 10.00 25.00
11 Roy Halladay/Adam
Wainwright/Ubaldo Jimenez LL 6.00 15.00
12 Carlos Marmol 8.00 20.00
13 Billy Wagner 6.00 15.00
14 Randy Wolf 6.00 15.00
15 David Wright 8.00 20.00
16 Aramis Ramirez 6.00 15.00
17 Mark Ellis 6.00 15.00
18 Kevin Millwood 6.00 15.00
19 Derek Lowe 6.00 15.00
20 Hanley Ramirez 6.00 15.00
21 Michael Cuddyer 6.00 15.00
22 Barry Zito 10.00 25.00
23 Jaime Garcia 8.00 20.00
24 Neil Walker 10.00 25.00
25 Carl Crawford 8.00 20.00
26 Neftali Feliz 6.00 15.00
27 Ben Zobrist 10.00 25.00
28 Carlos Carrasco 10.00 25.00
29 Josh Hamilton 6.00 15.00
30 Gio Gonzalez 10.00 25.00
31 Erick Aybar 6.00 15.00
32 Chris Johnson 6.00 15.00
33 Max Scherzer 15.00 40.00
34 Rick Ankiel 6.00 15.00
35 Shin-Soo Choo 6.00 15.00
36 Ted Lilly 6.00 15.00
37 Vicente Padilla 6.00 15.00
38 Ryan Dempster 6.00 15.00
39 Ian Kennedy 6.00 15.00
40 Justin Upton 10.00 25.00
41 Freddy Garcia 6.00 15.00
42 Mariano Rivera 12.00 30.00
43 Brendan Ryan 6.00 15.00
44 Martin Prado 6.00 15.00
45 Hunter Pence 8.00 20.00
46 Hong-Chih Kuo 6.00 15.00
47 Kevin Correia 6.00 15.00
48 Andrew Cashner 6.00 15.00
49 Los Angeles Angels TC 6.00 15.00
50 Alex Rodriguez 12.00 30.00
51 David Eckstein 6.00 15.00
52 Tampa Bay Rays TC 6.00 15.00
53 Arizona Diamondbacks TC 6.00 15.00
54 Brian Fuentes 6.00 15.00
55 Matt Joyce 6.00 15.00
56 Johan Santana 6.00 15.00
57 Mark Trumbo 12.00 30.00
58 Edgar Renteria 6.00 15.00
59 Gaby Sanchez 6.00 15.00
60 Andrew McCutchen 12.00 30.00
61 David Price 8.00 20.00
62 Jonathan Papelbon 8.00 20.00
63 Edinson Volquez 6.00 15.00
64 Yorvit Torrealba 6.00 15.00
65 Chris Sale 30.00 80.00
66 R.A. Dickey 10.00 25.00
67 Vladimir Guerrero 6.00 15.00
68 Cleveland Indians TC 6.00 15.00
69 Brett Gardner 10.00 25.00
70 Kyle Drabek 6.00 15.00
71 Trevor Hoffman 8.00 20.00
72 Jair Jurrjens 6.00 15.00
73 James McDonald 6.00 15.00
74 Tyler Clippard 6.00 15.00
75 Jered Weaver 10.00 25.00
76 Tom Gorzelanny 6.00 15.00
77 Tim Hudson 8.00 20.00
78 Mike Stanton 12.00 30.00
79 Kurt Suzuki 6.00 15.00
80 Desmond Jennings 6.00 15.00
81 Omar Infante 6.00 15.00
82 Josh Johnson/Adam
Wainwright/Roy Halladay LL 6.00 15.00
83 Greg Halman 6.00 15.00
84 Roger Bernadina 6.00 15.00
85 Jack Wilson 6.00 15.00
86 Carlos Silva 6.00 15.00
87 Daniel Descalso 6.00 15.00
88 Brian Bogusevic 6.00 15.00
89 Placido Polanco 6.00 15.00
90 Yadier Molina 15.00 40.00
91 Lucas May 6.00 15.00
92 Chris Narveson 6.00 15.00
93 Paul Konerko 10.00 25.00
94 Ryan Raburn 6.00 15.00
95 Pedro Alvarez 10.00 25.00
96 Zach Duke 6.00 15.00
97 Carlos Gomez 6.00 15.00
98 Bronson Arroyo 6.00 15.00
99 Ben Revere 8.00 20.00
100 Albert Pujols 12.00 30.00
101 Gregor Blanco 6.00 15.00
102 CC Sabathia 8.00 20.00
103 Cliff Lee 6.00 15.00
104 Ian Stewart 6.00 15.00
105 Jonathan Lucroy 10.00 25.00
106 Felix Pie 6.00 15.00
107 Aubrey Huff 6.00 15.00
108 Zack Greinke 12.00 30.00
109 Hamilton/Cabrera/Mauer LL 10.00 25.00
110 Aroldis Chapman 12.00 30.00
111 Kevin Gregg 6.00 15.00
112 Jorge Cantu 6.00 15.00
113 Arthur Rhodes 6.00 15.00
114 Russell Martin 6.00 15.00
115 Jason Varitek 10.00 25.00
116 Russell Branyan 6.00 15.00
117 Brett Sinkbeil 6.00 15.00
118 Howie Kendrick 6.00 15.00
119 Jason Bay 8.00 20.00
120 Mat Latos 10.00 25.00
121 Brandon Inge 6.00 15.00
122 Bobby Jenks 6.00 15.00
123 Mike Lowell 6.00 15.00
124 CC Sabathia/Jon Lester
David Price LL 8.00 20.00
125 Evan Meek 6.00 15.00
126 San Diego Padres TC 6.00 15.00
127 Chris Volstad 6.00 15.00
128 Manny Ramirez 10.00 25.00
129 Lucas Duda 15.00 40.00
130 Robinson Cano 6.00 15.00
131 Kevin Kouzmanoff 6.00 15.00
132 Brian Duensing 6.00 15.00
133 Miguel Tejada 8.00 20.00
134 Carlos Gonzalez/Joey Votto
Omar Infante LL 10.00 25.00
135 Mike Stanton 12.00 30.00
136 Jason Marquis 6.00 15.00
137 Xavier Nady 6.00 15.00
138 Pujols/Gonzalez/Votto LL 12.00 30.00
139 Eric Young Jr. 6.00 15.00
140 Brett Anderson 5.00 12.00
141 Ubaldo Jimenez 5.00 12.00
142 Johnny Cueto 10.00 25.00
143 Jeremy Jeffress 6.00 15.00
144 Lance Berkman 8.00 20.00
145 Freddie Freeman 125.00 300.00
146 Roy Halladay 6.00 15.00
147 Jon Niese 6.00 15.00
148 Ricky Romero 6.00 15.00
149 David Aardsma 6.00 15.00
150 Miguel Cabrera 10.00 25.00
151 Fausto Carmona 6.00 15.00
152 Baltimore Orioles TC 6.00 15.00
153 A.J. Pierzynski 6.00 15.00
154 Marlon Byrd 6.00 15.00
155 Alex Rodriguez 12.00 30.00
156 Josh Thole 6.00 15.00
157 New York Mets TC 8.00 20.00
158 Casey Blake 6.00 15.00
159 Chris Perez 6.00 15.00
160 Josh Tomlin 6.00 15.00
161 Chicago White Sox TC 6.00 15.00
162 Ronny Cedeno 6.00 15.00
163 Carlos Pena 8.00 20.00
164 Koji Uehara 6.00 15.00
165 Jeremy Hellickson 10.00 25.00
166 Josh Johnson 8.00 20.00
167 Clay Hensley 6.00 15.00
168 Felix Hernandez 6.00 15.00
169 Chipper Jones 10.00 25.00
170 David DeJesus 6.00 15.00
171 Garrett Jones 6.00 15.00
172 Lyle Overbay 6.00 15.00
173 Jose Lopez 6.00 15.00
174 Roy Oswalt 8.00 20.00
175 Brennan Boesch 8.00 20.00
176 Daniel Hudson 6.00 15.00
177 Brian Matusz 4.00 10.00
178 Heath Bell 6.00 15.00
179 Armando Galarraga 6.00 15.00
180 Paul Maholm 6.00 15.00
181 Magglio Ordonez 8.00 20.00
182 Jeremy Bonderman 6.00 15.00
183 Stephen Strasburg 10.00 25.00
184 Brandon Morrow 6.00 15.00
185 Peter Bourjos 8.00 20.00
186 Carl Pavano 6.00 15.00
187 Milwaukee Brewers TC 6.00 15.00
188 Pablo Sandoval 8.00 20.00
189 Kerry Wood 6.00 15.00
190 Coco Crisp 6.00 15.00
191 Jay Bruce 8.00 20.00
192 Cincinnati Reds TC 6.00 15.00
193 Cory Luebke 6.00 15.00
194 Andres Torres 6.00 15.00
195 Nick Markakis 8.00 20.00
196 Jose Ceda 5.00 12.00
197 Aaron Hill 6.00 15.00
198 Buster Posey 12.00 30.00
199 Jimmy Rollins 8.00 20.00
200 Ichiro Suzuki 12.00 30.00
201 Mike Napoli 6.00 15.00
202 Bautista/Konerko/Cabrera LL 10.00 25.00
203 Dillon Gee 10.00 25.00
204 Oakland Athletics TC 6.00 15.00
205 Ty Wigginton 6.00 15.00
206 Chase Headley 6.00 15.00
207 Angel Pagan 6.00 15.00
208 Clay Buchholz 5.00 12.00
209 Carlos Santana 10.00 25.00
210 Brian Wilson 10.00 25.00
211 Joey Votto 10.00 25.00
212 Pedro Feliz 6.00 15.00
213 Brandon Snyder 6.00 15.00
214 Chase Utley 6.00 15.00
215 Edwin Encarnacion 15.00 40.00

216 Jose Bautista 8.00 20.00
217 Yunel Escobar 6.00 15.00
218 Victor Martinez 8.00 20.00
219 Carlos Ruiz 6.00 15.00
220 Todd Helton 8.00 20.00
221 Scott Hairston 6.00 15.00
222 Matt Lindstrom 6.00 15.00
223 Gregory Infante 6.00 15.00
224 Milton Bradley 6.00 15.00
225 Josh Willingham 10.00 25.00
226 Jose Guillen 6.00 15.00
227 Nate McLouth 6.00 15.00
228 Scott Rolen 8.00 20.00
229 Jonathan Sanchez 6.00 15.00
230 Aaron Cook 6.00 15.00
231 Mark Buehrle 8.00 20.00
232 Jamie Moyer 6.00 15.00
233 Ramon Hernandez 6.00 15.00
234 Miguel Montero 6.00 15.00
235 Felix Hernandez/Clay Buchholz/David Price LL 8.00 20.00
236 Nelson Cruz 12.00 30.00
237 Jason Vargas 6.00 15.00
238 Pedro Ciriaco 10.00 25.00
239 Jhoulys Chacin 6.00 15.00
240 Andre Ethier 8.00 20.00
241 Wandy Rodriguez 6.00 15.00
242 Brad Lidge 6.00 15.00
243 Omar Vizquel 8.00 20.00
244 Mike Aviles 6.00 15.00
245 Neil Walker 10.00 25.00
246 John Lannan 6.00 15.00
247 Starlin Castro 6.00 15.00
248 Wade LeBlanc 6.00 15.00
249 Aaron Harang 6.00 15.00
250 Carlos Gonzalez 8.00 20.00
251 Alcides Escobar 10.00 25.00
252 Michael Saunders 10.00 25.00
253 Jim Thome 8.00 20.00
254 Lars Anderson 8.00 20.00
255 Torii Hunter 6.00 15.00
256 Tyler Colvin 5.00 12.00
257 Travis Hafner 6.00 15.00
258 Rafael Soriano 6.00 15.00
259 Kyle Davies 6.00 15.00
260 Freddy Sanchez 6.00 15.00
261 Alexei Ramirez 10.00 25.00
262 Alex Gordon 8.00 20.00
263 Joel Pineiro 6.00 15.00
264 Ryan Perry 6.00 15.00
265 John Danks 6.00 15.00
266 Rickie Weeks 5.00 12.00
267 Jose Contreras 6.00 15.00
268 Jake McGee 12.00 30.00
269 Stephen Drew 6.00 15.00
270 Ubaldo Jimenez 5.00 12.00
271 Adam Dunn 8.00 20.00
272 J.J. Hardy 6.00 15.00
273 Derrek Lee 6.00 15.00
274 Michael Brantley 6.00 15.00
275 Clayton Kershaw 15.00 40.00
276 Miguel Olivo 6.00 15.00
277 Trevor Hoffman 8.00 20.00
278 Marco Scutaro 10.00 25.00
279 Nick Swisher 6.00 15.00
280 Andrew Bailey 6.00 15.00
281 Kevin Slowey 6.00 15.00
282 Buster Posey 12.00 30.00
283 Colorado Rockies TC 6.00 15.00
284 Reid Brignac 6.00 15.00
285 Hank Conger 8.00 20.00
286 Melvin Mora 6.00 15.00
287 Scott Cousins 6.00 15.00
288 Matt Capps 6.00 15.00
289 Yuniesky Betancourt 6.00 15.00
290 Ike Davis 5.00 12.00
291 Juan Gutierrez 6.00 15.00
292 Darren Ford 6.00 15.00
293 Justin Morneau 6.00 15.00
294 Luke Scott 6.00 15.00
295 Jon Jay 6.00 15.00
296 John Buck 6.00 15.00
297 Jason Jaramillo 6.00 15.00
298 Jeff Keppinger 6.00 15.00
299 Chris Carpenter 6.00 15.00
300 Roy Halladay 6.00 15.00
301 Seth Smith 6.00 15.00
302 Adrian Beltre 15.00 40.00
303 Emilio Bonifacio 6.00 15.00
304 Jim Thome 8.00 20.00
305 James Loney 5.00 12.00
306 Cabrera/ARod/Bautista LL 12.00 30.00
307 Alex Rios 5.00 12.00
308 Ian Desmond 5.00 12.00
309 Chicago Cubs TC 8.00 20.00
310 Alex Gonzalez 6.00 15.00
311 James Shields 6.00 15.00
312 Gaby Sanchez 6.00 15.00
313 Chris Coghlan 6.00 15.00
314 Ryan Kalish 8.00 20.00
315 David Ortiz 12.00 30.00
316 Chris Young 6.00 15.00
317 Yonder Alonso 6.00 15.00
318 Pujols/Dunn/Votto LL 12.00 30.00
319 Atlanta Braves TC 6.00 15.00
320 Michael Young 6.00 15.00
321 Jeremy Guthrie 6.00 15.00
322 Brent Morel 6.00 15.00
323 C.J. Wilson 6.00 15.00
324 Boston Red Sox TC 8.00 20.00
325 Jayson Werth 8.00 20.00
326 Ozzie Martinez 6.00 15.00
327 Christian Guzman 6.00 15.00
328 David Price 8.00 20.00
329 Brett Wallace 6.00 15.00
330 Derek Jeter 25.00 60.00
331 Carlos Guillen 6.00 15.00
332 Melky Cabrera 6.00 15.00
333 Tom Wilhelmsen 20.00 50.00
334 St. Louis Cardinals 15.00 40.00
335 Buster Posey 12.00 30.00
336 Chris Heisey 6.00 15.00
337 Jordan Walden 15.00 40.00
338 Jason Hammel 10.00 25.00
339 Alexi Casilla 6.00 15.00
340 Evan Longoria 6.00 15.00
341 Kyle Kendrick 6.00 15.00
342 Jorge De La Rosa 6.00 15.00
343 Mason Tobin 6.00 15.00
344 Michael Kohn 6.00 15.00
345 Austin Jackson 6.00 15.00
346 Jose Bautista 8.00 20.00
347 Darwin Barney 12.00 30.00
348 Landon Powell 6.00 15.00
349 Drew Stubbs 6.00 15.00
350 Francisco Liriano 6.00 15.00
351 Jacoby Ellsbury 15.00 40.00
352 Colby Lewis 6.00 15.00
353 Cliff Pennington 6.00 15.00
354 Scott Baker 6.00 15.00
355 Justin Verlander 12.00 30.00
356 Alfonso Soriano 8.00 20.00
357 Mike Cameron 6.00 15.00
358 Paul Janish 6.00 15.00
359 Roy Halladay 6.00 15.00
360 Ivan Rodriguez 8.00 20.00
361 Florida Marlins 6.00 15.00
362 Doug Fister 6.00 15.00
363 Aaron Rowand 6.00 15.00
364 Tim Wakefield 10.00 25.00
365 Adam Lind 8.00 20.00
366 Joe Nathan 12.00 30.00
367 Hiroki Kuroda 15.00 40.00
368 Brian Broderick 6.00 15.00
369 Wilson Betemit 6.00 15.00
370 Matt Garza 6.00 15.00
371 Taylor Teagarden 6.00 15.00
372 Jarrod Saltalamacchia 6.00 15.00
373 Trever Miller 6.00 15.00
374 Washington Nationals 6.00 15.00
375 Matt Kemp 10.00 25.00
376 Clayton Richard 6.00 15.00
377 Esmil Rogers 6.00 15.00
378 Mark Reynolds 6.00 15.00
379 Ben Francisco 6.00 15.00
380 Jose Reyes 8.00 20.00
381 Michael Gonzalez 6.00 15.00
382 Travis Snider 6.00 15.00
383 Ryan Ludwick 6.00 15.00
384 Nick Hundley 6.00 15.00
385 Ichiro Suzuki 12.00 30.00
386 Barry Enright 6.00 15.00
387 Danny Valencia 8.00 20.00
388 Kenley Jansen 10.00 25.00
389 Carlos Quentin 5.00 12.00
390 Danny Valencia 12.00 30.00
391 Phil Coke 6.00 15.00
392 Kris Medlen 10.00 25.00
393 Jake Arrieta 6.00 15.00
394 Austin Jackson 6.00 15.00
395 Tyler Flowers 6.00 15.00
396 Adam Jones 8.00 20.00
397 Sean Rodriguez 6.00 15.00
398 Pittsburgh Pirates 30.00 80.00
399 Adam Moore 6.00 15.00
400 Troy Tulowitzki 20.00 50.00
401 Michael Crotta 6.00 15.00
402 Jack Cust 6.00 15.00
403 Felix Hernandez 6.00 15.00
404 Chris Capuano 6.00 15.00
405 Ian Kinsler 8.00 20.00
406 John Lackey 10.00 25.00
407 Jonathan Broxton 6.00 15.00
408 Denard Span 6.00 15.00
409 Vin Mazzaro 6.00 15.00
410 Prince Fielder 6.00 15.00
411 Josh Bell 6.00 15.00
412 Samuel Deduno 6.00 15.00
413 Derek Holland 6.00 15.00
414 Jose Molina 6.00 15.00
415 Brian McCann 8.00 20.00
416 Everth Cabrera 6.00 15.00
417 Miguel Cairo 6.00 15.00
418 Zach Britton 10.00 25.00
419 Kelly Johnson 6.00 15.00
420 Ryan Howard 8.00 20.00
421 Domonic Brown 8.00 20.00
422 Juan Pierre 6.00 15.00
423 Hideki Okajima 6.00 15.00
424 New York Yankees 12.00 30.00
425 Adrian Gonzalez 10.00 25.00
426 Travis Buck 6.00 15.00
427 Brad Emaus 6.00 15.00
428 Brett Myers 6.00 15.00
429 Skip Schumaker 6.00 15.00
430 Trevor Crowe 6.00 15.00
431 Marcos Mateo 12.00 30.00
432 Matt Harrison 6.00 15.00
433 Curtis Granderson 10.00 25.00
434 Mark DeRosa 6.00 15.00
435 Elvis Andrus 8.00 20.00
436 Trevor Cahill 6.00 15.00
437 Jordan Schafer 6.00 15.00
438 Ryan Theriot 6.00 15.00
439 Ervin Santana 6.00 15.00
440 Grady Sizemore 8.00 20.00
441 Rafael Furcal 6.00 15.00
442 Brad Bergesen 6.00 15.00
443 Brian Roberts 6.00 15.00
444 Brett Cecil 6.00 15.00
445 Mitch Talbot 6.00 15.00
446 Brandon Beachy 10.00 25.00
447 Toronto Blue Jays 6.00 15.00
448 Colby Rasmus 6.00 15.00
449 Austin Kearns 6.00 15.00
450 Mark Teixeira 6.00 15.00
451 Livan Hernandez 6.00 15.00
452 David Freese 6.00 15.00
453 Joe Saunders 12.00 30.00
454 Alberto Callaspo 6.00 15.00
455 Logan Morrison 6.00 15.00
456 Ryan Doumit 6.00 15.00
457 Brandon Allen 6.00 15.00
458 Javier Vazquez 6.00 15.00
459 Frank Francisco 6.00 15.00
460 Cole Hamels 8.00 20.00
461 Eric Sogard 6.00 15.00
462 Daric Barton 6.00 15.00
463 Will Venable 6.00 15.00
464 Daniel Bard 6.00 15.00
465 Yovani Gallardo 6.00 15.00
466 Johnny Damon 8.00 20.00
467 Wade Davis 6.00 15.00
468 Chone Figgins 6.00 15.00
469 Joe Blanton 6.00 15.00
470 Billy Butler 6.00 15.00
471 Tim Collins 5.00 12.00
472 Jason Kendall 6.00 15.00
473 Chad Billingsley 10.00 25.00
474 Jeff Mathis 6.00 15.00
475 Phil Hughes 6.00 15.00
476 Matt LaPorta 6.00 15.00
477 Franklin Gutierrez 6.00 15.00
478 Mike Minor 6.00 15.00
479 Justin Duchscherer 6.00 15.00
480 Dustin Pedroia 10.00 25.00
481 Randy Wells 6.00 15.00
482 Eric Hinske 6.00 15.00
483 Justin Smoak 25.00 60.00
484 Gerardo Parra 6.00 15.00
485 Delmon Young 8.00 20.00
486 Francisco Rodriguez 8.00 20.00
487 Chris Snyder 12.00 30.00
488 Brayan Villarreal 6.00 15.00
489 Marc Rzepczynski 6.00 15.00
490 Matt Holliday 10.00 25.00
491 Fernando Abad 5.00 12.00
492 A.J. Burnett 5.00 12.00
493 Ryan Sweeney 6.00 15.00
494 Drew Storen 6.00 15.00
495 Shane Victorino 8.00 20.00
496 Gavin Floyd 6.00 15.00
497 Alex Avila 12.00 30.00
498 Scott Feldman 6.00 15.00
499 J.A. Happ 8.00 20.00
500 Kevin Youkilis 5.00 12.00
501 Tsuyoshi Nishioka 12.00 30.00
502 Jeff Baker 6.00 15.00
503 Nathan Adcock 6.00 15.00
504 Jhonny Peralta 6.00 15.00
505 Tommy Hanson 5.00 12.00
506 Aneury Rodriguez 5.00 12.00
507 Huston Street 6.00 15.00
508 Homer Bailey 6.00 15.00
509 Michael Bourn 6.00 15.00
510 Jason Heyward 8.00 20.00
511 Philadelphia Phillies 12.00 30.00
512 Octavio Dotel 6.00 15.00
513 Adam LaRoche 6.00 15.00
514 Kelly Shoppach 6.00 15.00
515 Carlos Beltran 10.00 25.00
516 Mike Leake 8.00 20.00
517 Fred Lewis 6.00 15.00
518 Michael Morse 6.00 15.00
519 Corey Hart 6.00 15.00
520 Jorge Posada 15.00 40.00
521 Joaquin Benoit 6.00 15.00
522 Asdrubal Cabrera 10.00 25.00
523 Mike Nickeas 6.00 15.00
524 Michael Martinez 20.00 50.00
525 Vernon Wells 6.00 15.00
526 Jason Donald 6.00 15.00
527 Kila Ka'aihue 6.00 15.00
528 Bobby Abreu 6.00 15.00
529 Maicer Izturis 6.00 15.00
530 Felix Hernandez 6.00 15.00
531 Juan Rivera 6.00 15.00
532 Erik Bedard 6.00 15.00
533 Lorenzo Cain 6.00 15.00
534 Bud Norris 6.00 15.00
535 Rich Harden 6.00 15.00
536 Tony Sipp 15.00 40.00
537 Jake Peavy 6.00 15.00
538 Jason Motte 6.00 15.00
539 Brandon Lyon 6.00 15.00
540 Joakim Soria 6.00 15.00
541 John Jaso 6.00 15.00
542 Mike Pelfrey 6.00 15.00
543 Texas Rangers 6.00 15.00
544 Justin Masterson 6.00 15.00
545 Jose Tabata 5.00 12.00
546 Pat Burrell 6.00 15.00
547 Albert Pujols 30.00 80.00
548 Ryan Franklin 6.00 15.00
549 Jayson Nix 6.00 15.00
550 Joe Mauer 8.00 20.00
551 Marcus Thames 6.00 15.00
552 San Francisco Giants 6.00 15.00
553 Kyle Lohse 6.00 15.00
554 Cedric Hunter 6.00 15.00
555 Madison Bumgarner 12.00 30.00
556 B.J. Upton 8.00 20.00
557 Wes Helms 6.00 15.00
558 Carlos Zambrano 8.00 20.00
559 Reggie Willits 6.00 15.00
560 Chris Iannetta 6.00 15.00
561 Luke Gregerson 6.00 15.00
562 Gordon Beckham 5.00 12.00
563 Josh Rodriguez 6.00 15.00
564 Jeff Samardzija 12.00 30.00
565 Mark Teahen 6.00 15.00
566 Jordan Zimmermann 10.00 25.00
567 Dallas Braden 6.00 15.00
568 Kansas City Royals 6.00 15.00
569 Cameron Maybin 5.00 12.00
570 Matt Cain 8.00 20.00
571 Jeremy Affeldt 6.00 15.00
572 Brad Hawpe 6.00 15.00
573 Nyjer Morgan 6.00 15.00
574 Brandon Kintzler 6.00 15.00
575 Rod Barajas 6.00 15.00
576 Jed Lowrie 5.00 12.00
577 Mike Fontenot 6.00 15.00
578 Willy Aybar 6.00 15.00
579 Jeff Niemann 6.00 15.00
580 Chris Young 6.00 15.00
581 Fernando Rodney 6.00 15.00
582 Kosuke Fukudome 6.00 15.00
583 Ryan Spilborghs 6.00 15.00
584 Jason Bartlett 6.00 15.00
585 Dan Johnson 6.00 15.00
586 Carlos Lee 6.00 15.00
587 J.P. Arencibia 15.00 40.00
588 Rajai Davis 6.00 15.00
589 Seattle Mariners 25.00 60.00
590 Tim Lincecum 6.00 15.00
591 John Axford 6.00 15.00
592 Dayan Viciedo 6.00 15.00
593 Francisco Cordero 6.00 15.00
594 Jose Valverde 6.00 15.00
595 Michael Pineda 10.00 25.00
596 Anibal Sanchez 6.00 15.00
597 Rick Porcello 10.00 25.00
598 Jonny Gomes 6.00 15.00
599 Travis Ishikawa 6.00 15.00
600 Neftali Feliz 6.00 15.00
601 J.J. Putz 6.00 15.00
602 Ivan DeJesus 6.00 15.00
603 David Murphy 6.00 15.00
604 Joe Paterson 10.00 25.00
605 Brandon Belt 10.00 25.00
606 Juan Miranda 6.00 15.00
607 Daniel Murphy 12.00 30.00
608 Casey McGehee 6.00 15.00
609 Juan Francisco 6.00 15.00
610 Josh Beckett 5.00 12.00
611 Geovany Soto 8.00 20.00
612 Detroit Tigers 6.00 15.00
613 Dexter Fowler 10.00 25.00
614 Minnesota Twins 6.00 15.00
615 Shaun Marcum 6.00 15.00
616 Ross Ohlendorf 6.00 15.00
617 Joel Zumaya 6.00 15.00
618 Josh Lueke 6.00 15.00
619 Jonny Venters 6.00 15.00
620 Luke Hochevar 6.00 15.00
621 Omar Beltre 6.00 15.00
622 Matt Thornton 6.00 15.00
623 Leo Nunez 6.00 15.00
624 Luke French 6.00 15.00
625 Ruben Tejada 6.00 15.00
626 Dan Haren 6.00 15.00
627 Kyle Blanks 6.00 15.00
628 Blake DeWitt 6.00 15.00
629 Ivan Nova 10.00 25.00
630 Brandon Phillips 6.00 15.00
631 Houston Astros 6.00 15.00
632 Scott Kazmir 6.00 15.00
633 Aaron Crow 8.00 20.00
634 Mitch Moreland 6.00 15.00
635 Jason Heyward 25.00 60.00
636 Chris Tillman 6.00 15.00
637 Ricky Nolasco 6.00 15.00
638 Ryan Madson 6.00 15.00
639 Pedro Beato 4.00 10.00
640 Dan Uggla 5.00 12.00
641 Travis Wood 6.00 15.00
642 Jason Hammel 10.00 25.00
643 Jaime Garcia 30.00 80.00
644 Joel Hanrahan 10.00 25.00
645 Adam Wainwright 8.00 20.00
646 Los Angeles Dodgers 8.00 20.00
647 Jeanmar Gomez 6.00 15.00
648 Cody Ross 6.00 15.00
649 Joba Chamberlain 5.00 12.00
650 Josh Hamilton 6.00 15.00
651 Kendrys Morales 6.00 15.00
652 Edwin Jackson 6.00 15.00
653 J.D. Drew 6.00 15.00
654 Chris Getz 6.00 15.00
655 Starlin Castro 15.00 40.00
656 Raul Ibanez 8.00 20.00
657 Nick Blackburn 6.00 15.00
658 Mitch Maier 6.00 15.00
659 Clint Barmes 6.00 15.00
660 Ryan Zimmerman 8.00 20.00

2011 Topps Cognac Diamond Anniversary

*COGNAC VET: 1.5X TO 4X BASIC
*COGNAC RC: 1X TO 2.5X BASIC RC
*COGNAC SP: .2X TO .5X BASIC SP
STATED ODDS 1:2 UPDATE HOBBY
STATED SP ODDS 1:41 UPDATE HOBBY
145 Freddie Freeman 40.00 100.00

2011 Topps Diamond Anniversary

*DIAMOND VET: 2X TO 5X BASIC
*DIAMOND RC: 1.2X TO 3X BASIC RC
*DIAMOND SP: .3X TO .8X BASIC SP
SER.1 STATED ODDS 1:4 HOBBY
145 Freddie Freeman 25.00 60.00

2011 Topps Diamond Anniversary Factory Set Limited Edition

COMPLETE SET (660) 30.00 80.00
*FACT.SET LTD: .5X TO 1.2X BASIC
145 Freddie Freeman 40.00 100.00

2011 Topps Diamond Anniversary HTA

COMPLETE SET (25) 5.00 12.00
HTA1 Hank Aaron 1.00 2.50
HTA2 Ichiro Suzuki .60 1.50
HTA3 Babe Ruth 1.25 3.00
HTA4 Evan Longoria .30 .75
HTA5 Josh Hamilton .30 .75
HTA6 Jason Heyward .40 1.00
HTA7 Mickey Mantle 1.50 4.00
HTA8 Ryan Braun .30 .75
HTA9 Joey Votto .50 1.25
HTA10 Sandy Koufax 1.00 2.50
HTA11 David Wright .40 1.00
HTA12 Troy Tulowitzki .50 1.25
HTA13 Derek Jeter 1.25 3.00
HTA14 Tim Lincecum .30 .75
HTA15 Joe Mauer .40 1.00
HTA16 Mike Schmidt .75 2.00
HTA17 Ryan Howard .40 1.00
HTA18 Robinson Cano .30 .75
HTA19 Carl Crawford .30 .75
HTA20 Albert Pujols .60 1.50
HTA21 Roy Halladay .30 .75
HTA22 Miguel Cabrera .50 1.25
HTA23 Buster Posey .60 1.50
HTA24 Jackie Robinson .50 1.25
HTA25 Felix Hernandez .30 .75

2011 Topps Factory Set Red Border

*RED VET: 4X TO 10X BASIC
*RED RC: 2.5X TO 6X BASIC RC
ONE PACK OF FIVE RED PER FACT.SET
STATED PRINT RUN 245 SER.#'d SETS
145 Freddie Freeman 50.00 120.00

2011 Topps Gold

*GOLD VET: 2X TO 5X BASIC
*GOLD RC: 1.2X TO 3X BASIC RC
SER.1 ODDS 1:8 HOBBY
STATED PRINT RUN 2011 SER.#'d SETS
145 Freddie Freeman 25.00 60.00

2011 Topps Hope Diamond Anniversary

*HOPE VET: 8X TO 20X BASIC
*HOPE RC: 5X TO 12X BASIC RC
*HOPE SP: X TO X BASIC SP
STATED ODDS 1:35 UPDATE HOBBY
STATED SP ODDS 1:1340 UPDATE HOBBY
STATED PRINT RUN 60 SER.#'d SETS
145 Freddie Freeman 100.00 250.00

2011 Topps Sparkle

APPX.ODDDS ONE PER HOBBY CASE
1 Ryan Braun 12.50 30.00
3 Jon Lester 15.00 40.00
5 Joey Votto 12.50 30.00
15 David Wright 20.00 50.00
20 Hanley Ramirez 8.00 20.00
23 Jaime Garcia 8.00 20.00
25 Carl Crawford 20.00 50.00
35 Shin-Soo Choo 20.00 50.00
40 Justin Upton 10.00 25.00
42 Mariano Rivera 15.00 40.00
44 Martin Prado 10.00 25.00
50 Alex Rodriguez 20.00 50.00
60 Andrew McCutchen 12.50 30.00
61 David Price 8.00 20.00
67 Vladimir Guerrero 15.00 40.00
70 Kyle Drabek 12.50 30.00
75 Jered Weaver 10.00 25.00
78 Mike Stanton 12.50 30.00
80 Desmond Jennings 10.00 25.00
100 Albert Pujols 30.00 60.00
102 CC Sabathia 15.00 40.00
108 Zack Greinke 10.00 25.00
110 Aroldis Chapman 15.00 40.00
120 Mat Latos 10.00 25.00
128 Manny Ramirez 12.50 30.00
140 Brett Anderson 10.00 25.00
150 Miguel Cabrera 10.00 25.00
165 Jeremy Hellickson 10.00 25.00
166 Josh Johnson 10.00 25.00
169 Chipper Jones 12.50 30.00
174 Roy Oswalt 12.50 30.00
177 Brian Matusz 10.00 25.00
195 Nick Markakis 20.00 50.00
200 Ichiro Suzuki 12.50 30.00
208 Clay Buchholz 10.00 25.00
209 Carlos Santana 12.50 30.00
210 Brian Wilson 12.50 30.00
214 Chase Utley 12.50 30.00
216 Jose Bautista 12.50 30.00
218 Victor Martinez 10.00 25.00
236 Nelson Cruz 8.00 20.00
240 Andre Ethier 10.00 25.00
241 Wandy Rodriguez 12.50 30.00
247 Starlin Castro 20.00 50.00
250 Carlos Gonzalez 8.00 20.00
255 Torii Hunter 10.00 25.00
269 Stephen Drew 10.00 25.00
270 Ubaldo Jimenez 12.50 30.00
271 Adam Dunn 10.00 25.00
275 Clayton Kershaw 8.00 20.00
290 Ike Davis 12.50 30.00
293 Justin Morneau 12.50 30.00
294 Luke Scott 12.50 30.00
299 Chris Carpenter 8.00 20.00
300 Roy Halladay 20.00 50.00
307 Alex Rios 10.00 25.00
315 David Ortiz 10.00 25.00
320 Michael Young 12.50 30.00
322 Brent Morel 8.00 20.00
330 Derek Jeter 40.00 80.00
335 Buster Posey 12.50 30.00
340 Evan Longoria 10.00 25.00
345 Austin Jackson 12.50 30.00
350 Francisco Liriano 8.00 20.00
351 Jacoby Ellsbury 12.50 30.00
355 Justin Verlander 12.50 30.00
356 Alfonso Soriano 8.00 20.00
375 Matt Kemp 10.00 25.00
378 Mark Reynolds 10.00 25.00
380 Jose Reyes 10.00 25.00
389 Carlos Quentin 8.00 20.00
396 Adam Jones 8.00 20.00
400 Troy Tulowitzki 10.00 25.00
405 Ian Kinsler 10.00 25.00
407 Jonathan Broxton 8.00 20.00
410 Prince Fielder 15.00 40.00
415 Brian McCann 10.00 25.00
419 Kelly Johnson 8.00 20.00
420 Ryan Howard 10.00 25.00
425 Adrian Gonzalez 10.00 25.00
435 Elvis Andrus 8.00 20.00
436 Trevor Cahill 12.50 30.00
441 Rafael Furcal 10.00 25.00
450 Mark Teixeira 12.50 30.00
455 Logan Morrison 8.00 20.00
460 Cole Hamels 10.00 25.00
465 Yovani Gallardo 8.00 20.00
470 Billy Butler 8.00 20.00
473 Chad Billingsley 12.50 30.00
478 Mike Minor 8.00 20.00
480 Dustin Pedroia 10.00 25.00
485 Delmon Young 10.00 25.00
490 Matt Holliday 8.00 20.00
500 Kevin Youkilis 8.00 20.00
505 Tommy Hanson 10.00 25.00
510 Jason Heyward 10.00 25.00
519 Corey Hart 12.50 30.00
520 Jorge Posada 10.00 25.00
525 Vernon Wells 10.00 25.00
530 Felix Hernandez 10.00 25.00
545 Jose Tabata 12.50 30.00
550 Joe Mauer 12.50 30.00
555 Madison Bumgarner 12.50 30.00
560 Chris Iannetta 12.50 30.00
562 Gordon Beckham 12.50 30.00
567 Dallas Braden 10.00 25.00
570 Matt Cain 12.50 30.00
586 Carlos Lee 15.00 40.00
590 Tim Lincecum 20.00 50.00
610 Josh Beckett 10.00 25.00
613 Dexter Fowler 12.50 30.00
626 Dan Haren 10.00 25.00
627 Kyle Blanks 8.00 20.00
630 Brandon Phillips 10.00 25.00
640 Dan Uggla 8.00 20.00
645 Adam Wainwright 10.00 25.00
650 Josh Hamilton 12.50 30.00
651 Kendrys Morales 8.00 20.00
652 Edwin Jackson 8.00 20.00
660 Ryan Zimmerman 10.00 25.00

2011 Topps Target

*VETS: .5X TO 1.2X BASIC TOPPS CARDS
*RC: .5X TO 1.2X BASIC TOPPS RC CARDS
145 Freddie Freeman 10.00 25.00

2011 Topps Wal-Mart Black Border

*VETS: .5X TO 1.2X BASIC TOPPS CARDS
*RC: .5X TO 1.2X BASIC TOPPS RC CARDS
145 Freddie Freeman 10.00 25.00

2011 Topps 60

COMPLETE SET (150) 30.00 80.00
COMP.SER.1 SET (50) 10.00 25.00
COMP.SER.2 SET (50) 10.00 25.00
COMP.UPD.SET (50) 10.00 25.00
SER.1 ODDS 1:4 HOBBY
UPD.ODDS 1:4 HOBBY
1-50 ISSUED IN SERIES 1
51-100 ISSUED IN SERIES 2
101-150 ISSUED IN UPDATE
1 Ryan Howard .60 1.50
2 Andre Dawson .50 1.25
3 Babe Ruth 2.00 5.00
4 Gary Carter .50 1.25
5 Lou Gehrig 1.50 4.00
6 Robinson Cano .50 1.25
7 Mickey Mantle 2.50 6.00
8 Felix Hernandez .50 1.25
9 Ian Kinsler .50 1.25
10 Alex Rodriguez 1.00 2.50
11 Troy Tulowitzki .75 2.00
12 Prince Fielder .50 1.25
13 Jonathan Papelbon .50 1.25
14 Barry Larkin .50 1.25
15 Jason Heyward .60 1.50
16 Carl Crawford .50 1.25
17 Dale Murphy .75 2.00
18 Keith Hernandez .30 .75
19 Andre Ethier .50 1.25
20 Manny Ramirez .75 2.00
21 Tommy Hanson .30 .75
22 Clay Buchholz .30 .75
23 Neftali Feliz .30 .75
24 Josh Johnson .50 1.25
25 Orlando Cepeda .50 1.25
26 Derek Jeter 2.00 5.00
27 David Wright .60 1.50
28 Billy Butler .30 .75
29 Ryan Zimmerman .50 1.25
30 Nick Markakis .60 1.50
31 Justin Upton .50 1.25
32 Adam Dunn .50 1.25
33 Johan Santana .50 1.25
34 Mark Reynolds .30 .75
35 Frank Thomas .75 2.00
36 Adam Jones .50 1.25
37 Stephen Strasburg .75 2.00
38 Ryan Braun .50 1.25
39 Adam Wainwright .50 1.25
40 Michael Young .30 .75
41 Shin-Soo Choo .50 1.25
42 Mat Latos .50 1.25
43 Chipper Jones .75 2.00
44 Duke Snider .50 1.25
45 Hanley Ramirez .50 1.25
46 Ike Davis .30 .75
47 Nolan Ryan 2.50 6.00
48 Buster Posey 1.00 2.50
49 Josh Hamilton .50 1.25
50 Miguel Cabrera .75 2.00
51 Walter Johnson .75 2.00
52 Felix Hernandez .50 1.25
53 Jose Bautista .50 1.25
54 Ryan Zimmerman .50 1.25
55 Mariano Rivera 1.00 2.50
56 Roberto Alomar .50 1.25
57 Sandy Koufax 1.50 4.00
58 Hank Aaron 1.50 4.00
59 Roy Campanella .75 2.00
60 Mel Ott .75 2.00
61 Tom Seaver .50 1.25
62 Mike Stanton .75 2.00
63 Evan Longoria .50 1.25
64 Jorge Posada .50 1.25
65 Don Mattingly 1.50 4.00
66 Paul Molitor .75 2.00
67 Andrew McCutchen .75 2.00
68 Joey Votto .75 2.00
69 David Price .60 1.50
70 Chris Carpenter .50 1.25
71 Willie Stargell .50 1.25
72 Eddie Mathews .75 2.00
73 Nelson Cruz .75 2.00
74 Chase Utley .50 1.25
75 CC Sabathia .50 1.25
76 Joe Mauer .60 1.50
77 Dave Winfield .50 1.25
78 Francisco Liriano .30 .75
79 Rickey Henderson .75 2.00
80 Thurman Munson .75 2.00
81 Brian McCann .50 1.25
82 Shane Victorino .50 1.25
83 Hunter Pence .50 1.25
84 Starlin Castro .50 1.25
85 Johnny Bench .75 2.00
86 Dustin Pedroia .75 2.00
87 Clayton Kershaw 1.25 3.00
88 Mark Teixeira .50 1.25
89 Jered Weaver .50 1.25
90 Greg Maddux 1.00 2.50
91 David Ortiz .75 2.00
92 Alfonso Soriano .50 1.25
93 Carlos Gonzalez .50 1.25
94 Torii Hunter .30 .75
95 Jon Lester .50 1.25
96 Tim Lincecum .50 1.25
97 Jackie Robinson .75 2.00
98 Marlon Byrd .30 .75
99 Jacoby Ellsbury .60 1.50
100 Albert Pujols 1.00 2.50
101 Joe DiMaggio 1.50 4.00
102 Hank Aaron 1.50 4.00
103 Alex Rodriguez 1.00 2.50
104 Alex Rodriguez 1.00 2.50
105 Rogers Hornsby .50 1.25
106 Jimmie Foxx .75 2.00
107 Johnny Mize .50 1.25
108 Babe Ruth 2.00 5.00
109 Luis Aparicio .50 1.25
110 Carlton Fisk .50 1.25
111 Reggie Jackson .50 1.25
112 Reggie Jackson .50 1.25
113 Willie McCovey .50 1.25
114 Nolan Ryan 2.50 6.00
115 Nolan Ryan 2.50 6.00
116 Nolan Ryan 2.50 6.00
117 Fergie Jenkins .50 1.25
118 Joe Morgan .50 1.25
119 Tom Seaver .50 1.25
120 Ozzie Smith 1.00 2.50
121 Pee Wee Reese .50 1.25
122 Roberto Alomar .50 1.25
123 Andre Dawson .50 1.25
124 Rickey Henderson .75 2.00
125 Paul Molitor .75 2.00
126 Frank Robinson .50 1.25
127 Duke Snider .50 1.25
128 Frank Thomas .75 2.00
129 Ty Cobb 1.25 3.00
130 Lou Gehrig 1.50 4.00
131 Christy Mathewson .75 2.00
132 George Sisler .50 1.25
133 Tris Speaker .50 1.25
134 Honus Wagner .75 2.00
135 Cy Young .75 2.00
136 Bert Blyleven .50 1.25
137 Steve Garvey .30 .75
138 Roger Maris .75 2.00
139 Dan Uggla .30 .75
140 Eric Hosmer 2.00 5.00
141 Danny Duffy .50 1.25
142 Tyler Chatwood .30 .75
143 Lance Berkman .50 1.25
144 Zach Britton .75 2.00
145 Michael Pineda .75 2.00
146 Freddie Freeman 5.00 12.00
147 Kyle Drabek .50 1.25
148 Craig Kimbrel .75 2.00
149 Drew Storen .30 .75
150 Sandy Koufax 1.50 4.00

2011 Topps 60 Autograph Relics

COMMON CARD 6.00 15.00
SER.1 ODDS 1:3970 HOBBY
STATED PRINT RUN 50 SER.#'d SETS
AC Aroldis Chapman S2 15.00 40.00
AD Andre Dawson 50.00 100.00
AG Adrian Gonzalez S2 50.00 100.00
AK Al Kaline 20.00 50.00
BM Brian Matusz 6.00 15.00
BW Bernie Williams S2 50.00 100.00
CF Carlton Fisk S2 50.00 100.00
DP David Price S2 10.00 25.00
DS Duke Snider 10.00 25.00
FH Felix Hernandez 25.00 60.00
GC Gary Carter 20.00 50.00
HR Hanley Ramirez 6.00 15.00
IK Ian Kinsler 12.50 30.00
JH Jason Heyward S2 50.00 100.00
JV Joey Votto S2 20.00 50.00
RC Robinson Cano 50.00 100.00
RH Ryan Howard 20.00 50.00
RO Roy Oswalt S2 40.00 80.00
RS Ryne Sandberg S2 25.00 60.00
TS Tom Seaver S2 60.00 150.00

2011 Topps 60 Autographs

SER.1 ODDS 1:342 HOBBY
UPD.ODDS 1:620 HOBBY
EXCHANGE DEADLINE 1/31/2014
EXCH * IS PARTIAL EXCHANGE
AC Andrew Cashner S2 6.00 15.00
AC Andrew Cashner UPD 3.00 8.00
ACA Asdrubal Cabrera S2 5.00 12.00
AD Andre Dawson 10.00 25.00
AE Andre Ethier 8.00 20.00
AG Alex Gordon 6.00 15.00
AG Adrian Gonzalez UPD 8.00 20.00
AJ Adam Jones 6.00 15.00
AK Al Kaline EXCH * 12.00 30.00
AM Andrew McCutchen 20.00 50.00
AP Albert Pujols S2 100.00 200.00
AP Albert Pujols UPD 100.00 200.00
APA Angel Pagan UPD 5.00 12.00
APA Angel Pagan S2 5.00 12.00
AR Alex Rodriguez 60.00 120.00
AT Andres Torres S2 5.00 12.00
BA Brett Anderson UPD 4.00 10.00
BC Brett Cecil UPD 3.00 8.00
BD Blake DeWitt 8.00 20.00
BDU Brian Duensing 4.00 10.00
BJU B.J. Upton 5.00 12.00
BL Barry Larkin 30.00 60.00
BL Brandon League UPD 3.00 8.00
BM Brian McCann 6.00 15.00
BMA Brian Matusz 5.00 12.00
BP Buster Posey S2 30.00 80.00
CB Clay Buchholz 6.00 15.00
CB Clay Buchholz UPD 6.00 15.00
CC Carl Crawford 8.00 20.00
CCO Chris Coghlan 3.00 8.00
CD Chris Dickerson 8.00 20.00
CF Chone Figgins 4.00 10.00
CG Chris Getz 4.00 10.00
CH Chris Heisey UPD 5.00 12.00
CL Cliff Lee 10.00 25.00
CL Cliff Lee S2 10.00 25.00
CP Carlos Pena S2 5.00 12.00
CR Colby Rasmus UPD 10.00 25.00
CT Chris Tillman 6.00 15.00

CU Chase Utley S2 20.00 50.00
CV Chris Volstad EXCH * 3.00 8.00
CY Chris B. Young UPD 4.00 10.00
DB Daniel Bard UPD 6.00 15.00
DB Domonic Brown 10.00 25.00
DBA Daric Barton 3.00 8.00
DG Dwight Gooden S2 8.00 20.00
DM Daniel McCutchen UPD 3.00 8.00
DS Drew Stubbs UPD 5.00 12.00
DS Darryl Strawberry S2 8.00 20.00
DS Duke Snider 15.00 40.00
DSN Drew Storen EXCH 6.00 15.00
DST Drew Stubbs 6.00 15.00
DW David Wright S2 20.00 50.00
DW David Wright UPD 15.00 40.00
FCA Fausto Carmona EXCH 3.00 8.00
FD Felix Doubront 6.00 15.00
FF Freddie Freeman S2 15.00 40.00
FH Felix Hernandez S2 12.50 30.00
FH Felix Hernandez UPD 12.00 30.00
FR Fernando Rodney UPD 3.00 8.00
GB Gordon Beckham 5.00 12.00
GC Gary Carter 20.00 50.00
GC Gary Carter UPD 20.00 50.00
GG Gio Gonzalez S2 4.00 10.00
GP Glen Perkins 4.00 10.00
GS Gaby Sanchez S2 5.00 12.00
GS Gaby Sanchez UPD 3.00 8.00
HA Hank Aaron UPD 125.00 250.00
HP Hunter Pence 8.00 20.00
HR Hanley Ramirez 8.00 20.00
IK Ian Kinsler 3.00 8.00
IK Ian Kennedy S2 5.00 12.00
JB Jose Bautista S2 10.00 25.00
JB Jose Bautista UPD 10.00 25.00
JBR Jay Bruce UPD 6.00 15.00
JC Joba Chamberlain 3.00 8.00
JF Jeff Francis 3.00 8.00
JH Jason Heyward 10.00 25.00
JH Josh Hamilton UPD 20.00 50.00
JJ Josh Johnson UPD 4.00 10.00
JJ Josh Johnson 5.00 12.00
JJA Jon Jay UPD 4.00 10.00
JN Jon Niese UPD 4.00 10.00
JNI Jeff Niemann UPD 3.00 8.00
JP Jonathan Papelbon 3.00 8.00
JP Jhonny Peralta S2 4.00 10.00
JT Josh Tomlin S2 5.00 12.00
JT Josh Tomlin 5.00 12.00
JT Josh Thole UPD EXCH 4.00 10.00
JZ Jordan Zimmermann UPD EXCH 4.00 10.00
KD Kyle Drabek S2 3.00 8.00
KH Keith Hernandez 8.00 20.00
KJ Kevin Jepsen 3.00 8.00
KU Koji Uehara 8.00 20.00
LC Lorenzo Cain S2 8.00 20.00
LM Logan Morrison S2 3.00 8.00
LMA Lou Marson 15.00 40.00
MB Marlon Byrd 3.00 8.00
MB Madison Bumgarner S2 20.00 50.00
MC Miguel Cabrera UPD 75.00 150.00
MF Mark Fidrych 20.00 50.00
MH Matt Harrison 3.00 8.00
ML Mike Leake S2 3.00 8.00
MN Mike Napoli 5.00 12.00
MR Manny Ramirez 20.00 50.00
MR Mark Reynolds S2 3.00 8.00
MSC Max Scherzer 12.00 30.00
NW Neil Walker 5.00 12.00
OC Orlando Cepeda 6.00 15.00
PB Peter Bourjos EXCH 15.00 40.00
PF Prince Fielder 12.50 30.00
PS Pablo Sandoval UPD 10.00 25.00
RC Robinson Cano 12.00 30.00
RC Robinson Cano S2 12.00 30.00
RK Ryan Kalish 3.00 8.00
RK Ralph Kiner S2 15.00 40.00
RP Rick Porcello S2 5.00 12.00
RW Randy Wells 4.00 10.00
RZ Ryan Zimmerman S2 6.00 15.00
SC Starlin Castro S2 8.00 20.00
SK Sandy Koufax UPD 200.00 400.00
SSC Shin-Soo Choo S2 10.00 25.00
SV Shane Victorino S2 8.00 20.00
TB Taylor Buchholz S2 5.00 12.00
TC Trevor Cahill S2 3.00 8.00
TC Tyler Colvin 8.00 20.00
TH Tommy Hanson 8.00 20.00
TH Tim Hudson UPD 10.00 25.00
TT Troy Tulowitzki 12.50 30.00
TW Travis Wood 5.00 12.00
TW Travis Wood UPD 3.00 8.00
VM Vin Mazzaro 3.00 8.00
WD Wade Davis 4.00 10.00
WL Wade LeBlanc S2 3.00 8.00
WV Will Venable 6.00 15.00

2011 Topps 60 Dual Relics

STATED PRINT RUN 50 SER.#'d SETS
1 Josh Hamilton 6.00 15.00
2 J.Votto/M.Cabrera 20.00 50.00
3 R.Cano/D.Pedroia 20.00 50.00
4 J.Lester/C.Kershaw 15.00 40.00
5 B.Posey/J.Heyward 30.00 60.00
6 R.Alomar/B.Blyleven 15.00 40.00
7 H.Aaron/C.Jones 30.00 60.00
8 L.Gehrig/C.Ripken Jr. 100.00 175.00
9 B.Gibson/A.Wainwright 20.00 50.00
10 J.Morgan/C.Utley 20.00 50.00
11 Ichiro Suzuki
{Torii Hunter 12.50 30.00
12 M.Teixeira/J.Posada 50.00 100.00
13 Mariano Rivera
Carlos Marmol 12.50 30.00
14 Josh Beckett
John Lackey 6.00 15.00
15 Josh Johnson
Clay Buchholz 10.00 25.00

2011 Topps 60 Relics

SER.1 ODDS 1:47 HOBBY
AD Andre Dawson 2.50 6.00
AG Adrian Gonzalez 3.00 8.00
AJ Adam Jones S2 2.50 6.00
AR Aramis Ramirez 1.50 4.00
AR Aramis Ramirez S2 1.50 4.00
AS Alfonso Soriano S2 2.50 6.00
BL Barry Larkin 2.50 6.00
BR Babe Ruth 250.00 400.00
CB Carlos Beltran 2.50 6.00
CK Clayton Kershaw S2 6.00 15.00
CM Carlos Marmol 2.50 6.00
CM Carlos Marmol S2 2.50 6.00
CS Curt Schilling 2.50 6.00
CU1 Chase Utley Bat S2 2.50 6.00
CU2 Chase Utley Jsy S2 2.50 6.00
CZ Carlos Zambrano 2.50 6.00
DB Daniel Bard S2 1.50 4.00
DJ Derek Jeter 8.00 25.00
DJ Derek Jeter S2 8.00 20.00
DM Don Mattingly 6.00 15.00
DO David Ortiz S2 4.00 10.00
DP Dustin Pedroia 4.00 10.00
DW Dave Winfield 2.50 6.00
EL Evan Longoria 4.00 10.00
FC Fausto Carmona 1.50 4.00
FH Felix Hernandez 2.50 6.00
GC Gary Carter 2.50 6.00
GG Goose Gossage 2.50 6.00
GS Geovany Soto 2.50 6.00
GS Geovany Soto S2 2.50 6.00
HA Hank Aaron S2 12.00 30.00
HJ Howard Johnson 1.50 4.00
IK Ian Kinsler S2 2.50 6.00
IS Ichiro Suzuki 8.00 20.00
JA Jonathan Albaladejo 1.50 4.00
JB Josh Beckett S2 1.50 4.00
JC Joba Chamberlain 1.50 4.00
JE Jacoby Ellsbury 3.00 8.00
JH Josh Hamilton 2.50 6.00
JH Jason Heyward S2 3.00 8.00
JL Jon Lester S2 2.50 6.00
JM Joe Morgan 2.50 6.00
JR Jimmy Rollins 2.50 6.00
JR Jackie Robinson S2 8.00 20.00
JU Justin Upton 2.50 6.00
JW Jered Weaver 2.50 6.00
KF Kosuke Fukudome 2.50 6.00
LB Lew Burdette 1.50 4.00
MB Marlon Byrd S2 1.50 4.00
MG Matt Garza 1.50 4.00
MH Matt Holliday 4.00 10.00
MK Matt Kemp 3.00 8.00
ML Mat Latos S2 2.50 6.00
MP Mike Piazza 4.00 10.00
MR Manny Ramirez 4.00 10.00
MR Mark Reynolds S2 1.50 4.00
MS Marco Scutaro S2 2.50 6.00
MT Mark Teixeira 2.50 6.00
MT Mark Teixeira S2 2.50 6.00
MY Michael Young S2 1.50 4.00
NR Nolan Ryan 4.00 10.00
NS Nick Swisher S2 2.50 6.00
OS Ozzie Smith 5.00 12.00
PF Prince Fielder 2.50 6.00
PF Prince Fielder S2 2.50 6.00
PH Phil Hughes S2 1.50 4.00
PS Pablo Sandoval S2 2.50 6.00
RA Roberto Alomar 2.50 6.00
RC Roy Campanella S2 10.00 25.00
RD Ryan Dempster S2 1.50 4.00
RH Ryan Howard 3.00 8.00
RH Rickey Henderson S2 4.00 10.00
RI Raul Ibanez 2.50 6.00
RR Robin Roberts 6.00 15.00
RZ Ryan Zimmerman S2 2.50 6.00
SB Sal Bando 1.50 4.00
SC Starlin Castro S2 2.50 6.00
SG Steve Garvey 1.50 4.00
SV Shane Victorino S2 2.50 6.00
TC Tyler Colvin S2 1.50 4.00
TC Tyler Colvin 1.50 4.00
TG Tony Gwynn 4.00 10.00
TH Torii Hunter 1.50 4.00
TT Troy Tulowitzki 4.00 10.00
VG Vladimir Guerrero S2 2.50 6.00
VM Victor Martinez 2.50 6.00
WB Wade Boggs 2.50 6.00
YB Yogi Berra 8.00 20.00
ABE Adrian Beltre 4.00 10.00
AGO Alex Gordon 2.50 6.00
AJB A.J. Burnett 1.50 4.00
APE Andy Pettitte 2.50 6.00
ARO Alex Rodriguez 5.00 12.00
BGA Brett Gardner 2.50 6.00
BGA Brett Gardner S2 2.50 6.00
CCS CC Sabathia 2.50 6.00
DLE Derrek Lee 1.50 4.00
DMC Daniel McCutchen 1.50 4.00
DWR David Wright 3.00 8.00
JCH Joba Chamberlain S2 1.50 4.00
JDA Johnny Damon 2.50 6.00
JDD J.D. Drew 1.50 4.00
JDD J.D. Drew S2 1.50 4.00
JLA John Lackey S2 2.50 6.00
JLO Jed Lowrie S2 1.50 4.00
JPA Jonathan Papelbon 2.50 6.00
JPO Jorge Posada 2.50 6.00
MBY Marlon Byrd 1.50 4.00
MRI Mariano Rivera 5.00 12.00
PHU Phil Hughes 1.50 4.00
PWR Pee Wee Reese 8.00 20.00
RCA Robinson Cano 2.50 6.00
RCA Robinson Cano S2 2.50 6.00
RHE Rickey Henderson 4.00 10.00
RWE Randy Wells S2 1.50 4.00
SCA Starlin Castro 2.50 6.00
SSC Shin-Soo Choo 2.50 6.00

2011 Topps 60 Relics Diamond Anniversary

*DA: .75X TO 2X BASIC
STATED PRINT RUN 99 SER.#'d SETS
DJ Derek Jeter S2 20.00 50.00
HA Hank Aaron S2 15.00 40.00
RH Rickey Henderson S2 15.00 40.00

2011 Topps 60 Years of Topps

COMPLETE SET (118) 30.00 60.00
COMP.SER.1 SET (59) 12.50 30.00
COMP.SER.2 SET (59) 12.50 30.00
SER.1 ODDS 1:3 HOBBY
1-59 ISSUED IN SER.1
59-118 ISSUED IN SER.2
*ORIGINAL BACK: .6X TO 1.5X BASIC
ORIGINAL ODDS 1:36 HOBBY
1 Jackie Robinson .75 2.00
2 Roy Campanella .75 2.00
3 Monte Irvin .50 1.25
4 Ernie Banks .75 2.00
5 Phil Rizzuto .50 1.25
6 Mickey Mantle 2.50 6.00
7 Pee Wee Reese .50 1.25
8 Roger Maris .75 2.00
9 Stan Musial 1.25 3.00
10 Juan Marichal .50 1.25
11 Gaylord Perry .50 1.25
12 Frank Robinson .50 1.25
13 Bob Gibson .50 1.25
14 Lou Brock .50 1.25
15 Al Kaline .75 2.00
16 Tony Perez .50 1.25
17 Frank Robinson/Brooks Robinson .50 1.25
18 Tom Seaver .50 1.25
19 Reggie Jackson .50 1.25
20 Nolan Ryan 2.50 6.00
21 Rod Carew .50 1.25
22 Carlton Fisk .50 1.25
23 Mike Schmidt 1.25 3.00
24 Carl Yastrzemski 1.25 3.00
25 Robin Yount .75 2.00
26 Bruce Sutter .50 1.25
27 P.Niekro/N.Ryan 2.50 6.00
28 Eddie Murray .50 1.25
29 Paul Molitor .75 2.00
30 Andre Dawson .50 1.25
31 Jim Palmer .50 1.25
32 Ozzie Smith 1.00 2.50
33 Tony Gwynn .75 2.00
34 Steve Garvey .30 .75
35 Dave Winfield .50 1.25
36 Dennis Eckersley .50 1.25
37 Greg Maddux 1.00 2.50
38 Bo Jackson .75 2.00
39 Bernie Williams .50 1.25
40 Roberto Alomar .50 1.25
41 Frank Thomas .75 2.00
42 Jim Edmonds .50 1.25
43 Mike Piazza .75 2.00
44 Barry Larkin .50 1.25
45 Mickey Mantle 2.50 6.00
46 Mariano Rivera 1.00 2.50
47 Bob Abreu .30 .75
48 Mike Piazza/Ivan Rodriguez
Jason Kendall .75 2.00
49 Alex Rodriguez 1.00 2.50
50 Manny Ramirez .75 2.00
51 Vladimir Guerrero .50 1.25
52 Cliff Lee .50 1.25
53 Mark Teixeira .50 1.25
54 Justin Verlander .75 2.00
55 Ryan Howard .60 1.50
56 Troy Tulowitzki .75 2.00
57 Johnny Cueto .50 1.25
58 Joe Mauer .60 1.50
59 Albert Pujols 1.00 2.50
60 Yogi Berra .75 2.00
61 Warren Spahn .50 1.25
62 Jackie Robinson .75 2.00
63 Ed Mathews .75 2.00
64 Mickey Mantle 2.50 6.00
65 Brooks Robinson .50 1.25
66 Luis Aparicio .50 1.25
67 Richie Ashburn .50 1.25
68 Harmon Killebrew .75 2.00
69 Stan Musial 1.25 3.00
70 Orlando Cepeda .50 1.25
71 Duke Snider .50 1.25
72 Carl Yastrzemski 1.25 3.00
73 Frank Robinson .50 1.25
74 Roger Maris .75 2.00
75 Steve Carlton .50 1.25
76 Ernie Banks .75 2.00
77 Johnny Bench .75 2.00
78 Tom Seaver .50 1.25
79 Gaylord Perry .50 1.25
80 Nolan Ryan 2.50 6.00
81 Rich Gossage .50 1.25
82 Dave Parker .30 .75
83 Reggie Jackson .50 1.25
84 Dave Winfield .50 1.25
85 Don Sutton .50 1.25
86 Gary Carter .50 1.25
87 Eddie Murray .50 1.25
88 Ron Guidry .30 .75
89 Jim Palmer .50 1.25
90 Steve Garvey .30 .75
91 Cal Ripken Jr. 2.50 6.00
92 Rickey Henderson .75 2.00
93 Andre Dawson .50 1.25
94 Don Mattingly 1.50 4.00
95 Ozzie Smith 1.00 2.50
96 Dale Murphy .75 2.00
97 Paul Molitor .75 2.00
98 Curt Schilling .50 1.25
99 Larry Walker .50 1.25
100 Wade Boggs .50 1.25
101 Craig Biggio .50 1.25
102 Manny Ramirez .75 2.00
103 Frank Thomas .75 2.00
104 Derek Jeter 2.00 5.00
105 Tony Gwynn .75 2.00
106 Mariano Rivera 1.00 2.50
107 Roy Halladay .50 1.25
108 Chris Carpenter .50 1.25
109 David Ortiz .75 2.00
110 Josh Beckett .30 .75
111 Albert Pujols 1.00 2.50
112 A.Rodriguez/D.Jeter 2.00 5.00
113 Billy Butler .30 .75
114 Hanley Ramirez .50 1.25
115 Josh Hamilton .50 1.25
116 Ryan Braun .50 1.25
117 E.Longoria/D.Price .60 1.50
118 Buster Posey 1.00 2.50

2011 Topps 60 Years of Topps Original Back

*ORIGINAL BACK: .6X TO 1.5X BASIC
SER.1 ODDS 1:36 HOBBY
1-59 ISSUED IN SER.1
60-118 ISSUED IN SER.2

2011 Topps 60th Anniversary Reprint Autographs

SER.1 ODDS 1:14,750 HOBBY
EXCHANGE DEADLINE 1/31/2014
AK Al Kaline S2 60.00 150.00
BG Bob Gibson
'59 Topps/60 40.00 100.00
BR Brooks Robinson 40.00 80.00
EB Ernie Banks EXCH 40.00 80.00
EM Eddie Murray S2 60.00 120.00
FR Frank Robinson EXCH 40.00 80.00
HA Henry Aaron S2 250.00 350.00
MS Mike Schmidt S2 30.00 60.00
PM Paul Molitor S2 50.00 100.00
RJ Reggie Jackson 100.00 200.00
RS Ryne Sandberg 75.00 150.00
SK Sandy Koufax S2 200.00 400.00
SM Stan Musial S2 250.00 350.00
TG Tony Gwynn S2 50.00 100.00
TS Tom Seaver EXCH 60.00 150.00
WB Wade Boggs S2 50.00 100.00

2011 Topps 60th Anniversary Reprint Relics

SER.1 ODDS 1:7817 HOBBY
STATED PRINT RUN 60 SER.#'d SETS
AD Andre Dawson S2 60.00 120.00
AK Al Kaline S2 10.00 25.00
AR Alex Rodriguez 30.00 60.00
BB Bert Blyleven S2 10.00 25.00
BG Bob Gibson 25.00 60.00
BR Brooks Robinson 40.00 80.00
CF Carlton Fisk S2 10.00 25.00
CY Carl Yastrzemski 15.00 40.00
DJ Derek Jeter 75.00 150.00
DM Dale Murphy S2 10.00 25.00
DW Dave Winfield S2 30.00 60.00
EB Ernie Banks 50.00 100.00
EM Eddie Murray S2 10.00 25.00
FR Frank Robinson 10.00 25.00
FT Frank Thomas S2 30.00 60.00
HA Henry Aaron S2 10.00 25.00
HK Harmon Killebrew S2 10.00 25.00
JB Johnny Bench 30.00 60.00
JM Joe Morgan S2 50.00 100.00
JM Joe Mauer 12.00 30.00
JR Jackie Robinson 10.00 25.00
LB Lou Brock S2 10.00 25.00
MS Mike Schmidt S2 40.00 80.00
NR Nolan Ryan S2 10.00 25.00
NR Nolan Ryan 10.00 25.00
PM Paul Molitor S2 30.00 60.00
RA Roberto Alomar S2 10.00 25.00
RC Roy Campanella 10.00 25.00
RH Rickey Henderson 30.00 60.00
RJ Reggie Jackson 10.00 25.00
RS Ryne Sandberg 30.00 60.00
SK Sandy Koufax S2 50.00 100.00
SM Stan Musial S2 30.00 60.00
TG Tony Gwynn S2 40.00 80.00
TM Thurman Munson 10.00 25.00
TS Tom Seaver 40.00 80.00
WB Wade Boggs S2 10.00 25.00
WM Willie McCovey 30.00 60.00
YB Yogi Berra 10.00 25.00

2011 Topps Before There Was Topps

COMPLETE SET (7) 4.00 10.00
COMMON CARD .75 2.00
BTT1 American Tobacco 1909 T206 .75 2.00
BTT2 American Tobacco 1911 T205 .75 2.00
BTT3 American Tobacco 1911 T201 .75 2.00
BTT4 Exhibit Supply Company 1921 .75 2.00
BTT5 Goudey 1933 .75 2.00
BTT6 Gum Inc 1939 Play Ball .75 2.00
BTT7 Bowman 1948-1955 .75 2.00

2011 Topps Black Diamond Wrapper Redemption

COMPLETE SET (60) 60.00 120.00
1 Cliff Lee• 1.25 3.00
2 Roy Halladay 1.25 3.00
3 Zack Greinke 2.00 5.00
4 David Wright 1.50 4.00
5 Justin Upton 1.25 3.00
6 Joey Votto 2.00 5.00
7 CC Sabathia 1.25 3.00
8 Ichiro Suzuki 2.50 6.00
9 Jered Weaver 1.25 3.00
10 Adrian Gonzalez 1.50 4.00
11 Albert Pujols 2.50 6.00
12 Joe Mauer 1.50 4.00
13 Adam Dunn 1.25 3.00
14 Ryan Zimmerman 1.25 3.00
15 Adam Jones 1.25 3.00
16 Tim Lincecum 1.25 3.00
17 Carlos Gonzalez 1.25 3.00
18 Mark Teixeira 1.25 3.00
19 Mat Latos 1.25 3.00
20 Ubaldo Jimenez .75 2.00
21 Prince Fielder 1.25 3.00
22 Victor Martinez 1.25 3.00
23 Ian Kinsler 1.25 3.00
24 Dan Uggla .75 2.00
25 Justin Morneau 1.25 3.00
26 Brian McCann 1.25 3.00
27 Josh Johnson 1.25 3.00
28 Roy Oswalt 1.25 3.00
29 Chase Utley 1.25 3.00
30 Jose Reyes 1.25 3.00
31 Felix Hernandez 1.25 3.00
32 Alex Rodriguez 2.50 6.00
33 Troy Tulowitzki 2.00 5.00
34 Dustin Pedroia 2.00 5.00
35 Adam Wainwright 1.25 3.00
36 David Price 1.50 4.00
37 Jon Lester 1.25 3.00
38 Josh Hamilton 1.25 3.00
39 Aroldis Chapman 2.50 6.00
40 Jason Heyward 1.50 4.00
41 Ryan Braun 1.25 3.00
42 Matt Holliday 2.00 5.00
43 Buster Posey 2.50 6.00
44 Nick Markakis 1.50 4.00
45 Kevin Youkilis .75 2.00
46 Clayton Kershaw 3.00 8.00
47 Evan Longoria 1.25 3.00
48 Andre Ethier 1.25 3.00
49 Hanley Ramirez 1.25 3.00
50 Robinson Cano 1.25 3.00
51 Andrew McCutchen 2.00 5.00
52 Martin Prado .75 2.00
53 Carl Crawford 1.25 3.00
54 Derek Jeter 5.00 12.00
55 Torii Hunter .75 2.00
56 Mark Reynolds .75 2.00
57 Miguel Cabrera 2.00 5.00
58 Mike Stanton 2.00 5.00
59 Starlin Castro 1.25 3.00
60 Ryan Howard 1.50 4.00

2011 Topps Black Diamond Wrapper Redemption Autographs

STATED PRINT RUN 60 SER.#'d SETS
RA1 Monte Irvin 50.00 100.00
RA2 Irv Noren 12.50 30.00
RA3 Roy Sievers 15.00 40.00
RA4 Vernon Law 30.00 60.00
RA5 Bill Pierce 75.00 150.00
RA6 Eddie Yost 12.00 30.00
RA7 John Antonelli 30.00 60.00
RA8 Charlie Silvera 50.00 100.00
RA9 Roy Smalley 12.50 30.00
RA10 Curt Simmons 125.00 250.00
RA11 Ned Garver 40.00 80.00
RA12 Bobby Shantz 30.00 60.00
RA13 Joe Presko 75.00 150.00
RA14 Bob Friend 20.00 50.00
RA15 Jerry Coleman 100.00 200.00
RA16 Virgil Trucks 75.00 150.00
RA17 Chuck Diering 10.00 25.00
RA18 Lou Brissie 10.00 25.00
RA19 Joe DeMaestri 10.00 25.00
RA20 Randy Jackson 12.00 30.00
RA21 Ivan Delock 30.00 60.00
RA22 Bob DelGreco 75.00 150.00
RA23 Dick Groat 30.00 60.00
RA24 Johnny Groth 20.00 50.00
RA25 Eddie Robinson 12.50 30.00
RA26 Cloyd Boyer 20.00 50.00
RA29 Joe Astroth 10.00 25.00
RA30 Del Crandall 20.00 50.00
RA31 Ralph Branca 40.00 80.00
RA32 Red Schoendienst 25.00 60.00
RA33 Yogi Berra 60.00 150.00
RA34 Joe Garagiola 20.00 50.00

2011 Topps CMG Reprints

COMPLETE SET (30) 12.50 30.00
STATED ODDS 1:8 HOBBY
CMGR1 Babe Ruth 2.00 5.00
CMGR2 Babe Ruth 2.00 5.00
CMGR3 Hank Greenberg .75 2.00
CMGR4 Babe Ruth 2.00 5.00
CMGR5 Babe Ruth 2.00 5.00
CMGR6 Christy Mathewson .75 2.00
CMGR7 Jackie Robinson .75 2.00
CMGR8 Cy Young .75 2.00
CMGR9 George Sisler .50 1.25
CMGR10 Honus Wagner .75 2.00
CMGR11 Honus Wagner .75 2.00
CMGR12 Honus Wagner .75 2.00
CMGR13 Honus Wagner .75 2.00
CMGR14 Jackie Robinson .75 2.00
CMGR15 Jimmie Foxx .75 2.00
CMGR16 Jimmie Foxx .75 2.00
CMGR17 Jimmie Foxx .75 2.00
CMGR18 Johnny Mize
Enos Slaughter .50 1.25
CMGR19 Walter Johnson .75 2.00
CMGR20 Lou Gehrig 1.50 4.00
CMGR21 Lou Gehrig 1.50 4.00
CMGR22 Mel Ott .75 2.00
CMGR23 Rogers Hornsby .50 1.25
CMGR24 Lou Gehrig 1.50 4.00
CMGR25 Ty Cobb 1.25 3.00
CMGR26 Ty Cobb 1.25 3.00
CMGR27 Ty Cobb 1.25 3.00
CMGR28 Ty Cobb 1.25 3.00
CMGR29 Ty Cobb 1.25 3.00
CMGR30 Walter Johnson .75 2.00

2011 Topps Commemorative Patch

RANDOM INSERTS IN PACKS
AC Aroldis Chapman S2 5.00 12.00
AE Andre Ethier 4.00 10.00
AG Adrian Gonzalez S2 6.00 15.00
AG Adrian Gonzalez 6.00 15.00
AJ Adam Jones 5.00 12.00
AK Al Kaline UPD 10.00 25.00
AM Andrew McCutchen S2 5.00 12.00
AM Andrew McCutchen 5.00 12.00
AP Albert Pujols S2 8.00 20.00
AP Albert Pujols 8.00 20.00
AW Adam Wainwright 5.00 12.00
BA Brett Anderson S2 4.00 10.00
BB Brandon Belt UPD 8.00 20.00
BF Bob Feller S2 5.00 12.00
BG Bob Gibson UPD 8.00 20.00
BL Barry Larkin UPD 8.00 20.00
BM Bill Mazeroski UPD 8.00 20.00
BM Brian McCann S2 6.00 15.00
BM Brandon Morrow 4.00 10.00
BP Buster Posey S2 6.00 15.00
BP Buster Posey 6.00 15.00
BR Brian Roberts S2 5.00 12.00
BR Babe Ruth UPD 8.00 15.00
BW Brian Wilson S2 5.00 12.00
CB Chad Billingsley S2 5.00 12.00
CF Carlton Fisk UPD 6.00 15.00
CH Cole Hamels 5.00 12.00
CK Clayton Kershaw 5.00 12.00
CL Cliff Lee S2 6.00 15.00
CR Cal Ripken Jr. S2 8.00 20.00
CS Carlos Santana 5.00 12.00
CU Chase Utley 8.00 20.00
DG Dee Gordon UPD 5.00 12.00
DJ Derek Jeter 10.00 25.00
DL Derrek Lee S2 5.00 12.00
DO David Ortiz 6.00 15.00
DP David Price UPD 5.00 12.00
DW David Wright S2 5.00 12.00
DW David Wright 5.00 12.00
EH Eric Hosmer UPD 10.00 25.00
EL Evan Longoria 6.00 15.00
EM Eddie Murray UPD 4.00 10.00
FF Freddie Freeman UPD 8.00 20.00
FH Felix Hernandez S2 5.00 12.00
FH Felix Hernandez 5.00 12.00
FJ Fergie Jenkins UPD 5.00 12.00
FR Frank Robinson UPD 5.00 12.00
FT Frank Thomas UPD 8.00 20.00
GG Gio Gonzalez 4.00 10.00
GP Gaylord Perry UPD 5.00 12.00
GS Grady Sizemore S2 5.00 12.00
HA Hank Aaron S2 12.50 30.00
HA Hank Aaron UPD 8.00 20.00
HP Hunter Pence 5.00 12.00
ID Ian Desmond 4.00 10.00
IK Ian Kinsler S2 4.00 10.00
IS Ichiro Suzuki S2 8.00 20.00
IS Ichiro Suzuki 8.00 20.00
JB Jose Bautista S2 6.00 15.00
JB Johnny Bench UPD 5.00 12.00
JB Josh Bell 4.00 10.00
JF Jimmie Foxx UPD 6.00 15.00
JH Jason Heyward 6.00 15.00
JM Juan Marichal UPD 5.00 12.00
JM Joe Mauer 6.00 15.00
JP Jim Palmer S2 6.00 15.00
JR Jose Reyes S2 6.00 15.00
JR Jose Reyes 6.00 15.00
JS John Smoltz UPD 5.00 12.00
JU Justin Upton 4.00 10.00
JV Joey Votto 6.00 15.00
JW Jered Weaver S2 5.00 12.00
KS Kurt Suzuki 4.00 10.00
KU Koji Uehara 4.00 10.00
LA Luis Aparicio UPD 10.00 25.00
MB Madison Bumgarner S2 5.00 12.00
MC Miguel Cabrera 5.00 12.00
MG Matt Garza S2 5.00 12.00
MH Matt Holliday 4.00 10.00
MI Monte Irvin UPD 6.00 15.00
MK Matt Kemp S2 5.00 12.00
ML Mat Latos S2 4.00 10.00
ML Mat Latos 4.00 10.00
MP Martin Prado S2 5.00 12.00
MP Michael Pineda UPD 5.00 12.00
MR Mark Reynolds S2 5.00 12.00
MR Manny Ramirez 4.00 10.00
MS Mike Schmidt S2 8.00 20.00
MS Mike Schmidt UPD 8.00 20.00
NM Nick Markakis 5.00 12.00
NR Nolan Ryan UPD 12.50 30.00
NR Nolan Ryan S2 10.00 25.00
OS Ozzie Smith UPD 10.00 25.00
PA Pedro Alvarez S2 5.00 12.00
PF Prince Fielder S2 5.00 12.00
PM Paul Molitor UPD 6.00 15.00
PO Paul O'Neill UPD 4.00 10.00
PS Pablo Sandoval 5.00 12.00
RA Roberto Alomar UPD 6.00 15.00
RA Roberto Alomar S2 6.00 15.00
RB Ryan Braun S2 6.00 15.00
RB Ryan Braun UPD 5.00 12.00
RC Robinson Cano S2 6.00 15.00
RF Rollie Fingers UPD 6.00 15.00
RH Rickey Henderson UPD 6.00 15.00
RH Rickey Henderson S2 6.00 15.00
RH Roy Halladay 6.00 15.00
RJ Reggie Jackson S2 6.00 15.00
RJ Reggie Jackson UPD 10.00 25.00
RM Roger Maris UPD 8.00 20.00
RS Ryne Sandberg UPD 12.50 30.00
RZ Ryan Zimmerman S2 5.00 12.00
RZ Ryan Zimmerman 5.00 12.00
SC Starlin Castro 5.00 12.00
SD Stephen Drew S2 4.00 10.00
SG Steve Garvey UPD 12.50 30.00
SS Stephen Strasburg 6.00 15.00
TC Trevor Cahill 4.00 10.00
TG Tony Gwynn S2 6.00 15.00
TH Torii Hunter 4.00 10.00
TL Tim Lincecum 6.00 15.00
TS Tom Seaver S2 6.00 15.00
TS Tom Seaver UPD 6.00 15.00
VW Vernon Wells 4.00 10.00
WM Willie McCovey UPD 4.00 10.00
ZB Zach Britton UPD 4.00 10.00
BMA Brian Matusz 6.00 15.00
CFI Carlton Fisk UPD 6.00 15.00
CLE Carlos Lee S2 4.00 10.00
FJE Fergie Jenkins UPD 5.00 12.00
IDA Ike Davis 4.00 10.00
ISU Ichiro Suzuki S2 4.00 10.00
ISU Ichiro Suzuki 4.00 10.00
JBA Jose Bautista UPD 4.00 10.00
JHA Josh Hamilton 8.00 20.00
JMI Johnny Mize UPD 8.00 20.00
JMO Joe Morgan UPD 5.00 12.00
JWE Jayson Werth S2 5.00 12.00
JWR Jayson Werth S2 5.00 12.00
NRY Nolan Ryan S2 10.00 25.00
NRY Nolan Ryan UPD 12.50 30.00
PMO Paul Molitor UPD 6.00 15.00
RAL Roberto Alomar UPD 6.00 15.00
RAL Roberto Alomar S2 6.00 15.00
RED Red Schoendienst UPD 8.00 20.00
RHO Ryan Howard 6.00 15.00
RJA Reggie Jackson UPD 10.00 25.00
RZI Ryan Zimmerman S2 5.00 12.00
SSC Shin-Soo Choo 6.00 15.00
THA Tommy Hanson 4.00 10.00

2011 Topps Diamond Anniversary Autographs

SOME HARPER ISSUED IN 2010 BOW.STER.
STATED PRINT RUN 60 SER.#'d SETS
60AAK Al Kaline 25.00 50.00
60ANR Nolan Ryan 50.00 100.00
60AAC Andrew Cashner 40.00 80.00
60AAD1 Andre Dawson 50.00 100.00
60AAD2 Andre Dawson Expos 20.00 50.00
60AAE Andre Ethier 20.00 50.00
60AAJ Adam Jones 40.00 80.00
60ABG Bob Gibson 60.00 120.00
60ABH Bryce Harper 150.00 300.00
60ABM Brian McCann 75.00 150.00
60ABR Brooks Robinson 40.00 80.00
60ACB Clay Buchholz 20.00 50.00
60ACF Carlton Fisk 40.00 80.00
60ACG Carlos Gonzalez 10.00 25.00
60ACJ Chipper Jones 75.00 150.00
60ACR Cal Ripken Jr. 100.00 200.00
60ACS Charlie Sheen 250.00 500.00
60ACU Chase Utley 50.00 100.00
60ACY Carl Yastrzemski 75.00 150.00
60ADM Don Mattingly 75.00 150.00
60ADM Dale Murphy 20.00 50.00
60ADO David Ortiz 50.00 100.00
60ADW David Wright 60.00 120.00
60AEB Ernie Banks 75.00 150.00
60AEL Evan Longoria 30.00 60.00
60AEM Eddie Murray 60.00 120.00
60AFJ Fergie Jenkins 12.00 30.00
60AFR Frank Robinson 25.00 60.00
60AFT Frank Thomas 200.00 300.00
60AGB Gordon Beckham 10.00 25.00
60AGC Gary Carter 20.00 50.00
60AGC Gary Carter Expos 30.00 60.00
60AHA Hank Aaron 100.00 200.00
60AHR Hanley Ramirez 20.00 50.00
60AIK Ian Kinsler 30.00 60.00
60AJB Johnny Bench 40.00 80.00
60AJH Jason Heyward 20.00 40.00
60AJH Josh Hamilton 125.00 250.00
60AJJ Josh Johnson 30.00 60.00
60AJM Joe Morgan 40.00 80.00
60AJM Juan Marichal 15.00 40.00
60AJU Justin Upton 20.00 50.00
60AKO Keith Olbermann 40.00 80.00
60ALA Luis Aparicio 40.00 80.00
60AMK Matt Kemp 30.00 60.00
60AMR Mariano Rivera 100.00 200.00
60AMS Mike Schmidt 75.00 150.00
60AMS Mike Stanton 150.00 300.00
60ANC Nelson Cruz 12.00 30.00
60ANM Nick Markakis 20.00 50.00
60AOC Orlando Cepeda 20.00 50.00
60APG Peter Gammons 50.00 100.00
60APM Paul Molitor 20.00 50.00
60APS Pablo Sandoval 20.00 50.00
60ARA Roberto Alomar 50.00 100.00
60ARJ Reggie Jackson A's 30.00 60.00
60ARJ Reggie Jackson Yankees 30.00 60.00
60ARK Ralph Kiner 150.00 250.00
60ARO Ryan O'Hara 150.00 250.00
60ARS Ryne Sandberg 60.00 120.00
60ASB Sy Berger 75.00 150.00
60ASM Stan Musial 200.00 350.00
60ASS Stephen Strasburg 175.00 350.00
60ATG Tony Gwynn 40.00 80.00
60ATP Tony Perez 30.00 60.00

2011 Topps Diamond Die Cut

DDC1 Ryan Braun 3.00 8.00
DDC2 Mickey Mantle 15.00 40.00
DDC3 Aaron Hill 2.00 5.00
DDC4 Tim Hudson 3.00 8.00
DDC5 CC Sabathia 3.00 8.00
DDC6 Shin-Soo Choo 3.00 8.00
DDC7 Andrew McCutchen 5.00 12.00
DDC8 Hank Aaron 10.00 25.00
DDC9 Max Scherzer 5.00 12.00
DDC10 Miguel Cabrera 5.00 12.00
DDC11 Brian Matusz 2.00 5.00
DDC12 Jackie Robinson 5.00 12.00
DDC13 Chipper Jones 5.00 12.00
DDC14 Johan Santana 3.00 8.00
DDC15 Andre Ethier 3.00 8.00
DDC16 Justin Upton 3.00 8.00
DDC17 Johnny Cueto 3.00 8.00
DDC18 Gordon Beckham 2.00 5.00
DDC19 Alex Rios 2.00 5.00
DDC20 Nolan Ryan 15.00 40.00
DDC21 Rickey Henderson 5.00 12.00
DDC22 Carlos Marmol 3.00 8.00
DDC23 Matt Cain 3.00 8.00
DDC24 Adam Wainwright 3.00 8.00
DDC25 Vladimir Guerrero 3.00 8.00
DDC26 Mike Minor 2.00 5.00
DDC27 Ricky Romero 2.00 5.00
DDC28 Delmon Young 3.00 8.00
DDC29 Brett Anderson 2.00 5.00
DDC30 Evan Longoria 3.00 8.00
DDC31 Brett Wallace 2.00 5.00
DDC32 Cal Ripken Jr. 15.00 40.00
DDC33 Tommy Hanson 2.00 5.00
DDC34 Mark Buehrle 3.00 8.00
DDC35 Mariano Rivera 6.00 15.00
DDC36 Stephen Drew 2.00 5.00
DDC37 Ubaldo Jimenez 2.00 5.00
DDC38 Alexei Ramirez 3.00 8.00
DDC39 Thurman Munson 5.00 12.00
DDC40 Felix Hernandez 3.00 8.00
DDC41 Adrian Beltre 5.00 12.00
DDC42 Ian Kinsler 3.00 8.00
DDC43 Billy Butler 2.00 5.00
DDC44 Carlos Ruiz 2.00 5.00
DDC45 Stephen Strasburg 5.00 12.00
DDC46 Vernon Wells 2.00 5.00
DDC47 Ian Desmond 2.00 5.00
DDC48 Matt Holliday 5.00 12.00
DDC49 Ike Davis 2.00 5.00
DDC50 Ryan Howard 6.00 15.00
DDC51 Andrew Bailey 2.00 5.00
DDC52 David Ortiz 5.00 12.00
DDC53 Jimmy Rollins 3.00 8.00
DDC54 Ernie Banks 5.00 12.00
DDC55 Ryan Zimmerman 3.00 8.00
DDC56 Alex Rodriguez 6.00 15.00
DDC57 Brian McCann 3.00 8.00
DDC58 Tim Lincecum 3.00 8.00
DDC59 Freddie Freeman 30.00 80.00
DDC60 David Wright 4.00 10.00
DDC61 Carlos Quentin 2.00 5.00
DDC62 Adam Jones 3.00 8.00
DDC63 Brandon Morrow 2.00 5.00
DDC64 Chris Sale 15.00 40.00
DDC65 Reggie Jackson 3.00 8.00
DDC66 Carl Yastrzemski 8.00 20.00
DDC67 Sandy Koufax 10.00 25.00
DDC68 Nick Markakis 4.00 10.00
DDC69 Jair Jurrjens 2.00 5.00
DDC70 Josh Hamilton 3.00 8.00

DDC71 Prince Fielder 3.00 8.00
DDC72 Cole Hamels 4.00 10.00
DDC73 Kelly Johnson 2.00 5.00
DDC74 Colby Rasmus 3.00 8.00
DDC75 Tony Gwynn 5.00 12.00
DDC76 Hank Greenberg 5.00 12.00
DDC77 Tom Seaver 3.00 8.00
DDC78 Bob Gibson 3.00 8.00
DDC79 Fausto Carmona 2.00 5.00
DDC80 Joe Mauer 4.00 10.00
DDC81 Jose Bautista 3.00 8.00
DDC82 Yunel Escobar 2.00 5.00
DDC83 Jeremy Hellickson 5.00 12.00
DDC84 Josh Beckett 2.00 5.00
DDC85 Hanley Ramirez 3.00 8.00
DDC86 Yadier Molina 6.00 15.00
DDC87 Corey Hart 2.00 5.00
DDC88 Hunter Pence 3.00 8.00
DDC89 Roger Maris 5.00 12.00
DDC90 Ichiro Suzuki 6.00 15.00
DDC91 Martin Prado 2.00 5.00
DDC92 Starlin Castro 3.00 8.00
DDC93 Kendry Morales 2.00 5.00
DDC94 Marlon Byrd 2.00 5.00
DDC95 Domonic Brown 4.00 10.00
DDC96 Dave Winfield 3.00 8.00
DDC97 Wade Boggs 3.00 8.00
DDC98 Heath Bell 2.00 5.00
DDC99 Dan Haren 2.00 5.00
DDC100 Albert Pujols 6.00 15.00
DDC101 Nelson Cruz 5.00 12.00
DDC102 Yovani Gallardo 2.00 5.00
DDC103 Howie Kendrick 2.00 5.00
DDC104 Desmond Jennings 3.00 8.00
DDC105 Troy Tulowitzki 5.00 12.00
DDC106 Gaby Sanchez 2.00 5.00
DDC107 Joakim Soria 2.00 5.00
DDC108 Clayton Kershaw 8.00 20.00
DDC109 Mike Schmidt 8.00 20.00
DDC110 Roy Halladay 3.00 8.00
DDC111 Jered Weaver 3.00 8.00
DDC112 Babe Ruth 12.00 30.00
DDC113 Wandy Rodriguez 2.00 5.00
DDC114 Torii Hunter 2.00 5.00
DDC115 Josh Johnson 3.00 8.00
DDC116 Justin Verlander 5.00 12.00
DDC117 Clay Buchholz 2.00 5.00
DDC118 Danny Valencia 3.00 8.00
DDC119 Kurt Suzuki 2.00 5.00
DDC120 David Price 4.00 10.00
DDC121 Daniel Hudson 2.00 5.00
DDC122 Neftali Feliz 2.00 5.00
DDC123 Michael Young 2.00 5.00
DDC124 Jose Reyes 3.00 8.00
DDC125 Robinson Cano 3.00 8.00
DDC126 Billy Wagner 2.00 5.00
DDC127 Miguel Montero 2.00 5.00
DDC128 Kevin Youkilis 2.00 5.00
DDC129 Austin Jackson 2.00 5.00
DDC130 Chase Utley 3.00 8.00
DDC131 Rickie Weeks 2.00 5.00
DDC132 Manny Ramirez 5.00 12.00
DDC133 Carlos Santana 5.00 12.00
DDC134 Aramis Ramirez 2.00 5.00
DDC135 Jason Heyward 4.00 10.00
DDC136 Chris Young 2.00 5.00
DDC137 Tyler Colvin 2.00 5.00
DDC138 Jon Jay 2.00 5.00
DDC139 Nick Swisher 3.00 8.00
DDC140 Mark Teixeira 3.00 8.00
DDC141 Jose Tabata 2.00 5.00
DDC142 Francisco Liriano 2.00 5.00
DDC143 Mike Stanton 5.00 12.00
DDC144 Grady Sizemore 3.00 8.00
DDC145 Justin Morneau 3.00 8.00
DDC146 Jon Lester 3.00 8.00
DDC147 Chris Carpenter 3.00 8.00
DDC148 Mark Reynolds 2.00 5.00
DDC149 Scott Rolen 3.00 8.00
DDC150 Carlos Gonzalez 3.00 8.00
DDC151 Derek Jeter 12.00 30.00
DDC152 Lou Gehrig 10.00 25.00
DDC153 Ryne Sandberg 10.00 25.00
DDC154 Jay Bruce 3.00 8.00
DDC155 Eric Hosmer 12.00 30.00

2011 Topps Diamond Die Cut Black

*BLACK: 1X TO 2.5X BASIC
ISSUED VIA ONLINE REDEMPTION
STATED PRINT RUN 60 SER.#'D SETS

2011 Topps Diamond Duos

COMPLETE SET (30) 6.00 15.00
STATED ODDS 1:4 HOBBY
BD R.Braun/I.Davis .40 1.00
BW Lance Berkman/Brett Wallace .40 1.00
BY Wade Boggs/Kevin Youkilis .40 1.00
CC T.Cobb/M.Cabrera 1.00 2.50
CS Steve Carlton/CC Sabathia .40 1.00
GT Carlos Gonzalez/Troy Tulowitzki .60 1.50
HF J.Heyward/F.Freeman 4.00 10.00
HG Josh Hamilton/Vladimir Guerrero .40 1.00
HH R.Howard/J.Heyward .50 1.25
HJ Rickey Henderson/Desmond Jennings.60 1.50
HM Tommy Hanson/Mike Minor .25 .60
JC D.Jeter/R.Cano 1.50 4.00
JJ Reggie Jackson/Adam Jones .40 1.00
KA Ian Kinsler/Elvis Andrus .40 1.00
KL C.Kershaw/M.Latos 1.00 2.50
KT Harmon Killebrew/Jim Thome .60 1.50
LJ B.Larkin/D.Jeter 1.50 4.00
LZ E.Longoria/R.Zimmerman .40 1.00
MH G.Maddux/J.Hellickson .75 2.00
MP J.Mauer/B.Posey .75 2.00
PC A.Pujols/M.Cabrera .75 2.00
PG David Price/Matt Garza .50 1.25
RS Ramirez/Stanton .60 1.50
SC T.Seaver/A.Chapman .75 2.00
TR Frank Thomas/Manny Ramirez .60 1.50
TU Hisanori Takahashi/Koji Uehara .25 .60
UR Chase Utley/Jimmy Rollins .40 1.00
US Upton/Stanton .60 1.50
VG Joey Votto/Adrian Gonzalez .60 1.50
HHO Rogers Hornsby/Matt Holliday .60 1.50

2011 Topps Diamond Duos Series 2

COMPLETE SET (30) 6.00 15.00
DD1 Roy Halladay/Roy Oswalt .40 1.00
DD2 Chase Utley/Robinson Cano .40 1.00
DD3 Cliff Lee/Zack Greinke .60 1.50
DD4 Adrian Gonzalez/Carl Crawford .50 1.25
DD5 D.Uggla/J.Heyward .50 1.25
DD6 R.Braun/C.Gonzalez .40 1.00
DD7 Frank Thomas/Adam Dunn .60 1.50
DD8 Zack Greinke/Yovani Gallardo .60 1.50
DD9 Adrian Beltre/Elvis Andrus .60 1.50
DD10 Adrian Gonzalez/Kevin Youkilis .50 1.25
DD11 Carl Crawford/Jacoby Ellsbury .50 1.25
DD12 Troy Tulowitzki/Hanley Ramirez .60 1.50
DD13 A.Chapman/C.Sale 2.00 5.00
DD14 Ryan Zimmerman/Jayson Werth .40 1.00
DD15 T.Lincecum/B.Wilson .60 1.50
DD16 Josh Hamilton/Joey Votto .60 1.50
DD17 B.Posey/N.Feliz .75 2.00
DD18 Roy Halladay/Felix Hernandez .40 1.00
DD19 M.Cabrera/V.Martinez .60 1.50
DD20 Kershaw/Bumgarner 1.00 2.50
DD21 David Price/Jon Lester .50 1.25
DD22 Troy Tulowitzki/Ubaldo Jimenez .60 1.50
DD23 Cliff Lee/CC Sabathia .40 1.00
DD24 A.McCutchen/P.Alvarez .60 1.50
DD25 Mark Teixeira/Adrian Gonzalez .50 1.25
DD26 A.Rodriguez/E.Longoria .75 2.00
DD27 Johnson/Verlander .60 1.50
DD28 A.Pujols/M.Holliday .75 2.00
DD29 H.Aaron/J.Heyward 1.25 3.00
DD30 S.Koufax/C.Kershaw 1.25 3.00

2011 Topps Diamond Duos Relics

STATED ODDS 1:12,500 HOBBY
STATED PRINT RUN 50 SER.#'d SETS
DDR1 D.Jeter/R.Cano 12.00 30.00
DDR2 J.Mauer/B.Posey 50.00 100.00
DDR3 A.Pujols/M.Cabrera 30.00 60.00
DDR4 R.Howard/J.Heyward 40.00 80.00
DDR5 J.Hamilton/V.Guerrero 20.00 50.00
DDR6 E.Longoria/R.Zimmerman 10.00 25.00
DDR7 C.Utley/J.Rollins 30.00 60.00
DDR8 J.Votto/A.Gonzalez 10.00 25.00
DDR9 H.Ramirez/M.Stanton 15.00 40.00
DDR10 B.Larkin/D.Jeter 50.00 100.00
DDR11 R.Jackson/A.Jones 30.00 60.00
DDR12 T.Cobb/M.Cabrera 30.00 60.00
DDR13 W.Boggs/K.Youkilis 30.00 60.00
DDR14 C.Kershaw/M.Latos 30.00 60.00
DDR15 J.Upton/M.Stanton 10.00 25.00

2011 Topps Diamond Duos Relics Series 2

STATED PRINT RUN 50 SER.#'d SETS
DDR1 C.Utley/R.Cano 10.00 25.00
DDR2 H.Aaron/J.Heyward 40.00 80.00
DDR3 M.Cabrera/V.Martinez 12.50 30.00
DDR5 R.Braun/C.Gonzalez 12.50 30.00
DDR6 J.Lester/K.Youkilis 20.00 50.00
DDR7 R.Alomar/R.Cano 30.00 60.00
DDR8 I.Kinsler/N.Cruz 10.00 25.00
DDR9 T.Lincecum/B.Posey 50.00 100.00
DDR10 J.Hamilton/J.Votto 10.00 25.00
DDR11 B.Posey/N.Feliz 20.00 50.00
DDR12 R.Halladay/F.Hernandez 12.50 30.00
DDR13 A.Rodriguez/E.Longoria 40.00 80.00
DDR14 J.Johnson/J.Verlander 10.00 25.00
DDR15 A.Pujols/M.Holliday 20.00 50.00

2011 Topps Diamond Giveaway

COMPLETE SET (30) 40.00 100.00
COMP.SER.1 SET (10) 12.50 30.00
COMP.SER.2 SET (10) 12.50 30.00
COMP.UPD.SET (10) 12.50 30.00
APPX.SER.1 ODDS 1:9 HOBBY
TDG1 Mickey Mantle 2.00 5.00
TDG2 Jackie Robinson 2.00 5.00
TDG3 Reggie Jackson 2.00 5.00
TDG4 Albert Pujols 2.00 5.00
TDG5 Derek Jeter 2.00 5.00
TDG6 Roy Halladay 2.00 5.00
TDG7 Derek Jeter 2.00 5.00
TDG8 Albert Pujols 2.00 5.00
TDG9 Ryan Howard 2.00 5.00
TDG10 Tim Lincecum 2.00 5.00
TDG11 Tony Gwynn 2.00 5.00
TDG12 Mike Schmidt 2.00 5.00
TDG13 Nolan Ryan 2.00 5.00
TDG14 Jason Heyward 2.00 5.00
TDG15 Troy Tulowitzki 2.00 5.00
TDG16 Buster Posey 2.00 5.00
TDG17 Ryan Braun 2.00 5.00
TDG18 Evan Longoria 2.00 5.00
TDG19 Joe Mauer 2.00 5.00
TDG20 Kevin Youkilis 2.00 5.00
TDG21 Mickey Mantle 2.00 5.00
TDG22 Sandy Koufax 2.00 5.00
TDG23 Cal Ripken Jr. 2.00 5.00
TDG24 Adrian Gonzalez 2.00 5.00
TDG25 Adrian Beltre 2.00 5.00
TDG26 Carl Crawford 2.00 5.00
TDG27 Victor Martinez 2.00 5.00
TDG28 Cliff Lee 2.00 5.00
TDG29 Jose Bautista 2.00 5.00
TDG30 Prince Fielder 2.00 5.00

2011 Topps Diamond Stars

COMPLETE SET (25) 10.00 25.00
DS1 Evan Longoria .40 1.00
DS2 Troy Tulowitzki .60 1.50
DS3 Joe Mauer .50 1.25
DS4 Adrian Gonzalez .50 1.25
DS5 Joey Votto .60 1.50
DS6 Buster Posey .75 2.00
DS7 Chase Utley .40 1.00
DS8 David Wright .50 1.25
DS9 Hanley Ramirez .40 1.00
DS10 Albert Pujols .75 2.00
DS11 Roy Halladay .40 1.00
DS12 Alex Rodriguez .75 2.00
DS13 Jason Heyward .50 1.25
DS14 Miguel Cabrera .60 1.50
DS15 Cliff Lee .40 1.00
DS16 Felix Hernandez .40 1.00
DS17 Matt Holliday .60 1.50
DS18 Robinson Cano .40 1.00
DS19 Josh Hamilton .40 1.00
DS20 Ichiro Suzuki .75 2.00
DS21 Carl Crawford .40 1.00
DS22 Ryan Howard .50 1.25
DS23 Josh Johnson .40 1.00
DS24 Ryan Braun .40 1.00
DS25 Carlos Gonzalez .40 1.00

2011 Topps Factory Set All Star Bonus

COMPLETE SET (5) 3.00 8.00
1 Albert Pujols 1.25 3.00
2 Ichiro Suzuki 1.25 3.00
3 Roy Halladay .60 1.50
4 Tim Lincecum .60 1.50
5 Adrian Gonzalez .75 2.00

2011 Topps Factory Set Bonus

*BONUS: 5X TO 12X BASIC
*BONUS RC: 3X TO 8X BASIC
STATED PRINT RUN 75 SER.#'d SETS
145 Freddie Freeman 60.00 150.00

2011 Topps Factory Set Mantle Chrome Gold Refractors

200 Mickey Mantle 1963 Topps 6.00 15.00
200 Mickey Mantle 1962 Topps 6.00 15.00
300 Mickey Mantle 1961 Topps 6.00 15.00

2011 Topps Factory Set Mantle World Series Medallion

1 Mickey Mantle 1953 6.00 15.00
2 Mickey Mantle 1956 6.00 15.00
3 Mickey Mantle 1961 6.00 15.00

2011 Topps Glove Manufactured Leather Nameplates

SER.1 ODDS 1:461 HOBBY
BLACK: .5X TO 1.2X BASIC
SER.1 BLACK ODDS 1:1815 HOBBY
UPD.BLACK ODDS 1:935 HOBBY
BLACK PRINT RUN 99 SER.#'d SETS
SER.1 NICKNAME ODDS 1:200,000 HOBBY
UPD.NICKNAME ODDS 1:87,500 HOBBY
NICKNAME PRINT RUN 1 SER.#'d SET
NO NICKNAME PRICING AVAILABLE
AD Andre Dawson S2 4.00 10.00
AD Andre Dawson UPD 4.00 10.00
AE Andre Ethier 4.00 10.00
AG Adrian Gonzalez 4.00 10.00
AM Andrew McCutchen 4.00 10.00
AP Albert Pujols 8.00 20.00
AR Alex Rodriguez UPD 5.00 12.00
AR Alex Rodriguez 5.00 12.00
AW Adam Wainwright 6.00 15.00
BB Brandon Belt UPD 4.00 10.00
BB Billy Butler 4.00 10.00
BF Bob Feller S2 6.00 15.00
BG Bob Gibson S2 8.00 20.00
BM Bill Mazeroski S2 5.00 12.00
BP Buster Posey 10.00 25.00
BR Babe Ruth S2 10.00 25.00
BR Babe Ruth UPD 10.00 25.00
BW Brian Wilson UPD 4.00 10.00
BZ Ben Zobrist UPD 4.00 10.00
CC Carl Crawford 4.00 10.00
CF Carlton Fisk UPD 4.00 10.00
CF Carlton Fisk S2 4.00 10.00
CG Carlos Gonzalez 5.00 12.00
CH Cole Hamels UPD 4.00 10.00
CK Clayton Kershaw 4.00 10.00
CR Cal Ripken Jr. S2 5.00 12.00
CU Chase Utley 6.00 15.00
CY Carl Yastrzemski S2 6.00 15.00
DD Danny Duffy UPD 4.00 10.00
DJ Derek Jeter 10.00 25.00
DM Don Mattingly S2 6.00 15.00
DP David Price 4.00 10.00
DS Duke Snider UPD 4.00 10.00
DW David Wright 8.00 20.00
EH Eric Hosmer UPD 6.00 15.00
EL Evan Longoria 6.00 15.00
EM Eddie Murray S2 8.00 20.00
FH Felix Hernandez 4.00 10.00
FJ Fergie Jenkins S2 4.00 10.00
FJ Fergie Jenkins UPD 4.00 10.00
FR Frank Robinson UPD 4.00 10.00
FR Frank Robinson S2 4.00 10.00
FT Frank Thomas S2 4.00 10.00
FT Frank Thomas UPD 4.00 10.00
GM Greg Maddux S2 6.00 15.00
HA Hank Aaron S2 4.00 10.00
HA Hank Aaron UPD 4.00 10.00
HG Hank Greenberg S2 5.00 12.00
HK Harmon Killebrew S2 8.00 20.00
HP Hunter Pence 4.00 10.00
HR Hanley Ramirez 4.00 10.00
IS Ichiro Suzuki 8.00 20.00
JB Johnny Bench S2 8.00 20.00
JB Jose Bautista UPD 5.00 12.00
JD Joe DiMaggio UPD 6.00 15.00
JF Jimmie Foxx UPD 4.00 10.00
JF Jimmie Foxx S2 4.00 10.00
JH Jim Hunter S2 4.00 10.00
JH Josh Hamilton 6.00 15.00
JJ Josh Johnson 4.00 10.00
JL Jon Lester 5.00 12.00
JM Johnny Mize S2 4.00 10.00
JM Johnny Mize UPD 4.00 10.00
JM Joe Mauer 8.00 20.00
JP Jim Palmer S2 6.00 15.00
JS James Shields UPD 4.00 10.00
JT Julio Teheran UPD 4.00 10.00
JU Justin Upton 4.00 10.00
JV Joey Votto 8.00 20.00
JW Jayson Werth UPD 4.00 10.00
KY Kevin Youkilis UPD 4.00 10.00
LA Luis Aparicio UPD 4.00 10.00
LA Luis Aparicio S2 4.00 10.00
LB Lance Berkman UPD 4.00 10.00
LG Lou Gehrig S2 8.00 20.00
MC Miguel Cabrera UPD 4.00 10.00
MC Miguel Cabrera 4.00 10.00
MH Matt Holliday 6.00 15.00
MI Monte Irvin S2 5.00 12.00
MK Matt Kemp UPD 4.00 10.00
ML Mat Latos 4.00 10.00
MM Mickey Mantle S2 12.50 30.00
MO Mel Ott S2 5.00 12.00
MP Michael Pineda UPD 5.00 12.00
MP Martin Prado 4.00 10.00
MS Max Scherzer UPD 4.00 10.00
MS Mike Schmidt S2 8.00 20.00
MS Mike Stanton 5.00 12.00
MT Mark Teixeira 5.00 12.00
NC Nelson Cruz 6.00 15.00
NM Nick Markakis 6.00 15.00
NR Nolan Ryan S2 8.00 20.00
NR Nolan Ryan UPD 8.00 20.00
OC Orlando Cepeda S2 5.00 12.00
OS Ozzie Smith S2 4.00 10.00
OS Ozzie Smith UPD 4.00 10.00
PM Paul Molitor UPD 4.00 10.00
PN Phil Niekro S2 6.00 15.00
PR Phil Rizzuto S2 6.00 15.00
RA Richie Ashburn S2 5.00 12.00
RA Roberto Alomar UPD 4.00 10.00
RB Ryan Braun 5.00 12.00
RC Roy Campanella S2 5.00 12.00
RC Robinson Cano 6.00 15.00
RH Rogers Hornsby S2 4.00 10.00
RH Rogers Hornsby UPD 4.00 10.00
RH Ryan Howard 8.00 20.00
RJ Reggie Jackson UPD 4.00 10.00
RJ Reggie Jackson S2 4.00 10.00
RS Ryne Sandberg S2 6.00 15.00
RZ Ryan Zimmerman 4.00 10.00
SC Starlin Castro 6.00 15.00
SK Sandy Koufax S2 10.00 25.00
SM Stan Musial S2 10.00 25.00
SS Stephen Strasburg 10.00 25.00
TC Trevor Cahill 4.00 10.00
TG Tony Gwynn S2 5.00 12.00
TH Travis Hafner UPD 4.00 10.00
TH Torii Hunter 4.00 10.00
TL Tim Lincecum 8.00 20.00
TM Thurman Munson S2 6.00 15.00
TN Tsuyoshi Nishioka UPD 5.00 12.00
TS Tom Seaver UPD 5.00 12.00
TS Tom Seaver S2 5.00 12.00
UJ Ubaldo Jimenez 4.00 10.00
VM Victor Martinez 4.00 10.00
WF Whitey Ford S2 5.00 12.00
WM Willie McCovey S2 4.00 10.00
WM Willie McCovey UPD 4.00 10.00
WS Willie Stargell S2 5.00 12.00
ZB Zach Britton UPD 4.00 10.00
ADU Adam Dunn UPD 4.00 10.00
ARO Alex Rodriguez UPD 5.00 12.00
BRO Brooks Robinson S2 8.00 20.00
CCS CC Sabathia 5.00 12.00
DMU Dale Murphy S2 6.00 15.00
JAS Jerry Sands UPD 4.00 10.00
JHE Jason Heyward 10.00 25.00
JMA Juan Marichal S2 6.00 15.00
JMO Joe Morgan UPD 4.00 10.00
JVE Justin Verlander 5.00 12.00
JWE Jered Weaver UPD 4.00 10.00
NOR Nolan Ryan UPD 8.00 20.00
NRY Nolan Ryan UPD 8.00 20.00
PWR Pee Wee Reese UPD 4.00 10.00
RHA Roy Halladay 6.00 15.00
RHE Rickey Henderson UPD 4.00 10.00
RHE Rickey Henderson S2 4.00 10.00
RJA Reggie Jackson UPD 4.00 10.00
SSC Shin-Soo Choo 6.00 15.00

2011 Topps History of Topps

COMPLETE SET (10) 3.00 8.00
STATED ODDS 1:18 HOBBY

2011 Topps Kimball Champions

COMPLETE SET (150) 40.00 100.00
COMP.SER.1 SET (50) 12.50 30.00
COMP.SER.2 SET (50) 12.50 30.00
COMP.UPD SET (50) 12.50 30.00
SER.1 ODDS 1:4 HOBBY
UPD.ODDS 1:4 HOBBY
KC1 Ubaldo Jimenez .25 .60
KC2 Derek Jeter 1.50 4.00
KC3 Carlos Santana .60 1.50
KC4 Johan Santana .40 1.00
KC5 Carlos Gonzalez .40 1.00
KC6 Clay Buchholz .25 .60
KC7 Mickey Mantle 2.00 5.00
KC8 Ryan Braun .40 1.00
KC9 Chase Utley .40 1.00
KC10 Ichiro Suzuki .75 2.00
KC11 Starlin Castro .40 1.00
KC12 Torii Hunter .25 .60
KC13 Ty Cobb 1.00 2.50
KC14 Clayton Kershaw 1.00 2.50
KC15 David Price .50 1.25
KC16 Aroldis Chapman .75 2.00
KC17 Chris Carpenter .40 1.00
KC18 Andrew McCutchen .60 1.50
KC19 Brandon Morrow .25 .60
KC20 Roy Halladay .40 1.00
KC21 Shin-Soo Choo .40 1.00
KC22 Victor Martinez .40 1.00
KC23 Mat Latos .40 1.00
KC24 Josh Johnson .40 1.00
KC25 Vladimir Guerrero .40 1.00
KC26 Justin Morneau .40 1.00
KC27 Nick Markakis .50 1.25
KC28 Mike Stanton .60 1.50
KC29 Jered Weaver .40 1.00
KC30 David Wright .50 1.25
KC31 Nelson Cruz .60 1.50
KC32 Alex Rios .25 .60
KC33 Martin Prado .25 .60
KC34 Joey Votto .60 1.50
KC35 Jon Lester .40 1.00
KC36 Hanley Ramirez .40 1.00
KC37 Stephen Strasburg .60 1.50
KC38 Roy Oswalt .40 1.00
KC39 CC Sabathia .40 1.00
KC40 Albert Pujols .75 2.00
KC41 Pablo Sandoval .40 1.00
KC42 Mariano Rivera .75 2.00
KC43 Pee Wee Reese .40 1.00
KC44 Hunter Pence .40 1.00
KC45 David Ortiz .60 1.50
KC46 Mel Ott .60 1.50
KC47 Brett Anderson .25 .60
KC48 Justin Upton .40 1.00
KC49 Jose Bautista .40 1.00
KC50 Miguel Cabrera .60 1.50
KC51 Hank Aaron 1.25 3.00
KC52 Sandy Koufax 1.25 3.00
KC53 Carlton Fisk .40 1.00
KC54 Nolan Ryan 2.00 5.00
KC55 Stan Musial 1.00 2.50
KC56 Steve Carlton .40 1.00
KC57 Tom Seaver .40 1.00
KC58 Mel Ott .60 1.50
KC59 Tony Gwynn .60 1.50
KC60 Johnny Bench .60 1.50
KC61 Greg Maddux .75 2.00
KC62 Luis Aparicio .40 1.00
KC63 Juan Marichal .40 1.00
KC64 Jackie Robinson .60 1.50
KC65 Bob Gibson .40 1.00
KC66 Yogi Berra .60 1.50
KC67 Pee Wee Reese .40 1.00
KC68 Reggie Jackson .40 1.00
KC69 Robin Roberts .40 1.00
KC70 Roy Campanella .60 1.50
KC71 Brooks Robinson .40 1.00
KC72 Ernie Banks .60 1.50
KC73 Phil Rizzuto .40 1.00
KC74 Eddie Murray .40 1.00
KC75 Bob Feller .40 1.00
KC76 Lou Brock .40 1.00
KC77 Frank Robinson .40 1.00
KC78 Eddie Mathews .60 1.50
KC79 Barry Larkin .40 1.00
KC80 Roger Maris .60 1.50
KC81 Craig Biggio .40 1.00
KC82 Mike Schmidt 1.00 2.50
KC83 Don Mattingly 1.25 3.00
KC84 Ryne Sandberg 1.25 3.00
KC85 Willie McCovey .40 1.00
KC86 Whitey Ford .40 1.00
KC87 Andre Dawson .40 1.00
KC88 Jim Palmer .40 1.00
KC89 Duke Snider .40 1.00
KC90 Hank Greenberg .60 1.50
KC91 Dale Murphy .60 1.50
KC92 Frank Thomas .60 1.50
KC93 Wade Boggs .40 1.00
KC94 Carl Yastrzemski 1.00 2.50
KC95 Lou Gehrig 1.25 3.00
KC96 Cal Ripken Jr. 2.00 5.00
KC97 Paul Molitor .60 1.50
KC98 Gary Carter .40 1.00
KC99 Ty Cobb 1.00 2.50
KC100 Babe Ruth 1.50 4.00
KC101 Babe Ruth 1.50 4.00
KC102 Willie McCovey .40 1.00
KC103 Zach Britton .60 1.50
KC104 Jimmie Foxx .60 1.50
KC105 Honus Wagner .60 1.50
KC106 Gary Carter .40 1.00
KC107 Dan Uggla .25 .60
KC108 Lance Berkman .40 1.00
KC109 Trevor Cahill .25 .60
KC110 Hank Aaron 1.25 3.00
KC111 Tris Speaker .40 1.00
KC112 Cole Hamels .50 1.25
KC113 Alex Rodriguez .75 2.00
KC114 Felix Hernandez .40 1.00
KC115 Ty Cobb 1.00 2.50
KC116 Johnny Mize .40 1.00
KC117 Curtis Granderson .50 1.25
KC118 Cliff Lee .40 1.00
KC119 Matt Holliday .60 1.50
KC120 Frank Robinson .40 1.00
KC121 Luis Aparicio .40 1.00
KC122 Christy Mathewson .60 1.50
KC123 Bert Blyleven .40 1.00
KC124 Frank Thomas .60 1.50
KC125 Nolan Ryan 2.00 5.00
KC126 Danny Duffy .40 1.00
KC127 Justin Verlander .60 1.50
KC128 Carlton Fisk .40 1.00
KC129 George Sisler .40 1.00
KC130 Adrian Gonzalez .50 1.25
KC131 Adam Dunn .40 1.00
KC132 Tom Seaver .40 1.00
KC133 Ozzie Smith .75 2.00
KC134 Miguel Cabrera .60 1.50
KC135 Carl Crawford .40 1.00
KC136 Paul Molitor .60 1.50
KC137 Joe Morgan .40 1.00
KC138 Rogers Hornsby .40 1.00
KC139 James Shields .25 .60
KC140 Michael Pineda .60 1.50
KC141 Andre Dawson .40 1.00
KC142 Ryan Howard .50 1.25
KC143 Kyle Drabek .40 1.00
KC144 Reggie Jackson .40 1.00
KC145 Eric Hosmer 1.50 4.00
KC146 Vladimir Guerrero .40 1.00
KC147 Mark Teixeira .40 1.00
KC148 Jose Reyes .40 1.00
KC149 Cy Young .60 1.50
KC150 Joe DiMaggio 1.25 3.00

2011 Topps Lost Cards

COMPLETE SET (10) 6.00 15.00
STATED ODDS 1:12 HOBBY
*ORIGINAL BACK: .6X TO 1.5X BASIC
ORIGINAL ODDS 1:108 HOBBY
LC1 Stan Musial 53T 1.25 3.00
LC2 Duke Snider 53T .50 1.25
LC3 Mickey Mantle 54T 2.50 6.00
LC4 Roy Campanella 54T .75 2.00
LC5 Stan Musial 55T 1.25 3.00
LC6 Whitey Ford 55T .50 1.25
LC7 Bob Feller 55T .50 1.25
LC8 Mickey Mantle 55T 2.50 6.00
LC9 Stan Musial 56T 1.25 3.00
LC10 Stan Musial 57T 1.25 3.00

2011 Topps Mickey Mantle Reprint Relics

SER.1 ODDS 1:115,000 HOBBY
UPD.ODDS 1:52,500 HOBBY
PRINT RUNS B/WN 64-66 COPIES PER
MMRR2 Mickey Mantle Bat/65 30.00 60.00
MMRR1 Mickey Mantle Jsy/64 30.00 60.00
MMRR3 Mickey Mantle Jsy/66 30.00 60.00

2011 Topps Prime 9 Player of the Week Refractors

COMPLETE SET (9) 10.00 25.00
PNR1 Johnny Bench 1.00 2.50
PNR2 Albert Pujols 1.25 3.00
PNR3 Jackie Robinson 1.00 2.50
PNR4 Derek Jeter 2.50 6.00
PNR5 Mike Schmidt 1.50 4.00
PNR6 Hank Aaron 2.00 5.00
PNR7 Mickey Mantle 3.00 8.00
PNR8 Ichiro Suzuki 1.25 3.00
PNR9 Sandy Koufax 2.00 5.00

2011 Topps Silk Collection

SER.1 ODDS 1:396 HOBBY
UPD.ODDS 1:221 HOBBY
STATED PRINT RUN 50 SER.#'d SETS
1 Ryan Kalish 6.00 15.00
2 Jose Bautista 6.00 15.00
3 Carlos Gonzalez 6.00 15.00
4 Justin Upton 6.00 15.00
5 Chipper Jones 10.00 25.00
6 Ubaldo Jimenez 4.00 10.00
7 Brett Wallace 4.00 10.00
8 Roy Oswalt 6.00 15.00
9 Brennan Boesch 6.00 15.00
10 Albert Pujols 12.00 30.00
11 Jaime Garcia 6.00 15.00
12 Kevin Kouzmanoff 4.00 10.00
13 Brett Anderson 4.00 10.00
14 Ian Desmond 4.00 10.00
15 Adam Dunn 6.00 15.00
16 David Wright 8.00 20.00
17 Andrew Bailey 4.00 10.00
18 Torii Hunter 4.00 10.00
19 Max Scherzer 10.00 25.00
20 Carl Crawford 6.00 15.00
21 Michael Young 4.00 10.00
22 Chris Carpenter 6.00 15.00
23 Chase Utley 6.00 15.00
24 Clay Buchholz 4.00 10.00
25 Stephen Drew 4.00 10.00
26 Alex Gordon 6.00 15.00
27 Shin-Soo Choo 6.00 15.00
28 Miguel Cabrera 10.00 25.00
29 Andrew McCutchen 10.00 25.00
30 Victor Martinez 6.00 15.00
31 Jered Weaver 6.00 15.00
32 Clayton Kershaw 10.00 25.00
33 Ichiro Suzuki 12.00 30.00
34 Mike Stanton 10.00 25.00
35 Vladimir Guerrero 6.00 15.00
36 Cliff Lee 6.00 15.00
37 Miguel Montero 4.00 10.00
38 Howie Kendrick 4.00 10.00
39 Jon Lester 6.00 15.00
40 Nick Swisher 6.00 15.00
41 Magglio Ordonez 6.00 15.00
42 Carlos Santana 10.00 25.00
43 Ryan Braun 6.00 15.00
44 Carlos Pena 6.00 15.00
45 Tim Hudson 6.00 15.00
46 Alex Rodriguez 12.00 30.00
47 Aaron Hill 4.00 10.00
48 Chris Young 4.00 10.00
49 Johan Santana 6.00 15.00
50 James Shields 4.00 10.00
51 C.J. Wilson 4.00 10.00
52 Mariano Rivera 15.00 40.00
53 Marlon Byrd 4.00 10.00
54 Martin Prado 4.00 10.00
55 Joey Votto 10.00 25.00
56 Paul Konerko 6.00 15.00
57 Mark Buehrle 6.00 15.00
58 Fausto Carmona 4.00 10.00
59 Nelson Cruz 10.00 25.00
60 Wandy Rodriguez 4.00 10.00
61 Derrek Lee 4.00 10.00
62 Ricky Romero 4.00 10.00
63 Carlos Marmol 6.00 15.00
64 Johnny Cueto 6.00 15.00
65 Starlin Castro 6.00 15.00
66 Zack Greinke 10.00 25.00
67 Scott Rolen 6.00 15.00
68 Nick Markakis 8.00 20.00
69 Jimmy Rollins 6.00 15.00
70 John Danks 4.00 10.00
71 Ike Davis 4.00 10.00
72 Brandon Morrow 4.00 10.00
73 Derek Jeter 25.00 60.00
74 Peter Bourjos 6.00 15.00
75 Roy Halladay 6.00 15.00
76 Alex Rios 4.00 10.00
77 Hanley Ramirez 6.00 15.00
78 Jon Jay 4.00 10.00
79 Justin Morneau 6.00 15.00
80 Aramis Ramirez 4.00 10.00
81 Todd Helton 6.00 15.00
82 Andre Ethier 6.00 15.00
83 Stephen Strasburg 10.00 25.00
84 Adrian Beltre 10.00 25.00
85 Brian Wilson 10.00 25.00
86 Kurt Suzuki 4.00 10.00
87 David Price 8.00 20.00
88 Jason Kubel 4.00 10.00
89 Hunter Pence 6.00 15.00
90 Alexei Ramirez 6.00 15.00
91 Billy Wagner 4.00 10.00
92 Michael Cuddyer 4.00 10.00
93 Jeremy Hellickson 10.00 25.00
94 CC Sabathia 6.00 15.00
95 Josh Johnson 6.00 15.00
96 Brian Matusz 4.00 10.00
97 Mat Latos 6.00 15.00
98 Rickie Weeks 4.00 10.00
99 Heath Bell 4.00 10.00
100 David Ortiz 10.00 25.00
101 Trevor Cahill 4.00 10.00
102 Felix Hernandez 6.00 15.00
103 Shane Victorino 6.00 15.00
104 Michael Bourn 4.00 10.00
105 Josh Hamilton 6.00 15.00
106 Corey Hart 4.00 10.00
107 John Lackey 6.00 15.00
108 Kevin Youkilis 4.00 10.00
109 Daric Barton 4.00 10.00
110 Danny Valencia 6.00 15.00
111 Edwin Jackson 4.00 10.00
112 Jason Bartlett 4.00 10.00
113 Matt Cain 6.00 15.00
114 Rick Porcello 6.00 15.00
115 Huston Street 4.00 10.00
116 Dan Uggla 4.00 10.00
117 Ryan Ludwick 4.00 10.00
118 Elvis Andrus 6.00 15.00
119 Ivan Rodriguez 6.00 15.00
120 Casey McGehee 4.00 10.00
121 Adam Wainwright 6.00 15.00
122 Dustin Pedroia 10.00 25.00
123 Travis Snider 4.00 10.00
124 Jason Heyward 8.00 20.00
125 Phil Hughes 4.00 10.00
126 Dan Haren 4.00 10.00
127 J.P. Arencibia 4.00 10.00
128 Matt Kemp 8.00 20.00
129 Denard Span 4.00 10.00
130 Drew Storen 4.00 10.00
131 Jonathan Broxton 4.00 10.00
132 Adrian Gonzalez 8.00 20.00
133 Adam Jones 6.00 15.00
134 Joba Chamberlain 4.00 10.00
135 Carlos Beltran 6.00 15.00
136 Evan Longoria 6.00 15.00
137 Adam Lind 6.00 15.00
138 Joe Mauer 8.00 20.00
139 Brian McCann 6.00 15.00
140 Francisco Liriano 4.00 10.00
141 Chris Tillman 4.00 10.00
142 Troy Tulowitzki 10.00 25.00
143 Grady Sizemore 6.00 15.00
144 Jose Tabata 4.00 10.00
145 Drew Stubbs 4.00 10.00
146 Austin Jackson 4.00 10.00
147 Franklin Gutierrez 4.00 10.00
148 Kendrys Morales 4.00 10.00
149 Carlos Quentin 4.00 10.00
150 Wade Davis 4.00 10.00
151 Jose Valverde 4.00 10.00
152 Logan Morrison 4.00 10.00
153 Delmon Young 6.00 15.00
154 Alfonso Soriano 6.00 15.00
155 Colby Rasmus 6.00 15.00
156 Mike Minor 4.00 10.00
157 Yovani Gallardo 4.00 10.00
158 Chris Iannetta 4.00 10.00
159 Cody Ross 4.00 10.00
160 Jorge Posada 6.00 15.00
161 Dallas Braden 4.00 10.00
162 Dexter Fowler 6.00 15.00
163 Shaun Marcum 4.00 10.00
164 Kyle Blanks 4.00 10.00
165 B.J. Upton 6.00 15.00
166 Matt Holliday 10.00 25.00
167 Joakim Soria 4.00 10.00
168 Jake Arrieta 8.00 20.00
169 Ryan Doumit 4.00 10.00
170 Curtis Granderson 8.00 20.00
171 Madison Bumgarner 8.00 20.00
172 Buster Posey 12.00 30.00
173 Kelly Johnson 4.00 10.00
174 Chad Billingsley 6.00 15.00
175 Cole Hamels 8.00 20.00
176 Justin Verlander 10.00 25.00
177 Domonic Brown 8.00 20.00
178 Billy Butler 4.00 10.00
179 Jacoby Ellsbury 8.00 20.00
180 Will Venable 4.00 10.00
181 Ian Kinsler 6.00 15.00
182 Tommy Hanson 4.00 10.00
183 Kosuke Fukudome 6.00 15.00
184 Ryan Zimmerman 6.00 15.00
185 Geovany Soto 6.00 15.00
186 Matt Garza 4.00 10.00
187 Prince Fielder 6.00 15.00
188 Mark Reynolds 4.00 10.00
189 Mark Teixeira 6.00 15.00
190 Carlos Lee 4.00 10.00
191 Brian Roberts 4.00 10.00
192 Kila Ka'aihue 4.00 10.00
193 Brett Myers 4.00 10.00
194 Vernon Wells 4.00 10.00
195 Jose Reyes 6.00 15.00
196 Brandon Phillips 4.00 10.00
197 Josh Beckett 4.00 10.00
198 Gordon Beckham 4.00 10.00
199 Tim Lincecum 6.00 15.00
200 Jeff Niemann 4.00 10.00
201 Adrian Gonzalez 8.00 20.00
202 Josh Willingham 6.00 15.00
203 Jose Iglesias 6.00 15.00
204 Mike Napoli 4.00 10.00
205 Conor Jackson 4.00 10.00
206 Tim Stauffer 4.00 10.00
207 Carlos Pena 6.00 15.00
208 Rick Ankiel 4.00 10.00
209 Russell Martin 4.00 10.00
210 Zach Britton 10.00 25.00
211 Brian Fuentes 4.00 10.00
212 Angel Sanchez 4.00 10.00
213 Andruw Jones 4.00 10.00
214 Jerry Sands 10.00 25.00
215 Brandon Belt 10.00 25.00
216 Jonathan Herrera 4.00 10.00
217 Yuniesky Betancourt 4.00 10.00
218 Mitchell Boggs 4.00 10.00
219 Andy Dirks 10.00 25.00
220 Zack Greinke 10.00 25.00
221 Jeff Francis 4.00 10.00
222 Nolan Reimold 4.00 10.00
223 Freddy Garcia 4.00 10.00
224 Aaron Harang 4.00 10.00
225 Kerry Wood 4.00 10.00
226 Orlando Cabrera 4.00 10.00
227 Lyle Overbay 4.00 10.00
228 Scott Downs 4.00 10.00
229 Sean Burnett 4.00 10.00
230 Victor Martinez 6.00 15.00
231 Logan Forsythe 4.00 10.00
232 Brandon McCarthy 4.00 10.00
233 Joe Mather 4.00 10.00
234 Edgar Renteria 4.00 10.00
235 Scott Sizemore 4.00 10.00
236 Jeff Francoeur 6.00 15.00
237 Kyle Farnsworth 4.00 10.00
238 Jon Rauch 4.00 10.00
239 Brad Penny 4.00 10.00
240 Fernando Salas 6.00 15.00
241 Doug Davis 4.00 10.00
242 Pete Kozma 10.00 25.00
243 Alfredo Amezaga 4.00 10.00
244 Mark Melancon 4.00 10.00
245 Rafael Soriano 4.00 10.00
246 Alex White 4.00 10.00
247 Bartolo Colon 4.00 10.00
248 Trystan Magnuson 4.00 10.00

249 Omar Infante 4.00 10.00
250 Carl Crawford 6.00 15.00
251 Matt Guerrier 4.00 10.00
252 Alexi Amarista 4.00 10.00
253 Humberto Quintero 4.00 10.00
254 Reed Johnson 4.00 10.00
255 Darren Oliver 4.00 10.00
256 Alex Cobb 4.00 10.00
257 Josh Collmenter 4.00 10.00
258 Michael Pineda 10.00 25.00
259 Jon Garland 4.00 10.00
260 Lance Berkman 6.00 15.00
261 Eduardo Sanchez 6.00 15.00
262 John Mayberry 4.00 10.00
263 Brendan Ryan 4.00 10.00
264 Bruce Chen 4.00 10.00
265 Alexi Ogando 10.00 25.00
266 Brad Ziegler 4.00 10.00
267 Jason Giambi 4.00 10.00
268 Charlie Furbush 4.00 10.00
269 Julio Teheran 6.00 15.00
270 Vladimir Guerrero 6.00 15.00
271 Xavier Nady 4.00 10.00
272 Kevin Gregg 4.00 10.00
273 Jason Bourgeois 4.00 10.00
274 Derrek Lee 4.00 10.00
275 Adrian Beltre 10.00 25.00
276 Daniel Moskos 4.00 10.00
277 Carlos Peguero 6.00 15.00
278 Tyler Chatwood 4.00 10.00
279 Orlando Hudson 4.00 10.00
280 Jayson Werth 6.00 15.00
281 Philip Humber 4.00 10.00
282 Brandon League 4.00 10.00
283 J.P. Howell 4.00 10.00
284 Michael Dunn 4.00 10.00
285 Miguel Tejada 6.00 15.00
286 Jamey Carroll 4.00 10.00
287 Arthur Rhodes 4.00 10.00
288 Bill Hall 4.00 10.00
289 David DeJesus 4.00 10.00
290 Adam Dunn 6.00 15.00
291 Charlie Morton 10.00 25.00
292 J.J. Hardy 4.00 10.00
293 Kevin Correia 4.00 10.00
294 Alcides Escobar 6.00 15.00
295 Danny Duffy 6.00 15.00
296 Justin Turner 10.00 25.00
297 John Buck 4.00 10.00
298 Sergio Santos 4.00 10.00
299 Todd Frazier 10.00 25.00
300 Cliff Lee 6.00 15.00

2011 Topps Target Hanger Pack Exlcusives

ONE PER TARGET HANGER PACK
THP1 Albert Pujols 1.50 4.00
THP2 Derek Jeter 3.00 8.00
THP3 Mat Latos .75 2.00
THP4 Hanley Ramirez .75 2.00
THP5 Miguel Cabrera 1.25 3.00
THP6 Aroldis Chapman 1.50 4.00
THP7 Chase Utley .75 2.00
THP8 Ryan Braun .75 2.00
THP9 David Price 1.00 2.50
THP10 Joey Votto 1.25 3.00
THP11 David Wright 1.00 2.50
THP12 Carlos Gonzalez .75 2.00
THP13 David Ortiz 1.25 3.00
THP14 Andre Ethier .75 2.00
THP15 Roy Halladay .75 2.00
THP16 Cliff Lee .75 2.00
THP17 Dan Uggla .50 1.25
THP18 Mark Teixeira .75 2.00
THP19 Felix Hernandez .75 2.00
THP20 Buster Posey 1.50 4.00
THP21 Ryan Zimmerman .75 2.00
THP22 Ian Kinsler .75 2.00
THP23 Mike Stanton 1.25 3.00
THP24 Troy Tulowitzki 1.25 3.00
THP25 Zack Greinke 1.25 3.00
THP26 Pedro Alvarez 1.00 2.50
THP27 Jon Lester .75 2.00
THP28 Justin Upton .75 2.00
THP29 Clayton Kershaw 2.00 5.00
THP30 Carl Crawford .75 2.00

2011 Topps Target Red Diamond

COMPLETE SET (30) 40.00 80.00
RANDOM INSERTS IN TARGET PACKS
RDT1 Babe Ruth 3.00 8.00
RDT2 Derek Jeter 3.00 8.00
RDT3 Ty Cobb 2.00 5.00
RDT4 Josh Hamilton .75 2.00
RDT5 Albert Pujols 1.50 4.00
RDT6 Jason Heyward 1.00 2.50
RDT7 Mickey Mantle 4.00 10.00
RDT8 Ryan Braun .75 2.00
RDT9 Honus Wagner 1.25 3.00
RDT10 Jackie Robinson 1.25 3.00
RDT11 Roy Halladay .75 2.00
RDT12 Carlos Gonzalez .75 2.00
RDT13 Ichiro Suzuki 1.50 4.00
RDT14 Roy Campanella 1.25 3.00
RDT15 Miguel Cabrera 1.25 3.00
RDT16 Adrian Gonzalez 1.00 2.50
RDT17 CC Sabathia .75 2.00
RDT18 Ryan Howard 1.00 2.50
RDT19 Adrian Beltre 1.25 3.00
RDT20 Sandy Koufax 2.50 6.00
RDT21 Evan Longoria .75 2.00
RDT22 Robinson Cano .75 2.00
RDT23 Adam Dunn .75 2.00
RDT24 Joe Mauer 1.00 2.50
RDT25 Tim Lincecum .75 2.00
RDT26 Victor Martinez .75 2.00
RDT27 Ubaldo Jimenez .50 1.25
RDT28 Matt Holliday 1.25 3.00
RDT29 Josh Johnson .75 2.00
RDT30 Hank Aaron 2.50 6.00

2011 Topps Topps Town

COMPLETE SET (50) 6.00 15.00
STATED ODDS 1:1 HOBBY
TT1 Miguel Cabrera .50 1.25
TT2 Dan Haren .20 .50
TT3 Brett Wallace .20 .50
TT4 Brett Anderson .20 .50
TT5 Roy Halladay .30 .75
TT6 Vernon Wells .20 .50
TT7 Joe Mauer .40 1.00
TT8 Jose Reyes .30 .75
TT9 Adam Jones .30 .75
TT10 Josh Hamilton .30 .75
TT11 Chris Young .20 .50
TT12 Mat Latos .30 .75
TT13 Chase Utley .30 .75
TT14 Shin-Soo Choo .30 .75
TT15 David Wright .40 1.00
TT16 Nick Markakis .40 1.00
TT17 Aroldis Chapman .75 2.00
TT18 Ryan Zimmerman .30 .75
TT19 Andrew McCutchen .50 1.25
TT20 Ichiro Suzuki .60 1.50
TT21 Starlin Castro .30 .75
TT22 Jason Heyward .40 1.00
TT23 Evan Longoria .30 .75
TT24 Josh Johnson .30 .75
TT25 Ryan Howard .40 1.00
TT26 Matt Garza .20 .50
TT27 Andre Ethier .30 .75
TT28 David Ortiz .50 1.25
TT29 Carlos Gonzalez .30 .75
TT30 Ryan Braun .30 .75
TT31 Manny Ramirez .50 1.25
TT32 Mike Stanton .50 1.25
TT33 Victor Martinez .30 .75
TT34 Felix Hernandez .30 .75
TT35 David Price .40 1.00
TT36 Robinson Cano .30 .75
TT37 Billy Butler .20 .50
TT38 Justin Verlander .50 1.25
TT39 Adrian Gonzalez .40 1.00
TT40 Buster Posey .60 1.50
TT41 Carlos Santana .50 1.25
TT42 Kevin Youkilis .20 .50
TT43 Vladimir Guerrero .30 .75
TT44 Ubaldo Jimenez .20 .50
TT45 Hanley Ramirez .30 .75
TT46 Joey Votto .50 1.25
TT47 Dustin Pedroia .50 1.25
TT48 Troy Tulowitzki .50 1.25
TT49 CC Sabathia .30 .75
TT50 Albert Pujols .60 1.50

2011 Topps Topps Town Series 2

COMPLETE SET (50) 6.00 15.00
TT1 Tim Lincecum .30 .75
TT2 Mark Reynolds .20 .50
TT3 Cliff Lee .30 .75
TT4 Logan Morrison .20 .50
TT5 Grady Sizemore .30 .75
TT6 Todd Helton .30 .75
TT7 Adrian Gonzalez .40 1.00
TT8 Ryan Ludwick .20 .50
TT9 Dan Uggla .20 .50
TT10 Justin Upton .30 .75
TT11 Kendrys Morales .20 .50
TT12 Justin Morneau .30 .75
TT13 Zack Greinke .50 1.25
TT14 Derek Jeter 1.25 3.00
TT15 Jose Bautista .30 .75
TT16 Adam Wainwright .30 .75
TT17 Nelson Cruz .50 1.25
TT18 Brandon Phillips .20 .50
TT19 Victor Martinez .30 .75
TT20 Clayton Kershaw .75 2.00
TT21 Adam Dunn .30 .75
TT22 Chone Figgins .20 .50
TT23 Matt Holliday .50 1.25
TT24 Neftali Feliz .20 .50
TT25 Pedro Alvarez .40 1.00
TT26 Trevor Cahill .20 .50
TT27 Mark Teixeira .30 .75
TT28 Aramis Ramirez .20 .50
TT29 Chris Coghlan .20 .50
TT30 Carl Crawford .30 .75
TT31 Jon Lester .30 .75
TT32 Cole Hamels .40 1.00
TT33 Austin Jackson .20 .50
TT34 Ike Davis .20 .50
TT35 Ian Kinsler .30 .75
TT36 Hunter Pence .30 .75
TT37 Jeremy Hellickson .50 1.25
TT38 Brian Matusz .20 .50
TT39 Clay Buchholz .20 .50
TT40 Lance Berkman .30 .75
TT41 Angel Pagan .20 .50
TT42 Torii Hunter .20 .50
TT43 Chris Carpenter .30 .75
TT44 B.J. Upton .30 .75
TT45 Martin Prado .20 .50
TT46 Roy Oswalt .30 .75
TT47 Jay Bruce .30 .75
TT48 Joakim Soria .20 .50
TT49 Jayson Werth .30 .75
TT50 Phil Hughes .20 .50

2011 Topps Toys R Us Purple Diamond

COMPLETE SET (10) 12.50 30.00
RANDOM INSERTS IN TRU PACKS
PDC1 Buster Posey 6.00 15.00
PDC2 Troy Tulowitzki 1.25 3.00
PDC3 Evan Longoria .75 2.00
PDC4 Tim Lincecum .75 2.00
PDC5 Alex Rodriguez 1.50 4.00
PDC6 CC Sabathia .75 2.00
PDC7 Joe Mauer 1.00 2.50
PDC8 Robinson Cano .75 2.00
PDC9 Starlin Castro .75 2.00
PDC10 Ryan Howard 1.00 2.50

2011 Topps Value Box Chrome Refractors

COMPLETE SET (3) 4.00 10.00
ONE PER $14.99 RETAIL VALUE BOX
MBC1 Mickey Mantle 2.50 6.00
MBC2 Jackie Robinson .75 2.00
MBC3 Babe Ruth 2.00 5.00

2011 Topps Wal-Mart Blue Diamond

COMPLETE SET (30) 30.00 60.00
RANDOM INSERTS IN WAL MART PACKS
BDW1 Albert Pujols 1.50 4.00
BDW2 Derek Jeter 3.00 8.00
BDW3 Mat Latos .75 2.00
BDW4 Hanley Ramirez .75 2.00
BDW5 Miguel Cabrera 1.25 3.00
BDW6 Aroldis Chapman 1.50 4.00
BDW7 Chase Utley .75 2.00
BDW8 Ryan Braun .75 2.00
BDW9 David Price 1.00 2.50
BDW10 Joey Votto 1.25 3.00
BDW11 David Wright 1.00 2.50
BDW12 Carlos Gonzalez .75 2.00
BDW13 David Ortiz 1.25 3.00
BDW14 Andre Ethier .75 2.00
BDW15 Roy Halladay .75 2.00
BDW16 Cliff Lee .75 2.00
BDW17 Dan Uggla .50 1.25
BDW18 Mark Teixeira .75 2.00
BDW19 Felix Hernandez .75 2.00
BDW20 Buster Posey 1.50 4.00
BDW21 Ryan Zimmerman .75 2.00
BDW22 Ian Kinsler .75 2.00
BDW23 Mike Stanton 1.25 3.00
BDW24 Troy Tulowitzki 1.25 3.00
BDW25 Zack Greinke 1.25 3.00
BDW26 Pedro Alvarez 1.00 2.50
BDW27 Jon Lester .75 2.00
BDW28 Justin Upton .75 2.00
BDW29 Clayton Kershaw 2.00 5.00
BDW30 Carl Crawford .75 2.00

2011 Topps Wal-Mart Hanger Pack Exclusives

ONE PER WAL MART HANGER PACK
WHP1 Babe Ruth 6.00 15.00
WHP2 Derek Jeter 6.00 15.00
WHP3 Ty Cobb 4.00 10.00
WHP4 Josh Hamilton 1.50 4.00
WHP5 Albert Pujols 3.00 8.00
WHP6 Jason Heyward 2.00 5.00
WHP7 Mickey Mantle 8.00 20.00
WHP8 Ryan Braun 1.50 4.00
WHP9 Honus Wagner 2.50 6.00
WHP10 Jackie Robinson 2.50 6.00
WHP11 Roy Halladay 1.50 4.00
WHP12 Carlos Gonzalez 1.50 4.00
WHP13 Ichiro Suzuki 3.00 8.00
WHP14 Roy Campanella 2.50 6.00
WHP15 Miguel Cabrera 2.50 6.00
WHP16 Adrian Gonzalez 2.00 5.00
WHP17 CC Sabathia 1.50 4.00
WHP18 Ryan Howard 2.00 5.00
WHP19 Adrian Beltre 2.50 6.00
WHP20 Sandy Koufax 5.00 12.00
WHP21 Evan Longoria 1.50 4.00
WHP22 Robinson Cano 1.50 4.00
WHP23 Adam Dunn 1.50 4.00
WHP24 Joe Mauer 2.00 5.00
WHP25 Tim Lincecum 1.50 4.00
WHP26 Victor Martinez 1.50 4.00
WHP27 Ubaldo Jimenez 1.00 2.50
WHP28 Matt Holliday 2.50 6.00
WHP29 Josh Johnson 1.50 4.00
WHP30 Hank Aaron 5.00 12.00

2011 Topps World Champion Autograph Relics

STATED ODDS 1:7941 HOBBY
STATED PRINT RUN 50 SER.#'d SETS
EXCHANGE DEADLINE 1/31/2014
BP Buster Posey 300.00 600.00
CR Cody Ross EXCH 150.00 250.00
FS Freddy Sanchez EXCH 125.00 250.00
MB Madison Bumgarner 100.00 200.00
PS Pablo Sandoval 75.00 150.00

2011 Topps World Champion Autographs

STATED ODDS 1:33,000 HOBBY
STATED PRINT RUN 50 SER.#'d SETS
EXCHANGE DEADLINE 1/31/2014
WCA1 Buster Posey 175.00 350.00
WCA2 Madison Bumgarner 100.00 200.00
WCA3 Pablo Sandoval 100.00 200.00
WCA4 Cody Ross 100.00 200.00
WCA5 Freddy Sanchez 100.00 200.00

2011 Topps World Champion Relics

STATED ODDS 1:6250 HOBBY
STATED PRINT RUN 100 SER.#'d SETS
EXCHANGE DEADLINE 1/31/2014
WCR1 Buster Posey 100.00 200.00
WCR2 Madison Bumgarner 60.00 120.00
WCR3 Pablo Sandoval 50.00 100.00
WCR4 Cody Ross EXCH 75.00 150.00
WCR5 Freddy Sanchez 40.00 80.00
WCR6 Tim Lincecum 125.00 250.00
WCR7 Matt Cain 40.00 80.00
WCR8 Jonathan Sanchez EXCH 75.00 150.00
WCR9 Brian Wilson 75.00 150.00
WCR10 Juan Uribe EXCH 40.00 80.00
WCR11 Aubrey Huff EXCH 60.00 120.00
WCR12 Edgar Renteria 50.00 100.00
WCR13 Andres Torres EXCH 40.00 80.00
WCR14 Pat Burrell 60.00 120.00
WCR15 Mike Fontenot 40.00 80.00

2011 Topps Update

COMP.SET w/o SP's (330) 500.00 1200.00
COMMON CARD (1-330) .12 .30
COMMON SP VAR (1-330) 5.00 12.00
COMMON RC (1-330) .40 1.00
PRINTING PLATE ODDS 1:846 HOBBY
PLATE PRINT RUN 1 SET PER COLOR
BLACK-CYAN-MAGENTA-YELLOW ISSUED
NO PLATE PRICING DUE TO SCARCITY
US1 Adrian Gonzalez .25 .60
US2 Ty Wigginton .12 .30
US3 Blake Beavan .20 .50
US5 Josh Willingham .20 .50
US6 Prince Fielder .20 .50
US7 Nate Schierholtz .12 .30
US8 David Robertson .12 .30
US9 Jose Iglesias RC .60 1.50
US11 Jason Pridie .12 .30
US12 Greg Dobbs .12 .30
US13 Koyie Hill .12 .30
US14 Alex Avila .20 .50
US15 Aaron Heilman .12 .30
US16 Welington Castillo .12 .30
US17 Craig Gentry .12 .30
US18A Robinson Cano .20 .50
US18B Joe DiMaggio SP 12.50 30.00
US19 Mike Napoli .12 .30
US20 Adrian Gonzalez .25 .60
US22 Randall Delgado RC .60 1.50
US23 Chance Ruffin RC .40 1.00
US24 Rex Brothers RC .40 1.00
US25 Tim Stauffer .12 .30
US26 Jered Weaver .20 .50
US27 Joey Devine .12 .30
US28 Adam Kennedy .12 .30
US29 Mike MacDougal .12 .30
US30 Dustin Ackley RC .60 1.50
US32 Matt Stairs .12 .30
US33 Jayson Nix .12 .30
US34 David Ross .12 .30
US35 Eduardo Nunez RC 1.00 2.50
US36 Josh Judy RC .40 1.00
US37 Rick Ankiel .12 .30
US38A Josh Hamilton .20 .50
US38B Roger Maris SP 5.00 12.00
US39 Eduardo Sanchez RC .60 1.50
US40 Brian Fuentes .12 .30
US41 Lou Marson .12 .30
US42A David Ortiz .30 .75
US42B Frank Thomas SP 5.00 12.00
US43 Carlos Quentin .12 .30
US44 Matt Treanor .12 .30
US45 Peter Moylan .12 .30
US46 Angel Sanchez .12 .30
US47 Paul Goldschmidt RC 10.00 25.00
US48 Scott Hairston .12 .30
US49 Rickie Weeks .12 .30
US4A Brian McCann .20 .50
US4B Carlton Fisk SP 5.00 12.00
US50A Jered Weaver .20 .50
US50B Nolan Ryan SP 8.00 20.00
US51 Andruw Jones .12 .30
US52 Lance Berkman .20 .50
US53 Koji Uehara .12 .30
US54 Jerry Sands RC 1.00 2.50
US55 Anthony Rizzo RC 10.00 25.00
US56 Ryan Adams RC .40 1.00
US57 Tony Campana RC 1.00 2.50
US58A Tim Lincecum .20 .50
US58B Bert Blyleven SP 5.00 12.00
US59A Matt Kemp .25 .60
US59B Rickey Henderson SP 5.00 12.00
US60 Heath Bell .12 .30
US61 Nick Masset .12 .30
US62 Jason Marquis .12 .30
US63 Doug Fister .12 .30
US64 J.C. Romero .12 .30
US65 Mitchell Boggs .12 .30
US66 Andy Dirks RC 1.00 2.50
US67 Miguel Olivo .12 .30
US68 Tyler Clippard .12 .30
US69 Gerald Laird .12 .30
US70 Michael Wuertz .12 .30
US71 Jeff Francis .12 .30
US72 Colby Rasmus .20 .50
US73 Juan Nicasio .12 .30
US74 Henry Blanco .12 .30
US75 Gio Gonzalez .20 .50
US76 Nolan Reimold .12 .30
US77 Freddy Garcia .12 .30
US78 David Ortiz .30 .75
US79 Chris Dickerson .12 .30
US80 Jose Bautista .20 .50
US81 Aaron Harang .12 .30
US82 Mark Ellis .12 .30
US83 Brandon Belt .30 .75
US84 Pablo Sandoval .20 .50
US85A Roy Halladay .20 .50
US85B Tom Seaver SP 5.00 12.00
US86 Rafael Furcal .12 .30
US87 Clayton Mortensen .12 .30
US88 Orlando Cabrera .12 .30
US89 Sean O'Sullivan .12 .30
US90 James Russell .12 .30
US91 Brandon League .12 .30
US92 Hunter Pence .20 .50
US93 Matt Downs .12 .30
US94 Ryan Vogelsong .12 .30
US95 Lyle Overbay .12 .30
US96 Ryan Hanigan .12 .30
US97 Cody Eppley RC .40 1.00
US98 Alexi Ogando .30 .75
US99 Carlos Villanueva .12 .30
US100 Cliff Lee .20 .50
US101 Scott Downs .12 .30
US102 Sean Burnett .12 .30
US103 Josh Collmenter RC .40 1.00
US104 Logan Forsythe RC .40 1.00
US105 Joel Hanrahan .20 .50
US106 Ryan Ludwick .12 .30
US107 Brandon McCarthy .12 .30
US108 Ubaldo Jimenez .12 .30
US109 Jair Jurrjens .12 .30
US10A Jose Bautista .20 .50
US10B Hank Aaron SP 6.00 15.00
US110 Edgar Renteria .12 .30
US111 Scott Sizemore .12 .30
US112 Lonnie Chisenhall RC .60 1.50
US113 Chris Perez .12 .30
US114 Lance Lynn RC 1.00 2.50
US115 Kerry Wood .12 .30
US116 Shawn Camp .12 .30
US117 Michael Stutes RC .60 1.50
US118 Michael Pineda .30 .75
US119 Jeff Francoeur .20 .50
US120 Bobby Parnell .12 .30
US121 Jon Rauch .12 .30
US122 Alfredo Aceves .12 .30
US123 Brad Penny .12 .30
US124 Xavier Paul .12 .30
US125 Joel Peralta .12 .30
US126 Adrian Gonzalez .25 .60
US127 Rickie Weeks .12 .30
US128 Mariano Rivera .40 1.00
US129 Brooks Conrad .12 .30
US130 David Robertson .12 .30
US131 Jeff Keppinger .12 .30
US132 Jose Altuve RC 12.00 30.00
US133 Fernando Salas .20 .50
US134 Michael Bourn .12 .30
US135 Grant Balfour .12 .30
US136 Brandon Crawford .20 .50
US137 Willie Bloomquist .12 .30
US138A Michael Young .12 .30
US138B Paul Molitor SP 5.00 12.00
US139 Rafael Soriano .12 .30
US140A Clayton Kershaw .50 1.25
US140B Sandy Koufax SP 6.00 15.00
US141 Mike Cameron .12 .30
US142 Alex White RC .40 1.00
US143 Craig Kimbrel .30 .75
US144 Kevin Youkilis .12 .30
US145 Bartolo Colon .12 .30
US146 Jordan Walden .12 .30
US147 C.J. Wilson .12 .30
US148 Alex Presley RC .60 1.50
US149 Omar Infante .12 .30
US150 Adrian Beltre .30 .75
US151 Cory Gearrin RC .40 1.00
US152 Julio Teheran RC .60 1.50
US153 Matt Guerrier .12 .30
US154A Cliff Lee .20 .50
US154B Babe Ruth SP 6.00 15.00
US155 Eric Hosmer RC 2.50 6.00
US156 Humberto Quintero .12 .30
US157 Reed Johnson .12 .30
US158 Darren Oliver .12 .30
US159 Alex Cobb RC .40 1.00
US160 Victor Martinez .20 .50
US161 Conor Jackson .12 .30
US162 Troy Tulowitzki .30 .75
US163 Adrian Beltre .30 .75
US164 Hector Noesi .60 1.50
US165 Al Albuquerque RC .40 1.00
US166 David Ortiz .30 .75
US167 Brandan Ryan .12 .30
US168 Bruce Chen .12 .30
US169 Ezequiel Carrera RC .40 1.00
US170 Brad Ziegler .12 .30
US171 Matt Lindstrom .12 .30
US172 Jonny Venters .12 .30
US173 Charlie Furbush RC .40 1.00
US174 Jacob Turner RC 1.50 4.00
US175 Mike Trout RC 800.00 2000.00
US176 Xavier Nady .12 .30
US177 Rene Tosoni RC .40 1.00
US178 Jason Bourgeois .12 .30
US179 Michael Pineda .30 .75
US180 Daniel Moskos RC .40 1.00
US181 Jo Jo Reyes .12 .30
US182 Ronny Paulino .12 .30
US183 Carlos Peguero RC .60 1.50
US184 Tyler Chatwood RC .40 1.00
US185 Orlando Hudson .12 .30
US186 J.D. Martinez RC 10.00 25.00
US187 Bobby Wilson .12 .30
US188 Eric Hosmer .75 2.00
US189 Wilson Valdez .12 .30
US190 Alexi Ogando .30 .75
US191 Andy Sonnanstine .12 .30
US192 Mike Moustakas RC 1.00 2.50
US193 Lonnie Chisenhall .20 .50
US194 Jason Kipnis RC 1.25 3.00
US195A Joey Votto .30 .75
US195B Larry Walker SP 5.00 12.00
US196 Philip Humber .12 .30
US197 Brandon League .12 .30
US198 Kevin Jepsen .12 .30
US199 Micah Owings .12 .30
US200 Vladimir Guerrero .20 .50
US201 Hisanori Takahashi .12 .30
US202 Derrek Lee .12 .30
US203 Juan Nicasio RC .40 1.00
US204 Brian Wilson .30 .75
US205 D.J. LeMahieu RC 20.00 50.00
US206 J.P. Howell .12 .30
US207A Jay Bruce .20 .50
US207B Frank Robinson SP 5.00 12.00
US208 Javier Lopez .12 .30
US209 Rubby De La Rosa RC 1.00 2.50
US210 Jayson Werth .20 .50
US211 Dustin Moseley .12 .30
US212 Pat Neshek .12 .30
US213 Louis Coleman RC .40 1.00
US214 Matt Daley .12 .30
US215 Michael Dunn .12 .30
US216 Takashi Saito .12 .30
US217 Elliot Johnson .12 .30
US218 Matt Kemp .25 .60
US219 George Sherrill .12 .30
US21A Prince Fielder .20 .50
US21B Willie McCovey SP 5.00 12.00
US220 Adam Dunn .20 .50
US221 Jamey Carroll .12 .30
US222 Chris Gimenez .12 .30
US223 Arthur Rhodes .12 .30
US224 Bill Hall .12 .30
US225 David DeJesus .12 .30
US226 Steve Pearce .30 .75
US227 Kosuke Fukudome .20 .50
US228 Zach Britton .30 .75
US229A Asdrubal Cabrera .20 .50
US229B Roberto Alomar SP 8.00 20.00
US230A Miguel Cabrera .30 .75
US230B Al Kaline SP 5.00 12.00
US231 Charlie Blackmon RC 8.00 20.00
US232 Miguel Tejada .20 .50
US233 John McDonald .12 .30
US234 Brandon Crawford RC .60 1.50
US235 Charlie Morton .30 .75
US236 Jose Morales .12 .30
US237 Ryan Roberts .12 .30
US238A Carlos Beltran .20 .50
US238B Darryl Strawberry SP 5.00 12.00
US239 J.J. Hardy .12 .30
US240 Blake Tekotte RC .40 1.00
US241 Brandon Wood .12 .30
US242 Matt Holliday .30 .75
US243 Chris Denorfia .12 .30
US244 Francisco Rodriguez .20 .50
US245 Kevin Correia .12 .30
US246 Alcides Escobar .20 .50
US247 Zack Cozart RC 1.00 2.50
US248 Octavio Dotel .12 .30
US249A Starlin Castro .20 .50
US249B Ozzie Smith SP 5.00 12.00
US250 Zack Greinke .30 .75
US251 Justin Turner .30 .75
US252 Derek Jeter .75 2.00
US253 Scott Linebrink .12 .30
US254 Dustin Ackley .20 .50
US255 Allen Craig .25 .60
US256 Mark Kotsay .12 .30
US257 Erik Bedard .12 .30
US258A Andre Ethier .20 .50
US258B Monte Irvin SP 5.00 12.00
US259 Andre Ethier .20 .50
US260A Matt Holliday .30 .75
US260B Ty Cobb SP 5.00 12.00
US261 John Buck .12 .30
US262 Javy Guerra (RC) .60 1.50
US263 Chad Qualls .12 .30
US264 Alex White .12 .30
US265 Willie Harris .12 .30
US266 Jason Isringhausen .12 .30
US267 Sam Fuld .12 .30
US268 Yadier Molina .40 1.00
US269 Sergio Santos .12 .30
US270 Todd Frazier RC 1.00 2.50
US271 Eric O'Flaherty .12 .30
US272 Jorge Cantu .12 .30
US273 Miguel Montero .12 .30
US274 Jeff Karstens .12 .30
US275 Michael Cuddyer .12 .30
US276 Yuniesky Betancourt .12 .30
US277 Sam LeCure .12 .30
US278A Jacoby Ellsbury .25 .60
US278B Tris Speaker SP 5.00 12.00
US279 Trevor Plouffe .12 .30
US280 Kyle Farnsworth .12 .30
US281 Mark Melancon .12 .30
US282 Brad Hand RC .40 1.00
US283 Latroy Hawkins .12 .30
US284 Laynce Nix .12 .30
US285 David Purcey .12 .30
US286 Rich Thompson .12 .30
US287 Matt Joyce .12 .30
US288 Eric Thames RC 2.00 5.00
US289 Eric Chavez .12 .30
US290 Sean Burroughs .12 .30
US291A Andrew McCutchen .30 .75
US291B Andre Dawson SP 5.00 12.00
US292 Mike Adams .12 .30
US293 Howie Kendrick .12 .30
US294 Edwin Jackson .12 .30
US295 Wilson Ramos .12 .30
US296 Bobby Jenks .12 .30
US297 Chase D'Arnaud RC .40 1.00
US298 Yorvit Torrealba .12 .30
US299 Robinson Cano .20 .50
US300 Carl Crawford .20 .50
US301 Tom Gorzelanny .12 .30
US302 Alex Torres RC .40 1.00
US303 Juan Uribe .12 .30
US304 Hunter Pence .20 .50
US305 Carlos Beltran .20 .50
US306 Brandon Phillips .12 .30
US307 Casey Coleman .12 .30
US308 Kyle Seager RC 1.00 2.50
US309A Paul Konerko .20 .50
US309B Jimmie Foxx SP 5.00 12.00
US310 Scott Rolen .20 .50
US311 Drew Butera .12 .30
US312 Danny Duffy RC .60 1.50
US313 Tyson Ross .12 .30
US314 Armando Galarraga .12 .30
US315 Carlos Pena .20 .50
US316 Justin Upton .20 .50
US317 Craig Counsell .12 .30
US318 Brayan Pena .12 .30
US319 Corey Patterson .12 .30
US31A Curtis Granderson .25 .60
US31B Paul O'Neill SP 5.00 12.00
US320 Russell Martin .12 .30
US321 Gaby Sanchez .12 .30
US322 Fernando Martinez .12 .30
US323 Jhonny Peralta .12 .30
US324 Melvin Mora .12 .30
US325 Jason Giambi .12 .30
US326 Trevor Bell .12 .30
US327 Blake Beavan RC .60 1.50
US328 Kevin Gregg .12 .30
US329 Dee Gordon RC .60 1.50
US330 Lance Berkman .20 .50

2011 Topps Update Cognac Diamond Anniversary

*COGNAC VET: 2X TO 5X BASIC
*COGNAC RC: .6X TO 1.5X BASIC RC
*COGNAC SP: .25X TO .6X BASIC SP
STATED ODDS 1:3 HOBBY
STATED SP ODDS 1:81 HOBBY
US47 Paul Goldschmidt 30.00 80.00
US55 Anthony Rizzo 25.00 60.00
US132 Jose Altuve 50.00 120.00
US175 Mike Trout 2000.00 5000.00

2011 Topps Update Black

*BLACK: 12X TO 30X BASIC
*BLACK RC: 4X TP 10X BASIC
STATED ODDS 1:58 HOBBY
STATED PRINT RUN 60 SER.#'d SETS
US47 Paul Goldschmidt 300.00 800.00
US55 Anthony Rizzo 100.00 250.00
US132 Jose Altuve 1000.00 1500.00
US175 Mike Trout 10000.00 15000.00

2011 Topps Update Diamond Anniversary

*DIAMOND VET: 2X TO 5X BASIC
*DIAMOND RC: .6X TO 1.5X BASIC RC
*DIAMOND SP: .25X TO .6X BASIC SP
STATED ODDS 1:4 HOBBY
STATED SP ODDS 1:79 HOBBY
US47 Paul Goldschmidt 30.00 80.00
US55 Anthony Rizzo 25.00 60.00
US132 Jose Altuve 50.00 120.00
US175 Mike Trout 2000.00 5000.00

2011 Topps Update Gold

*GOLD VET: 2X TO 5X BASIC
*GOLD RC: .6X TO 1.5X BASIC RC
STATED ODDS 1:3 HOBBY
STATED PRINT RUN 2011 SER.#'d SETS
US47 Paul Goldschmidt 30.00 80.00
US55 Anthony Rizzo 25.00 60.00
US132 Jose Altuve 50.00 120.00
US175 Mike Trout 2000.00 5000.00

2011 Topps Update Hope Diamond Anniversary

*HOPE VET: 12X TO 30X BASIC
*HOPE RC: 4X TO 10X BASIC RC
*HOPE SP: .75X TO 2X BASIC SP
STATED ODDS 1:68 HOBBY
STATED SP ODDS 1:2627 HOBBY
STATED PRINT RUN 60 SER.#'d SETS
US47 Paul Goldschmidt 300.00 800.00
US55 Anthony Rizzo 100.00 250.00
US132 Jose Altuve 1000.00 1500.00
US175 Mike Trout 10000.00 15000.00

2011 Topps Update Target Red Border

*TARGET: 2X TO 5X BASIC
*TARGET RC: .6X TO 1.5X BASIC RC
FOUND IN TARGET RETAIL PACKS
US47 Paul Goldschmidt 30.00 80.00
US55 Anthony Rizzo 25.00 60.00
US132 Jose Altuve 150.00 400.00
US175 Mike Trout 2000.00 5000.00

2011 Topps Update Wal-Mart Blue Border

*WM: 2X TO 5X BASIC
*WM RC: .6X TO 1.5X BASIC RC
FOUND IN WAL MART RETAIL PACKS
US47 Paul Goldschmidt 30.00 80.00
US55 Anthony Rizzo 25.00 60.00
US132 Jose Altuve 75.00 200.00
US175 Mike Trout 2000.00 5000.00

2011 Topps Update All-Star Stitches

STATED ODDS 1:51 HOBBY
AS1 Jose Bautista 4.00 10.00
AS2 Alex Avila 4.00 10.00
AS3 Robinson Cano 5.00 12.00
AS4 Adrian Gonzalez 4.00 10.00
AS5 Curtis Granderson 4.00 10.00
AS6 Josh Hamilton 5.00 12.00
AS7 David Ortiz 4.00 10.00
AS8 Carlos Quentin 3.00 8.00
AS9 Jered Weaver 3.00 8.00
AS10 Tim Lincecum 5.00 12.00
AS11 Gio Gonzalez 3.00 8.00
AS12 Brandon League 3.00 8.00
AS13 Alexi Ogando 3.00 8.00
AS14 Chris Perez 4.00 10.00
AS15 Justin Verlander 5.00 12.00
AS16 David Robertson 4.00 10.00
AS17 Michael Young 3.00 8.00
AS18 Kevin Youkilis 3.00 8.00
AS19 Josh Beckett 4.00 10.00
AS20 C.J. Wilson 3.00 8.00
AS21 Adrian Beltre 3.00 8.00
AS22 Asdrubal Cabrera 4.00 10.00
AS23 Miguel Cabrera 5.00 12.00
AS24 Michael Cuddyer 4.00 10.00
AS25 Jacoby Ellsbury 4.00 10.00
AS26 Matt Joyce 4.00 10.00
AS27 Howie Kendrick 3.00 8.00
AS28 Paul Konerko 3.00 8.00
AS29 Justin Upton 4.00 10.00
AS30 Jhonny Peralta 4.00 10.00
AS31 Brian McCann 3.00 8.00
AS32 Prince Fielder 4.00 10.00
AS33 Rickie Weeks 3.00 8.00
AS34 Lance Berkman 4.00 10.00
AS35 Matt Kemp 5.00 12.00
AS36 Heath Bell 3.00 8.00
AS37 Tyler Clippard 3.00 8.00
AS38 Pablo Sandoval 4.00 10.00
AS39 Roy Halladay 5.00 12.00
AS40 Joel Hanrahan 4.00 10.00
AS41 Jair Jurrjens 4.00 10.00
AS42 Clayton Kershaw 4.00 10.00
AS43 Craig Kimbrel 5.00 12.00
AS44 Cliff Lee 5.00 12.00
AS45 Troy Tulowitzki 3.00 8.00
AS46 Jonny Venters 4.00 10.00
AS47 Joey Votto 5.00 12.00
AS48 Brian Wilson 5.00 12.00
AS49 Jay Bruce 4.00 10.00
AS50 Carlos Beltran 3.00 8.00
AS51 Starlin Castro 5.00 12.00
AS52 Andre Ethier 3.00 8.00
AS53 Matt Holliday 4.00 10.00
AS54 Yadier Molina 4.00 10.00
AS55 Miguel Montero 4.00 10.00
AS56 Andrew McCutchen 4.00 10.00
AS57 Hunter Pence 4.00 10.00
AS58 Brandon Phillips 4.00 10.00
AS59 Scott Rolen 4.00 10.00
AS60 Gaby Sanchez 3.00 8.00
AS61 Kevin Correia 4.00 10.00
AS62 Russell Martin 4.00 10.00
AS63 Jose Valverde 4.00 10.00
AS64 Jose Reyes 5.00 12.00
AS65 Ryan Braun 4.00 10.00
AS66 Felix Hernandez 3.00 8.00
AS67 Jon Lester 4.00 10.00
AS68 David Price 4.00 10.00
AS69 James Shields 3.00 8.00
AS70 Matt Cain 4.00 10.00
AS71 Cole Hamels 4.00 10.00
AS72 Ryan Vogelsong 4.00 10.00
AS73 Placido Polanco 4.00 10.00
AS74 Shane Victorino 4.00 10.00
AS75 Ricky Romero 3.00 8.00

2011 Topps Update All-Star Stitches Diamond Anniversary

*DIAMOND: .75X TO 2X BASIC
STATED ODDS 1:759 HOBBY
STATED PRINT RUN 60 SER.#'d SETS

2011 Topps Update Diamond Duos

COMPLETE SET (30) 6.00 15.00
STATED ODDS 1:8 HOBBY
DD1 F.Hernanez/M.Pineda .60 1.50
DD2 Andre Ethier/Matt Kemp .50 1.25
DD3 Jered Weaver/Dan Haren .40 1.00
DD4 A.Pujols/L.Berkman .75 2.00
DD5 E.Hosmer/B.Belt 1.50 4.00
DD6 Brett Anderson/Trevor Cahill .25 .60
DD7 S.Castro/D.Barney .75 2.00
DD8 Joey Votto/Jay Bruce .60 1.50
DD9 Zack Greinke/Shaun Marcum .60 1.50
DD10 M.Pineda/Z.Britton .60 1.50
DD11 Adam Dunn/Paul Konerko .40 1.00
DD12 Matt Holliday/Colby Rasmus .60 1.50
DD13 Stanton/Morrison .60 1.50
DD14 Jose Bautista/Adam Lind .40 1.00
DD15 J.DiMaggio/D.Jeter 1.50 4.00
DD16 E.Hosmer/D.Duffy 1.50 4.00
DD17 C.Kimbrel/J.Teheran .60 1.50
DD18 Adrian Gonzalez/Jose Bautista .50 1.25
DD19 J.Verlander/M.Scherzer .60 1.50
DD20 H.Aaron/J.Bautista 1.25 3.00
DD21 David Price/James Shields .50 1.25
DD22 Ricky Romero/Kyle Drabek .40 1.00
DD23 David Ortiz/Vladimir Guerrero .60 1.50
DD24 E.Longoria/B.Zobrist .40 1.00
DD25 E.Hosmer/F.Freeman 4.00 10.00
DD26 B.Posey/B.McCann .75 2.00
DD27 Grady Sizemore/Shin-Soo Choo .40 1.00
DD28 Brandon Phillips/Howie Kendrick .25 .60
DD29 M.Kemp/J.Sands .60 1.50
DD30 S.Koufax/R.Braun 1.25 3.00

2011 Topps Update Diamond Duos Dual Relics

STATED ODDS 1:4650 HOBBY
STATED PRINT RUN 50 SER.#'d SETS
DD1 F.Hernanez/M.Pineda 15.00 40.00
DD2 A.Ethier/M.Kemp 20.00 50.00
DD3 J.Weaver/D.Haren 20.00 50.00
DD4 A.Pujols/L.Berkman 40.00 80.00
DD5 E.Hosmer/B.Bell 50.00 100.00
DD6 B.Anderson/T.Cahill 6.00 15.00
DD7 S.Castro/D.Barney 30.00 60.00
DD8 J.Votto/J.Bruce 15.00 40.00
DD9 Z.Greinke/S.Marcum 15.00 40.00
DD10 M.Pineda/Z.Britton 15.00 40.00
DD11 A.Dunn/P.Konerko 20.00 50.00
DD12 M.Holliday/C.Rasmus 10.00 25.00
DD13 M.Stanton/L.Morrison 12.50 30.00
DD14 J.Bautista/A.Lind 15.00 40.00
DD15 J.DiMaggio/D.Jeter 100.00 175.00

2011 Topps Update Next 60 Autographs

STATED ODDS 1:566 HOBBY
EXCHANGE DEADLINE 9/30/2014
AC Aroldis Chapman 20.00 50.00
AJ Austin Jackson 6.00 15.00
AO Alexi Ogando 4.00 10.00
BB Brandon Belt 4.00 10.00
BW Brett Wallace 4.00 10.00
CK Craig Kimbrel 12.00 30.00
CS Chris Sale 8.00 20.00
DA Dustin Ackley 12.50 30.00
DD Danny Duffy 4.00 10.00
DH Daniel Hudson 3.00 8.00
EH Eric Hosmer 60.00 120.00
FF Freddie Freeman 10.00 25.00
JH Jeremy Hellickson 5.00 12.00
JJ Jeremy Jeffress 3.00 8.00
JS Jerry Sands 4.00 10.00
JW Jordan Walden 4.00 10.00
KD Kyle Drabek 3.00 8.00
MM Mike Moustakas 8.00 20.00
MP Michael Pineda 8.00 20.00
MS Mike Stanton 60.00 120.00
MT Mark Trumbo 8.00 20.00
NF Neftali Feliz 4.00 10.00
SC Starlin Castro 40.00 80.00
JT1 Jose Tabata 5.00 12.00
JT2 Julio Teheran 4.00 10.00

2011 Topps Update Topps Town

STATED ODDS 1:8 HOBBY
TTU1 Eric Hosmer 1.25 3.00
TTU2 Francisco Liriano .20 .50
TTU3 Prince Fielder .30 .75
TTU4 Carlos Beltran .30 .75
TTU5 Ricky Romero .20 .50
TTU6 Vernon Wells .20 .50
TTU7 Rickie Weeks .20 .50
TTU8 Brian Wilson .50 1.25
TTU9 Colby Rasmus .30 .75
TTU10 Zach Britton .50 1.25
TTU11 Wandy Rodriguez .20 .50
TTU12 Gaby Sanchez .20 .50
TTU13 Shane Victorino .30 .75
TTU14 Matt Garza .20 .50
TTU15 Francisco Rodriguez .30 .75
TTU16 Drew Stubbs .20 .50
TTU17 James Shields .20 .50
TTU18 Heath Bell .20 .50
TTU19 Fausto Carmona .20 .50
TTU20 Freddie Freeman 3.00 8.00
TTU21 Chad Billingsley .30 .75
TTU22 Stephen Drew .20 .50
TTU23 Jimmy Rollins .30 .75
TTU24 Vladimir Guerrero .30 .75
TTU25 Gio Gonzalez .30 .75
TTU26 Curtis Granderson .40 1.00
TTU27 Neil Walker .30 .75
TTU28 Alfonso Soriano .30 .75
TTU29 Michael Young .20 .50
TTU30 Paul Konerko .30 .75
TTU31 Adam Lind .30 .75
TTU32 Ben Zobrist .30 .75
TTU33 Travis Hafner .20 .50
TTU34 Jhoulys Chacin .20 .50
TTU35 Jaime Garcia .30 .75
TTU36 Jered Weaver .30 .75
TTU37 Max Scherzer .50 1.25
TTU38 Alex Rodriguez .60 1.50
TTU39 Jacoby Ellsbury .40 1.00
TTU40 Matt Kemp .40 1.00
TTU41 Michael Bourn .20 .50
TTU42 Kurt Suzuki .20 .50
TTU43 Brian McCann .30 .75
TTU44 CC Sabathia .30 .75
TTU45 Josh Beckett .20 .50
TTU46 Adrian Beltre .50 1.25
TTU47 Drew Storen .20 .50
TTU48 Ian Desmond .20 .50
TTU49 Matt Cain .30 .75
TTU50 Michael Pineda .50 1.25

2012 Topps

COMP.FACT.HOBBY.SET (661) 40.00 80.00
COMP.FACT.ALLSTAR.SET (661) 40.00 80.00
COMP.FACT.FENWAY SET(661) 40.00 80.00
COMP.FACT.HOLIDAY SET(661) 40.00 80.00
COMP.SER.1 w/o SP's (330) 12.50 30.00
COMP.SER.1 w/o SP's (330) 12.50 30.00
COMMON CARD (1-660) .15 .40
COMMON RC (1-660) .25 .60
COMMON SP VAR (1-660) 5.00 12.00
SER.1 PLATE ODDS 1:2331 HOBBY
SER.2 PLATE ODDS 1:1624 HOBBY
PLATE PRINT RUN 1 SET PER COLOR
BLACK-CYAN-MAGENTA-YELLOW ISSUED
NO PLATE PRICING DUE TO SCARCITY
1A Ryan Braun .15 .40
1B Ryan Braun VAR SP 5.00 12.00
2 Trevor Cahill .15 .40
3 Jaime Garcia .20 .50
4 Jeremy Guthrie .15 .40
5 Desmond Jennings .20 .50
6 Nick Hagadone RC .25 .60
7A Mickey Mantle .75 2.00
7B Mickey Mantle UER .75 2.00
8 Mike Adams .15 .40
9 Jesus Montero RC .25 .60
10 Jon Lester .15 .40
11 Hong-Chih Kuo .15 .40
12 Wilson Ramos .15 .40
13 Vernon Wells .15 .40
14 Jesus Guzman .15 .40
15 Melky Cabrera .15 .40
16 Desmond Jennings .20 .50
17 Alex Rios .20 .50
18 Colby Lewis .15 .40
19 Yonder Alonso .15 .40
20 Craig Kimbrel .20 .50
21 Chris Iannetta .15 .40
22 Alfredo Simon .15 .40
23 Cory Luebke .15 .40
24 Ike Davis .15 .40
25 Neil Walker .15 .40
26 Kyle Lohse .15 .40
27 John Buck .15 .40
28 Placido Polanco .15 .40
29 Livan Hernandez/Roy Oswalt Randy Wolf LDR .20 .50
30A Derek Jeter .60 1.50
30B Derek Jeter VAR SP 12.00 30.00
30C J.DiMaggio VAR SP 8.00 20.00
31 Brent Morel .15 .40
32 Detroit Tigers PS HL .15 .40
33 Curtis Granderson/Robinson Cano/Adrian Gonzalez LL .20 .50
34 Derek Holland .15 .40
35A Eric Hosmer .20 .50
35B Hosmer VAR Gatorade SP 5.00 12.00
35C Hosmer VAR Dugout SP 5.00 12.00
36 Michael Taylor RC .25 .60
37 Mike Napoli .15 .40
38 Felipe Paulino .15 .40
39 James Loney .15 .40
40 Tom Milone RC .25 .60
41 Devin Mesoraco RC .25 .60
42 Drew Pomeranz RC .25 .60
43 Brett Wallace .15 .40
44 Edwin Jackson .15 .40
45 Jhoulys Chacin .15 .40
46 Peter Bourjos .15 .40
47 Luke Hochevar .15 .40
48 Wade Davis .20 .50
49 Jon Niese .15 .40
50 Adrian Gonzalez .20 .50
51 Alcides Escobar .20 .50
52 Verland/Weaver/Shields LL .25 .60
53 St. Louis Cardinals WS HL .25 .60
54 Jhonny Peralta .15 .40
55 Michael Young .15 .40
56 Geovany Soto .20 .50
57 Yuniesky Betancourt .15 .40
58 Tim Hudson .20 .50
59 Texas Rangers PS HL .15 .40
60 Hanley Ramirez .20 .50
61 Daniel Bard .15 .40
62 Ben Revere .20 .50
63 Nate Schierholtz .15 .40
64 Michael Martinez .15 .40
65 Delmon Young .20 .50
66 Nyjer Morgan .15 .40
67 Aaron Crow .15 .40
68 Jason Hammel .20 .50
69 Dee Gordon .15 .40
70 Brett Pill RC .40 1.00
71 Jeff Karstens .15 .40
72 Rex Brothers .15 .40
73 Brandon McCarthy .15 .40
74 Kevin Correia .15 .40
75 Jordan Zimmermann .20 .50
76A Ian Kennedy .15 .40
76B Ian Kennedy VAR SP 5.00 12.00
77 Kemp/Prince/Pujols LL .30 .75
78 Erick Aybar .15 .40
79 Austin Romine RC .25 .60
80A David Price .20 .50
80B David Price VAR SP With trophy 5.00 12.00
81 Liam Hendriks RC .25 .60
82 Rick Porcello .15 .40
83 Bobby Parnell .15 .40
84 Brian Matusz .15 .40
85A Jason Heyward .20 .50
85B Jason Heyward VAR SP Throwback jersey 5.00 12.00
86 Brett Cecil .15 .40
87 Craig Kimbrel .20 .50
88 Javy Guerra .15 .40
89 Dontrelle Willis .15 .40
90 Adron Chambers RC .40 1.00
91 ARodr/Thome/Giambi LDR .30 .75
92 Tim Lincecum/Chris Carpenter Roy Oswalt LDR .20 .50
93A Skip Schumaker .15 .40
93B Schumaker Squirrel SP 30.00 80.00
94 Logan Forsythe .15 .40
95 Chris Parmelee RC .25 .60
96 Grady Sizemore .20 .50
97 Jim Thome RB .20 .50
98 Domonic Brown .20 .50
99 Michael McKenry .15 .40
100 Jose Bautista .20 .50
101 David Hernandez .15 .40
102 Chase d'Arnaud .15 .40
103 Madison Bumgarner .20 .50
104 Brett Anderson .15 .40
105 Paul Konerko .15 .40
106 Mark Trumbo .15 .40
107 Luke Scott .15 .40
108 Albert Pujols WS HL .30 .75
109 Mariano Rivera RB .30 .75
110 Mark Teixeira .20 .50
111 Kevin Slowey .15 .40
112 Juan Nicasio .15 .40
113 Craig Kimbrel RB .20 .50
114 Matt Garza .15 .40
115 Tommy Hanson .15 .40
116 A.J. Pierzynski .15 .40
117 Carlos Ruiz .15 .40
118 Miguel Olivo .15 .40
119 Ichiro/Mauer/Vlad LDR .30 .75
120 Hunter Pence .20 .50
121 Josh Bell .15 .40
122 Ted Lilly .15 .40
123 Scott Downs .15 .40
124 Pujols/Vlad/Helton LDR .30 .75
125 Adam Jones .20 .50
126 Eduardo Nunez .15 .40
127 Eli Whiteside .15 .40
128 Lucas Duda .20 .50
129A Matt Moore RC .40 1.00
129B Moore Leg Up FS .40 1.00
130 Asdrubal Cabrera .20 .50
131 Ian Desmond .15 .40
132 Will Venable .15 .40
133 Ivan Nova .20 .50
134 Stephen Lombardozzi RC .25 .60
135 Johnny Cueto .20 .50
136 Casey McGehee .15 .40
137 Jarrod Saltalamacchia .15 .40
138 Pedro Alvarez .15 .40
139 Scott Sizemore .15 .40
140 Troy Tulowitzki .25 .60
141 Brandon Belt .20 .50
142 Travis Wood .15 .40
143 George Kottaras .15 .40
144 Marlon Byrd .15 .40
145A Billy Butler .15 .40
145B Billy Butler VAR SP 5.00 12.00
146 Carlos Gomez .15 .40
147 Orlando Hudson .15 .40
148 Chris Getz .15 .40
149 Chris Sale .25 .60
150 Roy Halladay .20 .50
151 Chris Davis .15 .40
152 Chad Billingsley .15 .40
153 Mark Melancon .15 .40
154 Ty Wigginton .15 .40
155 Matt Cain .20 .50
156 Kenn/Kershaw/Halladay LL .40 1.00
157 Anibal Sanchez .15 .40
158A Josh Reddick .15 .40
158B Josh Reddick VAR SP Rookie Cup 5.00 12.00
159 Chipper/Pujols/Helton LDR .30 .75
160 Kevin Youkilis .25 .60
161 Dee Gordon .15 .40
162 Max Scherzer .25 .60
163 Justin Turner .25 .60
164 Carl Pavano .15 .40
165A Michael Morse .15 .40
165B Michael Morse VAR SP 5.00 12.00
166 Brennan Boesch .15 .40
167 Starlin Castro RB .20 .50
168 Blake Beavan .15 .40
169 Brett Myers .15 .40
170 Jacoby Ellsbury .20 .50
171 Koji Uehara .15 .40
172 Reed Johnson .15 .40
173A Ryan Roberts .15 .40
173B Ryan Roberts VAR SP 5.00 12.00
174 Yadier Molina .30 .75
175 Jared Hughes RC .25 .60
176 Nolan Reimold .15 .40
177 Josh Thole .15 .40
178 Edward Mujica .15 .40
179 Denard Span .15 .40
180 Mariano Rivera .30 .75
181 Reyes/Braun/Kemp LL .20 .50
182 Michael Brantley .15 .40
183 Addison Reed RC .25 .60
184 Wilin Rosario RC .25 .60
185A Pablo Sandoval .20 .50
185B Pablo Sandoval VAR SP 5.00 12.00
185C Pablo Sandoval VAR SP 5.00 12.00
186 John Lannan .15 .40
187 Jose Altuve .20 .50
188A Bobby Abreu .15 .40
188B Bobby Abreu VAR SP 5.00 12.00
189 Alberto Callaspo .15 .40
190 Cole Hamels .20 .50
191 Angel Pagan .15 .40
192 Chipper/Pujols/Jones LDR .30 .75
193 Kelly Shoppach .15 .40
194 Danny Duffy .15 .40
195 Ben Zobrist .20 .50
196 Matt Joyce .15 .40
197 Brendan Ryan .15 .40
198 Matt Dominguez RC .30 .75
199 Adam Dunn .20 .50
200 Miguel Cabrera .25 .60
201 Doug Fister .15 .40
202 Andrew Carignan RC .25 .60
203 Jeff Niemann .15 .40
204 Tom Gorzelanny .15 .40
205 Justin Masterson .15 .40
206 David Robertson .15 .40
207A J.P. Arencibia .15 .40
207B J.P. Arencibia VAR SP Rookie Cup 5.00 12.00
208 Mark Reynolds .15 .40
209 A.J. Burnett .15 .40
210 Zack Greinke .25 .60
211 Kelvin Herrera RC .25 .60
212 Tim Wakefield/CC Sabathia Mark Buehrle LDR .20 .50
213 Alex Avila .15 .40
214 Mike Pelfrey .15 .40
215A Freddie Freeman .30 .75
215B Freddie Freeman VAR SP 5.00 12.00
216 Jason Kipnis .20 .50
217 Texas Rangers PS HL .15 .40
218 Kyle Hudson RC .25 .60
219 Jordan Pacheco RC .25 .60
220 Jay Bruce .20 .50
221 Luke Gregerson .15 .40
222 Chris Coghlan .15 .40
223 Joe Saunders .15 .40
224 Kemp/Prince/Howard LL .20 .50
225 Michael Pineda .15 .40
226 Ryan Hanigan .15 .40
227 Mike Minor .15 .40
228 Brent Lillibridge .15 .40
229 Yunel Escobar .15 .40
230 Justin Morneau .20 .50
231 Dexter Fowler .20 .50
232 Rivera/Johan/Felix LDR .30 .75
233 St. Louis Cardianls PS HL .25 .60
234 Mark Teixeira RB .20 .50
235 Joe Benson RC .25 .60
236 Jose Tabata .15 .40
237 Russell Martin .15 .40
238 Emilio Bonifacio .15 .40
239 Cabrera/Young/Gonzalez .25 .60
240 David Wright .20 .50
241 James McDonald .15 .40
242 Eric Young .15 .40
243 Justin De Fratus RC .25 .60
244 Sergio Santos .15 .40
245 Adam Lind .20 .50
246 Bud Norris .15 .40
247 Clay Buchholz .15 .40
248 Stephen Drew .15 .40
249 Trevor Plouffe .15 .40
250 Jered Weaver .20 .50
251 Jason Bay .20 .50
252 Dellin Betances RC .40 1.00
253 Tim Federowicz RC .25 .60
254 Philip Humber .15 .40
255 Scott Rolen .20 .50
256A Mat Latos .20 .50
256B Mat Latos VAR SP 5.00 12.00
257 Seth Smith .15 .40
258 Jon Jay .25 .60
259 Michael Stutes .15 .40
260 Brian Wilson .25 .60
261 Kyle Blanks .15 .40
262 Shaun Marcum .15 .40
263 Steve Delabar RC .25 .60
264 Chris Carpenter PS HL .20 .50
265 Aroldis Chapman .25 .60
266 Carlos Corporan .15 .40
267 Joel Pineiro .15 .40
268 Miguel Cairo .15 .40
269 Jason Vargas .15 .40
270A Starlin Castro .20 .50
270B Starlin Castro VAR SP 5.00 12.00
271 John Jaso .15 .40
272 Nyjer Morgan PS HL .15 .40
273A David Freese .15 .40
273B David Freese VAR SP 8.00 20.00
273C S.Musial VAR SP 6.00 15.00
274 Alex Liddi RC .25 .60
275 Brad Peacock RC .25 .60
276 Scott Baker .15 .40
277 Jeremy Moore RC .25 .60
278 Randy Wells .15 .40
279 R.A. Dickey .20 .50
280A Ryan Howard .20 .50
280B Ryan Howard VAR SP Back of jersey 8.00 20.00
281 Mark Trumbo .15 .40
282 Ryan Raburn .15 .40
283 Brandon Allen .15 .40
284 Tony Gwynn .15 .40
285 Drew Storen .15 .40
286 Franklin Gutierrez .15 .40
287 Antonio Bastardo .15 .40
288 Miguel Montero .15 .40
289 Casey Kotchman .15 .40
290 Curtis Granderson .20 .50
291 David Freese WS HL .15 .40
292 Ben Revere .20 .50
293 Eric Thames .20 .50
294 John Axford .15 .40
295 Jayson Werth .20 .50
296 Brayan Pena .15 .40
297 Kershaw/Halladay/Lee LL .40 1.00
298 Jeff Keppinger .15 .40
299 Mitch Moreland .15 .40
300 Josh Hamilton .20 .50
301 Alexi Ogando .15 .40
302 Jose Bautista/Curtis Granderson/Mark Teixeira LL .20 .50
303 Danny Valencia .20 .50
304 Brandon Morrow .15 .40
305 Chipper Jones .25 .60
306 Ubaldo Jimenez .15 .40
307 Vance Worley .20 .50
308A Mike Leake .15 .40
308B Mike Leake VAR SP 5.00 12.00
309 Kurt Suzuki .15 .40
310 Adrian Beltre .25 .60
311 John Danks .15 .40
312 Nick Hundley .15 .40
313 Phil Hughes .15 .40
314 Matt LaPorta .15 .40
315 Dustin Ackley .15 .40
316 Nick Blackburn .15 .40
317 Tyler Chatwood .15 .40
318 Erik Bedard .15 .40
319 Verland/CC/Weaver LL .25 .60
320 Matt Holliday .25 .60
321 Jason Bourgeois .15 .40
322 Ricky Nolasco .15 .40
323 Jason Isringhausen .15 .40
324 ARod/Thme/Gmbi LDR .30 .75
325 Chris Schwinden RC .30 .75
326 Kevin Gregg .15 .40
327 Mark Kotsay .15 .40
328 John Lackey .20 .50
329 Allen Craig WS HL .20 .50
330A Matt Kemp .20 .50
330B Matt Kemp VAR SP 6.00 15.00
330C W.Mays VAR SP 6.00 15.00
331A A.Pujols w/Glove SP 40.00 80.00
331B Albert Pujols Swinging .30 .75
331C Pujols Wearing suit SP 8.00 20.00
331D Babe Ruth VAR SP 8.00 20.00
332A Jose Reyes .15 .40
332B Jose Reyes SP 30.00 60.00
333 Roger Bernadina .15 .40
334 Anthony Rizzo .30 .75
335 Josh Satin RC .30 .75
336 Gavin Floyd .15 .40
337 Glen Perkins .15 .40
338 Jose Constanza RC .25 .60
339 Clayton Richard .15 .40
340 Adam LaRoche .15 .40
341 Edwin Encarnacion .25 .60
342 Kosuke Fukudome .20 .50
343 Salvador Perez .20 .50
344 Nelson Cruz .25 .60
345 Jonathan Papelbon .20 .50
346 Dillon Gee .15 .40
347 Craig Gentry .15 .40
348 Alfonso Soriano .20 .50
349 Tim Lincecum .20 .50
350A Evan Longoria .20 .50
350B Evan Longoria VAR SP With fans 5.00 12.00
351 Corey Hart .15 .40
352 Julio Teheran .20 .50
353 John Mayberry .15 .40
354 Jeremy Hellickson .15 .40
355 Mark Buehrle .20 .50
356 Endy Chavez .15 .40
357 Aaron Harang .15 .40
358 Jacob Turner .20 .50
359 Danny Espinosa .15 .40
360 Nelson Cruz RB .25 .60
361 Chase Utley .20 .50
362 Dayan Viciedo .15 .40
363 Fernando Salas .15 .40
364 Brandon Beachy .15 .40
365 Aramis Ramirez .15 .40
366 Jose Molina .15 .40
367 Chris Volstad .15 .40
368 Carl Crawford .20 .50
369 Huston Street .15 .40
370 Lyle Overbay .15 .40
371 Jim Thome .20 .50
372 Daniel Descalso .15 .40
373 Carlos Gonzalez .20 .50
374 Coco Crisp .15 .40
375 Drew Stubbs .15 .40
376 Carlos Quentin .15 .40
377 Brandon Inge .15 .40
378 Brandon League .15 .40
379 Sergio Romo RC .30 .75
380 Daniel Murphy .20 .50
381 David DeJesus .15 .40
382 Wandy Rodriguez .15 .40
383 Andre Ethier .20 .50
384 Sean Marshall .15 .40
385 David Murphy .15 .40
386 Ryan Zimmerman .20 .50
387 Joakim Soria .15 .40
388 Chase Headley .15 .40
389 Alexi Casilla .15 .40
390 Taylor Green RC .25 .60
391 Rod Barajas .20 .50
392 Cliff Lee .20 .50
393 Manny Ramirez .25 .60
394 Bryan LaHair .15 .40
395A Jonathan Lucroy .20 .50
395B Rod Barajas .20 .50
396A Yoenis Cespedes RC .60 1.50
396B Cespedes Grey Jsy FS .60 1.50
397 Hector Noesi .15 .40
398A Buster Posey .30 .75
398B Buster Posey VAR SP 8.00 20.00
399 Brian McCann .20 .50
400A Robinson Cano VAR SP 5.00 12.00
400B Robinson Cano .20 .50
401 Kenley Jansen .20 .50
402 Allen Craig .20 .50
403 Bronson Arroyo .15 .40
404 Jonathan Sanchez .15 .40
405 Nathan Eovaldi .20 .50
406 Juan Rivera .15 .40
407 Torii Hunter .20 .50
408 Jonny Venters .15 .40
409 Greg Holland RC .30 .75
410 Jeff Locke RC .40 1.00
411A T.Nishioka VAR SP 5.00 12.00
411B Tsuyoshi Nishioka .20 .50
412 Don Kelly .15 .40
413 Frank Francisco .15 .40
414 Ryan Vogelsong .15 .40
415 Rafael Furcal .15 .40
416 Todd Helton .20 .50
417 Carlos Pena .20 .50
418 Jarrod Parker RC .30 .75
419 Cameron Maybin .15 .40
420 Barry Zito .20 .50
421A Heath Bell VAR SP 5.00 12.00
421B Heath Bell .15 .40
422 Austin Jackson .20 .50
423 Colby Rasmus .20 .50
424 Vladimir Guerrero RB .20 .50
425 Carlos Zambrano .20 .50
426 Eric Hinske .15 .40
427 Rafael Dolis RC .30 .75
428 Jordan Schafer .15 .40
429 Michael Bourn .15 .40
430A Felix Hernandez .20 .50
430B Felix Hernandez VAR SP Wearing glasses 5.00 12.00
431 Guillermo Moscoso .20 .50
432 Wei-Yin Chen RC .60 1.50
433 Nate McLouth .15 .40
434 Jason Motte .15 .40
435 Jeff Baker .15 .40
436 Chris Perez .15 .40
437 Yoshinori Tateyama RC .30 .75
438 Juan Uribe .15 .40
439 Elvis Andrus .20 .50
440 Chien-Ming Wang .20 .50
441 Mike Aviles .15 .40
442 Johnny Giavotella .15 .40
443 B.J. Upton .20 .50
444 Rafael Betancourt .15 .40
445 Ramon Santiago .15 .40
446 Mike Trout 10.00 25.00
447 Jair Jurrjens .15 .40
448 Dustin Moseley .15 .40
449 Shane Victorino .20 .50
450B Justin Upton .20 .50
450A Justin Upton VAR SP 5.00 12.00
451 Jeff Francoeur .20 .50
452 Robert Andino .15 .40
453 Garrett Jones .15 .40
454 Michael Cuddyer .15 .40
455 Jed Lowrie .15 .40
456 Omar Infante .15 .40
457 J.D. Martinez .25 .60
458 Kyle Kendrick .15 .40
459 Eric Surkamp RC .40 1.00
460 Thomas Field RC .25 .60
461 Victor Martinez .20 .50
462A Brett Lawrie RC .30 .75
462B Brett Lawrie VAR SP 5.00 12.00
462C B.Lawrie Fielding FS .30 .75
463 Francisco Cordero .15 .40
464 Joe Savery RC .30 .75
465 Michael Schwimer RC .30 .75
466 Lance Berkman .20 .50
467 Juan Francisco .20 .50
468 Nick Markakis .20 .50
469 Vinnie Pestano .15 .40
470A Howie Kendrick VAR SP 5.00 12.00
470B Howie Kendrick .15 .40
471 James Shields .15 .40
472 Mat Gamel .15 .40
473 Evan Meek .15 .40
474 Mitch Maier .15 .40
475 Chris Dickerson .15 .40
476 Ramon Hernandez .15 .40
477 Edinson Volquez .15 .40
478 Rajai Davis .15 .40
479 Johan Santana .20 .50
480 J.J. Putz .15 .40
481 Matt Harrison .15 .40
482 Chris Capuano .15 .40
483 Alex Gordon .20 .50
484 Hisashi Iwakuma RC .50 1.25
485 Carlos Marmol .15 .40
486 Jerry Sands .15 .40
487 Eric Sogard .15 .40
488 Nick Swisher .20 .50
489 Andres Torres .15 .40
490 Chris Carpenter .20 .50
491 Jose Valverde RB .20 .50
492 Rickie Weeks .15 .40
493 Ryan Madson .15 .40
494 Darwin Barney .15 .40
495 Adam Wainwright .20 .50
496 Jorge De La Rosa .15 .40
497A Andrew McCutchen .25 .60
497B Andrew McCutchen VAR SP 5.00 12.00
497C R.Clemente VAR SP 8.00 20.00
498 Joey Votto .25 .60
499 Francisco Rodriguez .20 .50
500 Alex Rodriguez .30 .75
501 Matt Capps .15 .40
502 Collin Cowgill RC .25 .60
503 Tyler Clippard .15 .40
504 Ryan Dempster .15 .40
505 Fautino De Los Santos .15 .40
506 David Ortiz .25 .60
507 Norichika Aoki RC .30 .75
508 Brandon Phillips .15 .40
509 Travis Snider .15 .40
510 Randall Delgado .15 .40
511 Ervin Santana .15 .40
512 Josh Willingham .20 .50
513 Gaby Sanchez .20 .50
514 Brian Roberts .15 .40
515 Willie Bloomquist .15 .40
516 Charlie Morton .25 .60
517 Francisco Liriano .15 .40
518 Jake Peavy .15 .40
519 Gio Gonzalez .20 .50
520 Ryan Adams .15 .40
521 Ruben Tejada .15 .40
522 Matt Downs .15 .40
523 Jim Johnson .15 .40
524 Martin Prado .15 .40
525 Paul Maholm .15 .40
526 Casper Wells .15 .40
527 Aaron Hill .15 .40
528 Bryan Petersen .15 .40
529 Luke Hughes .15 .40
530 Cliff Pennington .15 .40
531 Joel Hanrahan .15 .40
532 Tim Stauffer .15 .40
533 Ian Stewart .15 .40
534 Hector Gomez RC .25 .60
535 Joe Mauer .20 .50
536 Kendrys Morales .15 .40
537A Ichiro Suzuki .30 .75
537B I.Suzuki VAR SP 6.00 15.00
538 Wilson Betemit .15 .40
539 Andrew Bailey .15 .40
540A Dustin Pedroia .25 .60
540B D.Pedroia VAR SP 6.00 15.00
541 Jack Hannahan .15 .40
542 Jeff Samardzija .15 .40
543 Josh Johnson .20 .50
544 Josh Collmenter .20 .50
545 Randy Wolf .15 .40
546 Matt Thornton .15 .40
547 Jason Giambi .15 .40
548 Charlie Furbush .15 .40
549 Kelly Johnson .15 .40
550 Ian Kinsler .20 .50
551 Joe Blanton .15 .40
552 Kyle Drabek .15 .40
553 James Darnell RC .25 .60
554 Raul Ibanez .20 .50
555 Alex Presley .15 .40
556 Stephen Strasburg .25 .60
557 Zack Cozart .15 .40
558 Wade Miley RC .30 .75
559 Brandon Dickson RC .30 .75
560 J.A. Happ .20 .50
561 Freddy Sanchez .25 .60
562 Henderson Alvarez .15 .40
563 Alex White .15 .40
564 Jose Valverde .20 .50
565 Dan Uggla .20 .50
566 Jason Donald .15 .40
567 Mike Stanton .25 .60
568 Jason Castro .15 .40
569 Travis Hafner .15 .40
570 Zach McAllister RC .30 .75
571 J.J. Hardy .15 .40
572 Hiroki Kuroda .15 .40
573 Kyle Farnsworth .20 .50
574 Kerry Wood .15 .40
575 Garrett Richards RC .40 1.00
576 Jonathan Herrera .15 .40
577 Dallas Braden .15 .40
578 Wade Davis .20 .50
579 Dan Uggla RB .20 .50
580 Tony Campana .15 .40
581 Jason Kubel .15 .40
582 Shin-Soo Choo .20 .50
583 Josh Tomlin .15 .40
584 Daric Barton .15 .40
585 Jimmy Paredes .15 .40
586 Daisuke Matsuzaka .20 .50
587 Chris Johnson .15 .40
588 Mark Ellis .15 .40
589 Alex Gonzalez .15 .40
590 Humberto Quintero .15 .40
591 Aubrey Huff .15 .40
592 Carlos Lee .15 .40
593 Marco Scutaro .20 .50
594 Ricky Romero .15 .40
595 David Carpenter RC .30 .75
596 Freddy Garcia .15 .40
597 Hank Conger .15 .40
598 Reid Brignac .15 .40
599 Zach Britton .20 .50
600A Clayton Kershaw .40 1.00
600B Clayton Kershaw VAR SP Brooklyn jersey 5.00 12.00
601 Dan Haren .15 .40
602 Alejandro De Aza .15 .40
603 Lonnie Chisenhall .15 .40
604 Juan Abreu RC .30 .75
605 Jason Bartlett .15 .40
606 Mike Carp .15 .40
607 CC Sabathia .20 .50
608 Paul Goldschmidt .25 .60
609 Lorenzo Cain .15 .40
610 Cody Ross .15 .40
611 Neftali Feliz .15 .40
612 Carlos Beltran .20 .50
613 C.J. Wilson .15 .40
614 Andruw Jones .15 .40
615 Luis Marte RC .25 .60
616 Tyler Pastornicky RC .25 .60
617 Jimmy Rollins .20 .50
618 Eric Chavez .15 .40
619 Tyler Greene .15 .40
620 Trayvon Robinson .15 .40
621 Scott Hairston .15 .40
622 Daniel Hudson .15 .40
623 Clint Barmes .15 .40
624 Gerardo Parra .15 .40
625 Tommy Hunter .15 .40
626 Alexei Ramirez .20 .50
627 Justin Smoak .20 .50
628 Sean Rodriguez .15 .40
629 Gordon Beckham .15 .40
630 Logan Morrison .15 .40
631 Ryan Kalish .15 .40
632 Joe Nathan .15 .40
633 Chris Narveson .15 .40
634 Jose Contreras .15 .40
635 Brett Gardner .20 .50
636 Chris Heisey .15 .40
637 Brad Brach RC .25 .60
638 Derek Lowe .15 .40
639A Justin Verlander .25 .60
639B J.Verlander VAR SP 6.00 15.00
640 Jemile Weeks RC .15 .40
641 Derek Jeter RB .60 1.50
642 Mike Moustakas .20 .50
643 Chris Young .15 .40
644 Andy Dirks .15 .40
645 Kyle Seager .15 .40
646 Francisco Cervelli .15 .40
647 Bruce Chen .15 .40
648 Josh Beckett .15 .40
649 Brandon Crawford .15 .40
650A Prince Fielder .20 .50
650B Prince Fielder VAR SP 5.00 12.00
651 Ryan Sweeney .15 .40
652 Grant Balfour .15 .40
653 Jordan Walden .15 .40
654 Yovani Gallardo .20 .50
655 Ryan Doumit .15 .40
656 Carlos Santana .20 .50
657 Dave Sappelt RC .30 .75
658 Juan Pierre .15 .40
659 Homer Bailey .15 .40
660A Yu Darvish RC .60 1.50
660B Darvish Left Hand SP 5.00 12.00
660C Darvish Gray jsy SP .60 1.50
661A Bryce Harper SP RC 300.00 600.00
661B Bryce Harper AU 600.00 1000.00
661C B.Harper Leg up FS 8.00 20.00
661D B.Harper Yelling FS 8.00 20.00
NNO Fenway Park Dirt 8.00 20.00

2012 Topps Black

*BLACK VET: 10X TO 25X BASIC
*BLACK RC: 6X TO 15X BASIC RC
SER.1 ODDS 1:150 HOBBY
SER.2 ODDS 1:108 HOBBY
STATED PRINT RUN 61 SER.#'d SETS
7 Mickey Mantle 60.00 120.00
30 Derek Jeter 60.00 120.00

41 Devin Mesoraco 15.00 40.00
44 Edwin Jackson 30.00 60.00
53 St. Louis Cardinals WS HL 20.00 50.00
93 Skip Schumaker 12.50 30.00
97 Jim Thome RB 20.00 50.00
129 Matt Moore 40.00 80.00
164 Carl Pavano 6.00 15.00
179 Denard Span 15.00 40.00
305 Chipper Jones 20.00 50.00
307 Vance Worley 10.00 25.00
329 Allen Craig WS HL 12.50 30.00
330 Matt Kemp 15.00 40.00
377 Brandon Inge 10.00 25.00
380 Daniel Murphy 8.00 20.00
418 Jarrod Parker 8.00 20.00
432 Wei-Yin Chen 30.00 60.00
438 Juan Uribe 12.50 30.00
441 Mike Aviles 8.00 20.00
462 Brett Lawrie 12.50 30.00
475 Chris Dickerson 6.00 15.00
482 Chris Capuano 15.00 40.00
501 Matt Capps 6.00 15.00
518 Jake Peavy 6.00 15.00
531 Joel Hanrahan 8.00 20.00
539 Andrew Bailey 8.00 20.00
561 Freddy Sanchez 8.00 20.00
610 Cody Ross 6.00 15.00
613 C.J. Wilson 10.00 25.00
614 Andruw Jones 6.00 15.00
617 Jimmy Rollins 10.00 25.00
634 Jose Contreras 8.00 20.00
636 Chris Heisey 8.00 20.00
644 Andy Dirks 6.00 15.00
648 Josh Beckett 10.00 25.00
658 Juan Pierre 8.00 20.00

2012 Topps Factory Set Orange

*RED VET: 4X TO 10X BASIC
*RED RC: 2.5X TO 6X BASIC RC
ONE PACK OF FIVE RED PER FACT.SET
STATED PRINT RUN 190 SER.#'d SETS
661 Bryce Harper 30.00 60.00

2012 Topps Gold

*GOLD VET: 1X TO 2.5X BASIC
*GOLD RC: .6X TO 1.5X BASIC RC
STATED ODDS 1:3 UPD.HOBBY
STATED PRINT RUN 2012 SER.#'d SETS

2012 Topps Gold Sparkle

*GOLD VET: 1.5X TO 4X BASIC
*GOLD RC: 1X TO 2.5X BASIC RC
STATED ODDS 1:4 HOBBY
660 Yu Darvish 8.00 20.00

2012 Topps Target Red Border

*TARGET RED: 1.25X TO 3X BASIC
*TARGET RED RC: .75X TO 2X BASIC RC
FOUND IN TARGET RETAIL PACKS

2012 Topps Toys R Us Purple Border

*TRU PURPLE: 1.2X TO 3X BASIC
*TRU PURPLE RC: .75X TO 2X BASIC RC
FOUND IN TOYS R US RETAIL PACKS

2012 Topps Wal-Mart Blue Border

*WM BLUE: 1.25X TO 3X BASIC
*WM BLUE RC: .75X TO 2X BASIC RC
FOUND IN WALMART RETAIL PACKS

2012 Topps 1987 Topps Minis

COMPLETE SET (150) 50.00 100.00
COMP.SER.1 SET (50) 12.50 30.00
COMP.SER.2 SET (50) 15.00 40.00
COMP.UPD SET (50) 12.50 30.00
STATED ODDS 1:4 HOBBY
UPDATE ODDS 1:4 UPDATE
1-50 ISSUED IN SERIES 1
51-100 ISSUED IN SERIES 2
101-150 ISSUED IN UPDATE
TM1 Ryan Braun .40 1.00
TM2 Mike Stanton .60 1.50
TM3 Eric Hosmer .50 1.25
TM4 Michael Young .40 1.00
TM5 Howie Kendrick .40 1.00
TM6 Dustin Ackley .40 1.00
TM7 Joey Votto .60 1.50
TM8 Ian Kinsler .50 1.25
TM9 Jason Heyward .50 1.25
TM10 Roy Halladay .50 1.25
TM11 Ubaldo Jimenez .40 1.00
TM12 Shin-Soo Choo .50 1.25
TM13 Jayson Werth .50 1.25
TM14 Ichiro Suzuki .75 2.00
TM15 Robinson Cano .50 1.25
TM16 Derek Jeter 1.50 4.00
TM17 Craig Kimbrel .50 1.25
TM18 Michael Bourn .40 1.00
TM19 Lance Berkman .50 1.25
TM20 Evan Longoria .50 1.25
TM21 Matt Holliday .60 1.50
TM22 Brett Gardner .50 1.25
TM23 Dustin Pedroia .60 1.50
TM24 Dan Uggla .50 1.25
TM25 Hanley Ramirez .50 1.25
TM26 David Wright .50 1.25
TM27 Ryan Howard .50 1.25
TM28 Buster Posey .75 2.00
TM29 Adam Jones .50 1.25
TM30 Andre Ethier .50 1.25
TM31 Brandon Phillips .40 1.00
TM32 Tommy Hanson .40 1.00
TM33 Adrian Gonzalez .50 1.25
TM34 Josh Johnson .50 1.25
TM35 Zack Greinke .60 1.50
TM36 Mariano Rivera .75 2.00
TM37 CC Sabathia .50 1.25
TM38 Chase Utley .50 1.25
TM39 Jay Bruce .50 1.25
TM40 Andrew McCutchen .60 1.50
TM41 James Shields .40 1.00
TM42 Josh Hamilton .50 1.25
TM43 Mat Latos .50 1.25
TM44 Troy Tulowitzki .60 1.50
TM45 Shane Victorino .50 1.25
TM46 David Price .50 1.25
TM47 Starlin Castro .50 1.25
TM48 Paul Konerko .40 1.00
TM49 Jered Weaver .50 1.25
TM50 Curtis Granderson .50 1.25
TM51 Albert Pujols .75 2.00
TM52 Miguel Cabrera .60 1.50
TM53 Matt Kemp .50 1.25
TM54 Justin Upton .50 1.25
TM55 Justin Verlander .60 1.50
TM56 Jose Bautista .50 1.25
TM57 Jacoby Ellsbury .50 1.25
TM58 Prince Fielder .50 1.25
TM59 Cliff Lee .50 1.25
TM60 Clayton Kershaw 1.00 2.50
TM61 Carlos Gonzalez .50 1.25
TM62 Tim Lincecum .50 1.25
TM63 Felix Hernandez .50 1.25
TM64 Jose Reyes .40 1.00
TM65 Mark Teixeira .50 1.25
TM66 Cole Hamels .50 1.25
TM67 Adrian Beltre .60 1.50
TM68 Dan Haren .40 1.00
TM69 Ryan Zimmerman .50 1.25
TM70 Jon Lester .40 1.00
TM71 Carlos Santana .50 1.25
TM72 Hunter Pence .50 1.25
TM73 Alex Gordon .50 1.25
TM74 Nelson Cruz .60 1.50
TM75 Alex Rodriguez .75 2.00
TM76 Rickie Weeks .40 1.00
TM77 Mike Napoli .40 1.00
TM78 Brian McCann .50 1.25
TM79 Brian Wilson .60 1.50
TM80 Pablo Sandoval .50 1.25
TM81 David Price .50 1.25
TM82 Josh Beckett .40 1.00
TM83 Joe Mauer .50 1.25
TM84 Stephen Strasburg .60 1.50
TM85 Michael Pineda .40 1.00
TM86 Bob Gibson .40 1.00
TM87 Stan Musial 1.00 2.50
TM88 Brooks Robinson .50 1.25
TM89 Frank Robinson .40 1.00
TM90 Babe Ruth 1.50 4.00
TM91 Tom Seaver .40 1.00
TM92 Sandy Koufax 1.25 3.00
TM93 Warren Spahn .40 1.00
TM94 Jim Palmer .40 1.00
TM95 Roger Maris .60 1.50
TM96 Mickey Mantle 2.00 5.00
TM97 Ken Griffey Jr. 1.25 3.00
TM98 Joe DiMaggio 1.25 3.00
TM99 Roberto Clemente 1.50 4.00
TM100 Johnny Bench .60 1.50
TM101 Paul Goldschmidt .60 1.50
TM102 Reggie Jackson .40 1.00
TM103 Lance Lynn .40 1.00
TM104 Chipper Jones .60 1.50
TM105 Ichiro Suzuki .75 2.00
TM106 Al Kaline .60 1.50
TM107 Madison Bumgarner .50 1.25
TM108 Jesus Montero .40 1.00
TM109 Carl Yastrzemski 1.00 2.50
TM110 Asdrubal Cabrera .50 1.25
TM111 Andy Pettitte .50 1.25
TM112 Yu Darvish 1.00 2.50
TM113 Billy Butler .40 1.00
TM114 Jonathan Papelbon .40 1.00
TM115 Carlos Beltran .50 1.25
TM116 Ian Kennedy .40 1.00
TM117 Gary Carter .40 1.00
TM118 Austin Jackson .40 1.00
TM119 Gio Gonzalez .50 1.25
TM120 Matt Cain .50 1.25
TM121 Mat Latos .50 1.25
TM122 Yonder Alonso .40 1.00
TM123 C.J. Wilson .40 1.00
TM124 Yoenis Cespedes 1.00 2.50
TM125 Lou Gehrig 1.25 3.00
TM126 Jackie Robinson .60 1.50
TM127 Mike Trout 4.00 10.00
TM128 Freddie Freeman .75 2.00
TM129 Elvis Andrus .50 1.25
TM130 Ty Cobb 1.00 2.50
TM131 Jimmy Rollins .50 1.25
TM132 Jim Rice .40 1.00
TM133 Will Middlebrooks .50 1.25
TM134 Bryan LaHair .40 1.00
TM135 Mike Moustakas .50 1.25
TM136 Brandon Beachy .50 1.25
TM137 Cal Ripken Jr. 2.00 5.00
TM138 Ryan Dempster .40 1.00
TM139 Matt Moore .60 1.50
TM140 Don Mattingly 1.25 3.00
TM141 Nolan Ryan 2.00 5.00
TM142 Albert Belle .25 .60
TM143 R.A. Dickey .50 1.25
TM144 Mark Trumbo .40 1.00
TM145 Chris Sale .60 1.50
TM146 Brett Lawrie .60 1.50
TM147 Johan Santana .50 1.25
TM148 Justin Morneau .50 1.25
TM149 Giancarlo Stanton .60 1.50
TM150 Bryce Harper 4.00 10.00

2012 Topps A Cut Above

COMPLETE SET (25) 6.00 15.00
STATED ODDS 1:6 HOBBY
ACA1 Prince Fielder .50 1.25
ACA2 Albert Pujols .75 2.00
ACA3 Justin Verlander .60 1.50
ACA4 Ken Griffey Jr. 1.25 3.00
ACA5 Ryan Braun .40 1.00
ACA6 Evan Longoria .50 1.25
ACA7 Dustin Pedroia .60 1.50
ACA8 Hanley Ramirez .50 1.25
ACA9 Cal Ripken Jr. 2.00 5.00
ACA10 Miguel Cabrera .60 1.50
ACA11 Nolan Ryan 2.00 5.00
ACA12 Stan Musial 1.00 2.50
ACA13 Mike Schmidt 1.00 2.50
ACA14 Willie Mays 1.25 3.00
ACA15 Jose Bautista .50 1.25
ACA16 Sandy Koufax 1.25 3.00
ACA17 Tim Lincecum .50 1.25
ACA18 Roy Halladay .50 1.25
ACA19 Robinson Cano .50 1.25
ACA20 Johnny Bench .60 1.50
ACA21 Hank Aaron 1.25 3.00
ACA22 Jackie Robinson .60 1.50
ACA23 Matt Kemp .50 1.25
ACA24 Mickey Mantle 2.00 5.00
ACA25 Troy Tulowitzki .60 1.50

2012 Topps A Cut Above Relics

STATED ODDS 1:9525 HOBBY
STATED PRINT RUN 50 SER.#'d SETS
AP Albert Pujols 15.00 40.00
EL Evan Longoria 8.00 20.00
HA Hank Aaron 30.00 60.00
HR Hanley Ramirez 4.00 10.00
JB Johnny Bench 12.50 30.00
JR Jackie Robinson 12.00 30.00
JV Justin Verlander 12.50 30.00
NR Nolan Ryan 30.00 60.00
RB Ryan Braun 12.50 30.00
TL Tim Lincecum 10.00 25.00
WM Willie Mays 40.00 80.00

2012 Topps Babe Ruth Commemorative Rings

BR1 Babe Ruth 6.00 15.00
1923 World Series
BR2 Babe Ruth 6.00 15.00
1927 World Series
BR3 Babe Ruth 6.00 15.00
1928 World Series
BR4 Babe Ruth 6.00 15.00
1932 World Series
BR5 Babe Ruth 6.00 15.00
1918 World Series

2012 Topps Career Day

COMPLETE SET (25) 6.00 15.00
STATED ODDS 1:6 HOBBY
CD1 Albert Pujols .75 2.00
CD2 Ken Griffey Jr. 1.25 3.00
CD3 Al Kaline .60 1.50
CD4 Stan Musial 1.00 2.50
CD5 Sandy Koufax 1.25 3.00
CD6 Joe DiMaggio 1.25 3.00
CD7 Frank Robinson .40 1.00
CD8 Mike Schmidt 1.00 2.50
CD9 Johnny Bench .60 1.50
CD10 Ryan Braun .40 1.00
CD11 Miguel Cabrera .60 1.50
CD12 Reggie Jackson .40 1.00
CD13 Evan Longoria .50 1.25
CD14 Dustin Pedroia .60 1.50
CD15 Willie Mays 1.25 3.00
CD16 Ryan Howard .50 1.25
CD17 Joey Votto .60 1.50
CD18 Robinson Cano .50 1.25
CD19 Jackie Robinson .60 1.50
CD20 Josh Hamilton .50 1.25
CD21 Matt Kemp .50 1.25
CD22 Mickey Mantle 2.00 5.00
CD23 Roberto Clemente 1.50 4.00
CD24 Troy Tulowitzki .60 1.50
CD25 Yogi Berra .60 1.50

2012 Topps Classic Walk-Offs

COMPLETE SET (15) 5.00 12.00
STATED ODDS 1:8 HOBBY
CW1 Bill Mazeroski .40 1.00
CW2 Carlton Fisk .40 1.00
CW3 Johnny Bench .60 1.50
CW4 David Ortiz .60 1.50
CW5 Jay Bruce .50 1.25
CW6 Mark Teixeira .50 1.25
CW7 Mickey Mantle 2.00 5.00
CW8 Alfonso Soriano .50 1.25
CW9 Rafael Furcal .40 1.00
CW10 Jim Thome .50 1.25
CW11 Magglio Ordonez .40 1.00
CW12 Alex Gonzalez .40 1.00
CW13 Scott Podsednik .25 .60
CW14 David Ortiz .60 1.50
CW15 Derek Jeter 1.50 4.00

2012 Topps Classic Walk-Offs Relics

STATED ODDS 1:20,200 HOBBY
STATED PRINT RUN 50 SER.#'d SETS
BM Bill Mazeroski 40.00 80.00
CF Carlton Fisk 40.00 80.00
DJ Derek Jeter 50.00 100.00
DO David Ortiz 10.00 25.00
JB Johnny Bench 10.00 25.00
JB Jay Bruce 10.00 25.00
JT Jim Thome 10.00 25.00
MM Mickey Mantle 60.00 120.00
MT Mark Teixeira 30.00 60.00

2012 Topps Gold Futures

COMPLETE SET (50) 10.00 25.00
COMP.SER.1 SET (25) 5.00 12.00
COMP.SER.2 SET (25) 5.00 12.00
STATED ODDS 1:6 HOBBY
1-25 ISSUED IN SERIES 1
26-50 ISSUED IN SERIES 2
GF1 Michael Pineda .40 1.00
GF2 Zach Britton .40 1.00
GF3 Brandon Belt .50 1.25
GF4 Freddie Freeman .75 2.00
GF5 Eric Hosmer .50 1.25
GF6 Dustin Ackley .40 1.00
GF7 Starlin Castro .50 1.25
GF8 Aroldis Chapman .60 1.50
GF9 Jeremy Hellickson .40 1.00
GF10 Craig Kimbrel .50 1.25
GF11 Julio Teheran .50 1.25
GF12 J.P. Arencibia .40 1.00
GF13 Anthony Rizzo .75 2.00
GF14 Mike Stanton .60 1.50
GF15 Mark Trumbo .40 1.00
GF16 Mike Trout 8.00 20.00
GF17 Dee Gordon .40 1.00
GF18 Alexi Ogando .40 1.00
GF19 Jose Tabata .40 1.00
GF20 Mike Moustakas .50 1.25
GF21 Arodys Vizcaino .25 .60
GF22 Ryan Lavarnway .40 1.00
GF23 Ivan Nova .50 1.25
GF24 Paul Goldschmidt .60 1.50
GF25 Jason Kipnis .50 1.25
GF26 Jesus Montero .40 1.00
GF27 Matt Moore .60 1.50
GF28 Buster Posey .75 2.00
GF29 Chris Sale .60 1.50
GF30 Carlos Santana .50 1.25
GF31 Desmond Jennings .50 1.25
GF32 Drew Storen .40 1.00
GF33 Madison Bumgarner .50 1.25
GF34 Brandon Beachy .40 1.00
GF35 Randall Delgado .40 1.00
GF36 Brad Peacock .40 1.00
GF37 Jordan Walden .40 1.00
GF38 Domonic Brown .50 1.25
GF39 Drew Pomeranz .40 1.00
GF40 Jason Heyward .50 1.25
GF41 Neftali Feliz .40 1.00
GF42 Yonder Alonso .40 1.00
GF43 Stephen Strasburg .60 1.50
GF44 Matt Dominguez .50 1.25
GF45 Lonnie Chisenhall .40 1.00
GF46 Jemile Weeks .40 1.00
GF47 Jacob Turner .50 1.25
GF48 Dellin Betances .60 1.50
GF49 Liam Hendriks .40 1.00
GF50 Corey Luebke .40 1.00

2012 Topps Gold Futures Coins

UPDATE ODDS 1:9725 HOBBY
SER.2 ODDS 1:8,487 HOBBY
PRINT RUNS B/WN 5-58 COPIES PER
NO PRICING ON QTY 5 OR LESS
BH Bryce Harper/34 UPD 100.00 200.00
EH Eric Hosmer/35 12.50 30.00
JH Jeremy Hellickson/58 10.00 25.00
MM Matt Moore/55 12.50 30.00
MP Michael Pineda/36 12.50 30.00
MT Mike Trout/27 125.00 300.00
SS Stephen Strasburg/37 40.00 80.00
YC Yoenis Cespedes/52 UPD 12.00 30.00

2012 Topps Gold Futures Relics

SER.1 ODDS 1:13,400 HOBBY
SER.2 ODDS 1:9525 HOBBY
STATED PRINT RUN 50 SER.#'d SETS
AR Anthony Rizzo 10.00 25.00
BB Brandon Belt 6.00 15.00
BB Brandon Beachy S2 6.00 15.00
BP Buster Posey S2 12.50 30.00
CK Craig Kimbrel 5.00 12.00
CS Chris Sale S2 12.50 30.00
DA Dustin Ackley 30.00 60.00
DG Dee Gordon 6.00 15.00
DJ Desmond Jennings S2 5.00 12.00
DP Drew Pomeranz S2 10.00 25.00
DS Drew Storen S2 10.00 25.00
EH Eric Hosmer 10.00 25.00
JA J.P. Arencibia 8.00 20.00
JH Jeremy Hellickson 6.00 15.00
JM Jesus Montero S2 10.00 25.00
JT Julio Teheran 5.00 12.00
JW Jordan Walden S2 10.00 25.00
MB Madison Bumgarner S2 12.50 30.00
MM Matt Moore S2 8.00 20.00
MP Michael Pineda 10.00 25.00
MS Mike Stanton 10.00 25.00
MT Mark Trumbo 10.00 25.00
SC Starlin Castro 8.00 20.00
ZB Zach Britton 8.00 20.00
MTR Mike Trout 75.00 200.00

2012 Topps Gold Rush Wrapper Redemption

COMPLETE SET (100) 125.00 250.00
1 Albert Pujols 1.50 4.00
2 Adrian Gonzalez 1.00 2.50
3 Albert Belle .50 1.25
4 Allen Craig 1.00 2.50
5 Aroldis Chapman 1.25 3.00
6 Brandon Phillips .75 2.00
7 Brandon Belt 1.00 2.50
8 Brett Gardner 1.00 2.50
9 Nelson Cruz 1.25 3.00
10 Carl Yastrzemski 2.00 5.00
11 Carlos Gonzalez 1.00 2.50
12 Jay Bruce 1.00 2.50
13 Chris Young .75 2.00
14 Clayton Kershaw 2.00 5.00
15 Dan Uggla .75 2.00
16 Daniel Hudson .75 2.00
17 Danny Espinosa .75 2.00
18 Edgar Martinez .75 2.00
19 Felix Hernandez 1.00 2.50
20 Willie Mays 2.50 6.00
21 Frank Thomas 1.25 3.00
22 Jordan Zimmermann 1.00 2.50
23 Ian Kinsler 1.00 2.50
24 Tony Gwynn 1.25 3.00
25 Jason Motte .75 2.00
26 Jemile Weeks .75 2.00
27 Jered Weaver 1.00 2.50
28 Jesus Montero .75 2.00
29 Joe Mauer 1.00 2.50
30 Mariano Rivera 1.50 4.00
31 Jhonny Peralta .75 2.00
32 Tommy Hanson .75 2.00
33 Josh Hamilton 1.00 2.50
34 Andre Ethier 1.00 2.50
35 John Smoltz 1.25 3.00
36 Matt Kemp 1.00 2.50
37 Miguel Cabrera 1.25 3.00
38 Mitch Moreland .75 2.00
39 Roy Halladay 1.00 2.50
40 Ryan Braun .75 2.00
41 Dennis Eckersley .75 2.00
42 Ryne Sandberg 2.50 6.00
43 Salvador Perez 1.00 2.50
44 Starlin Castro 1.00 2.50
45 Tim Hudson 1.00 2.50
46 Tim Lincecum 1.00 2.50
47 Sandy Koufax 2.50 6.00
48 Warren Spahn .75 2.00
49 Yovani Gallardo .75 2.00
50 Hank Aaron 2.50 6.00
51 Harmon Killebrew 1.25 3.00
52 Stan Musial 2.00 5.00
53 Ken Griffey Jr. 2.50 6.00
54 Cal Ripken Jr. 4.00 10.00
55 Duke Snider .75 2.00
56 Evan Longoria 1.00 2.50
57 Justin Upton 1.00 2.50
58 Brett Lawrie 1.00 2.50
59 Jon Niese .75 2.00
60 Bryce Harper 10.00 25.00
61 Giancarlo Stanton 1.25 3.00
62 Ricky Romero .75 2.00
63 Rickie Weeks .75 2.00
64 Brian McCann 1.00 2.50
65 Ike Davis .75 2.00
66 Yonder Alonso .75 2.00
67 Alex Gordon 1.00 2.50
68 Aramis Ramirez .75 2.00
69 J.P. Arencibia .75 2.00
70 Ivan Nova 1.00 2.50
71 Pablo Sandoval 1.00 2.50
72 Matt Garza .75 2.00
73 Joe Saunders .75 2.00
74 Gio Gonzalez 1.00 2.50
75 Dee Gordon .75 2.00
76 Jeremy Hellickson .75 2.00
77 Derek Holland .75 2.00
78 Ervin Santana .75 2.00
79 Adam Lind 1.00 2.50
80 Nick Markakis 1.00 2.50
81 Billy Butler .75 2.00
82 Adam Jones 1.00 2.50
83 Rick Porcello .75 2.00
84 Brennan Boesch .75 2.00
85 David Price 1.00 2.50
86 Madison Bumgarner 1.00 2.50
87 Clay Buchholz .75 2.00
88 Yu Darvish 2.00 5.00
89 Mike Trout 75.00 200.00
90 Eric Hosmer 1.00 2.50
91 Craig Kimbrel 1.00 2.50
92 Elvis Andrus 1.00 2.50
93 Juan Marichal .75 2.00
94 Johnny Bench 1.25 3.00
95 Ozzie Smith 1.50 4.00
96 Willie Mays 2.50 6.00
97 Bob Gibson .75 2.00
98 Don Mattingly 2.50 6.00
99 Paul O'Neill .75 2.00
100 Gary Carter .75 2.00

2012 Topps Gold Rush Wrapper Redemption Autographs

PRINT RUNS B/WN 25-150 COPIES PER
2 Adrian Gonzalez/50 50.00 100.00
3 Albert Belle/50 12.50 30.00
4 Allen Craig/50 30.00 60.00
5 Aroldis Chapman/50 12.50 30.00
6 Brandon Phillips/50 20.00 50.00
7 Brandon Belt/50 10.00 25.00
8 Brett Gardner/50 10.00 25.00
9 Nelson Cruz/50 12.50 30.00
11 Carlos Gonzalez/50 30.00 60.00
12 Jay Bruce/50 30.00 60.00
13 Chris Young/50 12.50 30.00
15 Dan Uggla/50 6.00 15.00
16 Daniel Hudson/50 50.00 100.00
17 Danny Espinosa/50 10.00 25.00
22 Jordan Zimmermann/50 10.00 25.00
25 Jason Motte/50 10.00 25.00
27 Jered Weaver/50 20.00 50.00
28 Jesus Montero/50 15.00 40.00
34 Andre Ethier/50 30.00 60.00
36 Matt Kemp/50 100.00 200.00
38 Mitch Moreland/50 10.00 25.00
41 Dennis Eckersley/50 10.00 25.00
43 Salvador Perez/50 40.00 100.00
44 Starlin Castro/50 50.00 100.00
45 Tim Hudson/50 6.00 15.00
52 Stan Musial/50 50.00 100.00
55 Duke Snider/75 10.00 25.00
56 Evan Longoria/50 50.00 100.00
58 Brett Lawrie/60 20.00 50.00
59 Jon Niese/100 6.00 15.00
61 Giancarlo Stanton/70 25.00 60.00
62 Ricky Romero/135 6.00 15.00
63 Rickie Weeks/150 6.00 15.00
65 Ike Davis/100 6.00 15.00
66 Yonder Alonso/150 6.00 15.00
67 Alex Gordon/100 6.00 15.00
68 Aramis Ramirez/100 10.00 25.00
69 J.P. Arencibia/100 6.00 15.00
70 Ivan Nova/150 15.00 40.00
71 Pablo Sandoval/75 20.00 50.00
72 Matt Garza/100 6.00 15.00
73 Joe Saunders/100 6.00 15.00
74 Gio Gonzalez/100 12.50 30.00
75 Dee Gordon/100 6.00 15.00
76 Jeremy Hellickson/100 10.00 25.00
77 Derek Holland/100 12.50 30.00
78 Ervin Santana/100 10.00 25.00
79 Adam Lind/50 6.00 15.00
80 Nick Markakis/80 6.00 15.00
81 Billy Butler/100 6.00 15.00
87 Clay Buchholz/100 20.00 50.00
91 Craig Kimbrel/50 20.00 50.00
92 Elvis Andrus/100 10.00 25.00

2012 Topps Gold Standard

COMPLETE SET (50) 12.50 30.00
COMP.SER.1 SET (25) 6.00 15.00
COMP.SER.2 SET (25) 6.00 15.00
STATED ODDS 1:6 HOBBY
1-25 ISSUED IN SERIES 1
26-50 ISSUED IN SERIES 2
GS1 Nolan Ryan 2.00 5.00
GS2 Stan Musial 1.00 2.50
GS3 Paul Molitor .60 1.50
GS4 Cal Ripken Jr. 2.00 5.00
GS5 Bob Gibson .40 1.00
GS6 Mike Schmidt 1.00 2.50
GS7 Frank Robinson .40 1.00
GS8 Ernie Banks .60 1.50
GS9 Willie McCovey .40 1.00
GS10 Reggie Jackson .40 1.00
GS11 Tom Seaver .40 1.00
GS12 Al Kaline .60 1.50
GS13 Alex Rodriguez .75 2.00
GS14 Frank Thomas .60 1.50
GS15 Ty Cobb 1.00 2.50
GS16 John Smoltz .60 1.50
GS17 Jim Thome .50 1.25
GS18 Joe DiMaggio 1.25 3.00
GS19 Andre Dawson .40 1.00
GS20 Derek Jeter 1.50 4.00
GS21 Chipper Jones .60 1.50
GS22 Nolan Ryan 2.00 5.00
GS23 Tom Seaver .40 1.00
GS24 Mickey Mantle 2.00 5.00
GS25 Willie Mays 1.25 3.00
GS26 Andre Dawson .40 1.00
GS27 Jim Thome .50 1.25
GS28 Stan Musial 1.00 2.50
GS29 Cal Ripken Jr. 2.00 5.00
GS30 Willie Mays 1.25 3.00
GS31 Hank Aaron 1.25 3.00
GS32 Ernie Banks .60 1.50
GS33 Bob Gibson .40 1.00
GS34 Reggie Jackson .40 1.00
GS35 Chipper Jones .60 1.50
GS36 Al Kaline .60 1.50
GS37 Willie McCovey .40 1.00
GS38 Paul Molitor .60 1.50
GS39 Frank Robinson .40 1.00
GS40 Nolan Ryan 2.00 5.00
GS41 Mike Schmidt 1.00 2.50
GS42 John Smoltz .60 1.50
GS43 Tom Seaver .40 1.00
GS44 Alex Rodriguez .75 2.00
GS45 Derek Jeter 1.50 4.00
GS46 Joe DiMaggio 1.25 3.00
GS47 Mickey Mantle 2.00 5.00
GS48 Lou Gehrig 1.25 3.00
GS49 Roberto Clemente 1.50 4.00
GS50 Ty Cobb 1.00 2.50

2012 Topps Gold Standard Relics

SER.1 ODDS 1:20,200 HOBBY
SER.2 ODDS 1:9250 HOBBY
STATED PRINT RUN 50 SER.#'d SETS
EXCHANGE DEADLINE 12/31/2014
AD Andre Dawson S2 5.00 12.00
AR Alex Rodriguez 20.00 50.00
CR Cal Ripken Jr. 30.00 60.00
CR Cal Ripken Jr. S2 30.00 60.00
DJ Derek Jeter S2 40.00 80.00
DJ Derek Jeter 40.00 80.00
EB Ernie Banks 20.00 50.00
FR Frank Robinson S2 20.00 50.00
HA Hank Aaron S2 20.00 50.00
JD Joe DiMaggio S2 30.00 60.00
JD Joe DiMaggio 30.00 60.00
LG Lou Gehrig S2 40.00 80.00
MM Mickey Mantle S2 40.00 80.00
MM Mickey Mantle 40.00 80.00
MS Mike Schmidt S2 20.00 50.00
NR Nolan Ryan S2 30.00 60.00
NR Nolan Ryan 30.00 60.00
PM Paul Molitor S2 12.50 30.00
RC Roberto Clemente S2 30.00 60.00
TC Ty Cobb S2 30.00 60.00
TC Ty Cobb EXCH 30.00 60.00
TS Tom Seaver 10.00 25.00
TS Tom Seaver S2 10.00 25.00
WM Willie Mays S2 12.50 30.00
WM Willie Mays 12.50 30.00

2012 Topps Gold Team Coin Autographs

STATED PRINT RUN 30 SER.#'d SETS
KG Ken Griffey Jr./30 150.00 300.00
WM Willie Mays/30 150.00 300.00

2012 Topps Gold World Series Champion Pins

SER.1 ODDS 1:1000 HOBBY
SER.2 ODDS 1:1160 HOBBY
SER.1 PRINT RUN 736 SER.#'d SETS
AP Albert Pujols 10.00 25.00
AP Albert Pujols S2 8.00 20.00
BG Bob Gibson 8.00 20.00
BL Barry Larkin S2 8.00 20.00
BM Bill Mazeroski S2 10.00 25.00
BR Babe Ruth S2 12.50 30.00
BRO Brooks Robinson 8.00 20.00
CH Cole Hamels 8.00 20.00
CJ Chipper Jones 10.00 25.00
CR Cal Ripken Jr. S2 12.50 30.00
DJ Derek Jeter 10.00 25.00
DO David Ortiz 6.00 15.00
DP Dustin Pedroia 6.00 15.00
DS Darryl Strawberry S2 6.00 15.00
FR Frank Robinson S2 6.00 15.00
HA Hank Aaron S2 8.00 20.00
JB Johnny Bench 8.00 20.00
JD Joe DiMaggio S2 8.00 20.00
JR Jackie Robinson S2 6.00 15.00
LG Lou Gehrig 10.00 25.00
MC Miguel Cabrera S2 6.00 15.00
MM Mickey Mantle S2 12.50 30.00
MR Mariano Rivera S2 8.00 20.00
MS Mike Schmidt 10.00 25.00
OS Ozzie Smith S2 8.00 20.00
PM Paul Molitor 6.00 15.00
RA Roberto Alomar S2 6.00 15.00
RC Roberto Clemente 12.00 30.00
RH Rickey Henderson S2 10.00 25.00
RJ Reggie Jackson S2 6.00 15.00
RJ Reggie Jackson 6.00 15.00
SG Steve Garvey S2 5.00 12.00
SK Sandy Koufax S2 10.00 25.00
SK Sandy Koufax 10.00 25.00
SM Stan Musial 10.00 25.00
TL Tim Lincecum 10.00 25.00
TS Tom Seaver 8.00 20.00
WB Wade Boggs S2 6.00 15.00
WM Willie Mays 10.00 25.00
YB Yogi Berra S2 8.00 20.00

2012 Topps Golden Giveaway Code Cards

STATED ODDS 1:6 HOBBY
PRICING FOR UNUSED CODES
GGC1 Ryan Braun 1.00 2.50
GGC2 Troy Tulowitzki 1.00 2.50
GGC3 Miguel Cabrera 1.00 2.50
GGC4 Roy Halladay 1.00 2.50
GGC5 Matt Kemp 1.00 2.50
GGC6 Albert Pujols 1.00 2.50
GGC7 Willie Mays 1.00 2.50
GGC8 Roberto Clemente 1.00 2.50
GGC9 Ichiro Suzuki 1.00 2.50
GGC10 Sandy Koufax 1.00 2.50
GGC11 Albert Pujols 1.00 2.50
GGC12 Felix Hernandez 1.00 2.50
GGC13 Buster Posey 1.00 2.50
GGC14 Clayton Kershaw 1.00 2.50
GGC15 Carlos Gonzalez 1.00 2.50
GGC16 Johnny Bench 1.00 2.50
GGC17 Tim Lincecum 1.00 2.50
GGC18 Cal Ripken Jr. 1.00 2.50
GGC19 Derek Jeter 1.00 2.50
GGC20 Ken Griffey Jr. 1.25 3.00
GGC21 Bob Gibson 1.00 2.50
GGC22 Nolan Ryan 1.00 2.50
GGC23 Tony Gwynn 1.00 2.50
GGC24 Steve Carlton 1.00 2.50
GGC25 Warren Spahn 1.00 2.50
GGC26 Bryce Harper 1.00 2.50
GGC27 Trevor Bauer 1.00 2.50
GGC28 Yu Darvish 1.00 2.50
GGC29 Yoenis Cespedes 1.00 2.50
GGC30 Will Middlebrooks 1.00 2.50

2012 Topps Golden Greats

COMPLETE SET (100) 40.00 80.00
STATED ODDS 1:4 HOBBY
UPDATE ODDS 1:6 HOBBY
ALL VERSIONS PRICED EQUALLY
GG1 Lou Gehrig 1.00 2.50
GG2 Lou Gehrig 1.00 2.50
GG3 Lou Gehrig 1.00 2.50
GG4 Lou Gehrig 1.00 2.50
GG5 Lou Gehrig 1.00 2.50
GG6 Nolan Ryan 1.50 4.00
GG7 Nolan Ryan 1.50 4.00
GG8 Nolan Ryan 1.50 4.00
GG9 Nolan Ryan 1.50 4.00
GG10 Nolan Ryan 1.50 4.00
GG11 Willie Mays 1.00 2.50
GG12 Willie Mays 1.00 2.50
GG13 Willie Mays 1.00 2.50
GG14 Willie Mays 1.00 2.50
GG15 Willie Mays 1.00 2.50
GG16 Ty Cobb .75 2.00
GG17 Ty Cobb .75 2.00
GG18 Ty Cobb .75 2.00
GG19 Ty Cobb .75 2.00
GG20 Ty Cobb .75 2.00
GG21 Joe DiMaggio 1.00 2.50
GG22 Joe DiMaggio 1.00 2.50
GG23 Joe DiMaggio 1.00 2.50
GG24 Joe DiMaggio 1.00 2.50
GG25 Joe DiMaggio 1.00 2.50
GG26 Derek Jeter 1.25 3.00
GG27 Derek Jeter 1.25 3.00
GG28 Derek Jeter 1.25 3.00
GG29 Derek Jeter 1.25 3.00
GG30 Derek Jeter 1.25 3.00
GG31 Mickey Mantle 1.50 4.00
GG32 Mickey Mantle 1.50 4.00
GG33 Mickey Mantle 1.50 4.00
GG34 Mickey Mantle 1.50 4.00
GG35 Mickey Mantle 1.50 4.00
GG36 Roberto Clemente 1.25 3.00
GG37 Roberto Clemente 1.25 3.00
GG38 Roberto Clemente 1.25 3.00
GG39 Roberto Clemente 1.25 3.00
GG40 Roberto Clemente 1.25 3.00
GG41 Cal Ripken Jr. 1.50 4.00
GG42 Cal Ripken Jr. 1.50 4.00
GG43 Cal Ripken Jr. 1.50 4.00
GG44 Cal Ripken Jr. 1.50 4.00
GG45 Cal Ripken Jr. 1.50 4.00
GG46 Sandy Koufax 1.00 2.50
GG47 Sandy Koufax 1.00 2.50
GG48 Sandy Koufax 1.00 2.50
GG49 Sandy Koufax 1.00 2.50
GG50 Sandy Koufax 1.00 2.50
GG51 Hank Aaron 1.00 2.50
GG52 Hank Aaron 1.00 2.50
GG53 Hank Aaron 1.00 2.50
GG54 Hank Aaron 1.00 2.50
GG55 Hank Aaron 1.00 2.50
GG56 Tom Seaver .30 .75
GG57 Tom Seaver .30 .75
GG58 Tom Seaver .30 .75
GG59 Tom Seaver .30 .75
GG60 Tom Seaver .30 .75
GG61 Jackie Robinson .50 1.25
GG62 Jackie Robinson .50 1.25
GG63 Jackie Robinson .50 1.25
GG64 Jackie Robinson .50 1.25
GG65 Jackie Robinson .50 1.25
GG66 Albert Pujols .60 1.50
GG67 Albert Pujols .60 1.50
GG68 Albert Pujols .60 1.50
GG69 Albert Pujols .60 1.50
GG70 Albert Pujols .60 1.50
GG71 Babe Ruth 1.25 3.00
GG72 Babe Ruth 1.25 3.00
GG73 Babe Ruth 1.25 3.00
GG74 Babe Ruth 1.25 3.00
GG75 Babe Ruth 1.25 3.00
GG76 Andre Dawson .30 .75
GG77 Bob Gibson .30 .75
GG78 Brooks Robinson .30 .75
GG79 Dave Winfield .30 .75
GG80 Don Mattingly 1.00 2.50
GG81 Ernie Banks .50 1.25
GG82 Gary Carter .30 .75
GG83 Harmon Killebrew .50 1.25
GG84 Jim Palmer .30 .75
GG85 Joe Morgan .30 .75
GG86 John Smoltz .50 1.25
GG87 Johnny Bench .50 1.25

GG88 Ken Griffey Jr. 1.00 2.50
GG89 Lou Brock .30 .75
GG90 Mike Schmidt .75 2.00
GG91 Ozzie Smith .60 1.50
GG92 Reggie Jackson .30 .75
GG93 Rickey Henderson .50 1.25
GG94 Stan Musial .75 2.00
GG95 Tony Gwynn .50 1.25
GG96 Tony Perez .30 .75
GG97 Wade Boggs .30 .75
GG98 Warren Spahn .30 .75
GG99 Willie Stargell .30 .75
GG100 Yogi Berra .50 1.25

2012 Topps Golden Greats Autographs

STATED ODDS 1:39,990 HOBBY
UPDATE ODDS 1:34,350 HOBBY
STATED PRINT RUN 10 SER.#'d SETS
ALL VERSIONS EQUALLY PRICED
NO PRICING ON MOST DUE TO SCARCITY
EXCHANGE DEADLINE 12/31/2014
UPD.EXCH.DEADLINE 9/30/2015
SK1 Sandy Koufax 250.00 350.00
SK2 Sandy Koufax 250.00 350.00
SK3 Sandy Koufax 250.00 350.00
SK4 Sandy Koufax 250.00 350.00
SK5 Sandy Koufax 250.00 350.00
WM1 Willie Mays EXCH 150.00 250.00
WM2 Willie Mays EXCH 150.00 250.00
WM3 Willie Mays EXCH 150.00 250.00
WM4 Willie Mays EXCH 150.00 250.00
WM5 Willie Mays EXCH 150.00 250.00

2012 Topps Golden Greats Coins

SER.1 ODDS 1:52,700 HOBBY
SER.2 ODDS 1:15,560 HOBBY
PRINT RUNS B/WN 2-44 COPIES PER
NO PRICING ON QTY 24 OR LESS
HA Hank Aaron/44 75.00 150.00
JR Jackie Robinson/42 40.00 80.00
NR Nolan Ryan/34 100.00 200.00
RJ Reggie Jackson/44 S2 40.00 80.00
SK Sandy Koufax/32 150.00 250.00
TS Tom Seaver/41 40.00 80.00

2012 Topps Golden Greats Relics

STATED ODDS 1:13,400 HOBBY
UPDATE ODDS 1:22,400 HOBBY
STATED PRINT RUN 10 SER.#'d SETS
ALL VERSIONS EQUALLY PRICED
NO UPDATE CARD PRICING AVAILABLE
EXCHANGE DEADLINE 12/31/2014
GGR1 Lou Gehrig 40.00 80.00
GGR2 Lou Gehrig 40.00 80.00
GGR3 Lou Gehrig 40.00 80.00
GGR4 Lou Gehrig 40.00 80.00
GGR5 Lou Gehrig 40.00 80.00
GGR6 Nolan Ryan EXCH 60.00 120.00
GGR7 Nolan Ryan EXCH 60.00 120.00
GGR8 Nolan Ryan EXCH 60.00 120.00
GGR9 Nolan Ryan EXCH 60.00 120.00
GGR10 Nolan Ryan EXCH 60.00 120.00
GGR11 Willie Mays 40.00 80.00
GGR12 Willie Mays 40.00 80.00
GGR13 Willie Mays 40.00 80.00
GGR14 Willie Mays 40.00 80.00
GGR15 Willie Mays 40.00 80.00
GGR16 Ty Cobb EXCH 50.00 100.00
GGR17 Ty Cobb EXCH 50.00 100.00
GGR18 Ty Cobb EXCH 50.00 100.00
GGR19 Ty Cobb EXCH 50.00 100.00
GGR20 Ty Cobb EXCH 50.00 100.00
GGR21 Joe DiMaggio 40.00 80.00
GGR22 Joe DiMaggio 40.00 80.00
GGR23 Joe DiMaggio 40.00 80.00
GGR24 Joe DiMaggio 40.00 80.00
GGR25 Joe DiMaggio 40.00 80.00
GGR26 Derek Jeter 150.00 250.00
GGR27 Derek Jeter 150.00 250.00
GGR28 Derek Jeter 150.00 250.00
GGR29 Derek Jeter 150.00 250.00
GGR30 Derek Jeter 150.00 250.00
GGR31 Mickey Mantle 60.00 120.00
GGR32 Mickey Mantle 60.00 120.00
GGR33 Mickey Mantle 60.00 120.00
GGR34 Mickey Mantle 60.00 120.00
GGR35 Mickey Mantle 60.00 120.00
GGR36 Roberto Clemente 50.00 100.00
GGR37 Roberto Clemente 50.00 100.00
GGR38 Roberto Clemente 50.00 100.00
GGR39 Roberto Clemente 50.00 100.00
GGR40 Roberto Clemente 50.00 100.00
GGR41 Cal Ripken Jr. 75.00 150.00
GGR42 Cal Ripken Jr. 75.00 150.00
GGR43 Cal Ripken Jr. 75.00 150.00
GGR44 Cal Ripken Jr. 75.00 150.00
GGR45 Cal Ripken Jr. 75.00 150.00
GGR46 Sandy Koufax EXCH 75.00 150.00
GGR47 Sandy Koufax EXCH 75.00 150.00
GGR48 Sandy Koufax EXCH 75.00 150.00
GGR49 Sandy Koufax EXCH 75.00 150.00
GGR50 Sandy Koufax EXCH 75.00 150.00
GGR51 Hank Aaron 40.00 80.00
GGR52 Hank Aaron 40.00 80.00
GGR53 Hank Aaron 40.00 80.00
GGR54 Hank Aaron 40.00 80.00
GGR55 Hank Aaron 40.00 80.00
GGR56 Tom Seaver 40.00 80.00
GGR57 Tom Seaver 40.00 80.00
GGR58 Tom Seaver 40.00 80.00
GGR59 Tom Seaver 40.00 80.00
GGR60 Tom Seaver 40.00 80.00
GGR61 Jackie Robinson 30.00 60.00
GGR62 Jackie Robinson 30.00 60.00
GGR63 Jackie Robinson 30.00 60.00
GGR64 Jackie Robinson 30.00 60.00
GGR65 Jackie Robinson 30.00 60.00
GGR66 Albert Pujols 75.00 150.00
GGR67 Albert Pujols 75.00 150.00
GGR68 Albert Pujols 75.00 150.00
GGR69 Albert Pujols 75.00 150.00
GGR70 Albert Pujols 75.00 150.00
GGR71 Babe Ruth 100.00 200.00
GGR72 Babe Ruth 100.00 200.00
GGR73 Babe Ruth 100.00 200.00
GGR74 Babe Ruth 100.00 200.00
GGR75 Babe Ruth 100.00 200.00

2012 Topps Golden Moments

COMPLETE SET (50) 8.00 20.00
STATED ODDS 1:4 HOBBY
GM1 Tom Seaver .40 1.00
GM2 Jose Bautista .50 1.25
GM3 Derek Jeter 1.50 4.00
GM4 Josh Hamilton .50 1.25
GM5 Adrian Gonzalez .50 1.25
GM6 Red Schoendienst .40 1.00
GM7 Clayton Kershaw 1.00 2.50
GM8 Andre Dawson .40 1.00
GM9 Justin Verlander .60 1.50
GM10 Prince Fielder .50 1.25
GM11 Edgar Martinez .40 1.00
GM12 Andrew McCutchen .60 1.50
GM13 Don Mattingly 1.25 3.00
GM14 Felix Hernandez .50 1.25
GM15 Ryan Braun .40 1.00
GM16 Jim Rice .40 1.00
GM17 Jered Weaver .50 1.25
GM18 Barry Larkin .40 1.00
GM19 Andy Pettitte .50 1.25
GM20 Ryne Sandberg 1.25 3.00
GM21 Albert Belle .25 .60
GM22 Willie McCovey .40 1.00
GM23 Dennis Eckersley .40 1.00
GM24 Justin Upton .50 1.25
GM25 Ichiro Suzuki .75 2.00
GM26 Paul O'Neill .40 1.00
GM27 Lance Berkman .50 1.25
GM28 George Foster .25 .60
GM29 Albert Pujols .75 2.00
GM30 Jacoby Ellsbury .50 1.25
GM31 CC Sabathia .50 1.25
GM32 Roger Maris .60 1.50
GM33 Troy Tulowitzki .60 1.50
GM34 Brooks Robinson .40 1.00
GM35 Frank Thomas .60 1.50
GM36 John Smoltz .60 1.50
GM37 Asdrubal Cabrera .50 1.25
GM38 Matt Kemp .50 1.25
GM39 Robinson Cano .50 1.25
GM40 Miguel Cabrera .60 1.50
GM41 Joey Votto .60 1.50
GM42 Al Kaline .60 1.50
GM43 Curtis Granderson .50 1.25
GM44 Jim Thome .50 1.25
GM45 Joe Morgan .40 1.00
GM46 Dustin Pedroia .60 1.50
GM47 Carlton Fisk .40 1.00
GM48 Luis Aparicio .40 1.00
GM49 James Shields .40 1.00
GM50 Roy Halladay .50 1.25

2012 Topps Golden Moments Series 2

COMPLETE SET (50) 12.50 30.00
STATED ODDS 1:4 HOBBY
GM1 Adam Jones .50 1.25
GM2 Buster Posey .75 2.00
GM3 Eric Hosmer .50 1.25
GM4 Evan Longoria .50 1.25
GM5 Johnny Bench .60 1.50
GM6 Jose Bautista .50 1.25
GM7 Pablo Sandoval .50 1.25
GM8 Paul Molitor .60 1.50
GM9 Ryan Howard .50 1.25
GM10 Ryan Zimmerman .50 1.25
GM11 Stan Musial 1.00 2.50
GM12 Tim Lincecum .50 1.25
GM13 Alex Rodriguez .75 2.00
GM14 Cal Ripken Jr. 2.00 5.00
GM15 Carl Yastrzemski 1.00 2.50
GM16 Carlos Gonzalez .50 1.25
GM17 Cliff Lee .50 1.25
GM18 Cole Hamels .50 1.25
GM19 Craig Kimbrel .50 1.25
GM20 Dave Winfield .40 1.00
GM21 David Ortiz .60 1.50
GM22 David Wright .50 1.25
GM23 Don Mattingly 1.25 3.00
GM24 George Brett 1.25 3.00
GM25 Hanley Ramirez .50 1.25
GM26 Ian Kinsler .50 1.25
GM27 Jim Palmer .40 1.00
GM28 Joe Mauer .50 1.25
GM29 Mariano Rivera .75 2.00
GM30 Mark Teixeira .50 1.25
GM31 Giancarlo Stanton .60 1.50
GM32 Ozzie Smith .75 2.00
GM33 Reggie Jackson .40 1.00
GM34 Rickey Henderson .60 1.50
GM35 Starlin Castro .50 1.25
GM36 Stephen Strasburg .60 1.50
GM37 Tony Gwynn .40 1.00
GM38 Wade Boggs .40 1.00
GM39 Willie Mays 1.25 3.00
GM40 Adrian Gonzalez .50 1.25
GM41 Andre Dawson .40 1.00
GM42 Chase Utley .50 1.25
GM43 Gary Carter .40 1.00
GM44 Josh Hamilton .50 1.25
GM45 Miguel Cabrera .60 1.50
GM46 Mike Schmidt 1.00 2.50
GM47 Prince Fielder .50 1.25
GM48 Ryne Sandberg 1.25 3.00
GM49 Steve Garvey .25 .60
GM50 Ken Griffey Jr. 1.25 3.00

2012 Topps Golden Moments 24K Gold Embedded

STATED ODDS 1:147,500 HOBBY
STATED PRINT RUN 1 SER.#'d SET
NO PRICING DUE TO SCARCITY
EXCHANGE DEADLINE 12/31/2014

2012 Topps Golden Moments Die Cuts

GMDC1 Babe Ruth 8.00 20.00
GMDC2 Lou Gehrig 6.00 15.00
GMDC3 Ty Cobb 5.00 12.00
GMDC4 Stan Musial 5.00 12.00
GMDC5 Joe DiMaggio 6.00 15.00
GMDC6 Willie Mays 6.00 15.00
GMDC7 Mickey Mantle 10.00 25.00
GMDC8 Warren Spahn 2.00 5.00
GMDC9 Bob Gibson 2.00 5.00
GMDC10 Johnny Bench 3.00 8.00
GMDC11 Sandy Koufax 6.00 15.00
GMDC12 Frank Robinson 2.00 5.00
GMDC13 Tom Seaver 2.00 5.00
GMDC14 Roberto Clemente 8.00 20.00
GMDC15 Steve Carlton 2.00 5.00
GMDC16 Yogi Berra 3.00 8.00
GMDC17 Jim Thome 2.50 6.00
GMDC18 Jackie Robinson 3.00 8.00
GMDC19 Ken Griffey Jr. 6.00 15.00
GMDC20 Rickey Henderson 3.00 8.00
GMDC21 Nolan Ryan 10.00 25.00
GMDC22 Eddie Mathews 3.00 8.00
GMDC23 Cal Ripken Jr. 10.00 25.00
GMDC24 Tony Gwynn 2.00 5.00
GMDC25 Ichiro Suzuki 4.00 10.00
GMDC26 Carl Yastrzemski 5.00 12.00
GMDC27 Joe Mauer 2.50 6.00
GMDC28 Josh Hamilton 2.50 6.00
GMDC29 Ozzie Smith 4.00 10.00
GMDC30 Ryan Braun 2.00 5.00
GMDC31 Willie McCovey 2.00 5.00
GMDC32 Jim Palmer 2.00 5.00
GMDC33 Rod Carew 2.00 5.00
GMDC34 Derek Jeter 8.00 20.00
GMDC35 Duke Snider 2.00 5.00
GMDC36 Al Kaline 3.00 8.00
GMDC37 Alex Rodriguez 4.00 10.00
GMDC38 Harmon Killebrew 3.00 8.00
GMDC39 Reggie Jackson 2.00 5.00
GMDC40 Vladimir Guerrero 2.50 6.00
GMDC41 Albert Pujols 4.00 10.00
GMDC42 Robin Yount 3.00 8.00
GMDC43 Roy Halladay 2.50 6.00
GMDC44 Wade Boggs 2.00 5.00
GMDC45 Eddie Murray 2.00 5.00
GMDC46 Johan Santana 2.50 6.00
GMDC47 Mariano Rivera 4.00 10.00
GMDC48 Hanley Ramirez 2.50 6.00
GMDC49 Robinson Cano 2.50 6.00
GMDC50 Carlton Fisk 2.00 5.00
GMDC51 Don Mattingly 6.00 15.00
GMDC52 Justin Upton 2.50 6.00
GMDC53 Buster Posey 4.00 10.00
GMDC54 Clayton Kershaw 5.00 12.00
GMDC55 Matt Kemp 2.50 6.00
GMDC56 Ryne Sandberg 6.00 15.00
GMDC57 Joey Votto 3.00 8.00
GMDC58 Carlos Gonzalez 2.50 6.00
GMDC59 Craig Kimbrel 2.50 6.00
GMDC60 Stephen Strasburg 3.00 8.00
GMDC61 David Wright 2.50 6.00
GMDC62 Eric Hosmer 2.50 6.00
GMDC63 Evan Longoria 2.50 6.00
GMDC64 Mark Teixeira 2.50 6.00
GMDC65 Mike Stanton 3.00 8.00
GMDC66 CC Sabathia 2.50 6.00
GMDC67 Dustin Pedroia 3.00 8.00
GMDC68 Justin Verlander 3.00 8.00
GMDC69 David Price 2.50 6.00
GMDC70 Jered Weaver 2.50 6.00
GMDC71 Cliff Lee 2.50 6.00
GMDC72 Ian Kinsler 2.50 6.00
GMDC73 Roberto Alomar 2.00 5.00
GMDC74 Pablo Sandoval 2.50 6.00
GMDC75 Troy Tulowitzki 3.00 8.00
GMDC76 Felix Hernandez 2.50 6.00
GMDC77 Mike Trout 100.00 250.00
GMDC78 Starlin Castro 2.50 6.00
GMDC79 Brooks Robinson 2.00 5.00
GMDC80 Jacob Ellsbury 3.00 8.00
GMDC81 Jose Bautista 2.50 6.00
GMDC82 Tim Lincecum 2.50 6.00
GMDC83 Miguel Cabrera 3.00 8.00
GMDC84 Ryan Zimmerman 2.50 6.00
GMDC85 Nelson Cruz 3.00 8.00
GMDC86 Ryan Howard 2.50 6.00
GMDC87 Jason Heyward 2.50 6.00
GMDC88 David Ortiz 3.00 8.00
GMDC89 Adrian Gonzalez 2.50 6.00
GMDC90 Brian Wilson 3.00 8.00
GMDC91 Chris Carpenter 2.50 6.00
GMDC92 David Freese 2.00 5.00
GMDC93 Josh Johnson 2.50 6.00
GMDC94 Adam Jones 2.50 6.00
GMDC95 Jay Bruce 2.50 6.00
GMDC96 Shin-Soo Choo 2.50 6.00
GMDC97 Chase Utley 2.50 6.00
GMDC98 Mike Napoli 2.00 5.00
GMDC99 Jose Reyes 2.00 5.00
GMDC100 Jon Lester 2.00 5.00
GMDC101 Yoenis Cespedes 2.50 6.00
GMDC102 Yu Darvish 4.00 10.00
GMDC103 Bryce Harper 50.00 100.00

2012 Topps Golden Moments Die Cuts Gold

*GOLD: 1X TO 2.5X BASIC
PRINT RUNS B/WN 99-100 COPIES PER
GMDC101 Yoenis Cespedes/100 6.00 15.00
GMDC102 Yu Darvish/100 10.00 25.00
GMDC103 Bryce Harper/100 100.00 200.00

2012 Topps Golden Moments Autographs

SER.1 ODDS 1:322 HOBBY
SER.2 ODDS 1:335 HOBBY
UPDATE ODDS 1:531 HOBBY
SER.1 EXCH DEADLINE 12/31/2014
SER.2 EXCH DEADLINE 04/30/2015
UPD.EXCH DEADLINE 9/30/2015
AB Antonio Bastardo UPD 4.00 10.00
AB Albert Belle S2 10.00 25.00
AC Andrew Carignan UPD 3.00 8.00
AC Alex Cobb S2 5.00 12.00
ACA Andrew Carignan S2 5.00 12.00
AD Andre Dawson S2 6.00 15.00
AE A.J. Ellis UPD 5.00 12.00
AE Andre Ethier S2 5.00 12.00
AE Andre Ethier 5.00 12.00
AG Adrian Gonzalez 8.00 20.00
AG Adrian Gonzalez S2 8.00 20.00
AJ Adam Jones S2 6.00 15.00
AJ Adam Jones 6.00 15.00
AJA Austin Jackson S2 6.00 15.00
AL Tyler Pastornicky UPD 3.00 8.00
AL Adam Lind 3.00 8.00
AO Alexi Ogando 4.00 10.00
AP Andy Pettitte S2 50.00 100.00
AR Aramis Ramirez S2 4.00 10.00
BG Bob Gibson S2 30.00 60.00
BG Brett Gardner 8.00 20.00
BH Bryce Harper UPD 125.00 250.00
BL Brett Lawrie UPD 6.00 15.00
BM Brian McCann 4.00 10.00
BP Brandon Phillips 10.00 25.00
BP Brad Peacock S2 3.00 8.00
BPO Buster Posey S2 50.00 100.00
BS Bruce Sutter UPD 10.00 25.00
BU B.J. Upton S2 6.00 15.00
CB Clay Buchholz S2 10.00 25.00
CB Chad Billingsley 3.00 8.00
CC Chris Coghlan 4.00 10.00
CC Chris Coghlan S2 3.00 8.00
CG Carlos Gonzalez 6.00 15.00
CJ Chipper Jones 25.00 60.00
CK Clayton Kershaw 15.00 40.00
CR Cody Ross UPD 8.00 20.00
CR Cody Ross S2 10.00 25.00
CS Carlos Santana S2 3.00 8.00
CS Chris Sale 8.00 20.00
CU Chase Utley S2 20.00 50.00
CY Chris Young S2 5.00 12.00
CY Chris Young 4.00 10.00
DB Daniel Bard UPD 3.00 8.00
DB Domonic Brown S2 8.00 20.00
DG Dee Gordon S2 3.00 8.00
DGO Dwight Gooden S2 15.00 40.00
DH Derek Holland UPD 6.00 15.00
DJ David Justice S2 30.00 60.00
DP Drew Pomeranz S2 6.00 15.00
DP Dustin Pedroia 15.00 40.00
DS Drew Stubbs 5.00 12.00
DS Darryl Strawberry S2 6.00 15.00
DSN Duke Snider S2 12.00 30.00
DST Drew Storen S2 3.00 8.00
EA Elvis Andrus S2 5.00 12.00
EA Elvis Andrus 5.00 12.00
EH Eric Hosmer S2 5.00 12.00
EK Ed Kranepool UPD 3.00 8.00
EL Evan Longoria S2 15.00 40.00
EM Edgar Martinez 10.00 25.00
FF Freddie Freeman S2 8.00 20.00
FH Felix Hernandez 6.00 15.00
GB Gordon Beckham 6.00 15.00
GB Gordon Beckham S2 6.00 15.00
GC Gary Carter S2 20.00 50.00
GG Gio Gonzalez S2 6.00 15.00
GG Gio Gonzalez 6.00 15.00
GS Gary Sheffield S2 10.00 25.00
HR Hanley Ramirez 8.00 20.00
IK Ian Kinsler 10.00 30.00
IK Ian Kennedy S2 5.00 12.00
IKE Ian Kennedy 4.00 10.00
JA Jose Altuve S2 15.00 40.00
JB Johnny Bench S2 40.00 80.00
JB Jose Bautista 10.00 25.00
JBA Jose Bautista S2 15.00 40.00
JBR Jay Bruce 5.00 12.00
JC Johnny Cueto 8.00 20.00
JDM J.D. Martinez UPD 10.00 25.00
JG Jason Grilli UPD 3.00 8.00
JH Joel Hanrahan UPD 4.00 10.00
JH Josh Hamilton 15.00 40.00
JH Jason Heyward S2 8.00 20.00
JHA Josh Hamilton S2 60.00 120.00
JM Jesus Montero UPD 6.00 15.00
JM Jason Motte S2 3.00 8.00
JMO Jesus Montero S2 6.00 15.00
JN Jeff Niemann UPD 3.00 8.00
JP Jarrod Parker S2 5.00 12.00
JPO Johnny Podres S2 5.00 12.00
JS John Smoltz S2 40.00 80.00
JT Justin Turner UPD 10.00 25.00
JTA Jose Tabata S2 4.00 10.00
JV Justin Verlander UPD 20.00 50.00
JW Jordan Walden UPD 8.00 20.00
JW Jordan Walden S2 3.00 8.00
JW Jered Weaver 5.00 12.00
JZ Jordan Zimmermann 6.00 15.00
JZ Jordan Zimmermann S2 6.00 15.00
LA Luis Aparicio 40.00 80.00
LH Liam Hendriks S2 3.00 8.00
MB Madison Bumgarner S2 20.00 50.00
MB Madison Bumgarner 20.00 50.00
MBY Marlon Byrd 5.00 12.00
MC Miguel Cabrera 40.00 80.00
MC Miguel Cabrera S2 60.00 120.00
MG Matt Garza 3.00 8.00
MH Mark Hamburger UPD 3.00 8.00
MK Matt Kemp 8.00 20.00
MM Matt Moore UPD 6.00 15.00
MM Matt Moore S2 6.00 15.00
MMI Mike Minor S2 3.00 8.00
MMO Mike Morse S2 3.00 8.00
MP Michael Pineda UPD 8.00 20.00
MR Manny Ramirez UPD 60.00 150.00
MS Mike Schmidt S2 20.00 50.00
MT Mike Trout S2 200.00 500.00
NF Neftali Feliz S2 5.00 12.00
NF Neftali Feliz 6.00 15.00
NW Neil Walker 5.00 12.00
OC Orlando Cepeda S2 10.00 25.00
PF Prince Fielder S2 30.00 60.00
PM Paul Molitor S2 12.50 30.00
PO Paul O'Neill S2 10.00 25.00
PO Paul O'Neill 10.00 25.00
PS Pablo Sandoval 8.00 20.00
PS Pablo Sandoval S2 8.00 20.00
RB Ryan Braun 10.00 25.00
RD Rafael Dolis UPD 3.00 8.00
RD Randall Delgado S2 3.00 8.00
RH Ryan Howard S2 30.00 60.00
RK Ralph Kiner UPD 10.00 25.00
RK Ralph Kiner S2 10.00 25.00
RP Rick Porcello S2 5.00 12.00
RS Ryne Sandberg S2 30.00 60.00
RW Rickie Weeks UPD 4.00 10.00
RZ Ryan Zimmerman S2 6.00 15.00
RZ Ryan Zimmerman 6.00 15.00
SG Steve Garvey S2 10.00 25.00
SM Stan Musial S2 20.00 50.00
SP Salvador Perez UPD 10.00 25.00
SV Shane Victorino S2 8.00 20.00
TB Trevor Bauer UPD 15.00 40.00
TC Trevor Cahill S2 4.00 10.00
TC Trevor Cahill 5.00 12.00
TH Tommy Hanson 10.00 25.00
UJ Ubaldo Jimenez 6.00 15.00
UJ Ubaldo Jimenez S2 12.50 30.00
WM Will Middlebrooks UPD 30.00 60.00
WM Willie McCovey S2 20.00 50.00
WR Wilin Rosario S2 3.00 8.00
YD Yu Darvish S2 60.00 150.00
ZC Zack Cozart UPD 5.00 12.00

2012 Topps Golden Moments Dual Relics

STATED ODDS 1:9525 HOBBY
STATED PRINT 50 SER.#'d SETS
GBG J.Bruce/K.Griffey Jr. 20.00 50.00
GBM J.Bench/D.Mesoraco 12.00 30.00
GBP J.Bench/B.Posey 20.00 50.00
GCM R.Clemente/A.McCutchen 75.00 150.00
GDB A.Dawson/E.Banks 20.00 50.00
GHL J.Hellickson/E.Longoria 15.00 40.00
GIG I.Suzuki/K.Griffey Jr. 50.00 100.00
GJS C.Jones/M.Schmidt 20.00 50.00
GKV S.Koufax/J.Verlander 60.00 120.00
GML P.Molitor/A.Lind 10.00 25.00
GMM M.Mantle/R.Maris 75.00 150.00
GMP W.McCovey/B.Posey 60.00 120.00
GPF D.Pedroia/C.Fisk 20.00 50.00
GPM A.Pujols/S.Musial 50.00 100.00
GYE C.Yastrzemski/J.Ellsbury 30.00 60.00

2012 Topps Golden Moments Relics

SER.1 ODDS 1:47 HOBBY
SER.2 ODDS 1:50 HOBBY
I Ichiro Suzuki S2 6.00 15.00
AA Alex Avila S2 3.00 8.00
AA Alex Avila 3.00 8.00
AB A.J. Burnett S2 3.00 8.00
AC Asdrubal Cabrera 4.00 10.00
AD Adam Dunn 4.00 10.00
AG Adrian Gonzalez 4.00 10.00
AJ Austin Jackson 4.00 10.00
AL Adam Lind S2 4.00 10.00
AM Andrew McCutchen S2 5.00 12.00
AM Andrew McCutchen 5.00 12.00
AP Albert Pujols 12.00 30.00
AP Albert Pujols S2 12.00 30.00
BA Bobby Abreu S2 3.00 8.00
BA Brett Anderson 3.00 8.00
BB Billy Butler S2 3.00 8.00
BL Barry Larkin S2 6.00 15.00
BL Barry Larkin 6.00 15.00
BM Brian McCann 4.00 10.00
BM Bengie Molina S2 2.00 5.00
BP Brandon Phillips S2 3.00 8.00
BP Buster Posey 6.00 15.00
BU B.J. Upton 4.00 10.00
BU B.J. Upton S2 4.00 10.00
BW Brian Wilson S2 5.00 12.00
BW Brian Wilson 5.00 12.00
CB Chad Billingsley 3.00 8.00
CB Clay Buchholz S2 3.00 8.00
CG Curtis Granderson 4.00 10.00
CH Corey Hart 3.00 8.00
CH Corey Hart S2 3.00 8.00
CI Chris Iannetta S2 3.00 8.00
CJ Chipper Jones S2 5.00 12.00
CJ Chipper Jones 5.00 12.00
CL Carlos Lee S2 3.00 8.00
CM Casey McGehee S2 3.00 8.00
CM Casey McGehee 3.00 8.00
CP Carlos Pena 4.00 10.00
CP Carlos Pena S2 4.00 10.00
CQ Carlos Quentin 3.00 8.00
CS CC Sabathia 4.00 10.00
CS Chris Sale 5.00 12.00
CZ Carlos Zambrano S2 4.00 10.00
DD David DeJesus S2 3.00 8.00
DD Daniel Descalso 3.00 8.00
DG Dillon Gee S2 3.00 8.00
DH Daniel Hudson 3.00 8.00
DJ Derek Jeter 10.00 25.00
DM Don Mattingly 10.00 25.00
DM Don Mattingly S2 10.00 25.00
DO David Ortiz S2 5.00 12.00
DO David Ortiz 5.00 12.00
DP David Price 4.00 10.00
DS Drew Stubbs 3.00 8.00
DS Drew Stubbs S2 3.00 8.00
DU Dan Uggla S2 4.00 10.00
DU Dan Uggla 4.00 10.00
DW David Wright 4.00 10.00
DW David Wright S2 4.00 10.00
EA Elvis Andrus 4.00 10.00
EB Ernie Banks 8.00 20.00
EL Evan Longoria 4.00 10.00
EL Evan Longoria S2 4.00 10.00
With bat
EM Evan Meek S2 3.00 8.00
FR Frank Robinson 5.00 12.00
FT Frank Thomas S2 5.00 12.00
GB Gordon Beckham S2 3.00 8.00
GB Gordon Beckham 3.00 8.00
GC Gary Carter 4.00 10.00
GS Geovany Soto S2 4.00 10.00
HB Heath Bell S2 3.00 8.00
HC Hank Conger S2 3.00 8.00
HR Hanley Ramirez 4.00 10.00
ID Ivan DeJesus 2.00 5.00
ID Ian Desmond S2 3.00 8.00
IK Ian Kinsler S2 4.00 10.00
JA J.P. Arencibia S2 3.00 8.00
JA John Axford 3.00 8.00
JB Jose Bautista 4.00 10.00
JB Jay Bruce S2 4.00 10.00
JC Johnny Cueto S2 4.00 10.00
JC Jhoulys Chacin 3.00 8.00
JD Johnny Damon 4.00 10.00
JD Johnny Damon S2 4.00 10.00
JG Jaime Garcia S2 4.00 10.00
JH Jeremy Hellickson S2 3.00 8.00
JH Josh Hamilton 4.00 10.00
JJ Josh Johnson S2 4.00 10.00
JL James Loney S2 3.00 8.00
JL Jon Lester 3.00 8.00
JN Jon Niese 3.00 8.00
JP Jhonny Peralta 3.00 8.00
JP Jhonny Peralta S2 3.00 8.00
JR Jose Reyes 3.00 8.00
JU Justin Upton S2 4.00 10.00
JV Justin Verlander 5.00 12.00
JW Jered Weaver 4.00 10.00
JW Jayson Werth S2 4.00 10.00
JZ Jordan Zimmermann S2 4.00 10.00
KM Kendrys Morales 3.00 8.00
KS Kurt Suzuki 3.00 8.00
KY Kevin Youkilis 5.00 12.00
MB Madison Bumgarner 4.00 10.00
MB Marlon Byrd S2 3.00 8.00
MC Melky Cabrera S2 3.00 8.00
MC Miguel Cabrera 6.00 15.00
MH Matt Holliday 5.00 12.00
MK Matt Kemp 4.00 10.00
ML Mat Latos 4.00 10.00
ML Mat Latos S2 4.00 10.00
MM Mitch Moreland S2 3.00 8.00
MP Martin Prado 3.00 8.00
MR Mark Reynolds S2 3.00 8.00
MS Max Scherzer S2 5.00 12.00
MS Mike Schmidt 6.00 15.00
MT Mark Teixeira 4.00 10.00
NM Nick Markakis 4.00 10.00
NM Nick Markakis S2 4.00 10.00
PB Pat Burrell 2.00 5.00
PF Prince Fielder 4.00 10.00
PF Prince Fielder S2 4.00 10.00
PM Paul Molitor S2 5.00 12.00
PM Paul Molitor 5.00 12.00
PO Paul O'Neill S2 3.00 8.00
RA Roberto Alomar S2 3.00 8.00
RB Ryan Braun S2 3.00 8.00
RB Ryan Braun 3.00 8.00
RC Robinson Cano 4.00 10.00
RH Roy Halladay 4.00 10.00
RJ Reggie Jackson 3.00 8.00
RM Roger Maris 12.00 30.00
RM Roger Maris S2 12.00 30.00
RP Rick Porcello S2 3.00 8.00
RR Ricky Romero S2 3.00 8.00
RZ Ryan Zimmerman S2 4.00 10.00
RZ Ryan Zimmerman 4.00 10.00
SC Starlin Castro 4.00 10.00
SC Shin-Soo Choo S2 4.00 10.00
SM Shaun Marcum 3.00 8.00
SR Scott Rolen 4.00 10.00
SS Sergio Santos 3.00 8.00
SS Stephen Strasburg S2 8.00 20.00
TC Trevor Cahill 3.00 8.00
TH Tommy Hanson 3.00 8.00
TH Torii Hunter S2 4.00 10.00
TL Tim Lincecum 4.00 10.00
TT Troy Tulowitzki 5.00 12.00
TW Travis Wood 3.00 8.00
UJ Ubaldo Jimenez 3.00 8.00
UJ Ubaldo Jimenez S2 3.00 8.00
VM Victor Martinez S2 4.00 10.00
VW Vernon Wells S2 3.00 8.00
WB Wade Boggs S2 3.00 8.00
YG Yovani Gallardo S2 4.00 10.00
YG Yovani Gallardo 4.00 10.00
ZG Zack Greinke S2 5.00 12.00
AGR Alex Gordon 4.00 10.00
APA Angel Pagan S2 3.00 8.00
BMC Brian McCann S2 4.00 10.00
BWA Brett Wallace 3.00 8.00
CGE Craig Gentry 3.00 8.00
CGO Carlos Gonzalez 4.00 10.00
CZA Carlos Zambrano S2 4.00 10.00
DDE David DeJesus S2 3.00 8.00
DME Devin Mesoraco S2 3.00 8.00
DPE Dustin Pedroia 5.00 12.00
DST Drew Stubbs S2 3.00 8.00
ELO Evan Longoria S2 4.00 10.00
HCO Hank Conger S2 3.00 8.00
IDA Ike Davis S2 3.00 8.00
JCU Johnny Cueto 4.00 10.00
JJA Jon Jay S2 5.00 12.00
JLO Jed Lowrie S2 3.00 8.00
JLU Jonathan Lucroy 4.00 10.00
JPA Jonathan Papelbon 4.00 10.00
JPA Jonathan Papelbon S2 4.00 10.00
JPE Jake Peavy S2 3.00 8.00
JPO Jorge Posada S2 3.00 8.00
JVO Joey Votto 5.00 12.00
JWA Jordan Walden S2 3.00 8.00
JWE Jayson Werth 4.00 10.00
JZI Jordan Zimmermann S2 4.00 10.00
MBO Michael Bourn S2 3.00 8.00
MCA Melky Cabrera S2 3.00 8.00
MCA Matt Cain 4.00 10.00
MCB Miguel Cabrera S2 6.00 15.00
MLA Matt LaPorta 3.00 8.00
MSC Max Scherzer 5.00 12.00
MST Mike Stanton 5.00 12.00
RAL Roberto Alomar S2 3.00 8.00
RMA Russell Martin S2 3.00 8.00
SCA Starlin Castro S2 4.00 10.00
SMU Stan Musial 6.00 15.00
SST Stephen Strasburg 8.00 20.00
THU Tim Hudson 4.00 10.00
UJI Ubaldo Jimenez S2 3.00 8.00
VWE Vernon Wells S2 3.00 8.00
ZGR Zack Greinke S2 5.00 12.00

2012 Topps Golden Moments Relics Gold Sparkle

*GOLD: .6X TO 1.5X BASIC
STATED ODDS 1:953 HOBBY
STATED PRINT RUN 99 SER.#'d SETS
CY Carl Yastrzemski S2 10.00 25.00

2012 Topps Historical Stitches

RANDOM INSERTS IN RETAIL PACKS
I Ichiro Suzuki S2 3.00 8.00
AB Albert Belle S2 1.00 2.50
AD Andre Dawson S2 1.50 4.00
AK Al Kaline 2.50 6.00
AP Albert Pujols S2 3.00 8.00
AR Alex Rodriguez S2 3.00 8.00
BG Bob Gibson 1.50 4.00
CF Carlton Fisk 1.50 4.00
CJ Chipper Jones S2 2.50 6.00
CR Cal Ripken Jr. S2 8.00 20.00
CY Carl Yastrzemski S2 4.00 10.00
DJ Derek Jeter S2 12.50 30.00
DM Don Mattingly 5.00 12.00
FR Frank Robinson 1.50 4.00
GC Gary Carter S2 1.50 4.00
HA Hank Aaron 5.00 12.00
HK Harmon Killebrew S2 2.50 6.00
IR Ivan Rodriguez S2 1.50 4.00
JB Johnny Bench 2.50 6.00
JD Joe DiMaggio 5.00 12.00
JH Josh Hamilton S2 2.00 5.00
JM Juan Marichal S2 1.50 4.00
JM Joe Morgan 1.50 4.00
JR Jackie Robinson 2.50 6.00
JR Jim Rice S2 1.50 4.00
JS John Smoltz S2 2.50 6.00
JV Justin Verlander S2 2.50 6.00
KG Ken Griffey Jr. S2 12.50 30.00
LA Luis Aparicio 1.50 4.00
LG Lou Gehrig 5.00 12.00
MM Mickey Mantle 8.00 20.00
MR Mariano Rivera S2 3.00 8.00
MS Mike Schmidt 4.00 10.00
NR Nolan Ryan 8.00 20.00
NR Nolan Ryan S2 8.00 20.00
PM Paul Molitor S2 2.50 6.00
RC Roberto Clemente 10.00 25.00
RJ Reggie Jackson 1.50 4.00
RM Roger Maris 2.50 6.00
RM Roger Maris S2 2.50 6.00
RS Ryne Sandberg 5.00 12.00
SK Sandy Koufax 5.00 12.00
SM Stan Musial 4.00 10.00
TC Ty Cobb 4.00 10.00
TS Tom Seaver 1.50 4.00
VG Vladimir Guerrero S2 2.00 5.00
WM Willie Mays 5.00 12.00
WMC Willie McCovey 1.50 4.00
WS Warren Spahn S2 1.50 4.00
YB Yogi Berra S2 2.50 6.00

2012 Topps Mickey Mantle Reprint Relics

STATED ODDS 1:147,600 HOBBY
PRINT RUNS B/WN 67-69 COPIES PER
MMR67 Mickey Mantle/67 50.00 100.00
MMR68 Mickey Mantle/68 50.00 100.00
MMR69 Mickey Mantle/69 50.00 100.00

2012 Topps Mound Dominance

COMPLETE SET (15) 6.00 15.00
STATED ODDS 1:8 HOBBY
MD1 Tom Seaver .40 1.00
MD2 Justin Verlander .60 1.50
MD3 Sandy Koufax 1.25 3.00
MD4 Jim Palmer .40 1.00
MD5 Dennis Eckersley .40 1.00
MD6 Bob Gibson .40 1.00
MD7 Roy Halladay .50 1.25
MD8 Nolan Ryan 2.00 5.00
MD9 Phil Niekro .40 1.00
MD10 Armando Galarraga .25 .60
MD11 Warren Spahn .40 1.00
MD12 Bob Feller .40 1.00
MD13 Jon Lester .40 1.00
MD14 John Smoltz .60 1.50
MD15 Dwight Gooden .25 .60

2012 Topps Mound Dominance Relics

STATED ODDS 1:9525 HOBBY
STATED PRINT 50 SER.#'d SETS
CB Clay Buchholz 10.00 25.00
DE Dennis Eckersley 20.00 50.00
FH Felix Hernandez 5.00 12.00
JP Jim Palmer 6.00 15.00
JS John Smoltz 12.50 30.00
JV Justin Verlander 15.00 40.00
MG Matt Garza 4.00 10.00
NR Nolan Ryan 15.00 40.00
RH Roy Halladay 10.00 25.00
SC Steve Carlton 15.00 40.00
SK Sandy Koufax 20.00 50.00
TS Tom Seaver 15.00 40.00
UJ Ubaldo Jimenez 4.00 10.00

2012 Topps Prime Nine Home Run Legends

COMPLETE SET (9) 6.00 15.00
COMMON EXCHANGE 1.50 4.00
STATED ODDS 1:18 HOBBY
HRL1 Hank Aaron 1.50 4.00
HRL2 Babe Ruth 2.00 5.00
HRL3 Willie Mays 1.50 4.00
HRL4 Reggie Jackson .50 1.25
HRL5 Alex Rodriguez 1.00 2.50
HRL6 Mickey Mantle 2.50 6.00
HRL7 Ernie Banks .75 2.00
HRL8 Frank Robinson .50 1.25
HRL9 Albert Pujols 1.00 2.50

2012 Topps Retail Refractors

COMPLETE SET (3) 4.00 10.00
MBC1 Mickey Mantle 3.00 8.00
MBC2 Willie Mays 2.00 5.00
MBC3 Ken Griffey Jr. 2.00 5.00

2012 Topps Retired Number Patches

RANDOM INSERTS IN RETAIL PACKS
AD Andre Dawson 1.25 3.00
AK Al Kaline 2.00 5.00
BF Bob Feller S2 1.25 3.00
BG Bob Gibson 1.25 3.00
BR Brooks Robinson S2 1.25 3.00
CF Carlton Fisk S2 1.25 3.00
CF Carlton Fisk 1.25 3.00
CH Catfish Hunter S2 1.25 3.00
CR Cal Ripken Jr. 6.00 15.00
DW Dave Winfield S2 1.25 3.00
EB Ernie Banks S2 2.00 5.00
FR Frank Robinson 1.25 3.00
FT Frank Thomas 2.00 5.00
GB George Brett S2 4.00 10.00
GC Gary Carter S2 1.25 3.00
HA Hank Aaron S2 4.00 10.00
HA Hank Aaron 4.00 10.00

JB Johnny Bench 2.00 5.00
JD Joe DiMaggio 4.00 10.00
JM Joe Morgan 1.25 3.00
JP Jim Palmer S2 1.25 3.00
JR Jackie Robinson 2.00 5.00
JRI Jim Rice 1.25 3.00
LB Lou Boudreau S2 1.25 3.00
LG Lou Gehrig 4.00 10.00
MM Mickey Mantle 6.00 15.00
MS Mike Schmidt 3.00 8.00
NR Nolan Ryan 6.00 15.00
NR Nolan Ryan S2 6.00 15.00
PN Phil Niekro S2 1.25 3.00
PR Phil Rizzuto S2 1.25 3.00
RC Rod Carew S2 1.25 3.00
RC Roberto Clemente 5.00 12.00
RH Rickey Henderson S2 2.00 5.00
RJ Reggie Jackson S2 1.25 3.00
RJ Reggie Jackson 1.25 3.00
RJA Reggie Jackson 1.25 3.00
RM Roger Maris 2.00 5.00
RS Ryne Sandberg S2 4.00 10.00
RY Robin Yount S2 2.00 5.00
SA Sparky Anderson S2 1.25 3.00
SK Sandy Koufax 4.00 10.00
SM Stan Musial 3.00 8.00
TG Tony Gwynn S2 1.25 3.00
TL Tommy Lasorda S2 1.25 3.00
TS Tom Seaver 1.25 3.00
WB Wade Boggs S2 1.25 3.00
WM Willie Mays 4.00 10.00
WS Willie Stargell S2 1.25 3.00
YB Yogi Berra S2 2.00 5.00

2012 Topps Retired Rings

STATED ODDS 1:759 HOBBY
STATED PRINT RUN 736 SER.#'d SETS
BR Babe Ruth 12.00 30.00
CF Carlton Fisk 4.00 10.00
CR Cal Ripken Jr. 10.00 25.00
DM Don Mattingly 10.00 25.00
FR Frank Robinson 4.00 10.00
FRO Frank Robinson 4.00 10.00
FT Frank Thomas 6.00 15.00
HA Hank Aaron 10.00 25.00
JB Johnny Bench 6.00 15.00
JD Joe DiMaggio 10.00 25.00
JM Joe Morgan 4.00 10.00
JR Jackie Robinson 10.00 25.00
LA Luis Aparicio 4.00 10.00
LG Lou Gehrig 10.00 25.00
MM Mickey Mantle 20.00 50.00
MS Mike Schmidt 10.00 25.00
NR Nolan Ryan 12.00 30.00
NRY Nolan Ryan 12.00 30.00
RC Roberto Clemente 15.00 40.00
RJ Reggie Jackson 4.00 10.00
RM Roger Maris 10.00 25.00
RS Ryne Sandberg 10.00 25.00
SK Sandy Koufax 10.00 25.00
SM Stan Musial 10.00 25.00
TS Tom Seaver 4.00 10.00
WM Willie Mays 10.00 25.00

2012 Topps Silk Collection

SER.2 ODDS 1:425 HOBBY
UPDATE ODDS 1:240 HOBBY
STATED PRINT RUN 50 SER.#'d SETS
SC1 Ryan Braun 6.00 15.00
SC2 Jaime Garcia 8.00 20.00
SC3 Desmond Jennings 8.00 20.00
SC4 Mickey Mantle 40.00 100.00
SC5 Jon Lester 6.00 15.00
SC6 Vernon Wells 6.00 15.00
SC7 Melky Cabrera 6.00 15.00
SC8 Craig Kimbrel 8.00 20.00
SC9 Chris Iannetta 6.00 15.00
SC10 Ike Davis 6.00 15.00
SC11 Derek Jeter 25.00 60.00
SC12 Eric Hosmer 8.00 20.00
SC13 Mike Napoli 6.00 15.00
SC14 Jhoulys Chacin 6.00 15.00
SC15 Adrian Gonzalez 8.00 20.00
SC16 Michael Young 6.00 15.00
SC17 Geovany Soto 8.00 20.00
SC18 Hanley Ramirez 8.00 20.00
SC19 Jordan Zimmermann 8.00 20.00
SC20 Ian Kennedy 6.00 15.00
SC21 David Price 8.00 20.00
SC22 Jason Heyward 8.00 20.00
SC23 Jose Bautista 8.00 20.00
SC24 Madison Bumgarner 8.00 20.00
SC25 Brett Anderson 6.00 15.00
SC26 Paul Konerko 6.00 15.00
SC27 Mark Teixeira 8.00 20.00
SC28 Matt Garza 6.00 15.00
SC29 Tommy Hanson 6.00 15.00
SC30 Hunter Pence 8.00 20.00
SC31 Adam Jones 8.00 20.00
SC32 Asdrubal Cabrera 8.00 20.00
SC33 Johnny Cueto 8.00 20.00
SC34 Troy Tulowitzki 10.00 25.00
SC35 Brandon Belt 8.00 20.00
SC36 Roy Halladay 8.00 20.00
SC37 Matt Cain 8.00 20.00
SC38 Kevin Youkilis 10.00 25.00
SC39 Jacoby Ellsbury 8.00 20.00
SC40 Mariano Rivera 12.00 30.00
SC41 Pablo Sandoval 8.00 20.00
SC42 Cole Hamels 8.00 20.00
SC43 Ben Zobrist 8.00 20.00
SC44 Miguel Cabrera 10.00 25.00
SC45 Justin Masterson 6.00 15.00
SC46 David Robertson 6.00 15.00
SC47 Zack Greinke 10.00 25.00
SC48 Alex Avila 6.00 15.00
SC49 Freddie Freeman 12.00 30.00
SC50 Jason Kipnis 8.00 20.00
SC51 Jay Bruce 8.00 20.00
SC52 Ubaldo Jimenez 6.00 15.00
SC53 Mike Minor 6.00 15.00
SC54 Justin Morneau 8.00 20.00
SC55 David Wright 8.00 20.00
SC56 Adam Lind 8.00 20.00
SC57 Stephen Drew 6.00 15.00
SC58 Jered Weaver 8.00 20.00
SC59 Mat Latos 8.00 20.00
SC60 Brian Wilson 10.00 25.00
SC61 Kyle Blanks 6.00 15.00
SC62 Shaun Marcum 6.00 15.00
SC63 Aroldis Chapman 10.00 25.00
SC64 Starlin Castro 8.00 20.00
SC65 Dexter Fowler 8.00 20.00
SC66 David Freese 6.00 15.00
SC67 Scott Baker 6.00 15.00
SC68 Sergio Santos 6.00 15.00
SC69 R.A. Dickey 8.00 20.00
SC70 Ryan Howard 8.00 20.00
SC71 Mark Trumbo 8.00 20.00
SC72 Delmon Young 8.00 20.00
SC73 Erick Aybar 6.00 15.00
SC74 Tony Gwynn 6.00 15.00
SC75 Drew Storen 6.00 15.00
SC76 Antonio Bastardo 6.00 15.00
SC77 Miguel Montero 6.00 15.00
SC78 Casey Kotchman 6.00 15.00
SC79 Curtis Granderson 8.00 20.00
SC80 Eric Thames 8.00 20.00
SC81 John Axford 8.00 20.00
SC82 Jayson Werth 8.00 20.00
SC83 Mitch Moreland 6.00 15.00
SC84 Josh Hamilton 8.00 20.00
SC85 Alexi Ogando 6.00 15.00
SC86 Danny Valencia 8.00 20.00
SC87 Brandon Morrow 6.00 15.00
SC88 Chipper Jones 10.00 25.00
SC89 Emilio Bonifacio 6.00 15.00
SC90 Vance Worley 8.00 20.00
SC91 Mike Leake 6.00 15.00
SC92 Kurt Suzuki 6.00 15.00
SC93 Adrian Beltre 10.00 25.00
SC94 John Danks 6.00 15.00
SC95 Phil Hughes 6.00 15.00
SC96 Matt LaPorta 6.00 15.00
SC97 Tim Hudson 8.00 20.00
SC98 Erik Bedard 6.00 15.00
SC99 Matt Holliday 10.00 25.00
SC100 Matt Kemp 8.00 20.00
SC101 Brett Lawrie 8.00 20.00
SC102 Michael Cuddyer 6.00 15.00
SC103 Martin Prado 6.00 15.00
SC104 Anthony Rizzo 12.00 30.00
SC105 Victor Martinez 8.00 20.00
SC106 Michael Bourn 6.00 15.00
SC107 Elvis Andrus 8.00 20.00
SC108 Chris Carpenter 8.00 20.00
SC109 Joey Votto 10.00 25.00
SC110 Carlos Lee 6.00 15.00
SC111 Rickie Weeks 6.00 15.00
SC112 Todd Helton 8.00 20.00
SC113 Josh Johnson 8.00 20.00
SC114 Dustin Pedroia 10.00 25.00
SC115 J.J. Hardy 6.00 15.00
SC116 Brett Gardner 8.00 20.00
SC117 Gio Gonzalez 8.00 20.00
SC118 Dayan Viciedo 6.00 15.00
SC119 Albert Pujols 12.00 30.00
SC120 Cameron Maybin 6.00 15.00
SC121 Cliff Lee 8.00 20.00
SC122 Carlos Quentin 6.00 15.00
SC123 James Shields 6.00 15.00
SC124 Yovani Gallardo 8.00 20.00
SC125 Shin-Soo Choo 8.00 20.00
SC126 Darwin Barney 6.00 15.00
SC127 Alex Rodriguez 12.00 30.00
SC128 Carlos Santana 8.00 20.00
SC129 Chris Young 6.00 15.00
SC130 Travis Hafner 6.00 15.00
SC131 Ichiro Suzuki 12.00 30.00
SC132 David Ortiz 10.00 25.00
SC133 Corey Hart 6.00 15.00
SC134 Carl Crawford 8.00 20.00
SC135 Logan Morrison 6.00 15.00
SC136 Josh Beckett 6.00 15.00
SC137 Brandon Beachy 6.00 15.00
SC138 Ian Kinsler 8.00 20.00
SC139 Dan Haren 6.00 15.00
SC140 Felix Hernandez 8.00 20.00
SC141 Brandon Phillips 6.00 15.00
SC142 Evan Longoria 8.00 20.00
SC143 Nelson Cruz 10.00 25.00
SC144 Joe Mauer 8.00 20.00
SC145 Andrew McCutchen 10.00 25.00
SC146 Carlos Zambrano 8.00 20.00
SC147 Stephen Strasburg 10.00 25.00
SC148 Justin Verlander 10.00 25.00
SC149 Jose Valverde 8.00 20.00
SC150 CC Sabathia 8.00 20.00
SC151 Kerry Wood 6.00 15.00
SC152 Jeff Francoeur 8.00 20.00
SC153 Andrew Bailey 6.00 15.00
SC154 Alex Gordon 8.00 20.00
SC155 Howie Kendrick 6.00 15.00
SC156 Nick Markakis 8.00 20.00
SC157 Jimmy Rollins 8.00 20.00
SC158 Brian McCann 8.00 20.00
SC159 Jeremy Hellickson 8.00 20.00
SC160 Dan Uggla 8.00 20.00
SC161 Adam Wainwright 8.00 20.00
SC162 Ricky Romero 6.00 15.00
SC163 Daniel Hudson 6.00 15.00
SC164 Wandy Rodriguez 6.00 15.00
SC165 Andre Ethier 8.00 20.00
SC166 Lance Berkman 8.00 20.00
SC167 Alexei Ramirez 8.00 20.00
SC168 Mike Moustakas 8.00 20.00
SC169 Chase Utley 8.00 20.00
SC170 C.J. Wilson 6.00 15.00
SC171 Ervin Santana 6.00 15.00
SC172 Jair Jurrjens 6.00 15.00
SC173 Robinson Cano 8.00 20.00
SC174 Clayton Kershaw 15.00 40.00
SC175 Jose Reyes 6.00 15.00
SC176 Tsuyoshi Nishioka 8.00 20.00
SC177 Mike Stanton 10.00 25.00
SC178 Drew Stubbs 6.00 15.00
SC179 Jemile Weeks 6.00 15.00
SC180 Justin Upton 8.00 20.00
SC181 Carlos Beltran 8.00 20.00
SC182 Carlos Marmol 6.00 15.00
SC183 Shane Victorino 8.00 20.00
SC184 Nick Swisher 8.00 20.00
SC185 Tim Lincecum 8.00 20.00
SC186 Ryan Zimmerman 8.00 20.00
SC187 Aramis Ramirez 6.00 15.00
SC188 Jim Thome 8.00 20.00
SC189 Torii Hunter 8.00 20.00
SC190 Mike Trout 300.00 800.00
SC191 Paul Goldschmidt 10.00 25.00
SC192 Yu Darvish 15.00 40.00
SC193 Hiroki Kuroda 6.00 15.00
SC194 Johan Santana 8.00 20.00
SC195 Carlos Gonzalez 8.00 20.00
SC196 Prince Fielder 8.00 20.00
SC197 J.J. Putz 6.00 15.00
SC198 Neftali Feliz 6.00 15.00
SC199 Buster Posey 12.00 30.00
SC200 Alfonso Soriano 8.00 20.00
SC201 Bryce Harper 40.00 100.00
SC202 Jamey Carroll 6.00 15.00
SC203 Matt Treanor 6.00 15.00
SC204 Darren Oliver 6.00 15.00
SC205 Miguel Batista 6.00 15.00
SC206 Trevor Bauer 30.00 80.00
SC207 Luke Scott 6.00 15.00
SC208 Matt Lindstrom 6.00 15.00
SC209 A.J. Ellis 6.00 15.00
SC210 Giancarlo Stanton 10.00 25.00
SC211 Yu Darvish 15.00 40.00
SC212 Travis Ishikawa 6.00 15.00
SC213 Brian Duensing 6.00 15.00
SC214 Jonny Gomes 6.00 15.00
SC215 Gerald Laird 6.00 15.00
SC216 Ross Detwiler 6.00 15.00
SC217 Johnny Damon 8.00 20.00
SC218 Hector Santiago 8.00 20.00
SC219 Ernesto Frieri 6.00 15.00
SC220 Joel Peralta 6.00 15.00
SC221 Adam Kennedy 6.00 15.00
SC222 Jason Hammel 8.00 20.00
SC223 Javier Lopez 6.00 15.00
SC224 Ty Wigginton 6.00 15.00
SC225 Matt Moore 10.00 25.00
SC226 Kevin Millwood 6.00 15.00
SC227 Lucas Harrell 6.00 15.00
SC228 Chris Nelson 6.00 15.00
SC229 Erik Bedard 6.00 15.00
SC230 Fernando Rodney 6.00 15.00
SC231 Tom Milone 6.00 15.00
SC232 Brad Ziegler 6.00 15.00
SC233 Joe Smith 6.00 15.00
SC234 Casey Kotchman 6.00 15.00
SC235 Andrew Cashner 6.00 15.00
SC236 Drew Hutchinson 8.00 20.00
SC237 Brandon Inge 6.00 15.00
SC238 Todd Frazier 6.00 15.00
SC239 Xavier Nady 6.00 15.00
SC240 Will Middlebrooks 8.00 20.00
SC241 Jason Grilli 6.00 15.00
SC242 Trevor Cahill 6.00 15.00
SC243 Greg Dobbs 6.00 15.00
SC244 Ryan Theriot 20.00 50.00
SC245 Takashi Saito 6.00 15.00
SC246 Austin Kearns 6.00 15.00
SC247 Santiago Casilla 6.00 15.00
SC248 Manny Acosta 6.00 15.00
SC249 Edwin Jackson 6.00 15.00
SC250 Yoenis Cespedes 15.00 40.00
SC251 Matt Albers 6.00 15.00
SC252 Felix Doubront 6.00 15.00
SC253 Octavio Dotel 6.00 15.00
SC254 Rick Ankiel 6.00 15.00
SC255 Andy Pettitte 8.00 20.00
SC256 Brad Peacock 6.00 15.00
SC257 Phil Coke 6.00 15.00
SC258 Josh Harrison 8.00 20.00
SC259 Kyle McClellan 6.00 15.00
SC260 Rafael Soriano 6.00 15.00
SC261 Michael Saunders 8.00 20.00
SC262 Lance Lynn 8.00 20.00
SC263 Jesus Montero 6.00 15.00
SC264 Jose Arredondo 6.00 15.00
SC265 J.P. Howell 6.00 15.00
SC266 Maicer Izturis 6.00 15.00
SC267 Drew Smyly 6.00 15.00
SC268 Yuniesky Betancourt 6.00 15.00
SC269 A.J. Burnett 6.00 15.00
SC270 Casey McGehee 6.00 15.00
SC271 Mitchell Boggs 6.00 15.00
SC272 Michael Pineda 6.00 15.00
SC273 Dan Wheeler 6.00 15.00
SC274 Alfredo Aceves 6.00 15.00
SC275 Angel Pagan 6.00 15.00
SC276 Steve Cishek 6.00 15.00
SC277 Jack Wilson 6.00 15.00
SC278 Randy Choate 6.00 15.00
SC279 Joaquin Benoit 6.00 15.00
SC280 Bobby Abreu 8.00 20.00
SC281 A.J. Pollock 10.00 25.00
SC282 Will Ohman 6.00 15.00
SC283 Jonathan Broxton 6.00 15.00
SC284 Matt Diaz 6.00 15.00
SC285 Ryan Ludwick 6.00 15.00
SC286 Jerry Hairston 6.00 15.00
SC287 Brian Fuentes 6.00 15.00
SC288 Chone Figgins 6.00 15.00
SC289 Cesar Izturis 6.00 15.00
SC290 Eric Chavez 6.00 15.00
SC291 Mark Derosa 6.00 15.00
SC292 Jason Marquis 6.00 15.00
SC293 Jake Westbrook 6.00 15.00
SC294 Kevin Slowey 6.00 15.00
SC295 Alfredo Simon 6.00 15.00
SC296 John McDonald 6.00 15.00
SC297 Mat Latos 8.00 20.00
SC298 Henry Rodriguez 6.00 15.00
SC299 Sergio Santos 6.00 15.00
SC300 Melky Cabrera 6.00 15.00

2012 Topps Team Rings

SER.2 ODDS 1:774 HOBBY
BF Bob Feller 2.00 5.00
CJ Chipper Jones 3.00 8.00
CR Cal Ripken Jr. 10.00 25.00
CY Carl Yastrzemski 5.00 12.00
EB Ernie Banks 3.00 8.00
EL Evan Longoria 2.50 6.00
FT Frank Thomas 3.00 8.00
GB George Brett 6.00 15.00
HK Harmon Killebrew 3.00 8.00
HR Hanley Ramirez 2.50 6.00
JB Johnny Bench 3.00 8.00
JBA Jose Bautista 2.50 6.00
JH Josh Hamilton 2.50 6.00
JU Justin Upton 2.50 6.00
KG Ken Griffey Jr. 6.00 15.00
MM Mickey Mantle 10.00 25.00
MS Mike Schmidt 5.00 12.00
NR Nolan Ryan 10.00 25.00
RC Rod Carew 2.00 5.00
RCL Roberto Clemente 8.00 20.00
RH Rickey Henderson 3.00 8.00
RY Robin Yount 3.00 8.00
SK Sandy Koufax 6.00 15.00
SM Stan Musial 5.00 12.00
SS Stephen Strasburg 3.00 8.00
TC Ty Cobb 5.00 12.00
TG Tony Gwynn 2.00 5.00
TH Todd Helton 2.50 6.00
TS Tom Seaver 2.00 5.00
WM Willie Mays 6.00 15.00

2012 Topps Timeless Talents

COMPLETE SET (25) 5.00 12.00
STATED ODDS 1:6 HOBBY
TT1 P.Molitor/R.Braun .60 1.50
TT2 Chase Utley/Dustin Ackley .50 1.25
TT3 D.Mattingly/E.Hosmer 1.25 3.00
TT4 W.Mays/M.Kemp 1.25 3.00
TT5 N.Ryan/J.Verlander 2.00 5.00
TT6 Felix Hernandez/Michael Pineda .50 1.25
TT7 Frank Thomas/Paul Konerko .60 1.50
TT8 Frank Robinson/Jose Bautista .50 1.25
TT9 John Smoltz/Craig Kimbrel .60 1.50
TT10 R.Sandberg/D.Uggla 1.25 3.00
TT11 Johnny Bench/Brian McCann .60 1.50
TT12 Andy Pettitte/Cliff Lee .50 1.25
TT13 Barry Larkin/Asdrubal Cabrera .50 1.25
TT14 N.Ryan/J.Weaver 2.00 5.00
TT15 Bob Gibson/Roy Halladay .50 1.25
TT16 Andre Dawson/Justin Upton .50 1.25
TT17 Joe Morgan/Brandon Phillips .40 1.00
TT18 Albert Belle/Mike Stanton .60 1.50
TT19 S.Musial/L.Berkman 1.00 2.50
TT20 Ernie Banks/Troy Tulowitzki .60 1.50
TT21 Dennis Eckersley/Andrew Bailey .40 1.00
TT22 Luis Aparicio/Starlin Castro .50 1.25
TT23 Edgar Martinez/David Ortiz .60 1.50
TT24 Roger Maris/Curtis Granderson .60 1.50
TT25 C.Ripken/D.Jeter 2.00 5.00

2012 Topps Timeless Talents Dual Relics

STATED ODDS 1:17,000 HOBBY
STATED PRINT RUN 50 SER.#'d SETS
BM J.Bench/B.McCann 30.00 60.00
DU A.Dawson/J.Upton 30.00 60.00
HP Felix Hernandez 10.00 25.00
Michael Pineda
MK W.Mays/M.Kemp 50.00 100.00
RJ C.Ripken/D.Jeter 50.00 100.00
RV Ryan/Verlander EXCH 50.00 100.00
RW Ryan/Weaver 20.00 50.00
SU R.Sandberg/D.Uggla 20.00 50.00
MTT R.Maris/C.Granderson 40.00 80.00
TTH Gibson/Halladay EXCH 50.00 100.00

2012 Topps World Champion Autograph Relics

STATED ODDS 1:12,300 HOBBY
STATED PRINT RUN 50 SER.#'d SETS
EXCHANGE DEADLINE 12/31/2014
AC Allen Craig 100.00 200.00
AP Albert Pujols 125.00 250.00
JG Jaime Garcia 90.00 150.00
JM Jason Motte 50.00 100.00
MH Matt Holliday 100.00 200.00

2012 Topps World Champion Autographs

STATED ODDS 1:39,990 HOBBY
STATED PRINT RUN 50 SER.#'d SETS
EXCHANGE DEADLINE 12/31/2014
AC Allen Craig 60.00 120.00
AP Albert Pujols 150.00 300.00
JG Jaime Garcia 75.00 150.00
JM Jason Motte 60.00 120.00
MH Matt Holliday 60.00 120.00

2012 Topps World Champion Relics

STATED ODDS 1:6700 HOBBY
STATED PRINT RUN 100 SER.#'d SETS
EXCHANGE DEADLINE 12/31/2014
AC Allen Craig 40.00 80.00
AP Albert Pujols 75.00 150.00
CC Chris Carpenter 50.00 100.00
DD Daniel Descalso 40.00 80.00
DF David Freese 90.00 150.00
EJ Edwin Jackson 10.00 25.00
JG Jaime Garcia 40.00 80.00
JJ Jon Jay 50.00 100.00
JM Jason Motte 40.00 80.00
LB Lance Berkman 75.00 150.00
MH Matt Holliday 50.00 100.00
RF Rafael Furcal 40.00 80.00
RT Ryan Theriot 10.00 25.00
SS Skip Schumaker EXCH 60.00 120.00
YM Yadier Molina 75.00 150.00

2012 Topps Update

COMP.SET w/o SPs (330) 60.00 150.00
COMMON CARD (1-330) .12 .30
COMMON VAR SP (1-330) 1.50 4.00
COMMON RC (1-330) .40 1.00
PRINTING PLATE ODDS 1:911 HOBBY
PLATE PRINT RUN 1 SET PER COLOR
BLACK-CYAN-MAGENTA-YELLOW ISSUED
NO PLATE PRICING DUE TO SCARCITY
US1A Francisco Liriano .12 .30
US1B A.Gonzalez LAD SP 100.00 200.00
US2A Kris Medlen .12 .30
US2B C.Crawford LAD SP 40.00 80.00
US3A Adam Kennedy .12 .30
US3B J.Beckett LAD SP 60.00 120.00
US4A Matt Treanor .12 .30
US4B N.Punto LAD SP 75.00 150.00
US5A Wade Miley .15 .40
US5B J.Loney BOS SP 40.00 100.00
US6A Carlos Gonzalez .15 .40
US6B K.Youkilis CHI SP 20.00 50.00
US7A Joe Mauer .15 .40
US7B J.Thome BAL SP 75.00 150.00
US8 Luis Perez .12 .30
US9 Andrew McCutchen .20 .50
US10A Mark Trumbo .12 .30
US10B Mark Trumbo 1.50 4.00
With teammates SP
US11 Rick Ankiel .12 .30
US12 Jake Westbrook .12 .30
US13 Matt Lindstrom .12 .30
US14 Jeremy Hefner RC .40 1.00
US15A Justin Verlander .20 .50
US15B J.Verlander 2.50 6.00
ASG SP
US16 Patrick Corbin RC .50 1.25
US17 Joe Smith .12 .30
US18 Tom Wilhelmsen .12 .30
US19 Jonathan Broxton .12 .30
US20 Christian Friedrich RC .40 1.00
US21 Buster Posey .25 .60
US22 Chris Nelson .12 .30
US23 Matt Harvey RC 2.50 6.00
US24 J.P. Howell .12 .30
US25 Joe Mather .12 .30
US26 Santiago Casilla .12 .30
US27 Cesar Izturis .12 .30
US28 Matt Albers .12 .30
US29 Jonathan Sanchez .12 .30
US30 Jonny Gomes .12 .30
US31 Esmil Rogers .12 .30
US32 Adam Jones .15 .40
US33 Nathan Eovaldi .15 .40
US34 A.J. Griffin RC .50 1.25
US35 Craig Breslow .12 .30
US36 Juan Cruz .12 .30
US37A Billy Butler .12 .30
US37B Billy Butler 5.00 12.00
With George Brett SP
US37C George Brett SP 5.00 12.00
US38 Elian Herrera RC .60 1.50
US39 Cory Wade .12 .30
US40 Jose Bautista .15 .40
US41 Juan Francisco .15 .40
US42 Yoenis Cespedes RC 1.00 2.50
US43 Michael Bowden .12 .30
US44 Jeremy Hermida .12 .30
US45 Eric Chavez .12 .30
US46 Jamie Moyer .12 .30
US47 Yuniesky Betancourt .12 .30
US48 Asdrubal Cabrera .15 .40
US49 A.J. Burnett .12 .30
US50 C.J. Wilson .12 .30
US51 Manny Parra .12 .30
US52A Clayton Kershaw .30 .75
US52B Kershaw w/Kemp SP 4.00 10.00
US53 Omar Infante .12 .30
US54 Phil Coke .12 .30
US55 Austin Kearns .12 .30
US56 Matt Diaz .12 .30
US57 Hanley Ramirez .15 .40
US58 Manny Acosta .12 .30
US59 Jerome Williams .12 .30
US60 Edwin Jackson .12 .30
US61 Alfredo Simon .12 .30
US62A CC Sabathia .15 .40
US62B CC Sabathia 2.00 5.00
With Kemp SP
US63 Gerald Laird .12 .30
US64 Matt Moore .20 .50
US65 Derek Norris RC .40 1.00
US66 James Russell .12 .30
US67 Jamey Carroll .12 .30
US68 Fernando Rodney .12 .30
US69 Brett Jackson RC .60 1.50
US70 Will Middlebrooks RC .50 1.25
US71 Brett Myers .12 .30
US72 Carlos Beltran .15 .40
US73 Joel Peralta .12 .30
US74 Starlin Castro .15 .40
US75 Rafael Furcal .12 .30
US76 Adam Dunn .15 .40
US77 Miguel Batista .12 .30
US78 Chad Durbin .12 .30
US79 Mike Baxter RC .40 1.00
US80 Jered Weaver .15 .40
US81 Lou Marson .12 .30
US82 Ty Wigginton .12 .30
US83 Carlos Lee .12 .30
US84 Eric Thames .15 .40
US85 Jacob Diekman RC .50 1.25
US86 Anibal Sanchez .12 .30
US87A Andrew McCutchen .20 .50
US87B Andrew McCutchen 2.50 6.00
In Suit SP
US88 Will Ohman .12 .30
US89 Andrew Cashner .12 .30
US90 Michael Saunders .15 .40
US91 Jonathan Papelbon .15 .40
US92 Chone Figgins .12 .30
US93 Chris Iannetta .12 .30
US94 Kevin Slowey .12 .30
US95 Edward Mujica .12 .30
US96 Jose Mijares .12 .30
US97 Shelley Duncan .12 .30
US98 Hector Santiago RC .50 1.25
US99 Chris Johnson .12 .30
US100 Ryan Dempster .12 .30
US101 Casey McGehee .12 .30
US102 Brandon League .12 .30
US103 Jack Wilson .12 .30
US104 Yasmani Grandal RC .40 1.00
US105 Mat Latos .15 .40
US106 Pedro Strop .12 .30
US107 Randy Choate .12 .30
US108 Kameron Loe .12 .30
US109 Starling Marte RC .50 1.25
US110 Robinson Cano .15 .40
US111 Clay Rapada .12 .30
US112 Eduardo Escobar RC .50 1.25
US113 Scott Elbert .12 .30
US114 Jeremy Guthrie .12 .30
US115 Jason Grilli .12 .30
US116 Chris Denorfia .12 .30
US117 Chris Resop .12 .30
US118 David Freese .12 .30
US119 Derek Jeter .50 1.25
US120A Robinson Cano .15 .40
US120B Robinson Cano 2.00 5.00
In Suit SP
US121 Johnny Damon .15 .40
US122 Logan Ondrusek .12 .30
US123 Jamie Moyer .12 .30
US124 Brad Peacock .12 .30
US125 Mark Lowe .12 .30
US126 John McDonald .12 .30
US127 Josh Harrison RC .50 1.25
US128 Dan Straily RC .40 1.00
US129 Giancarlo Stanton .20 .50
US130 Laynce Nix .12 .30
US131 Mitchell Boggs .12 .30
US132 Tommy Milone .12 .30
US133A Matt Kemp .15 .40
US133B Matt Kemp 2.00 5.00
In Suit SP
US134 Ramon Ramirez .12 .30
US135 Clay Hensley .12 .30
US136 Reed Johnson .12 .30
US137A Josh Hamilton .15 .40
US137B Josh Hamilton 2.00 5.00
With teammates SP
US138 Ernesto Frieri .12 .30
US139 Zack Greinke .20 .50
US140 Brian Duensing .12 .30
US141 R.A. Dickey .15 .40
US142 Erik Bedard .12 .30
US143 Jose Veras .12 .30
US144A Mike Trout 25.00 60.00
US144B M.Trout w/team SP 6.00 15.00
US145 Joey Devine .12 .30
US146 Casey Kotchman .12 .30
US147 Steve Delabar .12 .30
US148 Paul Konerko .15 .40
US149 Octavio Dotel .12 .30
US150 Jake Arrieta .15 .40
US151 Jordany Valdespin RC .50 1.25
US152 Jim Thome .15 .40
US153 Paul Maholm .12 .30
US154 Giancarlo Stanton .20 .50
US155 Franklin Morales .12 .30
US156 Troy Patton .12 .30
US157 Kole Calhoun RC .50 1.25
US158 Jared Burton .12 .30
US159 Ben Sheets .12 .30
US160 Marco Scutaro .15 .40
US161 Brian Dozier RC 1.25 3.00
US162A Yu Darvish RC 1.00 2.50
US162B Darvish Dress shirt SP 5.00 12.00
US163 Scott Diamond RC .40 1.00
US164 Melky Cabrera .12 .30
US165 Jacob Turner .15 .40
US166A Chipper Jones .20 .50
US166B C.Jones w/sign SP 5.00 12.00
US167 Trevor Cahill .12 .30
US168 Yu Darvish .30 .75
US169 Steve Cishek .12 .30
US170 Jerry Hairston .12 .30
US171 Rhiner Cruz RC .40 1.00
US172 Wilson Valdez .12 .30
US173 Jose Bautista .15 .40
US174 Javier Lopez .12 .30
US175 Tim Byrdak .12 .30
US176 Brad Ziegler .12 .30
US177 Mike Napoli .12 .30
US178 Lance Lynn .12 .30
US179 Matt Adams RC .50 1.25
US180 Roy Oswalt .15 .40
US181 Takashi Saito .12 .30
US182 Pablo Sandoval .15 .40
US183 Bryce Harper RC 12.00 30.00
US184 Stephen Strasburg .20 .50
US185 Donovan Solano RC 3.00 8.00
US186 Jason Hammel .15 .40
US187 John Jaso .12 .30
US188 Dallas Keuchel RC 2.00 5.00
US189 Melky Cabrera .12 .30
US190 Francisco Cordero .12 .30
US191 Bobby Abreu .12 .30
US192 Josh Hamilton .15 .40
US193 Henry Blanco .12 .30
US194 Brad Lincoln .12 .30
US195 Chad Qualls .12 .30
US196 Seth Smith .12 .30
US197 Cody Ransom .12 .30
US198 Michael Pineda .12 .30
US199 Nate Schierholtz .12 .30
US200 Chris Perez .12 .30
US201 Jason Frasor .12 .30
US202 Mark Trumbo .12 .30
US203 Fernando Rodney .12 .30
US204 Jesus Montero RC .40 1.00
US205 Travis Ishikawa .12 .30
US206 Cole Hamels .15 .40
US207 Greg Dobbs .12 .30
US208 Tyler Moore RC .40 1.00
US209 Yasmani Grandal .12 .30
US210 Tyler Chatwood .12 .30
US211 Matt Cain .15 .40
US212 Trevor Bauer .60 1.50
US213 Trevor Bauer RC 2.50 6.00
US214 Jeremy Affeldt .12 .30
US215 Brian Bogusevic .12 .30
US216 Matt Cain .15 .40
US217 Matt Guerrier .12 .30
US218 Alfredo Aceves .12 .30
US219 Brian Fuentes .12 .30
US220 Adrian Beltre .20 .50
US221 Drew Smyly RC .40 1.00
US222 Jairo Asencio .12 .30
US223 Boone Logan .12 .30
US224 Matt Belisle .12 .30
US225 Josh Lindblom .12 .30
US226 Rafael Soriano .12 .30
US227 Mark DeRosa .12 .30
US228 Aaron Cunningham .12 .30
US229 Quintin Berry RC .60 1.50
US230 Xavier Nady .12 .30
US231 Tim Dillard .12 .30
US232 Andrelton Simmons RC .60 1.50
US233 Jose Arredondo .12 .30
US234 Jeff Keppinger .12 .30
US235 Marc Rzepczynski .12 .30
US236 Lucas Luetge RC .40 1.00
US237 Prince Fielder .15 .40
US238 Shawn Camp .12 .30
US239 Luke Scott .12 .30
US240 Ronny Paulino .12 .30
US241A Curtis Granderson .15 .40
US241B Curtis Granderson 2.00 5.00
In suit SP
US242 Joe Kelly RC .60 1.50
US243 Brandon Inge .12 .30
US244 Matt Downs .12 .30
US245 Erasmo Ramirez RC .40 1.00
US246 Miguel Cabrera .20 .50
US247 Ryan Ludwick .12 .30
US248 Felix Doubront .12 .30
US249 Angel Pagan .12 .30
US250 Cristhian Martinez .12 .30
US251 Kyle McClellan .12 .30
US252 Chad Gaudin .12 .30
US253 Ryan Webb .12 .30
US254 Jason Marquis .12 .30
US255A Joey Votto .20 .50
US255B Joey Votto 2.50 6.00
With teammates SP
US256 Joe Nathan .12 .30
US257 Jose Quintana RC .40 1.00
US258 Josh Vitters RC .50 1.25
US259A Carlos Gonzalez .15 .40
US259B Carlos Gonzalez 2.00 5.00
In suit SP
US260 Ryan Cook RC .40 1.00
US261 Darren Oliver .12 .30
US262 Matt Kemp .15 .40
US263 Travis Snider .12 .30
US264 Josh Edgin RC .40 1.00
US265 Will Middlebrooks .15 .40
US266 Brandon Lyon .12 .30
US267 Darren O'Day .12 .30
US268A Craig Kimbrel .15 .40
US268B Craig Kimbrel 2.00 5.00
Dress shirt SP
US269 Drew Hutchison RC .50 1.25
US270 Luis Ayala .12 .30
US271A Ryan Braun .12 .30
US271B Ryan Braun 1.50 4.00
With teammates SP
US272A Ichiro Suzuki .25 .60
US272B Ichiro Bowing SP 10.00 25.00
US273 Yadier Molina .25 .60
US274 Jeff Gray .12 .30
US275 Todd Frazier .12 .30
US276 Matt Harvey 2.50 6.00
US277 Ben Francisco .12 .30
US278 Andy Pettitte .15 .40
US279 Ryan Cook RC .40 1.00
US280A David Wright .15 .40
US280B David Wright 2.00 5.00
With R.A. Dickey SP
US281 Matt Reynolds RC .40 1.00
US282 Darnell McDonald .12 .30
US283 Elvis Andrus .15 .40
US284 R.A. Dickey .15 .40
US285 Ian Kinsler .15 .40
US286 J.A. Happ .15 .40
US287 Dan Wheeler .12 .30
US288 Maicer Izturis .12 .30
US289A Prince Fielder .15 .40
US289B Prince Fielder 2.00 5.00
In suit SP
US290 Joaquin Benoit .12 .30
US291 Jesus Montero .40 1.00
US292A David Ortiz .20 .50
US292B David Ortiz 2.50 6.00
With teammates SP
US293 Shane Victorino .15 .40
US294 Sergio Santos .12 .30
US295 Carlos Ruiz .12 .30
US296 Henry Rodriguez .12 .30
US297 Hunter Pence .15 .40
US298 Gaby Sanchez .15 .40
US299A Bryce Harper 6.00 15.00
US299B B.Harper Suit SP 10.00 25.00
US299C Harper w/Chipper SP 10.00 25.00
US300 Mark Kotsay .12 .30
US301 Carlos Beltran .15 .40
US302 Lucas Harrell .12 .30
US303 Kevin Millwood .12 .30
US304 A.J. Ellis .12 .30
US305 David Price .15 .40
US306 Joe Wieland RC .40 1.00
US307 Ryan Roberts .12 .30
US308 Jay Bruce .15 .40
US309 Chris Heisey .12 .30
US310 Kelly Shoppach .12 .30
US311 Dan Uggla .15 .40
US312 Craig Stammen .12 .30
US313 Wandy Rodriguez .12 .30
US314 Eric O'Flaherty .12 .30
US315 Ross Detwiler .12 .30
US316 Ryan Theriot .12 .30
US317 Marco Estrada RC .40 1.00
US318 Anthony Bass .12 .30
US319 A.J. Pollock RC .60 1.50
US320 Xavier Avery RC .40 1.00
US321 David Carpenter RC .50 1.25
US322 Jordan Danks RC .40 1.00
US323 Fernando Abad .12 .30
US324 Jamey Wright .12 .30
US325 Joel Hanrahan .12 .30
US326 Gio Gonzalez .15 .40
US327A Chris Sale .20 .50
US327B Sale w/Team SP 2.50 6.00
US328 Geovany Soto .15 .40
US329 Jason Isringhausen .12 .30
US330 Alex Burnett .12 .30

2012 Topps Update Black

*BLACK: 12X TO 30X BASIC
*BLACK RC: 4X TO 10X BASIC
STATED ODDS 1:59 HOBBY
STATED PRINT RUN 61 SER.#'d SETS
US144 Mike Trout 600.00 1500.00
US162 Yu Darvish 12.50 30.00
US168 Yu Darvish 12.50 30.00
US183 Bryce Harper 500.00 1200.00
US299 Bryce Harper 40.00 100.00

2012 Topps Update Gold

*GOLD VET: 1.5X TO 4X BASIC
*GOLD RC: .5X TO 1.2X BASIC RC
STATED ODDS 1:5 HOBBY
STATED PRINT RUN 2012 SER.#'d SETS
US183 Bryce Harper 40.00 100.00

2012 Topps Update Gold Sparkle

*GLD SPARKLE VET: 1.2X TO 3X BASIC
*GLD SPARKLE RC: 4X TO 1X BASIC RC
STATED ODDS 1:4 HOBBY
US299 Bryce Harper 10.00 25.00

2012 Topps Update Orange
*GOLD VET: 5X TO 12X BASIC
*GOLD RC: 1.5X TO 4X BASIC RC
STATED PRINT RUN 210 SER.#'d SETS
US183 Bryce Harper 100.00 250.00

2012 Topps Update Target Red Border
*TARGET: 1.5X TO 4X BASIC
*TARGET RC: .5X TO 1.2X BASIC RC
FOUND IN TARGET RETAIL PACKS
US183 Bryce Harper 125.00 300.00
US299 Bryce Harper 10.00 25.00

2012 Topps Update Wal-Mart Blue Border
*WM: 1.5X TO 4X BASIC
*WM RC: .5X TO 1.2X BASIC RC
FOUND IN WAL MART RETAIL PACKS
US183 Bryce Harper 50.00 120.00
US299 Bryce Harper 8.00 20.00

2012 Topps Update All-Star Stitches
STATED ODDS 1:49 HOBBY
AB Adrian Beltre 3.00 8.00
AJ Adam Jones 4.00 10.00
AM Andrew McCutchen 5.00 12.00
BB Billy Butler 4.00 10.00
BH Bryce Harper 12.50 30.00
BP Buster Posey 6.00 15.00
CAG Carlos Gonzalez 3.00 8.00
CB Carlos Beltran 4.00 10.00
CCS CC Sabathia 3.00 8.00
CH Cole Hamels 3.00 8.00
CHS Chris Sale 3.00 8.00
CJ Chipper Jones 8.00 20.00
CLK Clayton Kershaw 4.00 10.00
CP Chris Perez 3.00 8.00
CR Carlos Ruiz 4.00 10.00
CRK Craig Kimbrel 4.00 10.00
CUG Curtis Granderson 4.00 10.00
CW C.J. Wilson 3.00 8.00
DJ Derek Jeter 10.00 25.00
DO David Ortiz 3.00 8.00
DP David Price 3.00 8.00
DU Dan Uggla 3.00 8.00
DW David Wright 4.00 10.00
EA Elvis Andrus 3.00 8.00
FH Felix Hernandez 3.00 8.00
FR Fernando Rodney 3.00 8.00
GG Gio Gonzalez 3.00 8.00
IK Ian Kinsler 3.00 8.00
JAB Jay Bruce 4.00 10.00
JHM Josh Hamilton 5.00 12.00
JM Joe Mauer 4.00 10.00
JN Joe Nathan 3.00 8.00
JOB Jose Bautista 4.00 10.00
JOP Jonathan Papelbon 3.00 8.00
JOV Joey Votto 5.00 12.00
JW Jered Weaver 3.00 8.00
MAC Matt Cain 4.00 10.00
MAH Matt Harrison 3.00 8.00
MAT Mark Trumbo 4.00 10.00
MEC Melky Cabrera 4.00 10.00
MHO Matt Holliday 4.00 10.00
MIC Miguel Cabrera 6.00 15.00
MIT Mike Trout 25.00 60.00
MK Matt Kemp 4.00 10.00
MN Mike Napoli 3.00 8.00
PF Prince Fielder 4.00 10.00
PK Paul Konerko 3.00 8.00
PS Pablo Sandoval 4.00 10.00
RB Ryan Braun 4.00 10.00
RD R.A. Dickey 5.00 12.00
RF Rafael Furcal 3.00 8.00
ROC Robinson Cano 4.00 10.00
SC Starlin Castro 4.00 10.00
SS Stephen Strasburg 6.00 15.00
YD Yu Darvish 10.00 25.00

2012 Topps Update All-Star Stitches Gold Sparkle
*GOLD: 1X TO 2.5X BASIC
STATED ODDS 1:1216 HOBBY
STATED PRINT RUN 50 SER.#'d SETS

2012 Topps Update Award Winners Gold Rings
STATED ODDS 1:940 HOBBY
I Ichiro Suzuki 8.00 20.00
AD Andre Dawson 6.00 15.00
AP Albert Pujols 10.00 25.00
BR Babe Ruth 12.50 30.00
CF Carlton Fisk 6.00 15.00
CR Cal Ripken Jr. 12.50 30.00
CY Carl Yastrzemski 8.00 20.00
DJ Derek Jeter 15.00 40.00
FR Frank Robinson 6.00 15.00
JB Johnny Bench 6.00 15.00
JR Jackie Robinson 10.00 25.00
JV Justin Verlander 8.00 20.00
KG Ken Griffey Jr. 12.50 30.00
LG Lou Gehrig 12.50 30.00
MM Mickey Mantle 25.00 50.00
MS Mike Schmidt 8.00 20.00
RB Ryan Braun 6.00 15.00
RC Roberto Clemente 15.00 40.00
RH Roy Halladay 6.00 15.00
RJ Reggie Jackson 6.00 15.00
SK Sandy Koufax 8.00 20.00
SM Stan Musial 10.00 25.00
TL Tim Lincecum 6.00 15.00
TS Tom Seaver 6.00 15.00
WM Willie Mays 10.00 25.00

2012 Topps Update Blockbusters
COMPLETE SET (30) 6.00 15.00
STATED ODDS 1:4 HOBBY
BB1 Albert Pujols .75 2.00
BB2 CC Sabathia .50 1.25
BB3 Frank Robinson .40 1.00
BB4 Gary Carter .40 1.00
BB5 Hanley Ramirez .50 1.25
BB6 Jay Buhner .25 .60
BB7 Ken Griffey Jr. 1.25 3.00
BB8 Miguel Cabrera .60 1.50
BB9 Nolan Ryan 2.00 5.00
BB10 Prince Fielder .50 1.25
BB11 Rickey Henderson .60 1.50
BB12 Tom Seaver .40 1.00
BB13 Yoenis Cespedes 1.00 2.50
BB14 Yu Darvish 1.00 2.50
BB15 Babe Ruth 1.50 4.00
BB16 Ivan Rodriguez .40 1.00
BB17 Catfish Hunter .40 1.00
BB18 Carlton Fisk .40 1.00
BB19 Ryne Sandberg 1.25 3.00
BB20 David Ortiz .60 1.50
BB21 Roy Halladay .50 1.25
BB22 Josh Beckett .40 1.00
BB23 Ichiro Suzuki .75 2.00
BB24 Steve Carlton .40 1.00
BB25 Alex Rodriguez .75 2.00
BB26 Bruce Sutter .40 1.00
BB27 Carlos Gonzalez .50 1.25
BB28 Johan Santana .50 1.25
BB29 Manny Ramirez .60 1.50
BB30 Jose Bautista .50 1.25

2012 Topps Update Blockbusters Commemorative Hat Logo Patch
BP1 Albert Pujols 2.50 6.00
BP2 CC Sabathia 1.50 4.00
BP3 Frank Robinson 1.25 3.00
BP4 Gary Carter 1.25 3.00
BP5 Hanley Ramirez 1.50 4.00
BP6 Jay Buhner .75 2.00
BP7 Ken Griffey Jr. 4.00 10.00
BP8 Miguel Cabrera 2.00 5.00
BP9 Nolan Ryan 6.00 15.00
BP10 Prince Fielder 1.50 4.00
BP11 Rickey Henderson 2.00 5.00
BP12 Tom Seaver 1.25 3.00
BP13 Yoenis Cespedes 3.00 8.00
BP14 Yu Darvish 3.00 8.00
BP15 Babe Ruth 5.00 12.00
BP16 Ivan Rodriguez 1.25 3.00
BP17 Catfish Hunter 1.25 3.00
BP18 Carlton Fisk 1.25 3.00
BP19 Ryne Sandberg 4.00 10.00
BP20 David Ortiz 2.00 5.00
BP21 Roy Halladay 1.50 4.00
BP22 Josh Beckett 1.25 3.00
BP23 Ichiro Suzuki 2.50 6.00
BP24 Steve Carlton 1.25 3.00
BP25 Alex Rodriguez 2.50 6.00
BP26 Johan Santana 1.50 4.00
BP27 Carlos Gonzalez 1.50 4.00
BP28 John Smoltz 2.00 5.00
BP29 Jose Reyes 1.25 3.00
BP30 Jose Bautista 1.50 4.00

2012 Topps Update Blockbusters Relics
STATED ODDS 1:6700 HOBBY
STATED PRINT RUN 50 SER.#'d SETS
AP Albert Pujols 10.00 25.00
BR Babe Ruth 75.00 150.00
GC Gary Carter 15.00 40.00
HR Hanley Ramirez 10.00 25.00
JB Jose Bautista 30.00 60.00
KG Ken Griffey Jr. 30.00 60.00
MC Miguel Cabrera 15.00 40.00
NR Nolan Ryan 12.00 30.00
RH Roy Halladay 10.00 25.00
YD Yu Darvish 20.00 50.00

2012 Topps Update General Manager Autographs
STATED ODDS 1:1345 HOBBY
AF Andrew Friedman 6.00 15.00
DM Dayton Moore 10.00 25.00
DO Dan O'Dowd 6.00 15.00
FW Frank Wren 10.00 25.00
JB Josh Byrnes 8.00 20.00
JD Jon Daniels 8.00 20.00
JL Jeff Luhnow 10.00 25.00
JZ Jack Zduriencik 6.00 15.00
MR Mike Rizzo 12.00 30.00
NC Ned Colletti 20.00 50.00
NH Neal Huntington 8.00 20.00
SA Sandy Alderson 20.00 50.00
TR Terry Ryan 15.00 40.00
JDI Jerry Dipoto 10.00 25.00

2012 Topps Update Gold Engravings
STATED ODDS 1:8053 HOBBY
BR Brooks Robinson 50.00 100.00
DS Duke Snider 12.00 30.00
HA Hank Aaron 100.00 200.00

2012 Topps Update Gold Hall of Fame Plaque
STATED ODDS 1:940 HOBBY
HOFBR Babe Ruth 10.00 25.00
HOFCR Cal Ripken Jr. 12.50 30.00
HOFCY Carl Yastrzemski 10.00 25.00
HOFGB George Brett 8.00 20.00
HOFGC Gary Carter 6.00 15.00
HOFJB Johnny Bench 10.00 25.00
HOFJP Jim Palmer 6.00 15.00
HOFJR Jackie Robinson 10.00 25.00
HOFLG Lou Gehrig 12.50 30.00
HOFMM Mickey Mantle 20.00 50.00
HOFMS Mike Schmidt 8.00 20.00
HOFNR Nolan Ryan 10.00 25.00
HOFOS Ozzie Smith 8.00 20.00
HOFRC Roberto Clemente 15.00 40.00
HOFRH Rickey Henderson 8.00 20.00
HOFRJ Reggie Jackson 8.00 20.00
HOFRS Ryne Sandberg 12.50 30.00
HOFSK Sandy Koufax 15.00 40.00
HOFSM Stan Musial 6.00 15.00
HOFTC Ty Cobb 8.00 20.00
HOFTS Tom Seaver 6.00 15.00
HOFWB Wade Boggs 6.00 15.00
HOFWM Willie Mays 8.00 20.00
HOFWS Warren Spahn 6.00 15.00
HOFYB Yogi Berra 12.50 30.00

2012 Topps Update Golden Debut Autographs
STATED ODDS 1:915 HOBBY
AR Anthony Rizzo 40.00 100.00
BB Brandon Belt 6.00 15.00
DM Devin Mesoraco 6.00 15.00
HI Hisashi Iwakuma 15.00 40.00
JP Jordan Pacheco 3.00 8.00
JPA Jarrod Parker 8.00 20.00
JW Jemile Weeks 4.00 10.00
LH Liam Hendriks 4.00 10.00
MH Mark Hamburger 3.00 8.00
MM Matt Moore 5.00 12.00
NE Nathan Eovaldi 3.00 8.00
PG Paul Goldschmidt 12.00 30.00
TB Trevor Bauer 15.00 40.00
TM Tom Milone 3.00 8.00
TP Tyler Pastornicky 3.00 8.00
WM Will Middlebrooks 5.00 12.00
WR Wilin Rosario 3.00 8.00
YA Yonder Alonso 8.00 20.00
YC Yoenis Cespedes 12.00 30.00
YD Yu Darvish 100.00 200.00

2012 Topps Update Golden Moments
COMPLETE SET (50) 10.00 25.00
STATED ODDS 1:4 HOBBY
GMU1 Bryce Harper 6.00 15.00
GMU2 Mike Trout 20.00 50.00
GMU3 Jered Weaver .50 1.25
GMU4 Josh Hamilton .50 1.25
GMU5 Johan Santana .50 1.25
GMU6 Adam Jones .50 1.25
GMU7 Philip Humber .40 1.00
GMU8 Ian Kennedy .40 1.00
GMU9 Miguel Cabrera .60 1.50
GMU10 Justin Verlander .60 1.50
GMU11 Yu Darvish 1.00 2.50
GMU12 Curtis Granderson .50 1.25
GMU13 Matt Cain .50 1.25
GMU14 Yoenis Cespedes 1.00 2.50
GMU15 Starlin Castro .50 1.25
GMU16 Andre Ethier .50 1.25
GMU17 David Price .50 1.25
GMU18 Bob Feller .40 1.00
GMU19 Joey Votto .60 1.50
GMU20 David Ortiz .60 1.50
GMU21 Ernie Banks .60 1.50
GMU22 Albert Belle .25 .60
GMU23 Nolan Ryan 2.00 5.00
GMU24 Giancarlo Stanton .60 1.50
GMU25 Ryan Braun .40 1.00
GMU26 Robin Yount .60 1.50
GMU27 Matt Kemp .50 1.25
GMU28 Harmon Killebrew .60 1.50
GMU29 David Wright .50 1.25
GMU30 Cal Ripken Jr. 2.00 5.00
GMU31 Reggie Jackson .40 1.00
GMU32 Mike Schmidt 1.00 2.50
GMU33 Roy Halladay .50 1.25
GMU34 Andrew McCutchen .60 1.50
GMU35 Eric Hosmer .50 1.25
GMU36 Matt Holliday .60 1.50
GMU37 Tony Gwynn .60 1.50
GMU38 Tim Lincecum .50 1.25
GMU39 Ryan Zimmerman .50 1.25
GMU40 Johnny Bench .60 1.50
GMU41 Derek Jeter 1.50 4.00
GMU42 Billy Butler .40 1.00
GMU43 Jose Bautista .50 1.25
GMU44 Jake Peavy .40 1.00
GMU45 Troy Tulowitzki .60 1.50
GMU46 Jon Lester .40 1.00
GMU47 George Brett 1.25 3.00
GMU48 Madison Bumgarner .50 1.25
GMU49 Edgar Martinez .40 1.00
GMU50 Al Kaline .60 1.50

2012 Topps Update Ichiro Yankees Commemorative Logo Patch
STATED ODDS 1:23,400 HOBBY
STATED PRINT RUN 200 SER.#'d SETS
MPR1 Ichiro Suzuki 20.00 50.00

2012 Topps Update Obama Presidential Predictor
COMMON OBAMA 2.00 5.00
STATED ODDS 1:81 HOBBY
PRICING FOR CARDS W/UNUSED CODES
PP1 Barack Obama/50 40.00 80.00

2012 Topps Update Romney Presidential Predictor
COMMON ROMNEY 2.00 5.00
STATED ODDS 1:81 HOBBY
PRICING FOR CARDS W/UNUSED CODES

2013 Topps
COMP.FACT.HOBBY.SET (660) 40.00 80.00
COMP.FACT.RUTH.SET (660) 40.00 80.00
COMP.FACT.ROBINSON.SET (660) 40.00 80.00
COMP.FACT.ALLSTAR.SET (660) 40.00 80.00
COMP.FACT.AARON.SET (660) 40.00 80.00
COMP.SET w/o SP's (660) 30.00 60.00
COMP.SER.1 SET w/o SP's (330) 12.50 30.00
COMP.SER.2 SET w/o SP's (330) 12.50 30.00
SERIES 1 PLATE ODDS 1:2323 HOBBY
SERIES 2 PLATE ODDS 1:1578 HOBBY
PLATE PRINT RUN 1 SET PER COLOR
BLACK-CYAN-MAGENTA-YELLOW ISSUED
NO PLATE PRICING DUE TO SCARCITY
1A Bryce Harper .40 1.00
1B Bryce Harper SP 8.00 20.00
1C Bryce Harper SP 10.00 25.00
2A Derek Jeter .60 1.50
2B Jeter SP w/Award 30.00 80.00
3 Hunter Pence .20 .50
4 Yadier Molina .30 .75
5 Carlos Gonzalez .20 .50
6A Ryan Howard .20 .50
6B Ryan Howard SP 4.00 10.00
8 Ryan Braun .20 .50
9 Dee Gordon .15 .40
10A Adam Jones .20 .50
10B Adam Jones SP 4.00 10.00
11A Yu Darvish .25 .60
11B Yu Darvish SP 4.00 10.00
11C Yu Darvish SP 4.00 10.00
12 A.J. Pierzynski .15 .40
13A Brett Lawrie .20 .50
13B Brett Lawrie SP 4.00 10.00
14A Paul Konerko .20 .50
14B Paul Konerko SP 4.00 10.00
15 Dustin Pedroia .25 .60
16A Andre Ethier .20 .50
16B Andre Ethier SP 4.00 10.00
17 Shin-Soo Choo .20 .50
18 Mitch Moreland .15 .40
19 Joey Votto .25 .60
20A Kevin Youkilis .15 .40
20B Kevin Youkilis SP 4.00 10.00
21 Lucas Duda .20 .50
22A Clayton Kershaw .40 1.00
22B Clayton Kershaw SP 4.00 10.00
23 Jemile Weeks .15 .40
24 Dan Haren .15 .40
25 Mark Teixeira .20 .50
26A Chase Utley .20 .50
26B Chase Utley SP 4.00 10.00
27A Mike Trout 2.00 5.00
27B Mike Trout SP 8.00 20.00
27C Mike Trout SP 8.00 20.00
27D Mike Trout SP 8.00 20.00
28A Prince Fielder .20 .50
28B Prince Fielder SP 4.00 10.00
29 Adrian Beltre .25 .60
30 Neftali Feliz .15 .40
31 Jose Tabata .15 .40
32 Craig Breslow .15 .40
33 Cliff Lee .20 .50
34A Felix Hernandez .20 .50
34B Felix Hernandez SP 4.00 10.00
35 Justin Verlander .25 .60
36 Jered Weaver .20 .50
37 Max Scherzer .25 .60
38 Brian Wilson .25 .60
39 Scott Feldman .15 .40
40 Chien-Ming Wang .20 .50
41 Daniel Hudson .15 .40
42 Detroit Tigers .15 .40
43 R.A. Dickey .20 .50
44A Anthony Rizzo .30 .75
44B Anthony Rizzo SP 4.00 10.00
45 Travis Ishikawa .15 .40
46 Craig Kimbrel .20 .50
47 Howie Kendrick .15 .40
48 Ryan Cook .15 .40
49 Chris Sale .25 .60
50 Adam Wainwright .20 .50
51 Jonathan Broxton .15 .40
52 CC Sabathia .20 .50
53 Alex Cobb .15 .40
54 Jaime Garcia .20 .50
55A Tim Lincecum .20 .50
55B Tim Lincecum SP 4.00 10.00
56 Joe Blanton .15 .40
57 Mark Lowe .15 .40
58 Jeremy Hellickson .15 .40
59 John Axford .15 .40
60 Jon Rauch .15 .40
61 Trevor Bauer .30 .75
62 Tommy Hunter .15 .40
63 Justin Masterson .15 .40
64 Will Middlebrooks .15 .40
65 J.P. Howell .15 .40
66 Daniel Nava .15 .40
67 San Francisco Giants .15 .40
68 Colby Rasmus .20 .50
69 Marco Scutaro .20 .50
70A Todd Frazier .15 .40
70B Todd Frazier SP 4.00 10.00
71A Kyle Kendrick .15 .40
71B KendrickClose up 20.00 50.00
72 Gerardo Parra .15 .40
73 Brandon Crawford .20 .50
74 Kenley Jansen .20 .50
75 Barry Zito .20 .50
76 Brandon Inge .15 .40
77 Dustin Moseley .15 .40
78A Dylan Bundy RC .60 1.50
78B Dylan Bundy SP 4.00 10.00
79 Adam Eaton RC .40 1.00
80 Ryan Zimmerman .20 .50
81 Kershaw/Cueto/Dickey .40 1.00
82 Jason Vargas .15 .40
83 Darin Ruf RC .50 1.25
84 Adeiny Hechavarria (RC) .30 .75
85 Sean Doolittle RC .15 .40
86 Henry Rodriguez RC .25 .60
87 Mike Olt RC .30 .75
88 Jamey Carroll .15 .40
89 Johan Santana .20 .50
90 Andy Pettitte .20 .50
91 Alfredo Aceves .15 .40
92 Clint Barmes .15 .40
93 Austin Kearns .15 .40
94 Verland/Price/Weaver .25 .60
95 Matt Harrison .20 .50
David Price/Jered Weaver
96 Edward Mujica .15 .40
97 Danny Espinosa .15 .40
98 Gaby Sanchez .15 .40
99 Paco Rodriguez RC .40 1.00
100A Mike Moustakas .20 .50
100B Mike Moustakas SP 4.00 10.00
101 Bryan Shaw .15 .40
102 Denard Span .15 .40
103 Evan Longoria .20 .50
104 Jed Lowrie .15 .40
105A Freddie Freeman .30 .75
105B Freddie Freeman SP 4.00 10.00
106 Drew Stubbs .15 .40
107A Joe Mauer .20 .50
107B Joe Mauer SP 4.00 10.00
108 Kendrys Morales .15 .40
109 Kirk Nieuwenhuis .15 .40
110A Justin Upton .20 .50
110B Justin Upton SP 4.00 10.00
111 Casey Kelly RC .30 .75
112A Mark Reynolds .15 .40
112B Mark Reynolds SP 4.00 10.00
113 Starlin Castro .15 .40
114 Casey McGehee .15 .40
115 Tim Hudson .20 .50
116 Brian McCann .20 .50
117 Aubrey Huff .15 .40
118 Daisuke Matsuzaka .20 .50
119 Chris Davis .20 .50
120 Ian Desmond .15 .40
121 Delmon Young .20 .50
122A Andrew McCutchen .25 .60
122B Andrew McCutchen SP 6.00 15.00
122C Andrew McCutchen SP 5.00 12.00
123 Rickie Weeks .15 .40
124 Ricky Romero .15 .40
125 Matt Holliday .25 .60
126 Dan Uggla .15 .40
127A Giancarlo Stanton .25 .60
127B Giancarlo Stanton SP 4.00 10.00
128A Buster Posey .30 .75
128B Buster Posey SP 5.00 12.00
129 Ike Davis .15 .40
130 Jason Motte .15 .40
131 Ian Kennedy .15 .40
132 Ryan Vogelsong .15 .40
133 James Shields .15 .40
134 Jake Arrieta .20 .50
135A Eric Hosmer .20 .50
135B Eric Hosmer SP 4.00 10.00
136 Tyler Clippard .15 .40
137 Edinson Volquez .15 .40
138 Michael Morse .15 .40
139 Bobby Parnell .15 .40
140 Wade Davis .15 .40
141 Carlos Santana .20 .50
142 Tony Cingrani RC .50 1.25
143 Jim Johnson .15 .40
144 Jason Bay .20 .50
145 Anthony Bass .15 .40
146 Kyle McClellan .15 .40
147 Ivan Nova .20 .50
148 L.J. Hoes RC .30 .75
149 Yovani Gallardo .15 .40
150 John Danks .15 .40
151 Alex Rios .20 .50
152 Jose Contreras .15 .40
153 Cabrera/Hamilton/Granderson .25 .60
154 Sergio Romo .15 .40
155 Mat Latos .20 .50
156 Dillon Gee .15 .40
157 Carter Capps RC .25 .60
158 Chad Billingsley .20 .50
159 Felipe Paulino .15 .40
160 Stephen Drew .15 .40
161 Bronson Arroyo .15 .40
162 Kyle Seager .15 .40
163 J.A. Happ .20 .50
164 Lucas Harrell .15 .40
165 Ramon Hernandez .15 .40
166 Logan Ondrusek .15 .40
167 Luke Hochevar .15 .40
168 Kyle Farnsworth .15 .40
169 Brad Ziegler .15 .40
170 Eury Perez RC .30 .75
171 Brock Holt RC .30 .75
172 Nyjer Morgan .15 .40
173 Tyler Skaggs RC .40 1.00
174 Jason Grilli .15 .40
175 A.J. Ramos RC .30 .75
176 Robert Andino .15 .40
177 Elliot Johnson .15 .40
178 Justin Maxwell .15 .40
179 Detroit Tigers .15 .40
180 Casey Kotchman .15 .40
181 Jeff Keppinger .15 .40
182 Randy Choate .25 .60
183 Drew Hutchison .20 .50
184 Geovany Soto .20 .50
185 Rob Scahill RC .25 .60
186 Jordan Pacheco .15 .40
187 Nick Maronde RC .30 .75
188 Brian Fuentes .15 .40
189 Posey/McCutch/Braun .30 .75
190 Daniel Descalso .15 .40
191 Chris Capuano .15 .40
192 Javier Lopez .20 .50
193 Matt Carpenter .25 .60
194 Encarn/Cabrera/Hamilton .25 .60
195 Chris Heisey .15 .40
196 Ryan Vogelsong .15 .40
197 Tyler Cloyd RC .30 .75
198 Chris Coghlan .15 .40
199 Avisail Garcia RC .30 .75
200 Scott Downs .15 .40
201 Jonny Venters .15 .40
202 Zack Cozart .15 .40
203 Wilson Ramos .15 .40
204A Alex Gordon .20 .50
204B Alex Gordon SP 4.00 10.00
205 Ryan Theriot .15 .40
206 Jimmy Rollins .20 .50
207 Matt Holliday .25 .60
208 Kurt Suzuki .15 .40
209 David DeJesus .15 .40
210 Vernon Wells .15 .40
211 Jarrod Parker .15 .40
212 Eric Chavez .15 .40
213A Alex Rodriguez .30 .75
213B Alex Rodriguez SP 4.00 10.00
214 Curtis Granderson .20 .50
215 Gordon Beckham .15 .40
216A Josh Willingham .20 .50
216B Josh Willingham SP 4.00 10.00
217 Brian Matusz .15 .40
218 Ben Zobrist .20 .50
219 Josh Beckett .15 .40
220 Octavio Dotel .15 .40
221 Heath Bell .15 .40
222 Jason Heyward .20 .50
223 Yonder Alonso .15 .40
224 Jon Jay .15 .40
225 Will Venable .15 .40
226 Derek Lowe .15 .40
227 Jose Altuve .20 .50
228A Adrian Gonzalez .20 .50
228B Adrian Gonzalez SP 4.00 10.00
229 Jeff Samardzija .15 .40
230 David Robertson .15 .40
231 Melky Mesa RC .30 .75
232 Jake Odorizzi RC .30 .75
233 Edwin Jackson .15 .40
234 A.J. Burnett .15 .40
235 Jake Westbrook .15 .40
236 Joe Nathan .15 .40
237 Brandon Lyon .15 .40
238 Carlos Zambrano .20 .50
239 Ramon Santiago .15 .40
240 J.J. Putz .15 .40
241 Jacoby Ellsbury .20 .50
242A Matt Kemp .20 .50
242B Matt Kemp SP 4.00 10.00
242C Matt Kemp SP 4.00 10.00
243 Aaron Crow .15 .40
244 Lucas Luetge .15 .40
245 Jason Isringhausen .15 .40
246 Braun/Stanton/Bruce .25 .60
247 Luis Perez .15 .40
248 Colby Lewis .15 .40
249 Vance Worley .20 .50
250 Jonathon Niese .15 .40
251 Sean Marshall .15 .40
252 Dustin Ackley .15 .40
253 Adam Greenberg (RC) .30 .75
254 Sean Burnett .15 .40
255 Josh Johnson .20 .50
256 Madison Bumgarner .20 .50
257 Mike Minor .15 .40
258 Doug Fister .15 .40
259 Bartolo Colon .15 .40
260 San Francisco Giants .15 .40
261 Trevor Rosenthal (RC) .50 1.25
262 Kevin Correia .15 .40
263 Ted Lilly .15 .40
264 Roy Halladay .20 .50
265 Tyler Colvin .15 .40
266 Albert Pujols .30 .75
267 Jason Kipnis .20 .50
268 David Lough RC .25 .60
269 St. Louis Cardinals .25 .60
270A Manny Machado RC 1.50 4.00
270B Machado SP Blk jsy 25.00 60.00
271 Jeurys Familia RC .40 1.00
272 Ryan Braun .20 .50
Alfonso Soriano/Chase Headley
273 Dexter Fowler .20 .50
274 Miguel Montero .15 .40
275 Johnny Cueto .20 .50
276 Luis Ayala .15 .40
277 Brendan Ryan .15 .40
278 Christian Garcia (RC) .25 .60
279 Vicente Padilla .15 .40
280 Rafael Dolis .15 .40
281 David Hernandez .15 .40
282A Russell Martin .15 .40
282B Russell Martin SP 4.00 10.00
283 CC Sabathia .20 .50
284 Angel Pagan .15 .40
285 Addison Reed .15 .40
286A Jurickson Profar RC .30 .75
286B Profar SP Blue jsy 20.00 50.00
287 Johnny Cueto .20 .50
Gio Gonzalez/R.A. Dickey
288 Starling Marte .20 .50
289 Jeremy Guthrie .15 .40
290 Tom Layne RC .25 .60
291 Ryan Sweeney .15 .40
292 Matt Thornton .15 .40
293 Jeff Karstens .15 .40
294 Trout/Beltre/Miggy 2.00 5.00
295 Brandon League .15 .40
296 Didi Gregorius RC 1.00 2.50
297 Michael Saunders .20 .50
298 Pablo Sandoval .20 .50
299 Darwin Barney .15 .40
300 Daniel Murphy .20 .50
301 Jarrod Saltalamacchia .15 .40
302 Aaron Hill .15 .40
303 Alex Rodriguez .30 .75
304 Kyle Drabek .15 .40
305A Shelby Miller RC .60 1.50
305B Miller SP Blue cap 20.00 50.00
306 Jerry Hairston .15 .40
307 Norichika Aoki .15 .40
308 Desmond Jennings .20 .50
309 Endy Chavez .15 .40
310 Edwin Encarnacion .25 .60
311A Rajai Davis .15 .40
311B Rajai Davis SP 4.00 10.00
312 Scott Hairston .15 .40
313 Maicer Izturis .15 .40
314 A.J. Ellis .15 .40
315 Rafael Furcal .15 .40
316A Josh Reddick .15 .40
316B Josh Reddick SP 4.00 10.00
317 Baltimore Orioles .15 .40
318 Hiroki Kuroda .15 .40
319 Brian Bogusevic .15 .40
320 Michael Young .15 .40
321 Allen Craig .20 .50
322 Alex Gonzalez .15 .40
323 Michael Brantley .15 .40
324A Cameron Maybin .15 .40
324B Cameron Maybin SP 4.00 10.00
325 Kevin Millwood .15 .40
326 Andruw Jones .15 .40
327 Jhonny Peralta .15 .40
328 Jayson Werth .20 .50
329 Rafael Soriano .15 .40
330 Ryan Raburn .15 .40
331A Jose Reyes .20 .50
331B Jose Reyes SP 4.00 10.00
332 Cole Hamels .20 .50
333 Santiago Casilla .15 .40
334 Derek Norris .15 .40
335 Chris Herrmann RC .25 .60
336 Hank Conger .15 .40
337 Chris Iannetta .15 .40
338 Mike Trout 2.00 5.00
339 Nick Swisher .20 .50
340 Franklin Gutierrez .15 .40
341 Lonnie Chisenhall .15 .40
342 Matt Dominguez .15 .40
343 Alex Avila .20 .50
344 Kris Medlen .20 .50
345 Jenrry Mejia .15 .40
346 Aaron Hicks RC .40 1.00
347 Brett Anderson .15 .40
348 Jonny Gomes .15 .40
349 Ernesto Frieri .15 .40
350A Albert Pujols .30 .75
350B Albert Pujols SP 6.00 15.00
351 Asdrubal Cabrera .20 .50
352 Tommy Hanson .15 .40
353 Bud Norris .15 .40
354 Casey Janssen .15 .40
355 Carlos Marmol .15 .40
356 Greg Dobbs .15 .40
357 Juan Francisco .15 .40
358 Henderson Alvarez .15 .40
359 CC Sabathia .20 .50
360 Khristopher Davis RC .75 2.00
361 Erik Kratz .15 .40
362A Yoenis Cespedes .25 .60
362B Yoenis Cespedes SP 4.00 10.00
363 Sergio Santos .15 .40
364 Carlos Pena .20 .50
365 Mike Baxter .15 .40
366 Ervin Santana .15 .40
367 Carlos Ruiz .15 .40
368 Chris Young .15 .40
369 Bryce Harper .40 1.00
370 A.J. Griffin .15 .40
371 Jeremy Affeldt .15 .40
372 Jeff Locke .15 .40
373 Derek Jeter .60 1.50
374 Miguel Cabrera .25 .60
375 Wilin Rosario .15 .40
376 Juan Pierre .15 .40
377 J.D. Martinez .25 .60
378 Joe Kelly .15 .40
379 Madison Bumgarner .20 .50
380 Juan Nicasio .15 .40
381 Wily Peralta .15 .40
382 Jackie Bradley Jr. RC .60 1.50
383 Matt Harrison .15 .40
384 Jake McGee .20 .50
385 Brandon Belt .20 .50
386 Brandon Phillips .15 .40
387 Jean Segura .20 .50
388 Justin Turner .25 .60
389 Phil Hughes .15 .40
390 James McDonald .15 .40
391 Travis Wood .15 .40
392 Tom Koehler RC .25 .60
393 Andres Torres .15 .40
394 Ubaldo Jimenez .15 .40
395 Alexei Ramirez .20 .50
396 Aroldis Chapman .25 .60
397 Mike Aviles .15 .40
398 Mike Fiers .15 .40
399 Shane Victorino .20 .50
400A David Wright .20 .50
400B David Wright SP 6.00 15.00
401 Ryan Dempster .15 .40
402 Tom Wilhelmsen .15 .40
403 Hisashi Iwakuma .20 .50
404 Ryan Madson .15 .40
405 Hector Sanchez .15 .40
406 Brandon McCarthy .15 .40
407 Juan Pierre .15 .40
408 Coco Crisp .15 .40
409 Logan Morrison .15 .40
410 Roy Halladay .20 .50
411 Jesus Guzman .15 .40
412 Everth Cabrera .15 .40
413 Brett Gardner .20 .50
414 Mark Buehrle .20 .50
415 Leonys Martin .15 .40
416 Jordan Lyles .15 .40
417 Logan Forsythe .15 .40
418 Evan Gattis RC .50 1.25
419 Matt Moore .20 .50
420 Rick Porcello .20 .50
421 Jordy Mercer RC .25 .60
422 Alfredo Marte RC .25 .60
423 Miguel Gonzalez RC .15 .40
424 Steven Lerud (RC) .25 .60
425 Josh Donaldson .20 .50
426 Vinnie Pestano .15 .40
427 Chris Nelson .15 .40
428 Kyle McPherson RC .25 .60
429 David Price .20 .50
430 Josh Harrison .15 .40
431 Blake Beavan .15 .40
432 Jose Iglesias .20 .50
433 Andrew Werner RC .25 .60
434 Wei-Yin Chen .15 .40
435 Brandon Maurer RC .30 .75
436 Elvis Andrus .20 .50
437 Dayan Viciedo .15 .40
438 Yasmani Grandal .15 .40
439 Marco Estrada .15 .40
440 Ian Kinsler .20 .50
441 Jose Bautista .20 .50
442 Mike Leake .15 .40
443 Lou Marson .15 .40
444 Jordan Walden .15 .40
445 Joe Thatcher .15 .40
446 Chris Parmelee .15 .40
447 Jacob Turner .20 .50
448 Tim Hudson .20 .50
449 Michael Cuddyer .15 .40
450A Jay Bruce .20 .50
450B Jay Bruce SP 6.00 15.00
451 Pedro Florimon .15 .40
452 Raul Ibanez .20 .50
453 Troy Tulowitzki .25 .60
454 Paul Goldschmidt .25 .60
455 Buster Posey .30 .75
456A Pablo Sandoval .20 .50
456B Pablo Sandoval SP 4.00 10.00
457 Nate Schierholtz .15 .40
458 Jake Peavy .15 .40
459 Jesus Montero .15 .40
460 Ryan Doumit .15 .40
461 Drew Pomeranz .20 .50
462 Eduardo Nunez .15 .40
463 Jason Hammel .20 .50
464 Luis Jimenez RC .25 .60
465 Placido Polanco .15 .40
466 Jerome Williams .15 .40
467 Brian Duensing .15 .40
468 Anthony Gose .15 .40
469 Adam Warren RC .25 .60
470 Jeff Francoeur .20 .50
471 Trevor Cahill .15 .40
472 John Mayberry .15 .40
473 Josh Johnson .20 .50
474 Brian Omogrosso RC .25 .60
475 Garrett Jones .15 .40
476 John Buck .20 .50
477 Paul Maholm .15 .40
478 Gavin Floyd .15 .40
479 Kelly Johnson .15 .40
480 Lance Berkman .20 .50
481 Justin Wilson RC .25 .60
482 Emilio Bonifacio .15 .40
483 Jordany Valdespin .15 .40
484 Johan Santana .20 .50

485 Ruben Tejada .15 .40
486 Jason Kubel .15 .40
487 Hanley Ramirez .20 .50
488 Ryan Wheeler RC .25 .60
489 Erick Aybar .15 .40
490 Cody Ross .15 .40
491 Clayton Richard .15 .40
492 Jose Molina .15 .40
493 Johnny Giavotella .15 .40
494 Alberto Callaspo .15 .40
495 Joaquin Benoit .15 .40
496 Scott Sizemore .15 .40
497 Brett Myers .15 .40
498 Martin Prado .15 .40
499 Billy Butler .15 .40
500 Stephen Strasburg .25 .60
501 Tommy Milone .15 .40
502 Patrick Corbin .20 .50
503 Clay Buchholz .15 .40
504 Michael Bourn .15 .40
505 Ross Detwiler .15 .40
506 Andy Pettitte .20 .50
507 Lance Lynn .15 .40
508 Felix Doubront .15 .40
509 Brennan Boesch .15 .40
510 Nate McLouth .15 .40
511 Rob Brantly RC .25 .60
512 Justin Smoak .15 .40
513 Zach McAllister .15 .40
514 Jonathan Papelbon .20 .50
515 Brian Roberts .15 .40
516 Omar Infante .15 .40
517 Pedro Alvarez .15 .40
518 Nolan Reimold .15 .40
519 Zack Greinke .25 .60
520 Peter Bourjos .15 .40
521 Evan Scribner RC .25 .60
522 Dallas Keuchel .20 .50
523 Wandy Rodriguez .15 .40
524 Wade LeBlanc .15 .40
525 J.P. Arencibia .15 .40
526 Tyler Flowers .15 .40
527 Carlos Beltran .20 .50
528 Darin Mastroianni .15 .40
529 Collin McHugh RC .25 .60
530 Wade Miley .15 .40
531 Craig Gentry .15 .40
532 Todd Helton .20 .50
533 J.J. Hardy .15 .40
534 Alberto Cabrera RC .25 .60
535 Philip Humber .15 .40
536 Mike Trout 2.00 5.00
537 Neil Walker .15 .40
538 Brett Wallace .15 .40
539 Phil Coke .15 .40
540 Michael Bourn .15 .40
541 Jon Lester .20 .50
542 Jeff Niemann .15 .40
543 Donovan Solano .25 .60
544 Tyler Chatwood .15 .40
545 Alex Presley .15 .40
546 Carlos Quentin .15 .40
547 Glen Perkins .15 .40
548 John Lackey .20 .50
549 Huston Street .15 .40
550 Matt Joyce .15 .40
551 Wellington Castillo .15 .40
552 Francisco Cervelli .15 .40
553 Josh Rutledge .15 .40
554 R.A. Dickey .20 .50
555 Joel Hanrahan .15 .40
556 Nick Hundley .15 .40
557 Adam Lind .20 .50
558 David Murphy .15 .40
559 Travis Snider .15 .40
560 Yunel Escobar .15 .40
561 Josh Vitters .20 .50
562 Jason Marquis .15 .40
563 Nate Eovaldi .20 .50
564 Francisco Peguero RC .25 .60
565 Torii Hunter .15 .40
566 C.J. Wilson .15 .40
567 Alfonso Soriano .20 .50
568 Steve Lombardozzi .15 .40
569 Ryan Ludwick .15 .40
570 Devin Mesoraco .15 .40
571 Melky Cabrera .15 .40
572 Lorenzo Cain .15 .40
573 Ian Stewart .15 .40
574 Corey Hart .15 .40
575 Justin Morneau .20 .50
576 Julio Teheran .20 .50
577 Matt Harvey .20 .50
578 Brett Jackson .20 .50
579 Adam LaRoche .15 .40
580 Jordan Danks .15 .40
581 Andrelton Simmons .15 .40
582 Seth Smith .15 .40
583 Alejandro De Aza .15 .40
584 Alfonso Soriano .20 .50
585 Homer Bailey .15 .40
586 Jose Quintana .15 .40
587 Matt Cain .20 .50
588 Jordan Zimmermann .20 .50
589A Jose Fernandez RC .60 1.50
589B Fernandez SP w/Miggy 25.00 60.00
590 Liam Hendriks .15 .40
591 Derek Holland .15 .40
592 Nick Markakis .20 .50
593 James Loney .20 .50
594 Carl Crawford .20 .50
595A David Ortiz .25 .60
595B David Ortiz SP 25.00 60.00
596 Brian Dozier .20 .50
597 Marco Scutaro .20 .50
598 Fernando Martinez .15 .40
599 Carlos Carrasco .15 .40
600 Mariano Rivera .30 .75
601 Brandon Moss .15 .40
602 Anibal Sanchez .15 .40
603 Chris Perez .15 .40
604 Rafael Betancourt .15 .40
605 Aramis Ramirez .15 .40
606 Mark Trumbo .15 .40
607 Chris Carter .15 .40
608 Ricky Nolasco .15 .40
609 Scott Baker .15 .40
610 Brandon Beachy .15 .40
611 Drew Storen .15 .40
612 Robinson Cano .20 .50
613 Jhoulys Chacin .15 .40
614 B.J. Upton .20 .50
615 Mark Ellis .15 .40
616 Grant Balfour .15 .40
617 Fernando Rodney .15 .40
618 Koji Uehara .15 .40
619 Carlos Gomez .15 .40
620 Hector Santiago .15 .40
621 Steve Cishek .15 .40
622 Alcides Escobar .20 .50
623 Alexi Ogando .15 .40
624 Justin Ruggiano .15 .40
625 Domonic Brown .20 .50
626 Gio Gonzalez .20 .50
627 David Price .20 .50
628 Martin Maldonado (RC) .25 .60
629 Trevor Plouffe .15 .40
630 Andy Dirks .15 .40
631 Chris Carpenter .20 .50
632 R.A. Dickey .20 .50
633 Victor Martinez .20 .50
634 Drew Smyly .15 .40
635 Jedd Gyorko RC .30 .75
636 Cole De Vries RC .25 .60
637 Ben Revere .15 .40
638 Andrew Cashner .15 .40
639 Josh Hamilton .20 .50
640 Jason Castro .15 .40
641 Bruce Chen .15 .40
642 Austin Jackson .15 .40
643 Matt Garza .15 .40
644 Ryan Lavarnway .15 .40
645 Luis Cruz .15 .40
646 Phillippe Aumont RC .25 .60
647 Adam Dunn .20 .50
648 Dan Straily .15 .40
649 Ryan Hanigan .15 .40
650 Nelson Cruz .25 .60
651 Gregor Blanco .15 .40
652 Jonathan Lucroy .20 .50
653 Chase Headley .15 .40
654 Brandon Barnes RC .25 .60
655 Salvador Perez .20 .50
656 Scott Diamond .15 .40
657 Jorge De La Rosa .15 .40
658 David Freese .15 .40
659 Mike Napoli .15 .40
660A Miguel Cabrera .25 .60
660B Miguel Cabrera SP 5.00 12.00
661A Hyun-Jin Ryu RC .60 1.50
661B Hyun-Jin Ryu SP 4.00 10.00
661C Ryu SP Grey jsy 20.00 50.00
661D Ryu SP Batting 20.00 50.00

2013 Topps Black

*BLACK VET: 8X TO 20X BASIC
*BLACK RC: 5X TO 12X BASIC RC
SERIES 1 ODDS 1:150 HOBBY
SERIES 2 ODDS 1:104 HOBBY
STATED PRINT RUN 62 SER.#'d SETS
16 Andre Ethier 10.00 25.00
19 Joey Votto 15.00 40.00
28 Prince Fielder 10.00 25.00
67 San Francisco Giants 20.00 50.00
78 Dylan Bundy 30.00 80.00
122 Andrew McCutchen 20.00 50.00
128 Buster Posey 30.00 60.00
154 Sergio Romo 10.00 25.00
188 Brian Fuentes 10.00 25.00
190 Daniel Descalso 10.00 25.00
205 Ryan Theriot 10.00 25.00
224 Jon Jay 8.00 20.00
261 Trevor Rosenthal 15.00 40.00
294 Trout/Beltre/Cabrera 15.00 40.00
645 Luis Cruz 5.00 12.00
660 Miguel Cabrera 15.00 40.00
661 Hyun-Jin Ryu 30.00 60.00

2013 Topps Camo

*CAMO VET: 10X TO 25X BASIC
*CAMO RC: 6X TO 15X BASIC RC
SERIES 1 ODDS 1:286 HOBBY
SERIES 2 ODDS 1:195 HOBBY
STATED PRINT RUN 99 SER.#'d SETS
2 Derek Jeter 60.00 120.00
16 Andre Ethier 8.00 20.00
19 Joey Votto 12.50 30.00
27 Mike Trout 20.00 50.00
28 Prince Fielder 8.00 20.00
122 Andrew McCutchen 15.00 40.00
154 Sergio Romo 8.00 20.00
205 Ryan Theriot 8.00 20.00
266 Albert Pujols 10.00 25.00
270 Manny Machado 30.00 60.00
294 Trout/Beltre/Cabrera 12.50 30.00
317 Baltimore Orioles 10.00 25.00
338 Mike Trout 20.00 50.00
350 Albert Pujols 10.00 25.00
362 Yoenis Cespedes 10.00 25.00
536 Mike Trout 20.00 50.00

2013 Topps Emerald

COMPLETE SET (660) 200.00 500.00
*EMERALD VET: 1.2X TO 3X BASIC
*EMERALD RC: .75X TO 2X BASIC RC
STATED ODDS 1:6 HOBBY

2013 Topps Factory Set Orange

*ORANGE VET: 5X TO 12X BASIC
*ORANGE RC: 3X TO 8X BASIC RC
INSERTED IN FACTORY SETS
STATED PRINT RUN 230 SER.#'d SETS

2013 Topps Gold

COMPLETE SET (660) 250.00 500.00
*GOLD VET: 1.2X TO 3X BASIC
*GOLD RC: .75X TO 2X BASIC RC
SERIES 1 ODDS 1:9 HOBBY
SERIES 2 ODDS 1:7 HOBBY
STATED PRINT RUN 2013 SER.#'d SETS

2013 Topps Pink

*PINK VET: 6X TO 15X BASIC
*PINK RC: 4X TO 10X BASIC RC
SERIES 1 ODDS 1:566 HOBBY
SERIES 2 ODDS 1:391 HOBBY
STATED PRINT RUN 50 SER.#'d SETS
2 Derek Jeter 60.00 120.00
16 Andre Ethier 10.00 25.00
19 Joey Votto 15.00 40.00
28 Prince Fielder 10.00 25.00
67 San Francisco Giants 20.00 50.00
78 Dylan Bundy 30.00 60.00
122 Andrew McCutchen 20.00 50.00
128 Buster Posey 30.00 60.00
154 Sergio Romo 10.00 25.00
188 Brian Fuentes 10.00 25.00
190 Daniel Descalso 10.00 25.00
205 Ryan Theriot 10.00 25.00
224 Jon Jay 8.00 20.00
261 Trevor Rosenthal 15.00 40.00
294 Trout/Beltre/Cabrera 15.00 40.00
645 Luis Cruz 20.00 50.00
660 Miguel Cabrera 15.00 40.00
661 Hyun-Jin Ryu 30.00 60.00

2013 Topps Silver Slate Blue Sparkle Wrapper Redemption

*SLATE VET: 2.5X TO 6X BASIC
*SLATE RC: 1.5X TO 4X BASIC RC
1 Bryce Harper 25.00 60.00
2 Derek Jeter 10.00 25.00
294 Trout/Beltre/Cabrera 6.00 15.00

2013 Topps Silver Slate Wrapper Redemption Autographs

PRINT RUNS B/WN 5-170 COPIES PER
AG Adrian Gonzalez/35 30.00 60.00
BB Brandon Beachy/24 15.00 40.00
CC Chris Carpenter/50 20.00 50.00
CK Clayton Kershaw/35 30.00 60.00
DB Dylan Bundy/50 15.00 40.00
JN Jeff Niemann/114 4.00 10.00
JV Josh Vitters/102 4.00 10.00
MD Matt Dominguez/37 8.00 20.00
MM Manny Machado/50 75.00 150.00
NM Nick Markakis/100 10.00 25.00
RD R.A. Dickey/35 30.00 60.00
SP Salvador Perez/100 10.00 25.00
SV Shane Victorino/48 15.00 40.00
TS Tyler Skaggs/50 6.00 15.00
WR Wilin Rosario/170 6.00 15.00
YE Yunel Escobar/100 6.00 15.00

2013 Topps Target Red Border

*TARGET RED: .75X TO 2X BASIC
*TARGET RED RC: .5X TO 1.2X BASIC RC
FOUND IN TARGET RETAIL PACKS

2013 Topps Toys R Us Purple Border

*TRU PURPLE: 3X TO 8X BASIC
*TRU PURPLE RC: 2X TO 5X BASIC RC
FOUND IN TOYS R US RETAIL PACKS
2 Derek Jeter 20.00 50.00
234 A.J. Burnett 5.00 12.00

2013 Topps Wal-Mart Blue Border

*WM BLUE: .75X TO 2X BASIC
*WM BLUE RC: .5X TO 1.2X BASIC RC
FOUND IN WAL MART RETAIL PACKS

2013 Topps '72 Topps Minis

COMPLETE SET (100) 40.00 80.00
COMP.SERIES 1 SET (1-50) 12.50 30.00
COMP.SERIES 2 SET (51-100) 15.00 40.00
STATED ODDS 1:4 HOBBY
TM1 Buster Posey .75 2.00
TM2 Dan Haren .40 1.00
TM3 Jered Weaver .50 1.25
TM4 Mike Trout 5.00 12.00
TM5 Ian Kennedy .40 1.00
TM6 Trevor Bauer .75 2.00
TM7 Craig Kimbrel .50 1.25
TM8 Dan Uggla .40 1.00
TM9 Adam Jones .50 1.25
TM10 Adrian Gonzalez .50 1.25
TM11 Dustin Pedroia .60 1.50
TM12 Anthony Rizzo .75 2.00
TM13 Starlin Castro .40 1.00
TM14 Chris Sale .60 1.50
TM15 Paul Konerko .50 1.25
TM16 Joey Votto .60 1.50
TM17 Johnny Cueto .50 1.25
TM18 Carlos Santana .50 1.25
TM19 Carlos Gonzalez .50 1.25
TM20 Justin Verlander .60 1.50
TM21 Prince Fielder .50 1.25
TM22 Andre Ethier .50 1.25
TM23 Clayton Kershaw 1.00 2.50
TM24 Giancarlo Stanton .60 1.50
TM25 Jose Reyes .50 1.25
TM26 Ryan Braun .50 1.25
TM27 R.A. Dickey .50 1.25
TM28 Alex Rodriguez .75 2.00
TM29 CC Sabathia .50 1.25
TM30 Curtis Granderson .50 1.25
TM31 Mark Teixeira .50 1.25
TM32 Josh Reddick .40 1.00
TM33 Cliff Lee .50 1.25
TM34 Andrew McCutchen .60 1.50
TM35 Felix Hernandez .50 1.25
TM36 Matt Holliday .60 1.50
TM37 Evan Longoria .50 1.25
TM38 Adrian Beltre .60 1.50
TM39 Yu Darvish .60 1.50
TM40 Colby Rasmus .50 1.25
TM41 Bryce Harper 1.00 2.50
TM42 Willie Mays 1.25 3.00
TM43 Tony Gwynn .60 1.50
TM44 Nolan Ryan 2.00 5.00
TM45 Cal Ripken Jr. 2.00 5.00
TM46 Jim Rice .50 1.25
TM47 Roberto Clemente 1.50 4.00
TM48 Lou Gehrig 1.25 3.00
TM49 Matt Kemp .50 1.25
TM50 Ted Williams 1.25 3.00
TM51 Ken Griffey Jr. 1.25 3.00
TM52 David Freese .40 1.00
TM53 Gio Gonzalez .50 1.25
TM54 Roy Halladay .50 1.25
TM55 Miguel Cabrera .60 1.50
TM56 David Wright .50 1.25
TM57 Albert Pujols .75 2.00
TM58 James Shields .40 1.00
TM59 Shelby Miller 1.00 2.50
TM60 Yoenis Cespedes .60 1.50
TM61 Brooks Robinson .50 1.25
TM62 Paul O'Neill .50 1.25
TM63 Yogi Berra .60 1.50
TM64 David Price .50 1.25
TM65 Manny Machado 2.50 6.00
TM66 Troy Tulowitzki .60 1.50
TM67 Tim Lincecum .50 1.25
TM68 Matt Cain .50 1.25
TM69 Robin Yount .60 1.50
TM70 Justin Upton .50 1.25
TM71 Reggie Jackson .50 1.25
TM72 Brandon Phillips .40 1.00
TM73 Dylan Bundy 1.00 2.50
TM74 Johan Santana .50 1.25
TM75 Willie Stargell .50 1.25
TM76 Jose Altuve .50 1.25
TM77 Fred Lynn .40 1.00
TM78 R.A. Dickey .50 1.25
TM79 Josh Hamilton .50 1.25
TM80 Johnny Bench .60 1.50
TM81 Eric Davis .40 1.00
TM82 Gary Sheffield .40 1.00
TM83 Don Mattingly 1.25 3.00
TM84 Ryan Howard .50 1.25
TM85 Matt Williams .40 1.00
TM86 George Brett 1.25 3.00
TM87 Jurickson Profar .50 1.25
TM88 Jose Bautista .50 1.25
TM89 Will Middlebrooks .40 1.00
TM90 Joe Morgan .50 1.25
TM91 Stephen Strasburg .60 1.50
TM92 Cole Hamels .50 1.25
TM93 Robinson Cano .50 1.25
TM94 David Ortiz .60 1.50
TM95 B.J. Upton .50 1.25
TM96 Jason Heyward .50 1.25
TM97 Josh Johnson .50 1.25
TM98 Ernie Banks .60 1.50
TM99 Ozzie Smith .75 2.00
TM100 Eddie Mathews .60 1.50

2013 Topps Calling Cards

COMPLETE SET (15) 4.00 10.00
STATED ODDS 1:8 HOBBY
CC1 Prince Fielder .50 1.25
CC2 Brandon Phillips .40 1.00
CC3 Felix Hernandez .50 1.25
CC4 David Ortiz .60 1.50
CC5 Jonathan Papelbon .50 1.25
CC6 Willie Stargell .50 1.25
CC7 Mark Teixeira .50 1.25
CC8 CC Sabathia .50 1.25
CC9 R.A. Dickey .50 1.25
CC10 Tim Lincecum .50 1.25
CC11 Reggie Jackson .50 1.25
CC12 Kevin Youkilis .40 1.00
CC13 Aroldis Chapman .60 1.50
CC14 Pablo Sandoval .50 1.25
CC15 Albert Pujols .75 2.00

2013 Topps Chasing History

COMPLETE SET (100) 25.00 60.00
COMP.SER 1 SET (1-50) 8.00 20.00
COMP.SER 2 SET (51-100) 8.00 20.00
COMP UPDATE SET (101-150) 8.00 20.00
STATED ODDS 1:4 HOBBY
CH1 Roy Halladay .40 1.00
CH2 Roberto Clemente 1.25 3.00
CH3 Ian Kinsler .40 1.00
CH4 Cal Ripken Jr. 1.50 4.00
CH5 Yogi Berra .50 1.25
CH6 Rod Carew .40 1.00
CH7 Carlos Santana .40 1.00
CH8 Rickey Henderson .50 1.25
CH9 Mariano Rivera .60 1.50
CH10 Lou Gehrig 1.00 2.50
CH11 Babe Ruth 1.25 3.00
CH12 Evan Longoria .40 1.00
CH13 Don Mattingly 1.00 2.50
CH14 Lou Brock .40 1.00
CH15 Willie McCovey .40 1.00
CH16 Lance Berkman .40 1.00
CH17 R.A. Dickey .40 1.00
CH18 Ken Griffey Jr. 1.00 2.50
CH19 Harmon Killebrew .50 1.25
CH20 Reggie Jackson .40 1.00
CH21 Frank Robinson .40 1.00
CH22 Matt Kemp .40 1.00
CH23 George Brett 1.00 2.50
CH24 David Wright .40 1.00
CH25 Frank Thomas .50 1.25
CH26 Chipper Jones .50 1.25
CH27 Nolan Ryan 1.50 4.00
CH28 Tony Gwynn .50 1.25
CH29 Stan Musial .75 2.00
CH30 Adam Dunn .40 1.00
CH31 Warren Spahn .40 1.00
CH32 Brian Wilson .50 1.25
CH33 Ted Williams 1.00 2.50
CH34 Robin Yount .50 1.25
CH35 Hank Aaron 1.00 2.50
CH36 Kerry Wood .30 .75
CH37 Derek Jeter 1.25 3.00
CH38 Tom Seaver .40 1.00
CH39 Jim Thome .30 .75
CH40 Mike Schmidt .75 2.00
CH41 Johan Santana .40 1.00
CH42 Alex Rodriguez .60 1.50
CH43 CC Sabathia .40 1.00
CH44 Mark Buehrle .40 1.00
CH45 Bob Feller .40 1.00
CH46 Hanley Ramirez .40 1.00
CH47 Willie Mays 1.00 2.50
CH48 Paul Konerko .40 1.00
CH49 Jackie Robinson .50 1.25
CH50 Sandy Koufax 1.00 2.50
CH51 Jason Kipnis .40 1.00
CH52 Gary Sheffield .30 .75
CH53 Jered Weaver .40 1.00
CH54 Anthony Rizzo .60 1.50
CH55 Ken Griffey Jr. 1.00 2.50
CH56 Matt Holliday .40 1.00
CH57 Cal Ripken Jr. 1.50 4.00
CH58 Rickey Henderson .50 1.25
CH59 Fred Lynn .30 .75
CH60 Derek Jeter 1.25 3.00
CH61 David Price .40 1.00
CH62 Willie McCovey .40 1.00
CH63 Jordan Zimmermann .40 1.00
CH64 Mike Trout 4.00 10.00
CH65 Gary Carter .40 1.00
CH66 Adrian Gonzalez .40 1.00
CH67 Stephen Strasburg .50 1.25
CH68 John Smoltz .50 1.25
CH69 Sandy Koufax 1.00 2.50
CH70 Miguel Cabrera .50 1.25
CH71 Buster Posey .60 1.50
CH72 Carlos Gonzalez .40 1.00
CH73 Robinson Cano .40 1.00
CH74 Stan Musial .75 2.00
CH75 Dustin Pedroia .50 1.25
CH76 Tony Gwynn .50 1.25
CH77 Roberto Clemente 1.25 3.00
CH78 Mark Trumbo .30 .75
CH79 Hank Aaron 1.00 2.50
CH80 Yu Darvish .50 1.25
CH81 Cliff Lee .40 1.00
CH82 Felix Hernandez .40 1.00
CH83 Willie Mays 1.00 2.50
CH84 Mariano Rivera .60 1.50
CH85 Tim Lincecum .40 1.00
CH86 Roy Halladay .40 1.00
CH87 Lance Lynn .30 .75
CH88 Justin Verlander .50 1.25
CH89 Darryl Strawberry .30 .75
CH90 Prince Fielder .40 1.00
CH91 Joey Votto .50 1.25
CH92 Mike Schmidt .75 2.00
CH93 Manny Machado 2.00 5.00
CH94 Ty Cobb .75 2.00
CH95 Matt Cain .40 1.00
CH96 Dylan Bundy .75 2.00
CH97 Troy Tulowitzki .50 1.25
CH98 Carl Crawford .40 1.00
CH99 David Wright .40 1.00
CH100 Phil Niekro .40 1.00
CH101 Jackie Bradley Jr. .75 2.00
CH102 Reggie Jackson .40 1.00
CH103 Anthony Rizzo .60 1.50
CH104 Nomar Garciaparra .40 1.00
CH105 Carlos Santana .40 1.00
CH106 Edwin Encarnacion .50 1.25
CH107 Babe Ruth 1.25 3.00
CH108 Shelby Miller .75 2.00
CH109 Jurickson Profar .40 1.00
CH110 Ted Williams 1.00 2.50
CH111 Bo Jackson .50 1.25
CH112 Johnny Podres .20 .50
CH113 Ozzie Smith .60 1.50
CH114 Tom Seaver .40 1.00
CH115 Paul Goldschmidt .50 1.25
CH116 Mike Zunino .50 1.25
CH117 Anthony Rendon 2.00 5.00
CH118 Mike Mussina .40 1.00
CH119 Pedro Martinez .40 1.00
CH120 Miguel Cabrera .50 1.25
CH121 Mike Trout 4.00 10.00
CH122 Roberto Clemente 1.25 3.00
CH123 Robinson Cano .40 1.00
CH124 Joey Votto .50 1.25
CH125 Justin Upton .40 1.00
CH126 Andrew McCutchen .50 1.25
CH127 Prince Fielder .40 1.00
CH128 Troy Tulowitzki .50 1.25
CH129 Clayton Kershaw .75 2.00
CH130 Jackie Robinson .50 1.25
CH131 Hyun-Jin Ryu .75 2.00
CH132 Justin Verlander .50 1.25
CH133 Dustin Pedroia .50 1.25
CH134 Tony Cingrani .60 1.50
CH135 Bret Saberhagen .20 .50
CH136 Zack Wheeler .60 1.50
CH137 Wade Boggs .40 1.00
CH138 David Ortiz .50 1.25
CH139 Buster Posey .60 1.50
CH140 Wil Myers .50 1.25
CH141 Marcell Ozuna .75 2.00
CH142 Matt Harvey .40 1.00
CH143 Craig Biggio .40 1.00
CH144 Yasiel Puig 1.25 3.00
CH145 Jim Palmer .40 1.00
CH146 Joe Morgan .40 1.00
CH147 Bob Feller .40 1.00
CH148 Manny Machado 2.00 5.00
CH149 Tony Gwynn .50 1.25
CH150 Jose Fernandez .75 2.00

2013 Topps Chasing History Holofoil

*HOLOFOIL: .75X TO 2X BASIC

2013 Topps Chasing History Holofoil Gold

*GOLD: 1X TO 2.5X BASIC

2013 Topps Chasing History Autographs

SERIES 1 ODDS 1:498 HOBBY
SERIES 2 ODDS 1:435 HOBBY
UPDATE ODDS 1:384 HOBBY
SERIES 1 EXCH DEADLINE 01/31/2016
SERIES 2 EXCH DEADLINE 06/30/2016
UPDATE EXHC DEADLINE 09/30/2016
AC Alex Cobb S2 3.00 8.00
AE Adam Eaton S2 4.00 10.00
AE Adam Eaton UPD 3.00 8.00
AG Adrian Gonzalez S2 30.00 60.00
AR Anthony Rizzo 20.00 50.00
BH Brock Holt S2 12.00 30.00
BH Brock Holt UPD 12.00 30.00
BJ Bo Jackson UPD
BM Brandon Maurer UPD 3.00 8.00
BR Bruce Rondon UPD 4.00 10.00
BS Bret Saberhagen UPD 5.00 12.00
BT Bob Tewksbury UPD 4.00 10.00
CA Chris Archer UPD 4.00 10.00
CA Chris Archer S2 4.00 10.00
CB Craig Biggio UPD
CC Collin Cowgill UPD 3.00 8.00
CC Collin Cowgill S2 4.00 10.00
CCS CC Sabathia 10.00 25.00
CD Cole De Vries S2 4.00 10.00
CRJ Cal Ripken Jr. 150.00 250.00
CSA Chris Sale 8.00 20.00
CST Carlos Santana 4.00 10.00
DB Dylan Bundy S2 10.00 25.00
DBA Don Baylor UPD 6.00 15.00
DC David Cooper S2 4.00 10.00
DG Didi Gregorius S2 8.00 20.00
DG Didi Gregorius UPD 4.00 10.00
DG Dwight Gooden 6.00 15.00
DGO Dee Gordon 5.00 12.00
DJ David Justice 8.00 20.00
DM Don Mattingly S2 60.00 120.00
DM Don Mattingly 60.00 120.00
DS Duke Snider 10.00 25.00
DW David Wright 12.00 30.00
EL Evan Longoria 20.00 50.00
FL Fred Lynn S2 8.00 20.00
FR Fernando Rodney 4.00 10.00
FT Frank Thomas 40.00 80.00
GC Gary Carter S2 12.50 30.00
GC Gerrit Cole UPD 8.00 20.00
GC Gary Carter 12.50 30.00
GR Garrett Richards UPD 3.00 8.00
GS Gary Sheffield S2 8.00 20.00
GS Gary Sheffield 5.00 12.00
GST Giancarlo Stanton 30.00 80.00
HA Hank Aaron 100.00 250.00
HJ Howard Johnson UPD 5.00 12.00
HR Hanley Ramirez 10.00 25.00
IN Ivan Nova 3.00 8.00
JA Jose Altuve 15.00 40.00
JB Jay Bruce S2 10.00 25.00
JB Jose Bautista 8.00 20.00
JBA Jose Bautista S2 8.00 20.00
JG Jason Grilli S2 6.00 15.00
JH Joel Hanrahan 4.00 10.00
JK Jason Kipnis S2 5.00 12.00
JP Jim Palmer S2 10.00 25.00
JP Jarrod Parker 3.00 8.00
JPO Johnny Podres S2 6.00 15.00
JPO Johnny Podres 6.00 15.00
JPR Jurickson Profar S2 5.00 12.00
JS James Shields S2 6.00 15.00
JW Jered Weaver S2 10.00 25.00
KGJ Ken Griffey Jr. 100.00 200.00
KH Kelvin Herrera UPD 4.00 10.00
LB Larry Bowa UPD 6.00 15.00
MA Matt Adams UPD 8.00 20.00
MAM Matt Moore 5.00 12.00
MAT Mark Trumbo 8.00 20.00
MC Miguel Cabrera S2 75.00 150.00
MIT Mike Trout 100.00 200.00
MM Manny Machado S2 60.00 120.00
MM Mike Mussina UPD
MM Matt Magill UPD 3.00 8.00
MS Mike Schmidt S2 40.00 80.00
MS Mike Schmidt 50.00 100.00
MT Mark Trumbo S2 6.00 15.00
MTR Mike Trout S2 75.00 150.00
MZ Mike Zunino UPD 4.00 10.00
NM Nick Maronde UPD 3.00 8.00
NM Nick Maronde S2 4.00 10.00
NR Nolan Ryan 60.00 120.00
OC Orlando Cepeda 15.00 40.00
PF Prince Fielder S2 20.00 50.00
PM Pedro Martinez UPD
PR Paco Rodriguez S2 4.00 10.00
RD Rafael Dolis UPD 3.00 8.00
RH Rickey Henderson 75.00 150.00
RJ Reggie Jackson 50.00 100.00
RP Ryan Pressly UPD 3.00 8.00
RS Ruben Sierra UPD 4.00 10.00
SC Starlin Castro 5.00 12.00
SD Scott Diamond S2 3.00 8.00
SG Steve Garvey S2 20.00 50.00
SK Sandy Koufax EXCH 200.00 400.00
SM Starling Marte S2 6.00 15.00
SM Stan Musial 15.00 40.00
SMA Shaun Marcum S2 4.00 10.00
TC Tony Cingrani UPD 3.00 8.00
TG Tony Gwynn S2 EXCH 15.00 40.00
TG Tony Gwynn 50.00 100.00
TS Tyler Skaggs S2 4.00 10.00
WB Wade Boggs S2 30.00 60.00
WF Whitey Ford 30.00 60.00
WP Wily Peralta S2 4.00 10.00
WR Wilin Rosario S2 4.00 10.00
YG Yan Gomes UPD 3.00 8.00
ZC Zack Cozart S2 4.00 10.00
ZW Zack Wheeler UPD 8.00 20.00

2013 Topps Chasing History Dual Relics

STATED ODDS 1:7650 HOBBY
STATED PRINT RUN 50 SER.#'d SETS
CB S.Castro/E.Banks 20.00 50.00
CC R.Clemente/T.Cobb 100.00 250.00
DR Jose Reyes/R.A. Dickey 10.00 25.00
JH R.Henderson/R.Jackson 30.00 60.00
KM J.Morneau/H.Killebrew 20.00 50.00
MB R.Braun/P.Molitor 10.00 25.00
PT Albert Pujols/Mike Trout
RD Y.Darvish/N.Ryan 40.00 80.00
RJ C.Ripken/D.Jeter 60.00 120.00
RR A.Rodriguez/M.Rivera 12.50 30.00
SB G.Brett/M.Schmidt 30.00 60.00
SS G.Sheffield/G.Stanton 10.00 25.00
UU B.J. Upton/Justin Upton
VP J.Verlander/D.Price 20.00 50.00
WS Tom Seaver/David Wright

2013 Topps Chasing History Relics

SERIES 1 ODDS 1:70 HOBBY
SERIES 2 ODDS 1:68 HOBBY
AB Adrian Beltre S2 5.00 12.00
AB Albert Belle 3.00 8.00
AC Asdrubal Cabrera S2 4.00 10.00
AC Aroldis Chapman 5.00 12.00
AD Adam Dunn 4.00 10.00
AE Andre Ethier 4.00 10.00
AG Alex Gordon S2 4.00 10.00
AGO Adrian Gonzalez S2 4.00 10.00
AJ Adam Jones 4.00 10.00
AJA Austin Jackson 3.00 8.00
AM Andrew McCutchen 5.00 12.00
AP Andy Pettitte S2 4.00 10.00
AR Alex Rodriguez S2 5.00 12.00
AR Anthony Rizzo 4.00 10.00
AS Alfonso Soriano S2 4.00 10.00
BB Billy Butler S2 3.00 8.00
BM Brian McCann S2 4.00 10.00
BP Brandon Phillips S2 3.00 8.00
BPO Buster Posey S2 6.00 15.00
BS Bruce Sutter 4.00 10.00
BW Brian Wilson 5.00 12.00
CB Chad Billingsley S2 4.00 10.00
CC Carl Crawford S2 4.00 10.00
CF Carlton Fisk S2 4.00 10.00
CG Carlos Gonzalez S2 4.00 10.00
CG Curtis Granderson 4.00 10.00
CGO Carlos Gonzalez 4.00 10.00
CJW C.J. Wilson 3.00 8.00
CK Clayton Kershaw 5.00 12.00
CL Cliff Lee S2 4.00 10.00
CL Cliff Lee 4.00 10.00
CR Colby Rasmus S2 4.00 10.00
CRJ Cal Ripken Jr. 10.00 25.00
CS Carlos Santana 4.00 10.00
CSA Chris Sale 5.00 12.00
DG Dwight Gooden 3.00 8.00
DJ Derek Jeter S2 6.00 15.00
DM Don Mattingly S2 10.00 25.00
DO David Ortiz 5.00 12.00
DP David Price S2 4.00 10.00
DW David Wright S2 4.00 10.00
Facing right
DW David Wright 4.00 10.00
Facing left
EA Elvis Andrus S2 4.00 10.00
EL Evan Longoria 4.00 10.00
FH Felix Hernandez S2 4.00 10.00
FJ Fergie Jenkins S2 4.00 10.00
FT Frank Thomas 10.00 25.00
GB George Brett 10.00 25.00
GS Gary Sheffield S2 3.00 8.00
HK Harmon Killebrew 10.00 25.00
HP Hunter Pence S2 4.00 10.00
HP Hunter Pence 4.00 10.00
HR Hanley Ramirez 4.00 10.00
IK Ian Kinsler 4.00 10.00
IKE Ian Kennedy 3.00 8.00
JA John Axford S2 3.00 8.00
JAH Jason Heyward 4.00 10.00
JB Jose Bautista 4.00 10.00
JC Johnny Cueto 4.00 10.00
JH Josh Hamilton S2 4.00 10.00
JH Joel Hanrahan 3.00 8.00
JHA Josh Hamilton 4.00 10.00
JK Jason Kipnis S2 4.00 10.00
JOV Joey Votto 5.00 12.00
JS James Shields S2 3.00 8.00
JS Johan Santana 4.00 10.00
JSM John Smoltz S2 5.00 12.00
JUV Justin Verlander 5.00 12.00
JV Justin Verlander S2 5.00 12.00
JVO Joey Votto S2 5.00 12.00
JW Jered Weaver 4.00 10.00
JZ Jordan Zimmermann S2 4.00 10.00
KGJ Ken Griffey Jr. 8.00 20.00
LB Lance Berkman 4.00 10.00
LL Lance Lynn S2 3.00 8.00
MAM Matt Moore 4.00 10.00
MAT Mark Trumbo 3.00 8.00
MC Matt Cain S2 4.00 10.00
MEC Melky Cabrera 3.00 8.00
MH Matt Holliday S2 5.00 12.00
MIC Miguel Cabrera 5.00 12.00
MIM Mike Moustakas 4.00 10.00
MIT Mike Trout 12.00 30.00
MK Matt Kemp 4.00 10.00
MR Mariano Rivera S2 8.00 20.00
MS Max Scherzer S2 5.00 12.00
MS Mike Schmidt 5.00 12.00
NC Nelson Cruz S2 5.00 12.00
NR Nolan Ryan 10.00 25.00
OC Orlando Cepeda S2 5.00 12.00
PF Prince Fielder S2 4.00 10.00
PK Paul Konerko S2 4.00 10.00
PK Paul Konerko 4.00 10.00
PN Phil Niekro S2 4.00 10.00
PS Pablo Sandoval S2 4.00 10.00
RC Roberto Clemente S2 20.00 50.00
RH Rickey Henderson 5.00 12.00
RHA Roy Halladay S2 4.00 10.00
RHA Roy Halladay 4.00 10.00
RHO Ryan Howard S2 4.00 10.00
RJ Reggie Jackson 4.00 10.00
RZ Ryan Zimmerman S2 4.00 10.00
SC Starlin Castro S2 3.00 8.00
SC Starlin Castro 3.00 8.00
SM Stan Musial S2 12.00 30.00
SM Stan Musial 12.00 30.00
SR Scott Rolen S2 4.00 10.00
SS Stephen Strasburg S2 5.00 12.00
TC Ty Cobb S2 20.00 50.00
TG Tony Gwynn 5.00 12.00
TL Tim Lincecum S2 5.00 12.00
TT Troy Tulowitzki S2 5.00 12.00
TT Troy Tulowitzki 5.00 12.00
VW Vernon Wells S2 3.00 8.00
WM Willie McCovey S2 8.00 20.00
WMA Willie Mays S2 15.00 40.00
YB Yogi Berra S2 5.00 12.00
YG Yovani Gallardo 3.00 8.00

2013 Topps Chasing History Relics Gold

*GOLD: .6X TO 1.5X BASIC
STATED ODDS 1:969 HOBBY
STATED PRINT RUN 99 SER.#'d SETS

2013 Topps Chase It Down

COMPLETE SET (15) 5.00 12.00
STATED ODDS 1:8 HOBBY
CD1 Mike Trout 4.00 10.00
CD2 Pablo Sandoval .40 1.00
CD3 Ryan Zimmerman .40 1.00
CD4 Jason Heyward .40 1.00
CD5 Adam Jones .40 1.00
CD6 Mike Moustakas .40 1.00
CD7 Bryce Harper .75 2.00
CD8 Chase Headley .30 .75
CD9 Josh Reddick .30 .75
CD10 Jon Jay .30 .75
CD11 Alex Gordon .40 1.00
CD12 Carlos Gonzalez .40 1.00
CD13 Manny Machado 2.00 5.00
CD14 Cameron Maybin .30 .75
CD15 Giancarlo Stanton .50 1.25

2013 Topps Chasing the Dream

COMPLETE SET (25) 6.00 15.00
STATED ODDS 1:6 HOBBY
CD1 Bryce Harper 1.00 2.50
CD2 Mike Trout 5.00 12.00
CD3 Will Middlebrooks .40 1.00
CD4 Trevor Bauer .75 2.00

CD5 Matt Moore .50 1.25
CD6 Anthony Rizzo .75 2.00
CD7 Jesus Montero .40 1.00
CD8 Josh Reddick .40 1.00
CD9 Devin Mesoraco .40 1.00
CD10 Giancarlo Stanton .60 1.50
CD11 Jacob Turner .50 1.25
CD12 Casey Kelly .50 1.25
CD13 Drew Hutchison .50 1.25
CD14 Drew Pomeranz .50 1.25
CD15 Jonathon Niese .40 1.00
CD16 Yonder Alonso .40 1.00
CD17 Addison Reed .40 1.00
CD18 Chris Sale .60 1.50
CD19 Yu Darvish .60 1.50
CD20 Tommy Milone .40 1.00
CD21 Jarrod Parker .40 1.00
CD22 Drew Smyly .40 1.00
CD23 Jose Altuve .50 1.25
CD24 Brett Lawrie .50 1.25
CD25 Mike Moustakas .50 1.25

2013 Topps Chasing The Dream Autographs

STATED ODDS 1:996 HOBBY
EXCHANGE DEADLINE 01/31/2016
AR Anthony Rizzo 20.00 50.00
BH Bryce Harper 300.00 400.00
BL Brett Lawrie 6.00 15.00
BP Brad Peacock 4.00 10.00
CS Chris Sale 6.00 15.00
DG Dee Gordon 5.00 12.00
DH Drew Hutchison 4.00 10.00
EA Elvis Andrus 3.00 8.00
FD Felix Doubront 4.00 10.00
GS Giancarlo Stanton 20.00 50.00
JP Jarrod Parker 4.00 10.00
MAM Matt Moore 5.00 12.00
MB Madison Bumgarner 12.00 30.00
MT Mike Trout 75.00 150.00
PG Paul Goldschmidt 12.00 30.00
TB Trevor Bauer 8.00 20.00
TM Tommy Milone 4.00 10.00
WP Wily Peralta 4.00 10.00
YA Yonder Alonso 5.00 12.00
YD Yu Darvish 75.00 150.00

2013 Topps Chasing The Dream Relics

STATED ODDS 1:210 HOBBY
AR Anthony Rizzo 5.00 12.00
BH Bryce Harper 10.00 25.00
BIB Billy Butler 4.00 10.00
BL Brett Lawrie 5.00 12.00
BP Buster Posey 10.00 25.00
BRB Brandon Beachy 4.00 10.00
CS Chris Sale 4.00 10.00
DA Dustin Ackley 4.00 10.00
DF David Freese 4.00 10.00
DG Dee Gordon 4.00 10.00
DH Derek Holland 5.00 12.00
DJ Desmond Jennings 4.00 10.00
DP Drew Pomeranz 4.00 10.00
EA Elvis Andrus 4.00 10.00
GG Gio Gonzalez 4.00 10.00
JAP Jarrod Parker 4.00 10.00
JM Jesus Montero 4.00 10.00
JPA J.P. Arencibia 4.00 10.00
JR Josh Reddick 4.00 10.00
JSM Justin Smoak 4.00 10.00
JT Jacob Turner 4.00 10.00
JZ Jordan Zimmermann 5.00 12.00
LL Lance Lynn 4.00 10.00
MA Matt Adams 4.00 10.00
MAM Matt Moore 4.00 10.00
MAT Mark Trumbo 4.00 10.00
MB Madison Bumgarner 6.00 15.00
MIM Mike Morse 4.00 10.00
MIT Mike Trout 10.00 25.00
MMO Mike Moustakas 4.00 10.00
NF Neftali Feliz 4.00 10.00
PG Paul Goldschmidt 4.00 10.00
TM Tommy Milone 4.00 10.00
WM Will Middlebrooks 6.00 15.00
WMI Wade Miley 4.00 10.00
WR Wilin Rosario 4.00 10.00
YA Yonder Alonso 4.00 10.00
YC Yoenis Cespedes 6.00 15.00
YD Yu Darvish 6.00 15.00

2013 Topps Cut To The Chase

COMPLETE SET (48) 40.00 80.00
COMP.SERIES 1 SET (23) 15.00 40.00
COMP.SERIES 2 SET (25) 15.00 40.00
SERIES 1 ODDS 1:14 HOBBY
SERIES 2 ODDS 1:12 HOBBY
CTC1 Mike Trout 8.00 20.00
CTC2 Ken Griffey Jr. 2.00 5.00
CTC3 Derek Jeter 2.50 6.00
CTC4 Babe Ruth 2.50 6.00
CTC5 Paul Molitor 1.00 2.50
CTC6 Carlos Gonzalez .75 2.00
CTC7 Stan Musial 1.50 4.00
CTC8 Ryan Braun .75 2.00
CTC9 Ted Williams 2.00 5.00
CTC10 Adam Jones .75 2.00
CTC11 Yu Darvish 1.00 2.50
CTC12 Lance Berkman .75 2.00
CTC13 Brett Lawrie .75 2.00
CTC14 David Price .75 2.00
CTC15 Dustin Pedroia 1.00 2.50
CTC16 Nelson Cruz 1.00 2.50
CTC17 Matt Cain .75 2.00
CTC18 Tony Gwynn 1.00 2.50
CTC19 Mike Schmidt 1.50 4.00
CTC20 Roberto Clemente 2.50 6.00
CTC21 Andrew McCutchen 1.00 2.50
CTC22 Ryne Sandberg 2.00 5.00
CTC23 Willie Mays 2.00 5.00
CTC24 Buster Posey 1.25 3.00
CTC25 Josh Hamilton .75 2.00
CTC26 Albert Belle .60 1.50
CTC27 Ralph Kiner .60 1.50
CTC28 Al Kaline 1.00 2.50
CTC29 Tom Seaver .75 2.00
CTC30 Rickey Henderson 1.00 2.50
CTC31 Matt Holliday 1.00 2.50
CTC32 Harmon Killebrew 1.00 2.50
CTC33 Jered Weaver .75 2.00
CTC34 Ernie Banks 1.00 2.50
CTC35 Chris Sale 1.00 2.50
CTC36 Joe Morgan .75 2.00
CTC37 Albert Pujols 1.25 3.00
CTC38 Prince Fielder .75 2.00
CTC39 Yoenis Cespedes 1.00 2.50
CTC40 Cal Ripken Jr. 3.00 8.00
CTC41 Stephen Strasburg 1.00 2.50
CTC42 R.A. Dickey .75 2.00
CTC43 Miguel Cabrera 1.00 2.50
CTC44 Manny Machado 4.00 10.00
CTC45 Bryce Harper 1.50 4.00
CTC46 Duke Snider .75 2.00
CTC47 Alex Rodriguez 1.25 3.00
CTC48 Sandy Koufax 2.00 5.00

2013 Topps Cy Young Award Winners Trophy

STATED ODDS 1:1396 HOBBY
BC Bartolo Colon 6.00 15.00
BG Bob Gibson 10.00 25.00
BW Brandon Webb 6.00 15.00
BZ Barry Zito 6.00 15.00
CC Chris Carpenter 10.00 25.00
CH Catfish Hunter 8.00 20.00
CK Clayton Kershaw 8.00 20.00
CL Cliff Lee 6.00 15.00
CS CC Sabathia 8.00 20.00
DE Dennis Eckersley 6.00 15.00
DG Dwight Gooden 6.00 15.00
FH Felix Hernandez 8.00 20.00
FJ Fergie Jenkins 6.00 15.00
JP Jim Palmer 8.00 20.00
JPE Jake Peavy 6.00 15.00
JS Johan Santana 6.00 15.00
JSM John Smoltz 8.00 20.00
JV Justin Verlander 6.00 15.00
PM1 Pedro Martinez 8.00 20.00
PM2 Pedro Martinez 8.00 20.00
RH1 Roy Halladay 8.00 20.00
RH2 Roy Halladay 8.00 20.00
SK Sandy Koufax 12.50 30.00
TL Tim Lincecum 10.00 25.00
TS Tom Seaver 12.50 30.00
VB Vida Blue 6.00 15.00
WF Whitey Ford 10.00 25.00
WS Warren Spahn 10.00 25.00
ZG Zack Greinke 6.00 15.00

2013 Topps Making Their Mark

COMPLETE SET (25) 5.00 12.00
STATED ODDS 1:6 HOBBY
MM1 Yoenis Cespedes .50 1.25
MM2 Mike Trout 4.00 10.00
MM3 Andrelton Simmons .30 .75
MM4 Jason Kipnis .40 1.00
MM5 Jeremy Hellickson .30 .75
MM6 Ike Davis .30 .75
MM7 Mike Olt .40 1.00
MM8 Kris Medlen .40 1.00
MM9 Tyler Skaggs .50 1.25
MM10 Wilin Rosario .30 .75
MM11 Trevor Bauer .60 1.50
MM12 Zack Cozart .30 .75
MM13 Matt Moore .40 1.00
MM14 Lance Lynn .30 .75
MM15 Salvador Perez .40 1.00
MM16 Will Middlebrooks .30 .75
MM17 Anthony Rizzo .60 1.50
MM18 Wade Miley .30 .75
MM19 Bryce Harper .75 2.00
MM20 Dylan Bundy .75 2.00
MM21 Jurickson Profar .40 1.00
MM22 Yu Darvish .50 1.25
MM23 Todd Frazier .30 .75
MM24 Manny Machado 2.00 5.00
MM25 Stephen Strasburg .50 1.25
MM26 Jean Segura .40 1.00
MM27 Zack Wheeler .60 1.50
MM28 Nick Franklin .40 1.00
MM29 Marcell Ozuna .75 2.00
MM30 Wei-Yin Chen .30 .75
MM31 Mike Zunino .50 1.25
MM32 Matt Harvey .40 1.00
MM33 Starling Marte .40 1.00
MM34 Nolan Arenado 3.00 8.00
MM35 Aaron Hicks .50 1.25
MM36 Carlos Martinez .50 1.25
MM37 Matt Adams .30 .75
MM38 Yasiel Puig 1.25 3.00
MM39 Kevin Gausman 1.00 2.50
MM40 Jackie Bradley Jr. .75 2.00
MM41 Shelby Miller .75 2.00
MM42 Wil Myers .50 1.25
MM43 Jose Fernandez .75 2.00
MM44 Jedd Gyorko .40 1.00
MM45 Evan Gattis .60 1.50
MM46 Hyun-Jin Ryu .75 2.00
MM47 Tony Cingrani .60 1.50
MM48 Craig Kimbrel .40 1.00
MM49 Kyle Gibson .50 1.25
MM50 Patrick Corbin .40 1.00

2013 Topps Making Their Mark Autographs

SERIES 2 ODDS 1:1638 HOBBY
UPDATE ODDS 1:2525
SERIES 2 EXCH DEADLINE 06/30/2016
UPDATE EXCH DEADLINE 09/30/2016
AH Aaron Hicks UPD 5.00 12.00
BR Bruce Rondon UPD 5.00 12.00
BR Bruce Rondon 5.00 12.00
CM Carlos Martinez UPD 10.00 25.00
DB Dylan Bundy 30.00 60.00
EG Evan Gattis UPD 15.00 40.00
JG Jedd Gyorko UPD
KG Kevin Gausman UPD 20.00 50.00
MA Matt Adams UPD 6.00 15.00
MM Manny Machado 50.00 100.00
MO Mike Olt 5.00 12.00
TC Tony Cingrani UPD 5.00 12.00
TS Tyler Skaggs 5.00 10.00
WM Wade Miley 5.00 10.00
WMI Will Middlebrooks 8.00 20.00
YC Yoenis Cespedes 8.00 20.00
YD Yu Darvish 60.00 *120.00
YP Yasiel Puig UPD 125.00 250.00

2013 Topps Making Their Mark Relics

STATED ODDS 1:176 HOBBY
AS Andrelton Simmons 4.00 10.00
BH Bryce Harper 6.00 15.00
DB Darwin Barney 4.00 10.00
JH Jeremy Hellickson 4.00 10.00
JK Jason Kipnis 4.00 10.00
JPR Jurickson Profar 4.00 10.00
LL Lance Lynn 4.00 10.00
MO Mike Olt 4.00 10.00
PG Paul Goldschmidt 5.00 12.00
SC Starlin Castro 4.00 10.00
SS Stephen Strasburg 5.00 12.00
WR Wilin Rosario 4.00 10.00
YC Yoenis Cespedes 4.00 10.00
YD Yu Darvish 5.00 12.00
ZC Zack Cozart 4.00 10.00

2013 Topps Manufactured Commemorative Patch

CP1 Adam Jones 2.50 6.00
CP2 Dustin Pedroia 3.00 8.00
CP3 Mike Trout 25.00 60.00
CP4 Felix Hernandez 2.50 6.00
CP5 Yu Darvish 3.00 8.00
CP6 Jose Bautista 2.50 6.00
CP7 Trevor Bauer 4.00 10.00
CP8 Jason Heyward 2.50 6.00
CP9 Nolan Ryan 10.00 25.00
CP10 Adrian Gonzalez 2.50 6.00
CP11 Giancarlo Stanton 3.00 8.00
CP12 David Wright 2.50 6.00
CP13 Yonder Alonso 2.00 5.00
CP14 Matt Holliday 3.00 8.00
CP15 Bryce Harper 5.00 12.00
CP16 Billy Butler 2.00 5.00
CP17 Ryan Braun 2.50 6.00
CP18 Yoenis Cespedes 3.00 8.00
CP19 Will Clark 2.50 6.00
CP20 Chipper Jones 3.00 8.00
CP21 Anthony Rizzo 4.00 10.00
CP22 Chris Sale 3.00 8.00
CP23 Mike Schmidt 5.00 12.00
CP24 Stephen Strasburg 3.00 8.00
CP25 Joey Votto 3.00 8.00
CP26 Cal Ripken Jr. 10.00 25.00
CP27 Babe Ruth 8.00 20.00
CP28 Frank Thomas 3.00 8.00
CP29 Bob Feller 2.50 6.00
CP30 Miguel Cabrera 3.00 8.00
CP31 Josh Hamilton 2.50 6.00
CP32 Joe Mauer 2.50 6.00
CP33 Yogi Berra 3.00 8.00
CP34 Rickey Henderson 3.00 8.00
CP35 Ken Griffey Jr. 6.00 15.00
CP36 Evan Longoria 2.50 6.00
CP37 Ian Kinsler 2.50 6.00
CP38 Jose Reyes 2.50 6.00
CP39 Justin Upton 2.50 6.00
CP40 Ernie Banks 3.00 8.00
CP41 Johnny Bench 3.00 8.00
CP42 Carlos Gonzalez 2.50 6.00
CP43 Sandy Koufax 6.00 15.00
CP44 Jackie Robinson 3.00 8.00
CP45 Tom Seaver 2.50 6.00
CP46 Ryan Howard 2.50 6.00
CP47 Roberto Clemente 8.00 20.00
CP48 Andrew McCutchen 3.00 8.00
CP49 Buster Posey 4.00 10.00
CP50 Stan Musial 5.00 12.00

2013 Topps Manufactured Commemorative Rookie Patch

RCP1 Willie Mays 10.00 25.00
RCP2 Ernie Banks 6.00 15.00
RCP3 Roberto Clemente 10.00 25.00
RCP4 Sandy Koufax 10.00 25.00
RCP5 Bob Gibson 6.00 15.00
RCP6 Willie McCovey 6.00 15.00
RCP7 Reggie Jackson 5.00 12.00
RCP8 Ryne Sandberg 6.00 15.00
RCP9 George Brett 8.00 20.00
RCP10 Eddie Murray 5.00 12.00
RCP11 Ozzie Smith 6.00 15.00
RCP12 Rickey Henderson 6.00 15.00
RCP13 Jim Palmer 5.00 12.00
RCP14 Tony Gwynn 5.00 12.00
RCP15 Wade Boggs 6.00 15.00
RCP16 Don Mattingly 8.00 20.00
RCP17 Darryl Strawberry 5.00 12.00
RCP18 Dwight Gooden 5.00 12.00
RCP19 Ken Griffey Jr. 12.50 30.00
RCP20 Chipper Jones 10.00 25.00
RCP21 Derek Jeter 12.50 30.00
RCP22 Albert Pujols 8.00 20.00
RCP23 Mike Trout 15.00 40.00
RCP24 Bryce Harper 10.00 25.00
RCP25 Yu Darvish 5.00 12.00

2013 Topps Manufactured Patch

MCP1 Jackie Robinson 6.00 15.00
MCP2 Willie Mays 10.00 25.00
MCP3 Jackie Robinson 6.00 15.00
MCP4 Hank Aaron 8.00 20.00
MCP5 Willie Mays 10.00 25.00
MCP6 Ted Williams 10.00 25.00
MCP7 Al Kaline 8.00 20.00
MCP8 Ted Williams 10.00 25.00
MCP9 Roberto Clemente 10.00 25.00
MCP10 Sandy Koufax 10.00 25.00
MCP11 Ted Williams 10.00 25.00
MCP12 Sandy Koufax 10.00 25.00
MCP13 Stan Musial 8.00 20.00
MCP14 Nolan Ryan 10.00 25.00
MCP15 Roberto Clemente 10.00 25.00
MCP16 Joe Morgan 5.00 12.00
MCP17 Mike Schmidt 8.00 20.00
MCP18 Reggie Jackson 6.00 15.00
MCP19 Prince Fielder 5.00 12.00
MCP20 Frank Thomas 6.00 15.00
MCP21 Joe Mauer 5.00 12.00
MCP22 Justin Verlander 6.00 15.00
MCP23 Derek Jeter 10.00 25.00
MCP24 Buster Posey 12.50 30.00
MCP25 Yoenis Cespedes 5.00 12.00

2013 Topps MVP Award Winners Trophy

SERIES 1 ODDS 1:1396 HOBBY
SERIES 2 ODDS 1:3800 HOBBY
AP Albert Pujols 8.00 20.00
AR Alex Rodriguez 8.00 20.00
BP Buster Posey S2 12.50 30.00
BR Babe Ruth 12.50 30.00
CJ Chipper Jones 10.00 25.00
CR Cal Ripken Jr. 12.50 30.00
DE Dennis Eckersley 6.00 15.00
DM Dale Murphy 8.00 20.00
DMA Don Mattingly 10.00 25.00
DP Dustin Pedroia 8.00 20.00
EB Ernie Banks S2 6.00 15.00
FT Frank Thomas 8.00 20.00
GB George Brett 8.00 20.00
HK Harmon Killebrew 8.00 20.00
JB Johnny Bench 8.00 20.00
JH Josh Hamilton 10.00 25.00
JR Jackie Robinson S2 8.00 20.00
JR Jackie Robinson 8.00 20.00
JRO Jimmy Rollins 6.00 15.00
JV Joey Votto S2 6.00 15.00
JV Justin Verlander 10.00 25.00
JVO Joey Votto 8.00 20.00
KG Ken Griffey Jr. S2 12.50 30.00
KG Ken Griffey Jr. 12.50 30.00
LB Lou Boudreau S2 6.00 15.00
MC Miguel Cabrera S2 10.00 25.00
MS Mike Schmidt 10.00 25.00
RB Ryan Braun 6.00 15.00
RC Roberto Clemente 12.50 30.00
RH Ryan Howard 8.00 20.00
RJ Reggie Jackson 6.00 15.00
SK Sandy Koufax 8.00 20.00
SM Stan Musial S2 8.00 20.00
SM Stan Musial 8.00 20.00
TW Ted Williams S2 10.00 25.00
VG Vladimir Guerrero 6.00 15.00
WM Willie Mays 10.00 25.00
WS Willie Stargell 8.00 20.00
YB Yogi Berra S2 6.00 15.00
YB Yogi Berra 10.00 25.00

2013 Topps Proven Mettle Coins Copper

SERIES 1 ODDS 1:5622 HOBBY
SERIES 2 ODDS 1:1685 HOBBY
STATED PRINT RUN 99 SER.#'d SETS
AG Adrian Gonzalez S2 12.50 30.00
AM Andrew McCutchen S2 15.00 40.00
AP Albert Pujols 20.00 50.00
BH Bryce Harper S2 20.00 50.00
BR Babe Ruth S2 20.00 50.00
BR Babe Ruth 40.00 80.00
BRO Brooks Robinson S2 20.00 50.00
CK Clayton Kershaw 12.50 30.00
CL Cliff Lee 10.00 25.00
CR Cal Ripken Jr. S2 15.00 40.00
CS CC Sabathia S2 12.50 30.00
DJ Derek Jeter 15.00 40.00
DW David Wright S2 15.00 40.00
EL Evan Longoria 10.00 25.00
GB George Brett S2 20.00 50.00
HA Hank Aaron 15.00 40.00
HK Harmon Killebrew S2 12.50 30.00
JB Johnny Bench S2 10.00 25.00
JF Jimmie Foxx S2 15.00 40.00
JH Josh Hamilton S2 12.50 30.00
JH Josh Hamilton 12.50 30.00
JM Joe Morgan 12.50 30.00
JR Jackie Robinson 12.50 30.00
JV Joey Votto S2 12.00 30.00
JV Justin Verlander 15.00 40.00
JVO Joey Votto 12.00 30.00
KGJ Ken Griffey Jr. 25.00 60.00
LG Lou Gehrig 15.00 40.00
MC Miguel Cabrera 10.00 25.00
MK Matt Kemp 10.00 25.00
MM Manny Machado S2 10.00 25.00
MT Mike Trout S2 25.00 60.00
NR Nolan Ryan S2 20.00 50.00
OS Ozzie Smith S2 20.00 50.00
PF Prince Fielder S2 12.50 30.00
RB Ryan Braun 10.00 25.00
RC Roberto Clemente 30.00 60.00
RIH Rickey Henderson 12.50 30.00
RJ Reggie Jackson S2 10.00 25.00
ROC Robinson Cano 12.50 30.00
ROH Roy Halladay 10.00 25.00
SK Sandy Koufax 15.00 40.00
SM Stan Musial 15.00 40.00
TC Ty Cobb 15.00 40.00
TS Tom Seaver S2 15.00 40.00
TW Ted Williams S2 10.00 25.00
WM Willie Mays 15.00 40.00
WS Willie Stargell S2 10.00 25.00
WSP Warren Spahn S2 10.00 25.00
YD Yu Darvish S2 10.00 25.00

2013 Topps Proven Mettle Coins Wrought Iron

*IRON: .5X TO 1.2X BASIC
SERIES 1 ODDS 1:11,126 HOBBY
SERIES 2 ODDS 1:2850 HOBBY
STATED PRINT RUN 50 SER.#'d SETS

2013 Topps ROY Award Winners Trophy

STATED ODDS 1:1575 HOBBY
AD Andre Dawson 6.00 15.00
AP Albert Pujols 8.00 20.00
BH Bryce Harper 10.00 25.00
BP Buster Posey 8.00 20.00
BW Billy Williams 5.00 12.00
CF Carlton Fisk 5.00 12.00
CK Craig Kimbrel 6.00 15.00
CR Cal Ripken Jr. 12.50 30.00
DG Dwight Gooden 6.00 15.00
DJ Derek Jeter 15.00 40.00
DJU David Justice 5.00 12.00
DP Dustin Pedroia 6.00 15.00
DS Darryl Strawberry 6.00 15.00
EL Evan Longoria 5.00 12.00
EM Eddie Murray 6.00 15.00
FL Fred Lynn 5.00 12.00
HR Hanley Ramirez 5.00 12.00
JB Johnny Bench 8.00 20.00
JH Jeremy Hellickson 5.00 12.00
JR Jackie Robinson 8.00 20.00
JV Justin Verlander 6.00 15.00
LA Luis Aparicio 5.00 12.00
MT Mike Trout 10.00 25.00
RB Ryan Braun 5.00 12.00
RC Rod Carew 5.00 12.00
RH Ryan Howard 5.00 12.00
SR Scott Rolen 5.00 12.00
TS Tom Seaver 6.00 15.00
WM Willie Mays 8.00 20.00
WMC Willie McCovey 8.00 20.00

2013 Topps Spring Fever

COMPLETE SET (50) 10.00 25.00
SF1 Wally Joyner .30 .75
SF2 Dan Haren .30 .75
SF3 Mike Trout 4.00 10.00
SF4 Tyler Skaggs .50 1.25
SF5 Orlando Cepeda .40 1.00
SF6 Tommy Hanson .30 .75
SF7 Jason Heyward .40 1.00
SF8 Nick Markakis .40 1.00
SF9 Manny Machado 2.00 5.00
SF10 Cal Ripken Jr. 1.50 4.00
SF11 Dustin Pedroia .50 1.25
SF12 Will Middlebrooks .30 .75
SF13 Josh Vitters .40 1.00
SF14 Anthony Rizzo .60 1.50
SF15 Andre Dawson .40 1.00
SF16 Jake Peavy .30 .75
SF17 Todd Frazier .30 .75
SF18 Devin Mesoraco .30 .75
SF19 Prince Fielder .40 1.00
SF20 Miguel Cabrera .50 1.25
SF21 Salvador Perez .40 1.00
SF22 A.J. Ellis .30 .75
SF23 Adrian Gonzalez .40 1.00
SF24 Nate Eovaldi .40 1.00
SF25 Jean Segura .40 1.00
SF26 David Wright .40 1.00
SF27 Boone Logan .30 .75
SF28 Jeurys Familia .50 1.25
SF29 Raul Ibanez .40 1.00
SF30 Robinson Cano .40 1.00
SF31 Don Mattingly 1.00 2.50
SF32 Rickey Henderson .50 1.25
SF33 Starling Marte .40 1.00
SF34 Will Clark .40 1.00
SF35 Ken Griffey Jr. 1.00 2.50
SF36 Stan Musial .75 2.00
SF37 Jeff Niemann .30 .75
SF38 Fernando Rodney .30 .75
SF39 Carlos Pena .40 1.00
SF40 Evan Longoria .40 1.00
SF41 Mike Olt .40 1.00
SF42 Jurickson Profar .40 1.00
SF43 Josh Hamilton .40 1.00
SF44 Jose Bautista .40 1.00
SF45 Bryce Harper .75 2.00
SF46 Ted Williams 1.00 2.50
SF47 Joey Votto .50 1.25
SF48 Matt Kemp .40 1.00
SF49 Ryan Braun .40 1.00
SF50 Buster Posey .60 1.50

2013 Topps Spring Fever Autographs

PRINT RUNS B/WN 10-451 COPIES PER
NO PRICING ON QTY 15 OR LESS
AD Andre Dawson/51 20.00 50.00
AE A.J. Ellis/155 8.00 20.00
AG Adrian Gonzalez/51 4.00 10.00
AR Anthony Rizzo/68 15.00 40.00
BL Boone Logan/151 8.00 20.00
CP Carlos Pena/138 6.00 15.00
CR Cal Ripken Jr./26 75.00 150.00
DP Dustin Pedroia/101 12.00 30.00
EL Evan Longoria/51 40.00 80.00
FR Fernando Rodney/174 6.00 15.00
JB Jose Bautista/101 20.00 50.00
JF Jeurys Familia/152 6.00 15.00
JH Josh Hamilton/51 30.00 60.00
JN Jeff Niemann/192 6.00 15.00
JP Jake Peavy/51 6.00 15.00
JS Jean Segura/316 6.00 15.00
JV Josh Vitters/451 8.00 20.00
MM Manny Machado/72 40.00 80.00
MT Mike Trout/51 100.00 200.00
NM Nick Markakis/345 8.00 20.00
OC Orlando Cepeda/176 10.00 25.00
RC Robinson Cano/58 12.50 30.00
RH Rickey Henderson/26 30.00 80.00
RI Raul Ibanez/113 8.00 20.00
SM Starling Marte/29 15.00 40.00
SMU Stan Musial/26
SP Salvador Perez/169 12.50 30.00
TH Tommy Hanson/151 12.50 30.00
TS Tyler Skaggs/110 8.00 20.00
WC Will Clark/44 20.00 50.00

2013 Topps Silk Collection

SERIES 1 ODDS 1:614 HOBBY
UPDATE ODDS 1:313 HOBBY
STATED PRINT RUN 50 SER.#'d SETS
CARDS LISTED ALPHABETICALLY
SC1 Dustin Ackley S1 6.00 15.00
SC2 Matt Adams UPD 6.00 15.00
SC3 Mike Adams UPD 6.00 15.00
SC4 Al Alburquerque UPD 6.00 15.00
SC5 Yonder Alonso S1 6.00 15.00
SC6 Jose Altuve S1 8.00 20.00
SC7 Pedro Alvarez S2 6.00 15.00
SC8 Robert Andino UPD 6.00 15.00
SC9 Elvis Andrus S2 8.00 20.00
SC10 Nolan Arenado UPD 60.00 150.00
SC11 Dylan Axelrod UPD 6.00 15.00
SC12 John Axford S1 6.00 15.00
SC13 Andrew Bailey UPD 6.00 15.00
SC14 Grant Balfour S2 6.00 15.00
SC15 Daniel Bard UPD 6.00 15.00
SC16 Trevor Bauer S1 12.00 30.00
SC17 Trevor Bauer UPD 12.00 30.00
SC18 Jose Bautista S2 8.00 20.00
SC19 Jason Bay UPD 8.00 20.00
SC20 Josh Beckett S1 6.00 15.00
SC21 Erik Bedard UPD 6.00 15.00
SC22 Brandon Belt S2 8.00 20.00
SC23 Carlos Beltran S2 8.00 20.00
SC24 Adrian Beltre S1 10.00 25.00
SC25 Quintin Berry UPD 4.00 10.00
SC26 Wilson Betemit UPD 6.00 15.00
SC27 Chad Billingsley S1 8.00 20.00
SC28 Kyle Blanks UPD 6.00 15.00
SC29 Joe Blanton UPD 6.00 15.00
SC30 Willie Bloomquist UPD 6.00 15.00
SC31 Mitchell Boggs UPD 6.00 15.00
SC32 Ryan Braun S1 8.00 20.00
SC33 Zach Britton UPD 8.00 20.00
SC34 Jay Bruce S2 8.00 20.00
SC35 Mark Buehrle S2 8.00 20.00
SC36 Madison Bumgarner S2 8.00 20.00
SC37 Billy Butler S2 6.00 15.00
SC38 Asdrubal Cabrera S2 8.00 20.00
SC39 Melky Cabrera S2 6.00 15.00
SC40 Miguel Cabrera S2 10.00 25.00
SC41 Matt Cain S2 8.00 20.00
SC42 Robinson Cano S2 8.00 20.00
SC43 Chris Carpenter S2 8.00 20.00
SC44 Chris Carter UPD 6.00 15.00
SC45 Starlin Castro S1 6.00 15.00
SC46 Yoenis Cespedes S2 10.00 25.00
SC47 Joba Chamberlain UPD 6.00 15.00
SC48 Aroldis Chapman S2 10.00 25.00
SC49 Endy Chavez UPD 6.00 15.00
SC50 Eric Chavez UPD 6.00 15.00
SC51 Randy Choate UPD 10.00 25.00
SC52 Shin-Soo Choo S1 8.00 20.00
SC53 Shin-Soo Choo UPD 8.00 20.00
SC54 Tyler Clippard S1 6.00 15.00
SC55 Tim Collins UPD 6.00 15.00
SC56 Ryan Cook S1 6.00 15.00
SC57 Kevin Correia UPD 6.00 15.00
SC58 Carl Crawford S2 8.00 20.00
SC59 Nelson Cruz S2 10.00 25.00
SC60 Johnny Cueto S1 8.00 20.00
SC61 Yu Darvish S1 10.00 25.00
SC62 Wade Davis UPD 6.00 15.00
SC63 Ryan Dempster S2 6.00 15.00
SC64 Ian Desmond S1 6.00 15.00
SC65 Scott Diamond S2 6.00 15.00
SC66 R.A. Dickey S1 8.00 20.00
SC67 R.A. Dickey S2 8.00 20.00
SC68 Stephen Drew UPD 6.00 15.00
SC69 Danny Duffy UPD 6.00 15.00
SC70 Adam Dunn S2 8.00 20.00
SC71 Jacoby Ellsbury S1 8.00 20.00
SC72 Edwin Encarnacion S1 10.00 25.00
SC73 Andre Ethier S1 8.00 20.00
SC74 Scott Feldman UPD 6.00 15.00
SC75 Neftali Feliz S1 6.00 15.00
SC76 Prince Fielder S1 8.00 20.00
SC77 Nick Franklin UPD 8.00 20.00
SC78 Freddie Freeman S1 12.00 30.00
SC79 David Freese S2 6.00 15.00
SC80 Christian Friedrich UPD 6.00 15.00
SC81 Rafael Furcal S1 6.00 15.00
SC82 Yovani Gallardo S1 6.00 15.00
SC83 Mat Gamel UPD 4.00 10.00
SC84 Jaime Garcia S1 8.00 20.00
SC85 Matt Garza S2 6.00 15.00
SC86 Kevin Gausman UPD 20.00 50.00
SC87 Jason Giambi UPD 6.00 15.00
SC88 Paul Goldschmidt S2 10.00 25.00
SC89 Adrian Gonzalez S1 8.00 20.00
SC90 Carlos Gonzalez S1 8.00 20.00
SC91 Gio Gonzalez S2 8.00 20.00
SC92 Alex Gordon S1 8.00 20.00
SC93 Yasmani Grandal S2 6.00 15.00
SC94 Curtis Granderson S1 8.00 20.00
SC95 Kevin Gregg UPD 6.00 15.00
SC96 Didi Gregorius UPD 25.00 60.00
SC97 Zack Greinke S2 10.00 25.00
SC98 Justin Grimm UPD 6.00 15.00
SC99 Travis Hafner UPD 6.00 15.00
SC100 Scott Hairston UPD 6.00 15.00
SC101 Roy Halladay S2 8.00 20.00
SC102 Cole Hamels S2 8.00 20.00
SC103 Josh Hamilton S2 8.00 20.00
SC104 Aaron Harang UPD 6.00 15.00
SC105 Dan Haren S1 6.00 15.00
SC106 Dan Haren UPD 6.00 15.00
SC107 Bryce Harper S1 15.00 40.00
SC108 Corey Hart S2 6.00 15.00
SC109 Matt Harvey S2 8.00 20.00
SC110 Chase Headley S2 6.00 15.00
SC111 Adeiny Hechavarria UPD 8.00 20.00
SC112 Jeremy Hellickson S1 6.00 15.00
SC113 Todd Helton S2 8.00 20.00
SC114 Jim Henderson UPD 8.00 20.00
SC115 Felix Hernandez S1 8.00 20.00
SC116 Kelvin Herrera UPD 6.00 15.00
SC117 Jason Heyward S1 8.00 20.00
SC118 Greg Holland UPD 6.00 15.00
SC119 Matt Holliday S1 10.00 25.00
SC120 Eric Hosmer S1 8.00 20.00
SC121 Ryan Howard S1 8.00 20.00
SC122 Tim Hudson S1 8.00 20.00
SC123 Torii Hunter S2 6.00 15.00
SC124 Hisashi Iwakuma S2 8.00 20.00
SC125 Maicer Izturis UPD 6.00 15.00
SC126 Austin Jackson S2 6.00 15.00
SC127 Edwin Jackson S1 6.00 15.00
SC128 Edwin Jackson UPD 6.00 15.00
SC129 Desmond Jennings S1 8.00 20.00
SC130 Ubaldo Jimenez S2 6.00 15.00
SC131 Chris Johnson UPD 6.00 15.00
SC132 Elliot Johnson UPD 6.00 15.00
SC133 Jim Johnson S1 6.00 15.00
SC134 Josh Johnson S1 8.00 20.00
SC135 Josh Johnson S2 8.00 20.00
SC136 Adam Jones S1 8.00 20.00
SC137 Garrett Jones S2 6.00 15.00
SC138 Ryan Kalish UPD 6.00 15.00
SC139 Scott Kazmir UPD 6.00 15.00
SC140 Don Kelly UPD 6.00 15.00
SC141 Ian Kennedy S1 6.00 15.00
SC142 Clayton Kershaw S1
SC143 Craig Kimbrel S1 8.00 20.00
SC144 Ian Kinsler S2 8.00 20.00
SC145 Paul Konerko S1 8.00 20.00
SC146 Casey Kotchman UPD 6.00 15.00
SC147 Hiroki Kuroda S1 6.00 15.00
SC148 Mat Latos S1 8.00 20.00
SC149 Brett Lawrie S1 8.00 20.00
SC150 Cliff Lee S1 8.00 20.00
SC151 Jon Lester S2 8.00 20.00
SC152 Tim Lincecum S1 8.00 20.00
SC153 Francisco Liriano UPD 6.00 15.00
SC154 Kyle Lohse UPD 6.00 15.00
SC155 Evan Longoria S1 8.00 20.00
SC156 Jed Lowrie UPD 6.00 15.00
SC157 Jonathan Lucroy S2 8.00 20.00
SC158 Lance Lynn S2 6.00 15.00
SC159 Ryan Madson S2 6.00 15.00
SC160 Shaun Marcum UPD 6.00 15.00
SC161 Nick Markakis S2 8.00 20.00
SC162 Russell Martin UPD 6.00 15.00
SC163 Carlos Martinez UPD 10.00 25.00
SC164 J.D. Martinez S2 10.00 25.00
SC165 Justin Masterson S1 6.00 15.00
SC166 Daisuke Matsuzaka UPD 8.00 20.00
SC167 Brian McCann S1 8.00 20.00
SC168 Andrew McCutchen S1 10.00 25.00
SC169 James McDonald S2 6.00 15.00
SC170 Kris Medlen S2 8.00 20.00
SC171 Will Middlebrooks S1 6.00 15.00
SC172 Wade Miley S2 6.00 15.00
SC173 Tommy Milone S2 6.00 15.00
SC174 Yadier Molina S1 12.00 30.00
SC175 Jesus Montero S2 6.00 15.00
SC176 Matt Moore S2 8.00 20.00
SC177 Kendrys Morales S1 6.00 15.00
SC178 Kendrys Morales UPD 6.00 15.00
SC179 Justin Morneau S2 8.00 20.00
SC180 Logan Morrison S2 6.00 15.00
SC181 Brandon Morrow UPD 6.00 15.00
SC182 Michael Morse UPD 6.00 15.00
SC183 Charlie Morton UPD 10.00 25.00
SC184 Mike Moustakas S1 8.00 20.00
SC185 Joe Nathan S1 6.00 15.00
SC186 Laynce Nix UPD 6.00 15.00
SC187 Derek Norris S2 6.00 15.00
SC188 Ivan Nova S1 8.00 20.00
SC189 Miguel Olivo UPD 4.00 10.00
SC190 David Ortiz S2 10.00 25.00
SC191 Marcell Ozuna UPD 15.00 40.00
SC192 Jonathan Papelbon S2 8.00 20.00
SC193 Jake Peavy S2 6.00 15.00
SC194 Dustin Pedroia S1 10.00 25.00
SC195 Carlos Pena S2 8.00 20.00
SC196 Hunter Pence S1 8.00 20.00
SC197 Cliff Pennington UPD 6.00 15.00
SC198 Wily Peralta S2 6.00 15.00
SC199 Chris Perez S2 6.00 15.00
SC200 Salvador Perez S2 8.00 20.00
SC201 Andy Pettitte S2 8.00 20.00
SC202 Brandon Phillips S2 6.00 15.00
SC203 A.J. Pierzynski UPD 6.00 15.00
SC204 Trevor Plouffe S2 6.00 15.00
SC205 Buster Posey S1 12.00 30.00
SC206 David Price S2 8.00 20.00
SC207 Yasiel Puig UPD 25.00 60.00
SC208 Albert Pujols S2 12.00 30.00
SC209 Nick Punto UPD 6.00 15.00
SC210 Carlos Quentin S2 6.00 15.00
SC211 Ryan Raburn UPD 6.00 15.00
SC212 Aramis Ramirez S2 6.00 15.00
SC213 Hanley Ramirez S2 8.00 20.00
SC214 Colby Rasmus S1 8.00 20.00
SC215 Jon Rauch UPD 6.00 15.00
SC216 Josh Reddick S1 6.00 15.00
SC217 Anthony Rendon UPD 40.00 100.00
SC218 Ben Revere S2 6.00 15.00
SC219 Jose Reyes S1 8.00 20.00
SC220 Mark Reynolds S1 6.00 15.00
SC221 Mariano Rivera S2 12.00 30.00
SC222 Anthony Rizzo S1 12.00 30.00
SC223 Ryan Roberts UPD 6.00 15.00
SC224 Fernando Rodney S2 6.00 15.00
SC225 Alex Rodriguez S1 12.00 30.00
SC226 Jimmy Rollins S1 8.00 20.00
SC227 Bruce Rondon UPD 6.00 15.00
SC228 Wilin Rosario S2 6.00 15.00
SC229 Cody Ross S2 6.00 15.00
SC230 Carlos Ruiz S2 6.00 15.00
SC231 James Russell UPD 6.00 15.00
SC232 Hyun-Jin Ryu S2 15.00 40.00
SC233 CC Sabathia S1 8.00 20.00
SC234 Chris Sale S1 10.00 25.00
SC235 Jarrod Saltalamacchia S1 6.00 15.00
SC236 Jeff Samardzija S1 6.00 15.00
SC237 Alex Sanabia UPD 6.00 15.00
SC238 Anibal Sanchez S2 6.00 15.00
SC239 Jonathan Sanchez UPD 4.00 10.00
SC240 Pablo Sandoval S2 8.00 20.00
SC241 Carlos Santana S1 8.00 20.00
SC242 Ervin Santana S2 6.00 15.00
SC243 Johan Santana S2 8.00 20.00
SC244 Skip Schumaker UPD 6.00 15.00
SC245 Luke Scott UPD 6.00 15.00
SC246 Marco Scutaro S2 8.00 20.00
SC247 Jean Segura S2 8.00 20.00
SC248 James Shields S1 6.00 15.00
SC249 James Shields UPD 6.00 15.00
SC250 Andrelton Simmons S2 6.00 15.00
SC251 Eric Sogard UPD 6.00 15.00
SC252 Rafael Soriano S1 6.00 15.00
SC253 Rafael Soriano UPD 6.00 15.00
SC254 Denard Span UPD 6.00 15.00
SC255 Giancarlo Stanton S1 10.00 25.00
SC256 Stephen Strasburg S2 10.00 25.00
SC257 Huston Street S2 6.00 15.00
SC258 Drew Stubbs UPD 6.00 15.00
SC259 Nick Swisher S2 8.00 20.00
SC260 Mark Teixeira S1 8.00 20.00
SC261 Miguel Tejada UPD 6.00 15.00
SC262 Chris Tillman UPD 6.00 15.00
SC263 Mike Trout S1 80.00 200.00
SC264 Mark Trumbo S2 6.00 15.00
SC265 Troy Tulowitzki S2 10.00 25.00
SC266 Jacob Turner S2 8.00 20.00
SC267 Dan Uggla S1 6.00 15.00
SC268 B.J. Upton S2 8.00 20.00
SC269 Justin Upton S1 8.00 20.00
SC270 Justin Upton UPD 8.00 20.00
SC271 Juan Uribe UPD 6.00 15.00
SC272 Chase Utley S1 8.00 20.00
SC273 Jason Vargas UPD 6.00 15.00
SC274 Jose Veras UPD 6.00 15.00
SC275 Justin Verlander S1 10.00 25.00
SC276 Shane Victorino S2 8.00 20.00
SC277 Edinson Volquez S1 6.00 15.00
SC278 Joey Votto S1 10.00 25.00
SC279 Adam Wainwright S1 8.00 20.00
SC280 Neil Walker S2 6.00 15.00
SC281 Jered Weaver S1 8.00 20.00
SC282 Rickie Weeks S1 6.00 15.00
SC283 Vernon Wells UPD 6.00 15.00
SC284 Jayson Werth S1 8.00 20.00
SC285 Ty Wigginton UPD 6.00 15.00
SC286 Brian Wilson S1 10.00 25.00

SC287 C.J. Wilson S2 6.00 15.00
SC288 Dewayne Wise UPD 6.00 15.00
SC289 Vance Worley UPD 8.00 20.00
SC290 David Wright S2 8.00 20.00
SC291 Kevin Youkilis S1 6.00 15.00
SC292 Kevin Youkilis UPD 6.00 15.00
SC293 Delmon Young S1 8.00 20.00
SC294 Delmon Young UPD 8.00 20.00
SC295 Michael Young S1 6.00 15.00
SC296 Michael Young UPD 6.00 15.00
SC297 Ryan Zimmerman S1 8.00 20.00
SC298 Jordan Zimmermann S2 8.00 20.00
SC299 Barry Zito S1 8.00 20.00
SC300 Ben Zobrist S1 8.00 20.00

2013 Topps Silver Slugger Award Winners Trophy

STATED ODDS 1:1674 HOBBY
AB Adrian Beltre 6.00 15.00
ABE Albert Belle 4.00 10.00
AD Andre Dawson 5.00 12.00
AR Alex Rodriguez 8.00 20.00
CF Carlton Fisk 5.00 12.00
CG Curtis Granderson 5.00 12.00
CGO Carlos Gonzalez 5.00 12.00
DM Dale Murphy 6.00 15.00
DMA Don Mattingly 12.00 30.00
DO David Ortiz 6.00 15.00
DS Darryl Strawberry 4.00 10.00
EM Eddie Murray 5.00 12.00
JB Jose Bautista 5.00 12.00
JR Jim Rice 5.00 12.00
KG Ken Griffey Jr. 12.00 30.00
MK Matt Kemp 5.00 12.00
MR Manny Ramirez 4.00 10.00
MS Mike Schmidt 10.00 25.00
PF Prince Fielder 5.00 12.00
RH Ryan Howard 5.00 12.00
RY Robin Yount 6.00 15.00
TG Tony Gwynn 6.00 15.00
TH Todd Helton 5.00 12.00
TT Troy Tulowitzki 6.00 15.00
WB Wade Boggs 5.00 12.00

2013 Topps The Elite

COMPLETE SET (20) 10.00 25.00
STATED ODDS 1:18 HOBBY
TE1 Miguel Cabrera .75 2.00
TE2 Ryan Braun .60 1.50
TE3 Josh Hamilton .60 1.50
TE4 Tom Seaver .60 1.50
TE5 Sandy Koufax 1.50 4.00
TE6 Nolan Ryan 2.50 6.00
TE7 Reggie Jackson .60 1.50
TE8 Rickey Henderson .75 2.00
TE9 Johnny Bench .75 2.00
TE10 Ernie Banks .75 2.00
TE11 Ozzie Smith 1.00 2.50
TE12 Bob Gibson .60 1.50
TE13 Joe Morgan .60 1.50
TE14 Buster Posey 1.00 2.50
TE15 Willie Mays 1.50 4.00
TE16 Mike Schmidt 1.25 3.00
TE17 Babe Ruth 2.00 5.00
TE18 Ted Williams 1.50 4.00
TE19 Jackie Robinson .75 2.00
TE20 Lou Gehrig 1.50 4.00

2013 Topps The Elite Gold

*GOLD: 2.5X TO 6X BASIC
STATED ODDS 1:1050 HOBBY
STATED PRINT RUN 99 SER.#'d SETS

2013 Topps The Elite Red

*RED: 3X TO 8X BASIC
STATED PRINT RUN 50 SER.#'d SETS

2013 Topps The Greatest Chase Relic

STATED ODDS 1:119,550 HOBBY
STATED PRINT RUN 50 SER.#'d SETS
TW Ted Williams 50.00 100.00

2013 Topps The Greats

COMPLETE SET (30) 50.00 100.00
STATED ODDS 1:18 HOBBY
TG1 Roberto Clemente 2.50 6.00
TG2 Willie Mays 2.00 5.00
TG3 Babe Ruth 2.50 6.00
TG4 Ernie Banks 1.00 2.50
TG5 Ted Williams 2.00 5.00
TG6 Jimmie Foxx 1.00 2.50
TG7 Ken Griffey Jr. 2.00 5.00
TG8 Mike Schmidt 1.50 4.00
TG9 Rickey Henderson 1.00 2.50
TG10 Nolan Ryan 3.00 8.00
TG11 John Smoltz 1.00 2.50
TG12 Johnny Bench 1.00 2.50
TG13 Reggie Jackson .75 2.00
TG14 Stan Musial 1.50 4.00
TG15 Bob Gibson .75 2.00
TG16 Tom Seaver .75 2.00
TG17 Chipper Jones 1.00 2.50
TG18 Tony Gwynn 1.00 2.50
TG19 Willie McCovey .75 2.00
TG20 Tom Glavine .60 1.50
TG21 Joe Morgan .75 2.00
TG22 Hank Aaron 2.00 5.00
TG23 Yogi Berra 1.00 2.50
TG24 Sandy Koufax 2.00 5.00
TG25 Albert Pujols 1.25 3.00
TG26 Derek Jeter 2.50 6.00
TG27 Alex Rodriguez 1.25 3.00
TG28 Roy Halladay .75 2.00
TG29 Mariano Rivera 1.25 3.00
TG30 Cal Ripken Jr. 3.00 8.00

2013 Topps The Greats Gold

*GOLD: 2X TO 5X BASIC
STATED ODDS 1:1034 HOBBY
STATED PRINT RUN 99 SER.#'d SETS

2013 Topps The Greats Red

*RED: 3X TO 8X BASIC
STATED PRINT RUN 50 SER.#'d SETS

2013 Topps Triple Crown Relics

COMMON CARD 20.00 50.00
STATED ODDS 1:432 HOBBY
EXCHANGE DEADLINE 01/31/2016

2013 Topps WBC Stars

COMPLETE SET (15) 5.00 12.00
STATED ODDS 1:8
WBC1 Jose Reyes .40 1.00
WBC2 Anthony Rizzo .60 1.50
WBC3 Joey Votto .50 1.25
WBC4 Robinson Cano .40 1.00
WBC5 Hanley Ramirez .40 1.00
WBC6 Giancarlo Stanton .50 1.25
WBC7 Adrian Gonzalez .40 1.00
WBC8 Justin Morneau .40 1.00
WBC9 Carlos Beltran .40 1.00
WBC10 Miguel Cabrera .50 1.25
WBC11 Pablo Sandoval .40 1.00
WBC12 Carlos Gonzalez .40 1.00
WBC13 Joe Mauer .40 1.00
WBC14 David Wright .40 1.00
WBC15 Ryan Braun .40 1.00

2013 Topps World Champion Autograph Relics

STATED ODDS 1:12,247 HOBBY
STATED PRINT RUN 50 SER.#'d SETS
EXCHANGE DEADLINE 01/31/2016
BC Brandon Crawford EXCH 100.00 175.00
BP Buster Posey 250.00 400.00
MB Madison Bumgarner 75.00 200.00
MC Matt Cain EXCH 100.00 175.00
PS Pablo Sandoval 125.00 250.00

2013 Topps World Champion Autographs

STATED ODDS 1:23,579 HOBBY
STATED PRINT RUN 50 SER.#'d SETS
EXCHANGE DEADLINE 01/31/2016
BC Brandon Crawford EXCH 60.00 120.00
BP Buster Posey 150.00 300.00
MB Madison Bumgarner 75.00 150.00
MC Matt Cain 100.00 200.00
PS Pablo Sandoval EXCH 60.00 150.00

2013 Topps World Champion Relics

STATED ODDS 1:3940 HOBBY
STATED PRINT RUN 100 SER.#'d SETS
EXCHANGE DEADLINE 01/31/2016
AP Angel Pagan 20.00 50.00
BB Brandon Belt 30.00 60.00
BC Brandon Crawford EXCH 60.00 120.00
BP Buster Posey 75.00 150.00
BW Brian Wilson 20.00 50.00
BZ Barry Zito 12.50 30.00
HP Hunter Pence 30.00 60.00
MB Madison Bumgarner 40.00 80.00
MC Matt Cain 15.00 40.00
MS Marco Scutaro 20.00 50.00
PS Pablo Sandoval 60.00 120.00
RT Ryan Theriot 20.00 50.00
RV Ryan Vogelsong 12.50 30.00
TL Tim Lincecum 60.00 120.00
XN Xavier Nady 12.50 30.00

2013 Topps World Series MVP Award Winners Trophy

STATED ODDS 1:2300 HOBBY
BG Bob Gibson 8.00 20.00
BR Brooks Robinson 8.00 20.00
CH Cole Hamels 6.00 15.00
DF David Freese 6.00 15.00
DJ Derek Jeter 10.00 25.00
MR Mariano Rivera 8.00 20.00
MS Mike Schmidt 8.00 20.00
PM Paul Molitor 6.00 15.00
PS Pablo Sandoval 8.00 20.00
RC Roberto Clemente 12.50 30.00
RJ Reggie Jackson 6.00 15.00
RJA Reggie Jackson 6.00 15.00
SK Sandy Koufax 10.00 25.00
WF Whitey Ford 6.00 15.00
WS Willie Stargell 6.00 15.00

2013 Topps Update

COMPLETE SET w/o SP's (330) 60.00 150.00
PRINTING PLATE ODDS 1:1182 HOBBY
PLATE PRINT RUN 1 SET PER COLOR
BLACK-CYAN-MAGENTA-YELLOW ISSUED
NO PLATE PRICING DUE TO SCARCITY
US1A Matt Harvey .20 .50
US1B Harvey SP AS Jsy 4.00 10.00
US1C Tom Seaver SP 30.00 80.00
US2 Trevor Bauer .30 .75
US3 Chad Qualls .15 .40
US4 Matt Adams .15 .40
US5 Chris Sale .25 .60
US6 Joel Peralta .15 .40
US7A Yoenis Cespedes .25 .60
US7B Cespedes SP High five 4.00 10.00
US7C Cespedes SP Group pic 4.00 10.00
US8 Anthony Rendon RC 6.00 15.00
US9 Cody Allen RC .25 .60
US10 Kevin Youkilis .15 .40
US11 Joakim Soria .15 .40
US12 Brandon Phillips .15 .40
US13 Jose Fernandez .40 1.00
US14 Joe Saunders .15 .40
US15 DJ LeMahieu .25 .60
US16A Alex Gordon .20 .50
US16B Bo Jackson SP 4.00 10.00
US17 Justin Grimm RC .25 .60
US18 Ross Ohlendorf .15 .40
US19 Johnny Hellweg RC .25 .60
US20 Carlos Gomez .15 .40
US21 Junior Lake RC .25 .60
US22 Carlos Beltran .20 .50
US23 Mike Olt RC .30 .75
US24 Ryan Raburn .15 .40
US25 Wade Davis .15 .40
US26 Wil Myers .25 .60
US27 Eric Hinske .15 .40
US28 Pedro Alvarez .15 .40
US29 Scott Van Slyke RC .30 .75
US30 Mike Adams .15 .40
US31 Edwin Encarnacion .25 .60
US32 Adeiny Hechavarria RC .30 .75
US33 Garrett Richards .20 .50
US34 A.J. Pollock .20 .50
US35A Andrew McCutchen .25 .60
US35B McCutch SP Horizontal 4.00 10.00
US36 Daisuke Matsuzaka .20 .50
US37 Cliff Pennington .15 .40
US38 Denard Span .15 .40
US39 Shin-Soo Choo .20 .50
US40 Tim Collins .15 .40
US41 Dan Haren .15 .40
US42 Rafael Betancourt .15 .40
US43 Luke Putkonen .15 .40
US44 Jason Bay .20 .50
US45 Joey Terdoslavich RC .25 .60
US46 Yasiel Puig .60 1.50
US47 Matt Garza .15 .40
US48 Vance Worley .20 .50
US49 Marlon Byrd .15 .40
US50 Zack Wheeler RC .50 1.25
US51 Brett Marshall RC .30 .75
US52 Chris Davis .20 .50
US53A Craig Kimbrel .20 .50
US53B Kimbrel SP In dugout 4.00 10.00
US53C Hank Aaron SP 15.00 40.00
US53D Chipper Jones SP 4.00 10.00
US54 Jason Giambi .15 .40
US55 Pete Kozma .15 .40
US56 Kyuji Fujikawa RC .40 1.00
US57 Dayan Viciedo .15 .40
US58 Kevin Frandsen .15 .40
US59 Hisashi Iwakuma .20 .50
US60 Chris Tillman .15 .40
US61 Rafael Soriano .15 .40
US62 Carlos Villanueva .15 .40
US63 Clay Buchholz .15 .40
US64 Mark Reynolds .15 .40
US65 Ryan Roberts .15 .40
US66 James Russell .15 .40
US67 Kyle McClellan .15 .40
US68 Nick Franklin RC .30 .75
US69 Martin Perez .20 .50
US70 Joe Mauer .20 .50
US71 Cody Asche RC .40 1.00
US72 Adam Jones .20 .50
US73A Buster Posey .30 .75
US73B Will Clark SP 40.00 80.00
US73C Willie Mays SP 40.00 80.00
US74 Kyle Blanks .15 .40
US75 Ty Wigginton .15 .40
US76 Roy Oswalt .20 .50
US77 Kelvin Herrera .15 .40
US78 Francisco Rodriguez .20 .50
US79A Yu Darvish .25 .60
US79B Darvish SP Glasses on 4.00 10.00
US80 Zoilo Almonte RC .30 .75
US81 Casey Kotchman .15 .40
US82 Bryan Petersen .15 .40
US83 Alex Sanabia .15 .40
US84 Stephen Drew .15 .40
US85 Pedro Strop .15 .40
US86 Chad Gaudin .15 .40
US87 Evan Gattis .30 .75
US88A Troy Tulowitzki .25 .60
US88B Tulo SP w/Teammates 4.00 10.00
US89 Michael Pineda .15 .40
US90 Michael Young .15 .40
US91 Prince Fielder .20 .50
US92 Jeanmar Gomez .15 .40
US93 Adam Wainwright .20 .50
US94 Joba Chamberlain .15 .40
US95 Eric Chavez .15 .40
US96 Mark DeRosa .15 .40
US97 Alexi Amarista .15 .40
US98 Salvador Perez .20 .50
US99 Derrick Robinson RC .25 .60
US100 Bryce Harper .40 1.00
US101 Jonathan Villar RC .40 1.00
US102 Christian Friedrich .15 .40
US103 Michael Morse .15 .40
US104 Matt Carpenter .25 .60
US105 Corey Kluber RC .75 2.00
US106 Clayton Kershaw .40 1.00
US107 Andrew Bailey .15 .40
US108 Ryan Kalish .15 .40
US109 Jose Dominguez RC .25 .60
US110 Kole Calhoun .15 .40
US111 Scott Hairston .15 .40
US112 Luke Gregerson .15 .40
US113 Samuel Deduno .15 .40
US114A Dustin Pedroia .25 .60
US114B Nomar Garciaparra SP 4.00 10.00
US114C Wade Boggs SP 40.00 80.00
US115 Drew Stubbs .15 .40
US116 Mike Kickham RC .25 .60
US117 Willie Bloomquist .15 .40
US118 Joe Blanton .15 .40
US119A Felix Hernandez .20 .50
US119B Griffey Jr. SP Blk jsy 6.00 15.00
US119C Griffey Jr. SP Red jsy 20.00 50.00
US120 Matt Tuiasosopo .15 .40
US121 Jason Frasor .15 .40
US122 Danny Duffy .15 .40
US123 Tom Gorzelanny .15 .40
US124 Jason Kipnis .20 .50
US125 J.J. Hardy .15 .40
US126 Mike Zunino RC .40 1.00
US127 David Phelps .15 .40
US128 Bartolo Colon .15 .40
US129 David Wright .20 .50
US130 Jesse Chavez .15 .40
US131 Josh Phegley RC .25 .60
US132 Ronald Belisario .15 .40
US133 Jose Fernandez .40 1.00
US134A Justin Verlander .25 .60
US134B Verland SP Blue jsy 4.00 10.00
US135 Dewayne Wise .15 .40
US136 Travis Hafner .15 .40
US137 Yoervis Medina RC .25 .60
US138 Danny Salazar RC .50 1.25
US139 John Jaso .15 .40
US140A Justin Upton .20 .50
US140B Tony Gwynn SP 30.00 60.00
US141 Chris Carter .15 .40
US142A Yadier Molina .30 .75
US142B Molina SP Orange jsy 5.00 12.00
US143 Tim Lincecum .20 .50
US144 Drake Britton RC .30 .75
US145 Michael Cuddyer .15 .40
US146 Didi Gregorius RC 1.00 2.50
US147 Charlie Morton .25 .60
US148 Ben Zobrist .20 .50
US149 Daniel Bard .15 .40
US150A Gerrit Cole RC 5.00 12.00
US150B G.Cole SP Blk jsy 40.00 80.00
US151 Shawn Kelley .15 .40
US152 Randy Choate .25 .60
US153 Jeff Francoeur .20 .50
US154 Kyle Gibson RC .40 1.00
US155 J.B. Shuck RC .25 .60
US156 Laynce Nix .15 .40
US157 Marco Scutaro .20 .50
US158 Erasmo Ramirez .15 .40
US159 Donald Lutz RC .25 .60
US160 Lyle Overbay .15 .40
US161 Jim Henderson RC .30 .75
US162 Mark Melancon .15 .40
US163 Chris Davis .20 .50
US164 Robert Andino .15 .40
US165 A.J. Pierzynski .15 .40
US166 Kevin Gregg .15 .40
US167 Randall Delgado .15 .40
US168 Michael Wacha RC .30 .75
US169 Ezequiel Carrera .15 .40
US170 Miguel Tejada .15 .40
US171 Nick Punto .15 .40
US172 Blake Parker .15 .40
US173 Reed Johnson .15 .40
US174 Jose Mijares .15 .40
US175 Carlos Martinez RC .40 1.00
US176 Matt Lindstrom .15 .40
US177 David Ortiz .25 .60
US178 Derek Dietrich RC .30 .75
US179 Joe Smith .20 .50
US180A Bryce Harper .40 1.00
US180B Harper SP Group pic 4.00 10.00
US181 Oliver Perez .15 .40
US182 Luis Valbuena .15 .40
US183 Jeff Bianchi .15 .40
US184 Dioner Navarro .15 .40
US185 Daniel Nava .15 .40
US186 Jake Elmore .15 .40
US187 Wilson Betemit .15 .40
US188A Cliff Lee .20 .50
US188B John Kruk SP 15.00 40.00
US189 Kyle Lohse .15 .40
US190 Steve Delabar .15 .40
US191 Ricky Nolasco .15 .40
US192 Hyun-Jin Ryu .40 1.00
US193A Max Scherzer .25 .60
US193B Scherz SP Blue jsy 4.00 10.00
US194 Xavier Paul .15 .40
US195 Chris Johnson .15 .40
US196 Brayan Pena .15 .40
US197 Josh Collmenter .15 .40
US198 Brian Bogusevic .15 .40
US199 Juan Lagares RC .30 .75
US200A Wil Myers RC .40 1.00
US200B Myers SP Group pic 40.00 80.00
US201 Adam Ottavino .15 .40
US202 Yoenis Cespedes .25 .60
US203 Russell Martin .15 .40
US204 Mike Pelfrey .15 .40
US205A Prince Fielder .20 .50
US205B Prince George SP 40.00 80.00
US206 Reid Brignac .15 .40
US207 Matt Thornton .15 .40
US208 Juan Uribe .15 .40
US209 Anthony Swarzak .15 .40
US210 Matt Albers .15 .40
US211 Jarred Cosart RC .30 .75
US212 Alfonso Soriano .20 .50
US213 Matt Adams .15 .40
US214 Jean Segura .20 .50
US215 Travis Blackley .15 .40
US216A Manny Machado 1.00 2.50
US216B Ripken SP White jsy 40.00 80.00
US216C Ripken SP Blk jsy 6.00 15.00
US217 Elliot Johnson .15 .40
US218A Miguel Cabrera .25 .60
US218B Cabrera SP Group pic 4.00 10.00
US219 Pedro Alvarez .15 .40
US220 Zack Wheeler .30 .75
US221 Allen Craig .20 .50
US222 Erik Bedard .15 .40
US223 Jose Valverde .15 .40
US224 Brad Miller RC .30 .75
US225 Chris Getz .15 .40
US226 Michael Cuddyer .15 .40
US227 Carlos Gonzalez .20 .50
US228 Matt Moore .20 .50
US229 Jason Vargas .15 .40
US230 Scott Kazmir .15 .40
US231 Scott Feldman .15 .40
US232 Al Alburquerque .15 .40
US233 Anthony Rendon 3.00 8.00
US234 Jurickson Profar .20 .50
US235 Jose Iglesias .20 .50
US236 Shaun Marcum .15 .40
US237 Mariano Rivera .30 .75
US238 Eric Young Jr. .15 .40
US239 Justin Masterson .15 .40
US240 Paul Goldschmidt .25 .60
US241 Alberto Callaspo .15 .40
US242 Delmon Young .15 .40
US243 Marwin Gonzalez .15 .40
US244 Glen Perkins .15 .40
US245 James Shields .15 .40
US246 Don Kelly .15 .40
US247 Casper Wells .15 .40
US248 Jason Grilli .15 .40
US249 Madison Bumgarner .20 .50
US250A Yasiel Puig RC 1.00 2.50
US250B Puig SP Arms up 50.00 100.00
US250C Puig SP Big glove 12.00 30.00
US250D Puig SP Sliding 75.00 150.00
US251 Aaron Harang .15 .40
US252 Preston Claiborne .15 .40
US253 Shelby Miller .15 .40
US254 Brian Wilson .25 .60
US255 Alex Wood RC .30 .75
US256 Luke Scott .15 .40
US257 Bryan Shaw .15 .40
US258 Jose Bautista .20 .50
US259 Nolan Arenado RC 20.00 50.00
US260 Darren O'Day .15 .40
US261 Skip Schumaker .15 .40
US262 Jayson Nix .15 .40
US263 Austin Romine .15 .40
US264 Nate Freiman RC .25 .60
US265 Gerrit Cole 1.00 2.50
US266 Jed Lowrie .15 .40
US267 Nick Tepesch RC .25 .60
US268A Joey Votto .20 .50
US268B Votto SP Group pic 4.00 10.00
US268C Teddy Kremer SP 100.00 200.00
US269 Kendrys Morales .15 .40
US270 Edwin Jackson .15 .40
US271 Francisco Liriano .15 .40
US272 Josh Thole .15 .40
US273 Jeff Keppinger .15 .40
US274 Kevin Gausman RC .75 2.00
US275 Bud Norris .15 .40
US276A Torii Hunter .15 .40
US276B Hunter SP Group pic 4.00 10.00
US277 Sonny Gray RC .40 1.00
US278 Jose Alvarez RC .25 .60
US279 Marcell Ozuna RC .60 1.50
US280 John Lannan .15 .40
US281 Jonathan Pettibone RC .40 1.00
US282 Brock Peterson (RC) .30 .75
US283 Conor Gillaspie .20 .50
US284 Stephen Pryor .15 .40
US285A David Ortiz .25 .60
US285B Ortiz SP Group pic 5.00 12.00
US286 Aroldis Chapman .25 .60
US287 Brandon Morrow .15 .40
US288 Maicer Izturis .15 .40
US289 Kevin Correia .15 .40
US290 Christian Yelich RC 20.00 50.00
US291 Logan Schafer .15 .40
US292 Zach Britton .20 .50
US293 Robinson Cano .20 .50
US294 Chris Denorfia .15 .40
US295 Sean Burnett .15 .40
US296 Joe Nathan .15 .40
US297 Chris Narveson .15 .40
US298 Luis Avilan RC .25 .60
US299 Ian Kennedy .15 .40
US300A Mike Trout 2.00 5.00
US300B Trout SP w/Cano 5.00 12.00
US301 Juan Francisco .15 .40
US302 Yan Gomes .20 .50
US303 Jose Veras .15 .40
US304 Patrick Corbin .20 .50
US305 Dylan Axelrod .15 .40
US306 Pat Neshek .15 .40
US307 Mike Carp .15 .40
US308 J.P. Howell .15 .40
US309 Domonic Brown .20 .50
US310 Boone Logan .15 .40
US311 Craig Stammen .15 .40
US312 Nate Jones .15 .40
US313A Mariano Rivera .30 .75
US313B Rivera SP Running 5.00 12.00
US313C Rivera SP Out of pen 50.00 100.00
US314 Junichi Tazawa .15 .40
US315 Bruce Rondon RC .25 .60
US316A David Wright .20 .50
US316B Wright SP Group pic 4.00 10.00
US317 Oswaldo Arcia RC .25 .60
US318 Greg Holland .15 .40
US319 Jordan Schafer .15 .40
US320 Chris Archer .15 .40
US321 Grant Green RC .40 1.00
US322 Brandon Inge .15 .40
US323A Robinson Cano .20 .50
US323B Cano SP Glasses 4.00 10.00
US323C Don Mattingly SP 60.00 120.00
US323D Lou Gehrig SP 40.00 80.00
US324 Chris Colabello RC .40 1.00
US325 Vernon Wells .15 .40
US326 Jake Peavy .15 .40
US327 Endy Chavez .15 .40
US328 Eric Sogard .15 .40
US329 Henry Urrutia RC .30 .75
US330 Yasiel Puig .60 1.50

2013 Topps Update Black

*BLACK: 10X TO 25X BASIC
*BLACK RC: 3X TO 8X BASIC
STATED ODDS 1:77 HOBBY
STATED PRINT RUN 62 SER.#'d SETS
US46 Yasiel Puig 30.00 80.00
US205 Prince Fielder 12.50 30.00
US250 Yasiel Puig 30.00 80.00
US259 Nolan Arenado 250.00 600.00
US290 Christian Yelich 300.00 800.00
US330 Yasiel Puig 30.00 80.00

2013 Topps Update Boston Strong

15 Dustin Pedroia 40.00 80.00
32 Craig Breslow 20.00 50.00
64 Will Middlebrooks 15.00 40.00
241 Jacoby Ellsbury 20.00 50.00
301 Jarrod Saltalamacchia 50.00 100.00
348 Jonny Gomes 15.00 40.00
382 Jackie Bradley Jr. 12.50 30.00
399 Shane Victorino 20.00 50.00
401 Ryan Dempster 15.00 40.00
503 Clay Buchholz 10.00 25.00
508 Felix Doubront 12.50 30.00
541 Jon Lester 15.00 40.00
548 John Lackey 12.00 30.00
555 Joel Hanrahan 12.00 30.00
595 David Ortiz 75.00 150.00
618 Koji Uehara 20.00 50.00
644 Ryan Lavarnway 10.00 25.00
659 Mike Napoli 40.00 80.00
US84 Stephen Drew 10.00 25.00
US107 Andrew Bailey 10.00 25.00
US108 Ryan Kalish 10.00 25.00
US144 Drake Britton 30.00 60.00
US149 Daniel Bard 10.00 25.00
US185 Daniel Nava 50.00 100.00
US207 Matt Thornton 10.00 25.00
US307 Mike Carp 20.00 50.00
US314 Junichi Tazawa 10.00 25.00

2013 Topps Update Camo

*CAMO VET: 8X TO 20X BASIC
*CAMO RC: 1.5X TO 4X BASIC RC
STATED ODDS 1:125 HOBBY
STATED PRINT RUN 99 SER.#'d SETS
US35 Andrew McCutchen 12.00 30.00
US46 Yasiel Puig 25.00 60.00
US250 Yasiel Puig 25.00 60.00
US259 Nolan Arenado 200.00 500.00
US290 Christian Yelich 250.00 600.00

2013 Topps Update Emerald

*EMERALD VET: 1.2X TO 3X BASIC
*EMERALD RC: .4X TO 1X BASIC RC
STATED ODDS 1:6 HOBBY
US259 Nolan Arenado 75.00 200.00
US290 Christian Yelich 60.00 150.00

2013 Topps Update Gold

*GOLD VET: 1.2X TO 3X BASIC
*GOLD RC: .4X TO 1X BASIC RC
STATED ODDS 1:6 HOBBY
STATED PRINT RUN 2013 SER.#'d SETS
US259 Nolan Arenado 75.00 200.00
US290 Christian Yelich 75.00 200.00

2013 Topps Update Pink

*PINK VET: 8X TO 20X BASIC
*PINK RC: 2.5X TO 6X BASIC RC
STATED ODDS 1:250 HOBBY
STATED PRINT RUN 50 SER.#'d SETS
US35 Andrew McCutchen 30.00 60.00
US259 Nolan Arenado 200.00 500.00
US290 Christian Yelich 250.00 600.00

2013 Topps Update Target Red Border

*TARGET VET: 1.2X TO 3X BASIC
*TARGET RC: .4X TO 1X BASIC
US259 Nolan Arenado 75.00 200.00
US290 Christian Yelich 75.00 200.00

2013 Topps Update Wal-Mart Blue Border

*WM VET: 1.2X TO 3X BASIC
*WM RC: .4X TO 1X BASIC
US259 Nolan Arenado 75.00 200.00
US290 Christian Yelich 60.00 150.00

2013 Topps Update '71 Topps Minis

COMPLETE SET (50) 20.00 50.00
1 Bryce Harper 1.00 2.50
2 Babe Ruth 1.50 4.00
3 Derek Jeter 1.50 4.00
4 Bo Jackson .60 1.50
5 Ken Griffey Jr. 1.25 3.00
6 Miguel Cabrera .60 1.50
7 Mike Trout 5.00 12.00
8 Joe Mauer .50 1.25
9 Robinson Cano .50 1.25
10 Joey Votto .60 1.50
11 Justin Upton .50 1.25
12 Andrew McCutchen .60 1.50
13 Prince Fielder .50 1.25
14 Troy Tulowitzki .60 1.50
15 Clayton Kershaw 1.00 2.50
16 Jackie Robinson .60 1.50
17 Hyun-Jin Ryu 1.00 2.50
18 Justin Verlander .60 1.50
19 Dustin Pedroia .60 1.50
20 David Wright .50 1.25
21 Ian Kinsler .50 1.25
22 Evan Longoria .50 1.25
23 Adam Jones .50 1.25
24 Greg Maddux .75 2.00
25 Shelby Miller .50 1.25
26 Mariano Rivera .75 2.00
27 Stan Musial 1.00 2.50
28 Johnny Bench .60 1.50
29 Mike Schmidt 1.00 2.50
30 Cal Ripken Jr. 2.00 5.00
31 Yasiel Puig 1.50 4.00
32 Carlos Gonzalez .50 1.25
33 Buster Posey .75 2.00
34 Yu Darvish .60 1.50
35 Paul Goldschmidt .50 1.25
36 Felix Hernandez .50 1.25
37 David Ortiz .60 1.50
38 Will Clark .50 1.25
39 Giancarlo Stanton .50 1.25
40 Nomar Garciaparra .50 1.25
41 Yoenis Cespedes .60 1.50
42 Roberto Clemente 1.50 4.00
43 Frank Thomas .60 1.50
44 Wil Myers .60 1.50
45 Stephen Strasburg .60 1.50
46 George Brett 1.25 3.00
47 Don Mattingly 1.25 3.00
48 Jay Bruce .50 1.25
49 Matt Harvey .50 1.25
50 Manny Machado 2.50 6.00

2013 Topps Update All Star Game MVP Commemorative Patches

1 Willie Mays 8.00 20.00
2 Juan Marichal 4.00 10.00
3 Brooks Robinson 5.00 12.00
4 Tony Perez 4.00 10.00
5 Willie McCovey 4.00 10.00
6 Frank Robinson 4.00 10.00
7 Joe Morgan 4.00 10.00
8 Don Sutton 4.00 10.00
9 Gary Carter 4.00 10.00
10 Bo Jackson 4.00 10.00
11 Ken Griffey Jr. 6.00 15.00
12 Fred McGriff 4.00 10.00
13 Pedro Martinez 6.00 15.00
14 Derek Jeter 8.00 20.00
15 Cal Ripken Jr. 6.00 15.00

2013 Topps Update All Star Stitches

STATED ODDS 1:49 HOBBY
AC Allen Craig 5.00 12.00
ACH Aroldis Chapman 3.00 8.00
AG Alex Gordon 5.00 12.00
AJ Adam Jones 4.00 10.00
AW Adam Wainwright 5.00 12.00
BC Bartolo Colon 3.00 8.00
BH Bryce Harper 10.00 25.00
BP Buster Posey 6.00 15.00
BPH Brandon Phillips 4.00 10.00
BZ Ben Zobrist 3.00 8.00
CB Carlos Beltran 5.00 12.00
CBU Clay Buchholz 4.00 10.00
CD Chris Davis 6.00 15.00
CG Carlos Gonzalez 3.00 8.00
CK Clayton Kershaw 5.00 12.00
CKI Craig Kimbrel 4.00 10.00
CL Cliff Lee 5.00 12.00
CS Chris Sale 3.00 8.00
DB Domonic Brown 4.00 10.00
DO David Ortiz 5.00 12.00
DP Dustin Pedroia 5.00 12.00
DW David Wright 10.00 25.00
EE Edwin Encarnacion 3.00 8.00
FH Felix Hernandez 3.00 8.00
GP Glen Perkins 3.00 8.00
HI Hisashi Iwakuma 4.00 10.00
JB Jose Bautista 4.00 10.00
JF Jose Fernandez 5.00 12.00
JG Jason Grilli 4.00 10.00
JH J.J. Hardy 4.00 10.00
JK Jason Kipnis 4.00 10.00
JM Justin Masterson 4.00 10.00
JMA Joe Mauer 4.00 10.00
JN Joe Nathan 3.00 8.00
JP Jhonny Peralta 3.00 8.00
JS Jean Segura 4.00 10.00
JV Justin Verlander 6.00 15.00
JVO Joey Votto 5.00 12.00
JZ Jordan Zimmermann 4.00 10.00
MB Madison Bumgarner 6.00 15.00
MC Miguel Cabrera 6.00 15.00
MCA Matt Carpenter 4.00 10.00
MH Matt Harvey 8.00 20.00
MM Manny Machado 10.00 25.00
MMO Matt Moore 3.00 8.00
MR Mariano Rivera 10.00 25.00
MS Max Scherzer 5.00 12.00
MSC Marco Scutaro 4.00 10.00
MT Mike Trout 12.50 30.00
NC Nelson Cruz 3.00 8.00
PA Pedro Alvarez 4.00 10.00
PC Patrick Corbin 3.00 8.00
PF Prince Fielder 4.00 10.00
PG Paul Goldschmidt 3.00 8.00
RC Robinson Cano 4.00 10.00
SP Salvador Perez 4.00 10.00
TH Torii Hunter 4.00 10.00
TT Troy Tulowitzki 4.00 10.00
YD Yu Darvish 5.00 12.00
YM Yadier Molina 6.00 15.00

2013 Topps Update All-Star Stitches Chrome

ASRAC Allen Craig 5.00 12.00
ASRBH Bryce Harper 15.00 40.00
ASRBP Buster Posey
ASRCB Carlos Beltran 12.50 30.00
ASRCD Chris Davis 6.00 15.00
ASRCG Carlos Gonzalez
ASRCK Clayton Kershaw
ASRCL Cliff Lee
ASRDO David Ortiz 4.00 10.00
ASRDW David Wright 8.00 20.00
ASRFH Felix Hernandez 4.00 10.00
ASRJF Jose Fernandez
ASRJV Justin Verlander 10.00 25.00
ASRMC Miguel Cabrera
ASRMH Matt Harvey 12.50 30.00
ASRMM Manny Machado 10.00 25.00
ASRMR Mariano Rivera
ASRMT Mike Trout 15.00 40.00
ASRPF Prince Fielder
ASRPG Paul Goldschmidt 4.00 10.00
ASRRC Robinson Cano 4.00 10.00
ASRTT Troy Tulowitzki 6.00 15.00
ASRYM Yadier Molina 4.00 10.00
ASRJVO Joey Votto 10.00 25.00

2013 Topps Update All Star Stitches Gold

*GOLD: 1X TO 2.5X BASIC
STATED ODDS 1:1139 HOBBY
STATED PRINT RUN 50 SER.#'d SETS

2013 Topps Update Franchise Forerunners

COMPLETE SET (10) 5.00 12.00
1 H.J.Ryu/S.Koufax 1.25 3.00
2 Y.Puig/M.Kemp 1.50 4.00
3 C.Ripken/M.Machado 2.00 5.00
4 A.McCutchen/G.Cole 2.50 6.00
5 E.Longoria/W.Myers .60 1.50
6 B.Gibson/S.Miller .50 1.25
7 D.Wright/M.Harvey .50 1.25
8 Y.Darvish/N.Ryan 2.00 5.00
9 R.Henderson/Y.Cespedes .60 1.50
10 J.Fernandez/G.Stanton 1.00 2.50

2013 Topps Update League Leaders Pins

STATED ODDS 1:713 HOBBY
BG Bob Gibson 1.50 4.00
BP Buster Posey 2.50 6.00
BR Babe Ruth 5.00 12.00
CR Cal Ripken Jr. 6.00 15.00
DJ Derek Jeter 5.00 12.00
FH Felix Hernandez 1.50 4.00
JB Johnny Bench 2.00 5.00
JP Jim Palmer 1.50 4.00
JV Joey Votto 2.00 5.00
KG Ken Griffey Jr. 4.00 10.00
LG Lou Gehrig 4.00 10.00
MC Miguel Cabrera 2.00 5.00
MK Matt Kemp 1.50 4.00
MS Mike Schmidt 3.00 8.00
MT Mike Trout 15.00 40.00
NG Nomar Garciaparra 1.50 4.00
NR Nolan Ryan 6.00 15.00
RC Rod Carew 1.50 4.00
TC Ty Cobb 3.00 8.00
TW Ted Williams 4.00 10.00

2013 Topps Update Pennant Coins Copper

STATED ODDS 1:6300 HOBBY
STATED PRINT RUN 99 SER.#'d SETS
BR Brooks Robinson 12.50 30.00
BR Babe Ruth 10.00 25.00
DJ Derek Jeter 20.00 50.00
DO David Ortiz 8.00 20.00
GB George Brett 12.50 30.00
MR Mariano Rivera 15.00 40.00
OS Ozzie Smith 12.50 30.00
RC Roberto Clemente 20.00 50.00
RH Rickey Henderson 12.50 30.00
RY Robin Yount 8.00 20.00
SK Sandy Koufax 20.00 50.00
SM Stan Musial 20.00 50.00
TG Tom Glavine 8.00 20.00
TW Ted Williams 20.00 50.00
WM Willie Mays 15.00 40.00

2013 Topps Update Pennant Coins Wrought Iron

*WROUGHT IRON: .5X TO 1.2X BASIC

STATED ODDS 1:12,250 HOBBY
STATED PRINT RUN 50 SER.#'d SETS

2013 Topps Update Postseason Heroes

COMPLETE SET (20) 6.00 15.00
1 David Freese .40 1.00
2 Justin Verlander .60 1.50
3 George Brett 1.25 3.00
4 John Smoltz .60 1.50
5 Greg Maddux .75 2.00
6 Sandy Koufax 1.25 3.00
7 Reggie Jackson .50 1.25
8 Derek Jeter 1.50 4.00
9 Mariano Rivera .75 2.00
10 Bob Gibson .50 1.25
11 Buster Posey .75 2.00
12 Deion Sanders .40 1.00
13 David Ortiz .60 1.50
14 Roy Halladay .50 1.25
15 Evan Longoria .50 1.25
16 Nolan Ryan 2.00 5.00
17 Miguel Cabrera .60 1.50
18 Bret Saberhagen .25 .60
19 Jim Palmer .50 1.25
20 David Wright .50 1.25

2013 Topps Update Postseason Heroes Chrome

PH1 David Freese .60 1.50
PH2 Justin Verlander 1.00 2.50
PH3 George Brett 2.00 5.00
PH4 John Smoltz 1.00 2.50
PH5 Greg Maddux 1.25 3.00
PH6 Sandy Koufax 2.00 5.00
PH7 Reggie Jackson .75 2.00
PH8 Derek Jeter 2.50 6.00
PH9 Mariano Rivera 1.25 3.00
PH10 Bob Gibson .75 2.00
PH11 Buster Posey 1.25 3.00
PH12 Deion Sanders .60 1.50
PH13 David Ortiz 1.00 2.50
PH14 Roy Halladay .75 2.00
PH15 Evan Longoria .75 2.00
PH16 Nolan Ryan 3.00 8.00
PH17 Miguel Cabrera 1.00 2.50
PH18 Bret Saberhagen .40 1.00
PH19 Jim Palmer .75 2.00
PH20 David Wright .75 2.00

2013 Topps Update Record Holder Rings

STATED ODDS 1:1460 HOBBY
BR Babe Ruth 10.00 25.00
CR Cal Ripken Jr. 10.00 25.00
GB George Brett 10.00 25.00
NR Nolan Ryan 10.00 25.00
OS Ozzie Smith 8.00 20.00
RH Rickey Henderson 8.00 20.00
TC Ty Cobb 8.00 20.00
TW Ted Williams 10.00 25.00
WM Willie McCovey 6.00 15.00
YB Yogi Berra 8.00 20.00

2013 Topps Update Rookie Commemorative Patches

1 Cal Ripken Jr. 10.00 25.00
2 Will Clark 4.00 10.00
3 CC Sabathia 4.00 10.00
4 Josh Hamilton 4.00 10.00
5 Miguel Cabrera 5.00 12.00
6 Adrian Gonzalez 4.00 10.00
7 Robinson Cano 5.00 12.00
8 Felix Hernandez 4.00 10.00
9 Carl Crawford 4.00 10.00
10 Matt Kemp 4.00 10.00
11 Tim Lincecum 4.00 10.00
12 Ryan Zimmerman 4.00 10.00
13 Jose Reyes 4.00 10.00
14 Clayton Kershaw 4.00 10.00
15 Yasiel Puig 10.00 25.00

2014 Topps

COMP.ALLSTAR.FACT SET (660) 30.00 80.00
COMP.BLUE.RET.FACT SET (660) 30.00 80.00
COMP.GREEN.RET.FACT SET (660) 30.00 80.00
COMP.PURP.RET.FACT SET (660) 30.00 80.00
COMP.RED.HOB.FACT SET (660) 30.00 80.00
COMPLETE SET w/o SP's (660) 25.00 60.00
COMP.SERIES 1 SET w/o SP's (330) 12.00 30.00
COMP.SERIES 2 SET w/o SP's (330) 12.00 30.00
SER.1 PLATE ODDS 1:1610 HOBBY
SER.2 PLATE ODDS 1:874 HOBBY
PLATE PRINT RUN 1 SET PER COLOR
BLACK-CYAN-MAGENTA-YELLOW ISSUED
NO PLATE PRICING DUE TO SCARCITY
1A Mike Trout 1.25 3.00
1B Trout SP Gatorade 12.00 30.00
1C Trout SP Fut Star 12.00 30.00
1D Trout SP SABR 12.00 30.00
2 Jhonny Peralta .15 .40
3 Jarrod Dyson .15 .40
4 Cody Asche .20 .50
5 Lance Lynn .15 .40
6 Josh Beckett .15 .40
8 Coco Crisp .15 .40
9 Dustin Ackley .15 .40
10 Junior Lake .15 .40
11 Mike Carp .15 .40
12 Aaron Hicks .20 .50
13 Juan Nicasio .15 .40
14A Yoenis Cespedes .25 .60
14B Yoenis Cespedes SP 5.00 12.00
Celebrating
15A Paul Goldschmidt .25 .60
15B Paul Goldschmidt SP 2.50 6.00
Future Stars
15C Paul Goldschmidt SP 2.50 6.00
SABRmetrics
16 Johnny Cueto .20 .50
17 Todd Helton .20 .50
18A Jurickson Profar FS .20 .50
18B Jurickson Profar SP 2.00 5.00
Future Stars
19 Joey Votto .25 .60
20 Charlie Blackmon .25 .60
21 Alfredo Simon .15 .40
22 Mike Napoli WS .15 .40
23 Chris Heisey .15 .40
24A Manny Machado FS .25 .60
24B Manny Machado SP 2.50 6.00
Future Stars
24C Machado SP SABR 2.50 6.00
25A Troy Tulowitzki .25 .60
25B Troy Tulowitzki SP 2.50 6.00
SABRmetrics
26 Josh Phegley .15 .40
27 Michael Choice RC .25 .60
28 Brayan Pena .15 .40
29 Dvis/Cbrra/Encrncn LL .25 .60
30 Mark Buehrle .20 .50
31 Victor Martinez .20 .50
32 Reymond Fuentes RC .25 .60
33A Matt Harvey .20 .50
33B Pedro Alvarez SP 1.50 4.00
Future Stars
33C Pedro Alvarez SP 1.50 4.00
SABRmetrics
34 Buddy Boshers RC .25 .60
35 Trevor Cahill .15 .40
36A Billy Hamilton RC .30 .75
36B Hamilton SP Fut Star 2.00 5.00
36C Hamilton Swing FS 2.00 5.00
37 Nick Hundley .15 .40
38 Alvrz/Gldsmdt/Brce LL .25 .60
39 David Murphy .15 .40
40A Hyun-Jin Ryu .20 .50
40B Hyun-Jin Ryu SP 4.00 10.00
Celebrating
41 Adeiny Hechavarria .15 .40
42 Mariano Rivera .30 .75
43 Mark Trumbo .15 .40
44A Matt Carpenter .25 .60
44B Matt Carpenter SP 2.50 6.00
SABRmetrics
45 Jake Marisnick RC .25 .60
46A Kolten Wong RC .30 .75
46B K.Wong SP FS 2.00 5.00
47 Chris Davis HL .15 .40
48 Jarrod Saltalamacchia .15 .40
49 Enny Romero RC .25 .60
50A Buster Posey .30 .75
50B Posey SP SABR 3.00 8.00
51 Kyle Lohse .15 .40
52 Jim Adduci RC .25 .60
53 Clay Buchholz .15 .40
54 Andrew Lambo RC .25 .60
55 Chia-Jen Lo RC .25 .60
56A Taijuan Walker RC .25 .60
56B Taijuan Walker SP 1.50 4.00
Future Stars
57A Yadier Molina .30 .75
57B Yadier Molina SP 6.00 15.00
Celebrating
57C Yadier Molina SP 3.00 8.00
SABRmetrics
58 Dan Straily .15 .40
59 Nate Schierholtz .15 .40
60 Jon Niese .15 .40
61 Nick Markakis .20 .50
62 Joe Kelly .15 .40
63 Tyler Skaggs FS .15 .40
64 Will Venable .15 .40
65 Hisashi Iwakuma .20 .50
66 Kris Medlen .20 .50
67 Yasmani Grandal .15 .40
68 Sean Burnett .15 .40
69 Jhoulys Chacin .15 .40
70 Marcell Ozuna .25 .60
71 Anthony Rizzo .30 .75
72 Michael Young .15 .40
73 Kyle Seager .15 .40
74 John Mayberry .15 .40
75 Brandon Barnes .15 .40
76 Mike Aviles .15 .40
77 Aroldis Chapman .25 .60
78 Bronson Arroyo .15 .40
79 Garrett Jones .15 .40
80 Jack Hannahan .15 .40
81A Anibal Sanchez .15 .40
81B Anibal Sanchez SP 1.50 4.00
SABRmetrics
82A Leonys Martin .15 .40
82B Leonys Martin SP 1.50 4.00
SABRmetrics
83 Jonathan Schoop RC .25 .60
84 Todd Redmond .15 .40
85 Matt Joyce .15 .40
86 Wilmer Flores RC .30 .75
87 Tyson Ross .15 .40
88 Oswaldo Arcia .15 .40
89 Jarred Cosart FS .15 .40
90 Ethan Martin RC .25 .60
91 Starling Marte FS .20 .50
92 Martin Perez FS .20 .50
93 Ryan Sweeney .15 .40
94 Mitch Moreland .15 .40
95 Brandon Morrow .15 .40
96 Wily Peralta .15 .40
97A Alex Gordon .20 .50
97B Starling Marte SP 2.00 5.00
SABRmetrics
98 Edwin Encarnacion .25 .60
99 Melky Cabrera .15 .40
100A Bryce Harper .40 1.00
100B Harper SP Fut Star 4.00 10.00
101 Chris Nelson .15 .40
102 Matt Lindstrom .15 .40
103 Cbrra/Mauer/Trout LL 1.25 3.00
104 Kurt Suzuki .15 .40
105 Ryan Howard .20 .50
106 Shin-Soo Choo .20 .50
107 Jordan Zimmermann .20 .50
108 J.D. Martinez .25 .60
109 David Freese .15 .40
110A Wil Myers .15 .40
110B Wil Myers SP 1.50 4.00
Future Stars
111 Mark Ellis .15 .40
112 Torii Hunter .15 .40
113 Krshw/Frnndz/Hrvey LL .40 1.00
114 Francisco Liriano .15 .40
115 Brett Oberholtzer .15 .40
116 Hiroki Kuroda .15 .40
117 Snchz/Clon/Iwkma LL .20 .50
118A Ian Desmond .15 .40
118B Ian Desmond SP 1.50 4.00
SABRmetrics
119 Brandon Crawford .20 .50
120 Kevin Correia .15 .40
121 Franklin Gutierrez .15 .40
122 Jonathan Papelbon .20 .50
123 James Paxton RC .40 1.00
124A Jay Bruce .20 .50
124B Jay Bruce SP 2.00 5.00
SABRmetrics
125A Joe Mauer .20 .50
125B Joe Mauer SP 2.00 5.00
SABRmetrics
125C Joe Mauer SP 6.00 15.00
Snoopy
126 David DeJesus .15 .40
127 Yusmeiro Petit .15 .40
128 Erasmo Ramirez .15 .40
129 Yonder Alonso .15 .40
130 Scooter Gennett .20 .50
131 Junichi Tazawa .15 .40
132 Henderson Alvarez HL .15 .40
133A Xander Bogaerts RC .75 2.00
133B Bogaerts SP Fut Star 5.00 12.00
133C Bogaerts Gry Jsy FS 2.00 5.00
134A Josh Donaldson .20 .50
134B Josh Donaldson SP 2.00 5.00
SABRmetrics
135 Eric Sogard .15 .40
136A Will Middlebrooks FS .15 .40
136B Will Middlebrooks SP 1.50 4.00
Future Stars
137 Boone Logan .15 .40
138 Wei-Yin Chen .15 .40
139 Rafael Betancourt .15 .40
140 Jonathan Broxton .15 .40
141 Chris Tillman .15 .40
142 Zack Greinke .25 .60
143 Gldsmdt/Brce/Frman LL .30 .75
144 Joakim Soria .15 .40
145 Jason Castro .15 .40
146 Jonny Gomes WS .15 .40
147 Jason Frasor .15 .40
148 Chris Sale .25 .60
148B Sale SABR SP 2.50 6.00
149 Miguel Cabrera HL .25 .60
150A Andrew McCutchen .25 .60
150B McCutch SP Blk jsy 8.00 20.00
150C McCutch SP SABR 2.50 6.00
151 Bruce Chen .15 .40
152 Jonathan Herrera .15 .40
153 Dvis/Cbrra/Jones LL .25 .60
154 Chris Iannetta .15 .40
155 Daniel Murphy .20 .50
156 Kendrys Morales .15 .40
157 Matt Adams .15 .40
158 Nate McLouth .15 .40
159 Jason Grilli .15 .40
160 Bruce Rondon .15 .40
161A Adrian Beltre .25 .60
161B Adrian Beltre SP 2.50 6.00
SABRmetrics
162 Josmil Pinto RC .25 .60
163 Matt Shoemaker RC .40 1.00
164 Jaime Garcia .20 .50
165 Rajai Davis .15 .40
166A Dustin Pedroia .25 .60
166B Dustin Pedroia SP 5.00 12.00
In dugout
166C Dustin Pedroia SP 2.50 6.00
SABRmetrics
167 Jeremy Guthrie .15 .40
168 Alex Rodriguez .30 .75
169 Nick Franklin FS .15 .40
170 Wade Miley .15 .40
171 Trevor Rosenthal .20 .50
172 Rickie Weeks .15 .40
173 Brandon League .15 .40
174 Bobby Parnell .15 .40
175 Casey Janssen .15 .40
176 Alex Cobb .15 .40
177 Esmil Rogers .15 .40
178 Erik Johnson RC .25 .60
179A Gerrit Cole FS .25 .60
179B Gerrit Cole SP 2.50 6.00
Future Stars
180 Ben Revere .15 .40
181 Jim Henderson .15 .40
182 Carlos Ruiz .15 .40
183 Darwin Barney .15 .40
184 Yunel Escobar .15 .40
185 Howie Kendrick .15 .40
186 Clayton Richard .15 .40
187 Justin Turner .25 .60
188 Mark Melancon .15 .40
189 Adam LaRoche .15 .40
190 Kevin Gausman FS .25 .60
191 Chris Perez .15 .40
192A Pedro Alvarez .15 .40
192B Matt Harvey SP 2.00 5.00
Future Stars
192B Matt Harvey SP 2.00 5.00
SABRmetrics
193 Ricky Nolasco .15 .40
194 Joel Hanrahan .15 .40
195A Nick Castellanos RC .75 2.00
195B Castellanos SP Fut Star 5.00 12.00
195C Castellanos Gry Jsy FS 2.00 5.00
196 Cole Hamels .20 .50
197 Onelki Garcia RC .25 .60
198A Nick Swisher .20 .50
198B Nick Swisher SP 4.00 10.00
Celebrating
199 Matt Davidson RC .30 .75
200 Derek Jeter .60 1.50
201 Alex Rios .20 .50
202 Jeremy Hellickson .15 .40
203 Cliff Pennington .15 .40
204A Adrian Gonzalez .20 .50
204B Adrian Gonzalez SP 4.00 10.00
Celebrating
205 Seth Smith .15 .40
206 Jon Lester WS .20 .50
207 Jonathan Villar .15 .40
208 Dayan Viciedo .15 .40
209 Carlos Quentin .15 .40
210 Jose Altuve .20 .50
211 Dioner Navarro .15 .40
212A Jason Heyward .20 .50
212B Jason Heyward SP 4.00 10.00
High-five
212C Jason Heyward SP 2.00 5.00
Future Stars
213 Justin Smoak .15 .40
214 James Shields .15 .40
215 Jean Segura FS .20 .50
216 Ubaldo Jimenez .15 .40
217A Giancarlo Stanton .25 .60
217B Giancarlo Stanton SP 2.50 6.00
SABRmetrics
218 Matt Dominguez .15 .40
219 Charlie Morton .25 .60
220 Ryan Doumit .15 .40
221 Brian Dozier .20 .50
222 Vernon Wells .15 .40
223 Joaquin Benoit .15 .40
224 Michael Saunders .20 .50
225 Brian McCann .20 .50
226 Sean Doolittle .15 .40
227 Andrew Cashner .15 .40
228A Jayson Werth .20 .50
228B Jayson Werth SP 2.00 5.00
SABRmetrics
229A Justin Upton .20 .50
229B Justin Upton SP 4.00 10.00
High-five
230 Andre Rienzo RC .25 .60
231 J.R. Murphy RC .25 .60
232 Chris Owings RC .25 .60
233 Rafael Soriano .15 .40
234 Eric Stults .15 .40
235A Jason Kipnis .20 .50
235B Jason Kipnis SP 2.00 5.00
Future Stars
235C Jason Kipnis SP 2.00 5.00
SABRmetrics
236 Joel Peralta .15 .40
237 Cddyer/Jhnsn/Frman LL .30 .75
238 Alberto Callaspo .15 .40
239 Jeff Samardzija .15 .40
240 Ernesto Frieri .15 .40
241 Henderson Alvarez .15 .40
242 David Holmberg RC .25 .60
243 Ryan Cook .15 .40
244 Danny Farquhar .15 .40
245 Ross Detwiler .15 .40
246 Eduardo Nunez .15 .40
247 Anthony Gose .15 .40
248 Travis d'Arnaud RC .30 .75
249 Heath Hembree RC .50 1.25
250A Miguel Cabrera .25 .60
250B Miggy SP Look Up 5.00 12.00
250C Cabrera SP SABR 2.50 6.00
251 Sergio Romo .15 .40
252 Kevin Pillar RC .25 .60
253 Todd Helton HL .20 .50
254 Brett Gardner .20 .50
255 Billy Butler .15 .40
256 Abraham Almonte RC .25 .60
257 C.J. Wilson .15 .40
258 Jon Lester .20 .50
259 David Ortiz WS .25 .60
260 Zoilo Almonte .20 .50
261 Michael Brantley .20 .50
262 Jeff Keppinger .15 .40
263 Doug Fister .15 .40
264 Huston Street .15 .40
265 Yordano Ventura RC .30 .75
266 Zack Wheeler FS .20 .50
267 Ryan Vogelsong .15 .40
268 Don Kelly .15 .40
269 Joe Blanton .15 .40
270 Gregor Blanco .15 .40
271 Justin Ruggiano .15 .40
272A Carlos Villanueva .15 .40
272B Joey Votto SP 2.50 6.00
SABRmetrics
273 Mark DeRosa .15 .40
274 Jonny Gomes .15 .40
275A Nolan Arenado .40 1.00
275B Nolan Arenado SP 4.00 10.00
Future Stars
275C Nolan Arenado SP 4.00 10.00
SABRmetrics
276 Alfonso Soriano .20 .50
277 Mike Leake .15 .40
278 Tommy Medica RC .25 .60
279 Corey Kluber .20 .50
280 Everth Cabrera .15 .40
281 Robbie Erlin RC .25 .60
282 Rex Brothers .15 .40
283A Andrelton Simmons FS .15 .40
283B Andrelton Simmons SP 1.50 4.00
SABRmetrics
284 Brandon Belt .20 .50
285 Jonathan Lucroy .20 .50
286 Josh Fields RC .25 .60
287 Miguel Montero .15 .40
288A Julio Teheran FS .20 .50
288B Julio Teheran SP 2.00 5.00
Future Stars
289 Matt Thornton .15 .40
290 Chad Bettis RC .25 .60
291 Brandon McCarthy .15 .40
292 Aaron Hill .15 .40
293 Mike Zunino FS .15 .40
294 Wnwrght/Zmmrmnn/Krshw LL .40 1.00
295 Matt Tuiasosopo .15 .40
296 Domonic Brown .20 .50
297A Max Scherzer .25 .60
297B Max Scherzer SP 5.00 12.00
Celebrating
297C Max Scherzer SP 2.50 6.00
SABRmetrics
298 Chris Getz .15 .40
299 Schrzr/Clon/Moore LL .25 .60
300A Yu Darvish .25 .60
300B Yu Darvish SP 2.50 6.00
SABRmetrics
301A Shane Victorino .20 .50
301B Shane Victorino SP 2.00 5.00
SABRmetrics
302A Carlos Gomez .15 .40
302B Carlos Gomez SP 1.50 4.00
SABRmetrics
303 Andres Torres .15 .40
304 Juan Lagares .15 .40
305 Steve Cishek .15 .40
306 Garrett Richards .20 .50
307 Jake Peavy .15 .40
308 Alexei Ramirez .20 .50
309 Drew Stubbs .15 .40
310 Neftali Feliz .15 .40
311 Chris Young .15 .40
312 Jimmy Rollins .20 .50
313 Brad Peacock .15 .40
314A Hanley Ramirez .20 .50
314B Hanley Ramirez SP 4.00 10.00
Celebrating
315 Jose Quintana .15 .40
316 Mike Minor .15 .40
317 Lonnie Chisenhall .15 .40
318 Luis Valbuena .15 .40
319 Ryan Goins RC .30 .75
320 Hector Santiago .15 .40
321 Mariano Rivera HL .30 .75
322 Emilio Bonifacio .15 .40
323A Jose Bautista .20 .50
323B Jose Bautista SP 2.00 5.00
SABRmetrics
324 Elvis Andrus .20 .50
325 Trevor Plouffe .15 .40
326 Khris Davis .25 .60
327 Pablo Sandoval .20 .50
328 James Loney .15 .40
329A Matt Holliday .25 .60
329B Matt Holliday SP 2.50 6.00
SABRmetrics
330A Evan Longoria .20 .50
330B Evan Longoria SP 4.00 10.00
Celebrating
330C Evan Longoria SP 2.00 5.00
SABRmetrics
331A Yasiel Puig .25 .60
331B Puig SP FS 8.00 20.00
331C Puig SP Hands hips 8.00 20.00
332 Stephen Strasburg .25 .60
333 Wil Myers ERR .15 .40
Name spelled Will on back
334 Andy Dirks .15 .40
335 Miguel Cabrera .25 .60
336A Ben Zobrist .20 .50
336B Ben Zobrist SP 2.00 5.00
SABRmetrics
337 Zach Walters RC .25 .60
338 Carlos Santana .20 .50
339 Cody Ross .15 .40
340 Casey McGehee .15 .40
341 Mike Moustakas .20 .50
342 Brad Miller .20 .50
343 Nate Freiman .15 .40
344 Kevin Siegrist (RC) .25 .60
345 Darin Ruf .20 .50
346 Derek Norris .15 .40
347 Matt Cain .20 .50
348 Salvador Perez .20 .50
349 Martin Prado .15 .40
350 Carlos Gonzalez .20 .50
351 Matt Garza .15 .40
352 Ryan Wheeler .15 .40
353 A.J. Ramos .15 .40
354 Donnie Murphy .15 .40
355 Jarrod Parker .15 .40
356 Jose Reyes .20 .50
357 Lorenzo Cain .15 .40
358A Christian Yelich .30 .75
358B Yelich SP FS 3.00 8.00
359 Sean Rodriguez .15 .40
360 Russell Martin .15 .40
361 Edwin Jackson .15 .40
362 Daniel Nava .15 .40
363 David Hale RC .25 .60
364 Mike Trout 1.25 3.00
365 Dan Uggla .15 .40
366 Zack Cozart .15 .40
367 Brian Wilson .25 .60
368 Kyuji Fujikawa .20 .50
369 Erick Aybar .15 .40
370 Jerry Blevins .15 .40
371 Scott Kazmir .15 .40
372 Austin Jackson .15 .40
373 Kyle Drabek .15 .40
374 Taylor Jordan (RC) .20 .50
375A Adam Wainwright .20 .50
375AB Adam Wainwright SP 4.00 10.00
In front of fans
375C Adam Wainwright SP 4.00 10.00
Celebrating
375D Adam Wainwright SP 2.00 5.00
SABRmetrics
376 Jeurys Familia .20 .50
377 J.J. Hardy .15 .40
378 Ryan Zimmerman .20 .50
379 Gerardo Parra .15 .40
380 Tyler Chatwood .15 .40
381 Drew Smyly .15 .40
382 Michael Bourn .15 .40
383 Chris Archer .15 .40
384 Rick Porcello .20 .50
385 Josh Willingham .20 .50
386 Mike Olt .15 .40
387 Ed Lucas .15 .40
388 Yovani Gallardo .15 .40
389 Geovany Soto .20 .50
390 Bryce Harper .40 1.00
391 Blake Parker .15 .40
392 Jacob Turner .20 .50
393 Devin Mesoraco .15 .40
394 Sean Halton .15 .40
395 John Danks .15 .40
396 Brian Roberts .15 .40
397 Tim Lincecum .20 .50
398A Adam Jones .20 .50
398B Adam Jones SP 2.00 5.00
SABRmetrics
399 Hector Sanchez .15 .40
400 Clayton Kershaw .40 1.00
400A Kershaw SP Throw 8.00 20.00
400B Kershaw SP Celebrate 8.00 20.00
400C Kershaw SP SABR 4.00 10.00
401A Felix Hernandez .20 .50
401B Felix Hernandez SP 2.00 5.00
SABRmetrics
402 J.J. Putz .15 .40
403 Gordon Beckham .15 .40
404 C.C. Lee RC .25 .60
405 Jason Kubel .15 .40
406 Ramon Santiago .15 .40
407 John Jaso .15 .40
408 Joey Terdoslavich .15 .40
409 Ian Kennedy .15 .40
410 A.J. Griffin .15 .40
411 Josh Rutledge .15 .40
412A Hunter Pence .20 .50
412B Hunter Pence SP 2.00 5.00
SABRmetrics
413 Jose Fernandez .25 .60
414 Michael Wacha .20 .50
415 Andre Ethier .20 .50
416A Josh Reddick .15 .40
416B Josh Reddick SP 1.50 4.00
Future Stars
416C Josh Reddick SP 1.50 4.00
SABRmetrics
417 Chase Headley .15 .40
418 Jordy Mercer .15 .40
419 Lucas Harrell .15 .40
420 Lucas Duda .20 .50
421 R.A. Dickey .20 .50
422 Alexi Ogando .15 .40
423 Marco Scutaro .20 .50
424 Jose Ramirez RC 4.00 10.00
425A Craig Kimbrel .20 .50
425B Craig Kimbrel SP 4.00 10.00
Making fist
426 Koji Uehara .15 .40
427 Cameron Maybin .15 .40
428 Skip Schumaker .15 .40
429 Marcus Semien RC 1.25 3.00
430 Roger Kieschnick RC .25 .60
431 Brett Anderson .15 .40
432 Dillon Gee .15 .40
433 Omar Infante .15 .40
434 Miguel Gonzalez .15 .40
435 Ryan Braun .20 .50
436 Eric Young Jr. .15 .40
437 Alex Wood .15 .40
438 Jake Arrieta .20 .50
439 Jackie Bradley Jr. .25 .60
440 Ryan Raburn .15 .40
441 Mike Pelfrey .15 .40
442 Angel Pagan .15 .40
443 Jeff Kobernus RC .25 .60
444 Robbie Grossman .15 .40
445 Sean Marshall .15 .40
446 Tim Hudson .20 .50
447 Christian Bethancourt RC .25 .60
448 Brett Lawrie .20 .50
449 Jedd Gyorko .15 .40
450A Justin Verlander .25 .60
450B Verlander SP Celebrate 5.00 12.00
450C Verlander SP SABR 2.50 6.00
451 Luis Garcia RC .25 .60
452 Andrew McCutchen .25 .60
453 Nelson Cruz .25 .60
454 Brandon Beachy .15 .40
455 Danny Espinosa .15 .40
456 Eury De La Rosa RC .25 .60
457 CC Sabathia .20 .50
458 Vinnie Pestano .15 .40
459 Eric Hosmer .20 .50
460 Matt Kemp .20 .50
461 Steve Delabar .15 .40
462 J.A. Happ .20 .50
463 Samuel Deduno .15 .40
464 Evan Gattis .15 .40
465 Justin Morneau .20 .50
466 Ryan Dempster .15 .40
467 Scott Feldman .15 .40
468 Wilin Rosario .15 .40
469 Jesse Crain .15 .40
470 Kole Calhoun .15 .40
471 Brandon Moss .15 .40
472 Caleb Gindl .15 .40
473A Mike Napoli .15 .40
473B Mike Napoli SP 1.50 4.00
SABRmetrics
474 Carlos Martinez .20 .50
475A David Ortiz .25 .60
475B David Ortiz SP 5.00 12.00
Goggles on face
475C David Ortiz SP 5.00 12.00
Goggles on head
475D David Ortiz SP 2.50 6.00
SABRmetrics
476 D.J. LeMahieu .25 .60
477 Craig Gentry .15 .40
478 Billy Hamilton .20 .50
479 Ivan Nova .20 .50
480 Peter Bourjos .15 .40
481 Allen Craig .20 .50
482 Dallas Keuchel .20 .50
483 Shane Robinson .15 .40
484 Marlon Byrd .15 .40
485 Gonzalez Germen RC .30 .75
486 Drew Hutchison .15 .40
487 Jim Johnson .15 .40
488 Brian Duensing .15 .40
489 David Price .20 .50
490 Logan Morrison .15 .40
491 Felix Doubront .15 .40
492 Glen Perkins .15 .40
493 Ruben Tejada .15 .40
494 Rob Wooten RC .25 .60
495 John Axford .15 .40
496A Jose Abreu RC 2.00 5.00
496B Abreu Look left FS 4.00 10.00
497 Fernando Rodney .15 .40
498 Steve Susdorf RC .25 .60
499 Craig Kimbrel .20 .50
500 Robinson Cano .20 .50
501 Carlos Carrasco .15 .40
502 Chase Utley .20 .50
503 Kyle Kendrick .15 .40
504 Kelly Johnson .15 .40
505 Homer Bailey .15 .40
506 Rafael Furcal .15 .40
507 Justin Masterson .15 .40
508 Sonny Gray FS .20 .50
509A Brandon Phillips .15 .40
509B Brandon Phillips SP 1.50 4.00
SABRmetrics
510 Matt den Dekker RC .30 .75
511 Travis Wood .15 .40
512 Neil Walker .15 .40
513 Jordan Pacheco .15 .40
514 Alcides Escobar .20 .50
515 Curtis Granderson .20 .50
516 Mike Belfiore RC .25 .60
517 Norichika Aoki .15 .40
518 Chris Parmelee .15 .40
519 A.J. Ellis .15 .40
520 Jorge De La Rosa .15 .40
521 Anthony Rendon .25 .60
522 Wandy Rodriguez .15 .40
523 Gio Gonzalez .20 .50
524 Brian Bogusevic .15 .40
525A Chris Davis .15 .40
525B Chris Davis SP 1.50 4.00
SABRmetrics
526 Avisail Garcia .20 .50
527 Travis Snider .15 .40
528A Shelby Miller .20 .50
528B Shelby Miller SP 2.00 5.00
USA Jersey
529 Jesus Montero .15 .40
530 Danny Salazar .20 .50
531A Dylan Bundy .20 .50
531B Dylan Bundy SP 2.00 5.00
USA Jersey
532 Danny Duffy .15 .40
533 Jose Veras .15 .40
534 Ian Kinsler .20 .50
535 Juan Francisco .15 .40
536 Matt Harrison .15 .40
537 Madison Bumgarner .20 .50
538 Jon Jay .15 .40
539 Trevor Bauer .30 .75
540 Ike Davis .15 .40
541 Phil Hughes .15 .40
542 Josh Zeid RC .25 .60
543 Bud Norris .15 .40
544 Jason Vargas .15 .40
545 Jeremy Affeldt .15 .40
546 Heath Bell .15 .40
547 Brian Matusz .15 .40
548 Jered Weaver .20 .50
549 Hank Conger .15 .40
550A Prince Fielder .20 .50
550B Prince Fielder SP 4.00 10.00
Postseason sweatshirt
551 Addison Reed .15 .40
552 Yasiel Puig .25 .60
553 Michael Pineda .15 .40
554 Maicer Izturis .15 .40
555 Adam Eaton .15 .40
556 Brad Ziegler .15 .40
557 Vic Black RC .40 1.00
558 Nolan Reimold .15 .40
559 Asdrubal Cabrera .20 .50
560 Aramis Ramirez .15 .40
561 Wellington Castillo .15 .40
562 Didi Gregorius .20 .50
563 Colt Hynes RC .25 .60
564 Alejandro De Aza .15 .40
565 Roy Halladay .20 .50
566 Carl Crawford .20 .50
567 Donovan Solano .25 .60
568 Pedro Florimon .15 .40
569 Michael Morse .15 .40
570 Nathan Eovaldi .20 .50
571A Colby Rasmus .20 .50
571B Colby Rasmus SP 2.00 5.00
SABRmetrics
572 Tommy Milone .15 .40
573 Adam Lind .20 .50
574 Tyler Clippard .15 .40
575 Josh Hamilton .20 .50
576 David Robertson .15 .40
577 Steve Ames RC .25 .60
578 Tyler Thornburg .15 .40
579A Freddie Freeman .30 .75
579B Freeman SP SABR 3.00 8.00
580A Todd Frazier .15 .40
580B Todd Frazier SP 1.50 4.00
SABRmetrics
581 Tony Cingrani .20 .50
582 Desmond Jennings .20 .50
583 Ryan Ludwick .15 .40
584 Tyler Flowers .15 .40
585 Stephen Drew .15 .40
586 Luke Hochevar .15 .40
587 Dee Gordon .15 .40
588 Matt Moore .20 .50
589 Chris Carter .15 .40
590 Brett Cecil .15 .40
591 Jenrry Mejia .15 .40
592 Simon Castro RC .25 .60
593 Carlos Beltran .20 .50
594 Justin Maxwell .15 .40
595 A.J. Pierzynski .15 .40
596 Juan Uribe .15 .40
597 Mat Latos .20 .50
598 Marco Estrada .15 .40
599 Jason Motte .15 .40
600 David Wright .20 .50
601 Jason Hammel .15 .40
602 Tanner Roark RC .25 .60
603 Starlin Castro .15 .40
604 Clayton Kershaw .40 1.00
605 Tim Beckham RC .40 1.00
606 Kenley Jansen .20 .50
607 Jed Lowrie .15 .40
608 Jeff Locke .15 .40
609 Jonathan Pettibone .15 .40
610 Paul Konerko .20 .50
611 Patrick Corbin .20 .50
612 Jake Petricka RC .25 .60
613 Mark Teixeira .20 .50
614 Moises Sierra .15 .40
615 Drew Storen .15 .40
616 Zach McAllister .15 .40
617 Greg Holland .15 .40
618 Adam Dunn .20 .50
619 Chris Johnson .20 .50
620 Yan Gomes .20 .50
621 B.J. Upton .20 .50
622 Dexter Fowler .20 .50
623 Chad Billingsley .20 .50
624 Alex Presley .15 .40
625 Albert Pujols .30 .75
626 Tommy Hanson .10 .25
627 J.P. Arencibia .15 .40

628 Joe Nathan .15 .40
629A Cliff Lee .20 .50
629B Cliff Lee SP 2.00 5.00
SABRmetrics
630 Max Scherzer .25 .60
631 Bartolo Colon .15 .40
632 John Lackey .20 .50
633 Alex Avila .20 .50
634 Gaby Sanchez .15 .40
635 Josh Johnson .20 .50
636 Santiago Casilla .15 .40
637 Freddy Galvis .15 .40
638 Michael Cuddyer .15 .40
639 Conor Gillaspie .20 .50
640 Kyle Blanks .15 .40
641 A.J. Burnett .15 .40
642 Brandon Kintzler .15 .40
643 Alex Guerrero RC .30 .75
644 Grant Green .15 .40
645 Wilson Ramos .15 .40
646 Dan Haren .15 .40
647 L.J. Hoes .15 .40
648 A.J. Pollock .20 .50
649 Jordan Danks .15 .40
650 Jacoby Ellsbury .20 .50
651 Denard Span .15 .40
652 Edinson Volquez .15 .40
653 Jose Iglesias .20 .50
654 Jose Tabata .15 .40
655 Derek Holland .15 .40
656 Grant Balfour .15 .40
657 Corey Hart .15 .40
658 Wade Davis .15 .40
659 Ervin Santana .15 .40
660A Jose Fernandez .25 .60
660B Jose Fernandez SP 2.50 6.00
Future Stars
661A Masahiro Tanaka RC .75 2.00
661B Tanaka SP Press Conf 10.00 25.00
661C Tanaka Blue Jsy FS 1.50 4.00

2014 Topps Black

*BLACK VET: 10X TO 25X BASIC
*BLACK RC: 6X TO 15X BASIC RC
SERIES ONE ODDS 1:104 HOBBY
SERIES TWO ODDS 1:56 HOBBY
STATED PRINT RUN 63 SER.#'d SETS
42 Mariano Rivera 20.00 50.00
57 Yadier Molina 12.00 30.00
103 Cbrra/Mauer/Trout LL 10.00 25.00
133 Xander Bogaerts 40.00 100.00
150 Andrew McCutchen 20.00 50.00
179 Gerrit Cole FS 10.00 25.00
200 Derek Jeter 40.00 80.00
204 Adrian Gonzalez 12.50 30.00
248 Travis d'Arnaud 8.00 20.00
259 David Ortiz WS 10.00 25.00
274 Jonny Gomes 5.00 12.00

2014 Topps Camo

*CAMO VET: 8X TO 20X BASIC
*CAMO RC: 5X TO 12X BASIC RC
SERIES ONE ODDS 1:250 HOBBY
SERIES TWO ODDS 1:123 HOBBY
STATED PRINT RUN 99 SER.#'d SETS
19 Joey Votto 10.00 25.00
42 Mariano Rivera 20.00 50.00
44 Matt Carpenter 10.00 25.00
50 Buster Posey 15.00 40.00
56 Taijuan Walker 10.00 25.00
57 Yadier Molina 10.00 25.00
91 Starling Marte FS 8.00 20.00
105 Ryan Howard 8.00 20.00
110 Wil Myers 10.00 25.00
119 Brandon Crawford 8.00 20.00
125 Joe Mauer 12.00 30.00
133 Xander Bogaerts 30.00 60.00
146 Jonny Gomes WS 4.00 10.00
150 Andrew McCutchen 20.00 50.00
179 Gerrit Cole FS 8.00 20.00
192 Pedro Alvarez 6.00 15.00
200 Derek Jeter 30.00 60.00
259 David Ortiz WS 8.00 20.00
274 Jonny Gomes 4.00 10.00
283 Andrelton Simmons FS 6.00 15.00
321 Mariano Rivera HL 20.00 50.00
329 Matt Holliday 8.00 20.00

2014 Topps Factory Set Orange Border

*ORANGE VET: 6X TO 15X BASIC
*ORANGE RC: 4X TO 10X BASIC RC
INSERTED IN FACTORY SETS
STATED PRINT RUN 199 SER.#'d SETS
200 Derek Jeter 50.00 100.00

2014 Topps Gold

*GOLD VET: 1.5X TO 4X BASIC
*GOLD RC: .6X TO 1.5X BASIC RC
SERIES ONE ODDS 1:9 HOBBY
SERIES TWO ODDS 1:4 HOBBY
STATED PRINT RUN 2014 SER.#'d SETS

2014 Topps Green

*GREEN VET: 2.5X TO 6X BASIC
*GREEN RC: 1.5X TO 4X BASIC RC
42 Mariano Rivera 6.00 15.00
200 Derek Jeter 15.00 40.00
321 Mariano Rivera HL 6.00 15.00

2014 Topps Orange

*ORANGE VET: 4X TO 10X BASIC
*ORANGE RC: 2.5X TO 6X BASIC RC
496 Jose Abreu 8.00 20.00

2014 Topps Pink

*PINK VET: 12X TO 30X BASIC
*PINK RC: 8X TO 20X BASIC RC
SERIES ONE ODDS 1:501 HOBBY
SERIES TWO ODDS 1:501 HOBBY
STATED PRINT RUN 50 SER.#'d SETS
4 Cody Asche 15.00 40.00
12 Aaron Hicks 8.00 20.00
19 Joey Votto 10.00 25.00
42 Mariano Rivera 20.00 50.00
50 Buster Posey 20.00 50.00
55 Chia-Jen Lo 8.00 20.00
57 Yadier Molina 12.00 30.00
91 Starling Marte FS 10.00 25.00
105 Ryan Howard 10.00 25.00
110 Wil Myers 12.00 30.00
125 Joe Mauer 10.00 25.00
146 Jonny Gomes WS 12.50 30.00
150 Andrew McCutchen 20.00 50.00
179 Gerrit Cole FS 10.00 25.00
183 Darwin Barney 10.00 25.00
192 Pedro Alvarez 8.00 20.00
195 Nick Castellanos 15.00 40.00
200 Derek Jeter 40.00 80.00
206 Jon Lester WS 8.00 20.00
258 Jon Lester 8.00 20.00
259 David Ortiz WS 12.50 30.00
274 Jonny Gomes 12.50 30.00
283 Andrelton Simmons FS 8.00 20.00
321 Mariano Rivera HL 20.00 50.00
329 Matt Holliday 10.00 25.00

2014 Topps Red Foil

*RED FOIL VET: 1.5X TO 4X BASIC
*RED FOIL RC: 1X TO 2.5X BASIC RC
STATED ODDS 1:6 HOBBY

2014 Topps Sparkle

1 Mike Trout 30.00 80.00
14 Yoenis Cespedes 6.00 15.00
15 Paul Goldschmidt 6.00 15.00
18 Jurickson Profar FS 5.00 12.00
19 Joey Votto 25.00 60.00
24 Manny Machado FS 30.00 80.00
25 Troy Tulowitzki 6.00 15.00
33 Matt Harvey 5.00 12.00
36 Billy Hamilton 25.00 60.00
40 Hyun-Jin Ryu 5.00 12.00
42 Mariano Rivera 40.00 100.00
44 Matt Carpenter 25.00 60.00
50 Buster Posey 20.00 50.00
56 Taijuan Walker 12.00 30.00
57 Yadier Molina 20.00 50.00
71 Anthony Rizzo 8.00 20.00
77 Aroldis Chapman 6.00 15.00
97 Alex Gordon 15.00 40.00
100 Bryce Harper 10.00 25.00
106 Shin-Soo Choo 5.00 12.00
110 Wil Myers 4.00 10.00
124 Jay Bruce 5.00 12.00
125 Joe Mauer 25.00 60.00
133 Xander Bogaerts 30.00 80.00
148 Chris Sale 6.00 15.00
150 Andrew McCutchen 20.00 50.00
161 Adrian Beltre 6.00 15.00
166 Dustin Pedroia 20.00 50.00
179 Gerrit Cole FS 30.00 80.00
192 Pedro Alvarez 4.00 10.00
195 Nick Castellanos 12.00 30.00
196 Cole Hamels 5.00 12.00
204 Adrian Gonzalez 5.00 12.00
212 Jason Heyward 5.00 12.00
217 Giancarlo Stanton 6.00 15.00
229 Justin Upton 5.00 12.00
235 Jason Kipnis 12.00 30.00
250 Miguel Cabrera 20.00 50.00
251 Sergio Romo 4.00 10.00
266 Zack Wheeler FS 20.00 50.00
276 Alfonso Soriano 5.00 12.00
296 Domonic Brown 5.00 12.00
297 Max Scherzer 6.00 15.00
300 Yu Darvish 6.00 15.00
314 Hanley Ramirez 5.00 12.00
323 Jose Bautista 12.00 30.00
327 Pablo Sandoval 5.00 12.00
329 Matt Holliday 25.00 60.00
330 Evan Longoria 5.00 12.00
331 Yasiel Puig 6.00 15.00
332 Stephen Strasburg 6.00 15.00
338 Carlos Santana 12.00 30.00
347 Matt Cain 5.00 12.00
350 Carlos Gonzalez 5.00 12.00
356 Jose Reyes 5.00 12.00
358 Christian Yelich 8.00 20.00
375 Adam Wainwright 5.00 12.00
378 Ryan Zimmerman 5.00 12.00
383 Chris Archer 4.00 10.00
388 Yovani Gallardo 4.00 10.00
397 Tim Lincecum 8.00 20.00
398 Adam Jones 15.00 40.00
400 Clayton Kershaw 10.00 25.00
401 Felix Hernandez 5.00 12.00
412 Hunter Pence 20.00 50.00
414 Michael Wacha 5.00 12.00
421 R.A. Dickey 5.00 12.00
425 Craig Kimbrel 5.00 12.00
435 Ryan Braun 5.00 12.00
450 Justin Verlander 6.00 15.00
457 CC Sabathia 5.00 12.00
460 Matt Kemp 5.00 12.00
464 Evan Gattis 15.00 40.00
473 Mike Napoli 15.00 40.00
475 David Ortiz 20.00 50.00
481 Allen Craig 5.00 12.00
489 David Price 5.00 12.00
500 Robinson Cano 5.00 12.00
502 Chase Utley 30.00 80.00
509 Brandon Phillips 15.00 40.00
521 Anthony Rendon 6.00 15.00
525 Chris Davis 4.00 10.00
528 Shelby Miller 20.00 50.00
534 Ian Kinsler 5.00 12.00
537 Madison Bumgarner 8.00 20.00
548 Jered Weaver 5.00 12.00
550 Prince Fielder 5.00 12.00
555 Adam Eaton 4.00 10.00
579 Freddie Freeman 8.00 20.00
581 Tony Cingrani 5.00 12.00
597 Mat Latos 5.00 12.00
600 David Wright 15.00 40.00
613 Mark Teixeira 20.00 50.00
621 B.J. Upton 5.00 12.00
625 Albert Pujols 12.00 30.00
629 Cliff Lee 5.00 12.00
638 Michael Cuddyer 4.00 10.00
650 Jacoby Ellsbury 20.00 50.00
660 Jose Fernandez 6.00 15.00

2014 Topps Target Red Border

*TARGET RED VET: 1.2X TO 3X BASIC
*TARGET RED RC: .75X TO 2X BASIC RC
200 Derek Jeter 4.00 10.00

2014 Topps Toys R Us Purple Border

*TRU PURPLE VET: 4X TO 10X BASIC
*TRU PURPLE RC: 2.5X TO 6X BASIC RC
200 Derek Jeter 15.00 40.00

2014 Topps Wal-Mart Blue Border

*WALMART BLUE VET: 1.2X TO 3X BASIC
*WALMART BLUE RC: .75X TO 2X BASIC RC

2014 Topps Yellow

*YELLOW VET: 5X TO 12X BASIC
*YELLOW RC: 3X TO 8X BASIC RC
24 Manny Machado FS 8.00 20.00
42 Mariano Rivera 8.00 20.00
57 Yadier Molina 8.00 20.00
133 Xander Bogaerts 15.00 40.00
200 Derek Jeter 12.00 30.00
321 Mariano Rivera HL 8.00 20.00

2014 Topps '89 Topps Die Cut Mini Relics

SERIES ONE ODDS 1:19,275 HOBBY
SERIES TWO ODDS 1:9765 HOBBY
UPDATE ODDS 1:7334 HOBBY
STATED PRINT RUN 25 SER.#'d SETS
TMRAB Adrian Beltre S2 20.00 50.00
TMRAD Andre Dawson 15.00 40.00
TMRAM Andrew McCutchen UPD 20.00 50.00
TMRAR Alexei Ramirez UPD 15.00 40.00
TMRBH Bryce Harper S2 12.00 30.00
TMRBH Bryce Harper UPD 30.00 80.00
TMRBJ Bo Jackson 20.00 50.00
TMRCR Cal Ripken Jr. 75.00 150.00
TMRDM Don Mattingly 40.00 100.00
TMRDMU Dale Murphy 20.00 50.00
TMRDO David Ortiz S2 20.00 50.00
TMRFM Fred McGriff 15.00 40.00
TMRGM Greg Maddux 15.00 40.00
TMRGM Greg Maddux UPD 25.00 60.00
TMRIR Ivan Rodriguez UPD 15.00 40.00
TMRJH Jason Heyward UPD 15.00 40.00
TMRJR Jim Rice 15.00 40.00
TMRJV Joey Votto UPD 20.00 50.00
TMRMC Matt Cain UPD 15.00 40.00
TMRMM Mark McGwire S2 60.00 120.00
TMRMS Mike Schmidt 30.00 80.00
TMRMS Max Scherzer UPD 20.00 50.00
TMRSC Steve Carlton S2 15.00 40.00
TMRSM Shelby Miller S2 40.00 80.00
TMRTG Tom Glavine S2 15.00 40.00
TMRTG Tom Glavine 12.00 30.00
TMRTO Tony Gwynn 20.00 50.00
TMRTT Troy Tulowitzki S2 20.00 50.00
TMRVG Vladimir Guerrero UPD 15.00 40.00
TMRVM Victor Martinez UPD 15.00 40.00
TMRWB Wade Boggs 60.00 120.00
TMRYS Yangervis Solarte UPD 12.00 30.00
TMRBHA Billy Hamilton S2 15.00 40.00
TMRDJT Derek Jeter UPD 40.00 100.00
TMRGSP George Springer UPD 12.00 30.00
TMRGST Giancarlo Stanton UPD 20.00 50.00
TMRSMA Starling Marte S2 15.00 40.00

2014 Topps '89 Topps Die Cut Minis

STATED ODDS 1:8 HOBBY
TM1 Yasiel Puig .50 1.25
TM2 Clayton Kershaw .75 2.00
TM3 Fred Lynn .30 .75
TM4 Tony Gwynn .50 1.25
TM5 Tim Raines .40 1.00
TM6 Bo Jackson .50 1.25
TM7 Sandy Koufax 1.00 2.50
TM8 Babe Ruth 1.25 3.00
TM9 Nolan Ryan 1.50 4.00
TM10 Rickey Henderson .50 1.25
TM11 Fred McGriff .40 1.00
TM12 Lee Smith .30 .75
TM13 Don Mattingly 1.00 2.50
TM14 Wade Boggs .40 1.00
TM15 Andre Dawson .40 1.00
TM16 Mike Schmidt .75 2.00
TM17 Tom Glavine .40 1.00
TM18 George Brett 1.00 2.50
TM19 Lou Gehrig 1.00 2.50
TM20 Yogi Berra .50 1.25
TM21 Ted Williams 1.00 2.50
TM22 Jimmie Foxx .50 1.25
TM23 Roberto Clemente 1.25 3.00
TM24 Ozzie Smith .60 1.50
TM25 Greg Maddux .60 1.50
TM26 Jim Rice .40 1.00
TM27 Cal Ripken Jr. 1.50 4.00
TM28 Mike Trout 2.50 6.00
TM29 Josh Hamilton .40 1.00
TM30 Paul Goldschmidt .50 1.25
TM31 Manny Machado .50 1.25
TM32 Chris Davis .30 .75
TM33 Dustin Pedroia .50 1.25
TM34 David Ortiz .50 1.25
TM35 Ernie Banks .50 1.25
TM36 Randy Johnson .50 1.25
TM37 Joey Votto .50 1.25
TM38 Johnny Bench .50 1.25
TM39 Joe Morgan .40 1.00
TM40 Miguel Cabrera .50 1.25
TM41 Justin Verlander .50 1.25
TM42 Buster Posey .60 1.50
TM43 Joe Mauer .40 1.00
TM44 Matt Harvey .40 1.00
TM45 Felix Hernandez .40 1.00
TM46 Andrew McCutchen .50 1.25
TM47 Adam Wainwright .40 1.00
TM48 Yu Darvish .50 1.25
TM49 Bryce Harper .75 2.00
TM50 Robinson Cano .40 1.00
TM51 Ken Griffey Jr. 1.00 2.50
TM52 Mariano Rivera .60 1.50
TM53 Jose Canseco .40 1.00
TM54 Steve Carlton .40 1.00
TM55 Evan Longoria .40 1.00
TM56 Troy Tulowitzki .50 1.25
TM57 Deion Sanders .40 1.00
TM58 Mark McGwire 1.00 2.50
TM59 Chris Sale .50 1.25
TM60 Shelby Miller .40 1.00
TM61 Hanley Ramirez .40 1.00
TM62 Billy Hamilton .40 1.00
TM63 Juan Gonzalez .30 .75
TM64 Nomar Garciaparra .40 1.00
TM65 Ryan Braun .40 1.00
TM66 Max Scherzer .50 1.25
TM67 Freddie Freeman .60 1.50
TM68 Adam Jones .40 1.00
TM69 Giancarlo Stanton .50 1.25
TM70 Starlin Castro .30 .75
TM71 Jason Kipnis .40 1.00
TM72 Cliff Lee .40 1.00
TM73 Justin Upton .40 1.00
TM74 Carlos Gonzalez .40 1.00
TM75 Stephen Strasburg .50 1.25
TM76 Jose Altuve .40 1.00
TM77 Billy Butler .30 .75
TM78 Ivan Rodriguez .40 1.00
TM79 Albert Pujols .60 1.50
TM80 Jose Fernandez .50 1.25
TM81 Jean Segura .40 1.00
TM82 Robin Yount .50 1.25
TM83 David Wright .40 1.00
TM84 Derek Jeter 1.25 3.00
TM85 Yoenis Cespedes .50 1.25
TM86 Domonic Brown .40 1.00
TM87 Craig Kimbrel .40 1.00
TM88 Matt Kemp .40 1.00
TM89 Ryan Zimmerman .40 1.00
TM90 Hyun-Jin Ryu .40 1.00
TM91 Gerrit Cole .50 1.25
TM92 Wil Myers .30 .75
TM93 Prince Fielder .40 1.00
TM94 Jose Bautista .40 1.00
TM95 Jordan Zimmermann .40 1.00
TM96 Mark Teixeira .40 1.00
TM97 Darryl Strawberry .30 .75
TM98 Ryne Sandberg 1.00 2.50
TM99 Jorge Posada .40 1.00
TMAB Adrian Beltre UPD .50 1.25
TMAG Adrian Gonzalez UPD .40 1.00
TMAJ Adam Jones UPD .40 1.00
TMAM Andrew McCutchen UPD .50 1.25
TMAR Alexei Ramirez UPD .40 1.00
TMBB Billy Butler UPD .30 .75
TMBH Bryce Harper UPD .75 2.00
TMCB Clay Buchholz UPD .30 .75
TMCD Chris Davis UPD .30 .75
TMCG Carlos Gonzalez UPD .40 1.00
TMDC David Cone UPD .30 .75
TMDO David Ortiz UPD .50 1.25
TMDW David Wright UPD .40 1.00
TMEE Edwin Encarnacion UPD .50 1.25
TMEL Evan Longoria UPD .40 1.00
TMGM Greg Maddux UPD .60 1.50
TMHK Hiroki Kuroda UPD .30 .75
TMHR Hanley Ramirez UPD .40 1.00
TMIK Ian Kinsler UPD .40 1.00
TMIR Ivan Rodriguez UPD .40 1.00
TMJA Jose Abreu UPD 2.50 6.00
TMJC Jarred Cosart UPD .30 .75
TMJE Jacoby Ellsbury UPD .40 1.00
TMJF Jose Fernandez UPD .50 1.25
TMJH Jason Heyward UPD .40 1.00
TMJM Joe Mauer UPD .40 1.00
TMJV Joey Votto UPD .50 1.25
TMLG Luis Gonzalez UPD .30 .75
TMOV Omar Vizquel UPD .40 1.00
TMPF Prince Fielder UPD .40 1.00
TMPG Paul Goldschmidt UPD .50 1.25
TMRA Roberto Alomar UPD .40 1.00
TMRB Ryan Braun UPD .40 1.00
TMRC Robinson Cano UPD .40 1.00
TMRH Roy Halladay UPD .40 1.00
TMTT Troy Tulowitzki UPD .50 1.25
TMVG Vladimir Guerrero UPD .40 1.00
TMVM Victor Martinez UPD .40 1.00
TMYD Yu Darvish UPD .50 1.25
TMYS Yangervis Solarte UPD .30 .75
TM100 Will Clark .40 1.00
TMCKE Clayton Kershaw UPD .75 2.00
TMCKI Craig Kimbrel UPD .40 1.00
TMDJE Desmond Jennings UPD .40 1.00
TMDJT Derek Jeter UPD 1.25 3.00
TMGSP George Springer UPD 1.25 3.00
TMGST Giancarlo Stanton UPD .50 1.25
TMMCA Miguel Cabrera UPD .50 1.25
TMMCI Matt Cain UPD .40 1.00
TMMSC Max Scherzer UPD .50 1.25
TMMST Mel Stottlemyre UPD .30 .75

2014 Topps 50 Years of the Draft

COMPLETE SET (10) 5.00 12.00
STATED ODDS 1:18 HOBBY
50YD1 Joe Mauer .40 1.00
50YD2 Gerrit Cole .50 1.25
50YD3 David Price .40 1.00
50YD4 Don Mattingly 1.00 2.50
50YD5 Adrian Gonzalez .40 1.00
50YD6 Josh Hamilton .40 1.00
50YD7 Derek Jeter 1.25 3.00
50YD8 Ken Griffey Jr. 1.00 2.50
50YD9 Darryl Strawberry .30 .75
50YD10 Johnny Bench .50 1.25

2014 Topps All Rookie Cup

COMPLETE SET (10) 5.00 12.00
STATED ODDS 1:18 HOBBY
RCT1 Tom Seaver .40 1.00
RCT2 Willie McCovey .40 1.00
RCT3 Joe Morgan .40 1.00
RCT4 Albert Pujols .60 1.50
RCT5 Derek Jeter 1.25 3.00
RCT6 Jim Rice .40 1.00
RCT7 Mike Trout 2.50 6.00
RCT8 Ken Griffey Jr. 1.00 2.50
RCT9 Johnny Bench .50 1.25
RCT10 CC Sabathia .40 1.00

2014 Topps All Rookie Cup Team Autograph Relics

STATED ODDS 1:17,170 HOBBY
STATED PRINT RUN 25 SER.#'d SETS
EXCHANGE DEADLINE 1/31/2017
RCTARCS CC Sabathia EXCH 25.00 60.00
RCTARJR Jim Rice 25.00 60.00
RCTARKG Ken Griffey Jr. 100.00 200.00
RCTARMT Mike Trout 150.00 300.00

2014 Topps All Rookie Cup Team Autographs

STATED ODDS 1:29,500 HOBBY
STATED PRINT RUN 50 SER.#'d SETS
EXCHANGE DEADLINE 1/31/2017
RCTACS CC Sabathia 20.00 50.00
RCTAJB Johnny Bench 25.00 60.00
RCTAKG Ken Griffey Jr. 75.00 150.00
RCTAMT Mike Trout 125.00 250.00

2014 Topps All Rookie Cup Team Commemorative

STATED ODDS 1:10,700 HOBBY
STATED PRINT RUN 99 SER.#'d SETS
TARC1 Tom Seaver 15.00 40.00
TARC2 Willie McCovey 10.00 25.00
TARC3 Joe Morgan 10.00 25.00
TARC4 Albert Pujols 15.00 40.00
TARC5 Derek Jeter 25.00 60.00
TARC6 Jim Rice 8.00 20.00
TARC7 Mike Trout 12.00 30.00
TARC8 Ken Griffey Jr. 30.00 60.00
TARC9 Johnny Bench 10.00 25.00
TARC10 CC Sabathia 8.00 20.00

2014 Topps All Rookie Cup Team Commemorative Vintage

*VINTAGE: .75X TO 2X BASIC
STATED ODDS 1:42,925 HOBBY
STATED PRINT RUN 25 SER.#'d SETS
TARC8 Ken Griffey Jr. 75.00 150.00

2014 Topps All Rookie Cup Team Relics

STATED ODDS 1:14,750 HOBBY
STATED PRINT RUN 99 SER.#'d SETS
RCTRCK Craig Kimbrel 10.00 25.00
RCTRCS CC Sabathia 8.00 20.00
RCTRDJ Derek Jeter 15.00 40.00
RCTRJB Johnny Bench 15.00 40.00
RCTRJR Jim Rice 8.00 20.00

2014 Topps Before They Were Great

COMPLETE SET (30) 40.00 100.00
STATED ODDS 1:18 HOBBY
BG1 Johnny Bench .60 1.50
BG2 George Brett 1.25 3.00
BG3 Nomar Garciaparra .50 1.25
BG4 Bob Gibson .50 1.25
BG5 Tom Glavine .50 1.25
BG6 Ken Griffey Jr. 1.25 3.00
BG7 Tony Gwynn .60 1.50
BG8 Rickey Henderson .60 1.50
BG9 Reggie Jackson .50 1.25
BG10 Randy Johnson .60 1.50
BG11 Sandy Koufax 1.25 3.00
BG12 Greg Maddux .75 2.00
BG13 Pedro Martinez .50 1.25
BG14 Don Mattingly 1.25 3.00
BG15 Willie Mays 1.25 3.00
BG16 Mike Mussina .50 1.25
BG17 Jim Rice .50 1.25
BG18 Cal Ripken Jr. 2.00 5.00
BG19 Nolan Ryan 2.00 5.00
BG20 Mike Schmidt 1.00 2.50
BG21 Steve Carlton .50 1.25
BG22 Ted Williams 1.25 3.00
BG23 Jimmie Foxx .60 1.50
BG24 Roberto Clemente 1.50 4.00
BG25 Ty Cobb 1.00 2.50
BG26 Joe DiMaggio 1.25 3.00
BG27 Tom Seaver .50 1.25
BG28 Derek Jeter 1.50 4.00
BG29 Miguel Cabrera .60 1.50
BG30 Joe Morgan .50 1.25

2014 Topps Before They Were Great Gold

*GOLD: 2X TO 5X BASIC
STATED ODDS 1:715 HOBBY
STATED PRINT RUN 99 SER.#'d SETS

2014 Topps Before They Were Great Relics

STATED ODDS 1:3400 HOBBY
STATED PRINT RUN 25 SER.#'d SETS
EXCHANGE DEADLINE 1/31/2017
BGRBG Bob Gibson 12.00 30.00
BGRDJ Derek Jeter 30.00 60.00
BGRGM Greg Maddux 20.00 50.00
BGRJB Johnny Bench 15.00 40.00
BGRJM Joe Morgan 12.00 30.00
BGRJR Jim Rice 15.00 40.00
BGRKG Ken Griffey Jr. 40.00 100.00
BGRMC Miguel Cabrera 20.00 50.00
BGRMM Mike Mussina 12.00 30.00
BGRMS Mike Schmidt 10.00 25.00
BGRNG Nomar Garciaparra 12.00 30.00
BGRNR Nolan Ryan 40.00 80.00
BGRPM Pedro Martinez 20.00 50.00
BGRRC Roberto Clemente 75.00 150.00
BGRRH Rickey Henderson 20.00 50.00
BGRRJ Randy Johnson 15.00 40.00
BGRRJA Reggie Jackson 20.00 50.00
BGRSC Steve Carlton 12.00 30.00
BGRTG Tom Glavine 12.00 30.00
BGRTGW Tony Gwynn 20.00 50.00
BGRTS Tom Seaver EXCH 12.00 30.00
BGRTW Ted Williams 40.00 80.00
BGRWM Willie Mays 40.00 80.00

2014 Topps Breakout Moments

BM1 Buster Posey .75 2.00
BM2 Luis Gonzalez .40 1.00
BM3 Mark McGwire 1.25 3.00
BM4 Tony Gwynn .60 1.50
BM5 Zack Wheeler .50 1.25
BM6 Jayson Werth .50 1.25
BM7 Jean Segura .50 1.25
BM8 Clayton Kershaw 1.00 2.50
BM9 Max Scherzer .60 1.50
BM10 James Shields .40 1.00
BM11 Cal Ripken Jr. 2.00 5.00
BM12 Ivan Rodriguez .50 1.25
BM13 Adam Jones .50 1.25
BM14 Wil Myers .40 1.00
BM15 Tim Raines .50 1.25
BM16 Randy Johnson .60 1.50
BM17 Jeff Bagwell .50 1.25
BM18 Bryce Harper 1.00 2.50
BM19 Yoenis Cespedes .60 1.50
BM20 Matt Harvey .50 1.25
BM21 Shelby Miller .50 1.25
BM22 Michael Wacha .50 1.25
BM23 Derek Jeter 1.50 4.00
BM24 Ken Griffey Jr. 1.25 3.00
BM25 Robin Yount .60 1.50

2014 Topps Breakout Moments Relics

STATED PRINT RUN 25 SER.#'d SETS
BMRAJ Adam Jones 8.00 20.00
BMRBP Buster Posey 12.00 30.00
BMRCK Clayton Kershaw 40.00 80.00
BMRCR Cal Ripken Jr. 30.00 80.00
BMRJSH James Shields 6.00 15.00
BMRMM Mark McGwire 20.00 50.00
BMRYP Yasiel Puig 10.00 25.00
BMRZW Zack Wheeler 6.00 15.00

2014 Topps Class Rings Gold

*GOLD: ..75X TO 2X BASIC
SERIES ONE ODDS 1:4375 HOBBY
SERIES TWO ODDS 1:2200 HOBBY
STATED PRINT RUN 99 SER.#'d SETS
CR3 Derek Jeter 20.00 50.00
CR8 Lou Gehrig 12.00 30.00

2014 Topps Class Rings Gold Gems

*GOLD GEMS: 2.5X TO 6X BASIC
SERIES ONE ODDS 1:17,200 HOBBY
SERIES TWO ODDS 1:9410 HOBBY
STATED PRINT RUN 25 SER.#'d SETS
CR3 Derek Jeter 60.00 150.00

2014 Topps Class Rings Silver

SERIES ONE ODDS 1:610 HOBBY
SERIES TWO ODDS 1:1050 HOBBY
CR1 Sandy Koufax 6.00 15.00
CR2 Willie Mays 6.00 15.00
CR3 Derek Jeter 12.00 30.00
CR4 Randy Johnson 4.00 10.00
CR5 Ted Williams 4.00 10.00
CR6 Ty Cobb 4.00 10.00
CR7 Babe Ruth 6.00 15.00
CR8 Lou Gehrig 4.00 10.00
CR9 Roberto Clemente 6.00 15.00
CR10 Yogi Berra 4.00 10.00
CR11 Harmon Killebrew 4.00 10.00
CR12 Reggie Jackson 3.00 8.00
CR13 Cal Ripken Jr. 8.00 20.00
CR14 Rickey Henderson 4.00 10.00
CR15 Nolan Ryan 8.00 20.00
CR16 George Brett 4.00 10.00
CR17 Tony Gwynn 4.00 10.00
CR18 Jackie Robinson 4.00 10.00
CR19 Stan Musial 5.00 12.00
CR20 Miguel Cabrera 4.00 10.00
CR21 Mike Trout 10.00 25.00
CR22 Bryce Harper 6.00 15.00
CR23 Ken Griffey Jr. 8.00 20.00
CR24 Clayton Kershaw 6.00 15.00
CR25 Justin Verlander 4.00 10.00
CR26 Mike Schmidt 6.00 15.00
CR27 Tom Seaver 5.00 12.00
CR28 Buster Posey 5.00 12.00
CR29 Albert Pujols 5.00 12.00
CR30 Greg Maddux 5.00 12.00
CR31 Pedro Martinez 5.00 12.00
CR32 Johnny Bench 5.00 12.00
CR33 Steve Carlton 4.00 10.00
CR34 Ivan Rodriguez 3.00 8.00
CR35 Jeff Bagwell 4.00 10.00
CR36 Robin Yount 4.00 10.00
CR37 Deion Sanders 4.00 10.00
CR38 Mark McGwire 6.00 15.00
CR39 Rafael Palmeiro 4.00 10.00
CR40 Jose Canseco 4.00 10.00
CR41 Luis Gonzalez 4.00 10.00
CR42 Juan Gonzalez 4.00 10.00
CR43 Craig Biggio 4.00 10.00
CR44 Andre Dawson 3.00 8.00
CR45 Yoenis Cespedes 4.00 10.00
CR46 Ozzie Smith 5.00 12.00
CR47 Rod Carew 3.00 8.00
CR48 Jim Palmer 3.00 8.00
CR49 Eddie Murray 3.00 8.00
CR50 Joe Morgan 3.00 8.00

2014 Topps Factory Set All-Star Game Exclusive

AS1 Andrew McCutchen 4.00 10.00
AS2 Derek Jeter 10.00 25.00
AS3 Miguel Cabrera 4.00 10.00
AS4 Joe Mauer 3.00 8.00
AS5 Mike Trout 20.00 50.00

2014 Topps Factory Set Sandy Koufax Refractors

*GOLD REF: .75X TO 2X BASIC
79 Sandy Koufax 6.00 15.00
1956 Topps
187 Sandy Koufax 6.00 15.00
1958 Topps
302 Sandy Koufax 6.00 15.00
1957 Topps

2014 Topps Factory Set Ted Williams Refractors

*GOLD REF: .75X TO 2X BASIC
1 Ted Williams 6.00 15.00
1954 Topps
66 Ted Williams 6.00 15.00
1954 Bowman
165 Ted Williams 6.00 15.00
1951 Bowman

2014 Topps Future Stars That Never Were

STATED ODDS 1:18 HOBBY
FS1 Mike Schmidt 2.50 6.00
FS2 Jose Canseco 1.25 3.00
FS3 Eddie Murray 1.25 3.00
FS4 Robin Yount 1.50 4.00
FS5 Ozzie Smith 2.00 5.00
FS6 Joey Votto 1.50 4.00
FS7 Buster Posey 2.00 5.00
FS8 Evan Longoria 1.25 3.00
FS9 Jeff Bagwell 1.25 3.00
FS10 Mike Trout 8.00 20.00
FS11 Bryce Harper 2.50 6.00
FS12 Yoenis Cespedes 1.50 4.00
FS13 Mark McGwire 3.00 8.00
FS14 Randy Johnson 1.50 4.00
FS15 Hank Aaron 3.00 8.00
FS16 Willie Mays 3.00 8.00
FS17 Sandy Koufax 3.00 8.00
FS18 Greg Maddux 2.00 5.00
FS19 Steve Carlton 1.25 3.00
FS20 Chris Sale 1.50 4.00
FS21 Willie Stargell 1.25 3.00
FS22 R.A. Dickey 1.25 3.00
FS23 Tony Gwynn 1.50 4.00
FS24 Rickey Henderson 1.50 4.00
FS25 Ken Griffey Jr. 3.00 8.00
FS26 Stephen Strasburg 1.50 4.00
FS27 Wade Boggs 1.25 3.00
FS28 Darryl Strawberry 1.00 2.50
FS29 Don Mattingly 3.00 8.00
FS30 George Brett 3.00 8.00

2014 Topps Future Stars That Never Were Gold

*GOLD: 1X TO 2.5X BASIC
STATED ODDS 1:387 HOBBY
STATED PRINT RUN 99 SER.#'d SETS

2014 Topps Future Stars That Never Were Relics

STATED ODDS 1:1848 HOBBY
STATED PRINT RUN 25 SER.#'d SETS
FSRBH Bryce Harper 20.00 50.00
FSRBP Buster Posey 50.00 100.00
FSRCS Chris Sale 10.00 25.00
FSRDM Don Mattingly 50.00 100.00
FSRDS Darryl Strawberry 15.00 40.00
FSREL Evan Longoria 8.00 20.00
FSRGM Greg Maddux 12.00 30.00
FSRJB Jeff Bagwell 8.00 20.00
FSRJC Jose Canseco 15.00 40.00
FSRJS John Smoltz 15.00 40.00
FSRJV Joey Votto 15.00 40.00
FSRKG Ken Griffey Jr. 40.00 80.00
FSRMM Mark McGwire 50.00 100.00
FSRMS Mike Schmidt 15.00 40.00
FSRMT Mike Trout 50.00 100.00
FSRPO Paul O'Neill 8.00 20.00
FSRRD R.A. Dickey 12.00 30.00
FSRRH Rickey Henderson 20.00 50.00
FSRRY Robin Yount 30.00 60.00
FSRSC Steve Carlton 15.00 40.00
FSRSS Stephen Strasburg 10.00 25.00
FSRTG Tony Gwynn 20.00 50.00
FSRWB Wade Boggs 40.00 80.00
FSRYC Yoenis Cespedes 10.00 25.00

2014 Topps Gold Label

STATED ODDS 1:575 HOBBY
UPDATE ODDS 1:1005 HOBBY
STATED PRINT RUN 99 SER.#'d SETS
GL1 Greg Maddux 10.00 25.00
GL2 Rickey Henderson 8.00 20.00
GL3 Albert Pujols 10.00 25.00
GL4 Mike Schmidt 12.00 30.00
GL5 Joe Morgan 15.00 40.00
GL6 Randy Johnson 8.00 20.00
GL7 Tom Seaver 10.00 25.00
GL8 Steve Carlton 8.00 20.00
GL9 Johnny Bench 8.00 20.00
GL10 George Brett 15.00 40.00
GL11 Cal Ripken Jr. 20.00 50.00
GL12 Derek Jeter 40.00 80.00
GL13 Roberto Clemente 20.00 50.00
GL14 Ken Griffey Jr. 15.00 40.00
GL15 Nolan Ryan 30.00 60.00
GL16 Mike Trout 40.00 100.00
GL17 Andrew McCutchen 15.00 40.00
GL18 Miguel Cabrera 8.00 20.00
GL19 Clayton Kershaw 12.00 30.00
GL20 Joey Votto 15.00 40.00
GL21 Max Scherzer 8.00 20.00
GL22 Manny Machado 8.00 20.00
GL23 Felix Hernandez 6.00 15.00
GL24 Dustin Pedroia 8.00 20.00
GL25 Robinson Cano 6.00 15.00
GL26 Derek Jeter UPD 20.00 50.00
GL27 Mike Trout UPD 40.00 100.00
GL28 Bryce Harper UPD 20.00 50.00
GL29 Prince Fielder UPD 6.00 15.00
GL30 Andrew McCutchen UPD 8.00 20.00
GL31 Miguel Cabrera UPD 12.00 30.00
GL32 Yasiel Puig UPD 8.00 20.00
GL33 Albert Pujols UPD 12.00 30.00
GL34 Frank Thomas UPD 8.00 20.00
GL35 Jose Abreu UPD 20.00 50.00
GL36 Masahiro Tanaka UPD 20.00 50.00
GL37 Sandy Koufax UPD 15.00 40.00
GL38 Mark McGwire UPD 15.00 40.00
GL39 Roberto Clemente UPD 10.00 25.00
GL40 Cal Ripken Jr. UPD 20.00 50.00

2014 Topps Jackie Robinson Reprints Framed Black

COMMON CARD 8.00 20.00
STATED ODDS 1:2844 HOBBY

2014 Topps Jackie Robinson Reprints Framed Silver

*SILVER: .5X TO 1.2X BASIC
STATED ODDS 1:4750 HOBBY
STATED PRINT RUN 50 SER.#'d SETS

2014 Topps Manufactured Commemorative All Rookie Cup Patch

RCMPAM Andrew McCutchen 2.50 6.00
RCMPAP Albert Pujols 3.00 8.00
RCMPBP Buster Posey 3.00 8.00
RCMPCR Cal Ripken Jr. 8.00 20.00
RCMPDJ Derek Jeter 6.00 15.00
RCMPDS Darryl Strawberry 1.50 4.00
RCMPEM Eddie Murray 2.00 5.00
RCMPGC Gary Carter 2.00 5.00
RCMPJB Johnny Bench 2.50 6.00
RCMPJBA Jeff Bagwell 2.00 5.00
RCMPJC Jose Canseco 2.00 5.00
RCMPJM Joe Morgan 2.00 5.00
RCMPJV Joey Votto 2.50 6.00
RCMPJVE Justin Verlander 2.50 6.00
RCMPKG Ken Griffey Jr. 5.00 12.00
RCMPMM Mark McGwire 5.00 12.00
RCMPMR Manny Ramirez 2.50 6.00
RCMPMT Mike Trout 12.00 30.00
RCMPOS Ozzie Smith 3.00 8.00
RCMPRC Rod Carew 2.00 5.00
RCMPSS Stephen Strasburg 2.50 6.00
RCMPTS Tom Seaver 2.00 5.00

RCMPTT Troy Tulowitzki 2.50 6.00
RCMPWM Willie McCovey 2.00 5.00
RCMPYP Yasiel Puig 2.50 6.00

2014 Topps Manufactured Commemorative Team Logo Patch

CP1 Chris Davis 2.50 6.00
CP2 David Ortiz 4.00 10.00
CP3 Prince Fielder 3.00 8.00
CP4 Miguel Cabrera 4.00 10.00
CP5 Allen Craig 3.00 8.00
CP6 Bryce Harper 6.00 15.00
CP7 Mike Trout 20.00 50.00
CP8 Joe Mauer 3.00 8.00
CP9 Mariano Rivera 5.00 12.00
CP10 Derek Jeter 10.00 25.00
CP11 Felix Hernandez 3.00 8.00
CP12 David Price 3.00 8.00
CP13 Yu Darvish 4.00 10.00
CP14 Jose Bautista 3.00 8.00
CP15 Stephen Strasburg 4.00 10.00
CP16 Troy Tulowitzki 4.00 10.00
CP17 Yasiel Puig 4.00 10.00
CP18 Clayton Kershaw 6.00 15.00
CP19 Jose Fernandez 4.00 10.00
CP20 Anthony Rizzo 5.00 12.00
CP21 Matt Harvey 3.00 8.00
CP22 David Wright 3.00 8.00
CP23 Chase Utley 3.00 8.00
CP24 Buster Posey 5.00 12.00
CP25 Adam Wainwright 3.00 8.00
CP26 Chris Davis 2.50 6.00
CP27 David Ortiz 4.00 10.00
CP28 Chris Sale 4.00 10.00
CP29 Paul Goldschmidt 4.00 10.00
CP30 Freddie Freeman 5.00 12.00
CP31 Starlin Castro 2.50 6.00
CP32 Mike Trout 20.00 50.00
CP33 Jean Segura 3.00 8.00
CP34 Joe Mauer 3.00 8.00
CP35 Yoenis Cespedes 4.00 10.00
CP36 Domonic Brown 3.00 8.00
CP37 Jedd Gyorko 2.50 6.00
CP38 Buster Posey 5.00 12.00
CP39 Evan Longoria 3.00 8.00
CP40 David Wright 3.00 8.00
CP41 Jason Kipnis 3.00 8.00
CP42 Troy Tulowitzki 4.00 10.00
CP43 Jose Altuve 3.00 8.00
CP44 Alex Gordon 3.00 8.00
CP45 Hyun-Jin Ryu 3.00 8.00
CP46 Giancarlo Stanton 4.00 10.00
CP47 Andrew McCutchen 4.00 10.00
CP48 Felix Hernandez 3.00 8.00
CP49 Ryan Braun 3.00 8.00
CP50 Joey Votto 4.00 10.00

2014 Topps Manufactured Commemorative Rookie Card Patch

RCP1 Al Kaline 1.50 4.00
RCP2 Ernie Banks 1.50 4.00
RCP3 Sandy Koufax 3.00 8.00
RCP4 Harmon Killebrew 1.50 4.00
RCP5 Roberto Clemente 4.00 10.00
RCP6 Bill Mazeroski 1.25 3.00
RCP7 Frank Robinson 1.25 3.00
RCP8 Brooks Robinson 1.25 3.00
RCP9 George Brett 3.00 8.00
RCP10 Robin Yount 1.50 4.00
RCP11 Wade Boggs 1.25 3.00
RCP12 Ryne Sandberg 3.00 8.00
RCP13 Tony Gwynn 1.50 4.00
RCP14 Greg Maddux 2.00 5.00
RCP15 Bryce Harper 2.50 6.00
RCP16 Yu Darvish 1.50 4.00
RCP17 Yoenis Cespedes 1.50 4.00
RCP18 Matt Harvey 1.25 3.00
RCP19 Don Mattingly 3.00 8.00
RCP20 Dwight Gooden 1.00 2.50
RCP21 Randy Johnson 1.50 4.00
RCP22 Clayton Kershaw 2.50 6.00
RCP23 Joey Votto 1.50 4.00
RCP25 John Smoltz 1.50 4.00

2014 Topps Postseason Performance Autograph Relics

STATED ODDS 1:4250 HOBBY
STATED PRINT RUN 50 SER.#'d SETS
EXCHANGE DEADLINE 1/31/2017
PPARAS Anibal Sanchez EXCH 20.00 50.00
PPARCK Clayton Kershaw 60.00 150.00
PPARDO David Ortiz 60.00 150.00
PPAREL Evan Longoria 10.00 25.00
PPARMC Miguel Cabrera 60.00 150.00
PPARMH Matt Holliday EXCH 40.00 100.00
PPARMW Michael Wacha 100.00 200.00
PPARWM Wil Myers 8.00 20.00
PPARYC Yoenis Cespedes 12.00 30.00
PPARYP Yasiel Puig EXCH 75.00 200.00

2014 Topps Postseason Performance Autographs

STATED ODDS 1:14,250 HOBBY
STATED PRINT RUN 50 SER.#'d SETS
EXCHANGE DEADLINE 1/31/2017
PPAAS Anibal Sanchez EXCH 12.00 30.00
PPACK Clayton Kershaw 75.00 150.00
PPADF David Freese 40.00 80.00
PPADO David Ortiz EXCH 75.00 150.00
PPAFF Freddie Freeman 30.00 60.00
PPAMH Matt Holliday EXCH 30.00 60.00
PPAMW Michael Wacha 60.00 120.00
PPAWM Wil Myers 12.00 30.00
PPAYC Yoenis Cespedes 40.00 80.00

2014 Topps Postseason Performance Relics

STATED ODDS 1:2900 HOBBY
STATED PRINT RUN 100 SER.#'d SETS
EXCHANGE DEADLINE 1/31/2017
PPRAM Andrew McCutchen 12.00 30.00
PPRAS Anibal Sanchez 15.00 40.00
PPRCK Clayton Kershaw 10.00 25.00
PPRCKI Craig Kimbrel 12.00 30.00
PPRDF David Freese 10.00 25.00
PPRDO David Ortiz 10.00 25.00
PPRDP Dustin Pedroia 15.00 40.00
PPREL Evan Longoria 6.00 15.00
PPRFF Freddie Freeman 20.00 50.00
PPRHR Hanley Ramirez 12.00 30.00
PPRJE Jacoby Ellsbury 8.00 20.00
PPRJU Justin Upton 12.00 30.00
PPRJV Justin Verlander 8.00 20.00
PPRMC Miguel Cabrera 20.00 50.00
PPRMH Matt Holliday 20.00 50.00
PPRMW Michael Wacha 15.00 40.00
PPRPA Pedro Alvarez 15.00 40.00
PPRPF Prince Fielder 12.00 30.00
PPRVM Victor Martinez 12.00 30.00
PPRWMY Wil Myers 15.00 40.00
PPRXB Xander Bogaerts 40.00 80.00
PPRYC Yoenis Cespedes 12.00 30.00
PPRYM Yadier Molina 50.00 100.00
PPRYP Yasiel Puig 20.00 50.00
PPRZG Zack Greinke 10.00 25.00

2014 Topps Power Players

STATED ODDS 1:12 HOBBY
PP1 Bryce Harper 1.50 4.00
PP2 Cole Hamels .75 2.00
PP3 Wade Miley .60 1.50
PP4 Troy Tulowitzki 1.00 2.50
PP5 Andrew McCutchen 1.00 2.50
PP6 Nick Swisher .75 2.00
PP7 Aaron Hill .60 1.50
PP8 Alex Rios .75 2.00
PP9 Ernesto Frieri .60 1.50
PP10 Ben Revere .60 1.50
PP11 Chris Tillman .60 1.50
PP12 Clay Buchholz .60 1.50
PP13 Charlie Blackmon 1.00 2.50
PP14 Garrett Jones .60 1.50
PP15 Garrett Richards .75 2.00
PP16 Lonnie Chisenhall .60 1.50
PP17 Kolten Wong .75 2.00
PP18 Chris Perez .60 1.50
PP19 Matt Adams .60 1.50
PP20 Jason Heyward .75 2.00
PP21 Doug Fister .60 1.50
PP22 Jose Quintana .60 1.50
PP23 Mike Minor .60 1.50
PP24 Matt Holliday 1.00 2.50
PP25 Lance Lynn .60 1.50
PP26 Jon Lester .75 2.00
PP27 Onelki Garcia .60 1.50
PP28 Giancarlo Stanton 1.00 2.50
PP29 Kevin Pillar .60 1.50
PP30 Chad Bettis .60 1.50
PP31 Joe Blanton .60 1.50
PP32 Jason Kipnis .75 2.00
PP33 Ian Desmond .60 1.50
PP34 Adam LaRoche .60 1.50
PP35 David Freese .60 1.50
PP36 Martin Perez .75 2.00
PP37 Chris Iannetta .60 1.50
PP38 Sean Burnett .60 1.50
PP39 Adrian Gonzalez .75 2.00
PP40 Manny Machado 1.00 2.50
PP41 Matt Lindstrom .60 1.50
PP42 Matt Thornton .60 1.50
PP43 Trevor Cahill .60 1.50
PP44 Junior Lake .60 1.50
PP45 Johnny Cueto .75 2.00
PP46 Wei-Yin Chen .60 1.50
PP47 Carlos Villanueva .60 1.50
PP48 Max Scherzer 1.00 2.50
PP49 C.J. Wilson .60 1.50
PP50 Chris Owings .60 1.50
PP51 Shin-Soo Choo .75 2.00
PP52 Yadier Molina 1.25 3.00
PP53 Yonder Alonso .60 1.50
PP54 Ryan Howard .75 2.00
PP55 Jason Grilli .60 1.50
PP56 Zack Greinke 1.00 2.50
PP57 Justin Upton .75 2.00
PP58 Chris Sale 1.00 2.50
PP59 Yu Darvish 1.00 2.50
PP60 Carlos Gomez .60 1.50
PP61 Joey Votto 1.00 2.50
PP62 Pablo Sandoval .75 2.00
PP63 Matt Davidson .75 2.00
PP64 Jordan Zimmermann .75 2.00
PP65 Ethan Martin .60 1.50
PP66 Brandon McCarthy .60 1.50
PP67 Cliff Pennington .60 1.50
PP68 Torii Hunter .60 1.50
PP69 Dustin Pedroia 1.00 2.50
PP70 Mark Trumbo .60 1.50
PP71 Mike Zunino .60 1.50
PP72 Michael Brantley .75 2.00
PP73 Paul Goldschmidt 1.00 2.50
PP74 Erik Johnson .60 1.50
PP75 Marcell Ozuna 1.00 2.50
PP76 Mike Leake .60 1.50
PP77 Derek Jeter 2.50 6.00
PP78 Jake Peavy .60 1.50
PP79 Shane Victorino .75 2.00
PP80 Aroldis Chapman 1.00 2.50
PP81 Miguel Montero .60 1.50
PP82 Julio Teheran .75 2.00
PP83 Wilmer Flores .75 2.00
PP84 Alexei Ramirez .75 2.00
PP85 Melky Cabrera .60 1.50
PP86 Jhonny Peralta .60 1.50
PP87 Dayan Viciedo .60 1.50
PP88 Hiroki Kuroda .60 1.50
PP89 Brandon Belt .75 2.00
PP90 Brandon Crawford .75 2.00
PP91 Hector Santiago .60 1.50
PP92 Elvis Andrus .75 2.00
PP93 Jeff Samardzija .60 1.50
PP94 Kyle Lohse .60 1.50
PP95 James Shields .60 1.50
PP96 Darwin Barney .60 1.50
PP97 Nate McLouth .60 1.50
PP98 Tyler Skaggs .60 1.50
PP99 Jay Bruce .75 2.00
PP100 Hanley Ramirez .75 2.00
PP101 Brian McCann .75 2.00
PP102 Jurickson Profar .75 2.00
PP103 Jose Altuve .75 2.00
PP104 Joe Mauer .75 2.00
PP105 Carlos Ruiz .60 1.50
PP106 Edwin Encarnacion 1.00 2.50
PP107 Sergio Romo .60 1.50
PP108 Buster Posey 1.25 3.00
PP109 James Paxton 1.00 2.50
PP110 Chris Nelson .60 1.50
PP111 Matt Kemp .75 2.00
PP112 David Price .75 2.00
PP113 Evan Gattis .60 1.50
PP114 Nelson Cruz 1.00 2.50
PP115 Patrick Corbin .75 2.00
PP116 Colby Rasmus .75 2.00
PP117 Adam Wainwright .75 2.00
PP118 Brad Miller .75 2.00
PP119 Shelby Miller .75 2.00
PP120 Koji Uehara .60 1.50
PP121 Michael Bourn .60 1.50
PP122 Brad Ziegler .60 1.50
PP123 Scott Kazmir .60 1.50
PP124 Trevor Bauer 1.25 3.00
PP125 Aramis Ramirez .60 1.50
PP126 Jackie Bradley Jr. 1.00 2.50
PP127 Addison Reed .60 1.50
PP128 Ben Zobrist .75 2.00
PP129 Carlos Martinez .75 2.00
PP130 Martin Prado .60 1.50
PP131 Adam Eaton .60 1.50
PP132 Todd Frazier .60 1.50
PP133 Derek Holland .60 1.50
PP134 Carlos Santana .75 2.00
PP135 Marcus Semien 3.00 8.00
PP136 Masahiro Tanaka 4.00 10.00
PP137 Ryan Braun .75 2.00
PP138 Brandon Phillips .60 1.50
PP139 Ian Kennedy .60 1.50
PP140 Danny Salazar .75 2.00
PP141 CC Sabathia .75 2.00
PP142 Christian Yelich 1.25 3.00
PP143 Mat Latos .75 2.00
PP144 Stephen Strasburg 1.00 2.50
PP145 Ian Kinsler .75 2.00
PP146 Kyuji Fujikawa .75 2.00
PP147 Drew Storen .60 1.50
PP148 Mike Napoli .60 1.50
PP149 Prince Fielder .75 2.00
PP150 David Wright .75 2.00
PP151 Matt Cain .75 2.00
PP152 Justin Verlander 1.00 2.50
PP153 Jose Fernandez 1.00 2.50
PP154 Tim Hudson .75 2.00
PP155 Josh Reddick .60 1.50
PP156 Starlin Castro .60 1.50
PP157 Carlos Beltran .75 2.00
PP158 Ryan Zimmerman .75 2.00
PP159 Adam Dunn .75 2.00
PP160 Jose Reyes .75 2.00
PP161 Norichika Aoki .60 1.50
PP162 Albert Pujols 1.25 3.00
PP163 Wilin Rosario .60 1.50
PP164 Brian Wilson 1.00 2.50
PP165 Peter Bourjos .60 1.50
PP166 Jed Lowrie .60 1.50
PP167 Cliff Lee .75 2.00
PP168 Anthony Rendon 1.00 2.50
PP169 Freddie Freeman 1.25 3.00
PP170 Yovani Gallardo .60 1.50
PP171 Phil Hughes .60 1.50
PP172 Allen Craig .75 2.00
PP173 Gerardo Parra .60 1.50
PP174 Adam Jones .75 2.00
PP175 Jedd Gyorko .60 1.50
PP176 Chris Archer .60 1.50
PP177 Paul Konerko .75 2.00
PP178 Mike Moustakas .75 2.00
PP179 Chase Headley .60 1.50
PP180 Tim Lincecum .75 2.00
PP181 Dan Uggla .60 1.50
PP182 Corey Hart .60 1.50
PP183 Sonny Gray .75 2.00
PP184 Dylan Bundy .75 2.00
PP185 Jarrod Parker .60 1.50
PP186 Gio Gonzalez .75 2.00
PP187 J.J. Hardy .60 1.50
PP188 Michael Cuddyer .60 1.50
PP189 Madison Bumgarner .75 2.00
PP190 Rick Porcello .75 2.00
PP191 Salvador Perez .75 2.00
PP192 Ivan Nova .75 2.00
PP193 Jose Iglesias .75 2.00
PP194 Jacoby Ellsbury .75 2.00
PP195 Bartolo Colon .60 1.50
PP196 Carl Crawford .75 2.00
PP197 Christian Bethancourt .60 1.50
PP198 Matt Garza .60 1.50
PP199 Matt Moore .75 2.00
PP200 Clayton Kershaw 1.50 4.00
PP201 Mark Teixeira .75 2.00
PP202 Tony Cingrani .75 2.00
PP203 Hunter Pence .75 2.00
PP204 Michael Wacha .75 2.00
PP205 Curtis Granderson .75 2.00
PP206 Joe Nathan .60 1.50
PP207 B.J. Upton .75 2.00
PP208 Michael Pineda .60 1.50
PP209 Chris Davis .60 1.50
PP210 Andre Ethier .75 2.00
PP211 Jered Weaver .75 2.00
PP212 Brandon Beachy .60 1.50
PP213 Alex Wood .60 1.50
PP214 Felix Hernandez .75 2.00
PP215 Josh Hamilton .75 2.00
PP216 Homer Bailey .60 1.50
PP217 Glen Perkins .60 1.50
PP218 Chase Utley .75 2.00
PP219 Eric Hosmer .75 2.00
PP220 Jose Abreu 3.00 8.00

2014 Topps Power Players Autographs

UPDATE ODDS 1:7334 HOBBY
PRINT RUNS B/WN 15-40 COPIES PER
NO PRICING ON QTY 15
UPD EXCH DEADLINE 9/30/2017
PPAAG Adrian Gonzalez/25 UPD 50.00 100.00
PPAAJ Adam Jones/25 UPD 25.00 60.00
PPAAM A.McCutchen/25 UPD 60.00 120.00
PPAAR Anthony Rizzo/25 UPD 25.00 60.00
PPAGS Giancarlo Stanton/25 UPD 20.00 50.00
PPAJA J.Abreu/25 UPD EXCH 100.00 200.00
PPAJB Jose Bautista/25 UPD 15.00 40.00
PPAJL Junior Lake/40 12.00 30.00
PPAMS Max Scherzer/25 UPD 30.00 80.00
PPAPG Paul Goldschmidt/25 UPD 20.00 50.00
PPARC Robinson Cano/25 UPD 15.00 40.00
PPATT Troy Tulowitzki/25 UPD 20.00 50.00
PPAYV Yordano Ventura/25 UPD 15.00 40.00
PPACGN Carlos Gonzalez/25 UPD 15.00 40.00

2014 Topps Rookie Cup All Stars Commemorative

STATED ODDS 1:4375 HOBBY
STATED PRINT RUN 99 SER.#'d SETS
RCAS1 Cal Ripken Jr. 25.00 60.00
RCAS2 Tony Perez 12.00 30.00
RCAS3 Rod Carew 10.00 25.00
RCAS4 Carlton Fisk 10.00 25.00
RCAS5 Gary Carter 12.50 30.00
RCAS6 Andre Dawson 8.00 20.00
RCAS7 Paul Molitor 10.00 25.00
RCAS8 Ozzie Smith 10.00 25.00
RCAS9 Ryne Sandberg 12.00 30.00
RCAS10 Darryl Strawberry 8.00 20.00
RCAS11 Dwight Gooden 8.00 20.00
RCAS12 Nomar Garciaparra 10.00 25.00
RCAS13 Joe Mauer 12.50 30.00
RCAS14 Justin Verlander 8.00 20.00
RCAS15 Troy Tulowitzki 8.00 20.00
RCAS16 Ryan Braun 6.00 15.00
RCAS17 Dustin Pedroia 12.00 30.00
RCAS18 Joey Votto 8.00 20.00
RCAS19 Evan Longoria 6.00 15.00
RCAS20 Andrew McCutchen 12.00 30.00
RCAS21 Buster Posey 10.00 25.00
RCAS22 Stephen Strasburg 8.00 20.00
RCAS23 Bryce Harper 12.00 30.00
RCAS24 Yu Darvish 10.00 25.00
RCAS25 Fred Lynn 10.00 25.00

2014 Topps Rookie Cup All Stars Commemorative Vintage

*VINTAGE: .6X TO 1.5X BASIC
STATED ODDS 1:17,200 HOBBY
STATED PRINT RUN 25 SER.#'d SETS

2014 Topps Rookie Reprints Framed Black

STATED ODDS 1:428 HOBBY
STATED PRINT RUN 199 SER.#'d SETS
RCF1 Willie Mays 12.00 30.00
RCF2 Ernie Banks 10.00 25.00
RCF3 Sandy Koufax 12.00 30.00
RCF4 Roberto Clemente 12.00 30.00
RCF5 Brooks Robinson 8.00 20.00
RCF6 Frank Robinson 8.00 20.00
RCF7 Bob Gibson 8.00 20.00
RCF8 Willie McCovey 8.00 20.00
RCF9 Reggie Jackson 8.00 20.00
RCF10 Robin Yount 10.00 25.00
RCF11 George Brett 10.00 25.00
RCF12 Eddie Murray 8.00 20.00
RCF13 Ozzie Smith 10.00 25.00
RCF14 Rickey Henderson 10.00 25.00
RCF15 Cal Ripken Jr. 15.00 40.00
RCF16 Tony Gwynn 8.00 20.00
RCF17 Wade Boggs 8.00 20.00
RCF18 Don Mattingly 10.00 25.00
RCF19 Ken Griffey Jr. 10.00 25.00
RCF20 Derek Jeter 15.00 40.00
RCF21 Miguel Cabrera 10.00 25.00
RCF22 Justin Verlander 10.00 25.00
RCF23 Buster Posey 10.00 25.00
RCF24 Mike Trout 15.00 40.00
RCF25 Bryce Harper 15.00 40.00

2014 Topps Rookie Reprints Framed Gold

*GOLD: 1X TO 2.5X BASIC
STATED ODDS 1:3400 HOBBY
STATED PRINT RUN 25 SER.#'d SETS
RCF1 Willie Mays 75.00 150.00
RCF8 Willie McCovey 30.00 80.00
RCF9 Reggie Jackson 75.00 150.00
RCF14 Rickey Henderson 75.00 150.00
RCF15 Cal Ripken Jr. 60.00 120.00
RCF19 Ken Griffey Jr. 90.00 150.00
RCF20 Derek Jeter 100.00 200.00
RCF23 Buster Posey 90.00 150.00
RCF24 Mike Trout 90.00 150.00
RCF25 Bryce Harper 90.00 150.00

2014 Topps Rookie Reprints Framed Silver

*SILVER: .5X TO 1.2X BASIC
STATED ODDS 1:859 HOBBY
STATED PRINT RUN 99 SER.#'d SETS

2014 Topps Saber Stars

COMPLETE SET (25) 5.00 12.00
STATED ODDS 1:8 HOBBY
SST1 Mike Trout 2.00 5.00
SST2 Clayton Kershaw .60 1.50
SST3 Carlos Gomez .25 .60
SST4 Andrew McCutchen .40 1.00
SST5 Josh Donaldson .30 .75
SST6 Matt Carpenter .40 1.00
SST7 Robinson Cano .30 .75
SST8 Miguel Cabrera .40 1.00
SST9 Paul Goldschmidt .40 1.00
SST10 Evan Longoria .30 .75
SST11 Joe Mauer .30 .75
SST12 Michael Cuddyer .25 .60
SST13 Chris Davis .25 .60
SST14 Joey Votto .40 1.00
SST15 Freddie Freeman .50 1.25
SST16 Allen Craig .30 .75
SST17 Jacoby Ellsbury .30 .75
SST18 Juan Uribe .25 .60
SST19 Manny Machado .40 1.00
SST20 Shane Victorino .30 .75
SST21 Andrelton Simmons .25 .60
SST22 Matt Harvey .30 .75
SST23 Anibal Sanchez .25 .60
SST24 Adam Wainwright .30 .75
SST25 Felix Hernandez .30 .75

2014 Topps Saber Stars Autograph Relics

STATED ODDS 1:4620 HOBBY
STATED PRINT RUN 25 SER.#'d SETS
EXCHANGE DEADLINE 5/31/2017
SSTARAC Allen Craig 15.00 40.00
SSTARAS Andrelton Simmons EXCH 12.00 30.00
SSTARCK Clayton Kershaw 60.00 150.00
SSTAREL Evan Longoria 20.00 50.00
SSTARJV Joey Votto 40.00 100.00
SSTARMC Michael Cuddyer 12.00 30.00
SSTARMCA Miguel Cabrera 150.00 250.00
SSTARMM Manny Machado 60.00 150.00
SSTARMT Mike Trout EXCH 150.00 300.00
SSTARPG Paul Goldschmidt 20.00 50.00

2014 Topps Saber Stars Autographs

STATED ODDS 1:7290 HOBBY
STATED PRINT RUN 50 SER.#'d SETS
EXCHANGE DEADLINE 5/31/2017
SSTAAC Allen Craig 20.00 50.00
SSTAAS Andrelton Simmons EXCH 10.00 25.00
SSTACK Clayton Kershaw 60.00 150.00
SSTAEL Evan Longoria EXCH 12.00 30.00
SSTAFF Freddie Freeman 20.00 50.00
SSTAJV Joey Votto 20.00 50.00
SSTAMC Michael Cuddyer 10.00 25.00
SSTAMM Manny Machado 15.00 40.00
SSTAMT Mike Trout 150.00 250.00
SSTAPG Paul Goldschmidt 15.00 40.00

2014 Topps Saber Stars Relics

STATED ODDS 1:3697 HOBBY
STATED PRINT RUN 99 SER.#'d SETS
SSTRAC Allen Craig 25.00 60.00
SSTRCK Clayton Kershaw 25.00 60.00
SSTREL Evan Longoria 4.00 10.00
SSTRFF Freddie Freeman 6.00 15.00
SSTRJE Jacoby Ellsbury 10.00 25.00
SSTRJV Joey Votto 5.00 12.00
SSTRMC Michael Cuddyer 25.00 60.00
SSTRMM Manny Machado 5.00 12.00
SSTRMT Mike Trout 25.00 60.00
SSTRPG Paul Goldschmidt 5.00 12.00

2014 Topps Silk Collection

SERIES ONE ODDS 1:424 HOBBY
SERIES TWO ODDS 1:232 HOBBY
STATED PRINT RUN 50 SER.#'d SETS
CARDS LISTED ALPHABETICALLY
1 Matt Adams 4.00 10.00
2 Yonder Alonso 4.00 10.00
3 Jose Altuve 5.00 12.00
4 Pedro Alvarez 4.00 10.00
5 Elvis Andrus 5.00 12.00
6 Norichika Aoki S2 4.00 10.00
7 Chris Archer S2 4.00 10.00
8 Nolan Arenado 10.00 25.00
9 Homer Bailey S2 4.00 10.00
10 Jose Bautista 5.00 12.00
11 Brandon Beachy S2 4.00 10.00
12 Brandon Belt 5.00 12.00
13 Carlos Beltran S2 5.00 12.00
14 Adrian Beltre 6.00 15.00
15 Michael Bourn S2 4.00 10.00
16 Ryan Braun S2 5.00 12.00
17 Domonic Brown 5.00 12.00
18 Madison Bumgarner S2 5.00 12.00
19 Asdrubal Cabrera S2 5.00 12.00
20 Melky Cabrera 4.00 10.00
21 Miguel Cabrera 6.00 15.00
22 Matt Cain S2 5.00 12.00
23 Robinson Cano S2 5.00 12.00
24 Starlin Castro S2 4.00 10.00
25 Yoenis Cespedes 6.00 15.00
26 Aroldis Chapman 6.00 15.00
27 Shin-Soo Choo 5.00 12.00
28 Tony Cingrani S2 5.00 12.00
29 Gerrit Cole 6.00 15.00
30 Patrick Corbin S2 5.00 12.00
31 Allen Craig S2 5.00 12.00
32 Brandon Crawford 5.00 12.00
33 Carl Crawford S2 5.00 12.00
34 Michael Cuddyer S2 4.00 10.00
35 Johnny Cueto 5.00 12.00
36 Yu Darvish 6.00 15.00
37 Chris Davis S2 4.00 10.00
38 Ian Desmond 4.00 10.00
39 R.A. Dickey S2 5.00 12.00
40 Josh Donaldson 5.00 12.00
41 Adam Dunn S2 5.00 12.00
42 Adam Eaton S2 4.00 10.00
43 Jacoby Ellsbury S2 5.00 12.00
44 Edwin Encarnacion 6.00 15.00
45 Jose Fernandez S2 6.00 15.00
46 Prince Fielder S2 5.00 12.00
47 Doug Fister 4.00 10.00
48 Nick Franklin 4.00 10.00
49 Todd Frazier S2 4.00 10.00
50 Freddie Freeman S2 8.00 20.00
51 David Freese 4.00 10.00
52 Yovani Gallardo S2 4.00 10.00
53 Evan Gattis S2 4.00 10.00
54 Kevin Gausman 6.00 15.00
55 Paul Goldschmidt 6.00 15.00
56 Carlos Gomez 4.00 10.00
57 Adrian Gonzalez 5.00 12.00
58 Carlos Gonzalez S2 5.00 12.00
59 Gio Gonzalez S2 5.00 12.00
60 Curtis Granderson S2 5.00 12.00
61 Sonny Gray S2 5.00 12.00
62 Zack Greinke 6.00 15.00
63 Jason Grilli 4.00 10.00
64 Jedd Gyorko S2 4.00 10.00
65 Roy Halladay S2 5.00 12.00
66 Cole Hamels 5.00 12.00
67 Josh Hamilton S2 5.00 12.00
68 J.J. Hardy S2 4.00 10.00
69 Bryce Harper 10.00 25.00
70 Matt Harvey 5.00 12.00
71 Chase Headley S2 4.00 10.00
72 Jeremy Hellickson 4.00 10.00
73 Felix Hernandez S2 5.00 12.00
74 Jason Heyward 5.00 12.00
75 Aaron Hicks 5.00 12.00
76 Derek Holland S2 4.00 10.00
77 Greg Holland S2 4.00 10.00
78 Matt Holliday 6.00 15.00
79 Eric Hosmer S2 5.00 12.00
80 Ryan Howard 5.00 12.00
81 Torii Hunter 4.00 10.00
82 Jose Iglesias S2 5.00 12.00
83 Austin Jackson S2 4.00 10.00
84 Kenley Jansen S2 5.00 12.00
85 Desmond Jennings S2 5.00 12.00
86 Derek Jeter 15.00 40.00
87 Chris Johnson S2 4.00 10.00
88 Adam Jones S2 5.00 12.00
89 Garrett Jones 4.00 10.00
90 Joe Kelly 4.00 10.00
91 Matt Kemp S2 5.00 12.00
92 Clayton Kershaw S2 10.00 25.00
93 Craig Kimbrel S2 5.00 12.00
94 Ian Kinsler S2 5.00 12.00
95 Jason Kipnis 5.00 12.00
96 Paul Konerko S2 5.00 12.00
97 Hiroki Kuroda 4.00 10.00
98 John Lackey S2 5.00 12.00
99 Adam LaRoche 4.00 10.00
100 Mat Latos S2 5.00 12.00
101 Brett Lawrie S2 5.00 12.00
102 Mike Leake 4.00 10.00
103 Cliff Lee S2 5.00 12.00
104 Jon Lester 5.00 12.00
105 Tim Lincecum S2 5.00 12.00
106 Kyle Lohse 4.00 10.00
107 Evan Longoria 5.00 12.00
108 Jed Lowrie S2 4.00 10.00
109 Lance Lynn 4.00 10.00
110 Manny Machado 6.00 15.00
111 Nick Markakis 5.00 12.00
112 Starling Marte 5.00 12.00
113 Carlos Martinez S2 5.00 12.00
114 Victor Martinez 5.00 12.00
115 Justin Masterson S2 4.00 10.00
116 Joe Mauer 5.00 12.00
117 Brian McCann 5.00 12.00
118 Andrew McCutchen 6.00 15.00
119 Kris Medlen 5.00 12.00
120 Wade Miley 4.00 10.00
121 Shelby Miller S2 5.00 12.00
122 Yadier Molina 8.00 20.00
123 Matt Moore S2 5.00 12.00
124 Wil Myers 4.00 10.00
125 Mike Napoli S2 4.00 10.00
126 Joe Nathan S2 4.00 10.00
127 Ivan Nova S2 5.00 12.00
128 David Ortiz S2 6.00 15.00
129 Marcell Ozuna 6.00 15.00
130 Jarrod Parker S2 4.00 10.00
131 Dustin Pedroia 6.00 15.00
132 Hunter Pence S2 5.00 12.00
133 Jhonny Peralta 4.00 10.00
134 Chris Perez 4.00 10.00
135 Salvador Perez S2 5.00 12.00
136 Glen Perkins S2 4.00 10.00
137 Brandon Phillips S2 4.00 10.00
138 Buster Posey 8.00 20.00
139 Martin Prado S2 4.00 10.00
140 David Price S2 5.00 12.00
141 Jurickson Profar 5.00 12.00
142 Yasiel Puig 6.00 15.00
143 Albert Pujols S2 8.00 20.00
144 Aramis Ramirez S2 4.00 10.00
145 Hanley Ramirez 5.00 12.00
146 Colby Rasmus S2 5.00 12.00
147 Josh Reddick S2 4.00 10.00
148 Addison Reed S2 4.00 10.00
149 Anthony Rendon S2 6.00 15.00
150 Ben Revere 4.00 10.00
151 Jose Reyes S2 5.00 12.00
152 Anthony Rizzo 8.00 20.00
153 Jimmy Rollins 5.00 12.00
154 Sergio Romo 4.00 10.00
155 Wilin Rosario S2 4.00 10.00
156 Trevor Rosenthal 5.00 12.00
157 Carlos Ruiz 4.00 10.00
158 Hyun-Jin Ryu 5.00 12.00
159 CC Sabathia S2 5.00 12.00
160 Danny Salazar S2 5.00 12.00
161 Chris Sale 6.00 15.00
162 Jeff Samardzija 4.00 10.00
163 Pablo Sandoval 5.00 12.00
164 Carlos Santana S2 5.00 12.00
165 Max Scherzer 6.00 15.00
166 Kyle Seager 4.00 10.00
167 Jean Segura 5.00 12.00
168 James Shields 4.00 10.00
169 Tyler Skaggs 4.00 10.00
170 Rafael Soriano 4.00 10.00
171 Giancarlo Stanton 6.00 15.00
172 Stephen Strasburg S2 6.00 15.00
173 Nick Swisher 5.00 12.00
174 Julio Teheran 5.00 12.00
175 Mark Teixeira S2 5.00 12.00
176 Mike Trout 30.00 80.00
177 Mark Trumbo 4.00 10.00
178 Troy Tulowitzki 6.00 15.00
179 Koji Uehara S2 4.00 10.00
180 B.J. Upton S2 5.00 12.00
181 Justin Upton 5.00 12.00
182 Chase Utley S2 5.00 12.00
183 Justin Verlander S2 6.00 15.00
184 Shane Victorino 5.00 12.00
185 Joey Votto 6.00 15.00
186 Michael Wacha S2 5.00 12.00
187 Adam Wainwright S2 5.00 12.00
188 Neil Walker S2 4.00 10.00
189 Jered Weaver S2 5.00 12.00
190 Jayson Werth 5.00 12.00
191 Zack Wheeler 5.00 12.00
192 Brian Wilson S2 6.00 15.00
193 C.J. Wilson 4.00 10.00
194 Alex Wood S2 4.00 10.00
195 David Wright S2 5.00 12.00
196 Christian Yelich S2 8.00 20.00
197 Ryan Zimmerman S2 5.00 12.00
198 Jordan Zimmermann 5.00 12.00
199 Ben Zobrist S2 5.00 12.00
200 Mike Zunino 4.00 10.00

2014 Topps Spring Fever

COMPLETE SET (50) 12.00 30.00
SF1 Evan Longoria .25 .60
SF2 Mike Trout 1.50 4.00
SF3 Robinson Cano .25 .60
SF4 Miguel Cabrera .30 .75
SF5 Carlos Gonzalez .25 .60
SF6 Chris Davis .20 .50
SF7 Adam Jones .25 .60
SF8 Adrian Beltre .30 .75
SF9 Jose Bautista .25 .60
SF10 Clayton Kershaw .50 1.25
SF11 Hanley Ramirez .25 .60
SF12 Prince Fielder .25 .60
SF13 Adam Wainwright .25 .60
SF14 Felix Hernandez .25 .60
SF15 Ryan Braun .25 .60
SF16 Freddie Freeman .40 1.00
SF17 Billy Hamilton .25 .60
SF18 Giancarlo Stanton .30 .75
SF19 Mariano Rivera .40 1.00
SF20 Jose Fernandez .30 .75
SF21 Chris Sale .30 .75
SF22 Buster Posey .40 1.00
SF23 Joe Mauer .25 .60
SF24 Justin Verlander .30 .75
SF25 Yasiel Puig .30 .75
SF26 Albert Pujols .40 1.00
SF27 Jose Reyes .25 .60
SF28 Justin Upton .25 .60
SF29 David Ortiz .30 .75
SF30 Yoenis Cespedes .30 .75
SF31 Michael Wacha .25 .60
SF32 Xander Bogaerts .60 1.50
SF33 Max Scherzer .30 .75
SF34 Bryce Harper .50 1.25
SF35 Yu Darvish .30 .75
SF36 Andrew McCutchen .30 .75
SF37 Josh Hamilton .25 .60
SF38 Wil Myers .20 .50
SF39 Paul Goldschmidt .30 .75
SF40 Jason Heyward .25 .60
SF41 Craig Kimbrel .25 .60
SF42 Dustin Pedroia .30 .75
SF43 CC Sabathia .25 .60
SF44 Edwin Encarnacion .30 .75
SF45 Joey Votto .30 .75
SF46 Jason Kipnis .25 .60
SF47 Troy Tulowitzki .30 .75
SF48 Stephen Strasburg .30 .75
SF49 Adrian Gonzalez .25 .60
SF50 Derek Jeter 2.00 5.00

2014 Topps Spring Fever Autographs

PRINT RUNS B/WN 5-600 COPIES PER
NO PRICING ON QTY 10 OR LESS
SFAAW Allen Webster/150 10.00 25.00
SFABM Brad Miller/600 5.00 12.00
SFADB Domonic Brown/150 10.00 25.00
SFADS Duke Snider/20
SFAJK Joe Kelly/300 4.00 10.00
SFAJP Johnny Podres/30 20.00 50.00
SFANE Nate Eovaldi/300 5.00 12.00
SFASD Steve Delabar/300 4.00 10.00
SFATC Tony Cingrani/150 8.00 20.00
SFADBU Dylan Bundy/150 5.00 12.00

2014 Topps Strata Autograph Relics

SERIES ONE ODDS 1:3400 HOBBY
SERIES TWO ODDS 1:1850 HOBBY
UPDATE ODDS 1:26,002 HOBBY
STATED PRINT RUN 25 SER.#'d SETS
SER.1 EXCH DEADLINE 1/31/2017
SER.2 EXCH DEADLINE 5/31/2017
UPD EXCH DEADLINE 9/30/2017
SSRAJ A.Jones UPD EXCH 30.00 80.00
SSRBJ B.Jackson UPD EXCH 50.00 120.00
SSRBP Posey EXCH 200.00 300.00
SSRCB Craig Biggio S2 50.00 100.00
SSRCG Gonzalez EXCH 50.00 120.00
SSRCK Kershaw UPD EXCH 125.00 250.00
SSRCR Ripken Jr. S2 EXCH 150.00 250.00
SSRCS Chris Sale UPD 30.00 80.00
SSRDM Dale Murphy UPD 50.00 100.00
SSRDO David Ortiz S2 75.00 150.00
SSRDP Dustin Pedroia 200.00 400.00
SSRDP Pedroia S2 EXCH 75.00 150.00
SSRDPR Price EXCH 30.00 60.00
SSRDW Wright EXCH 200.00 300.00
SSRDW Wright S2 EXCH 75.00 150.00
SSREB Banks S2 EXCH 150.00 250.00
SSREL Longoria UPD EXCH 25.00 60.00
SSREM Edgar Martinez UPD 50.00 100.00
SSRFF Freddie Freeman UPD 30.00 80.00
SSRGG Gonzalez EXCH 75.00 150.00
SSRGM Maddux S2 EXCH 60.00 150.00
SSRGS Stanton EXCH 75.00 150.00
SSRHA Aaron S2 EXCH 200.00 300.00
SSRIR Rodriguez EXCH 75.00 150.00
SSRIR Rodriguez S2 EXCH 60.00 120.00
SSRJB Bautista EXCH 40.00 100.00
SSRJB Bench S2 EXCH 40.00 100.00
SSRJC Canseco EXCH 75.00 150.00
SSRJD Josh Donaldson UPD 25.00 60.00
SSRJF Fernandez EXCH 175.00 350.00
SSRJG Juan Gonzalez UPD 25.00 60.00
SSRJH Josh Hamilton 75.00 150.00
SSRJP Posada UPD EXCH 50.00 100.00
SSRJS Segura EXCH 60.00 120.00
SSRJT Teheran UPD EXCH 30.00 80.00
SSRJV Joey Votto UPD 30.00 80.00
SSRKG Griffey Jr. S2 EXCH 250.00 350.00
SSRKW Kolten Wong UPD 100.00 200.00
SSRLG L.Gonzalez UPD EXCH 20.00 50.00
SSRMC Cabrera EXCH 150.00 250.00
SSRMC Cabrera S2 EXCH 150.00 250.00
SSRMCA Cain EXCH 60.00 120.00
SSRMM Manny Machado 250.00 400.00
SSRMM McGwire UPD EXCH 100.00 200.00
SSRMR Rivera S2 EXCH 150.00 250.00
SSRMS Schmidt S2 EXCH 75.00 150.00
SSRMT Trout S2 EXCH 175.00 350.00
SSRNG Garciaparra UPD EXCH 30.00 80.00
SSRNR Nolan Ryan S2 75.00 200.00
SSROS Smith EXCH 150.00 300.00
SSROS Smith S2 EXCH 60.00 120.00
SSRPF Fielder EXCH 30.00 80.00
SSRPG Paul Goldschmidt 150.00 250.00
SSRPM Martinez S2 EXCH 75.00 150.00
SSRRB Ryan Braun UPD 25.00 60.00
SSRRC Cano UPD EXCH 50.00 100.00
SSRRH Rickey Henderson S2 30.00 80.00
SSRRJA Reggie Jackson S2 25.00 60.00
SSRSM Miller EXCH 100.00 200.00
SSRTD d'Arnaud EXCH 100.00 200.00
SSRTG Gwynn EXCH 75.00 150.00
SSRTG Tony Gwynn S2 75.00 150.00
SSRTR Raines UPD EXCH 25.00 60.00
SSRTS Tom Seaver S2 60.00 150.00
SSRTT Tulowitzki EXCH 30.00 80.00
SSRWB Boggs S2 EXCH 60.00 120.00
SSRWM Myers EXCH 100.00 200.00
SSRWM Mays S2 EXCH 250.00 350.00
SSRYD Darvish EXCH 300.00 400.00
SSRYM Yadier Molina UPD 75.00 150.00

SSRZW Zack Wheeler UPD 75.00 150.00
SSRJBA Bagwell S2 EXCH 40.00 100.00

2014 Topps Super Veteran

COMPLETE SET (15) 10.00 25.00
SV1 Albert Pujols .75 2.00
SV2 Miguel Cabrera .60 1.50
SV3 Derek Jeter 1.50 4.00
SV4 Adrian Beltre .60 1.50
SV5 Torii Hunter .40 1.00
SV6 David Ortiz .60 1.50
SV7 Carlos Beltran .50 1.25
SV8 Jimmy Rollins .50 1.25
SV9 Barry Zito .50 1.25
SV10 Andy Pettitte .50 1.25
SV11 Matt Holliday .60 1.50
SV12 Adam Wainwright .50 1.25
SV13 CC Sabathia .50 1.25
SV14 Roy Halladay .50 1.25
SV15 Mariano Rivera .75 2.00

2014 Topps Super Veteran Relics

STATED PRINT RUN 25 SER.#'d SETS
SVRAPE Andy Pettitte 12.00 30.00
SVRBZ Barry Zito 12.00 30.00
SVRCB Carlos Beltran 12.00 30.00
SVRDO David Ortiz 30.00 60.00
SVRJR Jimmy Rollins 20.00 50.00
SVRMC Miguel Cabrera 15.00 40.00
SVRMH Matt Holliday 40.00 80.00

2014 Topps The Future is Now

STATED ODDS 1:4 HOBBY
FN1 Shelby Miller .25 .60
FN2 Shelby Miller .25 .60
FN3 Shelby Miller .25 .60
FN4 Jurickson Profar .25 .60
FN5 Jurickson Profar .25 .60
FN6 Jurickson Profar .25 .60
FN7 Jean Segura .25 .60
FN8 Jean Segura .25 .60
FN9 Jean Segura .25 .60
FN10 Zack Wheeler .25 .60
FN11 Zack Wheeler .25 .60
FN12 Zack Wheeler .25 .60
FN13 Yoenis Cespedes .30 .75
FN14 Yoenis Cespedes .30 .75
FN15 Hyun-Jin Ryu .25 .60
FN16 Hyun-Jin Ryu .25 .60
FN17 Wil Myers .20 .50
FN18 Wil Myers .20 .50
FN19 Mike Trout 1.50 4.00
FN20 Mike Trout 1.50 4.00
FN21 Jose Fernandez .30 .75
FN22 Jose Fernandez .30 .75
FN23 Manny Machado .30 .75
FN24 Manny Machado .30 .75
FN25 Yasiel Puig .30 .75
FN26 Yasiel Puig .30 .75
FN27 Yu Darvish .30 .75
FN28 Yu Darvish .30 .75
FN29 Bryce Harper .50 1.25
FN30 Bryce Harper .50 1.25
FN31 Michael Wacha .25 .60
FN32 Michael Wacha .25 .60
FN33 Michael Wacha .25 .60
FN34 Billy Hamilton .25 .60
FN35 Billy Hamilton .25 .60
FN36 Billy Hamilton .25 .60
FN37 Kolten Wong .25 .60
FN38 Kolten Wong .25 .60
FN39 Kolten Wong .25 .60
FN40 Xander Bogaerts .60 1.50
FN41 Xander Bogaerts .60 1.50
FN42 Xander Bogaerts .60 1.50
FN43 Taijuan Walker .20 .50
FN44 Taijuan Walker .20 .50
FN45 Taijuan Walker .20 .50
FN46 Sonny Gray .25 .60
FN47 Sonny Gray .25 .60
FN48 Sonny Gray .25 .60
FN49 Jarrod Parker .20 .50
FN50 Jarrod Parker .20 .50
FN51 Jarrod Parker .20 .50
FN52 Freddie Freeman .40 1.00
FN53 Freddie Freeman .40 1.00
FN54 Freddie Freeman .40 1.00
FN55 Dylan Bundy .25 .60
FN56 Dylan Bundy .25 .60
FN57 Dylan Bundy .25 .60
FN58 Kevin Gausman .30 .75
FN59 Kevin Gausman .30 .75
FN60 Kevin Gausman .30 .75
FNCY1 Christian Yelich UPD UER .40 1.00
FNCY2 Christian Yelich UPD .40 1.00
FNCY3 Christian Yelich UPD .40 1.00
FNGP1 Gregory Polanco UPD .30 .75
FNGP2 Gregory Polanco UPD .30 .75
FNGP3 Gregory Polanco UPD .30 .75
FNGS1 George Springer UPD .75 2.00
FNGS2 George Springer UPD .75 2.00
FNGS3 George Springer UPD .75 2.00
FNJA1 Jose Abreu UPD 1.50 4.00
FNJA2 Jose Abreu UPD 1.50 4.00
FNJA3 Jose Abreu UPD 1.50 4.00
FNJS1 Jon Singleton UPD .25 .60
FNJS2 Jon Singleton UPD .25 .60
FNJS3 Jon Singleton UPD .25 .60
FNMB1 Mookie Betts UPD 4.00 10.00
FNMB2 Mookie Betts UPD 4.00 10.00
FNMB3 Mookie Betts UPD 4.00 10.00
FNMW1 Michael Wacha UPD .25 .60
FNMW2 Michael Wacha UPD .25 .60
FNMW3 Michael Wacha UPD .25 .60
FNNC1 Nick Castellanos UPD .60 1.50
FNNC2 Nick Castellanos UPD .60 1.50
FNNC3 Nick Castellanos UPD .60 1.50
FNOT1 Oscar Taveras UPD .25 .60
FNOT2 Oscar Taveras UPD .25 .60
FNOT3 Oscar Taveras UPD .25 .60
FNYV1 Yordano Ventura UPD .25 .60
FNYV2 Yordano Ventura UPD .25 .60
FNYV3 Yordano Ventura UPD .25 .60

2014 Topps The Future is Now Autographs

SERIES ONE ODDS 1:9736 HOBBY
SERIES TWO ODDS 1:4880 HOBBY
UPDATE ODDS 1:3667 HOBBY
STATED PRINT RUN 25 SER.#'d SETS
SER.1 EXCH DEADLINE 1/31/2017
SER.2 EXCH DEADLINE 5/31/2017
EXCHANGE DEADLINE 9/30/2017
ALL VERSIONS EQUALLY PRICED
FNAAA1 Arismendy Alcantara UPD 10.00 25.00
FNAAA2 Arismendy Alcantara UPD 10.00 25.00
FNAAA3 Arismendy Alcantara UPD 10.00 25.00
FNABH1 Bryce Harper 100.00 200.00
FNABH2 Bryce Harper 100.00 200.00
FNACY1 Christian Yelich UPD UER 25.00 60.00
FNACY2 Christian Yelich UPD 25.00 60.00
FNACY3 Christian Yelich UPD 25.00 60.00
FNADB1 Dylan Bundy S2 15.00 40.00
FNADB2 Dylan Bundy S2 15.00 40.00
FNADB3 Dylan Bundy S2 15.00 40.00
FNAFF1 Freddie Freeman S2 15.00 40.00
FNAFF2 Freddie Freeman S2 15.00 40.00
FNAFF3 Freddie Freeman S2 15.00 40.00
FNAGP1 Gregory Polanco UPD 25.00 60.00
FNAGP2 Gregory Polanco UPD 25.00 60.00
FNAGP3 Gregory Polanco UPD 25.00 60.00
FNAGS1 George Springer UPD 25.00 60.00
FNAGS2 George Springer UPD 25.00 60.00
FNAGS3 George Springer UPD 25.00 60.00
FNAJA1 Jose Abreu UPD 75.00 150.00
FNAJA2 Jose Abreu UPD 75.00 150.00
FNAJA3 Jose Abreu UPD 75.00 150.00
FNAJP1 Jurickson Profar 20.00 50.00
FNAJP1 Jarrod Parker S2 10.00 25.00
FNAJP2 Jurickson Profar 20.00 50.00
FNAJP2 Jarrod Parker S2 10.00 25.00
FNAJP3 Jurickson Profar 20.00 50.00
FNAJP3 Jarrod Parker S2 10.00 25.00
FNAJS1 Jean Segura EXCH 6.00 15.00
FNAJS1 Jon Singleton UPD 12.00 30.00
FNAJS2 Jean Segura EXCH 6.00 15.00
FNAJS2 Jon Singleton UPD 12.00 30.00
FNAJS3 Jean Segura EXCH 6.00 15.00
FNAJS3 Jon Singleton UPD 12.00 30.00
FNAJT1 Julio Teheran 30.00 60.00
FNAJT1 Julio Teheran S2 15.00 40.00
FNAJT2 Julio Teheran 30.00 60.00
FNAJT2 Julio Teheran S2 15.00 40.00
FNAJT3 Julio Teheran S2 15.00 40.00
FNAKG1 Kevin Gausman S2 20.00 50.00
FNAKG2 Kevin Gausman S2 20.00 50.00
FNAKG3 Kevin Gausman S2 20.00 50.00
FNAKW1 Kolten Wong S2 20.00 50.00
FNAKW2 Kolten Wong S2 20.00 50.00
FNAKW3 Kolten Wong S2 20.00 50.00
FNAMB1 Mookie Betts UPD 40.00 100.00
FNAMB2 Mookie Betts UPD 40.00 100.00
FNAMB3 Mookie Betts UPD 40.00 100.00
FNAMM1 Manny Machado 50.00 100.00
FNAMM2 Manny Machado 50.00 100.00
FNAMT1 Mike Trout 100.00 250.00
FNAMT2 Mike Trout 100.00 250.00
FNAMW1 Michael Wacha S2 20.00 50.00
FNAMW2 Michael Wacha S2 20.00 50.00
FNAMW3 Michael Wacha S2 20.00 50.00
FNAOT1 Oscar Taveras UPD 40.00 100.00
FNAOT2 Oscar Taveras UPD 40.00 100.00
FNAOT3 Oscar Taveras UPD 40.00 100.00
FNASG1 Sonny Gray S2 12.00 30.00
FNASG2 Sonny Gray S2 12.00 30.00
FNASG3 Sonny Gray S2 12.00 30.00
FNASM1 Shelby Miller EXCH 12.50 30.00
FNASM2 Shelby Miller EXCH 12.50 30.00
FNASM3 Shelby Miller EXCH 12.50 30.00
FNATW1 Taijuan Walker S2 15.00 40.00
FNATW2 Taijuan Walker S2 15.00 40.00
FNATW3 Taijuan Walker S2 15.00 40.00
FNAWM1 Wil Myers 40.00 80.00
FNAWM2 Wil Myers 40.00 80.00
FNAXB1 Xander Bogaerts S2 25.00 60.00
FNAXB2 Xander Bogaerts S2 25.00 60.00
FNAXB3 Xander Bogaerts S2 25.00 60.00
FNAYC1 Yoenis Cespedes 20.00 50.00
FNAYC2 Yoenis Cespedes 20.00 50.00
FNAYD1 Yu Darvish 50.00 100.00
FNAYD2 Yu Darvish 50.00 100.00
FNAYS1 Yangervis Solarte UPD 12.00 30.00
FNAYS2 Yangervis Solarte UPD 12.00 30.00
FNAYS3 Yangervis Solarte UPD 12.00 30.00
FNAYV1 Yordano Ventura UPD 15.00 40.00
FNAYV2 Yordano Ventura UPD 15.00 40.00
FNAYV3 Yordano Ventura UPD 15.00 40.00
FNAZW1 Zack Wheeler 20.00 50.00
FNAZW2 Zack Wheeler 20.00 50.00
FNAZW3 Zack Wheeler 20.00 50.00

2014 Topps The Future is Now National Promos

1 Mike Trout 6.00 15.00
2 Yasiel Puig 1.25 3.00
3 Xander Bogaerts 2.50 6.00
4 Yoenis Cespedes 1.25 3.00
5 Billy Hamilton 1.00 2.50
6 Bryce Harper 2.00 5.00

2014 Topps The Future is Now Relics

SERIES ONE ODDS 1:2425 HOBBY
SERIES TWO ODDS 1:1232 HOBBY
UPDATE ODDS 1:2777 HOBBY
STATED PRINT RUN 99 SER.#'d SETS
FNRBH1 Bryce Harper 10.00 25.00
FNRBH1 Billy Hamilton 5.00 12.00
FNRBH2 Billy Hamilton 5.00 12.00
FNRBH2 Bryce Harper 10.00 25.00
FNRBH3 Billy Hamilton 5.00 12.00
FNRCY1 Christian Yelich UPD 8.00 20.00
FNRDB1 Dylan Bundy 5.00 12.00
FNRDB2 Dylan Bundy 5.00 12.00
FNRDB3 Dylan Bundy 5.00 12.00
FNRFF1 Freddie Freeman 8.00 20.00
FNRFF2 Freddie Freeman 8.00 20.00
FNRFF3 Freddie Freeman 8.00 20.00
FNRGS1 George Springer UPD 8.00 20.00
FNRHR1 Hyun-Jin Ryu 5.00 12.00
FNRHR2 Hyun-Jin Ryu 5.00 12.00
FNRJF1 Jose Fernandez 6.00 15.00
FNRJF2 Jose Fernandez 6.00 15.00
FNRJP1 Jurickson Profar 5.00 12.00
FNRJP1 Jarrod Parker 4.00 10.00
FNRJP1 James Paxton UPD 6.00 15.00
FNRJP2 Jarrod Parker 4.00 10.00
FNRJP2 Jurickson Profar 5.00 12.00
FNRJP3 Jurickson Profar 5.00 12.00
FNRJP3 Jarrod Parker 4.00 10.00
FNRJS1 Jean Segura 5.00 12.00
FNRJS1 Jon Singleton UPD 5.00 12.00
FNRJS2 Jean Segura 5.00 12.00
FNRJS3 Jean Segura 5.00 12.00
FNRKG1 Kevin Gausman 6.00 15.00
FNRKG2 Kevin Gausman 6.00 15.00
FNRKG3 Kevin Gausman 6.00 15.00
FNRKW1 Kolten Wong 5.00 12.00
FNRKW2 Kolten Wong 5.00 12.00
FNRKW3 Kolten Wong 5.00 12.00
FNRMM1 Manny Machado 6.00 15.00
FNRMM2 Manny Machado 6.00 15.00
FNRMT1 Mike Trout 12.00 30.00
FNRMT2 Mike Trout 12.00 30.00
FNRMW1 Michael Wacha UPD 8.00 20.00
FNRNC1 Nick Castellanos UPD 12.00 30.00
FNROT1 Oscar Taveras UPD 15.00 40.00
FNRSG1 Sonny Gray 5.00 12.00
FNRSG2 Sonny Gray 5.00 12.00
FNRSG3 Sonny Gray 5.00 12.00
FNRSM1 Shelby Miller 8.00 20.00
FNRSM2 Shelby Miller 8.00 20.00
FNRSM3 Shelby Miller 8.00 20.00
FNRTD1 Travis d'Arnaud UPD 5.00 12.00
FNRTS1 Tyler Skaggs UPD 4.00 10.00
FNRTW1 Taijuan Walker 4.00 10.00
FNRTW2 Taijuan Walker 4.00 10.00
FNRTW3 Taijuan Walker 4.00 10.00
FNRWM1 Wil Myers 8.00 20.00
FNRWM2 Wil Myers 8.00 20.00
FNRWR1 Wilin Rosario 4.00 10.00
FNRWR2 Wilin Rosario 4.00 10.00
FNRWR3 Wilin Rosario 4.00 10.00
FNRXB1 Xander Bogaerts 12.00 30.00
FNRXB2 Xander Bogaerts 12.00 30.00
FNRXB3 Xander Bogaerts 12.00 30.00
FNRYC1 Yoenis Cespedes 6.00 15.00
FNRYC2 Yoenis Cespedes 6.00 15.00
FNRYD1 Yu Darvish 12.00 30.00
FNRYD2 Yu Darvish 12.00 30.00
FNRYP1 Yasiel Puig 15.00 40.00
FNRYP2 Yasiel Puig 15.00 40.00
FNRYV1 Yordano Ventura UPD 6.00 15.00
FNRZW1 Zack Wheeler 5.00 12.00
FNRZW2 Zack Wheeler 5.00 12.00
FNRZW3 Zack Wheeler 5.00 12.00

2014 Topps Trajectory Autographs

SERIES ONE ODDS 1:568 HOBBY
SERIES TWO ODDS 1:585 HOBBY
UPDATE ODDS 1:575 HOBBY
SER.1 EXCH DEADLINE 1/31/2017
SER.2 EXCH DEADLINE 5/31/2017
UPDATE EXCH DEADLINE 9/30/2017
TAAA Arismendy Alcantara UPD 3.00 8.00
TAAC Allen Craig S2 30.00 60.00
TAAE Adam Eaton S2 3.00 8.00
TAAGO Anthony Gose S2 3.00 8.00
TAAH Adeiny Hechavarria S2 3.00 8.00
TAAL Andrew Lambo 3.00 8.00
TAAR Andre Rienzo 3.00 8.00
TABBU Bill Buckner 5.00 12.00
TABH Bryce Harper 50.00 120.00
TABJ Bo Jackson 30.00 60.00
TACA Chris Archer 3.00 8.00
TACB Christian Bethancourt S2 3.00 8.00
TACB Cam Bedrosian UPD 3.00 8.00
TACBL Charlie Blackmon UPD 5.00 12.00
TACC Chris Colabello UPD 3.00 8.00
TACCR C.J. Cron UPD 3.00 8.00
TACF Cliff Floyd S2 3.00 8.00
TACO Chris Owings S2 3.00 8.00
TACO Chris Owings UPD 3.00 8.00
TACR Cal Ripken Jr. EXCH 60.00 120.00
TACS Carlos Santana S2 4.00 10.00
TACW Chase Whitley UPD 3.00 8.00
TACY Christian Yelich 20.00 50.00
TADB Dave Buchanan UPD 3.00 8.00
TADB Dusty Baker S2 3.00 8.00
TADD Derek Dietrich UPD 4.00 10.00
TADG Didi Gregorius 4.00 10.00
TADM Dale Murphy S2 10.00 25.00
TADN Daniel Nava S2 3.00 8.00
TADS Deion Sanders 20.00 50.00
TADW David Wright EXCH 15.00 40.00
TAEA Erisbel Arruebarrena UPD 3.00 8.00
TAEB Ernie Banks 20.00 50.00
TAED Eric Davis S2 3.00 8.00
TAEG Evan Gattis 3.00 8.00
TAFF Freddie Freeman S2 6.00 15.00
TAFM Fred McGriff S2 6.00 15.00
TAFV Fernando Valenzuela S2 25.00 60.00
TAGM Greg Maddux EXCH 40.00 80.00
TAGS George Springer UPD 6.00 15.00
TAHA Hank Aaron 100.00 200.00
TAHA Henderson Alvarez S2 3.00 8.00
TAIR Ivan Rodriguez EXCH 10.00 25.00
TAJA Jose Abreu S2 60.00 150.00
TAJA Jose Abreu UPD 40.00 80.00
TAJB Johnny Bench S2 40.00 80.00
TAJD Jake Diekman UPD 3.00 8.00
TAJDE Jacob deGrom UPD 200.00 500.00
TAJG Jason Grilli S2 3.00 8.00
TAJH Jason Heyward S2 8.00 20.00
TAJK Jason Kipnis 5.00 12.00
TAJK Joe Kelly UPD 3.00 8.00
TAJM Jake Marisnick 3.00 8.00
TAJR Junior Lake S2 3.00 8.00
TAJS Jean Segura S2 4.00 10.00
TAJS Jonathan Schoop UPD 3.00 8.00
TAJSI Jon Singleton UPD 6.00 15.00
TAKG Ken Griffey Jr. 75.00 150.00
TAKM Kris Medlen 4.00 10.00
TAKP Kyle Parker UPD 4.00 10.00
TAKS Kevin Siegrist S2 3.00 8.00
TAKW Kolten Wong 4.00 10.00
TAKW Kolten Wong S2 4.00 10.00
TALA Luis Aparicio 10.00 25.00
TALH Livan Hernandez S2 3.00 8.00
TAMA Matt Adams 3.00 8.00
TAMBE Mookie Betts UPD 50.00 120.00
TAMC Matt Cain EXCH 12.00 30.00
TAMD Matt Davidson 4.00 10.00
TAMM Mark McGwire S2 40.00 100.00
TAMMA Manny Machado S2 20.00 50.00
TAMMI Mike Minor S2 3.00 8.00
TAMN Mike Napoli S2 8.00 20.00
TAMS Marcus Stroman UPD 5.00 12.00
TAMT Mike Trout 100.00 200.00
TANG Nomar Garciaparra 12.50 30.00
TANM Nick Martinez UPD 3.00 8.00
TAOS Ozzie Smith S2 10.00 25.00
TAOT Oscar Taveras UPD 12.00 30.00
TAPB Peter Bourjos S2 3.00 8.00
TAPG Paul Goldschmidt 8.00 20.00
TAPG Paul Goldschmidt S2 8.00 20.00
TAPM Pedro Martinez 60.00 120.00
TARB Rex Brothers UPD 3.00 8.00
TARE Roenis Elias UPD 3.00 8.00
TARK Ralph Kiner S2 15.00 40.00
TARM Rafael Montero UPD 3.00 8.00
TARN Ricky Nolasco 3.00 8.00
TARO Rougned Odor UPD 8.00 20.00
TASC Steve Cishek S2 3.00 8.00
TASK Sandy Koufax 150.00 300.00
TASM Starling Marte S2 4.00 10.00
TASMI Shelby Miller S2 15.00 40.00
TASS Steven Souza UPD 4.00 10.00
TATC Tyler Chatwood S2 3.00 8.00
TATD Travis d'Arnaud 4.00 10.00
TATG Tom Glavine 20.00 50.00
TATK Tom Koehler UPD 3.00 8.00
TATL Tommy La Stella UPD 3.00 8.00
TATR Tim Raines S2 10.00 25.00
TATT Troy Tulowitzki S2 8.00 20.00
TATW Taijuan Walker 3.00 8.00
TAWM Wil Myers 3.00 8.00
TAWMI Wade Miley 3.00 8.00
TAYC Yoenis Cespedes 8.00 20.00
TAYD Yu Darvish EXCH 40.00 80.00
TAYS Yangervis Solarte UPD 3.00 8.00
TAZA Zoilo Almonte S2 4.00 10.00

2014 Topps Trajectory Jumbo Relics

STATED ODDS 1:2625 HOBBY
UPDATE ODDS 1:11,001 HOBBY
PRINT RUNS B/WN 25-99 COPIES PER
TJRAC Alex Cobb/99 10.00 25.00
TJRAW Adam Wainwright/99 25.00 60.00
TJRBH Billy Hamilton/99 20.00 50.00
TJRBHA Billy Hamilton/99 20.00 50.00
TJRBM Brian McCann/25 UPD 12.00 30.00
TJRBP Buster Posey/25 UPD 20.00 50.00
TJRBZ Ben Zobrist/99 8.00 20.00
TJRCC CC Sabathia/25 UPD 20.00 50.00
TJRCD Chris Davis/99 6.00 15.00
TJRCG Carlos Gonzalez/25 UPD 25.00 60.00
TJRCK Craig Kimbrel/99 8.00 20.00
TJRCS Chris Sale/99 10.00 25.00
TJRCS Chris Sale/25 UPD 15.00 40.00
TJRCW C.J. Wilson/99 10.00 25.00
TJRDF David Freese/99 6.00 15.00
TJRDG Didi Gregorius/99 8.00 20.00
TJRDJ Derek Jeter/25 UPD 40.00 100.00
TJRDM Devin Mesoraco/99 6.00 15.00
TJRDO David Ortiz/99 12.00 30.00
TJRDW David Wright/99 10.00 25.00
TJREE Edwin Encarnacion/99 10.00 25.00
TJREL Evan Longoria/99 8.00 20.00
TJREL Evan Longoria/25 UPD 12.00 30.00
TJREL1 Evan Longoria/99 8.00 20.00
TJREM Eddie Murray/99 10.00 25.00
TJRFF Freddie Freeman/99 12.00 30.00
TJRFH Felix Hernandez/99 8.00 20.00
TJRFH Felix Hernandez/25 UPD 12.00 30.00
TJRHR Hanley Ramirez/25 UPD 60.00 120.00
TJRJB Jay Bruce/25 UPD 12.00 30.00
TJRJC Jose Canseco/99 15.00 40.00
TJRJM Joe Morgan/99 10.00 25.00
TJRJM Joe Mauer/25 UPD 60.00 120.00
TJRJP Jorge Posada/25 UPD 12.00 30.00
TJRJS Justin Smoak/99 6.00 15.00
TJRJSE Jean Segura/99 8.00 20.00
TJRJT Julio Teheran/99 8.00 20.00
TJRJV Joey Votto/25 UPD 15.00 40.00
TJRJW Jayson Werth/99 8.00 20.00
TJRJWE Jayson Werth/99 8.00 20.00
TJRJZ Jordan Zimmermann/99 8.00 20.00
TJRKG Ken Griffey Jr./99 20.00 50.00
TJRMA Matt Adams/99 6.00 15.00
TJRMB Madison Bumgarner/99 12.00 30.00
TJRMCA Matt Cain/25 UPD 30.00 80.00
TJRMH Matt Holliday/99 8.00 20.00
TJRML Mike Leake/99 8.00 20.00
TJRMM Mike Minor/99 10.00 25.00
TJRMMC Mark McGwire/99 15.00 40.00
TJRMS Max Scherzer/99 10.00 25.00
TJRMT Mike Trout/99 40.00 80.00
TJRMT Mike Trout/25 UPD 30.00 80.00
TJRMTA Masahiro Tanaka/25 UPD 90.00 150.00
TJRNG Nomar Garciaparra/25 UPD 40.00 100.00
TJROT Oscar Taveras/99 8.00 20.00
TJRPA Pedro Alvarez/99 10.00 25.00
TJRPK Paul Konerko/99 8.00 20.00
TJRRZ Ryan Zimmerman/99 8.00 20.00
TJRSC Starlin Castro/99 8.00 20.00
TJRSC Shin-Soo Choo/25 UPD 12.00 30.00
TJRSCA Steve Carlton/99 10.00 25.00
TJRSM Shelby Miller/99 15.00 40.00
TJRSS Stephen Strasburg/99 10.00 25.00
TJRSV Shane Victorino/25 UPD 12.00 30.00
TJRTD Travis d'Arnaud/99 6.00 15.00
TJRTG Tom Glavine/99 12.00 30.00
TJRTGW Tony Gwynn/99 10.00 25.00
TJRTL Tim Lincecum/25 UPD 25.00 60.00
TJRTT Troy Tulowitzki/99 8.00 20.00
TJRVG Vladimir Guerrero/25 UPD 12.00 30.00
TJRWM Wil Myers/25 UPD 10.00 25.00
TJRWM Willie McCovey/99 15.00 40.00
TJRWMA Wade Miley/99 6.00 15.00
TJRWMI Will Middlebrooks/99 6.00 15.00
TJRWR Wilin Rosario/99 6.00 15.00
TJRXB Xander Bogaerts/99 20.00 50.00
TJRYA Yonder Alonso/99 6.00 15.00
TJRYP Yasiel Puig/25 UPD 15.00 40.00

2014 Topps Trajectory Relics

SERIES ONE ODDS 1:50 HOBBY
SERIES TWO ODDS 1:51 HOBBY
TRAB Adrian Beltre S2 3.00 8.00
TRAC Alex Cobb S2 2.00 5.00
TRAH Aaron Hicks S2 2.50 6.00
TRAP Andy Pettitte 2.50 6.00
TRAR Alex Rodriguez 4.00 10.00
TRARA Alexei Ramirez 2.50 6.00
TRAS Andrelton Simmons 2.00 5.00
TRAW Adam Wainwright S2 2.50 6.00
TRBB Brennan Boesch S2 2.00 5.00
TRBBE Brandon Belt 2.50 6.00
TRBG Brett Gardner S2 2.50 6.00
TRBH Bryce Harper 12.00 30.00
TRBM Brandon Morrow S2 2.00 5.00
TRBP Buster Posey 4.00 10.00
TRBR Babe Ruth 60.00 120.00
TRBRO Bruce Rondon 2.00 5.00
TRBS Bruce Sutter 2.00 5.00
TRBZ Ben Zobrist 2.50 6.00
TRCC CC Sabathia S2 2.50 6.00
TRCS Carlos Santana 2.50 6.00
TRCSA Chris Sale 3.00 8.00
TRDJ1 Derek Jeter Bat 20.00 50.00
TRDJ2 Derek Jeter Jsy 15.00 40.00
TRDPR David Price 2.50 6.00
TRDS Don Sutton 2.50 6.00
TREA Elvis Andrus 2.50 6.00
TREB Ernie Banks 10.00 25.00
TRGB Gordon Beckham S2 2.00 5.00
TRGS Gary Sheffield 2.00 5.00
TRHA Hank Aaron 40.00 80.00
TRHAL Henderson Alvarez 2.00 5.00
TRHW Hoyt Wilhelm 10.00 25.00
TRID Ian Desmond 2.00 5.00
TRID Ike Davis S2 2.00 5.00
TRIR Ivan Rodriguez 2.50 6.00
TRIR Ivan Rodriguez S2 2.50 6.00
TRJE Jacoby Ellsbury S2 2.50 6.00
TRJP Jorge Posada S2 2.50 6.00
TRJPE Jhonny Peralta 2.00 5.00
TRJR Jose Reyes 2.50 6.00
TRJS Jean Segura 2.50 6.00
TRJSH James Shields 2.00 5.00
TRJT Julio Teheran 2.50 6.00
TRJV Joey Votto S2 3.00 8.00
TRJVO Joey Votto 3.00 8.00
TRJW Jayson Werth 2.50 6.00
TRJZ Jordan Zimmermann 2.50 6.00
TRML Mike Leake S2 2.00 5.00
TRMM Mike Minor S2 2.00 5.00
TRMS Mike Schmidt 6.00 15.00
TRMS Max Scherzer S2 3.00 8.00
TRMT Mike Trout 12.00 30.00
TRMTE Mark Teixeira 2.50 6.00
TRMY Michael Young 2.00 5.00
TRNF Neftali Feliz S2 2.00 5.00
TRPA Pedro Alvarez 2.00 5.00
TRPF Prince Fielder 2.50 6.00
TRPS Pablo Sandoval 2.50 6.00
TRPS Pablo Sandoval S2 2.50 6.00
TRRC Roberto Clemente 40.00 80.00
TRRH Ryan Howard S2 2.50 6.00
TRRP Rick Porcello 2.50 6.00
TRRS Red Schoendienst 10.00 25.00
TRRW Rickie Weeks 2.00 5.00
TRRY Robin Yount 15.00 40.00
TRSC Starlin Castro S2 2.00 5.00
TRSM Shelby Miller S2 2.50 6.00
TRSP Salvador Perez 2.50 6.00
TRSS Stephen Strasburg 3.00 8.00
TRTL Tim Lincecum S2 2.50 6.00
TRTT Troy Tulowitzki 3.00 8.00
TRTW Ted Williams 40.00 80.00
TRVG Vladimir Guerrero S2 2.50 6.00
TRVM Victor Martinez S2 2.50 6.00
TRWM Willie Mays 25.00 60.00
TRWR Wilin Rosario 2.00 5.00
TRYA Yonder Alonso 2.00 5.00
TRYA Yonder Alonso S2 2.00 5.00
TRYP Yasiel Puig 10.00 25.00
TRZW Zack Wheeler 2.50 6.00
TRJPA Jordan Pacheco S2 2.00 5.00
TRJPR Jarrod Parker S2 2.00 5.00
TRMCA Matt Carpenter S2 3.00 8.00
TRMMA Manny Machado S2 3.00 8.00
TRMMO Mitch Moreland S2 2.00 5.00
TRSC1 Starlin Castro S2 2.00 5.00

2014 Topps Trajectory Relics Gold

*GOLD: .6X TO 1.5X BASIC
SERIES TWO ODDS 1:1155 HOBBY
STATED PRINT RUN 99 SER.#'d SETS

2014 Topps Upper Class

COMPLETE SET (50) 10.00 25.00
STATED ODDS 1:4 HOBBY
UC1 Bryce Harper .50 1.25
UC2 Mike Trout 1.50 4.00
UC3 Yu Darvish .30 .75
UC4 Yoenis Cespedes .30 .75
UC5 Matt Harvey .25 .60
UC6 Craig Kimbrel .25 .60
UC7 Freddie Freeman .40 1.00
UC8 Sandy Koufax .60 1.50
UC9 Roberto Clemente .75 2.00
UC10 Buster Posey .40 1.00
UC11 David Freese .20 .50
UC12 Giancarlo Stanton .30 .75
UC13 Stephen Strasburg .30 .75
UC14 Madison Bumgarner .25 .60
UC15 Evan Longoria .25 .60
UC16 Joey Votto .30 .75
UC17 Jay Bruce .25 .60
UC18 Ryan Braun .25 .60
UC19 Troy Tulowitzki .30 .75
UC20 Dustin Pedroia .30 .75
UC21 Hanley Ramirez .25 .60
UC22 Matt Cain .25 .60
UC23 Prince Fielder .25 .60
UC24 Justin Verlander .30 .75
UC25 Jered Weaver .25 .60
UC26 Ryan Howard .25 .60
UC27 Robinson Cano .25 .60
UC28 Brian McCann .25 .60
UC29 Felix Hernandez .25 .60
UC30 Matt Holliday .30 .75
UC31 David Wright .25 .60
UC32 Yadier Molina .40 1.00
UC33 Randy Johnson .30 .75
UC34 Gary Sheffield .20 .50
UC35 Ken Griffey Jr. .60 1.50
UC36 Albert Belle .20 .50
UC37 Jim Abbott .20 .50
UC38 Tom Glavine .25 .60
UC39 Greg Maddux .40 1.00
UC40 Bo Jackson .30 .75
UC41 Jacoby Ellsbury .25 .60
UC42 Jim Rice .25 .60
UC43 Fred Lynn .20 .50
UC44 Gary Carter .25 .60
UC45 Ryne Sandberg .60 1.50
UC46 Wade Boggs .25 .60
UC47 Cal Ripken Jr. 1.00 2.50
UC48 Hank Aaron .60 1.50
UC49 Al Kaline .30 .75
UC50 Ernie Banks .30 .75

2014 Topps Upper Class Autograph Relics

STATED ODDS 1:3400 HOBBY
STATED PRINT RUN 25 SER.#'d SETS
EXCHANGE DEADLINE 1/31/2017
UCARAB Albert Belle 12.00 30.00
UCARBH Bryce Harper 125.00 250.00
UCARBJ Bo Jackson 100.00 200.00
UCARDF David Freese 20.00 50.00
UCARDP Dustin Pedroia EXCH 60.00 120.00
UCAREB Ernie Banks EXCH 60.00 120.00
UCARFF Freddie Freeman 40.00 80.00
UCARFL Fred Lynn 12.00 30.00
UCARGC Gary Carter 40.00 80.00
UCARGS Giancarlo Stanton 75.00 150.00
UCARGSH Gary Sheffield 12.00 30.00
UCARHR Hanley Ramirez EXCH 15.00 40.00
UCARJH Jeremy Hellickson EXCH 12.00 30.00
UCARJR Jim Rice 12.00 30.00
UCARMB Madison Bumgarner 50.00 100.00
UCARMC Matt Cain 30.00 60.00
UCARMT Mike Trout 100.00 200.00
UCARMTR Mark Trumbo 20.00 50.00
UCARRB Ryan Braun 15.00 40.00
UCARRP Rafael Palmeiro EXCH 20.00 50.00
UCARTG Tom Glavine 20.00 50.00
UCARTT Troy Tulowitzki EXCH 20.00 50.00
UCARYC Yoenis Cespedes 20.00 50.00
UCARYD Yu Darvish EXCH 60.00 120.00
UCARYM Yadier Molina 25.00 60.00

2014 Topps Upper Class Autographs

STATED ODDS 1:5829 HOBBY
STATED PRINT RUN 50 SER.#'d SETS
EXCHANGE DEADLINE 1/31/2017
UCAAB Albert Belle EXCH 6.00 15.00
UCAAK Al Kaline 25.00 50.00
UCABH Bryce Harper 60.00 120.00
UCABP Buster Posey 75.00 200.00
UCADF David Freese 6.00 15.00
UCADP Dustin Pedroia EXCH 10.00 25.00
UCAEB Ernie Banks EXCH 60.00 120.00
UCAFF Freddie Freeman 30.00 60.00
UCAFL Fred Lynn 6.00 15.00
UCAGC Gary Carter 12.00 30.00
UCAGS Giancarlo Stanton 10.00 25.00
UCAGSH Gary Sheffield 6.00 15.00
UCAHR Hanley Ramirez EXCH 8.00 20.00
UCAJA Jim Abbott 6.00 15.00
UCAJH Jeremy Hellickson EXCH 6.00 15.00
UCAJR Jim Rice 15.00 40.00
UCAMB Madison Bumgarner 8.00 20.00
UCAMC Matt Cain EXCH 12.00 30.00
UCAMT Mike Trout 100.00 200.00
UCAMTR Mark Trumbo 10.00 25.00
UCARP Rafael Palmeiro 10.00 25.00
UCATG Tom Glavine 15.00 40.00
UCATT Troy Tulowitzki EXCH 10.00 25.00
UCAYC Yoenis Cespedes 10.00 25.00
UCAYD Yu Darvish EXCH 50.00 100.00

2014 Topps Upper Class Relics

STATED ODDS 1:2425 HOBBY
STATED PRINT RUN 99 SER.#'d SETS
UCRBP Buster Posey 15.00 40.00
UCRCK Craig Kimbrel 10.00 25.00
UCRCR Cal Ripken Jr. 40.00 80.00
UCRDF David Freese 6.00 15.00
UCREL Evan Longoria 4.00 10.00
UCRGM Greg Maddux 10.00 25.00
UCRGS Giancarlo Stanton 5.00 12.00
UCRHR Hanley Ramirez 4.00 10.00
UCRJB Jay Bruce 10.00 25.00
UCRJH Jeremy Hellickson 3.00 8.00
UCRJV Justin Verlander 8.00 20.00
UCRJVO Joey Votto 12.00 30.00
UCRMB Madison Bumgarner 15.00 40.00
UCRMC Matt Cain 6.00 15.00
UCRMH Matt Harvey 8.00 20.00
UCRMHO Matt Holliday 5.00 12.00
UCRMTR Mark Trumbo 3.00 8.00
UCRPF Prince Fielder 4.00 10.00
UCRRC Roberto Clemente 40.00 80.00
UCRRCA Robinson Cano 4.00 10.00
UCRRH Ryan Howard 4.00 10.00
UCRSS Stephen Strasburg 6.00 15.00
UCRTT Troy Tulowitzki 5.00 12.00
UCRYC Yoenis Cespedes 5.00 12.00
UCRYM Yadier Molina 6.00 15.00

2014 Topps World Champion Autograph Relics

STATED ODDS 1:8500 HOBBY
STATED PRINT RUN 50 SER.#'d SETS
EXCHANGE DEADLINE 1/31/2017
WCARDO David Ortiz EXCH 75.00 150.00
WCARDP Dustin Pedroia EXCH 75.00 150.00
WCARFD Felix Doubront 75.00 150.00
WCARMN Mike Napoli 100.00 200.00
WCARWM Will Middlebrooks 15.00 40.00

2014 Topps World Champion Autographs

STATED ODDS 1:29,500 HOBBY
STATED PRINT RUN 50 SER.#'d SETS
EXCHANGE DEADLINE 1/31/2017
WCADO David Ortiz 150.00 300.00
WCADP Dustin Pedroia EXCH 75.00 150.00
WCAFD Felix Doubront 30.00 80.00
WCAMN Mike Napoli 50.00 100.00
WCAWM Will Middlebrooks 50.00 100.00

2014 Topps World Champion Relics

STATED ODDS 1:4825 HOBBY
STATED PRINT RUN 100 SER.#'d SETS
EXCHANGE DEADLINE 1/31/2017
WCRCB Clay Buchholz 10.00 25.00
WCRDO David Ortiz 15.00 40.00
WCRDP Dustin Pedroia 15.00 40.00
WCRFD Felix Doubront 10.00 25.00
WCRJE Jacoby Ellsbury 12.00 30.00
WCRJG Jonny Gomes EXCH 30.00 80.00
WCRJL Jon Lester 20.00 50.00
WCRJLA John Lackey 12.00 30.00
WCRJP Jake Peavy 50.00 100.00
WCRJS Jarrod Saltalamacchia 10.00 25.00
WCRKU Koji Uehara 20.00 50.00
WCRMN Mike Napoli 20.00 50.00
WCRSD Stephen Drew EXCH 10.00 25.00
WCRSV Shane Victorino 20.00 50.00
WCRXB Xander Bogaerts 40.00 80.00

2014 Topps Update

COMPLETE SET w/o SP's (330) 60.00 150.00
PRINTING PLATE ODDS 1:970 HOBBY
PLATE PRINT RUN 1 SET PER COLOR
BLACK-CYAN-MAGENTA-YELLOW ISSUED
NO PLATE PRICING DUE TO SCARCITY
US1 Albert Pujols .25 .60
US2 Derek Jeter .50 1.25
US3 Tom Wilhelmsen .12 .30
US4 Mark Reynolds .12 .30
US5 Jair Jurrjens .12 .30
US6A Jose Molina .12 .30
US6B Jose Molina SP 1.50 4.00
White jersey
US7 David Price .15 .40
US8 Josh Harrison .12 .30
US9 Francisco Rodriguez .15 .40
US10A George Springer RC 1.50 4.00
US10B Springer SP Fldng 6.00 15.00
US11 Robbie Ross Jr. .12 .30
US12A Brian McCann .15 .40
US12B Brian McCann SP 2.00 5.00
With glove
US12C Brian McCann SP 2.00 5.00
SABRmetrics
US13 Andrew Heaney RC .40 1.00
US14 Justin Grimm .12 .30
US15A Joba Chamberlain .12 .30
US15B Joba Chamberlain SP 1.50 4.00
With teammate
US15C Joba Chamberlain SP 1.50 4.00
SABRmetrics
US16 Andrew Brown .12 .30
US17A Yangervis Solarte RC .40 1.00
US17B Yangervis Solarte SP 1.50 4.00
Blue jersey
US18 Aramis Ramirez .12 .30
US19A Bronson Arroyo .12 .30
US19B Bronson Arroyo SP 1.50 4.00
SABRmetrics
US20 Gregory Polanco RC .60 1.50
US22A Kendrys Morales .12 .30
US22B Kendrys Morales SP 1.50 4.00
SABRmetrics
US23A Ubaldo Jimenez .12 .30
US23B Ubaldo Jimenez SP 1.50 4.00
SABRmetrics
US24 Tony Sanchez RC .40 1.00
US25 Masahiro Tanaka RC 1.25 3.00
US26A Mookie Betts RC 50.00 120.00
US26B Betts SP In dugout 30.00 80.00
US27A Shin-Soo Choo .15 .40
US27B Shin-Soo Choo SP 2.00 5.00
In dugout
US27C Shin-Soo Choo SP 2.00 5.00
SABRmetrics
US28A David Freese .12 .30
US28B David Freese SP 1.50 4.00
SABRmetrics
US29 Tyler Skaggs .12 .30
US30 Elian Herrera .12 .30
US31 Francisco Rodriguez .15 .40
US32A Mark Trumbo .12 .30
US32B Mark Trumbo SP 1.50 4.00
SABRmetrics
US33 Grady Sizemore .15 .40
US34 Gavin Floyd .12 .30
US35 Marcus Stroman RC .60 1.50
US36 Vance Worley .12 .30
US37 Leury Garcia .12 .30
US38A Jason Giambi .12 .30
US38B Jason Giambi SP 1.50 4.00
With bat
US38C Jason Giambi SP 1.50 4.00
SABRmetrics
US39 Brock Holt .12 .30
US40 Stephen Vogt RC .50 1.25
US41A Drew Stubbs .12 .30
US41B Drew Stubbs SP 1.50 4.00
SABRmetrics
US42 J.D. Martinez .20 .50
US43 Pat Neshek .12 .30
US44 Jesus Guzman .12 .30
US45 Pedro Ciriaco .12 .30
US46 Jake Marisnick .12 .30
US47 Steve Tolleson .12 .30
US48A Scott Hairston .12 .30
US48B Scott Hairston SP 1.50 4.00
Red jersey
US49 Willie Bloomquist .12 .30
US50A Jacob deGrom RC 60.00 150.00
US50B deGrom SP Wht Jsy 400.00 1000.00
US51 Brandon Guyer RC .40 1.00
US52 Chase Anderson RC .40 1.00
US53 Miguel Cabrera .20 .50
US54 Mike Trout 1.00 2.50
US55 Jon Lester .15 .40
US56A Huston Street .12 .30
US56B Huston Street SP 1.50 4.00
SABRmetrics
US57 Jacob deGrom 40.00 100.00
US58 Raul Ibanez .15 .40
US59 Brandon McCarthy .12 .30
US60 David Ross .12 .30
US61 Ryan Kalish .12 .30
US62A Adam Eaton .12 .30
US62B Adam Eaton SP 1.50 4.00
With glove
US62C Adam Eaton SP 1.50 4.00
SABRmetrics
US63A David Murphy .12 .30
US63B David Murphy SP 1.50 4.00
SABRmetrics

US64 LaTroy Hawkins .12 .30
US65 Chad Qualls .12 .30
US66 Marc Krauss .12 .30
US67 Scott Van Slyke .12 .30
US68 Justin Turner .20 .50
US69A Dellin Betances .15 .40
US69B Dellin Betances SP 2.00 5.00
SABRmetrics
US70A Jarrod Saltalamacchia .12 .30
US70B Jarrod Saltalamacchia SP 1.50 4.00
Tossing bat
US70C Jarrod Saltalamacchia SP 1.50 4.00
SABRmetrics
US71 Justin Masterson .12 .30
US72A Chris Young .12 .30
US72B Chris Young SP 1.50 4.00
SABRmetrics
US73A Francisco Cervelli .12 .30
US73B Francisco Cervelli SP 1.50 4.00
SABRmetrics
US74 Antonio Bastardo .12 .30
US75 Nick Punto .12 .30
US76 Daric Barton .12 .30
US77 Wil Nieves .12 .30
US78 Reid Brignac .12 .30
US79 Clint Barmes .12 .30
US80A Josh Harrison .12 .30
US80B Josh Harrison SP 1.50 4.00
SABRmetrics
US81 Seth Smith .12 .30
US82A Joaquin Arias .12 .30
US82B Joaquin Arias SP 1.50 4.00
SABRmetrics
US83 Brandon Hicks .12 .30
US84 Brandon Maurer .12 .30
US85 Daniel Descalso .12 .30
US86 Cesar Ramos .12 .30
US87 Allen Craig .15 .40
US88 Jon Singleton RC .50 1.25
US89 Stephen Drew .12 .30
US90 Steve Lombardozzi .12 .30
US91A Nate McLouth .12 .30
US91B Nate McLouth SP 1.50 4.00
In dugout
US92 Jeff Samardzija .12 .30
US93 Troy Patton .12 .30
US94 Tuffy Gosewisch RC .40 1.00
US95 Vidal Nuno RC .40 1.00
US96 Eugenio Suarez RC 1.50 4.00
US97 Salvador Perez .15 .40
US98 Anthony Rizzo .25 .60
US99 Scott Kazmir .12 .30
US100 Jose Abreu RC 3.00 8.00
US101 Kyle Blanks .12 .30
US102 Daniel Murphy .15 .40
US103 Starlin Castro .12 .30
US104 Luis Sardinas RC .40 1.00
US105 Ehire Adrianza RC .40 1.00
US106A Collin Cowgill .12 .30
US106B Collin Cowgill SP 1.50 4.00
SABRmetrics
US107A Josh Collmenter .12 .30
US107B Josh Collmenter SP 1.50 4.00
SABRmetrics
US108 Ryan Doumit .12 .30
US109 David Lough .12 .30
US110 Jackie Bradley Jr. .20 .50
US111A Emilio Bonifacio .12 .30
US111B Emilio Bonifacio SP 1.50 4.00
SABRmetrics
US112 Alfredo Simon .12 .30
US113 Oscar Taveras RC .50 1.25
US114 Jeff Francis .12 .30
US115 Nyjer Morgan .12 .30
US116 Brett Anderson .12 .30
US117A John Lackey .15 .40
US117B Bryan Holaday .12 .30
US117C John Lackey SP 2.00 5.00
SABRmetrics
US118 Collin McHugh .12 .30
US119 Mike Dunn RC .40 1.00
US120 Randy Wolf .12 .30
US121 Kyle Crockett RC .50 1.25
US122 Jeff Baker .12 .30
US123 Lyle Overbay .12 .30
US124 Nick Tepesch .12 .30
US125 Jason Bartlett .12 .30
US126 Omar Quintanilla .12 .30
US127 David Phelps .12 .30
US128 Luke Gregerson .12 .30
US129 Mike Adams .12 .30
US130 Tony Watson .12 .30
US131 Chris Denorfia .12 .30
US132A Tyler Colvin .12 .30
US132B Tyler Colvin SP 1.50 4.00
SABRmetrics
US133 Chris Young .12 .30
US134 Tony Cruz .12 .30
US135A Jake Odorizzi .12 .30
US135B Jake Odorizzi SP 1.50 4.00
SABRmetrics
US136 Dioner Navarro .12 .30
US137A Doug Fister .12 .30
US137B Doug Fister SP 1.50 4.00
SABRmetrics
US138 Asdrubal Cabrera .15 .40
US139 Jason Hammel .15 .40
US140 Nick Hundley .12 .30
US141 Chris Dickerson .12 .30
US142 Jon Lester .15 .40
US143A Jake Peavy .12 .30
US143B Jake Peavy SP 1.50 4.00
SABRmetrics
US144 Hector Rondon RC .40 1.00
US145 A.J. Pierzynski .12 .30
US146 Neftali Soto RC .40 1.00
US147 James Jones RC .40 1.00
US148 Kyle Parker RC .50 1.25
US149 C.J. Cron RC .40 1.00
US150A Jon Singleton RC .50 1.25
US150B Jon Singleton SP 2.00 5.00
Orange jersey
US151 Robinson Cano .15 .40
US152 Josh Donaldson .15 .40
US153 Kurt Suzuki .12 .30
US154 Yu Darvish .20 .50
US155 Devin Mesoraco .12 .30
US156 Ronald Belisario .12 .30
US157 Joe Smith .12 .30
US158A Eric Chavez .12 .30
US158B Eric Chavez SP 1.50 4.00
SABRmetrics
US159 Tyler Pastornicky .12 .30
US160A Delmon Young .15 .40
US160B Delmon Young SP 2.00 5.00
SABRmetrics
US161 Edward Mujica .12 .30
US162 Yoenis Cespedes .20 .50
US163 Ramon Santiago .12 .30
US164A Joe Kelly .12 .30
US164B Josh Tomlin .12 .30
US164C Joe Kelly SP 1.50 4.00
SABRmetrics
US165A Justin Morneau .15 .40
US165B Justin Morneau SP 2.00 5.00
SABRmetrics
US166 Andrew Romine .12 .30
US167 Jeff Francoeur .15 .40
US168 Austin Jackson .12 .30
US169A Chone Figgins .12 .30
US169B Chone Figgins SP 1.50 4.00
SABRmetrics
US170 Matt Davidson RC .50 1.25
US171A Chase Whitley RC .40 1.00
US171B Chase Whitley SP 1.50 4.00
Grey jersey
US172 Tucker Barnhart RC .40 1.00
US173 Jose Bautista .15 .40
US174 Jace Peterson RC .40 1.00
US175 Oscar Taveras .15 .40
US176 Michael Brantley .15 .40
US177 Dee Gordon .12 .30
US178 Clayton Kershaw .30 .75
US179 John Baker .12 .30
US180 Chris Taylor RC 2.00 5.00
US181A Tony Gwynn Jr. .12 .30
US181B Tony Gwynn Jr. SP 1.50 4.00
SABRmetrics
US182 Chris Colabello .12 .30
US183 Kelly Johnson .12 .30
US184 Danny Santana RC .50 1.25
US185A Juan Francisco .12 .30
US185B Juan Francisco SP 1.50 4.00
SABRmetrics
US186 Arismendy Alcantara RC .40 1.00
US187 Jonathan Herrera .12 .30
US188 Paul Maholm .12 .30
US189 Brandon Cumpton RC .40 1.00
US190 Jose Altuve .15 .40
US191 Yoenis Cespedes .20 .50
US192 Pat Neshek .12 .30
US193 Robinson Chirinos .12 .30
US194A Hector Santiago .12 .30
US194B Hector Santiago SP 1.50 4.00
SABRmetrics
US195A Gerald Laird .12 .30
US195B Gerald Laird SP 1.50 4.00
SABRmetrics
US196A Erisbel Arruebarrena RC .40 1.00
US196B Erisbel Arruebarrena SP 1.50 4.00
Fielding
US197A Marcus Stroman .20 .50
US197B Marcus Stroman SP 2.50 6.00
Looking up
US198 Adam Jones .15 .40
US199 Julio Teheran .15 .40
US200 Masahiro Tanaka .40 1.00
US201 Derek Norris .12 .30
US202 Rubby De La Rosa (RC) .40 1.00
US203 Cole Figueroa RC .40 1.00
US204A Chris Capuano .12 .30
US204B Chris Capuano SP 1.50 4.00
SABRmetrics
US205 Reed Johnson .12 .30
US206 Chris Perez .12 .30
US207A Rajai Davis .12 .30
US207B Rajai Davis SP 1.50 4.00
SABRmetrics
US208 Joakim Soria .12 .30
US209 Roger Bernadina .12 .30
US210 George Springer .50 1.25
US211 Jordan Schafer .12 .30
US212 Randy Choate .12 .30
US213A Stefen Romero RC .40 1.00
US213B Stefen Romero SP 1.50 4.00
Fielding
US214 Tommy La Stella RC .40 1.00
US215 Paul Goldschmidt .20 .50
US216 Andrew McCutchen .20 .50
US217 Charlie Furbush .12 .30
US218 David Carpenter .12 .30
US219A Mike Olt .12 .30
US219B Mike Olt SP 1.50 4.00
SABRmetrics
US220A Roenis Elias RC .40 1.00
US220B Roenis Elias SP 1.50 4.00
With water
US221A Gregory Polanco .20 .50
US221B Polanco SP Blk Jsy 2.50 6.00
US222 Brandon Moss .12 .30
US223 Yasiel Puig .20 .50
US224 Jared Burton .12 .30
US225A Luis Avilan .12 .30
US225B Luis Avilan SP 1.50 4.00
SABRmetrics
US226 Chris Coghlan .12 .30
US227 Ryan Wheeler .12 .30
US228 Aaron Crow .12 .30
US229A Sam Fuld .12 .30
US229B Sam Fuld SP 1.50 4.00
SABRmetrics
US230 Kurt Suzuki .12 .30
US231 Brendan Ryan .12 .30
US232 Scott Carroll RC .40 1.00
US233 Nelson Cruz .20 .50
US234 Felix Hernandez .15 .40
US235A Tommy Hunter .12 .30
US235B Tommy Hunter SP 1.50 4.00
SABRmetrics
US236 Jerome Williams .12 .30
US237 Jorge Polanco RC 1.00 2.50
US238 Giancarlo Stanton .20 .50
US239 Jose Abreu 1.00 2.50
US240 Aaron Sanchez RC .40 1.00
US241A Michael Choice RC .40 1.00
US241B Michael Choice SP 1.50 4.00
Blue jersey
US242 Javier López .12 .30
US243 Jesse Chavez .12 .30
US244A Daisuke Matsuzaka .15 .40
US244B Daisuke Matsuzaka SP 2.00 5.00
White jersey
US244C Daisuke Matsuzaka SP 2.00 5.00
SABRmetrics
US245A Andrew Heaney .12 .30
US245B Andrew Heaney SP 1.50 4.00
Black jersey
US246 Erick Aybar .12 .30
US247 Tony Watson .12 .30
US248 Brayan Pena .12 .30
US249 Eduardo Nunez .12 .30
US250 Yu Darvish .20 .50
US251 Ike Davis .12 .30
US252 Adrian Nieto RC .40 1.00
US253 Kevin Kiermaier RC .60 1.50
US254 Adrian Beltre .20 .50
US255 Jonathan Lucroy .15 .40
US256 Garrett Jones .12 .30
US257 Eduardo Escobar .12 .30
US258 Matt Carpenter .20 .50
US259 Craig Kimbrel .15 .40
US260A Jhonny Peralta .12 .30
US260B Jhonny Peralta SP 1.50 4.00
SABRmetrics
US261 Rene Rivera .12 .30
US262 Eddie Butler RC .40 1.00
US263 Kyle Seager .12 .30
US264 Freddie Freeman .25 .60
US265 Yoervis Medina .12 .30
US266 Drew Smyly .12 .30
US267 Jonathan Diaz RC .40 1.00
US268 Matt Shoemaker RC .60 1.50
US269 Max Scherzer .20 .50
US270 Hunter Pence .15 .40
US271 Juan Perez RC .40 1.00
US272A Mark Ellis .12 .30
US272B Mark Ellis SP 1.50 4.00
SABRmetrics
US273 Martin Prado .12 .30
US274 Chris Withrow .12 .30
US275 Boone Logan .12 .30
US276 Rougned Odor RC 1.00 2.50
US277 Chris Sale .20 .50
US278A Rafael Montero RC .40 1.00
US278B Rafael Montero SP 1.50 4.00
Throwing underhand
US279 Kevin Frandsen .12 .30
US280 Cole Gillespie .12 .30
US281 David Buchanan RC .40 1.00
US282 Glen Perkins .12 .30
US283 Tyson Ross .12 .30
US284 Robbie Ray RC .40 1.00
US285 Cody Allen .12 .30
US286 Brandon Barnes .12 .30
US287 Mike Bolsinger RC .40 1.00
US288 Aroldis Chapman .20 .50
US289 Adam Wainwright .15 .40
US290 Cam Bedrosian RC .40 1.00
US291 Jake McGee .15 .40
US292 Chase Utley .15 .40
US293 Tom Koehler .12 .30
US294 Chris Martin RC .40 1.00
US295 Greg Holland .12 .30
US296 Tyler Moore .12 .30
US297 Zack Greinke .20 .50
US298A Bobby Abreu .12 .30
US298B Bobby Abreu SP 1.50 4.00
On deck
US299 Charlie Blackmon .20 .50
US300 Miguel Cabrera .20 .50
US301 Mookie Betts 2.50 6.00
US302 Tom Gorzelanny .12 .30
US303 Jarred Cosart .12 .30
US304 Nick Martinez RC .40 1.00
US305 Sean Doolittle .12 .30
US306 Logan Forsythe .12 .30
US307 Santiago Casilla .12 .30
US308 Zelous Wheeler RC .40 1.00
US309 Alexei Ramirez .15 .40
US310 Troy Tulowitzki .20 .50
US312 Matt Thornton .12 .30
US313 Derek Dietrich .15 .40
US314 Corey Dickerson .12 .30
US315 Carlos Gomez .12 .30
US316 Ian Krol .12 .30
US317 Marwin Gonzalez .12 .30
US318 Logan Schafer .12 .30
US319A Ricky Nolasco .12 .30
US319B Ricky Nolasco SP 1.50 4.00
SABRmetrics
US320 Koji Uehara .12 .30
US321 Josh Satin .12 .30
US322A Drew Pomeranz .15 .40
US322B Drew Pomeranz SP 2.00 5.00
SABRmetrics
US323A Chase Headley .12 .30
US323B Chase Headley SP 1.50 4.00
SABRmetrics
US324 Alexi Amarista .12 .30
US325 Jose Abreu 1.00 2.50
US326A Joaquin Benoit .12 .30
US326B Joaquin Benoit SP 1.50 4.00
SABRmetrics
US327 Jonny Gomes .12 .30
US328A Dustin Ackley .12 .30
US328B Dustin Ackley SP 1.50 4.00
SABRmetrics
US329 Todd Frazier .12 .30
US330 Daniel Webb RC .40 1.00

2014 Topps Update Black

*BLACK: 8X TO 20X BASIC
*BLACK RC: 2.5X TO 6X BASIC
STATED ODDS 1:62 HOBBY
STATED PRINT RUN 63 SER.#'d SETS
US2 Derek Jeter 25.00 60.00
US54 Mike Trout 20.00 50.00
US100 Jose Abreu 15.00 40.00
US178 Clayton Kershaw 20.00 50.00
US223 Yasiel Puig 15.00 40.00
US239 Jose Abreu 15.00 40.00
US325 Jose Abreu 15.00 40.00

2014 Topps Update Camo

*CAMO VET: 8X TO 20X BASIC
*CAMO RC: 2.5X TO 6X BASIC RC
STATED ODDS 1:103 HOBBY
STATED PRINT RUN 99 SER.#'d SETS
US2 Derek Jeter 25.00 60.00
US54 Mike Trout 20.00 50.00
US100 Jose Abreu 15.00 40.00
US178 Clayton Kershaw 20.00 50.00
US223 Yasiel Puig 15.00 40.00
US239 Jose Abreu 15.00 40.00
US325 Jose Abreu 15.00 40.00

2014 Topps Update Gold

*GOLD VET: 1.2X TO 3X BASIC
*GOLD RC: .4X TO 1X BASIC RC
STATED ODDS 1:3 HOBBY
STATED PRINT RUN 2014 SER.#'d SETS

2014 Topps Update Pink

*PINK VET: 10X TO 25X BASIC
*PINK RC: 3X TO 8X BASIC RC
STATED ODDS 1:203 HOBBY
STATED PRINT RUN 50 SER.#'d SETS
US2 Derek Jeter 30.00 80.00
US54 Mike Trout 25.00 60.00
US100 Jose Abreu 20.00 50.00
US178 Clayton Kershaw 25.00 60.00
US223 Yasiel Puig 20.00 50.00
US239 Jose Abreu 20.00 50.00
US325 Jose Abreu 20.00 50.00

2014 Topps Update Red Hot Foil

*RED FOIL VET: 1.5X TO 4X BASIC
*RED FOIL RC: .4X TO 1X BASIC RC
STATED ODDS 1:6 HOBBY

2014 Topps Update Sparkle

RANDOM INSERTS IN PACKS
US10 George Springer 15.00 40.00
US23 Ubaldo Jimenez 6.00 15.00
US37 Leury Garcia 6.00 15.00
US45 Pedro Ciriaco 6.00 15.00
US59 Brandon McCarthy 6.00 15.00
US63 David Murphy 6.00 15.00
US64 LaTroy Hawkins 6.00 15.00
US70 Jarrod Saltalamacchia 6.00 15.00
US95 Vidal Nuno 6.00 15.00
US106 Collin Cowgill 6.00 15.00
US107 Josh Collmenter 6.00 15.00
US109 David Lough 6.00 15.00
US114 Jeff Francis 6.00 15.00
US115 Nyjer Morgan 6.00 15.00
US116 Brett Anderson 6.00 15.00
US120 Randy Wolf 6.00 15.00
US122 Jeff Baker 6.00 15.00
US124 Nick Tepesch 6.00 15.00
US137 Doug Fister 6.00 15.00
US142 Jon Lester 8.00 20.00
US148 Kyle Parker 8.00 20.00
US157 Joe Smith 6.00 15.00
US161 Edward Mujica 6.00 15.00
US163 Ramon Santiago 6.00 15.00
US166 Andrew Romine 6.00 15.00
US169 Chone Figgins 6.00 15.00
US170 Matt Davidson 8.00 20.00
US188 Paul Maholm 6.00 15.00
US194 Hector Santiago 6.00 15.00
US203 Cole Figueroa 6.00 15.00
US205 Reed Johnson 6.00 15.00
US206 Chris Perez 6.00 15.00
US214 Tommy La Stella 6.00 15.00
US226 Chris Coghlan 6.00 15.00
US237 Jorge Polanco 15.00 40.00
US271 Juan Perez 6.00 15.00
US275 Boone Logan 6.00 15.00
US276 Rougned Odor 15.00 40.00
US278 Rafael Montero 6.00 15.00
US281 David Buchanan 6.00 15.00
US284 Robbie Ray 6.00 15.00
US287 Mike Bolsinger 6.00 15.00
US290 Cam Bedrosian 6.00 15.00
US291 Jake McGee 8.00 20.00
US302 Tom Gorzelanny 6.00 15.00
US316 Ian Krol 6.00 15.00
US317 Marwin Gonzalez 6.00 15.00
US328 Dustin Ackley 6.00 15.00
US330 Daniel Webb 6.00 15.00

2014 Topps Update Target Red Border

*TARGET VET: 1.2X TO 3X BASIC
*TARGET RC: .4X TO 1X BASIC

2014 Topps Update Wal-Mart Blue Border

*WM VET: 1.2X TO 3X BASIC
*WM RC: .4X TO 1X BASIC

2014 Topps Update All Star Access

RANDOM INSERTS IN PACKS
ASAAC Aroldis Chapman 2.50 6.00
ASAAJ Adam Jones 2.00 5.00
ASAAM Andrew McCutchen 2.50 6.00
ASAARA Alexei Ramirez 2.00 5.00
ASAARI Anthony Rizzo 3.00 8.00
ASABM Brandon Moss 1.50 4.00
ASADG Dee Gordon 1.50 4.00
ASADJ Derek Jeter 6.00 15.00
ASADM Daniel Murphy 2.00 5.00
ASAEA Erick Aybar 1.50 4.00
ASAFH Felix Hernandez 2.00 5.00
ASAGS Giancarlo Stanton 2.50 6.00
ASAJB Jose Bautista 2.00 5.00
ASAJS Jeff Samardzija 1.50 4.00
ASAKU Koji Uehara 1.50 4.00
ASAMCA Miguel Cabrera 2.50 6.00
ASAMCR Matt Carpenter 2.50 6.00
ASAMS Max Scherzer 2.50 6.00
ASAMT Mike Trout 12.00 30.00
ASARC Robinson Cano 2.00 5.00
ASASP Salvador Perez 2.00 5.00
ASATT Troy Tulowitzki 2.50 6.00
ASAYC Yoenis Cespedes 2.50 6.00
ASAYD Yu Darvish 2.50 6.00
ASAYP Yasiel Puig 2.50 6.00

2014 Topps Update All Star Access Autographs

RANDOM INSERTS IN PACKS
STATED PRINT RUN 25 SER.#'d SETS
EXCHANGE DEADLINE 9/30/2017
AAAJA Jose Abreu 100.00 200.00
AAANC Nelson Cruz 30.00 80.00
AAARC Robinson Cano 25.00 60.00
AAATF Todd Frazier 20.00 50.00

2014 Topps Update All Star Access Relics

RANDOM INSERTS IN PACKS
STATED PRINT RUN 99 SER.#'d SETS
ASARAM Andrew McCutchen 20.00 50.00
ASARCK Clayton Kershaw 15.00 40.00
ASARDJ Derek Jeter 25.00 60.00
ASARJB Jose Bautista 6.00 15.00
ASARMTT Mike Trout 40.00 100.00
ASARRC Robinson Cano 6.00 15.00
ASARTT Troy Tulowitzki 8.00 20.00
ASARYC Yoenis Cespedes 12.00 30.00
ASARYD Yu Darvish 8.00 20.00
ASARYP Yasiel Puig 12.00 30.00

2014 Topps Update All Star Stitches

STATED ODDS 1:52 HOBBY
*GOLD/50: .75X TO 2X BASIC
ASRAJ Adam Jones 3.00 8.00
ASRAM Andrew McCutchen 4.00 10.00
ASRARI Anthony Rizzo 5.00 12.00
ASRARR Aramis Ramirez 2.50 6.00
ASRAW Adam Wainwright 3.00 8.00
ASRCB Charlie Blackmon 4.00 10.00
ASRCG Carlos Gomez 2.50 6.00
ASRCKE Clayton Kershaw 5.00 12.00
ASRCKI Craig Kimbrel 3.00 8.00
ASRCS Chris Sale 4.00 10.00
ASRCU Chase Utley 3.00 8.00
ASRDG Dee Gordon 2.50 6.00
ASRDJ Derek Jeter 10.00 25.00
ASRDME Devin Mesoraco 2.50 6.00
ASRDMU Daniel Murphy 3.00 8.00
ASRFF Freddie Freeman 5.00 12.00
ASRFH Felix Hernandez 3.00 8.00
ASRFR Francisco Rodriguez 3.00 8.00
ASRGP Glen Perkins 2.50 6.00
ASRGS Giancarlo Stanton 4.00 10.00
ASRHP Hunter Pence 3.00 8.00
ASRJA Jose Abreu 6.00 15.00
ASRJB Jose Bautista 3.00 8.00
ASRJD Josh Donaldson 3.00 8.00
ASRJLU Jonathan Lucroy 3.00 8.00
ASRKSE Kyle Seager 2.50 6.00
ASRKU Koji Uehara 2.50 6.00
ASRMCA Matt Carpenter 4.00 10.00
ASRMCB Miguel Cabrera 5.00 12.00
ASRMS Max Scherzer 4.00 10.00
ASRMT Mike Trout 20.00 50.00
ASRNC Nelson Cruz 4.00 10.00
ASRPG Paul Goldschmidt 4.00 10.00
ASRRC Robinson Cano 3.00 8.00
ASRSC Starlin Castro 2.50 6.00
ASRTR Tyson Ross 2.50 6.00
ASRTT Troy Tulowitzki 4.00 10.00
ASRYC Yoenis Cespedes 4.00 10.00
ASRYD Yu Darvish 4.00 10.00
ASRYP Yasiel Puig 5.00 12.00

2014 Topps Update All Star Stitches Autographs

STATED ODDS 1:4146 HOBBY
STATED PRINT RUN 25 SER.#'d SETS
EXCHANGE DEADLINE 9/30/2017
ASTARAJ Adam Jones 30.00 80.00
ASTARBM Brandon Moss 20.00 50.00
ASTARCB Charlie Blackmon 30.00 80.00
ASTARGP Glen Perkins 25.00 60.00
ASTARGS Giancarlo Stanton 40.00 100.00
ASTARJA Jose Abreu 100.00 200.00
ASTARJD Josh Donaldson 30.00 80.00
ASTARJH Josh Harrison EXCH 30.00 80.00
ASTARJL Jonathan Lucroy 30.00 80.00
ASTARKS Kyle Seager 25.00 60.00
ASTARMC Matt Carpenter 30.00 80.00
ASTARMS Max Scherzer 50.00 120.00
ASTARNC Nelson Cruz 30.00 80.00
ASTARPG Paul Goldschmidt 30.00 80.00
ASTARTT Troy Tulowitzki 30.00 80.00

2014 Topps Update All Star Stitches Dual

STATED ODDS 1:11,001 HOBBY
STATED PRINT RUN 25 SER.#'d SETS
ASDAR J.Abreu/A.Ramirez 30.00 80.00
ASDBT T.Tulowitzki/C.Blackmon 20.00 50.00
ASDCD Y.Cespedes/J.Donaldson 20.00 50.00
ASDCG Cabrera/Goldschmidt 20.00 50.00
ASDGR A.Ramirez/C.Gomez 12.00 30.00
ASDJT Tulowitzki/Jeter 50.00 125.00
ASDKP Y.Puig/C.Kershaw 30.00 80.00
ASDMJ D.Murphy/D.Jeter 40.00 100.00
ASDTP M.Trout/Y.Puig 100.00 250.00

2014 Topps Update All Star Stitches Triple

STATED ODDS 1:5108 HOBBY
STATED PRINT RUN 25 SER.#'d SETS
ASTRACY McCtchn/Puig/Gmz 40.00 100.00
ASTRAJY McCtchn/Puig/Hrrsn 40.00 100.00
ASTRAYG McCtchn/Stntn/Puig 40.00 100.00
ASTRCJA Gomez/Ramirez/Lucroy 25.00 60.00
ASTRCYD Kershaw/Puig/Gordon 50.00 120.00
ASTRJCA Sale/Ramirez/Abreu 25.00 60.00
ASTRJMA Bautista/Trout/Jones 50.00 120.00
ASTRMIM Cbrr/Knslr/Schrzr 30.00 80.00
ASTRRKF Hernandez/Cano/Seager 25.00 60.00
ASTRYJB Moss/Cespedes/Donaldson 30.00 80.00

2014 Topps Update Fond Farewells

COMPLETE SET (15) 4.00 10.00
STATED ODDS 1:8 HOBBY
FFAK Al Kaline .40 1.00
FFCR Cal Ripken Jr. 1.25 3.00
FFDJ Derek Jeter 1.00 2.50
FFGB George Brett .75 2.00
FFJS John Smoltz .40 1.00
FFMM Mark McGwire .75 2.00
FFMR Mariano Rivera .50 1.25
FFOV Omar Vizquel .30 .75
FFPK Paul Konerko .30 .75
FFRC Rod Carew .30 .75
FFRH Roy Halladay .30 .75
FFRY Robin Yount .40 1.00
FFTH Todd Helton .30 .75
FFWS Willie Stargell .30 .75

2014 Topps Update Fond Farewells Autographs

STATED ODDS 1:22,002 HOBBY
STATED PRINT RUN 25 SER.#'d SETS
EXCHANGE DEADLINE 9/30/2017
FFAAK Al Kaline 30.00 80.00
FFAJS John Smoltz 40.00 100.00
FFAOV Omar Vizquel 150.00 250.00
FFAPM Paul Molitor 25.00 60.00

2014 Topps Update Fond Farewells Relics

STATED ODDS 1:2777 HOBBY
STATED PRINT RUN 99 SER.#'d SETS
FFRCR Cal Ripken Jr. 15.00 40.00
FFRDJ Derek Jeter 25.00 60.00
FFRJS John Smoltz 8.00 20.00
FFRMM Mark McGwire 15.00 40.00
FFRMR Mariano Rivera 10.00 25.00
FFRPK Paul Konerko 6.00 15.00
FFRPM Paul Molitor 8.00 20.00
FFRRH Roy Halladay 6.00 15.00
FFRRY Robin Yount 8.00 20.00
FFRTH Todd Helton 6.00 15.00

2014 Topps Update Framed Derek Jeter Reprints Black

STATED ODDS 1:1211 HOBBY
STATED PRINT RUN 75 SER.#'d SETS
*SILVER: .5X TO 1.2X BASIC
SILVER ODDS 1:2848 HOBBY
SILVER PRINT RUN 25 SER.#'d SETS
*GOLD: 1X TO 2.5X BASIC
GOLD ODDS 1:7067 HOBBY
SILVER PRINT RUN 10 SER.#'d SETS
1994 Derek Jeter 15.00 40.00
1995 Derek Jeter 15.00 40.00
1996 Derek Jeter 15.00 40.00
1997 Derek Jeter 15.00 40.00
1998 Derek Jeter 15.00 40.00
1999 Derek Jeter 15.00 40.00
2000 Derek Jeter 15.00 40.00
2001 Derek Jeter 15.00 40.00
2002 Derek Jeter 15.00 40.00
2003 Derek Jeter 15.00 40.00
2004 Derek Jeter 15.00 40.00
2005 Derek Jeter 15.00 40.00
2006 Derek Jeter 15.00 40.00
2007 Derek Jeter 15.00 40.00
2008 Derek Jeter 15.00 40.00
2009 Derek Jeter 15.00 40.00
2010 Derek Jeter 15.00 40.00
2011 Derek Jeter 15.00 40.00
2012 Derek Jeter 15.00 40.00
2013 Derek Jeter 15.00 40.00
2014 Derek Jeter 15.00 40.00

2014 Topps Update Power Players

COMPLETE SET (25) 4.00 10.00
STATED ODDS 1:6 HOBBY
PPAAG Adrian Gonzalez .30 .75
PPAAJ Adam Jones .30 .75
PPAAM Andrew McCutchen .40 1.00
PPAAP Albert Pujols .50 1.25
PPAAR Anthony Rizzo .50 1.25
PPAAW Adam Wainwright .30 .75
PPACK Clayton Kershaw .60 1.50
PPAFH Felix Hernandez .30 .75
PPAGS Giancarlo Stanton .40 1.00
PPAHR Hanley Ramirez .30 .75
PPAJA Jose Abreu 2.00 5.00
PPAJB Jose Bautista .30 .75
PPAJE Jacoby Ellsbury .30 .75
PPAJU Justin Upton .30 .75
PPAMC Miguel Cabrera .40 1.00
PPAMS Max Scherzer .40 1.00
PPAPG Paul Goldschmidt .40 1.00
PPARC Robinson Cano .30 .75
PPASR Sergio Romo .25 .60
PPATT Troy Tulowitzki .40 1.00
PPAYV Yordano Ventura .30 .75
PPACGN Carlos Gonzalez .30 .75
PPACGM Carlos Gomez .25 .60
PPAMTA Masahiro Tanaka .75 2.00
PPAMTR Mike Trout 2.00 5.00

2014 Topps Update Power Players Relics

STATED ODDS 1:2777 HOBBY
STATED PRINT RUN 99 SER.#'d SETS
PPRAP Albert Pujols 6.00 15.00
PPRAR Anthony Rizzo 6.00 15.00
PPRCGM Carlos Gomez 3.00 8.00
PPRCGN Carlos Gonzalez 4.00 10.00
PPRGS Giancarlo Stanton 5.00 12.00
PPRJB Jose Bautista 4.00 10.00
PPRMTA Masahiro Tanaka 10.00 25.00
PPRMTR Mike Trout 25.00 60.00
PPRPG Paul Goldschmidt 5.00 12.00
PPRTT Troy Tulowitzki 5.00 12.00

2014 Topps Update World Series Championship Trophies

STATED ODDS 1:2712 HOBBY
WSCTAP Albert Pujols 12.00 30.00
WSCTBRO Brooks Robinson 8.00 20.00
WSCTBRU Babe Ruth 15.00 40.00
WSCTCH Cole Hamels 8.00 20.00
WSCTCR Cal Ripken Jr. 15.00 40.00
WSCTDF David Freese 6.00 15.00
WSCTDJ Derek Jeter 20.00 50.00
WSCTDO David Ortiz 12.00 30.00
WSCTGB George Brett 10.00 25.00
WSCTGM Greg Maddux 12.00 30.00
WSCTJB Johnny Bench 10.00 25.00
WSCTJM Joe Morgan 8.00 20.00
WSCTJP Johnny Podres 6.00 15.00
WSCTMC Miguel Cabrera 10.00 25.00
WSCTMR Manny Ramirez 10.00 25.00
WSCTPM Pedro Martinez 8.00 20.00
WSCTPS Pablo Sandoval 8.00 20.00
WSCTRC Roberto Clemente 20.00 50.00
WSCTRJ Randy Johnson 10.00 25.00
WSCTSC Steve Carlton 8.00 20.00
WSCTSK Sandy Koufax 14.00 35.00
WSCTSM Stan Musial 15.00 40.00
WSCTTS Tom Seaver 12.00 30.00
WSCTWF Whitey Ford 8.00 20.00
WSCTWS Willie Stargell 8.00 20.00

2014 Topps Update World Series Heroes

STATED ODDS 1:8 HOBBY
WSHAP Albert Pujols .75 2.00
WSHBM Bill Mazeroski .50 1.25
WSHBR Brooks Robinson .50 1.25
WSHBSA Bret Saberhagen .40 1.00
WSHBSU Bruce Sutter .40 1.00
WSHCC Chris Carpenter .50 1.25
WSHCH Cole Hamels .50 1.25
WSHCS Chris Sabo .40 1.00
WSHDC Davd Cone .40 1.00
WSHDE David Eckstein .40 1.00
WSHDF David Freese .40 1.00
WSHDJ Derek Jeter 1.50 4.00
WSHDO David Ortiz .60 1.50
WSHDS Duke Snider .50 1.25
WSHEM Eddie Murray .50 1.25
WSHFV Fernando Valenzuela .40 1.00
WSHGB George Brett 1.25 3.00
WSHGC Gary Carter .50 1.25
WSHGS Gary Sheffield .40 1.00
WSHHA Hank Aaron 1.25 3.00
WSHIR Ivan Rodriguez .50 1.25
WSHJB Josh Beckett .40 1.00
WSHJBE Johnny Bench .60 1.50
WSHJL John Lackey .50 1.25
WSHJM Joe Morgan .50 1.25
WSHJP Jonathan Papelbon .50 1.25
WSHJS John Smoltz .60 1.50
WSHLH Livan Hernandez .40 1.00
WSHMRA Manny Ramirez .60 1.50
WSHMRI Mariano Rivera .75 2.00
WSHMS Mike Schmidt 1.00 2.50
WSHMW Mookie Wilson .40 1.00
WSHOH Orlando Hernandez .40 1.00
WSHPMA Pedro Martinez .50 1.25
WSHPMO Paul Molitor .60 1.50
WSHPS Pablo Sandoval .50 1.25
WSHRA Roberto Alomar .50 1.25
WSHRC Roberto Clemente 1.50 4.00
WSHRH Rickey Henderson .60 1.50
WSHRJ Reggie Jackson .50 1.25
WSHRJA Reggie Jackson .50 1.25
WSHRJO Randy Johnson .60 1.50
WSHSC Steve Carlton .50 1.25
WSHSK Sandy Koufax 1.25 3.00
WSHTG Tom Glavine .50 1.25
WSHTL Tim Lincecum .50 1.25
WSHTS Tom Seaver .50 1.25
WSHWF Whitey Ford .50 1.25
WSHWS Willie Stargell .50 1.25

2014 Topps Update World Series Heroes Autographs

STATED ODDS 1:4401 HOBBY
PRINT RUNS B/WN 25-200 COPIES PER
EXCHANGE DEADLINE 9/30/2017
WSHACS Chris Sabo/200 15.00 40.00
WSHADC David Cone/25 15.00 40.00
WSHADE David Eckstein/25 100.00 200.00
WSHAGC Gary Carter/25 25.00 60.00
WSHAJS John Smoltz/25 40.00 100.00
WSHALH Livan Hernandez/25 15.00 40.00
WSHAMW Mookie Wilson/200 15.00 40.00
WSHAOH Orlando Hernandez/25 25.00 60.00
WSHABSA Bret Saberhagen/50 15.00 40.00

2014 Topps Update World Series Heroes Relics

STATED ODDS 1:2777 HOBBY
STATED PRINT RUN 99 SER.#'d SETS
WSHRAP Albert Pujols 8.00 20.00
WSHRDJ Derek Jeter 15.00 40.00
WSHRDO David Ortiz 20.00 50.00
WSHRIR Ivan Rodriguez 5.00 12.00
WSHRJM Joe Morgan 5.00 12.00
WSHRMRI Mariano Rivera 8.00 20.00
WSHRMS Mike Schmidt 12.00 30.00
WSHRPS Pablo Sandoval 5.00 12.00
WSHRRA Roberto Alomar 5.00 12.00
WSHRTG Tom Glavine 5.00 12.00

2014 Topps Update World Series MVP Patches

RANDOM INSERTS IN PACKS
WSPBR Brooks Robinson 5.00 12.00
WSPBS Bret Saberhagen 4.00 10.00
WSPCH Cole Hamels 5.00 12.00
WSPDE David Eckstein 4.00 10.00
WSPDF David Freese 4.00 10.00
WSPDJ Derek Jeter 10.00 25.00
WSPDO David Ortiz 6.00 15.00
WSPJB Johnny Bench 6.00 15.00
WSPJBE Josh Beckett 4.00 10.00
WSPJP Johnny Podres 4.00 10.00
WSPLH Livan Hernandez 4.00 10.00
WSPMR Mariano Rivera 6.00 15.00
WSPMRA Manny Ramirez 6.00 15.00
WSPMS Mike Schmidt 6.00 15.00
WSPPM Paul Molitor 6.00 15.00
WSPPS Pablo Sandoval 5.00 12.00
WSPRC Roberto Clemente 10.00 25.00
WSPRF Rollie Fingers 5.00 12.00
WSPRJ Reggie Jackson 5.00 12.00
WSPRJA Reggie Jackson 5.00 12.00
WSPRJO Randy Johnson 6.00 15.00
WSPSK Sandy Koufax 8.00 20.00
WSPTG Tom Glavine 5.00 12.00
WSPWF Whitey Ford 5.00 12.00
WSPWS Willie Stargell 5.00 12.00

2014 Topps Update World Series Rings Gold Gems

*GOLD GEM: 2X TO 5X BASIC
STATED ODDS 1:10,794 HOBBY
STATED PRINT RUN 25 SER.#'d SETS

2014 Topps Update World Series Rings Silver

STATED ODDS 1:756 HOBBY
*GOLD: .6X TO 1.5X BASIC
GOLD STATED ODDS 1:2712 HOBBY
GOLD PRINT RUN 99 SER.#'d SETS
*GOLD GEM: 2X TO 5X BASIC
GOLD GEM STATED ODDS 1:10,794 HOBBY
GOLD GEM PRINT RUN 25 SER.#'d SETS

WSRBF Bob Feller 5.00 12.00
WSRBR Babe Ruth 10.00 25.00
WSRBS Bret Saberhagen 4.00 10.00
WSRDO David Ortiz 6.00 15.00
WSREM Eddie Murray 5.00 12.00
WSRFR Frank Robinson 5.00 12.00
WSRHA Hank Aaron 6.00 15.00
WSRJB Johnny Bench 6.00 15.00
WSRJF Jimmie Foxx 6.00 15.00
WSRJP Johnny Podres 4.00 10.00
WSRMR Mariano Rivera 6.00 15.00
WSRMS Mike Schmidt 5.00 12.00
WSROC Orlando Cepeda 5.00 12.00
WSROS Ozzie Smith 6.00 15.00
WSRRC Roberto Clemente 10.00 25.00
WSRRH Rickey Henderson 6.00 15.00
WSRRJA Reggie Jackson 5.00 12.00
WSRRJO Randy Johnson 6.00 15.00
WSRRM Roger Maris 6.00 15.00
WSRSK Sandy Koufax 6.00 15.00
WSRSM Stan Musial 8.00 20.00
WSRTG Tom Glavine 5.00 12.00
WSRWF Whitey Ford 5.00 12.00
WSRWS Willie Stargell 5.00 12.00
WSRYB Yogi Berra 6.00 15.00

2015 Topps

COMPLETE SET (755) 25.00 60.00
COMP.RED.HOB.FACT SET (700) 30.00 80.00
COMP.BLUE.RET.FACT SET (700) 30.00 80.00
COMP.PURP.RET.FACT SET (700) 30.00 80.00
COMP.SER.1 SET w/o SP's (350) 12.00 30.00
COMP.SER.2 SET w/o SP's (350) 12.00 30.00
SER.1 VAR RANDOMLY INSERTED
FIVE RC VAR PER FACTORY SET
SER.2 VAR STATED ODDS 1:67 HOBBY
SER.1 PLATE ODDS 1:1721 HOBBY
SER.2 PLATE ODDS 1:926 HOBBY
PLATE PRINT RUN 1 SET PER COLOR
BLACK-CYAN-MAGENTA-YELLOW ISSUED
NO PLATE PRICING DUE TO SCARCITY
1A Derek Jeter 1.50 4.00
1B Jeter SP Tipping cap 60.00 80.00
2 Altuve/Martinez/Brantley LL .20 .50
3 Rene Rivera .15 .40
4 Curtis Granderson .20 .50
5A Josh Donaldson .20 .50
5B Josh Donaldson Gatorade 3.00 8.00
6 Jayson Werth .20 .50
8 Miguel Gonzalez .15 .40
9 Hunter Pence WSH .20 .50
10 Cole Hamels .20 .50
11 Jon Jay .15 .40
12 James McCann RC .40 1.00
13 Toronto Blue Jays .15 .40
14 Kendall Graveman RC .25 .60
15 Joey Votto .25 .60
16 David DeJesus .15 .40
17 Brian McCann .20 .50
18 Cody Allen .15 .40
19 Baltimore Orioles .15 .40
20A Madison Bumgarner .20 .50
20B Bumgarner SP Batting 3.00 8.00
21 Brett Gardner .20 .50
22 Tyler Flowers .15 .40
23 Michael Bourn .15 .40
24 New York Mets .15 .40
25A Jose Bautista .20 .50
25B Jose Bautista Standing 3.00 8.00
26 Bryce Brentz RC .25 .60
27 Kendrys Morales .15 .40
28 Alex Cobb .15 .40
29 Brandon Belt BH .20 .50
30 Tanner Roark FS .15 .40
31 Nick Tropeano RC .25 .60
32 Carlos Quentin .15 .40
33 Oakland Athletics .15 .40
34 Charlie Blackmon .25 .60
35 Brandon Moss .15 .40
36 Julio Teheran .20 .50
37 Arismendy Alcantara FS .15 .40
38 Jordan Zimmermann .20 .50
39A Salvador Perez .20 .50
39B Salvador Perez Celebrating 3.00 8.00
40 Joakim Soria .15 .40
41 Chris Colabello .15 .40
42 Todd Frazier .15 .40
43 Starlin Castro .15 .40
44 Gio Gonzalez .20 .50
45 Carlos Beltran .20 .50
46A Wilson Ramos .15 .40
46B Wilson Ramos Gatorade 2.50 6.00
47 Anthony Rizzo .30 .75
48 John Axford .15 .40
49 Dominic Leone RC .25 .60
50A Yu Darvish .25 .60
50B Yu Darvish Batting 4.00 10.00
51 Ryan Howard .20 .50
52 Fernando Rodney .15 .40
53 Nathan Eovaldi .20 .50
54 Joe Nathan .15 .40
55 Trevor May RC .25 .60
56 Matt Garza .15 .40
57 Lyle Overbay .15 .40
58 Evan Gattis FS .15 .40
59 Jake Odorizzi .15 .40
60 Michael Wacha .20 .50
61 Cto/Krshw/Wnwrght LL .40 1.00
62 Nolan Arenado .40 1.00
63 Chris Owings FS .15 .40
64 Atlanta Braves .15 .40
65 Alexei Ramirez .20 .50
66 Vance Worley .15 .40
67 Hunter Pence .20 .50
68 Lonnie Chisenhall .15 .40
69 Justin Upton .20 .50
70 Charlie Furbush .15 .40
71 Adrian Beltre BH .25 .60
72 Jordan Lyles .15 .40
73 Freddie Freeman .30 .75
74 Tyler Skaggs .15 .40
75 Dustin Pedroia .25 .60
76 Ian Kennedy .15 .40
77 Edwin Escobar RC .25 .60
78 Yordano Ventura .20 .50
79 Starling Marte .20 .50
80 Adam Wainwright .20 .50
81 Chris Young .15 .40
82 Nick Tepesch .15 .40
83 David Wright .20 .50
84 Jonathan Schoop .15 .40
85 Wnwrght/Cto/Krshw LL .40 1.00
86 Tim Hudson .20 .50
87 Eric Sogard .15 .40
88 Madison Bumgarner WSH .20 .50
89 Michael Choice .15 .40
90 Marcus Stroman FS .20 .50
91 Corey Dickerson .15 .40
92A Ian Kinsler .20 .50
92B Ian Kinsler Facing right 3.00 8.00
93 Andre Ethier .20 .50
94 Tommy Kahnle RC .25 .60
95 Junior Lake .15 .40
96 Sergio Santos .15 .40
97 Dalton Pompey RC .30 .75
98 Trt/Crz/Cbrra LL 1.25 3.00
99 Yonder Alonso .15 .40
100A Clayton Kershaw .40 1.00
100B Kershaw SP Bubble 6.00 15.00
101 Scooter Gennett .20 .50
102 Gordon Beckham .15 .40
103 Guilder Rodriguez RC .25 .60
104 Bud Norris .15 .40
105 Jeff Baker .15 .40
106 Pedro Alvarez .15 .40
107 James Loney .15 .40
108A Jorge Soler RC .40 1.00
108B J.Soler No bat FS 1.50 4.00
109 Doug Fister .15 .40
110 Tony Sipp .15 .40
111 Trevor Bauer .30 .75
112 Daniel Nava .15 .40
113 Jason Castro .15 .40
114 Mike Zunino .15 .40
115 Khris Davis .25 .60
116 Vidal Nuno .15 .40
117 Sean Doolittle .15 .40
118 Domonic Brown .15 .40
119 Anibal Sanchez .15 .40
120 Yoenis Cespedes .20 .50
121 Garrett Jones .15 .40
122 Corey Kluber .20 .50
123 Ben Revere .15 .40
124 Mark Melancon .15 .40
125 Troy Tulowitzki .25 .60
126 Detroit Tigers .15 .40
127 McCtchn/Mrn/Hrrsn LL .25 .60
128 Anthony Swarzak .15 .40
129 Jacob deGrom FS .50 1.25
130 Mike Napoli .15 .40
131 Edward Mujica .15 .40
132 Michael Taylor RC .25 .60
133 Daisuke Matsuzaka .20 .50
134A Brett Lawrie .20 .50
134B Brett Lawrie Baseballs in air 3.00 8.00
135 Matt Dominguez .15 .40
136A Manny Machado .25 .60
136B Machado SP w/Trout 6.00 15.00
137 Alcides Escobar .20 .50
138 Tim Lincecum .20 .50
139 Gary Brown RC .25 .60
140 Alex Avila .20 .50
141 Cory Spangenberg RC .25 .60
142 Masahiro Tanaka FS .20 .50
143 Jonathan Papelbon .20 .50
144 Rusney Castillo RC .30 .75
145 Jesse Hahn .15 .40
146 Tony Watson .15 .40
147 Andrew Heaney FS .15 .40
148 J.D. Martinez .25 .60
149 Daniel Murphy .20 .50
150A Giancarlo Stanton .20 .50
150B Giancarlo Stanton Celebrating 4.00 10.00
151 C.J. Cron FS .15 .40
152 Michael Pineda .15 .40
153 Josh Reddick .15 .40
154 Brandon Finnegan RC .25 .60
155 Jesse Chavez .15 .40
156 Santiago Casilla .15 .40
157 Ubaldo Jimenez .15 .40
158 Kevin Kiermaier FS .20 .50
159 Brandon Crawford .20 .50
160 Washington Nationals .15 .40
161 Howie Kendrick .15 .40
162 Drew Pomeranz .20 .50
163A Chase Utley .20 .50
163B Utley SP Dugout 3.00 8.00
164 Brian Schlitter RC .25 .60
165 John Jaso .15 .40
166 Jenrry Mejia .15 .40
167 Matt Cain .20 .50
168 Colorado Rockies .15 .40
169A Adam Jones .20 .50
169B Adam Jones Bubble 3.00 8.00
170 Tommy Medica .15 .40
171 Mike Foltynewicz RC .25 .60
172 Didi Gregorius .20 .50
173 Carlos Torres .15 .40
174 Jesus Guzman .15 .40
175 Adrian Beltre .25 .60
176 Jose Abreu FS .25 .60
177A Paul Konerko .20 .50
177B Paul Konerko With fans 3.00 8.00
178 Christian Yelich .30 .75
179 Jason Vargas .15 .40
180 Steve Pearce .25 .60
181A Jason Heyward .20 .50
181B Jason Heyward Waving 3.00 8.00
182 Devin Mesoraco .15 .40
183 Craig Gentry .15 .40
184 B.J. Upton .20 .50
185 Ricky Nolasco .15 .40
186 Rex Brothers .15 .40
187 Marlon Byrd .15 .40
188 Madison Bumgarner WSH .20 .50
189 Dustin Ackley .15 .40
190 Zach Britton .20 .50
191 Yimi Garcia RC .25 .60
192B Pederson Running FS 4.00 10.00
192A Joc Pederson RC 1.00 2.50
193 Buck Farmer RC .25 .60
194 David Murphy .15 .40
195 Garrett Richards .20 .50
196 Chicago Cubs .15 .40
197 Glen Perkins .15 .40
198 Alexi Ogando .15 .40
199 Eric Young Jr. .15 .40
200A Miguel Cabrera .25 .60
200B Miggy SP Celebration 4.00 10.00
201 Tommy La Stella .15 .40
202 Mike Minor .15 .40
203 Paul Goldschmidt .25 .60
204 Eduardo Escobar .15 .40
205 Josh Harrison .15 .40
206 Rick Porcello .20 .50
207A Bryce Harper .40 1.00
207B Harper SP Scream 6.00 15.00
208 Wilin Rosario .15 .40
209 Daniel Corcino .15 .40
210 Salvador Perez BH .20 .50
211 Clay Buchholz .15 .40
212 Cliff Lee .20 .50
213 Jered Weaver .20 .50
214 Kluber/Scherzer/Weaver LL .25 .60
215 Alejandro De Aza .15 .40
216A Greg Holland .15 .40
216B Greg Holland Gatorade 2.50 6.00
217 Daniel Norris RC .25 .60
218 David Buchanan .15 .40
219A Kennys Vargas .15 .40
219B Kennys Vargas Flexing 2.50 6.00
220 Shelby Miller .20 .50
221A Jason Kipnis .20 .50
221B Jason Kipnis Sliding 3.00 8.00
222 Antonio Bastardo .15 .40
223 Los Angeles Angels .15 .40
224 Bryan Mitchell RC .25 .60
225 Jacoby Ellsbury .20 .50
226 Dioner Navarro .15 .40
227 Madison Bumgarner WSH .20 .50
228 Jake Peavy .15 .40
229 Bryan Morris .15 .40
230 Jean Segura .20 .50
231 Andrew Cashner .15 .40
232 Andrew Susac .15 .40
233 Carlos Ruiz .15 .40
234 Brandon Belt .20 .50
235 Jeremy Guthrie .15 .40
236 Zack Wheeler .20 .50
237 Lucas Duda .20 .50
238 Hyun-Jin Ryu .20 .50
239 Jose Iglesias .20 .50
240 Anthony Ranaudo RC .25 .60
241 Dilson Herrera RC .30 .75
242 Edwin Encarnacion .25 .60
243 Al Alburquerque .15 .40
244 Bartolo Colon .15 .40
245 Tyler Colvin .15 .40
246 Chris Carter .15 .40
247 Aaron Hill .15 .40
248 Addison Reed .15 .40
249 Jose Reyes .20 .50
250A Evan Longoria .20 .50
250B Evan Longoria No cap 3.00 8.00
251 Anthony Rendon .25 .60
252 Travis Wood .15 .40
253 Gregory Polanco FS .20 .50
254 Steve Cishek .15 .40
255 James Russell .15 .40
256 Adam Eaton .15 .40
257 Jarrod Saltalamacchia .15 .40
258 Kansas City Royals .15 .40
259 Brian Dozier .20 .50
260 David Peralta RC .25 .60
261 Lance Lynn .20 .50
262 Ryan Braun .20 .50
263 Dillon Gee .15 .40
264 Tony Cingrani .20 .50
265 Arizona Diamondbacks .15 .40
266 Brandon Phillips .15 .40
267 Zack Greinke .25 .60
268 Aroldis Chapman .25 .60
269 Jordy Mercer .15 .40
270 Steven Moya RC .30 .75
271 Pittsburgh Pirates .15 .40
272 Matt Kemp .20 .50
273 Brandon Hicks .15 .40
274 Ryan Zimmerman .20 .50
275 Buster Posey .30 .75
276 Conor Gillaspie .15 .40
277 Cincinnati Reds .15 .40
278 David Phelps .15 .40
279 Coco Crisp .15 .40
280 Miguel Montero .15 .40
281A Elvis Andrus .20 .50
281B Andrus SP w/Jeter 6.00 15.00
282 Alex Presley .15 .40
283 Chris Johnson .15 .40
284 Brandon League .15 .40
285 Crtr/Trt/Crz LL 1.25 3.00
286 Trevor Rosenthal .20 .50
287 Everth Cabrera .15 .40
288 Chris Parmelee .15 .40
289 Matt Joyce .15 .40
290 David Lough .15 .40
291 Mark Reynolds .15 .40
292 Neil Walker .15 .40
293 Zach Duke .15 .40
294 Aaron Sanchez FS .20 .50
295 Erick Aybar .15 .40
296 Charlie Morton .25 .60
297 Scott Kazmir .15 .40
298 Rymer Liriano RC .25 .60
299 Joaquin Arias .15 .40
300 Mike Trout 1.25 3.00
301 Zack Cozart .15 .40
302A Martin Prado .15 .40
302B Martin Prado Gatorade 2.50 6.00
303 Ike Davis .15 .40
304 Shawn Kelley .15 .40
305 Sonny Gray .20 .50
306 Juan Lagares FS .15 .40
307 Mark Teixeira .20 .50
308 Carl Crawford .20 .50
309 Maikel Franco RC .30 .75
310 Jake Lamb RC .40 1.00
311 Jhonny Peralta .15 .40
312 Kyle Lobstein RC .25 .60
313 Rzzo/Stntn/Duda LL .30 .75
314 Jackie Bradley Jr. .25 .60
315 Javier Baez RC 2.00 5.00
316 R.A. Dickey .20 .50
317 Clayton Kershaw BH .40 1.00
318A George Springer FS .20 .50
318B George Springer Gatorade 3.00 8.00
319 Derek Jeter BH 1.50 4.00
320 Shin-Soo Choo .20 .50
321 Josh Hamilton .20 .50
322 Phil Hughes .15 .40
323 Eric Hosmer .20 .50
324 Chris Archer .15 .40
325 Felix Hernandez .20 .50
326 C.J. Wilson .15 .40
327 Xander Bogaerts FS .25 .60
328 Adrian Gonzalez .20 .50
329 Logan Forsythe .15 .40
330 Brian Duensing .15 .40
331 Danny Espinosa .15 .40
332 Kyle Seager .15 .40
333 Billy Hamilton FS .20 .50
334 Gerardo Parra .15 .40
335 Matt Barnes RC .25 .60
336 Matt Carpenter .25 .60
337 Jedd Gyorko .15 .40
338 Yasmani Grandal .15 .40
339 Austin Jackson .15 .40
340 Carlos Gomez .15 .40
341 Kluber/Sale/Hernandez LL .25 .60
342 San Diego Padres .15 .40
343 Shane Greene .15 .40
344 Manny Parra .15 .40
345 Brandon Cumpton .15 .40
346 Trevor Cahill .15 .40
347 Dexter Fowler .20 .50
348 Carlos Santana .20 .50
349 Uptn/Gnzlz/Stntn LL .25 .60
350 Yasiel Puig .25 .60
351 Tom Koehler .15 .40
352 Jaime Garcia .15 .40
353 Mike Leake .15 .40
354 Kyle Hendricks .25 .60
355 Travis Snider .15 .40
356 Marcus Semien .25 .60
357 Derek Holland .15 .40
358 Jon Singleton FS .20 .50
359 Robinson Chirinos .15 .40
360 Adam LaRoche .15 .40
361 Matt Holliday .25 .60
362 Jason Bourgeois .15 .40
363 Avisail Garcia .25 .60
364A Travis Ishikawa .15 .40
364B Ishikawa Dugout 2.50 6.00
365 L.J. Hoes .15 .40
366 Jhoulys Chacin .15 .40
367 Sam Fuld .15 .40
368 David Robertson .20 .50
369 Aaron Loup .15 .40
370 Marcell Ozuna FS .25 .60
371 Koji Uehara .15 .40
372 Matt Adams .15 .40
373 Kurt Suzuki .15 .40
374 Nick Martinez .15 .40
375A Johnny Cueto .20 .50
375B Cueto Batting 3.00 8.00
376A Chris Sale .25 .60
376B Sale Dugout 4.00 10.00
377 Tommy Hunter .15 .40
378 Danny Duffy .15 .40
379 Phil Gosselin RC .25 .60
380 Hector Noesi .15 .40
381 Stephen Drew .15 .40
382 Ivan Nova .20 .50
383 Delmon Young .20 .50
384 Justin Ruggiano .15 .40
385 James Paxton FS .20 .50
386 Ben Zobrist .20 .50
387A Jacob deGrom ROY .50 1.25
387B deGrom Glasses 8.00 20.00
388 Francisco Liriano .15 .40
389A Mookie Betts FS .50 1.25
389B Betts Sliding 8.00 20.00
390 Cody Ross .15 .40
391 Hisashi Iwakuma .20 .50
392 Brandon Guyer .15 .40
393 Danny Salazar .20 .50
394 Marco Scutaro .15 .40
395 Chris Taylor .20 .50
396 Alex Colome .15 .40
397 Mike Aviles .15 .40
398 Jordan Zimmermann HL .20 .50
399 Josmil Pinto .15 .40
400A Andrew McCutchen .25 .60
400B McCutchen w/pic 4.00 10.00
401 Chris Coghlan .15 .40
402 Jeurys Familia .20 .50
403 Leury Garcia .15 .40
404 Tanner Scheppers .15 .40
405 Ross Detwiler .15 .40
406 Jon Lester .20 .50
407 Jed Lowrie .15 .40
408 Jake Smolinski .15 .40
409 Juan Uribe .15 .40
410 Kyle Lohse .15 .40
411 Nelson Cruz .25 .60
412 Hector Rondon .15 .40
413 Anthony Gose .15 .40
414 J.A. Happ .20 .50
415 Ervin Santana .20 .50
416 Francisco Cervelli .15 .40
417 Leonys Martin .15 .40
418 Jung Ho Kang RC .25 .60
419 Omar Infante .15 .40
420 Cody Asche .15 .40
421 Joe Kelly .20 .50
422 Prince Fielder .20 .50
423 Javy Guerra .15 .40
424 Michael Saunders .20 .50
425 Bryan Shaw .15 .40
426 Trevor Plouffe .15 .40
427 Raisel Iglesias RC .30 .75
428 Jon Niese .15 .40
429 A.J. Ellis .15 .40
430 Jarred Cosart .15 .40
431 Brandon McCarthy .15 .40
432 Alex Rios .20 .50
433 Justin Masterson .15 .40
434 Carlos Frias RC .40 1.00
435 Mike Fiers .15 .40
436 Russell Martin .15 .40
437 Jake Marisnick .15 .40
438 DJ LeMahieu .25 .60
439 Kenley Jansen .20 .50
440 Denard Span .15 .40
442 Tyler Matzek .15 .40
443 Maicer Izturis .15 .40
444 Lonnie Chisenhall HL .15 .40
445 Christian Vazquez .20 .50
446 Nick Franklin .15 .40
447 Jose Ramirez .20 .50
448 Ryan Hanigan .15 .40
449 Joe Panik HL .20 .50
450A Robinson Cano .20 .50
450B Cano Signing 3.00 8.00
451 Clayton Kershaw AW .40 1.00
452 Drew Smyly .15 .40
453 Elian Herrera .15 .40
454 Wade Davis .15 .40
455 Adam Lind .20 .50
456 Alex Gordon .20 .50
457 Aaron Hicks .25 .60
458 Junichi Tazawa .15 .40
459 Tuffy Gosewisch .15 .40
461A Mike Moustakas .20 .50
461B Moustakas w/fans 3.00 8.00
462 Shae Simmons RC .25 .60
463 Justin Verlander .25 .60
464 Brett Cecil .15 .40
465 Seattle Mariners .15 .40
466 A.J. Burnett .15 .40
467 Mat Latos .20 .50
468A CC Sabathia .20 .50
468B Sabathia w/Jeter 5.00 12.00
469 James Shields .15 .40
470 Mark Trumbo .25 .60
471 Pat Neshek .15 .40
472 T.J. House .15 .40
473 Ryan Raburn .15 .40
474 Alexi Amarista .15 .40
475 Juan Perez .25 .60
476 Jose Lobaton .15 .40
477 Dallas Keuchel .25 .60
478 Los Angeles Dodgers .15 .40
479A Carlos Gonzalez .20 .50
479B Gonzalez Glasses 3.00 8.00
480 Matt Harvey FS .20 .50
481 Freddy Galvis .15 .40
482 Joaquin Benoit .15 .40
483 Randal Grichuk .15 .40
484 Melvin Mercedes RC .25 .60
485 Daniel Hudson .15 .40
486 Erik Goeddel RC .30 .75
487A Corey Kluber AW .20 .50
487B Kluber High five 3.00 8.00
488 John Lackey .20 .50
489 Jeremy Hellickson .15 .40
490 Gavin Floyd .15 .40
491 Rougned Odor FS .20 .50
492 Brandon Barnes .15 .40
493 Alex Rodriguez .30 .75
494 James Jones .15 .40
495 Christian Colon .15 .40
496 Houston Astros .15 .40
497 Hunter Strickland RC .25 .60
498 Anthony Desclafani .15 .40
499 Eduardo Nunez .15 .40
500 David Ortiz .25 .60
501 Will Venable .15 .40
502 Kevin Frandsen .15 .40
503 Joe Panik FS .20 .50
503B Panik Smiling 3.00 8.00
504 Minnesota Twins .15 .40
505 Arodys Vizcaino .15 .40
506 Chase Anderson .15 .40
507 A.J. Pierzynski .15 .40
508 Collin McHugh .15 .40
509 Danny Santana FS .15 .40
510 Mike Trout MVP 1.25 3.00
511 Asdrubal Cabrera .20 .50
512 Jay Bruce .20 .50
513 Michael Cuddyer .15 .40
514 Will Smith .15 .40
515 Victor Martinez .20 .50
516A Lorenzo Cain .20 .50
516B Cain High five 2.50 6.00
517 Yusmeiro Petit .15 .40
518 Rajai Davis .15 .40
519A Archie Bradley RC .25 .60
519B Bradley Drk jsy FS 1.00 2.50
520 Brayan Pena .15 .40
521 Nick Castellanos FS .25 .60
522 Sam Tuivailala RC .25 .60
523 Christian Bethancourt FS .15 .40
524 John Danks .15 .40
525 Luke Gregerson .15 .40
526 Will Middlebrooks .15 .40
527 Carlos Martinez FS .20 .50
528 Brad Ziegler .15 .40
529 Ryan Flaherty RC .15 .40
530 Chris Heston RC .25 .60
531 Drew Hutchison .15 .40
532 Dellin Betances FS .20 .50
533 Marwin Gonzalez .15 .40
534 Chris Capuano .15 .40
535 Erik Cordier RC .25 .60
536 Logan Morrison .15 .40
537 Steven Souza Jr. .20 .50
538 Brad Boxberger RC .25 .60
539 Jimmy Nelson FS .15 .40
540 Drew Stubbs .15 .40
541 Homer Bailey .15 .40
542 Yasmany Tomas RC .30 .75
543 Alberto Callaspo .15 .40
544 Travis d'Arnaud FS .20 .50
545 Clayton Kershaw MVP .40 1.00
546 Tyler Clippard .15 .40
547 Kristopher Negron RC .25 .60
548 Cleveland Indians .15 .40
549 Christian Walker RC .50 1.25
550 David Price .20 .50
551 Corey Hart .15 .40
552 Yovani Gallardo .15 .40
553 Grady Sizemore .20 .50
554 A.J. Griffin .15 .40
555 Jake Arrieta .20 .50
556 Jake McGee .20 .50
557 Nick Markakis .20 .50
558 Patrick Corbin .20 .50
559 Dee Gordon .15 .40
560 Jerome Williams .15 .40
561 Ken Giles .15 .40
562 Wilmer Flores .20 .50
563 J.J. Hardy .15 .40
564 Jose Quintana .15 .40
565 Michael Morse .15 .40
566 Chris Davis .15 .40
567 Brennan Boesch .15 .40
568 Chris Tillman .15 .40
569 Marco Estrada .15 .40
570 Jarrod Dyson .15 .40
571A Devon Travis RC .25 .60
571B Travis Whte Jsy FS 1.00 2.50
572 A.J. Pollock .20 .50
573 Ryan Rua RC .25 .60
574 Mitch Moreland .15 .40
575 Kris Medlen .20 .50
576 Chase Headley .15 .40
577 Henderson Alvarez .15 .40
578 Ender Inciarte RC .25 .60
579 Jason Hammel .20 .50
580 Chris Bassitt RC .25 .60
581 John Holdzkom RC .25 .60
582 Wei-Yin Chen .15 .40
583 Jose Abreu ROY .25 .60
584 Danny Farquhar .15 .40
585 Matt Moore .20 .50
586A Max Scherzer .25 .60
586B Scherzer Red jrsy 4.00 10.00
587 Daniel Descalso .15 .40
588A Kolten Wong FS .20 .50
588B Wong Waving 3.00 8.00
589 Jeff Locke .15 .40
590 Torii Hunter .15 .40
591 Josh Collmenter .15 .40
592 Martin Maldonado .15 .40
593 Ruben Tejada .15 .40
594 Jose Pirela RC .25 .60
595A Craig Kimbrel .20 .50
595B Kimbrel Bullpen 3.00 8.00
596 Bronson Arroyo .20 .50
597 Matt Shoemaker FS .20 .50
598 Nick Swisher .20 .50
599A Michael Brantley .20 .50
599B Brantley Leg up 3.00 8.00
600A Albert Pujols .30 .75
600B Pujols Laughing 5.00 12.00
601 Wade Miley .15 .40
602 Drew Storen .15 .40
603A Jose Fernandez FS .25 .60
603B Fernandez Ornge jrsy 4.00 10.00
604 Jordan Schafer .15 .40
605 Huston Street .15 .40
606 Ian Desmond .15 .40
607 Jarrod Parker .15 .40
608 Justin Smoak .15 .40
609 Luke Hochevar .15 .40
610 David Freese .15 .40
611 Gregor Blanco .15 .40
612 Caleb Joseph RC .25 .60
613 Josh Beckett HL .15 .40
614 Jordan Walden .15 .40
615 Carlos Sanchez .15 .40
616A Kris Bryant RC 10.00 25.00
616B Bryant Face Left FS 15.00 40.00
617 Terrance Gore RC .25 .60
618 Billy Butler .15 .40
619 Kevin Gausman .25 .60
620 Jose Altuve .20 .50
621 Luis Valbuena .15 .40
622A Yan Gomes .15 .40
622B Gomes Dugout 2.50 6.00
623 Melky Cabrera .15 .40
624 Miguel Alfredo Gonzalez RC .25 .60
625 Mark Buehrle .20 .50
626 Hanley Ramirez .20 .50
627 Jason Grilli .15 .40
628 Peter Bourjos .20 .50
629 Robbie Grossman .15 .40
630 Carlos Carrasco .15 .40
631 Chris Iannetta .15 .40
632 Kyle Gibson .20 .50
633 Skip Schumaker .15 .40
634 Roenis Elias FS .15 .40
635 Scott Feldman .15 .40
636 Micah Johnson RC .25 .60
637 Matt Szczur RC .30 .75
638 Jimmy Rollins .20 .50
639 Cameron Maybin .15 .40
640 Matt Clark RC .25 .60
641 Yorman Rodriguez RC .25 .60
642 Alex Wood .15 .40
643 Oswaldo Arcia .15 .40
644 Chicago White Sox .15 .40
645A Neftali Feliz .15 .40
645B Feliz Hugging 2.50 6.00
646 Aramis Ramirez .15 .40
647A Yadier Molina .30 .75
647B Molina Celebrating 5.00 12.00
648 St. Louis Cardinals BB .15 .40
649 Emilio Bonifacio .15 .40
650 Pablo Sandoval .20 .50
651A Andrelton Simmons .15 .40
651B Simmons w/fans 2.50 6.00
652 Stephen Vogt .20 .50
653 Rafael Montero FS .15 .40
654 Alfredo Simon .15 .40
655 Taylor Hill .15 .40
656 Adeiny Hechavarria FS .15 .40
657 Justin Morneau .20 .50
658 Tsuyoshi Wada .30 .75
659 Jimmy Rollins HL .20 .50
660 Roberto Osuna RC .25 .60
661 Grant Balfour .15 .40
662 Darin Ruf .15 .40
663 Jake Diekman .15 .40
664 Hector Santiago .15 .40
665 Stephen Strasburg .25 .60
666 Jonathan Broxton .15 .40
667 Kole Calhoun .15 .40
668 Jairo Diaz RC .25 .60
669 Tampa Bay Rays .15 .40
670 Darren O'Day .15 .40
671 Gerrit Cole .25 .60
672 Wily Peralta .15 .40
673 Brett Oberholtzer .15 .40
674 Desmond Jennings .20 .50
675A Jonathan Lucroy .20 .50
675B Lucroy High five 3.00 8.00
676 Nate McLouth .15 .40
677 Ryan Goins .15 .40
678 Sam Freeman .15 .40
679 Jorge De La Rosa .15 .40
680 Nick Hundley .15 .40
681 Zoilo Almonte .15 .40
682 Christian Bergman .15 .40
683 LaTroy Hawkins .15 .40
684 Wil Myers .20 .50
685 Yangervis Solarte .15 .40
686 Tyson Ross .15 .40
687 Odubel Herrera RC .40 1.00
688 Angel Pagan .15 .40
689 R.J. Alvarez RC .25 .60
690 Brett Bochy RC .25 .60
691 Lisalverto Bonilla RC .25 .60
692 Andrew Chafin RC .25 .60
693 Jason Rogers RC .25 .60
694 Xavier Scruggs RC .25 .60
695 Rafael Ynoa RC .25 .60
696 Boston Red Sox .15 .40
697 New York Yankees .15 .40
698 Texas Rangers .15 .40
699 Miami Marlins .15 .40
700A Joe Mauer .20 .50
700B Mauer Dugout 3.00 8.00
701 Milwaukee Brewers .15 .40

2015 Topps Black

*BLACK: 10X TO 25X BASIC
*BLACK RC: 6X TO 15X BASIC RC
SER.1 STATED ODDS 1:108 HOBBY
SER.2 STATED ODDS 1:58 HOBBY
STATED PRINT RUN 64 SER.#'d SETS
1 Derek Jeter 15.00 40.00
98 Trout/Cruz/Cabrera LL 30.00 80.00
285 Carter/Trout/Cruz LL 30.00 80.00
319 Derek Jeter BH 15.00 40.00
400 Andrew McCutchen 15.00 40.00
530 Chris Heston 20.00 50.00
545 Clayton Kershaw 15.00 40.00
588 Kolten Wong 10.00 25.00
647 Yadier Molina 12.00 30.00

2015 Topps Factory Set Sparkle Foil

*SPARKLE: 8X TO 20X BASIC
*SPARKLE RC: 5X TO 12X BASIC RC
STATED PRINT RUN 179 SER.#'d SETS

2015 Topps Framed

*FRAMED: 20X TO 50X BASIC
*FRAMED RC: 12X TO 30X BASIC RC
SER.1 STATED ODDS 1:427 HOBBY
SER.2 STATED ODDS 1:186 HOBBY
STATED PRINT RUN 20 SER.#'d SETS
1 Derek Jeter 125.00 250.00
12 James McCann 15.00 40.00
15 Joey Votto 15.00 40.00
20 Madison Bumgarner 20.00 50.00
43 Starlin Castro 15.00 40.00
51 Ryan Howard 15.00 40.00
61 Cto/Krshw/Wnwrght LL 25.00 60.00
75 Dustin Pedroia 15.00 40.00
83 David Wright 15.00 40.00
85 Wnwrght/Cto/Krshw LL 25.00 60.00
88 Madison Bumgarner WSH 20.00 50.00
90 Marcus Stroman FS 20.00 50.00
97 Dalton Pompey 15.00 40.00
98 Trt/Crz/Cbrra LL 25.00 60.00
100 Clayton Kershaw 25.00 60.00
108 Jorge Soler 40.00 100.00
125 Troy Tulowitzki 15.00 40.00
127 McCtchn/Mrn/Hrrsn LL 15.00 40.00
129 Jacob deGrom FS 20.00 50.00
136 Manny Machado 15.00 40.00
144 Rusney Castillo 30.00 80.00
150 Giancarlo Stanton 15.00 40.00
176 Jose Abreu FS 25.00 60.00
188 Madison Bumgarner WSH 20.00 50.00
192 Joc Pederson 20.00 50.00
200 Miguel Cabrera 25.00 60.00
203 Paul Goldschmidt 15.00 40.00
207 Bryce Harper 50.00 120.00
219 Kennys Vargas 15.00 40.00
227 Madison Bumgarner WSH 20.00 50.00
253 Gregory Polanco FS 15.00 40.00
275 Buster Posey 25.00 60.00
285 Carter/Trout/Cruz LL 25.00 60.00
300 Mike Trout 50.00 120.00
309 Maikel Franco 20.00 50.00
313 Rzzo/Stntn/Dda LL 15.00 40.00
315 Javier Baez 15.00 40.00
317 Clayton Kershaw BH 25.00 60.00
318 George Springer FS 15.00 40.00
319 Derek Jeter BH 125.00 250.00
327 Xander Bogaerts FS 20.00 50.00
333 Billy Hamilton FS 20.00 50.00
336 Matt Carpenter 15.00 40.00
349 Uptn/Gnzlz/Stntn LL 15.00 40.00
350 Yasiel Puig 25.00 60.00
400 Andrew McCutchen 25.00 60.00
530 Chris Heston 20.00 50.00
588 Kolten Wong 15.00 40.00

2015 Topps Gold

*GOLD: 2X TO 5X BASIC
*GOLD RC: 1.2X TO 3X BASIC RC
SER.1 STATED ODDS 1:10 HOBBY
SER.2 STATED ODDS 1:4 HOBBY
STATED PRINT RUN 2015 SER.#'d SETS
1 Derek Jeter 12.00 30.00
319 Derek Jeter BH 12.00 30.00

2015 Topps Limited

*LIMITED: .75X TO 2X BASIC

2015 Topps Limited

*LIMITED RC: .75X TO 2X BASIC RC
ISSUED VIA TOPPS.COM
REPORTEDLY LESS THAN 1000 SETS MADE
616 Kris Bryant 8.00 20.00

2015 Topps Pink

*PINK: 10X TO 25X BASIC
*PINK RC: 6X TO 15X BASIC RC
SER.1 STATED ODDS 1:527 HOBBY
SER.2 STATED ODDS 1:284 HOBBY
STATED PRINT RUN 50 SER.#'d SETS
1 Derek Jeter 75.00 200.00
98 Trout/Cruz/Cabrera LL 12.00 30.00
285 Carter/Trout/Cruz LL 12.00 30.00
319 Derek Jeter BH 75.00 200.00
400 Andrew McCutchen 20.00 50.00
530 Chris Heston 15.00 40.00
588 Kolten Wong 12.00 30.00

2015 Topps Rainbow Foil

*RAINBOW: 2X TO 5X BASIC
*RAINBOW RC: 1.2X TO 6X BASIC RC
SER.1 STATED ODDS 1:10 HOBBY
SER.2 STATED ODDS 1:10 HOBBY

2015 Topps Snow Camo

*SNOW CAMO: 8X TO 20X BASIC
*SNOW CAMO RC: 5X TO 12X BASIC RC
SER.1 STATED ODDS 1:266 HOBBY
SER.2 STATED ODDS 1:144 HOBBY
STATED PRINT RUN 99 SER.#'d SETS
1 Derek Jeter 25.00 60.00
98 Trout/Cruz/Cabrera LL 10.00 25.00
285 Carter/Trout/Cruz LL 10.00 25.00
319 Derek Jeter BH 25.00 60.00

2015 Topps Sparkle

SER.1 RANDOMLY INSERTED
SER.2 STATED ODDS 1:331 HOBBY
5 Josh Donaldson 6.00 15.00
6 Jayson Werth 6.00 15.00
15 Joey Votto 8.00 20.00
20 Madison Bumgarner 6.00 15.00
25 Jose Bautista 6.00 15.00
34 Charlie Blackmon 8.00 20.00
42 Todd Frazier 5.00 12.00
43 Starlin Castro 5.00 12.00
47 Anthony Rizzo 10.00 25.00
50 Yu Darvish 8.00 20.00
60 Michael Wacha 6.00 15.00
62 Nolan Arenado 12.00 30.00
67 Hunter Pence 6.00 15.00
73 Freddie Freeman 20.00 50.00
75 Dustin Pedroia 20.00 50.00
80 Adam Wainwright 6.00 15.00
83 David Wright 6.00 15.00
92 Ian Kinsler 6.00 15.00
100 Clayton Kershaw 12.00 30.00
109 Doug Fister 5.00 12.00
120 Yoenis Cespedes 6.00 15.00
125 Troy Tulowitzki 8.00 20.00
136 Manny Machado 8.00 20.00
144 Rusney Castillo 40.00 100.00
149 Daniel Murphy 6.00 15.00
150 Giancarlo Stanton 8.00 20.00
163 Chase Utley 6.00 15.00
169 Adam Jones 6.00 15.00
175 Adrian Beltre 8.00 20.00
181 Jason Heyward 6.00 15.00
192 Joc Pederson 20.00 50.00
200 Miguel Cabrera 8.00 20.00
203 Paul Goldschmidt 8.00 20.00
205 Josh Harrison 5.00 12.00
207 Bryce Harper 12.00 30.00
225 Jacoby Ellsbury 6.00 15.00
242 Edwin Encarnacion 8.00 20.00
250 Evan Longoria 6.00 15.00
251 Anthony Rendon 8.00 20.00
262 Ryan Braun 6.00 15.00
272 Matt Kemp 6.00 15.00
275 Buster Posey 10.00 25.00
300 Mike Trout 40.00 100.00
315 Javier Baez 20.00 50.00
320 Shin-Soo Choo 6.00 15.00
321 Josh Hamilton 6.00 15.00
325 Felix Hernandez 6.00 15.00
336 Matt Carpenter 8.00 20.00
348 Carlos Santana 15.00 40.00
350 Yasiel Puig 8.00 20.00
360 Adam LaRoche 5.00 12.00
361 Matt Holliday 8.00 20.00
363 Avisail Garcia 6.00 15.00
372 Matt Adams 5.00 12.00
383 Delmon Young 6.00 15.00
386 Ben Zobrist 6.00 15.00
391 Hisashi Iwakuma 6.00 15.00
393 Danny Salazar 6.00 15.00
407 Jed Lowrie 5.00 12.00
411 Nelson Cruz 8.00 20.00
415 Ervin Santana 5.00 12.00
421 Joe Kelly 5.00 12.00
422 Prince Fielder 6.00 15.00
436 Russell Martin 5.00 12.00
438 DJ LeMahieu 8.00 20.00
445 Christian Vazquez 6.00 15.00
452 Drew Smyly 5.00 12.00
461 Mike Moustakas 6.00 15.00
463 Justin Verlander 8.00 20.00
468 CC Sabathia 6.00 15.00
469 James Shields 5.00 12.00
470 Mark Trumbo 5.00 12.00
475 Juan Perez 5.00 12.00
493 Alex Rodriguez 10.00 25.00
497 Hunter Strickland 5.00 12.00
507 A.J. Pierzynski 5.00 12.00
513 Michael Cuddyer 5.00 12.00
526 Will Middlebrooks 5.00 12.00
555 Jake Arrieta 6.00 15.00
557 Nick Markakis 6.00 15.00
568 Chris Tillman 5.00 12.00
579 Jason Hammel 6.00 15.00
586 Max Scherzer 8.00 20.00
590 Torii Hunter 5.00 12.00
596 Bronson Arroyo 5.00 12.00
606 Ian Desmond 5.00 12.00
610 David Freese 5.00 12.00
618 Billy Butler 5.00 12.00
620 Jose Altuve 6.00 15.00
624 Miguel Alfredo Gonzalez 5.00 12.00
638 Jimmy Rollins 6.00 15.00
645 Neftali Feliz 5.00 12.00
657 Justin Morneau 6.00 15.00
664 Hector Santiago 5.00 12.00
665 Stephen Strasburg 8.00 20.00
671 Gerrit Cole 8.00 20.00
674 Desmond Jennings 6.00 15.00
684 Wil Myers 6.00 15.00
690 Brett Bochy 5.00 12.00
691 Lisalverto Bonilla 5.00 12.00

2015 Topps Throwback Variations

RANDOM INSERT IN UPD PACKS
15 Joey Votto 3.00 8.00
23 Michael Bourn 2.00 5.00
42 Todd Frazier 2.00 5.00
43 Starlin Castro 2.00 5.00
47 Anthony Rizzo 4.00 10.00
78 Yordano Ventura 2.50 6.00
92 Ian Kinsler 2.50 6.00
200 Miguel Cabrera 3.00 8.00
239 Jose Iglesias 2.50 6.00
266 Brandon Phillips 2.00 5.00
286 Trevor Rosenthal 2.50 6.00
300 Mike Trout 15.00 40.00
301 Zack Cozart 2.00 5.00
311 Jhonny Peralta 2.00 5.00
318 George Springer FS 2.50 6.00
325 Felix Hernandez 2.50 6.00
326 C.J. Wilson 2.00 5.00
327 Xander Bogaerts FS 3.00 8.00
333 Billy Hamilton FS 2.50 6.00
336 Matt Carpenter 3.00 8.00
348 Carlos Santana 2.50 6.00
371 Koji Uehara 2.00 5.00
389 Mookie Betts FS 6.00 15.00
401 Chris Coghlan 2.00 5.00
406 Jon Lester 2.50 6.00
412 Hector Rondon 2.00 5.00
450 Robinson Cano 2.50 6.00
456 Alex Gordon 2.50 6.00
458 Junichi Tazawa 2.00 5.00
477 Dallas Keuchel 2.50 6.00
500 David Ortiz 3.00 8.00
515 Victor Martinez 2.50 6.00
518 Rajai Davis 2.00 5.00
525 Luke Gregerson 2.00 5.00
599 Michael Brantley 2.50 6.00
620 Jose Altuve 2.50 6.00
626 Hanley Ramirez 2.50 6.00
654 Alfredo Simon 2.00 5.00

2015 Topps Toys R Us Purple Border

*PURPLE: 5X TO 12X BASIC
*PURPLE RC: 3X TO 8X BASIC RC
INSERTED IN TOYS R US PACKS
1 Derek Jeter 25.00 60.00
98 Trout/Cruz/Cabrera LL 5.00 12.00
285 Carter/Trout/Cruz LL 5.00 12.00
319 Derek Jeter BH 15.00 40.00

2015 Topps 2632

COMPLETE SET (10) 20.00 50.00
RANDOM INSERTS IN RETAIL PACKS
26321 Cal Ripken Jr. 2.00 5.00
26322 Cal Ripken Jr. 2.00 5.00
26323 Cal Ripken Jr. 2.00 5.00
26324 Cal Ripken Jr. 2.00 5.00
26325 Cal Ripken Jr. 2.00 5.00
26326 Cal Ripken Jr. 2.00 5.00
26327 Cal Ripken Jr. 2.00 5.00
26328 Cal Ripken Jr. 2.00 5.00
26329 Cal Ripken Jr. 2.00 5.00
263210 Cal Ripken Jr. 2.00 5.00

2015 Topps Archetypes

COMPLETE SET (25) 8.00 20.00
STATED ODDS 1:6 HOBBY
A1 Rickey Henderson .50 1.25
A2 Mariano Rivera .60 1.50
A3 Steve Carlton .40 1.00
A4 Mike Trout 2.50 6.00
A5 Yasiel Puig .50 1.25
A6 Yoenis Cespedes .40 1.00
A7 Paul Goldschmidt .50 1.25
A8 Giancarlo Stanton .50 1.25
A9 Buster Posey .60 1.50
A10 Babe Ruth 1.25 3.00
A11 Mark McGwire .75 2.00
A12 Derek Jeter 1.25 3.00
A13 Cal Ripken Jr. 1.50 4.00
A14 Nolan Ryan 1.50 4.00
A15 Mike Piazza .50 1.25
A16 Johnny Bench .50 1.25
A17 Tony Gwynn .50 1.25
A18 Ted Williams 1.00 2.50
A19 Albert Pujols .60 1.50
A20 Greg Maddux .60 1.50
A21 Jackie Robinson .50 1.25
A22 Hank Aaron 1.00 2.50
A23 Willie Mays 1.00 2.50
A24 Ty Cobb .75 2.00
A25 Ken Griffey Jr. 1.00 2.50

2015 Topps Archetypes Autographs

STATED ODDS 1:31,455 HOBBY
STATED PRINT RUN 25 SER.#'d SETS
EXCHANGE DEADLINE 1/31/2018
AAMM Mark McGwire 100.00 200.00
AAMP Mike Piazza EXCH 60.00 150.00
AAYC Yoenis Cespedes 20.00 50.00

2015 Topps Archetypes Relics

STATED ODDS 1:5270 HOBBY
STATED PRINT RUN 99 SER.#'d SETS
ARAM Andrew McCutchen 10.00 25.00
ARAP Albert Pujols 10.00 25.00
ARBP Buster Posey 15.00 40.00
ARCK Clayton Kershaw 15.00 40.00
ARDJ Derek Jeter 30.00 80.00
ARGM Greg Maddux 10.00 25.00
ARGS Giancarlo Stanton 8.00 20.00
ARMM Mark McGwire 15.00 40.00
ARMP Mike Piazza 8.00 20.00
ARMR Mariano Rivera 10.00 25.00
ARMT Mike Trout 20.00 50.00
ARPG Paul Goldschmidt 8.00 20.00
ARRH Rickey Henderson 8.00 20.00
ARSC Steve Carlton 6.00 15.00
ARYP Yasiel Puig 8.00 20.00

2015 Topps Baseball History

COMPLETE SET (30) 8.00 20.00
STATED ODDS 1:8 HOBBY
1A Geneva Conference Begins .30 .75
1B Hank Aaron 1.00 2.50
2A Polio Vaccine Announced As Safe .30 .75
2B Robin Roberts .40 1.00
3A American Debuts .30 .75
3B Red Schoendienst .40 1.00
4A Nixon-Kennedy Debate .30 .75
4B Ted Williams 1.00 2.50
5A MLK Leads March On Washington .30 .75
5B Warren Spahn .40 1.00
6A Apollo 11 .30 .75
6B Tom Seaver .40 1.00
7A Top 40 Countdown Premiers .30 .75
7B Hank Aaron 1.00 2.50
8A Gerald Ford Sworn In As Of USA .30 .75
8B Nolan Ryan 1.50 4.00
9A Apple Founded .30 .75
9B Reggie Jackson .40 1.00
10A ESPN's First Broadcast .30 .75
10B Bruce Sutter .40 1.00
11A CNN Begins Broadcasting .30 .75
11B Darryl Strawberry .30 .75
12A Space Shuttle Columbia Launches .30 .75
12B Fernando Valenzuela .30 .75
13A Sandra Day O'Connor Sworn In .30 .75
13B Steve Carlton .40 1.00
14A Live Aid Concert .30 .75
14B Nolan Ryan 1.50 4.00
15A Clinton Earns Democratic Nomination .30 .75
15B Ken Griffey Jr. 1.00 2.50

2015 Topps Baseball Royalty

COMPLETE SET (25) 60.00 120.00
STATED ODDS 1:18 HOBBY
BR1 Babe Ruth 3.00 8.00
BR2 Sandy Koufax 2.50 6.00
BR3 Ted Williams 2.50 6.00
BR4 Joe DiMaggio 2.50 6.00
BR5 Jackie Robinson 1.25 3.00
BR6 Willie Mays 2.50 6.00
BR7 Hank Aaron 2.50 6.00
BR8 Mike Piazza 1.25 3.00
BR9 Roger Clemens 1.50 4.00
BR10 Cal Ripken Jr. 4.00 10.00
BR11 Greg Maddux 1.50 4.00
BR12 Ken Griffey Jr. 2.50 6.00
BR13 Randy Johnson 1.25 3.00
BR14 Nolan Ryan 4.00 10.00
BR15 Reggie Jackson 1.00 2.50
BR16 Ozzie Smith 1.50 4.00
BR17 Mark McGwire 2.00 5.00
BR18 Mariano Rivera 1.50 4.00
BR19 Frank Thomas 1.25 3.00
BR20 Miguel Cabrera 1.25 3.00
BR21 David Ortiz 1.25 3.00
BR22 Chipper Jones 1.25 3.00
BR23 Albert Pujols 1.50 4.00
BR24 Derek Jeter 3.00 8.00
BR25 John Smoltz 1.25 3.00

2015 Topps Baseball Royalty Silver

*SILVER: 1.2X TO 3X BASIC
STATED ODDS 1:524 HOBBY
STATED PRINT RUN 99 SER.#'d SETS
BR24 Derek Jeter 12.00 30.00

2015 Topps Birth Year Coin and Stamps Quarter

SER.1 ODDS 1:10,271 HOBBY
SER.2 ODDS 1:4935 HOBBY
UPD ODDS 1:11,193 HOBBY
STATED PRINT RUN 50 SER.#'d SETS
*PENNY/50: .4X TO 1X QUARTER
*NICKEL/50: .4X TO 1X QUARTER
*DIME/50: .4X TO 1X QUARTER
BYBB Brandon Belt UPD 10.00 25.00
BYCB Craig Biggio UPD 10.00 25.00
BYEE Edwin Encarnacion UPD 12.00 30.00
BYFF Freddie Freeman UPD 15.00 40.00
BYJD Jacob deGrom UPD 25.00 60.00
BYJL Jon Lester UPD 10.00 25.00
BYJS John Smoltz UPD 12.00 30.00
BYRC Rusney Castillo UPD 12.00 30.00
BYRJ Randy Johnson UPD 12.00 30.00
BYYT Yasmany Tomas UPD 12.00 30.00
CS01 Hank Aaron 25.00 60.00
CS02 Javier Baez 60.00 150.00
CS03 Madison Bumgarner 10.00 25.00
CS04 Miguel Cabrera 25.00 60.00
CS05 Roberto Clemente 30.00 80.00
CS06 Josh Donaldson 10.00 25.00
CS07 Lou Gehrig 60.00 150.00
CS08 Tom Glavine 10.00 25.00
CS09 Bo Jackson 25.00 60.00
CS10 Reggie Jackson 25.00 60.00
CS11 Derek Jeter 50.00 120.00
CS12 Sandy Koufax 25.00 60.00
CS13 Mike Piazza 12.00 30.00
CS14 Yasiel Puig 25.00 60.00
CS15 Albert Pujols 25.00 60.00
CS16 Jim Rice 20.00 50.00
CS17 Babe Ruth 60.00 150.00
CS18 Nolan Ryan 50.00 120.00
CS19 Chris Sale 12.00 30.00
CS20 Max Scherzer 12.00 30.00
CS21 Ozzie Smith 30.00 80.00
CS23 Julio Teheran 10.00 25.00
CS24 Mike Trout 40.00 100.00
CS25 David Wright 10.00 25.00
CS26 Jose Abreu 12.00 30.00
CS27 Jeff Bagwell 20.00 50.00
CS28 Mookie Betts 20.00 50.00
CS29 Wade Boggs 20.00 50.00
CS30 Paul Goldschmidt 20.00 50.00
CS31 Clayton Kershaw 20.00 50.00
CS32 Mark McGwire 20.00 50.00
CS33 Anthony Rizzo 15.00 40.00
CS34 Mike Schmidt 20.00 50.00
CS35 Giancarlo Stanton 12.00 30.00
CS36 Buster Posey 15.00 40.00
CS38 Roger Maris 30.00 80.00
CS39 Jorge Soler 12.00 30.00
CS40 Joc Pederson 30.00 80.00
CS41 Kennys Vargas 8.00 20.00
CS42 Evan Longoria 10.00 25.00
CS43 Yu Darvish 15.00 40.00
CS44 Cal Ripken Jr. 40.00 100.00
CS45 Tom Seaver 30.00 80.00
CS46 Lonnie Chisenhall 8.00 20.00
CS47 Ken Griffey Jr. 25.00 60.00
CS48 Andrew McCutchen 30.00 80.00
CS49 Felix Hernandez 15.00 40.00
CS50 Ted Williams 25.00 60.00

2015 Topps Bunt Player Code Cards

STATED ODDS 1:917 HOBBY
UPDATE ODDS 1:1030 HOBBY
STATED PRINT RUN 25 SER.#'d SETS
AC Aroldis Chapman 75.00 150.00
AM Andrew McCutchen 125.00 250.00
AR Anthony Rizzo 100.00 200.00
BH Bryce Harper 150.00 300.00
BP Buster Posey UPD 75.00 200.00
CG Carlos Gonzalez UPD 50.00 120.00
CG Carlos Gomez 75.00 150.00
CH Chris Heston UPD 15.00 40.00
CK Craig Kimbrel 75.00 150.00
CK Clayton Kershaw 150.00 300.00
CS Chris Sale 100.00 200.00
DG Dee Gordon UPD 12.00 30.00
DO David Ortiz 75.00 150.00
DP David Price 75.00 150.00
FH Felix Hernandez 100.00 200.00
GH Greg Holland 60.00 120.00
GS Giancarlo Stanton 100.00 200.00
JC Johnny Cueto 100.00 200.00
JE Jacoby Ellsbury 100.00 200.00
JK Jason Kipnis UPD 15.00 40.00
JL Jon Lester 75.00 150.00
KB Kris Bryant UPD 25.00 60.00
MB Madison Bumgarner 125.00 250.00
MH Matt Harvey UPD 40.00 100.00
MH Matt Harvey 100.00 200.00
MT Mike Trout UPD 50.00 120.00
MT Mark Teixeira UPD 8.00 20.00
MT Mike Trout 150.00 300.00
PF Prince Fielder UPD 12.00 30.00
RC Robinson Cano 100.00 200.00
SG Sonny Gray UPD 20.00 50.00
SS Stephen Strasburg 75.00 150.00
TT Troy Tulowitzki 50.00 120.00
YP Yasiel Puig 150.00 300.00
ZG Zack Greinke UPD 12.00 30.00

2015 Topps Career High Autographs

SER.1 STATED ODDS 1:405 HOBBY
SER.2 STATED ODDS 1:405 HOBBY
UPD STATED ODDS 1:253 HOBBY
SER.1 EXCH DEADLINE 1/31/2018
SER.2 EXCH DEADLINE 1/31/2018
UPD EXCH DEADLINE 9/30/2017
CHAA Arismendy Alcantara 3.00 8.00
CHAC Allen Craig 3.00 8.00
CHAD Andre Dawson 4.00 10.00
CHAE A.J. Ellis 3.00 8.00
CHAJ Adam Jones 4.00 10.00
CHARA Anthony Ranaudo 3.00 8.00
CHAS Aaron Sanchez 4.00 10.00
CHBC Brett Cecil 3.00 8.00
CHCB Charlie Blackmon 5.00 12.00
CHCC C.J. Cron 3.00 8.00
CHCJ Chipper Jones 25.00 60.00
CHCO Chris Owings 3.00 8.00
CHCS Carlos Santana 4.00 10.00
CHCSA Chris Sale 6.00 15.00
CHCSP Cory Spangenberg 3.00 8.00
CHCY Christian Yelich 20.00 50.00
CHDB Dellin Betances 4.00 10.00
CHDC David Cone 10.00 25.00
CHDM Daisuke Matsuzaka 6.00 15.00
CHDS Duke Snider 12.00 30.00
CHED Eric Davis 3.00 8.00
CHEF Erik Cordier 3.00 8.00
CHEL Evan Longoria 4.00 10.00
CHFJ Fergie Jenkins 4.00 10.00
CHGB Grant Balfour 3.00 8.00
CHGP Gregory Polanco 4.00 10.00
CHGS George Springer 10.00 25.00
CHGST Giancarlo Stanton 12.00 30.00
CHHA Hank Aaron 125.00 250.00
CHHI Hisashi Iwakuma 6.00 15.00
CHHK Hiroki Kuroda 50.00 120.00
CHIK Ian Kinsler 4.00 10.00
CHJB Javier Baez 8.00 20.00
CHJD Jacob deGrom 20.00 50.00
CHJH John Holdzkom 3.00 8.00
CHJJ John Jaso 3.00 8.00
CHJL Juan Lagares 6.00 15.00
CHJM J.D. Martinez 12.00 30.00
CHJP Johnny Podres 10.00 25.00
CHJPA Joe Panik 10.00 25.00
CHJPO Jorge Posada 15.00 40.00
CHJS Jonathan Schoop 3.00 8.00
CHJSM John Smoltz 12.00 30.00
CHJSO Jorge Soler 10.00 25.00
CHJT Julio Teheran 4.00 10.00
CHKW Kolten Wong 4.00 10.00
CHMA Mike Adams 3.00 8.00
CHMAD Matt Adams 3.00 8.00
CHMM Mike Minor 3.00 8.00
CHMT Mike Trout 100.00 200.00
CHMZ Mike Zunino 3.00 8.00
CHRC Rusney Castillo 12.00 30.00
CHRH Ryan Howard 4.00 10.00
CHSK Sandy Koufax 150.00 300.00
CHSM Shelby Miller 4.00 10.00
CHSMA Starling Marte 4.00 10.00
CHSS Scott Sizemore 3.00 8.00
CHST Sam Tuivailala 3.00 8.00
CHUJ Ubaldo Jimenez 3.00 8.00
CHYP Yasiel Puig 15.00 40.00
CHYV Yordano Ventura 8.00 20.00
CHAAB Archie Bradley S2 3.00 8.00
CHAAN Aaron Northcraft S2 3.00 8.00
CHAAR Anthony Ranaudo S2 6.00 15.00
CHAAS Andrew Susac UPD 3.00 8.00
CHABB Byron Buxton UPD 20.00 50.00
CHABH Brock Holt UPD 4.00 10.00
CHABS Blake Swihart UPD 4.00 10.00
CHABW Bernie Williams UPD 10.00 25.00
CHACC Carlos Correa UPD 75.00 200.00
CHACJ Chris Johnson S2 3.00 8.00
CHACM Carlos Martinez UPD 6.00 15.00
CHACR Carlos Rodon S2 8.00 20.00
CHACW Christian Walker S2 10.00 25.00
CHADG Dee Gordon UPD 3.00 8.00
CHADH Dilson Herrera S2 4.00 10.00
CHADL DJ LeMahieu UPD 10.00 25.00
CHADN Daniel Norris S2 3.00 8.00
CHADP David Peralta UPD 3.00 8.00
CHADP Dalton Pompey S2 4.00 10.00
CHADT Devon Travis UPD 3.00 8.00
CHAEC Eric Campbell UPD 3.00 8.00
CHAEC Erik Cordier S2 3.00 8.00
CHAEE Edwin Escobar S2 3.00 8.00
CHAFJ Fergie Jenkins S2 8.00 20.00
CHAFL Francisco Lindor UPD 8.00 20.00
CHAGB Gary Brown S2 3.00 8.00
CHAGS George Springer S2 8.00 20.00
CHAHK Hiroki Kuroda S2 50.00 120.00
CHAHS Hector Santiago UPD 3.00 8.00
CHAHS Hector Santiago S2 3.00 8.00
CHAIK Ian Kinsler S2 4.00 10.00
CHAJB Javier Baez S2 25.00 60.00
CHAJC Jose Canseco S2 30.00 80.00
CHAJJ Jon Jay S2 3.00 8.00
CHAJP Jose Pirela UPD 3.00 8.00
CHAJR Jason Rogers UPD 3.00 8.00
CHAJR Jason Rogers S2 3.00 8.00
CHAJS Jorge Soler S2 8.00 20.00
CHAJT Junichi Tazawa S2 3.00 8.00
CHAJW Josh Willingham S2 3.00 8.00
CHAKB Kris Bryant UPD 75.00 200.00
CHAKB Kris Bryant S2 75.00 200.00
CHAKG Kendall Graveman S2 3.00 8.00
CHAKL Kyle Lobstein UPD 3.00 8.00
CHAKP Kevin Plawecki UPD 3.00 8.00
CHAKS Kyle Seager UPD 3.00 8.00
CHALD Lucas Duda S2 4.00 10.00
CHALS Luis Sardinas UPD 3.00 8.00
CHAMB Matt Barnes UPD 3.00 8.00
CHAMT Michael Taylor S2 3.00 8.00
CHANC Nick Castellanos S2 5.00 12.00
CHANS Noah Syndergaard UPD 12.00 30.00
CHARC Rusney Castillo S2 12.00 30.00
CHARD Rubby De La Rosa S2 3.00 8.00
CHARP Rafael Palmeiro UPD 6.00 15.00
CHASG Shane Greene UPD 3.00 8.00
CHASH Slade Heathcott UPD 6.00 15.00
CHASM Steven Matz UPD 20.00 50.00
CHASP Spencer Patton UPD 3.00 8.00
CHATC Tyler Chatwood S2 3.00 8.00
CHATH T.J. House UPD 3.00 8.00
CHATM Trevor May S2 3.00 8.00
CHATP Tommy Pham S2 4.00 10.00
CHAWP Wily Peralta UPD 3.00 8.00
CHAYV Yordano Ventura S2 6.00 15.00
CHAZW Zach Walters UPD 3.00 8.00
CHAACL Alex Colome UPD 3.00 6.00
CHAAJC A.J. Cole UPD 3.00 8.00
CHABFA Buck Farmer S2 3.00 8.00
CHABFI Brandon Finnegan S2 3.00 8.00
CHACSA Carlos Santana S2 4.00 10.00
CHACSP Cory Spangenberg S2 3.00 8.00
CHAJGA Joey Gallo UPD 8.00 20.00
CHAJGR J.R. Graham UPD 3.00 6.00
CHAJHO John Holdzkom S2 3.00 8.00
CHAJLG Juan Lagares S2 3.00 8.00
CHAJMC James McCann S2 5.00 12.00
CHAJMR Jake Marisnick S2 3.00 8.00
CHAJPA Joe Panik S2 10.00 25.00
CHAJPE Joc Pederson S2 6.00 15.00
CHAJPO Johnny Podres S2 3.00 8.00
CHAMAN Matt Andriese UPD 3.00 8.00
CHAMBR Matt Barnes S2 3.00 8.00
CHAMCL Matt Clark S2 3.00 8.00
CHAMFO Mike Foltynewicz S2 3.00 8.00
CHAMFR Maikel Franco S2 4.00 10.00
CHAMSE Marcus Semien UPD 5.00 12.00
CHAYGA Yimi Garcia S2 3.00 8.00

2015 Topps Career High Relics

SER.1 STATED ODDS 1:49 HOBBY
SER.2 STATED ODDS 1:52 HOBBY
CHRAC Allen Craig S2 2.00 5.00
CHRAG Adrian Gonzalez S2 2.50 6.00
CHRAJ Adam Jones S2 2.50 6.00
CHRAS Andrelton Simmons S2 2.00 5.00
CHRBH Billy Hamilton S2 2.50 6.00
CHRCBI Craig Biggio S2 4.00 10.00
CHRCBL Charlie Blackmon S2 3.00 8.00
CHRCR Cal Ripken Jr. S2 12.00 30.00
CHRCU Chase Utley S2 2.50 6.00
CHRDJ Derek Jeter S2 8.00 20.00
CHRDM Don Mattingly S2 6.00 15.00
CHRDN Daniel Norris S2 2.00 5.00
CHRDW David Wright S2 2.50 6.00
CHREL Evan Longoria S2 2.50 6.00
CHRGC Gerrit Cole S2 3.00 8.00
CHRHP Hunter Pence S2 2.50 6.00
CHRHR Hanley Ramirez S2 2.50 6.00
CHRJA Jose Abreu S2 3.00 8.00
CHRJBA Jose Bautista S2 2.50 6.00
CHRJBR Javier Baez S2 15.00 40.00
CHRJH Josh Hamilton S2 2.50 6.00
CHRJM Joe Mauer S2 2.50 6.00
CHRJS Jon Singleton S2 2.50 6.00
CHRJVE Justin Verlander S2 3.00 8.00
CHRLL Lance Lynn S2 2.00 5.00
CHRMBU Madison Bumgarner S2 2.50 6.00
CHRMC Miguel Cabrera S2 3.00 8.00
CHRMH Matt Holliday S2 3.00 8.00
CHRMMC Mark McGwire S2 10.00 25.00
CHRMS Max Scherzer S2 3.00 8.00
CHRNC Nick Castellanos S2 3.00 8.00
CHRPS Pablo Sandoval S2 2.50 6.00
CHRRB Ryan Braun S2 2.50 6.00
CHRRC Roger Clemens S2 6.00 15.00
CHRRJ Randy Johnson S2 3.00 8.00
CHRRZ Ryan Zimmerman S2 2.50 6.00
CHRSC Shin-Soo Choo S2 2.50 6.00
CHRSS Stephen Strasburg S2 3.00 8.00
CHRVG Vladimir Guerrero S2 2.50 6.00
CHRVM Victor Martinez S2 2.50 6.00
CHRWB Wade Boggs S2 4.00 10.00
CHRYD Yu Darvish S2 3.00 8.00
CHRYP Yasiel Puig S2 3.00 8.00
CRHAC Allen Craig 2.00 5.00
CRHAJ Adam Jones 2.50 6.00
CRHAM Andrew McCutchen 6.00 15.00
CRHAP Albert Pujols 15.00 40.00
CRHAR Anthony Rizzo 4.00 10.00
CRHAW Adam Wainwright 5.00 12.00
CRHBH Bryce Harper 8.00 20.00
CRHBP Buster Posey 4.00 10.00
CRHCG Carlos Gomez 2.00 5.00
CRHCK Clayton Kershaw 5.00 12.00
CRHCS Carlos Santana 2.50 6.00
CRHDM Daisuke Matsuzaka 2.50 6.00
CRHDO David Ortiz 3.00 8.00
CRHDPA Dustin Pedroia 3.00 8.00
CRHDPE David Price 2.50 6.00
CRHDW David Wright 2.50 6.00
CRHEL Evan Longoria 2.50 6.00
CRHFF Freddie Freeman 4.00 10.00
CRHFH Felix Hernandez 2.50 6.00
CRHGP Gregory Polanco 2.50 6.00
CRHGSN Giancarlo Stanton 3.00 8.00
CRHGSR George Springer 2.50 6.00
CRHHI Hisashi Iwakuma 2.50 6.00
CRHHR Hanley Ramirez 2.50 6.00
CRHIK Ian Kinsler 2.50 6.00
CRHJA Jose Abreu 8.00 20.00
CRHJBA Jose Bautista 2.50 6.00
CRHJBZ Javier Baez 6.00 15.00
CRHJC Johnny Cueto 2.50 6.00
CRHJD Josh Donaldson 2.50 6.00
CRHJE Jacoby Ellsbury 2.50 6.00
CRHJT Julio Teheran 2.50 6.00
CRHMA Matt Adams 2.00 5.00
CRHMB Mookie Betts 6.00 15.00
CRHMC Miguel Cabrera 3.00 8.00
CRHMM Manny Machado 3.00 8.00
CRHMS Max Scherzer 3.00 8.00
CRHMTA Masahiro Tanaka 12.00 30.00
CRHMTT Mike Trout 15.00 40.00
CRHPG Paul Goldschmidt 3.00 8.00
CRHRB Ryan Braun 2.50 6.00
CRHRC Robinson Cano 2.50 6.00
CRHTT Troy Tulowitzki 3.00 8.00
CRHXB Xander Bogaerts 3.00 8.00
CRHYD Yu Darvish 3.00 8.00
CRHYM Yadier Molina 4.00 10.00
CRHYP Yasiel Puig 3.00 8.00

2015 Topps Commemorative Bat Knobs

STATED ODDS 1:10,956 HOBBY
*BLACK/99: .5X TO 1.2X BASIC
*PINK/25: .75X TO 2X BASIC
CBK01 Willie Mays 15.00 40.00
CBK02 Mike Trout 20.00 50.00
CBK03 Buster Posey 12.00 30.00
CBK04 Babe Ruth 20.00 50.00
CBK05 Mark McGwire 15.00 40.00
CBK06 Derek Jeter 20.00 50.00
CBK07 Jose Abreu 10.00 25.00
CBK08 Ty Cobb 10.00 25.00
CBK09 Jackie Robinson 12.00 30.00
CBK10 Yasiel Puig 10.00 25.00
CBK11 Albert Pujols 10.00 25.00
CBK12 Ken Griffey Jr. 15.00 40.00
CBK13 Giancarlo Stanton 10.00 25.00
CBK14 Andrew McCutchen 15.00 40.00
CBK15 Robinson Cano 8.00 20.00
CBK16 David Ortiz 10.00 25.00
CBK17 Ted Williams 12.00 30.00
CBK18 Adam Jones 10.00 25.00
CBK19 Jacoby Ellsbury 8.00 20.00
CBK20 Miguel Cabrera 12.00 30.00
CBK21 Hunter Pence 8.00 20.00
CBK22 Ryan Braun 8.00 20.00
CBK23 Prince Fielder 8.00 20.00
CBK24 Rusney Castillo 8.00 20.00
CBK25 Jorge Soler 8.00 20.00

2015 Topps Commemorative Patch Pins

STATED ODDS 1:1154 HOBBY
STATED PRINT RUN 199 SER.#'d SETS
CPP01 Ken Griffey Jr. 8.00 20.00
CPP02 Derek Jeter 10.00 25.00
CPP03 Greg Maddux 5.00 12.00
CPP04 Cal Ripken Jr. 12.00 30.00
CPP05 Roger Clemens 5.00 12.00
CPP06 David Ortiz 4.00 10.00
CPP07 Dustin Pedroia 4.00 10.00
CPP08 Frank Thomas 10.00 25.00
CPP09 Nolan Ryan 12.00 30.00
CPP10 George Brett 8.00 20.00
CPP11 Rod Carew 3.00 8.00
CPP12 Clayton Kershaw 6.00 15.00
CPP13 Ivan Rodriguez 3.00 8.00
CPP14 Joe Mauer 3.00 8.00
CPP15 Dwight Gooden 2.50 6.00
CPP16 David Wright 3.00 8.00
CPP17 Mariano Rivera 10.00 25.00
CPP18 Mark McGwire 6.00 15.00
CPP19 Tony Gwynn 4.00 10.00
CPP20 Johnny Bench 6.00 15.00
CPP21 Ted Williams 8.00 20.00
CPP22 Bob Feller 3.00 8.00
CPP23 Brooks Robinson 8.00 20.00
CPP24 Alex Rodriguez 5.00 12.00
CPP25 Don Mattingly 10.00 25.00

2015 Topps Eclipsing History

COMPLETE SET (10) 4.00 10.00
STATED ODDS 1:10 HOBBY
EH1 L.Brock/R.Henderson .50 1.25
EH2 S.Musial/H.Aaron 1.00 2.50
EH3 S.Koufax/N.Ryan 1.50 4.00
EH4 O.Smith/O.Vizquel .60 1.50
EH5 T.Seaver/D.Gooden .40 1.00
EH6 W.Ford/M.Rivera .60 1.50
EH7 R.Carew/M.Trout 2.50 6.00
EH8 J.Rice/N.Garciaparra .40 1.00
EH9 D.Jeter/L.Gehrig 1.25 3.00
EH10 D.Strawberry/D.Wright .40 1.00

2015 Topps Eclipsing History Dual Relics

STATED ODDS 1:17,118 HOBBY
STATED PRINT RUN 50 SER.#'d SETS
EHRGS T.Seaver/D.Gooden 10.00 25.00
EHRTC R.Carew/M.Trout 25.00 60.00
EHRVS O.Smith/O.Vizquel 20.00 50.00

2015 Topps Factory Set All Star Bonus

AS1 Clayton Kershaw .75 2.00
AS2 Buster Posey .60 1.50
AS3 Mike Trout 2.50 6.00
AS4 Jose Abreu .50 1.25
AS5 Miguel Cabrera .50 1.25

2015 Topps First Home Run

COMPLETE SET (40) 20.00 50.00
*GOLD: .5X TO 1.2X BASIC
*SILVER: .5X TO 1.2X BASIC
RANDOM INSERT IN RETAIL PACKS
FHR01 Jorge Soler .75 2.00
FHR02 Andrew McCutchen .75 2.00
FHR03 David Wright .60 1.50
FHR04 Robinson Cano .60 1.50
FHR05 Derek Jeter 2.00 5.00
FHR06 Bryce Harper 1.25 3.00
FHR07 Mike Moustakas .60 1.50
FHR08 Eric Hosmer .60 1.50
FHR09 Matt Carpenter .75 2.00
FHR10 Chipper Jones .75 2.00
FHR11 Anthony Rizzo 1.00 2.50
FHR12 Jason Heyward .60 1.50
FHR13 Javier Baez 4.00 10.00
FHR14 Yasiel Puig .75 2.00
FHR15 Alex Rodriguez 1.00 2.50
FHR16 Matt Adams .50 1.25
FHR17 Adam Dunn .60 1.50
FHR18 Buster Posey 1.00 2.50
FHR19 Paul Konerko .60 1.50
FHR20 Adrian Gonzalez .60 1.50
FHR21 Jose Bautista .60 1.50
FHR22 Josh Hamilton .60 1.50
FHR23 Chase Utley .60 1.50
FHR24 Ryan Howard .60 1.50
FHR25 Joey Votto .75 2.00
FHR26 Adam Jones .60 1.50
FHR27 Chris Davis .50 1.25
FHR28 Don Mattingly 1.50 4.00
FHR29 Joe Mauer .60 1.50
FHR30 Jose Abreu .75 2.00
FHR31 Yoenis Cespedes .60 1.50
FHR32 Paul Goldschmidt .75 2.00
FHR33 Freddie Freeman 1.00 2.50
FHR34 Mike Trout 4.00 10.00
FHR35 Evan Longoria .60 1.50
FHR36 Victor Martinez .60 1.50
FHR37 Mike Piazza .75 2.00
FHR38 Troy Tulowitzki .75 2.00
FHR39 Dustin Pedroia .75 2.00
FHR40 Deion Sanders .60 1.50

2015 Topps First Home Run Series 2

COMPLETE SET (40) 20.00 50.00
*GOLD: .5X TO 1.2X BASIC
*SILVER: .5X TO 1.2X BASIC
RANDOM INSERT IN RETAIL PACKS
FHR1 Eddie Murray .60 1.50
FHR2 Cal Ripken Jr. 2.50 6.00
FHR3 Brooks Robinson .60 1.50
FHR4 Babe Ruth 2.00 5.00
FHR5 Ted Williams 1.50 4.00
FHR6 Frank Thomas .75 2.00
FHR7 Johnny Bench .75 2.00
FHR8 Tony Perez .60 1.50
FHR9 Ty Cobb 1.25 3.00
FHR10 Miguel Cabrera .75 2.00
FHR11 Giancarlo Stanton .75 2.00
FHR12 Hunter Pence .60 1.50
FHR13 Reggie Jackson .60 1.50
FHR14 Carlos Beltran .60 1.50
FHR15 Bo Jackson .75 2.00
FHR16 David Ortiz .75 2.00
FHR17 Mark McGwire 1.25 3.00
FHR18 Tony Gwynn .75 2.00
FHR19 Jayson Werth .60 1.50
FHR20 Harmon Killebrew .75 2.00
FHR21 Clayton Kershaw 1.25 3.00
FHR22 Rusney Castillo .60 1.50
FHR23 Dwight Gooden .50 1.25
FHR24 Greg Maddux 1.00 2.50
FHR25 Pedro Alvarez .50 1.25
FHR26 Ryan Braun .60 1.50
FHR27 Albert Pujols 1.00 2.50
FHR28 Matt Kemp .60 1.50
FHR29 Prince Fielder .60 1.50
FHR30 Nelson Cruz .75 2.00
FHR31 Cliff Floyd .50 1.25
FHR32 Pablo Sandoval .60 1.50
FHR33 Yadier Molina 1.00 2.50
FHR34 Alex Gordon .60 1.50
FHR35 Lucas Duda .60 1.50

2015 Topps First Home Run Medallions

RANDOM INSERT IN RETAIL PACKS
FHRMAD Adam Dunn 2.50 6.00
FHRMAG Adrian Gonzalez 2.50 6.00
FHRMAG Alex Gordon S2 2.50 6.00
FHRMAJ Adam Jones 2.50 6.00
FHRMAM Andrew McCutchen 3.00 8.00
FHRMAP Albert Pujols S2 4.00 10.00
FHRMARI Anthony Rizzo 4.00 10.00
FHRMARO Alex Rodriguez 4.00 10.00
FHRMBH Bryce Harper 5.00 12.00
FHRMBJ Bo Jackson S2 3.00 8.00
FHRMBP Buster Posey 4.00 10.00
FHRMCB Carlos Beltran S2 2.50 6.00
FHRMCD Chris Davis 2.00 5.00
FHRMCF Cliff Floyd S2 2.00 5.00
FHRMCJ Chipper Jones 3.00 8.00
FHRMCK Clayton Kershaw S2 5.00 12.00
FHRMCR Cal Ripken Jr. S2 10.00 25.00
FHRMCU Chase Utley 2.50 6.00
FHRMDG Dwight Gooden S2 2.00 5.00
FHRMDJ Derek Jeter 8.00 20.00
FHRMDM Don Mattingly 6.00 15.00
FHRMDO David Ortiz S2 3.00 8.00
FHRMDP Dustin Pedroia 3.00 8.00
FHRMDS Deion Sanders 2.50 6.00
FHRMDW David Wright 2.50 6.00
FHRMEH Eric Hosmer 2.50 6.00
FHRMEL Evan Longoria 2.50 6.00
FHRMEM Eddie Murray S2 2.50 6.00
FHRMFF Freddie Freeman 4.00 10.00
FHRMFT Frank Thomas S2 3.00 8.00

FHRMGM Greg Maddux S2 4.00 10.00
FHRMGS Giancarlo Stanton S2 3.00 8.00
FHRMHK Harmon Killebrew S2 3.00 8.00
FHRMHP Hunter Pence S2 2.50 6.00
FHRMJA Jose Abreu 3.00 8.00
FHRMJB Johnny Bench S2 3.00 8.00
FHRMJBA Javier Baez 15.00 40.00
FHRMJBU Jose Bautista 2.50 6.00
FHRMJHA Josh Hamilton 2.50 6.00
FHRMJHE Jason Heyward 2.50 6.00
FHRMJM Joe Mauer 2.50 6.00
FHRMJS Jorge Soler 3.00 8.00
FHRMJV Joey Votto 3.00 8.00
FHRMJW Jayson Werth S2 2.50 6.00
FHRMLD Lucas Duda S2 2.50 6.00
FHRMMA Matt Adams 2.00 5.00
FHRMMC Matt Carpenter 3.00 8.00
FHRMMC Miguel Cabrera S2 3.00 8.00
FHRMMK Matt Kemp S2 2.50 6.00
FHRMMM Mark McGwire S2 5.00 12.00
FHRMMM Mike Moustakas 2.50 6.00
FHRMMP Mike Piazza 3.00 8.00
FHRMMT Mike Trout 15.00 40.00
FHRMNC Nelson Cruz S2 3.00 8.00
FHRMPA Pedro Alvarez S2 2.00 5.00
FHRMPF Prince Fielder S2 2.50 6.00
FHRMPG Paul Goldschmidt 3.00 8.00
FHRMPK Paul Konerko 2.50 6.00
FHRMPS Pablo Sandoval S2 2.50 6.00
FHRMRB Ryan Braun S2 2.50 6.00
FHRMRC Rusney Castillo S2 2.50 6.00
FHRMRC Robinson Cano 2.50 6.00
FHRMRH Ryan Howard 2.50 6.00
FHRMRJ Reggie Jackson S2 2.50 6.00
FHRMTC Ty Cobb S2 5.00 12.00
FHRMTG Tony Gwynn S2 3.00 8.00
FHRMTP Tony Perez S2 2.50 6.00
FHRMTT Troy Tulowitzki 3.00 8.00
FHRMTW Ted Williams S2 6.00 15.00
FHRMVM Victor Martinez 2.50 6.00
FHRMYC Yoenis Cespedes 2.50 6.00
FHRMYM Yadier Molina S2 4.00 10.00
FHRMYP Yasiel Puig 3.00 8.00
FHRMBRO Brooks Robinson S2 2.50 6.00
FHRMBRU Babe Ruth S2 8.00 20.00

2015 Topps First Home Run Relics

RANDOM INSERT IN RETAIL PACKS
STATED PRINT RUN 99 SER.#'d SETS
FHRRAD Adam Dunn 8.00 20.00
FHRRAG Adrian Gonzalez 8.00 20.00
FHRRAG Alex Gordon S2 5.00 12.00
FHRRAJ Adam Jones 5.00 12.00
FHRRAM Andrew McCutchen 15.00 40.00
FHRRAP Albert Pujols S2 8.00 20.00
FHRRBH Bryce Harper 12.00 30.00
FHRRCK Clayton Kershaw S2 6.00 15.00
FHRRDJ Derek Jeter 50.00 100.00
FHRRDO David Ortiz S2 6.00 15.00
FHRRDP Dustin Pedroia 30.00 80.00
FHRREH Eric Hosmer 5.00 12.00
FHRRFF Freddie Freeman 10.00 25.00
FHRRGS Giancarlo Stanton S2 6.00 15.00
FHRRHP Hunter Pence S2 8.00 20.00
FHRRJB Jose Bautista 5.00 12.00
FHRRJHA Josh Hamilton 8.00 20.00
FHRRJHE Jason Heyward 5.00 12.00
FHRRJV Joey Votto 10.00 25.00
FHRRMC Miguel Cabrera S2 6.00 15.00
FHRRMT Mike Trout 20.00 50.00
FHRRNC Nelson Cruz S2 6.00 15.00
FHRRPA Pedro Alvarez S2 10.00 25.00
FHRRPF Prince Fielder S2 5.00 12.00
FHRRPG Paul Goldschmidt 10.00 25.00
FHRRPS Pablo Sandoval S2 5.00 12.00
FHRRRB Ryan Braun S2 5.00 12.00
FHRRRC Rusney Castillo S2 5.00 12.00
FHRRRJ Reggie Jackson S2 10.00 25.00
FHRRTG Tony Gwynn S2 15.00 40.00
FHRRTT Troy Tulowitzki 6.00 15.00
FHRRYM Yadier Molina S2 8.00 20.00

2015 Topps First Pitch

COMPLETE SET (25) 10.00 25.00
SER.1 STATED ODDS 1:8 HOBBY
SER.2 STATED ODDS 1:8 HOBBY
FP01 Jeff Bridges .75 2.00
FP02 Jack White 1.25 3.00
FP03 McKayla Maroney .75 2.00
FP04 Eddie Vedder 1.50 4.00
FP05 Biz Markie .75 2.00
FP06 Agnes McKee .75 2.00
FP07 Austin Mahone .75 2.00
FP08 Jermaine Jones .75 2.00
FP09 Tom Willis .75 2.00
FP10 Graham Elliot .75 2.00
FP11 Tom Morello .75 2.00
FP12 Macklemore .75 2.00
FP13 Suzy 1.25 3.00
FP14 50 Cent .75 2.00
FP15 Meb Keflezighi .75 2.00
FP16 Kelsey Grammer .75 2.00
FP17 Chris Pratt .75 2.00
FP18 Jon Hamm .75 2.00
FP19 Melissa McCarthy .75 2.00
FP20 Chelsea Handler .75 2.00
FP21 Stan Lee .75 2.00
FP22 Lars Ulrich .75 2.00
FP23 Kevin Hart .75 2.00
FP24 Bill Kreutzmann .75 2.00
Mickey Hart
FP25 Gabriel Iglesias .75 2.00

2015 Topps Free Agent 40

COMPLETE SET (15) 5.00 12.00
STATED ODDS 1:8 HOBBY
F401 Albert Pujols .60 1.50
F402 Robinson Cano .60 1.50
F403 CC Sabathia .40 1.00
F404 Nolan Ryan 1.50 4.00
F405 Goose Gossage .40 1.00
F406 David Ortiz .50 1.25
F407 Andre Dawson .40 1.00
F408 Greg Maddux .60 1.50
F409 Alex Rodriguez .60 1.50
F4010 Randy Johnson .50 1.25
F4011 Reggie Jackson .40 1.00
F4012 Carlton Fisk .40 1.00
F4013 David Cone .30 .75
F4014 Roger Clemens .60 1.50
F4015 Ivan Rodriguez .40 1.00

2015 Topps Free Agent 40 Relics

STATED ODDS 1:31,455 HOBBY
STATED PRINT RUN 50 SER.#'d SETS
F40RAP Albert Pujols 20.00 50.00
F40RCS CC Sabathia 6.00 15.00
F40RRJ Reggie Jackson 10.00 25.00

2015 Topps Future Stars Pin

STATED ODDS 1:1896 HOBBY
*VINTAGE/99: .75X TO 2X BASIC
FS01 Xander Bogaerts 3.00 8.00
FS02 Billy Hamilton 2.50 6.00
FS03 George Springer 2.50 6.00
FS04 Gregory Polanco 2.50 6.00
FS05 Arismendy Alcantara 2.00 5.00
FS06 Jacob deGrom 6.00 15.00
FS07 Masahiro Tanaka 2.50 6.00
FS08 Dellin Betances 2.50 6.00
FS09 Tanner Roark 2.00 5.00
FS10 Jose Abreu 3.00 8.00

2015 Topps Gallery of Greats

COMPLETE SET (25) 40.00 100.00
STATED ODDS 1:18 HOBBY
GG1 Clayton Kershaw 2.00 5.00
GG2 Frank Thomas 1.25 3.00
GG3 Derek Jeter 3.00 8.00
GG4 Ken Griffey Jr. 2.50 6.00
GG5 Tom Glavine 1.00 2.50
GG6 Mike Piazza 1.25 3.00
GG7 Mark McGwire 2.00 5.00
GG8 Roger Clemens 1.50 4.00
GG9 Miguel Cabrera 1.25 3.00
GG10 Cal Ripken Jr. 4.00 10.00
GG11 Yasiel Puig 1.25 3.00
GG12 Steve Carlton 1.00 2.50
GG13 Hanley Ramirez 1.00 2.50
GG14 Willie Mays 2.50 6.00
GG15 Sandy Koufax 2.50 6.00
GG16 Hank Aaron 2.50 6.00
GG17 Albert Pujols 1.50 4.00
GG18 Bryce Harper 2.00 5.00
GG19 Mariano Rivera 1.50 4.00
GG20 Jackie Robinson 1.25 3.00
GG21 Joe DiMaggio 2.50 6.00
GG22 Babe Ruth 3.00 8.00
GG23 Roberto Clemente 3.00 8.00
GG24 Nolan Ryan 4.00 10.00
GG25 Tony Gwynn 1.25 3.00

2015 Topps Gallery of Greats Gold

*GOLD: 1.2X TO 3X BASIC
STATED ODDS 1:974 HOBBY
STATED PRINT RUN 99 SER.#'d SETS
GG3 Derek Jeter 20.00 50.00

2015 Topps Gallery of Greats Relics

STATED ODDS 1:6452 HOBBY
STATED PRINT RUN 25 SER.#'d SETS
GGRAP Albert Pujols 20.00 50.00
GGRCK Clayton Kershaw 10.00 25.00
GGRDJ Derek Jeter 25.00 60.00
GGRFT Frank Thomas 20.00 50.00
GGRHR Hanley Ramirez 20.00 50.00
GGRKG Ken Griffey Jr. 25.00 60.00
GGRMM Mark McGwire 60.00 150.00
GGRMP Mike Piazza 25.00 60.00
GGRRC Roger Clemens 10.00 25.00
GGRTG Tom Glavine 40.00 100.00
GGRYP Yasiel Puig 15.00 40.00

2015 Topps Hall of Fame Class of '14 Triple Autograph

ISSUED AS EXCH IN '14 SER.1
STATED PRINT RUN 50 SER.#'d SETS
HOF14 Thomas/Gravine/Maddux 125.00 300.00

2015 Topps Heart of the Order

COMPLETE SET (20) 5.00 12.00
STATED ODDS 1:6 HOBBY
HOR1 Ted Williams 1.00 2.50
HOR2 Mike Piazza .50 1.25
HOR3 Hank Aaron 1.00 2.50
HOR4 Ken Griffey Jr. 1.00 2.50
HOR5 Jose Canseco .40 1.00
HOR6 Yasiel Puig .50 1.25
HOR7 Mike Trout 2.50 6.00
HOR8 Gary Carter .40 1.00
HOR9 Chipper Jones .50 1.25
HOR10 Giancarlo Stanton .50 1.25
HOR11 Tony Gwynn .50 1.25
HOR12 Hanley Ramirez .40 1.00
HOR13 Prince Fielder .40 1.00
HOR14 Ryan Howard .40 1.00
HOR15 Matt Adams .30 .75
HOR16 Jeff Bagwell .40 1.00
HOR17 Edgar Martinez .40 1.00
HOR18 Freddie Freeman .60 1.50
HOR19 Paul Goldschmidt .50 1.25
HOR20 Adam Jones .40 1.00

2015 Topps Heart of the Order Relics

STATED ODDS 1:4280 HOBBY
STATED PRINT RUN 99 SER.#'d SETS
HTORCJ Chipper Jones 10.00 25.00
HTORDO David Ortiz 8.00 20.00
HTORGC Gary Carter 10.00 25.00
HTORGS Giancarlo Stanton 8.00 20.00
HTORHA Hank Aaron 15.00 40.00
HTORKG Ken Griffey Jr. 30.00 80.00
HTORMT Mike Trout 40.00 100.00
HTORTG Tony Gwynn 30.00 80.00
HTORTW Ted Williams 25.00 60.00
HTORYP Yasiel Puig 15.00 40.00

2015 Topps Hot Streak

COMPLETE SET (20) 12.00 30.00
RANDOM INSERTS IN RETAIL PACKS
HS1 Yasiel Puig .60 1.50
HS2 Jim Palmer .75 2.00
HS3 Sandy Koufax 2.00 5.00
HS4 Max Scherzer 1.00 2.50
HS5 Don Mattingly 2.00 5.00
HS6 Chipper Jones 1.00 2.50
HS7 Vinny Castilla .60 1.50
HS8 Nomar Garciaparra .75 2.00
HS9 Frank Robinson .75 2.00
HS10 Clayton Kershaw 1.50 4.00
HS11 Roger Clemens 1.25 3.00
HS12 Randy Johnson 1.00 2.50
HS13 Pablo Sandoval .75 2.00
HS14 George Brett 2.00 5.00
HS15 Ozzie Smith 1.25 3.00
HS16 David Cone .60 1.50
HS17 Corey Kluber .75 2.00
HS18 Livan Hernandez .60 1.50
HS19 Albert Pujols 1.25 3.00
HS20 Luis Gonzalez .60 1.50

2015 Topps Hot Streak Relics

RANDOM INSERTS IN PACKS
STATED PRINT RUN 50 SER.#'d SETS
HSRCK Clayton Kershaw 25.00 60.00
HSRDM Don Mattingly 20.00 50.00
HSRFR Frank Robinson 12.00 30.00
HSRJP Jim Palmer 12.00 30.00
HSRTS Tom Seaver 12.00 30.00
HSRYP Yasiel Puig 20.00 50.00

2015 Topps Highlight of the Year

COMPLETE SET (90) 15.00 40.00
SER.1 STATED ODDS 1:4 HOBBY
SER.2 STATED ODDS 1:4 HOBBY
UPD STATED ODDS 1:4 HOBBY
H1 Lou Gehrig 1.00 2.50
H2 Babe Ruth 1.25 3.00
H3 Babe Ruth 1.25 3.00
H4 Bob Feller .40 1.00
H5 Stan Musial .75 2.00
H6 Ted Williams 1.00 2.50
H7 New York Giants .30 .75
H8 Ted Williams 1.00 2.50
H9 Enos Slaughter .40 1.00
H10 Ernie Banks .50 1.25
H11 Roger Maris .50 1.25
H12 Roger Maris .50 1.25
H13 Warren Spahn .40 1.00
H14 Brooks Robinson .40 1.00
H15 Juan Marichal .40 1.00
H16 Catfish Hunter .40 1.00
H17 Nolan Ryan 1.50 4.00
H18 Willie McCovey .40 1.00
H19 Mike Schmidt .75 2.00
H20 Fergie Jenkins .40 1.00
H21 Fernando Valenzuela .30 .75
H22 Nolan Ryan 1.50 4.00
H23 Jose Canseco .40 1.00
H24 Derek Jeter 1.25 3.00
H25 Mark McGwire .75 2.00
H26 Nomar Garciaparra .40 1.00
H27 Cal Ripken Jr. 1.50 4.00
H28 Josh Beckett .30 .75
H29 Justin Verlander .50 1.25
H30 Miguel Cabrera .50 1.25
H31 Ty Cobb .75 2.00
H32 Babe Ruth 1.25 3.00
H33 Babe Ruth 1.25 3.00
H34 Babe Ruth 1.25 3.00
H35 Babe Ruth 1.25 3.00
H36 Enos Slaughter .40 1.00
H37 Lou Gehrig 1.00 2.50
H38 Ted Williams 1.00 2.50
H39 Bobby Doerr .40 1.00
H40 Jackie Robinson .50 1.25
H41 Joe DiMaggio 1.00 2.50
H42 Bob Feller .40 1.00
H43 Willie Mays 1.00 2.50
H44 Roberto Clemente 1.25 3.00
H45 Hank Aaron 1.00 2.50
H46 Sandy Koufax 1.00 2.50
H47 Jim Palmer .40 1.00
H48 Tom Seaver .40 1.00
H49 Rickey Henderson .50 1.25
H50 Andre Dawson .40 1.00
H51 Roger Clemens .60 1.50
H52 Don Mattingly 1.00 2.50
H53 Mark McGwire .75 2.00
H54 Nolan Ryan 1.50 4.00
H55 Ozzie Smith .60 1.50
H56 Cal Ripken Jr. 1.50 4.00
H57 Edgar Martinez .40 1.00
H58 Greg Maddux .60 1.50
H59 Mariano Rivera .60 1.50
H60 Clayton Kershaw .75 2.00
H61 Babe Ruth UPD 1.25 3.00
H62 Lou Gehrig UPD 1.00 2.50
H63 Babe Ruth UPD 1.25 3.00
H64 Joe DiMaggio UPD 1.00 2.50
H65 Bob Feller UPD .40 1.00
H66 Ted Williams UPD 1.00 2.50
H67 Red Schoendienst UPD .40 1.00
H68 Bob Lemon UPD .40 1.00
H69 Hank Aaron UPD 1.00 2.50
H70 Hoyt Wilhelm UPD .40 1.00
H71 Sandy Koufax UPD 1.00 2.50
H72 Tom Seaver UPD .40 1.00
H73 Tom Seaver UPD .40 1.00
H74 Harmon Killebrew UPD .50 1.25
H75 Willie Mays UPD 1.00 2.50
H76 Hank Aaron UPD 1.00 2.50
H77 Reggie Jackson UPD .40 1.00
H78 Lou Brock UPD .40 1.00
H79 Dwight Gooden UPD .30 .75
H80 Fernando Valenzuela UPD .30 .75
H81 Robin Yount UPD .50 1.25
H82 Ken Griffey Jr. UPD 1.00 2.50
H83 Ivan Rodriguez UPD .40 1.00
H84 Randy Johnson UPD .50 1.25
H85 John Smoltz UPD .50 1.25
H86 David Ortiz UPD .50 1.25
H87 Ivan Rodriguez UPD .40 1.00
H88 Ubaldo Jimenez UPD .30 .75
H89 Albert Pujols UPD .60 1.50
H90 Yasiel Puig UPD .50 1.25

2015 Topps Highlight of the Year Autographs

STATED ODDS 1:31,455 HOBBY
UPD ODDS 1:10,614 HOBBY
STATED PRINT RUN 25 SER.#'d SETS
EXCHANGE DEADLINE 1/31/2018
UPD.EXCHANGE 9/30/2017
HYAAD Andre Dawson S2 8.00 20.00
HYACK Clayton Kershaw S2 30.00 80.00
HYACR Cal Ripken Jr. S2 50.00 120.00
HYACR Cal Ripken Jr. 50.00 120.00
HYADM Don Mattingly S2 25.00 60.00
HYADO David Ortiz UPD 50.00 120.00
HYAEB Ernie Banks 50.00 120.00
HYAEM Edgar Martinez S2 20.00 50.00
HYAJC Jose Canseco 40.00 100.00
HYAJP Jim Palmer S2 12.00 30.00
HYAJS John Smoltz UPD 20.00 50.00
HYAKG Ken Griffey Jr. UPD 75.00 200.00
HYALB Lou Brock UPD 60.00 150.00
HYAMC Miguel Cabrera 60.00 150.00
HYAMM Mark McGwire 50.00 120.00
HYAMS Mike Schmidt 25.00 60.00
HYANG Nomar Garciaparra 60.00 150.00
HYANR Nolan Ryan S2 60.00 150.00
HYAOS Ozzie Smith S2 20.00 50.00
HYARC Roger Clemens S2 30.00 80.00
HYARH Rickey Henderson S2 30.00 80.00
HYARJ Reggie Jackson UPD 30.00 80.00
HYASM Stan Musial 60.00 150.00

2015 Topps Highlight of the Year Relics

SER.1 STATED ODDS 1:5270 HOBBY
SER.2 STATED ODDS 1:4280 HOBBY
STATED PRINT RUN 99 SER.#'d SETS
HYRAD Andre Dawson S2 4.00 10.00
HYRBR Brooks Robinson 10.00 25.00
HYRCH Catfish Hunter 4.00 10.00
HYRCR Cal Ripken Jr. 15.00 40.00
HYRCR Cal Ripken Jr. S2 15.00 40.00
HYRDJ Derek Jeter 25.00 60.00
HYRDM Don Mattingly S2 15.00 40.00
HYREB Ernie Banks 12.00 30.00
HYRFJ Fergie Jenkins 4.00 10.00
HYRFV Fernando Valenzuela 10.00 25.00
HYRJM Juan Marichal 4.00 10.00
HYRJP Jim Palmer S2 8.00 20.00
HYRJV Justin Verlander 5.00 12.00
HYRMC Miguel Cabrera 5.00 12.00
HYRMM Mark McGwire 15.00 40.00
HYRMM Mark McGwire S2 8.00 20.00
HYRMS Mike Schmidt 15.00 40.00
HYRNG Nomar Garciaparra 4.00 10.00
HYRNR Nolan Ryan S2 15.00 40.00
HYRNRC Nolan Ryan 15.00 40.00
HYRNRH Nolan Ryan 15.00 40.00
HYROS Ozzie Smith S2 6.00 15.00
HYRRC Roger Clemens S2 6.00 15.00
HYRRH Rickey Henderson S2 5.00 12.00
HYRTS Tom Seaver S2 5.00 12.00

2015 Topps Inspired Play Dual Relics

STATED ODDS 1:31,455 HOBBY
STATED PRINT RUN 50 SER.#'d SETS
IRCG R.Cano/K.Griffey Jr. 20.00 50.00
IRFM F.McGriff/F.Freeman 12.00 30.00
IRHC C.Hamels/S.Carlton 25.00 60.00
IRMR M.Machado/C.Ripken Jr. 40.00 100.00

2015 Topps Inspired Play

COMPLETE SET (15) 5.00 12.00
STATED ODDS 1:8 HOBBY
I1 M.Machado/C.Ripken Jr. 1.50 4.00
I2 K.Griffey Jr./R.Cano 1.00 2.50
I3 D.Mattingly/M.Teixeira 1.00 2.50
I4 A.Kaline/M.Cabrera .50 1.25
I5 S.Carlton/C.Hamels .40 1.00
I6 R.Carew/J.Mauer .40 1.00
I7 C.Kershaw/F.Valenzuela .75 2.00
I8 J.Rice/Y.Cespedes .40 1.00
I9 S.Musial/M.McGwire .75 2.00
I10 F.McGriff/F.Freeman .60 1.50
I11 T.Seaver/M.Harvey .40 1.00
I12 J.Abreu/F.Thomas .50 1.25
I13 C.Kimbrel/J.Smoltz .50 1.25
I14 R.Johnson/F.Hernandez .50 1.25
I15 McCutchen/Stargell .50 1.25

2015 Topps Logoman Pin

STATED ODDS 1:758 HOBBY
MSBL01 Yu Darvish 5.00 12.00
MSBL02 Bryce Harper 8.00 20.00
MSBL03 David Wright 4.00 10.00
MSBL04 David Ortiz 6.00 15.00
MSBL05 Albert Pujols 8.00 20.00
MSBL06 Buster Posey 8.00 20.00
MSBL07 Dustin Pedroia 5.00 12.00
MSBL08 Mike Trout 8.00 20.00
MSBL09 Yasiel Puig 8.00 20.00
MSBL10 Miguel Cabrera 8.00 20.00
MSBL11 Andrew McCutchen 5.00 12.00
MSBL12 Freddie Freeman 6.00 15.00
MSBL13 Robinson Cano 4.00 10.00
MSBL14 Masahiro Tanaka 8.00 20.00
MSBL15 Anthony Rizzo 6.00 15.00
MSBL16 Manny Machado 5.00 12.00
MSBL17 Yadier Molina 6.00 15.00
MSBL18 Javier Baez 25.00 60.00
MSBL19 Clayton Kershaw 8.00 20.00
MSBL20 Giancarlo Stanton 8.00 20.00
MSBL21 Jose Abreu 8.00 20.00
MSBL22 Jose Bautista 4.00 10.00
MSBL23 David Price 4.00 10.00
MSBL24 Adam Wainwright 4.00 10.00
MSBL25 Jacoby Ellsbury 4.00 10.00

2015 Topps Postseason Performance Autograph Relics

STATED ODDS 1:4840 HOBBY
STATED PRINT RUN 50 SER.#'d SETS
EXCHANGE DEADLINE 1/31/2018
PPARBH Bryce Harper EXCH 100.00 200.00
PPARCK Clayton Kershaw 60.00 150.00
PPARMC Matt Carpenter 30.00 80.00
PPARSP Salvador Perez 25.00 60.00
PPARYV Yordano Ventura 40.00 100.00
PPARJSC Jonathan Schoop 20.00 50.00

2015 Topps Postseason Performance Autographs

STATED ODDS 1:15,728 HOBBY
STATED PRINT RUN 50 SER.#'d SETS
EXCHANGE DEADLINE 1/31/2018
PPABH Bryce Harper EXCH 100.00 200.00
PPACK Clayton Kershaw 100.00 200.00
PPACT Chris Tillman 15.00 40.00
PPAMA Matt Adams 40.00 80.00
PPAMC Matt Carpenter 10.00 25.00
PPASP Salvador Perez 15.00 40.00
PPAYV Yordano Ventura 8.00 20.00
PPAJSC Jonathan Schoop 6.00 15.00

2015 Topps Postseason Performance Relics

STATED ODDS 1:3126 HOBBY
STATED PRINT RUN 100 SER.#'d SETS
PPRAE A.J. Ellis 4.00 10.00
PPRAGN Adrian Gonzalez 5.00 12.00
PPRAGO Alex Gordon 12.00 30.00
PPRAJ Adam Jones 5.00 12.00
PPRAR Anthony Rendon 6.00 15.00
PPRBBU Billy Butler 4.00 10.00
PPRBH Bryce Harper 12.00 30.00
PPRDG Dee Gordon 4.00 10.00
PPRDS Drew Storen 4.00 10.00
PPREH Eric Hosmer 20.00 50.00
PPRJJ Jon Jay 4.00 10.00
PPRJS Jonathan Schoop 4.00 10.00
PPRKW Kolten Wong 25.00 60.00
PPRLL Lance Lynn 15.00 40.00
PPRMH Matt Holliday 25.00 60.00
PPRMK Matt Kemp 5.00 12.00
PPRMM Mike Moustakas 5.00 12.00
PPRNC Nelson Cruz 6.00 15.00
PPRNM Nick Markakis 5.00 12.00
PPRSM Shelby Miller 5.00 12.00
PPRSP Salvador Perez 5.00 12.00
PPRWC Wei-Yin Chen 20.00 50.00
PPRYM Yadier Molina 25.00 60.00
PPRYV Yordano Ventura 20.00 50.00
PPRZG Zack Greinke 6.00 15.00

2015 Topps Robbed

COMPLETE SET (15) 12.00 30.00
RANDOM INSERTS IN RETAIL PACKS
R1 Dustin Ackley .50 1.25
R2 Alexi Amarista .50 1.25
R3 Jacoby Ellsbury .60 1.50
R4 Carlos Gomez .50 1.25
R5 Josh Hamilton .60 1.50
R6 Jason Heyward .60 1.50
R7 Ryan Ludwick .50 1.25
R8 Michael Morse .50 1.25
R9 Yasiel Puig .75 2.00
R10 Colby Rasmus .60 1.50
R11 Ben Revere .50 1.25
R12 George Springer .60 1.50
R13 Giancarlo Stanton .75 2.00
R14 Mike Trout 4.00 10.00
R15 Mookie Betts 1.50 4.00

2015 Topps Robbed Relics

RANDOM INSERTS IN RETAIL PACKS
STATED PRINT RUN 25 SER.#'d SETS
RRDA Dustin Ackley 12.00 30.00
RRGS Giancarlo Stanton 15.00 40.00
RRJHD Jason Heyward 20.00 50.00

2015 Topps Spring Fever

COMPLETE SET (50) 10.00 25.00
SF1 Albert Pujols .40 1.00
SF2 Mike Trout 1.50 4.00
SF3 Freddie Freeman .40 1.00
SF4 Adam Jones .25 .60
SF5 David Ortiz .30 .75
SF6 Dustin Pedroia .30 .75
SF7 Anthony Rizzo .30 .75
SF8 Javier Baez 1.50 4.00
SF9 Jose Abreu .30 .75
SF10 Miguel Cabrera .30 .75
SF11 Max Scherzer .30 .75
SF12 Yasiel Puig .30 .75
SF13 Clayton Kershaw .50 1.25
SF14 Giancarlo Stanton .30 .75
SF15 David Wright .25 .60
SF16 Masahiro Tanaka .25 .60
SF17 Jacoby Ellsbury .25 .60
SF18 Andrew McCutchen .30 .75
SF19 Buster Posey .40 1.00
SF20 Robinson Cano .25 .60
SF21 Yadier Molina .40 1.00
SF22 Adam Wainwright .25 .60
SF23 Yu Darvish .30 .75
SF24 Jose Bautista .25 .60
SF25 Bryce Harper .50 1.25
SF26 Chris Sale .30 .75
SF27 Felix Hernandez .25 .60
SF28 Adrian Beltre .30 .75
SF29 Ryan Braun .25 .60
SF30 Billy Hamilton .25 .60
SF31 Jose Altuve .25 .60
SF32 Ian Desmond .20 .50
SF33 Madison Bumgarner .25 .60
SF34 Edwin Encarnacion .30 .75
SF35 Stephen Strasburg .30 .75
SF36 Josh Donaldson .25 .60
SF37 Evan Longoria .25 .60
SF38 Jon Lester .25 .60
SF39 Michael Brantley .25 .60
SF40 Alex Gordon .25 .60
SF41 Jason Kipnis .25 .60
SF42 Adrian Gonzalez .25 .60
SF43 Prince Fielder .25 .60
SF44 Paul Goldschmidt .30 .75
SF45 Jason Heyward .25 .60
SF46 Joey Votto .30 .75
SF47 Troy Tulowitzki .30 .75
SF48 Hanley Ramirez .25 .60
SF49 Chase Utley .25 .60
SF50 Hunter Pence .25 .60

2015 Topps Spring Fever Autographs

PRINT RUNS B/WN 10-225 COPIES PER
NO PRICING ON QTY 10
EXCHANGE DEADLINE 1/31/2018
SFACB Charlie Blackmon/99 6.00 15.00
SFACC C.J. Cron/199 4.00 10.00
SFACOW Chris Owings/199 4.00 10.00
SFACSP Cory Spangenberg/199 4.00 10.00
SFADH Dilson Herrera/48 5.00 12.00
SFAFJ Fergie Jenkins/25 12.00 30.00
SFAIK Ian Kinsler/25 20.00 50.00
SFAJB Javier Baez/50 30.00 80.00
SFAJD Jacob deGrom/75 50.00 120.00
SFAJPA Joe Panik/75 30.00 80.00
SFAJPE Joc Pederson/99 6.00 15.00
SFAJPO Johnny Podres/50 8.00 20.00
SFAJS Jorge Soler/99 15.00 40.00
SFAKV Kennys Vargas/199 10.00 25.00
SFAMAA Mike Adams/200 10.00 25.00
SFAMAD Matt Adams/99 10.00 25.00
SFAMB Mookie Betts/225 40.00 100.00
SFAMFO Mike Foltynewicz/112 4.00 10.00
SFAMFR Maikel Franco/199 5.00 12.00
SFAMS Max Scherzer/25 30.00 80.00
SFARO Rougned Odor/92 10.00 25.00
SFASM Shelby Miller/50 20.00 50.00
SFAYS Yangervis Solarte/202 4.00 10.00

2015 Topps Stepping Up

COMPLETE SET (20) 5.00 12.00
STATED ODDS 1:6 HOBBY
SU1 Reggie Jackson .40 1.00
SU2 Duke Snider .40 1.00
SU3 Sandy Koufax 1.00 2.50
SU4 Johnny Podres .30 .75
SU5 David Ortiz .50 1.25
SU6 Mariano Rivera .60 1.50
SU7 Miguel Cabrera .60 1.50
SU8 Joey Votto .50 1.25
SU9 Adrian Gonzalez .40 1.00
SU10 Randy Johnson .50 1.25
SU11 Madison Bumgarner .40 1.00
SU12 Albert Pujols .60 1.50
SU13 Ryan Howard .40 1.00
SU14 Hunter Pence .40 1.00
SU15 Luis Gonzalez .30 .75
SU16 Mookie Wilson .30 .75
SU17 Fernando Valenzuela .30 .75
SU18 Corey Kluber .40 1.00
SU19 Joe Panik .40 1.00
SU20 Jacob deGrom 1.00 2.50

2015 Topps Stepping Up Relics

STATED ODDS 1:4280 HOBBY
STATED PRINT RUN 99 SER.#'d SETS
SURAG Adrian Gonzalez 8.00 20.00
SURDO David Ortiz 8.00 20.00
SURDS Duke Snider 8.00 20.00
SURJV Joey Votto 8.00 20.00
SURMB Madison Bumgarner 6.00 15.00
SURMC Miguel Cabrera 8.00 20.00
SURMR Mariano Rivera 10.00 25.00
SURRH Ryan Howard 6.00 15.00
SURRJA Reggie Jackson 10.00 25.00
SURRJO Randy Johnson 8.00 20.00

2015 Topps Strata Signature Relics

STATED ODDS 1:3857 HOBBY
STATED PRINT RUN 25 SER.#'d SETS
EXCHANGE DEADLINE 1/31/2018
SSRAJ Adam Jones 30.00 80.00
SSRBH Bryce Harper EXCH 150.00 300.00
SSRBP Buster Posey S2 100.00 250.00
SSRCG Carlos Gonzalez EXCH 30.00 80.00
SSRCK Clayton Kershaw EXCH 100.00 250.00
SSRCS CC Sabathia EXCH 30.00 80.00
SSRCS Chris Sale S2 30.00 80.00
SSREE Edwin Encarnacion S2 25.00 60.00
SSREL Evan Longoria EXCH 25.00 60.00
SSRFF Freddie Freeman 60.00 150.00
SSRGP Gregory Polanco EXCH 50.00 120.00
SSRGS George Springer EXCH 75.00 200.00
SSRGST Giancarlo Stanton EXCH 75.00 200.00
SSRHR Hanley Ramirez EXCH 25.00 60.00
SSRJA Jose Abreu EXCH 150.00 250.00
SSRJB Jay Bruce EXCH 25.00 60.00
SSRJB Javier Baez S2 40.00 100.00
SSRJG Juan Gonzalez S2 20.00 50.00
SSRJH Jason Heyward S2 30.00 80.00
SSRJV Joey Votto EXCH 40.00 100.00
SSRKU Koji Uehara S2 20.00 50.00
SSRMC Miguel Cabrera EXCH 150.00 250.00
SSRMM Mike Minor S2 20.00 50.00
SSRMP Mike Piazza EXCH 75.00 200.00
SSRMR Mariano Rivera 200.00 300.00
SSRMS Max Scherzer EXCH 75.00 200.00
SSRMT Mark Teixeira S2 50.00 120.00
SSRPF Prince Fielder S2 20.00 50.00
SSRPG Paul Goldschmidt EXCH 50.00 120.00
SSRRB Ryan Braun EXCH 15.00 40.00
SSRRC Robinson Cano EXCH 50.00 120.00
SSRRP Rafael Palmeiro S2 40.00 100.00
SSRSC Steve Carlton EXCH 50.00 120.00
SSRVG Vladimir Guerrero S2 40.00 100.00
SSRYC Yoenis Cespedes EXCH 40.00 100.00
SSRYP Yasiel Puig EXCH 75.00 200.00
SSRJDE Jacob deGrom S2 150.00 400.00
SSRJSO Jorge Soler S2 30.00 80.00

2015 Topps Sultan of Swat

COMPLETE SET (10) 15.00 40.00
RANDOM INSERTS IN TARGET PACKS
RUTH1 Babe Ruth 1.50 4.00
RUTH2 Babe Ruth 1.50 4.00
RUTH3 Babe Ruth 1.50 4.00
RUTH4 Babe Ruth 1.50 4.00
RUTH5 Babe Ruth 1.50 4.00
RUTH6 Babe Ruth 1.50 4.00
RUTH7 Babe Ruth 1.50 4.00
RUTH8 Babe Ruth 1.50 4.00
RUTH9 Babe Ruth 1.50 4.00
RUTH10 Babe Ruth 1.50 4.00

2015 Topps The Babe Ruth Story

COMPLETE SET (10) 10.00 25.00
RANDOM INSERTS IN WAL-MART PACKS
BR1 St. Mary's Industrial School Student 1.50 4.00
BR2 Hometown Hero Baltimore 1.50 4.00
BR3 Red Sox Double Threat 1.50 4.00
BR4 Postseason Pitching Phenom 1.50 4.00
BR5 From Hurler To Hitter 1.50 4.00
BR6 The Home Run King 1.50 4.00
BR7 MVP In '23 1.50 4.00
BR8 Murderer's Row Member 1.50 4.00
BR9 The Called Shot 1.50 4.00
BR10 The Babe Becomes A Media Star 1.50 4.00

2015 Topps The Jackie Robinson Story

COMPLETE SET (10) 15.00 40.00
RANDOM INSERTS IN TARGET PACKS
JR1 Two-Sport College Star 2.00 5.00
JR2 Serving His Country 2.00 5.00
JR3 .387 With Kansas City 2.00 5.00
JR4 Robinson Signs With The Dodgers 2.00 5.00
JR5 Robinson Travels North 2.00 5.00
JR6 Breaking The MLB Color Barrier 2.00 5.00
JR7 NL MVP In 1949 2.00 5.00
JR8 World Series Title In 1955 2.00 5.00
JR9 Call To The Hall 2.00 5.00
JR10 Number 42 Retired Across MLB 2.00 5.00

2015 Topps The Pennant Chase

STATED ODDS 1:6138 HOBBY
ANNOUNCED PRINT RUN OF 50 EACH
EXCHANGE DEADLINE 11/1/2015
1 Arizona Diamondbacks 10.00 25.00
2 Atlanta Braves 20.00 50.00
3 Boston Red Sox 20.00 50.00
4 Chicago Cubs 10.00 25.00
5 Chicago White Sox 10.00 25.00
6 Cincinnati Reds 10.00 25.00
7 Cleveland Indians 10.00 25.00
8 Colorado Rockies BB 10.00 25.00
9 Houston Astros 10.00 25.00
10 Miami Marlins 10.00 25.00
11 Milwaukee Brewers 10.00 25.00
12 Minnesota Twins 10.00 25.00
13 New York Mets 10.00 25.00
14 New York Yankees 40.00 100.00
15 Philadelphia Phillies 10.00 25.00
16 San Diego Padres 10.00 25.00
17 Seattle Mariners 10.00 25.00
18 Tampa Bay Rays 10.00 25.00
19 Texas Rangers 10.00 25.00
20 Toronto Blue Jays 10.00 25.00
21 Kansas City Royals 10.00 25.00
22 Oakland Athletics 10.00 25.00
23 Pittsburgh Pirates 10.00 25.00
24 San Francisco Giants 20.00 50.00
25 Baltimore Orioles 10.00 25.00
26 Detroit Tigers 40.00 100.00
27 Los Angeles Dodgers 40.00 100.00
28 St. Louis Cardinals BB 40.00 100.00
29 Los Angeles Angels 10.00 25.00
30 Washington Nationals 40.00 100.00

2015 Topps Til It's Over

COMPLETE SET (15) 4.00 10.00
STATED ODDS 1:8 HOBBY
TIO1 David Ortiz .50 1.25
TIO2 Ken Griffey Jr. 1.00 2.50
TIO3 Troy Tulowitzki .50 1.25
TIO4 Evan Longoria .40 1.00
TIO5 Omar Vizquel .40 1.00
TIO6 Joe Mauer .40 1.00
TIO7 Lou Brock .40 1.00
TIO8 Nolan Ryan 1.50 4.00
TIO9 Craig Biggio .40 1.00
TIO10 Tom Seaver .40 1.00
TIO11 Ivan Rodriguez .40 1.00
TIO12 Matt Cain .40 1.00
TIO13 Willie Mays 1.00 2.50
TIO14 David Freese .30 .75
TIO15 Salvador Perez .40 1.00

2015 Topps World Champion Autograph Relics

STATED ODDS 1:9678 HOBBY
STATED PRINT RUN 50 SER.#'d SETS
EXCHANGE DEADLINE 1/31/2018
WCARBC Brandon Crawford 150.00 300.00
WCARBP Buster Posey 75.00 200.00
WCARHP Hunter Pence 150.00 300.00
WCARJP Joe Panik 150.00 300.00

2015 Topps World Champion Autographs

STATED ODDS 1:31,455 HOBBY
STATED PRINT RUN 50 SER.#'d SETS
EXCHANGE DEADLINE 1/31/2018
WCARBC Brandon Crawford 150.00 250.00
WCARJP Joe Panik 200.00 300.00

2015 Topps World Champion Relics

STATED ODDS 1:5215 HOBBY
STATED PRINT RUN 100 SER.#'d SETS
WCRBB Brandon Belt 50.00 120.00
WCRBC Brandon Crawford 40.00 100.00
WCRBP Buster Posey 100.00 200.00
WCRGB Gregor Blanco 40.00 100.00
WCRHP Hunter Pence 75.00 200.00
WCRJP Joe Panik 30.00 80.00
WCRJPE Juan Perez 50.00 120.00
WCRMB Madison Bumgarner 60.00 150.00
WCRMM Michael Morse 40.00 100.00
WCRPS Pablo Sandoval 75.00 200.00
WCRRV Ryan Vogelsong 20.00 50.00
WCRSR Sergio Romo 40.00 80.00
WCRTH Tim Hudson 50.00 120.00
WCRTI Travis Ishikawa 40.00 100.00
WCRTL Tim Lincecum 50.00 120.00

2015 Topps Update

COMPLETE SET w/o SP's (400) 75.00 200.00
PHOTO VAR ODDS 1:45 HOBBY
PRINTING PLATE ODDS 1:758 HOBBY
PLATE PRINT RUN 1 SET PER COLOR
BLACK-CYAN-MAGENTA-YELLOW ISSUED
NO PLATE PRICING DUE TO SCARCITY
US1 Aaron Thompson .12 .30
US2 Wilmer Difo RC .40 1.00
US3 Tyler Wilson RC .40 1.00
US4 Jean Machi .12 .30
US5 Ryan Vogelsong .12 .30
US6 David DeJesus .12 .30
US7A Brad Miller .15 .40
US8 Alex Claudio RC .40 1.00
US9 Shane Greene FS .12 .30
US10 Bobby Parnell .12 .30
US11A Evan Gattis FS .12 .30
US12 Travis Ishikawa .12 .30
US13 Tommy Pham RC .50 1.25
US14 Joey Gallo RD .25 .60
US15 McCutchen/Harrison .20 .50
US16 John Axford .12 .30
US17 Manny Machado .20 .50
US18 Michael Blazek .12 .30
US19 Erasmo Ramirez .12 .30
US20 Cole Hamels .15 .40
US21 Posey/Bumgardner .25 .60
US22 Jake Diekman .12 .30
US23 Kevin Plawecki RC .40 1.00
US24 Chris Young .12 .30
US25 Byron Buxton RC 2.00 5.00
US26 Jack Leathersich RC .40 1.00
US27 Nathan Eovaldi .15 .40
US28 Miguel Cabrera .20 .50

Card	Low	High
US29 Ben Paulsen RC	.40	1.00
US30 David Phelps	.12	.30
US31 Gordon Beckham	.12	.30
US32A Blake Swihart RC	.50	1.25
US32B Blake Swihart SP VAR	1.50	4.00
Taking off mask		
US33 Alex Rodriguez	.25	.60
US34 Matt Andriese RC	.40	1.00
US35 Justin Bour RC	.60	1.50
US36 Roberto Perez RC	.12	.30
US37 Luis Avilan	.12	.30
US38 Michael Lorenzen RC	.40	1.00
US39 Potent Padres	.15	.40
Matt Kemp/Justin Upton./Wil Myers		
US40 Sam Dyson RC	.40	1.00
US41 T.Shaw RC/A.Dykstra RC	.40	1.00
US42 Madison Bumgarner	.15	.40
US43 Randall Delgado	.12	.30
US44 Tim Cooney RC	.40	1.00
US45 Ryan Lavarnway	.12	.30
US46 David Price	.15	.40
US47 Jeremy Jeffress	.12	.30
US48 Carlos Perez RC	.40	1.00
US49 Mark Canha RC	.60	1.50
US50 Alex Guerrero	.15	.40
US51 Yasmani Grandal	.12	.30
US52 C.Anderson RC/P.Klein RC	.40	1.00
US53 Daniel Norris RC	.40	1.00
US54 Ldndrf RC/Muncy RC	2.00	5.00
US55 Hank Conger	.12	.30
US56 Kevin Siegrist	.12	.30
US57 Nick Ahmed	.12	.30
US58 Josh Donaldson	.15	.40
US59 R.Martin RC/M.Grace RC	.40	1.00
US60 Branden Pinder RC	.60	1.50
US61 Dallas Keuchel	.15	.40
US62 Brian Dozier	.15	.40
US63 Kelvin Herrera	.12	.30
US64 David Price	.15	.40
US65 Todd Frazier	.12	.30
US66 Neftali Feliz	.12	.30
US67 Leonel Campos RC	.40	1.00
US68 Albert Pujols	.25	.60
US69A Zach McAllister	.12	.30
US70 Vance Worley	.12	.30
US71 Joakim Soria	.12	.30
US72 Brett Gardner	.15	.40
US73 Tyler Saladino RC	.50	1.25
US74 Giovanny Urshela RC	4.00	10.00
US75 Ross Detwiler	.12	.30
US76 Lorenzo Cain	.12	.30
US77 Joe Smith	.12	.30
US78 Kris Bryant RC	4.00	10.00
US79 Bryant/Russell	1.25	3.00
US80 Juan Uribe	.12	.30
US81 Pat Venditte RC	.40	1.00
US82 Francisco Lindor RC	20.00	50.00
US83 Mason Williams RC	.50	1.25
US84 Sean O'Sullivan	.12	.30
US85 Justin Nicolino RC	.40	1.00
US86 Chris Colabello	.12	.30
US87 Zack Greinke	.20	.50
US88 Marc Rzepczynski	.12	.30
US89 Kendall Graveman	.12	.30
US90 Jacob deGrom	.40	1.00
US91 Brad Boxberger	.12	.30
US92A Justin Upton	.15	.40
US92B Justin Upton SP VAR	1.50	4.00
With bats		
US93 Sonny Gray	.15	.40
US94 Shane Victorino	.15	.40
US95 Elvis Araujo RC	.40	1.00
US96 Ben Zobrist	.15	.40
US97 Josh Ravin RC	.60	1.50
US98 Josh Fields	.12	.30
US99 Daniel Fields RC	.40	1.00
US100 Andrew McCutchen	.20	.50
US101 Jumbo Diaz RC	.40	1.00
US102 Chi Chi Gonzalez RC	.60	1.50
US103A Joey Gallo RC	.75	2.00
US103B J.Gallo Smiling	2.50	6.00
US104 Steve Cishek	.12	.30
US105 Brandon Moss	.12	.30
US106 Shelby Miller	.15	.40
US107 Carlos Gomez	.12	.30
US108 A.Garcia RC/J.Marte RC	.40	1.00
US109 Anthony Ranaudo RC	.40	1.00
US110 A.McKirahan RC/S.Marimon RC	.40	1.00
US111 Todd Cunningham	.12	.30
US112 Conor Gillaspie	.15	.40
US113 Eric Campbell	.15	.40
US114 J.Garcia RC/S.Copeland RC	.40	1.00
US115 Stephen Vogt	.15	.40
US116 Miguel Castro RC	.40	1.00
US117 Enrique Hernandez RC	3.00	8.00
US118 Jason Frasor	.12	.30
US119 Jacob Lindgren RC	.50	1.25
US120 Brandon Cunniff RC	.40	1.00
US121 Alexi Ogando	.12	.30
US122 Marlon Byrd	.12	.30
US123 Felix Hernandez	.15	.40
US124 Preston Tucker RC	.60	1.50
US125 Ben Revere	.12	.30
US126 Tyler Olson RC	.40	1.00
US127A Eduardo Rodriguez RC	.40	1.00
US127B E.Rod High-five	1.25	3.00
US128 Brock Holt	.12	.30
US129A David Ross	.12	.30
US130 Jonathan Villar	.12	.30
US131 Jordan Pacheco	.12	.30
US132 Gerardo Parra	.12	.30
US133 Vinnie Pestano	.12	.30
US134 Steven Matz RD RC	.50	1.25
US135A Jason Heyward	.15	.40
US135B J.Hywrd Laughing	1.50	4.00
US136 Byron Buxton RD	.60	1.50
US137 Andrew Romine	.12	.30
US138 Dellin Betances	.15	.40
US139 Mike Moustakas	.15	.40
US140 Mark Melancon	.12	.30
US141 Glen Perkins	.12	.30
US142 Kendrys Morales	.12	.30
US143 Tommy Hunter	.12	.30
US144 Delino DeShields Jr. RC	.40	1.00
US145 Yasmany Tomas RD	.15	.40
US146 Aaron Harang	.12	.30
US147 Chris Archer	.12	.30
US148 Taylor Featherston RC	.40	1.00
US149 Thomas Field	.12	.30
US150 Eric Sogard	.12	.30
US151A Colby Lewis	.12	.30
US151B Lewis Rubbing ball	1.25	3.00
US152 J.R. Graham RC	.40	1.00
US153 Archie Bradley RD	.12	.30
US154 Paul Goldschmidt	.20	.50
US155A Yoenis Cespedes	.15	.40
US155B Cespedes Batting cage	6.00	15.00
US156 Amazing Astros	.15	.40
Colby Rasmus/George Springer/Jake Marisnick		
US157A Noah Syndergaard RC	.75	2.00
US157B Syndergaard Batting	2.50	6.00
US158 Jason Kipnis	.15	.40
US159 Darren O'Day	.12	.30
US160 Slade Heathcott RC	.50	1.25
US161A Jeff Samardzija	.12	.30
US161B Samardzija In dugout	1.25	3.00
US162 Jorge Soler RD	.20	.50
US163 Andrew Heaney	.12	.30
US164 Johnny Giavotella	.12	.30
US165 Seth Maness	.12	.30
US166 Severino Gonzalez RC	.40	1.00
US167A Derek Norris	.12	.30
US167B D.Norris Finger up	1.25	3.00
US168 George Kontos RC	.50	1.25
US169 Max Scherzer	.20	.50
US170 Mike Foltynewicz RC	.40	1.00
US171 Jhonny Peralta	.12	.30
US172 Adrian Gonzalez	.15	.40
US173 Salvador Perez	.15	.40
US174A Carlos Correa RC	2.00	5.00
US174B C.Correa In dugout	12.00	30.00
US175 Edinson Volquez	.12	.30
US176 Austin Hedges RC	.40	1.00
US177 Matt Holliday	.20	.50
US178 Zach Duke	.12	.30
US179 Adam Liberatore RC	.50	1.25
US180 Tyler Collins	.12	.30
US181 Jimmy Paredes FS	.12	.30
US182 Scott Van Slyke	.12	.30
US183 Justin Turner	.20	.50
US184 Sean Rodriguez	.12	.30
US185 David Murphy	.12	.30
US186 A.J. Pollock	.15	.40
US187 Heart of the Order	.15	.40
Jose Bautista/Josh Donaldson/Devon Travis		
US188 deGrom/Harvey	.40	1.00
US189 Adam Warren	.12	.30
US190A Shelby Miller	.15	.40
US190B S.Miller Black jersey	1.50	4.00
US191 Royals Crush	.15	.40
Eric Hosmer/Kendrys Morales/Mike Moustakas		
US192 Albert Pujols	.25	.60
US193 A.Castro RC/A.Leon RC	.40	1.00
US194 C.Rearick RC/C.Mazzoni RC	.40	1.00
US195 A.J. Ramos	.12	.30
US196 Paulo Orlando RC	.60	1.50
US197 Wandy Rodriguez	.12	.30
US198 Brett Anderson	.12	.30
US199 Troy Tulowitzki	.20	.50
US200 Adam Jones	.15	.40
US201 Jose Altuve	.15	.40
US202 Manny Machado	.20	.50
US203 Jesse Hahn	.12	.30
US204 Jeff Francoeur	.15	.40
US205 Andres Blanco	.12	.30
US206 Mike Pelfrey	.12	.30
US207 Chris Young	.12	.30
US208 Addison Russell RD	.40	1.00
US209 Prince Fielder	.15	.40
US210 Yunel Escobar	.12	.30
US211 Tommy Milone	.12	.30
US212 Scott Carroll	.12	.30
US213 Pujols/Trout	1.00	2.50
US214 Yadier Molina	.25	.60
US215 Jonathan Papelbon	.15	.40
US216 Carlos Peguero	.12	.30
US217 Franklin Morales	.12	.30
US218 Pedro Ciriaco	.12	.30
US219 Michael Morse	.12	.30
US220A Addison Russell RC	1.25	3.00
US220B A.Rssll Signing autos	4.00	10.00
US221 Francisco Rodriguez	.15	.40
US222 Arquimedes Caminero	.12	.30
US223 Kevin Jepsen	.12	.30
US224 Ezequiel Carrera	.12	.30
US225 Keone Kela RC	.50	1.25
US226 Josh Donaldson	.15	.40
US227 Mike Trout	1.00	2.50
US228 Geovany Soto	.15	.40
US229 Hector Gomez	.12	.30
US230 Shawn Tolleson	.12	.30
US231 Felipe Rivero RC	.60	1.50
US232 Hansel Robles RC	.40	1.00
US233 Danny Muno RC	.40	1.00
US234 Noah Syndergaard RD	.25	.60
US235 Anthony Rizzo	.25	.60
US236 Angel Nesbitt RC	.40	1.00
US237A Craig Kimbrel	.15	.40
US237B Kimbrel Shaking hands	1.50	4.00
US238 A.J. Cole RC	.40	1.00
US239 Michael McKenry	.12	.30
US240 Jonathan Papelbon	.15	.40
US241 Sluggers Supreme	.20	.50
David Ortiz/Pablo Sandoval/Hanley Ramirez		
US242 Kris Bryant	1.25	3.00
US243 Austin Adams	.12	.30
US244 Colby Rasmus	.15	.40
US245 Rubby De La Rosa	.12	.30
US246 Blaine Hardy RC	.40	1.00
US247 Ryan Braun	.15	.40
US248 Lance McCullers RC	.40	1.00
US249 Anthony Rizzo	.25	.60
US250 Danny Valencia	.15	.40
US251 Carlos Correa RD	.60	1.50
US252 Francisco Rodriguez	.15	.40
US253 Trevor Rosenthal	.15	.40
US254 Billy Burns	.12	.30
US255 Sean Gilmartin RC	.40	1.00
US256 D.Ceciliani RC/D.Dorn RC	.40	1.00
US257 Josh Hamilton	.15	.40
US258 V.Velasquez RC/R.O'Rourke RC	.60	1.50
US259 John Jaso	.12	.30
US260A Andrew Miller	.15	.40
US260B A.Miller In dugout	1.50	4.00
US261 R.J. Alvarez RC	.40	1.00
US262 Eric Young Jr.	.12	.30
US263 Pedro Strop	.12	.30
US264 Brock Holt FS	.12	.30
US265A Brett Lawrie	.15	.40
US265B Lawrie Hands together	1.50	4.00
US266 Ike Davis	.12	.30
US267 Joe Ross RC	.40	1.00
US268 Troy Tulowitzki	.20	.50
US269 Burke Badenhop	.12	.30
US270 Craig Breslow	.12	.30
US271 Mike Leake	.12	.30
US272 Matt Duffy FS RC	.50	1.25
US273 Justin Upton	.15	.40
US274 Tucker Barnhart	.12	.30
US275 Casey McGehee	.12	.30
US276 Alex Wilson	.12	.30
US277 Yasmani Grandal	.12	.30
US278 Rene Rivera	.12	.30
US279 Juan Nicasio	.12	.30
US280 Mike Bolsinger FS	.12	.30
US281 Manny Banuelos RC	.60	1.50
US282 Jose Iglesias	.15	.40
US283 Kris Bryant RD	1.25	3.00
US284 Matt Wisler RC	.40	1.00
US285 Josh Rutledge	.12	.30
US286 Francisco Lindor RD	1.00	2.50
US287 Jim Johnson	.12	.30
US288 Matt Joyce	.12	.30
US289 Williams Perez RC	.50	1.25
US290 Zach Britton	.15	.40
US291 Eddie Butler FS	.12	.30
US292 Chad Qualls	.12	.30
US293 Cesar Ramos	.12	.30
US294 Mark Trumbo	.12	.30
US295 Russell Martin	.12	.30
US296 J.B. Shuck	.12	.30
US297 Wade Davis	.12	.30
US298 R.Navarro RC/D.Coleman RC	.40	1.00
US299 Mikie Mahtook RC	.40	1.00
US300 Max Scherzer	.20	.50
US301 Carlos Villanueva	.12	.30
US302 Chris Sale	.20	.50
US303 Asher Wojciechowski RC	.40	1.00
US304 Johnny Cueto	.15	.40
US305 Ryan Tepera RC	.40	1.00
US306 Vidal Nuno	.12	.30
US307 Hector Santiago	.12	.30
US308 Joey Butler	.12	.30
US309A Howie Kendrick	.12	.30
US309B H.Kendrick No hat	1.25	3.00
US310 Clayton Kershaw	.30	.75
US311 Carlos Martinez	.15	.40
US312 S.Oberg RC/D.Guerra RC	.40	1.00
US313 Jose Urena RC	.40	1.00
US314 Rafael Betancourt	.12	.30
US315 Kyle Kendrick	.12	.30
US316 Tyler Clippard	.12	.30
US317 Luis Sardinas	.12	.30
US318A Phillippe Aumont	.12	.30
US318B Aumont Rally squirrel	5.00	12.00
US319 Will Harris FS RC	.40	1.00
US320 Josh Donaldson	.15	.40
US321 Chris Heston RC	.40	1.00
US322 Mat Latos	.15	.40
US323 Joc Pederson RC	1.50	4.00
US324A Carlos Rodon RC	1.00	2.50
US324B Rodon Wearing jacket	3.00	8.00
US325A Matt Kemp	.15	.40
US325B M.Kemp In dugout	1.50	4.00
US326 Jonathan Herrera	.12	.30
US327 Ryan Webb	.12	.30
US328 Brandon Morrow	.12	.30
US329 J.D. Martinez	.20	.50
US330 Nate Karns	.12	.30
US331 Orlando Calixte RC	.40	1.00
US332 Matt Boyd RC	.40	1.00
US333 Mark Reynolds	.12	.30
US334 Clint Barmes	.12	.30
US335A Norichika Aoki	.12	.30
US335B Aoki In on deck circle	1.25	3.00
US336 Mark Teixeira	.15	.40
US337A Martin Prado	.12	.30
US337B M.Prado w/fans	1.25	3.00
US338 Pete Kozma	.12	.30
US339 Jose Alvarez	.12	.30
US340 Fernando Salas	.12	.30
US341 Eddie Rosario RC	.75	2.00
US342 Todd Frazier	.12	.30
US343 A.J. Burnett	.12	.30
US344 Aramis Ramirez	.12	.30
US345 Blaine Boyer	.12	.30
US346 Brandon Crawford	.15	.40
US347 Joe Blanton	.12	.30
US348 Jonathan Broxton	.12	.30
US349 DJ LeMahieu	.20	.50
US350A Didi Gregorius	.15	.40
US350B Gregorius Throwing	1.50	4.00
US351 Mike Fiers	.12	.30
US352 Jose Reyes	.15	.40
US353 Michael Wacha	.15	.40
US354 Brandon Finnegan RC	.40	1.00
US355 Gerrit Cole	.20	.50
US356 Miguel Montero	.12	.30
US357 Joe Panik	.15	.40
US358 Nolan Arenado	.30	.75
US359 E.Burgos RC/O.Hernandez RC	.40	1.00
US360 Joc Pederson	.50	1.25
US361 LaTroy Hawkins	.12	.30
US362 Rick Porcello	.15	.40
US363 Chasen Shreve RC	.40	1.00
US364 Mike Trout	1.00	2.50
US365 J.P. Howell	.12	.30
US366 Kelly Johnson	.12	.30
US367 Frank Garces RC	.40	1.00
US368 Aroldis Chapman	.20	.50
US369 Cory Rasmus	.12	.30
US370 Prince Fielder	.15	.40
US371 Carson Smith RC	.40	1.00
US372 Alex Wood	.12	.30
US373 Mitch Harris RC	.50	1.25
US374 Tyler Moore	.12	.30
US375 Mark Lowe	.12	.30
US376 Joc Pederson RD	.50	1.25
US377 Taijuan Walker FS	.12	.30
US378 Devon Travis RD	.12	.30
US379 Cameron Maybin	.12	.30
US380 Buster Posey	.25	.60
US381 Sergio Romo	.12	.30
US382 Dan Uggla	.12	.30
US383 Nelson Cruz	.20	.50
US384 Melvin Upton Jr.	.15	.40
US385 Collin Cowgill	.12	.30
US386 Alcides Escobar	.15	.40
US387 Jonny Gomes	.12	.30
US388 Kevin Pillar FS	.12	.30
US389 Seth Smith	.12	.30
US390 Donovan Solano	.20	.50
US391 Clayton Richard	.12	.30
US392 Odrisamer Despaigne FS	.12	.30
US393 Dan Haren	.12	.30
US394 Scott Kazmir	.12	.30
US395A Dexter Fowler	.15	.40
US395B Fowler Holding cap	1.50	4.00
US396A Ichiro Suzuki	.25	.60
US396B Ichiro In on deck circle	2.50	6.00
US397 Bryce Harper	.30	.75
US398 J.T. Realmuto RC	2.50	6.00
US399 Jace Peterson	.12	.30
US400 Logan Verrett RC	.50	1.25

2015 Topps Update Black

*BLACK: 10X TO 25X BASIC
*BLACK RC: 3X TO 8X BASIC RC
STATED ODDS 1:48 HOBBY
STATED PRINT RUN 64 SER.#'d SETS

Card	Low	High
US25 Byron Buxton	15.00	40.00
US32 Blake Swihart	8.00	20.00
US90 Jacob deGrom	8.00	20.00
US100 Andrew McCutchen	10.00	25.00
US134 Steven Matz RD	20.00	50.00
US136 Byron Buxton RD	15.00	40.00
US155 Yoenis Cespedes	8.00	20.00
US157 Noah Syndergaard	12.00	30.00
US174 Carlos Correa	60.00	150.00
US234 Noah Syndergaard RD	12.00	30.00
US251 Carlos Correa RD	25.00	60.00
US310 Clayton Kershaw	10.00	25.00
US341 Eddie Rosario	10.00	25.00
US380 Buster Posey	6.00	15.00

2015 Topps Update Gold

*GOLD: 1.2X TO 3X BASIC
*GOLD RC: .4X TO 1X BASIC RC
STATED ODDS 1:3 HOBBY
STATED PRINT RUN 2015 SER.#'d SETS

Card	Low	High
US25 Byron Buxton	1.50	4.00
US78 Kris Bryant	10.00	258.00
US100 Andrew McCutchen	1.25	3.00
US157 Noah Syndergaard	1.50	4.00
US174 Carlos Correa	10.00	25.00
US234 Noah Syndergaard RD	1.50	4.00
US242 Kris Bryant	6.00	15.00
US251 Carlos Correa RD	8.00	20.00
US283 Kris Bryant RD	6.00	15.00

2015 Topps Update No Logo

*NO LOGO: 1.2X TO 3X BASIC
*NO LOGO RC: .75X TO 2X BASIC RC
RANDOM INSERTS IN RETAIL PACKS
CARDS MISSING THE TOPPS LOGO

2015 Topps Update Pink

*PINK: 12X TO 30X BASIC
*PINK RC: 4X TO 10X BASIC RC
STATED ODDS 1:169 HOBBY
STATED PRINT RUN 50 SER.#'d SETS

Card	Low	High
US25 Byron Buxton	20.00	50.00
US32 Blake Swihart	10.00	25.00
US90 Jacob deGrom	10.00	25.00
US100 Andrew McCutchen	12.00	30.00
US134 Steven Matz RD	25.00	60.00
US136 Byron Buxton RD	20.00	50.00
US155 Yoenis Cespedes	10.00	25.00
US157 Noah Syndergaard	15.00	40.00
US174 Carlos Correa	75.00	200.00
US234 Noah Syndergaard RD	15.00	40.00
US251 Carlos Correa RD	30.00	80.00
US310 Clayton Kershaw	12.00	30.00
US341 Eddie Rosario	12.00	30.00
US380 Buster Posey	8.00	20.00

2015 Topps Update Rainbow Foil

*FOIL: 2.5X TO 6X BASIC
*FOIL RC: 1.5X TO 4X BASIC RC
STATED ODDS 1:10 HOBBY

Card	Low	High
US25 Byron Buxton	3.00	8.00
US100 Andrew McCutchen	2.50	6.00
US157 Noah Syndergaard	3.00	8.00
US174 Carlos Correa	12.00	30.00
US234 Noah Syndergaard RD	3.00	8.00
US251 Carlos Correa RD	10.00	25.00

2015 Topps Update Sparkle

STATED ODDS 1:225 HOBBY

Card	Low	High
US16 John Axford	4.00	10.00
US23 Kevin Plawecki	4.00	10.00
US25 Byron Buxton	15.00	40.00
US31 Gordon Beckham	4.00	10.00
US32 Blake Swihart	10.00	25.00
US35 Justin Bour	10.00	25.00
US46 David Price	5.00	12.00
US49 Mark Canha	6.00	15.00
US50 Alex Guerrero	10.00	25.00
US51 Yasmani Grandal	8.00	20.00
US92 Justin Upton	5.00	12.00
US99 Daniel Fields	8.00	20.00
US122 Marlon Byrd	4.00	10.00
US124 Preston Tucker	6.00	15.00
US130 Jonathan Villar	4.00	10.00
US135 Jason Heyward	10.00	25.00
US148 Taylor Featherston	4.00	10.00
US155 Yoenis Cespedes	10.00	25.00
US157 Noah Syndergaard	15.00	40.00
US160 Slade Heathcott	5.00	12.00
US161 Jeff Samardzija	4.00	10.00
US167 Derek Norris	4.00	10.00
US170 Mike Foltynewicz	10.00	25.00
US176 Austin Hedges	4.00	10.00
US190 Shelby Miller	10.00	25.00
US203 Jesse Hahn	4.00	10.00
US224 Ezequiel Carrera	4.00	10.00
US228 Geovany Soto	5.00	12.00
US237 Craig Kimbrel	5.00	12.00
US244 Colby Rasmus	5.00	12.00
US245 Rubby De La Rosa	4.00	10.00
US257 Josh Hamilton	5.00	12.00
US260 Andrew Miller	10.00	25.00
US284 Matt Wisler	15.00	40.00
US315 Kyle Kendrick	4.00	10.00
US317 Luis Sardinas	4.00	10.00
US320 Josh Donaldson	10.00	25.00
US325 Matt Kemp	10.00	25.00
US335 Norichika Aoki	4.00	10.00
US341 Eddie Rosario	8.00	20.00
US350 Didi Gregorius		
US356 Miguel Montero	8.00	20.00
US362 Rick Porcello	5.00	12.00
US374 Tyler Moore	6.00	15.00
US379 Cameron Maybin		
US384 Melvin Upton Jr.	6.00	15.00
US387 Jonny Gomes	6.00	15.00
US395 Dexter Fowler	5.00	12.00
US396 Ichiro Suzuki	8.00	20.00

2015 Topps Update Snow Camo

*SNOW CAMO: 10X TO 25X BASIC
*SNOW CAMO RC: 6X TO 15X BASIC RC
STATED ODDS 1:86 HOBBY
STATED PRINT RUN 99 SER.#'d SETS

Card	Low	High
US25 Byron Buxton	12.00	30.00
US100 Andrew McCutchen	10.00	25.00
US134 Steven Matz RD	10.00	25.00
US155 Yoenis Cespedes	8.00	20.00
US157 Noah Syndergaard	12.00	30.00
US174 Carlos Correa	50.00	120.00
US234 Noah Syndergaard RD	12.00	30.00
US251 Carlos Correa RD	20.00	50.00
US310 Clayton Kershaw	10.00	25.00
US380 Buster Posey	6.00	15.00

2015 Topps Update Stat Back Variations

STATED ODDS 1:68 HOBBY

Card	Low	High
US17 Manny Machado	2.00	5.00
US42 Madison Bumgarner	1.50	4.00
US58 Josh Donaldson	1.50	4.00
US61 Dallas Keuchel	1.50	4.00
US64 David Price	1.50	4.00
US68 Albert Pujols	2.50	6.00
US72 Brett Gardner	1.50	4.00
US76 Lorenzo Cain	1.25	3.00
US87 Zack Greinke	2.00	5.00
US90 Jacob deGrom	4.00	10.00
US93 Sonny Gray	1.50	4.00
US100 Andrew McCutchen	2.00	5.00
US115 Stephen Vogt	1.50	4.00
US123 Felix Hernandez	1.50	4.00
US139 Mike Moustakas	1.50	4.00
US141 Glen Perkins	1.25	3.00
US147 Chris Archer	1.25	3.00
US154 Paul Goldschmidt	2.00	5.00
US158 Jason Kipnis	1.50	4.00
US171 Jhonny Peralta	1.25	3.00
US172 Adrian Gonzalez	1.50	4.00
US173 Salvador Perez	1.50	4.00
US186 A.J. Pollock	1.50	4.00
US199 Troy Tulowitzki	2.00	5.00
US200 Adam Jones	1.50	4.00
US201 Jose Altuve	1.50	4.00
US214 Yadier Molina	2.50	6.00
US240 Jonathan Papelbon	1.50	4.00
US247 Ryan Braun	1.50	4.00
US249 Anthony Rizzo	2.50	6.00
US252 Francisco Rodriguez	1.50	4.00
US273 Justin Upton	1.50	4.00
US295 Russell Martin	1.25	3.00
US300 Max Scherzer	2.00	5.00
US302 Chris Sale	2.00	5.00
US310 Clayton Kershaw	3.00	8.00
US336 Mark Teixeira	1.50	4.00
US342 Todd Frazier	1.25	3.00
US343 A.J. Burnett	1.25	3.00
US346 Brandon Crawford	1.50	4.00
US349 DJ LeMahieu	2.00	5.00
US353 Michael Wacha	1.50	4.00
US355 Gerrit Cole	2.00	5.00
US358 Nolan Arenado	3.00	8.00
US364 Mike Trout	10.00	25.00
US370 Prince Fielder	1.50	4.00
US380 Buster Posey	2.50	6.00
US383 Nelson Cruz	2.00	5.00
US386 Alcides Escobar	1.50	4.00
US397 Bryce Harper	3.00	8.00

2015 Topps Update Throwback Variations

RANDOM INSERTS IN PACKS

Card	Low	High
US7 Brad Miller	2.50	6.00
US11 Evan Gattis FS	2.00	5.00
US32 Blake Swihart	2.50	6.00
US69 Zach McAllister	2.00	5.00
US129 David Ross	2.00	5.00
US161 Jeff Samardzija	2.00	5.00
US362 Rick Porcello	2.50	6.00
US395 Dexter Fowler	2.50	6.00

2015 Topps Update All Star Access

Card	Low	High
COMPLETE SET (25)	30.00	80.00
INSERTED IN RETAIL PACKS		
MLB1 Mike Trout	5.00	12.00
MLB2 Albert Pujols	1.25	3.00
MLB3 Brock Holt	.60	1.50
MLB4 Yadier Molina	1.25	3.00
MLB5 Madison Bumgarner	1.25	3.00
MLB6 Joc Pederson	2.50	6.00
MLB7 Joe Panik	.75	2.00
MLB8 Kris Bryant	3.00	8.00
MLB9 Jacob deGrom	2.00	5.00
MLB10 Adam Jones	.75	2.00
MLB11 Manny Machado	1.00	2.50
MLB12 Zack Greinke	1.00	2.50
MLB13 Andrew McCutchen	1.00	2.50
MLB14 Anthony Rizzo	1.25	3.00
MLB15 Clayton Kershaw	1.50	4.00
MLB16 Sonny Gray	.75	2.00
MLB17 Prince Fielder	.75	2.00
MLB18 Max Scherzer	1.00	2.50
MLB19 Todd Frazier	.60	1.50
MLB20 Lorenzo Cain	.60	1.50
MLB21 Alcides Escobar	.75	2.00
MLB22 Nelson Cruz	1.00	2.50
MLB23 Jose Altuve	.75	2.00
MLB24 Josh Donaldson	.75	2.00
MLB25 Bryce Harper	1.50	4.00

2015 Topps Update All Star Access Autographs

INSERTED IN RETAIL PACKS
STATED PRINT RUN 25 SER.#'d SETS
EXCHANGE DEADLINE 9/30/2017

Card	Low	High
MLBAJA Jose Altuve	25.00	60.00
MLBASP Salvador Perez	25.00	60.00
MLBATF Todd Frazier	20.00	50.00

2015 Topps Update All Star Stitches

STATED ODDS 1:53 HOBBY
*GOLD/50: .75X TO 2X BASIC

Card	Low	High
STITAB A.J. Burnett	2.00	5.00
STITAC Aroldis Chapman	3.00	8.00
STITAE Alcides Escobar	2.50	6.00
STITAGN Adrian Gonzalez	2.50	6.00
STITAJ Adam Jones	2.50	6.00
STITAM Andrew McCutchen	3.00	8.00
STITAPO A.J. Pollock	2.50	6.00
STITAPU Albert Pujols	4.00	10.00
STITAR Anthony Rizzo	4.00	10.00
STITBB Brad Boxberger	2.00	5.00
STITBC Brandon Crawford	2.50	6.00
STITBD Brian Dozier	2.50	6.00
STITBG Brett Gardner	2.50	6.00
STITBHA Bryce Harper	8.00	20.00
STITBHO Brock Holt	2.00	5.00
STITBP Buster Posey	4.00	10.00
STITCA Chris Archer	2.00	5.00
STITCK Clayton Kershaw	5.00	12.00
STITCM Carlos Martinez	2.50	6.00
STITCS Chris Sale	3.00	8.00
STITDB Dellin Betances	2.50	6.00
STITDK Dallas Keuchel	2.50	6.00
STITDL DJ LeMahieu	3.00	8.00
STITDO Darren O'Day	2.00	5.00
STITDP David Price	2.50	6.00
STITFH Felix Hernandez	2.50	6.00
STITGC Gerrit Cole	3.00	8.00
STITGP Glen Perkins	2.00	5.00
STITJA Jose Altuve	2.50	6.00
STITJDE Jacob deGrom	6.00	15.00
STITJDO Josh Donaldson	2.50	6.00
STITJK Jason Kipnis	2.50	6.00
STITJM J.D. Martinez	3.00	8.00
STITJPA Joe Panik	2.50	6.00
STITJPD Joc Pederson	8.00	20.00
STITJPE Jhonny Peralta	2.00	5.00
STITJU Justin Upton	2.50	6.00
STITKB Kris Bryant	15.00	40.00
STITKH Kelvin Herrera	2.00	5.00
STITLC Lorenzo Cain	2.00	5.00
STITMB Madison Bumgarner	2.50	6.00
STITMMA Manny Machado	3.00	8.00
STITMME Mark Melancon	2.00	5.00
STITMTE Mark Teixeira	2.50	6.00
STITMTR Mike Trout	15.00	40.00
STITNA Nolan Arenado	5.00	12.00
STITNC Nelson Cruz	3.00	8.00
STITPF Prince Fielder	2.50	6.00
STITPG Paul Goldschmidt	3.00	8.00
STITRM Russell Martin	2.00	5.00
STITSM Shelby Miller	2.50	6.00
STITSP Salvador Perez	2.50	6.00
STITSV Stephen Vogt	2.50	6.00
STITTF Todd Frazier	2.00	5.00
STITTT Troy Tulowitzki	3.00	8.00
STITWD Wade Davis	2.00	5.00
STITYG Yasmani Grandal	2.00	5.00
STITYM Yadier Molina	4.00	10.00
STITZB Zach Britton	2.50	6.00
STITZG Zack Greinke	3.00	8.00

2015 Topps Update All Star Stitches Autographs

STATED ODDS 1:6996 HOBBY
STATED PRINT RUN 25 SER.#'d SETS
EXCHANGE DEADLINE 9/30/2017

Card	Low	High
ASTARAE Alcides Escobar	30.00	80.00
ASTARBC Brandon Crawford	30.00	80.00
ASTARBH Brock Holt	25.00	60.00
ASTARDL DJ LeMahieu	50.00	120.00
ASTARDP David Price	30.00	80.00
ASTARGC Gerrit Cole	40.00	100.00
ASTARJA Jose Altuve	30.00	80.00
ASTARJK Jason Kipnis	30.00	80.00
ASTARJM J.D. Martinez	40.00	100.00
ASTARPG Paul Goldschmidt	40.00	100.00
ASTARSP Salvador Perez	30.00	80.00
ASTARTF Todd Frazier	25.00	60.00
ASTARJPD Joc Pederson	60.00	150.00
ASTARJPR Jhonny Peralta	30.00	80.00

2015 Topps Update All Star Stitches Dual

STATED ODDS 1:10,800 HOBBY
STATED PRINT RUN 25 SER.#'d SETS

Card	Low	High
ASDCG L.Cain/M.Moustakas	15.00	40.00
ASDFC A.Chapman/T.Frazier	20.00	50.00
ASDGP J.Pederson/A.Gonzalez	15.00	40.00
ASDHP Peralta/Martinez	25.00	60.00
ASDHS Pederson/Harper	25.00	60.00
ASDMJ A.Jones/M.Machado	20.00	50.00
ASDPB Bumgarner/Posey	25.00	60.00
ASDRB Rizzo/Bryant	40.00	100.00

2015 Topps Update All Star Stitches Triple

STATED ODDS 1:4848 HOBBY
STATED PRINT RUN 25 SER.#'d SETS

Card	Low	High
ASTDPH Prz/Hrrra/Dvs	25.00	60.00
ASTGGP Pdrsn/Gnzlz/Grndl	30.00	80.00
ASTHMU Hrpr/Pdrsn/McCtchn	50.00	120.00
ASTMJB Jns/Brttn/Mchdo	20.00	50.00
ASTPBC Bmgrnr/Crwfrd/Psy	25.00	60.00
ASTPCG Cain/Prz/Mstks	50.00	120.00
ASTRMW Wcha/Rsnthl/Mlna	40.00	100.00

2015 Topps Update Career High Jumbo Relics

STATED ODDS 1:11,193 HOBBY
STATED PRINT RUN 25 SER.#'d SETS

Card	Low	High
CHJRAG Alex Gordon	15.00	40.00
CHJRAJ Adam Jones	12.00	30.00
CHJRAM Andrew McCutchen	60.00	150.00
CHJRBP Buster Posey	15.00	40.00
CHJRCB Clay Buchholz	15.00	40.00
CHJRCG Carlos Gomez	8.00	20.00
CHJRDJ Derek Jeter	25.00	60.00
CHJRFH Felix Hernandez	10.00	25.00
CHJRJBA Jose Bautista	10.00	25.00
CHJRJBZ Javier Baez	8.00	20.00
CHJRJE Jacoby Ellsbury	10.00	25.00
CHJRJM Joe Mauer	15.00	40.00
CHJRJPE Joc Pederson	15.00	40.00
CHJRMB Madison Bumgarner	20.00	50.00
CHJRMC Miguel Cabrera	30.00	80.00
CHJRMH Matt Harvey	20.00	50.00
CHJRMP Mike Piazza	20.00	50.00
CHJRMTE Mark Teixeira	10.00	25.00
CHJRRC Robinson Cano	8.00	20.00
CHJRYM Yadier Molina	20.00	50.00

2015 Topps Update Chrome

RANDOM INSERTS IN HOLIDAY MEGA BOXES
*GOLD/250: 2.5X TO 6X BASIC
*BLACK/99: 4X TO 10X BASIC

Card	Low	High
US9 Shane Greene	.50	1.25
US11 Evan Gattis	.50	1.25
US16 John Axford	.50	1.25
US23 Kevin Plawecki RC	.50	1.25
US32 Blake Swihart RC	.60	1.50
US46 David Price	.60	1.50
US102 Chi Chi Gonzalez RC	.75	2.00
US103 Joey Gallo RC	1.00	2.50
US119 Jacob Lindgren RC	.60	1.50
US127 Eduardo Rodriguez RC	.50	1.25
US135 Jason Heyward	.60	1.50
US136 Byron Buxton RD	2.50	6.00
US144 Delino DeShields Jr. RC	.50	1.25
US151 Colby Lewis	.50	1.25
US155 Yoenis Cespedes	.60	1.50
US157 Noah Syndergaard RC	1.00	2.50
US161 Jeff Samardzija	.50	1.25
US170 Mike Foltynewicz RC	.50	1.25
US174 Carlos Correa RC	6.00	15.00
US181 Jimmy Paredes	.50	1.25
US190 Shelby Miller	.60	1.50
US208 Addison Russell RD	1.50	4.00
US220 Addison Russell RC	1.50	4.00
US225 Keone Kela	.60	1.50
US237 Craig Kimbrel	.60	1.50
US238 A.J. Cole	.50	1.25
US257 Josh Hamilton	.60	1.50
US264 Brock Holt	.50	1.25
US272 Matt Duffy	.60	1.50
US280 Mike Bolsinger	.50	1.25
US283 Kris Bryant RD	5.00	12.00
US286 Francisco Lindor RD	6.00	15.00
US291 Eddie Butler	.50	1.25
US294 Mark Trumbo	.50	1.25
US308 Joey Butler	.50	1.25
US309 Howie Kendrick	.50	1.25
US319 Will Harris	.50	1.25
US320 Josh Donaldson	.60	1.50
US324 Carlos Rodon RC	1.25	3.00
US325 Matt Kemp	.60	1.50
US341 Eddie Rosario RC	1.00	2.50
US350 Didi Gregorius	.60	1.50
US362 Rick Porcello	.60	1.50
US376 Joc Pederson RD	2.00	5.00
US377 Taijuan Walker	.50	1.25
US388 Kevin Pillar	.50	1.25
US392 Odrisamer Despaigne	.50	1.25
US395 Dexter Fowler	.60	1.50
US396 Ichiro	1.00	2.50
US398 J.T. Realmuto	6.00	15.00

2015 Topps Update Chrome All Star Stiches

RANDOM INSERTS IN HOLIDAY MEGA BOXES

Card	Low	High
ASCRAE Alcides Escobar	4.00	10.00
ASCRAJ Adam Jones	4.00	10.00
ASCRAM Andrew McCutchen	5.00	12.00
ASCRAP Albert Pujols	6.00	15.00
ASCRBH Bryce Harper	10.00	25.00
ASCRBP Buster Posey	10.00	25.00
ASCRCS Chris Sale	8.00	20.00
ASCRJA Jose Altuve	4.00	10.00
ASCRKB Kris Bryant	25.00	60.00
ASCRLC Lorenzo Cain	8.00	20.00
ASCRMB Madison Bumgarner	4.00	10.00
ASCRMM Manny Machado	10.00	25.00
ASCRNC Nelson Cruz	5.00	12.00
ASCRPF Prince Fielder	4.00	10.00
ASCRPG Paul Goldschmidt	5.00	12.00
ASCRSM Shelby Miller	8.00	20.00
ASCRSP Salvador Perez	4.00	10.00
ASCRTF Todd Frazier	12.00	30.00
ASCRZG Zack Greinke	6.00	15.00
ASCRJDE Jacob deGrom	10.00	25.00
ASCRJDO Josh Donaldson	4.00	10.00
ASCRJPD Joc Pederson	12.00	30.00
ASCRJPR Jhonny Peralta	3.00	8.00
ASCRMTE Mark Teixeira	4.00	10.00
ASCRMTR Mike Trout	25.00	60.00

2015 Topps Update Chrome All Star Stiches Autographs

RANDOM INSERTS IN HOLIDAY MEGA BOXES
STATED PRINT RUN 25 SER.#'d SETS

Card	Low	High
ASCARAG Adrian Gonzalez	20.00	50.00
ASCARBP Buster Posey	150.00	250.00
ASCARDP David Price	30.00	80.00
ASCARJA Jose Altuve	20.00	50.00
ASCARJD Jacob deGrom	150.00	400.00
ASCARMM Manny Machado	150.00	250.00
ASCARMT Mike Trout	200.00	400.00
ASCARPG Paul Goldschmidt	60.00	150.00
ASCARSP Salvador Perez	20.00	50.00

2015 Topps Update Chrome Rookie Sensations

RANDOM INSERTS IN PACKS

Card	Low	High
RSC1 Hanley Ramirez	.75	2.00
RSC2 Ichiro	1.25	3.00
RSC3 Mike Trout	5.00	12.00
RSC4 Mike Piazza	1.00	2.50
RSC5 Carlton Fisk	.75	2.00
RSC6 Nomar Garciaparra	.75	2.00
RSC7 Troy Tulowitzki	1.00	2.50
RSC8 Jose Fernandez	1.00	2.50
RSC9 Jacob deGrom	2.00	5.00
RSC10 Fernando Valenzuela	.60	1.50
RSC11 Dwight Gooden	.60	1.50
RSC12 Ted Williams	2.00	5.00
RSC13 Jeff Bagwell	.75	2.00
RSC14 Jose Abreu	1.00	2.50
RSC15 Dustin Pedroia	1.00	2.50
RSC16 Jackie Robinson	1.00	2.50
RSC17 Cal Ripken Jr.	3.00	8.00
RSC18 Derek Jeter	2.50	6.00
RSC19 Neftali Feliz	.60	1.50
RSC20 Tom Seaver	.75	2.00
RSC21 Albert Pujols	1.25	3.00

RSC22 Bryce Harper 1.50 4.00
RSC23 Buster Posey 1.25 3.00
RSC24 Livan Hernandez .60 1.50
RSC25 Mark McGwire 1.50 4.00

2015 Topps Update Etched in History

STATED ODDS 1:621 HOBBY
*GOLD/50: 1.5X TO 4X BASIC
EIH1 Nolan Ryan 6.00 15.00
EIH2 Hank Aaron 4.00 10.00
EIH3 Rickey Henderson 2.00 5.00
EIH4 Ted Williams 4.00 10.00
EIH5 Babe Ruth 5.00 12.00
EIH6 Ichiro Suzuki 2.50 6.00
EIH7 Mariano Rivera 2.50 6.00
EIH8 Nolan Ryan 6.00 15.00
EIH9 Francisco Rodriguez 1.50 4.00
EIH10 Roger Clemens 2.50 6.00
EIH11 Alex Rodriguez 2.50 6.00
EIH12 Cal Ripken Jr. 6.00 15.00
EIH13 Nomar Garciaparra 1.50 4.00
EIH14 Roger Maris 2.00 5.00
EIH15 Ozzie Smith 2.50 6.00

2015 Topps Update First Home Run

COMPLETE SET (30) 20.00 50.00
*GOLD: .5X TO 1.2X BASIC
*SILVER: .5X TO 1.2X BASIC
*WHITE: .5X TO 1.2X BASIC
RANDOM INSERT IN RETAIL PACKS
FHR1 Ernie Banks .60 1.50
FHR2 Brandon Belt .50 1.25
FHR3 Adrian Beltre .60 1.50
FHR4 Craig Biggio .50 1.25
FHR5 Wade Boggs .50 1.25
FHR6 Kole Calhoun .40 1.00
FHR7 Roberto Clemente 2.00 5.00
FHR8 Jacoby Ellsbury .50 1.25
FHR9 Edwin Encarnacion .60 1.50
FHR10 Nomar Garciaparra .50 1.25
FHR11 Carlos Gomez .40 1.00
FHR12 Ken Griffey Jr. 1.25 3.00
FHR13 Jonathan Lucroy .50 1.25
FHR14 Starling Marte .50 1.25
FHR15 Edgar Martinez .50 1.25
FHR16 Willie Mays 1.25 3.00
FHR17 Devin Mesoraco .40 1.00
FHR18 Paul O'Neill .50 1.25
FHR19 Brandon Phillips .40 1.00
FHR20 Dalton Pompey .50 1.25
FHR21 Hanley Ramirez .50 1.25
FHR22 Jackie Robinson .60 1.50
FHR23 Ryne Sandberg 1.25 3.00
FHR24 Mike Schmidt 1.00 2.50
FHR25 Mark Teixeira .50 1.25
FHR26 Kennys Vargas .40 1.00
FHR27 Kolten Wong .50 1.25
FHR28 Mike Zunino .40 1.00
FHR29 Ichiro Suzuki .75 2.00
FHR30 Kris Bryant 3.00 8.00

2015 Topps Update First Home Run Medallions

RANDOM INSERT IN RETAIL PACKS
FHRM1 Brandon Phillips 2.00 5.00
FHRM2 Kolten Wong 2.50 6.00
FHRM3 Kole Calhoun 2.00 5.00
FHRM4 Craig Biggio 2.50 6.00
FHRM5 Mike Zunino 2.00 5.00
FHRM6 Devin Mesoraco 2.00 5.00
FHRM7 Kennys Vargas 2.00 5.00
FHRM8 Edwin Encarnacion 3.00 8.00
FHRM9 Wade Boggs 2.50 6.00
FHRM10 Edgar Martinez 2.50 6.00
FHRM11 Brandon Belt 2.50 6.00
FHRM12 Paul O'Neill 2.50 6.00
FHRM13 Jackie Robinson 6.00 15.00
FHRM14 Roberto Clemente 10.00 25.00
FHRM15 Willie Mays 6.00 15.00
FHRM16 Ernie Banks 5.00 12.00
FHRM17 Ken Griffey Jr. 6.00 15.00
FHRM18 Mike Schmidt 5.00 12.00
FHRM19 Ryne Sandberg 6.00 15.00
FHRM20 Nomar Garciaparra 2.50 6.00
FHRM21 Hanley Ramirez 2.50 6.00
FHRM22 Carlos Gomez 2.00 5.00
FHRM23 Adrian Beltre 3.00 8.00
FHRM24 Dalton Pompey 2.50 6.00
FHRM25 Jacoby Ellsbury 2.50 6.00
FHRM26 Starling Marte 2.50 6.00
FHRM27 Jonathan Lucroy 2.50 6.00
FHRM28 Mark Teixeira 2.50 6.00
FHRM29 Ichiro Suzuki 4.00 10.00
FHRM30 Kris Bryant 12.00 30.00

2015 Topps Update First Home Run Relics

INSERTED IN RETAIL PACKS
STATED PRINT RUN 99 SER.#'d SETS
FHRRAB Adrian Beltre 15.00 40.00
FHRRBB Brandon Belt 6.00 15.00
FHRRBP Brandon Phillips 6.00 15.00
FHRRCB Craig Biggio 8.00 20.00
FHRRDM Devin Mesoraco 6.00 15.00
FHRREB Ernie Banks 12.00 30.00
FHRRHR Hanley Ramirez 5.00 12.00
FHRRJE Jacoby Ellsbury 12.00 30.00
FHRRKB Kris Bryant 20.00 50.00
FHRRKC Kole Calhoun 10.00 25.00
FHRRMS Mike Schmidt 12.00 30.00
FHRRMT Mark Teixeira 5.00 12.00
FHRRMZ Mike Zunino 10.00 25.00
FHRRNG Nomar Garciaparra 10.00 25.00
FHRRPO Paul O'Neill 8.00 20.00

2015 Topps Update Pride and Perseverance

COMPLETE SET (12) 4.00 10.00
STATED ODDS 1:10 HOBBY
PP1 Buddy Carlyle .40 1.00
PP2 Curtis Pride .40 1.00
PP3 George Springer .50 1.25
PP4 Jake Peavy .40 1.00
PP5 Jason Johnson .40 1.00
PP6 Jim Abbott .40 1.00
PP7 Jim Eisenreich .40 1.00
PP8 Jon Lester .50 1.25
PP9 Pete Wyshner Gray .40 1.00
PP10 Sam Fuld .40 1.00
PP11 William Hoy .40 1.00
PP12 Anthony Rizzo .75 2.00

2015 Topps Update Rarities

COMPLETE SET (15) 5.00 12.00
STATED ODDS 1:8 HOBBY
R1 Frank Robinson .30 .75
R2 Shawn Green .25 .60
R3 Daniel Nava .25 .60
R4 Ted Williams .75 2.00
R5 Roberto Clemente 1.00 2.50
R6 Mariano Rivera .50 1.25
R7 Anibal Sanchez .25 .60
R8 Mike Mussina .30 .75
R9 George Brett .75 2.00
R10 Rod Carew .30 .75
R11 Asdrubal Cabrera .30 .75
R12 Don Mattingly .75 2.00
R13 Randy Johnson .40 1.00
R14 Ken Griffey Jr. .75 2.00
R15 Billy Williams .30 .75

2015 Topps Update Rarities Autographs

STATED ODDS 1:21,228 HOBBY
STATED PRINT RUN 25 SER.#'d SETS
EXCHANGE DEADLINE 9/30/2017
RADM Don Mattingly 30.00 80.00
RARC Rod Carew 40.00 100.00
RARJ Randy Johnson EXCH 75.00 200.00
RASG Shawn Green 10.00 25.00

2015 Topps Update Rookie Sensations

COMPLETE SET (25) 5.00 12.00
STATED ODDS 1:6 HOBBY
RS1 Hanley Ramirez .30 .75
RS2 Ichiro Suzuki .50 1.25
RS3 Mike Trout 2.00 5.00
RS4 Mike Piazza .40 1.00
RS5 Carlton Fisk .30 .75
RS6 Nomar Garciaparra .30 .75
RS7 Troy Tulowitzki .40 1.00
RS8 Jose Fernandez .40 1.00
RS9 Jacob deGrom .75 2.00
RS10 Fernando Valenzuela .25 .60
RS11 Dwight Gooden .25 .60
RS12 Ted Williams .75 2.00
RS13 Jeff Bagwell .30 .75
RS14 Jose Abreu .40 1.00
RS15 Dustin Pedroia .40 1.00
RS16 Jackie Robinson .40 1.00
RS17 Cal Ripken Jr. 1.25 3.00
RS18 Derek Jeter 1.00 2.50
RS19 Neftali Feliz .25 .60
RS20 Tom Seaver .30 .75
RS21 Albert Pujols .50 1.25
RS22 Bryce Harper .60 1.50
RS23 Buster Posey .50 1.25
RS24 Livan Hernandez .25 .60
RS25 Mark McGwire .60 1.50

2015 Topps Update Rookie Sensations Autographs

STATED ODDS 1:6996 HOBBY
STATED PRINT RUN 25 SER.#'d SETS
EXCHANGE DEADLINE 9/30/2017
RSACF Carlton Fisk 25.00 60.00
RSADP Dustin Pedroia 25.00 60.00
RSAFV Fernando Valenzuela 40.00 100.00
RSAJB Jeff Bagwell 40.00 100.00
RSAJF Jose Fernandez 15.00 40.00
RSALH Livan Hernandez 10.00 25.00
RSAMH Matt Harvey EXCH 30.00 80.00
RSANG Nomar Garciaparra 20.00 50.00
RSATT Troy Tulowitzki 25.00 60.00

2015 Topps Update Tape Measure Blasts

COMPLETE SET (15) 5.00 12.00
STATED ODDS 1:8 HOBBY
TMB1 Jose Canseco .30 .75
TMB2 Andres Galarraga .30 .75
TMB3 Mark McGwire .60 1.50
TMB4 Reggie Jackson .30 .75
TMB5 Mike Trout 2.00 5.00
TMB6 Ryan Howard .30 .75
TMB7 Giancarlo Stanton .40 1.00
TMB8 Adam Dunn .30 .75
TMB9 Bo Jackson .40 1.00
TMB10 David Ortiz .40 1.00
TMB11 Mark McGwire .60 1.50
TMB12 Roberto Clemente 1.00 2.50
TMB13 Albert Pujols .50 1.25
TMB14 Ted Williams .75 2.00
TMB15 Josh Gibson .40 1.00

2015 Topps Update Tape Measure Blasts Autographs

STATED ODDS 1:21,228 HOBBY
STATED PRINT RUN 25 SER.#'d SETS
EXCHANGE DEADLINE 9/30/2017
TMBAAG Andres Galarraga 12.00 30.00
TMBAJC Jose Canseco 20.00 50.00
TMBAMMC Mark McGwire 100.00 200.00
TMBARH Ryan Howard 12.00 30.00

2015 Topps Update Whatever Works

COMPLETE SET (15) 4.00 10.00
STATED ODDS 1:8 HOBBY
WW1 Mark Teixeira .30 .75
WW2 Tim Lincecum .30 .75
WW3 Wade Boggs .30 .75
WW4 Nomar Garciaparra .30 .75
WW5 Craig Biggio .30 .75
WW6 Max Scherzer .40 1.00
WW7 Joe DiMaggio .75 2.00
WW8 Roger Clemens .50 1.25
WW9 Richie Ashburn .30 .75
WW10 Jim Palmer .30 .75
WW11 Mike Napoli .25 .60
WW12 Justin Verlander .40 1.00
WW13 David Ortiz .40 1.00
WW14 Chipper Jones .40 1.00
WW15 Alex Gordon .30 .75

2015 Topps Update Whatever Works Autographs

STATED ODDS 1:21,228 HOBBY
STATED PRINT RUN 25 SER.#'d SETS
EXCHANGE DEADLINE 9/30/2017
WWAAG Alex Gordon 20.00 50.00
WWACB Craig Biggio 30.00 80.00
WWAMN Mike Napoli 20.00 50.00
WWAMT Mark Teixeira 40.00 100.00

2016 Topps

COMP.RED.HOB.FACT SET (700) 30.00 80.00
COMP.BLUE.RET.FACT SET (700) 30.00 80.00
COMP.SER 1 SET w/o SP's (350) 12.00 30.00
COMP.SER 2 SET w/o SP's (350) 12.00 30.00
CAMO ODDS 1:125 HOBBY; 1:25 JUMBO
42 SP ODDS 1:69 HOBBY
SER.1 VAR ODDS 1:1247 H; 1:250 JUMBO
SER.2 VAR ODDS 1:683 HOBBY
SER.1 PLATE ODDS 1:1350 HOBBY
SER.2 PLATE ODDS 1:803 HOBBY
PLATE PRINT RUN 1 SET PER COLOR
BLACK-CYAN-MAGENTA-YELLOW ISSUED
NO PLATE PRICING DUE TO SCARCITY
1A Mike Trout 1.25 3.00
1B Trout SP Camo 15.00 40.00
1C Trout SP Pointing bat 125.00 250.00
2 Jerad Eickhoff RC .40 1.00
3 Richie Shaffer RC .25 .60
4A Sonny Gray .20 .50
4B Sonny Gray SP 40.00 100.00
Sunglasses
5 Kyle Seager .15 .40
6 Jimmy Paredes .15 .40
8A Michael Brantley .20 .50
8B Michael Brantley SP 40.00 100.00
Sunglasses
9 Eric Hosmer .20 .50
10 Nelson Cruz .25 .60
11 Andre Ethier .20 .50
12A Nolan Arenado .40 1.00
12B Nolan Arenado SP Camo 6.00 15.00
13 Craig Kimbrel .20 .50
14 Chris Davis .15 .40
15 Ryan Howard .20 .50
16 Rougned Odor .20 .50
17 Billy Butler .15 .40
18 Francisco Rodriguez .20 .50
19 Delino DeShields Jr. FS .15 .40
20 Andrew McCutchen .25 .60
21 Mike Moustakas WSH .20 .50
22 John Hicks RC .25 .60
23 Jeff Francoeur .20 .50
24 Clayton Kershaw .40 1.00
25 Brad Ziegler .15 .40
26 Dvs/Trt/Cruz LL 1.25 3.00
27 Alec Asher RC .25 .60
28A Brian McCann .20 .50
28B Brian McCann SP Camo 3.00 8.00
29 Altve/Cbrra/Bgrts LL .25 .60
30 Yan Gomes .15 .40
31 Travis d'Arnaud .20 .50
32 Zack Greinke .25 .60
33 Edinson Volquez .15 .40
34 Omar Infante .15 .40
35 Luke Hochevar .15 .40
36 Miguel Montero .15 .40
37 C.J. Cron .15 .40
38 Jed Lowrie .15 .40
39 Mark Trumbo .15 .40
40 Jedd Gyorko .15 .40
41 Josh Harrison .15 .40
42 A.J. Ramos .15 .40
43 Noah Syndergaard FS .20 .50
44 David Freese .15 .40
45 Ryan Zimmerman .20 .50
46A Jhonny Peralta .15 .40
46B Jhonny Peralta SP Camo 2.50 6.00
47 Gio Gonzalez .20 .50
48 J.J. Hoover .15 .40
49 Ike Davis .15 .40
50A Salvador Perez .20 .50
50B Salvador Perez SP Camo 3.00 8.00
51 Dustin Garneau RC .25 .60
52 Julio Teheran .20 .50
53A George Springer .20 .50
53B George Springer SP Camo 3.00 8.00
54 Jung Ho Kang FS .15 .40
55 Jesus Montero .15 .40
56 Salvador Perez WSH .20 .50
57 Adam Lind .20 .50
58 Grnke/Krshw/Arrta LL .40 1.00
59 John Lamb RC .25 .60
60 Shelby Miller .20 .50
61 Johnny Cueto WSH .20 .50
62 Trayce Thompson RC .40 1.00
63 Zach Britton .20 .50
64 Corey Kluber .20 .50
65 Pittsburgh Pirates .15 .40
66A Kyle Schwarber RC .75 2.00
66B Schwarber Gry jrsy Fctry
67 Matt Harvey .20 .50
68 Odubel Herrera FS .20 .50
69 Anibal Sanchez .15 .40
70 Kendrys Morales .15 .40
71 John Danks .15 .40
72 Chris Young .15 .40
73 Ketel Marte RC .50 1.25
74 Troy Tulowitzki .25 .60
75 Rusney Castillo .15 .40
76 Glen Perkins .15 .40
77 Clay Buchholz .15 .40
78A Miguel Sano RC .40 1.00
78C Sano Drk jrsy Fctry
78B Sano SP Dugout 75.00 200.00
79 Seattle Mariners .15 .40
80 Carson Smith .15 .40
81 Alexei Ramirez .20 .50
82 Michael Bourn .15 .40
83 Starling Marte .20 .50
84A Mookie Betts .50 1.25
84B Betts SP Camo 8.00 20.00
85A Corey Seager RC 6.00 15.00
85B Seagr Fldng Fctry
86A Wilmer Flores .20 .50
86B Wilmer Flores SP Camo 3.00 8.00
87 Jorge De La Rosa .15 .40
88 Ubaldo Jimenez .15 .40
89 Edwin Encarnacion .25 .60
90 Koji Uehara .15 .40
91 Yasmani Grandal FS .15 .40
92 Darren O'Day .15 .40
93 Charlie Blackmon .25 .60
94 Miguel Cabrera .25 .60
95 Kole Calhoun FS .15 .40
96 Jose Bautista .20 .50
97 Ender Inciarte FS .15 .40
98 Garrett Richards .20 .50
99 Taijuan Walker .15 .40
100A Bryce Harper .40 1.00
100B Harper SP Camo 10.00 25.00
101 Justin Turner .25 .60
102 Doug Fister .15 .40
103 Trea Turner RC .75 2.00
104 Jeremy Hellickson .15 .40
105 Marcus Semien .25 .60
106 Jordan Walden .15 .40
107 Kevin Siegrist .15 .40
108 Ben Paulsen .15 .40
109 Henry Owens RC .30 .75
110 J.D. Martinez FS .25 .60
111 Coco Crisp .15 .40
112 Matt Kemp .20 .50
113 Aaron Sanchez .20 .50
114 Brett Lawrie .20 .50
115 Aaron Harang .15 .40
116 Brett Gardner .20 .50
117 Liam Hendriks .15 .40
118 Jose Fernandez .25 .60
119 Sean Doolittle .15 .40
120 Alcides Escobar WSH .20 .50
121 Roberto Osuna FS .15 .40
122 Melky Cabrera .15 .40
123 J.P. Howell .15 .40
124 Melvin Upton Jr. .20 .50
125 Grnke/Krshw/Arrta LL .40 1.00
126 David Ortiz .30 .75
Albert Pujols
127 Zach Lee RC .25 .60
128 Eddie Rosario .20 .50
129 Kendall Graveman .15 .40
130 A.J. Pollock .15 .40
131 Adam LaRoche .15 .40
132A Joe Ross FS .15 .40
132B Joe Ross FS SP 30.00 80.00
Sunglasses
133A Aaron Nola RC .50 1.25
133B Nola SP Dugout 50.00 125.00
134A Yadier Molina .30 .75
134B Yadier Molina SP 60.00 150.00
Glove out
135 Colby Rasmus .20 .50
136 Michael Cuddyer .15 .40
137 Joe Panik .20 .50
138 Francisco Liriano .15 .40
139A Yasiel Puig .25 .60
139B Puig SP w/bat 50.00 125.00
140 Carlos Carrasco FS .15 .40
141 Colin Rea RC .25 .60
142 CC Sabathia .20 .50
143 Oliver Perez .15 .40
144 Jose Iglesias .20 .50
145 Jon Niese .15 .40
146 Stephen Piscotty RC .40 1.00
147 Dee Gordon .15 .40
148 Yangervis Solarte .15 .40
149 Chad Bettis .15 .40
150A Clayton Kershaw .40 1.00
150B Kershaw SP W/bat 80.00 200.00
151 Jon Lester .20 .50
152 Kyle Lohse .15 .40
153 Jason Hammel .20 .50
154A Hunter Pence .20 .50
154B Hunter Pence SP Camo 3.00 8.00
155 New York Yankees .15 .40
156 Cameron Maybin .15 .40
157 Darnell Sweeney RC .25 .60
158 Henry Urrutia .15 .40
159 Erick Aybar .15 .40
160 Chris Sale .25 .60
161 Phil Hughes .15 .40
162 Bautista/Donaldson/Davis LL .20 .50
163 Joaquin Benoit .15 .40
164 Andrew Heaney .15 .40
165 Adam Eaton .15 .40
166 Gldschmdt/Rizzo/Arndo LL .40 1.00
167 Jacoby Ellsbury .20 .50
168 Nathan Eovaldi .20 .50
169 Charlie Morton .25 .60
170 Carlos Gomez .15 .40
171 Matt Cain .20 .50
172 Carter Capps .15 .40
173A Jose Abreu .25 .60
173B Abreu SP Camo 4.00 10.00
173C Abreu SP Blk jsy 40.00 100.00
174 Jered Weaver .20 .50
175A Manny Machado .25 .60
175B Manny Machado SP Camo 4.00 10.00
176 Brandon Phillips .15 .40
177 Gregor Blanco .15 .40
178 Rob Refsnyder RC .30 .75
179 Jose Peraza RC .30 .75
180 Kevin Gausman .25 .60
181 Minnesota Twins .15 .40
182 Kevin Pillar .15 .40
183 Andrelton Simmons .15 .40
184 Travis Jankowski RC .25 .60
185 Keuchel/Gray/Price LL .20 .50
186 Yasmany Tomas FS .15 .40
187 Keuchel/McHugh/Price LL .20 .50
188A Greg Bird RC .30 .75
188B Greg Bird SP 40.00 100.00
Tipping cap
189 Jake McGee .15 .40
190 Jeurys Familia .20 .50
191 Brian Johnson RC .25 .60
192 John Jaso .15 .40
193 Trevor Bauer .30 .75
194 Chase Headley .15 .40
195A Jason Kipnis .20 .50
195B Jason Kipnis SP Camo 3.00 8.00
196 Hunter Strickland .15 .40
197 Neil Walker .15 .40
198 Oakland Athletics .15 .40
199 Jay Bruce .20 .50
200A Josh Donaldson .20 .50
200B Josh Donaldson SP Camo 3.00 8.00
201 Adam Jones .20 .50
202 Colorado Rockies .15 .40
203 Aaron Hill .15 .40
204 Mark Teixeira .20 .50
205 Taylor Jungmann FS .15 .40
206A Alex Gordon .20 .50
206B Alex Gordon SP Camo 3.00 8.00
207 Maikel Franco FS .20 .50
208 Kurt Suzuki .15 .40
209 Max Scherzer .25 .60
210 Mike Zunino .15 .40
211 Nick Ahmed .15 .40
212 Starlin Castro .15 .40
213 Matt Shoemaker .20 .50
214 Chris Colabello .15 .40
215 Adrian Gonzalez .20 .50
216 Logan Forsythe .15 .40
217 Lance Lynn .15 .40
218 Andrew Miller .20 .50
219 Hector Olivera RC .30 .75
220 GreinkeCole/Arrieta LL .25 .60
221 Ryan LaMarre RC .25 .60
222 Homer Bailey .15 .40
223 Christian Yelich .30 .75
224 Billy Burns FS .15 .40
225 Scooter Gennett .20 .50
226 Brian Ellington RC .25 .60
227 David Murphy .15 .40
228 Matt Garza .15 .40
229 Jesse Hahn .15 .40
230 Ryan Vogelsong .15 .40
231 Chris Coghlan .15 .40
232A Michael Conforto RC .30 .75
232B Conforto SP Camo 10.00 25.00
232C Cnfrto Fldng Fctry
233 J.J. Hardy .15 .40
234 David Robertson .15 .40
235 Blaine Boyer .15 .40
236 Juan Lagares .15 .40
237 Carlos Ruiz .15 .40
238 Baltimore Orioles .15 .40
239 Huston Street .15 .40
240 Nick Markakis .20 .50
241 Freddie Freeman .30 .75
242 Matt Wisler FS .15 .40
243 Luke Gregerson .15 .40
244A Matt Carpenter .25 .60
244B Matt Carpenter SP Camo 4.00 10.00
245 Tommy Kahnle .15 .40
246 Dustin Pedroia .25 .60
247 Yunel Escobar .15 .40
248 Atlanta Braves .15 .40
249 Carlos Gomez .15 .40
250A Miguel Cabrera .25 .60
250B Cabrera SP Glasses 50.00 125.00
251 Silvino Bracho RC .25 .60
252 Jorge Soler .25 .60
253A Nick Castellanos .25 .60
253B Nick Castellanos SP 50.00 125.00
Blowing bubble
254 Matt Holliday .25 .60
255 Justin Verlander .25 .60
256 C.J. Wilson .15 .40
257 Jake Marisnick .15 .40
258 Devon Travis FS .15 .40
259A Paul Goldschmidt .25 .60
259B Paul Goldschmidt SP 40.00 100.00
Ceremony
260 Ryan Hanigan .15 .40
261A Russell Martin .15 .40
261B Russell Martin SP Camo 2.50 6.00
261C Russell Martin SP 30.00 80.00
Catcher's gear
262 Ervin Santana .15 .40
263 Joc Pederson FS .20 .50
264A Jake Arrieta .20 .50
264B Jake Arrieta SP 40.00 100.00
Blue jersey
265A Luis Severino RC .30 .75
265B Svrno Gry jrsy Fcty
266 Jonathan Papelbon .20 .50
267 Chris Heston FS .15 .40
268A Robinson Cano .20 .50
268B Robinson Cano SP 40.00 100.00
With base
269A Giancarlo Stanton .25 .60
269B Giancarlo Stanton SP Camo 4.00 10.00
270 Pat Neshek .15 .40
271 Kevin Kiermaier .20 .50
272 Denard Span .15 .40
273 New York Mets .15 .40
274 Ryan Goins .15 .40
275A Ian Kinsler .20 .50
275B Ian Kinsler SP Camo 3.00 8.00
276 Francisco Cervelli .15 .40
277 Elvis Andrus .20 .50
278 Evan Gattis .15 .40
279 Alex Guerrero FS .20 .50
280 Brock Holt .15 .40
281 Alex Dickerson RC .25 .60
282 Scott Feldman .15 .40
283 Felix Hernandez .20 .50
284 Jon Gray RC .25 .60
285 Pablo Sandoval .20 .50
286A Joe Mauer .20 .50
286B Joe Mauer SP Camo 3.00 8.00
286C Joe Mauer SP 40.00 100.00
On deck
287 Alcides Escobar .20 .50
288 Jake Lamb FS .20 .50
289 Nick Hundley .15 .40
290 Zack Godley RC .25 .60
291 Asdrubal Cabrera .20 .50
292A Todd Frazier .15 .40
292B Todd Frazier SP Camo 2.50 6.00
293 Hyun-Jin Ryu .20 .50
294 Chicago White Sox .15 .40
295 Jonathan Schoop .15 .40
296 Yordano Ventura .20 .50
297 Detroit Tigers .15 .40
298A Ryan Braun .20 .50
298B Ryan Braun SP 40.00 100.00
In dugout
299 Angel Pagan .15 .40
300A Buster Posey .30 .75
300B Posey SP Running 75.00 200.00
301 Wade Miley .15 .40
302 Houston Astros .15 .40
303 Steve Pearce .25 .60
304 Charlie Furbush .15 .40
305 Colby Lewis .15 .40
306 Jarrod Saltalamacchia .15 .40
307 Wade Davis .15 .40
308 Brian Dozier .20 .50
309 Shin-Soo Choo .20 .50
310 David Wright .20 .50
311 Dariel Alvarez RC .25 .60
312A Curtis Granderson .20 .50
312B Grndrsn SP Lckr room 60.00 150.00
313 Martin Maldonado .15 .40
314 Kyle Hendricks .25 .60
315 San Diego Padres .15 .40
316 Jake Odorizzi FS .15 .40
317A Jose Altuve .20 .50
317B Altuve SP Camo 3.00 8.00
317C Altuve SP Clap 40.00 100.00
318 Washington Nationals .15 .40
319 Adam Wainwright .20 .50
320 Jake Peavy .15 .40
321A Hanley Ramirez .20 .50
321B Hanley Ramirez SP 40.00 100.00
With glove
322 Kelby Tomlinson RC .25 .60
323 Jacob deGrom .50 1.25
324 Steven Souza Jr. .20 .50
325 Kaleb Cowart RC .25 .60
326 Kevin Plawecki FS .15 .40
327A Anthony Rizzo .30 .75
327B Rizzo SP Dugout 60.00 150.00
328 Anthony DeSclafani .15 .40
329 Alex Rodriguez .30 .75
330 Edward Mujica .15 .40
331 Will Harris .15 .40
332 Toronto Blue Jays .15 .40
333 Keyvius Sampson RC .25 .60
334 Brandon McCarthy .15 .40
335 Mitch Moreland .15 .40
336 Mark Melancon .15 .40
337 Arndo/Hrpr/Gnzlz LL .40 1.00
338 Gldschmdt/Grdn/Hrpr LL .40 1.00
339 Carlos Santana .20 .50
340 Victor Martinez .20 .50
341A Josh Hamilton .20 .50
341B Josh Hamilton SP Camo 3.00 8.00
342 Jayson Werth .20 .50
343 Drew Hutchison .15 .40
344 Jonathan Lucroy .20 .50
345 Yonder Alonso .15 .40
346 Kluber/Keuchel/Estrada LL .20 .50
347 Jason Grilli .15 .40
348 Seth Smith .15 .40
349 Ben Revere .15 .40
350A Kris Bryant FS .30 .75
350B Bryant FS SP Camo 15.00 40.00
350C Bryant FS SP Dugout 125.00 250.00
351 Chase Utley .20 .50
352 Carson Blair RC .25 .60
353 Joey Gallo .20 .50
354A Tyson Ross .15 .40
354B Tyson Ross SP 20.00 50.00
w/Catcher
355 Avisail Garcia .20 .50
356 Odrisamer Despaigne .15 .40
357 Jace Peterson .15 .40
358 Chris Young .15 .40
359 Christian Colon .15 .40
360 Eduardo Escobar .15 .40
361 Jeff Locke .15 .40
362 Cory Spangenberg .15 .40
363 Brett Cecil .15 .40
364 Keon Broxton RC .25 .60
365 James Pazos RC .30 .75
366 Scott Alexander RC .25 .60
367 Pedro Alvarez .15 .40
368A Xander Bogaerts .25 .60
368B Xander Bogaerts SP 3.00 8.00
42 jersey/Fielding
369 Dellin Betances .20 .50
370 Bud Norris .15 .40
371 Jason Heyward .20 .50
372 Zack Cozart .15 .40
373 Tucker Barnhart .15 .40
374 Zach McAllister .15 .40
375 Jordan Lyles .15 .40
376 Brandon Barnes .15 .40
377 Scott Kazmir .15 .40
378 Jeff Mathis .20 .50
379 Wei-Yin Chen .15 .40
380 Michael Blazek .15 .40
381 Bartolo Colon .15 .40
382 David Ortz .25 .60
David Price/Winning Formula
383 Andres Blanco .15 .40
384 Michael Morse .15 .40
385 Jon Jay .15 .40
386 Nori Aoki .15 .40
387 Kansas City Clutch .15 .40
388 Evan Longoria .20 .50
389 Sam Dyson .15 .40
390 Danny Espinosa .15 .40
391 Matt Boyd FS .15 .40
392 Jon Singleton .20 .50
393 Kelvin Herrera .15 .40
394 Abel De Los Santos RC .25 .60
395 Raul Mondesi RC .50 1.25
396 Matt Reynolds RC .25 .60
397 Mac Williamson RC .25 .60
398 Cleveland Indians .15 .40
399 Kansas City Royals .15 .40
400A David Ortiz .25 .60
400B David Ortiz SP 30.00 80.00
Hand goggles
401 Peter O'Brien RC .25 .60
402 Daniel Norris FS .15 .40
403 David Peralta .15 .40
404 Miami Marlins .15 .40
405A Ruben Tejada .15 .40
405B Ruben Tejada SP 30.00 80.00
No glasses
406 Marwin Gonzalez .15 .40
407A Yoenis Cespedes .25 .60
407B Yoenis Cespedes SP 30.00 80.00
w/Horse
408 Jason Castro .15 .40
409 Jean Segura .20 .50
410A Mike Moustakas .20 .50
410B Mike Moustakas SP 2.50 6.00
42 jersey
411 Brian Matusz .15 .40
412 Mark Lowe .15 .40
413 David Phelps .15 .40
414A Wily Peralta .15 .40
414B Wily Peralta SP 1.50 4.00
42 jersey
415 Brett Wallace .15 .40
416 Johnny Cueto .20 .50
417 Brad Boxberger .15 .40
418 Yu Darvish .25 .60
419 Aaron Altherr RC .25 .60
420 Pedro Severino RC .25 .60
421A Cesar Hernandez .15 .40
421B Cesar Hernandez SP 2.00 5.00
42 jersey
422 Miguel Gonzalez .15 .40
423A Carl Crawford .20 .50
423B Carl Crawford SP 2.50 6.00
42 jersey/White jersey
424 Brandon Belt .20 .50
425 Jackie Bradley Jr. .25 .60
426A Joey Votto .25 .60
426B Joey Votto SP 3.00 8.00
42 jersey/Diving
426C Joey Votto SP 30.00 80.00
All Star patch on sleeve
427 Travis Shaw .15 .40
428 Gregory Polanco .20 .50
429 Kenta Maeda RC .50 1.25
430 Ariel Pena RC .25 .60
431 Philadelphia Phillies .15 .40
432A Cameron Rupp .15 .40
432B Cameron Rupp SP 2.00 5.00
42 jersey
433 Trevor Brown RC .30 .75
434 Matt Adams .15 .40
435 Enrique Hernandez .25 .60
436 Raudel Lazo RC .25 .60
437 Michael Lorenzen .15 .40
438 Paulo Orlando .15 .40
439 Francisco Lindor FS .25 .60
440A Tommy Pham FS .15 .40
440B Tommy Pham SP 20.00 50.00
Batting
441 David Ross .15 .40
442A Brandon Crawford .20 .50
442B Brandon Crawford SP 25.00 60.00
Black shirt
443A Prince Fielder .20 .50
443B Prince Fielder SP 25.00 60.00
In dugout
444 Jordan Zimmermann .20 .50
445 Robbie Ray .15 .40
446 Tom Murphy RC .25 .60
447 Ben Zobrist .20 .50
448 St. Louis Cardinals .15 .40
449 J.A. Happ .20 .50
450A David Price .20 .50
450B Price SPw/Dog 40.00 100.00
451 Jose Reyes .20 .50
452A Gerrit Cole .25 .60
452B Gerrit Cole SP 30.00 80.00
No cap
453 A.Rizzo/K.Bryant .30 .75
454 Greg Holland .15 .40
455 Preston Tucker .15 .40
456 Gordon Beckham .15 .40
457 Nick Swisher .20 .50
458 Kenley Jansen .20 .50
459 James Loney .15 .40
460 Danny Salazar .20 .50
461 Freddy Galvis .15 .40
462 Jumbo Diaz .15 .40
463 Boston Red Sox .15 .40
464A Robinson Chirinos .15 .40
464B Robinson Chirinos SP 20.00 50.00
Red shirt
465 Jesse Chavez .15 .40
466 Marco Estrada .15 .40
467 Giovanny Urshela .25 .60
468 Rajai Davis .15 .40
469 Logan Morrison .15 .40
470 John Lackey .20 .50
471A Kolten Wong .20 .50
471B Kolten Wong SP 25.00 60.00
Wearing hoodie
472 Josh Reddick .15 .40
473 Robbie Erlin .15 .40
474 Chicago Cubs .15 .40
475 Max Kepler RC .40 1.00
476 Hisashi Iwakuma .20 .50
477 Chris Tillman .15 .40
478A Cody Asche .15 .40
478B Cody Asche SP 2.00 5.00
42 jersey
479A Marcus Stroman .20 .50
479B Marcus Stroman SP 25.00 60.00
w/Bobblehead
480 Mike Foltynewicz .15 .40
481 Hector Rondon .15 .40
482 Drew Smyly .15 .40
483 Erasmo Ramirez .15 .40
484A Trevor Rosenthal .20 .50
484B Trevor Rosenthal SP 2.50 6.00
42 jersey/Pitching
485 James Paxton .20 .50
486 Chris Rusin .15 .40
487 Martin Prado .15 .40
488 Colton Murray RC .25 .60
489A Adeiny Hechavarria .15 .40
489B Adeiny Hechavarria SP 2.00 5.00
42 jersey/w/Teammate
490 Guido Knudson RC .25 .60
491 Rich Hill .15 .40
492 Yadier Molina .15 .40
Randal Grichuk/Many Healthy Returns
493 R.A. Dickey .20 .50
494 Luis Avilan .15 .40
495 Luke Maile RC .25 .60
496A Brett Anderson .15 .40
496B Brett Anderson SP 2.00 5.00
42 jersey
497 Devin Mesoraco .15 .40
498 Steve Cishek .15 .40
499 Carlos Perez .15 .40
500A Albert Pujols .30 .75
500B Pujols SP 42 jersey 4.00 10.00
501 Alex Rios .20 .50
502 Austin Hedges .15 .40
503 Luis Valbuena .15 .40
504 Elias Diaz RC .25 .60

505 Frankie Montas RC .30 .75
506 Stephen Vogt .20 .50
507A Travis Wood .15 .40
507B Travis Wood SP 2.00 5.00
42 jersey/Mound meeting
508 Jaime Garcia .15 .40
509 Mark Canha .15 .40
510 Tony Watson .15 .40
511 Manny Banuelos .25 .60
512 Ryan Madson .15 .40
513 Caleb Joseph .15 .40
514 Michael Taylor .15 .40
515 Ryan Flaherty .15 .40
516 Steve Johnson .15 .40
517 Corey Knebel .15 .40
518A Matt Duffy .15 .40
518B Duffy SP 42 jersey 2.00 5.00
519 Kyle Barraclough RC .25 .60
520 Anthony Rendon .25 .60
521A Chris Archer .15 .40
521B Chris Archer SP 20.00 50.00
No cap
522 Alex Avila .20 .50
523 Blake Swihart FS .20 .50
524 Justin Nicolino FS .15 .40
525 Jurickson Profar .20 .50
526 T.J. McFarland .15 .40
527 Jordy Mercer .15 .40
528 Byron Buxton FS .25 .60
529 Zack Wheeler .20 .50
530 Caleb Cotham RC .30 .75
531 Cody Allen .15 .40
532 Matt Marksberry RC .25 .60
533 Jonathan Villar .15 .40
534 Eduardo Nunez .15 .40
535 Ivan Nova .20 .50
536 Alex Wood .15 .40
537 Tampa Bay Rays .15 .40
538 Michael Reed RC .25 .60
539 Nate Karns .15 .40
540 Curt Casali .15 .40
541 James Shields .15 .40
542A Scott Van Slyke .15 .40
542B Scott Van Slyke SP 2.00 5.00
42 jersey
543 Carlos Rodon FS .25 .60
544 Jeremy Jeffress .15 .40
545A Hector Santiago .15 .40
545B Hector Santiago SP 2.00 5.00
42 jersey
546 Ricky Nolasco .15 .40
547 Nick Goody RC .30 .75
548A Lucas Duda .20 .50
548B Lucas Duda SP 2.50 6.00
42 jersey/Entering dugout
548C Lucas Duda SP 30.00 80.00
Blue jersey
549 Luke Jackson RC .25 .60
550A Dallas Keuchel .20 .50
550B Dallas Keuchel SP 25.00 60.00
Jacket on shoulder
551 Steven Matz FS .15 .40
552 Texas Rangers .15 .40
553 Adrian Houser RC .25 .60
554A Daniel Murphy .20 .50
554B Murphy SP Press conf 60.00 150.00
555 Franklin Gutierrez .15 .40
556 Abraham Almonte .15 .40
557 Alexi Amarista .15 .40
558 Sean Rodriguez .15 .40
559 Cliff Pennington .15 .40
560 Kennys Vargas .15 .40
561 Kyle Gibson .20 .50
562 Addison Russell FS .25 .60
563 Lance McCullers FS .15 .40
564 Tanner Roark .15 .40
565 Matt den Dekker .15 .40
566 Alex Rodriguez .30 .75
567 Carlos Beltran .20 .50
568 Arizona Diamondbacks .15 .40
569 Los Angeles Dodgers .15 .40
570 Corey Dickerson .15 .40
571 Mark Reynolds .15 .40
572 Marcell Ozuna .25 .60
573 Tom Koehler .15 .40
574 Ryan Dull RC .25 .60
575 Ryan Strausborger RC .25 .60
576 Tyler Duffey RC .25 .60
577 Jason Gurka RC .25 .60
578 Mike Leake .15 .40
579A Michael Wacha .20 .50
579B Michael Wacha SP 25.00 60.00
Hand goggles
580 Socrates Brito RC .25 .60
581 Zach Davies RC .30 .75
582 Jose Quintana .15 .40
583A Didi Gregorius .20 .50
583B Didi Gregorius SP 25.00 60.00
Golden sky
584 Adam Duvall RC .60 1.50
585 Raisel Iglesias FS .20 .50
586 Chris Stewart .15 .40
587 Neftali Feliz .15 .40
588 Cole Hamels .20 .50
589 Derek Holland .15 .40
590 Anthony Gose .15 .40
591 Trevor Plouffe .15 .40
592 Adrian Beltre .25 .60
593 Alex Cobb .15 .40
594 Lonnie Chisenhall .15 .40
595 Mike Napoli .15 .40
596 Sergio Romo .15 .40
597 Chi Chi Gonzalez .15 .40
598 Khris Davis .25 .60
599 Domingo Santana .20 .50
600A Madison Bumgarner .20 .50
600B Bmgrnr SP Hoodie 30.00 80.00
601 Leonys Martin .15 .40
602 Keith Hessler RC .25 .60
603 Shawn Armstrong RC .25 .60
604 Jeff Samardzija .15 .40
605 Santiago Casilla .15 .40
606 Miguel Almonte RC .25 .60
607 Brandon Drury RC .40 1.00
608 Rick Porcello .20 .50
609A Billy Hamilton .20 .50
609B Billy Hamilton SP 30.00 80.00
w/Bat
610 Adam Morgan .15 .40
611 Darin Ruf .15 .40
612 Cincinnati Reds .15 .40
613 Milwaukee Brewers .15 .40
614 Dalton Pompey .20 .50
615 Miguel Castro .15 .40
616 Keone Kela .15 .40
617 Justin Smoak .15 .40
618 Desmond Jennings .20 .50
619 Dustin Ackley .15 .40
620 Daniel Hudson .15 .40
621 Zach Duke .15 .40
622 Ken Giles .15 .40
623 Tyler Saladino .15 .40
624 Tommy Milone .15 .40
625A Wil Myers .20 .50
625B Wil Myers SP 2.50 6.00
42 jersey
626 Danny Valencia .20 .50
627 Mike Fiers .15 .40
628 Wellington Castillo .15 .40
629 Patrick Corbin .20 .50
630 Michael Saunders .20 .50
631 Chris Reed RC .25 .60
632 Ramon Cabrera RC .25 .60
633 Martin Perez .20 .50
634 Jorge Lopez RC .25 .60
635 A.J. Pierzynski .15 .40
636 Arodys Vizcaino .15 .40
637 Stephen Strasburg .25 .60
638 Michael Pineda .15 .40
639 Rubby De La Rosa .15 .40
640 Carl Edwards Jr. RC .30 .75
641 Vidal Nuno .15 .40
642 Mike Pelfrey .15 .40
643 Yoenis Cespedes .25 .60
David Wright/Elite Meet and Greet
644 Los Angeles Angels .15 .40
645 Danny Santana .15 .40
646 Brad Miller .20 .50
647 Eduardo Rodriguez FS .15 .40
648 San Francisco Giants .15 .40
649 Aroldis Chapman .25 .60
650 Carlos Correa FS .25 .60
651 Dioner Navarro .15 .40
652A Collin McHugh .15 .40
652B Collin McHugh SP 2.00 5.00
42 jersey
653 Chris Iannetta .15 .40
654 Brandon Guyer .15 .40
655 Domonic Brown .20 .50
656 Randal Grichuk FS .15 .40
657 Johnny Giavotella .15 .40
658A Wilson Ramos .15 .40
658B Wilson Ramos SP 2.00 5.00
42 jersey
659 Adonis Garcia .15 .40
660 John Axford .15 .40
661A DJ LeMahieu .25 .60
661B DJ LeMahieu SP 3.00 8.00
42 jersey/Facing right
661C DJ LeMahieu SP 30.00 80.00
Black hoodie
662 Masahiro Tanaka .20 .50
663 Jake Petricka .15 .40
664 Mikie Mahtook .15 .40
665A Jared Hughes .15 .40
665B Jared Hughes SP 2.00 5.00
42 jersey
666 J.T. Realmuto FS .25 .60
667 James McCann FS .25 .60
668 Javier Baez FS .30 .75
669 Tyler Skaggs .15 .40
670 Will Smith .15 .40
671 Tony Cingrani .20 .50
672 Shane Peterson .15 .40
673A Justin Upton .20 .50
673B Justin Upton SP 30.00 80.00
w/Microphone
674 Tyler Chatwood .15 .40
675 Gary Sanchez RC .75 2.00
676 Jarred Cosart .15 .40
677 Derek Norris .15 .40
678A Carlos Martinez .20 .50
678B Carlos Martinez SP 30.00 80.00
Hands together
679 Nate Jones .15 .40
680 Tuffy Gosewisch .15 .40
681 Joe Smith .15 .40
682 Danny Duffy .15 .40
683A Carlos Gonzalez .20 .50
683B Carlos Gonzalez SP 2.50 6.00
42 jersey/Batting
684 Jarrod Dyson .15 .40
685 Kyle Waldrop RC .30 .75
686 Brandon Finnegan FS .15 .40
687 Chris Owings .15 .40
688 Shawn Tolleson .15 .40
689 Eugenio Suarez .20 .50
690 Jimmy Nelson .15 .40
691 Kris Medlen .20 .50
692 Giovanni Soto RC .30 .75
693 Josh Tomlin .15 .40
694 Scott McGough RC .25 .60
695 Kyle Crockett .15 .40
696A Lorenzo Cain .15 .40
696B Lorenzo Cain SP 2.00 5.00
42 jersey
696C Lorenzo Cain SP 20.00 50.00
Parade
697 Andrew Cashner .15 .40
698 Matt Moore .20 .50
699 Justin Bour FS .20 .50
700A Ichiro Suzuki .30 .75
700B Ichiro SP 42 jersey 4.00 10.00
701 Tyler Flowers .15 .40

2016 Topps Black

*BLACK: 10X TO 25X BASIC
*BLACK RC: 6X TO 15X BASIC RC
SER.1 ODDS 1:83 HOBBY; 1:17 JUMBO
SER.2 ODDS 1:50 HOBBY
STATED PRINT RUN 64 SER.#'d SETS
1 Mike Trout 30.00 80.00
2 Jerad Eickhoff 12.00 30.00
20 Andrew McCutchen 15.00 40.00
24 Clayton Kershaw 12.00 30.00
26 Dvs/Trt/Cruz LL 12.00 30.00
54 Jung Ho Kang FS 10.00 25.00
56 Salvador Perez WSH 10.00 25.00
66 Kyle Schwarber 30.00 80.00
78 Miguel Sano 25.00 60.00
100 Bryce Harper 15.00 40.00
134 Yadier Molina 12.00 30.00
137 Joe Panik 10.00 25.00
175 Manny Machado 8.00 20.00
254 Matt Holliday 10.00 25.00
255 Justin Verlander 6.00 15.00
337 Arndo/Hrpr/Gnzlz LL 6.00 15.00
338 Gldschmdt/Grdn/Hrpr LL 6.00 15.00
350 Kris Bryant FS 25.00 60.00
453 A.Rizzo/K.Bryant 8.00 20.00

2016 Topps Black and White Negative

*BW NEGATIVE: 8X TO 20X BASIC
*BW NEGATIVE RC: 5X TO 12X BASIC
SER.1 ODDS 1:1108 HOBBY, 1:22 J
SER.2 ODDS 1:65 HOBBY
1 Mike Trout 25.00 60.00
24 Clayton Kershaw 12.00 30.00
26 Dvs/Trt/Cruz LL 12.00 30.00
54 Jung Ho Kang FS 10.00 25.00
56 Salvador Perez WSH 10.00 25.00
78 Miguel Sano 20.00 50.00
100 Bryce Harper 15.00 40.00
134 Yadier Molina 12.00 30.00
137 Joe Panik 10.00 25.00
150 Clayton Kershaw 12.00 30.00
175 Manny Machado 6.00 15.00
254 Matt Holliday 10.00 25.00
255 Justin Verlander 6.00 15.00
337 Arndo/Hrpr/Gnzlz LL 6.00 15.00
338 Gldschmdt/Grdn/Hrpr LL 6.00 15.00
350 Kris Bryant FS 20.00 50.00
453 A.Rizzo/K.Bryant 6.00 15.00

2016 Topps Factory Set Sparkle Foil

*SPARKLE: 8X TO 20X BASIC
*SPARKLE RC: 5X TO 12X BASIC RC
STATED PRINT RUN 177 SER.#'d SETS
1 Mike Trout 25.00 60.00
24 Clayton Kershaw 10.00 25.00
26 Dvs/Trt/Cruz LL 10.00 25.00
54 Jung Ho Kang FS 8.00 20.00
56 Salvador Perez WSH 8.00 20.00
78 Miguel Sano 20.00 50.00
100 Bryce Harper 12.00 30.00
134 Yadier Molina 10.00 25.00
150 Clayton Kershaw 10.00 25.00
175 Manny Machado 6.00 15.00
254 Matt Holliday 8.00 20.00
255 Justin Verlander 5.00 12.00
337 Arndo/Hrpr/Gnzlz LL 5.00 12.00
338 Gldschmdt/Grdn/Hrpr LL 5.00 12.00
350 Kris Bryant FS 20.00 50.00
453 A.Rizzo/K.Bryant 6.00 15.00

2016 Topps Gold

*GOLD: 2X TO 5X BASIC
*GOLD RC: 1.2X TO 3X BASIC RC
SER.1 ODDS 1:11 HOBBY, 1:3 JUMBO
SER.2 ODDS 1:6 HOBBY
146 Stephen Piscotty 6.00 15.00

2016 Topps Limited

COMPLETE SET (700) 90.00 150.00
1 Mike Trout 5.00 12.00
2 Jerad Eickhoff 1.00 2.50
3 Richie Shaffer .60 1.50
4 Sonny Gray .75 2.00
5 Kyle Seager .60 1.50
6 Jimmy Paredes .60 1.50
8 Michael Brantley .75 2.00
9 Eric Hosmer .75 2.00
10 Nelson Cruz 1.00 2.50
11 Andre Ethier .75 2.00
12 Nolan Arenado 1.50 4.00
13 Craig Kimbrel .75 2.00
14 Chris Davis .60 1.50
15 Ryan Howard .75 2.00
16 Rougned Odor .60 1.50
17 Billy Butler .60 1.50
18 Francisco Rodriguez .75 2.00
19 Delino DeShields Jr. FS .60 1.50
20 Andrew McCutchen 1.00 2.50
21 Mike Moustakas WSH .75 2.00
22 John Hicks .60 1.50
23 Jeff Francoeur .75 2.00
24 Clayton Kershaw 1.50 4.00
25 Brad Ziegler .60 1.50
26 Chris Davis 5.00 12.00
Mike Trout/Nelson Cruz LL
27 Alec Asher .60 1.50
28 Brian McCann .75 2.00
29 Altuve/Cabrera/Bogaerts 1.00 2.50
30 Yan Gomes .60 1.50
31 Travis d'Arnaud .75 2.00
32 Zack Greinke 1.00 2.50
33 Edinson Volquez .60 1.50
34 Omar Infante .60 1.50
35 Luke Hochevar .60 1.50
36 Miguel Montero .60 1.50
37 C.J. Cron .60 1.50
38 Jed Lowrie .60 1.50
39 Mark Trumbo .60 1.50
40 Jedd Gyorko .60 1.50
41 Josh Harrison .60 1.50
42 A.J. Ramos .60 1.50
43 Noah Syndergaard FS .75 2.00
44 David Freese .60 1.50
45 Ryan Zimmerman .75 2.00
46 Jhonny Peralta .60 1.50
47 Gio Gonzalez .75 2.00
48 J.J. Hoover .60 1.50
49 Ike Davis .60 1.50
50 Salvador Perez .75 2.00
51 Dustin Garneau .60 1.50
52 Julio Teheran .75 2.00
53 George Springer .75 2.00
54 Jung Ho Kang FS .60 1.50
55 Jesus Montero .60 1.50
56 Salvador Perez WSH .75 2.00
57 Adam Lind .75 2.00
58 Zack Greinke 1.50 4.00
Clayton Kershaw/Jake Arrieta LL
59 John Lamb .60 1.50
60 Shelby Miller .75 2.00
61 Johnny Cueto WSH .75 2.00
62 Trayce Thompson 1.00 2.50
63 Zach Britton .75 2.00
64 Corey Kluber .75 2.00
65 Pittsburgh Pirates .60 1.50
66 Kyle Schwarber 2.00 5.00
67 Matt Harvey .75 2.00
68 Odubel Herrera FS .75 2.00
69 Anibal Sanchez .60 1.50
70 Kendrys Morales .60 1.50
71 John Danks .60 1.50
72 Chris Young .60 1.50
73 Ketel Marte 1.25 3.00
74 Troy Tulowitzki 1.00 2.50
75 Rusney Castillo .60 1.50
76 Glen Perkins .60 1.50
77 Clay Buchholz .60 1.50
78 Miguel Sano 1.00 2.50
79 Seattle Mariners .60 1.50
80 Carson Smith .60 1.50
81 Alexei Ramirez .75 2.00
82 Michael Bourn .60 1.50
83 Starling Marte .75 2.00
84 Mookie Betts 2.00 5.00
85 Corey Seager 15.00 40.00
86 Wilmer Flores .75 2.00
87 Jorge De La Rosa .60 1.50
88 Ubaldo Jimenez .60 1.50
89 Edwin Encarnacion 1.00 2.50
90 Koji Uehara .60 1.50
91 Yasmani Grandal FS .60 1.50
92 Darren O'Day .60 1.50
93 Charlie Blackmon 1.00 2.50
94 Miguel Cabrera 1.00 2.50
95 Kole Calhoun FS .60 1.50
96 Jose Bautista .75 2.00
97 Ender Inciarte FS .60 1.50
98 Garrett Richards .75 2.00
99 Taijuan Walker .60 1.50
100 Bryce Harper 1.50 4.00
101 Justin Turner 1.00 2.50
102 Doug Fister .60 1.50
103 Trea Turner 2.00 5.00
104 Jeremy Hellickson .60 1.50
105 Marcus Semien 1.00 2.50
106 Jordan Walden .60 1.50
107 Kevin Siegrist .60 1.50
108 Ben Paulsen .60 1.50
109 Henry Owens .75 2.00
110 J.D. Martinez FS 1.00 2.50
111 Coco Crisp .60 1.50
112 Matt Kemp .75 2.00
113 Aaron Sanchez .75 2.00
114 Brett Lawrie .75 2.00
115 Aaron Harang .60 1.50
116 Brett Gardner .75 2.00
117 Liam Hendriks .60 1.50
118 Jose Fernandez 1.00 2.50
119 Sean Doolittle .60 1.50
120 Alcides Escobar WSH .75 2.00
121 Roberto Osuna FS .60 1.50
122 Melky Cabrera .60 1.50
123 J.P. Howell .60 1.50
124 Melvin Upton Jr. .75 2.00
125 Zack Greinke 1.50 4.00
Clayton Kershaw/Jake Arrieta LL
126 David Ortiz 1.25 3.00
Albert Pujols
127 Zach Lee .60 1.50
128 Eddie Rosario .75 2.00
129 Kendall Graveman .60 1.50
130 A.J. Pollock .60 1.50
131 Adam LaRoche .60 1.50
132 Joe Ross FS .60 1.50
133 Aaron Nola 1.25 3.00
134 Yadier Molina 1.25 3.00
135 Colby Rasmus .75 2.00
136 Michael Cuddyer .60 1.50
137 Joe Panik .60 1.50
138 Francisco Liriano .60 1.50
139 Yasiel Puig 1.00 2.50
140 Carlos Carrasco FS .75 2.00
141 Colin Rea .60 1.50
142 CC Sabathia .75 2.00
143 Oliver Perez .60 1.50
144 Jose Iglesias .75 2.00
145 Jon Niese .60 1.50
146 Stephen Piscotty 1.00 2.50
147 Dee Gordon .60 1.50
148 Yangervis Solarte .60 1.50
149 Chad Bettis .60 1.50
150 Clayton Kershaw 1.50 4.00
151 Jon Lester .75 2.00
152 Kyle Lohse .60 1.50
153 Jason Hammel .60 1.50
154 Hunter Pence .75 2.00
155 New York Yankees .60 1.50
156 Cameron Maybin .60 1.50
157 Darnell Sweeney .60 1.50
158 Henry Urrutia .60 1.50
159 Erick Aybar .60 1.50
160 Chris Sale 1.00 2.50
161 Phil Hughes .60 1.50
162 Jose Bautista .75 2.00
Josh Donaldson/Chris Davis LL
163 Joaquin Benoit .60 1.50
164 Andrew Heaney .60 1.50
165 Adam Eaton .60 1.50
166 Gldschmdt/Rizzo/Arndo LL 1.50 4.00
167 Jacoby Ellsbury .75 2.00
168 Nathan Eovaldi .75 2.00
169 Charlie Morton 1.00 2.50
170 Carlos Gomez .60 1.50
171 Matt Cain .75 2.00
172 Carter Capps .60 1.50
173 Jose Abreu 1.00 2.50
174 Jered Weaver .75 2.00
175 Manny Machado 1.00 2.50
176 Brandon Phillips .60 1.50
177 Gregor Blanco .60 1.50
178 Rob Refsnyder .75 2.00
179 Jose Peraza .75 2.00
180 Kevin Gausman 1.00 2.50
181 Minnesota Twins .60 1.50
182 Kevin Pillar .60 1.50
183 Andrelton Simmons .60 1.50
184 Travis Jankowski .60 1.50
185 Dallas Keuchel .75 2.00
Sonny Gray/David Price LL
186 Yasmany Tomas FS .60 1.50
187 Dallas Keuchel .75 2.00
Collin McHugh/David Price LL
188 Greg Bird .75 2.00
189 Jake McGee .75 2.00
190 Jeurys Familia .75 2.00
191 Brian Johnson .60 1.50
192 John Jaso .60 1.50
193 Trevor Bauer 1.25 3.00
194 Chase Headley .60 1.50
195 Jason Kipnis .75 2.00
196 Hunter Strickland .60 1.50
197 Neil Walker .60 1.50
198 Oakland Athletics .60 1.50
199 Jay Bruce .75 2.00
200 Josh Donaldson .75 2.00
201 Adam Jones .75 2.00
202 Colorado Rockies .60 1.50
203 Aaron Hill .60 1.50
204 Mark Teixeira .75 2.00
205 Taylor Jungmann FS .60 1.50
206 Alex Gordon .75 2.00
207 Maikel Franco FS .75 2.00
208 Kurt Suzuki .60 1.50
209 Max Scherzer 1.00 2.50
210 Mike Zunino .60 1.50
211 Nick Ahmed .60 1.50
212 Starlin Castro .60 1.50
213 Matt Shoemaker .75 2.00
214 Chris Colabello .60 1.50
215 Adrian Gonzalez .75 2.00
216 Logan Forsythe .60 1.50
217 Lance Lynn .60 1.50
218 Andrew Miller .75 2.00
219 Hector Olivera .75 2.00
220 Zack Greinke 1.00 2.50
Gerrit Cole/Jake Arrieta LL
221 Ryan LaMarre .60 1.50
222 Homer Bailey .60 1.50
223 Christian Yelich 1.25 3.00
224 Billy Burns FS .60 1.50
225 Scooter Gennett .75 2.00
226 Brian Ellington .60 1.50
227 David Murphy .60 1.50
228 Matt Garza .60 1.50
229 Jesse Hahn .60 1.50
230 Ryan Vogelsong .60 1.50
231 Chris Coghlan .60 1.50
232 Michael Conforto .75 2.00
233 J.J. Hardy .60 1.50
234 David Robertson .60 1.50
235 Blaine Boyer .60 1.50
236 Juan Lagares .60 1.50
237 Carlos Ruiz .60 1.50
238 Baltimore Orioles .60 1.50
239 Huston Street .60 1.50
240 Nick Markakis .75 2.00
241 Freddie Freeman 1.25 3.00
242 Matt Wisler FS .60 1.50
243 Luke Gregerson .60 1.50
244 Matt Carpenter 1.00 2.50
245 Tommy Kahnle .60 1.50
246 Dustin Pedroia 1.00 2.50
247 Yunel Escobar .60 1.50
248 Atlanta Braves .60 1.50
249 Carlos Gomez .60 1.50
250 Miguel Cabrera 1.00 2.50
251 Silvino Bracho .60 1.50
252 Jorge Soler 1.00 2.50
253 Nick Castellanos 1.00 2.50
254 Matt Holliday 1.00 2.50
255 Justin Verlander 1.00 2.50
256 C.J. Wilson .60 1.50
257 Jake Marisnick .60 1.50
258 Devon Travis FS .60 1.50
259 Paul Goldschmidt 1.00 2.50
260 Ryan Hanigan .60 1.50
261 Russell Martin .60 1.50
262 Ervin Santana .60 1.50
263 Joc Pederson FS .75 2.00
264 Jake Arrieta .75 2.00
265 Luis Severino .75 2.00
266 Jonathan Papelbon .75 2.00
267 Chris Heston FS .60 1.50
268 Robinson Cano .75 2.00
269 Giancarlo Stanton 1.00 2.50
270 Pat Neshek .60 1.50
271 Kevin Kiermaier .75 2.00
272 Denard Span .60 1.50
273 New York Mets .60 1.50
274 Ryan Goins .60 1.50
275 Ian Kinsler .75 2.00
276 Francisco Cervelli .60 1.50
277 Elvis Andrus .75 2.00
278 Evan Gattis .60 1.50
279 Alex Guerrero FS .75 2.00
280 Brock Holt .60 1.50
281 Alex Dickerson .60 1.50
282 Scott Feldman .60 1.50
283 Felix Hernandez .75 2.00
284 Jon Gray .60 1.50
285 Pablo Sandoval .75 2.00
286 Joe Mauer .75 2.00
287 Alcides Escobar .75 2.00
288 Jake Lamb FS .75 2.00
289 Nick Hundley .60 1.50
290 Zack Godley .60 1.50
291 Asdrubal Cabrera .75 2.00
292 Todd Frazier .60 1.50
293 Hyun-Jin Ryu .75 2.00
294 Chicago White Sox .60 1.50
295 Jonathan Schoop .60 1.50
296 Yordano Ventura .75 2.00
297 Detroit Tigers .60 1.50
298 Ryan Braun .75 2.00
299 Angel Pagan .60 1.50
300 Buster Posey 1.25 3.00
301 Wade Miley .60 1.50
302 Houston Astros .60 1.50
303 Steve Pearce 1.00 2.50
304 Charlie Furbush .60 1.50
305 Colby Lewis .60 1.50
306 Jarrod Saltalamacchia .60 1.50
307 Wade Davis .60 1.50
308 Brian Dozier .75 2.00
309 Shin-Soo Choo .60 1.50
310 David Wright .75 2.00
311 Dariel Alvarez .60 1.50
312 Curtis Granderson .75 2.00
313 Martin Maldonado .60 1.50
314 Kyle Hendricks 1.00 2.50
315 San Diego Padres .60 1.50
316 Jake Odorizzi FS .60 1.50
317 Jose Altuve .75 2.00
318 Washington Nationals .60 1.50
319 Adam Wainwright .75 2.00
320 Jake Peavy .60 1.50
321 Hanley Ramirez .75 2.00
322 Kelby Tomlinson .60 1.50
323 Jacob deGrom 2.00 5.00
324 Steven Souza Jr. .75 2.00
325 Kaleb Cowart .60 1.50
326 Kevin Plawecki FS .75 2.00
327 Anthony Rizzo 1.25 3.00
328 Anthony DeSclafani .60 1.50
329 Alex Rodriguez 1.25 3.00
330 Edward Mujica .60 1.50
331 Will Harris .60 1.50
332 Toronto Blue Jays .60 1.50
333 Keyvius Sampson .60 1.50
334 Brandon McCarthy .60 1.50
335 Mitch Moreland .60 1.50
336 Mark Melancon .60 1.50
337 Nolan Arenado 1.50 4.00
Bryce Harper/Carlos Gonzalez LL
338 Paul Goldschmidt 1.50 4.00
Dee Gordon/Bryce Harper LL
339 Carlos Santana .75 2.00
340 Victor Martinez .75 2.00
341 Josh Hamilton .75 2.00
342 Jayson Werth .75 2.00
343 Drew Hutchison .60 1.50
344 Jonathan Lucroy .75 2.00
345 Yonder Alonso .60 1.50
346 Corey Kluber .75 2.00
Dallas Keuchel/Marco Estrada LL
347 Jason Grilli .60 1.50
348 Seth Smith .60 1.50
349 Ben Revere .60 1.50
350 Kris Bryant FS 1.25 3.00
351 Chase Utley .75 2.00
352 Carson Blair .60 1.50
353 Joey Gallo .75 2.00
354 Tyson Ross .60 1.50
355 Avisail Garcia .75 2.00
356 Odrisamer Despaigne .60 1.50
357 Jace Peterson .60 1.50
358 Chris Young .60 1.50
359 Christian Colon .60 1.50
360 Eduardo Escobar .60 1.50
361 Jeff Locke .60 1.50
362 Cory Spangenberg .60 1.50
363 Brett Cecil .60 1.50
364 Keon Broxton .60 1.50
365 James Pazos .75 2.00
366 Scott Alexander .60 1.50
367 Pedro Alvarez .60 1.50
368 Xander Bogaerts 1.00 2.50
369 Dellin Betances .75 2.00
370 Bud Norris .60 1.50
371 Jason Heyward .75 2.00
372 Zack Cozart .60 1.50
373 Tucker Barnhart .60 1.50
374 Zach McAllister .60 1.50
375 Jordan Lyles .60 1.50
376 Brandon Barnes .60 1.50
377 Scott Kazmir .60 1.50
378 Jeff Mathis .75 2.00
379 Wei-Yin Chen .60 1.50
380 Michael Blazek .60 1.50
381 Bartolo Colon .60 1.50
382 David Ortiz 1.00 2.50
David Price/Winning Formula
383 Andres Blanco .60 1.50
384 Michael Morse .60 1.50
385 Jon Jay .60 1.50
386 Nori Aoki .60 1.50
387 Kansas City Clutch .60 1.50
388 Evan Longoria .75 2.00
389 Sam Dyson .60 1.50
390 Danny Espinosa .60 1.50
391 Matt Boyd FS .60 1.50
392 Jon Singleton .75 2.00
393 Kelvin Herrera .60 1.50
394 Abel De Los Santos .60 1.50
395 Raul Mondesi 1.25 3.00
396 Matt Reynolds .60 1.50
397 Mac Williamson .60 1.50
398 Cleveland Indians .60 1.50
399 Kansas City Royals .60 1.50
400 David Ortiz 1.00 2.50
401 Peter O'Brien .60 1.50
402 Daniel Norris FS .60 1.50
403 David Peralta .60 1.50
404 Miami Marlins .60 1.50
405 Ruben Tejada .60 1.50
406 Marwin Gonzalez .60 1.50
407 Yoenis Cespedes 1.00 2.50
408 Jason Castro .60 1.50
409 Jean Segura .75 2.00
410 Mike Moustakas .75 2.00
411 Brian Matusz .60 1.50
412 Mark Lowe .60 1.50
413 David Phelps .60 1.50
414 Wily Peralta .60 1.50
415 Brett Wallace .60 1.50
416 Johnny Cueto .75 2.00
417 Brad Boxberger .60 1.50
418 Yu Darvish 1.00 2.50
419 Aaron Altherr .60 1.50
420 Pedro Severino .60 1.50
421 Cesar Hernandez .60 1.50
422 Miguel Gonzalez .60 1.50
423 Carl Crawford .75 2.00
424 Brandon Belt .75 2.00
425 Jackie Bradley Jr. 1.00 2.50
426 Joey Votto 1.00 2.50
427 Travis Shaw .60 1.50
428 Gregory Polanco .75 2.00
429 Kenta Maeda 1.25 3.00
430 Ariel Pena .60 1.50
431 Philadelphia Phillies .60 1.50
432 Cameron Rupp .60 1.50
433 Trevor Brown .75 2.00
434 Matt Adams .60 1.50
435 Enrique Hernandez 1.00 2.50
436 Raudel Lazo .60 1.50
437 Michael Lorenzen .60 1.50
438 Paulo Orlando .60 1.50
439 Francisco Lindor FS 1.00 2.50
440 Tommy Pham FS .60 1.50
441 David Ross .60 1.50
442 Brandon Crawford .75 2.00
443 Prince Fielder .75 2.00
444 Jordan Zimmermann .75 2.00
445 Robbie Ray .60 1.50
446 Tom Murphy .60 1.50
447 Ben Zobrist .75 2.00
448 St. Louis Cardinals .60 1.50
449 J.A. Happ .75 2.00
450 David Price .75 2.00
451 Jose Reyes .75 2.00
452 Gerrit Cole 1.00 2.50
453 Rizzo/Bryant 1.25 3.00
454 Greg Holland .60 1.50
455 Preston Tucker .60 1.50
456 Gordon Beckham .60 1.50
457 Nick Swisher .75 2.00
458 Kenley Jansen .75 2.00
459 James Loney .60 1.50
460 Danny Salazar .75 2.00
461 Freddy Galvis .60 1.50
462 Jumbo Diaz .60 1.50
463 Boston Red Sox .60 1.50
464 Robinson Chirinos .60 1.50
465 Jesse Chavez .60 1.50
466 Marco Estrada .60 1.50
467 Giovanny Urshela 1.00 2.50
468 Rajai Davis .60 1.50
469 Logan Morrison .60 1.50
470 John Lackey .75 2.00
471 Kolten Wong .75 2.00
472 Josh Reddick .60 1.50
473 Robbie Erlin .60 1.50
474 Chicago Cubs .60 1.50
475 Max Kepler 1.00 2.50
476 Hisashi Iwakuma .75 2.00
477 Chris Tillman .60 1.50
478 Cody Asche .60 1.50
479 Marcus Stroman .75 2.00
480 Mike Foltynewicz .60 1.50
481 Hector Rondon .60 1.50
482 Drew Smyly .60 1.50
483 Erasmo Ramirez .60 1.50
484 Trevor Rosenthal .75 2.00
485 James Paxton .75 2.00
486 Chris Rusin .60 1.50
487 Martin Prado .60 1.50
488 Colton Murray .60 1.50
489 Adeiny Hechavarria .60 1.50
490 Guido Knudson .60 1.50
491 Rich Hill .60 1.50
492 Yadier Molina 1.25 3.00
Randal Grichuk/Many Healthy Returns
493 R.A. Dickey .75 2.00
494 Luis Avilan .60 1.50
495 Luke Maile .60 1.50
496 Brett Anderson .60 1.50
497 Devin Mesoraco .60 1.50
498 Steve Cishek .60 1.50
499 Carlos Perez .60 1.50
500 Albert Pujols 1.25 3.00
501 Alex Rios .75 2.00
502 Austin Hedges .60 1.50
503 Luis Valbuena .60 1.50
504 Elias Diaz .60 1.50
505 Frankie Montas .75 2.00
506 Stephen Vogt .75 2.00
507 Travis Wood .60 1.50
508 Jaime Garcia .60 1.50
509 Mark Canha .60 1.50
510 Tony Watson .60 1.50
511 Manny Banuelos 1.00 2.50
512 Ryan Madson .60 1.50
513 Caleb Joseph .60 1.50
514 Michael Taylor .60 1.50
515 Ryan Flaherty .60 1.50
516 Steve Johnson .60 1.50
517 Corey Knebel .60 1.50
518 Matt Duffy .60 1.50
519 Kyle Barraclough .60 1.50
520 Anthony Rendon 1.00 2.50
521 Chris Archer .60 1.50
522 Alex Avila .75 2.00
523 Blake Swihart FS .75 2.00
524 Justin Nicolino FS .60 1.50
525 Jurickson Profar .75 2.00
526 T.J. McFarland .60 1.50
527 Jordy Mercer .60 1.50
528 Byron Buxton FS 1.00 2.50
529 Zack Wheeler .75 2.00
530 Caleb Cotham .60 1.50
531 Cody Allen .60 1.50
532 Matt Marksberry .60 1.50
533 Jonathan Villar .60 1.50
534 Eduardo Nunez .60 1.50
535 Ivan Nova .75 2.00
536 Alex Wood .60 1.50
537 Tampa Bay Rays .60 1.50
538 Michael Reed .60 1.50
539 Nate Karns .60 1.50
540 Curt Casali .60 1.50
541 James Shields .60 1.50
542 Scott Van Slyke .60 1.50
543 Carlos Rodon FS 1.00 2.50
544 Jeremy Jeffress .60 1.50
545 Hector Santiago .60 1.50
546 Ricky Nolasco .60 1.50
547 Nick Goody .75 2.00
548 Lucas Duda .75 2.00
549 Luke Jackson .60 1.50
550 Dallas Keuchel .75 2.00
551 Steven Matz FS .60 1.50
552 Texas Rangers .60 1.50
553 Adrian Houser .60 1.50
554 Daniel Murphy .75 2.00
555 Franklin Gutierrez .60 1.50
556 Abraham Almonte .60 1.50
557 Alexi Amarista .60 1.50
558 Sean Rodriguez .60 1.50
559 Cliff Pennington .60 1.50
560 Kennys Vargas .60 1.50
561 Kyle Gibson .75 2.00

562 Addison Russell FS 1.00 2.50
563 Lance McCullers FS .60 1.50
564 Tanner Roark .60 1.50
565 Matt den Dekker .60 1.50
566 Alex Rodriguez 1.25 3.00
567 Carlos Beltran .75 2.00
568 Arizona Diamondbacks .60 1.50
569 Los Angeles Dodgers .60 1.50
570 Corey Dickerson .60 1.50
571 Mark Reynolds .60 1.50
572 Marcell Ozuna 1.00 2.50
573 Tom Koehler .60 1.50
574 Ryan Dull .60 1.50
575 Ryan Strausborger .60 1.50
576 Tyler Duffey .60 1.50
577 Jason Gurka .60 1.50
578 Mike Leake .60 1.50
579 Michael Wacha .75 2.00
580 Socrates Brito .60 1.50
581 Zach Davies .75 2.00
582 Jose Quintana .60 1.50
583 Didi Gregorius .75 2.00
584 Adam Duvall 1.50 4.00
585 Raisel Iglesias FS .75 2.00
586 Chris Stewart .60 1.50
587 Neftali Feliz .60 1.50
588 Cole Hamels .75 2.00
589 Derek Holland .60 1.50
590 Anthony Gose .60 1.50
591 Trevor Plouffe .60 1.50
592 Adrian Beltre 1.00 2.50
593 Alex Cobb .60 1.50
594 Lonnie Chisenhall .60 1.50
595 Mike Napoli .60 1.50
596 Sergio Romo .60 1.50
597 Chi Chi Gonzalez .60 1.50
598 Khris Davis 1.00 2.50
599 Domingo Santana .75 2.00
600 Madison Bumgarner .75 2.00
601 Leonys Martin .60 1.50
602 Keith Hessler .60 1.50
603 Shawn Armstrong .60 1.50
604 Jeff Samardzija .60 1.50
605 Santiago Casilla .60 1.50
606 Miguel Almonte .60 1.50
607 Brandon Drury 1.00 2.50
608 Rick Porcello .75 2.00
609 Billy Hamilton .75 2.00
610 Adam Morgan .60 1.50
611 Darin Ruf .60 1.50
612 Cincinnati Reds .60 1.50
613 Milwaukee Brewers .60 1.50
614 Dalton Pompey .75 2.00
615 Miguel Castro .60 1.50
616 Keone Kela .60 1.50
617 Justin Smoak .60 1.50
618 Desmond Jennings .75 2.00
619 Dustin Ackley .60 1.50
620 Daniel Hudson .60 1.50
621 Zach Duke .60 1.50
622 Ken Giles .60 1.50
623 Tyler Saladino .60 1.50
624 Tommy Milone .60 1.50
625 Wil Myers .75 2.00
626 Danny Valencia .75 2.00
627 Mike Fiers .60 1.50
628 Wellington Castillo .60 1.50
629 Patrick Corbin .75 2.00
630 Michael Saunders .75 2.00
631 Chris Reed .60 1.50
632 Ramon Cabrera .60 1.50
633 Martin Perez .75 2.00
634 Jorge Lopez .60 1.50
635 A.J. Pierzynski .60 1.50
636 Arodys Vizcaino .60 1.50
637 Stephen Strasburg 1.00 2.50
638 Michael Pineda .60 1.50
639 Rubby De La Rosa .60 1.50
640 Carl Edwards Jr. .75 2.00
641 Vidal Nuno .60 1.50
642 Mike Pelfrey .60 1.50
643 Yoenis Cespedes 1.00 2.50
David Wright/Elite Meet and Greet
644 Los Angeles Angels .60 1.50
645 Danny Santana .60 1.50
646 Brad Miller .75 2.00
647 Eduardo Rodriguez FS .60 1.50
648 San Francisco Giants .60 1.50
649 Aroldis Chapman 1.00 2.50
650 Carlos Correa FS 1.00 2.50
651 Dioner Navarro .60 1.50
652 Collin McHugh .60 1.50
653 Chris Iannetta .60 1.50
654 Brandon Guyer .60 1.50
655 Domonic Brown .75 2.00
656 Randal Grichuk FS .75 2.00
657 Johnny Giavotella .60 1.50
658 Wilson Ramos .60 1.50
659 Adonis Garcia .60 1.50
660 John Axford .60 1.50
661 DJ LeMahieu 1.00 2.50
662 Masahiro Tanaka .75 2.00
663 Jake Petricka .60 1.50
664 Mikie Mahtook .60 1.50
665 Jared Hughes .60 1.50
666 J.T. Realmuto FS 1.00 2.50
667 James McCann FS .75 2.00
668 Javier Baez FS 1.25 3.00
669 Tyler Skaggs .60 1.50
670 Will Smith .60 1.50
671 Tony Cingrani .75 2.00
672 Shane Peterson .60 1.50
673 Justin Upton .75 2.00
674 Tyler Chatwood .60 1.50
675 Gary Sanchez 2.00 5.00
676 Jarred Cosart .60 1.50
677 Derek Norris .60 1.50
678 Carlos Martinez .75 2.00
679 Nate Jones .60 1.50
680 Tuffy Gosewisch .60 1.50
681 Joe Smith .60 1.50
682 Danny Duffy .60 1.50
683 Carlos Gonzalez .75 2.00
684 Jarrod Dyson .60 1.50
685 Kyle Waldrop .75 2.00
686 Brandon Finnegan FS .60 1.50
687 Chris Owings .60 1.50
688 Shawn Tolleson .60 1.50
689 Eugenio Suarez .75 2.00
690 Jimmy Nelson .60 1.50
691 Kris Medlen .75 2.00
692 Giovanni Soto .75 2.00
693 Josh Tomlin .60 1.50
694 Scott McGough .60 1.50
695 Kyle Crockett .60 1.50
696 Lorenzo Cain .60 1.50
697 Andrew Cashner .60 1.50
698 Matt Moore .75 2.00
699 Justin Bour FS .75 2.00
700 Ichiro Suzuki 1.25 3.00
701 Tyler Flowers .60 1.50

2016 Topps Pink

*PINK: 10X TO 25X BASIC
*PINK RC: 6X TO 15X BASIC RC
SER.1 ODDS 1:535 HOBBY; 1:107 JUMBO
SER.2 ODDS 1:293 HOBBY
STATED PRINT RUN 50 SER.#'d SETS
1 Mike Trout 30.00 80.00
20 Andrew McCutchen 15.00 40.00
24 Clayton Kershaw 12.00 30.00
26 Dvs/Trt/Cruz LL 12.00 30.00
54 Jung Ho Kang FS 10.00 25.00
56 Salvador Perez WSH 10.00 25.00
66 Kyle Schwarber 30.00 80.00
78 Miguel Sano 25.00 60.00
100 Bryce Harper 15.00 40.00
134 Yadier Molina 12.00 30.00
137 Joe Panik 10.00 25.00
150 Clayton Kershaw 12.00 30.00
175 Manny Machado 8.00 20.00
254 Matt Holliday 10.00 25.00
255 Justin Verlander 6.00 15.00
337 Arndo/Hrpr/Gnzlz LL 6.00 15.00
338 Gldschmdt/Grdn/Hrpr LL 6.00 15.00
350 Kris Bryant FS 25.00 60.00
453 A.Rizzo/K.Bryant 8.00 20.00

2016 Topps Rainbow Foil

*RAINBOW: 2X TO 5X BASIC
*RAINBOW RC: 1.2X TO 3X BASIC RC
SER.1 ODDS 1:10 HOBBY, 1:2 JUMBO
SER.2 ODDS 1:10 HOBBY

2016 Topps Toys R Us Purple

*PURPLE: 5X TO 12X BASIC
*PURPLE RC: 3X TO 8X BASIC RC
INSERTED IN TRU PACKS

2016 Topps Vintage Stock

*VINTAGE: 8X TO 20X BASIC
*VINTAGE RC: 5X TO 12X BASIC RC
SER.1 ODDS 1:270 HOBBY, 1:54 JUMBO
SER.2 ODDS 1:148 HOBBY
STATED PRINT RUN 99 SER.#'d SETS
1 Mike Trout 25.00 60.00
24 Clayton Kershaw 10.00 25.00
26 Dvs/Trt/Cruz LL 10.00 25.00
54 Jung Ho Kang FS 8.00 20.00
56 Salvador Perez WSH 8.00 20.00
78 Miguel Sano 20.00 50.00
100 Bryce Harper 12.00 30.00
134 Yadier Molina 10.00 25.00
150 Clayton Kershaw 10.00 25.00
175 Manny Machado 6.00 15.00
254 Matt Holliday 8.00 20.00
255 Justin Verlander 5.00 12.00
337 Arndo/Hrpr/Gnzlz LL 5.00 12.00
338 Gldschmdt/Grdn/Hrpr LL 5.00 12.00
350 Kris Bryant FS 20.00 50.00
453 A.Rizzo/K.Bryant 6.00 15.00

2016 Topps 100 Years at Wrigley Field

COMPLETE SET (50) 15.00 40.00
SER.1 ODDS 1:8 HOBBY; 1:2 JUMBO
SER.2 ODDS 1:8 HOBBY
WRIG1 Kris Bryant .60 1.50
WRIG2 Ryne Sandberg .60 1.50
WRIG3 Greg Maddux .60 1.50
WRIG4 Mark Grace .40 1.00
WRIG5 Jake Arrieta .40 1.00
WRIG6 Mark Prior .40 1.00
WRIG7 Bruce Sutter .40 1.00
WRIG8 Fergie Jenkins .40 1.00
WRIG9 Goose Gossage .40 1.00
WRIG10 Stan Musial .75 2.00
WRIG11 Andre Dawson .40 1.00
WRIG12 Anthony Rizzo .60 1.50
WRIG13 Addison Russell .50 1.25
WRIG14 Wrigley Field Marquee Installed .30 .75
WRIG15 Cubs Park
Becomes Wrigley Field .30 .75
WRIG16 Maddux/Jenkins .60 1.50
WRIG17 Jimmie Foxx .50 1.25
WRIG18 William Wrigley Jr. becomes majority shareholder of the Cubs .30 .75
WRIG19 Babe Ruth 1.25 3.00
WRIG20 Aramis Ramirez .30 .75
WRIG21 Cole Hamels .40 1.00
WRIG22 Rafael Palmeiro .40 1.00
WRIG23 Ted Williams 1.00 2.50
WRIG24 Clark
Mascot .30 .75
WRIG25 Kyle Schwarber 1.00 2.50
WRIG26 Mark Grace .40 1.00
WRIG27 Billy Williams .40 1.00
WRIG28 Fergie Jenkins .40 1.00
WRIG29 Anthony Rizzo .60 1.50
WRIG30 Mark Prior .40 1.00
WRIG31 Jorge Soler .50 1.25
WRIG32 Kyle Schwarber 1.00 2.50
WRIG33 Rafael Palmeiro .40 1.00
WRIG34 Andre Dawson .40 1.00
WRIG35 Kris Bryant .60 1.50
WRIG36 Ryne Sandberg 1.00 2.50
WRIG37 Ron Santo .40 1.00
WRIG38 Greg Maddux .60 1.50
WRIG39 Addison Russell .50 1.25
WRIG40 Jason Heyward .40 1.00
WRIG41 Jon Lester .40 1.00
WRIG42 Bruce Sutter .40 1.00
WRIG43 Tom Glavine .40 1.00
WRIG44 Bricks and Ivy .30 .75
WRIG45 Jackie Robinson .50 1.25
WRIG46 Weeghman Park .30 .75
WRIG47 Ronald Reagan .30 .75
WRIG48 The Friendly Confines .30 .75
WRIG49 Hal Newhouser .40 1.00
WRIG50 Lou Gehrig 1.00 2.50

2016 Topps 100 Years at Wrigley Field Autographs

SER.1 ODDS 1:30,058 HOBBY; 1:5942 JUMBO
SER.2 ODDS 1:16,848 HOBBY
STATED PRINT RUN 25 SER.#'d SETS
SER.1 EXCH DEADLINE 1/31/2018
WRIGAAD Andre Dawson S2 60.00 150.00
WRIGAARI Anthony Rizzo S2 75.00 200.00
WRIGABS Bruce Sutter 10.00 25.00
WRIGABW Billy Williams S2 25.00 60.00
WRIGAEB Ernie Banks 60.00 150.00
WRIGAFJ Fergie Jenkins S2 15.00 40.00
WRIGAFJ Fergie Jenkins
WRIGAGG Goose Gossage 25.00 60.00
WRIGAGM Greg Maddux
WRIGAJS Jorge Soler S2 40.00 100.00
WRIGAKB Bryant S2 Celebrate 200.00 300.00
WRIGAKB Kris Bryant 200.00 300.00
WRIGAKS Kyle Schwarber S2
WRIGAMG Grace S2 Face left 30.00 80.00
WRIGAMG Mark Grace 30.00 80.00
WRIGAMP Mark Prior 20.00 50.00
WRIGARP Rafael Palmeiro S2
WRIGARS Ryne Sandberg 60.00 150.00
WRIGARSN Ron Santo S2 60.00 150.00
WRIGASM Stan Musial 60.00 150.00

2016 Topps 100 Years at Wrigley Field Relics

SER.1 ODDS 1:5075 HOBBY; 1:1015 JUMBO
SER.2 ODDS 1:2856 HOBBY
STATED PRINT RUN 99 SER.#'d SETS
WRIGRAD Andre Dawson S2 8.00 20.00
Waist up
WRIGRAD Andre Dawson 8.00 20.00
Fully body
WRIGRAR Anthony Rizzo 12.00 30.00
w/Fan
WRIGRARA Aramis Ramirez 6.00 15.00
WRIGRARI Anthony Rizzo S2 12.00 30.00
Batting
WRIGRARU Addison Russell S2 10.00 25.00
Dugout
WRIGRARU Addison Russell 10.00 25.00
Batting
WRIGRBS Bruce Sutter 8.00 20.00
WRIGRCH Cole Hamels 12.00 30.00
WRIGRFJ Fergie Jenkins 8.00 20.00
WRIGRGG Goose Gossage 8.00 20.00
WRIGRGM Maddux Pitching 12.00 30.00
WRIGRGM Maddux Microphone 12.00 30.00
WRIGRJA Jake Arrieta S2 12.00 30.00
WRIGRJH Jason Heyward S2 8.00 20.00
WRIGRJL Jon Lester S2 8.00 20.00
WRIGRJS Jorge Soler S2 15.00 40.00
WRIGRKB Bryant Celebrate 20.00 50.00
WRIGRKB Bryant Face left 20.00 50.00
WRIGRKS Kyle Schwarber S2 12.00 30.00
WRIGRMG Mark Grace S2 10.00 25.00
Facing left
WRIGRMG Mark Grace 10.00 25.00
Facing right
WRIGRRP Rafael Palmeiro S2 8.00 20.00
Batting
WRIGRRP Rafael Palmeiro 8.00 20.00
Running
WRIGRRS Sandberg Whte jsy 15.00 40.00
WRIGRRSA Sandberg Blue jsy 15.00 40.00
WRIGRRSN Ron Santo S2 20.00 50.00
WRIGRSC Starlin Castro 6.00 15.00
WRIGRTG Tom Glavine S2 8.00 20.00
WRIGRTMO Greg Maddux 6.00 15.00
Fergie Jekins/Take Me Out to the Ballgame Tradition Begins

2016 Topps Amazing Milestones

COMPLETE SET (10) 10.00 25.00
RANDOM INSERTS IN PACKS
AM01 Warren Spahn .50 1.25
AM02 Alex Rodriguez .75 2.00
AM03 Carl Yastrzemski 1.00 2.50
AM04 Ted Williams 1.25 3.00
AM05 Nolan Ryan 2.00 5.00
AM06 Hank Aaron 1.25 3.00
AM07 Babe Ruth 1.50 4.00
AM08 Greg Maddux .75 2.00
AM09 Rickey Henderson .60 1.50
AM10 Willie Mays 1.25 3.00

2016 Topps Back to Back

COMPLETE SET (15) 3.00 8.00
STATED ODDS 1:8 HOBBY; 1:2 JUMBO
B2B1 R.Braun/P.Fielder .30 .75
B2B2 K.Bryant/A.Rizzo .50 1.25
B2B3 B.Posey/B.Belt .50 1.25
B2B4 Griffey Jr./Martinez .75 2.00
B2B5 B.Phillips/J.Votto .40 1.00
B2B6 J.Pederson/A.Gonzalez .30 .75
B2B7 J.Bagwell/C.Biggio .30 .75
B2B8 P.Molitor/R.Yount .40 1.00
B2B9 Schoendienst/Musial .60 1.50
B2B10 Martinez/Cabrera .40 1.00
B2B11 Pujols/Trout 2.00 5.00
B2B12 Ruth/Gehrig 1.00 2.50
B2B13 Doerr/Williams .75 2.00
B2B14 Murray/Ripken Jr. 1.25 3.00
B2B15 Tulowitzki/Donaldson .40 1.00

2016 Topps Back to Back Autographs

STATED ODDS 1:60,115 HOBBY; 1:12,233 JUMBO
STATED PRINT RUN 25 SER.#'d SETS
EXCHANGE DEADLINE 1/31/2018
B2BAFB R.Braun/P.Fielder
B2BAMG Martinez/Griffey Jr. 100.00 250.00
B2BAPB B.Belt/B.Posey 60.00 150.00
B2BARB K.Bryant/A.Rizzo
B2BAVP J.Votto/B.Phillips 50.00 120.00

2016 Topps Back to Back Relics

STATED ODDS 1:15,324 HOBBY; 1:3059 JUMBO
STATED PRINT RUN 99 SER.#'d SETS
B2BRFB P.Fielder/R.Braun 5.00 12.00
B2BRMG E.Martinez/K.Griffey Jr. 15.00 40.00
B2BRPB B.Posey/B.Belt 8.00 20.00
B2BRRB A.Rizzo/K.Bryant 30.00 80.00
B2BRVP J.Votto/B.Phillips 6.00 15.00

2016 Topps Berger's Best

COMPLETE SET (65) 25.00 60.00
STATED ODDS 1:4 HOBBY
BB1 Willie Mays .75 2.00
BB2 Satchel Paige .40 1.00
BB3 Henry Aaron .75 2.00
BB4 Sandy Koufax .75 2.00
BB5 Jackie Robinson .40 1.00
BB6 Ted Williams .75 2.00
BB7 Roger Maris .40 1.00
BB8 Roberto Clemente 1.00 2.50
BB9 Willie McCovey .30 .75
BB10 Bill Mazeroski .30 .75
BB11 Roger Maris .40 1.00
BB12 Brooks Robinson .30 .75
BB13 Whitey Ford .30 .75
BB14 Hank Aaron .75 2.00
BB15 Jim Palmer .30 .75
BB16 Steve Carlton .30 .75
BB17 Rod Carew .30 .75
BB18 Reggie Jackson .30 .75
BB19 Johnny Bench .40 1.00
BB20 Nolan Ryan 1.25 3.00
BB21 Tom Seaver .30 .75
BB22 Joe Morgan .30 .75
BB23 Dave Winfield .30 .75
BB24 George Brett .75 2.00
BB25 Dennis Eckersley .30 .75
BB26 Robin Yount .40 1.00
BB27 Eddie Murray .30 .75
BB28 Ozzie Smith .50 1.25
BB29 Rickey Henderson .40 1.00
BB30 Harold Baines .30 .75
BB31 Cal Ripken Jr. 1.25 3.00
BB32 Tony Gwynn .40 1.00
BB33 Don Mattingly .75 2.00
BB34 Dwight Gooden .25 .60
BB35 Roger Clemens .50 1.25
BB36 Bo Jackson .40 1.00
BB37 Wade Boggs .30 .75
BB38 Ken Griffey Jr. .75 2.00
BB39 George Brett .75 2.00
BB40 Frank Thomas .40 1.00
BB41 Cal Ripken Jr. 1.25 3.00
BB42 Randy Johnson .40 1.00
BB43 Mike Piazza .40 1.00
BB44 Barry Larkin .30 .75
BB45 John Smoltz .40 1.00
BB46 Livan Hernandez .25 .60
BB47 Alex Rodriguez .50 1.25
BB48 Josh Hamilton .30 .75
BB49 Miguel Cabrera .40 1.00
BB50 Albert Pujols .50 1.25
BB51 Joe Mauer .30 .75
BB52 Robinson Cano .30 .75
BB53 Yadier Molina .50 1.25
BB54 Justin Verlander .40 1.00
BB55 Hanley Ramirez .30 .75
BB56 Daisuke Matsuzaka .30 .75
BB57 Clayton Kershaw .60 1.50
BB58 David Price .30 .75
BB59 Stephen Strasburg .40 1.00
BB60 Mike Trout 2.00 5.00
BB61 Bryce Harper .60 1.50
BB62 Mike Trout 2.00 5.00
BB63 Masahiro Tanaka .30 .75
BB64 Kris Bryant .50 1.25
BB65 Buster Posey .50 1.25

2016 Topps Berger's Best Series 2

COMPLETE SET (65) 25.00 60.00
STATED ODDS 1:4 HOBBY
BB21952 Eddie Mathews .40 1.00
BB21953 Willie Mays .75 2.00
BB21954 Al Kaline .40 1.00
BB21955 Roberto Clemente 1.00 2.50
BB21956 Ted Williams .75 2.00
BB21957 Hank Aaron .75 2.00
BB21958 Roberto Clemente 1.00 2.50
BB21959 Sandy Koufax .75 2.00
BB21960 Carl Yastrzemski .60 1.50
BB21961 Roger Maris .40 1.00
BB21962 Lou Brock .30 .75
BB21963 Stan Musial .60 1.50
BB21964 H.Aaron/W.Mays .75 2.00
BB21965 Willie Mays .75 2.00
BB21966 Frank Robinson .30 .75
BB21967 Tony Perez .30 .75
BB21968 Tom Seaver .30 .75
BB21969 Johnny Bench .40 1.00
BB21970 Reggie Jackson .30 .75
BB21971 Bert Blyleven .30 .75
BB21972 Hank Aaron .75 2.00
BB21973 Rich Gossage .30 .75
BB21974 Hank Aaron .75 2.00
BB21975 Robin Yount .40 1.00
BB21976 Nolan Ryan 1.25 3.00
BB21977 Bruce Sutter .30 .75
BB21978 Brooks Robinson .30 .75
BB21979 Rollie Fingers .30 .75
BB21980 Ozzie Smith .50 1.25
BB21981 Fernando Valenzuela .25 .60
BB21982 Reggie Jackson .30 .75
BB21983 Wade Boggs .30 .75
BB21984 Dwight Gooden .25 .60
BB21985 Roger Clemens .50 1.25
BB21986 Cal Ripken Jr. 1.25 3.00
BB21987 Jose Canseco .30 .75
BB21988 Tom Glavine .30 .75
BB21989 Randy Johnson .40 1.00
BB21990 Bernie Williams .30 .75
BB21991 Nolan Ryan 1.25 3.00
BB21992 Ken Griffey Jr. .75 2.00
BB21993 Mike Piazza .40 1.00
BB21994 Ryne Sandberg .75 2.00
BB21995 Nomar Garciaparra .30 .75
BB21996 Cal Ripken Jr. 1.25 3.00
BB21997 Ken Griffey Jr. .75 2.00
BB21998 Greg Maddux .50 1.25
BB21999 Mark McGwire .60 1.50
BB22000 Adrian Gonzalez .30 .75
BB22001 Ichiro Suzuki .50 1.25
BB22002 Jose Bautista .30 .75
BB22003 Albert Pujols .50 1.25
BB22004 David Ortiz .40 1.00
BB22005 Andrew McCutchen .40 1.00
BB22006 Ryan Howard .30 .75
BB22007 Alex Gordon .30 .75
BB22008 Evan Longoria .30 .75
BB22009 Tim Lincecum .30 .75
BB22010 Buster Posey .50 1.25
BB22011 Eric Hosmer .30 .75
BB22012 Yu Darvish .40 1.00
BB22013 Yasiel Puig .40 1.00
BB22014 Jose Abreu .40 1.00
BB22015 Carlos Correa .40 1.00
BB22016 Kyle Schwarber .75 2.00

2016 Topps Berger's Best Autographs

SER.1 ODDS 1:30,058 HOBBY; 1:5942 JUMBO
SER.2 ODDS 1:16,848 HOBBY
STATED PRINT RUN 25 SER.#'d SETS
SER.1 EXCH DEADLINE 1/31/2018
BBABJ Bo Jackson 40.00 100.00
BBADM Don Mattingly 75.00 200.00
BBAHR Hanley Ramirez 50.00 120.00
BBAJS John Smoltz 60.00 150.00
BBAKB Kris Bryant 60.00 150.00
BBAOS Ozzie Smith 30.00 80.00
BBARY Robin Yount
BBASC Steve Carlton 30.00 80.00
BBARCN Robinson Cano
BBARCR Rod Carew 20.00 50.00
BB2A1957 Hank Aaron
BB2A1963 Stan Musial
BB2A1966 Frank Robinson 30.00 80.00
BB2A1981 Fernando Valenzuela
BB2A1990 Bernie Williams 15.00 40.00
BB2A1994 Ryne Sandberg
BB2A1995 Nomar Garciaparra 50.00 120.00
BB2A2008 Evan Longoria 15.00 40.00
BB2A2014 Jose Abreu 12.00 30.00
BB2A2015 Carlos Correa 150.00 250.00

2016 Topps Berger's Best Relics

SER.1 ODDS 1:3794 HOBBY; 1:759 JUMBO
SER.2 ODDS 1:2142 HOBBY
STATED PRINT RUN 99 SER.#'d SETS
BBRAP Albert Pujols 12.00 30.00
BBRBH Bryce Harper 8.00 20.00
BBRBP Buster Posey 12.00 30.00
BBRCK Clayton Kershaw 12.00 30.00
BBRDE Dennis Eckersley 10.00 25.00
BBRDP David Price 4.00 10.00
BBREM Eddie Murray 10.00 25.00
BBRHR Hanley Ramirez 4.00 10.00
BBRJM Joe Mauer 8.00 20.00
BBRJV Justin Verlander 10.00 25.00
BBRKB Kris Bryant 20.00 50.00
BBRKG Ken Griffey Jr. 12.00 30.00
BBRMC Miguel Cabrera 12.00 30.00
BBRMP Mike Piazza 5.00 12.00
BBRSC Steve Carlton 12.00 30.00
BBRSS Stephen Strasburg 5.00 12.00
BBRTG Tony Gwynn 12.00 30.00
BBRYM Yadier Molina 20.00 50.00
BBRRCA Robinson Cano 4.00 10.00
BBRRCL Roger Clemens 10.00 25.00
BB2R1957 Hank Aaron 12.00 30.00
BB2R1960 Carl Yastrzemski 10.00 25.00
BB2R1966 Frank Robinson 10.00 25.00
BB2R1975 Robin Yount 8.00 20.00
BB2R1981 Fernando Valenzuela 8.00 20.00
BB2R1983 Wade Boggs 10.00 25.00
BB2R1989 Randy Johnson 5.00 12.00
BB2R1990 Bernie Williams 4.00 10.00
BB2R1991 Nolan Ryan 25.00 60.00
BB2R1994 Ryne Sandberg 10.00 25.00
BB2R1995 Nomar Garciaparra 6.00 15.00
BB2R1997 Ken Griffey Jr. 10.00 25.00
BB2R1999 Mark McGwire 8.00 20.00
BB2R2003 Albert Pujols 6.00 15.00
BB2R2004 David Ortiz 10.00 25.00
BB2R2005 Andrew McCutchen 10.00 25.00
BB2R2008 Evan Longoria
BB2R2010 Buster Posey 6.00 15.00
BB2R2012 Yu Darvish 5.00 12.00
BB2R2014 Jose Abreu 8.00 20.00

2016 Topps Bunt Player Code Cards

SER.1 ODDS 1:3740 HOBBY; 1:519 JUMBO
SER.2 ODDS 1:8152 HOBBY
STATED PRINT RUN 25 SER.#'d SETS
AM Andrew McCutchen 50.00 120.00
MC Miguel Cabrera 60.00 150.00
FH Felix Hernandez 40.00 100.00
TF Todd Frazier 60.00 150.00
MT Mike Trout 75.00 200.00
KB Kris Bryant 75.00 200.00
AG Alex Gordon S2
CK Clayton Kershaw
MB Madison Bumgarner 60.00 150.00
AP A.J. Pollock S2 60.00 150.00
AR Alex Rodriguez S2 60.00 150.00
DO David Ortiz 60.00 150.00
AR Anthony Rizzo 60.00 150.00
KS Kyle Schwarber
CS Corey Seager S2 60.00 150.00
JD Josh Donaldson 40.00 100.00
TT Troy Tulowitzki 75.00 200.00
DG Dee Gordon S2 60.00 150.00
IS Ichiro Suzuki
DW David Wright 60.00 150.00
CC Carlos Correa 150.00 300.00
EH Eric Hosmer S2 60.00 150.00
EL Evan Longoria S2 60.00 150.00
FF Freddie Freeman S2
DP Dustin Pedroia 50.00 120.00
GC Gerrit Cole S2 75.00 200.00
GS Giancarlo Stanton S2 50.00 120.00
AG Adrian Gonzalez
BH Bryce Harper
JA Jake Arrieta S2
HP Hunter Pence
JF Jose Fernandez S2 60.00 150.00
JP Joe Panik S2 50.00 120.00
JV Joey Votto S2
MH Matt Harvey 75.00 200.00
BP Buster Posey
LS Luis Severino S2
AP Albert Pujols 60.00 150.00
YM Yadier Molina
MC Miguel Cabrera S2 150.00 300.00
MM Manny Machado S2 125.00 300.00
MSA Miguel Sano S2 50.00 120.00
MSC Max Scherzer S2
NA Nolan Arenado S2 50.00 120.00
NS Noah Syndergaard S2 125.00 250.00
PF Prince Fielder S2 50.00 120.00
PG Paul Goldschmidt S2
RB Ryan Braun S2 100.00 250.00
SG Sonny Gray S2
XB Xander Bogaerts S2 125.00 250.00

2016 Topps Celebrating 65 Years

COMPLETE SET (10) 20.00 50.00
INSERTED IN RETAIL PACKS
651952 Jackie Robinson .60 1.50
651953 Satchel Paige .60 1.50
651954 Ted Williams 1.25 3.00
651955 Willie Mays 1.25 3.00
651973 Roberto Clemente 1.50 4.00
651977 Reggie Jackson .50 1.25
651980 Rickey Henderson .60 1.50
651989 Ken Griffey Jr. 1.25 3.00
652011 Mike Trout 3.00 8.00
652012 Matt Harvey .50 1.25

2016 Topps Changing of the Guard

COMPLETE SET (10) 20.00 50.00
INSERTED IN RETAIL PACKS
CTG1 Mike Trout 3.00 8.00
CTG2 Kris Bryant .75 2.00
CTG3 Bryce Harper 1.00 2.50
CTG4 Buster Posey .75 2.00
CTG5 Carlos Correa .60 1.50
CTG6 Kyle Schwarber 1.25 3.00
CTG7 Giancarlo Stanton .60 1.50
CTG8 Manny Machado .60 1.50
CTG9 Madison Bumgarner .50 1.25
CTG10 Jose Fernandez .60 1.50

2016 Topps Chasing 3000

COMMON CARD .60 1.50
STATED ODDS 1:9 HOBBY

2016 Topps Chasing 3000 Relics

COMMON CARD 25.00 60.00
STATED ODDS 1:14,040 HOBBY
STATED PRINT RUN 10 SER.#'d SETS

2016 Topps First Pitch

COMPLETE SET (40) 12.00 30.00
SER.1 ODDS 1:8 HOBBY; 1:2 JUMBO
SER.2 ODDS 1:8 HOBBY
FP1 Abby Wambach .75 2.00
FP1 Tim McGraw S2 .75 2.00
FP2 Jimmy Kimmel S2 .75 2.00
FP2 Gabrielle Giffords .75 2.00
FP3 Don Cherry .75 2.00
FP3 Rosie Rios S2 .75 2.00
FP4 Billy Joe Armstrong S2 .75 2.00
FP4 Mo'ne Davis .75 2.00
FP5 Evelyn Jones .75 2.00
FP5 Nina Agdal S2 .75 2.00
FP6 Jeff Tweedy S2 .75 2.00
FP6 Bree Morse .75 2.00
FP7 Jordan Spieth 10.00 25.00
FP7 Jim Harbaugh S2 3.00 8.00
FP8 Jim Breuer S2 .75 2.00
FP8 Kristaps Porzingis .75 2.00
FP9 Victor Espinoza .75 2.00
FP9 Spencer Stone S2 .75 2.00
FP10 Kyle Larson S2 .75 2.00
FP10 Johnny Knoxville .75 2.00
FP11 James Taylor .75 2.00
FP11 Miguel Cotto S2 .75 2.00
FP12 Tom Watson S2 .75 2.00
FP12 Bud Selig .75 2.00
FP13 LeVar Burton .75 2.00
FP13 Edward Burns S2 .75 2.00
FP14 Geoff Britten S2 .75 2.00
FP14 Hayley Atwell .75 2.00
FP15 Bill Withers .75 2.00
FP15 Lea Thompson S2 .75 2.00
FP16 Jim Caviezel S2 .75 2.00
FP16 Steve Aoki .75 2.00
FP17 Carrie Brownstein .75 2.00
FP17 George H. W. Bush S2 .75 2.00
FP18 J.K. Simmons S2 .75 2.00
FP18 Rebekah Gregory .75 2.00
FP19 Tony Hawk .75 2.00
FP19 Kendrick Lamar S2 .75 2.00
FP20 David Hearn S2 .75 2.00
FP20 Iron E Singleton .75 2.00

2016 Topps Futures Game Pins

STATED ODDS 1:1620 HOBBY
FGPAM Andrew McCutchen 3.00 8.00
FGPBH Bryce Harper 5.00 12.00
FGPCC Carlos Correa 3.00 8.00
FGPCK Clayton Kershaw 5.00 12.00
FGPDW David Wright 2.50 6.00
FGPFH Felix Hernandez 2.50 6.00
FGPGS Giancarlo Stanton 3.00 8.00
FGPJA Jose Altuve 2.50 6.00
FGPJM Joe Mauer 2.50 6.00
FGPKB Kris Bryant 4.00 10.00
FGPKS Kyle Schwarber 6.00 15.00
FGPMB Madison Bumgarner 2.50 6.00
FGPMC Michael Conforto 2.50 6.00
FGPMT Mike Trout 15.00 40.00
FGPNS Noah Syndergaard 2.50 6.00

2016 Topps Futures Game Pins Autographs

STATED ODDS 1:9360 HOBBY
STATED PRINT RUN 25 SER.#'d SETS
FGPABH Bryce Harper
FGPACC Carlos Correa
FGPACK Clayton Kershaw 75.00 150.00
FGPADW David Wright 30.00 80.00
FGPAJA Jose Altuve 40.00 100.00
FGPAKB Kris Bryant 250.00 350.00
FGPAKS Kyle Schwarber 30.00 80.00
FGPAMT Mike Trout 200.00 300.00
FGPANS Noah Syndergaard 50.00 120.00

2016 Topps Hallowed Highlights

COMPLETE SET (15) 4.00 10.00
STATED ODDS 1:8 HOBBY
HH1 Stan Musial .60 1.50
HH2 Ozzie Smith .50 1.25
HH3 John Smoltz .40 1.00
HH4 Frank Thomas .40 1.00
HH5 Sandy Koufax .75 2.00
HH6 Mark McGwire .60 1.50
HH7 Willie Mays .75 2.00
HH8 Cal Ripken Jr. 1.25 3.00
HH9 Nolan Ryan 1.25 3.00
HH10 Ken Griffey Jr. .75 2.00
HH11 Don Mattingly .75 2.00
HH12 Tony Gwynn .40 1.00
HH13 Robin Yount .40 1.00
HH14 Wade Boggs .30 .75
HH15 Greg Maddux .50 1.25

2016 Topps Hallowed Highlights Relics

STATED ODDS 1:33,696 HOBBY
STATED PRINT RUN 25 SER.#'d SETS
HHKG Ken Griffey Jr.
HHMM Mark McGwire
HHNR Nolan Ryan 40.00 100.00
HHTG Tony Gwynn 25.00 60.00
HHWM Willie Mays

2016 Topps Laser

SER.1 ODDS 1:736 HOBBY; 1:153 JUMBO
SER.2 ODDS 1:454 HOBBY
TL1 Mike Trout 20.00 50.00
TL2 Paul Goldschmidt 8.00 20.00
TL3 Kyle Schwarber 20.00 50.00
TL4 David Ortiz 8.00 20.00
TL5 Hanley Ramirez 6.00 15.00
TL6 Kris Bryant 10.00 25.00
TL7 Jose Abreu 8.00 20.00
TL8 Ichiro Suzuki 12.00 30.00
TL9 Clayton Kershaw 12.00 30.00
TL10 Ryan Braun 6.00 15.00
TL11 Matt Harvey 6.00 15.00
TL12 Buster Posey 12.00 30.00
TL13 Robinson Cano 6.00 15.00
TL14 Prince Fielder 6.00 15.00
TL15 Jason Heyward 6.00 15.00
TL16 Bryce Harper 25.00 60.00
TL17 Miguel Cabrera 12.00 30.00
TL18 Eric Hosmer 6.00 15.00
TL19 Yasiel Puig 12.00 30.00
TL20 Giancarlo Stanton 8.00 20.00
TL21 Masahiro Tanaka 6.00 15.00
TL22 Andrew McCutchen 8.00 20.00
TL23 Madison Bumgarner 6.00 15.00
TL24 Yadier Molina 15.00 40.00
TL25 Jose Bautista 6.00 15.00
TLAG Adrian Gonzalez S2 6.00 15.00
TLAP Albert Pujols S2 10.00 25.00
TLARI Anthony Rizzo S2 12.00 30.00
TLARO Alex Rodriguez S2 10.00 25.00
TLCC Carlos Correa S2 10.00 25.00
TLCD Chris Davis S2 6.00 15.00
TLCS Corey Seager S2 50.00 120.00
TLDK Dallas Keuchel S2 6.00 15.00
TLDP Dustin Pedroia S2 8.00 20.00
TLDW David Wright S2 6.00 15.00
TLFF Freddie Freeman S2 12.00 30.00
TLFH Felix Hernandez S2 6.00 15.00
TLHOL Hector Olivera S2 6.00 15.00
TLHOW Henry Owens S2 6.00 15.00
TLHP Hunter Pence S2 6.00 15.00
TLJA Jake Arrieta S2 6.00 15.00
TLJDE Jacob deGrom S2 15.00 40.00
TLJDO Josh Donaldson S2 6.00 15.00
TLLC Lorenzo Cain S2 5.00 12.00
TLMSA Miguel Sano S2 8.00 20.00
TLMSC Max Scherzer S2 8.00 20.00
TLNS Noah Syndergaard S2 6.00 15.00
TLTF Todd Frazier S2 6.00 15.00
TLTT Trea Turner S2 15.00 40.00
TLYD Yu Darvish S2 8.00 20.00

2016 Topps Laser Autographs

SER.1 ODDS 1:7515 HOBBY; 1:1497 JUMBO
SER.2 ODDS 1:4680 HOBBY
STATED PRINT RUN 25 SER.#'d SETS
SER.1 EXCH DEADLINE 1/31/2018
TLAAG Adrian Gonzalez S2 25.00 60.00
TLACC Carlos Correa S2 100.00 200.00
TLACS Corey Seager S2 200.00 500.00
TLADK Dallas Keuchel S2 25.00 60.00
TLADO David Ortiz 125.00 250.00
TLADP Dustin Pedroia S2 60.00 150.00
TLADW David Wright S2 25.00 60.00
TLAFF Freddie Freeman S2 30.00 80.00
TLAHOL Hector Olivera S2 25.00 60.00
TLAHR Hanley Ramirez 25.00 60.00
TLAIC Ichiro Suzuki 200.00 400.00
TLAJA Jose Abreu 30.00 80.00
TLAKB Kris Bryant 75.00 200.00
TLAKS Kyle Schwarber
TLAMH Matt Harvey EXCH 60.00 150.00
TLAMT Mike Trout 175.00 350.00
TLANS Noah Syndergaard S2 50.00 120.00
TLAPG Paul Goldschmidt 30.00 80.00
TLARB Ryan Braun 25.00 60.00

2016 Topps Laser Relics

SER.1 ODDS 1:1271 HOBBY; 1:255 JUMBO
SER.2 ODDS 1:798 HOBBY
STATED PRINT RUN 99 SER.#'d SETS
TLRAG Adrian Gonzalez S2 8.00 20.00
TLRAM Andrew McCutchen 20.00 50.00
TLRBP Buster Posey 12.00 30.00
TLRCK Clayton Kershaw 20.00 50.00
TLRCS Corey Seager S2 60.00 150.00
TLRDK Dallas Keuchel S2 8.00 20.00
TLRDO David Ortiz 20.00 50.00
TLRDP Dustin Pedroia S2 20.00 50.00
TLRDW David Wright S2 12.00 30.00
TLRFF Freddie Freeman S2 6.00 15.00
TLRHP Hunter Pence S2 6.00 15.00
TLRJA Jose Abreu 20.00 50.00
TLRKB Kris Bryant 50.00 120.00
TLRKS Kyle Schwarber 10.00 25.00
TLRLC Lorenzo Cain S2 6.00 15.00
TLRMB Madison Bumgarner 8.00 20.00
TLRMC Miguel Cabrera 20.00 50.00
TLRMH Matt Harvey 30.00 80.00
TLRMT Mike Trout 50.00 125.00
TLRPF Prince Fielder 8.00 20.00
TLRYD Yu Darvish S2 10.00 25.00
TLRYM Yadier Molina 25.00 60.00
TLRHOL Hector Olivera S2 6.00 15.00
TLRHOW Henry Owens S2 8.00 20.00
TLRJDE Jacob deGrom S2. 15.00 40.00
TLRJDO Josh Donaldson S2 10.00 25.00

TLRMSA Miguel Sano S2 10.00 25.00
TLRMTA Masahiro Tanaka 8.00 20.00
TLRNSY Noah Syndergaard S2 20.00 50.00

2016 Topps MLB Debut Bronze
RANDOM INSERTS IN PACKS
*SILVER: .5X TO 1.2X BASIC
*GOLD: .6X TO 1.5X BASIC
MLBD1 Hank Aaron .75 2.00
MLBD2 Ryan Braun .30 .75
MLBD3 Kris Bryant .50 1.25
MLBD4 Miguel Cabrera .40 1.00
MLBD5 Robinson Cano .30 .75
MLBD6 Starlin Castro .25 .60
MLBD7 Yoenis Cespedes .40 1.00
MLBD8 Nelson Cruz .40 1.00
MLBD9 Yu Darvish .40 1.00
MLBD10 Josh Donaldson .30 .75
MLBD11 Jacoby Ellsbury .30 .75
MLBD12 Paul Goldschmidt .40 1.00
MLBD13 Adrian Gonzalez .30 .75
MLBD14 Dwight Gooden .25 .60
MLBD15 Matt Harvey .30 .75
MLBD16 Jason Heyward .30 .75
MLBD17 Ryan Howard .30 .75
MLBD18 Sandy Koufax .75 2.00
MLBD19 Evan Longoria .30 .75
MLBD20 Victor Martinez .30 .75
MLBD21 Joe Mauer .30 .75
MLBD22 Willie Mays .75 2.00
MLBD23 Andrew McCutchen .40 1.00
MLBD24 Satchel Paige .40 1.00
MLBD25 Mike Piazza .40 1.00
MLBD26 Buster Posey .50 1.25
MLBD27 Albert Pujols .50 1.25
MLBD28 Cal Ripken Jr. 1.25 3.00
MLBD29 Brooks Robinson .30 .75
MLBD30 Jackie Robinson .40 1.00
MLBD31 Alex Rodriguez .50 1.25
MLBD32 Babe Ruth 1.00 2.50
MLBD33 Nolan Ryan 1.25 3.00
MLBD34 Giancarlo Stanton .40 1.00
MLBD35 Mike Trout 2.00 5.00
MLBD36 Troy Tulowitzki .40 1.00
MLBD37 Justin Upton .30 .75
MLBD38 Fernando Valenzuela .25 .60
MLBD39 Jayson Werth .30 .75
MLBD40 Bernie Williams .30 .75
MLBD2-1 Carl Yastrzemski .60 1.50
MLBD2-2 Johnny Bench .40 1.00
MLBD2-3 Wade Boggs .30 .75
MLBD2-4 George Brett .75 2.00
MLBD2-5 Tony Gwynn .40 1.00
MLBD2-6 Ken Griffey Jr. .75 2.00
MLBD2-7 Tom Seaver .30 .75
MLBD2-8 Paul Molitor .40 1.00
MLBD2-9 Robin Yount .40 1.00
MLBD2-10 Warren Spahn .30 .75
MLBD2-11 Duke Snider .30 .75
MLBD2-12 Bill Mazeroski .30 .75
MLBD2-13 Madison Bumgarner .30 .75
MLBD2-14 Clayton Kershaw .60 1.50
MLBD2-15 David Ortiz .40 1.00
MLBD2-16 Anthony Rizzo .50 1.25
MLBD2-17 Dustin Pedroia .40 1.00
MLBD2-18 Felix Hernandez .30 .75
MLBD2-19 David Wright .30 .75
MLBD2-20 Jake Arrieta .30 .75
MLBD2-21 Carlos Correa .40 1.00
MLBD2-22 Rob Refsnyder .30 .75
MLBD2-23 Don Mattingly .75 2.00
MLBD2-24 David Price .30 .75
MLBD2-25 Jose Abreu .40 1.00
MLBD2-26 Ichiro Suzuki .50 1.25
MLBD2-27 Hanley Ramirez .30 .75
MLBD2-28 Mark McGwire .60 1.50
MLBD2-29 Rod Carew .30 .75
MLBD2-30 Jeff Bagwell .30 .75
MLBD2-31 Alex Gordon .30 .75
MLBD2-32 Mike Moustakas .30 .75
MLBD2-33 Noah Syndergaard .30 .75
MLBD2-34 Manny Machado .40 1.00
MLBD2-35 Carlos Gonzalez .30 .75
MLBD2-36 Zack Greinke .40 1.00
MLBD2-37 Joey Votto .40 1.00
MLBD2-38 Starling Marte .30 .75
MLBD2-39 Sonny Gray .30 .75
MLBD2-40 Tom Glavine .30 .75

2016 Topps MLB Debut Medallion
RANDOM INSERTS IN PACKS
MDMAG Adrian Gonzalez 1.50 4.00
MDMAM Andrew McCutchen 2.00 5.00
MDMAP Albert Pujols 2.50 6.00
MDMAR Alex Rodriguez 2.50 6.00
MDMBP Buster Posey 2.50 6.00
MDMBR Brooks Robinson 1.50 4.00
MDMBW Bernie Williams 1.50 4.00
MDMCR Cal Ripken Jr. 6.00 15.00
MDMDG Dwight Gooden 1.25 3.00
MDMEL Evan Longoria 1.50 4.00
MDMFV Fernando Valenzuela 1.25 3.00
MDMGS Giancarlo Stanton 2.00 5.00
MDMHA Hank Aaron 4.00 10.00
MDMJD Josh Donaldson 1.50 4.00
MDMJE Jacoby Ellsbury 1.50 4.00
MDMJH Jason Heyward 1.50 4.00
MDMJM Joe Mauer 1.50 4.00
MDMJR Jackie Robinson 2.00 5.00
MDMJU Justin Upton 1.50 4.00
MDMJW Jayson Werth 1.50 4.00
MDMKB Kris Bryant 2.50 6.00
MDMMC Miguel Cabrera 2.00 5.00
MDMMH Matt Harvey 1.50 4.00
MDMMP Mike Piazza 2.00 5.00
MDMMT Mike Trout 10.00 25.00
MDMNC Nelson Cruz 2.00 5.00
MDMNR Nolan Ryan 6.00 15.00
MDMPG Paul Goldschmidt 2.00 5.00
MDMRB Ryan Braun 1.50 4.00
MDMRC Robinson Cano 1.50 4.00
MDMRH Ryan Howard 1.50 4.00
MDMSC Starlin Castro 1.25 3.00
MDMSK Sandy Koufax 4.00 10.00
MDMSP Satchel Paige 2.00 5.00
MDMTT Troy Tulowitzki 2.00 5.00
MDMVM Victor Martinez 1.50 4.00
MDMWM Willie Mays 4.00 10.00
MDMYC Yoenis Cespedes 2.00 5.00
MDMYD Yu Darvish 2.00 5.00
MDMBRU Babe Ruth 5.00 12.00
MLBDM21 Carl Yastrzemski S2 3.00 8.00
MLBDM22 Johnny Bench S2 2.00 5.00
MLBDM23 Wade Boggs S2 1.50 4.00
MLBDM24 George Brett S2 4.00 10.00
MLBDM25 Tony Gwynn S2 2.00 5.00
MLBDM26 Ken Griffey Jr. S2 4.00 10.00
MLBDM27 Tom Seaver S2 1.50 4.00
MLBDM28 Paul Molitor S2 2.00 5.00
MLBDM29 Robin Yount S2 2.00 5.00
MLBDM210 Warren Spahn S2 1.50 4.00
MLBDM211 Duke Snider S2 1.50 4.00
MLBDM212 Bill Mazeroski S2 1.50 4.00
MLBDM213 Madison Bumgarner S2 1.50 4.00
MLBDM214 Clayton Kershaw S2 3.00 8.00
MLBDM215 David Ortiz S2 2.00 5.00
MLBDM216 Anthony Rizzo S2 2.50 6.00
MLBDM217 Dustin Pedroia S2 2.00 5.00
MLBDM218 Felix Hernandez S2 1.50 4.00
MLBDM219 David Wright S2 1.50 4.00
MLBDM220 Jake Arrieta S2 1.50 4.00
MLBDM221 Carlos Correa S2 2.00 5.00
MLBDM222 Rob Refsnyder S2 1.50 4.00
MLBDM223 Don Mattingly S2 4.00 10.00
MLBDM224 David Price S2 1.50 4.00
MLBDM225 Jose Abreu S2 2.00 5.00
MLBDM226 Ichiro Suzuki S2 2.50 6.00
MLBDM227 Hanley Ramirez S2 1.50 4.00
MLBDM228 Mark McGwire S2 3.00 8.00
MLBDM229 Rod Carew S2 1.50 4.00
MLBDM230 Jeff Bagwell S2 1.50 4.00
MLBDM231 Alex Gordon S2 1.50 4.00
MLBDM232 Mike Moustakas S2 1.50 4.00
MLBDM233 Noah Syndergaard S2 1.50 4.00
MLBD2M34 Manny Machado S2 2.00 5.00
MLBDM235 Carlos Gonzalez S2 1.50 4.00
MLBDM236 Zack Greinke S2 2.00 5.00
MLBDM237 Joey Votto S2 2.00 5.00
MLBDM238 Starling Marte S2 1.50 4.00
MLBDM239 Sonny Gray S2 1.50 4.00
MLBDM240 Tom Glavine S2 1.50 4.00

2016 Topps MLB Debut Relics
RANDOM INSERTS IN PACKS
STATED PRINT RUN 99 SER.#'d SETS
MDRAG Adrian Gonzalez
MDRAM Andrew McCutchen 6.00 15.00
MDRAP Albert Pujols 5.00 12.00
MDREL Evan Longoria
MDRJD Josh Donaldson 10.00 25.00
MDRJE Jacoby Ellsbury 5.00 12.00
MDRJH Jason Heyward 5.00 12.00
MDRJM Joe Mauer 8.00 20.00
MDRKB Kris Bryant 30.00 80.00
MDRMC Miguel Cabrera
MDRMH Matt Harvey
MDRNC Nelson Cruz 6.00 15.00
MDRPG Paul Goldschmidt 15.00 40.00
MDRRB Ryan Braun 5.00 12.00
MDRRC Robinson Cano 5.00 12.00
MDRRH Ryan Howard 5.00 12.00
MDRSC Starlin Castro 4.00 10.00
MDRVM Victor Martinez 5.00 12.00
MDRYC Yoenis Cespedes 6.00 15.00
MDRYD Yu Darvish 6.00 15.00
MLBD2RAG Alex Gordon S2 5.00 12.00
MLBD2RAR Anthony Rizzo S2 8.00 20.00
MLBD2RCG Carlos Gonzalez S2 5.00 12.00
MLBD2RCK Clayton Kershaw S2 10.00 25.00
MLBD2RDO David Ortiz S2 20.00 50.00
MLBD2RDPE Dustin Pedroia S2 15.00 40.00
MLBD2RDPR David Price S2 15.00 40.00
MLBD2RDW David Wright S2 5.00 12.00
MLBD2RFH Felix Hernandez S2
MLBD2RHR Hanley Ramirez S2
MLBD2RJA Jose Abreu S2
MLBD2RJV Joey Votto S2
MLBD2RMMA Manny Machado S2 12.00 30.00
MLBD2RMMO Mike Moustakas S2 5.00 12.00
MLBD2RNS Noah Syndergaard S2 5.00 12.00
MLBD2RPM Paul Molitor S2 15.00 40.00
MLBD2RRR Rob Refsnyder S2 5.00 12.00
MLBD2RSM Starling Marte S2 12.00 30.00
MLBD2RTGW Tony Gwynn S2 6.00 15.00
MLBD2RZG Zack Greinke S2 6.00 15.00

2016 Topps MLB Wacky Promos
COMPLETE SET (6) 2.00 5.00
RANDOM INSERTS IN PACKS
MLBW1 Giants .40 1.00
Magic Beans
MLBW2 Mets .40 1.00
Deli Meat
MLBW3 Royals .40 1.00
Blue Cheese
MLBW4 Dodgers .40 1.00
Sushi
MLBW5 Red Sox .40 1.00
Tea Bags
MLBW6 Cardinals .40 1.00
Eggs

2016 Topps No Hitter Pins
STATED ODDS 1:826 HOBBY; 1:43 JUMBO
NHPBF Bob Feller 4.00 10.00
NHPCK Clayton Kershaw 8.00 20.00
NHPFV Fernando Valenzuela 3.00 8.00
NHPHB Homer Bailey 3.00 8.00
NHPJL Jon Lester 4.00 10.00
NHPJP Jim Palmer 4.00 10.00
NHPJS Johan Santana 4.00 10.00
NHPJZ Jordan Zimmermann 4.00 10.00
NHPMC Matt Cain 4.00 10.00
NHPNR Nolan Ryan 8.00 20.00
NHPPN Phil Niekro 4.00 10.00
NHPRJ Randy Johnson 5.00 12.00
NHPSK Sandy Koufax 6.00 15.00
NHPTS Tom Seaver 4.00 10.00
NHPWS Warren Spahn 4.00 10.00

2016 Topps No Hitter Pins Autographs
STATED ODDS 1:78,148 HOBBY; 1:1857 JUMBO
STATED PRINT RUN 25 SER.#'d SETS
EXCHANGE DEADLINE 1/31/2018
NHPCK Clayton Kershaw 125.00 250.00
NHPJL Jon Lester 75.00 150.00
NHPNR Nolan Ryan 125.00 250.00
NHPRJ Randy Johnson EXCH 125.00 250.00
NHPSK Sandy Koufax EXCH 200.00 300.00

2016 Topps Perspectives
COMPLETE SET (25) 5.00 12.00
STATED ODDS 1:4 HOBBY
P1 Andrew McCutchen .40 1.00
P2 Adrian Gonzalez .30 .75
P3 Robinson Cano .30 .75
P4 Bryce Harper .60 1.50
P5 Rusney Castillo .25 .60
P6 Byron Buxton .40 1.00
P7 Yasiel Puig .40 1.00
P8 Troy Tulowitzki .40 1.00
P9 Jhonny Peralta .25 .60
P10 Jung Ho Kang .25 .60
P11 Kris Bryant .50 1.25
P12 David Ortiz .40 1.00
P13 Ichiro Suzuki .50 1.25
P14 Justin Upton .30 .75
P15 Yadier Molina .50 1.25
P16 Gregory Polanco .30 .75
P17 Evan Longoria .30 .75
P18 Mark Teixeira .30 .75
P19 Ryan Braun .30 .75
P20 Ryan Howard .30 .75
P21 Cal Ripken Jr. 1.25 3.00
P22 Randy Johnson .40 1.00
P23 Craig Biggio .30 .75
P24 Nolan Ryan 1.25 3.00
P25 Ozzie Smith .50 1.25

2016 Topps Postseason Performance Autograph Relics
STATED ODDS 1:14,746 HOBBY; 1:746 JUMBO
STATED PRINT RUN 50 SER.#'d SETS
EXCHANGE DEADLINE 1/31/2018
PPARARI Anthony Rizzo 40.00 100.00
PPARARU Addison Russell 40.00 100.00
PPARDW David Wright 40.00 100.00
PPARJD Jacob deGrom 75.00 200.00
PPARJF Jeurys Familia 30.00 80.00
PPARJLE Jon Lester 25.00 60.00
PPARLD Lucas Duda 25.00 60.00
PPARMS Marcus Stroman 25.00 60.00
PPARNS Noah Syndergaard 50.00 120.00
PPARWF Wilmer Flores 25.00 60.00

2016 Topps Postseason Performance Autographs
STATED ODDS 1:14,746 HOBBY; 1:3014 JUMBO
STATED PRINT RUN 50 SER.#'d SETS
EXCHANGE DEADLINE 1/31/2018
PPAJB Javier Baez 30.00 80.00
PPAJD Jacob deGrom 30.00 80.00
PPAJF Jeurys Familia 25.00 60.00
PPAKP Kevin Pillar 15.00 40.00
PPALD Lucas Duda 20.00 50.00
PPAMS Marcus Stroman 20.00 50.00
PPANS Noah Syndergaard 50.00 120.00
PPAWF Wilmer Flores
PPAARU Addison Russell
PPAJLE Jon Lester 20.00 50.00

2016 Topps Postseason Performance Relics
STATED ODDS 1:2506 HOBBY; 1:501 JUMBO
STATED PRINT RUN 100 SER.#'d SETS
PPRARI Anthony Rizzo 12.00 30.00
PPRARU Addison Russell 10.00 25.00
PPRAS Aaron Sanchez 12.00 30.00
PPRBC Bartolo Colon 10.00 25.00
PPRDF Dexter Fowler 8.00 20.00
PPRDM Daniel Murphy 20.00 50.00
PPRDP David Price 20.00 50.00
PPRDW David Wright 20.00 50.00
PPREE Edwin Encarnacion 10.00 25.00
PPRJBA Jose Bautista 8.00 20.00
PPRJBE Javier Baez 12.00 30.00
PPRJDE Jacob deGrom 20.00 50.00
PPRJDO Josh Donaldson 8.00 20.00
PPRJF Jeurys Familia 20.00 50.00
PPRJLA Juan Lagares 25.00 60.00
PPRJLE Jon Lester 8.00 20.00
PPRKB Kris Bryant 12.00 30.00
PPRKS Kyle Schwarber 20.00 50.00
PPRLD Lucas Duda 8.00 20.00
PPRMH Matt Harvey 40.00 100.00
PPRNS Noah Syndergaard 20.00 50.00
PPRRD R.A. Dickey 10.00 25.00
PPRRM Russell Martin 20.00 50.00
PPRRO Roberto Osuna 6.00 15.00
PPRSC Starlin Castro 6.00 15.00
PPRSM Steven Matz 40.00 100.00
PPRTD Travis d'Arnaud 25.00 60.00
PPRTT Troy Tulowitzki 25.00 60.00
PPRWF Wilmer Flores 15.00 40.00
PPRYC Yoenis Cespedes 20.00 50.00

2016 Topps Pressed Into Service
COMPLETE SET (10) 2.00 5.00
STATED ODDS 1:8 HOBBY; 1:2 JUMBO
PIS1 Mitch Moreland .25 .60
PIS2 Wade Boggs .30 .75
PIS3 Jose Canseco .30 .75
PIS4 Michael Cuddyer .25 .60
PIS5 Paul O'Neill .30 .75
PIS6 Stan Musial .60 1.50
PIS7 Josh Harrison .25 .60
PIS8 Garrett Jones .25 .60
PIS9 Ichiro Suzuki .50 1.25
PIS10 Nick Swisher .30 .75

2016 Topps Pressed Into Service Autographs
STATED ODDS 1:60,115 HOBBY; 1:12,233 JUMBO
STATED PRINT RUN 25 SER.#'d SETS
EXCHANGE DEADLINE 1/31/2018
PSAJC Jose Canseco
PSAMC Michael Cuddyer
PSAPO Paul O'Neill
PSASM Stan Musial
PSAWB Wade Boggs EXCH 40.00 100.00

2016 Topps Pressed Into Service Relics
STATED ODDS 1:30,058 HOBBY; 1:5942 JUMBO
STATED PRINT RUN 50 SER.#'d SETS
PISRI Ichiro Suzuki 15.00 40.00
PISRJC Jose Canseco 10.00 25.00
PISRMC Michael Cuddyer 15.00 40.00
PISRPO Paul O'Neill 20.00 50.00
PISRWB Wade Boggs 12.00 30.00

2016 Topps Record Setters
COMPLETE SET (25) 20.00 50.00
INSERTED IN RETAIL PACKS
RS1 Mike Trout 3.00 8.00
RS2 Adrian Gonzalez .50 1.25
RS3 David Ortiz .60 1.50
RS4 Carlos Correa .60 1.50
RS5 Max Scherzer .60 1.50
RS6 Steven Matz .40 1.00
RS7 Dallas Keuchel .50 1.25
RS8 Chris Sale .60 1.50
RS9 Alex Rodriguez .75 2.00
RS10 Chris Heston .40 1.00
RS11 Edwin Encarnacion .60 1.50
RS12 Bryce Harper 1.00 2.50
RS13 Kris Bryant .75 2.00
RS14 Josh Donaldson .50 1.25
RS15 Jose Altuve .50 1.25

2016 Topps Record Setters Relics
INSERTED IN RETAIL PACKS
STATED PRINT RUN 25 SER.#'d SETS
RSRAG Adrian Gonzalez
RSRAR Alex Rodriguez
RSRCS Chris Sale
RSRDK Dallas Keuchel
RSRDO David Ortiz
RSREE Edwin Encarnacion
RSREH Eric Hosmer
RSRJD Josh Donaldson 15.00 40.00
RSRKB Kris Bryant 15.00 40.00
RSRMT Mike Trout

2016 Topps Scouting Report Autographs
SER.1 ODDS 1:293 HOBBY; 1:11 JUMBO
SER.2 ODDS 1:313 HOBBY
SER.1 EXCH DEADLINE 1/31/2018
UPD EXCH DEADLINE 9/30/2018
SRAAA Albert Almora UPD 10.00 25.00
SRAAB Aaron Blair UPD 3.00 8.00
SRAAB Archie Bradley 3.00 8.00
SRAAC Adam Conley UPD 3.00 8.00
SRAAD Aledmys Diaz UPD 25.00 60.00
SRAAH Allen Hanson UPD 4.00 10.00
SRAAK Al Kaline 15.00 40.00
SRAAN Aaron Nola S2 6.00 15.00
SRAAN Aaron Nola 6.00 15.00
SRAARE A.J. Reed UPD 3.00 8.00
SRAAW Alex Wood S2 3.00 8.00
SRABC Brandon Crawford 15.00 40.00
SRABD Brandon Drury S2 5.00 12.00
SRABH Brock Holt UPD 3.00 8.00
SRABHA Bryce Harper 50.00 120.00
SRABH Brock Holt 5.00 12.00
SRABJ Brian Johnson S2 3.00 8.00
SRABJ Brian Johnson 3.00 8.00
SRABM Brian McCann 15.00 40.00
SRABP Byung-Ho Park S2 20.00 50.00
SRABP Byung-Ho Park UPD 4.00 10.00
SRABPO Buster Posey 30.00 80.00
SRABS Blake Snell UPD 4.00 10.00
SRABSN Blake Snell S2 4.00 10.00
SRACC Carlos Correa 30.00 80.00
SRACE Carl Edwards Jr. S2 4.00 10.00
SRACH Cody Hall S2 3.00 8.00
SRACR Cody Reed UPD 3.00 8.00
SRACR Cal Ripken Jr. 25.00 60.00
SRACRE Colin Rea S2 3.00 8.00
SRACRO Carlos Rodon S2 5.00 12.00
SRACRO Carlos Rodon UPD 5.00 12.00
SRACS Corey Seager S2 40.00 100.00
SRACS Corey Seager 40.00 100.00
SRACV Christian Vazquez UPD 4.00 10.00
SRADF Doug Fister 3.00 8.00
SRADG Didi Gregorius 5.00 12.00
SRADK Dallas Keuchel 10.00 25.00
SRADM Devin Mesoraco 3.00 8.00
SRADS Duke Snider 6.00 15.00
SRAEG Erik Goeddel S2 3.00 8.00
SRAEI Ender Inciarte 3.00 8.00
SRAER Eddie Rosario UPD 3.00 8.00
SRAFL Francisco Lindor UPD 20.00 50.00
SRAFM Frankie Montas S2 4.00 10.00
SRAGB Greg Bird S2 4.00 10.00
SRAGS George Springer S2 10.00 25.00
SRAGS George Springer 10.00 25.00
SRAHO Henry Owens 4.00 10.00
SRAHOL Hector Olivera S2 4.00 10.00
SRAHOL Hector Olivera 4.00 10.00
SRAHOW Henry Owens S2 4.00 10.00
SRAJBE Jose Berrios S2 5.00 12.00
SRAJF Jose Fernandez 10.00 25.00
SRAJG Jon Gray S2 3.00 8.00
SRAJG Jon Gray 3.00 8.00
SRAJH Jeremy Hazelbaker UPD 4.00 10.00
SRAJHM Jason Hammel 4.00 10.00
SRAJHR Josh Harrison 5.00 12.00
SRAJM James McCann 4.00 10.00
SRAJP Jose Peraza S2 3.00 8.00
SRAJP Jose Peraza UPD 3.00 8.00
SRAJR Joey Rickard UPD 4.00 10.00
SRAJR J.T. Realmuto 10.00 25.00
SRAJT Jameson Taillon UPD 4.00 10.00
SRAJU Julio Urias UPD EXCH 15.00 40.00
SRAKC Kole Calhoun 3.00 8.00
SRAKG Ken Giles UPD 3.00 8.00
SRAKH Kelvin Herrera UPD 4.00 10.00
SRAKK Kevin Kiermaier UPD 4.00 10.00
SRAKM Kenta Maeda UPD 20.00 50.00
SRAKM Ketel Marte 6.00 15.00
SRAKME Kenta Maeda S2 40.00 100.00
SRAKS Kyle Schwarber S2 30.00 80.00
SRAKSC Kyle Schwarber 30.00 80.00
SRAKSU Kurt Suzuki 3.00 8.00
SRAKW Kyle Waldrop S2 4.00 10.00
SRAKW Kyle Waldrop 4.00 10.00
SRALG Lucas Giolito UPD 5.00 12.00
SRALJ Luke Jackson S2 3.00 8.00
SRALS Luis Severino S2 10.00 25.00
SRALS Luis Severino UPD 4.00 10.00
SRALS Luis Severino 10.00 25.00
SRAMAL Miguel Almonte S2 3.00 8.00
SRAMB Mike Bolsinger UPD 4.00 10.00
SRAMC Mike Clevinger UPD 6.00 15.00
SRAMCA Matt Cain 4.00 10.00
SRAMCO Michael Conforto S2 20.00 50.00
SRAMCO Michael Conforto 20.00 50.00
SRAMDF Matt Duffy SF S2 20.00 50.00
SRAMDU Matt Duffy HOU S2 3.00 8.00
SRAMF Michael Fulmer UPD 8.00 20.00
SRAMG Mychal Givens S2 3.00 8.00
SRAMK Max Kepler S2 6.00 15.00
SRAMK Max Kepler UPD 5.00 12.00
SRAMP Mark Prior 4.00 10.00
SRAMRE Michael Reed S2 3.00 8.00
SRAMRY Matt Reynolds S2 3.00 8.00
SRAMS Miguel Sano S2 10.00 25.00
SRAMS Miguel Sano 10.00 25.00
SRAMT Mike Trout 100.00 200.00
SRAMW Mac Williamson S2 3.00 8.00
SRAMW Matt Wisler 3.00 8.00
SRANK Nate Karns S2 3.00 8.00
SRANM Nomar Mazara UPD 5.00 12.00
SRANV Nick Vincent UPD 3.00 8.00
SRAPM Paul Molitor 8.00 20.00
SRAPO Peter O'Brien S2 3.00 8.00
SRAPS Pablo Sandoval 6.00 15.00
SRAPV Pat Venditte UPD 3.00 8.00
SRARCR Rod Carew 15.00 40.00
SRARM Raul Mondesi S2 6.00 15.00
SRARR Rob Refsnyder S2 4.00 10.00
SRARR Rob Refsnyder 4.00 10.00
SRARS Richie Shaffer S2 3.00 8.00
SRARS Robert Stephenson UPD 3.00 8.00
SRARST Ross Stripling UPD 3.00 8.00
SRARY Robin Yount 20.00 50.00
SRASB Socrates Brito UPD 3.00 8.00
SRASK Sandy Koufax 150.00 250.00
SRASMA Steven Matz 3.00 8.00
SRASP Stephen Piscotty S2 8.00 20.00
SRASP Stephen Piscotty 8.00 20.00
SRATD Tyler Duffey S2 3.00 8.00
SRATH T.J. House S2 3.00 8.00
SRATJ Tyrell Jenkins UPD 8.00 20.00
SRATJ Taylor Jungmann 3.00 8.00
SRATM Tom Murphy S2 3.00 8.00
SRATN Tyler Naquin UPD 4.00 10.00
SRATP Tommy Pham S2 3.00 8.00
SRATP Tommy Pham UPD 3.00 8.00
SRATS Trevor Story UPD 6.00 15.00
SRATT Trea Turner S2 12.00 30.00
SRATT Trea Turner 12.00 30.00
SRATW Tyler White UPD 3.00 8.00
SRAWM Wil Myers 4.00 10.00
SRAYD Yu Darvish 30.00 80.00
SRAYG Yan Gomes 3.00 8.00
SRAZL Zach Lee S2 3.00 8.00
SRAZL Zach Lee 3.00 8.00

2016 Topps Scouting Report Relics
SER.1 ODDS 1:54 HOBBY; 1:12 JUMBO
SER.2 ODDS 1:61 HOBBY
SRRAG Adrian Gonzalez 2.50 6.00
SRRAJ Adam Jones S2 2.50 6.00
SRRAM Andrew McCutchen 5.00 12.00
SRRAPU Albert Pujols 4.00 10.00
SRRAPU Albert Pujols S2 4.00 10.00
SRRAR Anthony Rizzo 4.00 10.00
SRRARI Anthony Rizzo S2 4.00 10.00
SRRARU Addison Russell S2 3.00 8.00
SRRBH Bryce Harper 6.00 15.00
SRRBP Buster Posey 4.00 10.00
SRRCD Chris Davis 2.00 5.00
SRRCGM Carlos Gomez S2 2.00 5.00
SRRCGN Carlos Gonzalez S2 2.50 6.00
SRRCK Craig Kimbrel S2 2.50 6.00
SRRCKE Clayton Kershaw 5.00 12.00
SRRCKL Corey Kluber 2.50 6.00
SRRCS Corey Seager S2 5.00 12.00
SRRCSA CC Sabathia 2.50 6.00
SRRDG Dee Gordon S2 2.00 5.00
SRRDK Dallas Keuchel S2 2.50 6.00
SRRDO David Ortiz 4.00 10.00
SRRDP Dustin Pedroia S2 3.00 8.00
SRRDPR David Price 2.50 6.00
SRRDW David Wright S2 2.50 6.00
SRREE Edwin Encarnacion S2 2.50 6.00
SRREH Eric Hosmer S2 2.50 6.00
SRREL Evan Longoria S2 2.50 6.00
SRRFF Freddie Freeman 4.00 10.00
SRRFH Felix Hernandez 2.50 6.00
SRRGC Gerrit Cole S2 3.00 8.00
SRRGS Giancarlo Stanton 3.00 8.00
SRRGSP George Springer S2 2.50 6.00
SRRGST Giancarlo Stanton S2 3.00 8.00
SRRHR Hanley Ramirez 2.50 6.00
SRRI Ichiro Suzuki 4.00 10.00
SRRJAB Jose Abreu S2 3.00 8.00
SRRJC Johnny Cueto 2.50 6.00
SRRJDE Jacob deGrom 6.00 15.00
SRRJDO Josh Donaldson 2.50 6.00
SRRJF Jose Fernandez S2 3.00 8.00
SRRJH Jason Heyward S2 2.50 6.00
SRRJK Jason Kipnis S2 2.50 6.00
SRRJM Joe Mauer 2.50 6.00
SRRJP Joc Pederson 2.50 6.00
SRRJS Jorge Soler S2 3.00 8.00
SRRJU Justin Upton S2 2.50 6.00
SRRJV Joey Votto S2 3.00 8.00
SRRJVE Justin Verlander S2 3.00 8.00
SRRJVE Justin Verlander 3.00 8.00
SRRKB Kris Bryant S2 4.00 10.00
SRRKP Kevin Plawecki 2.00 5.00
SRRKS Kyle Schwarber S2 5.00 12.00
SRRLC Lorenzo Cain S2 2.50 6.00
SRRLM Leonys Martin 2.00 5.00
SRRMA Matt Adams 2.00 5.00
SRRMB Madison Bumgarner 2.50 6.00
SRRMBR Michael Brantley 2.50 6.00
SRRMC Miguel Cabrera 4.00 10.00
SRRMCA Miguel Cabrera S2 3.00 8.00
SRRMH Matt Harvey S2 2.50 6.00
SRRMHA Matt Harvey 2.50 6.00
SRRMHO Matt Holliday 2.50 6.00
SRRMK Matt Kemp S2 2.50 6.00
SRRMM Manny Machado S2 5.00 12.00
SRRMS Max Scherzer 3.00 8.00
SRRMSA Miguel Sano S2 3.00 8.00
SRRMT Mike Trout S2 12.00 30.00
SRRMT Mark Teixeira 2.50 6.00
SRRMW Michael Wacha 2.50 6.00
SRRNC Nelson Cruz 3.00 8.00
SRRNS Noah Syndergaard 2.50 6.00
SRRPF Prince Fielder 2.50 6.00
SRRPF Prince Fielder S2 2.50 6.00
SRRPG Paul Goldschmidt S2 3.00 8.00
SRRRB Ryan Braun S2
SRRRC Robinson Cano S2 2.50 6.00
SRRRP Rick Porcello 2.50 6.00
SRRSMA Starling Marte 2.50 6.00
SRRTT Troy Tulowitzki S2 3.00 8.00
SRRWM Wil Myers S2 2.50 6.00
SRRYC Yoenis Cespedes 3.00 8.00
SRRYD Yu Darvish 3.00 8.00
SRRYM Yadier Molina 4.00 10.00
SRRYP Yasiel Puig 3.00 8.00
SRRYT Yasmany Tomas 2.00 5.00
SRRZG Zack Greinke 3.00 8.00

2016 Topps Spring Fever
COMPLETE SET (50) 10.00 25.00
SF1 Mike Trout 1.50 4.00
SF2 Buster Posey .40 1.00
SF3 Jason Heyward .25 .60
SF4 Todd Frazier .20 .50
SF5 David Price .25 .60
SF6 Zack Greinke .30 .75
SF7 Yu Darvish .30 .75
SF8 Salvador Perez .25 .60
SF9 Johnny Cueto .25 .60
SF10 Jacob deGrom .60 1.50
SF11 Joey Votto .30 .75
SF12 Robinson Cano .25 .60
SF13 Josh Donaldson .25 .60
SF14 Madison Bumgarner .25 .60
SF15 Kris Bryant .40 1.00
SF16 Clayton Kershaw .50 1.25
SF17 Hunter Pence .25 .60
SF18 Matt Harvey .25 .60
SF19 David Ortiz .30 .75
SF20 Anthony Rizzo .40 1.00
SF21 Dustin Pedroia .30 .75
SF22 Yadier Molina .40 1.00
SF23 Miguel Cabrera .30 .75
SF24 Felix Hernandez .25 .60
SF25 Andrew McCutchen .30 .75
SF26 David Wright .25 .60
SF27 Albert Pujols .40 1.00
SF28 Max Scherzer .30 .75
SF29 Bryce Harper .50 1.25
SF30 Adrian Gonzalez .25 .60
SF31 Kyle Schwarber .60 1.50
SF32 Corey Seager 2.00 5.00
SF33 Jon Gray .20 .50
SF34 Luis Severino .25 .60
SF35 Miguel Sano .30 .75
SF36 Trea Turner .60 1.50
SF37 Aaron Nola .40 1.00
SF38 Hector Olivera .25 .60
SF39 Stephen Piscotty .30 .75
SF40 Joe Mauer .25 .60
SF41 Ichiro Suzuki .40 1.00
SF42 Giancarlo Stanton .30 .75
SF43 Carlos Correa .30 .75
SF44 Masahiro Tanaka .25 .60
SF45 Jose Bautista .25 .60
SF46 Jake Arrieta .25 .60
SF47 Paul Goldschmidt .30 .75
SF48 Francisco Lindor .30 .75
SF49 Dee Gordon .20 .50
SF50 Manny Machado .30 .75

2016 Topps Team Glove Leather Autographs
SER.1 ODDS 1:2995 HOBBY; 1:598 JUMBO
SER.2 ODDS 1:1872 HOBBY
STATED PRINT RUN 25 SER.#'d SETS
SER.1 EXCH DEADLINE 1/31/2018
GLAAGA Andres Galarraga S2 20.00 50.00
GLAAGO Alex Gordon S2 40.00 100.00
GLAAK Al Kaline 75.00 200.00
GLAAN Aaron Nola EXCH 40.00 100.00
GLABH Bryce Harper EXCH 100.00 250.00
GLABJ Bo Jackson S2 40.00 100.00
GLABM Brian McCann EXCH 50.00 120.00
GLABP Buster Posey EXCH 200.00 300.00
GLACC Carlos Correa 75.00 200.00
GLACJ Chipper Jones 60.00 150.00
GLACK Clayton Kershaw S2 75.00 200.00
GLACL Roger Clemens EXCH 60.00 150.00
GLACN Robinson Cano EXCH 40.00 100.00
GLACR Cal Ripken Jr. 200.00 300.00
GLACRA Rod Carew 25.00 60.00
GLACS Chris Sale EXCH 40.00 100.00
GLACS Corey Seager S2 40.00 100.00
GLACY Carl Yastrzemski S2 50.00 120.00
GLADK Dallas Keuchel S2 20.00 50.00
GLADW David Wright S2
GLAFM Frankie Montas S2 10.00 25.00
GLAFT Frank Thomas 200.00 300.00
GLAFV Fernando Valenzuela S2 40.00 100.00
GLAGR Ken Griffey Jr. 250.00 400.00
GLAHO Henry Owens S2 15.00 40.00
GLAI Ichiro Suzuki 300.00 500.00
GLAJA Jose Abreu S2 25.00 60.00
GLAJC Jose Canseco S2 40.00 100.00
GLAJF Jeurys Familia S2 20.00 50.00
GLAJG Jon Gray 25.00 60.00
GLAJP Joc Pederson S2 25.00 60.00
GLAJS Jorge Soler S2 40.00 100.00
GLALS Luis Severino 12.00 30.00
GLAMC Michael Conforto EXCH 150.00 300.00
GLAMC Matt Cain S2 40.00 100.00
GLAMP Mike Piazza 60.00 150.00
GLAMS Miguel Sano S2 12.00 30.00
GLAMT Mike Trout 250.00 400.00
GLANS Noah Syndergaard S2 50.00 120.00
GLAPM Paul Molitor
GLAPS Pablo Sandoval 40.00 100.00
GLARJ Randy Johnson S2 60.00 150.00
GLARY Robin Yount S2 30.00 80.00
GLASC Steve Carlton S2 30.00 80.00
GLASC Kyle Schwarber 200.00 300.00
GLASK Sandy Koufax 300.00 400.00
GLASP Stephen Piscotty S2 50.00 120.00
GLATT Troy Tulowitzki S2 30.00 80.00
GLAVG Vladimir Guerrero S2 60.00 150.00
GLAWM Wil Myers 10.00 25.00

2016 Topps Team Logo Pins
SER.1 ODDS 1:897 HOBBY; 1:19 JUMBO
SER.2 ODDS 1:1412 HOBBY
TLPI Ichiro Suzuki 3.00 8.00
TLPAD Andre Dawson 2.00 5.00
TLPAM Andrew McCutchen 2.50 6.00
TLPAN Aaron Nola 3.00 8.00
TLPAP Albert Pujols 3.00 8.00
TLPARI Anthony Rizzo 3.00 8.00
TLPARO Alex Rodriguez 3.00 8.00
TLPBH Bryce Harper 4.00 10.00
TLPBP Buster Posey 3.00 8.00
TLPBR Babe Ruth 6.00 15.00
TLPCA Chris Archer 1.50 4.00
TLPCC Carlos Correa 2.50 6.00
TLPCD Chris Davis 1.50 4.00
TLPCK Clayton Kershaw 4.00 10.00
TLPCR Cal Ripken Jr. 8.00 20.00
TLPCS Chris Sale 2.50 6.00
TLPCSE Corey Seager 15.00 40.00
TLPDK Dallas Keuchel 2.00 5.00
TLPDO David Ortiz 2.50 6.00
TLPDPE Dustin Pedroia 2.50 6.00
TLPDPR David Price 2.00 5.00
TLPDW David Wright 2.00 5.00
TLPDW Dave Winfield 2.00 5.00
TLPFF Freddie Freeman 3.00 8.00
TLPFH Felix Hernandez 2.00 5.00
TLPFL Francisco Lindor 2.50 6.00
TLPGB George Brett 5.00 12.00
TLPGM Greg Maddux 3.00 8.00
TLPGS Giancarlo Stanton 2.50 6.00
TLPHA Hank Aaron 5.00 12.00
TLPHP Hunter Pence 2.00 5.00
TLPJA Jake Arrieta 2.00 5.00
TLPJA Jose Abreu 2.50 6.00
TLPJB Jose Bautista 2.00 5.00
TLPJBE Johnny Bench 2.50 6.00
TLPJD Josh Donaldson 2.00 5.00
TLPJR Jackie Robinson 2.50 6.00
TLPJVE Justin Verlander 2.50 6.00
TLPJVO Joey Votto 2.50 6.00
TLPKB Kris Bryant 3.00 8.00
TLPKG Ken Griffey Jr. 5.00 12.00
TLPKS Kyle Schwarber 5.00 12.00
TLPLC Lorenzo Cain 1.50 4.00
TLPMB Madison Bumgarner 2.00 5.00
TLPMC Miguel Cabrera 2.50 6.00
TLPMH Matt Harvey 2.00 5.00
TLPMM Mark McGwire 4.00 10.00
TLPMS Miguel Sano 2.50 6.00
TLPMTA Masahiro Tanaka 2.00 5.00
TLPMTR Mike Trout 12.00 30.00
TLPNA Nolan Arenado 4.00 10.00
TLPNC Nelson Cruz 2.50 6.00
TLPNR Nolan Ryan 8.00 20.00
TLPOS Ozzie Smith 3.00 8.00
TLPPF Prince Fielder 2.50 6.00
TLPPG Paul Goldschmidt 2.50 6.00
TLPRC Roberto Clemente 6.00 15.00
TLPRJ Randy Johnson 2.50 6.00
TLPRY Robin Yount 2.50 6.00
TLPSC Steve Carlton 2.00 5.00
TLPSK Sandy Koufax 5.00 12.00
TLPSM Shelby Miller 2.00 5.00
TLPTF Todd Frazier 1.50 4.00
TLPTG Tony Gwynn 2.50 6.00
TLPTT Troy Tulowitzki 2.50 6.00
TLPTW Ted Williams 5.00 12.00
TLPWM Willie Mays 5.00 12.00
TLPYD Yu Darvish 2.50 6.00
TLPYM Yadier Molina 3.00 8.00

2016 Topps Team Logo Pins Autographs
SER.1 ODDS 1:42,131 HOBBY; 1:929 JUMBO
SER.2 ODDS 1:4680 HOBBY
STATED PRINT RUN 25 SER.#'d SETS
SER.1 EXCH DEADLINE 1/31/2018
TLPTT Troy Tulowitzki EXCH 100.00 250.00
TLPCK Clayton Kershaw 100.00 250.00
TLPCR Cal Ripken Jr. 150.00 300.00
TLPJA Jose Abreu EXCH 60.00 150.00
TLPKB Kris Bryant 150.00 300.00
TLPKS Kyle Schwarber 125.00 250.00
TLPMS Miguel Sano 40.00 100.00
TLPMTR Mike Trout 300.00 500.00
TLPNR Nolan Ryan 100.00 200.00
TLPRJ Randy Johnson EXCH 60.00 150.00
TLPABH Bryce Harper 150.00 250.00
TLPADK Dallas Keuchel 25.00 60.00
TLPADO David Ortiz 150.00 300.00
TLPADP Dustin Pedroia 60.00 150.00
TLPADW David Wright 12.00 30.00
TLPAGM Greg Maddux 150.00 250.00
TLPAMM Mark McGwire 100.00 250.00
TLPASC Steve Carlton 50.00 120.00

2016 Topps The Greatest Streaks
COMPLETE SET (10) 10.00 25.00
RANDOM INSERTS IN PACKS
GS01 Cal Ripken Jr. 2.00 5.00
GS02 Ken Griffey Jr. 1.25 3.00
GS03 Zack Greinke .60 1.50
GS04 Ichiro Suzuki .75 2.00
GS05 Babe Ruth 1.50 4.00
GS06 Chris Sale .60 1.50
GS07 Tom Seaver .50 1.25
GS08 Nolan Ryan 2.00 5.00
GS09 Ted Williams 1.25 3.00
GS10 Lou Gehrig 1.25 3.00

2016 Topps Tribute to the Kid
COMMON CARD .75 2.00
STATED ODDS 1:8 HOBBY

2016 Topps Tribute to the Kid Relics
COMMON CARD 12.00 30.00
STATED ODDS 1:2824 HOBBY
STATED PRINT RUN 50 SER.#'d SETS

2016 Topps Walk Off Wins
COMPLETE SET (15) 12.00 30.00
RANDOM INSERTS IN PACKS
WOW1 Luis Gonzalez 1.00 2.50
WOW2 David Ortiz 1.25 3.00
WOW3 Evan Longoria 1.00 2.50
WOW4 Bill Mazeroski 1.00 2.50
WOW5 David Freese .75 2.00
WOW6 Manny Machado 1.25 3.00
WOW7 Wilmer Flores 1.00 2.50
WOW8 Allen Craig .75 2.00
WOW9 Nomar Garciaparra 1.00 2.50

WOW10 Jose Abreu 1.25 3.00
WOW11 Todd Frazier .75 2.00
WOW12 Starling Marte 1.00 2.50
WOW13 Ozzie Smith 1.50 4.00
WOW14 Carlton Fisk 1.00 2.50
WOW15 Henry Urrutia .75 2.00

2016 Topps Walk Off Wins Autographs

RANDOM INSERTS IN PACKS
STATED PRINT RUN 25 SER.#'d SETS
EXCHANGE DEADLINE 1/31/2018
WOWABM Bill Mazeroski
WOWADO David Ortiz
WOWAEL Evan Longoria
WOWALG Luis Gonzalez
WOWAWF Wilmer Flores

2016 Topps Walk Off Wins Relics

RANDOM INSERTS IN PACKS
STATED PRINT RUN 25 SER.#'d SETS
WOWRAC Allen Craig
WOWRDF David Freese 15.00 40.00
WOWRDO David Ortiz
WOWREL Evan Longoria
WOWRJA Jose Abreu 15.00 40.00
WOWRLG Luis Gonzalez
WOWRMMA Manny Machado 12.00 30.00
WOWRNG Nomar Garciaparra
WOWRTF Todd Frazier 15.00 40.00
WOWRWF Wilmer Flores 25.00 60.00

2016 Topps World Champion Autograph Relics

STATED ODDS 1:7515 HOBBY; 1:1497 JUMBO
STATED PRINT RUN 50 SER.#'d SETS
EXCHANGE DEADLINE 1/31/2018
WCARAE Alcides Escobar 25.00 60.00
WCARAG Alex Gordon 60.00 120.00
WCARKM Kendrys Morales 40.00 80.00
WCARSP Salvador Perez 50.00 100.00

2016 Topps World Champion Autographs

STATED ODDS 1:30,058 HOBBY; 1:5942 JUMBO
STATED PRINT RUN 50 SER.#'d SETS
EXCHANGE DEADLINE 1/31/2018
WCAAE Alcides Escobar 40.00 80.00
WCAAG Alex Gordon 60.00 120.00
WCAKH Kelvin Herrera EXCH 40.00 80.00
WCAKM Kendrys Morales EXCH 25.00 60.00
WCASP Salvador Perez 40.00 80.00

2016 Topps World Champion Coin and Stamps Quarter

SER.1 ODDS 1:8057 HOBBY; 1:188 JUMBO
SER.2 ODDS 1:1921 HOBBY
SER.1 PRINT RUN 50 SER.#'d SETS
SER.2 PRINT RUN 25 SER.#'d SETS
*DIME/50: .4X TO 1X QUARTER
*NICKEL/50: .4X TO 1X QUARTER
*PENNY/50: .4X TO 1X QUARTER
WCCSAK Al Kaline 20.00 50.00
WCCSBL Barry Larkin 15.00 40.00
WCCSBP Buster Posey 15.00 40.00
WCCSBR Babe Ruth 60.00 150.00
WCCSCH Cole Hamels 10.00 25.00
WCCSCR Cal Ripken Jr. 20.00 50.00
WCCSCS CC Sabathia 10.00 25.00
WCCSDF David Freese 10.00 25.00
WCCSDO David Ortiz 15.00 40.00
WCCSDP Dustin Pedroia 20.00 50.00
WCCSGB George Brett 25.00 60.00
WCCSGC Gary Carter 12.00 30.00
WCCSLG Lou Gehrig 25.00 60.00
WCCSLGO Luis Gonzalez 10.00 25.00
WCCSMB Madison Bumgarner 10.00 25.00
WCCSOS Ozzie Smith 20.00 50.00
WCCSPM Paul Molitor 12.00 30.00
WCCSPS Pablo Sandoval 10.00 25.00
WCCSSK Sandy Koufax 25.00 60.00
WCCSTG Tom Glavine 10.00 25.00
WCCSTL Tommy Lasorda 10.00 25.00
WCCSWM Willie Mays 30.00 80.00
WCCSWS Warren Spahn 10.00 25.00
WCCSWST Willie Stargell 15.00 40.00
WCCSYM Yadier Molina 15.00 40.00
WCCSRAP Albert Pujols 20.00 50.00
WCCSRAR Alex Rodriguez 30.00 80.00
WCCSRBM Bill Mazeroski 30.00 80.00
WCCSRDG Dwight Gooden 8.00 20.00
WCCSRDO David Ortiz 25.00 60.00
WCCSRDP Dustin Pedroia 12.00 30.00
WCCSRDW Dave Winfield 20.00 50.00
WCCSRHP Hunter Pence 25.00 60.00
WCCSRHW Honus Wagner 75.00 200.00
WCCSRJB Johnny Bench 25.00 60.00
WCCSRJC Jose Canseco 30.00 80.00
WCCSRJE Jacoby Ellsbury 15.00 40.00
WCCSRJP Joe Panik 30.00 80.00
WCCSRMA Moises Alou 15.00 40.00
WCCSRMC Matt Cain 20.00 50.00
WCCSRMT Mark Teixeira 30.00 80.00
WCCSRNR Nolan Ryan 40.00 100.00
WCCSRPR Phil Rizzuto 25.00 60.00
WCCSRRC Roberto Clemente 30.00 80.00
WCCSRRF Rollie Fingers 10.00 25.00
WCCSRRJ Reggie Jackson 25.00 60.00
WCCSRSK Sandy Koufax 40.00 100.00
WCCSRTP Tony Perez 20.00 50.00
WCCSRBRO Brooks Robinson 20.00 50.00
WCCSRBRU Babe Ruth 100.00 250.00

2016 Topps World Champion Relics

STATED ODDS 1:7515 HOBBY; 1:1005 JUMBO
STATED PRINT RUN 100 SER.#'d SETS
WCRAE Alcides Escobar 8.00 20.00
WCRAG Alex Gordon 8.00 20.00
WCREH Eric Hosmer 30.00 80.00
WCRJC Johnny Cueto 25.00 60.00
WCRKM Kendrys Morales 6.00 15.00
WCRLC Lorenzo Cain 20.00 50.00
WCRMM Mike Moustakas 8.00 20.00
WCRSP Salvador Perez 20.00 50.00
WCRYV Yordano Ventura 25.00 60.00

2016 Topps Update

COMPLETE SET w/o SP's (300) 20.00 50.00
PLATE PRINT RUN 1 SET PER COLOR
BLACK-CYAN-MAGENTA-YELLOW ISSUED
NO PLATE PRICING DUE TO SCARCITY
US1A Manny Machado AS .20 .50
US2 Dean Kiekhefer RC .40 1.00
US3 C.Mullee/C.Green .40 1.00
US4 Jake Arrieta AS .15 .40
US5 B.Gamel/J.Barbato .50 1.25
US6 Chris Herrmann .12 .30
US7 Blaine Boyer .12 .30
US8 Pedro Alvarez .12 .30
US9 Ross Stripling RC .40 1.00
US10 John Jaso .12 .30
US11 Erick Aybar .12 .30
US12 Matt Szczur .15 .40
US13A Sean Manaea RC .40 1.00
US13B Sean Manaea SP 1.00 2.50
w/Catcher
US14 Chris Capuano .12 .30
US15 Wilson Ramos AS .12 .30
US16 Alexei Ramirez .15 .40
US17 Pat Dean RC .40 1.00
US18 Luis Cessa RC .40 1.00
US19 Max Scherzer AS .20 .50
US20 Junichi Tazawa .12 .30
US21 Austin Barnes RC .60 1.50
US22 Neil Walker .12 .30
US23 Ian Desmond AS .12 .30
US24 Jett Bandy RC .40 1.00
US25 Hyun-Soo Kim RD .20 .50
US26 Jose Lobaton .12 .30
US27 C.Correa/J.Altuve .20 .50
US28 Alfredo Simon .12 .30
US29 Jon Moscot RC .40 1.00
US30 J.Harrison/A.McCutchen .20 .50
US31 Eduardo Nunez AS .12 .30
US32 Juan Uribe .12 .30
US33 Aledmys Diaz AS .20 .50
US34A Cody Reed RC .40 1.00
US34B Cody Reed SP 1.00 2.50
Batting
US35 Joaquin Benoit .12 .30
US36 Yonder Alonso .12 .30
US37 Jeff Francoeur .12 .30
US38 Cole Hamels AS .15 .40
US39 Tommy Joseph RC .75 2.00
US40 Blake Snell RD .15 .40
US41 Mark Melancon .12 .30
US42 Andrew Miller .15 .40
US43 Michael Conforto RD .15 .40
US44 Aledmys Diaz RD .20 .50
US45A Julio Urias RC 1.25 3.00
US45B Julio Urias SP 3.00 8.00
US46 Steven Wright .12 .30
US47 Austin Romine .12 .30
US48 Kelvin Herrera AS .12 .30
US49 Ivan Nova .15 .40
US50 Ben Zobrist AS .15 .40
US51 Steve Pearce .20 .50
US52A Wil Myers AS .15 .40
US53 H.Cervenka/J.Gant .12 .30
US54 Adam Duvall AS .30 .75
US55 Vince Velasquez .12 .30
US56 Corey Kluber AS .15 .40
US57 B.Nicholas/D.Lee .60 1.50
US58A Jameson Taillon RC .50 1.25
US58B Jameson Taillon SP 1.25 3.00
Bullpen
US59 Steven Brault RC .40 1.00
US60 Daniel Hudson .12 .30
US61 Jed Lowrie .12 .30
US62 Jake Arrieta HL .15 .40
US63 G.Mahle/A.Triggs .40 1.00
US64 Steve Pearce .20 .50
US65A Byung-Ho Park RC .50 1.25
US65B Byung-Ho Park SP 1.25 3.00
In dugout
US66 Fernando Rodney .12 .30
US67A Blake Snell RC .50 1.25
US67B Blake Snell SP 1.25 3.00
In dugout
US68 Adam Duvall HRD .30 .75
US69A Mike Clevinger RC .75 2.00
US69B Mike Clevinger SP 2.00 5.00
Batting
US70 Brandon Belt AS .15 .40
US71 Kelly Johnson .12 .30
US72 Derek Law RC .50 1.25
US73 Scott Schebler RC .60 1.50
US74 Brandon Nimmo RC .60 1.50
US75 Alex Colome .12 .30
US76 Yunel Escobar .12 .30
US77 Wade Miley .12 .30
US78 Jay Bruce .15 .40
US79A Josh Donaldson AS .15 .40
US80 Aaron Hill .12 .30
US81 Jeimer Candelario RC .50 1.25
US82 Chad Qualls .12 .30
US83 Bud Norris .12 .30
US84 Marcell Ozuna AS .20 .50
US85 Shawn Morimando RC .40 1.00
US86 Stephen Vogt AS .15 .40
US87 Asdrubal Cabrera .15 .40
US88 Tyrell Jenkins RC .40 1.00
US89 A.J. Reed RD .12 .30
US90 Jake McGee .15 .40
US91 Dan Jennings RC .40 1.00
US92A A.J. Reed RC .40 1.00
US92B A.J. Reed SP 1.00 2.50
Running
US93 Addison Russell AS .20 .50
US94 Adam Lind .15 .40
US95 Hector Neris .12 .30
US96 Chad Kuhl RC .50 1.25
US97 Cameron Maybin .12 .30
US98 Mike Bolsinger .12 .30
US99A Jeremy Hazelbaker RC .50 1.25
US99B Jeremy Hazelbaker SP 1.25 3.00
Dugout
US100 Andrew Cashner .12 .30
US101 Brad Brach AS .12 .30
US102 Aaron Hicks .15 .40
US103 Matt Duffy .12 .30
US104 Matt Wieters .20 .50
US105 Joey Rickard RC .40 1.00
US106 Ji-Man Choi RC .50 1.25
US107 Rene Rivera .12 .30
US108 Keon Broxton RC .40 1.00
US109 Shelby Miller .15 .40
US110 Bryan Shaw .12 .30
US111 Josh Reddick .12 .30
US112 Ben Revere .12 .30
US113 Steven Wright AS .12 .30
US114 Trevor Story HL .60 1.50
US115 Xander Bogaerts AS .20 .50
US116 Jake Diekman .12 .30
US117A Tyler Naquin RC .60 1.50
US117B Tyler Naquin SP 1.50 4.00
Dugout
US118 Mark Trumbo HRD .12 .30
US119 Stephen Piscotty RD .20 .50
US120 C.Davis/M.Machado .20 .50
US121 Ender Inciarte .12 .30
US122 Oswaldo Arcia .12 .30
US123 J.Blash/L.Perdomo .40 1.00
US124 Junior Guerra RC .50 1.25
US125A Daniel Murphy AS .15 .40
US126 Bartolo Colon HL .12 .30
US127 Brad Ziegler .12 .30
US128 Denard Span .12 .30
US129 Peter Bourjos .12 .30
US130 Ryan Rua .12 .30
US131 Tyler Flowers .12 .30
US132 Jose Reyes .15 .40
US133 Odubel Herrera AS .15 .40
US134 Luis Severino RD .15 .40
US135 Tony Barnette RC .40 1.00
US136 Julio Urias RD .40 1.00
US137 Dexter Fowler .15 .40
US138 Kyle Schwarber RD .40 1.00
US139 Albert Almora RD .15 .40
US140 Eduardo Nunez .12 .30
US141 Buster Posey AS .25 .60
US142 Andrelton Simmons .12 .30
US143 Drew Stubbs .12 .30
US144 Giancarlo Stanton HRD .20 .50
US145 Aroldis Chapman .20 .50
US146 Alen Hanson RC .50 1.25
US147 T.Guerrero/M.Buschmann .40 1.00
US148 Matt Moore .15 .40
US149 Matt Bowman RC .40 1.00
US150 Trevor Story RD .60 1.50
US151 Taylor Motter RC .40 1.00
US152A Michael Fulmer RC .60 1.50
US152B Michael Fulmer SP 1.50 4.00
US153 Zach Duke .12 .30
US154 Trevor Cahill .12 .30
US155 Nolan Reimold .12 .30
US156 Geovany Soto .12 .30
US157 Jameson Taillon RD .15 .40
US158A Nomar Mazara RC .60 1.50
US158B Nomar Mazara SP 1.50 4.00
US159 Edwin Encarnacion AS .20 .50
US160 Jon Lester AS .15 .40
US161A Bartolo Colon AS .12 .30
US162 Drew Pomeranz .15 .40
US163 Matt Wieters AS .20 .50
US164 Todd Frazier HRD .15 .40
US165 Drew Butera .12 .30
US166 Starling Marte AS .15 .40
US167A Corey Seager AS 1.25 3.00
US168 Robbie Grossman .12 .30
US169 Max Scherzer HL .20 .50
US170 Addison Reed .12 .30
US171 Miguel Sano RD .12 .30
US172 Kenley Jansen AS .15 .40
US173 Fernando Rodney AS .12 .30
US174 Starlin Castro .12 .30
US175A Mike Trout AS 1.00 2.50
US176A Jose Berrios RC .60 1.50
US176B Jose Berrios SP 1.50 4.00
In Dugout
US177 Matt Joyce .12 .30
US178A Albert Almora RC .50 1.25
US178B Albert Almora SP 1.25 3.00
Gray jersey
US179 Ezequiel Carrera .12 .30
US180 Matt Andriese .15 .40
US181 Andrew Miller AS .15 .40
US182A Hyun-Soo Kim RC .60 1.50
US182B Hyun-Soo Kim SP 1.50 4.00
w/Fans
US183 Todd Frazier .12 .30
US184 Yovani Gallardo .12 .30
US185 Jeremy Hellickson .12 .30
US186 Melvin Upton Jr. .15 .40
US187 Justin Wilson .12 .30
US188 Shawn Kelley .12 .30
US189 Jonathan Lucroy .15 .40
US190A Trayce Thompson RC .60 1.50
US190B Trayce Thompson SP 1.50 4.00
Fielding
US191 Mark Trumbo AS .12 .30
US192 Jackie Bradley Jr. AS .20 .50
US193 Joakim Soria .12 .30
US194A Eric Hosmer AS .15 .40
US195 Carlos Beltran .15 .40
US196 Mark Trumbo .12 .30
US197 Brad Brach .12 .30
US198A Carlos Gonzalez AS .15 .40
US199 Brandon Moss .12 .30
US200 Alex Colome AS .12 .30
US201A Mookie Betts AS .40 1.00
US202 Jose Ramirez .15 .40
US203 Tony Kemp RC .40 1.00
US204 Michael Fulmer RD .20 .50
US205 Corey Seager HRD 1.25 3.00
US206A Salvador Perez AS .15 .40
US207 Jarrod Cosart .12 .30
US208 Pedro Strop .12 .30
US209 Tyler Clippard .12 .30
US210 James Shields .12 .30
US211A Tyler White RC .40 1.00
US211B Tyler White SP 1.00 2.50
In dugout
US212 Ian Kennedy .12 .30
US213 Lucas Giolito RD .20 .50
US214 Edwin Diaz RC .75 2.00
US215 Kirby Yates RC .60 1.50
US216A Robert Stephenson RC .50 1.25
US216B Robert Stephenson SP 1.00 2.50
Bunting
US217 J.Martinez/M.Cabrera .20 .50
US218 Carlos Gonzalez HRD .15 .40
US219 Tim Adleman RC .40 1.00
US220A Colin Moran RC .40 1.00
US220B Colin Moran SP 1.00 2.50
w/Bat
US221 D.Gregorius/S.Castro .15 .40
US222A Zach Britton AS .15 .40
US223A Jose Fernandez AS .20 .50
US224 Albert Suarez RC .40 1.00
US225 Tim Lincecum .15 .40
US226A Trevor Story RC 4.00 10.00
US226B Trevor Story SP 20.00 50.00
US227 Aaron Sanchez AS .15 .40
US228 Jose Berrios RD .20 .50
US229A Lucas Giolito RC .60 1.50
US229B Lucas Giolito SP 1.50 4.00
Batting
US230 Zack Greinke .20 .50
US231 Austin Jackson .12 .30
US232A Clayton Kershaw AS .30 .75
US233A Chris Sale AS .20 .50
US234 Carlos Beltran AS .15 .40
US235 Matt Bush (RC) .50 1.25
US236 Drew Pomeranz AS .15 .40
US237 Ian Desmond .12 .30
US238 Alejandro de Aza .12 .30
US239 Matt Kemp .15 .40
US240 Rickie Weeks Jr. .12 .30
US241 Jose Quintana AS .12 .30
US242 Joe Biagini RC .40 1.00
US243 Drew Storen .12 .30
US244A Mallex Smith RC .40 1.00
US244B Mallex Smith SP 1.00 2.50
No helmet
US245 Howie Kendrick .12 .30
US246 Jay Bruce AS .15 .40
US247 Tyler Goeddel RC .40 1.00
US248 Sam Dyson .12 .30
US249 Tony Wolters RC .40 1.00
US250 Jonathan Lucroy AS .15 .40
US251 Craig Kimbrel .15 .40
US252A Johnny Cueto AS .15 .40
US253 A.J. Ramos AS .12 .30
US254A David Ortiz AS .20 .50
US255 Adam Conley .12 .30
US256A Nolan Arenado AS .30 .75
US257 Jedd Gyorko .12 .30
US258A Seung-Hwan Oh RC 1.00 2.50
US258B Seung-Hwan Oh SP 2.50 6.00
US259 Chris Young .12 .30
US260 Ichiro Suzuki HL .25 .60
US261 Jarrod Saltalamacchia .12 .30
US262A Robinson Cano AS .15 .40
US263 Kirk Nieuwenhuis .12 .30
US264 Cody Anderson .12 .30
US265 Doug Fister .12 .30
US266 Willson Contreras RC 2.50 6.00
US267 Michael Saunders AS .15 .40
US268 Wil Myers HRD .15 .40
US269 Francisco Rodriguez .15 .40
US270 Chris Devenski RC .40 1.00
US271 Jeff Francoeur .15 .40
US272 Brett Lawrie .15 .40
US273 Paul Goldschmidt AS .20 .50
US274 Chris Coghlan .12 .30
US275 Francisco Lindor AS .20 .50
US276 Justin Grimm .12 .30
US277 Derek Dietrich .15 .40
US278 Mark Melancon AS .12 .30
US279 Corey Seager RD 2.50 6.00
US280 Robinson Cano HRD .15 .40
US281A Anthony Rizzo AS .25 .60
US282 Will Harris AS .12 .30
US283 David Freese .12 .30
US284 Aaron Nola RD .25 .60
US285 Kenta Maeda RD .25 .60
US286 Gerardo Parra .12 .30
US287A Tim Anderson RC 5.00 12.00
US287B Tim Anderson SP 50.00 120.00
Dugout
US288A Jose Altuve AS .15 .40
US289 Cesar Vargas RC .40 1.00
US290A Miguel Cabrera AS .20 .50
US291A Dellin Betances AS .15 .40
US292A Aledmys Diaz RC .60 1.50
US292B Aledmys Diaz SP 1.50 4.00
Tipping cap
US293 Hansel Robles .12 .30
US294A Kris Bryant AS .25 .60
US295 Nomar Mazara RD .20 .50
US296 Jeurys Familia AS .15 .40
US297A Bryce Harper AS .30 .75
US298 Jhoulys Chacin .12 .30
US299 Julio Teheran AS .15 .40
US300 A.J. Ellis .12 .30

2016 Topps Update Black

*BLACK: 10X TO 25X BASIC
*BLACK RC: 3X TO 8X BASIC RC
STATED PRINT RUN 65 SER.#'d SETS
US33 Aledmys Diaz AS 15.00 40.00
US44 Aledmys Diaz RD 15.00 40.00
US167 Corey Seager AS 20.00 50.00
US205 Corey Seager HRD 20.00 50.00
US232 Clayton Kershaw AS 20.00 50.00
US292 Aledmys Diaz 15.00 40.00
US294 Kris Bryant AS 15.00 40.00

2016 Topps Update Black and White Negative

*BW NEGATIVE: 6X TO 15X BASIC
*BW NEGATIVE RC: 2X TO 5X BASIC
US33 Aledmys Diaz AS 8.00 20.00
US44 Aledmys Diaz RD 8.00 20.00
US141 Buster Posey AS 10.00 25.00
US175 Mike Trout AS 15.00 40.00
US232 Clayton Kershaw AS 10.00 25.00
US266 Willson Contreras 8.00 20.00
US292 Aledmys Diaz 8.00 20.00

2016 Topps Update Gold

*GOLD: 2X TO 5X BASIC
*GOLD RC: .6X TO 1.5X BASIC RC
STATED PRINT RUN 2016 SER.#'d SETS

2016 Topps Update Pink

*PINK: 12X TO 30X BASIC
*PINK RC: 4X TO 10X BASIC RC
STATED PRINT RUN 50 SER.#'d SETS
US33 Aledmys Diaz AS 20.00 50.00
US44 Aledmys Diaz RD 20.00 50.00
US167 Corey Seager AS 25.00 60.00
US205 Corey Seager HRD 25.00 60.00
US232 Clayton Kershaw AS 25.00 60.00
US292 Aledmys Diaz 20.00 50.00
US294 Kris Bryant AS 20.00 50.00

2016 Topps Update Rainbow Foil

*FOIL: 3X TO 8X BASIC
*FOIL RC: 1X TO 2.5X BASIC RC

2016 Topps Update 3000 Hits Club

COMPLETE SET (20) 4.00 10.00
3000H1 Carl Yastrzemski .75 2.00
3000H2 Ty Cobb .75 2.00
3000H3 Hank Aaron 1.00 2.50
3000H4 Stan Musial .75 2.00
3000H5 Honus Wagner .50 1.25
3000H6 Paul Molitor .50 1.25
3000H7 Willie Mays 1.00 2.50
3000H8 Eddie Murray .40 1.00
3000H9 Cal Ripken Jr. 1.50 4.00
3000H10 George Brett 1.00 2.50
3000H11 Robin Yount .50 1.25
3000H12 Tony Gwynn .50 1.25
3000H13 Ichiro Suzuki .60 1.50
3000H14 Craig Biggio .40 1.00
3000H15 Rickey Henderson
3000H16 Rod Carew .40 1.00
3000H17 Lou Brock .40 1.00
3000H18 Wade Boggs .40 1.00
3000H19 Roberto Clemente 1.25 3.00
3000H20 Al Kaline .50 1.25

2016 Topps Update 3000 Hits Club Autographs

STATED PRINT RUN 25 SER.#'d SETS
EXCHANGE DEADLINE 9/30/2018
3000AI Ichiro Suzuki 200.00 400.00
3000AAK Al Kaline 25.00 50.00
3000ACB Craig Biggio
3000ACR Cal Ripken Jr. 40.00 100.00
3000ACY Carl Yastrzemski 30.00 80.00
3000APM Paul Molitor 20.00 50.00
3000ARC Rod Carew
3000ARH Rickey Henderson
3000AWB Wade Boggs

2016 Topps Update 3000 Hits Club Medallions

*GOLD/50: 1.2X TO 3X BASIC
3000M1 Ty Cobb 2.00 5.00
3000M2 Hank Aaron 2.50 6.00
3000M3 Stan Musial 2.00 5.00
3000M4 Honus Wagner 1.25 3.00
3000M5 Carl Yastrzemski 2.00 5.00
3000M6 Paul Molitor 1.25 3.00
3000M7 Willie Mays 2.50 6.00
3000M8 Eddie Murray 1.00 2.50
3000M9 Cal Ripken Jr. 4.00 10.00
3000M10 George Brett 2.50 6.00
3000M11 Robin Yount 1.25 3.00
3000M12 Tony Gwynn 1.25 3.00
3000M13 Alex Rodriguez 1.50 4.00
3000M14 Craig Biggio 1.00 2.50
3000M15 Rickey Henderson 1.25 3.00
3000M16 Rod Carew 1.00 2.50
3000M17 Lou Brock 1.00 2.50
3000M18 Wade Boggs 1.00 2.50
3000M19 Roberto Clemente 3.00 8.00
3000M20 Al Kaline 1.25 3.00

2016 Topps Update 500 Home Run Club Stamps

PRINT RUNS B/WN 220-375 COPIES PER
500SCAP Albert Pujols/375 20.00 50.00
500SCAR Alex Rodriguez/375 6.00 15.00
500SCBR Babe Ruth/375 12.00 30.00
500SCDO David Ortiz/375 8.00 20.00
500SCEM Eddie Murray/375 4.00 10.00
500SCFT Frank Thomas/375 8.00 20.00
500SCHA Hank Aaron/375 10.00 25.00
500SCHK Harmon Killebrew/375 5.00 12.00
500SCKG Ken Griffey Jr./375 10.00 25.00
500SCRJ Reggie Jackson/375 5.00 12.00
500SCRP Rafael Palmeiro/375 4.00 10.00
500SCTW Ted Williams/375 10.00 25.00
500SCWM Willie McCovey/375 4.00 10.00
500SCMMC Mark McGwire/220 8.00 20.00
500SCWMA Willie Mays/375 10.00 25.00

2016 Topps Update 500 HR Futures Club

COMPLETE SET (20) 10.00 25.00
*GOLD: .5X TO 1.2X BASIC
*SILVER: .5X TO 1.2X BASIC
5001 Miguel Cabrera .60 1.50
5002 Prince Fielder .50 1.25
5003 Ryan Braun .50 1.25
5004 Giancarlo Stanton .60 1.50
5005 Mike Trout 3.00 8.00
5006 Bryce Harper 1.00 2.50
5007 Adam Jones .50 1.25
5008 Nolan Arenado 1.00 2.50
5009 Adrian Gonzalez .50 1.25
50010 Jose Bautista .50 1.25
50011 Josh Donaldson .50 1.25
50012 Paul Goldschmidt .60 1.50
50013 Carlos Gonzalez .50 1.25
50014 Justin Upton .50 1.25
50015 Kyle Schwarber 1.25 3.00
50016 Chris Davis .40 1.00
50017 Anthony Rizzo .75 2.00
50018 Carlos Correa .60 1.50
50019 Joc Pederson .50 1.25
50020 Miguel Sano .60 1.50

2016 Topps Update 500 HR Futures Club Medallions

*GOLD/50: 1X TO 2.5X BASIC
500M1 Miguel Cabrera 4.00 10.00
500M2 Prince Fielder 3.00 8.00
500M3 Ryan Braun 3.00 8.00
500M4 Giancarlo Stanton 4.00 10.00
500M5 Mike Trout 6.00 15.00
500M6 Bryce Harper 5.00 12.00
500M7 Adam Jones 3.00 8.00
500M8 Nolan Arenado 6.00 15.00
500M9 Adrian Gonzalez 3.00 8.00
500M10 Jose Bautista 3.00 8.00
500M11 Josh Donaldson 3.00 8.00
500M12 Paul Goldschmidt 4.00 10.00
500M13 Carlos Gonzalez 3.00 8.00
500M14 Justin Upton 3.00 8.00
500M15 Kyle Schwarber 6.00 15.00
500M16 Chris Davis 2.50 6.00
500M17 Anthony Rizzo 5.00 12.00
500M18 Carlos Correa 4.00 10.00
500M19 Joc Pederson 3.00 8.00
500M20 Miguel Sano 4.00 10.00

2016 Topps Update 500 HR Futures Club Relics

STATED PRINT RUN 99 SER.#'d SETS
500RAG Adrian Gonzalez 12.00 30.00
500RAJ Adam Jones 5.00 12.00
500RAR Anthony Rizzo 8.00 20.00
500RBH Bryce Harper 10.00 25.00
500RCC Carlos Correa 6.00 15.00
500RGS Giancarlo Stanton 6.00 15.00
500RJU Justin Upton 5.00 12.00
500RKS Kyle Schwarber 10.00 25.00
500RMC Miguel Cabrera 6.00 15.00
500RMS Miguel Sano 6.00 15.00
500RMT Mike Trout 30.00 80.00
500RNA Nolan Arenado 10.00 25.00
500RPF Prince Fielder 5.00 12.00
500RPG Paul Goldschmidt 6.00 15.00
500RRB Ryan Braun 5.00 12.00

2016 Topps Update All-Star Game Access

COMPLETE SET (25) 25.00 60.00
MLB1 Clayton Kershaw 1.50 4.00
MLB2 Manny Machado 1.00 2.50
MLB3 Anthony Rizzo 1.25 3.00
MLB4 Nolan Arenado 1.50 4.00
MLB5 Kris Bryant 1.25 3.00
MLB6 Chris Sale 1.00 2.50
MLB7 Jose Altuve .75 2.00
MLB8 Mike Trout 5.00 12.00
MLB9 Robinson Cano .75 2.00
MLB10 Bryce Harper 1.50 4.00
MLB11 David Ortiz 1.00 2.50
MLB12 Buster Posey 1.25 3.00
MLB13 Corey Seager 6.00 15.00
MLB14 Wil Myers .75 2.00
MLB15 Dellin Betances .75 2.00
MLB16 Zach Britton .75 2.00
MLB17 Miguel Cabrera 1.00 2.50
MLB18 Bartolo Colon .60 1.50
MLB19 Johnny Cueto .75 2.00
MLB20 Josh Donaldson .75 2.00
MLB21 Edwin Encarnacion 1.00 2.50
MLB22 Carlos Gonzalez .75 2.00
MLB23 Eric Hosmer .75 2.00
MLB24 Daniel Murphy .75 2.00
MLB25 Salvador Perez .75 2.00

2016 Topps Update All-Star Stitches

*GOLD/50: .75X TO 2X BASIC
ASTITAD Adam Duvall 5.00 12.00
ASTITADI Aledmys Diaz 8.00 20.00
ASTITAM Andrew Miller 5.00 12.00
ASTITARI Anthony Rizzo 5.00 12.00
ASTITARU Addison Russell 5.00 12.00
ASTITAS Aaron Sanchez 4.00 10.00
ASTITBBE Brandon Belt 4.00 10.00
ASTITBC Bartolo Colon 4.00 10.00
ASTITBH Bryce Harper 5.00 12.00
ASTITBP Buster Posey 4.00 10.00
ASTITBZ Ben Zobrist 5.00 12.00
ASTITCB Carlos Beltran 4.00 10.00
ASTITCH Cole Hamels 2.50 6.00
ASTITCK Clayton Kershaw 6.00 15.00
ASTITCKL Corey Kluber 5.00 12.00
ASTITCS Corey Seager 10.00 25.00
ASTITCSA Chris Sale 3.00 8.00
ASTITDB Dellin Betances 4.00 10.00
ASTITDF Dexter Fowler 4.00 10.00
ASTITDM Daniel Murphy 4.00 10.00
ASTITDO David Ortiz 8.00 20.00
ASTITDP Drew Pomeranz 2.50 6.00
ASTITDS Danny Salazar 2.50 6.00
ASTITEE Edwin Encarnacion 4.00 10.00
ASTITEH Eric Hosmer 2.50 6.00
ASTITFL Francisco Lindor 8.00 20.00
ASTITID Ian Desmond 2.00 5.00
ASTITJA Jake Arrieta 4.00 10.00
ASTITJAL Jose Altuve 4.00 10.00
ASTITJB Jackie Bradley Jr. 4.00 10.00
ASTITJBR Jay Bruce 2.50 6.00
ASTITJC Johnny Cueto 2.50 6.00
ASTITJD Josh Donaldson 2.50 6.00
ASTITJF Jose Fernandez 6.00 15.00
ASTITJL Jon Lester 4.00 10.00
ASTITJT Julio Teheran 4.00 10.00
ASTITKB Kris Bryant 4.00 10.00
ASTITMB Madison Bumgarner 2.50 6.00
ASTITMBE Mookie Betts 5.00 12.00
ASTITMC Matt Carpenter 3.00 8.00
ASTITMCA Miguel Cabrera 5.00 12.00
ASTITMMA Manny Machado 5.00 12.00
ASTITMO Marcell Ozuna 3.00 8.00
ASTITMS Michael Saunders 2.50 6.00
ASTITMSC Max Scherzer 3.00 8.00
ASTITMT Mark Trumbo 3.00 8.00
ASTITMTR Mike Trout 15.00 40.00
ASTITMW Matt Wieters 3.00 8.00
ASTITNA Nolan Arenado 5.00 12.00
ASTITNS Noah Syndergaard 5.00 12.00
ASTITPG Paul Goldschmidt 4.00 10.00
ASTITRC Robinson Cano 2.50 6.00
ASTITSM Starling Marte 2.50 6.00
ASTITSP Salvador Perez 2.50 6.00
ASTITSS Stephen Strasburg 3.00 8.00
ASTITSV Stephen Vogt 2.50 6.00
ASTITSW Steven Wright 2.50 6.00
ASTITTF Todd Frazier 2.00 5.00
ASTITWR Wilson Ramos 4.00 10.00
ASTITXB Xander Bogaerts 5.00 12.00
ASTITZB Zach Britton 2.50 6.00

2016 Topps Update All-Star Stitches Autographs

STATED PRINT RUN 25 SER.#'d SETS
EXCHANGE DEADLINE 9/30/2018
ASAPAR Anthony Rizzo 100.00 250.00
ASAPBH Bryce Harper 125.00 300.00
ASAPBP Buster Posey 125.00 300.00
ASAPCK Clayton Kershaw 125.00 300.00
ASAPDO David Ortiz 100.00 250.00
ASAPJAR Jake Arrieta 100.00 250.00
ASAPKB Kris Bryant 150.00 400.00
ASAPMM Manny Machado 100.00 250.00
ASAPMT Mike Trout 150.00 400.00
ASAPNA Nolan Arenado 75.00 200.00
ASAPNS Noah Syndergaard 50.00 120.00
ASAPRC Robinson Cano 30.00 80.00

2016 Topps Update All-Star Stitches Dual

STATED PRINT RUN 25 SER.#'d SETS
ASDAR Rizzo/Arrieta 25.00 60.00
ASDBBR Bogaerts/Betts 25.00 60.00
ASDBC Cueto/Bumgarner 8.00 20.00
ASDBO Ortiz/Betts 30.00 80.00
ASDBR Rizzo/Bryant 30.00 80.00
ASDDE Encarnacion/Donaldson 25.00 60.00
ASDHS Strasburg/Harper 25.00 60.00
ASDHT Trout/Harper 40.00 100.00
ASDPB Bumgarner/Posey 30.00 80.00
ASDPH Hosmer/Perez 30.00 80.00

2016 Topps Update All-Star Stitches Triple

STATED PRINT RUN 25 SER.#'d SETS
ASTABR Brnt/Arrta/Rzzo 25.00 60.00
ASTBBB Bgrts/Btts/Brdly Jr. 40.00 100.00
ASTBOB Btts/Bgrts/Ortiz 40.00 100.00
ASTBRR Rzzo/Brnt/Rssll 40.00 100.00
ASTFSS Strsbrg/Sndrgrd/Frnndz 30.00 80.00
ASTHTB Brnt/Trt/Hrpr 100.00 250.00
ASTMAD Dnldsn/Mchdo/Arndo 30.00 80.00
ASTMTW Trumbo/Machado/Wieters 20.00 50.00
ASTPBC Cto/Psy/Bmgrnr 25.00 60.00
ASTRLS Rssll/Sgr/Lndr 30.00 80.00

2016 Topps Update Fire

COMPLETE SET (15) 4.00 10.00
F1 Kenta Maeda .60 1.50
F2 Michael Conforto .40 1.00
F3 Bryce Harper .75 2.00
F4 Mike Trout 2.50 6.00
F5 Carlos Correa .50 1.25
F6 Ken Griffey Jr. 1.00 2.50
F7 Clayton Kershaw .75 2.00
F8 Noah Syndergaard .40 1.00
F9 Kris Bryant .60 1.50
F10 Anthony Rizzo .60 1.50
F11 Corey Seager 3.00 8.00
F12 Miguel Sano .50 1.25
F13 Andrew McCutchen .50 1.25
F14 Josh Donaldson .40 1.00
F15 Giancarlo Stanton .50 1.25

2016 Topps Update Fire Autographs

STATED PRINT RUN 25 SER.#'d SETS
EXCHANGE DEADLINE 9/30/2018
FA1 Kenta Maeda 40.00 100.00
FA5 Carlos Correa 60.00 150.00
FA7 Clayton Kershaw
FA8 Noah Syndergaard 40.00 100.00
FA9 Kris Bryant 125.00 300.00
FA10 Anthony Rizzo 30.00 80.00
FA11 Corey Seager EXCH 75.00 200.00
FA12 Miguel Sano 20.00 50.00

2016 Topps Update First Pitch

COMPLETE SET (20) 3.00 8.00
FP1 Jeff Bauman .75 2.00
FP2 Jake Gyllenhaal .75 2.00
FP3 Warren G .75 2.00
FP4 Brady Kahle .75 2.00
FP5 Keith Urban .75 2.00
FP6 Aubrey Plaza .75 2.00
FP7 Chance the Rapper .75 2.00
FP8 Burke Waldron .75 2.00
FP9 Craig Sager .75 2.00
FP10 JoJo Fletcher .75 2.00

2016 Topps Update First Pitch Relics

STATED PRINT RUN 25 SER.#'d SETS
FPRAP Aubrey Plaza 20.00 50.00
FPRBW Burke Waldron 20.00 50.00
FPRCS Craig Sager 20.00 50.00
FPRCTR Chance the Rapper 20.00 50.00
FPRJF JoJo Fletcher 20.00 50.00
FPRKU Keith Urban 20.00 50.00
FPRWG Warren G 20.00 50.00

2016 Topps Update Target Exclusive Rookies

TAR1 Luis Severino 1.50 4.00
TAR2 Trea Turner 4.00 10.00
TAR3 Jose Berrios 2.00 5.00
TAR4 Trevor Story 6.00 15.00
TAR5 Nomar Mazara 2.00 5.00
TAR6 Julio Urias 4.00 10.00
TAR7 Blake Snell 1.50 4.00
TAR8 Jameson Taillon 1.50 4.00
TAR9 Hyun-Soo Kim 2.00 5.00
TAR10 Lucas Giolito 2.00 5.00
TAR11 Michael Fulmer 2.00 5.00
TAR12 Byung-Ho Park 1.50 4.00
TAR13 Michael Conforto 1.50 4.00
TAR14 Jon Gray 1.25 3.00
TAR15 Kenta Maeda 2.50 6.00
TAR16 Peter O'Brien 1.25 3.00
TAR17 Stephen Piscotty 2.00 5.00
TAR18 Miguel Sano 2.00 5.00
TAR19 Kyle Schwarber 4.00 10.00
TAR20 Corey Seager 12.00 30.00

2016 Topps Update Team Franklin

COMPLETE SET (20) 4.00 10.00
TF1 Miguel Cabrera .50 1.25
TF2 Yadier Molina .50 1.25
TF3 Robinson Cano .40 1.00
TF4 Salvador Perez .40 1.00
TF5 Paul Goldschmidt .50 1.25
TF6 Jose Altuve .40 1.00
TF7 Evan Longoria .40 1.00
TF8 Justin Upton .40 1.00
TF9 Joey Votto .50 1.25
TF10 Yoenis Cespedes .50 1.25
TF11 Hunter Pence .40 1.00
TF12 Dustin Pedroia .50 1.25
TF13 Ryan Braun .40 1.00
TF14 Starling Marte .50 1.25
TF15 Jose Abreu .50 1.25
TF16 Edwin Encarnacion .50 1.25

TF17 Hanley Ramirez .40 1.00
TF18 Miguel Sano .50 1.25
TF19 Josh Reddick .30 .75
TF20 Ben Zobrist .40 1.00

2016 Topps Update Team Franklin Autographs

STATED PRINT RUN 25 SER.#'d SETS
EXCHANGE DEADLINE 9/30/2018
TFADP Dustin Pedroia 20.00 50.00
TFAEL Evan Longoria
TFAHR Hanley Ramirez 10.00 25.00
TFAMS Miguel Sano 20.00 50.00
TFARC Robinson Cano 20.00 50.00

2016 Topps Update Walmart Exclusive Rookies

W1 Aaron Nola 2.50 6.00
W2 Henry Owens 1.50 4.00
W3 Jose Berrios 2.00 5.00
W4 Trevor Story 6.00 15.00
W5 Nomar Mazara 2.00 5.00
W6 Julio Urias 4.00 10.00
W7 Blake Snell 1.50 4.00
W8 Jameson Taillon 1.50 4.00
W9 Hyun-Soo Kim 2.00 5.00
W10 Lucas Giolito 2.00 5.00
W11 Michael Fulmer 2.00 5.00
W12 Byung-Ho Park 1.50 4.00
W13 Michael Conforto 1.50 4.00
W14 Jon Gray 1.25 3.00
W15 Kenta Maeda 2.50 6.00
W16 Peter O'Brien 1.25 3.00
W17 Stephen Piscotty 2.00 5.00
W18 Miguel Sano 2.00 5.00
W19 Kyle Schwarber 4.00 10.00
W20 Corey Seager 12.00 30.00

2016 Topps Walmart Holiday Snowflake

HMW1 Mike Trout 1.50 4.00
HMW2 Jose Berrios RC .30 .75
HMW3 Paul Goldschmidt .30 .75
HMW4 Jason Heyward .25 .60
HMW5 CC Sabathia .25 .60
HMW6 Starling Marte .25 .60
HMW7 George Springer .25 .60
HMW8 Jaime Garcia .20 .50
HMW9 Justin Upton .25 .60
HMW10 Brett Gardner .25 .60
HMW11 Jose Abreu .30 .75
HMW12 Dallas Keuchel .25 .60
HMW13 Aroldis Chapman .30 .75
HMW14 Andrelton Simmons .20 .50
HMW15 Adam Jones .25 .60
HMW16 Matt Holliday .30 .75
HMW17 Jacoby Ellsbury .25 .60
HMW18 Wade Davis .20 .50
HMW19 Joe Panik .25 .60
HMW20 Alex Rodriguez .40 1.00
HMW21 Matt Andriese .25 .60
HMW22 Byung-Ho Park RC .25 .60
HMW23 Carlos Gonzalez .25 .60
HMW24 Manny Machado .30 .75
HMW25 Noah Syndergaard .25 .60
HMW26 Julio Urias RC .60 1.50
HMW27 Dustin Pedroia .30 .75
HMW28 Jackie Bradley Jr. .30 .75
HMW29 Nelson Cruz .30 .75
HMW30 Jonathan Lucroy .25 .60
HMW31 Corey Kluber .25 .60
HMW32 Adeiny Hechavarria .20 .50
HMW33 Seung-Hwan Oh RC .50 1.25
HMW34 Michael Fulmer RC .30 .75
HMW35 Andrew Miller .25 .60
HMW36 Shelby Miller .25 .60
HMW37 Raisel Iglesias .25 .60
HMW38 Nori Aoki .20 .50
HMW39 Anthony Rizzo .40 1.00
HMW40 Byron Buxton .30 .75
HMW41 Jake Odorizzi .20 .50
HMW42 Madison Bumgarner .25 .60
HMW43 Masahiro Tanaka .25 .60
HMW44 Curtis Granderson .25 .60
HMW45 Aaron Nola RC .40 1.00
HMW46 Tyler White RC .20 .50
HMW47 Johnny Cueto .25 .60
HMW48 Andrew McCutchen .30 .75
HMW49 Francisco Rodriguez .25 .60
HMW50 Asdrubal Cabrera .25 .60
HMW51 Luis Severino RC .25 .60
HMW52 Marcell Ozuna .30 .75
HMW53 Vince Velasquez .20 .50
HMW54 Melvin Upton Jr. .25 .60
HMW55 Lorenzo Cain .20 .50
HMW56 David Price .25 .60
HMW57 Michael Conforto RC .25 .60
HMW58 Kris Bryant .40 1.00
HMW59 Kole Calhoun .20 .50
HMW60 Freddie Freeman .40 1.00
HMW61 Brandon Crawford .25 .60
HMW62 Aledmys Diaz RC .30 .75
HMW63 Ryan Howard .25 .60
HMW64 Giancarlo Stanton .30 .75
HMW65 Mark Teixeira .25 .60
HMW66 Marco Estrada .20 .50
HMW67 Mallex Smith RC .20 .50
HMW68 Mark Trumbo .20 .50
HMW69 Zack Greinke .30 .75
HMW70 Matt Wieters .30 .75
HMW71 Jon Lester .25 .60
HMW72 Jeremy Hazelbaker RC .25 .60
HMW73 Jacob deGrom .60 1.50
HMW74 Clayton Kershaw .50 1.25
HMW75 Max Scherzer .30 .75
HMW76 David Ortiz .30 .75
HMW77 Evan Gattis .20 .50
HMW78 Ichiro .40 1.00
HMW79 J.D. Martinez .30 .75
HMW80 Josh Donaldson .25 .60
HMW81 Kyle Schwarber RC .60 1.50
HMW82 Justin Verlander .30 .75
HMW83 Evan Longoria .25 .60
HMW84 Ian Desmond .20 .50
HMW85 Neil Walker .20 .50
HMW86 Matt Harvey .25 .60
HMW87 Steven Matz .20 .50
HMW88 Matt Adams .20 .50
HMW89 Hyun-Soo Kim RC .30 .75
HMW90 Dexter Fowler .25 .60
HMW91 Prince Fielder .25 .60
HMW92 Elvis Andrus .25 .60
HMW93 Cole Hamels .25 .60
HMW94 Albert Almora RC .25 .60
HMW95 Tanner Roark .20 .50
HMW96 Gerrit Cole .30 .75
HMW97 Matt Carpenter .30 .75
HMW98 Jason Kipnis .25 .60
HMW99 Miguel Cabrera .30 .75
HMW100 Carlos Martinez .25 .60
HMW101 Eric Hosmer .25 .60
HMW102 Maikel Franco .25 .60
HMW103 Jason Hammel .25 .60
HMW104 Xander Bogaerts .30 .75
HMW105 Dellin Betances .25 .60
HMW106 Hanley Ramirez .25 .60
HMW107 Joe Mauer .25 .60
HMW108 R.A. Dickey .25 .60
HMW109 Russell Martin .20 .50
HMW110 Bryce Harper .50 1.25
HMW111 Daniel Murphy .25 .60
HMW112 Bartolo Colon .20 .50
HMW113 Denard Span .20 .50
HMW114 Yu Darvish .30 .75
HMW115 Todd Frazier .20 .50
HMW116 Sonny Gray .25 .60
HMW117 Trayce Thompson RC .30 .75
HMW118 Adrian Beltre .30 .75
HMW119 Yunel Escobar .20 .50
HMW120 Trevor Rosenthal .25 .60
HMW121 James Shields .20 .50
HMW122 Joc Pederson .25 .60
HMW123 Josh Reddick .20 .50
HMW124 Doug Fister .20 .50
HMW125 Gregory Polanco .25 .60
HMW126 Henry Owens RC .25 .60
HMW127 Jose Bautista .25 .60
HMW128 Robert Stephenson RC .20 .50
HMW129 Corey Seager RC 2.00 5.00
HMW130 Eugenio Suarez .25 .60
HMW131 Tyler Naquin RC .30 .75
HMW132 Carlos Correa .30 .75
HMW133 Michael Brantley .25 .60
HMW134 Stephen Strasburg .30 .75
HMW135 Justin Bour .25 .60
HMW136 Trevor Story RC 1.00 2.50
HMW137 Josh Harrison .20 .50
HMW138 Stephen Piscotty RC .30 .75
HMW139 Cameron Maybin .20 .50
HMW140 Yovani Gallardo .20 .50
HMW141 Mookie Betts .60 1.50
HMW142 Michael Pineda .20 .50
HMW143 Adam Wainwright .25 .60
HMW144 Erick Aybar .20 .50
HMW145 Odubel Herrera .25 .60
HMW146 Addison Russell .30 .75
HMW147 Michael Wacha .25 .60
HMW148 Francisco Lindor .30 .75
HMW149 Kenta Maeda RC .40 1.00
HMW150 Yasiel Puig .30 .75
HMW151 Jeremy Hellickson .20 .50
HMW152 DJ LeMahieu .30 .75
HMW153 Adrian Gonzalez .25 .60
HMW154 Miguel Sano RC .30 .75
HMW155 Nomar Mazara RC .30 .75
HMW156 Jon Jay .20 .50
HMW157 Hunter Pence .25 .60
HMW158 Edwin Encarnacion .30 .75
HMW159 Didi Gregorius .25 .60
HMW160 Chris Archer .20 .50
HMW161 Buster Posey .40 1.00
HMW162 Salvador Perez .25 .60
HMW163 Felix Hernandez .25 .60
HMW164 Albert Pujols .40 1.00
HMW165 Mike Moustakas .25 .60
HMW166 Roberto Osuna .20 .50
HMW167 Craig Kimbrel .25 .60
HMW168 Jeff Samardzija .20 .50
HMW169 Jed Lowrie .20 .50
HMW170 Ian Kinsler .25 .60
HMW171 Jake Arrieta .25 .60
HMW172 Blake Snell RC .25 .60
HMW173 Ross Stripling RC .20 .50
HMW174 Martin Prado .20 .50
HMW175 Troy Tulowitzki .30 .75
HMW176 Ryan Braun .25 .60
HMW177 Chris Sale .30 .75
HMW178 Matt Duffy .20 .50
HMW179 Ender Inciarte .20 .50
HMW180 Wil Myers .25 .60
HMW181 Nolan Arenado .50 1.25
HMW182 Starlin Castro .20 .50
HMW183 Yadier Molina .40 1.00
HMW184 Javier Baez .40 1.00
HMW185 Carlos Rodon .30 .75
HMW186 Christian Yelich .40 1.00
HMW187 Stephen Vogt .25 .60
HMW188 Robinson Cano .25 .60
HMW189 Brandon Belt .25 .60
HMW190 Danny Salazar .25 .60
HMW191 Victor Martinez .25 .60
HMW192 Joey Votto .30 .75
HMW193 Rougned Odor .25 .60
HMW194 Kyle Seager .20 .50
HMW195 Marcus Stroman .25 .60
HMW196 Kenley Jansen .25 .60
HMW197 Jameson Taillon RC .25 .60
HMW198 David Wright .25 .60
HMW199 Yoenis Cespedes .30 .75
HMW200 Nick Castellanos .30 .75

2016 Topps Walmart Holiday Snowflake Metallic

*METALLIC: 1.5X TO 4X BASIC

2016 Topps Walmart Holiday Snowflake Relics

RAB Aaron Blair 2.50 6.00
RAC Aroldis Chapman 4.00 10.00
RAG Adrian Gonzalez 3.00 8.00
RAJ Adam Jones 3.00 8.00
RAN Aaron Nola 5.00 12.00
RBS Blake Snell 3.00 8.00
RCA Chris Archer 2.50 6.00
RCD Corey Dickerson 2.50 6.00
RCK Corey Kluber 3.00 8.00
RCM Colin Moran 2.50 6.00
RCR Carlos Rodon 4.00 10.00
RCS Chris Sale 4.00 10.00
RDP Dustin Pedroia 4.00 10.00
RDW David Wright 3.00 8.00
REH Eric Hosmer 3.00 8.00
REL Evan Longoria 3.00 8.00
RFF Freddie Freeman 5.00 12.00
RGC Gerrit Cole 4.00 10.00
RGS Giancarlo Stanton 4.00 10.00
RHR Hanley Ramirez 3.00 8.00
RIK Ian Kinsler 3.00 8.00
RJD Jacob deGrom 8.00 20.00
RJR Joey Rickard 2.50 6.00
RJS Jorge Soler 4.00 10.00
RJU Justin Upton 3.00 8.00
RKC Kole Calhoun 2.50 6.00
RKK Kevin Kiermaier 3.00 8.00
RLS Luis Severino 3.00 8.00
RMC Miguel Cabrera 4.00 10.00
RMD Matt Duffy 2.50 6.00
RMP Michael Pineda 2.50 6.00
RNM Nomar Mazara 4.00 10.00
RNS Noah Syndergaard 3.00 8.00
RRB Ryan Braun 3.00 8.00
RRC Robinson Cano 3.00 8.00
RSD Sean Doolittle 2.50 6.00
RSG Sonny Gray 3.00 8.00
RTT Troy Tulowitzki 4.00 10.00
RYC Yoenis Cespedes 4.00 10.00
RYP Yasiel Puig 4.00 10.00
RARI Anthony Rizzo 5.00 12.00
RARU Addison Russell 4.00 10.00
RCMA Carlos Martinez 3.00 8.00
RDPR David Price 3.00 8.00
RGSP George Springer 3.00 8.00
RJAB Jose Abreu 4.00 10.00
RJHE Jason Heyward 3.00 8.00
RJPE Joc Pederson 3.00 8.00
RMSA Miguel Sano 4.00 10.00
RSMA Starling Marte 3.00 8.00
RTWA Taijuan Walker 2.50 6.00

2016 Topps Walmart Holiday Snowflake Autographs

AAC Alex Cobb/100
AAN Aaron Nola/100
AARE A.J. Reed/100
ABPA Byung-Ho Park/50
ABS Blake Snell/25
ACKL Corey Kluber/100
ACR Carlos Rodon
AFL Francisco Lindor/25
AJB Jose Berrios/50
AJD Jacob deGrom/10
AJE Jerad Eickhoff/95
AJH Jason Heyward
AJP Joe Panik/100
AJS Jorge Soler/25
AJT Jameson Taillon/25
AKB Kris Bryant/10
AKK Kevin Kiermaier/100
AKM Kendrys Morales/100
AKS Kyle Schwarber
ALG Lucas Giolito/50
ALS Luis Severino
AMD Matt Duffy/200
AMF Michael Fulmer/25
AMFR Maikel Franco
AMP Michael Pineda
AMS Miguel Sano/25
ANM Nomar Mazara/25
ANS Noah Syndergaard/10
APO Peter O'Brien/200
ARST Ross Stripling
ASD Sean Doolittle/50
ASP Stephen Piscotty/100
ATS Trevor Story/50
ATT Trea Turner/100
ATW Taijuan Walker

2017 Topps

COMP.RED.HOB.FACT SET (700) 30.00 80.00
COMP.BLUE.RET.FACT SET (700) 30.00 80.00
COMP. SET w/o SP'S (700) 25.00 60.00
SP SER.1 ODDS 1:678 HOBBY
SP SER.1 ODDS 1:136 JUMBO
SP SER.1 ODDS 1:189 FAT PACK
SP SER.1 ODDS 1:566 RETAIL
SP SER.1 ODDS 1:95 ALL HANGERS
SP SER.1 ODDS 1:680 ALL BLASTERS
SP SER.2 ODDS 1:353 HOBBY
SER.1 PLATE ODDS 1:7286 HOBBY
SER.1 PLATE ODDS 1:2020 FAT PACK
SER.1 PLATE ODDS 1:1011 HANGER
SER.1 PLATE ODDS 1:7285 BLASTER
SER.1 PLATE ODDS 1:1454 JUMBO
SER.1 PLATE ODDS 1:6028 TAR. RETAIL
SER.1 PLATE ODDS 1:6042 WM. RETAIL
SER.2 PLATE ODDS 1:3773 WM. HOBBY
PLATE PRINT RUN 1 SET PER COLOR
BLACK-CYAN-MAGENTA-YELLOW ISSUED
NO PLATE PRICING DUE TO SCARCITY
1A Kris Bryant .30 .75
1B Bryant SP Dugout 30.00 80.00
1C Bryant UPD SP 1.25 3.00
2 Jason Hammel .20 .50
3 Chris Capuano .15 .40
4 Mark Reynolds .15 .40
5A Corey Seager .25 .60
5B Seager SP On-deck 25.00 60.00
6 Kevin Pillar .15 .40
7 Gary Sanchez .25 .60
8A Jose Berrios .20 .50
8B Jose Berrios SP 20.00 50.00
red jersey
9A Chris Sale .25 .60
9B Sale Blk jckt SP 25.00 60.00
10 Steven Souza Jr. .20 .50
11 Jake Smolinski .15 .40
12 Jerad Eickhoff .15 .40
13 Adeiny Hechavarria .15 .40
14 Travis d'Arnaud .20 .50
15 Braden Shipley RC .25 .60
16 Lance McCullers .15 .40
17 Daniel Descalso .15 .40
18 Jake Arrieta WS HL .20 .50
19 David Wright .20 .50
20A Mike Trout 1.25 3.00
20B Trout SP Dugout 125.00 300.00
20C Trout UPD SP 5.00 12.00
21 Robert Gsellman RC .25 .60
22 Keone Kela .15 .40
23 Marcell Ozuna .25 .60
24 Christian Friedrich .15 .40
25A Giancarlo Stanton .25 .60
25B Giancarlo Stanton SP 25.00 60.00
standing against fence
26 David Peralta .15 .40
27 Kurt Suzuki .15 .40
28 Rick Porcello LL .20 .50
29 Marco Estrada .15 .40
30A Josh Bell RC .60 1.50
30B Bell UPD SP 1.50 4.00
30C Bell UPD SP 1.50 4.00
31 Carlos Carrasco .15 .40
32 Syndergaard/Harvey .20 .50
33 Carson Fulmer RC .25 .60
34A Bryce Harper .40 1.00
34B Harper SP On-deck 40.00 100.00
35 Nolan Arenado LL .40 1.00
36 Machado/Trumbo/Jones .25 .60
37 Toronto Blue Jays .15 .40
38A Stephen Strasburg .25 .60
38B Stephen Strasburg SP 25.00 60.00
stepping out of dugout
39 Aroldis Chapman WS HL .25 .60
40 Jordan Zimmermann .20 .50
41 Paulo Orlando .15 .40
42 Trevor Story .25 .60
43 Tyler Austin RC .30 .75
44A Paul Goldschmidt .25 .60
44B Paul Goldschmidt SP 25.00 60.00
Double Bubble Bath
45 Joakim Soria .15 .40
46 Will Middlebrooks .15 .40
47 Gregor Blanco .15 .40
48 Brian McCann .20 .50
49 Scooter Gennett .20 .50
50A Clayton Kershaw .40 1.00
50B Krshw SP Cap on chest 40.00 100.00
51 Jake Barrett .15 .40
52 Neftali Feliz .15 .40
53A Ryon Healy RC .30 .75
53B Ryon Healy UPD SP .75 2.00
green jersey
53C Ryon Healy UPD SP .75 2.00
throwing helmet
54 Dellin Betances .20 .50
55 Mark Trumbo LL .15 .40
56 Danny Salazar .20 .50
57 C.J. Cron .15 .40
58 Starling Marte .20 .50
59 Carlos Rodon .25 .60
60A Jose Bautista .20 .50
60B Jose Bautista SP 20.00 50.00
pointing fingers
61 Xander Bogaerts .25 .60
62 Daniel Murphy .20 .50
63 Mike Moustakas .20 .50
64 Adam Eaton .25 .60
65A Madison Bumgarner .20 .50
65B Bmgrnr SP Cap at chest 20.00 50.00
66 Aaron Altherr .15 .40
67 Teoscar Hernandez RC 1.00 2.50
68 Zach Britton .20 .50
69 Henry Owens .15 .40
70 Wily Peralta .15 .40
71 Matt Shoemaker .20 .50
72 Chicago Cubs .15 .40
73 Kyle Schwarber .25 .60
74 Brett Lawrie .20 .50
75A Carlos Correa .25 .60
75B Correa SP Celebrate 25.00 60.00
76 Andre Ethier .20 .50
77 Austin Jackson .15 .40
78 Addison Russell WS HL .25 .60
79 Gabriel Ynoa RC .25 .60
80 Ivan Nova .20 .50
81 DJ LeMahieu LL .25 .60
82 Aaron Sanchez LL .20 .50
83 Anibal Sanchez .15 .40
84 Daniel Murphy LL .20 .50
85 Brandon Finnegan .15 .40
86 Asdrubal Cabrera .20 .50
87A Dansby Swanson RC .60 1.50
87B Swanson SP Red jsy 75.00 200.00
87C Swanson UPD SP 1.50 4.00
88 Freddy Galvis .15 .40
89 Brandon Moss .15 .40
90 Jason Grilli .15 .40
91A Troy Tulowitzki .25 .60
91B Troy Tulowitzki SP 25.00 60.00
blue jersey
92 Derek Norris .15 .40
93 Matt Joyce .15 .40
94 Kyle Barraclough .15 .40
95 Chris Davis .15 .40
96 Jose Quintana .15 .40
97 Marcus Semien .25 .60
98 Junior Guerra .15 .40
99 Michael Wacha .20 .50
100 Nate Jones .15 .40
101 Pedro Alvarez .15 .40
102 Cameron Maybin .15 .40
103 Alex Reyes RC .30 .75
104 Dioner Navarro .15 .40
105 Francisco Rodriguez .20 .50
106 Brandon Crawford .20 .50
107 Howie Kendrick .15 .40
108 Nick Hundley .15 .40
109A Nelson Cruz .25 .60
109B Nelson Cruz SP 25.00 60.00
blue hoodie
110 Joey Votto LL .25 .60
111 Edinson Volquez .15 .40
112 Angel Pagan .15 .40
113 Kyle Hendricks LL .25 .60
114 Colin Rea .15 .40
115 Joaquin Benoit .15 .40
116 Archie Bradley .15 .40
117 Adrian Gonzalez .20 .50
118 Billy Butler .15 .40
119A Francisco Lindor .25 .60
119B Lindor SP Running 60.00 150.00
120 Reynaldo Lopez RC .25 .60
121 Carlos Santana .20 .50
122 Cleveland Indians .15 .40
123 Jean Segura .20 .50
124 Travis Jankowski .15 .40
125 Yangervis Solarte .15 .40
126A Miguel Sano .20 .50
126B Miguel Sano SP 20.00 50.00
red jersey
127 Michael Bourn .15 .40
128 Adam Duvall .20 .50
129 Adonis Garcia .15 .40
130A Dustin Pedroia .25 .60
130B Dustin Pedroia SP 25.00 60.00
in dugout
131 J.A. Happ LL .20 .50
132 Randal Grichuk .15 .40
133 Jace Peterson .15 .40
134 Chase Utley .20 .50
135 Jered Weaver .20 .50
136 Matt Reynolds .15 .40
137 Yan Gomes .25 .60
138 Tyson Ross .15 .40
139 JaCoby Jones RC .30 .75
140 Jesse Hahn .15 .40
141 Baltimore Orioles .15 .40
142 Carlos Ruiz .15 .40
143 Nick Noonan .15 .40
144 Jon Lester LL .20 .50
145 Max Scherzer LL .25 .60
146 Chad Pinder RC .25 .60
147 Marcus Stroman .20 .50
148 Tim Anderson .25 .60
149 Gregory Polanco .20 .50
150A Miguel Cabrera .25 .60
150B Cabrera SP Dugout 60.00 150.00
150C Cabrera UPD SP 1.00 2.50
151 Jonathan Villar .15 .40
152 Nolan Arenado LL .40 1.00
153 Nori Aoki .15 .40
154 Kevin Kiermaier .20 .50
155A Jacob deGrom .50 1.25
155B Jacob deGrom SP 50.00 125.00
in dugout
156 Alex Colome .15 .40
157 Sean Doolittle .15 .40
158 Tommy Pham .15 .40
159 Justin Verlander LL .25 .60
160 Evan Gattis .15 .40
161A Mookie Betts .50 1.25
161B Betts SP Celebrate 50.00 125.00
162 Jon Lester LL .20 .50
163 Adam Conley .15 .40
164 Matt Harvey .20 .50
165 Corey Dickerson .15 .40
166 Jorge Soler .25 .60
167 Lorenzo Cain .15 .40
168 Ryan Zimmerman .20 .50
169 Steve Pearce .25 .60
170 Chris Carter LL .15 .40
171 Seth Smith .15 .40
172 Wilmer Flores .20 .50
173 Chicago White Sox .15 .40
174 Philadelphia Phillies .15 .40
175 Houston Astros .15 .40
176 Jaime Garcia .15 .40
177A Sonny Gray .20 .50
177B Sonny Gray SP 20.00 50.00
yellow jersey
178 Rick Porcello .20 .50
179 Matt Moore .20 .50
180 Jake McGee .20 .50
181 Aaron Hicks .20 .50
182 Keon Broxton .15 .40
183 Wade Miley .15 .40
184 Oswaldo Arcia .15 .40
185 Raisel Iglesias .20 .50
186 Andrew Cashner .15 .40
187 Sean Manaea .15 .40
188 Caleb Cotham .15 .40
189 Los Angeles Angels .15 .40
190 Blake Snell .20 .50
191 Wilson Ramos .15 .40
192 San Diego Padres .15 .40
193 Jimmy Nelson .15 .40
194 A.J. Ramos .15 .40
195 Edwin Encarnacion LL .25 .60
196 Colby Rasmus .20 .50
197 Jacoby Ellsbury .20 .50
198 Francisco Cervelli .15 .40
199A Johnny Cueto .20 .50
199B Johnny Cueto SP 20.00 50.00
blowing bubble
200 Homer Bailey .15 .40
201 Eddie Rosario .20 .50
202 Masahiro Tanaka LL .20 .50
203 Tyler Naquin .25 .60
204 Anthony Rizzo LL .30 .75
205 Kendrys Morales .15 .40
206 Chicago Cubs WS HL .15 .40
207A Justin Upton .20 .50
207B Justin Upton SP 20.00 50.00
Tigres jersey
208A Masahiro Tanaka .20 .50
208B Tanaka SP Hi Five 40.00 100.00
209 Jon Gray .15 .40
210A Yoan Moncada RC 2.00 5.00
210B Moncada SP Red jsy 60.00 150.00
211 Noah Syndergaard LL .20 .50
212 Tanner Roark .15 .40
213 Alex Wood .15 .40
214 Jose Altuve LL .20 .50
215 Johnny Giavotella .15 .40
216 Denard Span .15 .40
217 Miami Marlins .15 .40
218 Michael Saunders .20 .50
219 Joe Musgrove RC .75 2.00
220A Ryan Braun .20 .50
220B Ryan Braun SP 20.00 50.00
batting cage
221 Adam Wainwright .20 .50
222 Cesar Hernandez .15 .40
223 Jason Heyward .20 .50
224 Hector Rondon .15 .40
225 Wade Davis .15 .40
226 Logan Morrison .15 .40
227A Byron Buxton .25 .60
227B Buxton SP On-deck 50.00 120.00
228 Mike Foltynewicz .15 .40
229 David Ortiz LL .25 .60
230 Tulowitzki/Donaldson .25 .60
231 Rubby De La Rosa .15 .40
232 Geovany Soto .15 .40
233 Nomar Mazara .15 .40
234A Luke Weaver RC .30 .75
234B Luke Weaver UPD SP .75 2.00
head bowed
234C Luke Weaver UPD SP .75 2.00
in dugout
235 San Francisco Giants .15 .40
236 Lucas Duda UER .20 .50
Eric Campbell pictured
237 Joey Gallo .20 .50
238 Ben Zobrist .20 .50
239 Rajai Davis .15 .40
240 Mike Aviles .15 .40
241 Chris Young .15 .40
242 Mookie Betts LL .50 1.25
243A Felix Hernandez .20 .50
243B Felix Hernandez SP 20.00 50.00
hoodie
244A Freddie Freeman .30 .75
244B Freeman SP Water bath 30.00 80.00
244C Frmn UPD SP w/o Hat 1.25 3.00
245 Jackie Bradley Jr. .25 .60
246 Hunter Strickland .15 .40
247 Hector Neris .15 .40
248 Yasmany Tomas .15 .40
249 New York Yankees .15 .40
250 Sean Rodriguez .15 .40
251 Justin Turner .25 .60
252 Clint Robinson .15 .40
253 Tucker Barnhart .15 .40
254 Wade LeBlanc .15 .40
255A Orlando Arcia RC .40 1.00
255B Orlando Arcia UPD SP 1.00 2.50
fists out
255C Orlando Arcia UPD SP 1.00 2.50
in dugout
256 Tony Watson .15 .40
257 Corey Kluber LL .20 .50
258 Matt Adams .15 .40
259 Taijuan Walker .15 .40
260A Stephen Piscotty .20 .50
260B Stephen Piscotty SP 20.00 50.00
with team
261 Nathan Eovaldi .20 .50
262 Liam Hendriks .15 .40
263A Addison Russell .25 .60
263B Addison Russell SP 25.00 60.00
high fives
264 Cory Spangenberg .15 .40
265A Charlie Blackmon .25 .60
265B Charlie Blackmon SP 25.00 60.00
purple jersey
266 Tampa Bay Rays .15 .40
267 Clay Buchholz .15 .40
268 Anthony Gose .15 .40
269 Jose De Leon RC .25 .60
270 Jake Arrieta LL .20 .50
271 Nelson Cruz LL .25 .60
272 Pat Neshek .15 .40
273 A.J. Reed .15 .40
274 Matt Strahm RC .25 .60
275 Dallas Keuchel .20 .50
276 Yelich/Ozuna/Stanton .30 .75
277 Kris Bryant LL .30 .75
278 Julio Teheran .20 .50
279 Leonys Martin .15 .40
280 Adrian Beltre .25 .60
281 Coco Crisp .15 .40
282 Tyler Flowers .15 .40
283A Andrew Benintendi RC .75 2.00
283B Bnntndi SP Inteview 50.00 125.00
283C Bnntndi UPD SP 2.00 5.00
284 Elvis Andrus .20 .50
285 Tyler White .15 .40
286 Drew Pomeranz .20 .50
287A Aaron Judge RC 5.00 12.00
287B Judge SP w/Bat 200.00 500.00
287C Judge UPD SP 10.00 25.00
288A Joey Votto .25 .60
288B Joey Votto SP 25.00 60.00
Gatorade shower
289 Brian Goodwin RC .25 .60
290 Shin-Soo Choo .20 .50
291 Khris Davis LL .25 .60
292 Fernando Rodney .15 .40
293 Aledmys Diaz .20 .50
294 Kole Calhoun .15 .40
295 Matt Kemp LL .20 .50
296 Tyler Clippard .15 .40
297 Anthony DeSclafani .15 .40
298 Story/Arenado .40 1.00
299A Yulieski Gurriel RC .40 1.00
299B Yulieski Gurriel SP 25.00 60.00
dark blue jersey
299C Yulieski Gurriel UPD SP 1.00 2.50
no hat
299D Yulieski Gurriel UPD SP 1.00 2.50
orange jersey
300 Arodys Vizcaino .15 .40
301 Jeurys Familia .20 .50
302 David Freese .15 .40
303 Pedro Strop .15 .40
304 Minnesota Twins .15 .40
305 Tyler Duffey .15 .40
306A David Dahl RC .30 .75
306B David Dahl UPD SP .75 2.00
sunglasses on
306C David Dahl UPD SP .75 2.00
lowering bat
307 Zach Duke .15 .40
308 Yovani Gallardo .15 .40
309 Craig Kimbrel .20 .50
310 Scott Schebler .20 .50
311 Tyler Chatwood .15 .40
312 Brandon Guyer .15 .40
313 Robbie Grossman .15 .40
314 Ryan Flaherty .15 .40
315 Carlos Beltran .20 .50
316 Justin Smoak .15 .40
317 Mitch Moreland .15 .40
318 Matt Carasiti RC .25 .60
319 Seth Lugo RC .25 .60
320 Arizona Diamondbacks .15 .40
321 Dustin Pedroia LL .25 .60
322 Albert Pujols LL .30 .75
323 Jameson Taillon .20 .50
324 Ben Revere .15 .40
325 Chris Hatcher .15 .40
326 Chris Archer .15 .40
327 Danny Espinosa .15 .40
328 Adam Lind .20 .50
329 Josh Reddick .15 .40
330 Doug Fister .15 .40
331 Jake Lamb .20 .50
332 Huston Street .15 .40
333 Jarred Cosart .15 .40
334 Drew Smyly .15 .40
335A Jeff Hoffman RC .25 .60
335B Jeff Hoffman UPD SP .60 1.50
high five
336 Hector Santiago .15 .40
337 Scott Van Slyke .15 .40
338 Alcides Escobar .20 .50
339 Daniel Norris .15 .40
340A Aaron Nola .20 .50
340B Nola SP Thrbck 40.00 100.00
341A Alex Bregman RC 1.25 3.00
341B Bregman SP Kneeling 75.00 200.00
341C Bregman UPD SP 3.00 8.00
342 Josh Tomlin .15 .40
343 Mike Zunino .15 .40
344 Jake Thompson RC .25 .60
345 Kevin Gausman .25 .60
346 Jonathan Lucroy .20 .50
347 Brandon Belt .20 .50
348 Jeremy Hellickson .15 .40
349A Tyler Glasnow RC 1.00 2.50
349B Tyler Glasnow UPD SP 2.50 6.00
black jersey
350A David Ortiz .25 .60
350B Ortiz SP Door 25.00 60.00
350C Ortiz SP Cowboy 25.00 60.00
350D Ortiz SP Dugout 25.00 60.00
350E Ortiz SP Gatorade 25.00 60.00
350F Ortiz SP Tigers 25.00 60.00
350G Ortiz SP Lego 25.00 60.00
350H Ortiz SP Jacket 25.00 60.00
350I Ortiz SP Pujols 25.00 60.00
350J Ortiz SP Dodgers 25.00 60.00
350K Ortiz SP Helmet 25.00 60.00
351 German Marquez RC .40 1.00
352 Cameron Rupp .15 .40
353 Felipe Rivero .20 .50
354 Nick Tropeano .15 .40
355 Shelby Miller .20 .50
356 Brad Miller .20 .50
357 Kelvin Herrera .15 .40
358 Brad Boxberger .15 .40
359A Matt Carpenter .25 .60
359B Matt Carpenter SP 25.00 60.00
no hat
360 Jon Lester .20 .50
361 Dylan Bundy .20 .50
362 John Lackey .20 .50
363 Yunel Escobar .15 .40
364 Koda Glover RC .25 .60
365 Jorge De La Rosa .15 .40
366 Jayson Werth .20 .50
367 Jurickson Profar .20 .50
368 Jhonny Peralta .15 .40
369 Mark Canha .15 .40
370 St. Louis Cardinals .15 .40
371 Chad Bettis .15 .40
372 Ryan Schimpf .15 .40
373A Yadier Molina .30 .75
373B Yadier Molina SP 30.00 80.00
in gear
374 Jim Johnson .15 .40
375A Yasiel Puig .25 .60
375B Jackie Robinson SP 30.00 80.00
376 Chase Anderson .15 .40
377 Adam Rosales .15 .40
378 They Got Hops! .25 .60
Francisco Lindor/Tyler Naquin
379 Phil Hughes .15 .40
380A Albert Pujols .30 .75
380B Pujols SP Thrwng 30.00 80.00
381A Hunter Renfroe RC .30 .75
381B Hunter Renfroe UPD SP .75 2.00
camo jersey
382A Josh Harrison .15 .40
382B Honus Wagner SP 40.00 100.00
383 Adam Frazier .15 .40
384 Welington Castillo .15 .40
385 DJ LeMahieu .25 .60
386 Michael Lorenzen .15 .40
387 Zack Godley .15 .40
388 Yasmani Grandal .15 .40
389A George Springer .20 .50
389B George Springer SP 20.00 50.00
sitting
390A Evan Longoria .20 .50
390B Evan Longoria SP 20.00 50.00
throwback jersey
391 Jonathan Schoop .15 .40
392 Pablo Sandoval .20 .50
393 Koji Uehara .15 .40
394 Detroit Tigers .15 .40
395 Drew Storen .15 .40
396 J.T. Realmuto .25 .60
397 Stephen Cardullo RC .25 .60
398 Blake Treinen RC .40 1.00
399 Ender Inciarte .15 .40
400A Nolan Arenado .40 1.00
400B Arenado SP Dugout 40.00 100.00
401A Manny Margot RC .25 .60
401B Manny Margot UPD SP .60 1.50
brown jersey
401C Manny Margot UPD SP .60 1.50
gray jersey
402 Logan Forsythe .15 .40
403 John Axford .15 .40
404A Joe Mauer .20 .50
404B Mauer SP Pine tar 40.00 100.00
405 Max Kepler .20 .50
406 Stephen Vogt .20 .50
407 Eduardo Escobar .15 .40
408 Michael Conforto .20 .50
409 R.A. Dickey .20 .50
410 Jarrett Parker .15 .40
411 Maikel Franco .20 .50
412 Chris Iannetta .15 .40
413 Rob Segedin RC .25 .60
414 Zack Cozart .15 .40
415 Pat Valaika RC .30 .75
416 Neil Walker .15 .40

417 Darren O'Day .15 .40
418 James McCann .20 .50
419 Roberto Perez .15 .40
420 Matt Wisler .15 .40
421 Santiago Casilla .15 .40
422 Andrew Miller .20 .50
423 Sergio Romo .15 .40
424 Derek Dietrich .20 .50
425A Carlos Gonzalez .20 .50
425B Carlos Gonzalez SP 20.00 50.00
pinstripe jersey
426 New York Mets .15 .40
427 Carlos Gomez .15 .40
428 Jay Bruce .20 .50
429 Mark Melancon .15 .40
430 Texas Rangers .15 .40
431 Tommy Joseph .25 .60
432 Lucas Giolito .20 .50
433A Mitch Haniger RC .40 1.00
433B Mitch Haniger UPD SP 1.00 2.50
gray jersey
434 Tyler Saladino .15 .40
435 Robbie Ray .15 .40
436 Cody Allen .15 .40
437 Trevor Rosenthal .20 .50
438 Chris Carter .15 .40
439A Salvador Perez .20 .50
439B Salvador Perez SP 20.00 50.00
sunglasses on
440 Eduardo Rodriguez .15 .40
441 Jose Iglesias .20 .50
442A Javier Baez .30 .75
442B Baez SP In jckt 30.00 80.00
443 Dee Gordon .15 .40
444 Andrew Heaney .15 .40
445 Alex Gordon .20 .50
446 Dexter Fowler .20 .50
447 Scott Kazmir .15 .40
448 Jose Martinez RC .40 1.00
449 Ian Kennedy .15 .40
450A Justin Verlander .25 .60
450B Vrlndr SP Fist bump 40.00 100.00
451 Jharel Cotton RC .25 .60
452 Travis Shaw .15 .40
453 Danny Santana .15 .40
454 Andrew Toles RC .25 .60
455 Mauricio Cabrera RC .25 .60
456 Steve Cishek .15 .40
457 Brett Gardner .20 .50
458 Hernan Perez .15 .40
459A Wil Myers .20 .50
459B Wil Myers SP 20.00 50.00
sunglasses on
460 Alejandro De Aza .15 .40
461 Bruce Maxwell RC .25 .60
462 Rich Hill .15 .40
463 Jeff Samardzija .15 .40
464 Hisashi Iwakuma .20 .50
465 CC Sabathia .20 .50
466 David Robertson .15 .40
467 Adam Ottavino .15 .40
468 Kyle Hendricks .25 .60
469 Francisco Liriano .15 .40
470 Brandon Drury .15 .40
471 Nick Franklin .15 .40
472 Pittsburgh Pirates .15 .40
473 Eugenio Suarez .20 .50
474 Michael Pineda .15 .40
475 Peter O'Brien .15 .40
476 Matt Olson RC 1.25 3.00
477 Zach Davies .15 .40
478 Rob Zastryzny RC .25 .60
479 Ryan Madson .15 .40
480 Jason Kipnis .20 .50
481 Kansas City Royals .15 .40
482A Didi Gregorius .20 .50
482B Lou Gehrig SP 30.00 80.00
483 Anthony Rendon .25 .60
484 Yonder Alonso .15 .40
485A Greg Bird .20 .50
485B Roger Maris SP 40.00 100.00
486 Aroldis Chapman .25 .60
487 Jose Ramirez .20 .50
488 Jake Odorizzi .15 .40
489 Jarrod Dyson .15 .40
490 Joc Pederson .20 .50
491 Ryan Vogelsong .15 .40
492 Avisail Garcia .20 .50
493 Hunter Dozier RC .25 .60
494 Tom Murphy .15 .40
495 Adam Jones .20 .50
496 Mike Fiers .15 .40
497 Boston Red Sox .15 .40
498 Roman Quinn RC .25 .60
499 Danny Valencia .20 .50
500A Anthony Rizzo .30 .75
500C Ernie Banks SP 50.00 120.00
500B Rizzo SP Blue jrsy 30.00 80.00
500D Rizzo UPD SP Rnng 1.25 3.00
501 Ian Kinsler .20 .50
502 Willson Contreras .25 .60
503 Jesus Aguilar (RC) .60 1.50
504 Austin Hedges .15 .40
505 Seung-Hwan Oh .30 .75
506 Jose Peraza .20 .50
507 Matt Garza .15 .40
508A Hanley Ramirez .20 .50
508B Hanley Ramirez SP 20.00 50.00
kneeling
508C Ted Williams SP 60.00 150.00
509 Miguel Rojas RC .25 .60
510 Kelby Tomlinson .15 .40
511 Devin Mesoraco .15 .40
512 Mallex Smith .15 .40
513 Tony Kemp .15 .40
514 Jeremy Jeffress .15 .40
515 Nick Castellanos .25 .60
516 Tony Wolters .15 .40
517 Kolten Wong .20 .50
518 Christian Yelich .30 .75
519 Dan Vogelbach RC .40 1.00
520 Andrelton Simmons .15 .40
521 Brandon Phillips .15 .40
522 Edwin Diaz .20 .50
523A Carlos Martinez .20 .50
523B Carlos Martinez SP 20.00 50.00
no hat
524 James Loney .15 .40
525 Curtis Granderson .20 .50
526 Jake Marisnick .15 .40
527 Gio Gonzalez .20 .50
528A Jake Arrieta .20 .50
528B Jake Arrieta SP 20.00 50.00
with bat
529 J.J. Hardy .15 .40
530 Jabari Blash .15 .40
531 Nick Markakis .20 .50
532 Eduardo Nunez .15 .40
533 Trevor Bauer .30 .75
534 Cody Asche .15 .40
535 Lonnie Chisenhall .15 .40
536A Trey Mancini RC .50 1.25
536B Mancini UPD SP 1.25 3.00
537 Gerardo Parra .15 .40
538 Brad Ziegler .15 .40
539A Amir Garrett RC .25 .60
539B Amir Garrett UPD SP .60 1.50
gray jersey
540 Billy Hamilton .20 .50
541 Shawn Kelley .15 .40
542 Trevor Plouffe .15 .40
543 Brian Dozier .25 .60
544 Luis Severino .20 .50
545 Martin Perez .20 .50
546 Addison Reed .15 .40
547 Vince Velasquez .15 .40
548A David Price .20 .50
548B Price SP Dugout 30.00 80.00
549 Miguel Gonzalez .15 .40
550 Mikie Mahtook .15 .40
551 Matt Duffy .15 .40
552 Tom Koehler .15 .40
553 T.J. Rivera RC .40 1.00
554 Jason Castro .15 .40
555A Noah Syndergaard .20 .50
555B Sndrgrd SP Throwback 40.00 100.00
555C Noah Syndergaard UPD SP .75 2.00
bat in hand
556 Starlin Castro .15 .40
557 Milwaukee Brewers .15 .40
558 Oakland Athletics .15 .40
559 Jason Motte .15 .40
560 Zack Greinke .25 .60
561 Ricky Nolasco .15 .40
562 Nick Ahmed .15 .40
563 Marwin Gonzalez .15 .40
564 Washington Nationals .15 .40
565 J.D. Martinez .25 .60
566 Heart of Texas .20 .50
Elvis Andrus/Rougned Odor
567 Devon Travis .15 .40
568 Ryan Pressly .15 .40
569 Jorge Alfaro RC .30 .75
570A Josh Donaldson .20 .50
570B Josh Donaldson SP 20.00 50.00
camo hat
570C Josh Donaldson UPD SP .75 2.00
white jersey
571 J.C. Ramirez .15 .40
572 Atlanta Braves .15 .40
573 Bartolo Colon .15 .40
574 Trayce Thompson .20 .50
575 Chris Owings .15 .40
576 Russell Martin .15 .40
577 Chris Tillman .15 .40
578 Jed Lowrie .15 .40
579 Taylor Jungmann .15 .40
580 Matt Holliday .25 .60
581 Brock Holt .15 .40
582A Julio Urias .25 .60
582B Julio Urias SP 25.00 60.00
sunglasses on
583 Colorado Rockies .15 .40
584 Tater Triumph .40 1.00
Jayson Werth/Bryce Harper
585 Collin McHugh .15 .40
586A Aaron Sanchez .20 .50
586B Aaron Sanchez SP 20.00 50.00
patch on hat
587 Gerrit Cole .25 .60
588 Kirk Nieuwenhuis .15 .40
589 Ian Desmond .15 .40
590 Triplet of Twins .25 .60
Miguel Sano/Byron Buxton/Eduardo Escobar
591 Matt Bush .20 .50
592 Kendall Graveman .15 .40
593A Jose Abreu .25 .60
593B Jose Abreu SP 25.00 60.00
fingers over eye
594 Justin Bour .20 .50
595A Max Scherzer .25 .60
595B Schrzr SP Wht Jrsy 30.00 80.00
596 Ken Giles .15 .40
597A Kenta Maeda .20 .50
597B Kenta Maeda SP 20.00 50.00
warm-up on
597C Sandy Koufax SP 50.00 125.00
598 Michael Taylor .15 .40
599 Cincinnati Reds .15 .40
600A Yoenis Cespedes .25 .60
600B Yoenis Cespedes .25 .60
hands on lips
600C Yoenis Cespedes UPD SP 1.00 2.50
holding glove
601 Khris Davis .25 .60
602 Alex Dickerson .15 .40
603A Eric Thames .20 .50
603B Eric Thames UPD SP .75 2.00
blue and yellow hat
604 Gavin Cecchini RC .25 .60
605 Michael Brantley .20 .50
606 Glen Perkins .15 .40
607 Tyler Thornburg .15 .40
608 Los Angeles Dodgers .15 .40
609 Adalberto Mejia RC .25 .60
610 Ryan Buchter RC .25 .60
611A Victor Martinez .20 .50
611B Ty Cobb SP 75.00 200.00
612 Odubel Herrera .20 .50
613 Jonathan Broxton .15 .40
614 Shawn O'Malley .15 .40
615 John Jaso .15 .40
616 Mark Trumbo .15 .40
617 A.J. Pollock .15 .40
618 Kenley Jansen .20 .50
619 Brad Brach .15 .40
620 Sam Dyson .15 .40
621 Chase Headley .15 .40
622 Steven Wright .15 .40
623 Melvin Upton Jr. .20 .50
624 Brandon Maurer .15 .40
625 Ty Blach RC .25 .60
626 Roberto Osuna .15 .40
627 Zach Putnam .15 .40
628 Domingo Santana .20 .50
629 Jordy Mercer .15 .40
630A Edwin Encarnacion .25 .60
630B Edwin Encarnacion SP 25.00 60.00
standing at fence
631 Zack Wheeler .20 .50
632 Steven Matz .15 .40
633A Hunter Pence .20 .50
633B Pence SP No hat 30.00 80.00
634 Danny Duffy .15 .40
635A Michael Fulmer .15 .40
635B Michael Fulmer SP 15.00 40.00
high five
636 Allegheny Armada .25 .60
Andrew McCutchen/John Jaso
637 Ryan Rua .15 .40
638 Luis Valbuena .15 .40
639A Matt Kemp .20 .50
639B Matt Kemp SP 20.00 50.00
blue jersey
639C Hank Aaron SP 60.00 150.00
640 Cole Hamels .20 .50
641A Robinson Cano .20 .50
641B Robinson Cano SP 20.00 50.00
Albert Pujols pictured
642 Renato Nunez RC .50 1.25
643 Wei-Yin Chen .15 .40
644 Jose Altuve .20 .50
645A Trea Turner .20 .50
645B Turner SP High five 20.00 50.00
645C Turner UPD SP .75 2.00
646 Corey Knebel .15 .40
647 Jose Reyes .20 .50
648 Seattle Mariners .15 .40
649A Manny Machado .25 .60
649B Manny Machado SP 25.00 60.00
black t-shirt
649C Manny Machado UPD SP 1.00 2.50
black hoodie
650A Andrew McCutchen .25 .60
650B McCtchn SP Holding bat 40.00 100.00
650C Roberto Clemente SP 60.00 150.00
651 Jose Lobaton .15 .40
652A Kyle Seager .15 .40
652B Seager SP Teal jrsy 30.00 80.00
653 Cam Bedrosian .15 .40
654 Chris Young .15 .40
655 Garrett Richards .20 .50
656 Todd Frazier .15 .40
657 Kevin Quackenbush RC .25 .60
658 James Paxton .20 .50
659 Melky Cabrera .15 .40
660 Jeanmar Gomez .15 .40
661 Peter Bourjos .15 .40
662 J.A. Happ .20 .50
663 Ketel Marte .20 .50
664 Blake Swihart .20 .50
665 Yu Darvish .25 .60
666A Rougned Odor .20 .50
666B Rougned Odor SP 20.00 50.00
white jersey
667 Alex Cobb .15 .40
668 Jedd Gyorko .15 .40
669 Corey Kluber .20 .50
670 Martin Maldonado .15 .40
671 Joe Ross .15 .40
672 Luke Maile .15 .40
673 Joe Panik .20 .50
674 Martin Prado .15 .40
675A Buster Posey .30 .75
675B Posey SP Hand raised 30.00 80.00
676A Eric Hosmer .20 .50
676B Hosmer SP Glove 30.00 80.00
677 Cheslor Cuthbert .15 .40
678 Ervin Santana .15 .40
679 Jung Ho Kang .15 .40
680 Mike Pelfrey .15 .40
681 Mike Napoli .15 .40
682 James Shields .15 .40
683 Mac Williamson .15 .40
684 Jorge Polanco .20 .50
685 Enrique Hernandez .25 .60
686 Luis Sardinas .15 .40
687 Tyler Collins .15 .40
688 Mike Clevinger .20 .50
689 Jason Vargas .15 .40
690 Andres Blanco .15 .40
691 Richard Bleier RC .25 .60
692 Rob Refsnyder .15 .40
693 Matt Cain .20 .50
694 Matt Wieters .25 .60
695 Jon Jay .15 .40
696 Jeff Mathis .20 .50
697 Christian Bethancourt .15 .40
698 Tony Cingrani .20 .50
699 Ichiro .30 .75
700 Ryan Goins .15 .40

2017 Topps Black

*BLACK: 10X TO 25X BASIC
*BLACK RC: 6X TO 15X BASIC RC
SER.1 ODDS 1:102 HOBBY
SER.1 STATED ODDS 1:20 JUMBO
SER.2 STATED ODDS 1:60 HOBBY
STATED PRINT RUN 66 SER. #'d SETS
283 Andrew Benintendi 40.00 100.00
287 Aaron Judge 75.00 200.00
341 Alex Bregman 30.00 80.00

2017 Topps Black and White Negative

*BW NEGATIVE: 8X TO 20X BASIC
*BW NEGATIVE RC: 5X TO 12X BASIC
STATED ODDS 1:135 HOBBY
STATED ODDS 1:26 JUMBO
SER.2 ODDS 1:84 HOBBY
287 Aaron Judge 60.00 150.00

2017 Topps Factory Set Sparkle Foil

*SPARKLE: 8X TO 20X BASIC
*SPARKLE RC: 5X TO 12X BASIC RC
STATED PRINT RUN 175 SER.#'d SETS

2017 Topps Father's Day Blue

*BLUE: 10X TO 25X BASIC
*BLUE RC: 6X TO 15X BASIC RC
STATED ODDS 1:562 HOBBY
STATED ODDS 1:162 FAT PACK
STATED ODDS 1:485 TAR. RETAIL
STATED ODDS 1:81 HANGER
STATED ODDS 1:583 BLASTER
STATED ODDS 1:117 JUMBO
STATED ODDS 1:486 WM RETAIL
SER.2 ODDS 1:303 HOBBY
STATED PRINT RUN 50 SER. #'d SETS
283 Andrew Benintendi 40.00 100.00
287 Aaron Judge 75.00 200.00
341 Alex Bregman 30.00 80.00

2017 Topps Gold

*GOLD: 2X TO 5X BASIC
*GOLD RC: 1.2X TO 3X BASIC RC
STATED ODDS 1:15 HOBBY
STATED ODDS 1:5 FAT PACK
STATED ODDS 1:13 RETAIL
STATED ODDS 1:2 HANGER
STATED ODDS 1:15 BLASTER
STATED ODDS 1:3 JUMBO
SER.2 ODDS 1:8 HOBBY
STATED PRINT RUN 2017 SER. #'d SETS

2017 Topps Memorial Day Camo

COMPLETE SET (700)
*CAMO: 12X TO 30X BASIC
*CAMO RC: 8X TO 20X BASIC RC
STATED ODDS 1:1165 HOBBY
STATED ODDS 1:324 FAT PACK
STATED ODDS 1:969 TAR.RETAIL
STATED ODDS 1:161 HANGER
STATED ODDS 1:1165 BLASTER
STATED ODDS 1:233 JUMBO
STATED ODDS 1:971 WM RETAIL
SER.2 ODDS 1:605 HOBBY
STATED PRINT RUN 25 SER. #'d SETS
283 Andrew Benintendi 50.00 120.00
287 Aaron Judge 100.00 250.00
341 Alex Bregman 40.00 100.00

2017 Topps Mother's Day Pink

*PINK: 10X TO 25X BASIC
*PINK RC: 6X TO 15X BASIC RC
STATED ODDS 1:562 HOBBY
STATED ODDS 1:162 FAT PACK
STATED ODDS 1:485 TAR. RETAIL
STATED ODDS 1:81 HANGER
STATED ODDS 1:583 BLASTER
STATED ODDS 1:117 JUMBO
STATED ODDS 1:486 WM RETAIL
SER.2 ODDS 1:303 HOBBY
STATED PRINT RUN 50 SER. #'d SETS
283 Andrew Benintendi 40.00 100.00
287 Aaron Judge 75.00 200.00
341 Alex Bregman 30.00 80.00

2017 Topps Rainbow Foil

*RAINBOW: 2X TO 5X BASIC
*RAINBOW RC: 1.2X TO 3X BASIC RC
STATED ODDS 1:10 HOBBY
STATED ODDS 1:4 FAT PACK
STATED ODDS 1:10 RETAIL
STATED ODDS 1:2 HANGER
STATED ODDS 1:10 BLASTER
STATED ODDS 1:2 JUMBO
SER.2 ODDS 1:10 HOBBY
287 Aaron Judge 15.00 40.00

2017 Topps Toys R Us Purple Border

*PURPLE: 5X TO 12X BASIC
*PURPLE RC: 3X TO 8X BASIC RC
287 Aaron Judge 40.00 100.00

2017 Topps Vintage Stock

*VINTAGE: 8X TO 20X BASIC
*VINTAGE RC: 5X TO 12X BASIC RC
STATED ODDS 1:294 HOBBY
STATED ODDS 1:82 FAT PACK
STATED ODDS 1:245 RETAIL
STATED ODDS 1:41 HANGER
STATED ODDS 1:294 BLASTER
STATED ODDS 1:59 JUMBO
SER.2 ODDS 1:153 HOBBY
STATED PRINT RUN 99 SER. #'d SETS
287 Aaron Judge 60.00 150.00

2017 Topps '87 Topps

COMPLETE SET (200) 100.00 250.00
STATED ODDS 1:4 HOBBY
STATED ODDS 1:2 FAT PACK
STATED ODDS 1:4 WM/TAR. RETAIL
STATED ODDS 1:4 BLASTER
SER.2 ODDS 1:4 HOBBY
*RED/25: 6X TO 15X BASIC
871 Carlos Correa .40 1.00
872 Giancarlo Stanton .40 1.00
873 Nomar Mazara .25 .60
874 Carlos Gonzalez .30 .75
875 Kris Bryant .50 1.25
876 Ichiro Suzuki .50 1.25
877 Felix Hernandez .30 .75
878 Stephen Strasburg .40 1.00
879 Sandy Koufax .75 2.00
8710 Francisco Lindor .40 1.00
8711 Ozzie Smith .50 1.25
8712 Yoan Moncada .75 2.00
8713 David Wright .30 .75
8714 Henry Owens .25 .60
8715 Miguel Cabrera .40 1.00
8716 Miguel Sano .30 .75
8717 Anthony Rizzo .50 1.25
8718 Trea Turner .30 .75
8719 Adam Jones .30 .75
8720 Buster Posey .50 1.25
8721 Frank Thomas .40 1.00
8722 Carlos Rodon .40 1.00
8723 Luis Severino .30 .75
8724 Yoenis Cespedes .40 1.00
8725 Willson Contreras .40 1.00
8726 Robinson Cano .30 .75
8727 Reggie Jackson .30 .75
8728 Chris Sale .40 1.00
8729 Rickey Henderson .40 1.00
8730 Orlando Arcia .40 1.00
8731 Evan Longoria .30 .75
8732 Bo Jackson .40 1.00
8733 Alex Bregman 1.25 3.00
8734 David Price .30 .75
8735 Wil Myers .30 .75
8736 Josh Bell .60 1.50
8737 Randy Johnson .40 1.00
8738 Nolan Ryan 1.25 3.00
8739 Clayton Kershaw .60 1.50
8740 Corey Seager .40 1.00
8741 Troy Tulowitzki .40 1.00
8742 Nolan Arenado .60 1.50
8743 Hunter Pence .30 .75
8744 Max Scherzer .40 1.00
45 Eric Hosmer .30 .75
8746 Aledmys Diaz .30 .75
8747 Roger Clemens .50 1.25
8748 Cal Ripken Jr. 1.25 3.00
8749 Jake Arrieta .30 .75
8750 Mike Trout 2.00 5.00
8751 Trevor Story .40 1.00
8752 Jose Canseco .30 .75
8753 Yu Darvish .40 1.00
8754 Madison Bumgarner .30 .75
8755 Jose Altuve .30 .75
8756 Hank Aaron .75 2.00
8757 Mike Piazza .40 1.00
8758 Aaron Judge 10.00 25.00
8759 Ken Griffey Jr. .75 2.00
8760 Tyler Glasnow 1.00 2.50
8761 Dustin Pedroia .40 1.00
8762 Aaron Nola .30 .75
8763 Andrew Benintendi .75 2.00
8764 Manny Machado .40 1.00
8765 John Smoltz .40 1.00
8766 Gerrit Cole .40 1.00
8767 Don Mattingly .75 2.00
8768 Masahiro Tanaka .30 .75
8769 Kenta Maeda .30 .75
8770 Julio Urias .40 1.00
8771 Barry Larkin .30 .75
8772 Blake Snell .30 .75
8773 Mookie Betts .75 2.00
8774 Kyle Schwarber .40 1.00
8775 Bryce Harper .60 1.50
8776 David Ortiz .40 1.00
8777 Freddie Freeman .50 1.25
8778 Josh Donaldson .30 .75
8779 Alex Reyes .30 .75
8780 Greg Maddux .50 1.25
8781 Michael Conforto .30 .75
8782 Albert Pujols .50 1.25
8783 Lucas Giolito .30 .75
8784 Andrew McCutchen .40 1.00
8785 Ryne Sandberg .75 2.00
8786 Jacob deGrom .75 2.00
8787 Sonny Gray .30 .75
8788 Aroldis Chapman .40 1.00
8789 Mark McGwire .60 1.50
8790 David Dahl .30 .75
8791 Stephen Piscotty .30 .75
8792 Addison Russell .40 1.00
8793 Xander Bogaerts .40 1.00
8794 Noah Syndergaard .30 .75
8795 Johnny Cueto .30 .75
8796 Chipper Jones .40 1.00
8797 Yulieski Gurriel .40 1.00
8798 Justin Verlander .40 1.00
8799 Joc Pederson .30 .75
87100 Dansby Swanson .60 1.50
87101 Josh Donaldson .30 .75
87102 Manny Margot .25 .60
87103 Corey Seager .40 1.00
87104 Tyler Glasnow 1.00 2.50
87105 Alex Bregman 1.25 3.00
87106 Jose Altuve .30 .75
87107 Braden Shipley .25 .60
87108 Cal Ripken Jr. 1.25 3.00
87109 Matt Carpenter .40 1.00
87110 Gavin Cecchini .25 .60
87111 Chad Pinder .25 .60
87112 Reggie Jackson .30 .75
87113 Josh Bell .60 1.50
87114 Carl Yastrzemski .60 1.50
87115 Max Scherzer .40 1.00
87116 Jake Thompson .25 .60
87117 Kris Bryant .50 1.25
87118 Reynaldo Lopez .25 .60
87119 Buster Posey .50 1.25
87120 Clayton Kershaw .60 1.50
87121 David Ortiz .40 1.00
87122 Raimel Tapia .30 .75
87123 Bo Jackson .40 1.00
87124 Dustin Pedroia .40 1.00
87125 Ken Griffey Jr. .75 2.00
87126 Noah Syndergaard .30 .75
87127 Robert Gsellman .25 .60
87128 Ryne Sandberg .75 2.00
87129 Matt Strahm .25 .60
87130 Jose Canseco .30 .75
87131 Jose De Leon .25 .60
87132 Ivan Rodriguez .30 .75
87133 Francisco Lindor .40 1.00
87134 Miguel Cabrera .40 1.00
87135 Sandy Koufax .75 2.00
87136 Chipper Jones .40 1.00
87137 Yulieski Gurriel .40 1.00
87138 Corey Kluber .30 .75
87139 Dansby Swanson .60 1.50
87140 Jason Varitek .40 1.00
87141 Randy Johnson .40 1.00
87142 Matt Olson 1.25 3.00
87143 Hank Aaron .75 2.00
87144 Anthony Rizzo .50 1.25
87145 Chris Sale .40 1.00
87146 Omar Vizquel .30 .75
87147 Adam Jones .30 .75
87148 Roger Clemens .50 1.25
87149 Andrew Toles .25 .60
87150 Mike Trout 2.00 5.00
87151 Jorge Alfaro .30 .75
87152 Eric Hosmer .30 .75
87153 Don Mattingly .75 2.00
87154 John Smoltz .40 1.00
87155 Yoan Moncada .75 2.00
87156 Rickey Henderson .40 1.00
87157 Tom Glavine .30 .75
87158 Robinson Cano .30 .75
87159 Nolan Arenado .60 1.50
87160 Seth Lugo .25 .60
87161 David Dahl .30 .75
87162 Carlos Gonzalez .30 .75
87163 Dave Winfield .30 .75
87164 Andrew Benintendi .75 2.00
87165 Alex Reyes .30 .75
87166 German Marquez .40 1.00
87167 Manny Machado .40 1.00
87168 Mike Piazza .40 1.00
87169 Ozzie Smith .50 1.25
87170 Rob Zastryzny .25 .60
87171 Ichiro .50 1.25
87172 Bryce Harper .60 1.50
87173 Renato Nunez .50 1.25
87174 George Brett .75 2.00
87175 Frank Thomas .40 1.00
87176 Greg Maddux .50 1.25
87177 Aaron Judge 10.00 25.00
87178 Hunter Dozier .25 .60
87179 Johnny Damon .30 .75
87180 Andres Galarraga .30 .75
87181 Aledmys Diaz .30 .75
87182 Barry Larkin .30 .75
87183 Dan Vogelbach .40 1.00
87184 Bruce Maxwell .25 .60
87185 Roman Quinn .25 .60
87186 Ty Blach .25 .60
87187 Nolan Ryan 1.25 3.00
87188 Starling Marte .30 .75
87189 Teoscar Hernandez 1.00 2.50
87190 Mookie Betts .75 2.00
87191 Fernando Valenzuela .25 .60
87192 Dellin Betances .30 .75
87193 Addison Russell .40 1.00
87194 Derek Jeter 1.00 2.50
87195 Mark McGwire .60 1.50
87196 Jeff Hoffman .25 .60
87197 Trey Mancini .50 1.25
87198 Jacob deGrom .75 2.00
87199 JaCoby Jones .30 .75
87200 Jharel Cotton .25 .60

2017 Topps '87 Topps Autographs

STATED ODDS 1:465 HOBBY
STATED ODDS 1:681 FAT PACK
STATED ODDS 1:1770 TAR. RETAIL
STATED ODDS 1:2296 HANGER
STATED ODDS 1:15 JUMBO
STATED ODDS 1:1534 WM RETAIL
SER.2 ODDS 1:588 HOBBY
SER.1 EXCH DEADLINE 12/31/2018
SER.2 EXCH DEADLINE 5/31/2019
*MAPLE/25: .75X TO 2X BASIC
1987AAB Alex Bregman 40.00 100.00
1987AABE Andrew Benintendi 60.00 150.00
1987AABE Andrew Benintendi S2 75.00 200.00
1987AABR Alex Bregman S2 25.00 60.00
1987AAD Aledmys Diaz 15.00 40.00
1987AADI Aledmys Diaz S2 10.00 25.00
1987AAGA Andres Galarraga 15.00 40.00
1987AAGA Andres Galarraga S2 8.00 20.00
1987AAJU Aaron Judge 125.00 300.00
1987AAJU Aaron Judge S2 300.00 600.00
1987AAN Aaron Nola 6.00 15.00
1987AAR Alex Reyes 15.00 40.00
1987AARE Alex Reyes S2 10.00 25.00
1987AARI Anthony Rizzo
1987AARI Anthony Rizzo S2 40.00 100.00
1987AAT Andrew Toles S2 3.00 8.00
1987ABB Barry Bonds 250.00 500.00
1987ABD Brandon Drury 3.00 8.00
1987ABH Bryce Harper
1987ABHA Bryce Harper S2 250.00 400.00
1987ABJ Bo Jackson 60.00 150.00
1987ABJ Bo Jackson S2
1987ABL Barry Larkin 20.00 50.00
1987ABM Bruce Maxwell S2 3.00 8.00
1987ABP Buster Posey S2
1987ABS Blake Snell 4.00 10.00
1987ABS Braden Shipley S2 3.00 8.00
1987ABW Billy Wagner 6.00 15.00
1987ACC Carlos Correa 40.00 100.00
1987ACFU Carson Fulmer 6.00 15.00
1987ACKE Clayton Kershaw S2 100.00 250.00
1987ACM Carlos Martinez 4.00 10.00
1987ACP Chad Pinder S2 3.00 8.00
1987ACR Carlos Rodon 10.00 25.00
1987ACR Cal Ripken Jr. S2 150.00 300.00
1987ACRI Cal Ripken Jr.
1987ACSE Corey Seager 60.00 150.00
1987ACSE Corey Seager S2 60.00 150.00
1987ADD David Dahl 10.00 25.00
1987ADD David Dahl S2 4.00 10.00
1987ADJ Derek Jeter 400.00 800.00
1987ADJ Derek Jeter S2 500.00 800.00
1987ADMA Don Mattingly 100.00 250.00
1987ADO David Ortiz 150.00 300.00
1987ADS Dansby Swanson 60.00 150.00
1987ADST Darryl Strawberry S2
1987ADSW Dansby Swanson S2 40.00 100.00
1987ADV Dan Vogelbach S2 5.00 12.00
1987AFL Francisco Lindor 25.00 60.00
1987AFL Francisco Lindor S2 EXCH 20.00 50.00
1987AFT Frank Thomas 30.00 80.00
1987AFV Fernando Valenzuela 20.00 50.00
1987AGMR German Marquez S2 5.00 12.00
1987AGS George Springer 10.00 25.00
1987AHA Hank Aaron
1987AHA Hank Aaron S2 200.00 400.00
1987AHO Henry Owens 3.00 8.00
1987AHR Hunter Renfroe 12.00 30.00
1987AIR Ivan Rodriguez 20.00 50.00
1987AI Ichiro S2 250.00 500.00
1987AJA Jim Abbott 10.00 25.00
1987AJAF Jorge Alfaro S2 4.00 10.00
1987AJAL Jose Altuve 25.00 60.00
1987AJB Josh Bell 25.00 60.00
1987AJBE Jose Berrios 5.00 12.00
1987AJC Jose Canseco 10.00 25.00
1987AJCA Jose Canseco S2 6.00 15.00
1987AJCO Jharel Cotton S2 3.00 8.00
1987AJDE Jacob deGrom 50.00 120.00
1987AJDL Jose De Leon S2 3.00 8.00
1987AJH Jeremy Hazelbaker 4.00 10.00
1987AJH Jeff Hoffman S2 3.00 8.00
1987AJJ JaCoby Jones S2 4.00 10.00
1987AJMU Joe Musgrove 10.00 25.00
1987AJP Joc Pederson 8.00 20.00
1987AJP Joe Panik S2 4.00 10.00
1987AJT Jake Thompson S2 3.00 8.00
1987AJU Julio Urias 15.00 40.00
1987AKB Kris Bryant 300.00 500.00
1987AKB Kris Bryant S2 150.00 300.00
1987AKG Ken Griffey Jr.
1987AKG Ken Griffey Jr. S2 150.00 300.00
1987AKMA Kenta Maeda 30.00 80.00
1987AKS Kyle Schwarber 40.00 100.00
1987ALS Luis Severino 8.00 20.00
1987AMC Michael Conforto 20.00 50.00
1987AMM Manny Machado S2 75.00 200.00
1987AMMA Manny Machado S2 75.00 200.00
1987AMMC Mark McGwire 75.00 200.00
1987AMMG Mark McGwire S2
1987AMMR Manny Margot S2 6.00 15.00
1987AMO Matt Olson S2 10.00 25.00
1987AMP Mike Piazza S2 60.00 150.00
1987AMS Matt Strahm S2 3.00 8.00
1987AMSA Miguel Sano 10.00 25.00
1987AMSM Mallex Smith 3.00 8.00
1987AMT Mike Trout
1987AMTR Mike Trout S2 200.00 400.00
1987ANA Nolan Arenado 20.00 50.00
1987AND Norman Dale 250.00 500.00
Gene Hackman
1987ANM Nomar Mazara 8.00 20.00
1987ANR Nolan Ryan S2 100.00 250.00
1987ANS Noah Syndergaard 30.00 80.00
1987ANS Noah Syndergaard S2 25.00 60.00
1987AOS Ozzie Smith 60.00 150.00
1987AOV Omar Vizquel 15.00 40.00
1987AOV Omar Vizquel S2 10.00 25.00
1987APO Peter O'Brien 3.00 8.00
1987ARG Robert Gsellman S2 3.00 8.00
1987ARH Rickey Henderson 30.00 80.00
1987ARHE Ryon Healy 4.00 10.00
1987ARL Reynaldo Lopez S2 3.00 8.00
1987ARN Renato Nunez S2 6.00 15.00
1987ARQ Roman Quinn S2 3.00 8.00
1987ARTA Raimel Tapia S2 4.00 10.00
1987ARZ Rob Zastryzny S2 3.00 8.00
1987ASK Sandy Koufax EXCH 175.00 350.00
1987ASK Sandy Koufax S2 600.00 800.00
1987ASL Seth Lugo S2 3.00 8.00
1987ASM Starling Marte
1987ASMA Steven Matz 12.00 30.00
1987ASP Stephen Piscotty 10.00 25.00
1987ATA Tyler Austin 8.00 20.00
1987ATA Tyler Austin S2 6.00 15.00
1987ATB Ty Blach S2 3.00 8.00
1987ATG Tyler Glasnow S2 10.00 25.00
1987ATGS Tyler Glasnow S2 10.00 25.00
1987ATGV Tom Glavine S2 25.00 60.00
1987ATH Teoscar Hernandez S2 12.00 30.00
1987ATM Trey Mancini S2 20.00 50.00
1987ATN Tyler Naquin 5.00 12.00
1987ATS Trevor Story 15.00 40.00
1987ATT Trea Turner 10.00 25.00
1987AVG Vladimir Guerrero S2 50.00 120.00
1987AWCO Willson Contreras 30.00 80.00
1987AYG Yulieski Gurriel 30.00 80.00
1987AYG Yulieski Gurriel S2 8.00 20.00
1987AYM Yoan Moncada 150.00 300.00
1987AYM Yoan Moncada S2 60.00 150.00

2017 Topps '87 Topps Silver Pack Chrome

*GREEN/150: 1X TO 2.5X BASIC
*BLUE/99: 1.5X TO 4X BASIC
*ORANGE/75-99: 2X TO 5X BASIC
*GOLD/50: 2.5X TO 6X BASIC
87AB Andrew Benintendi 2.00 5.00
87ABR Alex Bregman 3.00 8.00
87AD Aledmys Diaz S2 .75 2.00
87AE Adam Eaton S2 1.00 2.50
87AJ Adam Jones S2 .75 2.00
87AJ Aaron Judge 30.00 80.00
87AM Andrew McCutchen 1.00 2.50
87AN Aaron Nola .75 2.00
87AR Alex Reyes .75 2.00
87ARI Anthony Rizzo S2 1.25 3.00
87ARU Addison Russell 1.00 2.50
87BB Byron Buxton 1.00 2.50
87BH Bryce Harper S2 1.50 4.00
87BJ Bo Jackson 1.00 2.50
87BP Buster Posey S2 1.25 3.00
87BR Babe Ruth S2 2.50 6.00
87CC Carlos Correa S2 1.00 2.50
87CK Clayton Kershaw 1.50 4.00
87CK Corey Kluber S2 .75 2.00
87CR Cal Ripken Jr. 3.00 8.00
87CS Chris Sale 1.00 2.50
87CSA Carlos Santana S2 .75 2.00
87CSE Corey Seager S2 1.00 2.50
87DB Dellin Betances S2 .75 2.00
87DD David Dahl .75 2.00
87DJ Derek Jeter S2 2.50 6.00
87DM Don Mattingly S2 2.00 5.00
87DP David Price .75 2.00
87DS Dansby Swanson 1.50 4.00
87EB Ernie Banks S2 1.00 2.50
87EH Eric Hosmer .75 2.00
87EL Evan Longoria .75 2.00
87FF Freddie Freeman 1.25 3.00
87FH Felix Hernandez .75 2.00
87FL Francisco Lindor 1.00 2.50
87FT Frank Thomas S2 1.00 2.50
87GB George Brett S2 2.00 5.00
87GS George Springer S2 .75 2.00
87GS Gary Sanchez 1.00 2.50
87GST Giancarlo Stanton 1.00 2.50
87HA Hank Aaron 2.00 5.00
87HR Hunter Renfroe S2 .75 2.00
87I Ichiro S2 1.25 3.00
87JA Jose Altuve .75 2.00
87JAR Jake Arrieta .75 2.00
87JBA Javier Baez S2 1.25 3.00
87JBE Johnny Bench S2 1.00 2.50
87JBU Jose Bautista S2 .75 2.00
87JD Josh Donaldson .75 2.00
87JDG Jacob deGrom S2 2.00 5.00
87JDL Jose De Leon S2 .60 1.50
87JL Jake Lamb S2 .75 2.00
87JR Jackie Robinson 1.00 2.50
87JS John Smoltz S2 1.00 2.50
87JU Julio Urias 1.00 2.50
87JV Joey Votto 1.00 2.50

87JV Justin Verlander S2 1.00 2.50
87KB Kris Bryant 1.25 3.00
87KG Ken Griffey Jr. 2.00 5.00
87KM Kenta Maeda .75 2.00
87KS Kyle Schwarber S2 1.00 2.50
87LW Luke Weaver .75 2.00
87MB Madison Bumgarner .75 2.00
87MB Mookie Betts S2 2.00 5.00
87MC Matt Carpenter S2 1.00 2.50
87MC Miguel Cabrera 1.00 2.50
87MM Manny Machado 1.00 2.50
87MM Manny Margot S2 .60 1.50
87MMG Mark McGwire S2 1.50 4.00
87MS Max Scherzer 1.00 2.50
87MSA Miguel Sano S2 .75 2.00
87MST Marcus Stroman S2 .75 2.00
87MT Masahiro Tanaka S2 .75 2.00
87MT Mike Trout 5.00 12.00
87NA Nolan Arenado 1.50 4.00
87NR Nolan Ryan 3.00 8.00
87NS Noah Syndergaard .75 2.00
87OA Orlando Arcia 1.00 2.50
87PG Paul Goldschmidt 1.00 2.50
87RCA Robinson Cano S2 .75 2.00
87RCL Roberto Clemente S2 2.50 6.00
87RH Ryon Healy S2 .75 2.00
87RP Rick Porcello S2 .75 2.00
87SG Sonny Gray .75 2.00
87SK Sandy Koufax S2 2.00 5.00
87SMR Starling Marte S2 .75 2.00
87SMZ Steven Matz S2 .60 1.50
87SP Stephen Piscotty S2 .75 2.00
87SS Stephen Strasburg S2 1.00 2.50
87TA Tyler Austin S2 .75 2.00
87TG Tyler Glasnow 2.50 6.00
87TM Trey Mancini S2 1.25 3.00
87TS Trevor Story 1.00 2.50
87TT Trea Turner .75 2.00
87TW Ted Williams S2 2.00 5.00
87WM Wil Myers .75 2.00
87YC Yoenis Cespedes 1.00 2.50
87YD Yu Darvish 1.00 2.50
87YG Yulieski Gurriel S2 1.00 2.50
87YM Yoan Moncada S2 2.00 5.00

2017 Topps '87 Topps Silver Pack Chrome Autographs

RANDOM INSERTS IN PACKS
PRINT RUNS B/WN 40-199 COPIES PER
87AI Ichiro S2
87AAB Andrew Benintendi/199 60.00 150.00
87AABR Alex Bregman/199 50.00 125.00
87AAE Adam Eaton S2/99
87AAJ Adam Jones S2/20
87AAJ Aaron Judge/199 200.00 400.00
87AAN Aaron Nola/40 10.00 25.00
87AAR Alex Reyes/199 15.00 40.00
87ABB Byron Buxton/149 15.00 40.00
87ABH Bryce Harper S2
87ACC Carlos Correa S2
87ACK Clayton Kershaw
87ADB Dellin Betances S2/99
87ADD David Dahl/199 15.00 40.00
87ADJ Derek Jeter S2
87ADM Don Mattingly S2
87AFL Francisco Lindor/199 20.00 50.00
87AFT Frank Thomas S2
87AJA Jake Arrieta
87AJAT Jose Altuve/199 25.00 60.00
87AJL Jake Lamb S2/99
87AJS John Smoltz S2
87AKB Kris Bryant/50
87AKM Kenta Maeda/50 15.00 40.00
87ALW Luke Weaver/199 8.00 20.00
87AMC Matt Carpenter S2/50
87AMM Manny Margot S2/50
87AMT Mike Trout
87ANA Nolan Arenado/50 25.00 60.00
87ANS Noah Syndergaard/50 30.00 80.00
87ARP Rick Porcello S2/50
87ASP Stephen Piscotty S2
87ATA Tyler Austin S2/50
87ATG Tyler Glasnow/199 20.00 50.00
87ATS Trevor Story/149 20.00 50.00
87ATT Trea Turner/149 15.00 40.00
87AYC Yoenis Cespedes
87AYG Yulieski Gurriel S2/50
87AYM Yoan Moncada S2
87AARI Anthony Rizzo S2/15
87ACSA Carlos Santana S2/99
87ACSE Corey Seager S2
87AJBA Javier Baez S2/14
87AMMG Mark McGwire S2
87AMST Marcus Stroman S2/99
87ASMZ Steven Matz S2/50

2017 Topps All Star Team Medallions

STATED ODDS 1:1274 HOBBY
STATED ODDS 1:30 JUMBO
*GOLD/99: .5X TO 1.2X BASIC
*BLACK/50: .6X TO 1.5X BASIC
MLBASARI Anthony Rizzo 5.00 12.00
MLBASARU Addison Russell 4.00 10.00
MLBASBH Bryce Harper 6.00 15.00
MLBASBP Buster Posey 5.00 12.00
MLBASCG Carlos Gonzalez 3.00 8.00
MLBASCH Chris Sale 4.00 10.00
MLBASCSA Matt Carpenter 4.00 10.00
MLBASCSE Corey Seager 6.00 15.00
MLBASDO David Ortiz 6.00 15.00
MLBASEE Edwin Encarnacion 4.00 10.00
MLBASEH Eric Hosmer 3.00 8.00
MLBASFL Francisco Lindor 6.00 15.00
MLBASJAL Jose Altuve 3.00 8.00
MLBASJAR Jake Arrieta 3.00 8.00
MLBASJB Jackie Bradley Jr. 4.00 10.00
MLBASJD Josh Donaldson 3.00 8.00
MLBASKB Kris Bryant 10.00 25.00
MLBASMBE Mookie Betts 8.00 20.00
MLBASMBU Madison Bumgarner 3.00 8.00
MLBASMCB Miguel Cabrera 4.00 10.00
MLBASMCP Cole Hamels 3.00 8.00
MLBASMM Manny Machado 4.00 10.00
MLBASMT Mike Trout 10.00 25.00
MLBASNA Nolan Arenado 6.00 15.00
MLBASNS Noah Syndergaard 5.00 12.00
MLBASRC Robinson Cano 3.00 8.00
MLBASSP Salvador Perez 5.00 12.00
MLBASSS Stephen Strasburg 4.00 10.00
MLBASWM Wil Myers 3.00 8.00
MLBASXB Xander Bogaerts 4.00 10.00

2017 Topps All Time All Stars

COMPLETE SET (50) 30.00 80.00
ATAS1 Johnny Bench .60 1.50
ATAS2 Gary Carter .50 1.25
ATAS3 Bryce Harper 1.00 2.50
ATAS4 Reggie Jackson .50 1.25
ATAS5 Edgar Martinez .50 1.25
ATAS6 Cal Ripken Jr. 2.00 5.00
ATAS7 Brooks Robinson .50 1.25
ATAS8 Bob Feller .50 1.25
ATAS9 Buster Posey .75 2.00
ATAS10 Ryne Sandberg 1.25 3.00
ATAS11 Pedro Martinez .50 1.25
ATAS12 Ken Griffey Jr. 1.25 3.00
ATAS13 Rod Carew .50 1.25
ATAS14 Albert Pujols .75 2.00
ATAS15 Harmon Killebrew .60 1.50
ATAS16 Joe Morgan .50 1.25
ATAS17 Nolan Ryan 2.00 5.00
ATAS18 Duke Snider .50 1.25
ATAS19 Don Mattingly 1.25 3.00
ATAS20 Ted Williams 1.25 3.00
ATAS21 Rickey Henderson .60 1.50
ATAS23 Mike Piazza .60 1.50
ATAS24 Roger Clemens .75 2.00
ATAS25 Steve Carlton .50 1.25
ATAS26 Ernie Banks .60 1.50
ATAS27 Clayton Kershaw 1.00 2.50
ATAS28 Derek Jeter 1.50 4.00
ATAS29 Hank Aaron 1.25 3.00
ATAS30 Jimmie Foxx .60 1.50
ATAS31 Wade Boggs .50 1.25
ATAS32 Ichiro .75 2.00
ATAS33 Tom Glavine .50 1.25
ATAS34 Carlton Fisk .50 1.25
ATAS35 George Brett 1.25 3.00
ATAS36 Eddie Mathews .60 1.50
ATAS37 Greg Maddux .75 2.00
ATAS38 Eddie Murray .50 1.25
ATAS39 Lou Gehrig 1.25 3.00
ATAS40 Justin Verlander .60 1.50
ATAS41 Nomar Garciaparra .50 1.25
ATAS42 Juan Marichal .50 1.25
ATAS43 Carl Yastrzemski 1.00 2.50
ATAS44 Al Kaline .60 1.50
ATAS45 Alex Rodriguez .75 2.00
ATAS46 Miguel Cabrera .60 1.50
ATAS47 Chipper Jones .60 1.50
ATAS48 Barry Larkin .50 1.25
ATAS49 John Smoltz .60 1.50
ATAS50 Roberto Alomar .50 1.25
ATAS61 Andre Dawson .50 1.25

2017 Topps All Star MVPs

*BLUE: .5X TO 1.2X BASIC
ASM1 Juan Marichal .50 1.25
ASM2 Brooks Robinson .50 1.25
ASM3 Tony Perez .50 1.25
ASM4 Willie McCovey .50 1.25
ASM5 Carl Yastrzemski 1.00 2.50
ASM6 Frank Robinson .50 1.25
ASM7 Joe Morgan .50 1.25
ASM8 Gary Carter .50 1.25
ASM9 Roger Clemens .75 2.00
ASM10 Bo Jackson .60 1.50
ASM11 Cal Ripken Jr. 2.00 5.00
ASM12 Ken Griffey Jr. 1.25 3.00
ASM13 Mike Piazza .60 1.50
ASM14 Roberto Alomar .50 1.25
ASM15 Pedro Martinez .50 1.25
ASM16 Derek Jeter 1.50 4.00
ASM17 Cal Ripken Jr. 2.00 5.00
ASM18 Ichiro .75 2.00
ASM19 Carl Crawford .50 1.25
ASM20 Brian McCann .50 1.25
ASM21 Prince Fielder .50 1.25
ASM22 Melky Cabrera .40 1.00
ASM23 Mike Trout 3.00 8.00
ASM24 Mike Trout 3.00 8.00
ASM25 Eric Hosmer .50 1.25

2017 Topps Reverence Patch Autographs

STATED ODDS 1:3629 HOBBY
STATED ODDS 1:680 JUMBO
STATED PRINT RUN 25 SER. #'d SETS
EXCHANGE DEADLINE 12/31/2018
TAPABE Andrew Benintendi 100.00 250.00
TAPABR Alex Bregman 75.00 200.00
TAPAP Andy Pettitte EXCH 30.00 80.00
TAPBL Barry Larkin EXCH 30.00 80.00
TAPCC Carlos Correa EXCH 75.00 200.00
TAPCJ Chipper Jones 75.00 200.00
TAPCK Clayton Kershaw 60.00 150.00
TAPCR Cal Ripken Jr. 150.00 400.00
TAPDM Don Mattingly 125.00 250.00
TAPDS Dansby Swanson EXCH 75.00 200.00
TAPFL Francisco Lindor
TAPI Ichiro Suzuki 300.00 500.00
TAPJS John Smoltz 30.00 80.00
TAPMP Mike Piazza 125.00 300.00
TAPMT Mike Trout 200.00 500.00
TAPNS Noah Syndergaard EXCH 30.00 80.00
TAPRH Rickey Henderson 60.00 150.00
TAPTS Trevor Story 30.00 80.00

2017 Topps Bowman Then and Now

COMPLETE SET (20) 5.00 12.00
STATED ODDS 1:8 HOBBY
STATED ODDS 1:3 FAT PACK
STATED ODDS 1:8 RETAIL
STATED ODDS 1:2 HANGER
STATED ODDS 1:8 BLASTER
STATED ODDS 1:2 JUMBO
BOWMAN1 Trout 2.00 5.00
BOWMAN2 Kershaw .60 1.50
BOWMAN3 Bryant .50 1.25
BOWMAN4 Manny Machado .40 1.00
BOWMAN5 Bumgarner .30 .75
BOWMAN6 Harper .60 1.50
BOWMAN7 Posey .50 1.25
BOWMAN8 Felix Hernandez .30 .75
BOWMAN9 Joe Mauer .30 .75
BOWMAN10 Pujols .50 1.25
BOWMAN11 Stephen Strasburg .40 1.00
BOWMAN12 Andrew McCutchen .40 1.00
BOWMAN13 Eric Hosmer .30 .75
BOWMAN14 David Price .30 .75
BOWMAN15 Joey Votto .40 1.00
BOWMAN16 Justin Verlander .40 1.00
BOWMAN17 Robinson Cano .30 .75
BOWMAN18 Correa .40 1.00
BOWMAN19 Seager .40 1.00
BOWMAN20 Cabrera .40 1.00

2017 Topps Factory Set Retail Bonus Rookie Variations

87 Dansby Swanson
210 Yoan Moncada
283 Andrew Benintendi
287 Aaron Judge
341 Alex Bregman

2017 Topps First Pitch

COMPLETE SET (40) 8.00 20.00
SER.1 ODDS 1:8 HOBBY
SER.1 ODDS 1:3 FAT PACK
SER.1 ODDS 1:8 RETAIL
SER.1 ODDS 1:2 HANGER
SER.1 ODDS 1:8 BLASTER
SER.1 ODDS 1:2 JUMBO
SER.2 ODDS 1:8 HOBBY
FP1 William Shatner .60 1.50
FP2 Bob Odenkirk .60 1.50
FP3 Judd Apatow .60 1.50
FP4 Jeremy Piven .60 1.50
FP5 Deshauna Barber .60 1.50
FP6 John Goodman .60 1.50
FP7 Keegan-Michael Key .60 1.50
FP8 Joan Jett .60 1.50
FP9 Joe Mantegna .60 1.50
FP10 Leslie Jordan .60 1.50
FP11 Paul Wall .60 1.50
FP12 Chris Lane .60 1.50
FP13 Luis Coronel .60 1.50
FP14 Brett Eldredge .60 1.50
FP15 Victoria Justice .60 1.50
FP16 Lou Ferrigno .60 1.50
FP17 Bethanie Mattek-Sands .60 1.50
FP21 Jon Lovitz .60 1.50
FP21 Bonnie Hunt .60 1.50
FP22 Stephen Colbert .60 1.50
FP22 Isaiah Mustafa .60 1.50
FP23 Mase .60 1.50
FP23 Ben Higgins .60 1.50
FP24 Gary Busey .60 1.50
FP25 Ben Gibbard .60 1.50
FP26 Josh Duhamel .60 1.50
FP27 Chace Crawford .60 1.50
FP28 Diplo .60 1.50
FP29 Donovan Bailey .60 1.50
FP30 Jabbawockeez .60 1.50
FP31 Morimoto .60 1.50
FP32 Brian Shaw .60 1.50
FP33 Anthony Rapp .60 1.50
FP34 Ty Pennington .60 1.50
FP35 Steve Bowen .60 1.50
FP36 Alex Curry .60 1.50
FP37 Camilla Luddington .60 1.50
FP38 Tom Lehman .60 1.50
FP39 Danny Willett .60 1.50
FP40 Luke Donald .60 1.50

2017 Topps Five Tool

STATED ODDS 1:8 HOBBY
STATED ODDS 1:3 FAT PACK
STATED ODDS 1:8 RETAIL
STATED ODDS 1:2 HANGER
STATED ODDS 1:8 BLASTER
STATED ODDS 1:2 JUMBO
5T1 Mike Trout 2.00 5.00
5T2 Bryce Harper .60 1.50
5T3 Kris Bryant .50 1.25
5T4 Manny Machado .40 1.00
5T5 Josh Donaldson .30 .75
5T6 Mookie Betts .75 2.00
5T7 Evan Longoria .30 .75
5T8 Francisco Lindor .40 1.00
5T9 Eric Hosmer .30 .75
5T10 Carlos Correa .40 1.00
5T11 Giancarlo Stanton .40 1.00
5T12 Kris Bryant .50 1.25
5T13 Andrew McCutchen .40 1.00
5T14 Ryan Braun .30 .75
5T15 Buster Posey .50 1.25
5T16 Wil Myers .30 .75
5T17 Nolan Arenado .60 1.50
5T18 Joey Votto .40 1.00
5T19 Paul Goldschmidt .40 1.00
5T20 Corey Seager .40 1.00
5T21 Robinson Cano .30 .75
5T22 Jose Altuve .30 .75
5T23 Yoenis Cespedes .40 1.00
5T24 Addison Russell .40 1.00
5T25 Carlos Gonzalez .30 .75
5T26 Xander Bogaerts .40 1.00
5T27 Ian Kinsler .30 .75
5T28 Dustin Pedroia .40 1.00
5T29 Trevor Story .40 1.00
5T30 George Springer .30 .75
5T31 Miguel Cabrera .40 1.00
5T32 Matt Kemp .30 .75
5T33 Ichiro Suzuki .50 1.25
5T34 Hanley Ramirez .30 .75
5T35 Noah Syndergaard .30 .75
5T36 Madison Bumgarner .30 .75
5T37 Jake Arrieta .30 .75
5T38 Jason Kipnis .30 .75
5T39 Adam Jones .30 .75
5T40 Kyle Seager .25 .60
5T41 Brian Dozier .40 1.00
5T42 Freddie Freeman .50 1.25
5T43 Yoan Moncada .75 2.00
5T44 Hunter Pence .30 .75
5T45 Edwin Encarnacion .40 1.00
5T46 Aaron Judge 3.00 8.00
5T47 Alex Bregman 1.25 3.00
5T48 Dansby Swanson .60 1.50
5T49 Andrew Benintendi .75 2.00
5T50 David Dahl .30 .75

2017 Topps Golden Glove Awards

COMPLETE SET (18) 10.00 25.00
STATED ODDS 1:5 TAR. RETAIL
STATED ODDS 1:5 TAR. BLASTER
GG1 Dallas Keuchel .50 1.25
GG2 Zack Greinke .60 1.50
GG3 Salvador Perez .50 1.25
GG4 Buster Posey .75 2.00
GG5 Mitch Moreland .40 1.00
GG6 Anthony Rizzo .75 2.00
GG7 Ian Kinsler .50 1.25
GG8 Joe Panik .50 1.25
GG9 Adrian Beltre .60 1.50
GG10 Nolan Arenado 1.00 2.50
GG11 Francisco Lindor .60 1.50
GG12 Brandon Crawford .50 1.25
GG13 Brett Gardner .50 1.25
GG14 Starling Marte .50 1.25
GG15 Kevin Kiermaier .50 1.25
GG16 Ender Inciarte .40 1.00
GG17 Mookie Betts 1.25 3.00
GG18 Jason Heyward .50 1.25

2017 Topps Home Run Derby Champions

COMPLETE SET (21) 30.00 80.00
HRD1 Andre Dawson .50 1.25
HRD5 Juan Gonzalez .60 1.50
HRD7 Frank Thomas .60 1.50
HRD10 Luis Gonzalez .40 1.00
HRD11 Bobby Abreu .40 1.00
HRD12 Ryan Howard .50 1.25
HRD13 Justin Morneau .50 1.25
HRD14 Prince Fielder .50 1.25
HRD15 David Ortiz .60 1.50
HRD16 Robinson Cano .50 1.25
HRD17 Prince Fielder .50 1.25
HRD18 Yoenis Cespedes .60 1.50
HRD19 Yoenis Cespedes .60 1.50
HRD20 Todd Frazier .40 1.00
HRD21 Giancarlo Stanton .60 1.50

2017 Topps Independence Day

COMPLETE SET (30) 15.00 40.00
ID1 Miguel Cabrera .60 1.50
ID2 Gregory Polanco .50 1.25
ID3 Evan Longoria .50 1.25
ID4 Jose Abreu .60 1.50
ID5 Khris Davis .60 1.50
ID6 Manny Machado .60 1.50
ID7 Corey Seager .60 1.50
ID8 Nolan Arenado 1.00 2.50
ID9 Trevor Story .60 1.50
ID10 Kyle Seager .40 1.00
ID11 Kris Bryant .75 2.00
ID12 Giancarlo Stanton .60 1.50
ID13 Miguel Sano .50 1.25
ID14 Anthony Rizzo .75 2.00
ID15 Carlos Correa .60 1.50
ID16 Julio Urias .60 1.50
ID17 Matt Carpenter .60 1.50
ID18 Max Scherzer .60 1.50
ID19 Yoenis Cespedes .60 1.50
ID20 Andrew McCutchen .60 1.50
ID21 Freddie Freeman .75 2.00
ID22 Jose Altuve .50 1.25
ID23 David Ortiz .60 1.50
ID24 Bryce Harper 1.00 2.50
ID25 Maikel Franco .50 1.25
ID26 Buster Posey .75 2.00
ID27 Francisco Lindor .60 1.50
ID28 Joe Mauer .50 1.25
ID29 Mookie Betts 1.25 3.00
ID30 Robinson Cano .50 1.25

2017 Topps Independence Day MLB Logo Patch

IDMLAB Adrian Beltre 4.00 10.00
IDMLAD Aledmys Diaz 3.00 8.00
IDMLAJ Adam Jones 3.00 8.00
IDMLAM Andrew McCutchen 4.00 10.00
IDMLAN Aaron Nola 3.00 8.00
IDMLAP Albert Pujols 5.00 12.00
IDMLAR Anthony Rizzo 6.00 15.00
IDMLBB Byron Buxton 4.00 10.00
IDMLBH Bryce Harper 6.00 15.00
IDMLBP Buster Posey 5.00 12.00
IDMLCCO Carlos Correa 4.00 10.00
IDMLCK Clayton Kershaw 6.00 15.00
IDMLCS Corey Seager 4.00 10.00
IDMLDO David Ortiz 4.00 10.00
IDMLDP Dustin Pedroia 4.00 10.00
IDMLEH Eric Hosmer 3.00 8.00
IDMLEL Evan Longoria 3.00 8.00
IDMLFF Freddie Freeman 5.00 12.00
IDMLFH Felix Hernandez 3.00 8.00
IDMLFL Francisco Lindor 4.00 10.00
IDMLGS Giancarlo Stanton 4.00 10.00
IDMLJAB Jose Abreu 4.00 10.00
IDMLJAL Jose Altuve 3.00 8.00
IDMLJB Javier Baez 5.00 12.00
IDMLJM Joe Mauer 3.00 8.00
IDMLJU Julio Urias 4.00 10.00
IDMLJVE Justin Verlander 4.00 10.00
IDMLJVO Joey Votto 4.00 10.00
IDMLKB Kris Bryant 5.00 12.00
IDMLKD Khris Davis 4.00 10.00
IDMLKS Kyle Seager 2.50 6.00
IDMLMBE Mookie Betts 8.00 20.00
IDMLMCB Miguel Cabrera 4.00 10.00
IDMLMCR Matt Carpenter 4.00 10.00
IDMLMF Maikel Franco 3.00 8.00
IDMLMM Manny Machado 4.00 10.00
IDMLMSA Miguel Sano 3.00 8.00
IDMLMSC Max Scherzer 4.00 10.00
IDMLMTA Masahiro Tanaka 3.00 8.00
IDMLMTR Mike Trout 15.00 40.00
IDMLNA Nolan Arenado 6.00 15.00
IDMLPG Paul Goldschmidt 4.00 10.00
IDMLRB Ryan Braun 3.00 8.00
IDMLRC Robinson Cano 3.00 8.00
IDMLRO Rougned Odor 3.00 8.00
IDMLTS Trevor Story 4.00 10.00
IDMLWM Wil Myers 3.00 8.00
IDMLYC Yoenis Cespedes 4.00 10.00
IDMLYD Yu Darvish 4.00 10.00
IDMLYM Yadier Molina 5.00 12.00

2017 Topps Jackie Robinson Day

COMPLETE SET (30) 15.00 40.00
STATED ODDS 1:2 BLASTER
*RED/25: 2.5X TO 6X BASIC
JRD1 Manny Machado .60 1.50
JRD2 Josh Donaldson .50 1.25
JRD3 Mookie Betts 1.25 3.00
JRD4 Evan Longoria .50 1.25
JRD5 Masahiro Tanaka .50 1.25
JRD6 Francisco Lindor .60 1.50
JRD7 Miguel Cabrera .60 1.50
JRD8 Todd Frazier .40 1.00
JRD9 Eric Hosmer .50 1.25
JRD10 Joe Mauer .50 1.25
JRD11 Yu Darvish .60 1.50
JRD12 Felix Hernandez .50 1.25
JRD13 Carlos Correa .60 1.50
JRD14 Sonny Gray .50 1.25
JRD15 Mike Trout 3.00 8.00
JRD16 Bryce Harper 1.00 2.50
JRD17 Giancarlo Stanton .60 1.50
JRD18 Miguel Sano .50 1.25
JRD19 Aaron Nola .50 1.25
JRD20 Yoenis Cespedes .60 1.50
JRD21 Kris Bryant .75 2.00
JRD22 Matt Carpenter .60 1.50
JRD23 Andrew McCutchen .60 1.50
JRD24 Ryan Braun .50 1.25
JRD25 Buster Posey .75 2.00
JRD26 Clayton Kershaw 1.00 2.50
JRD27 Wil Myers .50 1.25
JRD28 Nolan Arenado 1.00 2.50
JRD29 Joey Votto .60 1.50
JRD30 Paul Goldschmidt .60 1.50

2017 Topps Jackie Robinson Logo Patch

STATED ODDS 1:1 PER BLASTER BOX
*GOLD/99: .5X TO 1.2X BASIC
*BLACK/50: .6X TO 1.5X BASIC
JRPCABE Andrew Benintendi 6.00 15.00
JRPCABR Alex Bregman 3.00 8.00
JRPCAJO Adam Jones 3.00 8.00
JRPCAJU Aaron Judge 10.00 25.00
JRPCAM Andrew McCutchen 4.00 10.00
JRPCAN Aaron Nola 3.00 8.00
JRPCARI Anthony Rizzo 5.00 12.00
JRPCARU Addison Russell 4.00 10.00
JRPCBH Bryce Harper 6.00 15.00
JRPCBP Buster Posey 5.00 12.00
JRPCCC Carlos Correa 4.00 10.00
JRPCCG Carlos Gonzalez 3.00 8.00
JRPCCK Clayton Kershaw 5.00 12.00
JRPCCSA Chris Sale 4.00 10.00
JRPCCSE Corey Seager 6.00 15.00
JRPCDPE Dustin Pedroia 4.00 10.00
JRPCDPR David Price 3.00 8.00
JRPCEH Eric Hosmer 3.00 8.00
JRPCEL Evan Longoria 3.00 8.00
JRPCFF Freddie Freeman 5.00 12.00
JRPCFH Felix Hernandez 3.00 8.00
JRPCFL Francisco Lindor 4.00 10.00
JRPCGS Giancarlo Stanton 4.00 10.00
JRPCJA Jose Altuve 3.00 8.00
JRPCJBE Josh Bell 6.00 15.00
JRPCJD Josh Donaldson 3.00 8.00
JRPCJM Joe Mauer 3.00 8.00
JRPCJVE Justin Verlander 4.00 10.00
JRPCJVO Joey Votto 4.00 10.00
JRPCKB Kris Bryant 10.00 25.00
JRPCMBE Mookie Betts 8.00 20.00
JRPCMBU Madison Bumgarner 3.00 8.00
JRPCMCB Miguel Cabrera 4.00 10.00
JRPCMCR Matt Carpenter 4.00 10.00
JRPCMK Matt Kemp 3.00 8.00
JRPCMM Manny Machado 4.00 10.00
JRPCMSA Miguel Sano 3.00 8.00
JRPCMSC Max Scherzer 4.00 10.00
JRPCMTA Masahiro Tanaka 3.00 8.00
JRPCMTR Mike Trout 10.00 25.00
JRPCNA Nolan Arenado 6.00 15.00
JRPCNS Noah Syndergaard 5.00 12.00
JRPCPG Paul Goldschmidt 4.00 10.00
JRPCRB Ryan Braun 3.00 8.00
JRPCRC Robinson Cano 3.00 8.00
JRPCSG Sonny Gray 3.00 8.00
JRPCTF Todd Frazier 2.50 6.00
JRPCWM Wil Myers 3.00 8.00
JRPCYC Yoenis Cespedes 4.00 10.00
JRPCYD Yu Darvish 4.00 10.00

2017 Topps Major League Material Autographs

SER.1 ODDS 1:2387 HOBBY
SER.1 ODDS 1:1987 FAT PACK
SER.1 ODDS 1:5290 TAR. RETAIL
SER.1 ODDS 1:5323 HANGER
SER.1 ODDS 1:332 JUMBO
SER.1 ODDS 1:5317 WM RETAIL
SER.2 ODDS 1:5196 HOBBY
PRINT RUNS B/WN 15-50 COPIES PER
NO PRICING ON QTY 15
SER.1 EXCH DEADLINE 12/31/2018
SER.2 EXCH DEADLINE 5/31/2019
MLMAADI Aledmys Diaz S2
MLMAAG Alex Gordon/50
MLMAAJ Aaron Judge/50 75.00 200.00
MLMAAN Aaron Nola/50 20.00 50.00
MLMAARE Anthony Rendon/50 15.00 40.00
MLMABB Brandon Belt/50 10.00 25.00
MLMACC Carlos Correa/50 30.00 80.00
MLMACKL Corey Kluber/50 15.00 40.00
MLMACR Carlos Rodon/50 15.00 40.00
MLMADB Dellin Betances/25 S2 10.00 25.00
MLMADDU Danny Duffy/50 15.00 40.00
MLMADPO Drew Pomeranz/35 S2 10.00 25.00
MLMADPR David Price/50 20.00 50.00
MLMAFL Francisco Lindor/50 25.00 60.00
MLMAGS George Springer/50 12.00 30.00
MLMAGSA Gary Sanchez/50 60.00 150.00
MLMAHO Henry Owens/50 8.00 20.00
MLMAIK Ian Kinsler/50 12.00 30.00
MLMAJAL Jose Altuve/50 30.00 80.00
MLMAJB Jackie Bradley Jr./50 20.00 50.00
MLMAJB Javier Baez/50 15.00 40.00
MLMAJD Jacob deGrom/50 30.00 80.00
MLMAJH Jason Hammel/50 10.00 25.00
MLMAJP Joe Panik/35 S2 10.00 25.00
MLMAJPE Joc Pederson/50 20.00 50.00
MLMAJS Jorge Soler/50 12.00 30.00
MLMAKB Kris Bryant/50 75.00 200.00
MLMAKK Kevin Kiermaier/50 15.00 40.00
MLMAKM Kenta Maeda/50 15.00 40.00
MLMAKS Kyle Schwarber/50 30.00 80.00
MLMAKS Kyle Seager/35 S2 8.00 20.00
MLMALS Luis Severino/50 12.00 30.00
MLMAMCA Matt Carpenter/50 15.00 40.00
MLMAMF Maikel Franco/50
MLMAMF Michael Fulmer/35 S2 8.00 20.00
MLMAMSA Miguel Sano/50 15.00 40.00
MLMAMST Marcus Stroman/50
MLMANS Noah Syndergaard/50 20.00 50.00
MLMANS Noah Syndergaard/25 S2 25.00 60.00
MLMASMA Starling Marte/50 10.00 25.00
MLMASMZ Steven Matz/50 8.00 20.00
MLMASMZ Steven Matz/35 S2 8.00 20.00
MLMASP Stephen Piscotty/50 10.00 25.00
MLMATN Tyler Naquin/35 S2 12.00 30.00
MLMATS Trevor Story/50 20.00 50.00
MLMATT Trea Turner/35 S2 10.00 25.00
MLMAWC Willson Contreras/50 12.00 30.00
MLMAWM Wil Myers/50 10.00 25.00

2017 Topps Major League Materials

SER.1 ODDS 1:46 HOBBY
SER.1 ODDS 1:38 FAT PACK
SER.1 ODDS 1:101 WM/TAR. RETAIL
SER.1 ODDS 1:11 JUMBO
SER.1 ODDS 1:101 HANGER
SER.2 ODDS 1:49 HOBBY
*RED/25: .75X TO 2X BASIC
MLMAG Adrian Gonzalez 3.00 8.00
MLMAGO Alex Gordon S2 3.00 8.00
MLMAJ Adam Jones S2 3.00 8.00
MLMAJ Adam Jones 3.00 8.00
MLMAM Andrew McCutchen 4.00 10.00
MLMAM Andrew McCutchen S2 4.00 10.00
MLMAN Aaron Nola 3.00 8.00
MLMAP Albert Pujols 5.00 12.00
MLMAP Albert Pujols S2 5.00 12.00
MLMARI Anthony Rizzo S2 5.00 12.00
MLMARI Anthony Rizzo 5.00 12.00
MLMARU Addison Russell 4.00 10.00
MLMARU Addison Russell S2 4.00 10.00
MLMAW Adam Wainwright S2 3.00 8.00
MLMAW Adam Wainwright 3.00 8.00
MLMBH Bryce Harper S2 6.00 15.00
MLMBHM Billy Hamilton 3.00 8.00
MLMBPH Brandon Phillips 2.50 6.00
MLMBPO Buster Posey S2 5.00 12.00
MLMCA Chris Archer S2 2.50 6.00
MLMCB Carlos Beltran S2 3.00 8.00
MLMCC Carlos Correa S2 4.00 10.00
MLMCG Curtis Granderson 3.00 8.00
MLMCGO Carlos Gonzalez S2 3.00 8.00
MLMCGR Curtis Granderson S2 3.00 8.00
MLMCH Cole Hamels 3.00 8.00
MLMCKE Clayton Kershaw S2 5.00 12.00
MLMCKL Corey Kluber S2 3.00 8.00
MLMCKL Corey Kluber 3.00 8.00
MLMCM Carlos Martinez 3.00 8.00
MLMCSN Carlos Santana 3.00 8.00
MLMCY Christian Yelich 5.00 12.00
MLMCY Christian Yelich S2 5.00 12.00
MLMDB Dellin Betances S2 3.00 8.00
MLMDBE Dellin Betances 3.00 8.00
MLMDO David Ortiz S2 4.00 10.00
MLMDPE Dustin Pedroia 4.00 10.00
MLMDPR David Price 3.00 8.00
MLMDW David Wright 3.00 8.00
MLMDW David Wright S2 3.00 8.00
MLMEE Edwin Encarnacion 4.00 10.00
MLMEH Eric Hosmer 3.00 8.00
MLMEL Evan Longoria 3.00 8.00
MLMEL Evan Longoria S2 3.00 8.00
MLMFF Freddie Freeman S2 5.00 12.00
MLMFF Freddie Freeman 5.00 12.00
MLMFH Felix Hernandez S2 3.00 8.00
MLMGC Gerrit Cole 4.00 10.00
MLMGP Gregory Polanco 3.00 8.00
MLMGP Gregory Polanco S2 3.00 8.00
MLMGSA Gary Sanchez S2 4.00 10.00
MLMGSP George Springer 3.00 8.00
MLMGST Giancarlo Stanton 4.00 10.00
MLMGST Giancarlo Stanton S2 4.00 10.00
MLMHJR Hyun-Jin Ryu 3.00 8.00
MLMHR Hanley Ramirez 3.00 8.00
MLMHR Hanley Ramirez S2 3.00 8.00
MLMIK Ian Kinsler 3.00 8.00
MLMI Ichiro S2 5.00 12.00
MLMJAB Jose Abreu 4.00 10.00
MLMJAR Jake Arrieta 3.00 8.00
MLMJBA Javier Baez 5.00 12.00
MLMJBA Javier Baez S2 5.00 12.00
MLMJBR Jay Bruce S2 3.00 8.00
MLMJDG Jacob deGrom S2 8.00 20.00
MLMJDG Jacob deGrom 8.00 20.00
MLMJDO Josh Donaldson 3.00 8.00
MLMJE Jacoby Ellsbury S2 3.00 8.00
MLMJF Jeurys Familia S2 3.00 8.00
MLMJG Jon Gray S2 2.50 6.00
MLMJHA Josh Harrison 2.50 6.00
MLMJHE Jason Heyward 3.00 8.00
MLMJL Jon Lester 3.00 8.00
MLMJM J.D. Martinez S2 4.00 10.00
MLMJMR J.D. Martinez 4.00 10.00
MLMJPA Joe Panik S2 3.00 8.00
MLMJT Jameson Taillon S2 3.00 8.00
MLMJT Julio Teheran 3.00 8.00
MLMJU Justin Upton 3.00 8.00
MLMJUP Justin Upton S2 3.00 8.00
MLMJV Joey Votto S2 4.00 10.00
MLMJVE Justin Verlander 4.00 10.00
MLMJVO Joey Votto 4.00 10.00
MLMKB Kris Bryant 10.00 25.00
MLMKB Kris Bryant S2 10.00 25.00
MLMKK Kevin Kiermaier S2 3.00 8.00
MLMKS Kyle Seager S2 2.50 6.00
MLMKSC Kyle Schwarber 4.00 10.00
MLMKSE Kyle Seager 2.50 6.00
MLMKW Kolten Wong S2 3.00 8.00
MLMLC Lorenzo Cain S2 2.50 6.00
MLMLC Lorenzo Cain 2.50 6.00
MLMLS Luis Severino S2 3.00 8.00
MLMMBU Madison Bumgarner 3.00 8.00
MLMMCB Miguel Cabrera 4.00 10.00
MLMMCB Miguel Cabrera S2 4.00 10.00
MLMMCO Michael Conforto S2 3.00 8.00
MLMMH Matt Harvey S2 3.00 8.00
MLMMHA Matt Harvey 3.00 8.00
MLMMHO Matt Holliday 4.00 10.00
MLMMM Manny Machado 4.00 10.00
MLMMM Manny Machado S2 4.00 10.00
MLMMP Michael Pineda S2 2.50 6.00
MLMMS Miguel Sano S2 3.00 8.00
MLMMS Miguel Sano 3.00 8.00
MLMMT Mike Trout S2 10.00 25.00
MLMMTA Masahiro Tanaka S2 3.00 8.00
MLMMTE Mark Teixeira S2 3.00 8.00
MLMMTR Mike Trout 10.00 25.00
MLMMW Matt Wieters 4.00 10.00
MLMMW Michael Wacha S2 3.00 8.00
MLMNA Nolan Arenado S2 6.00 15.00
MLMNC Nelson Cruz S2 4.00 10.00
MLMNC Nelson Cruz 4.00 10.00
MLMNS Noah Syndergaard S2 3.00 8.00
MLMPF Prince Fielder S2 3.00 8.00
MLMPF Prince Fielder 3.00 8.00
MLMPG Paul Goldschmidt 4.00 10.00
MLMRB Ryan Braun 3.00 8.00
MLMRB Ryan Braun S2 3.00 8.00
MLMRC Robinson Cano S2 3.00 8.00
MLMRC Robinson Cano 3.00 8.00
MLMRO Rougned Odor 3.00 8.00
MLMRP Rick Porcello 3.00 8.00
MLMSC Starlin Castro S2 2.50 6.00
MLMSG Sonny Gray 3.00 8.00
MLMSM Starling Marte S2 3.00 8.00
MLMSPE Salvador Perez S2 3.00 8.00
MLMTT Troy Tulowitzki S2 4.00 10.00
MLMVM Victor Martinez 2.50 6.00
MLMWM Wil Myers 3.00 8.00
MLMWM Wil Myers S2 3.00 8.00
MLMYC Yoenis Cespedes S2 4.00 10.00
MLMYC Yoenis Cespedes 4.00 10.00
MLMYM Yadier Molina 5.00 12.00
MLMYMO Yadier Molina S2 5.00 12.00
MLMYP Yasiel Puig 4.00 10.00
MLMYT Yasmany Tomas 2.50 6.00
MLMYV Yordano Ventura 3.00 8.00
MLMZG Zack Greinke S2 4.00 10.00

2017 Topps Major League Milestones

COMPLETE SET (20) 6.00 15.00
STATED ODDS 1:8 HOBBY
MLM1 Miguel Cabrera .40 1.00
MLM2 Albert Pujols .50 1.25
MLM3 Trevor Story .40 1.00
MLM4 Adrian Gonzalez .30 .75
MLM5 Jose Bautista .30 .75
MLM6 Corey Seager .40 1.00
MLM7 Alex Rodriguez .50 1.25
MLM8 Miguel Cabrera .40 1.00
MLM9 Ichiro .50 1.25
MLM10 Max Scherzer .40 1.00
MLM11 Adrian Beltre .40 1.00
MLM12 Jake Arrieta .30 .75
MLM13 David Ortiz .40 1.00
MLM14 Justin Verlander .40 1.00
MLM15 Felix Hernandez .30 .75
MLM16 Cole Hamels .30 .75
MLM17 Kris Bryant .50 1.25
MLM18 Mark Teixeira .30 .75
MLM19 Ichiro .50 1.25
MLM20 David Ortiz .40 1.00

2017 Topps Major League Milestones Relics

STATED ODDS 1:1362 HOBBY
STATED PRINT RUN 100 SER.#'d SETS
*RED/25: .6X TO 1.5X BASIC
MLMRAB Adrian Beltre 5.00 12.00
MLMRAG Adrian Gonzalez 4.00 10.00
MLMRAP Albert Pujols 6.00 15.00
MLMRAR Alex Rodriguez 10.00 25.00
MLMRCS Corey Seager 5.00 12.00
MLMRDOR David Ortiz 6.00 15.00
MLMRDOT David Ortiz 6.00 15.00
MLMRFH Felix Hernandez 4.00 10.00
MLMRIC Ichiro 10.00 25.00
MLMRIH Ichiro 10.00 25.00
MLMRJA Jake Arrieta 8.00 20.00
MLMRJB Jose Bautista 4.00 10.00
MLMRJV Justin Verlander 5.00 12.00
MLMRKB Kris Bryant 6.00 15.00
MLMRMCA Miguel Cabrera 5.00 12.00
MLMRMCB Miguel Cabrera 5.00 12.00
MLMRMS Max Scherzer 5.00 12.00
MLMRMT Mark Teixeira 4.00 10.00
MLMRTS Trevor Story 5.00 12.00
MLMRZG Zack Greinke 5.00 12.00

2017 Topps Memorable Moments

COMPLETE SET (50) 10.00 25.00
STATED ODDS 1:8 HOBBY
MM1 Lou Gehrig .75 2.00
MM2 Anthony Rizzo .50 1.25
MM3 Babe Ruth 1.00 2.50
MM4 Steve Carlton .30 .75
MM5 Roger Clemens .50 1.25
MM6 Sandy Koufax .75 2.00
MM7 Roger Maris .40 1.00
MM8 Carlton Fisk .30 .75
MM9 Ted Williams .75 2.00
MM10 Aaron Boone .25 .60
MM11 Ichiro .50 1.25
MM12 Ozzie Smith .50 1.25
MM13 Roberto Clemente 1.00 2.50
MM14 Mark McGwire .60 1.50
MM15 Nolan Ryan 1.25 3.00
MM16 Bill Mazeroski .30 .75
MM17 Jackie Robinson .40 1.00
MM18 Bo Jackson .40 1.00
MM19 Ty Cobb .60 1.50
MM20 Ted Williams .75 2.00
MM21 Luis Gonzalez .25 .60
MM22 Willie Stargell .30 .75
MM23 Mike Piazza .40 1.00
MM24 Derek Jeter 1.00 2.50
MM25 Jackie Robinson .40 1.00
MM26 Jimmie Foxx .40 1.00
MM27 Nolan Ryan 1.25 3.00
MM28 Ken Griffey Jr. .75 2.00
MM29 Carl Yastrzemski .60 1.50
MM30 Miguel Cabrera .40 1.00
MM31 Derek Jeter 1.00 2.50
MM32 Ty Cobb .60 1.50
MM33 Jackie Robinson .40 1.00
MM34 Topps .25 .60

MM35 Lou Gehrig .75 2.00
MM36 Satchel Paige .40 1.00
MM37 Ted Williams .75 2.00
MM38 Brooks Robinson .30 .75
MM39 Fernando Valenzuela .25 .60
MM40 Cal Ripken Jr. 1.25 3.00
MM41 Reggie Jackson .30 .75
MM42 Babe Ruth 1.00 2.50
MM43 Rickey Henderson .40 1.00
MM44 Babe Ruth 1.00 2.50
MM45 Ichiro .50 1.25
MM46 Hank Aaron .75 2.00
MM47 Johnny Damon .30 .75
MM48 Ken Griffey Jr. .75 2.00
MM49 Cal Ripken Jr. 1.25 3.00
MM50 Mike Trout 2.00 5.00

2017 Topps Memorable Moments Autograph Relics

STATED ODDS 1:15,189 HOBBY
PRINT RUNS B/WN 10-35 COPIES PER
NO PRICING ON QTY 10
EXCHANGE DEADLINE 5/31/2019
MMARAD Aledmys Diaz/35 20.00 50.00
MMARCC Carlos Correa
MMARCF Carlton Fisk
MMARFV Fernando Valenzuela
MMARJD Josh Donaldson
MMAROS Ozzie Smith
MMARTN Tyler Naquin/35 12.00 30.00
MMARTS Trevor Story EXCH

2017 Topps Memorable Moments Autographs

STATED ODDS 1:14,809 HOBBY
PRINT RUNS B/WN 10-35 COPIES PER
NO PRICING ON QTY 15 OR LESS
EXCHANGE DEADLINE 5/31/2019
MMAAD Aledmys Diaz/35 20.00 50.00
MMALG Luis Gonzalez
MMATT Trea Turner
MMAKMA Kenta Maeda/15
MMAKMI Kevin Mitchell/25 10.00 25.00

2017 Topps Memorable Moments Relics

STATED ODDS 1:1818 HOBBY
STATED PRINT RUN 100 SER.#'d SETS
*RED/25: .6X TO 1.5X BASIC
MMRAR Anthony Rizzo 10.00 25.00
MMRBC Bartolo Colon 8.00 20.00
MMRCR Cal Ripken Jr. 15.00 40.00
MMRDG Dee Gordon 3.00 8.00
MMRDJ Derek Jeter 25.00 60.00
MMRI Ichiro 10.00 25.00
MMRJD Johnny Damon 6.00 15.00
MMRKGR Ken Griffey Jr. 10.00 25.00
MMRMC Miguel Cabrera 5.00 12.00
MMRMM Mark McGwire 15.00 40.00
MMRMPI Mike Piazza 10.00 25.00
MMRMT Mike Trout 25.00 60.00
MMRNR Nolan Ryan 15.00 40.00
MMROS Ozzie Smith 10.00 25.00
MMRRJ Reggie Jackson 12.00 30.00

2017 Topps MLB All Star Logo Patch

STATED ODDS 1:2219 HOBBY
*GOLD/75: .5X TO 1.2X BASIC
*BLACK/50: .5X TO 1.2X BASIC
ASLBJ Bo Jackson 10.00 25.00
ASLBL Barry Larkin 8.00 20.00
ASLBRO Brooks Robinson 10.00 25.00
ASLBRU Babe Ruth 10.00 25.00
ASLCJ Chipper Jones 8.00 20.00
ASLCR Cal Ripken Jr. 15.00 40.00
ASLCY Carl Yastrzemski 12.00 30.00
ASLDM Don Mattingly 10.00 25.00
ASLGB George Brett 10.00 25.00
ASLGM Greg Maddux 10.00 25.00
ASLHA Hank Aaron 10.00 25.00
ASLHK Harmon Killebrew 8.00 20.00
ASLIR Ivan Rodriguez 4.00 10.00
ASLJB Johnny Bench 5.00 12.00
ASLJM Joe Morgan 5.00 12.00
ASLKG Ken Griffey Jr. 10.00 25.00
ASLLG Lou Gehrig 10.00 25.00
ASLMM Mark McGwire 8.00 20.00
ASLMP Mike Piazza 6.00 15.00
ASLNR Nolan Ryan 15.00 40.00
ASLOS Ozzie Smith 8.00 20.00
ASLOV Omar Vizquel 4.00 10.00
ASLRC Roberto Clemente 12.00 30.00
ASLRCA Rod Carew 5.00 12.00
ASLRCL Roger Clemens 6.00 15.00
ASLRJ Reggie Jackson 10.00 25.00
ASLRS Ryne Sandberg 10.00 25.00
ASLSK Sandy Koufax 10.00 25.00
ASLWF Whitey Ford 4.00 10.00
ASLWS Willie Stargell 10.00 25.00

2017 Topps MLB Awards

COMPLETE SET (14) 8.00 20.00
STATED ODDS 1:4 RETAIL
STATED ODDS 1:4 BLASTER
CBP1 Mark Trumbo .40 1.00
CBP2 Jose Fernandez .60 1.50
CYA1 Rick Porcello .50 1.25
CYA2 Max Scherzer .60 1.50
HA1 David Ortiz .60 1.50
HA2 Kris Bryant .75 2.00
MOY1 Terry Francona .50 1.25
MOY2 Dave Roberts .50 1.25
MVP1 Mike Trout 3.00 8.00
MVP2 Kris Bryant .75 2.00
RLY1 Zach Britton .50 1.25
RLY2 Kenley Jansen .50 1.25
ROY1 Michael Fulmer .40 1.00
ROY2 Corey Seager .60 1.50

2017 Topps MLB Network

COMPLETE SET (29) 25.00 60.00
SER.1 ODDS 1:36 HOBBY
SER.1 ODDS 1:10 FAT PACK
SER.1 ODDS 1:24 RETAIL
SER.1 ODDS 1:24 BLASTER
SER.1 ODDS 1:5 HANGER
SER.1 ODDS 1:10 JUMBO
SER.2 ODDS 1:36 HOBBY
MLBN1 Kevin Millar 1.00 2.50
MLBN2 Mike Lowell 1.00 2.50
MLBN3 Greg Amsinger 1.00 2.50
MLBN4 Ryan Dempster 1.00 2.50
MLBN4 Tim Flannery UPD 1.00 2.50
MLBN5 MLB Tonight 1.00 2.50
MLBN6 Lauren Shehadi 1.00 2.50
MLBN7 Sean Casey 1.00 2.50
MLBN8 Harold Reynolds 1.00 2.50
MLBN8 Christopher Russo UPD 1.00 2.50
MLBN9 John Smoltz 1.50 4.00
MLBN10 Dan Plesac 1.00 2.50
MLBN11 Bob Costas 1.00 2.50
MLBN12 Tom Verducci UPD 1.00 2.50
MLBN13 Joel Sherman UPD 1.00 2.50
MLBN14 Brian Kenny 1.00 2.50
MLBN15 Bill Ripken 1.00 2.50
MLBN16 Carlos Pena 1.25 3.00
MLBN17 Eric Byrnes 1.00 2.50
MLBN20 Robert Flores 1.00 2.50
MLBN21 Matt Yallof UPD 1.00 2.50
MLBN23 Paul Severino UPD 1.00 2.50
MLBN25 Mark DeRosa 1.00 2.50
MLBN26 Scott Braun UPD 1.00 2.50
MLBN27 Kelly Nash 1.00 2.50
MLBN28 Heidi Watney UPD 1.00 2.50
MLBN29 Intentional Talk 1.00 2.50
MLBN30 Ken Rosenthal UPD 1.00 2.50
MLBN31 Peter Gammons 1.00 2.50

2017 Topps Postseason Performance Autograph Relics

STATED ODDS 1:8363 HOBBY
STATED ODDS 1:6976 FAT PACK
STATED ODDS 1:18,515 TAR. RETAIL
STATED ODDS 1:18,187 HANGER
STATED ODDS 1:18,988 WM RETAIL
STATED ODDS 1:1159 JUMBO
STATED PRINT RUN 50 SER. #'d SETS
EXCHANGE DEADLINE 12/31/2018
*RED/25: .5X TO 1.2X BASIC
PPARARU Addison Russell 50.00 120.00
PPARCK Clayton Kershaw 40.00 100.00
PPARCKL Corey Kluber 25.00 60.00
PPARDO David Ortiz
PPAREE Edwin Encarnacion
PPARFL Francisco Lindor 50.00 120.00
PPARJB Javier Baez 30.00 80.00
PPARJP Joe Panik 40.00 100.00
PPARJU Julio Urias EXCH 25.00 60.00
PPARKB Kris Bryant 150.00 300.00
PPARNS Noah Syndergaard
PPARTT Troy Tulowitzki 25.00 60.00

2017 Topps Postseason Performance Autographs

STATED ODDS 1:8363 HOBBY
STATED ODDS 1:6976 FAT PACK
STATED ODDS 1:18,515 TAR. RETAIL
STATED ODDS 1:18,187 HANGER
STATED ODDS 1:18,988 WM RETAIL
STATED ODDS 1:1159 JUMBO
STATED PRINT RUN 50 SER. #'d SETS
EXCHANGE DEADLINE 12/31/2018
*RED/25: .5X TO 1.2X BASIC
PPACKL Corey Kluber 12.00 30.00
PPADF Dexter Fowler 25.00 60.00
PPAFL Francisco Lindor 40.00 100.00
PPAJB Javier Baez 40.00 100.00
PPAJP Joe Panik
PPAJU Julio Urias 25.00 60.00
PPAKB Kris Bryant 125.00 300.00
PPANS Noah Syndergaard

2017 Topps Postseason Performance Relics

STATED ODDS 1:4332 HOBBY
STATED ODDS 1:9726 WM RETAIL
STATED ODDS 1:9600 TAR. RETAIL
STATED ODDS 1:9489 HANGER
STATED ODDS 1:1601 JUMBO
STATED PRINT RUN 100 SER. #'d SETS
*RED/25: .5X TO 1.2X BASIC
PPRAR Anthony Rizzo 10.00 25.00
PPRBP Buster Posey 20.00 50.00
PPRCK Clayton Kershaw 12.00 30.00
PPRCS Corey Seager 8.00 20.00
PPRDO David Ortiz 20.00 50.00
PPREE Edwin Encarnacion 8.00 20.00
PPRFL Francisco Lindor 12.00 30.00
PPRJU Julio Urias 8.00 20.00
PPRKB Kris Bryant 30.00 80.00
PPRMB Madison Bumgarner 20.00 50.00
PPRNS Noah Syndergaard 20.00 50.00

2017 Topps Rediscover Topps

COMPLETE SET (10) 4.00 10.00
STATED ODDS 1:8 HOBBY
STATED ODDS 1:3 FAT PACK
STATED ODDS 1:8 RETAIL
STATED ODDS 1:2 HANGER
STATED ODDS 1:8 BLASTER
STATED ODDS 1:2 JUMBO
RT1 Hank Aaron .75 2.00
RT2 Jackie Robinson .40 1.00
RT3 Reggie Jackson .30 .75
RT4 Nolan Ryan 1.25 3.00
RT5 Roberto Clemente 1.00 2.50
RT6 George Brett .75 2.00
RT7 Don Mattingly .75 2.00
RT8 Mark McGwire .60 1.50
RT9 Ken Griffey Jr. .75 2.00
RT10 Mike Trout 2.00 5.00

2017 Topps Reverance Autograph Patches

STATED ODDS 1:2645 HOBBY
STATED PRINT RUN 25 SER.#'d SETS
EXCHANGE DEADLINE 5/31/2019
TAPAR Anthony Rizzo EXCH 75.00 200.00
TAPARU Addison Russell EXCH 15.00 40.00
TAPBH Bryce Harper 150.00 300.00
TAPBP Buster Posey 75.00 200.00
TAPCS Corey Seager 75.00 200.00
TAPCY Carl Yastrzemski 60.00 150.00
TAPDO David Ortiz 75.00 200.00
TAPDP Dustin Pedroia 30.00 80.00
TAPGM Greg Maddux 75.00 200.00
TAPJAL Jose Altuve 75.00 200.00
TAPJU Julio Urias 20.00 50.00
TAPKM Kenta Maeda 20.00 50.00
TAPKS Kyle Schwarber 20.00 50.00
TAPMM Manny Machado 60.00 150.00
TAPMMG Mark McGwire 75.00 200.00
TAPRC Roger Clemens 40.00 100.00
TAPRJO Randy Johnson 60.00 150.00
TAPTT Troy Tulowitzki 10.00 25.00
TAPYM Yoan Moncada 60.00 150.00

2017 Topps Salute

COMPLETE SET (200) 75.00 200.00
STATED ODDS 1:4 HOBBY
STATED ODDS 1:2 FAT PACK
STATED ODDS 1:4 WM/TAR. RETAIL
STATED ODDS 1:4 BLASTER
SER.2 ODDS 1:4 HOBBY
*RED/25: 6X TO 15X BASIC
S1 Bryce Harper .60 1.50
S2 Miguel Cabrera .40 1.00
S3 Ty Cobb .60 1.50
S4 Paul Goldschmidt .40 1.00
S5 Braden Shipley .25 .60
S6 Jacob deGrom .75 2.00
S7 Johnny Bench .40 1.00
S8 Duke Snider .30 .75
S9 Freddie Freeman .50 1.25
S10 David Price .30 .75
S11 Orlando Arcia .40 1.00
S12 Alex Reyes .30 .75
S13 Kyle Seager .25 .60
S14 Francisco Lindor .40 1.00
S15 Al Kaline .40 1.00
S16 Sandy Koufax .75 2.00
S17 Robin Yount .40 1.00
S18 Roberto Clemente 1.00 2.50
S19 Ted Williams .75 2.00
S20 Gregory Polanco .30 .75
S21 Cal Ripken Jr. 1.25 3.00
S22 Addison Russell .40 1.00
S23 Honus Wagner .40 1.00
S24 Joey Votto .40 1.00
S25 Mike Trout 2.00 5.00
S26 Bo Jackson .40 1.00
S27 Jorge Soler .40 1.00
S28 Jose Altuve .30 .75
S29 Tyler Glasnow 1.00 2.50
S30 Matt Shoemaker .30 .75
S31 Frank Robinson .30 .75
S32 Jake Arrieta .30 .75
S33 Anthony Rendon .40 1.00
S34 Buster Posey .50 1.25
S35 Ian Kinsler .30 .75
S36 George Springer .30 .75
S37 Jim Palmer .30 .75
S38 Joe Mauer .30 .75
S39 Jackie Robinson .40 1.00
S40 David Ortiz .40 1.00
S41 Jason Hammel .30 .75
S42 Jose Peraza .30 .75
S43 Brandon Belt .30 .75
S44 Anthony Rizzo .50 1.25
S45 Noah Syndergaard .30 .75
S46 Alex Gordon .30 .75
S47 Trevor Story .40 1.00
S48 Yoenis Cespedes .40 1.00
S49 Luke Weaver .30 .75
S50 Brooks Robinson .30 .75
S51 Mookie Betts .75 2.00
S52 Babe Ruth 1.00 2.50
S53 Carlos Rodon .40 1.00
S54 Ryan Braun .30 .75
S55 Tyler Austin .30 .75
S56 Joe Morgan .30 .75
S57 Stephen Piscotty .30 .75
S58 Josh Donaldson .30 .75
S59 Carlos Gonzalez .30 .75
S60 Andrew McCutchen .40 1.00
S61 Jackie Bradley Jr. .40 1.00
S62 Manny Machado .40 1.00
S63 Willson Contreras .40 1.00
S64 Ken Griffey Jr. .75 2.00
S65 Kenta Maeda .30 .75
S66 Alex Bregman 1.25 3.00
S67 Todd Frazier .25 .60
S68 Josh Bell .60 1.50
S69 Ozzie Smith .50 1.25
S70 Giancarlo Stanton .40 1.00
S71 Justin Verlander .40 1.00
S72 Ichiro Suzuki .50 1.25
S73 Aaron Judge 3.00 8.00
S74 Rickey Henderson .40 1.00
S75 Dansby Swanson .60 1.50
S76 Miguel Sano .30 .75
S77 Ivan Rodriguez .30 .75
S78 Aaron Nola .30 .75
S79 Jameson Taillon .30 .75
S80 Kris Bryant .50 1.25
S81 Corey Seager .40 1.00
S82 Albert Pujols .50 1.25
S83 David Dahl .30 .75
S84 Carlos Correa .40 1.00
S85 Chris Sale .40 1.00
S86 Kendrys Morales .25 .60
S87 Wil Myers .30 .75
S88 Nolan Ryan 1.25 3.00
S89 Yulieski Gurriel .40 1.00
S90 Jose Abreu .40 1.00
S91 Rod Carew .30 .75
S92 Andrew Benintendi .75 2.00
S93 Jose Bautista .30 .75
S94 Brandon Phillips .25 .60
S95 Nolan Arenado .60 1.50
S96 Joe Musgrove .75 2.00
S97 Lou Brock .30 .75
S98 Hank Aaron .75 2.00
S99 Stan Musial .60 1.50
S100 Barry Larkin .30 .75
S101 Bobby Abreu .25 .60
S102 Hunter Dozier .25 .60
S103 Addison Russell .40 1.00
S104 Tyler Naquin .40 1.00
S105 Steven Matz .25 .60
S106 Jason Kipnis .30 .75
S107 Alex Gordon .30 .75
S108 Eddie Mathews .40 1.00
S109 Dave Winfield .30 .75
S110 Bryce Harper .60 1.50
S111 Aledmys Diaz .30 .75
S112 David Ortiz .40 1.00
S113 Jose Canseco .30 .75
S114 Yoan Moncada .75 2.00
S115 Trey Mancini .50 1.25
S116 Gary Sanchez .40 1.00
S117 Bob Feller .30 .75
S118 Joey Rickard .25 .60
S119 Orlando Cepeda .30 .75
S120 Kris Bryant .50 1.25
S121 Juan Marichal .30 .75
S122 Byron Buxton .40 1.00
S123 Matt Olson 1.25 3.00
S124 Matt Strahm .25 .60
S125 Mike Trout 2.00 5.00
S126 David Dahl .30 .75
S127 Warren Spahn .30 .75
S128 Trey Mancini .50 1.25
S129 Josh Donaldson .30 .75
S130 Carlos Correa .40 1.00
S131 Robert Gsellman .25 .60
S132 Aaron Judge 3.00 8.00
S133 Andrew Toles .25 .60
S134 Fergie Jenkins .30 .75
S135 Jake Thompson .25 .60
S136 Tyler Austin .30 .75
S137 Gary Carter .30 .75
S138 JaCoby Jones .30 .75
S139 Tim Anderson .40 1.00
S140 Todd Frazier .25 .60
S141 Alex Bregman 1.25 3.00
S142 Harmon Killebrew .40 1.00
S143 Brian Dozier .40 1.00
S144 Anthony Rizzo .50 1.25
S145 Ken Griffey Jr. .75 2.00
S146 Noah Syndergaard .30 .75
S147 Jorge Alfaro .30 .75
S148 Tommy Lasorda .30 .75
S149 Jeff Bagwell .30 .75
S150 Clayton Kershaw .60 1.50
S151 Joe Panik .30 .75
S152 Buster Posey .50 1.25
S153 Roberto Alomar .30 .75
S154 Josh Donaldson .30 .75
S155 Jose De Leon .25 .60
S156 Maikel Franco .30 .75
S157 Javier Baez .50 1.25
S158 Willie Stargell .30 .75
S159 Tim Raines .30 .75
S160 Dansby Swanson .60 1.50
S161 Stephen Piscotty .30 .75
S162 Yulieski Gurriel .40 1.00
S163 George Brett .75 2.00
S164 Eddie Murray .30 .75
S165 Jered Weaver .30 .75
S166 Adam Duvall .30 .75
S167 Joey Votto .40 1.00
S168 Frank Thomas .40 1.00
S169 Jharel Cotton .25 .60
S170 Tyler Glasnow 1.00 2.50
S171 Dan Vogelbach .40 1.00
S172 Ty Blach .25 .60
S173 Duke Snider .30 .75
S174 Willie McCovey .30 .75
S175 Anthony Rizzo .50 1.25
S176 Raimel Tapia .30 .75
S177 Starling Marte .30 .75
S178 Reynaldo Lopez .25 .60
S179 Jacob deGrom .75 2.00
S180 Corey Seager .40 1.00
S181 Anthony Rendon .40 1.00
S182 Manny Margot .25 .60
S183 Mookie Betts .75 2.00
S184 Manny Machado .40 1.00
S185 Braden Shipley .25 .60
S186 Addison Russell .40 1.00
S187 Kenny Lofton .25 .60
S188 Renato Nunez .50 1.25
S189 Alex Reyes .30 .75
S190 Teoscar Hernandez 1.00 2.50
S191 Jeff Hoffman .25 .60
S192 Francisco Lindor .40 1.00
S193 Aledmys Diaz .30 .75
S194 Josh Bell .60 1.50
S195 Tyler Glasnow 1.00 2.50
S196 Randal Grichuk .25 .60
S197 Gavin Cecchini .25 .60
S198 Gregory Polanco .30 .75
S199 Andrew Benintendi .75 2.00
S200 Derek Jeter 1.00 2.50

2017 Topps Salute Autographs

SER.1 ODDS 1:1987 HOBBY
SER.1 ODDS 1:1567 TAR. RETAIL
SER.1 ODDS 1:1284 HANGER
SER.1 ODDS 1:679 FAT PACK
SER.1 ODDS 1:68 JUMBO
SER.1 ODDS 1:1773 WM RETAIL
SER.2 ODDS 1:951 HOBBY
SER.1 EXCH DEADLINE 12/31/2018
SER.2 EXCH DEADLINE 5/31/2019
*RED/25: .6X TO 1.5X BASIC
TSAAB Alex Bregman 25.00 60.00
TSAABE Andrew Benintendi 75.00 200.00
TSAABE Andrew Benintendi S2 75.00 200.00
TSAABR Archie Bradley 3.00 8.00
TSAABR Alex Bregman S2 25.00 60.00
TSAADA Aledmys Diaz S2 10.00 25.00
TSAADI Aledmys Diaz S2 10.00 25.00
TSAADU Adam Duvall S2 20.00 50.00
TSAAG Andres Galarraga 12.00 30.00
TSAAGO Alex Gordon 20.00 50.00
TSAAGO Alex Gordon S2 20.00 50.00
TSAAJ Aaron Judge 125.00 300.00
TSAAJ Aaron Judge S2 125.00 300.00
TSAAK Al Kaline 25.00 50.00
TSAAN Aaron Nola 4.00 10.00
TSAAR Anthony Rendon 10.00 25.00
TSAARE Alex Reyes 4.00 10.00
TSAARE Anthony Rendon S2 10.00 25.00
TSAARI Anthony Rizzo 25.00 60.00
TSAARI Anthony Rizzo S2 25.00 60.00
TSAARS Addison Russell S2
TSAARU Addison Russell S2
TSAARY Alex Reyes S2 4.00 10.00
TSAAT Andrew Toles S2 3.00 8.00
TSABA Bobby Abreu S2 12.00 30.00
TSABB Brandon Belt 10.00 25.00
TSABB Byron Buxton S2 10.00 25.00
TSABH Bryce Harper
TSABJ Bo Jackson
TSABL Barry Larkin 30.00 80.00
TSABM Bill Mazeroski 20.00 50.00
TSABM Bruce Maxwell S2 3.00 8.00
TSABPH Brandon Phillips 8.00 20.00
TSABRO Brooks Robinson 20.00 50.00
TSABS Braden Shipley 3.00 8.00
TSABS Braden Shipley S2 3.00 8.00
TSACC Carlos Correa 40.00 100.00
TSACFI Carlton Fisk
TSACFU Carson Fulmer 3.00 8.00
TSACL Cliff Lee
TSACP Chad Pinder S2 3.00 8.00
TSACR Cal Ripken Jr.
TSACRO Carlos Rodon 5.00 12.00
TSADB Dellin Betances 6.00 15.00
TSADD David Dahl 3.00 8.00
TSADD David Dahl S2 4.00 10.00
TSADO David Ortiz S2
TSADS Dansby Swanson EXCH 60.00 150.00
TSADSA Danny Salazar 8.00 20.00
TSADSN Duke Snider
TSADSN Duke Snider S2
TSADSW Dansby Swanson S2
TSADV Dan Vogelbach S2 5.00 12.00
TSAEM Edgar Martinez 10.00 25.00
TSAFJ Fergie Jenkins 10.00 25.00
TSAFJ Fergie Jenkins S2 5.00 12.00
TSAFL Francisco Lindor 25.00 60.00
TSAFL Francisco Lindor S2 EXCH 20.00 50.00
TSAFM Fred McGriff
TSAFR Frank Robinson 40.00 100.00
TSAFV Fernando Valenzuela
TSAGCA Gary Carter S2 20.00 50.00
TSAGCE Gavin Cecchini S2 EXCH 3.00 8.00
TSAGG Goose Gossage 10.00 25.00
TSAGM German Marquez S2 5.00 12.00
TSAGP Gregory Polanco S2 4.00 10.00
TSAGPO Gregory Polanco 10.00 25.00
TSAGS George Springer 10.00 25.00
TSAHD Hunter Dozier S2 3.00 8.00
TSAHR Hunter Renfroe 6.00 15.00
TSAHS Hector Santiago 3.00 8.00
TSAIK Ian Kinsler 15.00 40.00
TSAIR Ivan Rodriguez
TSAJA Jose Abreu
TSAJA Jorge Alfaro S2 4.00 10.00
TSAJB Jackie Bradley Jr. 15.00 40.00
TSAJBA Javier Baez 20.00 50.00
TSAJBA Javier Baez S2 6.00 15.00
TSAJBAG Jeff Bagwell 30.00 80.00
TSAJBE Josh Bell 25.00 60.00
TSAJBER Jose Berrios 4.00 10.00
TSAJBL Josh Bell S2 8.00 20.00
TSAJBR Jay Bruce 10.00 25.00
TSAJCA Jose Canseco S2 15.00 40.00
TSAJCO Jharel Cotton S2 3.00 8.00
TSAJDA Johnny Damon
TSAJDE Jacob deGrom
TSAJDG Jacob deGrom S2 50.00 120.00
TSAJDL Jose De Leon S2 3.00 8.00
TSAJDO Josh Donaldson S2
TSAJH Jason Hammel 10.00 25.00
TSAJH Jeff Hoffman S2 3.00 8.00
TSAJJ JaCoby Jones S2 4.00 10.00
TSAJK Jason Kipnis S2 8.00 20.00
TSAJL Jake Lamb 4.00 10.00
TSAJM Joe Mauer
TSAJMA J.D. Martinez 12.00 30.00
TSAJMAR Juan Marichal 12.00 30.00
TSAJMO Joe Morgan
TSAJMU Joe Musgrove 10.00 25.00
TSAJO Jake Odorizzi 3.00 8.00
TSAJP Joe Panik 12.00 30.00
TSAJP Joe Panik S2 12.00 30.00
TSAJPA Jim Palmer 12.00 30.00
TSAJPE Joc Pederson 6.00 15.00
TSAJPER Jose Peraza 12.00 30.00
TSAJR Joey Rickard S2 10.00 25.00
TSAJS Jorge Soler 15.00 40.00
TSAJT Julio Teheran 10.00 25.00
TSAJT Jake Thompson S2 3.00 8.00
TSAJTA Jameson Taillon 4.00 10.00
TSAJTH Jake Thompson 10.00 25.00
TSAJW Jered Weaver S2
TSAKB Kris Bryant
TSAKG Ken Griffey Jr. S2
TSAKL Kenny Lofton S2 12.00 30.00
TSAKM Kendrys Morales 8.00 20.00
TSAKSE Kyle Seager 8.00 20.00
TSALB Lou Brock 25.00 60.00
TSALS Luis Severino 8.00 20.00
TSALW Luke Weaver 6.00 15.00
TSAMF Maikel Franco S2 8.00 20.00
TSAMM Manny Margot S2
TSAMO Matt Olson S2 6.00 15.00
TSAMS Matt Shoemaker 4.00 10.00
TSAMS Matt Strahm S2 10.00 25.00
TSAMSA Miguel Sano 8.00 20.00
TSAMT Mike Trout
TSANS Noah Syndergaard 15.00 40.00
TSAOAR Orlando Arcia 6.00 15.00
TSAOC Orlando Cepeda
TSAOC Orlando Cepeda S2 8.00 20.00
TSAOS Ozzie Smith
TSAPC Patrick Corbin 4.00 10.00
TSAPN Phil Niekro 12.00 30.00
TSAPO Paul O'Neill 12.00 30.00
TSARA Roberto Alomar 25.00 60.00
TSARA Roberto Alomar S2 30.00 80.00
TSARC Rod Carew
TSARF Rollie Fingers 15.00 40.00
TSARGR Randal Grichuk S2
TSARGS Robert Gsellman S2 3.00 8.00
TSARH Ryon Healy 4.00 10.00
TSARL Reynaldo Lopez S2 3.00 8.00
TSARN Renato Nunez S2 6.00 15.00
TSARQ Roman Quinn S2 3.00 8.00
TSARTA Raimel Tapia S2 4.00 10.00
TSARY Robin Yount 30.00 80.00
TSARZ Rob Zastryzny S2
TSASL Seth Lugo S2 10.00 25.00
TSASMR Starling Marte S2 4.00 10.00
TSASMT Steven Matz S2 12.00 30.00
TSASP Stephen Piscotty 8.00 20.00
TSASP Stephen Piscotty S2 6.00 15.00
TSATA Tyler Austin 8.00 20.00
TSATAN Tim Anderson S2 5.00 12.00
TSATAU Tyler Austin S2 8.00 20.00
TSATB Ty Blach S2 12.00 30.00
TSATF Todd Frazier S2
TSATGA Tyler Glasnow S2 EXCH 10.00 25.00
TSATGL Tyler Glasnow S2 EXCH 10.00 25.00
TSATH Teoscar Hernandez S2 12.00 30.00
TSATL Tommy Lasorda S2 20.00 50.00
TSATMA Trey Mancini S2 20.00 50.00
TSATMN Trey Mancini S2 20.00 50.00
TSATN Tyler Naquin S2 5.00 12.00
TSATST Trevor Story 15.00 40.00
TSATW Taijuan Walker 10.00 25.00
TSAVG Vladimir Guerrero S2 40.00 100.00
TSAWC Willson Contreras 15.00 40.00
TSAWD Wade Davis 10.00 25.00
TSAWM Wil Myers
TSAYG Yulieski Gurriel 30.00 80.00
TSAYG Yulieski Gurriel S2 5.00 12.00
TSAYM Yoan Moncada S2

2017 Topps Silver Slugger Awards

STATED ODDS 1:4 WM RETAIL
STATED ODDS 1:5 WM BLASTER
SS1 Salvador Perez .50 1.25
SS2 Wilson Ramos .40 1.00
SS3 Miguel Cabrera .60 1.50
SS4 Anthony Rizzo .75 2.00
SS5 Jose Altuve .50 1.25
SS6 Daniel Murphy .50 1.25
SS7 Josh Donaldson .50 1.25
SS8 Nolan Arenado 1.00 2.50
SS9 Xander Bogaerts .60 1.50
SS10 Corey Seager .60 1.50
SS11 Mike Trout 3.00 8.00
SS12 Charlie Blackmon .60 1.50
SS13 Mark Trumbo .40 1.00
SS14 Christian Yelich .75 2.00
SS15 Mookie Betts 1.25 3.00
SS16 Yoenis Cespedes .60 1.50
SS17 David Ortiz .60 1.50
SS18 Jake Arrieta .50 1.25

2017 Topps Spring Training Logo Patch

STATED ODDS 1:1295 HOBBY
STATED ODDS 1:30 JUMBO
*GOLD/99: .5X TO 1.2X BASIC
*BLACK/50: .6X TO 1.5X BASIC
MLBSTAM Andrew McCutchen 4.00 10.00
MLBSTAN Aaron Nola 3.00 8.00
MLBSTBH Bryce Harper 6.00 15.00
MLBSTBP Buster Posey 5.00 12.00
MLBSTCC Carlos Correa 4.00 10.00
MLBSTCK Clayton Kershaw 5.00 12.00
MLBSTCS Chris Sale 4.00 10.00
MLBSTEH Eric Hosmer 3.00 8.00
MLBSTEL Evan Longoria 3.00 8.00
MLBSTFF Freddie Freeman 5.00 12.00
MLBSTFL Francisco Lindor 4.00 10.00
MLBSTGS Giancarlo Stanton 4.00 10.00
MLBSTGSA Gary Sanchez 6.00 15.00
MLBSTJD Josh Donaldson 3.00 8.00
MLBSTJM Joe Mauer 3.00 8.00
MLBSTJV Joey Votto 4.00 10.00
MLBSTKB Kris Bryant 10.00 25.00
MLBSTMB Mookie Betts 8.00 20.00
MLBSTMCB Miguel Cabrera 4.00 10.00
MLBSTMCR Matt Carpenter 4.00 10.00
MLBSTMM Manny Machado 4.00 10.00
MLBSTMTR Mike Trout 8.00 20.00
MLBSTNA Nolan Arenado 6.00 15.00
MLBSTNS Noah Syndergaard 5.00 12.00
MLBSTPG Paul Goldschmidt 4.00 10.00
MLBSTRB Ryan Braun 3.00 8.00
MLBSTRC Robinson Cano 3.00 8.00
MLBSTSG Sonny Gray 3.00 8.00
MLBSTWM Wil Myers 3.00 8.00
MLBSTYD Yu Darvish 4.00 10.00

2017 Topps World Champion Autograph Relics

STATED ODDS 1:16,871 HOBBY
STATED ODDS 1:13,952 FAT PACK
STATED ODDS 1:37,029 TAR. RETAIL
STATED ODDS 1:36,374 HANGER
STATED ODDS 1:2328 JUMBO
STATED ODDS 1:36,249 WM RETAIL
STATED PRINT RUN 50 SER. #'d SETS
EXCHANGE DEADLINE 12/31/2018
*RED/25: .75X TO 2X BASIC
WCRAA Albert Almora 40.00 100.00
WCRARU Addison Russell 60.00 150.00
WCRJB Javier Baez
WCRJH Jason Heyward 30.00 80.00
WCRKB Kris Bryant 200.00 400.00
WCRKS Kyle Schwarber 50.00 120.00
WCRWC Willson Contreras 30.00 80.00

2017 Topps World Champion Autographs

STATED ODDS 1:16,871 HOBBY
STATED ODDS 1:13,952 FAT PACK
STATED ODDS 1:37,029 TAR. RETAIL
STATED ODDS 1:36,374 HANGER
STATED ODDS 1:2328 JUMBO
STATED ODDS 1:36,249 RETAIL
STATED PRINT RUN 50 SER. #'d SETS
EXCHANGE DEADLINE 12/31/2018
*RED/25: .5X TO 1.2X BASIC
WCAAA Albert Almora 30.00 80.00
WCAARU Addison Russell 60.00 150.00
WCAJB Javier Baez 25.00 60.00
WCAJH Jason Heyward
WCAKB Kris Bryant 250.00 400.00
WCAKS Kyle Schwarber 60.00 150.00
WCAWC Willson Contreras 40.00 100.00

2017 Topps World Champion Relics

STATED ODDS 1:2888 HOBBY
STATED ODDS 1:2408 FAT PACK
STATED ODDS 1:6400 TAR. RETAIL
STATED ODDS 1:6419 HANGER
STATED ODDS 1:6432 TAR. RETAIL
STATED ODDS 1:401 JUMBO
STATED PRINT RUN 100 SER. #'d SETS
*RED/25: .75X TO 2X BASIC
WCRAA Albert Almora 15.00 40.00
WCRAC Aroldis Chapman 15.00 40.00
WCRARI Anthony Rizzo 20.00 50.00
WCRARU Addison Russell 15.00 40.00
WCRBZ Ben Zobrist 20.00 50.00
WCRDF Dexter Fowler 12.00 30.00
WCRJA Jake Arrieta 15.00 40.00
WCRJB Javier Baez 20.00 50.00
WCRJH Jason Heyward 10.00 25.00
WCRJL Jon Lester 15.00 40.00
WCRJS Jorge Soler 12.00 30.00
WCRKB Kris Bryant 50.00 120.00
WCRKS Kyle Schwarber 12.00 30.00
WCRWC Willson Contreras 15.00 40.00

2017 Topps Update

COMPLETE SET w/o SP's (300) 20.00 50.00
PLATE PRINT RUN 1 SET PER COLOR
BLACK-CYAN-MAGENTA-YELLOW ISSUED
NO PLATE PRICING DUE TO SCARCITY
US1 Aaron Judge HRD 1.50 4.00
US2 Domingo German RC 1.25 3.00
US3 Paul Sewald RC .40 1.00
Tyler Pill RC
US4 Matt Chapman RC 4.00 10.00
US5 Casey Fien RC .40 1.00
US6 Ramon Torres RC .40 1.00
US7 Willy Garcia RC .40 1.00
Adam Engel RC
US8 Yulieski Gurriel RD .20 .50
US9A George Springer AS .15 .40
US9B George Springer SP .75 2.00
US10A Ian Happ RC .75 2.00
US10B Ernie Banks SP .75 2.00
US10C Ian Happ SP 1.25 3.00
US10D Ian Happ SP
US10E Ryne Sandberg SP 1.50 4.00
US11 Gary Sanchez HRD .20 .50
US12 Lisalverto Bonilla .12 .30
US13 Brian McCann .15 .40
US14 Blast Off! .20 .50
Carlos Correa/Jose Altuve
US15 Kyle Higashioka RC 2.50 6.00
US16 Rafael Bautista RC .40 1.00
US17 Chris Archer AS .12 .30
US18A Mookie Betts AS .40 1.00
US18B Mookie Betts SP 2.00 5.00
US18C Ted Williams SP 1.50 4.00
US19 Eric Skoglund RC .40 1.00
US20 Jason Vargas AS .12 .30
US21 Christian Arroyo RD .20 .50
US22A Hunter Renfroe RD .15 .40
US22B Hunter Renfroe SP .75 2.00
blue jersey
US23 Derek Holland .12 .30
US24 Joe Smith .12 .30
US25A Christian Arroyo RC .60 1.50
US25B Christian Arroyo SP 1.00 2.50
US25C Christian Arroyo SP
US26 Steve Pearce .20 .50
US27A Nolan Arenado AS .30 .75
US27B Nolan Arenado SP 1.50 4.00
US28 Drew Robinson RC .60 1.50
US29 Drew Steckenrider RC .40 1.00
US30 Danny Ortiz RC .40 1.00
US31 Danny Santana .12 .30
US32 Luis Torrens RC .40 1.00
US33A Salvador Perez AS .15 .40
US33B Bo Jackson SP .75 2.00
US33C Salvador Perez SP .75 2.00
US34 Nelson Cruz AS .20 .50
US35 Dinelson Lamet RC .40 1.00
US36 Adam Lind .15 .40
US37 Ian Happ RD .25 .60
US38A Cody Bellinger AS 2.00 5.00
US38B Cody Bellinger SP 5.00 12.00
US39 Charlie Morton .20 .50
US40 Pat Neshek .12 .30
US41A Mitch Haniger RD .20 .50
US41B Mitch Haniger SP
Mariners
US42A Seth Smith .12 .30
US42B Eddie Murray SP .60 1.50
US43A Joey Votto AS .20 .50
US43B Johnny Bench SP .75 2.00
US43C Joey Votto SP 1.00 2.50
US44 Chicago Cubs World Series Celebration .20
.50
US45 Johan Camargo RC .40 1.00
US46 Dylan Covey RC .40 1.00
US47A Yadier Molina AS .25 .60
US47B Yadier Molina SP 1.25 3.00
US47C Ozzie Smith SP 1.00 2.50
US48 Ariel Hernandez RC .40 1.00
US49 Austin Bibens-Dirkx RC .40 1.00
US50A Cody Bellinger RC 20.00 50.00
US50B Cody Bellinger SP 6.00 15.00
US50C Cody Bellinger SP
gray jersey
US50D Jackie Robinson SP .75 2.00
US51 Jorge Bonifacio RC .40 1.00
US52 Michael Fulmer AS .12 .30
US53 Barrett Astin RC .40 1.00
US54 Ronald Torreyes .12 .30
US55 Luis Severino AS .15 .40
US56 Jake Junis RC .60 1.50
US57 Charged-Up Battery .12 .30
Roberto Osuna/Russell Martin
US58 Ervin Santana .12 .30
US59 Matt Joyce .12 .30
US60 Kyle Freeland RC .50 1.25
US61 Matt Szczur .15 .40
US62 Travis Wood .12 .30
US63 Andrew Cashner .12 .30
US64 Corey Kluber AS .15 .40
US65 Giancarlo Stanton HRD .20 .50
US66 Jose Osuna RC .40 1.00
US67 Avisail Garcia AS .15 .40
US68 Jered Weaver .15 .40
US69 Alex Avila .15 .40
US70 Josh Reddick .12 .30
US71 Junichi Tazawa .12 .30
US72 Joaquin Benoit .12 .30
US73 Jason Grilli .12 .30
US74 Ryne Stanek RC .40 1.00
US75 Jake Buchanan RC .40 1.00
US76 Miguel Montero .12 .30
US77A Mike Moustakas AS .15 .40
US77B George Brett SP 1.50 4.00
US78 Jarlin Garcia RC .40 1.00
US79 Nick Goody .12 .30
US80 Ichiro .25 .60
US81 Clay Buchholz .12 .30
US82 Matt Boyd .12 .30
US83 Carlos Ruiz .12 .30
US84 Michael Brantley AS .15 .40

US85 Tommy Milone .12 .30
US86 Clayton Richard .12 .30
US87A Chris Sale AS .20 .50
US87B Roger Clemens SP 1.00 2.50
US87C Chris Sale SP 1.00 2.50
US88 Jorge Soler .20 .50
US89 Casey Lawrence RC .40 1.00
US90A Derek Fisher RC .50 1.25
US90B Derek Fisher SP .75 2.00
US90C Derek Fisher SP
US91A Jordan Montgomery RC .60 1.50
US91B Jordan Montgomery SP 1.00 2.50
US91C Jordan Montgomery SP
US92 Anthony Alford RC .40 1.00
US93 Jesse Chavez .12 .30
US94 Justin Upton AS .15 .40
US95 Stephen Strasburg AS .20 .50
US96A Brett Phillips RC .50 1.25
US96B Brett Phillips SP .75 2.00
US97 Alexi Amarista .12 .30
US98 Andrew Moore RC .50 1.25
US99A Aaron Judge RD 1.50 4.00
US99B Reggie Jackson SP .60 1.50
US99C Aaron Judge SP 75.00 200.00
US100 Chris Sale .20 .50
US101 Magneuris Sierra RC .40 1.00
US102 Dovydas Neverauskas RC .40 1.00
Gift Ngoepe RC
US103 Matt Adams .12 .30
US104 Sam Gaviglio RC .40 1.00
US105 John Brebbia RC .50 1.25
US106 Kendrys Morales .12 .30
US107 Andrew Bailey .12 .30
US108 Wilson Ramos .12 .30
US109 Ben Revere .12 .30
US110A Corey Seager AS .20 .50
US110B Corey Seager SP 1.00 2.50
US111 Meat of the Mets .15 .40
Wilmer Flores/Michael Conforto
US112A Ryan Zimmerman AS .15 .40
US112B Ryan Zimmerman SP .75 2.00
US113 Franklin Barreto RD .12 .30
US114 Pat Neshek AS .12 .30
US115 M Is For Mashing .40 1.00
Manny Machado/Mookie Betts
US116 Tyler Glasnow RD .50 1.25
US117 Neftali Feliz .12 .30
US118 Bradley Zimmer RD .15 .40
US119 Greg Holland .12 .30
US120 Carlos Beltran .15 .40
US121A Daniel Murphy AS .15 .40
US121B Daniel Murphy SP .75 2.00
US122 Coming to America .20 .50
Yu Darvish/Nori Aoki
US123 Colby Rasmus .15 .40
US124 Nick Hundley .12 .30
US125 Yoan Moncada RD .40 1.00
US126 Austin Slater RC .40 1.00
US127 Antonio Senzatela RC .40 1.00
US128 Ervin Santana AS .12 .30
US129 Brooks Pounders .12 .30
US130 Zack Greinke AS .20 .50
US131 Doug Fister .12 .30
US132 Dallas Keuchel AS .15 .40
US133 Keynan Middleton RC .60 1.50
US134 Justin Bour HRD .15 .40
US135 Chase De Jong RC .50 1.25
US136A Josh Harrison AS .12 .30
US136B Roberto Clemente SP 2.00 5.00
US137 Daniel Hudson .12 .30
US138 Logan Verrett .12 .30
US139 Luis Castillo RC 1.25 3.00
US140 Sal Romano RC .40 1.00
US141A Bryce Harper AS .30 .75
US141B Bryce Harper SP 1.50 4.00
US142 Tzu-Wei Lin RC .40 1.00
US143 Trevor Cahill .12 .30
US144 Charlie Blackmon AS .20 .50
US145 Dillon Overton RC .40 1.00
US146 David Dahl RD .15 .40
US147 Jose Alvarado RC .40 1.00
Austin Pruitt RC
US148 The Next Dynasty 1.50 4.00
Aaron Judge/Greg Bird
US149 James Pazos .12 .30
US150A Alex Bregman RD .60 1.50
US150B Alex Bregman SP
US151 Yandy Diaz RC .75 2.00
US152A Robinson Cano AS .15 .40
US152B Robinson Cano SP .75 2.00
US152C Ken Griffey Jr. SP 1.50 4.00
US153 Robbie Ray AS .12 .30
US154 Franklin Gutierrez .12 .30
US155 Run and Hit .20 .50
Joey Votto/Billy Hamilton
US156A Yu Darvish AS .20 .50
US156B Yu Darvish SP 1.00 2.50
US156C Yu Darvish SP 1.00 2.50
US156D Nolan Ryan SP 2.50 6.00
US157 Corey Dickerson AS .12 .30
US158 Phillip Ervin RC .40 1.00
US159 JT Riddle RC .40 1.00
US160 Ben Lively RC .40 1.00
Andrew Knapp RC
US161 Justin Haley RC .40 1.00
US162A Sean Newcomb RC .50 1.25
US162B Greg Maddux SP 1.00 2.50
US162C Sean Newcomb SP .75 2.00
in dugout
US162D Sean Newcomb SP
US163 Edinson Volquez .12 .30
US164 Carlos Martinez AS .15 .40
US165 Boone Logan .12 .30
US166A Aaron Judge AS 1.50 4.00
US166B Aaron Judge SP 8.00 20.00
US166C Babe Ruth SP 2.00 5.00
US167 Drew Smyly .12 .30
US168A Michael Conforto AS .15 .40
US168B Michael Conforto .15 .40
pinstripe jersey
US168C Mike Piazza SP .75 2.00
US169 A.J. Ellis .12 .30
US170 Cameron Maybin .12 .30
US171 Brock Stassi RC .50 1.25
US172 Jason Hammel .15 .40
US173 Chris Coghlan .12 .30
US174 Brandon Moss .12 .30
US175A Jose Altuve AS .15 .40
US175B Jose Altuve .15 .40
blue jersey
US176 History Makers .25 .60
Kris Bryant/Anthony Rizzo
US177 Jake Lamb AS .15 .40
US178 Stuart Turner RC .40 1.00
US179 Pierce Johnson RC .40 1.00
US180 Mike Moustakas HRD .15 .40
US181 Emilio Pagan RC .40 1.00
US182A Jaime Garcia .12 .30
US182B John Smoltz SP .75 2.00
US183 Taylor Motter .12 .30
US184 Jean Segura .15 .40
US185 Birds in the Garden
Stephen Piscotty .15 .40
Jason Heyward/Randal Grichuk
US186 Jose De Leon RC .40 1.00
US187 Jaycob Brugman RC .40 1.00
US188 Trevor Plouffe .12 .30
US189 Chad Bell RC .60 1.50
US190 Brad Goldberg RC .40 1.00
US191 Corey Knebel AS .12 .30
US192 Jacob May RC .40 1.00
US193 Orlando Arcia RD .20 .50
US194 Derek Fisher RD .15 .40
US195 Fernando Rodney .12 .30
US196 Brad Hand AS .12 .30
US197 Dellin Betances AS .15 .40
US198 Chih-Wei Hu RC .40 1.00
US199 Brett Cecil .12 .30
US200A Yoan Moncada RC 1.25 3.00
US200B Yoan Moncada SP 2.00 5.00
US200C Yoan Moncada SP
white wrist tape
US201 Nolan Fontana RC .40 1.00
US202 Kenley Jansen AS .15 .40
US203 Joe Blanton .12 .30
US204 Chris Heston .12 .30
US205A Zack Cozart AS .12 .30
US205B Barry Larkin SP .60 1.50
US206 Partners in Pop .15 .40
Eric Thames/Ryan Braun
US207 Kurt Suzuki .12 .30
US208 Randy Rosario RC .40 1.00
US209 Josh Hader RC .50 1.25
US210 Sammy Solis .12 .30
US211 Rookie Davis RC .40 1.00
US212 Jose Quintana .12 .30
US213 Yovani Gallardo .12 .30
US214 Cody Bellinger RD 2.00 5.00
US215 Joe Jimenez RC .50 1.25
US216 J.P. Howell .12 .30
US217 Howie Kendrick .12 .30
US218 Greg Holland AS .12 .30
US219 Paul DeJong RC 1.25 3.00
US220 Jeff Locke .12 .30
US221 Mark Zagunis RC .40 1.00
US222 Jose Ramirez AS .15 .40
US223A Clayton Kershaw AS .30 .75
US223B Clayton Kershaw SP 1.50 4.00
US223C Sandy Koufax SP 1.50 4.00
US224 Wade Davis AS .12 .30
US225A Andrew Benintendi RD .40 1.00
US225B Andrew Benintendi SP 2.00 5.00
US225C Andrew Benintendi SP
US226A Lewis Brinson RC .60 1.50
US226B Lewis Brinson SP 1.00 2.50
US226C Lewis Brinson SP
US227A Trey Mancini RD .25 .60
US227B Trey Mancini SP 1.25 3.00
US227C Cal Ripken Jr. SP 2.50 6.00
US228 Wade Davis .12 .30
US229 Tyson Ross .12 .30
US230 DJ LeMahieu AS .20 .50
US231 Reynaldo Lopez RC .40 1.00
US232A Marcell Ozuna AS .20 .50
US232B Marcell Ozuna SP 1.00 2.50
US233 Taijuan Walker .12 .30
US234A Francisco Lindor AS .20 .50
US234B Francisco Lindor SP 1.00 2.50
US235 Nick Pivetta RC .50 1.25
Ricardo Pinto RC
US236A Starlin Castro AS .12 .30
US236B Derek Jeter SP 2.00 5.00
US237A Buster Posey AS .25 .60
US237B Buster Posey SP 1.25 3.00
US238 Chris Bostick RC .50 1.25
US239 Neil Ramirez .12 .30
US240A Jacob Faria RC .40 1.00
US240B Jacob Faria SP .60 1.50
US241 Ryon Healy RD .15 .40
US242 Mike Hauschild RC .40 1.00
US243 Hector Velazquez RC .75 2.00
US244 Justin Turner AS .20 .50
US245A Yonder Alonso AS .12 .30
US245B Mark McGwire SP 1.25 3.00
US246 Marc Rzepczynski .12 .30
US247A Dansby Swanson RD .30 .75
US247B Hank Aaron SP 1.50 4.00
US247C Dansby Swanson SP
US248A Ender Inciarte AS .12 .30
US248B Chipper Jones SP .75 2.00
US249 Alex Reyes RD .15 .40
US250 Daniel Robertson RC .40 1.00
US251 Daniel Descalso .12 .30
US252 Mike Dunn .12 .30
US253 Matt Belisle .12 .30
US254 Amir Garrett RD .12 .30
US255 Stefan Crichton RC .40 1.00
US256 Mike Ohlman RC .40 1.00
US257 Alex Wood AS .12 .30
US258 Francis Martes RC .40 1.00
US259A Tyler Austin RD .15 .40
US259B Lou Gehrig SP 1.50 4.00
US260A Carlos Correa AS .20 .50
US260B Carlos Correa SP 1.00 2.50
US261A Max Scherzer AS .20 .50
US261B Max Scherzer SP 1.00 2.50
US262 Fernando Salas .12 .30
US263 Brian Duensing .12 .30
US264 Boog Powell RC .40 1.00
US265 Eric Young Jr. .12 .30
US266 Jett Bandy .12 .30
US267 Jhoulys Chacin .12 .30
US268 Miguel Sano HRD .15 .40
US269A Craig Kimbrel AS .15 .40
US269B Craig Kimbrel SP .75 2.00
US269C Pedro Martinez SP .60 1.50
US270A Gary Sanchez AS .20 .50
US270B Don Mattingly SP 1.50 4.00
US270C Gary Sanchez SP 1.00 2.50
US271A Jesse Winker RC 1.50 4.00
US271B Jesse Winker SP 2.50 6.00
US272 Justin Smoak AS .12 .30
US273 Dwight Smith RC .40 1.00
US274 Mitch Moreland .12 .30
US275A Bradley Zimmer .15 .40
US275B Bradley Zimmer SP .75 2.00
US275C Bradley Zimmer SP
US276 Allen Cordoba RC .40 1.00
Franchy Cordero RC
US277A Paul Goldschmidt AS .20 .50
US277B Paul Goldschmidt SP 1.00 2.50
US278 Rajai Davis .12 .30
US279A Franklin Barreto RC .40 1.00
US279B Franklin Barreto SP .60 1.50
US279C Franklin Barreto SP
on dugout steps
US279D Rickey Henderson SP .75 2.00
US280 Brett Anderson .12 .30
US281 Luke Voit RC 6.00 15.00
US282 Michael Martinez .12 .30
US283 Adam Eaton .20 .50
US284 Peter Bourjos .12 .30
US285 Scott Feldman .12 .30
US286 Jeff Hoffman RD .12 .30
US287 Mark Leiter Jr. RC .60 1.50
US288A Miguel Sano AS .15 .40
US288B Miguel Sano SP .75 2.00
US289 Sam Travis RC .50 1.25
US290 Anthony Rendon .20 .50
US291 Andrew Miller AS .15 .40
US292A Jonathan Schoop AS .12 .30
US292B Brooks Robinson SP .60 1.50
US293 Tuffy Gosewisch .12 .30
US294 Bobby Wahl RC .40 1.00
US295 Ben Taylor RC .50 1.25
US296A Giancarlo Stanton AS .20 .50
US296B Giancarlo Stanton SP 1.00 2.50
US297 Reymin Guduan RC .40 1.00
Jordan Jankowski RC
US298 Brett Eibner .12 .30
US299 Charlie Blackmon HRD .20 .50
US300 Cody Bellinger HRD 2.00 5.00

2017 Topps Update Black

*BLACK: 10X TO 25X BASIC
*BLACK RC: 3X TO 8X BASIC RC
STATED PRINT RUN 66 SER.#'d SETS
US50 Cody Bellinger 150.00 400.00
US148 The Next Dynasty 12.00 30.00
Aaron Judge/Greg Bird

2017 Topps Update Black and White Negative

*BW NEGATIVE: 5X TO 12X BASIC
*BW NEGATIVE RC: 1.5X TO 4X BASIC
US50 Cody Bellinger 75.00 200.00
US148 The Next Dynasty 10.00 25.00
Aaron Judge/Greg Bird

2017 Topps Update Father's Day Blue

*BLUE: 10X TO 25X BASIC
*BLUE RC: 3X TO 8X BASIC RC
STATED PRINT RUN 50 SER.#'d SETS
US50 Cody Bellinger 150.00 400.00
US148 The Next Dynasty 15.00 40.00
Aaron Judge/Greg Bird

2017 Topps Update Gold

*GOLD: 2.5X TO 6X BASIC
*GOLD RC: .75X TO 2X BASIC RC
STATED PRINT RUN 2017 SER.#'d SETS
US50 Cody Bellinger 40.00 100.00
US148 The Next Dynasty 4.00 10.00
Aaron Judge/Greg Bird

2017 Topps Update Memorial Day Camo

*CAMO: 12X TO 30X BASIC
*CAMO RC: 4X TO 10X BASIC RC
STATED PRINT RUN 25 SER.#'d SETS
US50 Cody Bellinger 200.00 500.00
US148 The Next Dynasty 20.00 50.00
Aaron Judge/Greg Bird

2017 Topps Update Mother's Day Pink

*PINK: 10X TO 25X BASIC
*PINK RC: 3X TO 8X BASIC RC
STATED PRINT RUN 50 SER.#'d SETS
US50 Cody Bellinger 150.00 400.00
US148 The Next Dynasty 15.00 40.00
Aaron Judge/Greg Bird

2017 Topps Update Rainbow Foil

*FOIL: 2X TO 5X BASIC
*FOIL RC: .6X TO 1.5X BASIC RC
US50 Cody Bellinger 30.00 80.00
US148 The Next Dynasty 3.00 8.00
Aaron Judge/Greg Bird

2017 Topps Update Salute

COMPLETE SET (50) 30.00 80.00
*RED/25: 5X TO 12X BASIC
USS1 Mike Trout 2.50 6.00
USS2 Jose Altuve .40 1.00
USS3 Nelson Cruz .50 1.25
USS4 Francisco Lindor .50 1.25
USS5 Koda Glover .30 .75
USS6 Manny Machado .50 1.25
USS7 Ichiro .60 1.50
USS8 Jesse Winker 1.25 3.00
USS9 Ian Happ .60 1.50
USS10 Clayton Kershaw .75 2.00
USS11 Mitch Haniger .50 1.25
USS12 Mitch Haniger .50 1.25
USS13 Tim Anderson .50 1.25
USS14 Franklin Barreto .30 .75
USS15 Jeff Hoffman .30 .75
USS16 Alex Bregman 1.50 4.00
USS17 George Springer .40 1.00
USS18 Antonio Senzatela .30 .75
USS19 Lewis Brinson .50 1.25
USS20 Chris Sale .50 1.25
USS21 Sean Newcomb .40 1.00
USS22 Manny Margot .30 .75
USS23 Bradley Zimmer .40 1.00
USS24 Javier Baez .60 1.50
USS25 Masahiro Tanaka .40 1.00
USS26 Gerrit Cole .50 1.25
USS27 Kendrys Morales .30 .75
USS28 Max Scherzer .50 1.25
USS29 Andrew Benintendi 1.00 2.50
USS30 Bryce Harper .75 2.00
USS31 Dansby Swanson .75 2.00
USS32 Josh Reddick .30 .75
USS33 Keon Broxton .30 .75
USS34 Amir Garrett .30 .75
USS35 Jordan Montgomery .50 1.25
USS36 Marcell Ozuna .50 1.25
USS37 Starling Marte .40 1.00
USS38 Michael Pineda .30 .75
USS39 Nomar Mazara .30 .75
USS40 Daniel Murphy .40 1.00
USS41 Christian Arroyo .50 1.25
USS42 Billy Hamilton .40 1.00
USS43 Cody Bellinger 5.00 12.00
USS44 Randal Grichuk .30 .75
USS45 Ryan Braun .40 1.00
USS46 Jose Bautista .40 1.00
USS47 Andrew McCutchen .50 1.25
USS48 Mark Trumbo .30 .75
USS49 Kyle Freeland .40 1.00
USS50 Anthony Rizzo .60 1.50

2017 Topps Update Toys R Us Purple

*PURPLE: 5X TO 12X BASIC
*PURPLE RC: 1.5X TO 4X BASIC
US38 Cody Bellinger 12.00 30.00
US50 Cody Bellinger 75.00 200.00
US148 The Next Dynasty 10.00 25.00
Aaron Judge/Greg Bird
US214 Cody Bellinger 12.00 30.00
US300 Cody Bellinger 12.00 30.00

2017 Topps Update Vintage Stock

*VINTAGE: 6X TO 15X BASIC
*VINTAGE RC: 2X TO 5X BASIC RC
STATED PRINT RUN 99 SER.#'d SETS
US38 Cody Bellinger 20.00 50.00
US50 Cody Bellinger 100.00 250.00
US148 The Next Dynasty 12.00 30.00
Aaron Judge/Greg Bird
US214 Cody Bellinger 20.00 50.00
US300 Cody Bellinger 20.00 50.00

2017 Topps Update '87 Topps

COMPLETE SET (50) 30.00 80.00
*RED/25: 5X TO 12X BASIC
US871 Bryce Harper .75 2.00
US872 Amir Garrett .30 .75
US873 Noah Syndergaard .40 1.00
US874 Manny Machado .50 1.25
US875 Adam Eaton .50 1.25
US876 Starlin Castro .30 .75
US877 Dexter Fowler .40 1.00
US878 Dallas Keuchel .40 1.00
US879 Brandon Phillips .30 .75
US8710 Mike Trout 2.50 6.00
US8711 Edwin Diaz .40 1.00
US8712 Dee Gordon .30 .75
US8713 Mitch Haniger .50 1.25
US8714 Koda Glover .30 .75
US8715 Jean Segura .40 1.00
US8716 Jeff Hoffman .30 .75
US8717 Antonio Senzatela .30 .75
US8718 Magneuris Sierra .30 .75
US8719 Matt Holliday .50 1.25
US8720 Kris Bryant .60 1.50
US8721 Matt Wieters .50 1.25
US8722 Dylan Bundy .40 1.00
US8723 Billy Hamilton .40 1.00
US8724 Orlando Arcia .50 1.25
US8725 Andrew Benintendi 1.00 2.50
US8726 Jake Lamb .40 1.00
US8727 Jesse Winker 1.25 3.00
US8728 Marcell Ozuna .50 1.25
US8729 Chris Sale .50 1.25
US8730 Christian Arroyo .50 1.25
US8731 Edwin Encarnacion .50 1.25
US8732 Yonder Alonso .30 .75
US8733 Jose Ramirez .40 1.00
US8734 Cody Bellinger 5.00 12.00
US8735 Aaron Judge 5.00 12.00
US8736 Eric Thames .40 1.00
US8737 Christian Yelich .60 1.50
US8738 Lucas Giolito .40 1.00
US8739 Corey Seager .50 1.25
US8740 Ian Desmond .30 .75
US8741 Aroldis Chapman .50 1.25
US8742 Jordan Montgomery .50 1.25
US8743 Khris Davis .50 1.25
US8744 Joey Gallo .40 1.00
US8745 Franklin Barreto .30 .75
US8746 Bradley Zimmer .40 1.00
US8747 Lewis Brinson .50 1.25
US8748 Ian Happ .60 1.50
US8749 Sean Newcomb .40 1.00
US8750 Adalberto Mejia .30 .75

2017 Topps Update '87 Topps Autographs

EXCHANGE DEADLINE 9/30/2019
87AAA Anthony Alford 3.00 8.00
87AABE Andrew Benintendi 40.00 100.00
87AABR Alex Bregman 15.00 40.00
87AAG Amir Garrett 3.00 8.00
87AAJ Aaron Judge
87AAS Antonio Senzatela 3.00 8.00
87ABH Bryce Harper
87ABPH Brett Phillips 4.00 10.00
87ABZ Bradley Zimmer 5.00 12.00
87ACA Christian Arroyo 5.00 12.00
87ACB Cody Bellinger 40.00 100.00
87ACE Carl Edwards Jr. 3.00 8.00
87ACSA Chris Sale 30.00 80.00
87ACSE Corey Seager
87ADL Dinelson Lamet 3.00 8.00
87AEE Edwin Encarnacion 75.00 200.00
87AERS Eddie Rosario 4.00 10.00
87AET Eric Thames 12.00 30.00
87AFB Franklin Barreto 3.00 8.00
87AIH Ian Happ 6.00 15.00
87AJBN Jorge Bonifacio 3.00 8.00
87AJJ Joe Jimenez 4.00 10.00
87AJM Jordan Montgomery 8.00 20.00
87AJW Jesse Winker 5.00 12.00
87AKB Kris Bryant
87AKD Khris Davis 5.00 12.00
87AKGL Koda Glover 3.00 8.00
87ALB Lewis Brinson 5.00 12.00
87AMS Magneuris Sierra 15.00 40.00
87AMT Mike Trout 500.00 700.00
87ANS Noah Syndergaard
87APD Paul DeJong 10.00 25.00
87APV Pat Valaika 4.00 10.00
87ARSE Rob Segedin 3.00 8.00
87ASN Sean Newcomb 4.00 10.00
87AST Sam Travis 4.00 10.00
87AYM Yoan Moncada

2017 Topps Update All Rookie Cup

COMPLETE SET (50) 20.00 50.00
ARC1 Chipper Jones .60 1.50
ARC2 Stephen Strasburg .60 1.50
ARC3 Eddie Murray .40 1.00
ARC4 Andre Dawson .50 1.25
ARC5 Mike Trout 3.00 8.00
ARC6 Ichiro .75 2.00
ARC7 Ryan Braun .50 1.25
ARC8 Derek Jeter 1.50 4.00
ARC9 Willie McCovey .50 1.25
ARC10 Joe Mauer .50 1.25
ARC11 Jeff Bagwell .50 1.25
ARC12 Evan Longoria .50 1.25
ARC13 Cal Ripken Jr. 2.00 5.00
ARC14 Cal Ripken Jr. 2.00 5.00
ARC15 Ivan Rodriguez .50 1.25
ARC16 Ryne Sandberg 1.25 3.00
ARC17 Johnny Bench .60 1.50
ARC18 Tom Seaver .50 1.25
ARC19 Andrew McCutchen .60 1.50
ARC20 Yasiel Puig .60 1.50
ARC21 Anthony Rizzo .75 2.00
ARC22 Ken Griffey Jr. 1.25 3.00
ARC23 Buster Posey .75 2.00
ARC24 Tony Perez .50 1.25
ARC25 Carlton Fisk .50 1.25
ARC26 Fernando Valenzuela .40 1.00
ARC27 Mike Piazza .60 1.50
ARC28 Dustin Pedroia .60 1.50
ARC29 Tim Raines .50 1.25
ARC30 Noah Syndergaard .50 1.25
ARC31 Billy Williams .50 1.25
ARC32 Joey Votto .60 1.50
ARC33 Justin Verlander .60 1.50
ARC34 George Springer .50 1.25
ARC35 Jose Canseco .50 1.25
ARC36 Nomar Garciaparra .50 1.25
ARC37 Gary Carter .50 1.25
ARC38 Kris Bryant .75 2.00
ARC39 Nolan Arenado 1.00 2.50
ARC40 Masahiro Tanaka .50 1.25
ARC41 Mark McGwire 1.00 2.50
ARC42 Giancarlo Stanton .60 1.50
ARC43 Ozzie Smith .75 2.00
ARC44 Prince Fielder .50 1.25
ARC45 Bryce Harper 1.00 2.50
ARC46 Yu Darvish .60 1.50
ARC47 Joe Morgan .50 1.25
ARC48 Rod Carew .50 1.25
ARC49 Albert Pujols .75 2.00
ARC50 Carlos Correa .60 1.50

2017 Topps Update All Star Stitches

*GOLD/50: .6X TO 1.5X BASIC
*ORANGE/25: .75X TO 2X BASIC
ASRAG Avisail Garcia 3.00 8.00
ASRAJ Aaron Judge 25.00 60.00
ASRAM Andrew Miller 3.00 8.00
ASRAW Alex Wood 2.50 6.00
ASRBH Bryce Harper 5.00 12.00
ASRBHA Brad Hand 2.50 6.00
ASRBK Brandon Kintzler 2.50 6.00
ASRBP Buster Posey 5.00 12.00
ASRCA Chris Archer 2.50 6.00
ASRCB Cody Bellinger 10.00 25.00
ASRCBL Charlie Blackmon 4.00 10.00
ASRCC Carlos Correa 4.00 10.00
ASRCD Corey Dickerson 2.50 6.00
ASRCK Clayton Kershaw 6.00 15.00
ASRCKI Craig Kimbrel 3.00 8.00
ASRCKL Corey Kluber 3.00 8.00
ASRCKN Corey Knebel 2.50 6.00
ASRCM Carlos Martinez 3.00 8.00
ASRCS Corey Seager 4.00 10.00
ASRCSA Chris Sale 4.00 10.00
ASRDB Dellin Betances 3.00 8.00
ASRDK Dallas Keuchel 3.00 8.00
ASRDL DJ LeMahieu 4.00 10.00
ASRDM Daniel Murphy 3.00 8.00
ASREI Ender Inciarte 3.00 8.00
ASRES Ervin Santana 2.50 6.00
ASRFL Francisco Lindor 4.00 10.00
ASRGH Greg Holland 2.50 6.00
ASRGS Giancarlo Stanton 4.00 10.00
ASRGSA Gary Sanchez 6.00 15.00
ASRGSP George Springer 5.00 12.00
ASRJA Jose Altuve 3.00 8.00
ASRJH Josh Harrison 2.50 6.00
ASRJL Jake Lamb 3.00 8.00
ASRJR Jose Ramirez 3.00 8.00
ASRJS Jonathan Schoop 2.50 6.00
ASRJSM Justin Smoak 2.50 6.00
ASRJT Justin Turner 5.00 12.00
ASRJU Justin Upton 3.00 8.00
ASRJV Jason Vargas 3.00 8.00
ASRJVO Joey Votto 4.00 10.00
ASRKJ Kenley Jansen 3.00 8.00
ASRLM Lance McCullers 2.50 6.00
ASRLS Luis Severino 3.00 8.00
ASRMB Mookie Betts 8.00 20.00
ASRMBR Michael Brantley 3.00 8.00
ASRMC Michael Conforto 3.00 8.00
ASRMF Michael Fulmer 2.50 6.00
ASRMM Mike Moustakas 3.00 8.00
ASRMO Marcell Ozuna 4.00 10.00
ASRMS Max Scherzer 4.00 10.00
ASRMSA Miguel Sano 4.00 10.00
ASRNA Nolan Arenado 6.00 15.00
ASRNC Nelson Cruz 4.00 10.00
ASRPG Paul Goldschmidt 4.00 10.00
ASRRC Robinson Cano 3.00 8.00
ASRRO Roberto Osuna 2.50 6.00
ASRRR Robbie Ray 2.50 6.00
ASRRZ Ryan Zimmerman 3.00 8.00
ASRSC Starlin Castro 2.50 6.00
ASRSP Salvador Perez 3.00 8.00
ASRSS Stephen Strasburg 4.00 10.00
ASRWD Wade Davis 2.50 6.00
ASRYA Yonder Alonso 2.50 6.00
ASRYD Yu Darvish 4.00 10.00
ASRYM Yadier Molina 5.00 12.00
ASRZC Zack Cozart 2.50 6.00
ASRZG Zack Greinke 4.00 10.00

2017 Topps Update All Star Stitches Autographs

STATED PRINT RUN 25 SER.#'d SETS
EXCHANGE DEADLINE 9/30/2019
ASARAJ Aaron Judge
ASARBH Bryce Harper
ASARBP Buster Posey EXCH 30.00 80.00
ASARCB Cody Bellinger EXCH 125.00 300.00
ASARCBL Charlie Blackmon 25.00 60.00
ASARCC Carlos Correa
ASARCK Clayton Kershaw
ASARCS Corey Seager EXCH 60.00 150.00
ASARCSA Chris Sale
ASARFL Francisco Lindor EXCH 40.00 100.00
ASARGS George Springer 20.00 50.00
ASARJA Jose Altuve 20.00 50.00
ASARJV Joey Votto
ASARMC Michael Conforto
ASARMS Miguel Sano 30.00 80.00

2017 Topps Update All Star Stitches Duals

STATED PRINT RUN 25 SER.#'d SETS
ASDAC Altuve/Correa
ASDBS Bellinger/Seager 30.00 80.00
ASDCS Springer/Correa 20.00 50.00
ASDJB Bellinger/Judge 60.00 150.00
ASDJS Sanchez Judge 80.00 200.00
ASDMC Betts/Sale 20.00 50.00
ASDOS Stanton/Ozuna 10.00 25.00
ASDSS Strasburg/Scherzer

2017 Topps Update All Star Stitches Triples

STATED PRINT RUN 25 SER.#'d SETS
ASTACS Springer/Altuve/Correa 25.00 60.00
ASTCMC Betts/Sale/Kimbrel 25.00 60.00
ASTGGL Goldschmidt Greinke Lamb 12.00 30.00
ASTKBS Bellinger/Kershaw/Seager 40.00 100.00
ASTKLR Ramirez/Kluber/Lindor 25.00 60.00
ASTPHB Posey/Bellinger/Harper 25.00 60.00
ASTSHS Harper/Strasburg/Scherzer 40.00 100.00
ASTSJS Sanchez/Judge/Severino 60.00 150.00
ASTSKS Sale/Scherzer/Kershaw 20.00 50.00
ASTZHM Zimmerman/Murphy/Harper

2017 Topps Update Hank Aaron Award Relics

*GOLD/99: .75X TO 2X BASIC
*BLACK/50: 1X TO 2.5X BASIC
HAAP Albert Pujols 2.00 5.00
HAAR Alex Rodriguez 2.00 5.00
HABH Bryce Harper 2.50 6.00
HABP Buster Posey 2.00 5.00
HADJE Derek Jeter 4.00 10.00
HADJT Derek Jeter 4.00 10.00
HADO David Ortiz 1.50 4.00
HAGS Giancarlo Stanton 1.50 4.00
HAJB Jose Bautista 1.25 3.00
HAJD Josh Donaldson 1.25 3.00
HAJV Joey Votto 1.50 4.00
HAKB Kris Bryant 2.00 5.00
HAMC Miguel Cabrera 1.50 4.00
HAMT Mike Trout 8.00 20.00
HAPG Paul Goldschmidt 1.50 4.00

2017 Topps Update Heroes of Autumn

COMPLETE SET (25) 60.00 150.00
*BLUE/500: .6X TO 1.5X BASIC
*RED/250: .75X TO 2X BASIC
*SILVER/50: 1X TO 2.5X BASIC
PLATE PRINT RUN 1 SET PER COLOR
BLACK-CYAN-MAGENTA-YELLOW ISSUED
NO PLATE PRICING DUE TO SCARCITY
HA1 Randy Johnson 1.25 3.00
HA2 Frank Robinson 1.00 2.50
HA3 Anthony Rizzo 1.50 4.00
HA4 Roberto Alomar 1.00 2.50
HA5 Albert Pujols 1.50 4.00
HA6 Luis Gonzalez .75 2.00
HA7 George Brett 2.50 6.00
HA8 Sandy Koufax 2.50 6.00
HA9 Andy Pettitte 1.00 2.50
HA10 Reggie Jackson 1.00 2.50
HA11 Babe Ruth 3.00 8.00
HA12 Ben Zobrist 1.00 2.50
HA13 Brooks Robinson 1.00 2.50
HA14 Willie Stargell 1.00 2.50
HA15 Dennis Eckersley 1.00 2.50
HA16 Pedro Martinez 1.00 2.50
HA17 Tom Glavine 1.00 2.50
HA18 Buster Posey 1.50 4.00
HA19 Johnny Bench 1.25 3.00
HA20 Rickey Henderson 1.25 3.00
HA21 Derek Jeter 3.00 8.00
HA22 Roger Clemens 1.50 4.00
HA23 John Smoltz 1.25 3.00
HA24 David Ortiz 1.25 3.00
HA25 Jackie Robinson 1.25 3.00

2017 Topps Update MVP Award

COMPLETE SET (30) 15.00 40.00
*RED/25: 5X TO 12X BASIC
MVP1 Mike Trout 2.50 6.00
MVP2 Roger Clemens .60 1.50
MVP3 Rickey Henderson .50 1.25
MVP4 Clayton Kershaw .75 2.00
MVP5 Frank Thomas .50 1.25
MVP6 Sandy Koufax 1.00 2.50
MVP7 Chipper Jones .50 1.25
MVP8 Ichiro .60 1.50
MVP9 Roger Maris .50 1.25
MVP10 Kris Bryant .60 1.50
MVP11 Ken Griffey Jr. 1.00 2.50
MVP12 Jackie Robinson .50 1.25
MVP13 Reggie Jackson .40 1.00
MVP14 Joey Votto .50 1.25
MVP15 Cal Ripken Jr. 1.50 4.00
MVP16 Brooks Robinson .40 1.00
MVP17 Babe Ruth 1.25 3.00
MVP18 Bryce Harper .75 2.00
MVP19 Roberto Clemente 1.25 3.00
MVP20 Carl Yastrzemski .75 2.00
MVP21 George Brett 1.00 2.50
MVP22 Josh Donaldson .40 1.00
MVP23 Don Mattingly 1.00 2.50
MVP24 Buster Posey .60 1.50
MVP25 Ty Cobb .75 2.00
MVP26 Ernie Banks .50 1.25
MVP27 Lou Gehrig 1.00 2.50
MVP28 Ted Williams 1.00 2.50
MVP29 Johnny Bench .50 1.25
MVP30 Hank Aaron 1.00 2.50

2017 Topps Update MVP Award Relics

*GOLD/99: ..6X TO 1.5X BASIC
*BLACK/50: .75X TO 2X BASIC
MVPRAD Andre Dawson 2.50 6.00
MVPRAM Andrew McCutchen 5.00 12.00
MVPRAP Albert Pujols 6.00 15.00
MVPRAR Alex Rodriguez 6.00 15.00
MVPRBH Bryce Harper 8.00 20.00
MVPRBL Barry Larkin 2.50 6.00
MVPRBP Buster Posey 6.00 15.00
MVPRBRO Brooks Robinson 2.50 6.00
MVPRCJ Chipper Jones 3.00 8.00
MVPRCK Clayton Kershaw 5.00 12.00
MVPRCRI Cal Ripken Jr. 8.00 20.00
MVPRCRJ Cal Ripken Jr. 8.00 20.00
MVPRCY Carl Yastrzemski 5.00 12.00
MVPRDM Don Mattingly 8.00 20.00
MVPREBA Ernie Banks 5.00 12.00
MVPREBN Ernie Banks 5.00 12.00
MVPRFRB Frank Robinson 2.50 6.00
MVPRFRO Frank Robinson 2.50 6.00
MVPRFT Frank Thomas 3.00 8.00
MVPRGB George Brett 6.00 15.00
MVPRHA Hank Aaron 6.00 15.00
MVPRIR Ivan Rodriguez 2.50 6.00
MVPRI Ichiro 6.00 15.00
MVPRJB2 Johnny Bench 3.00 8.00
MVPRJBA Jeff Bagwell 2.50 6.00
MVPRJBE Johnny Bench 3.00 8.00
MVPRJC Jose Canseco 2.50 6.00
MVPRJD Josh Donaldson 2.50 6.00
MVPRJM Joe Morgan 2.50 6.00
MVPRJR Jackie Robinson 3.00 8.00
MVPRJVE Justin Verlander 5.00 12.00
MVPRJVO Joey Votto 5.00 12.00
MVPRKB Kris Bryant 8.00 20.00
MVPRKG Ken Griffey Jr. 8.00 20.00
MVPRMC Miguel Cabrera 3.00 8.00
MVPRMTO Mike Trout 8.00 20.00
MVPRMTR Mike Trout 8.00 20.00
MVPRRCA Rod Carew 2.50 6.00
MVPRRCE Roberto Clemente 10.00 25.00
MVPRRCL Roger Clemens 6.00 15.00
MVPRRH Rickey Henderson 5.00 12.00
MVPRRJ Reggie Jackson 2.50 6.00
MVPRRM Roger Maris 3.00 8.00
MVPRRS Ryne Sandberg 10.00 25.00
MVPRRY Robin Yount 3.00 8.00
MVPRSK Sandy Koufax 8.00 20.00
MVPRTWI Ted Williams 8.00 20.00
MVPRTWL Ted Williams 8.00 20.00
MVPRWM Willie McCovey 2.50 6.00
MVPRWS Willie Stargell 2.50 6.00

2017 Topps Update Postseason Celebration

COMPLETE SET (25) 10.00 25.00
*BLUE/500: .6X TO 1.5X BASIC
*RED/250: .75X TO 2X BASIC
*SILVER/50: 1X TO 2.5X BASIC
PC1 Toronto Blue Jays 1.00 2.50
PC2 San Francisco Giants 1.00 2.50
PC3 Philadelphia Phillies 1.00 2.50
PC4 Detroit Tigers 1.00 2.50
PC5 Chicago White Sox 1.00 2.50
PC6 New York Mets 1.00 2.50
PC7 St. Louis Cardinals 1.00 2.50
PC8 New York Yankees 1.00 2.50
PC9 Oakland Athletics 1.00 2.50
PC10 St. Louis Cardinals 1.00 2.50
PC11 San Francisco Giants 1.00 2.50
PC12 Boston Red Sox 1.00 2.50
PC13 Oakland Athletics 1.00 2.50
PC14 Pittsburgh Pirates 1.00 2.50
PC15 Kansas City Royals 1.00 2.50
PC16 New York Yankees 1.00 2.50
PC17 Chicago Cubs 1.00 2.50
PC18 Los Angeles Angels 1.00 2.50
PC19 Philadelphia Phillies 1.00 2.50
PC20 Boston Red Sox 1.00 2.50
PC21 Boston Red Sox 1.00 2.50
PC22 San Francisco Giants 1.00 2.50
PC23 Pittsburgh Pirates 1.00 2.50
PC24 New York Yankees 1.00 2.50
PC25 Brooklyn Dodgers 1.00 2.50

2017 Topps Update Salute Autographs

EXCHANGE DEADLINE 9/30/2019
SAAB Andrew Benintendi 40.00 100.00
SAABE Andrew Benintendi 40.00 100.00
SAABR Alex Bregman 15.00 40.00
SAAG Amir Garrett 3.00 8.00
SAAJ Aaron Judge
SAARI Anthony Rizzo
SAAS Antonio Senzatela 3.00 8.00
SABHM Billy Hamilton 12.00 30.00
SABHR Bryce Harper
SABZ Bradley Zimmer 4.00 10.00
SACA Christian Arroyo 6.00 15.00
SACB Cody Bellinger EXCH 125.00 300.00
SACK Clayton Kershaw
SACS Chris Sale 30.00 80.00
SACSE Corey Seager
SADR Daniel Robertson 3.00 8.00
SAFL Francisco Lindor 60.00 150.00
SAGS George Springer 15.00 40.00
SAIH Ian Happ 12.00 30.00
SAJA Jose Altuve 25.00 60.00
SAJBZ Javier Baez
SAJH Jeff Hoffman 3.00 8.00

SAJJ Joe Jimenez 4.00 10.00
SAJM Jordan Montgomery 10.00 25.00
SAJR Josh Reddick 3.00 8.00
SAJW Jesse Winker 5.00 12.00
SAKM Kendrys Morales 6.00 15.00
SALB Lewis Brinson 5.00 12.00
SAMHN Mitch Haniger 6.00 15.00
SAMMA Manny Machado
SAMMR Manny Margot 8.00 20.00
SAMP Michael Pineda 3.00 8.00
SAMTO Mike Trout 500.00 700.00
SARG Randal Grichuk 3.00 8.00
SASM Starling Marte 4.00 10.00
SASN Sean Newcomb 4.00 10.00

2017 Topps Update Storied World Series

COMPLETE SET (25) 15.00 40.00
SWS1 1907 Chicago Cubs 1.00 2.50
SWS2 1999 New York Yankees 1.00 2.50
SWS3 1963 Los Angeles Dodgers 1.00 2.50
SWS4 1984 Detroit Tigers 1.00 2.50
SWS5 1905 New York Giants 1.00 2.50
SWS6 1967 St. Louis Cardinals 1.00 2.50
SWS7 1979 Pittsburgh Pirates 1.00 2.50
SWS8 2004 Boston Red Sox 1.00 2.50
SWS9 1932 New York Yankees 1.00 2.50
SWS10 1961 New York Yankees 1.00 2.50
SWS11 1995 Atlanta Braves 1.00 2.50
SWS12 1954 New York Giants 1.00 2.50
SWS13 1970 Baltimore Orioles 1.00 2.50
SWS14 2016 Chicago Cubs 1.00 2.50
SWS15 1936 New York Yankees 1.00 2.50
SWS16 1939 New York Yankees 1.00 2.50
SWS17 1989 Oakland Athletics 1.00 2.50
SWS18 1948 Cleveland Indians 1.00 2.50
SWS19 1969 New York Mets 1.00 2.50
SWS20 1986 New York Mets 1.00 2.50
SWS21 1955 Brooklyn Dodgers 1.00 2.50
SWS22 1942 St. Louis Cardinals 1.00 2.50
SWS23 1909 Pittsburgh Pirates 1.00 2.50
SWS24 1998 New York Yankees 1.00 2.50
SWS25 1927 New York Yankees 1.00 2.50

2017 Topps Update Untouchables

COMPLETE SET (30) 6.00 15.00
U1 Pedro Martinez .40 1.00
U2 Jake Arrieta .40 1.00
U3 Warren Spahn .40 1.00
U4 Justin Verlander .50 1.25
U5 Roy Halladay .40 1.00
U6 Tom Glavine .40 1.00
U7 CC Sabathia .40 1.00
U8 Bartolo Colon .30 .75
U9 Felix Hernandez .40 1.00
U10 Sandy Koufax 1.00 2.50
U11 Dallas Keuchel .40 1.00
U12 Greg Maddux .60 1.50
U13 John Smoltz .50 1.25
U14 Tim Lincecum .40 1.00
U15 Roger Clemens .60 1.50
U16 Steve Carlton .40 1.00
U17 Pedro Martinez .40 1.00
U18 Roy Halladay .40 1.00
U19 Randy Johnson .50 1.25
U20 Jim Palmer .40 1.00
U21 Clayton Kershaw .75 2.00
U22 Max Scherzer .50 1.25
U23 Tom Seaver .40 1.00
U24 Roger Clemens .60 1.50
U25 Randy Johnson .50 1.25
U26 Rick Porcello .40 1.00
U27 Corey Kluber .40 1.00
U28 Greg Maddux .60 1.50
U29 Whitey Ford .40 1.00
U30 Roger Clemens .60 1.50

2018 Topps

COMPLETE SET (700) 30.00 80.00
COMP.RED.HOB.FACT SET (700) 30.00 80.00
COMP.BLUE.RET.FACT SET (700) 30.00 80.00
COMP.SER.1 SET (350) 12.00 30.00
COMP.SER.2 SET (350) 15.00 40.00
SER.1 PLATE ODDS 1:8716 HOBBY
SER.2 PLATE ODDS 1:4730 HOBBY
PLATE PRINT RUN 1 SET PER COLOR
BLACK-CYAN-MAGENTA-YELLOW ISSUED
NO PLATE PRICING DUE TO SCARCITY
1 Aaron Judge .60 1.50
2 Clayton Kershaw LL .40 1.00
3 Dylan Bundy .20 .50
4 Kevin Pillar .15 .40
5 Chris Tillman .15 .40
6 Dominic Smith RC .30 .75
7 Clint Frazier RC .50 1.25
8 Detroit Tigers .15 .40
9 Jon Gray .15 .40
10 Francisco Lindor .25 .60
11 Aaron Nola .20 .50
12 Joey Gallo LL .20 .50
13 Jay Bruce .20 .50
14 Amir Garrett .15 .40
15 Andrelton Simmons .15 .40
16 Daniel Coulombe RC .40 1.00
17 Robbie Ray .15 .40
18 Rafael Devers RC .75 2.00
19 Garrett Richards .15 .40
20 Chris Sale .25 .60
21 Harrison Bader RC .40 1.00
22 Edinson Volquez .15 .40
23 Jordy Mercer .15 .40
24 Martin Maldonado .15 .40
25 Manny Machado .25 .60
26 Cesar Hernandez .15 .40
27 Josh Tomlin .15 .40
28 Jayson Werth .20 .50
29 Hunter Renfroe .15 .40
30 Carlos Correa .25 .60
31 Corey Kluber LL .20 .50
32 Jose Iglesias .20 .50
33 Dexter Fowler .20 .50
34 Luis Severino LL .20 .50
35 Logan Forsythe .15 .40
36 Anthony Rendon .25 .60
37 Corey Kluber LL .20 .50
38 Danny Salazar .20 .50
39 Alex Bregman WS HL .25 .60
40 Carlos Santana .20 .50
41 Daniel Norris .15 .40
42 Cody Bellinger .50 1.25
43 Eduardo Rodriguez .15 .40
44 Trea Turner .20 .50
45 Giancarlo Stanton LL .25 .60
46 Cam Bedrosian .15 .40
47 Hunter Pence .20 .50
48 Boston Red Sox .15 .40
49 Ervin Santana .15 .40
50 Anthony Rizzo .30 .75
51 Michael Wacha .20 .50
52 Brad Hand .15 .40
53 Alex Avila .20 .50
54 Chase Anderson .15 .40
55 Raisel Iglesias .20 .50
56 Rougned Odor .20 .50
57 Scott Feldman .15 .40
58 Ryan Zimmerman .20 .50
59 Clayton Kershaw LL .40 1.00
60 Starling Marte .20 .50
61 Keon Broxton .15 .40
62 Austin Hays RC .40 1.00
63 Amed Rosario RC .30 .75
64 Giancarlo Stanton LL .25 .60
65 Alex Wood .15 .40
66 Ian Kennedy .15 .40
67 Aledmys Diaz .20 .50
68 Billy Hamilton .20 .50
69 Jed Lowrie .15 .40
70 Johnny Cueto .20 .50
71 Mike Foltynewicz .15 .40
72 Cheslor Cuthbert .15 .40
73 Miami Marlins .15 .40
74 Roberto Osuna .15 .40
75 Andrew Miller .20 .50
76 Eduardo Nunez .15 .40
77 Martin Prado .15 .40
78 Carlos Carrasco LL .15 .40
79 J.T. Realmuto .25 .60
80 Dellin Betances .20 .50
81 Adam Wainwright .20 .50
82 Justin Smoak .15 .40
83 Howie Kendrick .15 .40
84 Todd Frazier .15 .40
85 Antonio Senzatela .15 .40
86 Eric Hosmer .20 .50
87 Brandon Phillips .15 .40
88 Michael Conforto .20 .50
89 Yasiel Puig .25 .60
90 Miguel Cabrera .25 .60
91 Travis d'Arnaud .20 .50
92 Charlie Blackmon LL .25 .60
93 Jack Flaherty RC 1.00 2.50
94 Robbie Grossman .15 .40
95 Tyler Mahle RC .30 .75
96 David Dahl .15 .40
97 Dinelson Lamet .15 .40
98 Chicago White Sox .15 .40
99 Greg Allen RC .25 .60
100 Giancarlo Stanton .25 .60
101 Avisail Garcia .20 .50
102 Wil Myers .20 .50
103 Christian Vazquez .20 .50
104 Mitch Moreland .15 .40
105 Daniel Murphy .20 .50
106 Jharel Cotton .15 .40
107 Jorge Polanco .20 .50
108 Justin Turner LL .25 .60
109 Starlin Castro .15 .40
110 Carlos Gonzalez .20 .50
111 Aaron Judge LL .60 1.50
112 Pat Valaika .15 .40
113 Gio Gonzalez .20 .50
114 Cody Bellinger LL .50 1.25
115 Zack Granite RC .25 .60
116 Ariel Miranda RC .40 1.00
117 Kendrys Morales .15 .40
118 Ian Happ .20 .50
119 Los Angeles Angels .15 .40
120 Carlos Carrasco .15 .40
121 Rich Hill .15 .40
122 Chris Owings .15 .40
123 A.J. Ramos .15 .40
124 Julio Urias .25 .60
125 Yoenis Cespedes .25 .60
126 A.Rizzo/B.Harper .40 1.00
127 Byron Buxton .25 .60
128 Jake Marisnick .15 .40
129 Chris Sale LL .25 .60
130 Brian Dozier .20 .50
131 Jonathan Schoop .15 .40
132 Marcell Ozuna .25 .60
133 Nomar Mazara .15 .40
134 Lance Lynn .15 .40
135 Atlanta Braves .15 .40
136 Raudy Read RC .25 .60
137 Michael Lorenzen .15 .40
138 Luiz Gohara RC .25 .60
139 Zach Davies LL .15 .40
140 Mookie Betts .50 1.25
141 Brandon Drury .15 .40
142 Adam Jones .20 .50
143 James Paxton .20 .50
144 Jean Segura .15 .40
145 Michael Fulmer .15 .40
146 Zack Greinke LL .25 .60
147 Randal Grichuk .15 .40
148 Richard Urena RC .25 .60
149 John Jaso .15 .40
150 Nolan Arenado .40 1.00
151 Ryan McMahon RC .60 1.50
152 Matt Barnes .15 .40
153 Scooter Gennett .20 .50
154 George Springer WS HL .20 .50
155 Matt Joyce .15 .40
156 Milwaukee Brewers .15 .40
157 Ichiro .30 .75
158 Stephen Piscotty .15 .40
159 Joc Pederson .20 .50
160 Masahiro Tanaka .20 .50
161 Matt Moore .20 .50
162 Matt Shoemaker .20 .50
163 Mike Leake .15 .40
164 Adeiny Hechavarria .15 .40
165 Ty Blach .15 .40
166 Victor Robles RC .60 1.50
167 Dansby Swanson .25 .60
168 Ricky Nolasco .15 .40
169 Khris Davis LL .25 .60
170 Christian Yelich .30 .75
171 John Lackey .20 .50
172 Willson Contreras .25 .60
173 Mike Moustakas .20 .50
174 Jimmie Sherfy RC .25 .60
175 Jose Quintana .15 .40
176 Seattle Mariners .15 .40
177 Walker Buehler RC 1.25 3.00
178 Matt Adams .15 .40
179 Brandon Woodruff RC .75 2.00
180 Ryan Braun .20 .50
181 Garrett Cooper RC .25 .60
182 Alex Bregman .25 .60
183 Matt Kemp .20 .50
184 Mike Fiers .15 .40
185 Chance Sisco RC .30 .75
186 Luis Perdomo .15 .40
187 Chad Kuhl .15 .40
188 Matt Harvey .20 .50
189 Jedd Gyorko .15 .40
190 Justin Upton .20 .50
191 Chris Archer .15 .40
192 Nolan Arenado LL .40 1.00
193 Aaron Judge LL .60 1.50
194 Lonnie Chisenhall .15 .40
195 Avisail Garcia LL .20 .50
196 Orlando Arcia .15 .40
197 Maikel Franco .20 .50
198 Marcus Semien .25 .60
199 Shin-Soo Choo .20 .50
200 Andrew McCutchen .25 .60
201 Gregory Polanco .20 .50
202 Brett Phillips .15 .40
203 Odubel Herrera .20 .50
204 Brett Gardner .20 .50
205 R.Cano/K.Seager .20 .50
206 Nick Markakis .20 .50
207 Jackson Stephens RC .25 .60
208 Andrew Cashner .15 .40
209 Eugenio Suarez .20 .50
210 Brandon Belt .20 .50
211 Btts/Brdly/Bnntndi .50 1.25
212 Lance McCullers WS HL .15 .40
213 J.A. Happ .20 .50
214 Corey Knebel .15 .40
215 Marwin Gonzalez .15 .40
216 A.J. Pollock .15 .40
217 Erick Fedde RC .25 .60
218 Khris Davis LL .25 .60
219 J.P. Crawford RC .25 .60
220 Nelson Cruz .25 .60
221 Steven Matz .15 .40
222 Ivan Nova .20 .50
223 Evan Longoria .20 .50
224 Dillon Peters RC .25 .60
225 Kyle Schwarber .25 .60
226 Nick Williams RC .30 .75
227 Corey Dickerson .15 .40
228 Zack Wheeler .20 .50
229 Texas Rangers .15 .40
230 Trevor Story .25 .60
231 Joe Mauer .20 .50
232 Nate Jones .15 .40
233 Stephen Strasburg .25 .60
234 Brian Anderson RC .30 .75
235 Mark Reynolds .15 .40
236 CC Sabathia .20 .50
237 Mike Clevinger .20 .50
238 Jose Bautista .20 .50
239 Cleveland Indians .15 .40
240 Robinson Cano .20 .50
241 Nick Pivetta .15 .40
242 Craig Kimbrel .20 .50
243 James McCann .20 .50
244 Francisco Mejia RC .30 .75
245 Willie Calhoun RC .40 1.00
246 Yangervis Solarte .15 .40
247 Anthony Banda RC .25 .60
248 Jake Lamb .20 .50
249 Christian Arroyo .15 .40
250 Buster Posey .30 .75
251 Aaron Sanchez .20 .50
252 Tim Anderson .25 .60
253 Nelson Cruz LL .25 .60
254 Adrian Beltre .25 .60
255 Zach Davies .15 .40
256 Eric Hosmer LL .20 .50
257 J.D. Martinez .25 .60
258 Tyler Saladino .15 .40
259 Rhys Hoskins RC 1.00 2.50
260 Rick Porcello .20 .50
261 Andrew Stevenson RC .25 .60
262 E.Hosmer/M.Sano .20 .50
263 Chase Utley .20 .50
264 Carlos Rodon .25 .60
265 Javier Baez .30 .75
266 Jon Lester .20 .50
267 Yoan Moncada .25 .60
268 Neil Walker .15 .40
269 Greg Holland .15 .40
270 Jackie Bradley Jr. .25 .60
271 Cam Gallagher RC .25 .60
272 Paul Blackburn RC .25 .60
273 Charlie Blackmon LL .25 .60
274 Jeff Samardzija .15 .40
275 George Springer .20 .50
276 Ozzie Albies RC .75 2.00
277 Aaron Slegers RC .40 1.00
278 Lucas Sims RC .25 .60
279 Jordan Zimmermann .20 .50
280 Jose Abreu .25 .60
281 Alex Verdugo RC .40 1.00
282 Ender Inciarte .15 .40
283 Koji Uehara .15 .40
284 Jose Pirela .15 .40
285 Trey Mancini .20 .50
286 New York Yankees .15 .40
287 Mark Trumbo .15 .40
288 Miguel Sano .20 .50
289 Jonathan Villar .15 .40
290 Salvador Perez .20 .50
291 Marcell Ozuna LL .25 .60
292 Baltimore Orioles .15 .40
293 Felipe Rivero .20 .50
294 Jose Altuve LL .20 .50
295 Zack Godley .15 .40
296 Lewis Brinson .15 .40
297 Kevin Kiermaier .20 .50
298 Y.Gurriel/J.Marisnick .20 .50
299 Luis Santos RC .40 1.00
300 Mike Trout 1.25 3.00
301 Brandon Finnegan .15 .40
302 Troy Tulowitzki .25 .60
303 Luis Severino .20 .50
304 Whit Merrifield .25 .60
305 Miguel Andujar RC 1.00 2.50
306 Nicky Delmonico RC .25 .60
307 Daniel Murphy LL .20 .50
308 Cameron Rupp .15 .40
309 Josh Reddick .15 .40
310 Jason Kipnis .20 .50
311 Yulieski Gurriel .20 .50
312 Carlos Asuaje .15 .40
313 Raimel Tapia .15 .40
314 Colorado Rockies .15 .40
315 Chris Rowley RC .40 1.00
316 Max Fried RC 1.00 2.50
317 Chase Headley .15 .40
318 Danny Duffy .15 .40
319 David Peralta .15 .40
320 Yasmani Grandal .15 .40
321 Edwin Diaz .20 .50
322 Parker Bridwell RC .25 .60
323 Elvis Andrus .20 .50
324 Jake Odorizzi .15 .40
325 Khris Davis .25 .60
326 Joey Gallo .20 .50
327 Jason Vargas LL .15 .40
328 Tyler Flowers .15 .40
329 George Springer WS HL .20 .50
330 Ian Kinsler .20 .50
331 Zack Cozart .15 .40
332 Alex Colome .15 .40
333 Joe Musgrove .25 .60
334 Eddie Rosario .25 .60
335 Stephen Strasburg LL .25 .60
336 Bruce Maxwell .15 .40
337 Nick Ahmed .15 .40
338 Brandon McCarthy .15 .40
339 Philadelphia Phillies .15 .40
340 Gary Sanchez .25 .60
341 J.D. Davis RC .30 .75
342 Sean Manaea .15 .40
343 Kevin Gausman .25 .60
344 Wilmer Flores .20 .50
345 Jose Reyes .20 .50
346 Max Scherzer LL .25 .60
347 Kolten Wong .20 .50
348 Hisashi Iwakuma .20 .50
349 Washington Nationals .15 .40
350 Clayton Kershaw .40 1.00
351 Bryce Harper .40 1.00
352 Cincinnati Reds Team Card .15 .40
353 Yan Gomes .25 .60
354 Robert Stephenson .15 .40
355 Joe Ross .15 .40
356 Jeff Hoffman .15 .40
357 Josh Hader .20 .50
358 Brad Brach .15 .40
359 Wade Miley .15 .40
360 Taijuan Walker .15 .40
361 J.Altuve/C.Correa .25 .60
362 Miguel Rojas .15 .40
363 Bryan Shaw .15 .40
365 Y.Puig/C.Bellinger .50 1.25
365 Mallex Smith .15 .40
366 Tyler Glasnow FS .25 .60
367 Liam Hendriks .15 .40
368 Matt Strahm .15 .40
369 Chris Taylor .20 .50
370 Steven Wright .15 .40
371 Cole Hamels .20 .50
372 Nick Tropeano .15 .40
373 Jorge Bonifacio .15 .40
374 Bradley Zimmer FS .15 .40
375 Evan Gattis .15 .40
376 Kyle McGrath RC .25 .60
377 Domingo Santana .20 .50
378 Aaron Wilkerson RC .25 .60
379 Zimmerman/Werth .20 .50
380 Kelby Tomlinson .15 .40
381 Kole Calhoun .15 .40
382 Brandon Guyer .15 .40
383 JaCoby Jones .20 .50
384 Addison Russell .20 .50
385 Jason Hammel .20 .50
386 James Shields .15 .40
387 Julio Teheran .20 .50
388 Taylor Motter .15 .40
389 Stanton/Judge .60 1.50
390 Jesse Chavez .15 .40
391 Ben Zobrist .20 .50
392 Marcus Stroman .20 .50
393 Corey Kluber .20 .50
394 Chad Pinder .15 .40
395 Martin Perez .20 .50
396 Matt Olson .25 .60
397 Dallas Keuchel .20 .50
398 Sam Dyson .15 .40
399 Chicago Cubs Team Card .15 .40
400 Jose Altuve .20 .50
401 Michael Brantley .20 .50
402 Adam Warren .15 .40
403 Luis Torrens .15 .40
404 Alex Claudio .15 .40
405 T.J. Rivera .15 .40
406 Kelvin Herrera .15 .40
407 Pat Neshek .15 .40
408 Mikie Mahtook .15 .40
409 Scott Kingery RC .40 1.00
410 Felix Jorge RC .25 .60
411 David Price .20 .50
412 Mike Minor .15 .40
413 Trevor Bauer .30 .75
414 Danny Valencia .20 .50
415 Jace Peterson .15 .40
416 Derek Fisher FS .15 .40
417 Yolmer Sanchez .15 .40
418 Jose Ramirez .20 .50
419 Fernando Rodney .15 .40
420 Alex Cobb .15 .40
421 Lorenzo Cain .15 .40
422 Victor Caratini RC .30 .75
423 Houston Astros .15 .40
424 Matt Wieters .25 .60
425 Shelby Miller .20 .50
426 Jacob Faria .15 .40
427 Jordan Montgomery .15 .40
428 Jakob Junis .15 .40
429 Victor Martinez .20 .50
430 Manny Margot FS .15 .40
431 Charlie Blackmon .25 .60
432 Albert Almora .20 .50
433 Anthony Santander RC .25 .60
434 Miguel Montero .15 .40
435 Matt Holliday .25 .60
436 Yu Darvish .25 .60
437 J.J. Hardy .15 .40
438 Stephen Vogt .20 .50
439 Dustin Pedroia .25 .60
440 Troy Scribner RC .25 .60
441 Danny Santana .15 .40
442 Jesus Aguilar .20 .50
443 Gerrit Cole .25 .60
444 Aaron Altherr .15 .40
445 Trevor Cahill .15 .40
446 Lucas Duda .20 .50
447 Carlos Gomez .15 .40
448 Max Kepler .20 .50
449 DJ LeMahieu .25 .60
450 Joey Votto .25 .60
451 Ubaldo Jimenez .15 .40
452 Tucker Barnhart .15 .40
453 Devon Travis .15 .40
454 Kyle Seager .15 .40
455 Hernan Perez .15 .40
456 Jimmy Nelson .15 .40
457 Hanley Ramirez .20 .50
458 Yovani Gallardo .15 .40
459 Breyvic Valera RC .25 .60
460 Robert Gsellman .15 .40
461 Michael Taylor .15 .40
462 Paul DeJong FS .25 .60
463 Cory Spangenberg .15 .40
464 Travis Jankowski .15 .40
465 San Diego Padres .15 .40
466 Tim Locastro RC .25 .60
467 Carlos Ramirez RC .25 .60
468 Tampa Bay Rays .15 .40
469 Sonny Gray .20 .50
470 Alex Mejia RC .25 .60
471 Josh Harrison .15 .40
472 Matt Garza .15 .40
473 Wilmer Difo .15 .40
474 Jeff Mathis .20 .50
475 Aroldis Chapman .25 .60
476 Wilson Ramos .15 .40
477 Logan Morrison .15 .40
478 Brad Miller .20 .50
479 Daniel Descalso .15 .40
480 Aaron Hicks .20 .50
481 Ronald Torreyes .15 .40
482 Delino DeShields .15 .40
483 Drew Pomeranz .15 .40
484 Kenta Maeda .20 .50
485 Kyle Farmer RC .25 .60
486 Tomas Nido RC .25 .60
487 Carl Edwards Jr. .15 .40
488 Joe Panik .20 .50
489 Blake Snell .20 .50
490 Jarrod Dyson .15 .40
491 Andrew Heaney .15 .40
492 Jon Jay .15 .40
493 Kyle Gibson .20 .50
494 Adalberto Mejia .15 .40
495 Aaron Bummer RC .25 .60
496 Leury Garcia .15 .40
497 Chasen Shreve .15 .40
498 Jen-Ho Tseng RC .25 .60
499 Justin Bour .15 .40
500 Kris Bryant .30 .75
501 Clayton Richard .15 .40
502 Xander Bogaerts .25 .60
503 Josh Donaldson .20 .50
504 Scott Schebler .20 .50
505 Taylor Williams RC .25 .60
506 Jose Berrios .20 .50
507 Zack Greinke .25 .60
508 Ryon Healy .15 .40
509 Santiago Casilla .15 .40
510 Freddie Freeman .30 .75
511 Wade Davis .15 .40
512 Mike Napoli .15 .40
513 Mike Zunino .15 .40
514 A.J. Minter RC .30 .75
515 Greg Bird .20 .50
516 Ken Giles .15 .40
517 Phillip Evans RC .25 .60
518 Andrew Toles .15 .40
519 Reyes Moronta RC .25 .60
520 Jim Johnson .15 .40
521 Jose Osuna .15 .40
522 Guillermo Heredia .15 .40
523 Matt Bush .15 .40
524 Steve Pearce .25 .60
525 Johan Camargo .15 .40
526 Tanner Roark .15 .40
527 Francisco Cervelli .15 .40
528 Marco Estrada .15 .40
529 Bryant/Schwarber .30 .75
530 Jason Vargas .15 .40
531 Chris O'Grady RC .25 .60
532 Tim Beckham .20 .50
533 Kennys Vargas .15 .40
534 German Marquez .15 .40
535 Jhoulys Chacin .15 .40
536 San Francisco Giants .15 .40
537 Phil Hughes .15 .40
538 Jason Castro .15 .40
539 Lance McCullers .15 .40
540 Mitch Garver RC .25 .60
541 Dwight Smith Jr. .15 .40
542 Pittsburgh Pirates .15 .40
543 Luis Castillo .20 .50
544 Yadier Molina .30 .75
545 Nicholas Castellanos .25 .60
546 Jordan Luplow RC .25 .60
547 Travis Wood .15 .40
548 Alex Meyer .15 .40
549 Alex Gordon .20 .50
550 Corey Seager .25 .60
551 Yacksel Rios RC .25 .60
552 Kyle Hendricks .25 .60
553 Denard Span .15 .40
554 Yonder Alonso .15 .40
555 Jacob deGrom .50 1.25
556 Andrew Benintendi FS .25 .60
557 Jacoby Ellsbury .20 .50
558 Ben Gamel .20 .50
559 Ian Desmond .15 .40
560 Mark Melancon .15 .40
561 Dan Straily .15 .40
562 Brian McCann .20 .50
563 Hector Neris .15 .40
564 Joey Rickard .15 .40
564 New York Mets .15 .40
566 Yasmany Tomas .15 .40
567 Felix Hernandez .20 .50
568 J.C. Ramirez .15 .40
569 Keone Kela .15 .40
570 Trevor Williams .15 .40
571 C.J. Cron .15 .40
572 Dillon Maples RC .25 .60
573 Mark Leiter Jr. .20 .50
574 Jared Hughes .15 .40
575 Adrian Gonzalez .20 .50
576 Didi Gregorius .20 .50
577 Yunel Escobar .15 .40
578 Melky Cabrera .15 .40
579 Carson Fulmer .15 .40
580 Oakland Athletics .15 .40
581 Jesse Winker .25 .60
582 Albert Pujols .30 .75
583 Tommy Joseph .25 .60
584 Toronto Blue Jays Team Card .15 .40
585 Brandon Crawford .20 .50
586 Kyle Freeland .20 .50
587 Chris Davis .15 .40
588 David Wright .20 .50
589 Adam Duvall .20 .50
590 Dee Gordon .15 .40
591 Daniel Nava .15 .40
592 Gorkys Hernandez .15 .40
593 Luke Weaver FS .20 .50
594 Sandy Alcantara RC .25 .60
595 Addison Reed .15 .40
596 Keury Mella RC .25 .60
597 Caleb Joseph .15 .40
598 David Robertson .15 .40
599 Justin Turner .25 .60
600 Noah Syndergaard .20 .50
601 Jose Peraza .20 .50
602 Michael Pineda .15 .40
603 Zach Britton .15 .40
604 Gerardo Parra .15 .40
605 Lucas Giolito .20 .50
606 Jake Arrieta .20 .50
607 Sean Newcomb FS .20 .50
608 Kurt Suzuki .15 .40
609 Austin Hedges .15 .40
610 Scott Kazmir .15 .40
611 Josh Bell FS .20 .50
612 Steven Souza Jr. .20 .50
613 Cory Gearrin .15 .40
614 Minnesota Twins .15 .40
615 Eric Thames .20 .50
616 Greg Garcia .15 .40
617 Doug Fister .15 .40
618 Paul Goldschmidt .25 .60
619 Jeremy Hellickson .15 .40
620 Chris Young .15 .40
621 Jerad Eickhoff .15 .40
622 Ryan Rua .15 .40
623 Josh Fields .15 .40
624 Franklin Barreto .15 .40
625 Los Angeles Dodgers .15 .40
626 Brandon Maurer .15 .40
627 Matthew Boyd .15 .40
628 Vince Velasquez .15 .40
629 Max Scherzer .25 .60
630 Alcides Escobar .20 .50
631 David Freese .15 .40
632 Edwin Encarnacion .25 .60
633 Jameson Taillon .20 .50
634 Carlos Martinez .20 .50
635 Cody Allen .15 .40
636 Freddy Galvis .15 .40
637 Manny Pina .15 .40
638 Travis Shaw .15 .40
639 Niko Goodrum RC .40 1.00
640 Seth Lugo .15 .40
641 Cameron Maybin .15 .40
642 Ben Revere .15 .40
643 Justin Wilson .15 .40
644 Carlos Perez .15 .40
645 Welington Castillo .15 .40
646 Jose de Leon .15 .40
647 Jose Urena .15 .40
648 Derek Holland .15 .40
649 Curtis Granderson .20 .50
650 Justin Verlander .25 .60
651 JT Riddle .15 .40
652 Matt Carpenter .25 .60
653 Jorge Soler .25 .60
654 Trayce Thompson .20 .50
655 Andre Ethier .20 .50
656 Brian Goodwin .15 .40
657 Derek Dietrich .20 .50
658 Tom Koehler .15 .40
659 Arizona Diamondbacks .15 .40
660 Mitch Haniger FS .20 .50
661 Christian Villanueva RC .25 .60
662 Patrick Corbin .20 .50
663 Seth Smith .15 .40
664 Gregor Blanco .15 .40
665 Tommy Pham .15 .40
666 Eric Sogard .15 .40
667 Jonathan Lucroy .20 .50
668 Tyler Anderson .15 .40
669 Matt Chapman .25 .60
670 Asdrubal Cabrera .20 .50
671 Tyler Clippard .15 .40
672 Brandon Nimmo .20 .50
673 Adam Frazier .15 .40
674 Jose Martinez .15 .40
675 Victor Arano RC .25 .60
676 Chad Green .15 .40
677 Brandon Moss .15 .40
678 Chad Bettis .15 .40
679 Tyson Ross .15 .40
680 Enrique Hernandez .25 .60
681 Ehire Adrianza .15 .40
682 Kansas City Royals .15 .40
683 Adam Eaton .25 .60
684 Hunter Strickland .15 .40
685 Russell Martin .15 .40
686 Bud Norris .15 .40
687 Blake Treinen .15 .40
688 Tony Wolters .15 .40
689 Jeurys Familia .20 .50
690 St. Louis Cardinals .15 .40
691 Jason Heyward .20 .50
692 Tony Watson .15 .40
693 Brandon Kintzler .15 .40
694 Anthony DeSclafani .15 .40
695 Matt Davidson .20 .50
696 Kenley Jansen .20 .50
697 Eduardo Escobar .15 .40
698 Ryan Sherriff RC .25 .60
699 Drew Smyly .15 .40
700 Shohei Ohtani RC 5.00 12.00

2018 Topps Black

*BLACK: 10X TO 25X BASIC
*BLACK RC: 6X TO 15X BASIC RC
SER.1 ODDS 1:169 HOBBY
SER.2 ODDS 1:114 HOBBY
STATED PRINT RUN 67 SER. #'d SETS
259 Rhys Hoskins 30.00 80.00
529 Bryant/Schwarber 8.00 20.00
700 Shohei Ohtani 200.00 500.00

2018 Topps Black and White Negative

*BW NEGATIVE: 8X TO 20X BASIC
*BW NEGATIVE RC: 5X TO 12X BASIC
SER.1 ODDS 1:230 HOBBY
SER.2 ODDS 1:155 HOBBY
259 Rhys Hoskins 15.00 40.00
700 Shohei Ohtani 150.00 400.00

2018 Topps Factory Set Foilboard

*FACT.FOIL: 6X TO 15X BASIC
*FACT.FOIL RC: 4X TO 10X BASIC RC
INSERTED IN FACTORY SETS
STATED PRINT RUN 190 SER. #'d SETS
698B Ronald Acuna Jr 1000.00 2500.00

2018 Topps Father's Day Blue

*BLUE: 10X TO 25X BASIC
*BLUE RC: 6X TO 15X BASIC RC
SER.1 ODDS 1:693 HOBBY
SER.2 ODDS 1:380 HOBBY
STATED PRINT RUN 50 SER. #'d SETS
259 Rhys Hoskins 30.00 80.00
529 Bryant/Schwarber 8.00 20.00
700 Shohei Ohtani 200.00 500.00

2018 Topps Gold

*GOLD: 2X TO 5X BASIC
*GOLD RC: 1.2X TO 3X BASIC RC
SER. 1 ODDS 1:18 HOBBY
SER.2 ODDS 1:10 HOBBY
STATED PRINT RUN 2018 SER. #'d SETS

2018 Topps Limited

*LTD: .1.5X TO 4X BASIC
LTD RC: 1X TO 2.5X BASIC RC
ANNCD PRINT RUN OF 1000

2018 Topps Memorial Day Camo

*CAMO: 12X TO 30X BASIC
*CAMO RC: 8X TO 20X BASIC RC
SER.1 ODDS 1:1388 HOBBY
SER.2 ODDS 1:759 HOBBY
STATED PRINT RUN 25 SER. #'d SETS
259 Rhys Hoskins 40.00 100.00
529 Bryant/Schwarber 10.00 25.00
700 Shohei Ohtani 250.00 600.00

2018 Topps Mother's Day Pink

*PINK: 10X TO 25X BASIC
*PINK RC: 6X TO 15X BASIC RC
SER.1 ODDS 1:693 HOBBY
SER.2 ODDS 1:380 HOBBY
STATED PRINT RUN 50 SER. #'d SETS
259 Rhys Hoskins 30.00 80.00
529 Bryant/Schwarber 8.00 20.00
700 Shohei Ohtani 200.00 500.00

2018 Topps Rainbow Foil

*RAINBOW: 2X TO 5X BASIC
*RAINBOW RC: 1.2X TO 3X BASIC RC
SER.1 ODDS 1:10 HOBBY
SER.2 ODDS 1:10 HOBBY
259 Rhys Hoskins 6.00 15.00

2018 Topps Toys R Us Purple

*PURPLE: 5X TO 12X BASIC
*PURPLE RC: 3X TO 8X BASIC RC
SER.1 ODDS 1:XX BLASTER
259 Rhys Hoskins 15.00 40.00

2018 Topps Vintage Stock

*VINTAGE: 8X TO 20X BASIC
*VINTAGE RC: 5X TO 12X BASIC RC
SER.1 ODDS 1:351 HOBBY
SER.2 ODDS 1:192 HOBBY
STATED PRINT RUN 99 SER. #'d SETS
259 Rhys Hoskins 25.00 60.00
529 Bryant/Schwarber 6.00 15.00
700 Shohei Ohtani 150.00 400.00

2018 Topps Base Set Factory Chrome Variations

RANDOMLY INSERTED IN FACTORY SETS
*GOLD/50: 1X TO 2.5X BASIC
*ORANGE/25: 2X TO 5X BASIC
7 Clint Frazier 5.00 12.00
18 Rafael Devers 8.00 20.00
63 Amed Rosario 3.00 8.00
166 Victor Robles 6.00 15.00
259 Rhys Hoskins 10.00 25.00
700 Shohei Ohtani 50.00 120.00

2018 Topps Base Set Photo Variations

SER.1 STATED ODDS 1:57 HOBBY
SER. 1 ODDS SSP 1:1619 HOBBY
SER.2 STATED ODDS 1:30 HOBBY
SER. 2 SSP ODDS SSP 1:886 HOBBY
1A Judge Blue pllvr 25.00 60.00
1B Judge Stripe jrsy 250.00 500.00
6A Dominic Smith 2.00 5.00
Blue and gray shirt
6B Smith Celebrating 75.00 200.00

7A Frazier Blue pllvr 10.00 25.00
7B Frazier Bttng glvs 125.00 300.00
7C Frazier One hand
10A Lindor No helmet 2.50 6.00
10B Lindor White Jrsy 100.00 250.00
11 Aaron Nola 2.00 5.00
Sitting in dugout
18A Devers Red pllvr 12.00 30.00
18B Devers Pointing 100.00 250.00
18C Devers Brwn bat
20A Sale Jckt 2.50 6.00
20B Sale Off mound 40.00 100.00
25A Machado Snglss 6.00 15.00
25B Machado Hand face 75.00 200.00
30A Correa Blue warmup 2.50 6.00
30B Correa White Jrsy 30.00 80.00
33 Dexter Fowler 2.00 5.00
Red pullover
42A Bllngr Blue gray shirt 6.00 15.00
42B Bllngr Gray Jrsy 75.00 200.00
44 Turner Red pllvr 2.00 5.00
50A Anthony Rizzo 3.00 8.00
Blue pullover
50B Rizzo Gray Jrsy 60.00 150.00
58 Ryan Zimmerman 2.00 5.00
Red pullover
63A Rosario Blue pllvr 10.00 25.00
63B Rosario Gray Jrsy 60.00 150.00
63C Rosario Pnstrp Jrsy
68 Hamilton Red hde 6.00 15.00
81 Adam Wainwright 2.00 5.00
Red hoodie
82 Justin Smoak 1.50 4.00
Blue pullover
86 Eric Hosmer 2.00 5.00
Blue shirt
88 Michael Conforto 2.00 5.00
Blue pullover
89 Yasiel Puig 2.50 6.00
Blue shirt
90 Cabrera Blue hde 2.50 6.00
100A Stanton Orange shirt 2.50 6.00
100B Stanton Gray Jrsy 100.00 250.00
102 Wil Myers 2.00 5.00
Blue shirt
105 Daniel Murphy 2.00 5.00
Red shirt
110 Carlos Gonzalez 2.00 5.00
Black pullover
118 Ian Happ 2.00 5.00
Blue pullover
125 Yoenis Cespedes 2.50 6.00
Blue sleevless shirt, black sleeves under
127 Byron Buxton 2.50 6.00
Blue and gray shirt
130 Brian Dozier 2.00 5.00
Blue pullover
132 Marcell Ozuna 2.50 6.00
Black pullover
140A Betts Blue hde 5.00 12.00
140B Betts On base 60.00 150.00
142 Adam Jones 2.00 5.00
Black and gray shirt
150A Nolan Arenado 4.00 10.00
Black pullover
150B Arndo Stripe Jrsy 75.00 200.00
157A Ichiro Black pllvr 3.00 8.00
157B Ichiro On base
160 Masahiro Tanaka 2.00 5.00
Dark blue pullover
166 Robles Hispanic Logo 15.00 40.00
172 Contreras Blue pllvr 2.50 6.00
173 Mike Moustakas 2.00 5.00
Blue hoodie
180 Ryan Braun 2.00 5.00
Blue pullover
182 Alex Bregman 2.50 6.00
Blue pullover
190 Justin Upton 2.00 5.00
Horziontal, bat next to head
191 Chris Archer 1.50 4.00
Blue sleevless shirt
196 Orlando Arcia 1.50 4.00
Blue and gray shirt
200A Andrew McCutchen 2.50 6.00
Black pullover
200B McCtchn Gray Jrsy 75.00 200.00
220 Nelson Cruz 2.50 6.00
Blue pullover
223 Evan Longoria 2.00 5.00
Blue and gray shirt
225A Kyle Schwarber 2.50 6.00
Blue and gray shirt
225B Schwarber Point 40.00 100.00
226A Williams Red shirt 2.00 5.00
226B Williams Stripe Jrsy 50.00 120.00
233 Stephen Strasburg 2.50 6.00
Blue and red pullover
238 Jose Bautista 2.00 5.00
Blue shirt
240A Robinson Cano 2.00 5.00
Blue pullover
240B Cano White Jrsy 75.00 200.00
245 Calhoun Red shirt 2.50 6.00
248 Jake Lamb 2.00 5.00
Black pullover
250A Posey Black pllvr 3.00 8.00
250B Posey White Jrsy 60.00 150.00
254 Beltre Blue pllvr 2.50 6.00
257 Martinez Pullover 2.50 6.00
259A Hoskins Red pllvr 15.00 40.00
259B Hoskins Red Jrsy 75.00 200.00
259C Hoskins Look at sky
264 Carlos Rodon 2.50 6.00
Black pullover
265A Baez Blue hde 3.00 8.00
265B Baez Pinstripe Jrsy 50.00 120.00
267 Moncada Black pllvr 2.50 6.00
275 Springer Hispanic Logo 2.00 5.00
276A Albies Blue pllvr 10.00 25.00
276B Albies Blue Jrsy 40.00 100.00
280 Jose Abreu 2.50 6.00
Black pullover
288 Sano Blue hde 2.00 5.00
290 Salvador Perez 2.00 5.00
Blue hoodie
297 Kevin Kiermaier 2.00 5.00
Blue shirt
300A Trout Gray red shirt 12.00 30.00
300B Trout Red Jrsy 150.00 400.00
303 Svrno Blue gray shirt 2.00 5.00
306 Dlmnco Black and gray 1.50 4.00
325 Khris Davis 2.50 6.00
Green pullover
326 Gallo Blue pllvr 2.00 5.00
330 Ian Kinsler 2.00 5.00
Blue pullover
340 Sanchez Blue pllvr 2.50 6.00
350A Kershaw Blue shirt 4.00 10.00
350B Kershaw Gray Jrsy 50.00 120.00
351A Harper Red shirt 4.00 10.00
351B Harper Clapping 60.00 150.00
351C Reggie Jackson 3.00 8.00
351D Ty Cobb 4.00 10.00
369 Chris Taylor 2.00 5.00
Blue shirt
384A Russell Blue pllvr 2.00 5.00
384B Russell Pointing
384C Ernie Banks 2.50 6.00
392 Marcus Stroman 2.00 5.00
Standing behing cage
393A Kluber Red shirt 2.00 5.00
393B Kluber Clench fist 20.00 50.00
397 Dallas Keuchel 2.00 5.00
Blue pullover
400A Altuve Blue shirt 2.00 5.00
400B Altuve Clapping 25.00 60.00
400C Honus Wagner 2.50 6.00
413 Trevor Bauer 3.00 8.00
Blue hoodie
416 Matt Olson 2.50 6.00
Green Pullover
418A Ramirez Hat 2.00 5.00
418B Ramirez Pointing 25.00 60.00
430 Manny Margot 1.50 4.00
Blue hoodie
431A Blackmon Blk hoodie 2.50 6.00
431B Blackmon Hand out 12.00 30.00
431C Rickey Henderson 2.50 6.00
436A Darvish Blue pllvr 2.50 6.00
436B Darvish Streching 15.00 40.00
436C Greg Maddux 3.00 8.00
439A Pedroia Blue pllvr 2.50 6.00
439B Pedroia Hand up 30.00 80.00
450A Votto Red pllvr 2.50 6.00
450B Votto Hands out 30.00 80.00
450C Johnny Bench 4.00 10.00
454 Kyle Seager 1.50 4.00
Blue shirt
462A Paul DeJong 2.50 6.00
Carrying bag
462B Ozzie Smith 3.00 8.00
469A Gray Interview 2.00 5.00
469B Gray Pointing 30.00 80.00
471 Josh Harrison 1.50 4.00
Standing behing cage
484 Kenta Maeda 2.00 5.00
Blue shirt
499 Justin Bour 1.50 4.00
Black shirt
500A Bryant Holding bat 3.00 8.00
500B Bryant Sliding 75.00 200.00
500C Ryne Sandberg 5.00 12.00
502 Xander Bogaerts 2.50 6.00
Red and blue pullover
503A Donaldson Cage 2.00 5.00
503B Donaldson Hand up 20.00 50.00
503C George Brett 5.00 12.00
506 Jose Berrios 2.00 5.00
Blue hoodie
507 Zack Greinke 2.50 6.00
Black shirt
510A Freeman Hat 3.00 8.00
510B Freeman Waving 25.00 60.00
510C Chipper Jones 2.50 6.00
515A Greg Bird 2.00 5.00
Blue shirt
515B Don Mattingly 5.00 12.00
544A Molina Behind cage 3.00 8.00
544B Molina Hands up 30.00 80.00
544C Roberto Clemente 6.00 15.00
545 Nicholas Castellanos 2.50 6.00
Blue shirt
550A Cal Ripken Jr. 6.00 15.00
550B Jackie Robinson 2.50 6.00
555A deGrom Blue shirt 5.00 12.00
555B deGrom Helmet 25.00 60.00
556A Benintendi Blue pllvr 2.50 6.00
556B Benintendi Arm up 40.00 100.00
556C C.Seager Blue pllvr 2.50 6.00
556D C.Seager Helmet 30.00 80.00
556E Ted Williams 5.00 12.00
567A Hernandez Gray shirt 2.00 5.00
567B Hernandez Point 20.00 50.00
576A Gregorius Blue pllvr 2.00 5.00
576B Gregorius Pointing 25.00 60.00
576C Derek Jeter 12.00 30.00
582A Pujols Red pllvr 3.00 8.00
582B Pujols Pointing up 50.00 120.00
582C Hank Aaron 5.00 12.00
585A Brandon Crawford 2.00 5.00
Black hat
585B Willie McCovey 2.00 5.00
589 Adam Duvall 2.00 5.00
Red jersey
593 Luke Weaver 2.00 5.00
Red hat
599 Justin Turner 2.50 6.00
Blue pullover
600A Syndrgrd Blue pllvr 2.00 5.00
600B Syndrgrd Fist 75.00 200.00
600C Tom Seaver 2.00 5.00
605A Lucas Giolito 2.00 5.00
No hat
605B Frank Thomas 2.50 6.00
611A Scherzer Red pllvr 2.50 6.00
611B Scherzer Fist 25.00 60.00
615 Eric Thames 2.00 5.00
Blue pullover
618A Gldschmdt Blk pllvr 2.50 6.00
618B Gldschmdt Hand out 30.00 80.00
618C Lou Gehrig 4.00 10.00
629 Sandy Koufax 4.00 10.00
632 Edwin Encarnacion 2.50 6.00
Red and blue pullover
650A Verlander Blue hoodie 3.00 8.00
650B Verlander Hand up 30.00 80.00
650C Bob Gibson 2.00 5.00
652 Matt Carpenter 2.50 6.00
Red shirt
665 Tommy Pham 1.50 4.00
Red shirt
698A Acuna Bat down 400.00 1000.00
698B Acuna Bat up 30.00 80.00
699A Torres Both hands 20.00 50.00
699B Torres One hand
700A Ohtani Red pllvr 30.00 80.00
700B Ohtani Hand on hlmt 150.00 400.00
700C Babe Ruth 6.00 15.00
700D Ohtani Red glv

2018 Topps '83 All Stars

STATED ODDS 1:4 HOBBY
*BLUE: 1.2X TO 3X BASIC
*BLACK/299: 1.5X TO 4X BASIC
*GOLD/50: 4X TO 10X BASIC
83AS1 Aaron Judge 1.00 2.50
83AS2 Giancarlo Stanton .40 1.00
83AS3 Carlos Correa .40 1.00
83AS4 Mike Trout 2.00 5.00
83AS5 Jose Altuve .30 .75
83AS6 Chris Sale .40 1.00
83AS7 George Springer .30 .75
83AS8 Francisco Lindor .40 1.00
83AS9 Miguel Sano .30 .75
83AS10 Luis Severino .30 .75
83AS11 Corey Kluber .30 .75
83AS12 Clayton Kershaw .60 1.50
83AS13 Bryce Harper .60 1.50
83AS14 Buster Posey .50 1.25
83AS15 Charlie Blackmon .40 1.00
83AS16 Cody Bellinger .75 2.00
83AS17 Paul Goldschmidt .40 1.00
83AS18 Corey Seager .40 1.00
83AS19 Joey Votto .40 1.00
83AS20 Max Scherzer .40 1.00
83AS21 Stephen Strasburg .40 1.00
83AS22 Mookie Betts .75 2.00
83AS23 Gary Sanchez .40 1.00
83AS24 Robinson Cano .30 .75
83AS25 Yadier Molina .50 1.25
83AS26 Salvador Perez .30 .75
83AS27 Craig Kimbrel .30 .75
83AS28 Jose Ramirez .30 .75
83AS29 Josh Harrison .25 .60
83AS30 Justin Upton .30 .75
83AS31 Justin Verlander .40 1.00
83AS32 Yu Darvish .40 1.00
83AS33 Kris Bryant .50 1.25
83AS34 Anthony Rizzo .50 1.25
83AS35 Addison Russell .30 .75
83AS36 Yoenis Cespedes .40 1.00
83AS37 Josh Donaldson .30 .75
83AS38 Manny Machado .40 1.00
83AS39 Starling Marte .30 .75
83AS40 Noah Syndergaard .30 .75
83AS41 Andrew McCutchen .40 1.00
83AS42 Adam Jones .30 .75
83AS43 Albert Pujols .50 1.25
83AS44 Brian Dozier .30 .75
83AS45 Miguel Cabrera .40 1.00
83AS46 Ichiro .50 1.25
83AS47 Wade Boggs .30 .75
83AS48 Cal Ripken Jr. 1.25 3.00
83AS49 Ryne Sandberg .75 2.00
83AS50 Rickey Henderson .40 1.00
83AS51 Don Mattingly .75 2.00
83AS52 Chipper Jones .40 1.00
83AS53 John Smoltz .40 1.00
83AS54 Greg Maddux .50 1.25
83AS55 Dwight Gooden .25 .60
83AS56 Darryl Strawberry .25 .60
83AS57 Roger Clemens .50 1.25
83AS58 Mark McGwire .60 1.50
83AS59 Jose Canseco .30 .75
83AS60 Randy Johnson .40 1.00
83AS61 Frank Thomas .40 1.00
83AS62 Mariano Rivera .50 1.25
83AS63 Mike Piazza .40 1.00
83AS64 Derek Jeter 1.00 2.50
83AS65 Pedro Martinez .30 .75
83AS66 Dave Winfield .30 .75
83AS67 Dennis Eckersley .30 .75
83AS68 Ozzie Smith .50 1.25
83AS69 Barry Larkin .30 .75
83AS70 Rod Carew .30 .75
83AS71 Reggie Jackson .30 .75
83AS72 Johnny Bench .40 1.00
83AS73 Gary Carter .30 .75
83AS74 George Brett .75 2.00
83AS75 Hideki Matsui .40 1.00

2018 Topps '83 Rookies

STATED ODDS 1:4 HOBBY
*BLUE: 1.2X TO 3X BASIC
*BLACK/299: 1.5X TO 4X BASIC
*GOLD/50: 4X TO 10X BASIC
831 Shohei Ohtani 5.00 12.00
832 Walker Buehler 1.25 3.00
833 Luiz Gohara .25 .60
834 Tyler Mahle .30 .75
835 Austin Hays .40 1.00
836 Chance Sisco .30 .75
837 Sandy Alcantara .25 .60
838 Jen-Ho Tseng .25 .60
839 Richard Urena .25 .60
8310 Greg Allen .25 .60
8311 Brian Anderson .30 .75
8312 Dillon Peters .25 .60
8313 A.J. Minter .30 .75
8314 Troy Scribner .25 .60
8315 Clint Frazier .50 1.25
8316 Ozzie Albies .75 2.00
8317 Amed Rosario .30 .75
8318 Rhys Hoskins 1.00 2.50
8319 Rafael Devers .75 2.00
8320 Dominic Smith .30 .75
8321 Victor Robles .60 1.50
8322 Dillon Maples .25 .60
8323 Christian Villanueva .25 .60
8324 Nick Williams .30 .75

2018 Topps '83 Topps

COMPLETE SET (100) 60.00 150.00
STATED ODDS 1:4 HOBBY
*BLUE: 2X TO 5X BASIC
*BLACK/299: 3X TO 8X BASIC
*GOLD/50: 4X TO 10X BASIC
831 Ryne Sandberg .75 2.00
832 Hank Aaron .75 2.00
833 Andrew McCutchen .40 1.00
834 Mookie Betts .75 2.00
835 Jacob deGrom .75 2.00
836 Noah Syndergaard .30 .75
837 Frank Thomas .40 1.00
838 Khris Davis .40 1.00
839 Alex Verdugo .40 1.00
8310 Eric Thames .30 .75
8311 Matt Carpenter .40 1.00
8312 Carlos Martinez .30 .75
8313 Mike Trout 2.00 5.00
8314 Rafael Devers .75 2.00
8315 Ian Happ .30 .75
8316 Clayton Kershaw .60 1.50
8317 Dominic Smith .30 .75
8318 Nolan Ryan 1.25 3.00
8319 Nick Williams .30 .75
8320 Alex Wood .25 .60
8321 Jake Arrieta .30 .75
8322 Giancarlo Stanton .40 1.00
8323 Kris Bryant .50 1.25
8324 Aaron Judge 1.00 2.50
8325 Yu Darvish .40 1.00
8326 Brian Dozier .30 .75
8327 Charlie Blackmon .40 1.00
8328 Luis Severino .30 .75
8329 Harrison Bader .40 1.00
8330 Rhys Hoskins 1.00 2.50
8331 Jose Altuve .30 .75
8332 Manny Machado .40 1.00
8333 Michael Fulmer .25 .60
8334 Kyle Seager .25 .60
8335 Nelson Cruz .40 1.00
8336 Stephen Strasburg .40 1.00
8337 Miguel Sano .30 .75
8338 Matt Kemp .30 .75
8339 Cal Ripken Jr. 1.25 3.00
8340 Ozzie Albies .75 2.00
8341 Miguel Cabrera .40 1.00
8342 Yadier Molina .50 1.25
8343 Andrew Benintendi .40 1.00
8344 Roy Halladay .30 .75
8345 Josh Donaldson .30 .75
8346 Dansby Swanson .40 1.00
8347 Jose Berrios .30 .75
8348 Darryl Strawberry .25 .60
8349 Freddie Freeman .50 1.25
8350 Amed Rosario .30 .75
8351 Buster Posey .50 1.25
8352 Jeff Bagwell .30 .75
8353 Willie Calhoun .40 1.00
8354 Anthony Rizzo .50 1.25
8355 Justin Upton .30 .75
8356 Don Mattingly .75 2.00
8357 Barry Larkin .30 .75
8358 Nolan Arenado .60 1.50
8359 Yoan Moncada .40 1.00
8360 Justin Turner .40 1.00
8361 Felix Hernandez .30 .75
8362 Sandy Koufax .75 2.00
8363 Kenta Maeda .30 .75
8364 Robinson Cano .30 .75
8365 Edwin Encarnacion .40 1.00
8366 Daniel Murphy .30 .75
8367 Ichiro .50 1.25
8368 Derek Jeter 1.00 2.50
8369 Tom Glavine .30 .75
8370 Clint Frazier .50 1.25
8371 Craig Kimbrel .30 .75
8372 Didi Gregorius .30 .75
8373 Adam Jones .30 .75
8374 Gary Sanchez .40 1.00
8375 Max Scherzer .40 1.00
8376 Ryan McMahon .60 1.50
8377 Byron Buxton .40 1.00
8378 Masahiro Tanaka .30 .75
8379 Jose Canseco .30 .75
8380 George Springer .30 .75
8381 Kyle Schwarber .40 1.00
8382 Trea Turner .30 .75
8383 Paul Goldschmidt .40 1.00
8384 Bryce Harper .60 1.50
8385 Victor Robles .60 1.50
8386 Javier Baez .50 1.25
8387 Cody Bellinger .75 2.00
8388 John Smoltz .40 1.00
8389 Bo Jackson .40 1.00
8390 J.P. Crawford .25 .60
8391 Eric Hosmer .30 .75
8392 Carlos Correa .40 1.00
8393 Chris Sale .40 1.00
8394 Wil Myers .30 .75
8395 Francisco Lindor .40 1.00
8396 Alex Bregman .40 1.00
8397 Corey Seager .40 1.00
8398 Justin Verlander .40 1.00
8399 Addison Russell .30 .75
83100 Wade Boggs .30 .75

2018 Topps '83 Topps Autographs

SER.1 ODDS 1:809 HOBBY
SER.2 ODDS 1:1233 HOBBY
UPD ODDS 1:1352 HOBBY
SER.1 EXCH.DEADLINE 12/31/2019
SER.2 EXCH.DEADLINE 5/31/2020
UPD EXCH.DEADLINE 9/30/2020
*BLACK/99: .5X TO 1.2X BASIC
*BLACK/50: .6X TO 1.5X BASIC
*BLACK/25: .75X TO 2X BASIC
*GOLD/50: .6X TO 1.5X BASIC
*GOLD/25: .75X TO 2X BASIC
*RED/25: .75X TO 2X BASIC
83AABA Anthony Banda 2.50 6.00
83AABE Andrew Benintendi UPD 40.00 100.00
83AABL Adrian Beltre S2 20.00 50.00
83AABR Alex Bregman 15.00 40.00
83AAC Andrew McCutchen UPD 25.00 60.00
83AADI Aledmys Diaz 3.00 8.00
83AADU Adam Duvall 8.00 20.00
83AAE Austin Meadows UPD 6.00 15.00
83AAGR Amir Garrett S2 2.50 6.00
83AAH Austin Hays S2 6.00 15.00
83AAJN Andruw Jones 10.00 25.00
83AAJO Adam Jones
83AAN Aaron Nola 8.00 20.00
83AAN A.J. Minter UPD 3.00 8.00
83AAO Adam Jones S2
83AAP Andy Pettitte
83AARI Anthony Rizzo UPD
83AARO Amed Rosario EXCH 25.00 60.00
83AARU Addison Russell S2 12.00 30.00
83AAS Amed Rosario S2 10.00 25.00
83AASL Aaron Slegers 6.00 15.00
83AAST Andrew Stevenson 8.00 20.00
83AAV Alex Verdugo 15.00 40.00
83AAW Alex Wood 8.00 20.00
83ABA Brian Anderson S2 8.00 20.00
83ABBU Byron Buxton UPD 6.00 15.00
83ABD Brian Dozier S2
83ABF Brandon Finnegan 2.50 6.00
83ABG Ben Gamel 3.00 8.00
83ABH Bryce Harper S2
83ABJ Bo Jackson S2 60.00 150.00
83ABL Barry Larkin
83ABL Barry Larkin S2 25.00 60.00
83ABP Boog Powell 2.50 6.00
83ABPH Brett Phillips 5.00 12.00
83ABPO Buster Posey UPD
83ABT Blake Treinen UPD 2.50 6.00
83ABW Brandon Woodruff 5.00 12.00
83ACAR Christian Arroyo S2 6.00 15.00
83ACCA Carlos Carrasco 8.00 20.00
83ACCO Carlos Correa S2
83ACF Clint Frazier 25.00 60.00
83ACG Chad Green UPD 6.00 15.00
83ACR Cal Ripken Jr.
83ACR Cal Ripken Jr. S2
83ACS Chris Sale S2 30.00 80.00
83ACS Chris Stratton UPD 2.50 6.00
83ACSA Chris Sale 15.00 40.00
83ACSE Corey Seager 40.00 100.00
83ACY Christian Yelich UPD 40.00 100.00
83ACY Clayton Kershaw S2
83ADA Don Mattingly S2 25.00 60.00
83ADCZ Dylan Cozens UPD 2.50 6.00
83ADD David Dahl 6.00 15.00
83ADE Dennis Eckersley UPD 6.00 15.00
83ADFI Derek Fisher S2 2.50 6.00
83ADFO Dexter Fowler S2
83ADFW Dustin Fowler S2 2.50 6.00
83ADG Dwight Gooden S2 20.00 50.00
83ADGF Domingo German 15.00 40.00
83ADI Dominic Smith S2 6.00 15.00
83ADJ Derek Jeter S2
83ADJE Derek Jeter S2
83ADMA Don Mattingly 100.00 250.00
83ADN Dennis Eckersley S2 15.00 40.00
83ADN Daniel Mengden UPD 4.00 10.00
83ADS Darryl Strawberry S2
83ADSI Dominic Smith 12.00 30.00
83ADSM Drew Smyly 2.50 6.00
83ADST Darryl Strawberry 30.00 80.00
83ADSW Dansby Swanson S2 12.00 30.00
83AED Eric Davis 10.00 25.00
83AET Eric Thames 3.00 8.00
83AFF Freddie Freeman S2 30.00 80.00
83AFH Frank Thomas S2
83AFJ Felix Jorge S2 2.50 6.00
83AFME Francisco Mejia 15.00 40.00
83AFO Fernando Romero UPD 2.50 6.00
83AFP Freddy Peralta UPD 2.50 6.00
83AFR Franmil Reyes UPD 4.00 10.00
83AFT Frank Thomas S2
83AGA Gary Sanchez S2 40.00 100.00
83AGB Greg Bird 3.00 8.00
83AGC Garrett Cooper 2.50 6.00
83AGL Greg Allen S2 2.50 6.00
83AGMA Greg Maddux
83AGO Gleyber Torres UPD 50.00 120.00
83AGS Gary Sanchez 40.00 100.00
83AGT Gleyber Torres S2 100.00 250.00
83AHA Hank Aaron 125.00 300.00
83AHB Harrison Bader 4.00 10.00
83AHR Hunter Renfroe 6.00 15.00
83AIF Ian Kinsler UPD 15.00 40.00
83AIH Ian Happ 12.00 30.00
83AIK Isiah Kiner-Falefa UPD 4.00 10.00
83AJBA Jeff Bagwell 40.00 100.00
83AJBE Johnny Bench S2
83AJBR Jose Berrios 10.00 25.00
83AJBZ Javier Baez 20.00 50.00
83AJC Jose Canseco S2 20.00 50.00
83AJCA Jose Canseco 15.00 40.00
83AJCR J.P. Crawford 8.00 20.00
83AJD J.D. Davis 3.00 8.00
83AJDO Josh Donaldson UPD 20.00 50.00
83AJE Jerad Eickhoff 2.50 6.00
83AJF Jacob Faria 2.50 6.00
83AJF Jack Flaherty UPD 10.00 25.00
83AJHA Josh Hader 6.00 15.00
83AJHO Jeff Hoffman 6.00 15.00
83AJK Jordan Hicks UPD 6.00 15.00
83AJL Joey Lucchesi UPD 6.00 15.00
83AJL Jake Lamb S2
83AJM John Smoltz S2
83AJMO Jordan Montgomery S2 2.50 6.00
83AJR Jose Ramirez S2 25.00 60.00
83AJS Justin Smoak S2 6.00 15.00
83AJS Jesse Biddle UPD 3.00 8.00
83AJSM John Smoltz S2
83AJST Jackson Stephens 2.50 6.00
83AJTH Jim Thome
83AJU Juan Soto UPD 150.00 300.00
83AJU Justin Upton S2
83AJV Joey Votto S2 60.00 150.00
83AJW Jesse Winker 10.00 25.00
83AJY Joey Votto S2 60.00 150.00
83AKB Kris Bryant S2
83AKBO Keon Broxton 2.50 6.00
83AKBR Kris Bryant 60.00 150.00
83AKD Khris Davis 8.00 20.00
83AKGI Ken Giles S2 2.50 6.00
83AKGL Koda Glover 4.00 10.00
83AKSE Kyle Seager 6.00 15.00
83ALC Luis Castillo UPD 3.00 8.00
83ALE Luis Severino S2 30.00 80.00
83ALG Lucas Giolito 8.00 20.00
83ALI Lucas Sims S2 2.50 6.00
83ALU Lourdes Gurriel Jr. UPD 10.00 25.00
83ALW Luke Weaver 3.00 8.00
83AMA Miguel Andujar 50.00 120.00
83AMC Mike Clevinger 4.00 10.00
83AMC Mike Clevinger UPD 3.00 8.00
83AMD Mike Soroka UPD 5.00 12.00
83AMF Max Fried 6.00 15.00
83AMF Michael Fulmer UPD 5.00 12.00
83AMG Mark McGwire S2
83AMK Max Kepler 5.00 12.00
83AML Mark Leiter 3.00 8.00
83AMM Manny Machado S2
83AMM Miles Mikolas UPD 6.00 15.00
83AMMA Manny Machado 60.00 150.00
83AMMG Mark McGwire
83AMMR Manny Margot S2 2.50 6.00
83AMN Miguel Andujar UPD 40.00 100.00
83AMO Matt Olson 8.00 20.00
83AMO Marcell Ozuna UPD 10.00 25.00
83AMO Miguel Gomez S2 2.50 6.00
83AMT Mike Trout S2
83AMTR Mike Trout 250.00 500.00
83AND Nicky Delmonico 8.00 20.00
83ANK Nick Kingham UPD 3.00 8.00
83ANP Nick Pivetta UPD 2.50 6.00
83ANR Nolan Ryan S2
83ANS Noah Syndergaard S2
83AOA Ozzie Albies UPD 20.00 50.00
83AOAL Ozzie Albies 20.00 50.00
83AOS Ozzie Smith S2 60.00 150.00
83AOV Omar Vizquel 25.00 60.00
83APB Paul Blackburn 2.50 6.00
83APBR Parker Bridwell 2.50 6.00
83APD Paul DeJong 10.00 25.00
83APG Paul Goldschmidt S2
83APN Pat Neshek UPD 4.00 10.00
83ARA Ronald Acuna S2 100.00 250.00
83ARD Rafael Devers 50.00 120.00
83ARHO Rhys Hoskins S2 30.00 80.00
83ARM Ryan McMahon 6.00 15.00
83ARR Rod Carew S2
83ARS Ryne Sandberg
83ARS Ryne Sandberg S2
83ARU Richard Urena S2 5.00 12.00
83ARU Ronald Acuna Jr. UPD 100.00 250.00
83ASA Sandy Alcantara S2 2.50 6.00
83ASD Sean Doolittle UPD 2.50 6.00
83ASI Scott Kingery UPD 4.00 10.00
83ASK Sandy Koufax UPD 300.00 600.00
83ASM Starling Marte UPD 5.00 12.00
83ASN Sean Newcomb S2 5.00 12.00
83ASO Shohei Ohtani S2 800.00 1200.00
83ASO Shohei Ohtani UPD EXCH 250.00 500.00
83ASS Steven Souza Jr. 3.00 8.00
83AST Sam Travis S2 3.00 8.00
83ATAN Tim Anderson 10.00 25.00
83ATAU Tyler Austin UPD 4.00 10.00
83ATB Tyler Beede UPD 2.50 6.00
83ATBK Tim Beckham S2 5.00 12.00
83ATGS Tyler Glasnow 4.00 10.00
83ATGV Tom Glavine S2
83ATL Tzu-Wei Lin UPD 3.00 8.00
83ATM Tyler Mahle UPD 3.00 8.00
83ATMA Trey Mancini S2 8.00 20.00
83ATN Tomas Nido S2 2.50 6.00
83ATO Tyler O'Neill UPD EXCH 4.00 10.00
83ATS Trevor Story 5.00 12.00
83ATS Troy Scribner S2 2.50 6.00
83ATU Torii Hunter UPD 6.00 15.00
83ATW Tyler Wade 12.00 30.00
83AVR Victor Robles 40.00 100.00
83AVR Victor Robles S2 20.00 50.00
83AWA Willy Adames UPD EXCH 10.00 25.00
83AWB Wade Boggs 40.00 100.00
83AWB Wade Boggs S2 40.00 100.00
83AWU Walker Buehler UPD 30.00 80.00
83AYM Yadier Molina S2
83AYO Yoan Moncada UPD
83AZG Zack Granite 8.00 20.00

2018 Topps '83 Topps Silver Pack Chrome

COMPLETE SET (150) 100.00 250.00
*BLUE/150: 1.5X TO 4X BASIC
*GREEN/99: 2X TO 5X BASIC
*BLUE WAVE/75: 2X TO 5X BASIC
*PURPLE/75: 2X TO 5X BASIC
*GOLD/50: 2.5X TO 6X BASIC
*ORANGE/25: 3X TO 8X BASIC
1 Derek Jeter 2.00 5.00
2 Mike Trout 4.00 10.00
3 Ichiro 1.00 2.50
4 Brandon Woodruff 1.50 4.00
5 Mark McGwire 1.25 3.00
6 Cal Ripken Jr. 2.50 6.00
7 Kris Bryant 1.00 2.50
8 Carlos Correa .75 2.00
9 Manny Machado .75 2.00
10 Clayton Kershaw 1.25 3.00
11 Anthony Rizzo 1.00 2.50
12 Nicky Delmonico .50 1.25
13 Aaron Judge 2.00 5.00
14 Jack Flaherty 2.00 5.00
15 Jose Altuve .60 1.50
16 Cody Bellinger 1.50 4.00
17 Noah Syndergaard .60 1.50
18 Andrew Benintendi .75 2.00
19 Clint Frazier 1.00 2.50
20 Rafael Devers 1.50 4.00
21 Garrett Cooper .50 1.25
22 Javier Baez 1.00 2.50
23 Giancarlo Stanton .75 2.00
24 Amed Rosario .60 1.50
25 Luis Severino .60 1.50
26 Ozzie Albies 1.50 4.00
27 Victor Robles 1.25 3.00
28 Trey Mancini .60 1.50
29 Ian Happ .60 1.50
30 Paul Goldschmidt .75 2.00
31 Harrison Bader .75 2.00
32 Zack Granite .50 1.25
33 Walker Buehler 2.50 6.00
34 Paul DeJong .75 2.00
35 Rhys Hoskins 2.00 5.00
36 Dominic Smith .60 1.50
37 Dustin Fowler .50 1.25
38 Miguel Andujar 2.00 5.00
39 Hank Aaron 1.50 4.00
40 Bryce Harper 1.25 3.00
41 J.P. Crawford .50 1.25
42 Joey Votto .75 2.00
43 Ryne Sandberg 1.50 4.00
44 Ryan McMahon 1.25 3.00
45 Andrew Stevenson .50 1.25
46 Alex Verdugo .75 2.00
47 Francisco Mejia .60 1.50
48 Wade Boggs .60 1.50
49 Max Fried 2.00 5.00
50 Parker Bridwell .50 1.25
51 Shohei Ohtani 12.00 30.00
52 Kyle Schwarber .75 2.00
53 Sandy Alcantara .50 1.25
54 Mookie Betts 1.50 4.00
55 Charlie Blackmon .75 2.00
56 Ozzie Smith 1.00 2.50
57 Tyler Mahle .60 1.50
58 Will Clark .60 1.50
59 Matt Olson .75 2.00
60 Lucas Sims .50 1.25
61 Nolan Ryan 2.50 6.00
62 Wil Myers .60 1.50
63 Gary Sanchez .75 2.00
64 Yu Darvish .75 2.00
65 Jose Ramirez .60 1.50
66 Rickey Henderson .75 2.00
67 Yadier Molina 1.00 2.50
68 Anthony Banda .50 1.25
69 Nick Williams .60 1.50
70 Alex Bregman .75 2.00
71 Darryl Strawberry .50 1.25
72 Robinson Cano .60 1.50
73 George Springer .60 1.50
74 Adrian Beltre .75 2.00
75 Don Mattingly 1.50 4.00
76 Chris Sale .75 2.00
77 J.D. Davis .60 1.50
78 Travis Shaw .50 1.25
79 Roberto Clemente 2.00 5.00
80 Francisco Lindor .75 2.00
81 A.J. Minter .60 1.50
82 Whit Merrifield .75 2.00
83 Austin Hays .75 2.00
84 Chance Sisco .60 1.50
85 Josh Donaldson .60 1.50
86 Victor Caratini .60 1.50
87 Trea Turner .60 1.50
88 Troy Scribner .50 1.25
89 Yoan Moncada .75 2.00
90 Justin Upton .60 1.50
91 Michael Conforto .60 1.50
92 Brian Anderson .60 1.50
93 George Brett 1.50 4.00
94 Paul Blackburn .50 1.25
95 Max Scherzer .75 2.00
96 Buster Posey 1.00 2.50
97 Tyler Wade .60 1.50
98 Corey Seager .75 2.00
99 Byron Buxton .75 2.00
100 Chipper Jones .75 2.00
101 Ronald Acuna Jr. 15.00 40.00
102 Nolan Arenado 1.25 3.00
103 David Ortiz .75 2.00
104 Jacob deGrom 1.50 4.00
105 Eddie Murray .60 1.50
106 Mike Piazza .75 2.00
107 Ichiro 1.00 2.50
108 Andrew McCutchen .75 2.00
109 Austin Meadows 1.25 3.00
110 Barry Larkin .60 1.50
111 Fernando Romero .50 1.25
112 Joey Lucchesi .50 1.25
113 Gerrit Cole .75 2.00
114 J.D. Martinez .75 2.00
115 Mike Soroka 1.50 4.00
116 Marcell Ozuna .75 2.00
117 Justin Verlander .75 2.00
118 Jake Lamb .60 1.50
119 Chris Stratton .50 1.25
120 Mariano Rivera 1.00 2.50
121 Corey Kluber .60 1.50
122 Masahiro Tanaka .60 1.50
123 Isiah Kiner-Falefa .75 2.00
124 Todd Frazier .50 1.25
125 Giancarlo Stanton .75 2.00
126 Ernie Banks .75 2.00
127 Bo Jackson .75 2.00
128 Chris Archer .50 1.25
129 Ian Kinsler .60 1.50
130 Dustin Pedroia .75 2.00
131 Freddie Freeman 1.00 2.50
132 Frank Thomas .75 2.00
133 Tyler O'Neill .75 2.00
134 Juan Soto 12.00 30.00
135 Stephen Strasburg .75 2.00
136 Daniel Mengden .50 1.25
137 Randy Johnson .75 2.00
138 Lourdes Gurriel Jr. 1.00 2.50
139 Christian Yelich 1.00 2.50
140 Starling Marte .60 1.50
141 Matt Kemp .60 1.50
142 Jordan Hicks 1.00 2.50
143 Albert Pujols 1.00 2.50
144 Didi Gregorius .60 1.50
145 Shohei Ohtani 12.00 30.00
146 Jackie Robinson .75 2.00
147 Gleyber Torres 5.00 12.00
148 Miles Mikolas .60 1.50
149 Nick Kingham .50 1.25
150 Scott Kingery .75 2.00

2018 Topps '83 Topps Silver Pack Chrome Autographs

RANDOM INSERTS IN SILVER PACKS
PRINT RUNS B/WN 10-199 COPIES PER
NO PRICING ON QTY 10
*ORANGE/25: .6X TO 1.5X BASIC
4 Brandon Woodruff/199 20.00 50.00
12 Nicky Delmonico/199 6.00 15.00
14 Jack Flaherty/199 25.00 60.00
17 Noah Syndergaard/50 12.00 30.00
19 Clint Frazier/99 50.00 120.00
20 Rafael Devers/99 60.00 150.00
21 Garrett Cooper/199 12.00 30.00
22 Javier Baez/50 20.00 50.00
24 Amed Rosario/99 20.00 50.00
25 Luis Severino/30 20.00 50.00
26 Ozzie Albies/99 40.00 100.00
27 Victor Robles/99 40.00 100.00
28 Trey Mancini/99 20.00 50.00
29 Ian Happ/99 15.00 40.00
30 Paul Goldschmidt/30 15.00 40.00
31 Harrison Bader/199 10.00 25.00

32 Zack Granite/199 6.00 15.00
34 Paul DeJong/99 30.00 80.00
36 Dominic Smith/50 12.00 30.00
37 Dustin Fowler/199 6.00 15.00
38 Miguel Andujar/199 60.00 150.00
41 J.P. Crawford/199 6.00 15.00
44 Ryan McMahon/199 15.00 40.00
45 Andrew Stevenson/199 6.00 15.00
46 Alex Verdugo/199 15.00 40.00
49 Max Fried/199 25.00 60.00
50 Parker Bridwell/199 6.00 15.00
51 Shohei Ohtani/25 150.00 400.00
53 Sandy Alcantara/99 6.00 15.00
57 Tyler Mahle/149 8.00 20.00
58 Will Clark/99 30.00 80.00
59 Matt Olson/149 10.00 25.00
68 Anthony Banda/149 6.00 15.00
70 Alex Bregman/50
71 Darryl Strawberry/99 25.00 60.00
73 George Springer/50 20.00 50.00
75 Don Mattingly/25 60.00 150.00
77 J.D. Davis/99 8.00 20.00
78 Travis Shaw/149 6.00 15.00
81 A.J. Minter/99 8.00 20.00
82 Whit Merrifield/149 10.00 25.00
83 Austin Hays/99 10.00 25.00
84 Chance Sisco/149 8.00 20.00
88 Troy Scribner/99 6.00 15.00
90 Justin Upton/50 8.00 20.00
91 Michael Conforto/50 15.00 40.00
92 Brian Anderson/99 8.00 20.00
94 Paul Blackburn/99 6.00 15.00
97 Tyler Wade/99 8.00 20.00
101 Ronald Acuna Jr./99 150.00 400.00
103 David Ortiz
104 Jacob deGrom/30
107 Ichiro
108 Andrew McCutchen/30 20.00 50.00
109 Austin Meadows
110 Barry Larkin/30
111 Fernando Romero/99 6.00 15.00
115 Mike Soroka/99 20.00 50.00
116 Marcell Ozuna/99 10.00 25.00
118 Jake Lamb/99 8.00 20.00
119 Chris Stratton/99 6.00 15.00
120 Mariano Rivera
121 Corey Kluber/30 8.00 20.00
123 Isiah Kiner-Falefa/99 10.00 25.00
127 Bo Jackson
129 Ian Kinsler/99 8.00 20.00
131 Freddie Freeman/30
132 Frank Thomas
134 Juan Soto/99 150.00 400.00
136 Daniel Mengden/99 6.00 15.00
138 Lourdes Gurriel Jr./99 12.00 30.00
139 Christian Yelich/50
145 Shohei Ohtani
147 Gleyber Torres/99 150.00 400.00
148 Miles Mikolas/99 8.00 20.00
149 Nick Kingham/99 6.00 15.00
150 Scott Kingery/99 10.00 25.00

2018 Topps '83 Topps Silver Pack Chrome Autographs Orange Refractors

*ORANGE REF: .6X TO 1.5X BASIC
RANDOM INSERTS IN SILVER PACKS
STATED PRINT RUN 25 SER.#'d SETS

2018 Topps Aaron Judge Highlights

INSERTED IN WALMART PACKS
*BLUE: .5X TO 1.2X BASIC
*BLACK: .6X TO 1.5X BASIC
*GOLD/50: 5X TO 12X BASIC
AJ1 Aaron Judge 1.00 2.50
AJ2 Aaron Judge 1.00 2.50
AJ3 Aaron Judge 1.00 2.50
AJ4 Aaron Judge 1.00 2.50
AJ5 Aaron Judge 1.00 2.50
AJ6 Aaron Judge 1.00 2.50
AJ7 Aaron Judge 1.00 2.50
AJ8 Aaron Judge 1.00 2.50
AJ9 Aaron Judge 1.00 2.50
AJ10 Aaron Judge 1.00 2.50
AJ11 Aaron Judge 1.00 2.50
AJ12 Aaron Judge 1.00 2.50
AJ13 Aaron Judge 1.00 2.50
AJ14 Aaron Judge 1.00 2.50
AJ15 Aaron Judge 1.00 2.50
AJ16 Aaron Judge 1.00 2.50
AJ17 Aaron Judge 1.00 2.50
AJ18 Aaron Judge 1.00 2.50
AJ19 Aaron Judge 1.00 2.50
AJ20 Aaron Judge 1.00 2.50
AJ21 Aaron Judge 1.00 2.50
AJ22 Aaron Judge 1.00 2.50
AJ23 Aaron Judge 1.00 2.50
AJ24 Aaron Judge 1.00 2.50
AJ25 Aaron Judge 1.00 2.50
AJ26 Aaron Judge 1.00 2.50
AJ27 Aaron Judge 1.00 2.50
AJ28 Aaron Judge 1.00 2.50
AJ29 Aaron Judge 1.00 2.50
AJ30 Aaron Judge 1.00 2.50

2018 Topps All Star Medallions

STATED ODDS 1:1537 HOBBY
*BLACK/99: .5X TO 1.2X BASIC
*GOLD/50: .75X TO 2X BASIC
*RED/25: 1X TO 2.5X BASIC
ASTMAJ Aaron Judge 6.00 15.00
ASTMBH Bryce Harper 4.00 10.00
ASTMBP Buster Posey 3.00 8.00
ASTMCBE Cody Bellinger 5.00 12.00
ASTMCBL Charlie Blackmon 2.50 6.00
ASTMCC Carlos Correa 2.50 6.00
ASTMCKE Clayton Kershaw 4.00 10.00
ASTMCKI Craig Kimbrel 2.00 5.00
ASTMCKL Corey Kluber 2.00 5.00
ASTMCSA Chris Sale 2.50 6.00
ASTMCSE Corey Seager 2.50 6.00
ASTMDM Daniel Murphy 2.00 5.00
ASTMFL Francisco Lindor 2.50 6.00
ASTMGSA Gary Sanchez 2.50 6.00
ASTMGSP George Springer 2.00 5.00
ASTMGST Giancarlo Stanton 2.50 6.00
ASTMJA Jose Altuve 2.00 5.00
ASTMJV Joey Votto 2.50 6.00
ASTMLS Luis Severino 2.00 5.00
ASTMMB Mookie Betts 5.00 12.00
ASTMMC Michael Conforto 2.00 5.00
ASTMMSA Miguel Sano 2.00 5.00
ASTMMSC Max Scherzer 2.50 6.00
ASTMNA Nolan Arenado 4.00 10.00
ASTMPG Paul Goldschmidt 2.50 6.00
ASTMRC Robinson Cano 2.00 5.00
ASTMRZ Ryan Zimmerman 2.00 5.00
ASTMSP Salvador Perez 2.00 5.00
ASTMSS Stephen Strasburg 2.50 6.00
ASTMYM Yadier Molina 3.00 8.00

2018 Topps Cody Bellinger Highlights

INSERTED IN TARGET PACKS
*BLUE: .5X TO 1.2X BASIC
*BLACK: .6X TO 1.5X BASIC
*GOLD/50: 5X TO 12X BASIC
CB1 Cody Bellinger .75 2.00
CB2 Cody Bellinger .75 2.00
CB3 Cody Bellinger .75 2.00
CB4 Cody Bellinger .75 2.00
CB5 Cody Bellinger .75 2.00
CB6 Cody Bellinger .75 2.00
CB7 Cody Bellinger .75 2.00
CB8 Cody Bellinger .75 2.00
CB9 Cody Bellinger .75 2.00
CB10 Cody Bellinger .75 2.00
CB11 Cody Bellinger .75 2.00
CB12 Cody Bellinger .75 2.00
CB13 Cody Bellinger .75 2.00
CB14 Cody Bellinger .75 2.00
CB15 Cody Bellinger .75 2.00
CB16 Cody Bellinger .75 2.00
CB17 Cody Bellinger .75 2.00
CB18 Cody Bellinger .75 2.00
CB19 Cody Bellinger .75 2.00
CB20 Cody Bellinger .75 2.00
CB21 Cody Bellinger .75 2.00
CB22 Cody Bellinger .75 2.00
CB23 Cody Bellinger .75 2.00
CB24 Cody Bellinger .75 2.00
CB25 Cody Bellinger .75 2.00
CB26 Cody Bellinger .75 2.00
CB27 Cody Bellinger .75 2.00
CB28 Cody Bellinger .75 2.00
CB29 Cody Bellinger .75 2.00
CB30 Cody Bellinger .75 2.00

2018 Topps Derek Jeter Highlights

INSERTED IN TARGET PACKS
*BLUE: .5X TO 1.2X BASIC
*BLACK: .6X TO 1.5X BASIC
*GOLD/50: 5X TO 12X BASIC
DJH1 Derek Jeter 1.00 2.50
DJH2 Derek Jeter 1.00 2.50
DJH3 Derek Jeter 1.00 2.50
DJH4 Derek Jeter 1.00 2.50
DJH5 Derek Jeter 1.00 2.50
DJH6 Derek Jeter 1.00 2.50
DJH7 Derek Jeter 1.00 2.50
DJH8 Derek Jeter 1.00 2.50
DJH9 Derek Jeter 1.00 2.50
DJH10 Derek Jeter 1.00 2.50
DJH11 Derek Jeter 1.00 2.50
DJH12 Derek Jeter 1.00 2.50
DJH13 Derek Jeter 1.00 2.50
DJH14 Derek Jeter 1.00 2.50
DJH15 Derek Jeter 1.00 2.50
DJH16 Derek Jeter 1.00 2.50
DJH17 Derek Jeter 1.00 2.50
DJH18 Derek Jeter 1.00 2.50
DJH19 Derek Jeter 1.00 2.50
DJH20 Derek Jeter 1.00 2.50
DJH21 Derek Jeter 1.00 2.50
DJH22 Derek Jeter 1.00 2.50
DJH23 Derek Jeter 1.00 2.50
DJH24 Derek Jeter 1.00 2.50
DJH25 Derek Jeter 1.00 2.50
DJH26 Derek Jeter 1.00 2.50
DJH27 Derek Jeter 1.00 2.50
DJH28 Derek Jeter 1.00 2.50
DJH29 Derek Jeter 1.00 2.50
DJH30 Derek Jeter 1.00 2.50

2018 Topps Future Stars

INSERTED IN RETAIL RELIC BOXES
*BLUE: .5X TO 1.2X BASIC
*BLACK: .75X TO 2X BASIC
*GOLD/50: 4X TO 10X BASIC
FS1 Rhys Hoskins 1.00 2.50
FS2 Victor Robles .60 1.50
FS3 Amed Rosario .30 .75
FS4 Dominic Smith .30 .75
FS5 Shohei Ohtani 6.00 15.00
FS6 Clint Frazier .50 1.25
FS7 Ozzie Albies .75 2.00
FS8 Nick Williams .30 .75
FS9 Alex Verdugo .40 1.00
FS10 Willie Calhoun .40 1.00
FS11 J.P. Crawford .25 .60
FS12 Francisco Mejia .30 .75
FS13 Austin Hays .40 1.00
FS14 Chance Sisco .30 .75
FS15 Walker Buehler 1.25 3.00
FS16 Ryan McMahon .60 1.50
FS17 Cody Bellinger .75 2.00
FS18 Trey Mancini .30 .75
FS19 Andrew Benintendi .40 1.00
FS20 Manny Margot .25 .60
FS21 Paul DeJong .40 1.00
FS22 Hunter Renfroe .25 .60
FS23 Ian Happ .30 .75
FS24 Matt Olson .40 1.00
FS25 Lucas Giolito .30 .75
FS26 Alex Bregman .40 1.00
FS27 Byron Buxton .40 1.00
FS28 Dansby Swanson .40 1.00
FS29 Lewis Brinson .25 .60
FS30 Gary Sanchez .40 1.00
FS31 Aaron Judge 1.00 2.50
FS32 Michael Conforto .30 .75
FS33 Addison Russell .30 .75
FS34 Trea Turner .30 .75
FS35 Javier Baez .50 1.25
FS36 Nomar Mazara .25 .60
FS37 Kyle Schwarber .40 1.00
FS38 Aaron Nola .30 .75
FS39 Rougned Odor .30 .75
FS40 Trevor Story .40 1.00
FS41 Franklin Barreto .25 .60
FS42 Jack Flaherty 1.00 2.50
FS43 Harrison Bader
FS44 Luiz Gohara .25 .60
FS45 Tyler Mahle .30 .75
FS46 Francisco Lindor .40 1.00
FS47 Corey Seager .40 1.00
FS48 Carlos Correa .40 1.00
FS49 Julio Urias .40 1.00
FS50 Matt Chapman .40 1.00

2018 Topps Home Run Challenge

SER.1 ODDS 1:36 HOBBY
GINTER ODDS 1:24 HOBBY
HRCAD Adam Duvall 1.50 4.00
HRCAE Anthony Rendon 2.00 5.00
HRCAJ Aaron Judge 5.00 12.00
HRCAM Andrew McCutchen 2.00 5.00
HRCAO Adam Jones 1.50 4.00
HRCAR Anthony Rizzo 2.50 6.00
HRCBD Brian Dozier 1.50 4.00
HRCBH Bryce Harper 3.00 8.00
HRCCB Cody Bellinger 4.00 10.00
HRCCD Corey Dickerson 1.25 3.00
HRCCL Charlie Blackmon 2.00 5.00
HRCEE Edwin Encarnacion 2.00 5.00
HRCET Eric Thames 1.50 4.00
HRCFF Freddie Freeman 2.50 6.00
HRCGA Gary Sanchez 2.00 5.00
HRCGP George Springer 1.50 4.00
HRCGS Giancarlo Stanton 2.00 5.00
HRCJA Jose Abreu 2.00 5.00
HRCJB Jay Bruce 1.50 4.00
HRCJC Jonathan Schoop 1.25 3.00
HRCJG Joey Gallo 1.50 4.00
HRCJL Jake Lamb 1.50 4.00
HRCJM J.D. Martinez 2.00 5.00
HRCJS Justin Smoak 1.25 3.00
HRCJU Justin Upton 1.50 4.00
HRCJV Joey Votto 2.00 5.00
HRCKB Kris Bryant 2.50 6.00
HRCKD Khris Davis 2.00 5.00
HRCLM Logan Morrison 1.25 3.00
HRCMA Manny Machado 2.00 5.00
HRCMC Michael Conforto 1.50 4.00
HRCMD Matt Davidson 1.50 4.00
HRCMM Mike Moustakas 1.50 4.00
HRCMN Mike Napoli 1.25 3.00
HRCMO Marcell Ozuna 2.00 5.00
HRCMR Mark Reynolds 1.25 3.00
HRCMS Miguel Sano 1.50 4.00
HRCMT Mike Trout 10.00 25.00
HRCNA Nolan Arenado 3.00 8.00
HRCNC Nelson Cruz 2.00 5.00
HRCPG Paul Goldschmidt 2.00 5.00
HRCRO Rougned Odor 1.50 4.00
HRCRZ Ryan Zimmerman 1.50 4.00
HRCSC Scott Schebler 1.50 4.00
HRCSS Steven Souza Jr. 1.50 4.00
HRCTM Trey Mancini 1.50 4.00
HRCTS Travis Shaw 1.25 3.00
HRCWC Willson Contreras 2.00 5.00
HRCWM Wil Myers 1.50 4.00
HRCYA Yonder Alonso 1.25 3.00

2018 Topps Independence Day

*INDPNDNCE: 10X TO 25X BASIC
*INDPNDNCE RC: 6X TO 15X BASIC RC
SER.1 ODDS 1:456 HOBBY
RANDOMLY INSERTED IN SER.2
STATED PRINT RUN 76 SER.#'d SETS
259 Rhys Hoskins 30.00 80.00
529 Bryant/Schwarber 8.00 20.00
700 Shohei Ohtani 200.00 500.00

2018 Topps Instant Impact

STATED ODDS 1:8 HOBBY
*BLUE: 1.2X TO 3X BASIC
*BLACK/299: 1.5X TO 4X BASIC
*GOLD/50: 4X TO 10X BASIC
II1 Ted Williams .75 2.00
II2 Al Kaline .40 1.00
II3 Nomar Garciaparra .30 .75
II4 Ichiro .50 1.25
II5 Mike Trout 2.00 5.00
II6 Albert Pujols .50 1.25
II7 Shohei Ohtani 6.00 15.00
II8 Rafael Devers .75 2.00
II9 Cody Bellinger .75 2.00
II10 Andrew Benintendi .40 1.00
II11 Corey Seager .40 1.00
II12 Aaron Judge 1.00 2.50
II13 Mark McGwire .60 1.50
II14 Dwight Gooden
II15 Mike Piazza .40 1.00
II16 Cal Ripken Jr. 1.25 3.00
II17 Andruw Jones .25 .60
II18 Billy Williams .30 .75
II19 Bryce Harper .60 1.50
II20 Buster Posey .50 1.25
II21 Carlos Correa .40 1.00
II22 Chipper Jones .40 1.00
II23 Carlton Fisk .30 .75
II24 Darryl Strawberry .25 .60
II25 Derek Jeter 1.00 2.50
II26 Dustin Pedroia .40 1.00
II27 Gary Sanchez .40 1.00
II28 Jackie Robinson .40 1.00
II29 Yasiel Puig .40 1.00
II30 Johnny Bench .40 1.00
II31 Jose Abreu .40 1.00
II32 Jose Canseco .30 .75
II33 Justin Verlander .40 1.00
II34 Evan Longoria .30 .75
II35 Willie McCovey .30 .75
II36 Jeff Bagwell .30 .75
II37 Joey Votto .40 1.00
II38 Masahiro Tanaka .30 .75
II39 Paul DeJong .40 1.00
II40 Trey Mancini .30 .75
II41 Ryan Braun .30 .75
II42 Stephen Strasburg .40 1.00
II43 Rod Carew .30 .75
II44 Tom Seaver .30 .75
II45 Trea Turner .30 .75
II46 Tim Raines .30 .75
II47 Amed Rosario .30 .75
II48 Rhys Hoskins 1.00 2.50
II49 Francisco Lindor .40 1.00
II50 Victor Robles .60 1.50

2018 Topps Instant Impact Autograph Relics

STATED ODDS 1:12,461 HOBBY
STATED PRINT RUN 25 SER.#'d SETS
EXCHANGE DEADLINE 5/31/2020
IARAO Andruw Jones
IARBP Buster Posey
IARCB Cody Bellinger
IARCJ Chipper Jones
IARCR Cal Ripken Jr.
IARDS Darryl Strawberry 40.00 100.00
IARGS Gary Sanchez
IARI Ichiro
IARJB Jeff Bagwell
IARJC Jose Canseco
IARMM Mark McGwire
IARMP Mike Piazza
IARMT Mike Trout
IARNG Nomar Garciaparra
IARPd Paul DeJong
IARRC Rod Carew
IARRD Rafael Devers 40.00 100.00
IARTM Trey Mancini
IARTR Tim Raines
IARVR Victor Robles

2018 Topps Instant Impact Relics

STATED ODDS 1:11,545 HOBBY
STATED PRINT RUN 100 SER.#'d SETS
*RED/25: .6X TO 1.5X BASIC
IIRAB Andrew Benintendi 5.00 12.00
IIRAO Andruw Jones 3.00 8.00
IIRAP Albert Pujols 12.00 30.00
IIRAR Amed Rosario 4.00 10.00
IIRBH Bryce Harper 8.00 20.00
IIRBP Buster Posey 12.00 30.00
IIRCB Cody Bellinger 8.00 20.00
IIRCC Carlos Correa 5.00 12.00
IIRCJ Chipper Jones 8.00 20.00
IIRCR Cal Ripken Jr. 15.00 40.00
IIRCS Corey Seager 8.00 20.00
IIRDJ Derek Jeter 20.00 50.00
IIRGS Gary Sanchez 5.00 12.00
IIRI Ichiro 6.00 15.00
IIRJB Jeff Bagwell 4.00 10.00
IIRJC Jose Canseco 12.00 30.00
IIRJV Joey Votto 5.00 12.00
IIRMK Masahiro Tanaka 4.00 10.00
IIRMM Mark McGwire 8.00 20.00
IIRMP Mike Piazza 8.00 20.00
IIRMT Mike Trout 25.00 60.00
IIRNG Nomar Garciaparra 6.00 15.00
IIRPd Paul DeJong 5.00 12.00
IIRRB Ryan Braun 4.00 10.00
IIRRD Rafael Devers 10.00 25.00
IIRSS Stephen Strasburg 5.00 12.00
IIRTR Tim Raines 4.00 10.00
IIRTT Trea Turner 4.00 10.00
IIRVR Victor Robles 8.00 20.00
IIRYP Yasiel Puig 6.00 15.00

2018 Topps Kris Bryant Highlights

INSERTED IN WALMART PACKS
*BLUE: .5X TO 1.2X BASIC
*BLACK: .6X TO 1.5X BASIC
*GOLD/50: 5X TO 12X BASIC
KB1 Kris Bryant .50 1.25
KB2 Kris Bryant .50 1.25
KB3 Kris Bryant .50 1.25
KB4 Kris Bryant .50 1.25
KB5 Kris Bryant .50 1.25
KB6 Kris Bryant .50 1.25
KB7 Kris Bryant .50 1.25
KB8 Kris Bryant .50 1.25
KB9 Kris Bryant .50 1.25
KB10 Kris Bryant .50 1.25
KB11 Kris Bryant .50 1.25
KB12 Kris Bryant .50 1.25
KB13 Kris Bryant .50 1.25
KB14 Kris Bryant .50 1.25
KB15 Kris Bryant .50 1.25
KB16 Kris Bryant .50 1.25
KB17 Kris Bryant .50 1.25
KB18 Kris Bryant .50 1.25
KB19 Kris Bryant .50 1.25
KB20 Kris Bryant .50 1.25
KB21 Kris Bryant .50 1.25
KB22 Kris Bryant .50 1.25
KB23 Kris Bryant .50 1.25
KB24 Kris Bryant .50 1.25
KB25 Kris Bryant .50 1.25
KB26 Kris Bryant .50 1.25
KB27 Kris Bryant .50 1.25
KB28 Kris Bryant .50 1.25
KB29 Kris Bryant .50 1.25
KB30 Kris Bryant .50 1.25

2018 Topps Legends in the Making

COMPLETE SET (30) 15.00 40.00
STATED ODDS 1:4 BLASTER
*BLUE: .6X TO 1.5X BASIC
*BLACK: 1.2X TO 3X BASIC
*GOLD/50: 2.5X TO 6X BASIC
LTMAB Andrew Benintendi .40 1.00
LTMAJ Aaron Judge 1.00 2.50
LTMAM Andrew McCutchen .40 1.00
LTMAR Anthony Rizzo .50 1.25
LTMBH Bryce Harper .60 1.50
LTMBP Buster Posey .50 1.25
LTMCB Cody Bellinger .75 2.00
LTMCC Carlos Correa .40 1.00
LTMCE Corey Seager .40 1.00
LTMCS Chris Sale .40 1.00
LTMFF Freddie Freeman .50 1.25
LTMFL Francisco Lindor .40 1.00
LTMGS Giancarlo Stanton .40 1.00
LTMJA Jose Altuve .30 .75
LTMJD Josh Donaldson .30 .75
LTMJV Joey Votto .40 1.00
LTMKB Kris Bryant .50 1.25
LTMMB Mookie Betts .75 2.00
LTMMC Miguel Cabrera .40 1.00
LTMMM Manny Machado .40 1.00
LTMMS Miguel Sano .30 .75
LTMMT Mike Trout 2.00 5.00
LTMNA Nolan Arenado .60 1.50
LTMNS Noah Syndergaard .30 .75
LTMPG Paul Goldschmidt .40 1.00
LTMRC Robinson Cano .30 .75
LTMWM Wil Myers .30 .75
LTMYD Yu Darvish .40 1.00
LTMYM Yadier Molina .50 1.25
LTMYO Yoan Moncada .40 1.00

2018 Topps Legends in the Making Series 2

INSERTED IN RETAIL PACKS
*BLUE: .5X TO 1.2X BASIC
*BLACK: .75X TO 2X BASIC
*GOLD/50: 4X TO 10X BASIC
LITM1 Rafael Devers .75 2.00
LITM2 Shohei Ohtani 6.00 15.00
LITM3 Byron Buxton .40 1.00
LITM4 Ozzie Albies .75 2.00
LITM5 Kyle Schwarber .40 1.00
LITM6 Addison Russell .30 .75
LITM7 Javier Baez .50 1.25
LITM8 Jose Abreu .40 1.00
LITM9 Charlie Blackmon .40 1.00
LITM10 George Springer .30 .75
LITM11 Alex Bregman .40 1.00
LITM12 Marcell Ozuna .40 1.00
LITM13 Clayton Kershaw .60 1.50
LITM14 Christian Yelich .50 1.25
LITM15 Michael Conforto .30 .75
LITM16 Jacob deGrom .75 2.00
LITM17 Gary Sanchez .40 1.00
LITM18 Luis Severino .30 .75
LITM19 Giancarlo Stanton .40 1.00
LITM20 Rhys Hoskins 1.00 2.50
LITM21 Trea Turner .30 .75
LITM22 Victor Robles .60 1.50
LITM23 Amed Rosario .30 .75
LITM24 Justin Verlander .40 1.00
LITM25 Felix Hernandez .30 .75
LITM26 Corey Kluber .30 .75
LITM27 Adrian Beltre .40 1.00
LITM28 Max Scherzer .40 1.00
LITM29 Albert Pujols .50 1.25
LITM30 Stephen Strasburg .40 1.00

2018 Topps Longball Legends

STATED ODDS 1:8 HOBBY
*BLUE: 1.2X TO 3X BASIC
*BLACK/299: 1.5X TO 4X BASIC
*GOLD/50: 4X TO 10X BASIC
LL1 Aaron Judge 1.00 2.50
LL2 Giancarlo Stanton .40 1.00
LL3 Babe Ruth 1.00 2.50
LL4 Willson Contreras .40 1.00
LL5 Ted Williams .75 2.00
LL6 Darryl Strawberry .25 .60
LL7 Mark McGwire .60 1.50
LL8 Jose Canseco .30 .75
LL9 Mike Piazza .40 1.00
LL10 Cecil Fielder .25 .60
LL11 Jim Thome .30 .75
LL12 Willie Stargell .30 .75
LL13 Reggie Jackson .30 .75
LL14 Joey Gallo .30 .75
LL15 Gary Sanchez .40 1.00
LL16 Charlie Blackmon .40 1.00
LL17 Paul Goldschmidt .40 1.00
LL18 Mark McGwire .60 1.50
LL19 Josh Donaldson .30 .75
LL20 Kris Bryant .50 1.25
LL21 Mike Trout 2.00 5.00
LL22 Harmon Killebrew .40 1.00
LL23 Roberto Clemente 1.00 2.50
LL24 Alex Rodriguez .50 1.25
LL25 Joey Votto .40 1.00
LL26 Anthony Rizzo .50 1.25
LL27 Bryce Harper .60 1.50
LL28 Manny Machado .40 1.00
LL29 Nelson Cruz .40 1.00
LL30 Joc Pederson .30 .75
LL31 Nomar Mazara .25 .60
LL32 Jon Gray .25 .60
LL33 Kyle Schwarber .40 1.00
LL34 Noah Syndergaard .30 .75
LL35 Aaron Judge 1.00 2.50
LL36 Matt Olson .40 1.00
LL37 Jake Lamb .30 .75
LL38 Giancarlo Stanton .40 1.00
LL39 Khris Davis .40 1.00
LL40 David Ortiz .40 1.00
LL41 Hank Aaron .75 2.00
LL42 Albert Pujols .50 1.25
LL43 Bo Jackson .40 1.00
LL44 Hank Aaron .75 2.00
LL45 Albert Pujols .50 1.25
LL46 Babe Ruth 1.00 2.50
LL47 Frank Thomas .40 1.00
LL48 Bryce Harper .60 1.50
LL49 Mike Trout 2.00 5.00
LL50 Nolan Arenado .60 1.50

2018 Topps Longball Legends Autograph Relics

STATED ODDS 1:11,091 HOBBY
STATED PRINT RUN 25 SER.#'d SETS
EXCHANGE DEADLINE 5/31/2020
LARAR Anthony Rizzo
LARBJ Bo Jackson
LARDO David Ortiz
LARDS Darryl Strawberry 40.00 100.00
LARFT Frank Thomas
LARGS Gary Sanchez
LARJC Jose Canseco
LARJG Joey Gallo
LARJL Jake Lamb
LARJP Joc Pederson 25.00 60.00
LARJR Jon Gray
LARJT Jim Thome
LARJV Joey Votto
LARKB Kris Bryant EXCH 100.00 250.00
LARKD Khris Davis
LARKS Kyle Schwarber
LARMA Manny Machado
LARMC Mark McGwire
LARMM Mark McGwire
LARMT Mike Trout
LARNS Noah Syndergaard
LARPG Paul Goldschmidt 15.00 40.00
LARRJ Reggie Jackson

2018 Topps Longball Legends Relics

STATED ODDS 1:1353 HOBBY
STATED PRINT RUN 100 SER.#'d SETS
*RED/25: .6X TO 1.5X BASIC
LLRAO Alex Rodriguez 10.00 25.00
LLRAR Anthony Rizzo 6.00 15.00
LLRBA Bryce Harper 8.00 20.00
LLRBH Bryce Harper 8.00 20.00
LLRBJ Bo Jackson 5.00 12.00
LLRCF Cecil Fielder 10.00 25.00
LLRDO David Ortiz 5.00 12.00
LLRFT Frank Thomas 8.00 20.00
LLRGA Gary Sanchez 5.00 12.00
LLRGS Giancarlo Stanton 5.00 12.00
LLRGT Giancarlo Stanton 5.00 12.00
LLRJC Jose Canseco 12.00 30.00
LLRJD Josh Donaldson 4.00 10.00
LLRJG Joey Gallo 4.00 10.00
LLRJP Joc Pederson 8.00 20.00
LLRJR Jon Gray 3.00 8.00
LLRJT Jim Thome 8.00 20.00
LLRJV Joey Votto 5.00 12.00
LLRKB Kris Bryant 10.00 25.00
LLRKS Kyle Schwarber 5.00 12.00
LLRMC Mark McGwire 8.00 20.00
LLRMG Mark McGwire 8.00 20.00
LLRMM Manny Machado 5.00 12.00
LLRMP Mike Piazza 8.00 20.00
LLRMR Mike Trout 25.00 60.00
LLRMT Mike Trout 25.00 60.00
LLRNA Nolan Arenado 8.00 20.00
LLRNS Noah Syndergaard 8.00 20.00
LLRPG Paul Goldschmidt 5.00 12.00
LLRWC Willson Contreras 5.00 12.00

2018 Topps Manufactured All Star Patches

STATED ODDS 1:1001 HOBBY
*BLACK/99: .5X TO 1.2X BASIC
*GOLD/50: .6X TO 1.5X BASIC
*RED/25: .75X TO 2X BASIC
ASPAK Al Kaline 8.00 20.00
ASPBR Brooks Robinson 6.00 15.00
ASPCF Carlton Fisk 8.00 20.00
ASPCJ Cal Ripken Jr. 10.00 25.00
ASPCR Cal Ripken Jr. 10.00 25.00
ASPDM Don Mattingly 10.00 25.00
ASPDG Dwight Gooden 8.00 20.00
ASPDK Duke Snider 8.00 20.00
ASPDM Don Mattingly 10.00 25.00
ASPDS Darryl Strawberry 8.00 20.00
ASPEM Eddie Mathews 6.00 15.00
ASPGR George Brett 12.00 30.00
ASPHA Hank Aaron 10.00 25.00
ASPHH Hank Aaron 10.00 25.00
ASPHK Harmon Killebrew 6.00 15.00
ASPJB Johnny Bench 6.00 15.00
ASPJR Jackie Robinson 8.00 20.00
ASPMM Mark McGwire 8.00 20.00
ASPOS Ozzie Smith 8.00 20.00
ASPRA Ryne Sandberg 6.00 15.00
ASPRC Rod Carew 5.00 12.00
ASPRH Rickey Henderson 8.00 20.00
ASPRJ Reggie Jackson 8.00 20.00
ASPRO Roberto Clemente 10.00 25.00
ASPRS Ryne Sandberg 6.00 15.00
ASPRY Robin Yount 6.00 15.00
ASPSK Sandy Koufax 8.00 20.00
ASPSP Satchel Paige 6.00 15.00
ASPTW Ted Williams 12.00 30.00
ASPWB Wade Boggs 6.00 15.00

2018 Topps Major League Material Autographs

SER.1 ODDS 1:5491 HOBBY
SER.2 ODDS 1:8873 HOBBY
PRINT RUNS B/WN 15-50 COPIES PER
NO PRICING ON QTY 15 OR LESS
SER.1 EXCH.DEADLINE 12/31/2019
SER.2 EXCH.DEADLINE 5/31/2020
*RED/25: .5X TO 1.2X BASIC
MLMAAI Aledmys Diaz/50
MLMAAI Anthony Rizzo S2
MLMAAN Aaron Nola/50 S2 12.00 30.00
MLMAAR Anthony Rizzo/25
MLMAAR Amed Rosario/30 S2 8.00 20.00
MLMAAW Alex Wood/50
MLMABD Brian Dozier S2
MLMABG Ben Gamel/50 8.00 20.00
MLMABH Bryce Harper S2
MLMABZ Bradley Zimmer/50 15.00 40.00
MLMACA Christian Arroyo/50
MLMACB Cody Bellinger EXCH
MLMACF Clint Frazier/50 20.00 50.00
MLMACL Charlie Blackmon/50 10.00 25.00
MLMACS Chris Sale
MLMACS Carlos Santana/30 S2 15.00 40.00
MLMACY Christian Yelich/50 S2 20.00 50.00
MLMADG Didi Gregorius/50
MLMAET Eric Thames/50
MLMAFB Franklin Barreto/50 12.00 30.00
MLMAGB Greg Bird/50 S2 8.00 20.00
MLMAGS George Springer/50
MLMAIH Ian Happ/50 20.00 50.00
MLMAJA Jose Altuve/25 20.00 50.00
MLMAJL Jake Lamb/30 S2 8.00 20.00
MLMAJO Justin Smoak/30 S2 8.00 20.00
MLMAJP Joc Pederson/30 S2 8.00 20.00
MLMAJR Jose Ramirez/30 S2 25.00 60.00
MLMAJS Jean Segura/50
MLMAJU Justin Upton S2
MLMAJV Joey Votto S2
MLMAJZ Javier Baez/50
MLMAKD Khris Davis/50 15.00 40.00
MLMAKE Kyle Seager/50
MLMAKS Kyle Schwarber S2
MLMALS Luis Severino/50
MLMAMT Mike Trout S2
MLMANS Noah Syndergaard/25
MLMAPD Paul DeJong/50 15.00 40.00
MLMARD Rafael Devers/50 20.00 50.00
MLMARG Randal Grichuk/50
MLMARH Ryon Healy/50 6.00 15.00
MLMASM Starling Marte/50 30.00 80.00
MLMATM Trey Mancini/50 20.00 50.00
MLMATP Tommy Pham/50 S2 15.00 40.00
MLMAWC Willson Contreras/50 S2 15.00 40.00
MLMAWM Whit Merrifield/50 S2

2018 Topps Major League Materials

SER.1 STATED ODDS 1:55 HOBBY
SER.2 STATED ODDS 1:68 HOBBY
*BLACK/99: .5X TO 1.2X BASIC
*GOLD/50: .6X TO 1.5X BASIC
*RED/25: .75X TO 2X BASIC
MLMAB Andrew Benintendi 5.00 12.00
MLMAB Andrew Benintendi S2 5.00 12.00
MLMAE Alex Bregman 4.00 10.00
MLMAG Adrian Gonzalez 3.00 8.00
MLMAI Anthony Rizzo S2 5.00 12.00
MLMAJ Adam Jones 3.00 8.00
MLMAJ Adam Jones S2 3.00 8.00
MLMAM Andrew McCutchen 4.00 10.00
MLMAN Aaron Nola S2 3.00 8.00
MLMAP Albert Pujols 5.00 12.00
MLMAP Albert Pujols S2 5.00 12.00
MLMAR Addison Russell 3.00 8.00
MLMAR Amed Rosario S2 3.00 8.00
MLMAU Addison Russell S2 3.00 8.00
MLMAZ Anthony Rizzo 5.00 12.00
MLMBC Brandon Crawford 3.00 8.00
MLMBH Bryce Harper 5.00 12.00
MLMBH Bryce Harper S2 5.00 12.00
MLMBP Buster Posey 5.00 12.00
MLMBP Buster Posey S2 5.00 12.00
MLMBZ Ben Zobrist 3.00 8.00
MLMCA Chris Sale 4.00 10.00
MLMCAR Chris Archer 2.50 6.00
MLMCB Cody Bellinger 5.00 12.00
MLMCB Charlie Blackmon S2 4.00 10.00
MLMCC Carlos Correa 4.00 10.00
MLMCC Carlos Correa S2 4.00 10.00
MLMCE Corey Seager S2 4.00 10.00
MLMCI Craig Kimbrel 3.00 8.00
MLMCK Clayton Kershaw 5.00 12.00
MLMCK Clayton Kershaw S2 5.00 12.00
MLMCL Charlie Blackmon 4.00 10.00
MLMCL Corey Kluber S2 3.00 8.00
MLMCM Carlos Martinez 3.00 8.00
MLMCS Corey Seager 4.00 10.00
MLMCS Carlos Santana S2 3.00 8.00
MLMCU Corey Kluber 3.00 8.00
MLMCY Christian Yelich S2 5.00 12.00
MLMDB Dellin Betances 3.00 8.00
MLMDE Dustin Pedroia 4.00 10.00
MLMDE Dustin Pedroia S2 4.00 10.00
MLMDF Dexter Fowler S2 3.00 8.00
MLMDG Didi Gregorius 3.00 8.00
MLMDG Dee Gordon S2 2.50 6.00
MLMDK Dallas Keuchel 3.00 8.00
MLMDM Daniel Murphy 3.00 8.00
MLMDP David Price 3.00 8.00
MLMDR Didi Gregorius S2 3.00 8.00
MLMDS Dansby Swanson 4.00 10.00
MLMDS Dominic Smith S2 3.00 8.00
MLMEE Edwin Encarnacion 4.00 10.00
MLMEH Eric Hosmer S2 3.00 8.00
MLMEL Evan Longoria 3.00 8.00
MLMEL Evan Longoria S2 3.00 8.00
MLMET Eric Thames 3.00 8.00
MLMFF Freddie Freeman 5.00 12.00
MLMFH Felix Hernandez S2 3.00 8.00
MLMFL Francisco Lindor S2 4.00 10.00
MLMGA Gary Sanchez 5.00 12.00
MLMGB Greg Bird S2 3.00 8.00
MLMGS George Springer 3.00 8.00
MLMGT Giancarlo Stanton 5.00 12.00
MLMHJR Hyun-Jin Ryu 3.00 8.00
MLMHP Hunter Pence S2 3.00 8.00
MLMHR Hanley Ramirez 3.00 8.00
MLMIH Ian Happ 3.00 8.00
MLMIK Ian Kinsler S2 3.00 8.00
MLMI Ichiro 5.00 12.00
MLMI Ichiro S2 5.00 12.00
MLMJA Jose Altuve 3.00 8.00
MLMJA Jose Abreu S2 4.00 10.00
MLMJB Javier Baez 5.00 12.00
MLMJD Josh Donaldson S2 3.00 8.00
MLMJE Josh Bell 3.00 8.00
MLMJE Jason Heyward S2 3.00 8.00
MLMJF Jack Flaherty S2 5.00 12.00
MLMJG Jon Gray 2.50 6.00
MLMJG Joey Gallo S2 3.00 8.00
MLMJH Jason Heyward 3.00 8.00
MLMJJ Jose Bautista 3.00 8.00
MLMJJ Jacob deGrom S2 8.00 20.00
MLMJL Justin Verlander 4.00 10.00
MLMJL Jose Altuve S2 3.00 8.00
MLMJM J.D. Martinez 4.00 10.00
MLMJM Joe Mauer S2 3.00 8.00
MLMJO Joey Votto S2 3.00 8.00
MLMJR Jackie Bradley Jr. 4.00 10.00
MLMJT Jameson Taillon 3.00 8.00
MLMJU Justin Upton 3.00 8.00
MLMJU Justin Upton S2 3.00 8.00
MLMJV Joey Votto 3.00 8.00
MLMJV Justin Verlander S2 4.00 10.00
MLMJZ Javier Baez S2 5.00 12.00
MLMKB Kris Bryant 6.00 15.00
MLMKD Khris Davis S2 3.00 8.00
MLMKE Kyle Seager 2.50 6.00
MLMKJ Kenley Jansen S2 3.00 8.00
MLMKK Kevin Kiermaier 3.00 8.00
MLMKM Kenta Maeda 3.00 8.00
MLMKS Kyle Schwarber 4.00 10.00
MLMLE Luis Severino S2 3.00 8.00
MLMLG Lucas Giolito S2 3.00 8.00
MLMLS Luis Severino 3.00 8.00
MLMLW Luke Weaver S2 3.00 8.00
MLMMA Masahiro Tanaka 3.00 8.00
MLMMA Miguel Cabrera S2 4.00 10.00
MLMMB Mookie Betts 8.00 20.00
MLMMC Miguel Cabrera 4.00 10.00
MLMMD Marcus Stroman S2 3.00 8.00
MLMMF Michael Fulmer 2.50 6.00
MLMMH Mitch Haniger S2 3.00 8.00
MLMMK Matt Kemp S2 3.00 8.00
MLMMM Manny Machado 4.00 10.00
MLMMM Manny Machado S2 4.00 10.00
MLMMN Michael Conforto 3.00 8.00
MLMMN Michael Conforto S2 3.00 8.00
MLMMO Marcell Ozuna 4.00 10.00
MLMMO Marcell Ozuna S2 4.00 10.00

MLMMOL Matt Olson 4.00 10.00
MLMMR Masahiro Tanaka S2 3.00 8.00
MLMMS Marcus Stroman 3.00 8.00
MLMMS Miguel Sano S2 3.00 8.00
MLMMT Mike Trout 10.00 25.00
MLMMT Mike Trout S2 10.00 25.00
MLMMX Max Scherzer S2 4.00 10.00
MLMNA Nolan Arenado 6.00 15.00
MLMNA Nolan Arenado S2 6.00 15.00
MLMNC Nelson Cruz 4.00 10.00
MLMNC Nicholas Castellanos S2 4.00 10.00
MLMNR Nelson Cruz S2 4.00 10.00
MLMNS Noah Syndergaard 3.00 8.00
MLMNS Noah Syndergaard S2 3.00 8.00
MLMOA Orlando Arcia 2.50 6.00
MLMPD Paul DeJong S2 4.00 10.00
MLMPG Paul Goldschmidt S2 4.00 10.00
MLMRB Ryan Braun 3.00 8.00
MLMRC Robinson Cano 3.00 8.00
MLMRC Robinson Cano S2 3.00 8.00
MLMRD Rafael Devers S2 5.00 12.00
MLMRZ Ryan Zimmerman 3.00 8.00
MLMSA Starling Marte 3.00 8.00
MLMSC Starlin Castro 2.50 6.00
MLMSG Sonny Gray S2 3.00 8.00
MLMSP Salvador Perez 3.00 8.00
MLMTB Trevor Bauer S2 5.00 12.00
MLMTP Tommy Pham 2.50 6.00
MLMTT Trea Turner 3.00 8.00
MLMTT Trea Turner S2 3.00 8.00
MLMTU Troy Tulowitzki 4.00 10.00
MLMVM Victor Martinez 3.00 8.00
MLMWC Willson Contreras 4.00 10.00
MLMWC Willson Contreras S2 4.00 10.00
MLMWM Wil Myers 3.00 8.00
MLMXB Xander Bogaerts 4.00 10.00
MLMXB Xander Bogaerts S2 4.00 10.00
MLMYC Yoenis Cespedes 4.00 10.00
MLMYC Yoenis Cespedes S2 4.00 10.00
MLMYM Yadier Molina 5.00 12.00
MLMYM Yadier Molina S2 5.00 12.00
MLMYP Yasiel Puig 4.00 10.00

2018 Topps MLB Awards

COMPLETE SET (50) 15.00 40.00
STATED ODDS 1:8
*BLUE: .75X TO 2X BASIC
*BLACK/299: 1.5X TO 4X BASIC
*GOLD/50: 4X TO 10X BASIC
MLBA1 Jose Altuve .30 .75
MLBA2 Giancarlo Stanton .40 1.00
MLBA3 Craig Kimbrel .30 .75
MLBA4 Kenley Jansen .30 .75
MLBA5 Anthony Rizzo .50 1.25
MLBA6 Mike Moustakas .30 .75
MLBA7 Ryan Zimmerman .30 .75
MLBA8 Aaron Judge 1.00 2.50
MLBA9 Cody Bellinger .75 2.00
MLBA10 Corey Kluber .30 .75
MLBA11 Max Scherzer .40 1.00
MLBA12 Jose Altuve .30 .75
MLBA13 Giancarlo Stanton .40 1.00
MLBA14 Martin Maldonado .25 .60
MLBA15 Tucker Barnhart .25 .60
MLBA16 Eric Hosmer .30 .75
MLBA17 Paul Goldschmidt .40 1.00
MLBA18 Brian Dozier .30 .75
MLBA19 DJ LeMahieu .40 1.00
MLBA20 Andrelton Simmons .25 .60
MLBA21 Brandon Crawford .30 .75
MLBA22 Evan Longoria .30 .75
MLBA23 Nolan Arenado .60 1.50
MLBA24 Alex Gordon .30 .75
MLBA25 Marcell Ozuna .40 1.00
MLBA26 Byron Buxton .40 1.00
MLBA27 Ender Inciarte .25 .60
MLBA28 Mookie Betts .75 2.00
MLBA29 Jason Heyward .30 .75
MLBA30 Marcus Stroman .30 .75
MLBA31 Zack Greinke .40 1.00
MLBA32 Buster Posey .50 1.25
MLBA33 Gary Sanchez .40 1.00
MLBA34 Eric Hosmer .30 .75
MLBA35 Paul Goldschmidt .40 1.00
MLBA36 Daniel Murphy .30 .75
MLBA37 Jose Altuve .30 .75
MLBA38 Corey Seager .40 1.00
MLBA39 Francisco Lindor .40 1.00
MLBA40 George Springer .30 .75
MLBA41 Justin Upton .30 .75
MLBA42 Aaron Judge 1.00 2.50
MLBA43 Marcell Ozuna .40 1.00
MLBA44 Giancarlo Stanton .40 1.00
MLBA45 Charlie Blackmon .40 1.00
MLBA46 Nolan Arenado .60 1.50
MLBA47 Jose Ramirez .30 .75
MLBA48 Adam Wainwright .30 .75
MLBA49 Nelson Cruz .40 1.00
MLBA50 George Springer .30 .75

2018 Topps Opening Day Insert

COMPLETE SET (30) 15.00 40.00
STATED ODDS 1:2 BLASTER
*BLUE: .75X TO 2X BASIC
*BLACK: 1X TO 2.5X BASIC
*GOLD/50: 3X TO 8X BASIC
OD1 Robinson Cano .30 .75
OD2 Adrian Beltre .40 1.00
OD3 Carlos Correa .40 1.00
OD4 Miguel Sano .30 .75
OD5 Cody Bellinger .75 2.00
OD6 Salvador Perez .30 .75
OD7 Wil Myers .30 .75
OD8 Mike Trout 2.00 5.00
OD9 Noah Syndergaard .30 .75
OD10 Yadier Molina .50 1.25
OD11 Giancarlo Stanton .40 1.00
OD12 Freddie Freeman .50 1.25
OD13 Buster Posey .50 1.25
OD14 Francisco Lindor .40 1.00
OD15 Andrew McCutchen .40 1.00
OD16 Miguel Cabrera .40 1.00
OD17 Kris Bryant .50 1.25
OD18 Josh Donaldson .30 .75
OD19 Nolan Arenado .60 1.50
OD20 Joey Votto .40 1.00
OD21 Evan Longoria .30 .75
OD22 Aaron Judge 1.00 2.50
OD23 Aaron Nola .30 .75
OD24 Khris Davis .40 1.00
OD25 Bryce Harper .60 1.50
OD26 Yoan Moncada .40 1.00
OD27 Andrew Benintendi .40 1.00
OD28 Eric Thames .30 .75
OD29 Manny Machado .40 1.00
OD30 Paul Goldschmidt .40 1.00

2018 Topps Players Weekend Patches

STATED ODDS 1:1 BLASTER
*BLUE/99: .5X TO 1.2X BASIC
*GOLD/50: .75X TO 2X BASIC
*RED/25: 1X TO 2.5X BASIC
PWPABL Adrian Beltre 2.00 5.00
PWPABN Andrew Benintendi 2.00 5.00
PWPAJO Adam Jones 1.50 4.00
PWPAJU Aaron Judge 5.00 12.00
PWPAM Andrew McCutchen 2.00 5.00
PWPAP Albert Pujols 2.50 6.00
PWPAR Amed Rosario 1.50 4.00
PWPARI Anthony Rizzo 2.50 6.00
PWPBB Byron Buxton 2.00 5.00
PWPBP Buster Posey 2.50 6.00
PWPCL Charlie Blackmon 2.00 5.00
PWPCSE Corey Seager 2.00 5.00
PWPDM Daniel Murphy 1.50 4.00
PWPEH Eric Hosmer 1.50 4.00
PWPEL Evan Longoria 1.50 4.00
PWPET Eric Thames 1.50 4.00
PWPFF Freddie Freeman 2.50 6.00
PWPFL Francisco Lindor 2.00 5.00
PWPGSA Gary Sanchez 2.00 5.00
PWPGSP George Springer 1.50 4.00
PWPGST Giancarlo Stanton 2.00 5.00
PWPI Ichiro 2.50 6.00
PWPJA Jose Altuve 1.50 4.00
PWPJB Jose Bautista 1.50 4.00
PWPJD Josh Donaldson 1.50 4.00
PWPJG Jacob deGrom 4.00 10.00
PWPJR Jose Abreu 2.00 5.00
PWPJVO Joey Votto 2.00 5.00
PWPJZ Javier Baez 2.50 6.00
PWPKB Kris Bryant 2.50 6.00
PWPKC Kyle Schwarber 2.00 5.00
PWPKD Khris Davis 2.00 5.00
PWPKS Kyle Seager 1.25 3.00
PWPMA Masahiro Tanaka 1.50 4.00
PWPMB Mookie Betts 4.00 10.00
PWPMCB Miguel Cabrera 2.00 5.00
PWPMK Matt Kemp 1.50 4.00
PWPMM Manny Machado 2.00 5.00
PWPMT Mike Trout 10.00 25.00
PWPNA Nolan Arenado 3.00 8.00
PWPNC Nelson Cruz 2.00 5.00
PWPPG Paul Goldschmidt 2.00 5.00
PWPRC Robinson Cano 1.50 4.00
PWPRD Rafael Devers 4.00 10.00
PWPRH Rhys Hoskins 6.00 15.00
PWPSP Salvador Perez 1.50 4.00
PWPWM Wil Myers 1.50 4.00
PWPYD Yu Darvish 2.00 5.00
PWPYML Yadier Molina 2.50 6.00
PWPYP Yasiel Puig 2.00 5.00

2018 Topps Postseason Performance Autograph Relics

STATED ODDS 1:12024 HOBBY
PRINT RUNS B/WN 35-50 COPIES PER
EXCHANGE DEADLINE 12/31/2019
*RED/25: X TO X BASIC
PSARAB Andrew Benintendi EXCH 75.00 200.00
PSARAR Anthony Rizzo
PSARCB Cody Bellinger EXCH 50.00 120.00
PSARCC Carlos Correa
PSARDG Didi Gregorius
PSARGB Greg Bird/40
PSARGS Gary Sanchez/50 60.00 150.00
PSARJA Jose Altuve/35
PSARJB Javier Baez/50 30.00 80.00
PSARJM J.D. Martinez
PSARJR Jay Bruce/50
PSARLS Luis Severino/50 15.00 40.00
PSARPG Paul Goldschmidt/50 20.00 50.00
PSARRD Rafael Devers/50 75.00 200.00
PSARWC Willson Contreras EXCH 20.00 50.00

2018 Topps Postseason Performance Autographs

STATED ODDS 1:10231 HOBBY
STATED PRINT RUN 50 SER.#'d SETS
EXCHANGE DEADLINE 12/31/2019
*RED/25: .6X TO 1.5X BASIC
PSPACB Cody Bellinger EXCH 50.00 120.00
PSPADG Didi Gregorius
PSPAGB Greg Bird 15.00 40.00
PSPAGS Gary Sanchez
PSPAJB Javier Baez 30.00 80.00
PSPAJL Jake Lamb 15.00 40.00
PSPAJR Jay Bruce 25.00 60.00
PSPAKB Kris Bryant
PSPAPG Paul Goldschmidt
PSPARD Rafael Devers 75.00 200.00

2018 Topps Postseason Performance Relics

STATED ODDS 1:2723 HOBBY
STATED PRINT RUN 100 SER.#'d SETS
*RED/25: .6X TO 1.5X BASIC
PSPAB Andrew Benintendi 12.00 30.00
PSPAC Aroldis Chapman 10.00 25.00
PSPAI Anthony Rizzo 10.00 25.00
PSPAR Addison Russell 6.00 15.00
PSPBH Bryce Harper 8.00 20.00
PSPCC Carlos Correa 8.00 20.00
PSPCK Clayton Kershaw 10.00 25.00
PSPCS Corey Seager 8.00 20.00
PSPDG Didi Gregorius
PSPDK Dallas Keuchel 10.00 25.00
PSPDM Daniel Murphy 6.00 15.00
PSPGS Gary Sanchez 10.00 25.00
PSPJA Jose Altuve 12.00 30.00
PSPJB Javier Baez 10.00 25.00
PSPJM J.D. Martinez
PSPJT Justin Turner 8.00 20.00
PSPJV Justin Verlander 8.00 20.00
PSPKB Kris Bryant 12.00 30.00
PSPLS Luis Severino
PSPMB Mookie Betts 15.00 40.00
PSPMT Masahiro Tanaka 6.00 15.00
PSPPG Paul Goldschmidt 6.00 15.00
PSPRD Rafael Devers 12.00 30.00
PSPTB Trevor Bauer 10.00 25.00
PSPWC Willson Contreras 8.00 20.00
PSPYD Yu Darvish 8.00 20.00
PSPYP Yasiel Puig 6.00 15.00

2018 Topps Salute

COMPLETE SET (100) 50.00 120.00
STATED ODDS 1:4 HOBBY
*BLUE: 1.2X TO 3X BASIC
*BLACK/299: 1.5X TO 4X BASIC
*GOLD/50: 4X TO 10X BASIC
TS1 Bryce Harper .60 1.50
TS2 Carlos Correa .40 1.00
TS3 Joey Votto .40 1.00
TS4 Corey Seager .40 1.00
TS5 Adam Jones .30 .75
TS6 Chris Sale .40 1.00
TS7 Jose Altuve .30 .75
TS8 Dexter Fowler .30 .75
TS9 George Springer .30 .75
TS10 Charlie Blackmon .40 1.00
TS11 Khris Davis .40 1.00
TS12 Trevor Story .40 1.00
TS13 Alex Wood .25 .60
TS14 Domingo Santana .30 .75
TS15 Anthony Rizzo .50 1.25
TS16 Paul Goldschmidt .40 1.00
TS17 Francisco Lindor .40 1.00
TS18 Javier Baez .50 1.25
TS19 Aaron Judge 1.00 2.50
TS20 Ryon Healy .25 .60
TS21 Trey Mancini .30 .75
TS22 Ben Gamel .30 .75
TS23 Mitch Haniger .30 .75
TS24 Matt Carpenter .40 1.00
TS25 Cody Bellinger .75 2.00
TS26 Cal Ripken Jr. 1.25 3.00
TS27 Don Mattingly .75 2.00
TS28 Frank Thomas .40 1.00
TS29 Barry Larkin .30 .75
TS30 John Smoltz .40 1.00
TS31 Brooks Robinson .30 .75
TS32 Craig Biggio .30 .75
TS33 Jim Palmer .30 .75
TS34 Roy Halladay .30 .75
TS35 Ivan Rodriguez .30 .75
TS36 Roberto Alomar .30 .75
TS37 Darryl Strawberry .25 .60
TS38 Johnny Damon .30 .75
TS39 Andres Galarraga .30 .75
TS40 Eric Davis .25 .60
TS41 George Brett .75 2.00
TS42 Willie McCovey .30 .75
TS43 Andre Dawson .30 .75
TS44 Tom Seaver .30 .75
TS45 Jose Canseco .30 .75
TS46 Nolan Arenado .60 1.50
TS47 Kris Bryant .50 1.25
TS48 Miguel Sano .30 .75
TS49 Eric Thames .30 .75
TS50 Kyle Seager .25 .60
TS51 Michael Fulmer .25 .60
TS52 Joe Panik .30 .75
TS53 Jean Segura .25 .60
TS54 Aledmys Diaz .30 .75
TS55 Kevin Kiermaier .30 .75
TS56 Keon Broxton .25 .60
TS57 Bradley Zimmer .25 .60
TS58 Christian Arroyo .25 .60
TS59 Mike Trout 2.00 5.00
TS60 Daniel Murphy .30 .75
TS61 Alex Bregman .40 1.00
TS62 Andrew Benintendi .40 1.00
TS63 Luis Severino .30 .75
TS64 Didi Gregorius .40 1.00
TS65 Dellin Betances .30 .75
TS66 Hunter Renfroe .25 .60
TS67 Jose Berrios .30 .75
TS68 Ken Giles .25 .60
TS69 Dansby Swanson .40 1.00
TS70 Ian Happ .30 .75
TS71 Rafael Devers .75 2.00
TS72 Amed Rosario .30 .75
TS73 Nick Williams .30 .75
TS74 Ozzie Albies .75 2.00
TS75 Clint Frazier .50 1.25
TS76 J.P. Crawford .25 .60
TS77 Dominic Smith .30 .75
TS78 Rhys Hoskins 1.00 2.50
TS79 Ryan McMahon .60 1.50
TS80 Alex Verdugo .40 1.00
TS81 Willie Calhoun .40 1.00
TS82 Victor Robles .60 1.50
TS83 Walker Buehler 1.25 3.00
TS84 Luiz Gohara .25 .60
TS85 Francisco Mejia .30 .75
TS86 Jack Flaherty 1.00 2.50
TS87 Tyler Mahle .30 .75
TS88 J.D. Davis .30 .75
TS89 Lucas Sims .25 .60
TS90 Max Fried 1.00 2.50
TS91 Brandon Woodruff .75 2.00
TS92 Nicky Delmonico .25 .60
TS93 Harrison Bader .40 1.00
TS94 Miguel Andujar 1.00 2.50
TS95 Parker Bridwell .25 .60
TS96 Zack Granite .25 .60
TS97 Andrew Stevenson .25 .60
TS98 Austin Hays .40 1.00
TS99 Chance Sisco .30 .75
TS100 Sandy Alcantara .25 .60

2018 Topps Salute Autographs

SER.1 ODDS 1:1100 HOBBY
SER.2 ODDS 1:1215 HOBBY
UPD ODDS 1:699 HOBBY
SER.1 EXCH.DEADLINE 12/31/2019
SER.2 EXCH.DEADLINE 5/31/2020
UPD EXCH.DEADLINE 9/30/2020
*RED/25: .75X TO 2X BASIC
SAAA Aaron Altherr S2 15.00 40.00
SAAB Alex Bregman S2 15.00 40.00
SAAC Austin Barnes S2 3.00 8.00
SAAD Adam Duvall S2 3.00 8.00
SAADA Andre Dawson
SAADI Aledmys Diaz 3.00 8.00
SAAE Alex Bregman S2 15.00 40.00
SAAE Austin Meadows UPD 5.00 12.00
SAAG Andres Galarraga 3.00 8.00
SAAH Austin Hays 15.00 40.00
SAAH Austin Hays S2 10.00 25.00
SAAI Anthony Rizzo S2
SAAJ Alex Mejia S2 15.00 40.00
SAAJ Aaron Judge UPD
SAAJO Adam Jones
SAAM Andrew McCutchen UPD 20.00 50.00
SAAN Aaron Nola S2
SAAR Amed Rosario S2 8.00 20.00
SAAR Alex Rodriguez UPD
SAARI Anthony Rizzo
SAARO Amed Rosario 20.00 50.00
SAAS Andrew Stevenson 8.00 20.00
SAAS Anthony Santander S2 2.50 6.00
SAAV Alex Verdugo 5.00 12.00
SAAW Alex Wood 4.00 10.00
SABG Ben Gamel 3.00 8.00
SABG Ben Gamel S2 3.00 8.00
SABJ Bo Jackson UPD 40.00 100.00
SABL Barry Larkin
SABP Brett Phillips S2 2.50 6.00
SABRO Brooks Robinson
SABW Brandon Woodruff 6.00 15.00
SABZ Bradley Zimmer 10.00 25.00
SABZ Bradley Zimmer S2 8.00 20.00
SACAR Christian Arroyo 2.50 6.00
SACBE Cody Bellinger EXCH
SACBI Craig Biggio
SACBL Charlie Blackmon 8.00 20.00
SACC Carlos Correa
SACC Carlos Carrasco S2
SACF Clint Frazier 20.00 50.00
SACF Clint Frazier S2 15.00 40.00
SACJ Chipper Jones
SACJ Chipper Jones S2
SACK Corey Kluber S2
SACR Cal Ripken Jr. 100.00 250.00
SACR Clint Frazier S2 15.00 40.00
SACR Cal Ripken Jr. UPD 75.00 200.00
SACS Chance Sisco S2 6.00 15.00
SACSA Chris Sale 15.00 40.00
SACSI Chance Sisco 15.00 40.00
SACT Chris Taylor S2 8.00 20.00
SACV Christian Villanueva S2 10.00 25.00
SACV Christian Villanueva UPD 2.50 6.00
SADB Dellin Betances 6.00 15.00
SADB Don Mattingly S2
SADFO Dexter Fowler 20.00 50.00
SADG Didi Gregorius 15.00 40.00
SADG Dwight Gooden UPD 20.00 50.00
SADM Dillon Maples S2 4.00 10.00
SADMA Don Mattingly
SADO David Ortiz
SADR Didi Gregorius UPD 8.00 20.00
SADS Domingo Santana S2 3.00 8.00
SADSA Domingo Santana 6.00 15.00
SADSM Dominic Smith 3.00 8.00
SADST Darryl Strawberry 30.00 80.00
SADSW Dansby Swanson 25.00 60.00
SAED Eric Davis 10.00 25.00
SAEE Edwin Encarnacion S2
SAEH Eric Thames S2 6.00 15.00
SAER Eddie Rosario S2 4.00 10.00
SAET Eric Thames 3.00 8.00
SAET Eric Thames S2 6.00 15.00
SAFB Franklin Barreto S2
SAFI Francisco Lindor S2
SAFL Francisco Lindor S2
SAFL Francisco Lindor UPD 15.00 40.00
SAFM Francisco Mejia 15.00 40.00
SAFM Francisco Mejia S2 6.00 15.00
SAFN Francisco Lindor S2
SAFP Freddy Peralta UPD 2.50 6.00
SAFR Franmil Reyes UPD 6.00 15.00
SAFT Frank Thomas
SAGS George Springer UPD 8.00 20.00
SAGT Gleyber Torres UPD 40.00 100.00
SAHB Harrison Bader 4.00 10.00
SAHR Hunter Renfroe 6.00 15.00
SAHR Hunter Renfroe S2 2.50 6.00
SAIH Ian Happ 3.00 8.00
SAIK Isiah Kiner-Falefa UPD 4.00 10.00
SAIR Ivan Rodriguez
SAJB Jaime Barria UPD 5.00 12.00
SAJB Jose Abreu S2
SAJB Jose Berrios
SAJBR Jose Berrios S2 10.00 25.00
SAJBZ Javier Baez 20.00 50.00
SAJC J.P. Crawford S2 6.00 15.00
SAJC Johan Camargo UPD 10.00 25.00
SAJCA Jose Canseco 8.00 20.00
SAJCR J.P. Crawford 10.00 25.00
SAJD J.D. Davis 3.00 8.00
SAJDA Johnny Damon 12.00 30.00
SAJE Jean Segura S2 2.50 6.00
SAJF Jack Flaherty S2 10.00 25.00
SAJF Jack Flaherty UPD 10.00 25.00
SAJH Josh Hader S2 6.00 15.00
SAJI Josh Harrison S2 20.00 50.00
SAJL Jack Flaherty 10.00 25.00
SAJL Jose Altuve S2
SAJM Joe Morgan UPD
SAJO Josh Harrison S2 20.00 50.00
SAJPL Jim Palmer 25.00 60.00
SAJPN Joe Panik 3.00 8.00
SAJR Jose Ramirez S2 12.00 30.00
SAJS Juan Soto UPD 75.00 200.00
SAJSE Jean Segura 5.00 12.00
SAJSM John Smoltz
SAJT Jim Thome S2
SAJTH Jim Thome
SAJV Joey Votto
SAKB Keon Broxton S2 2.50 6.00
SAKBO Keon Broxton 2.50 6.00
SAKBR Kris Bryant EXCH
SAKD Khris Davis 8.00 20.00
SAKD Khris Davis S2 4.00 10.00
SAKF Kyle Farmer S2 5.00 12.00
SAKM Kenny Mella S2 2.50 6.00
SAKP Kevin Pillar S2
SAKR Keon Broxton S2 2.50 6.00
SAKS Kyle Seager 6.00 15.00
SALG Lourdes Gurriel Jr. UPD 5.00 12.00
SALI Lucas Sims 5.00 12.00
SALS Luis Severino
SAMA Miguel Andujar 40.00 100.00
SAMA Manny Machado S2
SAMC Matt Carpenter
SAMC Mike Clevinger S2 3.00 8.00
SAMF Michael Fulmer 12.00 30.00
SAMH Mitch Haniger 3.00 8.00
SAMH Matt Chapman S2 4.00 10.00
SAMM Manny Machado S2
SAMM Miles Mikolas UPD 6.00 15.00
SAMMU Max Muncy UPD 10.00 25.00
SAMN Manny Margot S2
SAMR Max Fried 10.00 25.00
SAMR Mariano Rivera UPD
SAMT Mike Trout 250.00 500.00
SAMT Mike Trout UPD
SANC Nicholas Castellanos S2 10.00 25.00
SAND Nicky Delmonico 6.00 15.00
SANK Nick Kingham UPD 6.00 15.00
SAOA Ozzie Albies 15.00 40.00
SAOL Ozzie Albies S2 25.00 60.00
SAOS Ozzie Smith S2
SAOV Omar Vizquel 25.00 60.00
SAPB Parker Bridwell 2.50 6.00
SAPd Paul DeJong S2 4.00 10.00
SAPG Paul Goldschmidt 20.00 50.00
SAPM Pedro Martinez UPD
SARA Roberto Alomar
SARA Ronald Acuna Jr. UPD 150.00 400.00
SARB Ryan Braun S2
SARC Rod Carew EXCH
SARD Rafael Devers 30.00 80.00
SARD Rafael Devers S2
SARH Rhys Hoskins S2 50.00 120.00
SARH Rhys Hoskins UPD 15.00 40.00
SARHE Ryon Healy 4.00 10.00
SARHO Rhys Hoskins 75.00 200.00
SARJ Ryder Jones S2 4.00 10.00
SARM Ryan McMahon 6.00 15.00
SARO Randy Johnson UPD
SASA Sandy Alcantara 2.50 6.00
SASA Sandy Alcantara S2 2.50 6.00
SASK Scott Kingery UPD 4.00 10.00
SASO Shohei Ohtani UPD 150.00 400.00
SASO Shohei Ohtani S2 125.00 300.00
SATB Tyler Beede UPD 2.50 6.00
SATH Tyler Mahle 8.00 20.00
SATH Torii Hunter UPD 8.00 20.00
SATH Tommy Pham S2 10.00 25.00
SATM Trey Mancini 15.00 40.00
SATM Trey Mancini S2 6.00 15.00
SATP Tommy Pham S2 10.00 25.00
SATR Tim Raines UPD 10.00 25.00
SATS Travis Shaw S2 6.00 15.00
SATW Travis Shaw S2 6.00 15.00
SAVA Victor Arano S2 4.00 10.00
SAVR Victor Robles 30.00 80.00
SAVR Victor Robles S2 15.00 40.00
SAWB Walker Buehler S2 12.00 30.00
SAWC Willie Calhoun 8.00 20.00
SAWM Whit Merrifield S2 4.00 10.00
SAYM Yoan Moncada S2
SAZG Zack Granite 2.50 6.00
SAZG Zack Granite S2 3.00 8.00

2018 Topps Salute Series 2

STATED ODDS 1:4 HOBBY
*BLUE: 1.2X TO 3X BASIC
*BLACK/299: 1.5X TO 4X BASIC
*GOLD/50: 4X TO 10X BASIC
S1 Bryce Harper .60 1.50
S2 Francisco Lindor .40 1.00
S3 Tommy Pham .25 .60
S4 Trey Mancini .30 .75
S5 Manny Machado .40 1.00
S6 Eric Thames .30 .75
S7 Nolan Arenado .60 1.50
S8 Clint Frazier .50 1.25
S9 Franklin Barreto .25 .60
S10 Khris Davis .40 1.00
S11 Miguel Cabrera .40 1.00
S12 Edwin Encarnacion .40 1.00
S13 Josh Harrison .25 .60
S14 Jose Altuve .30 .75
S15 Manny Machado .40 1.00
S16 Alex Bregman .40 1.00
S17 Jose Altuve .30 .75
S18 Travis Shaw .25 .60
S19 Orlando Arcia .25 .60
S20 Adam Duvall .30 .75
S21 Mike Clevinger .30 .75
S22 Francisco Lindor .40 1.00
S23 Jose Ramirez .30 .75
S24 Edwin Encarnacion .40 1.00
S25 Chris Archer .25 .60
S26 Corey Kluber .30 .75
S27 Francisco Lindor .40 1.00
S28 Yoan Moncada .40 1.00
S29 Jose Abreu .40 1.00
S30 Nick Williams .30 .75
S31 Keon Broxton .25 .60
S32 Eric Thames .30 .75
S33 Aaron Nola .30 .75
S34 Travis Shaw .25 .60
S35 Ryan Braun .30 .75
S36 Domingo Santana .25 .60
S37 Carlos Carrasco .25 .60
S38 Nicholas Castellanos .40 1.00
S39 Nick Williams .30 .75
S40 Elvis Andrus .30 .75
S41 Robinson Cano .30 .75
S42 Josh Reddick .25 .60
S43 Lance McCullers .25 .60
S44 Ben Gamel .30 .75
S45 Alex Bregman .40 1.00
S46 Jean Segura .30 .75
S47 Hunter Renfroe .25 .60
S48 Wil Myers .30 .75
S49 Anthony Rizzo .50 1.25
S50 Addison Russell .30 .75
S51 Josh Bell .30 .75
S52 Josh Harrison .25 .60
S53 Andrew McCutchen .40 1.00
S54 Shohei Ohtani 5.00 12.00
S55 Dillon Maples .25 .60
S56 Rafael Devers .75 2.00
S57 Amed Rosario .30 .75
S58 Clint Frazier .50 1.25
S59 Willie Calhoun .40 1.00
S60 Ozzie Albies .75 2.00
S61 Rhys Hoskins 1.00 2.50
S62 J.P. Crawford .25 .60
S63 Francisco Mejia .30 .75
S64 Jack Flaherty 1.00 2.50
S65 Austin Hays .40 1.00
S66 Sandy Alcantara .25 .60
S67 Christian Villanueva .25 .60
S68 Kyle Farmer .25 .60
S69 Tim Locastro .25 .60
S70 Bob Gibson .30 .75
S71 Chipper Jones .40 1.00
S72 Jim Thome .30 .75
S73 Roberto Clemente 1.00 2.50
S74 Ted Williams .75 2.00
S75 Ernie Banks .40 1.00
S76 Wade Boggs .30 .75
S77 Reggie Jackson .30 .75
S78 Derek Jeter 1.00 2.50
S79 Nolan Ryan 1.25 3.00
S80 Rickey Henderson .40 1.00
S81 Ozzie Smith .50 1.25
S82 Mariano Rivera .50 1.25
S83 Sandy Koufax .75 2.00
S84 Jackie Robinson .40 1.00
S85 Hank Aaron .75 2.00
S86 Aaron Judge 1.00 2.50
S87 Billy Hamilton .30 .75
S88 Jackie Bradley Jr. .40 1.00
S89 Manny Margot .25 .60
S90 Javier Baez .50 1.25
S91 Addison Russell .30 .75
S92 Byron Buxton .40 1.00
S93 Kevin Kiermaier .30 .75
S94 Nolan Arenado .60 1.50
S95 Yasiel Puig .40 1.00
S96 Kevin Pillar .25 .60
S98 Chris Taylor .30 .75
S99 Tommy Pham .25 .60
S100 Justin Turner .40 1.00

2018 Topps Spring Training Logo Patches

STATED ODDS 1:832 HOBBY
*BLUE/99: .5X TO 1.2X BASIC
*GOLD/50: .75X TO 2X BASIC
*RED/25: 1X TO 2.5X BASIC
STPAB Andrew Benintendi
STPABE Adrian Beltre 2.50 6.00
STPAJ Aaron Judge 6.00 15.00
STPAM Andrew McCutchen 2.50 6.00
STPAN Aaron Nola 2.00 5.00
STPBH Bryce Harper 4.00 10.00
STPBP Buster Posey 3.00 8.00
STPCB Cody Bellinger 5.00 12.00
STPCC Carlos Correa 2.50 6.00
STPEL Evan Longoria 2.00 5.00
STPET Eric Thames 2.00 5.00
STPFF Freddie Freeman 3.00 8.00
STPFL Francisco Lindor 2.50 6.00
STPGS Giancarlo Stanton 2.50 6.00
STPJD Josh Donaldson 2.00 5.00
STPJV Joey Votto 2.50 6.00
STPKB Kris Bryant 3.00 8.00
STPKD Khris Davis 2.50 6.00
STPMCB Miguel Cabrera 2.50 6.00
STPMM Manny Machado 2.50 6.00
STPMS Miguel Sano 2.00 5.00
STPMT Mike Trout 12.00 30.00
STPNA Nolan Arenado 4.00 10.00
STPNS Noah Syndergaard 2.00 5.00
STPPG Paul Goldschmidt 2.50 6.00
STPRC Robinson Cano 2.00 5.00
STPSP Salvador Perez 2.00 5.00
STPWM Wil Myers 2.00 5.00
STPYML Yadier Molina 3.00 8.00
STPYM Yoan Moncada 2.50 6.00

2018 Topps Superstar Sensations

COMPLETE SET (50) 15.00 40.00
STATED ODDS 1:8
*BLUE: 1.2X TO 3X BASIC
*BLACK/299: 1.5X TO 4X BASIC
*GOLD/50: 3X TO 8X BASIC
SSS1 Mike Trout 2.00 5.00
SSS2 Jose Altuve .30 .75
SSS3 Josh Donaldson .30 .75
SSS4 Addison Russell .30 .75
SSS5 Carlos Correa .40 1.00
SSS6 Corey Seager .40 1.00
SSS7 Jose Bautista .30 .75
SSS8 Wil Myers .30 .75
SSS9 Manny Machado .40 1.00
SSS10 Trea Turner .30 .75
SSS11 Yu Darvish .30 .75
SSS12 Clayton Kershaw .60 1.50
SSS13 Miguel Sano .30 .75
SSS14 Nelson Cruz .40 1.00
SSS15 Chris Sale .40 1.00
SSS16 Yoan Moncada .40 1.00
SSS17 Miguel Cabrera .40 1.00
SSS18 Felix Hernandez .30 .75
SSS19 Freddie Freeman .50 1.25
SSS20 Noah Syndergaard .30 .75
SSS21 Adam Jones .30 .75
SSS22 Gary Sanchez .40 1.00
SSS23 Nolan Arenado .60 1.50
SSS24 Evan Longoria .30 .75
SSS25 Max Scherzer .40 1.00
SSS26 Justin Verlander .40 1.00
SSS27 Andrew Benintendi .40 1.00
SSS28 Khris Davis .40 1.00
SSS29 Eric Hosmer .30 .75
SSS30 Aaron Judge 1.00 2.50
SSS31 Bryce Harper .60 1.50
SSS32 Yadier Molina .50 1.25
SSS33 Joey Votto .40 1.00
SSS34 Paul Goldschmidt .40 1.00
SSS35 Francisco Lindor .40 1.00
SSS36 Michael Conforto .30 .75
SSS37 Robinson Cano .30 .75
SSS38 Eric Thames .30 .75
SSS39 George Springer .30 .75
SSS40 Cody Bellinger .75 2.00
SSS41 Daniel Murphy .30 .75
SSS42 Kris Bryant .50 1.25
SSS43 Giancarlo Stanton .50 1.25
SSS44 Anthony Rizzo .50 1.25
SSS45 Ichiro .50 1.25
SSS46 Andrew McCutchen .40 1.00
SSS47 Mookie Betts .75 2.00
SSS48 Matt Kemp .30 .75
SSS49 Yoenis Cespedes .40 1.00
SSS50 Buster Posey .50 1.25

2018 Topps Team MVP Medallions

STATED ODDS 1:1001 HOBBY
*BLACK/99: .75X TO 2X BASIC
*GOLD/50: 1X TO 2.5X BASIC
*RED/25: 1.2X TO 3X BASIC
MVPAB Adrian Beltre 2.50 6.00
MVPAJ Aaron Judge 5.00 12.00
MVPBB Byron Buxton 2.00 5.00
MVPBH Bryce Harper 3.00 8.00
MVPBP Buster Posey 2.50 6.00
MVPCA Chris Archer 1.25 3.00
MVPCK Clayton Kershaw 3.00 8.00
MVPFF Freddie Freeman 2.50 6.00
MVPFL Francisco Lindor 2.00 5.00
MVPJA Jose Altuve 1.50 4.00
MVPJB Josh Bell 1.50 4.00
MVPJBO Justin Bour 1.25 3.00
MVPJD Josh Donaldson 1.50 4.00
MVPJR Jose Abreu 2.00 5.00
MVPJV Joey Votto 2.00 5.00
MVPKB Kris Bryant 2.50 6.00
MVPKD Khris Davis 2.00 5.00
MVPMB Mookie Betts 4.00 10.00
MVPMC Miguel Cabrera 2.00 5.00
MVPMM Manny Machado 2.00 5.00
MVPMT Mike Trout 10.00 25.00
MVPNA Nolan Arenado 3.00 8.00
MVPNC Nelson Cruz 2.00 5.00
MVPNS Noah Syndergaard 1.50 4.00
MVPPG Paul Goldschmidt 2.00 5.00
MVPRB Ryan Braun 1.50 4.00
MVPRH Rhys Hoskins 5.00 12.00
MVPSP Salvador Perez 1.50 4.00
MVPWM Wil Myers 1.50 4.00
MVPYM Yadier Molina 2.50 6.00

2018 Topps Top 10 Topps Now Inserts

COMPLETE SET (10) 10.00 25.00
STATED ODDS 1:18
TN1 Aaron Judge 1.00 2.50
TN2 Aaron Judge 1.00 2.50
TN3 Aaron Judge 1.00 2.50
TN4 Aaron Judge 1.00 2.50
TN5 Derek Jeter 1.00 2.50
TN6 Derek Jeter 1.00 2.50
TN7 Cody Bellinger .75 2.00
TN8 Aaron Judge 1.00 2.50
TN9 A.Judge/B.Ruth 1.00 2.50
TN10 Aaron Judge 1.00 2.50

2018 Topps World Series Champions Autograph Relics

STATED ODDS 1:18719 HOBBY
PRINT RUNS B/WN 15-50 COPIES PER
EXCHANGE DEADLINE 12/31/2019
WCARAR Alex Bregman/50 60.00 150.00
WCARCC Carlos Correa/50 50.00 120.00
WCAREG Evan Gattis/15 50.00 120.00
WCARGS George Springer/50 40.00 100.00
WCARJM Joe Musgrove/50 20.00 50.00
WCARYU Yuli Gurriel/50 15.00 40.00

2018 Topps World Series Champions Autograph Relics Red

*RED: .75X TO 2X BASIC
STATED ODDS 1:32945 HOBBY
STATED PRINT RUN 25 SER.#'d SETS
EXCHANGE DEADLINE 12/31/2019
WCAREG Evan Gattis 50.00 120.00

2018 Topps World Series Champions Autographs

STATED ODDS 1:19380 HOBBY
STATED PRINT RUN 50 SER.#'d SETS
EXCHANGE DEADLINE 12/31/2019
*RED/25: .75X TO 2X BASIC
WCAAR Alex Bregman
WCACC Carlos Correa 50.00 120.00
WCAGS George Springer
WCAJM Joe Musgrove 20.00 50.00
WCAKG Ken Giles
WCAYG Yuli Gurriel

2018 Topps World Series Champions Relics

STATED ODDS 1:5821 HOBBY
STATED PRINT RUN 100 SER.#'d SETS
*RED/25: .6X TO 1.5X BASIC
WCRAB Alex Bregman 15.00 40.00
WCRCC Carlos Correa 15.00 40.00
WCRDK Dallas Keuchel 12.00 30.00
WCREG Evan Gattis 10.00 25.00
WCRGS George Springer 12.00 30.00
WCRJA Jose Altuve 12.00 30.00
WCRJM Joe Musgrove 15.00 40.00
WCRJR Josh Reddick 12.00 30.00
WCRJV Justin Verlander 15.00 40.00
WCRKG Ken Giles 10.00 25.00
WCRMG Marwin Gonzalez 20.00 50.00
WCRYG Yuli Gurriel 12.00 30.00

2018 Topps Update

COMPLETE SET (300) 20.00 50.00
PRINTING PLATE ODDS 1:5519 HOBBY
PLATE PRINT RUN 1 SET PER COLOR
BLACK-CYAN-MAGENTA-YELLOW ISSUED
NO PLATE PRICING DUE TO SCARCITY
US1 Shohei Ohtani RC 10.00 25.00
US2 Joe Jimenez .15 .40
US3 Jordan Lyles .15 .40
US4 Jorge Alfaro .15 .40
US5 James Paxton HL .20 .50
US6 Jacob Nottingham RC .25 .60
US7 Giancarlo Stanton .25 .60
US8 Manny Machado .25 .60
US9 Nick Kingham RD .15 .40
US10 Ian Kinsler .20 .50
US11 Adam Engel .15 .40
US12 Miles Mikolas RC .30 .75
US13 P.J. Conlon RC .25 .60
Corey Oswalt RC
US14 Scott Kingery RD .25 .60
US15 Kyle Barraclough .15 .40
US16 Brad Boxberger .15 .40
US17 Jason Vargas .15 .40

US18 Michael Soroka RD .50 1.25
US19 Billy McKinney RC .30 .75
US20 Jeurys Familia .20 .50
US21 Kenley Jansen AS .20 .50
US22 Tyler Chatwood .15 .40
US23 J.D. Martinez AS .25 .60
US24 Pablo Sandoval .20 .50
US25 Willy Adames RD .20 .50
US26 Felipe Vazquez .20 .50
US27 Christian Yelich AS .30 .75
US28 Alex Blandino RC .25 .60
Brandon Dixon RC
US29 David Hess RC .30 .75
Pedro Araujo RC
US30 Jon Lester AS .20 .50
US31 Jose Ramirez AS .20 .50
US32 Cole Hamels .20 .50
US33 Reynaldo Lopez .20 .50
US34 Austin Meadows RC 2.00 5.00
US35 Dan Otero .15 .40
US36 Mike Gerber RC .25 .60
Grayson Greiner RC
US37 Javier Baez HRD .30 .75
US38 Jose Berrios AS .20 .50
US39 Freddy Peralta RC .25 .60
US40 Jacob Barnes RC .25 .60
US41 Pedro Strop .15 .40
US42 Teoscar Hernandez .25 .60
US43 Albies/Acuna 5.00 12.00
US44 Freddie Freeman AS .30 .75
US45 Bartolo Colon .15 .40
US46 Carlos Gomez .15 .40
US47 Jake Odorizzi .15 .40
US48 Nick Markakis AS .20 .50
US49 Eugenio Suarez AS .20 .50
US50 Andrew Cashner .15 .40
US51 Nathan Eovaldi .20 .50
US52 Michael Hermosillo RC .25 .60
Justin Anderson RC
US53 Seung Hwan Oh .20 .50
US54 Denard Span .15 .40
US55 Mike Moustakas .20 .50
US56 Trevor Oaks RC .25 .60
Eric Stout RC
US57 Ryder Jones RC .25 .60
US58 Jordan Hicks RC .50 1.25
US59 Kyle Schwarber HRD .25 .60
US60 Yadier Molina AS .30 .75
US61 Mike Tauchman RC 1.25 3.00
US62 Mark Reynolds .15 .40
US63 Corey Dickerson .15 .40
US64 Mookie Betts AS .50 1.25
US65 Yelich/Cain .30 .75
US66 J.A. Happ AS .20 .50
US67 Alex Bregman AS .25 .60
US68 Michael Soroka RC .75 2.00
US69 Martinez/Betts .50 1.25
US70 Brad Hand AS .15 .40
US71 Logan Morrison .15 .40
US72 Mike Foltynewicz AS .15 .40
US73 Marcell Ozuna .25 .60
US74 Joey Votto AS .25 .60
US75 J.A. Happ .20 .50
US76 Salvador Perez AS .20 .50
US77 Merandy Gonzalez RC .25 .60
Eliezer Hernandez RC
US78 Luis Severino AS .20 .50
US79 Altuve/Judge .60 1.50
US80 Jonathan Villar .15 .40
US81 Sean Doolittle AS .15 .40
US82 Eric Lauer RC .30 .75
US83 Andrew McCutchen .25 .60
US84 Jack Reinheimer RC .30 .75
US85 Josh Hader AS .20 .50
US86 Randal Grichuk .15 .40
US87 Thunder and Lighting .25 .60
Joey Votto/Billy Hamilton
US88 Daniel Mengden RC .25 .60
US89 Justin Verlander HL .25 .60
US90 Ryan Yarbrough RC .40 1.00
US91 Zack Littell RC .25 .60
US92 Jeremy Hellickson .15 .40
US93 Daniel Winkler .15 .40
US94 Willson Contreras AS .25 .60
US95 Dustin Fowler RC .25 .60
US96 Tyler Clippard .15 .40
US97 Charlie Blackmon AS .25 .60
US98 Edwin Diaz AS .20 .50
US99 Gleyber Torres AS 1.50 4.00
US100 Ichiro .30 .75
US101 Chris Sale AS .30 .75
US102 Albert Pujols HL .30 .75
US103 Gerson Bautista .25 .60
Luis Guillorme RC
US104 Juan Soto RD 6.00 15.00
US105 Ronald Guzman RC .25 .60
US106 Jesmuel Valentin RC .25 .60
Mitch Walding RC
US107 Craig Kimbrel AS .20 .50
US108 Sean Rodriguez .15 .40
US109 Patrick Corbin AS .20 .50
US110 Lourdes Gurriel Jr. RC .50 1.25
US111 Jean Segura AS .15 .40
US112 J.T. Realmuto AS .25 .60
US113 Jesus Aguilar AS .20 .50
US114 Ildemaro Vargas RC .25 .60
US115 Eric Hosmer .20 .50
US116 Asdrubal Cabrera .20 .50
US117 Kyle Martin RC .25 .60
US118 Evan Longoria .20 .50
US119 Javier Baez AS .30 .75
US120 Joey Wendle RC .50 1.25
US121 George Springer AS .20 .50
US122 Jesus Aguilar HRD .20 .50
US123 Wade LeBlanc .15 .40
US124 Ariel Jurado RC .25 .60
US125 Carlos Santana .20 .50
US126 Joe Musgrove .25 .60
US127 Tyler Skaggs .15 .40
US128 Kingery/Hoskins .60 1.50
US129 Tyson Ross .15 .40
US130 Austin Meadows RD .40 1.00
US131 Zach Britton .15 .40
US132 Brandon Crawford AS .20 .50
US133 Devin Mesoraco .15 .40
US134 Brett Phillips .15 .40
US135 Sal Romano .15 .40
US136 Starlin Castro .15 .40
US137 Trevor Bauer AS .30 .75
US138 Junior Guerra .15 .40
US139 John Hicks .15 .40
US140 Clay Buchholz .15 .40
US141 Eduardo Escobar .15 .40
US142 Tyler Beede RC .25 .60
US143 Jeimer Candelario .20 .50
US144 Lou Trivino RC .30 .75
US145 Scooter Gennett AS .20 .50
US146 Blake Treinen AS .15 .40
US147 Matt Moore .20 .50
US148 Michael Brantley AS .20 .50
US149 Leonys Martin .15 .40
US150 Hosmer/Bellinger .50 1.25
US151 Matt Kemp .20 .50
US152 Steve Cishek .15 .40
US153 Ohtani/Ichiro 4.00 10.00
US154 Jaime Barria RC .30 .75
US155 Brad Ziegler .15 .40
US156 Paul Goldschmidt AS .25 .60
US157 Francisco Lindor AS .25 .60
US158 Upton/Ohtani/Trout 4.00 10.00
US159 Nolan Arenado AS .40 1.00
US160 Ryan Madson .15 .40
US161 Seranthony Dominguez RC .25 .60
US162 Ozzie Albies AS .50 1.25
US163 Danny Valencia .15 .40
US164 Jefry Marte .15 .40
US165 Matt Kemp AS .20 .50
US166 Juan Lagares .15 .40
US167 Sean Manaea HL .15 .40
US168 Freddie Freeman HRD .30 .75
US169 Jose Castillo RC .25 .60
Walker Lockett RC
US170 Wilson Ramos .15 .40
US171 Adam Duvall .20 .50
US172 Aaron Judge AS .60 1.50
US173 Tyler Wade RC .30 .75
US174 Fernando Romero RC .25 .60
US175 Dylan Cozens RC .25 .60
US176 Mike Trout AS 1.25 3.00
US177 Jacob deGrom AS .50 1.25
US178 Danny Farquhar .15 .40
US179 Hyun-Jin Ryu .20 .50
US180 Francisco Liriano .15 .40
US181 Gerson Bautista RC .25 .60
US182 Nelson Cruz AS .25 .60
US183 Mitch Moreland AS .15 .40
US184 Jurickson Profar .20 .50
US185 Corey Kluber AS .20 .50
US186 Lorenzo Cain AS .15 .40
US187 Jonathan Lucroy .20 .50
US188 Nick Gardewine RC .25 .60
US189 Shohei Ohtani HL 4.00 10.00
US190 Mike Montgomery .15 .40
US191 Gleyber Torres RD 1.50 4.00
US192 Daniel Palka RC .25 .60
US193 Christian Arroyo .15 .40
US194 Miguel Gomez RC .25 .60
US195 J.D. Martinez .25 .60
US196 Braxton Lee RC .25 .60
US197 Joe Jimenez AS .15 .40
US198 Shane Bieber RC 8.00 20.00
US199 Ramirez/Lindor .25 .60
US200 Gleyber Torres RC 6.00 15.00
US201 Nick Kingham RC .25 .60
US202 Bryce Harper HRD .40 1.00
US203 Roberto Osuna .15 .40
US204 Zack Cozart .15 .40
US205 Shin-Soo Choo AS .20 .50
US206 Neil Walker .15 .40
US207 Trevor Story AS .25 .60
US208 Brandon Mann RC .25 .60
US209 Bryce Harper AS .40 1.00
US210 Kirby Yates .20 .50
US211 Brandon Morrow .15 .40
US212 Alex Bregman HRD .25 .60
US213 Todd Frazier .15 .40
US214 Max Scherzer AS .25 .60
US215 Archie Bradley .15 .40
US216 Max Stassi .15 .40
US217 Justin Verlander AS .25 .60
US218 Tyler O'Neill RC .40 1.00
US219 Aroldis Chapman AS .25 .60
US220 Robinson Chirinos .15 .40
US221 Jose Bautista .20 .50
US222 Felipe Vazquez AS .20 .50
US223 Dominic Leone .15 .40
US224 Brandon McCarthy .15 .40
US225 Mike Fiers .15 .40
US226 Sean Doolittle .15 .40
US227 Ketel Marte .20 .50
US228 Colin Moran .15 .40
US229 Taylor Davis RC .25 .60
US230 Garrett Cooper RC .25 .60
US231 Jesse Biddle RC .30 .75
US232 Brad Hand .15 .40
US233 Tommy Pham .20 .50
US234 Jose Abreu AS .25 .60
US235 Trevor Cahill .15 .40
US236 Mitch Haniger AS .20 .50
US237 Carson Kelly .15 .40
US238 Matt Harvey .20 .50
US239 Mark Canha .15 .40
US240 Gerrit Cole AS .25 .60
US241 Chris Archer .15 .40
US242 Franmil Reyes RC .40 1.00
US243 Marco Gonzales .15 .40
US244 Daniel Robertson .15 .40
US245 Jose Pirela .15 .40
US246 Tony Kemp .15 .40
US247 Marcus Walden RC .30 .75
US248 Christian Yelich .30 .75
US249 Wander Suero RC .25 .60
US250 Ronald Acuna Jr. RC 40.00 100.00
US251 Aledmys Diaz .20 .50
US252 Ronald Acuna Jr. RD 5.00 12.00
US253 Manny Machado AS .25 .60
US254 Tommy Kahnle .15 .40
US255 Max Muncy HRD .20 .50
US256 Cameron Maybin .15 .40
US257 Chris Stratton RC .25 .60
US258 Lance Lynn .15 .40
US259 Stephen Piscotty .15 .40
US260 Lewis Brinson .15 .40
US261 Andrew Suarez RC .25 .60
US262 Sam Gaviglio .15 .40
US263 Brian Dozier .20 .50
US264 Jaime Garcia .15 .40
US265 Kevin Gausman .25 .60
US266 Austin Gomber RC .30 .75
US267 Alex Colome .15 .40
US268 Rhys Hoskins HRD .60 1.50
US269 Francisco Mejia RC .30 .75
US270 Dereck Rodriguez RC .30 .75
US271 Joey Lucchesi RC .25 .60
US272 Matt Duffy .15 .40
US273 David Bote RC .60 1.50
US274 Yairo Munoz RC .25 .60
US275 Jay Bruce .20 .50
US276 Hector Santiago .15 .40
US277 Ryan Tepera .15 .40
US278 Yan Gomes AS .25 .60
US279 Isiah Kiner-Falefa RC .40 1.00
US280 Ross Stripling .15 .40
US281 Willy Adames RC .30 .75
US282 Brian Flynn .15 .40
US283 Daniel Gossett RC .25 .60
US284 Arodys Vizcaino .15 .40
US285 Shohei Ohtani RD 4.00 10.00
US286 Shane Carle RC .30 .75
US287 Jonathan Schoop .15 .40
US288 Jordan Hicks RD .30 .75
US289 Matt Adams .15 .40
US290 Anthony Banda RC .25 .60
US291 Brent Suter .15 .40
US292 Brandon Drury .15 .40
US293 Charlie Culberson .15 .40
US294 Shane Greene .15 .40
US295 Yonny Chirinos RC .25 .60
US296 Aaron Nola AS .20 .50
US297 Luis Valbuena .15 .40
US298 Rajai Davis .15 .40
US299 Jose Altuve AS .20 .50
US300 Juan Soto RC 25.00 60.00

2018 Topps Update Black

*BLACK: 10X TO 25X BASIC
*BLACK RC: 6X TO 15X BASIC RC
STATED ODDS 1:94 HOBBY
STATED PRINT RUN 67 SER. #'d SETS
US250 Ronald Acuna Jr. 2500.00 6000.00
US300 Juan Soto 1000.00 2500.00

2018 Topps Update Black and White Negative

*BW NEGATIVE: 8X TO 20X BASIC
*BW NEGATIVE RC: 5X TO 12X BASIC
STATED ODDS 1:137 HOBBY
US250 Ronald Acuna Jr. 600.00 1500.00
US300 Juan Soto 750.00 2000.00

2018 Topps Update Father's Day Blue

*BLUE: 10X TO 25X BASIC
*BLUE RC: 6X TO 15X BASIC RC
STATED ODDS 1:442 HOBBY
STATED PRINT RUN 50 SER. #'d SETS
US250 Ronald Acuna Jr. 1500.00 4000.00
US300 Juan Soto 1000.00 2500.00

2018 Topps Update Gold

*GOLD: 2X TO 5X BASIC
*GOLD RC: 1.2X TO 3X BASIC RC
STATED ODDS 1:11 HOBBY
STATED PRINT RUN 2018 SER. #'d SETS
US99 Gleyber Torres AS 20.00 50.00
US250 Ronald Acuna Jr. 300.00 800.00
US300 Juan Soto 250.00 600.00

2018 Topps Update Independence Day

*INDPNDNCE: 10X TO 25X BASIC
*INDPNDNCE RC: 6X TO 15X BASIC RC
STATED ODDS 1:291 HOBBY
STATED PRINT RUN 76 SER. #'d SETS
US250 Ronald Acuna Jr. 1500.00 4000.00
US300 Juan Soto 1000.00 2500.00

2018 Topps Update Memorial Day Camo

*CAMO: 12X TO 30X BASIC
*CAMO RC: 8X TO 20X BASIC RC
STATED ODDS 1:884 HOBBY
STATED PRINT RUN 25 SER. #'d SETS
US250 Ronald Acuna Jr. 3000.00 8000.00
US300 Juan Soto 1250.00 3000.00

2018 Topps Update Mother's Day Pink

*PINK: 10X TO 25X BASIC
*PINK RC: 6X TO 15X BASIC RC
STATED ODDS 1:442 HOBBY
STATED PRINT RUN 50 SER. #'d SETS
US250 Ronald Acuna Jr. 1500.00 4000.00
US300 Juan Soto 1000.00 2500.00

2018 Topps Update Rainbow Foil

*RAINBOW: 2X TO 5X BASIC
*RAINBOW RC: 1.2X TO 3X BASIC RC
STATED ODDS 1:10 HOBBY
US99 Gleyber Torres AS 15.00 40.00
US250 Ronald Acuna Jr. 300.00 800.00
US300 Juan Soto 250.00 600.00

2018 Topps Update Vintage Stock

*VINTAGE: 8X TO 20X BASIC
*VINTAGE RC: 5X TO 12X BASIC RC
STATED ODDS 1:223 HOBBY
STATED PRINT RUN 99 SER. #'d SETS
US250 Ronald Acuna Jr. 600.00 1500.00
US300 Juan Soto 750.00 2000.00

2018 Topps Update Photo Variations

SP STATED ODDS 1:45 HOBBY
SSP STATED ODDS 1:273 HOBBY
US1A Ohtani Red pllvr 10.00 25.00
US1B Ohtani Wht jrsy 40.00 100.00
US1C Ohtani Bttng 40.00 100.00
US1D Nolan Ryan 5.00 12.00
US7A Stanton Blue pllvr 1.50 4.00
US7B Babe Ruth 4.00 10.00
US9 Roberto Clemente 4.00 10.00
US10 Kinsler w/Glv 2.50 6.00
US12A Mikolas Tip cap 1.25 3.00
US12B Mikolas w/ball 20.00 50.00
US14A Kingery Red pllvr 1.50 4.00
US14B Kingery Pnstpe jrsy 15.00 40.00
US20 Don Mattingly 3.00 8.00
US21 Sandy Koufax 3.00 8.00
US23A Wade Boggs 1.25 3.00
US23B Pedro Martinez 1.25 3.00
US31 Chipper Jones 1.50 4.00
US34A Austin Meadows 2.50 6.00
Blue jersey
US34B Meadows Fldng 12.00 30.00
US38 Torii Hunter 1.00 2.50
US39 Prlta Frnt jrsy shwn 10.00 25.00
US44 Hank Aaron 3.00 8.00
US58A Hicks w/team 2.00 5.00
US58B Hicks Leg out 15.00 40.00
US64 Ted Williams 3.00 8.00
US68A Michael Soroka 3.00 8.00
In dugout
US68B Soroka Hrzntl 12.00 30.00
US73 Marcell Ozuna 1.50 4.00
Red pullover
US76 George Brett 3.00 8.00
US83A Andrew McCutchen 1.50 4.00
Black pullover
US83B Andrew McCutchen 1.50 4.00
Yankees
US88 Mengden Hrzntl 8.00 20.00
US95A Dustin Fowler 1.00 2.50
In dugout
US95B Fowler Tan bat 12.00 30.00
US98 Randy Johnson 1.50 4.00
US100 Ichiro 2.00 5.00
Blue and teal pullover
US101 Roger Clemens 2.00 5.00
US107 Rally Goose 25.00 60.00
US110A Gurriel Dugout 2.00 5.00
US110B Gurriel Fldng 12.00 30.00
US111 Bob Gibson 1.25 3.00
US118A Evan Longoria 1.25 3.00
In dugout, leaning on bat rack
US118B Bo Jackson 1.50 4.00
US121 Rickey Henderson 1.50 4.00
US151 Matt Kemp 1.25 3.00
Batting cage, no helmet
US157 Ernie Banks 1.50 4.00
US174A Fernando Romero 1.00 2.50
Looking up
US174B Romero Knee up 12.00 30.00
US175 Cozens Running 12.00 30.00
US177 Mike Piazza 1.50 4.00
US195 Martinez Blue pllvr 1.50 4.00
US197 Will Clark 1.25 3.00
US198 Bieber Ball over head 30.00 80.00
US200A Torres Blk pllvr 10.00 25.00
US200B Torres Gry jrsy 40.00 100.00
US200C Torres Thrwng 40.00 100.00
US200D Lou Gehrig 3.00 8.00
US201A Nick Kingham 1.00 2.50
Walking
US201B Kingham Yllw jrsy 10.00 25.00
US213 Todd Frazier 1.00 2.50
Blue pullover
US217 Trevor Hoffman 1.25 3.00
US218A Tyler O'Neill 1.50 4.00
In dugout
US218B O'Neill Bttng 12.00 30.00
US232 Josh Donaldson 1.25 3.00
US242 Reyes Bttng 12.00 30.00
US246 Yelich Pllvr 2.00 5.00
US250A Acuna Pllvr 300.00 800.00
US250B Acuna bttng 1250.00 3000.00
US250C Acuna Hldng glv 800.00 1500.00
US250D Derek Jeter 4.00 10.00
US253 Cal Ripken Jr. 4.00 10.00
US257 Stratton Blck jrsy 20.00 50.00
US259 Mark McGwire 2.50 6.00
US271 Joey Lucchesi 1.00 2.50
Brown jersey
US281 Adames Vrtcle 12.00 30.00
US300A Soto Dugout 60.00 150.00
US300B Soto Glrde 400.00 800.00

2018 Topps Update '83 Topps

STATED ODDS 1:4 HOBBY
*BLUE: 1.2X TO 3X BASIC
*BLACK/299: 1.5X TO 4X BASIC
*GOLD/50: 3X TO 8X BASIC
831 Andrew McCutchen .40 1.00
832 Shohei Ohtani 6.00 15.00
833 Scott Kingery .40 1.00
834 Jordan Hicks .50 1.25
835 Joey Lucchesi .25 .60
836 Trevor Hoffman .30 .75
837 Torii Hunter .25 .60
838 Willy Adames .30 .75
839 Steven Souza Jr. .30 .75
8310 Marcell Ozuna .40 1.00
8311 Christian Yelich .50 1.25
8312 Juan Soto 6.00 15.00
8313 Ronald Acuna Jr. 8.00 20.00
8314 Austin Meadows .60 1.50
8315 Tyler O'Neill .50 1.25
8316 Gleyber Torres 2.50 6.00
8317 Lourdes Gurriel Jr. .50 1.25
8318 Mitch Haniger .30 .75
8319 Ian Kinsler .25 .60
8320 Tommy Pham .25 .60
8321 Todd Frazier .25 .60
8322 Matt Chapman .40 1.00
8323 J.D. Martinez .40 1.00
8324 Dee Gordon .25 .60
8325 Lorenzo Cain .25 .60
8326 Joey Gallo .30 .75
8327 Ichiro .50 1.25
8328 Giancarlo Stanton .40 1.00
8329 Patrick Corbin .30 .75
8330 Sean Manaea .25 .60
8331 Gerrit Cole .40 1.00
8332 Johnny Cueto .30 .75
8333 Evan Longoria .30 .75
8334 Sean Doolittle .25 .60
8335 Dylan Bundy .30 .75
8336 Miles Mikolas .30 .75
8337 Jack Flaherty 1.00 2.50
8338 Jose Bautista .30 .75
8339 Matt Kemp .30 .75
8340 Blake Snell .30 .75
8341 Hyun-Jin Ryu .30 .75
8342 Mike Trout 2.00 5.00
8343 Aaron Judge 1.00 2.50
8344 Kris Bryant .50 1.25
8345 Bryce Harper .60 1.50
8346 Rhys Hoskins 1.00 2.50
8347 Rafael Devers .75 2.00
8348 Michael Soroka .75 2.00
8349 Freddy Peralta .25 .60
8350 Fernando Romero .25 .60

2018 Topps Update All Star Stitches

STATED ODDS 1:59 HOBBY
*SILVER/50: .6X TO 1.5X BASIC
*RED/25: .75X TO 2X BASIC
ASTAB Alex Bregman 4.00 10.00
ASTAC Aroldis Chapman 4.00 10.00
ASTAJ Aaron Judge 10.00 25.00
ASTAN Aaron Nola 3.00 8.00
ASTBC Brandon Crawford 3.00 8.00
ASTBS Blake Snell 3.00 8.00
ASTBT Blake Treinen 2.50 6.00
ASTCB Charlie Blackmon 4.00 10.00
ASTCI Craig Kimbrel 3.00 8.00
ASTCK Corey Kluber 3.00 8.00
ASTCM Charlie Morton 4.00 10.00
ASTCS Chris Sale 4.00 10.00
ASTCY Christian Yelich 5.00 12.00
ASTED Edwin Diaz 3.00 8.00
ASTES Eugenio Suarez 3.00 8.00
ASTFF Freddie Freeman 5.00 12.00
ASTFL Francisco Lindor 4.00 10.00
ASTFV Felipe Vazquez 3.00 8.00
ASTGC Gerrit Cole 4.00 10.00
ASTGS George Springer 3.00 8.00
ASTGT Gleyber Torres 6.00 15.00
ASTJA Jose Abreu 4.00 10.00
ASTJB Javier Baez 5.00 12.00
ASTJD Jacob deGrom 8.00 20.00
ASTJE Jose Berrios 3.00 8.00
ASTJG Jesus Aguilar 3.00 8.00
ASTJH Josh Hader 3.00 8.00
ASTJI Jose Ramirez 3.00 8.00
ASTJL Jon Lester 3.00 8.00
ASTJLO Jed Lowrie 2.50 6.00
ASTJM J.D. Martinez 4.00 10.00
ASTJN Justin Verlander 4.00 10.00
ASTJP J.A. Happ 3.00 8.00
ASTJR J.T. Realmuto 4.00 10.00
ASTJS Jean Segura 2.50 6.00
ASTJT Jose Altuve 3.00 8.00
ASTJV Joey Votto 4.00 10.00
ASTKJ Kenley Jansen 3.00 8.00
ASTKS Kyle Schwarber 4.00 10.00
ASTLC Lorenzo Cain 2.50 6.00
ASTLS Luis Severino 3.00 8.00
ASTMA Manny Machado 4.00 10.00
ASTMB Mookie Betts 8.00 20.00
ASTMF Mike Foltynewicz 2.50 6.00
ASTMH Mitch Haniger 3.00 8.00
ASTMK Matt Kemp 3.00 8.00
ASTMM Max Muncy 3.00 8.00
ASTMO Mitch Moreland 2.50 6.00
ASTMR Michael Brantley 3.00 8.00
ASTMS Max Scherzer 4.00 10.00
ASTMT Mike Trout 10.00 25.00
ASTNA Nolan Arenado 6.00 15.00
ASTNC Nelson Cruz 4.00 10.00
ASTNM Nick Markakis 3.00 8.00
ASTOA Ozzie Albies 5.00 12.00
ASTPC Patrick Corbin 3.00 8.00
ASTPG Paul Goldschmidt 4.00 10.00
ASTRS Ross Stripling 2.50 6.00
ASTSC Shin-Soo Choo 3.00 8.00
ASTSD Sean Doolittle 2.50 6.00
ASTSG Scooter Gennett 3.00 8.00
ASTSP Salvador Perez 3.00 8.00
ASTTB Trevor Bauer 5.00 12.00
ASTTS Trevor Story 4.00 10.00
ASTWC Willson Contreras 4.00 10.00
ASTWR Wilson Ramos 2.50 6.00
ASTYG Yan Gomes 4.00 10.00
ASTYM Yadier Molina 5.00 12.00
ASTZG Zack Greinke 4.00 10.00

2018 Topps Update All Star Stitches Autographs

STATED ODDS 1:10,826 HOBBY
PRINT RUNS B/WN 10-25 COPIES PER
NO PRICING DUE TO SCARCITY
EXCHANGE DEADLINE 9/30/2020
SSAAB Alex Bregman EXCH 50.00 120.00
SSAAJ Aaron Judge
SSACK Corey Kluber 25.00 60.00
SSACS Chris Sale 12.00 30.00
SSAFF Freddie Freeman 25.00 60.00
SSAFL Francisco Lindor 50.00 120.00
SSAGS George Springer 15.00 40.00
SSAGT Gleyber Torres 40.00 100.00
SSAJA Jose Altuve 50.00 120.00
SSAJB Javier Baez EXCH 30.00 80.00
SSAJd Jacob deGrom 50.00 120.00
SSAJV Joey Votto
SSALS Luis Severino 20.00 50.00
SSAMH Mitch Haniger 25.00 60.00
SSAMM Manny Machado 25.00 60.00
SSAOA Ozzie Albies/25
SSAPG Paul Goldschmidt 12.00 30.00
SSAWC Willson Contreras/25 40.00 100.00
SSAYM Yadier Molina EXCH 40.00 100.00

2018 Topps Update All Star Stitches Dual Autographs

STATED ODDS 1:31,274 HOBBY
STATED PRINT RUN 25 SER.#'d SETS
EXHCANGE DEADLINE 9/30/2020
SSDAB Altuve/Bregman EXCH 60.00 150.00
SSDAS Altuve/Springer
SSDBS Story/Blackmon 20.00 50.00
SSDCB Baez/Contereas 50.00 120.00
SSDFA Freeman/Albies 60.00 150.00
SSDJT Torres/Judge
SSDLK Lindor/Kluber 60.00 150.00
SSDTJ Judge/Trout
SSDTS Severino/Torres

2018 Topps Update All Star Stitches Dual Relics

STATED ODDS 1:17,059 HOBBY
STATED PRINT RUN 25 SER.#'d SETS
EXHCANGE DEADLINE 9/30/2020
ASDAB Blackmon/Arenado 25.00 60.00
ASDAL Altuve/Bregman 25.00 60.00
ASDBS Betts/Sale 30.00 80.00
ASDCB Contreras/Baez 50.00 120.00
ASDCY Cain/Yelich 20.00 50.00
ASDFA Albies/Freeman 20.00 50.00
ASDJT Torres/Judge 30.00 80.00
ASDTJ Judge/Trout 60.00 150.00
ASDTS Severino/Torres 25.00 60.00
ASDVC Cole/Verlander 30.00 80.00

2018 Topps Update An International Affair

STATED ODDS 1:8 HOBBY
*BLUE: 1.2X TO 3X BASIC
*BLACK/299: 1.5X TO 4X BASIC
*GOLD/50: 3X TO 8X BASIC
IA1 Xander Bogaerts .40 1.00
IA2 Luiz Gohara .25 .60
IA3 Freddie Freeman .50 1.25
IA4 Joey Votto .40 1.00
IA5 Jose Quintana .25 .60
IA6 Yasiel Puig .40 1.00
IA7 Yoan Moncada .40 1.00
IA8 Yoenis Cespedes .40 1.00
IA9 Aroldis Chapman .40 1.00
IA10 Jose Abreu .40 1.00
IA11 Jonathan Schoop .25 .60
IA12 Ozzie Albies .75 2.00
IA13 Pedro Martinez .30 .75
IA14 Adrian Beltre .40 1.00
IA15 Albert Pujols .50 1.25
IA16 David Ortiz .40 1.00
IA17 Gary Sanchez .40 1.00
IA18 Manny Machado .40 1.00
IA19 Rafael Devers .75 2.00
IA20 Robinson Cano .30 .75
IA21 Victor Robles .60 1.50
IA22 Max Kepler .30 .75
IA23 Shohei Ohtani 2.00 5.00
IA24 Ichiro .50 1.25
IA25 Yu Darvish .40 1.00
IA26 Hideki Matsui .40 1.00
IA27 Masahiro Tanaka .30 .75
IA28 Julio Urias .40 1.00
IA29 Khris Davis .40 1.00
IA30 Didi Gregorius .30 .75
IA31 Mariano Rivera .50 1.25
IA32 Carlos Correa .40 1.00
IA33 Roberto Clemente 1.00 2.50
IA34 Francisco Lindor .40 1.00
IA35 Javier Baez .50 1.25
IA36 Yadier Molina .50 1.25
IA37 Gift Ngoepe .25 .60
IA38 Hyun-Jin Ryu .30 .75
IA39 Aaron Judge 1.00 2.50
IA40 Bryce Harper .60 1.50
IA41 Giancarlo Stanton .40 1.00
IA42 Kris Bryant .50 1.25
IA43 Mike Trout 2.00 5.00
IA44 Buster Posey .50 1.25
IA45 Mookie Betts .75 2.00
IA46 Jose Altuve .30 .75
IA47 Ronald Acuna Jr. 2.00 5.00
IA48 Miguel Cabrera .40 1.00
IA49 Willson Contreras .40 1.00
IA50 Gleyber Torres 2.50 6.00

2018 Topps Update Bryce Harper Highlights

RANDOM INSERTS IN PACKS
BH1 Bryce Harper 1.00 2.50
BH2 Bryce Harper 1.00 2.50
BH3 Bryce Harper 1.00 2.50
BH4 Bryce Harper 1.00 2.50
BH5 Bryce Harper 1.00 2.50
BH6 Bryce Harper 1.00 2.50
BH7 Bryce Harper 1.00 2.50
BH8 Bryce Harper 1.00 2.50
BH9 Bryce Harper 1.00 2.50
BH10 Bryce Harper 1.00 2.50
BH11 Bryce Harper 1.00 2.50
BH12 Bryce Harper 1.00 2.50
BH13 Bryce Harper 1.00 2.50
BH14 Bryce Harper 1.00 2.50
BH15 Bryce Harper 1.00 2.50
BH16 Bryce Harper 1.00 2.50
BH17 Bryce Harper 1.00 2.50
BH18 Bryce Harper 1.00 2.50
BH19 Bryce Harper 1.00 2.50
BH20 Bryce Harper 1.00 2.50

2018 Topps Update Don't Blink

STATED ODDS 1:8 HOBBY
*BLUE: 1.2X TO 3X BASIC
*BLACK/299: 1.5X TO 4X BASIC
*GOLD/50: 3X TO 8X BASIC
DB1 Rickey Henderson .40 1.00
DB2 Tim Raines .30 .75
DB3 Billy Hamilton .30 .75
DB4 Lou Brock .30 .75
DB5 Mike Trout 2.00 5.00
DB6 Byron Buxton .40 1.00
DB7 Ichiro .50 1.25
DB8 Dee Gordon .25 .60
DB9 Trea Turner .30 .75
DB10 Jose Altuve .30 .75
DB11 Bo Jackson .40 1.00
DB12 Ozzie Smith .50 1.25
DB13 Honus Wagner .40 1.00
DB14 Lorenzo Cain .25 .60
DB15 Andrew McCutchen .40 1.00
DB16 Jackie Robinson .40 1.00
DB17 Kris Bryant .50 1.25
DB18 Wil Myers .30 .75
DB19 Ty Cobb .60 1.50
DB20 Amed Rosario .30 .75
DB21 Bradley Zimmer .25 .60
DB22 Whit Merrifield .40 1.00
DB23 Kevin Kiermaier .30 .75
DB24 Yoan Moncada .40 1.00
DB25 Mookie Betts .75 2.00

2018 Topps Update Hall of Famer Highlights

RANDOM INSERTS IN PACKS
HFH1 Chipper Jones .60 1.50
HFH2 Chipper Jones .60 1.50
HFH3 Chipper Jones .60 1.50
HFH4 Chipper Jones .60 1.50
HFH5 Chipper Jones .60 1.50
HFH6 Chipper Jones .60 1.50
HFH7 Chipper Jones .60 1.50
HFH8 Vladimir Guerrero .50 1.25
HFH9 Vladimir Guerrero .50 1.25
HFH10 Vladimir Guerrero .50 1.25
HFH11 Vladimir Guerrero .50 1.25
HFH12 Jim Thome .50 1.25
HFH13 Jim Thome .50 1.25
HFH14 Jim Thome .50 1.25
HFH15 Jim Thome .50 1.25
HFH16 Jim Thome .50 1.25
HFH17 Trevor Hoffman .50 1.25
HFH18 Trevor Hoffman .50 1.25
HFH19 Trevor Hoffman .50 1.25
HFH20 Trevor Hoffman .50 1.25

2018 Topps Update Jackie Robinson Commemorative Patches

RANDOM INSERTS IN PACKS
*GOLD/99: .6X TO 1.5X BASIC
*BLUE/50: 1X TO 2.5X BASIC
JRPAB Andrew Benintendi 1.25 3.00
JRPAE Adrian Beltre 1.25 3.00
JRPAJ Aaron Judge 3.00 8.00
JRPAM Andrew McCutchen 1.25 3.00
JRPAP Albert Pujols 1.50 4.00
JRPAR Anthony Rizzo 1.50 4.00
JRPBA Billy Hamilton 1.00 2.50
JRPBD Brian Dozier 1.00 2.50
JRPBH Bryce Harper 2.00 5.00
JRPCA Chris Sale 1.25 3.00
JRPCB Charlie Blackmon 1.25 3.00
JRPCC Carlos Correa 1.25 3.00
JRPCE Cody Bellinger 2.50 6.00
JRPCI Craig Kimbrel 1.00 2.50
JRPCK Clayton Kershaw 2.00 5.00
JRPCM Carlos Martinez 1.00 2.50
JRPCS Corey Seager 1.25 3.00
JRPDG Dee Gordon .75 2.00
JRPFF Freddie Freeman 1.50 4.00
JRPFH Felix Hernandez 1.00 2.50
JRPFL Francisco Lindor 1.25 3.00
JRPGA Gary Sanchez 1.25 3.00
JRPGO Gleyber Torres 8.00 20.00
JRPGS George Springer 1.00 2.50
JRPGT Giancarlo Stanton 1.25 3.00
JRPIK Ian Kinsler 1.00 2.50
JRPJA Jose Altuve 1.00 2.50
JRPJB Josh Bell 1.00 2.50
JRPJD Josh Donaldson 1.00 2.50
JRPJO Joey Votto 1.25 3.00
JRPJR Jose Abreu 1.25 3.00
JRPJU Justin Upton 1.00 2.50
JRPJV Justin Verlander 1.25 3.00
JRPJZ Javier Baez 1.50 4.00
JRPKB Kris Bryant 1.50 4.00
JRPKS Kyle Schwarber 1.25 3.00
JRPMG Miguel Cabrera 1.25 3.00
JRPMK Matt Kemp 1.00 2.50
JRPMM Manny Machado 1.25 3.00
JRPMT Mike Trout 6.00 15.00
JRPNS Noah Syndergaard 1.00 2.50
JRPOA Ozzie Albies 2.50 6.00
JRPPG Paul Goldschmidt 1.25 3.00
JRPRH Rhys Hoskins 3.00 8.00
JRPSP Salvador Perez 1.00 2.50
JRPTS Trevor Story 1.25 3.00
JRPTT Trea Turner 1.00 2.50
JRPYM Yadier Molina 1.50 4.00
JRPYO Yoan Moncada 1.25 3.00
JRPYP Yasiel Puig 1.25 3.00

2018 Topps Update Legends in the Making

INSERTED IN RETAIL PACKS
*BLUE: .5X TO 1.2X BASIC
*BLACK: .75X TO 2X BASIC
*GOLD/50: 3X TO 8X BASIC
LITM1 Ronald Acuna Jr. 8.00 20.00
LITM2 Gleyber Torres 2.50 6.00
LITM3 Scott Kingery .40 1.00
LITM4 Austin Meadows .60 1.50
LITM5 Didi Gregorius .30 .75
LITM6 Matt Chapman .40 1.00
LITM7 Starling Marte .30 .75
LITM8 Juan Soto 6.00 15.00
LITM9 Jameson Taillon .30 .75
LITM10 Gerrit Cole .40 1.00
LITM11 Francisco Mejia .30 .75
LITM12 Justin Upton .30 .75
LITM13 Billy Hamilton .30 .75
LITM14 Lance McCullers .25 .60
LITM15 Ian Happ .30 .75
LITM16 Joey Gallo .30 .75
LITM17 Khris Davis .40 1.00
LITM18 J.D. Martinez .40 1.00
LITM19 Giancarlo Stanton .40 1.00
LITM20 Andrew McCutchen .40 1.00
LITM21 Shohei Ohtani 6.00 15.00
LITM22 Walker Buehler 1.25 3.00
LITM23 Xander Bogaerts .40 1.00
LITM24 Clint Frazier .50 1.25
LITM25 Miguel Sano .30 .75
LITM26 Yu Darvish .40 1.00
LITM27 Paul DeJong .40 1.00
LITM28 Jose Berrios .30 .75
LITM29 Craig Kimbrel .30 .75
LITM30 Luke Weaver .30 .75

2018 Topps Update Postseason Manufactured Relics

STATED ODDS 1:270 HOBBY
*GOLD/99: .6X TO 1.5X BASIC
*BLUE/50: 1X TO 2.5X BASIC
PSLAB Adrian Beltre 1.25 3.00
PSLAJ Aaron Judge 3.00 8.00
PSLAO Alex Rodriguez 1.50 4.00
PSLAP Albert Pujols 1.50 4.00
PSLAR Anthony Rizzo 1.50 4.00
PSLBC Brandon Crawford 1.00 2.50
PSLBH Bryce Harper 2.00 5.00
PSLBP Buster Posey 1.50 4.00
PSLCC Carlos Correa 1.25 3.00
PSLCK Clayton Kershaw 2.00 5.00
PSLCL Corey Kluber 1.00 2.50
PSLDF David Freese .75 2.00
PSLDG Didi Gregorius 1.00 2.50
PSLDJ Derek Jeter 3.00 8.00
PSLEH Eric Hosmer 1.00 2.50
PSLFL Francisco Lindor 1.25 3.00

PSLGS George Springer 1.00 2.50
PSLHM Hideki Matsui 1.25 3.00
PSLJA Jose Altuve 1.00 2.50
PSLJB Jose Bautista 1.00 2.50
PSLJD Josh Donaldson 1.00 2.50
PSLJE Jacob deGrom 2.50 6.00
PSLJV Justin Verlander 1.25 3.00
PSLKB Kris Bryant 1.50 4.00
PSLMC Miguel Cabrera 1.25 3.00
PSLMR Mariano Rivera 1.50 4.00
PSLNS Noah Syndergaard 1.00 2.50
PSLPS Pablo Sandoval 1.00 2.50
PSLSP Salvador Perez 1.00 2.50
PSLYM Yadier Molina 1.50 4.00

2018 Topps Update Postseason Preeminence

INSERTED IN RETAIL PACKS
*BLUE: .5X TO 1.2X BASIC
*BLACK: .75X TO 2X BASIC
*GOLD/50: 3X TO 8X BASIC
P01 Johnny Bench .40 1.00
P02 Lou Gehrig .75 2.00
P03 Roberto Alomar .30 .75
P04 Derek Jeter 1.00 2.50
P05 Ozzie Smith .50 1.25
P06 George Brett .75 2.00
P07 Brooks Robinson .30 .75
P08 Buster Posey .50 1.25
P09 Chipper Jones .40 1.00
P010 Reggie Jackson .30 .75
P011 Babe Ruth 1.00 2.50
P012 Lou Brock .30 .75
P013 David Ortiz .40 1.00
P014 Hideki Matsui .40 1.00
P015 Sandy Koufax .75 2.00
P016 Bob Gibson .30 .75
P017 John Smoltz .40 1.00
P018 Mariano Rivera .50 1.25
P019 Albert Pujols .50 1.25
P020 Rickey Henderson .40 1.00
P021 Justin Verlander .40 1.00
P022 Jose Altuve .30 .75
P023 George Springer .30 .75
P024 Kris Bryant .50 1.25
P025 Anthony Rizzo .50 1.25
P026 Corey Kluber .30 .75
P027 Jackie Robinson .40 1.00
P028 Jon Lester .30 .75
P029 Randy Johnson .40 1.00
P030 Andy Pettitte .30 .75

2018 Topps Update Salute

2018 Topps Update Salute Platinum
*BLUE: 1.2X TO 3X BASIC
*BLACK/299: 1.5X TO 4X BASIC
*GOLD/50: 3X TO 8X BASIC
S1 Babe Ruth 1.00 2.50
S2 Ted Williams .75 2.00
S3 Jackie Robinson .40 1.00
S4 Reggie Jackson .30 .75
S5 Bo Jackson .40 1.00
S6 Pedro Martinez .30 .75
S7 Randy Johnson .40 1.00
S8 Cal Ripken Jr. 1.25 3.00
S9 Torii Hunter .25 .60
S10 Ichiro .50 1.25
S11 Willie McCovey .30 .75
S12 Rod Carew .30 .75
S13 Tim Raines .30 .75
S14 Satchel Paige .40 1.00
S15 Joe Morgan .30 .75
S16 Dwight Gooden .25 .60
S17 Alex Rodriguez .50 1.25
S18 Aaron Judge 1.00 2.50
S19 Mike Trout 2.00 5.00
S20 Mariano Rivera .50 1.25
S21 Ronald Acuna Jr. 8.00 20.00
S22 Gleyber Torres 2.50 6.00
S23 Scott Kingery .40 1.00
S24 Jordan Hicks .50 1.25
S25 Austin Meadows .60 1.50
S26 Tyler O'Neill .40 1.00
S27 Lourdes Gurriel Jr. .50 1.25
S28 Isiah Kiner-Falefa .40 1.00
S29 Juan Soto 6.00 15.00
S30 Miles Mikolas .30 .75
S31 Jack Flaherty 1.00 2.50
S32 Dylan Cozens .25 .60
S33 Mike Soroka .75 2.00
S34 Shane Bieber 5.00 12.00
S35 Daniel Mengden .25 .60
S36 Freddy Peralta .25 .60
S37 Willy Adames .30 .75
S38 Sean Manaea .25 .60
S39 Shohei Ohtani 6.00 15.00
S40 Mookie Betts .75 2.00
S41 Didi Gregorius .30 .75
S42 Giancarlo Stanton .40 1.00
S43 Nick Kingham .25 .60
S44 Justin Verlander .40 1.00
S45 Willson Contreras .40 1.00
S46 George Springer .30 .75
S47 Francisco Lindor .40 1.00
S48 Edwin Encarnacion .40 1.00
S49 James Paxton .30 .75
S50 Andrew McCutchen .40 1.00

2018 Topps Update Storybook Endings

STATED ODDS 1:8 HOBBY
*BLUE: 1.2X TO 3X BASIC
*BLACK/299: 1.5X TO 4X BASIC
*GOLD/50: 3X TO 8X BASIC
SE1 Derek Jeter 1.00 2.50
SE2 David Ortiz .40 1.00
SE3 Sandy Koufax .75 2.00
SE4 Ted Williams .75 2.00
SE5 Jackie Robinson .40 1.00
SE6 Mariano Rivera .50 1.25
SE7 Cal Ripken Jr. 1.25 3.00
SE8 Chipper Jones .40 1.00
SE9 Will Clark .30 .75
SE10 Andy Pettitte .30 .75

2018 Topps Update Triple All Star Stitches

STATED ODDS 1:17,059 HOBBY
STATED PRINT RUN 25 SER.#'d SETS
ASTSABS Altuve/Bregman/Springer 40.00 100.00
ASTSASB Blackmon/Story/Arenado
ASTSAVC Verlander/Altuve/Cole 20.00 50.00
ASTSBMS Martinez/Sale/Betts 50.00 120.00
ASTSCBL Contreras/Baez/Lester
ASTSCYH Hader/Cain/Yelich 25.00 60.00
ASTSFAM Albies/Freeman/Markakis 40.00 100.00
ASTSHCD Cruz/Diaz/Haniger 40.00 100.00
ASTSJTS Judge/Torres/Severino 75.00 200.00
ASTSLRB Ramirez/Lindor/Bauer 25.00 60.00

2019 Topps

COMPLETE SET (702)
SER.1 PLATE ODDS 1:2369 HOBBY
SER.2 PLATE ODDS 1:3060 HOBBY
PLATE PRINT RUN 1 SET PER COLOR
BLACK-CYAN-MAGENTA-YELLOW ISSUED
NO PLATE PRICING DUE TO SCARCITY
1 Ronald Acuna Jr. 1.25 3.00
2 Tyler Anderson .15 .40
3 Eduardo Nunez WSH .15 .40
4 Dereck Rodriguez FS .15 .40
5 Chase Anderson .15 .40
6 Max Scherzer LL .25 .60
7 Gleyber Torres .50 1.25
8 Adam Jones .20 .50
9 Ben Zobrist .20 .50
10 Clayton Kershaw .40 1.00
11 Mike Zunino .15 .40
12 Rizzo/Perez .30 .75
13 David Price .20 .50
14 Judge/Gregorius .60 1.50
15 J.P. Crawford .15 .40
16 Charlie Blackmon .25 .60
17 Caleb Joseph .15 .40
18 Blake Parker .15 .40
19 Jacob deGrom LL .50 1.25
20 Jose Urena .15 .40
21 Jean Segura .25 .60
22 Adalberto Mondesi .30 .75
23 J.D. Martinez LL .25 .60
24 Blake Snell LL .20 .50
25 Chad Green .15 .40
26 Angel Stadium .15 .40
27 Mike Leake .15 .40
28 Betts/Benintendi .50 1.25
29 Eugenio Suarez .20 .50
30 Josh Hader .20 .50
31 Busch Stadium .15 .40
32 Carlos Correa .25 .60
33 Jacob Nix RC .30 .75
34 Josh Donaldson .20 .50
35 Joey Rickard .15 .40
36 Paul Blackburn .15 .40
37 Marcus Stroman .20 .50
38 Kolby Allard RC .40 1.00
39 Richard Urena .15 .40
40 Jon Lester .20 .50
41 Corey Seager .25 .60
42 Edwin Encarnacion .25 .60
43 Nick Burdi RC .25 .60
44 Jay Bruce .20 .50
45 Nick Pivetta .15 .40
46 Jose Abreu .25 .60
47 Yankee Stadium .15 .40
48 PNC Park .15 .40
49 Michael Kopech RC .75 2.00
50 Mookie Betts .50 1.25
51 Michael Brantley .20 .50
52 J.T. Realmuto .25 .60
53 Brandon Crawford .20 .50
54 Rick Porcello .20 .50
55 Yuli Gurriel .20 .50
56 Christian Villanueva .15 .40
57 Justin Verlander .25 .60
58 Carlos Martinez .20 .50
59 Zack Godley .15 .40
60 Kyle Tucker RC .60 1.50
61 Touki Toussaint RC .30 .75
62 Elvis Andrus .20 .50
63 Jake Odorizzi .15 .40
64 Ramon Laureano RC .50 1.25
65 Derek Dietrich .20 .50
66 Stephen Piscotty .15 .40
67 Danny Jansen RC .25 .60
68 Nick Ahmed .15 .40
69 Jorge Polanco .20 .50
70 Nolan Arenado LL .40 1.00
71 SunTrust Park .15 .40
72 Chris Taylor .20 .50
73 Jon Gray .15 .40
74 Chad Bettis .15 .40
75 Safeco Field .15 .40
76 J.D. Martinez WSH .25 .60
77 J.D. Martinez .25 .60
78 Francisco Arcia RC .40 1.00
79 Miller Park .15 .40
80 Tim Anderson .25 .60
81 Wade Davis .15 .40
82 Lourdes Gurriel Jr. FS .20 .50
83 Lou Trivino .15 .40
84 Matt Carpenter .25 .60
85 Garrett Hampson RC .40 1.00
86 David Bote .20 .50
87 Danny Duffy .15 .40
88 Jonathan Villar .15 .40
89 Corey Dickerson .15 .40
90 Javier Baez LL .30 .75
91 Hector Rondon .15 .40
92 Clayton Richard .15 .40
93 Matthew Boyd .15 .40
94 Corbin Burnes RC 2.00 5.00
95 Dennis Santana RC .25 .60
96 Trevor Williams .15 .40
97 Harrison Bader .20 .50
98 Chance Adams RC .25 .60
99 Aroldis Chapman .25 .60
100 Mike Trout 1.25 3.00
101 Michael Taylor .15 .40
102 Shin-Soo Choo .20 .50
103 Sean Manaea .15 .40
104 Joe Musgrove .25 .60
105 Jose Quintana .15 .40
106 Adam Ottavino .15 .40
107 Scooter Gennett .20 .50
108 Ian Kennedy .15 .40
109 Michael Conforto .20 .50
110 Trevor Bauer .30 .75
111 Reynaldo Lopez .20 .50
112 Joey Gallo .20 .50
113 Willie Calhoun FS .15 .40
114 Brandon Lowe RC .40 1.00
115 Tyler Glasnow .25 .60
116 Miguel Sano .20 .50
117 Enrique Hernandez .25 .60
118 Julio Teheran .20 .50
119 Willson Contreras .20 .50
120 Robert Gsellman .15 .40
121 Joey Wendle .20 .50
122 Zach Davies .15 .40
123 Jose Martinez .15 .40
124 Jason Kipnis .20 .50
125 Paul DeJong .25 .60
126 Oakland Coliseum .15 .40
127 Seranthony Dominguez .15 .40
128 Yoenis Cespedes .25 .60
129 Kenley Jansen .20 .50
130 Blake Snell .20 .50
131 Mark Trumbo .15 .40
132 Miguel Andujar .25 .60
133 Ryan Zimmerman .20 .50
134 Sean Reid-Foley RC .25 .60
135 Wade LeBlanc .15 .40
136 Brad Peacock .15 .40
137 Carlos Rodon .25 .60
138 Kyle Barraclough .15 .40
139 Mitch Haniger .20 .50
140 Daniel Poncedeleon RC .40 1.00
141 Ryon Healy .15 .40
142 Pedro Strop .15 .40
143 Yan Gomes .25 .60
144 Jake Arrieta .20 .50
145 Harper/ Gennett .40 1.00
146 Jesse Winker .25 .60
147 Blake Treinen .15 .40
148 Brandon Belt .20 .50
149 Khris Davis .25 .60
150 Aaron Judge .60 1.50
151 Pablo Lopez RC .25 .60
152 Teoscar Hernandez .25 .60
153 Hunter Strickland .15 .40
154 Johnny Cueto .20 .50
155 James McCann .20 .50
156 Luis Castillo .20 .50
157 Buster Posey .30 .75
158 Byron Buxton .25 .60
159 Minute Maid Park .15 .40
160 Fenway Park .15 .40
161 Eric Hosmer .20 .50
162 Yasiel Puig .25 .60
163 Aaron Nola .20 .50
164 Billy Hamilton .20 .50
165 Robbie Ray .15 .40
166 Matt Chapman .25 .60
167 Xander Bogaerts .25 .60
168 Salvador Perez .20 .50
169 Charlie Morton .25 .60
170 Manny Margot .15 .40
171 Kyle Hendricks .25 .60
172 Brandon Nimmo .20 .50
173 Michael Fulmer .15 .40
174 Jose Leclerc RC .25 .60
175 Tommy Pham .15 .40
176 Trea Turner .20 .50
177 Kohl Stewart RC .30 .75
178 Jose Altuve .20 .50
179 Jackie Bradley Jr. .25 .60
180 Justin Turner .25 .60
181 Antonio Senzatela .15 .40
182 Archie Bradley .15 .40
183 Freddie Freeman .30 .75
184 Ken Giles .15 .40
185 Matt Duffy .15 .40
186 Franmil Reyes FS .15 .40
187 Citizens Bank Park .15 .40
188 Matt Davidson .20 .50
189 Khris Davis LL .25 .60
190 Steven Duggar RC .30 .75
191 Dansby Swanson .25 .60
192 Luis Urias RC .40 1.00
193 Addison Reed .15 .40
194 Felipe Vazquez .15 .40
195 Brett Phillips .15 .40
196 Adam Engel .15 .40
197 Wrigley Field .15 .40
198 Gregory Polanco .20 .50
199 Mike Clevinger .20 .50
200 Jacob deGrom .50 1.25
201 Marcus Semien .25 .60
202 Muncy/Bellinger .50 1.25
203A Will Smith UER .15 .40
Tony Watson pictured
203B Will Smith COR
204 Zack Cozart .15 .40
205 Todd Frazier .15 .40
206 Jaime Barria .15 .40
207 Richard Bleier .15 .40
208 Josh Bell .20 .50
209 Nicholas Castellanos .25 .60
210 Kris Bryant .30 .75
211 Jeimer Candelario .15 .40
212 Brian Anderson FS .15 .40
213 Juan Soto .75 2.00
214 Colin Moran .15 .40
215 Didi Gregorius .20 .50
216 Arenado/Baez .40 1.00
217 Joe Jimenez .15 .40
218 Scott Schebler .20 .50
219 Martin Perez .20 .50
220 Alex Colome .15 .40
221 Luis Severino .20 .50
222 Zack Greinke .25 .60
223 Jose Ramirez .20 .50
224 Odubel Herrera .20 .50
225 Yadier Molina .30 .75
226 Albert Almora .20 .50
227 Adolis Garcia RC 4.00 10.00
228 Rafael Devers .30 .75
229 Shane Greene .15 .40
230 Miguel Cabrera .25 .60
231 Joc Pederson .20 .50
232 Kyle Seager .15 .40
233 Dylan Bundy .20 .50
234 Austin Hedges .15 .40
235 Luke Weaver .15 .40
236 Sean Doolittle .15 .40
237 Seth Lugo .15 .40
238 Whit Merrifield .25 .60
239 Christian Yelich LL .30 .75
240 Trey Mancini .20 .50
241 James Paxton .20 .50
242 Anthony Rendon .25 .60
243 Jonathan Loaisiga RC .30 .75
244 Tyler Flowers .15 .40
245 Rogers Centre .15 .40
246 Ryan Borucki RC .25 .60
247 Sam Tuivailala .15 .40
248 Justin Bour .15 .40
249 Jordan Zimmermann .20 .50
250 Shohei Ohtani .40 1.00
251 Niko Goodrum .20 .50
252 Jakob Junis .15 .40
253 Starling Marte .20 .50
254 Dodger Stadium .15 .40
255 Andrelton Simmons .15 .40
256 Cody Allen .15 .40
257 Andrew Heaney .15 .40
258 Eddie Rosario .20 .50
259 Jonathan Schoop .15 .40
260 Aaron Hicks .20 .50
261 Jedd Gyorko .15 .40
262 Mitch Moreland .15 .40
263 Gray/Gregorius .20 .50
264 Avisail Garcia .20 .50
265 Joey Lucchesi FS .15 .40
266 Ohtani/Bregman .40 1.00
267 Ross Stripling .15 .40
268 Blake Snell LL .20 .50
269 Francisco Lindor .25 .60
270 Brad Keller RC .25 .60
271 Shane Bieber FS .25 .60
272 Orlando Arcia .15 .40
273 Kole Calhoun .15 .40
274 Francisco Cervelli .15 .40
275 Steve Pearce WSH .25 .60
276 Nolan Arenado .40 1.00
277 Mitch Garver .15 .40
278 Mike Minor .15 .40
279 Rhys Hoskins .30 .75
280 Miles Mikolas .25 .60
281 Jeff McNeil RC .60 1.50
282 Tim Beckham .20 .50
283 Rich Hill .15 .40
284 Joey Votto .25 .60
285 Sonny Gray .20 .50
286 Taijuan Walker .15 .40
287 Jesus Aguilar .20 .50
288 Joe Panik .20 .50
289 Matt Olson .25 .60
290 Steven Souza Jr. .20 .50
291 Enyel De Los Santos RC .25 .60
292 Dee Gordon .15 .40
293 Andrew Miller .20 .50
294 Correa/Altuve .25 .60
295 Pujols/Betts .50 1.25
296 Lewis Brinson .15 .40
297 Paul Goldschmidt .25 .60
298 Devon Travis .15 .40
299 Edwin Diaz .20 .50
300 Christian Yelich .30 .75
301 Tanner Roark .15 .40
302 Jose Berrios .20 .50
303 Ranger Suarez RC .25 .60
304 Michael Lorenzen .15 .40
305 Brad Boxberger .15 .40
306 Justus Sheffield RC .40 1.00
307 Jorge Soler .25 .60
308 Yolmer Sanchez .15 .40
309 Randal Grichuk .15 .40
310 Javier Baez .30 .75
311 Jake Bauers RC .40 1.00
312 Mookie Betts LL .50 1.25
313 Robinson Cano .20 .50
314 David Price WSH .20 .50
315 Duane Underwood Jr. RC .25 .60
316 Adam Eaton .25 .60
317 Kevin Gausman .25 .60
318 Cedric Mullins RC .50 1.25
319 Alex Gordon .20 .50
320 Ronald Guzman FS .15 .40
321 Jack Flaherty FS .25 .60
322 Brian McCann .20 .50
323 George Springer .20 .50
324 Logan Morrison .15 .40
325 Dan Straily .15 .40
326 Heath Fillmyer RC .25 .60
327 Maikel Franco .20 .50
328 Yonder Alonso .15 .40
329 Jordan Hicks FS .20 .50
330 Lorenzo Cain .15 .40
331 Cesar Hernandez .15 .40
332 Ryan O'Hearn RC .25 .60
333 Ray Black RC .25 .60
334 Jake Lamb .20 .50
335 Ervin Santana .15 .40
336 Corey Kluber .20 .50
337 Mychal Givens .15 .40
338 Andrew Cashner .15 .40
339 Josh Harrison .15 .40
340 Tyler Skaggs .15 .40
341 Nationals Park .15 .40
342 Wilmer Difo .15 .40
343 Sal Romano .15 .40
344 Max Scherzer .25 .60
345 Justin Upton .20 .50
346 Chris Iannetta .15 .40
347 Kirby Yates .20 .50
348 Russell Martin .15 .40
349 Kyle Schwarber .25 .60
350 Nick Markakis .20 .50
351 Jarrod Dyson .15 .40
352 David Peralta .15 .40
353 Gary Sanchez .25 .60
354 Nomar Mazara .15 .40
355 Stephen Gonsalves RC .25 .60
356 Stephen Strasburg .25 .60
357 Chris Martin .15 .40
358 Leonys Martin .15 .40
359 Noah Syndergaard .20 .50
360 Mark Melancon .15 .40
361 Taylor Davis .15 .40
362 Jeremy Jeffress .15 .40
363 Max Stassi .15 .40
364 Kenta Maeda .20 .50
365 Ketel Marte .20 .50
366 Isiah Kiner-Falefa .20 .50
367 Ohtani/Trout 1.25 3.00
368 Brad Hand .15 .40
369 Charlie Culberson .15 .40
370 Jacoby Ellsbury .20 .50
371 Zack Wheeler .20 .50
372 Yu Darvish .25 .60
373 Christian Vazquez .20 .50
374 Alex Blandino .15 .40
375 Cody Reed .15 .40
376 Framber Valdez RC .25 .60
377 Yoan Moncada .25 .60
378 Brandon Workman .15 .40
379 Tim Hill RC .25 .60
380 Chris Archer .15 .40
381 Juan Lagares .15 .40
382 Daniel Norris .15 .40
383 Adalberto Mejia .15 .40
384 Dominic Leone .15 .40
385 Ender Inciarte .15 .40
386 Ryan Pressly .15 .40
387 Mike Foltynewicz .25 .60
388 Dominic Smith .15 .40
389 Victor Caratini .15 .40
390 Evan Longoria .20 .50
391 Jung Ho Kang .15 .40
392 Cionel Perez RC .25 .60
393 Hunter Renfroe .15 .40
394 Miguel Rojas .15 .40
395 Andrew McCutchen .25 .60
396 Masahiro Tanaka .20 .50
397 Lance McCullers Jr. .15 .40
398 Erick Fedde .15 .40
399 Tyler Mahle .15 .40
400 Bryce Harper .40 1.00
401 Tony Kemp .15 .40
402 Victor Robles FS .30 .75
403 Ivan Nova .20 .50
404 Jace Peterson .15 .40
405 Chaz Roe .15 .40
406 Jason Castro .15 .40
407 Eduardo Nunez .15 .40
408 Sean Newcomb .15 .40
409 Nate Jones .15 .40
410 Fernando Tatis Jr. RC 30.00 80.00
411 Magneuris Sierra .25 .60
412 Clint Frazier FS .20 .50
413 Mike Fiers .15 .40
414 Michael Soroka FS .25 .60
415 Bryan Shaw .15 .40
416 Keon Broxton .15 .40
417 Noel Cuevas RC .25 .60
418 Jason Vargas .15 .40
419 Sandy Leon .15 .40
420 Kevin Kiermaier .20 .50
421 Yoshihisa Hirano .15 .40
422 Matt Barnes .15 .40
423 Ji-Man Choi .15 .40
424 Target Field .15 .40
425 Steel City Slammers .15 .40
Corey Dickerson
426 Austin Romine .15 .40
427 Jorge Bonifacio .15 .40
428 Pablo Sandoval .20 .50
429 Wilmer Font .15 .40
430 Roman Quinn .15 .40
431 Lonnie Chisenhall .15 .40
432 Ryan Yarbrough .15 .40
433 Pedro Baez .15 .40
434 Roberto Osuna .15 .40
435 Steven Brault .15 .40
436 Kendrys Morales .15 .40
437 Albert Pujols .30 .75
438 Max Kepler .20 .50
439 Ryan McMahon .25 .60
440 Dustin Pedroia .25 .60
441 Oriole Park at Camden Yards .15 .40
442 Reese McGuire RC .40 1.00
443 Steven Matz .15 .40
444 Judge/Staton .60 1.50
445 Walker Buehler .30 .75
446 Francisco Mejia FS .20 .50
447 Up High, Down Low .20 .50
Jose Altuve/George Springer
448 Willians Astudillo RC .25 .60
449 Matt Moore .20 .50
450 Greg Garcia .15 .40
451 Jorge Alfaro .15 .40
452 Caleb Ferguson RC .30 .75
453 Taylor Rogers .15 .40
454 Matt Kemp .20 .50
455 Zach Eflin .15 .40
456 Austin Barnes .15 .40
457 Nick Ciuffo RC .25 .60
458 Alex Avila .20 .50
459 Trevor Hildenberger .15 .40
460 Trevor Story .25 .60
461 Eduardo Rodriguez .15 .40
462 Luke Voit .40 1.00
463 Wily Peralta .15 .40
464 Alex Wood .15 .40
465 Raisel Iglesias .15 .40
466 Yairo Munoz .15 .40
467 A.J. Minter .20 .50
468 Anthony DeSclafani .15 .40
469 Brandon Morrow .15 .40
470 Peter O'Brien .15 .40
471 Kevin Newman RC .40 1.00
472 Scott Kingery FS .20 .50
473 Kyle Wright RC .40 1.00
474 Carson Kelly .15 .40
475 Pete Alonso RC 5.00 12.00
476 Arodys Vizcaino .15 .40
477 Mikie Mahtook .15 .40
478 Alen Hanson .20 .50
479 Wei-Yin Chen .15 .40
480 Vince Velasquez .15 .40
481 J.A. Happ .20 .50
482 Starlin Castro .15 .40
483 Alex Cobb .15 .40
484 Andrew Chafin .15 .40
485 Wil Myers .20 .50
486 CC Sabathia .20 .50
487 San Diego Sluggers .20 .50
Hunter Renfroe/Eric Hosmer
488 Dexter Fowler .20 .50
489 Joe Ross .15 .40
490 Matt Harvey .20 .50
491 Comerica Park .15 .40
492 Adam Plutko .15 .40
493 JaCoby Jones .20 .50
494 Ian Desmond .15 .40
495 Progressive Field .15 .40
496 Buck Farmer .15 .40
497 Citi Field .15 .40
498 Pablo Reyes RC .25 .60
499 Daniel Murphy .20 .50
500 Manny Machado .25 .60
501 Carlos Carrasco .15 .40
502 Mike Montgomery .15 .40
503 Marcell Ozuna .25 .60
504 Stephen Tarpley RC .30 .75
505 Dellin Betances .20 .50
506 Ben Gamel .20 .50
507 Cody Bellinger .50 1.25
508 Albies/Acuna 1.25 3.00
509 Globe Life Park in Arlington .15 .40
510 Patrick Corbin .20 .50
511 Rougned Odor .20 .50
512 Franklin Barreto .15 .40
513 Brett Gardner .20 .50
514 Greg Allen .20 .50
515 Hyun-Jin Ryu .20 .50
516 Keone Kela .15 .40
517 Shawn Armstrong .15 .40
518 Steven Wright .15 .40
519 Julio Urias .25 .60
520 David Fletcher RC .75 2.00
521 Chase Field .15 .40
522 Brian Johnson .15 .40
523 Marco Gonzales .15 .40
524 Chad Pinder .15 .40
525 Ian Kinsler .20 .50
526 Sandy Alcantara .15 .40
527 Guaranteed Rate Field .15 .40
528 Jon Edwards RC .25 .60
529 Chance Sisco .15 .40
530 Ian Happ .20 .50
531 Josh Reddick .15 .40
532 Lance Lynn .15 .40
533 Matt Shoemaker .20 .50
534 Aaron Altherr .15 .40
535 Tyler Naquin .20 .50
536 Get Up! .30 .75
Yadier Molina/Marcell Ozuna
537 Ronald Torreyes .15 .40
538 Seung-Hwan Oh .20 .50
539 Franchy Cordero .15 .40
540 Cole Hamels .20 .50
541 Michael Wacha .20 .50
542 Chris Davis .15 .40
543 Nick Williams .15 .40
544 Jake Marisnick .15 .40
545 Tyler White .15 .40
546 Brock Holt .15 .40
547 Trevor Richards RC .25 .60
548 Chris Owings .15 .40
549 Sale/Vazquez
550 Adam Cimber RC .25 .60
551 Kolten Wong .20 .50
552 David Hess .15 .40
553 Daniel Mengden .15 .40
554 Corey Knebel .15 .40
555 Marlins Park .15 .40
556 Rowdy Tellez RC .40 1.00
557 Adam Duvall .25 .60
558 Phillip Ervin .15 .40
559 Ildemaro Vargas .15 .40
560 Victor Reyes RC .25 .60
561 Ozzie Albies FS .25 .60
562 Willy Adames .15 .40
563 Keynan Middleton .15 .40
564 Austin Meadows FS .25 .60
565 Andrew Triggs .15 .40
566 Tropicana Field .15 .40
567 Josh Rogers RC .25 .60
568 Giancarlo Stanton .25 .60
569 Carl Edwards Jr. .15 .40
570 Eduardo Escobar .15 .40
571 Bobby Poyner RC .30 .75
572 Gerrit Cole .25 .60
573 Tucker Barnhart .15 .40
574 Jeff Samardzija .15 .40
575 Jimmy Yacabonis RC .25 .60
576 Jake Cave RC .30 .75
577 Nicky Delmonico .15 .40
578 Patrick Wisdom RC .25 .60
579 Andrew Benintendi .25 .60
580 DJ Stewart RC .30 .75
581 Travis Jankowski .15 .40
582 Austin Wynns RC .25 .60
583 Yefry Ramirez RC .25 .60
584 Josh James RC .40 1.00
585 Carlos Santana .20 .50
586 Drew VerHagen RC .25 .60
587 Johan Camargo .15 .40
588 Taylor Ward RC .25 .60
589 Jeurys Familia .20 .50
590 Jose Peraza .20 .50
591 Wilson Ramos .15 .40
592 Eric Lauer .15 .40
593 John Hicks .15 .40
594 Austin Slater .15 .40
595 Yandy Diaz .20 .50
596 Anthony Rizzo .30 .75
597 Kyle Gibson .20 .50
598 Chris Devenski .15 .40
599 Daniel Palka .15 .40
600 Shohei Ohtani .40 1.00
601 David Dahl .15 .40
602 German Marquez .15 .40
603 J.D. Davis .15 .40
604 Coors Field .15 .40
605 Jeffrey Springs RC .25 .60
606 Johnny Field RC .30 .75
607 J.T. Riddle .15 .40
608 Ehire Adrianza .15 .40
609 Kauffman Stadium .15 .40
610 Howie Kendrick .15 .40
611 Chris Shaw RC .25 .60
612 Mark Canha .15 .40
613 Welington Castillo .15 .40
614 Ryan Braun .20 .50
615 Nick Tropeano .15 .40
616 Oracle Park .15 .40
617 Hernan Perez .15 .40
618 Nick Martini RC .25 .60
619 Tommy Hunter .15 .40
620 Jared Hughes .15 .40
621 Pat Valaika .15 .40
622 Troy Tulowitzki .25 .60
623 Kevin Pillar .15 .40
624 Amed Rosario FS .20 .50
625 Yelich/Arcia .30 .75
626 Robbie Erlin .15 .40
627 Freddy Peralta .25 .60
628 Roenis Elias .15 .40
629 Myles Straw RC .40 1.00
630 Dustin Fowler .15 .40
631 Tyler Austin .25 .60
632 Yusei Kikuchi RC .40 1.00
633 Addison Russell .20 .50
634 John Gant .15 .40
635 Adam Frazier .15 .40
636 Jace Fry RC .25 .60
637 Yusmeiro Petit .15 .40
638 Kristopher Negron .15 .40
639 Roberto Perez .15 .40
640 Brian Goodwin .15 .40
641 Bryse Wilson RC .30 .75
642 Jhoulys Chacin .15 .40
643 Chris Sale .25 .60
644 Delino DeShields .15 .40
645 Steve Cishek .15 .40
646 Jason Heyward .20 .50
647 Kyle Freeland .20 .50
648 Kevin Kramer RC .30 .75
649 Carlos Tocci RC .25 .60
650 Diego Castillo RC .25 .60
651 Jorge Lopez .15 .40
652 Rosell Herrera RC .25 .60
653 Greg Bird .20 .50
654 Kurt Suzuki .15 .40
655 Tyler O'Neill FS .20 .50
656 Jacob Faria .15 .40
657 JC Ramirez .15 .40
658 Max Muncy .20 .50
659 Aramis Garcia RC .25 .60
660 Dawel Lugo RC .40 1.00
661 Zack Greinke .25 .60
662 Jameson Taillon .20 .50
663 Adam Conley .15 .40
664 Lucas Giolito .20 .50
665 David Freese .15 .40
666 Cam Gallagher .15 .40
667 Ronny Rodriguez RC .25 .60
668 Pat Neshek .15 .40
669 Mallex Smith .15 .40
670 Eloy Jimenez RC 4.00 10.00
671 Alex Verdugo FS .20 .50
672 Christin Stewart RC .30 .75
673 Danny Salazar .20 .50
674 Collin McHugh .15 .40
675 Nelson Cruz .25 .60
676 Travis Shaw .15 .40
677 Aaron Sanchez .20 .50
678 Luis Ortiz RC .25 .60
679 Adam Wainwright .20 .50
680 Justin Smoak .15 .40
681 Jeff Mathis .20 .50
682 Petco Park .15 .40
683 Isaac Galloway RC .25 .60
684 Robert Stock RC .25 .60
685 Billy McKinney .15 .40
686 Brandon Drury .15 .40
687 Brandon Woodruff .25 .60
688 Jalen Beeks RC .25 .60
689 Jose Briceno RC .25 .60
690 Hunter Dozier .15 .40
691 Great American Ball Park .15 .40
692 Fernando Rodney .15 .40
693 Ryan Brasier RC .25 .60
694 Steve Pearce .25 .60
695 Eric Thames .15 .40
696 Sam Dyson .15 .40
697 Dakota Hudson RC .30 .75
698 Baez/Contreras .30 .75
699 Felix Hernandez .20 .50
700 Alex Bregman .25 .60
NNO Vladimir Guerrero Jr SP 25.00 60.00

2019 Topps 150th Anniversary

*150TH ANNV: 2X TO 5X BASIC
*150TH ANNV RC: 1.2X TO 3X BASIC RC
SER.1 ODDS 1:6 HOBBY
SER.2 ODDS 1:6 HOBBY
281 Jeff McNeil 8.00 20.00
475 Pete Alonso 15.00 40.00

2019 Topps Advanced Stats

*ADV STATS: 6X TO 15X BASIC
*ADV STATS RC: 4X TO 10X BASIC RC
SER.1 ODDS 1:75 HOBBY
SER.2 ODDS 1:89 HOBBY
STATED PRINT RUN 150 SER. #'d SETS
281 Jeff McNeil 12.00 30.00

2019 Topps Black

*BLACK: 10X TO 25X BASIC
*BLACK RC: 6X TO 15X BASIC RC
SER.1 ODDS 1:122 HOBBY
SER.2 ODDS 1:178 HOBBY
STATED PRINT RUN 67 SER. #'d SETS
1 Ronald Acuna Jr. 60.00 150.00
60 Kyle Tucker 40.00 100.00
100 Mike Trout 60.00 150.00
132 Miguel Andujar 25.00 60.00
250 Shohei Ohtani 25.00 60.00
281 Jeff McNeil 25.00 60.00
400 Bryce Harper 25.00 60.00
410 Fernando Tatis Jr. 1250.00 3000.00
445 Walker Buehler 30.00 80.00
473 Kyle Wright 12.00 30.00
475 Pete Alonso 200.00 500.00
560 Victor Reyes 8.00 20.00
588 Taylor Ward 6.00 15.00

2019 Topps Father's Day Blue

*BLUE: 10X TO 25X BASIC
*BLUE RC: 6X TO 15X BASIC RC
SER.1 ODDS 1:191 HOBBY
STATED PRINT RUN 50 SER. #'d SETS
1 Ronald Acuna Jr. 60.00 150.00
50 Mookie Betts 20.00 50.00
60 Kyle Tucker 40.00 100.00
100 Mike Trout 60.00 150.00
132 Miguel Andujar 25.00 60.00

250 Shohei Ohtani 25.00 60.00
281 Jeff McNeil 25.00 60.00
400 Bryce Harper 25.00 60.00
410 Fernando Tatis Jr. 1250.00 3000.00
445 Walker Buehler 30.00 80.00
473 Kyle Wright 12.00 30.00
475 Pete Alonso 200.00 500.00
560 Victor Reyes 8.00 20.00
588 Taylor Ward 6.00 15.00
632 Yusei Kikuchi 10.00 25.00

2019 Topps Gold

*GOLD: 2X TO 5X BASIC
*GOLD RC: 1.2X TO 3X BASIC RC
SER. 1 ODDS 1:5 HOBBY
SER. 2 ODDS 1:6 HOBBY
STATED PRINT RUN 2019 SER. #'d SETS
281 Jeff McNeil 8.00 20.00
410 Fernando Tatis Jr. 400.00 1000.00
475 Pete Alonso 30.00 80.00

2019 Topps Independence Day

*INDPNDNCE: 10X TO 25X BASIC
*INDPNDNCE RC: 6X TO 15X BASIC RC
SER.1 ODDS 1:126 HOBBY
SER.2 ODDS 1:160 HOBBY
STATED PRINT RUN 76 SER. #'d SETS
1 Ronald Acuna Jr. 60.00 150.00
60 Kyle Tucker 40.00 100.00
100 Mike Trout 60.00 150.00
132 Miguel Andujar 25.00 60.00
250 Shohei Ohtani 25.00 60.00
281 Jeff McNeil 25.00 60.00
400 Bryce Harper 25.00 60.00
410 Fernando Tatis Jr. 1250.00 3000.00
445 Walker Buehler 30.00 80.00
473 Kyle Wright 12.00 30.00
475 Pete Alonso 200.00 500.00
560 Victor Reyes 8.00 20.00
588 Taylor Ward 6.00 15.00

2019 Topps Meijer Purple

*PURPLE: 5X TO 12X BASIC
*PURPLE RC: 3X TO 8X BASIC RC
281 Jeff McNeil 10.00 25.00

2019 Topps Memorial Day Camo

*CAMO: 12X TO 30X BASIC
*CAMO RC: 8X TO 20X BASIC RC
SER.1 ODDS 1:381 HOBBY
SER.2 ODDS 1:486 HOBBY
STATED PRINT RUN 25 SER. #'d SETS
1 Ronald Acuna Jr. 75.00 200.00
50 Mookie Betts 25.00 60.00
60 Kyle Tucker 50.00 120.00
100 Mike Trout 75.00 200.00
132 Miguel Andujar 30.00 80.00
250 Shohei Ohtani 30.00 80.00
281 Jeff McNeil 30.00 80.00
400 Bryce Harper 30.00 80.00
410 Fernando Tatis Jr. 1500.00 4000.00
445 Walker Buehler 40.00 100.00
473 Kyle Wright 15.00 40.00
475 Pete Alonso 250.00 600.00
560 Victor Reyes 10.00 25.00
588 Taylor Ward 8.00 20.00
632 Yusei Kikuchi 12.00 30.00

2019 Topps Mother's Day Pink

*PINK: 10X TO 25X BASIC
*PINK RC: 6X TO 15X BASIC RC
SER.1 ODDS 1:191 HOBBY
STATED PRINT RUN 50 SER. #'d SETS
1 Ronald Acuna Jr. 60.00 150.00
50 Mookie Betts 20.00 50.00
60 Kyle Tucker 40.00 100.00
100 Mike Trout 60.00 150.00
132 Miguel Andujar 25.00 60.00
250 Shohei Ohtani 25.00 60.00
281 Jeff McNeil 25.00 60.00
400 Bryce Harper 25.00 60.00
410 Fernando Tatis Jr. 1250.00 3000.00
445 Walker Buehler 30.00 80.00
473 Kyle Wright 12.00 30.00
475 Pete Alonso 200.00 500.00
560 Victor Reyes 8.00 20.00
588 Taylor Ward 6.00 15.00
632 Yusei Kikuchi 10.00 25.00

2019 Topps Rainbow Foil

*RAINBOW: 2X TO 5X BASIC
*RAINBOW RC: 1.2X TO 3X BASIC RC
SER.1 ODDS 1:10 HOBBY
SER.2 ODDS 1:10 HOBBY
281 Jeff McNeil 6.00 15.00
410 Fernando Tatis Jr. 400.00 1000.00
475 Pete Alonso 20.00 50.00

2019 Topps Vintage Stock

*VINTAGE: 8X TO 20X BASIC
*VINTAGE RC: 5X TO 12X BASIC RC
SER.1 ODDS 1:97 HOBBY
SER.2 ODDS 1:123 HOBBY
STATED PRINT RUN 99 SER. #'d SETS
250 Shohei Ohtani 20.00 50.00
281 Jeff McNeil 25.00 60.00
410 Fernando Tatis Jr. 1000.00 2500.00
475 Pete Alonso 100.00 250.00

2019 Topps Walgreens Yellow

*YELLOW: 3X TO 8X BASIC
*YELLOW RC: 2X TO 5X BASIC RC
INSERTED IN WALGREENS PACKS
1 Ronald Acuna Jr. 20.00 50.00
213 Juan Soto 15.00 40.00

2019 Topps Base Set Legend Variations

SER.1 STATED ODDS 1:444 HOBBY
SER.2 STATED ODDS 1:20 HOBBY
SER.2 SSP ODDS 1:589 HOBBY
10 Sandy Koufax 25.00 60.00
21 Ozzie Smith 25.00 60.00
32 Cal Ripken Jr. 30.00 80.00
46 Frank Thomas 20.00 50.00
50 Ted Williams 40.00 100.00
57 Nolan Ryan 40.00 100.00
100 Hank Aaron 50.00 120.00
150 Don Mattingly 30.00 80.00
172 Mike Piazza 25.00 60.00
176 Ty Cobb 20.00 50.00
178 Jackie Robinson 30.00 80.00
215 Derek Jeter 40.00 100.00
230 Lou Gehrig 30.00 80.00
238 Rickey Henderson 20.00 50.00
250 Babe Ruth 50.00 120.00
253 Roberto Clemente 50.00 125.00
260 Reggie Jackson 30.00 80.00
262 Wade Boggs 25.00 60.00
276 Brooks Robinson 25.00 60.00
280 Bob Gibson 20.00 50.00
289 Mark McGwire 25.00 60.00
292 Ichiro 25.00 60.00
330 Bo Jackson 40.00 100.00
344 Pedro Martinez 20.00 50.00
350 Carl Yastrzemski 30.00 80.00
370 Lou Brock 2.00 5.00
373 Carlton Fisk 2.00 5.00
374 Joe Morgan 2.00 5.00
377 Roberto Alomar 2.00 5.00
381 Darryl Strawberry 1.50 4.00
385 Dale Murphy 2.50 6.00
387 Warren Spahn 20.00 50.00
428 Will Clark 2.00 5.00
431 Willie Stargell 2.00 5.00
436 Edgar Martinez 2.00 5.00
437 Johnny Mize 15.00 40.00
460 Ernie Banks 20.00 50.00
477 Al Kaline 20.00 50.00
486 Whitey Ford 15.00 40.00
488 Ken Griffey Jr. 5.00 12.00
501 Bob Feller 15.00 40.00
503 Roger Maris 40.00 100.00
505 Mariano Rivera 3.00 8.00
507 Pee Wee Reese 15.00 40.00
514 Tony Gwynn 2.50 6.00
518 Roger Clemens 3.00 8.00
525 Ryne Sandberg 5.00 12.00
529 Frank Robinson 2.00 5.00
542 Eddie Murray 2.00 5.00
545 Jeff Bagwell 2.00 5.00
551 Rogers Hornsby 20.00 50.00
564 Mel Ott 25.00 60.00
565 Catfish Hunter 2.00 5.00
568 Harmon Killebrew 20.00 50.00
573 Johnny Bench 2.50 6.00
574 Christy Mathewson 20.00 50.00
579 Tris Speaker 15.00 40.00
587 Chipper Jones 2.50 6.00
590 Barry Larkin 2.00 5.00
591 Gary Carter 2.00 5.00
594 Monte Irvin 25.00 60.00
622 Honus Wagner 20.00 50.00
623 Stan Musial 30.00 80.00
631 Rod Carew 2.00 5.00
646 Andre Dawson 2.00 5.00
653 Dave Winfield 2.00 5.00
665 Duke Snider 15.00 40.00
675 Vladimir Guerrero Sr. 2.00 5.00
676 Robin Yount 2.50 6.00
676 Eddie Mathews 25.00 60.00
679 Dizzy Dean 20.00 50.00
680 Willie McCovey 25.00 60.00
690 George Brett 5.00 12.00
692 Dennis Eckersley 2.00 5.00
694 David Ortiz 2.50 6.00

2019 Topps Base Set Photo Variations

SER.1 STATED ODDS 1:15 HOBBY
SER.2 STATED ODDS 1:20 HOBBY
SER.2 SSP ODDS 1:589 HOBBY
1 Ronald Acuna Jr. 15.00 40.00
7 Gleyber Torres 5.00 12.00
10 Clayton Kershaw 5.00 12.00
16 Charlie Blackmon 2.50 6.00
32 Carlos Correa 2.50 6.00
34 Josh Donaldson 2.00 5.00
37 Marcus Stroman 2.00 5.00
41 Corey Seager 2.50 6.00
46 Jose Abreu 2.50 6.00
49 Michael Kopech 5.00 12.00
50 Mookie Betts 6.00 15.00
52 J.T. Realmuto 2.50 6.00
53 Brandon Crawford 2.00 5.00
57 Justin Verlander 2.50 6.00
60 Kyle Tucker 15.00 40.00
62 Elvis Andrus 2.00 5.00
77 J.D. Martinez 2.50 6.00
84 Matt Carpenter 2.50 6.00
100 Mike Trout 12.00 30.00
107 Scooter Gennett 2.00 5.00
109 Michael Conforto 2.00 5.00
110 Trevor Bauer 3.00 8.00
112 Joey Gallo 2.00 5.00
119 Willson Contreras 2.00 5.00
125 Paul DeJong 2.50 6.00
128 Yoenis Cespedes 2.50 6.00
130 Blake Snell 2.00 5.00
133 Ryan Zimmerman 2.00 5.00
137 Carlos Rodon 2.50 6.00
139 Mitch Haniger 2.00 5.00
149 Khris Davis 2.50 6.00
150 Aaron Judge 6.00 15.00
157 Buster Posey 3.00 8.00
161 Eric Hosmer 2.00 5.00
163 Aaron Nola 2.00 5.00
166 Matt Chapman 2.50 6.00
168 Salvador Perez 2.00 5.00
176 Trea Turner 2.00 5.00
178 Jose Altuve 2.00 5.00
180 Justin Turner 2.50 6.00
183 Freddie Freeman 3.00 8.00
200 Jacob deGrom 5.00 12.00
209 Nicholas Castellanos 2.50 6.00
210 Kris Bryant 3.00 8.00
213 Juan Soto 20.00 50.00
215 Didi Gregorius 2.00 5.00
221 Luis Severino 2.00 5.00
222 Zack Greinke 2.50 6.00
223 Jose Ramirez 2.00 5.00
225 Yadier Molina 6.00 15.00
228 Rafael Devers 3.00 8.00
230 Miguel Cabrera 2.50 6.00
238 Whit Merrifield 2.50 6.00
250 Shohei Ohtani 10.00 25.00
253 Starling Marte 2.00 5.00
258 Eddie Rosario 2.00 5.00
262 Adam Jones 2.00 5.00
269 Francisco Lindor 5.00 12.00
276 Nolan Arenado 4.00 10.00
279 Rhys Hoskins 3.00 8.00
284 Joey Votto 2.50 6.00
287 Jesus Aguilar 2.00 5.00
292 Dee Gordon 1.50 4.00
297 Paul Goldschmidt 2.50 6.00
300 Christian Yelich 3.00 8.00
302 Jose Berrios 2.00 5.00
306 Justus Sheffield 2.50 6.00
310 Javier Baez 3.00 8.00
311 Jake Bauers 2.50 6.00
313 Robinson Cano 2.00 5.00
323 George Springer 2.00 5.00
330 Lorenzo Cain 1.50 4.00
336 Corey Kluber 2.00 5.00
344 Max Scherzer 2.50 6.00
349 Kyle Schwarber 2.50 6.00
353 Gary Sanchez 2.50 6.00
356 Stephen Strasburg 2.50 6.00
359 Noah Syndergaard 2.00 5.00
372 Yu Darvish 2.50 6.00
380 Chris Archer 1.50 4.00
390 Evan Longoria 2.00 5.00
395 Andrew McCutchen 2.50 6.00
396 Masahiro Tanaka 2.00 5.00
397 Lance McCullers 1.50 4.00
400A Bryce Harper 4.00 10.00
400B Bryce Harper 60.00 150.00
402 Victor Robles 3.00 8.00
410 Fernando Tatis Jr.
412 Clint Frazier 2.00 5.00
437 Albert Pujols 3.00 8.00
440 Dustin Pedroia 2.50 6.00
442 Reese McGuire 2.50 6.00
445 Walker Buehler 3.00 8.00
448 Willians Astudillo 1.50 4.00
460 Trevor Story 2.50 6.00
473 Kyle Wright 5.00 12.00
475 Pete Alonso
485 Wil Myers 2.00 5.00
486 CC Sabathia 2.00 5.00
500A Manny Machado 2.50 6.00
500B Manny Machado 12.00 30.00
503 Marcell Ozuna 2.50 6.00
507 Cody Bellinger 5.00 12.00
515 Hyun-Jin Ryu 2.00 5.00
540 Cole Hamels 2.00 5.00
556 Rowdy Tellez 2.50 6.00
561 Ozzie Albies 4.00 10.00
564 Austin Meadows 2.50 6.00
568 Giancarlo Stanton 2.50 6.00
572 Gerrit Cole 2.50 6.00
579 Andrew Benintendi 2.50 6.00
596A Anthony Rizzo 3.00 8.00
596B Anthony Rizzo 25.00 60.00
618 Nick Martini 1.50 4.00
624 Amed Rosario 2.00 5.00
629 Myles Straw 2.50 6.00
632A Yusei Kikuchi 2.50 6.00
632B Yusei Kikuchi 15.00 40.00
632C Yusei Kikuchi
643 Chris Sale 2.50 6.00
655 Tyler O'Neill 2.00 5.00
658 Max Muncy 2.00 5.00
661 Zack Greinke 2.50 6.00
670 Eloy Jimenez
672 Christin Stewart 2.00 5.00
680 Justin Smoak 1.50 4.00
699 Felix Hernandez 2.00 5.00
700A Alex Bregman 2.50 6.00
700B Alex Bregman 20.00 50.00
700C Vladimir Guerrero Jr
700D Vladimir Guerrero Jr

2019 Topps '18 Topps Now Review

STATED ODDS 1:18 HOBBY
TN1 Aaron Judge 1.00 2.50
TN2 Shohei Ohtani .60 1.50
TN3 Shohei Ohtani .60 1.50
TN4 Gleyber Torres .75 2.00
TN5 Juan Soto 1.25 3.00
TN6 Bryce Harper .60 1.50
TN7 Kyle Schwarber .40 1.00
TN8 Mike Trout 2.00 5.00
TN9 Trout/Pujols/Ohtani 2.00 5.00
TN10 Ronald Acuna Jr. 2.00 5.00

2019 Topps '84 Topps

STATED ODDS 1:4 HOBBY
*150TH/150: 2X TO 5X BASIC
T841 Don Mattingly .75 2.00
T842 Juan Soto 1.25 3.00
T843 Trea Turner .30 .75
T844 Rhys Hoskins .50 1.25
T845 Javier Baez .50 1.25
T846 Carlos Santana .30 .75
T847 Jake Bauers .40 1.00
T848 Max Scherzer .40 1.00
T849 Vladimir Guerrero .30 .75
T8410 J.T. Realmuto .40 1.00
T8411 Luis Urias .40 1.00
T8412 Trevor Hoffman .30 .75
T8413 Luke Weaver .25 .60
T8414 Paul Goldschmidt .40 1.00
T8415 Joey Votto .40 1.00
T8416 Whit Merrifield .40 1.00
T8417 Bob Gibson .30 .75
T8418 Gleyber Torres .75 2.00
T8419 Ronald Acuna Jr. 2.00 5.00
T8420 Mookie Betts .75 2.00
T8421 Andrew Benintendi .40 1.00
T8422 Jose Altuve .30 .75
T8423 Derek Jeter 1.00 2.50
T8424 Wade Boggs .30 .75
T8425 Nick Williams .25 .60
T8426 Luis Severino .30 .75
T8427 Chris Sale .40 1.00
T8428 Ramon Laureano .50 1.25
T8429 Pedro Martinez .30 .75
T8430 Frank Thomas .40 1.00
T8431 Will Clark .30 .75
T8432 Robin Yount .40 1.00
T8433 Dee Gordon .25 .60
T8434 Cody Bellinger .75 2.00
T8435 Ivan Rodriguez .30 .75
T8436 Jacob deGrom .75 2.00
T8437 Touki Toussaint .30 .75
T8438 Charlie Blackmon .40 1.00
T8439 Anthony Rizzo .50 1.25
T8440 Blake Snell .30 .75
T8441 Mike Trout 2.00 5.00
T8442 Clayton Kershaw .60 1.50
T8443 Mike Piazza .40 1.00
T8444 Kris Bryant .50 1.25
T8445 Zack Greinke .40 1.00
T8446 Kyle Seager .25 .60
T8447 Trey Mancini .30 .75
T8448 Eric Thames .25 .60
T8449 Dennis Eckersley .30 .75
T8450 Kyle Tucker .60 1.50
T8451 Matt Chapman .40 1.00
T8452 Ozzie Albies .40 1.00
T8453 Joey Gallo .30 .75
T8454 Dale Murphy .40 1.00
T8455 Matt Olson .40 1.00
T8456 Starling Marte .30 .75
T8457 Roberto Alomar .30 .75
T8458 Justin Verlander .40 1.00
T8459 Adrian Beltre .40 1.00
T8460 Eric Hosmer .30 .75
T8461 Mark McGwire .60 1.50
T8462 Tom Glavine .30 .75
T8463 Eddie Rosario .30 .75
T8464 Christian Yelich .50 1.25
T8465 Steve Carlton .30 .75
T8466 Jose Ramirez .30 .75
T8467 Buster Posey .50 1.25
T8468 Jesus Aguilar .30 .75
T8469 Shohei Ohtani .60 1.50
T8470 Albert Pujols .50 1.25
T8471 Nolan Arenado .60 1.50
T8472 Matt Carpenter .40 1.00
T8473 Ozzie Smith .50 1.25
T8474 Aaron Nola .30 .75
T8475 Bo Jackson .40 1.00
T8476 Willie McCovey .30 .75
T8477 Jose Abreu .40 1.00
T8478 Ryan O'Hearn .25 .60
T8479 Gary Sanchez .40 1.00
T8480 Jeff McNeil .60 1.50
T8481 Kolby Allard .40 1.00
T8482 Yadier Molina .50 1.25
T8483 Travis Shaw .25 .60
T8484 Jonathan Loaisiga .30 .75
T8485 Bert Blyleven .30 .75
T8486 Jose Berrios .30 .75
T8487 Wil Myers .30 .75
T8488 Brian Anderson .25 .60
T8489 Francisco Lindor .40 1.00
T8490 Noah Syndergaard .30 .75
T8491 Miles Mikolas .40 1.00
T8492 Carlos Correa .40 1.00
T8493 Mitch Haniger .30 .75
T8494 Corey Seager .40 1.00
T8495 Khris Davis .40 1.00
T8496 Nolan Ryan 1.25 3.00
T8497 Chance Adams .25 .60
T8498 David Ortiz .40 1.00
T8499 Trevor Bauer .50 1.25
T84100 Aaron Judge 1.00 2.50

2019 Topps '84 Topps All Star Relics

STATED ODDS 1:207 HOBBY
*150th/150: .6X TO 1.5X BASIC
*GOLD/50: 1X TO 2.5X BASIC
*RED/25: 2X TO 5X BASIC
ASRCF Carlton Fisk 2.00 5.00
ASRCR Cal Ripken Jr. 8.00 20.00
ASRCY Carl Yastrzemski 4.00 10.00
ASRDM Dale Murphy 2.50 6.00
ASRDT Don Mattingly 8.00 20.00
ASRDW Dave Winfield 2.00 5.00
ASRMM Mark McGwire 4.00 10.00
ASRNR Nolan Ryan 8.00 20.00
ASROS Ozzie Smith 3.00 8.00
ASRRA Rod Carew 2.00 5.00
ASRRC Roger Clemens 3.00 8.00
ASRRH Rickey Henderson 2.50 6.00
ASRRJ Reggie Jackson 2.00 5.00
ASRRS Ryne Sandberg 5.00 12.00
ASRRY Robin Yount 2.50 6.00
ASRSC Steve Carlton 2.00 5.00
ASRTG Tony Gwynn 2.50 6.00
ASRTS Tom Seaver 2.00 5.00
ASRWB Wade Boggs 2.00 5.00
ASRWC Will Clark 2.00 5.00

2019 Topps '84 Topps All Stars

84ASI Ichiro .50 1.25
84ASAB Alex Bregman .40 1.00
84ASAD Andre Dawson .30 .75
84ASAJ Aaron Judge 1.00 2.50
84ASBH Bryce Harper .60 1.50
84ASBJ Bo Jackson .40 1.00
84ASCB Charlie Blackmon .40 1.00
84ASCF Carlton Fisk .30 .75
84ASCR Cal Ripken Jr. 1.25 3.00
84ASCS Chris Sale .40 1.00
84ASCY Christian Yelich .50 1.25
84ASDG Dwight Gooden .25 .60
84ASDJ Derek Jeter 1.00 2.50
84ASDM Dale Murphy .40 1.00
84ASDS Darryl Strawberry .25 .60
84ASDW Dave Winfield .30 .75
84ASFF Freddie Freeman .50 1.25
84ASFL Francisco Lindor .40 1.00
84ASHM Hideki Matsui .40 1.00
84ASJA Jose Altuve .30 .75
84ASJB Javier Baez .50 1.25
84ASJD Jacob deGrom .75 2.00
84ASJM J.D. Martinez .40 1.00
84ASJV Joey Votto .40 1.00
84ASKG Ken Griffey Jr. .75 2.00
84ASLS Luis Severino .30 .75
84ASMB Mookie Betts .75 2.00
84ASMM Manny Machado .40 1.00
84ASMS Max Scherzer .40 1.00
84ASMT Mike Trout 2.00 5.00
84ASOA Ozzie Albies .40 1.00
84ASOS Ozzie Smith .50 1.25
84ASPG Paul Goldschmidt .40 1.00
84ASRC Rod Carew .30 .75
84ASRH Rickey Henderson .40 1.00
84ASRJ Reggie Jackson .30 .75
84ASRS Ryne Sandberg .75 2.00
84ASRY Robin Yount .40 1.00
84ASTG Tony Gwynn .40 1.00
84ASTS Trevor Story .40 1.00
84ASWB Wade Boggs .30 .75
84ASWC Willson Contreras .30 .75
84ASYM Yadier Molina .50 1.25
84ASCYA Carl Yastrzemski .60 1.50
84ASDMA Don Mattingly .75 2.00
84ASJBE Johnny Bench .40 1.00
84ASMAC Mark McGwire .60 1.50
84ASRCL Roger Clemens .50 1.25
84ASTGL Tom Glavine .30 .75
84ASWCL Will Clark .30 .75

2019 Topps '84 Topps All Stars 150th Anniversary

*150th/150: 2X TO 5X BASIC
STATED ODDS 1:284 HOBBY
STATED PRINT RUN 150 SER.#'d SETS
84ASDJ Derek Jeter 8.00 20.00
84ASMT Mike Trout 15.00 40.00

2019 Topps '84 Topps All Stars Black

*BLACK/299: 1.2X TO 3X BASIC
STATED ODDS 1:49 HOBBY
STATED PRINT RUN 299 SER.#'d SETS
84ASDJ Derek Jeter 5.00 12.00
84ASMT Mike Trout 10.00 25.00

2019 Topps '84 Topps All Stars Gold

*GOLD/50: 3X TO 8X BASIC
STATED ODDS 1:294 HOBBY
STATED PRINT RUN 50 SER.#'d SETS
84ASDJ Derek Jeter 12.00 30.00
84ASMT Mike Trout 25.00 60.00

2019 Topps '84 Topps Autographs

SER.1 ODDS 1:740 HOBBY
SER.2 ODDS 1:800 HOBBY
EXCHANGE DEADLINE 12/31/2020
84AAG Adolis Garcia 30.00 80.00
84AAK Al Kaline 15.00 40.00
84AARZ Anthony Rizzo 40.00 100.00
84ABHA Bryce Harper
84ABK Brad Keller 2.50 6.00
84ABL Brandon Lowe 15.00 40.00
84ABN Brandon Nimmo 3.00 8.00
84ABS Blake Snell 6.00 15.00
84ABT Blake Treinen 2.50 6.00
84ACA Chance Adams 5.00 12.00
84ACHE Cesar Hernandez 5.00 12.00
84ACJ Chipper Jones 60.00 150.00
84ACM Colin Moran 3.00 8.00
84ACMU Cedric Mullins 5.00 12.00
84ACR Cal Ripken Jr. 75.00 200.00
84ACT Chris Taylor S2 5.00 12.00
84ADBO David Bote 10.00 25.00
84ADJ Danny Jansen 2.50 6.00
84ADJ Derek Jeter 200.00 500.00
84ADM Daniel Mengden S2 4.00 10.00
84ADMA Don Mattingly 50.00 120.00
84ADMU Dale Murphy 25.00 60.00
84ADRO Dereck Rodriguez 10.00 25.00
84ADST Darryl Strawberry 15.00 40.00
84AEJ Eloy Jimenez S2 25.00 60.00
84AFL Francisco Lindor EXCH 20.00 50.00
84AFP Freddy Peralta 4.00 10.00
84AFR Fernando Romero S2 4.00 10.00
84AFT Fernando Tatis Jr. S2 60.00 150.00
84AFTH Frank Thomas 40.00 100.00
84AFV Felipe Vazquez 5.00 12.00
84AGSA Gary Sanchez 15.00 40.00
84AHA Hank Aaron 125.00 300.00
84AIR Ivan Rodriguez S2 15.00 40.00
84AJA Jose Altuve 30.00 80.00
84AJB Jake Bauers 5.00 12.00
84AJC Johan Camargo S2 6.00 15.00
84AJHA Josh Hader 3.00 8.00
84AJJ Jake Junis 4.00 10.00
84AJMC Jeff McNeil 15.00 40.00
84AJN Jacob Nix S2 4.00 10.00
84AJS Juan Soto 50.00 120.00
84AKA Kolby Allard 6.00 15.00
84AKB Kris Bryant 30.00 80.00
84AKD Khris Davis 8.00 20.00
84AKSC Kyle Schwarber 10.00 25.00
84AKT Kyle Tucker 25.00 60.00
84ALG Lourdes Gurriel Jr. 6.00 15.00
84ALS Luis Severino 3.00 8.00
84AMA Miguel Andujar 12.00 30.00
84AMCL Mike Clevinger 5.00 12.00
84AMF Mike Foltynewicz 4.00 10.00
84AMH Mitch Haniger 6.00 15.00
84AMKO Michael Kopech 15.00 40.00
84AMMG Mark McGwire 60.00 150.00
84AMMU Max Muncy 6.00 15.00
84AMO Matt Olson 6.00 15.00
84ANP Nick Pivetta S2 4.00 10.00
84ANR Nolan Ryan 75.00 200.00
84ANSY Noah Syndergaard 12.00 30.00
84AOS Ozzie Smith 40.00 100.00
84APD Paul DeJong S2 8.00 20.00
84APW Patrick Wisdom 4.00 10.00
84ARA Ronald Acuna Jr. 75.00 200.00
84ARHE Rickey Henderson 50.00 120.00
84ARO Ryan O'Hearn 2.50 6.00
84ARS Ryne Sandberg 40.00 100.00
84ARY Robin Yount 20.00 50.00
84ASD Steven Duggar 4.00 10.00
84ASN Sean Newcomb S2 2.50 6.00
84ASO Shohei Ohtani 125.00 300.00
84ASR Sean Reid-Foley 2.50 6.00
84ATAN Tim Anderson 8.00 20.00
84ATO Tyler O'Neill S2 6.00 15.00
84ATS Travis Shaw 5.00 12.00
84ATST Trevor Story 6.00 15.00
84ATT Touki Toussaint S2 3.00 8.00
84ATW Taylor Ward 2.50 6.00
84AVG Vladimir Guerrero Jr. S2 60.00 150.00
84AVR Victor Robles S2 8.00 20.00
84AWCL Will Clark 30.00 80.00
84AWM Whit Merrifield 6.00 15.00
84AYM Yadier Molina S2 25.00 60.00
84AZG Zack Godley 2.50 6.00
84AARS Amed Rosario S2 5.00 12.00
84AIKF Isiah Kiner-Falefa S2 3.00 8.00
84AJBE Johnny Bench S2 40.00 10.00
84AJBS Jose Berrios S2 3.00 8.00
84AMMI Miles Mikolas S2 5.00 12.00
84ARHY Rhys Hoskins S2 15.00 40.00
84ASAD Andre Dawson S2 15.00 40.00
84ASAJ Aaron Judge S2
84ASBB Bert Blyleven S2 3.00 8.00
84ASBG Bob Gibson S2 50.00 120.00
84ASBI Shane Bieber S2 12.00 30.00
84ASBJ Bo Jackson S2 40.00 100.00
84ASBS Blake Snell S2 6.00 15.00
84ASCF Carlton Fisk S2 20.00 50.00
84ASCK Corey Kluber S2 6.00 15.00
84ASCR Cal Ripken Jr. S2 75.00 200.00
84ASCS Chris Sale S2 10.00 25.00
84ASCY Christian Yelich S2 25.00 60.00
84ASDG Dwight Gooden S2 15.00 40.00
84ASDJ Derek Jeter S2 200.00 500.00
84ASDM Dale Murphy S2 25.00 60.00
84ASDS Darryl Strawberry S2 12.00 30.00
84ASDW Dave Winfield S2 10.00 25.00
84ASFL Francisco Lindor S2 20.00 50.00
84ASHM Hideki Matsui S2 40.00 100.00
84ASJB Johnny Bench S2 40.00 100.00
84ASJd Jacob deGrom S2
84ASJV Joey Votto S2
84ASLS Luis Severino S2 3.00 8.00
84ASMH Mitch Haniger S2 6.00 15.00
84ASMM Mark McGwire S2 30.00 80.00
84ASMT Mike Trout S2
84ASMZ Steven Matz S2 5.00 12.00
84ASOA Ozzie Albies S2 20.00 50.00
84ASOS Ozzie Smith S2 40.00 100.00
84ASPN Phil Niekro S2 10.00 25.00
84ASRC Roger Clemens S2
84ASRH Rickey Henderson S2 50.00 120.00
84ASRJ Reggie Jackson S2
84ASRS Ryne Sandberg S2 40.00 100.00
84ASRY Robin Yount S2 20.00 50.00
84ASTG Tom Glavine S2 25.00 60.00
84ASTR Tim Raines S2 3.00 8.00
84ASWB Wade Boggs S2 3.00 8.00
84ASWC Willson Contreras S2 10.00 25.00
84RAAD Austin Dean S2 2.50 6.00
84RAAG Aramis Garcia S2 2.50 6.00
84RABW Bryse Wilson S2 3.00 8.00
84RACB Corbin Burnes S2 8.00 20.00
84RACS Chris Shaw S2 4.00 10.00
84RADF David Fletcher S2 8.00 20.00
84RADH Dakota Hudson S2 5.00 12.00
84RADP Daniel Poncedeleon S2 4.00 10.00
84RADS Dennis Santana S2 2.50 6.00
84RAFV Framber Valdez S2 8.00 20.00
84RAHF Heath Fillmyer S2 5.00 12.00
84RAJB Jose Briceno S2 5.00 12.00
84RAJC Jake Cave S2 5.00 12.00
84RAJJ Josh James S2 5.00 12.00
84RAKK Kevin Kramer S2 3.00 8.00
84RAKN Kevin Newman S2 5.00 12.00
84RAKW Kyle Wright S2 4.00 10.00
84RAMS Myles Straw S2 8.00 20.00
84RANB Nick Burdi S2 2.50 6.00
84RANM Nick Martini S2 5.00 12.00
84RPA Peter Alonso 60.00 150.00
84RARB Ray Black S2 2.50 6.00
84RART Rowdy Tellez S2 6.00 15.00
84RASG Stephen Gonsalves S2 2.50 6.00
84RAWA Willians Astudillo S2 10.00 25.00
84ASBSU Bruce Sutter S2 10.00 25.00
84ASCYA Carl Yastrzemski S2 50.00 120.00
84ASDMA Don Mattingly S2 50.00 120.00
84ASJAL Jose Altuve S2 15.00 40.00
84ASJRI Jim Rice S2 8.00 20.00
84ASWCL Will Clark S2 30.00 80.00
84RACST Christin Stewart S2 3.00 8.00
84RAJBE Jalen Beeks S2 2.50 6.00
84RARMC Reese McGuire S2 5.00 12.00

2019 Topps '84 Topps Autographs 150th Anniversary

*150TH ANNV/150: .5X TO 1.2X BASIC
SER.1 ODDS 1:2431 HOBBY
SER.2 ODDS 1:1825 HOBBY
STATED PRINT RUN 150 SER.#'d SETS
EXCHANGE DEADLINE 12/31/2020
84AFT Fernando Tatis Jr. S2 125.00 300.00

2019 Topps '84 Topps Autographs Gold

*GOLD/50: .6X TO 1.5X BASIC
SER.1 ODDS 1:3808 HOBBY
SER.2 ODDS 1:5390 HOBBY
STATED PRINT RUN 50 SER.#'d SETS
EXCHANGE DEADLINE 12/31/2020
84ADMA Don Mattingly 100.00 250.00
84AFL Francisco Lindor EXCH 25.00 60.00
84AFT Fernando Tatis Jr. S2 150.00 400.00
84AJA Jose Altuve 50.00 120.00
84AOS Ozzie Smith 40.00 100.00
84ARY Robin Yount 30.00 80.00
84ASBG Bob Gibson S2 75.00 200.00

2019 Topps '84 Topps Autographs Red

*RED/25: .8X TO 2X BASIC
SER.1 ODDS 1:750 HOBBY
SER.2 ODDS 1:6274 HOBBY
STATED PRINT RUN 25 SER.#'d SETS
EXCHANGE DEADLINE 12/31/2020
84AARZ Anthony Rizzo 50.00 120.00
84ACJ Chipper Jones 75.00 200.00
84ACR Cal Ripken Jr. 100.00 250.00
84ADMA Don Mattingly 125.00 300.00
84AFL Francisco Lindor EXCH 30.00 80.00
84AFT Fernando Tatis Jr. S2 200.00 500.00
84AGSA Gary Sanchez 20.00 50.00
84AJA Jose Altuve 60.00 150.00
84AMMG Mark McGwire 75.00 200.00
84AMTR Mike Trout 400.00 800.00
84ANR Nolan Ryan 125.00 300.00
84AOS Ozzie Smith 50.00 120.00
84ARHE Rickey Henderson 60.00 150.00
84ARS Ryne Sandberg 50.00 120.00
84ARY Robin Yount 40.00 100.00
84RPA Peter Alonso 125.00 300.00

2019 Topps '84 Topps Relics

SER.1 ODDS 1:82 HOBBY
SER.2 ODDS 1:149 HOBBY
*150TH/150: .5X TO 1.2X BASIC
*GOLD/50: .6X TO 1.5X BASIC
*RED/25: .75X TO 2X BASIC
84RAB Adrian Beltre 3.00 8.00
84RAB Alex Bregman S2 3.00 8.00
84RABE Andrew Benintendi 3.00 8.00
84RAJ Aaron Judge 8.00 20.00
84RAJ Aaron Judge S2 8.00 20.00
84RAN Aaron Nola S2 2.50 6.00
84RAP Albert Pujols 4.00 10.00
84RAR Anthony Rizzo 4.00 10.00
84RBC Brandon Crawford 2.50 6.00
84RBH Bryce Harper S2 5.00 12.00
84RBP Buster Posey 4.00 10.00
84RCC Carlos Correa 3.00 8.00
84RCH Charlie Blackmon S2 3.00 8.00
84RCK Clayton Kershaw 5.00 12.00
84RCR Cal Ripken Jr. 6.00 15.00
84RCS Corey Seager 3.00 8.00
84RCSA Chris Sale 3.00 8.00
84RDJ Derek Jeter S2 8.00 20.00
84RDM Don Mattingly 8.00 20.00
84RDO David Ortiz S2 3.00 8.00
84REM Eddie Murray 6.00 15.00
84RFF Freddie Freeman 4.00 10.00
84RFL Francisco Lindor 3.00 8.00
84RGS George Springer S2 2.50 6.00
84RJA Jose Abreu 3.00 8.00
84RJAL Jose Altuve 2.50 6.00
84RJB Javier Baez 4.00 10.00
84RJd Jacob deGrom 6.00 15.00
84RJM Joe Mauer 2.50 6.00
84RJM J.D. Martinez S2 3.00 8.00
84RJS Juan Soto S2 4.00 10.00
84RJV Joey Votto 3.00 8.00
84RJVE Justin Verlander 3.00 8.00
84RKB Kris Bryant S2 4.00 10.00
84RKBR Kris Bryant 4.00 10.00
84RKD Khris Davis S2 3.00 8.00
84RMA Miguel Andujar S2 3.00 8.00
84RMB Mookie Betts 8.00 20.00
84RMB Mookie Betts S2 6.00 15.00
84RMC Matt Carpenter S2 3.00 8.00
84RMH Mitch Haniger 2.50 6.00
84RMI Miguel Cabrera S2 3.00 8.00
84RMK Masahiro Tanaka S2 2.50 6.00
84RMO Michael Conforto S2 2.50 6.00
84RMS Max Scherzer 3.00 8.00
84RMT Mike Trout 8.00 20.00
84RMT Mike Trout S2 15.00 40.00
84RNA Nolan Arenado 5.00 12.00
84RNC Nicholas Castellanos 3.00 8.00
84RNR Nolan Ryan 12.00 30.00
84RNS Noah Syndergaard 2.50 6.00
84ROA Ozzie Albies 3.00 8.00
84ROS Ozzie Smith 4.00 10.00
84RPG Paul Goldschmidt 3.00 8.00
84RRA Ronald Acuna Jr. 12.00 30.00
84RRH Rickey Henderson 4.00 10.00
84RRHO Rhys Hoskins 4.00 10.00
84RRJ Reggie Jackson 5.00 12.00
84RRY Robin Yount 3.00 8.00
84RSO Shohei Ohtani 10.00 25.00
84RTM Trey Mancini 2.50 6.00
84RTT Trea Turner 2.50 6.00
84RVR Victor Robles S2 4.00 10.00
84RWB Wade Boggs 5.00 12.00
84RWM Wil Myers 2.50 6.00
84RYM Yadier Molina 4.00 10.00

2019 Topps '84 Topps Rookies

STATED ODDS 1:4 HOBBY
*BLUE: .75X TO 2X BASIC
*BLACK/299: 1.2X TO 3X BASIC
*150th/150: 2X TO 5X BASIC
*GOLD/50: 3X TO 8X BASIC
84RAC Adam Cimber .25 .60
84RAD Austin Dean .25 .60
84RAG Aramis Garcia .25 .60
84RBK Brad Keller .25 .60
84RBL Brandon Lowe .40 1.00
84RBW Bryse Wilson .30 .75
84RCB Corbin Burnes 2.00 5.00
84RCM Cedric Mullins .50 1.25
84RCP Cionel Perez .25 .60
84RCS Christin Stewart .30 .75
84RCT Carlos Tocci .25 .60
84RDD Dean Deetz .25 .60
84RDF David Fletcher .75 2.00
84RDH Dakota Hudson .30 .75
84RDJ Danny Jansen .25 .60
84RDP Daniel Ponce De Leon .40 1.00
84RDS Dennis Santana .25 .60
84RED Enyel De Los Santos .25 .60
84RFV Framber Valdez .25 .60
84RHF Heath Fillmyer .25 .60
84RJB Jose Briceno .25 .60
84RJC Jake Cave .30 .75
84RJF Johnny Field .30 .75
84RJJ Josh James .40 1.00
84RJS Jeffrey Springs .25 .60
84RKK Kevin Kramer .30 .75
84RKN Kevin Newman .40 1.00
84RKW Kyle Wright .40 1.00
84RMK Michael Kopech .75 2.00
84RMS Myles Straw .40 1.00
84RNB Nick Burdi .25 .60
84RNC Noel Cuevas .25 .60
84RNM Nick Martini .25 .60
84RPL Pablo Lopez .25 .60
84RPW Patrick Wisdom .25 .60
84RRB Ryan Borucki .25 .60
84RRM Reese McGuire .40 1.00
84RRT Rowdy Tellez .40 1.00
84RSD Steven Duggar .30 .75
84RSG Stephen Gonsalves .25 .60
84RSR Sean Reid-Foley .25 .60
84RTR Trevor Richards .25 .60
84RTW Taylor Ward .25 .60
84RWA Willians Astudillo .25 .60
84RYK Yusei Kikuchi .40 1.00
84RCSH Chris Shaw .25 .60
84RDST DJ Stewart .30 .75
84RJBE Jalen Beeks .25 .60
84RJSH Justus Sheffield .40 1.00
84RRBL Ray Black .25 .60

2019 Topps '84 Topps Silver Pack Chrome

T841 Don Mattingly 1.25 3.00
T842 Mike Trout 3.00 8.00
T843 Ronald Acuna Jr. 3.00 8.00
T844 Javier Baez .75 2.00
T845 Mookie Betts 1.25 3.00

T846 Jackie Robinson .60 1.50
T847 Corey Kluber .50 1.25
T848 Kris Bryant .75 2.00
T849 Francisco Lindor .60 1.50
T8410 Charlie Blackmon .60 1.50
T8411 Jose Altuve .50 1.25
T8412 Noah Syndergaard .50 1.25
T8413 George Springer .50 1.25
T8414 Bo Jackson .60 1.50
T8415 Manny Machado .60 1.50
T8416 Christian Yelich .75 2.00
T8417 Shohei Ohtani 1.00 2.50
T8418 Aaron Judge 1.50 4.00
T8419 Derek Jeter 1.50 4.00
T8420 Ryne Sandberg 1.25 3.00
T8421 Gleyber Torres 1.25 3.00
T8422 Rickey Henderson .60 1.50
T8423 Rhys Hoskins .75 2.00
T8424 Yadier Molina .75 2.00
T8425 Jake Bauers .60 1.50
T8426 Juan Soto 2.00 5.00
T8427 Buster Posey .75 2.00
T8428 Kyle Schwarber .60 1.50
T8429 Will Clark .50 1.25
T8430 Darryl Strawberry .40 1.00
T8431 John Smoltz .60 1.50
T8432 Cedric Mullins .75 2.00
T8433 Jeff McNeil 1.00 2.50
T8434 Patrick Wisdom .40 1.00
T8435 Brad Keller .40 1.00
T8436 Chance Adams .40 1.00
T8437 Sean Reid-Foley .40 1.00
T8438 Ramon Laureano .75 2.00
T8439 Ryan O'Hearn .40 1.00
T8440 Justus Sheffield .60 1.50
T8441 Kevin Kramer .50 1.25
T8442 Bryse Wilson .50 1.25
T8443 Steven Matz .40 1.00
T8444 Jesus Aguilar .50 1.25
T8445 Jim Rice .50 1.25
T8446 Mark Grace .50 1.25
T8447 Adalberto Mondesi .50 1.25
T8448 Ozzie Smith .75 2.00
T8449 Mark McGwire 1.00 2.50
T8450 Cal Ripken Jr. 2.00 5.00

2019 Topps '84 Topps Silver Pack Chrome Blue Refractors

*BLUE REF: 1.5X TO 4X BASIC
RANDOM INSERTS IN SILVER PACKS
STATED PRINT RUN 150 SER.#'d SETS

2019 Topps '84 Topps Silver Pack Chrome Gold Refractors

*GOLD REF: 5X TO 12X BASIC
RANDOM INSERTS IN SILVER PACKS
STATED PRINT RUN 50 SER.#'d SETS

2019 Topps '84 Topps Silver Pack Chrome Green Refractors

*GREEN REF: 2X TO 5X BASIC
RANDOM INSERTS IN SILVER PACKS
STATED PRINT RUN 150 SER.#'d SETS

2019 Topps '84 Topps Silver Pack Chrome Orange Refractors

*ORANGE REF: 6X TO 15X BASIC
RANDOM INSERTS IN SILVER PACKS
STATED PRINT RUN 25 SER.#'d SETS

2019 Topps '84 Topps Silver Pack Chrome Purple Refractors

*PURPLE REF: 2X TO 5X BASIC
RANDOM INSERTS IN SILVER PACKS
STATED PRINT RUN 75 SER.#'d SETS

2019 Topps '84 Topps Silver Pack Chrome Autographs

RANDOM INSERTS IN SILVER PACKS
PRINT RUNS B/WN 10-299 COPIES PER
NO PRICING ON QTY 10
T84A1 Don Mattingly/30 75.00 200.00
T84A2 Mike Trout
T84A7 Corey Kluber/50 8.00 20.00
T84A11 Jose Altuve/50 20.00 50.00
T84A13 George Springer/50 15.00 40.00
T84A15 Manny Machado/30 25.00 60.00
T84A19 Derek Jeter
T84A20 Ryne Sandberg/30 40.00 100.00
T84A23 Rhys Hoskins/30 30.00 80.00
T84A24 Yadier Molina
T84A25 Jake Bauers/199 5.00 12.00
T84A28 Kyle Schwarber/30 15.00 40.00
T84A29 Will Clark
T84A30 Darryl Strawberry/50 15.00 40.00
T84A31 John Smoltz/50 15.00 40.00
T84A32 Cedric Mullins/199 10.00 25.00
T84A33 Jeff McNeil/299 15.00 40.00
T84A34 Patrick Wisdom/199 3.00 8.00
T84A35 Brad Keller/199 3.00 8.00
T84A36 Chance Adams/199 3.00 8.00
T84A37 Sean Reid-Foley/199 3.00 8.00
T84A38 Ramon Laureano/199 20.00 50.00
T84A39 Ryan O'Hearn/199 3.00 8.00
T84A40 Justus Sheffield/199 5.00 12.00
T84A41 Kevin Kramer/199 4.00 10.00
T84A42 Bryse Wilson/199 4.00 10.00
T84A43 Steven Matz/199 3.00 8.00
T84A44 Jesus Aguilar/199 5.00 12.00
T84A45 Jim Rice/199 10.00 25.00
T84A46 Mark Grace/199 10.00 25.00
T84A47 Adalberto Mondesi/199 10.00 25.00
T84A48 Ozzie Smith/30 30.00 80.00
T84A49 Mark McGwire/30 30.00 80.00

2019 Topps '84 Topps Silver Pack Chrome Autographs Orange Refractors

*ORANGE/25: 1X TO 2.5X p/r 199-299
*ORANGE/25: .75X TO 2X p/r 50
*ORANGE/25: .5X TO 1.2X p/r 30
RANDOM INSERTS IN SILVER PACKS
STATED PRINT RUN 25 SER.#'d SETS
T84A29 Will Clark 40.00 100.00

2019 Topps '84 Topps Silver Pack Chrome Series 2

T841 Clayton Kershaw 1.00 2.50
T842 Ken Griffey Jr. 1.25 3.00
T843 Alex Bregman .60 1.50
T844 Paul Goldschmidt .60 1.50
T845 Robinson Cano .50 1.25
T846 Anthony Rizzo .75 2.00
T847 Nolan Ryan 2.00 5.00
T848 Joey Votto .60 1.50
T849 Albert Pujols .75 2.00
T8410 Chipper Jones .60 1.50
T8411 Touki Toussaint .50 1.25
T8412 Kolby Allard .60 1.50
T8413 DJ Stewart .50 1.25
T8414 Wade Boggs .50 1.25
T8415 Chris Sale .60 1.50
T8416 Ernie Banks .60 1.50
T8417 Frank Thomas .60 1.50
T8418 Michael Kopech 1.25 3.00
T8419 Nolan Arenado 1.00 2.50
T8420 Eloy Jimenez 1.50 4.00
T8421 Kyle Tucker 1.00 2.50
T8422 George Brett 1.25 3.00
T8423 Cody Bellinger 1.25 3.00
T8424 Robin Yount .60 1.50
T8425 Willians Astudillo .40 1.00
T8426 Jacob deGrom 1.25 3.00
T8427 Miguel Andujar .60 1.50
T8428 Jonathan Loaisiga .50 1.25
T8429 Nick Martini .40 1.00
T8430 Khris Davis .60 1.50
T8431 Andrew McCutchen .60 1.50
T8432 Kevin Newman .60 1.50
T8433 Roberto Clemente 1.50 4.00
T8434 Luis Urias .60 1.50
T8435 Tony Gwynn .60 1.50
T8436 Steven Duggar .50 1.25
T8437 Yusei Kikuchi .60 1.50
T8438 Adrian Beltre .60 1.50
T8439 Dakota Hudson .50 1.25
T8440 Manny Machado .60 1.50
T8441 Bryce Harper 1.00 2.50
T8442 Rowdy Tellez .60 1.50
T8443 Danny Jansen .40 1.00
T8444 Roberto Alomar .50 1.25
T8445 Max Scherzer .60 1.50
T8446 Josh James .60 1.50
T8447 Daniel Ponce de Leon .60 1.50
T8448 Myles Straw .60 1.50
T8449 Kohl Stewart .50 1.25
T8450 Mariano Rivera .75 2.00

2019 Topps '84 Topps Silver Pack Chrome Series 2 Black Refractors

*BLACK REF: 1.2X TO 3X BASIC
RANDOM INSERTS IN SILVER PACKS
STATED PRINT RUN 199 SER.#'d SETS

2019 Topps '84 Topps Silver Pack Chrome Series 2 Blue Refractors

*BLUE REF: 1.5X TO 4X BASIC
RANDOM INSERTS IN SILVER PACKS
STATED PRINT RUN 150 SER.#'d SETS

2019 Topps '84 Topps Silver Pack Chrome Series 2 Gold Refractors

*GOLD REF: 5X TO 12X BASIC
RANDOM INSERTS IN SILVER PACKS
STATED PRINT RUN 50 SER.#'d SETS

2019 Topps '84 Topps Silver Pack Chrome Series 2 Green Refractors

*GREEN REF: 2X TO 5X BASIC
RANDOM INSERTS IN SILVER PACKS
STATED PRINT RUN 99 SER.#'d SETS

2019 Topps '84 Topps Silver Pack Chrome Series 2 Orange Refractors

*ORANGE REF: 6X TO 15X BASIC
RANDOM INSERTS IN SILVER PACKS
STATED PRINT RUN 25 SER.#'d SETS

2019 Topps '84 Topps Silver Pack Chrome Series 2 Purple Refractors

*PURPLE REF: 2X TO 5X BASIC
RANDOM INSERTS IN SILVER PACKS
STATED PRINT RUN 75 SER.#'d SETS

2019 Topps '84 Topps Silver Pack Chrome Series 2 Autographs

RANDOM INSERTS IN SILVER PACKS
PRINT RUNS B/WN 10-149 COPIES PER
NO PRICING ON QTY 10
*ORANGE/25: 1X TO 2.5X p/r 149
*ORANGE/25: .75X TO 2X p/r 50-99
T844 Paul Goldschmidt/30 20.00 50.00
T8411 Touki Toussaint/149 4.00 10.00
T8412 Kolby Allard/149 5.00 12.00
T8413 DJ Stewart/149 4.00 10.00
T8414 Wade Boggs
T8418 Michael Kopech/99 10.00 25.00
T8420 Eloy Jimenez/30 60.00 150.00
T8421 Kyle Tucker/50 25.00 60.00
T8425 Willians Astudillo/149 8.00 20.00
T8426 Jacob deGrom/30 30.00 80.00
T8427 Miguel Andujar/30 15.00 40.00
T8428 Jonathan Loaisiga/149 4.00 10.00
T8429 Nick Martini/149 3.00 8.00
T8432 Kevin Newman/149 6.00 15.00
T8436 Steven Duggar/149 4.00 10.00
T8437 Yusei Kikuchi/99 6.00 15.00
T8439 Dakota Hudson/149 5.00 12.00
T8442 Rowdy Tellez/149 5.00 12.00
T8446 Josh James/149 5.00 12.00
T8447 Daniel Ponce de Leon/149 5.00 12.00
T8448 Myles Straw/149 6.00 15.00
T8449 Kohl Stewart/149 4.00 10.00

2019 Topps 150 Years of Professional Baseball

STATED ODDS 1:7 HOBBY
*150TH/150: 2X TO 5X BASIC
*GREEN: .75X TO 2X BASIC
1501 Babe Ruth 1.00 2.50
1502 Babe Ruth 1.00 2.50
1503 Lou Gehrig .75 2.00
1504 Roger Maris .40 1.00
1505 Cal Ripken Jr. 1.25 3.00
1506 Carlton Fisk .30 .75
1507 Reggie Jackson .30 .75
1508 Jackie Robinson .40 1.00
1509 Babe Ruth 1.00 2.50
15010 Nolan Ryan 1.25 3.00
15011 Cal Ripken Jr. 1.25 3.00
15012 Babe Ruth 1.00 2.50
15013 Babe Ruth 1.00 2.50
15014 Ty Cobb 1.25 3.00
15015 Mike Piazza .40 1.00
15016 Nolan Ryan 1.25 3.00
15017 Rickey Henderson .40 1.00
15018 Ichiro .50 1.25
15019 Roberto Clemente 1.00 2.50
15020 David Ortiz .40 1.00
15021 Ty Cobb .60 1.50
15022 Cal Ripken Jr. 1.25 3.00
15023 Jackie Robinson .40 1.00
15024 Mariano Rivera .50 1.25
15025 Ozzie Smith .50 1.25
15026 Derek Jeter 1.00 2.50
15027 The Topps Company .25 .60
15028 Nolan Ryan 1.25 3.00
15029 Lou Brock .30 .75
15030 William Howard Taft .25 .60
15031 Catfish Hunter .30 .75
15032 Ted Williams .75 2.00
15033 Hank Aaron .75 2.00
15034 Ted Williams .75 2.00
15035 Hank Aaron .75 2.00
15036 Wrigley Field .25 .60
15037 Bill Mazeroski .30 .75
15038 Brooks Robinson .30 .75
15039 Phil Niekro .30 .75
15040 Duke Snider .30 .75
15041 Lou Gehrig .75 2.00
15042 Ted Williams .75 2.00
15043 Larry Doby .30 .75
15044 George Brett .75 2.00
15045 Sandy Koufax .75 2.00
15046 Enos Slaughter .30 .75
15047 Sandy Koufax .75 2.00
15048 Ted Williams .75 2.00
15049 Eddie Mathews .40 1.00
15050 Oriole Park at Camden Yards .25 .60
15051 Babe Ruth 1.00 2.50
15052 Jackie Robinson .40 1.00
15053 Lou Gehrig .75 2.00
15054 Clayton Kershaw .60 1.50
15055 Robin Yount .40 1.00
15056 Tom Glavine .30 .75
15057 Vladimir Guerrero .30 .75
15058 Don Mattingly .75 2.00
15059 Reggie Jackson .30 .75
15060 Ivan Rodriguez .30 .75
15061 Roger Maris .40 1.00
15062 Dennis Eckersley .30 .75
15063 Mariano Rivera .50 1.25
15064 Frank Thomas .40 1.00
15065 Adrian Beltre .40 1.00
15066 Justin Verlander .40 1.00
15067 Rod Carew .30 .75
15068 Bryce Harper .60 1.50
15069 Ernie Banks .40 1.00
15070 Mike Piazza .40 1.00
15071 Mark McGwire .60 1.50
15072 Roberto Clemente 1.00 2.50
15073 Derek Jeter 1.00 2.50
15074 Miguel Cabrera .40 1.00
15075 Mike Trout 2.00 5.00
15076 Bob Gibson .30 .75
15077 Al Kaline .40 1.00
15078 Albert Pujols .50 1.25
15079 Wade Boggs .30 .75
15080 David Ortiz .40 1.00
15081 Willie McCovey .30 .75
15082 Tom Seaver .30 .75
15083 Steve Carlton .30 .75
15084 Ty Cobb .60 1.50
15085 Carl Yastrzemski .60 1.50
15086 Pedro Martinez .30 .75
15087 Juan Marichal .30 .75
15088 Nolan Ryan 1.25 3.00
15089 Hank Aaron .75 2.00
15090 Ted Williams .75 2.00
15091 Bob Feller .30 .75
15092 Duke Snider .30 .75
15093 Eddie Mathews .40 1.00
15094 Warren Spahn .30 .75
15095 George Brett .75 2.00
15096 Brooks Robinson .30 .75
15097 Lou Brock .30 .75
15098 Jim Palmer .30 .75
15099 Harmon Killebrew .40 1.00
150100 Ichiro .50 1.25
150101 Ty Cobb .60 1.50
150102 Babe Ruth 1.00 2.50
150103 Jake Arrieta .30 .75
150104 Ichiro .50 1.25
150105 Rickey Henderson .40 1.00
150106 Rickey Henderson .40 1.00
150107 Frank Thomas .40 1.00
150108 Jeff Bagwell .30 .75
150109 Mookie Betts .75 2.00
150110 Albert Pujols .50 1.25
150111 Jacob deGrom .75 2.00
150112 Pedro Martinez .30 .75
150113 Bob Gibson .30 .75
150114 Ichiro .50 1.25
150115 Steve Carlton .30 .75
150116 Carl Yastrzemski .60 1.50
150117 Miguel Cabrera .40 1.00
150118 Lou Gehrig .75 2.00
150119 Tom Seaver .30 .75
150120 Roger Maris .40 1.00
150121 Clayton Kershaw .60 1.50
150122 Jackie Robinson .40 1.00
150123 Sandy Koufax .75 2.00
150124 Ted Williams .75 2.00
150125 Randy Johnson .40 1.00
150126 Juan Marichal .30 .75
150127 Ernie Banks .40 1.00
150128 Mark McGwire .60 1.50
150129 Todd Helton .30 .75
150130 Albert Pujols .50 1.25
150131 Bryce Harper .60 1.50
150132 Mike Trout 2.00 5.00
150133 Joe Morgan .30 .75
150134 Nolan Ryan 1.25 3.00
150135 Hank Aaron .75 2.00
150136 Mark McGwire .60 1.50
150137 Mike Trout 2.00 5.00
150138 Robin Yount .40 1.00
150139 Zack Greinke .40 1.00
150140 Nolan Ryan 1.25 3.00
150141 Mike Piazza .40 1.00
150142 Cal Ripken Jr. 1.25 3.00
150143 Willie McCovey .30 .75
150144 Rod Carew .30 .75
150145 Pedro Martinez .30 .75
150146 Babe Ruth 1.00 2.50
150147 Aaron Judge 1.00 2.50
150148 Lou Gehrig .75 2.00
150149 Babe Ruth 1.00 2.50
150150 Jim Rice .30 .75

2019 Topps 150 Years of Professional Baseball Autographs

STATED ODDS 1:13,136 HOBBY
PRINT RUNS B/WN 5-25 COPIES PER
NO PRICING ON QTY 15 OR LESS
EXCHANGE DEADLINE 12/30/2020
1506 Carlton Fisk/25 75.00 200.00
15015 Mike Piazza
15018 Ichiro
15020 David Ortiz
15024 Mariano Rivera
15025 Ozzie Smith/25 25.00 60.00
15037 Bill Mazeroski/25 25.00 60.00
15039 Phil Niekro/25 15.00 40.00
15058 Don Mattingly/25 60.00 150.00
15062 Dennis Eckersley/25 12.00 30.00
15076 Bob Gibson/25 30.00 80.00
15087 Juan Marichal/25 60.00 150.00

2019 Topps 150 Years of Professional Baseball Greatest Moments

STATED ODDS 1:14 HOBBY
*BLUE:.75X TO 2X BASIC
*GREEN:.75X TO 2X BASIC
*BLACK/299: 1.2X TO 3X BASIC
*150th/150: 2X TO 5X BASIC
*GOLD/50: 3X TO 8X BASIC
GM1 Don Larsen .25 .60
GM2 Christy Mathewson .40 1.00
GM3 Mel Ott .40 1.00
GM4 Roger Clemens .50 1.25
GM5 Mark McGwire .60 1.50
GM6 Bob Feller .30 .75
GM7 Ted Williams .75 2.00
GM8 Derek Jeter 1.00 2.50
GM9 Bartolo Colon .25 .60
GM10 Bo Jackson .40 1.00
GM11 Edgar Martinez .30 .75
GM12 Ken Griffey Jr. .75 2.00
GM13 Bob Gibson .30 .75
GM14 Christy Mathewson .40 1.00
GM15 Derek Jeter 1.00 2.50
GM16 Sandy Koufax .75 2.00
GM17 Albert Pujols .50 1.25
GM18 Aaron Judge 1.00 2.50
GM19 Bryce Harper .60 1.50
GM20 Mariano Rivera .50 1.25
GM21 Max Scherzer .40 1.00
GM22 Anthony Rizzo .50 1.25
GM23 Ted Williams .75 2.00
GM24 Edinson Volquez .25 .60
GM25 David Freese .25 .60

2019 Topps 150 Years of Professional Baseball Greatest Moments Autographs

STATED ODDS 1:12,167 HOBBY
PRINT RUNS B/WN 5-25 COPIES PER
NO PRICING ON QTY 15 OR LESS
EXCHANGE DEADLINE 12/31/2020
GM11 Edgar Martinez/25 15.00 40.00
GM18 Aaron Judge

2019 Topps 150 Years of Professional Baseball Greatest Players

STATED ODDS 1:14 HOBBY
*BLUE:.75X TO 2X BASIC
*GREEN:.75X TO 2X BASIC
*BLACK/299: 1.2X TO 3X BASIC
*150th/150: 2X TO 5X BASIC
*GOLD/50: 3X TO 8X BASIC
GP1 Max Scherzer .40 1.00
GP2 Barry Larkin .30 .75
GP3 Joey Votto .40 1.00
GP4 Johnny Bench .40 1.00
GP5 Rickey Henderson .40 1.00
GP6 Cal Ripken Jr. 1.25 3.00
GP7 Yadier Molina .50 1.25
GP8 Buster Posey .50 1.25
GP9 Honus Wagner .40 1.00
GP10 Sandy Koufax .75 2.00
GP11 Stan Musial .60 1.50
GP12 Chipper Jones .40 1.00
GP13 Ryne Sandberg .75 2.00
GP14 Ozzie Smith .50 1.25
GP15 John Smoltz .40 1.00
GP16 Alex Rodriguez .50 1.25
GP17 Jeff Bagwell .30 .75
GP18 Tony Gwynn .40 1.00
GP19 Rogers Hornsby .30 .75
GP20 Mel Ott .40 1.00
GP21 Christy Mathewson .40 1.00
GP22 Johnny Mize .30 .75
GP23 Lefty Grove .30 .75
GP24 Tris Speaker .30 .75
GP25 Dizzy Dean .30 .75
GP26 Don Larsen .25 .60
GP27 Pee Wee Reese .30 .75
GP28 Gil Hodges .30 .75
GP29 Whitey Ford .30 .75
GP30 Billy Williams .30 .75
GP31 Dave Winfield .30 .75
GP32 Tony Perez .30 .75
GP33 Bill Mazeroski .30 .75
GP34 Rollie Fingers .30 .75
GP35 Ken Griffey Jr. .75 2.00
GP36 Frank Robinson .30 .75
GP37 Phil Rizzuto .30 .75
GP38 Joe Morgan .30 .75
GP39 Eddie Murray .30 .75
GP40 Phil Niekro .30 .75
GP41 Red Schoendienst .30 .75
GP42 Enos Slaughter .30 .75
GP43 Willie Stargell .30 .75
GP44 Fergie Jenkins .30 .75
GP45 Ralph Kiner .30 .75
GP46 Catfish Hunter .30 .75
GP47 Monte Irvin .30 .75
GP48 Orlando Cepeda .30 .75
GP49 Larry Doby .30 .75
GP50 Roberto Alomar .30 .75

2019 Topps 150 Years of Professional Baseball Greatest Players Autographs

STATED ODDS 1:12,167 HOBBY
PRINT RUNS B/WN 5-25 COPIES PER
NO PRICING ON QTY 15 OR LESS
EXCHANGE DEADLINE 12/31/2020
GP5 Rickey Henderson
GP8 Buster Posey
GP31 Dave Winfield
GP33 Bill Mazeroski/25 50.00 120.00
GP34 Rollie Fingers/25 10.00 25.00
GP40 Phil Niekro/25 20.00 50.00
GP48 Orlando Cepeda/25 15.00 40.00

2019 Topps 150 Years of Professional Baseball Greatest Seasons

STATED ODDS 1:14 HOBBY
*BLUE:.75X TO 2X BASIC
2019 Topps 150 Years of Professional Baseball Green
*BLACK/299: 1.2X TO 3X BASIC
*150th/150: 2X TO 5X BASIC
*GOLD/50: 3X TO 8X BASIC
GS1 Dwight Gooden .25 .60
GS2 Roger Clemens .50 1.25
GS3 Tony Gwynn .40 1.00
GS4 Christy Mathewson .40 1.00
GS5 Tris Speaker .30 .75
GS6 Mel Ott .40 1.00
GS7 Frank Robinson .30 .75
GS8 David Ortiz .40 1.00
GS9 Roberto Clemente 1.00 2.50
GS10 Mariano Rivera .50 1.25
GS11 Lou Brock .30 .75
GS12 Brooks Robinson .30 .75
GS13 Duke Snider .30 .75
GS14 George Brett .75 2.00
GS15 Eddie Mathews .40 1.00
GS16 Reggie Jackson .30 .75
GS17 Al Kaline .40 1.00
GS18 Bob Feller .30 .75
GS19 Whitey Ford .30 .75
GS20 Stan Musial .60 1.50
GS21 Johnny Mize .30 .75
GS22 Honus Wagner .40 1.00
GS23 Dizzy Dean .30 .75
GS24 Aaron Judge 1.00 2.50
GS25 Ken Griffey Jr. .75 2.00

2019 Topps 150 Years of Professional Baseball Greatest Seasons Autographs

STATED ODDS 1:12,167 HOBBY
PRINT RUNS B/WN 5-25 COPIES PER
NO PRICING ON QTY 15 OR LESS
EXCHANGE DEADLINE 12/31/2020
GS1 Dwight Gooden/25 20.00 50.00
GS11 Lou Brock/25 25.00 60.00

2019 Topps 150th Anniversary Manufactured Medallions

SER.1 ODDS 1:1230 HOBBY
SER.2 ODDS 1:XX HOBBY
*150TH/150: .6X TO 1.5X BASIC
*GOLD/50: .75X TO 2X BASIC
*RED/25: 1.2X TO 3X BASIC
AMMAB Adrian Beltre 2.50 6.00
AMMAD Andre Dawson S2 4.00 10.00
AMMAJ Aaron Judge 6.00 15.00
AMMAK Al Kaline 2.50 6.00
AMMAP Albert Pujols 3.00 8.00
AMMAR Anthony Rizzo 3.00 8.00
AMMBF Bob Feller S2 5.00 12.00
AMMBG Bob Gibson 2.00 5.00
AMMBH Bryce Harper S2 4.00 10.00
AMMBJ Bo Jackson 2.50 6.00
AMMBL Barry Larkin S2 5.00 12.00
AMMBP Buster Posey 3.00 8.00
AMMBR Babe Ruth S2 6.00 15.00
AMMCB Charlie Blackmon S2 2.50 6.00
AMMCF Carlton Fisk S2 3.00 8.00
AMMCJ Chipper Jones S2 5.00 12.00
AMMCK Clayton Kershaw 4.00 10.00
AMMCR Cal Ripken Jr. 6.00 15.00
AMMCS Chris Sale S2 2.50 6.00
AMMCY Christian Yelich S2 5.00 12.00
AMMCY Carl Yastrzemski 4.00 10.00
AMMDE Dennis Eckersley S2 3.00 8.00
AMMDJ Derek Jeter 10.00 25.00
AMMDM Don Mattingly 5.00 12.00
AMMDO David Ortiz 2.50 6.00
AMMDS Duke Snider S2 2.00 5.00
AMMEB Ernie Banks S2 2.50 6.00
AMMEM Eddie Murray S2 5.00 12.00
AMMFF Freddie Freeman S2 3.00 8.00
AMMFH Felix Hernandez 2.00 5.00
AMMFL Francisco Lindor 2.50 6.00
AMMFT Frank Thomas 2.50 6.00
AMMGB George Brett S2 12.00 30.00
AMMHA Hank Aaron S2 10.00 25.00
AMMHW Honus Wagner S2 2.50 6.00
AMMI Ichiro 3.00 8.00
AMMIR Ivan Rodriguez 2.00 5.00
AMMJA Jose Altuve 2.00 5.00
AMMJB Javier Baez S2 3.00 8.00
AMMJd Jacob deGrom S2 5.00 12.00
AMMJM Juan Marichal S2 2.00 5.00
AMMJM Joe Mauer 2.00 5.00
AMMJR Jackie Robinson 2.50 6.00
AMMJR Jose Ramirez S2 2.00 5.00
AMMJS Juan Soto 8.00 20.00
AMMJT Joey Votto 2.50 6.00
AMMJV Justin Verlander 2.50 6.00
AMMKB Kris Bryant 3.00 8.00
AMMLB Lou Brock S2 6.00 15.00
AMMLG Lou Gehrig 5.00 12.00
AMMMB Mookie Betts 5.00 12.00
AMMMC Miguel Cabrera S2 2.50 6.00
AMMMG Mark McGwire 4.00 10.00
AMMMM Manny Machado 2.50 6.00
AMMMO Mel Ott S2 2.50 6.00
AMMMP Mike Piazza 2.50 6.00
AMMMR Mariano Rivera S2 3.00 8.00
AMMMS Max Scherzer 2.50 6.00
AMMMT Mike Trout 12.00 30.00
AMMNA Nolan Arenado 4.00 10.00
AMMNR Nolan Ryan S2 8.00 20.00
AMMOS Ozzie Smith S2 3.00 8.00
AMMPG Paul Goldschmidt 2.50 6.00
AMMPM Pedro Martinez S2 2.00 5.00
AMMRA Roberto Alomar 2.00 5.00
AMMRC Roberto Clemente 10.00 25.00
AMMRC Roger Clemens S2 3.00 8.00
AMMRCA Rod Carew 2.00 5.00
AMMRH Rogers Hornsby S2 3.00 8.00
AMMRJ Reggie Jackson 2.00 5.00
AMMRM Roger Maris S2 2.50 6.00
AMMRO Ronald Acuna Jr. 12.00 30.00
AMMRS Ryne Sandberg S2 5.00 12.00
AMMRY Robin Yount 5.00 12.00
AMMSC Steve Carlton 2.00 5.00
AMMSK Sandy Koufax S2 5.00 12.00
AMMSM Stan Musial S2 8.00 20.00
AMMSO Shohei Ohtani 4.00 10.00
AMMTC Ty Cobb 4.00 10.00
AMMTG Tom Glavine 2.00 5.00
AMMTG Tony Gwynn S2 5.00 12.00
AMMTH Todd Helton S2 4.00 10.00
AMMTS Tom Seaver 2.00 5.00
AMMTW Ted Williams S2 5.00 12.00
AMMVG Vladimir Guerrero S2 2.00 5.00
AMMVG Vladimir Guerrero 2.00 5.00
AMMWB Wade Boggs 2.00 5.00
AMMWC Will Clark S2 4.00 10.00
AMMWM Willie McCovey 2.00 5.00
AMMWS Willie Stargell S2 3.00 8.00
AMMYM Yadier Molina 3.00 8.00
AMMBRO Brooks Robinson S2 6.00 15.00
AMMBRU Babe Ruth S2 6.00 15.00
AMMEMA Eddie Mathews S2 2.50 6.00
AMMJMO Joe Morgan S2 2.00 5.00
AMMNRY Nolan Ryan S2 8.00 20.00
AMMRCA Rod Carew S2 2.00 5.00
AMMRHE Rickey Henderson S2 2.50 6.00
AMMRHO Rhys Hoskins S2 3.00 8.00
AMMWSP Warren Spahn S2 2.00 5.00

2019 Topps 150th Anniversary Manufactured Patches

ONE PER RETAIL BLASTER
*150TH/150: .75X TO 2X BASIC
*GOLD/50: 1X TO 2.5X BASIC
*RED/25: 1.5X TO 4X BASIC
AMPI Ichiro S2 2.00 5.00
AMPAB Adrian Beltre S2 1.50 4.00
AMPAB Alex Bregman 1.50 4.00
AMPABE Andrew Benintendi 1.50 4.00
AMPAJ Aaron Judge S2 4.00 10.00
AMPAK Al Kaline S2 1.50 4.00
AMPAP Albert Pujols S2 2.00 5.00
AMPAP Andy Pettitte 1.25 3.00
AMPAR Anthony Rizzo S2 2.00 5.00
AMPBG Bob Gibson S2 1.25 3.00
AMPBH Bryce Harper S2 2.50 6.00
AMPBJ Bo Jackson S2 1.50 4.00
AMPBL Barry Larkin 1.25 3.00
AMPBP Buster Posey S2 2.00 5.00
AMPBRU Babe Ruth 4.00 10.00
AMPCB Cody Bellinger 3.00 8.00
AMPCBL Charlie Blackmon 1.50 4.00
AMPCC Carlos Correa 1.50 4.00
AMPCJ Chipper Jones S2 1.50 4.00
AMPCK Clayton Kershaw 2.50 6.00
AMPCR Cal Ripken Jr. 5.00 12.00
AMPCS Corey Seager 1.50 4.00
AMPCSA Chris Sale 1.50 4.00
AMPCY Christian Yelich 2.00 5.00
AMPCY Carl Yastrzemski S2 2.50 6.00
AMPDE Dennis Eckersley 1.25 3.00
AMPDJ Derek Jeter S2 4.00 10.00
AMPDM Don Mattingly S2 3.00 8.00
AMPDO David Ortiz S2 1.50 4.00
AMPDP Dustin Pedroia 1.50 4.00
AMPDW David Wright S2 1.25 3.00
AMPEB Ernie Banks S2 1.50 4.00
AMPFF Freddie Freeman 2.00 5.00
AMPFL Francisco Lindor S2 1.50 4.00
AMPFT Frank Thomas S2 1.50 4.00
AMPGB George Brett S2 3.00 8.00
AMPGC Gerrit Cole 1.50 4.00
AMPGS Giancarlo Stanton 1.50 4.00
AMPGSP George Springer 1.25 3.00
AMPGT Gleyber Torres 3.00 8.00
AMPHA Hank Aaron S2 3.00 8.00
AMPHK Harmon Killebrew S2 1.50 4.00
AMPHW Honus Wagner S2 1.50 4.00
AMPIR Ivan Rodriguez S2 1.25 3.00
AMPJA Jose Altuve S2 1.25 3.00
AMPJA Jose Abreu 1.50 4.00
AMPJB Javier Baez 2.00 5.00
AMPJB Jeff Bagwell S2 1.25 3.00
AMPJDE Jacob deGrom 3.00 8.00
AMPJG Juan Gonzalez 1.00 2.50
AMPJR Jose Ramirez 1.25 3.00
AMPJR Jackie Robinson S2 1.50 4.00
AMPJS Juan Soto S2 5.00 12.00
AMPJU Justin Upton 1.25 3.00
AMPJV Justin Verlander S2 1.50 4.00
AMPKB Kris Bryant 2.00 5.00
AMPLG Lou Gehrig S2 3.00 8.00
AMPLS Luis Severino 1.25 3.00
AMPMB Mookie Betts S2 3.00 8.00
AMPMC Miguel Cabrera 1.50 4.00
AMPMM Mark McGwire 2.50 6.00
AMPMM Mark McGwire S2 2.50 6.00
AMPMMC Manny Machado 1.50 4.00
AMPMP Mike Piazza 1.50 4.00
AMPMP Mike Piazza S2 1.50 4.00
AMPMS Max Scherzer S2 1.50 4.00
AMPMS Max Scherzer 1.50 4.00
AMPMT Mike Trout 8.00 20.00
AMPNA Nolan Arenado S2 2.50 6.00
AMPNR Nolan Ryan 5.00 12.00
AMPNS Noah Syndergaard 1.25 3.00
AMPOA Ozzie Albies 1.50 4.00
AMPOS Ozzie Smith 2.00 5.00
AMPPG Paul Goldschmidt 1.50 4.00
AMPPM Pedro Martinez 1.25 3.00
AMPRA Ronald Acuna Jr. 8.00 20.00
AMPRA Roberto Alomar S2 1.25 3.00
AMPRC Rod Carew S2 1.25 3.00
AMPRC Roberto Clemente 4.00 10.00
AMPRCA Rod Carew 1.25 3.00
AMPRH Rhys Hoskins 2.00 5.00
AMPRHE Rickey Henderson 1.50 4.00
AMPRJ Randy Johnson 1.50 4.00
AMPRJ Reggie Jackson S2 1.25 3.00
AMPRM Roger Maris 1.50 4.00
AMPRY Robin Yount S2 1.50 4.00
AMPSC Steve Carlton S2 1.25 3.00
AMPSK Sandy Koufax S2 3.00 8.00
AMPSM Stan Musial S2 2.50 6.00
AMPSO Shohei Ohtani S2 2.50 6.00
AMPSP Salvador Perez 1.25 3.00
AMPTC Ty Cobb 2.50 6.00
AMPTG Tony Gwynn S2 1.50 4.00
AMPTT Trea Turner 1.25 3.00
AMPTW Ted Williams S2 3.00 8.00
AMPVG Vladimir Guerrero S2 1.25 3.00
AMPWS Willie Stargell S2 1.25 3.00
AMPYM Yadier Molina S2 2.00 5.00
AMPJVO Joey Votto S2 1.50 4.00
AMPTGL Tom Glavine S2 1.25 3.00

2019 Topps Aaron Judge Highlights

STATED ODDS 1:4 TAR.BLASTER
*150th/150: 1.25X TO 3X BASIC
AJ1 Aaron Judge 1.00 2.50
AJ2 Aaron Judge 1.00 2.50
AJ3 Aaron Judge 1.00 2.50
AJ4 Aaron Judge 1.00 2.50
AJ5 Aaron Judge 1.00 2.50
AJ6 Aaron Judge 1.00 2.50
AJ7 Aaron Judge 1.00 2.50
AJ8 Aaron Judge 1.00 2.50
AJ9 Aaron Judge 1.00 2.50
AJ10 Aaron Judge 1.00 2.50
AJ11 Aaron Judge 1.00 2.50
AJ12 Aaron Judge 1.00 2.50
AJ13 Aaron Judge 1.00 2.50
AJ14 Aaron Judge 1.00 2.50
AJ15 Aaron Judge 1.00 2.50
AJ16 Aaron Judge 1.00 2.50
AJ17 Aaron Judge 1.00 2.50
AJ18 Aaron Judge 1.00 2.50
AJ19 Aaron Judge 1.00 2.50
AJ20 Aaron Judge 1.00 2.50
AJ21 Aaron Judge 1.00 2.50
AJ22 Aaron Judge 1.00 2.50
AJ23 Aaron Judge 1.00 2.50
AJ24 Aaron Judge 1.00 2.50
AJ25 Aaron Judge 1.00 2.50
AJ26 Aaron Judge 1.00 2.50
AJ27 Aaron Judge 1.00 2.50
AJ28 Aaron Judge 1.00 2.50
AJ29 Aaron Judge 1.00 2.50
AJ30 Aaron Judge 1.00 2.50

2019 Topps Cactus League Legends

*150TH/150: 1.5X TO 4X BASIC
CLL1 Ernie Banks .50 1.25
CLL2 Mike Trout 2.50 6.00
CLL3 Rickey Henderson .50 1.25
CLL4 Juan Marichal .40 1.00
CLL5 Rod Carew .40 1.00
CLL6 Ichiro .60 1.50
CLL7 Clayton Kershaw .75 2.00
CLL8 Frank Thomas .50 1.25
CLL9 Reggie Jackson .40 1.00
CLL10 Brooks Robinson .40 1.00
CLL11 Corey Seager .50 1.25
CLL12 Paul Goldschmidt .50 1.25
CLL13 Buster Posey .60 1.50
CLL14 Trevor Hoffman .40 1.00
CLL15 Adrian Beltre .50 1.25
CLL16 Mark McGwire .75 2.00
CLL17 Will Clark .40 1.00
CLL18 Shohei Ohtani .75 2.00
CLL19 Willie McCovey .40 1.00
CLL20 Randy Johnson .50 1.25
CLL21 Fergie Jenkins .40 1.00
CLL22 Albert Pujols .60 1.50
CLL23 Kris Bryant .60 1.50
CLL24 Joey Votto .50 1.25
CLL25 Francisco Lindor .50 1.25
CLL26 Nolan Arenado .75 2.00
CLL27 Charlie Blackmon .50 1.25
CLL28 Khris Davis .50 1.25
CLL29 Robin Yount .50 1.25
CLL30 Cody Bellinger 1.00 2.50

2019 Topps Commemorative Retro Hat Logos

STATED ODDS 1:635 HOBBY
*150TH/150: .6X TO 1.5X BASIC
*GOLD/50: .75X TO 2X BASIC
*RED/25: 1.2X TO 3X BASIC
RHLPAB Alex Bregman 2.00 5.00
RHLPABR Alex Bregman 2.00 5.00
RHLPAN Aaron Nola 1.50 4.00
RHLPAR Anthony Rizzo 2.50 6.00
RHLPBS Blake Snell 1.50 4.00
RHLPCC Carlos Correa 2.00 5.00
RHLPCK Clayton Kershaw 3.00 8.00
RHLPCY Christian Yelich 2.50 6.00
RHLPDP Dustin Pedroia 2.00 5.00
RHLPDS Dansby Swanson 2.00 5.00
RHLPEA Elvis Andrus 1.50 4.00
RHLPFF Freddie Freeman 2.50 6.00
RHLPFL Francisco Lindor 2.00 5.00
RHLPGS George Springer 1.50 4.00
RHLPJAB Jose Abreu 2.00 5.00
RHLPJAL Jose Altuve 1.50 4.00
RHLPJD Jacob deGrom 4.00 10.00
RHLPJM Joe Mauer 1.50 4.00
RHLPJR Jose Ramirez 1.50 4.00
RHLPLC Lorenzo Cain 1.25 3.00
RHLPMB Mookie Betts 4.00 10.00
RHLPMC Michael Conforto 1.50 4.00
RHLPMK Matt Kemp 1.50 4.00
RHLPMT Mike Trout 10.00 25.00
RHLPMTR Mike Trout 10.00 25.00
RHLPNS Noah Syndergaard 1.50 4.00
RHLPOA Ozzie Albies 2.00 5.00
RHLPPG Paul Goldschmidt 2.00 5.00
RHLPRC Robinson Cano 1.50 4.00

RHLPRH Rhys Hoskins 2.50 6.00
RHLPSM Starling Marte 1.50 4.00
RHLPSO Shohei Ohtani 3.00 8.00
RHLPTMA Trey Mancini 1.50 4.00
RHLPTS Travis Shaw 1.25 3.00
RHLPWM Wil Myers 1.50 4.00
RHLPXB Xander Bogaerts 2.00 5.00
RHLPYM Yadier Molina 2.50 6.00
RHLPYMO Yoan Moncada 2.00 5.00
RHLPZG Zack Greinke 2.00 5.00

2019 Topps Evolution

STATED ODDS 1:42 HOBBY
*150TH/150: 2X TO 5X BASIC
EO1 Robinson/Kershaw 1.00 2.50
EO2 Aaron/Acuna 3.00 8.00
EO3 Harper/Guerrero 1.00 2.50
EO4 Harmon Killebrew .60 1.50
Joe Mauer
EO5 Blake Snell .50 1.25
Wade Boggs
EO6 Feller/Lindor .60 1.50
EO7 Ruth/Judge 1.50 4.00
EO8 Cobb/Cabrera 1.00 2.50
EO9 Benintendi/Williams 1.25 3.00
EO10 Bryant/Banks .75 2.00
EO11 Fenway Park .40 1.00
Fenway Park
EO12 Wrigley Field .40 1.00
Wrigley Field
EO13 Yankee Stadium .40 1.00
Yankee Stadium
EO14 Candlestick Park .40 1.00
At&t Park
EO15 Ebbets Field .40 1.00
Dodger Stadium
EO16 Forbes Field .40 1.00
PNC Park
EO17 Sportsman's Park .40 1.00
Busch Stadium
EO18 Shea Stadium .40 1.00
Citi Field
EO19 Memorial Stadium .40 1.00
Oriole Park at Camden Yards
EO20 Crosley Field .40 1.00
Great American Ball Park
EO21 Vintage Baseball .40 1.00
Modern Baseball
EO22 Vintage Catcher's Mask .40 1.00
Modern Catcher's Mask
EO23 Vintage Baseball Glove .40 1.00
Modern Baseball Glove
EO24 Vintage Sunglasses .40 1.00
Modern Sunglasses
EO25 Vintage Cleats .40 1.00
Modern Cleats

2019 Topps Evolution of Stadiums

STATED ODDS 1:56 HOBBY
*BLUE: .6X TO 1.5X BASIC
*BLACK/299: 1X TO 2.5X BASIC
*150th/150: 2X TO 5X BASIC
*GOLD/50: 3X TO 8X BASIC
ES1 T-Mobile Park .40 1.00
The Kingdome
ES2 Citizens Bank Park .40 1.00
Veterans Stadium
ES3 Minute Maid Park .40 1.00
Astrodome
ES4 Comerica Park .40 1.00
Tiger Stadium
ES5 Oracle Park .40 1.00
Polo Grounds
ES6 Guaranteed Rate Field .40 1.00
Comiskey Park
ES7 SunTrust Park .40 1.00
Turner Field
ES8 Miller Park .40 1.00
Milwaukee County Stadium
ES9 Municipal Stadium .40 1.00
Kauffman Stadium
ES10 Target Field .40 1.00
Hubert H. Humphrey Metrodome

2019 Topps Evolution of Team Logos

STATED ODDS 1:56 HOBBY
*BLUE: .6X TO 1.5X BASIC
*BLACK/299: 1X TO 2.5X BASIC
*150th/150: 2X TO 5X BASIC
*GOLD/50: 3X TO 8X BASIC
EL1 Yadier Molina .75 2.00
Bob Gibson
EL2 Lewis Brinson .60 1.50
Miguel Cabrera
EL3 Ichiro 1.25 3.00
Ken Griffey JR.
EL4 Rhys Hoskins .75 2.00
Steve Carlton
EL5 Buster Posey .75 2.00
Mel Ott
EL6 Joey Votto .60 1.50
Johnny Bench
EL7 Mike Trout 3.00 8.00
Rod Carew
EL8 Frank Thomas .60 1.50
Carlton Fisk
EL9 Roberto Clemente 1.50 4.00
Starling Marte
EL10 Jose Altuve 2.00 5.00
Nolan Ryan

2019 Topps Evolution of Technology

STATED ODDS 1:56 HOBBY
*BLUE: .6X TO 1.5X BASIC
*BLACK/299: 1X TO 2.5X BASIC
*150th/150: 2X TO 5X BASIC
*GOLD/50: 3X TO 8X BASIC
ET1 Ticket Stubs .40 1.00
Digital Mobile Ticket
ET2 Jumbotron .40 1.00
Scoreboard
ET3 Instant Replay Review .40 1.00
Field Umpire
ET4 Box Scores .40 1.00
MLB At Bat App
ET5 Television Broadcast .40 1.00
-Radio Broadcast

2019 Topps Franchise Feats

STATED ODDS 1:4 BLASTER
*BLUE: .6X TO 1.5X BASIC
*BLACK/299: 1X TO 2.5X BASIC
*150th/150: 1.5X TO 4X BASIC
*GOLD/50: 2.5X TO 6X BASIC
FF1 Hank Aaron 1.25 3.00
FF2 Randy Johnson .60 1.50
FF3 Mike Trout 3.00 8.00
FF4 Cal Ripken Jr. 2.00 5.00
FF5 Ted Williams 1.25 3.00
FF6 Ernie Banks .60 1.50
FF7 Frank Thomas .60 1.50
FF8 Johnny Bench .60 1.50
FF9 Bob Feller .50 1.25
FF10 Todd Helton .50 1.25
FF11 Al Kaline .60 1.50
FF12 Jose Altuve .50 1.25
FF13 George Brett 1.25 3.00
FF14 Sandy Koufax 1.25 3.00
FF15 Giancarlo Stanton .60 1.50
FF16 Robin Yount .60 1.50
FF17 Harmon Killebrew .60 1.50
FF18 Mike Piazza .60 1.50
FF19 Babe Ruth 1.50 4.00
FF20 Rickey Henderson .60 1.50
FF21 Steve Carlton .50 1.25
FF22 Roberto Clemente 1.50 4.00
FF23 Tony Gwynn .60 1.50
FF24 Buster Posey .75 2.00
FF25 Nolan Ryan 2.00 5.00
FF26 Ken Griffey Jr. 1.25 3.00
FF27 Stan Musial 1.00 2.50
FF28 Roberto Alomar .50 1.25
FF29 Max Scherzer .60 1.50
FF30 Evan Longoria .50 1.25

2019 Topps Gary Vee's Top Entrepreneurs in Baseball

STATED ODDS 1:18 HOBBY
*BLUE: .6X TO 1.5X BASIC
*BLACK/299: 1X TO 2.5X BASIC
*150th/150: 1.5X TO 4X BASIC
*GOLD/50: 3X TO 8X BASIC
GV1 Bryce Harper 1.00 2.50
GV2 Marcus Stroman .50 1.25
GV3 Ian Kinsler .50 1.25
GV4 Hunter Pence .50 1.25
GV5 Jose Ramirez .50 1.25
GV6 Alex Bregman .60 1.50
GV7 Chris Iannetta .40 1.00
GV8 Randy Johnson .60 1.50
GV9 Derek Jeter 1.50 4.00
GV10 Trevor May .40 1.00

2019 Topps Gary Vee's Top Entrepreneurs in Baseball 150th Anniversary

*150th/150: 1.5X TO 4X BASIC
STATED ODDS 1:3054 HOBBY
STATED PRINT RUN 150 SER.#'d SETS
GV1 Bryce Harper 8.00 20.00
GV9 Derek Jeter 20.00 50.00

2019 Topps Gary Vee's Top Entrepreneurs in Baseball Black

*BLACK/299: 1X TO 2.5X BASIC
STATED ODDS 1:49 HOBBY
STATED PRINT RUN 299 SER.#'d SETS
GV1 Bryce Harper 6.00 15.00
GV9 Derek Jeter 15.00 40.00

2019 Topps Gary Vee's Top Entrepreneurs in Baseball Gold

*GOLD/50: 3X TO 8X BASIC
STATED ODDS 1:294 HOBBY
STATED PRINT RUN 50 SER.#'d SETS
GV1 Bryce Harper 12.00 30.00
GV9 Derek Jeter 50.00 120.00

2019 Topps Gary Vee's Top Entrepreneurs in Baseball Dual Autographs

STATED ODDS 1:53,533 HOBBY
PRINT RUNS B/WN 5-25 COPIES PER
NO PRICING ON QTY 15 OR LESS
EXCHANGE DEADLINE 12/31/2020
GVIK Ian Kinsler 60.00 150.00
Gary Vaynerchuk/25
GVIR Jose Ramirez 60.00 150.00
Gary Vaynerchuk/25

2019 Topps Gleyber Torres Highlights

*150TH/150: 1.5X TO 4X BASIC
GT1 Gleyber Torres .75 2.00
GT2 Gleyber Torres .75 2.00
GT3 Gleyber Torres .75 2.00
GT4 Gleyber Torres .75 2.00
GT5 Gleyber Torres .75 2.00
GT6 Gleyber Torres .75 2.00
GT7 Gleyber Torres .75 2.00
GT8 Gleyber Torres .75 2.00
GT9 Gleyber Torres .75 2.00
GT10 Gleyber Torres .75 2.00
GT11 Gleyber Torres .75 2.00
GT12 Gleyber Torres .75 2.00
GT13 Gleyber Torres .75 2.00
GT14 Gleyber Torres .75 2.00
GT15 Gleyber Torres .75 2.00
GT16 Gleyber Torres .75 2.00
GT17 Gleyber Torres .75 2.00
GT18 Gleyber Torres .75 2.00
GT19 Gleyber Torres .75 2.00
GT20 Gleyber Torres .75 2.00
GT21 Gleyber Torres .75 2.00
GT22 Gleyber Torres .75 2.00
GT23 Gleyber Torres .75 2.00
GT24 Gleyber Torres .75 2.00
GT25 Gleyber Torres .75 2.00
GT26 Gleyber Torres .75 2.00
GT27 Gleyber Torres .75 2.00
GT28 Gleyber Torres .75 2.00
GT29 Gleyber Torres .75 2.00
GT30 Gleyber Torres .75 2.00

2019 Topps MLB Logo Golden Anniversary Commemorative Patches

STATED ODDS 1:2828 HOBBY
*150th/150: .6X TO 1.5X BASIC
*GOLD/50: .75X TO 2X BASIC
*RED/25: 1.2X TO 3X BASIC
GAPAB Alex Bregman 2.00 5.00
GAPAJ Aaron Judge 5.00 12.00
GAPAR Anthony Rizzo 2.50 6.00
GAPBH Bryce Harper 3.00 8.00
GAPBP Buster Posey 2.50 6.00
GAPBS Blake Snell 1.50 4.00
GAPCC Carlos Correa 2.00 5.00
GAPCS Chris Sale 2.00 5.00
GAPCY Christian Yelich 2.50 6.00
GAPFF Freddie Freeman 2.50 6.00
GAPFL Francisco Lindor 2.00 5.00
GAPGS Giancarlo Stanton 2.00 5.00
GAPGT Gleyber Torres 4.00 10.00
GAPJA Jose Altuve 1.50 4.00
GAPJB Jose Berrios 1.50 4.00
GAPJd Jacob deGrom 4.00 10.00
GAPJG Joey Gallo 1.50 4.00
GAPJM J.D. Martinez 2.00 5.00
GAPJR J.T. Realmuto 2.00 5.00
GAPJS Juan Soto 6.00 15.00
GAPJV Justin Verlander 2.00 5.00
GAPKB Kris Bryant 2.50 6.00
GAPKD Khris Davis 2.00 5.00
GAPMB Mookie Betts 4.00 10.00
GAPMC Matt Carpenter 2.00 5.00
GAPMH Mitch Haniger 1.50 4.00
GAPMS Max Scherzer 2.00 5.00
GAPMT Mike Trout 10.00 25.00
GAPNA Nolan Arenado 3.00 8.00
GAPNS Noah Syndergaard 1.50 4.00
GAPPG Paul Goldschmidt 2.00 5.00
GAPRA Ronald Acuna Jr. 10.00 25.00
GAPRH Rhys Hoskins 2.50 6.00
GAPSM Starling Marte 1.50 4.00
GAPSO Shohei Ohtani 3.00 8.00
GAPSP Salvador Perez 1.50 4.00
GAPTM Trey Mancini 1.50 4.00
GAPTS Trevor Story 2.00 5.00
GAPWM Wil Myers 1.50 4.00
GAPYM Yadier Molina 2.50 6.00
GAPABE Andrew Benintendi 2.00 5.00
GAPCBE Cody Bellinger 4.00 10.00
GAPCKE Clayton Kershaw 3.00 8.00
GAPJAB Jose Abreu 2.00 5.00
GAPJBZ Javier Baez 2.50 6.00
GAPJRA Jose Ramirez 1.50 4.00
GAPJSM Justin Smoak 1.25 3.00
GAPJVO Joey Votto 2.00 5.00
GAPMCA Miguel Cabrera 2.00 5.00
GAPMCH Matt Chapman 2.00 5.00

2019 Topps Grapefruit League Greats

STATED ODDS 1:2 BLASTER
*150TH/150: 1.5X TO 4X BASIC
GLG1 Hank Aaron 1.00 2.50
GLG2 Jackie Robinson .50 1.25
GLG3 Don Mattingly 1.00 2.50
GLG4 Cal Ripken Jr. 1.50 4.00
GLG5 Babe Ruth 1.25 3.00
GLG6 Ted Williams 1.00 2.50
GLG7 Ty Cobb .75 2.00
GLG8 Lou Gehrig 1.00 2.50
GLG9 Sandy Koufax 1.00 2.50
GLG10 Bob Gibson .40 1.00
GLG11 Roberto Clemente 1.25 3.00
GLG12 Nolan Ryan 1.50 4.00
GLG13 George Brett 1.00 2.50
GLG14 Max Scherzer .50 1.25
GLG15 Pedro Martinez .40 1.00
GLG16 Chipper Jones .50 1.25
GLG17 Wade Boggs .40 1.00
GLG18 Derek Jeter 1.25 3.00
GLG19 Carl Yastrzemski .75 2.00
GLG20 Al Kaline .50 1.25
GLG21 David Ortiz .50 1.25
GLG22 Vladimir Guerrero .40 1.00
GLG23 Bo Jackson .50 1.25
GLG24 Jose Altuve .40 1.00
GLG25 Mike Piazza .50 1.25
GLG26 Aaron Judge 1.25 3.00
GLG27 Gleyber Torres 1.00 2.50
GLG28 Mookie Betts 1.00 2.50
GLG29 Ronald Acuna Jr. 2.50 6.00
GLG30 Yadier Molina .60 1.50

2019 Topps Greatness Returns

STATED ODDS 1:42 HOBBY
*150TH/150: 1.5X TO 4X BASIC
GR1 Ryan/Verlander 2.00 5.00
GR2 Judge/Jeter 1.50 4.00
GR3 Kershaw/Koufax 1.25 3.00
GR4 Stanton/Jackson .60 1.50
GR5 Yount/Yelich .75 2.00
GR6 Benintendi/Yaz 1.00 2.50
GR7 Betts/Williams 1.25 3.00
GR8 Banks/Baez .75 2.00
GR9 Sale/Martinez .60 1.50
GR10 Jacob deGrom 1.25 3.00
Tom Seaver
GR11 Cobb/Harper 1.00 2.50
GR12 Ohtani/Ryan 2.00 5.00
GR13 Alomar/Lindor .60 1.50
GR14 Trout/Aaron 3.00 8.00
GR15 Ichiro/Ohtani 1.00 2.50
GR16 Clark/Posey .75 2.00
GR17 Trout/Acuna 3.00 8.00
GR18 Max Scherzer .60 1.50
Bob Gibson
GR19 Sale/Johnson .60 1.50
GR20 Jeter/Torres 1.50 4.00
GR21 Ripken/Correa 2.00 5.00
GR22 Charlie Blackmon .60 1.50
Todd Helton
GR23 Brooks Robinson 1.00 2.50
Nolan Arenado
GR24 Betts/Henderson 1.25 3.00
GR25 Pujols/Gehrig 1.25 3.00

2019 Topps Historic Homes Stadium Relics

STATED ODDS 1:6121 HOBBY
PRINT RUNS B/WN 40-99 COPIES PER
HHR1 Yankee Stadium/40 200.00 400.00
HHR2 Wrigley Field/99 75.00 200.00
HHR3 Fenway Park/99 75.00 200.00
HHR4 Memorial Stadium/99 75.00 200.00
HHR5 Tiger Stadium/99 60.00 150.00
HHR6 Metropolitan Stadium/99 50.00 120.00
HHR7 Three Rivers Stadium/90 60.00 150.00
HHR8 Atlanta Fulton County Stadium/99 50.00 120.00
HHR9 Cleveland Municipal Stadium/99 50.00 120.00
HHR10 Milwaukee County Stadium/99 50.00 120.00

2019 Topps Home Run Challenge

SER.1 ODDS 1:24 HOBBY
SER.2 ODDS 1:24 HOBBY
HRC1 Mike Trout 6.00 15.00
HRC2 J.D. Martinez 1.25 3.00
HRC3 Giancarlo Stanton 1.25 3.00
HRC4 Jose Ramirez 1.00 2.50
HRC5 Khris Davis 1.25 3.00
HRC6 Aaron Judge 3.00 8.00
HRC7 Bryce Harper 2.00 5.00
HRC8 Manny Machado 1.25 3.00
HRC9 Nolan Arenado 2.00 5.00
HRC10 Paul Goldschmidt 1.25 3.00
HRC11 Mookie Betts 2.50 6.00
HRC12 Kris Bryant 1.50 4.00
HRC13 Javier Baez 1.50 4.00
HRC14 Alex Bregman 1.25 3.00
HRC15 Francisco Lindor 1.25 3.00
HRC16 Ronald Acuna Jr. 6.00 15.00
HRC17 Rhys Hoskins 1.50 4.00
HRC18 Shohei Ohtani 2.00 5.00
HRC19 Carlos Correa 1.25 3.00
HRC20 Anthony Rizzo 1.50 4.00
HRC21 Gleyber Torres 2.50 6.00
HRC22 Andrew Benintendi 1.25 3.00
HRC23 Ozzie Albies 1.25 3.00
HRC24 Joey Votto 1.25 3.00
HRC25 Trevor Story 1.25 3.00
HRC26 Freddie Freeman 1.50 4.00
HRC27 Jose Altuve 1.00 2.50
HRC28 George Springer 1.00 2.50
HRC29 Matt Carpenter 1.25 3.00
HRC30 Gary Sanchez 1.25 3.00
HRC31 Kyle Schwarber 1.25 3.00
HRC32 Cody Bellinger 2.50 6.00
HRC33 Miguel Andujar 1.25 3.00
HRC34 Christian Yelich 1.50 4.00
HRC35 Juan Soto 4.00 10.00

2019 Topps Iconic Card Reprints

SER.1 ODDS 1:21 HOBBY
SER.2 ODDS 1:9 HOBBY
*150TH/150: 2X TO 5X BASIC
ICR1 Ty Cobb .75 2.00
ICR2 Ty Cobb .75 2.00
ICR3 Babe Ruth 1.25 3.00
ICR4 Babe Ruth 1.25 3.00
ICR5 Lou Gehrig 1.00 2.50
ICR6 Jackie Robinson .50 1.25
ICR7 Al Kaline .50 1.25
ICR8 Roberto Clemente 1.25 3.00
ICR9 Jackie Robinson .50 1.25
ICR10 Roberto Clemente 1.25 3.00
ICR11 Bob Gibson .40 1.00
ICR12 Carl Yastrzemski .75 2.00
ICR13 Rod Carew .40 1.00
ICR14 Robin Yount .50 1.25
ICR15 Don Mattingly 1.00 2.50
ICR16 Jose Canseco .40 1.00
ICR17 Bo Jackson .50 1.25
ICR18 Mike Piazza .50 1.25
ICR19 Derek Jeter 1.25 3.00
ICR20 Miguel Cabrera .50 1.25
ICR21 Albert Pujols .60 1.50
ICR22 Rickey Henderson .50 1.25
ICR23 Justin Verlander .50 1.25
ICR24 Clayton Kershaw .75 2.00
ICR25 Cal Ripken Jr. 1.50 4.00
ICR26 Buster Posey .60 1.50
ICR27 Stephen Strasburg .50 1.25
ICR28 Bryce Harper .75 2.00
ICR29 Mike Trout 2.50 6.00
ICR30 Mike Trout 2.50 6.00
ICR31 Mookie Betts 1.00 2.50
ICR32 Kris Bryant .60 1.50
ICR33 Aaron Judge 1.25 3.00
ICR34 Ichiro .60 1.50
ICR35 Tom Seaver .40 1.00
ICR36 Nolan Ryan 1.50 4.00
ICR37 Wade Boggs .40 1.00
ICR38 Mark McGwire .75 2.00
ICR39 Bob Feller .40 1.00
ICR40 Duke Snider .40 1.00
ICR41 Eddie Mathews .50 1.25
ICR42 Warren Spahn .40 1.00
ICR43 George Brett 1.00 2.50
ICR44 Brooks Robinson .40 1.00
ICR45 Hank Aaron 1.00 2.50
ICR46 Hank Aaron 1.00 2.50
ICR47 Frank Thomas .50 1.25
ICR48 Mariano Rivera .60 1.50
ICR49 Sandy Koufax 1.00 2.50
ICR50 Ted Williams 1.00 2.50
ICR51 Ty Cobb .75 2.00
ICR52 Ty Cobb .75 2.00
ICR53 Lou Gehrig 1.00 2.50
ICR54 Whitey Ford .40 1.00
ICR55 Lou Gehrig 1.00 2.50
ICR56 Monte Irvin .40 1.00
ICR57 Warren Spahn .40 1.00
ICR58 Duke Snider .40 1.00
ICR59 Bob Feller .40 1.00
ICR60 Jackie Robinson .50 1.25
ICR61 Ted Williams 1.00 2.50
ICR62 Ernie Banks .50 1.25
ICR63 Harmon Killebrew .50 1.25
ICR64 Jackie Robinson .50 1.25
ICR65 Roberto Clemente 1.25 3.00
ICR66 Ted Williams 1.00 2.50
ICR67 Sandy Koufax 1.00 2.50
ICR68 Hank Aaron 1.00 2.50
ICR69 Sandy Koufax 1.00 2.50
ICR70 Roger Maris .50 1.25
ICR71 Willie McCovey .40 1.00
ICR72 Carl Yastrzemski .75 2.00
ICR73 Juan Marichal .40 1.00
ICR74 Roger Maris .50 1.25
ICR75 Lou Brock .40 1.00
ICR76 Jim Palmer .40 1.00
ICR77 Joe Morgan .40 1.00
ICR78 Steve Carlton .40 1.00
ICR79 Reggie Jackson .40 1.00
ICR80 Nolan Ryan 1.50 4.00
ICR81 Bert Blyleven .40 1.00
ICR82 Carlton Fisk .40 1.00
ICR83 Roberto Clemente 1.25 3.00
ICR84 Hank Aaron 1.00 2.50
ICR85 Dennis Eckersley .40 1.00
ICR86 Eddie Murray .40 1.00
ICR87 Dale Murphy .50 1.25
ICR88 Ryne Sandberg 1.00 2.50
ICR89 Darryl Strawberry .30 .75
ICR90 Roger Clemens .60 1.50
ICR91 Will Clark .40 1.00
ICR92 Bo Jackson .50 1.25
ICR93 Roberto Alomar .40 1.00
ICR94 Randy Johnson .50 1.25
ICR95 Derek Jeter 1.25 3.00
ICR96 Derek Jeter 1.25 3.00
ICR97 Vladimir Guerrero .40 1.00
ICR98 Bryce Harper .75 2.00
ICR99 Mike Trout 2.50 6.00
ICR100 Manny Machado .50 1.25

2019 Topps Iconic Cards Reprints Autographs

SER.1 ODDS 1:23,858 HOBBY
SER.2 ODDS 1:18,250 HOBBY
PRINT RUNS B/WN 5-25 COPIES PER
NO PRICING ON QTY 15 OR LESS
EXCHANGE DEADLINE 12/31/2020
ICR16 Al Kaline/25 75.00 200.00
ICR17 Sandy Koufax EXCH
ICR23 Bob Gibson/25 60.00 150.00
ICR27 Nolan Ryan
ICR29 Robin Yount
ICR31 Rickey Henderson
ICR32 Cal Ripken Jr.
ICR34 Don Mattingly/25 75.00 200.00
ICR36 Bo Jackson
ICR38 Frank Thomas
ICR40 Mike Piazza
ICR41 Derek Jeter
ICR51 Bryce Harper
ICR56 Aaron Judge
ICR68 Hank Aaron S2
ICR73 Juan Marichal/25 S2
ICR75 Lou Brock/25 S2 25.00 60.00
ICR78 Steve Carlton/25 S2
ICR80 Nolan Ryan S2
ICR82 Carlton Fisk/25 S2 25.00 60.00
ICR84 Hank Aaron S2
ICR85 Dennis Eckersley/25 S2 10.00 25.00
ICR87 Dale Murphy/25 S2 50.00 120.00
ICR89 Darryl Strawberry/25 S2 25.00 60.00
ICR91 Will Clark/25 S2 40.00 100.00
ICR93 Roberto Alomar/25 S2 20.00 50.00
ICR94 Randy Johnson S2
ICR96 Derek Jeter S2
ICR97 Vladimir Guerrero/25 S2 100.00 250.00

2019 Topps Legacy of Baseball Autographs

STATED ODDS 1:1073 HOBBY
EXCHANGE DEADLINE 12/31/2020
LBAAD Aledmys Diaz 2.50 6.00
LBAAG Avisail Garcia 3.00 8.00
LBAAH Alen Hanson 3.00 8.00
LBAAM Adalberto Mondesi 5.00 12.00
LBAAS Antonio Senzatela 2.50 6.00
LBABJ Brian Johnson 2.50 6.00
LBABK Brad Keller 2.50 6.00
LBACMU Cedric Mullins 6.00 15.00
LBADJ Danny Jansen 6.00 15.00
LBADST Dan Straily 2.50 6.00
LBAED Edwin Diaz 6.00 15.00
LBAFM Frankie Montas 2.50 6.00
LBAFV Felipe Vazquez 5.00 12.00
LBAJB Jake Bauers 3.00 8.00
LBAJBO Justin Bour 4.00 10.00
LBAJC Johan Camargo 8.00 20.00
LBAJF Jake Faria 2.50 6.00
LBAJH Josh Hader 5.00 12.00
LBAJM Jeff McNeil 8.00 20.00
LBAJMA Jake Marisnick 2.50 6.00
LBAJP Jose Peraza 4.00 10.00
LBAKA Kolby Allard 4.00 10.00
LBAKB Kris Bryant
LBAKF Kyle Freeland 3.00 8.00
LBALB Lou Brock
LBALH Livan Hernandez 2.50 6.00
LBAMD Matt Duffy 2.50 6.00
LBAMFO Mike Foltynewicz 4.00 10.00
LBAMGO Marwin Gonzalez 2.50 6.00
LBAMI Monte Irvin 15.00 40.00
LBAMM Max Muncy 8.00 20.00
LBAMTR Mike Trout
LBANG Niko Goodrum 6.00 15.00
LBAPN Phil Niekro
LBARO Roy Oswalt 5.00 12.00
LBARS Ross Stripling 2.50 6.00
LBASD Steven Duggar 5.00 12.00
LBASO Shohei Ohtani
LBASR Sean Reid-Foley 2.50 6.00
LBATA Tyler Anderson 2.50 6.00
LBATL Tzu-Wei Lin 2.50 6.00
LBATS Tyler Skaggs 10.00 25.00
LBAYS Yangervis Solarte 2.50 6.00
LBAZG Zack Godley 2.50 6.00

2019 Topps Legacy of Baseball Autographs 150th Anniversary

*150TH ANNV/150: .5X TO 1.2X BASIC
SER.1 ODDS 1:1559 HOBBY
SER.2 ODDS 1:1998 HOBBY
STATED PRINT RUN 150 SER.#'d SETS
EXCHANGE DEADLINE 12/31/2020
LBAAG Adolis Garcia S2 25.00 60.00
LBABW Bryse Wilson S2 4.00 10.00
LBACM Colin Moran 6.00 15.00
LBACS Christin Stewart S2 4.00 10.00
LBACY Carl Yastrzemski S2 8.00 20.00
LBADC David Cone 8.00 20.00
LBADH Dakota Hudson S2 4.00 10.00
LBADP Daniel Ponce de Leon S2 5.00 12.00
LBADR Dereck Rodriguez S2 3.00 8.00
LBAEDA Eric Davis 8.00 20.00
LBAFV Framber Valdez S2 3.00 8.00
LBAHF Heath Fillmyer S2 3.00 8.00
LBAJK John Kruk S2 3.00 8.00
LBAJR Josh Rogers S2 3.00 8.00
LBAKG Ken Giles 3.00 8.00
LBAKK Kevin Kramer S2 4.00 10.00
LBAKS Kohl Stewart S2 4.00 10.00
LBAKT Kyle Tucker 25.00 60.00
LBALV Luke Voit S2 20.00 50.00
LBAMC Matt Chapman 8.00 20.00
LBAMCA Matt Carpenter 8.00 20.00
LBAMG Mark Grace 12.00 30.00
LBANB Nick Burdi S2 3.00 8.00
LBAPW Patrick Wisdom S2 3.00 8.00
LBARA Rick Ankiel 8.00 20.00
LBARL Ramon Laureano S2 8.00 20.00
LBATH Teoscar Hernandez 5.00 12.00
LBAYG Yasmani Grandal 3.00 8.00
LBADSA Dennis Santana S2 3.00 8.00
LBAJSP Jeffrey Springs S2 3.00 8.00

2019 Topps Legacy of Baseball Autographs Gold

*GOLD/50: .6X TO 1.5X BASIC
SER.1 ODDS 1:3897
SER.2 ODDS 1:4838
STATED PRINT RUN 50 SER.#'d SETS
EXCHANGE DEADLINE 12/31/2020
LBABB Bert Blyleven 10.00 25.00
LBABM Bill Mazeroski 25.00 60.00
LBACM Colin Moran 8.00 20.00
LBACR Carlos Rodon 6.00 15.00
LBADC David Cone 10.00 25.00
LBAEDA Eric Davis 10.00 25.00
LBAFT Fernando Tatis Jr. S2 100.00 250.00
LBAJA Jesus Aguilar 8.00 20.00
LBAKG Ken Giles 4.00 10.00
LBAKT Kyle Tucker 30.00 80.00
LBAMC Matt Chapman 10.00 25.00
LBAMCA Matt Carpenter 10.00 25.00
LBAMG Mark Grace 15.00 40.00
LBAPA Pete Alonso S2 75.00 200.00
LBARA Rick Ankiel 10.00 25.00
LBASG Shawn Green 8.00 20.00
LBATH Teoscar Hernandez 6.00 15.00
LBAVC Vinny Castilla 4.00 10.00
LBAYG Yasmani Grandal 4.00 10.00
LBAYK Yusei Kikuchi S2 8.00

2019 Topps Legacy of Baseball Autographs Red

*RED/25: .8X TO 2X BASIC
SER.1 ODDS 1:7794 HOBBY
SER.2 ODDS 1:6864 HOBBY
PRINT RUN BTW 10-25 COPIES PER
NO PRICING QTY 15 OR LESS
EXCHANGE DEADLINE 12/31/2020
LBABA Bobby Abreu 25.00 60.00
LBABB Bert Blyleven 12.00 30.00
LBABG Bob Gibson 50.00 120.00
LBABM Bill Mazeroski 30.00 80.00
LBACK Corey Kluber 25.00 60.00
LBACM Colin Moran 10.00 25.00
LBACR Carlos Rodon 8.00 20.00
LBADC David Cone. 12.00 30.00
LBAEDA Eric Davis 12.00 30.00
LBAFJ Fergie Jenkins 15.00 40.00
LBAFT Fernando Tatis Jr. S2 125.00 300.00
LBAGS George Springer 12.00 30.00
LBAJA Jesus Aguilar 10.00 25.00
LBAKG Ken Giles 5.00 12.00
LBAKL Kenny Lofton 25.00 60.00
LBAKT Kyle Tucker 40.00 100.00
LBALS Luis Severino 6.00 15.00
LBAMC Matt Chapman 12.00 30.00
LBAMCA Matt Carpenter 12.00 30.00
LBAMG Mark Grace 20.00 40.00
LBARA Rick Ankiel 12.00 30.00
LBARH Rhys Hoskins 25.00 60.00
LBASG Shawn Green 10.00 25.00
LBATH Teoscar Hernandez 8.00 20.00
LBAVC Vinny Castilla 5.00 12.00
LBAYG Yasmani Grandal 5.00 12.00

2019 Topps Major League Materials

SER.1 ODDS 1:70 HOBBY
SER.2 ODDS 1:111 HOBBY
*150TH/150: .5X TO 1.2X BASIC
*GOLD/50: .6X TO 1.5X BASIC
*RED/25: .75X TO 2X BASIC
MLMAB Adrian Beltre 3.00 8.00
MLMAB Alex Bregman S2 3.00 8.00
MLMABE Andrew Benintendi 3.00 8.00
MLMAJ Aaron Judge 8.00 20.00
MLMAM Andrew McCutchen S2 3.00 8.00
MLMAP Albert Pujols 4.00 10.00
MLMAR Anthony Rizzo S2 4.00 10.00
MLMARI Anthony Rizzo 4.00 10.00
MLMBB Byron Buxton S2 3.00 8.00
MLMBC Brandon Crawford 2.50 6.00
MLMBH Bryce Harper 5.00 12.00
MLMBH Bryce Harper S2 5.00 12.00
MLMBP Buster Posey 4.00 10.00
MLMCA Chris Archer S2 2.00 5.00
MLMCB Cody Bellinger S2 6.00 15.00
MLMCC Carlos Correa 3.00 8.00
MLMCK Clayton Kershaw 5.00 12.00
MLMCK Corey Kluber S2 2.50 6.00
MLMCS CC Sabathia S2 2.50 6.00
MLMCS Corey Seager 3.00 8.00
MLMCSA Chris Sale 3.00 8.00
MLMDG Didi Gregorius S2 2.50 6.00
MLMDO David Ortiz S2 3.00 8.00
MLMDP David Price S2 2.50 6.00
MLMDP Dustin Pedroia 3.00 8.00
MLMDS Dansby Swanson S2 3.00 8.00
MLMEA Elvis Andrus 2.50 6.00
MLMEL Evan Longoria S2 2.50 6.00
MLMFF Freddie Freeman 4.00 10.00
MLMFL Francisco Lindor 3.00 8.00
MLMGS George Springer S2 2.50 6.00
MLMGS Gary Sanchez 3.00 8.00
MLMGT Gleyber Torres 6.00 15.00
MLMJA Jose Altuve 2.50 6.00
MLMJAB Jose Abreu 3.00 8.00
MLMJB Javier Baez 4.00 10.00
MLMJD Josh Donaldson S2 2.50 6.00
MLMJD Josh Donaldson 2.50 6.00
MLMJDE Jacob deGrom 6.00 15.00
MLMJG Joey Gallo S2 2.50 6.00
MLMJH Jason Heyward S2 2.50 6.00
MLMJM Joe Mauer 2.50 6.00
MLMJR Jose Ramirez S2 2.50 6.00
MLMJS Justin Smoak S2 2.00 5.00
MLMJS Jean Segura 3.00 8.00
MLMJT Jameson Taillon S2 2.50 6.00
MLMJV Justin Verlander 3.00 8.00
MLMJVO Joey Votto 3.00 8.00
MLMKB Kris Bryant 4.00 10.00
MLMKS Kyle Schwarber S2 3.00 8.00
MLMLC Lorenzo Cain S2 2.00 5.00
MLMLS Luis Severino S2 2.50 6.00
MLMMA Miguel Andujar S2 3.00 8.00
MLMMB Mookie Betts 6.00 15.00
MLMMC Michael Conforto 2.50 6.00
MLMMCA Miguel Cabrera 3.00 8.00
MLMMH Mitch Haniger 2.50 6.00
MLMMS Miguel Sano S2 2.50 6.00
MLMMS Max Scherzer 3.00 8.00
MLMMT Mike Trout S2 15.00 40.00
MLMMT Mike Trout 10.00 25.00
MLMOA Ozzie Albies 3.00 8.00
MLMPG Paul Goldschmidt S2 3.00 8.00
MLMPG Paul Goldschmidt 3.00 8.00
MLMRA Ronald Acuna Jr. 12.00 30.00
MLMRD Rafael Devers S2 4.00 10.00
MLMRH Rhys Hoskins 4.00 10.00
MLMSG Scooter Gennett S2 2.50 6.00
MLMSO Shohei Ohtani 5.00 12.00
MLMSP Salvador Perez 2.50 6.00
MLMSS Stephen Strasburg S2 3.00 8.00
MLMTM Trey Mancini 2.50 6.00
MLMTS Trevor Story S2 3.00 8.00
MLMTS Travis Shaw 2.00 5.00
MLMTT Troy Tulowitzki S2 3.00 8.00
MLMTT Trea Turner 2.50 6.00
MLMVR Victor Robles S2 4.00 10.00
MLMWC Willson Contreras 2.50 6.00
MLMWM Wil Myers 2.50 6.00
MLMXB Xander Bogaerts S2 3.00 8.00
MLMYM Yoan Moncada 3.00 8.00
MLMYMO Yadier Molina 4.00 10.00
MLMYP Yasiel Puig S2 3.00 8.00
MLMABE Andrew Benintendi S2 3.00 8.00
MLMDPE Dustin Pedroia S2 3.00 8.00
MLMJTO Juan Soto S2 10.00 25.00
MLMMST Marcus Stroman S2 2.50 6.00

2019 Topps Major League Materials Autographs

SER.1 ODDS 1:3808 HOBBY
SER.2 ODDS 1:3432 HOBBY
PRINT RUNS B/WN 10-50 COPIES PER
NO PRICING ON QTY 15 OR LESS
EXCHANGE DEADLINE 12/31/2020
*RED/25: .5X TO 1.2X BASIC
MLARAJ Aaron Judge/10 S2
MLARBB Byron Buxton S2 10.00 25.00
MLARBN Brandon Nimmo S2 8.00 20.00
MLARBS Blake Snell/50
MLARCS Chris Sale EXCH 25.00 60.00
MLARCY Christian Yelich/50 20.00 50.00
MLARDB Dellin Betances S2 8.00 20.00
MLARDG Didi Gregorius/50 8.00 20.00
MLARER Eddie Rosario S2 8.00 20.00
MLARFF Freddie Freeman/50 25.00 60.00
MLARFL Francisco Lindor/30 S2 20.00 50.00
MLARFV Felipe Vazquez S2 6.00 15.00
MLARGS George Springer/50 8.00 20.00
MLARJA Jesus Aguilar/50 8.00 20.00
MLARJA Jose Altuve S2
MLARJd Jacob deGrom/50 30.00 80.00
MLARJF Jack Flaherty S2 10.00 25.00
MLARJH Josh Hader S2 8.00 20.00
MLARJM Jose Martinez S2 6.00 15.00
MLARJS Juan Soto S2 25.00 60.00
MLARJSO Juan Soto/50 60.00 150.00
MLARKB Kris Bryant S2
MLARKD Khris Davis/50
MLARKS Kyle Schwarber/50 15.00 40.00
MLARKT Kyle Tucker/50 40.00 100.00
MLARLS Luis Severino/50 15.00 40.00
MLARMA Miguel Andujar S2 10.00 25.00
MLARMC Matt Carpenter S2 10.00 25.00
MLARMH Mitch Haniger/50 12.00 30.00
MLARMM Manny Machado/30 S2 25.00 60.00
MLARMO Matt Olson/50 10.00 25.00
MLARNS Noah Syndergaard/50 20.00 50.00
MLAROA Ozzie Albies/50 25.00 60.00
MLARPD Paul DeJong S2 10.00 25.00
MLARPG Paul Goldschmidt
MLARRD Rafael Devers S2 25.00 60.00
MLARRH Rhys Hoskins S2 25.00 60.00
MLARRH Rhys Hoskins/50 40.00 100.00
MLARSMA Starling Marte/50 50.00 120.00
MLARSP Salvador Perez/50
MLARTB Trevor Bauer S2 12.00 30.00
MLARTM Trey Mancini S2 8.00 20.00
MLARTP Tommy Pham S2 6.00 15.00
MLARTS Travis Shaw/50
MLARTST Trevor Story/50
MLARVR Victor Robles S2 12.00 30.00
MLARWC Willson Contreras/25 15.00 40.00
MLARWM Whit Merrifield S2 10.00 25.00
MLARYM Yadier Molina/50 50.00 120.00
MLARAMC Andrew McCutchen S2
MLARARO Amed Rosario S2 8.00 20.00
MLARJMC Jeff McNeil S2 20.00 50.00
MLARJSM Justin Smoak S2 6.00 15.00
MLARMMU Max Muncy S2 8.00 20.00
MLARSMA Steven Matz S2 6.00 15.00

2019 Topps Mookie Betts Highlights

STATED ODDS 1:4 WM BLASTER
*150th/150: 1.25X TO 3X BASIC
MB1 Mookie Betts .75 2.00
MB2 Mookie Betts .75 2.00
MB3 Mookie Betts .75 2.00
MB4 Mookie Betts .75 2.00
MB5 Mookie Betts .75 2.00
MB6 Mookie Betts .75 2.00
MB7 Mookie Betts .75 2.00
MB8 Mookie Betts .75 2.00
MB9 Mookie Betts .75 2.00
MB10 Mookie Betts .75 2.00
MB11 Mookie Betts .75 2.00
MB12 Mookie Betts .75 2.00
MB13 Mookie Betts .75 2.00
MB14 Mookie Betts .75 2.00
MB15 Mookie Betts .75 2.00
MB16 Mookie Betts .75 2.00

MB17 Mookie Betts .75 2.00
MB18 Mookie Betts .75 2.00
MB19 Mookie Betts .75 2.00
MB20 Mookie Betts .75 2.00
MB21 Mookie Betts .75 2.00
MB22 Mookie Betts .75 2.00
MB23 Mookie Betts .75 2.00
MB24 Mookie Betts .75 2.00
MB25 Mookie Betts .75 2.00
MB26 Mookie Betts .75 2.00
MB27 Mookie Betts .75 2.00
MB28 Mookie Betts .75 2.00
MB29 Mookie Betts .75 2.00
MB30 Mookie Betts .75 2.00

2019 Topps Mystery Rookie Redemption Autographs

RANDOM INSERTS IN PACKS
EXCHANGE DEADLINE 12/31/2020
MRAA Vladimir Guerrero Jr. 150.00 400.00
MRAB Eloy Jimenez 50.00 120.00

2019 Topps Postseason Performance Autograph Relics

SER.1 ODDS 1:11,809 HOBBY
STATED PRINT RUN 50 SER.#'d SETS
EXCHANGE DEADLINE 12/31/2020
*RED/25: .75X TO 2X BASIC
PPARAR Anthony Rizzo
PPARCC Carlos Correa
PPARCS Chris Sale
PPARFF Freddie Freeman
PPARGS George Springer
PPARJA Jose Altuve 20.00 50.00
PPARJAG Jesus Aguilar
PPARJP Joc Pederson
PPARKF Kyle Freeland 10.00 25.00
PPARMCA Matt Chapman 12.00 30.00
PPARMG Marwin Gonzalez 15.00 40.00
PPARMK Matt Kemp
PPARMT Masahiro Tanaka
PPAROA Ozzie Albies
PPARRA Ronald Acuna Jr.
PPARTS Travis Shaw
PPARTST Trevor Story
PPAYG Yuli Gurriel

2019 Topps Postseason Performance Autographs

STATED ODDS 1:14,798 HOBBY
STATED PRINT RUN 50 SER.#'d SETS
EXCHANGE DEADLINE 12/31/2020
*RED/25: .6X TO 1.5X BASIC
PPAAJ Aaron Judge
PPAAR Anthony Rizzo
PPABW Brandon Woodruff 12.00 30.00
PPACT Chris Taylor EXCH 10.00 25.00
PPACY Christian Yelich
PPAFFR Freddie Freeman
PPAFL Francisco Lindor EXCH
PPAGSP George Springer
PPAJA Jose Altuve 15.00 40.00
PPAJAG Jesus Aguilar 12.00 30.00
PPAJH Josh Hader 15.00 40.00
PPAKD Khris Davis
PPAKF Kyle Freeland 10.00 25.00
PPAMCA Matt Chapman 12.00 30.00
PPAMG Marwin Gonzalez 8.00 20.00
PPAMM Manny Machado
PPAMMU Max Muncy
PPAMT Masahiro Tanaka
PPATS Travis Shaw
PPATST Trevor Story

2019 Topps Postseason Performance Relics

STATED ODDS 1:6058 HOBBY
STATED PRINT RUN 99 SER.#'d SETS
*RED/25: .6X TO 1.5X BASIC
PPRAB Alex Bregman 8.00 20.00
PPRABE Andrew Benintendi 10.00 25.00
PPRAJ Aaron Judge 25.00 60.00
PPRAR Anthony Rizzo 8.00 20.00
PPRCB Charlie Blackmon 5.00 12.00
PPRCC Carlos Correa 5.00 12.00
PPRCK Clayton Kershaw 8.00 20.00
PPRCS Chris Sale 5.00 12.00
PPRFF Freddie Freeman 6.00 15.00
PPRGS George Springer 4.00 10.00
PPRHR Hyun-Jin Ryu 4.00 10.00
PPRJA Jose Altuve 4.00 10.00
PPRJL Jon Lester 4.00 10.00
PPRJM J.D. Martinez 15.00 40.00
PPRJP Joc Pederson 4.00 10.00
PPRJT Justin Turner 6.00 15.00
PPRJV Justin Verlander 5.00 12.00
PPRKB Kris Bryant 6.00 15.00
PPRLS Luis Severino 10.00 25.00
PPRMB Mookie Betts 12.00 30.00
PPRMC Matt Chapman 5.00 12.00
PPRMT Masahiro Tanaka 15.00 40.00
PPROA Ozzie Albies 5.00 12.00
PPRTS Trevor Story 5.00 12.00
PPRXB Xander Bogaerts 10.00 25.00
PPRYP Yasiel Puig 5.00 12.00

2019 Topps Revolution of the Game

STATED ODDS 1:104 HOBBY
*150TH/150: 1.2X TO 3X BASIC
REV2 Kenesaw Mountain Landis .60 1.50
REV3 Casey Stengel .75 2.00
REV5 Albert Spalding .60 1.50
REV6 Tommy Lasorda .75 2.00
REV7 Tony LaRussa .75 2.00
REV7 Henry Chadwick .60 1.50
REV8 Joe Torre .75 2.00
REV9 Bill James .60 1.50
REV10 Branch Rickey .60 1.50
REV11 Happy Chandler .60 1.50

2019 Topps Revolution of the Game Autographs

STATED ODDS 1:13,920 HOBBY
STATED PRINT RUNS B/WN 99-199 COPIES PER
EXCHANGE DEADLINE 12/31/2020
REVBJ Bill James/199 10.00 25.00
REVBS Bud Selig/99 12.00 30.00
REVJT Joe Torre EXCH 25.00 60.00
REVTL Tony LaRussa/99 8.00 20.00
REVTO Tommy Lasorda/99 40.00 100.00

2019 Topps Ronald Acuna Highlights

STATED ODDS 1:4 BLASTER
*150TH/150: 1.5X TO 4X BASIC
RA1 Ronald Acuna Jr. 2.00 5.00
RA2 Ronald Acuna Jr. 2.00 5.00
RA3 Ronald Acuna Jr. 2.00 5.00
RA4 Ronald Acuna Jr. 2.00 5.00
RA5 Ronald Acuna Jr. 2.00 5.00
RA6 Ronald Acuna Jr. 2.00 5.00
RA7 Ronald Acuna Jr. 2.00 5.00
RA8 Ronald Acuna Jr. 2.00 5.00
RA9 Ronald Acuna Jr. 2.00 5.00
RA10 Ronald Acuna Jr. 2.00 5.00
RA11 Ronald Acuna Jr. 2.00 5.00
RA12 Ronald Acuna Jr. 2.00 5.00
RA13 Ronald Acuna Jr. 2.00 5.00
RA14 Ronald Acuna Jr. 2.00 5.00
RA15 Ronald Acuna Jr. 2.00 5.00
RA16 Ronald Acuna Jr. 2.00 5.00
RA17 Ronald Acuna Jr. 2.00 5.00
RA18 Ronald Acuna Jr. 2.00 5.00
RA19 Ronald Acuna Jr. 2.00 5.00
RA20 Ronald Acuna Jr. 2.00 5.00
RA21 Ronald Acuna Jr. 2.00 5.00
RA22 Ronald Acuna Jr. 2.00 5.00
RA23 Ronald Acuna Jr. 2.00 5.00
RA24 Ronald Acuna Jr. 2.00 5.00
RA25 Ronald Acuna Jr. 2.00 5.00
RA26 Ronald Acuna Jr. 2.00 5.00
RA27 Ronald Acuna Jr. 2.00 5.00
RA28 Ronald Acuna Jr. 2.00 5.00
RA29 Ronald Acuna Jr. 2.00 5.00
RA30 Ronald Acuna Jr. 2.00 5.00

2019 Topps Significant Statistics

STATED ODDS 1:56 HOBBY
*BLUE: .6X TO 1.5X BASIC
*BLACK/299: 1X TO 2.5X BASIC
*150th/150: 2X TO 5X BASIC
*GOLD/50: 3X TO 8X BASIC
SS1 Giancarlo Stanton .60 1.50
SS2 Khris Davis .60 1.50
SS3 Aaron Judge 1.50 4.00
SS4 Trevor Story .60 1.50
SS5 Aaron Judge 1.50 4.00
SS6 Manny Machado .60 1.50
SS7 Joey Gallo .50 1.25
SS8 Byron Buxton .60 1.50
SS9 Mookie Betts 1.25 3.00
SS10 Mookie Betts 1.25 3.00
SS11 J.D. Martinez .60 1.50
SS12 Edwin Diaz .50 1.25
SS13 Blake Treinen .40 1.00
SS14 Josh Hader .50 1.25
SS15 Edwin Diaz .50 1.25
SS16 Harrison Bader .50 1.25
SS17 Lorenzo Cain .40 1.00
SS18 J.T. Realmuto .60 1.50
SS19 Jordan Hicks .50 1.25
SS20 Jordan Hicks .50 1.25
SS21 Tyler Glasnow .60 1.50
SS22 Alex Colome .40 1.00
SS23 Kyle Crick .40 1.00
SS24 Jeremy Jeffress .40 1.00
SS25 Jacob deGrom 1.25 3.00

2019 Topps Significant Statistics Autograph Relics

STATED ODDS 1:10,165 HOBBY
PRINT RUN B/TW 10-50 COPIES PER
NO PRICING QTY 15 OR LESS
EXCHANGE DEADLINE 12/31/2020
*RED/25: .75X TO 2X BASIC
SSARAC Alex Colome/50 5.00 12.00
SSARBB Byron Buxton/30 8.00 20.00
SSARBT Blake Treinen/50 5.00 12.00
SSARHB Harrison Bader/50 6.00 15.00
SSARJH Jordan Hicks/50 6.00 15.00
SSARJJ Jeremy Jeffress/50 5.00 12.00
SSARKD Khris Davis/50 8.00 20.00
SSARJHA Josh Hader/50 6.00 15.00
SSARJHI Jordan Hicks/50 6.00 15.00

2019 Topps Significant Statistics Autograph Relics Red

*RED/25: .75X TO 2X BASIC
STATED ODDS 1:17,845 HOBBY
PRINT RUN B/TW X-25 COPIES PER
NO PRICING QTY 15 OR LESS
EXCHANGE DEADLINE 12/31/2020
SSARJd Jacob deGrom 40.00 100.00

2019 Topps Significant Statistics Autographs

STATED ODDS 1:11,310 HOBBY
STATED PRINT RUN 50 SER.#'d SETS
EXCHANGE DEADLINE 12/31/2020
*RED/25: .6X TO 1.5X BASIC
SSABT Blake Treinen 3.00 8.00
SSAHB Harrison Bader 4.00 10.00
SSAJJ Jeremy Jeffress 3.00 8.00
SSAKD Khris Davis 5.00 12.00
SSAJHA Josh Hader 4.00 10.00
SSAJHI Jordan Hicks 4.00 10.00
SSAJHK Jordan Hicks 4.00 10.00

2019 Topps Significant Statistics Relics

STATED ODDS 1:2760 HOBBY
STATED PRINT RUN 99 SER.#'d SETS
*RED/25: .75X TO 2X BASIC
SSRBB Byron Buxton 3.00 8.00
SSRBT Blake Treinen 2.00 5.00
SSRGS Giancarlo Stanton 3.00 8.00
SSRHB Harrison Bader 2.50 6.00
SSRJd Jacob deGrom 6.00 15.00
SSRJG Joey Gallo 2.50 6.00
SSRJH Josh Hader 2.50 6.00
SSRJM J.D. Martinez 3.00 8.00
SSRJR J.T. Realmuto 3.00 8.00
SSRKD Khris Davis 3.00 8.00
SSRLC Lorenzo Cain 2.00 5.00
SSRMB Mookie Betts 6.00 15.00
SSRMM Manny Machado 5.00 12.00
SSRTS Trevor Story 3.00 8.00
SSRAJD Aaron Judge 8.00 20.00
SSRAJU Aaron Judge 8.00 20.00
SSRJHI Jordan Hicks 2.50 6.00
SSRJHK Jordan Hicks 2.50 6.00
SSRJMA J.D. Martinez 3.00 8.00
SSRMBT Mookie Betts 6.00 15.00

2019 Topps Significant Statistics Relics Red

*RED/25: .75X TO 2X BASIC
STATED ODDS 1:10,429 HOBBY
STATED PRINT RUN 25 SER.#'d SETS
SSRJd Jacob deGrom 15.00 40.00
SSRJM J.D. Martinez 12.00 30.00
SSRMM Manny Machado 12.00 30.00
SSRJMA J.D. Martinez 12.00 30.00

2019 Topps Stars of the Game

INSERTED IN RETAIL PACKS
SSB1 Ronald Acuna Jr. 5.00 12.00
SSB2 Mike Trout 5.00 12.00
SSB3 J.D. Martinez 1.00 2.50
SSB4 Justin Verlander 1.00 2.50
SSB5 Luis Severino .75 2.00
SSB6 Edwin Encarnacion 1.00 2.50
SSB7 Christian Yelich 1.25 3.00
SSB8 Xander Bogaerts 1.00 2.50
SSB9 Eric Hosmer .75 2.00
SSB10 Charlie Blackmon 1.00 2.50
SSB11 Rafael Devers 1.25 3.00
SSB12 Trea Turner .75 2.00
SSB13 Gary Sanchez 1.00 2.50
SSB14 Kris Bryant 1.25 3.00
SSB15 Mookie Betts 2.00 5.00
SSB16 Michael Conforto .75 2.00
SSB17 Nolan Arenado 1.50 4.00
SSB18 Paul Goldschmidt 1.00 2.50
SSB19 Bryce Harper 1.50 4.00
SSB20 Justin Upton .75 2.00
SSB21 Francisco Lindor 1.00 2.50
SSB22 Eddie Rosario .75 2.00
SSB23 Gerrit Cole 1.00 2.50
SSB24 Eugenio Suarez .75 2.00
SSB25 Joey Gallo .75 2.00
SSB26 Andrew Benintendi 1.00 2.50
SSB27 Jose Berrios .75 2.00
SSB28 Rhys Hoskins 1.25 3.00
SSB29 Blake Snell .75 2.00
SSB30 Miguel Andujar 1.00 2.50
SSB31 Shohei Ohtani 1.50 4.00
SSB32 Matt Carpenter 1.00 2.50
SSB33 Anthony Rizzo 1.25 3.00
SSB34 Corey Seager 1.00 2.50
SSB35 Adrian Beltre 1.00 2.50
SSB36 Whit Merrifield 1.00 2.50
SSB37 Alex Bregman 1.00 2.50
SSB38 Max Scherzer 1.00 2.50
SSB39 Nicholas Castellanos 1.00 2.50
SSB40 Adam Jones .75 2.00
SSB41 Stephen Strasburg 1.00 2.50
SSB42 Scooter Gennett .75 2.00
SSB43 Manny Machado 1.00 2.50
SSB44 Lorenzo Cain .60 1.50
SSB45 Wil Myers .75 2.00
SSB46 Javier Baez 1.25 3.00
SSB47 Khris Davis 1.00 2.50
SSB48 Giancarlo Stanton 1.00 2.50
SSB49 Starling Marte .60 1.50
SSB50 Carlos Correa 1.00 2.50
SSB51 Aaron Nola .75 2.00
SSB52 Yoan Moncada 1.00 2.50
SSB53 Mitch Haniger .75 2.00
SSB54 Dee Gordon .60 1.50
SSB55 Jose Abreu 1.00 2.50
SSB56 Juan Soto 3.00 8.00
SSB57 Jose Altuve .75 2.00
SSB58 Zack Greinke 1.00 2.50
SSB59 Michael Kopech 2.00 5.00
SSB60 Miguel Cabrera 1.00 2.50
SSB61 Felix Hernandez .75 2.00
SSB62 Jacob deGrom 2.00 5.00
SSB63 Ozzie Albies 1.00 2.50
SSB64 Joey Votto 1.00 2.50
SSB65 Salvador Perez .75 2.00
SSB66 Cody Bellinger 2.00 5.00
SSB67 Trey Mancini .75 2.00
SSB68 Clayton Kershaw 1.50 4.00
SSB69 Trevor Bauer 1.25 3.00
SSB70 Jose Ramirez .75 2.00
SSB71 Kyle Schwarber 1.00 2.50
SSB72 Edwin Diaz .75 2.00
SSB73 Justin Smoak .60 1.50
SSB74 Yoenis Cespedes 1.00 2.50
SSB75 Andrew McCutchen 1.00 2.50
SSB76 Matt Chapman 1.00 2.50
SSB77 Corey Kluber .75 2.00
SSB78 Freddie Freeman 1.25 3.00
SSB79 Robinson Cano .75 2.00
SSB80 Masahiro Tanaka .75 2.00
SSB81 Paul DeJong 1.00 2.50
SSB82 Yadier Molina 1.25 3.00
SSB83 Gleyber Torres 2.00 5.00
SSB84 Jon Lester .75 2.00
SSB85 Marcell Ozuna 1.00 2.50
SSB86 Ichiro 1.25 3.00
SSB87 James Paxton .75 2.00
SSB88 Josh Donaldson .75 2.00
SSB89 Nelson Cruz 1.00 2.50
SSB90 J.T. Realmuto 1.00 2.50
SSB91 Yu Darvish 1.00 2.50
SSB92 Trevor Story 1.00 2.50
SSB93 Albert Pujols 1.25 3.00
SSB94 Noah Syndergaard .75 2.00
SSB95 Aaron Judge 2.50 6.00
SSB96 Daniel Murphy .75 2.00
SSB97 Buster Posey 1.25 3.00
SSB98 George Springer .75 2.00
SSB99 Chris Sale 1.00 2.50
SSB100 Kyle Tucker 1.50 4.00

2019 Topps World Series Champion Autograph Relics

STATED ODDS 1:15,798 HOBBY
STATED PRINT RUN 50 SER.#'d SETS
EXCHANGE DEADLINE 12/31/2020
*RED/25: ..6X TO 1.5X BASIC
WCARBH Brock Holt 40.00 100.00
WCARCS Chris Sale 40.00 100.00
WCARCV Christian Vazquez 50.00 120.00
WCARDP David Price 30.00 80.00
WCARER Eduardo Rodriguez 50.00 120.00
WCARMB Matt Barnes
WCARRP Rick Porcello EXCH 40.00 100.00

2019 Topps World Series Champion Autographs

STATED ODDS 1:14,798 HOBBY
STATED PRINT RUN 50 SER.#'d SETS
EXCHANGE DEADLINE 12/31/2020
*RED/25: .6X TO 1.5X BASIC
WCABH Brock Holt EXCH 30.00 80.00
WCABS Blake Swihart 30.00 80.00
WCACS Chris Sale EXCH 40.00 100.00
WCACV Christian Vazquez 40.00 100.00
WCADP David Price
WCAER Eduardo Rodriguez
WCAJB Jackie Bradley Jr.
WCANE Nathan Eovaldi
WCARB Ryan Brasier 40.00 100.00
WCARD Rafael Devers EXCH
WCARP Rick Porcello EXCH 30.00 80.00
WCASP Steve Pearce EXCH 50.00 120.00

2019 Topps World Series Champion Relics

STATED ODDS 1:6058 HOBBY
STATED PRINT RUN 99 SER.#'d SETS
*RED/25: .75X TO 2X BASIC
WCRAN Andrew Benintendi 20.00 50.00
WCRBR Brock Holt 10.00 25.00
WCRCS Chris Sale 12.00 30.00
WCRCV Christian Vazquez 20.00 50.00
WCRDP David Price 15.00 40.00
WCRIK Ian Kinsler 12.00 30.00
WCRJB Jackie Bradley Jr. 25.00 60.00
WCRJM J.D. Martinez 15.00 40.00
WCRKI Craig Kimbrel 12.00 30.00
WCRMB Matt Barnes 15.00 40.00
WCRMO Mookie Betts 30.00 80.00
WCRRD Rafael Devers 20.00 50.00
WCRRP Rick Porcello 20.00 50.00
WCRXB Xander Bogaerts 20.00 50.00

2019 Topps Update

COMPLETE SET (300) 20.00 50.00
PRINTING PLATE ODDS 1:3863 HOBBY
PLATE PRINT RUN 1 SET PER COLOR
BLACK-CYAN-MAGENTA-YELLOW ISSUED
NO PLATE PRICING DUE TO SCARCITY
US1 Vladimir Guerrero Jr. RC 4.00 10.00
US2 Mike Tauchman (RC) .40 1.00
US3 Curt Casali .15 .40
US4 Gary Sanchez AS .25 .60
US5 CC Sabathia HL CL .20 .50
US6 Yonder Alonso .15 .40
US7 Aroldis Chapman AS .25 .60
US8 Walker Buehler AS .30 .75
US9 Masahiro Tanaka AS .20 .50
US10 Jorge Polanco AS .20 .50
US11 Brandon Brennan RC .25 .60
US12 Paul Goldschmidt .25 .60
US13 Yasmani Grandal AS .15 .40
US14 Jose Suarez RC .25 .60
US15 James McCann AS .20 .50
US16 Martin Maldonado .15 .40
US17 Edwin Diaz .20 .50
US18 Christian Walker .20 .50
US19 Zach Plesac RC .60 1.50
US20 Mike Soroka AS .25 .60
US21 Melky Cabrera .15 .40
US22 Ian Kinsler .20 .50
US23 Cal Quantrill RC .25 .60
US24 Lucas Giolito AS .20 .50
US25 Cody Bellinger AS .50 1.25
US26 Mark Reynolds .15 .40
US27 JD Hammer RC .30 .75
US28 Oscar Mercado RC .60 1.50
US29 Tommy La Stella .15 .40
US30 Hanser Alberto RC .15 .40
US31 Joc Pederson HRD .20 .50
US32 Matt Albers .15 .40
US33 Josh Harrison .15 .40
US34 Griffin Canning RD .25 .60
US35 Derek Dietrich .20 .50
US36 Jake Odorizzi AS .15 .40
US37 Tim Beckham .20 .50
US38 Harold Ramirez RC .40 1.00
US39 Cavan Biggio RC 1.25 3.00
US40 Travis Bergen RC .25 .60
US41 Russell Martin .15 .40
US42 David Dahl AS .15 .40
US43 Josh Naylor RC .30 .75
US44 Trevor Story AS .25 .60
US45 Brendan Rodgers RD .25 .60
US46 Tanner Roark .15 .40
US47 Pete Alonso AS 1.25 3.00
US48 Matt Chapman HRD .25 .60
US49 Mike Moustakas AS .20 .50
US50 Nick Senzel RC .75 2.00
US51 Bryan Reynolds RC .75 2.00
US52 Keston Hiura RD 1.50 4.00
US53 P.Markel RC/D.McKay RC .25 .60
US54 Paul DeJong AS .25 .60
US55 Javier Baez AS .30 .75
US56 Fernando Tatis Jr. RD 10.00 25.00
US57 Clayton Richard .15 .40
US58 J.T. Realmuto AS .25 .60
US59 Jared Walsh RC 4.00 10.00
US60 Kyle Barraclough .15 .40
US61 Francisco Liriano .15 .40
US62 Vladimir Guerrero Jr. RD 1.00 2.50
US63 Trent Thornton RC .25 .60
US64 Junior Guerra .15 .40
US65 Brad Hand AS .15 .40
US66 J.T. Realmuto .25 .60
US67 Nick Ramirez RC .25 .60
US68 Yandy Diaz .20 .50
US69 Shed Long RC .40 1.00
US70 A.J. Pollock .15 .40
US71 D.Dietrich/Y.Puig .25 .60
US72 Albert Pujols HL CL .30 .75
US73 Peter Lambert RC .40 1.00
US74 Elvis Luciano RC .40 1.00
US75 Shane Bieber AS .25 .60
US76 Alex Colome .15 .40
US77 Drew Pomeranz .15 .40
US78 Mike Ford RC 1.25 3.00
US79 Jonathan Schoop .15 .40
US80 Kyle Bird RC .25 .60
US81 Jose Iglesias .20 .50
US82 Jose Alvarado .15 .40
US83 Whit Merrifield AS .25 .60
US84 Tommy Edman RC 1.25 3.00
US85 Robbie Grossman .15 .40
US86 Hunter Pence .20 .50
US87 Willson Contreras AS .20 .50
US88 Aaron Brooks RC .25 .60
US89 Carlos Santana AS .20 .50
US90 Blake Parker .15 .40
US91 Ketel Marte AS .20 .50
US92 George Springer AS .20 .50
US93 Michael Brantley .20 .50
US94 Gregory Soto RC .25 .60
US95 Nick Senzel RD .60 1.50
US96 Justin Verlander AS .25 .60
US97 Erik Swanson RC .25 .60
US98 Jones/Dyson/Peralta .20 .50
US99 T.Anderson/J.Harrison .25 .60
US100 Austin Riley RC 1.25 3.00
US101 Joe Kelly .15 .40
US102 Matt Strahm .15 .40
US103 Austin Allen RC .30 .75
US104 Sandy Alcantara AS .15 .40
US105 Luis Rengifo RC .40 1.00
US106 Yasiel Puig .25 .60
US107 Robinson Cano .20 .50
US108 Cole Irvin RC .25 .60
US109 Carter Kieboom RC .40 1.00
US110 Marwin Gonzalez .15 .40
US111 Matt Festa RC .25 .60
US112 Josh Bell HRD .20 .50
US113 Cody Bellinger HL CL .50 1.25
US114 Joey Gallo AS .20 .50
US115 Pedro Avila RC .25 .60
US116 Kelvin Gutierrez RC .40 1.00
US117 DJ LeMahieu AS .25 .60
US118 Freddy Galvis .15 .40
US119 Jesus Sucre .15 .40
US120 Billy Hamilton .20 .50
US121 Asdrubal Cabrera .20 .50
US122 Kris Bryant AS .30 .75
US123 Justus Sheffield RC .40 1.00
US124 Raimel Tapia .15 .40
US125 Braden Bishop RC .30 .75
US126 Luis Castillo AS .20 .50
US127 Kelvin Herrera .15 .40
US128 Gio Urshela .25 .60
US129 Ty France RC .75 2.00
US130 Devin Smeltzer RC .40 1.00
US131 Mike Moustakas .20 .50
US132 Neil Walker .15 .40
US133 Leury Garcia .15 .40
US134 J.D. Martinez AS .25 .60
US135 Will Smith AS .15 .40
US136 Austin Meadows AS .25 .60
US137 Hansel Robles .15 .40
US138 Adam Warren .15 .40
US139 Adam Haseley RC .40 1.00
US140 Michael Pineda .15 .40
US141 Brandon Woodruff AS .25 .60
US142 Shaun Anderson RC .25 .60
US143 Alex Bregman AS .25 .60
US144 Xander Bogaerts AS .25 .60
US145 Nick Anderson RC .25 .60
US146 Mike Trout AS 1.25 3.00
US147 Richie Martin RC .25 .60
US148 Gleyber Torres AS .50 1.25
US149 Corbin Martin RC .40 1.00
US150 Keston Hiura RC 3.00 8.00
US151 Mookie Betts AS .50 1.25
US152 Jordan Lyles .15 .40
US153 Tyler Austin .25 .60
US154 Sonny Gray .20 .50
US155 Charlie Morton .25 .60
US156 Jeurys Familia .20 .50
US157 Matt Chapman AS .25 .60
US158 Brian Dozier .20 .50
US159 Jordan Luplow .15 .40
US160 Jose Abreu AS .25 .60
US161 Tommy Kahnle .15 .40
US162 Scott Alexander .15 .40
US163 Miguel Castro .15 .40
US164 Sergio Romo .15 .40
US165 Dwight Smith Jr. .15 .40
US166 Andrew Miller .20 .50
US167 Nolan Arenado AS .40 1.00
US168 Thairo Estrada RC .40 1.00
US169 Taylor Clarke RC .25 .60
US170 Michael Chavis RC .40 1.00
US171 Corbin Martin RD .25 .60
US172 Y.Moncada/Y.Alonso .25 .60
US173 M.Gonzalez/G.Springer .20 .50
US174 Matthew Beaty RC .50 1.25
US175 Derek Holland .15 .40
US176 Anibal Sanchez .15 .40
US177 J.P. Crawford .15 .40
US178 Charlie Blackmon AS .25 .60
US179 Hector Neris .15 .40
US180 Josh VanMeter RC .40 1.00
US181 Scott Oberg .15 .40
US182 Andrew Knizner RC .40 1.00
US183 K.Dowdy/K.Bird
US184 Travis d'Arnaud .20 .50
US185 Christian Yelich AS .30 .75
US186 John Ryan Murphy .15 .40
US187 Curtis Granderson .20 .50
US188 Avisail Garcia .20 .50
US189 M.Trout/S.Ohtani 1.25 3.00
US190 Greg Holland .15 .40
US191 Brad Boxberger .15 .40
US192 Michael Chavis RD .25 .60
US193 Marcus Stroman AS .20 .50
US194 Max Muncy AS .20 .50
US195 Nick Hundley .15 .40
US196 Trevor May .15 .40
US197 Cole Tucker RC .40 1.00
US198 Pete Alonso RD 1.25 3.00
US199 Will Smith RC .60 1.50
US200 Griffin Canning RC .40 1.00
US201 Kevin Pillar .15 .40
US202 Nicky Lopez RC .40 1.00
US203 Wilmer Flores .20 .50
US204 Jason Martin RC .30 .75
US205 Darwinzon Hernandez RC .25 .60
US206 Dylan Moore RC .25 .60
US207 Chris Paddack RD .30 .75
US208 Carter Kieboom RD .25 .60
US209 Justin Bour .15 .40
US210 J.Noll RC/J.Bourque RC .25 .60
US211 Skye Bolt RC .30 .75
US212 Wei-Chieh Huang RC .30 .75
US213 Richard Lovelady RC .25 .60
US214 Zack Britton .15 .40
US215 Frankie Montas .15 .40
US216 Christian Yelich HL CL .30 .75
US217 David Robertson .15 .40
US218 Mitch Keller RC .30 .75
US219 Adrian Sampson RC .25 .60
US220 Ronald Acuna Jr. AS 1.25 3.00
US221 Shelby Miller .20 .50
US222 Martin Perez .20 .50
US223 John Means AS 2.00 5.00
US224 Yasmani Grandal .15 .40
US225 Kevin Plawecki .15 .40
US226 Ryne Harper RC .40 1.00
US227 Lane Thomas RC .40 1.00
US228 Montana DuRapau RC .25 .60
US229 Kyle Dowdy RC .30 .75
US230 Pedro Severino .15 .40
US231 Mike Shawaryn RC .25 .60
US232 Michael Brantley AS .20 .50
US233 DJ LeMahieu .25 .60
US234 Trevor Cahill .15 .40
US235 Alex Jackson RC .40 1.00
US236 Adam Ottavino .15 .40
US237 Domingo Santana .20 .50
US238 T.Bergen/S.Coonrod RC .25 .60
US239 Thomas Pannone RC .40 1.00
US240 Merrill Kelly RC .25 .60
US241 B.Drury/V.Guerrero Jr. .75 2.00
US242 Adam Jones .20 .50
US243 Eloy Jimenez RD .60 1.50
US244 Jon Duplantier RC .25 .60
US245 Mike Yastrzemski RC 1.50 4.00
US246 M.Betts/J.Martinez .50 1.25
US247 Luis Arraez RC 1.00 2.50
US248 Ryan Helsley RC .30 .75
US249 Nick Margevicius RC .25 .60
US250 Jonathan Lucroy .20 .50
US251 Bell/Marte/Cervelli .20 .50
US252 Austin Riley RD .75 2.00
US253 C.J. Cron .15 .40
US254 Shane Greene AS .15 .40
US255 Jurickson Profar .20 .50
US256 Jake Bauers RC .40 1.00
US257 Josh Donaldson .20 .50
US258 Lance Lynn .15 .40
US259 Alex Bregman HRD .25 .60
US260 F.Freeman/B.Harper .40 1.00
US261 Jeff McNeil AS .40 1.00
US262 Pete Alonso HRD 1.25 3.00
US263 Chris Paddack RC .50 1.25
US264 B.Kline RC/M.Wotherspoon RC .40 1.00
US265 Noah Syndergaard HL CL .20 .50
US266 Kevin Cron RC .75 2.00
US267 Jacob deGrom AS .50 1.25
US268 Jose Berrios AS .20 .50
US269 Craig Kimbrel .20 .50
US270 Homer Bailey .15 .40
US271 Ronald Acuna Jr. HRD 1.25 3.00
US272 Vladimir Guerrero Jr. HRD 1.00 2.50
US273 Wade Miley .15 .40
US274 Josh Bell AS .20 .50
US275 Brandon Kintzler .15 .40
US276 Spencer Turnbull RC .40 1.00
US277 Luke Weaver .15 .40
US278 Yusei Kikuchi RD .25 .60
US279 Freddie Freeman AS .30 .75
US280 Yan Gomes .25 .60
US281 Tyson Ross .15 .40
US282 Nathan Eovaldi .20 .50
US283 Omar Narvaez RC .30 .75
US284 Clayton Kershaw AS .40 1.00
US285 Dallas Keuchel .20 .50
US286 Luis Cessa .15 .40
US287 Edwin Encarnacion .25 .60
US288 Amir Garrett .15 .40
US289 Mike Zunino .15 .40
US290 Marco Estrada .15 .40
US291 Nate Lowe RC 1.25 3.00
US292 Joe Biagini .15 .40
US293 Francisco Lindor AS .25 .60
US294 Josh Fuentes RC .40 1.00
US295 Cavan Biggio RD .75 2.00
US296 Daniel Vogelbach AS .15 .40
US297 Hyun-Jin Ryu AS .20 .50
US298 Carlos Santana HRD .20 .50
US299 Brendan Rodgers RC .40 1.00
US300 Renato Nunez .20 .50

2019 Topps Update Advanced Stats

*ADV STATS: 5X TO 12X BASIC
*ADV STATS RC: 3X TO 8X BASIC RC
STATED ODDS 1:240 HOBBY
STATED PRINT RUN 150 SER.#'d SETS

2019 Topps Update Black

*BLACK: 8X TO 20X BASIC
*BLACK RC: 5X TO 12X BASIC RC
STATED ODDS 1:102 HOBBY
STATED PRINT RUN 67 SER. #'d SETS
US1 Vladimir Guerrero Jr. 500.00 800.00
US2 Mike Tauchman 12.00 30.00
US28 Oscar Mercado 15.00 40.00
US39 Cavan Biggio 25.00 60.00
US45 Brendan Rodgers RD 8.00 20.00
US50 Nick Senzel 40.00 100.00
US51 Bryan Reynolds 25.00 60.00
US52 Keston Hiura RD 20.00 50.00
US69 Shed Long 8.00 20.00
US84 Tommy Edman 50.00 120.00
US100 Austin Riley 100.00 250.00
US109 Carter Kieboom 75.00 200.00
US130 Devin Smeltzer 12.00 30.00
US139 Adam Haseley 12.00 30.00
US150 Keston Hiura 100.00 250.00
US170 Michael Chavis 60.00 150.00
US182 Andrew Knizner 12.00 30.00
US192 Michael Chavis RD 12.00 30.00
US197 Cole Tucker 8.00 20.00
US198 Pete Alonso RD 60.00 150.00
US199 Will Smith 50.00 120.00
US207 Chris Paddack RD 12.00 30.00
US208 Carter Kieboom RD 15.00 40.00
US218 Mitch Keller 12.00 30.00
US227 Lane Thomas 12.00 30.00
US243 Eloy Jimenez RD 30.00 80.00
US245 Mike Yastrzemski 30.00 80.00
US247 Luis Arraez 50.00 120.00
US252 Austin Riley RD 30.00 80.00
US261 Jeff McNeil AS 12.00 30.00
US263 Chris Paddack 40.00 100.00
US291 Nate Lowe 12.00 30.00
US295 Cavan Biggio RD 25.00 60.00
US299 Brendan Rodgers 50.00 120.00

2019 Topps Update Father's Day Blue

*BLUE: 8X TO 20X BASIC
*BLUE RC: 5X TO 12X BASIC RC
STATED ODDS 1:311 HOBBY
STATED PRINT RUN 50 SER. #'d SETS
US1 Vladimir Guerrero Jr. 200.00 500.00
US2 Mike Tauchman 12.00 30.00
US28 Oscar Mercado 15.00 40.00
US39 Cavan Biggio 25.00 60.00
US45 Brendan Rodgers RD 8.00 20.00
US50 Nick Senzel 40.00 100.00
US51 Bryan Reynolds 25.00 60.00
US52 Keston Hiura RD 20.00 50.00
US69 Shed Long 8.00 20.00
US84 Tommy Edman 50.00 120.00
US100 Austin Riley 100.00 250.00
US109 Carter Kieboom 75.00 200.00
US130 Devin Smeltzer 12.00 30.00
US139 Adam Haseley 12.00 30.00
US150 Keston Hiura 100.00 250.00
US170 Michael Chavis 20.00 50.00
US182 Andrew Knizner 12.00 30.00
US192 Michael Chavis RD 12.00 30.00
US197 Cole Tucker 8.00 20.00
US198 Pete Alonso RD 60.00 150.00
US199 Will Smith 50.00 120.00
US207 Chris Paddack RD 12.00 30.00
US208 Carter Kieboom RD 15.00 40.00
US218 Mitch Keller 12.00 30.00
US227 Lane Thomas 12.00 30.00
US243 Eloy Jimenez RD 30.00 80.00
US245 Mike Yastrzemski 30.00 80.00
US247 Luis Arraez 50.00 120.00
US252 Austin Riley RD 30.00 80.00
US261 Jeff McNeil AS 12.00 30.00
US263 Chris Paddack 12.00 30.00
US291 Nate Lowe 12.00 30.00
US295 Cavan Biggio RD 25.00 60.00
US299 Brendan Rodgers 30.00 80.00

2019 Topps Update Gold

*GOLD: 1.2X TO 3X BASIC
*GOLD RC: .75X TO 2X BASIC RC
STATED ODDS 1:8 HOBBY
STATED PRINT RUN 2018 SER. #'d SETS
US1 Vladimir Guerrero Jr. 50.00 120.00
US28 Oscar Mercado 6.00 15.00
US39 Cavan Biggio 4.00 10.00
US50 Nick Senzel 6.00 15.00
US52 Keston Hiura RD 3.00 8.00
US84 Tommy Edman 8.00 20.00
US100 Austin Riley 6.00 15.00
US109 Carter Kieboom 12.00 30.00
US150 Keston Hiura 30.00 80.00
US192 Michael Chavis RD 2.00 5.00
US198 Pete Alonso RD 10.00 25.00
US199 Will Smith 8.00 20.00
US208 Carter Kieboom RD 2.50 6.00
US227 Lane Thomas 2.00 5.00
US243 Eloy Jimenez RD 5.00 12.00
US247 Luis Arraez 8.00 20.00
US295 Cavan Biggio RD 4.00 10.00
US299 Brendan Rodgers 5.00 12.00

2019 Topps Update Independence Day

*INDPNDNCE: 8X TO 20X BASIC
*INDPNDNCE RC: 5X TO 12X BASIC RC
STATED ODDS 1:205 HOBBY
STATED PRINT RUN 76 SER. #'d SETS
US1 Vladimir Guerrero Jr. 200.00 500.00
US2 Mike Tauchman 12.00 30.00
US28 Oscar Mercado 15.00 40.00
US39 Cavan Biggio 25.00 60.00
US45 Brendan Rodgers RD 8.00 20.00
US50 Nick Senzel 40.00 100.00
US51 Bryan Reynolds 25.00 60.00
US52 Keston Hiura RD 20.00 50.00
US84 Tommy Edman 50.00 120.00
US100 Austin Riley 100.00 250.00
US109 Carter Kieboom 75.00 200.00
US130 Devin Smeltzer 12.00 30.00
US139 Adam Haseley 12.00 30.00
US150 Keston Hiura 100.00 250.00
US170 Michael Chavis 20.00 50.00
US182 Andrew Knizner 12.00 30.00
US192 Michael Chavis RD 12.00 30.00
US197 Cole Tucker 8.00 20.00
US198 Pete Alonso RD 60.00 150.00
US199 Will Smith 50.00 120.00
US207 Chris Paddack RD 12.00 30.00
US208 Carter Kieboom RD 15.00 40.00
US218 Mitch Keller 12.00 30.00
US227 Lane Thomas 12.00 30.00
US243 Eloy Jimenez RD 30.00 80.00
US245 Mike Yastrzemski 30.00 80.00
US247 Luis Arraez 50.00 120.00
US252 Austin Riley RD 30.00 80.00
US261 Jeff McNeil AS 12.00 30.00
US263 Chris Paddack 12.00 30.00
US291 Nate Lowe 12.00 30.00
US295 Cavan Biggio RD 25.00 60.00
US299 Brendan Rodgers 30.00 80.00

2019 Topps Update Memorial Day Camo

*CAMO: 12X TO 30X BASIC
*CAMO RC: 8X TO 20X BASIC RC
STATED ODDS 1:622 HOBBY
STATED PRINT RUN 25 SER. #'d SETS
US1 Vladimir Guerrero Jr. 600.00 1000.00
US28 Oscar Mercado 25.00 60.00
US39 Cavan Biggio 40.00 100.00
US45 Brendan Rodgers RD 12.00 30.00
US50 Nick Senzel 60.00 150.00
US51 Bryan Reynolds 40.00 100.00
US52 Keston Hiura RD 30.00 80.00
US69 Shed Long 12.00 30.00
US84 Tommy Edman 75.00 200.00
US100 Austin Riley 150.00 400.00
US109 Carter Kieboom 125.00 300.00
US130 Devin Smeltzer 20.00 50.00

US139 Adam Haseley 20.00 50.00
US150 Keston Hiura 150.00 400.00
US170 Michael Chavis 100.00 250.00
US182 Andrew Knizner 20.00 50.00
US192 Michael Chavis RD 20.00 50.00
US197 Cole Tucker 12.00 30.00
US198 Pete Alonso RD 100.00 250.00
US199 Will Smith 75.00 200.00
US207 Chris Paddack RD 20.00 50.00
US208 Carter Kieboom RD 25.00 60.00
US218 Mitch Keller 20.00 50.00
US227 Lane Thomas 20.00 50.00
US243 Eloy Jimenez RD 50.00 120.00
US245 Mike Yastrzemski 50.00 120.00
US247 Luis Arraez 75.00 200.00
US252 Austin Riley RD 50.00 120.00
US261 Jeff McNeil AS 20.00 50.00
US263 Chris Paddack 60.00 150.00
US291 Nate Lowe 20.00 50.00
US295 Cavan Biggio RD 40.00 100.00
US299 Brendan Rodgers 75.00 200.00

2019 Topps Update Mother's Day Pink

*PINK: 8X TO 20X BASIC
*PINK RC: 5X TO 12X BASIC RC
STATED ODDS 1:311 HOBBY
STATED PRINT RUN 50 SER. #'d SETS
US1 Vladimir Guerrero Jr. 200.00 500.00
US2 Mike Tauchman 12.00 30.00
US28 Oscar Mercado 15.00 40.00
US39 Cavan Biggio 25.00 60.00
US45 Brendan Rodgers RD 8.00 20.00
US50 Nick Senzel 40.00 100.00
US51 Bryan Reynolds 25.00 60.00
US52 Keston Hiura RD 20.00 50.00
US69 Shed Long 8.00 20.00
US84 Tommy Edman 50.00 120.00
US100 Austin Riley 100.00 250.00
US109 Carter Kieboom 75.00 200.00
US130 Devin Smeltzer 12.00 30.00
US139 Adam Haseley 12.00 30.00
US150 Keston Hiura 100.00 250.00
US170 Michael Chavis 20.00 50.00
US182 Andrew Knizner 12.00 30.00
US192 Michael Chavis RD 12.00 30.00
US197 Cole Tucker 8.00 20.00
US198 Pete Alonso RD 60.00 150.00
US199 Will Smith 50.00 120.00
US207 Chris Paddack RD 12.00 30.00
US208 Carter Kieboom RD 15.00 40.00
US218 Mitch Keller 12.00 30.00
US227 Lane Thomas 12.00 30.00
US243 Eloy Jimenez RD 30.00 80.00
US245 Mike Yastrzemski 30.00 80.00
US247 Luis Arraez 50.00 120.00
US252 Austin Riley RD 30.00 80.00
US261 Jeff McNeil AS 12.00 30.00
US263 Chris Paddack 12.00 30.00
US291 Nate Lowe 12.00 30.00
US295 Cavan Biggio RD 25.00 60.00
US299 Brendan Rodgers 30.00 80.00

2019 Topps Update Photo Variations

VAR STATED ODDS 1:32 HOBBY
RC VAR STATED ODDS 1:622 HOBBY
US1A Guerrero Jr. Point 40.00 100.00
US1B Guerrero Jr. w/Ball 150.00 400.00
US12 Paul Goldschmidt 1.50 4.00
arms streched out
US21 Willie Mays 3.00 8.00
US28A Mercado Crouch 2.50 6.00
US28B Mercado Point 25.00 60.00
US35 Derek Dietrich 1.25 3.00
red tank top
US39A Biggio Interview 5.00 12.00
US39B Biggio Trot 30.00 80.00
US50A Senzel Touch Hat 6.00 15.00
US50B Senzel Gatorade 50.00 120.00
US56 Tony Gwynn 1.50 4.00
US63A Trent Thornton 1.00 2.50
blue jersey
US63B Thornton Gray jrsy 15.00 40.00
US74 Luciano Tossing ball 25.00 60.00
US79 Jackie Robinson 1.50 4.00
US93 Ken Griffey Jr. 3.00 8.00
US100A Riley Jump 10.00 25.00
US100B Riley w/Blooper 40.00 100.00
US105 Rengifo Pullover 10.00 25.00
US106 Yasiel Puig 1.50 4.00
with Indians
US107 Robinson Cano 1.25 3.00
touching chest
US109A Kieboom Thrwng 8.00 20.00
US109B Kieboom Blue jrsy 30.00 80.00
US123A Justus Sheffield 1.50 4.00
Arm up
US123B Sheffield Arm down 15.00 40.00
US128 Thurman Munson 4.00 10.00
US133 Willie Mays 3.00 8.00
US147 Cal Ripken Jr. 4.00 10.00
US149A Corbin Martin 1.50 4.00
tipping hat
US149B Martin Clenched fist 15.00 40.00
US150A Hiura Thrwbck 40.00 100.00
US150B Hiura Hand helmet 40.00 100.00
US165 Eddie Murray 1.25 3.00
US168 Estrada Thrwng 40.00 100.00
US168 Robin Yount 1.50 4.00
US170A Chavis Wht jrsy 4.00 10.00
US170B Chavis Red jrsy 50.00 120.00
US179 Mariano Rivera 2.00 5.00
US182 Johnny Bench 1.50 4.00
US187 Roberto Clemente 4.00 10.00
US197A Cole Tucker 1.50 4.00
wearing costume
US197B Tucker Signs 30.00 80.00
US199A Smith Vertical 5.00 12.00
US199B Smith Horizontal 30.00 80.00
US200A Griffin Canning 1.50 4.00
red pullover
US200B Canning w/Catcher 15.00 40.00
US202 George Brett 3.00 8.00
US206 Ichiro 2.00 5.00
US218 Mitch Keller 1.25 3.00
sitting in dugout
US219 Nolan Ryan 5.00 12.00
US224 Yasmani Grandal 1.00 2.50
running
US227 Thomas w/Ozuna 20.00 50.00
US237 Randy Johnson 1.50 4.00
US242 Adam Jones 1.25 3.00
left foot off ground
US244A Duplantier Gray jrsy 1.00 2.50
US244B Duplantier Wht jrsy 15.00 40.00
US245 Carl Yastrzemski 2.50 6.00
US249A Nick Margevicius 1.00 2.50
brown jersey
US249B Margevicius Full mound 15.00 40.00
US256A Jake Bauers 1.50 4.00
white jersey
US256B Bauers Gray jrsy 15.00 40.00
US257 Josh Donaldson 1.25 3.00
ball visible
US263B Chris Paddack 2.00 5.00
with Machado
US263A Paddack Jckt 30.00 80.00
US266A Cron Dirt 3.00 8.00
US266B Cron Dugout 20.00 50.00
US269 Ryne Sandberg 3.00 8.00
US283 Edgar Martinez 1.25 3.00
US291A Nate Lowe 5.00 12.00
peace sign
US291B Lowe Bttng cage 15.00 40.00
US295 Roy Halladay 1.25 3.00
US299A Brendan Rodgers 1.50 4.00
coming out dugout
US299B Rodgers Barehand 30.00 80.00
US300 Mike Mussina 1.25 3.00

2019 Topps Update Rainbow Foil

*RAINBOW: 1.2X TO 3X BASIC
*RAINBOW RC: .75X TO 2X BASIC RC
STATED ODDS 1:10 HOBBY
US1 Vladimir Guerrero Jr. 30.00 80.00
US28 Oscar Mercado 2.50 6.00
US39 Cavan Biggio 4.00 10.00
US50 Nick Senzel 6.00 15.00
US52 Keston Hiura RD 3.00 8.00
US84 Tommy Edman 4.00 10.00
US100 Austin Riley 6.00 15.00
US109 Carter Kieboom 12.00 30.00
US150 Keston Hiura 30.00 80.00
US192 Michael Chavis RD 2.00 5.00
US198 Pete Alonso RD 10.00 25.00
US199 Will Smith 8.00 20.00
US208 Carter Kieboom RD 2.50 6.00
US227 Lane Thomas 2.00 5.00
US243 Eloy Jimenez RD 5.00 12.00
US247 Luis Arraez 8.00 20.00
US295 Cavan Biggio RD 4.00 10.00
US299 Brendan Rodgers 5.00 12.00

2019 Topps Update Vintage Stock

*VINTAGE: 6X TO 15X BASIC
*VINTAGE RC: 4X TO 10X BASIC RC
STATED ODDS 1:157 HOBBY
STATED PRINT RUN 99 SER. #'d SETS
US1 Vladimir Guerrero Jr. 150.00 400.00
US28 Oscar Mercado 12.00 30.00
US39 Cavan Biggio 20.00 50.00
US45 Brendan Rodgers RD 6.00 15.00
US50 Nick Senzel 30.00 80.00
US51 Bryan Reynolds 20.00 50.00
US52 Keston Hiura RD 15.00 40.00
US84 Tommy Edman 40.00 100.00
US100 Austin Riley 40.00 100.00
US109 Carter Kieboom 60.00 150.00
US139 Adam Haseley 10.00 25.00
US150 Keston Hiura 75.00 200.00
US170 Michael Chavis 15.00 40.00
US182 Andrew Knizner 10.00 25.00
US192 Michael Chavis RD 10.00 25.00
US197 Cole Tucker 6.00 15.00
US198 Pete Alonso RD 50.00 120.00
US199 Will Smith 40.00 100.00
US208 Carter Kieboom RD 12.00 30.00
US218 Mitch Keller 10.00 25.00
US227 Lane Thomas 10.00 25.00
US243 Eloy Jimenez RD 25.00 60.00
US245 Mike Yastrzemski 25.00 60.00
US247 Luis Arraez 40.00 100.00
US252 Austin Riley RD 25.00 60.00
US261 Jeff McNeil AS 10.00 25.00
US263 Chris Paddack 10.00 25.00
US291 Nate Lowe 10.00 25.00
US295 Cavan Biggio RD 20.00 50.00
US299 Brendan Rodgers 25.00 60.00

2019 Topps Update Walgreens Yellow

*YELLOW: 2.5X TO 6X BASIC
*YELLOW RC: 1.5X TO 4X BASIC RC
INSERTED IN WALGREENS PACKS
US1 Vladimir Guerrero Jr. 50.00 120.00
US28 Oscar Mercado 5.00 12.00
US39 Cavan Biggio 8.00 20.00
US50 Nick Senzel 12.00 30.00
US52 Keston Hiura RD 6.00 15.00
US84 Tommy Edman 8.00 20.00
US100 Austin Riley 12.00 30.00
US109 Carter Kieboom 25.00 60.00
US150 Keston Hiura 30.00 80.00
US192 Michael Chavis RD 4.00 10.00
US198 Pete Alonso RD 20.00 50.00
US199 Will Smith 15.00 40.00
US208 Carter Kieboom RD 5.00 12.00
US227 Lane Thomas 4.00 10.00
US243 Eloy Jimenez RD 10.00 25.00
US247 Luis Arraez 15.00 40.00
US295 Cavan Biggio RD 8.00 20.00
US299 Brendan Rodgers 10.00 25.00

2019 Topps Update '84 Oversized Box Toppers

84BT1 Yusei Kikuchi .60 1.50
84BT2 Mike Trout 5.00 12.00
84BT3 Noah Syndergaard .75 2.00
84BT4 Max Scherzer 1.00 2.50
84BT5 Juan Soto 3.00 8.00
84BT6 Aaron Judge 2.50 6.00
84BT7 Jacob deGrom 2.00 5.00
84BT8 Cody Bellinger 2.00 5.00
84BT9 Christian Yelich 1.25 3.00
84BT10 Clayton Kershaw 1.50 4.00
84BT11 Nolan Ryan 3.00 8.00
84BT12 Francisco Lindor 1.00 2.50
84BT13 Kris Bryant 1.25 3.00
84BT14 Mookie Betts 2.00 5.00
84BT15 Ronald Acuna Jr. 5.00 12.00
84BT16 Javier Baez 1.25 3.00
84BT17 Jose Altuve .75 2.00
84BT18 Don Mattingly 2.00 5.00
84BT19 Derek Jeter 2.50 6.00
84BT20 Mark McGwire 1.50 4.00
84BT21 Fernando Tatis Jr. 10.00 25.00
84BT22 Eloy Jimenez 2.50 6.00
84BT23 Vladimir Guerrero Jr. 4.00 10.00
84BT24 Pete Alonso 5.00 12.00
84BT25 Ted Williams 2.00 5.00
84BT26 Nick Senzel 2.00 5.00
84BT27 Carter Kieboom 1.00 2.50
84BT28 Chris Paddack 1.25 3.00
84BT29 Michael Chavis 1.00 2.50
84BT30 Austin Riley 3.00 8.00
84BT31 Keston Hiura 2.00 5.00
84BT32 Brendan Rodgers 1.00 2.50
84BT33 Willie Mays 2.00 5.00
84BT34 Bryce Harper 1.50 4.00
84BT35 Manny Machado 1.00 2.50
84BT36 Paul Goldschmidt 1.00 2.50
84BT37 Mariano Rivera 1.25 3.00
84BT38 Walker Buehler 1.25 3.00
84BT39 Alex Bregman 1.00 2.50
84BT40 Shohei Ohtani 1.50 4.00
84BT41 Roberto Clemente 2.50 6.00
84BT42 Jackie Robinson 1.00 2.50
84BT43 Thurman Munson 1.00 2.50
84BT44 Andrew McCutchen 1.00 2.50
84BT45 Mike Piazza 1.00 2.50
84BT46 Albert Pujols 1.25 3.00
84BT47 Pedro Martinez .75 2.00
84BT48 David Ortiz 1.00 2.50
84BT49 Frank Thomas 1.00 2.50
84BT50 Bo Jackson 1.00 2.50

2019 Topps Update '84 Topps

STATED ODDS 1:4 HOBBY
*BLUE: .6X TO 1.5X
*BLACK/299: 1X TO 2.5X
*150TH/150: 1X TO 2.5X
*GOLD/50: 5X TO 12X
841 Garrett Hampson .40 1.00
842 Kerry Wood .25 .60
843 J.D. Martinez .40 1.00
844 Gerrit Cole .40 1.00
845 Xander Bogaerts .40 1.00
846 Miguel Cabrera .40 1.00
847 CC Sabathia .30 .75
848 Fernando Tatis Jr. 4.00 10.00
849 Eloy Jimenez 1.00 2.50
8410 Vladimir Guerrero Jr. 1.50 4.00
8411 Pete Alonso 2.00 5.00
8412 Ted Williams .75 2.00
8413 Nick Senzel .75 2.00
8414 Carter Kieboom .40 1.00
8415 Chris Paddack .50 1.25
8416 Michael Chavis .40 1.00
8417 Nick Margevicius .25 .60
8418 Jon Duplantier .25 .60
8419 Mariano Rivera .50 1.25
8420 Roy Halladay .30 .75
8421 Griffin Canning .40 1.00
8422 Thairo Estrada .40 1.00
8423 Lane Thomas .40 1.00
8424 Cole Tucker .40 1.00
8425 Shohei Ohtani .60 1.50
8426 Corbin Martin .40 1.00
8427 Roberto Clemente 1.00 2.50
8428 Jackie Robinson .40 1.00
8429 Austin Riley 1.25 3.00
8430 Keston Hiura .75 2.00
8431 Willie Mays .75 2.00
8432 Oscar Mercado .60 1.50
8433 Ken Griffey Jr. .75 2.00
8434 Adam Jones .30 .75
8435 Patrick Corbin .30 .75
8436 Brendan Rodgers .40 1.00
8437 Will Smith .60 1.50
8438 Bryce Harper .60 1.50
8439 Manny Machado .40 1.00
8440 Andrew McCutchen .40 1.00
8441 Paul Goldschmidt .40 1.00
8442 Robinson Cano .30 .75
8443 Josh Donaldson .30 .75
8444 Nelson Cruz .40 1.00
8445 Yasmani Grandal .25 .60
8446 Michael Brantley .30 .75
8447 Victor Robles .50 1.25
8448 Walker Buehler .50 1.25
8449 Alex Bregman .40 1.00
8450 Thurman Munson .40 1.00

2019 Topps Update '84 Topps Autographs

STATED ODDS 1:431 HOBBY
EXCHANGE DEADLINE 9/30/2021
84AAME Austin Meadows 5.00 12.00
84ABBX Byron Buxton 8.00 20.00
84ABR Bryan Reynolds 6.00 15.00
84ACK Carter Kieboom 12.00 30.00
84ACP Chris Paddack 10.00 25.00
84ACS CC Sabathia
84ACT Cole Tucker 4.00 10.00
84ADH Darwinzon Hernandez 2.50 6.00
84ADP Dustin Pedroia 20.00 50.00
84AEJ Eloy Jimenez 40.00 100.00
84AEL Elvis Luciano 4.00 10.00
84AFT Fernando Tatis Jr. 125.00 300.00
84AGC Gerrit Cole 20.00 50.00
84AGH Garrett Hampson 4.00 10.00
84AJAG Jesus Aguilar 3.00 8.00
84AJCA Jose Canseco 10.00 25.00
84AJD Jon Duplantier 2.50 6.00
84AJM J.D. Martinez 25.00 60.00
84AJMA Jason Martin 3.00 8.00
84AJME John Means 60.00 150.00
84AJV Joey Votto 20.00 50.00
84AKW Kerry Wood 15.00 40.00
84ALBR Lou Brock 20.00 50.00
84ALT Lane Thomas 8.00 20.00
84AMBE Matthew Beaty 6.00 15.00
84AMC Miguel Cabrera 60.00 150.00
84AMCA Michael Chavis 12.00 30.00
84AMK Merrill Kelly 2.50 6.00
84AMM Mike Mussina 60.00 150.00
84AMS Max Scherzer
84AMS Mike Soroka 10.00 25.00
84ANA Nolan Arenado 40.00 100.00
84ANGA Nomar Garciaparra 25.00 60.00
84ANL Nate Lowe 12.00 30.00
84ANM Nick Margevicius 2.50 6.00
84APA Pete Alonso 60.00 150.00
84APAV Pedro Avila 2.50 6.00
84ARH Ryan Helsley 3.00 8.00
84ARL Richard Lovelady 2.50 6.00
84ASB Skye Bolt 3.00 8.00
84ASL Shed Long 4.00 10.00
84ASP Salvador Perez 8.00 20.00
84ATE Thairo Estrada 10.00 25.00
84ATG Tom Glavine 10.00 25.00
84ATM Trey Mancini 3.00 8.00
84ATT Trent Thornton 2.50 6.00
84AVG Vladimir Guerrero Jr. 75.00 200.00
84AVGU Vladimir Guerrero 20.00 50.00
84RAAR Austin Riley 15.00 40.00
84RJSH Justus Sheffield 4.00 10.00
84RKH Keston Hiura 30.00 80.00
84RRBO Ryan Borucki 2.50 6.00
84RWS Will Smith 12.00 30.00

2019 Topps Update '84 Topps Autographs 150th Anniversary

*150TH ANNV/150: .5X TO 1.2X BASIC
STATED ODDS 1:967 HOBBY
STATED PRINT RUN 150 SER.#'d SETS
EXCHANGE DEADLINE 9/30/2021
84AMKE Mitch Keller 4.00 10.00

2019 Topps Update '84 Topps Autographs Gold

*GOLD/50: .6X TO 1.5X BASIC
STATED ODDS 1:2681 HOBBY
STATED PRINT RUN 50 SER.#'d SETS
EXCHANGE DEADLINE 9/30/2021
84ACB Cavan Biggio EXCH 60.00 150.00
84AMKE Mitch Keller 5.00 12.00
84ANS Nick Senzel EXCH 40.00 100.00

2019 Topps Update '84 Topps Autographs Red

*RED/25: .8X TO 2X BASIC
STATED ODDS 1:637 HOBBY
STATED PRINT RUN 25 SER.#'d SETS
EXCHANGE DEADLINE 9/30/2021
84ACB Cavan Biggio EXCH 75.00 200.00
84AMKE Mitch Keller 6.00 15.00
84ANS Nick Senzel EXCH 50.00 120.00

2019 Topps Update '84 Topps Silver Pack Chrome

T84U1 Mike Trout 3.00 8.00
T84U2 Shohei Ohtani 1.00 2.50
T84U3 Griffin Canning .60 1.50
T84U4 Randy Johnson .60 1.50
T84U5 Jon Duplantier .40 1.00
T84U6 Ronald Acuna Jr. 3.00 8.00
T84U7 Austin Riley 2.00 5.00
T84U8 Michael Chavis .60 1.50
T84U9 J.D. Martinez .60 1.50
T84U10 Rafael Devers .75 2.00
T84U11 Kerry Wood .40 1.00
T84U12 Eloy Jimenez 1.50 4.00
T84U13 Nick Senzel 1.25 3.00
T84U14 Ken Griffey Jr. 1.25 3.00
T84U15 Trevor Bauer .75 2.00
T84U16 Brendan Rodgers .60 1.50
T84U17 Jeff Bagwell .50 1.25
T84U18 Justin Verlander .60 1.50
T84U19 Corbin Martin .60 1.50
T84U20 Walker Buehler .75 2.00
T84U21 Christian Yelich .75 2.00
T84U22 Keston Hiura 1.25 3.00
T84U23 Byron Buxton .60 1.50
T84U24 Pete Alonso 3.00 8.00
T84U25 Clint Frazier .50 1.25
T84U26 Gary Sanchez .60 1.50
T84U27 Giancarlo Stanton .60 1.50
T84U28 Thairo Estrada .60 1.50
T84U29 Aaron Judge 1.50 4.00
T84U30 Jose Canseco .50 1.25
T84U31 Aaron Nola .50 1.25
T84U32 Bryce Harper 1.00 2.50
T84U33 Cole Tucker .60 1.50
T84U34 Fernando Tatis Jr. 6.00 15.00
T84U35 Chris Paddack .75 2.00
T84U36 Willie Mays 1.25 3.00
T84U37 Edgar Martinez .50 1.25
T84U38 Ichiro Suzuki .75 2.00
T84U39 Will Smith 1.00 2.50
T84U40 Mitch Keller .50 1.25
T84U41 Lane Thomas .60 1.50
T84U42 Brandon Lowe .60 1.50
T84U43 Blake Snell .50 1.25
T84U44 Joey Gallo .50 1.25
T84U45 Cavan Biggio 2.00 5.00
T84U46 Vladimir Guerrero Jr. 2.50 6.00
T84U47 Trent Thornton .40 1.00
T84U48 Carter Kieboom .60 1.50
T84U49 Victor Robles .75 2.00
T84U50 Kevin Cron 1.25 3.00

2019 Topps Update '84 Topps Silver Pack Chrome Black Refractors

*BLACK REF: 1.2X TO 3X BASIC
RANDOM INSERTS IN SILVER PACKS
STATED PRINT RUN 199 SER.#'d SETS

2019 Topps Update '84 Topps Silver Pack Chrome Blue Refractors

*BLUE REF: 1.5X TO 4X BASIC
RANDOM INSERTS IN SILVER PACKS
STATED PRINT RUN 150 SER.#'d SETS

2019 Topps Update '84 Topps Silver Pack Chrome Gold Refractors

*GOLD REF: 5X TO 12X BASIC
RANDOM INSERTS IN SILVER PACKS
STATED PRINT RUN 50 SER.#'d SETS

2019 Topps Update '84 Topps Silver Pack Chrome Green Refractors

*GREEN REF: 2X TO 5X BASIC
RANDOM INSERTS IN SILVER PACKS
STATED PRINT RUN 150 SER.#'d SETS

2019 Topps Update '84 Topps Silver Pack Chrome Orange Refractors

*ORANGE REF: 6X TO 15X BASIC
RANDOM INSERTS IN SILVER PACKS
STATED PRINT RUN 25 SER.#'d SETS

2019 Topps Update '84 Topps Silver Pack Chrome Purple Refractors

*PURPLE REF: 2X TO 5X BASIC
RANDOM INSERTS IN SILVER PACKS
STATED PRINT RUN 75 SER.#'d SETS

2019 Topps Update '84 Topps Silver Pack Chrome Autographs

RANDOM INSERTS IN SILVER PACKS
PRINT RUNS B/WN 8-150 COPIES PER
NO PRICING ON QTY 10 OR LESS
T84U2 Shohei Ohtani
T84U3 Griffin Canning/149 6.00 15.00
T84U4 Randy Johnson
T84U6 Ronald Acuna Jr./25 75.00 200.00
T84U7 Austin Riley/149 30.00 80.00
T84U8 Michael Chavis/149 12.00 30.00
T84U10 Rafael Devers/25 30.00 80.00
T84U11 Kerry Wood/25 15.00 40.00
T84U12 Eloy Jimenez/50 40.00 100.00
T84U15 Trevor Bauer
T84U17 Jeff Bagwell
T84U19 Corbin Martin/150 5.00 12.00
T84U22 Keston Hiura/149 30.00 80.00
T84U23 Byron Buxton
T84U24 Pete Alonso/149 60.00 150.00
T84U25 Clint Frazier
T84U26 Gary Sanchez
T84U28 Thairo Estrada/149 10.00 25.00
T84U30 Jose Canseco
T84U33 Cole Tucker/149 6.00 15.00
T84U34 Fernando Tatis Jr./99 150.00 400.00
T84U35 Chris Paddack/99 20.00 50.00
T84U37 Edgar Martinez/25 20.00 50.00
T84U39 Will Smith/149 10.00 25.00
T84U40 Mitch Keller
T84U41 Lane Thomas/149 8.00 20.00
T84U42 Brandon Lowe/99 10.00 25.00
T84U43 Blake Snell
T84U45 Cavan Biggio
T84U46 Vladimir Guerrero Jr./99 75.00 200.00
T84U47 Trent Thornton
T84U48 Carter Kieboom/149 15.00 40.00
T84U49 Victor Robles

2019 Topps Update '84 Topps Silver Pack Chrome Autographs Orange Refractors

*ORANGE/25: 1X TO 2.5X p/r 149-150
*ORANGE/25: .6X TO 1.5X p/r 50
RANDOM INSERTS IN SILVER PACKS
STATED PRINT RUN 25 SER.#'d SETS
T84U30 Jose Canseco 30.00 80.00
T84U40 Mitch Keller 25.00 60.00
T84U43 Blake Snell 12.00 30.00
T84U45 Cavan Biggio 40.00 100.00
T84U47 Trent Thornton 6.00 15.00
T84U49 Victor Robles 12.00 30.00

2019 Topps Update 150 Years of Baseball

STATED ODDS 1:8 HOBBY
*BLUE: .6X TO 1.5X
*BLACK/299: 1X TO 2.5X
*150TH/150: 1X TO 2.5X
*GOLD/50: 1.5X TO 4X
1501 Gary Carter .30 .75
1502 Willie Mays .75 2.00
1503 Aaron Judge 1.00 2.50
1504 Alex Bregman .40 1.00
1505 Andre Dawson .30 .75
1506 Andy Pettitte .30 .75
1507 Anthony Rizzo .50 1.25
1508 Carlton Fisk .30 .75
1509 Chris Sale .40 1.00
15010 Christian Yelich .50 1.25
15011 Cody Bellinger .75 2.00
15012 Edgar Martinez .30 .75
15013 Eloy Jimenez 1.00 2.50
15014 Fernando Tatis Jr. 4.00 10.00
15015 Francisco Lindor .40 1.00
15016 Freddie Freeman .50 1.25
15017 George Springer .30 .75
15018 Giancarlo Stanton .40 1.00
15019 Gleyber Torres .75 2.00
15020 Jacob deGrom .75 2.00
15021 Javier Baez .50 1.25
15022 Jose Altuve .30 .75
15023 Kris Bryant .50 1.25
15024 Lou Boudreau .30 .75
15025 Manny Machado .40 1.00
15026 Mike Mussina .30 .75
15027 Mookie Betts .75 2.00
15028 Noah Syndergaard .30 .75
15029 Nolan Arenado .60 1.50
15030 Randy Johnson .40 1.00
15031 Pete Alonso 2.00 5.00
15032 Rhys Hoskins .50 1.25
15033 Robinson Cano .30 .75
15034 Roger Clemens .50 1.25
15035 Jim Bunning .30 .75
15036 Ronald Acuna Jr. 2.00 5.00
15037 Roy Halladay .30 .75
15038 Shohei Ohtani .60 1.50
15039 Stephen Strasburg .40 1.00
15040 Thurman Munson .40 1.00
15041 Tim Raines .30 .75
15042 Todd Helton .30 .75
15043 Tony Perez .30 .75
15044 Vladimir Guerrero Jr. 1.50 4.00
15045 Paul Molitor .40 1.00
15046 Luis Aparicio .30 .75
15047 Bert Blyleven .30 .75
15048 Bruce Sutter .30 .75
15049 Jim Thome .30 .75
15050 Goose Gossage .30 .75
15051 Willie Mays .75 2.00
15052 Willie Mays .75 2.00
15053 Babe Ruth 1.00 2.50
15054 Bud Selig .25 .60
15055 Warren Spahn .30 .75
15056 Willie Stargell .30 .75
15057 Sandy Alomar Jr. .25 .60
15058 Bo Jackson .40 1.00
15059 Willie Mays .75 2.00
15060 Chad Bettis .25 .60
15061 Marcus Stroman .30 .75
15062 Luis Gonzalez .25 .60
15063 John Ward .30 .75
15064 Hugh Duffy .30 .75
15065 Jose Canseco .30 .75
15066 Deion Sanders .30 .75
15067 Ken Griffey Jr. .75 2.00
15068 Dwight Gooden .25 .60
15069 Tris Speaker .30 .75
15070 George Springer .30 .75
15071 Casey Stengel .30 .75
15072 Phil Niekro .30 .75
15073 Jim Bunning .30 .75
15074 Randy Johnson .40 1.00
15075 Tom Seaver .30 .75
15076 Rogers Hornsby .30 .75
15077 Willie Mays .75 2.00
15078 Warren Spahn .30 .75
15079 Catfish Hunter .30 .75
15080 Derek Jeter 1.00 2.50
15081 Adrian Beltre .40 1.00
15082 Tom Glavine .30 .75
15083 Vladimir Guerrero .30 .75
15084 Wade Boggs .30 .75
15085 Orlando Cepeda .30 .75
15086 Jose Altuve .30 .75
15087 Johnny Bench .40 1.00
15088 Javier Baez .50 1.25
15089 Jim Palmer .30 .75
15090 Ivan Rodriguez .30 .75
15091 Willie Stargell .30 .75
15092 Max Scherzer .40 1.00
15093 Thurman Munson .40 1.00
15094 Ken Griffey Jr. .75 2.00
15095 Roger Clemens .50 1.25
15096 Jackie Robinson .40 1.00
15097 Sandy Koufax .75 2.00
15098 Randy Johnson .40 1.00
15099 Nolan Ryan 1.25 3.00
150100 David Ortiz .40 1.00

2019 Topps Update 150th Anniversary

*150TH: 1.2X TO 3X BASIC
*150TH RC: .75X TO 2X BASIC RC
STATED ODDS 1:6 HOBBY
US1 Vladimir Guerrero Jr. 30.00 80.00
US28 Oscar Mercado 2.50 6.00
US39 Cavan Biggio 4.00 10.00
US50 Nick Senzel 6.00 15.00
US52 Keston Hiura RD 3.00 8.00
US84 Tommy Edman 4.00 10.00
US100 Austin Riley 6.00 15.00
US109 Carter Kieboom 12.00 30.00
US150 Keston Hiura 30.00 80.00
US192 Michael Chavis RD 2.00 5.00
US198 Pete Alonso RD 10.00 25.00
US199 Will Smith 8.00 20.00
US208 Carter Kieboom RD 2.50 6.00
US227 Lane Thomas 2.00 5.00
US243 Eloy Jimenez RD 5.00 12.00
US247 Luis Arraez 8.00 20.00
US295 Cavan Biggio RD 4.00 10.00
US299 Brendan Rodgers 5.00 12.00

2019 Topps Update 150th Anniversary Manufactured Medallions

STATED ODDS 1:242 HOBBY
*150TH/150: .6X TO 1.5X BASIC
*GOLD/50: 1X TO 2.5X BASIC
*RED/25: 2X TO 5X BASIC
AMMAB Alex Bregman 1.25 3.00
AMMAD Andre Dawson 1.00 2.50
AMMAR Alex Rodriguez 1.50 4.00
AMMBB Bert Blyleven 1.00 2.50
AMMBS Blake Snell 1.00 2.50
AMMCB Cody Bellinger 2.50 6.00
AMMCC Carlos Correa 1.25 3.00
AMMCF Carlton Fisk 2.50 6.00
AMMCM Christy Mathewson 1.25 3.00
AMMDD Dizzy Dean 1.00 2.50
AMMDM Dale Murphy 2.50 6.00
AMMDW David Wright 2.50 6.00
AMMEJ Eloy Jimenez 3.00 8.00
AMMEM Edgar Martinez 1.00 2.50
AMMFR Frank Robinson 1.00 2.50
AMMFT Fernando Tatis Jr. 12.00 30.00
AMMGC Gary Carter 2.50 6.00
AMMGS Giancarlo Stanton 1.25 3.00
AMMHK Harmon Killebrew 2.50 6.00
AMMJB Jeff Bagwell 1.00 2.50
AMMJM J.D. Martinez 1.25 3.00
AMMJP Jim Palmer 2.50 6.00
AMMJS John Smoltz 1.25 3.00
AMMJT Jim Thome 1.00 2.50
AMMKD Khris Davis 1.25 3.00
AMMKG Ken Griffey Jr. 5.00 12.00
AMMMM Manny Machado 1.25 3.00
AMMMP Mike Piazza 2.50 6.00
AMMNS Nick Senzel 3.00 8.00
AMMPA Pete Alonso 6.00 15.00
AMMPG Paul Goldschmidt 1.25 3.00
AMMRC Roger Clemens 2.50 6.00
AMMRH Roy Halladay 1.00 2.50
AMMRJ Reggie Jackson 2.50 6.00
AMMTM Thurman Munson 2.50 6.00
AMMTP Tony Perez 2.50 6.00
AMMTR Tim Raines 1.00 2.50
AMMTS Tris Speaker 1.00 2.50
AMMVG Vladimir Guerrero Jr. 5.00 12.00
AMMVR Victor Robles 1.50 4.00
AMMWF Whitey Ford 2.50 6.00
AMMWM Willie Mays 3.00 8.00
AMMJBE Johnny Bench 2.50 6.00
AMMJBZ Javier Baez 2.50 6.00
AMMJMI Johnny Mize 1.00 2.50
AMMKGE Ken Griffey Jr. 5.00 12.00
AMMMMS Mike Mussina 2.00 5.00
AMMNSY Noah Syndergaard 1.00 2.50
AMMRJO Randy Johnson 1.25 3.00
AMMSSO Sammy Sosa 1.25 3.00

2019 Topps Update 150th Anniversary Manufactured Patches

RANDOM INSERTS IN PACKS
*150TH/150: .5X TO 1.2X BASIC
*GOLD/50: .75X TO 2X BASIC
*RED/25: 1.2X TO 3X BASIC
AMPAD Andre Dawson 1.00 2.50
AMPAR Alex Rodriguez 1.50 4.00
AMPBF Bob Feller 1.00 2.50
AMPBH Bryce Harper 2.00 5.00
AMPBR Brooks Robinson 1.00 2.50
AMPBS Blake Snell 1.00 2.50
AMPCM Christy Mathewson 1.25 3.00
AMPDS Darryl Strawberry .75 2.00
AMPEJ Eloy Jimenez 3.00 8.00
AMPEM Eddie Mathews 1.25 3.00
AMPFR Frank Robinson 1.00 2.50
AMPFT Fernando Tatis Jr. 4.00 10.00
AMPGC Gerrit Cole 1.25 3.00
AMPHM Hideki Matsui 1.25 3.00
AMPJM Joe Morgan 1.00 2.50
AMPJR Jim Rice 1.00 2.50
AMPKG Ken Griffey Jr. 2.50 6.00
AMPLB Lou Brock 1.00 2.50
AMPMC Matt Chapman 1.25 3.00
AMPMM Manny Machado 1.25 3.00
AMPMO Mel Ott 1.25 3.00
AMPMR Mariano Rivera 1.50 4.00
AMPNG Nomar Garciaparra 1.00 2.50
AMPNR Nolan Ryan 4.00 10.00
AMPNS Nick Senzel 2.50 6.00
AMPPA Pete Alonso 5.00 12.00
AMPPG Paul Goldschmidt 1.25 3.00
AMPPR Pee Wee Reese 1.00 2.50
AMPRC Robinson Cano 1.00 2.50
AMPRH Roy Halladay 1.00 2.50
AMPRS Ryne Sandberg 2.50 6.00
AMPSS Sammy Sosa 1.25 3.00
AMPTB Trevor Bauer 1.50 4.00
AMPTM Thurman Munson 1.25 3.00
AMPTS Trevor Story 1.25 3.00
AMPVG Vladimir Guerrero Jr. 6.00 15.00
AMPVR Victor Robles 1.50 4.00
AMPWB Walker Buehler 1.50 4.00
AMPWM Willie Mays 2.50 6.00
AMPWS Warren Spahn 1.00 2.50
AMPYK Yusei Kikuchi 1.25 3.00
AMPEMU Eddie Murray 1.00 2.50
AMPJBE Johnny Bench 1.25 3.00
AMPJMA J.D. Martinez 1.25 3.00
AMPNRY Nolan Ryan 4.00 10.00
AMPRHO Rogers Hornsby 1.00 2.50
AMPTSE Tom Seaver 1.00 2.50
AMPVGU Vladimir Guerrero 1.00 2.50
AMPWME Whit Merrifield 1.25 3.00
AMPWSP Warren Spahn 1.00 2.50

2019 Topps Update All Star Stitches

STATED ODDS 1:42 HOBBY
*GOLD/50: .6X TO 1.5X BASIC
*SILVER/50: .6X TO 1.5X BASIC
*RED/25: .75X TO 2X BASIC
ASSRAB Alex Bregman 3.00 8.00
ASSRAC Aroldis Chapman 3.00 8.00
ASSRAM Austin Meadows 3.00 8.00
ASSRCB Cody Bellinger 6.00 15.00
ASSRCBL Charlie Blackmon 3.00 8.00
ASSRCK Clayton Kershaw 5.00 12.00
ASSRCM Charlie Morton 3.00 8.00
ASSRCS Carlos Santana 2.50 6.00
ASSRCY Christian Yelich 4.00 10.00
ASSRDD David Dahl 2.00 5.00
ASSRDL DJ LeMahieu 3.00 8.00
ASSRDV Daniel Vogelbach 2.00 5.00
ASSRFF Freddie Freeman 4.00 10.00
ASSRFL Francisco Lindor 3.00 8.00
ASSRGC Gerrit Cole 3.00 8.00
ASSRGS Gary Sanchez 3.00 8.00
ASSRGSP George Springer 2.50 6.00
ASSRGT Gleyber Torres 5.00 12.00
ASSRHP Hunter Pence 2.50 6.00
ASSRHR Hyun-Jin Ryu 2.50 6.00
ASSRJA Jose Abreu 3.00 8.00
ASSRJB Javier Baez 4.00 10.00
ASSRJBE Josh Bell 2.50 6.00
ASSRJBR Jose Berrios 2.50 6.00
ASSRJd Jacob deGrom 6.00 15.00
ASSRJEM Jeff McNeil 5.00 12.00
ASSRJG Joey Gallo 2.50 6.00
ASSRJH Josh Hader 2.50 6.00
ASSRJM J.D. Martinez 3.00 8.00
ASSRJMC James McCann 2.50 6.00
ASSRJO Jake Odorizzi 2.00 5.00
ASSRJP Jorge Polanco 2.50 6.00
ASSRJR J.T. Realmuto 3.00 8.00
A9SRJV Justin Verlander 3.00 8.00
ASSRKB Kris Bryant 4.00 10.00
ASSRKM Ketel Marte 2.50 6.00
ASSRKY Kirby Yates 2.50 6.00
ASSRLC Luis Castillo 2.50 6.00
ASSRLG Lucas Giolito 2.50 6.00
ASSRMB Mookie Betts 6.00 15.00
ASSRMBR Michael Brantley 2.50 6.00
ASSRMC Matt Chapman 3.00 8.00
ASSRMMO Mike Moustakas 2.50 6.00
ASSRMMU Max Muncy 2.50 6.00
ASSRMS Max Scherzer 3.00 8.00
ASSRMSO Mike Soroka 3.00 8.00
ASSRMST Marcus Stroman 2.50 6.00
ASSRMT Mike Trout 10.00 25.00
ASSRMTA Masahiro Tanaka 2.50 6.00
ASSRNA Nolan Arenado 5.00 12.00
ASSRPA Pete Alonso 10.00 25.00
ASSRPD Paul DeJong 3.00 8.00
ASSRRA Ronald Acuna Jr. 8.00 20.00
ASSRSB Shane Bieber 3.00 8.00
ASSRSGR Sonny Gray 2.50 6.00
ASSRTS Trevor Story 3.00 8.00
ASSRWB Walker Buehler 5.00 12.00
ASSRWC Willson Contreras 2.50 6.00
ASSRWM Whit Merrifield 3.00 8.00
ASSRYG Yasmani Grandal 2.00 5.00

2019 Topps Update All Star Stitches Autographs

STATED ODDS 1:13,946 HOBBY
STATED PRINT RUN 25 SER.#'d SETS

EXCHANGE DEADLINE 9/30/2021
ASSAAM Austin Meadows 12.00 30.00
ASSACB Charlie Blackmon 12.00 30.00
ASSACS Carlos Santana 20.00 50.00
ASSAFL Francisco Lindor 25.00 60.00
ASSAGC Gerrit Cole 25.00 60.00
ASSAGS Gary Sanchez 20.00 50.00
ASSAGSP George Springer 25.00 60.00
ASSAJH Josh Hader 10.00 25.00
ASSAMS Max Scherzer 40.00 100.00
ASSANA Nolan Arenado 40.00 100.00
ASSAPA Pete Alonso 125.00 300.00
ASSAPD Paul DeJong 12.00 30.00
ASSARA Ronald Acuna Jr. 75.00 200.00
ASSAWB Walker Buehler
ASSAWC Willson Contreras 10.00 25.00
ASSAWM Whit Merrifield 15.00 40.00

2019 Topps Update All Star Stitches Dual Autographs

STATED ODDS 1:41,139 HOBBY
STATED PRINT RUN 25 SER.#'d SETS
EXCHANGE DEADLINE 9/30/2021
ASDARSC G.Sanchez/W.Contreras 25.00 60.00
ASDARSL F.Lindor/C.Santana 40.00 100.00
SADARAD D.Dahl/N.Arenado
SADARAM J.McNeil/P.Alonso 125.00 300.00
SADARCS M.Scherzer/G.Cole 75.00 200.00
SADARDA P.Alonso/J.deGrom 200.00 500.00
SADARMM C.Morton/A.Meadows 25.00 60.00

2019 Topps Update Bryce Harper Welcome to Philly

150TH/150: 2X TO 5X BASIC
*RED/10: 6X TO 15X BASIC
BH1 Bryce Harper .50 1.25
BH2 Bryce Harper .50 1.25
BH3 Bryce Harper .50 1.25
BH4 Bryce Harper .50 1.25
BH5 Bryce Harper .50 1.25
BH6 Bryce Harper .50 1.25
BH7 Bryce Harper .50 1.25
BH8 Bryce Harper .50 1.25
BH9 Bryce Harper .50 1.25
BH10 Bryce Harper .50 1.25
BH11 Bryce Harper .50 1.25
BH12 Bryce Harper .50 1.25
BH13 Bryce Harper .50 1.25
BH14 Bryce Harper .50 1.25
BH15 Bryce Harper .50 1.25
BH16 Bryce Harper .50 1.25
BH17 Bryce Harper .50 1.25
BH18 Bryce Harper .50 1.25
BH19 Bryce Harper .50 1.25
BH20 Bryce Harper .50 1.25

2019 Topps Update Dual All Star Stitches

STATED ODDS 1:21,652 HOBBY
STATED PRINT RUN 25 SER.#'d SETS
ASSDRBB K.Bryant/J.Baez 25.00 60.00
ASSDRBM M.Betts/J.Martinez 40.00 100.00
ASSDRBS G.Springer/A.Bregman 12.00 30.00
ASSDRCV J.Verlander/G.Cole 12.00 30.00
ASSDRDA P.Alonso/J.deGrom
ASSDRFA R.Acuna Jr./F.Freeman 30.00 80.00
ASSDRKB C.Bellinger/C.Kershaw 25.00 60.00
ASSDRLS C.Santana/F.Lindor 40.00 100.00
ASSDRSL G.Sanchez/D.LeMahieu 12.00 30.00
ASSDRTY C.Yelich/M.Trout 20.00 50.00

2019 Topps Update Est 1869

COMPLETE SET (13) 20.00 50.00
STATED ODDS 1:51 HOBBY
*BLUE: .6X TO 1.5X
*BLACK/299: 1X TO 2.5X
*150TH/150: 1X TO 2.5X
*GOLD/50: 5X TO 12X
EST1 Cincinnati Red Stockings .60 1.50
EST2 Joey Votto 1.00 2.50
EST3 Nick Senzel 2.00 5.00
EST4 George Foster .60 1.50
EST5 Frank Robinson .75 2.00
EST6 Joe Morgan .75 2.00
EST7 Johnny Bench 1.00 2.50
EST8 Tony Perez .75 2.00
EST9 Tom Seaver .75 2.00
EST10 Eric Davis .60 1.50
EST11 Tom Browning .60 1.50
EST12 Barry Larkin .75 2.00
EST13 Ken Griffey Jr. 2.00 5.00

2019 Topps Update Est 1869 Autographs

STATED ODDS 1:39,180 HOBBY
PRINT RUNS B/WN 5-25 COPIES PER
NO PRICING ON QTY 10 OR LESS
EXCHANGE DEADLINE 9/30/2021
EST4 George Foster/25 25.00 60.00
EST8 Tony Perez/25 25.00 60.00
EST10 Eric Davis/25 25.00 60.00
EST11 Tom Browning/25 25.00 60.00

2019 Topps Update Iconic Card Reprints

STATED ODDS 1:16 HOBBY
*150 ANN/150: 2.5X TO 6X HOBBY
ICR1 Johnny Bench .40 1.00
ICR2 Ozzie Smith .50 1.25
ICR3 Joey Votto .40 1.00
ICR4 Nolan Ryan 1.25 3.00
ICR5 Honus Wagner .40 1.00
ICR6 Tony Gwynn .40 1.00
ICR7 Ken Griffey Jr. .75 2.00
ICR8 Joe Mauer .30 .75
ICR9 Luis Aparicio .30 .75
ICR10 Frank Robinson .30 .75
ICR11 Orlando Cepeda .30 .75
ICR12 Roger Maris .40 1.00
ICR13 Sandy Koufax .75 2.00
ICR14 Dave Winfield .30 .75
ICR15 Paul Molitor .40 1.00
ICR16 Miguel Cabrera .40 1.00
ICR17 Johnny Mize .30 .75
ICR18 Gil Hodges .30 .75
ICR19 Willie Mays .75 2.00
ICR20 Phil Rizzuto .30 .75
ICR21 Pee Wee Reese .30 .75
ICR22 Stan Musial .60 1.50
ICR23 Stan Musial .60 1.50
ICR24 Stan Musial .60 1.50
ICR25 Bob Clemente 1.00 2.50
ICR26 Bob Gibson .30 .75
ICR27 Billy Williams .30 .75
ICR28 Bob Clemente 1.00 2.50
ICR29 Chipper Jones .40 1.00
ICR30 Tim Raines .30 .75
ICR31 Darryl Strawberry .25 .60
ICR32 Dwight Gooden .25 .60
ICR33 Jeff Bagwell .30 .75
ICR34 Ivan Rodriguez .30 .75
ICR35 Christy Mathewson .40 1.00
ICR36 Tris Speaker .30 .75
ICR37 Willie Stargell .30 .75
ICR38 Gary Carter .30 .75
ICR39 Ralph Kiner .30 .75
ICR40 Enos Slaughter .30 .75
ICR41 Red Schoendienst .30 .75
ICR42 Fergie Jenkins .30 .75
ICR43 Tony Perez .30 .75
ICR44 Ernie Banks .40 1.00
ICR45 Lefty Grove .30 .75
ICR46 Ken Griffey Jr. .75 2.00
ICR47 Mel Ott .40 1.00
ICR48 Frank Thomas .40 1.00
ICR49 Frank Thomas .40 1.00
ICR50 Chipper Jones .40 1.00

2019 Topps Update Iconic Card Reprints Autographs

STATED ODDS 1:24,200 HOBBY
PRINT RUNS B/WN 5-25 COPIES PER
NO PRICING ON QTY 10 OR LESS
EXCHANGE DEADLINE 9/30/2021
ICR1 Johnny Bench
ICR2 Ozzie Smith
ICR7 Ken Griffey Jr.
ICR31 Darryl Strawberry/25 40.00 100.00
ICR33 Jeff Bagwell/25 30.00 80.00
ICR34 Ivan Rodriguez/25 20.00 50.00
ICR43 Tony Perez/25 40.00 100.00
ICR46 Ken Griffey Jr

2019 Topps Update Legacy of Baseball Autographs 150th Anniversary

STATED ODDS 1:2177 HOBBY
STATED PRINT RUN 150 SER.#'d SETS
EXCHANGE DEADLINE 9/30/2021
LBABRE Bryan Reynolds 12.00 30.00
LBADH Darwinzon Hernandez 3.00 8.00
LBAGC Griffin Canning 5.00 12.00
LBAGH Garrett Hampson 5.00 12.00
LBAHRA Harold Ramirez 5.00 12.00
LBAJD Jon Duplantier 3.00 8.00
LBAJH JD Hammer 4.00 10.00
LBAJMA Jason Martin 4.00 10.00
LBALAR Luis Arraez 15.00 40.00
LBALT Lane Thomas 5.00 12.00
LBAMK Merrill Kelly 3.00 8.00
LBANLO Nate Lowe 15.00 40.00
LBARH Ryan Helsley 4.00 10.00
LBASA Shaun Anderson 3.00 8.00
LBASB Skye Bolt 4.00 10.00
LBATT Trent Thornton 3.00 8.00

2019 Topps Update Legacy of Baseball Autographs Gold

*GOLD/50: .6X TO 1.5X BASIC
STATED ODDS 1:3165 HOBBY
STATED PRINT RUN 50 SER.#'d SETS
EXCHANGE DEADLINE 9/30/2021
LBAAR Austin Riley 15.00 40.00
LBACK Carter Kieboom 15.00 40.00
LBACP Chris Paddack 12.00 30.00
LBACT Cole Tucker 20.00 50.00
LBAEJ Eloy Jimenez 20.00 50.00
LBAEL Elvis Luciano 12.00 30.00
LBAFT Fernando Tatis Jr. 75.00 200.00
LBAKH Keston Hiura 25.00 60.00
LBAMC Michael Chavis 10.00 25.00
LBANM Nick Margevicius 4.00 10.00
LBAPA Pete Alonso 75.00 200.00
LBAPC Patrick Corbin
LBATE Thairo Estrada 10.00 25.00
LBAVG Vladimir Guerrero Jr. 50.00 120.00
LBAWS Will Smith 15.00 40.00

2019 Topps Update Legacy of Baseball Autographs Red

*RED/25: .8X TO 2X BASIC
STATED ODDS 1:4472 HOBBY
PRINT RUNS B/WN 5-25 COPIES PER
NO PRICING ON QTY 5
EXCHANGE DEADLINE 9/30/2021
LBAAJ Adam Jones/25 10.00 25.00
LBAAR Austin Riley/25 20.00 50.00
LBACF Cecil Fielder/25 20.00 50.00
LBACFR Clint Frazier/25 6.00 15.00
LBACK Carter Kieboom/25 20.00 50.00
LBACP Chris Paddack/25 15.00 40.00
LBACS CC Sabathia/25
LBACT Cole Tucker/25 25.00 60.00
LBAEJ Eloy Jimenez/25 25.00 60.00
LBAEL Elvis Luciano/25 15.00 40.00
LBAFT Fernando Tatis Jr./25 100.00 250.00
LBAGCO Gerrit Cole/25 40.00 100.00
LBAKG Ken Griffey Jr./25
LBAKH Keston Hiura/25 30.00 80.00
LBAKW Kerry Wood/25 25.00 60.00
LBALM Lance McCullers Jr./25 10.00 25.00
LBAMC Michael Chavis/25 12.00 30.00
LBAMS Max Scherzer/25 40.00 100.00
LBANA Nolan Arenado/25 40.00 100.00
LBANM Nick Margevicius/25 5.00 12.00
LBAPA Pete Alonso/25 100.00 250.00
LBAPC Patrick Corbin/25
LBASC Shin-Soo Choo/25 20.00 50.00
LBATE Thairo Estrada/25 12.00 30.00
LBATM Tino Martinez/25 12.00 30.00
LBAVG Vladimir Guerrero Jr./25 60.00 150.00
LBAWS Will Smith/25 20.00 50.00

2019 Topps Update Major League Materials

STATED ODDS 1:425 HOBBY
*150TH/150: .5X TO 1.2X BASIC
*GOLD/50: .6X TO 1.5X BASIC
*RED/25: .75X TO 2X BASIC
MLMAB Alex Bregman 3.00 8.00
MLMAM Austin Meadows 3.00 8.00
MLMBP Buster Posey 4.00 10.00
MLMBR Brendan Rodgers 3.00 8.00
MLMBS Blake Snell 2.50 6.00
MLMCB Cody Bellinger 6.00 15.00
MLMCC Carlos Correa 3.00 8.00
MLMCR Cal Ripken Jr. 8.00 20.00
MLMCS Chris Sale 3.00 8.00
MLMDG Didi Gregorius 2.50 6.00
MLMFL Francisco Lindor 3.00 8.00
MLMFT Frank Thomas 3.00 8.00
MLMGC Gerrit Cole 3.00 8.00
MLMGS George Springer 2.50 6.00
MLMJB Javier Baez 4.00 10.00
MLMJL Jon Lester 2.50 6.00
MLMJM J.D. Martinez 3.00 8.00
MLMJR J.T. Realmuto 3.00 8.00
MLMJV Joey Votto 3.00 8.00
MLMKG Ken Griffey Jr. 6.00 15.00
MLMKH Keston Hiura 4.00 10.00
MLMLS Luis Severino 2.50 6.00
MLMMB Mookie Betts 4.00 10.00
MLMMC Michael Chavis 3.00 8.00
MLMMO Marcell Ozuna 3.00 8.00
MLMMT Mike Trout 10.00 25.00
MLMNA Nolan Arenado 5.00 12.00
MLMNS Nick Senzel 4.00 10.00
MLMPC Patrick Corbin 2.50 6.00
MLMRD Rafael Devers 4.00 10.00
MLMRH Rickey Henderson 3.00 8.00
MLMRZ Ryan Zimmerman 2.50 6.00
MLMSS Stephen Strasburg 3.00 8.00
MLMTB Trevor Bauer 4.00 10.00
MLMTG Tony Gwynn 3.00 8.00
MLMVG Vladimir Guerrero Jr. 6.00 15.00
MLMABE Andrew Benintendi 4.00 10.00
MLMFTJ Fernando Tatis Jr. 5.00 12.00
MLMGST Giancarlo Stanton 3.00 8.00
MLMRHA Roy Halladay 2.50 6.00

2019 Topps Update Perennial All Stars

PAS1 Babe Ruth 1.00 2.50
PAS2 Ted Williams .75 2.00
PAS3 Jackie Robinson .40 1.00
PAS4 Reggie Jackson .30 .75
PAS5 Pedro Martinez .30 .75
PAS6 Randy Johnson .40 1.00
PAS7 Cal Ripken Jr. 1.25 3.00
PAS8 Ichiro Suzuki .50 1.25
PAS9 Willie Mays .75 2.00
PAS10 Tony Gwynn .40 1.00
PAS11 Carl Yastrzemski .60 1.50
PAS12 Stan Musial .60 1.50
PAS13 Johnny Bench .40 1.00
PAS14 Ozzie Smith .50 1.25
PAS15 Al Kaline .40 1.00
PAS16 Brooks Robinson .30 .75
PAS17 Derek Jeter 1.00 2.50
PAS18 Ken Griffey Jr. .75 2.00
PAS19 George Brett .75 2.00
PAS20 Roberto Clemente 1.00 2.50
PAS21 Mel Ott .40 1.00
PAS22 Alex Rodriguez .50 1.25
PAS23 Ryne Sandberg .75 2.00
PAS24 Mariano Rivera .50 1.25
PAS25 Ernie Banks .40 1.00
PAS26 Mark McGwire .60 1.50
PAS27 Rickey Henderson .40 1.00
PAS28 David Ortiz .40 1.00
PAS29 Aaron Judge 1.00 2.50
PAS30 Mike Trout 2.00 5.00
PAS31 Bryce Harper .60 1.50
PAS32 Chris Sale .40 1.00
PAS33 Justin Verlander .40 1.00
PAS34 Clayton Kershaw .60 1.50
PAS35 Paul Goldschmidt .40 1.00
PAS36 Jose Altuve .30 .75
PAS37 Max Scherzer .40 1.00
PAS38 Buster Posey .50 1.25
PAS39 Vladimir Guerrero .30 .75
PAS40 Roy Halladay .30 .75
PAS41 Sandy Koufax .75 2.00
PAS42 Nolan Ryan 1.25 3.00
PAS43 Yadier Molina .50 1.25
PAS44 Javier Baez .50 1.25
PAS45 Nolan Arenado .60 1.50
PAS46 Francisco Lindor .40 1.00
PAS47 Christian Yelich .50 1.25
PAS48 Jacob deGrom .75 2.00
PAS49 Alex Bregman .40 1.00
PAS50 Mookie Betts .75 2.00

2019 Topps Update Shohei Ohtani Highlights

150TH/150: 2X TO 5X BASIC
*RED/10: 6X TO 15X BASIC
SO1 Shohei Ohtani .50 1.25
SO2 Shohei Ohtani .50 1.25
SO3 Shohei Ohtani .50 1.25
SO4 Shohei Ohtani .50 1.25
SO5 Shohei Ohtani .50 1.25
SO6 Shohei Ohtani .50 1.25
SO7 Shohei Ohtani .50 1.25
SO8 Shohei Ohtani .50 1.25
SO9 Shohei Ohtani .50 1.25
SO10 Shohei Ohtani .50 1.25
SO11 Shohei Ohtani .50 1.25
SO12 Shohei Ohtani .50 1.25
SO13 Shohei Ohtani .50 1.25
SO14 Shohei Ohtani .50 1.25
SO15 Shohei Ohtani .50 1.25
SO16 Shohei Ohtani .50 1.25
SO17 Shohei Ohtani .50 1.25
SO18 Shohei Ohtani .50 1.25
SO19 Shohei Ohtani .50 1.25
SO20 Shohei Ohtani .50 1.25

2019 Topps Update The Family Business

STATED ODDS 1:31 HOBBY
*BLUE: .6X TO 1.5X
*BLACK/299: 1X TO 2.5X
*150TH/150: 1X TO 2.5X
*GOLD/50: 1.5X TO 4X
FB1 Ken Griffey Jr. 1.25 3.00
FB2 Cal Ripken Jr. 1.25 3.00
FB3 Roberto Alomar .30 .75
FB4 Vladimir Guerrero .30 .75
FB5 Ivan Rodriguez .30 .75
FB6 Roger Clemens .50 1.25
FB7 Yadier Molina .50 1.25
FB8 Ronald Acuna Jr. 2.00 5.00
FB9 Cecil Fielder .25 .60
FB10 Mariano Rivera .50 1.25
FB11 Hank Aaron .75 2.00
FB12 Tim Raines .30 .75
FB13 Jose Canseco .30 .75
FB14 Bryce Harper .60 1.50
FB15 Fernando Tatis Jr. 4.00 10.00
FB16 Tony Gwynn .40 1.00
FB17 Corey Seager .40 1.00
FB18 Manny Machado .40 1.00
FB19 Dee Gordon .25 .60
FB20 Nolan Arenado .60 1.50
FB21 Pedro Martinez .30 .75
FB22 Cody Bellinger .75 2.00
FB23 Robinson Cano .30 .75
FB24 Vladimir Guerrero Jr. 1.50 4.00
FB25 Reggie Jackson .30 .75

2019 Topps Update The Family Business Autographs

STATED ODDS 1:34,282 HOBBY
PRINT RUNS B/WN 5-25 COPIES PER
NO PRICING ON QTY 5
EXCHANGE DEADLINE 9/30/2021
FB3 Roberto Alomar
FB4 Vladimir Guerrero
FB8 Ronald Acuna Jr.
FB9 Cecil Fielder/25 25.00 60.00
FB13 Jose Canseco/25 25.00 60.00
FB15 Fernando Tatis Jr./25
FB24 Vladimir Guerrero Jr./25 50.00 120.00

2019 Topps Update Triple All Star Stitches

STATED ODDS 1:21,652 HOBBY
STATED PRINT RUN 25 SER.#'d SETS
ASTRADM Alonso/deGrom/McNeil 50.00 120.00
ASTRBAS Story/Blackmon/Arenado 20.00 50.00
ASTRBCB Baez/Bryant/Contreras 60.00 150.00
ASTRFSA Acuna/Soroka/Freeman 30.00 80.00
ASTRGHY Hader/Grandal/Yelich 25.00 60.00
ASTRKBB Buehler/Kershaw/Bellinger 40.00 100.00
ASTRLHS Santana/Hand/Lindor 50.00 120.00
ASTRSCL LeMahieu/Sanchez/Chapman 12.00 30.00
ASTRSVB Verlander/Springer/Bregman
ASTRTYB Yelich/Trout/Bryant

2020 Topps

COMPLETE SET (700) 30.00 80.00
COMP.SER.1 SET (350) 15.00 40.00
COMP.SER.2 SET (350) 15.00 40.00
SER.1 GOLDEN TICKET ODDS 1:196,245 HOBBY
SER.2 GOLDEN TICKET ODDS 1:236,030 HOBBY
TICKET ANNCD PRINT RUN OF 50
NO TICKET PRICING DUE TO SCARCITY
1 Mike Trout 1.25 3.00
2 Gerrit Cole LL .40 1.00
3 Nicky Lopez .15 .40
4 Robinson Cano .20 .50
5 JaCoby Jones .20 .50
6 Juan Soto WSH .75 2.00
7 Aaron Judge .60 1.50
8 Jonathan Villar .15 .40
9 Trent Grisham RC 1.00 2.50
10 Austin Meadows .25 .60
11 Anthony Rendon LL .25 .60
12 Sam Hilliard RC .40 1.00
13 Miles Mikolas .15 .40
14 Anthony Rendon .25 .60
15 F.Tatis/M.Machado .30 .75
16 Gleyber Torres .50 1.25
17 Franmil Reyes .15 .40
18 Master and Apprentice .25 .60
Nelson Cruz/Mitch Garver
19 Los Angeles Angels TC .15 .40
20 Aristides Aquino RC .60 1.50
21 Shane Greene .15 .40
22 Emilio Pagan .15 .40
23 Christin Stewart .15 .40
24 Kenley Jansen .20 .50
25 Kirby Yates .15 .40
26 Kyle Hendricks .25 .60
27 Milwaukee Brewers TC .15 .40
28 Tim Anderson .25 .60
29 Starlin Castro .15 .40
30 Josh VanMeter .25 .60
31 Close Call .20 .50
Niko Goodrum/Jorge Polanco
32 Brandon Woodruff .25 .60
33 Houston Astros TC .15 .40
34 Ian Kinsler .20 .50
35 Adalberto Mondesi .20 .50
36 Sean Doolittle .15 .40
37 Albert Almora .20 .50
38 Austin Nola RC .40 1.00
39 Tyler O'Neill .20 .50
40 Bobby Bradley RC .25 .60
41 Brian Anderson .15 .40
42 Lewis Brinson .15 .40
43 Leury Garcia .15 .40
44 Tommy Edman FS .25 .60
45 Mitch Haniger .20 .50
46 Gary Sanchez .25 .60
47 Dansby Swanson .25 .60
48 Jeff McNeil FS .20 .50
49 Eloy Jimenez CUP .50 1.25
50 Cody Bellinger .50 1.25
51 Anthony Rizzo .30 .75
52 Yasmani Grandal .15 .40
53 Pete Alonso LL .60 1.50
54 Hunter Dozier .15 .40
55 Jose Martinez .15 .40
56 Andres Munoz RC .40 1.00
57 Travis Demeritte RC .40 1.00
58 Jesse Winker .25 .60
59 Chris Archer .15 .40
60 Matt Barnes .15 .40
61 C.Biggio/B.Bichette 1.00 2.50
62 Chase Anderson .15 .40
63 Christian Vazquez .20 .50
64 Kyle Lewis RC 2.00 5.00
65 Cleveland Indians TC .15 .40
66 Andrew Heaney .15 .40
67 Tyler Beede .15 .40
68 James Paxton .20 .50
69 Brendan McKay RC .40 1.00
70 Nico Hoerner RC 1.00 2.50
71 Sandy Alcantara .15 .40
72 K.Hiura/B.Gamel .30 .75
73 Oakland Athletics TC .15 .40
74 Bubba Starling RC .50 1.25
75 Michael Conforto .20 .50
76 Stephen Strasburg WSH .25 .60
77 Charlie Culberson .15 .40
78 Bo Bichette RC 2.00 5.00
79 Brad Keller .15 .40
80 Austin Barnes .15 .40
81 Ryan Yarbrough .15 .40
82 Jorge Polanco .20 .50
83 New York Yankees TC .15 .40
84 Ken Giles .15 .40
85 Tim and Yolmer .25 .60
Tim Anderson/Yolmer Sanchez
86 Hyun-Jin Ryu LL .20 .50
87 St. Louis Cardinals TC .15 .40
88 Jorge Alfaro .15 .40
89 Kurt Suzuki .15 .40
90 Brock Holt .15 .40
91 Yolmer Sanchez .15 .40
92 Blake Treinen .15 .40
93 Alex Colome .15 .40
94 Marwin Gonzalez .15 .40
95 Ian Kennedy .15 .40
96 Jose Abreu LL .25 .60
97 Lewis Thorpe RC .25 .60
98 Jesus Aguilar .20 .50
99 Dan Vogelbach .15 .40
100 Alex Bregman .25 .60
101 Brad Hand .15 .40
102 Josh Phegley .15 .40
103 Danny Hultzen RC .30 .75
104 Marco Gonzales .15 .40
105 Niko Goodrum .20 .50
106 Rogelio Armenteros RC .30 .75
107 Luis Castillo .20 .50
108 Josh Rojas RC .25 .60
109 Reese McGuire .20 .50
110 Jesus Luzardo RC .50 1.25
111 Buster Posey .30 .75
112 Max Stassi .15 .40
113 Matt Carpenter .25 .60
114 Ildemaro Vargas .15 .40
115 Matt Thaiss RC .30 .75
116 Daniel Murphy .20 .50
117 Max Kepler .20 .50
118 Clayton Kershaw .40 1.00
119 Kyle Schwarber .25 .60
120 Kenta Maeda .20 .50
121 DJ LeMahieu .25 .60
122 Caleb Smith .15 .40
123 Seth Brown RC .25 .60
124 Jose Berrios .20 .50
125 Shohei Ohtani .40 1.00
126 German Marquez .25 .60
127 Matt Chapman .25 .60
128 Steven Matz .15 .40
129 Yoan Moncada .25 .60
130 Michael Chavis FS .20 .50
131 Ketel Marte .20 .50
132 Jay Bruce .20 .50
133 Michael Brosseau RC .50 1.25
134 David Fletcher .25 .60
135 Enrique Hernandez .25 .60
136 Amed Rosario .20 .50
137 Merrill Kelly .15 .40
138 Jackie Bradley Jr. .25 .60
139 Jose Quintana .15 .40
140 Trevor Bauer .30 .75
141 Roberto Osuna .15 .40
142 Tyler Flowers .15 .40
143 Christian Yelich LL .30 .75
144 Jake Arrieta .20 .50
145 Paul Goldschmidt .25 .60
146 Dwight Smith Jr. .15 .40
147 Jake Rogers RC .25 .60
148 Willy Adames .15 .40
149 Orlando Arcia .15 .40
150 Ronald Acuna Jr. 1.00 2.50
151 Tommy La Stella .15 .40
152 Zack Wheeler .20 .50
153 Andrew Cashner .15 .40
154 C.J. Cron .15 .40
155 Jack Flaherty .25 .60
156 Nick Markakis .20 .50
157 G.Torres/D.Gregorius .30 .75
158 Jake Lamb .20 .50
159 Jorge Soler LL .25 .60
160 C.Yelich/N.Arenado .40 1.00
161 Aroldis Chapman .25 .60
162 Michel Baez RC .25 .60
163 Ryan Pressly .15 .40
164 Matt Strahm .15 .40
165 Matthew Boyd .15 .40
166 Nick Solak RC 1.00 2.50
167 Anthony Kay RC .25 .60
168 Fernando Tatis Jr. CUP 1.25 3.00
169 Jacob Waguespack RC .30 .75
170 Gregory Polanco .20 .50
171 Kole Calhoun .15 .40
172 Sonny Gray .20 .50
173 Yadier Molina .30 .75
174 Alex Verdugo .20 .50
175 Lucas Giolito .20 .50
176 Brandon Belt .20 .50
177 Craig Kimbrel .20 .50
178 Mauricio Dubon RC .30 .75
179 Ramon Laureano FS .20 .50
180 Max Scherzer .25 .60
181 Stephen Strasburg LL .25 .60
182 Vladimir Guerrero Jr. CUP .40 1.00
183 Starling Marte .20 .50
184 Mychal Givens .15 .40
185 Johnny Cueto .20 .50
186 Roberto Perez .15 .40
187 Chance Sisco .15 .40
188 Manny Machado .25 .60
189 Mike Moustakas .20 .50
190 Aaron Nola .20 .50
191 Jeremy Jeffress .15 .40
192 Yusei Kikuchi .20 .50
193 Anibal Sanchez .20 .50
194 Liam Hendriks .15 .40
195 Julio Teheran .20 .50
196 Andrew Benintendi .25 .60
197 Raisel Iglesias .15 .40
198 Erick Fedde .15 .40
199 Domingo Santana .20 .50
200 Christian Yelich .30 .75
201 Francisco Lindor .25 .60
202 New York Mets TC .15 .40
203 Joc Pederson .20 .50
204 Hector Neris .15 .40
205 Patrick Sandoval RC .40 1.00
206 Tommy Pham .15 .40
207 Zac Gallen RC .60 1.50
208 Zack Collins RC .30 .75
209 Derek Dietrich .20 .50
210 Mitch Garver .15 .40
211 Trevor Richards .15 .40
212 Mike Fiers .15 .40
213 Minnesota Twins TC .15 .40
214 Trea Turner .20 .50
215 Luke Jackson .15 .40
216 Scott Kingery .20 .50
217 Amir Garrett .15 .40
218 Atlanta Braves TC .15 .40
219 Jean Segura .20 .50
220 J.T. Realmuto .25 .60
221 Nick Pivetta .15 .40
222 Andrew Chafin .15 .40
223 Aaron Civale RC .50 1.25
224 Juan Soto .75 2.00
225 Oscar Mercado FS .25 .60
226 Trent Thornton .15 .40
227 David Peralta .15 .40
228 Logan Allen RC .25 .60
229 Randy Arozarena RC 2.00 5.00
230 Nolan Arenado .40 1.00
231 Randal Grichuk .15 .40
232 Justin Verlander LL .25 .60
233 David Dahl .15 .40
234 Cesar Hernandez .15 .40
235 Dustin May RC .75 2.00
236 Brandon Crawford .20 .50
237 Luis Garcia .15 .40
238 Freddy Peralta .15 .40
239 Anthony Rendon WSH .25 .60
240 Jameson Taillon .20 .50
241 Mike Clevinger .20 .50
242 Alex Young RC .25 .60
243 Jeimer Candelario .15 .40
244 Chris Paddack FS .25 .60
245 Los Angeles Dodgers TC .15 .40
246 Philadelphia Phillies TC .15 .40
247 Garrett Cooper .15 .40
248 Hunter Renfroe .15 .40
249 Jordan Yamamoto RC .25 .60
250 Bryce Harper .40 1.00
251 A.J. Puk RC .40 1.00
252 Aaron Hicks .20 .50
253 Brandon Drury .15 .40
254 Andrew Miller .20 .50
255 Max Muncy .20 .50
256 Roman Quinn .15 .40
257 Joey Lucchesi .15 .40
258 Max Scherzer WSH .25 .60
259 Jaylin Davis RC .40 1.00
260 Zack Greinke .25 .60
261 Daniel Mengden .15 .40
262 Anthony Santander .15 .40
263 J.P. Crawford .15 .40
264 Abraham Toro RC .30 .75
265 Patrick Corbin .20 .50
266 Austin Riley FS .30 .75
267 Joey Votto .25 .60
268 Ian Desmond .15 .40
269 J.D. Martinez .25 .60
270 Jose Urena .15 .40
271 Josh Bell .20 .50
272 Carlos Santana .20 .50
273 Bryan Abreu RC .25 .60
274 Boston Red Sox TC .15 .40
275 JT Riddle .15 .40
276 Yordan Alvarez RC 2.50 6.00
277 Dominic Smith .15 .40
278 Isan Diaz RC .40 1.00
279 Masahiro Tanaka .25 .60
280 Tony Gonsolin RC 1.00 2.50
281 Nelson Cruz .25 .60
282 Jake Marisnick .15 .40
283 Robel Garcia RC .25 .60
284 Jason Kipnis .20 .50
285 Tyler Alexander RC .40 1.00
286 Blake Parker .15 .40
287 Jose Peraza .20 .50
288 Jon Gray .15 .40
289 Yuli Gurriel .20 .50
290 Nick Senzel FS .25 .60
291 Tyler Naquin .20 .50
292 Gavin Lux RC 1.25 3.00
293 Wade Davis .15 .40
294 Jordan Zimmermann .20 .50
295 Jeff Samardzija .15 .40
296 Whit Merrifield .25 .60
297 Mike Yastrzemski FS .40 1.00
298 C.Bellinger/A.Verdugo .30 .75
299 David Price .20 .50
300 Javier Baez .30 .75
301 Mike Tauchman .25 .60
302 Tim Anderson LL .25 .60
303 Mallex Smith .15 .40
304 Shane Bieber .25 .60
305 Tyler Glasnow .25 .60
306 Jon Lester .20 .50
307 Daniel Palka .15 .40
308 Carlos Rodon .25 .60
309 Robbie Grossman .15 .40
310 Jose Urquidy RC .30 .75
311 David Bote .20 .50
312 Billy Hamilton .20 .50
313 Meiky Cabrera .15 .40
314 Rafael Devers .30 .75
315 Adam Frazier .15 .40
316 Justin Turner .25 .60
317 Sean Murphy RC .40 1.00
318 Omar Narvaez .15 .40
319 Matt Olson .25 .60
320 Austin Hedges .15 .40
321 Eduardo Rodriguez .15 .40
322 Dario Agrazal RC .30 .75
323 Tyler White .15 .40
324 Mike Soroka CUP .25 .60
325 Good-bye, Home Run .25 .60
Kyle Schwarber
326 Dylan Cease RC .40 1.00
327 Cavan Biggio FS .30 .75
328 Chris Davis .15 .40
329 Washington Nationals TC .15 .40
330 George Springer .20 .50
331 Kevin McCarthy RC .25 .60
332 Jacob deGrom .50 1.25
333 Evan Longoria .20 .50
334 Kevin Pillar .15 .40
335 Luke Voit .30 .75
336 Miguel Cabrera .25 .60
337 Michael Pineda .15 .40
338 Chicago Cubs TC .15 .40
339 Hansel Robles .15 .40
340 Adbert Alzolay RC .30 .75
341 Hanser Alberto .15 .40
342 Taylor Rogers .15 .40
343 Carson Kelly .15 .40
344 Ben Gamel .20 .50
345 Justin Verlander .25 .60
346 Lourdes Gurriel Jr. .20 .50
347 Ryan Braun .20 .50
348 Adrian Morejon RC .25 .60
349 Carlos Correa .25 .60
350 Pete Alonso CUP .60 1.50
351 Gerrit Cole .40 1.00
352 Tanner Roark .15 .40
353 DJ Stewart .15 .40
354 Luke Weaver .15 .40
355 Max Fried FS .25 .60
356 Franklin Barreto .15 .40
357 Homer Bailey .15 .40
358 Rio Ruiz .15 .40
359 Domingo Leyba RC .30 .75
360 Luis Rengifo .15 .40
361 Zach Eflin .15 .40
362 Chris Shaw .15 .40
363 Shed Long .20 .50
364 Hunter Harvey RC .40 1.00
365 Three's Company .25 .60
Elvis Andrus/Willie Calhoun/Joey Gallo
366 Marcus Semien .25 .60
367 Giancarlo Stanton .25 .60
368 Wade Miley .15 .40
369 Kolten Wong .20 .50
370 Seth Mejias-Brean RC .25 .60
371 Victor Caratini .15 .40
372 Josh Donaldson .20 .50
373 Kevin Cron .25 .60
374 Jose Ramirez .20 .50
375 Jose Osuna .15 .40
376 Shogo Akiyama RC .40 1.00
377 Phillip Ervin .15 .40
378 Nathan Eovaldi .20 .50
379 Ivan Nova .20 .50
380 James Karinchak RC .40 1.00
381 Kyle Garlick RC .40 1.00
382 Archie Bradley .15 .40
383 Steven Brault .15 .40
384 Carlos Carrasco .15 .40
385 Ryan Zimmerman .20 .50
386 Dakota Hudson FS .20 .50
387 Tony Wolters .15 .40
388 Dustin Pedroia .25 .60
389 Ryan O'Hearn .15 .40
390 Emmanuel Clase RC .40 1.00
391 Justin Upton .20 .50
392 Luis Robert RC 10.00 25.00
393 Dereck Rodriguez .15 .40
394 Keone Kela .15 .40
395 Scott Oberg .15 .40
396 Miami Marlins TC .15 .40
397 Charlie Blackmon .25 .60
398 Miguel Andujar .25 .60
399 Adrian Houser .15 .40
400 Hyun-Jin Ryu .20 .50
401 Jake Fraley RC .30 .75
402 Vince Velazquez .15 .40
403 Jose Trevino .15 .40
404 Raimel Tapia .15 .40
405 San Francisco Giants TC .15 .40
406 Charlie Morton .25 .60
407 T.J. Zeuch RC .25 .60
408 Brendan Rodgers FS .25 .60
409 Jake Odorizzi .15 .40
410 Luis Urias FS .20 .50
411 Mark Melancon .15 .40
412 Bomba Brothers .25 .60
Nelson Cruz/Miguel Sano
413 Rich Hill .15 .40
414 Gio Gonzalez .20 .50
415 Joey Gallo .25 .60
416 Chris Taylor .20 .50
417 Colorado Rockies TC .15 .40
418 Alex Dickerson .15 .40
419 J.A. Happ .20 .50
420 Mookie Betts .50 1.25
421 Garrett Stubbs RC .25 .60
422 Will Smith .15 .40
423 Andrelton Simmons .15 .40
424 Miguel Sano .20 .50
425 Mike Foltynewicz .15 .40
426 Yoenis Cespedes .25 .60
427 Edwin Diaz .20 .50
428 Jaime Barria .15 .40
429 Joe Musgrove .25 .60
430 Darwinzon Hernandez .15 .40
431 Cincinnati Reds TC .15 .40
432 Walker Buehler .30 .75
433 Noah Syndergaard .20 .50
434 Brusdar Graterol RC .40 1.00
435 Mitch Keller .25 .60
436 Travis d'Arnaud .20 .50
437 Scott Heineman RC .25 .60
438 Danny Duffy .15 .40
439 Dee Gordon .15 .40
440 Carter Kieboom FS .20 .50
441 Nick Wittgren .25 .60
442 Tom Eshelman RC .30 .75
443 Johan Camargo .15 .40
444 Martin Perez .20 .50
445 Spencer Turnbull .15 .40
446 B.Harper/R.Hoskins .40 1.00
447 Griffin Canning FS .25 .60
448 Ian Happ .20 .50
449 Shun Yamaguchi RC .30 .75
450 Jorge Soler .25 .60
451 Justus Sheffield .25 .60
452 Joe Jimenez .15 .40

453 Miguel Rojas .15 .40
454 Austin Voth .15 .40
455 Kris Bryant .30 .75
456 Dom Nunez RC .30 .75
457 Kevin Gausman .25 .60
458 Trey Mancini .25 .60
459 Kwang-Hyun Kim RC .50 1.25
460 Tyler Mahle .15 .40
461 Harrison Bader .20 .50
462 Tony Kemp .15 .40
463 Frankie Montas .15 .40
464 Randy Dobnak RC .50 1.25
465 Eugenio Suarez .20 .50
466 Garrett Hampson .15 .40
467 Andrew McCutchen .25 .60
468 Chad Green .15 .40
469 Kris Bryant .30 .75
470 Yan Gomes .25 .60
471 Lorenzo Cain .15 .40
472 Steven Duggar .15 .40
473 Lance McCullers Jr. .15 .40
474 Mark Canha .15 .40
475 Robert Dugger RC .25 .60
476 James Marvel RC .25 .60
477 Brent Suter .15 .40
478 Cole Tucker .25 .60
479 Dexter Fowler .20 .50
480 Ozzie Albies .25 .60
481 Victor Reyes .15 .40
482 Adam Duvall .20 .50
483 Eddie Rosario .20 .50
484 Brian Goodwin .15 .40
485 Jack Mayfield RC .25 .60
486 Dawel Lugo .15 .40
487 Yandy Diaz .20 .50
488 Reynaldo Lopez .20 .50
489 Colin Moran .15 .40
490 Austin Slater .15 .40
491 Will Smith .25 .60
492 Paul DeJong .25 .60
493 Christian Walker .20 .50
494 Rowan Wick .15 .40
495 Lamonte Wade Jr. RC .40 1.00
496 Lucas Sims .15 .40
497 Albert Pujols .30 .75
498 Brandon Workman .15 .40
499 Sam Tuivailala .15 .40
500 Nick Anderson .15 .40
501 Tampa Bay Rays TC .15 .40
502 Willians Astudillo .15 .40
503 Dylan Bundy .20 .50
504 Pablo Lopez .15 .40
505 Billy McKinney .15 .40
506 Delino DeShields .15 .40
507 Blake Snell .20 .50
508 Carlos Martinez .20 .50
509 Willi Castro RC .40 1.00
510 Michael Lorenzen .15 .40
511 Jordan Hicks .20 .50
512 Josh James .15 .40
513 Michael Brantley .20 .50
514 Logan Webb RC .40 1.00
515 Maikel Franco .20 .50
516 Texas Rangers TC .15 .40
517 Dylan Moore .15 .40
518 Shin-Soo Choo .20 .50
519 Didi Gregorius .20 .50
520 Justin Smoak .15 .40
521 Felix Hernandez .20 .50
522 J.D. Davis .15 .40
523 Corey Kluber .20 .50
524 Jurickson Profar .20 .50
525 Jake Cave .20 .50
526 Byron Buxton .25 .60
527 Khris Davis .25 .60
528 Harold Ramirez .15 .40
529 Ender Inciarte .15 .40
530 Xander Bogaerts .25 .60
531 David Bednar RC .25 .60
532 Robbie Ray .15 .40
533 Nick Castellanos .25 .60
534 Michael Wacha .20 .50
535 Avisail Garcia .20 .50
536 Elvis Luciano .15 .40
537 Marcell Ozuna .25 .60
538 O.Albies/R.Acuna 1.00 2.50
539 Tyrone Taylor RC .25 .60
540 Kean Wong RC .40 1.00
541 Danny Mendick RC .30 .75
542 Tom Murphy .15 .40
543 Harold Castro .20 .50
544 Wil Myers .20 .50
545 Kevin Kiermaier .20 .50
546 Ross Stripling .15 .40
547 Victor Robles .30 .75
548 Brian O'Grady RC .25 .60
549 Freddie Freeman .30 .75
550 John Means .25 .60
551 Clint Frazier .20 .50
552 Yu Darvish .25 .60
553 Salvador Perez .20 .50
554 Mike Zunino .15 .40
555 Marcus Stroman .20 .50
556 Josh Naylor .15 .40
557 Adam Ottavino .20 .50
558 Sean Manaea .15 .40
559 Josh Hader .20 .50
560 Chad Pinder .15 .40
561 Trevor Williams .15 .40
562 Gio Urshela .25 .60
563 Danny Jansen .15 .40
564 Matt Beaty .20 .50
565 Jordan Luplow .15 .40
566 Seattle Mariners TC .15 .40
567 Yonathan Daza RC .30 .75
568 Adam Eaton .25 .60
569 E.Jimenez/T.Anderson .50 1.25
570 Manny Pina .15 .40
571 Keston Hiura .30 .75
572 Manuel Margot .15 .40
573 Jason Heyward .20 .50
574 Brandon Lowe FS .20 .50
575 Kyle Seager .15 .40
576 Sergio Romo .15 .40
577 Elvis Andrus .20 .50
578 Chris Bassitt .15 .40
579 Kevin Kramer .15 .40
580 Dellin Betances .20 .50
581 Michael Taylor .15 .40
582 Willie Calhoun .15 .40
583 Josh Staumont RC .25 .60
584 Michael Kopech .30 .75
585 Kyle Tucker FS .25 .60
586 Stevie Wilkerson RC .40 1.00
587 Lou Trivino .15 .40
588 Tommy Kahnle .15 .40
589 Eric Lauer .15 .40
590 Yu Chang RC .40 1.00
591 A.Judge/G.Sanchez .60 1.50
592 Corey Dickerson .20 .50
593 Stephen Piscotty .15 .40
594 Pittsburgh Pirates TC .15 .40
595 Eduardo Escobar .15 .40
596 Daniel Norris .15 .40
597 Jonathan Hernandez RC .25 .60
598 Jacob Stallings RC .30 .75
599 Ryan McMahon .25 .60
600 Drew Steckenrider .15 .40
601 Tucker Barnhart .15 .40
602 Jose Altuve .20 .50
603 Dinelson Lamet .15 .40
604 Derek Fisher .15 .40
605 Stephen Vogt .20 .50
606 Martin Maldonado .15 .40
607 Cal Quantrill .15 .40
608 Sam Gaviglio .15 .40
609 Ronald Guzman .15 .40
610 Cole Hamels .20 .50
611 Braun/Cain/Yelich .30 .75
612 Luis Arraez FS .30 .75
613 Isiah Kiner-Falefa .20 .50
614 Brett Gardner .20 .50
615 Junior Fernandez RC .25 .60
616 Cam Gallagher .15 .40
617 Bryan Reynolds .20 .50
618 Joey Wendle .20 .50
619 Rick Porcello .20 .50
620 Corey Seager .25 .60
621 Dallas Keuchel .20 .50
622 Brett Phillips .15 .40
623 Mike Ford .25 .60
624 Renato Nunez .20 .50
625 Detroit Tigers TC .15 .40
626 Nate Lowe .40 1.00
627 Eric Hosmer .20 .50
628 Julio Urias .25 .60
629 Toronto Blue Jays TC .15 .40
630 Francisco Mejia .20 .50
631 Stephen Strasburg .25 .60
632 Austin Hays .25 .60
633 Lance Lynn .15 .40
634 San Diego Padres TC .15 .40
635 Sean Newcomb .15 .40
636 Jake Bauers .20 .50
637 Trevor Story .25 .60
638 Nomar Mazara .15 .40
639 Kolby Allard .15 .40
640 Rev'd Up .25 .60
Adam Eaton/Howie Kendrick
641 A.J. Pollock .15 .40
642 Ryan Borucki .15 .40
643 Wilson Ramos .15 .40
644 Teoscar Hernandez .25 .60
645 Jeff Mathis .20 .50
646 Kevin Newman FS .25 .60
647 Joe Ross .15 .40
648 Mike Leake .15 .40
649 Jed Lowrie .15 .40
650 Kelvin Herrera .15 .40
651 Arizona Diamondbacks TC .15 .40
652 Pedro Severino .15 .40
653 Zach Plesac .25 .60
654 Tim Lopes RC .30 .75
655 Howie Kendrick .15 .40
656 Alex Cobb .15 .40
657 Rougned Odor .20 .50
658 Chad Wallach RC .25 .60
659 Aledmys Diaz .15 .40
660 Brandon Nimmo .20 .50
661 Justin Dunn RC .30 .75
662 Andrew Knapp .15 .40
663 Chicago White Sox TC .15 .40
664 Yonny Chirinos .15 .40
665 Willson Contreras .25 .60
666 Kyle Freeland .20 .50
667 Adam Haseley .20 .50
668 Kansas City Royals TC .15 .40
669 Luis Severino .20 .50
670 Aaron Barrett RC .25 .60
671 Ryan McBroom RC .30 .75
672 Chris Sale .25 .60
673 Anthony DeSclafani .15 .40
674 Jose Abreu .25 .60
675 David Robertson .15 .40
676 Rangel Ravelo RC .30 .75
677 Ji-Man Choi .15 .40
678 Jose Rodriguez RC .25 .60
679 Glenn Sparkman .15 .40
680 Nick Ahmed .15 .40
681 Edwin Rios RC .60 1.50
682 Ronny Rodriguez .15 .40
683 Jakob Junis .15 .40
684 Mike Minor .15 .40
685 Freddy Galvis .15 .40
686 Josh Reddick .15 .40
687 Rhys Hoskins .30 .75
688 Austin Romine .15 .40
689 James McCann .20 .50
690 Ehire Adrianza .15 .40
691 Brock Burke RC .25 .60
692 Jonathan Schoop .15 .40
693 Jon Berti RC .25 .60
694 Baltimore Orioles TC .15 .40
695 Danny Santana .15 .40
696 G.Torres/F.Lindor .50 1.25
697 Eric Sogard .15 .40
698 Tyler Chatwood .15 .40
699 Sheldon Neuse RC .30 .75
700 Adam Wainwright .20 .50

2020 Topps Advanced Stats

*ADV STATS: 4X TO 10X BASIC
SER.1 STATED ODDS 1:107 HOBBY
SER.2 STATED ODDS 1:65 HOBBY
STATED PRINT RUN 300 SER. #'d SETS
69 Brendan McKay 10.00 25.00
70 Nico Hoerner 20.00 50.00
78 Bo Bichette 75.00 200.00
110 Jesus Luzardo 12.00 30.00
229 Randy Arozarena 20.00 50.00
235 Dustin May 10.00 25.00
276 Yordan Alvarez 40.00 100.00
292 Gavin Lux 60.00 150.00
376 Shogo Akiyama 25.00 60.00
392 Luis Robert 150.00 400.00
459 Kwang-Hyun Kim 6.00 15.00
681 Edwin Rios 6.00 15.00

2020 Topps Black

*BLACK: 10X TO 25X BASIC
*BLACK RC: 6X TO 15X BASIC RC
SER.1 ODDS 1:117 HOBBY
SER.2 ODDS 1:97 HOBBY
STATED PRINT RUN 69 SER. #'d SETS
1 Mike Trout 50.00 120.00
69 Brendan McKay 25.00 60.00
70 Nico Hoerner 50.00 125.00
78 Bo Bichette 200.00 500.00
110 Jesus Luzardo 30.00 80.00
178 Mauricio Dubon 20.00 50.00
229 Randy Arozarena 50.00 120.00
235 Dustin May 25.00 60.00
276 Yordan Alvarez 150.00 400.00
292 Gavin Lux 150.00 400.00
376 Shogo Akiyama 60.00 150.00
392 Luis Robert 1000.00 2000.00
459 Kwang-Hyun Kim 15.00 40.00
681 Edwin Rios 15.00 40.00

2020 Topps Father's Day Blue

*BLUE: 10X TO 25X BASIC
*BLUE RC: 6X TO 15X BASIC RC
SER.1 STATED ODDS 1:546 HOBBY
SER.2 STATED ODDS 1:358 HOBBY
STATED PRINT RUN 50 SER. #'d SETS
1 Mike Trout 50.00 120.00
69 Brendan McKay 25.00 60.00
70 Nico Hoerner 50.00 125.00
78 Bo Bichette 200.00 500.00
110 Jesus Luzardo 30.00 80.00
178 Mauricio Dubon 20.00 50.00
229 Randy Arozarena 50.00 120.00
235 Dustin May 25.00 60.00
276 Yordan Alvarez 150.00 400.00
292 Gavin Lux 150.00 400.00
376 Shogo Akiyama 30.00 80.00
392 Luis Robert 500.00 1200.00
459 Kwang-Hyun Kim 15.00 40.00
681 Edwin Rios 15.00 40.00

2020 Topps Gold

*GOLD: 2X TO 5X BASIC
*GOLD RC: 1.2X TO 3X BASIC RC
SER.1 STATED ODDS 1:14 HOBBY
SER.2 STATED ODDS 1:9 HOBBY
STATED PRINT RUN 2020 SER. #'d SETS
69 Brendan McKay 5.00 12.00
70 Nico Hoerner 10.00 25.00
78 Bo Bichette 40.00 100.00
110 Jesus Luzardo 6.00 15.00
229 Randy Arozarena 10.00 25.00
235 Dustin May 5.00 12.00
276 Yordan Alvarez 20.00 50.00
292 Gavin Lux 30.00 80.00
376 Shogo Akiyama 6.00 15.00
392 Luis Robert 75.00 200.00

2020 Topps Gold Foil

*GOLD FOIL: 2X TO 5X BASIC
*GOLD FOIL RC: 1.2X TO 3X BASIC RC
SER.1 STATED ODDS 1:2 HOBBY JUMBO
SER.2 STATED ODDS 1:2 HOBBY JUMBO
69 Brendan McKay 5.00 12.00
70 Nico Hoerner 10.00 25.00
78 Bo Bichette 40.00 100.00
235 Dustin May 5.00 12.00
276 Yordan Alvarez 20.00 50.00
292 Gavin Lux 30.00 80.00
376 Shogo Akiyama 6.00 15.00
392 Luis Robert 75.00 200.00

2020 Topps Independence Day

*INDPNDNCE: 10X TO 25X BASIC
*INDPNDNCE RC: 6X TO 15X BASIC RC
SER.1 STATED ODDS 1:359 HOBBY
SER.2 STATED ODDS 1:236 HOBBY
STATED PRINT RUN 76 SER. #'d SETS
1 Mike Trout 50.00 120.00
69 Brendan McKay 25.00 60.00
70 Nico Hoerner 50.00 125.00
78 Bo Bichette 200.00 500.00
110 Jesus Luzardo 30.00 80.00
178 Mauricio Dubon 20.00 50.00
229 Randy Arozarena 50.00 120.00
235 Dustin May 25.00 60.00
276 Yordan Alvarez 150.00 400.00
292 Gavin Lux 150.00 400.00
376 Shogo Akiyama 30.00 80.00
392 Luis Robert 400.00 1000.00
459 Kwang-Hyun Kim 15.00 40.00
681 Edwin Rios 15.00 40.00

2020 Topps Meijer Purple

*PURPLE: 5X TO 12X BASIC
*PURPLE RC: 3X TO 8X BASIC RC
STATED ODDS TWO PER BLISTER PACK
69 Brendan McKay 12.00 30.00
70 Nico Hoerner 25.00 60.00
78 Bo Bichette 100.00 250.00
110 Jesus Luzardo 15.00 40.00
229 Randy Arozarena 25.00 60.00
235 Dustin May 12.00 30.00
276 Yordan Alvarez 60.00 150.00
292 Gavin Lux 75.00 200.00

2020 Topps Memorial Day Camo

*CAMO: 12X TO 30X BASIC
*CAMO RC: 8X TO 20X BASIC RC
SER.1 STATED ODDS 1:1091 HOBBY
SER.2 STATED ODDS 1:715 HOBBY
STATED PRINT RUN 25 SER. #'d SETS
1 Mike Trout 60.00 150.00
69 Brendan McKay 30.00 80.00
70 Nico Hoerner 60.00 150.00
78 Bo Bichette 250.00 600.00
110 Jesus Luzardo 40.00 100.00
178 Mauricio Dubon 25.00 60.00
229 Randy Arozarena 60.00 150.00
235 Dustin May 30.00 80.00
276 Yordan Alvarez 200.00 500.00
292 Gavin Lux 200.00 500.00
376 Shogo Akiyama 40.00 100.00
392 Luis Robert 600.00 1500.00
459 Kwang-Hyun Kim 20.00 50.00
681 Edwin Rios 20.00 50.00

2020 Topps Mother's Day Pink

*PINK: 10X TO 25X BASIC
*PINK RC: 6X TO 15X BASIC RC
SER.1 STATED ODDS 1:546 HOBBY
SER.2 STATED ODDS 1:358 HOBBY
STATED PRINT RUN 50 SER. #'d SETS
1 Mike Trout 50.00 120.00
69 Brendan McKay 25.00 60.00
70 Nico Hoerner 50.00 125.00
78 Bo Bichette 200.00 500.00
110 Jesus Luzardo 30.00 80.00
178 Mauricio Dubon 20.00 50.00
229 Randy Arozarena 50.00 120.00
235 Dustin May 25.00 60.00
276 Yordan Alvarez 150.00 400.00
292 Gavin Lux 150.00 400.00
376 Shogo Akiyama 30.00 80.00
392 Luis Robert 500.00 1200.00
459 Kwang-Hyun Kim 15.00 40.00
681 Edwin Rios 15.00 40.00

2020 Topps Rainbow Foil

*RAINBOW: 2X TO 5X BASIC
*RAINBOW RC: 1.2X TO 3X BASIC RC
SER.1 STATED ODDS 1:10 HOBBY
SER.2 STATED ODDS 1:10 HOBBY
69 Brendan McKay 5.00 12.00
70 Nico Hoerner 10.00 25.00
78 Bo Bichette 40.00 100.00
235 Dustin May 5.00 12.00
276 Yordan Alvarez 20.00 50.00
292 Gavin Lux 30.00 80.00
376 Shogo Akiyama 6.00 15.00
392 Luis Robert 75.00 200.00

2020 Topps Vintage Stock

*VINTAGE: 8X TO 20X BASIC
*VINTAGE RC: 5X TO 12X BASIC RC
SER,1 STATED ODDS 1:186 HOBBY
SER,2 STATED ODDS 1:186 HOBBY
STATED PRINT RUN 99 SER. #'d SETS
1 Mike Trout 40.00 100.00
69 Brendan McKay 20.00 50.00
70 Nico Hoerner 40.00 100.00
78 Bo Bichette 150.00 400.00
110 Jesus Luzardo 25.00 60.00
178 Mauricio Dubon 15.00 40.00
229 Randy Arozarena 40.00 100.00
235 Dustin May 20.00 50.00
276 Yordan Alvarez 100.00 250.00
292 Gavin Lux 125.00 300.00
376 Shogo Akiyama 25.00 60.00
392 Luis Robert 250.00 600.00
459 Kwang-Hyun Kim 12.00 30.00
681 Edwin Rios 12.00 30.00

2020 Topps Walgreens Yellow

69 Brendan McKay 8.00 20.00
70 Nico Hoerner 15.00 40.00
78 Bo Bichette 60.00 150.00
110 Jesus Luzardo 10.00 25.00
229 Randy Arozarena 15.00 40.00
235 Dustin May 8.00 20.00
276 Yordan Alvarez 60.00 150.00
292 Gavin Lux 50.00 120.00

2020 Topps Base Set Photo Variations

SER.1 STATED ODDS 1:43 HOBBY
SER.2 STATED ODDS 1:28 HOBBY
SER.1 STATED SSP ODDS 1:1272 HOBBY
SER.2 STATED SSP ODDS 1:835 HOBBY
1A Trout Signing 10.00 25.00
1B Mike Trout SSP 800.00 1200.00
7A Judge Blue shirt 5.00 12.00
7B Aaron Judge SSP 300.00 600.00
8 Cal Ripken Jr. SSP 20.00 50.00
13 Stan Musial SSP 15.00 40.00
14 Anthony Rendon 2.00 5.00
Expos uniform
20A Aquino Flex 3.00 8.00
20B Aristides Aquino SSP 60.00 150.00
20C Aquino FACTORY 3.00 8.00
35 George Brett 4.00 10.00
46 Sanchez Dugout 3.00 8.00
47 Chipper Jones 3.00 8.00
49 Jimenez w/Ball 4.00 10.00
50A Bellinger Overhead 6.00 15.00
50B Cody Bellinger SSP 30.00 80.00
51 Rizzo Overhead 4.00 10.00
52 Mike Piazza 3.00 8.00
55 Ozzie Smith 3.00 8.00
60 Roger Clemens 2.50 6.00
64 Lewis Dugout 20.00 50.00
68 Gerrit Cole 3.00 8.00
69A McKay Wht jrsy 2.00 5.00
69B Brendan McKay SSP 25.00 60.00
70 Hoerner High-five 6.00 15.00
78A Bichette Wknd uni 60.00 150.00
78B Bo Bichette SSP 150.00 400.00
78C Bichette FACTORY 10.00 25.00
94 Brooks Robinson 1.50 4.00
100A Alex Bregman 2.00 5.00
iPad photo
100B Alex Bregman SSP 25.00 60.00
110 Luzardo Overhead 8.00 20.00
111 Posey Blck pants 5.00 12.00
117 Max Kepler 1.50 4.00
red jersey
118 Kershaw Blue shirt 5.00 12.00
119 Kyle Schwarber 2.00 5.00
pink sleeves
120 Sandy Koufax SSP 20.00 50.00
121 Lou Gehrig SSP 25.00 60.00
124 Randy Johnson 2.00 5.00
125 Ohtani Warmup 3.00 8.00
127 Chapman Wknd uni 2.00 5.00
129 Jackie Robinson SSP 25.00 60.00
138 Ty Cobb SSP 25.00 60.00
140 Trevor Bauer 2.50 6.00
camo hat
145 Goldschmidt Dive 2.50 6.00
149 Robin Yount• 2.00 5.00
150A Acuna Signing 15.00 40.00
150B Ronald Acuna Jr. SSP 100.00 250.00
156 Hank Aaron SSP 40.00 100.00
161 Mariano Rivera 3.00 8.00
168A Tatis Crouching 25.00 60.00
168B Fernando Tatis Jr. SSP 200.00 500.00
170 Roberto Clemente SSP 40.00 100.00
173 Molina Blue chest 2.50 6.00
175 Frank Thomas 6.00 15.00
179 Ramon Laureano 1.50 4.00
in dugout
180 Scherzer Expos 3.00 8.00
182A Guerrero Jr. Red hat 3.00 8.00
182B Vladimir Guerrero Jr. SSP 75.00 200.00
183 Vladimir Guerrero 1.50 4.00
186 Johnny Bench 3.00 8.00
188 Manny Machado 2.00 5.00
sunglasses on
192 Ichiro 3.00 8.00
196 Ted Williams SSP 25.00 60.00
200A Yelich Pinstripe 2.50 6.00
200B Christian Yelich SSP 25.00 60.00
201 Lindor Red carpet 2.50 6.00
206 Reggie Jackson• 1.50 4.00
219 Honus Wagner 3.00 8.00
224 Soto Expos 15.00 40.00
230 Arenado Prpl uni 2.50 6.00
235 May Glasses 10.00 25.00
248 Tony Gwynn 2.00 5.00
250A Harper Gatorade 3.00 8.00
250B Bryce Harper SSP 30.00 80.00
252 Roger Maris 6.00 15.00
253 Ernie Banks 4.00 10.00
260 Nolan Ryan 5.00 12.00
267 Votto Slvlss jrsy 3.00 8.00
269 J.D. Martinez 2.00 5.00
close-up
271 Josh Bell 1.50 4.00
Red Carpet Show
276A Alvarez Wlkng w/bat 40.00 100.00
276B Yordan Alvarez SSP 150.00 400.00
276C Alvarez FACTORY 12.00 30.00
279 Masahiro Tanaka 2.00 5.00
jacket on
289 Mark McGwire 3.00 8.00
292A Lux Jumping 40.00 100.00
292B Gavin Lux SSP 125.00 300.00
292C Gavin Lux 6.00 15.00
gray jsy FACTORY
296 Merrifield Wknd uni 3.00 8.00
299 Pedro Martinez 1.50 4.00
300A Baez Jumping 2.50 6.00
300B Javier Baez SSP 40.00 100.00
303 Ken Griffey Jr. SSP 30.00 80.00
306 Ryne Sandberg 4.00 10.00
309 Rickey Henderson 3.00 8.00
314 Devers Weights 2.50 6.00
317 Murphy Grn jrsy 4.00 10.00
330 George Springer 1.50 4.00
jumping
332 Jacob deGrom 6.00 15.00
batting
334 Willie Mays SSP 25.00 60.00
335A Don Mattingly 5.00 12.00
335B Babe Ruth SSP 40.00 100.00
341 Frank Robinson 1.50 4.00
345 Verlander Orng jrsy 2.00 5.00
349 Carlos Correa 2.00 5.00
blue jersey
350A Alonso Gatorade 3.00 8.00
350B Pete Alonso SSP 600.00 1000.00
351A Cole Blue jrsy 3.00 8.00
351B Cole SSP Pinstripe 40.00 100.00
354 Randy Johnson 2.00 5.00
361 Steve Carlton 1.50 4.00
362 Will Clark 1.50 4.00
363 Ichiro SSP 25.00 60.00
364 Hunter Harvey 2.00 5.00
black jsy
366 Marcus Semien 2.00 5.00
green jsy
367A Giancarlo Stanton 2.00 5.00
gray jsy, fielding
367B Stanton SSP Hggng 20.00 50.00
375A Willie Stargell 1.50 4.00
375B Robert Clemente SSP 40.00 100.00
378 Carl Yastrzemski 3.00 8.00
381 Sandy Koufax SSP 40.00 100.00
388A Carlton Fisk 1.50 4.00
388B Ted Williams SSP 40.00 100.00
392A Robert Snglsss 200.00 500.00
392B Robert SSP Rnnng 500.00 1200.00
392C Bichette/Robert/Alvarez SSP 1000.00 2000.00
392D Luis Robert NNOF 1500.00 3000.00
392E Robert FACTORY 6.00 15.00
397 Charlie Blackmon 2.00 5.00
pinstripe jsy
401 Fraley Hdbnd 1.50 4.00
408 Brendan Rodgers 2.00 5.00
dugout steps
416 Jackie Robinson SSP 25.00 60.00
418 Willie McCovey 1.50 4.00
419 Lou Gehrig SSP 40.00 100.00
420A Betts Hoodie 4.00 10.00
420B Betts SSP Blue jrsy 40.00 100.00
420C Betts SSP Hllywd 300.00 800.00
424 Rod Carew 1.50 4.00
427 Tom Seaver 1.50 4.00
432A Buehler Bttng 2.50 6.00
432B Buehler SSP Run 20.00 50.00
433 Noah Syndergaard 1.50 4.00
wearing helmet
434 Brusdar Graterol 2.00 5.00
white jsy
440 Carter Kieboom 1.50 4.00
red hoodie
455A Bryant Bttng 2.50 6.00
455B Kris Bryant SSP Glv 25.00 60.00
458 Trey Mancini 2.00 5.00
black jsy
461 Lou Brock 1.50 4.00
464 Dobnak Hoodie 2.50 6.00
465 Eugenio Suarez 1.50 4.00
white jsy
467A Andrew McCutchen 20.00 50.00
red jsy
467B McCtchn SSP Pnstrpe jrsy 25.00 60.00
469 Tom Glavine 1.50 4.00
472 Willie Mays SSP 25.00 60.00
480 Ozzie Albies 2.00 5.00
hoodie
482A Eddie Mathews 2.00 5.00
482B Hank Aaron SSP 30.00 80.00
483 Eddie Rosario 1.50 4.00
blue jsy
486 Al Kaline 4.00 10.00
497A Pujols Shkng hnds 2.50 6.00
497B Pujols SSP Cap chest 25.00 60.00
507 Blake Snell 1.50 4.00
wearing shirt
508 Bob Gibson 1.50 4.00
514 Logan Webb 2.00 5.00
batting
517 Ken Griffey Jr. SSP 30.00 80.00
519 Mike Schmidt 3.00 8.00
525A Harmon Killebrew 2.00 5.00
looking forward
525B Killebrew SSP Look up 25.00 60.00
530 Xander Bogaerts 2.00 5.00
tuxedo
533 Nick Castellanos 2.00 5.00
gray jsy
541 Danny Mendick 1.50 4.00
batting
549 Freeman Bttng 4.00 10.00
552 Yu Darvish 2.00 5.00
batting
556 Dave Winfield 1.50 4.00
557 Mariano Rivera SSP 40.00 100.00
558 Dennis Eckersley 1.50 4.00
559 Josh Hader 1.50 4.00
white plyr's wknd jsy
560 Reggie Jackson 1.50 4.00
561 Wade Boggs 1.50 4.00
562 Babe Ruth SSP 60.00 150.00
567 Yonathan Daza 1.50 4.00
jsy#2
571 Hiura Blue jrsy 12.00 30.00
577 Elvis Andrus 1.50 4.00
Gatorade shower
585 Kyle Tucker 2.00 5.00
swinging
586 Cal Ripken Jr. SSP 40.00 100.00
590 Yu Chang 2.00 5.00
wearing a hat
591 Craig Biggio 1.50 4.00
602A Jose Altuve 1.50 4.00
cap on chest
602B Altuve SSP Cage 25.00 60.00
609 Nolan Ryan SSP 30.00 80.00
615 Junior Fernandez 1.25 3.00
with catcher
620 Corey Seager 2.00 5.00
gray jsy
624 Eddie Murray 1.50 4.00
631A Stephen Strasburg 2.00 5.00
bunting
631B Strasburg SSP White House 25.00 60.00
637 Trevor Story 2.00 5.00
purple jsy
649 Gary Carter 1.50 4.00
660 Darryl Strawberry 1.25 3.00
661 Justin Dunn 1.50 4.00
Futures game jsy
665 Willson Contreras 2.00 5.00
in shorts
669 Luis Severino 1.50 4.00
locker room celebration
672 Chris Sale 2.00 5.00
Stars and Stripes hat
674 Jose Abreu 2.00 5.00
throwback jsy
676 Rangel Ravelo 1.50 4.00
in dugout
681 Edwin Rios 3.00 8.00
bat up
685 Frank Robinson 1.50 4.00
686 Jeff Bagwell 1.50 4.00
687A Hoskins Bubble 2.50 6.00
687B Hoskins SSP Sgnng 25.00 60.00
691 Brock Burke 1.25 3.00
blue jsy
699 Sheldon Neuse 1.50 4.00
gray jsy
NNO Rob Manfred SSSP 60.00 150.00

2020 Topps '19 Topps Now Review

COMPLETE SET (10) 4.00 10.00
STATED ODDS 1:18 HOBBY
TNR1 Mike Trout 1.50 4.00
TNR2 Vladimir Guerrero Jr. .50 1.25
TNR3 Albert Pujols .40 1.00
TNR4 Yordan Alvarez 2.00 5.00
TNR5 Shohei Ohtani .50 1.25
TNR6 Pete Alonso .75 2.00
TNR7 Mariano Rivera .40 1.00
TNR8 Bryce Harper .50 1.25
TNR9 Pete Alonso .75 2.00
TNR10 Justin Verlander .30 .75

2020 Topps '85 Topps

STATED ODDS 1:4 HOBBY
*BLUE: 1.2X TO 3X BASIC
*BLACK/299: 2X TO 5X BASIC
*GOLD/50: 5X TO 12X BASIC
851 Mike Trout 1.50 4.00
852 Shohei Ohtani .50 1.25
853 Albert Pujols .40 1.00
854 Matt Thaiss .25 .60
855 Alex Young .20 .50
856 Zac Gallen .50 1.25
857 Chipper Jones .30 .75
858 Dale Murphy .30 .75
859 Hank Aaron .60 1.50
8510 Mike Soroka .30 .75
8511 Ozzie Albies .30 .75
8512 Ronald Acuna Jr. 1.25 3.00
8513 Cal Ripken Jr. 1.00 2.50
8514 Mike Mussina .25 .60
8515 Chris Sale .30 .75
8516 J.D. Martinez .30 .75
8517 Rafael Devers .40 1.00
8518 Roger Clemens .40 1.00
8519 Wade Boggs .25 .60
8520 Xander Bogaerts .30 .75
8521 Mookie Betts .60 1.50
8522 Jackie Robinson .30 .75
8523 Rod Carew .25 .60
8524 Anthony Rizzo .40 1.00
8525 Kris Bryant .40 1.00
8526 Kyle Schwarber .30 .75
8527 Ryne Sandberg .60 1.50
8528 Willson Contreras .30 .75
8529 Robel Garcia .20 .50
8530 Dylan Cease .30 .75
8531 Eloy Jimenez .60 1.50
8532 Frank Thomas .30 .75
8533 Zack Collins .25 .60
8534 Joey Votto .30 .75
8535 Johnny Bench .30 .75
8536 Nick Senzel .30 .75
8537 Trevor Bauer .40 1.00
8538 Aristides Aquino .50 1.25
8539 Francisco Lindor .30 .75
8540 Shane Bieber .30 .75
8541 Nolan Arenado .50 1.25
8542 Al Kaline .30 .75
8543 Miguel Cabrera .30 .75
8544 Jake Rogers .20 .50
8545 George Springer .25 .60
8546 Gerrit Cole .50 1.25
8547 Jeff Bagwell .25 .60
8548 Jose Altuve .25 .60
8549 Nolan Ryan 1.00 2.50
8550 Yordan Alvarez 2.00 5.00
8551 Alex Bregman .30 .75
8552 Whit Merrifield .30 .75
8553 George Brett .60 1.50
8554 Clayton Kershaw .50 1.25
8555 Sandy Koufax .60 1.50
8556 Walker Buehler .40 1.00
8557 Dustin May .60 1.50
8558 Jordan Yamamoto .20 .50
8559 Christian Yelich .40 1.00
8560 Keston Hiura .40 1.00
8561 Robin Yount .30 .75
8562 Jose Berrios .25 .60
8563 Max Kepler .25 .60
8564 Vladimir Guerrero .25 .60
8565 Darryl Strawberry .20 .50
8566 Jacob deGrom .60 1.50
8567 Noah Syndergaard .25 .60
8568 Pete Alonso .75 2.00
8569 Aaron Judge .75 2.00
8570 Don Mattingly .60 1.50
8571 Luis Severino .25 .60
8572 Mariano Rivera .40 1.00
8573 Reggie Jackson .25 .60
8574 Gleyber Torres .60 1.50
8575 Mark McGwire .50 1.25
8576 Ramon Laureano .25 .60
8577 Rickey Henderson .30 .75
8578 Matt Chapman .30 .75
8579 Bryce Harper .50 1.25
8580 Rhys Hoskins .40 1.00
8581 Roberto Clemente .75 2.00
8582 Manny Machado .30 .75
8583 Chris Paddack .30 .75
8584 Fernando Tatis Jr. 1.50 4.00
8585 Tony Gwynn .30 .75
8586 Will Clark .25 .60
8587 Willie Mays .60 1.50
8588 Ichiro .40 1.00
8589 Ken Griffey Jr. .60 1.50
8590 Paul Goldschmidt .30 .75
8591 Ozzie Smith .40 1.00
8592 Gavin Lux 1.00 2.50
8593 Yadier Molina .40 1.00
8594 Blake Snell .25 .60
8595 Nico Hoerner .75 2.00
8596 Brendan McKay .30 .75
8597 Bo Bichette 1.50 4.00
8598 Vladimir Guerrero Jr. .50 1.25
8599 Juan Soto 1.00 2.50
85100 Max Scherzer .30 .75

2020 Topps '85 Topps Series 2

COMPLETE SET (50) 10.00 25.00
STATED ODDS 1:8 HOBBY
*BLUE: 1.2X TO 3X BASIC
*BLACK/299: 2X TO 5X BASIC
*GOLD/50: 5X TO 12X BASIC
85TB1 Anthony Rendon .30 .75
85TB2 Ketel Marte .25 .60
85TB3 Freddie Freeman .40 1.00
85TB4 Austin Riley .40 1.00
85TB5 Trey Mancini .30 .75
85TB6 Andrew Benintendi .30 .75
85TB7 David Ortiz .30 .75
85TB8 Javier Baez .40 1.00
85TB9 Tim Anderson .30 .75
85TB10 Jose Abreu .30 .75
85TB11 Sonny Gray .25 .60
85TB12 Eugenio Suarez .25 .60
85TB13 Barry Larkin .25 .60
85TB14 Mike Clevinger .25 .60
85TB15 Carlos Santana .25 .60
85TB16 Trevor Story .30 .75
85TB17 Charlie Blackmon .30 .75
85TB18 Gerrit Cole .50 1.25
85TB19 Carlos Correa .30 .75
85TB20 Jorge Soler .30 .75
85TB21 Cody Bellinger .60 1.50
85TB22 Corey Seager .30 .75
85TB23 Lorenzo Cain .20 .50
85TB24 Nelson Cruz .30 .75
85TB25 Miguel Sano .25 .60
85TB26 Robinson Cano .25 .60
85TB27 Marcus Stroman .25 .60
85TB28 Masahiro Tanaka .30 .75
85TB29 Giancarlo Stanton .30 .75
85TB30 DJ LeMahieu .30 .75
85TB31 Matt Olson .30 .75
85TB32 Mookie Betts .60 1.50
85TB33 Marcus Semien .30 .75
85TB34 Aaron Nola .25 .60
85TB35 J.T. Realmuto .30 .75
85TB36 Andrew McCutchen .30 .75
85TB37 Josh Bell .25 .60
85TB38 Trent Grisham .75 2.00
85TB39 Buster Posey .40 1.00
85TB40 Mike Yastrzemski .50 1.25
85TB41 Kyle Lewis 1.50 4.00
85TB42 Randy Johnson .30 .75
85TB43 Jack Flaherty .30 .75
85TB44 Jose Canseco .25 .60

85TB45 Tyler Glasnow .30 .75
85TB46 Joey Gallo .30 .75
85TB47 Luis Robert 1.50 4.00
85TB48 Roberto Alomar .25 .60
85TB49 Stephen Strasburg .30 .75
85TB50 Trea Turner .25 .60

2020 Topps '85 Topps All Stars

COMPLETE SET (50) 12.00 30.00
STATED ODDS 1:8 HOBBY
*BLUE: 1.2X TO 3X BASIC
*BLACK/299: 2X TO 5X BASIC
*GOLD/50: 5X TO 12X BASIC
85AS1 Mike Trout 1.50 4.00
85AS2 Aaron Judge .75 2.00
85AS3 Roger Clemens .40 1.00
85AS4 Cal Ripken Jr. 1.00 2.50
85AS5 Reggie Jackson .25 .60
85AS6 Rickey Henderson .30 .75
85AS7 Carl Yastrzemski .50 1.25
85AS8 Mark McGwire .50 1.25
85AS9 Johnny Bench
85AS10 Hideki Matsui .30 .75
85AS11 Bo Jackson .30 .75
85AS12 Ryne Sandberg .60 1.50
85AS13 Andre Dawson .25 .60
85AS14 Chris Sale .30 .75
85AS15 Tom Glavine .25 .60
85AS16 Willson Contreras .30 .75
85AS17 Jacob deGrom .60 1.50
85AS18 Francisco Lindor .30 .75
85AS19 Christian Yelich .40 1.00
85AS20 Luis Severino .25 .60
85AS21 Wade Boggs .25 .60
85AS22 Robin Yount .30 .75
85AS23 Don Mattingly .60 1.50
85AS24 Ozzie Smith .40 1.00
85AS25 Jose Altuve .25 .60
85AS26 Bob Gibson .25 .60
85AS27 Carlton Fisk .25 .60
85AS28 Dale Murphy .30 .75
85AS29 Will Clark .25 .60
85AS30 Darryl Strawberry .20 .50
85AS31 Edgar Martinez .25 .60
85AS32 Blake Snell .25 .60
85AS33 Ozzie Albies .30 .75
85AS34 Jim Rice .25 .60
85AS35 Rod Carew .25 .60
85AS36 Paul Goldschmidt .30 .75
85AS37 George Springer .25 .60
85AS38 Max Scherzer .30 .75
85AS39 Ronald Acuna Jr. 1.25 3.00
85AS40 Ken Griffey Jr. .60 1.50
85AS41 Ketel Marte .25 .60
85AS42 Nolan Arenado .50 1.25
85AS43 Gleyber Torres .60 1.50
85AS44 Pete Alonso .75 2.00
85AS45 Jeff McNeil .25 .60
85AS46 Lucas Giolito .25 .60
85AS47 Shane Bieber .30 .75
85AS48 Jose Berrios .25 .60
85AS49 Clayton Kershaw .50 1.25
85AS50 Kris Bryant .40 1.00

2020 Topps '85 Topps All Stars Autographs

STATED ODDS 1:591 HOBBY
EXCHANGE DEADLINE 4/30/2022
85ASAAD Andre Dawson 20.00 50.00
85ASAAJ Aaron Judge
85ASABGI Bob Gibson
85ASABJA Bo Jackson
85ASABS Blake Snell 4.00 10.00
85ASACFI Carlton Fisk 25.00 60.00
85ASACK Clayton Kershaw 40.00 100.00
85ASACRJ Cal Ripken Jr. 60.00 150.00
85ASACS Chris Sale 10.00 25.00
85ASACSA Carlos Santana 15.00 40.00
85ASACY Carl Yastrzemski 50.00 120.00
85ASACYE Christian Yelich 30.00 80.00
85ASADJL DJ LeMahieu 30.00 80.00
85ASADM Don Mattingly 40.00 100.00
85ASADMU Dale Murphy
85ASADS Darryl Strawberry 12.00 30.00
85ASAEM Edgar Martinez 15.00 40.00
85ASAGS George Springer 8.00 20.00
85ASAHM Hideki Matsui
85ASAJAL Jose Altuve 10.00 25.00
85ASAJB Johnny Bench
85ASAJM Jeff McNeil 15.00 40.00
85ASAJME John Means
85ASAKB Kris Bryant
85ASAKGJ Ken Griffey Jr.
85ASAKMA Ketel Marte 12.00 30.00
85ASALG Lucas Giolito 10.00 25.00
85ASAMM Mark McGwire 30.00 80.00
85ASAMMU Max Muncy 8.00 20.00
85ASAMS Max Scherzer 25.00 60.00
85ASAMSO Mike Soroka 15.00 40.00
85ASAMT Mike Trout
85ASANA Nolan Arenado
85ASAOS Ozzie Smith
85ASAPA Pete Alonso 50.00 120.00
85ASAPG Paul Goldschmidt 10.00 25.00
85ASARAJ Ronald Acuna Jr. 60.00 150.00
85ASARC Roger Clemens
85ASARH Rickey Henderson
85ASARJ Reggie Jackson
85ASARS Ryne Sandberg
85ASARYO Robin Yount 50.00 120.00
85ASASB Shane Bieber 20.00 50.00
85ASAWB Wade Boggs 30.00 80.00
85ASAWC Willson Contreras 8.00 20.00
85ASAWCL Will Clark 40.00 100.00

2020 Topps '85 Topps All Stars Autographs Gold

*GOLD: .5X TO 1.2X BASIC
STATED ODDS 1:2032 HOBBY
STATED PRINT RUN 50 SER.#'d SETS
EXCHANGE DEADLINE 4/30/2022

2020 Topps '85 Topps All Stars Autographs Red

*RED: .6X TO 1.5X BASIC
STATED ODDS 1:3216 HOBBY
STATED PRINT RUN 25 SER.#'d SETS
SER.1 EXCH DEADLINE 12/31/2021

2020 Topps '85 Topps All Stars Relics

STATED ODDS 1:74 HOBBY
85ASRAB Alex Bregman 2.50 6.00
85ASRAJ Aaron Judge 6.00 15.00
85ASRAP Albert Pujols 3.00 8.00
85ASRBL Barry Larkin 6.00 15.00
85ASRBP Buster Posey 3.00 8.00
85ASRCB Cody Bellinger 5.00 12.00
85ASRCF Carlton Fisk 6.00 15.00
85ASRCJ Chipper Jones 6.00 15.00
85ASRCK Clayton Kershaw 4.00 10.00
85ASRCR Cal Ripken Jr. 6.00 15.00
85ASRCY Christian Yelich 3.00 8.00
85ASRDM Don Mattingly 12.00 30.00
85ASRDO David Ortiz 4.00 10.00
85ASRDS Darryl Strawberry 6.00 15.00
85ASRDW David Wright 6.00 15.00
85ASRDWI Dave Winfield 4.00 10.00
85ASREM Eddie Murray 6.00 15.00
85ASRFL Francisco Lindor 2.50 6.00
85ASRFT Frank Thomas 4.00 10.00
85ASRGB George Brett 8.00 20.00
85ASRGS George Springer 2.00 5.00
85ASRGT Gleyber Torres 5.00 12.00
85ASRI Ichiro 3.00 8.00
85ASRJA Jose Altuve 2.00 5.00
85ASRJB Javier Baez 3.00 8.00
85ASRJM Joe Mauer 2.00 5.00
85ASRKB Kris Bryant 3.00 8.00
85ASRKG Ken Griffey Jr. 10.00 25.00
85ASRMC Miguel Cabrera 2.50 6.00
85ASRMM Mark McGwire 6.00 15.00
85ASRMS Max Scherzer 2.50 6.00
85ASRMT Masahiro Tanaka 6.00 15.00
85ASRMTR Mike Trout 10.00 25.00
85ASRNR Nolan Ryan 10.00 25.00
85ASROS Ozzie Smith 5.00 12.00
85ASRPA Pete Alonso 6.00 15.00
85ASRPM Paul Molitor
85ASRRA Ronald Acuna Jr. 6.00 15.00
85ASRRC Roger Clemens 5.00 12.00
85ASRRH Rickey Henderson 4.00 10.00
85ASRRS Ryne Sandberg 8.00 20.00
85ASRTG Tony Gwynn 4.00 10.00
85ASRWB Wade Boggs 5.00 12.00
85ASRWC Willson Contreras 2.50 6.00
85ASRWCL Will Clark 6.00 15.00
85ASRYM Yadier Molina 3.00 8.00

2020 Topps '85 Topps All Stars Relics Black

*BLACK: .6X TO 1.5X BASIC
STATED ODDS 1:193 HOBBY
STATED PRINT RUN 199 SER.#'d SETS
85ASRDG Dwight Gooden 6.00 15.00

2020 Topps '85 Topps All Stars Relics Gold

*GOLD: 1X TO 2.5X BASIC
STATED ODDS 1:1259 HOBBY
STATED PRINT RUN 50 SER.#'d SETS
85ASRDG Dwight Gooden 10.00 25.00
85ASRDMU Dale Murphy 10.00 25.00
85ASRJR Jim Rice 8.00 20.00
85ASRTR Tim Raines 5.00 12.00

2020 Topps '85 Topps All Stars Relics Red

*RED: 1.5X TO 4X BASIC
STATED ODDS 1:2517 HOBBY
STATED PRINT RUN 25 SER.#'d SETS
85ASRDG Dwight Gooden 15.00 40.00
85ASRDMU Dale Murphy 15.00 40.00
85ASRJR Jim Rice 12.00 30.00
85ASRTR Tim Raines 8.00 20.00

2020 Topps '85 Topps Autographs

SER.1 STATED ODDS 1:656 HOBBY
SER.2 STATED ODDS 1:591 HOBBY
SER.1 EXCH DEADLINE 12/31/2021
SER.2 EXCH DEADLINE 4/30/2022
85BAAKN Andrew Knizner S2 5.00 12.00
85BADJ Derek Jeter S2 EXCH 200.00 500.00
85BALA Luis Arraez S2 10.00 25.00
85BALTH Lane Thomas S2 5.00 12.00
85BAMBE Matt Beaty S2 3.00 8.00
85BAZP Zach Plesac S2 10.00 25.00
85AAA Adbert Alzolay S2 3.00 8.00
85AAAQ Aristides Aquino
85AAC Aaron Civale 5.00 12.00
85AAD Andre Dawson 20.00 50.00
85AAJ Aaron Judge EXCH 100.00 250.00
85AAJO Andruw Jones S2 12.00 30.00
85AAN Aaron Nola 6.00 15.00
85AAP A.J. Puk
85AARI Austin Riley 30.00 80.00
85AARZ Anthony Rizzo S2 20.00 50.00
85AAT Abraham Toro 3.00 8.00
85AAY Alex Young 2.50 6.00
85ABB Bo Bichette 150.00 400.00
85ABBE Brock Burke 2.50 6.00
85ABBU Byron Buxton S2 12.00 30.00
85ABHA Bryce Harper 125.00 300.00
85ABL Brandon Lowe S2 6.00 15.00
85ABM Brendan McKay S2 4.00 10.00
85ABO Bobby Bradley 2.50 6.00
85ACB Cavan Biggio 12.00 30.00
85ACC Carlos Carrasco S2 2.50 6.00
85ACF Carlton Fisk 25.00 60.00
85ACJ Chipper Jones S2 50.00 120.00
85ACK Carter Kieboom 10.00 25.00
85ACKE Clayton Kershaw 60.00 150.00
85ACP Chris Paddack S2 4.00 10.00
85ACR Cal Ripken Jr. 75.00 200.00
85ACY Christian Yelich S2 30.00 80.00
85ADC Dylan Cease 4.00 10.00
85ADE Dennis Eckersley 8.00 20.00
85ADH Dakota Hudson S2 3.00 8.00
85ADHA Darwinzon Hernandez S2 2.50 6.00
85ADJ Danny Jansen S2 2.50 6.00
85ADL DJ LeMahieu 25.00 60.00
85ADM Don Mattingly 50.00 120.00
85ADMA Dustin May 20.00 50.00
85ADMU Dale Murphy S2 12.00 30.00
85ADO David Ortiz 50.00 120.00
85ADPD Dustin Pedroia 20.00 50.00
85ADPE David Peralta S2 2.50 6.00
85ADS Dansby Swanson 12.00 30.00
85ADST Darryl Strawberry 30.00 80.00
85AEJ Eloy Jimenez 25.00 60.00
85AFT Fernando Tatis Jr. 100.00 250.00
85AFTH Frank Thomas 50.00 120.00
85AGC Gerrit Cole 30.00 80.00
85AGCA Griffin Canning S2 4.00 10.00
85AGL Gavin Lux 30.00 80.00
85AHA Hank Aaron 100.00 250.00
85AHH Hunter Harvey 6.00 15.00
85AHM Hideki Matsui 30.00 80.00
85AID Isan Diaz 6.00 15.00
85AJAA Jose Altuve 25.00 60.00
85AJB Jake Bauers S2 3.00 8.00
85AJBN Johnny Bench 25.00 60.00
85AJDA Jaylin Davis S2 4.00 10.00
85AJFE Junior Fernandez 2.50 6.00
85AJFR Jake Fraley S2 3.00 8.00
85AJL Jesus Luzardo S2 12.00 30.00
85AJMA J.D. Martinez S2 12.00 30.00
85AJR Jake Rogers 8.00 20.00
85AJRA Jose Ramirez S2 8.00 20.00
85AJRI Jim Rice S2 15.00 40.00
85AJS Juan Soto 50.00 120.00
85AJSM John Smoltz 40.00 100.00
85AJV Joey Votto 30.00 80.00
85AJVA Jason Varitek 20.00 50.00
85AJY Jordan Yamamoto 2.50 6.00
85AKB Kris Bryant S2 30.00 80.00
85AKHI Keston Hiura 12.00 30.00
85AKL Kyle Lewis 40.00 100.00
85AKT Kyle Tucker S2 8.00 20.00
85AKW Kerry Wood 10.00 25.00
85ALA Logan Allen 2.50 6.00
85ALB Lou Brock S2 30.00 80.00
85ALG Lourdes Gurriel Jr. S2 3.00 8.00
85ALM Lance McCullers Jr. 4.00 10.00
85ALR Luis Robert S2 100.00 250.00
85ALS Luis Severino S2 5.00 12.00
85ALW Logan Webb 4.00 10.00
85AMB Michel Baez S2 2.50 6.00
85AMCL Mike Clevinger 8.00 20.00
85AMD Mauricio Dubon S2 8.00 20.00
85AMG Mark Grace S2 30.00 80.00
85AM Mike Mussina S2 12.00 30.00
85AMMU Max Muncy 15.00 40.00
85AMR Mariano Rivera 100.00 250.00
85AMSO Mike Soroka 20.00 50.00
85AMT Mike Trout 300.00 600.00
85AMTH Matt Thaiss S2 5.00 12.00
85AMU Andres Munoz 4.00 10.00
85ANGA Nomar Garciaparra 25.00 60.00
85ANH Nico Hoerner 15.00 40.00
85ANR Nolan Ryan 100.00 250.00
85ANSE Nick Senzel S2 8.00 20.00
85ANSO Nick Solak 8.00 20.00
85AOS Ozzie Smith 40.00 100.00
85APAL Pete Alonso 40.00 100.00
85APS Patrick Sandoval 4.00 10.00
85ARAC Ronald Acuna Jr. 100.00 250.00
85ARAL Roberto Alomar 20.00 50.00
85ARCL Roger Clemens 75.00 200.00
85ARG Robel Garcia 6.00 15.00
85ARHO Rhys Hoskins S2 12.00 30.00
85ASB Shane Bieber S2 20.00 50.00
85ASB Seth Brown 2.50 6.00
85ASH Sam Hilliard 4.00 10.00
85ASM Sean Murphy 8.00 20.00
85ASO Shohei Ohtani 75.00 200.00
85ATA Tim Anderson 6.00 15.00
85ATB Trevor Bauer S2 8.00 20.00
85ATD Travis Demeritte 6.00 15.00
85ATG Trent Grisham S2 12.00 30.00
85ATG Tom Glavine 40.00 100.00
85ATJZ T.J. Zeuch S2 2.50 6.00
85ATTO Touki Toussaint S2 3.00 8.00
85AVG Vladimir Guerrero Jr. 40.00 100.00
85AVGJ Vladimir Guerrero S2 12.00 30.00
85AWB Wade Boggs 30.00 80.00
85AWBU Walker Buehler S2 40.00 100.00
85AWCA Willi Castro S2 10.00 25.00
85AWCO Willson Contreras 15.00 40.00
85AXB Xander Bogaerts 25.00 60.00
85AYA Yordan Alvarez 75.00 200.00

2020 Topps '85 Topps Autographs Black

*BLACK: .5X TO 1.2X BASIC
SER.1 STATED ODDS 1:1927 HOBBY
SER.2 STATED ODDS 1:765 HOBBY
PRINT RUNS B/WN 112-199 COPIES PER
SER.1 EXCH DEADLINE 12/31/2021
SER.2 EXCH DEADLINE 4/30/2022
85AAP A.J. Puk/199 15.00 40.00
85AJRA Jose Ramirez S2 12.00 30.00

2020 Topps '85 Topps Autographs Gold

*GOLD: .6X TO 1.5X BASIC
SER.1 STATED ODDS 1:6360 HOBBY
SER.2 STATED ODDS 1:2032 HOBBY
STATED PRINT RUN 50 SER.#'d SETS
SER.1 EXCH DEADLINE 12/31/2021
SER.2 EXCH DEADLINE 4/30/2022
85AAAQ Aristides Aquino/50 50.00 120.00
85ACF Carlton Fisk/50 30.00 80.00
85ADM Don Mattingly/50 60.00 150.00
85ADPD Dustin Pedroia/50 30.00 80.00
85AGC Gerrit Cole/50 40.00 100.00
85AHM Hideki Matsui/50 40.00 100.00
85AJRA Jose Ramirez S2 15.00 40.00
85AJS Juan Soto/50 60.00 150.00
85AJSM John Smoltz/50 60.00 150.00
85AJVA Jason Varitek/50 25.00 60.00
85ANGA Nomar Garciaparra/50 50.00 120.00
85AOS Ozzie Smith/50 60.00 150.00
85ARAC Ronald Acuna Jr./50 125.00 300.00
85ARAL Roberto Alomar/47 25.00 60.00
85AWCO Willson Contreras/50 25.00 60.00
85AXB Xander Bogaerts/50 30.00 80.00

2020 Topps '85 Topps Autographs Red

*RED: .75X TO 2X BASIC
SER.1 STATED ODDS 1:805 HOBBY
SER.2 STATED ODDS 1:3216 HOBBY
PRINT RUNS B/WN 21-25 COPIES PER
SER.1 EXCH DEADLINE 12/31/2021
SER.2 EXCH DEADLINE 4/30/2022
85AAAQ Aristides Aquino/25 60.00 150.00
85ABHA Bryce Harper/25 150.00 400.00
85ACF Carlton Fisk/25 40.00 100.00
85ACKE Clayton Kershaw/25 75.00 200.00
85ACR Cal Ripken Jr./25 150.00 400.00
85ADM Don Mattingly/25 75.00 200.00
85ADO David Ortiz/25 60.00 150.00
85ADPD Dustin Pedroia/25 40.00 100.00
85AGC Gerrit Cole/25 50.00 120.00
85AHA Hank Aaron/25 125.00 300.00
85AHM Hideki Matsui/25 50.00 120.00
85AJRA Jose Ramirez S2 20.00 50.00
85AJS Juan Soto/25 150.00 400.00
85AJSM John Smoltz/25 75.00 200.00
85AJVA Jason Varitek/25 30.00 80.00
85AMR Mariano Rivera/25 125.00 300.00
85AMT Mike Trout/25 40.00 800.00
85ANGA Nomar Garciaparra/25 60.00 150.00
85ANR Nolan Ryan/25 125.00 300.00
85AOS Ozzie Smith/24 75.00 200.00
85ARAC Ronald Acuna Jr./25 150.00 400.00
85ARAL Roberto Alomar/21 30.00 80.00
85ARCL Roger Clemens/25 100.00 250.00
85ASO Shohei Ohtani/25 100.00 250.00
85AWB Wade Boggs/25 40.00 100.00
85AWCO Willson Contreras/25 30.00 80.00
85AXB Xander Bogaerts/25 40.00 100.00

2020 Topps '85 Topps Relics

SER.1 STATED ODDS 1:49 HOBBY
SER.2 STATED ODDS 1:74 HOBBY
85RAB Alex Bregman 2.50 6.00
85RAJ Aaron Judge 6.00 15.00
85RAP Albert Pujols 3.00 8.00
85RBH Bryce Harper 6.00 15.00
85RBL Barry Larkin 6.00 15.00
85RBP Buster Posey 3.00 8.00
85RCB Charlie Blackmon 2.50 6.00
85RCBE Cody Bellinger 5.00 12.00
85RCR Cal Ripken Jr. 6.00 15.00
85RDM Don Mattingly 12.00 30.00
85REM Eddie Murray 6.00 15.00
85RFF Freddie Freeman 3.00 8.00
85RFL Francisco Lindor 2.50 6.00
85RFT Fernando Tatis Jr. 8.00 20.00
85RFTH Frank Thomas 4.00 10.00
85RGB George Brett 8.00 20.00
85RGS George Springer 2.00 5.00
85RGT Gleyber Torres 5.00 12.00
85RHR Hyun-Jin Ryu 2.00 5.00
85RJBZ Javier Baez 3.00 8.00
85RJS Juan Soto 8.00 20.00
85RKB Kris Bryant 3.00 8.00
85RKG Ken Griffey Jr. 10.00 25.00
85RKH Keston Hiura 3.00 8.00
85RMC Miguel Cabrera 4.00 10.00
85RMK Max Kepler 2.00 5.00
85RMM Manny Machado 2.50 6.00
85RMMG Mark McGwire 6.00 15.00
85RMS Max Scherzer 4.00 10.00
85RMT Mike Trout 10.00 25.00
85RNA Nolan Arenado 4.00 10.00
85RNR Nolan Ryan 10.00 25.00
85ROS Ozzie Smith 5.00 12.00
85RPA Pete Alonso 6.00 15.00
85RPG Paul Goldschmidt 4.00 10.00
85RRA Ronald Acuna Jr. 6.00 15.00
85RRC Roger Clemens 5.00 12.00
85RRD Rafael Devers 3.00 8.00
85RRH Rickey Henderson 4.00 10.00
85RRHO Rhys Hoskins 4.00 10.00
85RRJ Reggie Jackson 6.00 15.00
85RRS Ryne Sandberg 8.00 20.00
85RRY Robin Yount 5.00 12.00
85RTG Tony Gwynn 4.00 10.00
85RVG Vladimir Guerrero Jr. 4.00 10.00
85RWB Wade Boggs 5.00 12.00
85RWC Will Clark 6.00 15.00
85RWM Whit Merrifield 2.50 6.00
85RXB Xander Bogaerts 2.50 6.00
85TRAJ Aaron Judge S2 6.00 15.00
85TRAM Andrew McCutchen S2 2.50 6.00
85TRAN Aaron Nola S2 2.00 5.00
85TRAR Anthony Rizzo S2 3.00 8.00
85TRBB Bo Bichette S2 12.00 30.00
85TRCK Clayton Kershaw S2 4.00 10.00
85TRCP Chris Paddack S2 2.50 6.00
85TRCS Corey Seager S2 2.50 6.00
85TRCSA Chris Sale S2 2.50 6.00
85TRCSO Carlos Santana S2 2.00 5.00
85TRCY Christian Yelich S2 3.00 8.00
85TRDV Dan Vogelbach S2 1.50 4.00
85TREA Elvis Andrus S2 2.00 5.00
85TRES Eugenio Suarez S2 2.00 5.00
85TRGS Gary Sanchez S2 2.50 6.00
85TRGSA Giancarlo Stanton S2 2.50 6.00
85TRJA Jose Altuve S2 2.00 5.00
85TRJd Jacob deGrom S2 4.00 10.00
85TRJF Jack Flaherty S2 2.50 6.00
85TRJG Joey Gallo S2 2.50 6.00
85TRJM J.D. Martinez S2 2.50 6.00
85TRJR J.T. Realmuto S2 2.50 6.00
85TRJS Jorge Soler S2 2.50 6.00
85TRJV Joey Votto S2 4.00 10.00
85TRJVE Justin Verlander S2 2.50 6.00
85TRKS Kyle Schwarber S2 2.50 6.00
85TRLC Lorenzo Cain S2 1.50 4.00
85TRLG Lourdes Gurriel Jr. S2 2.00 5.00
85TRLS Luis Severino S2 2.00 5.00
85TRMCO Michael Conforto S2 2.00 5.00
85TRMO Matt Olson S2 2.50 6.00
85TRMS Marcus Semien S2 2.50 6.00
85TRMSA Miguel Sano S2 2.00 5.00
85TRMT Mike Trout S2 10.00 25.00
85TRNS Noah Syndergaard S2 2.00 5.00
85TROA Ozzie Albies S2 2.50 6.00
85TRPD Paul DeJong S2 2.50 6.00
85TRRA Ronald Acuna Jr. S2 6.00 15.00
85TRRC Robinson Cano S2 2.00 5.00
85TRSB Shane Bieber S2 2.50 6.00
85TRSG Sonny Gray S2 2.00 5.00
85TRSO Shohei Ohtani S2 6.00 15.00
85TRSS Stephen Strasburg S2 2.50 6.00
85TRTS Trevor Story S2 2.50 6.00
85TRWB Walker Buehler S2 3.00 8.00
85TRYA Yordan Alvarez S2 10.00 25.00
85TRYM Yadier Molina S2 4.00 10.00

2020 Topps '85 Topps Relics Black

*BLACK: .6X TO 1.5X BASIC
SER.1 STATED ODDS 1:717 HOBBY
SER.2 STATED ODDS 1:193 HOBBY
STATED PRINT RUN 199 SER.#'d SETS
85RMB Mookie Betts 8.00 20.00
85TRER Eddie Rosario S2 3.00 8.00
85TRMY Mike Yastrzemski S2 6.00 15.00

2020 Topps '85 Topps Relics Gold

*GOLD: 1X TO 2.5X BASIC
SER.1 STATED ODDS 1:2856 HOBBY
SER.2 STATED ODDS 1:1259 HOBBY
STATED PRINT RUN 50 SER.#'d SETS
85RMB Mookie Betts 12.00 30.00
85TRER Eddie Rosario S2 5.00 12.00
85TRMY Mike Yastrzemski S2 10.00 25.00
85TRSB Shane Bieber S2 6.00 15.00

2020 Topps '85 Topps Relics Red

*RED: 1.5X TO 4X BASIC
SER.1 STATED ODDS 1:5701 HOBBY
SER.2 STATED ODDS 1:2517 HOBBY
STATED PRINT RUN 25 SER.#'d SETS
85RMB Mookie Betts 20.00 50.00
85TRBB Bo Bichette S2 40.00 100.00
85TRER Eddie Rosario S2 8.00 20.00
85TRMY Mike Yastrzemski S2 15.00 40.00
85TRSB Shane Bieber S2 10.00 25.00

2020 Topps '85 Topps Silver Pack Chrome

85C1 Mike Trout 5.00 12.00
85C2 Shohei Ohtani 1.50 4.00
85C3 Ronald Acuna Jr. 4.00 10.00
85C4 Cal Ripken Jr. 3.00 8.00
85C5 Rafael Devers 1.25 3.00
85C6 Nico Hoerner 2.50 6.00
85C7 Mookie Betts 2.00 5.00
85C8 Kris Bryant 1.25 3.00
85C9 Ryne Sandberg 2.00 5.00
85C10 Dylan Cease 1.00 2.50
85C11 Frank Thomas 1.00 2.50
85C12 Francisco Lindor 1.00 2.50
85C13 Nolan Arenado 1.50 4.00
85C14 Jose Altuve .75 2.00
85C15 Nolan Ryan 3.00 8.00
85C16 Yordan Alvarez 6.00 15.00
85C17 Whit Merrifield 1.00 2.50
85C18 Clayton Kershaw 1.50 4.00
85C19 Dustin May 2.00 5.00
85C20 Jordan Yamamoto .60 1.50
85C21 Christian Yelich 1.25 3.00
85C22 Keston Hiura 1.25 3.00
85C23 Max Kepler .75 2.00
85C24 Darryl Strawberry .60 1.50
85C25 Jacob deGrom 2.00 5.00
85C26 Pete Alonso 2.50 6.00
85C27 Aaron Judge 2.50 6.00
85C28 Don Mattingly 3.00 8.00
85C29 Gleyber Torres 2.00 5.00
85C30 Mark McGwire 1.50 4.00
85C31 Bryce Harper 1.50 4.00
85C32 Manny Machado 1.00 2.50
85C33 Fernando Tatis Jr. 5.00 12.00
85C34 Sean Murphy 1.00 2.50
85C35 Will Clark 2.50 6.00
85C36 Ichiro 1.25 3.00
85C37 Ken Griffey Jr. 3.00 8.00
85C38 Paul Goldschmidt 1.00 2.50
85C39 Kyle Lewis 5.00 12.00
85C40 Brendan McKay 1.00 2.50
85C41 Bo Bichette 5.00 12.00
85C42 Vladimir Guerrero Jr. 1.50 4.00
85C43 Juan Soto 3.00 8.00
85C44 Matt Thaiss .75 2.00
85C45 Zac Gallen 1.50 4.00
85C46 Aristides Aquino 1.50 4.00
85C47 Robel Garcia .60 1.50
85C48 Gavin Lux 3.00 8.00
85C49 Jesus Luzardo 1.25 3.00
85C50 Trent Grisham 2.50 6.00

2020 Topps '85 Topps Silver Pack Chrome Black Refractors

*BLACK REF: .75X TO 2X BASIC
RANDOM INSERTS IN PACKS
STATED PRINT RUN 199 SER.#'d SETS
85C16 Yordan Alvarez 12.00 30.00
85C41 Bo Bichette 15.00 40.00
85C48 Gavin Lux 15.00 40.00

2020 Topps '85 Topps Silver Pack Chrome Blue Refractors

*BLUE REF: 1X TO 2.5X BASIC
RANDOM INSERTS IN PACKS
STATED PRINT RUN 150 SER.#'d SETS
85C16 Yordan Alvarez 15.00 40.00
85C41 Bo Bichette 20.00 50.00
85C48 Gavin Lux 20.00 50.00

2020 Topps '85 Topps Silver Pack Chrome Gold Refractors

*GOLD REF: 2.5X TO 6X BASIC
RANDOM INSERTS IN PACKS
STATED PRINT RUN 50 SER.#'d SETS
85C1 Mike Trout 40.00 100.00
85C16 Yordan Alvarez 40.00 100.00
85C37 Ken Griffey Jr. 30.00 80.00
85C41 Bo Bichette 50.00 120.00
85C48 Gavin Lux 50.00 120.00

2020 Topps '85 Topps Silver Pack Chrome Green Refractors

*GREEN REF: 1.2X TO 3X BASIC
RANDOM INSERTS IN PACKS
STATED PRINT RUN 99 SER.#'d SETS
85C16 Yordan Alvarez 20.00 50.00
85C41 Bo Bichette 25.00 60.00
85C48 Gavin Lux 25.00 60.00

2020 Topps '85 Topps Silver Pack Chrome Orange Refractors

*ORANGE REF: 4X TO 10X BASIC
RANDOM INSERTS IN PACKS
STATED PRINT RUN 25 SER.#'d SETS
85C1 Mike Trout 60.00 150.00
85C16 Yordan Alvarez 60.00 150.00
85C37 Ken Griffey Jr. 50.00 120.00
85C41 Bo Bichette 75.00 200.00
85C48 Gavin Lux 75.00 200.00

2020 Topps '85 Topps Silver Pack Chrome Purple Refractors

*PURPLE REF: 1.2X TO 3X BASIC
RANDOM INSERTS IN PACKS
STATED PRINT RUN 75 SER.#'d SETS
85C16 Yordan Alvarez 20.00 50.00
85C41 Bo Bichette 25.00 60.00
85C48 Gavin Lux 25.00 60.00

2020 Topps '85 Topps Silver Pack Chrome Series 2

85TC1 Ketel Marte .75 2.00
85TC2 Shogo Akiyama 1.00 2.50
85TC3 Chipper Jones 1.00 2.50
85TC4 Ozzie Albies 1.00 2.50
85TC5 Hunter Harvey 1.00 2.50
85TC6 Xander Bogaerts 1.00 2.50
85TC7 Adbert Alzolay .75 2.00
85TC8 Anthony Rizzo 1.25 3.00
85TC9 Javier Baez 1.25 3.00
85TC10 Eloy Jimenez 2.00 5.00
85TC11 Zack Collins .75 2.00
85TC12 Joey Votto 1.00 2.50
85TC13 Aaron Civale 1.25 3.00
85TC14 Kwang-Hyun Kim 1.25 3.00
85TC15 Sam Hilliard 1.00 2.50
85TC16 Jake Rogers .60 1.50
85TC17 Alex Bregman 1.00 2.50
85TC18 Justin Verlander 1.00 2.50
85TC19 Abraham Toro .75 2.00
85TC20 Jose Urquidy .75 2.00
85TC21 George Brett 2.00 5.00
85TC22 Jorge Soler 1.00 2.50
85TC23 Cody Bellinger 2.00 5.00
85TC24 Isan Diaz 1.00 2.50
85TC25 Robin Yount 1.00 2.50
85TC26 Noah Syndergaard .75 2.00
85TC27 Shun Yamaguchi .75 2.00
85TC28 Masahiro Tanaka 1.00 2.50
85TC29 A.J. Puk 1.00 2.50
85TC30 Sheldon Neuse .75 2.00
85TC31 Matt Chapman 1.00 2.50
85TC32 Rickey Henderson 1.00 2.50
85TC33 Roberto Clemente 2.50 6.00
85TC34 Tony Gwynn 1.00 2.50
85TC35 Giancarlo Stanton 1.00 2.50
85TC36 Mauricio Dubon .75 2.00
85TC37 Jaylin Davis 1.00 2.50
85TC38 Buster Posey 1.25 3.00
85TC39 Justin Dunn .75 2.00
85TC40 Randy Johnson 1.00 2.50
85TC41 Randy Arozarena 5.00 12.00
85TC42 Yadier Molina 1.25 3.00
85TC43 Brandon Lowe .75 2.00
85TC44 Nick Solak 2.50 6.00
85TC45 Josh Rojas .60 1.50
85TC46 Danny Mendick .75 2.00
85TC47 Anthony Kay .60 1.50
85TC48 Luis Robert 20.00 50.00
85TC49 Carter Kieboom .75 2.00
85TC50 Max Scherzer 1.00 2.50

2020 Topps '85 Topps Silver Pack Chrome Series 2 Black Refractors

*BLACK REF: .75X TO 2X BASIC
RANDOM INSERTS IN PACKS
STATED PRINT RUN 199 SER.#'d SETS
85TC2 Shogo Akiyama 10.00 25.00
85TC3 Chipper Jones 5.00 12.00
85TC21 George Brett 6.00 15.00
85TC32 Rickey Henderson 8.00 20.00
85TC33 Roberto Clemente 8.00 20.00
85TC34 Tony Gwynn 6.00 15.00
85TC38 Buster Posey 3.00 8.00

2020 Topps '85 Topps Silver Pack Chrome Series 2 Blue Refractors

*BLUE REF: 1X TO 2.5X BASIC
RANDOM INSERTS IN PACKS
STATED PRINT RUN 150 SER.#'d SETS
85TC2 Shogo Akiyama 12.00 30.00
85TC3 Chipper Jones 6.00 15.00
85TC21 George Brett 8.00 20.00
85TC32 Rickey Henderson 10.00 25.00
85TC33 Roberto Clemente 10.00 25.00
85TC34 Tony Gwynn 8.00 20.00
85TC38 Buster Posey 4.00 10.00

2020 Topps '85 Topps Silver Pack Chrome Series 2 Gold Refractors

*GOLD REF: 2.5X TO 6X BASIC
RANDOM INSERTS IN PACKS
STATED PRINT RUN 50 SER.#'d SETS
85TC2 Shogo Akiyama 30.00 80.00
85TC3 Chipper Jones 15.00 40.00
85TC21 George Brett 20.00 50.00
85TC32 Rickey Henderson 25.00 60.00
85TC33 Roberto Clemente 25.00 60.00
85TC34 Tony Gwynn 20.00 50.00
85TC38 Buster Posey 10.00 25.00
85TC48 Luis Robert 150.00 400.00

2020 Topps '85 Topps Silver Pack Chrome Series 2 Green Refractors

*GREEN REF: 1.2X TO 3X BASIC
RANDOM INSERTS IN PACKS
STATED PRINT RUN 99 SER.#'d SETS
85TC2 Shogo Akiyama 15.00 40.00
85TC3 Chipper Jones 8.00 20.00
85TC21 George Brett 10.00 25.00
85TC32 Rickey Henderson 12.00 30.00
85TC33 Roberto Clemente 12.00 30.00
85TC34 Tony Gwynn 10.00 25.00
85TC38 Buster Posey 5.00 12.00
85TC48 Luis Robert 75.00 200.00

2020 Topps '85 Topps Silver Pack Chrome Series 2 Orange Refractors

*ORANGE REF: 4X TO 10X BASIC
RANDOM INSERTS IN PACKS
STATED PRINT RUN 25 SER.#'d SETS
85TC2 Shogo Akiyama 50.00 120.00
85TC3 Chipper Jones 25.00 60.00
85TC21 George Brett 30.00 80.00
85TC32 Rickey Henderson 40.00 100.00
85TC33 Roberto Clemente 40.00 100.00
85TC34 Tony Gwynn 30.00 80.00
85TC38 Buster Posey 15.00 40.00
85TC48 Luis Robert 250.00 600.00

2020 Topps '85 Topps Silver Pack Chrome Series 2 Purple Refractors

*PURPLE REF: 1.2X TO 3X BASIC
RANDOM INSERTS IN PACKS
STATED PRINT RUN 75 SER.#'d SETS
85TC2 Shogo Akiyama 15.00 40.00
85TC3 Chipper Jones 8.00 20.00
85TC21 George Brett 10.00 25.00
85TC32 Rickey Henderson 12.00 30.00
85TC33 Roberto Clemente 12.00 30.00
85TC34 Tony Gwynn 10.00 25.00
85TC38 Buster Posey 5.00 12.00
85TC48 Luis Robert 75.00 200.00

2020 Topps '85 Topps Silver Pack Chrome Autographs

RANDOM INSERTS IN SILVER PACKS
PRINT RUNS B/WN 10-299 COPIES PER
NO PRICING ON QTY 15 OR LESS
85C3 Ronald Acuna Jr./30 200.00 500.00
85C5 Rafael Devers/30 25.00 60.00
85C6 Nico Hoerner/299 15.00 40.00
85C10 Dylan Cease/299 5.00 12.00
85C16 Yordan Alvarez/199 50.00 120.00
85C17 Whit Merrifield/50 12.00 30.00
85C19 Dustin May/299 25.00 60.00
85C20 Jordan Yamamoto/199 3.00 8.00
85C22 Keston Hiura/50
85C23 Max Kepler/30 15.00 40.00
85C24 Darryl Strawberry/30 20.00 50.00
85C25 Jacob deGrom/30 50.00 120.00
85C26 Pete Alonso/30 50.00 120.00
85C27 Aaron Judge
85C33 Fernando Tatis Jr./30 100.00 250.00
85C34 Sean Murphy/299 8.00 20.00
85C39 Kyle Lewis/299 25.00 60.00
85C40 Brendan McKay/199 10.00 25.00
85C41 Bo Bichette/199 100.00 250.00
85C42 Vladimir Guerrero Jr./30 40.00 100.00
85C43 Juan Soto/30 150.00 400.00
85C44 Matt Thaiss/299 4.00 10.00
85C46 Aristides Aquino/299 20.00 50.00
85C47 Robel Garcia/299 3.00 8.00
85C48 Gavin Lux/199 40.00 100.00
85C49 Jesus Luzardo/299 15.00 40.00
85C50 Trent Grisham/299 20.00 50.00

2020 Topps '85 Topps Silver Pack Chrome Autographs Orange Refractors

*ORANGE/25: .75X TO 2X p/r 199-299
*ORANGE/25: .6X TO 1.5X p/r 50
*ORANGE/25: .5X TO 1.2X p/r 30
RANDOM INSERTS IN SILVER PACKS
STATED PRINT RUN 25 SER.#'d SETS
85C6 Nico Hoerner 60.00 150.00
85C10 Dylan Cease 30.00 80.00
85C16 Yordan Alvarez 150.00 400.00
85C22 Keston Hiura 30.00 80.00
85C33 Fernando Tatis Jr. 200.00 500.00
85C41 Bo Bichette 400.00 800.00
85C48 Gavin Lux 125.00 300.00

2020 Topps '85 Topps Silver Pack Chrome Series 2 Autographs

RANDOM INSERTS IN SILVER PACKS
PRINT RUNS B/WN 25-199 COPIES PER
85TC2 Shogo Akiyama/149 8.00 20.00
85TC3 Chipper Jones/25 100.00 250.00
85TC5 Hunter Harvey/199 5.00 12.00
85TC6 Xander Bogaerts/35
85TC7 Adbert Alzolay/199 4.00 10.00
85TC8 Anthony Rizzo/25 25.00 60.00
85TC10 Eloy Jimenez/30 40.00 100.00
85TC11 Zack Collins/199 4.00 10.00
85TC12 Joey Votto/25 40.00 100.00
85TC13 Aaron Civale/199 6.00 15.00
85TC14 Kwang-Hyun Kim/99 8.00 20.00
85TC15 Sam Hilliard/199 12.00 30.00
85TC16 Jake Rogers/199 3.00 8.00
85TC19 Abraham Toro/199 4.00 10.00
85TC20 Jose Urquidy/99 5.00 12.00
85TC24 Isan Diaz/199 5.00 12.00
85TC25 Robin Yount/25 40.00 100.00
85TC26 Noah Syndergaard/35
85TC27 Shun Yamaguchi/99 5.00 12.00
85TC28 Masahiro Tanaka/25
85TC30 Sheldon Neuse/199 4.00 10.00
85TC32 Rickey Henderson/25 50.00 120.00
85TC36 Mauricio Dubon/199 4.00 10.00
85TC37 Jaylin Davis/199 6.00 15.00
85TC38 Buster Posey/25
85TC39 Justin Dunn/199 4.00 10.00
85TC40 Randy Johnson/25 60.00 150.00
85TC41 Randy Arozarena/199 75.00 200.00
85TC44 Nick Solak/199 15.00 40.00
85TC46 Danny Mendick/199 4.00 10.00
85TC47 Anthony Kay/199 3.00 8.00
85TC48 Luis Robert/149 150.00 400.00

2020 Topps '85 Topps Silver Pack Chrome Series 2 Autographs Orange Refractors

*ORANGE/25: .75X TO 2X p/r 149-199
*ORANGE/25: .6X TO 1.5X p/r 99
*ORANGE/25: .5X TO 1.2X p/r 30-35
RANDOM INSERTS IN SILVER PACKS
STATED PRINT RUN 25 SER.#'d SETS
85TC48 Luis Robert 400.00 800.00

2020 Topps 2030

COMPLETE SET (20) 12.00 30.00
STATED ODDS 1:6 HOBBY
T20301 Mike Trout 1.50 4.00
T20302 Aaron Judge .75 2.00
T20303 Luis Robert 6.00 15.00
T20304 Francisco Lindor .30 .75
T20305 Christian Yelich .40 1.00
T20306 Gavin Lux 1.00 2.50
T20307 Ronald Acuna Jr. 1.25 3.00
T20308 Bo Bichette 4.00 10.00
T20309 Kris Bryant .40 1.00
T203010 Nolan Arenado .50 1.25
T203011 Pete Alonso .75 2.00

T203012 Juan Soto 1.00 2.50
T203013 Fernando Tatis Jr. 1.50 4.00
T203014 Bryce Harper .50 1.25
T203015 Alex Bregman .30 .75
T203016 Mookie Betts .60 1.50
T203017 Cody Bellinger .60 1.50
T203018 Vladimir Guerrero Jr. .50 1.25
T203019 Javier Baez .40 1.00
T203020 Shohei Ohtani .50 1.25

2020 Topps Baseball Stars Autographs

STATED ODDS 1:580 HOBBY
EXCHANGE DEADLINE 12/31/2021
*BLACK/199: .5X TO 1.2X BASIC
*GOLD/50: .6X TO 1.5X BASIC
*RED/25: .75X TO 2X BASIC
BSAAA Adbert Alzolay 3.00 8.00
BSAAAQ Aristides Aquino 15.00 40.00
BSAAC Aaron Civale 5.00 12.00
BSAAM Andres Munoz
BSAAN Austin Nola 4.00 10.00
BSAAR Austin Riley 15.00 40.00
BSAARI Anthony Rizzo 20.00 50.00
BSAAT Abraham Toro 3.00 8.00
BSABA Bryan Abreu 2.50 6.00
BSABB Bobby Bradley 2.50 6.00
BSABBU Brock Burke 2.50 6.00
BSABO Bo Bichette 60.00 150.00
BSABR Bryan Reynolds 3.00 8.00
BSACD Corey Dickerson 3.00 8.00
BSACF Cecil Fielder 15.00 40.00
BSACH Cesar Hernandez 2.50 6.00
BSACK Clayton Kershaw
BSACKE Clayton Kershaw
BSACP Chris Paddack 12.00 30.00
BSACW Christian Walker 3.00 8.00
BSACY Christian Yelich
BSADF David Fletcher 8.00 20.00
BSADM Daniel Mengden 2.50 6.00
BSADM Dustin May 12.00 30.00
BSADME Danny Mendick 3.00 8.00
BSADPD Daniel Ponce de Leon 2.50 6.00
BSADR Dereck Rodriguez 2.50 6.00
BSADSR Darryl Strawberry 20.00 50.00
BSAEE Eduardo Escobar 2.50 6.00
BSAFP Freddy Peralta 2.50 6.00
BSAFT Fernando Tatis Jr. 60.00 150.00
BSAFT Frank Thomas 30.00 80.00
BSAGH Garrett Hampson 2.50 6.00
BSAGL Gavin Lux 40.00 100.00
BSAGL Gavin Lux 40.00 100.00
BSAGS George Springer 8.00 20.00
BSAGU Gio Urshela 12.00 30.00
BSAHH Hunter Harvey
BSAHR Harold Ramirez 2.50 6.00
BSAID Isan Diaz 4.00 10.00
BSAJB Jake Bauers 3.00 8.00
BSAJD Jaylin Davis
BSAJDU Justin Dunn 3.00 8.00
BSAJF Junior Fernandez
BSAJF Jack Flaherty 10.00 25.00
BSAJRA Jose Ramirez 8.00 20.00
BSAJFR Jake Fraley 3.00 8.00
BSAJJ Josh James 2.50 6.00
BSAJL Jesus Luzardo 10.00 25.00
BSAJM Jordan Montgomery 4.00 10.00
BSAJR Jake Rogers 5.00 12.00
BSAJSM John Smoltz 12.00 30.00
BSAJSO Juan Soto 40.00 100.00
BSAJST Josh Staumont
BSAJY Jordan Yamamoto 2.50 6.00
BSAKB Kris Bryant 50.00 120.00
BSAKB Kris Bryant
BSAKGJ Ken Griffey Jr. 100.00 250.00
BSAKH Keston Hiura 10.00 25.00
BSAKK Kwang-Hyun Kim 10.00 25.00
BSAKL Kyle Lewis 30.00 80.00
BSALA Logan Allen 2.50 6.00
BSALAR Luis Arraez 10.00 25.00
BSALGJ Lourdes Gurriel Jr. 3.00 8.00
BSALMJ Lance McCullers Jr. 2.50 6.00
BSALR Luis Robert 100.00 250.00
BSALTH Lewis Thorpe
BSAMB Michael Brosseau 5.00 12.00
BSAMC Michael Chavis 5.00 12.00
BSAMM Mitch Moreland 2.50 6.00
BSAMMA Manny Machado
BSAMMC Mark McGwire
BSAMO Matt Olson 8.00 20.00
BSAMS Max Scherzer 25.00 60.00
BSAMT Mike Trout 125.00 300.00
BSANA Nolan Arenado 40.00 100.00
BSANH Nico Hoerner 20.00 50.00
BSANH Nico Hoerner 20.00 50.00
BSANL Nate Lowe 6.00 15.00
BSANLA Aaron Nola 8.00 20.00
BSANS Noah Syndergaard 12.00 30.00
BSANSO Nick Solak 10.00 25.00
BSAPA Pete Alonso 30.00 80.00
BSAPG Paul Goldschmidt
BSARA Rogelio Armenteros 3.00 8.00
BSARAR Randy Arozarena 40.00 100.00
BSARF Rollie Fingers 6.00 15.00
BSARH Rhys Hoskins 10.00 25.00
BSARMC Ryan McMahon 4.00 10.00
BSARY Ryan Yarbrough 2.50 6.00
BSASA Shogo Akiyama 5.00 12.00
BSASB Seth Brown 2.50 6.00
BSASH Sam Hilliard
BSASL Shed Long
BSASM Sean Murphy 4.00 10.00
BSASMU Sean Murphy 4.00 10.00
BSASN Sheldon Neuse 3.00 8.00
BSASO Shohei Ohtani 75.00 200.00
BSASSC Shin-Soo Choo 10.00 25.00
BSASY Shun Yamaguchi 10.00 25.00
BSATA Tim Anderson 10.00 25.00
BSATB Trevor Bauer
BSATD Travis Demeritte
BSATE Tommy Edman 12.00 30.00
BSATG Tony Gonsolin 8.00 20.00
BSATG Trent Grisham 12.00 30.00
BSATK Tommy Kahnle
BSATM Tino Martinez 25.00 60.00
BSAVG Vladimir Guerrero Jr. EXCH 25.00 60.00
BSAVR Victor Robles 12.00 30.00
BSAWA Williams Astudillo 2.50 6.00
BSAWC Willson Contreras 8.00 20.00
BSAWM Whit Merrifield 6.00 15.00
BSAWS Will Smith 8.00 20.00
BSAYA Yordan Alvarez
BSAYA Yordan Alvarez 30.00 80.00
BSAYC Yu Chang 8.00 20.00

2020 Topps Best of Topps Now

COMPLETE SET (10) 5.00 12.00
STATED ODDS 1:18 HOBBY
BTN1 Juan Soto 1.00 2.50
BTN2 Howie Kendrick .20 .50
BTN3 Juan Soto 1.00 2.50
BTN4 Justin Verlander .30 .75
BTN5 Mike Trout 1.50 4.00
BTN6 Yordan Alvarez 2.00 5.00
Pete Alonso
BTN7 Anthony Rendon .30 .75
BTN8 Gerrit Cole .50 1.25
BTN9 Luis Robert 1.50 4.00
BTN10 Mookie Betts .60 1.50

2020 Topps Decade of Dominance

STATED ODDS 1:35 HOBBY
*BLUE: 1X TO 2.5X BASIC
*BLACK/299: 1.5X TO 4X BASIC
*GOLD/50: 3X TO 8X BASIC
DOD1 Babe Ruth 1.00 2.50
DOD2 Willie Mays .75 2.00
DOD3 Hank Aaron .75 2.00
DOD4 Mark McGwire .60 1.50
DOD5 Ken Griffey Jr. .75 2.00
DOD6 Roger Clemens .50 1.25
DOD7 Sandy Koufax .75 2.00
DOD8 Ty Cobb .60 1.50
DOD9 Mike Trout 2.00 5.00
DOD10 Lou Gehrig .75 2.00
DOD11 Tony Gwynn .40 1.00
DOD12 Ichiro .50 1.25
DOD13 Alex Rodriguez .50 1.25
DOD14 Randy Johnson .40 1.00
DOD15 Mariano Rivera .50 1.25
DOD16 Ted Williams .75 2.00
DOD17 Honus Wagner .40 1.00
DOD18 Nolan Ryan 1.25 3.00
DOD19 Rickey Henderson .40 1.00
DOD20 Johnny Bench .40 1.00

2020 Topps Decade's Next

STATED ODDS 1:24 HOBBY
*BLUE: 1X TO 2.5X BASIC
*BLACK/299: 1.2X TO 3X BASIC
*GOLD/50: 3X TO 8X BASIC
DN1 Vladimir Guerrero Jr. .50 1.25
DN2 Austin Riley .40 1.00
DN3 Fernando Tatis Jr. 1.50 4.00
DN4 Yordan Alvarez 2.00 5.00
DN5 Ronald Acuna Jr. 1.25 3.00
DN6 Gleyber Torres .60 1.50
DN7 Keston Hiura .40 1.00
DN8 Brendan Rodgers .30 .75
DN9 Eloy Jimenez .60 1.50
DN10 Gavin Lux 1.00 2.50
DN11 Pete Alonso .75 2.00
DN12 Juan Soto 1.00 2.50
DN13 Bo Bichette 1.50 4.00
DN14 Kyle Tucker .30 .75
DN15 Nick Senzel .30 .75
DN16 Ozzie Albies .30 .75
DN17 Walker Buehler .40 1.00
DN18 Rafael Devers .40 1.00
DN19 Cody Bellinger .60 1.50
DN20 Victor Robles .40 1.00
DN21 Lucas Giolito .25 .60
DN22 Nico Hoerner .75 2.00
DN23 Shohei Ohtani .50 1.25
DN24 Julio Urias .30 .75
DN25 Chris Paddack .30 .75
DN26 Brendan McKay .30 .75
DN27 Ramon Laureano .25 .60
DN28 Jesus Luzardo .40 1.00
DN29 Carter Kieboom .25 .60
DN30 Mike Soroka .30 .75

2020 Topps Decade's Next Autographs

STATED ODDS 1:23,284 HOBBY
PRINT RUNS B/WN 5-25 COPIES PER
NO PRICING ON QTY 5
EXCHANGE DEADLINE 12/31/2021
DN1 Vladimir Guerrero Jr./25 50.00 120.00
DN2 Austin Riley/25 25.00 60.00
DN3 Fernando Tatis Jr./25 75.00 200.00
DN4 Yordan Alvarez/25 100.00 250.00
DN5 Ronald Acuna Jr./25 100.00 250.00
DN6 Gleyber Torres/25 60.00 150.00
DN7 Keston Hiura/25 30.00 80.00
DN9 Eloy Jimenez/25 20.00 50.00
DN10 Gavin Lux/25 100.00 250.00
DN11 Pete Alonso/25 75.00 200.00
DN12 Juan Soto/25 75.00 200.00
DN13 Bo Bichette/25 100.00 250.00
DN14 Kyle Tucker/25 15.00 40.00
DN16 Ozzie Albies/25 20.00 50.00
DN18 Rafael Devers/25 25.00 60.00
DN20 Victor Robles/25 20.00 50.00
DN21 Lucas Giolito/25 10.00 25.00
DN22 Nico Hoerner/25 30.00 80.00
DN24 Julio Urias/25 15.00 40.00
DN25 Chris Paddack/25 15.00 40.00
DN26 Brendan McKay/25 25.00 60.00
DN27 Ramon Laureano/25 20.00 50.00
DN28 Jesus Luzardo/25 30.00 80.00
DN30 Mike Soroka/25 15.00 40.00

2020 Topps Decades' Best

STATED ODDS 1:7 HOBBY
*BLUE: 1X TO 2.5X BASIC
*CHROME: 1X TO 2.5X BASIC
*BLACK/299: 1.2X TO 3X BASIC
*GREEN: 1.5X TO 4X BASIC
*CHR.GOLD/50: 3X TO 8X BASIC
*GOLD/50: 3X TO 8X BASIC
DB1 Willie Mays .60 1.50
DB2 Ernie Banks .30 .75
DB3 Ernie Banks .30 .75
DB4 Hank Aaron .60 1.50
DB5 Warren Spahn .25 .60
DB6 Willie Mays .60 1.50
DB7 Frank Robinson .25 .60
DB8 Orlando Cepeda .25 .60
DB9 Luis Aparicio .25 .60
DB10 Phil Rizzuto .25 .60
DB11 Larry Doby .25 .60
DB12 Eddie Mathews .30 .75
DB13 Duke Snider .25 .60
DB14 Ted Williams .60 1.50
DB15 Stan Musial .50 1.25
DB16 Jackie Robinson .30 .75
DB17 Willie Mays .60 1.50
DB18 Monte Irvin .25 .60
DB19 Ralph Kiner .25 .60
DB20 Hank Aaron .60 1.50
DB21 Pittsburgh Pirates .20 .50
DB22 New York Yankees .30 .75
DB23 San Francisco Giants .30 .75
DB24 Los Angeles Dodgers .30 .75
DB25 St. Louis Cardinals .30 .75
DB26 Minnesota Twins .20 .50
DB27 Baltimore Orioles .20 .50
DB28 Cincinnati Reds .20 .50
DB29 Detroit Tigers .20 .50
DB30 New York Mets .30 .75
DB31 Bob Gibson .25 .60
DB32 Jim Palmer .25 .60
DB33 Tom Seaver .25 .60
DB34 Fergie Jenkins .25 .60
DB35 Catfish Hunter .25 .60
DB36 Steve Carlton .25 .60
DB37 Nolan Ryan 1.00 2.50
DB38 Bert Blyleven .25 .60
DB39 Don Sutton .25 .60
DB40 Phil Niekro .25 .60
DB41 Wade Boggs .25 .60
DB42 Don Mattingly .60 1.50
DB43 Ryne Sandberg .60 1.50
DB44 Cal Ripken Jr. 1.00 2.50
DB45 Darryl Strawberry .20 .50
DB46 Eddie Murray .25 .60
DB47 Dale Murphy .30 .75
DB48 George Brett .60 1.50
DB49 Robin Yount .30 .75
DB50 Andre Dawson .25 .60
DB51 Ken Griffey Jr. .60 1.50
DB52 Frank Thomas .30 .75
DB53 Sammy Sosa .30 .75
DB54 Mark McGwire .50 1.25
DB55 Jeff Bagwell .25 .60
DB56 Tony Gwynn .30 .75
DB57 Roberto Alomar .25 .60
DB58 Barry Larkin .25 .60
DB59 Chipper Jones .30 .75
DB60 Edgar Martinez .25 .60
DB61 Cal Ripken Jr. 1.00 2.50
DB62 Pedro Martinez .25 .60
DB63 Rickey Henderson .30 .75
DB64 Roger Clemens .40 1.00
DB65 Sammy Sosa .30 .75
DB66 Ken Griffey Jr. .60 1.50
DB67 Chipper Jones .30 .75
DB68 Jeff Bagwell .25 .60
DB69 Barry Larkin .25 .60
DB70 Frank Thomas .30 .75
DB71 Pedro Martinez .25 .60
DB72 Randy Johnson .30 .75
DB73 Andy Pettitte .25 .60
DB74 Roger Clemens .40 1.00
DB75 Mike Mussina .25 .60
DB76 Mariano Rivera .40 1.00
DB77 Tom Glavine .25 .60
DB78 John Smoltz .30 .75
DB79 CC Sabathia .25 .60
DB80 Roy Oswalt .25 .60
DB81 Boston Red Sox .30 .75
DB82 New York Yankees .30 .75
DB83 Chicago Cubs .30 .75
DB84 Houston Astros .20 .50
DB85 Los Angeles Dodgers .30 .75
DB86 Cleveland Indians .20 .50
DB87 San Francisco Giants .30 .75
DB88 St. Louis Cardinals .30 .75
DB89 Texas Rangers .20 .50
DB90 Kansas City Royals .20 .50
DB91 Miguel Cabrera .30 .75
DB92 Shohei Ohtani .50 1.25
DB93 Mike Trout 1.50 4.00
DB94 Kris Bryant .40 1.00
DB95 Jacob DeGrom .60 1.50
DB96 Bryce Harper .50 1.25
DB97 Max Scherzer .30 .75
DB98 Felix Hernandez .25 .60
DB99 Mookie Betts .60 1.50
DB100 Aaron Judge .75 2.00

2020 Topps Decades' Best Series 2

STATED ODDS 1:7 HOBBY
*BLUE: 1X TO 2.5X BASIC
*CHROME: 1X TO 2.5X BASIC
*BLACK/299: 1.2X TO 3X BASIC
*GREEN: 1.5X TO 4X BASIC
*CHR.GOLD/50: 3X TO 8X BASIC
*GOLD/50: 3X TO 8X BASIC
DB1 Detroit Tigers .20 .50
DB2 Philadelphia Phillies .20 .50
DB3 St. Louis Cardinals .20 .50
DB4 Boston Red Sox .20 .50
DB5 New York Giants .20 .50
DB6 New York Yankees .20 .50
DB7 Brooklyn Dodgers .20 .50
DB8 Milwaukee Braves .20 .50
DB9 Cleveland Indians .20 .50
DB10 Chicago White Sox .20 .50
DB11 Whitey Ford .25 .60
DB12 Juan Marichal .25 .60
DB13 Jim Bunning .25 .60
DB14 Bob Gibson .25 .60
DB15 Sandy Koufax .60 1.50
DB16 Warren Spahn .25 .60
DB17 Hoyt Wilhelm .25 .60
DB18 Fergie Jenkins .25 .60
DB19 Phil Niekro .25 .60
DB20 Don Sutton .25 .60
DB21 Hank Aaron .60 1.50
DB22 Frank Robinson .25 .60
DB23 Brooks Robinson .25 .60
DB24 Carl Yastrzemski .50 1.25
DB25 Harmon Killebrew .30 .75
DB26 Willie Mays .60 1.50
DB27 Willie McCovey .25 .60
DB28 Orlando Cepeda .25 .60
DB29 Roberto Clemente .75 2.00
DB30 Roger Maris .30 .75
DB31 Eddie Murray .25 .60
DB32 Carlton Fisk .25 .60
DB33 Andre Dawson .25 .60
DB34 Johnny Bench .30 .75
DB35 Joe Morgan .25 .60
DB36 Rod Carew .25 .60
DB37 Steve Carlton .25 .60
DB38 Tom Seaver .25 .60
DB39 Jim Palmer .25 .60
DB40 Catfish Hunter .25 .60
DB41 Johnny Bench .30 .75
DB42 Jim Rice .25 .60
DB43 Willie Stargell .25 .60
DB44 Rod Carew .25 .60
DB45 Joe Morgan .25 .60
DB46 Reggie Jackson .25 .60
DB47 Mike Schmidt .50 1.25
DB48 Willie McCovey .25 .60
DB49 George Foster .20 .50
DB50 Hank Aaron .60 1.50
DB51 New York Yankees .20 .50
DB52 Oakland Athletics .20 .50
DB53 St. Louis Cardinals .20 .50
DB54 Detroit Tigers .20 .50
DB55 New York Mets .20 .50
DB56 Kansas City Royals .20 .50
DB57 Los Angeles Dodgers .20 .50
DB58 Philadelphia Phillies 5.00 12.00
DB59 Minnesota Twins .20 .50
DB60 Baltimore Orioles .20 .50
DB61 Bert Blyleven .25 .60
DB62 Steve Carlton .25 .60
DB63 Dwight Gooden .20 .50
DB64 Roger Clemens .40 1.00
DB65 Nolan Ryan 1.00 2.50
DB66 Jack Morris .25 .60
DB67 Rollie Fingers .25 .60
DB68 Goose Gossage .25 .60
DB69 Bruce Sutter .25 .60
DB70 Dennis Eckersley .25 .60
DB71 Houston Astros .20 .50
DB72 Montreal Expos .20 .50
DB73 Cleveland Indians .20 .50
DB74 Atlanta Braves .20 .50
DB75 New York Yankees .20 .50
DB76 Toronto Blue Jays .20 .50
DB77 Cincinnati Reds .20 .50
DB78 Pittsburgh Pirates .20 .50
DB79 Texas Rangers .20 .50
DB80 Boston Red Sox .20 .50
DB81 Albert Pujols .40 1.00
DB82 Joe Mauer .25 .60
DB83 Ryan Howard .25 .60
DB84 Alex Rodriguez .40 1.00
DB85 Ichiro .40 1.00
DB86 Albert Pujols .40 1.00
DB87 Randy Johnson .30 .75
DB88 Tim Lincecum .25 .60
DB89 Barry Zito .25 .60
DB90 Pedro Martinez .25 .60
DB91 Justin Verlander .30 .75
DB92 Clayton Kershaw .50 1.25
DB93 Max Scherzer .30 .75
DB94 Stephen Strasburg .30 .75
DB95 Felix Hernandez .25 .60
DB96 Chris Sale .30 .75
DB97 Zack Greinke .30 .75
DB98 Jacob deGrom .60 1.50
DB99 Corey Kluber .25 .60
DB100 Jon Lester .25 .60

2020 Topps Decades' Best Autographs

SER.1 STATED ODDS 1:25,440 HOBBY
SER.2 STATED ODDS 1:8808 HOBBY
PRINT RUNS B/WN 5-25 COPIES PER
NO PRICING ON QTY 15 OR LESS
SER.1 EXCH DEADLINE 12/31/2021
SER.2 EXCH DEADLINE 4/30/2022
DB12 Juan Marichal S2 30.00 80.00
DB14 Bob Gibson/25 S2 30.00 80.00
DB20 Don Sutton/25 S2 20.00 50.00
DB28 Orlando Cepeda/25 S2 25.00 60.00
DB32 Carlton Fisk/25 S2 25.00 60.00
DB33 Andre Dawson/25 S2 15.00 40.00
DB37 Steve Carlton/25 S2 25.00 60.00
DB38 Bert Blyleven/25 15.00 40.00
DB39 Don Sutton/25 20.00 50.00
DB42 Jim Rice/25 S2 25.00 60.00
DB45 Darryl Strawberry/25 30.00 80.00
DB47 Dale Murphy/25 30.00 80.00
DB49 George Foster/25 S2 20.00 50.00
DB50 Andre Dawson/25 15.00 40.00
DB57 Roberto Alomar/25 40.00 100.00
DB58 Barry Larkin/25 25.00 60.00
DB60 Edgar Martinez/25 25.00 60.00
DB61 Bert Blyleven/25 S2 15.00 40.00
DB62 Steve Carlton/25 S2 25.00 60.00
DB63 Dwight Gooden/25 S2 25.00 60.00
DB66 Jack Morris/25 S2 30.00 80.00
DB66 Ken Griffey Jr.
DB67 Rollie Fingers/25 S2 15.00 40.00
DB68 Goose Gossage/25 S2 25.00 60.00
DB69 Bruce Sutter/25 S2 10.00 25.00
DB70 Dennis Eckersley/25 S2 15.00 40.00
DB83 Ryan Howard/25 S2 30.00 80.00
DB88 Tim Lincecum/25 S2 60.00 150.00
DB89 Barry Zito/25 S2 15.00 40.00
DB92 Clayton Kershaw S2
DB93 Max Scherzer/25 S2 40.00 100.00
DB95 Jacob DeGrom/25 30.00 80.00
DB96 Chris Sale/25 S2 25.00 60.00
DB97 Max Scherzer/25 40.00 100.00
DB98 Jacob deGrom/25 S2 30.00 80.00
DB99 Corey Kluber/25 S2 20.00 50.00

2020 Topps Draft Day Medallions

STATED ODDS 1:739 HOBBY
*BLACK/50: .75X TO 2X BASIC
*GOLD/25: 1X TO 2.5X BASIC
DDMAB Alex Bregman 2.00 5.00
DDMABE Andrew Benintendi 2.00 5.00
DDMAJ Aaron Judge 5.00 12.00
DDMAR Anthony Rizzo 2.50 6.00
DDMARE Anthony Rendon 2.00 5.00
DDMBB Byron Buxton 2.00 5.00
DDMBBI Bo Bichette 4.00 10.00
DDMBH Bryce Harper 5.00 12.00
DDMBR Brendan Rodgers 2.00 5.00
DDMCB Cody Bellinger 4.00 10.00
DDMCC Carlos Correa 2.00 5.00
DDMCK Clayton Kershaw 3.00 8.00
DDMCKI Carter Kieboom 1.50 4.00
DDMCS Corey Seager 2.00 5.00
DDMCSA Chris Sale 2.00 5.00
DDMCY Christian Yelich 2.50 6.00
DDMDS Dansby Swanson 2.00 5.00
DDMEL Evan Longoria 1.50 4.00
DDMFF Freddie Freeman 2.50 6.00
DDMFL Francisco Lindor 2.00 5.00
DDMGC Gerrit Cole 3.00 8.00
DDMGL Gavin Lux 6.00 15.00
DDMGS Giancarlo Stanton 2.00 5.00
DDMGSA George Springer 1.50 4.00
DDMJB Javier Baez 3.00 8.00
DDMJD Josh Donaldson 1.50 4.00
DDMJdG Jacob deGrom 4.00 10.00
DDMJF Jack Flaherty 2.00 5.00
DDMKB Kris Bryant 2.50 6.00
DDMKL Kyle Lewis 10.00 25.00
DDMKS Kyle Schwarber 2.00 5.00
DDMLG Lucas Giolito 1.50 4.00
DDMMB Mookie Betts 3.00 8.00
DDMMC Michael Conforto 1.50 4.00
DDMMCH Matt Chapman 2.00 5.00
DDMMM Manny Machado 2.00 5.00
DDMMS Max Scherzer 2.00 5.00
DDMMSO Mike Soroka 2.00 5.00
DDMMT Mike Trout 10.00 25.00
DDMNA Nolan Arenado 3.00 8.00
DDMNS Nick Senzel 2.00 5.00
DDMPA Pete Alonso 5.00 12.00
DDMPG Paul Goldschmidt 2.00 5.00
DDMRH Rhys Hoskins 2.50 6.00
DDMSS Stephen Strasburg 2.00 5.00
DDMTA Tim Anderson 2.00 5.00
DDMTL Tim Lincecum 1.50 4.00
DDMTS Trevor Story 2.00 5.00
DDMTT Trea Turner 1.50 4.00
DDMWB Walker Buehler 2.50 6.00

2020 Topps Empire State Award Winners Pete Alonso

COMMON CARD .60 1.50
RANDOM INSERTS IN PACKS
*BLUE: 1.2X TO 3X BASIC
*BLACK/299: 1.5X TO 4X BASIC
*GOLD/50: 3X TO 8X BASIC
*RED/10: 8X TO 20X BASIC

2020 Topps Empire State Award Winners Pete Alonso Autographs

COMMON CARD 75.00 200.00
RANDOM INSERTS IN PACKS
STATED PRINT RUN 5 SER.#'d SETS
EXCHANGE DEADLINE 4/30/2022

2020 Topps Fernando Tatis Jr. Highlights

COMPLETE SET (30) 15.00 40.00
STATED ODDS 1:4 GRAVITY
*BLUE: 1.2X TO 3X BASIC
*BLACK/299: 1.5X TO 4X BASIC
*GOLD/50: 3X TO 8X BASIC
*RED/10: 8X TO 20X BASIC
FTH1 Fernando Tatis Jr. 1.50 4.00
FTH2 Fernando Tatis Jr. 1.50 4.00
FTH3 Fernando Tatis Jr. 1.50 4.00
FTH4 Fernando Tatis Jr. 1.50 4.00
FTH5 Fernando Tatis Jr. 1.50 4.00
FTH6 Fernando Tatis Jr. 1.50 4.00
FTH7 Fernando Tatis Jr. 1.50 4.00
FTH8 Fernando Tatis Jr. 1.50 4.00
FTH9 Fernando Tatis Jr. 1.50 4.00
FTH10 Fernando Tatis Jr. 1.50 4.00
FTH11 Fernando Tatis Jr. 1.50 4.00
FTH12 Fernando Tatis Jr. 1.50 4.00
FTH13 Fernando Tatis Jr. 1.50 4.00
FTH14 Fernando Tatis Jr. 1.50 4.00
FTH15 Fernando Tatis Jr. 1.50 4.00
FTH16 Fernando Tatis Jr. 1.50 4.00
FTH17 Fernando Tatis Jr. 1.50 4.00
FTH18 Fernando Tatis Jr. 1.50 4.00
FTH19 Fernando Tatis Jr. 1.50 4.00
FTH20 Fernando Tatis Jr. 1.50 4.00
FTH21 Fernando Tatis Jr. 1.50 4.00
FTH22 Fernando Tatis Jr. 1.50 4.00
FTH23 Fernando Tatis Jr. 1.50 4.00
FTH24 Fernando Tatis Jr. 1.50 4.00
FTH25 Fernando Tatis Jr. 1.50 4.00
FTH26 Fernando Tatis Jr. 1.50 4.00
FTH27 Fernando Tatis Jr. 1.50 4.00
FTH28 Fernando Tatis Jr. 1.50 4.00
FTH29 Fernando Tatis Jr. 1.50 4.00
FTH30 Fernando Tatis Jr. 1.50 4.00

2020 Topps Fernando Tatis Jr. Highlights Autographs

STATED ODDS 1:5410 GRAVITY
STATED PRINT RUN 5 SER.#'d SETS
EXCHANGE DEADLINE 4/30/2022
FTJHA1 Fernando Tatis Jr. 125.00 300.00
FTJHA2 Fernando Tatis Jr. 125.00 300.00
FTJHA3 Fernando Tatis Jr. 125.00 300.00
FTJHA4 Fernando Tatis Jr. 125.00 300.00
FTJHA5 Fernando Tatis Jr. 125.00 300.00
FTJHA6 Fernando Tatis Jr. 125.00 300.00
FTJHA7 Fernando Tatis Jr. 125.00 300.00
FTJHA8 Fernando Tatis Jr. 125.00 300.00
FTJHA9 Fernando Tatis Jr. 125.00 300.00
FTJHA10 Fernando Tatis Jr. 125.00 300.00
FTJHA11 Fernando Tatis Jr. 125.00 300.00
FTJHA12 Fernando Tatis Jr. 125.00 300.00
FTJHA13 Fernando Tatis Jr. 125.00 300.00
FTJHA14 Fernando Tatis Jr. 125.00 300.00
FTJHA15 Fernando Tatis Jr. 125.00 300.00
FTJHA16 Fernando Tatis Jr. 125.00 300.00
FTJHA17 Fernando Tatis Jr. 125.00 300.00
FTJHA18 Fernando Tatis Jr. 125.00 300.00
FTJHA19 Fernando Tatis Jr. 125.00 300.00
FTJHA20 Fernando Tatis Jr. 125.00 300.00
FTJHA21 Fernando Tatis Jr. 125.00 300.00
FTJHA22 Fernando Tatis Jr. 125.00 300.00
FTJHA23 Fernando Tatis Jr. 125.00 300.00
FTJHA24 Fernando Tatis Jr. 125.00 300.00
FTJHA25 Fernando Tatis Jr. 125.00 300.00
FTJHA26 Fernando Tatis Jr. 125.00 300.00
FTJHA27 Fernando Tatis Jr. 125.00 300.00
FTJHA28 Fernando Tatis Jr. 125.00 300.00
FTJHA29 Fernando Tatis Jr. 125.00 300.00
FTJHA30 Fernando Tatis Jr. 125.00 300.00

2020 Topps Global Game Medallions

STATED ODDS 1:2213 HOBBY
*BLACK/149: .5X TO 1.2X BASIC
*GOLD/50: .6X TO 1.5X BASIC
GGMAB Alex Bregman 2.50 6.00
GGMAC Aroldis Chapman 2.50 6.00
GGMAJ Aaron Judge 6.00 15.00
GGMAP Albert Pujols 3.00 8.00
GGMAV Alex Verdugo 2.00 5.00
GGMBH Bryce Harper 4.00 10.00
GGMBP Buster Posey 3.00 8.00
GGMCB Cody Bellinger 5.00 12.00
GGMCC Carlos Correa 4.00 10.00
GGMCK Clayton Kershaw 4.00 10.00
GGMCY Christian Yelich 3.00 8.00
GGMDG Didi Gregorius 2.00 5.00
GGMDO David Ortiz 2.50 6.00
GGMEJ Eloy Jimenez 5.00 12.00
GGMFF Freddie Freeman 3.00 8.00
GGMFL Francisco Lindor 2.50 6.00
GGMGS Gary Sanchez 2.50 6.00
GGMGT Gleyber Torres 5.00 12.00
GGMHM Hideki Matsui 2.50 6.00
GGMI Ichiro 5.00 12.00
GGMJA Jose Altuve 2.00 5.00
GGMJB Javier Baez 3.00 8.00
GGMJS Juan Soto 8.00 20.00
GGMJT Jameson Taillon 2.00 5.00
GGMJU Julio Urias 2.50 6.00
GGMJV Joey Votto 2.50 6.00
GGMKB Kris Bryant 3.00 8.00
GGMKD Khris Davis 2.50 6.00
GGMKG Ken Griffey Jr. 6.00 15.00
GGMLU Luis Urias 2.00 5.00
GGMMA Masahiro Tanaka 2.50 6.00
GGMMB Mookie Betts 5.00 12.00
GGMMC Miguel Cabrera 2.50 6.00
GGMMM Manny Machado 2.50 6.00
GGMMT Mike Trout 12.00 30.00
GGMOA Ozzie Albies 2.50 6.00
GGMRA Ronald Acuna Jr. 10.00 25.00
GGMRC Roberto Clemente 10.00 25.00
GGMRD Rafael Devers 3.00 8.00
GGMRO Robinson Cano 2.00 5.00
GGMSO Shohei Ohtani 5.00 12.00
GGMVG Vladimir Guerrero Jr. 4.00 10.00
GGMWC Willson Contreras 2.50 6.00
GGMXB Xander Bogaerts 2.50 6.00
GGMYA Yordan Alvarez 8.00 20.00
GGMYD Yu Darvish 2.50 6.00
GGMYG Yasmani Grandal 1.50 4.00
GGMYM Yadier Molina 3.00 8.00
GGMYO Yoan Moncada 2.50 6.00
GGMYP Yasiel Puig 2.50 6.00

2020 Topps Home Run Challenge Code Cards

STATED ODDS 1:24 HOBBY
HRC1 Bryce Harper 1.25 3.00
HRC2 Ronald Acuna Jr. 3.00 8.00
HRC3 J.D. Martinez .75 2.00
HRC4 Freddie Freeman 1.00 2.50
HRC5 Mookie Betts 1.50 4.00
HRC6 Nolan Arenado 1.25 3.00
HRC7 Javier Baez 1.00 2.50
HRC8 Kris Bryant 1.00 2.50
HRC9 Anthony Rizzo 1.00 2.50
HRC10 Francisco Lindor .75 2.00
HRC11 Aaron Judge 2.00 5.00
HRC12 Giancarlo Stanton .75 2.00
HRC13 Vladimir Guerrero Jr. 1.25 3.00
HRC14 George Springer .60 1.50
HRC15 Juan Soto 2.50 6.00
HRC16 Joey Gallo .75 2.00
HRC17 Paul Goldschmidt .75 2.00
HRC18 Manny Machado .75 2.00
HRC19 Fernando Tatis Jr. 4.00 10.00
HRC20 Josh Bell .60 1.50
HRC21 Pete Alonso 2.00 5.00
HRC22 Gleyber Torres 1.50 4.00
HRC23 Christian Yelich 1.00 2.50
HRC24 Mike Trout 4.00 10.00
HRC25 Cody Bellinger 1.50 4.00
HRC26 Alex Bregman .75 2.00
HRC27 Yordan Alvarez 5.00 12.00
HRC28 Max Kepler .60 1.50
HRC29 Max Muncy .60 1.50
HRC30 Rhys Hoskins 1.00 2.50

2020 Topps Home Run Challenge Code Cards Series 2

STATED ODDS 1:24 HOBBY
HRC1 Bryce Harper .75 2.00
HRC2 Ronald Acuna Jr. 2.00 5.00
HRC3 J.D. Martinez .50 1.25
HRC4 Freddie Freeman .60 1.50
HRC5 Mookie Betts 1.00 2.50
HRC6 Nolan Arenado .75 2.00
HRC7 Javier Baez .60 1.50
HRC8 Kris Bryant .60 1.50
HRC9 Anthony Rizzo .60 1.50
HRC10 Francisco Lindor .50 1.25
HRC11 Aaron Judge 1.25 3.00
HRC12 Giancarlo Stanton .50 1.25
HRC13 Vladimir Guerrero Jr. .75 2.00
HRC14 George Springer .40 1.00
HRC15 Juan Soto 1.50 4.00
HRC16 Joey Gallo .50 1.25
HRC17 Paul Goldschmidt .50 1.25
HRC18 Manny Machado .50 1.25
HRC19 Fernando Tatis Jr. 2.50 6.00
HRC20 Josh Bell .40 1.00
HRC21 Pete Alonso 1.25 3.00
HRC22 Gleyber Torres 1.00 2.50
HRC23 Christian Yelich .60 1.50
HRC24 Mike Trout 2.50 6.00
HRC25 Cody Bellinger 1.00 2.50
HRC26 Alex Bregman .50 1.25
HRC27 Yordan Alvarez 3.00 8.00
HRC28 Max Kepler .40 1.00
HRC29 Max Muncy .40 1.00
HRC30 Rhys Hoskins .60 1.50

2020 Topps Jumbo Jersey Sleeve Patches

STATED ODDS 1:1963 HOBBY
*BLACK/149: .5X TO 1.2X BASIC
*GOLD/50: .75X TO 2X BASIC
JJSPAA Aristides Aquino 12.00 30.00
JJSPABR Alex Bregman 3.00 8.00
JJSPAM Adalberto Mondesi 2.50 6.00
JJSPAP Albert Pujols 4.00 10.00
JJSPARI Anthony Rizzo 10.00 25.00
JJSPBH Bryce Harper 5.00 12.00
JJSPBM Brendan McKay 4.00 10.00
JJSPBP Buster Posey 4.00 10.00
JJSPBS Blake Snell 2.50 6.00
JJSPCB Cody Bellinger 5.00 12.00
JJSPCK Clayton Kershaw 6.00 15.00
JJSPDV Daniel Vogelbach 2.00 5.00
JJSPEA Elvis Andrus 2.50 6.00
JJSPEJ Eloy Jimenez 6.00 15.00
JJSPFF Freddie Freeman 4.00 10.00
JJSPJB Javier Baez 6.00 15.00
JJSPJBE Josh Bell 2.50 6.00
JJSPJD Jacob deGrom 5.00 12.00
JJSPJG Joey Gallo 3.00 8.00
JJSPJL Jesus Luzardo 4.00 10.00
JJSPJS Juan Soto 10.00 25.00
JJSPJV Justin Verlander 3.00 8.00
JJSPJVO Joey Votto 3.00 8.00
JJSPJY Jordan Yamamoto 2.00 5.00
JJSPKB Kris Bryant 6.00 15.00
JJSPKL Kyle Lewis 15.00 40.00
JJSPKM Ketel Marte 2.50 6.00
JJSPMB Mookie Betts 4.00 10.00
JJSPMC Matt Chapman 3.00 8.00
JJSPMK Max Kepler 2.50 6.00
JJSPMS Max Scherzer 3.00 8.00
JJSPMT Mike Trout 15.00 40.00
JJSPNA Nolan Arenado 5.00 12.00
JJSPOA Ozzie Albies 3.00 8.00
JJSPPA Pete Alonso 10.00 25.00
JJSPRA Ronald Acuna Jr. 10.00 25.00
JJSPRD Rafael Devers 4.00 10.00
JJSPRH Rhys Hoskins 4.00 10.00
JJSPSO Shohei Ohtani 10.00 25.00
JJSPTM Trey Mancini 3.00 8.00
JJSPTS Trevor Story 3.00 8.00
JJSPWB Walker Buehler 4.00 10.00
JJSPWM Whit Merrifield 3.00 8.00
JJSPXB Xander Bogaerts 3.00 8.00
JJSPYA Yordan Alvarez 12.00 30.00
JJSPZG Zac Gallen 5.00 12.00

2020 Topps Major League Material Autographs

SER.1 STATED ODDS 1:8,326 HOBBY
SER.2 STATED ODDS 1:2583 HOBBY
PRINT RUNS B/WN 8-50 COPIES PER
NO PRICING ON QTY 8
SER.1 EXCH DEADLINE 12/31/2021
SER.2 EXCH DEADLINE 4/30/2022
MJMABB Bo Bichette/50 S2 50.00 120.00
MJMABS Blake Snell/50 S2 8.00 20.00
MJMABZ Barry Zito S2
MJMACB Cavan Biggio/50 S2 12.00 30.00
MJMACC Carlos Carrasco S2
MJMACF Clint Frazier/50 S2 8.00 20.00
MJMADL DJ LeMahieu/50 S2 30.00 80.00
MJMADW David Wright/25 S2 20.00 50.00
MJMAEJ Eloy Jimenez/50 S2 20.00 50.00
MJMAFT Fernando Tatis Jr./25 S2 125.00 300.00
MJMAGL Gavin Lux/50 S2 50.00 120.00
MJMAJR J.T. Realmuto/50 S2 15.00 40.00
MJMAJS Juan Soto/25 S2 60.00 150.00
MJMAKH Kyle Hendricks/50 S2 12.00 30.00
MJMAKY Kirby Yates/50 S2 6.00 15.00
MJMALM Lance McCullers Jr./50 S2 10.00 25.00
MJMAMC Michael Chavis/50 S2 8.00 20.00
MJMAMG Mitch Garver/50 S2 10.00 25.00
MJMAMM Miles Mikolas/21 S2 8.00 20.00
MJMAMMU Max Muncy/50 S2 8.00 20.00
MJMAMT Mike Trout/25 S2 250.00 600.00
MJMAMV Mo Vaughn/25 S2 30.00 80.00
MJMAMY Mike Yastrzemski/50 S2 15.00 40.00
MJMANH Nico Hoerner/50 S2 25.00 60.00
MJMANS Nick Solak/50 S2 12.00 30.00
MJMANSE Nick Senzel/50 S2 10.00 25.00
MJMANSY Noah Syndergaard/25 S2 15.00 40.00
MJMAPA Pete Alonso/25 S2 50.00 120.00
MJMAPC Patrick Corbin/50 S2 8.00 20.00
MJMARA Ronald Acuna Jr./25 S2 125.00 300.00
MJMARD Rafael Devers/25 S2 30.00 80.00
MJMARH Ryan Howard/50 S2 12.00 30.00
MJMARHO Rhys Hoskins/25 S2 25.00 60.00
MJMASB Shane Bieber/50 S2 15.00 40.00
MJMASC Shin-Soo Choo/50 S2 15.00 40.00
MJMASM Sean Murphy/50 S2 10.00 25.00
MJMATLI Tim Lincecum/50 S2 30.00 80.00
MJMAVG Vladimir Guerrero Jr./25 S2 30.00 80.00
MJMAWC Willson Contreras/50 S2 12.00 30.00
MJMAWCL Will Clark/25 S2 40.00 100.00
MJMAXB Xander Bogaerts S2 10.00 25.00
MLMAAN Aaron Nola/50 15.00 40.00
MLMAAR Austin Riley/50 25.00 60.00
MLMABL Brandon Lowe/50 10.00 25.00
MLMABM Brendan McKay/50 10.00 25.00
MLMABR Brendan Rodgers/50 10.00 25.00
MLMACCS CC Sabathia/30 25.00 60.00
MLMACP Chris Paddack/50 10.00 25.00
MLMACY Christian Yelich/30 30.00 80.00
MLMAFR Franmil Reyes/50 6.00 15.00
MLMAFTJ Fernando Tatis Jr./50 100.00 250.00
MLMAGT Gleyber Torres/30 40.00 100.00
MLMAGU Gio Urshela/50 25.00 60.00
MLMAJA Jose Altuve/30 15.00 40.00
MLMAJB Jose Berrios/50 8.00 20.00
MLMAJDM J.D. Martinez/50 10.00 25.00
MLMAJF Jack Flaherty/50 15.00 40.00
MLMAJS Juan Soto/50 50.00 120.00
MLMAJSH Justus Sheffield/50 10.00 25.00
MLMAKH Keston Hiura/50 15.00 40.00
MLMAKS Kyle Schwarber/50 15.00 40.00
MLMALGJ Lourdes Gurriel Jr./50 10.00 25.00
MLMALV Luke Voit/50 12.00 30.00
MLMAMCH Matt Chapman/50 10.00 25.00
MLMAMCL Mike Clevinger/50 12.00 30.00

MLMAMK Max Kepler/50 10.00 25.00
MLMAMS Max Scherzer/50 20.00 50.00
MLMAMSO Mike Soroka/50 10.00 25.00
MLMANA Nolan Arenado/30 30.00 80.00
MLMAPA Pete Alonso/50 40.00 100.00
MLMARAJ Ronald Acuna Jr./30 75.00 200.00
MLMARH Rhys Hoskins/50 20.00 50.00
MLMAVGJ Vladimir Guerrero Jr./50 25.00 60.00
MLMAVR Victor Robles/50 12.00 30.00
MLMAWA Willians Astudillo/50 10.00 25.00
MLMAYA Yordan Alvarez/50 60.00 150.00

2020 Topps Major League Material Autographs Red

*RED/25: .5X TO 1.2X BASIC
SER.1 STATED ODDS 1:14,932 HOBBY
SER.2 STATED ODDS 1:5341 HOBBY
PRINT RUNS B/WN 10-25 COPIES PER
NO PRICING ON QTY 10
SER.1 EXCH DEADLINE 12/31/2021
SER.2 EXCH DEADLINE 4/30/2022
MJMABZ Barry Zito/25 S2 10.00 25.00
MJMACC Carlos Carrasco/25 S2 15.00 40.00

2020 Topps Major League Materials

SER.1 STATED ODDS 1:136 HOBBY
SER.2 STATED ODDS 1:171 HOBBY
*BLACK/199: .5X TO 1.2X BASIC
*GOLD/50: .6X TO 1.5X BASIC
*RED/25: .75X TO 2X BASIC
MLMAA Aristides Aquino S2 4.00 10.00
MLMAB Alex Bregman S2 3.00 8.00
MLMAB Andrew Benintendi 3.00 8.00
MLMAJ Aaron Judge 8.00 20.00
MLMAM Austin Meadows 3.00 8.00
MLMAR Anthony Rizzo 4.00 10.00
MLMARI Austin Riley 4.00 10.00
MLMARO Amed Rosario 2.50 6.00
MLMBB Byron Buxton 3.00 8.00
MLMBH Bryce Harper S2 6.00 15.00
MLMBP Buster Posey 4.00 10.00
MLMBS Blake Snell 2.50 6.00
MLMCB Charlie Blackmon 3.00 8.00
MLMCBE Cody Bellinger 6.00 15.00
MLMCK Clayton Kershaw S2 5.00 12.00
MLMCP Chris Paddack S2 3.00 8.00
MLMCS CC Sabathia S2 2.50 6.00
MLMCS Corey Seager 3.00 8.00
MLMCSA Carlos Santana 2.50 6.00
MLMCY Christian Yelich S2 4.00 10.00
MLMDD David Dahl 2.00 5.00
MLMDG Didi Gregorius 2.50 6.00
MLMDO David Ortiz S2 5.00 12.00
MLMDS Dansby Swanson 3.00 8.00
MLMDV Daniel Vogelbach 2.00 5.00
MLMEA Elvis Andrus S2 2.50 6.00
MLMEJ Eloy Jimenez S2 6.00 15.00
MLMES Eugenio Suarez S2 2.50 6.00
MLMET Eric Thames 2.00 5.00
MLMFF Freddie Freeman 4.00 10.00
MLMFL Francisco Lindor 3.00 8.00
MLMFT Fernando Tatis Jr. S2 5.00 12.00
MLMGS George Springer 2.50 6.00
MLMGSA Gary Sanchez 3.00 8.00
MLMGT Gleyber Torres S2 5.00 12.00
MLMJA Jose Altuve 2.50 6.00
MLMJB Javier Baez S2 4.00 10.00
MLMJB Jose Berrios 2.50 6.00
MLMJF Jack Flaherty S2 3.00 8.00
MLMJG Joey Gallo 3.00 8.00
MLMJH Josh Hader 2.50 6.00
MLMJR J.T. Realmuto 3.00 8.00
MLMJS Jorge Soler S2 3.00 8.00
MLMJSO Juan Soto S2 5.00 12.00
MLMJV Justin Verlander S2 3.00 8.00
MLMJVO Joey Votto S2 3.00 8.00
MLMKB Kris Bryant S2 4.00 10.00
MLMKH Keston Hiura S2 4.00 10.00
MLMKW Kolten Wong S2 2.50 6.00
MLMLC Lorenzo Cain 2.00 5.00
MLMLG Lucas Giolito S2 2.50 6.00
MLMLG Lourdes Gurriel Jr. 2.50 6.00
MLMLV Luke Voit 4.00 10.00
MLMMB Matthew Boyd 2.00 5.00
MLMMC Miguel Cabrera S2 3.00 8.00
MLMMCO Michael Conforto 2.50 6.00
MLMMK Max Kepler S2 2.50 6.00
MLMMM Manny Machado S2 3.00 8.00
MLMMO Matt Olson S2 3.00 8.00
MLMMS Max Scherzer S2 3.00 8.00
MLMMSA Miguel Sano 2.50 6.00
MLMMSE Marcus Semien S2 3.00 8.00
MLMMT Mike Trout 12.00 30.00
MLMMTA Masahiro Tanaka S2 3.00 8.00
MLMMTR Mike Trout S2 12.00 30.00
MLMNA Nolan Arenado S2 5.00 12.00
MLMNC Nick Castellanos S2 3.00 8.00
MLMNS Nick Senzel 3.00 8.00
MLMNSY Noah Syndergaard 2.50 6.00
MLMOA Ozzie Albies 3.00 8.00
MLMPA Pete Alonso 8.00 20.00
MLMPD Paul DeJong 3.00 8.00
MLMPG Paul Goldschmidt S2 3.00 8.00
MLMRC Robinson Cano S2 2.50 6.00
MLMRH Rhys Hoskins S2 4.00 10.00
MLMSB Shane Bieber S2 3.00 8.00
MLMSG Sonny Gray 2.50 6.00
MLMSO Shohei Ohtani S2 5.00 12.00
MLMSS Stephen Strasburg 3.00 8.00
MLMTA Tim Anderson 3.00 8.00
MLMTM Trey Mancini 3.00 8.00
MLMTS Trevor Story 3.00 8.00
MLMTT Trea Turner 2.50 6.00
MLMVG Vladimir Guerrero Jr. S2 4.00 10.00
MLMWB Walker Buehler 4.00 10.00
MLMWC Willson Contreras 3.00 8.00
MLMWM Whit Merrifield 3.00 8.00
MLMXB Xander Bogaerts 3.00 8.00
MLMYM Yoan Moncada 3.00 8.00
MLMYM Yadier Molina S2 4.00 10.00

2020 Topps Player Medallions

ONE PER BLASTER
*BLACK/199: .6X TO 1.5X BASIC
*GOLD/50: 1X TO 2.5X BASIC
TPMAA Aristides Aquino 2.50 6.00
TPMAB Alex Bregman 1.50 4.00
TPMAJ Aaron Judge 4.00 10.00
TPMAR Anthony Rendon 1.50 4.00
TPMARZ Anthony Rizzo 2.00 5.00
TPMBB Bo Bichette 4.00 10.00
TPMBH Bryce Harper 2.50 6.00
TPMBM Brendan McKay 1.50 4.00
TPMBP Buster Posey 2.00 5.00
TPMCB Cody Bellinger 3.00 8.00
TPMCK Clayton Kershaw 2.50 6.00
TPMCY Christian Yelich 2.00 5.00
TPMEJ Eloy Jimenez 3.00 8.00
TPMFF Freddie Freeman 2.00 5.00
TPMFL Francisco Lindor 1.50 4.00
TPMFT Fernando Tatis Jr. 8.00 20.00
TPMGC Gerrit Cole 2.50 6.00
TPMGL Gavin Lux 4.00 10.00
TPMGT Gleyber Torres 3.00 8.00
TPMJA Jose Altuve 1.25 3.00
TPMJB Josh Bell 1.25 3.00
TPMJBA Javier Baez 2.00 5.00
TPMJd Jacob deGrom 3.00 8.00
TPMJG Joey Gallo 1.50 4.00
TPMJL Jesus Luzardo 2.00 5.00
TPMJS Juan Soto 5.00 12.00
TPMJV Justin Verlander 1.50 4.00
TPMKB Kris Bryant 2.00 5.00
TPMKH Keston Hiura 2.00 5.00
TPMKL Kyle Lewis 8.00 20.00
TPMKM Ketel Marte 1.25 3.00
TPMLR Luis Robert 8.00 20.00
TPMMB Mookie Betts 3.00 8.00
TPMMC Matt Chapman 1.50 4.00
TPMMCA Miguel Cabrera 1.50 4.00
TPMMK Max Kepler 1.25 3.00
TPMMS Max Scherzer 1.50 4.00
TPMMT Mike Trout 8.00 20.00
TPMNA Nolan Arenado 2.50 6.00
TPMPA Pete Alonso 4.00 10.00
TPMPG Paul Goldschmidt 1.50 4.00
TPMRA Ronald Acuna Jr. 5.00 12.00
TPMRD Rafael Devers 2.00 5.00
TPMRH Rhys Hoskins 2.00 5.00
TPMSO Shohei Ohtani 2.50 6.00
TPMTM Trey Mancini 1.50 4.00
TPMVG Vladimir Guerrero Jr. 2.50 6.00
TPMWM Whit Merrifield 1.50 4.00
TPMYA Yordan Alvarez 10.00 25.00
TPMYM Yadier Molina 2.00 5.00

2020 Topps Player of the Decade Mike Trout

STATED ODDS 1:32 HOBBY
*BLUE: 1X TO 2.5X BASIC
*BLACK/299: 1.2X TO 3X BASIC
*GOLD/50: 4X TO 10X BASIC
*RED/10: 6X TO 15X BASIC
MT1 Mike Trout 1.50 4.00
MT2 Mike Trout 1.50 4.00
MT3 Mike Trout 1.50 4.00
MT4 Mike Trout 1.50 4.00
MT5 Mike Trout 1.50 4.00
MT6 Mike Trout 1.50 4.00
MT7 Mike Trout 1.50 4.00
MT8 Mike Trout 1.50 4.00
MT9 Mike Trout 1.50 4.00
MT10 Mike Trout 1.50 4.00
MT11 Mike Trout 1.50 4.00
MT12 Mike Trout 1.50 4.00
MT13 Mike Trout 1.50 4.00
MT14 Mike Trout 1.50 4.00
MT15 Mike Trout 1.50 4.00
MT16 Mike Trout 1.50 4.00
MT17 Mike Trout 1.50 4.00
MT18 Mike Trout 1.50 4.00
MT19 Mike Trout 1.50 4.00
MT20 Mike Trout 1.50 4.00
MT21 Mike Trout 1.50 4.00
MT22 Mike Trout 1.50 4.00
MT23 Mike Trout 1.50 4.00
MT24 Mike Trout 1.50 4.00
MT25 Mike Trout 1.50 4.00

2020 Topps Postseason Performance Autograph Relics

STATED ODDS 1:57,238 HOBBY
PRINT RUNS B/WN 30-50 COPIES PER
EXCHANGE DEADLINE 12/31/2021
PPARDS Dansby Swanson/25 20.00 50.00
PPARGC Gerrit Cole/50 20.00 50.00
PPARGS George Springer/35 15.00 40.00
PPARJA Jose Altuve/35 20.00 50.00
PPARJF Jack Flaherty/50 15.00 40.00
PPARJP Joc Pederson/25 12.00 30.00
PPARMSO Mike Soroka/50 20.00 50.00
PPARPG Paul Goldschmidt/50 20.00 50.00
PPARRA Ronald Acuna Jr./25 75.00 200.00
PPARSD Sean Doolittle/50 12.00 30.00

2020 Topps Postseason Performance Autograph Relics Red

*RED/25: .5X TO 1.2X BASIC
STATED ODDS 1:57,238 HOBBY
PRINT RUNS B/WN 10-25 COPIES PER
NO PRICING ON QTY 10
EXCHANGE DEADLINE 12/31/2021
PPARBS Blake Snell/25 10.00 25.00
PPARMM Max Muncy/25 10.00 25.00

2020 Topps Postseason Performance Autographs

STATED ODDS 1:28,035 HOBBY
PRINT RUNS B/WN 25-50 COPIES PER
EXCHANGE DEADLINE 12/31/2021
*RED/25: .5X TO 1.2X BASIC
PPAAJ Aaron Judge
PPABS Blake Snell/50 8.00 20.00
PPADS Dansby Swanson/25 15.00 40.00
PPAGL Gavin Lux/25 30.00 80.00
PPAGS George Springer/25 15.00 40.00
PPAGT Gleyber Torres/25 40.00 100.00
PPAJA Jose Altuve/25 15.00 40.00
PPAJF Jack Flaherty/50 20.00 50.00
PPAJP Joc Pederson/25 10.00 25.00
PPAJS Juan Soto/25 50.00 120.00
PPAMM Max Muncy/50 8.00 20.00
PPAMS Max Scherzer/25 20.00 50.00
PPAMSO Mike Soroka/50 15.00 40.00
PPAOA Ozzie Albies
PPAPC Patrick Corbin/25 20.00 50.00
PPAPG Paul Goldschmidt/25 20.00 50.00
PPARA Ronald Acuna Jr./25 60.00 150.00
PPASD Sean Doolittle/50 12.00 30.00

2020 Topps Postseason Performance Relics

STATED ODDS 1:3606 HOBBY
STATED PRINT RUN 99 SER.#'d SETS
*RED/25: .75X TO 2X BASIC
PPRAB Alex Bregman 4.00 10.00
PPRAJ Aaron Judge 20.00 50.00
PPRAR Anthony Rendon 8.00 20.00
PPRCB Cody Bellinger 8.00 20.00
PPRCC Carlos Correa 4.00 10.00
PPRDS Dansby Swanson 5.00 12.00
PPRFF Freddie Freeman 8.00 20.00
PPRGC Gerrit Cole 6.00 15.00
PPRGS Giancarlo Stanton 4.00 10.00
PPRGSP George Springer 3.00 8.00
PPRJA Jose Altuve 3.00 8.00
PPRJF Jack Flaherty 4.00 10.00
PPRJP Joc Pederson 3.00 8.00
PPRJS Juan Soto 12.00 30.00
PPRJV Justin Verlander 4.00 10.00
PPRMS Max Scherzer 4.00 10.00
PPRMSO Mike Soroka 5.00 12.00
PPROA Ozzie Albies 4.00 10.00
PPRPC Patrick Corbin 3.00 8.00
PPRPG Paul Goldschmidt 4.00 10.00
PPRRA Ronald Acuna Jr. 10.00 25.00
PPRRZ Ryan Zimmerman 10.00 25.00
PPRSD Sean Doolittle 6.00 15.00
PPRSS Stephen Strasburg 6.00 15.00
PPRTG Tyler Glasnow 4.00 10.00
PPRTT Trea Turner 6.00 15.00
PPRWB Walker Buehler 5.00 12.00
PPRYM Yadier Molina 10.00 25.00

2020 Topps Rhys Hoskins Highlights

COMPLETE SET (30) 8.00 20.00
RANDOM INSERTS IN PACKS
*BLUE: 1.2X TO 3X BASIC
*BLACK/299: 1.5X TO 4X BASIC
*GOLD/50: 4X TO 10X BASIC
*RED/10: 8X TO 20X BASIC
RH1 Rhys Hoskins .40 1.00
RH2 Rhys Hoskins .40 1.00
RH3 Rhys Hoskins .40 1.00
RH4 Rhys Hoskins .40 1.00
RH5 Rhys Hoskins .40 1.00
RH6 Rhys Hoskins .40 1.00
RH7 Rhys Hoskins .40 1.00
RH8 Rhys Hoskins .40 1.00
RH9 Rhys Hoskins .40 1.00
RH10 Rhys Hoskins .40 1.00
RH11 Rhys Hoskins .40 1.00
RH12 Rhys Hoskins .40 1.00
RH13 Rhys Hoskins .40 1.00
RH14 Rhys Hoskins .40 1.00
RH15 Rhys Hoskins .40 1.00
RH16 Rhys Hoskins .40 1.00
RH17 Rhys Hoskins .40 1.00
RH18 Rhys Hoskins .40 1.00
RH19 Rhys Hoskins .40 1.00
RH20 Rhys Hoskins .40 1.00
RH21 Rhys Hoskins .40 1.00
RH22 Rhys Hoskins .40 1.00
RH23 Rhys Hoskins .40 1.00
RH24 Rhys Hoskins .40 1.00
RH25 Rhys Hoskins .40 1.00
RH26 Rhys Hoskins .40 1.00
RH27 Rhys Hoskins .40 1.00
RH28 Rhys Hoskins .40 1.00
RH29 Rhys Hoskins .40 1.00
RH30 Rhys Hoskins .40 1.00

2020 Topps Rhys Hoskins Highlights Autographs

RANDOM INSERTS IN PACKS
STATED PRINT RUN 10 SER.#'d SETS
EXCHANGE DEADLINE 12/31/2021
RHA1 Rhys Hoskins 40.00 100.00
RHA2 Rhys Hoskins 40.00 100.00
RHA3 Rhys Hoskins 40.00 100.00
RHA4 Rhys Hoskins 40.00 100.00
RHA5 Rhys Hoskins 40.00 100.00
RHA6 Rhys Hoskins 40.00 100.00
RHA7 Rhys Hoskins 40.00 100.00
RHA8 Rhys Hoskins 40.00 100.00
RHA9 Rhys Hoskins 40.00 100.00
RHA10 Rhys Hoskins 40.00 100.00
RHA11 Rhys Hoskins 40.00 100.00
RHA12 Rhys Hoskins 40.00 100.00
RHA13 Rhys Hoskins 40.00 100.00
RHA14 Rhys Hoskins 40.00 100.00
RHA15 Rhys Hoskins 40.00 100.00
RHA16 Rhys Hoskins 40.00 100.00
RHA17 Rhys Hoskins 40.00 100.00
RHA18 Rhys Hoskins 40.00 100.00
RHA19 Rhys Hoskins 40.00 100.00
RHA20 Rhys Hoskins 40.00 100.00
RHA21 Rhys Hoskins 40.00 100.00
RHA22 Rhys Hoskins 40.00 100.00
RHA23 Rhys Hoskins 40.00 100.00
RHA24 Rhys Hoskins 40.00 100.00
RHA25 Rhys Hoskins 40.00 100.00
RHA26 Rhys Hoskins 40.00 100.00
RHA27 Rhys Hoskins 40.00 100.00
RHA28 Rhys Hoskins 40.00 100.00
RHA29 Rhys Hoskins 40.00 100.00
RHA30 Rhys Hoskins 40.00 100.00

2020 Topps Rookie Card Retrospective RC Logo Medallions

ONE PER BLASTER BOX
*BLACK/199: 1X TO 2.5X BASIC
*GOLD/50: 1.5X TO 4X BASIC
RCRAJ Aaron Judge 5.00 12.00
RCRAK Al Kaline 2.00 5.00
RCRAP Albert Pujols 3.00 8.00
RCRBG Bob Gibson 1.50 4.00
RCRBH Bryce Harper 3.00 8.00
RCRBJ Bo Jackson 4.00 10.00
RCRBP Buster Posey 4.00 10.00
RCRBR Brooks Robinson 1.50 4.00
RCRCA Jose Canseco 1.50 4.00
RCRCB Cody Bellinger 4.00 10.00
RCRCC Carlos Correa 2.00 5.00
RCRCJ Chipper Jones 3.00 8.00
RCRCK Clayton Kershaw 3.00 8.00
RCRCR Cal Ripken Jr. 6.00 15.00
RCRCY Christian Yelich 2.50 6.00
RCRDG Dwight Gooden
RCRDM Don Mattingly 5.00 12.00
RCRDS Darryl Strawberry 1.25 3.00
RCRDY Dennis Eckersley 1.50 4.00
RCREB Ernie Banks 2.00 5.00
RCREM Eddie Murray 1.50 4.00
RCRFA Frank Thomas 4.00 10.00
RCRFR Frank Robinson 1.50 4.00
RCRFT Fernando Tatis Jr. 10.00 25.00
RCRHA Hank Aaron 5.00 12.00
RCRIS Ichiro 4.00 10.00
RCRJA Jose Altuve 1.50 4.00
RCRJB Jeff Bagwell 1.50 4.00
RCRJS John Smoltz 2.00 5.00
RCRKB Kris Bryant 4.00 10.00
RCRKG Ken Griffey Jr. 6.00 15.00
RCRMC Miguel Cabrera 2.00 5.00
RCRMS Giancarlo Stanton 2.00 5.00
RCRMT Mike Trout 12.00 30.00
RCROS Ozzie Smith 2.50 6.00
RCRPA Pete Alonso 5.00 12.00
RCRRC Roger Clemens 2.50 6.00
RCRRH Rickey Henderson 5.00 12.00
RCRRJ Reggie Jackson 4.00 10.00
RCRRO Roberto Clemente 5.00 12.00
RCRRS Ryne Sandberg 4.00 10.00
RCRRY Rhys Hoskins 2.50 6.00
RCRSA Sandy Alomar Jr. 1.25 3.00
RCRSK Sandy Koufax 4.00 10.00
RCRSO Shohei Ohtani 3.00 8.00
RCRSS Sammy Sosa 2.00 5.00
RCRST Stephen Strasburg 2.00 5.00
RCRTG Tony Gwynn 2.00 5.00
RCRTR Tim Raines 1.50 4.00
RCRVG Vladimir Guerrero Jr. 3.00 8.00

2020 Topps Significant Statistics

STATED ODDS 1:32 HOBBY
*GOLD/50: 1.5X TO 4X BASIC
SS1 Vladimir Guerrero Jr. .50 1.25
SS2 Aaron Judge .75 2.00
SS3 Mike Trout 1.50 4.00
SS4 Mike Trout 1.50 4.00
SS5 Mike Trout 1.50 4.00
SS6 Miguel Sano .25 .60
SS7 Jorge Soler .30 .75
SS8 Nelson Cruz .30 .75
SS9 Joey Gallo .30 .75
SS10 Rafael Devers .40 1.00
SS11 Cody Bellinger .60 1.50
SS12 Mike Trout 1.50 4.00
SS13 Nomar Mazara .20 .50
SS14 Christian Yelich .40 1.00
SS15 Mike Trout 1.50 4.00
SS16 Josh Hader .25 .60
SS17 Jordan Hicks .25 .60
SS18 Jacob deGrom .60 1.50
SS19 Victor Robles .40 1.00
SS20 Harrison Bader .25 .60
SS21 Byron Buxton .30 .75
SS22 Lorenzo Cain .20 .50
SS23 J.T. Realmuto .30 .75
SS24 Trea Turner .25 .60
SS25 Austin Hedges .20 .50

2020 Topps Significant Statistics Autographs

STATED ODDS 1:11,458 HOBBY
PRINT RUNS B/WN 10-50 COPIES PER
NO PRICING ON QTY 10
EXCHANGE DEADLINE 4/30/2022
*RED/25: .5X TO 1.2X BASIC
SSAAMU Andres Munoz/50 5.00 12.00
SSABB Byron Buxton/25 15.00 40.00
SSACY Christian Yelich/25 30.00 80.00
SSAJd Jacob deGrom/25 50.00 120.00
SSAJH Josh Hader/50 6.00 15.00
SSAJR J.T. Realmuto/50 15.00 40.00
SSAJS Jorge Soler/50 5.00 12.00
SSARD Rafael Devers/25 20.00 50.00
SSAVG Vladimir Guerrero Jr. EXCH 40.00 100.00
SSAVR Victor Robles/50 12.00 30.00

2020 Topps Significant Statistics Relic Autographs

STATED ODDS 1:11,458 HOBBY
PRINT RUNS B/WN 10-50 COPIES PER
NO PRICING ON QTY 10 OR LESS
EXCHANGE DEADLINE 4/30/2022
*RED/25: .5X TO 1.2X BASIC
SSARAM Andres Munoz/50 6.00 15.00
SSARJH Josh Hader/50 8.00 20.00
SSARJR J.T. Realmuto/50 20.00 50.00
SSARJR2 J.T. Realmuto/50 20.00 50.00
SSARJS Jorge Soler/50 6.00 15.00
SSARVG Vladimir Guerrero Jr. EXCH 50.00 120.00
SSARVR Victor Robles/50 15.00 40.00

2020 Topps Significant Statistics Relics

STATED ODDS 1:5729 HOBBY
STATED PRINT RUN 99 SER.#'d SETS
*RED/25: .6X TO 1.5X BASIC
SSRAJ Aaron Judge 8.00 20.00
SSRCB Cody Bellinger 6.00 15.00
SSRCY Christian Yelich 4.00 10.00
SSRHB Harrison Bader 2.50 6.00
SSRJd Jacob deGrom 6.00 15.00
SSRJG Joey Gallo 3.00 8.00
SSRJR J.T. Realmuto 3.00 8.00
SSRJS Jorge Soler 3.00 8.00
SSRLC Lorenzo Cain 2.00 5.00
SSRMS Miguel Sano 2.50 6.00
SSRMT Mike Trout 15.00 40.00
SSRNC Nelson Cruz 3.00 8.00
SSRRD Rafael Devers 4.00 10.00
SSRTT Trea Turner 2.50 6.00
SSRVG Vladimir Guerrero Jr. 5.00 12.00
SSRVR Victor Robles 4.00 10.00
SSRMT2 Mike Trout 15.00 40.00
SSRMT3 Mike Trout 15.00 40.00
SSRMT4 Mike Trout 15.00 40.00
SSRMT5 Mike Trout 15.00 40.00

2020 Topps Topps Choice

STATED ODDS 1:28 HOBBY
*BLUE: 1.2X TO 3X BASIC
*BLACK/299: 1.5X TO 4X BASIC
*GOLD/50: 4X TO 10X BASIC
TC1 Vladimir Guerrero Jr. .50 1.25
TC2 Yordan Alvarez 2.00 5.00
TC3 Gavin Lux 1.00 2.50
TC4 Babe Ruth .75 2.00
TC5 Pete Alonso .75 2.00
TC6 Ronald Acuna Jr. 1.25 3.00
TC7 Mike Trout 1.50 4.00
TC8 Clayton Kershaw .50 1.25
TC9 Ichiro .40 1.00
TC10 Don Mattingly .60 1.50
TC11 Randy Johnson .30 .75
TC12 Ty Cobb .50 1.25
TC13 Fernando Tatis Jr. 1.50 4.00
TC14 Mookie Betts .60 1.50
TC15 Yadier Molina .40 1.00
TC16 Kris Bryant .40 1.00
TC17 Christian Yelich .40 1.00
TC18 Aaron Judge .75 2.00
TC19 Cody Bellinger .60 1.50
TC20 Bryce Harper .50 1.25
TC21 Jose Altuve .25 .60
TC22 Cal Ripken Jr. 1.00 2.50
TC23 Ken Griffey Jr. .60 1.50
TC24 Shohei Ohtani .50 1.25
TC25 Ryne Sandberg .60 1.50

2020 Topps Topps Choice Autographs

STATED ODDS 1:57,238 HOBBY
PRINT RUNS B/WN 5-25 COPIES PER
NO PRICING ON QTY 15 OR LESS
EXCHANGE DEADLINE 12/31/2021
TC1 Vladimir Guerrero Jr./25 100.00 250.00
TC2 Yordan Alvarez/25 150.00 400.00
TC3 Gavin Lux/25 125.00 300.00
TC5 Pete Alonso/25 100.00 250.00
TC6 Ronald Acuna Jr./25 100.00 250.00
TC10 Don Mattingly/25 75.00 200.00
TC13 Fernando Tatis Jr./25 150.00 400.00

2020 Topps Turkey Red '20

STATED ODDS ONE PER BLASTER PACK
*BLUE/50: 4X TO 10X BASIC
TR1 Bryce Harper .50 1.25
TR2 Ronald Acuna Jr. 1.25 3.00
TR3 Ketel Marte .25 .60
TR4 Adam Jones .25 .60
TR5 Zack Greinke .30 .75
TR6 Freddie Freeman .40 1.00
TR7 Nick Markakis .25 .60
TR8 Ozzie Albies .30 .75
TR9 Trey Mancini .30 .75
TR10 Sean Murphy .30 .75
TR11 Dustin May .60 1.50
TR12 John Means .30 .75
TR13 Mookie Betts .60 1.50
TR14 J.D. Martinez .30 .75
TR15 Chris Sale .30 .75
TR16 Tim Anderson .30 .75
TR17 Yoan Moncada .30 .75
TR18 Eloy Jimenez .60 1.50
TR19 Willson Contreras .30 .75
TR20 Javier Baez .40 1.00
TR21 Kris Bryant .40 1.00
TR22 Kyle Schwarber .30 .75
TR23 Nick Senzel .30 .75
TR24 Yasiel Puig .30 .75
TR25 Luis Castillo .25 .60
TR26 Francisco Lindor .30 .75
TR27 Rafael Devers .40 1.00
TR28 Jose Ramirez .25 .60
TR29 Nolan Arenado .50 1.25
TR30 Charlie Blackmon .30 .75
TR31 Brendan Rodgers .30 .75
TR32 Brendan McKay .30 .75
TR33 Matthew Boyd .20 .50
TR34 Miguel Cabrera .30 .75
TR35 Jose Altuve .25 .60
TR36 Alex Bregman .30 .75
TR37 Yordan Alvarez 2.00 5.00
TR38 Justin Verlander .30 .75
TR39 A.J. Puk .30 .75
TR40 Whit Merrifield .30 .75
TR41 Nico Hoerner .75 2.00
TR42 Cody Bellinger .60 1.50
TR43 Clayton Kershaw .50 1.25
TR44 Walker Buehler .40 1.00
TR45 Albert Pujols .40 1.00
TR46 Mike Trout 1.50 4.00
TR47 Shohei Ohtani .50 1.25
TR48 Brian Anderson .20 .50
TR49 Jesus Luzardo .40 1.00
TR50 Zac Gallen .50 1.25
TR51 Christian Yelich .40 1.00
TR52 Lorenzo Cain .20 .50
TR53 Josh Hader .25 .60
TR54 Eddie Rosario .25 .60
TR55 Nelson Cruz .30 .75
TR56 Xander Bogaerts .30 .75
TR57 Max Kepler .25 .60
TR58 Gary Sanchez .30 .75
TR59 Gleyber Torres .60 1.50
TR60 Aaron Judge .75 2.00
TR61 Giancarlo Stanton .30 .75
TR62 Masahiro Tanaka .30 .75
TR63 Pete Alonso .75 2.00
TR64 Jeff McNeil .25 .60
TR65 Jacob deGrom .60 1.50
TR66 Matt Chapman .30 .75
TR67 Khris Davis .30 .75
TR68 Matt Olson .30 .75
TR69 Rhys Hoskins .40 1.00
TR70 Aaron Nola .25 .60
TR71 Gerrit Cole .50 1.25
TR72 Josh Bell .25 .60
TR73 Gavin Lux 1.00 2.50
TR74 Chris Archer .20 .50
TR75 Manny Machado .30 .75
TR76 Fernando Tatis Jr. 1.50 4.00
TR77 Buster Posey .40 1.00
TR78 Brandon Crawford .25 .60
TR79 Yusei Kikuchi .25 .60
TR80 Keston Hiura .40 1.00
TR81 Yadier Molina .40 1.00
TR82 Marcell Ozuna .30 .75
TR83 Paul Goldschmidt .30 .75
TR84 Austin Meadows .30 .75
TR85 Blake Snell .25 .60
TR86 Charlie Morton .30 .75
TR87 Joey Gallo .30 .75
TR88 Shin-Soo Choo .25 .60
TR89 Kyle Lewis 1.50 4.00
TR90 Cavan Biggio .40 1.00
TR91 Vladimir Guerrero Jr. .50 1.25
TR92 Marcus Stroman .25 .60
TR93 Aristides Aquino .50 1.25
TR94 Bo Bichette 1.50 4.00
TR95 Juan Soto 1.00 2.50
TR96 Max Scherzer .30 .75
TR97 Anthony Rendon .30 .75
TR98 Sean Doolittle .20 .50
TR99 Gio Urshela .30 .75
TR100 George Springer .25 .60

2020 Topps Turkey Red '20 Series 2

STATED ODDS ONE PER BLASTER PACK
*BLUE/50: 4X TO 10X BASIC
TR1 Ken Griffey Jr. .60 1.50
TR2 Stephen Strasburg .30 .75
TR3 Joey Votto .30 .75
TR4 Noah Syndergaard .25 .60
TR5 Chris Paddack .30 .75
TR6 Jack Flaherty .30 .75
TR7 Don Mattingly .60 1.50
TR8 Frank Thomas .30 .75
TR9 Cal Ripken Jr. 1.00 2.50
TR10 Matt Thaiss .25 .60
TR11 Randy Johnson .30 .75
TR12 Alex Young .20 .50
TR13 Josh Rojas .20 .50
TR14 Chipper Jones .30 .75
TR15 Hank Aaron .60 1.50
TR16 Hunter Harvey .30 .75
TR17 Andrew Benintendi .30 .75
TR18 Roger Clemens .40 1.00
TR19 Ted Williams .60 1.50
TR20 Jackie Robinson .30 .75
TR21 Rod Carew .25 .60
TR22 Nolan Ryan 1.00 2.50
TR23 Robel Garcia .20 .50
TR24 Adbert Alzolay .25 .60
TR25 Anthony Rizzo .40 1.00
TR26 Ryne Sandberg .60 1.50
TR27 Ernie Banks .30 .75
TR28 Dylan Cease .30 .75
TR29 Zack Collins .25 .60
TR30 Lucas Giolito .25 .60
TR31 Barry Larkin .25 .60
TR32 Sonny Gray .25 .60
TR33 Eugenio Suarez .25 .60
TR34 Shane Bieber .30 .75
TR35 Jim Thome .25 .60
TR36 Trevor Story .30 .75
TR37 Sam Hilliard .30 .75
TR38 David Dahl .20 .50
TR39 Jake Rogers .20 .50
TR40 Nolan Ryan 1.00 2.50
TR41 Jeff Bagwell .25 .60
TR42 George Brett .60 1.50
TR43 Jorge Soler .30 .75
TR44 Hyun-Jin Ryu .25 .60
TR45 Corey Seager .30 .75
TR46 Joc Pederson .25 .60
TR47 Sandy Koufax .60 1.50
TR48 Isan Diaz .30 .75
TR49 Jordan Yamamoto .20 .50
TR50 Trent Grisham .75 2.00
TR51 Robin Yount .30 .75
TR52 Brusdar Graterol .30 .75
TR53 Jose Berrios .25 .60
TR54 Vladimir Guerrero .50 1.25
TR55 Michael Conforto .25 .60
TR56 Darryl Strawberry .20 .50
TR57 Luis Severino .25 .60
TR58 Babe Ruth .75 2.00
TR59 Reggie Jackson .25 .60
TR60 Lou Gehrig .60 1.50
TR61 Rickey Henderson .30 .75
TR62 Mark McGwire .50 1.25
TR63 Seth Brown .20 .50
TR64 Sheldon Neuse .25 .60
TR65 Mike Schmidt .50 1.25
TR66 J.T. Realmuto .30 .75
TR67 Steve Carlton .25 .60
TR68 Bryan Reynolds .25 .60
TR69 Roberto Clemente .75 2.00
TR70 Tony Gwynn .30 .75
TR71 Mauricio Dubon .25 .60
TR72 Jaylin Davis .30 .75
TR73 Ty Cobb .50 1.25
TR74 Honus Wagner .30 .75
TR75 Max Muncy .25 .60
TR76 Will Clark .25 .60
TR77 Willie Mays .60 1.50
TR78 Ichiro .40 1.00
TR79 Edgar Martinez .25 .60
TR80 Justin Dunn .25 .60
TR81 Jake Fraley .25 .60
TR82 Junior Fernandez .20 .50
TR83 Randy Arozarena 1.50 4.00
TR84 Ozzie Smith .40 1.00
TR85 Tommy Edman .30 .75
TR86 Tyler Glasnow .30 .75
TR87 Nick Solak .75 2.00
TR88 Brock Burke .20 .50
TR89 Elvis Andrus .25 .60
TR90 Roberto Alomar .25 .60
TR91 Anthony Kay .20 .50
TR92 T.J. Zeuch .20 .50
TR93 Lourdes Gurriel Jr. .25 .60
TR94 Victor Robles .40 1.00
TR95 Patrick Corbin .25 .60
TR96 Ryan Zimmerman .25 .60
TR97 Stan Musial .50 1.25
TR98 Mariano Rivera .40 1.00
TR99 Joe Mauer .25 .60
TR100 Andres Munoz .30 .75

2020 Topps Turkey Red '20 Chrome

STATED ODDS 1:10 BLASTER PACKS
*BLUE REF/50: 3X TO 8X BASIC
TRC1 Bryce Harper 1.50 4.00
TRC2 Ronald Acuna Jr. 4.00 10.00
TRC3 Ketel Marte .75 2.00
TRC4 Adam Jones .75 2.00
TRC5 Zack Greinke 1.00 2.50
TRC6 Freddie Freeman 1.25 3.00
TRC7 Nick Markakis .75 2.00
TRC8 Ozzie Albies 1.00 2.50
TRC9 Trey Mancini 1.00 2.50
TRC10 Sean Murphy 1.00 2.50
TRC11 Dustin May 2.00 5.00
TRC12 John Means 1.00 2.50
TRC13 Mookie Betts 2.00 5.00
TRC14 J.D. Martinez 1.00 2.50
TRC15 Chris Sale 1.00 2.50
TRC16 Tim Anderson 1.00 2.50
TRC17 Yoan Moncada 1.00 2.50
TRC18 Eloy Jimenez 2.00 5.00
TRC19 Willson Contreras 1.00 2.50
TRC20 Javier Baez 1.25 3.00
TRC21 Kris Bryant 1.25 3.00
TRC22 Kyle Schwarber 1.00 2.50
TRC23 Nick Senzel 1.00 2.50
TRC24 Yasiel Puig 1.00 2.50
TRC25 Luis Castillo .75 2.00
TRC26 Francisco Lindor 1.00 2.50
TRC27 Rafael Devers 1.25 3.00
TRC28 Jose Ramirez .75 2.00
TRC29 Nolan Arenado 1.50 4.00
TRC30 Charlie Blackmon 1.00 2.50
TRC31 Brendan Rodgers 1.00 2.50
TRC32 Brendan McKay 1.00 2.50
TRC33 Matthew Boyd .60 1.50
TRC34 Miguel Cabrera 1.00 2.50
TRC35 Jose Altuve .75 2.00
TRC36 Alex Bregman 1.00 2.50
TRC37 Yordan Alvarez 6.00 15.00
TRC38 Justin Verlander 1.00 2.50
TRC39 A.J. Puk 1.00 2.50
TRC40 Whit Merrifield 1.00 2.50
TRC41 Nico Hoerner 2.50 6.00
TRC42 Cody Bellinger 2.00 5.00
TRC43 Clayton Kershaw 1.50 4.00
TRC44 Walker Buehler 1.25 3.00
TRC45 Albert Pujols 1.25 3.00
TRC46 Mike Trout 5.00 12.00
TRC47 Shohei Ohtani 1.50 4.00
TRC48 Brian Anderson .60 1.50
TRC49 Jesus Luzardo 1.25 3.00
TRC50 Zac Gallen 1.50 4.00
TRC51 Christian Yelich 1.25 3.00
TRC52 Lorenzo Cain .60 1.50
TRC53 Josh Hader .75 2.00
TRC54 Eddie Rosario .75 2.00
TRC55 Nelson Cruz 1.00 2.50
TRC56 Xander Bogaerts 1.00 2.50
TRC57 Max Kepler .75 2.00
TRC58 Gary Sanchez 1.00 2.50
TRC59 Gleyber Torres 2.00 5.00
TRC60 Aaron Judge 2.50 6.00
TRC61 Giancarlo Stanton 1.00 2.50
TRC62 Masahiro Tanaka 1.00 2.50
TRC63 Pete Alonso 2.50 6.00
TRC64 Jeff McNeil .75 2.00
TRC65 Jacob deGrom 2.00 5.00
TRC66 Matt Chapman 1.00 2.50
TRC67 Khris Davis 1.00 2.50
TRC68 Matt Olson 1.00 2.50
TRC69 Rhys Hoskins 1.25 3.00
TRC70 Aaron Nola .75 2.00
TRC71 Gerrit Cole 1.50 4.00
TRC72 Josh Bell .75 2.00
TRC73 Gavin Lux 3.00 8.00
TRC74 Chris Archer .60 1.50
TRC75 Manny Machado 1.00 2.50
TRC76 Fernando Tatis Jr. 5.00 12.00
TRC77 Buster Posey 1.25 3.00
TRC78 Brandon Crawford .75 2.00
TRC79 Yusei Kikuchi .75 2.00
TRC80 Keston Hiura 1.25 3.00
TRC81 Yadier Molina 1.25 3.00
TRC82 Marcell Ozuna 1.00 2.50
TRC83 Paul Goldschmidt 1.00 2.50
TRC84 Austin Meadows 1.00 2.50
TRC85 Blake Snell .75 2.00
TRC86 Charlie Morton 1.00 2.50
TRC87 Joey Gallo 1.00 2.50
TRC88 Shin-Soo Choo .75 2.00
TRC89 Kyle Lewis 5.00 12.00
TRC90 Cavan Biggio 1.25 3.00
TRC91 Vladimir Guerrero Jr. 1.50 4.00
TRC92 Marcus Stroman .75 2.00
TRC93 Aristides Aquino 1.50 4.00
TRC94 Bo Bichette 5.00 12.00
TRC95 Juan Soto 3.00 8.00
TRC96 Max Scherzer 1.00 2.50
TRC97 Anthony Rendon 1.00 2.50
TRC98 Sean Doolittle .60 1.50
TRC99 Gio Urshela 1.00 2.50
TRC100 George Springer .75 2.00

2020 Topps Turkey Red '20 Chrome Series 2

STATED ODDS 1:10 BLASTER PACKS
*BLUE REF/50: 3X TO 8X BASIC
TRC1 Ken Griffey Jr. 2.00 5.00
TRC2 Stephen Strasburg 1.00 2.50
TRC3 Joey Votto 1.00 2.50
TRC4 Noah Syndergaard .75 2.00
TRC5 Chris Paddack 1.00 2.50
TRC6 Jack Flaherty 1.00 2.50
TRC7 Don Mattingly 2.00 5.00
TRC8 Frank Thomas 1.00 2.50
TRC9 Cal Ripken Jr. 3.00 8.00
TRC10 Matt Thaiss .75 2.00
TRC11 Randy Johnson 1.00 2.50
TRC12 Alex Young .60 1.50
TRC13 Josh Rojas .60 1.50
TRC14 Chipper Jones 1.00 2.50
TRC15 Hank Aaron 2.00 5.00
TRC16 Hunter Harvey 1.00 2.50
TRC17 Andrew Benintendi 1.00 2.50
TRC18 Roger Clemens 1.25 3.00
TRC19 Ted Williams 2.00 5.00
TRC20 Jackie Robinson 1.00 2.50
TRC21 Rod Carew .75 2.00
TRC22 Nolan Ryan 3.00 8.00
TRC23 Robel Garcia .60 1.50
TRC24 Adbert Alzolay .75 2.00
TRC25 Anthony Rizzo 1.25 3.00
TRC26 Ryne Sandberg 2.00 5.00
TRC27 Ernie Banks 1.00 2.50

TRC28 Dylan Cease 1.00 2.50
TRC29 Zack Collins .75 2.00
TRC30 Lucas Giolito .75 2.00
TRC31 Barry Larkin .75 2.00
TRC32 Sonny Gray .75 2.00
TRC33 Eugenio Suarez .75 2.00
TRC34 Shane Bieber 1.00 2.50
TRC35 Jim Thome .75 2.00
TRC36 Trevor Story 1.00 2.50
TRC37 Sam Hilliard 1.00 2.50
TRC38 David Dahl .60 1.50
TRC39 Jake Rogers .60 1.50
TRC40 Nolan Ryan 3.00 8.00
TRC41 Jeff Bagwell .75 2.00
TRC42 George Brett 2.00 5.00
TRC43 Jorge Soler 1.00 2.50
TRC44 Hyun-Jin Ryu .75 2.00
TRC45 Corey Seager 1.00 2.50
TRC46 Joc Pederson .75 2.00
TRC47 Sandy Koufax 2.00 5.00
TRC48 Isan Diaz 1.00 2.50
TRC49 Jordan Yamamoto .60 1.50
TRC50 Trent Grisham 2.50 6.00
TRC51 Robin Yount 1.00 2.50
TRC52 Brusdar Graterol 1.00 2.50
TRC53 Jose Berrios .75 2.00
TRC54 Vladimir Guerrero 1.50 4.00
TRC55 Michael Conforto .75 2.00
TRC56 Darryl Strawberry .60 1.50
TRC57 Luis Severino .75 2.00
TRC58 Babe Ruth 2.50 6.00
TRC59 Reggie Jackson .75 2.00
TRC60 Lou Gehrig 2.00 5.00
TRC61 Rickey Henderson 1.00 2.50
TRC62 Mark McGwire 1.50 4.00
TRC63 Seth Brown .60 1.50
TRC64 Sheldon Neuse .75 2.00
TRC65 Mike Schmidt 1.50 4.00
TRC66 J.T. Realmuto 1.00 2.50
TRC67 Steve Carlton .75 2.00
TRC68 Bryan Reynolds .75 2.00
TRC69 Roberto Clemente 2.50 6.00
TRC70 Tony Gwynn 1.00 2.50
TRC71 Ty Cobb 1.50 4.00
TRC72 Honus Wagner 1.00 2.50
TRC73 Mauricio Dubon .75 2.00
TRC74 Jaylin Davis 1.00 2.50
TRC75 Max Muncy .75 2.00
TRC76 Will Clark .75 2.00
TRC77 Willie Mays 2.00 5.00
TRC78 Ichiro 1.25 3.00
TRC79 Edgar Martinez .75 2.00
TRC80 Justin Dunn .75 2.00
TRC81 Jake Fraley .75 2.00
TRC82 Junior Fernandez .60 1.50
TRC83 Randy Arozarena 5.00 12.00
TRC84 Ozzie Smith 1.25 3.00
TRC85 Tommy Edman 1.00 2.50
TRC86 Tyler Glasnow 1.00 2.50
TRC87 Nick Solak 2.50 6.00
TRC88 Brock Burke .60 1.50
TRC89 Elvis Andrus .75 2.00
TRC90 Roberto Alomar .75 2.00
TRC91 Anthony Kay .60 1.50
TRC92 T.J. Zeuch .60 1.50
TRC93 Lourdes Gurriel Jr. .75 2.00
TRC94 Victor Robles 1.25 3.00
TRC95 Patrick Corbin .75 2.00
TRC96 Ryan Zimmerman .75 2.00
TRC97 Stan Musial 1.50 4.00
TRC98 Mariano Rivera 1.25 3.00
TRC99 Joe Mauer .75 2.00
TRC100 Andres Munoz 1.00 2.50

2020 Topps Turkey Red '20 Box Toppers

RANDOM INSERTS IN BOXES
OTR1 Mike Trout 3.00 8.00
OTR2 Shohei Ohtani 1.00 2.50
OTR3 Ketel Marte .50 1.25
OTR4 Ronald Acuna Jr. 2.50 6.00
OTR5 Freddie Freeman .75 2.00
OTR6 Trey Mancini .60 1.50
OTR7 Mookie Betts 1.25 3.00
OTR8 Rafael Devers .75 2.00
OTR9 Javier Baez .75 2.00
OTR10 Kris Bryant .75 2.00
OTR11 Nico Hoerner 1.50 4.00
OTR12 Eloy Jimenez 1.25 3.00
OTR13 Aristides Aquino 1.00 2.50
OTR14 Francisco Lindor .60 1.50
OTR15 Nolan Arenado 1.00 2.50
OTR16 Miguel Cabrera .60 1.50
OTR17 Jose Altuve .50 1.25
OTR18 Alex Bregman .60 1.50
OTR19 Yordan Alvarez 4.00 10.00
OTR20 Justin Verlander .60 1.50
OTR21 Whit Merrifield .60 1.50
OTR22 Cody Bellinger 1.25 3.00
OTR23 Clayton Kershaw 1.00 2.50
OTR24 Gavin Lux 2.00 5.00
OTR25 Christian Yelich .75 2.00
OTR26 Keston Hiura .75 2.00
OTR27 Max Kepler .50 1.25
OTR28 Pete Alonso 1.50 4.00
OTR29 Jacob deGrom 1.25 3.00
OTR30 Gleyber Torres 1.25 3.00
OTR31 Aaron Judge 1.50 4.00
OTR32 Giancarlo Stanton .60 1.50
OTR33 Matt Chapman .60 1.50
OTR34 Jesus Luzardo .75 2.00
OTR35 Bryce Harper 1.00 2.50
OTR36 Rhys Hoskins .75 2.00
OTR37 Josh Bell .50 1.25
OTR38 Manny Machado .60 1.50
OTR39 Fernando Tatis Jr. 3.00 8.00
OTR40 Buster Posey .75 2.00
OTR41 Kyle Lewis 3.00 8.00
OTR42 Yadier Molina .75 2.00
OTR43 Paul Goldschmidt .60 1.50
OTR44 Brendan McKay .60 1.50
OTR45 Joey Gallo .60 1.50
OTR46 Vladimir Guerrero Jr. 1.00 2.50
OTR47 Bo Bichette 3.00 8.00
OTR48 Juan Soto 2.00 5.00
OTR49 Max Scherzer .60 1.50
OTR50 Anthony Rendon .60 1.50

2020 Topps Warriors of the Diamond

STATED ODDS 1:16 HOBBY
*BLUE: 1.2X TO 3X BASIC
*BLACK/299: 2X TO 5X BASIC
*GOLD/50: 5X TO 12X BASIC
WOD1 Babe Ruth .75 2.00
WOD2 Joe Morgan .25 .60
WOD3 Hank Aaron .60 1.50
WOD4 Willie Mays .60 1.50
WOD5 Roger Clemens .40 1.00
WOD6 Tom Seaver .25 .60
WOD7 Rickey Henderson .30 .75
WOD8 Lou Gehrig .60 1.50
WOD9 Alex Rodriguez .40 1.00
WOD10 Honus Wagner .30 .75
WOD11 Stan Musial .50 1.25
WOD12 Ted Williams .60 1.50
WOD13 Ty Cobb .50 1.25
WOD14 Mike Schmidt .50 1.25
WOD15 Randy Johnson .30 .75
WOD16 Albert Pujols .40 1.00
WOD17 Carl Yastrzemski .50 1.25
WOD18 Warren Spahn .25 .60
WOD19 Mike Trout 1.50 4.00
WOD20 Dwight Gooden .20 .50
WOD21 Steve Carlton .25 .60
WOD22 Bob Gibson .25 .60
WOD23 Pedro Martinez .25 .60
WOD24 Sandy Koufax .60 1.50
WOD25 Jacob deGrom .60 1.50
WOD26 Justin Verlander .30 .75
WOD27 Max Scherzer .30 .75
WOD28 Nolan Ryan 1.00 2.50
WOD29 Clayton Kershaw .50 1.25
WOD30 Tom Glavine .25 .60
WOD31 Cal Ripken Jr. 1.00 2.50
WOD32 Mookie Betts .60 1.50
WOD33 Chipper Jones .30 .75
WOD34 Ernie Banks .30 .75
WOD35 Cody Bellinger .60 1.50
WOD36 Christian Yelich .40 1.00
WOD37 Alex Bregman .30 .75
WOD38 Bryce Harper .50 1.25
WOD39 Ken Griffey Jr. .60 1.50
WOD40 George Brett .60 1.50
WOD41 Jackie Robinson .30 .75
WOD42 Roberto Clemente .75 2.00
WOD43 Frank Robinson .25 .60
WOD44 Frank Thomas .30 .75
WOD45 Johnny Bench .30 .75
WOD46 Eddie Mathews .30 .75
WOD47 Rod Carew .25 .60
WOD48 Robin Yount .30 .75
WOD49 Al Kaline .30 .75
WOD50 Wade Boggs .25 .60

2020 Topps Vladimir Guerrero Jr. Highlights

COMPLETE SET (30) 20.00 50.00
RANDOM INSERTS IN PACKS
*BLUE: 1.2X TO 3X BASIC
*BLACK/299: 1.5X TO 4X BASIC
*GOLD/50: 4X TO 10X BASIC
*RED/10: 8X TO 20X BASIC
VGJ1 Vladimir Guerrero Jr. .50 1.25
VGJ2 Vladimir Guerrero Jr. .50 1.25
VGJ3 Vladimir Guerrero Jr. .50 1.25
VGJ4 Vladimir Guerrero Jr. .50 1.25
VGJ5 Vladimir Guerrero Jr. .50 1.25
VGJ6 Vladimir Guerrero Jr. .50 1.25
VGJ7 Vladimir Guerrero Jr. .50 1.25
VGJ8 Vladimir Guerrero Jr. .50 1.25
VGJ9 Vladimir Guerrero Jr. .50 1.25
VGJ10 Vladimir Guerrero Jr. .50 1.25
VGJ11 Vladimir Guerrero Jr. .50 1.25
VGJ12 Vladimir Guerrero Jr. .50 1.25
VGJ13 Vladimir Guerrero Jr. .50 1.25
VGJ14 Vladimir Guerrero Jr. .50 1.25
VGJ15 Vladimir Guerrero Jr. .50 1.25
VGJ16 Vladimir Guerrero Jr. .50 1.25
VGJ17 Vladimir Guerrero Jr. .50 1.25
VGJ18 Vladimir Guerrero Jr. .50 1.25
VGJ19 Vladimir Guerrero Jr. .50 1.25
VGJ20 Vladimir Guerrero Jr. .50 1.25
VGJ21 Vladimir Guerrero Jr. .50 1.25
VGJ22 Vladimir Guerrero Jr. .50 1.25
VGJ23 Vladimir Guerrero Jr. .50 1.25
VGJ24 Vladimir Guerrero Jr. .50 1.25
VGJ25 Vladimir Guerrero Jr. .50 1.25
VGJ26 Vladimir Guerrero Jr. .50 1.25
VGJ27 Vladimir Guerrero Jr. .50 1.25
VGJ28 Vladimir Guerrero Jr. .50 1.25
VGJ29 Vladimir Guerrero Jr. .50 1.25
VGJ30 Vladimir Guerrero Jr. .50 1.25

2020 Topps Vladimir Guerrero Jr. Highlights Autographs

RANDOM INSERTS IN PACKS
STATED PRINT RUN 10 SER.#'d SETS
EXCHANGE DEADLINE 12/31/2021
VGJA1 Vladimir Guerrero Jr. 40.00 100.00
VGJA2 Vladimir Guerrero Jr. 40.00 100.00
VGJA3 Vladimir Guerrero Jr. 40.00 100.00
VGJA4 Vladimir Guerrero Jr. 40.00 100.00
VGJA5 Vladimir Guerrero Jr. 40.00 100.00
VGJA6 Vladimir Guerrero Jr. 40.00 100.00
VGJA7 Vladimir Guerrero Jr. 40.00 100.00
VGJA8 Vladimir Guerrero Jr. 40.00 100.00
VGJA9 Vladimir Guerrero Jr. 40.00 100.00
VGJA10 Vladimir Guerrero Jr. 40.00 100.00
VGJA11 Vladimir Guerrero Jr. 40.00 100.00
VGJA12 Vladimir Guerrero Jr. 40.00 100.00
VGJA13 Vladimir Guerrero Jr. 40.00 100.00
VGJA14 Vladimir Guerrero Jr. 40.00 100.00
VGJA15 Vladimir Guerrero Jr. 40.00 100.00
VGJA16 Vladimir Guerrero Jr. 40.00 100.00
VGJA17 Vladimir Guerrero Jr. 40.00 100.00
VGJA18 Vladimir Guerrero Jr. 40.00 100.00
VGJA19 Vladimir Guerrero Jr. 40.00 100.00
VGJA20 Vladimir Guerrero Jr. 40.00 100.00
VGJA21 Vladimir Guerrero Jr. 40.00 100.00
VGJA22 Vladimir Guerrero Jr. 40.00 100.00
VGJA23 Vladimir Guerrero Jr. 40.00 100.00
VGJA24 Vladimir Guerrero Jr. 40.00 100.00
VGJA25 Vladimir Guerrero Jr. 40.00 100.00
VGJA26 Vladimir Guerrero Jr. 40.00 100.00
VGJA27 Vladimir Guerrero Jr. 40.00 100.00
VGJA28 Vladimir Guerrero Jr. 40.00 100.00
VGJA29 Vladimir Guerrero Jr. 40.00 100.00
VGJA30 Vladimir Guerrero Jr. 40.00 100.00

2020 Topps World Series Champion Autograph Relics

STATED ODDS 1:28,035 HOBBY
PRINT RUNS B/WN 35-50 COPIES PER
EXCHANGE DEADLINE 12/31/2021
WCARJS Juan Soto EXCH 100.00 250.00
WCARKS Kurt Suzuki/35 30.00 80.00
WCARMS Max Scherzer
WCARPC Patrick Corbin EXCH 25.00 60.00
WCARRZ Ryan Zimmerman/35 60.00 150.00
WCARSD Sean Doolittle/50 15.00 40.00
WCARVR Victor Robles/50 12.00 30.00
WCARYG Yan Gomes

2020 Topps World Series Champion Autograph Relics Red

*RED: .5X TO 1.2X BASIC
STATED ODDS 1:57,238 HOBBY
STATED PRINT RUN 25 SER.#'d SETS
EXCHANGE DEADLINE 12/31/2021
WCARMS Max Scherzer 125.00 300.00
WCARYG Yan Gomes 30.00 80.00

2020 Topps World Series Champion Autographs

STATED ODDS 1:28,035 HOBBY
STATED PRINT RUN 50 SER.#'d SETS
EXCHANGE DEADLINE 12/31/2021
*RED/25: .5X TO 1.2X BASIC
WCAFR Fernando Rodney 25.00 60.00
WCAHK Howie Kendrick 50.00 120.00
WCAJR Joe Ross 25.00 60.00
WCAJS Juan Soto EXCH 125.00 300.00
WCAMS Max Scherzer 25.00 60.00
WCAPC Patrick Corbin 40.00 100.00
WCASD Sean Doolittle 20.00 50.00
WCAVR Victor Robles 40.00 100.00

2020 Topps World Series Champion Relics

STATED ODDS 1:3606 HOBBY
STATED PRINT RUN 99 SER.#'d SETS
*RED/25: .75X TO 2X BASIC
WCRAC Asdrubal Cabrera 15.00 40.00
WCRAR Anthony Rendon 20.00 50.00
WCRAS Anibal Sanchez 10.00 25.00
WCRBD Brian Dozier 10.00 25.00
WCRJS Juan Soto 30.00 80.00
WCRKS Kurt Suzuki 10.00 25.00
WCRMS Max Scherzer
WCRMT Michael Taylor 8.00 20.00
WCRPC Patrick Corbin 10.00 25.00
WCRRZ Ryan Zimmerman 15.00 40.00
WCRSD Sean Doolittle 8.00 20.00
WCRSS Stephen Strasburg 15.00 40.00
WCRTT Trea Turner 12.00 30.00
WCRVR Victor Robles 12.00 30.00
WCRYG Yan Gomes 10.00 25.00

2020 Topps Update

PRINTING PLATE ODDS 1:7828 HOBBY
PLATE PRINT RUN 1 SET PER COLOR
BLACK-CYAN-MAGENTA-YELLOW ISSUED
NO PLATE PRICING DUE TO SCARCITY
U1 Bo Bichette 3.00 8.00
U2 Adam Engel .15 .40
U3 Trea Turner .20 .50
Wilmer Difo
U4 Mike Trout AS 1.25 3.00
U5 Starlin Castro .15 .40
U6 Mike Moustakas .20 .50
U7 Alex Bregman .60 1.50
Yordan Alvarez
U8 Buster Posey AS .30 .75
U9 Ken Griffey Jr. HRD .50 1.25
U10 Anthony Alford .15 .40
U11 Chris Owings .15 .40
U12 Aaron Bummer .15 .40
U13 Jose Martinez .15 .40
U14 Giancarlo Stanton HRD .25 .60
U15 Aaron Judge AS .60 1.50
U16 Phillip Diehl RC .30 .75
U17 Josh Fuentes .15 .40
U18 Felix Pena .15 .40
U19 Yasmani Grandal .15 .40
U20 Francisco Cervelli .15 .40
U21 Kyle Lewis 4.00 10.00
U22 Cody Stashak RC .25 .60
U23 Cheslor Cuthbert .15 .40
U24 Buck Farmer .15 .40
U25 Josh Taylor RC .40 1.00
U26 Kyle Gibson .15 .40
U27 Kyle Ryan .15 .40
U28 Eduardo Nunez .15 .40
U29 Aristides Aquino .40 1.00
U30 Yasmany Tomas .15 .40
U31 Curt Casali .15 .40
U32 Drew Pomeranz .15 .40
U33 Alex Verdugo .20 .50
U34 Justin Verlander .25 .60
U35 Kyle Farmer .15 .40
U36 Robinson Cano HRD .20 .50
U37 Yoenis Cespedes HRD .25 .60
U38 Albert Pujols .30 .75
U39 Kevin Plawecki .15 .40
U40 Antonio Senzatela .15 .40
U41 Josh Lindblom .15 .40
U42 Kris Bryant AS .30 .75
U43 Alex Blandino .15 .40
U44 Jorge Alcala RC .25 .60
U45 Zack Wheeler .20 .50
U46 Jose Suarez .15 .40
U47 Jose Peraza .20 .50
U48 Sandy Leon .15 .40
U49 Jared Walsh 1.00 2.50
U50 Nolan Arenado AS .40 1.00
U51 Matt Davidson .20 .50
U52 Kyle Higashioka .25 .60
U53 Brad Miller .15 .40
U54 Alex Avila .15 .40
U55 Miguel Cabrera AS .25 .60
U56 Lane Thomas .20 .50
U57 Yoan Lopez .15 .40
U58 Erick Mejia RC .40 1.00
U59 Ryan Howard HRD .20 .50
U60 Brendan McKay .25 .60
U61 Jedd Gyorko .15 .40
U62 David Ortiz HRD .25 .60
U63 Terrance Gore .15 .40
U64 Alex Bregman AS .25 .60
U65 Yoshi Tsutsugo RC .60 1.50
U66 Max Scherzer .25 .60
U67 Michael Fulmer .15 .40
U68 Greg Garcia .15 .40
U69 Derek Holland .15 .40
U70 Skye Bolt .15 .40
U71 Jesus Aguilar .20 .50
U72 Drew Butera .15 .40
U73 Todd Frazier .15 .40
U74 Bryce Harper .40 1.00
Jean Segura
U75 Pedro Martinez AS .20 .50
U76 Edwin Encarnacion .25 .60
U77 Jalen Beeks .15 .40
U78 Joe Jimenez .15 .40
U79 Sean Poppen RC .40 1.00
U80 Cody Bellinger AS .50 1.25
U81 Junior Guerra .15 .40
U82 Kenley Jansen .20 .50
U83 Trent Grisham RC 1.50 4.00
U84 Yusmeiro Petit .15 .40
U85 Felix Hernandez AS .20 .50
U86 Josh Harrison .15 .40
U87 Zack Greinke .25 .60
U88 Craig Kimbrel .20 .50
U89 Brian Johnson .15 .40
U90 Clayton Kershaw .40 1.00
U91 Julio Teheran .20 .50
U92 Jacob deGrom .50 1.25
U93 Tyler White .15 .40
U94 Jesus Luzardo .30 .75
U95 Domingo Santana .20 .50
U96 Logan Morrison .15 .40
U97 Donovan Solano .25 .60
U98 Jose Iglesias .20 .50
U99 Cesar Hernandez .15 .40
U100 David Price .20 .50
U101 Nick Dini RC .30 .75
U102 Kevin Ginkel RC .25 .60
U103 Michael Hermosillo .15 .40
U104 Grayson Greiner .15 .40
U105 Jake Newberry RC .25 .60
U106 Meibrys Viloria .15 .40
U107 Eric Thames .15 .40
U108 Taylor Ward .25 .60
U109 Pedro Strop .15 .40
U110 Mark McGwire HRD .40 1.00
U111 Rich Hill .15 .40
U112 Nik Turley RC .25 .60
U113 Devin Williams RC 1.50 4.00
U114 Josh Phegley .15 .40
U115 Brad Peacock .15 .40
U116 Robinson Chirinos .15 .40
U117 Cameron Maybin .15 .40
U118 Frank Schwindel RC .40 1.00
U119 Mike Trout 1.25 3.00
U120 Stevie Wilkerson .25 .60
U121 Ichiro AS .30 .75
U122 Tino Martinez HRD .20 .50
U123 Neil Walker .15 .40
U124 David Ortiz AS .25 .60
U125 Chris Martin .15 .40
U126 Jhoulys Chacin .15 .40
U127 Ryan Weber .15 .40
U128 Jonathan Davis .20 .50
U129 Hunter Pence .20 .50
U130 Richie Martin .15 .40
U131 Alex Reyes .20 .50
U132 Daniel Descalso .15 .40
U133 Chris Iannetta .15 .40
U134 Gleyber Torres AS .50 1.25
U135 Brandon Dixon .15 .40
U136 David McKay .15 .40
U137 Touki Toussaint .20 .50
U138 Tommy Pham .15 .40
U139 Greg Allen .20 .50
U140 Clayton Kershaw .40 1.00
U141 Jonathan Villar .15 .40
U142 Albert Pujols .30 .75
U143 Francisco Lindor AS .25 .60
U144 Mookie Betts .50 1.25
Gleyber Torres
U145 Ronald Acuna Jr. AS 1.00 2.50
U146 Andrew Knizner .15 .40
U147 Robinson Cano .20 .50
U148 Pete Alonso HRD .60 1.50
U149 Nick Solak .60 1.50
U150 Ken Griffey Jr. HRD .50 1.25
U151 Jairo Diaz .15 .40
U152 Sam Haggerty RC .40 1.00
U153 Robert Stephenson .15 .40
U154 Mariano Rivera AS .30 .75
U155 Zach Davies .15 .40
U156 Wilmer Flores .20 .50
U157 Deivy Grullon RC .25 .60
U158 Jason Kipnis .20 .50
U159 Steven Souza Jr. .15 .40
U160 Richard Bleier .15 .40
U161 Jake Marisnick .15 .40
U162 Giovanny Gallegos .15 .40
U163 JT Riddle .15 .40
U164 Sam Travis .15 .40
U165 Kyle Wright .25 .60
U166 Adolis Garcia .50 1.25
U167 Yoshi Hirano .15 .40
U168 Keynan Middleton .15 .40
U169 Yadier Molina AS .30 .75
U170 Travis Shaw .15 .40
U171 Bryse Wilson .20 .50
U172 Tyler Wade .15 .40
U173 Edwin Encarnacion .25 .60
U174 Logan Forsythe .15 .40
U175 Diego Castillo .15 .40
U176 Brock Holt .15 .40
U177 Andy Burns RC .25 .60
U178 Jarrod Dyson .15 .40
U179 Jeff Hoffman .15 .40
U180 C.J. Cron .15 .40
U181 Mitch Moreland .15 .40
U182 Josh Tomlin .15 .40
U183 Steve Cishek .15 .40
U184 Miguel Cabrera .25 .60
U185 Max Scherzer AS .25 .60
U186 Rowdy Tellez .20 .50
U187 Pete Alonso AS .60 1.50
U188 Luis Severino .20 .50
U189 Johnny Davis RC .25 .60
U190 Ken Griffey Jr. AS .50 1.25
U191 Zack Greinke .25 .60
U192 Ian Miller RC .25 .60
U193 Miguel Cabrera .25 .60
U194 Justin Verlander AS .25 .60
U195 Daniel Hudson .15 .40
U196 Nestor Cortes RC .25 .60
U197 Zach Green RC .25 .60
U198 Hunter Renfroe .15 .40
U199 Adeiny Hechavarria .15 .40
U200 Anthony Rendon .25 .60
U201 Anthony Rizzo AS .30 .75
U202 Asdrubal Cabrera .20 .50
U203 Austin Pruitt .15 .40
U204 Eric Davis HRD .15 .40
U205 Kenta Maeda .20 .50
U206 Asher Wojciechowski .15 .40
U207 Jorge Lopez .15 .40
U208 Randy Arozarena RC 5.00 12.00
U209 Cal Ripken Jr. AS .75 2.00
U210 Gabe Speier RC .25 .60
U211 Drew Smyly .15 .40
U212 Jordan Lyles .15 .40
U213 Keury Mella .15 .40
U214 Kendall Graveman .15 .40
U215 Joey Votto .25 .60
U216 Sean Murphy .25 .60
U217 Andrew Suarez .15 .40
U218 Matt Chapman .25 .60
Matt Olson
U219 Zack Greinke .25 .60
U220 Alec Mills RC .25 .60
U221 Joe Panik .20 .50
U222 Scott Barlow .15 .40
U223 Chris Devenski .15 .40
U224 Cy Sneed RC .25 .60
U225 Jharel Cotton .15 .40
U226 Franchy Cordero .15 .40
U227 Garrett Richards .20 .50
U228 Starling Marte .20 .50
U229 Giancarlo Stanton AS .25 .60
U230 Cal Ripken Jr. HRD .75 2.00
U231 Jordy Mercer .15 .40
U232 Jason Castro .15 .40
U233 Mike Montgomery .15 .40
U234 Gavin Lux .75 2.00
U235 Javier Baez AS .30 .75
U236 Bartolo Colon .15 .40
U237 Clayton Kershaw AS .40 1.00
U238 Tim Locastro .15 .40
U239 Jefry Rodriguez .15 .40
U240 Justin Verlander .25 .60
U241 Tyler Heineman RC .25 .60
U242 Ty France .25 .60
U243 Mike Trout 1.25 3.00
U244 Wade LeBlanc .15 .40
U245 Justin Verlander .25 .60
U246 Greg Holland .15 .40
U247 Kole Calhoun .15 .40
U248 Miguel Cabrera .25 .60
U249 Aroldis Chapman .25 .60
U250 Omar Narvaez .15 .40
U251 Nico Hoerner .60 1.50
U252 Alex Wood .15 .40
U253 Peter Lambert .20 .50
U254 Taijuan Walker .15 .40
U255 Bryce Harper HRD .40 1.00
U256 Jose Ramirez .25 .60
Francisco Lindor
U257 Derek Jeter AS .60 1.50
U258 Todd Frazier HRD .15 .40
U259 Albert Pujols .30 .75
U260 Kyle Crick .15 .40
U261 Mike Trout .75 2.00
Justin Upton
U262 Ty Buttrey .15 .40
U263 Miguel Cabrera .25 .60
U264 Aaron Judge HRD .60 1.50
U265 Dario Agrazal RC .30 .75
U266 Andrew McCutchen AS .25 .60
U267 Albert Pujols AS .30 .75
U268 Mookie Betts AS .50 1.25
U269 Christian Yelich AS .30 .75
U270 Dustin Garneau .15 .40
U271 Kevin Pillar .15 .40
U272 Joey Votto AS .25 .60
U273 Rafael Devers .30 .75
Xander Bogaerts
U274 Jordan Montgomery .15 .40
U275 Brett Anderson .15 .40
U276 Joe Kelly .15 .40
U277 Jose Altuve AS .20 .50
U278 Austin Allen .20 .50
U279 Bryce Harper AS .40 1.00
U280 Albert Pujols .30 .75
U281 Joel Kuhnel RC .25 .60
U282 Christian Arroyo .15 .40
U283 Tomas Nido .15 .40
U284 Walker Buehler .30 .75
Russell Martin
U285 Billy Hamilton .20 .50
U286 Chase Anderson .15 .40
U287 Chris Sale AS .25 .60
U288 Giancarlo Stanton .25 .60
U289 Myles Straw .20 .50
U290 Pete Alonso .40 1.00
Jeff McNeil
U291 Trayce Thompson .15 .40
U292 Mike Trout 1.25 3.00
U293 Mike King RC .40 1.00
U294 Adam Plutko .15 .40
U295 Chris Sale .25 .60
U296 Mark McGwire HRD .40 1.00
U297 Jesus Tinoco RC .25 .60
U298 Magneuris Sierra .15 .40
U299 Jacob deGrom AS .50 1.25
U300 Yordan Alvarez 2.00 5.00

2020 Topps Update Advanced Stats

*ADVANCED: 3X TO 8X BASIC
*ADVANCED RC: 2X TO 5X BASIC RC
STATED ODDS 1:157 HOBBY
STATED PRINT RUN 300 SER. #'d SETS
U9 Ken Griffey Jr. HRD 12.00 30.00
U83 Trent Grisham 15.00 40.00
U113 Devin Williams 15.00 40.00
U145 Ronald Acuna Jr. AS 15.00 40.00
U150 Ken Griffey Jr. HRD 12.00 30.00
U190 Ken Griffey Jr. AS 12.00 30.00
U208 Randy Arozarena 40.00 100.00

2020 Topps Update Black

*BLACK: 8X TO 20X BASIC
*BLACK RC: 5X TO 12X BASIC RC
STATED ODDS 1:113 HOBBY
STATED PRINT RUN 69 SER. #'d SETS
U4 Mike Trout AS 40.00 100.00
U9 Ken Griffey Jr. HRD 40.00 100.00
U15 Aaron Judge AS 20.00 50.00
U83 Trent Grisham 30.00 80.00
U113 Devin Williams 40.00 100.00
U119 Mike Trout 40.00 100.00
U121 Ichiro AS 20.00 50.00
U145 Ronald Acuna Jr. AS 40.00 100.00
U148 Pete Alonso HRD 15.00 40.00
U150 Ken Griffey Jr. HRD 40.00 100.00
U187 Pete Alonso AS 15.00 40.00
U190 Ken Griffey Jr. AS 40.00 100.00
U208 Randy Arozarena 100.00 250.00
U243 Mike Trout 40.00 100.00
U251 Nico Hoerner 25.00 60.00
U257 Derek Jeter AS 25.00 60.00
U261 Mike Trout 25.00 60.00
Justin Upton
U264 Aaron Judge HRD 20.00 50.00
U292 Mike Trout 40.00 100.00

2020 Topps Update Father's Day Blue

*FD BLUE: 8X TO 20X BASIC
*FD BLUE RC: 5X TO 12X BASIC RC
STATED ODDS 1:626 HOBBY
STATED PRINT RUN 50 SER. #'d SETS
U1 Bo Bichette 60.00 150.00
U4 Mike Trout AS 40.00 100.00
U9 Ken Griffey Jr. HRD 40.00 100.00
U15 Aaron Judge AS 20.00 50.00
U83 Trent Grisham 30.00 80.00
U113 Devin Williams 40.00 100.00
U119 Mike Trout 40.00 100.00
U121 Ichiro AS 20.00 50.00
U145 Ronald Acuna Jr. AS 40.00 100.00
U148 Pete Alonso HRD 15.00 40.00
U150 Ken Griffey Jr. HRD 40.00 100.00
U187 Pete Alonso AS 15.00 40.00
U190 Ken Griffey Jr. AS 40.00 100.00
U208 Randy Arozarena 100.00 250.00
U234 Gavin Lux 40.00 100.00
U243 Mike Trout 40.00 100.00
U251 Nico Hoerner 25.00 60.00
U257 Derek Jeter AS 25.00 60.00
U261 Mike Trout 25.00 60.00
Justin Upton
U264 Aaron Judge HRD 20.00 50.00
U292 Mike Trout 40.00 100.00

2020 Topps Update Gold

*GOLD: 1.5X TO 4X BASIC
*GOLD RC: 1X TO 2.5X BASIC RC
STATED ODDS 1:16 HOBBY
STATED PRINT RUN 2020 SER. #'d SETS
U9 Ken Griffey Jr. HRD 6.00 15.00
U83 Trent Grisham 10.00 25.00
U113 Devin Williams 8.00 20.00
U145 Ronald Acuna Jr. AS 8.00 20.00
U150 Ken Griffey Jr. HRD 6.00 15.00
U190 Ken Griffey Jr. AS 6.00 15.00
U208 Randy Arozarena 20.00 50.00

2020 Topps Update Gold Foil

*GOLD FOIL: 1.2X TO 3X BASIC
*GOLD FOIL RC: .8X TO 2X BASIC RC
STATED ODDS 1:2 JUMBO
U83 Trent Grisham 6.00 15.00
U113 Devin Williams 6.00 15.00
U208 Randy Arozarena 15.00 40.00

2020 Topps Update Independence Day

*INDPNDNCE: 8X TO 20X BASIC
*INDPNDNCE RC: 5X TO 12X BASIC RC
STATED ODDS 1:412 HOBBY
STATED PRINT RUN 76 SER. #'d SETS
U4 Mike Trout AS 40.00 100.00
U9 Ken Griffey Jr. HRD 40.00 100.00
U15 Aaron Judge AS 15.00 40.00
U83 Trent Grisham 30.00 80.00
U113 Devin Williams 40.00 100.00
U119 Mike Trout 40.00 100.00
U121 Ichiro AS 20.00 50.00
U145 Ronald Acuna Jr. AS 40.00 100.00
U148 Pete Alonso HRD 15.00 40.00
U150 Ken Griffey Jr. HRD 40.00 100.00
U187 Pete Alonso AS 15.00 40.00
U190 Ken Griffey Jr. AS 40.00 100.00
U208 Randy Arozarena 100.00 250.00
U243 Mike Trout 40.00 100.00
U257 Derek Jeter AS 25.00 60.00
U264 Aaron Judge HRD 15.00 40.00
U292 Mike Trout 40.00 100.00

2020 Topps Update Meijer Purple

*PURPLE: 1.2X TO 3X BASIC
*PURPLE RC: .8X TO 2X BASIC RC
EXCLUSIVE TO MEIJER PACKS
U83 Trent Grisham 8.00 20.00
U113 Devin Williams 5.00 12.00
U208 Randy Arozarena 25.00 60.00

2020 Topps Update Memorial Day Camo

*MD CAMO: 12X TO 30X BASIC
*MD CAMO RC: 8X TO 20X BASIC RC
STATED ODDS 1:1252 HOBBY
STATED PRINT RUN 25 SER. #'d SETS
U1 Bo Bichette 100.00 250.00
U4 Mike Trout AS 60.00 150.00
U9 Ken Griffey Jr. HRD 60.00 150.00
U15 Aaron Judge AS 40.00 100.00
U83 Trent Grisham 50.00 120.00
U110 Mark McGwire HRD 20.00 50.00
U113 Devin Williams 60.00 150.00
U119 Mike Trout 60.00 150.00
U121 Ichiro AS 30.00 80.00
U145 Ronald Acuna Jr. AS 60.00 150.00
U148 Pete Alonso HRD 25.00 60.00
U150 Ken Griffey Jr. HRD 60.00 150.00
U187 Pete Alonso AS 25.00 60.00
U190 Ken Griffey Jr. AS 60.00 150.00
U208 Randy Arozarena 150.00 400.00
U234 Gavin Lux 60.00 150.00
U243 Mike Trout 60.00 150.00
U251 Nico Hoerner 40.00 100.00
U257 Derek Jeter AS 40.00 100.00
U261 Mike Trout 40.00 100.00
Justin Upton
U264 Aaron Judge HRD 40.00 100.00
U292 Mike Trout 60.00 150.00
U296 Mark McGwire HRD 20.00 50.00

2020 Topps Update Mother's Day Pink

*MD PINK: 8X TO 20X BASIC
*MD PINK RC: 5X TO 12X BASIC RC
STATED ODDS 1:626 HOBBY
STATED PRINT RUN 50 SER. #'d SETS
U1 Bo Bichette 60.00 150.00
U4 Mike Trout AS 40.00 100.00
U9 Ken Griffey Jr. HRD 40.00 100.00
U15 Aaron Judge AS 20.00 50.00
U83 Trent Grisham 30.00 80.00
U113 Devin Williams 40.00 100.00
U119 Mike Trout 40.00 100.00
U121 Ichiro AS 20.00 50.00
U145 Ronald Acuna Jr. AS 40.00 100.00
U148 Pete Alonso HRD 15.00 40.00
U150 Ken Griffey Jr. HRD 40.00 100.00
U187 Pete Alonso AS 15.00 40.00
U190 Ken Griffey Jr. AS 40.00 100.00
U208 Randy Arozarena 100.00 250.00
U234 Gavin Lux 40.00 100.00
U243 Mike Trout 40.00 100.00
U251 Nico Hoerner 25.00 60.00
U257 Derek Jeter AS 25.00 60.00
U261 Mike Trout 25.00 60.00
Justin Upton
U264 Aaron Judge HRD 20.00 50.00
U292 Mike Trout 40.00 100.00

2020 Topps Update Rainbow Foil

*RNBW FOIL: 1.2X TO 3X BASIC
*RNBW FOIL RC: .8X TO 2X BASIC RC
STATED ODDS 1:10 HOBBY
U83 Trent Grisham 6.00 15.00
U113 Devin Williams 6.00 15.00
U208 Randy Arozarena 15.00 40.00

2020 Topps Update Target Red

*RED: 1.2X TO 3X BASIC
*RED RC: .8X TO 2X BASIC RC
EXCLUSIVE TO TARGET PACKS
U83 Trent Grisham 8.00 20.00
U113 Devin Williams 5.00 12.00
U208 Randy Arozarena 25.00 60.00

2020 Topps Update Vintage Stock

*VINTAGE: 6X TO 15X BASIC
*VINTAGE RC: 4X TO 10X BASIC RC
STATED ODDS 1:317 HOBBY
STATED PRINT RUN 99 SER. #'d SETS
U9 Ken Griffey Jr. HRD 30.00 80.00
U15 Aaron Judge AS 12.00 30.00
U83 Trent Grisham 30.00 80.00
U113 Devin Williams 30.00 80.00
U145 Ronald Acuna Jr. AS 30.00 80.00
U150 Ken Griffey Jr. HRD 30.00 80.00
U190 Ken Griffey Jr. AS 30.00 80.00
U208 Randy Arozarena 75.00 200.00
U264 Aaron Judge HRD 12.00 30.00

2020 Topps Update Walgreens Yellow

*YELLOW: 1.2X TO 3X BASIC
*YELLOW RC: .8X TO 2X BASIC RC
EXCLUSIVE TO WALGREENS PACKS
U83 Trent Grisham 8.00 20.00
U113 Devin Williams 5.00 12.00
U208 Randy Arozarena 15.00 40.00

2020 Topps Update Walmart Royal Blue

*ROYAL BLUE: 1.2X TO 3X BASIC
*ROYAL BLUE RC: .8X TO 2X BASIC RC
EXCLUSIVE TO WALMART PACKS
U83 Trent Grisham 8.00 20.00
U113 Devin Williams 5.00 12.00
U208 Randy Arozarena 15.00 40.00

2020 Topps Update Photo Variations

STATED ODDS 1:63 HOBBY
STATED SSP ODDS 1:1252 HOBBY
STATED SSSP ODDS 1:XX HOBBY
NO PRICING SSSP DUE TO SCARCITY
U1A Bichette ls shirt 25.00 60.00
U1B Bichette SSP 150.00 400.00
U4A Trout interview 20.00 50.00
U4B Trout SSP 150.00 400.00
U8 Posey waving 6.00 15.00
U15A Judge locker 12.00 30.00
U15B Judge SSP 125.00 300.00
U21 Lewis dugout 12.00 30.00
U29 Aquino white 8.00 20.00
U33 Verdugo interview 4.00 10.00
U42 Bryant red carpet 5.00 12.00
U50 Arenado red carper 4.00 10.00
U52 Ruth SSP 100.00 250.00
U55 Cabrera dugout 3.00 8.00
U60 Brendan McKay 2.00 5.00
holding bat
U63 Robinson SSP 30.00 80.00
U64 Bregman interview 4.00 10.00
U65 Tsutsugo interview 4.00 10.00
U68 Tatis Jr. SSP 100.00 250.00
U80A Bellinger podium 4.00 10.00
U80B Bellinger SSP 30.00 80.00
U83 Grisham interview 15.00 40.00
U90 Koufax SSP 25.00 60.00
U94 Luzardo signing 6.00 15.00
U100 Price hard hat 3.00 8.00
U121A Ichiro interview 8.00 20.00
U121B Ichiro SSP 75.00 200.00
U122 Gehrig SSP 40.00 100.00
U124A Ortiz interview 5.00 12.00
U129 Mays SSP 25.00 60.00
U134 Torres interview 5.00 12.00
U143 Lindor interview 5.00 12.00
U145A Acuna Jr. portrait 20.00 50.00

U145B Acuna Jr. SSP 50.00 120.00
U149 Solak high-five 6.00 15.00
U154A Rivera smiling 6.00 15.00
U154B Rivera SSP 125.00 300.00
U158 Banks SSP 20.00 50.00
U169 Molina interview 4.00 10.00
U173A Robert suit 60.00 150.00
U173B Robert SSP 300.00 800.00
U178 Clemente SSP 60.00 150.00
U185 Scherzer trophy 5.00 12.00
U187 Alonso podium 5.00 12.00
U190A Griffey Jr. interview 10.00 25.00
U190B Griffey Jr. SSP 75.00 200.00
U194 Verlander interview 4.00 10.00
U199 Aaron SSP 25.00 60.00
U200 Rendon jsy 3.00 8.00
U201 Rizzo smiling 3.00 8.00
U209A Ripken interview 8.00 20.00
U209B Ripken SSP 60.00 150.00
U216 Murphy cream 3.00 8.00
U229 Stanton goggles 4.00 10.00
U234A Lux dugout 12.00 30.00
U234B Lux SSP 50.00 120.00
U235 Baez interview 6.00 15.00
U237 Kershaw podium 5.00 12.00
U251 Hoerner signing 8.00 20.00
U255 Soto SSP 40.00 100.00
U257A Jeter interview 10.00 25.00
U257B Jeter SSP 100.00 250.00
U266 Andrew McCutchen press conference 2.00 5.00
U267 Pujols interview 4.00 10.00
U268 Betts hard hat 8.00 20.00
U269 Yelich red carpet 2.50 6.00
U269A Yelich SSP 20.00 50.00
U271 Williams SSP 100.00 250.00
U272 Joey Votto interview 2.00 5.00
U277 Jose Altuve in t-shirt 1.50 4.00
U279A Harper interview 8.00 20.00
U279B Harper SSP 100.00 250.00
U287 Chris Sale in t-shirt 2.00 5.00
U299 deGrom interview 6.00 15.00
U300 Alvarez podium 12.00 30.00

2020 Topps Update '85 Topps

STATED ODDS 1:XX HOBBY
85TB1 Derek Jeter 1.00 2.50
85TB2 Josh Donaldson .30 .75
85TB3 Yoshi Tsutsugo .60 1.50
85TB4 Shogo Akiyama .40 1.00
85TB5 Mike Trout 2.00 5.00
85TB6 Starling Marte .30 .75
85TB7 Ronald Acuna Jr. 1.50 4.00
85TB8 Fred McGriff .30 .75
85TB9 Eddie Murray .30 .75
85TB10 Jackie Robinson .40 1.00
85TB11 Ernie Banks .40 1.00
85TB12 Andre Dawson .30 .75
85TB13 Javier Baez .50 1.25
85TB14 Luis Robert 2.00 5.00
85TB15 Yoan Moncada .40 1.00
85TB16 Frank Robinson .30 .75
85TB17 Joe Morgan .30 .75
85TB18 Yordan Alvarez 2.50 6.00
85TB19 Gavin Lux 1.25 3.00
85TB20 Cody Bellinger .75 2.00
85TB21 David Price .30 .75
85TB22 Mookie Betts .75 2.00
85TB23 Christian Yelich .50 1.25
85TB24 Tim Raines .30 .75
85TB25 Willie Mays .75 2.00
85TB26 Dwight Gooden .25 .60
85TB27 David Wright .30 .75
85TB28 Pete Alonso 1.00 2.50
85TB29 Aaron Judge 1.00 2.50
85TB30 Thurman Munson .40 1.00
85TB31 Jesus Luzardo .50 1.25
85TB32 A.J. Puk .40 1.00
85TB33 Bryce Harper .60 1.50
85TB34 Ryan Howard .30 .75
85TB35 Mike Schmidt .60 1.50
85TB36 Willie Stargell .30 .75
85TB37 Fernando Tatis Jr. 2.00 5.00
85TB38 Dave Winfield .30 .75
85TB39 Willie McCovey .30 .75
85TB40 Tim Lincecum .30 .75
85TB41 Ken Griffey Jr. .75 2.00
85TB42 Bob Gibson .30 .75
85TB43 Lou Brock .30 .75
85TB44 Nolan Ryan 1.25 3.00
85TB45 Bo Bichette 2.00 5.00
85TB46 Juan Soto 1.25 3.00
85TB47 Shohei Ohtani .60 1.50
85TB48 Austin Meadows .40 1.00
85TB49 Roberto Clemente 1.00 2.50
85TB50 Lewis Brinson .25 .60

2020 Topps Update '85 Topps Black

*BLACK: 1X TO 2.5X
STATED ODDS 1:XX HOBBY
STATED PRINT RUN 299 SER.#'d SETS
85TB1 Derek Jeter 6.00 15.00
85TB10 Jackie Robinson 3.00 8.00
85TB22 Mookie Betts 4.00 10.00
85TB29 Aaron Judge 8.00 20.00
85TB37 Fernando Tatis Jr. 6.00 15.00
85TB41 Ken Griffey Jr. 5.00 12.00
85TB45 Bo Bichette 8.00 20.00

2020 Topps Update '85 Topps Blue

*BLUE: .6X TO 1.5X
STATED ODDS 1:XX HOBBY
85TB41 Ken Griffey Jr. 3.00 8.00
85TB45 Bo Bichette 5.00 12.00

2020 Topps Update '85 Topps Gold

*GOLD: 2.5X TO 6X
STATED ODDS 1:XX HOBBY
STATED PRINT RUN 50 SER.#'d SETS
85TB1 Derek Jeter 15.00 40.00
85TB10 Jackie Robinson 8.00 20.00
85TB22 Mookie Betts 10.00 25.00
85TB29 Aaron Judge 20.00 50.00
85TB37 Fernando Tatis Jr. 15.00 40.00
85TB41 Ken Griffey Jr. 12.00 30.00
85TB45 Bo Bichette 20.00 50.00

2020 Topps Update '85 Topps Autographs

STATED ODDS 1:XX HOBBY
EXCHANGE DEADLINE 8/31/2022
85ABR Bryan Reynolds 8.00 20.00
85ADJ Derek Jeter
85AGS George Springer 25.00 60.00
85AJC Jose Canseco 12.00 30.00
85AJH Josh Hader 5.00 12.00
85AJJ Josh James 2.50 6.00
85AJM Joe Mauer EXCH 40.00 100.00
85AKS Kyle Schwarber 8.00 20.00
85ALR Luis Robert EXCH 75.00 200.00
85AMA Max Kepler 5.00 12.00
85AMK Mitch Keller 4.00 10.00
85AMO Matt Olson 6.00 15.00
85AMS Max Scherzer 25.00 60.00
85AMT Mike Trout EXCH
85AOM Oscar Mercado 4.00 10.00
85APA Pete Alonso EXCH 25.00 60.00
85APC Patrick Corbin 3.00 8.00
85ARD Rafael Devers 20.00 50.00
85ARM Ryan McBroom 12.00 30.00
85ASC Shin-Soo Choo 6.00 15.00
85ASG Sonny Gray EXCH 8.00 20.00
85ATA Tyler Alexander EXCH 4.00 10.00
85ATL Tim Lincecum EXCH 40.00 100.00
85AYD Yonathan Daza 3.00 8.00
85AYT Yoshi Tsutsugo EXCH 10.00 25.00
85AZG Zac Gallen 10.00 25.00
85AAKA Anthony Kay 2.50 6.00
85AARE Anthony Rendon 4.00 10.00
85ADGO Dwight Gooden 12.00 30.00
85AJMA James Marvel 2.50 6.00
85AJRO Josh Rojas 2.50 6.00
85AMCA Miguel Cabrera
85ARDO Randy Dobnak EXCH 12.00 30.00
85ARHE Rickey Henderson
85ARLA Ramon Laureano 8.00 20.00
85BAAO Adam Ottavino 5.00 12.00
85BADL Domingo Leyba 3.00 8.00
85BADV Dan Vogelbach 2.50 6.00
85BAGU Gio Urshela 10.00 25.00
85BAHD Hunter Dozier 2.50 6.00
85BAJA Jim Abbott 10.00 25.00
85BAJD Justin Dunn 5.00 12.00
85BAJS Jorge Soler 8.00 20.00
85BAMB Mike Brosseau 5.00 12.00
85BASL Shed Long 3.00 8.00
85BASN Sheldon Neuse 3.00 8.00
85BAYC Yu Chang 5.00 12.00
85BAJBU Jay Buhner 10.00 25.00
85BATLS Tommy La Stella 2.50 6.00

2020 Topps Update '85 Topps Autographs Black

*BLACK: .5X TO 1.2X
STATED ODDS 1:XX HOBBY
STATED PRINT RUN 199 SER.#'d SETS
EXCHANGE DEADLINE 8/31/2022
85AMA Max Kepler 8.00 20.00
85ASC Shin-Soo Choo 12.00 30.00
85AYT Yoshi Tsutsugo EXCH 15.00 40.00

2020 Topps Update '85 Topps Autographs Gold

*GOLD: .6X TO 1.5X
STATED ODDS 1:XX HOBBY
STATED PRINT RUN 50 SER.#'d SETS
EXCHANGE DEADLINE 8/31/2022
85ABR Bryan Reynolds 15.00 40.00
85AMA Max Kepler 15.00 40.00
85ASC Shin-Soo Choo 20.00 50.00
85AYT Yoshi Tsutsugo EXCH 20.00 50.00
85ARHE Rickey Henderson 40.00 100.00
85BAYC Yu Chang 12.00 30.00

2020 Topps Update '85 Topps Autographs Red

*RED: .8X TO 2X
STATED ODDS 1:XX HOBBY
STATED PRINT RUN 25 SER.#'d SETS
EXCHANGE DEADLINE 8/31/2022
85ABR Bryan Reynolds 20.00 50.00
85ALR Luis Robert EXCH 400.00 1000.00
85AMA Max Kepler 25.00 60.00
85ASC Shin-Soo Choo 30.00 80.00
85AYD Yonathan Daza 10.00 25.00
85AYT Yoshi Tsutsugo EXCH 25.00 60.00
85AMCA Miguel Cabrera 125.00 300.00
85ARHE Rickey Henderson 50.00 120.00
85BAJA Jim Abbott 25.00 60.00
85BAJD Justin Dunn 12.00 30.00
85BAYC Yu Chang 15.00 40.00

2020 Topps Update '85 Topps Silver Pack Chrome

STATED ODDS 1:XX HOBBY
CPC1 Yordan Alvarez 6.00 15.00
CPC2 Derek Jeter 4.00 10.00
CPC3 Mariano Rivera 2.00 5.00
CPC4 Rhys Hoskins 1.25 3.00
CPC5 Travis Demeritte 1.00 2.50
CPC6 Walker Buehler 1.25 3.00
CPC7 Shohei Ohtani 1.50 4.00
CPC8 Michael Brosseau 1.25 3.00
CPC9 Luis Robert 10.00 25.00
CPC10 Sonny Gray .75 2.00
CPC11 Cody Bellinger 2.00 5.00
CPC12 Nick Castellanos 1.00 2.50
CPC13 Willson Contreras 1.00 2.50
CPC14 Bo Bichette 6.00 15.00
CPC15 Hyun-Jin Ryu .75 2.00
CPC16 Jesus Luzardo 1.25 3.00
CPC17 Josh Staumont .60 1.50
CPC18 Yoshi Tsutsugo 1.50 4.00
CPC19 Mookie Betts 4.00 10.00
CPC20 Shogo Akiyama 1.00 2.50
CPC21 A.J. Puk 1.00 2.50
CPC22 Gerrit Cole 1.50 4.00
CPC23 Gavin Lux 3.00 8.00
CPC24 Willi Castro 1.00 2.50
CPC25 Roger Clemens 1.25 3.00
CPC26 Andrew Benintendi 1.00 2.50
CPC27 Brusdar Graterol 1.00 2.50
CPC28 Zac Gallen 1.50 4.00
CPC29 Rangel Ravelo .75 2.00
CPC30 Ronald Acuna Jr. 5.00 12.00
CPC31 Stephen Strasburg 1.00 2.50
CPC32 Cavan Biggio 1.25 3.00
CPC33 Shane Bieber 1.00 2.50
CPC34 Josh Donaldson .75 2.00
CPC35 Fernando Tatis Jr. 5.00 12.00
CPC36 Brock Burke .60 1.50
CPC37 Tommy Edman 1.00 2.50
CPC38 Tony Gonsolin 2.50 6.00
CPC39 Genesis Cabrera 1.00 2.50
CPC40 Bobby Bradley .60 1.50
CPC41 George Springer .75 2.00
CPC42 Mike Yastrzemski 1.50 4.00
CPC43 Trent Grisham 2.50 6.00
CPC44 Dale Murphy 1.00 2.50
CPC45 Mike Trout 5.00 12.00
CPC46 Anthony Rendon 1.00 2.50
CPC47 Yonathan Daza .75 2.00
CPC48 Seth Brown .60 1.50
CPC49 Juan Soto 3.00 8.00
CPC50 Christian Yelich 1.25 3.00

2020 Topps Update '85 Topps Silver Pack Chrome Black Refractors

*BLACK: .8X TO 2X
STATED ODDS 1:XX HOBBY
STATED PRINT RUN 199 SER.#'d SETS
CPC2 Derek Jeter 12.00 30.00
CPC9 Luis Robert 30.00 80.00
CPC14 Bo Bichette 15.00 40.00
CPC45 Mike Trout 15.00 60.00

2020 Topps Update '85 Topps Silver Pack Chrome Blue Refractors

*BLUE: 1X TO 2.5X
STATED ODDS 1:XX HOBBY
STATED PRINT RUN 150 SER.#'d SETS
CPC2 Derek Jeter 15.00 40.00
CPC9 Luis Robert 40.00 100.00
CPC14 Bo Bichette 25.00 60.00
CPC30 Ronald Acuna Jr. 15.00 40.00
CPC35 Fernando Tatis Jr. 15.00 40.00
CPC45 Mike Trout 20.00 50.00

2020 Topps Update '85 Topps Silver Pack Chrome Gold Refractors

*GOLD: 2.5X TO 6X
STATED ODDS 1:XX HOBBY
STATED PRINT RUN 50 SER.#'d SETS
CPC2 Derek Jeter 40.00 100.00
CPC3 Mariano Rivera 15.00 40.00
CPC9 Luis Robert 100.00 250.00
CPC14 Bo Bichette 60.00 150.00
CPC30 Ronald Acuna Jr. 40.00 100.00
CPC35 Fernando Tatis Jr. 75.00 200.00
CPC45 Mike Trout 50.00 120.00
CPC49 Juan Soto 25.00 60.00

2020 Topps Update '85 Topps Silver Pack Chrome Green Refractors

*GREEN: 1.2X TO 3X
STATED ODDS 1:XX HOBBY
STATED PRINT RUN 99 SER.#'d SETS
CPC2 Derek Jeter 20.00 50.00
CPC9 Luis Robert 50.00 120.00
CPC14 Bo Bichette 30.00 80.00
CPC30 Ronald Acuna Jr. 20.00 50.00
CPC35 Fernando Tatis Jr. 20.00 50.00
CPC45 Mike Trout 25.00 60.00

2020 Topps Update '85 Topps Silver Pack Chrome Orange Refractors

*ORANGE: 4X TO 10X
STATED ODDS 1:XX HOBBY
STATED PRINT RUN 25 SER.#'d SETS
CPC2 Derek Jeter 60.00 150.00
CPC3 Mariano Rivera 25.00 60.00
CPC9 Luis Robert 150.00 400.00
CPC14 Bo Bichette 100.00 250.00
CPC30 Ronald Acuna Jr. 100.00 250.00
CPC35 Fernando Tatis Jr. 125.00 300.00
CPC45 Mike Trout 75.00 200.00
CPC49 Juan Soto 40.00 100.00

2020 Topps Update '85 Topps Silver Pack Chrome Purple Refractors

*PURPLE: 1.2X TO 3X
STATED ODDS 1:XX HOBBY
STATED PRINT RUN 75 SER.#'d SETS
CPC2 Derek Jeter 20.00 50.00
CPC9 Luis Robert 50.00 120.00
CPC14 Bo Bichette 30.00 80.00
CPC30 Ronald Acuna Jr. 20.00 50.00
CPC35 Fernando Tatis Jr. 30.00 80.00
CPC45 Mike Trout 25.00 60.00

2020 Topps Update '85 Topps Silver Pack Chrome Autographs

RANDOM INSERTS IN SILVER PACKS
PRINT RUNS B/WN 10-149 COPIES PER
NO PRICING ON QTY 15 OR LESS
EXCHANGE DEADLINE 8/31/22
CPC1 Yordan Alvarez/99 60.00 150.00
CPC2 Derek Jeter
CPC4 Rhys Hoskins/30 10.00 25.00
CPC6 Walker Buehler/50 40.00 100.00
CPC8 Michael Brosseau/149 6.00 15.00
CPC9 Luis Robert/99 200.00 500.00
CPC10 Sonny Gray/99 10.00 25.00
CPC11 Cody Bellinger/30
CPC12 Nick Castellanos/99 10.00 25.00
CPC14 Bo Bichette EXCH
CPC15 Hyun-Jin Ryu/50 30.00 80.00
CPC16 Jesus Luzardo/99 20.00 50.00
CPC17 Josh Staumont/149 12.00 30.00
CPC18 Yoshi Tsutsugo/99 15.00 40.00
CPC20 Shogo Akiyama/99 10.00 25.00
CPC22 Gerrit Cole/30
CPC23 Gavin Lux/99 50.00 120.00
CPC24 Willi Castro/149 20.00 50.00
CPC26 Andrew Benintendi/30 30.00 80.00
CPC27 Brusdar Graterol/99 20.00 50.00
CPC28 Zac Gallen/99 25.00 60.00
CPC29 Rangel Ravelo/75 5.00 12.00
CPC30 Ronald Acuna Jr./30 200.00 500.00
CPC31 Stephen Strasburg/30 25.00 60.00
CPC32 Cavan Biggio/50 12.00 30.00
CPC33 Shane Bieber/99 15.00 40.00
CPC35 Fernando Tatis Jr./30 100.00 250.00
CPC36 Brock Burke/149 3.00 8.00
CPC37 Tommy Edman/149 25.00 60.00
CPC38 Tony Gonsolin/149 12.00 30.00
CPC39 Genesis Cabrera/149 5.00 12.00
CPC41 George Springer
CPC42 Mike Yastrzemski/99 25.00 60.00
CPC43 Trent Grisham/99 25.00 60.00
CPC44 Dale Murphy/50 30.00 80.00
CPC46 Anthony Rendon/30 25.00 60.00
CPC47 Yonathan Daza/149 4.00 10.00
CPC48 Seth Brown/149 3.00 8.00
CPC49 Juan Soto/30 150.00 400.00
CPC50 Christian Yelich/30

2020 Topps Update '85 Topps Silver Pack Chrome Autographs Orange Refractors

*ORANGE/25: .75X TO 2X p/r 149
*ORANGE/25: .6X TO 1.5X p/r 75-99
*ORANGE/25: .5X TO 1.2X p/r 30-50
RANDOM INSERTS IN SILVER PACKS
STATED PRINT RUN 25 SER.#'d SETS
EXCHANGE DEADLINE 8/31/22
CPC1 Yordan Alvarez 150.00 400.00
CPC9 Luis Robert 400.00 800.00
CPC11 Cody Bellinger 75.00 200.00
CPC14 Bo Bichette EXCH 400.00 800.00
CPC18 Yoshi Tsutsugo 40.00 100.00
CPC22 Gerrit Cole 75.00 200.00
CPC23 Gavin Lux 125.00 300.00
CPC24 Willi Castro 100.00 250.00
CPC32 Cavan Biggio 25.00 60.00
CPC33 Shane Bieber 30.00 80.00
CPC35 Fernando Tatis Jr. 200.00 500.00
CPC41 George Springer 50.00 120.00

2020 Topps Update 20 Years of The Captain

STATED ODDS 1:XX HOBBY
*BLUE: .6X TO 1.5X
*BLACK/299: 1X TO 2.5X
*GOLD/50: 2.5X TO 6X
*RED/10: 12X TO 30X
YOC00 Derek Jeter 1.00 2.50
YOC01 Derek Jeter 1.00 2.50
YOC02 Derek Jeter 1.00 2.50
YOC03 Derek Jeter 1.00 2.50
YOC04 Derek Jeter 1.00 2.50
YOC05 Derek Jeter 1.00 2.50
YOC06 Derek Jeter 1.00 2.50
YOC07 Derek Jeter 1.00 2.50
YOC08 Derek Jeter 1.00 2.50
YOC09 Derek Jeter 1.00 2.50
YOC10 Derek Jeter 1.00 2.50
YOC11 Derek Jeter 1.00 2.50
YOC12 Derek Jeter 1.00 2.50
YOC13 Derek Jeter 1.00 2.50
YOC14 Derek Jeter 1.00 2.50
YOC95 Derek Jeter 1.00 2.50
YOC96 Derek Jeter 1.00 2.50
YOC97 Derek Jeter 1.00 2.50
YOC98 Derek Jeter 1.00 2.50
YOC99 Derek Jeter 1.00 2.50

2020 Topps Update 20 Years of The Captain Commemorative Patches

STATED ODDS 1:XX HOBBY
*BLACK/50: 1X TO 2.5X
*GOLD/25: 1.5X TO 4X
*RED/10 5X TO 12X
20YCC00 Derek Jeter 3.00 8.00
20YCC01 Derek Jeter 3.00 8.00
20YCC02 Derek Jeter 3.00 8.00
20YCC03 Derek Jeter 3.00 8.00
20YCC04 Derek Jeter 3.00 8.00
20YCC05 Derek Jeter 3.00 8.00
20YCC06 Derek Jeter 3.00 8.00
20YCC07 Derek Jeter 3.00 8.00
20YCC08 Derek Jeter 3.00 8.00
20YCC09 Derek Jeter 3.00 8.00
20YCC10 Derek Jeter 3.00 8.00
20YCC11 Derek Jeter 3.00 8.00
20YCC12 Derek Jeter 3.00 8.00
20YCC13 Derek Jeter 3.00 8.00
20YCC14 Derek Jeter 3.00 8.00
20YCC95 Derek Jeter 3.00 8.00
20YCC96 Derek Jeter 3.00 8.00
20YCC97 Derek Jeter 3.00 8.00
20YCC98 Derek Jeter 3.00 8.00
20YCC99 Derek Jeter 3.00 8.00

2020 Topps Update A Numbers Game

STATED ODDS 1:XX HOBBY
NG1 Roberto Alomar .30 .75
NG2 Ryne Sandberg .75 2.00
NG3 Roberto Clemente 1.00 2.50
NG4 Randy Johnson .40 1.00
NG5 Rickey Henderson .40 1.00
NG6 Nolan Ryan 1.25 3.00
NG7 Jackie Robinson .40 1.00
NG8 Jeff Bagwell .30 .75
NG9 Chipper Jones .60 1.50
NG10 Ken Griffey Jr. .75 2.00
NG11 Stan Musial .60 1.50
NG12 Robin Yount .40 1.00
NG13 Mariano Rivera .50 1.25
NG14 Ted Williams .75 2.00
NG15 Tony Gwynn .40 1.00
NG16 Cal Ripken Jr. 1.25 3.00
NG17 Mike Piazza .40 1.00
NG18 Willie Mays .75 2.00
NG19 Ernie Banks .40 1.00
NG20 Sandy Koufax .75 2.00
NG21 Ozzie Smith .50 1.25
NG22 Derek Jeter 1.00 2.50
NG23 Mike Schmidt .60 1.50
NG24 Johnny Bench .40 1.00
NG25 Hank Aaron .75 2.00

2020 Topps Update A Numbers Game Black

*BLACK: 1X TO 2.5X
STATED ODDS 1:XX HOBBY
STATED PRINT RUN 299 SER.#'d SETS
NG6 Nolan Ryan 4.00 10.00
NG7 Jackie Robinson 3.00 8.00
NG10 Ken Griffey Jr. 5.00 12.00
NG22 Derek Jeter 6.00 15.00

2020 Topps Update A Numbers Game Blue

*BLUE: .6X TO 1.5X
STATED ODDS 1:XX HOBBY
NG10 Ken Griffey Jr. 3.00 8.00

2020 Topps Update A Numbers Game Gold

*GOLD: 2.5X TO 6X
STATED ODDS 1:XX HOBBY
STATED PRINT RUN 50 SER.#'d SETS
NG6 Nolan Ryan 10.00 25.00
NG7 Jackie Robinson 8.00 20.00
NG10 Ken Griffey Jr. 12.00 30.00
NG16 Cal Ripken Jr. 12.00 30.00
NG22 Derek Jeter 15.00 40.00

2020 Topps Update All Star Stitches

STATED ODDS 1:XX HOBBY
ASSCAJ Aaron Judge 8.00 20.00
ASSCAP Albert Pujols 4.00 10.00
ASSCAR Anthony Rizzo 4.00 10.00
ASSCBC Bartolo Colon 4.00 10.00
ASSCBG Brett Gardner 6.00 15.00
ASSCBH Bryce Harper 5.00 12.00
ASSCBL Brandon Lowe 2.50 6.00
ASSCBP Buster Posey 4.00 10.00
ASSCCB Charlie Blackmon 3.00 8.00
ASSCCC Carlos Correa 3.00 8.00
ASSCCK Clayton Kershaw 5.00 12.00
ASSCCS Corey Seager 3.00 8.00
ASSCDG Dee Gordon 2.00 5.00
ASSCDO David Ortiz 3.00 8.00
ASSCFL Francisco Lindor 5.00 12.00
ASSCGC Gerrit Cole 5.00 12.00
ASSCGS Giancarlo Stanton 3.00 8.00
ASSCJA Jose Altuve 4.00 10.00
ASSCJB Jose Berrios 2.50 6.00
ASSCJC Johnny Cueto 4.00 10.00
ASSCJD Josh Donaldson 2.50 6.00
ASSCJP Joc Pederson 2.50 6.00
ASSCJR Jose Ramirez 2.50 6.00
ASSCJT Justin Turner 4.00 10.00
ASSCJV Joey Votto 3.00 8.00
ASSCKB Kris Bryant 4.00 10.00
ASSCLC Lorenzo Cain 2.00 5.00
ASSCLM Lance McCullers Jr. 2.00 5.00
ASSCLS Luis Severino 2.50 6.00
ASSCMB Mookie Betts 8.00 20.00
ASSCMC Miguel Cabrera 3.00 8.00
ASSCMM Manny Machado 3.00 8.00
ASSCMS Max Scherzer 3.00 8.00
ASSCMT Mike Trout 15.00 40.00
ASSCNA Nolan Arenado 5.00 12.00
ASSCNC Nelson Cruz 3.00 8.00
ASSCPG Paul Goldschmidt 3.00 8.00
ASSCRC Robinson Cano 2.50 6.00
ASSCRZ Ryan Zimmerman 4.00 10.00
ASSCSG Sonny Gray 2.50 6.00
ASSCSP Salvador Perez 5.00 12.00
ASSCSS Stephen Strasburg 3.00 8.00
ASSCTS Trevor Story 3.00 8.00
ASSCXB Xander Bogaerts 5.00 12.00
ASSCYD Yu Darvish 3.00 8.00
ASSCYM Yadier Molina 4.00 10.00
ASSCZG Zack Greinke 4.00 10.00
ASSCAJU Aaron Judge 8.00 20.00
ASSCARI Anthony Rizzo 4.00 10.00
ASSCBHA Bryce Harper 5.00 12.00
ASSCBPO Buster Posey 4.00 10.00
ASSCCCS CC Sabathia 2.50 6.00
ASSCCHS Chris Sale 5.00 12.00
ASSCCKE Clayton Kershaw 5.00 12.00
ASSCCLK Clayton Kershaw 5.00 12.00
ASSCCSA Chris Sale 5.00 12.00
ASSCCSE Corey Seager 3.00 8.00
ASSCDJE Jacob deGrom 8.00 20.00
ASSCGSA Gary Sanchez 3.00 8.00
ASSCGSP George Springer 2.50 6.00
ASSCJAL Jose Altuve 4.00 10.00
ASSCJOA Jose Altuve 4.00 10.00
ASSCJUV Justin Verlander 3.00 8.00
ASSCJVE Justin Verlander 3.00 8.00
ASSCJVO Joey Votto 3.00 8.00
ASSCMBE Mookie Betts 8.00 20.00
ASSCMCO Michael Conforto 2.50 6.00
ASSCMIT Mike Trout 15.00 40.00
ASSCMMA Manny Machado 3.00 8.00
ASSCMSA Miguel Sano 2.50 6.00
ASSCMSC Max Scherzer 3.00 8.00
ASSCMTA Masahiro Tanaka 3.00 8.00
ASSCMTR Mike Trout 15.00 40.00
ASSCNAR Nolan Arenado 5.00 12.00
ASSCNOA Nolan Arenado 5.00 12.00
ASSCPGO Paul Goldschmidt 3.00 8.00
ASSCSAL Chris Sale 5.00 12.00
ASSCTRO Mike Trout 15.00 40.00
ASSCXBO Xander Bogaerts 5.00 12.00
ASSCYMO Yadier Molina 4.00 10.00

2020 Topps Update All Star Stitches Red

*RED: .8X TO 2X
STATED ODDS 1:XX HOBBY
STATED PRINT RUN 25 SER.#'d SETS
ASSCAP Albert Pujols 20.00 50.00
ASSCAR Anthony Rizzo 20.00 50.00
ASSCCK Clayton Kershaw 25.00 60.00
ASSCJR Jose Ramirez 10.00 25.00
ASSCJT Justin Turner 15.00 40.00
ASSCJV Joey Votto 12.00 30.00
ASSCMC Miguel Cabrera 15.00 40.00
ASSCMT Mike Trout 40.00 100.00
ASSCPG Paul Goldschmidt 12.00 30.00
ASSCSG Sonny Gray 10.00 25.00
ASSCXB Xander Bogaerts 12.00 30.00
ASSCYM Yadier Molina 12.00 30.00
ASSCARI Anthony Rizzo 20.00 50.00
ASSCCKE Clayton Kershaw 25.00 60.00
ASSCCLK Clayton Kershaw 25.00 60.00
ASSCJUV Justin Verlander 12.00 30.00
ASSCJVE Justin Verlander 12.00 30.00
ASSCJVO Joey Votto 12.00 30.00
ASSCMIT Mike Trout 40.00 100.00
ASSCMTR Mike Trout 40.00 100.00
ASSCPGO Paul Goldschmidt 12.00 30.00
ASSCTRO Mike Trout 40.00 100.00
ASSCXBO Xander Bogaerts 12.00 30.00
ASSCYMO Yadier Molina 12.00 30.00

2020 Topps Update All Star Stitches Silver

*SILVER: .6X TO 1.5X
STATED ODDS 1:XX HOBBY
STATED PRINT RUN 50 SER.#'d SETS
ASSCAR Anthony Rizzo 10.00 25.00
ASSCJT Justin Turner 12.00 30.00
ASSCJV Joey Votto 10.00 25.00
ASSCMC Miguel Cabrera 12.00 30.00
ASSCSG Sonny Gray 8.00 20.00
ASSCARI Anthony Rizzo 10.00 25.00
ASSCJUV Justin Verlander 10.00 25.00
ASSCJVE Justin Verlander 10.00 25.00
ASSCJVO Joey Votto 10.00 25.00

2020 Topps Update All Star Stitches Autographs

STATED ODDS 1:XX HOBBY
PRINT RUNS B/WN 10-25 COPIES PER
NO PRICING ON QTY 15 OR LESS
EXCHANGE DEADLINE 8/31/2022
ASSAAB Alex Bregman/25 15.00 40.00
ASSAAM Andrew McCutchen/25 40.00 100.00
ASSACS Chris Sale/25
ASSAGC Gerrit Cole/25 20.00 50.00
ASSAGS George Springer/25 10.00 25.00
ASSAGT Gleyber Torres/25
ASSAJA Jose Altuve/25 10.00 25.00
ASSAJD Jacob deGrom/25 60.00 150.00
ASSAMC Miguel Cabrera/25
ASSAMT Mike Trout/25
ASSANA Nolan Arenado/25 25.00 60.00
ASSARA Ronald Acuna Jr./25 60.00 150.00
ASSASS Stephen Strasburg/25 20.00 50.00
ASSAWC Willson Contreras/25 12.00 30.00
ASSAXB Xander Bogaerts/25 12.00 30.00
ASSAYM Yadier Molina/25
ASSACSA CC Sabathia/25 15.00 40.00
ASSAJBE Jose Berrios/25 10.00 25.00

2020 Topps Update All Star Stitches Dual Autographs

STATED ODDS 1:XX HOBBY
PRINT RUNS B/WN 10-25 COPIES PER
NO PRICING ON QTY 15 OR LESS
EXCHANGE DEADLINE 8/31/2022
ASDAAS Springer/Altuve/25 20.00 50.00
ASDAAT Acuna/Torres/25
ASDABS Springer/Bregman/25 25.00 60.00
ASDAMC McCutchen/Cole
ASDATA Acuna/Trout/25
ASDAYW Molina/Contreras/25 40.00 100.00

2020 Topps Update All Star Stitches Jumbo

STATED ODDS 1:XX HOBBY
PRINT RUNS B/WN 10-25 COPIES PER
NO PRICING ON QTY 15 OR LESS
ASJAC Aroldis Chapman/25 10.00 25.00
ASJAN Aaron Nola/25 15.00 40.00
ASJAR Anthony Rizzo/25 40.00 100.00
ASJBC Bartolo Colon/20 8.00 20.00
ASJBH Bryce Harper/25 40.00 100.00
ASJBP Buster Posey/25 15.00 40.00
ASJBS Blake Snell/25 15.00 40.00
ASJCB Charlie Blackmon/25 15.00 40.00
ASJCC Carlos Correa/25
ASJCK Clayton Kershaw/25 40.00 100.00
ASJCS Chris Sale/25 8.00 20.00
ASJCY Christian Yelich/20 20.00 50.00
ASJDO David Ortiz
ASJES Eugenio Suarez
ASJFF Freddie Freeman 20.00 50.00
ASJFL Francisco Lindor/25 12.00 30.00
ASJGC Gerrit Cole/25 12.00 30.00
ASJGS Giancarlo Stanton
ASJGT Gleyber Torres
ASJHR Hyun-Jin Ryu/20 8.00 20.00
ASJJA Jose Abreu/25 25.00 60.00
ASJJB Jose Berrios
ASJJD Josh Donaldson/20 6.00 15.00
ASJJM J.D. Martinez
ASJJT Justin Turner/25 25.00 60.00
ASJJV Joey Votto/25 30.00 80.00
ASJKS Kyle Schwarber/25 20.00 50.00
ASJLS Luis Severino/25 15.00 40.00
ASJMB Mookie Betts/25 25.00 60.00
ASJMC Matt Chapman
ASJMM Max Muncy/25 15.00 40.00
ASJMS Max Scherzer/25 15.00 40.00
ASJNA Nolan Arenado
ASJNS Noah Syndergaard
ASJPG Paul Goldschmidt/25
ASJRZ Ryan Zimmerman
ASJSG Sonny Gray/25 20.00 50.00
ASJSP Salvador Perez
ASJTB Trevor Bauer/25 20.00 50.00
ASJTS Trevor Story
ASJWC Willson Contreras/25 30.00 80.00
ASJXB Xander Bogaerts/25 20.00 50.00
ASJYD Yu Darvish
ASJZG Zack Greinke/25 15.00 40.00
ASJALT Jose Altuve/25 15.00 40.00
ASJBPO Buster Posey/25 15.00 40.00
ASJCBL Charlie Blackmon/25 15.00 40.00
ASJCCS CC Sabathia
ASJCHS Chris Sale
ASJCLK Clayton Kershaw
ASJCSA Chris Sale
ASJCSE Corey Seager/25 20.00 50.00
ASJGCO Gerrit Cole/25 12.00 30.00
ASJGSA Gary Sanchez/25 8.00 20.00
ASJGSP George Springer/25 6.00 15.00
ASJGTO Gleyber Torres
ASJJAL Jose Altuve/25 15.00 40.00
ASJJOA Jose Altuve
ASJJRA Jose Ramirez
ASJJUV Justin Verlander/25 15.00 40.00
ASJJVE Justin Verlander
ASJLSE Luis Severino/25 15.00 40.00
ASJMAM Manny Machado/20 12.00 30.00
ASJMAX Max Scherzer/25 15.00 40.00
ASJMBE Mookie Betts/25 25.00 60.00
ASJMMA Manny Machado/25 12.00 30.00
ASJMOB Mookie Betts/25 25.00 60.00
ASJMSA Miguel Sano/25 6.00 15.00
ASJMSO Mike Soroka
ASJMTA Masahiro Tanaka
ASJMTR Mike Trout/25 40.00 100.00
ASJNAR Nolan Arenado
ASJPGO Paul Goldschmidt/25
ASJSST Stephen Strasburg/25
ASJTRO Mike Trout
ASJYAM Yadier Molina
ASJYMO Yadier Molina

2020 Topps Update Baseball Stars Autographs

STATED ODDS 1:XX HOBBY
EXCHANGE DEADLINE 8/31/2022
BSAAK Andrew Knapp 2.50 6.00
BSAAR Anthony Rendon 10.00 25.00
BSABO Brian O'Grady 2.50 6.00
BSACD Corey Dickerson 3.00 8.00
BSACM Charlie Morton 4.00 10.00
BSADA Dario Agrazal 3.00 8.00
BSADB David Bote 3.00 8.00
BSADJ Danny Jansen 2.50 6.00
BSADP David Price 10.00 25.00
BSAER Eduardo Rodriguez 4.00 10.00
BSAET Eric Thames 2.50 6.00
BSAGC Gerrit Cole 20.00 50.00
BSAHR Hyun-Jin Ryu 20.00 50.00
BSAJB Jon Berti 2.50 6.00
BSAJG Joey Gallo 10.00 25.00
BSAJH J.D. Hammer 4.00 10.00
BSAJM Jack Mayfield 8.00 20.00
BSAJS Juan Soto 60.00 150.00
BSAKK Kwang-Hyun Kim 12.00 30.00
BSAKM Ketel Marte 3.00 8.00
BSAKN Kevin Newman 5.00 12.00
BSAKW Kolten Wong 3.00 8.00
BSALB Lewis Brinson 2.50 6.00
BSALR Luis Robert 100.00 250.00
BSALW LaMonte Wade Jr. 4.00 10.00
BSAMM Mike Moustakas
BSAMS Marcus Stroman 10.00 25.00
BSANC Nick Castellanos 8.00 20.00
BSAPS Patrick Sandoval 4.00 10.00
BSARG Robel Garcia 2.50 6.00
BSARM Ryan McMahon 4.00 10.00
BSARV Daniel Vogelbach 2.50 6.00
BSASA Shogo Akiyama 8.00 20.00
BSASH Scott Heineman 2.50 6.00
BSATE Tom Eshelman 3.00 8.00
BSATP Tommy Pham 2.50 6.00
BSAYD Yonathan Daza 3.00 8.00
BSAYG Yasmani Grandal 2.50 6.00
BSAZG Zac Gallen 6.00 15.00
BSAKMA Kenta Maeda 25.00 60.00
BSAMSE Marcus Semien 4.00 10.00
BSAMST Myles Straw 3.00 8.00
BSASMA Sean Manaea 2.50 6.00

2020 Topps Update Baseball Stars Autographs Black

*BLACK: .5X TO 1.2X
STATED ODDS 1:XX HOBBY
STATED PRINT RUN 199 SER.#'d SETS
EXCHANGE DEADLINE 8/31/2022
BSAKW Kolten Wong 6.00 15.00
BSASA Shogo Akiyama 12.00 30.00
BSAMSE Marcus Semien 5.00 12.00

2020 Topps Update Baseball Stars Autographs Gold

*GOLD: .6X TO 1.5X
STATED ODDS 1:XX HOBBY
STATED PRINT RUN 50 SER.#'d SETS
EXCHANGE DEADLINE 8/31/2022
BSAET Eric Thames 10.00 25.00
BSAKK Kwang-Hyun Kim 30.00 80.00
BSAKW Kolten Wong 12.00 30.00
BSAMM Mike Moustakas 10.00 25.00
BSASA Shogo Akiyama 15.00 40.00
BSAMSE Marcus Semien 6.00 15.00

2020 Topps Update Baseball Stars Autographs Red

*RED: .8X TO 2X
STATED ODDS 1:XX HOBBY
STATED PRINT RUN 25 SER.#'d SETS
EXCHANGE DEADLINE 8/31/2022
BSAAR Anthony Rendon 40.00 100.00
BSAET Eric Thames 12.00 30.00
BSAKK Kwang-Hyun Kim 40.00 100.00
BSAKW Kolten Wong 15.00 40.00
BSAMM Mike Moustakas 12.00 30.00
BSASA Shogo Akiyama 20.00 50.00
BSAMSE Marcus Semien 8.00 20.00

2020 Topps Update Boxloader Patches

STATED ODDS 1 PER HOBBY
BPAA Aristides Aquino 4.00 10.00
BPAB Alex Bregman 2.50 6.00
BPAJ Aaron Judge 10.00 25.00
BPAM Andrew McCutchen 2.50 6.00
BPAR Anthony Rizzo 6.00 15.00
BPBB Bo Bichette 20.00 50.00
BPBH Bryce Harper 8.00 20.00
BPBM Brendan McKay 2.50 6.00
BPBP Buster Posey 8.00 20.00
BPCB Cody Bellinger 6.00 15.00
BPCK Clayton Kershaw 6.00 15.00
BPCY Christian Yelich 6.00 15.00
BPEJ Eloy Jimenez 5.00 12.00
BPFF Freddie Freeman 8.00 20.00
BPFL Francisco Lindor 2.50 6.00
BPFT Fernando Tatis Jr. 15.00 40.00
BPGL Gavin Lux 8.00 20.00
BPGS Giancarlo Stanton 2.50 6.00
BPGT Gleyber Torres 8.00 20.00
BPJB Javier Baez 3.00 8.00
BPJD Jacob deGrom 5.00 12.00
BPJL Jesus Luzardo 3.00 8.00
BPJS Juan Soto 8.00 20.00
BPJV Joey Votto 2.50 6.00
BPKA Jose Altuve 2.00 5.00
BPKB Kris Bryant 6.00 15.00
BPKL Kyle Lewis 12.00 30.00
BPLR Luis Robert 40.00 100.00
BPMB Mookie Betts 10.00 25.00
BPMC Matt Chapman 2.50 6.00
BPMK Max Kepler 2.00 5.00
BPMS Max Scherzer 2.50 6.00
BPMT Mike Trout 25.00 60.00

BPNA Nolan Arenado 6.00 15.00
BPNH Nico Hoerner 6.00 15.00
BPNS Nick Solak 6.00 15.00
BPPA Pete Alonso 6.00 15.00
BPPG Paul Goldschmidt 2.50 6.00
BPRA Ronald Acuna Jr. 15.00 40.00
BPRD Rafael Devers 3.00 8.00
BPRH Rhys Hoskins 8.00 20.00
BPSM Sean Murphy 2.50 6.00
BPSO Shohei Ohtani 5.00 12.00
BPTS Trevor Story 2.50 6.00
BPVG Vladimir Guerrero Jr. 10.00 25.00
BPWM Whit Merrifield 2.50 6.00
BPYA Yordan Alvarez 15.00 40.00
BPYM Yadier Molina 3.00 8.00
BPJBE Josh Bell 4.00 10.00
BPJVE Justin Verlander 2.50 6.00

2020 Topps Update Coin Cards

STATED ODDS 1:XX HOBBY
TBCAA Aristides Aquino 2.00 5.00
TBCAB Alex Bregman 1.25 3.00
TBCAJ Aaron Judge 3.00 8.00
TBCAR Anthony Rendon 1.25 3.00
TBCBB Bo Bichette 4.00 10.00
TBCBH Bryce Harper 4.00 10.00
TBCBM Brendan McKay 4.00 10.00
TBCBP Buster Posey 1.50 4.00
TBCCB Cody Bellinger 2.50 6.00
TBCCK Clayton Kershaw 2.00 5.00
TBCCY Christian Yelich 1.50 4.00
TBCEJ Eloy Jimenez 2.50 6.00
TBCFF Freddie Freeman 1.50 4.00
TBCFL Francisco Lindor 1.25 3.00
TBCFT Fernando Tatis Jr. 10.00 25.00
TBCGC Gerrit Cole 4.00 10.00
TBCGL Gavin Lux 4.00 10.00
TBCGT Gleyber Torres 2.50 6.00
TBCJB Javier Baez 1.50 4.00
TBCJD Jacob deGrom 4.00 10.00
TBCJG Joey Gallo 1.25 3.00
TBCJL Jesus Luzardo 1.50 4.00
TBCJS Juan Soto 4.00 10.00
TBCJV Justin Verlander 1.25 3.00
TBCKB Kris Bryant 1.50 4.00
TBCKH Keston Hiura 1.50 4.00
TBCKL Kyle Lewis 6.00 15.00
TBCKM Ketel Marte 1.00 2.50
TBCLR Luis Robert 6.00 15.00
TBCMB Mookie Betts 5.00 12.00
TBCMC Matt Chapman 1.25 3.00
TBCMM Manny Machado 1.25 3.00
TBCMS Max Scherzer 1.25 3.00
TBCMT Mike Trout 6.00 15.00
TBCNA Nolan Arenado 2.50 6.00
TBCNH Nico Hoerner 3.00 8.00
TBCPA Pete Alonso 3.00 8.00
TBCPG Paul Goldschmidt 1.25 3.00
TBCRA Ronald Acuna Jr. 5.00 12.00
TBCRD Rafael Devers 1.50 4.00
TBCRH Rhys Hoskins 1.50 4.00
TBCSO Shohei Ohtani 2.50 6.00
TBCVG Vladimir Guerrero Jr. 4.00 10.00
TBCWB Walker Buehler 1.50 4.00
TBCWM Whit Merrifield 1.25 3.00
TBCYA Yordan Alvarez 10.00 25.00
TBCYM Yadier Molina 3.00 8.00
TBCANR Anthony Rizzo 3.00 8.00
TBCJOD Josh Donaldson 1.00 2.50
TBCJOV Joey Votto 1.25 3.00

2020 Topps Update Coin Cards Black

*BLACK: .6X TO 1.5X
STATED ODDS 1:XX HOBBY
STATED PRINT RUN 199 SER.#'d SETS
TBCCY Christian Yelich 8.00 20.00
TBCFF Freddie Freeman 5.00 12.00
TBCLR Luis Robert 15.00 40.00
TBCNA Nolan Arenado 8.00 20.00
TBCRA Ronald Acuna Jr. 10.00 25.00

2020 Topps Update Coin Cards Gold

*GOLD: 1X TO 2.5X
STATED ODDS 1:XX HOBBY
STATED PRINT RUN 50 SER.#'d SETS
TBCCY Christian Yelich 12.00 30.00
TBCFF Freddie Freeman 8.00 20.00
TBCJD Jacob deGrom 10.00 25.00
TBCLR Luis Robert 60.00 150.00
TBCNA Nolan Arenado 12.00 30.00
TBCRA Ronald Acuna Jr. 15.00 40.00
TBCSO Shohei Ohtani 8.00 20.00
TBCVG Vladimir Guerrero Jr. 12.00 30.00

2020 Topps Update Decades' Best

STATED ODDS 1:XX HOBBY
DB1 Whitey Ford .30 .75
DB2 Bob Lemon .30 .75
DB3 Early Wynn .30 .75
DB4 Robin Roberts .30 .75
DB5 Warren Spahn .30 .75
DB6 Hoyt Wilhelm .30 .75
DB7 Bob Feller .30 .75
DB8 Jim Bunning .30 .75
DB9 Sandy Koufax .75 2.00
DB10 Hal Newhouser .30 .75
DB11 Rod Carew .30 .75
DB12 Tom Seaver .30 .75
DB13 Frank Robinson .30 .75
DB14 Carl Yastrzemski .60 1.50
DB15 Brooks Robinson .30 .75
DB16 Sandy Koufax .75 2.00
DB17 Bob Gibson .30 .75
DB18 Roberto Clemente 1.00 2.50
DB19 Willie Mays .75 2.00
DB20 Sandy Koufax .75 2.00
DB21 Cincinnati Reds .25 .60
DB22 Baltimore Orioles .25 .60
DB23 Pittsburgh Pirates .25 .60
DB24 Los Angeles Dodgers .25 .60
DB25 Boston Red Sox .25 .60
DB26 New York Yankees .25 .60
DB27 Oakland Athletics .25 .60
DB28 Philadelphia Phillies .25 .60
DB29 Kansas City Royals .25 .60
DB30 New York Mets .25 .60
DB31 Mike Schmidt .60 1.50
DB32 Ryne Sandberg .75 2.00
DB33 Cal Ripken Jr. 1.25 3.00
DB34 Dale Murphy .40 1.00
DB35 Dwight Gooden .25 .60
DB36 Jose Canseco .30 .75
DB37 Roger Clemens .50 1.25
DB38 Don Mattingly .75 2.00
DB39 Steve Carlton .30 .75
DB40 Mark McGwire .60 1.50
DB41 Roger Clemens .50 1.25
DB42 Randy Johnson .40 1.00
DB43 Tom Glavine .30 .75
DB44 Pedro Martinez .30 .75
DB45 Mike Mussina .30 .75
DB46 John Smoltz .40 1.00
DB47 David Cone .25 .60
DB48 Dennis Eckersley .30 .75
DB49 Andy Pettitte .30 .75
DB50 Mariano Rivera .50 1.25
DB51 Boston Red Sox .25 .60
DB52 New York Yankees .25 .60
DB53 St. Louis Cardinals .25 .60
DB54 Los Angeles Angels .25 .60
DB55 Philadelphia Phillies .25 .60
DB56 Arizona Diamondbacks .25 .60
DB57 Chicago White Sox .25 .60
DB58 Atlanta Braves .25 .60
DB59 Oakland Athletics .25 .60
DB60 Houston Astros .25 .60
DB61 Albert Pujols .50 1.25
DB62 Ichiro .50 1.25
DB63 Miguel Cabrera .40 1.00
DB64 Ryan Howard .30 .75
DB65 Alex Rodriguez .50 1.25
DB66 Vladimir Guerrero .30 .75
DB67 Jim Thome .30 .75
DB68 David Ortiz .40 1.00
DB69 Todd Helton .30 .75
DB70 Chipper Jones .60 1.50
DB71 Mike Trout 2.00 5.00
DB72 Andrew McCutchen .40 1.00
DB73 Joey Votto .40 1.00
DB74 Paul Goldschmidt .40 1.00
DB75 Mookie Betts .75 2.00
DB76 Miguel Cabrera .40 1.00
DB77 Christian Yelich .50 1.25
DB78 Nolan Arenado .60 1.50
DB79 Freddie Freeman .50 1.25
DB80 Jose Altuve .30 .75

2020 Topps Update Decades' Best Black

*BLACK: 1X TO 2.5X
STATED ODDS 1:XX HOBBY
STATED PRINT RUN 299 SER.#'d SETS
DB7 Bob Feller 4.00 10.00
DB14 Carl Yastrzemski 5.00 12.00
DB34 Dale Murphy 4.00 10.00
DB36 Jose Canseco 4.00 10.00
DB38 Don Mattingly 5.00 12.00
DB62 Ichiro 2.50 6.00
DB75 Mookie Betts 4.00 10.00

2020 Topps Update Decades' Best Blue

*BLUE: .6X TO 1.5X
STATED ODDS 1:XX HOBBY
DB7 Bob Feller 2.50 6.00
DB14 Carl Yastrzemski 3.00 8.00
DB36 Jose Canseco 2.50 6.00

2020 Topps Update Decades' Best Gold

*GOLD: 2.5X TO 6X
STATED ODDS 1:XX HOBBY
STATED PRINT RUN 50 SER.#'d SETS
DB7 Bob Feller 10.00 25.00
DB14 Carl Yastrzemski 12.00 30.00
DB33 Cal Ripken Jr. 12.00 30.00
DB34 Dale Murphy 15.00 40.00
DB36 Jose Canseco 10.00 25.00
DB38 Don Mattingly 20.00 50.00
DB62 Ichiro 6.00 15.00
DB75 Mookie Betts 10.00 25.00

2020 Topps Update Dual All Star Stitches

STATED ODDS 1:XX HOBBY
STATED PRINT RUN 50 SER.#'d SETS
ASSDAC Correa/Altuve 6.00 15.00
ASSDDA Alonso/deGrom
ASSDDC deGrom/Colon 20.00 50.00
ASSDJJ Jeter/Judge 40.00 100.00
ASSDJS Stanton/Judge 12.00 30.00
ASSDKT Kershaw/Trout 30.00 80.00
ASSDPT Trout/Pujols 20.00 50.00
ASSDTA Trout/Acuna 30.00 80.00
ASSDTH Trout/Harper 30.00 80.00

2020 Topps Update Jeter's Final Season Commemorative Patch Autographs

STATED ODDS 1:XX HOBBY
PRINT RUNS B/WN 5-25 COPIES PER
NO PRICING ON QTY 15 OR LESS
EXCHANGE DEADLINE 8/31/2022
JFPAAS Alfonso Soriano/25 40.00 100.00
JFPACS CC Sabathia/25
JFPAMT Mark Teixeira/25 50.00 120.00
JFPAMTA Masahiro Tanaka/25 50.00 120.00

2020 Topps Update Jeter's Final Season Commemorative Patches

STATED ODDS 1:XX HOBBY
*BLACK: 1X TO 2.5X
*GOLD: 1.5X TO 4X
JFPI Ichiro 4.00 10.00
JFPAS Alfonso Soriano 1.00 2.50
JFPCS CC Sabathia 1.00 2.50
JFPJG Joe Girardi 1.00 2.50
JFPMT Mark Teixeira 1.00 2.50
JFPDJ1 Derek Jeter 3.00 8.00
JFPDJ2 Derek Jeter 3.00 8.00
JFPDJ3 Derek Jeter 3.00 8.00
JFPDJ4 Derek Jeter 3.00 8.00
JFPMTA Masahiro Tanaka 1.25 3.00

2020 Topps Update Major League Material Autographs

STATED ODDS 1:XX HOBBY
PRINT RUNS B/WN 25-50 COPIES PER
EXCHANGE DEADLINE 8/31/2022
MLAAB Alex Bregman/50 12.00 30.00
MLAAJ Aaron Judge/25
MLAAR Anthony Rendon/50 8.00 20.00
MLABB Bo Bichette/50
MLABM Brendan McKay/50
MLACB Cody Bellinger/25
MLADJ David Justice/50 15.00 40.00
MLAEA Elvis Andrus/50 6.00 15.00
MLAEH Eric Hosmer/50 10.00 25.00
MLAFT Fernando Tatis Jr./50 60.00 150.00
MLAGT Gleyber Torres/50 25.00 60.00
MLAJG Joey Gallo/50 10.00 25.00
MLAJR J.T. Realmuto/50 15.00 40.00
MLAKH Keston Hiura/50
MLALG Lucas Giolito/50 12.00 30.00
MLALR Luis Robert/50 100.00 250.00
MLAMC Matt Chapman/50 12.00 30.00
MLAMG Mark Grace/50 30.00 80.00
MLAMT Mike Trout/25
MLANC Nick Castellanos/50 15.00 40.00
MLANS Noah Syndergaard/30 30.00 80.00
MLAPA Pete Alonso/50 25.00 60.00
MLARA Ronald Acuna Jr./50 50.00 120.00
MLARD Rafael Devers/50 20.00 50.00
MLARH Rhys Hoskins/50 25.00 60.00
MLASG Sonny Gray/50 10.00 25.00
MLATE Tommy Edman/50 15.00 40.00
MLAVG Vladimir Guerrero Jr./50 20.00 50.00
MLAWB Walker Buehler/50 25.00 60.00
MLAWC Willson Contreras/50 8.00 20.00
MLAXB Xander Bogaerts/50 20.00 50.00
MLAYA Yordan Alvarez/50
MLAZG Zac Gallen/50 12.00 30.00
MLAAJO Andruw Jones/50 20.00 50.00
MLAJSO Jorge Soler/50 8.00 20.00

2020 Topps Update Major League Materials

STATED ODDS 1:XX HOBBY
MLMAA Aristides Aquino 5.00 12.00
MLMAB Alex Bregman 3.00 8.00
MLMAP Albert Pujols 4.00 10.00
MLMAR Anthony Rizzo 4.00 10.00
MLMBH Bryce Harper 5.00 12.00
MLMCK Clayton Kershaw 5.00 12.00
MLMCS CC Sabathia 2.50 6.00
MLMCY Christian Yelich 4.00 10.00
MLMDO David Ortiz 3.00 8.00
MLMEA Elvis Andrus 2.50 6.00
MLMGT Gleyber Torres 6.00 15.00
MLMJB Javier Baez 4.00 10.00
MLMJS Jorge Soler 3.00 8.00
MLMKH Keston Hiura 4.00 10.00
MLMLG Lucas Giolito 2.50 6.00
MLMMC Miguel Cabrera 3.00 8.00
MLMMK Max Kepler 4.00 10.00
MLMMO Matt Olson 3.00 8.00
MLMMS Max Scherzer 3.00 8.00
MLMNA Nolan Arenado 5.00 12.00
MLMPG Paul Goldschmidt 3.00 8.00
MLMRD Rafael Devers 4.00 10.00
MLMRH Rhys Hoskins 4.00 10.00
MLMSG Sonny Gray 2.50 6.00
MLMVG Vladimir Guerrero Jr. 5.00 12.00
MLMVR Victor Robles 4.00 10.00
MLMYM Yadier Molina 4.00 10.00
MLMAMC Andrew McCutchen 3.00 8.00
MLMDJL DJ LeMahieu 3.00 8.00
MLMFTJ Fernando Tatis Jr. 8.00 20.00
MLMGSP George Springer 2.50 6.00
MLMJTR J.T. Realmuto 3.00 8.00
MLMJVO Joey Votto 3.00 8.00
MLMKBR Kris Bryant 4.00 10.00
MLMLCA Lorenzo Cain 2.00 5.00
MLMMCH Matt Chapman 4.00 10.00
MLMMCO Michael Conforto 2.50 6.00
MLMMTR Mike Trout 12.00 30.00
MLMOHT Shohei Ohtani 5.00 12.00

2020 Topps Update Major League Materials Black

*BLACK: .5X TO 1.2X
STATED ODDS 1:XX HOBBY
STATED PRINT RUN 199 SER.#'d SETS
MLMMC Miguel Cabrera 10.00 25.00

2020 Topps Update Major League Materials Gold

*GOLD: .6X TO 1.5X
STATED ODDS 1:XX HOBBY
STATED PRINT RUN 50 SER.#'d SETS
MLMAR Anthony Rizzo 10.00 25.00
MLMMC Miguel Cabrera 12.00 30.00
MLMSG Sonny Gray 8.00 20.00

2020 Topps Update Major League Materials Red

*RED: .8X TO 2X
STATED ODDS 1:XX HOBBY
STATED PRINT RUN 25 SER.#'d SETS
MLMAA Aristides Aquino 12.00 30.00
MLMAP Albert Pujols 20.00 50.00
MLMAR Anthony Rizzo 20.00 50.00
MLMCK Clayton Kershaw 15.00 40.00
MLMMC Miguel Cabrera 15.00 40.00
MLMMK Max Kepler 10.00 25.00
MLMPG Paul Goldschmidt 12.00 30.00
MLMSG Sonny Gray 10.00 25.00
MLMYM Yadier Molina 12.00 30.00
MLMFTJ Fernando Tatis Jr. 20.00 50.00

2020 Topps Update Prospects

STATED ODDS 1:XX HOBBY
P1 Evan White .60 1.50
P2 Nate Pearson .75 2.00
P3 Wander Franco 5.00 12.00
P4 Jo Adell 1.00 2.50
P5 Tyler Stephenson .60 1.50
P6 MacKenzie Gore .50 1.25
P7 Cristian Pache .75 2.00
P8 Josh Jung .60 1.50
P9 Ke'Bryan Hayes 1.25 3.00
P10 Bobby Dalbec 1.50 4.00
P11 Colton Welker .25 .60
P12 Alec Bohm 1.50 4.00
P13 Nick Allen .25 .60
P14 Ethan Small .30 .75
P15 Ryan Mountcastle 1.25 3.00
P16 Andres Gimenez .60 1.50
P17 Brady Singer 1.25 3.00
P18 Casey Mize .75 2.00
P19 Alex Kirilloff .50 1.25
P20 Forrest Whitley .40 1.00
P21 Keibert Ruiz 1.25 3.00
P22 Brennen Davis .50 1.25
P23 Sixto Sanchez .75 2.00
P24 Nick Madrigal 1.00 2.50
P25 Joey Bart .75 2.00
P26 Daulton Varsho .40 1.00
P27 Dylan Carlson 1.00 2.50
P28 Nolan Jones .40 1.00
P29 Luis Garcia 1.00 2.50
P30 Clarke Schmidt .40 1.00

2020 Topps Update Prospects Black

*BLACK: 1X TO 2.5X
STATED ODDS 1:XX HOBBY
STATED PRINT RUN 299 SER.#'d SETS
P3 Wander Franco 40.00 100.00
P4 Jo Adell 12.00 30.00
P6 MacKenzie Gore 10.00 25.00
P7 Cristian Pache 15.00 40.00
P8 Josh Jung 6.00 15.00
P10 Bobby Dalbec 4.00 10.00
P12 Alec Bohm 20.00 50.00
P19 Alex Kirilloff 6.00 15.00
P21 Keibert Ruiz 5.00 12.00
P22 Brennen Davis 5.00 12.00
P24 Nick Madrigal 8.00 20.00
P25 Joey Bart 8.00 20.00
P27 Dylan Carlson 15.00 40.00

2020 Topps Update Prospects Blue

*BLUE: .6X TO 1.5X
STATED ODDS 1:XX HOBBY
P3 Wander Franco 25.00 60.00
P7 Cristian Pache 10.00 25.00
P8 Josh Jung 4.00 10.00
P12 Alec Bohm 12.00 30.00
P19 Alex Kirilloff 3.00 8.00
P21 Keibert Ruiz 2.50 6.00
P22 Brennen Davis 3.00 8.00
P24 Nick Madrigal 4.00 10.00
P25 Joey Bart 3.00 8.00
P27 Dylan Carlson 5.00 12.00

2020 Topps Update Prospects Gold

*GOLD: 2.5X TO 6X
STATED ODDS 1:XX HOBBY
STATED PRINT RUN 50 SER.#'d SETS
P3 Wander Franco 100.00 250.00
P4 Jo Adell 30.00 80.00
P6 MacKenzie Gore 25.00 60.00
P7 Cristian Pache 40.00 100.00
P8 Josh Jung 20.00 50.00
P10 Bobby Dalbec 15.00 40.00
P12 Alec Bohm 50.00 120.00
P19 Alex Kirilloff 15.00 40.00
P21 Keibert Ruiz 12.00 30.00
P22 Brennen Davis 12.00 30.00
P24 Nick Madrigal 20.00 50.00
P25 Joey Bart 20.00 50.00
P27 Dylan Carlson 60.00 150.00

2020 Topps Update Prospects Autographs

STATED ODDS 1:XX HOBBY
STATED PRINT RUN 25 SER.#'d SETS
EXCHANGE DEADLINE 8/31/2022
PAAB Alec Bohm 150.00 400.00
PABD Bobby Dalbec
PABS Brady Singer 60.00 150.00
PACM Casey Mize 50.00 120.00
PACP Cristian Pache
PACS Clarke Schmidt 25.00 60.00
PACW Colton Welker 25.00 60.00
PAES Ethan Small
PAEW Evan White 30.00 80.00
PAJA Jo Adell 100.00 250.00
PAJB Joey Bart 100.00 250.00
PAJJ Josh Jung 40.00 100.00
PAKR Keibert Ruiz 15.00 40.00
PALG Luis Garcia 60.00 150.00
PAMG MacKenzie Gore
PANM Nick Madrigal 50.00 120.00
PANP Nate Pearson
PARM Ryan Mountcastle 100.00 250.00
PAWF Wander Franco 200.00 500.00
PABDA Brennen Davis 60.00 150.00

2020 Topps Update Ronald Acuna Jr. Highlights

*BLACK: 1X TO 2.5X BASIC
*GOLD: 2.5X TO 6X BASIC
TRA1 Ronald Acuna Jr. 1.50 4.00
TRA2 Ronald Acuna Jr. 1.50 4.00
TRA3 Ronald Acuna Jr. 1.50 4.00
TRA4 Ronald Acuna Jr. 1.50 4.00
TRA5 Ronald Acuna Jr. 1.50 4.00
TRA6 Ronald Acuna Jr. 1.50 4.00
TRA7 Ronald Acuna Jr. 1.50 4.00
TRA8 Ronald Acuna Jr. 1.50 4.00
TRA9 Ronald Acuna Jr. 1.50 4.00
TRA10 Ronald Acuna Jr. 1.50 4.00
TRA11 Ronald Acuna Jr. 1.50 4.00
TRA12 Ronald Acuna Jr. 1.50 4.00
TRA13 Ronald Acuna Jr. 1.50 4.00
TRA14 Ronald Acuna Jr. 1.50 4.00
TRA15 Ronald Acuna Jr. 1.50 4.00
TRA16 Ronald Acuna Jr. 1.50 4.00
TRA17 Ronald Acuna Jr. 1.50 4.00
TRA18 Ronald Acuna Jr. 1.50 4.00
TRA19 Ronald Acuna Jr. 1.50 4.00
TRA20 Ronald Acuna Jr. 1.50 4.00

2020 Topps Update Triple All Star Stitches

STATED ODDS 1:XX HOBBY
STATED PRINT RUN 50 SER.#'d SETS
ASSTASA Springer/Altuve/Correa
ASSTKDS DeGrom/Kershaw/Strasburg 25.00 60.00
ASSTPCO Cabrera/Pujols/Ortiz 25.00 60.00
ASSTPMC Posey/Contreras/Molina 20.00 50.00
ASSTTJA Acuna/Judge/Trout
ASSTZSS Strasburg/Scherzer/Zimmerman 20.0050.00

2020 Topps Update Turkey Red '20

STATED ODDS 1:XX HOBBY
TR1 CC Sabathia .30 .75
TR2 Willie McCovey .30 .75
TR3 Ozzie Albies .40 1.00
TR4 Hunter Pence .30 .75
TR5 Mookie Betts .75 2.00
TR6 Yordan Alvarez 2.50 6.00
TR7 David Price .30 .75
TR8 Gavin Lux 1.25 3.00
TR9 Craig Biggio .30 .75
TR10 Dave Winfield .30 .75
TR11 Bo Bichette 2.00 5.00
TR12 Carlton Fisk .30 .75
TR13 Andrew McCutchen .40 1.00
TR14 Shogo Akiyama .40 1.00
TR15 Ken Griffey Jr. .75 2.00
TR16 Thurman Munson .40 1.00
TR17 Shun Yamaguchi .30 .75
TR18 Gary Carter .30 .75
TR19 Lewis Brinson .25 .60
TR20 Kwang-Hyun Kim .50 1.25
TR21 Tom Seaver .30 .75
TR22 Gerrit Cole .60 1.50
TR23 Trea Turner .30 .75
TR24 Yoshi Tsutsugo .60 1.50
TR25 Marcus Semien .40 1.00
TR26 Nick Castellanos .40 1.00
TR27 Luis Robert 2.00 5.00
TR28 Andy Pettitte .30 .75
TR29 Anthony Rendon .40 1.00
TR30 Ron Santo .30 .75
TR31 Johnny Bench .40 1.00
TR32 Mike Piazza .40 1.00
TR33 Yasmani Grandal .25 .60
TR34 Eddie Murray .30 .75
TR35 Dale Murphy .40 1.00
TR36 Mark Grace .30 .75
TR37 Mike Clevinger .30 .75
TR38 Mike Mussina .30 .75
TR39 Trevor Bauer .50 1.25
TR40 Kerry Wood .25 .60
TR41 Corey Kluber .30 .75
TR42 Brooks Robinson .30 .75
TR43 John Smoltz .40 1.00
TR44 Byron Buxton .40 1.00
TR45 Carter Kieboom .30 .75
TR46 Wade Boggs .30 .75
TR47 Larry Walker .30 .75
TR48 Willie Stargell .30 .75
TR49 Derek Jeter 1.00 2.50
TR50 Nolan Ryan 1.25 3.00

2020 Topps Update Turkey Red '20 Blue

*BLUE: 4X TO 10X
STATED ODDS 1:XX HOBBY
STATED PRINT RUN 50 SER.#'d SETS
TR11 Bo Bichette 25.00 60.00
TR15 Ken Griffey Jr. 15.00 40.00
TR49 Derek Jeter 40.00 100.00
TR50 Nolan Ryan 20.00 50.00

2020 Topps Update Turkey Red '20 Chrome

STATED ODDS 1:XX HOBBY
TRC1 CC Sabathia .75 2.00
TRC2 Willie McCovey .75 2.00
TRC3 Ozzie Albies 1.00 2.50
TRC4 Hunter Pence .75 2.00
TRC5 Mookie Betts 2.00 5.00
TRC6 Yordan Alvarez 6.00 15.00
TRC7 David Price .75 2.00
TRC8 Gavin Lux 3.00 8.00
TRC9 Craig Biggio .75 2.00
TRC10 Dave Winfield .75 2.00
TRC11 Bo Bichette 3.00 8.00
TRC12 Carlton Fisk .75 2.00
TRC13 Andrew McCutchen 1.00 2.50
TRC14 Shogo Akiyama 1.00 2.50
TRC15 Ken Griffey Jr. 2.00 5.00
TRC16 Thurman Munson 2.00 5.00
TRC17 Shun Yamaguchi .75 2.00
TRC18 Gary Carter .75 2.00
TRC19 Lewis Brinson .60 1.50
TRC20 Kwang-Hyun Kim 1.25 3.00
TRC21 Tom Seaver .75 2.00
TRC22 Gerrit Cole 1.50 4.00
TRC23 Trea Turner .75 2.00
TRC24 Yoshi Tsutsugo 1.50 4.00
TRC25 Marcus Semien 1.00 2.50
TRC26 Nick Castellanos 1.00 2.50
TRC27 Luis Robert 5.00 12.00
TRC28 Andy Pettitte .75 2.00
TRC29 Anthony Rendon 1.00 2.50
TRC30 Ron Santo .75 2.00
TRC31 Johnny Bench 1.00 2.50
TRC32 Mike Piazza 1.00 2.50
TRC33 Yasmani Grandal .60 1.50
TRC34 Eddie Murray .75 2.00
TRC35 Dale Murphy 1.00 2.50
TRC36 Mark Grace .75 2.00
TRC37 Mike Clevinger .75 2.00
TRC38 Mike Mussina .75 2.00
TRC39 Trevor Bauer 1.25 3.00
TRC40 Kerry Wood .60 1.50
TRC41 Corey Kluber .75 2.00
TRC42 Brooks Robinson .75 2.00
TRC43 John Smoltz 1.00 2.50
TRC44 Byron Buxton 1.00 2.50
TRC45 Carter Kieboom .75 2.00
TRC46 Wade Boggs .75 2.00
TRC47 Larry Walker .75 2.00
TRC48 Willie Stargell .75 2.00
TRC49 Derek Jeter 4.00 10.00
TRC50 Nolan Ryan 3.00 8.00

2020 Topps Update Turkey Red '20 Chrome Blue Refractors

*BLUE: 3X TO 8X
STATED ODDS 1:XX HOBBY
STATED PRINT RUN 50 SER.#'d SETS
TRC5 Mookie Betts 100.00 250.00
TRC8 Gavin Lux 50.00 120.00
TRC11 Bo Bichette 60.00 150.00
TRC15 Ken Griffey Jr. 30.00 80.00
TRC18 Gary Carter 10.00 25.00
TRC49 Derek Jeter 100.00 250.00

2021 Topps

SER. 1 PLATE ODDS 1:13,324 HOBBY
PLATE PRINT RUN 1 SET PER COLOR
BLACK-CYAN-MAGENTA-YELLOW ISSUED
NO PLATE PRICING DUE TO SCARCITY
1 Fernando Tatis Jr. 1.25 3.00
2 Roberto Osuna .15 .40
3 Matt Chapman .25 .60
4 David Bote .20 .50
5 Julio Urias .25 .60
6 Justus Sheffield .25 .60
7 Dab on 'Em .15 .40
Orlando Arcia
8 Mauricio Dubon .15 .40
9 Max Fried .25 .60
10 Daulton Varsho RC .60 1.50
11 Max Kepler .20 .50
12 Joey Bart RC 2.50 6.00
13 Mookie Betts .50 1.25
14 Robert/Jimenez .30 .75
15 Mookie Betts WSH .50 1.25
16 Patrick Sandoval .20 .50
17 Sean Doolittle .15 .40
18 Shun Yamaguchi .15 .40
19 Jakob Junis .15 .40
20 J.D. Martinez .25 .60
21 Eric Sogard .15 .40
22 Pedro Severino .15 .40
23 Nomar Mazara .15 .40
24 Nolan Arenado .40 1.00
25 Sixto Sanchez RC 2.50 6.00
26 Bobby Dalbec RC 2.00 5.00
27 Mike Trout 1.25 3.00
28 Luke Weaver .15 .40
29 Chris Davis .15 .40
30 Miguel Andujar .25 .60
31 Brandon Kintzler .15 .40
32 Edward Olivares RC .60 1.50
33 Yonathan Daza .15 .40
34 Roberto Perez .15 .40
35 Danny Santana .15 .40
36 Charlie Morton .25 .60
37 Jose Quintana .15 .40
38 Mitch Moreland .15 .40
39 New York Yankees TC .15 .40
40 Joc Pederson .20 .50
41 Deivi Garcia RC 2.00 5.00
42 Kyle Lewis .60 1.50
43 Jo Adell RC 3.00 8.00
44 Walker Buehler WSH .30 .75
45 Wade LeBlanc .15 .40
46 Jesus Luzardo FS .25 .60
47 Ketel Marte .20 .50
48 Maikel Franco .20 .50
49 Starling Marte .20 .50
50 Cody Bellinger .50 1.25
51 Sean Manaea .15 .40
52 Archie Bradley .15 .40
53 Andres Gimenez RC .60 1.50
54 Joakim Soria .15 .40
55 Nick Senzel .25 .60
56 Steven Matz .15 .40
57 Will Smith .25 .60
58 Washington Nationals TC .15 .40
59 Milwaukee Brewers TC .15 .40
60 Yu Darvish LL .25 .60
61 Acuna/Guerrero .50 1.25
62 Stephen Vogt .20 .50
63 Ronald Guzman .15 .40
64 Chris Taylor .20 .50
65 Isaac Paredes RC 1.00 2.50
66 Ryan Brasier .15 .40
67 Clayton Kershaw .40 1.00
68 Charlie Blackmon .25 .60
69 Gio Gonzalez .20 .50
70 Detroit Tigers TC .15 .40
71 Randy Dobnak .25 .60
72 Shane Bieber LL .25 .60
73 Colorado Rockies TC .15 .40
74 Byron Buxton .25 .60
75 Kolten Wong .20 .50
76 Jon Gray .15 .40
77 Jack Flaherty .25 .60
78 David Peterson RC 1.25 3.00
79 Roman Quinn .15 .40
80 Liam Hendriks .15 .40
81 Brett Gardner .20 .50
82 Michael Lorenzen .15 .40
83 Gavin Lux FS .50 1.25
84 Pete Alonso .60 1.50
85 Brusdar Graterol FS .20 .50
86 Austin Meadows .25 .60
87 Jorge Alfaro .15 .40
88 Albert Abreu RC .25 .60
89 Lucas Giolito .20 .50
90 Shane Bieber LL .25 .60
91 Orlando Arcia .15 .40
92 Tarik Skubal RC 1.25 3.00
93 Hunter Harvey .15 .40
94 Josh Donaldson .20 .50
95 Gerrit Cole .40 1.00
96 Brian Goodwin .15 .40
97 Niko Goodrum .20 .50
98 Lourdes Gurriel Jr. .20 .50
99 Aaron Judge .60 1.50
100 Christian Yelich .30 .75
101 Travis d'Arnaud .20 .50
102 Paul DeJong .25 .60
103 Daniel Johnson RC .40 1.00
104 Kenta Maeda .20 .50
105 Shane Bieber LL .25 .60
106 Brandon Nimmo .20 .50
107 David Dahl .15 .40
108 DJ LeMahieu LL .25 .60
109 Jean Segura .20 .50
110 Ian Happ .20 .50
111 Austin Riley .30 .75
112 Justin Verlander .25 .60
113 Nate Pearson RC 1.25 3.00
114 Colin Moran .15 .40
115 Willie Calhoun .15 .40
116 Nico Hoerner FS .40 1.00
117 Gio Urshela .25 .60
118 Carter Kieboom .20 .50
119 Dee Strange-Gordon .15 .40
120 Freddie Freeman .30 .75
121 Matthew Boyd .15 .40
122 Nick Heath RC .50 1.25
123 Beau Burrows RC .40 1.00
124 Amir Garrett .15 .40
125 Adalberto Mondesi .20 .50
126 Monte Harrison RC .40 1.00
127 Wilson Ramos .15 .40
128 Dylan Bundy .20 .50
129 Daniel Murphy .20 .50
130 Josh Bell .20 .50
131 Joey Gallo .25 .60
132 Marwin Gonzalez .15 .40
133 Mitch Keller .25 .60
134 Jose Urena .15 .40
135 Brandon Woodruff .25 .60
136 Marco Gonzales .15 .40
137 Trevor Bauer LL .30 .75
138 Tim Anderson .25 .60
139 Humberto Mejia RC .40 1.00
140 Garrett Richards .20 .50
141 Caleb Smith .15 .40
142 Jake Odorizzi .15 .40
143 Ryan Mountcastle RC 2.50 6.00
144 Anderson Tejeda RC .60 1.50
145 Kodi Whitley RC .40 1.00
146 Patrick Corbin .20 .50
147 Yuli Gurriel .20 .50
148 Chris Archer .15 .40
149 Mitch Haniger .20 .50
150 Shohei Ohtani .40 1.00
151 Evan White RC 1.50 4.00
152 Motor City Mashers .25 .60
Miguel Cabrera/Jonathan Schoop
153 Tyler Stephenson RC 1.25 3.00
154 Andrew Benintendi .25 .60
155 Seth Lugo .15 .40
156 Minnesota Twins TC .15 .40
157 Aroldis Chapman .25 .60
158 Buck Farmer .15 .40
159 Jansen/Guerrero .30 .75
160 Brandon Workman .15 .40
161 Lewis Brinson .15 .40
162 Rhys Hoskins .30 .75
163 J.D. Davis .15 .40
164 Jesus Aguilar .20 .50
165 Willson Contreras .25 .60
166 Upton/Trout .60 1.50
167 James Kaprielian RC .40 1.00
168 Max Stassi .15 .40
169 Brady Singer RC 1.25 3.00
170 Jacob deGrom LL .50 1.25
171 Hector Neris .15 .40
172 Miami Marlins TC .15 .40
173 Evan Longoria .20 .50
174 Raisel Iglesias .15 .40
175 Brad Hand .15 .40
176 Jake Bauers .20 .50
177 Ryan Castellani RC .40 1.00
178 Albert Pujols .30 .75
179 Clayton Kershaw WSH .40 1.00
180 Jose Abreu LL .25 .60
181 Miles Mikolas .15 .40
182 Eduardo Rodriguez .15 .40
183 Cristian Javier RC .60 1.50
184 Tyler Chatwood .15 .40
185 Amed Rosario .20 .50
186 Luke Voit .30 .75
187 Cristian Pache RC 2.50 6.00
188 Brandon Drury .15 .40
189 Adam Plutko .15 .40
190 Sonny Gray .20 .50
191 Wilmer Flores .20 .50
192 Manny Machado .25 .60
193 Brandon Bielak RC .40 1.00
194 Atlanta Braves TC .15 .40
195 Baltimore Orioles TC .15 .40
196 Ryan Yarbrough .15 .40
197 Nick Madrigal RC 2.00 5.00
198 Corey Seager WSH .25 .60
199 Trevor Williams .15 .40
200 Jacob deGrom .50 1.25
201 Los Angeles Dodgers TC .15 .40
202 Howie Kendrick .15 .40
203 Trea Turner .20 .50
204 Kyle Seager .15 .40
205 Luis Patino RC 1.00 2.50
206 Wade Davis .15 .40
207 Yadier Molina .30 .75
208 Griffin Canning .25 .60
209 Mike Foltynewicz .15 .40
210 Alonso/Conforto .30 .75
211 Salvador Perez .20 .50
212 Robbie Ray .15 .40
213 JaCoby Jones .20 .50
214 Alex Verdugo .20 .50
215 Justin Dunn FS .15 .40
216 Adam Frazier .15 .40
217 Jeimer Candelario .15 .40
218 Matt Olson .25 .60
219 Nelson Cruz .25 .60
220 Marcell Ozuna LL .25 .60
221 Chadwick Tromp RC .40 1.00
222 Tampa Bay Rays TC .15 .40
223 Luis Robert .75 2.00
224 Vladimir Guerrero Jr. .40 1.00
225 Juan Soto LL .75 2.00
226 Rafael Devers .30 .75
227 Mike Yastrzemski .40 1.00
228 Blake Taylor RC .40 1.00
229 Paul Goldschmidt .25 .60
230 Tony Gonsolin .25 .60
231 Dane Dunning RC .75 2.00
232 Albert Almora Jr. .20 .50
233 Dansby Swanson .25 .60
234 Lorenzo Cain .15 .40
235 A.J. Pollock .15 .40
236 Ian Kennedy .15 .40
237 Willy Adames .15 .40
238 Kris Bubic RC .40 1.00
239 Ian Anderson RC 1.50 4.00
240 Jose Urquidy FS .15 .40
241 Anthony Rizzo .30 .75
242 Gleyber Torres .50 1.25
243 Santiago Espinal RC .40 1.00
244 Spencer Howard RC .75 2.00
245 Aristides Aquino FS .25 .60
246 Cavan Biggio .30 .75
247 Mallex Smith .15 .40
248 Francisco Mejia .20 .50
249 Trent Grisham FS .30 .75
250 Bryce Harper .40 1.00
251 Pittsburgh Pirates TC .15 .40
252 Luke Voit LL .30 .75

253 Carlos Correa .25 .60
254 Zack Britton .15 .40
255 Austin Hays .25 .60
256 Keibert Ruiz RC .75 2.00
257 Brendan McKay FS .20 .50
258 Mike Yaztrzemski .30 .75
259 Chris Paddack .25 .60
260 Eduardo Escobar .15 .40
261 Blake Snell .20 .50
262 Mark Canha .15 .40
263 Ronald Acuna Jr. 1.00 2.50
264 Leody Taveras RC .75 2.00
265 Mike Clevinger .20 .50
266 Jurickson Profar .20 .50
267 Kirby Yates .15 .40
268 Johnny Cueto .20 .50
269 Jesus Sanchez RC .75 2.00
270 Mitch White RC .40 1.00
271 Luis Castillo .20 .50
272 John Means .25 .60
273 Oliver Perez .15 .40
274 Freddy Galvis .15 .40
275 Joey Votto .25 .60
276 Marcus Semien .25 .60
277 Alec Bohm RC 3.00 8.00
278 Jon Lester .20 .50
279 Danny Mendick .15 .40
280 Kevin Kiermaier .20 .50
281 Jesse Winker .25 .60
282 Omar Narvaez .15 .40
283 Texas Rangers TC .15 .40
284 Eloy Jimenez .50 1.25
285 Dylan Carlson RC 2.00 5.00
286 Harrison Bader .20 .50
287 Arizona Diamondbacks TC .15 .40
288 Miguel Rojas .15 .40
289 Josh Reddick .15 .40
290 Josh Harrison .15 .40
291 Miguel Cabrera .25 .60
292 Oscar Mercado .20 .50
293 Rougned Odor .20 .50
294 Leury Garcia .15 .40
295 Hunter Renfroe .15 .40
296 Joey Wendle .20 .50
297 Alex Bregman .25 .60
298 Luis Garcia RC 1.25 3.00
299 Teoscar Hernandez .25 .60
300 Yordan Alvarez .60 1.50
301 Buster Posey .30 .75
302 Max Muncy .20 .50
303 Betts/Bellinger .30 .75
304 Danny Duffy .15 .40
305 Tony Kemp .15 .40
306 Michael Taylor .15 .40
307 Avisail Garcia .20 .50
308 Jay Bruce .20 .50
309 Francisco Lindor .25 .60
310 Bo Bichette FS .60 1.50
311 Codi Heuer RC .40 1.00
312 Marcell Ozuna LL .25 .60
313 Matt Shoemaker .20 .50
314 Tommy Edman .25 .60
315 Brandon Crawford .20 .50
316 Alex Gordon .20 .50
317 Jake Arrieta .20 .50
318 Chicago White Sox TC .15 .40
319 Triston McKenzie RC .75 2.00
320 Anthony Santander .15 .40
321 Casey Mize RC 2.00 5.00
322 Javier Baez .30 .75
323 Machado/Tatis .60 1.50
324 Nick Neidert RC .40 1.00
325 Max Scherzer .25 .60
326 Eddy Alvarez RC .40 1.00
327 Whit Merrifield .25 .60
328 Kevin Gausman .25 .60
329 Mike Minor .15 .40
330 Juan Soto .75 2.00

2021 Topps Advanced Stats

*ADV STATS: 6X TO 15X BASIC
*ADV STATS RC: 4X TO 10X BASIC RC
STATED ODDS 1:228 HOBBY
STATED PRINT RUN 300 SER.#'d SETS
1 Fernando Tatis Jr. 40.00 100.00
12 Joey Bart 40.00 100.00
26 Bobby Dalbec 75.00 200.00
27 Mike Trout 40.00 100.00
43 Jo Adell 60.00 150.00
143 Ryan Mountcastle 60.00 150.00
187 Cristian Pache 50.00 120.00
197 Nick Madrigal 30.00 80.00
239 Ian Anderson 40.00 100.00
277 Alec Bohm 125.00 300.00
285 Dylan Carlson 75.00 200.00
298 Luis Garcia 30.00 80.00
321 Casey Mize 30.00 80.00

2021 Topps Black

*BLACK: 10X TO 25X BASIC
*BLACK RC: 6X TO 15X BASIC RC
STATED ODDS 1:175 HOBBY
STATED PRINT RUN 70 SER.#'d SETS
1 Fernando Tatis Jr. 60.00 150.00
12 Joey Bart 60.00 150.00
26 Bobby Dalbec 125.00 300.00
27 Mike Trout 60.00 150.00
43 Jo Adell 100.00 250.00
113 Nate Pearson 60.00 150.00
143 Ryan Mountcastle 100.00 250.00
187 Cristian Pache 150.00 400.00
197 Nick Madrigal 100.00 250.00
205 Luis Patino 30.00 80.00
228 Blake Taylor 12.00 30.00
239 Ian Anderson 60.00 150.00
244 Spencer Howard 30.00 80.00
256 Keibert Ruiz 40.00 100.00
264 Leody Taveras 25.00 60.00
269 Jesus Sanchez 25.00 60.00
277 Alec Bohm 300.00 800.00
285 Dylan Carlson 200.00 500.00
298 Luis Garcia 125.00 300.00
321 Casey Mize 50.00 120.00

2021 Topps Father's Day Blue

*FD BLUE: 10X TO 25X BASIC
*FD BLUE RC: 6X TO 15X BASIC RC
STATED ODDS 1:1067 HOBBY
STATED PRINT RUN 50 SER.#'d SETS
1 Fernando Tatis Jr. 60.00 150.00
12 Joey Bart 60.00 150.00
26 Bobby Dalbec 125.00 300.00
27 Mike Trout 60.00 150.00
42 Kyle Lewis 30.00 80.00
43 Jo Adell 100.00 250.00
113 Nate Pearson 60.00 150.00
143 Ryan Mountcastle 100.00 250.00
187 Cristian Pache 150.00 400.00
197 Nick Madrigal 100.00 250.00
205 Luis Patino 30.00 80.00
228 Blake Taylor 12.00 30.00
239 Ian Anderson 60.00 150.00
244 Spencer Howard 30.00 80.00
256 Keibert Ruiz 40.00 100.00
264 Leody Taveras 25.00 60.00
269 Jesus Sanchez 25.00 60.00
277 Alec Bohm 500.00 1200.00
285 Dylan Carlson 200.00 500.00
298 Luis Garcia 125.00 300.00
321 Casey Mize 50.00 120.00
330 Juan Soto 50.00 120.00

2021 Topps Gold

*GOLD: 2.5X TO 6X BASIC
*GOLD RC: 1.5X TO 4X BASIC RC
STATED ODDS 1:27 HOBBY
STATED PRINT RUN 2021 SER.#'d SETS
1 Fernando Tatis Jr. 15.00 40.00
12 Joey Bart 12.00 30.00
26 Bobby Dalbec 25.00 60.00
27 Mike Trout 12.00 30.00
43 Jo Adell 25.00 60.00
143 Ryan Mountcastle 25.00 60.00
187 Cristian Pache 20.00 50.00
197 Nick Madrigal 15.00 40.00
239 Ian Anderson 15.00 40.00
277 Alec Bohm 50.00 120.00
285 Dylan Carlson 30.00 80.00
298 Luis Garcia 12.00 30.00

2021 Topps Gold Foil

*GLD FOIL: 2X TO 5X BASIC
*GLD FOIL RC: 1.2X TO 3X BASIC RC
STATED ODDS 1:2 HOBBY JUMBO
1 Fernando Tatis Jr. 12.00 30.00
12 Joey Bart 12.00 30.00
26 Bobby Dalbec 15.00 40.00
27 Mike Trout 8.00 20.00
187 Cristian Pache 15.00 40.00
197 Nick Madrigal 12.00 30.00
239 Ian Anderson 12.00 30.00
277 Alec Bohm 30.00 80.00
285 Dylan Carlson 25.00 60.00
298 Luis Garcia 10.00 25.00

2021 Topps Green Foil

*GRN FOIL: 5X TO 12X BASIC
*GRN FOIL RC: 3X TO 8X BASIC RC
RANDOM INSERTS IN PACKS
STATED PRINT RUN 499 SER.#'d SETS
1 Fernando Tatis Jr. 30.00 80.00
12 Joey Bart 30.00 80.00
26 Bobby Dalbec 50.00 150.00
27 Mike Trout 40.00 100.00
43 Jo Adell 50.00 120.00
143 Ryan Mountcastle 50.00 120.00
187 Cristian Pache 40.00 100.00
197 Nick Madrigal 30.00 80.00
239 Ian Anderson 30.00 80.00
277 Alec Bohm 100.00 250.00
285 Dylan Carlson 60.00 150.00
298 Luis Garcia 30.00 80.00
321 Casey Mize 20.00 50.00

2021 Topps Independence Day

*VINTAGE: 10X TO 25X BASIC
*VINTAGE RC: 6X TO 15X BASIC RC
STATED ODDS 1:703 HOBBY
STATED PRINT RUN 76 SER.#'d SETS
1 Fernando Tatis Jr. 60.00 150.00
12 Joey Bart 60.00 150.00
26 Bobby Dalbec 125.00 300.00
27 Mike Trout 60.00 150.00
43 Jo Adell 100.00 250.00
113 Nate Pearson 60.00 150.00
143 Ryan Mountcastle 100.00 250.00
187 Cristian Pache 150.00 400.00
197 Nick Madrigal 100.00 250.00
205 Luis Patino 30.00 80.00
228 Blake Taylor 12.00 30.00
239 Ian Anderson 60.00 150.00
244 Spencer Howard 30.00 80.00
256 Keibert Ruiz 40.00 100.00
264 Leody Taveras 25.00 60.00
269 Jesus Sanchez 25.00 60.00
277 Alec Bohm 300.00 800.00
285 Dylan Carlson 200.00 500.00
298 Luis Garcia 125.00 300.00
321 Casey Mize 50.00 120.00

2021 Topps Meijer Purple

*PURPLE: 1.5X TO 4X BASIC
*PURPLE RC: 1X TO 2.5X BASIC RC
STATED ODDS 1:2 MEIJER BLASTER
1 Fernando Tatis Jr. 10.00 25.00
12 Joey Bart 10.00 25.00
26 Bobby Dalbec 12.00 30.00
27 Mike Trout 8.00 20.00
143 Ryan Mountcastle 15.00 40.00
187 Cristian Pache 8.00 20.00
197 Nick Madrigal 10.00 25.00
239 Ian Anderson 10.00 25.00
277 Alec Bohm 25.00 60.00
285 Dylan Carlson 20.00 50.00

2021 Topps Memorial Day Camo

*CAMO: 12X TO 30X BASIC
*CAMO RC: 8X TO 20X BASIC RC
STATED ODDS 1:2134 HOBBY
STATED PRINT RUN 25 SER.#'d SETS
1 Fernando Tatis Jr. 75.00 200.00
12 Joey Bart 75.00 200.00
25 Sixto Sanchez 100.00 250.00
26 Bobby Dalbec 150.00 400.00
27 Mike Trout 75.00 200.00
42 Kyle Lewis 40.00 100.00
43 Jo Adell 125.00 300.00
113 Nate Pearson 75.00 200.00
143 Ryan Mountcastle 125.00 300.00
151 Evan White 50.00 120.00
187 Cristian Pache 200.00 500.00
197 Nick Madrigal 125.00 300.00
205 Luis Patino 40.00 100.00
228 Blake Taylor 15.00 40.00
239 Ian Anderson 75.00 200.00
244 Spencer Howard 40.00 100.00
256 Keibert Ruiz 50.00 120.00
264 Leody Taveras 30.00 80.00
269 Jesus Sanchez 30.00 80.00
277 Alec Bohm 600.00 1500.00
285 Dylan Carlson 250.00 600.00
298 Luis Garcia 150.00 400.00
321 Casey Mize 60.00 150.00
330 Juan Soto 60.00 150.00

2021 Topps Mother's Day Pink

*MD.PINK: 10X TO 25X BASIC
*MD.PINK RC: 6X TO 15X BASIC RC
STATED ODDS 1:1067 HOBBY
STATED PRINT RUN 50 SER.#'d SETS
1 Fernando Tatis Jr. 60.00 150.00
12 Joey Bart 60.00 150.00
26 Bobby Dalbec 125.00 300.00
27 Mike Trout 60.00 150.00
42 Kyle Lewis 30.00 80.00
43 Jo Adell 100.00 250.00
113 Nate Pearson 60.00 150.00
143 Ryan Mountcastle 100.00 250.00
187 Cristian Pache 150.00 400.00
197 Nick Madrigal 100.00 250.00
205 Luis Patino 30.00 80.00
228 Blake Taylor 12.00 30.00
239 Ian Anderson 60.00 150.00
244 Spencer Howard 30.00 80.00
256 Keibert Ruiz 40.00 100.00
264 Leody Taveras 25.00 60.00
269 Jesus Sanchez 25.00 60.00
277 Alec Bohm 500.00 1200.00
285 Dylan Carlson 200.00 500.00
298 Luis Garcia 125.00 300.00
321 Casey Mize 50.00 120.00
330 Juan Soto 50.00 120.00

2021 Topps Orange Foil

*ORNG FOIL: 6X TO 15X BASIC
*ORNG FOIL RC: 4X TO 10X BASIC RC
RANDOM INSERTS IN PACKS
STATED PRINT RUN 299 SER.#'d SETS
1 Fernando Tatis Jr. 40.00 100.00
12 Joey Bart 40.00 100.00
26 Bobby Dalbec 75.00 200.00
27 Mike Trout 40.00 100.00
43 Jo Adell 60.00 150.00
143 Ryan Mountcastle 60.00 150.00
187 Cristian Pache 50.00 120.00
197 Nick Madrigal 30.00 80.00
239 Ian Anderson 40.00 100.00
277 Alec Bohm 125.00 300.00
285 Dylan Carlson 75.00 200.00
298 Luis Garcia 30.00 80.00
321 Casey Mize 30.00 80.00

2021 Topps Platinum Anniversary

*PLAT.ANN: 10X TO 25X BASIC
*PLAT.ANN RC: 6X TO 15X BASIC RC
STATED ODDS 1:763 HOBBY
STATED PRINT RUN 70 SER.#'d SETS
1 Fernando Tatis Jr. 50.00 120.00
43 Jo Adell 100.00 250.00
113 Nate Pearson 60.00 150.00
143 Ryan Mountcastle 100.00 250.00
187 Cristian Pache 125.00 300.00
197 Nick Madrigal 100.00 250.00
205 Luis Patino 30.00 80.00
228 Blake Taylor 12.00 30.00
244 Spencer Howard 30.00 80.00
256 Keibert Ruiz 40.00 100.00
264 Leody Taveras 25.00 60.00
269 Jesus Sanchez 25.00 60.00
277 Alec Bohm 300.00 800.00
285 Dylan Carlson 150.00 400.00
298 Luis Garcia 125.00 300.00
321 Casey Mize 50.00 120.00

2021 Topps Rainbow Foil

*FOIL: 2X TO 5X BASIC
*FOIL RC: 1.2X TO 3X BASIC RC
STATED ODDS 1:10 HOBBY
1 Fernando Tatis Jr. 12.00 30.00
12 Joey Bart 12.00 30.00
26 Bobby Dalbec 15.00 40.00
27 Mike Trout 8.00 20.00
187 Cristian Pache 10.00 25.00
197 Nick Madrigal 12.00 30.00
239 Ian Anderson 12.00 30.00
277 Alec Bohm 30.00 80.00
285 Dylan Carlson 25.00 60.00
298 Luis Garcia 10.00 25.00

2021 Topps Red Foil

*RED FOIL: 8X TO 20X BASIC
*RED FOIL RC: 5X TO 12X BASIC RC
RANDOM INSERTS IN PACKS
STATED PRINT RUN 199 SER.#'d SETS
1 Fernando Tatis Jr. 40.00 100.00
12 Joey Bart 50.00 120.00
26 Bobby Dalbec 75.00 200.00
27 Mike Trout 50.00 120.00
43 Jo Adell 60.00 150.00
143 Ryan Mountcastle 60.00 150.00
187 Cristian Pache 50.00 120.00
197 Nick Madrigal 30.00 80.00
239 Ian Anderson 40.00 100.00
256 Keibert Ruiz 30.00 80.00
277 Alec Bohm 150.00 400.00
285 Dylan Carlson 125.00 300.00
298 Luis Garcia 40.00 100.00
321 Casey Mize 30.00 80.00

2021 Topps Vintage Stock

*VINTAGE: 8X TO 20X BASIC
*VINTAGE RC: 5X TO 12X BASIC RC
STATED ODDS 1:554 HOBBY
STATED PRINT RUN 199 SER.#'d SETS
1 Fernando Tatis Jr. 50.00 120.00
12 Joey Bart 50.00 120.00
26 Bobby Dalbec 100.00 250.00
27 Mike Trout 50.00 120.00
43 Jo Adell 75.00 200.00
113 Nate Pearson 50.00 120.00
143 Ryan Mountcastle 75.00 200.00
187 Cristian Pache 75.00 200.00
197 Nick Madrigal 40.00 100.00
228 Blake Taylor 10.00 25.00
239 Ian Anderson 50.00 120.00
256 Keibert Ruiz 30.00 80.00
277 Alec Bohm 250.00 600.00
285 Dylan Carlson 150.00 400.00
298 Luis Garcia 40.00 100.00
321 Casey Mize 40.00 100.00

2021 Topps Walgreens Yellow

*WG YELLOW: 1.2X TO 3X BASIC
*WG YELLOW RC: .8X TO 2X BASIC RC
STATED ODDS 6 PER WG HANGER
1 Fernando Tatis Jr. 8.00 20.00
12 Joey Bart 6.00 15.00
187 Cristian Pache 6.00 15.00
197 Nick Madrigal 6.00 15.00
239 Ian Anderson 6.00 15.00
277 Alec Bohm 20.00 50.00
285 Dylan Carlson 10.00 25.00

2021 Topps Walmart Royal Blue

*WM BLUE: 1.2X TO 3X BASIC
*WM BLUE RC: .8X TO 2X BASIC RC
STATED ODDS 2 PER WM HANGER
1 Fernando Tatis Jr. 8.00 20.00
12 Joey Bart 6.00 15.00
187 Cristian Pache 6.00 15.00
197 Nick Madrigal 6.00 15.00
239 Ian Anderson 6.00 15.00
277 Alec Bohm 20.00 50.00
285 Dylan Carlson 10.00 25.00

2021 Topps Base Set Photo Variations

SER.1 STATED ODDS 1:79 HOBBY
SER.1 STATED SSP ODDS 1:2348 HOBBY
SER.1 STATED USP ODDS 1:88,187 HOBBY
1A Fernando Tatis Jr. sliding 25.00 60.00
1B Fernando Tatis Jr. SSP 100.00 250.00
3 Matt Chapman shirt 4.00 10.00
4 Ernie Banks 8.00 20.00
10 Daulton Varsho grey jsy 8.00 20.00
12A Joey Bart orange jsy 15.00 40.00
12B Joey Bart SSP 100.00 250.00
13A Mookie Betts pointing 4.00 10.00
13B Mookie Betts SSP 40.00 100.00
24 Nolan Arenado black jsy 3.00 8.00
25 Sixto Sanchez white jsy 10.00 25.00
26 Bobby Dalbec blue shirt 40.00 100.00
27A Mike Trout back swing 15.00 40.00
27B Mike Trout SSP 300.00 600.00
29 Cal Ripken Jr. 8.00 20.00
41 Deivi Garcia grey jsy 12.00 30.00
42 Kyle Lewis green jsy 6.00 15.00
43A Jo Adell no hat 30.00 80.00
43B Jo Adell SSP 150.00 400.00
50 Cody Bellinger blue shirt 4.00 10.00
53 Andres Gimenez pinstripe 10.00 25.00
65 Isaac Paredes black shirt 10.00 25.00
67 Clayton Kershaw overhead 8.00 20.00
81 Babe Ruth 10.00 25.00
84A Pete Alonso helmet off 5.00 12.00
84B Pete Alonso SSP 50.00 125.00
team celebration
92A Tarik Skubal leg up 12.00 30.00
92B Tarik Skubal SSP 60.00 150.00
95 Gerrit Cole overhead 3.00 8.00
99A Aaron Judge grey shirt 5.00 12.00
99B Aaron Judge SSP 50.00 125.00
100A Christian Yelich no helmet 5.00 12.00
100B Christian Yelich SSP 25.00 60.00
112 Justin Verlander blue shirt 2.00 5.00
113A Nate Pearson white jsy back 12.00 30.00
113B Nate Pearson SSP 40.00 100.00
120 Hank Aaron 6.00 15.00
130 Roberto Clemente 8.00 20.00
143A Ryan Mountcastle black jsy 25.00 60.00
143B Ryan Mountcastle SSP 100.00 250.00
150 Shohei Ohtani red shirt 5.00 12.00
151 Evan White blue jsy 8.00 20.00
153 Tyler Stephenson batting 8.00 20.00
154 Ted Williams 6.00 15.00
169 Brady Singer jsy back 8.00 20.00
186 Lou Gehrig 6.00 15.00
187A Cristian Pache red jsy 50.00 120.00
187B Cristian Pache SSP 200.00 500.00
192 Manny Machado shorts 4.00 10.00
197A Nick Madrigal pinstripe 15.00 40.00
197B Nick Madrigal SSP 100.00 250.00
200 Jacob deGrom NYPD hat 5.00 12.00
205 Luis Patino grey jsy 4.00 10.00
207 Yadier Molina gear 6.00 15.00
223A Luis Robert no hat 15.00 40.00
223B Luis Robert SSP 100.00 250.00
224A Vladimir Guerrero Jr. blue shirt 3.00 8.00
224B Vladimir Guerrero USP 200.00 500.00
226 Rafael Devers blue shirt 2.50 6.00
227A Willie Mays 6.00 15.00
227B Mike Yastrzemski USP 300.00 800.00
229 Stan Musial 8.00 20.00
231 Dane Dunning throwback 4.00 10.00
239A Ian Anderson SSP 8.00 20.00
239B Ian Anderson SSP#(no hat 60.00 150.00
240 Nolan Ryan 6.00 15.00
241 Anthony Rizzo dugout 6.00 15.00
242 Derek Jeter 10.00 25.00
244 Spencer Howard pinstripe 6.00 15.00
246 Cavan Biggio USP 100.00 250.00
247A Ken Griffey Jr. 12.00 30.00
247B Ken Griffey Jr. USP 300.00 600.00
250A Bryce Harper white headband 10.00 25.00
250B Bryce Harper SSP 40.00 100.00
256 Keibert Ruiz helmet off 6.00 15.00
263A Ronald Acuna Jr. wall jump 12.00 30.00
263B Ronald Acuna SSP 100.00 250.00
265 Mike Clevinger skateboard 4.00 10.00
266A Tony Gwynn 4.00 10.00
266B Roberto Alomar USP 150.00 400.00
269 Jesus Sanchez black shirt 5.00 12.00
275 Joey Votto grey 8.00 20.00
277A Alec Bohm looking up 50.00 120.00
277B Alec Bohm SSP 200.00 500.00
285A Dylan Carlson blue jsy 40.00 100.00
285B Dylan Carlson SSP 150.00 400.00
291 Miguel Cabrera grey shirt 4.00 10.00
297A Alex Bregman smiling 2.00 5.00
297B Alex Bregman SSP 20.00 50.00
298A Luis Garcia red shirt 20.00 50.00
298B Luis Garcia SSP 60.00 150.00
301 Buster Posey mask 4.00 10.00
302 Jackie Robinson 6.00 15.00
309 Francisco Lindor no hat 2.00 5.00
310 Bo Bichette knee up 8.00 20.00
319A Triston McKenzie front of net 4.00 10.00
319B Triston McKenzie SSP 50.00 120.00
321A Casey Mize blue jsy 12.00 30.00
321B Casey Mize SSP 100.00 250.00
322A Javier Baez w/Heyward 5.00 12.00
322B Javier Baez SSP 50.00 120.00
325 Max Scherzer sitting 2.00 5.00
327 George Brett 8.00 20.00
330A Juan Soto cutout 12.00 30.00
330B Juan Soto SSP 100.00 250.00

2021 Topps '51 All Star Box Toppers

ONE PER HOBBY JUMBO BOX
51BT1 Ronald Acuna Jr. 6.00 15.00
51BT2 Mike Trout 8.00 20.00
51BT3 Shohei Ohtani 2.50 6.00
51BT4 Rafael Devers 2.00 5.00
51BT5 Kris Bryant 2.00 5.00
51BT6 Javier Baez 2.00 5.00
51BT7 Luis Robert 5.00 12.00
51BT8 Francisco Lindor 1.50 4.00
51BT9 Nolan Arenado 2.50 6.00
51BT10 Alex Bregman 1.50 4.00
51BT11 Justin Verlander 1.50 4.00
51BT12 Mookie Betts 3.00 8.00
51BT13 Cody Bellinger 3.00 8.00
51BT14 Christian Yelich 2.00 5.00
51BT15 Pete Alonso 4.00 10.00
51BT16 Jacob deGrom 3.00 8.00
51BT17 Aaron Judge 4.00 10.00
51BT18 Gerrit Cole 2.50 6.00
51BT19 Bryce Harper 2.50 6.00
51BT20 Fernando Tatis Jr. 8.00 20.00
51BT21 Buster Posey 2.00 5.00
51BT22 Yadier Molina 2.00 5.00
51BT23 Vladimir Guerrero Jr. 2.50 6.00
51BT24 Juan Soto 5.00 12.00
51BT25 Matt Chapman 1.50 4.00

2021 Topps '52 Topps Redux

STATED ODDS 1:10 RETAIL
T521 Aaron Judge 1.25 3.00
T522 Miguel Cabrera .50 1.25
T523 Yordan Alvarez 1.25 3.00
T524 Javier Baez .60 1.50
T525 Josh Donaldson .40 1.00
T526 Mookie Betts 1.00 2.50
T527 Casey Mize 2.50 6.00
T528 Buster Posey .60 1.50
T529 Juan Soto 1.50 4.00
T5210 Francisco Lindor .50 1.25
T5211 Alex Bregman .50 1.25
T5212 J.D. Martinez .50 1.25
T5213 Max Scherzer .50 1.25
T5214 Alec Bohm 3.00 8.00
T5215 Jacob deGrom 1.00 2.50
T5216 Justin Verlander .50 1.25
T5217 Evan White 2.00 5.00
T5218 Nate Pearson 1.50 4.00
T5219 Luis Robert 1.50 4.00
T5220 Pete Alonso 1.25 3.00
T5221 Bryce Harper .75 2.00
T5222 Cody Bellinger 1.00 2.50
T5223 Josh Bell .40 1.00
T5224 Manny Machado .50 1.25
T5225 Gerrit Cole .75 2.00
T5226 Jo Adell 2.00 5.00
T5227 Mike Trout 2.50 6.00
T5228 Bo Bichette 1.25 3.00
T5229 Rafael Devers .60 1.50
T5230 Yadier Molina .60 1.50
T5231 Paul Goldschmidt .50 1.25
T5232 Fernando Tatis Jr. 2.50 6.00
T5233 Dylan Carlson 2.50 6.00
T5234 Albert Pujols .60 1.50
T5235 Nolan Arenado .75 2.00
T5236 Blake Snell .40 1.00
T5237 Eloy Jimenez 1.00 2.50
T5238 Gleyber Torres 1.00 2.50
T5239 Kris Bryant .60 1.50
T5240 Clayton Kershaw .75 2.00
T5241 Stephen Strasburg .50 1.25
T5242 Freddie Freeman .60 1.50
T5243 Shohei Ohtani .75 2.00
T5244 Matt Chapman .50 1.25
T5245 Ronald Acuna Jr. 2.00 5.00
T5246 Vladimir Guerrero Jr. .75 2.00
T5247 Sonny Gray .40 1.00
T5248 Joey Votto .50 1.25
T5249 Joey Bart 1.00 2.50
T5250 Christian Yelich .60 1.50

2021 Topps '52 Topps Redux Black

*BLACK.: 4X TO 10X BASIC
STATED ODDS 1:9867 RETAIL
STATED PRINT RUN 25 SER.#'d SETS
T521 Aaron Judge 50.00 120.00
T529 Juan Soto 30.00 80.00
T5214 Alec Bohm 100.00 250.00
T5219 Luis Robert 25.00 60.00
T5227 Mike Trout 60.00 150.00
T5232 Fernando Tatis Jr. 60.00 150.00
T5233 Dylan Carlson 60.00 150.00
T5245 Ronald Acuna Jr. 30.00 80.00

2021 Topps '52 Topps Redux Red

*RED.: 2.5X TO 6X BASIC
STATED ODDS 1:3504 RETAIL
STATED PRINT RUN 70 SER.#'d SETS
T529 Juan Soto 20.00 50.00
T5214 Alec Bohm 60.00 150.00
T5227 Mike Trout 40.00 100.00
T5232 Fernando Tatis Jr. 40.00 100.00
T5233 Dylan Carlson 40.00 100.00
T5245 Ronald Acuna Jr. 20.00 50.00

2021 Topps '52 Topps Redux Chrome

STATED ODDS 1:10 RETAIL
TC521 Aaron Judge 2.50 6.00
TC522 Miguel Cabrera 1.00 2.50
TC523 Yordan Alvarez 2.50 6.00
TC524 Javier Baez 1.25 3.00
TC525 Josh Donaldson .75 2.00
TC526 Mookie Betts 2.00 5.00
TC527 Casey Mize 5.00 12.00
TC528 Buster Posey 1.25 3.00
TC529 Juan Soto 3.00 8.00
TC5210 Francisco Lindor 1.00 2.50
TC5211 Alex Bregman 1.00 2.50
TC5212 J.D. Martinez 1.00 2.50
TC5213 Max Scherzer 1.00 2.50
TC5214 Alec Bohm 6.00 15.00
TC5215 Jacob deGrom 2.00 5.00
TC5216 Justin Verlander 1.00 2.50
TC5217 Evan White 4.00 10.00
TC5218 Nate Pearson 4.00 10.00
TC5219 Luis Robert 3.00 8.00
TC5220 Pete Alonso 2.50 6.00
TC5221 Bryce Harper 1.50 4.00
TC5222 Cody Bellinger 2.00 5.00
TC5223 Josh Bell .75 2.00
TC5224 Manny Machado 1.00 2.50
TC5225 Gerrit Cole 1.50 4.00
TC5226 Jo Adell 4.00 10.00
TC5227 Mike Trout 5.00 12.00
TC5228 Bo Bichette 2.50 6.00
TC5229 Rafael Devers 1.25 3.00
TC5230 Yadier Molina 1.25 3.00
TC5231 Paul Goldschmidt 1.00 2.50
TC5232 Fernando Tatis Jr. 5.00 12.00
TC5233 Dylan Carlson 5.00 12.00
TC5234 Albert Pujols 1.25 3.00
TC5235 Nolan Arenado 1.50 4.00
TC5236 Blake Snell .75 2.00
TC5237 Eloy Jimenez 2.00 5.00
TC5238 Gleyber Torres 2.00 5.00
TC5239 Kris Bryant 1.25 3.00
TC5240 Clayton Kershaw 1.50 4.00
TC5241 Stephen Strasburg 1.00 2.50
TC5242 Freddie Freeman 1.25 3.00
TC5243 Shohei Ohtani 1.50 4.00
TC5244 Matt Chapman 1.00 2.50
TC5245 Ronald Acuna Jr. 4.00 10.00
TC5246 Vladimir Guerrero Jr. 1.50 4.00
TC5247 Sonny Gray .75 2.00
TC5248 Joey Votto 1.00 2.50
TC5249 Joey Bart 2.00 5.00
TC5250 Christian Yelich 1.25 3.00

2021 Topps '52 Topps Redux Chrome Black Refractors

*BLACK.: 6X TO 15X BASIC
STATED ODDS 1:9867 RETAIL
STATED PRINT RUN 25 SER.#'d SETS
TC521 Aaron Judge 75.00 200.00
TC526 Mookie Betts 50.00 120.00
TC5214 Alec Bohm 200.00 500.00
TC5219 Luis Robert 200.00 500.00
TC5226 Jo Adell 40.00 100.00
TC5227 Mike Trout 150.00 400.00
TC5228 Bo Bichette 60.00 150.00
TC5232 Fernando Tatis Jr. 200.00 500.00
TC5233 Dylan Carlson 100.00 250.00
TC5238 Gleyber Torres 30.00 80.00
TC5245 Ronald Acuna Jr. 60.00 150.00

2021 Topps '52 Topps Redux Chrome Red Refractors

*RED.: 3X TO 8X BASIC
STATED ODDS 1:3504 RETAIL
STATED PRINT RUN 70 SER.#'d SETS
TC521 Aaron Judge 40.00 100.00
TC526 Mookie Betts 25.00 60.00
TC5214 Alec Bohm 100.00 250.00
TC5219 Luis Robert 100.00 250.00
TC5226 Jo Adell 20.00 50.00
TC5227 Mike Trout 75.00 200.00
TC5228 Bo Bichette 30.00 80.00
TC5233 Dylan Carlson 50.00 120.00
TC5238 Gleyber Torres 15.00 40.00
TC5245 Ronald Acuna Jr. 30.00 80.00

2021 Topps '86 Topps

STATED ODDS 1:4 HOBBY
*BLUE: .8X TO 2X BASIC
*BLACK/299: 1.2X TO 3X BASIC
*PLAT.ANN./70: 2.5X TO 6X BASIC
86B1 Mike Trout 2.50 6.00
86B1 Brady Singer
86B2 Willie Mays 1.00 2.50
86B2 Triston McKenzie
86B3 Brady Singer 1.50 4.00
86B3 Jose Garcia
86B4 Clayton Kershaw .75 2.00
86B4 J.D. Martinez
86B5 Gerrit Cole .75 2.00
86B5 Shane McClanahan
86B6 Austin Meadows .50 1.25
86B6 Aaron Nola
86B7 Hank Aaron 1.00 2.50
86B7 Yu Darvish
86B8 Ryan Mountcastle 3.00 8.00
86B8 Sixto Sanchez
86B9 Blake Snell .40 1.00
86B9 Jazz Chisholm
86B10 Joey Gallo .50 1.25
86B10 Nick Madrigal
86B11 Cody Bellinger 1.00 2.50
86B11 Michael Conforto
86B12 Freddie Freeman .60 1.50
86B12 Francisco Lindor
86B13 Mookie Betts 1.00 2.50
86B13 Yordan Alvarez
86B14 Joey Bart 1.00 2.50
86B14 Joey Bart
86B15 Ryne Sandberg 1.00 2.50
86B15 Byron Buxton
86B16 David Ortiz .50 1.25
86B16 Carlos Correa
86B17 Christian Yelich .60 1.50
86B17 Dylan Carlson
86B18 Walker Buehler .60 1.50
86B18 Jose Abreu
86B19 Yadier Molina .60 1.50
86B19 Jose Ramirez
86B20 Bryce Harper .75 2.00
86B20 Ian Anderson
86B21 Josh Bell .40 1.00
86B21 Dane Dunning
86B22 Shohei Ohtani .75 2.00
86B22 Jose Canseco
86B23 Eddie Murray .40 1.00
86B23 Jo Adell
86B24 Jose Altuve .40 1.00
86B24 Randy Johnson
86B25 Greg Maddux .60 1.50
86B25 Deivi Garcia
86B26 Miguel Cabrera .50 1.25
86B26 Charlie Blackmon
86B27 Josh Donaldson .40 1.00
86B27 Corey Seager
86B28 Xander Bogaerts .50 1.25
86B28 Ozzie Albies
86B29 Trevor Story .50 1.25
86B29 Luke Voit
86B30 Alex Bregman .50 1.25
86B30 Cristian Pache
86B31 Keston Hiura .60 1.50
86B31 Sam Huff
86B32 Andrew McCutchen .50 1.25
86B32 Dean Kremer
86B33 Anthony Rendon .50 1.25
86B33 Bobby Dalbec
86B34 Nolan Ryan 1.50 4.00
86B34 Ke'Bryan Hayes
86B35 Vladimir Guerrero Jr. .75 2.00
86B35 Mike Yastrzemski
86B36 Javier Baez .60 1.50
86B36 Daulton Varsho
86B37 Shane Bieber .50 1.25
86B37 Manny Machado
86B38 Jesus Luzardo .50 1.25
86B38 Tanner Houck
86B39 Tyler Stephenson 1.50 4.00
86B39 Garrett Crochet
86B40 Roger Clemens .60 1.50
86B40 Luis Garcia
86B41 Cal Ripken Jr. 1.50 4.00
86B41 George Springer
86B42 Starling Marte .40 1.00
86B42 Willson Contreras
86B43 Alec Bohm 3.00 8.00
86B43 Jake Cronenworth
86B44 Kris Bryant .60 1.50
86B44 Matt Olson
86B45 Whit Merrifield .50 1.25
86B45 Brailyn Marquez
86B46 Andres Gimenez .75 2.00
86B46 Mike Schmidt
86B47 Don Mattingly 1.00 2.50
86B47 Tarik Skubal
86B48 George Brett 1.00 2.50
86B48 Alex Kirilloff
86B49 Johnny Bench .50 1.25
86B49 Max Muncy
86B50 Frank Thomas .50 1.25
86B50 Kris Bubic
86B51 Will Clark .40 1.00
86B52 Eloy Jimenez 1.00 2.50
86B53 Justin Verlander .50 1.25
86B54 Randy Johnson .50 1.25
86B55 Bo Bichette 1.25 3.00
86B56 Brooks Robinson .40 1.00
86B57 Nolan Arenado .75 2.00
86B58 Buster Posey .60 1.50
86B59 Rafael Devers .60 1.50
86B60 Ken Griffey Jr. 1.00 2.50
86B61 Roberto Clemente 1.25 3.00
86B62 Jacob deGrom 1.00 2.50
86B63 Mike Clevinger .40 1.00
86B64 Chipper Jones .50 1.25
86B65 Pete Alonso 1.25 3.00
86B66 Francisco Lindor .50 1.25
86B67 Kirby Puckett .50 1.25
86B68 Vladimir Guerrero .40 1.00
86B69 Nate Pearson 1.50 4.00
86B70 Cristian Javier .75 2.00
86B71 Gleyber Torres 1.00 2.50
86B72 Sonny Gray .40 1.00
86B73 Jack Flaherty .50 1.25
86B74 Matt Chapman .50 1.25
86B75 Luis Robert 1.50 4.00
86B76 Mark McGwire .75 2.00
86B77 Tony Gwynn .50 1.25
86B78 Ichiro .60 1.50
86B79 Barry Larkin .40 1.00
86B80 Rickey Henderson .50 1.25
86B81 Joey Votto .50 1.25
86B82 Evan White 2.00 5.00
86B83 Dylan Carlson 2.50 6.00
86B84 Stephen Strasburg .50 1.25
86B85 Casey Mize 2.50 6.00
86B86 Kyle Lewis 1.25 3.00
86B87 Mike Piazza .50 1.25
86B88 Jackie Robinson .50 1.25
86B89 Ketel Marte .40 1.00
86B90 Jo Adell 2.00 5.00
86B91 Anthony Rizzo .60 1.50
86B92 Giancarlo Stanton .50 1.25
86B93 Albert Pujols .60 1.50
86B94 Ronald Acuna Jr. 2.00 5.00
86B95 Max Scherzer .50 1.25
86B96 Juan Soto 1.50 4.00
86B97 Paul Goldschmidt .50 1.25
86B98 Derek Jeter 1.25 3.00
86B99 Aaron Judge 1.25 3.00
86B100 Fernando Tatis Jr. 2.50 6.00

2021 Topps '86 Topps Autographs

STATED ODDS 1:371 HOBBY
EXCHANGE DEADLINE 1/31/2023
86AI Ichiro 150.00 400.00
86AAD Andre Dawson 30.00 80.00
86AAG Alex Gordon 20.00 50.00
86AAJ Aaron Judge 100.00 250.00
86AAP A.J. Puk 8.00 20.00
86AAY Andy Young 6.00 15.00
86ABD Bobby Dalbec 50.00 120.00
86ABL Brandon Lowe 8.00 20.00
86ACF Carlton Fisk 20.00 50.00
86ACM Casey Mize 40.00 100.00
86ACT Chadwick Tromp 8.00 20.00
86ADC Dylan Carlson 50.00 120.00
86ADE Dennis Eckersley 20.00 50.00
86ADM Don Mattingly 40.00 100.00
86AEA Elvis Andrus 3.00 8.00
86AEM Edgar Martinez 20.00 50.00
86AEW Evan White 20.00 50.00
86AFF Freddie Freeman 40.00 100.00
86AFT Fernando Tatis Jr. 200.00 500.00
86AGC Gerrit Cole 30.00 80.00
86AHA Hank Aaron

86AHR Hyun-Jin Ryu 20.00 50.00
86AJA Jim Abbott 20.00 50.00
86AJB Joey Bart 25.00 60.00
86AJC Jose Canseco 20.00 50.00
86AJG Joey Gallo 20.00 50.00
86AKL Kenny Lofton 15.00 40.00
86AKM Ketel Marte 10.00 25.00
86AKS Kyle Schwarber 15.00 40.00
86AKW Kerry Wood 12.00 30.00
86ALR Luis Robert 100.00 250.00
86ALW Larry Walker 25.00 60.00
86AMH Monte Harrison 8.00 20.00
86AMM Mike Moustakas
86AMT Mike Trout 400.00 1000.00
86AMY Mike Yastrzemski 15.00 40.00
86ANC Nick Castellanos
86ANH Nico Hoerner 20.00 50.00
86ANM Nick Madrigal 50.00 120.00
86ANN Nick Neidert
86ANP Nate Pearson 25.00 60.00
86ANR Nolan Ryan 100.00 250.00
86AOS Ozzie Smith 30.00 80.00
86APD Paul DeJong 12.00 30.00
86APG Paul Goldschmidt 20.00 50.00
86ARC Ryan Castellani
86ARD Rafael Devers
86ARH Ryan Howard 50.00 120.00
86ARS Ryne Sandberg
86ARY Robin Yount 60.00 150.00
86ASA Shogo Akiyama 10.00 25.00
86ASB Shane Bieber 15.00 40.00
86ASC Shin-Soo Choo 15.00 40.00
86ASE Santiago Espinal 6.00 15.00
86ASH Spencer Howard 20.00 50.00
86ASR Scott Rolen 15.00 40.00
86ATM Tino Martinez 25.00 60.00
86AWB Wade Boggs 30.00 80.00
86AWM Whit Merrifield 12.00 30.00
86AZB Zack Burdi 8.00 20.00
86AZM Zach McKinstry 50.00 120.00
86AABO Alec Bohm 100.00 250.00
86AABR Alex Bregman 25.00 60.00
86AARE Anthony Rendon 20.00 50.00
86AAVE Alex Verdugo
86ABBI Brandon Bielak 4.00 10.00
86ABBU Beau Burrows 8.00 20.00
86ABBU Byron Buxton
86ABHA Bryce Harper 100.00 250.00
86ABSI Brady Singer 12.00 30.00
86ACBI Cavan Biggio 12.00 30.00
86ACCS CC Sabathia 25.00 60.00
86ACJA Cristian Javier
86ACPA Cristian Pache 75.00 200.00
86ADAS Dave Stewart 10.00 25.00
86ADGO Dwight Gooden 30.00 80.00
86ADJA Danny Jansen
86ADJO Daniel Johnson 8.00 20.00
86ADMU Dale Murphy 40.00 100.00
86ADST Darryl Strawberry 30.00 80.00
86ADVA Daulton Varsho 10.00 25.00
86AEAL Eddy Alvarez 4.00 10.00
86AFTH Frank Thomas 60.00 150.00
86AJAA Jose Altuve 20.00 50.00
86AJAD Jo Adell 100.00 250.00
86AJBN Johnny Bench 100.00 250.00
86AJKE Jarred Kelenic
86AJKR John Kruk 15.00 40.00
86AJMA Jorge Mateo 6.00 15.00
86AJRA Jose Ramirez
86AJSM John Smoltz 30.00 80.00
86AJSO Juan Soto 100.00 250.00
86AJVA Jason Varitek
86AKBU Kris Bubic 10.00 25.00
86AKHI Keston Hiura 8.00 20.00
86AKLE Kyle Lewis
86AKWH Kodi Whitley
86AKWO Kolten Wong 3.00 8.00
86ALCA Luis Castillo 6.00 15.00
86ALGA Luis Garcia
86ALPA Luis Patino 15.00 40.00
86AMAB Matthew Boyd
86AMCA Miguel Cabrera
86AMCH Michael Chavis 6.00 15.00
86AMCP Matt Chapman 20.00 50.00
86AMMG Mark McGwire 60.00 150.00
86AMMU Max Muncy
86AMSO Mike Soroka
86AMST Marcus Stroman 20.00 50.00
86APAL Pete Alonso 60.00 150.00
86ARAC Ronald Acuna Jr. 100.00 250.00
86ARAL Roberto Alomar 25.00 60.00
86ARHE Rickey Henderson
86ARMO Ryan Mountcastle 40.00 100.00
86ASGR Sonny Gray 12.00 30.00
86ASST Stephen Strasburg 25.00 60.00
86ATGL Tyler Glasnow 10.00 25.00
86ATSK Tarik Skubal
86ATST Tyler Stephenson 12.00 30.00
86AWBU Walker Buehler
86AWCO Willson Contreras 12.00 30.00
86AWIC William Contreras 25.00 60.00
86AYMO Yoan Moncada 15.00 40.00
86BDCA Dylan Carlson
86BEMU Eddie Murray
86BJDO Dontrelle Willis
86BJHE Jonah Heim
86BJON Jorge Ona
86BJST Jonathan Stiever
86BRAR Randy Arozarena
86BTHO Tanner Houck
86ABELL Josh Bell 10.00 25.00

2021 Topps '86 Topps Autographs Black

*BLACK/199: .5X TO 1.2X BASIC
STATED ODDS 1:1327 HOBBY
STATED PRINT RUN 199 SER.#'d SETS
EXCHANGE DEADLINE 1/31/2023
86AEA Elvis Andrus 10.00 25.00
86AEW Evan White 30.00 80.00
86ACPA Cristian Pache 125.00 300.00
86ARMO Ryan Mountcastle 50.00 120.00

2021 Topps '86 Topps Autographs Gold

*GOLD/50: ..6X TO 1.5X BASIC
*GOLD/25: .8X TO 2X BASIC
STATED ODDS 1:2681 HOBBY
PRINT RUN B/TW 10-50 COPIES PER
NO PRICING QTY 15 OR LESS
EXCHANGE DEADLINE 1/31/2023
86AEA Elvis Andrus/50 12.00 30.00
86AEW Evan White/50 40.00 100.00
86ASR Scott Rolen/50 30.00 80.00
86ATG Tom Glavine/50 40.00 100.00
86AABO Alec Bohm/50 200.00 500.00
86ACPA Cristian Pache/50 150.00 400.00

2021 Topps '86 Topps Autographs Red

*RED/25: .8X TO 2X BASIC
STATED ODDS 1:7178 HOBBY
PRINT RUN B/TW 3-25 COPIES PER
NO PRICING QTY 15 OR LESS
EXCHANGE DEADLINE 1/31/2023
86AEA Elvis Andrus/25 15.00 40.00
86AEW Evan White/25 60.00 150.00
86ASR Scott Rolen/25 40.00 100.00
86ATG Tom Glavine/25 50.00 120.00
86AABO Alec Bohm/25 400.00 800.00
86ACPA Cristian Pache/25 200.00 500.00
86ARMO Ryan Mountcastle/25 125.00 300.00

2021 Topps '86 Topps Relics

STATED ODDS 1:94 HOBBY
*BLACK/199: .5X TO 1.2X BASE
*GOLD/50: .6X TO 1.5X BASE
*RED/25: .75X TO 2X BASE
86RAB Alex Bregman 3.00 8.00
86RAJ Aaron Judge 8.00 20.00
86RAN Aaron Nola 2.50 6.00
86RBB Bo Bichette 6.00 15.00
86RBL Brandon Lowe 2.50 6.00
86RBP Buster Posey 4.00 10.00
86RBS Blake Snell 2.50 6.00
86RCC Carlos Correa 3.00 8.00
86RCR Cal Ripken Jr. 12.00 30.00
86RCS Corey Seager 3.00 8.00
86RDJ Derek Jeter 30.00 80.00
86RDM Don Mattingly 12.00 30.00
86RFL Francisco Lindor 3.00 8.00
86RFT Fernando Tatis Jr. 10.00 25.00
86RGT Gleyber Torres 8.00 20.00
86RJA Jose Altuve 2.50 6.00
86RJB Javier Baez 4.00 10.00
86RJF Jack Flaherty 3.00 8.00
86RJL Jesus Luzardo 3.00 8.00
86RJS Jorge Soler 3.00 8.00
86RJV Joey Votto 3.00 8.00
86RKB Kris Bryant 4.00 10.00
86RKG Ken Griffey Jr. 20.00 50.00
86RKH Keston Hiura 4.00 10.00
86RKL Kyle Lewis 6.00 15.00
86RLR Luis Robert 10.00 25.00
86RMB Mookie Betts 8.00 20.00
86RMC Miguel Cabrera 3.00 8.00
86RMM Mark McGwire 10.00 25.00
86RMO Matt Olson 3.00 8.00
86RMS Miguel Sano 2.50 6.00
86RMT Mike Trout 12.00 30.00
86RNA Nolan Arenado 4.00 10.00
86RNR Nolan Ryan 15.00 40.00
86ROA Ozzie Albies 6.00 15.00
86RPA Pete Alonso 5.00 12.00
86RPD Paul DeJong 3.00 8.00
86RRA Ronald Acuna Jr. 8.00 20.00
86RRD Rafael Devers 4.00 10.00
86RRH Rhys Hoskins 4.00 10.00
86RSA Shogo Akiyama 3.00 8.00
86RSO Shohei Ohtani 6.00 15.00
86RTG Tony Gwynn 6.00 15.00
86RTS Trevor Story 3.00 8.00
86RVG Vladimir Guerrero Jr. 5.00 12.00
86RVR Victor Robles 4.00 10.00
86RWB Walker Buehler 4.00 10.00
86RWC Willson Contreras 3.00 8.00
86RXB Xander Bogaerts 3.00 8.00
86RYM Yoan Moncada 3.00 8.00
86RJBE Josh Bell 2.50 6.00
86RJSO Juan Soto 6.00 15.00
86RYMO Yadier Molina 4.00 10.00

2021 Topps '86 Topps Silver Pack Chrome

86BC1 Mike Trout 10.00 25.00
86BC2 Jose Canseco .75 2.00
86BC3 Brady Singer 3.00 8.00
86BC4 Clayton Kershaw 1.50 4.00
86BC5 Gerrit Cole 1.50 4.00
86BC6 Austin Meadows 1.00 2.50
86BC7 Hank Aaron 2.00 5.00
86BC8 Ryan Mountcastle 6.00 15.00
86BC9 Yoan Moncada 1.00 2.50
86BC10 Joey Gallo 1.00 2.50
86BC11 Cody Bellinger 2.00 5.00
86BC12 Freddie Freeman 1.25 3.00
86BC13 Mookie Betts 2.00 5.00
86BC14 Ke'Bryan Hayes 6.00 15.00
86BC15 Kris Bubic 1.00 2.50
86BC16 Nick Madrigal 5.00 12.00
86BC17 Christian Yelich 1.25 3.00
86BC18 Leody Taveras 2.00 5.00
86BC19 Yadier Molina 1.25 3.00
86BC20 Bryce Harper 1.50 4.00
86BC21 Deivi Garcia 5.00 12.00
86BC22 Shohei Ohtani 1.50 4.00
86BC23 Dylan Carlson 8.00 20.00
86BC24 Luis Patino 2.50 6.00
86BC25 Greg Maddux 1.25 3.00
86BC26 Miguel Cabrera 1.00 2.50
86BC27 Josh Donaldson .75 2.00
86BC28 Xander Bogaerts 1.00 2.50
86BC29 Trevor Story 1.00 2.50
86BC30 Alex Bregman 1.00 2.50
86BC31 Keston Hiura 1.25 3.00
86BC32 Ozzie Smith 1.25 3.00
86BC33 Keibert Ruiz 2.00 5.00
86BC34 Nolan Ryan 3.00 8.00
86BC35 Vladimir Guerrero Jr. 1.50 4.00
86BC36 Javier Baez 1.25 3.00
86BC37 Shane Bieber 1.00 2.50
86BC38 Jesus Luzardo 1.00 2.50
86BC39 Tyler Stephenson 3.00 8.00
86BC40 Roger Clemens 1.25 3.00
86BC41 Cal Ripken Jr. 3.00 8.00
86BC42 Sixto Sanchez 3.00 8.00
86BC43 Ian Anderson 4.00 10.00
86BC44 Kris Bryant 1.25 3.00
86BC45 Anderson Tejeda 1.50 4.00
86BC46 Andres Gimenez 1.50 4.00
86BC47 Don Mattingly 2.00 5.00
86BC48 George Brett 2.00 5.00
86BC49 Jorge Soler 1.00 2.50
86BC50 Frank Thomas 1.00 2.50
86BC51 Will Clark .75 2.00
86BC52 Monte Harrison 1.00 2.50
86BC53 Justin Verlander 1.00 2.50
86BC54 Randy Johnson 1.00 2.50
86BC55 Bo Bichette 2.50 6.00
86BC56 Shogo Akiyama 1.00 2.50
86BC57 Nolan Arenado 1.50 4.00
86BC58 Buster Posey 1.25 3.00
86BC59 Rafael Devers 1.25 3.00
86BC60 Ken Griffey Jr. 8.00 20.00
86BC61 Mike Yastrzemski 1.50 4.00
86BC62 Jacob deGrom 2.00 5.00
86BC63 Triston McKenzie 3.00 8.00
86BC64 Chipper Jones 1.00 2.50
86BC65 Pete Alonso 2.50 6.00
86BC66 Francisco Lindor 1.00 2.50
86BC67 Yordan Alvarez 2.50 6.00
86BC68 Alec Bohm 12.00 30.00
86BC69 Nate Pearson 3.00 8.00
86BC70 Cristian Javier 1.50 4.00
86BC71 Brandon Lowe .75 2.00
86BC72 Sonny Gray .75 2.00
86BC73 Jack Flaherty 1.00 2.50
86BC74 Matt Chapman 1.00 2.50
86BC75 Luis Robert 6.00 15.00
86BC76 Mark McGwire 1.50 4.00
86BC77 Tony Gwynn 1.00 2.50
86BC78 Ichiro 1.25 3.00
86BC79 Spencer Howard 2.00 5.00
86BC80 Robin Yount 1.00 2.50
86BC81 Joey Votto 1.00 2.50
86BC82 Evan White 4.00 10.00
86BC83 Byron Buxton 1.00 2.50
86BC84 Stephen Strasburg 1.00 2.50
86BC85 Casey Mize 5.00 12.00
86BC86 Manny Machado 1.00 2.50
86BC87 Jonathan Arauz .75 2.00
86BC88 Jackie Robinson 1.00 2.50
86BC89 Bobby Dalbec 6.00 15.00
86BC90 Jo Adell 8.00 20.00
86BC91 Joey Bart 2.00 5.00
86BC92 Luis Garcia 3.00 8.00
86BC93 Daulton Varsho 1.50 4.00
86BC94 Ronald Acuna Jr. 4.00 10.00
86BC95 Max Scherzer 1.00 2.50
86BC96 Juan Soto 5.00 12.00
86BC97 Paul Goldschmidt 1.00 2.50
86BC98 Roberto Clemente 2.50 6.00
86BC99 Aaron Judge 2.50 6.00
86BC100 Fernando Tatis Jr. 8.00 20.00

2021 Topps '86 Topps Silver Pack Chrome Blue Refractors

*BLUE/150: 1X TO 2.5X BASIC
RANDOM INSERTS IN SILVER PACKS
STATED PRINT RUN 150 SER.#'d SETS
86BC1 Mike Trout 30.00 80.00
86BC60 Ken Griffey Jr. 30.00 80.00

2021 Topps '86 Topps Silver Pack Chrome Gold Refractors

*GOLD/50: 2.5X TO 6X BASIC
RANDOM INSERTS IN SILVER PACKS
STATED PRINT RUN 50 SER.#'d SETS
86BC1 Mike Trout 100.00 250.00
86BC23 Dylan Carlson 60.00 150.00
86BC60 Ken Griffey Jr. 75.00 200.00

2021 Topps '86 Topps Silver Pack Chrome Green Refractors

*GREEN/99: 1.2X TO 3X BASIC
RANDOM INSERTS IN SILVER PACKS
STATED PRINT RUN 99 SER.#'d SETS
86BC1 Mike Trout 40.00 100.00
86BC23 Dylan Carlson 30.00 80.00
86BC60 Ken Griffey Jr. 40.00 100.00

2021 Topps '86 Topps Silver Pack Chrome Orange Refractors

*ORANGE/25: 4X TO 10X BASIC
RANDOM INSERTS IN SILVER PACKS
STATED PRINT RUN 25 SER.#'d SETS
86BC1 Mike Trout 150.00 400.00
86BC23 Dylan Carlson 100.00 250.00
86BC60 Ken Griffey Jr. 125.00 300.00

2021 Topps '86 Topps Silver Pack Chrome Purple Refractors

*PURPLE/75: 1.2X TO 3X BASIC
RANDOM INSERTS IN SILVER PACKS
STATED PRINT RUN 75 SER.#'d SETS
86BC1 Mike Trout 40.00 100.00
86BC23 Dylan Carlson 30.00 80.00
86BC60 Ken Griffey Jr. 40.00 100.00

2021 Topps '86 Topps Silver Pack Chrome Autographs

RANDOM INSERTS IN SILVER PACKS
PRINT RUNS B/WN 10-199 COPIES PER
NO PRICING ON QTY 15 OR LESS
EXCHANGE DEADLINE 12/31/22
86BC3 Brady Singer/30 40.00 100.00
86BC6 Austin Meadows/50 12.00 30.00
86BC8 Ryan Mountcastle/99 60.00 150.00
86BC9 Yoan Moncada/50 25.00 60.00
86BC10 Joey Gallo/30 15.00 40.00
86BC12 Freddie Freeman/30 60.00 150.00
86BC14 Ke'Bryan Hayes/99 200.00 500.00
86BC15 Kris Bubic/199 10.00 25.00
86BC16 Nick Madrigal/199 50.00 120.00
86BC19 Yadier Molina/30 75.00 200.00
86BC21 Deivi Garcia/99 50.00 120.00
86BC23 Dylan Carlson/99 100.00 250.00
86BC24 Luis Patino/199 20.00 50.00
86BC25 Greg Maddux/20 75.00 200.00
86BC28 Xander Bogaerts/30 40.00 100.00
86BC31 Keston Hiura/50 20.00 50.00
86BC35 Vladimir Guerrero Jr./30 75.00 200.00
86BC37 Shane Bieber/50 30.00 80.00
86BC39 Tyler Stephenson/199 20.00 50.00
86BC44 Kris Bryant
86BC45 Anderson Tejeda/150 15.00 40.00
86BC49 Jorge Soler/50 8.00 20.00
86BC50 Frank Thomas
86BC51 Will Clark/30 60.00 150.00
86BC56 Shogo Akiyama
86BC59 Rafael Devers/30 20.00 50.00
86BC60 Ken Griffey Jr.
86BC61 Mike Yastrzemski/99 25.00 60.00
86BC62 Jacob deGrom/30 100.00 250.00
86BC65 Pete Alonso/30 40.00 100.00
86BC68 Alec Bohm/99 125.00 300.00
86BC69 Nate Pearson/199 40.00 100.00
86BC70 Cristian Javier/199 15.00 40.00
86BC72 Sonny Gray/50 10.00 25.00
86BC74 Matt Chapman/99 20.00 50.00
86BC79 Spencer Howard/199 20.00 50.00
86BC81 Joey Votto
86BC82 Evan White/199 25.00 60.00
86BC84 Stephen Strasburg
86BC85 Casey Mize/99 75.00 200.00
86BC86 Manny Machado
86BC89 Bobby Dalbec/99 50.00 120.00
86BC90 Jo Adell/99 100.00 250.00
86BC91 Joey Bart/99 50.00 120.00
86BC93 Daulton Varsho/99 20.00 50.00
86BC94 Ronald Acuna Jr./30 100.00 250.00
86BC96 Juan Soto/30 125.00 300.00
86BC99 Aaron Judge
86BC100 Fernando Tatis Jr./99 150.00 400.00

2021 Topps '86 Topps Silver Pack Chrome Autographs Orange Refractors

*ORANGE/25: .75X TO 2X p/r 150-199
*ORANGE/25: .6X TO 1.5X p/r 99
*ORANGE/25: .5X TO 1.2X p/r 30
RANDOM INSERTS IN SILVER PACKS
STATED PRINT RUN 25 SER.#'d SETS
EXCHANGE DEADLINE 12/31/22
86BC6 Austin Meadows 20.00 50.00
86BC8 Ryan Mountcastle 125.00 300.00
86BC10 Joey Gallo 25.00 60.00
86BC14 Ke'Bryan Hayes 500.00 1000.00
86BC16 Nick Madrigal 150.00 400.00
86BC23 Dylan Carlson 200.00 500.00
86BC31 Keston Hiura 30.00 80.00
86BC37 Shane Bieber 60.00 150.00
86BC51 Will Clark 100.00 250.00
86BC56 Shogo Akiyama
86BC59 Rafael Devers 30.00 80.00
86BC62 Jacob deGrom 150.00 400.00
86BC65 Pete Alonso 100.00 250.00
86BC68 Alec Bohm 250.00 600.00
86BC70 Cristian Javier 40.00 100.00
86BC74 Matt Chapman 40.00 100.00
86BC89 Bobby Dalbec 150.00 400.00
86BC91 Joey Bart 150.00 400.00
86BC94 Ronald Acuna Jr. 200.00 500.00
86BC96 Juan Soto 200.00 500.00

2021 Topps 70 Years of Baseball Autographs

STATED ODDS 1:140 HOBBY
EXCHANGE DEADLINE 1/31/2023
*BLACK/50: .6X TO 1.5X BASIC
*GOLD/25: .8X TO 2X BASIC
70YAAB Alec Bohm 125.00 300.00
70YAAB Adrian Beltre
70YAAK Alejandro Kirk
70YAAM Austin Meadows 8.00 20.00
70YAAM Adonis Medina
70YABB Brandon Bielak
70YABG Bob Gibson 30.00 80.00
70YABG Bob Gibson
70YABK Brad Keller 2.50 6.00
70YABZ Barry Zito
70YACB Corbin Burnes 12.00 30.00
70YACS Clarke Schmidt 10.00 25.00
70YACY Christian Yelich
70YADC Dylan Carlson 60.00 150.00
70YADD Dane Dunning 5.00 12.00
70YADJ Danny Jansen 2.50 6.00
70YADJ Daulton Jefferies
70YADL Derrek Lee
70YADM Dale Murphy
70YADS Darryl Strawberry
70YADV Daulton Varsho
70YAED Eric Davis 15.00 40.00
70YAEH Eric Hosmer
70YAEO Edward Olivares 6.00 15.00
70YAEW Evan White
70YAFJ Fergie Jenkins 20.00 50.00
70YAFK Franklyn Kilome 6.00 15.00
70YAFR Franmil Reyes
70YAFT Frank Thomas
70YAHR Hyun-Jin Ryu
70YAIA Ian Anderson
70YAIP Isaac Paredes 10.00 25.00
70YAJA Jo Adell 50.00 120.00
70YAJB Joey Bart 25.00 60.00
70YAJB Josh Bell
70YAJD J.D. Davis
70YAJG Joey Gallo
70YAJH Jonah Heim
70YAJJ Josh James 2.50 6.00
70YAJJ Jahmai Jones
70YAJK John Kruk 12.00 30.00
70YAJM Jordan Montgomery 6.00 15.00
70YAJO Johan Oviedo 10.00 25.00
70YAJO Jared Oliva
70YAJR Jim Rice 15.00 40.00
70YAJR J.T. Realmuto
70YAJS Juan Soto
70YAJS Juan Soto
70YAJV Jason Varitek
70YAJW Jake Woodford
70YAKA Keegan Akin 5.00 12.00
70YAKB Kris Bubic
70YAKL Kenny Lofton
70YAKR Keibert Ruiz
70YAKW Kerry Wood 12.00 30.00
70YALA Luis Arraez
70YALD Lewin Diaz
70YALG Luis Gonzalez 5.00 12.00
70YALG Luis Garcia
70YALM Lance McCullers Jr. 5.00 12.00
70YALP Luis Patino
70YALW Larry Walker
70YAMG Mitch Garver 10.00 25.00
70YAMH Monte Harrison
70YAMK Mitch Keller 5.00 12.00
70YAMM Mike Mussina
70YAMM Manny Machado
70YAMS Marcus Semien
70YAMT Mike Trout 200.00 500.00
70YAMT Mike Trout
70YAMW Mitch White
70YAMY Mike Yastrzemski
70YANG Nomar Garciaparra 20.00 50.00
70YANH Nick Heath
70YANM Nick Madrigal
70YANP Nate Pearson 12.00 30.00
70YAOA Ozzie Albies
70YAOC Orlando Cepeda
70YAOV Omar Vizquel 15.00 40.00
70YAPS Pavin Smith
70YARA Ronald Acuna Jr. 50.00 120.00
70YARA Ronald Acuna Jr.
70YARH Ryan Howard 15.00 40.00
70YARM Ryan Mountcastle 40.00 100.00
70YARM Rafael Marchan
70YASE Santiago Espinal
70YASG Steve Garvey 12.00 30.00
70YASH Sam Hilliard 3.00 8.00
70YASH Spencer Howard
70YASM Sean Murphy 6.00 15.00
70YASR Seth Romero 2.50 6.00
70YASS Sterling Sharp 2.50 6.00
70YASS Stephen Strasburg
70YATA Tim Anderson 20.00 50.00
70YATB Trevor Bauer
70YATE Tommy Edman 12.00 30.00
70YATG Tony Gonsolin 4.00 10.00
70YATH Trevor Hoffman 20.00 50.00
70YATM Tino Martinez 15.00 40.00
70YATM Triston McKenzie
70YATR Tim Raines 10.00 25.00
70YATR Trevor Rogers
70YATS Tyler Stephenson
70YATT Touki Toussaint 5.00 12.00
70YATW Taylor Widener 8.00 20.00
70YAWB Wade Boggs
70YAYK Yusei Kikuchi 12.00 30.00
70YAYM Yermin Mercedes 100.00 250.00
70YAYM Yoan Moncada
70YAYR Yohan Ramirez 6.00 15.00
70YAZB Zack Burdi
70YAZP Zach Plesac 6.00 15.00
70YABBR Ben Braymer
70YABBU Beau Burrows
70YABDA Bobby Dalbec 40.00 10.00
70YABOR Ryan Borucki
70YACMI Casey Mize 30.00 80.00
70YACPA Cristian Pache
70YADFL David Fletcher
70YADGA Deivi Garcia 20.00 50.00
70YADJO Daniel Johnson 8.00 20.00
70YADKR Dean Kremer 6.00 15.00
70YAJAR Jonathan Arauz 5.00 12.00
70YAJAZ Jazz Chisholm 25.00 60.00
70YAJBJ Jackie Bradley Jr.
70YAJGA Jose Garcia 15.00 40.00
70YAJSO Jorge Soler 10.00 25.00
70YAJST Jonathan Stiever
70YAKBH Ke'Bryan Hayes 50.00 120.00
70YAMMA Mark Mathias 8.00 20.00
70YAMMO Mickey Moniak 30.00 80.00
70YAMST Marcus Stroman
70YAMYA Miguel Yajure
70YASHU Sam Huff 15.00 40.00
70YASSO Sammy Sosa
70YATAN Tejay Antone 12.00 30.00
70YATHA Tom Hatch 3.00 8.00
70YAWCA Willi Castro
70YAYMO Yadier Molina

2021 Topps 70 Years of Topps Baseball

STATED ODDS 1:11 HOBBY
70YT1 Mookie Betts 1.00 2.50
70YT1 Willie Mays
70YT2 Aaron Judge 1.25 3.00
70YT2 Derek Jeter
70YT3 Clayton Kershaw .75 2.00
70YT3 Mookie Betts
70YT4 Derek Jeter 1.25 3.00
70YT4 Casey Mize
70YT5 Andrew McCutchen .50 1.25
70YT5 Javier Baez
70YT6 Mike Trout 2.50 6.00
70YT6 Ken Griffey Jr.
70YT7 Cal Ripken Jr. 1.50 4.00
70YT7 Barry Larkin
70YT8 Paul Goldschmidt .50 1.25
70YT8 Max Scherzer
70YT9 Yadier Molina .60 1.50
70YT9 Aaron Judge
70YT10 Buster Posey .60 1.50
70YT10 Anthony Rizzo
70YT11 Anthony Rizzo .60 1.50
70YT11 Ke'Bryan Hayes
70YT12 Ronald Acuna Jr. 2.00 5.00
70YT12 Walker Buehler
70YT13 Bryce Harper .75 2.00
70YT13 Christian Yelich
70YT14 Will Clark .40 1.00
70YT14 Corey Seager
70YT15 Johnny Bench .50 1.25
70YT15 Gary Carter
70YT16 Gerrit Cole .75 2.00
70YT16 Alex Kirilloff
70YT17 Gleyber Torres 1.00 2.50
70YT17 Luis Garcia
70YT18 Pete Alonso 1.25 3.00
70YT18 Jose Garcia
70YT19 Mark McGwire .75 2.00
70YT19 Rickey Henderson
70YT20 Rickey Henderson .50 1.25
70YT20 Kirby Puckett
70YT21 Mike Piazza .50 1.25
70YT21 Anthony Rendon
70YT22 Robin Yount .50 1.25
70YT22 Jo Adell
70YT23 Jacob deGrom 1.00 2.50
70YT23 Alec Bohm
70YT24 Tony Gwynn .50 1.25
70YT24 Brady Singer
70YT25 Christian Yelich .60 1.50
70YT25 Yordan Alvarez
70YT26 Francisco Lindor .50 1.25
70YT26 Eddie Murray
70YT27 Ken Griffey Jr. 1.00 2.50
70YT27 Shane Bieber
70YT28 Shohei Ohtani .75 2.00
70YT28 Cal Ripken Jr.
70YT29 Fernando Tatis Jr. 2.50 6.00
70YT29 Mark McGwire
70YT30 Justin Verlander .50 1.25
70YT30 Cristian Pache
70YT31 Miguel Cabrera .50 1.25
70YT31 Tarik Skubal
70YT32 Frank Robinson .40 1.00
70YT32 Ryan Mountcastle
70YT33 Javier Baez .60 1.50
70YT33 Bobby Dalbec
70YT34 Bo Bichette 1.25 3.00
70YT34 Nate Pearson
70YT35 Chipper Jones .50 1.25
70YT35 Craig Biggio
70YT36 Vladimir Guerrero .40 1.00
70YT36 David Wright
70YT37 Willie Mays 1.00 2.50
70YT37 Yu Darvish
70YT38 Vladimir Guerrero Jr. .75 2.00
70YT38 Ian Anderson
70YT39 Cody Bellinger 1.00 2.50
70YT39 Fernando Tatis Jr.
70YT40 Kris Bryant .60 1.50
70YT40 Bryce Harper
70YT41 Luis Robert 1.50 4.00
70YT41 Ronald Acuna Jr.
70YT42 Alex Bregman .50 1.25
70YT42 Nick Madrigal
70YT43 Mariano Rivera .60 1.50
70YT43 Trevor Story
70YT44 Jackie Robinson .50 1.25
70YT44 David Ortiz
70YT45 Ichiro .60 1.50
70YT45 Michael Conforto
70YT46 Albert Pujols .60 1.50
70YT46 Eloy Jimenez
70YT47 Joey Votto .50 1.25
70YT47 Tyler Stephenson
70YT48 Jose Altuve .40 1.00
70YT48 Sixto Sanchez
70YT49 Blake Snell .40 1.00
70YT49 Tim Lincecum
70YT50 Ryne Sandberg 1.00 2.50
70YT50 Jack Flaherty
70YT51 Bob Gibson .40 1.00
70YT51 Sam Huff
70YT52 Nolan Arenado .75 2.00
70YT52 Randy Arozarena
70YT53 Rafael Devers .60 1.50
70YT53 Bo Bichette
70YT54 Don Mattingly 1.00 2.50
70YT54 Dylan Carlson
70YT55 Stephen Strasburg .50 1.25
70YT55 Mike Trout
70YT56 George Brett 1.00 2.50
70YT56 Whit Merrifield
70YT57 Ozzie Smith .60 1.50
70YT57 Tyler Glasnow
70YT58 Al Kaline .50 1.25
70YT58 Xander Bogaerts
70YT59 Mike Schmidt .75 2.00
70YT59 Giancarlo Stanton
70YT60 Juan Soto 1.50 4.00
70YT60 Joey Bart
70YT61 Reggie Jackson .40 1.00
70YT61 Deivi Garcia
70YT62 Matt Chapman .50 1.25
70YT62 Juan Soto
70YT63 Roberto Clemente 1.25 3.00
70YT63 Jazz Chisholm
70YT64 Roger Clemens .60 1.50
70YT64 Stan Musial
70YT65 Ernie Banks .50 1.25
70YT65 Greg Maddux
70YT66 Frank Thomas .50 1.25
70YT66 Luis Robert
70YT67 Nolan Ryan 1.50 4.00
70YT67 Roger Maris
70YT68 Randy Johnson .50 1.25
70YT68 Hank Aaron
70YT69 Brooks Robinson .40 1.00
70YT69 Mike Piazza
70YT70 Hank Aaron 1.00 2.50
70YT70 Jackie Robinson

2021 Topps 70th Anniversary Commemorative Logo Patches

STATED ODDS 1 PER BLASTER
*BLUE: .5X TO 1.2X BASIC
*BLACK/299: .6X TO 1.5X BASIC
*PLAT.ANN./70: .8X TO 2X BASIC
70LPI Ichiro 3.00 8.00
70LPBG Bob Gibson 2.00 5.00
70LPCJ Chipper Jones 2.50 6.00
70LPCK Clayton Kershaw 4.00 10.00
70LPCR Cal Ripken Jr. 4.00 10.00
70LPDJ Derek Jeter 6.00 15.00
70LPEB Ernie Banks 2.50 6.00
70LPEM Eddie Mathews 2.50 6.00
70LPFT Frank Thomas 2.50 6.00
70LPGB George Brett 5.00 12.00
70LPHA Hank Aaron 3.00 8.00
70LPJB Johnny Bench 2.50 6.00
70LPJM Joe Morgan 2.00 5.00
70LPJR Jackie Robinson 4.00 10.00
70LPKG Ken Griffey Jr. 4.00 10.00
70LPMC Miguel Cabrera 2.50 6.00
70LPMR Mariano Rivera 3.00 8.00
70LPMT Mike Trout 12.00 30.00
70LPNR Nolan Ryan 8.00 20.00
70LPPM Pedro Martinez 2.00 5.00
70LPRJ Reggie Jackson 2.00 5.00
70LPSC Steve Carlton 2.00 5.00
70LPTS Tom Seaver 2.00 5.00
70LPVG Vladimir Guerrero 2.00 5.00
70LPWM Willie Mays 5.00 12.00

2021 Topps Cody Bellinger Highlights

STATED ODDS 1:4 BLASTERS
*BLUE: 1.2X TO 3X BASIC
*BLACK/299: 1.5X TO 4X BASIC
*PLAT.ANNV/70: 3X TO 8X BASIC
*RED/10: 6X TO 15X BASIC
TE1 Cody Bellinger .60 1.50
TE2 Cody Bellinger .60 1.50
TE3 Cody Bellinger .60 1.50
TE4 Cody Bellinger .60 1.50
TE5 Cody Bellinger .60 1.50
TE6 Cody Bellinger .60 1.50
TE7 Cody Bellinger .60 1.50
TE8 Cody Bellinger .60 1.50
TE9 Cody Bellinger .60 1.50
TE10 Cody Bellinger .60 1.50
TE11 Cody Bellinger .60 1.50
TE12 Cody Bellinger .60 1.50
TE13 Cody Bellinger .60 1.50
TE14 Cody Bellinger .60 1.50
TE15 Cody Bellinger .60 1.50
TE16 Cody Bellinger .60 1.50
TE17 Cody Bellinger .60 1.50
TE18 Cody Bellinger .60 1.50
TE19 Cody Bellinger .60 1.50
TE20 Cody Bellinger .60 1.50
TE21 Cody Bellinger .60 1.50
TE22 Cody Bellinger .60 1.50
TE23 Cody Bellinger .60 1.50
TE24 Cody Bellinger .60 1.50
TE25 Cody Bellinger .60 1.50
TE26 Cody Bellinger .60 1.50
TE27 Cody Bellinger .60 1.50
TE28 Cody Bellinger .60 1.50
TE29 Cody Bellinger .60 1.50
TE30 Cody Bellinger .60 1.50

2021 Topps Cody Bellinger Highlights Autographs

STATED ODDS 1:11,207 BLASTER
STATED PRINT RUN 5 SER.#'d SETS
EXCHANGE DEADLINE 1/31/2023

2021 Topps Double Headers

STATED ODDS 1:30 HOBBY
TDH1 Tony Gwynn .50 1.25
TDH2 Don Mattingly 1.00 2.50
TDH3 Hank Aaron 1.00 2.50
TDH4 Willie Mays 1.00 2.50
TDH5 Roberto Clemente 1.25 3.00
TDH6 Jeff Bagwell .40 1.00
TDH7 Wade Boggs .40 1.00
TDH8 Bob Gibson .40 1.00
TDH9 Reggie Jackson .40 1.00
TDH10 Nolan Ryan 1.50 4.00
TDH11 Barry Larkin .40 1.00
TDH12 Eddie Murray .40 1.00
TDH13 Jim Palmer .40 1.00
TDH14 Cal Ripken Jr 1.50 4.00
TDH15 Mike Piazza .50 1.25
TDH16 Pedro Martinez .40 1.00
TDH17 Mariano Rivera .60 1.50
TDH18 Jackie Robinson .50 1.25
TDH19 Ernie Banks .50 1.25
TDH20 Thurman Munson .50 1.25
TDH21 Ted Williams 1.00 2.50
TDH22 Johnny Bench .50 1.25
TDH23 Ichiro .60 1.50
TDH24 Derek Jeter 1.25 3.00
TDH25 Ken Griffey Jr. 1.00 2.50

2021 Topps Home Run Challenge Code Cards

STATED ODDS 1:24 HOBBY
HRC1 Mike Trout
HRC1 Mike Trout 3.00 8.00
HRC2 Ronald Acuna Jr. 2.50 6.00
HRC2 Ronald Acuna Jr.
HRC3 Freddie Freeman
HRC3 Freddie Freeman .75 2.00
HRC4 J.D. Martinez .60 1.50
HRC4 J.D. Martinez
HRC5 Rafael Devers
HRC5 Rafael Devers .75 2.00
HRC6 Javier Baez .75 2.00
HRC6 Javier Baez
HRC7 Kyle Schwarber
HRC7 Kyle Schwarber .60 1.50
HRC8 Eloy Jimenez 1.25 3.00
HRC8 Eloy Jimenez
HRC9 Francisco Lindor
HRC9 Francisco Lindor .60 1.50
HRC10 Nolan Arenado 1.00 2.50
HRC10 Nolan Arenado
HRC11 Yordan Alvarez
HRC11 Yordan Alvarez 1.50 4.00
HRC12 Alex Bregman .60 1.50
HRC12 Alex Bregman
HRC13 Jorge Soler
HRC13 Jorge Soler .60 1.50
HRC14 Mookie Betts 1.25 3.00
HRC14 Mookie Betts
HRC15 Cody Bellinger
HRC15 Cody Bellinger 1.25 3.00
HRC16 Christian Yelich .75 2.00
HRC16 Christian Yelich
HRC17 Josh Donaldson
HRC17 Josh Donaldson .50 1.25
HRC18 Pete Alonso 1.50 4.00
HRC18 Pete Alonso
HRC19 Aaron Judge
HRC19 Aaron Judge 1.50 4.00
HRC20 Gleyber Torres 1.25 3.00
HRC20 Gleyber Torres
HRC21 Bryce Harper
HRC21 Bryce Harper 1.00 2.50
HRC22 Giancarlo Stanton .60 1.50
HRC22 Giancarlo Stanton
HRC23 Fernando Tatis Jr.
HRC23 Fernando Tatis Jr. 3.00 8.00
HRC24 Paul Goldschmidt .60 1.50
HRC24 Paul Goldschmidt
HRC25 Joey Gallo
HRC25 Joey Gallo .60 1.50
HRC26 Vladimir Guerrero Jr. 1.00 2.50
HRC26 Vladimir Guerrero Jr.
HRC27 Juan Soto
HRC27 Juan Soto 2.00 5.00
HRC28 Eugenio Suarez .50 1.25
HRC28 Eugenio Suarez
HRC29 Kris Bryant
HRC29 Kris Bryant .75 2.00
HRC30 Matt Chapman .75 2.00
HRC30 Matt Chapman

2021 Topps Iconic Card Patches

STATED ODDS 1:1385 HOBBY
ICPAJ Aaron Judge 10.00 25.00
ICPAP Albert Pujols 12.00 30.00

ICPBG Bob Gibson 8.00 20.00
ICPBH Bryce Harper 8.00 20.00
ICPBJ Bo Jackson 15.00 40.00
ICPBL Barry Larkin 8.00 20.00
ICPBP Buster Posey 12.00 30.00
ICPBR Brooks Robinson 8.00 20.00
ICPCB Cody Bellinger 8.00 20.00
ICPCJ Chipper Jones 10.00 25.00
ICPCK Clayton Kershaw 12.00 30.00
ICPCR Cal Ripken Jr. 12.00 30.00
ICPCY Christian Yelich 6.00 15.00
ICPDG Dwight Gooden 8.00 20.00
ICPDJ Derek Jeter 15.00 40.00
ICPDM Don Mattingly 20.00 50.00
ICPDS Darryl Strawberry 4.00 15.00
ICPEB Ernie Banks 15.00 40.00
ICPEM Eddie Murray 10.00 25.00
ICPFT Frank Thomas 12.00 30.00
ICPFTJ Fernando Tatis Jr. 25.00 60.00
ICPGB George Brett 10.00 25.00
ICPHA Hank Aaron 20.00 50.00
ICPI Ichiro 10.00 25.00
ICPJB Johnny Bench 12.00 30.00
ICPJC Jose Canseco 10.00 25.00
ICPJP Jim Palmer 8.00 20.00
ICPJR Jackie Robinson 12.00 30.00
ICPJV Justin Verlander 4.00 10.00
ICPKB Kris Bryant 6.00 15.00
ICPKG Ken Griffey Jr. 15.00 40.00
ICPMM Mark McGwire 10.00 25.00
ICPMT Mike Trout 30.00 80.00
ICPNR Nolan Ryan 15.00 40.00
ICPOS Ozzie Smith 10.00 25.00
ICPPA Pete Alonso 10.00 25.00
ICPRA Ronald Acuna Jr 10.00 25.00
ICPRC Roberto Clemente 20.00 50.00
ICPRH Rickey Henderson 20.00 50.00
ICPRJ Reggie Jackson 8.00 20.00
ICPSO Shohei Ohtani 10.00 25.00
ICPSS Stephen Strasburg 8.00 20.00
ICPTG Tony Gwynn 12.00 10.00
ICPTM Thurman Munson 15.00 40.00
ICPTS Tom Seaver 12.00 30.00
ICPTW Ted Williams 15.00 40.00
ICPWB Wade Boggs 8.00 20.00
ICPWM Willie Mays 8.00 20.00
ICPYA Yordan Alvarez 8.00 20.00
ICPYMO Yadier Molina 12.00 30.00

2021 Topps Major League Material Autographs

STATED ODDS 1:9123 HOBBY
PRINT RUN B/TW 10-50 COPIES PER
NO PRICING QTY 15 OR LESS
EXCHANGE DEADLINE 1/31/2023
MLMAAB Alec Bohm
MLMAAG Andres Gimenez
MLMAAJ Aaron Judge
MLMAAM Andrew McCutchen
MLMAAV Alex Verdugo
MLMABB Byron Buxton
MLMABD Bobby Dalbec
MLMABH Bryce Harper
MLMABL Brandon Lowe/50 12.00 30.00
MLMABS Brady Singer
MLMACB Cody Bellinger
MLMACC Carlos Correa
MLMACM Casey Mize
MLMACP Cristian Pache
MLMACS Corey Seager/30 60.00 150.00
MLMADC Dylan Carlson
MLMADG Deivi Garcia
MLMAEW Evan White/50 60.00 150.00
MLMAFF Freddie Freeman
MLMAFT Fernando Tatis Jr.
MLMAFT Fernando Tatis Jr.
MLMAGT Gleyber Torres/25
MLMAIA Ian Anderson
MLMAJA Jo Adell
MLMAJB Joey Bart
MLMAJB Josh Bell/50 30.00 80.00
MLMAJC Jake Cronenworth
MLMAJF Jack Flaherty/50 25.00 60.00
MLMAJL Jesus Luzardo
MLMAJS Juan Soto
MLMAJS Juan Soto/30 125.00 300.00
MLMAKH Keston Hiura/50 12.00 30.00
MLMAKH Ke'Bryan Hayes
MLMAKL Kyle Lewis
MLMAKL Kyle Lewis/50 40.00 100.00
MLMAKR Keibert Ruiz
MLMAKS Kyle Schwarber/30 12.00 30.00
MLMALG Luis Garcia
MLMALR Luis Robert
MLMAMC Miguel Cabrera
MLMAMK Max Kepler/50 15.00 40.00
MLMAMT Mike Trout
MLMAMT Mike Trout
MLMANA Nolan Arenado
MLMANC Nick Castellanos
MLMANH Nico Hoerner/50 15.00 40.00
MLMANM Nick Madrigal
MLMANP Nate Pearson
MLMAPA Pete Alonso
MLMAPA Pete Alonso/25 50.00 120.00
MLMAPD Paul DeJong/50 20.00 50.00
MLMARA Ronald Acuna Jr.
MLMARA Ronald Acuna Jr.
MLMARD Rafael Devers
MLMARH Rhys Hoskins/30 30.00 80.00
MLMARM Ryan Mountcastle
MLMASG Sonny Gray/50 15.00 40.00
MLMASH Sam Huff
MLMASM Starling Marte/50 8.00 20.00
MLMASS Sixto Sanchez
MLMATB Trevor Bauer
MLMATH Tanner Houck
MLMATS Trevor Story
MLMAVG Vladimir Guerrero Jr.
MLMAVG Vladimir Guerrero Jr./30 30.00 80.00
MLMAWB Walker Buehler/30 40.00 100.00
MLMAWC Willson Contreras/30 12.00 30.00
MLMAWM Whit Merrifield
MLMAXB Xander Bogaerts/30 25.00 60.00
MLMAYM Yadier Molina/25 75.00 200.00
MLMAYM Yadier Molina
MLMAABR Alex Bregman
MLMAJCH Jazz Chisholm
MLMAJSO Jorge Soler/50 10.00 25.00
MLMATSK Tarik Skubal
MLMATST Tyler Stephenson
MLMAYMO Yoan Moncada/30 25.00 60.00

2021 Topps Major League Material Autographs Red

*RED/25: .5X TO 1.2X p/r 50
*RED/25: .4X TO 1X p/r 30
STATED ODDS 1:10,404 HOBBY
PRINT RUN B/TW 5-25 COPIES PER
NO PRICING QTY 15 OR LESS
EXCHANGE DEADLINE 1/31/2023
MLMAKS Kyle Schwarber/25 20.00 50.00

2021 Topps Major League Material Relics

STATED ODDS 1:97 HOBBY
*BLACK/199: .5X TO 1.2X BASE
*GOLD/50: .6X TO 1.5X BASE
*RED/25: .75X TO 2X BASE
MLMAB Alex Bregman 3.00 8.00
MLMAB Alec Bohm
MLMAJ Aaron Judge 8.00 20.00
MLMAJ Aaron Judge
MLMAN Aaron Nola 2.50 6.00
MLMAR Amed Rosario 2.50 6.00
MLMAV Alex Verdugo
MLMBB Bo Bichette 5.00 12.00
MLMBD Bobby Dalbec
MLMBL Brandon Lowe 2.50 6.00
MLMBS Blake Snell 2.50 6.00
MLMBS Brady Singer
MLMCB Cavan Biggio
MLMCC Carlos Correa 3.00 8.00
MLMCM Casey Mize 5.00 12.00
MLMCM Casey Mize
MLMCP Cristian Pache
MLMCS Corey Seager 3.00 8.00
MLMCY Christian Yelich
MLMDC Dylan Carlson
MLMDG Deivi Garcia
MLMDM Dustin May
MLMDS Dansby Swanson 3.00 8.00
MLMEW Evan White 5.00 12.00
MLMFL Francisco Lindor
MLMFT Fernando Tatis Jr. 10.00 25.00
MLMFT Fernando Tatis Jr.
MLMGC Gerrit Cole
MLMGT Gleyber Torres 4.00 10.00
MLMIA Ian Anderson
MLMJA Jo Adell
MLMJB Javier Baez 4.00 10.00
MLMJB Javier Baez
MLMJC Jake Cronenworth
MLMJF Jack Flaherty 3.00 8.00
MLMJL Jesus Luzardo 3.00 8.00
MLMJL Jesus Luzardo
MLMJS Juan Soto 4.00 10.00
MLMJS Juan Soto
MLMKB Kris Bryant 4.00 10.00
MLMKH Keston Hiura 4.00 10.00
MLMKH Ke'Bryan Hayes
MLMKL Kyle Lewis 5.00 12.00
MLMKT Kyle Tucker
MLMLG Luis Garcia
MLMLR Luis Robert 8.00 20.00
MLMLR Luis Robert
MLMLV Luke Voit
MLMMC Miguel Cabrera 3.00 8.00
MLMMC Miguel Cabrera
MLMMO Matt Olson 3.00 8.00
MLMMS Miguel Sano 2.50 6.00
MLMMT Mike Trout 12.00 30.00
MLMMT Mike Trout
MLMNA Nolan Arenado 4.00 10.00
MLMNM Nick Madrigal
MLMNP Nate Pearson
MLMOA Ozzie Albies 3.00 8.00
MLMPA Pete Alonso 5.00 12.00
MLMPA Pete Alonso
MLMPD Paul DeJong 3.00 8.00
MLMRA Ronald Acuna Jr. 5.00 12.00
MLMRA Ronald Acuna Jr.
MLMRD Rafael Devers 4.00 10.00
MLMRH Rhys Hoskins 4.00 10.00
MLMRM Ryan Mountcastle
MLMSA Shogo Akiyama 3.00 8.00
MLMSH Spencer Howard
MLMSS Sixto Sanchez
MLMTS Trevor Story 3.00 8.00
MLMTS Tarik Skubal
MLMTT Trea Turner
MLMVG Vladimir Guerrero Jr. 5.00 12.00
MLMVG Vladimir Guerrero Jr.
MLMWB Walker Buehler 4.00 10.00
MLMWC Willson Contreras 3.00 8.00
MLMWS Will Smith
MLMXB Xander Bogaerts 3.00 8.00
MLMXB Xander Bogaerts
MLMYM Yoan Moncada 3.00 8.00
MLMABR Alex Bregman
MLMJAL Jose Altuve 2.50 6.00
MLMJBA Joey Bart
MLMJBE Josh Bell 2.50 6.00
MLMJCH Jazz Chisholm
MLMMMU Max Muncy
MLMSHU Sam Huff

2021 Topps Platinum Players Die Cuts

STATED ODDS 1:30 HOBBY
*BLUE: .8X TO 2X BASIC
*BLACK/299: 1.2X TO 3X BASIC
*PLAT.ANN./70: 2.5X TO 6X BASIC
PDC1 Mike Trout 2.50 6.00
PDC2 Hank Aaron 1.00 2.50
PDC3 Cal Ripken Jr. 1.50 4.00
PDC4 Pedro Martinez .40 1.00
PDC5 Jackie Robinson .50 1.25
PDC6 Johnny Bench .50 1.25
PDC7 Nolan Ryan 1.50 4.00
PDC8 George Brett 1.00 2.50
PDC9 Clayton Kershaw .75 2.00
PDC10 Frank Thomas .50 1.25
PDC11 Reggie Jackson .40 1.00
PDC12 Derek Jeter 1.25 3.00
PDC13 Willie Mays 1.00 2.50
PDC14 Ken Griffey Jr. 1.00 2.50
PDC15 Ichiro .60 1.50
PDC16 Mariano Rivera .60 1.50
PDC17 Justin Verlander .50 1.25
PDC18 Mike Piazza .50 1.25
PDC19 Brooks Robinson .40 1.00
PDC20 Wade Boggs .40 1.00
PDC21 Ozzie Smith .60 1.50
PDC22 Robin Yount .50 1.25
PDC23 Willie McCovey .40 1.00
PDC24 Ernie Banks .50 1.25
PDC25 Albert Pujols .60 1.50

2021 Topps Postseason Performance Autograph Relics

STATED ODDS 1:18,156 HOBBY
PRINT RUN B/TW 15-30 COPIES PER
NO PRICING QTY 15 OR LESS
EXCHANGE DEADLINE 1/31/2023
PPARGS George Springer/30 12.00 30.00
PPARGT Gleyber Torres/25 40.00 100.00
PPARJA Jesus Aguilar/30
PPARKH Kyle Hendricks/30 15.00 40.00
PPARLV Luke Voit/30 20.00 50.00
PPARPG Paul Goldschmidt/25 40.00 100.00
PPARRA Ronald Acuna Jr./30 100.00 250.00
PPARWB Walker Buehler/30 40.00 100.00
PPARYM Yadier Molina/25 60.00 150.00
PPARBLO Brandon Lowe/30
PPARCSE Corey Seager/30 75.00 200.00
PPARDJL DJ LeMahieu/30 40.00 100.00
PPAREHO Eric Hosmer/30 25.00 60.00
PPARFFR Freddie Freeman/30
PPARFTJ Fernando Tatis Jr./25 200.00 500.00
PPARJAL Jose Altuve/30 25.00 60.00
PPARLCA Luis Castillo/30 20.00 50.00
PPARLGI Lucas Giolito/30 20.00 50.00
PPARMMA Manny Machado/25 50.00 120.00
PPARMMU Max Muncy/30 20.00 50.00
PPARMSE Marcus Semien/30 15.00 40.00
PPARSMU Sean Murphy/30 15.00 40.00
PPARTGL Tyler Glasnow/30 15.00 40.00

2021 Topps Postseason Performance Autograph Relics Red

*RED/25: .4X TO 1X p/r 30
STATED ODDS 1:36,312 HOBBY
PRINT RUN B/TW 10-25 COPIES PER
NO PRICING QTY 15 OR LESS
EXCHANGE DEADLINE 1/31/2023
PPARJA Jesus Aguilar/25 12.00 30.00
PPARWB Walker Buehler/25 75.00 200.00
PPARFFR Freddie Freeman/25 50.00 120.00
PPARLGI Lucas Giolito/25 40.00 100.00

2021 Topps Postseason Performance Autographs

STATED ODDS 1:18,156 HOBBY
PRINT RUN B/TW 15-30 COPIES PER
EXCHANGE DEADLINE 1/31/2023
PPAGC Gerrit Cole/25 75.00 200.00
PPAGS George Springer/30 12.00 30.00
PPAGT Gleyber Torres/25 40.00 100.00
PPAJA Jesus Aguilar/30
PPAKH Kyle Hendricks/30 15.00 40.00
PPALV Luke Voit/30 20.00 50.00
PPAPG Paul Goldschmidt/25 40.00 100.00
PPARA Ronald Acuna Jr./25 100.00 250.00
PPAWB Walker Buehler/30 40.00 100.00
PPAYM Yadier Molina/25 60.00 150.00
PPABLO Brandon Lowe/30 12.00 30.00
PPACSE Corey Seager/30 75.00 200.00
PPADJL DJ LeMahieu/30 40.00 100.00
PPAEHO Eric Hosmer/30 25.00 60.00
PPAFFR Freddie Freeman/30 40.00 100.00
PPAFTJ Fernando Tatis Jr./25 200.00 500.00
PPAJAL Jose Altuve/30 25.00 60.00
PPALCA Luis Castillo/30 20.00 50.00
PPALGI Lucas Giolito/30 20.00 50.00
PPAMMA Manny Machado/25 50.00 120.00
PPAMMU Max Muncy/30 20.00 50.00
PPAMSE Marcus Semien/30 15.00 40.00
PPASMU Sean Murphy/30 15.00 40.00
PPATGL Tyler Glasnow/30 15.00 40.00

2021 Topps Postseason Performance Autographs Red

*RED/25: .4X TO 1X p/r 30
STATED ODDS 1:36,312 HOBBY
PRINT RUN B/TW 10-25 COPIES PER
NO PRICING QTY 15 OR LESS
EXCHANGE DEADLINE 1/31/2023
PPAJA Jesus Aguilar/25 12.00 30.00
PPAWB Walker Buehler/25 75.00 200.00
PPABLO Brandon Lowe/25 20.00 50.00
PPAFFR Freddie Freeman/25 50.00 120.00

2021 Topps Postseason Performance Relics

STATED ODDS 1:4689 HOBBY
STATED PRINT RUN 99 SER.#'d SETS
PPRAB Alex Bregman 4.00 10.00
PPRAJ Aaron Judge 30.00 80.00
PPRBL Brandon Lowe 3.00 8.00
PPRBS Blake Snell 3.00 8.00
PPRCB Cody Bellinger 10.00 25.00
PPRCK Clayton Kershaw 12.00 30.00
PPRCS Corey Seager 4.00 10.00
PPRDL DJ LeMahieu 4.00 10.00
PPREH Eric Hosmer 3.00 8.00
PPRFF Freddie Freeman 12.00 30.00
PPRFT Fernando Tatis Jr. 30.00 80.00
PPRGS George Springer 3.00 8.00
PPRGT Gleyber Torres 12.00 30.00
PPRIA Ian Anderson 15.00 40.00
PPRJA Jose Altuve 3.00 8.00
PPRLG Lucas Giolito 3.00 8.00
PPRLV Luke Voit 6.00 15.00
PPRMF Max Fried 4.00 10.00
PPRMM Manny Machado 4.00 10.00
PPRMO Matt Olson 4.00 10.00
PPRMS Marcus Semien 4.00 10.00
PPROA Ozzie Albies 4.00 10.00
PPRPG Paul Goldschmidt 4.00 10.00
PPRRA Ronald Acuna Jr. 20.00 50.00
PPRSM Sean Murphy 2.50 6.00
PPRTB Trevor Bauer 15.00 40.00
PPRTG Tyler Glasnow 4.00 10.00
PPRWB Walker Buehler 10.00 25.00
PPRYM Yadier Molina 5.00 12.00
PPRMMU Max Muncy 3.00 8.00

2021 Topps Postseason Performance Relics Red

*RED/25: .8X TO 2X BASIC
STATED ODDS 1:18,520 HOBBY
STATED PRINT RUN 25 SER.#'d SETS
PPRCK Clayton Kershaw 40.00 100.00

2021 Topps Spring Training Cap Logos

STATED ODDS 1:505 HOBBY
STCLAB Alex Bregman 3.00 8.00
STCLAJ Aaron Judge 8.00 20.00
STCLBB Bo Bichette 8.00 20.00
STCLBH Bryce Harper 10.00 25.00
STCLBP Buster Posey 6.00 15.00
STCLBS Blake Snell 2.50 6.00
STCLCB Cody Bellinger 6.00 15.00
STCLCK Clayton Kershaw 12.00 30.00
STCLCY Christian Yelich 4.00 10.00
STCLEJ Eloy Jimenez 6.00 15.00
STCLFF Freddie Freeman 4.00 10.00
STCLFL Francisco Lindor 3.00 8.00
STCLFT Fernando Tatis Jr. 15.00 40.00
STCLGC Gerrit Cole 5.00 12.00
STCLGT Gleyber Torres 6.00 15.00
STCLJB Javier Baez 4.00 10.00
STCLJD Josh Donaldson 2.50 6.00
STCLJG Joey Gallo 3.00 8.00
STCLJV Joey Votto 3.00 8.00
STCLKB Kris Bryant 4.00 10.00
STCLKL Kyle Lewis 8.00 20.00
STCLKM Ketel Marte 2.50 6.00
STCLLR Luis Robert 10.00 25.00
STCLMB Mookie Betts 12.00 30.00
STCLMC Miguel Cabrera 3.00 8.00
STCLMM Manny Machado 3.00 8.00
STCLMS Max Scherzer 3.00 8.00
STCLMT Mike Trout 20.00 50.00
STCLNA Nolan Arenado 5.00 12.00
STCLPA Pete Alonso 8.00 20.00
STCLPG Paul Goldschmidt 3.00 8.00
STCLRA Ronald Acuna Jr. 20.00 50.00
STCLRD Rafael Devers 4.00 10.00
STCLSO Shohei Ohtani 5.00 12.00
STCLVG Vladimir Guerrero Jr. 5.00 12.00
STCLYM Yadier Molina 4.00 10.00
STCLABO Alec Bohm 15.00 40.00
STCLBDA Bobby Dalbec 15.00 40.00
STCLBSI Brady Singer 10.00 25.00
STCLCMI Casey Mize 8.00 20.00
STCLJAD Jo Adell 15.00 40.00
STCLJBA Joey Bart 6.00 15.00
STCLJDE Jacob deGrom 6.00 15.00
STCLJSO Juan Soto 10.00 25.00
STCLJVE Justin Verlander 3.00 8.00
STCLKBH Ke'Bryan Hayes 15.00 40.00
STCLMCH Matt Chapman 3.00 8.00
STCLRMO Ryan Mountcastle 10.00 25.00
STCLSBI Shane Bieber 3.00 8.00
STCLSSA Sixto Sanchez 10.00 25.00

2021 Topps Spring Training Cap Logos Black

*BLACK/299: .5X TO 1.2X BASIC
STATED ODDS 1:1621 HOBBY
STATED PRINT RUN 299 SER.#'d SETS
STCLRMO Ryan Mountcastle 15.00 40.00

2021 Topps Spring Training Cap Logos Platinum Anniversary

*PLAT.ANN./70: .6X TO 1.5X BASIC
STATED ODDS 1:6911 HOBBY
STATED PRINT RUN 70 SER.#'d SETS
STCLABO Alec Bohm 30.00 80.00
STCLRMO Ryan Mountcastle 25.00 60.00

2021 Topps Stars in Service

STATED ODDS 1:30 HOBBY
*BLUE: .8X TO 2X BASIC
*BLACK/299: 1.2X TO 3X BASIC
*PLAT.ANN./70: 2.5X TO 6X BASIC
SIS1 Christian Yelich .60 1.50
SIS2 Clayton Kershaw .75 2.00
SIS3 Aaron Judge 1.25 3.00
SIS4 Adam Wainwright .40 1.00
SIS5 Cal Ripken Jr. 1.50 4.00
SIS6 Anthony Rizzo .60 1.50
SIS7 Mookie Betts 1.00 2.50
SIS8 Carlos Carrasco .30 .75
SIS9 Pete Alonso 1.25 3.00
SIS10 Albert Pujols .60 1.50
SIS11 Derek Jeter 1.25 3.00
SIS12 Yadier Molina .60 1.50
SIS13 Don Mattingly 1.00 2.50
SIS14 Roberto Clemente 1.25 3.00
SIS15 Pedro Martinez .40 1.00
SIS16 CC Sabathia .40 1.00
SIS17 Sean Doolittle .30 .75
SIS18 Jon Lester .40 1.00
SIS19 Ken Griffey Jr. 1.00 2.50
SIS20 David Ortiz .50 1.25
SIS21 Andrew McCutchen .50 1.25
SIS22 Francisco Lindor .50 1.25
SIS23 Mike Piazza .50 1.25
SIS24 Justin Verlander .50 1.25
SIS25 Edgar Martinez .40 1.00

2021 Topps The History of Topps

STATED ODDS 1:75 HOBBY
*BLUE: .8X TO 2X BASIC
*BLACK/299: 1.2X TO 3X BASIC
*PLAT.ANN./70: 2.5X TO 6X BASIC
HOT1 Topps is Founded by the Shorin Family 1.25 3.00
HOT2 First Baseball Playing Cards Are Sold 1.25 3.00
HOT3 Sy Berger Creates the First Complete Set 1.25 3.00
HOT4 First Topps All-Rookie Team 1.25 3.00
HOT5 GPK Introduced 4.00 10.00
HOT6 Topps Re-Introduces Bowman 1.25 3.00
HOT7 Topps receives MLB exclusive 1.25 3.00
HOT8 Topps Digital Apps Launched 1.25 3.00
HOT9 Topps Now Introduced 1.25 3.00
HOT10 Project 2020 Takes Off 2.00 5.00

2021 Topps Through the Years

STATED ODDS 1:25 HOBBY
*BLUE: .8X TO 2X BASIC
*BLACK/299: 1.2X TO 3X BASIC
*PLAT.ANN./70: 2.5X TO 6X BASIC
TTY1 Juan Soto 1.50 4.00
TTY2 Cal Ripken Jr. 1.50 4.00
TTY3 Nolan Ryan 1.50 4.00
TTY4 Derek Jeter 1.25 3.00
TTY5 Cody Bellinger 1.00 2.50
TTY6 Pete Alonso 1.25 3.00
TTY7 Ken Griffey Jr. 1.00 2.50
TTY8 Bryce Harper .75 2.00
TTY9 Mike Trout 2.50 6.00
TTY10 Mark McGwire .75 2.00
TTY11 Clayton Kershaw .75 2.00
TTY12 Fernando Tatis Jr. 2.50 6.00
TTY13 David Ortiz .50 1.25
TTY14 Cal Ripken Jr. 1.50 4.00
TTY15 Hank Aaron 1.00 2.50
TTY16 Ken Griffey Jr. 1.00 2.50
TTY17 Shohei Ohtani .75 2.00
TTY18 Hank Aaron 1.00 2.50
TTY19 Kris Bryant .60 1.50
TTY20 Aaron Judge 1.25 3.00
TTY21 Derek Jeter 1.25 3.00
TTY22 Shohei Ohtani .75 2.00
TTY23 Cal Ripken Jr. 1.50 4.00
TTY24 Ronald Acuna Jr. 2.00 5.00
TTY25 Aaron Judge 1.25 3.00
TTY26 Chipper Jones .50 1.25
TTY27 Stephen Strasburg .50 1.25
TTY28 Mike Trout 2.50 6.00
TTY29 Justin Verlander .50 1.25
TTY30 Bo Bichette 1.25 3.00

2021 Topps World Series Champion Autograph Relics

STATED ODDS 1:18,156 HOBBY
STATED PRINT RUN 50 SER.#'d SETS
EXCHANGE DEADLINE 1/31/2023
WCARBG Brusdar Graterol 25.00 60.00
WCARCS Corey Seager 75.00 200.00
WCARCT Chris Taylor 30.00 80.00
WCARMM Max Muncy 30.00 80.00
WCARWB Walker Buehler 75.00 200.00
WCARWS Will Smith 40.00 100.00

2021 Topps World Series Champion Autograph Relics Red

*RED/25: .5X TO 1.2X BASIC
STATED ODDS 1:36,312 HOBBY
STATED PRINT RUN 25 SER.#'d SETS
EXCHANGE DEADLINE 1/31/2023
WCARCB Cody Bellinger 125.00 300.00
WCARDM Dustin May 60.00 150.00
WCARJU Julio Urias 60.00 150.00
WCARTG Tony Gonsolin 40.00 100.00

2021 Topps World Series Champion Autographs

STATED ODDS 1:18,156 HOBBY
STATED PRINT RUN 50 SER.#'d SETS
EXCHANGE DEADLINE 1/31/2023
WCAAB Austin Barnes 40.00 100.00
WCABG Brusdar Graterol 25.00 60.00
WCABT Blake Treinen 40.00 100.00
WCACS Corey Seager 75.00 200.00
WCACT Chris Taylor 30.00 80.00
WCAMM Max Muncy 25.00 60.00
WCAWB Walker Buehler 60.00 150.00

2021 Topps World Series Champion Autographs Red

*RED/25: .5X TO 1.2X BASIC
STATED ODDS 1:24,368 HOBBY
STATED PRINT RUN 25 SER.#'d SETS
EXCHANGE DEADLINE 1/31/2023
WCACB Cody Bellinger 125.00 300.00
WCADM Dustin May 60.00 150.00
WCAJU Julio Urias 60.00 150.00
WCATG Tony Gonsolin 40.00 100.00

2021 Topps World Series Champion Relics

STATED ODDS 1:4689 HOBBY
STATED PRINT RUN 99 SER.#'d SETS
WCRAP A.J. Pollock 12.00 30.00
WCRBG Brusdar Graterol 10.00 25.00
WCRCB Cody Bellinger 30.00 80.00
WCRCK Clayton Kershaw 30.00 80.00
WCRCS Corey Seager 30.00 80.00
WCRCT Chris Taylor 15.00 40.00
WCRDM Dustin May 15.00 40.00
WCRJP Joc Pederson 12.00 30.00
WCRJU Julio Urias 20.00 50.00
WCRKJ Kenley Jansen 15.00 40.00
WCRMB Mookie Betts 40.00 100.00
WCRMM Max Muncy 12.00 30.00
WCRTG Tony Gonsolin 10.00 25.00
WCRWB Walker Buehler 25.00 60.00
WCRWS Will Smith 25.00 60.00

2021 Topps World Series Champion Relics Red

*RED/25: .8X TO 2X BASIC
STATED ODDS 1:18,520 HOBBY
STATED PRINT RUN 25 SER.#'d SETS
WCRDM Dustin May 50.00 120.00

1952 Topps Advertising Panels

These three card strips feature a regular 1952 Topps card and ad information on the back. These cards are not numbered in the traditional sense. Any additions to this list or any Advertising Panel list will be appreciated

COMPLETE SET 100.00 200.00
1 Bob Mahoney 75.00 150.00
Robin Roberts/Sid Hudson
2 Bob Wellman 50.00 100.00
Lou Kretlow/Ray Scarborough
3 Wally Westlake 50.00 100.00
Dizzy Trout/Irv Noren
4 Eddie Joost 50.00 100.00
Willie Jones/Gordon Goldsberry

1953 Topps Advertising Panels

These three card strips feature a regular 53 Topps card on the front and advertising information on the back.

COMPLETE SET 300.00 600.00
1 Johnny Mize 60.00 120.00
Clem Koshorek/Toby Atwell
2 Jim Hearn 50.00 100.00
Johnny Groth/Sherm Lollar
3 Mickey Mantle 250.00 500.00
Johnny Wyrostek/Sal Yvars

1954 Topps Advertising Panels

1 Granny Hamner 50.00 100.00
Richie Ashburn/Johnny Schmitz

1955 Topps Advertising Panels

These panels feature regular 1955 Topps cards on the front and advertising information on the back. These items have been seen with advertising for the 1955 Topps Double Header set affixed as well.

COMPLETE SET 150.00 300.00
1 Dave Jolly 25.00 50.00
Jim Pendleton/Karl Spooner
2 Danny Schell 25.00 50.00
Jake Thies/Howie Pollet
3 Jackie Robinson 125.00 250.00
Bill Taylor/Curt Roberts

1956 Topps Advertising Panels

These panels feature regular 1956 Topps cards on the front and advertising information on the back.

COMPLETE SET 25.00 50.00
1 Bob Grim 25.00 50.00
Dusty Rhodes/Each Card is printed twice
2 Johnny O'Brien 25.00 50.00
Harvey Haddix/Frank House

1957 Topps Advertising Panels

Issued in three card strips to promote the upcoming 1957 Topps set, these three card panels are somewhat different in that the backs of these cards were composites of other cards as well as an advertisment for Topps/Bazooka bubble gum.

COMPLETE SET 200.00 400.00
1 Dick Williams 30.00 60.00
Brooks Lawrence/Lou Skizas
2 Jim Piersall 75.00 150.00
Pee Wee Reese/Harvey Kuenn
3 Hector Lopez 40.00 80.00
Johnny Logan/Billy Martin
4 Tom Sturdivant 50.00 100.00
Elston Howard/Clem Labine
5 Brooks Lawrence 30.00 60.00
Lou Skizas/Bob Boyd

1959 Topps Advertising Panels

The fronts of these cards feature standard 1959 Topps cards while the backs feature cards of either Nellie Fox or Ted Kluszewski.

COMPLETE SET 400.00 800.00
1 Don McMahon 25.00 50.00
Red Wilson/Bob Boyd
2 Joe Pignatano 25.00 50.00
Sam Jones/Jack Urban
3 Billy Hunter 25.00 50.00
Chuck Stobbs/Carl Sawatski
4 Vito Valentinelli 25.00 50.00
Ken Lehman/Ed Bouchee
5 Mel Roach 50.00 100.00
Brooks Lawrence/Warren Spahn
6 Harvey Kuenn 25.00 50.00
Alex Grammas/Bob Cerv
7 Bob Cerv 250.00 500.00
Jim Bolger/Mickey Mantle

1960 Topps Advertising Panels

These panels were issued to promote the upcoming Topps set. The fronts feature standard 1960 Topps cards while the backs feature advertising information.

COMPLETE SET 200.00 400.00
1 Wayne Terwilliger 20.00 50.00
Kent Hadley/Faye Throneberry
2 Hank Foiles 20.00 50.00
Hobie Landrith/Hal Smith
3 Cal McLish 150.00 300.00
Hal Smith/Ernie Banks/Jim Grant/Al Kaline/Jerry Casale/Milt Pappas/Wally Moon

1961 Topps Advertising Panels

Used to promote the upcoming Topps sets; these fronts show standard 1961 Topps cards on the front with advertising information on the back.

COMPLETE SET 100.00 200.00
1 Dan Dobbek 20.00 50.00
Russ Nixon/1960 NL Pitching Leaders
2 Jack Kralick 20.00 50.00
Dick Stigman/Joe Christopher
3 Ed Roebuck 20.00 50.00
Bob Schmidt/Zoilo Versalles
4 Lindy Shows Larry 20.00 50.00
Johnny Blanchard/Johnny Kucks

1962 Topps Advertising Panels

These panels feature standard 1962 Topps cards on the front as well as a Roger Maris card back.

COMPLETE SET 75.00 150.00
1 AL Home Run Leaders 50.00 100.00
Barney Schultz/Carl Sawatski
2 NL Strikeout Leaders 50.00 100.00
Carroll Hardy/Carl Sawatski
3 Darrell Johnson 50.00 100.00
AL Strikeout Leaders/Jim Kaat
4 Norm Larker 50.00 100.00
Al Schroll/Jim King

1963 Topps Advertising Panels

These Panels features regular 1963 Topps cards on the front and a Stan Musial ad/endorsement on the back.

COMPLETE SET 75.00 150.00
1 Elston Howard 40.00 80.00
Bob Veale/Cal Koonce
2 Hoyt Wilhelm 50.00 100.00
Don Lock/Bob Duliba

1964 Topps Advertising Panels

These panels, which were used to promote the 1964 Topps set; feature standard 1964 Topps cards on the front and a Mickey Mantle card back.

COMPLETE SET 150.00 300.00
1 Walt Alston 40.00 80.00
Bill Henry/Vada Pinson
2 Jimmie Hall 20.00 50.00
Ernie Broglio/A.L. ERA Leaders
3 Mickey Mantle 250.00 500.00
Jim Davenport/Boog Powell
4 Denis Menke 20.00 50.00
Dean Chance/Tim Harkness
5 Hoyt Wilhelm 40.00 80.00
Curt Flood/Bill Bruton
6 Carl Willey 20.00 50.00
White Sox Rookies/Bob Friend

1965 Topps Advertising Panels

This panel features three players on the front and an advertising for the upcoming Topps Embossed insert set.

1 Ron Herbel 20.00 50.00
Joe Gibbon/Ed Charles

1966 Topps Advertising Panels

This panel was issued to preview the 1966 Topps baseball set. As is traditional for these panels, they were issued in three card strips. The back of these inserts features information on the upcoming "rub-off" insert set

1 Sandy Koufax 125.00 250.00
Jim Fregosi/Don Mossi
2 Jim Lonborg 50.00 100.00
Howie Koplitz/Luis Aparicio

1967 Topps Advertising Panels

Described as a salesman's sample; the front of this panel features standard 1967 Topps cards on the front and advertising information on the back

COMPLETE SET 50.00 100.00
1 Earl Battey 20.00 50.00
Manny Mota/Gene Brabender
2 Ron Fairly 30.00 60.00
Bobby Murcer/Stan Bahnsen/Curt Simmo

2003 Topps 205

COMPLETE SERIES 1 (165) 15.00 40.00
COMPLETE SERIES 2 (175) 75.00 125.00
COMP.SERIES 2 w/o SP's (155) 15.00 40.00
COM (1-130/161-169/193-315) .20 .50
COMMON (131-145/170-192) .20 .50
COMMON CARD (146-160) .40 1.00
COMMON SP 1.00 2.50
COMMON SP RC 1.00 2.50
SERIES 2 SP STATED ODDS 1:5
SP CL: 152/157/171-177/180-181/184-185
SP CL: 187-192/300
SER.1 VINTAGE BUYBACKS ODDS 1:336
SER.2 VINTAGE BUYBACK ODDS 1:295
1A Barry Bonds w/Cap .75 2.00
1B Barry Bonds w/Helmet .75 2.00
2 Bret Boone .20 .50
3A Albert Pujols Clear Logo .60 1.50
3B Albert Pujols White Logo .60 1.50
4 Carl Crawford .30 .75
5 Bartolo Colon .20 .50
6 Cliff Floyd .20 .50
7 John Olerud .20 .50
8A Jason Giambi Full Jkt .20 .50
8B Jason Giambi Partial Jkt .20 .50
9 Edgardo Alfonzo .20 .50
10 Ivan Rodriguez .30 .75
11 Jim Edmonds .30 .75
12A Mike Piazza Orange .50 1.25
12B Mike Piazza Yellow .50 1.25
13 Greg Maddux .60 1.50
14 Jose Vidro .20 .50
15A Vlad Guerrero Clear Logo .30 .75
15B Vlad Guerrero White Logo .30 .75
16 Bernie Williams .30 .75
17 Roger Clemens .60 1.50
18A Miguel Tejada Blue .30 .75
18B Miguel Tejada Green .30 .75
19 Carlos Delgado .20 .50
20A Alfonso Soriano w/Bat .30 .75
20B Alfonso Soriano Sunglasses .30 .75
21 Bobby Cox MG .20 .50
22 Mike Scioscia .20 .50
23 John Smoltz .50 1.25
24 Luis Gonzalez .20 .50
25 Shawn Green .20 .50
26 Raul Ibanez .30 .75
27 Andruw Jones .20 .50
28 Josh Beckett .20 .50
29 Derek Lowe .20 .50
30 Todd Helton .30 .75
31 Barry Larkin .30 .75
32 Jason Jennings .20 .50
33 Darin Erstad .20 .50
34 Magglio Ordonez .30 .75
35 Mike Sweeney .20 .50
36 Kazuhisa Ishii .20 .50
37 Ron Gardenhire MG .20 .50
38 Tim Hudson .30 .75
39 Tim Salmon .20 .50
40A Pat Burrell Black Bat .20 .50
40B Pat Burrell Brown Bat .20 .50
41 Manny Ramirez .50 1.25
42 Nick Johnson .20 .50
43 Tom Glavine .30 .75
44 Mark Mulder .20 .50
45 Brian Jordan .20 .50
46 Rafael Palmeiro .30 .75
47 Vernon Wells .20 .50
48 Bob Brenly MG .20 .50
49 C.C. Sabathia .30 .75
50A Alex Rodriguez Look Ahead .60 1.50
50B Alex Rodriguez Look Away .60 1.50
51A Sammy Sosa Head Duck .50 1.25
51B Sammy Sosa Head Left .50 1.25
52 Paul Konerko .30 .75
53 Craig Biggio .30 .75
54 Moises Alou .20 .50
55 Johnny Damon .30 .75
56 Torii Hunter .20 .50
57 Omar Vizquel .30 .75
58 Orlando Hernandez .20 .50
59 Barry Zito .30 .75
60 Lance Berkman .30 .75

61 Carlos Beltran .30 .75
62 Edgar Renteria .20 .50
63 Ben Sheets .20 .50
64 Doug Mientkiewicz .20 .50
65 Troy Glaus .20 .50
66 Preston Wilson .20 .50
67 Kerry Wood .20 .50
68 Frank Thomas .50 1.25
69 Jimmy Rollins .30 .75
70 Brian Giles .20 .50
71 Bobby Higginson .20 .50
72 Larry Walker .30 .75
73 Randy Johnson .50 1.25
74 Tony LaRussa MG .20 .50
75A Derek Jeter w/Gold Trim 1.25 3.00
75B Derek Jeter w/o Gold Trim 1.25 3.00
76 Bobby Abreu .20 .50
77A Adam Dunn Closed Mouth .30 .75
77B Adam Dunn Open Mouth .30 .75
78 Ryan Klesko .20 .50
79 Francisco Rodriguez .30 .75
80 Scott Rolen .30 .75
81 Roberto Alomar .30 .75
82 Joe Torre MG .30 .75
83 Jim Thome .30 .75
84 Kevin Millwood .20 .50
85 J.T. Snow .20 .50
86 Trevor Hoffman .30 .75
87 Jay Gibbons .20 .50
88A Mark Prior New Logo .30 .75
88B Mark Prior Old Logo .30 .75
89 Rich Aurilia .20 .50
90 Chipper Jones .50 1.25
91 Richie Sexson .20 .50
92 Gary Sheffield .20 .50
93 Pedro Martinez .30 .75
94 Rodrigo Lopez .20 .50
95 Al Leiter .20 .50
96 Jorge Posada .30 .75
97 Luis Castillo .20 .50
98 Aubrey Huff .20 .50
99 A.J. Pierzynski .20 .50
100A Ichiro Suzuki Look Ahead .60 1.50
100B Ichiro Suzuki Look Right .60 1.50
101 Eric Chavez .20 .50
102 Brett Myers .20 .50
103 Jason Kendall .20 .50
104 Jeff Kent .20 .50
105 Eric Hinske .20 .50
106 Jacque Jones .20 .50
107 Phil Nevin .20 .50
108 Roy Oswalt .30 .75
109 Curt Schilling .30 .75
110A N.Garciaparra w/Gold Trim .30 .75
110B N.Garciaparra w/o Gold Trim .30 .75
111 Garret Anderson .20 .50
112 Eric Gagne .20 .50
113 Javier Vazquez .20 .50
114 Jeff Bagwell .30 .75
115 Mike Lowell .20 .50
116 Carlos Pena .30 .75
117 Ken Griffey Jr. 1.00 2.50
118 Tony Batista .20 .50
119 Edgar Martinez .30 .75
120 Austin Kearns .20 .50
121 Jason Stokes PROS .20 .50
122 Jose Reyes PROS .50 1.25
123 Rocco Baldelli PROS .20 .50
124 Joe Borchard PROS .20 .50
125 Joe Mauer PROS .50 1.25
126 Gavin Floyd PROS .20 .50
127 Mark Teixeira PROS .30 .75
128 Jeremy Guthrie PROS .20 .50
129 B.J. Upton PROS .30 .75
130 Khalil Greene PROS .30 .75
131 Hanley Ramirez FY RC 1.50 4.00
132 Andy Marte FY RC .20 .50
133 J.D. Durbin FY RC .20 .50
134 Jason Kubel FY RC .60 1.50
135 Craig Brazell FY RC .20 .50
136 Bryan Bullington FY RC .20 .50
137 Jose Contreras FY RC .50 1.25
138 Brian Burgamy FY RC .20 .50
139 Evel Bastida-Martinez FY RC .20 .50
140 Joey Gomes FY RC .20 .50
141 Ismael Castro FY RC .20 .50
142 Travis Wong FY RC .20 .50
143 Michael Garciaparra FY RC .20 .50
144 Arnaldo Munoz FY RC .20 .50
145 Louis Sockalexis FY XRC .20 .50
146 Richard Hoblitzell REP .40 1.00
147 George Graham REP .40 1.00
148 Hal Chase REP .40 1.00
149 John McGraw REP .60 1.50
150 Bobby Wallace REP .40 1.00
151 David Shean REP .40 1.00
152 Richard Hoblitzell REP SP 1.00 2.50
153 Hal Chase REP .40 1.00
154 Hooks Wiltse REP .40 1.00
155 George Brett RET 2.00 5.00
156 Willie Mays RET 2.00 5.00
157 Honus Wagner RET SP 2.50 6.00
158 Nolan Ryan RET 3.00 8.00
159 Reggie Jackson RET .60 1.50
160 Mike Schmidt RET 1.50 4.00
161 Josh Barfield PROS .20 .50
162 Grady Sizemore PROS .30 .75
163 Justin Morneau PROS .30 .75
164 Laynce Nix PROS .20 .50
165 Zack Greinke PROS 2.50 6.00
166 Victor Martinez PROS .30 .75
167 Jeff Mathis PROS .20 .50
168 Casey Kotchman PROS .20 .50
169 Gabe Gross PROS .20 .50
170 Edwin Jackson FY RC .20 .50
171 Delmon Young FY SP RC 4.00 10.00
172 Eric Duncan FY SP RC 1.00 2.50
173 Brian Snyder FY SP RC 1.00 2.50
174 Chris Lubanski FY SP RC 1.00 2.50
175 Ryan Harvey FY SP RC 1.00 2.50
176 Nick Markakis FY SP RC 5.00 12.00
177 Chad Billingsley FY SP RC 3.00 8.00
178 Elizardo Ramirez FY RC .20 .50
179 Ben Francisco FY RC .20 .50
180 Franklin Gutierrez FY SP RC 2.50 6.00
181 Aaron Hill FY SP RC 2.50 6.00
182 Kevin Correia FY RC .20 .50
183 Kelly Shoppach FY RC .30 .75
184 Felix Pie FY SP RC 1.50 4.00
185 Adam Loewen FY SP RC 1.00 2.50
186 Danny Garcia FY RC .20 .50
187 Rickie Weeks FY SP RC 3.00 8.00
188 Robby Hammock FY SP RC 1.00 2.50
189 Ryan Wagner FY SP RC 1.00 2.50
190 Matt Kata FY SP RC 1.00 2.50
191 Bo Hart FY SP RC 1.00 2.50
192 Brandon Webb FY SP RC 2.50 6.00
193 Bengie Molina .20 .50
194 Junior Spivey .20 .50
195 Gary Sheffield .20 .50
196 Jason Johnson .20 .50
197 David Ortiz .50 1.25
198 Roberto Alomar .30 .75
199 Wily Mo Pena .20 .50
200 Sammy Sosa .50 1.25
201 Jay Payton .20 .50
202 Dmitri Young .20 .50
203 Derrek Lee .30 .75
204A Jeff Bagwell w/Hat .30 .75
204B Jeff Bagwell w/o Hat .30 .75
205 Runelvys Hernandez .20 .50
206 Kevin Brown .20 .50
207 Wes Helms .20 .50
208 Eddie Guardado .20 .50
209 Orlando Cabrera .20 .50
210 Alfonso Soriano .30 .75
211 Ty Wigginton .20 .50
212A Rich Harden Look Left .30 .75
212B Rich Harden Look Right .30 .75
213 Mike Lieberthal .20 .50
214 Brian Giles .20 .50
215 Jason Schmidt .20 .50
216 Jamie Moyer .20 .50
217 Matt Morris .20 .50
218 Victor Zambrano .20 .50
219 Roy Halladay .30 .75
220 Mike Hampton .20 .50
221 Kevin Millar Sox .20 .50
222 Hideo Nomo .50 1.25
223 Milton Bradley .20 .50
224 Jose Guillen .20 .50
225 Derek Jeter 1.25 3.00
226 Rondell White .20 .50
227A Hank Blalock Blue Jsy .20 .50
227B Hank Blalock White Jsy .20 .50
228 Shigetoshi Hasegawa .20 .50
229 Mike Mussina .30 .75
230 Cristian Guzman .20 .50
231A Todd Helton Blue .30 .75
231B Todd Helton Green .30 .75
232 Kenny Lofton .20 .50
233 Carl Everett .20 .50
234 Shea Hillenbrand .20 .50
235 Brad Fullmer .20 .50
236 Bernie Williams .30 .75
237 Vicente Padilla .20 .50
238 Tim Worrell .20 .50
239 Juan Gonzalez .20 .50
240 Ichiro Suzuki .60 1.50
241 Aaron Boone .20 .50
242 Shannon Stewart .20 .50
243A Barry Zito Blue .30 .75
243B Barry Zito Green .30 .75
244 Reggie Sanders .20 .50
245 Scott Podsednik .20 .50
246 Miguel Cabrera 2.50 6.00
247 Angel Berroa .20 .50
248 Carlos Zambrano .30 .75
249 Marlon Byrd .20 .50
250 Mark Prior .30 .75
251 Esteban Loaiza .20 .50
252 David Eckstein .20 .50
253 Alex Cintron .20 .50
254 Melvin Mora .20 .50
255 Russ Ortiz .20 .50
256 Carlos Lee .20 .50
257 Tino Martinez .20 .50
258 Randy Wolf .20 .50
259 Jason Phillips .20 .50
260 Vladimir Guerrero .30 .75
261 Brad Wilkerson .20 .50
262 Ivan Rodriguez .30 .75
263 Matt Lawton .20 .50
264 Adam Dunn .20 .50
265 Joe Borowski .20 .50
266 Jody Gerut .20 .50
267 Alex Rodriguez .60 1.50
268 Brendan Donnelly .20 .50
269A Randy Johnson Grey .50 1.25
269B Randy Johnson Pink .50 1.25
270 Nomar Garciaparra .30 .75
271 Javy Lopez .20 .50
272 Travis Hafner .20 .50
273 Juan Pierre .20 .50
274 Morgan Ensberg .20 .50
275 Albert Pujols .60 1.50
276 Jason LaRue .20 .50
277 Paul Lo Duca .20 .50
278 Andy Pettitte .30 .75
279 Mike Piazza .50 1.25
280A Jim Thome Blue .30 .75
280B Jim Thome Green .30 .75
281 Marquis Grissom .20 .50
282 Woody Williams .20 .50
283A Curt Schilling Look Ahead .30 .75
283B Curt Schilling Look Right .30 .75
284A Chipper Jones Blue .50 1.25
284B Chipper Jones Yellow .50 1.25
285 Deivi Cruz .20 .50
286 Johnny Damon .30 .75
287 Chin-Hui Tsao .20 .50
288 Alex Gonzalez .20 .50
289 Billy Wagner .20 .50
290 Jason Giambi .20 .50
291 Keith Foulke .20 .50
292 Jerome Williams .20 .50
293 Livan Hernandez .20 .50
294 Aaron Guiel .20 .50
295 Randall Simon .20 .50
296 Byung-Hyun Kim .20 .50
297 Jorge Julio .20 .50
298 Miguel Batista .20 .50
299 Rafael Furcal .20 .50
300A Dontrelle Willis No Smile .20 .50
300B Dontrelle Willis Smile SP 1.00 2.50
301 Alex Sanchez .20 .50
302 Shawn Chacon .20 .50
303 Matt Clement .20 .50
304 Luis Matos .20 .50
305 Steve Finley .20 .50
306 Marcus Giles .20 .50
307 Boomer Wells .20 .50
308 Jeromy Burnitz .20 .50
309 Mike MacDougal .20 .50
310 Mariano Rivera .60 1.50
311 Adrian Beltre .50 1.25
312 Mark Loretta .20 .50
313 Ugueth Urbina .20 .50
314 Bill Mueller .20 .50
315 Johan Santana .30 .75

2003 Topps 205 American Beauty

*AMER.BTY: 1.25X TO 3X BASIC
RANDOM INSERTS IN PACKS
*AMER.BTY PURPLE: 4X TO 10X BASIC
PURPLE CARDS ARE 10% OF PRINT RUN
CL: 1/20/50/51/100/146-150

2003 Topps 205 Brooklyn

COMMON C (1-150) .40 1.00
COMMON U (1-150) .60 1.50
COMMON R (1-150) 1.00 2.50
1-150 RANDOM INSERTS IN SER.1 PACKS
COMMON CARD (151-315) 1.00 2.50
151-315 SERIES 2 STATED ODDS 1:12
151-315 STATED PRINT RUN 205 SETS
151-315 ARE NOT SERIAL-NUMBERED
151-315 PRINT RUN PROVIDED BY TOPPS
BROOKLYN 5 PRINT RUN 5 SETS
NO BROOKLYN 5 PRICING DUE TO SCARCITY
SEE BECKETT.COM FOR C/U/R/5 SCHEMATIC
SCHEMATIC IS IN OPG SUBSCRIPTION AREA
1 Barry Bonds w/Helmet U 2.50 6.00
2 Bret Boone U .60 1.50
3 Albert Pujols Clear Logo U 2.00 5.00
4 Carl Crawford U 1.00 2.50
5 Bartolo Colon R 1.00 2.50
6 Cliff Floyd R 1.00 2.50
7 John Olerud R 1.00 2.50
8 Jason Giambi Full Jkt U .60 1.50
11 Jim Edmonds U 1.00 2.50
12 Mike Piazza Orange C 1.00 2.50
13 Greg Maddux U 2.00 5.00
14 Jose Vidro U .60 1.50
15 Vlad Guerrero Clear Logo R 1.50 4.00
16 Bernie Williams R 1.50 4.00
17 Roger Clemens C 1.25 3.00
18 Miguel Tejada Blue U 1.00 2.50
19 Carlos Delgado U .60 1.50
20 Alfonso Soriano w/Bat C .60 1.50
21 Bobby Cox MG U .60 1.50
22 Mike Scioscia R 1.00 2.50
23 John Smoltz U 1.50 4.00
24 Luis Gonzalez C .40 1.00
25 Shawn Green C .40 1.00
26 Raul Ibanez C .60 1.50
27 Andruw Jones U .60 1.50
28 Josh Beckett C .40 1.00
30 Todd Helton C .60 1.50
31 Barry Larkin U 1.00 2.50
32 Jason Jennings U .60 1.50
33 Darin Erstad U .60 1.50
34 Magglio Ordonez C .60 1.50
35 Mike Sweeney U .60 1.50
36 Kazuhisa Ishii U .60 1.50
37 Ron Gardenhire MG C .40 1.00
38 Tim Hudson U 1.00 2.50
39 Tim Salmon C .40 1.00
40 Pat Burrell Black Bat R 1.00 2.50
41 Manny Ramirez C 1.00 2.50
42 Nick Johnson U .60 1.50
43 Tom Glavine U 1.00 2.50
44 Mark Mulder R 1.00 2.50
45 Brian Jordan U .60 1.50
46 Rafael Palmeiro R 1.50 4.00
47 Vernon Wells C .40 1.00
48 Bob Brenly MG U .60 1.50
49 C.C. Sabathia U 1.00 2.50
50 Alex Rodriguez Look Away C 1.25 3.00
51 Sammy Sosa Head Left R 2.50 6.00
52 Paul Konerko R 1.50 4.00
53 Craig Biggio U 1.00 2.50
54 Moises Alou R 1.00 2.50
55 Johnny Damon U 1.00 2.50
56 Torii Hunter C .40 1.00
57 Omar Vizquel C .60 1.50
59 Barry Zito U 1.00 2.50
60 Lance Berkman C .60 1.50
61 Carlos Beltran U 1.00 2.50
62 Edgar Renteria U .60 1.50
63 Ben Sheets U .60 1.50
64 Doug Mientkiewicz U .60 1.50
65 Troy Glaus R 1.00 2.50
66 Preston Wilson U .60 1.50
67 Kerry Wood C .40 1.00
68 Frank Thomas U 1.50 4.00
69 Jimmy Rollins U 1.00 2.50
70 Brian Giles U .60 1.50
71 Bobby Higginson U .60 1.50
72 Larry Walker C .60 1.50
73 Randy Johnson C 1.00 2.50
74 Tony LaRussa MG R 1.50 4.00
75 Derek Jeter w/Gold Trim U 4.00 10.00
76 Bobby Abreu U .60 1.50
77 Adam Dunn Open Mouth U 1.00 2.50
78 Ryan Klesko R 1.00 2.50
79 Francisco Rodriguez U 1.00 2.50
80 Scott Rolen R 1.50 4.00
81 Roberto Alomar C .60 1.50
82 Joe Torre MG R 1.50 4.00
85 J.T. Snow U .60 1.50
86 Trevor Hoffman R 1.50 4.00
87 Jay Gibbons U .60 1.50
88 Mark Prior New Logo C .60 1.50
89 Rich Aurilia R 1.00 2.50
90 Chipper Jones U 1.00 2.50
91 Richie Sexson R 1.00 2.50
92 Gary Sheffield U .60 1.50
93 Pedro Martinez R 1.50 4.00
94 Rodrigo Lopez U .60 1.50
95 Al Leiter U .60 1.50
96 Jorge Posada C .60 1.50
97 Luis Castillo R 1.00 2.50
98 Aubrey Huff C .40 1.00
99 A.J. Pierzynski U .60 1.50
100 Ichiro Suzuki Look Ahead U 2.00 5.00
101 Eric Chavez U .60 1.50
102 Brett Myers U .60 1.50
103 Jason Kendall U .60 1.50
105 Eric Hinske U .60 1.50
106 Jacque Jones U .60 1.50
107 Phil Nevin R 1.00 2.50
108 Roy Oswalt R 1.50 4.00
109 Curt Schilling U 1.00 2.50
110 N.Garciaparra w/Gold Trim R 1.50 4.00
111 Garret Anderson U .60 1.50
112 Eric Gagne U .60 1.50
113 Javier Vazquez U .60 1.50
114 Jeff Bagwell U 1.00 2.50
115 Mike Lowell C .40 1.00
116 Carlos Pena U 1.00 2.50
117 Ken Griffey Jr. R 5.00 12.00
118 Tony Batista R 1.00 2.50
119 Edgar Martinez U 1.00 2.50
120 Austin Kearns C .40 1.00
129 B.J. Upton PROS U 1.00 2.50
131 Hanley Ramirez FY R 8.00 20.00
132 Andy Marte FY U .60 1.50
136 Bryan Bullington FY R 1.00 2.50
138 Brian Burgamy FY R 1.00 2.50
144 Arnaldo Munoz FY U .60 1.50
151 David Shean REP 1.00 2.50
152 Richard Hoblitzell REP 1.00 2.50
153 Hal Chase REP 1.00 2.50
154 Hooks Wiltse REP 1.00 2.50
155 George Brett RET 5.00 12.00
156 Willie Mays RET 5.00 12.00
157 Honus Wagner RET 2.50 6.00
158 Nolan Ryan RET 8.00 20.00
159 Reggie Jackson RET 1.50 4.00
160 Mike Schmidt RET 4.00 10.00
161 Josh Barfield PROS 1.00 2.50
162 Grady Sizemore PROS 1.50 4.00
163 Justin Morneau PROS 1.50 4.00
164 Laynce Nix PROS 1.00 2.50
165 Zack Greinke PROS 12.00 30.00
166 Victor Martinez PROS 1.50 4.00
167 Jeff Mathis PROS 1.00 2.50
168 Casey Kotchman PROS 1.00 2.50
169 Gabe Gross PROS 1.00 2.50
170 Edwin Jackson FY 1.50 4.00
171 Delmon Young FY 6.00 15.00
172 Eric Duncan FY 1.00 2.50
173 Brian Snyder FY 1.00 2.50
174 Chris Lubanski FY 1.00 2.50
175 Ryan Harvey FY 1.00 2.50
176 Nick Markakis FY 8.00 20.00
177 Chad Billingsley FY 5.00 12.00
178 Elizardo Ramirez FY 1.00 2.50
179 Ben Francisco FY 1.00 2.50
180 Franklin Gutierrez FY 2.50 6.00
181 Aaron Hill FY 3.00 8.00
182 Kevin Correia FY 1.00 2.50
183 Kelly Shoppach FY 1.50 4.00
184 Felix Pie FY 1.50 4.00
185 Adam Loewen FY 1.00 2.50
186 Danny Garcia FY 1.00 2.50
187 Rickie Weeks FY 3.00 8.00
188 Robby Hammock FY 1.00 2.50
189 Ryan Wagner FY 1.00 2.50
190 Matt Kata FY 1.00 2.50
191 Bo Hart FY 1.00 2.50
192 Brandon Webb FY 3.00 8.00
193 Bengie Molina 1.00 2.50
194 Junior Spivey 1.00 2.50
195 Gary Sheffield 1.00 2.50
196 Jason Johnson 1.00 2.50
197 David Ortiz 2.50 6.00
198 Roberto Alomar 1.50 4.00
199 Wily Mo Pena 1.00 2.50
200 Sammy Sosa 2.50 6.00
201 Jay Payton 1.00 2.50
202 Dmitri Young 1.00 2.50
203 Derrek Lee 1.50 4.00
204A Jeff Bagwell w/Hat 1.50 4.00
204B Jeff Bagwell w/o Hat 1.50 4.00
205 Runelvys Hernandez 1.00 2.50
206 Kevin Brown 1.00 2.50
207 Wes Helms 1.00 2.50
208 Eddie Guardado 1.00 2.50
209 Orlando Cabrera 1.00 2.50
210 Alfonso Soriano 1.50 4.00
211 Ty Wigginton 1.00 2.50
212A Rich Harden Look Left 1.50 4.00
212B Rich Harden Look Right 1.50 4.00
213 Mike Lieberthal 1.00 2.50
214 Brian Giles 1.00 2.50
215 Jason Schmidt 1.00 2.50
216 Jamie Moyer 1.00 2.50
217 Matt Morris 1.00 2.50
218 Victor Zambrano 1.00 2.50
219 Roy Halladay 1.50 4.00
220 Mike Hampton 1.00 2.50
221 Kevin Millar Sox 1.00 2.50
222 Hideo Nomo 2.50 6.00
223 Milton Bradley 1.00 2.50
224 Jose Guillen 1.00 2.50
225 Derek Jeter 6.00 15.00
226 Rondell White 1.00 2.50
227A Hank Blalock Blue Jsy 1.00 2.50
227B Hank Blalock White Jsy 1.00 2.50
228 Shigetoshi Hasegawa 1.00 2.50
229 Mike Mussina 1.50 4.00
230 Cristian Guzman 1.00 2.50
231A Todd Helton Blue 1.50 4.00
231B Todd Helton Green 1.50 4.00
232 Kenny Lofton 1.00 2.50
233 Carl Everett 1.00 2.50
234 Shea Hillenbrand 1.00 2.50
235 Brad Fullmer 1.00 2.50
236 Bernie Williams 1.50 4.00
237 Vicente Padilla 1.00 2.50
238 Tim Worrell 1.00 2.50
239 Juan Gonzalez 1.00 2.50
240 Ichiro Suzuki 3.00 8.00
241 Aaron Boone 1.00 2.50
242 Shannon Stewart 1.00 2.50
243A Barry Zito Blue 1.50 4.00
243B Barry Zito Green 1.50 4.00
244 Reggie Sanders 1.00 2.50
245 Scott Podsednik 1.00 2.50
246 Miguel Cabrera 12.00 30.00
247 Angel Berroa 1.00 2.50
248 Carlos Zambrano 1.50 4.00
249 Marlon Byrd 1.00 2.50
250 Mark Prior 1.50 4.00
251 Esteban Loaiza 1.00 2.50
252 David Eckstein 1.00 2.50
253 Alex Cintron 1.00 2.50
254 Melvin Mora 1.00 2.50
255 Russ Ortiz 1.00 2.50
256 Carlos Lee 1.00 2.50
257 Tino Martinez 1.00 2.50
258 Randy Wolf 1.00 2.50
259 Jason Phillips 1.00 2.50
260 Vladimir Guerrero 1.50 4.00
261 Brad Wilkerson 1.00 2.50
262 Ivan Rodriguez 1.50 4.00
263 Matt Lawton 1.00 2.50
264 Adam Dunn 1.50 4.00
265 Joe Borowski 1.00 2.50
266 Jody Gerut 1.00 2.50
267 Alex Rodriguez 3.00 8.00
268 Brendan Donnelly 1.00 2.50
269A Randy Johnson Grey 2.50 6.00
269B Randy Johnson Pink 2.50 6.00
270 Nomar Garciaparra 1.50 4.00
271 Javy Lopez 1.00 2.50
272 Travis Hafner 1.00 2.50
273 Juan Pierre 1.00 2.50
274 Morgan Ensberg 1.00 2.50
275 Albert Pujols 3.00 8.00
276 Jason LaRue 1.00 2.50
277 Paul Lo Duca 1.00 2.50
278 Andy Pettitte 1.50 4.00
279 Mike Piazza 2.50 6.00
280A Jim Thome Blue 1.50 4.00
280B Jim Thome Green 1.50 4.00
281 Marquis Grissom 1.00 2.50
282 Woody Williams 1.00 2.50
283A Curt Schilling Look Ahead 1.50 4.00
283B Curt Schilling Look Right 1.50 4.00
284A Chipper Jones Blue 2.50 6.00
284B Chipper Jones Yellow 2.50 6.00
285 Deivi Cruz 1.00 2.50
286 Johnny Damon 1.50 4.00
287 Chin-Hui Tsao 1.00 2.50
288 Alex Gonzalez 1.00 2.50
289 Billy Wagner 1.00 2.50
290 Jason Giambi 1.00 2.50
291 Keith Foulke 1.00 2.50
292 Jerome Williams 1.00 2.50
293 Livan Hernandez 1.00 2.50
294 Aaron Guiel 1.00 2.50
295 Randall Simon 1.00 2.50
296 Byung-Hyun Kim 1.00 2.50
297 Jorge Julio 1.00 2.50
298 Miguel Batista 1.00 2.50
299 Rafael Furcal 1.00 2.50
300A Dontrelle Willis No Smile 1.00 2.50
300B Dontrelle Willis Smile 1.00 2.50
301 Alex Sanchez 1.00 2.50
302 Shawn Chacon 1.00 2.50
303 Matt Clement 1.00 2.50
304 Luis Matos 1.00 2.50
305 Steve Finley 1.00 2.50
306 Marcus Giles 1.00 2.50
307 Boomer Wells 1.00 2.50
308 Jeromy Burnitz 1.00 2.50
309 Mike MacDougal 1.00 2.50
310 Mariano Rivera 3.00 8.00
311 Adrian Beltre 2.50 6.00
312 Mark Loretta 1.00 2.50
313 Ugueth Urbina 1.00 2.50
314 Bill Mueller 1.00 2.50
315 Johan Santana 1.50 4.00

2003 Topps 205 Brooklyn Exclusive Pose

*BROOKLYN EP: 1X TO 2.5X POLAR EP
OVERALL BROOKLYN SERIES 2 ODDS 1:12
STATED PRINT RUN 205 SETS
CARDS ARE NOT SERIAL-NUMBERED
PRINT RUN PROVIDED BY TOPPS

2003 Topps 205 Cycle

*CYCLE 121-145: 1.25X TO 3X BASIC
RANDOM INSERTS IN PACKS
*CYCLE PURPLE 121-130: 3X TO 8X BASIC
*CYCLE PURPLE 131-145: 3X TO 8X BASIC
PURPLE CARDS ARE 10% OF PRINT RUN

2003 Topps 205 Drum

*DRUM: 2X TO 5X BASIC
*DRUM: .6X TO 1.5X BASIC SP
RANDOM INSERTS IN PACKS

2003 Topps 205 Drum Exclusive Pose

*DRUM EP: 1X TO 2.5X POLAR EP
RANDOM INSERTS IN SERIES 2 PACKS

2003 Topps 205 Honest

*HONEST: 1.25X TO 3X BASIC
RANDOM INSERTS IN PACKS
*HONEST PURPLE: 4X TO 10X BASIC
PURPLE CARDS ARE 10% OF PRINT RUN
CL: 1/3/8/12/15/18/20/40/50/51/75/77/88
CL: 100/110

2003 Topps 205 Piedmont

*PIEDMONT: 1.25X TO 3X BASIC
RANDOM INSERTS IN PACKS
*PIEDMONT PURPLE: 4X TO 10X BASIC
PURPLE CARDS ARE 10% OF PRINT RUN
CL: 2-19/21-49/52-69

2003 Topps 205 Polar Bear

*POLAR BEAR: .75X TO 2X BASIC
*POLAR BEAR: .25X TO .6X BASIC SP
RANDOM INSERTS IN PACKS

2003 Topps 205 Polar Bear Exclusive Pose

316 Willie Mays EP 2.50 6.00
317 Delmon Young EP 3.00 8.00
318 Rickie Weeks EP 1.50 4.00
319 Ryan Wagner EP .50 1.25
320 Brandon Webb EP 1.50 4.00
321 Chris Lubanski EP .50 1.25
322 Ryan Harvey EP .50 1.25
323 Nick Markakis EP 4.00 10.00
324 Chad Billingsley EP 2.00 5.00
325 Aaron Hill EP 1.50 4.00
326 Brian Snyder EP .50 1.25
327 Eric Duncan EP .50 1.25
328 Sammy Sosa EP 1.25 3.00
329 Alfonso Soriano EP .75 2.00
330 Ichiro Suzuki EP 1.50 4.00
331 Alex Rodriguez EP 1.50 4.00
332 Nomar Garciaparra EP .75 2.00
333 Albert Pujols EP 1.50 4.00
334 Jim Thome EP .75 2.00
335 Dontrelle Willis EP .50 1.25

2003 Topps 205 Sovereign

*SOVEREIGN: 1.25X TO 3X BASIC
*SOVEREIGN: .4X TO 1X BASIC SP
RANDOM INSERTS IN PACKS
*SOV.GREEN: 2.5X TO 6X BASIC
*SOV.GREEN: 1.25X TO 3X BASIC SP
SOV.GREEN CARDS ARE 25% OF PRINT RUN

2003 Topps 205 Sovereign Exclusive Pose

*SOVEREIGN EP: .6X TO 1.5X POLAR EP
RANDOM INSERTS IN SERIES 2 PACKS
*SOV.GREEN EP: 1.25X TO 3X POLAR EP
SOV.GREEN CARDS ARE 25% OF PRINT RUN

2003 Topps 205 Sweet Caporal

*SWEET CAP: 1.25X TO 3X BASIC
RANDOM INSERTS IN PACKS
*SWEET CAP PURPLE: 4X TO 10X BASIC
PURPLE CARDS ARE 10% OF PRINT RUN
CL: 70-99/101-120

2003 Topps 205 Autographs

SER.1 GROUP A1 ODDS 1:2434
SER.1 GROUP B1 ODDS 1:608
SER.1 GROUP C1 ODDS 1:1460
SER.1 GROUP D1 ODDS 1:122
SER.2 GROUP A2 ODDS 1:5816
SER.2 GROUP B2 ODDS 1:646
SER.2 GROUP C2 ODDS 1:49
A2 STATED PRINT RUN 50 CARDS
A2 IS NOT SERIAL-NUMBERED
A2 PRINT RUN PROVIDED BY TOPPS
CF Cliff Floyd B1 8.00 20.00
DW Dontrelle Willis C2 8.00 20.00
ED Eric Duncan C2 8.00 20.00
FP Felix Pie C2 4.00 10.00
HA Hank Aaron A2 SP/50 150.00 250.00
JR Jose Reyes D1 6.00 15.00
JW Jerome Williams B2 6.00 15.00
LB Lance Berkman B1 6.00 15.00
LC Luis Castillo C2 4.00 10.00
MB Marlon Byrd D1 4.00 10.00
MO Magglio Ordonez C1 8.00 20.00
MS Mike Sweeney B1 8.00 20.00
PL Paul Lo Duca D1 6.00 15.00
RH Rich Harden C2 12.50 30.00
RWA Ryan Wagner C2 6.00 15.00
SR Scott Rolen A1 6.00 15.00
TH Torii Hunter D1 6.00 15.00

2003 Topps 205 Relics

COM.UNI A1/RELIC A2 6.00 15.00
COM.BAT B-D1/UNI E1/RELIC B2 4.00 10.00
BAT B-D1/UNI E1/RELIC B2 SEMI 6.00 15.00
COMMON BAT E-H1/UNI F-M1 3.00 8.00
SER.1 BAT GROUP A1 ODDS 1:1216
SER.1 BAT GROUP B1 ODDS 1:972
SER.1 BAT GROUP C1 ODDS 1:270
SER.1 BAT GROUP D1 ODDS 1:365
SER.1 BAT GROUP E1 ODDS 1:561
SER.1 BAT GROUP F1 ODDS 1:486
SER.1 BAT GROUP G1 ODDS 1:91
SER.1 BAT GROUP H1 ODDS 1:203
SER.1 UNI GROUP A1 ODDS 1:4884
SER.1 UNI GROUP B1 ODDS 1:456
SER.1 UNI GROUP C1 ODDS 1:1460
SER.1 UNI GROUP D1 ODDS 1:1216
SER.1 UNI GROUP E1 ODDS 1:973
SER.1 UNI GROUP F1 ODDS 1:608
SER.1 UNI GROUP G1 ODDS 1:61
SER.1 UNI GROUP H1 ODDS 1:183
SER.1 UNI GROUP I1 ODDS 1:83
SER.1 UNI GROUP J1 ODDS 1:324
SER.1 UNI GROUP K1 ODDS 1:317
SER.1 UNI GROUP L1 ODDS 1:243
SER.1 UNI GROUP M1 ODDS 1:221
SER.2 RELIC GROUP A ODDS 1:79
SER.2 RELIC GROUP B ODDS 1:16
AB A.J. Burnett Jsy G1 3.00 8.00
AD Adam Dunn Bat G1 3.00 8.00
AJ Andruw Jones Jsy B2 6.00 15.00
AL Al Leiter Jsy I1 3.00 8.00
APB Albert Pujols Bat A2 10.00 25.00
AP1 Albert Pujols Uni E1 8.00 20.00
AP2 Albert Pujols Hat A2 10.00 25.00
ARA Aramis Ramirez Bat B2 4.00 10.00
AR1 Alex Rodriguez Jsy H1 6.00 15.00
AR2 Alex Rodriguez Bat B2 6.00 15.00
AS1 Alfonso Soriano Uni G1 3.00 8.00
AS2 Alfonso Soriano Bat A2 6.00 15.00
BB1 Barry Bonds Uni B1 10.00 25.00
BB2 Bret Boone Bat A2 6.00 15.00
BD Brandon Duckworth Jsy B2 4.00 10.00
BG1 Brian Giles Bat G1 3.00 8.00
BG2 Brian Giles Bat A2 6.00 15.00
BP Brad Penny Jsy B2 4.00 10.00
BW1 Bernie Williams Bat D1 6.00 15.00
BW2 Bernie Williams Jsy A2 8.00 20.00
BZ Barry Zito Jsy K1 3.00 8.00
CB Craig Biggio Uni D1 6.00 15.00
CD Carlos Delgado Jsy B2 4.00 10.00
CG Cristian Guzman Jsy B2 4.00 10.00
CJB Chipper Jones Bat A2 8.00 20.00
CP Corey Patterson Bat A2 6.00 15.00
CS1 Curt Schilling Jsy B1 4.00 10.00
CS2 Curt Schilling Bat B2 4.00 10.00
DE Darin Erstad Uni A2 6.00 15.00
DL Derek Lowe Hat A1 6.00 15.00
DW Dontrelle Willis Uni B2 6.00 15.00
EC Eric Chavez Bat G1 3.00 8.00
EG Eric Gagne Jsy G1 3.00 8.00
EMA Edgar Martinez Jsy B2 6.00 15.00
EMU Eddie Murray Bat A2 10.00 25.00
FM Fred McGriff Bat B2 6.00 15.00
FR Frank Robinson Bat A2 8.00 20.00
FT Frank Thomas Jsy B2 6.00 15.00
GA Garret Anderson Uni L1 3.00 8.00
GB George Brett Jsy A2 12.50 30.00
GC Gary Carter Bat A2 6.00 15.00
GM1 Greg Maddux Jsy B1 6.00 15.00
GM2 Greg Maddux Bat A2 8.00 20.00
GS Gary Sheffield Bat B2 4.00 10.00
HB Hank Blalock Bat B2 4.00 10.00
IR Ivan Rodriguez Bat A2 8.00 20.00
JB1 Jeff Bagwell Uni G1 4.00 10.00
JB2 Jeff Bagwell Bat A2 8.00 20.00
JC Jose Canseco Bat B2 6.00 15.00
JD Johnny Damon Bat B1 6.00 15.00
JE Jim Edmonds Jsy A2 6.00 15.00
JG Jason Giambi Bat A2 6.00 15.00
JGI Jeremy Giambi Jsy B2 4.00 10.00
JGO Juan Gonzalez Bat B2 4.00 10.00
JJ Jason Jennings Jsy G1 3.00 8.00
JK Jeff Kent Bat C1 4.00 10.00
JO John Olerud Jsy B2 4.00 10.00
JP Jorge Posada Bat A2 8.00 20.00
JS John Smoltz Jsy B1 6.00 15.00
JT Jim Thome Bat F1 4.00 10.00
KB Kevin Brown Jsy B2 4.00 10.00
KI Kazuhisa Ishii Jsy I1 3.00 8.00
KL1 Kenny Lofton Bat G1 3.00 8.00
KL2 Kenny Lofton Uni B2 4.00 10.00
LB Lance Berkman Bat C1 4.00 10.00
LC Luis Castillo Jsy G1 3.00 8.00
LG1 Luis Gonzalez Jsy J1 3.00 8.00
LG2 Luis Gonzalez Bat A2 6.00 15.00
LW Larry Walker Jsy B2 4.00 10.00
MC Mike Cameron Jsy B2 4.00 10.00
MG Mark Grace Bat A2 8.00 20.00
MGR Marquis Grissom Bat B2 4.00 10.00
MM Mark Mulder Uni A2 6.00 15.00
MO Magglio Ordonez Jsy M1 3.00 8.00
MP1 Mike Piazza Bat C1 6.00 15.00
MP2 Mike Piazza Bat A2 8.00 20.00
MR Manny Ramirez Bat H1 4.00 10.00
MSC Mike Schmidt Bat A2 15.00 40.00
MSW Mike Sweeney Bat H1 3.00 8.00
MTE Miguel Tejada Bat B2 4.00 10.00
MTI Mark Teixeira Bat B2 6.00 15.00
MV Mo Vaughn Jsy I1 3.00 8.00
NG1 Nomar Garciaparra Jsy G1 6.00 15.00
NG2 Nomar Garciaparra Bat A2 8.00 20.00
NJ Nick Johnson Bat D1 4.00 10.00
NR Nolan Ryan Uni A2 30.00 60.00
PM1 Pedro Martinez Jsy F1 4.00 10.00
PM2 Pedro Martinez Jsy A2 8.00 20.00
PO Paul O'Neill Uni B2 6.00 15.00
RA1 Roberto Alomar Bat G1 4.00 10.00
RA2 Roberto Alomar Uni B2 6.00 15.00
RBB Rocco Baldelli Bat B2 4.00 10.00
RBJ Rocco Baldelli Jsy B2 4.00 10.00
RC Roger Clemens Uni A2 8.00 20.00
RF1 Rafael Furcal Bat E1 3.00 8.00
RF2 Rafael Furcal Bat A2 6.00 15.00
RH Rickey Henderson Bat B2 6.00 15.00
RJ1 Randy Johnson Jsy C1 6.00 15.00
RJ2 Randy Johnson Jsy A2 8.00 20.00
RO Roy Oswalt Jsy I1 3.00 8.00
RP1 Rafael Palmeiro Jsy H1 4.00 10.00
RP2 Rafael Palmeiro Bat A2 8.00 20.00
RV Robin Ventura Bat B2 4.00 10.00
SB Sean Burroughs Bat B2 4.00 10.00
SR1 Scott Rolen Bat A1 6.00 15.00
SR2 Scott Rolen Uni A2 8.00 20.00
SS Sammy Sosa Jsy A2 8.00 20.00
SST Shannon Stewart Bat B2 4.00 10.00
TG Troy Glaus Uni A2 6.00 15.00
TH Todd Helton Jsy D1 6.00 15.00
TM Tino Martinez Bat B2 6.00 15.00
TP Troy Percival Uni G1 3.00 8.00
TS Tsuyoshi Shinjo Bat B2 4.00 10.00
VG Vladimir Guerrero Bat A2 8.00 20.00
VW Vernon Wells Jsy A2 6.00 15.00
WB Wade Boggs Bat A2 8.00 20.00

2003 Topps 205 Triple Folder Polar Bear

COMPLETE SET (100) 20.00 50.00
COMPLETE SERIES 1 (50) 10.00 25.00
COMPLETE SERIES 2 (50) 10.00 25.00
ONE PER PACK
*BROOKLYN: 3X TO 8X BASIC
SERIES 1 BROOKLYN ODDS 1:72
SERIES 2 BROOKLYN ODDS 1:29
TF1 B.Bonds/J.LaRue .75 2.00
TF2 A.Soriano/D.Jeter 1.25 3.00
TF3 A.Rodriguez/M.Tejada .60 1.50
TF4 N.Garciaparra/D.Jeter 1.25 3.00
TF5 O.Vizquel/A.Rodriguez .60 1.50
TF6 P.Konerko/O.Vizquel .30 .75
TF7 P.Konerko/M.Ordonez .30 .75
TF8 D.Mientkiewicz/D.Erstad .20 .50
TF9 J.Kendall/J.Rollins .30 .75
TF10 S.Green/R.Alomar .30 .75
TF11 D.Jeter/R.Alomar 1.25 3.00
TF12 B.Abreu/L.Castillo .20 .50
TF13 R.Johnson/C.Schilling .50 1.25
TF14 M.Piazza/K.Wood .50 1.25
TF15 R.Clemens/J.Posada .60 1.50
TF16 I.Suzuki/R.Klesko .60 1.50
TF17 A.Soriano/C.Jones .50 1.25
TF18 B.Bonds/N.Johnson .75 2.00
TF19 C.Jones/A.Jones .50 1.25
TF20 B.Abreu/P.Konerko .30 .75
TF21 R.Palmeiro/A.Rodriguez .60 1.50
TF22 E.Hinske/C.Delgado .20 .50
TF23 N.Garciaparra/J.Gibbons .30 .75
TF24 M.Piazza/L.Gonzalez .50 1.25
TF25 J.Snow/V.Guerrero .30 .75
TF26 J.Giambi/B.Williams .30 .75
TF27 M.Tejada/R.Sexson .30 .75
TF28 D.Mientkiewicz/J.Rollins .30 .75

TF29 E.Chavez/D.Jeter 1.25 3.00
TF30 A.Soriano/B.Boone .30 .75
TF31 C.Jones/M.Piazza .50 1.25
TF32 I.Suzuki/B.Boone .60 1.50
TF33 B.Abreu/M.Piazza .50 1.25
TF34 J.Rollins/P.Burrell .30 .75
TF35 I.Suzuki/M.Tejada .60 1.50
TF36 J.LaRue/B.Bonds .75 2.00
TF37 D.Jeter/A.Soriano 1.25 3.00
TF38 M.Tejada/A.Rodriguez .60 1.50
TF39 D.Jeter/N.Garciaparra 1.25 3.00
TF40 A.Rodriguez/O.Vizquel .60 1.50
TF41 C.Schilling/R.Johnson .50 1.25
TF42 J.Posada/R.Clemens .60 1.50
TF43 R.Klesko/I.Suzuki .60 1.50
TF44 N.Johnson/B.Bonds .75 2.00
TF45 A.Rodriguez/R.Palmeiro .60 1.50
TF46 V.Guerrero/J.Snow .30 .75
TF47 D.Jeter/E.Chavez 1.25 3.00
TF48 B.Boone/I.Suzuki .60 1.50
TF49 M.Piazza/B.Abreu .50 1.25
TF50 M.Tejada/I.Suzuki .60 1.50
TF51 J.Pierre/J.Thome .30 .75
TF52 K.Millwood/J.Thome .30 .75
TF53 H.Blalock/J.Posada .30 .75
TF54 D.Cruz/H.Blalock .20 .50
TF55 R.Furcal/T.Wigginton .20 .50
TF56 J.Thome/N.Garciaparra .30 .75
TF57 C.Biggio/J.Giambi .30 .75
TF58 A.Boone/J.Giambi .20 .50
TF59 J.Giambi/B.Williams .30 .75
TF60 C.Guzman/J.Gerut .20 .50
TF61 T.Helton/J.Reyes .50 1.25
TF62 D.Jeter/H.Blalock 1.25 3.00
TF63 M.Piazza/J.Rollins .50 1.25
TF64 B.Williams/D.Jeter 1.25 3.00
TF65 A.Jones/R.Furcal .20 .50
TF66 M.Piazza/A.Jones .50 1.25
TF67 M.Piazza/C.Floyd .50 1.25
TF68 J.Kendall/A.Pujols .60 1.50
TF69 N.Garciaparra/M.Ramirez .50 1.25
TF70 J.Posada/A.Rodriguez .60 1.50
TF71 D.Jeter/A.Rodriguez 1.25 3.00
TF72 M.Sweeney/A.Rodriguez .60 1.50
TF73 M.Grissom/I.Rodriguez .30 .75
TF74 J.Phillips/G.Sheffield .20 .50
TF75 C.Jones/G.Sheffield .50 1.25
TF76 J.Spivey/G.Sheffield .20 .50
TF77 A.Leiter/I.Suzuki .60 1.50
TF78 J.Vidro/J.Thome .30 .75
TF79 J.Rollins/P.Lo Duca .30 .75
TF80 A.Rodriguez/R.Palmeiro .60 1.50
TF81 A.Pujols/J.Edmonds .60 1.50
TF82 E.Chavez/M.Sweeney .20 .50
TF83 C.Guzman/J.Rollins .30 .75
TF84 A.Soriano/B.Williams .30 .75
TF85 I.Suzuki/D.Jeter 1.25 3.00
TF86 J.Rollins/D.Lee .30 .75
TF87 S.Green/P.Lo Duca .20 .50
TF88 C.Delgado/J.Posada .30 .75
TF89 D.Young/C.Sabathia .30 .75
TF90 D.Willis/S.Chacon .20 .50
TF91 E.Martinez/A.Rodriguez .60 1.50
TF92 E.Martinez/C.Delgado .30 .75
TF93 E.Martinez/E.Loaiza .30 .75
TF94 R.Halladay/C.Sabathia .30 .75
TF95 I.Suzuki/A.Pujols .60 1.50
TF96 I.Suzuki/S.Hasegawa .60 1.50
TF97 G.Jenkins/A.Boone .20 .50
TF98 N.Garciaparra/A.Soriano .30 .75
TF99 J.Posada/A.Soriano .30 .75
TF100 V.Wells/G.Anderson .20 .50

2003 Topps 205 Triple Folder Autographs

SERIES 2 STATED ODDS 1:355 HOBBY
STATED PRINT RUN 205 SETS
CARDS ARE NOT SERIAL-NUMBERED
PRINT RUN PROVIDED BY TOPPS
DW Dontrelle Willis 10.00 25.00
JW Jerome Williams 15.00 40.00
RH Rich Harden 30.00 60.00
RW Ryan Wagner 15.00 40.00

2002 Topps 206 Olbermann Promos

COMPLETE SET 2.00 5.00
COMMON CARD .40 1.00

2002 Topps 206

COMPLETE SET (525) 110.00 220.00
COMPLETE SERIES 1 (180) 25.00 60.00
COMPLETE SERIES 2 (180) 25.00 60.00
COMPLETE SERIES 3 (165) 50.00 100.00
COM(1-140/181-270/308-418) .20 .50
COMMON (141-155/271-285) .20 .50
141-155/271-285 STATED ODDS 1:2
COMMON RC (308-418) .20 .50
COMMON SP (308-398) .75 2.00
COMMON FYP SP (419-432) .40 1.00
COMMON RET SP (433-447) .75 2.00
SER.3 SP STATED ODDS ONE PER PACK
REPURCHASED CARD SER.1 ODDS 1:110
REPURCHASED CARD SER.2 ODDS 1:179
REPURCHASED CARD SER.2 ODDS 1:101
1 Vladimir Guerrero .50 1.25
2 Sammy Sosa .50 1.25
3 Garret Anderson .20 .50
4 Rafael Palmeiro .30 .75
5 Juan Gonzalez .20 .50
6 John Smoltz .30 .75
7 Mark Mulder .20 .50
8 Jon Lieber .20 .50
9 Greg Maddux .75 2.00
10 Moises Alou .20 .50
11 Joe Randa .20 .50
12 Bobby Abreu .20 .50
13 Juan Pierre .20 .50
14 Kerry Wood .20 .50
15 Craig Biggio .30 .75
16 Curt Schilling .20 .50
17 Brian Jordan .20 .50
18 Edgardo Alfonzo .20 .50
19 Darren Dreifort .20 .50
20 Todd Helton .30 .75
21 Ramon Ortiz .20 .50
22 Ichiro Suzuki 1.00 2.50
23 Jimmy Rollins .20 .50
24 Darin Erstad .20 .50
25 Shawn Green .20 .50
26 Tino Martinez .30 .75
27 Bret Boone .20 .50
28 Alfonso Soriano .20 .50
29 Chan Ho Park .20 .50
30 Roger Clemens 1.00 2.50
31 Cliff Floyd .20 .50
32 Johnny Damon .30 .75
33 Frank Thomas .50 1.25
34 Barry Bonds 1.25 3.00
35 Luis Gonzalez .20 .50
36 Carlos Lee .20 .50
37 Roberto Alomar .30 .75
38 Carlos Delgado .20 .50
39 Nomar Garciaparra .75 2.00
40 Jason Kendall .20 .50
41 Scott Rolen .30 .75
42 Tom Glavine .30 .75
43 Ryan Klesko .20 .50
44 Brian Giles .20 .50
45 Bud Smith .20 .50
46 Charles Nagy .20 .50
47 Tony Gwynn .60 1.50
48 C.C. Sabathia .20 .50
49 Frank Catalanotto .20 .50
50 Jerry Hairston .20 .50
51 Jeromy Burnitz .20 .50
52 David Justice .20 .50
53 Bartolo Colon .20 .50
54 Andres Galarraga .20 .50
55 Jeff Weaver .20 .50
56 Terrence Long .20 .50
57 Tsuyoshi Shinjo .20 .50
58 Barry Zito .20 .50
59 Mariano Rivera .50 1.25
60 John Olerud .20 .50
61 Randy Johnson .50 1.25
62 Kenny Lofton .20 .50
63 Jermaine Dye .20 .50
64 Troy Glaus .20 .50
65 Larry Walker .20 .50
66 Hideo Nomo .50 1.25
67 Mike Mussina .30 .75
68 Paul LoDuca .20 .50
69 Magglio Ordonez .20 .50
70 Paul O'Neill .30 .75
71 Sean Casey .20 .50
72 Lance Berkman .20 .50
73 Adam Dunn .20 .50
74 Aramis Ramirez .20 .50
75 Rafael Furcal .20 .50
76 Gary Sheffield .20 .50
77 Todd Hollandsworth .20 .50
78 Chipper Jones .50 1.25
79 Bernie Williams .30 .75
80 Richard Hidalgo .20 .50
81 Eric Chavez .20 .50
82 Mike Piazza .75 2.00
83 J.D. Drew .20 .50
84 Ken Griffey Jr. 1.00 2.50
85 Joe Kennedy .20 .50
86 Joel Pineiro .20 .50
87 Josh Towers .20 .50
88 Andruw Jones .30 .75
89 Carlos Beltran .20 .50
90 Mike Cameron .20 .50
91 Albert Pujols 1.00 2.50
92 Alex Rodriguez .60 1.50
93 Omar Vizquel .30 .75
94 Juan Encarnacion .20 .50
95 Jeff Bagwell .30 .75
96 Jose Canseco .30 .75
97 Ben Sheets .20 .50
98 Mark Grace .30 .75
99 Mike Sweeney .20 .50
100 Mark McGwire 1.25 3.00
101 Ivan Rodriguez .30 .75
102 Rich Aurilia .20 .50
103 Cristian Guzman .20 .50
104 Roy Oswalt .20 .50
105 Tim Hudson .20 .50
106 Brent Abernathy .20 .50
107 Mike Hampton .20 .50
108 Miguel Tejada .20 .50
109 Bobby Higginson .20 .50
110 Edgar Martinez .30 .75
111 Jorge Posada .30 .75
112 Jason Giambi Yankees .20 .50
113 Pedro Astacio .20 .50
114 Kazuhiro Sasaki .20 .50
115 Preston Wilson .20 .50
116 Jason Bere .20 .50
117 Mark Quinn .20 .50
118 Pokey Reese .20 .50
119 Derek Jeter 1.25 3.00
120 Shannon Stewart .20 .50
121 Jeff Kent .20 .50
122 Jeremy Giambi .20 .50
123 Pat Burrell .20 .50
124 Jim Edmonds .20 .50
125 Mark Buehrle .20 .50
126 Kevin Brown .20 .50
127 Raul Mondesi .20 .50
128 Pedro Martinez .30 .75
129 Jim Thome .30 .75
130 Russ Ortiz .20 .50
131 Brandon Duckworth PROS .20 .50
132 Ryan Jamison PROS .20 .50
133 Brandon Inge PROS .20 .50
134 Felipe Lopez PROS .20 .50
135 Jason Lane PROS .20 .50
136 Forrest Johnson PROS RC .20 .50
137 Greg Nash PROS .20 .50
138 Covelli Crisp PROS .75 2.00
139 Nick Neugebauer PROS .20 .50
140 Dustan Mohr PROS .20 .50
141 Freddy Sanchez FYP RC .75 2.00
142 Justin Backsmeyer FYP RC .20 .50
143 Jorge Julio FYP .20 .50
144 Ryan Motti FYP RC .20 .50
145 Chris Tritle FYP RC .20 .50
146 Noochie Varner FYP RC .20 .50
147 Brian Rogers FYP .20 .50
148 Michael Hill FYP RC .20 .50
149 Luis Pineda FYP .20 .50
150 Rich Thompson FYP RC .20 .50
151 Bill Hall FYP .20 .50
152 Juan Dominguez FYP RC .20 .50
153 Justin Woodrow FYP .20 .50
154 Nic Jackson FYP RC .20 .50
155 Laynce Nix FYP RC .60 1.50
156 Hank Aaron RET 2.00 5.00
157 Ernie Banks RET 1.00 2.50
158 Johnny Bench RET 1.00 2.50
159 George Brett RET 2.00 5.00
160 Carlton Fisk RET .60 1.50
161 Bob Gibson RET .60 1.50
162 Reggie Jackson RET .60 1.50
163 Don Mattingly RET 2.00 5.00
164 Kirby Puckett RET 1.00 2.50
165 Frank Robinson RET .60 1.50
166 Nolan Ryan RET 2.50 6.00
167 Tom Seaver RET .60 1.50
168 Mike Schmidt RET 2.00 5.00
169 Dave Winfield RET .40 1.00
170 Carl Yastrzemski RET 1.25 3.00
171 Frank Chance REP .40 1.00
172 Ty Cobb REP 2.00 5.00
173 Sam Crawford REP .40 1.00
174 Johnny Evers REP .40 1.00
175 John McGraw REP .60 1.50
176 Eddie Plank REP 1.00 2.50
177 Tris Speaker REP 1.00 2.50
178 Joe Tinker REP .40 1.00
179 H.Wagner Orange REP 3.00 8.00
180 Cy Young REP 1.00 2.50
181 Javier Vazquez .20 .50
182A Mark Mulder Green Jsy .20 .50
182B Mark Mulder White Jsy .20 .50
183A Roger Clemens Blue Jsy 1.00 2.50
183B Roger Clemens Pinstripes 1.00 2.50
184 Kazuhisa Ishii RC .30 .75
185 Roberto Alomar .30 .75
186 Lance Berkman .20 .50
187A Adam Dunn Arms Folded .20 .50
187B Adam Dunn w/Bat .20 .50
188A Aramis Ramirez w/Bat .20 .50
188B Aramis Ramirez w/o Bat .20 .50
189 Chuck Knoblauch .20 .50
190 Nomar Garciaparra .75 2.00
191 Brad Penny .20 .50
192A Gary Sheffield w/Bat .20 .50
192B Gary Sheffield w/o Bat .20 .50
193 Alfonso Soriano .20 .50
194 Andruw Jones .30 .75
195A Randy Johnson Black Jsy .50 1.25
195B Randy Johnson Purple Jsy .50 1.25
196A Corey Patterson Blue Jsy .20 .50
196B Corey Patterson Pinstripes .20 .50
197 Milton Bradley .20 .50
198A J.Damon Blue Jsy Cap .30 .75
198B J.Damon Blue Jsy Hlmt .30 .75
198C J.Damon White Jsy .30 .75
199A Paul Lo Duca Blue Jsy .20 .50
199B Paul Lo Duca White Jsy .20 .50
200A Albert Pujols Red Jsy 1.00 2.50
200B Albert Pujols Running 1.00 2.50
200C Albert Pujols w/Bat 1.00 2.50
201 Scott Rolen .30 .75
202A J.D. Drew Running .20 .50
202B J.D. Drew w/Bat .20 .50
202C J.D. Drew White Jsy .20 .50
203 Vladimir Guerrero .50 1.25
204A Jason Giambi Blue Jsy .20 .50
204B Jason Giambi Grey Jsy .20 .50
204C Jason Giambi Pinstripes .20 .50
205A Moises Alou Grey Jsy .20 .50
205B Moises Alou Pinstripes .20 .50
206A Magglio Ordonez Signing .20 .50
206B Magglio Ordónez w/Bat .20 .50
207 Carlos Febles .20 .50
208 So Taguchi RC .30 .75
209A Rafael Palmeiro One Hand .30 .75
209B Rafael Palmeiro Two Hands .30 .75
210 David Wells .20 .50
211 Orlando Cabrera .20 .50
212 Sammy Sosa .50 1.25
213 Armando Benitez .20 .50
214 Wes Helms .20 .50
215A Mariano Rivera Arms Folded .50 1.25
215B Mariano Rivera Holding Ball .50 1.25
216 Jimmy Rollins .20 .50
217 Matt Lawton .20 .50
218A Shawn Green w/Bat .20 .50
218B Shawn Green w/o Bat .20 .50
219A Bernie Williams w/Bat .30 .75
219B Bernie Williams w/o Bat .30 .75
220A Bret Boone Blue Jsy .20 .50
220B Bret Boone White Jsy .20 .50
221A Alex Rodriguez Blue Jsy .60 1.50
221B Alex Rodriguez One Hand .60 1.50
221C Alex Rodriguez Two Hands .60 1.50
222 Roger Cedeno .20 .50
223 Marty Cordova .20 .50
224 Fred McGriff .30 .75
225A Chipper Jones Batting .50 1.25
225B Chipper Jones Running .50 1.25
226 Kerry Wood .20 .50
227A Larry Walker Grey Jsy .20 .50
227B Larry Walker Purple Jsy .20 .50
228 Robin Ventura .20 .50
229 Robert Fick .20 .50
230A Tino Martinez Black Glove .30 .75
230B Tino Martinez Throwing .30 .75
230C Tino Martinez w/Bat .30 .75
231 Ben Petrick .20 .50
232 Neifi Perez .20 .50
233 Pedro Martinez .30 .75
234A Brian Jordan Grey Jsy .20 .50
234B Brian Jordan White Jsy .20 .50
235 Freddy Garcia .20 .50
236A Derek Jeter Batting 1.25 3.00
236B Derek Jeter Blue Jsy 1.25 3.00
236C Derek Jeter Kneeling 1.25 3.00
237 Ben Grieve .20 .50
238A Barry Bonds Black Jsy 1.25 3.00
238B Barry Bonds w/Wrist Band 1.25 3.00
238C B.Bonds w/o Wrist Band 1.25 3.00
239 Luis Gonzalez .20 .50
240 Shane Halter .20 .50
241A Brian Giles Black Jsy .20 .50
241B Brian Giles Grey Jsy .20 .50
242 Bud Smith .20 .50
243 Richie Sexson .20 .50
244A Barry Zito Green Jsy .20 .50
244B Barry Zito White Jsy .20 .50
245 Eric Milton .20 .50
246A Ivan Rodriguez Blue Jsy .30 .75
246B Ivan Rodriguez Grey Jsy .30 .75
246C Ivan Rodriguez White Jsy .30 .75
247 Toby Hall .20 .50
248A Mike Piazza Black Jsy .75 2.00
248B Mike Piazza Grey Jsy .75 2.00
249 Ruben Sierra .20 .50
250A Tsuyoshi Shinjo Cap .20 .50
250B Tsuyoshi Shinjo Helmet .20 .50
251A Jermaine Dye Green Jsy .20 .50
251B Jermaine Dye White Jsy .20 .50
252 Roy Oswalt .20 .50
253 Todd Helton .30 .75
254 Adrian Beltre .20 .50
255 Doug Mientkiewicz .20 .50
256A Ichiro Suzuki Blue Jsy 1.00 2.50
256B Ichiro Suzuki w/Bat 1.00 2.50
256C Ichiro Suzuki White Jsy 1.00 2.50
257A C.C. Sabathia Blue Jsy .20 .50
257B C.C. Sabathia White Jsy .20 .50
258 Paul Konerko .20 .50
259 Ken Griffey Jr. 1.00 2.50
260A Jeromy Burnitz w/Bat .20 .50
260B Jeromy Burnitz w/o Bat .20 .50
261 Hank Blalock PROS .30 .75
262 Mark Prior PROS .30 .75
263 Josh Beckett PROS .20 .50
264 Carlos Pena PROS .20 .50
265 Sean Burroughs PROS .20 .50
266 Austin Kearns PROS .20 .50
267 Chin-Hui Tsao PROS .20 .50
268 Dewon Brazelton PROS .20 .50
269 J.D. Martin PROS .20 .50
270 Marlon Byrd PROS .20 .50
271 Joe Mauer FYP RC 5.00 12.00
272 Jason Botts FYP RC .20 .50
273 Mauricio Lara FYP RC .20 .50
274 Jonny Gomes FYP RC 1.00 2.50
275 Gavin Floyd FYP RC .40 1.00
276 Alex Requena FYP RC .20 .50
277 Jimmy Gobble FYP RC .20 .50
278 Chris Duffy FYP RC .20 .50
279 Colt Griffin FYP RC .20 .50
280 Ryan Church FYP RC .40 1.00
281 Beltran Pérez FYP RC .20 .50
282 Clint Nageotte FYP RC .30 .75
283 Justin Schuda FYP RC .20 .50
284 Scott Hairston FYP RC .30 .75
285 Mario Ramos FYP RC .20 .50
286A Tom Seaver White Sox RET .60 1.50
286B Tom Seaver Mets RET .60 1.50
287A Hank Aaron White Jsy RET 2.00 5.00
287B Hank Aaron Blue Jsy RET 2.00 5.00
288 Mike Schmidt RET 2.00 5.00
289A Robin Yount Blue Jsy RET 1.00 2.50
289B Robin Yount P'stripes RET 1.00 2.50
290 Joe Morgan RET .40 1.00
291 Frank Robinson RET .60 1.50
292A Reggie Jackson A's RET .60 1.50
292B Reggie Jackson Yanks RET .60 1.50
293A Nolan Ryan Astros RET 2.50 6.00
293B Nolan Ryan Rangers RET 2.50 6.00
294 Dave Winfield RET .40 1.00
295 Willie Mays RET 2.00 5.00
296 Brooks Robinson RET .60 1.50
297A Mark McGwire A's RET 2.50 6.00
297B Mark McGwire Cards RET 2.50 6.00
298 Honus Wagner RET 1.00 2.50
299A Sherry Magee REP .40 1.00
299B Sherry Magie UER REP .40 1.00
300 Frank Chance REP .40 1.00
301A Joe Doyle NY REP .40 1.00
301B Joe Doyle NY Nat'l REP .40 1.00
302 John McGraw REP .60 1.50
303 Jimmy Collins REP .40 1.00
304 Buck Herzog REP .40 1.00
305 Sam Crawford REP .40 1.00
306 Cy Young REP 1.00 2.50
307 Honus Wagner Blue REP 3.00 8.00
308A A.Rodriguez Blue Jsy SP 1.25 3.00
308B A.Rodriguez White Jsy .60 1.50
309 Vernon Wells .20 .50
310A B.Bonds w/Elbow Pad 1.25 3.00
310B B.Bonds w/o Elbow Pad SP 2.50 6.00
311 Vicente Padilla .20 .50
312A A.Soriano w/Wristband .20 .50
312B A.Soriano w/o Wristband SP .75 2.00
313 Mike Piazza .75 2.00
314 Jacque Jones .20 .50
315 Shawn Green SP .75 2.00
316 Paul Byrd .20 .50
317 Lance Berkman .20 .50
318 Larry Walker .20 .50
319 Ken Griffey Jr. SP 2.00 5.00
320 Shea Hillenbrand .20 .50
321 Jay Gibbons .20 .50
322 Andruw Jones .30 .75
323 Luis Gonzalez SP .75 2.00
324 Garret Anderson .20 .50
325 Roy Halladay .20 .50
326 Randy Winn .20 .50
327 Matt Morris .20 .50
328 Robb Nen .20 .50
329 Trevor Hoffman .20 .50
330 Kip Wells .20 .50
331 Orlando Hernandez .20 .50
332 Rey Ordonez .20 .50
333 Torii Hunter .20 .50
334 Geoff Jenkins .20 .50
335 Eric Karros .20 .50
336 Mike Lowell .20 .50
337 Nick Johnson .20 .50
338 Randall Simon .20 .50
339 Ellis Burks .20 .50
340A Sammy Sosa Blue Jsy SP 1.00 2.50
340B Sammy Sosa White Jsy .50 1.25
341 Pedro Martinez .30 .75
342 Junior Spivey .20 .50
343 Vinny Castilla .20 .50
344 Randy Johnson SP 1.00 2.50
345 Chipper Jones SP 1.00 2.50
346 Orlando Hudson .20 .50
347 Albert Pujols SP 2.00 5.00
348 Rondell White .20 .50
349 Vladimir Guerrero .50 1.25
350A Mark Prior Red SP .60 1.50
350B Mark Prior Yellow .30 .75
351 Eric Gagne .20 .50
352 Todd Zeile .20 .50
353 Manny Ramirez SP .75 2.00
354 Kevin Millwood .20 .50
355 Troy Percival .20 .50
356A Jason Giambi Batting SP .75 2.00
356B Jason Giambi Throwing .20 .50
357 Bartolo Colon .20 .50
358 Jeremy Giambi .20 .50
359 Jose Cruz Jr. .20 .50
360A I.Suzuki Blue Jsy SP 2.00 5.00
360B I.Suzuki White Jsy 1.00 2.50
361 Eddie Guardado .20 .50
362 Ivan Rodriguez .30 .75
363 Carl Crawford .20 .50
364 Jason Simontacchi RC .20 .50
365 Kenny Lofton .20 .50
366 Raul Mondesi .20 .50
367 A.J. Pierzynski .20 .50
368 Ugueth Urbina .20 .50
369 Rodrigo Lopez .20 .50
370A N.Garciaparra One Bat SP 1.50 4.00
370B N.Garciaparra Two Bats .75 2.00
371 Craig Counsell .20 .50
372 Barry Larkin .30 .75
373 Carlos Pena .20 .50
374 Luis Castillo .20 .50
375 Raul Ibanez .20 .50
376 Kazuhisa Ishii SP .75 2.00
377 Derek Lowe .20 .50
378 Curt Schilling .20 .50
379 Jim Thome Phillies .30 .75
380A Derek Jeter Blue SP 2.50 6.00
380B Derek Jeter Seats 1.25 3.00
381 Pat Burrell .20 .50
382 Jamie Moyer .20 .50
383 Eric Hinske .20 .50
384 Scott Rolen .30 .75
385 Miguel Tejada SP .75 2.00
386 Andy Pettitte .30 .75
387 Mike Lieberthal .20 .50
388 Al Leiter .20 .50
389 Todd Helton SP .75 2.00
390A Adam Dunn Bat SP .75 2.00
390B Adam Dunn Glove .20 .50
391 Cliff Floyd .20 .50
392 Tim Salmon .30 .75
393 Joe Torre MG .30 .75
394 Bobby Cox MG .20 .50
395 Tony LaRussa MG .20 .50
396 Art Howe MG .20 .50
397 Bob Brenly MG .20 .50
398 Ron Gardenhire MG .20 .50
399 Mike Cuddyer PROS .20 .50
400 Joe Mauer PROS 5.00 12.00
401 Mark Teixeira PROS .50 1.25
402 Hee Seop Choi PROS .20 .50
403 Angel Berroa PROS .20 .50
404 Jesse Foppert PROS RC .30 .75
405 Bobby Crosby PROS .50 1.25
406 Jose Reyes PROS .30 .75
407 Casey Kotchman PROS RC .40 1.00
408 Aaron Heilman PROS .20 .50
409 Adrian Gonzalez PROS .20 .50
410 Delwyn Young PROS RC .40 1.00
411 Brett Myers PROS .20 .50
412 Justin Huber PROS RC .30 .75
413 Drew Henson PROS .20 .50
414 Taggert Bozied PROS RC .30 .75
415 Dontrelle Willis PROS RC 1.25 3.00
416 Rocco Baldelli PROS .20 .50
417 Jason Stokes PROS RC .20 .50
418 Brandon Phillips PROS .20 .50
419 Jake Blalock FYP RC .20 .50
420 Micah Schilling FYP RC .40 1.00
421 Denard Span FYP RC .40 1.00
422A J.Loney Red FYP RC 1.50 4.00
422B J.Loney w/Sky FYP RC 1.50 4.00
423A W.Bankston Blue FYP RC .75 2.00
423B W.Bankston w/Sky FYP RC .75 2.00
424 Jeremy Hermida FYP RC 2.00 5.00
425 Curtis Granderson FYP RC 2.00 5.00
426A J.Pridie Red FYP RC .40 1.00
426B J.Pridie w/Sky FYP RC .40 1.00
427 Larry Broadway FYP RC .20 .50
428A K.Greene Green FYP RC 3.00 8.00
428B K.Greene Red FYP RC 3.00 8.00
429 Joey Votto FYP RC 25.00 60.00
430A B.Upton Grey FYP RC 2.00 5.00
430B B.Upton w/People FYP RC 2.00 5.00
431A S.Santos Gold FYP RC .40 1.00
431B S.Santos Grey FYP RC .40 1.00
432 Brian Dopirak FYP RC .40 1.00
433 Ozzie Smith RET SP 1.50 4.00
434 Wade Boggs RET SP 1.00 2.50
435 Yogi Berra RET SP 1.50 4.00
436 Al Kaline RET SP 1.50 4.00
437 Robin Roberts RET SP .75 2.00
438 Roberto Clemente RET SP 3.00 8.00
439 Gary Carter RET SP .75 2.00
440 Fergie Jenkins RET SP .75 2.00
441 Orlando Cepeda RET SP .75 2.00
442 Rod Carew RET SP 1.00 2.50
443 Harmon Killebrew RET SP 1.50 4.00
444 Duke Snider RET SP 1.00 2.50
445 Stan Musial RET SP 2.50 6.00
446 Hank Greenberg RET SP 1.50 4.00
447 Lou Brock RET SP 1.00 2.50
448 Jim Palmer RET .40 1.00
449 John McGraw REP .60 1.50
450 Mordecai Brown REP .40 1.00
451 Christy Mathewson REP .60 1.50
452 Sam Crawford REP .40 1.00
453 Bill O'Hara REP .40 1.00
454 Joe Tinker REP .40 1.00
455 Nap Lajoie REP .60 1.50
456 Honus Wagner Red REP 3.00 8.00

2002 Topps 206 Carolina Brights

*CAROLINA 181-270: 3X TO 8X BASIC
*CAROLINA RC's 181-270: 1X TO 2.5X
*CAROLINA 271-285: 1.25X TO 3X BASIC
*CAROLINA 286-307: 2X TO 5X BASIC
RANDOM INSERTS IN PACKS

2002 Topps 206 Cycle

*CYCLE 1-140: 5X TO 12X BASIC CARDS
*CYCLE 141-155: 1.25X TO 3X BASIC
*CYCLE 156-180: 3X TO 8X BASIC
RANDOM INSERTS IN PACKS

2002 Topps 206 Piedmont Black

*P'MONT.BLACK 181-270: 1.5X TO 4X BASIC
*P'MONT.BLACK RC's 181-270: .5X TO 1.2X
*P'MONT.BLACK 271-285: .6X TO 1.5X
*P'MONT.BLACK 286-307: 1X TO 2.5X
RANDOM INSERTS IN PACKS

2002 Topps 206 Piedmont Red

*P'MONT.RED 181-270: 3X TO 8X BASIC
*P'MONT.RED RC's 181-270: 1X TO 2.5X
*P'MONT.RED 271-285: 1.25X TO 3X
*P'MONT.RED 286-307: 2X TO 5X BASIC
RANDOM INSERTS IN PACKS

2002 Topps 206 Polar Bear

*POLAR 1-140/181-270/308-418: 1.25X TO 3X
*RC 1-140/181-270/308-418: .5X TO 1.2X
*FYP 141-155/271-285: .5X TO 1.2X
*SP 308-418: .6X TO 1.5X SP
*FYP 419-432: .5X TO 1.2X
*RT/RP 156-180/286-307/448-456: .75X TO 2X
*RET 443-447: .75X TO 2X
RANDOM INSERTS IN PACKS

2002 Topps 206 Sweet Caporal Black

*BLACK 308-418: 2.5X TO 6X BASIC
*BLACK SP 308-418: 1.25X TO 3X BASIC
*BLACK RC 308-418: 1X TO 2.5X BASIC
*BLACK 419-432: 1.25X TO 3X BASIC
*BLACK 433-447: .75X TO 2X BASIC
*BLACK 448-456: 1.5X TO 4X BASIC
RANDOM INSERTS IN PACKS

2002 Topps 206 Sweet Caporal Blue

*BLUE 308-418: 2X TO 5X BASIC
*BLUE SP 308-418: 1X TO 2.5X BASIC
*BLUE RC 308-418: .75X TO 2X BASIC
*BLUE 419-432: 1X TO 2.5X BASIC
*BLUE 433-447: .6X TO 1.5X BASIC
*BLUE 448-456: 1.25X TO 3X BASIC
RANDOM INSERTS IN PACKS

2002 Topps 206 Sweet Caporal Red

*RED 308-418: 1.5X TO 4X BASIC
*RED SP 308-418: .75X TO 2X BASIC
*RED RC 308-418: .6X TO 1.5X BASIC
*RED 419-432: .75X TO 2X BASIC
*RED 433-447: .5X TO 1.2X BASIC
*RED 448-456: 1X TO 2.5X BASIC
RANDOM INSERTS IN PACKS

2002 Topps 206 Tolstoi

*TOLSTOI 1-140: 1.5X TO 4X BASIC
*TOLSTOI 141-155: .4X TO 1X BASIC
*TOLSTOI 156-180: 1X TO 2.5X BASIC
RANDOM INSERTS IN PACKS
75% OF ALL TOLSTOI ARE BLACK BACKS

2002 Topps 206 Tolstoi Red

*TOLSTOI RED 1-140: 3X TO 8X BASIC
*TOLSTOI RED 141-155: .6X TO 1.5X BASIC
*TOLSTOI RED 156-180: 2X TO 5X BASIC
RANDOM INSERTS IN PACKS
25% OF ALL TOLSTOI ARE RED BACKS

2002 Topps 206 Uzit

*UZIT 308-418: 3X TO 8X BASIC
*UZIT SP 308-418: 1.5X TO 4X BASIC
*UZIT RC 308-418: 1.5X TO 4X BASIC
*UZIT 419-432: 1.5X TO 4X BASIC
*UZIT 433-447: 1X TO 2.5X BASIC
*UZIT 448-456: 2X TO 5X BASIC
RANDOM INSERTS IN PACKS

2002 Topps 206 Autographs

SER.1 GROUP A1 ODDS 1:1067
SER.1 GROUP B1 ODDS 1:1122
SER.1 GROUP C1 ODDS 1:532
SER.1 GROUP D1 ODDS 1:444
SER.1 GROUP E1 ODDS 1:532
SER.1 GROUP F1 ODDS 1:121
SER.1 GROUP G1 ODDS 1:118
SER.1 OVERALL AUTO ODDS 1:41
SER.2 GROUP A2 ODDS 1:511
SER.2 GROUP B2 ODDS 1:893
SER.2 GROUP C2 ODDS 1:1557
SER.2 GROUP D2 ODDS 1:106
SER.2 GROUP E2 ODDS 1:638
SER.2 GROUP F2 ODDS 1:596
SER.2 GROUP G2 ODDS 1:526
SER.2 OVERALL AUTO ODDS 1:55
SER.3 GROUP A3 ODDS 1:810
SER.3 GROUP B3 ODDS 1:442
SER.3 GROUP C3 ODDS 1:411
SER.3 GROUP D3 ODDS 1:393
SER.3 GROUP E3 ODDS 1:393
SER.3 GROUP F3 ODDS 1:384
SER.3 GROUP G3 ODDS 1:383
AP Albert Pujols A2 125.00 300.00
AR Alex Rodriguez A1 30.00 80.00
BB Barry Bonds A1 100.00 250.00
BG Brian Giles G1 6.00 15.00
BI Brandon Inge D1 6.00 15.00
BS Ben Sheets E2 6.00 15.00
BSM Bud Smith B2 6.00 15.00
BZ Barry Zito D1 4.00 10.00
CG Cristian Guzman G1 4.00 10.00
CT Chris Tritle G2 4.00 10.00
DB Dewon Brazelton D2 4.00 10.00
DE David Eckstein G3 6.00 15.00
DH Drew Henson D3 4.00 10.00
EC Eric Chavez A2 10.00 25.00
FJ Forrest Johnson F1 4.00 10.00
FL Felipe Lopez C1 4.00 10.00
GF Gavin Floyd D2 4.00 10.00
GN Greg Nash F1 4.00 10.00
HB Hank Blalock D2 4.00 10.00
JC Jose Cruz Jr. A3 4.00 10.00
JD Johnny Damon Sox B2 10.00 25.00
JDM J.D. Martin D2 4.00 10.00
JE Jim Edmonds C1 15.00 40.00
JJ Jorge Julio F1 4.00 10.00
JM Joe Mauer D2 25.00 60.00
JR Jimmy Rollins G1 10.00 25.00
JV Jose Vidro B3 6.00 15.00
KI Kazuhisa Ishii A2 15.00 40.00
LB Lance Berkman A2 20.00 50.00
LG Luis Gonzalez C2 6.00 15.00
MA Moises Alou A2 10.00 25.00
MB Milton Bradley C3 6.00 15.00
MB Marlon Byrd D2 4.00 10.00
ML Mike Lamb F3 4.00 10.00
MO Magglio Ordonez E1 6.00 15.00
MP Mark Prior D2 6.00 15.00
MT Marcus Thames E3 4.00 10.00
RC Roger Clemens B1 30.00 60.00
RJ Ryan Jamison F1 4.00 10.00
RS Richie Sexson F2 6.00 15.00
SR Scott Rolen A2 12.00 30.00
ST So Taguchi A2 15.00 40.00

2002 Topps 206 Relics

SER.1 BAT GROUP A1 ODDS 1:166
SER.1 BAT GROUP B1 ODDS 1:1780
SER.2 BAT GROUP A2 ODDS 1:35,217
SER.2 BAT GROUP B2 ODDS 1:8991
SER.2 BAT GROUP C2 ODDS 1:2097
SER.2 BAT GROUP D2 ODDS 1:75
SER.2 BAT GROUP E2 ODDS 1:1377
SER.2 BAT GROUP F2 ODDS 1:893
SER.2 BAT GROUP G2 ODDS 1:248
SER.2 BAT GROUP H2 ODDS 1:319
SER.2 BAT GROUP I2 ODDS 1:447
SER.2 BAT OVERALL ODDS 1:40
SER.3 BAT GROUP A3 ODDS 1:15,316
SER.3 BAT GROUP B3 ODDS 1:390
SER.3 BAT GROUP C3 ODDS 1:370
SER.3 BAT GROUP D3 ODDS 1:34
SER.3 BAT GROUP E3 ODDS 1:187
SER.3 BAT GROUP F3 ODDS 1:185
SER.1 UNI GROUP A1 ODDS 1:14
SER.1 UNI GROUP B1 ODDS 1:74
SER.2 UNI GROUP A2 ODDS 1:372
SER.2 UNI GROUP B2 ODDS 1:27
SER.2 UNI GROUP C2 ODDS 1:62
SER.2 UNI GROUP D2 ODDS 1:447
SER.2 UNI OVERALL ODDS 1:18
SER.3 UNI GROUP A3 ODDS 1:247
SER.3 UNI GROUP B3 ODDS 1:185
SER.3 UNI GROUP C3 ODDS 1:62
SER.3 UNI GROUP D3 ODDS 1:187
SER.3 UNI GROUP E3 ODDS 1:27
SER.3 UNI GROUP F3 ODDS 1:176
SER.1 OVERALL RELICS ODDS 1:11
SER.2 OVERALL RELICS ODDS 1:12
COBB PRINT RUN PROVIDED BY TOPPS
WAGNER PRINT RUN PROVIDED BY TOPPS
SER.1 RELICS HAVE LIGHT YELLOW FRAMES
SER.2 RELICS HAVE LIGHT BLUE FRAMES
SER.3 RELICS HAVE LIGHT PINK FRAMES
AB A.J. Burnett Jsy B2 3.00 8.00
AD2 Adam Dunn Bat D2 6.00 15.00
AD3 Adam Dunn Bat C3 6.00 15.00
AJ1 Andruw Jones Jsy A1 4.00 10.00
AJ2 Andruw Jones Jsy C2 4.00 10.00
AJ3 Andruw Jones Uni E3 4.00 10.00
AP1 Albert Pujols Bat A1 10.00 25.00
AP2 Albert Pujols Jsy B2 10.00 25.00
AP3 Albert Pujols Bat D3 10.00 25.00
ARA Aramis Ramirez Bat D2 6.00 15.00
AR2 Alex Rodriguez Bat D2 8.00 20.00
AR3 Alex Rodriguez Bat D3 6.00 15.00
AS1 Alfonso Soriano Bat A1 6.00 15.00
AS2 Alfonso Soriano Bat I2 3.00 8.00
AS3 Alfonso Soriano Bat D3 3.00 8.00
BB1 Barry Bonds Jsy A1 10.00 25.00
BB2 Barry Bonds Uni C2 10.00 25.00
BD Brandon Duckworth Jsy B2 3.00 8.00
BH Buck Herzog Bat G2 12.00 30.00
BL Barry Larkin Jsy B2 4.00 10.00
BP Brad Penny Jsy B2 3.00 8.00
BW1 Bernie Williams Jsy A1 4.00 10.00
BW2 Bernie Williams Jsy B2 4.00 10.00
BW3 Bernie Williams Uni A3 6.00 15.00
BZ1 Barry Zito Jsy A1 3.00 8.00
BZ3 Barry Zito Uni C3 3.00 8.00
CB Craig Biggio Jsy B1 4.00 10.00
CD Carlos Delgado Jsy A1 3.00 8.00
CF1 Cliff Floyd Jsy A1 3.00 8.00
CF2 Cliff Floyd Jsy B2 3.00 8.00
CG Cristian Guzman Jsy B2 3.00 8.00
CJ1 Chipper Jones Jsy A1 6.00 15.00
CJ2 Chipper Jones Jsy B2 6.00 15.00
CJ3 Chipper Jones Uni B3 6.00 15.00
CL Carlos Lee Jsy A1 3.00 8.00
CP Corey Patterson Bat F3 3.00 6.00
CS2 Curt Schilling Bat D2 6.00 15.00
CS3 Curt Schilling Bat D3 3.00 8.00
DE Darin Erstad Jsy B2 3.00 8.00
DM Doug Mientkiewicz Uni D3 3.00 8.00
EC2 Eric Chavez Bat H2 3.00 8.00
EC3 Eric Chavez Uni E3 3.00 8.00
EM1 Edgar Martinez Jsy A1 4.00 10.00
EM2 Edgar Martinez Jsy B2 4.00 10.00
FM Fred McGriff Bat D2 6.00 15.00
FT1 Frank Thomas Jsy A1 6.00 15.00
FT2 Frank Thomas Jsy B2 6.00 15.00
FT3 Frank Thomas Uni C3 6.00 15.00
GM1 Greg Maddux Jsy A1 6.00 15.00
GM2 Greg Maddux Jsy C2 6.00 15.00
GS2 Gary Sheffield Bat D2 6.00 15.00
GS3 Gary Sheffield Bat B3 6.00 15.00
HW1 H.Wag Oran Bat B1/300 * 300.00 500.00
IR1 Ivan Rodriguez Jsy A1 4.00 10.00
IR2 Ivan Rodriguez Uni A2 4.00 10.00
IR3 Ivan Rodriguez Bat D3 4.00 10.00
JB1 Jeff Bagwell Jsy A1 4.00 10.00
JB2 Jeff Bagwell Uni C2 4.00 10.00
JB3 Jeff Bagwell Bat D3 4.00 10.00
JD Johnny Damon Sox Bat D2 4.00 10.00
JE1 Jim Edmonds Jsy A1 3.00 8.00
JE3 Jim Edmonds Uni F3 3.00 8.00

JG Juan Gonzalez Bat D2 6.00 15.00
JH Josh Hamilton 8.00 20.00
JJ Jason Jennings Jsy B2 3.00 8.00
JK Jeff Kent Uni B2 3.00 8.00
JO1 John Olerud Jsy A1 3.00 8.00
JO2 John Olerud Jsy B2 3.00 8.00
JT Joe Tinker Bat G2 25.00 60.00
JW Jeff Weaver Jsy A1 3.00 8.00
KB Kevin Brown Jsy B2 3.00 8.00
KL Kenny Lofton Jsy B1 3.00 8.00
LG Luis Gonzalez Uni E3 3.00 8.00
LW1 Larry Walker Jsy A1 3.00 8.00
LW2 Larry Walker Jsy B2 3.00 8.00
MC Mike Cameron Jsy A1 3.00 8.00
MG Mark Grace Bat D2 6.00 15.00
MO Magglio Ordonez Jsy A1 3.00 8.00
MP1 Mike Piazza Jsy A1 6.00 15.00
MP2 Mike Piazza Uni C2 w/Bat 6.00 15.00
MP3 Mike Piazza Uni C3 Catching gear 6.00 15.00
MT2 Miguel Tejada Bat H2 3.00 8.00
MT3 Miguel Tejada Uni E3 3.00 8.00
MV2 Mo Vaughn Bat D2 6.00 15.00
MV3 Mo Vaughn Uni E3 3.00 8.00
MW Matt Williams Jsy B2 3.00 8.00
NG Nomar Garciaparra Bat C3 8.00 20.00
NJ Nick Johnson Bat E3 3.00 8.00
PB Pat Burrell Bat B3 6.00 15.00
PM Pedro Martinez Uni A3 6.00 15.00
PO Paul O'Neill Jsy A1 4.00 10.00
PW Preston Wilson Jsy B2 3.00 8.00
RA1 Roberto Alomar Jsy A1 4.00 10.00
RA2 Roberto Alomar Bat D2 6.00 15.00
RA3 Roberto Alomar Bat D3 4.00 10.00
RD Ryan Dempster Jsy B2 3.00 8.00
RH2 Rickey Henderson Bat D2 8.00 20.00
RH3 Rickey Henderson Bat D3 6.00 15.00
RJ1 Randy Johnson Jsy A1 6.00 15.00
RJ2 Randy Johnson Jsy C2 6.00 15.00
RJ3 Randy Johnson Uni A3 8.00 20.00
RP2 Rafael Palmeiro Jsy B2 4.00 10.00
RP3 Rafael Palmeiro Uni B3 4.00 10.00
RV Robin Ventura Bat D2 6.00 15.00
SB Sean Burroughs Bat D2 4.00 10.00
SC Sam Crawford Bat A1 20.00 50.00
SCR Sam Crawford Bat C2 20.00 50.00
SG1 Shawn Green Jsy A1 3.00 8.00
SG2 Shawn Green Jsy C2 3.00 8.00
SR Scott Rolen Bat D3 4.00 10.00
SS Shannon Stewart Bat A1 6.00 15.00
TC Ty Cobb Bat B2/100 * 150.00 300.00
TL Travis Lee Bat D2 4.00 10.00
TM1 Tino Martinez Jsy A1 4.00 10.00
TM2 Tino Martinez Bat D2 6.00 15.00
WB Wilson Betemit Bat D3 3.00 8.00
BBO1 Bret Boone Jsy B1 3.00 8.00
BBO2 Bret Boone Jsy D2 3.00 8.00
CHP Chan Ho Park Bat A1 6.00 15.00
JCA Jose Canseco Bat A1 6.00 15.00
JCO Jimmy Collins Bat F2 UER 25.00 60.00
JEV1 Johnny Evers Jsy A1 20.00 50.00
JEV Johnny Evers Bat G2 20.00 50.00
JMA Joe Mays Jsy B2 3.00 8.00
JMC1 John McGraw Bat A1 30.00 60.00
JMC2 John McGraw Bat E2 30.00 60.00
JTH1 Jim Thome Jsy A1 4.00 10.00
JTH2 Jim Thome Bat D2 6.00 15.00
JTH3 Jim Thome Uni C3 4.00 10.00
TGL1 Tom Glavine Jsy A1 4.00 10.00
TGL2 Tom Glavine Jsy A2 4.00 10.00
TGW Tony Gwynn Jsy A1 6.00 15.00
TGW Tony Gwynn Jsy B2 6.00 15.00
TGW Tony Gwynn Uni E3 6.00 15.00
THA Toby Hall Jsy B2 3.00 8.00
THE1 Todd Helton Jsy A1 4.00 10.00
THE2 Todd Helton Jsy C2 4.00 10.00
THE3 Todd Helton Uni E3 4.00 10.00
TSH2 Tsuyoshi Shinjo Bat D2 6.00 15.00
TSH3 Tsuyoshi Shinjo Bat D3 3.00 8.00
TSP Tris Speaker Bat A1 40.00 80.00
JAGI Jason Giambi Jsy A1 3.00 8.00
JEGI Jeremy Giambi Jsy A1 3.00 8.00

2002 Topps 206 Team 206 Series 1

COMPLETE SET (20) 6.00 15.00
ONE TEAM 206 OR AUTO/RELIC PER PACK
T2061 Barry Bonds 1.00 2.50
T2062 Ivan Rodriguez .25 .60
T2063 Luis Gonzalez .20 .50
T2064 Jason Giambi Yankees .20 .50
T2065 Pedro Martinez .25 .60
T2066 Larry Walker .20 .50
T2067 Bob Abreu .20 .50
T2068 Derek Jeter 1.00 2.50
T2069 Bret Boone .20 .50
T20610 Mike Piazza .60 1.50
T20611 Alex Rodriguez .50 1.50
T20612 Roger Clemens .75 2.00
T20613 Albert Pujols .75 2.00
T20614 Randy Johnson .40 1.00
T20615 Sammy Sosa .40 1.00
T20616 Cristian Guzman .20 .50
T20617 Shawn Green .20 .50
T20618 Curt Schilling .20 .50
T20619 Ichiro Suzuki .75 2.00
T20620 Chipper Jones .40 1.00

2002 Topps 206 Team 206 Series 2

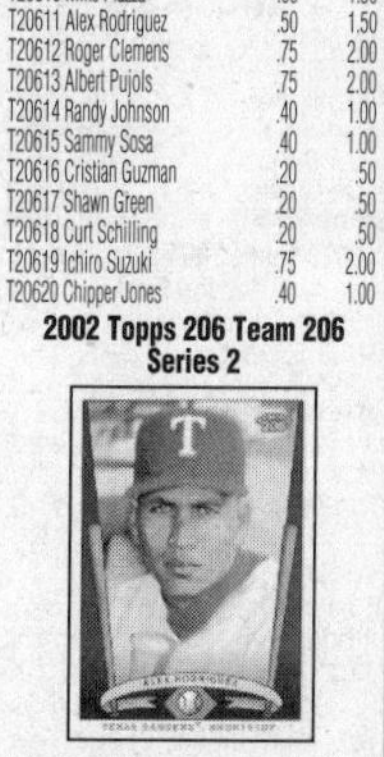

COMPLETE SET (25) 6.00 15.00
ONE TEAM 206 OR AUTO/RELIC PER PACK
T2061 Alex Rodriguez .50 1.50
T2062 Sammy Sosa .40 1.00
T2063 Jason Giambi .20 .50
T2064 Nomar Garciaparra .60 1.50
T2065 Ichiro Suzuki .75 2.00
T2066 Chipper Jones .40 1.00
T2067 Derek Jeter 1.00 2.50
T2068 Barry Bonds 1.00 2.50
T2069 Mike Piazza .60 1.50
T20610 Randy Johnson .40 1.00
T20611 Shawn Green .20 .50
T20612 Todd Helton .25 .60
T20613 Luis Gonzalez .20 .50
T20614 Albert Pujols .75 2.00
T20615 Curt Schilling .20 .50
T20616 Scott Rolen .25 .60
T20617 Ivan Rodriguez .25 .60
T20618 Roberto Alomar .25 .60
T20619 Cristian Guzman .20 .50
T20620 Bret Boone .20 .50
T20621 Barry Zito .20 .50
T20622 Larry Walker .20 .50
T20623 Eric Chavez .20 .50
T20624 Roger Clemens .75 2.00
T20625 Pedro Martinez .25 .60

2002 Topps 206 Team 206 Series 3

COMPLETE SET (30) 6.00 15.00
ONE TEAM 206 OR AUTO/RELIC PER PACK
1 Ichiro Suzuki .75 2.00
2 Kazuhisa Ishii .25 .60
3 Alex Rodriguez .50 1.50
4 Mark Prior .25 .60
5 Derek Jeter 1.00 2.50
6 Sammy Sosa .40 1.00
7 Nomar Garciaparra .60 1.50
8 Mike Piazza .60 1.50
9 Jason Giambi .20 .50
10 Vladimir Guerrero .40 1.00
11 Curt Schilling .20 .50
12 Jim Thome Phillies .25 .60
13 Adam Dunn .20 .50
14 Albert Pujols .75 2.00
15 Pat Burrell .20 .50
16 Chipper Jones .40 1.00
17 Randy Johnson .40 1.00
18 Todd Helton .25 .60
19 Luis Gonzalez .20 .50
20 Alfonso Soriano .20 .50
21 Shawn Green .20 .50
22 Pedro Martinez .25 .60
23 Lance Berkman .20 .50
24 Ivan Rodriguez .25 .60
25 Larry Walker .20 .50
26 Andruw Jones .25 .60
27 Ken Griffey Jr. .75 2.00
28 Manny Ramirez .25 .60
29 Barry Bonds 1.00 2.50
30 Miguel Tejada .20 .50

2009 Topps 206

COMPLETE SET (350) 100.00 200.00
COMP.SET w/o SP's (300) 20.00 50.00
COMMON CARD (1-300) .15 .40
COMMON ROOKIE (1-300) .30 .75
COMMON SP VAR (1-300) .75 2.00
SP VAR ODDS 1:4 HOBBY
SP VAR HAVE NO CARD NUMBERS
OVERALL PLATE ODDS 1:285 HOBBY
PLATE PRINT RUN 1 SET PER COLOR
BLACK-CYAN-MAGENTA-YELLOW ISSUED
NO PLATE PRICING DUE TO SCARCITY
1a Ryan Howard .30 .75
1b Ryan Howard VAR SP 1.50 4.00
2 Erick Aybar .15 .40
3 Carlos Quentin .15 .40
4 Juan Pierre .15 .40
5 Chris Young .15 .40
6 John Mayberry (RC) .50 1.25
7 Rocco Baldelli .15 .40
8 Dan Uggla .15 .40
9 Matt Holliday .40 1.00
10a Andrew McCutchen (RC) 1.50 4.00
10b McCutchen VAR SP 4.00 10.00
11 Adam Jones .25 .60
12 Ian Stewart .15 .40
13 Bobby Parnell RC .50 1.25
14 Scott Rolen .25 .60
15 Max Scherzer .40 1.00
16 Jonny Gomes .15 .40
17 Jonathan Broxton .15 .40
18 Kenji Johjima .25 .60
19a Mel Ott .40 1.00
19b Mel Ott VAR SP 2.00 5.00
20 Geovany Soto .25 .60
21 Ivan Rodriguez .25 .60
22 Josh Reddick RC .50 1.25
23a Koji Uehara RC .75 2.00
23b Koji Uehara VAR SP 2.00 5.00
24 David Ortiz .40 1.00
25 Magglio Ordonez .25 .60
26 Chien-Ming Wang .25 .60
27 Andrew Carpenter RC .50 1.25
28a Kenshin Kawakami RC .50 1.25
28b Kenshin Kawakami VAR SP 1.25 3.00
29 Kerry Wood .15 .40
30 Justin Morneau .25 .60
31 Andy Sonnanstine .15 .40
32 Stephen Drew .15 .40
33 Jay Bruce .25 .60
34 Andre Ethier .25 .60
35 Erik Bedard .15 .40
36a Jimmie Foxx .40 1.00
36b Jimmie Foxx VAR SP 2.00 5.00
37 Rich Harden .15 .40
38 Hunter Pence .25 .60
39 Jayson Werth .25 .60
40 Daniel Schlereth RC .30 .75
41a David Hernandez RC .30 .75
41b David Hernandez VAR SP .75 2.00
42 Jason Marquis .15 .40
43 Hideki Matsui .40 1.00
44a Michael Bowden (RC) .30 .75
44b Michael Bowden VAR SP .75 2.00
45 Derek Lowe .15 .40
46 Cliff Lee .25 .60
47 Rickie Weeks .15 .40
48 Carlos Pena .25 .60
49a Walter Johnson .40 1.00
49b Walter Johnson VAR SP 2.00 5.00
50 Joe Crede .25 .60
51 Zack Greinke .40 1.00
52 Kevin Kouzmanoff .15 .40
53 Wilkin Ramirez RC .30 .75
54 Jonathan Papelbon .25 .60
55 Chris Volstad .15 .40
56 Robinson Cano .25 .60
57a Matt LaPorta RC .50 1.25
57b Matt LaPorta VAR SP 1.25 3.00
58 Brian Roberts .15 .40
59 David Huff RC .30 .75
60 Daniel Murphy RC 1.25 3.00
61a Derek Holland RC .50 1.25
61b Derek Holland VAR SP 1.25 3.00
62 Dan Haren .15 .40
63 Bronson Arroyo .15 .40
64 Corey Hart .15 .40
65 Troy Glaus .15 .40
66a Ty Cobb .60 1.50
66b Ty Cobb VAR SP 3.00 8.00
67 Alfonso Soriano .25 .60
68 Luke Hochevar .15 .40
69 Jimmy Rollins .25 .60
70 Matt Tuiasosopo (RC) .30 .75
71a Dustin Pedroia .40 1.00
71b Dustin Pedroia VAR SP 2.00 5.00
72a Rick Porcello RC 1.00 2.50
72b Rick Porcello VAR SP 2.50 6.00
73 Joba Chamberlain .15 .40
74 Greg Golson (RC) .30 .75
75 Jair Jurrjens .15 .40
76 Trevor Crowe RC .30 .75
77 Joe Nathan .15 .40
78 Hank Blalock .15 .40
79 Bobby Abreu .15 .40
80 Jim Thome .25 .60
81 Orlando Hudson .15 .40
82 Randy Johnson .40 1.00
83a Rogers Hornsby .25 .60
83b Rogers Hornsby VAR SP 1.25 3.00
84 Mike Fontenot .15 .40
85 Kazuo Matsui .15 .40
86 Kurt Suzuki .15 .40
87a Ryan Perry RC .75 2.00
87b Ryan Perry VAR SP 2.00 5.00
88 Melvin Mora .15 .40
89 Ubaldo Jimenez .15 .40
90a Alex Rodriguez .50 1.25
90b Alex Rodriguez VAR SP 2.50 6.00
91 John Lannan .15 .40
92 Javier Vazquez .15 .40
93 Victor Martinez .25 .60
94 Francisco Liriano .15 .40
95 Matt Garza .15 .40
96 Vladimir Guerrero .25 .60
97 Gavin Floyd .15 .40
98 Matt Kemp .30 .75
99 Adrian Gonzalez .30 .75
100 Ramiro Pena RC .50 1.25
101 J.D. Drew .15 .40
102a Hanley Ramirez .25 .60
102b Hanley Ramirez VAR SP 1.25 3.00
103a Andrew Bailey RC .75 2.00
103b Andrew Bailey VAR SP 2.00 5.00
104 Mark Melancon RC .30 .75
105 Lou Montanez .15 .40
106 Jeff Francis .15 .40
107a Fernando Martinez RC .75 2.00
107b Fernando Martinez VAR SP 2.00 5.00
108 Alex Rios .15 .40
109 Justin Upton .25 .60
110 Chris Dickerson .15 .40
111 Mike Cameron .15 .40
112 Felix Hernandez .25 .60
113a Tris Speaker .25 .60
113b Tris Speaker VAR SP 1.25 3.00
114 Carlos Zambrano .25 .60
115 Michael Bourn .15 .40
116a Chase Utley .25 .60
116b Chase Utley VAR SP 1.25 3.00
117 Jordan Schafer (RC) .50 1.25
118 Kevin Youkilis .15 .40
119 Curtis Granderson .30 .75
120a Derek Jeter 1.00 2.50
120b Derek Jeter VAR SP 5.00 12.00
121 Francisco Cervelli RC .75 2.00
122 Nick Markakis .30 .75
123 Brad Hawpe .15 .40
124 Johan Santana .25 .60
125 Adam Lind .15 .40
126 Brandon Webb .25 .60
127 Javier Valentin .15 .40
128 James Loney .15 .40
129a Ichiro Suzuki .50 1.25
129b Ichiro Suzuki VAR SP 2.50 6.00
130a Honus Wagner .40 1.00
130b Honus Wagner VAR SP 2.00 5.00
131 Kosuke Fukudome .25 .60
132 Carlos Lee .15 .40
133 Shane Victorino .15 .40
134 Travis Snider RC .50 1.25
135 Jon Lester .25 .60
136 Edgar Renteria .15 .40
137a Mark Teixeira .25 .60
137b Mark Teixeira VAR SP 1.25 3.00
138a Elvis Andrus RC .75 2.00
138b Elvis Andrus VAR SP 2.00 5.00
139 Chipper Jones .40 1.00
140 Jeremy Sowers .15 .40
141 Prince Fielder .25 .60
142a Evan Longoria .25 .60
142b Evan Longoria VAR SP 1.25 3.00
143a Cy Young .40 1.00
143b Cy Young VAR SP 2.00 5.00
144 Neftali Feliz RC .50 1.25
145 David DeJesus .15 .40
146 Tony Gwynn Jr. .15 .40
147 Fernando Perez (RC) .30 .75
148 Josh Beckett .15 .40
149 Josh Johnson .25 .60
150 A.J. Burnett .15 .40
151 Wade LeBlanc RC .50 1.25
152 Luke Scott .15 .40
153 Dexter Fowler (RC) .50 1.25
154a Mickey Mantle 1.25 3.00
154b Mickey Mantle VAR SP 6.00 15.00
155 Adam Dunn .25 .60
156 Brian McCann .25 .60
157 Brandon Phillips .15 .40
158 Mat Gamel RC .75 2.00
159 Rick Ankiel .15 .40
160a Thurman Munson .40 1.00
160b Thurman Munson VAR SP 2.00 5.00
161 Jermaine Dye .15 .40
162 Billy Butler .15 .40
163 Cole Hamels .30 .75
164 Luis Valbuena RC .50 1.25
165 John Smoltz .40 1.00
166 Joel Zumaya .15 .40
167 Nick Swisher .25 .60
168 Aaron Cunningham RC .30 .75
169 Carlos Beltran .25 .60
170 Jhonny Peralta .15 .40
171a David Wright .30 .75
171b David Wright VAR SP 1.50 4.00
172 Michael Young .15 .40
173 Howie Kendrick .15 .40
174a Gordon Beckham RC .50 1.25
174b Gordon Beckham VAR SP 1.25 3.00
175a Manny Ramirez .40 1.00
175b Manny Ramirez VAR SP 2.00 5.00
176 Barry Zito .25 .60
177a Pee Wee Reese .25 .60
177b Pee Wee Reese VAR SP 1.25 3.00
178 Bobby Scales RC .50 1.25
179 Roy Oswalt .25 .60
180 Jack Cust .15 .40
181a David Price RC .60 1.50
181b David Price VAR SP 1.50 4.00
182 Daisuke Matsuzaka .25 .60
183 Jeremy Bonderman .15 .40
184 Jorge Posada .25 .60
185 Brian Duensing RC .50 1.25
186 Yunel Escobar .15 .40
187 Travis Hafner .15 .40
188 Glen Perkins .15 .40
189 Scott Kazmir .15 .40
190 Jon Garland .15 .40
191 Paul Konerko .25 .60
192 Rafael Furcal .15 .40
193 Jake Peavy .15 .40
194 George Kottaras (RC) .30 .75
195 Jacoby Ellsbury .30 .75
196 Jeremy Hermida .15 .40
197 Brett Anderson RC .50 1.25
198 Brad Nelson (RC) .30 .75
199 Nolan Reimold (RC) .30 .75
200 Todd Helton .25 .60
201 John Maine .15 .40
202 Vernon Wells .15 .40
203 Chris Young .15 .40
204 Johnny Cueto .25 .60
205 J.J. Hardy .15 .40
206 Yadier Molina .50 1.25
207a Jackie Robinson .40 1.00
207b Jackie Robinson VAR SP 2.00 5.00
208 Derrek Lee .15 .40
209 Gil Meche .15 .40
210 Pat Burrell .15 .40
211 Jordan Zimmermann RC .75 2.00
212 Jason Bay .25 .60
213 Chris Coghlan RC .75 2.00
214 Jason Giambi .15 .40
215 Vin Mazzaro RC .30 .75
216 Ryan Freel .15 .40
217 Garrett Atkins .15 .40
218 Francisco Rodriguez .25 .60
219 Roy Halladay .25 .60
220 Conor Jackson .15 .40
221 Joey Votto .40 1.00
222 Clayton Kershaw .60 1.50
223 Ken Griffey Jr. .75 2.00
224a Roy Campanella .40 1.00
224b Roy Campanella VAR SP 2.00 5.00
225 Jeff Samardzija .25 .60
226 Lance Berkman .25 .60
227 Brad Lidge .15 .40
228 Will Venable RC .30 .75
229 Mike Lowell .15 .40
230 Miguel Cabrera .40 1.00
231a CC Sabathia .25 .60
231b CC Sabathia VAR SP 1.25 3.00
232 Daniel Bard RC .30 .75
233 Garret Anderson .15 .40
234a Grady Sizemore .25 .60
234b Grady Sizemore VAR SP 1.25 3.00
235 Yovani Gallardo .15 .40
236 James Shields .15 .40
237a Christy Mathewson .40 1.00
237b Christy Mathewson VAR SP 2.00 5.00
238 Mark Buehrle .25 .60
239 Joakim Soria .15 .40
240 Kyle Blanks RC .50 1.25
241 Kris Medlen RC .75 2.00
242 Milton Bradley .15 .40
243 Miguel Tejada .25 .60
244 Daric Barton .15 .40
245 Ricky Romero (RC) .50 1.25
246 Felix Pie .15 .40
247 Huston Street .15 .40
248 Mariano Rivera .50 1.25
249 Ryan Zimmerman .25 .60
250 Tim Hudson .25 .60
251 Francisco Cordero .15 .40
252 Ryan Braun .25 .60
253 Akinori Iwamura .15 .40
254a Johnny Mize .25 .60
254b Johnny Mize VAR SP 1.25 3.00
255 A.J. Pierzynski .15 .40
256 Alex Gordon .25 .60
257 Nate McLouth .15 .40
258 Aaron Bates RC .30 .75
259 Jason Varitek 2.00 5.00
260 Andrew Miller .25 .60
261 Johnny Damon .25 .60
262a Tommy Hanson RC .75 2.00
262b Tommy Hanson VAR SP 2.00 5.00
263 Aubrey Huff .15 .40
264 Ryan Garko .15 .40
265 Carlos Delgado .15 .40
266 Josh Hamilton .25 .60
267 Jered Weaver .25 .60
268a Aaron Poreda RC .30 .75
268b Aaron Poreda VAR SP .75 2.00
269 Russell Martin .15 .40
270 Matt Cain .25 .60
271a Lou Gehrig .75 2.00
271b Lou Gehrig VAR SP 4.00 10.00
272 Aramis Ramirez .15 .40
273 Brian Bannister .15 .40
274a Colby Rasmus (RC) .50 1.25
274b Colby Rasmus VAR SP 1.25 3.00
275 Justin Masterson .15 .40
276 Justin Verlander .40 1.00
277 Andy Pettitte .25 .60
278 David Freese RC 1.00 2.50
279 Casey Kotchman .15 .40
280 Fausto Carmona .15 .40
281 Joe Mauer .30 .75
282 Ian Kinsler .25 .60
283 Joe Saunders .15 .40
284 Alexei Ramirez .25 .60
285 Chad Billingsley .25 .60
286a Tim Lincecum .25 .60
286b Tim Lincecum VAR SP 1.25 3.00
287a Babe Ruth 1.00 2.50
287b Babe Ruth VAR SP 5.00 12.00
288 Ryan Theriot .15 .40
289 Josh Whitesell RC .50 1.25
290 Trevor Cahill RC .40 1.00
291 Jonathan Niese RC .50 1.25
292 Jeremy Guthrie .15 .40
293 Troy Tulowitzki .40 1.00
294 Jose Reyes .25 .60
295 Cristian Guzman .15 .40
296 Mat Latos RC 1.00 2.50
297 Micah Owings .15 .40
298 Trevor Hoffman .25 .60
299a Albert Pujols .50 1.25
299b Albert Pujols VAR SP 2.50 6.00
300a George Sisler .25 .60
300b George Sisler VAR SP 1.25 3.00

2009 Topps 206 Bronze

*BRONZE VET: .6X TO 1.5X BASIC
*BRONZE RC: .5X TO 1.2X BASIC RC
APPX.ODDS 1 PER HOBBY PACK

2009 Topps 206 Mini Piedmont

*PIEDMONT VET: .75X TO 2X BASIC
*PIEDMONT RC: .6X TO 1.5X BASIC RC
*PIEDMONT VAR: .5X TO 1.2X BASIC VAR
OVERALL ONE MINI PER PACK
VARIATION ODDS 1:20 HOBBY
OVERALL PLATE ODDS 1:332 HOBBY
PLATE PRINT RUN 1 SET PER COLOR
BLACK-CYAN-MAGENTA-YELLOW ISSUED
NO PLATE PRICING DUE TO SCARCITY

2009 Topps 206 Mini Carolina Brights

STATED ODDS 1:1331 HOBBY
STATED PRINT RUN 1 SER.#'d SETS
NO PRICING DUE TO SCARCITY

2009 Topps 206 Mini Cycle

*CYCLE VET: 6X TO 15X BASIC VET
*CYCLE RC: 3X TO 8X BASIC RC
STATED ODDS 1:22 HOBBY
STATED PRINT RUN 99 SER.#'d SETS

2009 Topps 206 Mini Framed Cloth

STATED ODDS 1:160 HOBBY
STATED PRINT RUN 50 SER.#'d SETS
1 Ryan Howard 8.00 20.00
10 Andrew McCutchen 20.00 50.00
19 Mel Ott 10.00 25.00
23 Koji Uehara 10.00 25.00
28 Kenshin Kawakami 6.00 15.00
36 Jimmie Foxx 10.00 25.00
41 David Hernandez 4.00 10.00
44 Michael Bowden 4.00 10.00
49 Walter Johnson 10.00 25.00
57 Matt LaPorta 6.00 15.00
61 Derrek Holland 6.00 15.00
66 Ty Cobb 15.00 40.00
71 Dustin Pedroia 10.00 25.00
72 Rick Porcello 12.00 30.00
83 Rogers Hornsby 6.00 15.00
87 Ryan Perry 10.00 25.00
90 Alex Rodriguez 12.00 30.00
102 Hanley Ramirez 6.00 15.00
103 Andrew Bailey 10.00 25.00
107 Fernando Martinez 10.00 25.00
113 Tris Speaker 6.00 15.00
116 Chase Utley 6.00 15.00
120 Derek Jeter 25.00 60.00
129 Ichiro Suzuki 12.00 30.00
130 Honus Wagner 10.00 25.00
137 Mark Teixeira 6.00 15.00
138 Elvis Andrus 10.00 25.00
142 Evan Longoria 6.00 15.00
143 Cy Young 10.00 25.00
154 Mickey Mantle 30.00 80.00
160 Thurman Munson 10.00 25.00
171 David Wright 8.00 20.00
174 Gordon Beckham 6.00 15.00
175 Manny Ramirez 10.00 25.00
177 Pee Wee Reese 6.00 15.00
181 David Price 8.00 20.00
207 Jackie Robinson 10.00 25.00
224 Roy Campanella 10.00 25.00
231 CC Sabathia 6.00 15.00
234 Grady Sizemore 6.00 15.00
237 Christy Mathewson 10.00 25.00
254 Johnny Mize 6.00 15.00
262 Tommy Hanson 10.00 25.00
268 Aaron Poreda 4.00 10.00
271 Lou Gehrig 20.00 50.00
274 Colby Rasmus 6.00 15.00
286 Tim Lincecum 6.00 15.00
287 Babe Ruth 25.00 60.00
299 Albert Pujols 12.00 30.00
300 George Sisler 6.00 15.00

2009 Topps 206 Mini Old Mill

*OLD MILL: 3X TO 8X BASIC VET
*OLD MILL RC: 1.5X TO 4X BASIC RC
STATED ODDS 1:20 HOBBY
120 Derek Jeter 8.00 20.00

2009 Topps 206 Mini Piedmont Gold

*GOLD VET: 8X TO 20X BASIC VET
*GOLD RC: 4X TO 10X BASIC RC
STATED ODDS 1:159 HOBBY
STATED PRINT RUN 50 SER.#'d SETS

2009 Topps 206 Mini Polar Bear

*POLAR VET: 2X TO 5X BASIC VET
*POLAR RC: 1X TO 2.5X BASIC RC
STATED ODDS 1:10 HOBBY
120 Derek Jeter 6.00 15.00

2009 Topps 206 Autographs

STATED ODDS 1:66 HOBBY
EXCHANGE DEADLINE 11/30/2012
NFA1 David Wright 10.00 25.00
NFA2 Johnny Cueto 4.00 10.00
NFA3 Evan Longoria 6.00 15.00
NFA4 Gio Gonzalez 5.00 12.00
NFA5 Juan Rivera 3.00 8.00
NFA6 Ryan Braun 6.00 15.00
NFA7 Joba Chamberlain 6.00 15.00
NFA8 Dustin Pedroia 10.00 25.00
NFA9 Jay Bruce 10.00 25.00
NFA10 Jordan Zimmermann 5.00 12.00
NFA11 Ryan Howard 10.00 25.00
NFA12 Max Scherzer 30.00 80.00
NFA13 Heath Bell 3.00 8.00
NFA14 Jonathan Papelbon 8.00 20.00
NFA15 Jhonny Peralta 3.00 8.00
NFA16 Milton Bradley 3.00 8.00

2009 Topps 206 Checklists

COMPLETE SET (7) 5.00 12.00
APPX.ODDS 1:3 HOBBY
1 Mickey Mantle 1.00 2.50
2 Mickey Mantle 1.00 2.50
3 Mickey Mantle 1.00 2.50
4 Mickey Mantle 1.00 2.50
5 Mickey Mantle 1.00 2.50
6 Mickey Mantle 1.00 2.50
7 Mickey Mantle 1.00 2.50

2009 Topps 206 Mini Framed Autograph

STATED ODDS 1:18 HOBBY
EXCHANGE DEADLINE 11/30/2012
FMA1 Gordon Beckham 3.00 8.00
FMA2 Koji Uehara 4.00 10.00
FMA3 Ryan Perry 8.00 20.00
FMA4 Elvis Andrus 3.00 8.00
FMA5 Jonathan Van Every 3.00 8.00
FMA6 Glen Perkins 3.00 8.00
FMA7 Jordan Zimmermann 6.00 15.00
FMA8 Daniel Schlereth 3.00 8.00
FMA9 Chris Volstad 3.00 8.00
FMA10 Ryan Braun 6.00 15.00
FMA11 Nick Evans 4.00 10.00
FMA12 Fernando Martinez 5.00 12.00
FMA13 Shairon Martis 3.00 8.00
FMA14 James Parr 3.00 8.00
FMA15 Mat Gamel 4.00 10.00
FMA16 Michael Bowden 5.00 12.00
FMA17 David Hernandez 4.00 10.00
FMA18 Chris Young 4.00 10.00
FMA19 Denard Span 3.00 8.00
FMA20 Phil Hughes 4.00 10.00
FMA21 Jason Motte 8.00 20.00
FMA22 Clayton Kershaw 40.00 100.00
FMA23 Justin Masterson 4.00 10.00
FMA24 Vinny Mazzaro 3.00 8.00
FMA25 Scott Elbert 4.00 10.00
FMA26 Rich Hill 3.00 8.00
FMA27 Luke Montz 3.00 8.00
FMA28 Curtis Granderson 4.00 10.00
FMA29 Kila Ka'aihue 3.00 8.00
FMA30 Josh Outman 3.00 8.00

2009 Topps 206 Mini Framed Relics Piedmont

STATED ODDS 1:71 HOBBY
FR1 Alex Rodriguez Bat 8.00 20.00
FR2 Ryan Howard 6.00 15.00
FR3 David Wright 5.00 12.00
FR4 Albert Pujols 10.00 25.00
FR5 Evan Longoria 6.00 15.00
FR6 Chipper Jones 6.00 15.00
FR7 Carlos Beltran 3.00 8.00
FR8 Ichiro Suzuki 6.00 15.00
FR9 Hanley Ramirez 3.00 8.00
FR10 Carl Crawford 3.00 8.00
FR11 David Ortiz Jsy 3.00 8.00
FR12 Nick Markakis 4.00 10.00
FR13 Michael Young 3.00 8.00
FR14 Hideki Matsui 6.00 15.00
FR15 Ryan Braun 5.00 12.00
FR16 Robinson Cano 5.00 12.00
FR17 Miguel Tejada 3.00 8.00
FR18 Phil Hughes 3.00 8.00
FR19 Cole Hamels 4.00 10.00
FR20 James Loney 3.00 8.00
FR21 Brian McCann 4.00 10.00
FR22 Ty Cobb Bat 30.00 60.00
FR23 Jimmie Foxx Bat 10.00 25.00
FR24 Jackie Robinson Bat 25.00 60.00
FR25 Babe Ruth 50.00 100.00

2009 Topps 206 Mini Framed Relics Old Mill

*OLD MILL: .4X TO 1X PIEDMONT
STATED ODDS 1:105 HOBBY

2009 Topps 206 Mini Framed Relics Polar Bear

*POLAR: .6X TO 1.5X PIEDMONT
RANDOM INSERTS IN PACKS

2010 Topps 206

COMPLETE SET (350) 100.00 200.00
COMP.SET w/o SP's (300) 20.00 50.00
COMMON CARD (1-300) .15 .40
COMMON ROOKIE (1-300) .30 .75
COMMON SP VAR (301-350) .60 1.50
SP VAR HAVE NO CARD NUMBERS
1 Matt Holliday .40 1.00
2 Willie Stargell .25 .60
3 Nate McLouth .15 .40
4 David Ortiz .40 1.00
5 Will Venable .15 .40
6 Denard Span .15 .40
7 Ted Lilly .15 .40
8 Shane Victorino .25 .60
9 Zack Greinke .40 1.00
10 Conor Jackson .15 .40
11 Brandon Inge .25 .60
12 Chris Iannetta .15 .40
13 Tim Hudson .25 .60
14 Rafael Furcal .15 .40
15 Mordecai Brown .15 .40
16 Johan Santana .25 .60
17 Mike Leake RC 1.00 2.50
18 Travis Snider .15 .40
19 Carlos Ruiz .15 .40
20 Mark DeRosa .15 .40
21 Jason Kubel .15 .40
22 Kevin Kouzmanoff .15 .40
23 Matt Cain .25 .60
24 Starlin Castro RC .75 2.00
25 Jackie Robinson .40 1.00
26 Stan Musial .60 1.50
27 Derek Holland .15 .40
28 Chris Young .15 .40
29 John Lackey .25 .60
30 Yunel Escobar .15 .40
31 Colby Rasmus .25 .60
32 Brad Hawpe .15 .40
33 Justin Upton .25 .60
34 Zach Duke .15 .40
35 Ryan Dempster .15 .40
36 Mark Reynolds .15 .40
37 Gordon Beckham .15 .40
38 Derrek Lee .15 .40
39 Yovani Gallardo .15 .40
40 Hiroki Kuroda .15 .40
41 Brian McCann .25 .60
42 A.J. Burnett .15 .40
43 Martin Prado .15 .40
44 Bryan Anderson (RC) .30 .75
45 Adrian Gonzalez .30 .75
46 Carlos Quentin .15 .40
47 Rickie Weeks .15 .40
48 David Price .30 .75
49 Vernon Wells .15 .40
50 Ricky Nolasco .15 .40
51 Asdrubal Cabrera .25 .60
52 Ichiro Suzuki .50 1.25
53 Felix Hernandez .25 .60
54 Kevin Slowey .15 .40
55 Stephen Strasburg RC 2.50 6.00
56 Nick Markakis .30 .75
57 Aaron Harang .15 .40
58 Justin Verlander .40 1.00
59 Thurman Munson .40 1.00
60 Jason Heyward RC 1.25 3.00
61 Carlos Zambrano .25 .60
62 Geovany Soto .25 .60
63 Fausto Carmona .15 .40
64 Bobby Abreu .15 .40
65 Aaron Hill .15 .40
66 Marco Scutaro .25 .60
67 Cristian Guzman .15 .40
68 Garrett Atkins .15 .40
69 Honus Wagner .40 1.00
70 Luke Hochevar .15 .40
71 Paul Maholm .15 .40
72 Pablo Sandoval .25 .60
73 Dustin Pedroia .40 1.00
74 Carlos Gomez .15 .40
75 Jeff Francis .15 .40
76 Clay Buchholz .15 .40
77 Scott Sizemore RC .50 1.25
78 Placido Polanco .15 .40
79 Shin-Soo Choo .25 .60
80 Akinori Iwamura .15 .40
81 Adam Lind .25 .60
82 Nick Swisher .25 .60
83 Carlos Lee .15 .40
84 Cal Ripken Jr. 1.25 3.00
85 Josh Beckett .15 .40
86 Chris Carpenter .25 .60
87 Cole Hamels .30 .75
88 Jeremy Bonderman .15 .40
89 Matt Kemp .30 .75
90 Jon Lester .25 .60
91 Mickey Mantle 1.25 3.00
92 Andre Ethier .25 .60
93 Cody Ross .15 .40
94 Jorge Posada .25 .60
95 Grady Sizemore .25 .60
96 Evan Longoria .25 .60
97 Javier Vazquez .15 .40
98 Nolan Ryan 1.25 3.00
99 Christy Mathewson .40 1.00
100 Howie Kendrick .15 .40
101 Andy Pettitte .25 .60
102 Kevin Millwood .15 .40
103 James Shields .15 .40
104 Joey Votto .40 1.00
105 Brian Roberts .15 .40
106 Kazuo Matsui .15 .40
107 Derek Lowe .15 .40
108 Alexei Ramirez .25 .60
109 Carlos Beltran .25 .60
110 Mike Napoli .15 .40
111 Mark Teixeira .25 .60
112 Ryan Zimmerman .25 .60
113 Chase Utley .25 .60
114 Alex Rodriguez .50 1.25
115 Yadier Molina .50 1.25
116 B.J. Upton .25 .60
117 Freddy Sanchez .15 .40
118 Roy Oswalt .25 .60
119 Matt Garza .15 .40
120 Ken Griffey Jr. .75 2.00
121 Orlando Cabrera .15 .40
122 Cy Young .40 1.00
123 Kurt Suzuki .15 .40
124 Josh Hamilton .25 .60
125 Prince Fielder .25 .60
126 Jason Marquis .15 .40
127 Nick Blackburn .15 .40
128 Mat Latos .25 .60
129 John Maine .15 .40
130 Nelson Cruz .40 1.00
131 Troy Tulowitzki .40 1.00
132 Mike Cameron .15 .40
133 Edwin Jackson .15 .40
134 Todd Helton .25 .60
135 Delmon Young .25 .60

136 Chris Volstad .15 .40
137 Troy Glaus .15 .40
138 J.A. Happ .25 .60
139 Barry Zito .25 .60
140 Ian Kinsler .25 .60
141 Ivan Rodriguez .25 .60
142 Bengie Molina .15 .40
143 Michael Cuddyer .15 .40
144 Curtis Granderson .30 .75
145 Jay Bruce .25 .60
146 Brett Anderson .15 .40
147 Roy Halladay .25 .60
148 Andre Dawson .25 .60
149 Scott Kazmir .15 .40
150 Ryan Ludwick .15 .40
151 Chris Getz .15 .40
152 Cliff Lee .25 .60
153 Ryan Braun .25 .60
154 Orlando Hudson .15 .40
155 Jake Peavy .15 .40
156 Chris Tillman .15 .40
157 Edinson Volquez .15 .40
158 Jenrry Mejia RC .50 1.25
159 Frank Robinson .25 .60
160 Erick Aybar .15 .40
161 Neftali Feliz .15 .40
162 Derek Jeter 1.00 2.50
163 Max Scherzer .40 1.00
164 Joba Chamberlain .15 .40
165 Ty Cobb .60 1.50
166 Austin Jackson RC .50 1.25
167 Mike Pelfrey .15 .40
168 Nolan Reimold .15 .40
169 Michael Bourn .15 .40
170 Ian Stewart .15 .40
171 Ian Desmond (RC) .50 1.25
172 Kid Elberfeld .15 .40
173 Aramis Ramirez .15 .40
174 Clayton Kershaw .60 1.50
175 Dan Haren .15 .40
176 Hanley Ramirez .25 .60
177 Gavin Floyd .15 .40
178 Jimmy Rollins .25 .60
179 Drew Stubbs RC .75 2.00
180 Gil Meche .15 .40
181 Wade Davis (RC) .50 1.25
182 Lou Gehrig .75 2.00
183 Carlos Pena .25 .60
184 Chipper Jones .40 1.00
185 Babe Ruth 1.00 2.50
186 Mark Buehrle .25 .60
187 Chris Coghlan .15 .40
188 Rich Harden .15 .40
189 Nick Johnson .15 .40
190 Kenshin Kawakami .25 .60
191 Victor Martinez .25 .60
192 Johnny Cueto .25 .60
193 Buster Posey RC 2.50 6.00
194 Brett Myers .15 .40
195 Stephen Drew .15 .40
196 Adam Jones .25 .60
197 Travis Hafner .15 .40
198 David DeJesus .15 .40
199 Vladimir Guerrero .25 .60
200 Corey Hart .15 .40
201 Franklin Gutierrez .15 .40
202 Alex Gordon .25 .60
203 Allen Craig RC .75 2.00
204 Justin Morneau .25 .60
205 Koji Uehara .15 .40
206 Jacoby Ellsbury .30 .75
207 Carlos Guillen .15 .40
208 Chone Figgins .15 .40
209 Torii Hunter .15 .40
210 Hunter Pence .25 .60
211 Jered Weaver .25 .60
212 Pedro Feliz .15 .40
213 Joel Pineiro .15 .40
214 John Danks .15 .40
215 Jason Bay .25 .60
216 Wandy Rodriguez .15 .40
217 Alex Rios .15 .40
218 Joe Mauer .30 .75
219 Edgar Renteria .15 .40
220 Rick Porcello .25 .60
221 Albert Pujols .50 1.25
222 Tom Seaver .25 .60
223 Kyle Blanks .15 .40
224 Tommy Hanson .15 .40
225 Adam Wainwright .25 .60
226 Jonathan Sanchez .15 .40
227 Chad Billingsley .25 .60
228 Francisco Liriano .15 .40
229 Jose Lopez .15 .40
230 Jair Jurrjens .15 .40
231 Justin Masterson .15 .40
232 Joe Saunders .15 .40
233 Frank Chance .25 .60
234 Dan Uggla .15 .40
235 Jeff Francoeur .25 .60
236 Johnny Bench .40 1.00
237 Carl Pavano .15 .40
238 Ubaldo Jimenez .15 .40
239 Lance Berkman .25 .60
240 Casey McGehee .15 .40
241 Manny Ramirez .40 1.00
242 Julio Borbon .15 .40
243 Alcides Escobar .25 .60
244 Russell Martin .15 .40
245 Chien-Ming Wang .25 .60
246 Raul Ibanez .25 .60
247 Jhoulys Chacin .15 .40
248 Yogi Berra .40 1.00
249 Rick Ankiel .15 .40
250 Ryan Doumit .15 .40
251 Hideki Matsui .40 1.00
252 Michael Young .15 .40
253 Elvis Andrus .25 .60
254 Reggie Jackson .25 .60
255 Tim Lincecum .25 .60
256 Brandon Webb .25 .60
257 Ryan Howard .30 .75
258 Scott Rolen .25 .60
259 Carlos Gonzalez .25 .60
260 Billy Butler .15 .40
261 Daniel McCutchen RC .50 1.25
262 Melvin Mora .15 .40
263 CC Sabathia .25 .60
264 Al Kaline .40 1.00
265 James Loney .15 .40
266 Rajai Davis .15 .40
267 Manny Parra .15 .40
268 Kosuke Fukudome .25 .60
269 Miguel Cabrera .40 1.00
270 Ricky Romero .15 .40
271 Chris Davis .25 .60
272 Carl Crawford .25 .60
273 Robinson Cano .25 .60
274 Adrian Beltre .40 1.00
275 Andrew McCutchen .40 1.00
276 Jason Bartlett .15 .40
277 Johnny Evers .15 .40
278 Adam Dunn .25 .60
279 Glen Perkins .15 .40
280 Ben Zobrist .25 .60
281 Melky Cabrera .15 .40
282 Jose Reyes .25 .60
283 Ervin Santana .15 .40
284 Alfonso Soriano .25 .60
285 Jayson Werth .25 .60
286 Kevin Youkilis .15 .40
287 Daisuke Matsuzaka .25 .60
288 Scott Baker .15 .40
289 David Wright .30 .75
290 Magglio Ordonez .25 .60
291 Daniel Murphy .30 .75
292 Josh Johnson .25 .60
293 Jeff Niemann .15 .40
294 Willie Keeler .15 .40
295 Tommy Manzella (RC) .30 .75
296 Brandon Phillips .15 .40
297 Miguel Montero .15 .40
298 Kendry Morales .15 .40
299 Dexter Fowler .25 .60
300 Trevor Cahill .15 .40
301 Kendry Morales SP .60 1.50
302 Alex Rodriguez SP 2.00 5.00
303 Brian McCann SP 1.00 2.50
304 Roy Halladay SP 1.00 2.50
305 Jacoby Ellsbury SP 1.25 3.00
306 Adrian Gonzalez SP 1.25 3.00
307 Gordon Beckham SP .60 1.50
308 Cliff Lee SP 1.00 2.50
309 Shin-Soo Choo SP 1.00 2.50
310 Evan Longoria SP 1.00 2.50
311 Rick Porcello SP 1.00 2.50
312 Ian Kinsler SP 1.00 2.50
313 Zack Greinke SP 1.50 4.00
314 Hunter Pence SP 1.00 2.50
315 Ryan Braun SP 1.00 2.50
316 Joe Mauer SP 1.25 3.00
317 Ryan Zimmerman SP 1.00 2.50
318 Matt Kemp SP 1.25 3.00
319 Aaron Hill SP .60 1.50
320 Chris Coghlan SP .60 1.50
321 Albert Pujols SP 2.00 5.00
322 Ubaldo Jimenez SP .60 1.50
323 Pablo Sandoval SP 1.00 2.50
324 Joey Votto SP 1.50 4.00
325 Andrew McCutchen SP 1.50 4.00
326 Carlos Zambrano SP 1.00 2.50
327 Rajai Davis SP .60 1.50
328 Adam Jones SP 1.00 2.50
329 Jason Bay SP 1.00 2.50
330 Justin Upton SP 1.00 2.50
331 Stephen Strasburg SP 5.00 12.00
332 Babe Ruth SP 4.00 10.00
333 Tim Lincecum SP 1.00 2.50
334 Tom Seaver SP 1.00 2.50
335 Wade Davis SP 1.00 2.50
336 Ryan Howard SP 1.25 3.00
337 Ian Desmond SP 1.00 2.50
338 Austin Jackson SP 1.00 2.50
339 Neftali Feliz SP .60 1.50
340 Mickey Mantle SP 5.00 12.00
341 Jason Heyward SP 2.50 6.00
342 Stephen Drew SP .60 1.50
343 Stan Musial SP 2.50 6.00
344 Tim Lincecum SP 1.00 2.50
345 Mickey Mantle SP 5.00 12.00
346 Justin Upton SP 1.00 2.50
347 Albert Pujols SP 2.00 5.00
348 Ryan Braun SP 1.00 2.50
349 Joe Mauer SP 1.25 3.00
350 Roy Halladay SP 1.00 2.50

2010 Topps 206 Bronze

COMPLETE SET (300) 50.00 100.00
*BRONZE VET: .6X TO 1.5X BASIC
*BRONZE RC: .5X TO 1.2X BASIC RC

2010 Topps 206 Mini Piedmont

*PIEDMONT VET: 1X TO 2.5X BASIC
*PIEDMONT RC: .6X TO 1.5X BASIC RC
84 Cal Ripken Jr. 5.00 12.00

2010 Topps 206 Mini American Caramel

*AC VET: 1.5X TO 4X BASIC VET
*AC RC: .75X TO 2X BASIC RC

2010 Topps 206 Mini Cycle

*CYCLE VET: 6X TO 15X BASIC VET
*CYCLE RC: 3X TO 8X BASIC RC
STATED PRINT RUN 99 SER.#'d SETS
84 Cal Ripken Jr. 50.00 100.00

2010 Topps 206 Mini Old Mill

*OLD MILL: 2.5X TO 6X BASIC VET
*OLD MILL RC: 1.2X TO 3X BASIC RC
84 Cal Ripken Jr. 20.00 50.00

2010 Topps 206 Mini Polar Bear

*POLAR VET: 2X TO 5X BASIC VET
*POLAR RC: 1X TO 2.5X BASIC RC
84 Cal Ripken Jr. 15.00 40.00

2010 Topps 206 Cut Signatures

STATED PRINT RUN 1 SER.#'d SET

2010 Topps 206 Dual Relics

STATED PRINT RUN 99 SER.#'d SETS
AD Adam Dunn 8.00 20.00
AP Albert Pujols 15.00 40.00
APE Andy Pettitte 6.00 15.00
AR Alex Rodriguez 8.00 20.00
BM Brian McCann 5.00 12.00
CC Carl Crawford 5.00 12.00
DW David Wright 5.00 12.00
GS Grady Sizemore 5.00 12.00
JB Johnny Bench 10.00 25.00
JH Josh Hamilton 8.00 20.00
JRO Jimmy Rollins 8.00 20.00
MM Mickey Mantle 100.00 175.00
MR Manny Ramirez 5.00 12.00
NM Nick Markakis 12.50 30.00
NR Nolan Ryan 12.50 30.00
PF Prince Fielder 5.00 12.00
RH Ryan Howard 12.50 30.00
RS Ryne Sandberg 12.50 30.00
SV Shane Victorino 8.00 20.00
WS Willie Stargell 8.00 20.00

2010 Topps 206 Mini Framed American Caramel Autographs

EXCH DEADLINE 8/31/2013
AC Asdrubal Cabrera 10.00 25.00
AR Alex Rios 12.50 30.00
ARO Alex Rodriguez 60.00 120.00
BU B.J. Upton 5.00 12.00
CB Chad Billingsley 6.00 15.00
CG Chris Getz 4.00 10.00
CS CC Sabathia 15.00 40.00
CT Chris Tillman 4.00 10.00
DB Dallas Braden 4.00 10.00
DS Duke Snider 12.50 30.00
EC Eric Chavez 3.00 8.00
FM Franklin Morales 3.00 8.00
FP Felipe Paulino 3.00 8.00
HR Hanley Ramirez 10.00 25.00
JD Joey Devine 3.00 8.00
JH Joel Hanrahan 3.00 8.00
JL Jed Lowrie 4.00 10.00
JP Johnny Podres 6.00 15.00
JU Justin Upton 8.00 20.00
KS Kurt Suzuki 3.00 8.00
MB Milton Bradley 3.00 8.00
MBU Madison Bumgarner 20.00 50.00
MC Melky Cabrera 6.00 15.00
MCA Matt Cain 10.00 25.00
MM Miguel Montero 3.00 8.00
MY Michael Young 6.00 15.00
NM Nick Markakis 6.00 15.00
OC Orlando Cabrera 4.00 10.00
PF Prince Fielder 12.50 30.00
PP Placido Polanco 8.00 20.00
RC Robinson Cano 125.00 250.00
RG Ryan Garko 3.00 8.00
RI Raul Ibanez 6.00 15.00
SP Steve Pearce 5.00 12.00
SR Sean Rodriguez 3.00 8.00
SS Stephen Strasburg 60.00 150.00
TC Tyler Colvin 8.00 20.00
TH Torii Hunter 10.00 25.00
VM Vin Mazzaro 3.00 8.00

2010 Topps 206 Mini Dual Relics Booklet

STATED PRINT RUN 99 SER.#'d SETS
MBR1 A.Pujols/R.Howard 40.00 80.00
MBR2 Prince Fielder 10.00 25.00
Ryan Braun
MBR3 E.Longoria/D.Wright 15.00 40.00
MBR4 I.Suzuki/A.Pujols 60.00 120.00
MBR5 J.Mauer/J.Bench 15.00 40.00
MBR6 Hanley Ramirez 10.00 25.00
Jimmy Rollins
MBR7 A.Jones/N.Markakis 15.00 40.00
MBR8 Tim Lincecum 10.00 25.00
Zack Greinke
MBR9 G.Sizemore/I.Suzuki 20.00 50.00
MBR10 T.Lincecum/R.Halladay 15.00 40.00
MBR11 I.Kinsler/G.Beckham 12.50 30.00
MBR12 C.Utley/R.Howard 15.00 40.00
MBR13 S.Choo/G.Sizemore 20.00 50.00
MBR14 Miguel Cabrera 10.00 25.00
Prince Fielder
MBR15 Justin Upton 10.00 25.00
Matt Kemp
MBR16 Carlton Fisk 10.00 25.00
Ivan Rodriguez
MBR17 D.Wright/J.Reyes 15.00 40.00
MBR18 M.Kemp/A.Ethier 12.50 30.00
MBR19 C.Sabathia/A.Pettitte 15.00 40.00
MBR20 Hanley Ramirez 10.00 25.00
Dan Uggla
MBR21 D.Pedroia/K.Youkilis 12.50 30.00
MBR22 Hunter Pence 10.00 25.00
Josh Hamilton
MBR23 Prince Fielder 10.00 25.00
Pablo Sandoval
MBR24 J.Mauer/B.McCann 15.00 40.00
MBR25 M.Mantle/B.Ruth 125.00 250.00

2010 Topps 206 Mini Framed Relics Piedmont

AG Alex Gordon 3.00 8.00
AJ Adam Jones 3.00 8.00
AP Albert Pujols 12.50 30.00
BM Bobby Murcer 6.00 15.00
BP Brandon Phillips 3.00 8.00
CB Clint Barmes 3.00 8.00
CC Carl Crawford 3.00 8.00
CG Curtis Granderson 4.00 10.00
CJ Conor Jackson 3.00 8.00
CM Carlos Marmol 3.00 8.00
CR Cal Ripken Jr. 8.00 20.00
CS Curt Schilling 3.00 8.00
CU Chase Utley 5.00 12.00
CZ Carlos Zambrano 3.00 8.00
DO David Ortiz 3.00 8.00
DU Dan Uggla 3.00 8.00
EJ Edwin Jackson 3.00 8.00
EV Edinson Volquez 3.00 8.00
FT Frank Thomas 4.00 10.00
GS Geovany Soto 3.00 8.00
IK Ian Kinsler 3.00 8.00
JD Johnny Damon 3.00 8.00
JE Johnny Evers 20.00 50.00
JR Jimmy Rollins 3.00 8.00
JV Jason Varitek 3.00 8.00
JW Josh Willingham 3.00 8.00
KJ Kelly Johnson 3.00 8.00
KM Kevin Millwood 3.00 8.00
KS Kevin Slowey 3.00 8.00
KW Kerry Wood 3.00 8.00
LC Luis Castillo 3.00 8.00
LH Livan Hernandez 3.00 8.00
MC Miguel Cabrera 4.00 10.00
MM Mickey Mantle 20.00 50.00
MR Mariano Rivera 4.00 10.00
MT Miguel Tejada 3.00 8.00
NS Nate Schierholtz 3.00 8.00
PK Paul Konerko 3.00 8.00
RH Rickey Henderson 6.00 15.00
SC Shin-Soo Choo 3.00 8.00
TG Tony Gwynn Jr. 3.00 8.00
YB Yogi Berra 8.00 20.00
YE Yunel Escobar 3.00 8.00
YG Yovani Gallardo 3.00 8.00
ZG Zack Greinke 3.00 8.00
BMC Brian McCann 3.00 8.00
GSI Grady Sizemore 3.00 8.00
JVO Joey Votto 6.00 15.00
RHO Ryan Howard 6.00 15.00
TGL Troy Glaus 3.00 8.00

2010 Topps 206 Mini Framed Relics Old Mill

*OLD MILL: .75X TO 2X PIEDMONT
CR Cal Ripken Jr. 25.00 60.00

2010 Topps 206 Mini Framed Relics Polar Bear

*POLAR BEAR: .6X TO 1.5X PIEDMONT

2010 Topps 206 Mini Framed Autographs Piedmont

EXCH DEADLINE 8/31/2013
AJ Adam Jones 8.00 20.00
AL Adam Lind 3.00 8.00
BM Bengie Molina 6.00 15.00
BS Brian Schneider 3.00 8.00
CC Chris Coghlan 3.00 8.00
CF Chone Figgins 5.00 12.00
CP Cliff Pennington 3.00 8.00
CR Colby Rasmus 3.00 8.00
CT Clete Thomas 3.00 8.00
CY Chris Young 3.00 8.00
DB Daric Barton 3.00 8.00
DM Daniel Murphy 8.00 20.00
DP Dustin Pedroia 40.00 80.00
EC Everth Cabrera 3.00 8.00
EV Eugenio Velez 3.00 8.00
FC Francisco Cervelli 6.00 15.00
FM Fernando Martinez 3.00 8.00
GB Gordon Beckham 10.00 25.00
HB Heath Bell 4.00 10.00
JB Gregor Blanco 4.00 10.00
JC Jeff Clement 3.00 8.00
JF Jeff Francis 3.00 8.00
JK Jason Kubel 3.00 8.00
JL John Lannan 3.00 8.00
JP Jhonny Peralta 3.00 8.00
JT J.R. Towles 3.00 8.00
JW Josh Willingham 3.00 8.00
JZ Jordan Zimmermann 8.00 20.00
MB Mitch Boggs 3.00 8.00
MS Max Scherzer 15.00 40.00
MT Matt Tolbert 3.00 8.00
NC Nelson Cruz 6.00 15.00
NF Neftali Feliz 5.00 12.00
NM Nyjer Morgan 4.00 10.00
PP Placido Polanco 5.00 12.00
PS Pablo Sandoval 10.00 25.00
RB Ryan Braun EXCH 15.00 40.00
RH Ryan Howard 20.00 50.00
RP Ryan Perry 3.00 8.00
RZ Ryan Zimmerman 10.00 25.00
SC Shin-Soo Choo 6.00 15.00
SG Sammy Gervacio 5.00 12.00
SS Scott Sizemore 3.00 8.00
SS Stephen Strasburg 30.00 80.00
TC Trevor Crowe 3.00 8.00
TG Tom Gorzelanny 4.00 10.00
TH Tommy Hanson 5.00 12.00
TT T.Tulowitzki EXCH 8.00 20.00
WV Will Venable 3.00 8.00
CRI C.Ripken Jr. 30.00 80.00
RPO R.Porcello EXCH 8.00 20.00

2010 Topps 206 Mini Framed Autographs Polar Bear

*POLAR BEAR: .5X TO 1.2X PIEDMONT
EXCH DEADLINE 8/31/2013

2010 Topps 206 Mini Framed Silk

STATED PRINT RUN 50 SER.#'d SETS
S1 Jackie Robinson 8.00 20.00
S2 Will Venable 3.00 8.00
S3 Cy Young 8.00 20.00
S4 Lou Gehrig 15.00 40.00
S5 Johan Santana 5.00 12.00
S6 Matt Cain 5.00 12.00
S7 John Lackey 5.00 12.00
S8 Honus Wagner 8.00 20.00
S9 David Price 6.00 15.00
S10 Ichiro Suzuki 10.00 25.00
S11 Felix Hernandez 5.00 12.00
S12 Nick Markakis 6.00 15.00
S13 Jason Heyward 12.00 30.00
S14 Shin-Soo Choo 5.00 12.00
S15 Christy Mathewson 8.00 20.00
S16 Adam Lind 5.00 12.00
S17 Chris Carpenter 5.00 12.00
S18 Andre Ethier 5.00 12.00
S19 Grady Sizemore 5.00 12.00
S20 Nolan Ryan 25.00 60.00
S21 Ty Cobb 12.00 30.00
S22 Chase Utley 5.00 12.00
S23 Thurman Munson 8.00 20.00
S24 Babe Ruth 20.00 50.00
S25 Mordecai Brown 3.00 8.00
S26 Josh Hamilton 5.00 12.00
S27 Prince Fielder 5.00 12.00
S28 Mat Latos 5.00 12.00
S29 Nelson Cruz 8.00 20.00
S30 Kid Elberfeld 3.00 8.00
S31 Curtis Granderson 6.00 15.00
S32 Frank Chance 5.00 12.00
S33 Johnny Evers 3.00 8.00
S34 Chipper Jones 8.00 20.00
S35 Buster Posey 25.00 60.00
S36 Justin Morneau 5.00 12.00
S37 Torii Hunter 3.00 8.00
S38 Jason Bay 5.00 12.00
S39 Tommy Hanson 3.00 8.00
S40 Adam Wainwright 5.00 12.00
S41 Ubaldo Jimenez 3.00 8.00
S42 Manny Ramirez 8.00 20.00
S43 Willie Keeler 3.00 8.00
S44 CC Sabathia 5.00 12.00
S45 Miguel Cabrera 8.00 20.00
S46 Adam Dunn 5.00 12.00
S47 Daisuke Matsuzaka 5.00 12.00
S48 David Wright 6.00 15.00
S49 Josh Johnson 5.00 12.00
S50 Kendry Morales 3.00 8.00

2010 Topps 206 Mini Historical Events

COMPLETE SET (20) 5.00 12.00
COMMON CARD .60 1.50

2010 Topps 206 Mini Piedmont Gold Chrome

STATED PRINT RUN 50 SER.#'d SETS
C1 Jackie Robinson 8.00 20.00
C2 Will Venable 3.00 8.00
C3 Cy Young 8.00 20.00
C4 Lou Gehrig 15.00 40.00
C5 Johan Santana 5.00 12.00
C6 Matt Cain 5.00 12.00
C7 John Lackey 5.00 12.00
C8 Honus Wagner 8.00 20.00
C9 David Price 6.00 15.00
C10 Ichiro Suzuki 10.00 25.00
C11 Felix Hernandez 5.00 12.00
C12 Nick Markakis 6.00 15.00
C13 Jason Heyward 12.00 30.00
C14 Shin-Soo Choo 5.00 12.00
C15 Christy Mathewson 8.00 20.00
C16 Adam Lind 5.00 12.00
C17 Chris Carpenter 5.00 12.00
C18 Andre Ethier 5.00 12.00
C19 Grady Sizemore 5.00 12.00
C20 Nolan Ryan 25.00 60.00
C21 Ty Cobb 12.00 30.00
C22 Chase Utley 5.00 12.00
C23 Thurman Munson 8.00 20.00
C24 Babe Ruth 20.00 50.00
C25 Mordecai Brown 3.00 8.00
C26 Josh Hamilton 5.00 12.00
C27 Prince Fielder 5.00 12.00
C28 Mat Latos 5.00 12.00
C29 Nelson Cruz 8.00 20.00
C30 Kid Elberfeld 3.00 8.00
C31 Curtis Granderson 6.00 15.00
C32 Frank Chance 5.00 12.00
C33 Johnny Evers 3.00 8.00
C34 Chipper Jones 8.00 20.00
C35 Buster Posey 25.00 60.00
C36 Justin Morneau 5.00 12.00
C37 Torii Hunter 3.00 8.00
C38 Jason Bay 5.00 12.00
C39 Tommy Hanson 3.00 8.00
C40 Adam Wainwright 5.00 12.00
C41 Ubaldo Jimenez 3.00 8.00
C42 Manny Ramirez 8.00 20.00
C43 Willie Keeler 3.00 8.00
C44 CC Sabathia 5.00 12.00
C45 Miguel Cabrera 8.00 20.00
C46 Adam Dunn 5.00 12.00
C47 Daisuke Matsuzaka 5.00 12.00
C48 David Wright 6.00 15.00
C49 Josh Johnson 5.00 12.00
C50 Kendry Morales 3.00 8.00

2010 Topps 206 Mini Personalities

COMPLETE SET (10) 40.00 80.00
STATED PRINT RUN 206 SER.#'d SETS
TP1 Chris Holmes 4.00 10.00
TP2 Jim McKenna 4.00 10.00
TP3 Loretta Micali 4.00 10.00
TP4 Clay Luraschi 4.00 10.00
TP5 Joe Del Toro 4.00 10.00
TP6 Tom Mozeleski 4.00 10.00
TP7 Ed Yablonski 4.00 10.00
TP8 Olga M. Vega 4.00 10.00
TP9 Adam Gandolfo 4.00 10.00
TP10 Kathy Szulewski 4.00 10.00

2010 Topps 206 Stamps

SR1 Honus Wagner 20.00 50.00
SR3 Babe Ruth 50.00 100.00
SR4 Babe Ruth 50.00 100.00
SR5 Babe Ruth 50.00 100.00
SR6 Babe Ruth 50.00 100.00
SR7 Babe Ruth 50.00 100.00
SR8 Babe Ruth 50.00 100.00
SR9 Ty Cobb 15.00 40.00
SR10 Ty Cobb 15.00 40.00
SR11 Johnny Mize 15.00 40.00
SR12 Johnny Mize 15.00 40.00
SR13 Johnny Mize 15.00 40.00
SR14 Johnny Mize 15.00 40.00
SR18 Jimmie Foxx 15.00 40.00
SR19 Jimmie Foxx 15.00 40.00
SR20 Jimmie Foxx 15.00 40.00
SR21 Lou Gehrig 20.00 50.00
SR22 Lou Gehrig 20.00 50.00
SR23 Lou Gehrig 20.00 50.00
SR24 Lou Gehrig 20.00 50.00
SR25 Lou Gehrig 20.00 50.00
SR26 Lou Gehrig 20.00 50.00
SR27 Lou Gehrig 20.00 50.00
SR28 Lou Gehrig 20.00 50.00
SR29 Lou Gehrig 20.00 50.00
SR30 Lou Gehrig 20.00 50.00
SR31 Lou Gehrig 20.00 50.00
SR32 Jackie Robinson 15.00 40.00
SR33 Jackie Robinson 15.00 40.00
SR34 Jackie Robinson 15.00 40.00
SR35 Jackie Robinson 15.00 40.00
SR36 Jackie Robinson 15.00 40.00
SR37 Jackie Robinson 15.00 40.00
SR38 Mickey Mantle 60.00 120.00
SR39 Mickey Mantle 60.00 120.00
SR40 Mickey Mantle 60.00 120.00
SR41 Mickey Mantle 60.00 120.00
SR42 Mickey Mantle 60.00 120.00
SR43 Mickey Mantle 60.00 120.00
SR44 Mickey Mantle 60.00 120.00
SR45 Mickey Mantle 60.00 120.00
SR46 Stan Musial 15.00 40.00
SR47 Thurman Munson 15.00 40.00
SR48 Thurman Munson 15.00 40.00
SR49 Nolan Ryan 40.00 80.00
SR50 Nolan Ryan 40.00 80.00
SR51 Cal Ripken Jr. 50.00 100.00
SR52 Cal Ripken Jr. 50.00 100.00

2020 Topps 206 Wave 1

RANDOM INSERTS IN PACKS
1 Gerrit Cole 1.00 2.50
2 Charlie Morton .60 1.50
3 Patrick Corbin .50 1.25
4 Noah Syndergaard .50 1.25
5 Mike Trout 3.00 8.00
6 Gleyber Torres 1.25 3.00
7 Freddie Freeman .75 2.00
8 Pete Alonso 1.50 4.00
9 D.J. LeMahieu .60 1.50
10 Xander Bogaerts .60 1.50
11 Max Kepler .50 1.25
12 Manny Machado .60 1.50
13 Andrew Benintendi .60 1.50
14 Brandon Lowe .50 1.25
15 George Springer .50 1.25
16 Buster Posey .75 2.00
17 Carlos Correa .60 1.50
18 Hunter Dozier .40 1.00
19 Tyler Glasnow .60 1.50
20 Scott Kingery .50 1.25
21 Randal Grichuk .40 1.00
22 J.T. Realmuto .60 1.50
23 Carlos Santana .50 1.25
24 Blake Snell .50 1.25
25 Jorge Alfaro .40 1.00
26 David Dahl .40 1.00
27 Robbie Ray .40 1.00
28 Amed Rosario .50 1.25
29 Corey Seager .60 1.50
30 Jon Lester .50 1.25
31 Kevin Kiermaier .50 1.25
32 J.D. Martinez .60 1.50
33 Babe Ruth 1.50 4.00
34 Mariano Rivera .75 2.00
35 Reggie Jackson .50 1.25
36 Tony Gwynn 1.50 4.00
37 Carl Yastrzemski 1.00 2.50
38 Mike Schmidt 1.00 2.50
39 Roberto Clemente 1.50 4.00
40 Johnny Bench .60 1.50
41 Vladimir Guerrero .50 1.25
42 Larry Doby .50 1.25
43 Justin Dunn .50 1.25
44 Sean Murphy .60 1.50
45 Gavin Lux 2.00 5.00
46 Logan Webb .60 1.50
47 Randy Dobnak .75 2.00
48 Dillon Tate .40 1.00
49 Bobby Bradley .40 1.00
50 Zack Collins .50 1.25

2020 Topps 206 Wave 1 Cycle Back

*CYCLE/25: 4X TO 10X BASIC
RANDOM INSERTS IN PACKS
STATED PRINT RUN 25 SER.#'d SETS
1 Gerrit Cole 30.00 80.00
5 Mike Trout 200.00 500.00
6 Gleyber Torres 60.00 150.00
8 Pete Alonso 40.00 100.00
33 Babe Ruth 6.00 150.00
35 Reggie Jackson 30.00 80.00
36 Tony Gwynn 25.00 60.00
37 Carl Yastrzemski 30.00 80.00
38 Mike Schmidt 30.00 80.00
39 Roberto Clemente 60.00 150.00
41 Vladimir Guerrero 25.00 60.00
42 Larry Doby 30.00 80.00
45 Gavin Lux 125.00 300.00

2020 Topps 206 Wave 1 Old Mill Back

*OLD MILL: 2.5X TO 6X BASIC
STATED ODDS 1:30 PACKS
1 Gerrit Cole 12.00 30.00
5 Mike Trout 75.00 200.00
6 Gleyber Torres 20.00 50.00
8 Pete Alonso 25.00 60.00
33 Babe Ruth 25.00 60.00
35 Reggie Jackson 12.00 30.00
36 Tony Gwynn 12.00 30.00
37 Carl Yastrzemski 20.00 50.00
38 Mike Schmidt 25.00 60.00
39 Roberto Clemente 25.00 60.00
41 Vladimir Guerrero 10.00 25.00
42 Larry Doby 15.00 40.00
45 Gavin Lux 60.00 150.00

2020 Topps 206 Wave 1 Piedmont Back

*PIEDMONT: .5X TO 1.2X BASIC
INSERTED 2 PER PACK
5 Mike Trout 8.00 20.00

2020 Topps 206 Wave 1 Polar Bear Back

*POLAR BEAR: 2.5X TO 6X BASIC
STATED ODDS 1:18 PACKS
1 Gerrit Cole 12.00 30.00
5 Mike Trout 75.00 200.00
6 Gleyber Torres 20.00 50.00
8 Pete Alonso 25.00 60.00
33 Babe Ruth 20.00 50.00
35 Reggie Jackson 12.00 30.00
36 Tony Gwynn 12.00 30.00
37 Carl Yastrzemski 12.00 30.00
38 Mike Schmidt 12.00 30.00
39 Roberto Clemente 25.00 60.00
41 Vladimir Guerrero 6.00 15.00
42 Larry Doby 12.00 30.00
45 Gavin Lux 30.00 80.00

2020 Topps 206 Wave 1 Sovereign Back

*SOVEREIGN: 1X TO 2.5X BASIC
STATED ODDS 1:6 PACKS
5 Mike Trout 30.00 80.00
6 Gleyber Torres 8.00 20.00
33 Babe Ruth 6.00 15.00
38 Mike Schmidt 5.00 12.00
39 Roberto Clemente 10.00 25.00

2020 Topps 206 Wave 1 Sweet Caporal Back

*S.CAPORAL: .75X TO 2X BASIC
STATED ODDS 1:3 PACKS
5 Mike Trout 15.00 40.00
6 Gleyber Torres 5.00 12.00
33 Babe Ruth 5.00 12.00

2020 Topps 206 Wave 1 Autographs

RANDOM INSERTS IN PACKS
1 Brandon Lowe 20.00 50.00
2 Johnny Bench
3 Mike Trout
4 Patrick Corbin
5 Reggie Jackson 125.00 300.00
6 Zack Collins 20.00 50.00

2020 Topps 206 Wave 2

RANDOM INSERTS IN PACKS
1 Anthony Rendon .60 1.50
2 Ketel Marte .50 1.25
3 Zac Gallen 1.00 2.50
4 Chipper Jones .60 1.50
5 Mike Soroka .60 1.50
6 Cal Ripken Jr. 2.00 5.00
7 John Means .60 1.50
8 Pedro Martinez .50 1.25
9 Kyle Schwarber .60 1.50
10 Yoan Moncada .60 1.50
11 Joey Votto .60 1.50
12 Aristides Aquino 1.00 2.50
13 Shane Bieber .60 1.50
14 Nolan Arenado 1.00 2.50
15 Jorge Soler .60 1.50
16 Sandy Koufax 1.25 3.00
17 Cody Bellinger 1.25 3.00
18 Max Muncy .50 1.25
19 Brusdar Graterol .60 1.50
20 Isan Diaz .60 1.50
21 Jorge Polanco .50 1.25
22 David Wright .50 1.25
23 Aaron Judge 1.50 4.00
24 Rickey Henderson .60 1.50
25 Jesus Luzardo .75 2.00
26 Chris Paddack .60 1.50
27 Tommy Pham .40 1.00
28 Brandon Belt .50 1.25
29 Ken Griffey Jr. 1.25 3.00
30 Ozzie Smith .75 2.00
31 Ivan Rodriguez .50 1.25
32 Nick Solak 1.50 4.00
33 Hyun-Jin Ryu .50 1.25
34 Max Scherzer .60 1.50
35 Albert Pujols .75 2.00
36 Ted Williams 1.25 3.00
37 Jackie Robinson .60 1.50
38 Jose Abreu .60 1.50
39 Charlie Blackmon .60 1.50
40 Al Kaline .60 1.50
41 Keston Hiura .75 2.00
42 Jose Berrios .50 1.25
43 Giancarlo Stanton .60 1.50
44 Didi Gregorius .50 1.25
45 Honus Wagner .60 1.50
46 Chris Archer .40 1.00
47 Eric Hosmer .50 1.25
48 Stan Musial 1.00 2.50
49 Trea Turner .50 1.25
50 Eric Thames .40 1.00

2020 Topps 206 Wave 2 Cycle Back

*CYCLE/25: 4X TO 10X BASIC
RANDOM INSERTS IN PACKS
STATED PRINT RUN 25 SER.#'d SETS
16 Sandy Koufax 60.00 150.00
29 Ken Griffey Jr. 125.00 300.00
36 Ted Williams 40.00 100.00
37 Jackie Robinson 60.00 150.00
45 Honus Wagner 60.00 150.00
48 Stan Musial 40.00 100.00

2020 Topps 206 Wave 2 Polar Bear Back

*POLAR BEAR: 2.5X TO 6X BASIC
STATED ODDS 1:18 PACKS
16 Sandy Koufax 40.00 100.00
29 Ken Griffey Jr. 40.00 100.00
36 Ted Williams 30.00 80.00
37 Jackie Robinson 25.00 60.00
45 Honus Wagner 40.00 100.00
48 Stan Musial 15.00 40.00

2020 Topps 206 Wave 2 Sovereign Back

*SOVEREIGN: 1X TO 2.5X BASIC
STATED ODDS 1:6 PACKS
16 Sandy Koufax 20.00 50.00
29 Ken Griffey Jr. 15.00 40.00
36 Ted Williams 12.00 30.00
37 Jackie Robinson 8.00 20.00
45 Honus Wagner 12.00 30.00

2020 Topps 206 Wave 2 Sweet Caporal Back

*S.CAPORAL: .75X TO 2X BASIC
STATED ODDS 1:3 PACKS
29 Ken Griffey Jr. 8.00 20.00
36 Ted Williams 8.00 20.00
37 Jackie Robinson 6.00 15.00
45 Honus Wagner 6.00 15.00

2020 Topps 206 Wave 2 Autographs

1 Chipper Jones
2 David Wright 150.00 400.00
3 Max Muncy 50.00 120.00
4 Nick Solak 30.00 80.00

2020 Topps 206 Wave 3

RANDOM INSERTS IN PACKS
1 Adley Rutschman 2.50 6.00
2 Wander Franco 4.00 10.00
3 Alex Kirilloff .75 2.00
4 Cristian Pache 1.25 3.00
5 Jarred Kelenic 2.00 5.00

6 Grayson Rodriguez .60 1.50
7 Braden Shewmake .60 1.50
8 Brett Baty 1.25 3.00
9 Alec Bohm 2.50 6.00
10 JJ Bleday 1.25 3.00
11 Riley Greene 1.50 4.00
12 Marco Luciano 1.50 4.00
13 MacKenzie Gore .75 2.00
14 Nolan Jones .60 1.50
15 Andrew Vaughn 1.50 4.00
16 Vidal Brujan 3.00 8.00
17 Sam Huff .75 2.00
18 Matt Manning .50 1.25
19 Nick Madrigal 1.50 4.00
20 CJ Abrams 1.25 3.00
21 Nolan Gorman .75 2.00
22 Ronny Mauricio 1.00 2.50
23 Nate Pearson 1.25 3.00
24 Kristian Robinson 1.25 3.00
25 Luis Patino .60 1.50
26 Josh Jung 1.00 2.50
27 Jo Adell 1.50 4.00
28 Spencer Howard 1.25 3.00
29 Ryan Mountcastle 2.00 5.00
30 Julio Rodriguez 2.50 6.00
31 Ian Anderson 1.25 3.00
32 Andy Pages .50 1.25
33 Ke'Bryan Hayes 2.00 5.00
34 Tarik Skubal 2.00 5.00
35 Royce Lewis 1.00 2.50
36 Brady Singer 2.00 5.00
37 Jarren Duran 1.50 4.00
38 Keibert Ruiz 2.00 5.00
39 Sixto Sanchez 1.25 3.00
40 Trevor Larnach .75 2.00
41 Joey Bart 1.25 3.00
42 Deivi Garcia 2.00 5.00
43 Triston Casas 1.00 2.50
44 Bobby Witt Jr. 3.00 8.00
45 Nick Lodolo .60 1.50
46 Daniel Lynch .40 1.00
47 Casey Mize 1.25 3.00
48 Miguel Amaya .40 1.00
49 Drew Waters 1.00 2.50
50 Hunter Greene .60 1.50

2020 Topps 206 Wave 3 Carolina Brights Back

*CAR.BRIGHTS: 2.5X TO 6X BASIC
STATED ODDS 1:20 PACKS
1 Adley Rutschman 25.00 60.00
2 Wander Franco 50.00 120.00
4 Cristian Pache 15.00 40.00
9 Alec Bohm 25.00 60.00
10 JJ Bleday 15.00 40.00
15 Andrew Vaughn 20.00 50.00
16 Vidal Brujan 25.00 60.00
19 Nick Madrigal 15.00 40.00
26 Josh Jung 20.00 50.00
27 Jo Adell 25.00 60.00
41 Joey Bart 15.00 40.00
42 Deivi Garcia 15.00 40.00
43 Triston Casas 12.00 30.00
44 Bobby Witt Jr. 40.00 100.00

2020 Topps 206 Wave 3 Cycle Back

*CYCLE/25: 4X TO 10X BASIC
RANDOM INSERTS IN PACKS
STATED PRINT RUN 25 SER.#'d SETS
1 Adley Rutschman 40.00 100.00
2 Wander Franco 100.00 250.00
4 Cristian Pache 25.00 60.00
9 Alec Bohm 40.00 100.00
10 JJ Bleday 25.00 60.00
11 Riley Greene 25.00 60.00
15 Andrew Vaughn 30.00 80.00
16 Vidal Brujan 40.00 100.00
19 Nick Madrigal 25.00 60.00
20 CJ Abrams 25.00 60.00
21 Nolan Gorman 20.00 50.00
26 Josh Jung 30.00 80.00
27 Jo Adell 40.00 100.00
30 Julio Rodriguez 30.00 80.00
35 Royce Lewis 30.00 80.00
41 Joey Bart 25.00 60.00
42 Deivi Garcia 25.00 60.00
43 Triston Casas 20.00 50.00
44 Bobby Witt Jr. 40.00 100.00

2020 Topps 206 Wave 3 Old Mill Back

*OLD MILL: 2.5X TO 6X BASIC
STATED ODDS 1:30 PACKS
1 Adley Rutschman 25.00 60.00
2 Wander Franco 50.00 120.00
4 Cristian Pache 15.00 40.00
9 Alec Bohm 25.00 60.00
10 JJ Bleday 15.00 40.00
15 Andrew Vaughn 20.00 50.00
16 Vidal Brujan 25.00 60.00
19 Nick Madrigal 15.00 40.00
21 Nolan Gorman 12.00 30.00
26 Josh Jung 20.00 50.00
27 Jo Adell 25.00 60.00
41 Joey Bart 15.00 40.00
42 Deivi Garcia 15.00 40.00
43 Triston Casas 12.00 30.00
44 Bobby Witt Jr. 40.00 100.00

2020 Topps 206 Wave 3 Sovereign Back

*SOVEREIGN: 1X TO 2.5X BASIC
STATED ODDS 1:6 PACKS
9 Alec Bohm 10.00 25.00
44 Bobby Witt Jr. 12.00 30.00

2020 Topps 206 Wave 3 Autographs

RANDOM INSERTS IN PACKS
1 Adley Rutschman 125.00 300.00
2 Andy Pages 75.00 200.00
3 Bobby Witt Jr. 125.00 300.00
4 Brett Baty 50.00 120.00
5 Jarren Duran 40.00 100.00
6 Sam Huff 150.00 400.00

2020 Topps 206 Wave 4

RANDOM INSERTS IN PACKS
1 Christian Yelich .75 2.00
2 Fernando Tatis Jr. 4.00 10.00
3 Bryce Harper 1.00 2.50
4 Josh Donaldson .50 1.25
5 Sonny Gray .50 1.25
6 George Brett 1.25 3.00
7 Mike Piazza 1.50 4.00
8 Lou Brock 1.00 2.50
9 Hank Aaron 1.25 3.00
10 Tim Anderson .80 2.00
11 Shin Soo Choo .50 1.25
12 Trevor Story .60 1.50
13 Willson Contreras .60 1.50
14 Gary Sanchez .60 1.50
15 Ty Cobb 1.00 2.50
16 Yordan Alvarez 4.00 10.00
17 Javier Baez .75 2.00
18 Frank Thomas 1.50 4.00
19 Josh Hader .50 1.25
20 Clayton Kershaw 1.00 2.50
21 Josh Bell .50 1.25
22 Eloy Jimenez 1.25 3.00
23 Tom Glavine .50 1.25
24 Luke Voit .75 2.00
25 Kyle Lewis 3.00 8.00
26 Randy Johnson 1.50 4.00
27 Matt Olson .60 1.50
28 Jeff McNeil .50 1.25
29 Eddie Rosario .50 1.25
30 Miguel Cabrera .60 1.50
31 Francisco Lindor .60 1.50
32 Evan Longoria .50 1.25
33 Michael Conforto .50 1.25
34 David Ortiz 1.00 2.50
35 Alex Bregman .60 1.50
36 Howie Kendrick .40 1.00
37 Nick Senzel .60 1.50
38 Nelson Cruz .60 1.50
39 Kris Bryant .75 2.00
40 Cavan Biggio .75 2.00
41 Nico Hoerner 1.50 4.00
42 Nolan Ryan 2.00 5.00
43 Michael Chavis .50 1.25
44 Justin Turner .60 1.50
45 Ryne Sandberg 1.25 3.00
46 Paul Goldschmidt .60 1.50
47 Max Fried .60 1.50
48 James Karinchak .60 1.50
49 Brendan McKay .60 1.50
50 Ozzie Albies .60 1.50

2020 Topps 206 Wave 4 Background Variation

*BKGRND VAR/25: 4X TO 10X BASIC
RANDOM INSERTS IN PACKS
STATED PRINT RUN 25 SER.#'d SETS
2 Fernando Tatis Jr. 75.00 200.00
6 George Brett 60.00 150.00
7 Mike Piazza 30.00 80.00
8 Lou Brock 40.00 100.00
9 Hank Aaron 40.00 100.00
10 Tim Anderson 25.00 60.00
14 Gary Sanchez 20.00 50.00
15 Ty Cobb 40.00 100.00
16 Yordan Alvarez 30.00 80.00
18 Frank Thomas 30.00 80.00
20 Clayton Kershaw 30.00 80.00
24 Luke Voit 30.00 80.00
25 Kyle Lewis 60.00 150.00
26 Randy Johnson 40.00 100.00
30 Miguel Cabrera 40.00 100.00
34 David Ortiz 25.00 60.00
39 Kris Bryant 100.00 250.00
40 Cavan Biggio 30.00 80.00
42 Nolan Ryan 60.00 150.00
45 Ryne Sandberg 40.00 100.00
46 Paul Goldschmidt 15.00 40.00
50 Ozzie Albies 20.00 50.00

2020 Topps 206 Wave 4 Old Mill Back

*OLD MILL: 2.5X TO 6X BASIC
STATED ODDS 1:30 PACKS
2 Fernando Tatis Jr. 50.00 120.00
6 George Brett 40.00 100.00
7 Mike Piazza 20.00 50.00
8 Lou Brock 25.00 60.00
9 Hank Aaron 25.00 60.00
10 Tim Anderson 15.00 40.00
14 Gary Sanchez 12.00 30.00
15 Ty Cobb 25.00 60.00
16 Yordan Alvarez 20.00 50.00
18 Frank Thomas 20.00 50.00
20 Clayton Kershaw 20.00 50.00
24 Luke Voit 15.00 40.00
25 Kyle Lewis 40.00 100.00
26 Randy Johnson 25.00 60.00
30 Miguel Cabrera 25.00 60.00
34 David Ortiz 15.00 40.00
39 Kris Bryant 25.00 60.00
40 Cavan Biggio 20.00 50.00
42 Nolan Ryan 30.00 80.00
45 Ryne Sandberg 25.00 60.00
46 Paul Goldschmidt 10.00 25.00
50 Ozzie Albies 10.00 25.00

2020 Topps 206 Wave 4 Polar Bear Back

*POLAR BEAR: 2.5X TO 6X BASIC
STATED ODDS 1:18 PACKS
2 Fernando Tatis Jr. 50.00 120.00
6 George Brett 40.00 100.00
7 Mike Piazza 20.00 50.00
8 Lou Brock 25.00 60.00
9 Hank Aaron 25.00 60.00
10 Tim Anderson 15.00 40.00
14 Gary Sanchez 12.00 30.00
15 Ty Cobb 25.00 60.00
16 Yordan Alvarez 20.00 50.00
18 Frank Thomas 20.00 50.00
20 Clayton Kershaw 20.00 50.00
24 Luke Voit 15.00 40.00
25 Kyle Lewis 40.00 100.00
26 Randy Johnson 25.00 60.00
30 Miguel Cabrera 25.00 60.00
34 David Ortiz 15.00 40.00
39 Kris Bryant 25.00 60.00
40 Cavan Biggio 20.00 50.00
42 Nolan Ryan 30.00 80.00
45 Ryne Sandberg 25.00 60.00
46 Paul Goldschmidt 10.00 25.00
50 Ozzie Albies 10.00 25.00

2020 Topps 206 Wave 4 Sovereign Back

*SOVEREIGN: 1X TO 2.5X BASIC
STATED ODDS 1:6 PACKS
2 Fernando Tatis Jr. 15.00 40.00
6 George Brett 12.00 30.00
8 Lou Brock 5.00 12.00
9 Hank Aaron 8.00 20.00
18 Frank Thomas 8.00 20.00
26 Randy Johnson 8.00 20.00
34 David Ortiz 5.00 12.00
42 Nolan Ryan 15.00 40.00

2020 Topps 206 Wave 4 Sweet Caporal Back

*S.CAPORAL: .75X TO 2X BASIC
STATED ODDS 1:3 PACKS
6 George Brett 10.00 25.00
8 Lou Brock 4.00 10.00
9 Hank Aaron 6.00 15.00
34 David Ortiz 4.00 10.00
42 Nolan Ryan 10.00 25.00

2020 Topps 206 Wave 4 Autographs

RANDOM INSERTS IN PACKS
1 Bryce Harper 150.00 400.00
2 David Ortiz 150.00 400.00
3 Nico Hoerner 75.00 200.00
4 Nolan Ryan
5 Tom Glavine 125.00 300.00
6 Trevor Story 50.00 120.00

2020 Topps 206 Wave 5

RANDOM INSERTS IN PACKS
1 Dansby Swanson .60 1.50
2 Derek Jeter 1.50 4.00
3 Yu Darvish .60 1.50
4 Will Smith .60 1.50
5 John Smoltz .60 1.50
6 Rafael Devers .75 2.00
7 Jack Flaherty .60 1.50
8 Luis Robert 5.00 12.00
9 Matt Chapman .60 1.50
10 Kwang-Hyun Kim .75 2.00
11 Jacob deGrom 1.25 3.00
12 Ernie Banks 1.50 4.00
13 Aaron Nola .50 1.25
14 Juan Soto 2.00 5.00
15 Lou Gehrig 2.00 5.00
16 Roger Clemens .75 2.00
17 Harmon Killebrew .60 1.50
18 Bo Bichette 3.00 8.00
19 Jose Canseco .50 1.25
20 Anthony Rizzo .75 2.00
21 Andrew McCutchen .60 1.50
22 Tom Seaver .50 1.25
23 Jim Thome .50 1.25
24 Ronald Acuna Jr. 2.50 6.00
25 Zack Greinke .60 1.50
26 Willie McCovey .50 1.25
27 Yadier Molina .75 2.00
28 Mookie Betts 1.25 3.00
29 Willie Stargell .50 1.25
30 Dominic Smith .40 1.00
31 Greg Maddux .75 2.00
32 Don Mattingly 1.25 3.00
33 Barry Zito .50 1.25
34 Kirby Puckett 1.50 4.00
35 Dave Winfield .50 1.25
36 Eddie Murray .50 1.25
37 Justin Verlander .60 1.50
38 Lucas Giolito .50 1.25
39 Brooks Robinson .50 1.25
40 Mark McGwire 1.00 2.50
41 Andres Galarraga .50 1.25
42 CC Sabathia .50 1.25
43 Gary Carter .50 1.25
44 Wade Boggs .50 1.25
45 Joe Mauer .50 1.25
46 Dustin May 1.25 3.00
47 Dennis Eckersley .50 1.25
48 Andre Dawson .50 1.25
49 Trevor Bauer .75 2.00
50 Willie Mays 1.25 3.00

2020 Topps 206 Wave 5 Cycle Back

*CYCLE/25: 4X TO 10X BASIC
RANDOM INSERTS IN PACKS
STATED PRINT RUN 25 SER.#'d SETS
2 Derek Jeter 40.00 100.00
5 John Smoltz 25.00 60.00
8 Luis Robert 125.00 300.00
14 Juan Soto 30.00 80.00
15 Lou Gehrig 40.00 100.00
16 Roger Clemens 20.00 50.00
17 Harmon Killebrew 20.00 50.00
18 Bo Bichette 50.00 120.00
19 Jose Canseco 20.00 50.00
20 Anthony Rizzo 50.00 120.00
23 Jim Thome 15.00 40.00
24 Ronald Acuna Jr. 40.00 100.00
26 Willie McCovey 20.00 50.00
28 Mookie Betts 40.00 100.00
29 Willie Stargell 20.00 50.00
31 Greg Maddux 50.00 120.00
32 Don Mattingly 50.00 120.00
33 Barry Zito 10.00 25.00
34 Kirby Puckett 60.00 150.00
35 Dave Winfield 30.00 80.00
36 Eddie Murray 15.00 40.00
39 Brooks Robinson 30.00 80.00
40 Mark McGwire 20.00 50.00
43 Gary Carter 25.00 60.00
44 Wade Boggs 30.00 80.00
45 Joe Mauer 10.00 25.00
48 Andre Dawson 30.00 80.00
50 Willie Mays 30.00 80.00

2020 Topps 206 Wave 5 Old Mill Back

*OLD MILL: 2.5X TO 6X BASIC
STATED ODDS 1:30 PACKS
2 Derek Jeter 25.00 60.00
8 Luis Robert 75.00 200.00
14 Juan Soto 20.00 50.00
15 Lou Gehrig 25.00 60.00
16 Roger Clemens 12.00 30.00
17 Harmon Killebrew 12.00 30.00
18 Bo Bichette 30.00 80.00
19 Jose Canseco 12.00 30.00
20 Anthony Rizzo 30.00 80.00
24 Ronald Acuna Jr. 25.00 60.00
26 Willie McCovey 12.00 30.00
28 Mookie Betts 15.00 40.00
29 Willie Stargell 12.00 30.00
31 Greg Maddux 30.00 80.00
32 Don Mattingly 30.00 80.00
33 Barry Zito 5.00 12.00
34 Kirby Puckett 40.00 100.00
35 Dave Winfield 20.00 50.00
36 Eddie Murray 6.00 15.00
39 Brooks Robinson 10.00 25.00
40 Mark McGwire 12.00 30.00
43 Gary Carter 15.00 40.00
44 Wade Boggs 20.00 50.00
48 Andre Dawson 12.00 30.00
50 Willie Mays 20.00 50.00

2020 Topps 206 Wave 5 Piedmont Back

*PIEDMONT: .5X TO 1.2X BASIC
INSERTED 2 PER PACK
34 Kirby Puckett 2.50 6.00

2020 Topps 206 Wave 5 Polar Bear Back

*POLAR BEAR: 2.5X TO 6X BASIC
STATED ODDS 1:18 PACKS
2 Derek Jeter 25.00 60.00
8 Luis Robert 75.00 200.00
14 Juan Soto 20.00 50.00
15 Lou Gehrig 25.00 60.00
16 Roger Clemens 12.00 30.00
17 Harmon Killebrew 12.00 30.00
18 Bo Bichette 30.00 80.00
19 Jose Canseco 12.00 30.00
20 Anthony Rizzo 30.00 80.00
24 Ronald Acuna Jr. 25.00 60.00
26 Willie McCovey 12.00 30.00
28 Mookie Betts 15.00 40.00
29 Willie Stargell 12.00 30.00
31 Greg Maddux 15.00 40.00
32 Don Mattingly 30.00 80.00
33 Barry Zito 5.00 12.00
34 Kirby Puckett 40.00 100.00
35 Dave Winfield 12.00 30.00
36 Eddie Murray 6.00 15.00
39 Brooks Robinson 10.00 25.00
43 Gary Carter 15.00 40.00
44 Wade Boggs 20.00 50.00
48 Andre Dawson 12.00 30.00
50 Willie Mays 20.00 50.00

2020 Topps 206 Wave 5 Sovereign Back

*SOVEREIGN: 1X TO 2.5X BASIC
STATED ODDS 1:6 PACKS
15 Lou Gehrig 8.00 20.00
17 Harmon Killebrew 4.00 10.00
32 Don Mattingly 6.00 15.00
34 Kirby Puckett 12.00 30.00
50 Willie Mays 8.00 20.00

2020 Topps 206 Wave 5 Sweet Caporal Back

*S.CAPORAL: .75X TO 2X BASIC
STATED ODDS 1:3 PACKS
15 Lou Gehrig 6.00 15.00
32 Don Mattingly 5.00 12.00
34 Kirby Puckett 5.00 12.00
50 Willie Mays 5.00 12.00

2020 Topps 206 Wave 5 Autographs

RANDOM INSERTS IN PACKS
1 Andres Galarraga 75.00 200.00
2 Barry Zito 30.00 80.00
3 Juan Soto 125.00 300.00
4 Ronald Acuna Jr. 200.00 500.00
5 Will Smith 25.00 60.00

2020 Topps 52-Card Baseball Game

2 Yordan Alvarez 4.00 10.00
2 Dylan Cease .60 1.50
2 Nico Hoerner 1.50 4.00
2 Gavin Lux 2.00 5.00
3 Brendan McKay .60 1.50
3 Bo Bichette 3.00 8.00
3 Jesus Luzardo .75 2.00
3 Aristides Aquino 1.00 2.50
4 Luis Robert 8.00 20.00
4 AJ Puk .60 1.50
4 Gleyber Torres 1.25 3.00
4 Shohei Ohtani 1.00 2.50
5 DJ LeMahieu .60 1.50
5 Buster Posey .75 2.00
5 Andrew Benintendi .60 1.50
5 Shane Bieber .60 1.50
6 Jorge Soler .60 1.50
6 Ketel Marte .50 1.25
6 Joey Votto .60 1.50
6 Stephen Strasburg .60 1.50
7 Josh Donaldson .50 1.25
7 Gary Sanchez .60 1.50
7 Walker Buehler .75 2.00
7 Miguel Cabrera .60 1.50
8 Matt Chapman .60 1.50
8 Rafael Devers .75 2.00
8 Ozzie Albies .60 1.50
8 Mookie Betts 1.25 3.00
9 Josh Bell .50 1.25
9 Josh Hader .50 1.25
9 Joey Gallo .60 1.50
9 Austin Riley .75 2.00
A Juan Soto 2.00 5.00
A Gerrit Cole 1.00 2.50
A Mike Trout 3.00 8.00
A Christian Yelich .75 2.00
J Bryce Harper 1.00 2.50
J Clayton Kershaw 1.00 2.50
J Jacob DeGrom 1.25 3.00
J Fernando Tatis Jr 3.00 8.00
K Nolan Arenado 1.00 2.50
K Jose Altuve .50 1.25
K Vladimir Guerrero Jr 1.00 2.50
K Javier Baez .75 2.00
Q Pete Alonso 1.50 4.00
Q Aaron Judge 1.50 4.00
Q Ronald Acuna Jr 2.50 6.00
Q Cody Bellinger 1.25 3.00
10 Masahiro Tanaka .60 1.50
10 Whit Merrifield .60 1.50
10 Anthony Rizzo .75 2.00
10 Trevor Story .60 1.50

2020 Topps 52-Card Baseball Game Variations

2 Derek Jeter 1.50 4.00
2 Mike Schmidt 1.00 2.50
3 Roberto Clemente 1.50 4.00
3 Pedro Martinez .50 1.25
4 Carl Yastrzemski 1.00 2.50
4 Rickey Henderson .60 1.50
5 George Brett 1.25 3.00
5 Ozzie Smith .75 2.00
6 Brooks Robinson .50 1.25
6 Randy Johnson .60 1.50
7 Mariano Rivera .75 2.00
7 Robin Yount .60 1.50
8 Hank Aaron 1.25 3.00
8 Nolan Ryan 2.00 5.00
9 Darryl Strawberry .40 1.00
9 Ryne Sandberg 1.25 3.00
A Jeff Bagwell .50 1.25
A Tom Seaver .50 1.25
J Will Clark .50 1.25
J Frank Robinson .50 1.25
K Mike Mussina .50 1.25
K Ernie Banks .60 1.50
Q Wade Boggs .50 1.25
Q Ichiro .75 2.00
10 Willie Mays 1.25 3.00
10 Rod Carew .50 1.25

2021 Topps '51 Topps Blake Jamieson

ANNCD P/R B/WN 5634-7725 COPIES PER
1 Mike Trout/7679* 2.00 5.00
2 Willie Mays/7679* .75 2.00
3 Duke Snider/7679* .30 .75
4 Babe Ruth/7679* 1.00 2.50
5 Cal Ripken Jr./7679* 1.25 3.00
6 Javier Baez/7679* .50 1.25
7 Greg Maddux/7679* .50 1.25
8 Albert Pujols/7679* .50 1.25
9 George Brett/7679* .75 2.00
10 Yordan Alvarez/7679* 1.00 2.50
11 Wade Boggs/7679* .30 .75
12 Juan Soto/7679* 1.25 3.00
13 Tom Seaver/7679* .30 .75
14 Fernando Tatis Jr./7725* 2.00 5.00
15 Ken Griffey Jr./7725* .75 2.00
16 Shohei Ohtani/7725* .60 1.50
17 Ronald Acuna Jr./7725* 1.50 4.00
18 Warren Spahn/7725* .30 .75
19 Al Kaline/7725* .40 1.00
20 Tony Gwynn/7725* .40 1.00
21 Reggie Jackson/7725* .30 .75
22 Clayton Kershaw/7725* .60 1.50
23 Kris Bryant/7725* .50 1.25
24 Nolan Ryan/7725* 1.25 3.00
25 Pete Alonso/7725* 1.00 2.50
26 Luis Robert/7725* 1.25 3.00
27 Derek Jeter/5634* 1.00 2.50
28 Cody Bellinger/5634* .75 2.00
29 Frank Thomas/5634* .40 1.00
30 Mike Piazza/5634* .40 1.00
31 Max Scherzer/5634* .40 1.00
32 Johnny Bench/5634* .40 1.00
33 Phil Rizzuto/5634* .30 .75
34 Ozzie Smith/5634* .50 1.25
35 Jacob deGrom/5634* .75 2.00
36 Justin Verlander/5634* .40 1.00
37 Christian Yelich/5634* .50 1.25
38 Nolan Arenado/5634* .60 1.50
39 Ernie Banks/5634* .40 1.00
40 Mookie Betts/7085* .75 2.00
41 Bob Feller/7085* .30 .75
42 Jackie Robinson/7085* .40 1.00
43 Aaron Judge/7085* 1.00 2.50
44 Bryce Harper/7085* .60 1.50
45 Ichiro/7085* .50 1.25
46 Hank Aaron/7085* .75 2.00
47 Gerrit Cole/7085* .60 1.50
48 Alec Bohm/7085* 2.50 6.00
49 Casey Mize/7085* 2.00 5.00
50 Joey Bart/7085* .75 2.00
51 Jo Adell/7085* 1.50 4.00
52 Dylan Carlson/7085* 2.00 5.00

2021 Topps '51 Topps Blake Jamieson Blue Back

*BLUE BACK: 8X TO 20X BASIC
RANDOM INSERTS IN BOXES
STATED PRINT RUN 51 SER.#'d SETS

2021 Topps '51 Topps Blake Jamieson Green Back

*GREEN BACK: 12X TO 30X BASIC
RANDOM INSERTS IN BOXES
STATED PRINT RUN 25 SER.#'d SETS

2021 Topps '51 Topps Blake Jamieson Artist Cards

RANDOM INSERTS IN BOXES
STATED PRINT RUN 100 SER.#'d SET
BJ1 Blake Jamieson 60.00 150.00
BJ2 Blake Jamieson 60.00 150.00
BJ3 Blake Jamieson 60.00 150.00
BJ4 Blake Jamieson 60.00 150.00

2021 Topps '51 Topps Blake Jamieson Autographs

SOLD DIRECTLY BY TOPPS ONLINE
STATED PRINT RUN 51 SER.#'d SETS
NO PRICING DUE TO LACK OF MARKET INFO
1 Mike Trout
5 Cal Ripken Jr.
12 Juan Soto
15 Ken Griffey Jr.
17 Ronald Acuna Jr.
26 Luis Robert
28 Cody Bellinger
35 Jacob deGrom
38 Nolan Arenado
44 Bryce Harper
48 Alec Bohm
51 Jo Adell

2021 Topps '51 Topps Blake Jamieson Autographs Green Back

*GREEN BACK: X TO X BASIC
SOLD DIRECTLY BY TOPPS ONLINE
STATED PRINT RUN 25 SER.#'d SETS
NO PRICING DUE TO LACK OF MARKET INFO

2006 Topps '52

COMP.SET w/o SPs (275) 40.00 80.00
COMMON CARD (1-275) .20 .50
COMMON LOGO VAR. 1.25 3.00
LOGO VAR.STATED ODDS 1:5 H,1:5 R
COMMON SP 1.00 2.50
SP STATED ODDS 1:5 H, 1:5 R
1 Howie Kendrick (RC) .40 1.00
2 Enrique Gonzalez (RC) .20 .50
3 Chuck James (RC) .20 .50
4 Chris Britton RC .20 .50
5 David Pauley (RC) .20 .50
6 Angel Pagan (RC) .20 .50
7 Pat Neshek RC 2.00 5.00
8 Walter Young (RC) .20 .50
9 Chris Denorfia (RC) .20 .50
10 Rafael Perez RC .20 .50
11 Ryan Spilborghs (RC) .20 .50
12 Jon Huber RC .20 .50
13 Jordan Tata RC .20 .50
14 Eric Reed (RC) .20 .50
15 Norris Hopper RC .20 .50
16 Scott Olsen (RC) .20 .50
17 Fernando Nieve (RC) .20 .50
18 Chris Booker (RC) .20 .50
19 Chad Billingsley (RC) .30 .75
20 Carlos Villanueva RC .20 .50
21 Craig Hansen RC .50 1.25
22 Dave Gassner (RC) .20 .50
23 Mike Pelfrey RC .50 1.25
24 Matt Smith RC .30 .75
25 Chris Roberson (RC) .20 .50
26 John Van Benschoten (RC) .20 .50
27 Kevin Frandsen (RC) .20 .50
28 Les Walrond (RC) .20 .50
29 James Shields RC .60 1.50
30 Russell Martin (RC) .30 .75
31 Ben Zobrist (RC) 1.00 2.50
32 John Rheinecker (RC) .20 .50
33 Francisco Rosario (RC) .20 .50
34 Santiago Ramirez (RC) .20 .50
35 Mike Napoli RC .30 .75
36 Tony Pena Jr. (RC) .20 .50
37A Jeff Karstens RC .20 .50
37B Jeff Karstens 52 Logo 1.25 3.00
38 Phil Stockman (RC) .20 .50
39 Kurt Birkins RC .20 .50
40 Dustin Pedroia (RC) 6.00 15.00
41 Buck Coats (RC) .20 .50
42 Jim Johnson RC .75 2.00
43 Angel Guzman (RC) .20 .50
44 Kelly Shoppach (RC) .20 .50
45 Josh Wilson (RC) .20 .50
46 Jack Hannahan RC .20 .50
47 Ricky Nolasco (RC) .20 .50
48 T.J. Bohn (RC) .20 .50
49 Joel Zumaya (RC) .50 1.25
50 Phil Barzilla RC .20 .50
51 Justin Huber (RC) .20 .50
52A Willy Aybar (RC) .20 .50
52B Willy Aybar 52 Logo 1.25 3.00
53 Tony Gwynn Jr. (RC) .20 .50
54 Chris Barnwell RC .20 .50
55 Henry Owens RC .20 .50
56 Jeff Bajenaru (RC) .20 .50
57 Jonah Bayliss RC .20 .50
58 Josh Sharpless RC .20 .50
59 Eliezer Alfonzo RC .20 .50
60 Bobby Livingston (RC) .20 .50
61 John Gall (RC) .20 .50
62 Ruddy Lugo (RC) .20 .50
63 Fabio Castro RC .20 .50
64 Casey Janssen RC .20 .50
65 Mike O'Connor RC .20 .50
66 Kendry Morales (RC) .50 1.25
67 James Hoey RC .20 .50
68 Dustin Moseley (RC) .20 .50
69 Peter Moylan RC .20 .50
70 Manny Delcarmen (RC) .20 .50
71 Rich Hill (RC) .50 1.25
72 Boone Logan RC .20 .50
73 Cody Ross (RC) .50 1.25
74 Fausto Carmona (RC) .20 .50
75 Ramon Ramirez (RC) .20 .50
76 Zach Miner (RC) .20 .50
77 Hanley Ramirez UER (RC) .30 .75
78 Josh Johnson (RC) .50 1.25
79 Taylor Buchholz (RC) .20 .50
80 Joe Nelson (RC) .20 .50
81 Hong-Chih Kuo (RC) .50 1.25
82 Chris Mabeus (RC) .20 .50
83 Willie Eyre (RC) .20 .50
84 John Maine (RC) .30 .75
85 Yurendell DeCaster (RC) .20 .50
86 Mike Thompson RC .20 .50
87 Brian Wilson RC 3.00 8.00
88A Matt Cain (RC) 1.25 3.00
88B Matt Cain 52 Logo 8.00 20.00
89 Sean Green RC .20 .50
90 Tyler Johnson (RC) .20 .50
91 Jason Childers RC .20 .50
92 Wes Littleton (RC) .20 .50
93 Ty Taubenheim RC .30 .75
94 Saul Rivera (RC) .20 .50
95 Reggie Willits RC .50 1.25
96 Carlos Quentin (RC) .30 .75
97 Macay McBride (RC) .20 .50
98 Brandon Fahey RC .20 .50
99 Sean Marshall (RC) .20 .50
100 Sean Tracey (RC) .20 .50
101 Brian Slocum (RC) .20 .50
102 Choo Freeman (RC) .20 .50
103 Brent Clevlen (RC) .30 .75
104 Josh Willingham (RC) .30 .75
105 Chris Resop (RC) .20 .50
106 Chris Sampson RC .20 .50
107A James Loney (RC) .30 .75
107B James Loney 52 Logo 2.00 5.00
108 Matt Kemp (RC) .50 1.25
109 Jason Kubel (RC) .20 .50
110 Brian Bannister (RC) .20 .50
111 Kevin Thompson (RC) .20 .50
112 Jeremy Brown (RC) .20 .50
113 Brian Sanches (RC) .20 .50
114 Nate McLouth (RC) .20 .50
115 Ben Johnson (RC) .20 .50
116 Jonathan Sanchez (RC) .50 1.25
117 Mark Lowe (RC) .20 .50
118 Skip Schumaker (RC) .20 .50
119 Jason Hammel (RC) .50 1.25
120 Drew Meyer (RC) .20 .50
121 Melvin Dorta RC .20 .50
122 Jeff Mathis (RC) .20 .50
123 Davis Romero (RC) .20 .50
124 Joey Devine RC .20 .50
125 Sendy Rleal RC .20 .50
126 Freddie Bynum (RC) .20 .50
127 Brian Anderson (RC) .20 .50
128 Jeremy Sowers (RC) .20 .50
129 Ryan Shealy (RC) .20 .50
130 Reggie Abercrombie (RC) .20 .50
131 Matt Albers (RC) .20 .50
132 Lastings Milledge (RC) .20 .50
133 Robert Andino RC .20 .50
134 Chris Demaria RC .20 .50
135 Boof Bonser (RC) .30 .75
136 Alay Soler RC .20 .50
137 Wil Nieves (RC) .20 .50
138 Mike Rouse (RC) .20 .50
139 Carlos Ruiz (RC) .20 .50
140 Matt Capps (RC) .20 .50
141 Travis Ishikawa (RC) .30 .75
142 Josh Kinney RC .20 .50
143 Josh Rupe (RC) .20 .50
144 Shaun Marcum (RC) .20 .50
145 Jason Bergmann RC .20 .50
146 Tommy Murphy (RC) .20 .50
147 Martin Prado (RC) .30 .75
148 Val Majewski (RC) .20 .50
149 Ian Kinsler (RC) .60 1.50
150 Joe Winkelsas (RC) .20 .50
151 Agustin Montero (RC) .20 .50
152 Joe Inglett RC .20 .50
153 Manuel Corpas RC .20 .50
154 Yusmeiro Petit (RC) .20 .50
155 Mark Woodyard (RC) .20 .50
156 Jeff Fulchino RC .20 .50
157 Stephen Andrade (RC) .20 .50
158 Tim Hamulack (RC) .20 .50
159 Colter Bean (RC) .20 .50
160 Anderson Hernandez (RC) .20 .50
161 Kevin Reese (RC) .20 .50
162 Jason Windsor (RC) .20 .50
163A Paul Maholm (RC) .20 .50
163B Paul Maholm 52 Logo 1.25 3.00
164 Jeremy Accardo RC .20 .50
165 Joel Guzman (RC) .20 .50
166 Erick Aybar (RC) .20 .50
167 Scott Thorman (RC) .20 .50
168 Adam Loewen (RC) .20 .50
169 Carlos Marmol RC .60 1.50
170 Bill Bray (RC) .20 .50
171 Edward Mujica RC .20 .50
172 Jeremy Hermida (RC) .20 .50
173 Taylor Tankersley (RC) .20 .50
174 Bobby Keppel (RC) .20 .50
175 Chris B. Young (RC) .50 1.25
176 Josh Rabe RC .20 .50
177 T.J. Beam (RC) .20 .50
178A Shane Komine RC .30 .75
178B Shane Komine 52 Logo 2.00 5.00
179 Scott Mathieson (RC) .20 .50
180 Josh Barfield (RC) .20 .50
181 Justin Knoedler (RC) .20 .50
182 Emiliano Fruto RC .20 .50
183 Adam Wainwright (RC) .30 .75
184 Nick Masset (RC) .20 .50
185 Ryan Roberts RC .20 .50
186 Brandon Watson (RC) .20 .50
187 Chris Bootcheck (RC) .20 .50
188 Dan Ortmeier (RC) .20 .50
189 Kevin Barry (RC) .20 .50
190 Cory Morris RC .20 .50
191 Kason Gabbard (RC) .20 .50
192 Tom Mastny (RC) .20 .50
193 David Aardsma (RC) .20 .50
194 Anthony Reyes (RC) .20 .50
195 Mike Jacobs (RC) .20 .50
196 Conor Jackson (RC) .30 .75
197 Kenji Johjima RC .50 1.25
198 Jack Taschner (RC) .20 .50
199 Renyel Pinto (RC) .20 .50
200 Chad Santos (RC) .20 .50
201 Aaron Rakers (RC) .20 .50
202 Franklin Gutierrez (RC) .20 .50
203 Chris Coste RC .50 1.25
204 Chris Iannetta RC .20 .50
205 Mike Vento (RC) .20 .50
206 Ryan O'Malley RC .20 .50
207 Jason Botts (RC) .20 .50
208 John Hattig (RC) .20 .50
209 Brandon Harper RC .20 .50
210 Ryan Theriot RC .60 1.50
211 Travis Hughes (RC) .20 .50
212 Paul Hoover (RC) .20 .50
213 Brayan Pena (RC) .20 .50
214 Craig Breslow RC .20 .50
215 Eude Brito (RC) .20 .50
216A Melky Cabrera (RC) .30 .75
216B Melky Cabrera 52 Logo 2.00 5.00
217A Jonathan Broxton (RC) .20 .50
217B Jonathan Broxton 52 Logo 1.25 3.00
218 Bryan Corey (RC) .20 .50
219 Ron Flores RC .20 .50
220 Andrew Brown (RC) .20 .50
221 Jaime Bubela (RC) .20 .50
222 Jason Bulger (RC) .20 .50
223 Alberto Callaspo (RC) .20 .50
224 Jose Capellan (RC) .20 .50
225A Cole Hamels (RC) .60 1.50
225B Cole Hamels 52 Logo 4.00 10.00
226 Bernie Castro (RC) .20 .50
227 Shin-Soo Choo (RC) .30 .75
228 Doug Clark (RC) .20 .50
229 Roy Corcoran RC .20 .50
230 Tim Corcoran RC .20 .50

231 Nelson Cruz (RC) .75 2.00
232 Rajai Davis (RC) .20 .50
233A Chris Duncan (RC) .30 .75
233B Chris Duncan 52 Logo 2.00 5.00
234 Scott Dunn (RC) .20 .50
235 Mike Esposito (RC) .20 .50
236 Scott Feldman RC .20 .50
237 Luis Figueroa RC .20 .50
238 Bartolome Fortunato (RC) .20 .50
239 Alejandro Freire RC .20 .50
240 J.J. Furmaniak (RC) .20 .50
241 Nick Markakis (RC) .40 1.00
242 Matt Garza (RC) .20 .50
243 Justin Germano (RC) .20 .50
244 Alexis Gomez (RC) .20 .50
245 Tom Gorzelanny (RC) .20 .50
246 Dan Uggla (RC) .30 .75
247 Jeremy Guthrie (RC) .20 .50
248 Stephen Drew (RC) .40 1.00
249 Brendan Harris (RC) .20 .50
250 Jeff Harris RC .20 .50
251 Corey Hart (RC) .20 .50
252 Chris Heintz RC .20 .50
253 Prince Fielder (RC) 1.00 2.50
254 Francisco Liriano (RC) .50 1.25
255 Jason Hirsh (RC) .20 .50
256 J.R. House (RC) .20 .50
257 Zach Jackson (RC) .20 .50
258 Charlton Jimerson (RC) .20 .50
259 Greg Jones (RC) .20 .50
260 Mitch Jones (RC) .20 .50
261 Ryan Jorgensen RC .20 .50
262 Logan Kensing (RC) .20 .50
263 John Koronka (RC) .20 .50
264 Anthony Lerew (RC) .20 .50
265 Anibal Sanchez (RC) .20 .50
266 Juan Mateo RC .20 .50
267 Paul McAnulty (RC) .20 .50
268 Dustin McGowan (RC) .20 .50
269 Marty McLeary (RC) .20 .50
270 Ryan Zimmerman (RC) .60 1.50
271 Dustin Nippert (RC) .20 .50
272 Eric O'Flaherty RC .20 .50
273 Ronny Paulino (RC) .20 .50
274 Tony Pena (RC) .20 .50
275 Hayden Penn (RC) .20 .50
276 Miguel Perez SP (RC) 1.00 2.50
277 Paul Phillips SP (RC) 1.00 2.50
278 Omar Quintanilla SP (RC) 1.00 2.50
279 Guillermo Quiroz SP (RC) 1.00 2.50
280 Darrell Rasner SP (RC) 1.00 2.50
281 Kenny Ray SP (RC) 1.00 2.50
282 Royce Ring SP (RC) 1.00 2.50
283 Brian Rogers SP RC 1.00 2.50
284 Ed Rogers SP (RC) 1.00 2.50
285 Danny Sandoval SP RC 1.00 2.50
286 Joe Saunders SP (RC) 1.00 2.50
287 Chris Schroder SP RC 1.00 2.50
288 Mike Smith SP (RC) 1.00 2.50
289 Travis Smith SP (RC) 1.00 2.50
290 Geovany Soto SP (RC) 2.50 6.00
291 Brian Sweeney SP (RC) 1.00 2.50
292 Jon Switzer SP (RC) 1.00 2.50
293 Joe Thurston SP (RC) 1.00 2.50
294 Jermaine Van Buren SP (RC) 1.00 2.50
295 Ryan Garko SP (RC) 1.00 2.50
296 Cla Meredith SP (RC) 1.00 2.50
297 Luke Scott SP (RC) 1.00 2.50
298 Andy Marte SP (RC) 1.00 2.50
299 Jered Weaver SP (RC) 3.00 8.00
300 Freddy Guzman SP (RC) 1.00 2.50
301 Jonathan Papelbon SP (RC) 5.00 12.00
302 John-Ford Griffin SP (RC) 1.00 2.50
303 Jon Lester SP RC 4.00 10.00
304 Shawn Hill SP (RC) 1.00 2.50
305 Brian Myrow SP RC 1.00 2.50
306 Anderson Garcia SP RC 1.00 2.50
307 Andre Ethier SP (RC) 3.00 8.00
308 Ben Hendrickson SP (RC) 1.00 2.50
309 Alejandro Machado SP (RC) 1.00 2.50
310 Justin Verlander SP (RC) 8.00 20.00
311A Mickey Mantle SP Blue 12.00 30.00
311B Mickey Mantle Black 2.50 6.00
311C Mickey Mantle Green 2.50 6.00
311D Mickey Mantle Orange 2.50 6.00
311E Mickey Mantle Red 2.50 6.00
311F Mickey Mantle Yellow 2.50 6.00
312 Steve Stemle SP RC 1.00 2.50

2006 Topps '52 Chrome

COMMON CARD .75 2.00
SEMISTARS 1.25 3.00
UNLISTED STARS 2.00 5.00
STATED ODDS 1:5 H, 1:7 R
STATED PRINT RUN 1952 SER.#'d SETS
1 Howie Kendrick 1.50 4.00
2 David Pauley .75 2.00
3 Chris Denorfia .75 2.00
4 Jordan Tata .75 2.00
5 Fernando Nieve .75 2.00
6 Craig Hansen 2.00 5.00
7 Mickey Mantle 6.00 15.00
8 James Shields 2.50 6.00
9 Francisco Rosario .75 2.00
10 Jeff Karstens .75 2.00
11 Buck Coats .75 2.00
12 Josh Wilson .75 2.00
13 Joel Zumaya 2.00 5.00
14 Tony Gwynn Jr. .75 2.00
15 Jonah Bayliss .75 2.00
16 John Gall .75 2.00
17 Mike O'Connor .75 2.00
18 Peter Moylan .75 2.00
19 Cody Ross 2.00 5.00
20 Hanley Ramirez UER 1.25 3.00
21 Hong-Chih Kuo 2.00 5.00
22 Yurendell DeCaster .75 2.00
23 Sean Green .75 2.00
24 Ty Taubenheim 1.25 3.00
25 Macay McBride .75 2.00
26 Brian Slocum .75 2.00
27 Chris Resop .75 2.00
28 Jason Kubel .75 2.00
29 Brian Sanches .75 2.00
30 Mark Lowe .75 2.00
31 Melvin Dorta .75 2.00
32 Sendy Rleal .75 2.00
33 Ryan Shealy .75 2.00
34 Robert Andino .75 2.00
35 Wil Nieves .75 2.00
36 Travis Ishikawa 1.25 3.00
37 Jason Bergmann .75 2.00
38 Ian Kinsler 2.50 6.00
39 Manuel Corpas .75 2.00
40 Stephen Andrade .75 2.00
41 Kevin Reese .75 2.00
42 Joel Guzman .75 2.00
43 Carlos Marmol 2.50 6.00
44 Taylor Tankersley .75 2.00
45 T.J. Beam .75 2.00
46 Justin Knoedler .75 2.00
47 Ryan Roberts .75 2.00
48 Kevin Barry .75 2.00
49 David Aardsma .75 2.00
50 Kenji Johjima 2.00 5.00
51 Aaron Rakers .75 2.00
52 Mike Vento .75 2.00
53 Brandon Harper .75 2.00
54 Brayan Pena .75 2.00
55 Jonathan Broxton .75 2.00
56 Jaime Bubela .75 2.00
57 Cole Hamels 2.50 6.00
58 Roy Corcoran .75 2.00
59 Chris Duncan 1.25 3.00
60 Luis Figueroa .75 2.00
61 Kendry Morales 2.00 5.00
62 Tom Gorzelanny .75 2.00
63 Brendan Harris .75 2.00
64 Anibal Sanchez .75 2.00
65 Zach Jackson .75 2.00
66 Ryan Jorgensen .75 2.00
67 Josh Johnson 2.00 5.00
68 Marty McLeary .75 2.00
69 Ronny Paulino .75 2.00
70 Tyler Johnson .75 2.00
71 Reggie Abercrombie .75 2.00
72 Nick Markakis 1.50 4.00
73 J.J. Furmaniak .75 2.00
74 Prince Fielder 4.00 10.00
75 Enrique Gonzalez .75 2.00
76 Angel Pagan .75 2.00
77 Rafael Perez .75 2.00
78 Eric Reed .75 2.00
79 Chris Booker .75 2.00
80 Dave Gassner .75 2.00
81 John Van Benschoten .75 2.00
82 Russell Martin 1.25 3.00
83 Santiago Ramirez .75 2.00
84 Phil Stockman .75 2.00
85 Jim Johnson 3.00 8.00
86 Jack Hannahan .75 2.00
87 Phil Barzilla .75 2.00
88 Chris Barnwell .75 2.00
89 Josh Sharpless .75 2.00
90 Chris Roberson .75 2.00

2006 Topps '52 Chrome Refractors

*CHROME REF: .6X TO 1.5X CHROME
STATED ODDS 1:19 H, 1:20 R
STATED PRINT RUN 552 SER.#'d SETS

2006 Topps '52 Chrome Gold Refractors

COMMON CARD 5.00 12.00
SEMISTARS 8.00 20.00
UNLISTED STARS 12.50 30.00
STATED ODDS 1:207 H, 1:207 R
STATED PRINT RUN 52 SER.#'d SETS
7 Mickey Mantle 200.00 300.00

2006 Topps '52 Debut Flashbacks

COMPLETE SET (20) 15.00 40.00
STATED ODDS 1:6 H, 1:6 R
*CHROME: .75X TO 2X BASIC
CHROME ODDS 1:25 H, 1:25 R
CHR.PRINT RUN 1952 SER.#'d SETS
CHROME REF.ODDS 1:87 H, 1:88 R
GOLD REF: 4X TO 10X BASIC
GOLD REF. ODDS 1:931 H, 1:931 R
DF1 Dontrelle Willis .50 1.25
DF2 Carlos Beltran .75 2.00
DF3 Albert Pujols 1.50 4.00
DF4 Ichiro Suzuki 1.50 4.00
DF5 Mike Piazza 1.25 3.00
DF6 Nomar Garciaparra .75 2.00
DF7 Scott Rolen .75 2.00
DF8 Mariano Rivera 1.50 4.00
DF9 David Ortiz 1.25 3.00
DF10 Johnny Damon .75 2.00
DF11 Tom Glavine .75 2.00
DF12 David Wright 1.00 2.50
DF13 Greg Maddux 1.50 4.00
DF14 Manny Ramirez 1.25 3.00
DF15 Alex Rodriguez 1.50 4.00
DF16 Roger Clemens 1.50 4.00
DF17 Alfonso Soriano .75 2.00
DF18 Frank Thomas 1.25 3.00
DF19 Chipper Jones 1.25 3.00
DF20 Ivan Rodriguez .75 2.00

2006 Topps '52 Debut Flashbacks Chrome Refractors

*CHROME REF: 1.25X TO 3X BASIC
STATED ODDS 1:87 H, 1:88 R
STATED PRINT RUN 552 SER.#'d SETS

2006 Topps '52 Debut Flashbacks Chrome Gold Refractors

GOLD REF: 4X TO 10X BASIC
STATED ODDS 1:931 H, 1:931 R
STATED PRINT RUN 52 SER.#'d SETS

2006 Topps '52 Dynamic Duos

COMPLETE SET (15) 8.00 20.00
STATED ODDS 1:4 H, 1:4 R
DD1 S.Drew/C.Quentin 1.00 2.50
DD2 J.Papelbon/J.Lester 2.50 6.00
DD3 J.Zumaya/J.Verlander 4.00 10.00
DD4 D.Uggla/H.Ramirez .75 2.00
DD5 J.Broxton/C.Billingsley .75 2.00
DD6 F.Liriano/M.Garza 1.25 3.00
DD7 L.Milledge/J.Maine .75 2.00
DD8 C.Coste/C.Hamels 1.50 4.00
DD9 M.Napoli/H.Kendrick 1.00 2.50
DD10 J.Inglett/A.Marte .50 1.25
DD11 J.Hermida/J.Willingham .75 2.00
DD12 M.Kemp/J.Loney 1.25 3.00
DD13 A.Ethier/R.Martin 1.50 4.00
DD14 M.Cabrera/J.Karstens .75 2.00
DD15 R.Nolasco/S.Olsen
J.Johnson/A.Sanchez 1.25 3.00

2006 Topps '52 Signatures

GROUP A ODDS 1:11,000 H, 1:52,000 R
GROUP B ODDS 1:2580 H, 1:9500 R
GROUP C ODDS 1:130 H, 1:410 R
GROUP D ODDS 1:912 H, 1:3000 R
GROUP E ODDS 1:111 H, 1:372 R
GROUP F ODDS 1:104 H, 1:358 R
GROUP G ODDS 1:32 H, 1:115 R
GROUP H ODDS 1:85 H, 1:300 R
GROUP I ODDS 1:30 H, 1:111 R
GROUP J ODDS 1:20 H, 1:76 R
NO A-B PRICING DUE TO SCARCITY
EXCH DEADLINE 12/31/08
ASTERISK = PARTIAL EXCHANGE
AG Angel Guzman E 3.00 8.00
AL Anthony Lerew H 3.00 8.00
AP Angel Pagan F 5.00 12.00
AS Anibal Sanchez H 5.00 12.00
BA Brian Anderson D 3.00 8.00
BB Boof Bonser C 5.00 12.00
BC Buck Coats G 3.00 8.00
BPB Brian Bannister E 5.00 12.00
BS Brian Slocum I 3.00 8.00
BZ Ben Zobrist J 5.00 12.00
CHJ Chuck James F 5.00 12.00
CI Chris Iannetta E 3.00 8.00
CJ C.Jones B 75.00 150.00
CM Chris Mabeus I 3.00 8.00
DO D.Ortiz B EXCH 40.00 80.00
DU Dan Uggla E 3.00 8.00
EA Erick Aybar J 3.00 8.00
EF E.Fruto J EXCH * 3.00 8.00
EG Enrique Gonzalez J 3.00 8.00
EM Edward Mujica J 5.00 12.00
FC Fabio Castro G 3.00 8.00
FG Franklin Gutierrez H 5.00 12.00
HCK Hong-Chih Kuo G 8.00 20.00
HK Howie Kendrick C 3.00 8.00
JFS Joe Saunders C 5.00 12.00
JG Joel Guzman F 3.00 8.00
JK Josh Kinney J 3.00 8.00
JM Jeff Mathis F EXCH 3.00 8.00
JP Jonathan Papelbon G 8.00 20.00
JS Josh Sharpless I 3.00 8.00
JV Justin Verlander C 60.00 150.00
JVB John Van Benschoten I 3.00 8.00
JW J.Weaver C EXCH 15.00 40.00
JWK Jeff Karstens G 5.00 12.00
JZ Joel Zumaya C 5.00 12.00
KM Kendry Morales G 3.00 8.00
MA Matt Albers I 3.00 8.00
MC M.Cabrera C 3.00 8.00
MG Matt Garza C 5.00 12.00
MK Matt Kemp G 8.00 20.00
MN M.Napoli G 3.00 8.00
MTC Matt Cain C 5.00 12.00
RA Reggie Abercrombie G 3.00 8.00
RO Ryan O'Malley G 3.00 8.00
SD Stephen Drew C 3.00 8.00
SM Scott Mathieson I 3.00 8.00
TJB T.J. Bohn I 3.00 8.00
TM Tom Mastny J 3.00 8.00
WB Bill Bray E 3.00 8.00
YD Yurendell DeCaster J 3.00 8.00
YP Yusmeiro Petit E 3.00 8.00

2006 Topps 52 Signatures Red Ink

STATED ODDS 1:235 H, 1:840 R
STATED PRINT RUN 52 SER.#'d SETS
EXCH DEADLINE 12/31/08

2007 Topps '52

COMP.SET w/o SPs (202) 20.00 50.00
COMMON CARD (1-227) .25 .60
COMMON ACTION VARIATION 2.00 5.00
ACT.VAR.STATED ODDS 1:6 H, 1:6 R
COMMON SP 2.00 5.00
SP STATED ODDS 1:6 H, 1:6 R
1 Akinori Iwamura RC .60 1.50
2 Angel Sanchez RC .25 .60
3 Luis Hernandez (RC) .25 .60
4 Joaquin Arias (RC) .25 .60
5a Troy Tulowitzki (RC) .75 2.00
5b Tulowitzki Action SP 2.50 6.00
6 Jesus Flores RC .25 .60
7 Mickey Mantle 2.00 5.00
8 Kory Casto (RC) .25 .60
9 Tony Abreu RC .60 1.50
10 Kevin Kouzmanoff (RC) .25 .60
11 Travis Buck (RC) .25 .60
12 Kurt Suzuki (RC) .25 .60
13 Matt DeSalvo (RC) .25 .60
14 Jerry Owens (RC) .25 .60
15 Alex Gordon RC .75 2.00
16 Jeff Baker (RC) .25 .60
17 Ben Francisco (RC) .25 .60
18 Nate Schierholtz (RC) .25 .60
19 Nathan Haynes (RC) .25 .60
20a Ryan Braun (RC) 1.25 3.00
20b R.Braun Action SP 3.00 8.00
21 Brian Barden RC .25 .60
22 Sean Barker RC .25 .60
23 Alejandro De Aza RC .40 1.00
24 Jamie Burke (RC) .25 .60
25 Michael Bourn (RC) .40 1.00
26 Jeff Salazar (RC) .25 .60
27 Chase Headley (RC) .25 .60
28 Chris Basak RC .25 .60
29 Mike Fontenot (RC) .25 .60
30a Hunter Pence (RC) .75 2.00
30b H.Pence Action SP 3.00 8.00
31 Masumi Kuwata RC .25 .60
32 Ryan Rowland-Smith RC .25 .60
33 Tyler Clippard (RC) .40 1.00
34 Matt Lindstrom (RC) .25 .60
35 Fred Lewis (RC) .40 1.00
36 Brett Carroll RC .25 .60
37 Alexi Casilla RC .40 1.00
38 Nick Gorneault (RC) .25 .60
39 Dennis Sarfate (RC) .25 .60
40 Felix Pie (RC) .25 .60
41 Miguel Montero (RC) .25 .60
42 Danny Putnam (RC) .25 .60
43 Shane Youman RC .25 .60
44 Andy LaRoche (RC) .25 .60
45 Jarrod Saltalamacchia (RC) .40 1.00
46 Kei Igawa RC .60 1.50
47 Don Kelly (RC) .25 .60
48 Fernando Cortez (RC) .25 .60
49 Travis Metcalf RC .40 1.00
50a Daisuke Matsuzaka RC 1.00 2.50
50b D.Matsuzaka Action SP 3.00 8.00
51 Edwar Ramirez RC .60 1.50
52 Ryan Sweeney (RC) .25 .60
53 Shawn Riggans (RC) .25 .60
54 Billy Sadler (RC) .25 .60
55 Billy Butler (RC) .40 1.00
56 Andy Cavazos RC .25 .60
57 Sean Henn (RC) .25 .60
58 Brian Esposito (RC) .25 .60
59 Brandon Morrow RC 1.25 3.00
60 Adam Lind (RC) .25 .60
61 Joe Smith RC .25 .60
62 Chris Stewart RC .25 .60
63 Eulogio De La Cruz (RC) .40 1.00
64 Sean Gallagher (RC) .25 .60
65 Carlos Gomez RC .50 1.25
66 Jailen Peguero RC .25 .60
67 Juan Perez RC .25 .60
68 Levale Speigner RC .25 .60
69 Jamie Vermilyea RC .25 .60
70a Delmon Young (RC) .40 1.00
70b D.Young Action SP 2.00 5.00
71 Jo-Jo Reyes (RC) .25 .60
72 Zack Segovia (RC) .25 .60
73 Andy Sonnanstine RC .25 .60
74 Chase Wright RC .60 1.50
75 Josh Fields (RC) .25 .60
76 Jon Knott (RC) .25 .60
77 Guillermo Rodriguez RC .25 .60
78 Jon Coutlangus (RC) .25 .60
79 Kevin Cameron RC .25 .60
80 Mark Reynolds RC .75 2.00
81 Brian Stokes (RC) .25 .60
82 Alberto Arias RC .25 .60
83 Yoel Hernandez RC .25 .60
84 David Murphy (RC) .25 .60
85 Josh Hamilton (RC) .75 2.00
86 Justin Hampson (RC) .25 .60
87 Doug Slaten RC .25 .60
88 Joseph Bisenius RC .25 .60
89 Troy Cate RC .25 .60
90 Homer Bailey (RC) .40 1.00
91 Jacoby Ellsbury (RC) 1.50 4.00
92 Devern Hansack RC .25 .60
93 Zach McClellan RC .25 .60
94 Vinny Rottino (RC) .25 .60
95 Elijah Dukes RC .40 1.00
96 Ryan Z. Braun UER RC .25 .60
97 Lee Gardner (RC) .25 .60
98 Joakim Soria RC .25 .60
99 Jason Miller (RC) .25 .60
100a Hideki Okajima RC 1.25 3.00
100b H.Okajima Action SP 3.00 8.00
101 John Danks RC .40 1.00
102 Garrett Jones (RC) .60 1.50
103 Jensen Lewis RC .25 .60
104 Clay Rapada RC .25 .60
105 Kyle Kendrick RC .60 1.50
106 Eric Stults RC .25 .60
107 Jared Burton RC .25 .60
108 Julio DePaula RC .40 1.00
109 Jesse Litsch RC .40 1.00
110 Micah Owings (RC) .25 .60
111 Cory Doyne (RC) .25 .60
112 Jay Marshall RC .25 .60
113 Mike Schultz RC .25 .60
114 Juan Salas (RC) .25 .60
115 Matt Chico (RC) .25 .60
116 Brad Salmon RC .25 .60
117 Jeff Bailey (RC) .25 .60
118 Gustavo Molina RC .25 .60
119 Brian Burres (RC) .25 .60
120 Yovani Gallardo (RC) .60 1.50
121 Hector Gimenez (RC) .25 .60
122 Kelvin Jimenez RC .25 .60
123 Rick Vanden Hurk RC .25 .60
124 Billy Petrick (RC) .25 .60
125 Andrew Miller RC 1.00 2.50
126 Rocky Cherry RC .60 1.50
127 Jordan De Jong RC .25 .60
128 Eric Hull RC .25 .60
129 Kevin Mahar RC .25 .60
130a Tim Lincecum RC 1.25 3.00
130b T.Lincecum Action SP 3.00 8.00
131 Garrett Olson (RC) .25 .60
132 Neal Musser RC .25 .60
133 Mike Rabelo RC .25 .60
134 Dennis Dove (RC) .25 .60
135 J.D. Durbin (RC) .25 .60
136 Jose Garcia RC .25 .60
137 Marcus McBeth (RC) .25 .60
138 Curtis Thigpen (RC) .25 .60
139 Mike Zagurski RC .25 .60
140 Kevin Slowey (RC) .60 1.50
141 Dewon Day RC .25 .60
142 Glen Perkins (RC) .25 .60
143 Brian Wolfe (RC) .25 .60
144 Dallas Braden RC .40 1.00
145 J.A. Happ (RC) 1.00 2.50
146 Lee Gronkiewicz RC .25 .60
147 Cesar Jimenez RC .25 .60
148 Mark McLemore (RC) .25 .60
149 Connor Robertson RC .25 .60
150a Phil Hughes (RC) .60 1.50
150b P.Hughes Action SP 3.00 8.00
151 Matt Brown (RC) .25 .60
152 Ryan Feierabend (RC) .25 .60
153 Brendan Ryan (RC) .25 .60
154 Terry Evans RC .25 .60
155 Eric Patterson (RC) .25 .60
156 Patrick Misch (RC) .25 .60
157 Darren Clarke RC .25 .60
158 Kevin Melillo (RC) .25 .60
159 Edwin Bellorin RC .25 .60
160 Ubaldo Jimenez (RC) .75 2.00
161 Ryan Budde (RC) .25 .60
162 Brian Buscher RC .40 1.00
163 Juan Gutierrez RC .25 .60
164 Franklin Morales (RC) .40 1.00
165 Carmen Pignatiello (RC) .25 .60
166 Jair Jurrjens (RC) .40 1.00
167 Manny Acosta (RC) .25 .60
168 Ian Stewart RC .25 .60
169 Daniel Barone (RC) .25 .60
170a Justin Upton RC .75 2.00
170b J.Upton Action SP 3.00 8.00
171 Tommy Watkins RC .40 1.00
172 Ross Wolf RC .25 .60
173 Jack Cassel RC .25 .60
174 Asdrubal Cabrera RC 1.25 3.00
175 Mauro Zarate RC .25 .60
176 Aaron Laffey RC .60 1.50
177 Marcus Gwyn RC .25 .60
178 Danny Richar RC .25 .60
179 Joel Hanrahan (RC) .40 1.00
180 Cameron Maybin RC .40 1.00
181 John Lannan RC .25 .60
182 Shelley Duncan (RC) .60 1.50
183 Brandon Wood (RC) .25 .60
184 Delwyn Young (RC) .25 .60
185 Manny Parra (RC) .25 .60
186 Ehren Wassermann RC .25 .60
187 Jose A. Reyes RC .25 .60
188 Jose Ascanio RC .25 .60
190a Alvin Colina RC .60 1.50
190b J.Chamberlain Action SP 5.00 12.00
191 Yunel Escobar (RC) .25 .60
192 Carlos Maldonado (RC) .25 .60
193 Dan Meyer (RC) .25 .60
194 Scott Moore (RC) .25 .60
195 Romulo Sanchez RC .25 .60
196 Tom Shearn (RC) .25 .60
197 Craig Stansberry (RC) .25 .60
201 Joba Chamberlain RC .40 1.00
202 John Nelson SP (RC) 2.00 5.00
203 Phil Dumatrait (RC) .25 .60
204 Brandon Moss (RC) .25 .60
205 Beltran Perez (RC) .25 .60
206 Drew Anderson RC .25 .60
207 Brett Campbell RC .25 .60
208 Andy Cannizaro SP RC 2.00 5.00
209 Travis Chick SP (RC) 2.00 5.00
210 Francisco Cruceta SP (RC) 2.00 5.00
211 Jose Diaz SP (RC) 2.00 5.00
212 Jeff Fiorentino SP (RC) 2.00 5.00
213 Tim Gradoville SP RC 2.00 5.00
214 Kevin Hooper SP (RC) 2.00 5.00
215 Philip Humber SP (RC) 2.00 5.00
216 Juan Lara SP RC 2.00 5.00
217 Mitch Maier SP RC 2.00 5.00
218 Juan Morillo SP (RC) 2.00 5.00
219 A.J. Murray SP RC 2.00 5.00
220 Chris Narveson SP (RC) 2.00 5.00
221 Oswaldo Navarro SP RC 2.00 5.00

2007 Topps '52 Black Back

STATED ODDS 1:6 HOBBY
1 Akinori Iwamura 2.50 6.00
2 Angel Sanchez 1.00 2.50
3 Luis Hernandez 1.00 2.50
4 Joaquin Arias 1.00 2.50
5 Troy Tulowitzki 3.00 8.00
6 Jesus Flores 1.00 2.50
7 Mickey Mantle 8.00 20.00
8 Kory Casto 1.00 2.50
9 Tony Abreu 2.50 6.00
10 Kevin Kouzmanoff 1.00 2.50
11 Travis Buck 1.00 2.50
12 Kurt Suzuki 1.00 2.50
13 Matt DeSalvo 1.00 2.50
14 Jerry Owens 1.00 2.50
15 Alex Gordon 3.00 8.00
16 Jeff Baker 1.00 2.50
17 Ben Francisco 1.00 2.50
18 Nate Schierholtz 1.00 2.50
19 Nathan Haynes 1.00 2.50
20 Ryan Braun 5.00 12.00
21 Brian Barden 1.00 2.50
22 Sean Barker 1.00 2.50
23 Alejandro De Aza 1.50 4.00
24 Jamie Burke 1.00 2.50
25 Michael Bourn 1.50 4.00
26 Jeff Salazar 1.00 2.50
27 Chase Headley 1.00 2.50
28 Chris Basak 1.00 2.50
29 Mike Fontenot 1.00 2.50
30 Hunter Pence 3.00 8.00
31 Masumi Kuwata 1.00 2.50
32 Ryan Rowland-Smith 1.00 2.50
33 Tyler Clippard 1.50 4.00
34 Matt Lindstrom 1.00 2.50
35 Fred Lewis 1.50 4.00
36 Brett Carroll 1.00 2.50
37 Alexi Casilla 1.50 4.00
38 Nick Gorneault 1.00 2.50
39 Dennis Sarfate 1.00 2.50
40 Felix Pie 1.00 2.50
41 Miguel Montero 1.00 2.50
42 Danny Putnam 1.00 2.50
43 Shane Youman 1.00 2.50
44 Andy LaRoche 1.00 2.50
45 Jarrod Saltalamacchia 1.50 4.00
46 Kei Igawa 2.50 6.00
47 Don Kelly 1.00 2.50
48 Fernando Cortez 1.00 2.50
49 Travis Metcalf 1.50 4.00
50 Daisuke Matsuzaka 4.00 10.00
51 Edwar Ramirez 2.50 6.00
52 Ryan Sweeney 1.00 2.50
53 Shawn Riggans 1.00 2.50
54 Billy Sadler 1.00 2.50
55 Billy Butler 1.50 4.00
56 Andy Cavazos 1.00 2.50
57 Sean Henn 1.00 2.50
58 Brian Esposito 1.00 2.50
59 Brandon Morrow 5.00 12.00
60 Adam Lind 1.00 2.50
61 Joe Smith 1.00 2.50
62 Chris Stewart 1.00 2.50
63 Eulogio De La Cruz 1.50 4.00
64 Sean Gallagher 1.00 2.50
65 Carlos Gomez 2.00 5.00
66 Jailen Peguero 1.00 2.50
67 Juan Perez 1.00 2.50
68 Levale Speigner 1.00 2.50
69 Jamie Vermilyea 1.00 2.50
70 Delmon Young 1.50 4.00
71 Jo-Jo Reyes 1.00 2.50
72 Zack Segovia 1.00 2.50
73 Andy Sonnanstine 1.00 2.50
74 Chase Wright 2.50 6.00
75 Josh Fields 1.00 2.50
76 Jon Knott 1.00 2.50
77 Guillermo Rodriguez 1.00 2.50
78 Jon Coutlangus 1.00 2.50
79 Kevin Cameron 1.00 2.50
80 Mark Reynolds 3.00 8.00
81 Brian Stokes 1.00 2.50
82 Alberto Arias 1.00 2.50
83 Yoel Hernandez 1.00 2.50
84 David Murphy 1.00 2.50
85 Josh Hamilton 3.00 8.00
86 Justin Hampson 1.00 2.50
87 Doug Slaten 1.00 2.50
88 Joseph Bisenius 1.00 2.50
89 Troy Cate 1.00 2.50
90 Homer Bailey 1.50 4.00
91 Jacoby Ellsbury 6.00 15.00
92 Devern Hansack 1.00 2.50
93 Zach McClellan 1.00 2.50
94 Vinny Rottino 1.00 2.50
95 Elijah Dukes 1.50 4.00
96 Ryan Z. Braun UER 1.00 2.50
97 Lee Gardner 1.00 2.50
98 Joakim Soria 1.00 2.50
99 Jason Miller 1.00 2.50
100 Hideki Okajima 5.00 12.00
101 John Danks 1.50 4.00
102 Garrett Jones 2.50 6.00
103 Jensen Lewis 1.00 2.50
104 Clay Rapada 1.00 2.50
105 Kyle Kendrick 2.50 6.00
106 Eric Stults 1.00 2.50
110 Micah Owings 1.00 2.50
113 Mike Schultz 1.00 2.50
115 Matt Chico 1.00 2.50
120 Yovani Gallardo 2.50 6.00
125 Andrew Miller 4.00 10.00

2007 Topps '52 Chrome

STATED ODDS 1:3 H, 1:6 R
STATED PRINT RUN 1952 SER.#'d SETS
1 Akinori Iwamura 1.50 4.00
2 Angel Sanchez .60 1.50
3 Luis Hernandez .60 1.50
4 Troy Tulowitzki 2.00 5.00
5 Joaquin Arias .60 1.50
6 Jesus Flores .60 1.50
7 Brandon Wood .60 1.50
8 Kory Casto .60 1.50
9 Kevin Kouzmanoff .60 1.50
10 Tony Abreu 1.50 4.00
11 Travis Buck .60 1.50
12 Kurt Suzuki .60 1.50
13 Alejandro De Aza 1.00 2.50
14 Alex Gordon 2.00 5.00
15 Jerry Owens .60 1.50
16 Ryan J. Braun 3.00 8.00
17 Michael Bourn 1.00 2.50
18 Hunter Pence 2.00 5.00
19 Jeff Baker .60 1.50
20 Ben Francisco .60 1.50
21 Nate Schierholtz .60 1.50
22 Nathan Haynes .60 1.50
23 Andrew Miller 2.50 6.00
24 Sean Barker .60 1.50
25 Matt DeSalvo .60 1.50
26 Fred Lewis 1.00 2.50
27 Jamie Burke .60 1.50
28 Jeff Salazar .60 1.50
29 Chase Headley .60 1.50
30 Chris Basak .60 1.50
31 Mike Fontenot .60 1.50
32 Felix Pie .60 1.50
33 Masumi Kuwata .60 1.50
34 Daisuke Matsuzaka 2.50 6.00
35 Tim Lincecum 3.00 8.00
36 Jarrod Saltalamacchia 1.00 2.50
37 Tyler Clippard 1.00 2.50
38 Billy Butler 1.00 2.50
39 Matt Lindstrom .60 1.50
40 Brett Carroll .60 1.50
41 Alexi Casilla 1.00 2.50
42 Nick Gorneault .60 1.50
43 Matt Chico .60 1.50
44 Adam Lind .60 1.50
45 Miguel Montero .60 1.50
46 Danny Putnam .60 1.50
47 Delmon Young 1.00 2.50
48 Josh Fields .60 1.50
49 Carlos Gomez 1.25 3.00
50 Mark Reynolds 2.00 5.00
51 Shane Youman .60 1.50
52 Andy LaRoche .60 1.50
53 Kei Igawa 1.50 4.00
54 Don Kelly .60 1.50
55 Cameron Maybin 1.00 2.50
56 Travis Metcalf 1.00 2.50
57 Ubaldo Jimenez 2.00 5.00
58 Ryan Sweeney .60 1.50
59 Shawn Riggans .60 1.50
60 Jacoby Ellsbury 4.00 10.00
61 Andy Cavazos .60 1.50
62 Josh Hamilton 2.00 5.00
63 Homer Bailey 1.00 2.50
64 Sean Henn .60 1.50
65 Elijah Dukes 1.00 2.50
66 Brian Esposito .60 1.50
67 Brandon Morrow 3.00 8.00
68 Joe Smith .60 1.50
69 Chris Stewart .60 1.50
70 Eulogio De La Cruz 1.00 2.50
71 Sean Gallagher -.60 1.50
72 Jailen Peguero .60 1.50
73 Juan Perez .60 1.50
74 Levale Speigner .60 1.50
75 Jamie Vermilyea .60 1.50
76 Hideki Okajima 3.00 8.00
77 Eric Patterson .60 1.50
78 Zack Segovia .60 1.50
79 Kyle Kendrick 1.50 4.00
80 Andy Sonnanstine .60 1.50
81 Chase Wright 1.50 4.00
82 Jon Knott .60 1.50
83 Guillermo Rodriguez .60 1.50
84 Jon Coutlangus .60 1.50
85 Kevin Cameron .60 1.50
86 Brian Stokes .60 1.50
87 Alberto Arias .60 1.50
88 Delwyn Young .60 1.50
89 David Murphy .60 1.50
90 Micah Owings .60 1.50
91 Yovani Gallardo 1.50 4.00
92 Justin Hampson .60 1.50
93 Doug Slaten .60 1.50
94 Justin Upton 2.00 5.00
95 Joba Chamberlain 1.00 2.50

2007 Topps '52 Chrome Refractors

*CHR.REF: .75X TO 2X BASIC CHROME
STATED ODDS 1:9 H, 1:25 R
STATED PRINT RUN 552 SER.#'d SETS

2007 Topps '52 Chrome Gold Refractors

STATED ODDS 1:89 H, 1:300 R
STATED PRINT RUN 52 SER.#'d SETS
1 Akinori Iwamura 10.00 25.00
2 Angel Sanchez 4.00 10.00
3 Luis Hernandez 4.00 10.00
4 Troy Tulowitzki 12.00 30.00
5 Joaquin Arias 4.00 10.00
6 Jesus Flores 4.00 10.00
7 Brandon Wood 4.00 10.00
8 Kory Casto 4.00 10.00
9 Kevin Kouzmanoff 4.00 10.00
10 Tony Abreu 10.00 25.00
11 Travis Buck 4.00 10.00
12 Kurt Suzuki 4.00 10.00
13 Alejandro De Aza 6.00 15.00
14 Alex Gordon 12.00 30.00
15 Jerry Owens 4.00 10.00
16 Ryan J. Braun 20.00 50.00
17 Michael Bourn 6.00 15.00
18 Hunter Pence 12.00 30.00
19 Jeff Baker 4.00 10.00
20 Ben Francisco 4.00 10.00
21 Nate Schierholtz 4.00 10.00
22 Nathan Haynes 4.00 10.00
23 Andrew Miller 15.00 40.00
24 Sean Barker 4.00 10.00
25 Matt DeSalvo 4.00 10.00
26 Fred Lewis 6.00 15.00
27 Jamie Burke 4.00 10.00
28 Jeff Salazar 4.00 10.00
29 Chase Headley 4.00 10.00
30 Chris Basak 4.00 10.00
31 Mike Fontenot 4.00 10.00
32 Felix Pie 4.00 10.00
33 Masumi Kuwata 4.00 10.00
34 Daisuke Matsuzaka 15.00 40.00
35 Tim Lincecum 20.00 50.00
36 Jarrod Saltalamacchia 6.00 15.00
37 Tyler Clippard 6.00 15.00
38 Billy Butler 6.00 15.00
39 Matt Lindstrom 4.00 10.00
40 Brett Carroll 4.00 10.00
41 Alexi Casilla 6.00 15.00
42 Nick Gorneault 4.00 10.00
43 Matt Chico 4.00 10.00
44 Adam Lind 4.00 10.00
45 Miguel Montero 4.00 10.00
46 Danny Putnam 4.00 10.00
47 Delmon Young 6.00 15.00
48 Josh Fields 4.00 10.00
49 Carlos Gomez 8.00 20.00
50 Mark Reynolds 12.00 30.00
51 Shane Youman 4.00 10.00
52 Andy LaRoche 4.00 10.00
53 Kei Igawa 10.00 25.00
54 Don Kelly 4.00 10.00
55 Cameron Maybin 6.00 15.00
56 Travis Metcalf 6.00 15.00
57 Ubaldo Jimenez 12.00 30.00
58 Ryan Sweeney 4.00 10.00
59 Shawn Riggans 4.00 10.00
60 Jacoby Ellsbury 25.00 60.00
61 Andy Cavazos 4.00 10.00
62 Josh Hamilton 12.00 30.00
63 Homer Bailey 6.00 15.00
64 Sean Henn 4.00 10.00
65 Elijah Dukes 6.00 15.00
66 Brian Esposito 4.00 10.00
67 Brandon Morrow 20.00 50.00
68 Joe Smith 4.00 10.00
69 Chris Stewart 4.00 10.00
70 Eulogio De La Cruz 6.00 15.00
71 Sean Gallagher 4.00 10.00
72 Jailen Peguero 4.00 10.00
73 Juan Perez 4.00 10.00
74 Levale Speigner 4.00 10.00
75 Jamie Vermilyea 4.00 10.00
76 Hideki Okajima 20.00 50.00
77 Eric Patterson 4.00 10.00
78 Zack Segovia 4.00 10.00
79 Kyle Kendrick 10.00 25.00
80 Andy Sonnanstine 4.00 10.00
81 Chase Wright 10.00 25.00
82 Jon Knott 4.00 10.00
83 Guillermo Rodriguez 4.00 10.00
84 Jon Coutlangus 4.00 10.00
85 Kevin Cameron 4.00 10.00
86 Brian Stokes 4.00 10.00
87 Alberto Arias 4.00 10.00
88 Delwyn Young 4.00 10.00
89 David Murphy 4.00 10.00
90 Micah Owings 4.00 10.00
91 Yovani Gallardo 10.00 25.00
92 Justin Hampson 4.00 10.00
93 Doug Slaten 4.00 10.00
94 Justin Upton 12.00 30.00
95 Joba Chamberlain 6.00 15.00

2007 Topps '52 Debut Flashbacks

COMPLETE SET (15) 6.00 15.00
STATED ODDS 1:6 H, 1:6 R
COMPLETE CHR.SET (15) 10.00 25.00
*CHROME: .6X TO 1.5X BASIC
CHROME ODDS 1:16 H, 1:46 R
CHR.PRINT RUN 1952 SER.#'d SETS
CHR.REF: 1X TO 2.5X BASIC
CHR.REF ODDS 1:55 H, 1:170 R
CHR.REF PRINT RUN 552 SER.#'d SETS
DF1 Vladimir Guerrero .60 1.50
DF2 Ken Griffey Jr. 2.00 5.00
DF3 Pedro Martinez .60 1.50
DF4 Carlos Delgado .40 1.00
DF5 Gary Sheffield .40 1.00
DF6 Curt Schilling .60 1.50
DF7 Jorge Posada .40 1.00
DF8 Miguel Tejada .60 1.50
DF9 Trevor Hoffman .60 1.50
DF10 Francisco Cordero .40 1.00
DF11 Travis Hafner .40 1.00
DF12 Paul Lo Duca .60 1.50
DF13 Jimmy Rollins .60 1.50
DF14 Magglio Ordonez .60 1.50
DF15 Jim Edmonds .60 1.50

2007 Topps '52 Debut Flashbacks Chrome Gold Refractors

*GOLD REF: 3X TO 8X BASIC
STATED ODDS 1:609 H, 1:1700 R
STATED PRINT RUN 52 SER.#'d SETS

2007 Topps '52 Dynamic Duos

COMPLETE SET (15) 6.00 15.00
STATED ODDS 1:4 H, 1:4 R
DD1 T.Lincecum/N.Schierholtz 2.00 5.00
DD2 J.Chamberlain/P.Hughes 1.00 2.50
DD3 R.Braun/Y.Gallardo 2.00 5.00
DD4 K.Kendrick/M.Bourn 1.00 2.50
DD5 D.Young/E.Dukes .60 1.50
DD6 H.Okajima/D.Matsuzaka 2.00 5.00
DD7 J.Upton/M.Reynolds 1.25 3.00
DD8 E.Patterson/F.Pie .40 1.00
DD9 J.Hamilton/H.Bailey 1.25 3.00
DD10 U.Jimenez/T.Tulowitzki 1.25 3.00
DD11 A.Gordon/B.Butler 1.25 3.00
DD12 D.Young/A.LaRoche .40 1.00
DD13 A.Miller/C.Maybin 1.50 4.00
DD14 J.Smith/C.Gomez .75 2.00
DD15 D.Murphy/J.Saltalamacchia .60 1.50

2007 Topps '52 Signatures

GROUP A ODDS 1:4750 H, 1:13,401 R
GROUP B ODDS 1:150 H, 1:429 R
GROUP C ODDS 1:3149 H, 1:19,065 R
GROUP D ODDS 1:1049 H, 1:3000 R
GROUP E ODDS 1:54 H, 1:162 R
GROUP F ODDS 1:9 H, 1:29 R
EXCHANGE DEADLINE 11/30/09
AA Alberto Arias F 3.00 8.00
AC Alexi Casilla F 3.00 8.00
AG Alex Gordon B 30.00 60.00
AL Andy LaRoche B 10.00 25.00
AS Angel Sanchez E 3.00 8.00
ASL Aaron Laffey F 3.00 8.00
BB Brian Barden F 3.00 8.00
BC Brett Carroll F 3.00 8.00
BE Brian Esposito F 3.00 8.00
BF Ben Francisco F 3.00 8.00
BP Billy Petrick E 3.00 8.00
BPB Brian Buscher E 3.00 8.00
BW Brian Wolfe E 3.00 8.00
CD Cory Doyne F 3.00 8.00
CH Chase Headley E 6.00 15.00
CM Cameron Maybin B 20.00 50.00
CS Chris Stewart B 3.00 8.00
CW Chase Wright B 8.00 20.00
DC Darren Clarke F 3.00 8.00
ER Edwar Ramirez F 5.00 12.00
FC Francisco Cordero A 50.00 100.00
FL Fred Lewis B 5.00 12.00
FP Felix Pie B 10.00 25.00
GS Gary Sheffield A 20.00 50.00
HO Hideki Okajima B 30.00 60.00
HP Hunter Pence B 8.00 20.00
JA Joaquin Arias B 3.00 8.00
JB Jared Burton B 8.00 20.00
JC Jon Coutlangus B 3.00 8.00
JCH Joba Chamberlain B 6.00 15.00
JH Joel Hanrahan D 10.00 25.00
JJR Jo-Jo Reyes B 3.00 8.00
JL Jensen Lewis F 3.00 8.00
JM Jason Miller D 3.00 8.00
JP Jorge Posada A 40.00 100.00
JRB Joseph Bisenius F 3.00 8.00
JSS J.Saltalamacchia B 3.00 8.00
JU Justin Upton B 12.00 30.00
KS Kurt Suzuki B 3.00 8.00
LS Levale Speigner F 3.00 8.00
MB Michael Bourn B 10.00 25.00
MBB Matthew Brown F 3.00 8.00
MJZ Mike Zagurski E 3.00 8.00
ML Matt Lindstrom B 6.00 15.00
MM Mark McLemore E 3.00 8.00
NG Nick Gorneault B 6.00 15.00
NH Nathan Haynes F 3.00 8.00
PD Phil Dumatrait E 3.00 8.00
PH P.Hughes B EXCH 30.00 60.00
RB Ryan Braun B 20.00 50.00
RC Rocky Cherry C 5.00 12.00
RDB Ryan Budde E 3.00 8.00
RZB Ryan Z. Braun B 3.00 8.00
TB Travis Buck B 5.00 12.00
TL Tim Lincecum B 75.00 150.00
TM Travis Metcalf B 10.00 25.00
TPC Troy Cate F 3.00 8.00
YG Yovani Gallardo B 3.00 8.00
ZS Zack Segovia E 3.00 8.00

2007 Topps '52 Signatures Red Ink

STATED ODDS 1:88 HOBBY
STATED PRINT RUN 52 SER.#'d SETS
EXCH DEADLINE 12/31/08
AA Alberto Arias 10.00 25.00
AC Alexi Casilla 10.00 25.00
AG Alex Gordon 60.00 120.00
AI Akinori Iwamura 30.00 60.00
AL Andy LaRoche 30.00 60.00
AM Andrew Miller 30.00 60.00
AS Angel Sanchez 10.00 25.00
ASL Aaron Laffey 20.00 50.00
BB Brian Barden 10.00 25.00
BC Brett Carroll 10.00 25.00
BE Brian Esposito 10.00 25.00
BF Ben Francisco 10.00 25.00
BP Billy Petrick 10.00 25.00
BPB Brian Buscher 10.00 25.00
BS Brian Stokes 10.00 25.00
BW Brian Wolfe 10.00 25.00
CD Cory Doyne 10.00 25.00
CH Chase Headley 30.00 60.00
CM Cameron Maybin 40.00 80.00
CS Chris Stewart 10.00 25.00
CW Chase Wright 30.00 60.00
DC Darren Clarke 10.00 25.00
ER Edwar Ramirez 15.00 40.00
FC Francisco Cordero 100.00 200.00
FL Fred Lewis 10.00 25.00
FP Felix Pie 20.00 50.00
GS Gary Sheffield 40.00 80.00
HO Hideki Okajima 50.00 100.00
HP Hunter Pence 75.00 150.00
JA Joaquin Arias 10.00 25.00
JB Jared Burton 15.00 40.00
JC Jon Coutlangus 10.00 25.00
JCH Joba Chamberlain 20.00 50.00
JH Joel Hanrahan 20.00 50.00
JJR Jo-Jo Reyes 10.00 25.00
JL Jensen Lewis 10.00 25.00
JM Jason Miller 10.00 25.00
JP Jorge Posada 60.00 150.00
JRB Joseph Bisenius 10.00 25.00
JSS Jarrod Saltalamacchia 10.00 25.00
JU Justin Upton 30.00 80.00
KK Kevin Kouzmanoff 10.00 25.00
KS Kurt Suzuki 20.00 50.00
LS Levale Speigner 10.00 25.00
MB Michael Bourn 30.00 60.00
MBB Matthew Brown 10.00 25.00
MJZ Mike Zagurski 20.00 50.00
ML Matt Lindstrom 15.00 40.00
MM Mark McLemore 10.00 25.00
NG Nick Gorneault 15.00 40.00
NH Nathan Haynes 10.00 25.00
PD Phil Dumatrait 10.00 25.00
PH Phil Hughes 60.00 120.00
PL Paul Lo Duca 20.00 50.00
RB Ryan Braun 50.00 100.00
RC Rocky Cherry 20.00 50.00
RDB Ryan Budde 10.00 25.00
RZB Ryan Braun 15.00 40.00
TB Travis Buck 15.00 40.00
TC Tyler Clippard 30.00 60.00
TL Tim Lincecum 150.00 300.00
TM Travis Metcalf 20.00 50.00
TPC Troy Cate 10.00 25.00
YG Yovani Gallardo 10.00 25.00
ZS Zack Segovia 20.00 50.00

2017 Topps 65th Anniversary Party Kris Bryant

COMMON CARD 30.00 80.00
STATED PRINT RUN 65 SER.#'D SETS
KB1952 Kris Bryant 12.00 30.00
KB1953 Kris Bryant 12.00 30.00
KB1954 Kris Bryant 12.00 30.00
KB1955 Kris Bryant 12.00 30.00
KB1956 Kris Bryant 12.00 30.00
KB1957 Kris Bryant 12.00 30.00
KB1958 Kris Bryant 12.00 30.00
KB1959 Kris Bryant 12.00 30.00
KB1960 Kris Bryant 12.00 30.00
KB1961 Kris Bryant 12.00 30.00
KB1962 Kris Bryant 12.00 30.00
KB1963 Kris Bryant 12.00 30.00
KB1964 Kris Bryant 12.00 30.00
KB1965 Kris Bryant 12.00 30.00
KB1966 Kris Bryant 12.00 30.00
KB1967 Kris Bryant 12.00 30.00
KB1968 Kris Bryant 12.00 30.00
KB1969 Kris Bryant 12.00 30.00
KB1970 Kris Bryant 12.00 30.00
KB1971 Kris Bryant 12.00 30.00
KB1972 Kris Bryant 12.00 30.00
KB1973 Kris Bryant 12.00 30.00
KB1974 Kris Bryant 12.00 30.00
KB1975 Kris Bryant 12.00 30.00
KB1976 Kris Bryant 12.00 30.00
KB1977 Kris Bryant 12.00 30.00
KB1978 Kris Bryant 12.00 30.00
KB1979 Kris Bryant 12.00 30.00
KB1980 Kris Bryant 12.00 30.00
KB1981 Kris Bryant 12.00 30.00
KB1982 Kris Bryant 12.00 30.00
KB1983 Kris Bryant 12.00 30.00
KB1984 Kris Bryant 12.00 30.00
KB1985 Kris Bryant 12.00 30.00
KB1986 Kris Bryant 12.00 30.00
KB1987 Kris Bryant 12.00 30.00
KB1988 Kris Bryant 12.00 30.00
KB1989 Kris Bryant 12.00 30.00
KB1990 Kris Bryant 12.00 30.00
KB1991 Kris Bryant 12.00 30.00
KB1992 Kris Bryant 12.00 30.00
KB1993 Kris Bryant 12.00 30.00
KB1994 Kris Bryant 12.00 30.00
KB1995 Kris Bryant 12.00 30.00
KB1996 Kris Bryant 12.00 30.00
KB1997 Kris Bryant 12.00 30.00
KB1998 Kris Bryant 12.00 30.00
KB1999 Kris Bryant 12.00 30.00
KB2000 Kris Bryant 12.00 30.00
KB2001 Kris Bryant 12.00 30.00
KB2002 Kris Bryant 12.00 30.00
KB2003 Kris Bryant 12.00 30.00
KB2004 Kris Bryant 12.00 30.00
KB2005 Kris Bryant 12.00 30.00
KB2006 Kris Bryant 12.00 30.00
KB2007 Kris Bryant 12.00 30.00
KB2008 Kris Bryant 12.00 30.00
KB2009 Kris Bryant 12.00 30.00
KB2010 Kris Bryant 12.00 30.00
KB2011 Kris Bryant 12.00 30.00
KB2012 Kris Bryant 12.00 30.00
KB2013 Kris Bryant 12.00 30.00
KB2014 Kris Bryant 12.00 30.00
KB2015 Kris Bryant 12.00 30.00
KB2016 Kris Bryant 12.00 30.00

2017 Topps 65th Anniversary Party Transcendent Kris Bryant Autographs

STATED PRINT RUN 15 SER.#'d SETS
VEGASKB1 Kris Bryant 150.00 400.00
VEGASKB2 Kris Bryant 150.00 400.00
VEGASKB3 Kris Bryant 150.00 400.00
VEGASKB4 Kris Bryant 150.00 400.00
VEGASKB5 Kris Bryant 150.00 400.00

2006 Topps AFLAC

COMMON CARD 5.00 12.00
EACH PLAYER ISSUED 100 OF OWN CARD
APPX.250 SETS DIST.AT 06 AFLAC GAME
BB Blake Beavan 12.50 30.00
BK Brett Krill 6.00 15.00
CC Christian Colon 5.00 12.00
CR Cameron Rupp 6.00 15.00
DB Drake Britton 5.00 12.00
DD Derek Dietrich 10.00 25.00
DM D.J. LeMahieu 25.00 60.00
DR Danny Rams 5.00 12.00
ED Evan Danieli 6.00 15.00
EG Erik Goeddel 6.00 15.00
FF Freddie Freeman 20.00 50.00
GP Greg Peavey 8.00 20.00
HM Hunter Morris 10.00 25.00
JG Jon Gilmore 8.00 20.00
JH Jason Heyward 40.00 80.00
JL Joe Leftridge 5.00 12.00
JS Josh Smoker 12.50 30.00
JT John Tolisano 8.00 20.00
JV Josh Vitters 12.50 30.00
KB Kyle Blair 5.00 12.00
KK Kevin Keyes 5.00 12.00
MB Madison Bumgarner 20.00 50.00
MH Matt Harvey 20.00 50.00
MM Michael Main 12.50 30.00
NN Nick Noonan 8.00 20.00
NR Neil Ramirez 10.00 25.00
PD Paul Demny 5.00 12.00
RP Rick Porcello 20.00 50.00
RS Robert Stock 12.50 30.00
SB Steven Brooks 6.00 15.00
SS Sequoyah Stonecipher 12.50 30.00
TA Tim Alderson 5.00 12.00
YG Yasmani Grandal 6.00 15.00

2006 Topps AFLAC Autographs

08 BOW.DFT.ODDS 1:215 HOBBY
09 BOW.DFT.ODDS 1:238 HOBBY
PRINT RUNS B/WN 43-248 COPIES PER
08 BOW.DFT CARDS NOT NUMBERED
BB Blake Beavan 12.00 30.00
CC Christian Colon/49 150.00 250.00
CR Cameron Rupp/43 8.00 20.00
DB Drake Britton 15.00 40.00
DL D.J. Lemahieu/142 60.00 150.00
DR Danny Rams 8.00 20.00
FF Freddie Freeman 75.00 200.00
JG Jon Gilmore 4.00 10.00
JH Jason Heyward 20.00 50.00
JS Josh Smoker 4.00 10.00
JT John Tolisano 8.00 20.00
JV Josh Vitters 10.00 25.00
MB Madison Bumgarner 50.00 120.00
MH Matt Harvey/230 100.00 200.00
MM Michael Main 12.00 30.00
NN Nick Noonan 8.00 20.00
NR Neil Ramirez/240 6.00 15.00
PD Paul Demny 4.00 10.00
RP Rick Porcello 10.00 25.00
RS Robert Stock/236 15.00 40.00
SS Sequoyah Stonecipher/248 12.00 30.00
TA Tim Alderson 10.00 25.00
YG Yasmani Grandal/230 10.00 25.00

2006 Topps AFLAC Promo

BB Blake Beavan 5.00 12.00
BK Brett Krill 3.00 8.00
CC Christian Colon 2.50 6.00
CR Cameron Rupp 3.00 8.00
DB Drake Britton 3.00 8.00
DD Derek Dietrich 5.00 12.00
DM D.J. LeMahieu 10.00 25.00
DR Danny Rams 4.00 10.00
ED Evan Danieli 2.50 6.00
EG Erik Goeddel 3.00 8.00
FF Freddie Freeman 15.00 40.00
GP Greg Peavey 4.00 10.00
HM Hunter Morris 4.00 10.00
JG Jon Gilmore 5.00 12.00
JH Jason Heyward 40.00 80.00
JJ Justin Jackson 5.00 12.00
JL Joe Leftridge 3.00 8.00
JS Josh Smoker 10.00 25.00
JT John Tolisano 4.00 10.00
JV Josh Vitters 20.00 50.00
KB Kyle Blair 2.50 6.00
KD Kentrail Davis 4.00 10.00
KK Kevin Keyes 2.50 6.00
MB Madison Bumgarner 20.00 50.00
MB2 Michael Burgess 10.00 25.00
MH Matt Harvey 20.00 50.00
MM Michael Main 4.00 10.00
NN Nick Noonan 5.00 12.00
NR Neil Ramirez 3.00 8.00
PD Paul Demny 5.00 12.00
RP Rick Porcello 20.00 50.00
RS Robert Stock 6.00 15.00
SB Steven Brooks 2.50 6.00
SR Sam Runion 4.00 10.00
SS Sequoyah Stonecipher 3.00 8.00
TA Tim Alderson 6.00 15.00
TR Tanner Robles 2.50 6.00
YG Yasmani Grandal 8.00 20.00

2007 Topps AFLAC

AB Andy Burns 4.00 10.00
AF Anthony Ferrara 10.00 25.00
AH Aaron Hicks 12.50 30.00
AM Alex Meyer 6.00 15.00
AN Adrian Nieto 6.00 15.00
AW Austin Wright 6.00 15.00
BD Brett DeVall 6.00 15.00
BH B.J. Hermsen 4.00 10.00
BN Billy Nicholson CO 4.00 10.00
BW Brett Warren 6.00 15.00
CA Chris Amezquita 4.00 10.00
CE Cecil Espy CO 4.00 10.00
CM Clark Murphy 4.00 10.00
DH Destin Hood 6.00 15.00
DM Daniel Marrs 4.00 10.00
EM Ethan Martin 10.00 25.00
GC Gerrit Cole 15.00 40.00
GL Garrison Lassiter 4.00 10.00
HM Harold Martinez 6.00 15.00
IG Isaac Galloway 4.00 10.00
JA Jack Armstrong 4.00 10.00
JC Jarred Cosart 12.50 30.00
JS Jordan Swagerty 4.00 10.00
KM Kevin Maris CO 4.00 10.00
KS Kyle Skipworth 15.00 40.00
MH Manny Hermosillo CO 4.00 10.00
MP Michael Palazzone 4.00 10.00
MS Mike Sheppard Jr. CO 6.00 15.00
QM Quinton Miller 10.00 25.00
RO Ricky Oropesa 4.00 10.00
ROS Ryan O'Sullivan 4.00 10.00
SG Sonny Gray 4.00 10.00
SS Scott Silverstein 6.00 15.00
TB Tim Beckham 5.00 12.00
TH Taylor Hightower 4.00 10.00
TM Tim Melville 6.00 15.00
WF Wesley Freeman 4.00 10.00
WK Walker Kelly 10.00 25.00
XA Xavier Avery 6.00 15.00

2007 Topps AFLAC Autographs

08 BOW.DFT.ODDS 1:215 HOBBY
09 BOW.DFT.ODDS 1:238 HOBBY
12 BOW.ODDS 1:703 HOBBY
PRINT RUNS B/WN 127-231 COPIES PER
08 BOW.DFT CARDS NOT NUMBERED
AF Anthony Ferrara 6.00 15.00
AN Adrian Nieto 4.00 10.00
BH B.J. Hermsen/127 8.00 20.00
GH Gerrit Cole/225 60.00 150.00
IG Isaac Galloway 10.00 25.00
JS Jordan Swagerty/210 10.00 25.00
QM Quinton Miller 6.00 15.00
SG Sonny Gray/200 40.00 80.00
TB Tim Beckham/127 25.00 60.00
WF Wesley Freeman/231 8.00 20.00
XA Xavier Avery 4.00 10.00

2003 Topps All-Time Fan Favorites

COMPLETE SET (150) 20.00 50.00
COMMON CARD (1-150) .25 .60
MONTE IRVIN UER 50% OF PRINT RUN
SET IS COMPLETE W/EITHER M.IRVIN
1 Willie Mays 1.25 3.00
2 Whitey Ford .40 1.00
3 Stan Musial 1.00 2.50
4 Paul Blair .25 .60
5 Harold Reynolds .25 .60
6 Bob Friend .25 .60
7 Rod Carew .40 1.00
8 Kirk Gibson .25 .60
9 Graig Nettles .25 .60
10 Ozzie Smith .75 2.00
11 Tony Perez .40 1.00
12 Tim Wallach .25 .60
13 Bert Campaneris .25 .60
14 Cory Snyder .25 .60
15 Dave Parker .25 .60
16 Darrell Evans .25 .60
17 Joe Pepitone .25 .60
18 Don Sutton .40 1.00
19 Dale Murphy .60 1.50
20 George Brett 1.25 3.00
21 Carlton Fisk .40 1.00
22 Bob Watson .25 .60
23 Wally Joyner .25 .60
24 Paul Molitor .60 1.50
25 Keith Hernandez .25 .60
26 Jerry Koosman .25 .60
27 George Bell .25 .60
28 Boog Powell .25 .60
29 Bruce Sutter .40 1.00
30 Ernie Banks .60 1.50
31 Steve Lyons .25 .60
32 Earl Weaver .40 1.00
33 Dave Stieb .25 .60
34 Alan Trammell .40 1.00
35 Bret Saberhagen .25 .60
36 J.R. Richard .25 .60
37 Mickey Rivers .25 .60
38 Juan Marichal .40 1.00
39 Gaylord Perry .40 1.00
40 Don Mattingly 1.25 3.00
41 Bob Grich .25 .60
42 Steve Sax .25 .60
43 Sparky Anderson .40 1.00
44 Luis Aparicio .40 1.00
45 Fergie Jenkins .40 1.00
46 Jim Palmer .40 1.00
47 Howard Johnson .25 .60
48 Dwight Evans .25 .60
49 Bill Buckner .25 .60
50 Cal Ripken 2.00 5.00
51 Jose Cruz .25 .60
52 Tony Oliva .25 .60
53 Bobby Richardson .25 .60
54 Luis Tiant .25 .60
55 Warren Spahn .40 1.00
56 Phil Rizzuto .40 1.00
57 Eric Davis .25 .60
58 Vida Blue .25 .60
59 Steve Balboni .25 .60
60 Mike Schmidt 1.00 2.50
61 Ken Griffey Sr. .25 .60
62 Jim Abbott .25 .60
63 Whitey Herzog .25 .60
64 Rich Gossage .40 1.00
65 Tony Armas .25 .60
66 Bill Skowron .25 .60
67 Don Newcombe .25 .60
68 Bill Madlock .25 .60
69 Lance Parrish .25 .60
70 Reggie Jackson .40 1.00
71 Willie Wilson .25 .60
72 Terry Pendleton .25 .60
73 Jim Piersall .25 .60
74 George Foster .25 .60
75 Bob Horner .25 .60
76 Chris Sabo .25 .60
77 Fred Lynn .25 .60
78 Jim Rice .40 1.00
79 Maury Wills .25 .60
80 Yogi Berra .60 1.50
81 Johnny Sain .25 .60
82 Tom Lasorda .40 1.00
83 Bill Mazeroski .40 1.00
84 John Kruk .25 .60
85 Bob Feller .40 1.00
86 Frank Robinson .40 1.00
87 Red Schoendienst .40 1.00
88 Gary Carter .40 1.00
89 Andre Dawson .40 1.00
90 Tim McCarver .25 .60
91 Robin Yount .60 1.50
92 Phil Niekro .40 1.00
93 Joe Morgan .40 1.00
94 Darren Daulton .25 .60
95 Bobby Thomson .40 1.00
96 Alvin Davis .25 .60
97 Robin Roberts .40 1.00
98 Kirby Puckett .60 1.50
99 Jack Clark .25 .60
100 Hank Aaron 1.25 3.00
101 Orlando Cepeda .40 1.00
102 Vern Law .25 .60
103 Cecil Cooper .25 .60
104 Don Larsen .25 .60
105 Mario Mendoza .25 .60
106 Tony Gwynn .60 1.50
107 Ernie Harwell .40 1.00
108A Monte Irvin .40 1.00
108B Monte Irvin NO AU ERR .40 1.00
109 Tommy John .25 .60
110 Rollie Fingers .40 1.00
111 Johnny Podres .25 .60
112 Jeff Reardon .25 .60
113 Buddy Bell .25 .60
114 Dwight Gooden .25 .60
115 Garry Templeton .25 .60
116 Johnny Bench .60 1.50
117 Joe Rudi .25 .60
118 Ron Guidry .25 .60
119 Vince Coleman .25 .60
120 Al Kaline .40 1.00
121 Carl Yastrzemski 1.00 2.50
122 Hank Bauer .25 .60
123 Mark Fidrych .25 .60
124 Paul O'Neill .40 1.00
125 Ron Cey .25 .60
126 Willie McGee .25 .60
127 Harmon Killebrew .60 1.50
128 Dave Concepcion .25 .60
129 Harold Baines .40 1.00
130 Lou Brock .40 1.00
131 Lee Smith .25 .60
132 Willie McCovey .40 1.00
133 Steve Garvey .25 .60
134 Kent Tekulve .25 .60
135 Tom Seaver .40 1.00
136 Bo Jackson .60 1.50
137 Walt Weiss .25 .60
138 Brook Jacoby .25 .60
139 Dennis Eckersley .40 1.00
140 Duke Snider .40 1.00
141 Lenny Dykstra .25 .60
142 Greg Luzinski .25 .60
143 Jim Bunning .40 1.00
144 Jose Canseco .40 1.00
145 Ron Santo .40 1.00
146 Bert Blyleven .40 1.00
147 Wade Boggs .40 1.00
148 Brooks Robinson .40 1.00
149 Ray Knight .25 .60
150 Nolan Ryan 2.00 5.00

2003 Topps All-Time Fan Favorites Chrome Refractors

*CHROME REF: 2X TO 5X BASIC
STATED ODDS 1:18
STATED PRINT RUN 299 SERIAL #'d SETS

2003 Topps All-Time Fan Favorites Archives Autographs

GROUP A STATED ODDS 1:218
GROUP B STATED ODDS 1:759
GROUP C STATED ODDS 1:116
GROUP D STATED ODDS 1:45
GROUP E STATED ODDS 1:87
GROUP F STATED ODDS 1:1028
GROUP G STATED ODDS 1:838
GROUP H STATED ODDS 1:818
GROUP I STATED ODDS 1:796
GROUP J STATED ODDS 1:111
GROUP K STATED ODDS 1:759
GROUP L STATED ODDS 1:744
AD Alvin Davis D 6.00 15.00
ADA Andre Dawson A 6.00 15.00
AK Al Kaline A 75.00 200.00
AO Al Oliver D 6.00 15.00
AT Alan Trammell C 8.00 20.00
BB Bert Blyleven D 8.00 20.00
BBE Buddy Bell C 6.00 15.00
BBI Buddy Biancalana D 6.00 15.00
BBU Bill Buckner C 8.00 20.00
BC Bert Campaneris E 6.00 15.00
BF Bob Feller C 10.00 25.00
BFR Bob Friend D 8.00 20.00
BGR Bob Grich D 6.00 15.00
BH Bob Horner J 6.00 15.00
BJ Bo Jackson A 40.00 80.00
BJA Brook Jacoby E 6.00 15.00
BL Bill Lee D 6.00 15.00
BMA Bill Madlock D 6.00 15.00
BMZ Bill Mazeroski A 15.00 40.00
BP Boog Powell D 6.00 15.00
BRO Brooks Robinson A 20.00 50.00
BS Bill Skowron D 8.00 20.00
BSA Bret Saberhagen A 20.00 50.00
BSU Bruce Sutter C 10.00 25.00
BT Bobby Thomson A 40.00 80.00
BW Bob Watson C 6.00 15.00
CC Cecil Cooper E 10.00 25.00
CF Carlton Fisk A 50.00 100.00
CL Carney Lansford C 6.00 15.00
CLE Chet Lemon D 6.00 15.00
CN Cory Snyder C 6.00 15.00
CR Cal Ripken A 75.00 150.00
CS Chris Sabo H 10.00 25.00
CSP Chris Speier C 10.00 25.00
CY Carl Yastrzemski A 50.00 100.00
DC Dave Concepcion A 40.00 80.00
DD Darren Daulton C 8.00 20.00
DDE Doug DeCinces C 10.00 25.00
DE Darrell Evans D 6.00 15.00
DEC Dennis Eckersley A 40.00 80.00
DEV Dwight Evans A 10.00 25.00
DG Dwight Gooden A 40.00 80.00
DL Don Larsen D 8.00 20.00
DM Dale Murphy A 50.00 100.00
DN Don Newcombe A 10.00 25.00
DON Don Mattingly A 75.00 150.00
DP Dave Parker A 20.00 50.00
DS Dave Stieb C 10.00 25.00
DSN Duke Snider A 50.00 100.00
DSU Don Sutton A 40.00 80.00
EB Ernie Banks A 40.00 80.00
ED Eric Davis I 6.00 15.00
EH Ernie Harwell C 20.00 50.00
EW Earl Weaver D 10.00 25.00
FJ Fergie Jenkins C 8.00 20.00
FL Fred Lynn A 30.00 60.00
FR Frank Robinson A 20.00 50.00
GB George Bell D 6.00 15.00
GBR George Brett A 175.00 350.00
GC Gary Carter A 15.00 40.00
GF George Foster D 6.00 15.00
GL Greg Luzinski C 6.00 15.00
GN Graig Nettles D 8.00 20.00
GP Gaylord Perry B 8.00 20.00
GT Garry Templeton C 6.00 15.00
HA Hank Aaron A 175.00 300.00
HB Hank Bauer A 12.50 30.00
HBA Harold Baines C 10.00 25.00
HJ Howard Johnson K 6.00 15.00
HK Harmon Killebrew A 50.00 100.00
HR Harold Reynolds A 15.00 40.00
JA Jim Abbott D 6.00 15.00
JB Jim Bunning A 30.00 60.00
JBE Johnny Bench A 75.00 150.00
JC Jack Clark B 8.00 20.00
JCA Joe Carter A 40.00 80.00
JCR Jose Cruz D 8.00 20.00
JK Jerry Koosman F 8.00 20.00
JKR John Kruk A 12.50 30.00
JM Joe Morgan A 40.00 80.00
JMA Juan Marichal A 50.00 100.00
JMO John Montefusco D 8.00 20.00
JOS Jose Canseco A 50.00 100.00
JP Jim Palmer A 75.00 150.00
JPE Joe Pepitone E 6.00 15.00
JR J.R. Richard E 10.00 25.00
JRE Jeff Reardon D 6.00 15.00
JRI Jim Rice A 40.00 80.00
JRU Joe Rudi E 8.00 20.00
KG Ken Griffey Sr. A 40.00 80.00
KGI Kirk Gibson A 20.00 50.00
KH Keith Hernandez A 40.00 80.00
KM Kevin Mitchell L 6.00 15.00
KP Kirby Puckett A 125.00 250.00
KS Kevin Seitzer D 6.00 15.00
KT Kent Tekulve C 10.00 25.00
LA Luis Aparicio D 10.00 25.00
LB Lou Brock A 50.00 100.00
LD Lenny Dykstra G 6.00 15.00
LDU Leon Durham D 6.00 15.00
LP Lance Parrish D 10.00 25.00
LS Lee Smith J 4.00 10.00
LT Luis Tiant A 12.50 30.00
MCG Willie McGee A 50.00 100.00
MF Mark Fidrych J 12.50 30.00
MI Monte Irvin A 40.00 80.00
MM Mario Mendoza E 6.00 15.00
MP Mike Pagliarulo E 6.00 15.00
MR Mickey Rivers E 6.00 15.00
MS Mike Schmidt A 100.00 200.00
MW Maury Wills E 6.00 15.00
NR Nolan Ryan A 175.00 300.00
OC Orlando Cepeda A 50.00 100.00
OS Ozzie Smith A 50.00 100.00
PB Paul Blair J 6.00 15.00
PM Paul Molitor A 40.00 80.00
PN Phil Niekro A 12.50 30.00
PO Paul O'Neill A 50.00 100.00
PR Phil Rizzuto A 50.00 100.00
RCA Rod Carew A 50.00 100.00
RCE Ron Cey D 6.00 15.00
RD Rob Dibble C 10.00 25.00
RDA Ron Darling C 6.00 15.00
RF Rollie Fingers A 40.00 80.00
RG Rich Gossage A 10.00 25.00
RGU Ron Guidry C 6.00 15.00
RJ Reggie Jackson A 30.00 60.00
RK Ralph Kiner A 50.00 100.00
RKI Ron Kittle D 6.00 15.00
RR Robin Roberts B 15.00 40.00
RS Red Schoendienst C 10.00 25.00
RSA Ron Santo D 12.50 30.00
RY Ray Knight J 6.00 15.00
RYO Robin Yount A 75.00 150.00
SA Sparky Anderson A 75.00 150.00
SB Steve Balboni E 6.00 15.00
SG Steve Garvey B 12.50 30.00
SL Steve Lyons C 6.00 15.00
SM Stan Musial A 100.00 200.00
SS Steve Sax D 6.00 15.00
SY Steve Yeager E 8.00 20.00
TA Tony Armas D 6.00 15.00
TG Tony Gwynn A 75.00 150.00
TH Tom Herr D 6.00 15.00
TJ Tommy John B 6.00 15.00
TL Tom Lasorda A 75.00 200.00
TM Tim McCarver A 20.00 50.00
TMC Tug McGraw D 10.00 25.00
TP Terry Pendleton B 6.00 15.00
TPE Tony Perez A 50.00 100.00
TSE Tom Seaver A 60.00 150.00
TW Tim Wallach E 10.00 25.00
VB Vida Blue C 6.00 15.00
VC Vince Coleman J 8.00 20.00
WB Wade Boggs A 50.00 100.00
WF Whitey Ford A 75.00 150.00
WH Whitey Herzog C 10.00 25.00
WHE Willie Hernandez D 6.00 15.00
WJ Wally Joyner J 6.00 15.00
WM Willie Mays A 175.00 300.00
WMC Willie McCovey A 75.00 150.00
WS Warren Spahn D 15.00 40.00
WW Walt Weiss D 6.00 15.00
WWI Willie Wilson A 40.00 80.00
YB Yogi Berra A 75.00 200.00

2003 Topps All-Time Fan Favorites Best Seat in the House Relics

STATED ODDS 1:13 RELIC PACKS
BS1 Brooks 10.00 25.00
F.Robinson/Palmer
BS2 Grich 10.00 25.00
Carew/Joyner
BS3 Parker 10.00 25.00
Tek/Stargell/Garner
BS4 Molitor 10.00 25.00
Yount/Fingers
BS5 Horner 10.00 25.00
Murphy/Niekro

2003 Topps All-Time Fan Favorites Relics

ONE PER RELIC PACK
ADA Andre Dawson Bat 4.00 10.00
AT Alan Trammell Bat 4.00 10.00
BFR Bob Friend Jsy 4.00 10.00
BH Bob Horner Bat 4.00 10.00
BJ Bo Jackson Bat 10.00 25.00
BR Bobby Richardson Bat 6.00 15.00
CF Curt Flood Bat 4.00 10.00
CS Chris Sabo Bat 4.00 10.00
DEC Dennis Eckersley Uni 4.00 10.00
DM Dale Murphy Bat 6.00 15.00
DON Don Mattingly Bat 12.50 30.00
DP Dave Parker Bat 4.00 10.00
FL Fred Lynn Bat 4.00 10.00
GBR George Brett Uni 12.50 30.00
GC Gary Carter Bat 4.00 10.00
GF George Foster Bat 4.00 10.00
GL Greg Luzinski Bat 4.00 10.00
HBA Harold Baines Bat 6.00 15.00
HR Harold Reynolds Bat 4.00 10.00
JCR Jose Cruz Bat 4.00 10.00
JM Joe Morgan Bat 4.00 10.00
JOS Jose Canseco Bat 6.00 15.00
JRI Jim Rice Bat 4.00 10.00
JRU Joe Rudi Bat 4.00 10.00
KGI Kirk Gibson Bat 4.00 10.00
KH Keith Hernandez Bat 4.00 10.00
KM Kevin Mitchell Bat 4.00 10.00
KP Kirby Puckett Bat 10.00 25.00
LD Lenny Dykstra Bat 4.00 10.00
LP Lance Parrish Bat 6.00 15.00
MCG Willie McGee Bat 6.00 15.00
MS Mike Schmidt Bat 12.50 30.00
MW Maury Wills Bat 4.00 10.00
NC Norm Cash Jsy 10.00 25.00
PO Paul O'Neill Bat 6.00 15.00
RCA Rod Carew Bat 6.00 15.00
RDA Ron Darling Jsy 4.00 10.00
SG Steve Garvey Bat 4.00 10.00
TMC Tug McGraw Jsy 4.00 10.00
VC Vince Coleman Bat 10.00 25.00
WHE Willie Hernandez Jsy 4.00 10.00
WJ Wally Joyner Bat 4.00 10.00
WS Willie Stargell Bat 6.00 15.00

2004 Topps All-Time Fan Favorites

COMPLETE SET (150) 20.00 50.00
1 Willie Mays 1.50 4.00
2 Bob Gibson .50 1.25
3 Dave Stieb .30 .75
4 Tim McCarver .30 .75
5 Reggie Jackson .50 1.25
6 John Candelaria .30 .75
7 Lenny Dykstra .30 .75
8 Tony Oliva .30 .75
9 Frank Viola .30 .75
10 Don Mattingly 1.50 4.00
11 Garry Maddox .30 .75
12 Randy Jones .30 .75
13 Joe Carter .30 .75
14 Orlando Cepeda .50 1.25
15 Bob Sheppard ANC .50 1.25
16 Bobby Grich .30 .75
17 George Scott .30 .75
18 Mickey Rivers .30 .75
19 Ron Santo .50 1.25
20 Mike Schmidt 1.25 3.00
21 Luis Aparicio .50 1.25
22 Cesar Geronimo .30 .75
23 Jack Morris .50 1.25
24 Jeffrey Loria OWNER .30 .75
25 George Brett 1.50 4.00
26 Paul O'Neill .50 1.25
27 Reggie Smith .30 .75
28 Robin Yount .75 2.00
29 Andre Dawson .50 1.25
30 Whitey Ford .50 1.25
31 Ralph Kiner .50 1.25
32 Will Clark .50 1.25
33 Keith Hernandez .30 .75
34 Tony Fernandez .30 .75
35 Willie McGee .30 .75
36 Harmon Killebrew .75 2.00
37 Dave Kingman .30 .75
38 Kirk Gibson .30 .75
39 Terry Steinbach .30 .75
40 Frank Robinson .50 1.25
41 Chet Lemon .30 .75
42 Mike Cuellar .30 .75
43 Darrell Evans .30 .75
44 Don Kessinger .30 .75
45 Dave Concepcion .30 .75
46 Sparky Anderson .50 1.25
47 Bret Saberhagen .30 .75
48 Brett Butler .30 .75
49 Kent Hrbek .30 .75
50 Hank Aaron 1.50 4.00
51 Rudolph Giuliani .75 2.00
52 Clete Boyer .30 .75
53 Mookie Wilson .30 .75
54 Dave Stewart .30 .75
55 Gary Matthews Sr. .30 .75
56 Roy Face .30 .75
57 Vida Blue .30 .75
58 Jimmy Key .30 .75
59 Al Hrabosky .30 .75

60 Al Kaline .75 2.00
61 Mike Scott .30 .75
62 Jack McDowell .30 .75
63 Reggie Jackson .50 1.25
64 Earl Weaver .50 1.25
65 Ernie Harwell ANC .50 1.25
66 David Justice .30 .75
67 Wilbur Wood .30 .75
68 Mike Boddicker .30 .75
69 Don Zimmer .30 .75
70 Jim Palmer .50 1.25
71 Doug DeCinces .30 .75
72 Ryne Sandberg 1.50 4.00
73 Don Newcombe .30 .75
74 Denny Martinez .30 .75
75 Carl Yastrzemski .75 2.00
76 Bake McBride .30 .75
77 Andy Van Slyke .30 .75
78 Bruce Sutter .50 1.25
79 Bobby Valentine .30 .75
80 Johnny Bench .75 2.00
81 Orel Hershiser .30 .75
82 Cecil Fielder .30 .75
83 Lou Whitaker .30 .75
84 Alan Trammell .50 1.25
85 Sam McDowell .30 .75
86 Ray Knight .30 .75
87 Gregg Jefferies .30 .75
88 Ben Oglivie .30 .75
89 Billy Beane .30 .75
90 Yogi Berra .75 2.00
91 Jose Canseco .50 1.25
92 Bobby Bonilla .30 .75
93 Darren Daulton .30 .75
94 Harold Reynolds .30 .75
95 Lou Brock .50 1.25
96 Pete Incaviglia .30 .75
97 Eric Gregg UMP .30 .75
98 Devon White .30 .75
99 Kelly Gruber .30 .75
100 Nolan Ryan 2.50 6.00
101 Carlton Fisk .50 1.25
102 George Foster .30 .75
103 Dennis Eckersley .50 1.25
104 Rick Sutcliffe .30 .75
105 Cal Ripken 2.50 6.00
106 Norm Cash .30 .75
107 Charlie Hough .30 .75
108 Paul Molitor .75 2.00
109 Maury Wills .30 .75
110 Tom Seaver .50 1.25
111 Brooks Robinson .50 1.25
112 Jim Rice .50 1.25
113 Dwight Gooden .30 .75
114 Harold Baines .50 1.25
115 Tim Raines .50 1.25
116 Roy Smalley .30 .75
117 Richie Allen .30 .75
118 Ron Swoboda .30 .75
119 Ron Guidry .30 .75
120 Duke Snider .50 1.25
121 Ferguson Jenkins .50 1.25
122 Mark Fidrych .30 .75
123 Buddy Bell .30 .75
124 Bo Jackson .75 2.00
125 Stan Musial 1.25 3.00
126 Jesse Barfield .30 .75
127 Tony Gwynn .75 2.00
128 Phil Garner .30 .75
129 Dale Murphy .75 2.00
130 Wade Boggs .50 1.25
131 Sid Fernandez .30 .75
132 Monte Irvin .50 1.25
133 Peter Ueberroth COM .30 .75
134 Gary Gaetti .30 .75
135 Gorman Thomas .30 .75
136 Dave Lopes .30 .75
137 Sy Berger .75 2.00
138 Buck O'Neil .30 .75
139 Herb Score .30 .75
140 Rod Carew .50 1.25
141 Joe Buck ANC .50 1.25
142 Willie Horton .30 .75
143 Hal McRae .30 .75
144 Rollie Fingers .50 1.25
145 Tom Brunansky .30 .75
146 Fay Vincent COM .30 .75
147 Gary Carter .50 1.25
148 Bobby Richardson .30 .75
149 Steve Garvey .30 .75
150 Don Larsen .30 .75

2004 Topps All-Time Fan Favorites Refractors

*REFRACTORS: 1.2X TO 3X BASIC
STATED ODDS 1:19
STATED PRINT RUN 299 SERIAL #'d SETS

2004 Topps All-Time Fan Favorites Autographs

GROUP A ODDS 1:69,360
GROUP B ODDS 1:648
GROUP C ODDS 1:102
GROUP D ODDS 1:5662
GROUP E ODDS 1:181
GROUP F ODDS 1:208
GROUP G ODDS 1:509
GROUP H ODDS 1:356
GROUP I ODDS 1:58
GROUP J ODDS 1:148
GROUP K ODDS 1:128
GROUP L ODDS 1:135
GROUP M ODDS 1:104
GROUP N ODDS 1:228
OVERALL AUTO ODDS 1:12
GROUP A PRINT RUN 10 CARDS
GROUP B PRINT RUN 50 SETS
GROUP C PRINT RUN 100 SETS
GROUP D PRINT RUN 250 CARDS
CARDS ARE NOT SERIAL-NUMBERED
PRINT RUNS PROVIDED BY TOPPS
NO GROUP A PRICING DUE TO SCARCITY
EXCHANGE DEADLINE 05/31/06
R.ALLEN EXCH UNABLE TO BE FULFILLED
04 WS HL AU'S REPLACE ALLEN EXCH
AD Andre Dawson C 15.00 40.00
AH Al Hrabosky L 6.00 15.00
AK Al Kaline B 15.00 40.00
AT Alan Trammell C 40.00 100.00
AV Andy Van Slyke C 25.00 60.00
BB Billy Beane C 25.00 60.00
BBE Buddy Bell N 6.00 15.00
BG Bob Gibson C 25.00 60.00
BGR Bobby Grich I 8.00 20.00
BJ Bo Jackson B 40.00 100.00
BO Ben Oglivie I 6.00 15.00
BON Buck O'Neil K 12.00 30.00
BR Bobby Richardson F 6.00 15.00
BRO Brooks Robinson B 20.00 50.00
BSA Bret Saberhagen C 12.00 30.00
BSU Bruce Sutter F 15.00 40.00
BV Bobby Valentine C 15.00 40.00
CF Carlton Fisk B 25.00 60.00
CG Cesar Geronimo C 20.00 50.00
CH Charlie Hough G 6.00 15.00
CL Chet Lemon M 6.00 15.00
CR Cal Ripken B 75.00 200.00
CY Carl Yastrzemski B 50.00 120.00
DC Dave Concepcion C 15.00 40.00
DD Darren Daulton L 8.00 20.00
DDE Doug DeCinces E 6.00 15.00
DE Darrell Evans I 6.00 15.00
DEC Dennis Eckersley C 20.00 50.00
DG Dwight Gooden B 20.00 50.00
DJ David Justice E 12.00 30.00
DK Dave Kingman E 25.00 60.00
DKE Don Kessinger M 6.00 15.00
DL Dave Lopes M 6.00 15.00
DLA Don Larsen L 8.00 20.00
DM Dale Murphy B 40.00 100.00
DON Don Mattingly B 50.00 120.00
DS Dave Stewart H 6.00 15.00
DSN Duke Snider C 15.00 40.00
DST Dave Stieb J 6.00 15.00
DZ Don Zimmer I 12.00 30.00
EG Eric Gregg I 6.00 15.00
EH Ernie Harwell E 30.00 80.00
EW Earl Weaver M 10.00 25.00
FJ Ferguson Jenkins F 10.00 25.00
FR Frank Robinson C 25.00 60.00
FVI Fay Vincent C 50.00 120.00
FVI1 Frank Viola I 8.00 30.00
GB George Brett B 75.00 200.00
GC Gary Carter B 25.00 60.00
GF George Foster I 8.00 20.00
GMA Gary Matthews Sr. J 6.00 15.00
GS George Scott K 6.00 15.00
HA Hank Aaron B 60.00 150.00
HB Harold Baines C 15.00 40.00
HK Harmon Killebrew C 30.00 80.00
HR Harold Reynolds C 10.00 25.00
JB Jesse Barfield J 6.00 15.00
JB1 Joe Buck C 20.00 50.00
JBE Johnny Bench C 50.00 120.00
JC Joe Carter C 10.00 25.00
JCA Jose Canseco C 40.00 100.00
JKE Jimmy Key C 10.00 25.00
JM Jack McDowell K 6.00 15.00
JMO Jack Morris K 12.00 30.00
JP Jim Palmer B 40.00 100.00
JR Jim Rice C 25.00 60.00
KG Kirk Gibson B 20.00 50.00
KH Keith Hernandez B 20.00 50.00
LA Luis Aparicio C 15.00 40.00
LB Lou Brock C 20.00 50.00
LD Lenny Dykstra C 10.00 25.00
MB Mike Boddicker J 6.00 15.00
MF Mark Fidrych C 25.00 60.00
MI Monte Irvin C 8.00 20.00
MR Mickey Rivers M 6.00 15.00
MS Mike Schmidt B 40.00 100.00
MSC Mike Scott M 6.00 15.00
MW Maury Wills I 6.00 15.00
MWI Mookie Wilson L 8.00 20.00
NR Nolan Ryan D 75.00 200.00
OC Orlando Cepeda C 15.00 40.00
OH Orel Hershiser E 15.00 40.00
PI Pete Incaviglia E 6.00 15.00
PM Paul Molitor B 20.00 50.00
PO Paul O'Neill B 25.00 60.00
PU Peter Ueberroth C 60.00 150.00
RC Rod Carew C 25.00 60.00
RF Rollie Fingers C 8.00 20.00
RG Ron Guidry C 15.00 40.00
RJO Randy Jones L 6.00 15.00
RJ2 Reggie Jackson C 20.00 50.00
RK Ralph Kiner G 15.00 40.00
RKN Ray Knight C 10.00 25.00
RS Ron Santo I 20.00 50.00
RSU Rick Sutcliffe C 15.00 40.00
RSW Ron Swoboda N 6.00 15.00
RY Robin Yount B 30.00 80.00
RYN Ryne Sandberg C 50.00 120.00
SA Sparky Anderson C 20.00 50.00
SB Sy Berger H 40.00 100.00
SF Sid Fernandez C 10.00 25.00
SG Steve Garvey C 15.00 40.00
SM Stan Musial C 12.00 30.00
SM1 Sam McDowell C 15.00 40.00
TB Tom Brunansky F 10.00 25.00
TF Tony Fernandez F 6.00 15.00
TG Tony Gwynn B 50.00 120.00
TM Tim McCarver E 12.00 30.00
TO Tony Oliva E 15.00 40.00
TR Tim Raines E 10.00 25.00
TSE Tom Seaver B 60.00 150.00
VB Vida Blue F 8.00 20.00
WB Wade Boggs B 25.00 60.00
WF Whitey Ford C 30.00 80.00
WH Willie Horton K 6.00 15.00
WMC Willie McGee C 15.00 40.00
WW Wilbur Wood I 6.00 15.00
YB Yogi Berra C 12.00 30.00

2004 Topps All-Time Fan Favorites Best Seat in the House Relics

STATED ODDS 1:10 RELIC PACKS
BS1 Seaver/Foster/Bench 10.00 25.00
BS2 F.Rob/Palmer/B.Rob 6.00 15.00
BS3 Parker/Madlock/Mazeroski 6.00 15.00
BS4 Hrbek/Carew/Killebrew 10.00 25.00

2004 Topps All-Time Fan Favorites Relics

ONE PER RELIC PACK
BR Brooks Robinson Bat 4.00 10.00
BS Bret Saberhagen Jsy 3.00 8.00
CF Carlton Fisk Bat 4.00 10.00
CY Carl Yastrzemski Bat 10.00 25.00
DE Dennis Eckersley Uni 4.00 10.00
DJ David Justice Bat 3.00 8.00
DP Dave Parker Uni 3.00 8.00
DS Darryl Strawberry Bat 3.00 8.00
EW Earl Weaver Jsy 3.00 8.00
FR Frank Robinson Jsy 3.00 8.00
FRB Frank Robinson Bat 3.00 8.00
GB George Brett Uni 8.00 20.00
GC Gary Carter Jsy 3.00 8.00
GF George Foster Bat 3.00 8.00
GN Graig Nettles Bat 3.00 8.00
HK Harmon Killebrew Jsy 6.00 15.00
HR Harold Reynolds Bat 3.00 8.00
JC Jose Canseco Jsy 4.00 10.00
JCB Jose Canseco Bat 4.00 10.00
JM Joe Morgan Bat 3.00 8.00
JP Jim Palmer Uni 3.00 8.00
JR Jim Rice Jsy 3.00 8.00
KG Kirk Gibson Bat 3.00 8.00
KH Keith Hernandez Bat 3.00 8.00
KP Kirby Puckett Jsy 6.00 15.00
LB Lou Brock Jsy 4.00 10.00
MS Mike Schmidt Bat 8.00 20.00
MW Maury Wills Jsy 3.00 8.00
NR Nolan Ryan Jsy 15.00 40.00
RC Rod Carew Bat 4.00 10.00
RJ Reggie Jackson Bat 4.00 10.00
TP Tony Perez Bat 3.00 8.00
WB Wade Boggs Uni 4.00 10.00
WM Willie Mays Uni 20.00 50.00

2005 Topps All-Time Fan Favorites

COMPLETE SET (142) 20.00 50.00
COMMON CARD (1-142) .25 .60
OVERALL PLATE ODDS 1:1414 HOB/RET
PLATE PRINT RUN 1 SET PER COLOR
BLACK-CYAN-MAGENTA-YELLOW ISSUED
NO PLATE PRICING DUE TO SCARCITY
1 Andy Van Slyke .25 .60
2 Bill Freehan .25 .60
3 Bo Jackson .60 1.50
4 Mark Grace .40 1.00
5 Chuck Knoblauch .25 .60
6 Candy Maldonado .25 .60
7 David Cone .25 .60
8 Don Mattingly 1.25 3.00
9 Darryl Strawberry .25 .60
10 Dick Williams .25 .60
11 Frank Robinson .40 1.00
12 Glenn Hubbard .25 .60
13 Jim Abbott .25 .60
14 Jeff Brantley .25 .60
15 John Elway 1.50 4.00
16 Jim Leyland .25 .60
17 Jesse Orosco .25 .60
18 Joe Pepitone .25 .60
19 J.R. Richard .25 .60
20 Jerome Walton .25 .60
21 Kevin Maas .25 .60
22 Lou Brock .40 1.00
23 Lou Whitaker .25 .60
24 Carl Erskine .25 .60
25 John Candelaria .25 .60
26 Mike Norris .25 .60
27 Nolan Ryan 2.00 5.00
28 Pedro Guerrero .25 .60
29 Roger Craig .25 .60
30 Ron Gant .25 .60
31 Sid Bream .25 .60
32 Sid Fernandez .25 .60
33 Tony LaRussa .40 1.00
34 Tom Seaver .40 1.00
35 Yogi Berra .60 1.50
36 Andre Dawson .40 1.00
37 Al Kaline .60 1.50
38 Brett Butler .25 .60
39 Bob Gibson .40 1.00
40 Bill Mazeroski .40 1.00
41 Matty Alou .25 .60
42 Chet Lemon .25 .60
43 Cal Ripken 2.00 5.00
44 Dusty Baker .25 .60
45 Dwight Gooden .25 .60
46 Dave Winfield .40 1.00
47 Ernie Banks .60 1.50
48 Gary Carter .40 1.00
49 Howard Johnson .25 .60
50 Mike Schmidt 1.00 2.50
51 Matt Williams .25 .60
52 Ozzie Smith .75 2.00
53 Atlee Hammaker .25 .60
54 Cleon Jones .25 .60
55 Dave Johnson .25 .60
56 Denny McLain .25 .60
57 Don Zimmer .25 .60
58 Gregg Jefferies .25 .60
59 Jay Buhner .25 .60
60 Johnny Bench .60 1.50
61 George Brett 1.25 3.00
62 Dale Murphy .60 1.50
63 Bob Welch .25 .60
64 Paul O'Neill .40 1.00
65 Mark Lemke .25 .60
66 Kevin McReynolds .25 .60
67 Jesus Alou .25 .60
68 Joe Pignatano .25 .60
69 Jim Lonborg .25 .60
70 Jerry Grote .25 .60
71 Joaquin Andujar .25 .60
72 Gary Gaetti .25 .60
73 Edgar Martinez .40 1.00
74 Ron Darling .25 .60
75 Duke Snider .40 1.00
76 Dave Magadan .25 .60
77 Doug Drabek .25 .60
78 Carl Yastrzemski .75 2.00
79 Mitch Williams .25 .60
80 Marvin Miller PA .25 .60
81 Michael Kay ANC .25 .60
82 Lonnie Smith .25 .60
83 John Wetteland .25 .60
84 Johnny Podres .25 .60
85 Joe Morgan .40 1.00
86 Juan Marichal .40 1.00
87 Jeffrey Leonard .25 .60
88 Bob Feller .40 1.00
89 Brooks Robinson .40 1.00
90 Clem Labine .25 .60
91 Barry Lyons .25 .60
92 Harmon Killebrew .60 1.50
93 Jim Frey .25 .60
94 John Kruk .25 .60
95 Ed Kranepool .25 .60
96 Jose Oquendo .25 .60
97 Johnny Pesky .25 .60
98 John Tudor .25 .60
99 Keith Hernandez .25 .60
100 Monte Irvin .40 1.00
101 Marty Barrett .25 .60
102 Oscar Gamble .25 .60
103 Hank Bauer .25 .60
104 Ron Blomberg .25 .60
105 Rod Carew .40 1.00
106 Rick Dempsey .25 .60
107 Walt Jockety GM .25 .60
108 Tom Kelly .25 .60
109 Steve Carlton .40 1.00
110 Rick Monday .25 .60
111 Rob Dibble .25 .60
112 Shawon Dunston .25 .60
113 Tony Gwynn .75 2.00
114 Tom Niedenfuer .25 .60
115 Bob Dernier .25 .60
116 Anthony Young .25 .60
117 Reggie Jackson .40 1.00
118 Steve Garvey .25 .60
119 Tim Raines .40 1.00
120 Whitey Ford .40 1.00
121 Rafael Santana .25 .60
122 Scott Brosius .25 .60
123 Stan Musial 1.00 2.50
124 Ron Santo .40 1.00
125 Wade Boggs .40 1.00
126 Jose Canseco .40 1.00
127 Brady Anderson .25 .60
128 Vida Blue .25 .60
129 Charlie Hough .25 .60
130 Jim Kaat .25 .60
131 Zane Smith .25 .60
132 Bob Boone .25 .60
133 Travis Fryman .25 .60
134 Harold Baines .40 1.00
135 Orlando Cepeda .40 1.00
136 Mike Cuellar .25 .60
137 Tito Fuentes .25 .60
138 Daryl Boston .25 .60
139 Jim Leyritz .25 .60
140 Moose Skowron .25 .60
141 Theo Epstein GM .25 .60
142 Barry Bonds 1.00 2.50

2005 Topps All-Time Fan Favorites Refractors

*REF: 2.5X TO 6X BASIC
STATED ODDS 1:19 H, 1:19 R
STATED PRINT RUN 299 SERIAL #'d SETS

2005 Topps All-Time Fan Favorites Autographs

GROUP A ODDS 1:34,438 H, 1:93,312 R
GROUP B ODDS 1:1456 H, 1:1421 R
GROUP C ODDS 1:397 H, 1:462 R
GROUP D ODDS 1:1467 H, 1:1414 R
GROUP E ODDS 1:43 H, 1:233 R
GROUP F ODDS 1:37 H, 1:122 R
GROUP G ODDS 1:1165 H, 1079 R
GROUP H ODDS 1:57 H, 1:97 R
GROUP I ODDS 1:108 H, 1:153 R
OVERALL AUTO ODDS 1:12
GROUP A PRINT RUN 15 CARDS
GROUP B PRINT RUN 40 SETS
GROUP C PRINT RUN 90 SETS
CARDS ARE NOT SERIAL-NUMBERED
PRINT RUNS PROVIDED BY TOPPS
NO GROUP A PRICING DUE TO SCARCITY
EXCHANGE DEADLINE 05/31/07
AH Atlee Hammaker H 6.00 15.00
AK Al Kaline E 25.00 50.00
AV Andy Van Slyke F 12.50 30.00
AY Anthony Young F 4.00 10.00
BB Brett Butler F 6.00 15.00
BF Bill Freehan H 8.00 20.00
BFE Bob Feller E 30.00 60.00
BG Bob Gibson C/90 * 50.00 100.00
BJ Bo Jackson E 40.00 80.00
BL Barry Lyons G 4.00 10.00
BM Bill Mazeroski E 15.00 40.00
BR Brooks Robinson C/90 * 75.00 150.00
BW Bob Welch F 8.00 20.00
CH Charlie Hayes F 4.00 10.00
CJ Cleon Jones H 10.00 25.00
CK Chuck Knoblauch E 20.00 50.00
CL Clem Labine E 10.00 25.00
CLE Chet Lemon H 6.00 15.00
CM Candy Maldonado H 4.00 10.00
CR Cal Ripken C/90 * 50.00 120.00
CY Carl Yastrzemski C/90 * 75.00 150.00
DC David Cone E 8.00 20.00
DD Doug Drabek E 6.00 15.00
DG Dwight Gooden D 12.00 30.00
DJ Dave Johnson E 10.00 25.00
DM Don Mattingly D 50.00 100.00
DMA Dave Magadan F 4.00 10.00
DMC Denny McLain F 10.00 25.00
DMU Dale Murphy F 10.00 25.00
DS Darryl Strawberry E 12.50 30.00
DW Dave Winfield C/90 * 50.00 100.00
DWI Dick Williams C/90 * 15.00 40.00
EM Edgar Martinez E 10.00 25.00
FR Frank Robinson D 30.00 60.00
GC Gary Carter E 20.00 50.00
GG Gary Gaetti H 4.00 10.00
GH Glenn Hubbard F 4.00 10.00
GJ Gregg Jefferies E 6.00 15.00
HJ Howard Johnson F 4.00 10.00
HK Harmon Killebrew E 40.00 80.00
JA Jim Abbott E 10.00 25.00
JAN Joaquin Andujar H 10.00 25.00
JBE Dr. Jim Beckett C/90 * 50.00 100.00
JBR Jeff Brantley E 10.00 25.00
JBU Jay Buhner E 10.00 25.00
JG Jerry Grote F 10.00 25.00
JK John Kruk F 4.00 10.00
JLE Jim Leyland F 4.00 10.00
JLO Jim Lonborg F 6.00 15.00
JMA Juan Marichal C/90 * 20.00 50.00
JO Jesse Orosco E 10.00 25.00
JOQ Jose Oquendo I 4.00 10.00
JP Joe Pignatano F 8.00 20.00
JPE Joe Pepitone F 6.00 15.00
JPY Johnny Pesky F 10.00 25.00
JR J.R. Richard E 10.00 25.00
JT John Tudor F 6.00 15.00
JW Jerome Walton F 8.00 20.00
JWE John Wetteland E 10.00 25.00
KM Kevin Maas E 6.00 15.00
KMC Kevin McReynolds F 6.00 15.00
LS Lonnie Smith I 6.00 15.00
LW Lou Whitaker C/90 * 10.00 25.00
MB Marty Barrett H 4.00 10.00
MI Monte Irvin E 10.00 25.00
MK Michael Kay ANC C/90 * 12.00 30.00
MLE Mark Lemke H 6.00 15.00
MM Marvin Miller PA C/90 * 40.00 80.00
MNO Mike Norris I 6.00 15.00
MW Matt Williams F 10.00 25.00
MWI Mitch Williams E 6.00 15.00
OG Oscar Gamble H 6.00 15.00
OS Ozzie Smith E 20.00 50.00
PO Paul O'Neill E 15.00 40.00
RB Ron Blomberg F 6.00 15.00
RCR Roger Craig E 6.00 15.00
RD Rick Dempsey I 6.00 15.00
RG Ron Gant C/90 * 6.00 15.00
RM Rick Monday E 10.00 25.00
RS Rafael Santana F 4.00 10.00
RSA Ron Santo C/90 * 20.00 50.00
SB Sid Bream F 6.00 15.00
SBR Scott Brosius C/90 * 20.00 50.00
SC Steve Carlton C/90 * 30.00 60.00
SD Shawon Dunston E 10.00 25.00
SF Sid Fernandez E 8.00 20.00
SG Steve Garvey E 12.00 30.00
SM Stan Musial B/40 * 150.00 300.00
TG Tony Gwynn C/90 * 50.00 100.00
TK Tom Kelly F 4.00 10.00
TL Tony LaRussa E 20.00 50.00
TN Tom Niedenfuer H 4.00 10.00
TR Tim Raines E 10.00 25.00
WF Whitey Ford C/90 * 40.00 80.00
YB Yogi Berra C/90 * 40.00 100.00

2005 Topps All-Time Fan Favorites Best Seat in the House Relics

GROUP A ODDS 1:170 BOX LOADER
GROUP B ODDS 1:14 BOX LOADER
GROUP A PRINT RUN 50 CARDS
GROUP B PRINT RUN 125 SETS
RAINBOW ODDS 1:56 BOX LOADER
RAINBOW PRINT RUN 25 SERIAL #'d SETS
NO RAINBOW PRICING DUE TO SCARCITY
CR C.Ripken 10.00 25.00
F.Robinson B/125
JD D.Johnson 6.00 15.00
R.Demp B/125
KMLW Kal/Lou/Chet/McL B/125 10.00 25.00
MFBJ Matt/Ford/Berra/Reg A/50 15.00 40.00
RR B.Robinson 12.00 30.00
C.Ripken B/125
RRRD Rob 10.00 25.00
Dem/Rob/Rip B/125

2005 Topps All-Time Fan Favorites Jim Beckett Promo

PROMO ISSUED IN BECKETT BASEBALL
JB Dr. Jim Beckett 2.00 5.00

2005 Topps All-Time Fan Favorites League Leaders Tri-Signers

STATED ODDS 1:5194 H, 1:5632 R
STATED PRINT RUN 50 SERIAL #'d SETS
EXCHANGE DEADLINE 05/31/07
JSB Reggie/Schmidt/Brett 300.00 500.00
MBG Mattingly/Boggs/Gooden 150.00 250.00

2005 Topps All-Time Fan Favorites Originals Relics

STATED ODDS 1:17 BOX-LOADER
STATED PRINT RUN 50 SERIAL #'d SETS
PRINT RUNS INTERMINGLE DIFT.CARDS
ACTUAL VINTAGE CARDS USED
AD Andre Dawson Bat 10.00 25.00
BJ Bo Jackson Jsy 12.50 30.00
DM Dale Murphy Bat 15.00 40.00
GC Gary Carter Bat 10.00 25.00
JR Jim Rice Bat 10.00 25.00
NR Nolan Ryan Jsy 30.00 60.00
RC Rod Carew Bat 15.00 40.00
RJ Reggie Jackson Bat 15.00 40.00
TG Tony Gwynn Jsy 20.00 50.00
WB Wade Boggs Bat 15.00 40.00

2005 Topps All-Time Fan Favorites Relics

GROUP A ODDS 1:83 BOX-LOADER
GROUP B ODDS 1:31 BOX-LOADER
GROUP C ODDS 1:3 BOX-LOADER
GROUP D ODDS 1:3 BOX-LOADER
GROUP A PRINT RUN 50 SERIAL #'d SETS
GROUP B PRINT RUN 135 SERIAL #'d SETS
GROUP C PRINT RUN 200 SERIAL #'d SETS
GROUP D PRINT RUN 350 SERIAL #'d SETS
RAINBOW ODDS 1:13 BOX-LOADER
RAINBOW PRINT RUN 25 SERIAL #'d SETS
NO RAINBOW PRICING DUE TO SCARCITY
AD Andre Dawson Bat D/350 4.00 10.00
BD Bucky Dent Bat C/200 4.00 10.00
BJ Bo Jackson Bat C/200 6.00 15.00
BR Brooks Robinson Bat D/350 6.00 15.00
BS Bruce Sutter Jsy D/350 4.00 10.00
CF Cecil Fielder Bat C/200 8.00 20.00
DM Dale Murphy Bat C/200 6.00 15.00
DS Darryl Strawberry Bat D/350 4.00 10.00
ED Eric Davis Bat C/200 4.00 10.00
GC Gary Carter Bat D/350 4.00 10.00
JC Joe Carter Bat D/350 4.00 10.00
JCC Jose Canseco Bat D/350 5.00 15.00
JR Jim Rice Bat C/200 4.00 10.00
KH Keith Hernandez Bat C/200 4.00 10.00
LD Lenny Dykstra Bat C/200 4.00 10.00
MW Mookie Wilson Bat B/135 4.00 10.00
NR Nolan Ryan Jsy B/135 15.00 40.00
PO Paul O'Neill Bat C/200 6.00 15.00
RC Rod Carew Bat C/200 6.00 15.00
RJ Reggie Jackson Bat D/350 6.00 15.00
TG Tony Gwynn Jsy C/200 6.00 15.00
VC Vince Coleman Bat C/200 4.00 10.00
WB Wade Boggs Bat C/200 6.00 15.00
WJ Wally Joyner Bat C/200 4.00 10.00
WM Willie McGee Bat D/350 6.00 15.00

2007 Topps All-Star FanFest

COMPLETE SET (7) 3.00 8.00
1 Tim Lincecum .40 1.00
2 Barry Bonds .30 .75
3 Alex Rodriguez .25 .60
4 David Wright .15 .40
5 Ryan Howard .15 .40
6 Daisuke Matsuzaka .30 .75
7 Mickey Mantle .60 1.50

2008 Topps All-Star FanFest

COMPLETE SET (8) 20.00 50.00
1 Babe Ruth 5.00 12.00
2 Jackie Robinson 2.00 5.00
3 Alex Rodriguez 2.50 6.00
4 David Wright 1.25 3.00
5 Lou Gehrig 4.00 10.00
6 Joba Chamberlain .75 2.00
7 Mickey Mantle 6.00 15.00
8 Johan Santana 1.25 3.00

2008 Topps All-Star FanFest Patch

STATED PRINT RUN 375 SER.#'d SETS
NO CARD NUMBERS
CARDS LISTED ALPHABETICALLY
1 Lou Gehrig 20.00 50.00
2 Mickey Mantle 30.00 60.00
3 Thurman Munson 15.00 40.00
4 Jose Reyes 12.50 30.00
5 Babe Ruth 10.00 25.00
6 Johan Santana 12.50 30.00
7 Tom Seaver 12.50 30.00
8 David Wright 12.50 30.00

2010 Topps All-Star FanFest

COMPLETE SET (6) 15.00 40.00
WR1 Torii Hunter 1.25 3.00
WR2 Hideki Matsui 3.00 8.00
WR3 Kendry Morales 1.25 3.00
WR4 Nolan Ryan 10.00 25.00
WR5 Rod Carew 2.00 5.00
WR6 Stephen Strasburg 10.00 25.00

2012 Topps All-Star FanFest

COMPLETE SET (6) 15.00 40.00
FF1 Eric Hosmer 2.00 5.00
FF2 Billy Butler 1.50 4.00
FF3 Mike Moustakas 2.00 5.00
FF4 Yu Darvish 4.00 10.00
FF5 Bryce Harper 25.00 60.00
FF6 Josh Hamilton 2.00 5.00

2013 Topps All-Star FanFest

COMPLETE SET (6) 25.00 60.00
WR1 Matt Harvey 10.00 25.00
WR2 David Wright 6.00 15.00
WR3 Mariano Rivera 10.00 25.00
WR4 Robinson Cano 3.00 8.00
WR5 Mike Trout 15.00 40.00
WR6 Bryce Harper 3.00 8.00

2013 Topps All-Star FanFest Patches

STATED PRINT RUN 150 SER.#'d SETS
PC1 Tom Seaver 40.00 100.00
PC2 Darryl Strawberry 30.00 80.00
PC3 Mariano Rivera 40.00 100.00
PC4 Babe Ruth 20.00 50.00
PC5 David Wright 40.00 100.00
PC6 Gary Carter 100.00 250.00

2014 Topps All-Star FanFest

WR01 Mike Trout 10.00 25.00
WR02 Andrew McCutchen 1.50 4.00
WR03 Miguel Cabrera 1.50 4.00
WR04 Derek Jeter 10.00 25.00
WR05 Clayton Kershaw 2.50 6.00
WR06 Joe Mauer 1.25 3.00
WRCB Charlie Brown 1.50 4.00

2014 Topps All-Star FanFest Patches

STATED PRINT RUN 150 SER.#'d SETS
PC01 Harmon Killebrew 20.00 50.00
PC02 Ty Cobb 20.00 50.00
PC03 Derek Jeter 50.00 100.00
PC04 Rod Carew 20.00 50.00
PC05 Robin Yount 20.00 50.00
PC06 Joe Mauer 30.00 60.00

2017 Topps All Star FanFest

ASG1 Mike Trout 8.00 20.00
ASG2 Clayton Kershaw 2.50 6.00
ASG3 Kris Bryant 2.00 5.00
ASG4 Buster Posey 2.00 5.00
ASG5 Bryce Harper 2.50 6.00
ASG6 Giancarlo Stanton 1.50 4.00

2017 Topps All-Star Game Silver

*AS SILVER: .75X TO 2X BASIC
*AS SILVER RC: 2X TO 5X BASIC RC
INSERTED IN AS FACTORY SETS

2006 Topps Allen and Ginter National Promos

COMPLETE SET (8) 15.00 30.00
*MINIS: .5X TO 1.5X BASE CARDS
NCC2 Kirk Gibson 1.25 3.00
NCC4 Vladimir Guerrero 1.00 2.50
NCC6 Nolan Ryan 4.00 10.00
NCC7 Jered Weaver .75 2.00
NCC8 Matt Kemp .75 2.00

2006 Topps Allen and Ginter

COMPLETE SET (350) 60.00 120.00
COMP.SET w/o SP's (300) 15.00 40.00
SP STATED ODDS 1:2 HOBBY, 1:2 RETAIL
SP CL: 5/15/25/35/45/50-59/65/85/105/115
SP CL: 125/135/145/150-159/165/175/185
SP CL: 205/215/235/245/251/255-256/265
SP CL: 285/295/305/315/325/335/345
FRAMED ORIGINALS ODDS 1:3227 H, 1:3227 R
1 Albert Pujols .50 1.25
2 Aubrey Huff .15 .40
3 Mark Teixeira .25 .60
4 Vernon Wells .15 .40
5 Ken Griffey Jr. SP 2.50 6.00
6 Nick Swisher .25 .60
7 Jose Reyes .25 .60
8 David Wright .30 .75
9 Vladimir Guerrero .25 .60
10 Andruw Jones .15 .40
11 Ramon Hernandez .15 .40
12 Miguel Tejada .25 .60
13 Juan Pierre .15 .40
14 Jim Thome .25 .60
15 Austin Kearns SP 1.25 3.00
16 Jhonny Peralta .15 .40
17 Clint Barmes .15 .40
18 Angel Berroa .15 .40
19 Nomar Garciaparra .25 .60
20 Joe Nathan .15 .40
21 Brandon Webb .25 .60
22 Chad Tracy .15 .40
23 Derek Jeter 1.00 2.50
24 Conor Jackson (RC) .25 .60
25 Jason Giambi SP 1.25 3.00
26 Johnny Estrada .15 .40
27 Luis Gonzalez .15 .40
28 Javier Vazquez .15 .40
29 Orlando Hudson .15 .40
30 Shawn Green .15 .40
31 Mark Buehrle .25 .60
32 Wily Mo Pena .15 .40
33 C.C. Sabathia .25 .60
34 Ronnie Belliard .15 .40
35 Travis Hafner SP 1.25 3.00
36 Mike Jacobs (RC) .15 .40
37 Roy Oswalt .25 .60
38 Zack Greinke .40 1.00
39 J.D. Drew .15 .40
40 Jeff Kent .15 .40
41 Ben Sheets .15 .40
42 Luis Castillo .15 .40
43 Carlos Delgado .15 .40
44 Cliff Floyd .15 .40
45 Danny Haren SP 1.25 3.00
46 Bobby Abreu .15 .40
47 Jeromy Burnitz .15 .40
48 Khalil Greene .15 .40
49 Moises Alou .15 .40
50 Alex Rodriguez SP 2.00 5.00
51 Ervin Santana SP 1.25 3.00
52 Bartolo Colon SP 1.25 3.00
53 John Smoltz SP 1.25 3.00
54 David Ortiz SP 1.25 3.00
55 Hideki Matsui SP 1.25 3.00
56 Jermaine Dye SP 1.25 3.00
57 Victor Martinez SP 1.25 3.00
58 Willy Taveras SP 1.25 3.00
59 Brady Clark SP 1.25 3.00
60 Justin Morneau .25 .60
61 Xavier Nady .15 .40
62 Rich Harden .15 .40
63 Jack Wilson .15 .40
64 Brian Giles .15 .40
65 Jon Lieber SP 1.25 3.00
66 Dan Johnson .15 .40
67 Billy Wagner .15 .40
68 Rickie Weeks .15 .40
69 Chris Ray (RC) .15 .40
70 Chris Shelton .15 .40
71 Dmitri Young .15 .40
72 Ivan Rodriguez .25 .60
73 Jeremy Bonderman .15 .40
74 Justin Verlander (RC) 1.25 3.00
75 Randy Johnson .40 1.00
76 Magglio Ordonez .25 .60
77 Brandon Inge .15 .40
78 Placido Polanco .15 .40
79 Ryan Howard .30 .75
80 Jason Bay .15 .40
81 Sean Casey .15 .40
82 Jeremy Hermida (RC) .15 .40
83 Mike Cameron .15 .40
84 Trevor Hoffman .25 .60
85 Mike Matheny SP 1.25 3.00
86 Steve Finley .15 .40
87 Adam Everett .15 .40
88 Jason Isringhausen .15 .40
89 Jonny Gomes .15 .40
90 Barry Zito .25 .60
91 Bobby Crosby .15 .40
92 Eric Chavez .15 .40
93 Frank Thomas .40 1.00
94 Huston Street .15 .40
95 Jorge Posada .25 .60
96 Casey Kotchman .15 .40
97 Darin Erstad .15 .40
98 Chipper Jones .40 1.00
99 Jeff Francoeur .40 1.00
100 Barry Bonds .60 1.50
101 Alfonso Soriano .25 .60
102 Brandon Claussen .15 .40
103 Aaron Boone .15 .40
104 Roger Clemens .50 1.25
105 Andy Pettitte SP 1.25 3.00
106 Nick Johnson .15 .40
107 Tom Gordon .15 .40
108 Orlando Hernandez .15 .40
109 Francisco Rodriguez .25 .60
110 Orlando Cabrera .15 .40
111 Edgar Renteria .15 .40
112 Tim Hudson .25 .60
113 Coco Crisp .15 .40
114 Matt Clement .15 .40
115 Greg Maddux SP 2.00 5.00
116 Paul Konerko .25 .60
117 Felipe Lopez .15 .40
118 Garrett Atkins .15 .40
119 Akinori Otsuka .15 .40

120 Craig Biggio .25 .60
121 Danys Baez .15 .40
122 Brad Penny .15 .40
123 Eric Gagne .15 .40
124 Lew Ford .15 .40
125 Mariano Rivera SP 1.25 3.00
126 Carlos Beltran .25 .60
127 Pedro Martinez .25 .60
128 Todd Helton .25 .60
129 Aaron Rowand .15 .40
130 Mike Lieberthal .15 .40
131 Oliver Perez .15 .40
132 Ryan Klesko .15 .40
133 Randy Winn .15 .40
134 Yuniesky Betancourt .15 .40
135 David Eckstein SP 1.25 3.00
136 Chad Orvella .15 .40
137 Toby Hall .15 .40
138 Hank Blalock .15 .40
139 B.J. Ryan .15 .40
140 Roy Halladay .25 .60
141 Livan Hernandez .15 .40
142 John Patterson .15 .40
143 Bengie Molina .15 .40
144 Brad Wilkerson .15 .40
145 Jorge Cantu SP 1.25 3.00
146 Mark Mulder .15 .40
147 Felix Hernandez .25 .60
148 Paul Lo Duca .15 .40
149 Prince Fielder (RC) .75 2.00
150 Johnny Damon SP 1.25 3.00
151 Ryan Langerhans SP 1.25 3.00
152 Kris Benson SP 1.25 3.00
153 Curt Schilling SP 1.25 3.00
154 Manny Ramirez SP 1.25 3.00
155 Robinson Cano SP 1.25 3.00
156 Derrek Lee SP 1.25 3.00
157 A.J. Pierzynski SP 1.25 3.00
158 Adam Dunn SP 1.25 3.00
159 Cliff Lee SP 1.25 3.00
160 Grady Sizemore .25 .60
161 Jeff Francis .15 .40
162 Dontrelle Willis .15 .40
163 Brad Ausmus .15 .40
164 Preston Wilson .15 .40
165 Derek Lowe SP 1.25 3.00
166 Chris Capuano .15 .40
167 Joe Mauer .25 .60
168 Torii Hunter .15 .40
169 Chase Utley .25 .60
170 Zach Duke .15 .40
171 Jason Schmidt .15 .40
172 Adrian Beltre .40 1.00
173 Eddie Guardado .15 .40
174 Richie Sexson .15 .40
175 Miguel Cabrera SP 1.25 3.00
176 Julio Lugo .15 .40
177 Francisco Cordero .15 .40
178 Kevin Millwood .15 .40
179 A.J. Burnett .15 .40
180 Jose Guillen .15 .40
181 Larry Bigbie .15 .40
182 Raul Ibanez .25 .60
183 Jake Peavy .15 .40
184 Pat Burrell .15 .40
185 Tom Glavine SP 1.25 3.00
186 J.J. Hardy .15 .40
187 Emil Brown .15 .40
188 Lance Berkman .25 .60
189 Marcus Giles .15 .40
190 Scott Podsednik .15 .40
191 Chone Figgins .15 .40
192 Melvin Mora .15 .40
193 Mark Loretta .15 .40
194 Carlos Zambrano .25 .60
195 Chien-Ming Wang .25 .60
196 Mark Prior .25 .60
197 Bobby Jenks .15 .40
198 Brian Fuentes .15 .40
199 Garret Anderson .15 .40
200 Ichiro Suzuki .50 1.25
201 Brian Roberts .15 .40
202 Jason Kendall .15 .40
203 Milton Bradley .15 .40
204 Jimmy Rollins .25 .60
205 Brett Myers SP 1.25 3.00
206 Joe Randa .15 .40
207 Mike Piazza .40 1.00
208 Matt Morris .15 .40
209 Omar Vizquel .25 .60
210 Jeremy Reed .15 .40
211 Chris Carpenter .25 .60
212 Jim Edmonds .25 .60
213 Scott Kazmir .25 .60
214 Travis Lee .15 .40
215 Michael Young SP 1.25 3.00
216 Rod Barajas .15 .40
217 Gustavo Chacin .15 .40
218 Lyle Overbay .15 .40
219 Troy Glaus .15 .40
220 Chad Cordero .15 .40
221 Jose Vidro .15 .40
222 Scott Rolen .25 .60
223 Carl Crawford .25 .60
224 Rocco Baldelli .15 .40
225 Mike Mussina .25 .60
226 Kelvim Escobar .15 .40
227 Corey Patterson .15 .40
228 Javy Lopez .15 .40
229 Jonathan Papelbon (RC) .75 2.00
230 Aramis Ramirez .15 .40
231 Tadahito Iguchi .15 .40
232 Morgan Ensberg .15 .40
233 Mark Grudzielanek .15 .40
234 Mike Sweeney .15 .40
235 Shawn Chacon SP 1.25 3.00
236 Nick Punto .15 .40
237 Geoff Jenkins .15 .40
238 Carlos Lee .15 .40
239 David DeJesus .15 .40
240 Brad Lidge .15 .40
241 Bob Wickman .15 .40
242 Jon Garland .15 .40
243 Kerry Wood .15 .40
244 Bronson Arroyo .15 .40
245 Matt Holliday SP 1.50 4.00
246 Josh Beckett .15 .40
247 Johan Santana .25 .60
248 Rafael Furcal .15 .40
249 Shannon Stewart .15 .40
250 Gary Sheffield .15 .40
251 Josh Barfield SP (RC) 1.25 3.00
252 Kenji Johjima RC .40 1.00
253 Ian Kinsler (RC) .50 1.25
254 Brian Anderson (RC) .15 .40
255 Matt Cain SP (RC) 1.25 3.00
256 Josh Willingham SP (RC) 1.25 3.00
257 John Koronka (RC) .15 .40
258 Chris Duffy (RC) .15 .40
259 Brian McCann (RC) .15 .40
260 Hanley Ramirez (RC) .25 .60
261 Hong-Chih Kuo (RC) .40 1.00
262 Francisco Liriano (RC) .40 1.00
263 Anderson Hernandez (RC) .15 .40
264 Ryan Zimmerman (RC) .50 1.25
265 Brian Bannister SP (RC) 1.25 3.00
266 Nolan Ryan 1.25 3.00
267 Frank Robinson .25 .60
268 Roberto Clemente 1.00 2.50
269 Hank Greenberg .40 1.00
270 Napolean Lajoie .40 1.00
271 Lloyd Waner .25 .60
272 Paul Waner .25 .60
273 Frankie Frisch .25 .60
274 Moose Skowron .15 .40
275 Mickey Mantle 1.25 3.00
276 Brooks Robinson .25 .60
277 Carl Yastrzemski .60 1.50
278 Johnny Pesky .15 .40
279 Stan Musial .60 1.50
280 Bill Mazeroski .25 .60
281 Harmon Killebrew .40 1.00
282 Monte Irvin .15 .40
283 Bob Gibson .25 .60
284 Ted Williams .75 2.00
285 Yogi Berra SP 1.25 3.00
286 Ernie Banks .40 1.00
287 Bobby Doerr .15 .40
288 Josh Gibson .40 1.00
289 Bob Feller .25 .60
290 Cal Ripken 1.25 3.00
291 Bobby Cox MG .15 .40
292 Terry Francona MG .15 .40
293 Dusty Baker MG .15 .40
294 Ozzie Guillen MG .15 .40
295 Jim Leyland MG SP 1.25 3.00
296 Willie Randolph MG .15 .40
297 Joe Torre MG .25 .60
298 Felipe Alou MG .15 .40
299 Tony La Russa MG .25 .60
300 Frank Robinson MG .25 .60
301 Mike Tyson .60 1.50
302 Duke Paoa Kahanamoku .15 .40
303 Jennie Finch 1.00 2.50
304 Brandi Chastain .15 .40
305 Danica Patrick SP 8.00 20.00
306 Wendy Guey .15 .40
307 Hulk Hogan .50 1.25
308 Carl Lewis .15 .40
309 John Wooden .25 .60
310 Randy Couture .75 2.00
311 Andy Irons .15 .40
312 Takeru Kobayashi .50 1.25
313 Leon Spinks .15 .40
314 Jim Thorpe .25 .60
315 Jerry Bailey SP 1.25 3.00
316 Adrian C. Anson REP .25 .60
317 John M. Ward REP .25 .60
318 Mike Kelly REP .15 .40
319 Capt. Jack Glasscock REP .15 .40
320 Aaron Hill .15 .40
321 Derrick Turnbow .15 .40
322 Nick Markakis (RC) .30 .75
323 Brad Hawpe .15 .40
324 Kevin Mench .15 .40
325 John Lackey SP 1.25 3.00
326 Chester A. Arthur .15 .40
327 Ulysses S. Grant .15 .40
328 Abraham Lincoln .15 .40
329 Grover Cleveland .15 .40
330 Benjamin Harrison .15 .40
331 Theodore Roosevelt .15 .40
332 Rutherford B. Hayes .15 .40
333 Chancellor Otto Von Bismarck .15 .40
334 Kaiser Wilhelm II .15 .40
335 Queen Victoria SP 1.25 3.00
336 Pope Leo XIII .15 .40
337 Thomas Edison .15 .40
338 Orville Wright .15 .40
339 Wilbur Wright .15 .40
340 Nathaniel Hawthorne .15 .40
341 Herman Melville .15 .40
342 Stonewall Jackson .15 .40
343 Robert E. Lee .15 .40
344 Andrew Carnegie .15 .40
345 John Rockefeller SP 1.25 3.00
346 Bob Fitzsimmons .15 .40
347 Billy The Kid .15 .40
348 Buffalo Bill .15 .40
349 Jesse James
350 Statue Of Liberty .15 .40
NNO Framed Originals 60.00 120.00

2006 Topps Allen and Ginter Mini

*MINI 1-350: 1X TO 2.5X BASIC
*MINI 1-350: 1X TO 2.5X BASIC RC's
APPX.15 MINIS PER 24-CT SEALED BOX
*MINI SP 1-350: .6X TO 1.5X BASIC SP
*MINI SP 1-350: .6X TO 1.5X BASIC SP RC's
MINI SP ODDS 1:13 H, 1:13 R
COMMON CARD (351-375) 20.00 50.00
SEMISTARS 351-375 30.00 60.00
UNLISTED STARS 351-375 30.00 60.00
351-375 RANDOM WITHIN RIP CARDS
OVERALL PLATE ODDS 1:865 H, 1:865 R
PLATE PRINT RUN 1 SET PER COLOR
BLACK-CYAN-MAGENTA-YELLOW ISSUED
NO PLATE PRICING DUE TO SCARCITY
351 Albert Pujols EXT 75.00 150.00
352 Alex Rodriguez EXT 30.00 60.00
353 Andruw Jones EXT 20.00 50.00
354 Barry Bonds EXT 20.00 50.00
355 Cal Ripken EXT 75.00 150.00
356 David Ortiz EXT 40.00 80.00
357 David Wright EXT 20.00 50.00
358 Derek Jeter EXT 75.00 150.00
359 Derrek Lee EXT 20.00 50.00
360 Hideki Matsui EXT 30.00 60.00
361 Ichiro Suzuki EXT 40.00 80.00
362 Johan Santana EXT 30.00 60.00
363 Josh Gibson EXT 20.00 50.00
364 Ken Griffey Jr. EXT 30.00 80.00
365 Manny Ramirez EXT 20.00 50.00
366 Mickey Mantle EXT 75.00 150.00
367 Miguel Cabrera EXT 20.00 50.00
368 Miguel Tejada EXT 20.00 50.00
369 Mike Piazza EXT 30.00 60.00
370 Nolan Ryan EXT 75.00 150.00
371 Roberto Clemente EXT 125.00 200.00
372 Roger Clemens EXT 40.00 80.00
373 Scott Rolen EXT 20.00 50.00
374 Ted Williams EXT 50.00 100.00
375 Vladimir Guerrero EXT 30.00 60.00

2006 Topps Allen and Ginter Mini A and G Back

*A & G BACK: 2X TO 5X BASIC
*A & G BACK: 1.5X TO 4X BASIC RC's
STATED ODDS 1:5 H, 1:5 R
*A & G BACK SP: 1X TO 2.5X BASIC SP
*A & G BACK SP: 1X TO 2.5X BASIC SP RC's
SP STATED ODDS 1:65 H, 1:65 R

2006 Topps Allen and Ginter Mini Black

*BLACK: 4X TO 10X BASIC
*BLACK: 2.5X TO 6X BASIC RC's
STATED ODDS 1:10 H, 1:10 R
*BLACK SP: 1.5X TO 4X BASIC SP
*BLACK SP: 1.5X TO 4X BASIC SP RC's
SP STATED ODDS 1:130 H, 1:130 R

2006 Topps Allen and Ginter Mini No Card Number

*NO NBR: 6X TO 15X BASIC
*NO NBR: 4X TO 10X BASIC RC's
*NO NBR: 2X TO 5X BASIC SP
*NO NBR: 2X TO 5X BASIC SP RC's
STATED ODDS 1:60 H, 1:168 R
STATED PRINT RUN 50 SETS
CARDS ARE NOT SERIAL-NUMBERED
PRINT RUN INFO PROVIDED BY TOPPS

2006 Topps Allen and Ginter Autographs

GROUP A ODDS 1:2467 H, 1:3850 R
GROUP B ODDS 1:14,500 H, 1:32,000 R
GROUP C ODDS 1:2200 H, 1:4300 R
GROUP D ODDS 1:548 H, 1:1090 R
GROUP E ODDS 1:473 H, 1:1000 R
GROUP F ODDS 1:250 H, 1:520 R
GROUP G ODDS 1:158 H, 1:299 R
GROUP A PRINT RUN 50 CARDS PER
GROUP A BONDS PRINT RUN 25 CARDS
GROUP B PRINT RUN 75 CARDS PER
GROUP C PRINT RUN 100 CARDS PER
GROUP D PRINT RUN 200 CARDS PER
GROUP A-D ARE NOT SERIAL-NUMBERED
A-D PRINT RUNS PROVIDED BY TOPPS
NO BONDS PRICING DUE TO SCARCITY
AI Andy Irons D/200 * 100.00 175.00
AR Alex Rodriguez A/50 * 400.00 500.00
BC Brandi Chastain D/200 * 40.00 80.00
BF Bob Feller E 30.00 80.00
BJR B.J. Ryan E 8.00 20.00
BW Billy Wagner F 5.00 12.00
CB Clint Barmes F 5.00 12.00
CL Carl Lewis D/200 * 60.00 120.00
CMW C.Wang C/100 * 500.00 600.00
CR Cal Ripken A/50 * 350.00 400.00
CU Chase Utley E 20.00 50.00
CY Carl Yastrzemski A/50 * 300.00 500.00
DL Derrek Lee E 6.00 15.00
DP Danica Patrick C/100 * 400.00 600.00
DW David Wright E 50.00 100.00
DWI Dontrelle Willis C/100 * 15.00 40.00
EC Eric Chavez G 5.00 12.00
ES Ervin Santana F 5.00 12.00
FL Francisco Liriano G 6.00 15.00
GS Gary Sheffield A/50 * 60.00 120.00
HH Hulk Hogan D/200 * 125.00 250.00
HS Huston Street E 10.00 25.00
JB Jerry Bailey D/200 * 30.00 60.00
JB1 Josh Barfield G 6.00 15.00
JF Jennie Finch D/200 * 50.00 100.00
JG Jonny Gomes G 6.00 15.00
JS Johan Santana C/100 * 75.00 150.00
JW John Wooden D/200 * 125.00 250.00
KJ Kenji Johjima A/50 * 50.00 100.00
LF Lew Ford G 5.00 12.00
LS Leon Spinks D/200 * 30.00 80.00
MC Miguel Cabrera C/100 * 75.00 150.00
MT Mike Tyson D/200 * 250.00 350.00
MY Michael Young E 5.00 12.00
NR Nolan Ryan A/50 * 350.00 450.00
OS Ozzie Smith B/75 * 125.00 250.00
PF Prince Fielder F 5.00 12.00
RA Randy Couture E 50.00 100.00
RC Robinson Cano G 15.00 40.00
RH Ryan Howard F 6.00 15.00
RZ Ryan Zimmerman F 15.00 40.00
SK Scott Kazmir F 5.00 12.00
SM Stan Musial A/50 * 300.00 500.00
TG Tony Gwynn A/50 * 200.00 300.00
TH Travis Hafner F 5.00 12.00
TK Takeru Kobayashi D/200 * 60.00 150.00
VG Vladimir Guerrero A/50 * 30.00 60.00
VM Victor Martinez E 5.00 12.00
WG Wendy Guey F 8.00 20.00
WMP Wily Mo Pena G 5.00 12.00

2006 Topps Allen and Ginter Autographs Red Ink

RANDOM INSERTS WITHIN RIP CARDS
STATED PRINT RUN 10 SETS
CARDS ARE NOT SERIAL-NUMBERED
PRINT RUN IFNO PROVIDED BY TOPPS
NO PRICING DUE TO SCARCITY

2006 Topps Allen and Ginter N43

COMPLETE SET (15) 50.00 100.00
STATED ODDS 1:2 SEALED HOBBY BOXES
1 Alex Rodriguez 2.50 6.00
2 Barry Bonds 3.00 8.00
3 Albert Pujols 2.50 6.00
4 Josh Gibson 2.00 5.00
5 Nolan Ryan 6.00 15.00
6 Ichiro Suzuki 2.50 6.00
7 Mickey Mantle 6.00 15.00
8 Ted Williams 4.00 10.00
9 David Wright 1.50 4.00
10 Ken Griffey Jr. 4.00 10.00
11 Mark Teixeira 1.25 3.00
12 Adrian C. Anson 1.25 3.00
13 Mike Tyson 3.00 8.00
14 Kenji Johjima 2.00 5.00
15 Ryan Zimmerman 2.50 6.00

2006 Topps Allen and Ginter N43 Autographs

STATED ODDS 1:1970 HOBBY BOXES
STATED PRINT RUN 10 SERIAL #'d SETS
NO PRICING DUE TO SCARCITY

2006 Topps Allen and Ginter N43 Relics

STATED ODDS 1:379 HOBBY BOXES
STATED PRINT RUN 50 SERIAL #'d SETS
AP Albert Pujols Uni 40.00 80.00
JG Josh Gibson Model Bat 200.00 300.00

2006 Topps Allen and Ginter Dick Perez

COMPLETE SET (30) 10.00 25.00
ONE PEREZ OR DECOY PER PACK
ORIGINALS RANDOM WITHIN RIP CARDS
ORIGINALS PRINT RUN 1 SERIAL #'d SET
NO ORIG. PRICING DUE TO SCARCITY
1 Shawn Green .25 .60
2 Andruw Jones .25 .60
3 Miguel Tejada .40 1.00
4 David Ortiz .60 1.50
5 Derrek Lee .25 .60
6 Paul Konerko .40 1.00
7 Ken Griffey Jr. 1.25 3.00
8 Travis Hafner .25 .60
9 Todd Helton .40 1.00
10 Ivan Rodriguez .40 1.00
11 Miguel Cabrera .60 1.50
12 Lance Berkman .40 1.00
13 Mike Sweeney .25 .60
14 Vladimir Guerrero .40 1.00
15 Rafael Furcal .25 .60
16 Carlos Lee .25 .60
17 Johan Santana .40 1.00
18 David Wright .50 1.25
19 Alex Rodriguez .75 2.00
20 Huston Street .25 .60
21 Bobby Abreu .25 .60
22 Jason Bay .25 .60
23 Jake Peavy .25 .60
24 Ichiro Suzuki .75 2.00
25 Barry Bonds 1.00 2.50
26 Albert Pujols .75 2.00
27 Aubrey Huff .25 .60
28 Mark Teixeira .40 1.00
29 Vernon Wells .25 .60
30 Alfonso Soriano .40 1.00

2006 Topps Allen and Ginter Postcards

COMPLETE SET (15) 20.00 50.00
STATED ODDS 1:2 HOBBY BOXES
PERSONALIZED ODDS 1:3000 HOB.BOXES
PERSONALIZED PRINT RUN 1 #'d SET
NO PERSONALIZED PRICING AVAILABLE
AP Albert Pujols 2.00 5.00
AR Alex Rodriguez 2.00 5.00
BB Barry Bonds 2.50 6.00
CR Cal Ripken 5.00 12.00
DJ Derek Jeter 4.00 10.00
DO David Ortiz 1.50 4.00
DW David Wright 1.25 3.00
IS Ichiro Suzuki 2.00 5.00
JG Josh Gibson 1.50 4.00
KG Ken Griffey Jr. 3.00 8.00
MM Mickey Mantle 5.00 12.00
MR Manny Ramirez 1.50 4.00
MT Miguel Tejada 1.00 2.50
TW Ted Williams 3.00 8.00
VG Vladimir Guerrero 1.00 2.50

2006 Topps Allen and Ginter Relics

GROUP A ODDS 1:2800 H, 1:4950 R
GROUP B ODDS 1:2000 H, 1:3900 R
GROUP C ODDS 1:140 H, 1:248 R
GROUP D ODDS 1:178 H, 1:413 R
GROUP E ODDS 1:128 H, 1:275 R
GROUP F ODDS 1:60 H, 1:118 R
GROUP G ODDS 1:66 H, 1:152 R
GROUP H ODDS 1:111 H, 1:174 R
GROUP I ODDS 1:178 H, 1:413 R
GROUP A ARE NOT SERIAL-NUMBERED
GROUP A QTY PROVIDED BY TOPPS
AP Albert Pujols Uni F 8.00 20.00
APE Andy Pettitte Jsy F 4.00 10.00
AR Alex Rodriguez Jsy C 4.00 10.00
BB Barry Bonds Uni G 10.00 25.00
BC Bobby Crosby Uni E 3.00 8.00
BM Brandon McCarthy Jsy E 3.00 8.00
CB Carlos Beltran Jsy H 3.00 8.00
CBA Clint Barmes Jsy G 3.00 8.00
CD Carlos Delgado Jsy F 3.00 8.00
CMW Chien-Ming Wang Jsy F 20.00 50.00
CS Curt Schilling Jsy F 4.00 10.00
CU Chase Utley Jsy G 6.00 15.00
DO David Ortiz Jsy G 4.00 10.00
DW David Wright Jsy H 6.00 15.00
DWI Dontrelle Willis Jsy I 3.00 8.00
EC Eric Chavez Uni E 3.00 8.00
FH Felix Hernandez Jsy C 4.00 10.00
FT Frank Thomas Bat F 6.00 15.00
GB G.W. Bush Tie A/150 * 200.00 300.00
GS Gary Sheffield Bat E 3.00 8.00
HCK Hong-Chih Kuo Jsy D 3.00 8.00
HM Hideki Matsui Uni G 6.00 15.00
HS Huston Street Jsy D 3.00 8.00
JC Jorge Cantu Jsy E 3.00 8.00
JD Johnny Damon Jsy C 4.00 10.00
JDY Jermaine Dye Uni G 3.00 8.00
JF Jeff Francouer Bat C 3.00 8.00
JG Jonny Gomes Jsy F 3.00 8.00
JK J.F.K. Sweater A/250 * 200.00 300.00
JP Jake Peavy Jsy C 3.00 8.00
JS Johan Santana Jsy G 4.00 10.00
JT Jim Thome Uni C 4.00 10.00
MB Mark Buehrle Uni F 3.00 8.00
MC Miguel Cabrera Uni B 6.00 15.00
MH Matt Holliday Jsy F 4.00 10.00
MM Mickey Mantle Uni D 30.00 80.00
MP Mark Prior Jsy G 3.00 8.00
MPZ Mike Piazza Bat C 4.00 10.00
MR Manny Ramirez Jsy H 4.00 10.00
MT Miguel Tejada Uni E 3.00 8.00
NS Nick Swisher Jsy E 3.00 8.00
PK Paul Konerko Uni D 3.00 8.00
PM Pedro Martinez Jsy I 4.00 10.00
RC Robinson Cano Uni F 4.00 10.00
RH Ryan Howard Bat C 12.00 30.00
RL Ryan Langerhans Bat C 3.00 8.00
RO Roy Oswalt Jsy G 3.00 8.00
TH Travis Hafner Jsy D 3.00 8.00
VG Vladimir Guerrero Bat F 4.00 10.00
VM Victor Martinez Jsy D 3.00 8.00
WT Willy Taveras Jsy H 3.00 8.00
ZD Zach Duke Jsy C 3.00 8.00

2006 Topps Allen and Ginter Rip Cards

1-50 STATED ODDS 1:265 HOBBY
1-4 PRINT RUN 10 SERIAL #'d SETS
5-9 PRINT RUN 15 SERIAL #'d SETS
10-19 PRINT RUN 25 SERIAL #'d SETS
20-50 PRINT RUN 99 SERIAL #'d SETS
1-19 NO PRICING DUE TO SCARCITY
ALL LISTED PRICES ARE FOR RIPPED
UNRIPPED HAVE ADD'L CARDS WITHIN
COMMON UNRIPPED (20-50) 75.00 150.00
UNRIPPED (30/35/43) 100.00 200.00
UNRIPPED (45/47/49) 100.00 200.00
RIP1 Mickey Mantle Back/10
RIP2 Dontrelle Willis/10
RIP3 Ivan Rodriguez/10
RIP4 Johan Santana/10
RIP5 Mike Piazza/15
RIP6 Randy Johnson/15
RIP7 Robinson Cano/15
RIP8 Scott Rolen/15
RIP9 Todd Helton/15
RIP10 Alex Rodriguez Back/25
RIP11 Alfonso Soriano/25
RIP12 D.Ortiz/A.Rodriguez/25
RIP13 Barry Bonds Back/25
RIP14 C.Beltran/C.Delgado/25
RIP15 David Wright/25
RIP16 Derrek Lee/25
RIP17 Huston Street/25
RIP18 Mariano Rivera/25
RIP19 Nolan Ryan/25
RIP20 Kenji Johjima/99 15.00 40.00
RIP21 Cap Anson/99 15.00 40.00
RIP22 Ryan Zimmerman/99 20.00 50.00
RIP23 Andruw Jones/99 10.00 25.00
RIP24 Barry Bonds at Wall/99 15.00 40.00
RIP25 Cal Ripken/99 30.00 60.00
RIP26 David Ortiz/99 10.00 25.00
RIP27 Hideki Matsui/99 10.00 25.00
RIP28 Ken Griffey Jr./99 20.00 50.00
RIP29 Manny Ramirez/99 10.00 25.00
RIP30 M.Mantle w/Bat/99 50.00 100.00
RIP31 A.Rod Bat Out/99 15.00 40.00
RIP32 Miguel Cabrera/99 6.00 15.00
RIP33 Miguel Tejada/99 6.00 15.00
RIP34 Pedro Martinez/99 10.00 25.00
RIP35 Albert Pujols w/Bat/99 30.00 60.00
RIP36 A.Rod Hands Out/99 15.00 40.00
RIP37 A.Rodriguez/D.Jeter/99 15.00 40.00
RIP38 Barry Bonds 700/99 15.00 40.00
RIP39 Derek Jeter/99 20.00 50.00
RIP40 Ichiro Suzuki/99 15.00 40.00
RIP41 I.Suzuki/H.Matsui/99 15.00 40.00
RIP42 Josh Gibson/99 15.00 40.00
RIP43 M.Mantle Swing/99 50.00 100.00
RIP44 Jonathan Papelbon/99 20.00 50.00
RIP45 M.Mantle/T.Williams/99 50.00 100.00
RIP46 Albert Pujols Back/99 30.00 60.00
RIP47 Roberto Clemente/99 30.00 60.00
RIP48 Roger Clemens/99 15.00 40.00
RIP49 Ted Williams/99 30.00 60.00
RIP50 Vladimir Guerrero/99 10.00 25.00

2007 Topps Allen and Ginter

COMPLETE SET (350) 60.00 120.00
COMP.SET w/o SP's (300) 20.00 50.00
SP STATED ODDS 1:2 HOBBY, 1:2 RETAIL
SP CL: 5/43/48/58/63/107/110/119/130/137
SP CL: 152/159/178/193/194/203/219/222
SP CL: 224/243/263/301/302/303/306/307
SP CL: 308/309/310/316/317/318/319/320
SP CL: 321/322/325/326/327/330/331/334
SP CL: 335/336/339/340/345/348/349/350
FRAMED ORIGINALS ODDS 1:17,072 HOBBY
FRAMED ORIGINALS ODDS 1:34,654 RETAIL
1 Ryan Howard .25 .60
2 Mike Gonzalez .12 .30
3 Austin Kearns .12 .30
4 Josh Hamilton .60 1.50
5 Stephen Drew SP 1.25 3.00
6 Matt Murton .12 .30
7 Mickey Mantle 1.00 2.50
8 Howie Kendrick .12 .30
9 Alexander Graham Bell .12 .30
10 Jason Bay .20 .50
11 Hank Blalock .12 .30
12 Johan Santana .20 .50
13 Eleanor Roosevelt .12 .30
14 Kei Igawa RC .50 1.25
15 Jeff Francoeur .30 .75
16 Carl Crawford .20 .50
17 Jhonny Peralta .12 .30
18 Mariano Rivera .40 1.00
19 Mario Andretti .30 .75
20 Vladimir Guerrero .20 .50
21 Adam Wainwright .20 .50
22 Huston Street .12 .30
23 Cael Sanderson .12 .30
24 Susan B. Anthony .12 .30
25 Jay Payton .12 .30
26 P.T. Barnum .12 .30
27 Scott Podsednik .12 .30
28 Willie Randolph .12 .30
29 Sean Casey .12 .30
30 Eiffel Tower .12 .30
31 Kenji Johjima .30 .75
32 Felix Hernandez .20 .50
33 Elijah Dukes RC .30 .75
34 Mark Grudzielanek .12 .30
35 J.D. Drew .12 .30
36 Kevin Kouzmanoff .12 .30
37 Jonathan Papelbon .30 .75
38 Bobby Crosby .12 .30
39 Brooklyn Bridge .12 .30
40 Adam Dunn .20 .50
41 Lyle Overbay .12 .30
42 Brian Fuentes .12 .30
43 Scott Rolen SP 1.25 3.00
44 Matt Lindstrom (RC) .20 .50
45 Carlos Zambrano .20 .50
46 Cole Hamels .25 .60
47 Matt Kemp .25 .60
48 Gary Matthews SP 1.25 3.00
49 J.J. Putz .12 .30
50 Albert Pujols .40 1.00
51 Dan Haren .12 .30
52 Aaron Harang .12 .30
53 Ferris Wheel .12 .30
54 Juan Rivera .12 .30
55 Ken Griffey Jr. .60 1.50
56 Chien-Ming Wang .20 .50
57 Sean Henn (RC) .20 .50
58 Mike Mussina SP 1.25 3.00
59 Ian Snell .12 .30
60 Josh Barfield .12 .30
61 Justin Morneau .20 .50
62 Dwight D. Eisenhower .12 .30
63 Bengie Molina SP 1.25 3.00
64 Brett Myers .12 .30
65 Andy Marte .12 .30
66 Bill Hall .12 .30
67 Ryan Shealy .12 .30
68 Joe B. Scott .12 .30
69 Mike Rabelo RC .20 .50
70 Jermaine Dye .12 .30
71 Andre Ethier .20 .50
72 Bruce Lee .12 .30
73 Nick Punto .12 .30
74 Ervin Santana .12 .30
75 Troy Tulowitzki (RC) .60 1.50
76 Garret Anderson .12 .30
77 Ryan Freel .12 .30
78 Carlos Guillen .12 .30
79 John Smoltz .30 .75
80 Chase Utley .20 .50
81 Mike Sweeney .12 .30
82 Joe Frazier .30 .75
83 Brad Lidge .12 .30
84 Casey Blake .12 .30
85 Ivan Rodriguez .20 .50
86 Roy Oswalt .20 .50
87 Akinori Iwamura RC .50 1.25
88 Francisco Rodriguez .20 .50
89 John Lackey .20 .50
90 Miguel Cabrera .30 .75
91 Kevin Mench .12 .30
92 Victor Martinez .20 .50
93 Chad Tracy .12 .30
94 Charlie Manuel .12 .30
95 Hanley Ramirez .20 .50
96 Dontrelle Willis .12 .30
97 Doug Slaten RC .20 .50
98 Noah Lowry .12 .30
99 Shawn Green .12 .30
100 David Ortiz .30 .75
101 Mark Reynolds RC .60 1.50
102 Preston Wilson .12 .30
103 Mohandas Gandhi .12 .30
104 Jeff Kent .12 .30
105 Lance Berkman .20 .50
106 C.C. Sabathia .20 .50
107 Jason Varitek SP 1.25 3.00
108 Mark Twain .12 .30
109 Melvin Mora .12 .30
110 Michael Young SP 1.25 3.00
111 Scott Hatteberg .12 .30
112 Erik Bedard .12 .30
113 Sitting Bull .12 .30
114 Homer Bailey (RC) .30 .75
115 Mark Teahen .12 .30
116 Ryan Braun (RC) 1.00 2.50
117 John Miles .12 .30
118 Coco Crisp .12 .30
119 Hunter Pence SP (RC) 2.00 5.00
120 Delmon Young (RC) .30 .75
121 Aramis Ramirez .12 .30
122 Magglio Ordonez .20 .50
123 Tadahito Iguchi .12 .30
124 Mark Selby .12 .30
125 Gil Meche .12 .30
126 Curt Schilling .20 .50
127 Brandon Phillips .12 .30
128 Milton Bradley .12 .30
129 Craig Monroe .12 .30
130 Jason Schmidt SP 1.25 3.00
131 Nick Markakis .25 .60
132 Paul Konerko .20 .50
133 Carlos Gomez RC .40 1.00
134 Garrett Atkins .12 .30
135 Jered Weaver .20 .50
136 Edgar Renteria .12 .30
137 Jason Isringhausen SP 1.25 3.00
138 Ray Durham .12 .30
139 Bob Baffert .12 .30
140 Nick Swisher .20 .50
141 Brian McCann .12 .30
142 Orlando Hudson .12 .30
143 Brian Bannister .12 .30
144 Manny Acta .12 .30
145 Jose Vidro .12 .30
146 Carlos Quentin .12 .30
147 Billy Butler (RC) .30 .75
148 Kenny Rogers .12 .30
149 Tom Gordon .12 .30
150 Derek Jeter .75 2.00
151 Bob Wickman .12 .30
152 Carlos Lee SP 1.25 3.00
153 Willy Taveras .12 .30
154 Paul LoDuca .12 .30
155 Ben Sheets .12 .30
156 Brian Roberts .12 .30
157 Freddy Adu .12 .30
158 Jason Kendall .12 .30
159 Michael Barrett SP 1.25 3.00
160 Frank Thomas .30 .75
161 Manny Ramirez .30 .75
162 Stanley Glenn .12 .30
163 Robinson Cano .20 .50
164 Phil Hughes (RC) .50 1.25
165 Joe Mauer .25 .60
166 Derrek Lee .12 .30
167 Jeff Weaver .12 .30
168 Joe Smith RC .12 .30
169 Louis Pasteur .12 .30
170 Gary Sheffield .12 .30
171 Luis Castillo .12 .30
172 Joe Torre .20 .50
173 Andy LaRoche (RC) .20 .50
174 Jamie Fischer .12 .30
175 Carlos Beltran .20 .50
176 Bronson Arroyo .12 .30
177 Rafael Furcal .12 .30
178 Juan Pierre SP 1.25 3.00
179 Matt Cain .20 .50
180 Alfonso Soriano .20 .50
181 Joe Borowski .12 .30
182 Conor Jackson .12 .30
183 Groundhog Day .12 .30
184 Pat Burrell .12 .30
185 Troy Glaus .12 .30
186 Joel Zumaya .12 .30
187 Russell Martin .12 .30
188 Josh Willingham .20 .50
189 Jarrod Saltalamacchia (RC) .30 .75
190 Scott Kazmir .20 .50
191 Jeremy Hermida .12 .30
192 Tower Bridge .12 .30
193 Rich Hill SP 1.25 3.00
194 Francisco Cordero SP 1.25 3.00
195 Mike Piazza .30 .75
196 Brad Ausmus .12 .30
197 Greg Louganis .12 .30
198 Frank Catalanotto .12 .30
199 Alejandro De Aza RC .30 .75
200 David Wright .25 .60
201 Freddy Sanchez .12 .30
202 Shea Hillenbrand .12 .30
203 Justin Verlander SP 1.25 3.00
204 Alex Gordon RC .60 1.50
205 Jimmy Rollins .20 .50
206 Mike Napoli .12 .30
207 Chris Burke .12 .30
208 Chipper Jones .30 .75
209 Randy Johnson .30 .75
210 Daisuke Matsuzaka RC .75 2.00
211 Orlando Cabrera .12 .30
212 B.J. Upton .12 .30
213 Lou Piniella MG .12 .30
214 Mike Cameron .12 .30
215 Luis Gonzalez .12 .30
216 Rickie Weeks .12 .30
217 Hideki Okajima RC 1.00 2.50
218 Johnny Estrada .12 .30
219 Dan Uggla SP 1.25 3.00
220 Ryan Zimmerman .20 .50
221 Tony Gwynn Jr. .12 .30
222 Rocco Baldelli SP 1.25 3.00
223 Xavier Nady .12 .30
224 Josh Bard SP 1.25 3.00
225 Raul Ibanez .20 .50
226 Chris Carpenter .20 .50
227 Matt DeSalvo (RC) .20 .50
228 Jack the Ripper .12 .30
229 Eric Chavez .12 .30
230 Jose Reyes .20 .50
231 Glen Perkins (RC) .20 .50
232 Gregg Zaun .12 .30
233 Jim Thome .20 .50
234 Joe Crede .12 .30
235 Barry Zito .20 .50
236 Yoel Hernandez RC .20 .50
237 Kelly Johnson .12 .30
238 Chris Young .12 .30
239 Fyodor Dostoevsky .12 .30
240 Miguel Tejada .20 .50
241 Doug Mientkiewicz .12 .30
242 Bobby Jenks .12 .30
243 Brad Hawpe SP 1.25 3.00
244 Jay Marshall RC .20 .50
245 Brad Penny .12 .30
246 Johnny Damon .20 .50
247 Dave Roberts .20 .50
248 Ron Washington .12 .30
249 Mike Aponte .12 .30
250 Brandon Webb .20 .50
251 Andy Pettitte .20 .50
252 Bud Black .12 .30
253 Michael Cuddyer .12 .30
254 Chris Stewart RC .20 .50
255 Mark Teixeira .20 .50
256 Hideki Matsui .30 .75
257 Curtis Granderson .25 .60
258 A.J. Pierzynski .12 .30
259 Tony La Russa .20 .50
260 Andruw Jones .12 .30
261 Torii Hunter .12 .30
262 Mark Loretta .12 .30
263 Jim Edmonds SP 1.25 3.00
264 Aaron Rowand .12 .30
265 Roy Halladay .20 .50
266 Freddy Garcia .12 .30
267 Reggie Sanders .12 .30
268 Washington Monument .12 .30
269 Franklin D. Roosevelt .12 .30
270 Alex Rodriguez .40 1.00
271 Wes Helms .12 .30
272 Mia Hamm .12 .30
273 Jorge Posada .20 .50
274 Tim Lincecum RC 1.00 2.50
275 Bobby Abreu .12 .30
276 Zach Duke .12 .30

277 Carlos Delgado .12 .30
278 Julio Juarez .12 .30
279 Brandon Inge .12 .30
280 Todd Helton .20 .50
281 Marcus Giles .12 .30
282 Josh Johnson .30 .75
283 Chris Capuano .12 .30
284 B.J. Ryan .12 .30
285 Nick Johnson .12 .30
286 Khalil Greene .12 .30
287 Travis Hafner .12 .30
288 Ted Lilly .12 .30
289 Jim Leyland .12 .30
290 Prince Fielder .20 .50
291 Trevor Hoffman .20 .50
292 Brian Giles .12 .30
293 Omar Vizquel .20 .50
294 Julio Lugo .12 .30
295 Jake Peavy .12 .30
296 Adrian Beltre .30 .75
297 Josh Beckett .12 .30
298 Harry S. Truman .12 .30
299 Mark Buehrle .20 .50
300 Ichiro Suzuki .40 1.00
301 Chris Duncan SP 1.25 3.00
302 Augie Garrido SP CO 1.25 3.00
303 Tyler Clippard SP (RC) 1.25 3.00
304 Ramon Hernandez .12 .30
305 Jeremy Bonderman .12 .30
306 Morgan Ensberg SP 1.25 3.00
307 J.J. Hardy SP 1.25 3.00
308 Mark Zupan SP 1.25 3.00
309 Laila Ali SP 1.25 3.00
310 Greg Maddux SP 1.50 4.00
311 David Ross .12 .30
312 Chris Duffy .12 .30
313 Moises Alou .12 .30
314 Yadier Molina .40 1.00
315 Corey Patterson .12 .30
316 Dan O'Brien SP 1.25 3.00
317 Michael Bourn SP (RC) 1.25 3.00
318 Jonny Gomes SP 1.25 3.00
319 Ken Jennings SP 1.25 3.00
320 Barry Bonds SP 1.50 4.00
321 Gary Hall Jr. SP 1.25 3.00
322 Kerri Walsh SP 1.25 3.00
323 Craig Biggio .20 .50
324 Ian Kinsler .20 .50
325 Grady Sizemore SP 1.25 3.00
326 Alex Rios SP 1.25 3.00
327 Ted Toles SP 1.25 3.00
328 Jason Jennings .12 .30
329 Vernon Wells .12 .30
330 Bob Geren SP MG 1.25 3.00
331 Dennis Rodman SP 1.25 3.00
332 Tom Glavine .20 .50
333 Pedro Martinez .20 .50
334 Gustavo Molina SP RC 1.25 3.00
335 Bartolo Colon SP 1.25 3.00
336 Misty May-Treanor SP 1.25 3.00
337 Randy Winn .12 .30
338 Eric Byrnes .12 .30
339 Jason McElwain SP 1.25 3.00
340 Placido Polanco SP 1.25 3.00
341 Adrian Gonzalez .25 .60
342 Chad Cordero .12 .30
343 Jeff Francis .12 .30
344 Lastings Milledge .20 .50
345 Sammy Sosa SP 1.25 3.00
346 Jacque Jones .12 .30
347 Anibal Sanchez .12 .30
348 Roger Clemens SP 1.50 4.00
349 Jesse Litsch SP RC 1.25 3.00
350 Adam LaRoche SP 1.25 3.00
NNO Framed Originals 50.00 100.00

2007 Topps Allen and Ginter Mini

*MINI 1-350: 1X TO 2.5X BASIC
*MINI 1-350: .6X TO 1.5X BASIC RC's
APPX. ONE MINI PER PACK
*MINI SP 1-350: .6X TO 1.5X BASIC SP
*MINI SP 1-350: .6X TO 1.5X BASIC SP RC's
MINI SP ODDS 1:13 H, 1:13 R
COMMON CARD (351-390) 15.00 40.00
351-390 RANDOM WITHIN RIP CARDS
OVERALL PLATE ODDS 1:788 HOBBY
PLATE PRINT RUN 1 SET PER COLOR
BLACK-CYAN-MAGENTA-YELLOW ISSUED
NO PLATE PRICING DUE TO SCARCITY
351 Alex Rodriguez EXT 20.00 50.00
352 Ryan Zimmerman EXT 20.00 50.00
353 Prince Fielder EXT 40.00 80.00
354 Gary Sheffield EXT 15.00 40.00
355 Jermaine Dye EXT 15.00 40.00
356 Hanley Ramirez EXT 15.00 40.00
357 Jose Reyes EXT 30.00 60.00
358 Miguel Tejada EXT 20.00 50.00
359 Elijah Dukes EXT 15.00 40.00
360 Ryan Howard EXT 15.00 40.00
361 Vladimir Guerrero EXT 15.00 40.00
362 Ichiro Suzuki EXT 30.00 60.00
363 Jason Bay EXT 15.00 40.00
364 Justin Morneau EXT 15.00 40.00
365 Michael Young EXT 15.00 40.00
366 Adam Dunn EXT 15.00 40.00
367 Alfonso Soriano EXT 20.00 50.00
368 Jake Peavy EXT 20.00 50.00
369 Nick Swisher EXT 20.00 50.00
370 David Wright EXT 30.00 60.00
371 Brandon Webb EXT 20.00 50.00
372 Brian McCann EXT 20.00 50.00
373 Frank Thomas EXT 20.00 50.00
374 Albert Pujols EXT 30.00 60.00
375 Russell Martin EXT 20.00 50.00
376 Felix Hernandez EXT 15.00 40.00
377 Barry Bonds EXT 40.00 80.00
378 Lance Berkman EXT 15.00 40.00
379 Joe Mauer EXT 30.00 60.00
380 B.J. Upton EXT 15.00 40.00
381 Todd Helton EXT 15.00 40.00
382 Paul Konerko EXT 15.00 40.00
383 Grady Sizemore EXT 20.00 50.00
384 Magglio Ordonez EXT 15.00 40.00
385 Dan Uggla EXT 20.00 50.00
386 J.D. Drew EXT 15.00 40.00
387 Adam LaRoche EXT 15.00 40.00
388 Carlos Beltran EXT 15.00 40.00
389 Derek Jeter EXT 40.00 80.00
390 Daisuke Matsuzaka EXT 30.00 60.00

2007 Topps Allen and Ginter Mini A and G Back

*A & G BACK: 1.25X TO 3X BASIC
*A & G BACK: .75X TO 2X BASIC RC's
STATED ODDS 1:5 H, 1:5 R
*A & G BACK SP: .75X TO 2X BASIC SP
*A & G BACK SP: .75X TO 2X BASIC SP RC's
SP STATED ODDS 1:65 H, 1:65 R

2007 Topps Allen and Ginter Mini Black

*BLACK: 2X TO 5X BASIC
*BLACK: 1.5X TO 4X BASIC RC's
STATED ODDS 1:10 H, 1:10 R
*BLACK SP: 1.5X TO 4X BASIC SP
*BLACK SP: 1.5X TO 4X BASIC SP RC's
SP STATED ODDS 1:130 H, 1:130 R

2007 Topps Allen and Ginter Mini Black No Number

*BLK NO NBR: 2.5X TO 6X BASIC
*BLK NO NBR: 2X TO 5X BASIC RC's
*BLK NO NBR: 1.5X TO 4X BASIC SP
*BLK NO NBR: 1.5X TO 4X BASIC SP RC's
RANDOM INSERTS IN PACKS
210 Daisuke Matsuzaka 6.00 15.00

2007 Topps Allen and Ginter Mini No Card Number

*NO NBR: 10X TO 25X BASIC
*NO NBR: 6X TO 15X BASIC RC's
*NO NBR: 2.5X TO 6X BASIC SP
*NO NBR: 2.5X TO 6X BASIC SP RC's
STATED ODDS 1:106 H, 1:108 R
STATED PRINT RUN 50 SETS
CARDS ARE NOT SERIAL-NUMBERED
PRINT RUN INFO PROVIDED BY TOPPS
7 Mickey Mantle 40.00 80.00
50 Albert Pujols 30.00 60.00
55 Ken Griffey Jr. 40.00 100.00
56 Chien-Ming Wang 30.00 60.00
150 Derek Jeter 40.00 80.00
270 Alex Rodriguez 30.00 60.00
300 Ichiro Suzuki 40.00 80.00
320 Barry Bonds SP 40.00 80.00

2007 Topps Allen and Ginter Autographs

GROUP A ODDS 1:64,496 H, 1:122200 R
GROUP B ODDS 1:3261 H, 1:6522 R
GROUP C ODDS 1:13,987 H, 1:27,642 R
GROUP D ODDS 1:288 H, 1:578 R
GROUP E ODDS 1:6789 H, 1:13,578 R
GROUP F ODDS 1:162 H, 1:324 R
GROUP G ODDS 1:680 H, 1:1362 R
GROUP A PRINT RUN 25 CARDS PER
GROUP B PRINT RUN 100 CARDS PER
GROUP C PRINT RUN 120 CARDS PER
GROUP D PRINT RUN 200 CARDS PER
GROUP A-D ARE NOT SERIAL-NUMBERED
A-D PRINT RUNS PROVIDED BY TOPPS
NO PUJOLS PRICING DUE TO SCARCITY
EXCH DEADLINE 7/31/2009
AE Andre Ethier F 5.00 12.00
AG Augie Garrido D/200 * 10.00 25.00
AG2 Adrian Gonzalez F 6.00 15.00
AI Akinori Iwamura F 5.00 12.00
AR Alex Rodriguez E/225 * 60.00 120.00
BB Bob Baffert D/200 * 30.00 60.00
BC Brian Cashman B/100 * 40.00 80.00
BH Bill Hall G 6.00 15.00
BPB Brian Bannister F 10.00 25.00
CG Curtis Granderson F 8.00 20.00
CH Cole Hamels F 10.00 25.00
CMW Chien-Ming Wang D/200 * 60.00 120.00
CS Cael Sanderson D/200 * 30.00 60.00
DO Dan O'Brien D/200 * 12.50 30.00
DR Dennis Rodman D/200 * 30.00 60.00
DW David Wright/200 * 20.00 50.00
ES Ervin Santana F 6.00 15.00
FA Freddy Adu D/200 * 10.00 25.00
GH Gary Hall Jr. D/200 * 10.00 25.00
GL Greg Louganis D/200 * 15.00 40.00
HK Howie Kendrick F 6.00 15.00
HR Hanley Ramirez F 8.00 20.00
JBS Joe B. Scott D/200 * 20.00 50.00
JF Jamie Fischer D/200 * 8.00 20.00
JH Jeremy Hermida G 5.00 12.00
JJ Julio Juarez D/200 * 8.00 20.00
JM Justin Morneau F 12.50 30.00
JMC Jason McElwain D/200 * 12.00 30.00
JMM John Miles D/200 * 15.00 40.00
JP Jonathan Papelbon F 15.00 40.00
JS Johan Santana B/100 * 20.00 50.00
JT Jim Thome B/100 * 50.00 100.00
KJ Ken Jennings D/200 * 50.00 120.00
KW Kerri Walsh D/200 * 40.00 80.00
LA Laila Ali D/200 * 50.00 120.00
MA Mike Aponte D/200 * 10.00 25.00
MEI Maicer Izturis F 6.00 15.00
MGA Mario Andretti D/200 * 40.00 80.00
MH Mia Hamm D/200 * 50.00 100.00
MMT Misty May-Treanor D/200 * 50.00 100.00
MN Mike Napoli F 6.00 15.00
MS Mark Selby D/200 * 15.00 40.00
MZ Mark Zupan D/200 * 5.00 12.00
NL Nook Logan G 5.00 12.00
NM Nick Markakis F 5.00 12.00
RH Ryan Howard B/100 * 10.00 25.00
RM Russell Martin F 5.00 12.00
RZ Ryan Zimmerman F 6.00 15.00
SG Stanley Glenn D/200 * 20.00 50.00
SJF Joe Frazier C/120 * 150.00 250.00
TH Torii Hunter F 8.00 20.00
TS Tommie Smith D/200 * 20.00 50.00
TT Ted Toles D/200 * 20.00 50.00
TTT Troy Tulowitzki F 6.00 15.00

2007 Topps Allen and Ginter Dick Perez

COMPLETE SET (30) 6.00 15.00
APPX.ONE PEREZ PER PACK
ORIGINALS RANDOM WITHIN RIP CARDS
ORIGINALS PRINT RUN 1 SERIAL #'d SET
NO ORIG. PRICING DUE TO SCARCITY
1 Brandon Webb .30 .75
2 Chipper Jones .50 1.25
3 Nick Markakis .40 1.00
4 Daisuke Matsuzaka .75 2.00
5 Alfonso Soriano .30 .75
6 Jermaine Dye .20 .50
7 Adam Dunn .30 .75
8 Grady Sizemore .30 .75
9 Troy Tulowitzki .60 1.50
10 Gary Sheffield .20 .50
11 Hanley Ramirez .30 .75
12 Carlos Lee .20 .50
13 Mark Teahen .20 .50
14 Gary Matthews .20 .50
15 Andre Ethier .30 .75
16 Prince Fielder .30 .75
17 Joe Mauer .40 1.00
18 Jose Reyes .30 .75
19 Derek Jeter 1.25 3.00
20 Nick Swisher .30 .75
21 Ryan Howard .40 1.00
22 Freddy Sanchez .20 .50
23 Greg Maddux .60 1.50
24 Raul Ibanez .30 .75
25 Barry Zito .30 .75
26 Jim Edmonds .30 .75
27 Delmon Young .30 .75
28 Michael Young .20 .50
29 Roy Halladay .30 .75
30 Ryan Zimmerman .30 .75

2007 Topps Allen and Ginter Mini Emperors

STATED ODDS 1:72 H, 1:72 R
1 Julius Caesar 2.00 5.00
2 Caesar Augustus 2.00 5.00
3 Tiberius 2.00 5.00
4 Caligula 2.00 5.00
5 Claudius 2.00 5.00
6 Nero 2.00 5.00
7 Titus 2.00 5.00
8 Hadrian 2.00 5.00
9 Marcus Aurelius 2.00 5.00
10 Septimus Severus 2.00 5.00

2007 Topps Allen and Ginter Mini Flags

COMPLETE SET (50) 100.00 175.00
STATED ODDS 1:12 H, 1:12 R
1 Algeria 1.50 4.00
2 Argentina 1.50 4.00
3 Australia 1.50 4.00
4 Austria 1.50 4.00
5 Belgium 1.50 4.00
6 Brazil 1.50 4.00
7 Bulgaria 1.50 4.00
8 Canada 1.50 4.00
9 Chile 1.50 4.00
10 China 1.50 4.00
11 Colombia 1.50 4.00
12 Costa Rica 1.50 4.00
13 Denmark 1.50 4.00
14 Dominican Republic 1.50 4.00
15 Ecuador 1.50 4.00
16 Egypt 1.50 4.00
17 France 1.50 4.00
18 Germany 1.50 4.00
19 Greece 1.50 4.00
20 Greenland 1.50 4.00
21 Honduras 1.50 4.00
22 Iceland 1.50 4.00
23 India 1.50 4.00
24 Indonesia 1.50 4.00
25 Ireland 1.50 4.00
26 Israel 1.50 4.00
27 Italy 1.50 4.00
28 Ivory Coast 1.50 4.00
29 Jamaica 1.50 4.00
30 Japan 1.50 4.00
31 Kenya 1.50 4.00
32 Mexico 1.50 4.00
33 Morocco 1.50 4.00
34 Netherlands 1.50 4.00
35 Nigeria 1.50 4.00
36 Norway 1.50 4.00
37 Panama 1.50 4.00
38 Peru 1.50 4.00
39 Philippines 1.50 4.00
40 Portugal 1.50 4.00
41 Puerto Rico 1.50 4.00
42 Russian Federation 1.50 4.00
43 Spain 1.50 4.00
44 Switzerland 1.50 4.00
45 Taiwan 1.50 4.00
46 Thailand 1.50 4.00
47 Turkey 1.50 4.00
48 United Arab Emirates 1.50 4.00
49 United Kingdom 1.50 4.00
50 United States of America 1.50 4.00

2007 Topps Allen and Ginter Mini Snakes

STATED ODDS 1:144 H, 1:144 R
1 Arizona Coral Snake 8.00 20.00
2 Copperhead 8.00 20.00
3 Black Mamba 8.00 20.00
4 King Cobra 8.00 20.00
5 Cottonmouth 8.00 20.00

2007 Topps Allen and Ginter N43

STATED ODDS 1:3 HOBBY BOX LOADER
AP Albert Pujols 1.25 3.00
AR Alex Rodriguez 1.25 3.00
BB Barry Bonds 1.50 4.00
BL Bruce Lee .40 1.00
DJ Ch Felicity's Diamond Jim 4.00 10.00
DM Daisuke Matsuzaka 1.50 4.00
DW David Wright .75 2.00
GL Greg Louganis .40 1.00
IS Ichiro Suzuki 1.25 3.00
JF Joe Frazier 1.00 2.50
MA Mario Andretti 1.00 2.50
PF Prince Fielder .60 1.50
RH Ryan Howard .75 2.00
RZ Ryan Zimmerman .60 1.50
VG Vladimir Guerrero .60 1.50

2007 Topps Allen and Ginter N43 Autographs

GROUP A ODDS 1:1747 HOBBY BOX LOADER
GROUP B ODDS 1:1034 HOBBY BOX LOADER
GROUP A PRINT RUN 10 SER.#'d SETS
GROUP B PRINT RUN 50 SER.#'d SETS
NO GROUP A PRICING AVAILABLE
DJ Ch Felicity's Diamond Jim B/50 30.00 60.00

2007 Topps Allen and Ginter National Pride

STATED ODDS 1:2 HOBBY BOX LOADER
1 Igawa/Matsuzaka/Matsui/Ichiro 2.00 5.00
2 Okajima/Iwamura/Johjima/Iguchi 2.50 6.00
3 Abreu/Cabrera/King Felix/Johan 1.25 3.00
4 Choo/Park/Kim/Ryu .75 2.00
5 Bay/Russ.Martin/Morneau/Harden .75 2.00
6 Hanley/Manny/Aramis/Vlad 1.25 3.00
7 J.Reyes/Pedro/Papi/Pujols 1.50 4.00
8 Beltran/Delgado/Pudge/Posada .75 2.00
9 Prince/ARod/Howard/Wright 1.50 4.00
10 Webb/Verlander/Maddux/Smoltz 1.50 4.00

2007 Topps Allen and Ginter Relics

GROUP A ODDS 1:1,160,000 H
GROUP A ODDS 1:243,648 R
GROUP B ODDS 1:31,376 H, 1:62,750 R
GROUP C ODDS 1:15,275 H, 1:30,550 R
GROUP D ODDS 1:383 H, 1:766 R
GROUP E ODDS 1:1530 H, 1:3068 R
GROUP F ODDS 1:510 H, 1:1022 R
GROUP G ODDS 1:109 H, 1:218 R
GROUP H ODDS 1:69 H, 1:140 R
GROUP I ODDS 1:340 H, 1:680 R
GROUP J ODDS 1:25 H, 1:48 R
GROUP B PRINT RUN 50 COPIES PER
GROUP C PRINT RUN 100 COPIES PER
GROUP D PRINT RUN 250 COPIES PER
GROUP B-D ARE NOT SERIAL-NUMBERED
GROUP B-D QTY PROVIDED BY TOPPS
NO WASHINGTON PRICING AVAILABLE
AER Alex Rodriguez Bat D/250 * 15.00 40.00
AL Adam LaRoche J 3.00 8.00
AP Albert Pujols Bat E 8.00 20.00
AR Aramis Ramirez J 3.00 8.00
AS Arthur Shorin B/50 * 150.00 300.00
BB Barry Bonds Pants D/250 * 6.00 15.00
BC Brian Cashman D/250 * 15.00 40.00
BL Bruce Lee D/250 * 200.00 400.00
BR Brian Roberts J 3.00 8.00
BZ Barry Zito Pants J 3.00 8.00
CB Carlos Beltran Bat I 3.00 8.00
CC Carl Crawford Bat H 3.00 8.00
CK Casey Kotchman J 3.00 8.00
CLC Coco Crisp Bat D 3.00 8.00
CMS Curt Schilling J 4.00 10.00
CP Corey Patterson Bat F 3.00 8.00
CT Chad Tracy Bat G 3.00 8.00
DAO David Ortiz Bat D/250 * 6.00 15.00
DL Derrek Lee Bat H 3.00 8.00
DO Dan O'Brien D/250 * 10.00 25.00
DW Dontrelle Willis J 3.00 8.00
EC Eric Chavez Pants J 3.00 8.00
EG Eric Gagne J 3.00 8.00
GH Gary Hall Jr. D/250 * 10.00 25.00
HB Hank Blalock J 3.00 8.00
HR Hanley Ramirez Bat G 4.00 10.00
IR Ivan Rodriguez J 4.00 10.00
JB Jason Bay Bat H 3.00 8.00
JF Jamie Fischer D/250 * 10.00 25.00
JG Jason Giambi Bat H 3.00 8.00
JJ Julio Juarez D/250 * 8.00 20.00
KJ Ken Jennings D/250 * 12.00 30.00
KO Keith Olbermann C/100 * 75.00 200.00
KW Kerri Walsh D/250 * 10.00 25.00
LA Laila Ali D/250 * 10.00 25.00
MC1 Miguel Cabrera G 4.00 10.00
MC2 Miguel Cabrera Bat G 4.00 10.00
MCM Mike Mussina Pants J 4.00 10.00
MG Marcus Giles J 3.00 8.00
MH Mia Hamm D/250 * 12.00 30.00
MM Mickey Mantle Bat D/250 * 40.00 80.00
MMU Mark Mulder Pants J 3.00 8.00
MP Mike Piazza Bat H 4.00 10.00
MR Manny Ramirez Bat H 4.00 10.00
MT Miguel Tejada J 3.00 8.00
NS Nick Swisher Bat H 3.00 8.00
PF Prince Fielder Bat G 6.00 15.00
PK Paul Konerko Bat H 3.00 8.00
PL Paul LoDuca J 3.00 8.00
RA Rich Aurilia Bat G 3.00 8.00
RC Robinson Cano Bat F 4.00 10.00
RH Rich Harden Pants J 3.00 8.00
RW Randy Winn J 3.00 8.00
SD Stephen Drew J 3.00 8.00
SJF Joe Frazier D/250 * 20.00 50.00
SP Scott Podsednik Bat G 3.00 8.00
SR1 Scott Rolen G 4.00 10.00
SR2 Scott Rolen Bat G 4.00 10.00
SS Sammy Sosa Bat I 4.00 10.00
TG Troy Glaus Bat H 3.00 8.00
TN Trot Nixon Bat G 3.00 8.00
TS Tommie Smith D/250 * 12.50 30.00
VG Vladimir Guerrero Bat H 4.00 10.00

2007 Topps Allen and Ginter Rip Card

STATED ODDS 1:285 HOBBY
PRINT RUNS B/WN 10-99 COPIES PER
NO PRICING ON QTY 10 OR LESS
ALL LISTED PRICED ARE FOR RIPPED
UNRIPPED HAVE ADD'L CARDS WITHIN
1 Grady Sizemore/90 10.00 25.00
2 Miguel Cabrera/75 10.00 25.00
3 Adam Dunn/95 6.00 15.00
4 Jose Reyes/99 10.00 25.00
5 Alfonso Soriano/90 6.00 15.00
6 Chase Utley/99 10.00 25.00
7 Frank Thomas/95 10.00 25.00
8 Andruw Jones/95 10.00 25.00
9 Nick Markakis/75 10.00 25.00
10 Felix Hernandez/99 10.00 25.00
11 Jered Weaver/99 10.00 25.00
12 Ivan Rodriguez/99 10.00 25.00
13 Joe Mauer/99 10.00 25.00
14 Derek Jeter/99 20.00 50.00
15 Delmon Young/
16 Brandon Webb/10
17 Miguel Tejada/95 6.00 15.00
18 Vladimir Guerrero/75 10.00 25.00
19 Greg Maddux/99 15.00 40.00
20 Michael Young/99 6.00 15.00
21 Barry Zito/99 6.00 15.00
22 Russell Martin/95 6.00 15.00
23 Daisuke Matsuzaka/99 90.00 150.00
24 Stephen Drew/95 10.00 25.00
25 Alex Rodriguez/99 15.00 40.00
26 J.D. Drew/99 6.00 15.00
27 Paul Konerko/99 6.00 15.00
28 Josh Hamilton /90 20.00 50.00
29 Mike Piazza /99 10.00 25.00
30 Ryan Howard/10
31 Carl Crawford/99 6.00 15.00
32 Adam LaRoche/99 6.00 15.00
33 Bill Hall/95 6.00 15.00
34 Scott Kazmir/95 10.00 25.00
35 Gary Matthews/99 6.00 15.00
36 Gary Sheffield/99 6.00 15.00
37 Francisco Rodriguez/95 6.00 15.00
38 Todd Helton/99 10.00 25.00
39 Dontrelle Willis/10
40 David Wright/99 15.00 40.00
41 David Ortiz/10
42 Barry Bonds/99 20.00 50.00
43 Johan Santana/75 10.00 25.00
44 Albert Pujols/90 20.00 50.00
45 Carlos Lee/99 6.00 15.00
46 Cole Hamels/95 10.00 25.00
47 Prince Fielder/99 10.00 25.00
48 Hanley Ramirez/99 10.00 25.00
49 Ryan Zimmerman/90 10.00 25.00
50 Kei Igawa/75 10.00 25.00

2007 Topps Allen and Ginter National Mini Promos

NCC4 Grady Sizemore .75 2.00
NCC5 C.C. Sabathia .60 1.50
NCC6 Victor Martinez .60 1.50

2007 Topps Allen and Ginter National Promos

NCC4 Grady Sizemore .75 2.00
NCC5 C.C. Sabathia .60 1.50
NCC6 Victor Martinez .60 1.50

2008 Topps Allen and Ginter

COMP.SET w/o FUKU.(350) 30.00 60.00
COMP.SET w/o SPs (300) 15.00 40.00
COMMON CARD (1-300) .15 .40
COMMON RC (1-300) .40 1.00
COMMON SP (301-350) 1.25 3.00
SP STATED ODDS 1:2 HOBBY
FRAMED ORIG.ODDS 1:26,500 HOBBY
1 Alex Rodriguez .50 1.25
2 Juan Pierre .15 .40
3 Benjamin Franklin .25 .60
4 Roy Halladay .25 .60
5 C.C. Sabathia .25 .60
6 Brian Barton RC .60 1.50
7 Mickey Mantle 1.25 3.00
8 Brian Bass (RC) .40 1.00
9 Ian Kinsler .25 .60
10 Manny Ramirez .40 1.00
11 Michael Cuddyer .15 .40
12 Ian Snell .15 .40
13 Mike Lowell .15 .40
14 Adrian Gonzalez .25 .60
15 B.J. Upton .25 .60
16 Hiroki Kuroda RC 1.00 2.50
17 Kenji Johjima .15 .40
18 James Loney .15 .40
19 Albert Einstein .25 .60
20 Vladimir Guerrero .25 .60
21 Miguel Tejada .25 .60
22 Chin-Lung Hu (RC) .40 1.00
23 A.J. Burnett .15 .40
24 Bobby Jenks .15 .40
25 Aramis Ramirez .15 .40
26 Corey Hart .15 .40
27 Brad Hawpe .15 .40
28 Adam LaRoche .15 .40
29 Empire State Building .25 .60
30 Miguel Cabrera .40 1.00
31 Ryan Zimmerman .25 .60
32 Mark Ellis .15 .40
33 Nick Swisher .25 .60
34 Bill Hall .15 .40
35 Eric Byrnes .15 .40
36 Michael Young .15 .40
37 Pedro Martinez .25 .60
38 Andruw Jones .15 .40
39 J.R. Towles RC .60 1.50
40 Justin Upton .25 .60
41 Paul Konerko .25 .60
42 Luke Scott .15 .40
43 Rickie Weeks .15 .40
44 Adam Wainwright .25 .60
45 Justin Morneau .25 .60
46 Chris Young .15 .40
47 Chad Billingsley .25 .60
48 Kazuo Matsui .15 .40
49 Shane Victorino .15 .40
50 Albert Pujols .50 1.25
51 Brian McCann .25 .60
52 Carlos Delgado .15 .40
53 Chien-Ming Wang .25 .60
54 Takashi Saito .15 .40
55 Josh Beckett .15 .40
56 Nick Johnson .15 .40
57 Ben Sheets .15 .40
58 Johnny Damon .25 .60
59 Nicky Hayden .25 .60
60 Prince Fielder .25 .60
61 Adam Dunn .25 .60
62 Dustin Pedroia .40 1.00
63 Jacoby Ellsbury .30 .75
64 Brad Penny .15 .40
65 Victor Martinez .25 .60
66 Joe Mauer .30 .75
67 Kevin Kouzmanoff .15 .40
68 Frank Thomas .40 1.00
69 Stevie Williams .25 .60
70 Matt Holliday .40 1.00
71 Fausto Carmona .15 .40
72 Clayton Kershaw RC 12.00 30.00
73 Tadahito Iguchi .15 .40
74 Khalil Greene .15 .40
75 Travis Hafner .15 .40
76 Jim Thome .25 .60
77 Joba Chamberlain .15 .40
78 Ivan Rodriguez .25 .60
79 Jose Guillen .15 .40
80 Hanley Ramirez .25 .60
81 Vernon Wells .15 .40
82 Jayson Nix (RC) .40 1.00
83 Masahide Kobayashi RC .60 1.50
84 Bonnie Blair .25 .60
85 Curtis Granderson .25 .60
86 Kelvim Escobar .25 .60
87 Aaron Rowand .15 .40
88 Troy Glaus .25 .60
89 Billy Wagner .15 .40
90 Jose Reyes .25 .60
91 Scott Rolen .25 .60
92 Dan Jansen .25 .60
93 David Eckstein .15 .40
94 Tom Gorzelanny .15 .40
95 Garrett Atkins .15 .40
96 Carlos Zambrano .25 .60
97 Jeff Francis .15 .40
98 Kazuo Fukumori RC .60 1.50
99 John Bowker (RC) .40 1.00
100 David Wright .25 .60
101 Adrian Beltre .40 1.00
102 Ray Durham .15 .40
103 Kerri Strug .25 .60
104 Orlando Hudson .15 .40
105 Jonathan Papelbon .25 .60
106 Brian Schneider .15 .40
107 Matt Biondi .25 .60
108 Alex Romero (RC) .60 1.50
109 Joey Chestnut .25 .60
110 Chase Utley .25 .60
111 Dan Uggla .15 .40
112 Akinori Iwamura .15 .40
113 Curt Schilling .25 .60
114 Trevor Hoffman .25 .60
115 Alex Rios .15 .40
116 Mariano Rivera .50 1.25
117 Jeff Niemann (RC) .40 1.00
118 Geovany Soto .40 1.00
119 Billy Mitchell .25 .60
120 Derek Jeter 1.00 2.50
121 Yovani Gallardo .15 .40
122 The Gateway Arch .25 .60
123 Josh Willingham .25 .60
124 Greg Maddux .50 1.25
125 John Lackey .25 .60
126 Chris Young .15 .40
127 Billy Butler .15 .40
128 Golden Gate Bridge .25 .60
129 Joey Votto (RC) 3.00 8.00
130 Tim Wakefield .25 .60
131 Todd Helton .25 .60
132 Gary Matthews .15 .40
133 Wild Bill Hickok .25 .60
134 Jason Varitek .40 1.00
135 Robinson Cano .25 .60
136 Javier Vazquez .15 .40
137 Annie Oakley .25 .60
138 Andy Pettitte .25 .60
139 Greg Reynolds RC .60 1.50
140 Jimmy Rollins .25 .60
141 Jermaine Dye .15 .40
142 Eugenio Velez RC .40 1.00
143 J.J. Hardy .15 .40
144 Grand Canyon .25 .60
145 Bobby Abreu .15 .40
146 Scott Kazmir .25 .60
147 James Fenimore Cooper .25 .60
148 Mark Buehrle .25 .60
149 Freddy Sanchez .15 .40
150 Johan Santana .25 .60
151 Orlando Cabrera .25 .60
152 Lyle Overbay .15 .40
153 Clay Buchholz (RC) .60 1.50
154 Jesse Carlson RC .60 1.50
155 Troy Tulowitzki .40 1.00
156 Delmon Young .25 .60
157 Ross Ohlendorf RC .60 1.50
158 Mary Shelley .25 .60
159 James Shields .15 .40
160 Alfonso Soriano .25 .60
161 Randy Winn .15 .40
162 Austin Kearns .15 .40
163 Jeremy Hermida .15 .40
164 Jorge Posada .25 .60
165 Justin Verlander .40 1.00
166 Bram Stoker .25 .60
167 Marie Curie .25 .60
168 Melky Cabrera .15 .40
169 Howie Kendrick .15 .40
170 Jake Peavy .15 .40
171 J.D. Drew .15 .40
172 Pablo Picasso .25 .60
173 Rick Ankiel .15 .40
174 Jose Valverde .15 .40
175 Chipper Jones .40 1.00
176 Claude Monet .25 .60
177 Evan Longoria RC 2.00 5.00
178 Jose Vidro .15 .40
179 Hideki Matsui .40 1.00
180 Ryan Braun .25 .60
181 Moises Alou .15 .40
182 Nate McLouth .15 .40
183 Harriet Tubman .25 .60
184 Felix Hernandez .25 .60
185 Carlos Pena .25 .60
186 Jarrod Saltalamacchia .15 .40
187 Les Miles .25 .60
188 Kelly Johnson .15 .40
189 Rampage Jackson .40 1.00
190 Grady Sizemore .25 .60
191 Francisco Cordero .15 .40
192 Yunel Escobar .15 .40
193 Edwin Encarnacion .40 1.00
194 Melvin Mora .15 .40
195 Russ Martin .15 .40
196 Edgar Renteria .15 .40
197 Bigfoot .40 1.00
198 Steve Holm RC .40 1.00
199 Daric Barton (RC) .40 1.00
200 David Ortiz .40 1.00
201 Tim Lincecum .25 .60
202 Jeff King .25 .60
203 Jhonny Peralta .15 .40
204 Julio Lugo .15 .40
205 J.J. Putz .15 .40
206 Jeff Francoeur .25 .60
207 Yuniesky Betancourt .15 .40
208 Bruce Jenner .25 .60
209 Clete Thomas RC .60 1.50
210 Carlos Lee .15 .40
211 Josh Hamilton .25 .60
212 Pyotr Ilyich Tchaikovsky .25 .60
213 Brendan Harris .15 .40
214 Dustin McGowan .15 .40
215 Aaron Harang .15 .40
216 Brett Myers .15 .40
217 Friedrich Nietzsche .25 .60
218 John Maine .15 .40
219 Charles Dickens .25 .60
220 Erik Bedard .15 .40
221 Tim Hudson .25 .60
222 Jeremy Bonderman .15 .40
223 Nyjer Morgan (RC) .40 1.00
224 Johnny Cueto RC 1.00 2.50
225 Roy Oswalt .25 .60
226 Rich Hill .15 .40
227 Frederick Douglass .25 .60
228 Derek Lowe .15 .40
229 Joe Blanton .15 .40
230 Carlos Beltran .25 .60
231 Huston Street .25 .60
232 Davy Crockett .25 .60
233 Pluto .25 .60
234 Jered Weaver .25 .60
235 Dan Haren .15 .40
236 Alex Gordon .25 .60
237 Zack Greinke .40 1.00
238 Todd Clever .25 .60
239 Brian Bannister .15 .40
240 Magglio Ordonez .25 .60
241 Ryan Garko .15 .40
242 Takudzwa Ngwenya .25 .60
243 Gil Meche .15 .40
244 Mark Teahen .15 .40
245 Carlos Guillen .15 .40
246 Jeff Kent .15 .40
247 Lisa Leslie .40 1.00
248 Lastings Milledge .15 .40
249 Serena Williams .50 1.25
250 Ichiro Suzuki .50 1.25
251 Matt Cain .25 .60
252 Callix Crabbe (RC) .40 1.00
253 Nick Blackburn RC .60 1.50
254 Hunter Pence .25 .60
255 Cole Hamels .30 .75
256 Garret Anderson .15 .40
257 Luis Gonzalez .15 .40
258 Eric Chavez .15 .40
259 Francisco Rodriguez .25 .60
260 Mark Teixeira .25 .60
261 Bob Motley .25 .60
262 Mark Spitz .25 .60
263 Yadier Molina .50 1.25
264 Adam Jones .25 .60
265 Brian Roberts .15 .40
266 Matt Kemp .30 .75
267 Andrew Miller .25 .60
268 Dean Karnazes .25 .60
269 Gary Sheffield .15 .40
270 Lance Berkman .25 .60
271 Paul Lo Duca .15 .40
272 Matt Tolbert RC .60 1.50
273 Jay Bruce (RC) 1.25 3.00
274 John Smoltz .40 1.00
275 Nick Markakis .30 .75
276 Oscar Wilde .25 .60
277 Dontrelle Willis .15 .40
278 Kevin Van Dam .25 .60
279 Jim Edmonds .25 .60
280 Brandon Webb .25 .60
281 Joe Nathan .15 .40
282 Jeanette Lee .25 .60
283 Andrew Litz .25 .60
284 Daisuke Matsuzaka .25 .60
285 Brandon Phillips .15 .40
286 Pat Burrell .15 .40
287 Chris Carpenter .25 .60
288 Pete Weber .25 .60
289 Derrek Lee .15 .40
290 Ken Griffey Jr. .75 2.00
291 Rich Thompson RC .60 1.50
292 Elijah Dukes .15 .40
293 Pedro Feliz .15 .40
294 Torii Hunter .15 .40
295 Chone Figgins .15 .40
296 Hideki Okajima .15 .40
297 Max Scherzer RC 4.00 10.00
298 Greg Smith RC .40 1.00
299 Rafael Furcal .15 .40
300 Ryan Howard .25 .60
301 Felix Pie SP 1.25 3.00
302 Brad Lidge SP 1.25 3.00
303 Jason Bay SP 1.25 3.00
304 Victor Hugo SP 1.25 3.00
305 Randy Johnson SP 1.25 3.00
306 Carlos Gomez SP 1.25 3.00
307 Pat Neshek SP 1.25 3.00
308 Jed Lowrie SP (RC) 1.25 3.00
309 Ryan Church SP 1.25 3.00
310 Michael Bourn SP 1.25 3.00
311 B.J. Ryan SP 1.25 3.00
312 Brandon Wood SP 1.25 3.00
313 Harriet Beecher Stowe SP 1.25 3.00

314 Mike Cameron SP 1.25 3.00
315 Tom Glavine SP 1.25 3.00
316 Ervin Santana SP 1.25 3.00
317 Geoff Jenkins SP 1.25 3.00
318 Andre Ethier SP 1.25 3.00
319 Jason Giambi SP 1.25 3.00
320 Dmitri Young SP 1.25 3.00
321 Wily Mo Pena SP 1.25 3.00
322 Hank Blalock SP 1.25 3.00
323 James Bowie SP 1.25 3.00
324 Casey Kotchman SP 1.25 3.00
325 Stephen Drew SP 1.25 3.00
326 Adam Kennedy SP 1.25 3.00
327 A.J. Pierzynski SP 1.25 3.00
328 Richie Sexson SP 1.25 3.00
329 Jeff Clement SP (RC) 1.25 3.00
330 Luke Hochevar SP RC 1.25 3.00
331 Luis Castillo SP 1.25 3.00
332 Dave Roberts SP 1.25 3.00
333 Coco Crisp SP 1.25 3.00
334 Jo-Jo Reyes SP 1.25 3.00
335 Phil Hughes SP 1.25 3.00
336 Allen Fisher SP 1.25 3.00
337 Jason Schmidt SP 1.25 3.00
338 Placido Polanco SP 1.25 3.00
339 Jack Cust SP 1.25 3.00
340 Carl Crawford SP 1.25 3.00
341 Ty Wigginton SP 1.25 3.00
342 Aubrey Huff SP 1.25 3.00
343 Bengie Molina SP 1.25 3.00
344 Matt Diaz SP 1.25 3.00
345 Francisco Liriano SP 1.25 3.00
346 Brandon Boggs SP (RC) 1.25 3.00
347 David DeJesus SP 1.25 3.00
348 Justin Masterson SP RC 1.50 4.00
349 Frank Morris SP 1.25 3.00
350 Kevin Youkilis SP 1.25 3.00
NNO Framed Original 50.00 100.00
NNO Kosuke Fukudome 10.00 25.00

2008 Topps Allen and Ginter Mini

*MINI 1-300: .75X TO 2X BASIC
*MINI 1-300 RC: .5X TO 1.2X BASIC RC's
APPX. ONE MINI PER PACK
*MINI SP 300-350: .75X TO 2X BASIC SP
MINI SP ODDS 1:13 HOBBY
351-390 RANDOM WITHIN RIP CARDS
OVERALL PLATE ODDS 1:961 HOBBY
PLATE PRINT RUN 1 SET PER COLOR
BLACK-CYAN-MAGENTA-YELLOW ISSUED
NO PLATE PRICING DUE TO SCARCITY
351 Prince Fielder EXT 20.00 50.00
352 Justin Upton EXT 20.00 50.00
353 Russell Martin EXT 30.00 60.00
354 Cy Young EXT 15.00 40.00
355 Hanley Ramirez EXT 20.00 50.00
356 Grady Sizemore EXT 10.00 25.00
357 David Ortiz EXT 10.00 25.00
358 Dan Haren EXT 15.00 40.00
359 Honus Wagner EXT 30.00 60.00
360 Albert Pujols EXT 30.00 60.00
361 Hiroki Kuroda EXT 15.00 40.00
362 Evan Longoria EXT 30.00 60.00
363 Tris Speaker EXT 20.00 50.00
364 Josh Hamilton EXT 10.00 25.00
365 Johan Santana EXT 10.00 25.00
366 Derek Jeter EXT 50.00 100.00
367 Jake Peavy EXT 10.00 25.00
368 Troy Glaus EXT 15.00 40.00
369 Nick Swisher EXT 10.00 25.00
370 George Sisler EXT 20.00 50.00
371 Ichiro Suzuki EXT 40.00 80.00
372 Mark Teixeira EXT 20.00 50.00
373 Justin Verlander EXT 15.00 40.00
374 Jackie Robinson EXT 12.00 30.00
375 Vladimir Guerrero EXT 30.00 60.00
376 Delmon Young EXT 10.00 25.00
377 Lou Gehrig EXT 15.00 40.00
378 Tim Lincecum EXT 20.00 50.00
379 Ryan Zimmerman EXT 15.00 40.00
380 David Wright EXT 15.00 40.00
381 Matt Holliday EXT 10.00 25.00
382 Jose Reyes EXT 30.00 60.00
383 Christy Mathewson EXT 30.00 60.00
384 Hunter Pence EXT 20.00 50.00
385 Chase Utley EXT 20.00 50.00
386 Daisuke Matsuzaka EXT 10.00 25.00
387 Miguel Cabrera EXT 15.00 40.00
388 Torii Hunter EXT 15.00 40.00
389 Carlos Zambrano EXT 20.00 50.00
390 Alex Rodriguez EXT 20.00 50.00
391 Victor Martinez EXT 10.00 25.00
392 Justin Morneau EXT 10.00 25.00
393 Carlos Beltran EXT 10.00 25.00
394 Ryan Braun EXT 20.00 50.00
395 Alfonso Soriano EXT 10.00 25.00
396 Joba Chamberlain EXT 12.50 30.00
397 Nick Markakis EXT 20.00 50.00
398 Ty Cobb EXT 15.00 40.00
399 B.J. Upton EXT 10.00 25.00
400 Ryan Howard EXT 20.00 50.00

2008 Topps Allen and Ginter Mini A and G Back

*A & G BACK: 1X TO 2.5X BASIC
*A & G BACK RCs: .6X TO 1.5X BASIC RCs
STATED ODDS 1:5 HOBBY
*A & G BACK SP: 1X TO 2.5X BASIC SP
SP STATED ODDS 1:65 HOBBY

2008 Topps Allen and Ginter Mini Black

*BLACK: 1.5X TO 4X BASIC
*BLACK RCs: .75X TO 2X BASIC RCs
STATED ODDS 1:10 HOBBY
*BLACK SP: 1.2X TO 3X BASIC SP
SP STATED ODDS 1:130 HOBBY

2008 Topps Allen and Ginter Mini No Card Number

*NO NBR: 10X TO 25X BASIC
*NO NBR RCs: 4X TO 10X BASIC RCs
*NO NBR: 1.5X TO 4X BASIC SP
STATED ODDS 1:151 HOBBY
STATED PRINT RUN 50 SETS
CARDS ARE NOT SERIAL-NUMBERED
PRINT RUN INFO PROVIDED BY TOPPS
7 Mickey Mantle 30.00 60.00
16 Hiroki Kuroda 6.00 15.00
22 Chin-Lung Hu 6.00 15.00
39 J.R. Towles 6.00 15.00
153 Clay Buchholz 10.00 25.00
177 Evan Longoria 15.00 40.00
224 Johnny Cueto 10.00 25.00
253 Nick Blackburn 6.00 15.00
273 Jay Bruce 10.00 25.00
297 Max Scherzer 6.00 15.00

2008 Topps Allen and Ginter Autographs

GROUP A ODDS 1:277 HOBBY
GROUP B ODDS 1:256 HOBBY
GROUP C ODDS 1:135 HOBBY
GRP A PRINT RUNS B/W 90-240 COPIES PER
CARDS ARE NOT SERIAL-NUMBERED
PRINT RUNS PROVIDED BY TOPPS
EXCHANGE DEADLINE 7/31/2010
AE Andre Ethier C 6.00 15.00
AF Andrea Farina A/190 * 15.00 40.00
AFI Allen Fisher A/190 * 6.00 15.00
AIR Alex Rios B 6.00 15.00
AL Andrew Litz A/190 * 15.00 40.00
AM Adriano Moraes A/190 * EXCH 15.00 40.00
BB Bonnie Blair A/190 * 10.00 25.00
BJ Bruce Jenner A/190 * 15.00 40.00
BM Bob Motley A/190 * 30.00 60.00
BP Brad Penny A/240 * 12.50 30.00
BPB Brian Bannister C 5.00 12.00
BPM Billy Mitchell A/190 * 20.00 50.00
CB Clay Buchholz B 6.00 25.00
CC Carl Crawford A/240 * 6.00 15.00
CG Curtis Granderson B 6.00 15.00
DB Murray Campbell A/190 * 50.00 100.00
DJ Dan Jansen A/190 * 12.50 30.00
DK Dean Karnazes A/190 * 20.00 50.00
DO David Ortiz A/90 * 30.00 60.00
DW David Wright A/240 * 20.00 50.00
ES Ervin Santana C 5.00 12.00
FC Francisco Cordero C EXCH 5.00 12.00
FCC Fausto Carmona C 5.00 12.00
FM Frank Morris A/190 * 10.00 25.00
GJ Geoff Jenkins B 5.00 12.00
HP Hunter Pence A/90 * 30.00 60.00
HR Hanley Ramirez A/240 * 12.50 30.00
IK Ian Kinsler C 6.00 15.00
JBF Jeff Francoeur C 6.00 15.00
JC Joba Chamberlain B 6.00 25.00
JF Jeff Francis B 5.00 12.00
JJC Joey Chestnut A/190 * 20.00 50.00
JK Jeff King A/190 * EXCH 12.50 30.00
JL Jeanette Lee A/190 * 40.00 80.00
JR Jose Reyes A/90 * 25.00 60.00
JS Jarrod Saltalamacchia C 5.00 12.00
KS Kerri Strug A/190 * 30.00 60.00
KVD Kevin Van Dam A/190 * 20.00 50.00
LL Lisa Leslie A/190 * 12.50 30.00
LM Les Miles A/190 * 15.00 40.00
MB Matt Biondi A/190 * 20.00 50.00
MK Matt Kemp B 8.00 20.00
MR Manny Ramirez A/90 * 50.00 100.00
MS Mark Spitz A/190 * 10.00 25.00
MTH Matt Holliday A/90 * 30.00 60.00
NH Nicky Hayden A/240 * 20.00 50.00
NM Nick Markakis B 5.00 12.00
OH Orlando Hudson B 5.00 12.00
PF Prince Fielder A/90 * 40.00 100.00
PW Pete Weber A/190 * 12.50 30.00
RH Ryan Howard A/90 * 40.00 80.00
RJ Rampage Jackson A/190 * 60.00 120.00
SJW Serena Williams A/190 * 1500.00 3000.00
SW Stevie Williams A/240 * 10.00 25.00
TC Todd Clever A/190 * 4.00 10.00
TH Torii Hunter A/240 * 8.00 20.00
TLH Travis Hafner A/240 * 10.00 25.00
TN Takudzwa Ngwenya A/190 * 12.50 30.00

2008 Topps Allen and Ginter Cabinet Boxloader

STATED ODDS 1:3 HOBBY BOXES
BH1 Matt Holliday/Jamey Carroll
Michael Barrett/Brian Giles 3.00 8.00
BH2 Lowell/Manny/Papel/Beckett 4.00 10.00
BH3 Howard /Rollins/Utley/Hamels 4.00 10.00
BH4 ARod/Big Hurt/Thome 5.00 12.00
BH5 Verlan/Buehrle/Buchholz 4.00 10.00
HB1 General George Washington
General Nathanael Greene 3.00 8.00
HB2 General Horatio Gates
General John Burgoyne 3.00 8.00
HB3 General George Meade
General Robert E. Lee 3.00 8.00
HB4 Lt. Col. William B. Travis/Colonel James Bowie
Colonel Davy Crockett/Genera 3.00 8.00
HB5 General Dwight Eisenhower/Field Marshal
Bernard Montgomery 3.00 8.00

2008 Topps Allen and Ginter Cabinet Boxloader Autograph

STATED ODDS 1:322 HOBBY BOXES
STATED PRINT RUN 200 SER.#'d SETS
BF Bigfoot 30.00 60.00

2008 Topps Allen and Ginter Mini Ancient Icons

COMPLETE SET (20) 60.00 120.00
STATED ODDS 1:48 HOBBY
A1 Gilgamesh 3.00 8.00
A2 Marduk 3.00 8.00
A3 Beowulf 3.00 8.00
A4 Poseidon 3.00 8.00
A5 The Sphinx 3.00 8.00
A6 Tutankhamen 3.00 8.00
A7 Alexander the Great 3.00 8.00
A8 Cleopatra 3.00 8.00
A9 Sun Tzu 3.00 8.00
A10 Quetzalcoatl 3.00 8.00
A11 Isis 3.00 8.00
A12 Hercules 3.00 8.00
A13 King Arthur 3.00 8.00
A14 Miyamoto Musashi 3.00 8.00
A15 Genghis Khan 3.00 8.00
A16 Zeus 3.00 8.00
A17 Achilles 3.00 8.00
A18 Confucius 3.00 8.00
A19 Attila the Hun 3.00 8.00
A20 Romulus and Remus 3.00 8.00

2008 Topps Allen and Ginter Mini Baseball Icons

COMPLETE SET (17) 20.00 50.00
STATED ODDS 1:48 HOBBY
BI1 Cy Young 4.00 10.00
BI2 Walter Johnson 4.00 10.00
BI3 Jackie Robinson 5.00 12.00
BI4 Thurman Munson 4.00 10.00
BI5 Mel Ott 3.00 8.00
BI6 Honus Wagner 4.00 10.00
BI7 Pee Wee Reese 3.00 8.00
BI8 Tris Speaker 3.00 8.00
BI9 Christy Mathewson 4.00 10.00
BI10 Ty Cobb 4.00 10.00
BI11 Johnny Mize 3.00 8.00
BI12 Jimmie Foxx 4.00 10.00
BI13 Lou Gehrig 5.00 12.00
BI14 Roy Campanella 3.00 8.00
BI15 George Sisler 3.00 8.00
BI16 Rogers Hornsby 3.00 8.00
BI17 Babe Ruth 8.00 20.00

2008 Topps Allen and Ginter Mini Pioneers of Aviation

COMPLETE SET (5) 15.00 40.00
STATED ODDS 1:XX
PA1 Ornithopter 4.00 10.00
PA2 Linen Balloon 4.00 10.00
PA3 Piloted Glider 4.00 10.00
PA4 Aerial Steam Carriage 4.00 10.00
PA5 Aerodrome 4.00 10.00

2008 Topps Allen and Ginter Mini Team Orange

COMPLETE SET (10) 50.00 100.00
STATED ODDS 1:144 HOBBY
TO1 Cornelius Franks 4.00 10.00
TO2 Mittens McCluskey 4.00 10.00
TO3 Capt. W.P. Mantooth 4.00 10.00
TO4 Wheelbarrow Walker 4.00 10.00
TO5 Archibald Clinker 4.00 10.00
TO6 Minty Beans 4.00 10.00
TO7 Francisco Fiasco 4.00 10.00
TO8 Thurgood Cartwright IV 4.00 10.00
TO9 Enzo DiStubbs 4.00 10.00
TO10 Sir Wagonwheel Stevens 4.00 10.00

2008 Topps Allen and Ginter Mini World's Deadliest Sharks

COMPLETE SET (5) 20.00 50.00
STATED ODDS 1:XX
WDS1 Great White Shark 5.00 12.00
WDS2 Tiger Shark 5.00 12.00
WDS3 Bull Shark 5.00 12.00
WDS4 Oceanic Whitetip Shark 5.00 12.00
WDS5 Mako Shark 5.00 12.00

2008 Topps Allen and Ginter Mini World Leaders

COMPLETE SET (50) 30.00 60.00
STATED ODDS 1:12 HOBBY
WL1 Cristina Fernandez de Kirchner 1.50 4.00
WL2 Kevin Rudd 1.50 4.00
WL3 Guy Verhofstadt 1.50 4.00
WL4 Luiz Inacio Lula da Silva 1.50 4.00
WL5 Stephen Harper 1.50 4.00
WL6 Michelle Bachelet Jeria 1.50 4.00
WL7 Oscar Arias Sanchez 1.50 4.00
WL8 Mirek Topolanek 1.50 4.00
WL9 Anders Fogh Rasmussen 1.50 4.00
WL10 Leonel Fernandez Reyna 1.50 4.00
WL11 Mohamed Hosni Mubarak 1.50 4.00
WL12 Tarja Halonen 1.50 4.00
WL13 Nicolas Sarkozy 1.50 4.00
WL14 Yahya A.J.J. Jammeh 1.50 4.00
WL15 Angela Merkel 1.50 4.00
WL16 Konstandinos Karamanlis 1.50 4.00
WL17 Benedict XVI 2.00 5.00
WL18 Geir H. Haarde 1.50 4.00
WL19 Manmohan Singh 1.50 4.00
WL20 Susilo Bambang Yudhoyono 1.50 4.00
WL21 Bertie Ahern 1.50 4.00
WL22 Ehud Olmert 1.50 4.00
WL23 Bruce Golding 1.50 4.00
WL24 Yasuo Fukuda 1.50 4.00
WL25 Mwai Kibaki 1.50 4.00
WL26 Felipe de Jesus Calderon Hinojosa 1.50 4.00
WL27 Sanjaa Bayar 1.50 4.00
WL28 Armando Guebuza 1.50 4.00
WL29 Girija Prasad Koirala 1.50 4.00
WL30 Jan Peter Balkenende 1.50 4.00
WL31 Helen Clark 1.50 4.00
WL32 Jens Stoltenberg 1.50 4.00
WL33 Qaboos bin Said al-Said 1.50 4.00
WL34 Alan Garcia Perez 1.50 4.00
WL35 Gloria Macapagal-Arroyo 1.50 4.00
WL36 Donald Tusk 1.50 4.00
WL37 Vladimir Vladimirovich Putin 2.50 6.00
WL38 Robert Fico 1.50 4.00
WL39 Thabo Mbeki 1.50 4.00
WL40 Lee Myung-bak 1.50 4.00
WL41 Jose Luis Rodriguez Zapatero 1.50 4.00
WL42 Fredrik Reinfeldt 1.50 4.00
WL43 Pascal Couchepin 1.50 4.00
WL44 Jakaya Kikwete 1.50 4.00
WL45 Samak Sundaravej 1.50 4.00
WL46 Tenzin Gyatso 1.50 4.00
WL47 Patrick Manning 1.50 4.00
WL48 Gordon Brown 2.50 6.00
WL49 George W. Bush 3.00 8.00
WL50 Nguyen Tan Dung 1.50 4.00

2008 Topps Allen and Ginter N43

STATED ODDS 1:3 HOBBY BOXES
CG Curtis Granderson 2.00 5.00
CU Chase Utley 3.00 8.00
DO David Ortiz 3.00 8.00
DW David Wright 2.00 5.00
HR Hanley Ramirez 2.00 5.00
IS Ichiro Suzuki 4.00 10.00
JC Joba Chamberlain 1.25 3.00
JR Jose Reyes 2.00 5.00
MH Matt Holliday 3.00 8.00
MR Manny Ramirez 3.00 8.00
PF Prince Fielder 2.00 5.00
RB Ryan Braun 2.00 5.00
RH Ryan Howard 2.00 5.00
RZ Ryan Zimmerman 2.00 5.00
VG Vladimir Guerrero 2.00 5.00

2008 Topps Allen and Ginter N43 Autographs

STATED PRINT RUN 15 SER.#'d SETS
STATED ODDS 1:426 HOBBY BOXES
NO PRICING DUE TO SCARCITY
EXCHANGE DEADLINE 7/31/2010

2008 Topps Allen and Ginter National Convention

COMPLETE SET (7) 8.00 20.00
1 Babe Ruth 3.00 8.00
2 Lou Gehrig 2.50 6.00
3 Jackie Robinson 1.25 3.00
4 Don Larsen .50 1.25
5 Johnny Unitas 2.50 6.00
6 Roger Maris 1.25 3.00
7 Mickey Mantle 4.00 10.00

2008 Topps Allen and Ginter Relics

GROUP A ODDS 1:280 HOBBY
GROUP B ODDS 1:71 HOBBY
GROUP C ODDS 1:20 HOBBY
RELIC AU ODDS 1:26,431 HOBBY
GROUP A B/W 100-250 COPIES PER
CARDS ARE NOT SERIAL NUMBERED
PRINT RUN INFO PROVIDED BY TOPPS
AD1 Adam Dunn Jsy 3.00 8.00
AD2 Adam Dunn Bat 3.00 8.00
AER Alex Rodriguez Bat A 10.00 25.00
AF Andrea Farina A/250 * 5.00 12.00
AFI Allen Fisher A/250 * 8.00 20.00
AIR Alex Rios Bat B 3.00 8.00
AJP A.J. Pierzynski Jsy C 3.00 8.00
AK Austin Kearns Bat B 3.00 8.00
AL Andrew Litz A/250 * 8.00 20.00
AM Archie Moore A/100 * 15.00 40.00
AP1 Albert Pujols Jsy 6.00 15.00
AP2 Albert Pujols Bat 10.00 25.00
APB Aaron Pryor A/100 * 30.00 60.00
AR Aramis Ramirez Jsy B 3.00 8.00
ASM Adriano Moraes A/250 * 5.00 12.00
ATK Adam Kennedy Jsy C 3.00 8.00
AW Andre Ward A/100 * 15.00 40.00
BA Bobby Abreu Bat B 3.00 8.00
BB Bonnie Blair A/250 * 10.00 25.00
BC Bobby Crosby Jsy C 3.00 8.00
BF Bigfoot A/250 * 30.00 60.00
BH Brad Hawpe Jsy C 3.00 8.00
BJ Bruce Jenner A/250 * 10.00 25.00
BM Billy Mitchell A/250 * 12.00 30.00
BMM Brian McCann Jsy C 3.00 8.00
BR1 Brian Roberts Jsy 3.00 8.00
BR2 Brian Roberts Bat 3.00 8.00
CAM Carlos Marmol Jsy C 3.00 8.00
CC1 Carl Crawford Jsy 3.00 8.00
CC2 Carl Crawford Bat 3.00 8.00
CG Curtis Granderson Jsy C 3.00 8.00
CJ Chipper Jones Jsy C 4.00 10.00
CK Casey Kotchman Jsy B 3.00 8.00
CS Curt Schilling Jsy B 3.00 8.00
CU Chase Utley Jsy C 4.00 10.00
CZ Carlos Zambrano Jsy C 3.00 8.00
DG Danny Green A/100 * 30.00 60.00
DJ Dan Jansen A/250 * 8.00 20.00
DK Dean Karnazes A/250 * 12.50 30.00
DM Daisuke Matsuzaka Jsy A 6.00 15.00
DO1 David Ortiz Jsy 4.00 10.00
DO2 David Ortiz Bat 4.00 10.00
DRY Delwyn Young Jsy C 3.00 8.00
DW David Wright Jsy C 6.00 15.00
DY Dmitri Young Bat B 3.00 8.00
EC Eric Chavez Jsy A 3.00 8.00
EM Edison Miranda A/100 * 15.00 40.00
ER Edgar Renteria Bat B 3.00 8.00
FM Frank Morris A/250 * 6.00 15.00
GA Garret Anderson Jsy C 3.00 8.00
HB Hank Blalock Jsy B 3.00 8.00
IR1 Ivan Rodriguez Jsy B 3.00 8.00
IR2 Ivan Rodriguez Bat B 3.00 8.00
IS Ichiro Suzuki Jsy C 6.00 15.00
JB Jason Bay Jsy C 4.00 10.00
JC Joey Chestnut A/250 * 8.00 20.00
JCJ Joel Casamayor A/100 * 30.00 60.00
JD J.D. Drew Bat B 3.00 8.00
JDD Johnny Damon Bat C 3.00 8.00
JF Jeff Francoeur Jsy C 3.00 8.00
JFB Jeff Fenech A/100 * 15.00 40.00
JG Jay Gibbons Bat B 3.00 8.00
JJH J.J. Hardy Jsy C 3.00 8.00
JK Jeff Kent Bat B 3.00 8.00
JKI Jeff King A/250 * 10.00 25.00
JL Jeanette Lee A/250 * 30.00 60.00
JM Joe Mauer Jsy C 4.00 10.00
JS John Smoltz Jsy C 3.00 8.00
JT Jim Thome Jsy C 4.00 10.00
JTD Jermaine Dye Jsy C 3.00 8.00
JV1 Jason Varitek Bat 4.00 10.00
JV2 Jason Varitek Jsy 4.00 10.00
KP Kelly Pavlik A/100 * 40.00 80.00
KS Kerri Strug A/250 * 15.00 40.00
KVD Kevin Van Dam A/250 * 10.00 25.00
LB Lance Berkman Jsy C 3.00 8.00
LL Lisa Leslie A/250 * 12.50 30.00
LM Les Miles A/250 * 10.00 25.00
MB Matt Biondi A/250 * 8.00 20.00
MC Melky Cabrera Jsy C 3.00 8.00
MDC Matt Capps Jsy C 3.00 8.00
MH Mike Hampton Jsy C 3.00 8.00
MH Marcus Henderson AU/100 * 60.00 120.00
MK Matt Kemp Jsy C 3.00 8.00
MR Manny Ramirez Jsy C 4.00 10.00
MS Mark Spitz A/250 * 12.50 30.00
MT Mark Teixeira Jsy C 3.00 8.00
MY Michael Young Jsy C 3.00 8.00
NH Nicky Hayden A/250 * 10.00 25.00
PF Prince Fielder Bat B 3.00 8.00
PK Paul Konerko Jsy C 3.00 8.00
PL Paul Lo Duca Bat B 3.00 8.00
PW Pete Weber A/250 * 8.00 20.00
RF Rafael Furcal Bat B 3.00 8.00
RH Ryan Howard Jsy C 3.00 8.00
RJ Rampage Jackson A/250 * 15.00 40.00
RM Ray Mancini A/100 * 40.00 80.00
RO Roy Oswalt Jsy C 3.00 8.00
RS Richie Sexson Jsy C 3.00 8.00
SD Stephen Drew Jsy B 3.00 8.00
SJW Serena Williams A/250 * 12.50 30.00
SP Samuel Peter A/100 * 20.00 50.00
SW Stevie Williams A/250 * 8.00 20.00
TC Todd Clever A/250 * 10.00 25.00
TG Tom Glavine Jsy C 3.00 8.00
TH Tim Hudson Jsy C 3.00 8.00
TLH Todd Helton Jsy C 3.00 8.00
TN Takudzwa Ngwenya A/250 * 8.00 20.00
TPH Travis Hafner Jsy C 3.00 8.00
TSG Tom Gorzelanny Jsy C 3.00 8.00
TT Troy Tulowitzki Jsy C 3.00 8.00
VG Vladimir Guerrero Bat B 3.00 8.00
VM Victor Martinez Jsy C 3.00 8.00
WMP Wily Mo Pena Bat B 3.00 8.00

2008 Topps Allen and Ginter Rip Cards

STATED ODDS 1:189 HOBBY
PRINT RUNS B/WN 10-99 COPIES PER
NO PRICING ON QTY 10 OR LESS
ALL LISTED PRICED ARE FOR RIPPED
UNRIPPED HAVE ADD'L CARDS WITHIN
COMMON UNRIPPED p/r 99 50.00 120.00
COMMON UNRIPPED p/r 75 60.00 150.00
COMMON UNRIPPED p/r 50 75.00 200.00
COMMON UNRIPPED p/r 28 100.00 250.00
RC1 Erik Bedard/99 6.00 15.00
RC2 Jacoby Ellsbury/75 10.00 25.00
RC3 Chris Carpenter/99 6.00 15.00
RC4 Brandon Phillips/99 6.00 15.00
RC5 Daric Barton/99 6.00 15.00
RC6 Brian McCann/99 6.00 15.00
RC7 Mickey Mantle/10
RC8 Dan Uggla/75 6.00 15.00
RC9 James Loney/99 10.00 25.00
RC10 James Shields/99 6.00 15.00
RC11 Curtis Granderson/75 10.00 25.00
RC12 Jason Bay/99 6.00 15.00
RC13 Alex Gordon/75 10.00 25.00
RC14 Travis Hafner/99 6.00 15.00
RC15 Derek Jeter/28
RC16 Pedro Feliz/99 6.00 15.00
RC17 Thurman Munson/50 10.00 25.00
RC18 Grady Sizemore/75 10.00 25.00
RC19 Alex Rios/99 6.00 15.00
RC20 David Ortiz/50 10.00 25.00
RC21 Walter Johnson/28
RC22 Scott Rolen/99 10.00 25.00
RC23 John Smoltz/99 10.00 25.00
RC24 Mel Ott/28
RC25 Ryan Howard/50 10.00 25.00
RC26 Hiroki Kuroda/99 10.00 25.00
RC27 Johnny Damon/99 6.00 15.00
RC28 Jose Reyes/75 10.00 25.00
RC29 Felix Hernandez/99 10.00 25.00
RC30 John Lackey/99 6.00 15.00
RC31 Albert Pujols/10
RC32 Mark Teixeira/99 10.00 25.00
RC33 Jim Edmonds/99 6.00 15.00
RC34 Prince Fielder/50 10.00 25.00
RC35 Brian Bannister/99 6.00 15.00
RC36 Chipper Jones/50 10.00 25.00
RC37 Edgar Renteria/99 6.00 15.00
RC38 Roy Campanella/50 10.00 25.00
RC39 Troy Tulowitzki/99 10.00 25.00
RC40 Adam LaRoche/99 6.00 15.00
RC41 Phil Hughes/99 10.00 25.00
RC42 Pee Wee Reese/50 10.00 25.00
RC43 Adam Jones/99 6.00 15.00
RC44 Huston Street/99 6.00 15.00
RC45 Cliff Lee/99 6.00 15.00
RC46 Delmon Young/99 6.00 15.00
RC47 Joe Mauer/99 10.00 25.00
RC48 Johan Santana/28
RC49 Dmitri Young/99 6.00 15.00
RC50 Todd Helton/99 10.00 25.00
RC51 Carlos Beltran/75 6.00 15.00
RC52 J.J. Putz/99 6.00 15.00
RC53 Carlos Lee/99 6.00 15.00
RC54 Billy Butler/99 6.00 15.00
RC55 Miguel Cabrera/99 10.00 25.00
RC56 Derrek Lee/99 6.00 15.00
RC57 Alfonso Soriano/75 10.00 25.00
RC58 Cole Hamels/99 10.00 25.00
RC59 Hanley Ramirez/75 10.00 25.00
RC60 Adrian Gonzalez/99 6.00 15.00
RC61 B.J. Upton/99 6.00 15.00
RC62 Tim Lincecum/75 10.00 25.00
RC63 Gary Matthews/99 6.00 15.00
RC64 Justin Upton/75 10.00 25.00
RC65 Zack Greinke/99 6.00 15.00
RC66 Roy Oswalt/75 6.00 15.00
RC67 Jimmy Rollins/28
RC68 Miguel Tejada/99 6.00 15.00
RC69 Clay Buchholz/99 10.00 25.00
RC70 Andruw Jones/99 6.00 15.00
RC71 Chase Utley/75 10.00 25.00
RC72 Aaron Rowand/99 6.00 15.00
RC73 Johnny Mize/50 10.00 25.00
RC74 Jonathan Papelbon/75 10.00 25.00
RC75 Jarrod Saltalamacchia/99 6.00 15.00
RC76 Lance Berkman/50 6.00 15.00
RC77 Vernon Wells/99 6.00 15.00
RC78 Dontrelle Willis/99 6.00 15.00
RC79 Jim Thome/99 10.00 25.00
RC80 Torii Hunter/99 6.00 15.00
RC81 Russ Martin/75 6.00 15.00
RC82 Jake Peavy/99 10.00 25.00
RC83 Carlos Zambrano/99 6.00 15.00
RC84 Troy Glaus/99 6.00 15.00
RC85 Ryan Zimmerman/75 10.00 25.00
RC86 Evan Longoria/75 10.00 25.00
RC87 Yovani Gallardo/99 6.00 15.00
RC88 Jimmie Foxx/10
RC89 Josh Hamilton/75 10.00 25.00
RC90 Matt Holliday/50 10.00 25.00
RC91 Matt Cain/99 6.00 15.00
RC92 Francisco Cordero/99 6.00 15.00
RC93 Derek Lowe/99 6.00 15.00
RC94 Brandon Webb/75 6.00 15.00
RC95 Carlos Pena/99 6.00 15.00
RC96 Ichiro Suzuki/10
RC97 Khalil Greene/99 10.00 25.00
RC98 Rogers Hornsby/10
RC99 C.C. Sabathia/75 6.00 15.00
RC100 Victor Martinez/99 6.00 15.00

2008 Topps Allen and Ginter United States

COMPLETE SET (50) 10.00 25.00
STATED ODDS 1:XX
US1 Alex Rios .25 .60
US2 Curt Schilling .40 1.00
US3 Brian Bannister .25 .60
US4 Torii Hunter .25 .60
US5 Chase Utley .40 1.00
US6 Roy Halladay .40 1.00
US7 Brad Ausmus .25 .60
US8 Ian Snell .25 .60
US9 Lastings Milledge .25 .60
US10 Nick Markakis .50 1.25
US11 Shane Victorino .25 .60
US12 Jason Schmidt .25 .60
US13 Curtis Granderson .40 1.00
US14 Scott Rolen .40 1.00
US15 Casey Blake .25 .60
US16 Nate Robertson .25 .60
US17 Brandon Webb .40 1.00
US18 Jonathan Papelbon .40 1.00
US19 Tim Stauffer .25 .60
US20 Mark Teixeira .40 1.00
US21 Chris Capuano .25 .60
US22 Jason Varitek .60 1.50
US23 Joe Mauer .50 1.25
US24 Dmitri Young .25 .60
US25 Ryan Howard .40 1.00
US26 Taylor Tankersley .25 .60
US27 Alex Gordon .25 .60
US28 Barry Zito .40 1.00
US29 Chris Carpenter .40 1.00
US30 Derek Jeter 1.50 4.00
US31 Cody Ross .25 .60
US32 Alex Rodriguez .75 2.00
US33 Ryan Zimmerman .40 1.00
US34 Travis Hafner .25 .60
US35 Nick Swisher .40 1.00
US36 Matt Holliday .60 1.50
US37 Jacoby Ellsbury .50 1.25
US38 Ken Griffey Jr. 1.25 3.00
US39 Paul Konerko .40 1.00
US40 Orlando Hudson .25 .60
US41 Mark Ellis .25 .60
US42 Todd Helton .40 1.00
US43 Adam Dunn .40 1.00
US44 Brandon Lyon .25 .60
US45 Daric Barton .25 .60
US46 David Wright .40 1.00
US47 Grady Sizemore .40 1.00
US48 Seth McClung .25 .60
US49 Pat Neshek .40 1.00
US50 John Buck .25 .60

2008 Topps Allen and Ginter World's Greatest Victories

COMPLETE SET (20) 30.00 60.00
STATED ODDS 1:24 HOBBY
WGV1 Kerri Strug 2.50 6.00
WGV2 Mark Spitz 2.50 6.00
WGV3 Jonas Salk 2.00 5.00
WGV4 Man Walks on the Moon 2.00 5.00
WGV5 Jon Lester 3.00 8.00
WGV6 The Fall of the Berlin Wall 2.00 5.00
WGV7 David and Goliath 2.00 5.00
WGV8 Gary Carter and the '86 Mets 2.50 6.00
WGV9 The Battle of Gettysburg 2.00 5.00
WGV10 Deep Blue 2.00 5.00
WGV11 The Allied Forces 2.00 5.00
WGV12 Don Larsen 2.50 6.00
WGV13 Truman Defeats Dewey 2.00 5.00
WGV14 The American Revolution 2.00 5.00
WGV15 2004 ALCS 3.00 8.00
WGV16 The Battle of Thermopylae 2.00 5.00
WGV17 Brown v. Board of Education 2.00 5.00
WGV18 Team Orange 2.50 6.00
WGV19 Bill Mazeroski 2.50 6.00
WGV20 Cinderella 2.00 5.00

2009 Topps Allen and Ginter

COMPLETE SET (350) 30.00 60.00
COMP.SET w/o SP's (300) 12.50 30.00
COMMON CARD (1-300) .15 .40
COMMON RC (1-300) .40 1.00
COMMON SP (301-350) 1.25 3.00
SP STATED ODDS 1:2 HOBBY
1 Jay Bruce .25 .60
2 Zack Greinke .40 1.00
3 Manny Parra .15 .40
4 Jorge Posada .25 .60
5 Luke Hochevar .15 .40
6 Adam Eaton .15 .40
7 John Smoltz .40 1.00
8 Matt Cain .25 .60
9 Ryan Theriot .15 .40
10 Chone Figgins .15 .40
11 Jacoby Ellsbury .30 .75
12 Jermaine Dye .15 .40
13 Travis Hafner .15 .40
14 Troy Tulowitzki .40 1.00
15 Alfred Nobel .15 .40
16 Josh Johnson .25 .60
17 Manny Ramirez .40 1.00
18 Clyde Parris .40 1.00
19 Mike Pelfrey .15 .40
20 Adam Jones .25 .60
21 Robinson Cano .25 .60
22 Mariano Rivera .50 1.25
23 Kristin Armstrong .15 .40
24 Steve Wiebe .15 .40
25 Evan Longoria .25 .60
26 Charles Goodyear .15 .40
27 Chien-Ming Wang .25 .60
28 Ervin Santana .15 .40
29 Jonathan Papelbon .25 .60
30 Ryan Howard .30 .75
31 Nick Markakis .30 .75
32 Jeremy Bonderman .15 .40
33 Florence Nightingale .15 .40
34 Ryan Dempster .15 .40
35 Geovany Soto .25 .60
36 Joba Chamberlain .25 .60
37 Andre Ethier .25 .60
38 Troy Glaus .15 .40
39 Hanley Ramirez .25 .60
40 Jeremy Hermida .15 .40
41 Victor Martinez .25 .60
42 Mark Buehrle .25 .60
43 Koji Uehara RC 1.00 2.50
44 Freddy Sanchez .15 .40
45 Derrek Lee .15 .40
46 Brian Roberts .15 .40
47 J.J. Hardy .15 .40
48 Brigham Young .15 .40
49 Ubaldo Jimenez .15 .40
50 Pat Neshek .25 .60
51 Ryan Perry RC 1.00 2.50
52 Aaron Hill .15 .40
53 Clayton Kershaw .60 1.50
54 Carlos Guillen .15 .40
55 Alex Rios .15 .40
56 Daniel Murphy RC 1.50 4.00
57 Frank Evans .25 .60
58 Brad Hawpe .15 .40
59 Mark Reynolds .15 .40
60 Matt Holliday .40 1.00
61 Burke Kenny .15 .40
62 Dan Uggla .15 .40
63 Andrew Miller .25 .60
64 Jordan Zimmermann RC 1.00 2.50
65 Dexter Fowler (RC) .60 1.50
66 Alex Rodriguez .50 1.25
67 Ian Kinsler .25 .60
68 Jamie Moyer .15 .40
69 James Loney .15 .40
70 Rick Ankiel .15 .40
71 Albert Pujols .50 1.25
72 Carlos Lee .15 .40
73 Vernon Wells .15 .40
74 Matt Tuiasosopo (RC) .40 1.00
75 David Wright .30 .75
76 Brandon Phillips .15 .40
77 Francisco Liriano .15 .40
78 Eric Byrnes .15 .40
79 Electron .15 .40
80 Joe Martinez RC .60 1.50
81 Willie Williams .40 1.00
82 Justin Verlander .40 1.00
83 Ludwig van Beethoven .15 .40
84 Justin Upton .25 .60
85 Jason Jaramillo (RC) .40 1.00
86 Michael Cuddyer .15 .40
87 Aaron Cook .15 .40
88 Brad Penny .15 .40
89 Elvis Andrus RC 1.00 2.50
90 Bobby Crosby .15 .40
91 Alex Gordon .25 .60
92 Joe Mauer .30 .75
93 David DeJesus .15 .40
94 Paul Maholm .15 .40
95 David Patton RC .60 1.50
96 Geronimo .15 .40
97 Art Pennington .40 1.00
98 Josh Whitesell RC .60 1.50
99 Chris Duncan .15 .40
100 Ichiro Suzuki .50 1.25
101 Andrew Bailey RC 1.00 2.50
102 Edinson Volquez .15 .40
103 Aaron Harang .15 .40
104 Jeff Francoeur .25 .60
105 Kurt Suzuki .15 .40
106 Mike Jacobs .15 .40
107 Bryan Berg .15 .40
108 Alamo .15 .40
109 Samuel Morse .15 .40
110 Kevin Youkilis .15 .40
111 Jason Giambi .15 .40
112 Milito Navarro .40 1.00
113 Rafael Furcal .15 .40
114 Hideki Matsui .40 1.00
115 Ryan Doumit .15 .40
116 Charles Darwin .15 .40
117 Blake DeWitt .15 .40
118 Scott Olsen .15 .40
119 Scott Lewis (RC) .40 1.00
120 Edwin Moreno (RC) .40 1.00
121 Ryan Church .15 .40
122 Dontrelle Willis .15 .40
123 Barry Zito .25 .60
124 Donald Veal RC .60 1.50
125 Randy Johnson .40 1.00
126 Trevor Crowe RC .40 1.00
127 J.D. Drew .15 .40
128 Red Moore .40 1.00
129 Brian Giles .15 .40
130 Johnny Damon .25 .60
131 Rickie Weeks .15 .40
132 Anna Tunnicliffe .15 .40
133 Roy Halladay .25 .60
134 Jered Weaver .25 .60
135 Jeff Suppan .15 .40
136 Mickey Mantle 1.25 3.00
137 Mark Teixeira .25 .60
138 Garrett Atkins .15 .40
139 Daisuke Matsuzaka .25 .60
140 Loren Opstedahl .40 1.00
141 Carlos Zambrano .25 .60
142 LaShawn Merritt .15 .40
143 Robbie Maddison .15 .40
144 Joakim Soria .15 .40
145 Todd Wellemeyer .15 .40
146 Rich Harden .15 .40
147 Coco Crisp .15 .40
148 Brad Lidge .15 .40
149 Chipper Jones .40 1.00
150 Prince Fielder .25 .60
151 Cole Hamels .30 .75
152 Phil Coke RC .60 1.50
153 CC Sabathia .25 .60
154 Corey Hart .15 .40
155 Yadier Molina .50 1.25
156 Jayson Werth .25 .60
157 Jason Motte (RC) .60 1.50
158 Sigmund Freud .15 .40
159 Denard Span .15 .40
160 Max Scherzer .40 1.00
161 Justin Morneau .25 .60
162 Shane Victorino .15 .40
163 Matt Garza .15 .40
164 Erik Bedard .15 .40
165 Chase Utley .25 .60
166 Gil Meche .15 .40
167 Jim Thome .25 .60
168 Adrian Gonzalez .30 .75
169 Kazuo Matsui .15 .40
170 Lance Berkman .25 .60
171 Brett Anderson RC .60 1.50
172 Jarrod Saltalamacchia .15 .40
173 Francisco Rodriguez .25 .60
174 John Lannan .15 .40
175 Alfonso Soriano .25 .60
176 Ramiro Pena RC .60 1.50
177 David Freese RC 1.25 3.00

178 Adam LaRoche .15 .40
179 Trevor Hoffman .25 .60
180 Russell Martin .15 .40
181 Aaron Rowand .15 .40
182 Jose Reyes .25 .60
183 Pedro Feliz .15 .40
184 Chris Young .15 .40
185 Dustin Pedroia .40 1.00
186 Adrian Beltre .40 1.00
187 Brett Myers .15 .40
188 Chris Davis .25 .60
189 Casey Kotchman .15 .40
190 B.J. Upton .25 .60
191 Hiroki Kuroda .15 .40
192 Ryan Zimmerman .25 .60
193 Khalil Greene .15 .40
194 Brandon Morrow .15 .40
195 Kevin Kouzmanoff .15 .40
196 Joey Votto .40 1.00
197 Jhonny Peralta .15 .40
198 Raul Ibanez .25 .60
199 James McDonald RC 1.00 2.50
200 Carlos Quentin .15 .40
201 Travis Snider RC .60 1.50
202 Conor Jackson .15 .40
203 Scott Kazmir .15 .40
204 Casey Blake .15 .40
205 Ryan Braun .25 .60
206 Miguel Tejada .25 .60
207 Jack Cust .15 .40
208 Michael Young .15 .40
209 St. Patrick's Cathedral .15 .40
210 Johan Santana .25 .60
211 Kevin Millwood .15 .40
212 Mariel Zagunis .15 .40
213 Stephanie Brown Trafton .15 .40
214 Adam Dunn .25 .60
215 Jed Lowrie .15 .40
216 Derek Lowe .15 .40
217 Jorge Cantu .15 .40
218 Bobby Parnell RC .60 1.50
219 Nate McLouth .15 .40
220 Suez Canal .15 .40
221 Brandon Webb .25 .60
222 Akinori Iwamura .15 .40
223 Scott Rolen .25 .60
224 Tim Lincecum .25 .60
225 David Price RC .75 2.00
226 Ricky Romero (RC) .60 1.50
227 Nelson Cruz .40 1.00
228 Will Simpson .15 .40
Archie Bunker
229 Mark Ellis .15 .40
230 Torii Hunter .15 .40
231 David Murphy .15 .40
232 Everth Cabrera RC .60 1.50
233 John Lackey .25 .60
234 Wyatt Earp .15 .40
235 Roy Oswalt .25 .60
236 Edgar Renteria .15 .40
237 Walton Glenn Eller .15 .40
238 Vincent Van Gogh .15 .40
239 Chris Carpenter .25 .60
240 Hank Blalock .15 .40
241 Trevor Cahill RC 1.00 2.50
242 Mark Teahen .15 .40
243 Alexander Cartwright .25 .60
244 Carlos Beltran .25 .60
245 Todd Helton .25 .60
246 General Custer .15 .40
247 Jeff Clement .15 .40
248 Colby Rasmus (RC) .60 1.50
249 John Higby .15 .40
250 Grady Sizemore .25 .60
251 Carl Crawford .25 .60
252 Lastings Milledge .15 .40
253 Miguel Cabrera .40 1.00
254 John Maine .15 .40
255 Aramis Ramirez .15 .40
256 Jose Lopez .15 .40
257 Heinrich Hertz .15 .40
258 Felix Hernandez .25 .60
259 Napoleon Bonaparte .15 .40
260 Louis Braille .15 .40
261 John Danks .15 .40
262 Magglio Ordonez .25 .60
263 Brian Duensing RC .60 1.50
264 Carlos Pena .25 .60
265 Paul Konerko .25 .60
266 Johnny Cueto .25 .60
267 Melvin Mora .15 .40
268 Andy Pettitte .25 .60
269 Brian McCann .25 .60
270 Josh Outman RC .60 1.50
271 Jair Jurrjens .15 .40
272 Brad Nelson (RC) .40 1.00
273 Jason Bay .25 .60
274 Josh Hamilton .25 .60
275 Vladimir Guerrero .25 .60
276 Michael Phelps .75 2.00
277 Kerry Wood .15 .40
278 Herb Simpson .40 1.00
279 Jon Lester .25 .60
280 Shin-Soo Choo .25 .60
281 Jake Peavy .15 .40
282 Eric Chavez .15 .40
283 Mike Aviles .15 .40
284 Kenshin Kawakami RC .60 1.50
285 George Kottaras (RC) .40 1.00
286 Matt Kemp .30 .75
287 James Shields .15 .40
288 Joe Saunders .15 .40
289 Milky Way .15 .40
290 Cat Osterman .50 1.25
291 Josh Beckett .15 .40
292 Oliver Perez .15 .40
293 Ian Snell .15 .40
294 Tim Hudson .25 .60
295 Brett Gardner .25 .60
296 Bobby Abreu .15 .40
297 Kolan McConiughey .15 .40
298 Dan Haren .15 .40
299 Shairon Martis RC .60 1.50
300 David Ortiz .40 1.00
301 Jonathan Sanchez SP 1.25 3.00
302 Stephen Drew SP 1.25 3.00
303 Rocco Baldelli SP 1.25 3.00
304 Yunel Escobar SP 1.25 3.00
305 Javier Vazquez SP 1.25 3.00
306 Cliff Lee SP 1.25 3.00
307 Hunter Pence SP 1.25 3.00
308 Fausto Carmona SP 1.25 3.00
309 Kosuke Fukudome SP 1.25 3.00
310 Old Faithful SP 1.25 3.00
311 Gavin Floyd SP 1.25 3.00
312 A.J. Burnett SP 1.25 3.00
313 Jeff Francis SP 1.25 3.00
314 Chad Billingsley SP 1.25 3.00
315 Andy LaRoche SP 1.25 3.00
316 Rick Porcello SP RC 2.50 6.00
317 John Baker SP 1.25 3.00
318 Delmon Young SP 1.25 3.00
319 Gary Sheffield SP 1.25 3.00
320 B.J. Ryan SP 1.25 3.00
321 Kelly Shoppach SP 1.25 3.00
322 Chris Volstad SP 1.25 3.00
323 Derek Jeter SP 3.00 8.00
324 Wladimir Balentien SP 1.25 3.00
325 Dioner Navarro SP 1.25 3.00
326 Cameron Maybin SP 1.25 3.00
327 Kenji Johjima SP 1.25 3.00
328 Matt LaPorta SP RC 2.00 5.00
329 Carlos Gomez SP 1.25 3.00
330 Cristian Guzman SP 1.25 3.00
331 Jeff Samardzija SP 1.25 3.00
332 Curtis Granderson SP 1.25 3.00
333 Nick Swisher SP 1.25 3.00
334 Pat Burrell SP 1.25 3.00
335 Justin Duchscherer SP 1.25 3.00
336 Ryan Ludwick SP 1.25 3.00
337 Billy Butler SP 1.25 3.00
338 Jason Wong SP 1.25 3.00
339 Jordan Schafer SP (RC) 1.25 3.00
340 Richard Gatling SP 1.25 3.00
341 Edgar Gonzalez SP 1.25 3.00
342 Sitting Bull SP 1.25 3.00
343 Doc Holliday SP 1.25 3.00
344 Chris Young SP 1.25 3.00
345 Carlos Delgado SP 1.25 3.00
346 Dominique Wilkins SP 1.25 3.00
347 Yovani Gallardo SP 1.25 3.00
348 Justin Masterson SP 1.25 3.00
349 Aubrey Huff SP 1.25 3.00
350 Jimmy Rollins SP 1.25 3.00

2009 Topps Allen and Ginter Code

*CODE: 2X TO 5X BASIC
STATED ODDS 1:12 HOBBY

2009 Topps Allen and Ginter Mini

COMP.SET w/o EXT (350) 125.00 250.00
*MINI 1-300: .75X TO 2X BASIC
*MINI 1-300 RC: .5X TO 1.2X BASIC RC's
APPX. ONE MINI PER PACK
*MINI SP 301-350: .5X TO 1.2X BASIC SP
MINI SP ODDS 1:13 HOBBY
351-390 RANDOM WITHIN RIP CARDS
OVERALL PLATE ODDS 1:608 HOBBY
PLATE PRINT RUN 1 SET PER COLOR
BLACK-CYAN-MAGENTA-YELLOW ISSUED
NO PLATE PRICING DUE TO SCARCITY
351 Manny Ramirez EXT 20.00 50.00
352 Travis Snider EXT 12.00 30.00
353 CC Sabathia EXT 12.00 30.00
354 Nick Markakis EXT 15.00 40.00
355 Jon Lester EXT 12.00 30.00
356 Cole Hamels EXT 15.00 40.00
357 Edinson Volquez EXT 8.00 20.00
358 Hanley Ramirez EXT 12.00 30.00
359 Alex Rodriguez EXT 25.00 60.00
360 Francisco Rodriguez EXT 12.00 30.00
361 Albert Pujols EXT 25.00 60.00
362 Matt Holliday EXT 20.00 50.00
363 Max Scherzer EXT 20.00 50.00
364 Adam Dunn EXT 12.00 30.00
365 Randy Johnson EXT 20.00 50.00
366 Roy Halladay EXT 12.00 30.00
367 Joe Mauer EXT 15.00 40.00
368 Roy Oswalt EXT 12.00 30.00
369 Grady Sizemore EXT 12.00 30.00
370 Jacoby Ellsbury EXT 15.00 40.00
371 Nate McLouth EXT 8.00 20.00
372 Josh Johnson EXT 12.00 30.00
373 Geovany Soto EXT 12.00 30.00
374 Josh Beckett EXT 8.00 20.00
375 Brian McCann EXT 12.00 30.00
376 David Wright EXT 15.00 40.00
377 Adrian Gonzalez EXT 15.00 40.00
378 Tim Lincecum EXT 12.00 30.00
379 Dan Haren EXT 8.00 20.00
380 Alex Rios EXT 8.00 20.00
381 Rich Harden EXT 8.00 20.00
382 Victor Martinez EXT 12.00 30.00
383 Carlos Lee EXT 8.00 20.00
384 Chipper Jones EXT 20.00 50.00
385 Clayton Kershaw EXT 30.00 80.00
386 Daisuke Matsuzaka EXT 12.00 30.00
387 Carlos Beltran EXT 12.00 30.00
388 Scott Kazmir EXT 8.00 20.00
389 Mark Teixeira EXT 12.00 30.00
390 Justin Upton EXT 12.00 30.00
391 David Price EXT 15.00 40.00
392 Felix Hernandez EXT 12.00 30.00
393 Mariano Rivera EXT 25.00 60.00
394 Joba Chamberlain EXT 8.00 20.00
395 Justin Morneau EXT 12.00 30.00
396 Ryan Howard EXT 15.00 40.00
397 Evan Longoria EXT 12.00 30.00
398 Ryan Zimmerman EXT 12.00 30.00
399 Jason Bay EXT 12.00 30.00
400 Miguel Cabrera EXT 20.00 50.00

2009 Topps Allen and Ginter Mini A and G Back

*A & G BACK: 1X TO 2.5X BASIC
*A & G BACK RCs: .6X TO 1.5X BASIC RCs
STATED ODDS 1:5 HOBBY
*A & G BACK SP: .6X TO 1.5X BASIC SP
SP STATED ODDS 1:65 HOBBY

2009 Topps Allen and Ginter Mini Black

*BLACK: 2X TO 5X BASIC
*BLACK RCs: .75X TO 2X BASIC RCs
STATED ODDS 1:10 HOBBY
*BLACK SP: .75X TO 2X BASIC SP
SP STATED ODDS 1:130 HOBBY

2009 Topps Allen and Ginter Mini No Card Number

*NO NBR: 8X TO 20X BASIC
*NO NBR RCs: 3X TO 8X BASIC RCs
*NO NBR SP: 1.2X TO 3X BASIC SP
STATED ODDS 1:95 HOBBY
STATED PRINT RUN 50 SETS
11 Jacoby Ellsbury 20.00 50.00
22 Mariano Rivera 12.50 30.00
66 Alex Rodriguez 20.00 50.00
136 Mickey Mantle 40.00 80.00
149 Chipper Jones 20.00 50.00
246 General Custer 12.50 30.00
316 Rick Porcello 10.00 25.00
323 Derek Jeter 30.00 60.00
328 Matt LaPorta 6.00 15.00
332 Curtis Granderson 10.00 25.00
338 Jason Wong 10.00 25.00
348 Justin Masterson 10.00 25.00

2009 Topps Allen and Ginter Autographs

GROUP A ODDS 1:2730 HOBBY
GROUP B ODDS 1:51 HOBBY
CARDS ARE NOT SERIAL-NUMBERED
PRINT RUNS PROVIDED BY TOPPS
NO PHELPS PRICING DUE TO SCARCITY
EXCHANGE DEADLINE 6/30/2012
AC Alexi Casilla B 4.00 10.00
AP Pennington/239 * B 10.00 25.00
AR Alex Rios B 6.00 15.00
AT A.Tunnicliffe/239 * B 8.00 20.00
BBE Bryan Berg/239 * B 5.00 12.00
BC B.Crowley/239 * B 6.00 15.00
BCA Cappelletto/239 * B 8.00 20.00
BK B.Kenny/239 * B 10.00 25.00
BM The Marlin/239 * B 15.00 40.00
BW Blake DeWitt B 4.00 10.00
BY B.Yates/239 * B 5.00 12.00
CG Carlos Gomez B 4.00 10.00
CJ Conor Jackson B 4.00 10.00
CK Clayton Kershaw B 60.00 150.00
CM C.Maybin B 5.00 12.00
CO C.Osterman/239 * B 12.00 30.00
CP C.Parris/239 * B 10.00 25.00
DO D.Ortiz/49 * A 100.00 200.00
DOW D.Wilkins/239 * B 15.00 40.00
DS Denard Span B 4.00 10.00
DW D.Wright/49 * A 15.00 40.00
EL Evan Longoria B 4.00 10.00
ES Ervin Santana B 4.00 10.00
FE F.Evans/239 * B 15.00 40.00
HR Hanley Ramirez B 5.00 12.00
HS H.Simpson/239 * B 15.00 40.00
HT H.Teter/239 * B 5.00 12.00
IK I.Kyle SP/239 * B 8.00 20.00
JB Jay Bruce B 8.00 20.00
JC Chamberlain/49 * A 30.00 60.00
JCU Jack Cust B 4.00 10.00
JF Jeff Francoeur B 4.00 10.00
JH J.Higby/239 * B 8.00 20.00
JJ Josh Johnson B 8.00 20.00
JM J.Masterson B 4.00 10.00
JOC Johnny Cueto B 4.00 10.00
JP J.Papelbon B 4.00 10.00
JR Jose Reyes/49 * A 8.00 20.00
JRI Juan Rivera B 4.00 10.00
JW J.Werth/49 * A 90.00 150.00
KA K.Armstrong/239 * B 10.00 25.00
KM McConiughey/239 * B 8.00 20.00
LC L.Cox/239 * B 12.50 30.00
LM L.Merritt/239 * B 8.00 20.00
LO L.Opstedahl/239 * B 5.00 12.00
MC M.Cabrera/49 * A 60.00 150.00
MH M.Holliday/49 * A 30.00 60.00
MK Matt Kemp B 5.00 12.00
MLO Mike Lowell B 8.00 20.00
MM M.Metzger/239 * B 6.00 15.00
MN M.Navarro/239 * B 20.00 50.00
MS Max Scherzer B 30.00 80.00
MZ M. Zagunis/239 * B 6.00 15.00
PH Phil Hughes B 8.00 20.00
RB Ryan Braun B 12.50 30.00
RC Ryan Church B 4.00 10.00
RF R.Fosbury/239 * B 12.50 30.00
RH Ryan Howard/49 * A 15.00 40.00
RJH Rich Hill B 4.00 10.00
RM R.Moore/239 * B 12.50 30.00
RMA R.Maddison/239 * B 10.00 25.00
SB S.Trafton/239 * B 8.00 20.00
SD S.Davis/239 * B 8.00 20.00
SO Scott Olsen B 4.00 10.00
SW S.Wiebe/239 * B 15.00 40.00
TT Troy Tulowitzki B 5.00 12.00
WE W.Eller/239 * B 10.00 25.00
WS W.Simpson/239 * B 12.50 30.00
WW W.Williams/239 * B 15.00 40.00
YM Y.Miyazawa/239 * B 10.00 25.00

2009 Topps Allen and Ginter Cabinet Boxloaders

COMPLETE SET (10) 20.00 50.00
ONE CABINET/N43 PER HOBBY BOX
CB1 Yurendell de Caster/Gene Kingsale 2.50 6.00
CB2 Frederich Cepeda/Yulieski Gourriel 3.00 8.00
CB3 D.Wright/B.Roberts 4.00 10.00
CB4 N.Aoki/D.Matsuzaka 4.00 10.00
CB5 H.Iwakuma/I.Suzuki 4.00 10.00
CB6 Thomas Jefferson/John Hancock 2.50 6.00
CB7 George Washington/Alexander Hamilton 3.00
8.00
CB8 Harry S Truman/Lester B. Pearson 3.00 8.00
CB9 Abraham Lincoln/Ulysses S. Grant 3.00 8.00
CB10 John F. Kennedy/Nikita Khrushchev 3.00 8.00

2009 Topps Allen and Ginter Baseball Highlights

COMPLETE SET (25) 10.00 25.00
STATED ODDS 1:6 HOBBY
AGHS1 Aaron Boone .40 1.00
AGHS2 Ken Griffey Jr. 2.00 5.00
AGHS3 Randy Johnson 1.00 2.50
AGHS4 Carlos Zambrano .60 1.50
AGHS5 Josh Hamilton .60 1.50
AGHS6 Josh Beckett .40 1.00
AGHS7 Manny Ramirez 1.00 2.50
AGHS8 Derek Jeter 2.50 6.00
AGHS9 Frank Thomas 1.00 2.50
AGHS10 Jim Thome .60 1.50
AGHS11 Francisco Rodriguez .60 1.50
AGHS12 New York Yankees 1.00 2.50
AGHS13 David Wright .75 2.00
AGHS14 Ichiro Suzuki 1.25 3.00
AGHS15 Jon Lester .60 1.50
AGHS16 Alex Rodriguez 1.25 3.00
AGHS17 Chipper Jones 1.00 2.50
AGHS18 Derek Jeter 2.50 6.00
AGHS19 Albert Pujols 1.25 3.00
AGHS20 CC Sabathia .60 1.50
AGHS21 David Price .75 2.00
AGHS22 Ken Griffey Jr. 2.00 5.00
AGHS23 Brad Lidge .40 1.00
AGHS24 Mariano Rivera 1.25 3.00
AGHS25 Evan Longoria .60 1.50

2009 Topps Allen and Ginter Mini Creatures

COMPLETE SET (20) 75.00 150.00
STATED ODDS 1:48 HOBBY
LMT1 Bigfoot 3.00 8.00
LMT2 The Loch Ness Monster 3.00 8.00
LMT3 Grendel 3.00 8.00
LMT4 Unicorn 3.00 8.00
LMT5 The Invisible Man 3.00 8.00
LMT6 Kraken 3.00 8.00
LMT7 Medusa 3.00 8.00
LMT8 Sphinx 3.00 8.00
LMT9 Minotaur 3.00 8.00
LMT10 Dragon 3.00 8.00
LMT11 Leviathan 3.00 8.00
LMT12 Cyclops 3.00 8.00
LMT13 Vampire 3.00 8.00
LMT14 Griffin 3.00 8.00
LMT15 Chupacabra 3.00 8.00
LMT16 Cerberus 3.00 8.00
LMT17 Hydra 3.00 8.00
LMT18 Werewolf 3.00 8.00
LMT19 Fairy 3.00 8.00
LMT20 Yeti 3.00 8.00

2009 Topps Allen and Ginter Mini Extinct Creatures

RANDOM INSERTS IN PACKS
EA1 Velociraptor 12.50 30.00
EA2 Dodo 12.50 30.00
EA3 Xerces Blue 12.50 30.00
EA4 Labrador Duck 12.50 30.00
EA5 Eastern Elk 12.50 30.00

2009 Topps Allen and Ginter Mini Inventions of the Future

RANDOM INSERTS IN PACKS
FI1 Aeromobile 10.00 25.00
FI2 Clock Defier 10.00 25.00
FI3 Protecto-Bubble 10.00 25.00
FI4 Here-To-There-O-Matic 10.00 25.00
FI5 Mental Movies 10.00 25.00

2009 Topps Allen and Ginter Mini National Heroes

COMPLETE SET (40) 30.00 60.00
STATED ODDS 1:12 HOBBY
NH1 George Washington 2.00 5.00
NH2 Haile Selassie I 1.25 3.00
NH3 Toussaint L'Ouverture 1.25 3.00
NH4 Rigas Feraios 1.25 3.00
NH5 Yi Sun-sin 1.25 3.00
NH6 Giuseppe Garibaldi 1.25 3.00
NH7 Juan Santamaria 1.25 3.00
NH8 Tecun Uman 1.25 3.00
NH9 Jon Sigurosson 1.25 3.00
NH10 Mohandas Gandhi 2.00 5.00
NH11 Simon Bolivar 1.25 3.00
NH12 Alexander Nevsky 1.25 3.00
NH13 Lim Bo Seng 1.25 3.00
NH14 Sun Yat-sen 1.25 3.00
NH15 Tiradentes 1.25 3.00
NH16 Chiang Kai-Shek 1.25 3.00
NH17 William I 1.25 3.00
NH18 Severyn Nalyvaiko 1.25 3.00
NH19 Vasil Levski 1.25 3.00
NH20 Tadeusz Kosciuszko 1.25 3.00
NH21 Andranik Toros Ozanian 1.25 3.00
NH22 William Wallace 1.25 3.00
NH23 Oda Nobunaga 1.25 3.00
NH24 Milos Obilic 1.25 3.00
NH25 Niels Ebbeson 1.25 3.00
NH26 Jose Rizal 1.25 3.00
NH27 Alfonso Ugarte 1.25 3.00
NH28 Mustafa Ataturk 1.25 3.00
NH29 Nelson Mandela 1.25 3.00
NH30 El Cid 1.25 3.00
NH31 William Tell 1.25 3.00
NH32 Winston Churchill 1.25 3.00
NH33 Skanderbeg 1.25 3.00
NH34 General Jose de San Martin 1.25 3.00
NH35 Janos Damjanich 1.25 3.00
NH36 Joan of Arc 1.25 3.00
NH37 Abd al-Qadir 1.25 3.00
NH38 David Ben-Gurion 1.25 3.00
NH39 Benito Juarez 1.25 3.00
NH40 Marcus Garvey 1.25 3.00

2009 Topps Allen and Ginter Mini World's Biggest Hoaxes

COMPLETE SET (20) 12.50 30.00
STATED ODDS 1:12 HOBBY
HHB1 Charles Ponzi 1.25 3.00
HHB2 Alabama Changes Value of Pi 1.25 3.00
HHB3 The Runaway Bride 1.25 3.00
HHB4 Idaho 1.25 3.00
HHB5 The Turk 1.25 3.00
HHB6 Enron 1.25 3.00
HHB7 Anna Anderson 1.25 3.00
HHB8 Ferdinand Waldo Demara 1.25 3.00
HHB9 San Serriffe 1.25 3.00
HHB10 D.B. Cooper 1.25 3.00
HHB11 Wisconsin State Capitol Collapses 1.25 3.00
HHB12 Victor Lustig 1.25 3.00
HHB13 The War of the Worlds 1.25 3.00
HHB14 George Parker 1.25 3.00
HHB15 The Bathtub Hoax 1.25 3.00
HHB16 The Cottingley Fairies 1.25 3.00
HHB17 James Reavis 1.25 3.00
HHB18 The Piltdown Man 1.25 3.00
HHB19 The Cardiff Giant 1.25 3.00
HHB20 Cold Fusion 1.25 3.00

2009 Topps Allen and Ginter N43

COMPLETE SET (15) 20.00 50.00
ONE CABINET/N43 PER HOBBY BOX
AP Albert Pujols 3.00 8.00
AR Alex Rodriguez 3.00 8.00
CJ Chipper Jones 2.50 6.00
DM Daisuke Matsuzaka 1.50 4.00
DW David Wright 2.00 5.00
EL Evan Longoria 1.50 4.00
GS Grady Sizemore 1.50 4.00
JB Jay Bruce 1.50 4.00
JH Josh Hamilton 1.50 4.00
JU Justin Upton 1.50 4.00
MC Miguel Cabrera 2.50 6.00
MR Manny Ramirez 2.50 6.00
RH Ryan Howard 2.00 5.00
TL Tim Lincecum 1.50 4.00
RHA Roy Halladay 1.50 4.00

2009 Topps Allen and Ginter National Pride

COMPLETE SET (75) 10.00 25.00
APPX.ODDS ONE PER HOBBY PACK
NP1 Ervin Santana .30 .75
NP2 Justin Upton .50 1.25
NP3 Jason Bay .50 1.25
NP4 Geovany Soto .50 1.25
NP5 Ryan Dempster .30 .75
NP6 Johnny Cueto .50 1.25
NP7 Chipper Jones .75 2.00
NP8 Fausto Carmona .30 .75
NP9 Carlos Guillen .30 .75
NP10 Jose Reyes .50 1.25
NP11 Hiroki Kuroda .30 .75
NP12 Prince Fielder .50 1.25
NP13 Justin Morneau .50 1.25
NP14 Fransisco Rodriguez .50 1.25
NP15 Jorge Posada .50 1.25
NP16 Jake Peavy .30 .75
NP17 Felix Hernandez .50 1.25
NP18 Robinson Cano .50 1.25
NP19 Erik Bedard .30 .75
NP20 Akinori Iwamura .30 .75
NP21 Scott Hairston .30 .75
NP22 David Wright .60 1.50
NP23 Chien-Ming Wang .50 1.25
NP24 Chase Utley .50 1.25
NP25 Jonathan Sanchez .30 .75
NP26 Yunel Escobar .30 .75
NP27 John Lackey .50 1.25
NP28 Melvin Mora .30 .75
NP29 Alfonso Soriano .50 1.25
NP30 Jose Contreras .30 .75
NP31 Grady Sizemore .50 1.25
NP32 Rich Harden .30 .75
NP33 Hanley Ramirez .50 1.25
NP34 Nick Markakis .60 1.50
NP35 Manny Ramirez .75 2.00
NP36 Yovani Gallardo .30 .75
NP37 Johan Santana .50 1.25
NP38 Mariano Rivera 1.00 2.50
NP39 Shin-Soo Choo .50 1.25
NP40 Hideki Matsui .75 2.00
NP41 Raul Ibanez .50 1.25
NP42 Edgar Renteria .30 .75
NP43 Jose Lopez .30 .75
NP44 Yuniesky Betancourt .30 .75
NP45 Evan Longoria .50 1.25
NP46 Carlos Ruiz .30 .75
NP47 Ryan Howard .60 1.50
NP48 Jorge Cantu .30 .75
NP49 Max Scherzer .75 2.00
NP50 Jair Jurrjens .30 .75
NP51 Albert Pujols 1.00 2.50
NP52 Daisuke Matsuzaka .50 1.25
NP53 Vladimir Guerrero .50 1.25
NP54 Carlos Zambrano .50 1.25
NP55 Kosuke Fukudome .50 1.25
NP56 Edinson Volquez .30 .75
NP57 Victor Martinez .50 1.25
NP58 Derek Jeter 2.00 5.00
NP59 Miguel Cabrera .75 2.00
NP60 Stephen Drew .30 .75
NP61 Mark Teahen .30 .75
NP62 Ryan Braun .50 1.25
NP63 Carlos Beltran .50 1.25
NP64 Francisco Liriano .30 .75
NP65 Carlos Delgado .30 .75
NP66 Joba Chamberlain .30 .75
NP67 Adrian Gonzalez .60 1.50
NP68 Ichiro Suzuki 1.00 2.50
NP69 Ryan Rowland-Smith .30 .75
NP70 Carlos Pena .50 1.25
NP71 Josh Hamilton .50 1.25
NP72 Edgar Gonzalez .30 .75
NP73 Carlos Lee .30 .75
NP74 Yadier Molina 1.00 2.50
NP75 Alex Rodriguez 1.00 2.50

2009 Topps Allen and Ginter Relics

GROUP A ODDS 1:100 HOBBY
GROUP B ODDS 1:215 HOBBY
GROUP D ODDS 1:17 HOBBY
GROUP C ODDS 1:39 HOBBY
CARDS ARE NOT SERIAL-NUMBERED
PRINT RUNS PROVIDED BY TOPPS
AER Alex Rodriguez Pants 12.50 30.00
AL Adam LaRoche Jsy C 3.00 8.00
AP Albert Pujols Bat 15.00 40.00
AP2 A.Pujols Hat/190 * 20.00 50.00
AP3 A.Pujols Jsy/255 * 15.00 40.00
AR Alex Rios Bat/90 * A 30.00 60.00
AS Alfonso Soriano Bat/191 * A 4.00 10.00
AT A.Rashguard/250 * A 10.00 25.00
BBE B.Berg Card/250 * A 15.00 40.00
BC Bob Crowley A 10.00 25.00
BCA Cappelletto Shirt/250 * A 8.00 20.00
BD Blake DeWitt Bat C 4.00 10.00
BK B.Kenny Hair/250 * A 30.00 60.00
BTM Marlin Jsy/250 * A 10.00 25.00
BU B.J. Upton Jsy D 3.00 8.00
BY Brock Yates/250 * A 8.00 20.00
BZ Barry Zito Pants A 3.00 8.00
CB Carlos Beltran Jsy C 3.00 8.00
CC Coco Crisp Bat A 5.00 12.00
CJ Chipper Jones Jsy C 4.00 10.00
CK Casey Kotchman Jsy A 3.00 8.00
CM Cameron Maybin Bat C 3.00 8.00
CO Osterman/250 * A 15.00 40.00
CP Corey Patterson Bat C 3.00 8.00
CQ Carlos Quentin Jsy D 3.00 8.00
CS CC Sabathia Jsy 3.00 8.00
CU Chase Utley Jsy D 3.00 8.00
CW Chien-Ming Wang Jsy A 4.00 10.00
DAW D.Wright Btg Glv 12.50 30.00
DAW2 David Wright Jsy 3.00 8.00
DM Matsuzaka Jsy/110 * A 20.00 50.00
DO David Ortiz Jsy A 4.00 10.00
DOW D.Wilkins/250 * A 10.00 25.00
DW Dontrelle Willis Pants D 3.00 8.00
EC Chavez Pants/210 * A 12.50 30.00
EG Eric Gagne Jsy B 3.00 8.00
EL Evan Longoria Jsy D 5.00 12.00
FL Fred Lewis Bat C 3.00 8.00
GS Gary Sheffield Bat A 3.00 8.00
GSI Grady Sizemore Jsy D 3.00 8.00
HB Hank Blalock Bat A 3.00 8.00
HM Hideki Matsui Jsy B 10.00 25.00
HR Ramirez Bat/199 * A 12.50 30.00
HT H.Teter/250 * A 12.50 30.00
IK Iris Kyle Suit/250 * A 12.50 30.00
IS Ichiro Suzuki Jsy 6.00 15.00
IS2 Ichiro Suzuki Bat 6.00 15.00
JB Jay Bruce Jsy D 3.00 8.00
JD Jermaine Dye Bat C 3.00 8.00
JHI J.Higby/250 * A 10.00 25.00
JM Joe Mauer Jsy D 3.00 8.00
JR Jimmy Rollins Jsy D 3.00 8.00
JRH Rich Harden Pants A 3.00 8.00
JT Jim Thome Bat B 3.00 8.00
JU Justin Upton Jsy D 3.00 8.00
JW Jered Weaver Jsy D 3.00 8.00
KA Armstrong Jsy/250 * A 6.00 15.00
KF Kosuke Fukudome Jsy D 3.00 8.00
KM McConiughey/250 * A 8.00 20.00
LC Lynne Cox/250 * A 10.00 25.00
LM L.Merritt/250 * A 8.00 20.00
LO Opstedahl/250 * A 12.50 30.00
MC Mike Cameron Bat C 3.00 8.00
MCA Miguel Cabrera Jsy C 3.00 8.00
MH Matt Holliday Jsy D 3.00 8.00
MM Mantle Pants/250 * A 60.00 150.00
MME M.Metzger/250 * A 10.00 25.00
MMO Melvin Mora Bat C 3.00 8.00
MMU Mark Mulder Pants C 3.00 8.00
MO Magglio Ordonez Jsy D 3.00 8.00
MP M.Phelps/250 * A 20.00 50.00
MR Manny Ramirez Jsy A 4.00 10.00
MR2 M.Ramirez Bat/190 * C 8.00 20.00
MT Mark Teixeira Jsy 4.00 10.00
MTE Miguel Tejada Jsy B 3.00 8.00
MZ M.Lame/250 * A 12.50 30.00
NM Nate McLouth Jsy D 3.00 8.00
NS Swisher Bat/164 * A 15.00 40.00
PF Prince Fielder Bat C 3.00 8.00
RB Rocco Baldelli Bat 3.00 8.00
RB2 Rocco Baldelli Jsy 3.00 8.00
RC Robinson Cano Bat/195 * A 10.00 25.00
RD Ryan Doumit Jsy D 3.00 8.00
RF Richard Fosbury A 8.00 20.00
RH Ryan Howard Jsy 4.00 10.00
RH2 Ryan Howard Bat 5.00 12.00
RJB Ryan Braun Jsy D 4.00 10.00
RL Ryan Ludwick Jsy D 3.00 8.00
RMA R.Maddison/250 * A 8.00 20.00
RO Roy Oswalt Jsy A 8.00 20.00
RZ Ryan Zimmerman Bat C 3.00 8.00
SB S.Trafton/250 * A 8.00 20.00
SD S.Davis/250 * A 8.00 20.00
SR Scott Rolen Jsy C 3.00 8.00
SW S.Wiebe/250 * A 8.00 20.00
TH Travis Hafner Jsy C 3.00 8.00
THU Tim Hudson Jsy A 3.00 8.00
TL Tim Lincecum Jsy D 4.00 10.00
TLH Todd Helton Jsy C 3.00 8.00
VG Vladimir Guerrero Bat C 3.00 8.00
VW Vernon Wells Jsy A 3.00 8.00
WE W.Eller/250 * A 12.50 30.00
WS Simpson/250 * A 30.00 60.00
YE Yunel Escobar Jsy D 3.00 8.00
YG Yovani Gallardo Jsy D 3.00 8.00

2009 Topps Allen and Ginter Rip Cards

STATED ODDS 1:257 HOBBY
PRINT RUNS B/WN 5-99 COPIES PER
NO PRICING ON QTY 25 OR LESS
ALL LISTED PRICED ARE FOR RIPPED
UNRIPPED HAVE ADD'L CARDS WITHIN
COMMON UNRIPPED p/r 99 40.00 80.00
COMMON UNRIPPED p/r 50 50.00 100.00
RC4 Paul Konerko/99 6.00 15.00
RC9 Pat Neshek/99 6.00 15.00
RC10 Brian Giles/99 6.00 15.00
RC11 Jeff Francis/99 6.00 15.00
RC12 Jermaine Dye/50 6.00 15.00
RC13 Dan Uggla/50 6.00 15.00
RC14 Tim Hudson/50 6.00 15.00
RC15 Chris Young/50 6.00 15.00
RC19 John Lackey/99 6.00 15.00
RC23 Rafael Furcal/50 6.00 15.00
RC26 Derrek Lee/50 6.00 15.00
RC27 Cameron Maybin/99 6.00 15.00
RC28 Ryan Dempster/50 6.00 15.00
RC31 Yunel Escobar/99 6.00 15.00
RC34 Joakim Soria/50 6.00 15.00
RC38 Miguel Tejada/50 6.00 15.00
RC40 Shane Victorino/99 6.00 15.00
RC43 Garrett Atkins/50 6.00 15.00
RC44 Fausto Carmona/99 6.00 15.00
RC45 Mike Jacobs/99 6.00 15.00
RC47 Oliver Perez/99 6.00 15.00
RC49 James Loney/50 6.00 15.00
RC52 Rickie Weeks/99 6.00 15.00
RC56 Aubrey Huff/99 6.00 15.00
RC57 Chad Billingsley/50 6.00 15.00
RC58 Carlos Gomez/99 6.00 15.00
RC60 Mike Aviles/99 6.00 15.00
RC62 Joe Saunders/99 6.00 15.00
RC63 Derek Lowe/50 6.00 15.00
RC64 Travis Hafner/99 6.00 15.00
RC69 Kevin Kouzmanoff/50 6.00 15.00
RC71 Ryan Ludwick/50 6.00 15.00
RC74 Melvin Mora/99 6.00 15.00
RC76 Yadier Molina/99 6.00 15.00
RC77 Carlos Pena/50 6.00 15.00
RC80 Aramis Ramirez/50 6.00 15.00
RC81 Rocco Baldelli/50 6.00 15.00
RC85 Brandon Phillips/50 6.00 15.00
RC93 Eric Chavez/99 6.00 15.00
RC99 Mark Buehrle/50 6.00 15.00

2010 Topps Allen and Ginter

COMPLETE SET (350) 60.00 120.00
COMP.SET w/o SPs (300) 15.00 40.00
COMMON CARD (1-300) .15 .40
COMMON RC (1-300) .40 1.00
COMMON SP (301-350) 1.25 3.00
SP STATED ODDS 1:2 HOBBY
1 Adam Lind .25 .60
2 Everth Cabrera .15 .40
3 Ryan Braun .25 .60
4 Prince Fielder .25 .60
5 Edwin Jackson .15 .40
6 Madison Bumgarner RC 4.00 10.00
7 Ryan Howard .30 .75
8 Miguel Tejada .25 .60
9 Kelly Kulick .15 .40
10 Gary Stewart .15 .40
11 Wade Davis (RC) .60 1.50
12 Jesus Flores .15 .40
13 B.J. Upton .25 .60
14 Shane Victorino .25 .60
15 Carlos Quentin .15 .40
16 Carl Pavano .15 .40
17 Johan Santana .25 .60
18 Jose Lopez .15 .40
19 Tommy Hanson .15 .40
20 Sacagawea .15 .40
21 Ryan Kennelly .15 .40
22 Lucy .15 .40
23 Joe Mauer .30 .75
24 Brandon Webb .25 .60
25 Max Scherzer .40 1.00
26 Andy Pettitte .25 .60
27 Brad Hawpe .15 .40
28 Felipe Lopez .15 .40
29 Cole Hamels .30 .75
30 Rafael Furcal .15 .40
31 Miguel Montero .15 .40
32 Joba Chamberlain .15 .40
33 Bengie Molina .15 .40
34 Delmon Young .25 .60
35 John Lackey .25 .60
36 Victor Martinez .25 .60
37 Daniel McCutchen RC .60 1.50
38 Tiago Della Vega .15 .40
39 Josh Johnson .25 .60
40 Carlos Beltran .25 .60
41 Daniel Hudson RC .60 1.50
42 Mark DeRosa .15 .40
43 Yovani Gallardo .15 .40
44 Chris Coghlan .15 .40
45 Justin Verlander .40 1.00
46 Chad Billingsley .25 .60
47 Drew Stubbs RC 1.00 2.50
48 Alan Francis .15 .40
49 Jenrry Mejia RC .60 1.50
50 Jason Bay .25 .60
51 Matt Holliday .40 1.00
52 Gavin Floyd .15 .40
53 Jason Heyward RC 1.50 4.00
54 Tony Hawk .40 1.00
55 Esmil Rogers RC .40 1.00
56 Shin-Soo Choo .25 .60
57 Jacoby Ellsbury .30 .75
58 Colby Rasmus .25 .60
59 Ivory Crockett .15 .40
60 Chris Davis .25 .60
61 Michael Cuddyer .15 .40
62 Matt Kemp .30 .75
63 Matt Carson (RC) .40 1.00
64 Josh Beckett .15 .40
65 Andre Ethier .25 .60
66 Orlando Hudson .15 .40
67 Carl Crawford .25 .60
68 Betelgeuse .15 .40
69 Clay Buchholz .15 .40
70 Joey Votto .40 1.00
71 Hunter Pence .25 .60
72 Erick Aybar .15 .40
73 Avery Jenkins .15 .40
74 Ryan Ludwick .15 .40
75 Jayson Werth .25 .60
76 Joakim Soria .15 .40
77 Ricky Romero .15 .40
78 Leonardo da Vinci .15 .40
79 James Loney .15 .40
80 Will Venable .15 .40
81 Cliff Lee .25 .60
82 Justin Upton .25 .60
83 David Wright .30 .75
84 Elvis Andrus .25 .60
85 Yunel Escobar .15 .40
86 Andrew Bailey .15 .40
87 Alexei Ramirez .25 .60
88 Kosuke Fukudome .25 .60
89 Joel Pineiro .15 .40
90 Kevin Kouzmanoff .15 .40
91 Carlos Zambrano .25 .60
92 Randy Oitker .15 .40
93 Brandon Inge .25 .60
94 Luke Hochevar .15 .40
95 Judson Laipply .15 .40
96 Roy Halladay .25 .60
97 Zach Duke .15 .40
98 Johnny Cueto .25 .60
99 Anthony Gatto .15 .40
100 Matt LaPorta .15 .40
101 Mark Buehrle .25 .60
102 Torii Hunter .15 .40
103 Niccolo Machiavelli .15 .40

104 Mahlon Duckett .15 .40
105 Nicolaus Copernicus .15 .40
106 Dustin Pedroia .40 1.00
107 Adam Dunn .25 .60
108 Paul Konerko .25 .60
109 Ian Kinsler .25 .60
110 Sherlock Holmes .15 .40
111 Josh Willingham .25 .60
112 Tyler Bradt .15 .40
113 Billy Butler .15 .40
114 Milton Bradley .15 .40
115 Trevor Hoffman .25 .60
116 Galileo Galilei .15 .40
117 Neil Walker (RC) .60 1.50
118 Eric Young Jr. (RC) .40 1.00
119 Dan Uggla .15 .40
120 Nick Swisher .25 .60
121 Francisco Rodriguez .25 .60
122 Yadier Molina .50 1.25
123 Mariano Rivera .50 1.25
124 Andrew McCutchen .40 1.00
125 Hideki Matsui .40 1.00
126 Chipper Jones .40 1.00
127 Albert Pujols .50 1.25
128 Hans Florine .15 .40
129 Johannes Gutenberg .15 .40
130 Area 51 .15 .40
131 Tyler Flowers RC .60 1.50
132 David Price .30 .75
133 Nelson Cruz .40 1.00
134 Vladimir Guerrero .25 .60
135 Ken Blackburn .15 .40
136 Garrett Jones .15 .40
137 Ryan Zimmerman .25 .60
138 Javier Vazquez .15 .40
139 Miguel Cabrera .40 1.00
140 Brandon Allen (RC) .40 1.00
141 Matt Cain .25 .60
142 Ubaldo Jimenez .15 .40
143 Jorge Posada .25 .60
144 Stuart Scott .40 1.00
145 Jim Thome .25 .60
146 Carlos Lee .15 .40
147 Cristian Guzman .15 .40
148 Anne Donovan .15 .40
149 Ichiro Suzuki .50 1.25
150 Grady Sizemore .25 .60
151 Kanekoa Texeira RC .40 1.00
152 The Parthenon .15 .40
153 Jay Bruce .25 .60
154 Juan Francisco RC .60 1.50
155 Carlos Carrasco (RC) 1.00 2.50
156 Cameron Maybin .15 .40
157 Kevin Youkilis .15 .40
158 Mark Teixeira .25 .60
159 Denard Span .15 .40
160 Derrek Lee .15 .40
161 Luis Durango RC .40 1.00
162 Juan Pierre .15 .40
163 Raul Ibanez .25 .60
164 Kyle Blanks .15 .40
165 Nick Jacoby .15 .40
166 Chris Tillman .15 .40
167 Dan Haren .15 .40
168 Rickie Weeks .15 .40
169 Felix Hernandez .25 .60
170 Adrian Gonzalez .30 .75
171 Michael Young .15 .40
172 Ian Desmond (RC) .60 1.50
173 Jimmy Rollins .25 .60
174 Eric Byrnes .15 .40
175 Tim Lincecum .25 .60
176 Preston Pittman .15 .40
177 Pedro Feliz .15 .40
178 Josh Hamilton .25 .60
179 Ben Zobrist .25 .60
180 Gordon Beckham .15 .40
181 Tyler Colvin RC .60 1.50
182 Chris Carpenter .25 .60
183 Tommy Manzella (RC) .40 1.00
184 Jake Peavy .15 .40
185 X-Rays .15 .40
186 Jose Reyes .25 .60
187 Jair Jurrjens .15 .40
188 Jason Bartlett .15 .40
189 Howie Kendrick .15 .40
190 Randy Wolf .15 .40
191 Justin Morneau .25 .60
192 Tom Knapp .15 .40
193 Tony Hoard/Rory .15 .40
194 Nyjer Morgan .15 .40
195 Sergio Santos (RC) .40 1.00
196 Scott Baker .15 .40
197 Johnny Damon .25 .60
198 A.J. Pierzynski .15 .40
199 Summer Sanders .15 .40
200 Lance Berkman .25 .60
201 Pablo Sandoval .25 .60
202 Aramis Ramirez .15 .40
203 Sig Hansen .15 .40
204 Russell Martin .15 .40
205 Meb Keflezighi .15 .40
206 J.D. Drew .15 .40
207 Wandy Rodriguez .15 .40
208 Evan Longoria .25 .60
209 Alex Gordon .25 .60
210 Chris Johnson RC .60 1.50
211 Johnny Strange .15 .40
212 Ken Griffey Jr. .75 2.00
213 Mark Reynolds .15 .40
214 CC Sabathia .25 .60
215 Daniel Murphy .30 .75
216 Jordin Sparks .15 .40
217 James Shields .15 .40
218 Todd Helton .25 .60
219 Adam Wainwright .25 .60
220 Manny Ramirez .40 1.00
221 Mike Leake RC 1.25 3.00
222 Craig Gentry RC .40 1.00
223 Jason Kubel .15 .40
224 Ian Stewart .15 .40
225 Mark Teahen .15 .40
226 Brian McCann .25 .60
227 Henry Rodriguez RC .40 1.00
228 Chase Utley .25 .60
229 Franklin Gutierrez .15 .40
230 Brian Roberts .15 .40
231 Travis Snider .15 .40
232 Hubertus Wawra .15 .40
233 Rick Ankiel .15 .40
234 Nick Johnson .15 .40
235 Carlos Guillen .15 .40
236 Shawn Johnson .40 1.00
237 Kevin Millwood .15 .40
238 Michael Brantley RC .60 1.50
239 Mike Cameron .15 .40
240 Aaron Hill .15 .40
241 Derek Lowe .15 .40
242 Jules Verne .15 .40
243 Jim Zapp .15 .40
244 Aaron Cook .15 .40
245 Michael Dunn RC .40 1.00
246 Geovany Soto .25 .60
247 Rajai Davis .15 .40
248 Jason Marquis .15 .40
249 Alfonso Soriano .25 .60
250 Magglio Ordonez .25 .60
251 Chase Headley .15 .40
252 Matt Garza .15 .40
253 Adam Moore RC .40 1.00
254 Rich Harden .15 .40
255 Robert Scott .15 .40
256 Rick Porcello .25 .60
257 Ervin Santana .15 .40
258 Ryan Dempster .15 .40
259 Scott Feldman .15 .40
260 Chris Young .15 .40
261 Adam Jones .25 .60
262 Zack Greinke .40 1.00
263 Ruben Tejada RC .60 1.50
264 Captain Nemo .15 .40
265 Kendry Morales .15 .40
266 Adam LaRoche .15 .40
267 Martin Prado .15 .40
268 Brad Kilby RC .40 1.00
269 A.J. Burnett .15 .40
270 Max Poser .15 .40
271 King Tut .15 .40
272 David Blaine .15 .40
273 David DeJesus .15 .40
274 Nick Markakis .30 .75
275 Clayton Kershaw .60 1.50
276 Daniel Runzler RC .60 1.50
277 Regis Philbin .15 .40
278 Jeff Francoeur .25 .60
279 Curtis Granderson .30 .75
280 Koji Uehara .25 .60
281 Kurt Suzuki .15 .40
282 Tyson Ross RC .40 1.00
283 Hank Presswood .15 .40
284 Dustin Richardson RC .40 1.00
285 Alex Rodriguez .50 1.25
286 Revolving Door .25 .60
287 Drew Brees .40 1.00
288 Bobby Jenks .15 .40
289 Hanley Ramirez .25 .60
290 Jon Lester .25 .60
291 Ron Teasley .15 .40
292 Chris Pettit RC .40 1.00
293 Troy Tulowitzki .25 .60
294 Buster Posey RC 3.00 8.00
295 Josh Thole RC .60 1.50
296 Barry Zito .25 .60
297 Isaac Newton .15 .40
298 Jorge Cantu .15 .40
299 Robinson Cano .25 .60
300 Nolan Reimold .15 .40
301 Gaby Sanchez SP 1.25 3.00
302 Daric Barton SP 1.25 3.00
303 Trevor Cahill SP 1.25 3.00
304 Carlos Pena SP 1.25 3.00
305 Kelly Johnson SP 1.25 3.00
306 Brandon Phillips SP 1.25 3.00
307 Akinori Iwamura SP 1.25 3.00
308 Adrian Beltre SP 3.00 8.00
309 Casey McGehee SP 1.25 3.00
310 Placido Polanco SP 1.25 3.00
311 Chone Figgins SP 1.25 3.00
312 Carlos Ruiz SP 1.25 3.00
313 Ryan Doumit SP 1.25 3.00
314 Ivan Rodriguez SP 1.25 3.00
315 Bobby Abreu SP 1.25 3.00
316 Nate McLouth SP 1.25 3.00
317 Alex Rios SP .75 2.00
318 Carlos Gonzalez SP 2.00 5.00
319 Austin Jackson SP RC 1.25 3.00
320 Scott Sizemore SP RC 1.25 3.00
321 Carlos Gomez SP 1.25 3.00
322 Gary Matthews SP 1.25 3.00
323 Angel Pagan SP 1.25 3.00
324 Randy Winn SP 1.25 3.00
325 Brett Gardner SP 2.00 5.00
326 Aaron Rowand SP 1.25 3.00
327 Vernon Wells SP 1.25 3.00
328 Jered Weaver SP 2.00 5.00
329 Troy Glaus SP 1.25 3.00
330 Jonathan Papelbon SP 1.25 3.00
331 Huston Street SP 1.25 3.00
332 Ricky Nolasco SP 1.25 3.00
333 Roy Oswalt SP 1.25 3.00
334 Brett Myers SP 1.25 3.00
335 Jonathan Broxton SP 1.25 3.00
336 Hiroki Kuroda SP 1.25 3.00
337 Joe Nathan SP 1.25 3.00
338 Francisco Liriano SP 1.25 3.00
339 Ben Sheets SP 1.25 3.00
340 Brad Lidge SP 1.25 3.00
341 Jon Garland SP 1.25 3.00
342 Erik Bedard SP 1.25 3.00
343 Brad Penny SP 1.25 3.00
344 Derek Holland SP 1.25 3.00
345 Stephen Drew SP 1.25 3.00
346 Ryan Theriot SP 1.25 3.00
347 Orlando Cabrera SP 1.25 3.00
348 Asdrubal Cabrera SP 2.00 5.00
349 Yuniesky Betancourt SP 1.25 3.00
350 Alcides Escobar SP 1.25 3.00

2010 Topps Allen and Ginter Mini

*MINI 1-300: .75X TO 2X BASIC
*MINI 1-300 RC: .5X TO 1.2X BASIC RC's
APPX. ONE MINI PER PACK
*MINI SP 301-350: .5X TO 1.2X BASIC SP
MINI SP ODDS 1:13 HOBBY
COMMON CARD (351-400) 6.00 15.00
351-400 RANDOM WITHIN RIP CARDS
STRASBURG 401 ISSUED IN PACKS
OVERALL PLATE ODDS 1:799 HOBBY
351 Cole Hamels EXT 12.00 30.00
352 Billy Butler EXT 30.00 60.00
353 Daisuke Matsuzaka EXT 30.00 60.00
354 Stephen Drew EXT 30.00 60.00
355 Ryan Braun EXT 20.00 50.00
356 Mark Teixeira EXT 20.00 50.00
357 Chipper Jones EXT 40.00 80.00
358 Justin Morneau EXT 20.00 50.00
359 Adrian Gonzalez EXT 6.00 15.00
360 Dustin Pedroia EXT 30.00 60.00
361 Miguel Cabrera EXT 30.00 60.00
362 Carlos Beltran EXT 10.00 25.00
363 Lance Berkman EXT 30.00 60.00
364 Kevin Kouzmanoff EXT 10.00 25.00
365 A.J. Burnett EXT 20.00 50.00
366 Tim Lincecum EXT 12.50 30.00
367 Francisco Rodriguez EXT 6.00 15.00
368 Zack Greinke EXT 20.00 50.00
369 Andre Ethier EXT 6.00 15.00
370 Hideki Matsui EXT 6.00 15.00
371 Alexei Ramirez EXT 6.00 15.00
372 Grady Sizemore EXT 20.00 50.00
373 Joe Mauer EXT 20.00 50.00
374 Adam Lind EXT 12.00 30.00
375 Kurt Suzuki EXT 10.00 25.00
376 Rick Porcello EXT 20.00 50.00
377 Felix Hernandez EXT 6.00 15.00
378 Albert Pujols EXT 20.00 50.00
379 Adam Dunn EXT 10.00 25.00
380 Brandon Webb EXT 20.00 50.00
381 Pablo Sandoval EXT 12.50 30.00
382 Chris Young EXT 20.00 50.00
383 Tommy Hanson EXT 30.00 60.00
384 Adam Jones EXT 20.00 50.00
385 Joe Nathan EXT 20.00 50.00
386 Andy Pettitte EXT 15.00 40.00
387 Gordon Beckham EXT 20.00 50.00
388 Alfonso Soriano EXT 6.00 15.00
389 Hanley Ramirez EXT 30.00 60.00
390 Torii Hunter EXT 20.00 50.00
391 Matt Garza EXT 6.00 15.00
392 Johnny Cueto EXT 20.00 50.00
393 Prince Fielder EXT 30.00 60.00
394 Andrew McCutchen EXT 30.00 60.00
395 Ken Griffey Jr. EXT 50.00 120.00
396 Ryan Howard EXT 10.00 25.00
397 Todd Helton EXT 6.00 15.00
398 Kosuke Fukudome EXT 30.00 60.00
399 Roy Halladay EXT 20.00 50.00
400 Matt Kemp EXT 40.00 80.00
401 Stephen Strasburg 12.00 30.00

2010 Topps Allen and Ginter Mini A and G Back

*A & G BACK: 1X TO 2.5X BASIC
*A & G BACK RCs: .6X TO 1.5X BASIC RCs
STATED ODDS 1:5 HOBBY
*A & G BACK SP: .6X TO 1.5X BASIC SP
SP STATED ODDS 1:65 HOBBY

2010 Topps Allen and Ginter Mini Black

*BLACK: 2X TO 5X BASIC
*BLACK RCs: .75X TO 2X BASIC RCs
STATED ODDS 1:10 HOBBY
*BLACK SP: .75X TO 2X BASIC SP
SP STATED ODDS 1:130 HOBBY

2010 Topps Allen and Ginter Mini No Card Number

*NO NBR: 8X TO 20X BASIC
*NO NBR RCs: 3X TO 8X BASIC RCs
*NO NBR SP: 1.2X TO 3X BASIC SP
STATED ODDS 1:140 HOBBY

2010 Topps Allen and Ginter Autographs

STATED ODDS 1:HOBBY
ASTERISK EQUALS PARTIAL EXCHANGE
AD Anne Donovan 6.00 15.00
AE Alcides Escobar 4.00 10.00
AEI Andre Ethier EXCH * 4.00 10.00
AF Alan Francis 6.00 15.00
AG Alex Gordon 40.00 80.00
AGA Anthony Gatto 6.00 15.00
AGO Adrian Gonzalez 8.00 20.00
AJ Adam Jones 6.00 15.00
AJE Avery Jenkins 30.00 60.00
AL Adam Lind 5.00 12.00
AM Andrew McCutchen 25.00 60.00
AR Alexei Ramirez 8.00 20.00
BD Brian Duensing 5.00 12.00
BJU B.J. Upton 10.00 25.00
CC Chris Coghlan 6.00 15.00
CK Clayton Kershaw 40.00 100.00
CM Cameron Maybin 4.00 10.00
CP Cliff Pennington 6.00 15.00
CR Colby Rasmus 4.00 10.00
CV Chris Volstad 4.00 10.00
CY Chris Young 4.00 10.00
DB David Blaine 40.00 80.00
DBR Drew Brees 75.00 200.00
DD Dale Davis 8.00 20.00
DM Daniel McCutchen 4.00 10.00
DP Dustin Pedroia 20.00 50.00
DS Drew Stubbs 4.00 10.00
DT Darren Taylor 4.00 10.00
EC Everth Cabrera 4.00 10.00
GS Gary Stewart 10.00 25.00
GSI Glenn Singleman 8.00 20.00
HF Hans Florine 8.00 20.00
HP Hank Presswood 10.00 25.00
HW Hubertus Wawra 5.00 12.00
IC Ivory Crockett 12.50 30.00
IK Ian Kinsler 5.00 12.00
JC Johnny Cueto 6.00 15.00
JCL Jeff Clement 5.00 12.00
JF Jeff Francis 4.00 10.00
JH Jason Heyward 10.00 25.00
JK Jason Kubel 6.00 15.00
JL Judson Laipply 6.00 15.00
JM Jason Motte 5.00 12.00
JO Josh Outman 4.00 10.00
JP Jonathan Papelbon 12.00 30.00
JR Juan Rivera 5.00 12.00
JRT J.R. Towles 4.00 10.00
JS Jordin Sparks 30.00 60.00
JST Johnny Strange 6.00 15.00
JU Justin Upton 8.00 20.00
JW Josh Willingham 5.00 12.00
JZ Jim Zapp 12.00 30.00
KB Ken Blackburn 10.00 25.00
KK Kelly Kulick 10.00 25.00
KU Koji Uehara 8.00 20.00
MB Michael Bourn 5.00 12.00
MC Miguel Cabrera 75.00 150.00
MD Mahlon Duckett 20.00 50.00
MH Matt Holliday 50.00 100.00
MK Matt Kemp 12.50 30.00
MKE Meb Keflezighi 10.00 25.00
MM Marvin Miller 40.00 80.00
MP Mike Parsons 8.00 20.00
MPO Max Poser 4.00 10.00
MS Max Scherzer 25.00 60.00
MTB Mitchell Boggs 5.00 12.00
NF Neftali Feliz 4.00 10.00
PP Placido Polanco 5.00 12.00
PPI Preston Pittman 8.00 20.00
PS Pablo Sandoval 12.00 30.00
RB Ryan Braun 15.00 40.00
RH Ryan Howard 12.00 30.00
RHI Rich Hill 5.00 12.00
RK Ryan Kennelly 10.00 25.00
RN Ricky Nolasco 4.00 10.00
RO Ross Ohlendorf 4.00 10.00
ROI Randy Oitker 5.00 12.00
RP Rick Porcello 6.00 15.00
RPE Ryan Perry 4.00 10.00
RPH Regis Philbin 12.00 50.00
RS Robert Scott 15.00 40.00
RT Ron Teasley 10.00 25.00
RTH Tony Hoard/Rory 8.00 20.00
RZ Ryan Zimmerman 8.00 20.00
SH Sig Hansen 30.00 60.00
SJ Shawn Johnson 50.00 100.00
SK Scott Kazmir 50.00 100.00
SS Stephen Strasburg 400.00 600.00
SS Stuart Scott 50.00 120.00
SSA Summer Sanders 15.00 40.00
SV Shane Victorino 10.00 25.00
TB Tyler Bradt 4.00 10.00
TC Trevor Crowe 4.00 10.00
TDV Tiago Della Vega 4.00 10.00
TH Tommy Hanson 5.00 12.00
THA Tony Hawk 75.00 150.00
TK Tom Knapp 12.50 30.00
TT Troy Tulowitzki 12.50 30.00
VW Vernon Wells 40.00 80.00
YE Yunel Escobar 5.00 12.00
YG Yovani Gallardo 4.00 10.00
ZS Zac Sunderland 4.00 10.00

2010 Topps Allen and Ginter Baseball Highlights

COMPLETE SET (15) 8.00 20.00
STATED ODDS 1:10 HOBBY
AGHS1 Chase Utley .60 1.50
AGHS2 Mark Buehrle .60 1.50
AGHS3 Derek Jeter 2.50 6.00
AGHS4 Mariano Rivera 1.25 3.00
AGHS5 Ichiro Suzuki 1.25 3.00
AGHS6 Johnny Damon .60 1.50
AGHS7 Carl Crawford .60 1.50
AGHS8 Dewayne Wise .40 1.00
AGHS9 Jimmy Rollins .60 1.50
AGHS10 Hideki Matsui 1.00 2.50
AGHS11 Andre Ethier .60 1.50
AGHS12 Troy Tulowitzki 1.00 2.50
AGHS13 Jonathan Sanchez .40 1.00
AGHS14 Mark Teixeira .60 1.50
AGHS15 Daniel Murphy .75 2.00

2010 Topps Allen and Ginter Cabinets

NCCB1 President Chester A. Arthur/Washington Roebling/John A. Roebling/Emily Roeb 2.00 5.00
NCCB2 Andrew McCutchen 2.50 6.00
NCCB3 President Herbert Hoover Elwood Mead 2.00 5.00
NCCB4 Lance Berkman/Ivan Rodriguez Carlos Lee 2.00 5.00
NCCB5 President Theodore Roosevelt/John Frank Stevens/George Washington Goethals/ 2.00 5.00
NCCB6 CC/Rivera/Hideki/Jeter 4.00 10.00
NCCB7 Joe Mauer 3.00 8.00
NCCB8 George Washington/Thomas Jefferson/Theodore Roosevelt Abraham Lincoln 2.00 5.00
NCCB9 Ellsbury/Pettitte/Posada 2.50 6.00
NCCB10 Gerald R. Ford/Richard M. Nixon/Wally Hickel 2.00 5.00

2010 Topps Allen and Ginter Mini Celestial Stars

RANDOM INSERTS IN PACKS
CS1 Mark Teixeira 1.50 4.00
CS2 Prince Fielder 1.50 4.00
CS3 Tim Lincecum 1.50 4.00
CS4 Derek Jeter 6.00 15.00
CS5 Dustin Pedroia 2.50 6.00
CS6 Cliff Lee 1.50 4.00
CS7 Evan Longoria 1.50 4.00
CS8 Ryan Howard 2.00 5.00
CS9 David Wright 2.00 5.00
CS10 Albert Pujols 3.00 8.00
CS11 Vladimir Guerrero 1.50 4.00
CS12 Johan Santana 1.50 4.00

2010 Topps Allen and Ginter Mini Creatures of Legend, Myth and Joy

STATED ODDS 1:288 HOBBY
CLMJ1 Santa Claus 10.00 25.00
CLMJ2 The Easter Bunny 10.00 25.00
CLMJ3 The Tooth Fairy 10.00 25.00
CLMJ4 Goldilocks 10.00 25.00
CLMJ5 Little Red Riding Hood 10.00 25.00
CLMJ6 Paul Bunyan 10.00 25.00
CLMJ7 Jack and the Beanstalk 10.00 25.00
CLMJ8 Peter Pan 10.00 25.00
CLMJ9 Three Little Pigs 10.00 25.00
CLMJ10 The Little Engine That Could 10.00 25.00

2010 Topps Allen and Ginter Mini Lords of Olympus

COMPLETE SET (25) 12.50 30.00
STATED ODDS 1:12 HOBBY
LO1 Zeus 1.25 3.00
LO2 Poseidon 1.25 3.00
LO3 Hades 1.25 3.00
LO4 Hera 1.25 3.00
LO5 Athena 1.25 3.00
LO6 Apollo 1.25 3.00
LO7 Aphrodite 1.25 3.00
LO8 Hermes 1.25 3.00
LO9 Artemis 1.25 3.00
LO10 Gaea 1.25 3.00
LO11 Uranus 1.25 3.00
LO12 Cronos 1.25 3.00
LO13 Prometheus 1.25 3.00
LO14 Phoebe 1.25 3.00
LO15 Demeter 1.25 3.00
LO16 Persephone 1.25 3.00
LO17 Dionysus 1.25 3.00
LO18 Eros 1.25 3.00
LO19 Helios 1.25 3.00
LO20 Thanatos 1.25 3.00
LO21 Pan 1.25 3.00
LO22 Nemesis 1.25 3.00
LO23 The Fates 1.25 3.00
LO24 The Muses 1.25 3.00
LO25 Atlas 1.25 3.00

2010 Topps Allen and Ginter Mini Monsters of the Mesozoic

COMPLETE SET (25) 12.50 30.00
STATED ODDS 1:12 HOBBY
MM1 Tyrannosaurus Rex 1.25 3.00
MM2 Triceratops 1.25 3.00
MM3 Stegosaurus 1.25 3.00
MM4 Velociraptor 1.25 3.00
MM5 Allosaurus 1.25 3.00
MM6 Megalosaurus 1.25 3.00
MM7 Spinosaurus 1.25 3.00
MM8 Ankylosaurus 1.25 3.00
MM9 Apatosaurus 1.25 3.00
MM10 Brachiosaurus 1.25 3.00
MM11 Diplodocus 1.25 3.00
MM12 Iguanodon 1.25 3.00
MM13 Pachycephalosaurus 1.25 3.00
MM14 Pentaceratops 1.25 3.00
MM15 Protoceratops 1.25 3.00
MM16 Ultrasaurus 1.25 3.00
MM17 Dilophosaurus 1.25 3.00
MM18 Supersaurus 1.25 3.00
MM19 Nomingia 1.25 3.00
MM20 Oviraptor 1.25 3.00
MM21 Bambiraptor 1.25 3.00
MM22 Protarchaeopteryx 1.25 3.00
MM23 Carcharodontosaurus 1.25 3.00
MM24 Carnotaurus 1.25 3.00
MM25 Giganotosaurus 1.25 3.00

2010 Topps Allen and Ginter Mini National Animals

COMPLETE SET (50) 12.50 30.00
STATED ODDS 1:8 HOBBY
NA1 Cougar 1.25 3.00
NA2 Cuban Crocodile 1.25 3.00
NA3 Falcon 1.25 3.00
NA4 Cheetah 1.25 3.00
NA5 Cow 1.25 3.00
NA6 Kangaroo 1.25 3.00
NA7 Ostrich 1.25 3.00
NA8 Chihuahua 1.25 3.00
NA9 Jaguar 1.25 3.00
NA10 Bull 1.25 3.00
NA11 Harpy Eagle 1.25 3.00
NA12 Markhor 1.25 3.00
NA13 African Elephant 1.25 3.00
NA14 Barbary Macaque 1.25 3.00
NA15 Giant Panda 1.25 3.00
NA16 Leopard 1.25 3.00
NA17 Camel 1.25 3.00
NA18 Beaver 1.25 3.00
NA19 Alpaca 1.25 3.00
NA20 Lion 1.25 3.00
NA21 Lynx 1.25 3.00
NA22 Slag 1.25 3.00
NA23 Elk 1.25 3.00
NA24 Condor 1.25 3.00
NA25 Wisent 1.25 3.00
NA26 Gray Wolf 1.25 3.00
NA27 Gallic Rooster 1.25 3.00
NA28 Sable Antelope 1.25 3.00
NA29 Flamingo 1.25 3.00
NA30 Koi 1.25 3.00
NA31 Ashy-faced Owl 1.25 3.00
NA32 Bulldog 1.25 3.00
NA33 Brown Bear 1.25 3.00
NA34 White-tailed Deer 1.25 3.00
NA35 Russian Bear 1.25 3.00
NA36 Dolphin 1.25 3.00
NA37 Komodo Dragon 1.25 3.00
NA38 Llama 1.25 3.00
NA39 Sheep 1.25 3.00
NA40 King Cobra 1.25 3.00
NA41 Green-and-black Streamertail 1.25 3.00
NA42 Carabao 1.25 3.00
NA43 Water Buffalo 1.25 3.00
NA44 Israeli Gazelle 1.25 3.00
NA45 Italian Wolf 1.25 3.00
NA46 Ring Tailed Lemur 1.25 3.00
NA47 Tiger 1.25 3.00
NA48 Dalmatian 1.25 3.00
NA49 Zebra 1.25 3.00
NA50 Bald Eagle 1.50 4.00

2010 Topps Allen and Ginter Mini Saltiest Sailors

RANDOM INSERTS IN PACKS
WSS1 Blackbeard 20.00 50.00
WSS2 Ned Low 20.00 50.00
WSS3 Jack Rackham 20.00 50.00
WSS4 Stede Bonnet 20.00 50.00
WSS5 Black Bart 20.00 50.00
WSS6 Captain Kidd 20.00 50.00
WSS7 Henry Morgan 20.00 50.00
WSS8 Edward England 20.00 50.00
WSS9 Thomas Tew 20.00 50.00
WSS10 Charles Vane 20.00 50.00

2010 Topps Allen and Ginter Mini Sailors of the Seven Seas

COMPLETE SET (10) 10.00 25.00
STATED ODDS 1:24 HOBBY
SSS1 Christopher Columbus 1.50 4.00
SSS2 Sir Francis Drake 1.50 4.00
SSS3 Sir Walter Raleigh 1.50 4.00
SSS4 Vasco Nunez de Balboa 1.50 4.00
SSS5 Francisco Vasquez de Coronado 1.50 4.00
SSS6 Hernando de Cortes 1.50 4.00
SSS7 Hernando de Soto 1.50 4.00
SSS8 Henry Hudson 1.50 4.00
SSS9 Francisco Pizarro 1.50 4.00
SSS10 Juan Ponce de Leon 1.50 4.00

2010 Topps Allen and Ginter Mini World's Biggest

RANDOM INSERTS IN RETAIL PACKS
WB1 Blue Whale 2.00 5.00
WB2 Burj Khalifa 2.00 5.00
WB3 Prague Castle 2.00 5.00
WB4 General Sherman Sequoia 2.00 5.00
WB5 Mount Everest 2.00 5.00
WB6 Antarctica 6.00 15.00
WB7 Sahara 6.00 15.00
WB8 Angel Falls 6.00 15.00
WB9 The Amazon 6.00 15.00
WB10 Steamboat Geyser 6.00 15.00
WB11 Lake Pontchartrain Causeway 6.00 15.00
WB12 The Nile 6.00 15.00
WB13 Russia 6.00 15.00
WB14 Three Gorges Dam 6.00 15.00
WB15 Golden Jubilee 6.00 15.00
WB16 Polar Bear 6.00 15.00
WB17 African Elephant 6.00 15.00
WB18 Eastern Lowland Gorilla 6.00 15.00
WB19 Goliath Birdeater 6.00 15.00
WB20 World's Largest Collection of World's Smallest Versions of World's Largest 6.00 15.00
WB21 Large Hadron Collider 6.00 15.00
WB22 1966 Leonid Meteor Shower 6.00 15.00
WB23 Sedan Crater 6.00 15.00
WB24 Kuthodaw Pagoda 6.00 15.00
WB25 Spring Temple Buddha 6.00 15.00

2010 Topps Allen and Ginter Mini World's Greatest Word Smiths

COMPLETE SET (15) 12.50 30.00
STATED ODDS 1:24 HOBBY
WGWS1 Homer 1.50 4.00
WGWS2 William Shakespeare 1.50 4.00
WGWS3 Washington Irving 1.50 4.00
WGWS4 Miguel de Cervantes 1.50 4.00
WGWS5 Fyodor Dostoevsky 1.50 4.00
WGWS6 Victor Hugo 1.50 4.00
WGWS7 Shen Kuo 1.50 4.00
WGWS8 John Milton 1.50 4.00
WGWS9 Dante Alighieri 1.50 4.00
WGWS10 Edgar Allan Poe 1.50 4.00
WGWS11 Marcus Aurelius 1.50 4.00
WGWS12 Virgil 1.50 4.00
WGWS13 John Bunyan 1.50 4.00
WGWS14 Plato 1.50 4.00
WGWS15 Confucius 1.50 4.00

2010 Topps Allen and Ginter N43

AE Andre Ethier 1.25 3.00
AM Andrew McCutchen 2.00 5.00
AP Albert Pujols 2.50 6.00
AR Alex Rodriguez 2.50 6.00
BU B.J. Upton 1.25 3.00
EL Evan Longoria 1.25 3.00
HP Hunter Pence 1.25 3.00
HR Hanley Ramirez 1.25 3.00
JM Joe Mauer 1.50 4.00
JU Justin Upton 1.25 3.00
MT Mark Teixeira 1.25 3.00
NM Nick Markakis 1.50 4.00
PF Prince Fielder 1.25 3.00
RB Ryan Braun 1.25 3.00
RH Ryan Howard 1.50 4.00

2010 Topps Allen and Ginter Relics

STATED ODDS 1:11 HOBBY
AD Adam Dunn 3.00 8.00
AD Anne Donovan 5.00 12.00
AE Andre Ethier 3.00 8.00
AF Alan Francis 6.00 15.00
AG Adrian Gonzalez Bat 3.00 8.00
AGA Anthony Gatto 5.00 12.00
AH Aaron Hill 3.00 8.00
AJ Adam Jones 3.00 8.00
AJ Avery Jenkins 20.00 50.00
AL Adam Lind 3.00 8.00
ARA Aramis Ramirez 3.00 8.00
AS Alfonso Soriano 3.00 8.00
BA Brett Anderson 3.00 8.00
BB Billy Butler 3.00 8.00
BM Brian McCann 3.00 8.00
BP Buster Posey 10.00 25.00
BR Brian Roberts 3.00 8.00
BU B.J. Upton 3.00 8.00
CC Chris Coghlan 3.00 8.00
CL Carlos Lee 3.00 8.00
CM Carlos Marmol 3.00 8.00
CQ Carlos Quentin 3.00 8.00
CR Colby Rasmus Bat 3.00 8.00
DB David Blaine 15.00 40.00
DBR Drew Brees 10.00 25.00
DD Dale Davis 4.00 10.00
DH Dan Haren 3.00 8.00
DT Darren Taylor 5.00 12.00
DU Dan Uggla 3.00 8.00
DW David Wright 5.00 12.00
DWR David Wright 3.00 8.00
EL Evan Longoria 3.00 8.00
GB Gordon Beckham 3.00 8.00
GS Grady Sizemore 3.00 8.00
GS Gary Stewart 5.00 12.00
GSI Glenn Singleman 4.00 10.00
HF Hans Florine 10.00 25.00
HR Hanley Ramirez 3.00 8.00
HW Hubertus Wawra 6.00 15.00
IC Ivory Crockett 5.00 12.00
IK Ian Kinsler 3.00 8.00
IR Ivan Rodriguez 3.00 8.00
IS Ichiro Suzuki 4.00 10.00
JB Jay Bruce 3.00 8.00
JD John Danks 3.00 8.00
JH Josh Hamilton 3.00 8.00
JJ Josh Johnson 3.00 8.00
JL Judson Laipply 5.00 12.00
JS Jordin Sparks 8.00 20.00
JS Johnny Strange 3.00 8.00
JSA Jeff Samardzija 3.00 8.00
JV Joey Votto 3.00 8.00
KB Kyle Blanks 3.00 8.00
KB Ken Blackburn 4.00 10.00
KF Kosuke Fukudome 3.00 8.00
KK Kelly Kulick 8.00 20.00
KM Kendry Morales 3.00 8.00
LB Lance Berkman 6.00 15.00
MC Matt Cain 3.00 8.00
MCA Miguel Cabrera 6.00 15.00
MCAB Melky Cabrera 3.00 8.00
MK Matt Kemp 3.00 8.00
MK Meb Keflezighi 5.00 12.00
ML Mat Latos 3.00 8.00
MM Marvin Miller 5.00 12.00
MP Mike Parsons 4.00 10.00
MPO Max Poser 6.00 15.00
MR Mark Reynolds 3.00 8.00
NC Nelson Cruz 3.00 8.00
NF Neftali Feliz 30.00 60.00
NM Nick Markakis 3.00 8.00
PF Prince Fielder 3.00 8.00
PP Preston Pittman 6.00 15.00
RB Ryan Braun 3.00 8.00
RC Robinson Cano 3.00 8.00
RH Ryan Howard 4.00 10.00
RK Ryan Kennelly 4.00 10.00
RN Ricky Nolasco 3.00 8.00
RO Randy Oitker 6.00 15.00
RP Regis Philbin 12.50 30.00
RTH Tony Hoard/Rory 12.50 30.00
RZ Ryan Zimmerman 3.00 8.00
SD Stephen Drew 3.00 8.00
SH Sig Hansen 30.00 60.00
SJ Shawn Johnson 15.00 40.00
SS Stuart Scott 15.00 40.00
SSA Summer Sanders 6.00 15.00
SV Shane Victorino 3.00 8.00
TB Tyler Bradt 6.00 15.00
TDV Tiago Della Vega 5.00 12.00
TH Tony Hawk 20.00 50.00
THE Todd Helton 3.00 8.00
THU Torii Hunter 3.00 8.00
TK Tom Knapp 12.50 30.00
TT Troy Tulowitzki 3.00 8.00
UJ Ubaldo Jimenez 3.00 8.00
YE Yunel Escobar 3.00 8.00
YG Yovani Gallardo 15.00 40.00
ZS Zac Sunderland 4.00 10.00

2010 Topps Allen and Ginter Rip Cards

STATED ODDS 1:285 HOBBY
PRINT RUNS B/WN 5-99 COPIES PER
ALL LISTED PRICED ARE FOR RIPPED
UNRIPPED HAVE ADD'L CARDS WITHIN
COMMON UNRIPPED p/r 99 40.00 80.00
COMMON UNRIPPED p/r 50 50.00 100.00
RC1 Rick Ankiel/99 6.00 15.00
RC4 Elijah Dukes/99 6.00 15.00
RC5 Carlos Gomez/99 6.00 15.00
RC7 Erik Bedard/50 6.00 15.00
RC11 Troy Glaus/50 6.00 15.00
RC14 Aramis Ramirez/50 6.00 15.00
RC15 Colby Rasmus/99 6.00 15.00
RC19 Mike Cameron/99 6.00 15.00
RC20 Corey Hart/99 6.00 15.00
RC24 Yunel Escobar/99 6.00 15.00
RC25 Nick Swisher/50 10.00 25.00
RC28 Nate McLouth/99 6.00 15.00
RC31 Jay Bruce/50 10.00 25.00
RC33 Hunter Pence/50 10.00 25.00
RC34 Kendry Morales/50 6.00 15.00
RC35 James Loney/99 6.00 15.00
RC36 Brandon Phillips/50 6.00 15.00
RC38 Carlos Lee/50 6.00 15.00
RC43 Russ Martin/99 6.00 15.00
RC44 Derrek Lee/50 6.00 15.00
RC45 Orlando Hudson/99 6.00 15.00
RC48 Lastings Milledge/99 6.00 15.00
RC50 Denard Span/99 6.00 15.00
RC52 Tim Hudson/50 10.00 25.00
RC53 Joakim Soria/50 6.00 15.00
RC54 Chad Billingsley/99 10.00 25.00
RC58 Tyler Flowers/99 10.00 25.00
RC60 Kyle Blanks/99 6.00 15.00
RC62 Carlos Pena/50 10.00 25.00
RC63 Magglio Ordonez/50 10.00 25.00
RC64 Elvis Andrus/99 10.00 25.00
RC66 Joey Votto/50 10.00 25.00
RC67 Yovani Gallardo/50 6.00 15.00
RC69 Delmon Young/99 10.00 25.00
RC71 Scott Kazmir/99 6.00 15.00
RC74 Tommy Manzella/99 6.00 15.00
RC76 Jim Thome/50 10.00 25.00
RC80 Michael Brantley/99 10.00 25.00
RC81 Franklin Gutierrez/50 6.00 15.00
RC82 Jered Weaver/50 10.00 25.00
RC85 Chris Coghlan/99 6.00 15.00
RC86 Nelson Cruz/50 15.00 40.00
RC87 Aaron Rowand/99 6.00 15.00
RC88 Ben Sheets/50 6.00 15.00
RC89 James Shields/50 6.00 15.00
RC91 Travis Snider/99 6.00 15.00
RC92 Jonathan Broxton/50 6.00 15.00
RC93 Carlos Zambrano/99 10.00 25.00
RC94 Rich Harden/50 6.00 15.00
RC98 Vernon Wells/50 6.00 15.00

2010 Topps Allen and Ginter This Day in History

COMPLETE SET (75) 10.00 25.00
TDH1 Chase Utley .40 1.00
TDH2 Stephen Drew .25 .60
TDH3 Aramis Ramirez .25 .60
TDH4 Lance Berkman .40 1.00
TDH5 Chipper Jones .60 1.50
TDH6 Brian Roberts .25 .60
TDH7 Jason Heyward 1.00 2.50
TDH8 Yunel Escobar .25 .60
TDH9 Pablo Sandoval .40 1.00
TDH10 David Ortiz .60 1.50
TDH11 Jason Bay .40 1.00
TDH12 Andre Ethier .40 1.00
TDH13 Adam Dunn .40 1.00
TDH14 Justin Verlander .60 1.50
TDH15 Manny Ramirez .60 1.50
TDH16 Carlos Gonzalez .40 1.00
TDH17 Joe Mauer .50 1.25

2010 Topps Allen and Ginter This Day in History

TDH18 Felix Hernandez .40 1.00
TDH19 Robinson Cano .40 1.00
TDH20 CC Sabathia .40 1.00
TDH21 Magglio Ordonez .40 1.00
TDH22 Grady Sizemore .40 1.00
TDH23 Dan Haren .25 .60
TDH24 Joey Votto .60 1.50
TDH25 Ryan Zimmerman .40 1.00
TDH26 Francisco Rodriguez .40 1.00
TDH27 Ken Griffey Jr. 1.25 3.00
TDH28 Jose Reyes .40 1.00
TDH29 Adam Jones .40 1.00
TDH30 Hideki Matsui .60 1.50
TDH31 Mark Teixeira .40 1.00
TDH32 Adrian Gonzalez .50 1.25
TDH33 Kosuke Fukudome .40 1.00
TDH34 Troy Tulowitzki .60 1.50
TDH35 Josh Johnson .40 1.00
TDH36 Hanley Ramirez .40 1.00
TDH37 Ichiro Suzuki .75 2.00
TDH38 Jim Thome .40 1.00
TDH39 Torii Hunter .25 .60
TDH40 Jake Peavy .25 .60
TDH41 Aaron Hill .25 .60
TDH42 Jorge Posada .40 1.00
TDH43 Jonathan Broxton .25 .60
TDH44 B.J. Upton .40 1.00
TDH45 Miguel Cabrera .60 1.50
TDH46 Yovani Gallardo .25 .60
TDH47 Brandon Phillips .25 .60
TDH48 Matt Holliday .60 1.50
TDH49 Justin Morneau .40 1.00
TDH50 Alex Rodriguez .75 2.00
TDH51 Gordon Beckham .25 .60
TDH52 Justin Upton .40 1.00
TDH53 Nick Markakis .50 1.25
TDH54 Derrek Lee .25 .60
TDH55 Ryan Braun .40 1.00
TDH56 Jimmy Rollins .40 1.00
TDH57 Miguel Tejada .40 1.00
TDH58 Dan Uggla .25 .60
TDH59 Hunter Pence .40 1.00
TDH60 Roy Halladay .40 1.00
TDH61 James Shields .25 .60
TDH62 Kevin Youkilis .25 .60
TDH63 Alfonso Soriano .40 1.00
TDH64 Josh Hamilton .40 1.00
TDH65 Zack Greinke .60 1.50
TDH66 Curtis Granderson .50 1.25
TDH67 Josh Beckett .25 .60
TDH68 Brian McCann .40 1.00
TDH69 Alexei Ramirez .40 1.00
TDH70 Andrew McCutchen .60 1.50
TDH71 Billy Butler .25 .60
TDH72 Jay Bruce .40 1.00
TDH73 Ian Kinsler .40 1.00
TDH74 Carlos Lee .25 .60
TDH75 Mariano Rivera .75 2.00

2011 Topps Allen and Ginter

COMPLETE SET (350) 50.00 100.00
COMP.SET w/o SP's (300) 12.50 30.00
COMMON CARD (1-300) .15 .40
COMMON RC (1-300) .40 1.00
COMMON SP (301-350) 1.25 3.00
SP ODDS 1:2 HOBBY
1 Carlos Gonzalez .25 .60
2 Ty Wigginton .15 .40
3 Lou Holtz .15 .40
4 Jhoulys Chacin .15 .40
5 Aroldis Chapman RC 1.25 3.00
6 Micky Ward .15 .40
7 Mickey Mantle 1.25 3.00
8 Alexei Ramirez .25 .60
9 Joe Saunders .15 .40
10 Miguel Cabrera .40 1.00
11 Marc Forgione .15 .40
12 Hope Solo .60 1.50
13 Brett Anderson .15 .40
14 Adrian Beltre .40 1.00
15 Diana Taurasi .15 .40
16 Gordon Beckham .15 .40
17 Jonathan Papelbon .25 .60
18 Daniel Hudson .15 .40
19 Daniel Bard .15 .40
20 Jeremy Hellickson RC 1.00 2.50
21 Logan Morrison .15 .40
22 Michael Bourn .15 .40
23 Aubrey Huff .15 .40
24 Kristi Yamaguchi .15 .40
25 Nelson Cruz .40 1.00
26 Edwin Jackson .15 .40
27 Dillon Gee RC .60 1.50
28 John Lindsey RC .40 1.00
29 Johnny Cueto .25 .60
30 Hanley Ramirez .25 .60
31 Jimmy Rollins .25 .60
32 Dirk Hayhurst .15 .40
33 Curtis Granderson .30 .75
34 Pedro Ciriaco RC .60 1.50
35 Adam Dunn .25 .60
36 Eric Sogard RC .40 1.00
37 Fausto Carmona .15 .40
38 Angel Pagan .15 .40
39 Stephen Drew .15 .40
40 John McEnroe .15 .40
41 Carlos Santana .40 1.00
42 Heath Bell .15 .40
43 Jake LaMotta .15 .40
44 Ozzie Martinez RC .40 1.00
45 Annika Sorenstam .15 .40
46 Edinson Volquez .15 .40
47 Phil Hughes .15 .40
48 Francisco Liriano .15 .40
49 Javier Vazquez .15 .40
50 Carl Crawford .25 .60
51 Tim Collins RC .40 1.00
52 Francisco Cordero .15 .40
53 Chipper Jones .40 1.00
54 Austin Jackson .15 .40
55 Dustin Pedroia .40 1.00
56 Scott Kazmir .15 .40
57 Derek Jeter 1.00 2.50
58 Alcides Escobar .25 .60
59 Jeremy Jeffress RC .40 1.00
60 Brandon Belt RC 1.00 2.50
61 Brian Roberts .15 .40
62 Alfonso Soriano .25 .60
63 Neil Walker .25 .60
64 Ricky Romero .15 .40
65 Ryan Howard .30 .75
66 Starlin Castro .25 .60
67 Delmon Young .25 .60
68 Max Scherzer .40 1.00
69 Neftali Feliz .15 .40
70 Evan Longoria .25 .60
71 Chris Perez .15 .40
72 Maxim Shmyrev .15 .40
73 Brandon Morrow .15 .40
74 Torii Hunter .15 .40
75 Jose Reyes .25 .60
76 Chase Headley .15 .40
77 Rafael Furcal .15 .40
78 Luke Scott .15 .40
79 Aimee Mullins .15 .40
80 Joey Votto .40 1.00
81 Yonder Alonso RC .60 1.50
82 Scott Rolen .25 .60
83 Mat Hoffman .15 .40
84 Gregory Infante RC .40 1.00
85 Chris Sale RC 3.00 8.00
86 Greg Halman RC .60 1.50
87 Colby Lewis .15 .40
88 David Ortiz .40 1.00
89 John Axford .15 .40
90 Roy Halladay .25 .60
91 Joel Pineiro .15 .40
92 Michael Pineda RC 1.00 2.50
93 Evan Lysacek .15 .40
94 Josh Rodriguez RC .40 1.00
95 Dan Uggla .15 .40
96 Daniel Boulud .15 .40
97 Zach Britton RC 1.00 2.50
98 Jason Bay .25 .60
99 Placido Polanco .15 .40
100 Albert Pujols .50 1.25
101 Peter Bourjos .25 .60
102 Wandy Rodriguez .15 .40
103 Andres Torres .15 .40
104 Huston Street .15 .40
105 Ubaldo Jimenez .15 .40
106 Jonathan Broxton .15 .40
107 L.L. Zamenhof .15 .40
108 Roy Oswalt .25 .60
109 Martin Prado .15 .40
110 Jake McGee (RC) .75 2.00
111 Pablo Sandoval .25 .60
112 Timothy Shieff .15 .40
113 Miguel Montero .15 .40
114 Brandon Phillips .15 .40
115 Shin-Soo Choo .25 .60
116 Josh Beckett .15 .40
117 Jonathan Sanchez .15 .40
118 Rafael Soriano .15 .40
119 Nancy Lopez .15 .40
120 Adrian Gonzalez .30 .75
121 J.D. Drew .15 .40
122 Ryan Dempster .15 .40
123 Rajai Davis .15 .40
124 Chad Billingsley .25 .60
125 Clayton Kershaw .60 1.50
126 Jair Jurrjens .15 .40
127 James Loney .15 .40
128 Michael Cuddyer .15 .40
129 Kelly Johnson .15 .40
130 Robinson Cano .25 .60
131 Chris Iannetta .15 .40
132 Colby Rasmus .25 .60
133 Geno Auriemma .25 .60
134 Matt Cain .25 .60
135 Kyle Petty .15 .40
136 Dick Vitale .15 .40
137 Carlos Beltran .25 .60
138 Matt Garza .15 .40
139 Tim Howard .15 .40
140 Felix Hernandez .25 .60
141 Vernon Wells .15 .40
142 Michael Young .15 .40
143 Carlos Zambrano .25 .60
144 Jorge Posada .25 .60
145 Victor Martinez .25 .60
146 John Danks .15 .40
147 George Bush .25 .60
148 Sanya Richards .15 .40
149 Lars Anderson RC .60 1.50
150 Troy Tulowitzki .40 1.00
151 Brandon Beachy RC 1.00 2.50
152 Jordan Zimmermann .25 .60
153 Scott Cousins RC .40 1.00
154 Todd Helton .25 .60
155 Josh Johnson .25 .60
156 Marlon Byrd .15 .40
157 Corey Hart .15 .40
158 Billy Butler .15 .40
159 Shawn Michaels .15 .40
160 David Wright .30 .75
161 Casey McGehee .15 .40
162 Mat Latos .25 .60
163 Ian Kennedy .15 .40
164 Heather Mitts .25 .60
165 Jo Frost .15 .40
166 Geovany Soto .25 .60
167 Adam LaRoche .15 .40
168 Carlos Marmol .25 .60
169 Dan Haren .15 .40
170 Tim Lincecum .25 .60
171 John Lackey .25 .60
172 Yunesky Maya RC .40 1.00
173 Mariano Rivera .50 1.25
174 Joakim Soria .15 .40
175 Jose Bautista .25 .60
176 Brian Bogusevic (RC) .40 1.00
177 Aaron Crow RC .60 1.50
178 Ben Revere RC .60 1.50
179 Shane Victorino .25 .60
180 Kyle Drabek RC .60 1.50
181 Mark Buehrle .25 .60
182 Clay Buchholz .15 .40
183 Mike Napoli .15 .40
184 Pedro Alvarez RC .30 .75
185 Justin Upton .25 .60
186 Yunel Escobar .15 .40
187 Jim Nantz .15 .40
188 Daniel Descalso RC .40 1.00
189 Dexter Fowler .25 .60
190 Sue Bird .15 .40
191 Matt Guy .15 .40
192 Carl Pavano .15 .40
193 Jorge De La Rosa .15 .40
194 Rick Porcello .25 .60
195 Tommy Hanson .15 .40
196 Jered Weaver .25 .60
197 Jay Bruce .25 .60
198 Freddie Freeman RC 6.00 15.00
199 Jake Peavy .15 .40
200 Josh Hamilton .25 .60
201 Andrew Romine RC .40 1.00
202 Nick Swisher .25 .60
203 Aaron Hill .15 .40
204 Jim Thome .25 .60
205 Kendrys Morales .15 .40
206 Tsuyoshi Nishioka RC 1.25 3.00
207 Kosuke Fukudome .25 .60
208 Marco Scutaro .25 .60
209 Guy Fieri .15 .40
210 Chase Utley .25 .60
211 Francisco Rodriguez .25 .60
212 Aramis Ramirez .15 .40
213 Xavier Nady .15 .40
214 Elvis Andrus .25 .60
215 Andrew McCutchen .40 1.00
216 Jose Tabata .15 .40
217 Shaun Marcum .15 .40
218 Bobby Abreu .15 .40
219 Johan Santana .25 .60
220 Prince Fielder .25 .60
221 Mark Rogers (RC) .40 1.00
222 James Shields .15 .40
223 Chuck Woolery .15 .40
224 Jason Kubel .15 .40
225 Jack LaLanne .15 .40
226 Andre Ethier .25 .60
227 Lucas Duda RC 1.00 2.50
228 Brandon Snyder (RC) .40 1.00
229 Juan Pierre .15 .40
230 Mark Teixeira .25 .60
231 C.J. Wilson .15 .40
232 Picabo Street .15 .40
233 Ben Zobrist .25 .60
234 Chrissie Wellington .15 .40
235 Cole Hamels .30 .75
236 B.J. Upton .25 .60
237 Carlos Quentin .15 .40
238 Rudy Ruettiger .15 .40
239 Brett Myers .15 .40
240 Matt Holliday .40 1.00
241 Ike Davis .15 .40
242 Cheryl Burke .15 .40
243 Mike Nickeas (RC) .40 1.00
244 Chone Figgins .15 .40
245 Brian McCann .25 .60
246 Ian Kinsler .25 .60
247 Yadier Molina .50 1.25
248 Ervin Santana .15 .40
249 Carlos Ruiz .15 .40
250 Ichiro Suzuki .50 1.25
251 Ian Desmond .15 .40
252 Omar Infante .15 .40
253 Mike Minor .15 .40
254 Denard Span .15 .40
255 David Price .30 .75
256 Hunter Pence .25 .60
257 Andrew Bailey .15 .40
258 Howie Kendrick .15 .40
259 Tim Hudson .25 .60
260 Alex Rodriguez .50 1.25
261 Carlos Pena .25 .60
262 Manny Pacquiao 2.50 6.00
263 Mark Trumbo (RC) 1.00 2.50
264 Adam Jones .25 .60
265 Buster Posey .50 1.25
266 Chris Coghlan .15 .40
267 Brett Sinkbeil RC .40 1.00
268 Dallas Braden .15 .40
269 Derrek Lee .15 .40
270 Kevin Youkilis .15 .40
271 Chris Young .15 .40
272 Wee Man .15 .40
273 Brent Morel RC .40 1.00
274 Stan Lee .15 .40
275 Justin Verlander .40 1.00
276 Desmond Jennings RC .60 1.50
277 Hank Conger RC .60 1.50
278 Travis Snider .15 .40
279 Brian Wilson .40 1.00
280 Adam Wainwright .25 .60
281 Adam Lind .25 .60
282 Reid Brignac .15 .40
283 Daric Barton .15 .40
284 Eric Jackson .15 .40
285 Alex Rios .15 .40
286 Cory Luebke RC .40 1.00
287 Yovani Gallardo .15 .40
288 Rickie Weeks .15 .40
289 Paul Konerko .25 .60
290 Cliff Lee .25 .60
291 Grady Sizemore .25 .60
292 Wade Davis .15 .40
293 William/K.Middleton .40 1.00
294 Jacoby Ellsbury .30 .75
295 Chris Carpenter .25 .60
296 Derek Lowe .15 .40
297 Travis Hafner .15 .40
298 Peter Gammons .15 .40
299 Ana Julaton .15 .40
300 Ryan Braun .25 .60
301 Gio Gonzalez SP 1.25 3.00
302 John Buck SP 1.25 3.00
303 Jaime Garcia SP 1.25 3.00
304 Madison Bumgarner SP 1.25 3.00
305 Justin Morneau SP 1.25 3.00
306 Josh Willingham SP 1.25 3.00
307 Ryan Ludwick SP 1.25 3.00
308 Jhonny Peralta SP 1.25 3.00
309 Kurt Suzuki SP 1.25 3.00
310 Matt Kemp SP 1.25 3.00
311 Ian Stewart SP 1.25 3.00
312 Cody Ross SP 1.25 3.00
313 Leo Nunez SP 1.25 3.00
314 Nick Markakis SP 1.25 3.00
315 Jayson Werth SP 1.25 3.00
316 Manny Ramirez SP 1.25 3.00
317 Brian Matusz SP 1.25 3.00
318 Brett Wallace SP 1.25 3.00
319 Jon Niese SP 1.25 3.00
320 Jon Lester SP 1.25 3.00
321 Mark Reynolds SP 1.25 3.00
322 Trevor Cahill SP 1.25 3.00
323 Orlando Hudson SP 1.25 3.00
324 Domonic Brown SP 1.25 3.00
325 Mike Stanton SP 1.25 3.00
326 Jason Castro SP 1.25 3.00
327 David DeJesus SP 1.25 3.00
328 Chris Johnson SP 1.25 3.00
329 Alex Gordon SP 1.25 3.00
330 CC Sabathia SP 1.25 3.00
331 Carlos Gomez SP 1.25 3.00
332 Luke Hochevar SP 1.25 3.00
333 Carlos Lee SP 1.25 3.00
334 Gaby Sanchez SP 1.25 3.00
335 Jason Heyward SP 1.50 4.00
336 Kevin Kouzmanoff SP 1.25 3.00
337 Drew Storen SP 1.25 3.00
338 Lance Berkman SP 1.25 3.00
339 Miguel Tejada SP 1.25 3.00
340 Ryan Zimmerman SP 1.25 3.00
341 Ricky Nolasco SP 1.25 3.00
342 Mike Pelfrey SP 1.25 3.00
343 Drew Stubbs SP 1.25 3.00
344 Danny Valencia SP 1.25 3.00
345 Zack Greinke SP 1.25 3.00
346 Brett Gardner SP 1.25 3.00
347 Josh Thole SP 1.25 3.00
348 Russell Martin SP 1.25 3.00
349 Yuniesky Betancourt SP 1.25 3.00
350 Joe Mauer SP 1.25 3.00

2011 Topps Allen and Ginter Code Cards

*MINI 1-300: 1.5X TO 4X BASIC
*MINI 1-300 RC: .75X TO 2X BASIC RC's
OVERALL CODE ODDS 1:8 HOBBY
301 Gio Gonzalez 1.25 3.00
302 John Buck .75 2.00
303 Jaime Garcia 1.25 3.00
304 Madison Bumgarner 1.50 4.00
305 Justin Morneau 1.25 3.00
306 Josh Willingham 1.25 3.00
307 Ryan Ludwick .75 2.00
308 Jhonny Peralta .75 2.00
309 Kurt Suzuki .75 2.00
310 Matt Kemp 1.50 4.00
311 Ian Stewart .75 2.00
312 Cody Ross .75 2.00
313 Leo Nunez .75 2.00
314 Nick Markakis 1.50 4.00
315 Jayson Werth 1.25 3.00
316 Manny Ramirez 2.00 5.00
317 Brian Matusz .75 2.00
318 Brett Wallace .75 2.00
319 Jon Niese .75 2.00
320 Jon Lester 1.25 3.00
321 Mark Reynolds .75 2.00
322 Trevor Cahill .75 2.00
323 Orlando Hudson .75 2.00
324 Domonic Brown 1.50 4.00
325 Mike Stanton 2.00 5.00
326 Jason Castro .75 2.00
327 David DeJesus .75 2.00
328 Chris Johnson .75 2.00
329 Alex Gordon 1.25 3.00
330 CC Sabathia 1.25 3.00
331 Carlos Gomez .75 2.00
332 Luke Hochevar .75 2.00
333 Carlos Lee .75 2.00
334 Gaby Sanchez .75 2.00
335 Jason Heyward 1.50 4.00
336 Kevin Kouzmanoff .75 2.00
337 Drew Storen .75 2.00
338 Lance Berkman 1.25 3.00
339 Miguel Tejada 1.25 3.00
340 Ryan Zimmerman 1.25 3.00
341 Ricky Nolasco .75 2.00
342 Mike Pelfrey .75 2.00
343 Drew Stubbs .75 2.00
344 Danny Valencia 1.25 3.00
345 Zack Greinke 2.00 5.00
346 Brett Gardner 1.25 3.00
347 Josh Thole .75 2.00
348 Russell Martin .75 2.00
349 Yuniesky Betancourt .75 2.00
350 Joe Mauer 1.50 4.00

2011 Topps Allen and Ginter Mini

*MINI 1-300: .75X TO 2X BASIC
*MINI 1-300 RC: .5X TO 1.2X BASIC RC's
*MINI SP 301-350: .5X TO 1.2X BASIC SP
MINI SP ODDS 1:13 HOBBY
COMMON CARD (351-400) 10.00 25.00
351-400 RANDOM WITHIN RIP CARDS
STATED PLATE ODDS 1:751 HOBBY
PLATE PRINT RUN 1 SET PER COLOR
BLACK-CYAN-MAGENTA-YELLOW ISSUED
NO PLATE PRICING DUE TO SCARCITY
352 Jason Heyward EXT 10.00 25.00
353 Ichiro Suzuki EXCH 10.00 25.00
354 Kevin Youkilis EXT 10.00 25.00
355 Roy Halladay EXT 10.00 25.00
356 Starlin Castro EXT 10.00 25.00
357 Mickey Mantle EXT 40.00 80.00
358 Robinson Cano EXT 40.00 80.00
359 Dan Uggla EXT 10.00 25.00
360 Carl Crawford EXT 10.00 25.00
361 Hunter Pence EXT 10.00 25.00
362 Chase Utley EXT 10.00 25.00
363 Justin Upton EXT 10.00 25.00
364 Pedro Alvarez EXT 10.00 25.00
365 Dustin Pedroia EXT 10.00 25.00
366 Albert Pujols EXT 10.00 25.00
367 Mike Stanton EXT 10.00 25.00
368 Joe Mauer EXT 10.00 25.00
369 Evan Longoria EXT 10.00 25.00
370 Carlos Gonzalez EXT 10.00 25.00
371 Adam Dunn EXT 30.00 60.00
372 Derek Jeter EXT 100.00 175.00
373 Jose Bautista EXT 10.00 25.00
374 Ryan Zimmerman EXT 30.00 60.00
375 Troy Tulowitzki EXT 10.00 25.00
376 Mat Latos EXT 10.00 25.00
377 Clayton Kershaw EXT 10.00 25.00
378 Shin-Soo Choo EXT 10.00 25.00
379 Cliff Lee EXT 10.00 25.00
380 Adrian Gonzalez EXT 10.00 25.00
381 Tim Lincecum EXT 10.00 25.00
382 Zack Greinke EXT 10.00 25.00
383 Torii Hunter EXT 10.00 25.00
384 Felix Hernandez EXT 10.00 25.00
385 Aroldis Chapman EXT 10.00 25.00
386 Josh Hamilton EXT 30.00 60.00
387 Hanley Ramirez EXT 10.00 25.00
388 Jon Lester EXT 10.00 25.00
389 Billy Butler EXT 10.00 25.00
390 Miguel Cabrera EXT 12.50 30.00
391 Justin Morneau EXT 30.00 60.00
392 Ubaldo Jimenez EXT 10.00 25.00
393 Alex Rodriguez EXT 10.00 25.00
394 CC Sabathia EXT 10.00 25.00
395 Buster Posey EXT 10.00 25.00
396 Ryan Howard EXT 10.00 25.00
397 Mark Teixeira EXT 40.00 80.00
398 Brett Anderson EXT 10.00 25.00
399 David Wright EXT 10.00 25.00
400 Joey Votto EXT 10.00 25.00

2011 Topps Allen and Ginter Mini A and G Back

*A & G BACK: 1X TO 2.5X BASIC
*A & G BACK RCs: .6X TO 1.5X BASIC RCs
A & G BACK ODDS 1:5 HOBBY
*A & G BACK SP: .6X TO 1.5X BASIC SP
A & G BACK SP ODDS 1:65 HOBBY

2011 Topps Allen and Ginter Mini Black

*BLACK: 2X TO 5X BASIC
*BLACK RCs: .75X TO 2X BASIC RCs
BLACK ODDS 1:10 HOBBY
BLACK SP ODDS 1:130 HOBBY
*BLACK SP: .75X TO 2X BASIC SP

2011 Topps Allen and Ginter Mini No Card Number

*NO NBR: 8X TO 20X BASIC
*NO NBR RCs: 3X TO 8X BASIC RCs
*NO NBR SP: 1.2X TO 3X BASIC SP
STATED ODDS 1:142 HOBBY

2011 Topps Allen and Ginter Glossy

ISSUED VIA TOPPS ONLINE STORE
STATED PRINT RUN 999 SER.#'d SETS
1 Carlos Gonzalez 1.25 3.00
2 Ty Wigginton .75 2.00
3 Lou Holtz .75 2.00
4 Jhoulys Chacin .75 2.00
5 Aroldis Chapman 2.50 6.00
6 Micky Ward .75 2.00
7 Mickey Mantle 6.00 15.00
8 Alexei Ramirez 1.25 3.00
9 Joe Saunders .75 2.00
10 Miguel Cabrera 2.00 5.00
11 Marc Forgione .75 2.00
12 Hope Solo .75 2.00
13 Brett Anderson .75 2.00
14 Adrian Beltre 2.00 5.00
15 Diana Taurasi .75 2.00
16 Gordon Beckham .75 2.00
17 Jonathan Papelbon 1.25 3.00
18 Daniel Hudson .75 2.00
19 Daniel Bard .75 2.00
20 Jeremy Hellickson 2.00 5.00
21 Logan Morrison .75 2.00
22 Michael Bourn .75 2.00
23 Aubrey Huff .75 2.00
24 Kristi Yamaguchi .75 2.00
25 Nelson Cruz 2.00 5.00
26 Edwin Jackson .75 2.00
27 Dillon Gee 1.25 3.00
28 John Lindsey .75 2.00
29 Johnny Cueto 1.25 3.00
30 Hanley Ramirez 1.25 3.00
31 Jimmy Rollins 1.25 3.00
32 Dirk Hayhurst .75 2.00
33 Curtis Granderson 1.50 4.00
34 Pedro Ciriaco 1.25 3.00
35 Adam Dunn 1.25 3.00
36 Eric Sogard .75 2.00
37 Fausto Carmona .75 2.00
38 Angel Pagan .75 2.00
39 Stephen Drew .75 2.00
40 John McEnroe .75 2.00
41 Carlos Santana 2.00 5.00
42 Heath Bell .75 2.00
43 Jake LaMotta .75 2.00
44 Ozzie Martinez .75 2.00
45 Annika Sorenstam .75 2.00
46 Edinson Volquez .75 2.00
47 Phil Hughes .75 2.00
48 Francisco Liriano .75 2.00
49 Javier Vazquez .75 2.00
50 Carl Crawford 1.25 3.00
51 Tim Collins .75 2.00
52 Francisco Cordero .75 2.00
53 Chipper Jones 2.00 5.00
54 Austin Jackson .75 2.00
55 Dustin Pedroia 2.00 5.00
56 Scott Kazmir .75 2.00
57 Derek Jeter 5.00 12.00
58 Alcides Escobar 1.25 3.00
59 Jeremy Jeffress .75 2.00
60 Brandon Belt 2.00 5.00
61 Brian Roberts .75 2.00
62 Alfonso Soriano 1.25 3.00
63 Neil Walker 1.25 3.00
64 Ricky Romero .75 2.00
65 Ryan Howard 1.50 4.00
66 Starlin Castro 1.25 3.00
67 Delmon Young 1.25 3.00
68 Max Scherzer 2.00 5.00
69 Neftali Feliz .75 2.00
70 Evan Longoria 1.25 3.00
71 Chris Perez .75 2.00
72 Maxim Shmyrev .75 2.00
73 Brandon Morrow .75 2.00
74 Torii Hunter .75 2.00
75 Jose Reyes 1.25 3.00
76 Chase Headley .75 2.00
77 Rafael Furcal .75 2.00
78 Luke Scott .75 2.00
79 Aimee Mullins .75 2.00
80 Joey Votto 2.00 5.00
81 Yonder Alonso 1.25 3.00
82 Scott Rolen 1.25 3.00
83 Mat Hoffman .75 2.00
84 Gregory Infante .75 2.00
85 Chris Sale 6.00 15.00
86 Greg Halman 1.25 3.00
87 Colby Lewis .75 2.00
88 David Ortiz 2.00 5.00
89 John Axford .75 2.00
90 Roy Halladay 1.25 3.00
91 Joel Pineiro .75 2.00
92 Michael Pineda 2.00 5.00
93 Evan Lysacek .75 2.00
94 Josh Rodriguez .75 2.00
95 Dan Uggla .75 2.00
96 Daniel Boulud .75 2.00
97 Zach Britton 2.00 5.00
98 Jason Bay 1.25 3.00
99 Placido Polanco .75 2.00
100 Albert Pujols 2.50 6.00
101 Peter Bourjos 1.25 3.00
102 Wandy Rodriguez .75 2.00
103 Andres Torres .75 2.00
104 Huston Street .75 2.00
105 Ubaldo Jimenez .75 2.00
106 Jonathan Broxton .75 2.00
107 L.L. Zamenhof .75 2.00
108 Roy Oswalt 1.25 3.00
109 Martin Prado .75 2.00
110 Jake McGee (RC) 1.50 4.00
111 Pablo Sandoval 1.25 3.00
112 Timothy Shieff .75 2.00
113 Miguel Montero .75 2.00
114 Brandon Phillips .75 2.00
115 Shin-Soo Choo 1.25 3.00
116 Josh Beckett .75 2.00
117 Jonathan Sanchez .75 2.00
118 Rafael Soriano .75 2.00
119 Nancy Lopez .75 2.00
120 Adrian Gonzalez 1.50 4.00
121 J.D. Drew .75 2.00
122 Ryan Dempster .75 2.00
123 Rajai Davis .75 2.00
124 Chad Billingsley 1.25 3.00
125 Clayton Kershaw 3.00 8.00
126 Jair Jurrjens .75 2.00
127 James Loney .75 2.00
128 Michael Cuddyer .75 2.00
129 Kelly Johnson .75 2.00
130 Robinson Cano 1.25 3.00
131 Chris Iannetta .75 2.00
132 Colby Rasmus 1.25 3.00
133 Geno Auriemma 1.25 3.00
134 Matt Cain 1.25 3.00
135 Kyle Petty .75 2.00
136 Dick Vitale .75 2.00
137 Carlos Beltran 1.25 3.00
138 Matt Garza .75 2.00
139 Tim Howard .75 2.00
140 Felix Hernandez 1.25 3.00
141 Vernon Wells .75 2.00
142 Michael Young .75 2.00
143 Carlos Zambrano 1.25 3.00
144 Jorge Posada 1.25 3.00
145 Victor Martinez 1.25 3.00
146 John Danks .75 2.00
147 George Bush 1.25 3.00
148 Sanya Richards .75 2.00
149 Lars Anderson 1.25 3.00
150 Troy Tulowitzki 2.00 5.00
151 Brandon Beachy 2.00 5.00
152 Jordan Zimmermann 1.25 3.00
153 Scott Cousins .75 2.00
154 Todd Helton 1.25 3.00
155 Josh Johnson 1.25 3.00
156 Marlon Byrd .75 2.00
157 Corey Hart .75 2.00
158 Billy Butler .75 2.00
159 Shawn Michaels .75 2.00
160 David Wright 1.50 4.00
161 Casey McGehee .75 2.00
162 Mat Latos 1.25 3.00
163 Ian Kennedy .75 2.00
164 Heather Mitts 1.25 3.00
165 Jo Frost .75 2.00
166 Geovany Soto 1.25 3.00
167 Adam LaRoche .75 2.00
168 Carlos Marmol 1.25 3.00
169 Dan Haren .75 2.00
170 Tim Lincecum 1.25 3.00
171 John Lackey 1.25 3.00
172 Yunesky Maya .75 2.00
173 Mariano Rivera 2.50 6.00
174 Joakim Soria .75 2.00
175 Jose Bautista 1.25 3.00
176 Brian Bogusevic (RC) .75 2.00
177 Aaron Crow 1.25 3.00
178 Ben Revere 1.25 3.00
179 Shane Victorino 1.25 3.00
180 Kyle Drabek 1.25 3.00
181 Mark Buehrle 1.25 3.00
182 Clay Buchholz .75 2.00
183 Mike Napoli .75 2.00
184 Pedro Alvarez 1.50 4.00
185 Justin Upton 1.25 3.00
186 Yunel Escobar .75 2.00
187 Jim Nantz .75 2.00
188 Daniel Descalso .75 2.00
189 Dexter Fowler 1.25 3.00
190 Sue Bird .75 2.00
191 Matt Guy .75 2.00
192 Carl Pavano .75 2.00
193 Jorge De La Rosa .75 2.00
194 Rick Porcello 1.25 3.00
195 Tommy Hanson .75 2.00
196 Jered Weaver 1.25 3.00
197 Jay Bruce 1.25 3.00
198 Freddie Freeman 12.00 30.00
199 Jake Peavy .75 2.00
200 Josh Hamilton 1.25 3.00
201 Andrew Romine .75 2.00
202 Nick Swisher 1.25 3.00
203 Aaron Hill .75 2.00
204 Jim Thome 1.25 3.00
205 Kendrys Morales .75 2.00
206 Tsuyoshi Nishioka 2.50 6.00
207 Kosuke Fukudome 1.25 3.00
208 Marco Scutaro 1.25 3.00
209 Guy Fieri .75 2.00
210 Chase Utley 1.25 3.00
211 Francisco Rodriguez 1.25 3.00
212 Aramis Ramirez .75 2.00
213 Xavier Nady .75 2.00
214 Elvis Andrus 1.25 3.00
215 Andrew McCutchen 2.00 5.00
216 Jose Tabata .75 2.00
217 Shaun Marcum .75 2.00
218 Bobby Abreu .75 2.00
219 Johan Santana 1.25 3.00
220 Prince Fielder 1.25 3.00
221 Mark Rogers (RC) .75 2.00
222 James Shields .75 2.00
223 Chuck Woolery .75 2.00
224 Jason Kubel .75 2.00
225 Jack LaLanne .75 2.00
226 Andre Ethier 1.25 3.00
227 Lucas Duda 2.00 5.00
228 Brandon Snyder (RC) .75 2.00
229 Juan Pierre .75 2.00
230 Mark Teixeira 1.25 3.00
231 C.J. Wilson .75 2.00
232 Picabo Street .75 2.00
233 Ben Zobrist 1.25 3.00
234 Chrissie Wellington .75 2.00
235 Cole Hamels 1.50 4.00
236 B.J. Upton 1.25 3.00
237 Carlos Quentin .75 2.00
238 Rudy Ruettiger .75 2.00
239 Brett Myers .75 2.00
240 Matt Holliday 2.00 5.00
241 Ike Davis .75 2.00
242 Cheryl Burke .75 2.00
243 Mike Nickeas (RC) .75 2.00
244 Chone Figgins .75 2.00
245 Brian McCann 1.25 3.00
246 Ian Kinsler 1.25 3.00
247 Yadier Molina 2.50 6.00
248 Ervin Santana .75 2.00
249 Carlos Ruiz .75 2.00
250 Ichiro Suzuki 2.50 6.00
251 Ian Desmond .75 2.00
252 Omar Infante .75 2.00
253 Mike Minor .75 2.00
254 Denard Span .75 2.00
255 David Price 1.50 4.00
256 Hunter Pence 1.25 3.00
257 Andrew Bailey .75 2.00
258 Howie Kendrick .75 2.00
259 Tim Hudson 1.25 3.00
260 Alex Rodriguez 2.50 6.00
261 Carlos Pena 1.25 3.00
262 Manny Pacquiao 15.00 40.00
263 Mark Trumbo (RC) 2.00 5.00
264 Adam Jones 1.25 3.00
265 Buster Posey 2.50 6.00
266 Chris Coghlan .75 2.00
267 Brett Sinkbeil .75 2.00
268 Dallas Braden .75 2.00
269 Derrek Lee .75 2.00
270 Kevin Youkilis .75 2.00
271 Chris Young .75 2.00
272 Wee Man .75 2.00
273 Brent Morel .75 2.00
274 Stan Lee .75 2.00
275 Justin Verlander 2.00 5.00
276 Desmond Jennings 1.25 3.00
277 Hank Conger 1.25 3.00
278 Travis Snider .75 2.00
279 Brian Wilson 2.00 5.00
280 Adam Wainwright 1.25 3.00
281 Adam Lind 1.25 3.00
282 Reid Brignac .75 2.00
283 Daric Barton .75 2.00
284 Eric Jackson .75 2.00
285 Alex Rios .75 2.00
286 Cory Luebke .75 2.00
287 Yovani Gallardo .75 2.00
288 Rickie Weeks .75 2.00
289 Paul Konerko 1.25 3.00
290 Cliff Lee 1.25 3.00
291 Grady Sizemore 1.25 3.00
292 Wade Davis .75 2.00
293 Prince William/Kate Middleton 2.00 5.00
294 Jacoby Ellsbury 1.50 4.00
295 Chris Carpenter 1.25 3.00
296 Derek Lowe .75 2.00
297 Travis Hafner .75 2.00
298 Peter Gammons .75 2.00
299 Ana Julaton .75 2.00
300 Ryan Braun 1.25 3.00
301 Gio Gonzalez 1.25 3.00
302 John Buck .75 2.00
303 Jaime Garcia 1.25 3.00
304 Madison Bumgarner 1.50 4.00
305 Justin Morneau 1.25 3.00
306 Josh Willingham 1.25 3.00
307 Ryan Ludwick .75 2.00
308 Jhonny Peralta .75 2.00
309 Kurt Suzuki .75 2.00
310 Matt Kemp 1.50 4.00
311 Ian Stewart .75 2.00
312 Cody Ross .75 2.00
313 Leo Nunez .75 2.00
314 Nick Markakis 1.50 4.00
315 Jayson Werth 1.25 3.00
316 Manny Ramirez 2.00 5.00
317 Brian Matusz .75 2.00
318 Brett Wallace .75 2.00
319 Jon Niese .75 2.00
320 Jon Lester 1.25 3.00
321 Mark Reynolds .75 2.00
322 Trevor Cahill .75 2.00
323 Orlando Hudson .75 2.00
324 Domonic Brown 1.50 4.00
325 Mike Stanton 2.00 5.00

326 Jason Castro .75 2.00
327 David DeJesus .75 2.00
328 Chris Johnson .75 2.00
329 Alex Gordon 1.25 3.00
330 CC Sabathia 1.25 3.00
331 Carlos Gomez .75 2.00
332 Luke Hochevar .75 2.00
333 Carlos Lee .75 2.00
334 Gaby Sanchez .75 2.00
335 Jason Heyward 1.50 4.00
336 Kevin Kouzmanoff .75 2.00
337 Drew Storen .75 2.00
338 Lance Berkman 1.25 3.00
339 Miguel Tejada 1.25 3.00
340 Ryan Zimmerman 1.25 3.00
341 Ricky Nolasco .75 2.00
342 Mike Pelfrey .75 2.00
343 Drew Stubbs .75 2.00
344 Danny Valencia 1.25 3.00
345 Zack Greinke 2.00 5.00
346 Brett Gardner 1.25 3.00
347 Josh Thole .75 2.00
348 Russell Martin .75 2.00
349 Yuniesky Betancourt .75 2.00
350 Joe Mauer 1.50 4.00

2011 Topps Allen and Ginter Glossy Rookie Exclusive

STATED PRINT RUN 999 SER.#'d SETS
AGS1 Eric Hosmer 8.00 20.00
AGS2 Dustin Ackley 2.00 5.00
AGS3 Mike Moustakas 3.00 8.00
AGS4 Dee Gordon 2.00 5.00
AGS5 Anthony Rizzo 12.00 30.00
AGS6 Charlie Blackmon 25.00 60.00
AGS7 Brandon Crawford 2.00 5.00
AGS8 Juan Nicasio 1.25 3.00
AGS9 Prince William/Kate Middleton 5.00 12.00
AGS10 U.S. Navy SEALs 2.00 5.00

2011 Topps Allen and Ginter Ascent of Man

COMPLETE SET (26) 10.00 25.00
STATED ODDS 1:6 HOBBY
AOM1 Prokaryotes .60 1.50
AOM2 Eukaryotes .60 1.50
AOM3 Choanoflagellates .60 1.50
AOM4 Porifera .60 1.50
AOM5 Cnidarians .60 1.50
AOM6 Platyhelminthes .60 1.50
AOM7 Chordates .60 1.50
AOM8 Ostracoderms .60 1.50
AOM9 Placoderms .60 1.50
AOM10 Sarcopterygii .60 1.50
AOM11 Amphibians .60 1.50
AOM12 Reptiles .60 1.50
AOM13 Eutherians .60 1.50
AOM14 Haplorrhini .60 1.50
AOM15 Catarrhini .60 1.50
AOM16 Hominoidea .60 1.50
AOM17 Hominidae .60 1.50
AOM18 Homininae .60 1.50
AOM19 Hominini .60 1.50
AOM20 Hominina .60 1.50
AOM21 Australopithecus .60 1.50
AOM22 Homo habilis .60 1.50
AOM23 Homo erectus .60 1.50
AOM24 Homo sapiens .60 1.50
AOM25 Cro-Magnon Man .60 1.50
AOM26 Modern Man .60 1.50

2011 Topps Allen and Ginter Autographs

STATED ODDS 1:68 HOBBY
DUAL AUTO ODDS 1:56,000 HOBBY
EXCHANGE DEADLINE 6/30/2014
AC Aroldis Chapman 10.00 25.00
ADU Angelo Dundee 20.00 50.00
AG Adrian Gonzalez 6.00 15.00
AJU Ana Julaton 6.00 15.00
AMU Aimee Mullins 10.00 25.00
APA Angel Pagan 6.00 15.00
ASO Annika Sorenstam 10.00 25.00
AT Andres Torres 6.00 15.00
BMO Brent Morel 4.00 10.00
BW Brett Wallace 4.00 10.00
CBU Cheryl Burke 20.00 50.00
CCS CC Sabathia 40.00 100.00
CF Chone Figgins 4.00 10.00
CS Chris Sale 12.00 30.00
CU Chase Utley 75.00 200.00
CWE Chrissie Wellington 10.00 25.00
CWO Chuck Woolery 12.50 30.00
DBO Daniel Boulud 12.50 30.00
DD David DeJesus 4.00 10.00
DH Daniel Hudson 6.00 15.00
DHA Dirk Hayhurst 20.00 50.00
DTU Diana Taurasi 12.50 30.00
DVI Dick Vitale 10.00 25.00
EJA Eric Jackson 12.50 30.00
ELY Evan Lysacek 6.00 15.00
FS Freddy Sanchez 5.00 12.00
GAU Geno Auriemma 12.50 30.00
GFI Guy Fieri 20.00 50.00
GG Gio Gonzalez 8.00 20.00
GO A.Gore/K.Olbermann 300.00 400.00
GWB George W. Bush 300.00 600.00
HMI Heather Mitts 10.00 25.00
HSO Hope Solo 30.00 80.00
JB Jose Bautista 12.50 30.00
JH Jason Heyward 10.00 25.00
JHA Josh Hamilton 6.00 15.00
JJ Josh Johnson 6.00 15.00
JLA Jake LaMotta 20.00 50.00
JM Joe Mauer 50.00 200.00
JMC John McEnroe 50.00 120.00
JNA Jim Nantz 10.00 25.00

JOF Jo Frost 12.50 30.00
JT Jose Tabata 6.00 15.00
KPE Kyle Petty 10.00 25.00
KYA Kristi Yamaguchi 40.00 100.00
LH Lou Holtz 25.00 80.00
LHO Larry Holmes 12.50 30.00
MC Miguel Cabrera 60.00 200.00
MFA Marc Forgione 6.00 15.00
MGU Matt Guy 10.00 25.00
MHO Mat Hoffman 8.00 20.00
MMO Mike Morse 4.00 10.00
MPA Manny Pacquiao 350.00 700.00
MSH Maxim Shmyrev 8.00 20.00
MWA Micky Ward 10.00 25.00
NC Nelson Cruz 6.00 15.00
NJA Nick Jacoby 8.00 20.00
NLO Nancy Lopez 10.00 25.00
PGA Peter Gammons 20.00 50.00
PST Picabo Street 12.00 30.00
RH Roy Halladay 200.00 350.00
RJO Rafer Johnson 12.50 30.00
RRU Rudy Ruettiger 10.00 25.00
RTU Ron Turcotte 20.00 50.00
RW Randy Wells 4.00 10.00
SBI Sue Bird 20.00 50.00
SC Starlin Castro 6.00 15.00
SLE Stan Lee 100.00 250.00
SM Sergio Mitre 6.00 15.00
SMI Shawn Michaels 40.00 100.00
SRI Sanya Richards 10.00 25.00
THO Tim Howard 12.00 30.00
TSC Timothy Shieff 10.00 25.00
UJ Ubaldo Jimenez 5.00 12.00
WEE Wee Man 12.00 30.00

2011 Topps Allen and Ginter Baseball Highlight Sketches

COMPLETE SET (25) 6.00 15.00
STATED ODDS 1:6 HOBBY
BHS1 Minnesota Twins .30 .75
BHS2 Jay Bruce .50 1.25
BHS3 Starlin Castro .50 1.25
BHS4 Roy Halladay .50 1.25
BHS5 Albert Pujols 1.00 2.50
BHS6 Jose Bautista .50 1.25
BHS7 CC Sabathia .50 1.25
BHS8 Cody Ross .30 .75
BHS9 Edwin Jackson .30 .75
BHS10 Ryan Howard .60 1.50
BHS11 Trevor Hoffman .50 1.25
BHS12 Armando Galarraga .30 .75
BHS13 San Francisco Giants .30 .75
BHS14 Mariano Rivera 1.00 2.50
BHS15 Aroldis Chapman 1.00 2.50
BHS16 Dallas Braden .30 .75
BHS17 Texas Rangers .30 .75
BHS18 Stephen Strasburg .75 2.00
BHS19 Matt Garza .30 .75
BHS20 Alex Rodriguez 1.00 2.50
BHS21 David Wright .60 1.50
BHS22 Ubaldo Jimenez .30 .75
BHS23 Mark Teixeira .50 1.25
BHS24 Jason Heyward .60 1.50
BHS25 Ichiro Suzuki 1.00 2.50

2011 Topps Allen and Ginter Cabinet Baseball Highlights

STATED ODDS 1:2 HOBBY BOXES
CB1 Galarraga/Miggy/Donald 2.50 6.00
CB2 Halladay/Ruiz/Howard 1.50 4.00
CB3 Dallas Braden/Landon Powell/Daric Barton 2.00 5.00
CB4 Ichiro/Bautista/King Felix 2.00 5.00
CB5 ARod/Jeter/Marcum 4.00 10.00
CB6 Pujols/La Russa/Dempster 2.00 5.00
CB7 Grand Canyon/Woodrow Wilson/Benjamin Harrison/Theodore Roosevelt 2.00 5.00
CB8 Yosemite National Park/Abraham Lincoln/John Conness 2.00 5.00
CB9 Yellowstone National Park/Ulysses S. Grant/Old Faithful 2.00 5.00
CB10 Redwood National Park/Lyndon B. Johnson/John E. Raker 2.00 5.00

2011 Topps Allen and Ginter Floating Fortresses

COMPLETE SET (20) 8.00 20.00
STATED ODDS 1:8 HOBBY
FF1 HMS Victory .60 1.50
FF2 Mary Rose .60 1.50
FF3 Henri Grace a Dieu .60 1.50
FF4 Michael .60 1.50
FF5 Sovereign of the Seas .60 1.50
FF6 HMS Indefatigable .60 1.50
FF7 Mahmudiye .60 1.50
FF8 Le Napoleon .60 1.50
FF9 USS Merrimack .60 1.50
FF10 USS Monitor .60 1.50
FF11 Lave .60 1.50
FF12 La Gloire .60 1.50
FF13 HMS Warrior .60 1.50
FF14 Solferino .60 1.50
FF15 USS Cairo .60 1.50
FF16 HMS Dreadnought .60 1.50
FF17 USS Texas .60 1.50
FF18 HMS Devastation .60 1.50
FF19 HMS Revenge .60 1.50
FF20 USS Pennsylvania .60 1.50

2011 Topps Allen and Ginter Hometown Heroes

COMPLETE SET (100) 10.00 25.00
HH1 Buster Posey .60 1.50
HH2 Colby Rasmus .30 .75
HH3 Brian Wilson .50 1.25
HH4 Jason Kubel .20 .50
HH5 Chase Utley .30 .75
HH6 Dan Haren .20 .50
HH7 CC Sabathia .30 .75
HH8 Stephen Drew .20 .50
HH9 Adam Wainwright .30 .75
HH10 Ryan Braun .30 .75
HH11 Jason Heyward .40 1.00
HH12 Andrew McCutchen .50 1.25
HH13 Shane Victorino .30 .75
HH14 Carl Pavano .20 .50
HH15 Matt Holliday .50 1.25
HH16 Dan Uggla .20 .50
HH17 Scott Rolen .30 .75
HH18 Zack Greinke .50 1.25

HH19 Nick Swisher .30 .75
HH20 David Price .40 1.00
HH21 Jon Lester .30 .75
HH22 John Danks .20 .50
HH23 Dustin Pedroia .50 1.25
HH24 Ryan Zimmerman .30 .75
HH25 Adam Dunn .30 .75
HH26 Torii Hunter .30 .75
HH27 Brandon Phillips .20 .50
HH28 Grady Sizemore .30 .75
HH29 Rick Porcello .30 .75
HH30 Dexter Fowler .20 .50
HH31 Jake Peavy .20 .50
HH32 Roy Halladay .30 .75
HH33 Austin Jackson .20 .50
HH34 Chipper Jones .50 1.25
HH35 Alex Gordon .30 .75
HH36 Gordon Beckham .20 .50
HH37 Clayton Kershaw .75 2.00
HH38 Andre Ethier .30 .75
HH39 Tim Lincecum .30 .75
HH40 Prince Fielder .30 .75
HH41 David DeJesus .20 .50
HH42 David Wright .40 1.00
HH43 Joba Chamberlain .20 .50
HH44 Delmon Young .30 .75
HH45 Ike Davis .20 .50
HH46 Jacoby Ellsbury .40 1.00
HH47 Phil Hughes .20 .50
HH48 Evan Longoria .30 .75
HH49 Danny Valencia .30 .75
HH50 Josh Hamilton .30 .75
HH51 Josh Beckett .20 .50
HH52 Ian Kinsler .30 .75
HH53 Justin Verlander .50 1.25
HH54 Joe Mauer .40 1.00
HH55 Justin Upton .30 .75
HH56 Brett Anderson .20 .50
HH57 Jordan Zimmermann .30 .75
HH58 Jimmy Rollins .30 .75
HH59 Brett Gardner .30 .75
HH60 Alex Rodriguez .60 1.50
HH61 Corey Hart .20 .50
HH62 Pedro Alvarez .40 1.00
HH63 Cody Ross .20 .50
HH64 Matt Cain .30 .75
HH65 Adrian Gonzalez .40 1.00
HH66 Derek Lowe .20 .50
HH67 Jon Jay .20 .50
HH68 Johnny Damon .20 .50
HH69 Yovani Gallardo .30 .75
HH70 Troy Tulowitzki .50 1.25
HH71 Chris Carpenter .30 .75
HH72 Billy Butler .20 .50
HH73 Mark Teixeira .30 .75
HH74 Jayson Werth .30 .75
HH75 Carl Crawford .30 .75
HH76 Adam Lind .20 .50
HH77 Mark Buehrle .30 .75
HH78 Manny Ramirez .50 1.25
HH79 Derek Jeter 1.25 3.00
HH80 Cliff Lee .30 .75
HH81 Neil Walker .30 .75
HH82 Jim Thome .30 .75
HH83 Travis Hafner .20 .50
HH84 Matt Kemp .40 1.00
HH85 Michael Young .20 .50
HH86 Kevin Youkilis .20 .50
HH87 Jeremy Hellickson .50 1.25
HH88 Roy Oswalt .30 .75
HH89 Todd Helton .30 .75
HH90 Ryan Howard .40 1.00
HH91 Madison Bumgarner .40 1.00
HH92 Mike Napoli .20 .50
HH93 Lance Berkman .30 .75
HH94 C.J. Wilson .20 .50
HH95 Kyle Drabek .30 .75
HH96 Brian McCann .30 .75
HH97 Brandon Morrow .20 .50
HH98 Clay Buchholz .20 .50
HH99 Andrew Bailey .20 .50
HH100 Travis Snider .20 .50

2011 Topps Allen and Ginter Minds that Made the Future

COMPLETE SET (40) 20.00 50.00
STATED ODDS 1:8 HOBBY
MMF1 Leonardo da Vinci .60 1.50
MMF2 Alexander Graham Bell .60 1.50
MMF3 Eli Whitney .60 1.50
MMF4 Nicolaus Copernicus .60 1.50
MMF5 Johannes Gutenberg .60 1.50
MMF6 George Washington Carver .60 1.50
MMF7 Samuel Morse .60 1.50
MMF8 Granville Woods .60 1.50
MMF9 Elisha Otis .60 1.50
MMF10 Alessandro Volta .60 1.50
MMF11 Tycho Brahe .60 1.50
MMF12 Gregor Mendel .60 1.50
MMF13 Carl Linnaeus .60 1.50
MMF14 Johannes Kepler .60 1.50
MMF15 Isaac Newton .60 1.50
MMF16 Marie Curie .60 1.50
MMF17 Carl Friedrich Gauss .60 1.50
MMF18 Sigmund Freud .60 1.50
MMF19 Bernhard Riemann .60 1.50
MMF20 Leonhard Euler .60 1.50
MMF21 Robert Fulton .60 1.50
MMF22 Ada Lovelace .60 1.50
MMF23 Florence Nightingale .60 1.50
MMF24 Nikola Tesla .60 1.50
MMF25 Galileo Galilei .60 1.50
MMF26 Charles Darwin .60 1.50
MMF27 Louis Pasteur .60 1.50
MMF28 Guglielmo Marconi .60 1.50
MMF29 Antoine Lavoisier .60 1.50
MMF30 Michael Faraday .60 1.50
MMF31 Dmitri Mendeleev .60 1.50
MMF32 Robert Koch .60 1.50
MMF33 Euclid .60 1.50
MMF34 Archimedes .60 1.50
MMF35 Jagadish Chandra Bose .60 1.50
MMF36 Aristotle .60 1.50
MMF37 John Deere .60 1.50
MMF38 George Eastman .60 1.50
MMF39 Samuel Colt .60 1.50
MMF40 Benjamin Franklin .60 1.50

2011 Topps Allen and Ginter Mini Animals in Peril

COMPLETE SET (30) 10.00 25.00
STATED ODDS 1:12 HOBBY
AP1 Siberian Tiger .75 2.00
AP2 Mountain Gorilla .75 2.00
AP3 Arakan Forest Turtle .75 2.00
AP4 Darwin's Fox .75 2.00
AP5 Gharial .75 2.00
AP6 Vaquita .75 2.00
AP7 Dhole .75 2.00
AP8 Blue Whale .75 2.00
AP9 Bonobo .75 2.00
AP10 Ethiopian Wolf .75 2.00
AP11 Giant Panda .75 2.00
AP12 Snow Leopard .75 2.00
AP13 African Wild Dog .75 2.00
AP14 Indian Rhinoceros .75 2.00
AP15 Philippine Eagle .75 2.00
AP16 Markhor .75 2.00
AP17 Orangutan .75 2.00
AP18 Grevy's Zebra .75 2.00
AP19 Tasmanian Devil .75 2.00
AP20 Bengal Tiger .75 2.00
AP21 Whooping Crane .75 2.00
AP22 Sea Otter .75 2.00
AP23 Red Wolf .75 2.00
AP24 Key Deer .75 2.00
AP25 Black-Footed Ferret .75 2.00
AP26 Amur Leopard .75 2.00
AP27 Anderson's Salamander .75 2.00
AP28 Greater Bamboo Lemur .75 2.00
AP29 Hawaiian Monk Seal .75 2.00
AP30 Kakapo .75 2.00

2011 Topps Allen and Ginter Mini Fabulous Face Flocculence

FFF1 A.Lincoln/The Lincoln 10.00 25.00
FFF2 The Ironing Board 8.00 20.00
FFF3 The Conscientious Objector 8.00 20.00
FFF4 The Bib 8.00 20.00
FFF5 Charles Darwin/The Darwin 8.00 20.00
FFF6 The Neckbeard 8.00 20.00
FFF7 The Goat Patch 8.00 20.00
FFF8 Ambrose Burnside/Burnside's Sideburns 8.00 20.00
FFF9 Thunderchops 8.00 20.00
FFF10 B.Wilson/The Closer 10.00 25.00

2011 Topps Allen and Ginter Mini Flora of the World

COMPLETE SET (5) 20.00 50.00
STATED ODDS 1:144 HOBBY
FOW1 Black-Eyed Susan 6.00 15.00
FOW2 Spurred Snapdragon 6.00 15.00
FOW3 Shirley Poppy 6.00 15.00
FOW4 Mexican Hat 6.00 15.00
FOW5 Sweet Alyssum 6.00 15.00

2011 Topps Allen and Ginter Mini Fortunes for the Taking

FFT1 The Oak Island Money Pit 6.00 15.00
FFT2 Captain Kidd's Treasure 6.00 15.00
FFT3 The Beale Ciphers 6.00 15.00
FFT4 The Amber Room 6.00 15.00
FFT5 The Devonshire Treasure of Cocos Island 6.00 15.00
FFT6 Blackbeard's Treasure 6.00 15.00
FFT7 The Treasure of Lima 6.00 15.00
FFT8 Montezuma's Treasure 6.00 15.00
FFT9 Butch Cassidy's Loot 6.00 15.00
FFT10 The Lost French Gold of Ohio 6.00 15.00

2011 Topps Allen and Ginter Mini Portraits of Penultimacy

COMPLETE SET (10) 5.00 12.00
STATED ODDS 1:12 HOBBY
PP1 Antonio Meucci .60 1.50
PP2 Mike Gellner .60 1.50
PP3 Dr. Watson .60 1.50
PP4 Igor .60 1.50
PP5 The Hare .60 1.50
PP6 Tonto .60 1.50
PP7 Antonio Salieri .60 1.50
PP8 Sancho Panza .60 1.50
PP9 Thomas E. Dewey .60 1.50
PP10 Toto .60 1.50

2011 Topps Allen and Ginter Mini Step Right Up

COMPLETE SET (10) 5.00 12.00
STATED ODDS 1:15 HOBBY
SRU1 The Bed of Nails .60 1.50
SRU2 Fire Breathing .60 1.50
SRU3 Fire Eating .60 1.50
SRU4 The Flea Circus .60 1.50
SRU5 The Human Cannonball .60 1.50
SRU6 The Human Blockhead .60 1.50
SRU7 Snake Charming .60 1.50
SRU8 The Strongman .60 1.50
SRU9 Knife Throwing .60 1.50
SRU10 Tightrope Walking .60 1.50

2011 Topps Allen and Ginter Mini Uninvited Guests

COMPLETE SET (10) 5.00 12.00
STATED ODDS 1:12 HOBBY
UG1 Bachelor's Grove Cemetery .60 1.50
UG2 The White House .60 1.50
UG3 Waverly Hills Sanatorium .60 1.50
UG4 The Villisca Axe Murder House .60 1.50
UG5 The Amityville Haunting .60 1.50
UG6 The Lemp Mansion .60 1.50
UG7 Alcatraz .60 1.50
UG8 The Winchester Mystery House .60 1.50
UG9 RMS Queen Mary .60 1.50
UG10 The Lizzie Borden House .60 1.50

2011 Topps Allen and Ginter Mini World's Most Mysterious Figures

COMPLETE SET (10) 5.00 12.00
STATED ODDS 1:15 HOBBY
WMF1 Rasputin .60 1.50
WMF2 The Poe Toaster .60 1.50
WMF3 Kasper Hauser .60 1.50
WMF4 Fulcanelli .60 1.50
WMF5 D.B. Cooper .60 1.50
WMF6 The Count of St. Germain .60 1.50
WMF7 The Man in the Iron Mask .60 1.50
WMF8 Nostradamus .60 1.50
WMF9 The Babushka Lady .60 1.50
WMF10 Captain Charles Johnson .60 1.50

2011 Topps Allen and Ginter N43

STATED ODDS 1:2 HOBBY BOXES
AC Aroldis Chapman 2.00 5.00
AP Albert Pujols 4.00 10.00
AW Adam Wainwright 1.25 3.00
CC Carl Crawford 1.25 3.00
CG Carlos Gonzalez 1.25 3.00
DP David Price 1.50 4.00
DW David Wright 1.50 4.00
HR Hanley Ramirez 1.25 3.00
JJ Josh Johnson 1.25 3.00
JV Joey Votto 2.00 5.00
MT Mark Teixeira 1.25 3.00
RC Robinson Cano 1.25 3.00
RH Roy Halladay 1.25 3.00
TL Tim Lincecum 1.25 3.00
UJ Ubaldo Jimenez .75 2.00

2011 Topps Allen and Ginter Relics

STATED ODDS 1:10 HOBBY
EXCHANGE DEADLINE 6/30/2014
AB1 Adrian Beltre Bat 10.00 25.00
AB2 Adrian Beltre Jsy 3.00 8.00
AD1 Adam Dunn Bat 3.00 8.00
AD2 Adam Dunn Jsy 3.00 8.00
ADU Angelo Dundee 4.00 10.00
AE Andre Ethier 3.00 8.00
AES Alcides Escobar 4.00 10.00
AG Adrian Gonzalez 4.00 10.00
AH Aaron Hill 3.00 8.00
AJ Adam Jones 3.00 8.00
AJA1 Austin Jackson Bat 3.00 8.00
AJA2 Austin Jackson Jsy 3.00 8.00
AJB A.J. Burnett 3.00 8.00
AJP A.J. Pierzynski 12.00 30.00
AJU Ana Julaton 10.00 25.00
AL1 Adam Lind Bat 3.00 8.00
AL2 Adam Lind Jsy 3.00 8.00
AM1 Andrew McCutchen Bat 6.00 15.00
AM2 Andrew McCutchen Jsy 12.00 30.00
AMU Aimee Mullins 4.00 10.00
AP1 Albert Pujols Bat 10.00 25.00
AP2 Albert Pujols Jsy 30.00 60.00
AR Alex Rodriguez 5.00 12.00
ARA1 Alexei Ramirez Bat 3.00 8.00
ARA2 Alexei Ramirez Jsy 3.00 8.00
ARM2 Aramis Ramirez Jsy 3.00 8.00
ARM1 Aramis Ramirez Bat 15.00 40.00
AS Alfonso Soriano 4.00 10.00
ASA Anibal Sanchez 3.00 8.00
ASO Annika Sorenstam 12.00 30.00
BB Billy Butler 3.00 8.00
BBO Brennan Boesch 3.00 8.00
BD Blake DeWitt 3.00 8.00
BG Brett Gardner 3.00 8.00
BJU B.J. Upton 3.00 8.00
BM Brian McCann 3.00 8.00
CB Carlos Beltran 10.00 25.00
CBU Cheryl Burke 10.00 25.00
CG Carlos Gomez 3.00 8.00
CJ Chipper Jones 5.00 12.00
CJO Chris Johnson 3.00 8.00
CM Casey McGehee 3.00 8.00
CP Carlos Pena 3.00 8.00
CQ Carlos Quentin 3.00 8.00
CR Cody Ross 5.00 12.00
CRA Colby Rasmus 5.00 12.00
CU Chase Utley 4.00 10.00
CWE Chrissie Wellington 5.00 12.00
CWO Chuck Woolery 5.00 12.00
DBO Daniel Boulud 6.00 15.00
DH Daniel Hudson 3.00 8.00
DJ Derek Jeter 10.00 25.00
DL Derrek Lee 3.00 8.00
DO David Ortiz 3.00 8.00
DP Dustin Pedroia 5.00 12.00
DS1 Drew Stubbs Bat 4.00 10.00
DS2 Drew Stubbs Jsy 3.00 8.00
DTU Diana Taurasi 6.00 15.00
DU1 Dan Uggla Bat 3.00 8.00
DU2 Dan Uggla Jsy 10.00 25.00
DVA Dick Vitale 10.00 25.00
EA Elvis Andrus 3.00 8.00
EJA Eric Jackson 6.00 15.00
EL1 Evan Longoria Bat 3.00 8.00
EL2 Evan Longoria Jsy 5.00 12.00
ELY Evan Lysacek 5.00 12.00
EV Edinson Volquez 3.00 8.00
FC Francisco Cervelli 3.00 8.00
FH Felix Hernandez 3.00 8.00
GAU Geno Auriemma 8.00 20.00
GB Gordon Beckham 3.00 8.00
GFI Guy Fieri 10.00 25.00
GS Grady Sizemore 8.00 20.00
GSO Geovany Soto 3.00 8.00
HK Howie Kendrick 3.00 8.00
HMI Heather Mitts 10.00 25.00
HP Hunter Pence 3.00 8.00
HR1 Hanley Ramirez Bat 3.00 8.00
HR2 Hanley Ramirez Jsy 3.00 8.00
HSO Hope Solo 20.00 50.00
ID1 Ike Davis Bat 3.00 8.00
ID2 Ike Davis Jsy 3.00 8.00
IDE Ian Desmond 3.00 8.00
IR Ivan Rodriguez 3.00 8.00
IS Ichiro Suzuki 6.00 15.00
JB Jason Bay 5.00 12.00
JBA Jose Bautista 4.00 10.00
JBE Josh Beckett 3.00 8.00
JBR Jay Bruce 5.00 12.00
JC Joba Chamberlain 3.00 8.00
JD Johnny Damon 3.00 8.00
JDD J.D. Drew 3.00 8.00
JE1 Jacoby Ellsbury Bat 5.00 12.00
JE2 Jacoby Ellsbury Jsy 3.00 8.00
JH Josh Hamilton 6.00 15.00
JJ Josh Johnson 3.00 8.00
JJA Jon Jay 3.00 8.00
JL James Loney 3.00 8.00
JLA John Lackey 3.00 8.00
JLA Jake LaMotta 15.00 40.00
JLL Jack LaLanne 6.00 15.00
JLO Jed Lowrie 3.00 8.00
JM Joe Maddon 3.00 8.00
JMC John McEnroe 20.00 50.00
JMO Justin Morneau 3.00 8.00
JNA Jim Nantz 6.00 15.00
JOF Jo Frost 6.00 15.00
JP1 Jorge Posada Bat 4.00 10.00
JP2 Jorge Posada Jsy 4.00 10.00
JPA Jonathan Papelbon 3.00 8.00
JR Jimmy Rollins 5.00 12.00
JRE Jose Reyes 6.00 15.00
JS Jarrod Saltalamacchia 3.00 8.00
JSA Jeff Samardzija 4.00 10.00
JT Jose Tabata 4.00 10.00
JU Justin Upton 3.00 8.00
JV1 Joey Votto Bat 4.00 10.00
JV2 Joey Votto Jsy 8.00 20.00
JVE Justin Verlander 6.00 15.00
JW Jayson Werth 3.00 8.00
KB Kyle Blanks 3.00 8.00
KF Kosuke Fukudome 4.00 10.00
KM Kendrys Morales 3.00 8.00
KPE Kyle Petty 10.00 25.00
KS Kurt Suzuki 3.00 8.00
KY Kevin Youkilis 4.00 10.00
KYA Kristi Yamaguchi 10.00 25.00
LHO Lou Holtz 20.00 50.00
LHO Larry Holmes 10.00 25.00
MB Mark Buehrle 3.00 8.00
MBY Marlon Byrd 3.00 8.00
MC Matt Cain 4.00 10.00
MCA1 Melky Cabrera Bat 6.00 15.00
MCA2 Melky Cabrera Jsy 6.00 15.00
MCB Miguel Cabrera 4.00 10.00
MFA Marc Forgione 6.00 15.00
MGU Matt Guy 5.00 12.00
MHO Mat Hoffman 3.00 8.00
MPA Manny Pacquiao 25.00 60.00
MR Mark Reynolds 3.00 8.00
MSH Maxim Shmyrev 8.00 20.00
MT Mark Teixeira 3.00 8.00
MWA Micky Ward 5.00 12.00
MY1 Michael Young Bat 3.00 8.00
MY2 Michael Young Jsy 3.00 8.00
NC Nelson Cruz 4.00 10.00
NF Neftali Feliz 3.00 8.00
NLO Nancy Lopez 12.00 30.00
NM Nick Markakis 5.00 12.00
NS Nick Swisher 3.00 8.00
PF Prince Fielder 3.00 8.00
PGA Peter Gammons 10.00 25.00
PH Phil Hughes 3.00 8.00
PK Paul Konerko 6.00 15.00
PS1 Pablo Sandoval Bat 4.00 10.00
PS2 Pablo Sandoval Jsy 4.00 10.00
PST Picabo Street 10.00 25.00
RB1 Ryan Braun Bat 6.00 15.00
RB2 Ryan Braun Jsy 4.00 10.00
RC Robinson Cano 3.00 8.00
RD Ryan Dempster 3.00 8.00
RDO Ryan Doumit 3.00 8.00
RH Ryan Howard 3.00 8.00
RJO Rafer Johnson 6.00 15.00
RM1 Russell Martin Bat 3.00 8.00
RM2 Russell Martin Jsy 3.00 8.00
RN Ricky Nolasco 3.00 8.00
RP Ryan Perry 3.00 8.00
RRU Rudy Ruettiger 12.00 30.00
RTU Ron Turcotte 8.00 20.00
RW1 Rickie Weeks Bat 3.00 8.00
RW2 Rickie Weeks Jsy 3.00 8.00
RZ Ryan Zimmerman 3.00 8.00
SBI Sue Bird 6.00 15.00
SC1 Starlin Castro Bat 5.00 12.00
SC2 Starlin Castro Jsy 5.00 12.00
SD Stephen Drew 10.00 25.00
SLE Stan Lee 20.00 50.00
SMI Shawn Michaels 10.00 25.00
SR Scott Rolen 8.00 20.00
SRI Sanya Richards 8.00 20.00
SV1 Shane Victorino Bat 4.00 10.00
SV2 Shane Victorino Jsy 3.00 8.00
TC Tyler Colvin 3.00 8.00
TG Tony Gwynn Jr. 10.00 25.00
TH Tim Hudson 3.00 8.00
THA Tommy Hanson 3.00 8.00
THE Todd Helton 3.00 8.00
THO Tim Howard 8.00 20.00
TSC Timothy Shieff 6.00 15.00
TT Troy Tulowitzki 3.00 8.00
TW Tim Wakefield 3.00 8.00
WEE Wee Man 5.00 12.00
WV Will Venable 3.00 8.00
XN Xavier Nady 3.00 8.00
YE Yunel Escobar 4.00 10.00

2011 Topps Allen and Ginter Rip Cards

OVERALL RIP ODDS 1:276 HOBBY
PRINT RUNS B/WN 10-99 COPIES PER
NO PRICING ON QTY 25 OR LESS
ALL LISTED PRICED ARE FOR RIPPED
UNRIPPED HAVE ADD'L CARDS WITHIN
COMMON UNRIPPED p/r 99 60.00 120.00
COMMON UNRIPPED p/r 75 60.00 120.00
COMMON UNRIPPED p/r 50 60.00 120.00
COMMON UNRIPPED p/r 25 100.00 250.00
COMMON UNRIPPED p/r 10 350.00 700.00
RC54 Jayson Werth/50 6.00 15.00
RC55 Jered Weaver/50 6.00 15.00
RC56 Francisco Liriano/50 4.00 10.00
RC57 Zack Greinke/50 10.00 25.00
RC58 Roy Oswalt/50 6.00 15.00
RC59 Hunter Pence/50 6.00 15.00
RC60 Adrian Beltre/50 10.00 25.00
RC61 Martin Prado/50 4.00 10.00
RC62 Jay Bruce/50 6.00 15.00
RC63 Jimmy Rollins/50 6.00 15.00
RC64 Paul Konerko/50 6.00 15.00
RC65 Brandon Phillips/50 4.00 10.00
RC66 Dan Haren/50 4.00 10.00
RC67 Andre Ethier/50 6.00 15.00
RC68 Matt Cain/50 6.00 15.00
RC69 Elvis Andrus/75 6.00 15.00
RC70 Jason Heyward/75 5.00 12.00
RC71 Ian Kinsler/75 6.00 15.00
RC72 Joakim Soria/75 4.00 10.00
RC73 Michael Young/75 4.00 10.00
RC74 Delmon Young/75 6.00 15.00
RC75 Mariano Rivera/75 10.00 25.00
RC76 Mat Latos/75 6.00 15.00
RC77 Colby Rasmus/75 5.00 12.00
RC78 Heath Bell/75 4.00 10.00
RC79 Shane Victorino/75 6.00 15.00
RC80 Derek Jeter/75 15.00 40.00
RC81 Billy Butler/75 4.00 10.00
RC82 Neftali Feliz/75 4.00 10.00
RC83 Carlos Santana/75 8.00 20.00
RC84 Gordon Beckham/99 4.00 10.00
RC85 Mike Stanton/99 10.00 25.00
RC86 Yovani Gallardo/99 4.00 10.00
RC87 Clay Buchholz/99 4.00 10.00
RC88 Pedro Alvarez/99 8.00 20.00
RC89 Matt Garza/99 4.00 10.00
RC90 Aroldis Chapman/99 8.00 20.00
RC91 David Ortiz/99 10.00 25.00
RC92 Jeremy Hellickson/99 6.00 15.00
RC93 Jacoby Ellsbury/99 6.00 15.00
RC94 Stephen Drew/99 4.00 10.00
RC95 Starlin Castro/99 5.00 12.00
RC96 Torii Hunter/99 4.00 10.00
RC97 Madison Bumgarner/99 8.00 20.00
RC99 Vernon Wells/99 4.00 10.00

2011 Topps Allen and Ginter State Map Relics

STATED PRINT RUN 50 SER.#'d SETS
1 New England 90.00 150.00
2 New York 90.00 150.00
3 Penn/N.Jersey 60.00 120.00
4 VA/WV/MD/DE 100.00 200.00
5 N.Carolina/S.Carolina 60.00 120.00
6 Kentucky/Tenn. 50.00 100.00
7 Michigan 50.00 100.00
8 Ohio 50.00 100.00
9 Indiana 60.00 120.00
10 Georgia 40.00 80.00
11 Florida 90.00 150.00
12 Alabama 50.00 100.00
13 Mississippi 50.00 100.00
14 Wisconsin 50.00 100.00
15 Illinois 50.00 100.00
16 Minnesota 60.00 120.00
17 Iowa 60.00 120.00
18 Arkansas 60.00 120.00
19 Missouri 50.00 100.00
20 Louisiana 60.00 120.00
21 North Dakota 40.00 80.00
22 South Dakota 50.00 100.00
23 Nebraska 60.00 120.00
24 Kansas 50.00 100.00
25 Oklahoma 50.00 100.00
26 Texas 90.00 150.00
27 Montana 40.00 80.00
28 Wyoming 30.00 60.00
29 Colorado 50.00 100.00
30 New Mexico 40.00 80.00
31 Idaho 50.00 100.00
32 Utah 75.00 150.00
33 Arizona 40.00 80.00
34 Washington 50.00 100.00
35 Oregon 25.00 60.00
36 Nevada 40.00 80.00
37 California 60.00 120.00
38 Alaska 50.00 100.00
39 Hawaii 75.00 150.00

2012 Topps Allen and Ginter

COMPLETE SET (350) 30.00 60.00
COMP.SET w/o SP's (300) 15.00 40.00
SP ODDS 1:2 HOBBY
1 Albert Pujols .50 1.25
2 Juan Pierre .25 .60
3 Miguel Cabrera .40 1.00
4 Yu Darvish RC 1.50 4.00
5 David Price .30 .75
6 Johnny Bench .40 1.00
7 Mickey Mantle 1.25 3.00
8 Mitch Moreland .25 .60
9 Yonder Alonso .25 .60
10 Dustin Pedroia .40 1.00
11 Eric Hosmer .30 .75
12 Bryce Harper RC 6.00 15.00
13 Drew Stubbs .25 .60
14 Nick Markakis .30 .75
15 Joel Hanrahan .25 .60
16 Rulon Gardner .15 .40
17 Lonnie Chisenhall .25 .60
18 Kevin Youkilis .40 1.00
19 Bob Knight .50 1.25
20 Miguel Montero .25 .60
21 Matt Moore RC 1.00 2.50
22 Jair Jurrjens .25 .60
23 Yogi Berra .40 1.00
24 Paul Goldschmidt .40 1.00
25 Shin-Soo Choo .30 .75
26 Hunter Pence .30 .75
27 Ricky Nolasco .25 .60
28 Dustin Ackley .25 .60
29 Hanley Ramirez .30 .75
30 Carlos Zambrano .30 .75
31 Jackie Robinson .40 1.00
32 Ben Zobrist .30 .75
33 Chipper Jones .40 1.00
34 Alex Gordon .30 .75
35 David Ortiz .40 1.00
36 Kirk Herbstreit .15 .40
37 James McDonald .25 .60
38 Pablo Sandoval .30 .75
39 Brad Peacock RC .60 1.50
40 Jimmy Rollins .30 .75
41 Clayton Kershaw .60 1.50
42 Justin Upton .30 .75
43 Josh Johnson .30 .75
44 Brandon League .25 .60
45 Ewa Malaya .15 .40
46 Jarrod Saltalamacchia .25 .60
47 Buster Posey .50 1.25
48 Jordan Walden .25 .60
49 Jeremy Hellickson .25 .60
50 Clay Buchholz .25 .60
51 Don Denkinger .15 .40
52 Cameron Maybin .25 .60
53 Hisashi Iwakuma RC 1.25 3.00
54 Al Kaline .40 1.00
55 Colin Montgomerie .40 1.00
56 Jordan Pacheco RC .60 1.50
57 Michael Pineda .25 .60
58 Ryan Braun .25 .60
59 Johnny Damon .30 .75

2011 Topps Allen and Ginter

60 Reggie Jackson .25 .60
61 Richard Petty .50 1.25
62 Michael Cuddyer .25 .60
63 Zach Britton .30 .75
64 Mat Latos .30 .75
65 Alex Rios .30 .75
66 Yadier Molina .50 1.25
67 Desmond Jennings .30 .75
68 Rickie Weeks .25 .60
69 Kurt Suzuki .25 .60
70 Aroldis Chapman .40 1.00
71 Curtis Granderson .30 .75
72 Joakim Soria .25 .60
73 Jordan Zimmermann .30 .75
74 Johnny Cueto .30 .75
75 Erin Andrews .75 2.00
76 Michael Bourn .25 .60
77 Chris Young .25 .60
78 Joe Mauer .30 .75
79 Yoenis Cespedes RC 1.50 4.00
80 Brooks Robinson .25 .60
81 Jerry Bailey .15 .40
82 Giancarlo Stanton .40 1.00
83 Matt Joyce .25 .60
84 Andre Ethier .30 .75
85 Curly Neal .40 1.00
86 Nyjer Morgan .25 .60
87 Annie Duke .15 .40
88 Stan Musial .60 1.50
89 Edwin Jackson .25 .60
90 Roy Halladay .30 .75
91 Grady Sizemore .30 .75
92 Craig Kimbrel .30 .75
93 Jose Bautista .30 .75
94 Geovany Soto .30 .75
95 Felix Hernandez .30 .75
96 Gavin Floyd .25 .60
97 Max Scherzer .40 1.00
98 Nelson Cruz .40 1.00
99 Sandy Koufax .75 2.00
100 Troy Tulowitzki .40 1.00
101 James Loney .25 .60
102 Huston Street .25 .60
103 Alexi Ogando .25 .60
104 Ian Desmond .25 .60
105 Arnold Palmer .60 1.50
106 Bud Norris .25 .60
107 C.J. Wilson .25 .60
108 J.P. Arencibia .25 .60
109 Tim Lincecum .30 .75
110 Heath Bell .25 .60
111 Wandy Rodriguez .25 .60
112 Chris Carpenter .30 .75
113 Meadowlark Lemon .40 1.00
114 Johan Santana .30 .75
115 Carlos Santana .30 .75
116 Brandon Beachy .25 .60
117 Nick Swisher .30 .75
118 Carl Yastrzemski .60 1.50
119 Asdrubal Cabrera .30 .75
120 Mariano Rivera .50 1.25
121 David Wright .30 .75
122 Brett Lawrie RC .75 2.00
123 Adam Lind .30 .75
124 Jered Weaver .30 .75
125 Ben Revere .25 .60
126 Justin Masterson .25 .60
127 Erick Aybar .25 .60
128 Andrew McCutchen .40 1.00
129 Michael Phelps .50 1.25
130 Madison Bumgarner .30 .75
131 Jim Palmer .25 .60
132 Daniel Hudson .25 .60
133 Carlos Beltran .30 .75
134 David Freese .25 .60
135 Michael Morse .25 .60
136 Jacoby Ellsbury .30 .75
137 George Brett .75 2.00
138 Josh Willingham .30 .75
139 Tim Hudson .30 .75
140 Mike Trout 12.00 30.00
141 Vance Worley .30 .75
142 Jose Reyes .30 .75
143 Nick Hagadone .25 .60
144 Joe Benson RC .60 1.50
145 Drew Storen .25 .60
146 Josh Beckett .25 .60
147 Tsuyoshi Nishioka .30 .75
148 Carlos Gonzalez .30 .75
149 Wilson Ramos .25 .60
150 Norichika Aoki RC .75 2.00
151 Jose Valverde .30 .75
152 Ryan Vogelsong .25 .60
153 Robinson Cano .30 .75
154 Bob Hurley Sr. .15 .40
155 Edinson Volquez .25 .60
156 Trevor Cahill .25 .60
157 Roger Federer .75 2.00
158 Melky Cabrera .25 .60
159 Devin Mesoraco RC .60 1.50
160 Shane Victorino .30 .75
161 Freddie Freeman .50 1.25
162 Jeff Francoeur .25 .60
163 Tom Seaver .25 .60
164 Ike Davis .25 .60
165 Alex Avila .25 .60
166 Ervin Santana .25 .60
167 J.J. Putz .25 .60
168 Jason Kipnis .30 .75
169 Mark Teixeira .30 .75
170 Don Mattingly .75 2.00
171 Stephen Strasburg .40 1.00
172 Chris Perez .25 .60
173 Jay Bruce .30 .75
174 Ubaldo Jimenez .25 .60
175 Luke Hochevar .25 .60
176 Babe Ruth 1.00 2.50
177 Stephen Drew .25 .60
178 Wei-Yin Chen RC 1.50 4.00
179 Cole Hamels .30 .75
180 Tim Federowicz RC .60 1.50
181 Joe DiMaggio .75 2.00
182 Colby Rasmus .30 .75
183 Darwin Barney .25 .60
184 Ara Parseghian .25 .60
185 Starlin Castro .30 .75
186 Jemile Weeks RC .25 .60
187 John Axford .25 .60
188 Tom Milone RC .60 1.50
189 Lance Berkman .30 .75
190 Addison Reed RC .60 1.50
191 Jason Bay .30 .75
192 Brett Pill RC 1.00 2.50
193 Jackie Joyner-Kersee .25 .60
194 J.J. Hardy .25 .60
195 Jhoulys Chacin .25 .60
196 Lou Gehrig .75 2.00
197 Ty Cobb .60 1.50
198 Phil Pfister .15 .40
199 Ricky Romero .25 .60
200 Matt Kemp .30 .75
201 Tommy Hanson .25 .60
202 Jaime Garcia .30 .75
203 Ian Kinsler .30 .75
204 Adam Dunn .30 .75
205 Tony Gwynn .40 1.00
206 Joey Votto .40 1.00
207 Cory Luebke .25 .60
208 Martin Prado .25 .60
209 Coco Crisp .25 .60
210 Willie Mays .75 2.00
211 Keegan Bradley .15 .40
212 Ken Griffey Jr. .75 2.00
213 Joe Nathan .25 .60
214 Yunel Escobar .25 .60
215 Dan Haren .25 .60
216 Corey Hart .25 .60
217 Brian Wilson .40 1.00
218 John Danks .25 .60
219 Ian Kennedy .25 .60
220 James Brown .15 .40
221 Carlos Marmol .25 .60
222 Yovani Gallardo .30 .75
223 CC Sabathia .30 .75
224 Adam Jones .30 .75
225 Roger Maris .40 1.00
226 Jim Thome .30 .75
227 Michael Young .25 .60
228 Dexter Fowler .30 .75
229 Ichiro Suzuki .50 1.25
230 Evan Longoria .30 .75
231 Todd Helton .30 .75
232 Kate Upton .50 1.25
233 Shaun Marcum .25 .60
234 Carlos Lee .25 .60
235 Victor Martinez .30 .75
236 Scott Rolen .25 .60
237 Al Unser Sr. .25 .60
238 Austin Jackson .30 .75
239 Liam Hendriks RC .60 1.50
240 Steve Lombardozzi RC .60 1.50
241 Andrew Bailey .25 .60
242 Alfonso Soriano .30 .75
243 Aramis Ramirez .25 .60
244 Brett Anderson .25 .60
245 Hank Haney .25 .60
246 Torii Hunter .30 .75
247 Hank Aaron .75 2.00
248 Jed Lowrie .25 .60
249 Phil Hughes .25 .60
250 Brennan Boesch .25 .60
251 B.J. Upton .30 .75
252 Tsuyoshi Wada RC .60 1.50
253 Jorge De La Rosa .25 .60
254 Rickey Henderson .40 1.00
255 Dayan Viciedo .25 .60
256 Brandon Morrow .25 .60
257 Dan Uggla .30 .75
258 Doug Fister .25 .60
259 Wade Davis .25 .60
260 Alex Liddi RC .60 1.50
261 Michael Taylor RC .60 1.50
262 Justin Verlander .40 1.00
263 Jason Motte .25 .60
264 Brian McCann .30 .75
265 Chris Parmelee RC .60 1.50
266 Carlos Ruiz .25 .60
267 Neftali Feliz .25 .60
268 Angel Pagan .25 .60
269 Mike Schmidt .60 1.50
270 Anthony Rizzo .50 1.25
271 Mark Reynolds .25 .60
272 Jose Tabata .25 .60
273 Gaby Sanchez .30 .75
274 Derek Jeter 1.00 2.50
275 Kerry Wood .25 .60
276 James Shields .25 .60
277 Jesus Montero RC .60 1.50
278 Fatal1ty .15 .40
279 Brett Gardner .30 .75
280 Brandon Belt .30 .75
281 Matt Cain .30 .75
282 Carlos Quentin .25 .60
283 Dale Webster .15 .40
284 Pedro Alvarez .25 .60
285 Ryan Zimmerman .30 .75
286 Neil Walker .25 .60
287 Hiroki Kuroda .25 .60
288 Alex Rodriguez .50 1.25
289 Brandon Phillips .25 .60
290 Derek Holland .25 .60
291 Chase Utley .30 .75
292 Greg Gumbel .15 .40
293 Cliff Lee .30 .75
294 Elvis Andrus .30 .75
295 Drew Pomeranz RC .60 1.50
296 Mark Trumbo .30 .75
297 Justin Morneau .30 .75
298 Dee Gordon .25 .60
299 Jeff Niemann .25 .60
300 Roberto Clemente 1.00 2.50
301 Adron Chambers SP RC 1.25 3.00
302 Jayson Werth SP 1.50 4.00
303 Ivan Nova SP 1.50 4.00
304 Kyle Farnsworth SP 2.50 6.00
305 Wilin Rosario SP RC 2.00 5.00
306 Ryan Howard SP 1.00 2.50
307 Jhonny Peralta SP 2.00 5.00
308 Paul Konerko SP 1.25 3.00
309 Bela Karolyi SP 1.25 3.00
310 Russell Martin SP 2.00 5.00
311 Bob Gibson SP 1.25 3.00
312 Anibal Sanchez SP 1.25 3.00
313 Carlos Pena SP 2.00 5.00
314 Michael Buffer SP 1.50 4.00
315 Dellin Betances SP RC 1.25 3.00
316 Adrian Gonzalez SP 1.50 4.00
317 Jason Heyward SP 1.00 2.50
318 Mike Moustakas SP 1.50 4.00
319 Adam Wainwright SP 1.50 4.00
320 Jonathan Papelbon SP 1.50 4.00
321 Chad Billingsley SP 2.00 5.00
322 Sergio Santos SP 2.00 5.00
323 Ryan Roberts SP 2.00 5.00
324 Cal Ripken Jr. SP 2.00 5.00
325 Frank Robinson SP 1.25 3.00
326 Logan Morrison SP 2.00 5.00
327 Jon Lester SP 1.25 3.00
328 Josh Hamilton SP 1.00 2.50
329 Billy Butler SP 2.00 5.00
330 Mike Napoli SP 1.25 3.00
331 Carl Crawford SP 1.50 4.00
332 Guy Bluford SP 1.25 3.00
333 Kelly Johnson SP 2.00 5.00
334 Adrian Beltre SP 3.00 8.00
335 Alexei Ramirez SP 2.50 6.00
336 Gio Gonzalez SP 2.50 6.00
337 Matt Holliday SP 1.25 3.00
338 Prince Fielder SP 1.50 4.00
339 Swin Cash SP 3.00 8.00
340 Marty Hogan SP 1.25 3.00
341 Colby Lewis SP 2.00 5.00
342 Ryan Dempster SP 2.00 5.00
343 Zack Greinke SP 2.00 5.00
344 Matt Dominguez SP RC 2.50 6.00
345 Nolan Ryan SP 2.00 5.00
346 Lefty Kreh SP 1.25 3.00
347 Matt Garza SP 2.00 5.00
348 Chase Headley SP 2.00 5.00
349 Danny Espinosa SP 2.00 5.00
350 Howie Kendrick SP 2.00 5.00

2012 Topps Allen and Ginter Mini

*MINI 1-300: .75X TO 2X BASIC
*MINI 1-300 RC: .5X TO 1.2X BASIC RC's
*MINI SP 301-350: .5X TO 1.2X BASIC SP
MINI SP ODDS 1:13 HOBBY
351-400 RANDOM WITHIN RIP CARDS
STATED PLATE ODDS 1:564 HOBBY
PLATE PRINT RUN 1 SET PER COLOR
NO PLATE PRICING DUE TO SCARCITY
352 Matt Kemp EXT 20.00 50.00
353 Ryan Zimmerman EXT 15.00 40.00
354 Derek Jeter EXT 100.00 175.00
355 Carlos Gonzalez EXT 15.00 40.00
356 Mark Teixeira EXT 15.00 40.00
357 Justin Upton EXT 30.00 60.00
358 Ian Kinsler EXT 15.00 40.00
359 Cole Hamels EXT 15.00 40.00
360 Cliff Lee EXT 40.00 80.00
361 James Shields EXT 30.00 60.00
362 Roy Halladay EXT 20.00 50.00
363 Miguel Cabrera EXT 20.00 50.00
364 Josh Hamilton EXT 20.00 50.00
365 Giancarlo Stanton EXT 20.00 50.00
366 Jacoby Ellsbury EXT 30.00 60.00
367 Starlin Castro EXT 20.00 50.00
368 Adrian Gonzalez EXT 15.00 40.00
369 Evan Longoria EXT 40.00 80.00
370 Felix Hernandez EXT 30.00 60.00
371 Ken Griffey Jr. EXT 60.00 150.00
372 Andrew McCutchen EXT 30.00 60.00
373 Ryan Howard EXT 30.00 60.00
374 Tim Lincecum EXT 40.00 80.00
375 Robinson Cano EXT 20.00 50.00
376 Justin Verlander EXT 20.00 50.00
377 Nolan Ryan EXT 125.00 250.00
378 Sandy Koufax EXT 30.00 60.00
379 CC Sabathia EXT 50.00 100.00
380 Dustin Pedroia EXT 20.00 50.00
381 Willie Mays EXT 30.00 60.00
382 Hanley Ramirez EXT 15.00 40.00
383 Ryan Braun EXT 30.00 60.00
384 Alex Rodriguez EXT 30.00 60.00
385 Jered Weaver EXT 20.00 50.00
386 Buster Posey EXT 20.00 50.00
387 Jose Bautista EXT 15.00 40.00
388 Stephen Strasburg EXT 40.00 80.00
389 Ichiro Suzuki EXT 20.00 50.00
390 Reggie Jackson EXT 20.00 50.00
392 Curtis Granderson EXT 50.00 100.00
393 Eric Hosmer EXT 15.00 40.00
394 David Wright EXT 30.00 60.00
395 Jose Reyes EXT 30.00 60.00
396 Troy Tulowitzki EXT 15.00 40.00
397 Clayton Kershaw EXT 20.00 50.00
398 Jose Valverde EXT 20.00 50.00
399 Albert Pujols EXT 40.00 80.00
400 Jay Bruce EXT 20.00 50.00

2012 Topps Allen and Ginter Mini A and G Back

*A & G BACK: 1X TO 2.5X BASIC
*A & G BACK RCs: .6X TO 1.5X BASIC RCs
A & G BACK ODDS 1:5 HOBBY
*A & G BACK SP: .6X TO 1.5X BASIC SP
A & G BACK SP ODDS 1:65 HOBBY

2012 Topps Allen and Ginter Mini Black

*BLACK: 1.5X TO 4X BASIC
*BLACK RCs: .6X TO 1.5X BASIC RCs
BLACK ODDS 1:10 HOBBY
*BLACK SP: 1X TO 2.5X BASIC SP
BLACK SP ODDS 1:130 HOBBY
140 Mike Trout 10.00 25.00

2012 Topps Allen and Ginter Mini Gold Border

*GOLD: .5X TO 1.2X BASIC
*GOLD RCs: .5X TO 1.2X BASIC RCs
COMMON SP (301-350) .40 1.00
SP SEMIS .60 1.50
SP UNLISTED 1.00 2.50
301 Adron Chambers 1.00 2.50
302 Jayson Werth .75 2.00
303 Ivan Nova .75 2.00
304 Kyle Farnsworth .75 2.00
305 Wilin Rosario .60 1.50
306 Ryan Howard .75 2.00
307 Jhonny Peralta .60 1.50
308 Paul Konerko .60 1.50
309 Bela Karolyi .40 1.00
310 Russell Martin .60 1.50
311 Bob Gibson .60 1.50
312 Anibal Sanchez .60 1.50
313 Carlos Pena .75 2.00
314 Michael Buffer .40 1.00
315 Dellin Betances 1.00 2.50
316 Adrian Gonzalez .75 2.00
317 Jason Heyward .75 2.00
318 Mike Moustakas .75 2.00
319 Adam Wainwright .75 2.00
320 Jonathan Papelbon .75 2.00
321 Chad Billingsley .60 1.50
322 Sergio Santos .60 1.50
323 Ryan Roberts .60 1.50
324 Cal Ripken Jr. 3.00 8.00
325 Frank Robinson .60 1.50
326 Logan Morrison .60 1.50
327 Jon Lester .60 1.50
328 Josh Hamilton .75 2.00
329 Billy Butler .60 1.50
330 Mike Napoli .60 1.50
331 Carl Crawford .75 2.00
332 Guy Bluford .40 1.00
333 Kelly Johnson .60 1.50
334 Adrian Beltre 1.00 2.50
335 Alexei Ramirez .75 2.00
336 Gio Gonzalez .75 2.00
337 Matt Holliday 1.00 2.50
338 Prince Fielder .75 2.00
339 Swin Cash 1.00 2.50
340 Marty Hogan .40 1.00
341 Colby Lewis .60 1.50
342 Ryan Dempster .60 1.50
343 Zack Greinke 1.00 2.50
344 Matt Dominguez .75 2.00
345 Nolan Ryan 3.00 8.00
346 Lefty Kreh .40 1.00
347 Matt Garza .60 1.50
348 Chase Headley .60 1.50
349 Danny Espinosa .60 1.50
350 Howie Kendrick .60 1.50

2012 Topps Allen and Ginter Mini No Card Number

*NO NBR: 5X TO 12X BASIC
*NO NBR RCs: 2X TO 5X BASIC RCs
*NO NBR SP: 1.2X TO 3X BASIC SP
STATED ODDS 1:111 HOBBY
ANNC'D PRINT RUN OF 50 SETS
274 Derek Jeter 40.00 80.00
324 Cal Ripken Jr. 40.00 80.00
345 Nolan Ryan 15.00 40.00

2012 Topps Allen and Ginter Autographs

STATED ODDS 1:51 HOBBY
EXCHANGE DEADLINE 06/30/2015
AC Allen Craig 8.00 20.00
AC Aroldis Chapman 12.00 30.00
ADK Annie Duke 12.00 30.00
AG Adrian Gonzalez 10.00 25.00
AJ Adam Jones 10.00 25.00
AK Al Kaline 100.00 250.00
AMC Andrew McCutchen 30.00 60.00
AO Alexi Ogando 4.00 10.00
APA Ara Parseghian 15.00 40.00
APL Arnold Palmer 100.00 200.00
AR Anthony Rizzo 15.00 40.00
AUS Al Unser Sr. 6.00 15.00
BA Brett Anderson 4.00 10.00
BB Brandon Belt 4.00 10.00
BG Bob Gibson 100.00 200.00
BHS Bob Hurley Sr. 8.00 20.00
BK Bela Karolyi 10.00 25.00
BKN Bob Knight 40.00 80.00
BL Brett Lawrie 6.00 15.00
BM Brian McCann 10.00 25.00
BP Buster Posey 100.00 200.00
BP Brad Peacock 4.00 10.00
BY Bryce Harper 125.00 300.00
CC Carl Crawford 10.00 25.00
CG Craig Gentry 4.00 10.00
CG Carlos Gonzalez 30.00 60.00
CK Clayton Kershaw 40.00 100.00
CMO Colin Montgomerie 8.00 20.00
CNE Curly Neal 20.00 50.00
CRJ Cal Ripken Jr. 300.00 400.00
DB Daniel Bard 4.00 10.00
DDK Don Denkinger 6.00 15.00
DF Dexter Fowler 4.00 10.00
DG Dee Gordon 8.00 20.00
DG Dillon Gee 4.00 10.00
DM Don Mattingly 200.00 300.00
DP David Price 10.00 25.00
DP Dustin Pedroia 20.00 50.00
DU Dan Uggla 8.00 20.00
DW Dale Webster 5.00 12.00
EA Elvis Andrus 6.00 15.00
EAN Erin Andrews 50.00 100.00
EB Ernie Banks 200.00 300.00
EH Eric Hosmer 30.00 60.00
EL Evan Longoria 90.00 150.00
EMA Ewa Mataya 10.00 25.00
FH Felix Hernandez 30.00 60.00
FR Frank Robinson 100.00 200.00
FT1 Fatal1ty 6.00 15.00
GB Gordon Beckham 5.00 12.00
GBL Guy Bluford 10.00 25.00
GGU Greg Gumbel 10.00 25.00
HA Hank Aaron 500.00 700.00
HH Hank Haney 8.00 20.00
JB Johnny Bench 100.00 200.00
JBA Jose Bautista 15.00 40.00
JBA Jerry Bailey 10.00 25.00
JBR Jay Bruce 12.50 30.00
JBR James Brown 10.00 25.00
JC Johnny Cueto 6.00 15.00
JDM J.D. Martinez 15.00 40.00
JE John McEnroe 30.00 80.00
JH Joel Hanrahan 6.00 15.00
JHE Jeremy Hellickson 6.00 15.00
JKJ Jackie Joyner-Kersee 12.50 30.00
JM Joe Mauer 50.00 120.00
JPA J.P. Arencibia 5.00 12.00
JPA Jimmy Paredes 4.00 10.00
JS Jordan Schafer 5.00 12.00
JT Julio Teheran 6.00 15.00
JT Jose Tabata 6.00 15.00
JV Jose Valverde 4.00 10.00
JW Jered Weaver 12.50 30.00
JZ Jordan Zimmermann 6.00 15.00
KBR Keegan Bradley 10.00 25.00
KGJ Ken Griffey Jr. EXCH 125.00 300.00
KH Kirk Herbstreit 10.00 25.00
KUP Kate Upton 250.00 500.00
LKR Lefty Kreh 6.00 15.00
MBF Michael Buffer 12.00 30.00
MC Miguel Cabrera 75.00 150.00
MH Mark Hamburger 4.00 10.00
MHO Marty Hogan 4.00 10.00
MK Matt Kemp 10.00 25.00
MLE Meadowlark Lemon 20.00 50.00
MM Matt Moore 5.00 12.00
MMO Mitch Moreland 4.00 10.00
MMR Mike Morse 5.00 12.00
MP Michael Pineda 4.00 10.00
MPH Michael Phelps 200.00 300.00
MS Max Scherzer 20.00 50.00
MSC Mike Schmidt 100.00 200.00
MST Giancarlo Stanton 75.00 200.00
MT Mark Trumbo 8.00 20.00
MTR Mike Trout 250.00 400.00
NE Nathan Eovaldi 4.00 10.00
NR Nolan Ryan 400.00 600.00
PF Prince Fielder 12.00 30.00
PG Paul Goldschmidt 15.00 40.00
PPF Phil Pfister 5.00 12.00
RB Ryan Braun 20.00 50.00
RC Robinson Cano 20.00 50.00
RFD Roger Federer 175.00 350.00
RG Rulon Gardner 8.00 20.00
RH Roy Halladay EXCH 100.00 200.00
RJ Reggie Jackson 150.00 300.00
RPT Richard Petty 15.00 40.00
RS Ryne Sandberg 150.00 300.00
RZ Ryan Zimmerman 15.00 40.00
SC Starlin Castro 10.00 25.00
SCA Swin Cash 8.00 20.00
SK Sandy Koufax EXCH 350.00 700.00
SM Stan Musial 75.00 200.00
TG Tony Gwynn 75.00 150.00
TH Torii Hunter 10.00 25.00
VW Vernon Wells 40.00 80.00
VW Vance Worley 6.00 15.00
WM Willie Mays EXCH 300.00 500.00
YC Yoenis Cespedes 60.00 120.00
YD Yu Darvish 75.00 150.00
YG Yovani Gallardo 10.00 25.00
ZB Zach Britton 6.00 15.00

2012 Topps Allen and Ginter Baseball Highlights Cabinets

COMPLETE SET (5) 12.50 30.00
STATED ODDS 1:5 HOBBY BOX TOPPER
BH1 D.Jeter/D.Price 2.50 6.00
BH2 David Freese 1.00 2.50
Jaime Garcia/Lance Berkman/Matt Holliday
BH3 C.Ripken Jr./L.Gehrig 3.00 8.00
BH4 Riv/Plou/Cud/Parm 1.25 3.00
BH5 Jeremy Hellickson .75 2.00
Craig Kimbrel

2012 Topps Allen and Ginter Baseball Highlights Sketches

COMPLETE SET (24) 8.00 20.00
STATED ODDS 1:8 HOBBY
BH1 Roger Maris .60 1.50
BH2 Tom Seaver .40 1.00
BH3 Ichiro Suzuki .75 2.00
BH4 Ryne Sandberg 1.25 3.00
BH5 Brooks Robinson .40 1.00
BH6 Frank Thomas .60 1.50
BH7 John Smoltz .75 2.00
BH8 Derek Jeter 1.50 4.00
BH9 Ryan Braun .40 1.00
BH10 Albert Pujols .75 2.00
BH11 Nolan Ryan 2.00 5.00
BH12 Justin Verlander .60 1.50
BH13 Matt Moore .60 1.50
BH14 Mickey Mantle 2.00 5.00
BH15 Ken Griffey Jr. 1.25 3.00
BH16 David Freese .40 1.00
BH17 Cal Ripken Jr. 2.00 5.00
BH18 Ozzie Smith .75 2.00
BH19 Carlton Fisk .40 1.00
BH20 Ichiro Suzuki .50 1.25
BH21 Willie Mays 1.25 3.00
BH22 Joe DiMaggio 1.25 3.00
BH23 Jackie Robinson .60 1.50
BH24 Roberto Clemente 1.50 4.00

2012 Topps Allen and Ginter Colony In A Card

STATED ODDS 1:288 HOBBY
AS Artemia Salina 6.00 15.00

2012 Topps Allen and Ginter Currency of the World Cabinet Relics

STATED ODDS 1:25 HOBBY BOX TOPPER
STATED PRINT RUN 50 SER.#'d SETS
CW1 Austria 20.00 50.00
CW2 Argentina 15.00 40.00
CW3 Belgium 15.00 40.00
CW4 Brazil 20.00 50.00
CW5 Colombia 20.00 50.00
CW6 Ecuador 15.00 40.00
CW7 East Caribbean 15.00 40.00
CW8 Germany 40.00 80.00
CW9 Great Britain 20.00 50.00
CW10 Guatemala 15.00 40.00
CW11 Greece 15.00 40.00
CW12 Falkland Islands 15.00 40.00
CW13 France 20.00 50.00
CW14 Ireland 15.00 40.00
CW15 Israel 20.00 50.00
CW16 Isle of Man 15.00 40.00
CW17 Italy 20.00 50.00
CW18 Jamaica 15.00 40.00
CW19 Mexico 15.00 40.00
CW20 Nicaragua 15.00 40.00
CW21 New Zealand 15.00 40.00
CW22 Pakistan 15.00 40.00
CW23 Poland 20.00 50.00
CW24 Russia 20.00 50.00
CW25 Romania 15.00 40.00
CW26 Turkey 15.00 40.00
CW27 Spain 20.00 50.00
CW28 St. Helena 20.00 50.00
CW29 Venezuela 15.00 40.00
CW30 El Salvador 30.00 60.00

2012 Topps Allen and Ginter Historical Turning Points

COMPLETE SET (20) 4.00 10.00
STATED ODDS 1:8 HOBBY
HTP1 Signing of Declaration of Independence .25 .60
HTP2 The Battle Waterloo .25 .60
HTP3 The Fall the Roman Empire .25 .60
HTP4 The Reformation .25 .60
HTP5 The Fall the Berlin Wall .25 .60
HTP6 The Treaty Versailles .25 .60
HTP7 Invention of Printing Press .25 .60
HTP8 Allied Victory World War II .25 .60
HTP9 Discovery of New World .25 .60
HTP10 Discovery of Electricity .25 .60
HTP11 Signing of Magna Carta .25 .60
HTP12 The Renaissance .25 .60
HTP13 The Industrial Revolution .25 .60
HTP14 The Emancipation Proclamation .25 .60
HTP15 The First at Kitty Hawk .25 .60
HTP16 The French Revolution .25 .60
HTP17 The Great Depression .25 .60
HTP18 On the Origin of Species .25 .60
HTP19 Sputnik I .25 .60
HTP20 The Agricultural Revolution .25 .60

2012 Topps Allen and Ginter Mini Culinary Curiosities

COMPLETE SET (10) 10.00 25.00
STATED ODDS 1:5 HOBBY
CC1 Nutria 1.00 2.50
CC2 Haggis 1.00 2.50
CC3 Kopi Luwak 1.00 2.50
CC4 Casu Marzu 1.00 2.50
CC5 Rocky Moutain Oysters 1.00 2.50
CC6 Hakarl 1.00 2.50
CC7 Fugu 1.00 2.50
CC8 Sannakji 1.00 2.50
CC9 Balut 1.00 2.50
CC10 Muktuk 1.00 2.50

2012 Topps Allen and Ginter Mini Fashionable Ladies

COMPLETE SET (10) 75.00 150.00
FL1 The First Lady 6.00 15.00
FL2 The Flapper 6.00 15.00
FL3 The Queen 6.00 15.00
FL4 The Victorian 6.00 15.00
FL5 The Bustle 6.00 15.00
FL6 The Weekender 6.00 15.00
FL7 The Bride 6.00 15.00
FL8 The Sportswoman 6.00 15.00
FL9 The Ingenue 6.00 15.00
FL10 The Icon 6.00 15.00

2012 Topps Allen and Ginter Mini Giants of the Deep

COMPLETE SET (15) 12.50 30.00
STATED ODDS 1:5 HOBBY
GD1 Humpback Whale .75 2.00
GD2 Sperm Whale .75 2.00
GD3 Blue Whale .75 2.00
GD4 Narwhal .75 2.00
GD5 Beluga Whale .75 2.00
GD6 Bowhead Whale .75 2.00
GD7 Right Whale .75 2.00
GD8 Fin Whale .75 2.00
GD9 Orca .75 2.00
GD10 Pilot Whale .75 2.00
GD11 Pygmy Sperm Whale .75 2.00
GD12 Minke Whale .75 2.00
GD13 Gray Whale .75 2.00
GD14 Bottlenose Whale .75 2.00
GD15 Bryde's Whale .75 2.00

2012 Topps Allen and Ginter Mini Guys in Hats

COMPLETE SET (10) 75.00 150.00
GH1 The Bowler 6.00 15.00
GH2 The Boater 6.00 15.00
GH3 The Fedora 6.00 15.00
GH4 The Fez 6.00 15.00
GH5 The Pith Helmet 6.00 15.00
GH6 The Top Hat 6.00 15.00
GH7 The Mortarboard 6.00 15.00
GH8 The Flat Cap 6.00 15.00
GH9 The Garrison Cap 6.00 15.00
GH10 The Bicorne 6.00 15.00

2012 Topps Allen and Ginter Mini Man's Best Friend

COMPLETE SET (20) 15.00 40.00
STATED ODDS 1:5 HOBBY
MBF1 Siberian Husky .75 2.00
MBF2 Dalmatian .75 2.00
MBF3 Golden Retriever .75 2.00
MBF4 German Shepherd .75 2.00
MBF5 Beagle .75 2.00
MBF6 Dachshund .75 2.00
MBF7 Yorkshire Terrier .75 2.00
MBF8 Labrador Retriever .75 2.00
MBF9 Boxer .75 2.00
MBF10 Poodle .75 2.00
MBF11 Chihuahua .75 2.00
MBF12 Shih Tzu .75 2.00
MBF13 Collie .75 2.00
MBF14 Pug .75 2.00
MBF15 Cocker Spaniel .75 2.00
MBF16 Saint Bernard .75 2.00
MBF17 Bulldog .75 2.00
MBF18 Boston Terrier .75 2.00
MBF19 Basset Hound .75 2.00
MBF20 Shetland Sheepdog .75 2.00

2012 Topps Allen and Ginter Mini Musical Masters

COMPLETE SET (16) 12.50 30.00
STATED ODDS 1:5 HOBBY
MM1 Johann Sebastian Bach .75 2.00
MM2 Wolfgang Amadeus Mozart .75 2.00
MM3 Ludwig van Beethoven .75 2.00
MM4 Richard Wagner .75 2.00
MM5 Joseph Haydn .75 2.00
MM6 Johannes Brahms .75 2.00
MM7 Franz Schubert .75 2.00
MM8 George Frideric Handel .75 2.00
MM9 Pyotr Ilyich Tchaikovsky .75 2.00
MM10 Sergei Prokofiev .75 2.00
MM11 Antonin Dvorak .75 2.00
MM12 Franz Liszt .75 2.00
MM13 Frederic Chopin .75 2.00
MM14 Igor Stravinsky .75 2.00
MM15 Giuseppe Verdi .75 2.00
MM16 Gustav Mahler .75 2.00

2012 Topps Allen and Ginter Mini People of the Bible

COMPLETE SET (15) 12.50 30.00
STATED ODDS 1:5 HOBBY
PB1 David 1.25 3.00
PB2 Moses 1.25 3.00
PB3 Abraham 1.25 3.00
PB4 Job 1.25 3.00
PB5 Jonah 1.25 3.00
PB6 Daniel 1.25 3.00
PB7 Mary Magdalene 1.25 3.00
PB8 Peter 1.25 3.00
PB9 Jesus 1.25 3.00
PB10 Luke 1.25 3.00
PB11 Adam and Eve 1.25 3.00
PB12 Isaiah 1.25 3.00
PB13 Joseph 1.25 3.00
PB14 Mary 1.25 3.00
PB15 John the Baptist 1.25 3.00

2012 Topps Allen and Ginter Mini World's Greatest Military Leaders

COMPLETE SET (20) 12.50 30.00
STATED ODDS 1:5 HOBBY
ML1 Alexander the Great .60 1.50
ML2 Simon Bolivar .60 1.50
ML3 Oliver Cromwell .60 1.50
ML4 Julius Caesar .60 1.50
ML5 Cyrus the Great .60 1.50
ML6 Hannibal Barca .60 1.50
ML7 Napoleon Bonaparte .60 1.50
ML8 George Washington .60 1.50
ML9 Ulysses S. Grant .60 1.50
ML10 Dwight D. Eisenhower .60 1.50
ML11 Leonidas .60 1.50
ML12 Charlemagne .60 1.50
ML13 Saladin .60 1.50
ML14 Duke of Wellington .60 1.50
ML15 Horatio Nelson .60 1.50
ML16 Frederick the Great .60 1.50
ML17 Duke of Marlborough .60 1.50
ML18 William Wallace .60 1.50
ML19 Darius the Great .60 1.50
ML20 Sun Tzu .60 1.50

2012 Topps Allen and Ginter N43

COMPLETE SET (15) 20.00 50.00
STATED ODDS 1:3 HOBBY BOX TOPPER
1 Albert Pujols 1.25 3.00
2 Brian Wilson 1.00 2.50
3 Don Mattingly 2.00 5.00
4 Eric Hosmer .75 2.00
5 Ernie Banks 1.00 2.50
6 Evan Longoria .75 2.00
7 Hanley Ramirez .75 2.00
8 Joe Mauer .75 2.00
9 Johnny Bench 1.00 2.50
10 Josh Hamilton .75 2.00
11 Ken Griffey Jr. 2.00 5.00
12 Matt Moore 1.00 2.50
13 Miguel Cabrera 1.00 2.50
14 Mike Schmidt 1.50 4.00
15 Tony Gwynn 1.00 2.50

2012 Topps Allen and Ginter Relics

STATED ODDS 1:10 HOBBY
EXCHANGE DEADLINE 06/30/2015
AA Alex Avila 3.00 8.00
AB A.J. Burnett 3.00 8.00
ABA Andrew Bailey 3.00 8.00
ABE Adrian Beltre 3.00 8.00
AD Annie Duke 3.00 8.00
AG Adrian Gonzalez 3.00 8.00
AH Aubrey Huff 3.00 8.00
AL Adam Lind 3.00 8.00
AM Andrew McCutchen 4.00 10.00
AP Albert Pujols 6.00 15.00
AP Arnold Palmer 8.00 20.00
APG Angel Pagan 3.00 8.00
AUS Al Unser Sr. 4.00 10.00
BA Bobby Abreu 3.00 8.00
BB Balloon Boy 5.00 12.00
BBU Billy Butler 3.00 8.00
BH Bob Hurley Sr. 3.00 8.00
BK Bob Knight 5.00 12.00
BL Barry Larkin 5.00 12.00
BM Brian McCann 3.00 8.00
BP Brandon Phillips 3.00 8.00
BU B.J. Upton 3.00 8.00
BW Brian Wilson 5.00 12.00
CB Clay Buchholz 3.00 8.00
CBI Chad Billingsley 3.00 8.00
CH Corey Hart 3.00 8.00
CI Chris Iannetta 3.00 8.00
CJ Chipper Jones 5.00 12.00
CL Carlos Lee 3.00 8.00
CM Casey McGehee 3.00 8.00
CMO Colin Montgomerie 6.00 15.00
CMR Carlos Marmol 3.00 8.00
CN Curly Neal EXCH 6.00 15.00
CP Carlos Pena 3.00 8.00
CQ Carlos Quentin 3.00 8.00
CY Chris Young 3.00 8.00
CZ Carlos Zambrano 3.00 8.00
CZA Carlos Zambrano 3.00 8.00
DD David DeJesus 3.00 8.00
DDE Don Denkinger 3.00 8.00
DG Dillon Gee 3.00 8.00
DJ Derek Jeter 10.00 25.00
DM Don Mattingly 10.00 25.00
DO David Ortiz 3.00 8.00
DP Dustin Pedroia 4.00 10.00
DS Drew Stubbs 3.00 8.00
DU Dan Uggla 3.00 8.00
DW David Wright 4.00 10.00
DWE Dale Webster 4.00 10.00
EA Elvis Andrus 3.00 8.00
EAN Erin Andrews 60.00 120.00
EH1 Eric Hosmer Bat 5.00 12.00
EH2 Eric Hosmer Jsy 20.00 50.00
EL Evan Longoria 3.00 8.00
ELO Evan Longoria 3.00 8.00
EM Evan Meek 3.00 8.00

EMA Ewa Mataya 5.00 12.00
EV Edinson Volquez 3.00 8.00
FF Freddie Freeman 3.00 8.00
FT1 Fatal1ty 4.00 10.00
GB Gordon Beckham 3.00 8.00
GBL Guy Bluford 5.00 12.00
GG Greg Gumbel 3.00 8.00
GS Geovany Soto 3.00 8.00
HA Hank Aaron 150.00 250.00
HB Heath Bell 3.00 8.00
HC Hank Conger 3.00 8.00
HCO Hank Conger 3.00 8.00
HH Hank Haney 3.00 8.00
HR Hanley Ramirez 3.00 8.00
I Ichiro Suzuki 5.00 12.00
ID Ike Davis 3.00 8.00
IK Ian Kinsler 3.00 8.00
JA J.P. Arencibia 3.00 8.00
JB Jose Bautista 4.00 10.00
JBA Jerry Bailey 4.00 10.00
JBE Johnny Bench 30.00 60.00
JBR James Brown 6.00 15.00
JC Johnny Cueto 3.00 8.00
JD Joe DiMaggio 40.00 80.00
JDA Johnny Damon 3.00 8.00
JG Jaime Garcia 3.00 8.00
JH Josh Hamilton 4.00 10.00
JHE Jeremy Hellickson 3.00 8.00
JJ Jon Jay 3.00 8.00
JJK Jackie Joyner-Kersee 3.00 8.00
JL James Loney 3.00 8.00
JLO Jed Lowrie 3.00 8.00
JM John McEnroe 4.00 10.00
JP Jhonny Peralta 3.00 8.00
JPA Jonathan Papelbon 3.00 8.00
JPE Jake Peavy 3.00 8.00
JPO Jorge Posada 3.00 8.00
JR Jackie Robinson 40.00 80.00
JU Justin Upton 3.00 8.00
JW Jayson Werth 3.00 8.00
JWA Jordan Walden 3.00 8.00
JZ Jordan Zimmermann 3.00 8.00
KB Keegan Bradley EXCH 6.00 15.00
KF Kosuke Fukudome 3.00 8.00
KG Ken Griffey Jr. 50.00 100.00
KH Kirk Herbstreit 4.00 10.00
KU Kate Upton 40.00 100.00
LG Lou Gehrig 75.00 150.00
LK Lefty Kreh EXCH 5.00 12.00
MB Marlon Byrd 3.00 8.00
MBO Michael Bourn 3.00 8.00
MBU Michael Buffer 8.00 20.00
MC Melky Cabrera 3.00 8.00
MCA Melky Cabrera 3.00 8.00
MCB Miguel Cabrera 6.00 15.00
MCN Matt Cain 3.00 8.00
MH Marty Hogan 3.00 8.00
MK Matt Kemp 5.00 12.00
ML Mike Leake 3.00 8.00
MLA Mat Latos 3.00 8.00
MLE Meadowlark Lemon 6.00 15.00
MM Mike Morse 3.00 8.00
MMA Mickey Mantle 125.00 250.00
MMO Mitch Moreland 3.00 8.00
MP Michael Pineda 3.00 8.00
MPH Michael Phelps 20.00 50.00
MPR Martin Prado 3.00 8.00
MR Mark Reynolds 3.00 8.00
MSC Max Scherzer 3.00 8.00
MY Michael Young 3.00 8.00
NM Nick Markakis 3.00 8.00
NR Nolan Ryan 50.00 100.00
PF Prince Fielder 4.00 10.00
PO Paul O'Neill 3.00 8.00
PP Phil Pfister 3.00 8.00
RA Roberto Alomar 4.00 10.00
RB Ryan Braun 5.00 12.00
RC Roberto Clemente 40.00 80.00
RD Ryan Dempster 3.00 8.00
RDA Rajai Davis 3.00 8.00
RF Roger Federer 6.00 15.00
RG Rulon Gardner 4.00 10.00
RJ Reggie Jackson 12.50 30.00
RM Roger Maris 60.00 120.00
RMA Russell Martin 3.00 8.00
RP Rick Porcello 3.00 8.00
RPE Richard Petty 4.00 10.00
RR Ricky Romero 3.00 8.00
RS Ryne Sandberg 15.00 40.00
RT Ryan Theriot 3.00 8.00
RZ Ryan Zimmerman 3.00 8.00
SC Starlin Castro 6.00 15.00
SCA Swin Cash 3.00 8.00
SCH Shin-Soo Choo 3.00 8.00
SK Sandy Koufax 40.00 80.00
SS Stephen Strasburg 3.00 8.00
TC Ty Cobb 100.00 200.00
TH Torii Hunter 3.00 8.00
UJ Ubaldo Jimenez 3.00 8.00
VM Victor Martinez 3.00 8.00
VW Vernon Wells 3.00 8.00
VWE Vernon Wells 3.00 8.00
WM Willie Mays 75.00 150.00
ZG Zack Greinke 3.00 8.00

2012 Topps Allen and Ginter Rip Cards

OVERALL RIP ODDS 1:287 HOBBY
PRINT RUNS B/WN 10-99 COPIES PER
NO PRICING ON QTY 25 OR LESS
ALL LISTED PRICED ARE FOR RIPPED
UNRIPPED HAVE ADD'L CARDS WITHIN
RC3 Brandon Phillips 6.00 15.00
RC4 Brett Lawrie 6.00 15.00
RC5 Ian Kinsler 6.00 15.00
RC6 Michael Pineda 6.00 15.00
RC12 Jacoby Ellsbury 6.00 15.00
RC22 Ryan Zimmerman 6.00 15.00
RC23 Carlos Gonzalez 6.00 15.00
RC26 Kevin Youkilis 6.00 15.00
RC31 Hunter Pence 6.00 15.00
RC34 Mike Trout 20.00 50.00
RC36 Josh Johnson 6.00 15.00
RC38 Carl Crawford 6.00 15.00
RC41 Starlin Castro 6.00 15.00
RC42 Josh Beckett 6.00 15.00
RC45 David Freese 6.00 15.00
RC46 Jason Heyward 6.00 15.00
RC50 Craig Kimbrel 6.00 15.00
RC51 Carlos Santana 6.00 15.00
RC56 Nelson Cruz 6.00 15.00
RC58 Madison Bumgarner 6.00 15.00
RC59 Adam Jones 6.00 15.00
RC60 Shin-Soo Choo 6.00 15.00
RC62 Giancarlo Stanton 6.00 15.00
RC65 Jesus Montero 6.00 15.00
RC66 Andrew McCutchen 6.00 15.00
RC69 Freddie Freeman 6.00 15.00
RC75 Brian McCann 6.00 15.00
RC78 Tommy Hanson 6.00 15.00
RC79 Jon Lester 6.00 15.00
RC98 David Price 6.00 15.00

2012 Topps Allen and Ginter Rollercoaster Cabinets

COMPLETE SET (5) 10.00 25.00
STATED ODDS 1:4 HOBBY BOX TOPPER
RC1 Leap-the-Dips 2.00 5.00
RC2 Scenic Railway 2.00 5.00
RC3 Rutschebanen 2.00 5.00
RC4 The Wild One 2.00 5.00
RC5 Jack Rabbit 2.00 5.00

2012 Topps Allen and Ginter What's in a Name

COMPLETE SET (100) 12.50 30.00
STATED ODDS 1:2 HOBBY
WIN1 Joe DiMaggio 1.25 3.00
WIN2 Carlos Eduardo Gonzalez .50 1.25
WIN3 Ryan Howard .50 1.25
WIN4 Paul Henry Konerko .40 1.00
WIN5 Troy Trevor Tulowitzki .60 1.50
WIN6 Ryan Braun .40 1.00
WIN7 Chase Cameron Utley .50 1.25
WIN8 Clifton Phifer Lee .50 1.25
WIN10 Lawrence Peter Berra .60 1.50
WIN11 Torii Kedar Hunter .50 1.25
WIN12 Saturnino Orestes Armas Minoso .25 .60
WIN13 Carl Demonte Crawford .50 1.25
WIN14 Larry Wayne Jones .60 1.50
WIN15 Michael Francisco Pineda .40 1.00
WIN16 Jose Miguel Cabrera .60 1.50
WIN17 Dustin Pedroia .60 1.50
WIN18 Stan Musial 1.00 2.50
WIN19 David Allen Wright .50 1.25
WIN20 Don Richard Ashburn .40 1.00
WIN21 Jack Roosevelt Robinson .60 1.50
WIN22 Matthew Ryan Kemp .50 1.25
WIN23 Giancarlo Cruz Michael Stanton .60 1.50
WIN24 Ian Michael Kinsler .50 1.25
WIN25 Daniel Cooley Uggla .50 1.25
WIN26 Orlando Manuel Pennes Cepeda .40 1.00
WIN27 Starlin DeJesus Castro .50 1.25
WIN28 Elvis Augusto Andrus .50 1.25
WIN29 Nolan Ryan 2.00 5.00
WIN30 Hunter Andrew Pence .50 1.25
WIN31 Andrew Stefan McCutchen .60 1.50
WIN32 Frederick Charles Freeman .75 2.00
WIN33 Atanasio Perez Rigal .40 1.00
WIN34 Clayton Kershaw 1.00 2.50
WIN35 Brooks Calbert Robinson .40 1.00
WIN36 Jose Antonio Bautista .50 1.25
WIN37 Jason Alias Heyward .50 1.25
WIN38 Harry Leroy Halladay .50 1.25
WIN39 Montford Merrill Irvin .40 1.00
WIN40 Jemile Nykiwa Weeks .40 1.00
WIN41 Timothy LeRoy Lincecum .50 1.25
WIN42 Cal Ripken Jr. 2.00 5.00
WIN43 Justin Verlander .60 1.50
WIN44 James Calvin Rollins .50 1.25
WIN45 Don Mattingly 1.25 3.00
WIN46 James Augustus Hunter .40 1.00
WIN47 Jacoby McCabe Ellsbury .50 1.25
WIN48 Anthony Keith Gwynn Sr. .60 1.50
WIN49 Edwin Donald Snider .40 1.00
WIN50 Mike Schmidt 1.00 2.50
WIN51 Joshua Holt Hamilton .50 1.25
WIN52 Derek Jeter 1.50 4.00
WIN53 Justin Ernest George Morneau .50 1.25
WIN54 Juan D'Vaughn Pierre .40 1.00
WIN55 Robinson Jose Cano .50 1.25
WIN56 Albertin Aroldis de la Cruz Chapman .60 1.50
WIN57 Joshua Patrick Beckett .40 1.00
WIN58 Rickey Nelson Henley Henderson .60 1.50
WIN59 Buster Posey .75 2.00
WIN60 Jay Allen Bruce .50 1.25
WIN61 James Howard Thome .50 1.25
WIN62 Jered David Weaver .50 1.25
WIN63 Rodney Cline Carew .40 1.00
WIN64 David Americo Ortiz .60 1.50
WIN65 Nicholas Thompson Swisher .50 1.25
WIN66 George Lee Anderson .40 1.00
WIN67 Wilver Dornel Stargell .40 1.00
WIN68 Prince Semien Fielder .50 1.25
WIN69 Felix Abraham Hernandez .50 1.25
WIN70 Jonathan Tyler Lester .40 1.00
WIN71 Joseph Patrick Mauer .50 1.25
WIN72 Carsten Charles Sabathia .50 1.25
WIN73 Ryan Wallace Zimmerman .50 1.25
WIN74 George Thomas Seaver .25 .60
WIN75 Colbert Michael Hamels .50 1.25
WIN76 Melvin Emanuel Upton .50 1.25
WIN77 David Taylor Price .50 1.25
WIN78 Jose Bernabe Reyes .40 1.00
WIN79 Mickey Mantle 2.00 5.00
WIN80 Matthew Thomas Holliday .60 1.50
WIN81 Covelli Loyce Crisp .40 1.00
WIN82 Ty Cobb 1.00 2.50
WIN83 Mark Charles Teixeira .50 1.25
WIN84 Albert Pujols .75 2.00
WIN85 Michael Anthony Napoli .40 1.00
WIN86 Daniel John Haren .40 1.00
WIN87 Joseph Daniel Votto .60 1.50
WIN88 Alex Jonathan Gordon .50 1.25
WIN89 Stephen Strasburg .60 1.50
WIN90 Evan Longoria .50 1.25
WIN91 Alex Rodriguez .75 2.00
WIN92 Paul Edward Goldschmidt .60 1.50
WIN93 Billy Ray Butler .40 1.00
WIN94 Reginald Martinez Jackson .40 1.00
WIN95 Ken Griffey Jr. 1.25 3.00
WIN96 Ozzie Smith .75 2.00
WIN97 Justin Irvin Upton .50 1.25
WIN98 Edward Charles Ford .40 1.00
WIN99 Babe Ruth 1.50 4.00
WIN100 Donald Zackary Greinke .60 1.50

2012 Topps Allen and Ginter World's Tallest Buildings

COMPLETE SET (10) 4.00 10.00
COMMON CARD .40 1.00
STATED ODDS 1:8 HOBBY
WTB1 Burj Khalifa .40 1.00
WTB2 Taipei 101 .40 1.00
WTB3 Petronas Towers .40 1.00
WTB4 Willis Tower .40 1.00
WTB5 1 World Trade Center .40 1.00
WTB6 Empire State Building .40 1.00
WTB7 Chrysler Building .40 1.00
WTB8 40 Wall Street .40 1.00
WTB9 Woolworth Building .40 1.00
WTB10 MetLife Building .40 1.00

2013 Topps Allen and Ginter

COMPLETE SET (350) 20.00 50.00
COMP.SET w/o SP's (300) 12.00 30.00
SP ODDS 1:2 HOBBY
1 Miguel Cabrera .25 .60
2 Derek Jeter .60 1.50
3 Babe Ruth .60 1.50
4 Ty Cobb .40 1.00
5 Albert Pujols .30 .75
6 Chanel Iman .15 .40
7 Mike Trout 2.00 5.00
8 Gary Carter .20 .50
9 Giancarlo Stanton .25 .60
10 Sandy Koufax .50 1.25
11 Robin van Persie .75 2.00
12 Dan Haren .15 .40
13 Adrian Gonzalez .20 .50
14 Ben Revere .15 .40
15 Julia Mancuso .15 .40
16 Amelia Boone .15 .40
17 Roy Jones Jr. .75 2.00
18 Matt Harrison .15 .40
19 Bobby Doerr .15 .40
20 John Smoltz .25 .60
21 Byamba .40 1.00
22 Bob Feller .20 .50
23 Adrian Beltre .25 .60
24 Anthony Gose .15 .40
25 Ernie Banks .25 .60
26 Elvis Andrus .20 .50
27 Shelby Miller RC .60 1.50
28 Paul O'Neill .20 .50
29 Jordan Zimmermann .20 .50
30 Bert Blyleven .20 .50
31 Ian Kennedy .15 .40
32 Aaron Hill .15 .40
33 Nana Meriwether .15 .40
34 Robin Roberts .20 .50
35 Kevin Harvick .60 1.50
36 Early Wynn .20 .50
37 Nelson Cruz .25 .60
38 Johnny Bench .25 .60
39 Desmond Jennings .20 .50
40 Will Middlebrooks .15 .40
41 Hisashi Iwakuma .20 .50
42 Jackie Robinson .25 .60
43 Hunter Pence .20 .50
44 Yasiel Puig RC 1.00 2.50
45 Shawn Nadelen .15 .40
46 Colby Rasmus .20 .50
47 Robin Ventura .15 .40
48 Starling Marte .20 .50
49 Kris Medlen .20 .50
50 Willie Mays .50 1.25
51 Jason Kipnis .20 .50
52 Scott Diamond .15 .40
53 Mark Teixeira .20 .50
54 B.J. Upton .20 .50
55 Fergie Jenkins .20 .50
56 Whitey Ford .20 .50
57 Mike Olt RC .30 .75
58 Shin-Soo Choo .20 .50
59 Joey Votto .25 .60
60 Yoenis Cespedes .25 .60
61 Alex Gordon .20 .50
62 McKayla Maroney .25 .60
63 Jose Bautista .20 .50
64 Neil Walker .15 .40
65 Jose Reyes .20 .50
66 Howie Kendrick .15 .40
67 Hank Aaron .50 1.25
68 Chrissy Teigen .25 .60
69 Jake Peavy .15 .40
70 CC Sabathia .20 .50
71 Ben Zobrist .20 .50
72 Matt Moore .20 .50
73 Tim Hudson .20 .50
74 Yu Darvish .25 .60
75 Lou Gehrig .50 1.25
76 Jim Abbott .15 .40
77 Frank Robinson .30 .75
78 Carlos Santana .20 .50
79 Dylan Bundy RC .60 1.50
80 Willie McCovey .20 .50
81 Al Kaline .40 1.00
82 Roberto Clemente .60 1.50
83 Ted Williams .60 1.50
84 Jason Vargas .15 .40
85 Phil Heath .25 .60
86 Warren Spahn .20 .50
87 Ken Griffey Jr. .75 2.00
88 Clayton Kershaw .40 1.00
89 Michael Brantley .15 .40
90 Jon Lester .20 .50
91 Carlos Ruiz .25 .60
92 Paco Rodriguez RC .40 1.00
93 A.J. Pierzynski .15 .40
94 Billy Butler .15 .40
95 Curtis Granderson .30 .75
96 Jason Heyward .40 1.00
97 Tony Gwynn .40 1.00
98 Darryl Strawberry .15 .40
99 Barry Zito .20 .50
100 Bill Walton .40 1.00
101 Yonder Alonso .15 .40
102 Ian Kinsler .30 .75
103 Bronson Arroyo .15 .40
104 Mike Richter .40 1.00
105 Tyler Skaggs .25 .60
106 Mike Minor .15 .40
107 Trevor Bauer .30 .75
108 Bob Gibson .30 .75
109 Asdrubal Cabrera .20 .50
110 Daniel Murphy .30 .75
111 Corey Hart .15 .40
112 Ziggy Marley .25 .60
113 Brandon Beachy .15 .40
114 Yasmani Grandal .25 .60
115 Stan Musial .40 1.00
116 Lindsey Vonn .25 .60
117 Penny Marshall .25 .60
118 Cal Ripken Jr. .75 2.00
119 Adam Richman .25 .60
120 Manny Machado RC 1.50 4.00
121 Hiroki Kuroda .15 .40
122 Jay Bruce .20 .50
123 Matt Garza .15 .40
124 Olivia Culpo .25 .60
125 Matt Holliday .25 .60
126 Jon Niese .15 .40
127 Doug Fister .15 .40
128 Joe Mauer .20 .50
129 Miguel Montero .15 .40
130A Pele .75 2.00
130B Pele UER 2.00 5.00
131 Brian Kelly .40 1.00
132 Ryne Sandberg .50 1.25
133 David Ortiz .25 .60
134 Roy Halladay .20 .50
135 Vance Worley .20 .50
136 Panama Canal .25 .60
137 Pedro Alvarez .15 .40
138 Anibal Sanchez .15 .40
139 Red Schoendienst .20 .50
140 Tommy Lee .25 .60
141 Trevor Cahill .15 .40
142 Garrett Jones .15 .40
143 Mike Schmidt .40 1.00
144 Torii Hunter .15 .40
145 Harmon Killebrew .25 .60
146 Vida Blue .15 .40
147 Ian Desmond .15 .40
148 Justin Upton .30 .75
149 Ed O'Neill .25 .60
150 Reggie Jackson .30 .75
151 R.A. Dickey .20 .50
152 Anthony Rendon RC 1.50 4.00
153 Alex Cobb .15 .40
154 Mike Morse .15 .40
155 Austin Jackson .15 .40
156 Jurickson Profar RC .30 .75
157 Adam Jones .20 .50
158 Brooks Robinson .20 .50
159 Jose Altuve .20 .50
160 Brian McCann .20 .50
161 Enos Slaughter .20 .50
162 Ivan Nova .20 .50
163 Don Mattingly .50 1.25
164 Chris Mortensen .25 .60
165 Felix Hernandez .20 .50
166 Jim Johnson .15 .40
167 Rod Carew .20 .50
168 Jesus Montero .15 .40
169 Todd Frazier .15 .40
170 Hanley Ramirez .20 .50
171 Chad Billingsley .20 .50
172 Jon Jay .15 .40
173 Coco Crisp .15 .40
174 Nathan Eovaldi .20 .50
175 Monty Hall .25 .60
176 Abe Vigoda .25 .60
177 Joe Morgan .20 .50
178 Carlos Gonzalez .20 .50
179 Bonnie Bernstein .25 .60
180 Nik Wallenda .25 .60
181 Wade Boggs .20 .50
182 Cody Ross .15 .40
183 Ryan Ludwick .15 .40
184 Mike Joy .25 .60
185 Guillaume Robert-Demolaize .25 .60
186 Andy Pettitte .30 .75
187 Scott Hamilton .25 .60
188 Bill Buckner .15 .40
189 David Freese .15 .40
190 David Murphy .25 .60
191 Bryce Harper .40 1.00
192 Anthony Rizzo .30 .75
193 Josh Hamilton .30 .75
194 Juan Marichal .20 .50
195 Derek Norris .20 .50
196 Josh Willingham .20 .50
197 Dexter Fowler .20 .50
198 Jayson Werth .20 .50
199 A.J. Burnett .15 .40
200 Dustin Pedroia .25 .60
201 Mike Moustakas .30 .75
202 Angel Pagan .15 .40
203 Adam Eaton .25 .60
204 Phil Niekro .30 .75
205 Justin Verlander .25 .60
206 Tony Perez .20 .50
207 Troy Tulowitzki .40 1.00
208 Allen Craig .20 .50
209 Ike Davis .15 .40
210 Madison Bumgarner .20 .50
211 Jacoby Ellsbury .25 .60
212 Barry Melrose .40 1.00
213 Jim Bunning .20 .50
214 Alexei Ramirez .30 .75
215 Aroldis Chapman .40 1.00
216 Jered Weaver .15 .40
217 Pope Francis I .20 .50
218 Zack Cozart .15 .40
219 Freddie Roach .40 1.00
220 Jim Rice .20 .50
221 Salvador Perez .20 .50
222 Andre Ethier .30 .75
223 Matthew Berry .30 .75
224 Brett Lawrie .30 .75
225 David Wright .20 .50
226 Willie Stargell .20 .50
227 Fernando Rodney .20 .50
228 Cecil Fielder .15 .40
229 C.J. Wilson .15 .40
230 Derek Holland .15 .40
231 Artie Lange .25 .60
232 Andre Dawson .20 .50
233 Starlin Castro .15 .40
234 Death Valley .25 .60
235 Carlos Beltran .20 .50
236 Brandon Morrow .25 .60
237 Chris Sale .25 .60
238 Ryan Braun .20 .50
239 Craig Kimbrel .30 .75
240 Mike Leake .15 .40
241 Matt Cain .20 .50
242 Robinson Cano .20 .50
243 Jason Dufner .25 .60
244 Nick Saban .40 1.00
245 Mark Buehrle .20 .50
246 Hyun-Jin Ryu RC 1.00 2.50
247 Ryan Howard .30 .75
248 Mariano Rivera .50 1.25
249 Nick Swisher .30 .75
250 John Calipari .40 1.00
251 Frank Thomas .25 .60
252 Catfish Hunter .20 .50
253 Mark Trumbo .25 .60
254 Lou Brock .20 .50
255 Bobby Bowden .40 1.00
256 Rickie Weeks .25 .60
257 Michael Young .15 .40
258 Billy Williams .15 .40
259 Matthias Blonski .25 .60
260 Duke Snider .20 .50
261 Dwight Gooden .25 .60
262 Jean Segura .20 .50
263 Ralph Kiner .15 .40
264 Adam Dunn .20 .50
265 A.J. Ellis .20 .50
266 Henry Rollins .25 .60
267 Grand Central Terminal .15 .40
268 Denard Span .15 .40
269 Tom Seaver .30 .75
270 James Shields .25 .60
271 Prince Fielder .30 .75
272 Josh Reddick .15 .40
273 Alcides Escobar .30 .75
274 Raul Ibanez .30 .75
275 Josh Beckett .15 .40
276 Lance Lynn .15 .40
277 Paul Goldschmidt .25 .60
278 Mike McCarthy .40 1.00
279 Gio Gonzalez .20 .50
280 Kendrys Morales .15 .40
281 Cliff Lee .20 .50
282 Tim Lincecum .20 .50
283 Jason Motte .15 .40
284 Will Clark .25 .60
285 Jose Fernandez RC .60 1.50
286 Alfonso Soriano .20 .50
287 Bill Mazeroski .20 .50
288 Chris Davis .20 .50
289 Edinson Volquez .15 .40
290 Eddie Murray .20 .50
291 Edwin Encarnacion .25 .60
292 Yovani Gallardo .15 .40
293 Jim Palmer .20 .50
294 Johnny Cueto .15 .40
295 Dan Uggla .15 .40
296 Ekolu Kalama .25 .60
297 Jeff Samardzija .15 .40
298 Evan Longoria .20 .50
299 Ryan Zimmerman .20 .50
300 Bud Selig .15 .40
301 Tommy Hanson SP .75 2.00
302 Brandon McCarthy SP .75 2.00
303 Wade Miley SP .75 2.00
304 Freddie Freeman SP 1.50 4.00
305 Wei-Yin Chen SP .75 2.00
306 Carlton Fisk SP 1.00 2.50
307 Darwin Barney SP .75 2.00
308 Alex Rios SP 1.00 2.50
309 Mat Latos SP 1.00 2.50
310 Brandon Phillips SP .75 2.00
311 Bob Lemon SP 1.00 2.50
312 Wilin Rosario SP .75 2.00
313 Josh Rutledge SP .75 2.00
314 Avisail Garcia SP .75 2.00
315 Omar Infante SP .75 2.00
316 Hal Newhouser SP 1.00 2.50
317 George Brett SP 2.50 6.00
318 Eric Hosmer SP 1.00 2.50
319 Matt Kemp SP 1.00 2.50
320 Shaun Marcum SP .75 2.00
321 Wily Peralta SP .75 2.00
322 Robin Yount SP 1.25 3.00
323 Paul Molitor SP 1.25 3.00
324 Justin Morneau SP 1.00 2.50
325 Johan Santana SP 1.00 2.50
326 Ruben Tejada SP .75 2.00
327 Yogi Berra SP 1.25 3.00
328 Alex Rodriguez SP 1.50 4.00
329 Kevin Youkilis SP .75 2.00
330 Rickey Henderson SP 1.25 3.00
331 Tommy Milone SP .75 2.00
332 Cole Hamels SP 1.00 2.50
333 John Kruk SP .75 2.00
334 Russell Martin SP .75 2.00
335 Andrew McCutchen SP 1.25 3.00
336 Chase Headley SP .75 2.00
337 Buster Posey SP 1.50 4.00
338 Marco Scutaro SP 1.00 2.50
339 Kyle Seager SP .75 2.00
340 Yadier Molina SP 1.50 4.00
341 Ozzie Smith SP 1.50 4.00
342 Adam Wainwright SP 1.00 2.50
343 David Price SP 1.00 2.50
344 Nolan Ryan SP 4.00 10.00
345 Melky Cabrera SP .75 2.00
346 Josh Johnson SP 1.00 2.50
347 Stephen Strasburg SP 1.25 3.00
348 Henry Rollins SP .75 2.00
349 Jason Dufner SP .75 2.00
350 Bill Walton SP 1.25 3.00

2013 Topps Allen and Ginter Mini

*MINI 1-300: .75X TO 2X BASIC
*MINI 1-300 RC: .5X TO 1.2X BASIC RC's
*MINI SP 301-350: .5X TO 1.2X BASIC SP
MINI SP ODDS 1:13 HOBBY
351-400 RANDOM WITHIN RIP CARDS
STATED PLATE ODDS 1:594 HOBBY
PLATE PRINT RUN 1 SET PER COLOR
BLACK-CYAN-MAGENTA-YELLOW ISSUED
NO PLATE PRICING DUE TO SCARCITY
351 Mariano Rivera EXT 10.00 25.00
352 Ted Williams EXT 20.00 50.00
353 CC Sabathia EXT 20.00 50.00
354 Ty Cobb EXT 12.50 30.00
355 Justin Verlander EXT 20.00 50.00
356 Prince Fielder EXT 10.00 25.00
357 Cal Ripken Jr. EXT 20.00 50.00
358 Adrian Gonzalez EXT 10.00 25.00
359 Ernie Banks EXT 20.00 50.00
360 Joe Morgan EXT 10.00 25.00
361 Bryce Harper EXT 30.00 80.00
362 Jurickson Profar EXT 20.00 50.00
363 Matt Cain EXT 20.00 50.00
364 Don Mattingly EXT 25.00 60.00
365 Roberto Clemente EXT 30.00 60.00
366 Josh Hamilton EXT 10.00 25.00
367 Jackie Robinson EXT 25.00 60.00
368 David Ortiz EXT 20.00 50.00
369 Cliff Lee EXT 10.00 25.00
370 Jered Weaver EXT 10.00 25.00
371 Mike Trout EXT 25.00 60.00
372 Felix Hernandez EXT 10.00 25.00
373 Joey Votto EXT 20.00 50.00
374 R.A. Dickey EXT 10.00 25.00
375 Dylan Bundy EXT 10.00 25.00
376 Evan Longoria EXT 20.00 50.00
377 Clayton Kershaw EXT 15.00 40.00
378 Manny Machado EXT 15.00 40.00
379 Miguel Cabrera EXT 20.00 50.00
380 Willie Mays EXT 15.00 40.00
381 David Wright EXT 20.00 50.00
382 Babe Ruth EXT 50.00 120.00
383 Troy Tulowitzki EXT 20.00 50.00
384 Ryan Braun EXT 20.00 50.00
385 Frank Thomas EXT 30.00 80.00
386 Stan Musial EXT 25.00 60.00
387 Robinson Cano EXT 15.00 40.00
388 Johnny Bench EXT 20.00 50.00
389 Joe Mauer EXT 20.00 50.00
390 Giancarlo Stanton EXT 12.50 30.00
391 Ken Griffey Jr. EXT 40.00 100.00
392 Yu Darvish EXT 20.00 50.00
393 Mike Schmidt EXT 20.00 50.00
394 Sandy Koufax EXT 15.00 40.00
395 Tom Seaver EXT 15.00 40.00
396 Derek Jeter EXT 30.00 60.00
397 Bob Gibson EXT 10.00 25.00
398 Harmon Killebrew EXT 20.00 50.00
399 Craig Kimbrel EXT 15.00 40.00
400 Jose Reyes EXT 20.00 50.00

2013 Topps Allen and Ginter Mini A and G Back

*A & G BACK: 1X TO 2.5X BASIC
*A & G BACK RCs: .6X TO 1.5X BASIC RCs
A & G BACK ODDS 1:5 HOBBY
*A & G BACK SP: .6X TO 1.5X BASIC SP
A & G BACK SP ODDS 1:65 HOBBY

2013 Topps Allen and Ginter Mini Black

*BLACK: 1.5X TO 4X BASIC
*BLACK RCs: 1X TO 2.5X BASIC RCs
BLACK ODDS 1:10 HOBBY
*BLACK SP: 1X TO 2.5X BASIC SP
BLACK SP ODDS 1:130 HOBBY

2013 Topps Allen and Ginter Across the Years

COMPLETE SET (100) 10.00 25.00
AB Adrian Beltre .50 1.25
AC Aroldis Chapman .50 1.25
AE Andre Ethier .40 1.00
AG Adrian Gonzalez .40 1.00
AJ Adam Jones .40 1.00
AP Andy Pettitte .40 1.00
AR Anthony Rizzo .60 1.50
BG Bob Gibson .40 1.00
BH Bryce Harper .75 2.00
BJU B.J. Upton .40 1.00
BR Brooks Robinson .40 1.00
BRT Babe Ruth 1.25 3.00
CB Carlos Beltran .40 1.00
CCS CC Sabathia .40 1.00
CG Carlos Gonzalez .40 1.00
CGR Curtis Granderson .40 1.00
CJW C.J. Wilson .30 .75
CK Craig Kimbrel .40 1.00
CKW Clayton Kershaw .75 2.00
CL Cliff Lee .40 1.00
CRJ Cal Ripken Jr. 1.50 4.00
CS Chris Sale .50 1.25
DB Dylan Bundy .75 2.00
DJ Derek Jeter 1.25 3.00
DM Don Mattingly 1.00 2.50
DO David Ortiz .50 1.25
DP Dustin Pedroia .50 1.25
DW David Wright .40 1.00
EB Ernie Banks .50 1.25
EL Evan Longoria .40 1.00
FH Felix Hernandez .40 1.00
FT Frank Thomas .50 1.25
GG Gio Gonzalez .40 1.00
GS Giancarlo Stanton .50 1.25
HK Harmon Killebrew .50 1.25
IK Ian Kinsler .40 1.00
JA Jose Altuve .40 1.00
JB Johnny Bench .50 1.25
JBR Jay Bruce .40 1.00
JBT Jose Bautista .40 1.00
JC Johnny Cueto .40 1.00
JE Jacoby Ellsbury .40 1.00
JH Josh Hamilton .40 1.00
JHY Jason Heyward .40 1.00
JK Jason Kipnis .40 1.00
JM Joe Morgan .40 1.00
JMR Joe Mauer .40 1.00
JMT Jesus Montero .30 .75
JP Jurickson Profar .40 1.00
JR Jim Rice .40 1.00
JRB Jackie Robinson .50 1.25
JRD Josh Reddick .30 .75
JRY Jose Reyes .40 1.00
JS James Shields .30 .75
JU Justin Upton .40 1.00
JV Joey Votto .50 1.25
JVL Justin Verlander .50 1.25
JW Jered Weaver .40 1.00
JWR Jayson Werth .40 1.00
KGR Ken Griffey Jr. 1.00 2.50
LG Lou Gehrig 1.00 2.50
MC Miguel Cabrera .50 1.25
MCN Matt Cain .40 1.00
MM Manny Machado 2.00 5.00
MR Mariano Rivera .60 1.50
MS Mike Schmidt .75 2.00
MT Mike Trout 4.00 10.00
MTR Mark Trumbo .30 .75
NS Nick Swisher .40 1.00
PF Prince Fielder .40 1.00
PG Paul Goldschmidt .50 1.25
RAD R.A. Dickey .40 1.00
RB Ryan Braun .40 1.00
RC Robinson Cano .40 1.00
RCL Roberto Clemente 1.25 3.00
RH Roy Halladay .40 1.00
RHO Ryan Howard .40 1.00
RJ Reggie Jackson .40 1.00
RS Ryne Sandberg 1.00 2.50
RZ Ryan Zimmerman .40 1.00
SC Starlin Castro .30 .75
SKX Sandy Koufax 1.00 2.50
SM Shelby Miller .75 2.00
SMU Stan Musial .75 2.00
SP Salvador Perez .40 1.00
TB Trevor Bauer .60 1.50
TC Ty Cobb .75 2.00
TG Tony Gwynn .50 1.25
TL Tim Lincecum .40 1.00
TS Tyler Skaggs .50 1.25
TSV Tom Seaver .40 1.00
TT Troy Tulowitzki .50 1.25
TW Ted Williams 1.00 2.50
WB Wade Boggs .40 1.00
WM Will Middlebrooks .30 .75
WMY Willie Mays 1.00 2.50
WS Willie Stargell .40 1.00
YC Yoenis Cespedes .50 1.25
YD Yu Darvish .50 1.25

2013 Topps Allen and Ginter Autographs

STATED ODDS 1:49 HOBBY
EXCHANGE DEADLINE 07/31/2016
AB Amelia Boone 4.00 10.00
AC Alex Cobb 4.00 10.00
AE Adam Eaton 4.00 10.00
AG Avisail Garcia 4.00 10.00
AGO Anthony Gose 4.00 10.00
AGZ Adrian Gonzalez 15.00 40.00
AJ Adam Jones 12.00 30.00
ALA Artie Lange 15.00 40.00
AR Adam Richman 12.00 30.00
ARO Axl Rose 200.00 400.00
ARZ Anthony Rizzo 20.00 50.00
AV Abe Vigoda 4.00 10.00
B Byamba 5.00 12.00
BB Bobby Bowden 15.00 40.00
BBE Bonnie Bernstein 8.00 20.00
BBU Bill Buckner 8.00 20.00
BJ Brett Jackson 4.00 10.00
BK Brian Kelly 6.00 15.00
BL Brett Lawrie EXCH 12.00 30.00
BM Barry Melrose 8.00 20.00
BP Brandon Phillips 10.00 25.00
BS Bud Selig 12.00 30.00
BSU Bruce Sutter EXCH 20.00 50.00
BW Bill Walton 12.00 30.00
CA Chris Archer 6.00 15.00
CF Cecil Fielder 15.00 40.00
CG Carlos Gonzalez 10.00 25.00
CH Chase Headley 30.00 60.00
CI Chanel Iman 6.00 15.00
CK Casey Kelly 4.00 10.00
CKM Craig Kimbrel 40.00 80.00
CM Chris Mortensen 4.00 10.00
CR Cal Ripken Jr. 75.00 200.00
CT Chrissy Teigen 15.00 40.00
DB Dylan Bundy 10.00 25.00
DM Dale Murphy 60.00 120.00
DMT Don Mattingly 50.00 120.00
DP Dustin Pedroia 30.00 60.00
DS Don Sutton 50.00 100.00
EK Ekolu Kalama 5.00 12.00
EO Ed O'Neill 40.00 80.00
FD Felix Doubront 4.00 10.00
FR Freddie Roach 15.00 40.00
GRD Guillaume Robert-Demolaize 10.00 25.00
HA Hank Aaron EXCH 175.00 350.00
HR Henry Rollins 25.00 60.00
JC John Calipari 20.00 50.00
JCU Johnny Cueto 10.00 25.00
JD Jason Dufner 12.00 30.00
JH Josh Hamilton EXCH 40.00 80.00
JK Jason Kipnis 10.00 25.00
JM Julia Mancuso 10.00 25.00
JML Juan Marichal 40.00 80.00
JP Jurickson Profar 8.00 20.00
JPA Jarrod Parker 4.00 10.00
JR Josh Reddick 4.00 10.00
JRC Jim Rice 12.00 30.00
JS Jean Segura 4.00 10.00
JSD James Shields 10.00 25.00
JZ Jordan Zimmermann 4.00 10.00
KH Kevin Harvick 10.00 25.00
LA Luis Aparicio 60.00 120.00
LL Lance Lynn 4.00 10.00
LV Lindsey Vonn 30.00 80.00
MB Matthias Blonski 5.00 12.00
MBU Madison Bumgarner 25.00 60.00
MBY Matthew Berry 10.00 25.00
MC Mark Cuban 30.00 80.00
MCN Matt Cain
MH Mike Richter 6.00 15.00
MHL Monty Hall 8.00 20.00
MJO Mike Joy 6.00 15.00
MM McKayla Maroney 12.00 30.00
MMC Mike McCarthy 30.00 80.00
MMD Manny Machado EXCH 60.00 120.00
MO Mike Olt 6.00 15.00
MS Mike Schmidt 75.00 150.00
MT Mark Trumbo 12.00 30.00
MTT Mike Trout EXCH
MW Maury Wills 4.00 10.00
NM Nana Meriwether 6.00 15.00
NS Nick Saban 100.00 250.00
NW Nik Wallenda 5.00 12.00
OC Olivia Culpo 10.00 25.00
P Pele 250.00 400.00
PF Prince Fielder EXCH 50.00 100.00

PG Paul Goldschmidt 10.00 25.00
PH Phil Heath 12.00 30.00
PM Penny Marshall 25.00 60.00
PO Paul O'Neill EXCH 25.00 60.00
RD R.A. Dickey
RJR Roy Jones Jr. 20.00 50.00
RVP Robin van Persie 50.00 100.00
RZ Ryan Zimmerman 12.00 30.00
SD Scott Diamond 4.00 10.00
SH Scott Hamilton 8.00 20.00
SK Sandy Koufax 300.00 500.00
SM Starling Marte 4.00 20.00
SMI Shelby Miller 4.00 10.00
SN Shawn Nadelen 5.00 12.00
SP Salvador Perez 15.00 40.00
TB Trevor Bauer EXCH 8.00 20.00
TCG Tony Cingrani 5.00 12.00
TL Tommy Lee EXCH 25.00 60.00
TM Tommy Milone 4.00 10.00
TS Tyler Skaggs 4.00 10.00
VB Vida Blue 4.00 10.00
WC Will Clark 20.00 50.00
WJ Wally Joyner 8.00 20.00
WM Wil Myers 4.00 10.00
WMB Will Middlebrooks EXCH 12.00 30.00
WP Wily Peralta 4.00 10.00
WR Wilin Rosario 4.00 10.00
YC Yoenis Cespedes 40.00 80.00
YD Yu Darvish EXCH 75.00 150.00
YG Yasmani Grandal 4.00 10.00
YP Yasiel Puig 125.00 300.00
ZC Zack Cozart 4.00 10.00
ZM Ziggy Marley 20.00 50.00

2013 Topps Allen and Ginter Autographs Red Ink

STATED ODDS 1:931 HOBBY
PRINT RUNS B/WN 10-409 SER.#'d SETS
NO PRICING ON MOST DUE TO SCARCITY
EXCHANGE DEADLINE 07/31/2013
DS Don Sutton/66 20.00 50.00
MO Mike Olt/373 4.00 10.00
MTT Mike Trout/31 250.00 500.00
WR Wilin Rosario/409 4.00 10.00

2013 Topps Allen and Ginter Civilizations of Ages Past

COMPLETE SET (20) 5.00 12.00
STATED ODDS 1:8 HOBBY
ASY Assyrians .60 1.50
AZ Aztecs .60 1.50
BAY Babylonians .60 1.50
BYZ Byzantine .60 1.50
EG Egyptians .60 1.50
GRK Greeks .60 1.50
HT Hittites .60 1.50
IN Inca .60 1.50
IRV Indus River Valley .60 1.50
MES Mesopotamians .60 1.50
MY Mayans .60 1.50
OL Olmecs .60 1.50
OTT Ottoman .60 1.50
PER Persians .60 1.50
PH Phoenicians .60 1.50
ROM Romans .60 1.50
SD Shang Dynasty .60 1.50
SU Sumerians .60 1.50
SWA Swahili .60 1.50
VK Vikings .60 1.50

2013 Topps Allen and Ginter Curious Cases

COMPLETE SET (10) 15.00 40.00
H HAARP 3.00 8.00
A51 Roswell 3.00 8.00
Area 51
CH Chemtrails 3.00 8.00
DA Denver Airport 3.00 8.00
FM Faked moon landings 3.00 8.00
JFK Assassination of JFK 3.00 8.00
MK MKULTRA 3.00 8.00
NOW The Illuminati 3.00 8.00
New World Order
PE The Philadelphia Experiment 3.00 8.00
UVB UVB-76 3.00 8.00

2013 Topps Allen and Ginter Framed Mini Relics

VERSION A ODDS 1:29 HOBBY
VERSION B ODDS 1:27 HOBBY
B Byamba 3.00 8.00
P Pele 10.00 25.00
AA Alex Avila 3.00 8.00
AB Albert Belle 3.00 8.00
ABB Amelia Boone 3.00 8.00
ABT Adrian Beltre 3.00 8.00
AC Asdrubal Cabrera 3.00 8.00
AG Alex Gordon 3.00 8.00
AGZ Adrian Gonzalez 3.00 8.00
AL Artie Lange 6.00 15.00
AR Aramis Ramirez 3.00 8.00
AR Adam Richman 10.00 25.00
AV Abe Vigoda 3.00 8.00
AW Adam Wainwright 4.00 10.00
BB Brandon Belt 3.00 8.00
BBR Bonnie Bernstein 6.00 15.00
BBW Bobby Bowden 4.00 10.00
BG Brett Gardner 3.00 8.00
BK Brian Kelly 4.00 10.00
BM Barry Melrose 6.00 15.00
BMC Brian McCann 3.00 8.00
BP Buster Posey 4.00 10.00
BR Babe Ruth 150.00 300.00
BW Bill Walton 3.00 8.00
CB Clay Buchholz 3.00 8.00
CBL Chad Billingsley 3.00 8.00
CF Cecil Fielder 3.00 8.00
CI Chanel Iman 4.00 10.00
CKM Craig Kimbrel 3.00 8.00
CL Cory Luebke 3.00 8.00
CM Cameron Maybin 3.00 8.00
CMO Chris Mortensen 3.00 8.00
CMR Carlos Marmol 3.00 8.00
CP Carlos Pena 3.00 8.00
CR Cody Ross 3.00 8.00
CT Chrissy Teigen 50.00 100.00
DA Dustin Ackley 3.00 8.00
DF Dexter Fowler 3.00 8.00
DJ Desmond Jennings 3.00 8.00
DP David Price 3.00 8.00
DS Drew Stubbs 3.00 8.00
DW David Wright 50.00 100.00
EA Elvis Andrus 3.00 8.00
EH Eric Hosmer 3.00 8.00
EON Ed O'Neill 6.00 15.00
FH Felix Hernandez 3.00 8.00
FL Fred Lynn 3.00 8.00
FR Frank Robinson 40.00 80.00
FR Freddie Roach 4.00 10.00
GB Gordon Beckham 3.00 8.00
GBR George Brett 60.00 120.00
GC Gary Carter 20.00 50.00
GS Gary Sheffield 3.00 8.00
HA Henderson Alvarez 3.00 8.00
HI Hisashi Iwakuma 3.00 8.00
HK Harmon Killebrew 15.00 40.00
HP Hunter Pence 3.00 8.00
HR Hanley Ramirez 3.00 8.00
ID Ike Davis 3.00 8.00
IDS Ian Desmond 3.00 8.00
IK Ian Kennedy 3.00 8.00
JA Jose Altuve 3.00 8.00
JAX John Axford 3.00 8.00
JBR Jay Bruce 3.00 8.00
JC Johnny Cueto 3.00 8.00
JCA John Calipari 4.00 10.00
JCH Jhoulys Chacin 3.00 8.00
JD Jason Dufner 4.00 10.00
JDM J.D. Martinez 3.00 8.00
JH Josh Hamilton 3.00 8.00
JHK Jeremy Hellickson 3.00 8.00
JHY Jason Heyward 3.00 8.00
JJ Jon Jay 3.00 8.00
JJY Jon Jay 3.00 8.00
JL Jon Lester 3.00 8.00
JM Justin Morneau 3.00 8.00
JMA Julia Mancuso 3.00 8.00
JMD James McDonald 3.00 8.00
JR Jimmy Rollins 3.00 8.00
JT Jose Tabata 3.00 8.00
JV Joey Votto 4.00 10.00
JVR Justin Verlander 4.00 10.00
JW Jered Weaver 3.00 8.00
JZ Jordan Zimmermann 3.00 8.00
KH Kevin Harvick 5.00 12.00
KM Kendrys Morales 3.00 8.00
LB Lou Brock 8.00 20.00
LG Lou Gehrig 50.00 100.00
LLN Lance Lynn 3.00 8.00
LM Logan Morrison 3.00 8.00
LV Lindsey Vonn 6.00 15.00
MB Michael Bourn 3.00 8.00
MBL Matthias Blonski 3.00 8.00
MBU Madison Bumgarner 3.00 8.00
MBY Matthew Berry 6.00 15.00
MC Matt Cain 3.00 8.00
MCU Mark Cuban 4.00 10.00
MH Matt Holliday 3.00 8.00
MHA Monty Hall 3.00 8.00
MJ Mike Joy 3.00 8.00
MKP Matt Kemp 3.00 8.00
ML Mat Latos 3.00 8.00
MM Matt Moore 3.00 8.00
MMA McKayla Maroney 10.00 25.00
MMC Mike McCarthy 6.00 15.00
MSZ Max Scherzer 3.00 8.00
NC Nelson Cruz 3.00 8.00
NM Nana Meriwether 4.00 10.00
NS Nick Saban 12.00 30.00
NW Neil Walker 3.00 8.00
NWA Nik Wallenda 4.00 10.00
OC Olivia Culpo 3.00 8.00
PF Prince Fielder 3.00 8.00
PH Phil Heath 4.00 10.00
PM Paul Molitor 20.00 50.00
PMA Penny Marshall 4.00 10.00
PON Paul O'Neill 4.00 10.00
PS Pablo Sandoval 3.00 8.00
RF Rafael Furcal 3.00 8.00
RH Roy Halladay 3.00 8.00
RHD Ryan Howard 3.00 8.00
RJJ Roy Jones Jr. 3.00 8.00
RN Ricky Nolasco 3.00 8.00
RR Ricky Romero 3.00 8.00
SC Starlin Castro 3.00 8.00
SG Steve Garvey 15.00 40.00
SH Scott Hamilton 3.00 8.00
SM Stan Musial 60.00 120.00
SN Shawn Nadelen 3.00 8.00
TH Tim Hudson 3.00 8.00
TL Tim Lincecum 3.00 8.00
TW Ted Williams 60.00 120.00
WM Willie Mays 30.00 60.00
WR Wilin Rosario 3.00 8.00
YD Yu Darvish 4.00 10.00
YG Yovani Gallardo 3.00 8.00
ZG Zack Greinke 3.00 8.00
ZM Ziggy Marley 3.00 8.00

2013 Topps Allen and Ginter Martial Mastery

COMPLETE SET (10) 4.00 10.00
STATED ODDS 1:8 HOBBY
AMZ Amazons .60 1.50
AP Apache .60 1.50
AZ Aztecs .60 1.50
GD Gladiators .60 1.50
KN Knights .60 1.50
RM Romans .60 1.50
SM Samurai .60 1.50
SP Spartans .60 1.50
VK Vikings .60 1.50
ZU Zulu .60 1.50

2013 Topps Allen and Ginter Mini All in a Days Work

B Butcher 6.00 15.00
C Clergy 6.00 15.00
F Firefighter 6.00 15.00
N Nurse 6.00 15.00
P Pilot 6.00 15.00
S Soldier 6.00 15.00
CW Construction Worker 6.00 15.00
PB Paperboy 6.00 15.00
PO Police Officer 6.00 15.00
ST Schoolteacher 6.00 15.00

2013 Topps Allen and Ginter Mini Famous Finds

COMPLETE SET (10) 8.00 20.00
STATED ODDS 1:5 HOBBY
L Olduvai Gorge 1.00 2.50
Lucy
P Pompeii 1.00 2.50
CA The Cave of Altamira 1.00 2.50
CG Cairo Geniza 1.00 2.50
DSS Dead Sea Scrolls 1.00 2.50
KTT King Tut's Tomb 1.00 2.50
NHL Nag Hammadi Library 1.00 2.50
PS The Pilate Stone 1.00 2.50
QSH The Tomb of the Qin Shi Huang 1.00 2.50
RS Rosetta Stone 1.00 2.50

2013 Topps Allen and Ginter Mini Heavy Hangs the Head

COMPLETE SET (30) 12.50 30.00
STATED ODDS 1:5 HOBBY
ALX Alexander I 1.25 3.00
ATG Alexander the Great 1.25 3.00
AUG Augustus 1.25 3.00
CHR Charlemagne 1.25 3.00
CLE Cleopatra 1.25 3.00
CON Constantine 1.25 3.00
CTG Cyrus the Great 1.25 3.00
DK King David 1.25 3.00
EM Emperor Meiji 1.25 3.00
FA Ferdinand & Isabella 1.25 3.00
FRD Frederick II 1.25 3.00
GA Gustavus Adolphus 1.25 3.00
ITT Ivan the Terrible 1.25 3.00
JC Julius Caesar 1.25 3.00
KH King Henry VIII 1.25 3.00
KHN King Henry V 1.25 3.00
KJ King James I 1.25 3.00
KL King Louis XIV 1.25 3.00
KR King Richard I 1.25 3.00
KW Krishnaraja Wadiyar III 1.25 3.00
NP Napoleon 1.25 3.00
PW Prince William 1.25 3.00
QB Queen Beatrix 1.25 3.00
QE Queen Elizabeth II 1.25 3.00
QSH Qin Shi Huang 1.25 3.00
QV Queen Victoria 1.25 3.00
RAM Ramses II 1.25 3.00
SLM Solomon 1.25 3.00
STM Suleiman the Magnificent 1.25 3.00
TUT Tutankhamun 1.25 3.00

2013 Topps Allen and Ginter Mini Inquiring Minds

COMPLETE SET (21) 10.00 25.00
AR Aristotle 1.00 2.50
AS Arthur Schopenhauer 1.00 2.50
AUG St. Augustine 1.00 2.50
BS Baruch Spinoza 1.00 2.50
EP Epicurus 1.00 2.50
FB Francis Bacon 1.00 2.50
FN Friedrich Nietzsche 1.00 2.50
GH Georg Wilhelm Friedrich Hegel 1.00 2.50
HA Hannah Arendt 1.00 2.50
IK Immanuel Kant 1.00 2.50
JL John Locke 1.00 2.50
JPS Jean-Paul Sartre 1.00 2.50
KM Karl Marx 1.00 2.50
NM Niccolo Machiavelli 1.00 2.50
PTO Plato 1.00 2.50
RD Rene Descartes 1.00 2.50
SCR Socrates 1.00 2.50
SDB Simone de Beauvoir 1.00 2.50
ST Sun Tzu 1.00 2.50
TA Thomas Aquinas 1.00 2.50
TH Thomas Hobbes 1.00 2.50

2013 Topps Allen and Ginter Mini No Card Number

*NO NBR: 4X TO 10X BASIC
*NO NBR RCs: 2.5X TO 6X BASIC RCs
*NO NBR SP: 1.2X TO 3X BASIC SP
STATED ODDS 1:102 HOBBY
ANNC'D PRINT RUN OF 50 SETS
2 Derek Jeter 30.00 60.00
344 Nolan Ryan 12.50 30.00

2013 Topps Allen and Ginter Mini Peacemakers

COMPLETE SET (10) 10.00 25.00
STATED ODDS 1:5 HOBBY
AL Abraham Lincoln 1.25 3.00
BC Bill Clinton 1.25 3.00
DL Dalai Lama 1.25 3.00
GND Gandhi 1.25 3.00
GW George Washington 1.25 3.00
HT Harriet Tubman 1.25 3.00
JA Jane Addams 1.25 3.00
JC Jimmy Carter 1.25 3.00
MT Mother Teresa 1.25 3.00
NM Nelson Mandela 1.25 3.00

2013 Topps Allen and Ginter Mini People on Bicycles

A Amphibious 6.00 15.00
M Messenger 6.00 15.00
T Tricycle 6.00 15.00
BR Brief Respite 6.00 15.00
NH No Hands 6.00 15.00
PF Penny-Farthing 6.00 15.00
QT Quadracycle for Two 6.00 15.00
TT Tricycle for Two 6.00 15.00
WE Woodland Excursion 6.00 15.00
TRI Triathlete 6.00 15.00

2013 Topps Allen and Ginter Mini The First Americans

COMPLETE SET (15) 10.00 25.00
STATED ODDS 1:5 HOBBY
WCT Wichita 1.00 2.50
ALG Algonquian 1.00 2.50
AP Apache 1.00 2.50
BNK Bannock 1.00 2.50
CHK Cherokee 1.00 2.50
CHY Cheyenne 1.00 2.50
CM Comanche 1.00 2.50
HPI Hopi 1.00 2.50
IRQ Iroquois 1.00 2.50
LK Lakota 1.00 2.50
NV Navajo 1.00 2.50
PUB Pueblo 1.00 2.50
PWN Pawnee 1.00 2.50
SX Sioux 1.00 2.50
ZN Zuni 1.00 2.50

2013 Topps Allen and Ginter N43 Autographs

STATED PRINT RUN 40 SER.#'d SETS
N43AP Pele 300.00 500.00

2013 Topps Allen and Ginter Box Toppers

AP Albert Pujols 2.00 5.00
BH Bryce Harper 2.50 6.00
DW David Wright 1.25 3.00
GS Giancarlo Stanton 1.50 4.00
JH Josh Hamilton 1.25 3.00
JV Joey Votto 1.50 4.00
MC Miguel Cabrera 1.50 4.00
MK Matt Kemp 1.25 3.00
MT Mike Trout 12.00 30.00
PF Prince Fielder 1.25 3.00
RAD R.A. Dickey 1.25 3.00
RB Ryan Braun 1.25 3.00
RC Robinson Cano 1.25 3.00
SS Stephen Strasburg 1.50 4.00
TT Troy Tulowitzki 1.50 4.00

2013 Topps Allen and Ginter Box Topper Relics

STATED PRINT RUN 25 SER.#'d SETS
AR Alex Rodriguez 30.00 60.00
BP Brandon Phillips 15.00 40.00
DJ Derek Jeter 100.00 200.00
HC Hank Conger 6.00 15.00
JB Jay Bruce 15.00 40.00
JV Justin Verlander 20.00 50.00
MC Matt Cain 20.00 50.00
SC Starlin Castro 20.00 50.00

2013 Topps Allen and Ginter Oddity Relics

STATED ODDS 1:7,150 HOBBY
PRINT RUNS B/WN 25-125 COPIES PER
BK Grassy Knoll/25 300.00 400.00
WF Wrigley Field/125 40.00 80.00
KHW Kim and Kris/50 60.00 120.00
OIT President Obama/50 125.00 250.00

2013 Topps Allen and Ginter One Little Corner

COMPLETE SET (20) 5.00 12.00
STATED ODDS 1:8 HOBBY
NPT Neptune .60 1.50
PTO Pluto .60 1.50
SDN Sedna .60 1.50
STN Saturn .60 1.50
SUN Sun .60 1.50
URN Uranus .60 1.50
AB Asteroid Belt .60 1.50
CM Comet .60 1.50
CR Ceres .60 1.50
CT Centaur .60 1.50
ER Eris .60 1.50
ERT Earth .60 1.50
HAU Haumea .60 1.50
JPT Jupiter .60 1.50
MK Makemake .60 1.50
MN Moon .60 1.50
MS Mars .60 1.50
MY Mercury .60 1.50
SD Scattered Disc .60 1.50
VN Venus .60 1.50

2013 Topps Allen and Ginter Palaces and Strongholds

COMPLETE SET (20) 5.00 12.00
STATED ODDS 1:8 HOBBY
ALH Alhambra .60 1.50
BP Buckingham Palace .60 1.50
CC Chateau de Chambord .60 1.50
FC Forbidden City .60 1.50
FK Fort Knox .60 1.50
GY Gyeongbokgung .60 1.50
HP Hohenschwangau Castle .60 1.50
LC Leeds Castle .60 1.50
MP Mysore Palace .60 1.50
NC Neuschwanstein Castle .60 1.50
PNP Pena National Palace .60 1.50
PP Peterhof Palace .60 1.50
PPC Potala Palace .60 1.50
SB Schonbrunn Palace .60 1.50
SP Summer Palace .60 1.50
TA The Alamo .60 1.50
TB The Bastille .60 1.50
TM Taj Mahal .60 1.50
TP Topkapi Palace .60 1.50
VSL Palace of Versailles .60 1.50

2013 Topps Allen and Ginter Relics

STATED ODDS 1:37 HOBBY
AC Aroldis Chapman 3.00 8.00
AD Adam Dunn 3.00 8.00
AE Andre Ethier 3.00 8.00
AG Adrian Gonzalez 3.00 8.00
AJ Austin Jackson 3.00 8.00
AL Adam Lind 3.00 8.00
BB Brandon Beachy 3.00 8.00
BBT Billy Butler 3.00 8.00
BD Bobby Doerr 10.00 25.00
BP Brandon Phillips 3.00 8.00
BS Bruce Sutter 20.00 50.00
CCS CC Sabathia 3.00 8.00
CG Carlos Gonzalez 3.00 8.00
CH Chris Heisey 3.00 8.00
CK Craig Kimbrel 3.00 8.00
CL Cliff Lee 3.00 8.00
DB Darwin Barney 3.00 8.00
DDJ David DeJesus 3.00 8.00
DM Don Mattingly 20.00 50.00
DW David Wright 12.50 30.00
GG Goose Gossage 20.00 50.00
HA Hank Aaron 50.00 100.00
HN Hal Newhouser 8.00 20.00
IK Ian Kinsler 3.00 8.00
JG Johnny Giavotella 3.00 8.00
JH Jason Heyward 3.00 8.00
JJH J.J. Hardy 3.00 8.00
JM Justin Masterson 3.00 8.00
JMA Joe Mauer 3.00 8.00
JP Jake Peavy 3.00 8.00
JPA J.P. Arencibia 3.00 8.00
JU Justin Upton 3.00 8.00
JZ Jordan Zimmermann 3.00 8.00
LD Lucas Duda 3.00 8.00
MM Miguel Montero 3.00 8.00
MR Mariano Rivera 6.00 15.00
RB Ryan Braun 3.00 8.00
RC Rod Carew 12.50 30.00
RJ Reggie Jackson 20.00 50.00
RK Ralph Kiner 10.00 25.00
RW Rickie Weeks 3.00 8.00
RY Robin Yount 20.00 50.00
RZ Ryan Zimmerman 3.00 8.00
SC Steve Carlton 30.00 60.00
SMC Shaun Marcum 3.00 8.00
SR Scott Rolen 3.00 8.00
SS Stephen Strasburg 3.00 8.00
TG Tony Gwynn 3.00 8.00
TH Todd Helton 3.00 8.00
UJ Ubaldo Jimenez 3.00 8.00

2013 Topps Allen and Ginter Rip Cards

OVERALL RIP ODDS 1:287 HOBBY
PRINT RUNS B/WN 10-99 COPIES PER
NO PRICING ON QTY 25 OR LESS
ALL LISTED PRICED ARE FOR RIPPED
UNRIPPED HAVE ADD'L CARDS WITHIN
RC1 Duke Snider/50 6.00 15.00
RC2 Cliff Lee/25 6.00 15.00
RC4 Ralph Kiner/25 6.00 15.00
RC6 Jason Heyward/50 6.00 15.00
RC7 Mike Olt/50 6.00 15.00
RC8 Yoenis Cespedes/25 10.00 25.00
RC12 Darryl Strawberry/25 6.00 15.00
RC13 Carlos Gonzalez/50 6.00 15.00
RC19 Tim Lincecum/50 6.00 15.00
RC21 David Wright/25 10.00 25.00
RC23 C.J. Wilson/50 6.00 15.00
RC24 David Freese/50 6.00 15.00
RC26 R.A. Dickey/25 6.00 15.00
RC27 Clayton Kershaw/25 10.00 25.00
RC28 Dwight Gooden/50 10.00 25.00
RC29 Giancarlo Stanton/50 6.00 15.00
RC30 Paul O'Neill/50 6.00 15.00
RC33 Jered Weaver/50 6.00 15.00
RC34 Anthony Rizzo/25 10.00 25.00
RC38 Nick Swisher/50 6.00 15.00
RC40 Evan Longoria/25 6.00 15.00
RC41 Torii Hunter/50 6.00 15.00
RC42 Dustin Pedroia/25 10.00 25.00
RC43 Paul Goldschmidt/50 10.00 25.00
RC45 James Shields/50 6.00 15.00
RC46 Matt Cain/50 6.00 15.00
RC47 Gio Gonzalez/50 6.00 15.00
RC50 Lou Gehrig
RC51 Allen Craig/25 6.00 15.00
RC52 Chris Sale/25 6.00 15.00
RC54 Mark Trumbo/50 6.00 15.00
RC55 Harmon Killebrew/25 10.00 25.00
RC56 Tony Gwynn/25 10.00 25.00
RC57 Justin Upton/25 6.00 15.00
RC58 Gary Carter/25 10.00 25.00
RC59 Warren Spahn/25 6.00 15.00
RC60 Wade Boggs/25 10.00 25.00
RC63 Matt Holliday/25 6.00 15.00
RC64 Ian Kinsler/50 6.00 15.00
RC66 Joey Votto/25 10.00 25.00
RC67 Hanley Ramirez/50 6.00 15.00
RC68 Jose Reyes/50 6.00 15.00
RC70 B.J. Upton/50 6.00 15.00
RC71 Joe Mauer/25 10.00 25.00
RC73 Troy Tulowitzki/50 6.00 15.00
RC74 Bob Gibson/25 6.00 15.00
RC75 Madison Bumgarner/50 6.00 15.00
RC77 Al Kaline/25 10.00 25.00
RC80 Will Middlebrooks/25 6.00 15.00
RC81 Tyler Skaggs/50 6.00 15.00
RC84 Adrian Gonzalez/25 6.00 15.00
RC85 Trevor Bauer/50 6.00 15.00
RC86 Carlos Beltran/50 6.00 15.00
RC88 Roy Halladay/50 6.00 15.00
RC90 Andy Pettitte/25 6.00 15.00
RC91 John Smoltz/25 6.00 15.00
RC93 Adam Eaton/50 6.00 15.00
RC95 Prince Fielder/25 6.00 15.00
RC96 Josh Hamilton/25 6.00 15.00
RC97 Willie Stargell/25 6.00 15.00
RC98 Josh Beckett/50 6.00 15.00
RC99 Starlin Castro/50 6.00 15.00

2013 Topps Allen and Ginter Wonders of the World Cabinets

1 Great Pyramid of Giza 3.00 8.00
2 Hanging Gardens of Babylon 3.00 8.00
3 Statue of Zeus at Olympia 3.00 8.00
4 Temple of Artemis at Ephesus 3.00 8.00
5 Mausoleum at Halicarnassus 3.00 8.00
6 Colossus of Rhodes 3.00 8.00
7 Lighthouse of Alexandria 3.00 8.00
8 Channel Tunnel 3.00 8.00
9 CN Tower 3.00 8.00
10 Empire State Building 3.00 8.00
11 Golden Gate Bridge 3.00 8.00
12 Itaipu Dam 3.00 8.00
13 Delta Works 3.00 8.00
14 Panama Canal 3.00 8.00
15 Grand Canyon 3.00 8.00
16 Great Barrier Reef 3.00 8.00
17 Harbor of Rio de Janeiro 3.00 8.00
18 Mount Everest 3.00 8.00
19 Aurora 3.00 8.00
20 Paricutin Volcano 3.00 8.00
21 Victoria Falls 3.00 8.00

2014 Topps Allen and Ginter

COMPLETE SET (350) 25.00 60.00
COMP.SET w/o SP's (300) 12.00 30.00
SP ODDS 1:2 HOBBY
1 Roger Maris .25 .60
2 Don Mattingly .50 1.25
3 Matt Davidson RC .30 .75
4 Edwin Encarnacion .25 .60
5 Jurickson Profar .20 .50
6 Laura Phelps Sweatt .15 .40
7 Hector Santiago .15 .40
8 Bob Feller .20 .50
9 Koji Uehara .15 .40
10 Andrew McCutchen .25 .60
11 Nick Franklin .15 .40
12 Jedd Gyorko .15 .40
13 Gary Sheffield .15 .40
14 Michael Cuddyer .15 .40
15 Matt Williams .15 .40
16 Bartolo Colon .15 .40
17 Travis d'Arnaud RC .30 .75
18 Ryne Sandberg .50 1.25
19 Pablo Sandoval .20 .50
20 Babe Ruth .60 1.50
21 Rafael Palmeiro .20 .50
22 Michael Eisner .15 .40
23 Snoop Lion .15 .40
24 Jorge Posada .20 .50
25 Joe DiMaggio .50 1.25
26 Fergie Jenkins .20 .50
27 David Ortiz .25 .60
28 Mark Trumbo .15 .40
29 Shelby Miller .20 .50
30 Judah Friedlander .15 .40
31 Michael Choice RC .25 .60
32 Tim Lincecum .20 .50
33 Alex Avila .20 .50
34 Felix Hernandez .20 .50
35 Brooks Robinson .20 .50
36 Yadier Molina .30 .75
37 Wil Myers .15 .40
38 Don Sutton .20 .50
39 Chris Sale .25 .60
40 Steve Delabar .15 .40
41 Lou Gehrig .50 1.25
42 Junior Lake .15 .40
43 Craig Kimbrel .20 .50
44 Ty Cobb .40 1.00
45 Nomar Garciaparra .20 .50
46 John L. Sullivan .15 .40
47 Wilmer Flores RC .30 .75
48 Alex Rodriguez .30 .75
49 Felix Doubront .15 .40
50 Orlando Hernandez .15 .40
51 Oswaldo Arcia .15 .40
52 Kevin Smith .15 .40
53 Sandy Koufax .50 1.25
54 Yordano Ventura RC .30 .75
55 Andrew Lambo RC .15 .40
56 Jason Heyward .20 .50
57 Carlos Beltran .20 .50
58 Tyler Skaggs .15 .40
59 Hal Newhouser .20 .50
60 Ryan Zimmerman .20 .50
61 Bo Jackson .25 .60
62 Diana Nyad .15 .40
63 Bill Buckner .15 .40
64 Taijuan Walker RC .25 .60
65 Fred McGriff .20 .50
66 Roger Clemens .30 .75
67 Omar Vizquel .20 .50
68 Gio Gonzalez .20 .50
69 Johnny Cueto .20 .50
70 Dr. James Andrews .15 .40
71 Wade Boggs .20 .50
72 Ralph Kiner .20 .50
73 Joe Morgan .20 .50
74 Adrian Gonzalez .20 .50
75 Rod Carew .20 .50
76 Cal Ripken Jr. .75 2.00
77 Stan Musial .40 1.00
78 Zack Greinke .25 .60
79 Matt Adams .15 .40
80 Justin Verlander .25 .60
81 Larry King .15 .40
82 Jackie Robinson .25 .60
83 Giancarlo Stanton .25 .60
84 Francisco Liriano .15 .40
85 Carlos Santana .20 .50
86 Randy Johnson .25 .60
87 Alex Gordon .20 .50
88 Buffalo Bill Cody .15 .40
89 Chuck Todd .15 .40
90 Roy Halladay .20 .50
91 Clay Buchholz .15 .40
92 Ernie Banks .25 .60
93 Willie Mays .50 1.25
94 Lou Brock .20 .50
95 Austin Wierschke .15 .40
96 Madison Bumgarner .20 .50
97 Sparky Anderson .20 .50
98 David Wright .20 .50
99 Wilin Rosario .15 .40
100 Queen Victoria .15 .40
101 Mike Trout 1.25 3.00
102 Todd Frazier .15 .40
103 Jon Lester .20 .50
104 Troy Tulowitzki .25 .60
105 Cole Hamels .20 .50
106 Patrick Corbin .20 .50
107 Will Middlebrooks .15 .40
108 Nolan Ryan .75 2.00
109 Jhoulys Chacin .15 .40
110 Jeremy Hellickson .15 .40
111 Frank Robinson .20 .50
112 Erin Brady .15 .40
113 Shin-Soo Choo .20 .50
114 Desmond Jennings .20 .50
115 Dustin Pedroia .25 .60
116 Brett Gardner .20 .50
117 Yu Darvish .25 .60
118 Adam Schefter .15 .40
119 Felicia Day .15 .40
120 Tom Seaver .20 .50
121 Freddie Freeman .30 .75
122 Craig Biggio .20 .50
123 Matt Carpenter .25 .60
124 Jonathan Schoop .15 .40
125 Glen Waggoner .15 .40
126 Willie Stargell .20 .50
127 Greg Maddux .30 .75
128 Bill Rancic .15 .40
129 Hank Aaron .50 1.25
130 Mike Zunino .15 .40
131 Buster Posey .30 .75
132 Ted Williams .50 1.25
133 Xander Bogaerts RC .75 2.00
134 Jordan Zimmermann .20 .50
135 Grant Balfour .15 .40
136 Carlos Gonzalez .20 .50
137 Reggie Jackson .20 .50
138 Mariano Rivera .30 .75
139 Jacoby Ellsbury .20 .50
140 Matt Moore .20 .50
141 Starlin Castro .15 .40
142 Hiroki Kuroda .15 .40
143 Eddie Mathews .25 .60
144 Brett Oberholtzer .15 .40
145 Derek Jeter .60 1.50
146 Max Scherzer .25 .60
147 Mark McGwire .50 1.25
148 Bryce Harper .40 1.00
149 Jose Canseco .20 .50
150 Mike Schmidt .40 1.00
151 James Paxton RC .40 1.00
152 Vince Gilligan .15 .40
153 The Iron Sheik .15 .40
154 Eric Hosmer .20 .50
155 Yogi Berra .25 .60
156 Jean Segura .20 .50
157 Hisashi Iwakuma .20 .50
158 Carlton Fisk .20 .50
159 George Brett .50 1.25
160 Daniel Okrent .15 .40
161 Tommy Lasorda .20 .50
162 George Kell .20 .50
163 Paul Molitor .25 .60
164 Jenny Dell .15 .40
165 Brad Miller .20 .50
166 Mike Napoli .15 .40
167 Nick Castellanos RC .75 2.00
168 Miguel Cabrera .25 .60
169 Dale Murphy .25 .60
170 Matt Holliday .25 .60
171 Dusty Baker .15 .40
172 Andrelton Simmons .15 .40
173 Jose Fernandez .25 .60
174 Ben Zobrist .20 .50
175 Chase Utley .20 .50
176 Anthony Robles .15 .40
177 Anthony Rizzo .30 .75
178 Domonic Brown .20 .50
179 Chris Archer .15 .40
180 Ryan Riess .15 .40
181 Jose Reyes .20 .50
182 Starling Marte .20 .50
183 Jim Palmer .20 .50
184 Gerrit Cole .25 .60
185 Jose Bautista .20 .50
186 Billy Hamilton RC .30 .75
187 David Price .20 .50
188 Jordan Oliver .15 .40
189 Clayton Kershaw .40 1.00
190 Kolten Wong RC .30 .75
191 Jordan Burfoughs .15 .40
192 Daniel Nava .15 .40
193 Tom Glavine .20 .50
194 Avisail Garcia .20 .50
195 Chris Carpenter .20 .50
196 Eddie Murray .20 .50
197 Wade Miley .15 .40
198 Jeff Locke .15 .40
199 Joe Mauer .20 .50
200 Zack Wheeler .20 .50
201 Paul O'Neill .20 .50
202 Jim Rice .20 .50
203 Jered Weaver .20 .50
204 Albert Pujols .30 .75
205 Robin Yount .25 .60
206 Willie McCovey .20 .50
207 Justin Upton .20 .50
208 Al Kaline .25 .60
209 Vladimir Guerrero .20 .50
210 Anthony Bourdain .15 .40
211 Mark Roth .15 .40
212 Doug Fister .15 .40
213 Allyson Felix .15 .40
214 Carli Lloyd .15 .40
215 Johnny Bench .25 .60
216 Matt Besser .15 .40
217 Jose Iglesias .20 .50
218 Casey Kelly .20 .50
219 Evan Gattis .15 .40
220 Josh Hamilton .20 .50
221 Adam Eaton .15 .40
222 Danny Salazar .20 .50
223 Tony Gwynn .25 .60
224 Tanner Foust .15 .40
225 Pedro Martinez .20 .50
226 Bob Gibson .20 .50
227 Jimmy Rollins .20 .50
228 Orlando Cepeda .20 .50
229 Julio Teheran .20 .50
230 Ivan Rodriguez .20 .50
231 Carlos Gomez .15 .40
232 Ozzie Smith .30 .75
233 Dan Straily .15 .40
234 Roberto Clemente .60 1.50
235 Masahiro Tanaka RC .75 2.00
236 J.D. Martinez .25 .60
237 James Shields .15 .40
238 Bert Kreischer .15 .40
239 Jose Altuve .20 .50
240 Tony Cingrani .20 .50
241 Dave Portnoy .15 .40
242 Warren Spahn .20 .50
243 Hellen Keller .15 .40
244 Jake Marisnick RC .25 .60
245 Matt Harvey .20 .50
246 Dwight Gooden .15 .40
247 Billy Williams .20 .50
248 Mark Teixeira .20 .50
249 Aroldis Chapman .25 .60
250 Steve Cishek .15 .40
251 Jason Castro .15 .40
252 Didi Gregorius .20 .50
253 Rickey Henderson .25 .60
254 Maria Gabriela Isler .15 .40
255 Andre Rienzo RC .25 .60
256 Juan Marichal .20 .50
257 Adrian Beltre .25 .60
258 Ricky Nolasco .15 .40
259 Jim Calhoun .15 .40
260 Jay Bruce .20 .50
261 Duke Snider .20 .50
262 Mike Pereira .15 .40
263 Alfonso Soriano .20 .50
264 Mike Piazza .25 .60
265 Sam Calagione .15 .40
266 Prince Fielder .20 .50
267 Kevin Clancy .15 .40
268 Jarrod Parker .15 .40
269 Jose Abreu RC 2.00 5.00
270 Ryan Howard .20 .50
271 Chuck Klosterman .15 .40

272 Tim Raines .20 .50
273 Danielle Kang .15 .40
274 Justin Masterson .15 .40
275 Robinson Cano .20 .50
276 Samantha Briggs .15 .40
277 Trevor Rosenthal .20 .50
278 CC Sabathia .20 .50
279 Steve Carlton .20 .50
280 Whitey Ford .20 .50
281 Yoenis Cespedes .25 .60
282 Salvador Perez .20 .50
283 Gar Ryness .15 .40
284 Will Clark .20 .50
285 Carl Crawford .20 .50
286 Kris Medlen .20 .50
287 Chuck Zito .15 .40
288 Evan Longoria .20 .50
289 Kyle Seager .15 .40
290 Hanley Ramirez .20 .50
291 Aramis Ramirez .15 .40
292 Andre Dawson .20 .50
293 Manny Ramirez .25 .60
294 David Freese .15 .40
295 Ryan Braun .20 .50
296 Joey Votto .25 .60
297 Brian McCann .20 .50
298 Deion Sanders .20 .50
299 Enny Romero RC .25 .60
300 R.A. Dickey .20 .50
301 Matt Kemp SP .75 2.00
302 Polar Vortex SP .60 1.50
303 Ian Kinsler SP .75 2.00
304 Matt Cain SP .75 2.00
305 Jayson Werth SP .75 2.00
306 Hyun-Jin Ryu SP .75 2.00
307 Cliff Lee SP .75 2.00
308 Pedro Alvarez SP .60 1.50
309 Hunter Pence SP .75 2.00
310 Yonder Alonso SP .60 1.50
311 Anibal Sanchez SP .60 1.50
312 Mike Mussina SP .75 2.00
313 Juan Gonzalez SP .60 1.50
314 Nolan Arenado SP 1.50 4.00
315 Brandon Phillips SP .60 1.50
316 Ken Griffey Jr. SP 2.00 5.00
317 Paul Goldschmidt SP 1.00 2.50
318 Jason Kipnis SP .75 2.00
319 Sonny Gray SP .75 2.00
320 Christian Yelich SP 1.25 3.00
321 Adam Jones SP .75 2.00
322 Paul Konerko SP .75 2.00
323 Harmon Killebrew SP 1.00 2.50
324 Adam Wainwright SP .75 2.00
325 Darryl Strawberry SP .60 1.50
326 Mike Olt SP .60 1.50
327 Brett Lawrie SP .75 2.00
328 C.J. Wilson SP .60 1.50
329 Michael Wacha SP .75 2.00
330 Joe Kelly SP .60 1.50
331 Curtis Granderson SP .75 2.00
332 Victor Martinez SP .75 2.00
333 Stephen Strasburg SP 1.00 2.50
334 Erik Johnson SP RC .60 1.50
335 Elvis Andrus SP .75 2.00
336 Wily Peralta SP .60 1.50
337 Josh Donaldson SP .75 2.00
338 Andy Pettitte SP .75 2.00
339 Jeff Samardzija SP .60 1.50
340 Dennis Eckersley SP .75 2.00
341 Barbed Wire SP .60 1.50
342 Chris Davis SP .60 1.50
343 Phil Niekro SP .75 2.00
344 Jason Grilli SP .60 1.50
345 Yasiel Puig SP 1.00 2.50
346 Ivan Nova SP .75 2.00
347 Allen Craig SP .75 2.00
348 Billy Butler SP .60 1.50
349 John Smoltz SP 1.00 2.50
350 Manny Machado SP 1.00 2.50

2014 Topps Allen and Ginter Mini

*MINI 1-300: 1X TO 2.5X BASIC
*MINI 1-300 RC: .6X TO 1.5X BASIC RCs
*MINI SP 301-350: .6X TO 1.5X BASIC SP
MINI SP ODDS 1:13 HOBBY
351-400 RANDOM WITHIN RIP CARDS
STATED PLATE ODDS 1:412 HOBBY
PLATE PRINT RUN 1 SET PER COLOR
BLACK-CYAN-MAGENTA-YELLOW ISSUED
NO PLATE PRICING DUE TO SCARCITY
351 Mark McGwire EXT 50.00 100.00
352 Bob Gibson EXT 10.00 25.00
353 Jose Fernandez EXT 12.00 30.00
354 Nolan Ryan EXT 50.00 100.00
355 Mike Trout EXT 30.00 80.00
356 Adam Jones EXT 10.00 25.00
357 Bryce Harper EXT 20.00 50.00
358 Andrew McCutchen EXT 12.00 30.00
359 Jayson Werth EXT 10.00 25.00
360 Evan Longoria EXT 10.00 25.00
361 Tony Gwynn EXT 12.00 30.00
362 Robinson Cano EXT 10.00 25.00
363 Brooks Robinson EXT 10.00 25.00
364 Pedro Martinez EXT 10.00 25.00
365 Derek Jeter EXT 30.00 80.00
366 Jacoby Ellsbury EXT 10.00 25.00
367 Bo Jackson EXT 12.00 30.00
368 Clayton Kershaw EXT 20.00 50.00
369 Joey Votto EXT 12.00 30.00
370 Cliff Lee EXT 10.00 25.00
371 Buster Posey EXT 15.00 40.00
372 Cal Ripken Jr. EXT 50.00 100.00
373 Matt Carpenter EXT 12.00 30.00
374 David Ortiz EXT 12.00 30.00
375 Justin Verlander EXT 12.00 30.00
376 Miguel Cabrera EXT 20.00 50.00
377 Johnny Bench EXT 12.00 30.00
378 Roberto Clemente EXT 40.00 100.00
379 Max Scherzer EXT 12.00 30.00
380 Giancarlo Stanton EXT 12.00 30.00
381 Stephen Strasburg EXT 12.00 30.00
382 Chris Davis EXT 8.00 20.00
383 Hyun-Jin Ryu EXT 10.00 25.00
384 Paul Goldschmidt EXT 12.00 30.00
385 Jason Kipnis EXT 10.00 25.00
386 Jackie Robinson EXT 12.00 30.00
387 Carlos Gomez EXT 8.00 20.00
388 Dustin Pedroia EXT 12.00 30.00
389 Paul O'Neill EXT 10.00 25.00
390 Tom Seaver EXT 10.00 25.00
391 Yasiel Puig EXT 30.00 60.00
392 Ozzie Smith EXT 15.00 40.00
393 George Brett EXT 25.00 60.00
394 Yu Darvish EXT 12.00 30.00
395 Ken Griffey Jr. EXT 25.00 60.00
396 Troy Tulowitzki EXT 12.00 30.00
397 Darryl Strawberry EXT 8.00 20.00
398 Prince Fielder EXT 10.00 25.00
399 Matt Harvey EXT 10.00 25.00
400 Wil Myers EXT 8.00 20.00

2014 Topps Allen and Ginter Mini A and G Back

*A & G BACK: 1.2X TO 3X BASIC
*A & G BACK RCs: .75X TO 2X BASIC RCs
A & G BACK ODDS 1:5 HOBBY
*A & G BACK SP: .75X TO 2X BASIC SP
A & G BACK SP ODDS 1:65 HOBBY

2014 Topps Allen and Ginter Mini Black

*BLACK: 2X TO 5X BASIC
*BLACK RCs: 1.2X TO 3X BASIC RCs
BLACK ODDS 1:10 HOBBY
*BLACK SP: 1.2X TO 3X BASIC SP
BLACK SP ODDS 1:130 HOBBY

2014 Topps Allen and Ginter Mini Gold

*GOLD: 1.5X TO 4X BASIC
*GOLD RCs: 1X TO 2.5X BASIC RCs
*GOLD SP: 1X TO 2.5X BASIC SP
RANDOM INSERTS IN BACKS

2014 Topps Allen and Ginter Mini No Card Number

*NO NBR: 5X TO 12X BASIC
*NO NBR RCs: 3X TO 8X BASIC RCs
*NO NBR SP: 1.2X TO 3X BASIC SP
STATED ODDS 1:64 HOBBY
ANNC'D PRINT RUN OF 50 SETS
20 Babe Ruth 20.00 50.00
36 Yadier Molina 6.00 15.00
61 Bo Jackson 10.00 25.00
93 Willie Mays 15.00 40.00
127 Greg Maddux 10.00 25.00
129 Hank Aaron 10.00 25.00
145 Derek Jeter 20.00 50.00
147 Mark McGwire 10.00 25.00
159 George Brett 10.00 25.00
168 Miguel Cabrera 8.00 20.00
189 Clayton Kershaw 10.00 25.00
264 Mike Piazza 8.00 20.00
269 Jose Abreu 12.00 30.00
316 Ken Griffey Jr. 12.00 30.00

2014 Topps Allen and Ginter Mini Red

*RED: 12X TO 30X BASIC
*RED RCs: 8X TO 20X BASIC RCs
*RED SP: 5X TO 12X BASIC SP
STATED PRINT RUN 33 SER.#'d SETS
1 Roger Maris 12.00 30.00
20 Babe Ruth 40.00 100.00
36 Yadier Molina 12.00 30.00
53 Sandy Koufax 20.00 50.00
61 Bo Jackson 20.00 50.00
82 Jackie Robinson 12.00 30.00
93 Willie Mays 30.00 80.00
104 Troy Tulowitzki 10.00 25.00
121 Freddie Freeman 10.00 25.00
127 Greg Maddux 20.00 50.00
129 Hank Aaron 20.00 50.00
145 Derek Jeter 60.00 120.00
147 Mark McGwire 20.00 50.00
159 George Brett 20.00 50.00
168 Miguel Cabrera 15.00 40.00
186 Billy Hamilton 12.00 30.00
189 Clayton Kershaw 15.00 40.00
204 Albert Pujols 20.00 50.00
234 Roberto Clemente 20.00 50.00
264 Mike Piazza 15.00 40.00
313 Juan Gonzalez 10.00 25.00
316 Ken Griffey Jr. 60.00 150.00
345 Yasiel Puig 20.00 50.00

2014 Topps Allen and Ginter Air Supremacy

COMPLETE SET (20) 8.00 20.00
STATED ODDS 1:2 HOBBY
AS01 B-17 Bomber .60 1.50
AS02 F-22 Raptor .60 1.50
AS03 Supermarine Spitfire .60 1.50
AS04 P-51 Mustang .60 1.50
AS05 B-52 Stratofortress .60 1.50
AS06 AC-47 Spooky .60 1.50
AS07 F-16 Fighting Falcon .60 1.50
AS08 F/A-18 Hornet .60 1.50
AS09 Republic P-47 Thunderbolt .60 1.50
AS10 Sea Harrier FA2 .60 1.50
AS11 Sopwith Camel .60 1.50
AS12 F-86 Sabre .60 1.50
AS13 F-15C Eagle .60 1.50
AS14 EA-18G Growler .60 1.50
AS15 V-22 Osprey .60 1.50
AS16 Curtiss P-40 Warhawk .60 1.50
AS17 B-25 Mitchell Launch .60 1.50
AS18 MiG-15 .60 1.50
AS19 Hawker Hurricane .60 1.50
AS20 F-15 Eagle .60 1.50

2014 Topps Allen and Ginter Autographs

RANDOM INSERTS IN PACKS
AGFADM Doug McDermott 15.00 40.00

2014 Topps Allen and Ginter Box Topper Relics

STATED ODDS 1:110 HOBBY BOXES
STATED PRINT RUN 25 SER.#'d SETS
BLRAG Adrian Gonzalez 8.00 20.00
BLRAJ Adam Jones 15.00 40.00
BLRDW David Wright 15.00 40.00
BLRJG Juan Gonzalez 12.00 30.00
BLRMM Manny Machado 50.00 100.00
BLRMR Mariano Rivera 20.00 50.00
BLRMT Mike Trout 60.00 120.00
BLRPG Paul Goldschmidt 10.00 25.00
BLRSC Steve Carlton 15.00 40.00
BLRYP Yasiel Puig 10.00 25.00

2014 Topps Allen and Ginter Box Toppers

OVERALL ONE PER HOBBY BOX
BL01 Bo Jackson 2.50 6.00
BL02 Pedro Martinez 2.00 5.00
BL03 Wil Myers 1.50 4.00
BL04 Willie Mays 5.00 12.00
BL05 Mike Trout 6.00 15.00
BL06 Clayton Kershaw 4.00 10.00
BL07 Jose Canseco 2.00 5.00
BL08 Mark McGwire 5.00 12.00
BL09 Jose Abreu 6.00 15.00
BL10 Chris Davis 1.50 4.00
BL11 Bryce Harper 4.00 10.00
BL12 Albert Pujols 3.00 8.00
BL13 Andrew McCutchen 2.50 6.00
BL14 Miguel Cabrera 2.50 6.00
BL15 Jacoby Ellsbury 2.00 5.00

2014 Topps Allen and Ginter Coincidence

RANDOM INSERTS IN RETAIL PACKS
AGC01 Kennedy and Lincoln 4.00 10.00
AGC02 King Umberto and The Waiter from Monza 2.00 5.00
AGC03 1895 Car Crash in Ohio 2.00 5.00
AGC04 Hendrix and Handel were neighbors 2.00 5.00
AGC05 Hugh Williams: Sole Survivor 2.00 5.00
AGC06 RMS Carmania and SMS Cap Trafalgar 2.00 5.00
AGC07 Wilmer McLean and The Civil War 2.00 5.00
AGC08 Mark Twain and Halley's Comet 2.00 5.00
AGC09 Oregon newspaper predicts future lottery numbers 2.00 5.00
AGC10 Morgan Robertson: Novels predict future disasters 2.00 5.00
AGC11 4th of July: Jefferson, Adams, and Monroe 2.00 5.00

2014 Topps Allen and Ginter Double Rip Cards

STATED ODDS 1:714 HOBBY
PRINT RUNS B/WN 5-25 COPIES PER
NO PRICING ON QTY 10 OR LESS
PRICED WITH CLEANLY RIPPED BACKS
DRIP03 W.Myers/M.Trout/25 30.00 80.00
DRIP04 P.Corbin/W.Miley/25 5.00 12.00
DRIP06 T.Tulowitzki/C.Gonzalez/25 6.00 15.00
DRIP08 M.Trout/J.Fernandez/20 30.00 80.00
DRIP10 J.Segura/R.Braun/20 5.00 12.00
DRIP14 B.Hamilton/J.Morgan/20 5.00 12.00
DRIP15 Z.Wheeler/M.Harvey/25 5.00 12.00
DRIP20 McCutchen/Cole/20 6.00 15.00
DRIP23 Posey/Bumgarner/25 8.00 20.00
DRIP25 H.Iwakuma/H.Ryu/25 5.00 12.00
DRIP26 F.Hernandez/T.Walker/20 5.00 12.00
DRIP27 M.Wacha/S.Miller/20 5.00 12.00
DRIP28 Y.Molina/A.Wainwright/20 8.00 20.00
DRIP29 M.Moore/D.Price/20 5.00 12.00
DRIP30 E.Longoria/D.Wright/25 5.00 12.00
DRIP32 F.Freeman/J.Teheran/15 8.00 20.00
DRIP33 J.Reyes/J.Bautista/25 5.00 12.00
DRIP35 G.Gonzalez/J.Zimmermann/15 5.00 12.00
DRIP38 H.Iwakuma/Y.Darvish/15 6.00 15.00
DRIP40 C.Davis/A.Jones/15 5.00 12.00
DRIP44 J.Upton/J.Heyward/15 5.00 12.00
DRIP56 J.Teheran/K.Medlen/15 5.00 12.00
DRIP60 J.Lake/S.Castro/15 4.00 10.00
DRIP66 T.Cingrani/J.Cueto/15 5.00 12.00

2014 Topps Allen and Ginter Festivals and Fairs

COMPLETE SET (10) 3.00 8.00
STATED ODDS 1:2 HOBBY
FAF01 La Tomatina .40 1.00
FAF02 Carnivale .40 1.00
FAF03 Mardi Gras .40 1.00
FAF04 Holi Festival .40 1.00
FAF05 Pingxi Lantern Festival .40 1.00
FAF06 Songkran Water Festival .40 1.00
FAF07 San Fermin Festival .40 1.00
FAF08 Dia de los Muertos .40 1.00
FAF09 Diwali Festival of Lights .40 1.00
FAF10 Junkanoo .40 1.00

2014 Topps Allen and Ginter Fields of Yore

COMPLETE SET (10) 6.00 15.00
STATED ODDS 1:2 HOBBY
FOY01 Ebbets Field .75 2.00
FOY02 Cleveland Municipal Stadium .75 2.00
FOY03 Griffith Stadium .75 2.00
FOY04 Metropolitan Stadium .75 2.00
FOY05 Wrigley Field .75 2.00
FOY06 Yankee Stadium .75 2.00
FOY07 Tiger Stadium .75 2.00
FOY08 Sportsman's Park .75 2.00
FOY09 Astrodome .75 2.00
FOY10 Shea Stadium .75 2.00

2014 Topps Allen and Ginter Fields of Yore Relics

STATED ODDS 1:900 HOBBY
STATED PRINT RUN 250 SER.#'d SETS
FOYRCS Cleveland Municipal Stadium 10.00 25.00
FOYRGS Griffith Stadium 10.00 25.00
FOYRMS Metropolitan Stadium 10.00 25.00
FOYRSP Sportsman's Park 10.00 25.00
FOYRWS Wrigley Field 15.00 40.00

2014 Topps Allen and Ginter Framed Mini Autographs

STATED ODDS 1:52 HOBBY
EXCHANGE DEADLINE 6/30/2017
AGAABO Anthony Bourdain 30.00 80.00
AGAAC Allen Craig 5.00 12.00
AGAAE Adam Eaton 5.00 12.00
AGAAF Allyson Felix 25.00 60.00
AGAAL Andrew Lambo 4.00 10.00
AGAARI Andre Rienzo 4.00 10.00
AGAARO Anthony Robles 6.00 15.00
AGAAS Adam Schefter 6.00 15.00
AGAAWI Austin Wierschke 5.00 12.00
AGABBU Bill Buckner 8.00 20.00
AGABJ Bo Jackson 90.00 150.00
AGABK Bert Kreischer 5.00 12.00
AGABR Bill Rancic 4.00 10.00
AGACA Chris Archer 4.00 10.00
AGACB Craig Biggio 50.00 120.00
AGACKE Casey Kelly 5.00 12.00
AGACKL Chuck Klosterman 12.00 30.00
AGACKR Clayton Kershaw 90.00 150.00
AGACL Carli Lloyd 25.00 60.00
AGACT Chuck Todd 10.00 25.00
AGACY Christian Yelich 20.00 50.00
AGACZ Chuck Zito 10.00 25.00
AGADG Didi Gregorius 5.00 12.00
AGADK Danielle Kang 8.00 20.00
AGADME Devin Mesoraco 10.00 25.00
AGADN Diana Nyad 8.00 20.00
AGADO Daniel Okrent 8.00 20.00
AGADPO David Portnoy 10.00 25.00
AGADR Darin Ruf 5.00 12.00
AGADST Dan Straily 4.00 10.00
AGADW David Wright 90.00 150.00
AGAEB Erin Brady 10.00 25.00
AGAFD Felix Doubront 4.00 10.00
AGAFDA Felicia Day 12.00 30.00
AGAGI Maria Gabriela Isler 15.00 40.00
AGAGR Gar Ryness 6.00 15.00
AGAGSP George Springer 15.00 40.00
AGAGW Glen Waggoner 6.00 15.00
AGAHS Hector Santiago 4.00 10.00
AGAJA Jose Abreu 200.00 300.00
AGAJAN Dr. James Andrews 15.00 40.00
AGAJB Jordan Burroughs 15.00 40.00
AGAJCA Jose Canseco 60.00 120.00
AGAJCL Jim Calhoun 8.00 20.00
AGAJD Jenny Dell 15.00 40.00
AGAJFR Judah Friedlander 5.00 12.00
AGAJGO Juan Gonzalez 20.00 50.00
AGAJGR Jason Grilli 6.00 15.00
AGAJGY Jedd Gyorko 4.00 10.00
AGAJKE Joe Kelly 4.00 10.00
AGAJKI Jason Kipnis 8.00 20.00
AGAJMA Jake Marisnick 4.00 10.00
AGAJO Jordan Oliver 12.00 30.00
AGAJSC Jonathan Schoop 4.00 10.00
AGAJSE Jean Segura 5.00 12.00
AGAKC Kevin Clancy 10.00 25.00
AGAKSM Kevin Smith 30.00 80.00
AGAKW Kolten Wong 10.00 25.00
AGALB Lou Brock 100.00 175.00
AGALK Larry King 15.00 40.00
AGALP Laura Phelps Sweatt 4.00 10.00
AGAMA Matt Adams 8.00 20.00
AGAMB Matt Besser 6.00 15.00
AGAMD Matt Davidson 5.00 12.00
AGAME Michael Eisner 8.00 20.00
AGAMMC Mark McGwire 150.00 300.00
AGAMO Mike Olt 4.00 10.00
AGAMPE Mike Pereira 8.00 20.00
AGAMRO Mark Roth 8.00 20.00
AGAMTR Mike Trout 250.00 350.00
AGAMW Michael Wacha 12.00 30.00
AGAMZ Mike Zunino 8.00 20.00
AGANC Nick Castellanos 15.00 40.00
AGANG Nomar Garciaparra 90.00 150.00
AGAOH Orlando Hernandez 15.00 40.00
AGAPG Paul Goldschmidt 20.00 50.00
AGARR Ryan Riess 6.00 15.00
AGASB Samantha Briggs 6.00 15.00
AGASCA Steve Carlton 60.00 120.00
AGASCI Steve Cishek 4.00 10.00
AGASCL Sam Calagione 10.00 25.00
AGASD Steve Delabar 4.00 10.00
AGASDO Snoop Lion 75.00 200.00
AGASG Sonny Gray 10.00 25.00
AGASMI Shelby Miller 5.00 12.00
AGASN Shabazz Napier 10.00 25.00
AGATC Tony Cingrani 5.00 12.00
AGATD Travis d'Arnaud 12.00 30.00
AGATFO Tanner Foust 4.00 10.00
AGATSH The Iron Sheik 20.00 50.00
AGATW Taijuan Walker 10.00 25.00
AGAVG Vince Gilligan 40.00 80.00
AGAWF Wilmer Flores 5.00 12.00
AGAWMD Will Middlebrooks 10.00 25.00
AGAWMY Wil Myers 12.00 30.00
AGAWP Wily Peralta 4.00 10.00
AGAXB Xander Bogaerts 12.00 30.00

2014 Topps Allen and Ginter Framed Mini Topps Employee Autographs

STATED ODDS 1:7800 HOBBY
EEAAC Arvin Catriz 40.00 100.00
EEAAK Ann Marie Klebon 40.00 100.00
EEAAS Ari Sirner 40.00 100.00
EEAET Evan Tanelli 40.00 100.00
EEAJB Jason Berger 40.00 100.00
EEAJS Ungmoon Sprance 40.00 100.00
EEALL Lance Lubin 40.00 100.00
EEASR Sam Roberts 40.00 100.00
EEAVC Vincent Carbellano 40.00 100.00
EEAMSM Michelle Smith 40.00 100.00

2014 Topps Allen and Ginter Jumbo Relics

FSJRVG V.Gilligan Storyboard 75.00 150.00

2014 Topps Allen and Ginter Landmarks and Monuments Cabinet Box Toppers

ONE TOPPER PER HOBBY BOX
LMC01 Jefferson Memorial 2.00 5.00
LMC02 Mount Rushmore 2.00 5.00
LMC03 Washington Monument 2.00 5.00
LMC04 Lincoln Memorial 2.00 5.00
LMC05 Yosemite Falls 2.00 5.00
LMC06 Statue of Liberty 2.00 5.00
LMC07 One World Trade Center 2.00 5.00
LMC08 The U.S. Capitol 2.00 5.00
LMC09 The Liberty Bell 2.00 5.00
LMC10 World War II Memorial 2.00 5.00

2014 Topps Allen and Ginter Mini Athletic Endeavors

STATED ODDS 1:288 HOBBY
AE01 Shovel Racing 6.00 15.00
AE02 Wife Carrying Championship 6.00 15.00
AE03 Rock Paper Scissors 6.00 15.00
AE04 Royal Shrovetide Football 6.00 15.00
AE05 Cheese Rolling 6.00 15.00
AE06 Poohsticks 6.00 15.00
AE07 Chess Boxing 6.00 15.00
AE08 Caber Toss 6.00 15.00
AE09 Sack Races 6.00 15.00
AE10 Roller Derby 6.00 15.00

2014 Topps Allen and Ginter Mini Framed Relics

GROUP A ODDS 1:174 HOBBY
GROUP B ODDS 1:175 HOBBY
RAABC Adrian Beltre A 4.00 10.00
RAAJ Adam Jones A 3.00 8.00
RAAP Andy Pettitte A 5.00 12.00
RAARI Anthony Rizzo A 8.00 20.00
RABH Billy Hamilton A 3.00 8.00
RABPO Buster Posey A 5.00 12.00
RABR Brooks Robinson A 30.00 80.00
RACK Clayton Kershaw A 4.00 10.00
RACKI Craig Kimbrel A 3.00 8.00
RACL Cliff Lee A 3.00 8.00
RADM Don Mattingly A 20.00 50.00
RAEA Elvis Andrus A 3.00 8.00
RAGG Gio Gonzalez A 3.00 8.00
RAHA Hank Aaron A 150.00 250.00
RAHI Hisashi Iwakuma A 3.00 8.00
RAHK Harmon Killebrew A 20.00 50.00
RAHR Hanley Ramirez A 3.00 8.00
RAID Ian Desmond A 2.50 6.00
RAJDI Joe DiMaggio A 90.00 150.00
RAJH Josh Hamilton A 3.00 8.00
RAJR Jackie Robinson A 50.00 120.00
RAJSE Jean Segura A 3.00 8.00
RAMMO Matt Moore A 3.00 8.00
RAMS Max Scherzer A 4.00 10.00
RAPO Paul O'Neill A 6.00 15.00
RARZ Ryan Zimmerman A 3.00 8.00
RASK Sandy Koufax A 60.00 150.00
RASS Stephen Strasburg A 4.00 10.00
RAWB Wade Boggs A 40.00 80.00
RBAR Alex Rodriguez B 15.00 40.00
RBBH Bryce Harper B 15.00 40.00
RBCGN Carlos Gonzalez B 3.00 8.00
RBDJ Derek Jeter B 30.00 60.00
RBDO David Ortiz B 4.00 10.00
RBDPR David Price B 3.00 8.00
RBEE Edwin Encarnacion B 4.00 10.00
RBEL Evan Longoria B 3.00 8.00
RBFF Freddie Freeman B 5.00 12.00
RBFH Felix Hernandez B 3.00 8.00
RBJB Jay Bruce B 3.00 8.00
RBJH Jason Heyward B 3.00 8.00
RBJRI Jim Rice B 10.00 25.00
RBJVO Joey Votto B 4.00 10.00
RBJZ Jordan Zimmermann B 3.00 8.00
RBKS Kyle Seager B 2.50 6.00
RBMCI Matt Cain B 3.00 8.00
RBMTR Mike Trout B 15.00 40.00
RBMTU Mark Trumbo B 2.50 6.00
RBPF Prince Fielder B 3.00 8.00
RBRB Ryan Braun B 3.00 8.00
RBRCE Roberto Clemente B 75.00 150.00
RBRCR Rod Carew B 10.00 25.00
RBTG Tony Gwynn B 15.00 40.00
RBTT Troy Tulowitzki B 4.00 10.00
RBYD Yu Darvish B 4.00 10.00
RBYM Yadier Molina B 8.00 20.00
RBYP Yasiel Puig B 10.00 25.00
RBZWH Zack Wheeler B 3.00 8.00

2014 Topps Allen and Ginter Mini Into the Unknown

COMPLETE SET (16) 8.00 20.00
STATED ODDS 1:5 HOBBY
ITU01 Christopher Columbus 1.00 2.50
ITU02 Ferdinand Magellan 1.00 2.50
ITU03 Vasco da Gama 1.00 2.50
ITU04 Leif Ericson 1.00 2.50
ITU05 John C. Fremont 1.00 2.50
ITU06 Vitus Bering 1.00 2.50
ITU07 Louis Hennepin 1.00 2.50
ITU08 Henry Hudson 1.00 2.50
ITU09 Pedro Teixeira 1.00 2.50
ITU10 Marco Polo 1.00 2.50
ITU11 Francisco Pizarro 1.00 2.50
ITU12 Lewis and Clark 1.00 2.50
ITU13 Amerigo Vespucci 1.00 2.50
ITU14 John Cabot 1.00 2.50
ITU15 Jacques Marquette 1.00 2.50
ITU16 Hernan Cortes 1.00 2.50

2014 Topps Allen and Ginter Mini Larger Than Life

COMPLETE SET (11) 8.00 20.00
STATED ODDS 1:5 HOBBY
LTL01 Paul Bunyan 1.00 2.50
LTL02 Casey Jones 1.00 2.50
LTL04 John Henry 1.00 2.50
LTL05 Rip Van Winkle 1.00 2.50
LTL06 Johnny Appleseed 1.00 2.50
LTL07 Davy Crockett 1.00 2.50
LTL08 Giacomo Casanova 1.00 2.50
LTL09 William Tell 1.00 2.50
LTL10 Hiawatha 1.00 2.50
LTL11 Sasquatch 1.00 2.50
LTL12 Pocahontas 1.00 2.50

2014 Topps Allen and Ginter Mini Little Lions

COMPLETE SET (16) 15.00 40.00
STATED ODDS 1:5 HOBBY
LL01 Persian Cat 1.25 3.00
LL02 Japanese Bobtail 1.25 3.00
LL03 American Shorthair 1.25 3.00
LL04 Siamese 1.25 3.00
LL05 Cornish Rex 1.25 3.00
LL06 Maine Coon 1.25 3.00
LL07 Oriental Bicolor 1.25 3.00
LL08 Russian Blue 1.25 3.00
LL09 Sphynx 1.25 3.00
LL10 Savannah 1.25 3.00
LL11 Scottish Fold 1.25 3.00
LL12 Norwegian Forest Cat 1.25 3.00
LL13 Exotic 1.25 3.00
LL14 Birman 1.25 3.00
LL15 Abyssinian 1.25 3.00
LL16 Turkish Van 1.25 3.00

2014 Topps Allen and Ginter Mini Urban Fauna

STATED ODDS 1:288 HOBBY
UF01 Sciurus Carolinensis 5.00 12.00
UF02 Periplaneta Americana 5.00 12.00
UF03 Procyon Lotor 5.00 12.00
UF04 Didelphis Virginiana 5.00 12.00
UF05 Anolis Equestris 5.00 12.00
UF06 Tadarida brasiliensis 5.00 12.00
UF07 Mephitis Mephitis 5.00 12.00
UF08 Lymantria Dispar Dispar 5.00 12.00
UF09 Rattus Norvegicus 5.00 12.00
UF10 Columba Livia 5.00 12.00

2014 Topps Allen and Ginter Mini Where Nature Ends

STATED ODDS 1:5 MINI
WNE01 Leonardo da Vinci 1.00 2.50
WNE02 Michelangelo 1.00 2.50
WNE03 Donatello 1.00 2.50
WNE04 Raphael 1.00 2.50
WNE05 Rembrandt van Rijn 1.00 2.50
WNE06 Masaccio 1.00 2.50
WNE07 Vincent van Gogh 1.00 2.50
WNE08 Edgar Degas 1.00 2.50
WNE09 Sandro Botticelli 1.00 2.50
WNE10 John Trumbull 1.00 2.50
WNE11 Gilbert Stuart 1.00 2.50
WNE12 Francisco de Goya 1.00 2.50
WNE13 Martin Johnson Heade 1.00 2.50
WNE14 Winslow Homer 1.00 2.50
WNE15 James Whistler 1.00 2.50
WNE16 Pieter Bruegel 1.00 2.50
WNE17 Diego Velazquez 1.00 2.50
WNE18 Albrecht Durer 1.00 2.50
WNE19 Edouard Manet 1.00 2.50
WNE20 Paul Cezanne 1.00 2.50
WNE21 Giotto di Bondone 1.00 2.50
WNE22 Claude Monet 1.00 2.50
WNE23 J.M.W. Turner 1.00 2.50
WNE24 Paul Gauguin 1.00 2.50
WNE25 William Blake 1.00 2.50
WNE26 Jan Vermeer 1.00 2.50

2014 Topps Allen and Ginter Mini World's Deadliest Predators

COMPLETE SET (22) 15.00 40.00
STATED ODDS 1:5 HOBBY
WDP01 Polar Bear 1.00 2.50
WDP02 Hippopotamus 1.00 2.50
WDP03 Blue-Ringed Octopus 1.00 2.50
WDP04 Lonomia 1.00 2.50
WDP05 Great White Shark 1.00 2.50
WDP06 African Lion 1.00 2.50
WDP07 Black Mamba 1.00 2.50
WDP08 Cape Buffalo 1.00 2.50
WDP09 Poison Dart Frog 1.00 2.50
WDP10 Hyena 1.00 2.50
WDP11 Komodo Dragon 1.00 2.50
WDP12 Clouded Leopard 1.00 2.50
WDP13 Brazilian Wandering Spider 1.00 2.50
WDP14 Saltwater Crocodile 1.00 2.50
WDP15 American Alligator 1.00 2.50
WDP16 Piranha 1.00 2.50
WDP17 Black Eagle 1.00 2.50
WDP18 Gray Wolf 1.00 2.50
WDP19 Wolverine 1.00 2.50
WDP20 Honey Badger 1.00 2.50
WDP21 Australian Box Jellyfish 1.00 2.50
WDP22 Cone Snail 1.00 2.50

2014 Topps Allen and Ginter National Convention Mini

NCCSAB Albert Belle 2.50 6.00
NCCSBF Bob Feller 3.00 8.00
NCCSDJ Derek Jeter 6.00 15.00
NCCSJA Jose Abreu 8.00 20.00
NCCSMT Masahiro Tanaka 6.00 15.00
NCCSMT Mike Trout 4.00 10.00

2014 Topps Allen and Ginter Natural Wonders

COMPLETE SET (20) 6.00 15.00
STATED ODDS 1:2 HOBBY
NW01 The Blue Hole .40 1.00
NW02 The Shilin Stone Forest .40 1.00
NW03 Cave of Crystals .40 1.00
NW04 Iguazu Falls .40 1.00
NW05 Door to Hell .40 1.00
NW06 Puerto Princesa Subterranean River .40 1.00
NW07 Table Mountain .40 1.00
NW08 Ha Long Bay .40 1.00
NW09 Marble Caves .40 1.00
NW10 Lake Retba .40 1.00
NW11 Travertine Pools .40 1.00
NW12 Sailing Stones of Racetrack Playa .40 1.00
NW13 Moeraki Boulders .40 1.00
NW14 Half Dome .40 1.00
NW15 Giant's Causeway .40 1.00
NW16 The Wave at Coyote Buttes .40 1.00
NW17 Luray Caverns .40 1.00
NW18 Socotra Archipelago .40 1.00
NW19 McWay Falls .40 1.00
NW20 Punalu'u Beach .40 1.00

2014 Topps Allen and Ginter Oddity Relics

STATED ODDS 1:51,250 HOBBY
STATED PRINT RUN 25 SER.#'d SETS
AGOR01 Daniel Nava 125.00 250.00

2014 Topps Allen and Ginter Mini Outlaws, Bandits and All-Around Neer Do Wells

COMPLETE SET (11) 10.00 25.00
STATED ODDS 1:5 HOBBY
OBA01 Robin Hood 1.25 3.00
OBA02 Jesse James 1.25 3.00
OBA03 Billy the Kid 1.25 3.00
OBA04 Butch Cassidy 1.25 3.00
OBA05 Juro Janosik 1.25 3.00
OBA06 Bonnie and Clyde 1.25 3.00
OBA07 William Kidd 1.25 3.00
OBA08 Edward Blackbeard Teach 1.25 3.00
OBA09 Jean Lafitte 1.25 3.00
OBA10 Ishikawa Goemon 1.25 3.00
OBA11 Ned Kelly 1.25 3.00

2014 Topps Allen and Ginter Oversized Reprint Cabinet Box Toppers

OVERALL ONE PER HOBBY BOX
ORCBLBH Bryce Harper 3.00 8.00
ORCBLJR Jackie Robinson 2.00 5.00
ORCBLMC Miguel Cabrera 2.00 5.00
ORCBLMT Mike Trout 5.00 12.00
ORCBLNR Nolan Ryan 5.00 12.00
ORCBLRC Roberto Clemente 5.00 12.00
ORCBLSK Sandy Koufax 4.00 10.00
ORCBLSS Stephen Strasburg 2.00 5.00
ORCBLWM Wil Myers 1.25 3.00
ORCBLYP Yasiel Puig 2.00 5.00

2014 Topps Allen and Ginter Pop Star Relics

STATED ODDS 1:4475 HOBBY
STATED PRINT RUN 25 SER.#'d SETS
PSRAP Albert Pujols 15.00 40.00
PSRBH Bryce Harper 20.00 50.00
PSRCK Clayton Kershaw 60.00 150.00
PSRDO David Ortiz 10.00 25.00
PSRDW David Wright 25.00 60.00
PSRMT Mike Trout 90.00 150.00
PSRPF Prince Fielder 10.00 25.00
PSRRC Robinson Cano 10.00 25.00
PSRYD Yu Darvish 25.00 60.00
PSRYP Yasiel Puig 12.00 30.00

2014 Topps Allen and Ginter Relics

GROUP A ODDS 1:24 HOBBY
GROUP B ODDS 1:24 HOBBY
FRBAA Alex Avila B 3.00 8.00
FRBAC Allen Craig B 3.00 8.00
FRBAF Allyson Felix B 5.00 12.00
FRBAJ Adam Jones B 3.00 8.00
FRBAR Anthony Rizzo B 5.00 12.00
FRBARO Anthony Robles B 2.50 6.00
FRBAS Adam Schefter B 2.50 6.00
FRBCB Carlos Beltran B 3.00 8.00
FRBCBU Clay Buchholz B 2.50 6.00
FRBCG Carlos Gonzalez B 3.00 8.00
FRBCGO Carlos Gomez B 2.50 6.00
FRBCK Clayton Kershaw B 6.00 15.00
FRBCKL Chuck Klosterman B 2.50 6.00
FRBCL Cliff Lee B 3.00 8.00
FRBCS Chris Sale B 4.00 10.00
FRBCT Chuck Todd B 4.00 10.00
FRBDB Domonic Brown B 3.00 8.00
FRBDP David Price B 3.00 8.00
FRBDPE Dustin Pedroia B 5.00 12.00
FRBDPO Dave Portnoy B 4.00 10.00
FRBEA Elvis Andrus B 3.00 8.00
FRBEE Edwin Encarnacion B 4.00 10.00
FRBFH Felix Hernandez B 3.00 8.00
FRBGB Grant Balfour B 2.50 6.00
FRBGW Glen Waggoner B 2.50 6.00
FRBID Ian Desmond B 2.50 6.00
FRBJB Jay Bruce B 3.00 8.00
FRBJF Jose Fernandez B 4.00 10.00
FRBJFR Judah Friedlander B 2.50 6.00
FRBJV Joey Votto B 4.00 10.00
FRBKS Kevin Smith B 5.00 12.00
FRBLK Larry King B 10.00 25.00
FRBME Michael Eisner B 5.00 12.00
FRBMM Matt Moore B 3.00 8.00
FRBMR Mark Roth B 2.50 6.00
FRBPA Pedro Alvarez B 2.50 6.00
FRBRB Ryan Braun B 3.00 8.00
FRBRR Ryan Riess B 2.50 6.00
FRBSC Sam Calagione B 2.50 6.00
FRBSL Snoop Lion B 5.00 12.00
FRBSM Starling Marte B 3.00 8.00
FRBTG Tony Gwynn B 8.00 20.00
FRBTT Troy Tulowitzki B 4.00 10.00
FRBYD Yu Darvish B 4.00 10.00
FRBYM Yadier Molina B 5.00 12.00
FRBZG Zack Greinke B 4.00 10.00
FRBZW Zack Wheeler B 3.00 8.00
FRAB Adrian Beltre A 4.00 10.00
FSRABO Anthony Bourdain A 5.00 12.00
FSRAC Aroldis Chapman A 4.00 10.00
FSRAD Andre Dawson A 6.00 15.00
FSRAG Adrian Gonzalez A 3.00 8.00
FSRAM Andrew McCutchen A 4.00 10.00
FSRAP Andy Pettitte A 5.00 12.00
FSRARO Alex Rodriguez A 4.00 10.00
FSRAW Austin Wierschke A 2.50 6.00
FSRBH Bryce Harper A 8.00 20.00
FSRBK Bert Kreischer A 2.50 6.00
FSRBM Brian McCann A 3.00 8.00
FSRBP Buster Posey A 5.00 12.00
FSRCH Cole Hamels A 3.00 8.00
FSRCKI Craig Kimbrel A 3.00 8.00
FSRCS CC Sabathia A 3.00 8.00
FSRCZ Chuck Zito A 2.50 6.00
FSRDA Dr. James Andrews A 5.00 12.00
FSRDJ Derek Jeter A 10.00 25.00
FSRDK Danielle Kang A 3.00 8.00
FSRDO David Ortiz A 4.00 10.00
FSRDOK Daniel Okrent A 4.00 10.00
FSREB Erin Brady A 4.00 10.00
FSREL Evan Longoria A 3.00 8.00
FSRFD Felicia Day A 5.00 12.00
FSRFF Freddie Freeman A 5.00 12.00
FSRGC Gerrit Cole A 4.00 10.00
FSRGI Maria Gabriela Isler A 4.00 10.00
FSRIS The Iron Sheik A 5.00 12.00
FSRJB Jose Bautista A 3.00 8.00
FSRJH Jason Heyward A 3.00 8.00
FSRJS Jean Segura A 3.00 8.00
FSRJZ Jordan Zimmermann A 3.00 8.00
FSRKC Kevin Clancy A 2.50 6.00
FSRKS Kyle Seager A 2.50 6.00
FSRLP Laura Phelps Sweatt A 2.50 6.00
FSRMA Matt Adams A 2.50 6.00
FSRMB Madison Bumgarner A 6.00 15.00
FSRMBE Matt Besser A 2.50 6.00
FSRMC Miguel Cabrera A 6.00 15.00
FSRMCA Matt Cain A 3.00 8.00
FSRMCR Matt Carpenter A 4.00 10.00
FSRMH Matt Harvey A 3.00 8.00
FSRMK Matt Kemp A 3.00 8.00
FSRMP Mike Pereira A 2.50 6.00
FSRMT Mike Trout A 10.00 25.00
FSRMTA Masahiro Tanaka A 15.00 40.00
FSRPF Prince Fielder A 3.00 8.00
FSRRC Robinson Cano A 3.00 8.00
FSRRZ Ryan Zimmerman A 3.00 8.00
FSRTF Tanner Foust A 2.50 6.00
FSRYP Yasiel Puig A 4.00 10.00

2014 Topps Allen and Ginter Rip Cards Ripped

STATED ODDS 1:178 HOBBY
PRINT RUNS B/WN 5-75 COPIES PER
NO PRICING ON QTY 10 OR LESS
PRICED WITH CLEANLY RIPPED BACKS
RIP01 Mike Trout/25 30.00 80.00

Card	Low	High
RIP02 Jered Weaver/75	5.00	12.00
RIP03 Paul Goldschmidt/50	6.00	15.00
RIP04 Freddie Freeman/75	8.00	20.00
RIP05 Julio Teheran/75	5.00	12.00
RIP06 Craig Kimbrel/50	5.00	12.00
RIP07 Chris Davis/50	4.00	10.00
RIP08 Manny Machado/50	6.00	15.00
RIP09 Xander Bogaerts/50	12.00	30.00
RIP10 Dustin Pedroia/50	6.00	15.00
RIP11 David Ortiz/25	6.00	15.00
RIP12 Starlin Castro/75	4.00	10.00
RIP13 Anthony Rizzo/75	8.00	20.00
RIP14 Chris Sale/75	6.00	15.00
RIP15 Shin-Soo Choo/75	5.00	12.00
RIP16 Brandon Phillips/75	4.00	10.00
RIP17 Joey Votto/50	6.00	15.00
RIP18 Justin Masterson/75	4.00	10.00
RIP19 Carlos Santana/50	5.00	12.00
RIP20 Carlos Gonzalez/50	5.00	12.00
RIP21 Troy Tulowitzki/50	6.00	15.00
RIP22 Billy Hamilton/50	5.00	12.00
RIP23 Miguel Cabrera/25	6.00	15.00
RIP24 Prince Fielder/50	5.00	12.00
RIP25 Justin Verlander/25	6.00	15.00
RIP26 Jose Altuve/75	5.00	12.00
RIP27 James Shields/75	4.00	10.00
RIP29 Yasiel Puig/50	6.00	15.00
RIP30 Clayton Kershaw/25	10.00	25.00
RIP31 Hyun-Jin Ryu/75	5.00	12.00
RIP32 Giancarlo Stanton/50	6.00	15.00
RIP33 Jose Fernandez/50	6.00	15.00
RIP34 Jean Segura/75	5.00	12.00
RIP35 Ryan Braun/50	5.00	12.00
RIP36 Joe Mauer/75	5.00	12.00
RIP37 David Wright/25	5.00	12.00
RIP38 Matt Harvey/50	5.00	12.00
RIP39 Robinson Cano/50	5.00	12.00
RIP40 Derek Jeter/25	15.00	40.00
RIP41 CC Sabathia/25	5.00	12.00
RIP42 Alex Rodriguez/25	8.00	20.00
RIP43 Yoenis Cespedes/50	6.00	15.00
RIP44 Chase Utley/50	5.00	12.00
RIP45 Cliff Lee/75	5.00	12.00
RIP46 Jedd Gyorko/75	4.00	10.00
RIP47 Pablo Sandoval/50	5.00	12.00
RIP48 Buster Posey/25	8.00	20.00
RIP49 Madison Bumgarner/75	5.00	12.00
RIP50 Felix Hernandez/50	5.00	12.00
RIP51 Hisashi Iwakuma/50	5.00	12.00
RIP52 Allen Craig/75	5.00	12.00
RIP53 Shelby Miller/75	5.00	12.00
RIP54 Wil Myers/50	4.00	10.00
RIP55 Evan Longoria/25	5.00	12.00
RIP56 David Price/50	5.00	12.00
RIP57 Adrian Beltre/50	6.00	15.00
RIP58 Yu Darvish/25	6.00	15.00
RIP59 Jose Reyes/25	5.00	12.00
RIP60 Jose Bautista/25	5.00	12.00
RIP62 Stephen Strasburg/25	6.00	15.00
RIP63 Gio Gonzalez/75	5.00	12.00
RIP65 Gerrit Cole/50	6.00	15.00
RIP66 Taijuan Walker/50	4.00	10.00
RIP67 Travis d'Arnaud/50	5.00	12.00
RIP68 Nick Castellanos/50	12.00	30.00
RIP71 George Brett/25	12.00	30.00
RIP80 Mike Schmidt/25	10.00	25.00
RIP92 Darryl Strawberry/25	4.00	10.00
RIP95 John Smoltz/25	6.00	15.00
RIP96 Dwight Gooden/25	4.00	10.00

2014 Topps Allen and Ginter The Amateur Osteologist

STATED ODDS 1:6600 HOBBY
EXCHANGE DEADLINE 7/31/2015

Card	Low	High
01 Amateur Osteologist EXCH	75.00	150.00

2014 Topps Allen and Ginter The Pastime's Pastime

Card	Low	High
COMPLETE SET (100)	20.00	50.00
STATED ODDS 1:2 HOBBY		
PPAB Adrian Beltre	.40	1.00
PPAC Allen Craig	.30	.75
PPAJ Adam Jones	.30	.75
PPAK Al Kaline	.40	1.00
PPAM Andrew McCutchen	.40	1.00
PPAP Albert Pujols	.50	1.25
PPAR Anthony Rizzo	.50	1.25
PPAW Adam Wainwright	.30	.75
PPBG Bob Gibson	.30	.75
PPBH Bryce Harper	.60	1.50
PPBR Babe Ruth	1.00	2.50
PPCB Clay Buchholz	.25	.60
PPCC CC Sabathia	.30	.75
PPCD Chris Davis	.25	.60
PPCG Carlos Gonzalez	.30	.75
PPCH Cole Hamels	.30	.75
PPCK Clayton Kershaw	.60	1.50
PPCR Cal Ripken Jr.	1.25	3.00
PPCS Chris Sale	.40	1.00
PPCU Chase Utley	.30	.75
PPDB Domonic Brown	.30	.75
PPDG Dwight Gooden	.25	.60
PPDJ Derek Jeter	1.00	2.50
PPDM Don Mattingly	.75	2.00
PPDO David Ortiz	.40	1.00
PPDP Dustin Pedroia	.40	1.00
PPDW David Wright	.30	.75
PPEB Ernie Banks	.40	1.00
PPEL Evan Longoria	.30	.75
PPFF Freddie Freeman	.50	1.25
PPFH Felix Hernandez	.30	.75
PPGC Gerrit Cole	.40	1.00
PPGG Gio Gonzalez	.30	.75
PPGS Giancarlo Stanton	.40	1.00
PPHA Hank Aaron	.75	2.00
PPHI Hisashi Iwakuma	.30	.75
PPHK Harmon Killebrew	.40	1.00
PPHR Hyun-Jin Ryu	.30	.75
PPJA Jose Altuve	.30	.75
PPJB Jose Bautista	.30	.75
PPJE Jacoby Ellsbury	.30	.75
PPJF Jose Fernandez	.40	1.00
PPJG Jedd Gyorko	.25	.60
PPJK Jason Kipnis	.30	.75
PPJM Justin Masterson	.25	.60
PPJR Jose Reyes	.30	.75
PPJS James Shields	.25	.60
PPJT Julio Teheran	.30	.75
PPJU Justin Upton	.30	.75
PPJV Joey Votto	.40	1.00
PPJW Jered Weaver	.30	.75
PPJZ Jordan Zimmermann	.30	.75
PPKG Ken Griffey Jr.	.75	2.00
PPLB Lou Brock	.30	.75
PPLG Lou Gehrig	.75	2.00
PPMB Madison Bumgarner	.30	.75
PPMC Miguel Cabrera	.40	1.00
PPMH Matt Harvey	.30	.75
PPMM Manny Machado	.40	1.00
PPMS Max Scherzer	.40	1.00
PPMT Mike Trout	2.00	5.00
PPNR Nolan Ryan	1.25	3.00
PPOS Ozzie Smith	.50	1.25
PPPF Prince Fielder	.30	.75
PPPG Paul Goldschmidt	.40	1.00
PPPS Pablo Sandoval	.30	.75
PPRB Ryan Braun	.30	.75
PPRC Robinson Cano	.30	.75
PPRD R.A. Dickey	.30	.75
PPRH Ryan Howard	.30	.75
PPRJ Reggie Jackson	.30	.75
PPRM Roger Maris	.40	1.00
PPSC Starlin Castro	.25	.60
PPSK Sandy Koufax	.75	2.00
PPSM Shelby Miller	.30	.75
PPSS Stephen Strasburg	.40	1.00
PPTC Ty Cobb	.60	1.50
PPTG Tom Glavine	.30	.75
PPTL Tim Lincecum	.30	.75
PPTT Troy Tulowitzki	.40	1.00
PPWM Wil Myers	.25	.60
PPYC Yoenis Cespedes	.40	1.00
PPYD Yu Darvish	.40	1.00
PPYP Yasiel Puig	.40	1.00
PPZW Zack Wheeler	.30	.75
PPARO Alex Rodriguez	.50	1.25
PPCBE Carlos Beltran	.30	.75
PPDPR David Price	.30	.75
PPHRA Hanley Ramirez	.30	.75
PPJMA Joe Mauer	.30	.75
PPJMO Joe Morgan	.30	.75
PPJRO Jackie Robinson	.40	1.00
PPJSE Jean Segura	.30	.75
PPJSM John Smoltz	.40	1.00
PPJVE Justin Verlander	.40	1.00
PPMMA Mark McGwire	.75	2.00
PPRHE Rickey Henderson	.40	1.00
PPRJO Randy Johnson	.40	1.00
PPTWI Ted Williams	.75	2.00
PPWMA Willie Mays	.75	2.00

2014 Topps Allen and Ginter The World's Capitals

Card	Low	High
COMPLETE SET (20)	5.00	12.00
STATED ODDS 1:2 HOBBY		
WC01 Jerusalem Israel	.40	1.00
WC02 New Delhi India	.40	1.00
WC03 Moscow Russia	.40	1.00
WC04 Beijing China	.40	1.00
WC05 Cairo Egypt	.40	1.00
WC06 Brasilia Brazil	.40	1.00
WC07 Washington D.C. USA	.40	1.00
WC08 London UK	.40	1.00
WC09 Paris France	.40	1.00
WC10 Berlin Germany	.40	1.00
WC11 Buenos Aires Argentina	.40	1.00
WC12 Brussels Belgium	.40	1.00
WC13 Rome Italy	.40	1.00
WC14 Tokyo Japan	.40	1.00
WC15 Ottawa Canada	.40	1.00
WC16 Mexico City Mexico	.40	1.00
WC17 Taipei Taiwan	.40	1.00
WC18 Bangkok Thailand	.40	1.00
WC19 Johannesburg South Africa	.40	1.00
WC20 Athens Greece	.40	1.00

2015 Topps Allen and Ginter

Card	Low	High
COMPLETE SET (350)	30.00	80.00
ORIGINAL BUYBACK ODDS 1:7958 HOBBY		
ORIG.BUYBACK PRINT RUN 1 SER.#'d SET		
1 Madison Bumgarner	.20	.50
2 Nick Markakis	.20	.50
3 Adrian Gonzalez	.20	.50
4 Wilmer Flores	.20	.50
5 Craig Kimbrel	.20	.50
6 Lucas Duda	.20	.50
7 Eric Hosmer	.20	.50
8 Garrett Richards	.20	.50
9 Jeff Samardzija	.15	.40
10 Curtis Granderson	.20	.50
11 Carlos Santana	.20	.50
12 Nelson Cruz	.25	.60
13 Koji Uehara	.15	.40
14 LaTroy Hawkins	.15	.40
15 Justin Verlander	.25	.60
16 Felix Hernandez	.20	.50
17 Yadier Molina	.30	.75
18 Adam Eaton	.15	.40
19 Charlie Blackmon	.25	.60
20 Leonys Martin	.15	.40
21 Kolten Wong	.20	.50
22 Trevor Rosenthal	.20	.50
23 Johnny Cueto	.20	.50
24 Appomattox Court House	.15	.40
25 Mark Trumbo	.15	.40
26 Steven Souza Jr.	.20	.50
27 Maikel Franco RC	.40	1.00
28 Jayson Werth	.20	.50
29 Nick Swisher	.20	.50
30 Megan Kalmoe	.15	.40
31 Frank Caliendo	.15	.40
32 James Murray	.15	.40
33 Michael Wacha	.20	.50
34 Buster Olney	.15	.40
35 Paul Goldschmidt	.25	.60
36 Anthony Ranaudo RC	.30	.75
37 Mike Mills	.15	.40
38 Evan Longoria	.20	.50
39 Jon Singleton	.20	.50
40 J.J. Hardy	.15	.40
41 Brandon Finnegan RC	.30	.75
42 Max Scherzer	.25	.60
43 Adam Jones	.20	.50
44 Sal Vulcano	.15	.40
45 Chris Owings	.15	.40
46 Andrew McCutchen	.25	.60
47 Lance Lynn	.15	.40
48 Coco Crisp	.15	.40
49 Hisashi Iwakuma	.20	.50
50 Francisco Rodriguez	.20	.50
51 Matt Garza	.15	.40
52 Jake Marisnick	.15	.40
53 Brandon Crawford	.20	.50
54 Javier Baez RC	2.50	6.00
55 Jonah Keri	.15	.40
56 Apollo Creed	.25	.60
57 David Cross	.15	.40
58 Jacob deGrom	.50	1.25
59 Hector Rondon	.15	.40
60 Marcus Semien	.25	.60
61 Domonic Brown	.20	.50
62 Andrelton Simmons	.15	.40
63 Edwin Escobar RC	.30	.75
64 Austin Jackson	.15	.40
65 David Ortiz	.25	.60
66 Billy Butler	.15	.40
67 Malcolm Gladwell	.15	.40
68 Matt Barnes RC	.30	.75
69 Christian Bethancourt	.15	.40
70 Kyle Seager	.15	.40
71 J.D. Martinez	.25	.60
72 Joe Panik	.20	.50
73 Daniel Murphy	.20	.50
74 Casey McGehee	.15	.40
75 Brandon Phillips	.15	.40
76 Jake Arrieta	.20	.50
77 Jason Hammel	.20	.50
78 Carlos Gonzalez	.20	.50
79 Grant Miller	.15	.40
80 Joe Gatto	.15	.40
81 Buck Farmer RC	.30	.75
82 Dalton Pompey RC	.40	1.00
83 Matt Harvey	.20	.50
84 Josh Harrison	.15	.40
85 Kris Bryant RC	3.00	8.00
86 Rick Porcello	.20	.50
87 Francisco Liriano	.15	.40
88 Carl Crawford	.20	.50
89 Jonathan Papelbon	.20	.50
90 Darren Rovell	.15	.40
91 Howie Kendrick	.15	.40
92 Michelle Beadle	.15	.40
93 Kelia Moniz	.15	.40
94 Xander Bogaerts	.25	.60
95 Kole Calhoun	.15	.40
96 Tim Hudson	.20	.50
97 Kendall Graveman RC	.30	.75
98 Yimi Garcia RC	.30	.75
99 Yan Gomes	.15	.40
100 Greg Holland	.15	.40
101 Stephen Strasburg	.25	.60
102 James Clubber Lang	.25	.60
103 Salvador Perez	.20	.50
104 Didi Gregorius	.20	.50
105 Daniel Norris RC	.30	.75
106 Yunel Escobar	.15	.40
107 Giancarlo Stanton	.25	.60
108 Prince Fielder	.20	.50
109 Troy Tulowitzki	.25	.60
110 Victor Martinez	.20	.50
111 Dellin Betances	.20	.50
112 Buck 65	.15	.40
113 Ryan Braun	.20	.50
114 Brian McCann	.20	.50
115 Dustin Pedroia	.25	.60
116 Freddie Freeman	.30	.75
117 Corey Kluber	.20	.50
118 Adam Lind	.20	.50
119 Paul Scheer	.15	.40
120 Matt Adams	.15	.40
121 Wei-Yin Chen	.15	.40
122 Jesse Hahn	.15	.40
123 Micah Johnson RC	.30	.75
124 Lakey Peterson	.15	.40
125 Nori Aoki	.15	.40
126 Alexei Ramirez	.20	.50
127 Nick Castellanos	.25	.60
128 R.A. Dickey	.20	.50
129 Yovani Gallardo	.15	.40
130 Juan Lagares	.15	.40
131 Josh Reddick	.15	.40
132 Dilson Herrera RC	.40	1.00
133 Addison Russell RC	1.00	2.50
134 Joc Pederson RC	1.25	3.00
135 Mark Teixeira	.20	.50
136 Tyson Ross	.15	.40
137 Marlon Byrd	.15	.40
138 Michael Pineda	.15	.40
139 Chris Sale	.25	.60
140 Jose Altuve	.20	.50
141 Justin Upton	.20	.50
142 Yasiel Puig	.25	.60
143 Mike Zunino	.15	.40
144 Brandon Belt	.20	.50
145 Santiago Casilla	.15	.40
146 Michael Morse	.15	.40
147 Yoenis Cespedes	.20	.50
148 Yasmany Tomas RC	.40	1.00
149 Andrew Heaney	.15	.40
150 Brody Stevens	.15	.40
151 Jorge Soler RC	.50	1.25
152 Jacoby Ellsbury	.20	.50
153 Brandon Moss	.15	.40
154 Rusney Castillo RC	.40	1.00
155 Mike Moustakas	.20	.50
156 Brian Dozier	.20	.50
157 Jose Reyes	.20	.50
158 Kurt Suzuki	.15	.40
159 Devin Mesoraco	.15	.40
160 Danny Santana	.15	.40
161 Bartolo Colon	.15	.40
162 Anthony Rizzo	.30	.75
163 Zach Lowe	.15	.40
164 Adrian Beltre	.25	.60
165 Jonathan Lucroy	.20	.50
166 Carlos Gomez	.15	.40
167 Julie Foudy	.15	.40
168 Clay Buchholz	.15	.40
169 Yordano Ventura	.20	.50
170 Chris Davis	.15	.40
171 Anthony Rendon	.25	.60
172 Matt Carpenter	.25	.60
173 Buster Posey	.30	.75
174 Joe Mauer	.20	.50
175 DJ LeMahieu	.25	.60
176 Jon Niese	.15	.40
177 Bernie Williams	.20	.50
178 Travis d'Arnaud	.20	.50
179 Manny Machado	.25	.60
180 Scott Kazmir	.15	.40
181 Drew Hutchison	.15	.40
182 Todd Frazier	.15	.40
183 Edwin Encarnacion	.25	.60
184 Marcell Ozuna	.25	.60
185 Gus Malzahn	.15	.40
186 Desmond Jennings	.20	.50
187 Miguel Cabrera	.25	.60
188 Shelby Miller	.20	.50
189 Kennys Vargas	.15	.40
190 Michael Bourn	.15	.40
191 John Lackey	.20	.50
192 Fernando Rodney	.15	.40
193 Aramis Ramirez	.15	.40
194 Zack Cozart	.15	.40
195 Torii Hunter	.15	.40
196 Ian Kinsler	.20	.50
197 Melky Cabrera	.15	.40
198 Albert Pujols	.30	.75
199 Zack Greinke	.25	.60
200 Jose Abreu	.25	.60
201 Joe Buck	.15	.40
202 Travis Ishikawa	.15	.40
203 David Wright	.20	.50
204 Chase Headley	.15	.40
205 Dustin Ackley	.15	.40
206 Erick Aybar	.15	.40
207 Derek Norris	.15	.40
208 Jose Fernandez	.25	.60
209 Hanley Ramirez	.20	.50
210 Starling Marte	.20	.50
211 Kyle Lohse	.15	.40
212 Chris Tillman	.15	.40
213 Elvis Andrus	.20	.50
214 Corey Dickerson	.15	.40
215 Joey Votto	.25	.60
216 Jake Lamb RC	.50	1.25
217 Wade Miley	.15	.40
218 Carlos Rodon RC	.75	2.00
219 Huston Street	.15	.40
220 Yasmani Grandal	.15	.40
221 Doug Fister	.15	.40
222 Gregory Polanco	.20	.50
223 Incredibeard	.15	.40
224 Edinson Volquez	.15	.40
225 Thunderlips	.25	.60
226 Nolan Arenado	.40	1.00
227 Christian Yelich	.30	.75
228 Robb Wolf	.15	.40
229 Ivan Drago	.25	.60
230 Keith Law	.15	.40
231 Henderson Alvarez	.15	.40
232 Matt Holliday	.25	.60
233 Ike Davis	.15	.40
234 Michael Cuddyer	.15	.40
235 Michael Taylor RC	.30	.75
236 Julio Teheran	.20	.50
237 Hyun-Jin Ryu	.20	.50
238 Dee Gordon	.15	.40
239 Zach Britton	.20	.50
240 Trevor May RC	.30	.75
241 CC Sabathia	.20	.50
242 James McCann RC	.50	1.25
243 Jean Segura	.20	.50
244 Jason Kipnis	.20	.50
245 Ryan Howard	.20	.50
246 Andrew Cashner	.15	.40
247 George Springer	.20	.50
248 Jose Bautista	.20	.50
249 Bryce Harper	.40	1.00
250 Jimmy Rollins	.20	.50
251 Adam LaRoche	.15	.40
252 Mike Trout	1.25	3.00
253 Carlos Beltran	.20	.50
254 Alex Gordon	.20	.50
255 Steven Moya RC	.40	1.00
256 Sonny Gray	.20	.50
257 Pablo Sandoval	.20	.50
258 Rocky Balboa	.25	.60
259 Jonathan Schoop	.15	.40
260 Hunter Pence	.20	.50
261 Yu Darvish	.25	.60
262 Alex Cobb	.15	.40
263 Pedro Alvarez	.15	.40
264 Matt Kemp	.20	.50
265 Jung Ho Kang RC	.30	.75
266 Drew Storen	.15	.40
267 Jered Weaver	.20	.50
268 Jimbo Fisher	.15	.40
269 Jeremy Roenick	.25	.60
270 Mike Foltynewicz RC	.30	.75
271 Dexter Fowler	.20	.50
272 Glen Perkins	.15	.40
273 Cole Hamels	.20	.50
274 Mookie Betts	.50	1.25
275 Billy Hamilton	.20	.50
276 Alex Rodriguez	.30	.75
277 Starlin Castro	.15	.40
278 Cliff Lee	.20	.50
279 Jon Jay	.15	.40
280 Jenrry Mejia	.15	.40
281 Cory Spangenberg RC	.30	.75
282 Adeiny Hechavarria	.15	.40
283 Aaron Hill	.15	.40
284 Jay Bruce	.20	.50
285 Ichiro	.30	.75
286 Addison Reed	.15	.40
287 Jon Lester	.20	.50
288 Robinson Cano	.20	.50
289 Wil Myers	.20	.50
290 Ryan Zimmerman	.20	.50
291 James Shields	.15	.40
292 Grant Balfour	.15	.40
293 Philae Probe	.15	.40
294 Adam Wainwright	.20	.50
295 Joe Nathan	.15	.40
296 Kenley Jansen	.20	.50
297 Magna Carta	.15	.40
298 Rubby De La Rosa	.15	.40
299 Brian Quinn	.15	.40
300 Bryce Brentz RC	.30	.75
301 Justin Morneau	.20	.50
302 Fall of the Berlin Wall	.15	.40
303 Denard Span	.15	.40
304 Gary Brown RC	.15	.40
305 Chris Carter	.15	.40
306 Stephen Drew	.15	.40
307 Jorge De La Rosa	.15	.40
308 David Freese	.15	.40
309 Gabe Kapler	.15	.40
310 Chris Coghlan	.15	.40
311 Michael Brantley	.20	.50
312 Gerrit Cole	.25	.60
313 Jhonny Peralta	.15	.40
314 Ian Desmond	.15	.40
315 Steve Cishek	.15	.40
316 Evan Gattis	.15	.40
317 Hunter Strickland RC	.15	.40
318 David Price	.20	.50
319 Brian Windhorst	.15	.40
320 Dallas Keuchel	.20	.50
321 Ben Zobrist	.20	.50
322 Mark Melancon	.15	.40
323 Joaquin Benoit	.15	.40
324 Will Middlebrooks	.15	.40
325 Aroldis Chapman	.25	.60
326 Mitch Moreland	.15	.40
327 Jeff Mauro	.15	.40
328 Val Kilmer	.15	.40
329 Brett Gardner	.20	.50
330 Jason Heyward	.20	.50
331 Alcides Escobar	.20	.50
332 Matt Cain	.20	.50
333 Chase Utley	.20	.50
334 Nick Tropeano	.15	.40
335 Collin Cowgill	.15	.40
336 Shane Victorino	.20	.50
337 Mike Olt	.15	.40
338 Mike Napoli	.15	.40
339 Clayton Kershaw	.40	1.00
340 Neftali Feliz	.15	.40
341 Malala Yousafzai	.15	.40
342 Josh Donaldson	.20	.50
343 Angel Pagan	.15	.40
344 Jordan Zimmermann	.20	.50
345 Lonnie Chisenhall	.15	.40
346 Shin-Soo Choo	.20	.50
347 Aaron Paul	.15	.40
348 Aaron Sanchez	.20	.50
349 Sam Tuivailala RC	.15	.40
350 Masahiro Tanaka	.20	.50

2015 Topps Allen and Ginter Mini

*MINI 1-300: 1X TO 2.5X BASIC
*MINI 1-300 RC: .5X TO 1.2X BASIC RCs
*MINI SP 301-350: .6X TO 1.5X BASIC
MINI SP ODDS 1:13 HOBBY
351-400 RANDOM WITHIN RIP CARDS
STATED PLATE ODDS 1:495 HOBBY
PLATE PRINT RUN 1 SET PER COLOR
BLACK-CYAN-MAGENTA-YELLOW ISSUED
NO PLATE PRICING DUE TO SCARCITY

Card	Low	High
351 Joey Votto EXT	25.00	60.00
352 Mike Moustakas EXT	20.00	50.00
353 Javier Baez EXT	125.00	300.00
354 Yasiel Puig EXT	30.00	80.00
355 Prince Fielder EXT	20.00	50.00
356 Stephen Strasburg EXT	25.00	60.00
357 Yoenis Cespedes EXT	25.00	60.00
359 Miguel Cabrera EXT	30.00	80.00
360 Adam Jones EXT	20.00	50.00
361 Jacoby Ellsbury EXT	20.00	50.00
363 Hunter Pence EXT	20.00	50.00
364 Jon Lester EXT	20.00	50.00
365 Jacob deGrom EXT	50.00	125.00
366 Troy Tulowitzki EXT	25.00	60.00
367 Clayton Kershaw EXT	40.00	100.00
368 Matt Harvey EXT	20.00	50.00
369 Rusney Castillo EXT	20.00	50.00
370 Madison Bumgarner EXT	20.00	50.00
371 David Wright EXT	20.00	50.00
372 Corey Kluber EXT	20.00	50.00
373 Joc Pederson EXT	40.00	100.00
374 Joe Mauer EXT	20.00	50.00
375 Edwin Encarnacion EXT	25.00	60.00
376 Eric Hosmer EXT	20.00	50.00
377 Giancarlo Stanton EXT	25.00	60.00
378 Pablo Sandoval EXT	20.00	50.00
379 Yu Darvish EXT	25.00	60.00
381 Matt Kemp EXT	20.00	50.00
382 Bryce Harper EXT	40.00	100.00
383 Andrew McCutchen EXT	25.00	60.00
384 Evan Longoria EXT	20.00	50.00
385 Paul Goldschmidt EXT	25.00	60.00
386 Jose Abreu EXT	30.00	80.00
388 Adam Wainwright EXT	20.00	50.00
389 Victor Martinez EXT	20.00	50.00
390 Mike Trout EXT	40.00	100.00
391 Anthony Rendon EXT	25.00	60.00
392 Robinson Cano EXT	20.00	50.00
393 Nelson Cruz EXT	25.00	60.00
394 Buster Posey EXT	30.00	80.00
395 Jose Bautista EXT	20.00	50.00
396 Brandon Belt EXT	25.00	60.00
397 Jason Heyward EXT	20.00	50.00
398 Alex Gordon EXT	20.00	50.00
399 Hanley Ramirez EXT	20.00	50.00
400 David Ortiz EXT	25.00	60.00

2015 Topps Allen and Ginter Mini A and G Back

*MINI AG 1-300: 1.2X TO 3X BASIC
*MINI AG 1-300 RC: .6X TO 1.5X BASIC RCs
*MINI AG SP 301-350: .75X TO 2X BASIC
MINI AG ODDS 1:5 HOBBY
MINI AG SP ODDS 1:65 HOBBY

2015 Topps Allen and Ginter Mini Black

*MINI BLK 1-300: 2X TO 5X BASIC
*MINI BLK 1-300 RC: 1X TO 2.5X BASIC RCs
*MINI BLK SP 301-350: 1.2X TO 3X BASIC
MINI BLK ODDS 1:10 HOBBY
MINI BLK SP ODDS 1:130 HOBBY

2015 Topps Allen and Ginter Mini Flag Back

*MINI FLAG: 5X TO 12X BASIC
*MINI FLAG RC: 2.5X TO 6X BASIC RCs
MINI FLAG ODDS 1:157 HOBBY
STATED PRINT RUN 25 SER.#'d SETS

Card	Low	High
1 Madison Bumgarner	10.00	25.00
3 Adrian Gonzalez	8.00	20.00
6 Lucas Duda	6.00	15.00
15 Justin Verlander	6.00	15.00
16 Felix Hernandez	10.00	25.00
17 Yadier Molina	10.00	25.00
27 Maikel Franco	10.00	25.00
35 Paul Goldschmidt	15.00	40.00
56 Apollo Creed	10.00	25.00
72 Joe Panik	12.00	30.00
85 Kris Bryant	100.00	200.00
104 Didi Gregorius	6.00	15.00
111 Dellin Betances	6.00	15.00
113 Ryan Braun	6.00	15.00
116 Freddie Freeman	10.00	25.00
134 Joc Pederson	20.00	50.00
151 Jorge Soler	12.00	30.00
173 Buster Posey	30.00	80.00
187 Miguel Cabrera	10.00	25.00
199 Zack Greinke	6.00	15.00
215 Joey Votto	6.00	15.00
225 Thunderlips	10.00	25.00
237 Hyun-Jin Ryu	6.00	15.00
241 CC Sabathia	6.00	15.00
249 Bryce Harper	15.00	40.00
252 Mike Trout	25.00	60.00
258 Rocky Balboa	15.00	40.00
339 Clayton Kershaw	20.00	50.00

2015 Topps Allen and Ginter Mini No Card Number

*MINI NNO: 6X TO 15X BASIC
*MINI NNO RC: 3X TO 8X BASIC RCs
MINI NNO ODDS 1:79 HOBBY
ANNCD PRINT RUN OF 50 COPIES EACH

2015 Topps Allen and Ginter Mini Red

*MINI RED: 5X TO 12X BASIC
*MINI RED RC: 2.5X TO 6X BASIC RCs
MINI RED ODDS 1:12 HOBBY BOXES
STATED PRINT RUN 40 SER.#'d SETS

Card	Low	High
1 Madison Bumgarner	10.00	25.00
3 Adrian Gonzalez	8.00	20.00
6 Lucas Duda	6.00	15.00
15 Justin Verlander	6.00	15.00
16 Felix Hernandez	10.00	25.00
17 Yadier Molina	10.00	25.00
27 Maikel Franco	10.00	25.00
35 Paul Goldschmidt	15.00	40.00
56 Apollo Creed	10.00	25.00
72 Joe Panik	12.00	30.00
85 Kris Bryant	100.00	200.00
104 Didi Gregorius	6.00	15.00
111 Dellin Betances	6.00	15.00
113 Ryan Braun	6.00	15.00
116 Freddie Freeman	10.00	25.00
134 Joc Pederson	20.00	50.00
151 Jorge Soler	12.00	30.00
173 Buster Posey	30.00	80.00
187 Miguel Cabrera	10.00	25.00
199 Zack Greinke	6.00	15.00
215 Joey Votto	6.00	15.00
225 Thunderlips	10.00	25.00
237 Hyun-Jin Ryu	6.00	15.00
241 CC Sabathia	6.00	15.00
249 Bryce Harper	15.00	40.00
252 Mike Trout	25.00	60.00
258 Rocky Balboa	15.00	40.00
339 Clayton Kershaw	20.00	50.00

2015 Topps Allen and Ginter Ancient Armory

Card	Low	High
COMPLETE SET (20)	3.00	8.00
OVERALL INSERT ODDS 1:2 HOBBY		
AA1 Catapult	.30	.75
AA2 Katana	.30	.75
AA3 Quarterstaff	.30	.75
AA4 Gauntlet	.30	.75
AA5 Chu Ko Nu	.30	.75
AA6 Katar	.30	.75
AA7 Dane Axe	.30	.75
AA8 War Hammer	.30	.75
AA9 Flail	.30	.75
AA10 Flanged Mace	.30	.75
AA11 Claymore	.30	.75
AA12 Shuriken	.30	.75
AA13 Taiaha	.30	.75
AA14 Atlatl	.30	.75
AA15 Sling	.30	.75
AA16 Tomahawk	.30	.75
AA17 Trident	.30	.75
AA18 Dory Spear	.30	.75
AA19 Cutlass	.30	.75
AA20 Shamshir	.30	.75

2015 Topps Allen and Ginter Box Topper Autographs

STATED ODDS 1:220 HOBBY BOXES
STATED PRINT RUN 15 SER.#'d SETS
EXCHANGE DEADLINE 6/30/2018

Card	Low	High
BLADW David Wright	100.00	250.00
BLAFF Freddie Freeman	50.00	120.00
BLAJB Javier Baez	100.00	250.00
BLAJS Jorge Soler	25.00	60.00
BLARC Rusney Castillo EXCH	15.00	40.00
BLACKE Clayton Kershaw EXCH	125.00	300.00
BLACKL Corey Kluber	15.00	40.00

2015 Topps Allen and Ginter Box Topper Relics

STATED ODDS 1:132 HOBBY BOXES
STATED PRINT RUN 25 SER.#'d SETS

Card	Low	High
BRDW David Wright	15.00	40.00
BRJA Jose Abreu	30.00	80.00
BRJS Jorge Soler	12.00	30.00
BRMB Madison Bumgarner	15.00	40.00
BRRB Ryan Braun	12.00	30.00
BRRC Rusney Castillo	6.00	15.00
BRCKE Clayton Kershaw	20.00	50.00
BRJBU Jose Bautista	6.00	15.00
BRMTA Masahiro Tanaka	15.00	40.00
BRMTR Mike Trout	40.00	100.00

2015 Topps Allen and Ginter Box Toppers

STATED ODDS 1:3 HOBBY BOXES

Card	Low	High
B1 Mike Trout	8.00	20.00
B2 Jose Abreu	1.50	4.00
B3 Rusney Castillo	1.25	3.00
B4 Jorge Soler	1.50	4.00
B5 Corey Kluber	1.25	3.00
B6 Clayton Kershaw	2.50	6.00
B7 David Wright	1.25	3.00
B8 Yasiel Puig	1.50	4.00
B9 Freddie Freeman	2.00	5.00
B10 Javier Baez	8.00	20.00
B11 Buster Posey	2.00	5.00
B12 Evan Longoria	1.25	3.00
B13 Troy Tulowitzki	1.50	4.00
B14 Joey Votto	1.50	4.00
B15 Giancarlo Stanton	1.50	4.00

2015 Topps Allen and Ginter Framed Mini Autographs

STATED ODDS 1:54 HOBBY
EXCHANGE DEADLINE 6/30/2018

Card	Low	High
AGAAB Archie Bradley	3.00	8.00
AGAAP Aaron Paul	20.00	50.00
AGAARA Anthony Ranaudo	3.00	8.00
AGAB6 Buck 65	12.00	30.00
AGABBR Bryce Brentz	3.00	8.00
AGABC Brandon Crawford	6.00	15.00
AGABEW Bernie Williams	20.00	50.00
AGABF Brandon Finnegan	3.00	8.00
AGABFA Buck Farmer	3.00	8.00
AGABH Bryce Harper	150.00	300.00
AGABM Brian McCann	30.00	80.00
AGABO Buster Olney	10.00	25.00
AGABQ Brian Quinn	15.00	40.00
AGABS Brody Stevens	6.00	15.00
AGABW Brian Windhorst	4.00	10.00
AGACB Charlie Blackmon	10.00	25.00
AGACKL Corey Kluber	12.00	30.00
AGACR Carlos Rodon	15.00	40.00
AGACSP Cory Spangenberg	3.00	8.00
AGACW Christian Walker	6.00	15.00
AGADB Dellin Betances	4.00	10.00
AGADC David Cross	25.00	60.00
AGADG Didi Gregorius	4.00	10.00
AGADH Dilson Herrera	4.00	10.00
AGADN Daniel Norris	3.00	8.00
AGADPE Dustin Pedroia	40.00	100.00
AGADPO Dalton Pompey	4.00	10.00
AGADR Darren Rovell	3.00	8.00
AGADW David Wright	60.00	150.00
AGAEE Edwin Encarnacion	6.00	15.00
AGAFC Frank Caliendo	8.00	20.00
AGAFF Freddie Freeman	15.00	40.00
AGAGB Gary Brown	3.00	8.00
AGAGK Gabe Kapler	3.00	8.00
AGAGM Gus Malzahn	12.00	30.00
AGAID Ivan Drago	100.00	200.00
AGAIMM Ichiro	300.00	600.00
AGAINY Ichiro	300.00	600.00
AGAISM Ichiro	300.00	600.00
AGAIW Incredibeard	6.00	15.00
AGAJBU Joe Buck	15.00	40.00
AGAJDE Jacob deGrom	40.00	100.00
AGAJF Jimbo Fisher	8.00	20.00
AGAJFO Julie Foudy	12.00	30.00
AGAJGA Joe Gatto	15.00	40.00
AGAJH Jason Heyward	30.00	80.00
AGAJK Jung-Ho Kang	60.00	150.00
AGAJKE Jonah Keri	4.00	10.00
AGAJMA Jeff Mauro	6.00	15.00
AGAJMU James Murray	20.00	50.00
AGAJPA Joe Panik	10.00	25.00
AGAJPE Joc Pederson	10.00	25.00
AGAJR Jeremy Roenick	12.00	30.00
AGAJSO Jorge Soler	10.00	25.00
AGAJW Justise Winslow	10.00	25.00
AGAKB Kris Bryant	100.00	250.00
AGAKG Kendall Graveman	3.00	8.00
AGAKL Keith Law	4.00	10.00
AGAKM Kelia Moniz	12.00	30.00
AGAKOU Kelly Oubre	10.00	25.00
AGALP Lakey Peterson	6.00	15.00
AGAMA Matt Adams	3.00	8.00
AGAMBA Matt Barnes	3.00	8.00
AGAMBE Michelle Beadle	15.00	40.00
AGAMFR Maikel Franco	6.00	15.00
AGAMG Malcolm Gladwell	8.00	20.00
AGAMK Megan Kalmoe	4.00	10.00
AGAMM Mike Mills	15.00	40.00
AGAMTA Michael Taylor	3.00	8.00
AGANS Noah Syndergaard	30.00	80.00
AGAPSC Paul Scheer	6.00	15.00
AGARB Ryan Braun	30.00	80.00
AGARCN Robinson Cano	12.00	30.00
AGARJH R.J. Hunter	12.00	30.00
AGARW Robb Wolf	4.00	10.00
AGASD Sam Dekker	12.00	30.00
AGASJ Stanley Johnson	25.00	60.00
AGAST Sam Tuivailala	3.00	8.00
AGASV Sal Vulcano	20.00	50.00
AGATH Thunderlips	200.00	300.00
AGATM Trevor May	3.00	8.00
AGAVK Val Kilmer	30.00	80.00
AGAWCS Willie Cauley-Stein	25.00	60.00
AGAWM Wil Myers	10.00	25.00
AGAYGA Yimi Garcia	3.00	8.00
AGAYT Yasmany Tomas	6.00	15.00
AGAZL Zach Lowe	6.00	15.00

2015 Topps Allen and Ginter Framed Mini Relics

STATED ODDS 1:61 HOBBY

Card	Low	High
FMRAB Adrian Beltre	4.00	10.00
FMRAG Alex Gordon	3.00	8.00
FMRAJ Adam Jones	3.00	8.00
FMRAM Andrew McCutchen	6.00	15.00
FMRAP Angel Pagan	2.50	6.00
FMRAS Aaron Sanchez	3.00	8.00
FMRAW Alex Wood	2.50	6.00
FMRBB Brandon Belt	3.00	8.00
FMRBM Brian McCann	3.00	8.00
FMRCB Charlie Blackmon	4.00	10.00
FMRCG Carlos Gonzalez	3.00	8.00
FMRCH Cole Hamels	3.00	8.00
FMRCK Clayton Kershaw	6.00	15.00
FMRCS CC Sabathia	3.00	8.00
FMRCT Chris Tillman	2.50	6.00
FMRCU Chase Utley	3.00	8.00
FMRDB Domonic Brown	3.00	8.00
FMRDMU Daniel Murphy	3.00	8.00
FMRDO David Ortiz	4.00	10.00
FMRDS Drew Storen	2.50	6.00
FMRDW David Wright	3.00	8.00
FMREH Eric Hosmer	3.00	8.00
FMRFF Freddie Freeman	5.00	12.00
FMRFH Felix Hernandez	3.00	8.00
FMRGC Gerrit Cole	4.00	10.00

FMRGP Gregory Polanco 3.00 8.00
FMRGS Giancarlo Stanton 4.00 10.00
FMRHA Henderson Alvarez 2.50 6.00
FMRHP Hunter Pence 3.00 8.00
FMRJB Jose Bautista 3.00 8.00
FMRJME Jenrry Mejia 2.50 6.00
FMRJMO Justin Morneau 3.00 8.00
FMRJPE Joc Pederson 10.00 25.00
FMRJT Julio Teheran 3.00 8.00
FMRJV Justin Verlander 6.00 15.00
FMRLM Leonys Martin 2.50 6.00
FMRMCA Matt Carpenter 4.00 10.00
FMRMCB Miguel Cabrera 4.00 10.00
FMRMH Matt Holliday 4.00 10.00
FMRMMO Matt Moore 3.00 8.00
FMRMMR Michael Morse 2.50 6.00
FMRMMU Mike Moustakas 3.00 8.00
FMRMTE Mark Teixeira 3.00 8.00
FMRMTR Mike Trout 12.00 30.00
FMRMZ Mike Zunino 2.50 6.00
FMRPA Pedro Alvarez 2.50 6.00
FMRRB Ryan Braun 3.00 8.00
FMRRH Ryan Howard 3.00 8.00
FMRRO Rougned Odor 3.00 8.00
FMRRZ Ryan Zimmerman 3.00 8.00
FMRSCA Starlin Castro 2.50 6.00
FMRSCH Shin-Soo Choo 3.00 8.00
FMRSM Starling Marte 3.00 8.00
FMRSP Salvador Perez 3.00 8.00
FMRTR Tyson Ross 2.50 6.00
FMRTW Taijuan Walker 2.50 6.00
FMRWC Wei-Yin Chen 2.50 6.00
FMRWF Wilmer Flores 3.00 8.00
FMRWM Wil Myers 3.00 8.00
FMRYM Yadier Molina 5.00 12.00
FMRYP Yasiel Puig 4.00 10.00
FMRZC Zack Cozart 2.50 6.00
FMRZW Zack Wheeler 3.00 8.00

2015 Topps Allen and Ginter Great Scott

COMPLETE SET (20) 3.00 8.00
OVERALL INSERT ODDS 1:2 HOBBY
GS1 X-Ray Diffraction .30 .75
GS2 Big Bang .30 .75
GS3 Polio Vaccine .30 .75
GS4 Large Hadron Collider .30 .75
GS5 Artificial Heart .30 .75
GS6 Deoxyribonucleic Acid .30 .75
GS7 Continental Drift .30 .75
GS8 Search Engine .30 .75
GS9 Fingerprints .30 .75
GS10 Dolly the Sheep .30 .75

2015 Topps Allen and Ginter Keys to the City

COMPLETE SET (10) 12.00 30.00
RANDOM INSERTS IN RETAIL PACKS
KTC1 Statue of Liberty 1.25 3.00
KTC2 Gateway Arch 1.25 3.00
KTC3 Liberty Bell 1.25 3.00
KTC4 Willis Tower 1.25 3.00
KTC5 Portland Light Head 1.25 3.00
KTC6 The Alamo 1.25 3.00
KTC7 Golden Gate Bridge 1.25 3.00
KTC8 The Space Needle 1.25 3.00
KTC9 Welcome Sign 1.25 3.00
KTC10 Empire State Building 1.25 3.00

2015 Topps Allen and Ginter Menagerie of the Mind

COMPLETE SET (20) 3.00 8.00
OVERALL INSERT ODDS 1:2 HOBBY
MM1 Troll .30 .75
MM2 Elf .30 .75
MM3 Dragon .30 .75
MM4 Phoenix .30 .75
MM5 Griffin .30 .75
MM6 Pegasus .30 .75
MM7 Unicorn .30 .75
MM8 Werewolf .30 .75
MM9 Hydra .30 .75
MM10 Cerberus .30 .75
MM11 Zombie .30 .75
MM12 Bunyip .30 .75
MM13 Cyclops .30 .75
MM14 Djinn .30 .75
MM15 Banshee .30 .75
MM16 Leprechaun .30 .75
MM17 Chimera .30 .75
MM18 Mermaid .30 .75
MM19 Sphinx .30 .75
MM20 Centaur .30 .75

2015 Topps Allen and Ginter Mini 10th Anniversary '06 Autographs

STATED ODDS 1:1375 HOBBY PACKS
STATED PRINT RUN 10 SER.#'d SETS
*07-15 AUTOS: .4X TO 1X '06 AUTOS
AGA06BB Bonnie Blair 20.00 50.00
AGA06DP Danica Patrick 150.00 250.00
AGA06GL Greg Louganis 20.00 50.00
AGA06HH Hulk Hogan 150.00 250.00
AGA06JC Joey Chestnut 25.00 60.00
AGA06JF Jennie Finch 60.00 120.00
AGA06JL Jeanette Lee 30.00 80.00
AGA06KS Kerri Strug 25.00 60.00
AGA06MA Mario Andretti 25.00 60.00
AGA06MH Mia Hamm 40.00 100.00
AGA06MS Mark Spitz 20.00 50.00
AGA06WG Wendy Guey 12.00 30.00

2015 Topps Allen and Ginter Mini A Healthy Mind

STATED ODDS 1:288 HOBBY
MIND1 Rowing a Boat 3.00 8.00
MIND2 Flying a Kite 3.00 8.00
MIND3 Riding a Bicycle 3.00 8.00
MIND4 Reading a Book 3.00 8.00
MIND5 Picnicking 3.00 8.00
MIND6 Bird Watching 3.00 8.00
MIND7 Shuffle Board 3.00 8.00
MIND8 Skipping Rocks 3.00 8.00
MIND9 Bocce 3.00 8.00
MIND10 Chess 3.00 8.00

2015 Topps Allen and Ginter Mini A Healthy Body

STATED ODDS 1:288 HOBBY
BODY1 Vibrating Belt Machine 3.00 8.00
BODY2 Persian Clubs 3.00 8.00
BODY3 Nauheim Baths 3.00 8.00
BODY4 Gymnasticon 3.00 8.00
BODY5 The Turnplatz 3.00 8.00
BODY6 Herbert's Natural Method 3.00 8.00
BODY7 Rope Climbing 3.00 8.00
BODY8 Barbell Lifts 3.00 8.00
BODY9 Caber Tossing 3.00 8.00
BODY10 Grappling 3.00 8.00

2015 Topps Allen and Ginter Mini A World Beneath Our Feet

COMPLETE SET (15) 8.00 20.00
OVERALL MINI INSERT ODDS 1:5 HOBBY
BUG1 Borneo Walking Stick 1.00 2.50
BUG2 Goliath Beetle 1.00 2.50
BUG3 Assassin Bug 1.00 2.50
BUG4 Devil's Flower Mantis 1.00 2.50
BUG5 Seven-Spotted Ladybug 1.00 2.50
BUG6 Monarch Butterfly 1.00 2.50
BUG7 European Honeybee 1.00 2.50
BUG8 Death's Head Hawkmoth 1.00 2.50
BUG9 Deer Tick 1.00 2.50
BUG10 Pennsylvania Firefly 1.00 2.50
BUG11 White-Legged Snake Millipede 1.00 2.50
BUG12 Green-Striped Darner 1.00 2.50
BUG13 Calleta Silkmoth Caterpillar 1.00 2.50
BUG14 Madagascar Hissing Cockroach 1.00 2.50
BUG15 Tsetse Fly 1.00 2.50

2015 Topps Allen and Ginter Mini Birds of Prey

COMPLETE SET (10) 10.00 25.00
OVERALL MINI INSERT ODDS 1:5 HOBBY
BP1 Red-tailed Hawk 1.50 4.00
BP2 Bald Eagle 1.50 4.00
BP3 Great Horned Owl 1.50 4.00
BP4 Burrowing Owl 1.50 4.00
BP5 Black Vulture 1.50 4.00
BP6 Crested Caracara 1.50 4.00
BP7 California Condor 1.50 4.00
BP8 Peregrine Falcon 1.50 4.00
BP9 Osprey 1.50 4.00
BP10 Barn Owl 1.50 4.00

2015 Topps Allen and Ginter Mini First Ladies

COMPLETE SET (41) 30.00 80.00
OVERALL MINI INSERT ODDS 1:5 HOBBY
FIRST1 Eleanor Roosevelt 1.25 3.00
FIRST2 Martha Washington 1.25 3.00
FIRST3 Abigail Adams 1.25 3.00
FIRST4 Dolley Madison 1.25 3.00
FIRST5 Elizabeth Monroe 1.25 3.00
FIRST6 Louisa Adams 1.25 3.00
FIRST7 Anna Harrison 1.25 3.00
FIRST8 Letitia Tyler 1.25 3.00
FIRST9 Julia Tyler 1.25 3.00
FIRST10 Sarah Polk 1.25 3.00
FIRST11 Margaret Taylor 1.25 3.00
FIRST12 Abigail Fillmore 1.25 3.00
FIRST13 Jane Pierce 1.25 3.00
FIRST14 Harriet Lane 1.25 3.00
FIRST15 Mary Lincoln 1.25 3.00
FIRST16 Eliza Johnson 1.25 3.00
FIRST17 Julia Grant 1.25 3.00
FIRST18 Lucy Hayes 1.25 3.00
FIRST19 Lucretia Garfield 1.25 3.00
FIRST20 Frances Cleveland 1.25 3.00
FIRST21 Caroline Harrison 1.25 3.00
FIRST22 Ida McKinley 1.25 3.00
FIRST23 Edith Roosevelt 1.25 3.00
FIRST24 Helen Taft 1.25 3.00
FIRST25 Ellen Wilson 1.25 3.00
FIRST26 Edith Wilson 1.25 3.00
FIRST27 Florence Harding 1.25 3.00
FIRST28 Grace Coolidge 1.25 3.00
FIRST29 Lou Hoover 1.25 3.00
FIRST30 Bess Truman 1.25 3.00
FIRST31 Mamie Eisenhower 1.25 3.00
FIRST32 Jacqueline Kennedy 1.25 3.00
FIRST33 Lady Bird Johnson 1.25 3.00
FIRST34 Pat Nixon 1.25 3.00
FIRST35 Betty Ford 1.25 3.00
FIRST36 Rosalynn Carter 1.25 3.00
FIRST37 Nancy Reagan 1.25 3.00
FIRST38 Barbara Bush 1.25 3.00
FIRST39 Hillary Clinton 1.25 3.00
FIRST40 Laura Bush 1.25 3.00
FIRST41 Michelle Obama 1.25 3.00

2015 Topps Allen and Ginter Mini Hoist the Black Flag

COMPLETE SET (10) 12.00 30.00
OVERALL MINI INSERT ODDS 1:5 HOBBY
HBF1 Blackbeard 1.50 4.00
HBF2 Anne Bonny 1.50 4.00
HBF3 Charles Vane 1.50 4.00
HBF4 Calico Jack Rackham 1.50 4.00
HBF5 Captain William Kidd 1.50 4.00
HBF6 Benjamin Hornigold 1.50 4.00
HBF7 Mary Read 1.50 4.00
HBF8 Stede Bonnet 1.50 4.00
HBF9 Black Bart 1.50 4.00
HBF10 Henry Every 1.50 4.00

2015 Topps Allen and Ginter Mini Magnates Barons and Tycoons

COMPLETE SET (10) 6.00 15.00
OVERALL MINI INSERT ODDS 1:5 HOBBY
MBT1 John D. Rockefeller 1.00 2.50
MBT2 Cornelius Vanderbilt 1.00 2.50
MBT3 James J. Hill 1.00 2.50
MBT4 Andrew Carnegie 1.00 2.50
MBT5 J.P. Morgan 1.00 2.50
MBT6 John Jacob Astor 1.00 2.50
MBT7 James Buchanan Duke 1.00 2.50
MBT8 Henry Flagler 1.00 2.50
MBT9 John W. Gates 1.00 2.50
MBT10 Andrew W. Mellon 1.00 2.50

2015 Topps Allen and Ginter Mini Mythological Menaces

COMPLETE SET (10) 6.00 15.00
OVERALL MINI INSERT ODDS 1:5 HOBBY
MM1 Loki 1.00 2.50
MM2 Pan 1.00 2.50
MM3 The Monkey King 1.00 2.50
MM4 Puck 1.00 2.50
MM5 Prometheus 1.00 2.50
MM6 Wisakedjak 1.00 2.50
MM7 Hermes 1.00 2.50
MM8 Eris 1.00 2.50
MM9 Coyote 1.00 2.50
MM10 Nanabozho 1.00 2.50

2015 Topps Allen and Ginter Oversized Reprint Cabinet Box Toppers

STATED ODDS 1:4 HOBBY BOXES
1 Madison Bumgarner 1.25 3.00
46 Andrew McCutchen 1.50 4.00
85 Kris Bryant 6.00 15.00
151 Jorge Soler 1.50 4.00
154 Rusney Castillo 1.25 3.00
173 Buster Posey 2.00 5.00
187 Miguel Cabrera 1.50 4.00
252 Mike Trout 8.00 20.00
288 Robinson Cano 1.25 3.00
339 Clayton Kershaw 2.50 6.00

2015 Topps Allen and Ginter Pride of the People Cabinet Box Toppers

STATED ODDS 1:4 HOBBY BOXES
PCB1 Christ the Redeemer 2.00 5.00
PCB2 The Great Wall 2.00 5.00
PCB3 Mount Rushmore 2.00 5.00
PCB4 St. Basil's Cathedral 2.00 5.00
PCB5 Eiffel Tower 2.00 5.00
PCB6 Mount Fuji 2.00 5.00
PCB7 Big Ben 2.00 5.00
PCB8 Angkor Wat 2.00 5.00
PCB9 Colosseum 2.00 5.00
PCB10 Great Pyramid of Giza 2.00 5.00

2015 Topps Allen and Ginter Relics

GROUP A ODDS 1:24 HOBBY
GROUP B ODDS 1:24 HOBBY
FSRAAB Adrian Beltre A 3.00 8.00
FSRAAG Adrian Gonzalez A 2.50 6.00
FSRAAJ Adam Jones A 2.50 6.00
FSRAAPA Aaron Paul A 2.50 6.00
FSRAAPU Albert Pujols A 5.00 12.00
FSRAAR Anthony Rizzo A 4.00 10.00
FSRAAS Aaron Sanchez A 2.50 6.00
FSRAAW Adam Wainwright A 2.50 6.00
FSRABHA Bryce Harper A 5.00 12.00
FSRABHM Billy Hamilton A 2.50 6.00
FSRABO Buster Olney A 2.50 6.00
FSRABP Brandon Phillips A 2.00 5.00
FSRABS Brody Stevens A 2.50 6.00
FSRABW Brian Windhorst A 2.50 6.00
FSRACD Chris Davis A 2.00 5.00
FSRACS CC Sabathia A 2.50 6.00
FSRACU Chase Utley A 2.50 6.00
FSRADB Domonic Brown A 2.50 6.00
FSRADP Dustin Pedroia A 3.00 8.00
FSRAEA Elvis Andrus A 2.50 6.00
FSRAEG Evan Gattis A 2.00 5.00
FSRAFC Frank Caliendo A 2.50 6.00
FSRAFH Felix Hernandez A 2.50 6.00
FSRAJBA Jose Bautista A 2.50 6.00
FSRAJBR Jay Bruce A 2.50 6.00
FSRAJBU Joe Buck A 2.50 6.00
FSRAJD Jacob deGrom A 6.00 15.00
FSRAJF Jose Fernandez A 3.00 8.00
FSRAJG Joe Gatto A 2.50 6.00
FSRAJK Jonah Keri A 2.50 6.00
FSRAJMA Jeff Mauro A 2.50 6.00
FSRAJR Jeremy Roenick A 2.50 6.00
FSRAJT Julio Teheran A 2.50 6.00
FSRAMCA Miguel Cabrera A 5.00 12.00
FSRAMCP Matt Carpenter A 3.00 8.00
FSRAMG Malcom Gladwell A 2.50 6.00
FSRAMMI Mike Minor A 2.00 5.00
FSRAMTA Masahiro Tanaka A 2.50 6.00
FSRAMTE Mark Teixeira A 2.50 6.00
FSRAPF Prince Fielder A 2.50 6.00
FSRAPS Paul Scheer A 2.50 6.00
FSRARC Rusney Castillo A 2.50 6.00
FSRARW Robb Wolf A 2.50 6.00
FSRASCA Starlin Castro A 2.00 5.00
FSRASCI Steve Cishek A 2.00 5.00
FSRASM Starling Marte A 2.50 6.00
FSRATR Tyson Ross A 2.00 5.00
FSRATT Troy Tulowitzki A 3.00 8.00
FSRATW Taijuan Walker A 2.00 5.00
FSRAVK Val Kilmer A 2.50 6.00
FSRAVM Victor Martinez A 2.50 6.00
FSRAWF Wilmer Flores A 2.50 6.00
FSRAYC Yoenis Cespedes A 2.50 6.00
FSRAYD Yu Darvish A 3.00 8.00
FSRAYP Yasiel Puig A 4.00 10.00
FSRAYV Yordano Ventura A 2.50 6.00
FSRBAC Aroldis Chapman B 3.00 8.00
FSRBAM Andrew McCutchen B 3.00 8.00
FSRBAS Andrelton Simmons B 2.00 5.00
FSRBBB Brandon Belt B 2.50 6.00
FSRBBM Brian McCann B 2.50 6.00
FSRBBP Buster Posey B 4.00 10.00
FSRBBQ Brian Quinn B 2.50 6.00
FSRBCBE Carlos Beltran B 2.50 6.00
FSRBCBL Charlie Blackmon B 3.00 8.00
FSRBCK Craig Kimbrel B 2.50 6.00
FSRBCT Chris Tillman B 2.00 5.00
FSRBCY Christian Yelich B 4.00 10.00
FSRBDO David Ortiz B 3.00 8.00
FSRBDR Darren Rovell B 2.50 6.00
FSRBDS Drew Storen B 2.00 5.00
FSRBDW David Wright B 2.50 6.00
FSRBEL Evan Longoria B 2.50 6.00
FSRBFF Freddie Freeman B 4.00 10.00
FSRBGK Gabe Kapler B 2.00 5.00
FSRBGS Giancarlo Stanton B 3.00 8.00
FSRBHRA Hanley Ramirez B 2.50 6.00
FSRBHRY Hyun-Jin Ryu B 2.50 6.00
FSRBJA Jose Abreu B 3.00 8.00
FSRBJE Jacoby Ellsbury B 2.50 6.00
FSRBJFO Julie Foudy B 2.50 6.00
FSRBJHA Josh Hamilton B 2.50 6.00
FSRBJHE Jason Heyward B 2.50 6.00
FSRBJMU James Murray B 5.00 12.00
FSRBJSC Jonathan Schoop B 2.00 5.00
FSRBJSO Jorge Soler B 3.00 8.00
FSRBJVE Justin Verlander B 3.00 8.00
FSRBJVO Joey Votto B 3.00 8.00
FSRBKL Keith Law B 2.50 6.00
FSRBKM Kelia Moniz B 4.00 10.00
FSRBLM Leonys Martin B 2.00 5.00
FSRBLP Lakey Peterson B 2.50 6.00
FSRBMBE Michelle Beadle B 2.50 6.00
FSRBMBU Madison Bumgarner B 4.00 10.00
FSRBMH Matt Holliday B 3.00 8.00
FSRBMKA Megan Kalmoe B 2.50 6.00
FSRBMKE Matt Kemp B 2.50 6.00
FSRBMT Mike Trout B 15.00 40.00
FSRBMZ Mike Zunino B 2.00 5.00
FSRBNA Nolan Arenado B 5.00 12.00
FSRBNC Nick Castellanos B 3.00 8.00
FSRBPA Pedro Alvarez B 2.00 5.00
FSRBPS Pablo Sandoval B 2.50 6.00
FSRBRB Ryan Braun B 2.50 6.00
FSRBSP Salvador Perez B 2.50 6.00
FSRBSS Stephen Strasburg B 3.00 8.00
FSRBSV Sal Vulcano B 2.50 6.00
FSRBTD Travis d'Arnaud B 2.50 6.00
FSRBWM Wil Myers B 2.50 6.00
FSRBXB Xander Bogaerts B 3.00 8.00
FSRBYM Yadier Molina B 4.00 10.00
FSRBZL Zach Lowe B 2.50 6.00

2015 Topps Allen and Ginter Starting Points

COMPLETE SET (100) 10.00 25.00
STATED ODDS 1:2 HOBBY
SP1 Felix Hernandez .40 1.00
SP2 Albert Pujols .60 1.50
SP3 Mike Trout 2.50 6.00
SP4 Paul Goldschmidt .50 1.25
SP5 Freddie Freeman .60 1.50
SP6 Craig Kimbrel .40 1.00
SP7 Chris Davis .30 .75
SP8 Adam Jones .40 1.00
SP9 Clay Buchholz .30 .75
SP10 Rusney Castillo .40 1.00
SP11 David Ortiz .50 1.25
SP12 Dustin Pedroia .50 1.25
SP13 Hanley Ramirez .40 1.00
SP14 Pablo Sandoval .40 1.00
SP15 Jon Lester .40 1.00
SP16 Anthony Rizzo .60 1.50
SP17 Jorge Soler .50 1.25
SP18 Jose Abreu .50 1.25
SP19 Chris Sale .50 1.25
SP20 Jeff Samardzija .30 .75
SP21 Aroldis Chapman .50 1.25
SP22 Johnny Cueto .40 1.00
SP23 Joey Votto .50 1.25
SP24 Corey Kluber .40 1.00
SP25 Carlos Gonzalez .40 1.00
SP26 Troy Tulowitzki .50 1.25
SP27 Miguel Cabrera .50 1.25
SP28 Yoenis Cespedes .40 1.00
SP29 Victor Martinez .40 1.00
SP30 David Price .40 1.00
SP31 Justin Verlander .50 1.25
SP32 Jose Altuve .40 1.00
SP33 George Springer .40 1.00
SP34 Alex Gordon .40 1.00
SP35 Eric Hosmer .40 1.00
SP36 Mike Moustakas .40 1.00
SP37 Salvador Perez .40 1.00
SP38 Adrian Gonzalez .40 1.00
SP39 Clayton Kershaw .75 2.00
SP40 Yasiel Puig .50 1.25
SP41 Jimmy Rollins .40 1.00
SP42 Hyun-Jin Ryu .40 1.00
SP43 Jose Fernandez .50 1.25
SP44 Dee Gordon .30 .75
SP45 Giancarlo Stanton .50 1.25
SP46 Ryan Braun .40 1.00
SP47 Carlos Gomez .30 .75
SP48 Torii Hunter .30 .75
SP49 Joe Mauer .40 1.00
SP50 Kennys Vargas .30 .75
SP51 Michael Cuddyer .30 .75
SP52 Jacob deGrom 1.00 2.50
SP53 Lucas Duda .40 1.00
SP54 Matt Harvey .40 1.00
SP55 David Wright .40 1.00
SP56 Carlos Beltran .40 1.00
SP57 Jacoby Ellsbury .40 1.00
SP58 Brian McCann .40 1.00
SP59 Alex Rodriguez .60 1.50
SP60 CC Sabathia .40 1.00
SP61 Billy Butler .30 .75
SP62 Coco Crisp .30 .75
SP63 Sonny Gray .40 1.00
SP64 Josh Reddick .30 .75
SP65 Maikel Franco .40 1.00
SP66 Cole Hamels .40 1.00
SP67 Ryan Howard .40 1.00
SP68 Cliff Lee .40 1.00
SP69 Chase Utley .40 1.00
SP70 Starling Marte .40 1.00
SP71 Andrew McCutchen .50 1.25
SP72 Matt Kemp .40 1.00
SP73 Brandon Belt .40 1.00
SP74 Madison Bumgarner .40 1.00
SP75 Hunter Pence .40 1.00
SP76 Buster Posey .60 1.50
SP77 Robinson Cano .40 1.00
SP78 Nelson Cruz .50 1.25
SP79 Hisashi Iwakuma .40 1.00
SP80 Fernando Rodney .30 .75
SP81 Matt Adams .30 .75
SP82 Jason Heyward .40 1.00
SP83 Matt Holliday .50 1.25
SP84 Yadier Molina .60 1.50
SP85 Adam Wainwright .40 1.00
SP86 Evan Longoria .40 1.00
SP87 Adrian Beltre .50 1.25
SP88 Shin-Soo Choo .40 1.00
SP89 Yu Darvish .50 1.25
SP90 Prince Fielder .40 1.00
SP91 Jose Bautista .40 1.00
SP92 Josh Donaldson .40 1.00
SP93 Edwin Encarnacion .50 1.25
SP94 Jose Reyes .40 1.00
SP95 Ian Desmond .30 .75
SP96 Doug Fister .30 .75
SP97 Bryce Harper .75 2.00
SP98 Max Scherzer .50 1.25
SP99 Stephen Strasburg .50 1.25
SP100 Jayson Werth .40 1.00

2015 Topps Allen and Ginter What Once Was Believed

COMPLETE SET (10) 3.00 8.00
OVERALL INSERT ODDS 1:2 HOBBY
WAS1 Flat Earth .30 .75
WAS2 Open Polar Sea .30 .75
WAS3 Ether .30 .75
WAS4 The Four Classical Elements .30 .75
WAS5 Alchemy .30 .75
WAS6 Brontosaurus .30 .75
WAS7 Rain follows the plow .30 .75
WAS8 Phrenology .30 .75
WAS9 California Island .30 .75
WAS10 Geocentric Solar System .30 .75

2015 Topps Allen and Ginter What Once Would Be

COMPLETE SET (10) 3.00 8.00
OVERALL INSERT ODDS 1:2 HOBBY
WOULD1 Flying Car .30 .75
WOULD2 Jetpacks .30 .75
WOULD3 Robot Housekeepers .30 .75
WOULD4 Automated Kitchen .30 .75
WOULD5 Food in pill form .30 .75
WOULD6 Giant Airliners .30 .75
WOULD7 Easy-clean furniture .30 .75
WOULD8 Mail Via Parachute .30 .75
WOULD9 Vacuum Tube trains .30 .75
WOULD10 Lunar Colonization .30 .75

2015 Topps Allen and Ginter X 10th Anniversary

COMPLETE SET (350)
COMMON CARD (1-350) .25 .60
SEMISTARS .30 .75
UNLISTED STARS .40 1.00
COMMON RC (1-300) .40 1.00
RC SEMIS .50 1.25
RC UNLISTED .60 1.50
COMMON SP (301-350) .50 1.25
SP SEMIS .60 1.50
SP UNLISTED .75 2.00
1 Madison Bumgarner .30 .75
2 Nick Markakis .30 .75
3 Adrian Gonzalez .30 .75
4 Wilmer Flores .30 .75
5 Craig Kimbrel .30 .75
6 Lucas Duda .30 .75
7 Eric Hosmer .30 .75
8 Garrett Richards .30 .75
9 Jeff Samardzija .25 .60
10 Curtis Granderson .30 .75
11 Carlos Santana .30 .75
12 Nelson Cruz .40 1.00
13 Koji Uehara .25 .60
14 LaTroy Hawkins .25 .60
15 Justin Verlander .40 1.00
16 Felix Hernandez .30 .75
17 Yadier Molina .50 1.25
18 Adam Eaton .25 .60
19 Charlie Blackmon .40 1.00
20 Leonys Martin .25 .60
21 Kolten Wong .30 .75
22 Trevor Rosenthal .30 .75
23 Johnny Cueto .30 .75
24 Appomattox Court House .25 .60
25 Mark Trumbo .25 .60
26 Steven Souza Jr. .30 .75
27 Maikel Franco RC .50 1.25
28 Jayson Werth .30 .75
29 Nick Swisher .30 .75
30 Megan Kalmoe .25 .60
31 Frank Caliendo .25 .60
32 James Murray .25 .60
33 Michael Wacha .30 .75
34 Buster Olney .25 .60
35 Paul Goldschmidt .40 1.00
36 Anthony Ranaudo RC .40 1.00
37 Mike Mills .25 .60
38 Evan Longoria .30 .75
39 Jon Singleton .30 .75
40 J.J. Hardy .25 .60
41 Brandon Finnegan RC .40 1.00
42 Max Scherzer .40 1.00
43 Adam Jones .30 .75
44 Sal Vulcano .25 .60
45 Chris Owings .25 .60
46 Andrew McCutchen .40 1.00
47 Lance Lynn .25 .60
48 Coco Crisp .25 .60
49 Hisashi Iwakuma .30 .75
50 Francisco Rodriguez .30 .75
51 Matt Garza .25 .60
52 Jake Marisnick .25 .60
53 Brandon Crawford .30 .75
54 Javier Baez RC 4.00 10.00
55 Jonah Keri .25 .60
56 Apollo Creed .25 .60
57 David Cross .25 .60
58 Jacob deGrom .75 2.00
59 Hector Rondon .25 .60
60 Marcus Semien .40 1.00
61 Domonic Brown .30 .75
62 Andrelton Simmons .25 .60
63 Edwin Escobar RC .40 1.00
64 Austin Jackson .25 .60
65 David Ortiz .40 1.00
66 Billy Butler .25 .60
67 Malcolm Gladwell .25 .60
68 Matt Barnes RC .40 1.00
69 Christian Bethancourt .25 .60
70 Kyle Seager .25 .60
71 J.D. Martinez .40 1.00
72 Joe Panik .30 .75
73 Daniel Murphy .30 .75
74 Casey McGehee .25 .60
75 Brandon Phillips .25 .60
76 Jake Arrieta .30 .75
77 Jason Hammel .30 .75
78 Carlos Gonzalez .30 .75
79 Grant Miller .25 .60
80 Joe Gatto .25 .60
81 Buck Farmer RC .40 1.00
82 Dalton Pompey RC .50 1.25
83 Matt Harvey .30 .75
84 Josh Harrison .25 .60
85 Kris Bryant RC 6.00 15.00
86 Rick Porcello .30 .75
87 Francisco Liriano .25 .60
88 Carl Crawford .30 .75
89 Jonathan Papelbon .30 .75
90 Darren Rovell .25 .60
91 Howie Kendrick .25 .60
92 Michelle Beadle .25 .60
93 Kelia Moniz .25 .60
94 Xander Bogaerts .40 1.00
95 Kole Calhoun .25 .60
96 Tim Hudson .30 .75
97 Kendall Graveman RC .40 1.00
98 Yimi Garcia RC .40 1.00
99 Yan Gomes .25 .60
100 Greg Holland .25 .60
101 Stephen Strasburg .40 1.00
102 James Clubber Lang .25 .60
103 Salvador Perez .30 .75
104 Didi Gregorius .30 .75
105 Daniel Norris RC .40 1.00
106 Yunel Escobar .25 .60
107 Giancarlo Stanton .40 1.00
108 Prince Fielder .30 .75
109 Troy Tulowitzki .40 1.00
110 Victor Martinez .30 .75
111 Dellin Betances .30 .75
112 Buck 65 .25 .60
113 Ryan Braun .30 .75
114 Brian McCann .30 .75
115 Dustin Pedroia .40 1.00
116 Freddie Freeman .50 1.25
117 Corey Kluber .30 .75
118 Adam Lind .30 .75
119 Paul Scheer .25 .60
120 Matt Adams .25 .60
121 Wei-Yin Chen .25 .60
122 Jesse Hahn .25 .60
123 Micah Johnson RC .40 1.00
124 Lakey Peterson .25 .60
125 Nori Aoki .25 .60
126 Alexei Ramirez .30 .75
127 Nick Castellanos .40 1.00
128 R.A. Dickey .30 .75
129 Yovani Gallardo .25 .60
130 Juan Lagares .25 .60
131 Josh Reddick .25 .60
132 Dilson Herrera RC .50 1.25
133 Addison Russell RC 1.25 3.00
134 Joc Pederson RC 1.50 4.00
135 Mark Teixeira .30 .75
136 Tyson Ross .25 .60
137 Marlon Byrd .25 .60
138 Michael Pineda .25 .60
139 Chris Sale .40 1.00
140 Jose Altuve .30 .75
141 Justin Upton .30 .75
142 Yasiel Puig .40 1.00
143 Mike Zunino .25 .60
144 Brandon Belt .30 .75
145 Santiago Casilla .25 .60
146 Michael Morse .25 .60
147 Yoenis Cespedes .30 .75
148 Yasmany Tomas RC .50 1.25
149 Andrew Heaney .25 .60
150 Brody Stevens .25 .60
151 Jorge Soler RC .60 1.50
152 Jacoby Ellsbury .30 .75
153 Brandon Moss .25 .60
154 Rusney Castillo RC .50 1.25
155 Mike Moustakas .30 .75
156 Brian Dozier .30 .75
157 Jose Reyes .30 .75
158 Kurt Suzuki .25 .60
159 Devin Mesoraco .25 .60
160 Danny Santana .25 .60
161 Bartolo Colon .25 .60
162 Anthony Rizzo .50 1.25
163 Zach Lowe .25 .60
164 Adrian Beltre .40 1.00
165 Jonathan Lucroy .30 .75
166 Carlos Gomez .25 .60
167 Julie Foudy .25 .60
168 Clay Buchholz .25 .60
169 Yordano Ventura .30 .75
170 Chris Davis .25 .60
171 Anthony Rendon .40 1.00
172 Matt Carpenter .40 1.00
173 Buster Posey .50 1.25
174 Joe Mauer .30 .75
175 DJ LeMahieu .40 1.00
176 Jon Niese .25 .60
177 Bernie Williams .30 .75
178 Travis d'Arnaud .30 .75
179 Manny Machado .40 1.00
180 Scott Kazmir .25 .60
181 Drew Hutchison .25 .60
182 Todd Frazier .25 .60
183 Edwin Encarnacion .40 1.00
184 Marcell Ozuna .40 1.00
185 Gus Malzahn .25 .60
186 Desmond Jennings .30 .75
187 Miguel Cabrera .40 1.00
188 Shelby Miller .30 .75
189 Kennys Vargas .25 .60
190 Michael Bourn .25 .60
191 John Lackey .30 .75
192 Fernando Rodney .25 .60
193 Aramis Ramirez .25 .60
194 Zack Cozart .25 .60
195 Torii Hunter .25 .60
196 Ian Kinsler .30 .75
197 Melky Cabrera .25 .60
198 Albert Pujols .50 1.25
199 Zack Greinke .40 1.00
200 Jose Abreu .40 1.00
201 Joe Buck .25 .60
202 Travis Ishikawa .25 .60
203 David Wright .30 .75
204 Chase Headley .25 .60
205 Dustin Ackley .25 .60
206 Erick Aybar .25 .60
207 Derek Norris .25 .60
208 Jose Fernandez .40 1.00
209 Hanley Ramirez .30 .75
210 Starling Marte .30 .75
211 Kyle Lohse .25 .60
212 Chris Tillman .25 .60
213 Elvis Andrus .30 .75
214 Corey Dickerson .25 .60
215 Joey Votto .40 1.00
216 Jake Lamb RC .60 1.50
217 Wade Miley .25 .60
218 Carlos Rodon RC 1.00 2.50
219 Huston Street .25 .60
220 Yasmani Grandal .25 .60
221 Doug Fister .25 .60
222 Gregory Polanco .30 .75
223 Incredibeard .25 .60
224 Edinson Volquez .25 .60
225 Thunderlips .25 .60
226 Nolan Arenado .60 1.50
227 Christian Yelich .50 1.25
228 Robb Wolf .25 .60
229 Ivan Drago .25 .60
230 Keith Law .25 .60
231 Henderson Alvarez .25 .60
232 Matt Holliday .40 1.00
233 Ike Davis .25 .60
234 Michael Cuddyer .25 .60
235 Michael Taylor RC .40 1.00
236 Julio Teheran .30 .75
237 Hyun-Jin Ryu .30 .75
238 Dee Gordon .25 .60
239 Zach Britton .30 .75
240 Trevor May RC .40 1.00
241 CC Sabathia .30 .75
242 James McCann RC .60 1.50
243 Jean Segura .30 .75
244 Jason Kipnis .30 .75
245 Ryan Howard .30 .75
246 Andrew Cashner .25 .60
247 George Springer .30 .75
248 Jose Bautista .30 .75
249 Bryce Harper .60 1.50
250 Jimmy Rollins .30 .75
251 Adam LaRoche .25 .60
252 Mike Trout 2.00 5.00
253 Carlos Beltran .30 .75
254 Alex Gordon .30 .75
255 Steven Moya RC .50 1.25
256 Sonny Gray .30 .75
257 Pablo Sandoval .30 .75
258 Rocky Balboa .25 .60
259 Jonathan Schoop .25 .60
260 Hunter Pence .30 .75
261 Yu Darvish .40 1.00
262 Alex Cobb .25 .60
263 Pedro Alvarez .25 .60
264 Matt Kemp .30 .75
265 Jung Ho Kang RC .40 1.00
266 Drew Storen .25 .60
267 Jered Weaver .30 .75
268 Jimbo Fisher .25 .60
269 Jeremy Roenick .25 .60
270 Mike Foltynewicz RC .40 1.00
271 Dexter Fowler .30 .75
272 Glen Perkins .25 .60
273 Cole Hamels .30 .75
274 Mookie Betts .75 2.00
275 Billy Hamilton .30 .75
276 Alex Rodriguez .50 1.25
277 Starlin Castro .25 .60
278 Cliff Lee .30 .75
279 Jon Jay .25 .60
280 Jenrry Mejia .25 .60
281 Cory Spangenberg RC .40 1.00
282 Adeiny Hechavarria .25 .60
283 Aaron Hill .25 .60
284 Jay Bruce .30 .75
285 Ichiro .50 1.25
286 Addison Reed .25 .60
287 Jon Lester .30 .75
288 Robinson Cano .30 .75
289 Wil Myers .30 .75
290 Ryan Zimmerman .30 .75
291 James Shields .25 .60
292 Grant Balfour .25 .60
293 Philae Probe .25 .60
294 Adam Wainwright .30 .75
295 Joe Nathan .25 .60
296 Kenley Jansen .30 .75
297 Magna Carta .25 .60
298 Rubby De La Rosa .25 .60
299 Brian Quinn .25 .60
300 Bryce Brentz RC .40 1.00
301 Justin Morneau .60 1.50
302 Fall of the Berlin Wall .50 1.25
303 Denard Span .50 1.25
304 Gary Brown RC .50 1.25
305 Chris Carter .50 1.25
306 Stephen Drew .50 1.25
307 Jorge De La Rosa .50 1.25
308 David Freese .50 1.25
309 Gabe Kapler .50 1.25
310 Chris Coghlan .50 1.25
311 Michael Brantley .60 1.50
312 Gerrit Cole .75 2.00
313 Jhonny Peralta .50 1.25
314 Ian Desmond .50 1.25
315 Steve Cishek .50 1.25
316 Evan Gattis .50 1.25
317 Hunter Strickland RC .50 1.25
318 David Price .60 1.50
319 Brian Windhorst .50 1.25
320 Dallas Keuchel .60 1.50
321 Ben Zobrist .60 1.50
322 Mark Melancon .50 1.25
323 Joaquin Benoit .50 1.25
324 Will Middlebrooks .50 1.25
325 Aroldis Chapman .75 2.00
326 Mitch Moreland .50 1.25
327 Jeff Mauro .50 1.25
328 Val Kilmer .50 1.25
329 Brett Gardner .60 1.50
330 Jason Heyward .60 1.50
331 Alcides Escobar .60 1.50
332 Matt Cain .60 1.50
333 Chase Utley .60 1.50
334 Nick Tropeano .50 1.25
335 Collin Cowgill .50 1.25
336 Shane Victorino .60 1.50
337 Mike Olt .50 1.25
338 Mike Napoli .50 1.25
339 Clayton Kershaw 1.25 3.00
340 Neftali Feliz .50 1.25
341 Malala Yousafzai .50 1.25
342 Josh Donaldson .60 1.50
343 Angel Pagan .50 1.25

344 Jordan Zimmermann .60 1.50
345 Lonnie Chisenhall .50 1.25
346 Shin-Soo Choo .60 1.50
347 Aaron Paul .50 1.25
348 Aaron Sanchez .60 1.50
349 Sam Tuivailala RC .50 1.25
350 Masahiro Tanaka .60 1.50

2015 Topps Allen and Ginter X 10th Anniversary Mini

*MINI 1-300: 1X TO 2.5X BASIC
*MINI RC 1-300: .6X TO 1.5X BASIC RCs
*MINI SP 301-350: 1X TO 2.5X BASIC
252 Mike Trout 10.00 25.00

2015 Topps Allen and Ginter X 10th Anniversary Mini A and G Back

*MINI AG BACK 1-300: 1.2X TO 3X BASIC
*MINI AG BACK RC 1-300: .75X TO 2X BASIC RCs
*MINI AG BACK SP 301-350: 1.2X TO 3X BASIC
252 Mike Trout 12.00 30.00

2015 Topps Allen and Ginter X 10th Anniversary Mini Silver

*MINI SLVR 1-300: 2X TO 5X BASIC
*MINI SLVR RC 1-300: 1.2X TO 3X BASIC RCs
*MINI SLVR SP 301-350: 2X TO 5X BASIC
54 Javier Baez 40.00 100.00
85 Kris Bryant 60.00 150.00
252 Mike Trout 20.00 50.00

2016 Topps Allen and Ginter

COMPLETE SET (350) 20.00 50.00
COMP.SET w/o SP's (300) 12.00 30.00
SP ODDS 1:2 HOBBY
ORIGINAL BUYBACK ODDS 1:6679 HOBBY
ORIG.BUYBACK PRINT RUN 1 SER.#'d SET
1 Jorge Soler .25 .60
2 Ryan Braun .20 .50
3 Joey Gallo .20 .50
4 Justin Verlander .25 .60
5 Kyle Waldrop RC .30 .75
6 Luke Maile RC .25 .60
7 John Lamb RC .25 .60
8 Denise Austin .20 .50
9 Tom Glavine .20 .50
10 Jason Sklar .20 .50
11 Howie Kendrick .15 .40
12 Trevor Story RC 1.25 3.00
13 Kevin Gausman .25 .60
14 Kendrys Morales .15 .40
15 Mark Trumbo .15 .40
16 Trayce Thompson RC .40 1.00
17 Ian Desmond .15 .40
18 Kolten Wong .20 .50
19 Rollie Fingers .20 .50
20 Michael Pineda .15 .40
21 Ben Zobrist .20 .50
22 Francisco Rodriguez .20 .50
23 Addison Russell .25 .60
24 Max Kepler RC .40 1.00
25 Charlie Blackmon .25 .60
26 John Lackey .20 .50
27 Matt Duffy .15 .40
28 Elvis Andrus .20 .50
29 Jay Bruce .20 .50
30 Curtis Granderson .20 .50
31 Brad Ziegler .15 .40
32 Falcon 9 Rocket .20 .50
33 Ender Inciarte .15 .40
34 Rick Klein .20 .50
35 Jayson Werth .20 .50
36 Alex Rodriguez .30 .75
37 Dawn Spacecraft .20 .50
38 David Peralta .15 .40
39 Paul Goldschmidt .25 .60
40 Jordan Zimmermann .20 .50
41 Drew Smyly .15 .40
42 Cuban Embassy .20 .50
43 Jake Odorizzi .15 .40
44 Miguel Castro RC .25 .60
45 Laurence Leavy .20 .50
46 Ben Revere .15 .40
47 Corey Dickerson .15 .40
48 J.T. Realmuto .25 .60
49 Ketel Marte RC .50 1.25
50 Daniel Murphy .20 .50
51 A.J. Ramos .15 .40
52 Adam Eaton .15 .40
53 Logan Forsythe .15 .40
54 Jose Abreu .25 .60
55 Hector Rondon .15 .40
56 Carlos Correa .25 .60
57 Jim Rice .20 .50
58 Freddie Freeman .30 .75
59 Billy Hamilton .20 .50
60 Devin Mesoraco .15 .40
61 Miguel Cabrera .25 .60
62 Dellin Betances .20 .50
63 Monica Abbott .20 .50
64 Steve Schirripa .20 .50
65 Hisashi Iwakuma .20 .50
66 Miguel Sano RC .40 1.00
67 Melky Cabrera .15 .40
68 Dexter Fowler .20 .50
69 Roberto Alomar .20 .50
70 Chase Headley .15 .40
71 Matt Reynolds RC .25 .60
72 Jake McGee .20 .50
73 James Shields .15 .40
74 Brian Dozier .20 .50
75 Mike Moustakas .20 .50
76 Collin McHugh .15 .40
77 Kevin Pillar .15 .40
78 Jose Berrios RC .40 1.00
79 Dustin Garneau RC .25 .60
80 Edwin Encarnacion .25 .60
81 Brian Johnson RC .25 .60
82 Gerardo Parra .15 .40
83 David Wright .20 .50
84 Robinson Cano .20 .50
85 Prince Fielder .20 .50
86 Adam Jones .20 .50
87 Craig Kimbrel .20 .50
88 Jose Fernandez .25 .60
89 Dallas Keuchel .20 .50
90 George Lopez .20 .50
91 Nick Hundley .15 .40
92 Steven Matz .15 .40
93 Mike Piazza .25 .60
94 Todd Frazier .15 .40
95 Jimmy Nelson .15 .40
96 Jason Kipnis .20 .50
97 Kyle Schwarber RC .75 2.00
98 Michael Conforto RC .30 .75
99 Luis Severino RC .30 .75
100 Rob Refsnyder RC .30 .75
101 Roger Clemens .30 .75
102 Aaron Nola RC .50 1.25
103 Carlos Martinez .20 .50
104 Byron Buxton .25 .60
105 Alex Dickerson RC .25 .60
106 Steve Spurrier .20 .50
107 Matt Stonie .20 .50
108 Justin Turner .25 .60
109 Eduardo Rodriguez .15 .40
110 Michele Steele .20 .50
111 Lorenzo Cain .15 .40
112 Kris Bryant .30 .75
113 Alcides Escobar .20 .50
114 Randy Sklar .20 .50
115 Brad Miller .20 .50
116 Jose Reyes .20 .50
117 Robin Yount .25 .60
118 Evan Gattis .15 .40
119 Gennady Golovkin 4.00 10.00
120 K.Maeda RC/J.Urias RC .50 1.25
121 Corey Seager RC 2.50 6.00
122 Andrew Heaney .15 .40
123 Alex Cobb .15 .40
124 Jonathan Lucroy .20 .50
125 Carl Edwards Jr. RC .30 .75
126 Greg Bird RC .30 .75
127 Lucas Duda .20 .50
128 Aroldis Chapman .25 .60
129 Zack Greinke .25 .60
130 Gregory Polanco .20 .50
131 Brooks Robinson .20 .50
132 Leigh Steinberg .20 .50
133 Joc Pederson .20 .50
134 Henry Owens .20 .50
135 Luis Gonzalez .20 .50
136 Matt Kemp .20 .50
137 Marcus Semien .25 .60
138 Cord McCoy .20 .50
139 Gio Gonzalez .20 .50
140 Caleb Cotham RC .30 .75
141 Colin Rea RC .25 .60
142 Jake Arrieta .20 .50
143 Adrian Gonzalez .20 .50
144 Matt Holliday .25 .60
145 Mike Greenberg .20 .50
146 Evan Longoria .20 .50
147 Martin Prado .15 .40
148 Kole Calhoun .15 .40
149 Michael Brantley .20 .50
150 Eric Hosmer .20 .50
151 David Ortiz .25 .60
152 Gary Sanchez RC .75 2.00
153 Jung Ho Kang .15 .40
154 Ervin Santana .15 .40
155 Brandon Phillips .15 .40
156 Jason Heyward .20 .50
157 Gerrit Cole .25 .60
158 Joe McKeehen .20 .50
159 Brett Gardner .20 .50
160 Steve Kerr .20 .50
161 Vinny G .20 .50
162 Josh Harrison .15 .40
163 Zach Lee RC .25 .60
164 Steven Souza Jr. .20 .50
165 Nelson Cruz .25 .60
166 Morgan Spurlock .20 .50
167 Jeff Samardzija .15 .40
168 Don Mattingly .50 1.25
169 Adrian Beltre .25 .60
170 Max Scherzer .25 .60
171 Brandon Crawford .20 .50
172 Joe Morgan .20 .50
173 Billy Burns .15 .40
174 Frankie Montas RC .30 .75
175 Jonathan Schoop .15 .40
176 Neil Walker .15 .40
177 Mark Teixeira .20 .50
178 David Robertson .15 .40
179 Jen Welter .20 .50
180 Ryne Sandberg .50 1.25
181 Alex Wood .15 .40
182 Nolan Arenado .40 1.00
183 Andrew McCutchen .25 .60
184 Mookie Betts .50 1.25
185 J.D. Martinez .25 .60
186 Alex Gordon .20 .50
187 Carl Yastrzemski .40 1.00
188 Edgar Martinez .20 .50
189 Buster Posey .30 .75
190 Jon Gray RC .25 .60
191 Anthony Anderson .20 .50
192 Dennis Eckersley .20 .50
193 Huston Street .15 .40
194 Mike Trout 1.25 3.00
195 Joey Votto .25 .60
196 Josh Reddick .15 .40
197 George Springer .20 .50
198 Ari Shaffir .20 .50
199 Carlton Fisk .20 .50
200 Carlos Gomez .15 .40
201 Byung Ho Park RC .30 .75
202 Missy Franklin .20 .50
203 Ernie Johnson .20 .50
204 Drew Storen .15 .40
205 Carlos Santana .20 .50
206 Bob Gibson .20 .50
207 Brandon Belt .20 .50
208 Joe Panik .20 .50
209 Andrew Miller .20 .50
210 Michael Breed .20 .50
211 Albert Pujols .30 .75
212 Maria Sharapova .20 .50
213 Heidi Watney .20 .50
214 Justin Bour .20 .50
215 Khris Davis .25 .60
216 Hannah Storm .20 .50
217 Julio Teheran .20 .50
218 Masahiro Tanaka .20 .50
219 Delino DeShields .15 .40
220 Matt Duffy .15 .40
221 Brian McCann .20 .50
222 Nomar Mazara RC .40 1.00
223 Erick Aybar .15 .40
224 Gary Carter .20 .50
225 Brandon Drury RC .40 1.00
226 Luke Jackson RC .25 .60
227 Timothy Busfield .20 .50
228 Colin Cowherd .20 .50
229 Mitch Moreland .15 .40
230 Jessica Mendoza .20 .50
231 Kaleb Cowart RC .25 .60
232 Hector Olivera RC .30 .75
233 Adam Lind .20 .50
234 Glen Perkins .15 .40
235 Cheyenne Woods .20 .50
236 Brad Boxberger .15 .40
237 Dustin Pedroia .25 .60
238 Tyler White RC .25 .60
239 Brandon Moss .15 .40
240 Robert Raiola .20 .50
241 Orlando Jones .20 .50
242 DJ LeMahieu .25 .60
243 Jay Oakerson .20 .50
244 Gravitational Waves .20 .50
245 Dwier Brown .20 .50
246 Mike Francesa .20 .50
247 Papal Visit .20 .50
248 Jill Martin .20 .50
249 Paul McBeth 1.25 3.00
250 Jose Canseco .20 .50
251 Stephen Piscotty RC .40 1.00
252 Cole Hamels .20 .50
253 Ozzie Smith .30 .75
254 Bryce Harper .40 1.00
255 Nomar Garciaparra .20 .50
256 Starling Marte .20 .50
257 Chris Archer .15 .40
258 Kenley Jansen .20 .50
259 Jose Peraza RC .30 .75
260 Anthony Rizzo .30 .75
261 Carlos Carrasco .15 .40
262 Giancarlo Stanton .25 .60
263 Hanley Ramirez .20 .50
264 Xander Bogaerts .25 .60
265 Felix Hernandez .20 .50
266 Anthony Rendon .25 .60
267 Sonny Gray .20 .50
268 Frank Thomas .25 .60
269 Maikel Franco .20 .50
270 David Price .20 .50
271 A.J. Pollock .15 .40
272 Troy Tulowitzki .25 .60
273 Dee Gordon .15 .40
274 Chris Sale .25 .60
275 Jacob deGrom .50 1.25
276 Matt Harvey .20 .50
277 Manny Machado .25 .60
278 Madison Bumgarner .20 .50
279 Paul Molitor .25 .60
280 Paul O'Neill .20 .50
281 Jose Bautista .20 .50
282 Stephen Strasburg .25 .60
283 Michael Wacha .20 .50
284 Orlando Cepeda .20 .50
285 Josh Donaldson .20 .50
286 Guido Knudson RC .25 .60
287 Andre Dawson .20 .50
288 Lance McCullers .15 .40
289 Jose Quintana .15 .40
290 Andrew Faulkner RC .30 .75
291 Kevin Kiermaier .20 .50
292 Marcell Ozuna .25 .60
293 Jonathan Papelbon .20 .50
294 Carlos Rodon .25 .60
295 Jose Altuve .20 .50
296 Rickey Henderson .25 .60
297 Corey Kluber .20 .50
298 Jacoby Ellsbury .20 .50
299 Clayton Kershaw .40 1.00
300 Trea Turner RC .75 2.00
301 Tyson Ross SP .40 1.00
302 Trevor Brown SP RC .50 1.25
303 Wei-Yin Chen SP .40 1.00
304 Yasmani Grandal SP .40 1.00
305 Tyler Duffey SP RC .40 1.00
306 Yu Darvish SP .60 1.50
307 Russell Martin SP .40 1.00
308 Andy Pettitte SP .50 1.25
309 Yasmany Tomas SP .40 1.00
310 Patrick Corbin SP .50 1.25
311 Wellington Castillo SP .40 1.00
312 Carlos Beltran SP .50 1.25
313 Stephen Vogt SP .50 1.25
314 Starlin Castro SP .40 1.00
315 Santiago Casilla SP .40 1.00
316 Ryan Weber SP RC .40 1.00
317 Yordano Ventura SP .50 1.25
318 Pedro Severino SP RC .40 1.00
319 Yasiel Puig SP .60 1.50
320 Roberto Clemente SP 1.50 4.00
321 Nick Castellanos SP .60 1.50
322 Ryan LaMarre SP RC .40 1.00
323 Victor Martinez SP .50 1.25
324 Rob Refsnyder SP .50 1.25
325 Raisel Iglesias SP .50 1.25
326 Peter O'Brien SP RC .40 1.00
327 Raul Mondesi SP RC .75 2.00
328 Randal Grichuk SP .40 1.00
329 Andre Ethier SP .50 1.25
330 Zack Godley SP RC .40 1.00
331 Taijuan Walker SP .40 1.00
332 Yan Gomes SP .40 1.00
333 Shin-Soo Choo SP .50 1.25
334 Scott Kazmir SP .40 1.00
335 Shawn Tolleson SP .40 1.00
336 Tom Murphy SP RC .40 1.00
337 Steve Cishek SP .40 1.00
338 Stephen Piscotty SP .60 1.50
339 Salvador Perez SP .50 1.25
340 Roberto Osuna SP .40 1.00
341 Richie Shaffer SP RC .40 1.00
342 Trea Turner SP 1.25 3.00
343 Shelby Miller SP .50 1.25
344 Ryan Zimmerman SP .50 1.25
345 Wil Myers SP .50 1.25
346 Pablo Sandoval SP .50 1.25
347 Sean Doolittle SP .40 1.00
348 Trevor Plouffe SP .40 1.00
349 Travis d'Arnaud SP .50 1.25
350 Steve Carlton SP .50 1.25
NNO Julio Urias 4.00 10.00

2016 Topps Allen and Ginter Mini

COMP.SET w/o EXT (350) 100.00 250.00
*MINI 1-300: 1X TO 2.5X BASIC
*MINI 1-300 RC: .6X TO 1.5X BASIC RCs
*MINI SP 301-350: .6X TO 1.5X BASIC
MINI SP ODDS 1:13 HOBBY
351-400 RANDOM WITHIN RIP CARDS
STATED PLATE ODDS 1:415 HOBBY
PLATE PRINT RUN 1 SET PER COLOR
BLACK-CYAN-MAGENTA-YELLOW ISSUED
NO PLATE PRICING DUE TO SCARCITY
351 Stephen Piscotty EXT 20.00 50.00
352 Rickey Henderson EXT 25.00 60.00
353 Carlos Correa EXT 25.00 60.00
354 Andrew McCutchen EXT 20.00 50.00
355 Mike Piazza EXT 20.00 50.00
356 Jason Kipnis EXT 25.00 60.00
357 Adrian Gonzalez EXT 15.00 40.00
358 Clayton Kershaw EXT 30.00 80.00
359 Matt Harvey EXT 20.00 50.00
360 Ryne Sandberg EXT 25.00 60.00
361 Ryan Braun EXT 15.00 40.00
362 Corey Seager EXT 50.00 120.00
363 Adrian Beltre EXT 20.00 50.00
364 Kyle Schwarber EXT 25.00 60.00
365 Dallas Keuchel EXT 15.00 40.00
366 David Price EXT 15.00 40.00
367 Joey Votto EXT 20.00 50.00
368 Jacoby Ellsbury EXT 15.00 40.00
369 Mike Trout EXT 100.00 250.00
370 Jason Heyward EXT 15.00 40.00
371 Todd Frazier EXT 12.00 30.00
372 Nolan Arenado EXT 30.00 80.00
373 Bryce Harper EXT 30.00 80.00
374 Manny Machado EXT 20.00 50.00
375 Felix Hernandez EXT 20.00 50.00
376 Matt Kemp EXT 20.00 50.00
377 Lorenzo Cain EXT 12.00 30.00
378 Luis Severino EXT 15.00 40.00
379 Trea Turner EXT 40.00 100.00
380 Maikel Franco EXT 15.00 40.00
381 Freddie Freeman EXT 25.00 60.00
382 Madison Bumgarner EXT 15.00 40.00
383 Sonny Gray EXT 15.00 40.00
384 Edwin Encarnacion EXT 20.00 50.00
385 J.D. Martinez EXT 20.00 50.00
386 Tom Glavine EXT 20.00 50.00
387 Jake Arrieta EXT 15.00 40.00
388 Zack Greinke EXT 20.00 50.00
389 Brian Dozier EXT 15.00 40.00
390 Michael Conforto EXT 25.00 60.00
391 Corey Dickerson EXT 20.00 50.00
392 Xander Bogaerts EXT 20.00 50.00
393 Robinson Cano EXT 20.00 50.00
394 Paul Molitor EXT 20.00 50.00
395 Joe Morgan EXT 30.00 80.00
396 Max Scherzer EXT 20.00 50.00
397 Dee Gordon EXT 12.00 30.00
398 Joey Gallo EXT 15.00 40.00
399 Chris Archer EXT 12.00 30.00
400 Jose Bautista EXT 15.00 40.00

2016 Topps Allen and Ginter Mini A and G Back

*MINI AG 1-300: 1.2X TO 3X BASIC
*MINI AG 1-300 RC: .75X TO 2X BASIC RCs
*MINI AG SP 301-350: .75X TO 2X BASIC
MINI AG ODDS 1:5 HOBBY
MINI AG SP ODDS 1:65 HOBBY

2016 Topps Allen and Ginter Mini Black

*MINI BLK 1-300: 1.5X TO 4X BASIC
*MINI BLK 1-300 RC: 1X TO 2.5X BASIC RCs
*MINI BLK SP 301-350: 1X TO 2.5X BASIC
MINI BLK ODDS 1:10 HOBBY
MINI BLK SP ODDS 1:130 HOBBY

2016 Topps Allen and Ginter Mini Brooklyn Back

*MINI BRK 1-300: 12X TO 30X BASIC
*MINI BRK 1-300 RC: 8X TO 20X BASIC RCs
*MINI BRK SP 301-350: 5X TO 12X BASIC
MINI BRK ODDS 1:146 HOBBY
STATED PRINT RUN 25 SER.#'d SETS

2016 Topps Allen and Ginter Mini No Card Number

*MINI NNO 1-300: 5X TO 12X BASIC
*MINI NNO 1-300 RC: 3X TO 8X BASIC RCs
*MINI NNO SP 301-350: 2X TO 5X BASIC
MINI NNO ODDS 1:73 HOBBY

2016 Topps Allen and Ginter Ancient Rome Coin Relics

STATED ODDS 1:1110 HOBBY
ARR1 The Colosseum 75.00 200.00
ARR2 Arch of Septimius Severus 50.00 100.00
ARR3 Verona Arena 50.00 100.00
ARR4 Pont du Gard Aqueduct 50.00 100.00
ARR5 Aqueduct of Segovia 50.00 100.00
ARR6 Roman Baths 50.00 100.00
ARR7 Palmyra 50.00 100.00
ARR8 The Pantheon 60.00 150.00
ARR9 Tower of Hercules 50.00 100.00
ARR10 Hadrian's Wall 50.00 100.00
ARR11 Castel Sant'Angelo 50.00 100.00
ARR12 Porta Nigra 50.00 100.00
ARR13 Arch of Constantine 50.00 100.00
ARR14 Arch of Titus 50.00 100.00
ARR15 Baths of Caracalla 50.00 100.00
ARR16 Pompeii 75.00 200.00
ARR17 Arena in Arles 50.00 100.00
ARR18 Pula Arena 50.00 100.00
ARR19 Library of Celsus 50.00 100.00
ARR20 Theatre of Bosra 50.00 100.00
ARR21 Maison Carree 50.00 100.00
ARR22 Curia Julia 50.00 100.00
ARR23 Alcantara Bridge 50.00 120.00
ARR24 Baalbek 50.00 120.00

2016 Topps Allen and Ginter Baseball Legends

COMPLETE SET (25) 6.00 15.00
STATED ODDS 1:5 HOBBY
BL1 Al Kaline .40 1.00
BL2 Carl Yastrzemski .60 1.50
BL3 Babe Ruth 1.00 2.50
BL4 Jackie Robinson .40 1.00
BL5 Ty Cobb .60 1.50
BL6 Duke Snider .30 .75
BL7 Johnny Bench .40 1.00
BL8 George Brett .75 2.00
BL9 Roberto Clemente 1.00 2.50
BL10 Hank Aaron .75 2.00
BL11 Ted Williams .75 2.00
BL12 Reggie Jackson .30 .75
BL13 Jim Palmer .30 .75
BL14 Larry Doby .30 .75
BL15 Whitey Ford .30 .75
BL16 Bob Feller .30 .75
BL17 Honus Wagner .40 1.00
BL18 Willie Mays .75 2.00
BL19 Ken Griffey Jr. .75 2.00
BL20 Willie Stargell .30 .75
BL21 Cal Ripken Jr. 1.25 3.00
BL22 Rod Carew .30 .75
BL23 Nolan Ryan 1.25 3.00
BL24 Sandy Koufax .75 2.00
BL25 Eddie Mathews .40 1.00

2016 Topps Allen and Ginter Box Topper Relics

STATED ODDS 1:111 HOBBY BOXES
STATED PRINT RUN 25 SER.#'d SETS
BLRAM Andrew McCutchen 30.00 80.00
BLRAP Albert Pujols 12.00 30.00
BLRDO David Ortiz 30.00 80.00
BLRDW David Wright 30.00 80.00
BLRGS Giancarlo Stanton 12.00 30.00
BLRJD Jacob deGrom 20.00 50.00
BLRMC Miguel Cabrera 25.00 60.00
BLRMH Matt Harvey 8.00 20.00
BLRMTA Masahiro Tanaka 8.00 20.00
BLRMTR Mike Trout 60.00 150.00

2016 Topps Allen and Ginter Box Toppers

BLAM Andrew McCutchen 1.50 4.00
BLAP Albert Pujols 2.00 5.00
BLAR Anthony Rizzo 2.00 5.00
BLBH Bryce Harper 2.50 6.00
BLBP Buster Posey 2.00 5.00
BLCK Clayton Kershaw 2.50 6.00
BLDO David Ortiz 1.50 4.00
BLDW David Wright 1.25 3.00
BLFH Felix Hernandez 1.25 3.00
BLGS Giancarlo Stanton 1.50 4.00
BLJD Jacob deGrom 3.00 8.00
BLMH Matt Harvey 1.25 3.00
BLMT Mike Trout 8.00 20.00
BLPG Paul Goldschmidt 1.50 4.00
BLTT Troy Tulowitzki 1.50 4.00

2016 Topps Allen and Ginter Double Rip Cards

STATED ODDS 1:720 HOBBY
PRINT RUNS B/WN 25-50 COPIES PER
PRICING FOR UNRIPPED
UNRIPPED HAVE ADD'L CARDS WITHIN
DRIP1 M.Bumgarner/B.Posey 75.00 200.00
DRIP2 K.Schwarber/K.Bryant 75.00 200.00
DRIP3 C.Correa/K.Bryant 75.00 200.00
DRIP4 M.Harvey/J.deGrom 75.00 200.00
DRIP5 B.Harper/M.Trout 75.00 200.00
DRIP6 J.Bautista/J.Donaldson 75.00 200.00
DRIP7 H.Aaron/B.Ruth 175.00 350.00
DRIP8 M.Piazza/K.Griffey Jr. 75.00 200.00
DRIP9 D.Ortiz/H.Owens 75.00 200.00
DRIP10 M.Machado/C.Ripken Jr. 75.00 200.00
DRIP11 S.Perez/A.Gordon 75.00 200.00
DRIP12 J.Arrieta/D.Keuchel 75.00 200.00
DRIP13 J.Verlander/M.Cabrera 75.00 200.00
DRIP14 O.Smith/Y.Molina 75.00 200.00
DRIP15 A.McCutchen/W.Stargell 75.00 200.00
DRIP16 A.Nola/C.Schilling 75.00 200.00
DRIP17 L.Severino/M.Tanaka 75.00 200.00
DRIP18 K.Maeda/C.Kershaw 75.00 200.00
DRIP19 Z.Greinke/R.Johnson 75.00 200.00
DRIP20 I.Suzuki/G.Stanton 75.00 200.00

2016 Topps Allen and Ginter Double Rip Cards Ripped

UNRIPPED ODDS 1:720 HOBBY
PRINT RUNS B/WN 25-50 COPIES PER
PRICING FOR CLEANLY RIPPED CARDS
DRIP1 Bumgarner/Posey/50 4.00 10.00
DRIP2 Schwarber/Bryant/50 6.00 15.00
DRIP3 Correa/Bryant/50 4.00 10.00
DRIP4 Harvey/deGrom/50 6.00 15.00
DRIP5 Harper/Trout/50 15.00 40.00
DRIP6 J.Bautista/J.Donaldson/50 2.50 6.00
DRIP7 Aaron/Ruth/50 8.00 20.00
DRIP8 Piazza/Griffey Jr./50 6.00 15.00
DRIP9 D.Ortiz/H.Owens/50 3.00 8.00
DRIP10 Machado/Ripken/50 10.00 25.00
DRIP11 S.Perez/A.Gordon/25 2.50 6.00
DRIP12 J.Arrieta/D.Keuchel/25 2.50 6.00
DRIP13 Verlander/Cabrera/50 3.00 8.00
DRIP14 Smith/Molina/50 4.00 10.00
DRIP15 A.McCutchen/W.Stargell/50 3.00 8.00
DRIP16 A.Nola/C.Schilling/50 4.00 10.00
DRIP17 L.Severino/M.Tanaka/50 2.50 6.00
DRIP18 Maeda/Kershaw/50 5.00 12.00
DRIP19 Z.Greinke/R.Johnson/50 3.00 8.00
DRIP20 Suzuki/Stanton/50 4.00 10.00

2016 Topps Allen and Ginter Framed Mini Autographs

STATED ODDS 1:48 HOBBY
EXCHANGE DEADLINE 6/30/2018
AGAAA Anthony Anderson 8.00 20.00
AGAAG Andres Galarraga 5.00 12.00
AGAAN Aaron Nola 20.00 50.00
AGAAS Ari Shaffir 4.00 10.00
AGABD Brandon Drury 6.00 15.00
AGABH Bryce Harper 125.00 300.00
AGABHP Byung-Ho Park 5.00 12.00
AGABJ Brian Johnson 4.00 10.00
AGABM Brandon Moss 4.00 10.00
AGABP Buster Posey 40.00 100.00
AGABS Blake Snell 10.00 25.00
AGACA Canelo Alvarez 60.00 150.00
AGACC Colin Cowherd 10.00 25.00
AGACC Carlos Correa 40.00 100.00
AGACE Carl Edwards Jr. 5.00 12.00
AGACM Cord McCoy 4.00 10.00
AGACR Colin Rea 4.00 10.00
AGACSA Chris Sale 10.00 25.00
AGACSE Corey Seager 30.00 80.00
AGACW Cheyenne Woods 8.00 20.00
AGADA Denise Austin 6.00 15.00
AGADB Dwier Brown 4.00 10.00
AGADK Dallas Keuchel 12.00 30.00
AGADL DJ LeMahieu 10.00 25.00
AGAEJ Ernie Johnson 25.00 60.00
AGAES Errol Spence Jr. 25.00 60.00
AGAFH Felix Hernandez 12.00 30.00
AGAFM Frankie Montas 5.00 12.00
AGAFV Fernando Valenzuela 20.00 50.00
AGAFW Frank Whaley 8.00 20.00
AGAGB Greg Bird 5.00 12.00
AGAGG Gennady Golovkin 150.00 400.00
AGAGL George Lopez 12.00 30.00
AGAHA Hank Aaron 120.00 300.00
AGAHOL Hector Olivera 5.00 12.00
AGAHS Hannah Storm 8.00 20.00
AGAHW Heidi Watney 15.00 40.00
AGAJBA Javier Baez 25.00 60.00
AGAJBE Jose Berrios 6.00 15.00
AGAJC Jose Canseco 12.00 30.00
AGAJD Jacob deGrom 30.00 80.00
AGAJM Jill Martin 4.00 10.00
AGAJME Jessica Mendoza 6.00 15.00
AGAJMK Joe McKeehen 6.00 15.00
AGAJO Jay Oakerson 6.00 15.00
AGAJP Jose Peraza 5.00 12.00
AGAJS Jorge Soler 6.00 15.00
AGAJS Jason Sklar 8.00 20.00
AGAJW Jen Welter 4.00 10.00
AGAKB Kris Bryant 75.00 200.00
AGAKG Ken Griffey Jr. 125.00 300.00
AGAKMA Kenta Maeda 20.00 50.00
AGAKMR Ketel Marte 8.00 20.00
AGAKS Kyle Schwarber 20.00 50.00
AGAKW Kyle Waldrop 5.00 12.00
AGALG Luis Gonzalez 5.00 12.00
AGALJ Luke Jackson 4.00 10.00
AGALL Laurence Leavy 4.00 10.00
AGALS Leigh Steinberg 6.00 15.00
AGALS Luis Severino 20.00 50.00
AGAMAB Monica Abbott 6.00 15.00
AGAMB Mike Breed 4.00 10.00
AGAMCA Miguel Castro 4.00 10.00
AGAMCO Michael Conforto 12.00 30.00
AGAMFA Mike Francesa 10.00 25.00
AGAMFR Missy Franklin 10.00 25.00
AGAMG Mike Greenberg 10.00 25.00
AGAMIS Michele Steele 8.00 20.00
AGAMP Mike Piazza 40.00 100.00
AGAMPH Michael Phelps 125.00 300.00
AGAMRE Michael Reed 4.00 10.00
AGAMRY Matt Reynolds 4.00 10.00
AGAMS Miguel Sano 6.00 15.00
AGAMSH Maria Sharapova 60.00 150.00
AGAMSP Morgan Spurlock 6.00 15.00
AGAMST Matt Stonie 12.00 30.00
AGAMST Marcus Stroman 5.00 12.00
AGAMT Mike Trout 150.00 400.00
AGANG Nomar Garciaparra 15.00 40.00
AGANL Nancy Lieberman 10.00 25.00
AGANM Nomar Mazara 12.00 30.00
AGAOJO Orlando Jones 8.00 20.00
AGAPM Paul Molitor 20.00 50.00
AGAPMB Paul McBeth 30.00 80.00
AGARC Ricky Craven 4.00 10.00
AGARC Robinson Cano 8.00 20.00
AGARKI Kevin Costner 175.00 350.00
AGARK Rick Klein 4.00 10.00
AGARR Rob Refsnyder 5.00 12.00
AGARRO Robert Raiola 4.00 10.00
AGARS Richie Shaffer 4.00 10.00
AGARSK Randy Sklar 10.00 25.00
AGASK Steve Kerr 12.00 30.00
AGASP Stephen Piscotty 8.00 20.00
AGASS Steve Spurrier 15.00 40.00
AGASSA Susan Sarandon 50.00 120.00
AGASSC Steve Schirripa 4.00 10.00
AGATB Timothy Busfield 10.00 25.00
AGATM Tom Murphy 4.00 10.00
AGATS Trevor Story 15.00 40.00
AGATT Trea Turner 12.00 30.00
AGATW Tyler White 4.00 10.00
AGAVGU Vinny G 10.00 25.00
AGAZL Zach Lee 4.00 10.00
AGAZW Zack Wheeler 5.00 12.00

2016 Topps Allen and Ginter Framed Mini Autographs Black

*BLACK: .75X TO 2X BASIC
STATED ODDS 1:382 HOBBY
STATED PRINT RUN 25 SER.#'d SETS
EXCHANGE DEADLINE 6/30/2018

2016 Topps Allen and Ginter Framed Mini Relics

STATED ODDS 1:122 HOBBY
AGRI Ichiro Suzuki 6.00 15.00
AGRAG Adrian Gonzalez 4.00 10.00
AGRAJ Adam Jones 4.00 10.00
AGRAM Andrew McCutchen
AGRAPU Albert Pujols 6.00 15.00
AGRARI Anthony Rizzo 5.00 15.00
AGRARU Addison Russell 5.00 12.00
AGRAW Adam Wainwright 4.00 10.00
AGRBH Bryce Harper 6.00 15.00
AGRBL Barry Larkin 8.00 20.00
AGRBP Buster Posey 6.00 15.00
AGRBR Babe Ruth 150.00 300.00
AGRCBE Carlos Beltran 4.00 10.00
AGRCBI Craig Biggio 4.00 10.00
AGRCKE Clayton Kershaw 6.00 15.00
AGRCKL Corey Kluber 4.00 10.00
AGRCR Cal Ripken Jr. 10.00 25.00
AGRCY Carl Yastrzemski 8.00 20.00
AGRDO David Ortiz 5.00 12.00
AGRDPE Dustin Pedroia 5.00 12.00
AGRDW David Wright 4.00 10.00
AGREL Evan Longoria 4.00 10.00
AGRFH Felix Hernandez 4.00 10.00
AGRGB George Brett 8.00 20.00
AGRGST Giancarlo Stanton 5.00 12.00
AGRJAB Jose Abreu 5.00 12.00
AGRJD Josh Donaldson 4.00 10.00
AGRJDG Jacob deGrom 10.00 25.00
AGRJE Jacoby Ellsbury 4.00 10.00
AGRJF Jose Fernandez 5.00 12.00
AGRJL Jon Lester 4.00 10.00
AGRJV Joey Votto 5.00 12.00
AGRKB Kris Bryant 8.00 20.00
AGRMC Miguel Cabrera 5.00 12.00
AGRMH Matt Harvey 4.00 10.00
AGRMMA Manny Machado 5.00 12.00
AGRMMG Mark McGwire 6.00 15.00
AGRMP Mike Piazza 8.00 20.00
AGRMTA Masahiro Tanaka 4.00 10.00
AGRMTR Mike Trout 12.00 30.00
AGRPS Pablo Sandoval 4.00 10.00
AGRRC Rod Carew 4.00 10.00
AGRTC Ty Cobb 125.00 250.00
AGRTL Tim Lincecum 4.00 10.00
AGRTR Tyson Ross 3.00 8.00
AGRTW Ted Williams
AGRVM Victor Martinez 4.00 10.00
AGRYM Yadier Molina 6.00 15.00
AGRYP Yasiel Puig 5.00 12.00
AGRYV Yordano Ventura 4.00 10.00

2016 Topps Allen and Ginter Mascots in the Wild

INSERTED IN RETAIL PACKS
MIW1 Bobcat 1.00 2.50
MIW2 Tiger 1.00 2.50
MIW3 Eagle 1.00 2.50
MIW4 Cardinal 1.00 2.50
MIW5 Bear 1.00 2.50
MIW6 Horse 1.00 2.50
MIW7 Moose 1.00 2.50
MIW8 Elephant 1.00 2.50
MIW9 Parrot 1.00 2.50

2016 Topps Allen and Ginter Mini Ferocious Felines

COMPLETE SET (15) 8.00 20.00
STATED ODDS 1:25 HOBBY
FF1 Bengal Tiger .75 2.00
FF2 Clouded Leopard .75 2.00
FF3 Canadian Lynx .75 2.00
FF4 Jaguar .75 2.00
FF5 African Lion .75 2.00
FF6 North American Cougar .75 2.00
FF7 South African Cheetah .75 2.00
FF8 Cheetah .75 2.00
FF9 Classic Tabby .75 2.00
FF10 Sand Cat .75 2.00
FF11 Manx Cat .75 2.00
FF12 Serval .75 2.00
FF13 Ocelot .75 2.00
FF14 Caracal .75 2.00
FF15 Siberian Tiger .75 2.00

2016 Topps Allen and Ginter Mini Greenland Explorer

STATED ODDS 1:26,436 HOBBY
GE Greenland Explorer 300.00 500.00

2016 Topps Allen and Ginter Mini Laureates of Peace

COMPLETE SET (10) 6.00 15.00
STATED ODDS 1:38 HOBBY
LP1 Martin Luther King, Jr. 1.00 2.50
LP2 Nelson Mandela 1.00 2.50
LP3 Baron Philip Noel-Baker 1.00 2.50
LP4 Ralph Bunche 1.00 2.50
LP5 Henry Dunant 1.00 2.50
LP6 Malala Yousafzai 1.00 2.50
LP7 Shirin Ebadi 1.00 2.50
LP8 Jane Addams 1.00 2.50
LP9 Frank B. Kellogg 1.00 2.50
LP10 Jimmy Carter 1.00 2.50

2016 Topps Allen and Ginter Rip Cards Ripped

UNRIPPED ODDS 1:180 HOBBY
PRINT RUNS B/WN 10-50 COPIES PER
PRICING FOR CLEANLY RIPPED CARDS
NO PRICING ON QTY 10
RIP1 Warren Spahn/50 2.50 6.00
RIP2 Zack Greinke/50 3.00 8.00
RIP3 Reggie Jackson/50 2.50 6.00
RIP4 Matt Kemp/50 2.50 6.00
RIP6 Buster Posey/25 4.00 10.00
RIP7 Rod Carew/50 2.50 6.00
RIP8 Justin Upton/50 2.50 6.00
RIP9 Miguel Cabrera/50 3.00 8.00
RIP11 Adam Jones/20 2.50 6.00
RIP12 Yoenis Cespedes/50 3.00 8.00
RIP13 Albert Pujols/25 4.00 10.00
RIP14 Anthony Rizzo/50 4.00 10.00
RIP15 Troy Tulowitzki/50 3.00 8.00
RIP16 Adam Wainwright/50 2.50 6.00
RIP17 David Price/25 2.50 6.00
RIP18 Jason Kipnis/25 2.50 6.00
RIP19 Sonny Gray/25 2.50 6.00
RIP21 Michael Wacha/25 2.50 6.00
RIP22 Freddie Freeman/25 4.00 10.00
RIP23 Willie Mays/50 6.00 15.00
RIP24 Clayton Kershaw/50 5.00 12.00
RIP25 Hank Aaron/50 6.00 15.00
RIP26 Kris Bryant/50 4.00 10.00
RIP27 Corey Seager/50 20.00 50.00
RIP28 Dee Gordon/25 2.00 5.00
RIP29 Giancarlo Stanton/50 3.00 8.00
RIP30 Yasiel Puig/50 3.00 8.00
RIP31 Joe Morgan
RIP32 Lorenzo Cain/25 2.00 5.00
RIP34 Roberto Clemente/50 8.00 20.00
RIP35 Cole Hamels/50 2.50 6.00
RIP36 Paul Goldschmidt/50 3.00 8.00
RIP37 Wade Boggs/50 2.50 6.00
RIP38 Rickey Henderson/50 3.00 8.00
RIP39 Brian Dozier/25 2.50 6.00
RIP40 Tyson Ross/25 2.00 5.00
RIP41 Adrian Gonzalez
RIP42 David Ortiz/50 3.00 8.00
RIP43 Mookie Betts/25 6.00 15.00
RIP44 J.D. Martinez/25 3.00 8.00
RIP45 Joey Votto/50 3.00 8.00
RIP46 Jackie Robinson/50 3.00 8.00
RIP47 Jeff Bagwell/50 2.50 6.00
RIP48 Tom Seaver/50 2.50 6.00
RIP49 Nolan Arenado/50 5.00 12.00
RIP50 Jose Abreu/50 3.00 8.00
RIP51 Bryce Harper/50 5.00 12.00
RIP52 Mike Trout/25 15.00 40.00
RIP53 Johnny Bench/25 3.00 8.00
RIP54 Carlos Correa/25 3.00 8.00
RIP55 Corey Kluber/25 2.50 6.00

RIP56 Robin Yount/25 3.00 8.00
RIP57 George Springer/50 2.50 6.00
RIP58 Jackie Bradley Jr./25 3.00 8.00
RIP60 Ozzie Smith/50 4.00 10.00
RIP61 Dallas Keuchel/50 2.50 6.00
RIP62 Manny Machado
RIP63 Roger Clemens/50 4.00 10.00
RIP64 Edwin Encarnacion/25 3.00 8.00
RIP65 Masahiro Tanaka/50 2.50 6.00
RIP66 Jacob deGrom/50 6.00 15.00
RIP67 Max Scherzer/50 3.00 8.00
RIP68 Eric Hosmer/50 2.50 6.00
RIP69 Cal Ripken Jr./50 8.00 20.00
RIP70 A.J. Pollock
RIP71 Josh Donaldson/50 2.50 6.00
RIP72 Ken Griffey Jr./50 6.00 15.00
RIP73 Johnny Cueto/25 2.50 6.00
RIP74 Evan Longoria/25 2.50 6.00
RIP76 Felix Hernandez/50 2.50 6.00
RIP77 Chipper Jones/25 3.00 8.00
RIP79 James Shields/25 2.00 5.00
RIP80 Jose Bautista/50 2.50 6.00
RIP81 Matt Harvey/50 2.50 6.00
RIP82 Jose Fernandez/50 3.00 8.00
RIP83 Madison Bumgarner/50 2.50 6.00
RIP85 Ty Cobb/50 5.00 12.00
RIP86 Adrian Beltre/50 3.00 8.00
RIP87 Robinson Cano/50 2.50 6.00
RIP88 Gerrit Cole/50 3.00 8.00
RIP90 Jose Reyes/50 2.50 6.00
RIP91 Andrew McCutchen/50 3.00 8.00
RIP93 Chris Sale/50 3.00 8.00
RIP94 Harmon Killebrew/50 3.00 8.00
RIP95 Prince Fielder/25 2.50 6.00
RIP96 Francisco Lindor/25 3.00 8.00
RIP97 Ryan Braun/25 2.50 6.00
RIP98 Chris Davis/25 2.00 5.00
RIP99 Alex Rodriguez/25 4.00 10.00
RIP100 Frank Robinson/50 2.50 6.00

2016 Topps Allen and Ginter Mini Skippers

STATED ODDS 1:288 HOBBY
S1 Pete Mackanin 6.00 15.00
S2 Bryan Price 6.00 15.00
S3 Dave Roberts 10.00 25.00
S4 Robin Ventura 6.00 15.00
S5 Terry Collins 8.00 20.00
S6 Craig Counsell 6.00 15.00
S7 Mike Matheny 6.00 15.00
S8 Joe Maddon 20.00 50.00
S9 Jeff Banister 6.00 15.00
S10 Dusty Baker 10.00 25.00
S11 Buck Showalter 10.00 25.00
S12 Mike Scioscia 6.00 15.00
S13 Andy Green 6.00 15.00
S14 Brad Ausmus 8.00 20.00
S15 A.J. Hinch 6.00 15.00
S16 Walt Weiss 10.00 25.00
S17 Bruce Bochy 8.00 20.00
S18 John Gibbons 6.00 15.00
S19 Paul Molitor 10.00 25.00
S20 Fredi Gonzalez 6.00 15.00
S21 Scott Servais 6.00 15.00
S22 Terry Francona 8.00 20.00
S23 Chip Hale 10.00 25.00
S24 John Farrell 6.00 15.00
S25 Kevin Cash 8.00 20.00
S26 Clint Hurdle 8.00 20.00
S27 Bob Melvin 6.00 15.00
S28 Don Mattingly 12.00 30.00
S29 Joe Girardi 12.00 30.00
S30 Ned Yost 8.00 20.00

2016 Topps Allen and Ginter Mini Subways and Streetcars

COMPLETE SET (12) 5.00 12.00
STATED ODDS 1:25 HOBBY
SS1 7 Train .60 1.50
SS2 Red Line .60 1.50
SS3 Metromover .60 1.50
SS4 Duquesne Incline .60 1.50
SS5 Market St. Cable Car .60 1.50
SS6 Duck Boat .60 1.50
SS7 Passenger Train .60 1.50
SS8 Aerial Tram .60 1.50
SS9 Motorcycle .60 1.50
SS10 City Bus .60 1.50
SS11 R.V. .60 1.50
SS12 Bikeshare .60 1.50

2016 Topps Allen and Ginter Mini US Mayors

COMPLETE SET (35) 20.00 50.00
STATED ODDS 1:11 HOBBY
USM1 Mick Cornett .75 2.00
USM2 Sylvester Turner .75 2.00
USM3 Sam Liccardo .75 2.00
USM4 Greg Stanton .75 2.00
USM5 Betsy Hodges .75 2.00
USM6 Muriel Bowser .75 2.00
USM7 Kasim Reed .75 2.00
USM8 Frank G. Jackson .75 2.00
USM9 Edwin M. Lee .75 2.00
USM10 Charlie Hales .75 2.00
USM11 Marty Walsh .75 2.00
USM12 Tom Barrett .75 2.00
USM13 Tom Tait .75 2.00
USM14 Mike Duggan .75 2.00
USM15 Tomas Regalado .75 2.00
USM16 Bob Buckhorn .75 2.00
USM17 Jim Kenney .75 2.00
USM18 Stephanie Rawlings-Blake .75 2.00
USM19 Andrew Ginther .75 2.00
USM20 Bill de Blasio .75 2.00
USM21 Ed Murray .75 2.00
USM22 Steven Fulop .75 2.00
USM23 Carolyn Goodman .75 2.00
USM24 Rahm Emanuel .75 2.00
USM25 Mitch Landrieu .75 2.00
USM26 Libby Schaaf .75 2.00
USM27 Kevin Faulconer .75 2.00
USM28 Bill Peduto .75 2.00
USM29 Eric Garcetti .75 2.00
USM30 Francis G. Slay .75 2.00
USM31 Michael Hancock .75 2.00
USM32 Greg Fischer .75 2.00
USM33 Sly James .75 2.00
USM34 Oscar Leeser .75 2.00
USM35 Mike Rawlings .75 2.00

2016 Topps Allen and Ginter Natural Wonders

COMPLETE SET (20) 3.00 8.00
STATED ODDS 1:5 HOBBY
NW1 Grand Canyon .25 .60
NW2 Great Barrier Reef .25 .60
NW3 Mount Everest .25 .60
NW4 Victoria Falls .25 .60
NW5 Amazon Rainforest .25 .60
NW6 Old Faithful .25 .60
NW7 Natural Bridge .25 .60
NW8 Aurora Borealis .25 .60
NW9 Eye of the Sahara .25 .60
NW10 Marble Caves .25 .60
NW11 Baobab Forest .25 .60
NW12 Dead Sea .25 .60
NW13 Komodo Island .25 .60
NW14 Punalu'u Beach .25 .60
NW15 Devils Tower .25 .60
NW16 Pulpit Rock .25 .60
NW17 Cliffs of Moher .25 .60
NW18 Cave of the Crystals .25 .60
NW19 Ngorongoro Crater .25 .60
NW20 Harbor of Rio de Janeiro .25 .60

2016 Topps Allen and Ginter Relics

VERSION A ODDS 1:24 HOBBY
VERSION B ODDS 1:24 HOBBY
FSRAAA Anthony Anderson A 2.50 6.00
FSRAAMI Andrew Miller A 2.50 6.00
FSRAAR Addison Russell A 3.00 8.00
FSRAAW Adam Wainwright A 2.50 6.00
FSRABB Brandon Belt A 2.50 6.00
FSRABC Brandon Crawford A 2.50 6.00
FSRABG Brett Gardner A 2.50 6.00
FSRACB Carlos Beltran A 2.50 6.00
FSRACGO Carlos Gonzalez A 2.50 6.00
FSRACGR Curtis Granderson A 2.50 6.00
FSRACK Corey Kluber A 2.50 6.00
FSRACMA Carlos Martinez A 2.50 6.00
FSRACMC Cord McCoy A 2.00 5.00
FSRACSA Carlos Santana A 2.50 6.00
FSRACSL Chris Sale A 3.00 8.00
FSRADBE Dellin Betances A 2.50 6.00
FSRADBR Dwier Brown A 2.00 5.00
FSRADPE Dustin Pedroia A 3.00 8.00
FSRAEH Eric Hosmer A 2.50 6.00
FSRAFH Felix Hernandez A 2.50 6.00
FSRAGL George Lopez A 2.50 6.00
FSRAGS Giancarlo Stanton A 3.00 8.00
FSRAHS Hannah Storm A 3.00 8.00
FSRAJA Jose Abreu A 3.00 8.00
FSRAJD Jacob deGrom A 6.00 15.00
FSRAJE Jacoby Ellsbury A 2.50 6.00
FSRAJF Jose Fernandez A 3.00 8.00
FSRAJHA Josh Harrison A 2.00 5.00
FSRAJM Joe McKeehen A 2.50 6.00
FSRAJSK Jason Sklar A 2.50 6.00
FSRAJSO Jorge Soler A 3.00 8.00
FSRAJV Joey Votto A 3.00 8.00
FSRAJW Jen Welter A 2.50 6.00
FSRAKC Kole Calhoun A 2.00 5.00
FSRAKSE Kyle Seager A 2.00 5.00
FSRAKW Kolten Wong A 2.50 6.00
FSRALC Lorenzo Cain A 2.00 5.00
FSRAMB Mookie Betts A 6.00 15.00
FSRAMC Miguel Cabrera A 3.00 8.00
FSRAMF Missy Franklin A 2.50 6.00
FSRAMP Michael Phelps A 5.00 12.00
FSRAMS Matt Stonie A 2.50 6.00
FSRANS Noah Syndergaard A 2.50 6.00
FSRAPF Prince Fielder A 2.50 6.00
FSRARCA Rusney Castillo A 2.00 5.00
FSRARCR Ricky Craven A 2.00 5.00
FSRARR Robert Raiola A 3.00 8.00
FSRARS Randy Sklar A 2.50 6.00
FSRASK Steve Kerr A 4.00 10.00
FSRATB Timothy Busfield A 2.50 6.00
FSRATD Travis d'Arnaud A 2.50 6.00
FSRAYM Yadier Molina A 4.00 10.00
FSRBAG Adrian Gonzalez B 2.50 6.00
FSRBAP Albert Pujols B 4.00 10.00
FSRBARI Anthony Rizzo B 4.00 10.00
FSRBAS Ari Shaffir B 2.00 5.00
FSRBBH Bryce Harper B 5.00 12.00
FSRBBM Brian McCann B 2.50 6.00
FSRBBP Buster Posey B 4.00 10.00
FSRBCK Clayton Kershaw B 4.00 10.00
FSRBCW Cheyenne Woods B 2.50 6.00
FSRBDA Denise Austin B 2.00 5.00
FSRBDG Dee Gordon B 2.00 5.00
FSRBDW David Wright B 2.50 6.00
FSRBEL Evan Longoria B 2.50 6.00
FSRBGC Gerrit Cole B 3.00 8.00
FSRBGG Gennady Golovkin B 10.00 25.00
FSRBHO Hector Olivera B 2.50 6.00
FSRBHR Hanley Ramirez B 2.50 6.00
FSRBI Ichiro Suzuki B 4.00 10.00
FSRBJAB Jose Abreu B 3.00 8.00
FSRBJAR Jake Arrieta B 2.50 6.00
FSRBJK Jung Ho Kang B 2.00 5.00
FSRBJL Jon Lester B 2.50 6.00
FSRBJMA Jill Martin B 2.50 6.00
FSRBJME Jessica Mendoza B 2.00 5.00
FSRBJO Jay Oakerson B 2.50 6.00
FSRBJP Joc Pederson B 2.50 6.00
FSRBJSH James Shields B 2.00 5.00
FSRBJV Justin Verlander B 3.00 8.00
FSRBJW Jayson Werth B 2.50 6.00
FSRBLD Lucas Duda B 2.50 6.00
FSRBLL Laurence Leavy B 3.00 8.00
FSRBLS Leigh Steinberg B 2.00 5.00
FSRBMBR Mike Breed B 2.00 5.00
FSRBMF Mike Francesa B 2.50 6.00
FSRBMG Mike Greenberg B 2.50 6.00
FSRBMH Matt Harvey B 2.50 6.00
FSRBMP Michael Pineda B 2.00 5.00
FSRBMSC Max Scherzer B 3.00 8.00
FSRBMSH Maria Sharapova B 5.00 12.00
FSRBMSP Morgan Spurlock B 2.00 5.00
FSRBMST Michele Steele B 2.00 5.00
FSRBMTA Masahiro Tanaka B 2.50 6.00
FSRBMTR Mike Trout B 6.00 15.00
FSRBMW Michael Wacha B 2.50 6.00
FSRBPM Paul McBeth B 8.00 20.00
FSRBPS Pablo Sandoval B 2.50 6.00
FSRBRB Ryan Braun B 2.50 6.00
FSRBRC Robinson Cano B 2.50 6.00
FSRBRK Rick Klein B 3.00 8.00
FSRBSP Salvador Perez B 2.50 6.00
FSRBVM Victor Martinez B 2.50 6.00
FSRBWM Wil Myers B 2.50 6.00
FSRBXB Xander Bogaerts B 3.00 8.00
FSRBYC Yoenis Cespedes B 3.00 8.00
FSRBYP Yasiel Puig B 3.00 8.00

2016 Topps Allen and Ginter The Numbers Game

COMPLETE SET (100) 20.00 50.00
STATED ODDS 1:2 HOBBY
NG1 Noah Syndergaard .25 .60
NG2 Mark McGwire .50 1.25
NG3 Buster Posey .40 1.00
NG4 Hank Aaron .60 1.50
NG5 Carl Yastrzemski .50 1.25
NG6 Corey Seager 2.00 5.00
NG7 Jason Heyward .25 .60
NG8 Mark Teixeira .25 .60
NG9 Nolan Ryan 1.00 2.50
NG10 Andrew McCutchen .30 .75
NG11 Stephen Piscotty .30 .75
NG12 Willie Stargell .25 .60
NG13 Max Scherzer .30 .75
NG14 David Price .25 .60
NG15 David Ortiz .30 .75
NG16 Frank Thomas .30 .75
NG17 Yasiel Puig .30 .75
NG18 Dennis Eckersley .25 .60
NG19 Felix Hernandez .25 .60
NG20 George Springer .25 .60
NG21 Mookie Betts .60 1.50
NG22 Giancarlo Stanton .30 .75
NG23 Manny Machado .30 .75
NG24 Madison Bumgarner .25 .60
NG25 Evan Longoria .25 .60
NG26 Randy Johnson .30 .75
NG27 Jon Lester .25 .60
NG28 Rollie Fingers .25 .60
NG29 Cal Ripken Jr. 1.00 2.50
NG30 Chipper Jones .30 .75
NG31 Mike Trout 1.50 4.00
NG32 Troy Tulowitzki .30 .75
NG33 Yoenis Cespedes .30 .75
NG34 Eric Hosmer .25 .60
NG35 Joe Morgan .25 .60
NG36 Steve Carlton .25 .60
NG37 Matt Harvey .25 .60
NG38 Anthony Rizzo .40 1.00
NG39 Ken Griffey Jr. .60 1.50
NG40 Paul Goldschmidt .30 .75
NG41 Jackie Robinson .30 .75
NG42 Roberto Alomar .25 .60
NG43 Roger Clemens .40 1.00
NG44 Dustin Pedroia .30 .75
NG45 Curt Schilling .25 .60
NG46 Chris Sale .30 .75
NG47 Kris Bryant .40 1.00
NG48 Ozzie Smith .40 1.00
NG49 Babe Ruth .75 2.00
NG50 Jose Abreu .30 .75
NG51 John Smoltz .30 .75
NG52 Jose Altuve .25 .60
NG53 Zack Greinke .30 .75
NG54 Albert Pujols .40 1.00
NG55 Ryan Braun .25 .60
NG56 Miguel Cabrera .30 .75
NG57 Jose Fernandez .30 .75
NG58 A.J. Pollock .20 .50
NG59 Adam Wainwright .25 .60
NG60 Roberto Clemente .75 2.00
NG61 Mike Piazza .30 .75
NG62 Jose Bautista .25 .60
NG63 Jake Arrieta .25 .60
NG64 Dallas Keuchel .25 .60
NG65 Clayton Kershaw .50 1.25
NG66 Reggie Jackson .25 .60
NG67 Ichiro Suzuki .40 1.00
NG68 Johnny Bench .30 .75
NG69 Jacob deGrom .60 1.50
NG70 Willie McCovey .25 .60
NG71 Billy Williams .25 .60
NG72 Don Mattingly .60 1.50
NG73 Nomar Garciaparra .25 .60
NG74 Jim Rice .25 .60
NG75 Kyle Seager .20 .50
NG76 Willie Mays .60 1.50
NG77 Robinson Cano .25 .60
NG78 Bill Mazeroski .25 .60
NG79 Rickey Henderson .30 .75
NG80 Greg Maddux .40 1.00
NG81 Wade Boggs .25 .60
NG82 Kenta Maeda .40 1.00
NG83 Matt Kemp .25 .60
NG84 Joey Votto .30 .75
NG85 Rod Carew .25 .60
NG86 Tom Seaver .25 .60
NG87 Carlton Fisk .25 .60
NG88 Prince Fielder .25 .60
NG89 Josh Donaldson .25 .60
NG90 Tom Glavine .25 .60
NG91 Paul Molitor .30 .75
NG92 Andy Pettitte .25 .60
NG93 Miguel Sano .30 .75
NG94 Bryce Harper .50 1.25
NG95 Carlos Correa .30 .75
NG96 Dee Gordon .25 .60
NG97 Stephen Strasburg .30 .75
NG98 Robin Yount .30 .75
NG99 George Brett .60 1.50
NG100 Ryne Sandberg .60 1.50

2017 Topps Allen and Ginter

COMPLETE SET (350) 30.00 80.00
COMP.SET w/o SP's (300) 20.00 50.00
SP ODDS 1:2 HOBBY
1 Kris Bryant .30 .75
2 Albert Pujols .30 .75
3 Tyler Naquin .25 .60
4 Babe Ruth .60 1.50
5 Adrian Gonzalez .20 .50
6 DJ LeMahieu .25 .60
7 Derek Jeter .60 1.50
8 Kevin Gausman .25 .60
9 Ryan Schimpf .15 .40
10 Mike Trout 1.25 3.00
11 Brandon Finnegan .15 .40
12 Corey Bellemore .15 .40
13 Jake Arrieta .20 .50
14 Robert Gsellman RC .25 .60
15 Gary Sanchez .25 .60
16 Garrett Richards .20 .50
17 Jose De Leon RC .25 .60
18 Marcus Semien .25 .60
19 Giancarlo Stanton .25 .60
20 Brooke Hogan .15 .40
21 Eric Hosmer .20 .50
22 Albert Almora .15 .40
23 John Smoltz .25 .60
24 Ken Griffey Jr. .50 1.25
25 Alexa Datt .15 .40
26 Matt Wieters .25 .60
27 Yulieski Gurriel RC .40 1.00
28 Andrew McCutchen .25 .60
29 Maikel Franco .20 .50
30 Jorge Soler .20 .50
31 Carlos Santana .20 .50
32 Peter Rosenberg .15 .40
33 Byron Buxton .25 .60
34 Billy Hamilton .20 .50
35 Johnny Damon .20 .50
36 Edwin Encarnacion .25 .60
37 Devon Travis .15 .40
38 Craig Kimbrel .20 .50
39 Yu Darvish .25 .60
40 Dansby Swanson RC .60 1.50
41 Chris Sale .25 .60
42 Mark Trumbo .15 .40
43 Tanner Roark .15 .40
44 Anthony Rizzo .30 .75
45 Harriet Tubman .15 .40
46 Chris Archer .15 .40
47 Omar Vizquel .20 .50
48 Carlos Correa .25 .60
49 David Wright .20 .50
50 Bryce Harper .40 1.00
51 Buster Posey .30 .75
52 Trees in India .15 .40
53 Brandon Belt .20 .50
54 Rickey Henderson .25 .60
55 Andre Dawson .20 .50
56 Rick Porcello .20 .50
57 Jharel Cotton RC .25 .60
58 Elfren Reyes .15 .40
59 Gary Stevens .15 .40
60 Nolan Ryan .75 2.00
61 Tommy Joseph .25 .60
62 Joc Pederson .20 .50
63 Barry Larkin .20 .50
64 Luis Severino .20 .50
65 Kyle Freeland RC .30 .75
66 Kenta Maeda .25 .60
67 Allie LaForce .15 .40
68 J.D. Martinez .25 .60
69 Carl Yastrzemski .40 1.00
70 Vashti Cunningham .15 .40
71 Julio Teheran .20 .50
72 Dustin Pedroia .25 .60
73 Starling Marte .20 .50
74 Cal Ripken Jr. .75 2.00
75 Max Scherzer .25 .60
76 David Dahl RC .30 .75
77 Brian Dozier .25 .60
78 Greg Maddux .30 .75
79 Rod Carew .20 .50
80 Mookie Betts .50 1.25
81 Carlos Carrasco .15 .40
82 Bobby Abreu .15 .40
83 Ichiro .30 .75
84 Ian Desmond .15 .40
85 Dave Winfield .20 .50
86 Aledmys Diaz .20 .50
87 Henry Owens .15 .40
88 Tyler Austin RC .30 .75
89 Ken Rosenthal .15 .40
90 Gavin Cecchini RC .25 .60
91 Nomar Mazara .15 .40
92 Hunter Dozier RC .25 .60
93 Chad Pinder RC .25 .60
94 Justin Upton .20 .50
95 Dee Gordon .15 .40
96 Kendrys Morales .15 .40
97 Aroldis Chapman .25 .60
98 Stephen Piscotty .20 .50
99 Teoscar Hernandez RC 1.00 2.50
100 Ty Cobb .40 1.00
101 Jay Bruce .20 .50
102 Honus Wagner .25 .60
103 Jose Reyes .20 .50
104 Dexter Fowler .20 .50
105 Brett Gardner .20 .50
106 Sean Manaea .15 .40
107 Pedro Martinez .20 .50
108 Ryon Healy RC .30 .75
109 Cole Hamels .20 .50
110 Ted Williams .50 1.25
111 Alex Gordon .20 .50
112 Jayson Werth .20 .50
113 Adam Jones .20 .50
114 Yasiel Puig .25 .60
115 Carlos Rodon .25 .60
116 Aaron Sanchez .20 .50
117 Joe Musgrove RC .75 2.00
118 Cameron Maybin .15 .40
119 Garrett McNamara .15 .40
120 Vince Velasquez .15 .40
121 Randal Grichuk .15 .40
122 Reggie Jackson .20 .50
123 George Springer .20 .50
124 Kyle Schwarber .25 .60
125 Paul Goldschmidt .25 .60
126 Adrian Beltre .25 .60
127 Ollie Schniederjans .15 .40
128 Tyler Glasnow RC 1.00 2.50
129 Ozzie Smith .30 .75
130 Renato Nunez RC .50 1.25
131 Dan Jennings EXEC .15 .40
132 Corey Seager .25 .60
133 Addison Russell .25 .60
134 Steven Matz .15 .40
135 Josh Donaldson .20 .50
136 Bo Jackson .25 .60
137 Nolan Arenado .40 1.00
138 Adam Duvall .20 .50
139 David Price .20 .50
140 Ryan Braun .20 .50
141 Michael Fulmer .15 .40
142 Tom Anderson .15 .40
143 Paris Locks .15 .40
144 Frank Thomas .25 .60
145 A.J. Reed .15 .40
146 Justin Verlander .25 .60
147 Salvador Perez .20 .50
148 Jesse Winker RC 1.00 2.50
149 Mike Piazza .25 .60
150 Sandy Koufax .50 1.25
151 Jacoby Ellsbury .20 .50
152 Jackie Robinson .25 .60
153 Sean Doolittle .15 .40
154 David Ortiz .25 .60
155 Joey Votto .25 .60
156 Daniel Murphy .20 .50
157 Carson Fulmer RC .25 .60
158 Xander Bogaerts .25 .60
159 Yoenis Cespedes .25 .60
160 Michal Kapral .15 .40
161 Ernie Banks .25 .60
162 Sonny Gray .20 .50
163 Wesley Bryan .15 .40
164 Gerrit Cole .25 .60
165 Jayson Stark .15 .40
166 Manny Margot RC .25 .60
167 Andres Galarraga .20 .50
168 Robbie Ray .15 .40
169 Antonio Senzatela RC .25 .60
170 Jackie Bradley Jr. .25 .60
171 Jose Canseco .20 .50
172 Aaron Judge RC 5.00 12.00
173 Odubel Herrera .20 .50
174 Danny Duffy .15 .40
175 Noah Syndergaard .20 .50
176 Marcus Stroman .20 .50
177 Valarie Jenkins .15 .40
178 Clayton Kershaw .40 1.00
179 Kirby Smart CO .15 .40
180 Corey Kluber .20 .50
181 Mark McGwire .40 1.00
182 Kyle Hendricks .25 .60
183 Amir Garrett RC .25 .60
184 Jose Altuve .20 .50
185 Wil Myers .20 .50
186 Josh Bell RC .60 1.50
187 Eric LeGrand .15 .40
188 Gregory Polanco .20 .50
189 Joe Manganiello .15 .40
190 Matt Carpenter .25 .60
191 Jay Glazer .15 .40
192 Willson Contreras .25 .60
193 Todd Frazier .15 .40
194 A.J. Pollock .15 .40
195 Matt Kemp .20 .50
196 Jose Bautista .20 .50
197 Ben Zobrist .20 .50
198 Javier Baez .30 .75
199 Curtis Granderson .20 .50
200 Francisco Lindor .25 .60
201 Orlando Arcia RC .40 1.00
202 Jurickson Profar .20 .50
203 Carlos Gonzalez .20 .50
204 Manny Machado .25 .60
205 Alex Bregman RC 1.25 3.00
206 Aaron Nola .20 .50
207 Edwin Diaz .20 .50
208 Felix Hernandez .20 .50
209 Mitch Haniger RC .40 1.00
210 Didi Gregorius .20 .50
211 Ben Smith .15 .40
212 Don Mattingly .50 1.25
213 Blake Snell .20 .50
214 Nick Jonas .15 .40
215 Yasmany Tomas .15 .40
216 Michael Conforto .20 .50
217 Brooks Robinson .20 .50
218 Tim Anderson .25 .60
219 Johnny Cueto .20 .50
220 Chipper Jones .25 .60
221 Yadier Molina .30 .75
222 Jake Thompson RC .25 .60
223 Lucas Giolito .20 .50
224 U.S. National Park Service .15 .40
225 Ian Kinsler .20 .50
226 Ryne Sandberg .50 1.25
227 Jon Gray .15 .40
228 Ryan Zimmerman .20 .50
229 Rougned Odor .20 .50
230 Kyle Seager .15 .40
231 Hank Aaron .50 1.25
232 Jose Abreu .25 .60
233 Jake Lamb .20 .50
234 Charlie Blackmon .25 .60
235 Roger Clemens .30 .75
236 Jason Kipnis .20 .50
237 Andrew Benintendi RC .75 2.00
238 Andrew Miller .20 .50
239 Jameson Taillon .20 .50
240 Masahiro Tanaka .20 .50
241 Zach Britton .20 .50
242 Luke Weaver RC .30 .75
243 Alex Reyes RC .30 .75
244 Khris Davis .25 .60
245 Roman Quinn RC .25 .60
246 William Shatner .15 .40
247 Victor Martinez .20 .50
248 Wilson Ramos .15 .40
249 Sage Steele .15 .40
250 Lyle Thompson .15 .40
251 Matt Harvey .20 .50
252 George Brett .50 1.25
253 Brandon Phillips .15 .40
254 Hunter Pence .20 .50
255 Trea Turner .20 .50
256 Andy Katz .15 .40
257 Lou Gehrig .50 1.25
258 Jose Peraza .20 .50
259 Roger Maris .25 .60
260 Jonathan Villar .15 .40
261 Mike Moustakas .20 .50
262 JaCoby Jones RC .30 .75
263 Kevin Kelley CO .15 .40
264 Robinson Cano .20 .50
265 Kevin Kiermaier .20 .50
266 Greg Bird .20 .50
267 Dellin Betances .20 .50
268 Matt Olson RC 1.25 3.00
269 Krazy George MAS .15 .40
270 Jason Heyward .20 .50
271 Stephen Strasburg .25 .60
272 J.T. Realmuto .25 .60
273 Jean Segura .20 .50
274 Laurie Hernandez .15 .40
275 Joe Panik .20 .50
276 Giant Panda .15 .40
277 Miguel Sano .20 .50
278 Trevor Story .25 .60
279 Randy Johnson .25 .60
280 Freddie Freeman .30 .75
281 Yoan Moncada RC .75 2.00
282 Christian Yelich .30 .75
283 Chris Davis .15 .40
284 Miguel Cotto .15 .40
285 Hunter Renfroe RC .30 .75
286 Roberto Clemente .60 1.50
287 Elvis Andrus .20 .50
288 Jorge Alfaro RC .30 .75
289 Julio Urias .25 .60
290 Jacob deGrom .50 1.25
291 Ender Inciarte .15 .40
292 Evan Longoria .20 .50
293 Johnny Bench .25 .60
294 Miguel Cabrera .25 .60
295 James Shields .15 .40
296 Zack Greinke .25 .60
297 Troy Tulowitzki .25 .60
298 Nelson Cruz .25 .60
299 Stephen A. Smith .15 .40
300 Max Kepler .20 .50
301 Trey Mancini SP RC .75 2.00
302 Jon Lester SP .50 1.25
303 Tim Raines SP .50 1.25
304 Whitey Ford SP .50 1.25
305 Ty Blach SP RC .40 1.00
306 Marcell Ozuna SP .60 1.50
307 J.J. Hardy SP .40 1.00
308 Jordan Zimmermann SP .50 1.25
309 Fernando Rodney SP .40 1.00
310 Brandon Crawford SP .50 1.25
311 Adam Eaton SP .60 1.50
312 Raimel Tapia SP RC .50 1.25
313 Matt Strahm SP RC .40 1.00
314 Dan Vogelbach SP RC .60 1.50
315 Willie McCovey SP .50 1.25
316 Adam Wainwright SP .50 1.25
317 Martin Prado SP .40 1.00
318 Harmon Killebrew SP .60 1.50
319 Seth Lugo SP RC .40 1.00
320 Jeff Hoffman SP RC .40 1.00
321 Drew Pomeranz SP .50 1.25
322 Justin Turner SP .60 1.50
323 Drew Smyly SP .40 1.00
324 Gary Carter SP .50 1.25
325 Danny Salazar SP .50 1.25
326 German Marquez SP RC .60 1.50
327 Steven Wright SP .40 1.00
328 Carlos Martinez SP .50 1.25
329 Jonathan Lucroy SP .50 1.25
330 Mark Melancon SP .40 1.00
331 Corey Dickerson SP .40 1.00
332 Yangervis Solarte SP .40 1.00
333 Dallas Keuchel SP .50 1.25
334 Joe Mauer SP .50 1.25
335 Lorenzo Cain SP .40 1.00
336 Kenley Jansen SP .50 1.25
337 Seung-Hwan Oh SP .75 2.00
338 Stephen Vogt SP .50 1.25
339 Reynaldo Lopez SP RC .40 1.00
340 Hanley Ramirez SP .50 1.25
341 Matt Moore SP .50 1.25
342 Braden Shipley SP RC .40 1.00
343 Brian McCann SP .50 1.25
344 Bartolo Colon SP .40 1.00
345 Lance McCullers SP .40 1.00
346 Hisashi Iwakuma SP .50 1.25
347 Warren Spahn SP .50 1.25
348 Logan Forsythe SP .40 1.00
349 Willie Stargell SP .50 1.25
350 Jeff Bagwell SP .50 1.25

2017 Topps Allen and Ginter Hot Box Foil

*FOIL 1-300: 2X TO 5X BASIC
*FOIL 1-300 RC: 1.2X TO 3X BASIC RCs
*FOIL SP 301-350: .75X TO 2X BASIC
INSERTED IN HOT HOBBY BOXES

2017 Topps Allen and Ginter Mini

*MINI 1-300: 1X TO 2.5X BASIC
*MINI 1-300 RC: .6X TO 1.5X BASIC RCs
*MINI SP 301-350: .6X TO 1.5X BASIC
MINI SP ODDS 1:13 HOBBY
351-400 RANDOM WITHIN RIP CARDS
STATED PLATE ODDS 1:1058 HOBBY
PLATE PRINT RUN 1 SET PER COLOR
BLACK-CYAN-MAGENTA-YELLOW ISSUED
NO PLATE PRICING DUE TO SCARCITY
351 Max Scherzer EXT 25.00 60.00
352 Cal Ripken Jr. EXT 25.00 60.00
353 Justin Verlander EXT 20.00 50.00
354 Yu Darvish EXT 20.00 50.00
355 Francisco Lindor EXT 20.00 50.00
356 Mookie Betts EXT 40.00 100.00
357 Andrew Benintendi EXT 50.00 120.00
358 Robinson Cano EXT 15.00 40.00
359 Aledmys Diaz EXT 15.00 40.00
360 Ernie Banks EXT 20.00 50.00
361 Aaron Judge EXT 150.00 400.00
362 Roberto Clemente EXT 40.00 100.00
363 Bryce Harper EXT 30.00 80.00
364 Buster Posey EXT 25.00 60.00
365 Joey Votto EXT 20.00 50.00
366 Dansby Swanson EXT 20.00 50.00
367 Alex Bregman EXT 20.00 50.00
368 Nolan Arenado EXT 30.00 80.00
369 Miguel Cabrera EXT 30.00 80.00
370 Yoenis Cespedes EXT 15.00 40.00
371 Giancarlo Stanton EXT 20.00 50.00
372 Masahiro Tanaka EXT 15.00 40.00
373 Ken Griffey Jr. EXT 40.00 100.00
374 Josh Donaldson EXT 15.00 40.00
375 Julio Urias EXT 20.00 50.00
376 Mike Trout EXT 40.00 100.00
377 Babe Ruth EXT 30.00 80.00
378 Noah Syndergaard EXT 15.00 40.00
379 Alex Reyes EXT 15.00 40.00
380 Kyle Schwarber EXT 20.00 50.00
381 Clayton Kershaw EXT 20.00 50.00
382 Ted Williams EXT 25.00 60.00
383 Paul Goldschmidt EXT 20.00 50.00
384 Manny Machado EXT 20.00 50.00
385 Derek Jeter EXT 30.00 80.00
386 Hunter Renfroe EXT 20.00 50.00
387 Tyler Glasnow EXT 50.00 120.00
388 Kris Bryant EXT 30.00 80.00
389 Jose Bautista EXT 15.00 40.00
390 Corey Seager EXT 20.00 50.00
391 Felix Hernandez EXT 20.00 50.00
392 Hank Aaron EXT 30.00 80.00
393 Yoan Moncada EXT 25.00 60.00
394 Ichiro EXT 25.00 60.00
395 Sandy Koufax EXT 30.00 80.00
396 Gary Sanchez EXT 25.00 60.00
397 Jackie Robinson EXT 25.00 60.00
398 Anthony Rizzo EXT 25.00 60.00
399 Eric Hosmer EXT 15.00 40.00
400 Carlos Correa EXT 20.00 50.00

2017 Topps Allen and Ginter Mini A and G Back

*MINI AG 1-300: 1.2X TO 3X BASIC
*MINI AG 1-300 RC: .75X TO 2X BASIC RCs
*MINI AG SP 301-350: .75X TO 2X BASIC
MINI AG ODDS 1:5 HOBBY
MINI AG SP ODDS 1:65 HOBBY

2017 Topps Allen and Ginter Mini Black Border

*MINI BLK 1-300: 2X TO 5X BASIC
*MINI BLK 1-300 RC: 1.2X TO 3X BASIC RCs
*MINI BLK SP 301-350: 1.2X TO 3X BASIC
MINI BLK ODDS 1:10 HOBBY
MINI BLK SP ODDS 1:130 HOBBY

2017 Topps Allen and Ginter Mini Brooklyn Back

*MINI BRK 1-300: 12X TO 30X BASIC
*MINI BRK 1-300 RC: 8X TO 20X BASIC RCs
*MINI BRK SP 301-350: 5X TO 12X BASIC
MINI BRK ODDS 1:170 HOBBY
STATED PRINT RUN 25 SER.#'d SETS
7 Derek Jeter 40.00 100.00
172 Aaron Judge 175.00 350.00

2017 Topps Allen and Ginter Mini Gold Border

*MINI GOLD 1-300: 2.5X TO 6X BASIC
*MINI GOLD 1-300 RC: 1.5X TO 4X BASIC RCs
*MINI GOLD 301-350: 1X TO 2.5X BASIC
RANDOMLY INSERTED IN RETAIL PACKS

2017 Topps Allen and Ginter Mini No Number

*MINI NNO 1-300: 5X TO 12X BASIC
*MINI NNO 1-300 RC: 3X TO 8X BASIC RCs
*MINI NNO SP 301-350: 2X TO 5X BASIC
MINI NNO ODDS 1:85 HOBBY
7 Derek Jeter 15.00 40.00

2017 Topps Allen and Ginter Autographs

STATED ODDS 1:731 HOBBY
EXCHANGE DEADLINE 6/30/2019
AGACA Christian Arroyo EXCH 6.00 15.00
AGACB Cody Bellinger 75.00 200.00
AGAIH Ian Happ 15.00 40.00

2017 Topps Allen and Ginter Box Toppers

BLAB Alex Bregman 4.00 10.00
BLAR Anthony Rizzo 1.50 4.00
BLBH Bryce Harper 2.00 5.00
BLBP Buster Posey 1.50 4.00
BLCK Clayton Kershaw 2.00 5.00
BLCS Corey Seager 1.25 3.00
BLDJ Derek Jeter 3.00 8.00
BLDS Dansby Swanson 2.00 5.00
BLGSA Gary Sanchez 1.25 3.00
BLGST Giancarlo Stanton 1.25 3.00
BLJD Josh Donaldson 1.00 2.50
BLKB Kris Bryant 1.50 4.00
BLMM Manny Machado 1.25 3.00
BLMT Mike Trout 6.00 15.00
BLNS Noah Syndergaard 1.00 2.50

2017 Topps Allen and Ginter Framed Mini Autographs

STATED ODDS 1:65 HOBBY
EXCHANGE DEADLINE 6/30/2019
MAABE Andrew Benintendi 25.00 60.00
MAABR Alex Bregman 25.00 60.00
MAADA Alexa Datt 6.00 15.00
MAADI Aledmys Diaz 5.00 12.00
MAADU Adam Duvall 5.00 12.00
MAAG Andres Galarraga 6.00 15.00
MAAJ Aaron Judge 75.00 200.00
MAAK Andy Katz 4.00 10.00
MAAL Allie LaForce 15.00 40.00
MAAN Aaron Nola 8.00 20.00
MAARE Alex Reyes 8.00 20.00
MAAT Andrew Toles 4.00 10.00
MABH Bryce Harper 100.00 250.00
MABHG Brooke Hogan 15.00 40.00
MABJ Bo Jackson EXCH 75.00 200.00
MABP Buster Posey 40.00 100.00
MABSM Ben Smith 4.00 10.00
MABST Bo Steil 4.00 10.00
MABZ Bradley Zimmer 5.00 12.00
MACB Corey Bellemore 4.00 10.00
MACC Carlos Correa EXCH 40.00 100.00
MACF Chris Fehn 20.00 50.00
MACFU Carson Fulmer 4.00 10.00
MACKE Clayton Kershaw 50.00 120.00
MACKL Corey Kluber 10.00 25.00
MACSA Chris Sale 15.00 40.00
MACSE Corey Seager 20.00 50.00
MADB Dellin Betances 5.00 12.00
MADCK David Castor Keene 4.00 10.00
MADF Dexter Fowler 5.00 12.00
MADJ Derek Jeter
MADJE Dan Jennings 4.00 10.00
MADS Dansby Swanson 20.00 50.00
MADV Dan Vogelbach 6.00 15.00
MAEL Eric LeGrand 5.00 12.00
MAFF Freddie Freeman 15.00 40.00
MAFL Francisco Lindor 20.00 50.00

MAFM Floyd Mayweather 150.00 400.00
MAFPJ Freddie Prinze Jr. 25.00 60.00
MAGC Gavin Cecchini 5.00 12.00
MAGM Garrett McNamara 4.00 10.00
MAGSP George Springer 10.00 25.00
MAGST Gary Stevens 5.00 12.00
MAHA Hank Aaron
MAHD Hunter Dozier 4.00 10.00
MAHO Henry Owens 4.00 10.00
MAI Ichiro
MAJAF Jorge Alfaro 5.00 12.00
MAJAL Jose Altuve 15.00 40.00
MAJBA Javier Baez 12.00 30.00
MAJCO Jharel Cotton 4.00 10.00
MAJDG Jacob deGrom 30.00 80.00
MAJDL Jose De Leon 4.00 10.00
MAJDO Josh Donaldson 8.00 20.00
MAJG Jay Glazer 4.00 10.00
MAJM Joe Musgrove 12.00 30.00
MAJMA Joe Manganiello 6.00 15.00
MAJS Jayson Stark 4.00 10.00
MAJTA Jameson Taillon 5.00 12.00
MAJTH Jake Thompson 4.00 10.00
MAJTS Joe Thomas Sr. 5.00 12.00
MAJU Julio Urias 6.00 15.00
MAKB Kris Bryant EXCH
MAKG Krazy George 5.00 12.00
MAKKL Kevin Kelley CO 5.00 12.00
MAKMA Kenta Maeda 6.00 15.00
MAKR Ken Rosenthal 10.00 25.00
MAKSC Kyle Schwarber EXCH 12.00 30.00
MAKSE Kyle Seager EXCH 12.00 30.00
MALH Laurie Hernandez 15.00 40.00
MALT Lyle Thompson EXCH 8.00 20.00
MALW Luke Weaver 5.00 12.00
MAMC Matt Carpenter EXCH 15.00 40.00
MAMCO Miguel Cotto 20.00 50.00
MAMF Michael Fulmer 4.00 10.00
MAMJA Mike Jaspersen
MAMKA Michal Kapral 4.00 10.00
MAMM Manny Machado 15.00 40.00
MAMTA Masahiro Tanaka 50.00 120.00
MAMTR Mike Trout 200.00 500.00
MAND Gene Hackman 60.00 150.00
MANJ Nick Jonas 15.00 40.00
MANS Noah Syndergaard 15.00 40.00
MAOS Ollie Schniederjans 5.00 12.00
MAOV Omar Vizquel 6.00 15.00
MAPF Paul Finebaum 5.00 12.00
MAPR Peter Rosenberg 5.00 12.00
MARGR Randal Grichuk 4.00 10.00
MARGS Robert Gsellman 4.00 10.00
MARH Ryon Healy 5.00 12.00
MARL Reynaldo Lopez 4.00 10.00
MARQ Roman Quinn 4.00 10.00
MART Raimel Tapia 5.00 12.00
MASK Sandy Koufax 200.00 400.00
MASM Starling Marte 5.00 12.00
MASMG Sarah Michelle Gellar 150.00 300.00
MASR Sierra Romero 5.00 12.00
MASS Stephen A. Smith 12.00 30.00
MASST Sage Steele 5.00 12.00
MASW Steven Wright 6.00 15.00
MATA Tyler Austin 5.00 12.00
MATAN Tom Anderson 12.00 30.00
MATAR Tom Arnold 8.00 20.00
MATB Ty Blach 4.00 10.00
MATM Trey Mancini 8.00 20.00
MATR Tom Rinaldi 4.00 10.00
MATS Trevor Story 6.00 15.00
MAVC Vashti Cunningham 4.00 10.00
MAVJ Valarie Jenkins 10.00 25.00
MAWB Wesley Bryan 4.00 10.00
MAWS William Shatner 60.00 150.00
MAYG Yulieski Gurriel 6.00 15.00
MAYM Yoan Moncada 40.00 100.00

2017 Topps Allen and Ginter Framed Mini Autographs Black Border

*BLACK: .75X TO 2X BASIC
STATED ODDS 1:423 HOBBY
STATED PRINT RUN 25 SER.#'d SETS
EXCHANGE DEADLINE 6/30/2019
MAFM Floyd Mayweather 300.00 600.00
MAKB Kris Bryant EXCH 100.00 250.00
MASMG Sarah Michelle Gellar 250.00 500.00

2017 Topps Allen and Ginter Framed Mini Gems and Ancient Fossil Relics

STATED ODDS 1:3600 HOBBY
PRINT RUNS B/WN 2-25 COPIES PER
NO PRICING ON QTY 16 OR LESS
GAFA Amethyst/25 75.00 200.00
GAFC Crystal/25
GAFG Gold/25
GAFP Peridot/25 75.00 200.00
GAFS Sapphire/25
GAFSTT Shark Tooth/25 150.00 300.00
GAFT Tourmaline/21 100.00 250.00

2017 Topps Allen and Ginter Framed Mini Relics

STATED ODDS 1:105 HOBBY
MRABE Andrew Benintendi 10.00 25.00
MRABR Alex Bregman 12.00 30.00
MRAJ Aaron Judge 30.00 80.00
MRAM Andrew McCutchen 4.00 10.00
MRAP Albert Pujols 5.00 12.00
MRARI Anthony Rizzo 5.00 12.00
MRARU Addison Russell 4.00 10.00
MRBB Byron Buxton 4.00 10.00
MRBH Bryce Harper 6.00 15.00
MRBP Buster Posey 5.00 12.00
MRCC Carlos Correa 4.00 10.00
MRCJ Chipper Jones 15.00 40.00
MRCK Clayton Kershaw 6.00 15.00
MRCR Cal Ripken Jr. 30.00 80.00
MRCS Corey Seager 4.00 10.00
MRDJ Derek Jeter 20.00 50.00
MRDM Don Mattingly 20.00 50.00
MRDO David Ortiz 4.00 10.00
MRDS Dansby Swanson 6.00 15.00
MREB Ernie Banks 60.00 150.00
MRFH Felix Hernandez 3.00 8.00
MRFL Francisco Lindor 4.00 10.00
MRFT Frank Thomas 30.00 80.00
MRGSA Gary Sanchez 4.00 10.00
MRGST Giancarlo Stanton 4.00 10.00
MRIC Ichiro 5.00 12.00
MRJD Josh Donaldson 3.00 8.00
MRJR Jackie Robinson
MRJS John Smoltz 6.00 15.00
MRJU Julio Urias 4.00 10.00
MRJVE Justin Verlander 4.00 10.00
MRJVO Joey Votto 4.00 10.00
MRKB Kris Bryant 10.00 25.00
MRKGF Ken Griffey Jr. 25.00 60.00
MRKGR Ken Griffey Jr. 25.00 60.00
MRMB Mookie Betts 8.00 20.00
MRMC Miguel Cabrera 4.00 10.00
MRMMA Manny Machado 4.00 10.00
MRMMG Mark McGwire 20.00 50.00
MRMP Mike Piazza 15.00 40.00
MRMTA Masahiro Tanaka 3.00 8.00
MRMTR Mike Trout 20.00 50.00
MRNA Nolan Arenado 6.00 15.00
MRNS Noah Syndergaard 3.00 8.00
MRPM Pedro Martinez 8.00 20.00
MRRCA Robinson Cano 3.00 8.00
MRRCL Roberto Clemente 50.00 120.00
MRTT Trea Turner 3.00 8.00
MRTW Ted Williams 75.00 200.00
MRYC Yoenis Cespedes 4.00 10.00

2017 Topps Allen and Ginter Mini Bust a Move

COMPLETE SET (15) 12.00 30.00
STATED ODDS 1:20 HOBBY
BAM1 Ballet Dance 1.00 2.50
BAM2 Bavarian Polka Dance 1.00 2.50
BAM3 Belly Dance 1.00 2.50
BAM4 Break Dance 1.00 2.50
BAM5 Charleston Dance 1.00 2.50
BAM6 Cossack Dance 1.00 2.50
BAM7 Flamenco Dance 1.00 2.50
BAM8 Hula Dance 1.00 2.50
BAM9 Irish Dance 1.00 2.50
BAM10 Jitterbug Dance 1.00 2.50
BAM11 Salsa Dance 1.00 2.50
BAM12 Tango Dance 1.00 2.50
BAM13 Twist Dance 1.00 2.50
BAM14 Waltz Dance 1.00 2.50
BAM15 Whirling Dervish Dance 1.00 2.50

2017 Topps Allen and Ginter Mini Constellations

COMPLETE SET (10) 12.00 30.00
STATED ODDS 1:50 HOBBY
C1 Orion 1.25 3.00
C2 Ursa Major 1.25 3.00
C3 Ursa Minor 1.25 3.00
C4 Scorpius 1.25 3.00
C5 Cygnus 1.25 3.00
C6 Leo 1.25 3.00
C7 Perseus 1.25 3.00
C8 Hercules 1.25 3.00
C9 Aquarius 1.25 3.00
C10 Libra 1.25 3.00

2017 Topps Allen and Ginter Mini Horse in the Race

RANDOM INSERTS IN RETAIL PACKS
HR1 Friesian Horse 1.50 4.00
HR2 Exmoor Pony 1.50 4.00
HR3 Shetland Pony 1.50 4.00
HR4 American Quarter Horse 1.50 4.00
HR5 Camargue Horse 1.50 4.00
HR6 American Miniature Horse 1.50 4.00
HR7 Grayson Highland Pony 1.50 4.00
HR8 Palomino Horse 1.50 4.00
HR9 Belgian Horse 1.50 4.00
HR10 Bavarian Warmblood Horse 1.50 4.00
HR11 East Bulgarian Horse 1.50 4.00
HR12 Clydesdale Horse 1.50 4.00
HR13 Arabian Horse 1.50 4.00
HR14 Shire Horse 1.50 4.00
HR15 Andalusian Horse 1.50 4.00
HR16 Barb Horse 1.50 4.00
HR17 Marwari Horse 1.50 4.00
HR18 Scandinavian Coldblood Trotter 1.50 4.00
HR19 Arabian Berber Horse 1.50 4.00
HR20 Bosnian Pony 1.50 4.00
HR21 Percheron Horse 1.50 4.00
HR22 Ardennais Horse 1.50 4.00
HR23 Mustang Horse 1.50 4.00
HR24 Pinto Horse 1.50 4.00
HR25 Norwegian Fjord Horse 1.50 4.00

2017 Topps Allen and Ginter Mini Magicians and Illusionists

COMPLETE SET (15) 15.00 40.00
STATED ODDS 1:34 HOBBY
MI1 Papus 1.25 3.00
MI2 Pamela Colman Smith 1.25 3.00
MI3 Arthur Edward Waite 1.25 3.00
MI4 Jean Eugene Robert-Houdin 1.25 3.00
MI5 P. T. Selbit 1.25 3.00
MI6 William Ellsworth Robinson 1.25 3.00
MI7 Thomas Nelson Downs 1.25 3.00
MI8 Horace Goldin 1.25 3.00
MI9 Alexander Herrmann 1.25 3.00
MI10 John Nevil Maskelyne 1.25 3.00
MI11 John Henry Anderson 1.25 3.00
MI12 Howard Thurston 1.25 3.00
MI13 Harry Kellar 1.25 3.00
MI14 Robert Heller 1.25 3.00
MI15 Georges Melies 1.25 3.00

2017 Topps Allen and Ginter Mini Required Reading

COMPLETE SET (15) 15.00 40.00
STATED ODDS 1:50 HOBBY
RR1 Walden 1.25 3.00
RR2 On the Origin of Species 1.25 3.00
RR3 Jane Eyre 1.25 3.00
RR4 A Tale of Two Cities 1.25 3.00
RR5 War and Peace 1.25 3.00
RR6 20,000 Leagues Under the Sea 1.25 3.00
RR7 Heart of Darkness 1.25 3.00
RR8 Moby Dick 1.25 3.00
RR9 Wuthering Heights 1.25 3.00
RR10 The Canterbury Tales 1.25 3.00
RR11 The Illiad 1.25 3.00
RR12 The Prince 1.25 3.00
RR13 The Adventures of Tom Sawyer 1.25 3.00
RR14 The Count of Monte Cristo 1.25 3.00
RR15 Dr. Jekyll and Mr. Hyde 1.25 3.00

2017 Topps Allen and Ginter Relics

VERSION A ODDS 1:24 HOBBY
VERSION B ODDS 1:24 HOBBY
FSRAAB Andrew Benintendi A 6.00 15.00
FSRAAG Adrian Gonzalez A 2.50 6.00
FSRAAJ Aaron Judge A 20.00 50.00
FSRAAK Andy Katz A 2.50 6.00
FSRAAM Andrew McCutchen A 3.00 8.00
FSRAAR Anthony Rizzo A 4.00 10.00
FSRABSM Ben Smith A 2.50 6.00
FSRACB Corey Bellemore A 2.50 6.00
FSRACK Craig Kimbrel A 2.50 6.00
FSRADJ Dan Jennings EXEC A 2.50 6.00
FSRADO David Ortiz A 3.00 8.00
FSRADP Dustin Pedroia A 3.00 8.00
FSRADW David Wright A 2.50 6.00
FSRAEL Evan Longoria A 2.50 6.00
FSRAELG Eric LeGrand A 2.50 6.00
FSRAGP Gregory Polanco A 2.50 6.00
FSRAGS Giancarlo Stanton A 3.00 8.00
FSRAGST Gary Stevens A 2.50 6.00
FSRAHP Hunter Pence A 2.50 6.00
FSRAJG Jay Glazer A 2.50 6.00
FSRAJH Jason Heyward A 2.50 6.00
FSRAJL Jon Lester A 2.50 6.00
FSRAJM Joe Manganiello A 2.50 6.00
FSRAJST Jayson Stark A 2.50 6.00
FSRAJT Jameson Taillon A 2.50 6.00
FSRAJU Justin Upton A 2.50 6.00
FSRAJV Justin Verlander A 3.00 8.00
FSRAKB Kris Bryant A 6.00 15.00
FSRAKK Kevin Kelley A 2.50 6.00
FSRAKR Ken Rosenthal A 2.50 6.00
FSRALH Laurie Hernandez A 3.00 8.00
FSRALT Lyle Thompson A 2.50 6.00
FSRAMB Mookie Betts A 6.00 15.00
FSRAMCA Miguel Cabrera A 3.00 8.00
FSRAMCO Miguel Cotto A 2.50 6.00
FSRAMF Michael Fulmer A 2.00 5.00
FSRAMKA Michal Kapral A 2.50 6.00
FSRAMM Manny Machado A 3.00 8.00
FSRAMT Masahiro Tanaka A 2.50 6.00
FSRANJ Nick Jonas A 2.50 6.00
FSRAPG Paul Goldschmidt A 3.00 8.00
FSRAPR Peter Rosenberg A 2.50 6.00
FSRARB Ryan Braun A 2.50 6.00
FSRARO Rougned Odor A 2.50 6.00
FSRASP Salvador Perez A 2.50 6.00
FSRATAN Tom Anderson A 4.00 10.00
FSRATG Tyler Glasnow A 8.00 20.00
FSRAVJ Valarie Jenkins A 8.00 20.00
FSRAVM Victor Martinez A 2.50 6.00
FSRAWS William Shatner A 4.00 10.00
FSRAYC Yoenis Cespedes A 3.00 8.00
FSRBABR Alex Bregman B 10.00 25.00
FSRBAC Aroldis Chapman B 3.00 8.00
FSRBAJO Adam Jones B 2.50 6.00
FSRBAJU Aaron Judge B 20.00 50.00
FSRBAM Andrew McCutchen B 3.00 8.00
FSRBAP Albert Pujols B 4.00 10.00
FSRBARI Anthony Rizzo B 4.00 10.00
FSRBARU Addison Russell B 3.00 8.00
FSRBAW Adam Wainwright B 2.50 6.00
FSRBBH Bryce Harper B 5.00 12.00
FSRBBP Buster Posey B 4.00 10.00
FSRBCC Carlos Correa B 3.00 8.00
FSRBCG Carlos Gonzalez B 2.50 6.00
FSRBCH Cole Hamels B 2.50 6.00
FSRBCKE Clayton Kershaw B 5.00 12.00
FSRBCKL Corey Kluber B 2.50 6.00
FSRBCSA Chris Sale B 3.00 8.00
FSRBCSE Corey Seager B 3.00 8.00
FSRBCY Christian Yelich B 4.00 10.00
FSRBDPR David Price B 2.50 6.00
FSRBDS Dansby Swanson B 5.00 12.00
FSRBEH Eric Hosmer B 2.50 6.00
FSRBFF Freddie Freeman B 4.00 10.00
FSRBFH Felix Hernandez B 2.50 6.00
FSRBFL Francisco Lindor B 3.00 8.00
FSRBGSA Gary Sanchez B 3.00 8.00
FSRBGSP George Springer B 2.50 6.00
FSRBHR Hanley Ramirez B 2.50 6.00
FSRBIC Ichiro B 4.00 10.00
FSRBIH Ichiro B 4.00 10.00
FSRBJAL Jose Altuve B 2.50 6.00
FSRBJAR Jake Arrieta B 2.50 6.00
FSRBJBA Javier Baez B 4.00 10.00
FSRBJBR Jackie Bradley Jr B 3.00 8.00
FSRBJBU Jose Bautista B 2.50 6.00
FSRBJD Josh Donaldson B 2.50 6.00
FSRBJDG Jacob deGrom B 6.00 15.00
FSRBJU Julio Urias B 3.00 8.00
FSRBJVE Justin Verlander B 3.00 8.00
FSRBJVO Joey Votto B 3.00 8.00
FSRBKM Kenta Maeda B 2.50 6.00
FSRBKS Kyle Seager B 2.00 5.00
FSRBMCA Matt Carpenter B 3.00 8.00
FSRBMCB Miguel Cabrera B 3.00 8.00
FSRBMH Matt Harvey B 2.50 6.00
FSRBMM Manny Machado B 3.00 8.00
FSRBMSA Miguel Sano B 2.50 6.00
FSRBMST Marcus Stroman B 2.50 6.00
FSRBMTA Masahiro Tanaka B 2.50 6.00
FSRBMTR Mike Trout B 8.00 20.00
FSRBNA Nolan Arenado B 5.00 12.00
FSRBNC Nelson Cruz B 3.00 8.00
FSRBNS Noah Syndergaard B 2.50 6.00
FSRBSM Starling Marte B 2.50 6.00
FSRBSP Stephen Piscotty B 2.50 6.00
FSRBTS Trevor Story B 3.00 8.00
FSRBWM Wil Myers B 2.50 6.00
FSRBXB Xander Bogaerts B 3.00 8.00
FSRBYM Yadier Molina B 4.00 10.00

2017 Topps Allen and Ginter Revolutionary Battles

COMPLETE SET (10) 4.00 10.00
STATED ODDS 1:10 HOBBY
RB1 Battle of Lexington .75 2.00
RB2 Battle of Bunker Hill .75 2.00
RB3 Battle of Quebec .75 2.00
RB4 Battle of Long Island .75 2.00
RB5 Battle of Trenton .75 2.00
RB6 Battle of Princeton .75 2.00
RB7 Surrender of General Burgoyne .75 2.00
RB8 Battle of Cowpens .75 2.00
RB9 Battle of Guilford Court House .75 2.00
RB10 Battle of the Chesapeake .75 2.00

2017 Topps Allen and Ginter Rip Cards

OVERALL RIP ODDS 1:160 HOBBY
PRINT RUNS B/WN 30-99 COPIES PER
UNRIPPED HAVE ADD'L CARDS WITHIN
RIP1 Gary Sanchez/60 50.00 120.00
RIP2 Jackie Robinson/60 60.00 150.00
RIP3 Ty Cobb/60 50.00 120.00
RIP4 Johnny Bench/60 50.00 120.00
RIP5 Ernie Banks/60
RIP6 Reggie Jackson/60 50.00 120.00
RIP7 Nolan Arenado/60 40.00 100.00
RIP8 Sandy Koufax/60 60.00 150.00
RIP9 Stephen Strasburg/60 50.00 120.00
RIP10 Don Mattingly/60 50.00 120.00
RIP11 Roger Maris/60 50.00 120.00
RIP12 Cal Ripken Jr./60 50.00 120.00
RIP13 Ichiro/60 50.00 120.00
RIP14 Andrew McCutchen/60 40.00 100.00
RIP15 Felix Hernandez/60 40.00 100.00
RIP16 Robinson Cano/60 40.00 100.00
RIP17 Roberto Clemente/60 75.00 200.00
RIP18 Ryan Braun/60 40.00 100.00
RIP19 Adrian Beltre/30 60.00 150.00
RIP20 George Brett/60 50.00 120.00
RIP21 David Ortiz/60 50.00 120.00
RIP22 Corey Seager/60 50.00 120.00
RIP23 Albert Pujols/30 100.00 250.00
RIP24 Nolan Ryan/60 60.00 150.00
RIP25 Mookie Betts/60 75.00 200.00
RIP26 Aaron Judge/60 300.00 600.00
RIP27 Ken Griffey Jr./60 75.00 200.00
RIP28 Xander Bogaerts/30 60.00 150.00
RIP29 Clayton Kershaw/60 60.00 150.00
RIP30 Honus Wagner/60 60.00 150.00
RIP31 Yoenis Cespedes/60 40.00 100.00
RIP32 Buster Posey/60 60.00 150.00
RIP33 Mike Trout/60 75.00 200.00
RIP34 Kenta Maeda/60 40.00 100.00
RIP35 Corey Kluber/60 40.00 100.00
RIP36 Kyle Schwarber/60 50.00 120.00
RIP37 Joey Votto/60 50.00 120.00
RIP38 Manny Machado/60 60.00 150.00
RIP39 Barry Larkin/60 50.00 120.00
RIP40 Adam Jones/30 40.00 100.00
RIP41 Trea Turner/60 40.00 100.00
RIP42 Jacob deGrom/60 40.00 100.00
RIP43 Bryce Harper/60 75.00 200.00
RIP44 Ozzie Smith/60 60.00 150.00
RIP45 Jake Arrieta/30
RIP46 Dave Winfield/60 50.00 120.00
RIP47 Mark McGwire/60
RIP48 Noah Syndergaard/60 50.00 120.00
RIP49 Paul Goldschmidt/30 100.00 250.00
RIP50 Anthony Rizzo/60 50.00 120.00
RIP51 Aledmys Diaz/60 50.00 120.00
RIP52 Alex Bregman/60 50.00 120.00
RIP53 Ted Williams/60 60.00 150.00
RIP54 Andrew Benintendi/60 50.00 120.00
RIP55 Randy Johnson/60
RIP56 Max Scherzer/60 50.00 120.00
RIP57 Jose Canseco/60 50.00 120.00
RIP58 Kris Bryant/60 75.00 200.00
RIP59 Yu Darvish/60 40.00 100.00
RIP60 Hank Aaron/60 75.00 200.00
RIP61 Mike Piazza/60 50.00 120.00
RIP62 Giancarlo Stanton/60 40.00 100.00
RIP63 Matt Kemp/30 60.00 150.00
RIP64 Yoan Moncada/60 50.00 120.00
RIP65 Hunter Pence/30 60.00 150.00
RIP66 Dansby Swanson/60 40.00 100.00
RIP67 Miguel Cabrera/60 40.00 100.00
RIP68 Wil Myers/40 40.00 100.00
RIP69 Chris Sale/60 40.00 100.00
RIP70 Francisco Lindor/60 50.00 120.00
RIP71 Derek Jeter/60 75.00 200.00
RIP72 Greg Maddux/60 50.00 120.00
RIP73 Justin Verlander/60 50.00 120.00
RIP74 Brooks Robinson/60 50.00 120.00
RIP75 Dustin Pedroia/60 40.00 100.00
RIP76 Babe Ruth/60 75.00 200.00
RIP77 Roger Clemens/60 40.00 100.00
RIP78 John Smoltz/60 60.00 150.00
RIP79 Addison Russell/60 50.00 120.00
RIP80 Jose Altuve/60 40.00 100.00
RIP81 Carlos Correa/60 50.00 120.00
RIP83 Freddie Freeman/30 60.00 150.00
RIP84 Chipper Jones/60 60.00 150.00
RIP85 Lou Gehrig/60 60.00 150.00
RIP86 Frank Thomas/60 50.00 120.00
RIP87 Eric Hosmer/30
RIP88 Masahiro Tanaka/60
RIP89 Bo Jackson/60 50.00 120.00
RIP90 Josh Donaldson/60 40.00 100.00
RIP96 Julio Urias/60 50.00 120.00

2017 Topps Allen and Ginter Rip Cards Ripped

UNRIPPED ODDS 1:160 HOBBY
PRINT RUNS B/WN 30-50 COPIES PER
PRICING FOR CLEANLY RIPPED CARDS
RIP1 Gary Sanchez/60 3.00 8.00
RIP2 Jackie Robinson/60 3.00 8.00
RIP3 Ty Cobb/60 5.00 12.00
RIP4 Johnny Bench/60 3.00 8.00
RIP5 Ernie Banks/60 3.00 8.00
RIP6 Reggie Jackson/60 2.50 6.00
RIP7 Nolan Arenado/60 5.00 12.00
RIP8 Sandy Koufax/60 6.00 15.00
RIP9 Stephen Strasburg/60 3.00 8.00
RIP10 Don Mattingly/60 6.00 15.00
RIP11 Roger Maris/60 3.00 8.00
RIP12 Cal Ripken Jr./60 10.00 25.00
RIP13 Ichiro/60 4.00 10.00
RIP14 Andrew McCutchen/60 3.00 8.00
RIP15 Felix Hernandez/60 2.50 6.00
RIP16 Robinson Cano/60 2.50 6.00
RIP17 Roberto Clemente/60 8.00 20.00
RIP18 Ryan Braun/60 2.50 6.00
RIP19 Adrian Beltre/30 3.00 8.00
RIP20 George Brett/60 6.00 15.00
RIP21 David Ortiz/60 3.00 8.00
RIP22 Corey Seager/60 3.00 8.00
RIP23 Albert Pujols/30 4.00 10.00
RIP24 Nolan Ryan/60 10.00 25.00
RIP25 Mookie Betts/60 6.00 15.00
RIP26 Aaron Judge/60 25.00 60.00
RIP27 Ken Griffey Jr./60 6.00 15.00
RIP28 Xander Bogaerts/30 3.00 8.00
RIP29 Clayton Kershaw/60 5.00 12.00
RIP30 Honus Wagner/60 3.00 8.00
RIP31 Yoenis Cespedes/60 3.00 8.00
RIP32 Buster Posey/60 4.00 10.00
RIP33 Mike Trout/60 15.00 40.00
RIP34 Kenta Maeda/60 2.50 6.00
RIP35 Corey Kluber/60 2.50 6.00
RIP36 Kyle Schwarber/60 3.00 8.00
RIP37 Joey Votto/60 3.00 8.00
RIP38 Manny Machado/60 3.00 8.00
RIP39 Barry Larkin/60 3.00 8.00
RIP40 Adam Jones/30 2.50 6.00
RIP41 Trea Turner/60 2.50 6.00
RIP42 Jacob deGrom/60 6.00 15.00
RIP43 Bryce Harper/60 5.00 12.00
RIP44 Ozzie Smith/60 4.00 10.00
RIP45 Jake Arrieta/30 2.50 6.00
RIP46 Dave Winfield/60 2.50 6.00
RIP47 Mark McGwire/60 5.00 12.00
RIP48 Noah Syndergaard/60 2.50 6.00
RIP49 Paul Goldschmidt/30 3.00 8.00
RIP50 Anthony Rizzo/60 4.00 10.00
RIP51 Aledmys Diaz/60 2.50 6.00
RIP52 Alex Bregman/60 10.00 25.00
RIP53 Ted Williams/60 6.00 15.00
RIP54 Andrew Benintendi/60 6.00 15.00
RIP55 Randy Johnson/60 3.00 8.00
RIP56 Max Scherzer/60 3.00 8.00
RIP57 Jose Canseco/60 2.50 6.00
RIP58 Kris Bryant/60 4.00 10.00
RIP59 Yu Darvish/60 3.00 8.00
RIP60 Hank Aaron/60 6.00 15.00
RIP61 Mike Piazza/60 3.00 8.00
RIP62 Giancarlo Stanton/60 3.00 8.00
RIP63 Matt Kemp/30 2.50 6.00
RIP64 Yoan Moncada/60 6.00 15.00
RIP65 Hunter Pence/30 2.50 6.00
RIP66 Dansby Swanson/60 5.00 12.00
RIP67 Miguel Cabrera/60 3.00 8.00
RIP68 Wil Myers/40 2.50 6.00
RIP69 Chris Sale/60 3.00 8.00
RIP70 Francisco Lindor/60 8.00 20.00
RIP71 Derek Jeter/60 8.00 20.00
RIP72 Greg Maddux/60 4.00 10.00
RIP73 Justin Verlander/60 3.00 8.00
RIP74 Brooks Robinson/60 2.50 6.00
RIP75 Dustin Pedroia/60 3.00 8.00
RIP76 Babe Ruth/60 8.00 20.00
RIP77 Roger Clemens/60 4.00 10.00
RIP78 John Smoltz/60 3.00 8.00
RIP79 Addison Russell/60 3.00 8.00
RIP80 Jose Altuve/60 2.50 6.00
RIP81 Carlos Correa/60 3.00 8.00
RIP83 Freddie Freeman/30 4.00 10.00
RIP84 Chipper Jones/60 3.00 8.00
RIP85 Lou Gehrig/60 6.00 15.00
RIP86 Frank Thomas/60 3.00 8.00
RIP87 Eric Hosmer/30 2.50 6.00
RIP88 Masahiro Tanaka/60 2.50 6.00
RIP89 Bo Jackson/60 3.00 8.00
RIP90 Josh Donaldson/60 2.50 6.00
RIP96 Julio Urias/60 3.00 8.00

2017 Topps Allen and Ginter Sport Fish and Fishing Lures

COMPLETE SET (20) 6.00 15.00
STATED ODDS 1:5 HOBBY
SFL1 Northern Pike .60 1.50
SFL2 Walleye .60 1.50
SFL3 Bluegill .60 1.50
SFL4 Bass .60 1.50
SFL5 Salmon .60 1.50
SFL6 Largemouth Bass .60 1.50
SFL7 Trout .60 1.50
SFL8 Rainbow Trout .60 1.50
SFL9 Tarpon .60 1.50
SFL10 Redfish .60 1.50
SFL11 Spotted Sea Trout .60 1.50
SFL12 Grouper .60 1.50
SFL13 Sailfish .60 1.50
SFL14 Giant Trevally .60 1.50
SFL15 Bluefin Tuna .60 1.50
SFL16 Yellowfin Tuna .60 1.50
SFL17 Dorado (Mahi Mahi) .60 1.50
SFL18 Wahoo .60 1.50
SFL19 Barracuda .60 1.50
SFL20 Smallmouth Bass .60 1.50

2017 Topps Allen and Ginter What a Day

COMPLETE SET (100) 25.00 60.00
STATED ODDS 1:2 HOBBY
WAD1 Kris Bryant .50 1.25
WAD2 Buster Posey .50 1.25
WAD3 Hank Aaron .75 2.00
WAD4 Chris Sale .40 1.00
WAD5 Anthony Rizzo .50 1.25
WAD6 Nolan Ryan 1.25 3.00
WAD7 Dansby Swanson .60 1.50
WAD8 Aledmys Diaz .30 .75
WAD9 David Price .30 .75
WAD10 Dustin Pedroia .40 1.00
WAD11 Ryan Braun .30 .75
WAD12 Roger Maris .40 1.00
WAD13 Jose Canseco .30 .75
WAD14 Mike Piazza .40 1.00
WAD15 Brooks Robinson .30 .75
WAD16 Xander Bogaerts .40 1.00
WAD17 Carlos Correa .40 1.00
WAD18 Masahiro Tanaka .30 .75
WAD19 Kyle Schwarber .40 1.00
WAD20 George Brett .75 2.00
WAD21 Stephen Strasburg .40 1.00
WAD22 Honus Wagner .30 .75
WAD23 Kenta Maeda .30 .75
WAD24 Carl Yastrzemski .60 1.50
WAD25 Andrew McCutchen .40 1.00
WAD26 Frank Thomas .40 1.00
WAD27 Mike Trout 2.00 5.00
WAD28 Daniel Murphy .30 .75
WAD29 Sandy Koufax .75 2.00
WAD30 Carlos Gonzalez .30 .75
WAD31 Matt Kemp .30 .75
WAD32 Lou Gehrig .75 2.00
WAD33 Nolan Arenado .60 1.50
WAD34 Yu Darvish .40 1.00
WAD35 Jose Bautista .30 .75
WAD36 George Springer .30 .75
WAD37 Bo Jackson .40 1.00
WAD38 Chris Davis .25 .60
WAD39 John Smoltz .40 1.00
WAD40 Gary Sanchez .40 1.00
WAD41 Eric Hosmer .30 .75
WAD42 Francisco Lindor .40 1.00
WAD43 Adrian Beltre .40 1.00
WAD44 Pedro Martinez .30 .75
WAD45 Clayton Kershaw .60 1.50
WAD46 Chipper Jones .40 1.00
WAD47 Ted Williams .75 2.00
WAD48 Albert Pujols .50 1.25
WAD49 Wil Myers .30 .75
WAD50 Trea Turner .30 .75
WAD51 Joey Votto .40 1.00
WAD52 David Dahl .30 .75
WAD53 Robinson Cano .30 .75
WAD54 Ozzie Smith .50 1.25
WAD55 David Wright .30 .75
WAD56 Don Mattingly .75 2.00
WAD57 Noah Syndergaard .30 .75
WAD58 Corey Seager .40 1.00
WAD59 Andrew Benintendi .75 2.00
WAD60 Ty Cobb .60 1.50
WAD61 Greg Maddux .50 1.25
WAD62 David Ortiz .40 1.00
WAD63 Reggie Jackson .30 .75
WAD64 Adam Jones .30 .75
WAD65 Yoenis Cespedes .40 1.00
WAD66 Justin Verlander .40 1.00
WAD67 Mookie Betts .75 2.00
WAD68 Max Scherzer .40 1.00
WAD69 Johnny Bench .40 1.00
WAD70 Troy Tulowitzki .40 1.00
WAD71 Matt Carpenter .40 1.00
WAD72 Edwin Encarnacion .40 1.00
WAD73 Ken Griffey Jr. .75 2.00
WAD74 Miguel Cabrera .40 1.00
WAD75 Randy Johnson .40 1.00
WAD76 Jake Arrieta .30 .75
WAD77 Felix Hernandez .30 .75
WAD78 Manny Machado .40 1.00
WAD79 Freddie Freeman .50 1.25
WAD80 Derek Jeter 1.00 2.50
WAD81 Addison Russell .40 1.00
WAD82 Ernie Banks .40 1.00
WAD83 Bryce Harper .60 1.50
WAD84 Cal Ripken Jr. 1.25 3.00
WAD85 Corey Kluber .30 .75
WAD86 Roberto Clemente 1.00 2.50
WAD87 Ichiro .50 1.25
WAD88 Babe Ruth 1.00 2.50
WAD89 Roger Clemens .50 1.25
WAD90 Jackie Robinson .40 1.00
WAD91 Jose Altuve .30 .75
WAD92 Javier Baez .50 1.25
WAD93 Josh Donaldson .30 .75
WAD94 Alex Bregman 1.25 3.00
WAD95 Byron Buxton .40 1.00
WAD96 Julio Urias .40 1.00
WAD97 Jacob deGrom .75 2.00
WAD98 Giancarlo Stanton .40 1.00
WAD99 Mark McGwire .60 1.50
WAD100 Paul Goldschmidt .40 1.00

2017 Topps Allen and Ginter World Baseball Classic Relics

STATED ODDS 1:274 HOBBY
STATED PRINT RUN 99 SER.#'d SETS
WBCRAB Adrian Beltre 6.00 15.00
WBCRABR Alex Bregman 8.00 20.00
WBCRAG Adrian Gonzalez 5.00 12.00
WBCRAJ Adam Jones 5.00 12.00
WBCRAM Andrew McCutchen 8.00 20.00
WBCRAV Alex Verdugo 8.00 20.00
WBCRBP Buster Posey 8.00 20.00
WBCRCC Carlos Correa 15.00 40.00
WBCRCG Carlos Gonzalez 5.00 12.00
WBCREH Eric Hosmer 10.00 25.00
WBCRFH Felix Hernandez 5.00 12.00
WBCRFL Francisco Lindor 12.00 30.00
WBCRGC Gavin Cecchini 4.00 10.00
WBCRGS Giancarlo Stanton 8.00 20.00
WBCRJA Jose Altuve 6.00 15.00
WBCRJBA Javier Baez 8.00 20.00
WBCRJBU Jose Bautista 5.00 12.00
WBCRMCB Miguel Cabrera 6.00 15.00
WBCRMM Manny Machado 6.00 15.00
WBCRNA Nolan Arenado 10.00 25.00
WBCRPG Paul Goldschmidt 6.00 15.00
WBCRRC Robinson Cano 5.00 12.00
WBCRSF Shintaro Fujinami 6.00 15.00
WBCRSP Salvador Perez 5.00 12.00
WBCRTN Takahiro Norimoto 4.00 10.00
WBCRTS Tomoyuki Sugano 6.00 15.00
WBCRTY Tetsuto Yamada 8.00 20.00
WBCRXB Xander Bogaerts 8.00 20.00
WBCRYM Yadier Molina 12.00 30.00
WBCRYT Yoshitomo Tsutsugoh 10.00 25.00

2017 Topps Allen and Ginter Mini World's Dudes

COMPLETE SET (45) 40.00 100.00
STATED ODDS 1:13 HOBBY
WD1 Surgeon Dude 1.00 2.50
WD2 Conductor Dude 1.00 2.50
WD3 Pilot Dude 1.00 2.50
WD4 Polo Dude 1.00 2.50
WD5 Traffic Cop Dude 1.00 2.50
WD6 Hunting Guide Dude 1.00 2.50
WD7 Deep Sea Dude 1.00 2.50
WD8 Scholar Dude 1.00 2.50
WD9 Japanese Sumo Dude 1.00 2.50
WD10 Algerian Lawyer Dude 1.00 2.50
WD11 Tennis Dude 1.00 2.50
WD12 New York Ferreter Dude 1.00 2.50
WD13 Tunisian Editor Dude 1.00 2.50
WD14 Packer Dude 1.00 2.50
WD15 Barber Dude 1.00 2.50
WD16 Chef Dude 1.00 2.50
WD17 Newsboy Dude 1.00 2.50
WD18 Egyptian Sultan Dude 1.00 2.50
WD19 German Snow Patrol Dude 1.00 2.50
WD20 English Chimney Sweep Dude 1.00 2.50
WD21 Chilean Sailor Dude 1.00 2.50
WD22 University Track Dude 1.00 2.50
WD23 Lumberjack Dude 1.00 2.50
WD24 Violin Dude 1.00 2.50
WD25 American Football Dude 1.00 2.50
WD26 Farmhand Dude 1.00 2.50
WD27 Steel Worker Dude 1.00 2.50
WD28 Irish Golfer Dude 1.00 2.50
WD29 Boxing Dude 1.00 2.50
WD30 Machinist Dude 1.00 2.50
WD31 German Cyclist Dude 1.00 2.50
WD32 Concession Dude 1.00 2.50
WD33 Zookeeper Dude 1.00 2.50
WD34 Ornithology Dude 1.00 2.50
WD35 Camping Dude 1.00 2.50
WD36 Circus Clown Dude 1.00 2.50
WD37 Artist Dude 1.00 2.50
WD38 Polish Prince Dude 1.00 2.50
WD39 Scottish Dude 1.00 2.50
WD40 Park Avenue Dude 1.00 2.50
WD41 Russian Peddler Dude 1.00 2.50
WD42 Scout Dude 1.00 2.50
WD43 Fisherman Dude 1.00 2.50
WD44 Gardener Dude 1.00 2.50
WD45 Secretary to the Sultan Dude 1.00 2.50

2017 Topps Allen and Ginter World's Fair

COMPLETE SET (20) 3.00 8.00
STATED ODDS 1:5 HOBBY
WF1 Life Savers Parachute Jump New York World's Fair .30 .75
WF2 X-Ray Machine Pan-American Exposition .30 .75
WF3 The Atomium Expo '58 .30 .75
WF4 The Great Wharf World's Columbian Exposition .30 .75
WF5 Westinghouse Tower New York World's Fair .30 .75
WF6 Eiffel Tower Exposition Universelle .30 .75
WF7 Diesel Engine Exposition Universelle .30 .75
WF8 Facsimile Machine The Great Exhibition .30 .75
WF9 Sunsphere 82 World's Fair .30 .75
WF10 Conical Pendulum Clock Exposition Universelle .30 .75
WF11 Space Needle Century 21 Exposition .30 .75
WF12 Unisphere 64-'65 World's Fair .30 .75
WF13 Solar Generator Exposition Universelle .30 .75
WF14 Monorail Centennial Exposition .30 .75
WF15 Ferris Wheel World's Columbian Exposition .30 .75
WF16 Biosphere Expo 67 .30 .75
WF17 Statue of Liberty Exposition Universelle .30 .75
WF18 Statue of the Republic World's Columbian Exposition .30 .75
WF19 Habitat 67 Expo 67 .30 .75
WF20 Telephone Centennial Exposition .30 .75

2016 Topps Allen and Ginter X

COMPLETE SET (350)
1 Jorge Soler .40 1.00
2 Ryan Braun .30 .75
3 Joey Gallo .30 .75
4 Justin Verlander .40 1.00
5 Kyle Waldrop RC .50 1.25
6 Luke Maile RC .40 1.00
7 John Lamb RC .40 1.00
8 Denise Austin .25 .60
9 Tom Glavine .30 .75
10 Jason Sklar .25 .60
11 Howie Kendrick .25 .60
12 Trevor Story RC 2.00 5.00
13 Kevin Gausman .40 1.00
14 Kendrys Morales .25 .60
15 Mark Trumbo .25 .60
16 Trayce Thompson RC .60 1.50
17 Ian Desmond .30 .75
18 Kolten Wong .30 .75
19 Rollie Fingers .30 .75
20 Michael Pineda .25 .60
21 Ben Zobrist .30 .75
22 Francisco Rodriguez .30 .75
23 Addison Russell .40 1.00
24 Max Kepler RC .60 1.50
25 Charlie Blackmon .40 1.00
26 John Lackey .30 .75
27 Matt Duffy .25 .60
28 Elvis Andrus .30 .75
29 Jay Bruce .30 .75
30 Curtis Granderson .30 .75
31 Brad Ziegler .25 .60
32 Falcon 9 Rocket .25 .60
33 Ender Inciarte .25 .60
34 Rick Klein .25 .60
35 Jayson Werth .30 .75
36 Alex Rodriguez .50 1.25
37 Dawn Spacecraft .25 .60
38 David Peralta .25 .60
39 Paul Goldschmidt .40 1.00
40 Jordan Zimmermann .30 .75
41 Drew Smyly .25 .60
42 Cuban Embassy .25 .60
43 Jake Odorizzi .25 .60
44 Miguel Castro RC .40 1.00
45 Laurence Leavy .25 .60
46 Ben Revere .25 .60
47 Corey Dickerson .25 .60
48 J.T. Realmuto .40 1.00
49 Ketel Marte RC .75 2.00
50 Daniel Murphy .30 .75
51 A.J. Ramos .25 .60
52 Adam Eaton .25 .60
53 Logan Forsythe .25 .60
54 Jose Abreu .40 1.00
55 Hector Rondon .25 .60
56 Carlos Correa .40 1.00
57 Jim Rice .30 .75
58 Freddie Freeman .50 1.25
59 Billy Hamilton .30 .75

60 Devin Mesoraco .25 .60
61 Miguel Cabrera .40 1.00
62 Dellin Betances .30 .75
63 Monica Abbott .25 .60
64 Steve Schirripa .25 .60
65 Hisashi Iwakuma .25 .60
66 Miguel Sano RC .60 1.50
67 Melky Cabrera .25 .60
68 Dexter Fowler .30 .75
69 Roberto Alomar .30 .75
70 Chase Headley .25 .60
71 Matt Reynolds RC .40 1.00
72 Jake McGee .30 .75
73 James Shields .25 .60
74 Brian Dozier .30 .75
75 Mike Moustakas .30 .75
76 Collin McHugh .25 .60
77 Kevin Pillar .25 .60
78 Jose Berrios RC .60 1.50
79 Dustin Garneau RC .40 1.00
80 Edwin Encarnacion .40 1.00
81 Brian Johnson RC .40 1.00
82 Gerardo Parra .25 .60
83 David Wright .30 .75
84 Robinson Cano .30 .75
85 Prince Fielder .30 .75
86 Adam Jones .30 .75
87 Craig Kimbrel .30 .75
88 Jose Fernandez .40 1.00
89 Dallas Keuchel .30 .75
90 George Lopez .25 .60
91 Nick Hundley .25 .60
92 Steven Matz .25 .60
93 Mike Piazza .40 1.00
94 Todd Frazier .25 .60
95 Jimmy Nelson .25 .60
96 Jason Kipnis .30 .75
97 Kyle Schwarber RC 1.25 3.00
98 Michael Conforto RC .50 1.25
99 Luis Severino RC .50 1.25
100 Rob Refsnyder RC .50 1.25
101 Roger Clemens .50 1.25
102 Aaron Nola RC .75 2.00
103 Carlos Martinez .30 .75
104 Byron Buxton .40 1.00
105 Alex Dickerson RC .40 1.00
106 Steve Spurrier .25 .60
107 Matt Stonie .25 .60
108 Justin Turner .40 1.00
109 Eduardo Rodriguez .25 .60
110 Michele Steele .25 .60
111 Lorenzo Cain .25 .60
112 Kris Bryant .50 1.25
113 Alcides Escobar .30 .75
114 Randy Sklar .25 .60
115 Brad Miller .30 .75
116 Jose Reyes .30 .75
117 Robin Yount .40 1.00
118 Evan Gattis .25 .60
119 Gennady Golovkin 6.00 15.00
120 Kenta Maeda .50 1.25
121 Corey Seager RC 4.00 10.00
122 Andrew Heaney .25 .60
123 Alex Cobb .25 .60
124 Jonathan Lucroy .30 .75
125 Carl Edwards Jr. RC .50 1.25
126 Greg Bird RC .50 1.25
127 Lucas Duda .30 .75
128 Aroldis Chapman .40 1.00
129 Zack Greinke .40 1.00
130 Gregory Polanco .30 .75
131 Brooks Robinson .30 .75
132 Leigh Steinberg .25 .60
133 Joc Pederson .30 .75
134 Henry Owens .30 .75
135 Luis Gonzalez .30 .75
136 Matt Kemp .30 .75
137 Marcus Semien .40 1.00
138 Cord McCoy .25 .60
139 Gio Gonzalez .30 .75
140 Caleb Cotham RC .50 1.25
141 Colin Rea RC .40 1.00
142 Jake Arrieta .30 .75
143 Adrian Gonzalez .30 .75
144 Matt Holliday .40 1.00
145 Mike Greenberg .25 .60
146 Evan Longoria .25 .60
147 Martin Prado .25 .60
148 Kole Calhoun .25 .60
149 Michael Brantley .30 .75
150 Eric Hosmer .30 .75
151 David Ortiz .40 1.00
152 Gary Sanchez RC 1.25 3.00
153 Jung Ho Kang .25 .60
154 Ervin Santana .25 .60
155 Brandon Phillips .25 .60
156 Jason Heyward .30 .75
157 Gerrit Cole .40 1.00
158 Joe McKeehen .25 .60
159 Brett Gardner .30 .75
160 Steve Kerr .25 .60
161 Vinny G .25 .60
162 Josh Harrison .25 .60
163 Zach Lee RC .40 1.00
164 Steven Souza Jr. .30 .75
165 Nelson Cruz .40 1.00
166 Morgan Spurlock .25 .60
167 Jeff Samardzija .25 .60
168 Don Mattingly .75 2.00
169 Adrian Beltre .40 1.00
170 Max Scherzer .40 1.00
171 Brandon Crawford .30 .75
172 Joe Morgan .30 .75
173 Billy Burns .25 .60
174 Frankie Montas RC .50 1.25
175 Jonathan Schoop .25 .60
176 Neil Walker .25 .60
177 Mark Teixeira .30 .75
178 David Robertson .25 .60
179 Jen Welter .25 .60
180 Ryne Sandberg .75 2.00
181 Alex Wood .25 .60
182 Nolan Arenado .60 1.50
183 Andrew McCutchen .40 1.00
184 Mookie Betts .75 2.00
185 J.D. Martinez .40 1.00
186 Alex Gordon .30 .75
187 Carl Yastrzemski .60 1.50
188 Edgar Martinez .30 .75
189 Buster Posey .50 1.25
190 Jon Gray RC .40 1.00
191 Anthony Anderson .25 .60
192 Dennis Eckersley .30 .75
193 Huston Street .25 .60
194 Mike Trout 5.00 12.00
195 Joey Votto .40 1.00
196 Josh Reddick .25 .60
197 George Springer .30 .75
198 Ari Shaffir .25 .60
199 Carlton Fisk .30 .75
200 Carlos Gomez .25 .60
201 Byung Ho Park RC .50 1.25
202 Missy Franklin .25 .60
203 Ernie Johnson .25 .60
204 Drew Storen .25 .60
205 Carlos Santana .30 .75
206 Bob Gibson .30 .75
207 Brandon Belt .30 .75
208 Joe Panik .30 .75
209 Andrew Miller .30 .75
210 Michael Breed .25 .60
211 Albert Pujols .50 1.25
212 Maria Sharapova .25 .60
213 Heidi Watney .25 .60
214 Justin Bour .30 .75
215 Khris Davis .40 1.00
216 Hannah Storm .25 .60
217 Julio Teheran .30 .75
218 Masahiro Tanaka .30 .75
219 Delino DeShields .25 .60
220 Matt Duffy .25 .60
221 Brian McCann .25 .60
222 Nomar Mazara RC .60 1.50
223 Erick Aybar .25 .60
224 Gary Carter .30 .75
225 Brandon Drury RC .60 1.50
226 Luke Jackson RC .40 1.00
227 Timothy Busfield .25 .60
228 Colin Cowherd .25 .60
229 Mitch Moreland .25 .60
230 Jessica Mendoza .25 .60
231 Kaleb Cowart RC .40 1.00
232 Hector Olivera RC .50 1.25
233 Adam Lind .30 .75
234 Glen Perkins .25 .60
235 Cheyenne Woods .25 .60
236 Brad Boxberger .25 .60
237 Dustin Pedroia .40 1.00
238 Tyler White RC .40 1.00
239 Brandon Moss .25 .60
240 Robert Raiola .25 .60
241 Orlando Jones .25 .60
242 DJ LeMahieu .40 1.00
243 Jay Oakerson .25 .60
244 Gravitational Waves .25 .60
245 Dwier Brown .25 .60
246 Mike Francesa .25 .60
247 Papal Visit .25 .60
248 Jill Martin .25 .60
249 Paul McBeth 1.50 4.00
250 Jose Canseco .30 .75
251 Stephen Piscotty RC .60 1.50
252 Cole Hamels .30 .75
253 Ozzie Smith .50 1.25
254 Bryce Harper .60 1.50
255 Nomar Garciaparra .30 .75
256 Starling Marte .30 .75
257 Chris Archer .25 .60
258 Kenley Jansen .30 .75
259 Jose Peraza RC .50 1.25
260 Anthony Rizzo .50 1.25
261 Carlos Carrasco .25 .60
262 Giancarlo Stanton .40 1.00
263 Hanley Ramirez .30 .75
264 Xander Bogaerts .40 1.00
265 Felix Hernandez .30 .75
266 Anthony Rendon .40 1.00
267 Sonny Gray .30 .75
268 Frank Thomas .40 1.00
269 Maikel Franco .30 .75
270 David Price .30 .75
271 A.J. Pollock .30 .75
272 Troy Tulowitzki .40 1.00
273 Dee Gordon .25 .60
274 Chris Sale .40 1.00
275 Jacob deGrom .75 2.00
276 Matt Harvey .30 .75
277 Manny Machado .40 1.00
278 Madison Bumgarner .30 .75
279 Paul Molitor .40 1.00
280 Paul O'Neill .30 .75
281 Jose Bautista .30 .75
282 Stephen Strasburg .40 1.00
283 Michael Wacha .30 .75
284 Orlando Cepeda .30 .75
285 Josh Donaldson .30 .75
286 Guido Knudson RC .40 1.00
287 Andre Dawson .30 .75
288 Lance McCullers .25 .60
289 Jose Quintana .25 .60
290 Andrew Faulkner RC .50 1.25
291 Kevin Kiermaier .30 .75
292 Marcell Ozuna .40 1.00
293 Jonathan Papelbon .30 .75
294 Carlos Rodon .40 1.00
295 Jose Altuve .30 .75
296 Rickey Henderson .40 1.00
297 Corey Kluber .30 .75
298 Jacoby Ellsbury .30 .75
299 Clayton Kershaw .60 1.50
300 Trea Turner RC 1.25 3.00
301 Tyson Ross SP .50 1.25
302 Trevor Brown SP RC .60 1.50
303 Wei-Yin Chen SP .50 1.25
304 Yasmani Grandal SP .50 1.25
305 Tyler Duffey SP RC .60 1.50
306 Yu Darvish SP .75 2.00
307 Russell Martin SP .50 1.25
308 Andy Pettitte SP .60 1.50
309 Yasmany Tomas SP .50 1.25
310 Patrick Corbin SP .60 1.50
311 Wellington Castillo SP .50 1.25
312 Carlos Beltran SP .60 1.50
313 Stephen Vogt SP .60 1.50
314 Starlin Castro SP .50 1.25
315 Santiago Casilla SP .50 1.25
316 Ryan Weber SP RC .50 1.25
317 Yordano Ventura SP .60 1.50
318 Pedro Severino SP RC .60 1.50
319 Yasiel Puig SP .75 2.00
320 Roberto Clemente SP 2.00 5.00
321 Nick Castellanos SP .75 2.00
322 Ryan LaMarre SP RC .50 1.25
323 Victor Martinez SP .60 1.50
324 Rob Refsnyder SP .60 1.50
325 Raisel Iglesias SP .60 1.50
326 Peter O'Brien SP RC .50 1.25
327 Raul Mondesi SP RC 1.00 2.50
328 Randal Grichuk SP .50 1.25
329 Andre Ethier SP .60 1.50
330 Zack Godley SP RC .60 1.50
331 Taijuan Walker SP .50 1.25
332 Yan Gomes SP .50 1.25
333 Shin-Soo Choo SP .60 1.50
334 Scott Kazmir SP .50 1.25
335 Shawn Tolleson SP .50 1.25
336 Tom Murphy SP RC .50 1.25
337 Steve Cishek SP .50 1.25
338 Stephen Piscotty SP .75 2.00
339 Salvador Perez SP .60 1.50
340 Roberto Osuna SP .50 1.25
341 Richie Shaffer SP RC .50 1.25
342 Trea Turner SP 1.50 4.00
343 Shelby Miller SP .60 1.50
344 Ryan Zimmerman SP .60 1.50
345 Wil Myers SP .60 1.50
346 Pablo Sandoval SP .60 1.50
347 Sean Doolittle SP .50 1.25
348 Trevor Plouffe SP .50 1.25
349 Travis d'Arnaud SP .60 1.50
350 Steve Carlton SP .60 1.50

2016 Topps Allen and Ginter X Silver Framed Mini Autographs

EXCHANGE DEADLINE 6/30/2018
AGAA Anthony Anderson 8.00 20.00
AGAAN Aaron Nola 20.00 50.00
AGABH Bryce Harper 125.00 300.00
AGABP Buster Posey 40.00 100.00
AGABS Blake Snell 10.00 25.00
AGACA Canelo Alvarez 60.00 150.00
AGACC Colin Cowherd 10.00 25.00
AGACC Carlos Correa 40.00 100.00
AGACM Cord McCoy 8.00 20.00
AGACSA Chris Sale 10.00 25.00
AGACSE Corey Seager 30.00 80.00
AGADK Dallas Keuchel 12.00 30.00
AGAEJ Ernie Johnson 25.00 60.00
AGAES Errol Spence Jr. 25.00 60.00
AGAFH Felix Hernandez 12.00 30.00
AGAFV Fernando Valenzuela 20.00 50.00
AGAFW Frank Whaley 8.00 20.00
AGAGG Gennady Golovkin 150.00 400.00
AGAGL George Lopez 12.00 30.00
AGAHA Hank Aaron 150.00 300.00
AGAHS Hannah Storm 8.00 20.00
AGAHW Heidi Watney 12.00 30.00
AGAJBA Javier Baez 25.00 60.00
AGAJBE Jose Berrios 10.00 25.00
AGAJC Jose Canseco 12.00 30.00
AGAJD Jacob deGrom 30.00 80.00
AGAJS Jason Sklar 15.00 40.00
AGAKB Kris Bryant 75.00 200.00
AGAKG Ken Griffey Jr. 125.00 300.00
AGAKMA Kenta Maeda 20.00 50.00
AGAKS Kyle Schwarber 20.00 50.00
AGALS Luis Severino 20.00 50.00
AGAMCO Michael Conforto 12.00 30.00
AGAMFA Mike Francesa 10.00 25.00
AGAMFR Missy Franklin 10.00 25.00
AGAMG Mike Greenberg 10.00 25.00
AGAMIS Michele Steele 8.00 20.00
AGAMP Mike Piazza 40.00 100.00
AGAMPH Michael Phelps 125.00 300.00
AGAMSH Maria Sharapova 60.00 150.00
AGAMST Matt Stonie 12.00 30.00
AGAMT Mike Trout 150.00 400.00
AGANG Nomar Garciaparra 15.00 40.00
AGANL Nancy Lieberman 10.00 25.00
AGANM Nomar Mazara 12.00 30.00
AGAOJO Orlando Jones 8.00 20.00
AGAPM Paul Molitor 20.00 50.00
AGAPMB Paul McBeth 30.00 80.00
AGARC Robinson Cano 8.00 20.00
AGARSK Randy Sklar 10.00 25.00
AGASK Steve Kerr 12.00 30.00
AGASP Stephen Piscotty 8.00 20.00
AGASS Steve Spurrier 15.00 40.00
AGASSA Susan Sarandon 50.00 120.00
AGATB Timothy Busfield 10.00 25.00
AGATS Trevor Story 10.00 25.00
AGATT Trea Turner 12.00 30.00
AGAVGU Vinny G 10.00 25.00

2018 Topps Allen and Ginter

COMPLETE SET (350) 25.00 60.00
COMP.SET w/o SP's (300) 15.00 40.00
SP ODDS 1:2 HOBBY
1 Mike Trout 1.25 3.00
2 Derek Jeter .60 1.50
3 Babe Ruth .60 1.50
4 Cameron Maybin .15 .40
5 Kris Bryant .30 .75
6 Chris Taylor .20 .50
7 Aaron Judge .60 1.50
8 Ryan Sickler .15 .40
9 Francisco Mejia RC .30 .75
10 Jose Altuve .20 .50
11 Jose Abreu .25 .60
12 Eddie Rosario .25 .60
13 Sonny Fredrickson .15 .40
14 Craig Kimbrel .20 .50
15 Giancarlo Stanton .25 .60
16 Austin Hays RC .40 1.00
17 Kyle Seager .15 .40
18 Bullpen Car .15 .40
19 Yoan Moncada .25 .60
20 Joey Votto .25 .60
21 Noah Syndergaard .20 .50
22 Michael Conforto .20 .50
23 Jordan Montgomery .15 .40
24 Trey Mancini .20 .50
25 Andre Dawson .20 .50
26 Marwin Gonzalez .15 .40
27 Sean Manaea .15 .40
28 Jack Flaherty RC 1.00 2.50
29 H. Jon Benjamin .15 .40
30 Carlos Correa .25 .60
31 Joc Pederson .25 .60
32 Anthony Rizzo .30 .75
33 Nicky Delmonico RC .25 .60
34 Scott Blumstein .15 .40
35 Robinson Cano .20 .50
36 Trevor Story .25 .60
37 Yu Darvish .25 .60
38 Jonathan Lucroy .20 .50
39 Trea Turner .20 .50
40 Max Scherzer .25 .60
41 Didi Gregorius .20 .50
42 Jackie Robinson .20 .50
43 Champ Pederson .15 .40
44 Aaron Hicks .20 .50
45 Dexter Fowler .20 .50
46 Kole Calhoun .15 .40
47 Dansby Swanson .25 .60
48 Manny Margot .15 .40
49 Luke Weaver .20 .50
50 Hank Aaron .50 1.25
51 J.D. Martinez .25 .60
52 Robbie Ray .15 .40
53 Mike Zunino .15 .40
54 Carlos Gonzalez .20 .50
55 Biz Markie .15 .40
56 Justin Bour .15 .40
57 Lindsey Vonn .25 .60
58 Andrelton Simmons .15 .40
59 J.D. Davis RC .30 .75
60 Cal Ripken Jr. .75 2.00
61 Randal Grichuk .15 .40
62 Justin Upton .20 .50
63 Luiz Gohara RC .30 .75
64 Daniel Murphy .20 .50
65 Clint Frazier RC .50 1.25
66 Paul Goldschmidt .25 .60
67 Ozzie Smith .30 .75
68 Yasiel Puig .25 .60
69 Anthony Banda RC .25 .60
70 Jason Heyward .20 .50
71 Matt Carpenter .25 .60
72 Nelson Cruz .25 .60
73 Adrian Beltre .25 .60
74 Eric Hosmer .20 .50
75 Christian Yelich .30 .75
76 Ryan Zimmerman .20 .50
77 Adam Duvall .20 .50
78 Jason Kipnis .20 .50
79 Jonathan Schoop .15 .40
80 Ryan Braun .20 .50
81 Yulli Gurriel .20 .50
82 Method Man .15 .40
83 Cryptocurrency 30.00 80.00
84 Marine National Monument .15 .40
85 Mariano Rivera .30 .75
86 Nicholas Castellanos .25 .60
87 Alex Wood .15 .40
88 Kenta Maeda .20 .50
89 Mike Moustakas .20 .50
90 Avisail Garcia .20 .50
91 Victor Caratini RC .30 .75
92 Barry Larkin .20 .50
93 Stephen Strasburg .25 .60
94 George Brett .50 1.25
95 Victor Robles RC .60 1.50
96 Wil Myers .20 .50
97 Mike Piazza .25 .60
98 A.J. Pollock .15 .40
99 Pedro Martinez .20 .50
100 Shohei Ohtani RC 6.00 15.00
101 Matt Kemp .20 .50
102 Josh Bell .20 .50
103 Lucas Sims RC .25 .60
104 Michael Fulmer .15 .40
105 Jacob deGrom .50 1.25
106 David Ortiz .25 .60
107 Roberto Clemente .60 1.50
108 Tommy Pham .15 .40
109 Sonny Gray .20 .50
110 Honus Wagner .25 .60
111 Brian Dozier .20 .50
112 Yadier Molina .30 .75
113 Randy Johnson .25 .60
114 Jim Thome .20 .50
115 Ian Happ .20 .50
116 Ozzie Albies RC .75 2.00
117 Corey Kluber .20 .50
118 Sean Doolittle .15 .40
119 Javier Baez .30 .75
120 Cody Bellinger .50 1.25
121 Dustin Pedroia .25 .60
122 Jimmy Nelson .15 .40
123 John Smoltz .20 .50
124 Nolan Ryan .75 2.00
125 Brian McCann .20 .50
126 Jon Lester .20 .50
127 J.P. Crawford RC .25 .60
128 Dellin Betances .20 .50
129 Stephen Piscotty .15 .40
130 Gary Sanchez .25 .60
131 Greg Maddux .30 .75
132 Masahiro Tanaka .20 .50
133 Johnny Bench .25 .60
134 Trevor Bauer .30 .75
135 Chris Sale .25 .60
136 Maikel Franco .20 .50
137 Josh Donaldson .20 .50
138 Ernie Banks .25 .60
139 Michael Rapaport .15 .40
140 Alex Bregman .25 .60
141 Archie Bradley .15 .40
142 Kevin Pillar .15 .40
143 Hunter Pence .20 .50
144 CC Sabathia .20 .50
145 Genie Bouchard .15 .40
146 Billy Hamilton .20 .50
147 Walker Buehler RC 1.25 3.00
148 Luis Severino .20 .50
149 Steve Simeone .15 .40
150 Ervin Santana .15 .40
151 Don Mattingly .50 1.25
152 Ben Lecomte .15 .40
153 Sloane Stephens .15 .40
154 Raisel Iglesias .15 .40
155 Hunter Renfroe .15 .40
156 Edwin Encarnacion .25 .60
157 Bill James .15 .40
158 Yonder Alonso .15 .40
159 Bob Gibson .20 .50
160 Matt Olson .25 .60
161 Austin Rogers .15 .40
162 Chipper Jones .25 .60
163 Byron Buxton .25 .60
164 Manny Machado .25 .60
165 Ben Zobrist .20 .50
166 Johnny Cueto .20 .50
167 Scott Kingery RC .40 1.00
168 Andrew Benintendi .25 .60
169 Mike Clevinger .20 .50
170 Bradley Zimmer .15 .40
171 Rougned Odor .20 .50
172 Buster Posey .30 .75
173 Nolan Arenado .40 1.00
174 Corey Seager .25 .60
175 Lincoln Riley .15 .40
176 Claire Smith .15 .40
177 Dallas Keuchel .20 .50
178 Jon Gray .15 .40
179 Tyronn Lue .15 .40
180 Willson Contreras .25 .60
181 Khris Davis .25 .60
182 Greg Bird .20 .50
183 Dee Gordon .15 .40
184 Andrew McCutchen .25 .60
185 Joe Panik .20 .50
186 George Springer .20 .50
187 Albert Pujols .30 .75
188 Zack Cozart .15 .40
189 Ichiro .25 .60
190 Ted Williams .50 1.25
191 Freddie Freeman .30 .75
192 Chris Archer .15 .40
193 Zack Granite RC .25 .60
194 Justin Smoak .15 .40
195 Tim Anderson .20 .50
196 Tyler Mahle RC .30 .75
197 Kenley Jansen .20 .50
198 Tom Segura .15 .40
199 Garrett Cooper RC .25 .60
200 Sandy Koufax .50 1.25
201 Miguel Andujar RC 1.00 2.50
202 Stugotz .15 .40
203 Amed Rosario RC .30 .75
204 Samesong Park .15 .40
205 Scott Rogowsky .15 .40
206 Paul Blackburn RC .25 .60
207 Ronald Acuna Jr. RC 8.00 20.00
208 Kelsey Plum .15 .40
209 Fernando Rodney .15 .40
210 Francisco Lindor .25 .60
211 Rhys Hoskins RC 1.00 2.50
212 Mark McGwire .40 1.00
213 Ryne Sandberg .50 1.25
214 Josh Reddick .15 .40
215 Brandon Crawford .20 .50
216 Rafael Devers RC .75 2.00
217 Dominic Smith RC .30 .75
218 Christopher McDonald .15 .40
219 Gerrit Cole .25 .60
220 Theo Epstein .25 .60
221 Jeff Bagwell .25 .60
222 Total Solar Eclipse .15 .40
223 Dave Winfield .20 .50
224 Starling Marte .20 .50
225 Lou Gehrig .50 1.25
226 Lucas Giolito .20 .50
227 Aaron Altherr .15 .40
228 Tommy Wiseau .15 .40
229 Roger Maris .25 .60
230 Tim Beckham .20 .50
231 Michael Brantley .20 .50
232 Chance Sisco RC .30 .75
233 Roger Clemens .30 .75
234 Adam Wainwright .20 .50
235 Marcell Ozuna .25 .60
236 Luis Castillo .20 .50
237 Brian Anderson RC .30 .75
238 Pat Neshek .15 .40
239 Evan Longoria .20 .50
240 Gleyber Torres RC 2.50 6.00
241 Jesse Winker .25 .60
242 Yoenis Cespedes .25 .60
243 Yuli Gurriel .20 .50
244 Orlando Arcia .15 .40
245 Mookie Betts .50 1.25
246 Travis Shaw .15 .40
247 Lance McCullers .15 .40
248 Aaron Nola .20 .50
249 Kyle Schwarber .25 .60
250 Bryce Harper .40 1.00
251 Charlie Blackmon .25 .60
252 Gio Gonzalez .20 .50
253 Hanley Ramirez .20 .50
254 Jackie Bradley Jr. .25 .60
255 Willie Calhoun RC .40 1.00
256 Jake Arrieta .20 .50
257 Andrew Stevenson RC .25 .60
258 Parker Bridwell RC .25 .60
259 Bomb Cyclone .15 .40
260 Sean Evans .15 .40
261 Brooks Robinson .20 .50
262 Felix Hernandez .20 .50
263 Jose Ramirez .20 .50
264 Reggie Jackson .20 .50
265 Carlos Rodon .20 .50
266 Franklin Barreto .15 .40
267 Garrett Richards .20 .50
268 Jose Berrios .20 .50
269 Phil Coyne USHER .15 .40
270 Eric Thames .20 .50
271 Jose Canseco .20 .50
272 Ryan McMahon RC .60 1.50
273 Jake Lamb .20 .50
274 Domingo Santana .20 .50
275 Justin Verlander .25 .60
276 Chris Davis .15 .40
277 Willie McCovey .20 .50
278 Pal DeJong .25 .60
279 Miguel Sano .20 .50
280 Clayton Kershaw .40 1.00
281 Salvador Perez .20 .50
282 Joey Gallo .20 .50
283 Addison Russell .20 .50
284 Ian Kinsler .20 .50
285 Jackson Stephens RC .25 .60
286 Frank Thomas .25 .60
287 Paige Spiranac .15 .40
288 Mike Leake .15 .40
289 Wade Boggs .20 .50
290 Ty Cobb .40 1.00
291 Albert Almora .20 .50
292 Marcus Stroman .20 .50
293 Alex Verdugo RC .40 1.00
294 Steven Matz .15 .40
295 Xander Bogaerts .25 .60
296 Taijuan Walker .15 .40
297 Miguel Cabrera .25 .60
298 Jameson Taillon .20 .50
299 Adam Jones .20 .50
300 Bo Jackson .25 .60
301 Whit Merrifield SP .60 1.50
302 Justin Turner SP .60 1.50
303 Hyun-Jin Ryu SP .50 1.25
304 Brandon Woodruff SP RC 1.25 3.00
305 Lewis Brinson SP .40 1.00
306 Joe Mauer SP .50 1.25
307 Hideki Matsui SP .60 1.50
308 Brett Gardner SP .50 1.25
309 Aroldis Chapman SP .60 1.50
310 Matt Chapman SP .60 1.50
311 Dustin Fowler SP RC .40 1.00
312 Carlos Santana SP .40 1.00
313 Nick Williams SP RC .50 1.25
314 Gregory Polanco SP .50 1.25
315 Christian Villanueva SP RC .40 1.00
316 Will Clark SP .50 1.25
317 Mitch Haniger SP .50 1.25
318 Carlos Martinez SP .50 1.25
319 Harrison Bader SP RC .60 1.50
320 Corey Dickerson SP .40 1.00
321 Nomar Mazara SP .40 1.00
322 Richard Urena SP RC .40 1.00
323 Erick Fedde SP RC .40 1.00
324 Anthony Rendon SP .60 1.50
325 Cole Hamels SP .50 1.25
326 Elvis Andrus SP .50 1.25
327 Kevin Kiermaier SP .50 1.25
328 Edwin Diaz SP .50 1.25
329 Josh Harrison SP .40 1.00
330 Ryder Jones SP RC .40 1.00
331 Todd Frazier SP .40 1.00
332 Max Kepler SP .50 1.25
333 Zach Davies SP .40 1.00
334 Sandy Alcantara SP RC .40 1.00
335 Julio Urias SP .60 1.50
336 Lorenzo Cain SP .40 1.00
337 Dennis Eckersley SP .50 1.25
338 Darryl Strawberry SP .40 1.00
339 Starlin Castro SP .40 1.00
340 Andy Pettitte SP .50 1.25
341 Rickey Henderson SP .60 1.50
342 Carlos Carrasco SP .40 1.00
343 Sean Newcomb SP .50 1.25
344 Ender Inciarte SP .40 1.00
345 Tyler Glasnow SP .60 1.50
346 Dwight Gooden SP .40 1.00
347 Jay Bruce SP .50 1.25
348 Josh Hader SP .50 1.25
349 German Marquez SP .40 1.00
350 Jen-Ho Tseng SP RC .40 1.00

2018 Topps Allen and Ginter Glossy Silver

*GLS SLVR 1-300: 2X TO 5X BASIC
*GLS SLVR 1-300 RC: 1.2X TO 3X BASIC RCs
*GLS SLVR 301-350: .75X TO 2X BASIC
FOUND ONLY IN HOBBY HOT BOXES

2018 Topps Allen and Ginter Mini

*MINI 1-300: 1X TO 2.5X BASIC
*MINI 1-300 RC: .6X TO 1.5X BASIC RCs
*MINI SP 301-350: .6X TO 1.5X BASIC
MINI SP ODDS 1:13 HOBBY
351-400 RANDOM WITHIN RIP CARDS
STATED PLATE ODDS 1:1328 HOBBY
PLATE PRINT RUN 1 SET PER COLOR
BLACK-CYAN-MAGENTA-YELLOW ISSUED
NO PLATE PRICING DUE TO SCARCITY
351 Mike Trout EXT 30.00 80.00
352 Shohei Ohtani EXT 125.00 300.00
353 Paul Goldschmidt EXT 12.00 30.00
354 Hank Aaron EXT 15.00 40.00
355 Ozzie Albies EXT 20.00 50.00
356 Manny Machado EXT 15.00 40.00
357 Cal Ripken Jr. EXT 30.00 80.00
358 Mookie Betts EXT 25.00 60.00
359 Andrew Benintendi EXT 25.00 60.00
360 Rafael Devers EXT 15.00 40.00
361 Jackie Robinson EXT 15.00 40.00
362 Sandy Koufax EXT 15.00 40.00
363 Anthony Rizzo EXT 15.00 40.00
364 Kris Bryant EXT 15.00 40.00
365 Joey Votto EXT 15.00 4.00
366 Francisco Lindor EXT 12.00 30.00
367 Nolan Arenado EXT 15.00 40.00
368 Miguel Cabrera EXT 12.00 30.00
369 Justin Verlander EXT 12.00 30.00
370 Carlos Correa EXT 12.00 30.00
371 Jose Altuve EXT 25.00 60.00
372 Nolan Ryan EXT 25.00 60.00
373 Bo Jackson EXT 25.00 60.00
374 Cody Bellinger EXT 25.00 60.00
375 Clayton Kershaw EXT 20.00 50.00
376 Corey Seager EXT 12.00 30.00
377 Yu Darvish EXT 12.00 30.00
378 Ichiro EXT 20.00 50.00
379 Byron Buxton EXT 15.00 40.00
380 Noah Syndergaard EXT 10.00 25.00
381 Amed Rosario EXT 10.00 25.00
382 Giancarlo Stanton EXT 12.00 30.00
383 Aaron Judge EXT 40.00 100.00
384 Clint Frazier EXT 15.00 40.00
385 Babe Ruth EXT 20.00 50.00
386 Derek Jeter EXT 20.00 50.00
387 Mariano Rivera EXT 20.00 50.00
388 Mark McGwire EXT 15.00 40.00
389 Rhys Hoskins EXT 20.00 50.00
390 Andrew McCutchen EXT 15.00 40.00
391 Roberto Clemente EXT 30.00 80.00
392 Buster Posey EXT 20.00 50.00
393 Robinson Cano EXT 10.00 25.00
394 Josh Donaldson EXT 10.00 25.00
395 Bryce Harper EXT 15.00 40.00
396 Max Scherzer EXT 15.00 40.00
397 Victor Robles EXT 15.00 40.00
398 Honus Wagner EXT 20.00 50.00
399 George Brett EXT 25.00 60.00
400 Frank Thomas EXT 20.00 50.00

2018 Topps Allen and Ginter Mini A and G Back

*MINI AG 1-300: 1.2X TO 3X BASIC
*MINI AG 1-300 RC: .75X TO 2X BASIC RCs
*MINI AG SP 301-350: .75X TO 2X BASIC
STATED ODDS 1:5 HOBBY

2018 Topps Allen and Ginter Mini Black Border

*MINI BLK 1-300: 2X TO 5X BASIC
*MINI BLK 1-300 RC: 1.2X TO 3X BASIC RCs
*MINI BLK SP 301-350: 1.2X TO 3X BASIC
MINI BLK ODDS 1:10 HOBBY

2018 Topps Allen and Ginter Mini Brooklyn Back

*MINI BRKLN 1-300: 12X TO 30X BASIC
*MINI BRKLN 1-300 RC: 8X TO 20X BASIC RCs
*MINI BRKLN 301-350: 5X TO 12X BASIC
STATED ODDS 1:248 HOBBY
STATED PRINT RUN 25 SER.#'d SETS

2018 Topps Allen and Ginter Mini Glow in the Dark

*MINI GLOW 1-300: 12X TO 30X BASIC
*MINI GLOW 1-300 RC: 8X TO 20X BASIC RCs
*MINI GLOW 301-350: 5X TO 12X BASIC
RANDOM INSERTS IN PACKS

2018 Topps Allen and Ginter Mini Gold

*MINI GOLD 1-300: 2.5X TO 6X BASIC
*MINI GOLD 1-300 RC: 1.5X TO 4X BASIC RCs
*MINI GOLD 301-350: 1X TO 2.5X BASIC
RANDOMLY INSERTED IN RETAIL PACKS

2018 Topps Allen and Ginter Mini No Number

*MINI NNO 1-300: 5X TO 12X BASIC
*MINI NNO 1-300 RC: 3X TO 8X BASIC RCs
*MINI NNO 301-350: 2X TO 5X BASIC
MINI NNO ODDS 1:124 HOBBY
ANNCD PRINT RUN 50 COPIES PER

2018 Topps Allen and Ginter Autographs

STATED ODDS 1:4163 HOBBY
EXCHANGE DEADLINE 6/30/2020
FSACE Chris Evans 300.00 600.00
FSACH Chris Hemsworth 300.00 600.00
FSAMB Mikal Bridges 12.00 30.00

2018 Topps Allen and Ginter Baseball Equipment of the Ages

COMPLETE SET (30) 12.00 30.00
STATED ODDS 1:6 HOBBY
BEA1 Vintage Glove .40 1.00
BEA2 The Catch Glove .40 1.00
BEA3 Modern Glove .40 1.00
BEA4 Vintage Bat .40 1.00
BEA5 Modern Bat .40 1.00
BEA6 Early Catcher's Mask .40 1.00
BEA7 Modern Catcher's Mask .40 1.00
BEA8 Batting Gloves .40 1.00
BEA9 Vintage Catcher's Mitt .40 1.00
BEA10 Modern Catcher's Mitt .40 1.00
BEA11 Vintage Baseball .40 1.00
BEA12 Modern Baseball .40 1.00
BEA13 Catcher's Chest Protector .40 1.00
BEA14 Flip-Up Sunglasses .40 1.00
BEA15 Vintage Cleats .40 1.00
BEA16 Modern Cleats .40 1.00
BEA17 Baseball Donut .40 1.00
BEA18 Fungo Bat .40 1.00
BEA19 Pitch Counter .40 1.00
BEA20 Rosin Bag .40 1.00
BEA21 Batting Shin Guards .40 1.00
BEA22 Catching Shin Guards .40 1.00
BEA23 Modern Baseball Sunglasses .40 1.00
BEA24 Baseball Hat .40 1.00
BEA25 Batting Helmet .40 1.00
BEA26 Radar Gun .40 1.00
BEA27 Bases .40 1.00
BEA28 Eye Black .40 1.00
BEA29 Baseball Sweater .40 1.00
BEA30 Vintage Uniform .40 1.00

2018 Topps Allen and Ginter Box Toppers

INSERTED IN HOBBY BOXES
BL1 Kris Bryant 2.50 6.00
BL2 Mike Trout 3.00 8.00
BL3 Jose Altuve 1.25 3.00
BL4 Aaron Judge 4.00 10.00
BL5 Clayton Kershaw 2.50 6.00
BL6 Bryce Harper 2.50 6.00
BL7 Shohei Ohtani 5.00 12.00
BL8 Ronald Acuna Jr. 5.00 12.00
BL9 Gleyber Torres 5.00 12.00
BL10 Cal Ripken Jr. 2.50 6.00
BL11 Don Mattingly 2.50 6.00
BL12 Mark McGwire 2.50 6.00
BL13 Chipper Jones 1.50 4.00
BL14 Babe Ruth 2.50 6.00
BL15 Honus Wagner 1.50 4.00

2018 Topps Allen and Ginter Fabled Relics

RANDOM INSERTS IN PACKS
STATED PRINT RUN 25 SER.#'d SETS
MFARC Cupid 75.00 200.00
MFARE El Dorado 75.00 200.00
MFARP Phoenix 75.00 200.00
MFARS Shangri-La 75.00 200.00
MFARKA King Arthur 150.00 300.00
MFARPE Pegasus 75.00 200.00

2018 Topps Allen and Ginter Fantasy Goldmine

COMPLETE SET (50) 15.00 40.00
STATED ODDS 1:4 HOBBY
FG1 Hank Aaron .75 2.00
FG2 Cal Ripken Jr. 1.25 3.00
FG3 Jackie Robinson .40 1.00
FG4 Sandy Koufax .75 2.00
FG5 Nolan Ryan 1.25 3.00

FG6 Bo Jackson .40 1.00
FG7 Babe Ruth 1.00 2.50
FG8 Derek Jeter 1.00 2.50
FG9 Mariano Rivera .50 1.25
FG10 Mark McGwire .60 1.50
FG11 Roberto Clemente 1.00 2.50
FG12 Honus Wagner .40 1.00
FG13 George Brett .75 2.00
FG14 Frank Thomas .40 1.00
FG15 Greg Maddux .50 1.25
FG16 Randy Johnson .40 1.00
FG17 Pedro Martinez .30 .75
FG18 Reggie Jackson .30 .75
FG19 Ted Williams .75 2.00
FG20 Jimmie Foxx .40 1.00
FG21 Ernie Banks .40 1.00
FG22 Ryne Sandberg .75 2.00
FG23 Chipper Jones .40 1.00
FG24 Wade Boggs .30 .75
FG25 Don Mattingly .75 2.00
FG26 Barry Larkin .30 .75
FG27 Nomar Garciaparra .30 .75
FG28 Ozzie Smith .50 1.25
FG29 John Smoltz .40 1.00
FG30 Andy Pettitte .30 .75
FG31 Roberto Alomar .30 .75
FG32 Ty Cobb .60 1.50
FG33 Lou Gehrig .75 2.00
FG34 Johnny Bench .40 1.00
FG35 Rickey Henderson .40 1.00
FG36 Hideki Matsui .40 1.00
FG37 Tom Seaver .30 .75
FG38 Jim Palmer .30 .75
FG39 Willie McCovey .30 .75
FG40 Jim Thome .30 .75
FG41 Brooks Robinson .30 .75
FG42 Al Kaline .40 1.00
FG43 Lou Brock .30 .75
FG44 Mike Piazza .40 1.00
FG45 Roger Clemens .50 1.25
FG46 Rod Carew .30 .75
FG47 Steve Carlton .30 .75
FG48 Ivan Rodriguez .30 .75
FG49 Ichiro .50 1.25
FG50 Bob Gibson .30 .75

2018 Topps Allen and Ginter Framed Mini Autographs

STATED ODDS 1:58 HOBBY
EXCHANGE DEADLINE 6/30/2020
MAAA Aaron Altherr 4.00 10.00
MAAE Austin Meadows 15.00 40.00
MAAH Austin Hays 10.00 25.00
MAAJ Aaron Judge 75.00 200.00
MAAL Alison Lee 10.00 25.00
MAAM A.J. Minter 5.00 12.00
MAAN Anthony Banda 4.00 10.00
MAAO Austin Rogers 6.00 15.00
MAAR Amed Rosario 5.00 12.00
MAAS Andrew Stevenson 4.00 10.00
MABD Brian Dozier 10.00 25.00
MABH Bryce Harper 100.00 250.00
MABI Bill James 10.00 25.00
MABJ Bo Jackson
MABL Ben Lecomte 4.00 10.00
MABM Biz Markie 20.00 50.00
MABW Brandon Woodruff 12.00 30.00
MACM Claire Smith 5.00 12.00
MACO Christopher McDonald 5.00 12.00
MACP Champ Pederson 6.00 15.00
MACS Chance Sisco 5.00 12.00
MADC Dominic Smith 5.00 12.00
MADF Dustin Fowler 4.00 10.00
MADM Don Mattingly 40.00 100.00
MADP Dillon Peters 4.00 10.00
MADS Darryl Strawberry 6.00 15.00
MADU Doris Burke 20.00 50.00
MAFJ Felix Jorge 4.00 10.00
MAFM Francisco Mejia
MAFT Frank Thomas 40.00 100.00
MAGC Garrett Cooper 4.00 10.00
MAGT Gleyber Torres 60.00 150.00
MAGU Genie Bouchard 15.00 40.00
MAHB Harrison Bader 6.00 15.00
MAHJ H. Jon Benjamin 20.00 50.00
MAIH Ian Happ 5.00 12.00
MAJA Jose Altuve 20.00 50.00
MAJB Justin Bour 4.00 10.00
MAJB John Boyega 20.00 50.00
'17 Card in '18 Frame
MAJC J.P. Crawford 4.00 10.00
MAJCK Jack Sock 6.00 15.00
MAJD J.D. Davis 5.00 12.00
MAJH Jordan Hicks 10.00 25.00
MAJI Jose Berrios 5.00 12.00
MAJJ Jaren Jackson Jr. 30.00 80.00
MAJM J.D. Martinez EXCH 20.00 50.00
MAJO Jose Canseco 12.00 30.00
MAJR Jose Ramirez 12.00 30.00
MAJS Jackson Stephens 4.00 10.00
MAJV Joey Votto 25.00 60.00
MAJZ Jon Lovitz 40.00 100.00
MAKB Keon Broxton 4.00 10.00
MAKD Khris Davis 6.00 15.00
MAKP Kelsey Plum 5.00 12.00
MAKR Kris Bryant 60.00 150.00
MALC Luis Castillo 5.00 12.00
MALR Lincoln Riley 25.00 60.00
MALV Lindsey Vonn 25.00 60.00
MAMF Max Fried 25.00 60.00
MAMG Miguel Gomez 4.00 10.00
MAMH Molly McGrath 12.00 30.00
MAMIII Marvin Bagley III 40.00 100.00
MAMM Manny Machado 30.00 80.00
MAMMI Miles Mikolas 5.00 12.00
MAMN Method Man EXCH 30.00 80.00
MAMO Matt Olson 6.00 15.00
MAMR Michael Rapaport 12.00 30.00
MAMT Mike Trout 300.00 500.00
MAMW Mark McGwire
MAMY Madison Keys 8.00 20.00
MANY Noah Syndergaard 12.00 30.00
MAOA Ozzie Albies 25.00 60.00
MAPB Parker Bridwell 4.00 10.00
MAPD Paul DeJong 6.00 15.00
MAPG Paul Goldschmidt 15.00 40.00
MAPL Paul Blackburn 4.00 10.00
MAPSP Paige Spiranac 15.00 40.00
MARA Ronald Acuna 75.00 200.00
MARD Rafael Devers 20.00 50.00
MARI Ryan Sickler 12.00 30.00
MARK Rhys Hoskins 20.00 50.00
MARR Raudy Read 4.00 10.00
MARU Richard Urena 4.00 10.00
MAS Stugotz 20.00 50.00
MASA Sandy Alcantara 4.00 10.00
MASB Scott Blumstein 4.00 10.00
MASE Sean Evans 12.00 30.00
MASF Sonny Fredrickson 5.00 12.00
MASG Sonny Gray
MASKI Scott Kingery 8.00 20.00
MASN Sean Newcomb 5.00 12.00
MASO Shohei Ohtani 150.00 400.00
MASR Scott Rogowsky 10.00 25.00
MASS Steve Simeone 4.00 10.00
MASST Sloane Stephens 6.00 15.00
MASX Collin Sexton 30.00 80.00
MATE Theo Epstein 50.00 120.00
MATG Tom Segura 12.00 30.00
MATH Tony Hawk 50.00 120.00
MATI Tommy Wiseau 20.00 50.00
MATL Tzu-Wei Lin 5.00 12.00
MATLU Tyronn Lue 4.00 10.00
MATM Tyler Mahle 5.00 12.00
MATN Tomas Nido 4.00 10.00
MATS Troy Scribner 4.00 10.00
MATV Travis Shaw 4.00 10.00
MAVC Victor Caratini 6.00 15.00
MAVR Victor Robles 20.00 50.00
MAWB Walker Buehler 25.00 60.00
MAWM Whit Merrifield 8.00 20.00
MAWO Willson Contreras 10.00 25.00

2018 Topps Allen and Ginter Framed Mini Autographs Black Frame

*BLACK: .75X TO 2X BASIC
STATED ODDS 1:527 HOBBY
PRINT RUN B/WN 10-25 SETS PER
NO PRICING QTY 15 OR LESS
EXCHANGE DEADLINE 6/30/2020
MABJ Bo Jackson 60.00 150.00

2018 Topps Allen and Ginter Magnificent Moons

COMPLETE SET (10) 4.00 10.00
STATED ODDS 1:6 HOBBY
MM1 Moon - Earth .40 1.00
MM2 Europa - Jupiter .40 1.00
MM3 Io - Jupiter .40 1.00
MM4 Mimas - Saturn .40 1.00
MM5 Enceladus - Saturn .40 1.00
MM6 Triton - Neptune .40 1.00
MM7 Phobos - Mars .40 1.00
MM8 Titan - Saturn .40 1.00
MM9 Miranda - Uranus .40 1.00
MM10 Ganymede - Jupiter .40 1.00

2018 Topps Allen and Ginter Mini Baseball Superstitions

COMPLETE SET (15) 15.00 40.00
STATED ODDS 1:50 HOBBY
MBS1 No talking about a No-hitter 1.25 3.00
MBS2 Batting Gloves 1.25 3.00
MBS3 Wearing the same Helmet 1.25 3.00
MBS4 Postseason Beards 1.25 3.00
MBS5 Leaping over the Foul line 1.25 3.00
MBS6 Pre-Game Meal 1.25 3.00
MBS7 Rally Caps 1.25 3.00
MBS8 Wearing The Same Hat 1.25 3.00
MBS9 Drawing in the Batter's Box Dirt 1.25 3.00
MBS10 Between-Inning Routine 1.25 3.00
MBS11 Curse of the Bambino 1.25 3.00
MBS12 Not changing seats 1.25 3.00
MBS13 Lucky Jersey Numbers 1.25 3.00
MBS14 Mismatched Socks 1.25 3.00
MBS15 Baseball cards 1.25 3.00

2018 Topps Allen and Ginter Mini DNA Relics

STATED ODDS 1:9666 HOBBY
PRINT RUNS B/WN 2-25 COPIES PER
NO PRICING ON QTY 17 OR LESS
DNARMO Mosasaur Tooth/25 250.00 500.00
DNARMT Megalodon Tooth/25 250.00 500.00

2018 Topps Allen and Ginter Mini Exotic Sports

COMPLETE SET (25) 25.00 60.00
INSERTED IN RETAIL PACKS
MES1 Tug-O-War 1.25 3.00
MES2 Ostrich Racing 1.25 3.00
MES3 Chess Boxing 1.25 3.00
MES4 Underwater Hockey 1.25 3.00
MES5 Zorbing 1.25 3.00
MES6 Sumo Wrestling 1.25 3.00
MES7 Sepak Takraw 1.25 3.00
MES8 Cheese Rolling 1.25 3.00
MES9 Dog Surfing 1.25 3.00
MES10 Cornhole 1.25 3.00
MES11 Downhill Boxcar Racing 1.25 3.00
MES12 Hot Dog Eating Contest 1.25 3.00
MES13 Drone Racing 1.25 3.00
MES14 Elephant Polo 1.25 3.00
MES15 Armwrestling 1.25 3.00
MES16 Disc Golf 1.25 3.00
MES17 Roller Derby 1.25 3.00
MES18 Ultimate 1.25 3.00
MES19 Quidditch 1.25 3.00
MES20 Beer Pong 1.25 3.00
MES21 Belly Flopping 1.25 3.00
MES22 Watercross 1.25 3.00
MES23 Speed Stacking 1.25 3.00
MES24 Redbull Flugtag 1.25 3.00
MES25 Bo-taoshi 1.25 3.00

2018 Topps Allen and Ginter Mini Flags of Lost Nations

COMPLETE SET (25) 25.00 60.00
STATED ODDS 1:50 HOBBY
FLN1 USSR 1.25 3.00
FLN2 Yugoslavia 1.25 3.00
FLN3 Tibet 1.25 3.00
FLN4 Sikkim 1.25 3.00
FLN5 United Arab Republic 1.25 3.00
FLN6 Ceylon 1.25 3.00
FLN7 Republic of Salo 1.25 3.00
FLN8 West Germany 1.25 3.00
FLN9 East Germany 1.25 3.00
FLN10 Czechoslovakia 1.25 3.00
FLN11 Zanzibar 1.25 3.00
FLN12 Zaire 1.25 3.00
FLN13 Tanganyika 1.25 3.00
FLN14 Abyssinia 1.25 3.00
FLN15 Siam 1.25 3.00
FLN16 Rhodesia 1.25 3.00
FLN17 Prussia 1.25 3.00
FLN18 Persia 1.25 3.00
FLN19 Newfoundland 1.25 3.00
FLN20 New Granada 1.25 3.00
FLN21 Hawaii 1.25 3.00
FLN22 Texas 1.25 3.00
FLN23 Vermont 1.25 3.00
FLN24 Ottoman Empire 1.25 3.00
FLN25 Corsica 1.25 3.00

2018 Topps Allen and Ginter Mini Folio of Fears

COMPLETE SET (10) 12.00 30.00
STATED ODDS 1:50 HOBBY
MFF1 Arachnophobia 1.25 3.00
MFF2 Acrophobia 1.25 3.00
MFF3 Entomophobia 1.25 3.00
MFF4 Aviophobia 1.25 3.00
MFF5 Ophidiophobia 1.25 3.00
MFF6 Astraphobia 1.25 3.00
MFF7 Coulrophobia 1.25 3.00
MFF8 Claustrophobia 1.25 3.00
MFF9 Phasmophobia 1.25 3.00
MFF10 Scotophobia 1.25 3.00

2018 Topps Allen and Ginter Mini Framed Relics

STATED ODDS 1:56 HOBBY
MFRAB Andrew Benintendi 5.00 12.00
MFRAE Adrian Beltre 4.00 10.00
MFRAI Anthony Rizzo 5.00 12.00
MFRAJ Adam Jones 3.00 8.00
MFRAO Alex Rodriguez 5.00 12.00
MFRAP Albert Pujols 5.00 12.00
MFRAS Amed Rosario 3.00 8.00
MFRAU Aaron Judge 15.00 40.00
MFRBB Byron Buxton 4.00 10.00
MFRBH Bryce Harper 6.00 15.00
MFRBJ Bo Jackson 12.00 30.00
MFRBL Barry Larkin 3.00 8.00
MFRBP Buster Posey 5.00 12.00
MFRCA Corey Seager 4.00 10.00
MFRCC Carlos Correa 4.00 10.00
MFRCF Clint Frazier 5.00 12.00
MFRCJ Chipper Jones 4.00 10.00
MFRCK Clayton Kershaw 6.00 15.00
MFRCR Cal Ripken Jr. 12.00 30.00
MFRCS Chris Sale 4.00 10.00
MFRDJ Derek Jeter 12.00 30.00
MFRDM Don Mattingly 10.00 25.00
MFRDO David Ortiz 4.00 10.00
MFRDP Dustin Pedroia 4.00 10.00
MFREL Evan Longoria 3.00 8.00
MFRFF Freddie Freeman 5.00 12.00
MFRFT Frank Thomas 8.00 20.00
MFRGA Gary Sanchez 4.00 10.00
MFRGB George Brett 8.00 20.00
MFRGM Greg Maddux 5.00 12.00
MFRI Ichiro 5.00 12.00
MFRJA Jose Altuve 3.00 8.00
MFRJB Javier Baez 5.00 12.00
MFRJC Jose Canseco 3.00 8.00
MFRJD Jacob deGrom 8.00 20.00
MFRJL Justin Verlander 4.00 10.00
MFRJR Jackie Robinson 100.00 250.00
MFRJS John Smoltz 4.00 10.00
MFRJT Jim Thome 3.00 8.00
MFRJU Justin Upton 3.00 8.00
MFRJV Joey Votto 4.00 10.00
MFRKB Kris Bryant 5.00 12.00
MFRMB Mookie Betts 5.00 12.00
MFRMC Mark McGwire 15.00 40.00
MFRMG Mark McGwire 10.00 25.00
MFRMM Manny Machado 4.00 10.00
MFRMP Mike Piazza 4.00 10.00
MFRMR Mariano Rivera 5.00 12.00
MFRMS Miguel Sano 3.00 8.00
MFRMT Mike Trout 20.00 50.00
MFRNR Nolan Ryan 12.00 30.00
MFROA Ozzie Albies 6.00 15.00
MFRPG Paul Goldschmidt 4.00 10.00
MFRPM Pedro Martinez 6.00 15.00
MFRRA Robinson Cano 3.00 8.00
MFRRC Roberto Clemente 125.00 300.00
MFRRD Rafael Devers 5.00 12.00
MFRRH Rickey Henderson 10.00 25.00
MFRYD Yu Darvish 4.00 10.00
MFRYM Yadier Molina 5.00 12.00

2018 Topps Allen and Ginter Mini Indigenous Heroes

COMPLETE SET (25) 20.00 50.00
STATED ODDS 1:10 HOBBY
MIH1 Mangas Coloradas .75 2.00
MIH2 Sitting Bull .75 2.00
MIH3 Cochise .75 2.00
MIH4 Chief Seattle .75 2.00
MIH5 Crazy Horse .75 2.00
MIH6 Geronimo .75 2.00
MIH7 Tecumseh .75 2.00
MIH8 Black Hawk .75 2.00
MIH9 Chief Cornstalk .75 2.00
MIH10 Victorio .75 2.00
MIH11 Red Cloud .75 2.00
MIH12 Squanto .75 2.00
MIH13 Sacajawea .75 2.00
MIH14 Chief Pontiac .75 2.00
MIH15 Will Rogers .75 2.00
MIH16 Sequoyah "George Guess" .75 2.00
MIH17 Pocahontas .75 2.00
MIH18 Hiawatha .75 2.00
MIH19 John Ross .75 2.00
MIH20 Joseph the Younger .75 2.00
MIH21 Jim Thorpe .75 2.00
MIH22 Powhatan .75 2.00
MIH23 Ben Nighthorse Campbell .75 2.00
MIH24 Charles Eastman .75 2.00
MIH25 Maria Tallchief .75 2.00

2018 Topps Allen and Ginter Mini Postage Required

COMPLETE SET (15) 15.00 40.00
STATED ODDS 1:50 HOBBY
MPR1 Hawaiian Missionaries Stamp 1.25 3.00
MPR2 Benjamin Franklin 1.25 3.00
MPR3 Landing of Columbus 1.25 3.00
MPR4 George Washington 1.25 3.00
MPR5 Two Penny Blue 1.25 3.00
MPR6 The Declaration of Independence 1.25 3.00
MPR7 Abraham Lincoln 1.25 3.00
MPR8 Inverted Jenny 1.25 3.00
MPR9 Benjamin Franklin 1.25 3.00
MPR10 Swedish Three Skilling
Banco Yellow 1.25 3.00
MPR11 Benjamin Franklin 1.25 3.00
MPR12 British Guiana Magenta 1.25 3.00
MPR13 Baden 9 Kreuzer Error 1.25 3.00
MPR14 Penny Black 1.25 3.00
MPR15 Post Office Mauritius 1.25 3.00

2018 Topps Allen and Ginter Mini Surprise

RANDOM INSERTS IN PACKS
MS1 Cuddy Calabrese 2.00 5.00
MS2 Benjamin Geaux-Homme 2.00 5.00
MS3 Dennis the Rash 2.00 5.00

2018 Topps Allen and Ginter Mini World Hottest Peppers

COMPLETE SET (15) 15.00 40.00
STATED ODDS 1:50 HOBBY
WHP1 Pepper X 1.25 3.00
WHP2 Carolina Reaper 1.25 3.00
WHP3 Trinidad Moruga Scorpion 1.25 3.00
WHP4 7 Pot Douglah 1.25 3.00
WHP5 Primo 1.25 3.00
WHP6 Butch T Trinidad Scorpion 1.25 3.00
WHP7 Naga Viper 1.25 3.00
WHP8 Ghost Pepper 1.25 3.00
WHP9 Komodo Dragon 1.25 3.00
WHP10 Trinidad 7 Pot 1.25 3.00
WHP11 Infinity Pepper 1.25 3.00
WHP12 7 Pot Barrackpore 1.25 3.00
WHP13 Red Savina Habanero 1.25 3.00
WHP14 Naga Morich 1.25 3.00
WHP15 Dorset Naga 1.25 3.00

2018 Topps Allen and Ginter N43 Box Toppers

STATED ODDS 1:6 HOBBY BOXES
ANNCD PRINT RUN 500 SER.#'d SETS
N431 Mike Trout 8.00 20.00
N432 Jose Altuve 1.25 3.00
N433 Carlos Correa 1.50 4.00
N434 Aaron Judge 4.00 10.00
N435 Francisco Lindor 1.50 4.00
N436 Clayton Kershaw 2.50 6.00
N437 Bryce Harper 2.50 6.00
N438 Cody Bellinger 3.00 8.00
N439 Joey Votto 1.50 4.00
N4310 Andrew Benintendi 1.50 4.00
N4311 Kris Bryant 2.00 5.00
N4312 Manny Machado 1.50 4.00
N4313 Rafael Devers 3.00 8.00
N4314 Amed Rosario 1.25 3.00
N4315 Victor Robles 2.50 6.00
N4316 Ozzie Albies 3.00 8.00
N4317 Noah Syndergaard 1.25 3.00
N4318 Paul Goldschmidt 1.50 4.00
N4319 Gary Sanchez 1.50 4.00
N4320 Shohei Ohtani 25.00 60.00

2018 Topps Allen and Ginter Natural Wonders Box Toppers

STATED ODDS 1:8 HOBBY BOXES
ANNCD PRINT RUN 500 COPIES PER
NWB1 Big Sur 3.00 8.00
NWB2 Mount Kilimanjaro 3.00 8.00
NWB3 Zion National Park 3.00 8.00
NWB4 Vatnajokull Glacier Cave 3.00 8.00
NWB5 Amazon Rainforest 3.00 8.00
NWB6 Na Pali Coast 3.00 8.00
NWB7 Phang Nga Bay 3.00 8.00
NWB8 The Antarctic 3.00 8.00
NWB9 Banff National Park 3.00 8.00
NWB10 Seljalandsfoss Waterfall 3.00 8.00

2018 Topps Allen and Ginter Relics

VERSION A ODDS 1:37 HOBBY
VERSION B ODDS 1:20 HOBBY
FSRAAE Anthony Rendon A 3.00 8.00
FSRAAN Aaron Nola A 2.50 6.00
FSRAAR Austin Rogers A 3.00 8.00
FSRAAW Alex Wood A 2.00 5.00
FSRABC Brandon Crawford A 2.50 6.00
FSRABD Brian Dozier A 2.50 6.00
FSRABH Billy Hamilton A 2.50 6.00
FSRABJ Bill James A 3.00 8.00
FSRABL Ben Lecomte A 3.00 8.00
FSRACA Chris Archer A 2.00 5.00
FSRACSM Claire Smith A 3.00 8.00
FSRADF Dexter Fowler A 2.50 6.00
FSRADG Dee Gordon A 2.00 5.00
FSRADR Didi Gregorius A 2.50 6.00
FSRADS Domingo Santana A 2.50 6.00
FSRAEA Elvis Andrus A 2.50 6.00
FSRAET Eric Thames A 2.50 6.00
FSRAGB Greg Bird A 2.50 6.00
FSRAHB H. Jon Benjamin A 3.00 8.00
FSRAIH Ian Happ A 2.50 6.00
FSRAJA Jose Abreu A 3.00 8.00
FSRAJB Jose Berrios A 2.50 6.00
FSRAJC Jonathan Schoop A 2.00 5.00
FSRAJE Jason Heyward A 2.50 6.00
FSRAJH Josh Harrison A 2.00 5.00
FSRAJM Justin Smoak A 2.00 5.00
FSRAKJ Kenley Jansen A 2.50 6.00
FSRAKM Kenta Maeda A 2.50 6.00
FSRALB Lewis Brinson A 2.00 5.00
FSRALS Luis Severino A 2.50 6.00
FSRAMR Michael Rapaport A 5.00 12.00
FSRAPS Paige Spiranac A 4.00 10.00
FSRARH Rhys Hoskins A 6.00 15.00
FSRARO Rougned Odor A 2.50 6.00
FSRARS Ryan Sickler A 3.00 8.00
FSRARZ Ryan Zimmerman A 2.50 6.00
FSRASB Scott Blumstein A 3.00 8.00
FSRASE Sean Evans A 3.00 8.00
FSRASF Sonny Fredrickson A 3.00 8.00
FSRASG Sonny Gray A 2.50 6.00
FSRASM Starling Marte A 2.50 6.00
FSRASP Salvador Perez A 2.50 6.00
FSRASR Scott Rogowsky A 5.00 12.00
FSRASSI Steve Simeone A 3.00 8.00
FSRATA Travis Shaw A 2.00 5.00
FSRATE Theo Epstein A 3.00 8.00
FSRATF Todd Frazier A 2.00 5.00
FSRATS Tom Segura A 5.00 12.00
FSRATW Tommy Wiseau A 5.00 12.00
FSRAWC Willson Contreras A 3.00 8.00
FSRAWM Whit Merrifield A 3.00 8.00
FSRAYM Yoan Moncada A 3.00 8.00
FSRBAB Andrew Benintendi B 3.00 8.00
FSRBAC Aroldis Chapman B 3.00 8.00
FSRBAE Adrian Beltre B 3.00 8.00
FSRBAJ Aaron Judge B 12.00 30.00
FSRBAM Andrew McCutchen B 3.00 8.00
FSRBAP Albert Pujols B 4.00 10.00
FSRBAR Anthony Rizzo B 4.00 10.00
FSRBAU Addison Russell B 2.50 6.00
FSRBBB Byron Buxton B 3.00 8.00
FSRBBH Bryce Harper B 5.00 12.00
FSRBBP Buster Posey B 4.00 10.00
FSRBCA Corey Seager B 3.00 8.00
FSRBCB Charlie Blackmon B 3.00 8.00
FSRBCC Carlos Correa B 3.00 8.00
FSRBCG Carlos Gonzalez B 2.50 6.00
FSRBCR Clayton Kershaw B 5.00 12.00
FSRBCS Chris Sale B 3.00 8.00
FSRBCY Christian Yelich B 4.00 10.00
FSRBDE Dustin Pedroia B 3.00 8.00
FSRBDM Daniel Murphy B 2.50 6.00
FSRBDO David Ortiz B 3.00 8.00
FSRBDP David Price B 2.50 6.00
FSRBEE Edwin Encarnacion B 3.00 8.00
FSRBEL Evan Longoria B 2.50 6.00
FSRBFF Freddie Freeman B 4.00 10.00
FSRBFH Felix Hernandez B 2.50 6.00
FSRBGA Gary Sanchez B 3.00 8.00
FSRBGS George Springer B 2.50 6.00
FSRBGT Giancarlo Stanton B 3.00 8.00
FSRBIK Ian Kinsler B 2.50 6.00
FSRBI Ichiro B 4.00 10.00
FSRBJB Javier Baez B 4.00 10.00
FSRBJd Jacob deGrom B 6.00 15.00
FSRBJE Josh Bell B 2.50 6.00
FSRBJG Joey Gallo B 2.50 6.00
FSRBJL Jake Lamb B 2.50 6.00
FSRBJM J.D. Martinez B 3.00 8.00
FSRBJN Justin Verlander B 3.00 8.00
FSRBJO Josh Donaldson B 2.50 6.00
FSRBJT Jose Altuve B 2.50 6.00
FSRBJU Justin Upton B 2.50 6.00
FSRBJV Joey Votto B 3.00 8.00
FSRBKB Kris Bryant B 4.00 10.00
FSRBKD Khris Davis B 3.00 8.00
FSRBKE Kyle Seager B 2.00 5.00
FSRBKS Kyle Schwarber B 3.00 8.00
FSRBMA Matt Carpenter B 3.00 8.00
FSRBMB Mookie Betts B 4.00 10.00
FSRBMC Miguel Cabrera B 3.00 8.00
FSRBMH Max Scherzer B 3.00 8.00
FSRBMK Masahiro Tanaka B 2.50 6.00
FSRBMM Manny Machado B 3.00 8.00
FSRBMN Michael Conforto B 2.50 6.00
FSRBMS Miguel Sano B 2.50 6.00
FSRBMT Mike Trout B 10.00 25.00
FSRBMZ Marcell Ozuna B 3.00 8.00
FSRBNA Nolan Arenado B 5.00 12.00
FSRBNC Nelson Cruz B 3.00 8.00
FSRBNS Noah Syndergaard B 2.50 6.00
FSRBPG Paul Goldschmidt B 3.00 8.00
FSRBRB Ryan Braun B 2.50 6.00
FSRBRC Robinson Cano B 2.50 6.00
FSRBSS Stephen Strasburg B 3.00 8.00
FSRBTM Trey Mancini B 2.50 6.00
FSRBTP Tommy Pham B 2.00 5.00
FSRBTT Trea Turner B 2.50 6.00
FSRBWM Wil Myers B 2.50 6.00
FSRBXB Xander Bogaerts B 3.00 8.00
FSRBYC Yoenis Cespedes B 3.00 8.00
FSRBYD Yu Darvish B 3.00 8.00
FSRBYM Yadier Molina B 4.00 10.00
FSRBYP Yasiel Puig B 3.00 8.00

2018 Topps Allen and Ginter Rip Cards

STATED UNRIPPED ODDS 1:161 HOBBY
PRINT RUNS B/WN 50-75 COPIES PER
RIP1 Derek Jeter/75 60.00 150.00
RIP2 Mariano Rivera/50 40.00 100.00
RIP3 Brooks Robinson/50 40.00 100.00
RIP4 Byron Buxton/50 40.00 100.00
RIP5 Corey Kluber/50 40.00 100.00
RIP6 Yoan Moncada/50 40.00 100.00
RIP7 Chris Archer/50 40.00 100.00
RIP8 Eric Hosmer/50 40.00 100.00
RIP9 J.D. Martinez/50 40.00 100.00
RIP10 Evan Longoria/50 40.00 100.00
RIP11 Khris Davis/50 40.00 100.00
RIP12 Michael Conforto/50 40.00 100.00
RIP13 Nelson Cruz/50 40.00 100.00
RIP14 Adrian Beltre/50 40.00 100.00
RIP15 Albert Pujols/50 50.00 120.00
RIP16 Alex Bregman/50 40.00 100.00
RIP17 Andrew McCutchen/50 40.00 100.00
RIP18 Barry Larkin/50 40.00 100.00
RIP19 Dustin Pedroia/50 40.00 100.00
RIP20 Felix Hernandez/50 40.00 100.00
RIP21 Freddie Freeman/50 40.00 100.00
RIP22 George Springer/50 40.00 100.00
RIP23 Jacob deGrom/50 40.00 100.00
RIP24 Javier Baez/50 40.00 100.00
RIP25 Johnny Bench/50 40.00 100.00
RIP26 John Smoltz/50 40.00 100.00
RIP27 Jose Canseco/50 60.00 150.00
RIP28 Kyle Schwarber/50 40.00 100.00
RIP29 Marcell Ozuna/50 40.00 100.00
RIP30 Miguel Cabrera/50 40.00 100.00
RIP31 Robinson Cano/50 40.00 100.00
RIP32 Salvador Perez/50 40.00 100.00
RIP33 Starling Marte/50 40.00 100.00
RIP34 Stephen Strasburg/50 40.00 100.00
RIP35 Will Clark/50 50.00 120.00
RIP36 Wil Myers/50 40.00 100.00
RIP37 Yadier Molina/50 40.00 100.00
RIP38 Ozzie Albies/50 50.00 120.00
RIP39 Ty Cobb/50 40.00 100.00
RIP40 Honus Wagner/50 40.00 100.00
RIP41 Chris Sale/50 50.00 120.00
RIP42 Clint Frazier/50 50.00 120.00
RIP43 Cody Bellinger/50 50.00 120.00
RIP44 Corey Seager/50 40.00 100.00
RIP45 Don Mattingly/50 50.00 120.00
RIP46 Francisco Lindor/50 40.00 100.00
RIP47 Frank Thomas/50 50.00 120.00
RIP48 Gary Sanchez/50 40.00 100.00
RIP49 Josh Donaldson/50 40.00 100.00
RIP50 Justin Upton/50 40.00 100.00
RIP51 Nolan Arenado/50 40.00 100.00
RIP52 Ozzie Smith/50 50.00 120.00
RIP53 Paul Goldschmidt/50 40.00 100.00
RIP54 Roger Clemens/50 40.00 100.00
RIP55 Trea Turner/50 40.00 100.00
RIP56 Ernie Banks/60 40.00 100.00
RIP57 Bo Jackson/75 50.00 120.00
RIP58 David Ortiz/75 40.00 100.00
RIP59 Adam Jones/50 40.00 100.00
RIP60 Aaron Judge/75 40.00 100.00
RIP61 Andrew Benintendi/75 40.00 100.00
RIP62 Anthony Rizzo/75 40.00 100.00
RIP63 Babe Ruth/75 50.00 120.00
RIP64 Bryce Harper/75 40.00 100.00
RIP65 Buster Posey/75 40.00 100.00
RIP66 Cal Ripken Jr./75 40.00 100.00
RIP67 Carlos Correa/75 40.00 100.00
RIP68 Chipper Jones/75 40.00 100.00
RIP69 Clayton Kershaw/75 40.00 100.00
RIP70 George Brett/75 50.00 120.00
RIP71 Giancarlo Stanton/75 50.00 120.00
RIP72 Greg Maddux/75 50.00 120.00
RIP73 Hank Aaron/75 50.00 120.00
RIP74 Ichiro/75 50.00 120.00
RIP75 Joey Votto/75 60.00 150.00
RIP76 Jose Altuve/75 40.00 100.00
RIP77 Justin Verlander/75 40.00 100.00
RIP78 Kris Bryant/75 50.00 120.00
RIP79 Lou Gehrig/75 50.00 120.00
RIP80 Manny Machado/75 40.00 100.00
RIP81 Mark McGwire/75 50.00 120.00
RIP82 Masahiro Tanaka/75 40.00 100.00
RIP83 Max Scherzer/75 40.00 100.00
RIP84 Mike Piazza/75 40.00 100.00
RIP85 Mike Trout/75 75.00 200.00
RIP86 Mookie Betts/75 50.00 120.00
RIP87 Noah Syndergaard/75 40.00 100.00
RIP88 Nolan Ryan/75 50.00 120.00
RIP89 Rafael Devers/75 50.00 120.00
RIP90 Randy Johnson/75 40.00 100.00
RIP91 Reggie Jackson/75 40.00 100.00
RIP92 Rhys Hoskins/75 50.00 120.00
RIP93 Roberto Clemente 75.00 200.00
RIP94 Sandy Koufax/75 40.00 100.00
RIP95 Shohei Ohtani/75 60.00 150.00
RIP96 Ted Williams/75 50.00 120.00
RIP97 Victor Robles/75 40.00 100.00
RIP98 Yu Darvish/75 40.00 100.00
RIP99 Amed Rosario/75 40.00 100.00
RIP100 Jackie Robinson/75 50.00 120.00

2018 Topps Allen and Ginter Rip Cards Ripped

STATED UNRIPPED ODDS 1:161 HOBBY
PRINT RUNS B/WN 50-75 COPIES PER
PRICED WITH CLEANLY RIPPED BACKS
RIP1 Derek Jeter/75 6.00 15.00
RIP2 Mariano Rivera/50 3.00 8.00
RIP3 Brooks Robinson/50 2.00 5.00
RIP4 Byron Buxton/50 2.50 6.00
RIP5 Corey Kluber/50 2.00 5.00
RIP6 Yoan Moncada/50 2.50 6.00
RIP7 Chris Archer/50 1.50 4.00
RIP8 Eric Hosmer/50 2.00 5.00
RIP9 J.D. Martinez/50 2.50 6.00
RIP10 Evan Longoria/50 2.00 5.00
RIP11 Khris Davis/50 2.50 6.00
RIP12 Michael Conforto/50 2.00 5.00
RIP13 Nelson Cruz/50 2.50 6.00
RIP14 Adrian Beltre/50 2.50 6.00
RIP15 Albert Pujols/50 3.00 8.00
RIP16 Alex Bregman/50 2.50 6.00
RIP17 Andrew McCutchen/50 2.50 6.00
RIP18 Barry Larkin/50 2.00 5.00
RIP19 Dustin Pedroia/50 2.50 6.00
RIP20 Felix Hernandez/50 2.00 5.00
RIP21 Freddie Freeman/50 3.00 8.00
RIP22 George Springer/50 2.00 5.00
RIP23 Jacob deGrom/50 5.00 12.00
RIP24 Javier Baez/50 3.00 8.00
RIP25 Johnny Bench/50 2.50 6.00
RIP26 John Smoltz/50 2.50 6.00
RIP27 Jose Canseco/50 2.00 5.00
RIP28 Kyle Schwarber/50 2.50 6.00
RIP29 Marcell Ozuna/50 2.50 6.00
RIP30 Miguel Cabrera/50 2.50 6.00
RIP31 Robinson Cano/50 2.00 5.00
RIP32 Salvador Perez/50 2.00 5.00
RIP33 Starling Marte/50 2.00 5.00
RIP34 Stephen Strasburg/50 2.50 6.00
RIP35 Will Clark/50 2.00 5.00
RIP36 Wil Myers/50 2.00 5.00
RIP37 Yadier Molina/50 3.00 8.00
RIP38 Ozzie Albies/50 5.00 12.00
RIP39 Ty Cobb/50 4.00 10.00
RIP40 Honus Wagner/50 2.50 6.00
RIP41 Chris Sale/50 2.50 6.00
RIP42 Clint Frazier/50 3.00 8.00
RIP43 Cody Bellinger/50 5.00 12.00
RIP44 Corey Seager/50 2.50 6.00
RIP45 Don Mattingly/50 5.00 12.00
RIP46 Francisco Lindor/50 2.50 6.00
RIP47 Frank Thomas/50 2.50 6.00
RIP48 Gary Sanchez/50 2.50 6.00
RIP49 Josh Donaldson/50 2.00 5.00
RIP50 Justin Upton/50 2.00 5.00
RIP51 Nolan Arenado/50 4.00 10.00
RIP52 Ozzie Smith/50 3.00 8.00
RIP53 Paul Goldschmidt/50 2.50 6.00
RIP54 Roger Clemens/50 3.00 8.00
RIP55 Trea Turner/50 2.00 5.00
RIP56 Ernie Banks/60 2.50 6.00
RIP57 Bo Jackson/75 2.50 6.00
RIP58 David Ortiz/75 2.50 6.00
RIP59 Adam Jones/50 2.00 5.00
RIP60 Aaron Judge/75 6.00 15.00
RIP61 Andrew Benintendi/75 2.50 6.00
RIP62 Anthony Rizzo/75 3.00 8.00
RIP63 Babe Ruth/75 6.00 15.00
RIP64 Bryce Harper/75 4.00 10.00
RIP65 Buster Posey/75 3.00 8.00
RIP66 Cal Ripken Jr./75 8.00 20.00
RIP67 Carlos Correa/75 2.50 6.00
RIP68 Chipper Jones/75 2.50 6.00
RIP69 Clayton Kershaw/75 4.00 10.00
RIP70 George Brett/75 5.00 12.00
RIP71 Giancarlo Stanton/75 2.50 6.00
RIP72 Greg Maddux/75 3.00 8.00
RIP73 Hank Aaron/75 5.00 12.00
RIP74 Ichiro/75 3.00 8.00
RIP75 Joey Votto/75 2.50 6.00
RIP76 Jose Altuve/75 2.00 5.00
RIP77 Justin Verlander/75 2.50 6.00
RIP78 Kris Bryant/75 3.00 8.00
RIP79 Lou Gehrig/75 5.00 12.00
RIP80 Manny Machado/75 2.50 6.00
RIP81 Mark McGwire/75 4.00 10.00
RIP82 Masahiro Tanaka/75 2.00 5.00
RIP83 Max Scherzer/75 2.50 6.00
RIP84 Mike Piazza/75 2.50 6.00
RIP85 Mike Trout/75 12.00 30.00
RIP86 Mookie Betts/75 5.00 12.00
RIP87 Noah Syndergaard/75 2.00 5.00
RIP88 Nolan Ryan/75 8.00 20.00
RIP89 Rafael Devers/75 5.00 12.00
RIP90 Randy Johnson/75 2.50 6.00
RIP91 Reggie Jackson/75 2.00 5.00
RIP92 Rhys Hoskins/75 6.00 15.00
RIP93 Roberto Clemente/75 6.00 15.00
RIP94 Sandy Koufax/75 5.00 12.00
RIP95 Shohei Ohtani/75 40.00 100.00
RIP96 Ted Williams/75 5.00 12.00
RIP97 Victor Robles/75 4.00 10.00
RIP98 Yu Darvish/75 2.50 6.00
RIP99 Amed Rosario/75 2.00 5.00
RIP100 Jackie Robinson/75 2.50 6.00

2018 Topps Allen and Ginter World Talent

COMPLETE SET (50) 15.00 40.00
STATED ODDS 1:4 HOBBY
WT1 Gleyber Torres 2.50 6.00
WT2 Ronald Acuna Jr. 8.00 20.00
WT3 Xander Bogaerts .40 1.00
WT4 Luiz Gohara .25 .60
WT5 Freddie Freeman .50 1.25
WT6 Joey Votto .40 1.00
WT7 Jose Quintana .25 .60
WT8 Aroldis Chapman .40 1.00
WT9 Jose Abreu .40 1.00
WT10 Yasiel Puig .40 1.00
WT11 Yoan Moncada .40 1.00
WT12 Yoenis Cespedes .40 1.00
WT13 Andruw Jones .25 .60
WT14 Jonathan Schoop .25 .60
WT15 Adrian Beltre .40 1.00
WT16 Albert Pujols .50 1.25
WT17 David Ortiz .40 1.00
WT18 Gary Sanchez .40 1.00
WT19 Manny Machado .40 1.00
WT20 Pedro Martinez .30 .75
WT21 Max Kepler .30 .75
WT22 Brandon Nimmo .30 .75
WT23 Masahiro Tanaka .30 .75
WT24 Shohei Ohtani 6.00 15.00
WT25 Yu Darvish .40 1.00
WT26 Ichiro .50 1.25
WT27 Dovydas Neverauskas .25 .60
WT28 Julio Urias .40 1.00
WT29 Khris Davis .40 1.00
WT30 Didi Gregorius .30 .75
WT31 Erasmo Ramirez .25 .60
WT32 Mariano Rivera .50 1.25
WT33 Rod Carew .30 .75
WT34 Carlos Correa .40 1.00
WT35 Francisco Lindor .40 1.00
WT36 Javier Baez .50 1.25
WT37 Yadier Molina
WT38 Jharel Cotton .25 .60
WT39 Gift Ngoepe .25 .60
WT40 Hyun-Jin Ryu .30 .75
WT41 Shin-Soo Choo .30 .75
WT42 Tzu-Wei Lin .30 .75
WT43 Jose Altuve .30 .75
WT44 Felix Hernandez .30 .75
WT45 Salvador Perez .30 .75
WT46 Aaron Judge 1.00 2.50
WT47 Bryce Harper .60 1.50
WT48 Clayton Kershaw .60 1.50
WT49 Kris Bryant .50 1.25
WT50 Mike Trout 2.00 5.00

2018 Topps Allen and Ginter Worlds Greatest Beaches

COMPLETE SET (10) 4.00 10.00
STATED ODDS 1:6 HOBBY
WGB1 Paradise Island .40 1.00
WGB2 Bora Bora .40 1.00
WGB3 Trunk Bay .40 1.00
WGB4 Roatan .40 1.00
WGB5 South Beach .40 1.00
WGB6 Bondi Beach .40 1.00
WGB7 Venice Beach .40 1.00
WGB8 Bay of Angels .40 1.00
WGB9 Cozumel .40 1.00
WGB10 Harbour Island .40 1.00

2018 Topps Allen and Ginter Worlds Greatest Beaches Relics

STATED ODDS 1:8086 HOBBY
PRINT RUNS B/WN 10-25 COPIES PER
NO PRICING ON QTY 10 OR LESS
WGBR1 Paradise Island/20 60.00 150.00
WGBR2 Bora Bora/25 50.00 120.00
WGBR5 South Beach/25 50.00 120.00
WGBR7 Venice Beach
WGBR10 Harbour Island/20 60.00 150.00

2019 Topps Allen and Ginter

COMPLETE SET (350) 25.00 60.00
COMP.SET w/o SP's (300) 15.00 40.00
SP ODDS 1:2 HOBBY
1 Mookie Betts .50 1.25
2 Christian Yelich .30 .75
3 Babe Ruth .60 1.50
4 Lou Gehrig .50 1.25
5 Shohei Ohtani .40 1.00
6 Luis Gonzalez .15 .40
7 Albert Pujols .30 .75
8 Reggie Jackson .20 .50
9 Zack Greinke .25 .60
10 Mike Trout 1.25 3.00
11 Nolan Ryan .75 2.00

12 Blake Treinen .15 .40
13 Ozzie Albies .25 .60
14 Chipper Jones .25 .60
15 Freddie Freeman .30 .75
16 Kris Bryant .30 .75
17 Anthony Rizzo .30 .75
18 Ryne Sandberg .50 1.25
19 Javier Baez .30 .75
20 Ernie Banks .25 .60
21 Francisco Lindor .25 .60
22 Jose Ramirez .20 .50
23 Bob Feller .20 .50
24 A.J. Burnett .15 .40
25 Ronald Acuna Jr. 1.25 3.00
26 Justin Verlander .25 .60
27 Gerrit Cole .25 .60
28 Jose Altuve .20 .50
29 Alex Bregman .25 .60
30 George Springer .20 .50
31 Jeff Bagwell .20 .50
32 Sandy Koufax .50 1.25
33 Walker Buehler .30 .75
34 Cody Bellinger .50 1.25
35 Mike Piazza .25 .60
36 Starlin Castro .15 .40
37 Josh Hader .20 .50
38 Lorenzo Cain .15 .40
39 Jesus Aguilar .20 .50
40 Ryan Braun .20 .50
41 Robinson Cano .20 .50
42 Jacob deGrom .50 1.25
43 Edwin Diaz .20 .50
44 Noah Syndergaard .20 .50
45 Amed Rosario .20 .50
46 Rickey Henderson .25 .60
47 Matt Chapman .25 .60
48 Dennis Eckersley .20 .50
49 Khris Davis .25 .60
50 Hank Aaron .50 1.25
51 Paul Molitor .25 .60
52 Buster Posey .30 .75
53 Willie McCovey .20 .50
54 Juan Marichal .20 .50
55 Evan Longoria .20 .50
56 J.D. Martinez .25 .60
57 Felix Hernandez .20 .50
58 Edgar Martinez .20 .50
59 Justus Sheffield RC .40 1.00
60 Ichiro .30 .75
61 Mark McGwire .40 1.00
62 Paul Goldschmidt .25 .60
63 Yadier Molina .30 .75
64 Stan Musial .40 1.00
65 Ozzie Smith .30 .75
66 Roger Clemens .30 .75
67 Roberto Alomar .20 .50
68 Justin Smoak .15 .40
69 Danny Jansen RC .25 .60
70 Max Scherzer .25 .60
71 Patrick Corbin .20 .50
72 Stephen Strasburg .25 .60
73 Trea Turner .20 .50
74 Cal Ripken Jr. .75 2.00
75 Brooks Robinson .20 .50
76 Jim Palmer .20 .50
77 Tony Gwynn .25 .60
78 Trevor Hoffman .20 .50
79 Luis Urias RC .40 1.00
80 Eric Hosmer .20 .50
81 Andrew McCutchen .25 .60
82 Rhys Hoskins .30 .75
83 Aaron Nola .20 .50
84 Roberto Clemente .60 1.50
85 Chris Archer .15 .40
86 Felipe Vazquez .15 .40
87 Willie Stargell .20 .50
88 Ralph Kiner .20 .50
89 Adrian Beltre .25 .60
90 Ivan Rodriguez .20 .50
91 Elvis Andrus .20 .50
92 Joey Gallo .20 .50
93 Blake Snell .20 .50
94 Willy Adames .15 .40
95 Jose Canseco .20 .50
96 Andrew Benintendi .25 .60
97 Rafael Devers .30 .75
98 Ted Williams .50 1.25
99 Chris Sale .25 .60
100 Ken Griffey Jr. .50 1.25
101 David Price .20 .50
102 Joey Votto .25 .60
103 Johnny Bench .25 .60
104 Tony Perez .20 .50
105 Todd Helton .20 .50
106 Trevor Story .25 .60
107 Nolan Arenado .40 1.00
108 Charlie Blackmon .25 .60
109 George Brett .50 1.25
110 Salvador Perez .20 .50
111 Bo Jackson .25 .60
112 Miguel Cabrera .25 .60
113 Al Kaline .25 .60
114 Jose Berrios .20 .50
115 Rod Carew .20 .50
116 Tony Oliva .15 .40
117 Harmon Killebrew .25 .60
118 Frank Thomas .25 .60
119 Michael Kopech RC .75 2.00
120 Yoan Moncada .25 .60
121 Jose Abreu .25 .60
122 Isiah Kiner-Falefa .20 .50
123 Gleyber Torres .50 1.25
124 Miguel Andujar .25 .60
125 Giancarlo Stanton .25 .60
126 Clayton Kershaw .40 1.00
127 Juan Soto .75 2.00
128 Roger Maris .25 .60
129 Jackie Robinson .25 .60
130 Torii Hunter .15 .40
131 Juan Gonzalez .15 .40
132 David Ortiz .25 .60
133 Don Mattingly .50 1.25
134 Derek Jeter .60 1.50
135 Dale Murphy .25 .60
136 Mariano Rivera .30 .75
137 Vladimir Guerrero .20 .50
138 Gary Carter .20 .50
139 Harold Baines .20 .50
140 Luis Severino .20 .50
141 Miles Mikolas .25 .60
142 Mitch Haniger .20 .50
143 Max Muncy .20 .50
144 Whit Merrifield .25 .60
145 Xander Bogaerts .25 .60
146 Josh Donaldson .20 .50
147 J.T. Realmuto .25 .60
148 Corey Kluber .20 .50
149 Manny Machado .25 .60
150 Steve Carlton .20 .50
151 Marc Summers .25 .60
152 Augie Carton .15 .40
153 Jay Larson .20 .50
154 Hailey Dawson .25 .60
155 Gary Vaynerchuk .25 .60
156 Vincent Stio .25 .60
157 Mike Oz .25 .60
158 Kyle Snyder .25 .60
159 Rodney Mullen .25 .60
160 Matthew Mercer .25 .60
161 Sister Mary Jo Sobieck .25 .60
162 Mason Cox .25 .60
163 Loretta Claiborne .20 .50
164 Justin Bonomo .25 .60
165 John Cynn .20 .50
166 1st Tiger Mask .25 .60
Satoru Sayama
167 Mayumi Seto .25 .60
168 Rhea Butcher .20 .50
169 Drew Drechsel .25 .60
170 Lawrence Rocks .15 .40
171 Charles Martinet .25 .60
172 Tyler Kepner .15 .40
173 Ben Schwartz .25 .60
174 Dan Rather .25 .60
175 Danielle Colby .25 .60
176 Post Malone .25 .60
177 Robert Oberst .25 .60
178 Brian Fallon .25 .60
179 Burton Rocks .15 .40
180 Quinn XCII .25 .60
181 Emily Jaenson .25 .60
182 Pete Alonso RC 3.00 8.00
183 Fernando Tatis Jr. RC 6.00 15.00
184 Travis Pastrana .25 .60
185 Hilary Knight .25 .60
186 Wade Boggs .20 .50
187 Jason Varitek .25 .60
188 Didi Gregorius .20 .50
189 Tyler O'Neill .20 .50
190 Eddie Rosario .20 .50
191 Brandon Nimmo .20 .50
192 Lourdes Gurriel Jr. .20 .50
193 Jack Flaherty .25 .60
194 Kevin Newman RC .40 1.00
195 Dakota Hudson RC .30 .75
196 Cedric Mullins RC .50 1.25
197 Brad Keller RC .25 .60
198 David Bote .20 .50
199 Dereck Rodriguez .15 .40
200 Aaron Judge .60 1.50
201 Sean Reid-Foley RC .25 .60
202 Luke Voit .40 1.00
203 Jeff McNeil RC .60 1.50
204 Cionel Perez RC .25 .60
205 Chance Adams RC .25 .60
206 Corbin Burnes RC 2.00 5.00
207 Ramon Laureano RC .50 1.25
208 Dawel Lugo RC .40 1.00
209 Ryan O'Hearn RC .25 .60
210 Framber Valdez RC .25 .60
211 Patrick Wisdom RC .25 .60
212 Dylan Cozens .15 .40
213 Egg 10.00 25.00
214 Jonathan Lucroy .20 .50
215 Cody Allen .15 .40
216 Justin Bour .15 .40
217 Andrelton Simmons .15 .40
218 Michael Brantley .20 .50
219 Yuli Gurriel .20 .50
220 Josh James RC .40 1.00
221 Stephen Piscotty .15 .40
222 Matt Olson .25 .60
223 Jurickson Profar .20 .50
224 Matt Shoemaker .20 .50
225 Brandon Drury .15 .40
226 Dansby Swanson .25 .60
227 Touki Toussaint RC .30 .75
228 Yasmani Grandal .15 .40
229 Orlando Arcia .15 .40
230 Matt Carpenter .25 .60
231 Paul DeJong .25 .60
232 Willson Contreras .20 .50
233 Cole Hamels .20 .50
234 A.J. Pollock .15 .40
235 Corey Seager .25 .60
236 Brandon Crawford .20 .50
237 Carlos Santana .20 .50
238 Trevor Bauer .30 .75
239 Starling Marte .20 .50
240 Dee Gordon .15 .40
241 Kyle Seager .15 .40
242 Brian Anderson .15 .40
243 Michael Conforto .20 .50
244 Brian Dozier .20 .50
245 Wil Myers .20 .50
246 Odubel Herrera .20 .50
247 Maikel Franco .20 .50
248 David Robertson .15 .40
249 Jake Arrieta .20 .50
250 Yusei Kikuchi RC .40 1.00
251 Gregory Polanco .20 .50
252 Nomar Mazara .15 .40
253 Kevin Kiermaier .20 .50
254 Charlie Morton .25 .60
255 Matt Kemp .20 .50
256 Yasiel Puig .25 .60
257 Sonny Gray .20 .50
258 Daniel Murphy .20 .50
259 David Dahl .15 .40
260 Billy Hamilton .20 .50
261 Nicholas Castellanos .25 .60
262 Willians Astudillo RC .25 .60
263 Byron Buxton .25 .60
264 Yonder Alonso .15 .40
265 Troy Tulowitzki .25 .60
266 DJ LeMahieu .25 .60
267 James Paxton .20 .50
268 Adam Ottavino .15 .40
269 Scooter Gennett .20 .50
270 Ben Zobrist .20 .50
271 Carl Yastrzemski .40 1.00
272 Carlton Fisk .20 .50
273 Fred McGriff .20 .50
274 Dwight Gooden .15 .40
275 Deion Sanders .20 .50
276 Hideki Matsui .25 .60
277 Frank Robinson .20 .50
278 Vladimir Guerrero Jr. RC 1.50 4.00
279 Kolby Allard RC .40 1.00
280 Bryce Harper .40 1.00
281 Bob Gibson .20 .50
282 A.J. Andrews .25 .60
283 Andy Pettitte .20 .50
284 Roy Halladay .20 .50
285 Jorge Alfaro .15 .40
286 Harrison Bader .20 .50
287 Catfish Hunter .20 .50
288 Ryan Yarbrough .15 .40
289 Whitey Ford .20 .50
290 Pee Wee Reese .20 .50
291 Cespedes Family BBQ .25 .60
Jake Mintz/Jordan Shusterman
292 Eddie Murray .20 .50
293 Jon Lester .20 .50
294 German Marquez .15 .40
295 Franmil Reyes .15 .40
296 Cincinnati Red Stockings .25 .60
297 Boston Red Sox .25 .60
298 Ian Happ .20 .50
299 J.A. Happ .20 .50
300 Tino Martinez .20 .50
351 Carlos Correa SP .60 1.50
352 Robin Yount SP .60 1.50
353 Shane Bieber SP .60 1.50
354 Rowdy Tellez SP RC .60 1.50
355 Jordan Hicks SP .50 1.25
356 Kyle Schwarber SP .60 1.50
357 Kenley Jansen SP .50 1.25
358 John Smoltz SP .60 1.50
359 Larry Doby SP .50 1.25
360 Jorge Posada SP .50 1.25
361 Victor Robles SP .75 2.00
362 Fergie Jenkins SP .50 1.25
363 Austin Meadows SP .60 1.50
364 Dustin Pedroia SP .60 1.50
365 Ty Cobb SP 1.00 2.50
366 Daniel Palka SP .40 1.00
367 Masahiro Tanaka SP .50 1.25
368 Eddie Murray SP .50 1.25
369 Rick Porcello SP .50 1.25
370 Marcell Ozuna SP .60 1.50
371 Yu Darvish SP .60 1.50
372 Justin Turner SP .60 1.50
373 Edwin Encarnacion SP .60 1.50
374 Yoenis Cespedes SP .60 1.50
375 Pat Neshek SP .40 1.00
376 Wade Davis SP .40 1.00
377 Christin Stewart SP RC .50 1.25
378 Aroldis Chapman SP .60 1.50
379 Darryl Strawberry SP .40 1.00
380 Nomar Garciaparra SP .50 1.25
381 Scott Kingery SP .50 1.25
382 Dave Winfield SP .50 1.25
383 Sean Doolittle SP .40 1.00
384 Rogers Hornsby SP .50 1.25
385 Gil Hodges SP .50 1.25
386 Eddie Mathews SP .60 1.50
387 Warren Spahn SP .50 1.25
388 Casey Stengel SP .50 1.25
389 Lou Brock SP .50 1.25
390 Phil Rizzuto SP .50 1.25
391 Phil Niekro SP .50 1.25
392 Sammy Sosa SP .60 1.50
393 Alex Rodriguez SP .75 2.00
394 Tom Seaver SP .50 1.25
395 Barry Larkin SP .50 1.25
396 Tommy Lasorda SP .50 1.25
397 Orlando Cepeda SP .50 1.25
398 Eloy Jimenez SP RC 1.50 4.00
399 Tim Raines SP .50 1.25
400 Randy Johnson SP .60 1.50

2019 Topps Allen and Ginter Gold Border

*GLS SLVR 1-300: 1.5X TO 4X BASIC
*GLS SLVR 1-300 RC: 1X TO 2.5X BASIC RCs
*GLS SLVR 351-400: .6X TO 1.5X BASIC
FOUND ONLY IN HOBBY HOT BOXES

2019 Topps Allen and Ginter Autographs

STATED ODDS 1:555 HOBBY
EXCHANGE DEADLINE 6/30/2021
FSA1TM 1st Tiger Mask 30.00 80.00
FSAJH James Holzhauer 20.00 50.00
FSAKB Ken Burns 15.00 40.00
FSANB Nathan Burns 100.00 250.00
FSAPM Post Malone 200.00 400.00
FSATP Travis Pastrana 40.00 100.00
FSAVG Vladimir Guerrero Jr. 60.00 150.00
FSAYK Yusei Kikuchi EXCH 15.00 40.00

2019 Topps Allen and Ginter Baseball Star Signs

COMPLETE SET (50) 12.00 30.00
STATED ODDS 1:4 HOBBY
BSS1 Ronald Acuna Jr. 2.00 5.00
BSS2 Hank Aaron .75 2.00
BSS3 Cal Ripken Jr. 1.25 3.00
BSS4 Mookie Betts .75 2.00
BSS5 Ted Williams .75 2.00
BSS6 David Ortiz .40 1.00
BSS7 Frank Thomas .40 1.00
BSS8 Francisco Lindor .40 1.00
BSS9 Miguel Cabrera .40 1.00
BSS10 Al Kaline .40 1.00
BSS11 Jose Altuve .30 .75
BSS12 Carlos Correa .40 1.00
BSS13 Alex Bregman .40 1.00
BSS14 George Brett .75 2.00
BSS15 Mike Trout 2.00 5.00
BSS16 Shohei Ohtani .60 1.50
BSS17 Rod Carew .30 .75
BSS18 Babe Ruth 1.00 2.50
BSS19 Derek Jeter 1.00 2.50
BSS20 Aaron Judge 1.00 2.50
BSS21 Mariano Rivera .50 1.25
BSS22 Reggie Jackson .30 .75
BSS23 Rickey Henderson .40 1.00
BSS24 Ken Griffey Jr. .75 2.00
BSS25 Ichiro .50 1.25
BSS26 Randy Johnson .40 1.00
BSS27 Blake Snell .30 .75
BSS28 Nolan Ryan 1.25 3.00
BSS29 Kris Bryant .50 1.25
BSS30 Anthony Rizzo .50 1.25
BSS31 Joey Votto .40 1.00
BSS32 Johnny Bench .40 1.00
BSS33 Nolan Arenado .60 1.50
BSS34 Clayton Kershaw .60 1.50
BSS35 Sandy Koufax .75 2.00
BSS36 Jackie Robinson .40 1.00
BSS37 Christian Yelich .50 1.25
BSS38 Jacob deGrom .75 2.00
BSS39 Noah Syndergaard .30 .75
BSS40 Rhys Hoskins .50 1.25
BSS41 Roberto Clemente 1.00 2.50
BSS42 Tony Gwynn .40 1.00
BSS43 Buster Posey .50 1.25
BSS44 Yadier Molina .50 1.25
BSS45 Ozzie Smith .50 1.25
BSS46 Paul Goldschmidt .40 1.00
BSS47 Juan Soto 1.25 3.00
BSS48 Max Scherzer .40 1.00
BSS49 Bryce Harper .60 1.50
BSS50 Manny Machado .40 1.00

2019 Topps Allen and Ginter Box Topper Rip Cards

STATED UNRIPPED ODDS 1:24 HOBBY BOXES
PRINT RUNS B/WN 47-65 COPIES PER
UNRIPPED HAVE ADD'L CARDS WITHIN
BRIP1 Mike Trout/65 150.00 400.00
BRIP2 Shohei Ohtani/65 150.00 400.00
BRIP3 Ichiro/65 100.00 250.00
BRIP4 Ken Griffey Jr./60 125.00 300.00
BRIP5 Clayton Kershaw/65 100.00 250.00
BRIP6 Kris Bryant/65
BRIP7 Derek Jeter/60 150.00 400.00
BRIP8 Aaron Judge/65 150.00 400.00
BRIP9 Hank Aaron/55 100.00 250.00
BRIP10 Ronald Acuna Jr./65 125.00 300.00
BRIP11 Jose Altuve/65 100.00 250.00
BRIP12 Nolan Ryan/60 125.00 300.00
BRIP13 Babe Ruth/50 125.00 300.00
BRIP14 Ted Williams/47 125.00 300.00
BRIP15 Sandy Koufax/55 100.00 250.00
BRIP16 Jackie Robinson/55 100.00 250.00
BRIP17 Cal Ripken Jr./60 125.00 300.00
BRIP18 Roberto Clemente/55 125.00 300.00
BRIP19 Juan Soto/65 100.00 250.00
BRIP20 Mookie Betts/65 100.00 250.00
BRIP21 Tony Gwynn/60 100.00 250.00
BRIP22 Reggie Jackson/60 100.00 250.00
BRIP23 Ozzie Smith/60 100.00 250.00
BRIP24 Frank Thomas/60 100.00 250.00
BRIP25 George Brett/60 125.00 300.00
BRIP26 Randy Johnson/60 100.00 250.00
BRIP27 Bryce Harper/65 100.00 250.00
BRIP28 Francisco Lindor/65 100.00 250.00
BRIP29 Carlos Correa/65 125.00 300.00
BRIP30 Manny Machado/65 100.00 250.00

2019 Topps Allen and Ginter Box Topper Rip Cards Ripped

UNRIPPED STATED ODDS 1:24 HOBBY BOXES
PRINT RUNS B/WN 47-65 COPIES PER
PRICED WITH CLEANLY RIPPED BACKS
BRIP1 Mike Trout/65 15.00 40.00
BRIP2 Shohei Ohtani/65 5.00 12.00
BRIP3 Ichiro/65 4.00 10.00
BRIP4 Ken Griffey Jr./60 6.00 15.00
BRIP5 Clayton Kershaw/65 5.00 12.00
BRIP6 Kris Bryant/65 4.00 10.00
BRIP7 Derek Jeter/60 8.00 20.00
BRIP8 Aaron Judge/65 8.00 20.00
BRIP9 Hank Aaron/55 6.00 15.00
BRIP10 Ronald Acuna Jr./65 15.00 40.00
BRIP11 Jose Altuve/65 2.50 6.00
BRIP12 Nolan Ryan/60 10.00 25.00
BRIP13 Babe Ruth/50 8.00 20.00
BRIP14 Ted Williams/47 6.00 15.00
BRIP15 Sandy Koufax/55 6.00 15.00
BRIP16 Jackie Robinson/55 3.00 8.00
BRIP17 Cal Ripken Jr./60 10.00 25.00
BRIP18 Roberto Clemente/55 8.00 20.00
BRIP19 Juan Soto/65 10.00 25.00
BRIP20 Mookie Betts/65 6.00 15.00
BRIP21 Tony Gwynn/60 3.00 8.00
BRIP22 Reggie Jackson/60 2.50 6.00
BRIP23 Ozzie Smith/60 4.00 10.00
BRIP24 Frank Thomas/60 3.00 8.00
BRIP25 George Brett/60 6.00 15.00
BRIP26 Randy Johnson/60 3.00 8.00
BRIP27 Bryce Harper/65 5.00 12.00
BRIP28 Francisco Lindor/65 3.00 8.00
BRIP29 Carlos Correa/65 3.00 8.00
BRIP30 Manny Machado/65 3.00 8.00

2019 Topps Allen and Ginter Box Toppers

INSERTED IN HOBBY BOXES
BL1 Kris Bryant .75 2.00
BL2 Shohei Ohtani 1.00 2.50
BL3 Gleyber Torres 1.25 3.00
BL4 Mike Trout 3.00 8.00
BL5 Juan Soto 2.00 5.00
BL6 Ronald Acuna Jr. 3.00 8.00
BL7 Christian Yelich .75 2.00
BL8 Jose Altuve .50 1.25
BL9 Jacob deGrom 1.25 3.00
BL10 Aaron Judge 1.50 4.00
BL11 Francisco Lindor .60 1.50
BL12 Mookie Betts 1.25 3.00
BL13 Javier Baez .75 2.00
BL14 Bryce Harper 1.00 2.50
BL15 Clayton Kershaw 1.00 2.50

2019 Topps Allen and Ginter Double Rip Cards

STATED UNRIPPED ODDS 1:1440 HOBBY
PRINT RUNS B/WN 10-26 COPIES PER
NO PRICING ON QTY 15 OR LESS
UNRIPPED HAVE ADD'L CARDS WITHIN
DRIP1 Aaron/Acuna
DRIP2 Correa/Altuve/25
DRIP3 Arenado/Helton/20
DRIP4 Banks/Bryant/20 100.00 250.00
DRIP5 Votto/Bench/20 75.00 200.00
DRIP6 Betts/Benintendi/25 75.00 200.00
DRIP7 Ohtani/Trout/25
DRIP10 Ripken/Robinson
DRIP11 Yelich/Yount/20
DRIP13 Soto/Scherzer/25
DRIP14 Stargell/Clemente
DRIP15 Judge/Ruth/20 100.00 250.00
DRIP16 deGrom/Seaver/20 75.00 200.00
DRIP17 Kikuchi/Ichiro/20 75.00 200.00
DRIP18 McCutchen/Hoskins/25 50.00 120.00
DRIP23 Verlander/Ryan/20
DRIP25 Posey/Piazza/20
DRIP28 Nola/Carlton/20 60.00 150.00
DRIP29 Syndergaard/Ryan
DRIP30 Cabrera/Kaline/20
DRIP31 Torres/Andujar/26
DRIP34 Piazza/Carter
DRIP37 Fisk/Thomas
DRIP38 McGwire/Goldschmidt/20
DRIP39 Dawson/Sandberg
DRIP40 Matsui/Ichiro/20 100.00 250.00
DRIP45 Doby/Robinson

2019 Topps Allen and Ginter Double Rip Cards Ripped

UNRIPPED STATED ODDS 1:1440 HOBBY
PRINT RUNS B/WN 10-26 COPIES PER
NO PRICING ON QTY 15 OR LESS
PRICED WITH CLEANLY RIPPED BACKS
DRIP1 Aaron/Acuna
DRIP2 Correa/Altuve/25 5.00 12.00
DRIP3 Arenado/Helton/20 8.00 20.00
DRIP4 Banks/Bryant/20 6.00 15.00
DRIP5 Votto/Bench/20 5.00 12.00
DRIP6 Betts/Benintendi/25 10.00 25.00
DRIP7 Ohtani/Trout/25 25.00 60.00
DRIP10 Ripken/Robinson
DRIP11 Yelich/Yount/20 6.00 15.00
DRIP13 Soto/Scherzer/25 15.00 40.00
DRIP14 Stargell/Clemente
DRIP15 Judge/Ruth/20 12.00 30.00
DRIP16 deGrom/Seaver/20 10.00 25.00
DRIP17 Kikuchi/Ichiro/20 5.00 12.00
DRIP18 McCutchen/Hoskins/25 6.00 15.00
DRIP23 Verlander/Ryan/20 15.00 40.00
DRIP25 Posey/Piazza/20 6.00 15.00
DRIP28 Nola/Carlton/20 4.00 10.00
DRIP29 Syndergaard/Ryan
DRIP30 Cabrera/Kaline/20 5.00 12.00
DRIP31 Torres/Andujar/26 10.00 25.00
DRIP34 Piazza/Carter
DRIP37 Fisk/Thomas
DRIP38 McGwire/Goldschmidt/20 8.00 20.00
DRIP39 Dawson/Sandberg
DRIP40 Matsui/Ichiro/20 5.00 12.00
DRIP45 Doby/Robinson

2019 Topps Allen and Ginter Dual Autographs

STATED ODDS 1:5550 HOBBY
EXCHANGE DEADLINE 6/30/2021
DABBH B.Hull/B.Hull 100.00 250.00
DACFB H.Mintz/J.Shusterman 25.00 60.00

2019 Topps Allen and Ginter Framed Mini Autographs

STATED ODDS 1:63 HOBBY
EXCHANGE DEADLINE 6/30/2021
*BLACK/25: .75X TO 2X BASIC
MAAA A.J. Andrews 6.00 15.00
MAAC Augie Carton 4.00 10.00
MAAD Austin Dean 4.00 10.00
MAAG Jeff Bagwell 20.00 50.00
MAAJ Aaron Judge 75.00 200.00
MABB Bert Blyleven 8.00 20.00
MABF Brian Fallon 25.00 60.00
MABK Brad Keller 4.00 10.00
MABN Brandon Nimmo 5.00 12.00
MABRO Burton Rocks 4.00 10.00
MABS Ben Schwartz 15.00 40.00
MABSN Blake Snell 6.00 15.00
MABT Blake Treinen 4.00 10.00
MACA Chance Adams 4.00 10.00
MACBU Corbin Burnes 12.00 30.00
MACM Charles Martinet 12.00 30.00
MACMU Cedric Mullins 12.00 30.00
MACP Cionel Perez 4.00 10.00
MACY Christian Yelich 30.00 80.00
MADB David Bote 5.00 12.00
MADC Danielle Colby 30.00 80.00
MADCO Dylan Cozens 4.00 10.00
MADD Drew Drechsel 8.00 20.00
MADG Didi Gregorius 5.00 12.00
MADH Dakota Hudson 5.00 12.00
MADL Dawel Lugo 6.00 15.00
MADR Dan Rather 40.00 100.00
MADRO Dereck Rodriguez 4.00 10.00
MAEJ Eloy Jimenez 25.00 60.00
MAEJA Emily Jaenson 12.00 30.00
MAER Eddie Rosario 5.00 12.00
MAFM Fred McGriff 20.00 50.00
MAFR Franmil Reyes 4.00 10.00
MAFT Fernando Tatis Jr. 150.00 400.00
MAFV Framber Valdez 4.00 10.00
MAGE Graham Elliot 6.00 15.00
MAGV Gary Vaynerchuk 50.00 120.00
MAHD Hailey Dawson 15.00 40.00
MAHF Harrison Ford 800.00 1500.00
MAHK Hilary Knight 8.00 20.00
MAIK Isiah Kiner-Falefa 5.00 12.00
MAJA Jesus Aguilar 5.00 12.00
MAJAL Jose Altuve 15.00 40.00
MAJB Justin Bonomo 6.00 15.00
MAJC John Cynn 5.00 12.00
MAJD Jacob deGrom 20.00 50.00
MAJFL Jack Flaherty 12.00 30.00
MAJH Josh Hader 5.00 12.00
MAJL Jay Larson 5.00 12.00
MAJP Jorge Posada 20.00 50.00
MAJS Justus Sheffield 6.00 15.00
MAJSO Juan Soto 50.00 120.00
MAJV Jason Varitek 25.00 60.00
MAKB Kris Bryant 50.00 120.00
MAKGJ Ken Griffey Jr. 125.00 300.00
MAKN Kevin Newman 6.00 15.00
MAKS Kyle Snyder 30.00 80.00
MALC Loretta Claiborne 5.00 12.00
MALG Lourdes Gurriel Jr. 6.00 15.00
MALR Lawrence Rocks 4.00 10.00
MALS Luis Severino 8.00 20.00
MALU Luis Urias 12.00 30.00
MALV Luke Voit 15.00 40.00
MAMA Miguel Andujar 12.00 30.00
MAMCO Mason Cox 6.00 15.00
MAMK Michael Kopech 12.00 30.00
MAMM Matthew Mercer 30.00 80.00
MAMMI Miles Mikolas 6.00 15.00
MAMMU Max Muncy 6.00 15.00
MAMO Mike Oz 6.00 15.00
MAMS Mayumi Seto 10.00 25.00
MAMSU Marc Summers 12.00 30.00
MAMT Mike Trout 300.00 600.00
MANR Nolan Ryan 75.00 200.00
MAOA Ozzie Albies 12.00 30.00
MAPA Peter Alonso 75.00 200.00
MAPW Patrick Wisdom 4.00 10.00
MAQX Quinn XCII 6.00 15.00
MARA Ronald Acuna Jr. 75.00 200.00
MARAN Rick Ankiel 5.00 12.00
MARB Rhea Butcher 5.00 12.00
MARL Ramon Laureano 8.00 20.00
MARM Rodney Mullen 10.00 25.00
MARO Robert Oberst 10.00 25.00
MAROH Ryan O'Hearn 4.00 10.00
MASB Shane Bieber 15.00 40.00
MASMJ Sister Mary Jo Sobieck 25.00 60.00
MASO Shohei Ohtani 100.00 250.00
MASR Sean Reid-Foley 4.00 10.00
MATF Thomas Fish
MATH Todd Helton 10.00 25.00
MATHO Trevor Hoffman 8.00 20.00
MATK Tyler Kepner 4.00 10.00
MATO Tyler O'Neill 5.00 12.00
MAVG Vladimir Guerrero 20.00 50.00
MAVS Vincent Stio 4.00 10.00
MAWA Willy Adames 6.00 15.00
MAWB Wade Boggs 30.00 80.00

2019 Topps Allen and Ginter Ginter Greats

COMPLETE SET (50) 12.00 30.00
STATED ODDS 1:4 HOBBY
GG1 Hank Aaron .75 2.00
GG2 Ernie Banks .40 1.00
GG3 Johnny Bench .40 1.00
GG4 George Brett .75 2.00
GG5 Rod Carew .30 .75
GG6 Roger Clemens .50 1.25
GG7 Roberto Clemente 1.00 2.50
GG8 Ty Cobb .60 1.50
GG9 Bob Feller .30 .75
GG10 Lou Gehrig .75 2.00
GG11 Bob Gibson .30 .75
GG12 Ken Griffey Jr .75 2.00
GG13 Tony Gwynn .40 1.00
GG14 Rickey Henderson .40 1.00
GG15 Rogers Hornsby .30 .75
GG16 Reggie Jackson .30 .75
GG17 Derek Jeter 1.00 2.50
GG18 Randy Johnson .40 1.00
GG19 Chipper Jones .40 1.00
GG20 Al Kaline .40 1.00
GG21 Clayton Kershaw .60 1.50
GG22 Harmon Killebrew .40 1.00
GG23 Sandy Koufax .75 2.00
GG24 Pedro Martinez .30 .75
GG25 Willie McCovey .30 .75
GG26 Joe Morgan .30 .75
GG27 Stan Musial .60 1.50
GG28 David Ortiz .40 1.00
GG29 Mel Ott .40 1.00
GG30 Jim Palmer .30 .75
GG31 Mike Piazza .40 1.00
GG32 Albert Pujols .50 1.25
GG33 Cal Ripken Jr. 1.25 3.00
GG34 Mariano Rivera .50 1.25
GG35 Brooks Robinson .30 .75
GG36 Frank Robinson .30 .75
GG37 Jackie Robinson .40 1.00
GG38 Babe Ruth 1.00 2.50
GG39 Nolan Ryan 1.25 3.00
GG40 Ryne Sandberg .75 2.00
GG41 Tom Seaver .30 .75
GG42 Ozzie Smith .50 1.25
GG43 Tris Speaker .30 .75
GG44 Ichiro .50 1.25
GG45 Frank Thomas .40 1.00
GG46 Mike Trout 2.00 5.00
GG47 Honus Wagner .40 1.00
GG48 Ted Williams .75 2.00
GG49 Carl Yastrzemski .60 1.50
GG50 Robin Yount .40 1.00

2019 Topps Allen and Ginter History of Flight

COMPLETE SET (15) 6.00 15.00
STATED ODDS 1:6 HOBBY
HOF1 Wright Flyer .75 2.00
HOF2 A Vlaicu III .75 2.00
HOF3 Demoiselle Monoplane .75 2.00
HOF4 Supermarine S.6B .75 2.00
HOF5 Me 262 .75 2.00
HOF6 Sikorsky R-4 .75 2.00
HOF7 B-17 Flying Fortress .75 2.00
HOF8 DH 106 Comet .75 2.00
HOF9 Boeing 707 .75 2.00
HOF10 Bell X-1 .75 2.00
HOF11 Harrier Jet .75 2.00
HOF12 SR-71 .75 2.00
HOF13 Concorde Jet .75 2.00
HOF14 Shuttle Discovery .75 2.00
HOF15 Shuttle Endeavour .75 2.00

2019 Topps Allen and Ginter Incredible Equipment

COMPLETE SET (20) 6.00 15.00
STATED ODDS 1:6 HOBBY
IE1 Thor's Hammer .75 2.00
IE2 Robin Hood's Bow .75 2.00
IE3 Pecos Bill's Lasso .75 2.00
IE4 Paul Bunyan's Axe .75 2.00
IE5 Old Stormalong's Harpoon .75 2.00
IE6 David's Slingshot .75 2.00
IE7 Rosie the Riveter's Work Gloves .75 2.00
IE8 Don Quixote's Lance .75 2.00
IE9 William Tell's Crossbow .75 2.00
IE10 Achilles's Armor .75 2.00
IE11 Hermes's Sandals .75 2.00
IE12 King Arthur's Sword .75 2.00
IE13 Heracles's Club .75 2.00
IE14 Merlin's Staff .75 2.00
IE15 Poseidon's Trident .75 2.00
IE16 Cupid's Bow .75 2.00
IE17 Santa's Sleigh .75 2.00
IE18 Pied Piper's Pipe .75 2.00
IE19 Odin's Throne .75 2.00
IE20 Johnny Kaw's Scythe .75 2.00

2019 Topps Allen and Ginter Incredible Equipment Relics

STATED ODDS 1:1560 HOBBY
IERDS David's Slingshot 15.00 40.00
IERTH Thor's Hammer 15.00 40.00
IERDQL Don Quixote's Lance 15.00 40.00
IEROSH Old Stormalong's Harpoon 15.00 40.00
IERPBA Paul Bunyan's Axe 15.00 40.00
IERPBL Pecos Bill's Lasso 15.00 40.00
IERRHB Robin Hood's Bow 15.00 40.00
IERRWG Rosie the Riveter's Work Gloves 15.00 40.00
IERWTCB William Tell's Crossbow 15.00 40.00

2019 Topps Allen and Ginter Look Out Below Box Toppers

STATED ODDS 1:8 HOBBY BOXES
LOBB1 Niagara Falls 2.00 5.00
LOBB2 Victoria Falls 2.00 5.00
LOBB3 Angel Falls 2.00 5.00
LOBB4 Iguazu Falls 2.00 5.00
LOBB5 Yosemite Falls 2.00 5.00
LOBB6 Ruby Falls 2.00 5.00
LOBB7 Horseshoe Falls 2.00 5.00
LOBB8 Ban Gioc-Detian Falls 2.00 5.00
LOBB9 Havasu Falls 2.00 5.00
LOBB10 Palouse Falls 2.00 5.00

2019 Topps Allen and Ginter Mares and Stallions

COMPLETE SET (15) 6.00 15.00
STATED ODDS 1:6 HOBBY
MS1 Arabian Horse .75 2.00
MS2 Quarter Horse .75 2.00
MS3 Thoroughbred Horse .75 2.00
MS4 Tennessee Walking Horse .75 2.00
MS5 Morgan Horse .75 2.00
MS6 American Paint Horse .75 2.00
MS7 Appaloosa .75 2.00
MS8 Miniature Horse .75 2.00
MS9 Andalusian Horse .75 2.00
MS10 Kentucky Mountain Horse .75 2.00
MS11 Clydesdale .75 2.00
MS12 Cleveland Bay Horse .75 2.00
MS13 Irish Cob Horse .75 2.00
MS14 Mustang Horse .75 2.00
MS15 Holsteiner Horse .75 2.00

2019 Topps Allen and Ginter Mini

*MINI 1-300: 1X TO 2.5X BASIC
*MINI 1-300 RC: .6X TO 1.5X BASIC RCs
*MINI SP 350-351: .6X TO 1.5X BASIC
MINI SP ODDS 1:13 HOBBY
STATED PLATE ODDS 1:1347 HOBBY
PLATE PRINT RUN 1 SET PER COLOR
BLACK-CYAN-MAGENTA-YELLOW ISSUED
NO PLATE PRICING DUE TO SCARCITY
213 Egg 12.00 30.00
MS1 Thomas Fish SP 10.00 25.00

2019 Topps Allen and Ginter Mini A and G Back

*MINI AG 1-300: 1.2X TO 3X BASIC
*MINI AG 1-300 RC: .75X TO 2X BASIC RCs
*MINI AG SP 351-400: .75X TO 2X BASIC
STATED ODDS 1:5 HOBBY

2019 Topps Allen and Ginter Mini Black Border

*MINI BLK 1-300: 1.5X TO 4X BASIC
*MINI BLK 1-300 RC: 1X TO 2.5X BASIC RCs
*MINI BLK SP 351-400: 1X TO 2.5X BASIC
MINI BLK ODDS 1:10 HOBBY

2019 Topps Allen and Ginter Mini Brooklyn Back

*MINI BRKLN 1-300: 10X TO 25X BASIC
*MINI BRKLN 1-300 RC: 6X TO 15X BASIC RCs
*MINI BRKLN 351-400: 4X TO 10X BASIC
STATED ODDS 1:264 HOBBY
STATED PRINT RUN 25 SER.#'d SETS

2019 Topps Allen and Ginter Mini Gold Border

*MINI GOLD 1-300: 1.2X TO 3X BASIC
*MINI GOLD 1-300 RC: .75X TO 2X BASIC RCs
*MINI GOLD 351-400: .5X TO 1.2X BASIC
RANDOMLY INSERTED IN RETAIL PACKS

2019 Topps Allen and Ginter Mini No Number

*MINI NNO 1-300: 5X TO 12X BASIC
*MINI NNO 1-300 RC: 3X TO 8X BASIC RCs
*MINI NNO 351-400: 2X TO 5X BASIC
MINI NNO ODDS 1:132 HOBBY
ANNCD PRINT RUN 50 COPIES PER

2019 Topps Allen and Ginter Mini Stained Glass

*MINI STND GLSS: 50X TO 120X BASIC
*MINI STND GLSS RC: 25X TO 60X BASIC RCs
STATED ODDS 1:527 HOBBY
ANNCD PRINT RUN 25 SER.#'d SETS

2019 Topps Allen and Ginter Mini Chugging Along

COMPLETE SET (15) 15.00 40.00
STATED ODDS 1:50 HOBBY
CA1 Monorail Train 1.25 3.00
CA2 Steam Train 1.25 3.00
CA3 Bullet Train 1.25 3.00
CA4 Cable Car 1.25 3.00
CA5 Electric Train 1.25 3.00
CA6 Commuter Train 1.25 3.00
CA7 Subway Train 1.25 3.00
CA8 Trolley 1.25 3.00
CA9 Combined Train 1.25 3.00
CA10 Freight Train 1.25 3.00
CA11 Mine Train 1.25 3.00
CA12 Yard Goat Train 1.25 3.00
CA13 Long-Distance Train 1.25 3.00
CA14 Heritage Train 1.25 3.00
CA15 Overland Train 1.25 3.00

2019 Topps Allen and Ginter Mini Collectible Canines
COMPLETE SET (25) 10.00 25.00
STATED ODDS 1:10 HOBBY
CC1 Beagle .75 2.00
CC2 Boxer .75 2.00
CC3 Vizsla .75 2.00
CC4 German Shepherd .75 2.00
CC5 Siberian Husky .75 2.00
CC6 Golden Retriever .75 2.00
CC7 Great Dane .75 2.00
CC8 Borzoi .75 2.00
CC9 Dachshund .75 2.00
CC10 Black Labrador .75 2.00
CC11 English Bulldog .75 2.00
CC12 English Springer Spaniel .75 2.00
CC13 Rhodesian Ridgeback .75 2.00
CC14 Papillon .75 2.00
CC15 Yellow Labrador .75 2.00
CC16 Chihuahua .75 2.00
CC17 French Bulldog .75 2.00
CC18 Bernese Mountain Dog .75 2.00
CC19 Corgi .75 2.00
CC20 Bullmastiff .75 2.00
CC21 Weimaraner .75 2.00
CC22 Shih Tzu .75 2.00
CC23 West Highland Terrier .75 2.00
CC24 Boston Terrier .75 2.00
CC25 Maltese .75 2.00

2019 Topps Allen and Ginter Mini DNA Relics
STATED ODDS 1:8451 HOBBY
PRINT RUNS BW/N 6-25 COPIES PER
NO PRICING ON QTY 6
DNARFA Fossilized Ammonite/17
DNARFN Fossilized Nautiloid/25 200.00 400.00
DNARFT Fossilized Trilobite/22 200.00 400.00
DNARFDB Fossilized Dinosaur Bone/25 200.00400.00
DNARFWB Fossilized Whale Bone/25 200.00 400.00

2019 Topps Allen and Ginter Mini Dreams of Blue Ribbons
STATED ODDS 1:50 HOBBY
DBR1 Partner Carrying Contest 1.25 3.00
DBR2 Chili Pepper Eating Contest 1.25 3.00
DBR3 Pie Eating Contest 1.25 3.00
DBR4 Marshmallow-Stuffing Contest 1.25 3.00
DBR5 Toe Wrestling Contest 1.25 3.00
DBR6 Sand Castle Building Contest 1.25 3.00
DBR7 Potato Sack Racing Contest 1.25 3.00
DBR8 Dizzy Bat Contest 1.25 3.00
DBR9 Stocking Challenge Contest 1.25 3.00
DBR10 Pig Racing Contest 1.25 3.00
DBR11 Frog Jumping Contest 1.25 3.00
DBR12 Wheelbarrow Racing Contest 1.25 3.00
DBR13 Giant Pumpkin Contest 1.25 3.00
DBR14 Hot Dog Eating Contest 1.25 3.00
DBR15 Three-legged Race Contest 1.25 3.00

2019 Topps Allen and Ginter Mini Framed Presidential Pieces Relics
STATED ODDS 1:10,837 HOBBY
PRINT RUNS B/WN 5-25 COPIES PER
NO PRICING ON QTY 5
PPRGC Grover Cleveland/25 100.00 250.00
PPRFDR Franklin D. Roosevelt/25 75.00 200.00
PPRJFK John F. Kennedy/25 300.00 600.00
PPRJQA John Quincy Adams

2019 Topps Allen and Ginter Mini Framed Relics
STATED ODDS 1:55 HOBBY
MFRAB Adrian Beltre 4.00 10.00
MFRABE Andrew Benintendi 4.00 10.00
MFRAD Andre Dawson 3.00 8.00
MFRAP Andy Pettitte 3.00 8.00
MFRBJ Bo Jackson 8.00 20.00
MFRBP Buster Posey 5.00 12.00
MFRCC Carlos Correa 4.00 10.00
MFRCF Carlton Fisk 3.00 8.00
MFRCJ Chipper Jones 6.00 15.00
MFRCK Clayton Kershaw 6.00 15.00
MFRCR Cal Ripken Jr. 5.00 12.00
MFRCY Carl Yastrzemski 6.00 15.00
MFRDJ Derek Jeter 12.00 30.00
MFRDM Don Mattingly 8.00 20.00
MFRDO David Ortiz 4.00 10.00
MFRGB George Brett 6.00 15.00
MFRGH Gil Hodges 10.00 25.00
MFRIR Ivan Rodriguez 3.00 8.00
MFRI Ichiro 5.00 12.00
MFRJA Jose Altuve 3.00 8.00
MFRJB Jeff Bagwell 3.00 8.00
MFRJC Jose Canseco 3.00 8.00
MFRJS John Smoltz 4.00 10.00
MFRJV Justin Verlander 4.00 10.00
MFRKB Kris Bryant 5.00 12.00
MFRKG Ken Griffey Jr. 8.00 20.00
MFRMB Mookie Betts 5.00 12.00
MFRMM Mark McGwire 6.00 15.00
MFRMP Mike Piazza 4.00 10.00
MFRMR Mariano Rivera 6.00 15.00
MFRMT Mike Trout 12.00 30.00
MFRNG Nomar Garciaparra 3.00 8.00
MFROA Ozzie Albies 4.00 10.00
MFROS Ozzie Smith 5.00 12.00
MFRPM Pedro Martinez 3.00 8.00
MFRRA Roberto Alomar 3.00 8.00
MFRRC Roberto Clemente 150.00 400.00
MFRRCL Roger Clemens 5.00 12.00
MFRRD Rafael Devers 5.00 12.00
MFRRH Rickey Henderson 6.00 15.00
MFRRHH Rhys Hoskins 5.00 12.00
MFRRHO Rogers Hornsby 10.00 25.00
MFRRJ Reggie Jackson 3.00 8.00
MFRRY Robin Yount 4.00 10.00
MFRSC Steve Carlton 3.00 8.00
MFRSO Shohei Ohtani 10.00 25.00
MFRTG Tony Gwynn 4.00 10.00
MFRTH Todd Helton 3.00 8.00
MFRTM Thurman Munson 30.00 80.00
MFRVG Vladimir Guerrero 3.00 8.00
MFRWB Wade Boggs 3.00 8.00

2019 Topps Allen and Ginter Mini In Bloom
STATED ODDS 1:50 HOBBY
IB1 Black-Eyed Susan 1.50 4.00
IB2 Spurred Snapdragon 1.50 4.00
IB3 Shirley Poppy 1.50 4.00
IB4 Mexican Hat 1.50 4.00
IB5 Sweet Alyssum 1.50 4.00
IB6 Lily of the Valley 1.50 4.00
IB7 Begonia 1.50 4.00
IB8 Moth Orchid 1.50 4.00
IB9 Skaapbos 1.50 4.00
IB10 Flowering Crassula 1.50 4.00
IB11 Crown of Thorns 1.50 4.00
IB12 White Candles 1.50 4.00
IB13 Golden Shrimp 1.50 4.00
IB14 Brazilian Plume 1.50 4.00
IB15 Butterfly Bush 1.50 4.00
IB16 Camellia 1.50 4.00
IB17 Chinese Rain Bell 1.50 4.00
IB18 Natal Lily 1.50 4.00
IB19 Bird of Paradise 1.50 4.00
IB20 Caricature Plant 1.50 4.00
IB21 Tulip 1.50 4.00
IB22 Rose 1.50 4.00
IB23 Johnny Jump Up 1.50 4.00
IB24 Marigold 1.50 4.00
IB25 Oriental Poppy 1.50 4.00

2019 Topps Allen and Ginter Mini In Bloom Plant Me
STATED ODDS 1:2327 HOBBY
IBPMMH Mexican Hat 20.00 50.00
IBPMOP Oriental Poppy 20.00 50.00
IBPMSA Sweet Alyssum 20.00 50.00
IBPMSP Shirley Poppy 20.00 50.00
IBPMSS Spurred Snapdragon 20.00 50.00
IBPMBES Black-Eyed Susan 20.00 50.00

2019 Topps Allen and Ginter Mini Look Out Below
COMPLETE SET (15) 15.00 40.00
STATED ODDS 1:50 HOBBY
LOB1 Niagara Falls 1.25 3.00
LOB2 Victoria Falls 1.25 3.00
LOB3 Iguazu Falls 1.25 3.00
LOB4 Kaieteur Falls 1.25 3.00
LOB5 Gullfoss 1.25 3.00
LOB6 Angel Falls 1.25 3.00
LOB7 Yosemite Falls 1.25 3.00
LOB8 Ban Gioc-Detian Falls 1.25 3.00
LOB9 Horseshoe Falls 1.25 3.00
LOB10 Devil's Throat 1.25 3.00
LOB11 Huangguoshu Waterfall 1.25 3.00
LOB12 Cuquenan Falls 1.25 3.00
LOB13 Havasu Falls 1.25 3.00
LOB14 Palouse Falls 1.25 3.00
LOB15 Ruby Falls 1.25 3.00

2019 Topps Allen and Ginter Mini Lost Languages
COMPLETE SET (10) 15.00 40.00
STATED ODDS 1:50 HOBBY
LL1 Narragansett Language 1.25 3.00
LL2 Tasmanian Language 1.25 3.00
LL3 Martha's Vineyard Sign Language 1.25 3.00
LL4 Upper Chinook Language 1.25 3.00
LL5 Plains Apache Language 1.25 3.00
LL6 Klallam Language 1.25 3.00
LL7 Chiwere Language 1.25 3.00
LL8 Shasta Language 1.25 3.00
LL9 Jersey Dutch Language 1.25 3.00
LL10 Carolina Algonquian Language 1.25 3.00

2019 Topps Allen and Ginter Mini New to the Zoo
COMPLETE SET (15) 15.00 40.00
STATED ODDS 1:8 RETAIL
NTTZ1 Elephant Calf 1.25 3.00
NTTZ2 Hippo Calf 1.25 3.00
NTTZ3 Giraffe Calf 1.25 3.00
NTTZ4 Rhino Calf 1.25 3.00
NTTZ5 Lion Cub 1.25 3.00
NTTZ6 Panda Cub 1.25 3.00
NTTZ7 Fox Pup 1.25 3.00
NTTZ8 Penguin Chick 1.25 3.00
NTTZ9 Orangutan Baby 1.25 3.00
NTTZ10 Baby Shark 1.25 3.00
NTTZ11 Seal Pup 1.25 3.00
NTTZ12 Gorilla Infant 1.25 3.00
NTTZ13 Kangaroo Joey 1.25 3.00
NTTZ14 Tiger Cub 1.25 3.00
NTTZ15 Zebra Foal 1.25 3.00
NTTZ16 Otter Pup 1.25 3.00
NTTZ17 Polar Bear Cub 1.25 3.00
NTTZ18 Koala Joey 1.25 3.00
NTTZ19 Goat Kid 1.25 3.00
NTTZ20 Monkey Infant 1.25 3.00

2019 Topps Allen and Ginter N43 Box Toppers
STATED ODDS 1:5 HOBBY BOXES
N431 Mike Trout 3.00 8.00
N432 Aaron Judge 1.50 4.00
N433 Kris Bryant .75 2.00
N434 Rhys Hoskins .75 2.00
N435 Juan Soto 2.00 5.00
N436 Mookie Betts 1.25 3.00
N437 Shohei Ohtani 1.00 2.50
N438 Bryce Harper 1.00 2.50
N439 Anthony Rizzo .75 2.00
N4310 Jacob deGrom 1.25 3.00
N4311 J.D. Martinez .60 1.50
N4312 Jose Altuve .50 1.25
N4313 Ronald Acuna Jr. 3.00 8.00
N4314 Max Scherzer .60 1.50
N4315 Manny Machado .60 1.50
N4316 Buster Posey .75 2.00
N4317 Alex Bregman .60 1.50
N4318 Clayton Kershaw 1.00 2.50
N4319 Miguel Cabrera .60 1.50
N4320 Justin Verlander .60 1.50

2019 Topps Allen and Ginter Relics
VERSION A ODDS 1:26 HOBBY
VERSION B ODDS 1:26 HOBBY
FSRAAA A.J. Andrews A 3.00 8.00
FSRAAC Augie Carton A 2.00 5.00
FSRAACH Aroldis Chapman A 3.00 8.00
FSRAAJ Aaron Judge A 8.00 20.00
FSRABB Brandon Belt A 2.50 6.00
FSRABC Brandon Crawford A 2.50 6.00
FSRABF Brian Fallon A 6.00 15.00
FSRABR Burton Rocks A 2.00 5.00
FSRABS Ben Schwartz A 3.00 8.00
FSRACA Chris Archer A 2.00 5.00
FSRACB Cody Bellinger A 6.00 15.00
FSRACM Charles Martinet A 3.00 8.00
FSRADC Danielle Colby A 6.00 15.00
FSRADD David Dahl A 2.00 5.00
FSRADDR Drew Drechsel A 3.00 8.00
FSRADG Dee Gordon A 2.00 5.00
FSRADR Dan Rather A 6.00 15.00
FSRAEA Elvis Andrus A 2.50 6.00
FSRAEJ Emily Jaenson A 3.00 8.00
FSRAGE Graham Elliot A 3.00 8.00
FSRAGV Gary Vaynerchuk A 60.00 150.00
FSRAHD Hailey Dawson A 3.00 8.00
FSRAHK Hilary Knight A 3.00 8.00
FSRAIH Ian Happ A 2.50 6.00
FSRAJB Javier Baez A 4.00 10.00
FSRAJBE Josh Bell A 2.50 6.00
FSRAJBO Justin Bonomo A 3.00 8.00
FSRAJBR Jackie Bradley Jr. A 3.00 8.00
FSRAJC Johnny Cueto A 2.50 6.00
FSRAJCY John Cynn A 2.50 6.00
FSRAJF Jeurys Familia A 2.50 6.00
FSRAJH Jason Heyward A 2.50 6.00
FSRAJL Jay Larson A 2.50 6.00
FSRAJM Jake Mintz A 3.00 8.00
FSRAJS Jordan Shusterman A 3.00 8.00
FSRAKD Khris Davis A 3.00 8.00
FSRAKS Kyle Snyder A 3.00 8.00
FSRALC Lorenzo Cain A 2.00 5.00
FSRALCL Loretta Claiborne A 2.50 6.00
FSRALR Lawrence Rocks A 2.00 5.00
FSRAMC Michael Conforto A 2.50 6.00
FSRAMCO Mason Cox A 3.00 8.00
FSRAMF Maikel Franco A 2.50 6.00
FSRAMM Matthew Mercer A 3.00 8.00
FSRAMO Mike Oz A 3.00 8.00
FSRAMS Mayumi Seto A 3.00 8.00
FSRAMSU Marc Summers A 3.00 8.00
FSRANC Nicholas Castellanos A 3.00 8.00
FSRAOA Orlando Arcia A 2.00 5.00
FSRAOH Odubel Herrera A 2.50 6.00
FSRAQX Quinn XCII A 3.00 8.00
FSRARB Ryan Braun A 2.50 6.00
FSRARBU Rhea Butcher A 2.50 6.00
FSRARH Ryon Healy A 2.00 5.00
FSRARM Rodney Mullen A 6.00 15.00
FSRARO Robert Oberst A 3.00 8.00
FSRASD Sean Doolittle A 2.00 5.00
FSRASS Sister Mary Jo Sobieck A 6.00 15.00
FSRATG Tyler Glasnow A 3.00 8.00
FSRATK Tyler Kepner A 2.00 5.00
FSRATM 1st Tiger Mask A 20.00 50.00
Satoru Sayama
FSRATP Travis Pastrana A 3.00 8.00
FSRAVS Vincent Stio A 3.00 8.00
FSRAWC Willson Contreras A 2.50 6.00
FSRBAA Albert Almora B 2.50 6.00
FSRBAB Andrew Benintendi B 3.00 8.00
FSRBABR Alex Bregman B 3.00 8.00
FSRBAN Aaron Nola B 2.50 6.00
FSRBAP Albert Pujols B 4.00 10.00
FSRBAR Anthony Rizzo B 4.00 10.00
FSRBARO Amed Rosario B 2.50 6.00
FSRBBP Buster Posey B 4.00 10.00
FSRBBZ Ben Zobrist B 2.50 6.00
FSRBCC Carlos Correa B 3.00 8.00
FSRBCK Clayton Kershaw B 5.00 12.00
FSRBCS Chris Sale B 3.00 8.00
FSRBCT Chris Taylor B 2.50 6.00
FSRBDB Dellin Betances B 2.50 6.00
FSRBDG Didi Gregorius B 2.50 6.00
FSRBDP Dustin Pedroia B 3.00 8.00
FSRBDPR David Price B 2.50 6.00
FSRBDS Dansby Swanson B 3.00 8.00
FSRBEL Evan Longoria B 2.50 6.00
FSRBFF Freddie Freeman B 4.00 10.00
FSRBFL Francisco Lindor B 3.00 8.00
FSRBJA Jose Altuve B 2.50 6.00
FSRBJB Jose Berrios B 2.50 6.00
FSRBJG Joey Gallo B 2.50 6.00
FSRBJL Jake Lamb B 2.50 6.00
FSRBJLE Jon Lester B 2.50 6.00
FSRBJM J.D. Martinez B 3.00 8.00
FSRBJMO Jordan Montgomery B 2.50 6.00
FSRBJR Jose Ramirez B 2.50 6.00
FSRBJS Justin Smoak B 2.00 5.00
FSRBJV Justin Verlander B 3.00 8.00
FSRBKB Kris Bryant B 4.00 10.00
FSRBKF Kyle Freeland B 2.50 6.00
FSRBKS Kyle Schwarber B 3.00 8.00
FSRBLS Luis Severino B 2.50 6.00
FSRBMA Miguel Andujar B 3.00 8.00
FSRBMB Mookie Betts B 6.00 15.00
FSRBMC Miguel Cabrera B 3.00 8.00
FSRBMCA Matt Carpenter B 3.00 8.00
FSRBMM Miles Mikolas B 3.00 8.00
FSRBNA Nolan Arenado B 5.00 12.00
FSRBNM Nomar Mazara B 2.00 5.00
FSRBNS Noah Syndergaard B 2.50 6.00
FSRBOA Ozzie Albies B 3.00 8.00
FSRBRD Rafael Devers B 4.00 10.00
FSRBRH Rhys Hoskins B 4.00 10.00
FSRBRO Rougned Odor B 2.50 6.00
FSRBRP Rick Porcello B 2.50 6.00
FSRBSK Scott Kingery B 2.50 6.00
FSRBSN Sean Newcomb B 2.00 5.00
FSRBSP Salvador Perez B 2.50 6.00
FSRBTS Trevor Story B 3.00 8.00
FSRBTT Trea Turner B 2.50 6.00
FSRBVR Victor Robles B 4.00 10.00
FSRBXB Xander Bogaerts B 3.00 8.00
FSRBYM Yadier Molina B 4.00 10.00

2019 Topps Allen and Ginter Rip Cards
STATED UNRIPPED ODDS 1:160 HOBBY
PRINT RUNS B/WN 25-90 COPIES PER
UNRIPPED HAVE ADD'L CARDS WITHIN
RIP1 Hank Aaron/50 60.00 150.00
RIP2 Ronald Acuna Jr/75 60.00 150.00
RIP3 Jose Altuve/75 40.00 100.00
RIP4 Nolan Arenado/75 40.00 100.00
RIP5 Jeff Bagwell/75 40.00 100.00
RIP6 Ernie Banks/50 40.00 100.00
RIP7 Adrian Beltre/75 40.00 100.00
RIP8 Johnny Bench/50 40.00 100.00
RIP9 Andrew Benintendi/75 40.00 100.00
RIP10 Mookie Betts/75 50.00 120.00
RIP11 Alex Bregman/75 50.00 120.00
RIP12 George Brett/75 50.00 120.00
RIP13 Lou Brock/50 40.00 100.00
RIP14 Kris Bryant/75 50.00 120.00
RIP15 Miguel Cabrera/75 40.00 100.00
RIP16 Rod Carew/50 40.00 100.00
RIP17 Steve Carlton/50 40.00 100.00
RIP18 Roberto Clemente/50 60.00 150.00
RIP19 Ty Cobb/25 60.00 150.00
RIP20 Carlos Correa/75
RIP21 Jacob deGrom/75
RIP22 Rafael Devers/75 40.00 100.00
RIP23 Larry Doby/50 40.00 100.00
RIP24 Bob Feller/50
RIP25 Carlton Fisk/75 40.00 100.00
RIP26 Whitey Ford/50 40.00 100.00
RIP27 Lou Gehrig/25 60.00 150.00
RIP28 Bob Gibson/50 40.00 100.00
RIP29 Paul Goldschmidt/75 40.00 100.00
RIP30 Zack Greinke/75 40.00 100.00
RIP31 Ken Griffey Jr/75 60.00 150.00
RIP32 Vladimir Guerrero/75 40.00 100.00
RIP33 Tony Gwynn/75 60.00 150.00
RIP34 Roy Halladay/75
RIP35 Todd Helton/75 40.00 100.00
RIP36 Rickey Henderson/75 50.00 120.00
RIP37 Trevor Hoffman/75 40.00 100.00
RIP38 Rhys Hoskins/75 40.00 100.00
RIP39 Reggie Jackson/50 50.00 120.00
RIP40 Derek Jeter/75 60.00 150.00
RIP41 Randy Johnson/75 50.00 120.00
RIP42 Chipper Jones/75 50.00 120.00
RIP43 Aaron Judge/75 60.00 150.00
RIP44 Al Kaline/50 75.00 200.00
RIP45 Clayton Kershaw/75 40.00 100.00
RIP46 Harmon Killebrew/50 60.00 150.00
RIP47 Sandy Koufax/50 50.00 120.00
RIP48 Barry Larkin/75 40.00 100.00
RIP49 Francisco Lindor/75 40.00 100.00
RIP50 Edgar Martinez/75 50.00 120.00
RIP51 Pedro Martinez/75 50.00 120.00
RIP52 Don Mattingly/75 60.00 150.00
RIP53 Willie McCovey/50
RIP54 Mark McGwire/75 40.00 100.00
RIP55 Yadier Molina/75 60.00 150.00
RIP56 Paul Molitor/75
RIP57 Thurman Munson/50 50.00 120.00
RIP58 Stan Musial/45 60.00 150.00
RIP59 Shohei Ohtani/75 60.00 150.00
RIP60 David Ortiz/75 40.00 100.00
RIP61 Jim Palmer/50
RIP62 Salvador Perez/75
RIP63 Andy Pettitte/75 40.00 100.00
RIP64 Mike Piazza/75
RIP65 Buster Posey/75 50.00 120.00
RIP66 David Price/75
RIP67 Albert Pujols/75 50.00 120.00
RIP68 Jose Ramirez/75 40.00 100.00
RIP69 Cal Ripken Jr/75 50.00 120.00
RIP70 Mariano Rivera/75 50.00 120.00
RIP71 Anthony Rizzo/75 40.00 100.00
RIP72 Jackie Robinson/45 60.00 150.00
RIP73 Brooks Robinson/50 40.00 100.00
RIP74 Frank Robinson/50 40.00 100.00
RIP75 Alex Rodriguez/75 40.00 100.00
RIP76 Ivan Rodriguez/75 40.00 100.00
RIP77 Babe Ruth/25 60.00 150.00
RIP78 Nolan Ryan/75 50.00 120.00
RIP79 Chris Sale/75 40.00 100.00
RIP80 Ryne Sandberg/75 40.00 100.00
RIP81 Max Scherzer/75 40.00 100.00
RIP82 Tom Seaver/75 40.00 100.00
RIP83 Ozzie Smith/75 40.00 100.00
RIP84 Blake Snell/75 40.00 100.00
RIP85 Duke Snider/45 50.00 120.00
RIP86 Sammy Sosa/75 40.00 100.00
RIP87 Juan Soto/75 40.00 100.00
RIP88 Willie Stargell/50 40.00 100.00
RIP89 Trevor Story/75 40.00 100.00
RIP90 Noah Syndergaard/75 40.00 100.00
RIP91 Frank Thomas/75 40.00 100.00
RIP92 Mike Trout/90 75.00 200.00
RIP93 Justin Verlander/75
RIP94 Joey Votto/75
RIP95 Honus Wagner/25 60.00 150.00
RIP96 Ted Williams/45
RIP97 Carl Yastrzemski/75 40.00 100.00
RIP98 Christian Yelich/75 50.00 120.00
RIP99 Robin Yount/75 40.00 100.00
RIP100 Ichiro/75 40.00 100.00

2019 Topps Allen and Ginter Rip Cards Mini
RANDOMLY INSERTED IN RIP PACKS
*RIP STND GLSS: 1.5X TO 4X RIP MINI
351 Aaron Judge 20.00 50.00
352 Al Kaline 10.00 25.00
353 Albert Pujols 12.00 30.00
354 Babe Ruth 20.00 50.00
355 Brooks Robinson 8.00 20.00
356 Javier Baez 12.00 30.00
357 Buster Posey 12.00 30.00
358 Cal Ripken Jr. 15.00 40.00
359 Carl Yastrzemski 15.00 40.00
360 Carlos Correa 15.00 40.00
361 Chipper Jones 10.00 25.00
362 Clayton Kershaw 15.00 40.00
363 David Ortiz 10.00 25.00
364 Derek Jeter 25.00 60.00
365 Francisco Lindor 10.00 25.00
366 Frank Thomas 10.00 25.00
367 George Brett 12.00 30.00
368 Hank Aaron 12.00 30.00
369 Ichiro 12.00 30.00
370 Jackie Robinson 10.00 25.00
371 Johnny Bench 10.00 25.00
372 Jose Altuve 12.00 30.00
373 Juan Soto 15.00 40.00
374 Justin Verlander 20.00 50.00
375 Ken Griffey Jr. 20.00 50.00
376 Kris Bryant 12.00 30.00
377 Lou Gehrig 15.00 40.00
378 Manny Machado 10.00 25.00
379 Mariano Rivera 20.00 50.00
380 Mark McGwire 12.00 30.00
381 Max Scherzer 10.00 25.00
382 Miguel Cabrera 10.00 25.00
383 Mike Trout 40.00 100.00
384 Mike Piazza 10.00 25.00
385 Mookie Betts 12.00 30.00
386 Nolan Ryan 15.00 40.00
387 Pedro Martinez 8.00 20.00
388 Reggie Jackson 12.00 30.00
389 Rickey Henderson 20.00 50.00
390 Roberto Clemente 20.00 50.00
391 Roger Clemens 12.00 30.00
392 Ronald Acuna Jr. 25.00 60.00
393 Ryne Sandberg 15.00 40.00
394 Sandy Koufax 20.00 50.00
395 Shohei Ohtani 20.00 50.00
396 Stan Musial 15.00 40.00
397 Steve Carlton 10.00 25.00
398 Ted Williams 15.00 40.00
399 Tony Gwynn 15.00 40.00
400 Paul Molitor 15.00 40.00

2019 Topps Allen and Ginter Rip Cards Ripped
UNRIPPED STATED ODDS 1:160 HOBBY
PRINT RUNS B/WN 25-90 COPIES PER
PRICED WITH CLEANLY RIPPED BACKS
RIP1 Hank Aaron/50 6.00 15.00
RIP2 Ronald Acuna Jr/75 15.00 40.00
RIP3 Jose Altuve/75 2.50 6.00
RIP4 Nolan Arenado/75 5.00 12.00
RIP5 Jeff Bagwell/75 2.50 6.00
RIP6 Ernie Banks/50 3.00 8.00
RIP7 Adrian Beltre/75 3.00 8.00
RIP8 Johnny Bench/50 3.00 8.00
RIP9 Andrew Benintendi/75 3.00 8.00
RIP10 Mookie Betts/75 6.00 15.00
RIP11 Alex Bregman/75 3.00 8.00
RIP12 George Brett/75 6.00 15.00
RIP13 Lou Brock/50 2.50 6.00
RIP14 Kris Bryant/75 4.00 10.00
RIP15 Miguel Cabrera/75 3.00 8.00
RIP16 Rod Carew/50 2.50 6.00
RIP17 Steve Carlton/50 2.50 6.00
RIP18 Roberto Clemente/50 8.00 20.00
RIP19 Ty Cobb/25 5.00 12.00
RIP20 Carlos Correa/75 3.00 8.00
RIP21 Jacob deGrom/75 6.00 15.00
RIP22 Rafael Devers/75 4.00 10.00
RIP23 Larry Doby/50 2.50 6.00
RIP24 Bob Feller/50 2.50 6.00
RIP25 Carlton Fisk/75 2.50 6.00
RIP26 Whitey Ford/50 2.50 6.00
RIP27 Lou Gehrig/25 6.00 15.00
RIP28 Bob Gibson/50 2.50 6.00
RIP29 Paul Goldschmidt/75 3.00 8.00
RIP30 Zack Greinke/75 3.00 8.00
RIP31 Ken Griffey Jr/75 6.00 15.00
RIP32 Vladimir Guerrero/75 2.50 6.00
RIP33 Tony Gwynn/75 3.00 8.00
RIP34 Roy Halladay/75 2.50 6.00
RIP35 Todd Helton/75 2.50 6.00
RIP36 Rickey Henderson/75 3.00 8.00
RIP37 Trevor Hoffman/75 2.50 6.00
RIP38 Rhys Hoskins/75 4.00 10.00
RIP39 Reggie Jackson/50 2.50 6.00
RIP40 Derek Jeter/75 8.00 20.00
RIP41 Randy Johnson/75 3.00 8.00
RIP42 Chipper Jones/75 3.00 8.00
RIP43 Aaron Judge/75 8.00 20.00
RIP44 Al Kaline/50 3.00 8.00
RIP45 Clayton Kershaw/75 5.00 12.00
RIP46 Harmon Killebrew/50 3.00 8.00
RIP47 Sandy Koufax/50 6.00 15.00
RIP48 Barry Larkin/75 2.50 6.00
RIP49 Francisco Lindor/75 3.00 8.00
RIP50 Edgar Martinez/75 2.50 6.00
RIP51 Pedro Martinez/75 2.50 6.00
RIP52 Don Mattingly/75 6.00 15.00
RIP53 Willie McCovey/50 2.50 6.00
RIP54 Mark McGwire/75 5.00 12.00
RIP55 Yadier Molina/75 4.00 10.00
RIP56 Paul Molitor/75 3.00 8.00
RIP57 Thurman Munson/50 3.00 8.00
RIP58 Stan Musial/45 5.00 12.00
RIP59 Shohei Ohtani/75 5.00 12.00
RIP60 David Ortiz/75 3.00 8.00
RIP61 Jim Palmer/50 2.50 6.00
RIP62 Salvador Perez/75 2.50 6.00
RIP63 Andy Pettitte/75 2.50 6.00
RIP64 Mike Piazza/75 3.00 8.00
RIP65 Buster Posey/75 4.00 10.00
RIP66 David Price/75 2.50 6.00
RIP67 Albert Pujols/75 4.00 10.00
RIP68 Jose Ramirez/75 2.50 6.00
RIP69 Cal Ripken Jr/75 10.00 25.00
RIP70 Mariano Rivera/75 4.00 10.00
RIP71 Anthony Rizzo/75 4.00 10.00
RIP72 Jackie Robinson/45 3.00 8.00
RIP73 Brooks Robinson/50 2.50 6.00
RIP74 Frank Robinson/50 2.50 6.00
RIP75 Alex Rodriguez/75 4.00 10.00
RIP76 Ivan Rodriguez/75 2.50 6.00
RIP77 Babe Ruth/25 8.00 20.00
RIP78 Nolan Ryan/75 10.00 25.00
RIP79 Chris Sale/75 3.00 8.00
RIP80 Ryne Sandberg/75 6.00 15.00
RIP81 Max Scherzer/75 3.00 8.00
RIP82 Tom Seaver/75 2.50 6.00
RIP83 Ozzie Smith/75 4.00 10.00
RIP84 Blake Snell/75 2.50 6.00
RIP85 Duke Snider/45 2.50 6.00
RIP86 Sammy Sosa/75 3.00 8.00
RIP87 Juan Soto/75 10.00 25.00
RIP88 Willie Stargell/50 2.50 6.00
RIP89 Trevor Story/75 3.00 8.00
RIP90 Noah Syndergaard/75 2.50 6.00
RIP91 Frank Thomas/75 3.00 8.00
RIP92 Mike Trout/90 15.00 40.00
RIP93 Justin Verlander/75 3.00 8.00
RIP94 Joey Votto/75 3.00 8.00
RIP95 Honus Wagner/25 3.00 8.00
RIP96 Ted Williams/45 6.00 15.00
RIP97 Carl Yastrzemski/75 5.00 12.00
RIP98 Christian Yelich/75 4.00 10.00
RIP99 Robin Yount/75 3.00 8.00
RIP100 Ichiro/75 4.00 10.00

2020 Topps Allen and Ginter
COMPLETE SET (350) 25.00 60.00
COMP.SET w/o SP's (300) 15.00 40.00
SP ODDS 1:2 HOBBY
1 Tom Glavine .20 .50
2 Randy Johnson .25 .60
3 Paul Goldschmidt .25 .60
4 Larry Doby .20 .50
5 Walker Buehler .30 .75
6 John Smoltz .25 .60
7 Tim Lincecum .20 .50
8 Jeff Bagwell .20 .50
9 Rhys Hoskins .30 .75
10 Rod Carew .20 .50
11 Lou Gehrig .50 1.25
12 George Springer .20 .50
13 Aaron Judge .60 1.50
14 Aaron Nola .20 .50
15 Kris Bryant .30 .75
16 Bryce Harper .40 1.00
17 Ken Griffey Jr. .50 1.25
18 George Brett .50 1.25
19 Keston Hiura .30 .75
20 Joe Mauer .20 .50
21 Ted Williams .50 1.25
22 Eddie Mathews .25 .60
23 Jorge Soler .25 .60
24 Shohei Ohtani .40 1.00
25 Carl Yastrzemski .40 1.00
26 Willie McCovey .20 .50
27 Joe Morgan .20 .50
28 Juan Soto .75 2.00
29 Willie Mays .50 1.25
30 Eloy Jimenez .50 1.25
31 Babe Ruth .60 1.50
32 Ichiro .30 .75
33 Edgar Martinez .20 .50
34 Pete Alonso .60 1.50
35 Rickey Henderson .25 .60
36 Alex Bregman .25 .60
37 Mike Mussina .20 .50
38 Miguel Cabrera .25 .60
39 Andy Pettitte .20 .50
40 Mariano Rivera .30 .75
41 David Ortiz .25 .60
42 Jackie Robinson .25 .60
43 Matt Chapman .25 .60
44 Rafael Devers .30 .75
45 Yoan Moncada .25 .60
46 Pedro Martinez .20 .50
47 Freddie Freeman .30 .75
48 Ketel Marte .20 .50
49 Roger Clemens .30 .75
50 Vladimir Guerrero Jr. .40 1.00
51 Roberto Clemente .60 1.50
52 Ivan Rodriguez .20 .50
53 Mike Soroka .25 .60
54 Victor Robles .30 .75
55 Nick Senzel .25 .60
56 Ozzie Albies .25 .60
57 Eddie Murray .20 .50
58 Christian Yelich .30 .75
59 Duke Snider .20 .50
60 Steve Carlton .20 .50
61 Jim Thome .20 .50
62 Whitey Ford .20 .50
63 Marcus Semien .25 .60
64 Andre Dawson .20 .50
65 Cody Bellinger .50 1.25
66 Darryl Strawberry .15 .40
67 Mookie Betts .50 1.25
68 Nomar Garciaparra .20 .50
69 Al Kaline .25 .60
70 Don Mattingly .50 1.25
71 Vladimir Guerrero .20 .50
72 Johnny Bench .25 .60
73 Mark McGwire .40 1.00
74 Ty Cobb .40 1.00
75 Joey Votto .25 .60
76 Chipper Jones .25 .60
77 Javier Baez .30 .75
78 Xander Bogaerts .25 .60
79 Sandy Koufax .50 1.25
80 DJ LeMahieu .25 .60
81 Barry Zito .20 .50
82 Andrew Benintendi .25 .60
83 J.D. Martinez .25 .60
84 Clayton Kershaw .40 1.00
85 Mike Trout 1.25 3.00
86 Anthony Rizzo .30 .75
87 Trevor Story .25 .60
88 Ronald Acuna Jr. 1.00 2.50
89 Paul Molitor .25 .60
90 Jack Flaherty .25 .60
91 Dave Winfield .20 .50
92 Barry Larkin .20 .50
93 Francisco Lindor .25 .60
94 Max Fried .25 .60
95 Manny Machado .25 .60
96 Frank Thomas .25 .60
97 Aristides Aquino RC .60 1.50
98 Cal Ripken Jr. .75 2.00
99 Gavin Lux RC 1.25 3.00
100 Max Scherzer .25 .60
101 Brooks Robinson .20 .50
102 Robin Yount .25 .60
103 Tim Anderson .25 .60
104 Hank Aaron .50 1.25
105 Todd Helton .20 .50
106 Willie Stargell .20 .50
107 Roger Maris .25 .60
108 Gary Carter .20 .50
109 Reggie Jackson .20 .50
110 Albert Pujols .30 .75
111 Buster Posey .30 .75
112 Bo Bichette RC 2.00 5.00
113 Luis Gonzalez .15 .40
114 Gleyber Torres .50 1.25
115 Fernando Tatis Jr. 1.25 3.00
116 Honus Wagner .25 .60
117 Ernie Banks .25 .60
118 Yordan Alvarez RC 2.50 6.00
119 Giancarlo Stanton .25 .60
120 Bob Gibson .20 .50
121 Zack Greinke .25 .60
122 Trea Turner .20 .50
123 Mike Piazza .25 .60
124 Juan Marichal .20 .50
125 Craig Biggio .20 .50
126 Wade Boggs .20 .50
127 Jose Altuve .20 .50
128 Tony Gwynn .25 .60
129 Josh Bell .20 .50
130 Nolan Arenado .40 1.00
131 Stan Musial .40 1.00
132 Jim Palmer .20 .50
133 Justin Verlander .25 .60
134 Roberto Alomar .20 .50
135 Harmon Killebrew .25 .60
136 Carlos Correa .25 .60
137 Yadier Molina .30 .75
138 Tom Seaver .20 .50
139 Nolan Ryan .75 2.00
140 Joe Torre .20 .50
141 Mike Schmidt .40 1.00
142 Patrick Corbin .20 .50
143 Carlton Fisk .20 .50
144 Warren Spahn .20 .50
145 Alex Rodriguez .30 .75
146 Jacob deGrom .50 1.25
147 Jose Berrios .20 .50
148 David Wright .20 .50
149 Ryne Sandberg .50 1.25
150 Ozzie Smith .30 .75
151 Kenley Jansen .20 .50
152 J.K. Dobbins .40 1.00
153 Starling Marte .20 .50
154 Tommy La Stella .15 .40
155 Chip Gaines .50 1.25
156 Lourdes Gurriel Jr. .20 .50
157 Jeff McNeil .20 .50
158 Kwang-Hyun Kim RC .50 1.25
159 Kyle Lewis RC 2.00 5.00
160 Lorenzo Cain .15 .40
161 Jackie Bradley Jr. .25 .60
162 Kyle Tucker .25 .60
163 Cole Hamels .20 .50
164 Kolten Wong .20 .50
165 Hugo Juice Tandron .25 .60
166 Briana Scurry .25 .60
167 Ken Jeong .25 .60
168 Willson Contreras .25 .60
169 Carter Kieboom .20 .50
170 Nick Thune .25 .60
171 Hunter Pence .20 .50
172 Baseball Brit .25 .60
Joey Mellows
173 Evan Longoria .20 .50
174 Anthony Kay RC .25 .60
175 Kirby Yates .15 .40
176 Justin Dunn RC .30 .75
177 Hunter Harvey RC .40 1.00
178 Marcell Ozuna .25 .60
179 Dallas Keuchel .20 .50
180 Khris Davis .25 .60
181 Adbert Alzolay RC .30 .75
182 Kelsey Cook .25 .60
183 Lucas Giolito .20 .50
184 Joc Pederson .20 .50
185 Austin Meadows .25 .60
186 Bryan Reynolds .20 .50
187 Masahiro Tanaka .25 .60
188 Eugenio Suarez .20 .50
189 Brandon Lowe .20 .50
190 Yuli Gurriel .20 .50
191 Nelson Cruz .25 .60
192 Jose Abreu .25 .60
193 Nyjah Huston 6.00 15.00
194 Mike Doc Emrick .20 .50
195 Robinson Cano .20 .50
196 Noah Syndergaard .20 .50
197 Matt Thaiss RC .30 .75
198 Will Smith .25 .60
199 Nico Hoerner RC 1.00 2.50
200 Jim Abbott .15 .40
201 Sakura Kokumai .25 .60
202 Tino Martinez .20 .50
203 Tony Dunst .25 .60
204 Jared Carrabis .25 .60
205 Salvador Perez .20 .50
206 C.J. Cron .15 .40
207 Brendan McKay RC .40 1.00
208 Mike Moustakas .20 .50
209 Johnny Bananas .75 2.00
210 Jose Ramirez .20 .50
211 Ryan Braun .20 .50
212 Chris Paddack .25 .60
213 Oscar Mercado .25 .60
214 Ryan McMahon .25 .60
215 Paul DeJong .25 .60
216 Shun Yamaguchi RC .30 .75
217 Aaron Wheelz Fotheringham .25 .60
218 Andrelton Simmons .15 .40
219 Josh Hader .20 .50
220 Eric Hosmer .20 .50
221 Mike Foltynewicz .15 .40
222 Isan Diaz RC .40 1.00
223 Shane Bieber .25 .60
224 Kole Calhoun .15 .40
225 Austin Riley .30 .75
226 A.J. Puk RC .40 1.00
227 Max Muncy .20 .50
228 Justine Siegal .25 .60
229 Jordan Yamamoto RC .25 .60
230 Matt Olson .25 .60
231 Bucky Lasek .25 .60
232 Dakota Hudson .20 .50
233 Howie Kendrick .15 .40
234 Jorge Alfaro .15 .40
235 Jesus Luzardo RC .50 1.25
236 Alex Verdugo .20 .50
237 Nick Ahmed .15 .40
238 Gerrit Cole .40 1.00
239 Kyle Schwarber .25 .60
240 Luis Arraez .30 .75
241 Michael Brantley .20 .50
242 Andy Cohen .25 .60
243 Max Kepler .20 .50
244 Brandon Woodruff .25 .60
245 Josh Donaldson .20 .50
246 Mike Clevinger .20 .50
247 Yusei Kikuchi .20 .50
248 Rob Friedman .25 .60
249 Stephen Strasburg .25 .60
250 Charlie Blackmon .25 .60
251 Corey Kluber .20 .50
252 Steve Byrne .25 .60
253 David Price .20 .50
254 Ryan Nyquist .25 .60
255 David Dahl .15 .40
256 Luis Robert RC 4.00 10.00
257 Corey Seager .25 .60

258 Cavan Biggio .30 .75
259 Whit Merrifield .25 .60
260 J.T. Realmuto .25 .60
261 Joey Gallo .25 .60
262 Zac Gallen RC .60 1.50
263 Dansby Swanson .25 .60
264 Abraham Toro RC .30 .75
265 Tommy Edman .25 .60
266 Didi Gregorius .20 .50
267 Elvis Andrus .20 .50
268 Eduardo Escobar .15 .40
269 Miguel Sano .20 .50
270 Luis Castillo .20 .50
271 Michael Conforto .20 .50
272 Jon Lester .20 .50
273 Gregory Polanco .20 .50
274 Steven Tefft .25 .60
275 Jeff Dye .25 .60
276 Jose Urquidy RC .30 .75
277 John Means .25 .60
278 Nick Castellanos .25 .60
279 Maikel Franco .20 .50
280 Jean Segura .20 .50
281 Derrick Goold .25 .60
282 Matthew Boyd .15 .40
283 Nomar Mazara .15 .40
284 Julian Edwards .25 .60
285 Orlando Arcia .15 .40
286 Trey Mancini .25 .60
287 Aroldis Chapman .25 .60
288 Courtney Hansen .25 .60
289 Anthony Rendon .25 .60
290 Ramon Laureano .20 .50
291 Sonny Gray .20 .50
292 Hyun-Jin Ryu .20 .50
293 Daniel Vogelbach .15 .40
294 Mauricio Dubon RC .30 .75
295 Zack Wheeler .20 .50
296 Trevor Bauer .30 .75
297 R.L. Stine .25 .60
298 Adalberto Mondesi .20 .50
299 Blake Snell .20 .50
300 Andres Munoz RC .40 1.00
301 Tim Raines SP .50 1.25
302 Thurman Munson SP .60 1.50
303 Earl Weaver SP .50 1.25
304 Darin Erstad SP .40 1.00
305 Bill Mazeroski SP .50 1.25
306 Moises Alou SP .40 1.00
307 Miguel Tejada SP .40 1.00
308 Phil Rizzuto SP .50 1.25
309 Alan Trammell SP .50 1.25
310 Sean Casey SP .40 1.00
311 Bert Blyleven SP .50 1.25
312 Dennis Eckersley SP .50 1.25
313 Fred McGriff SP .50 1.25
314 Dwight Gooden SP .40 1.00
315 Juan Gonzalez SP .40 1.00
316 Billy Williams SP .50 1.25
317 Cecil Fielder SP .40 1.00
318 Andruw Jones SP .40 1.00
319 Tony LaRussa SP .40 1.00
320 Orlando Cepeda SP .50 1.25
321 Trevor Hoffman SP .50 1.25
322 Catfish Hunter SP .50 1.25
323 Bernie Williams SP .50 1.25
324 Lou Brock SP .50 1.25
325 Mark Grace SP .50 1.25
326 Monte Irvin SP .50 1.25
327 Jose Canseco SP .50 1.25
328 Bobby Doerr SP .50 1.25
329 Ryan Howard SP .50 1.25
330 Bob Feller SP .50 1.25
331 Gary Sheffield SP .40 1.00
332 Shawn Green SP .40 1.00
333 Kenny Lofton SP .40 1.00
334 Rollie Fingers SP .50 1.25
335 Tony Perez SP .50 1.25
336 Jermaine Dye SP .40 1.00
337 Ralph Kiner SP .50 1.25
338 Fergie Jenkins SP .50 1.25
339 Kerry Wood SP .40 1.00
340 Magglio Ordonez SP .50 1.25
341 Jim Bunning SP .50 1.25
342 Mo Vaughn SP .40 1.00
343 Jack Morris SP .50 1.25
344 Phil Niekro SP .50 1.25
345 Larry Walker SP .50 1.25
346 Sparky Anderson SP .50 1.25
347 Tommy Lasorda SP .50 1.25
348 Luis Aparicio SP .50 1.25
349 Jay Buhner SP .40 1.00
350 Goose Gossage SP .50 1.25

2020 Topps Allen and Ginter Silver

*GLS SLVR 1-300: 1.5X TO 4X BASIC
*GLS SLVR 1-300 RC: 1X TO 2.5X BASIC RCs
*GLS SLVR 301-350: .6X TO 1.5X BASIC
FOUND ONLY IN HOBBY HOT BOXES

2020 Topps Allen and Ginter A Debut to Remember

COMPLETE SET (30) 10.00 25.00
STATED ODDS 1:XX
DTR1 Yordan Alvarez 2.50 6.00
DTR2 Miguel Cabrera .40 1.00
DTR3 Starlin Castro .25 .60
DTR4 Will Clark .30 .75
DTR5 Brandon Crawford .30 .75
DTR6 Johnny Cueto .30 .75
DTR7 Kyle Farmer .25 .60
DTR8 Joey Gallo .40 1.00
DTR9 Dwight Gooden .25 .60
DTR10 Ken Griffey Jr. .75 2.00
DTR11 Vladimir Guerrero Jr. .60 1.50
DTR12 Jason Heyward .30 .75
DTR13 Nico Hoerner 1.00 2.50
DTR14 Aaron Judge 1.00 2.50
DTR15 Ramon Laureano .30 .75
DTR16 Juan Marichal .30 .75
DTR17 Steven Matz .25 .60
DTR18 Willie McCovey .30 .75
DTR19 Brendan McKay .40 1.00
DTR20 Shohei Ohtani .60 1.50
DTR21 Chris Paddack .40 1.00
DTR22 Freddy Peralta .25 .60
DTR23 Daniel Ponce de Leon .25 .60
DTR24 Nick Solak 1.00 2.50
DTR25 Trevor Story .40 1.00
DTR26 Stephen Strasburg .40 1.00
DTR27 Ross Stripling .25 .60
DTR28 Fernando Tatis Jr. 2.00 5.00
DTR29 Luis Tiant .25 .60
DTR30 Ichiro .50 1.25

2020 Topps Allen and Ginter Autographs

STATED ODDS 1:XXX HOBBY
EXCHANGE DEADLINE 7/31/2020
FSAALM Alex Morgan 75.00 200.00
FSACD Charlie Day 60.00 150.00
FSACG Chip Gaines 50.00 120.00
FSACLB Ludacris 75.00 200.00
FSADMC Danny McBride 150.00 400.00
FSAMR Megan Rapinoe 40.00 100.00
FSAMSM Simone Manuel 8.00 20.00
FSAPR Paul Rudd 100.00 250.00
FSASL Spike Lee 60.00 150.00

2020 Topps Allen and Ginter Box Topper Rip Cards

STATED UNRIPPED ODDS 1:XX HOBBY BOXES
UNRIPPED HAVE ADD'L CARDS WITHIN
BRIP1 Hank Aaron 125.00 300.00
BRIP2 Ronald Acuna Jr. 100.00 250.00
BRIP3 Pete Alonso 100.00 250.00
BRIP4 Yordan Alvarez 125.00 300.00
BRIP5 Cody Bellinger 100.00 250.00
BRIP6 Johnny Bench 125.00 300.00
BRIP7 Bo Bichette 125.00 300.00
BRIP8 George Brett 100.00 250.00
BRIP9 Roberto Clemente 125.00 300.00
BRIP10 Ken Griffey Jr. 125.00 300.00
BRIP11 Vladimir Guerrero Jr. 100.00 250.00
BRIP12 Tony Gwynn 100.00 250.00
BRIP13 Bryce Harper 125.00 300.00
BRIP14 Reggie Jackson 100.00 250.00
BRIP15 Aaron Judge 125.00 300.00
BRIP16 Clayton Kershaw 125.00 300.00
BRIP17 Sandy Koufax 125.00 300.00
BRIP18 Willie Mays 125.00 300.00
BRIP19 Shohei Ohtani 125.00 300.00
BRIP20 Mike Piazza 125.00 300.00
BRIP21 Cal Ripken Jr. 125.00 300.00
BRIP22 Mariano Rivera 100.00 250.00
BRIP23 Brooks Robinson 100.00 250.00
BRIP24 Jackie Robinson 125.00 300.00
BRIP25 Babe Ruth 125.00 300.00
BRIP26 Juan Soto 100.00 250.00
BRIP27 Fernando Tatis Jr. 125.00 300.00
BRIP28 Mike Trout 150.00 400.00
BRIP29 Ted Williams 100.00 250.00
BRIP30 Ichiro 100.00 250.00

2020 Topps Allen and Ginter Box Topper Rip Cards Ripped

UNRIPPED STATED ODDS 1:XXX HOBBY
PRICED WITH CLEANLY RIPPED BACKS
BRIP1 Hank Aaron 6.00 15.00
BRIP2 Ronald Acuna Jr. 12.00 30.00
BRIP3 Pete Alonso 8.00 20.00
BRIP4 Yordan Alvarez 20.00 50.00
BRIP5 Cody Bellinger 6.00 15.00
BRIP6 Johnny Bench 3.00 8.00
BRIP7 Bo Bichette 15.00 40.00
BRIP8 George Brett 6.00 15.00
BRIP9 Roberto Clemente 8.00 20.00
BRIP10 Ken Griffey Jr. 6.00 15.00
BRIP11 Vladimir Guerrero Jr. 5.00 12.00
BRIP12 Tony Gwynn 3.00 8.00
BRIP13 Bryce Harper 5.00 12.00
BRIP14 Reggie Jackson 2.50 6.00
BRIP15 Aaron Judge 8.00 20.00
BRIP16 Clayton Kershaw 5.00 12.00
BRIP17 Sandy Koufax 6.00 15.00
BRIP18 Willie Mays 6.00 15.00
BRIP19 Shohei Ohtani 5.00 12.00
BRIP20 Mike Piazza 3.00 8.00
BRIP21 Cal Ripken Jr. 10.00 25.00
BRIP22 Mariano Rivera 4.00 10.00
BRIP23 Brooks Robinson 2.50 6.00
BRIP24 Jackie Robinson 3.00 8.00
BRIP25 Babe Ruth 8.00 20.00
BRIP26 Juan Soto 10.00 25.00
BRIP27 Fernando Tatis Jr. 15.00 40.00
BRIP28 Mike Trout 15.00 40.00
BRIP29 Ted Williams 6.00 15.00
BRIP30 Ichiro 4.00 10.00

2020 Topps Allen and Ginter Box Toppers

INSERTED IN HOBBY BOXES
BLAJ Aaron Judge 1.50 4.00
BLBB Bo Bichette 3.00 8.00
BLBH Bryce Harper 1.00 2.50
BLCB Cody Bellinger 1.25 3.00
BLCK Clayton Kershaw 1.00 2.50
BLCY Christian Yelich .75 2.00
BLFF Freddie Freeman .75 2.00
BLJB Javier Baez .75 2.00
BLJD Jacob deGrom 1.25 3.00
BLJS Juan Soto 3.00 8.00
BLMT Mike Trout 3.00 8.00
BLPA Pete Alonso 1.50 4.00
BLRA Ronald Acuna Jr. 2.50 6.00
BLYA Yordan Alvarez 4.00 10.00
BLYM Yadier Molina .75 2.00

2020 Topps Allen and Ginter Digging Deep

COMPLETE SET (20) 4.00 10.00
STATED ODDS 1:XX HOBBY
DD1 Red Beryl .40 1.00
DD2 Blue Apatite .40 1.00
DD3 Painite .40 1.00
DD4 Diamond .40 1.00
DD5 Ruby .40 1.00
DD6 Labradorite .40 1.00
DD7 Platinum .40 1.00
DD8 Pyrite .40 1.00
DD9 Chrysoberyl .40 1.00
DD10 Garnet .40 1.00
DD11 Sapphire .40 1.00
DD12 Gold .40 1.00
DD13 Jade .40 1.00
DD14 Pink Opal .40 1.00
DD15 Turquoise .40 1.00
DD16 Silver .40 1.00
DD17 Quartz .40 1.00
DD18 Lapis .40 1.00
DD19 Tanzanite .40 1.00
DD20 Copper .40 1.00

2020 Topps Allen and Ginter Double Rip Cards

DRIP1 O.Smith/Y.Molina/21 125.00 300.00
DRIP2 J.Baez/A.Rizzo
DRIP3 B.Harper/R.Hoskins/25 100.00 250.00
DRIP11 A.Benintendi/R.Devers/25 100.00 250.00
DRIP13 R.Clemente/R.Kiner
DRIP16 M.Rivera/W.Ford
DRIP17 Y.Alvarez/J.Altuve
DRIP18 W.Boggs/C.Yastrzemski
DRIP19 R.Yount/C.Yelich/20 100.00 250.00
DRIP20 P.Alonso/M.Piazza/20 100.00 250.00
DRIP22 C.Bellinger/C.Kershaw/25 100.00 250.00
DRIP23 V.Guerrero Jr./V.Guerrero
DRIP24 K.Griffey Jr./Ichiro
DRIP25 A.Judge/G.Torres/25 100.00 250.00
DRIP26 M.McGwire/R.Henderson
DRIP27 M.Trout/S.Ohtani/25 150.00 400.00
DRIP28 F.Tatis Jr./T.Gwynn
DRIP29 A.Kaline/M.Cabrera/20
DRIP30 G.Springer/A.Bregman
DRIP31 M.Scherzer/J.Soto/25 100.00 250.00
DRIP32 G.Brett/M.Schmidt
DRIP33 L.Gonzalez/R.Johnson/20 100.00 250.00
DRIP34 I.Rodriguez/N.Ryan
DRIP35 F.Thomas/E.Jimenez
DRIP36 G.Carter/A.Dawson
DRIP38 W.McCovey/W.Mays
DRIP39 T.Cobb/H.Wagner
DRIP40 A.Aquino/N.Senzel/25
DRIP41 T.Seaver/J.deGrom/20 100.00 250.00
DRIP43 T.Williams/C.Yastrzemski
DRIP44 R.Acuna Jr./H.Aaron
DRIP45 B.Posey/T.Lincecum

2020 Topps Allen and Ginter Double Rip Cards Ripped

UNRIPPED STATED ODDS 1:XXX HOBBY
PRINT RUNS B/WN 10-26 COPIES PER
NO PRICING ON QTY 15 OR LESS
PRICED WITH CLEANLY RIPPED BACKS
DRIP1 O.Smith/Y.Molina 6.00 15.00
DRIP2 J.Baez/A.Rizzo
DRIP3 B.Harper/R.Hoskins 8.00 20.00
DRIP11 A.Benintendi/R.Devers
DRIP13 R.Clemente/R.Kiner
DRIP16 M.Rivera/W.Ford
DRIP17 Y.Alvarez/J.Altuve
DRIP18 W.Boggs/C.Yastrzemski
DRIP19 R.Yount/C.Yelich
DRIP20 P.Alonso/M.Piazza
DRIP22 C.Bellinger/C.Kershaw
DRIP23 V.Guerrero Jr./V.Guerrero
DRIP24 K.Griffey Jr./Ichiro
DRIP25 A.Judge/G.Torres
DRIP26 M.McGwire/R.Henderson
DRIP27 M.Trout/S.Ohtani
DRIP28 F.Tatis Jr./T.Gwynn
DRIP29 A.Kaline/M.Cabrera
DRIP30 G.Springer/A.Bregman
DRIP31 M.Scherzer/J.Soto
DRIP32 G.Brett/M.Schmidt
DRIP33 L.Gonzalez/R.Johnson
DRIP34 I.Rodriguez/N.Ryan
DRIP35 F.Thomas/E.Jimenez
DRIP36 G.Carter/A.Dawson
DRIP38 W.McCovey/W.Mays
DRIP39 T.Cobb/H.Wagner
DRIP40 A.Aquino/N.Senzel
DRIP41 T.Seaver/J.deGrom
DRIP43 T.Williams/C.Yastrzemski
DRIP44 R.Acuna Jr./H.Aaron
DRIP45 B.Posey/T.Lincecum

2020 Topps Allen and Ginter Down on the Farm

COMPLETE SET (15) 4.00 10.00
COMMON CARD .40 1.00
STATED ODDS 1:XX HOBBY
DFB Bale of Hay .40 1.00
DFBA Barn .40 1.00
DFC Cow .40 1.00
DFCH Chicken .40 1.00
DFCO Combine .40 1.00
DFCS Corn Stalks .40 1.00
DFD Dog .40 1.00
DFF Farmer .40 1.00
DFG Garden .40 1.00
DFH Horse .40 1.00
DFI Irrigator .40 1.00
DFP Pig .40 1.00
DFR Rooster .40 1.00
DFS Silo .40 1.00
DFT Tractor .40 1.00

2020 Topps Allen and Ginter Dual Autographs

STATED ODDS 1:XX HOBBY
EXCHANGE DEADLINE 7/31/2020
DACJ J.Gaines/C.Gaines 300.00 800.00
DADM Kid/Desus 150.00 400.00

2020 Topps Allen and Ginter Field Generals

COMPLETE SET (20) 5.00 12.00
STATED ODDS 1:XX
FG1 Sandy Alomar Jr. .25 .60
FG2 Johnny Bench .40 1.00
FG3 Gary Carter .30 .75
FG4 Willson Contreras .40 1.00
FG5 Carlton Fisk .30 .75
FG6 Joe Girardi .30 .75
FG7 Yasmani Grandal .25 .60
FG8 Joe Mauer .30 .75
FG9 Yadier Molina .50 1.25
FG10 Thurman Munson .40 1.00
FG11 Salvador Perez .30 .75
FG12 Mike Piazza .40 1.00
FG13 Jorge Posada .30 .75
FG14 Buster Posey .50 1.25
FG15 J.T. Realmuto .40 1.00
FG16 Ivan Rodriguez .30 .75
FG17 Gary Sanchez .40 1.00
FG18 Benito Santiago .25 .60
FG19 Joe Torre .30 .75
FG20 Jason Varitek .40 1.00

2020 Topps Allen and Ginter Framed Mini Autographs

STATED ODDS 1:XX HOBBY
EXCHANGE DEADLINE 7/31/2020
*BLACK/25: .6X TO 1.5X BASIC
MAAA Aristides Aquino 15.00 40.00
MAACO Andy Cohen 30.00 80.00
MAAJ Aaron Judge 100.00 250.00
MAAK Anthony Kay 4.00 10.00
MAAN Austin Nola 6.00 15.00
MAAO Adam Ottavino 5.00 12.00
MAAR Austin Riley 8.00 20.00
MAAWF Aaron Fotheringham 8.00 20.00
MABABR Baseball Britt 8.00 20.00
MABB Bo Bichette 60.00 150.00
MABBR Bobby Bradley 4.00 10.00
MABH Bryce Harper 100.00 250.00
MABL Brandon Lowe 8.00 20.00
MABM Brendan McKay
MABR Bryan Reynolds 5.00 12.00
MABS Blake Snell 6.00 15.00
MABSC Briana Scurry 12.00 30.00
MABUL Bucky Lasek 30.00 80.00
MABZ Barry Zito 8.00 20.00
MACB Cavan Biggio 12.00 30.00
MACF Cecil Fielder 15.00 40.00
MACH Courtney Hansen 20.00 50.00
MACK Carter Kieboom 10.00 25.00
MACM Charlie Morton 6.00 15.00
MACP Chris Paddack 6.00 15.00
MACR Cal Ripken Jr. 100.00 250.00
MACY Christian Yelich 30.00 80.00
MADC David Cone 15.00 40.00
MADE Doc Emrick 25.00 60.00
MADG Derrick Goold 8.00 20.00
MADL DJ LeMahieu 30.00 80.00
MADN Desus Nice 30.00 80.00
MADSW Dansby Swanson 15.00 40.00
MADV Daniel Vogelbach 10.00 25.00
MAEJ Eloy Jimenez 20.00 50.00
MAFT Fernando Tatis Jr. 75.00 200.00
MAFTH Frank Thomas 75.00 200.00
MAGL Gavin Lux 40.00 100.00
MAHJT Juice Tandron EXCH 10.00 25.00
MAJA Jim Abbott 10.00 25.00
MAJBA Johnny Bananas 50.00 120.00
MAJBU Joe Burrow 200.00 500.00
MAJC Jose Canseco 10.00 25.00
MAJCA Jared Carrabis 20.00 50.00
MAJDUN Justin Dunn 10.00 25.00
MAJDY Jeff Dye 4.00 10.00
MAJE Julian Edwards 4.00 10.00
MAJF Junior Fernandez 4.00 10.00
MAJKD J.K. Dobbins 25.00 60.00
MAJL Jesus Luzardo 12.00 30.00
MAJM John Means 50.00 120.00
MAJP Jeff Passan 12.00 30.00
MAJS Juan Soto 50.00 120.00
MAJSI Justine Siegal 10.00 25.00
MAJU Jose Urquidy 5.00 12.00
MAJY Jordan Yamamoto 4.00 10.00
MAKC Kelsey Cook 15.00 40.00
MAKH Keston Hiura 12.00 30.00
MAKJ Ken Jeong 60.00 150.00
MAKL Kyle Lewis 40.00 100.00
MAKW Kerry Wood 15.00 40.00
MALA Luis Arraez 8.00 20.00
MALGU Lourdes Gurriel Jr. 5.00 12.00
MALR Luis Robert 100.00 250.00
MALT Lane Thomas 5.00 12.00
MAMB Matt Beaty 5.00 12.00
MAMC Michael Chavis 5.00 12.00
MAMG Mitch Garver 8.00 20.00
MAMM Max Muncy 10.00 25.00
MAMP Maria Pepe 10.00 25.00
MAMT Mike Trout
MAMTA Mike Tauchman 6.00 15.00
MAMY Mike Yastrzemski 15.00 40.00
MANH Nico Hoerner 20.00 50.00
MANHO Nyjah Huston 125.00 300.00
MANK Najah Knight 10.00 25.00
MANS Nick Senzel 6.00 15.00
MANSO Nick Solak 8.00 20.00
MANT Nick Thune 10.00 25.00
MAPA Pete Alonso 30.00 80.00
MAPC Patrick Corbin 5.00 12.00
MAPD Paul DeJong 6.00 15.00
MAPN Rob Friedman 10.00 25.00
MARA Ronald Acuna Jr. 75.00 200.00
MARNY Ryan Nyquist 12.00 30.00
MARS R.L. Stine 50.00 120.00
MASB Seth Brown 4.00 10.00
MASBR Sky Brown 40.00 100.00
MASH Sam Hilliard 10.00 25.00
MASK Sakura Kokumai 12.00 30.00
MASO Shohei Ohtani 60.00 150.00
MAST Steven Tefft 6.00 15.00
MASTB Steve Byrne 8.00 20.00
MATA Tim Anderson 10.00 25.00
MATD Tony Dunst 12.00 30.00
MATE Thairo Estrada 8.00 20.00
MATKM The Kid Mero 50.00 120.00
MAVR Victor Robles 8.00 20.00
MAWA Willians Astudillo 4.00 10.00
MAWB Walker Buehler 25.00 60.00
MAWS Will Smith 10.00 25.00
MAYA Yordan Alvarez 40.00 100.00
MAZP Zach Plesac 10.00 25.00

2020 Topps Allen and Ginter Longball Lore

COMPLETE SET (50) 20.00 50.00
STATED ODDS 1:XX
LL1 Hank Aaron .75 2.00
LL2 Ronald Acuna Jr. 1.50 4.00
LL3 Pete Alonso 1.00 2.50
LL4 Nolan Arenado .60 1.50
LL5 Jeff Bagwell .30 .75
LL6 Ernie Banks .40 1.00
LL7 Cody Bellinger .75 2.00
LL8 Kris Bryant .50 1.25
LL9 Miguel Cabrera .40 1.00
LL10 Robinson Cano .30 .75
LL11 Andre Dawson .30 .75
LL12 Cecil Fielder .25 .60
LL13 Lou Gehrig .75 2.00
LL14 Juan Gonzalez .25 .60
LL15 Ken Griffey Jr. .75 2.00
LL16 Vladimir Guerrero .30 .75
LL17 Vladimir Guerrero Jr. .60 1.50
LL18 Bryce Harper .60 1.50
LL19 Ryan Howard .30 .75
LL20 Reggie Jackson .30 .75
LL21 Chipper Jones .40 1.00
LL22 Aaron Judge 1.00 2.50
LL23 Harmon Killebrew .40 1.00
LL24 J.D. Martinez .40 1.00
LL25 Eddie Mathews .40 1.00
LL26 Hideki Matsui .40 1.00
LL27 Willie Mays .75 2.00
LL28 Willie McCovey .30 .75
LL29 Mark McGwire .60 1.50
LL30 Stan Musial .60 1.50
LL31 David Ortiz .40 1.00
LL32 Mike Piazza .40 1.00
LL33 Albert Pujols .50 1.25
LL34 Anthony Rizzo .50 1.25
LL35 Alex Rodriguez .50 1.25
LL36 Babe Ruth 1.00 2.50
LL37 Mike Schmidt .60 1.50
LL38 Gary Sheffield .25 .60
LL39 Giancarlo Stanton .40 1.00
LL40 Willie Stargell .30 .75
LL41 Darryl Strawberry .25 .60
LL42 Frank Thomas .40 1.00
LL43 Jim Thome .30 .75
LL44 Mike Trout 2.00 5.00
LL45 Mo Vaughn .25 .60
LL46 Larry Walker .30 .75
LL47 Ted Williams .75 2.00
LL48 Dave Winfield .30 .75
LL49 Carl Yastrzemski .60 1.50
LL50 Christian Yelich .50 1.25

2020 Topps Allen and Ginter Mini

*MINI 1-300: 1X TO 2.5X BASIC
*MINI 1-300 RC: .6X TO 1.5X BASIC RCs
*MINI SP 301-350: .6X TO 1.5X BASIC
MINI ODDS 1:XX HOBBY
MINI SP ODDS 1:XX HOBBY
EXT CARDS FOUND IN RIP PACKS
STATED PLATE ODDS 1:XXXX HOBBY
PLATE PRINT RUN 1 SET PER COLOR
BLACK-CYAN-MAGENTA-YELLOW ISSUED
NO PLATE PRICING DUE TO SCARCITY
351 Albert Pujols EXT 10.00 25.00
352 Mike Trout EXT 40.00 100.00
353 Shohei Ohtani EXT 12.00 30.00
354 Chipper Jones EXT 8.00 20.00
355 John Smoltz EXT 8.00 20.00
356 Ronald Acuna Jr. EXT 15.00 40.00
357 Brooks Robinson EXT 20.00 50.00
358 Cal Ripken Jr. EXT 20.00 50.00
359 Carl Yastrzemski EXT 12.00 30.00
360 Ted Williams EXT 15.00 40.00
361 David Ortiz EXT 8.00 20.00
362 Roger Clemens EXT 10.00 25.00
363 Jackie Robinson EXT 12.00 30.00
364 Sandy Koufax EXT 15.00 40.00
365 Kris Bryant EXT 10.00 25.00
366 Ryne Sandberg EXT 10.00 25.00
367 Frank Thomas EXT 12.00 30.00
368 Johnny Bench EXT 8.00 20.00
369 Francisco Lindor EXT 8.00 20.00
370 Carlos Correa EXT 8.00 20.00
371 Jose Altuve EXT 6.00 15.00
372 Justin Verlander EXT 8.00 20.00
373 George Brett EXT 15.00 40.00
374 Clayton Kershaw EXT 12.00 30.00
375 Cody Bellinger EXT 12.00 30.00
376 Mike Piazza EXT 12.00 30.00
377 Hank Aaron EXT 15.00 40.00
378 Christian Yelich EXT 15.00 40.00
379 Pedro Martinez EXT 8.00 20.00
380 Jacob deGrom EXT 15.00 40.00
381 Pete Alonso EXT 15.00 40.00
382 Aaron Judge EXT 20.00 50.00
383 Babe Ruth EXT 20.00 50.00
384 Mariano Rivera EXT 15.00 40.00
385 Reggie Jackson EXT 10.00 25.00
386 Rickey Henderson EXT 15.00 40.00
387 Bryce Harper EXT 12.00 30.00
388 Roberto Clemente EXT 20.00 50.00
389 Fernando Tatis Jr. EXT 25.00 60.00
390 Buster Posey EXT 10.00 25.00
391 Willie Mays EXT 15.00 40.00
392 Alex Rodriguez EXT 10.00 25.00
393 Ichiro EXT 12.00 30.00
394 Ken Griffey Jr. EXT 15.00 40.00
395 Randy Johnson EXT 8.00 20.00
396 Mark McGwire EXT 12.00 30.00
397 Nolan Ryan EXT 25.00 60.00
398 Vladimir Guerrero Jr. EXT 12.00 30.00
399 Juan Soto EXT 25.00 60.00
400 Max Scherzer EXT 8.00 20.00

2020 Topps Allen and Ginter Mini Black Border

*MINI BLK 1-300: 1.5X TO 4X BASIC
*MINI BLK 1-300 RC: 1X TO 2.5X BASIC RCs
*MINI BLK SP 301-350: 1X TO 2.5X BASIC
MINI BLK ODDS 1:XXX HOBBY

2020 Topps Allen and Ginter Mini Brooklyn Back

*MINI BRKLN 1-300: 12X TO 30X BASIC
*MINI BRKLN 1-300 RC: 8X TO 20X BASIC RCs
*MINI BRKLN 301-350: 5X TO 12X BASIC
STATED ODDS 1:XXX HOBBY
STATED PRINT RUN 25 SER.#'d SETS
17 Ken Griffey Jr. 40.00 100.00
18 George Brett 25.00 60.00
29 Willie Mays 25.00 60.00
32 Ichiro 30.00 80.00
35 Rickey Henderson 20.00 50.00
40 Mariano Rivera 30.00 80.00
51 Roberto Clemente 30.00 80.00
80 DJ LeMahieu 20.00 50.00

2020 Topps Allen and Ginter Mini Gold Border

*MINI GOLD 1-300: 1.2X TO 3X BASIC
*MINI GOLD 1-300 RC: .75X TO 2X BASIC RCs
*MINI GOLD 301-350: .75X TO 2X BASIC
RANDOMLY INSERTED IN RETAIL PACKS

2020 Topps Allen and Ginter Mini No Number

*MINI NNO 1-300: 5X TO 12X BASIC
*MINI NNO 1-300 RC: 3X TO 8X BASIC RCs
*MINI NNO 301-350: 2X TO 5X BASIC

2020 Topps Allen and Ginter Mini Stained Glass

*MINI STND GLS 1-150: 30X TO 80X BASIC
*MINI STND GLS 1-150 RC: 25X TO 60X BASIC RCs
*MINI STND GLS 351-400: 1.5X TO 4X BASIC
STATED ODDS 1:XXX HOBBY
ANNCD PRINT RUN OF 25 SETS
17 Ken Griffey Jr. 75.00 200.00
18 George Brett 60.00 150.00
29 Willie Mays 50.00 120.00
32 Ichiro 60.00 150.00
35 Rickey Henderson 40.00 100.00
40 Mariano Rivera 30.00 80.00
51 Roberto Clemente 60.00 150.00
79 Sandy Koufax 60.00 150.00
80 DJ LeMahieu 100.00 250.00
85 Mike Trout 125.00 300.00
110 Albert Pujols 60.00 150.00

2020 Topps Allen and Ginter Mini 9 Ways to First Base

COMPLETE SET (9) 8.00 20.00
STATED ODDS 1:XX HOBBY
M9WF1 Dropped Third Strike 1.25 3.00
M9WF2 Single 1.25 3.00
M9WF3 Base On Balls 1.25 3.00
M9WF4 Hit By Pitch 1.25 3.00
M9WF5 Fielder Interference 1.25 3.00
M9WF6 Fielder's Choice 1.25 3.00
M9WF7 Fielding Error 1.25 3.00
M9WF8 Catcher's Interference 1.25 3.00
M9WF9 Batted Ball hits another runner before a fielder touches it 1.25 3.00

2020 Topps Allen and Ginter Mini Behemoths Beneath

2019 Topps Allen and Ginter Mini Chugging Along 15.00 40.00
2019 Topps Allen and Ginter Mini Chugging Along
MGB1 Colossal Squid 1.25 3.00
MGB2 Blue Whale 1.25 3.00
MGB3 Fin Whale 1.25 3.00
MGB4 Whale Shark 1.25 3.00
MGB5 Sperm Whale 1.25 3.00
MGB6 Giant Manta Ray 1.25 3.00
MGB7 Lion's Mane Jelly 1.25 3.00
MGB8 Orca Whale 1.25 3.00
MGB9 Great White Shark 1.25 3.00
MGB10 Giant Oarfish 1.25 3.00
MGB11 Japanese Spider Crab 1.25 3.00
MGB12 Ocean Sunfish 1.25 3.00
MGB13 Giant Pacific Octopus 1.25 3.00
MGB14 Basking Shark 1.25 3.00
MGB15 Portuguese Man-of-War 1.25 3.00
MGB16 Giant Sea Star 1.25 3.00
MGB17 Giant Clam 1.25 3.00
MGB18 Anglerfish 1.25 3.00
MGB19 Sea Anemone 1.25 3.00
MGB20 Beluga Whale 1.25 3.00

2020 Topps Allen and Ginter Mini Booming Cities

COMPLETE SET (15) 12.00 30.00
STATED ODDS 1:XX HOBBY
BC1 Dubai United Arab Emirates 1.25 3.00
BC2 Shanghai China 1.25 3.00
BC3 Lagos Nigeria 1.25 3.00
BC4 Dar es Salaam Tanzania 1.25 3.00
BC5 Kampala Uganda 1.25 3.00
BC6 Karachi Pakistan 1.25 3.00
BC7 Dhaka Bangladesh 1.25 3.00
BC8 Istanbul Turkey 1.25 3.00
BC9 Sao Paulo Brazil 1.25 3.00
BC10 Jakarta Indonesia 1.25 3.00
BC11 Singapore 1.25 3.00
BC12 Riyadh Saudi Arabia 1.25 3.00
BC13 Tokyo Japan 1.25 3.00
BC14 Shenzhen China 1.25 3.00
BC15 Seattle Washington, USA 1.25 3.00

2020 Topps Allen and Ginter Mini Buggin Out

COMPLETE SET (20) 15.00 40.00
STATED ODDS 1:XX HOBBY
MBO1 Ladybird Beetle 1.25 3.00
MBO2 Monarch Butterfly 1.25 3.00
MBO3 Praying Mantis 1.25 3.00
MBO4 Hercules Beetle 1.25 3.00
MBO5 Thorn Bug 1.25 3.00
MBO6 Australian Walking Stick 1.25 3.00
MBO7 Atlas Moth 1.25 3.00
MBO8 Calleta Silkmoth 1.25 3.00
MBO9 Scorpion Fly 1.25 3.00
MBO10 Peacock Spider 1.25 3.00
MBO11 Spiny Orb Weaver 1.25 3.00
MBO12 Leafcutter Ant 1.25 3.00
MBO13 Red Postman Butterfly 1.25 3.00
MBO14 Giraffe Weevil 1.25 3.00
MBO15 Bumblebee 1.25 3.00
MBO16 Fire Ant 1.25 3.00
MBO17 Old World Swallowtail 1.25 3.00
MBO18 Caterpillar 1.25 3.00
MBO19 Dragonfly 1.25 3.00
MBO20 Treehopper 1.25 3.00

2020 Topps Allen and Ginter Mini Citadels and Safeholds

COMPLETE SET (20) 15.00 40.00
STATED ODDS 1:XX HOBBY
MCS1 Moorish Castle 1.25 3.00
MCS2 Rumeli Castle 1.25 3.00
MCS3 Dover Castle 1.25 3.00
MCS4 Murud-Janjira 1.25 3.00
MCS5 Prague Castle 1.25 3.00
MCS6 The Tower of London 1.25 3.00
MCS7 Citadel of Aleppo 1.25 3.00
MCS8 Bourtange Fort 1.25 3.00
MCS9 Caerphilly Castle 1.25 3.00
MCS10 Ankara Castle 1.25 3.00
MCS11 Spis Castle 1.25 3.00
MCS12 Mehrangarh Fort 1.25 3.00
MCS13 Krak Des Chevaliers 1.25 3.00
MCS14 Conwy Castle 1.25 3.00
MCS15 Fort de Douaumont 1.25 3.00
MCS16 Alcazar of Toledo 1.25 3.00
MCS17 Edinburgh Castle 1.25 3.00
MCS18 Malbork Castle 1.25 3.00
MCS19 Konigstein Fortress 1.25 3.00
MCS20 Balmoral Castle 1.25 3.00

2020 Topps Allen and Ginter Mini DNA Relics

STATED ODDS 1:XX HOBBY
PRINT RUNS B/WN 17-25 COPIES PER
MDNARFB Fossilized Bison/25 100.00 250.00
MDNARFC Fossilized Crocodile/25 100.00 250.00
MDNARFM Fossilized Mammoth/25 125.00 300.00
MDNARFP Fossilized Pterosaur
MDNARFS Fossilized Spinosaurus/17 200.00 500.00
MDNARFSF Fossilized Sawfish
MDNARFSH Fossilized Shark/25 100.00 250.00
MDNARFT Fossilized Turtle/20 100.00 250.00
MDNARFW Fossilized Whale/25 100.00 250.00

2020 Topps Allen and Ginter Mini Framed Relics

STATED ODDS 1:XX HOBBY
MFRAA Aristides Aquino 6.00 15.00
MFRAB Andrew Benintendi 4.00 10.00
MFRABR Alex Bregman 4.00 10.00
MFRAJ Aaron Judge 10.00 25.00
MFRAP Andy Pettitte 3.00 8.00
MFRAPU Albert Pujols 5.00 12.00
MFRAR Anthony Rizzo 5.00 12.00
MFRARO Alex Rodriguez 5.00 12.00
MFRBB Bo Bichette 10.00 25.00
MFRBF Bob Feller 25.00 60.00
MFRBH Bryce Harper 6.00 15.00
MFRBL Barry Larkin 3.00 8.00
MFRBP Buster Posey 5.00 12.00
MFRCB Cody Bellinger 5.00 12.00
MFRCBI Craig Biggio 3.00 8.00
MFRCC Carlos Correa 4.00 10.00
MFRCJ Chipper Jones 10.00 25.00
MFRCK Clayton Kershaw 8.00 20.00
MFRCR Cal Ripken Jr. 10.00 25.00
MFRCS CC Sabathia 3.00 8.00
MFRDL DJ LeMahieu 4.00 10.00
MFRDO David Ortiz 4.00 10.00
MFRDP David Price 3.00 8.00
MFREJ Eloy Jimenez 5.00 12.00
MFRFL Francisco Lindor 4.00 10.00
MFRFT Fernando Tatis Jr. 15.00 40.00
MFRGB George Brett 12.00 30.00
MFRGT Gleyber Torres 5.00 12.00
MFRHA Hank Aaron 25.00 60.00
MFRIR Ivan Rodriguez 3.00 8.00
MFRI Ichiro 8.00 20.00
MFRJA Jose Altuve 3.00 8.00
MFRJB Javier Baez 10.00 25.00
MFRJBA Jeff Bagwell 3.00 8.00
MFRJBE Johnny Bench 20.00 50.00
MFRJM J.D. Martinez 4.00 10.00
MFRJV Justin Verlander 4.00 10.00
MFRKB Kris Bryant 5.00 12.00
MFRKG Ken Griffey Jr. 15.00 40.00
MFRKH Keston Hiura 5.00 12.00
MFRLR Luis Robert 20.00 50.00
MFRMB Mookie Betts 10.00 25.00
MFRMC Miguel Cabrera 4.00 10.00
MFRMM Manny Machado 4.00 10.00
MFRMMC Mark McGwire 8.00 20.00
MFRMP Mike Piazza 4.00 10.00
MFRMR Mariano Rivera 6.00 15.00
MFRMT Mike Trout 15.00 40.00
MFRNG Nomar Garciaparra 3.00 8.00
MFRNS Nick Senzel 4.00 10.00
MFRPA Pete Alonso 8.00 20.00
MFRPG Paul Goldschmidt 4.00 10.00
MFRPM Pedro Martinez 3.00 8.00
MFRRA Ronald Acuna Jr. 15.00 40.00
MFRRAL Roberto Alomar 3.00 8.00
MFRRC Roger Clemens 6.00 15.00
MFRRD Rafael Devers 5.00 12.00
MFRRH Rickey Henderson 6.00 15.00
MFRRHO Rhys Hoskins 5.00 12.00
MFRRJ Reggie Jackson 10.00 25.00
MFRRJO Randy Johnson 6.00 15.00
MFRSO Shohei Ohtani 10.00 25.00
MFRTG Tom Glavine 3.00 8.00
MFRTGW Tony Gwynn 6.00 15.00
MFRTW Ted Williams 100.00 250.00
MFRVG Vladimir Guerrero Jr. 6.00 15.00
MFRWB Wade Boggs 5.00 12.00
MFRWM Willie Mays 300.00 800.00
MFRYA Yordan Alvarez 5.00 12.00
MFRYM Yadier Molina 5.00 12.00

2020 Topps Allen and Ginter Mini Safari Sights

COMPLETE SET (15) 12.00 30.00
STATED ODDS 1:XX HOBBY
SS1 Elephant 1.25 3.00
SS2 Cheetah 1.25 3.00
SS3 Crocodile 1.25 3.00
SS4 Gazelle 1.25 3.00
SS5 Gray Crowned Crane 1.25 3.00
SS6 Hyena 1.25 3.00
SS7 Lion 1.25 3.00
SS8 Warthog 1.25 3.00
SS9 Vervet Monkey 1.25 3.00
SS10 Giraffe 1.25 3.00
SS11 Zebra 1.25 3.00
SS12 Leopard 1.25 3.00
SS13 Hippo 1.25 3.00
SS14 Lion Cub 1.25 3.00
SS15 Safari Truck 1.25 3.00

2020 Topps Allen and Ginter Mini Where Monsters Live

COMPLETE SET (10) 8.00 20.00
STATED ODDS 1:XX HOBBY
MWML1 The Attic 1.25 3.00
MWML2 A Cave 1.25 3.00
MWML3 The Closet 1.25 3.00
MWML4 The Ocean 1.25 3.00
MWML5 An Old Trunk 1.25 3.00
MWML6 A Sewer Drain 1.25 3.00
MWML7 The Swamp 1.25 3.00
MWML8 A Dark Tunnel 1.25 3.00
MWML9 Under the Bed 1.25 3.00
MWML10 Under the Stairs 1.25 3.00

2020 Topps Allen and Ginter N43 Box Toppers

STATED ODDS 1:XX HOBBY BOXES

BLNAB Alex Bregman .60 1.50
BLNBB Bo Bichette 3.00 8.00
BLNBH Bryce Harper 1.00 2.50
BLNCY Christian Yelich .75 2.00
BLNFL Francisco Lindor .60 1.50
BLNFT Fernando Tatis Jr. 3.00 8.00
BLNGC Gerrit Cole 1.00 2.50
BLNGT Gleyber Torres 1.25 3.00
BLNJB Javier Baez .75 2.00
BLNJBE Jose Berrios .50 1.25
BLNJV Joey Votto .60 1.50
BLNKB Kris Bryant .75 2.00
BLNLR Luis Robert 3.00 8.00
BLNMB Mookie Betts 1.25 3.00
BLNMT Mike Trout 3.00 8.00
BLNNA Nolan Arenado 1.00 2.50
BLNPA Pete Alonso 1.50 4.00
BLNRA Ronald Acuna Jr. 2.50 6.00
BLNWB Walker Buehler .75 2.00
BLNYA Yordan Alvarez 4.00 10.00

2020 Topps Allen and Ginter Presidential Pin Relics

STATED ODDS 1:XX HOBBY
PRINT RUNS BW/N 15-25 COPIES PER
FPRBC Bill Clinton/25 50.00 120.00
FPRBO Barack Obama/24 200.00 500.00
FPRDE Dwight D. Eisenhower/25 100.00 250.00
FPRGF Gerald Ford/25 100.00 250.00
FPRGHWB George H.W. Bush/24 100.00 250.00
FPRGWB George W. Bush/15 100.00 250.00
FPRJC Jimmy Carter/20 100.00 250.00
FPRJFK John F. Kennedy/25 200.00 500.00
FPRLBJ Lyndon B. Johnson/25 100.00 250.00
FPRRN Richard Nixon/25 100.00 250.00
FPRRR Ronald Reagan/20 125.00 300.00

2020 Topps Allen and Ginter Reach for the Sky

COMPLETE SET (15) 3.00 8.00
STATED ODDS 1:XX
RFTS1 John Hancock Center .30 .75
RFTS2 Chrysler Building .30 .75
RFTS3 Wilshire Grand Center .30 .75
RFTS4 Comcast Tech Tower .30 .75
RFTS5 Empire State Building .30 .75
RFTS6 432 Park Avenue .30 .75
RFTS7 Steinway Tower .30 .75
RFTS8 Willis Tower .30 .75
RFTS9 Petronas Towers .30 .75
RFTS10 Lakhta Center .30 .75
RFTS11 Taipei 101 .30 .75
RFTS12 One World Trade Center .30 .75
RFTS13 Abraj Al-Bait Clock Tower .30 .75
RFTS14 Shanghai Tower .30 .75
RFTS15 Burj Khalifa .30 .75

2020 Topps Allen and Ginter Relics

VERSION A ODDS 1:XX HOBBY
VERSION B ODDS 1:XX HOBBY
FSRAAA Albert Almora Jr. A 2.50 6.00
FSRAAC Andy Cohen A 3.00 8.00
FSRAAF Aaron Wheelz Fotheringham A 3.00 8.00
FSRAAG Alex Gordon A 2.50 6.00
FSRAAO Adam Ottavino A 2.50 6.00
FSRAAR Austin Riley A 4.00 10.00
FSRABB Baseball Brit 2.50 6.00
Joey Mellows A
FSRABL Bucky Lasek A 3.00 8.00
FSRABS Briana Scurry A 2.50 6.00
FSRACF Clint Frazier A 2.50 6.00
FSRACH Courtney Hansen A 4.00 10.00
FSRACS Chris Sale A 3.00 8.00
FSRACV Christian Vazquez A 2.50 6.00
FSRADG Derrick Goold A 2.50 6.00
FSRADGR Didi Gregorius A 2.50 6.00
FSRADP Dustin Pedroia A 3.00 8.00
FSRAEL Evan Longoria A 2.50 6.00
FSRAGU Gio Urshela A 3.00 8.00
FSRAJB Johnny Bananas A 10.00 25.00
FSRAJBJ Jackie Bradley Jr. A 3.00 8.00
FSRAJC Jared Carrabis A 15.00 40.00
FSRAJCU Johnny Cueto A 2.50 6.00
FSRAJD Jeff Dye A 2.50 6.00
FSRAJH J.A. Happ A 2.50 6.00
FSRAJJ Josh James A 2.00 5.00
FSRAJLU Joey Lucchesi A 2.00 5.00
FSRAJM John Means A 3.00 8.00
FSRAJP Jeff Passan A 2.50 6.00
FSRAJS Justine Siegal A 3.00 8.00
FSRAJSE Jean Segura A 2.50 6.00
FSRAKC Kelsey Cook A 3.00 8.00
FSRAKD Khris Davis A 3.00 8.00
FSRAKW Kolten Wong A 2.50 6.00
FSRALG Lourdes Gurriel Jr. A 2.50 6.00
FSRALV Luke Voit A 4.00 10.00
FSRAMC Michael Conforto A 2.50 6.00
FSRAMCA Matt Carpenter A 3.00 8.00
FSRAMDE Mike Doc Emrick A 3.00 8.00
FSRAMG Mitch Garver A 4.00 10.00
FSRAMO Marcell Ozuna A 3.00 8.00
FSRAMP Maria Pepe A 3.00 8.00
` Nyjah Huston A 20.00 50.00
FSRANT Nick Thune A 2.50 6.00
FSRAOA Orlando Arcia A 4.00 10.00
FSRARF Rob Friedman A 2.50 6.00
FSRARL Ramon Laureano A 2.50 6.00
FSRARS R.L. Stine A 5.00 12.00
FSRASB Steve Byrne A 2.50 6.00
FSRASK Sakura Kokumai A 3.00 8.00
FSRASKI Scott Kingery A 2.50 6.00
FSRAST Steven Tefft A 2.50 6.00
FSRATD Tony Dunst A 2.50 6.00
FSRAWB Walker Buehler A 8.00 20.00
FSRAYK Yusei Kikuchi A 2.50 6.00
FSRBAB Andrew Benintendi B 3.00 8.00
FSRBAC Aroldis Chapman B 3.00 8.00
FSRBAM Andrew McCutchen B 3.00 8.00
FSRBAME Austin Meadows B 3.00 8.00
FSRBAN Aaron Nola B 5.00 12.00
FSRBBG Brett Gardner B 3.00 8.00
FSRBBL Brandon Lowe B 2.50 6.00
FSRBBR Brendan Rodgers B 3.00 8.00
FSRBCBL Charlie Blackmon B 3.00 8.00
FSRBCC Carlos Carrasco B 2.00 5.00
FSRBCY Christian Yelich B 4.00 10.00
FSRBDD David Dahl B 2.00 5.00
FSRBDH Dakota Hudson B 2.50 6.00
FSRBDS Dansby Swanson B 3.00 8.00
FSRBEA Elvis Andrus B 2.50 6.00
FSRBER Eduardo Rodriguez B 2.00 5.00
FSRBES Eugenio Suarez B 4.00 10.00
FSRBGP Gregory Polanco B 2.50 6.00
FSRBGS Gary Sanchez B 3.00 8.00
FSRBGSP George Springer B 2.50 6.00
FSRBGST Giancarlo Stanton B 3.00 8.00
FSRBJB Jose Berrios B 2.50 6.00
FSRBJF Jack Flaherty B 3.00 8.00
FSRBJG Joey Gallo B 3.00 8.00
FSRBJH Josh Hader B 2.50 6.00
FSRBJHE Jason Heyward B 2.50 6.00
FSRBJL Jon Lester B 2.50 6.00
FSRBJM Jeff McNeil B 2.50 6.00
FSRBJP James Paxton B 2.50 6.00
FSRBJPE Joc Pederson B 2.50 6.00
FSRBJPO Jorge Polanco B 2.50 6.00
FSRBJR J.T. Realmuto B 3.00 8.00
FSRBJS Jorge Soler B 3.00 8.00
FSRBJV Joey Votto B 3.00 8.00
FSRBKJ Kenley Jansen B 2.50 6.00
FSRBKS Kyle Schwarber B 3.00 8.00
FSRBLC Lorenzo Cain B 2.00 5.00
FSRBLCA Luis Castillo B 2.50 6.00
FSRBLS Luis Severino B 2.50 6.00
FSRBMA Miguel Andujar B 3.00 8.00
FSRBMC Michael Chavis B 2.50 6.00
FSRBMMU Max Muncy B 2.50 6.00
FSRBMO Matt Olson B 3.00 8.00
FSRBMS Miguel Sano B 2.50 6.00
FSRBMSO Mike Soroka B 3.00 8.00
FSRBMST Marcus Stroman B 2.50 6.00
FSRBMT Masahiro Tanaka B 3.00 8.00
FSRBOA Ozzie Albies B 3.00 8.00
FSRBPD Paul DeJong B 3.00 8.00
FSRBRB Ryan Braun B 2.50 6.00
FSRBSC Shin-Soo Choo B 2.50 6.00
FSRBSG Sonny Gray B 2.50 6.00
FSRBTA Tim Anderson B 3.00 8.00
FSRBTS Trevor Story B 3.00 8.00
FSRBWA Willians Astudillo B 2.00 5.00
FSRBWC Willson Contreras B 3.00 8.00
FSRBXB Xander Bogaerts B 3.00 8.00
FSRBYG Yuli Gurriel B 2.50 6.00

2020 Topps Allen and Ginter Rip Cards

RIP1 Hank Aaron/75
RIP2 Ronald Acuna Jr./99
RIP3 Roberto Alomar/75
RIP4 Pete Alonso/99
RIP5 Jose Altuve/99
RIP6 Yordan Alvarez/99
RIP7 Nolan Arenado/99
RIP8 Javier Baez/99
RIP9 Jeff Bagwell/75
RIP10 Ernie Banks/75
RIP11 Cody Bellinger/99
RIP12 Johnny Bench/75
RIP13 Bo Bichette/99
RIP14 Craig Biggio/90
RIP15 Wade Boggs
RIP16 Alex Bregman/99
RIP17 George Brett/75
RIP18 Kris Bryant/99
RIP19 Walker Buehler/99
RIP20 Miguel Cabrera/99
RIP21 Rod Carew/75
RIP22 Steve Carlton/75
RIP23 Roger Clemens/75
RIP24 Roberto Clemente/75
RIP25 Ty Cobb
RIP26 Gerrit Cole/99
RIP27 Jacob deGrom/99
RIP28 Rafael Devers/99
RIP29 Whitey Ford/75
RIP30 Lou Gehrig
RIP31 Bob Gibson/75
RIP32 Paul Goldschmidt/99
RIP33 Gavin Lux/99
RIP34 Ken Griffey Jr./75
RIP35 Vladimir Guerrero/90
RIP36 Vladimir Guerrero Jr./99
RIP37 Tony Gwynn/75
RIP38 Bryce Harper/99
RIP39 Rickey Henderson/75
RIP40 Keston Hiura/99
RIP41 Rhys Hoskins/99
RIP42 Reggie Jackson/75
RIP43 Eloy Jimenez/99
RIP44 Randy Johnson/75
RIP45 Chipper Jones/99
RIP46 Aaron Judge/99
RIP47 Al Kaline/75
RIP48 Clayton Kershaw/99
RIP49 Harmon Killebrew/75
RIP50 Sandy Koufax/50
RIP51 Barry Larkin/90
RIP52 Manny Machado/99
RIP53 Pedro Martinez/75
RIP54 Don Mattingly/75
RIP55 Willie Mays/50
RIP56 Willie McCovey/75
RIP57 Mark McGwire/75
RIP58 Yadier Molina/99
RIP59 Joe Morgan/75
RIP60 Thurman Munson/75
RIP61 Eddie Murray/75
RIP62 Stan Musial/75
RIP63 Shohei Ohtani/99
RIP64 David Ortiz/90
RIP65 Jim Palmer/75
RIP66 Andy Pettitte/90
RIP67 Mike Piazza/75
RIP68 Buster Posey/99
RIP69 Albert Pujols/99
RIP70 Cal Ripken Jr./75
RIP71 Mariano Rivera/90
RIP72 Anthony Rizzo/99
RIP73 Jackie Robinson/42
RIP74 Brooks Robinson/75
RIP75 Frank Robinson/75
RIP76 Alex Rodriguez/90
RIP77 Ivan Rodriguez/75
RIP78 Babe Ruth/25
RIP79 Nolan Ryan/75
RIP80 Ryne Sandberg/75
RIP81 Max Scherzer/99
RIP82 Mike Schmidt/75
RIP83 Tom Seaver/75
RIP84 Ozzie Smith/90
RIP85 John Smoltz/75
RIP86 Duke Snider/75
RIP87 Juan Soto/99
RIP88 Willie Stargell/75
RIP89 Stephen Strasburg/99
RIP90 Ichiro/99
RIP91 Fernando Tatis Jr./99
RIP92 Frank Thomas/75
RIP93 Jim Thome/75
RIP94 Gleyber Torres/99
RIP95 Mike Trout/99
RIP96 Justin Verlander/99
RIP97 Ted Williams/39
RIP98 Carl Yastrzemski/75
RIP99 Christian Yelich/99
RIP100 Robin Yount/75

2020 Topps Allen and Ginter Rip Cards Ripped

UNRIPPED STATED ODDS 1:XXX HOBBY
PRINT RUNS B/WN XX-XX COPIES PER
PRICED WITH CLEANLY RIPPED BACKS
RIP1 Hank Aaron/75 6.00 15.00
RIP2 Ronald Acuna Jr./99 12.00 30.00
RIP3 Roberto Alomar/75 2.50 6.00
RIP4 Pete Alonso/99 8.00 20.00
RIP5 Jose Altuve/99 2.50 6.00
RIP6 Yordan Alvarez/99 20.00 50.00
RIP7 Nolan Arenado/99 5.00 12.00
RIP8 Javier Baez/99 4.00 10.00
RIP9 Jeff Bagwell/75 2.50 6.00
RIP10 Ernie Banks/75 3.00 8.00
RIP11 Cody Bellinger/99 6.00 15.00
RIP12 Johnny Bench/75 3.00 8.00
RIP13 Bo Bichette/99 15.00 40.00
RIP14 Craig Biggio/90 2.50 6.00
RIP15 Wade Boggs 2.50 6.00
RIP16 Alex Bregman/99 3.00 8.00
RIP17 George Brett/75 6.00 15.00
RIP18 Kris Bryant/99 4.00 10.00
RIP19 Walker Buehler/99 4.00 10.00
RIP20 Miguel Cabrera/99 3.00 8.00
RIP21 Rod Carew/75 2.50 6.00
RIP22 Steve Carlton/75 2.50 6.00
RIP23 Roger Clemens/75 4.00 10.00
RIP24 Roberto Clemente/75 8.00 20.00
RIP25 Ty Cobb 5.00 12.00
RIP26 Gerrit Cole/99 5.00 12.00
RIP27 Jacob deGrom/99 6.00 15.00
RIP28 Rafael Devers/99 4.00 10.00
RIP29 Whitey Ford/75 2.50 6.00
RIP30 Lou Gehrig 6.00 15.00
RIP31 Bob Gibson/75 2.50 6.00
RIP32 Paul Goldschmidt/99 3.00 8.00
RIP33 Gavin Lux/99 10.00 25.00
RIP34 Ken Griffey Jr./75 6.00 15.00
RIP35 Vladimir Guerrero/90 2.50 6.00
RIP36 Vladimir Guerrero Jr./99 5.00 12.00
RIP37 Tony Gwynn/75 3.00 8.00
RIP38 Bryce Harper/99 5.00 12.00
RIP39 Rickey Henderson/75 3.00 8.00
RIP40 Keston Hiura/99 4.00 10.00
RIP41 Rhys Hoskins/99 4.00 10.00
RIP42 Reggie Jackson/75 2.50 6.00
RIP43 Eloy Jimenez/99 6.00 15.00
RIP44 Randy Johnson/75 3.00 8.00
RIP45 Chipper Jones/99 3.00 8.00
RIP46 Aaron Judge/99 8.00 20.00
RIP47 Al Kaline/75 3.00 8.00
RIP48 Clayton Kershaw/99 5.00 12.00
RIP49 Harmon Killebrew/75 3.00 8.00
RIP50 Sandy Koufax/50 6.00 15.00
RIP51 Barry Larkin/90 2.50 6.00
RIP52 Manny Machado/99 3.00 8.00
RIP53 Pedro Martinez/75 2.50 6.00
RIP54 Don Mattingly/75 6.00 15.00
RIP55 Willie Mays/50 6.00 15.00
RIP56 Willie McCovey/75 2.50 6.00
RIP57 Mark McGwire/75 5.00 12.00
RIP58 Yadier Molina/99 4.00 10.00
RIP59 Joe Morgan/75 2.50 6.00
RIP60 Thurman Munson/75 3.00 8.00
RIP61 Eddie Murray/75 2.50 6.00
RIP62 Stan Musial/75 5.00 12.00
RIP63 Shohei Ohtani/99 5.00 12.00
RIP64 David Ortiz/90 3.00 8.00
RIP65 Jim Palmer/75 2.50 6.00
RIP66 Andy Pettitte/90 2.50 6.00
RIP67 Mike Piazza/75 3.00 8.00
RIP68 Buster Posey/99 4.00 10.00
RIP69 Albert Pujols/99 4.00 10.00
RIP70 Cal Ripken Jr./75 10.00 25.00
RIP71 Mariano Rivera/90 4.00 10.00
RIP72 Anthony Rizzo/99 4.00 10.00
RIP73 Jackie Robinson/42 3.00 8.00
RIP74 Brooks Robinson/75 2.50 6.00
RIP75 Frank Robinson/75 2.50 6.00
RIP76 Alex Rodriguez/90 4.00 10.00
RIP77 Ivan Rodriguez/75 2.50 6.00
RIP78 Babe Ruth/25 8.00 20.00
RIP79 Nolan Ryan/75 10.00 25.00
RIP80 Ryne Sandberg/75 6.00 15.00
RIP81 Max Scherzer/99 3.00 8.00
RIP82 Mike Schmidt/75 5.00 12.00
RIP83 Tom Seaver/75 2.50 6.00
RIP84 Ozzie Smith/90 4.00 10.00
RIP85 John Smoltz/75 3.00 8.00
RIP86 Duke Snider/75 2.50 6.00
RIP87 Juan Soto/99 10.00 25.00
RIP88 Willie Stargell/75 2.50 6.00
RIP89 Stephen Strasburg/99 3.00 8.00
RIP90 Ichiro/99 4.00 10.00
RIP91 Fernando Tatis Jr./99 15.00 40.00
RIP92 Frank Thomas/75 3.00 8.00
RIP93 Jim Thome/75 2.50 6.00
RIP94 Gleyber Torres/99 6.00 15.00
RIP95 Mike Trout/99 15.00 40.00
RIP96 Justin Verlander/99 3.00 8.00
RIP97 Ted Williams/39 6.00 15.00
RIP98 Carl Yastrzemski/75 5.00 12.00
RIP99 Christian Yelich/99 4.00 10.00
RIP100 Robin Yount/75 3.00 8.00

2020 Topps Allen and Ginter Chrome

1 Tom Glavine .30 .75
2 Randy Johnson .40 1.00
3 Paul Goldschmidt .40 1.00
4 Larry Doby .30 .75
5 Walker Buehler .50 1.25
6 John Smoltz .40 1.00
7 Tim Lincecum .30 .75
8 Jeff Bagwell .30 .75
9 Rhys Hoskins .50 1.25
10 Rod Carew .30 .75
11 Lou Gehrig .75 2.00
12 George Springer .30 .75
13 Aaron Judge 1.00 2.50
14 Aaron Nola .30 .75
15 Kris Bryant .50 1.25
16 Bryce Harper .60 1.50
17 Ken Griffey Jr. .75 2.00
18 George Brett .75 2.00
19 Keston Hiura .50 1.25
20 Joe Mauer .30 .75
21 Ted Williams .75 2.00
22 Eddie Mathews .40 1.00
23 Jorge Soler .40 1.00
24 Shohei Ohtani .60 1.50
25 Carl Yastrzemski .60 1.50
26 Willie McCovey .30 .75
27 Joe Morgan .30 .75
28 Juan Soto 1.25 3.00
29 Willie Mays .75 2.00
30 Eloy Jimenez .75 2.00
31 Babe Ruth 1.00 2.50
32 Ichiro .50 1.25
33 Edgar Martinez .30 .75
34 Pete Alonso 1.00 2.50
35 Rickey Henderson .40 1.00
36 Alex Bregman .40 1.00
37 Mike Mussina .30 .75
38 Miguel Cabrera .40 1.00
39 Andy Pettitte .30 .75
40 Mariano Rivera .50 1.25
41 David Ortiz .40 1.00
42 Jackie Robinson .40 1.00
43 Matt Chapman .40 1.00
44 Rafael Devers .50 1.25
45 Yoan Moncada .40 1.00
46 Pedro Martinez .30 .75
47 Freddie Freeman .50 1.25
48 Ketel Marte .30 .75
49 Roger Clemens .50 1.25
50 Vladimir Guerrero Jr. .60 1.50
51 Roberto Clemente 1.00 2.50
52 Ivan Rodriguez .30 .75
53 Mike Soroka .40 1.00
54 Victor Robles .50 1.25
55 Nick Senzel .40 1.00
56 Ozzie Albies .40 1.00
57 Eddie Murray .30 .75
58 Christian Yelich .50 1.25
59 Duke Snider .30 .75
60 Steve Carlton .30 .75
61 Jim Thome .30 .75
62 Whitey Ford .30 .75
63 Marcus Semien .40 1.00
64 Andre Dawson .30 .75
65 Cody Bellinger .75 2.00
66 Darryl Strawberry .25 .60
67 Mookie Betts .75 2.00
68 Nomar Garciaparra .30 .75
69 Al Kaline .40 1.00
70 Don Mattingly .75 2.00
71 Vladimir Guerrero .30 .75
72 Johnny Bench .40 1.00
73 Mark McGwire .60 1.50
74 Ty Cobb .60 1.50
75 Joey Votto .40 1.00
76 Chipper Jones .40 1.00
77 Javier Baez .50 1.25
78 Xander Bogaerts .40 1.00
79 Sandy Koufax .75 2.00
80 DJ LeMahieu .40 1.00
81 Barry Zito .30 .75
82 Andrew Benintendi .40 1.00
83 J.D. Martinez .40 1.00
84 Clayton Kershaw .60 1.50
85 Mike Trout 2.00 5.00
86 Anthony Rizzo .50 1.25
87 Trevor Story .40 1.00
88 Ronald Acuna Jr. 1.50 4.00
89 Paul Molitor .40 1.00
90 Jack Flaherty .40 1.00
91 Dave Winfield .30 .75
92 Barry Larkin .30 .75
93 Francisco Lindor .40 1.00
94 Max Fried .40 1.00
95 Manny Machado .40 1.00
96 Frank Thomas .40 1.00
97 Aristides Aquino RC 1.50 4.00
98 Cal Ripken Jr. 1.25 3.00
99 Gavin Lux RC 3.00 8.00
100 Max Scherzer .40 1.00
101 Brooks Robinson .30 .75
102 Robin Yount .40 1.00
103 Tim Anderson .40 1.00
104 Hank Aaron .75 2.00
105 Todd Helton .30 .75
106 Willie Stargell .30 .75
107 Roger Maris .40 1.00
108 Gary Carter .30 .75
109 Reggie Jackson .30 .75
110 Albert Pujols .50 1.25
111 Buster Posey .50 1.25
112 Bo Bichette RC 6.00 15.00
113 Luis Gonzalez .25 .60
114 Gleyber Torres .75 2.00
115 Fernando Tatis Jr. 2.00 5.00
116 Honus Wagner .40 1.00
117 Ernie Banks .40 1.00
118 Yordan Alvarez RC 6.00 15.00
119 Giancarlo Stanton .40 1.00
120 Bob Gibson .30 .75
121 Zack Greinke .40 1.00
122 Trea Turner .30 .75
123 Mike Piazza .40 1.00
124 Juan Marichal .30 .75
125 Craig Biggio .30 .75
126 Wade Boggs .30 .75
127 Jose Altuve .30 .75
128 Tony Gwynn .40 1.00
129 Josh Bell .30 .75
130 Nolan Arenado .60 1.50
131 Stan Musial .60 1.50
132 Jim Palmer .30 .75
133 Justin Verlander .40 1.00
134 Roberto Alomar .30 .75
135 Harmon Killebrew .40 1.00
136 Carlos Correa .40 1.00
137 Yadier Molina .50 1.25
138 Tom Seaver .30 .75
139 Nolan Ryan 1.25 3.00
140 Joe Torre .30 .75
141 Mike Schmidt .60 1.50
142 Patrick Corbin .30 .75
143 Carlton Fisk .30 .75
144 Warren Spahn .30 .75
145 Alex Rodriguez .50 1.25
146 Jacob deGrom .75 2.00
147 Jose Berrios .30 .75
148 David Wright .30 .75
149 Ryne Sandberg .75 2.00
150 Ozzie Smith .50 1.25
151 Kenley Jansen .30 .75
152 J.K. Dobbins .60 1.50
153 Starling Marte .30 .75
154 Tommy La Stella .25 .60
155 Chip Gaines .75 2.00
156 Lourdes Gurriel Jr. .30 .75
157 Jeff McNeil .30 .75
158 Kwang-Hyun Kim RC 1.25 3.00
159 Kyle Lewis RC 5.00 12.00
160 Lorenzo Cain .25 .60
161 Jackie Bradley Jr. .40 1.00
162 Kyle Tucker .40 1.00
163 Cole Hamels .30 .75
164 Kolten Wong .30 .75
165 Hugo Juice Tandron .30 .75
166 Briana Scurry .30 .75
167 Ken Jeong .30 .75
168 Willson Contreras .40 1.00
169 Carter Kieboom .30 .75
170 Nick Thune .30 .75
171 Hunter Pence .30 .75
172 Baseball Brit .30 .75
Joey Mellows
173 Evan Longoria .30 .75
174 Anthony Kay RC .60 1.50
175 Kirby Yates .25 .60
176 Justin Dunn RC .75 2.00
177 Hunter Harvey RC 1.00 2.50
178 Marcell Ozuna .40 1.00
179 Dallas Keuchel .30 .75
180 Khris Davis .40 1.00
181 Adbert Alzolay RC .75 2.00
182 Kelsey Cook .40 1.00
183 Lucas Giolito .30 .75
184 Joc Pederson .30 .75
185 Austin Meadows .40 1.00
186 Bryan Reynolds .30 .75
187 Masahiro Tanaka .40 1.00
188 Eugenio Suarez .30 .75
189 Brandon Lowe .30 .75
190 Yuli Gurriel .30 .75
191 Nelson Cruz .40 1.00
192 Jose Abreu .40 1.00
193 Nyjah Huston 10.00 25.00
194 Mike Doc Emrick .30 .75
195 Robinson Cano .30 .75
196 Noah Syndergaard .30 .75
197 Matt Thaiss RC .75 2.00
198 Will Smith .40 1.00
199 Nico Hoerner RC 2.50 6.00
200 Jim Abbott .25 .60
201 Sakura Kokumai .30 .75
202 Tino Martinez .30 .75
203 Tony Dunst .30 .75
204 Jared Carrabis .40 1.00
205 Salvador Perez .30 .75
206 C.J. Cron .25 .60
207 Brendan McKay RC 1.00 2.50
208 Mike Moustakas .30 .75
209 Johnny Bananas 1.00 2.50
210 Jose Ramirez .30 .75
211 Ryan Braun .30 .75
212 Chris Paddack .40 1.00
213 Oscar Mercado .40 1.00
214 Derek Jeter 2.00 5.00
215 Paul DeJong .40 1.00
216 Shun Yamaguchi RC .75 2.00
217 Aaron Wheelz Fotheringham .40 1.00
218 Andrelton Simmons .25 .60
219 Josh Hader .30 .75
220 Eric Hosmer .30 .75
221 Mike Foltynewicz .25 .60
222 Isan Diaz RC 1.00 2.50
223 Shane Bieber .40 1.00
224 Kole Calhoun .25 .60
225 Austin Riley .50 1.25
226 A.J. Puk RC 1.00 2.50
227 Max Muncy .30 .75
228 Justine Siegal .40 1.00
229 Jordan Yamamoto RC .60 1.50
230 Matt Olson .40 1.00
231 Bucky Lasek .40 1.00
232 Dakota Hudson .30 .75
233 Howie Kendrick .25 .60
234 Jorge Alfaro .25 .60
235 Jesus Luzardo RC 1.25 3.00
236 Alex Verdugo .30 .75
237 Nick Ahmed .25 .60
238 Gerrit Cole .60 1.50
239 Kyle Schwarber .40 1.00
240 Luis Arraez .50 1.25
241 Michael Brantley .30 .75
242 Andy Cohen .30 .75
243 Max Kepler .30 .75
244 Brandon Woodruff .40 1.00
245 Josh Donaldson .30 .75
246 Mike Clevinger .30 .75
247 Yusei Kikuchi .30 .75
248 Rob Friedman .30 .75
249 Stephen Strasburg .40 1.00
250 Charlie Blackmon .40 1.00
251 Corey Kluber .30 .75
252 Steve Byrne .30 .75
253 David Price .30 .75
254 Ryan Nyquist .30 .75
255 David Dahl .25 .60
256 Luis Robert RC 5.00 12.00
257 Corey Seager .40 1.00
258 Cavan Biggio .50 1.25
259 Whit Merrifield .40 1.00
260 J.T. Realmuto .40 1.00
261 Joey Gallo .40 1.00
262 Zac Gallen RC 1.50 4.00
263 Dansby Swanson .40 1.00
264 Abraham Toro RC .75 2.00
265 Tommy Edman .40 1.00
266 Didi Gregorius .30 .75
267 Elvis Andrus .30 .75
268 Eduardo Escobar .25 .60
269 Miguel Sano .30 .75
270 Luis Castillo .30 .75
271 Michael Conforto .30 .75
272 Jon Lester .30 .75
273 Gregory Polanco .30 .75
274 Steven Tefft .30 .75
275 Jeff Dye .30 .75
276 Jose Urquidy RC .75 2.00
277 John Means .40 1.00
278 Nick Castellanos .40 1.00
279 Maikel Franco .30 .75
280 Jean Segura .30 .75
281 Derrick Goold .30 .75
282 Matthew Boyd .25 .60
283 Nomar Mazara .25 .60
284 Julian Edwards .30 .75
285 Orlando Arcia .25 .60
286 Trey Mancini .40 1.00
287 Aroldis Chapman .40 1.00
288 Courtney Hansen .30 .75
289 Anthony Rendon .40 1.00
290 Ramon Laureano .30 .75
291 Sonny Gray .30 .75
292 Hyun-Jin Ryu .30 .75
293 Daniel Vogelbach .25 .60
294 Mauricio Dubon RC .75 2.00
295 Zack Wheeler .30 .75
296 Trevor Bauer .50 1.25
297 R.L. Stine .40 1.00
298 Adalberto Mondesi .30 .75
299 Blake Snell .30 .75
300 Andres Munoz RC 1.00 2.50

2020 Topps Allen and Ginter Chrome Gold Refractors

*GOLD REF.: 4X TO 10X BASIC
*GOLD REF. RC: 1.5X TO 4X BASIC
RANDOM INSERTS IN PACKS
STATED PRINT RUN 50 SER.#'d SETS
13 Aaron Judge 25.00 60.00
14 Aaron Nola 6.00 15.00
15 Kris Bryant 10.00 25.00
16 Bryce Harper 20.00 50.00
17 Ken Griffey Jr. 40.00 100.00
29 Willie Mays 25.00 60.00
31 Babe Ruth 20.00 50.00
32 Ichiro 20.00 50.00
35 Rickey Henderson 15.00 40.00
41 David Ortiz 10.00 25.00
42 Jackie Robinson 12.00 30.00
51 Roberto Clemente 30.00 80.00
67 Mookie Betts 30.00 80.00
70 Don Mattingly 25.00 60.00
74 Ty Cobb 10.00 25.00
76 Chipper Jones 12.00 30.00
79 Sandy Koufax 20.00 50.00
85 Mike Trout 75.00 200.00
86 Anthony Rizzo 10.00 25.00
88 Ronald Acuna Jr. 40.00 100.00
92 Barry Larkin 8.00 20.00
98 Cal Ripken Jr. 30.00 80.00
99 Gavin Lux 20.00 50.00
104 Hank Aaron 25.00 60.00
110 Albert Pujols 20.00 501.00
112 Bo Bichette 75.00 200.00
114 Gleyber Torres 15.00 40.00
115 Fernando Tatis Jr. 25.00 60.00
118 Yordan Alvarez 40.00 100.00
128 Tony Gwynn 15.00 40.00
137 Yadier Molina 12.00 30.00
139 Nolan Ryan 25.00 60.00
141 Mike Schmidt 20.00 50.00
144 Warren Spahn 12.00 30.00
145 Alex Rodriguez 15.00 40.00
149 Ryne Sandberg 15.00 40.00
159 Kyle Lewis 30.00 80.00
167 Ken Jeong 6.00 15.00
214 Derek Jeter 25.00 60.00
222 Isan Diaz 6.00 15.00
223 Shane Bieber 8.00 20.00
256 Luis Robert 100.00 250.00
294 Mauricio Dubon 10.00 25.00
297 R.L. Stine 8.00 20.00

2020 Topps Allen and Ginter Chrome Green Refractors

*GRN REF.: 3X TO 8X BASIC
*GRN REF. RC: 1.2X TO 3X BASIC
RANDOM INSERTS IN PACKS
STATED PRINT RUN 99 SER.#'d SETS
13 Aaron Judge 10.00 25.00
16 Bryce Harper 8.00 20.00
17 Ken Griffey Jr. 25.00 60.00
29 Willie Mays 20.00 50.00
32 Ichiro 15.00 40.00
35 Rickey Henderson 8.00 20.00
42 Jackie Robinson 5.00 12.00
51 Roberto Clemente 15.00 40.00
67 Mookie Betts 10.00 25.00
70 Don Mattingly 20.00 50.00
74 Ty Cobb 8.00 20.00
85 Mike Trout 30.00 80.00
98 Cal Ripken Jr. 15.00 40.00
104 Hank Aaron 12.00 30.00
110 Albert Pujols 8.00 20.00
112 Bo Bichette 40.00 100.00
114 Gleyber Torres 8.00 20.00
115 Fernando Tatis Jr. 20.00 501.00
118 Yordan Alvarez 20.00 50.00
128 Tony Gwynn 8.00 20.00
139 Nolan Ryan 12.00 30.00
141 Mike Schmidt 8.00 20.00
145 Alex Rodriguez 5.00 12.00
159 Kyle Lewis 25.00 60.00
256 Luis Robert 60.00 150.00

2020 Topps Allen and Ginter Chrome Orange Refractors

*ORNG REF.: 5X TO 12X BASIC
*ORNG REF. RC: 2X TO 5X BASIC
RANDOM INSERTS IN PACKS
STATED PRINT RUN 25 SER.#'d SETS
13 Aaron Judge 60.00 150.00
14 Aaron Nola 10.00 25.00
15 Kris Bryant 12.00 30.00
16 Bryce Harper 25.00 60.00
17 Ken Griffey Jr. 60.00 150.00
29 Willie Mays 30.00 80.00
31 Babe Ruth 100.00 250.00
32 Ichiro 25.00 60.00
35 Rickey Henderson 20.00 50.00
41 David Ortiz 12.00 30.00
42 Jackie Robinson 25.00 60.00
51 Roberto Clemente 50.00 120.00
67 Mookie Betts 40.00 100.00
70 Don Mattingly 30.00 80.00
74 Ty Cobb 12.00 30.00
76 Chipper Jones 15.00 40.00
79 Sandy Koufax 25.00 60.00
85 Mike Trout 125.00 300.00
86 Anthony Rizzo 20.00 50.00
88 Ronald Acuna Jr. 50.00 120.00
92 Barry Larkin 8.00 20.00
98 Cal Ripken Jr. 60.00 150.00
99 Gavin Lux 50.00 120.00
104 Hank Aaron 30.00 80.00
110 Albert Pujols 25.00 60.00
112 Bo Bichette 100.00 250.00
114 Gleyber Torres 25.00 60.00
115 Fernando Tatis Jr. 40.00 100.00
118 Yordan Alvarez 50.00 120.00
128 Tony Gwynn 40.00 100.00
137 Yadier Molina 40.00 100.00
139 Nolan Ryan 30.00 80.00
141 Mike Schmidt 25.00 60.00
143 Carlton Fisk 20.00 50.00
144 Warren Spahn 15.00 40.00
145 Alex Rodriguez 20.00 50.00
149 Ryne Sandberg 20.00 50.00
159 Kyle Lewis 50.00 120.00
167 Ken Jeong 15.00 40.00
214 Derek Jeter 60.00 150.00
217 Aaron Wheelz Fotheringham 8.00 20.00
222 Isan Diaz 12.00 30.00
223 Shane Bieber 10.00 25.00
256 Luis Robert 200.00 500.00
294 Mauricio Dubon 12.00 30.00
297 R.L. Stine 10.00 25.00

2020 Topps Allen and Ginter Chrome Refractors

*REF.: 1.5X TO 4X BASIC
*REF. RC: .6X TO 1.5X BASIC
RANDOM INSERTS IN PACKS
17 Ken Griffey Jr. 8.00 20.00
85 Mike Trout 15.00 40.00
112 Bo Bichette 15.00 40.00
118 Yordan Alvarez 8.00 20.00
159 Kyle Lewis 12.00 30.00
256 Luis Robert 25.00 60.00

2020 Topps Allen and Ginter Chrome Autographs

STATED ODDS 1:XX HOBBY
EXCHANGE DEADLINE 10/31/22
ACGI Ichiro 200.00 500.00
ACGAA Aristides Aquino 20.00 50.00
ACGAJ Aaron Judge 75.00 200.00
ACGAP Albert Pujols 200.00 500.00
ACGBB Bo Bichette 150.00 400.00
ACGCB Cody Bellinger 60.00 150.00
ACGCJ Chipper Jones 75.00 200.00
ACGCR Cal Ripken Jr. 100.00 250.00
ACGDJ Derek Jeter 300.00 600.00
ACGDO David Ortiz 60.00 150.00
ACGHA Hank Aaron 200.00 500.00
ACGJB Johnny Bench 60.00 150.00
ACGJS Juan Soto 100.00 250.00
ACGJV Joey Votto 50.00 120.00
ACGKG Ken Griffey Jr. 300.00 600.00
ACGLR Luis Robert EXCH
ACGMM Mark McGwire 60.00 150.00
ACGMR Mariano Rivera 100.00 250.00
ACGMT Mike Trout 600.00 1200.00
ACGNH Nico Hoerner 40.00 100.00
ACGNR Nolan Ryan 125.00 300.00
ACGOS Ozzie Smith 60.00 150.00
ACGPA Pete Alonso 40.00 100.00
ACGPC Patrick Corbin 12.00 30.00
ACGRA Ronald Acuna Jr. 100.00 250.00
ACGRJ Randy Johnson 40.00 100.00
ACGSK Sandy Koufax 200.00 500.00
ACGYA Yordan Alvarez 125.00 300.00
ACGVGU Vladimir Guerrero 40.00 100.00

2020 Topps Allen and Ginter Chrome Mini

*MINI: 1.2X TO 3X BASIC
*MINI RC: .5X TO 1.2X BASIC
RANDOM INSERTS IN PACKS
17 Ken Griffey Jr. 2.50 6.00
256 Luis Robert 12.00 30.00

2020 Topps Allen and Ginter Chrome Mini Booming Cities

COMPLETE SET (15)
STATED ODDS 1:9 HOBBY
BCC1 Dubai United Arab Emirates 1.50 4.00
BCC2 Shanghai China 1.50 4.00
BCC3 Lagos Nigeria 1.50 4.00
BCC4 Dar es Salaam Tanzania 1.50 4.00
BCC5 Kampala Uganda 1.50 4.00
BCC6 Karachi Pakistan 1.50 4.00
BCC7 Dhaka Bangladesh 1.50 4.00
BCC8 Istanbul Turkey 1.50 4.00
BCC9 Sao Paulo Brazil 1.50 4.00
BCC10 Jakarta Indonesia 1.50 4.00
BCC11 Singapore Singapore 1.50 4.00
BCC12 Riyadh Saudi Arabia 1.50 4.00
BCC13 Tokyo Japan 1.50 4.00
BCC14 Shenzhen China 1.50 4.00
BCC15 Seattle Washington USA 1.50 4.00

2020 Topps Allen and Ginter Chrome Mini Buggin Out

COMPLETE SET (20)
STATED ODDS 1:6 HOBBY
MBOC1 Ladybird Beetle 1.50 4.00
MBOC2 Monarch Butterfly 1.50 4.00
MBOC3 Praying Mantis 1.50 4.00

MBOC4 Hercules Beetle 1.50 4.00
MBOC5 Thorn Bug 1.50 4.00
MBOC6 Australian Walking Stick 1.50 4.00
MBOC7 Atlas Moth 1.50 4.00
MBOC8 Calleta Silkmoth 1.50 4.00
MBOC9 Scorpion Fly 1.50 4.00
MBOC10 Peacock Spider 1.50 4.00
MBOC11 Leafcutter Ant 1.50 4.00
MBOC12 Spiny Orb Weaver 1.50 4.00
MBOC13 Red Postman Butterfly 1.50 4.00
MBOC14 Giraffe Weevil 1.50 4.00
MBOC15 Bumblebee 1.50 4.00
MBOC16 Fire Ant 1.50 4.00
MBOC17 Old World Swallowtail 1.50 4.00
MBOC18 Caterpillar 1.50 4.00
MBOC19 Dragonfly 1.50 4.00
MBOC20 Treehopper 1.50 4.00

2020 Topps Allen and Ginter Chrome Mini Safari Sights

COMPLETE SET (15)
STATED ODDS 1:9 HOBBY
SSC1 Elephant 1.50 4.00
SSC2 Cheetah 1.50 4.00
SSC3 Crocodile 1.50 4.00
SSC4 Gazelle 1.50 4.00
SSC5 Gray Crowned Crane 1.50 4.00
SSC6 Hyena 1.50 4.00
SSC7 Lion 1.50 4.00
SSC8 Warthog 1.50 4.00
SSC9 Vervet Monkey 1.50 4.00
SSC10 Giraffe 1.50 4.00
SSC11 Zebra 1.50 4.00
SSC12 Leopard 1.50 4.00
SSC13 Hippo 1.50 4.00
SSC14 Lion Cub 1.50 4.00
SSC15 Safari Truck 1.50 4.00

2018 Topps Allen and Ginter X Mini Framed Autographs

PRINT RUN B/WN 5-25 SETS PER
NO PRICING QTY 15 OR LESS
EXCHANGE DEADLINE 6/30/2020
MAAA Aaron Altherr 8.00 20.00
MAAE Austin Meadows 20.00 50.00
MAAH Austin Hays
MAAL Alison Lee 20.00 50.00
MAAM A.J. Minter 10.00 25.00
MAAN Anthony Banda 8.00 20.00
MAAO Austin Rogers 12.00 30.00
MAAR Amed Rosario 10.00 25.00
MAAS Andrew Stevenson 8.00 20.00
MABD Brian Dozier 10.00 25.00
MABH Bryce Harper
MABI Bill James 20.00 50.00
MABJ Bo Jackson 60.00 150.00
MABL Ben Lecomte 8.00 20.00
MABW Brandon Woodruff 25.00 60.00
MACM Claire Smith 10.00 25.00
MACO Christopher McDonald 10.00 25.00
MACP Champ Pederson 12.00 30.00
MACS Chance Sisco 10.00 25.00
MADC Dominic Smith 10.00 25.00
MADF Dustin Fowler 8.00 20.00
MADM Don Mattingly 75.00 200.00
MADP Dillon Peters 8.00 20.00
MADS Darryl Strawberry
MADU Doris Burke
MAFJ Felix Jorge 8.00 20.00
MAFM Francisco Mejia
MAFT Frank Thomas 75.00 200.00
MAGC Garrett Cooper 8.00 20.00
MAGT Gleyber Torres 75.00 200.00
MAGU Genie Bouchard
MAHB Harrison Bader 12.00 30.00
MAHJ H. Jon Benjamin 40.00 100.00
MAIH Ian Happ 10.00 25.00
MAJA Jose Altuve 40.00 100.00
MAJB Justin Bour 8.00 20.00
MAJC J.P. Crawford 8.00 20.00
MAJCK Jack Sock 12.00 30.00
MAJD J.D. Davis 10.00 25.00
MAJH Jordan Hicks 15.00 40.00
MAJI Jose Berrios 10.00 25.00
MAJM J.D. Martinez EXCH 40.00 100.00
MAJO Jose Canseco 25.00 60.00
MAJR Jose Ramirez 25.00 60.00
MAJS Jackson Stephens 8.00 20.00
MAJV Joey Votto 75.00 200.00
MAJZ Jon Lovitz
MAKB Keon Broxton 8.00 20.00
MAKD Khris Davis
MAKP Kelsey Plum 10.00 25.00
MAKR Kris Bryant 125.00 300.00
MALC Luis Castillo 10.00 25.00
MALR Lincoln Riley
MALV Lindsey Vonn 50.00 120.00
MAMF Max Fried 30.00 80.00
MAMG Miguel Gomez 8.00 20.00
MAMH Molly McGrath 25.00 60.00
MAMM Manny Machado 60.00 150.00
MAMMI Miles Mikolas 15.00 40.00
MAMN Method Man EXCH 60.00 150.00
MAMO Matt Olson 12.00 30.00
MAMR Michael Rapaport 25.00 60.00
MAMT Mike Trout
MAMW Mark McGwire 50.00 120.00
MAMY Madison Keys 15.00 40.00
MANY Noah Syndergaard 25.00 60.00
MAOA Ozzie Albies 50.00 120.00
MAPB Parker Bridwell
MAPD Paul DeJong 12.00 30.00
MAPG Paul Goldschmidt 30.00 80.00
MAPL Paul Blackburn 8.00 20.00
MAPSP Paige Spiranac 30.00 80.00
MARA Ronald Acuna 150.00 400.00
MARD Rafael Devers 30.00 80.00
MARI Ryan Sickler
MARK Rhys Hoskins 60.00 150.00
MARR Raudy Read 8.00 20.00
MARU Richard Urena 8.00 20.00
MAS Stugotz
MASA Sandy Alcantara 8.00 20.00
MASB Scott Blumstein 8.00 20.00
MASE Sean Evans
MASF Sonny Fredrickson 10.00 25.00
MASG Sonny Gray
MASKI Scott Kingery 15.00 40.00
MASN Sean Newcomb 10.00 25.00
MASO Shohei Ohtani 300.00 800.00
MASR Scott Rogowsky 20.00 50.00
MASS Steve Simeone
MASST Sloane Stephens
MATG Tom Segura
MATH Tony Hawk
MATI Tommy Wiseau
MATL Tzu-Wei Lin 10.00 25.00
MATLU Tyronn Lue 8.00 20.00
MATM Tyler Mahle 10.00 25.00
MATN Tomas Nido 8.00 20.00
MATS Troy Scribner 8.00 20.00
MATV Travis Shaw 8.00 20.00
MAVC Victor Caratini 12.00 30.00
MAVR Victor Robles 40.00 100.00
MAWB Walker Buehler 50.00 120.00
MAWM Whit Merrifield 15.00 40.00
MAWO Willson Contreras 20.00 50.00

2019 Topps Allen and Ginter X

1 Mookie Betts .75 2.00
2 Christian Yelich .50 1.25
3 Babe Ruth 1.00 2.50
4 Lou Gehrig .75 2.00
5 Shohei Ohtani .60 1.50
6 Luis Gonzalez .25 .60
7 Albert Pujols .50 1.25
8 Reggie Jackson .30 .75
9 Zack Greinke .40 1.00
10 Mike Trout 2.00 5.00
11 Nolan Ryan 1.25 3.00
12 Blake Treinen .25 .60
13 Ozzie Albies .40 1.00
14 Chipper Jones .40 1.00
15 Freddie Freeman .50 1.25
16 Kris Bryant .50 1.25
17 Anthony Rizzo .50 1.25
18 Ryne Sandberg .75 2.00
19 Javier Baez .50 1.25
20 Ernie Banks .40 1.00
21 Francisco Lindor .40 1.00
22 Jose Ramirez .30 .75
23 Bob Feller .30 .75
24 A.J. Burnett .25 .60
25 Ronald Acuna Jr. 2.00 5.00
26 Justin Verlander .40 1.00
27 Gerrit Cole .40 1.00
28 Jose Altuve .30 .75
29 Alex Bregman .40 1.00
30 George Springer .30 .75
31 Jeff Bagwell .30 .75
32 Sandy Koufax .75 2.00
33 Walker Buehler .50 1.25
34 Cody Bellinger .75 2.00
35 Mike Piazza .40 1.00
36 Starlin Castro .25 .60
37 Josh Hader .30 .75
38 Lorenzo Cain .25 .60
39 Jesus Aguilar .30 .75
40 Ryan Braun .30 .75
41 Robinson Cano .30 .75
42 Jacob deGrom .75 2.00
43 Edwin Diaz .30 .75
44 Noah Syndergaard .30 .75
45 Amed Rosario .30 .75
46 Rickey Henderson .40 1.00
47 Matt Chapman .40 1.00
48 Dennis Eckersley .30 .75
49 Khris Davis .40 1.00
50 Hank Aaron .75 2.00
51 Paul Molitor .40 1.00
52 Buster Posey .50 1.25
53 Willie McCovey .30 .75
54 Juan Marichal .30 .75
55 Evan Longoria .30 .75
56 J.D. Martinez .40 1.00
57 Felix Hernandez .30 .75
58 Edgar Martinez .30 .75
59 Justus Sheffield RC .60 1.50
60 Ichiro .50 1.25
61 Mark McGwire .60 1.50
62 Paul Goldschmidt .40 1.00
63 Yadier Molina .50 1.25
64 Stan Musial .60 1.50
65 Ozzie Smith .50 1.25
66 Roger Clemens .50 1.25
67 Roberto Alomar .30 .75
68 Justin Smoak .25 .60
69 Danny Jansen RC .40 1.00
70 Max Scherzer .40 1.00
71 Patrick Corbin .30 .75
72 Stephen Strasburg .40 1.00
73 Trea Turner .30 .75
74 Cal Ripken Jr. 1.25 3.00
75 Brooks Robinson .30 .75
76 Jim Palmer .30 .75
77 Tony Gwynn .40 1.00
78 Trevor Hoffman .30 .75
79 Luis Urias RC .60 1.50
80 Eric Hosmer .30 .75
81 Andrew McCutchen .40 1.00
82 Rhys Hoskins .50 1.25
83 Aaron Nola .30 .75
84 Roberto Clemente 1.00 2.50
85 Chris Archer .25 .60
86 Felipe Vazquez .25 .60
87 Willie Stargell .30 .75
88 Ralph Kiner .30 .75
89 Adrian Beltre .40 1.00
90 Ivan Rodriguez .30 .75
91 Elvis Andrus .30 .75
92 Joey Gallo .30 .75
93 Blake Snell .30 .75
94 Willy Adames .25 .60
95 Jose Canseco .30 .75
96 Andrew Benintendi .40 1.00
97 Rafael Devers .50 1.25
98 Ted Williams .75 2.00
99 Chris Sale .40 1.00
100 Ken Griffey Jr. .75 2.00
101 David Price .30 .75
102 Joey Votto .40 1.00
103 Johnny Bench .40 1.00
104 Tony Perez .30 .75
105 Todd Helton .30 .75
106 Trevor Story .40 1.00
107 Nolan Arenado .60 1.50
108 Charlie Blackmon .40 1.00
109 George Brett .75 2.00
110 Salvador Perez .30 .75
111 Bo Jackson .40 1.00
112 Miguel Cabrera .40 1.00
113 Al Kaline .40 1.00
114 Jose Berrios .30 .75
115 Rod Carew .30 .75
116 Tony Oliva .25 .60
117 Harmon Killebrew .40 1.00
118 Frank Thomas .40 1.00
119 Michael Kopech RC 1.25 3.00
120 Yoan Moncada .40 1.00
121 Jose Abreu .40 1.00
122 Isiah Kiner-Falefa .30 .75
123 Gleyber Torres .75 2.00
124 Miguel Andujar .40 1.00
125 Giancarlo Stanton .40 1.00
126 Clayton Kershaw .60 1.50
127 Juan Soto 1.25 3.00
128 Roger Maris .40 1.00
129 Jackie Robinson .40 1.00
130 Torii Hunter .25 .60
131 Juan Gonzalez .25 .60
132 David Ortiz .40 1.00
133 Don Mattingly .75 2.00
134 Derek Jeter 1.00 2.50
135 Dale Murphy .40 1.00
136 Mariano Rivera .50 1.25
137 Vladimir Guerrero .30 .75
138 Gary Carter .30 .75
139 Harold Baines .30 .75
140 Luis Severino .30 .75
141 Miles Mikolas .40 1.00
142 Mitch Haniger .30 .75
143 Max Muncy .30 .75
144 Whit Merrifield .40 1.00
145 Xander Bogaerts .40 1.00
146 Josh Donaldson .30 .75
147 J.T. Realmuto .40 1.00
148 Corey Kluber .30 .75
149 Manny Machado .40 1.00
150 Steve Carlton .30 .75
151 Marc Summers .40 1.00
152 Augie Carton .25 .60
153 Jay Larson .30 .75
154 Hailey Dawson .40 1.00
155 Gary Vaynerchuk .40 1.00
156 Vincent Stio .40 1.00
157 Mike Oz .40 1.00
158 Kyle Snyder .40 1.00
159 Rodney Mullen .40 1.00
160 Matthew Mercer .40 1.00
161 Sister Mary Jo Sobieck .40 1.00
162 Mason Cox .40 1.00
163 Loretta Claiborne .30 .75
164 Justin Bonomo .40 1.00
165 John Cynn .30 .75
166 1st Tiger Mask .40 1.00
Satoru Sayama
167 Mayumi Seto .40 1.00
168 Rhea Butcher .30 .75
169 Drew Drechsel .40 1.00
170 Lawrence Rocks .25 .60
171 Charles Martinet .40 1.00
172 Tyler Kepner .25 .60
173 Ben Schwartz .40 1.00
174 Dan Rather .40 1.00
175 Danielle Colby .40 1.00
176 Post Malone .40 1.00
177 Robert Oberst .40 1.00
178 Brian Fallon .40 1.00
179 Burton Rocks .25 .60
180 Quinn XCII .40 1.00
181 Emily Jaenson .40 1.00
182 Pete Alonso RC 6.00 15.00
183 Fernando Tatis Jr. RC 6.00 15.00
184 Travis Pastrana .40 1.00
185 Hilary Knight .40 1.00
186 Wade Boggs .30 .75
187 Jason Varitek .40 1.00
188 Didi Gregorius .30 .75
189 Tyler O'Neill .30 .75
190 Eddie Rosario .30 .75
191 Brandon Nimmo .30 .75
192 Lourdes Gurriel Jr. .30 .75
193 Jack Flaherty .40 1.00
194 Kevin Newman RC .60 1.50
195 Dakota Hudson RC
196 Cedric Mullins RC .75 2.00
197 Brad Keller RC .40 1.00
198 David Bote .30 .75
199 Dereck Rodriguez .25 .60
200 Aaron Judge 1.00 2.50
201 Sean Reid-Foley RC .40 1.00
202 Luke Voit .60 1.50
203 Jeff McNeil RC 1.00 2.50
204 Cionel Perez RC .40 1.00
205 Chance Adams RC
206 Corbin Burnes RC 3.00 8.00
207 Ramon Laureano RC .75 2.00
208 Dawel Lugo RC .60 1.50
209 Ryan O'Hearn RC .40 1.00
210 Framber Valdez RC .40 1.00
211 Patrick Wisdom RC .40 1.00
212 Dylan Cozens .25 .60
213 Egg 30.00 80.00
214 Jonathan Lucroy .30 .75
215 Cody Allen .25 .60
216 Justin Bour .25 .60
217 Andrelton Simmons .25 .60
218 Michael Brantley .30 .75
219 Yuli Gurriel .30 .75
220 Josh James RC
221 Stephen Piscotty .25 .60
222 Matt Olson .40 1.00
223 Jurickson Profar .30 .75
224 Matt Shoemaker .30 .75
225 Brandon Drury .25 .60
226 Dansby Swanson .40 1.00
227 Touki Toussaint RC .50 1.25
228 Yasmani Grandal .25 .60
229 Orlando Arcia .25 .60
230 Matt Carpenter .40 1.00
231 Paul DeJong .40 1.00
232 Willson Contreras .30 .75
233 Cole Hamels .30 .75
234 A.J. Pollock .25 .60
235 Corey Seager .40 1.00
236 Brandon Crawford .30 .75
237 Carlos Santana .30 .75
238 Trevor Bauer .50 1.25
239 Starling Marte .30 .75
240 Dee Gordon .25 .60
241 Kyle Seager .25 .60
242 Brian Anderson .25 .60
243 Michael Conforto .30 .75
244 Brian Dozier .30 .75
245 Wil Myers .30 .75
246 Odubel Herrera .30 .75
247 Maikel Franco .30 .75
248 David Robertson .25 .60
249 Jake Arrieta .30 .75
250 Yusei Kikuchi RC .60 1.50
251 Gregory Polanco .30 .75
252 Nomar Mazara .25 .60
253 Kevin Kiermaier .30 .75
254 Charlie Morton .40 1.00
255 Matt Kemp .30 .75
256 Yasiel Puig .40 1.00
257 Sonny Gray .30 .75
258 Daniel Murphy .30 .75
259 David Dahl .25 .60
260 Billy Hamilton .30 .75
261 Nicholas Castellanos .40 1.00
262 Willians Astudillo RC .40 1.00
263 Byron Buxton .40 1.00
264 Yonder Alonso .25 .60
265 Troy Tulowitzki .40 1.00
266 DJ LeMahieu .40 1.00
267 James Paxton .30 .75
268 Adam Ottavino .25 .60
269 Scooter Gennett .30 .75
270 Ben Zobrist .30 .75
271 Carl Yastrzemski .60 1.50
272 Carlton Fisk .30 .75
273 Fred McGriff .30 .75
274 Dwight Gooden .25 .60
275 Deion Sanders .30 .75
276 Hideki Matsui .40 1.00
277 Frank Robinson .30 .75
278 Vladimir Guerrero Jr. RC 8.00 20.00
279 Kolby Allard RC .60 1.50
280 Bryce Harper .60 1.50
281 Bob Gibson .30 .75
282 A.J. Andrews .40 1.00
283 Andy Pettitte .30 .75
284 Roy Halladay .30 .75
285 Jorge Alfaro .25 .60
286 Harrison Bader .30 .75
287 Catfish Hunter .30 .75
288 Ryan Yarbrough .25 .60
289 Whitey Ford .30 .75
290 Pee Wee Reese .30 .75
291 Cespedes Family BBQ .40 1.00
Jake Mintz/Jordan Shusterman
292 Eddie Murray .30 .75
293 Jon Lester .30 .75
294 German Marquez .25 .60
295 Franmil Reyes .25 .60
296 Cincinnati Red Stockings .25 .60
297 Boston Red Sox .25 .60
298 Ian Happ .30 .75
299 J.A. Happ .30 .75
300 Tino Martinez .30 .75
351 Carlos Correa SP .75 2.00
352 Robin Yount SP .75 2.00
353 Shane Bieber SP .75 2.00
354 Rowdy Tellez SP RC .75 2.00
355 Jordan Hicks SP .60 1.50
356 Kyle Schwarber SP .75 2.00
357 Kenley Jansen SP .60 1.50
358 John Smoltz SP .75 2.00
359 Larry Doby SP .60 1.50
360 Jorge Posada SP .60 1.50
361 Victor Robles SP 1.00 2.50
362 Fergie Jenkins SP .60 1.50
363 Austin Meadows SP .75 2.00
364 Dustin Pedroia SP .75 2.00
365 Ty Cobb SP 1.25 3.00
366 Daniel Palka SP .50 1.25
367 Masahiro Tanaka SP .60 1.50
368 Eddie Murray SP .60 1.50
369 Rick Porcello SP .60 1.50
370 Marcell Ozuna SP .75 2.00
371 Yu Darvish SP .75 2.00
372 Justin Turner SP .75 2.00
373 Edwin Encarnacion SP .75 2.00
374 Yoenis Cespedes SP .75 2.00
375 Pat Neshek SP .50 1.25
376 Wade Davis SP .50 1.25
377 Christin Stewart SP RC .60 1.50
378 Aroldis Chapman SP .75 2.00
379 Darryl Strawberry SP .50 1.25
380 Nomar Garciaparra SP .60 1.50
381 Scott Kingery SP .60 1.50
382 Dave Winfield SP .60 1.50
383 Sean Doolittle SP .50 1.25
384 Rogers Hornsby SP .60 1.50
385 Gil Hodges SP .60 1.50
386 Eddie Mathews SP .75 2.00
387 Warren Spahn SP .60 1.50
388 Casey Stengel SP .60 1.50
389 Lou Brock SP .60 1.50
390 Phil Rizzuto SP .60 1.50
391 Phil Niekro SP .60 1.50
392 Sammy Sosa SP .75 2.00
393 Alex Rodriguez SP 1.00 2.50
394 Tom Seaver SP .60 1.50
395 Barry Larkin SP .60 1.50
396 Tommy Lasorda SP .60 1.50
397 Orlando Cepeda SP .60 1.50
398 Eloy Jimenez SP RC 4.00 10.00
399 Tim Raines SP .60 1.50
400 Randy Johnson SP .75 2.00

2009 Topps American Heritage American Icons

COMPLETE SET (10)
STATED ODDS 1:487 H, 1:655 R
PRINT RUN 99 SER #'d SETS
AI1 Babe Ruth 25.00 60.00
AI2 Jackie Robinson 10.00 25.00
AI3 Lou Gehrig 20.00 50.00
AI4 Honus Wagner 10.00 25.00
AI5 Ty Cobb 15.00 40.00
AI6 Cy Young 10.00 25.00
AI7 Roy Campanella 10.00 25.00
AI8 Walter Johnson 10.00 25.00
AI9 Johnny Mize 6.00 15.00
AI10 Christy Mathewson 10.00 25.00

2009 Topps American Heritage American Legends

COMPLETE SET (18)
STATED ODDS 1:119 H, 1:200 R
PRINT RUN 199 SER #'d SETS
AL1 Walter Johnson 6.00 15.00
AL2 George Sisler 4.00 10.00
AL3 Ty Cobb 10.00 25.00
AL4 Thurman Munson 6.00 15.00
AL5 Christy Mathewson 6.00 15.00
AL6 Johnny Mize 4.00 10.00
AL7 Mickey Mantle 15.00 40.00
AL8 Babe Ruth 8.00 20.00
AL9 Rogers Hornsby 4.00 10.00
AL10 Pee Wee Reese 4.00 10.00
AL11 Lou Gehrig 12.50 30.00
AL12 Cy Young 6.00 15.00
AL13 Jimmie Foxx 6.00 15.00
AL14 Honus Wagner 6.00 15.00
AL15 Roy Campanella 6.00 15.00
AL16 Jackie Robinson 6.00 15.00
AL17 Mel Ott 4.00 10.00
AL18 Tris Speaker 4.00 10.00

2009 Topps American Heritage American Legends Relics

STATED ODDS 1:1472 H, 1:1590 R
PRINT RUN 25 SER #'d SETS
BR Babe Ruth Bat 100.00 200.00
JF Jimmie Foxx Bat 25.00 60.00
JM Johnny Mize Bat 15.00 40.00
JR Jackie Robinson Bat 15.00 40.00
LG Lou Gehrig Pants 75.00 150.00
MM Mickey Mantle Pants 50.00 100.00
PR Pee Wee Reese Bat 25.00 60.00
RC Roy Campanella Pants 15.00 40.00
RH Rogers Hornsby Bat 25.00 60.00
TC Ty Cobb Bat 50.00 100.00
TM Thurman Munson Jsy 25.00 60.00
TS Tris Speaker Bat 25.00 60.00

2009 Topps American Heritage Heroes

COMPLETE SET (150) 20.00 50.00
COMP.SET w/o SPs (125) 8.00 20.00
SP STATED ODDS 1:4
24 Frank Robinson .20 .50
26 Jackie Robinson .40 1.00
122 Jackie Robinson .40 1.00

2009 Topps American Heritage Heroes Chrome

COMPLETE SET (100)
*CHROME: .8X TO 2X BASIC CARDS
STATED PRINT RUN 1776 SER.#'d SETS
STATED ODDS 1:4

2009 Topps American Heritage Heroes Chrome Refractor

*REFRACTORS: 8X TO 20X BASIC CARDS
STATED ODDS 1:72
STATED PRINT RUN 76 SER.#'d SETS

2009 Topps American Heritage Heroes Heroes of Sport

COMPLETE SET (25) 12.50 25.00
STATED ODDS 1:4
*GOLD/199: 3X TO 8X BASIC INSERTS
*PLATINUM/25: 5X TO 12X BASIC INSERTS
HS1 Jackie Robinson .60 1.50
HS2 Babe Ruth 1.50 4.00
HS4 Cy Young .60 1.50
HS6 Tris Speaker .40 1.00
HS7 Mickey Mantle 1.50 4.00
HS8 Thurman Munson .60 1.50
HS10 Frank Robinson .40 1.00
HS11 Christy Mathewson .60 1.50
HS12 Roy Campanella .60 1.50
HS14 Lou Gehrig 1.25 3.00
HS16 Rogers Hornsby .40 1.00
HS17 Stan Musial .60 1.50
HS18 Honus Wagner .60 1.50
HS19 Jimmie Foxx .60 1.50
HS20 Walter Johnson .60 1.50
HS22 Reggie Jackson .40 1.00
HS23 Ty Cobb 1.00 2.50
HS25 George Sisler .40 1.00

2009 Topps American Heritage Heroes Heroes of Sport Relics

STATED ODDS 1:234
HSR1 Jackie Robinson Bat 15.00 40.00
HSR2a Babe Ruth Bat 50.00 100.00
HSR2b Babe Ruth Jsy 60.00 150.00
HSR3 Mickey Mantle Pants 30.00 60.00
HSR4 Johnny Mize Bat 10.00 25.00
HSR7 Rogers Hornsby Bat 10.00 25.00
HSR9 Jimmie Foxx Bat 10.00 25.00
HSR10 Ty Cobb Bat 50.00 100.00
HSR11 Lou Gehrig Pants 50.00 100.00
HSR12 Frank Robinson Bat 10.00 25.00

2009 Topps American Heritage Heroes Presidential Medal of Freedom

COMPLETE SET (25) 8.00 20.00
STATED ODDS 1:4
MOF23 Frank Robinson .60 1.50

2001 Topps American Pie

COMPLETE SET (150) 20.00 50.00
1 Al Kaline .50 1.25
2 Al Oliver .20 .50
3 Andre Dawson .20 .50
4 Bert Blyleven .20 .50
5 Bill Buckner .20 .50
6 Bill Mazeroski .30 .75
7 Bob Gibson .30 .75
8 Bill Freehan .20 .50
9 Bobby Grich .20 .50
10 Bobby Murcer .20 .50
11 Bobby Richardson .20 .50
12 Boog Powell .30 .75
13 Brooks Robinson .30 .75
14 Carl Yastrzemski .75 2.00
15 Carlton Fisk .30 .75
16 Clete Boyer .10 .30
17 Curt Flood .20 .50
18 Dale Murphy .30 .75
19 Tony Conigliaro .30 .75
20 Dave Parker .20 .50
21 Dave Winfield .20 .50
22 Dick Allen .20 .50
23 Dick Groat .20 .50
24 Don Drysdale .30 .75
25 Don Sutton .20 .50
26 Dwight Evans .30 .75
27 Eddie Mathews .50 1.25
28 Elston Howard .30 .75
29 Frank Howard .20 .50
30 Frank Robinson .30 .75
31 Fred Lynn .20 .50
32 Gary Carter .20 .50
33 Gaylord Perry .20 .50
34 Norm Cash .20 .50
35 George Brett 1.00 2.50
36 George Foster .20 .50
37 Goose Gossage .20 .50
38 Graig Nettles .20 .50
39 Greg Luzinski .20 .50
40 Hank Aaron 1.00 2.50
41 Harmon Killebrew .50 1.25
42 Jack Clark .20 .50
43 Jack Morris .20 .50
44 Jim Wynn .20 .50
45 Jim Kaat .20 .50
46 Jim Palmer .20 .50
47 Joe Pepitone .10 .30
48 Joe Rudi .20 .50
49 Johnny Bench .50 1.25
50 Juan Marichal .20 .50
51 Keith Hernandez .20 .50
52 Bucky Dent .20 .50
53 Lou Brock .30 .75
54 Ron Cey .20 .50
55 Luis Aparicio .20 .50
56 Luis Tiant .20 .50
57 Mark Fidrych .20 .50
58 Maury Wills .20 .50
59 Mickey Lolich .20 .50
60 Mickey Rivers .10 .30
61 Mike Schmidt 1.00 2.50
62 Moose Skowron .20 .50
63 Nolan Ryan 1.25 3.00
64 Orlando Cepeda .20 .50
65 Ozzie Smith .75 2.00
66 Phil Niekro .20 .50
67 Reggie Jackson .30 .75
68 Reggie Smith .20 .50
69 Rico Carty .10 .30
70 Roberto Clemente 1.25 3.00
71 Robin Yount .50 1.25
72 Roger Maris .50 1.25
73 Rollie Fingers .20 .50
74 Ron Guidry .20 .50
75 Ron Santo .30 .75
76 Ron Swoboda .20 .50
77 Sal Bando .20 .50
78 Sam McDowell .20 .50
79 Steve Carlton .20 .50
80 Thurman Munson .50 1.25
81 Tim McCarver .20 .50
82 Tom Seaver .30 .75
83 Mike Cuellar .20 .50
84 Tony Kubek .30 .75
85 Tommy John .20 .50
86 Tony Perez .20 .50
87 Tug McGraw .20 .50
88 Vida Blue .20 .50
89 Warren Spahn .30 .75
90 Whitey Ford .30 .75
91 Willie Mays 1.00 2.50
92 Willie McCovey .20 .50
93 Willie Stargell .30 .75
94 Yogi Berra .50 1.25
95 Stan Musial .75 2.00
96 Jim Piersall .20 .50
97 Duke Snider .30 .75
98 Bruce Sutter .20 .50
99 Dave Concepcion .20 .50
100 Darrell Evans .20 .50
101 Dennis Eckersley .20 .50
102 Hoyt Wilhelm .20 .50
103 Minnie Minoso .20 .50
104 Don Newcombe .20 .50
105 Richie Ashburn .30 .75
106 Alan Trammell .20 .50
107 Jim Hunter .30 .75
108 Lou Whitaker .20 .50
109 Johnny Podres .20 .50
110 Denny Martinez .20 .50
111 Willie Horton .20 .50
112 Dean Chance .10 .30
113 Fergie Jenkins .20 .50
114 Cecil Cooper .20 .50
115 Rick Reuschel .10 .30
116 Civil Rights Movement .10 .30
117 Bay of Pigs .10 .30
118 Cuban Missile Crisis .10 .30
119 N.Y. World's Fair .10 .30
120 Atomic Bomb Test Ban Treaty .10 .30
121 Kennedy Assassination .50 1.25
122 Lyndon Johnson Signs .10 .30
123 The Motown Sound .10 .30
124 British Music Invasion .20 .50
125 U.S. Troops in Vietnam .10 .30
126 Space Race .10 .30
127 Robert F. Kennedy .20 .50
128 Peace Movement .10 .30
129 Man On The Moon .20 .50
130 Woodstock .10 .30
131 Flower Power .10 .30
132 Women's Lib Movement .10 .30
133 Vietnam Cease Fire .10 .30
134 U.S. Gas Shortage .10 .30
135 Watergate .20 .50
136 Nixon Resigns .20 .50
137 Bicentennial .10 .30
138 Disco .10 .30
139 Three Mile Island .10 .30
140 Iran Hostage Crisis .10 .30
141 John F. Kennedy .75 2.00
142 Marilyn Monroe .75 2.00
143 Elvis Presley .75 2.00
144 Jimi Hendrix .50 1.25
145 Arthur Ashe .20 .50
146 Richard Nixon .50 1.25
147 James Dean .50 1.25
148 Janis Joplin .20 .50
149 Frank Sinatra .50 1.25
150 Malcolm X .20 .50

2001 Topps American Pie Decade Leaders

COMPLETE SET (10) 12.50 30.00
STATED ODDS 1:12
DL1 Willie Stargell .60 1.50
DL2 Harmon Killebrew 1.00 2.50
DL3 Johnny Bench 1.00 2.50
DL4 Hank Aaron 2.00 5.00
DL5 Rod Carew .60 1.50
DL6 Roberto Clemente 2.50 6.00
DL7 Nolan Ryan 2.50 6.00
DL8 Bob Gibson .60 1.50
DL9 Jim Palmer .60 1.50
DL10 Juan Marichal .60 1.50

2001 Topps American Pie Entertainment Star Autographs

STATED ODDS 1:1071
STATED PRINT RUN 500 SERIAL #'d SETS
1 Danny Bonaduce 12.00 30.00
2 Lou Ferrigno 12.00 30.00
3 Adam West 20.00 50.00

2001 Topps American Pie Profiles in Courage

COMPLETE SET (20) 20.00 50.00
STATED ODDS 1:8
PIC1 Roger Maris 1.25 3.00
PIC2 Lou Brock .75 2.00
PIC3 Brooks Robinson .75 2.00
PIC4 Carl Yastrzemski 1.50 4.00
PIC5 Mike Schmidt 2.50 6.00
PIC6 Hank Aaron 2.50 6.00
PIC7 Tom Seaver .75 2.00
PIC8 Willie Mays 2.50 6.00
PIC9 Graig Nettles .60 1.50
PIC10 Frank Robinson .75 2.00
PIC11 Rollie Fingers .60 1.50
PIC12 Tony Perez .60 1.50
PIC13 George Brett 2.50 6.00
PIC14 Robin Yount 1.25 3.00
PIC15 Nolan Ryan 3.00 8.00
PIC16 Warren Spahn .75 2.00
PIC17 Johnny Bench 1.25 3.00
PIC18 Vida Blue .60 1.50
PIC19 Roberto Clemente 3.00 8.00
PIC20 Thurman Munson 1.25 3.00

2001 Topps American Pie Relics

STATED ODDS 1:29
PAPM1 Frank Sinatra Jkt 20.00 50.00
PAPM2 JFK 6.00 15.00
Berlin Wall
PAPM3 Elvis Presley Jkt 25.00 60.00
PAPM4 Janis Joplin Dress 25.00 60.00

2001 Topps American Pie Rookie Reprint Relics

STATED ODDS 1:116
BBRRAD Andre Dawson Bat 10.00 25.00
BBRRAO Al Oliver Jsy 6.00 15.00
BBRRBG Bobby Grich Jsy 6.00 15.00
BBRRBM Bobby Murcer Bat 8.00 20.00
BBRRBP Boog Powell Bat 6.00 15.00
BBRRDE Dennis Eckersley Bat 6.00 15.00
BBRRDS Don Sutton Jsy 6.00 15.00
BBRRDW Dave Winfield Bat 6.00 15.00
BBRRGB George Brett Jsy 15.00 40.00
BBRRGC Gary Carter Bat 6.00 15.00
BBRRJB Johnny Bench Bat 10.00 25.00
BBRRJK Jim Kaat Bat 6.00 15.00
BBRRJM Joe Morgan Jsy 6.00 15.00
BBRRMF Mark Fidrych Jsy 6.00 15.00
BBRROS Ozzie Smith Bat 10.00 25.00
BBRRRJ Reggie Jackson Jsy 10.00 25.00
BBRRRY Robin Yount Jsy 10.00 25.00
BBRRSC Steve Carlton Bat 6.00 15.00
BBRRTM Tim McCarver Bat 6.00 15.00
BBRRTM Thurman Munson Jsy 15.00 40.00

2001 Topps American Pie Timeless Classics Relics

STATED ODDS 1:80
BBTC1 Sam McDowell 66 Jsy 6.00 15.00
BBTC2 Sam McDowell 70 Jsy 6.00 15.00
BBTC3 Frank Howard 60 Jsy 6.00 15.00
BBTC4 Dick Groat 61 Bat 6.00 15.00
BBTC5 Roger Maris 62 Bat 10.00 25.00
BBTC6 Orlando Cepeda 62 Jsy 6.00 15.00
BBTC7 Willie Mays 63 Jsy 20.00 50.00
BBTC8 C.Yaz 64 Jsy 12.00 30.00
BBTC9 Roberto Clemente 65 Bat 20.00 50.00
BBTC10 H.Killebrew 65 Bat 10.00 25.00
BBTC11 Br.Robinson 65 Jsy 10.00 25.00
BBTC12 Willie Mays 66 Jsy 12.00 30.00
BBTC13 Tony Conigliaro 66 Jsy 10.00 25.00
BBTC14 Frank Robinson 66 Jsy 10.00 25.00
BBTC15 C.Yaz 68 HR Jsy 15.00 40.00
BBTC16 C.Yaz 68 RBI Jsy 15.00 40.00
BBTC17 C.Yaz 68 BA Jsy 15.00 40.00
BBTC18 Hank Aaron 66 Bat 20.00 50.00
BBTC19 Frank Howard 69 Bat 6.00 15.00
BBTC20 C.Yaz 69 Bat 15.00 40.00
BBTC21 Willie McCovey 70 Jsy 6.00 15.00
BBTC22 Rico Carty 71 Bat 6.00 15.00
BBTC23 Frank Howard 71 Bat 6.00 15.00
BBTC24 Johnny Bench 71 Bat 10.00 25.00
BBTC25 Willie Stargell 72 Bat 10.00 25.00
BBTC26 Steve Carlton 73 Jsy 6.00 15.00
BBTC27 Norm Cash 62 Jsy 10.00 25.00
BBTC28 Reggie Jackson 74 Jsy 10.00 25.00
BBTC29 Willie Stargell 74 Jsy 10.00 25.00
BBTC30 Mike Schmidt 75 Jsy 15.00 40.00
BBTC31 Mike Schmidt 76 Jsy 15.00 40.00

BBTC32 Mickey Rivers 76 Bat 6.00 15.00
BBTC33 Tom Seaver 77 Jsy 10.00 25.00
BBTC34 George Brett 77 Bat 15.00 40.00
BBTC35 George Foster 77 Bat 6.00 15.00
BBTC36 Graig Nettles 77 Bat 6.00 15.00
BBTC37 Nolan Ryan 77 Jsy 12.50 30.00
BBTC38 Nolan Ryan 79 Jsy 12.50 30.00
BBTC39 Dave Parker 78 Bat 6.00 15.00
BBTC40 George Foster 78 Bat 6.00 15.00
BBTC41 Dick Allen 73 Bat 6.00 15.00
BBTC42 Dave Parker 79 Bat 6.00 15.00
BBTC43 Fred Lynn 80 Jsy 6.00 15.00
BBTC44 Keith Hernandez 80 Bat 6.00 15.00
BBTC45 Dave Winfield 80 Bat 6.00 15.00

2001 Topps American Pie Woodstock Relics

BAT STATED ODDS 1:167
DIRT STATED ODDS 1:806
OVERALL STATED ODDS 1:138
BBWMBB Bill Buckner Bat 6.00 15.00
BBWMBF Bill Freehan Bat 6.00 15.00
BBWMBR Brooks Robinson Bat 10.00 25.00
BBWMCF Carlton Fisk Bat 10.00 25.00
BBWMCY Carl Yastrzemski Bat 12.00 30.00
BBWMDE Dwight Evans Bat 10.00 25.00
BBWMDG Dick Groat Bat 6.00 15.00
BBWMDS Duke Snider Bat 10.00 25.00
BBWMDW Dave Winfield Bat 6.00 15.00
BBWMFL Fred Lynn Bat 6.00 15.00
BBWMFR Frank Robinson Bat 10.00 25.00
BBWMGB George Brett Bat 15.00 40.00
BBWMJP Jimmy Piersall Bat 6.00 15.00
BBWMJR Joe Rudi Bat 6.00 15.00
BBWMJW Jim Wynn Bat 6.00 15.00
BBWMMW Maury Wills Bat 6.00 15.00
BBWMOC Orlando Cepeda Bat 6.00 15.00
BBWMRJ Reggie Jackson Bat 10.00 25.00
BBWMRY Robin Yount Bat 10.00 25.00
BBWMSM Stan Musial Bat 6.00 15.00
BBWMTK Ted Kluszewski Bat 10.00 25.00
BBWMTP Tony Perez Bat 6.00 15.00
BBWMWM Willie Mays Bat 12.00 30.00
BBWMWS Woodstock Dirt 10.00 25.00
BBWMWS Willie Stargell Bat 10.00 25.00

2002 Topps American Pie

COMPLETE SET (150) 15.00 40.00
1 Warren Spahn .30 .75
2 Reggie Jackson .30 .75
3 Bill Mazeroski .30 .75
4 Carl Yastrzemski .75 2.00
5 Whitey Ford .30 .75
6 Ralph Houk .20 .50
7 Rod Carew .30 .75
8 Kirk Gibson .20 .50
9 Bobby Thomson .20 .50
10 Don Newcombe .20 .50
11 Gaylord Perry .20 .50
12 Bruce Sutter .20 .50
13 Bob Gibson .30 .75
14 Brooks Robinson .30 .75
15 Steve Carlton .20 .50
16 Robin Yount .50 1.25
17 Ernie Banks .50 1.25
18 Lou Brock .30 .75
19 Al Kaline .50 1.25
20 Carlton Fisk .30 .75
21 Frank Robinson .30 .75
22 Bobby Bonds .20 .50
23 Andre Dawson .20 .50
24 Goose Gossage .20 .50
25 Fred Lynn .20 .50
26 Keith Hernandez .20 .50
27 Rollie Fingers .20 .50
28 Juan Marichal .20 .50
29 Maury Wills .20 .50
30 Dave Winfield .20 .50
31 Frank Howard .20 .50
32 Tony Gwynn .60 1.50
33 Jim Palmer .20 .50
34 Mike Schmidt 1.00 2.50
35 Bo Jackson .50 1.25
36 Ferguson Jenkins .20 .50
37 Bobby Richardson .20 .50
38 Harmon Killebrew .50 1.25
39 Monte Irvin .20 .50
40 Jim Abbott .30 .75
41 Wade Boggs .30 .75
42 Jackie Robinson .50 1.25
43 Ralph Branca .20 .50
44 Minnie Minoso .20 .50
45 Tug McGraw .20 .50
46 Willie Mays 1.00 2.50
47 Nolan Ryan 1.25 3.00
48 Duke Snider .30 .75
49 Tom Seaver .30 .75
50 Casey Stengel .30 .75
51 D-Day .20 .50
52 Gulf War .20 .50
53 Vietnam War .20 .50
54 Korean War .20 .50
55 Secret Service .20 .50
56 Crayons .20 .50
57 Hoover Dam .20 .50
58 Penicillin .20 .50
59 Polio Vaccine .20 .50
60 Empire State Building .20 .50
61 Television .20 .50
62 Duke Ellington .30 .75
63 Voyager Mission .20 .50
64 Space Shuttle .20 .50
65 Ellis Island .20 .50
66 Statue Of Liberty .20 .50
67 Battle Of The Bulge .20 .50
68 Battle Of Midway .20 .50
69 Iwo Jima .20 .50
70 Panama Canal .20 .50
71 Spirit Of St. Louis Lindbergh .20 .50
72 Civil Rights We Shall Overcome .20 .50
73 Space Race .20 .50
74 Alaska Pipeline .20 .50
75 Teddy Bear .20 .50
76 Seabiscuit .20 .50
77 Bazooka Joe .20 .50
78 Mt. Rushmore .20 .50
79 Yellowstone Park .20 .50
80 Niagara Falls .20 .50
81 Grand Canyon .20 .50
82 Hoola Hoop .20 .50
83 George Patton .30 .75
84 Florence Griffith Joyner .20 .50
85 Amelia Earhart .20 .50
86 Glen Miller .20 .50
87 Rick Monday .20 .50
88 Buzz Aldrin .20 .50
89 Rosa Parks .20 .50
90 Edward R. Murrow .20 .50
91 Susan B. Anthony .20 .50
92 Bobby Kennedy .20 .50
93 Gloria Steinem .20 .50
94 Hank Greenberg .50 1.25
95 Jimmy Doolittle .20 .50
96 Thurgood Marshall .20 .50
97 Ernest Hemingway .50 1.25
98 Henry Ford .30 .75
99 Wright Brothers .20 .50
100 Thomas Edison .20 .50
101 Albert Einstein .50 1.25
102 Will Rogers .20 .50
103 George Gershwin .20 .50
104 Irving Berlin .20 .50
105 Frank Lloyd Wright .20 .50
106 Howard Hughes .30 .75
107 George M. Cohan .20 .50
108 Jack Kerouac .30 .75
109 Harry Houdini .30 .75
110 Helen Keller .20 .50
111 John McCain .75 2.00
112 Andrew Carnegie .20 .50
113 Sandra Day O'Connor .20 .50
114 Brooklyn Bridge .20 .50
115 Douglas MacArthur .30 .75
116 Elvis Presley .75 2.00
117 George Burns .20 .50
118 Judy Garland .50 1.25
119 Buddy Holly .20 .50
120 Don McLean .20 .50
121 Marilyn Monroe .75 2.00
122 Humphrey Bogart .60 1.50
123 Gary Cooper .30 .75
124 The Andrews Sisters .20 .50
125 Jim Thorpe .75 2.00
126 Joe Louis .50 1.25
127 Jesse Owens .30 .75
128 Kate Smith .20 .50
129 W.C. Fields .20 .50
130 Bette Davis .30 .75
131 Jayne Mansfield .30 .75
132 William McKinley .20 .50
133 Teddy Roosevelt .50 1.25
134 William Taft .20 .50
135 Woodrow Wilson .20 .50
136 Warren Harding .20 .50
137 Calvin Coolidge .20 .50
138 Herbert Hoover .20 .50
139 Franklin D. Roosevelt .30 .75
140 Harry Truman .30 .75
141 Dwight Eisenhower .30 .75
142 John F. Kennedy .75 2.00
143 Lyndon B. Johnson .30 .75
144 Richard Nixon .50 1.25
145 Gerald Ford .30 .75
146 Jimmy Carter .30 .75
147 Ronald Reagan 2.00 5.00
148 George H.W. Bush .20 .50
149 Bill Clinton 1.25 3.00
150 George W. Bush 1.25 3.00

2002 Topps American Pie First Pitch Seat Relics

STATED ODDS 1:32 HOBBY, 1:156 RETAIL
BC Bill Clinton 12.50 30.00
CC Calvin Coolidge 10.00 25.00
DE Dwight Eisenhower 10.00 25.00
FDR Franklin D. Roosevelt 10.00 25.00
GF Gerald Ford 15.00 40.00
GHWB George H.W. Bush 15.00 40.00
GWB George W. Bush 12.50 30.00
HH Herbert Hoover 15.00 40.00
HT Harry Truman 10.00 25.00
JFK John F. Kennedy 12.50 30.00
RN Richard Nixon 8.00 20.00
RR Ronald Reagan 12.00 30.00
WH Warren Harding 10.00 25.00
WT William Taft 6.00 15.00
WW Woodrow Wilson 6.00 15.00
LBJ Lyndon B. Johnson 10.00 25.00

2002 Topps American Pie Piece of American Pie

H.BOGART SCARF ODDS 1:1074 H, 1:1930 R
G.BURNS COAT ODDS 1:680 H, 1:1218 R
G.COOPER SCARF ODDS 1:414 H, 1:739 R
B.DAVIS JACKET ODDS 1:680 H, 1:1218 R
J.GARLAND SCARF ODDS 1:680 H, 1:1218 R
J.MANSFIELD PANTS ODDS 1:680 H, 11218 R
M.MONROE DRESS ODDS 1:684 H, 1:1221 R
E.PRESLEY COAT ODDS 1:684 H, 1:1221 R
E.PRESLEY SHIRT ODDS 1:684 H, 1:1221 R
R.REAGAN WALL ODDS 1:675 H, 1:1218 R
BD Bette Davis Jacket 10.00 25.00
EP Elvis Presley Army Shirt 30.00 60.00
EP2 Elvis Presley Jacket 25.00 60.00
GB George Burns Coat 30.00 60.00
GC Gary Cooper Scarf 10.00 25.00
HB H.Bogart Handkerchief 100.00 200.00
JD Judy Garland Scarf 20.00 50.00
JM Jayne Mansfield Shirt 12.00 30.00
MM Marilyn Monroe Dress 60.00 150.00
RR Ronald Reagan Wall 20.00 50.00

2002 Topps American Pie Sluggers Blue

COMPLETE SET (25) 20.00 50.00
*RED/GOLD/SILVER: EQUAL VALUE
ODDS: ONE SLUGGER PER PACK
1 Rod Carew 1.00 2.50
2 Brooks Robinson 1.00 2.50
3 Mike Schmidt 3.00 8.00
4 Carlton Fisk 1.00 2.50
5 Reggie Jackson 1.00 2.50
6 Carl Yastrzemski 2.50 6.00
7 Kirk Gibson .60 1.50
8 Al Kaline 1.50 4.00
9 Frank Robinson 1.00 2.50
10 Fred Lynn .60 1.50
11 Dave Winfield .60 1.50
12 Harmon Killebrew 1.50 4.00
13 Monte Irvin .60 1.50
14 Willie Mays 3.00 8.00
15 Duke Snider 1.00 2.50
16 George Foster .60 1.50
17 Joe Carter .60 1.50
18 Eddie Mathews 1.50 4.00
19 George Brett 3.00 8.00
20 Frank Howard .60 1.50
21 Andre Dawson .60 1.50
22 Ted Kluszewski 1.00 2.50
23 Ryne Sandberg 2.50 6.00
24 Jack Clark .60 1.50
25 Cecil Cooper .60 1.50

2002 Topps American Pie Through the Years Relics

BAT STATED ODDS 1:211 H, 1:377 R
JERSEY STATED ODDS 1:32 H, 1:58 R
UNIFORM STATED ODDS 1:60 H, 1:107 R
AD Andre Dawson Bat 6.00 15.00
AL Al Oliver Jsy 6.00 15.00
BB Bill Buckner Jsy 6.00 15.00
CY Carl Yastrzemski Jsy 10.00 25.00
DA Dick Allen Bat 6.00 15.00
DM Don Mattingly Bat 15.00 40.00
DP Dave Parker Jsy 6.00 15.00
DS Darryl Strawberry Bat 6.00 15.00
DW Dave Winfield Bat 6.00 15.00
EM Eddie Mathews Uniform 10.00 25.00
FR Frank Robinson Jsy 8.00 20.00
GP Gaylord Perry Uniform 6.00 15.00
JA Jim Abbott Jsy 8.00 20.00
JB Johnny Bench Uniform 10.00 25.00
JC Jack Clark Jsy 6.00 15.00
JK Jim Kaat Uniform 6.00 15.00
JM Joe Morgan Jsy 6.00 15.00
JR Joe Rudi Jsy 6.00 15.00
MM Minnie Minoso Jsy 6.00 15.00
NR Nolan Ryan Uniform 10.00 25.00
RM Rick Monday Jsy 6.00 15.00
TM Thurman Munson Bat 15.00 40.00
TS Tom Seaver Jsy 8.00 20.00
WB Wade Boggs Jsy 8.00 20.00
WM Willie Mays Uniform 10.00 25.00
WS Willie Stargell Uniform 8.00 20.00

1991 Topps Archives '53

The 1953 Topps Archive set is a reprint of the original 274-card 1953 Topps set. The only card missing from the reprint set is that of Billy Loes (174), who did not give Topps permission to reprint his card. Moreover, the set has been extended by 57 cards, with cards honoring Mrs. Eleanor Engle, Hoyt Wilhelm (who had already been included in the set as card number 151), 1953 HOF inductees Dizzy Dean and Al Simmons, and "prospect" Hank Aaron. Although the original cards measured 2 5/8" by 3 3/4", the reprint cards measure the modern standard size. Production quantities were supposedly limited to not more than 18,000 cases.

COMPLETE SET (330) 20.00 50.00
COMMON PLAYER (1-220) .05 .15
COMMON PLAYER (221-280) .08 .25
COMMON PLAYER (281-337) .10 .30
1 Jackie Robinson .30 .75
2 Luke Easter .10 .30
3 George Crowe .05 .15
4 Ben Wade .05 .15
5 Joe Dobson .05 .15
6 Sam Jones .05 .15
7 Bob Borkowski .05 .15
8 Clem Koshorek .05 .15
9 Joe Collins .10 .30
10 Smoky Burgess .10 .30
11 Sal Yvars .05 .15
12 Howie Judson .05 .15
13 Conrado Marrero .05 .15
14 Clem Labine .20 .50
15 Bobo Newsom .10 .30
16 Peanuts Lowrey .05 .15
17 Billy Hitchcock .05 .15
18 Ted Lepcio .05 .15
19 Mel Parnell .05 .15
20 Hank Thompson .05 .15
21 Billy Johnson .05 .15
22 Howie Fox .05 .15
23 Toby Atwell .05 .15
24 Ferris Fain .05 .15
25 Ray Boone .05 .15
26 Dale Mitchell .10 .30
27 Roy Campanella .30 .75
28 Eddie Pellagrini .05 .15
29 Hal Jeffcoat .05 .15
30 Willard Nixon .05 .15
31 Ewell Blackwell .10 .30
32 Clyde Vollmer .05 .15
33 Bob Kennedy .05 .15
34 George Shuba .05 .15
35 Irv Noren .05 .15
36 Johnny Groth .05 .15
37 Eddie Mathews .30 .75
38 Jim Hearn .05 .15
39 Eddie Miksis .05 .15
40 John Lipon .05 .15
41 Enos Slaughter .10 .30
42 Gus Zernial .10 .30
43 Gil McDougald .10 .30
44 Ellis Kinder .05 .15
45 Grady Hatton .05 .15
46 Johnny Klippstein .05 .15
47 Bubba Church .05 .15
48 Bob Del Greco .05 .15
49 Faye Throneberry .05 .15
50 Chuck Dressen MG .05 .15
51 Frank Campos .05 .15
52 Ted Gray .05 .15
53 Sherm Lollar .10 .30
54 Bob Feller .10 .30
55 Maurice McDermott .05 .15
56 Gerry Staley .05 .15
57 Carl Scheib .05 .15
58 George Metkovich .05 .15
59 Karl Drews .05 .15
60 Cloyd Boyer .05 .15
61 Early Wynn .20 .50
62 Monte Irvin .10 .30
63 Gus Niarhos .05 .15
64 Dave Philley .05 .15
65 Earl Harrist .05 .15
66 Minnie Minoso .10 .30
67 Roy Sievers .10 .30
68 Del Rice .05 .15
69 Dick Brodowski .05 .15
70 Ed Yuhas .05 .15
71 Tony Bartirome .05 .15
72 Fred Hutchinson .10 .30
73 Eddie Robinson .05 .15
74 Joe Rossi .05 .15
75 Mike Garcia .10 .30
76 Pee Wee Reese .30 .75
77 Johnny Mize .10 .30
78 Red Schoendienst .10 .30
79 Johnny Wyrostek .05 .15
80 Jim Hegan .05 .15
81 Joe Black .10 .30
82 Mickey Mantle 8.00 20.00
83 Howie Pollet .05 .15
84 Bob Hooper .05 .15
85 Bobby Morgan .05 .15
86 Billy Martin .20 .50
87 Ed Lopat .10 .30
88 Willie Jones .05 .15
89 Chuck Stobbs .05 .15
90 Hank Edwards .05 .15
91 Ebba St.Claire .05 .15
92 Paul Minner .05 .15
93 Hal Rice .05 .15
94 Bill Kennedy .05 .15
95 Willard Marshall .05 .15
96 Virgil Trucks .05 .15
97 Don Kolloway .05 .15
98 Cal Abrams .05 .15
99 Dave Madison .05 .15
100 Bill Miller .05 .15
101 Ted Wilks .05 .15
102 Connie Ryan .05 .15
103 Joe Astroth .05 .15
104 Yogi Berra 1.00 2.50
105 Joe Nuxhall .10 .30
106 Johnny Antonelli .10 .30
107 Danny O'Connell .05 .15
108 Bob Porterfield .05 .15
109 Alvin Dark .10 .30
110 Herman Wehmeier .05 .15
111 Hank Sauer .10 .30
112 Ned Garver .05 .15
113 Jerry Priddy .05 .15
114 Phil Rizzuto .30 .75
115 George Spencer .05 .15
116 Frank Smith .05 .15
117 Sid Gordon .05 .15
118 Gus Bell .10 .30
119 Johnny Sain .10 .30
120 Davey Williams .05 .15
121 Walt Dropo .05 .15
122 Elmer Valo .05 .15
123 Tommy Byrne .05 .15
124 Sibby Sisti .05 .15
125 Dick Williams .10 .30
126 Bill Connelly .05 .15
127 Clint Courtney .05 .15
128 Wilmer Mizell .10 .30
129 Keith Thomas .05 .15
130 Turk Lown .05 .15
131 Harry Byrd .05 .15
132 Tom Morgan .05 .15
133 Gil Coan .05 .15
134 Rube Walker .05 .15
135 Al Rosen .10 .30
136 Ken Heintzelman .05 .15
137 John Rutherford .05 .15
138 George Kell .10 .30
139 Sammy White .05 .15
140 Tommy Glaviano .05 .15
141 Allie Reynolds .30 .75
142 Vic Wertz .10 .30
143 Billy Pierce .10 .30
144 Bob Schultz .05 .15
145 Harry Dorish .05 .15
146 Granny Hamner .10 .30
147 Warren Spahn .20 .50
148 Mickey Grasso .05 .15
149 Dom DiMaggio .30 .75
150 Harry Simpson .05 .15
151 Hoyt Wilhelm .10 .30
152 Bob Adams .05 .15
153 Andy Seminick .10 .30
154 Dick Groat .10 .30
155 Dutch Leonard .05 .15
156 Jim Rivera .05 .15
157 Bob Addis .05 .15
158 Johnny Logan .10 .30
159 Wayne Terwilliger .05 .15
160 Bob Young .05 .15
161 Vern Bickford .05 .15
162 Ted Kluszewski .20 .50
163 Fred Hatfield .05 .15
164 Frank Shea .05 .15
165 Billy Hoeft .05 .15
166 Billy Hunter .05 .15
167 Art Schult .05 .15
168 Willard Schmidt .05 .15
169 Dizzy Trout .05 .15
170 Bill Werle .05 .15
171 Bill Glynn .05 .15
172 Rip Repulski .05 .15
173 Preston Ward .05 .15
174 Billy Loes Not Printed
175 Ron Kline .05 .15
176 Don Hoak .05 .15
177 Jim Dyck .05 .15
178 Jim Waugh .05 .15
179 Gene Hermanski .05 .15
180 Virgil Stallcup .05 .15
181 Al Zarilla .05 .15
182 Bobby Hofman .05 .15
183 Stu Miller .05 .15
184 Hal Brown .05 .15
185 Jim Pendleton .05 .15
186 Charlie Bishop .05 .15
187 Jim Fridley .05 .15
188 Andy Carey .10 .30
189 Ray Jablonski .05 .15
190 Dixie Walker CO .10 .30
191 Ralph Kiner .20 .50
192 Wally Westlake .05 .15
193 Mike Clark .05 .15
194 Eddie Kazak .05 .15
195 Ed McGhee .05 .15
196 Bob Keegan .05 .15
197 Del Crandall .10 .30
198 Forrest Main .05 .15
199 Marion Fricano .05 .15
200 Gordon Goldsberry .05 .15
201 Paul LaPalme .05 .15
202 Carl Sawatski .05 .15
203 Cliff Fannin .05 .15
204 Dick Bokelman .05 .15
205 Vern Benson .05 .15
206 Ed Bailey .05 .15
207 Whitey Ford .20 .50
208 Jim Wilson .05 .15
209 Jim Greengrass .05 .15
210 Bob Cerv .05 .15
211 J.W. Porter .05 .15
212 Jack Dittmer .05 .15
213 Ray Scarborough .05 .15
214 Bill Bruton .05 .15
215 Gene Conley .05 .15
216 Jim Hughes .05 .15
217 Murray Wall .05 .15
218 Les Fusselman .05 .15
219 Pete Runnels UER .10 .30
220 Satchel Paige UER .30 .75
221 Bob Milliken .08 .25
222 Vic Janowicz .20 .50
223 Johnny O'Brien .20 .50
224 Lou Sleater .08 .25
225 Bobby Shantz .20 .50
226 Ed Erautt .08 .25
227 Morrie Martin .08 .25
228 Hal Newhouser .30 .75
229 Rocky Krsnich .08 .25
230 Johnny Lindell .08 .25
231 Solly Hemus .08 .25
232 Dick Kokos .08 .25
233 Al Aber .08 .25
234 Ray Murray .08 .25
235 John Hetki .08 .25
236 Harry Perkowski .08 .25
237 Bud Podbielan .08 .25
238 Cal Hogue .08 .25
239 Jim Delsing .08 .25
240 Fred Marsh .08 .25
241 Al Sima .08 .25
242 Charlie Silvera .20 .50
243 Carlos Bernier .08 .25
244 Willie Mays 5.00 12.00
245 Bill Norman CO .08 .25
246 Roy Face .20 .50
247 Mike Sandlock .08 .25
248 Gene Stephens .08 .25
249 Eddie O'Brien .20 .50
250 Bob Wilson .08 .25
251 Sid Hudson .08 .25
252 Hank Foiles .08 .25
253 Does not exist
254 Preacher Roe .20 .50
255 Dixie Howell .08 .25
256 Les Peden .08 .25
257 Bob Boyd .08 .25
258 Jim Gilliam .20 .50
259 Roy McMillan .20 .50
260 Sam Calderone .08 .25
261 Does not exist
262 Bob Oldis .08 .25
263 Johnny Podres .20 .50
264 Gene Woodling .20 .50
265 Jackie Jensen .20 .50
266 Bob Cain .08 .25
269 Duane Pillette .08 .25
270 Vern Stephens .20 .50
272 Bill Antonello .08 .25
273 Harvey Haddix .20 .50
274 John Riddle .08 .25
276 Ken Raffensberger .08 .25
277 Don Lund .08 .25
278 Willie Miranda .08 .25
279 Joe Coleman .08 .25
280 Milt Bolling .08 .25
281 Jimmie Dykes MG .20 .50
282 Ralph Houk .20 .50
283 Frank Thomas .20 .50
284 Bob Lemon .50 1.25
285 Joe Adcock .20 .50
286 Jimmy Piersall .20 .50
287 Mickey Vernon .20 .50
288 Robin Roberts .20 .50
289 Rogers Hornsby MG .30 .75
290 Hank Bauer .20 .50
291 Hoot Evers .10 .30
292 Whitey Lockman .20 .50
293 Ralph Branca .20 .50
294 Wally Post .20 .50
295 Phil Cavarretta MG .20 .50
296 Gil Hodges .50 1.25
297 Roy Smalley .10 .30
298 Bob Friend .20 .50
299 Dusty Rhodes .10 .30
300 Eddie Stanky .10 .30
301 Harvey Kuenn .20 .50
302 Marty Marion .10 .30
303 Sal Maglie .20 .50
304 Lou Boudreau MG .20 .50
305 Carl Furillo .30 .75
306 Bobo Holloman .10 .30
307 Steve O'Neill MG .10 .30
308 Carl Erskine .30 .75
309 Leo Durocher MG .20 .50
310 Lew Burdette .20 .50
311 Richie Ashburn .30 .75
312 Hoyt Wilhelm .20 .50
313 Bucky Harris MG .20 .50
314 Joe Garagiola .20 .50
315 Johnny Pesky .20 .50
316 Fred Haney MG .10 .30
317 Hank Aaron 4.00 10.00
318 Curt Simmons .20 .50
319 Ted Williams 4.00 10.00
320 Don Newcombe .20 .50
321 Charlie Grimm MG .20 .50
322 Paul Richards MG .20 .50
323 Wes Westrum .10 .30
324 Vern Law .10 .30
325 Casey Stengel MG .50 1.25
326 D.Dean A.Simmons HOF .30 .75
327 Duke Snider .20 .50
328 Bill Rigney .20 .50
329 Al Lopez MG .20 .50
330 Bobby Thomson .20 .50
331 Nellie Fox .30 .75
332 Eleanor Engle .20 .50
333 Larry Doby .20 .50
334 Billy Goodman .20 .50
335 Checklist 1-140 .10 .30
336 Checklist 141-280 .10 .30
337 Checklist 281-337 .10 .30

1994 Topps Archives '54

The 1954 Archives set includes 248 reprint cards from the original set, plus eight specially created prospect cards (Roberto Clemente, Harmon Killebrew, Bob Grim, Camilo Pascual, Herb Score, Elston Howard, Bill Virdon, and Don Zimmer). No factory sets were sold. Randomly inserted were 1,954 redemption cards good for actual 1954 Topps cards; 1,954 Hank Aaron autographed gold cards; and 1,954 redemption cards for full sets of ToppsGold Archives cards. Each 12-card pack contains 11 Archives cards plus one ToppsGold Archives card. A random insert card replaced the gold card in every 2,210 packs. Ted Williams' cards numbers 1 and 250, as well as a new Mickey Mantle's card number 259, were issued as inserts in the 1994 Upper Deck All-Time Heroes series.

COMPLETE SET (256) 60.00 120.00
COMMON PLAYER (1-250) .05 .15
COMMON PLAYER (251-258) .06 .15
AARON AU RANDOM INSERT IN PACKS
CARDS 1/250/259 ISSUED IN 94 UD ATG
SET PRICE EXCLUDES CARDS 1/250/259
1 Not Issued
2 Gus Zernial .10 .30
3 Monte Irvin .10 .30
4 Hank Sauer .10 .30
5 Ed Lopat .10 .30
6 Pete Runnels .10 .30
7 Ted Kluszewski .20 .50
8 Bobby Young .05 .15
9 Harvey Haddix .10 .30
10 Jackie Robinson .30 .75
11 Paul Smith .05 .15
12 Del Crandall .10 .30
13 Billy Martin .20 .50
14 Preacher Roe .10 .30
15 Al Rosen .10 .30
16 Vic Janowicz .10 .30
17 Phil Rizzuto .30 .75
18 Walt Dropo .05 .15
19 Johnny Lipon .05 .15
20 Warren Spahn .20 .50
21 Bobby Shantz .10 .30
22 Jim Greengrass .05 .15
23 Luke Easter .10 .30
24 Granny Hamner .10 .30
25 Harvey Kuenn .10 .30
26 Ray Jablonski .05 .15
27 Ferris Fain .05 .15
28 Paul Minner .05 .15
29 Jim Hegan .05 .15
30 Ed Mathews .30 .75
31 Johnny Klippstein .05 .15
32 Duke Snider .20 .50
33 Johnny Schmitz .05 .15
34 Jim Rivera .05 .15
35 Jim Gilliam .10 .30
36 Hoyt Wilhelm .10 .30
37 Whitey Ford .20 .50
38 Eddie Stanky MG .10 .30
39 Sherm Lollar .10 .30
40 Mel Parnell .05 .15
41 Willie Jones .05 .15
42 Don Mueller .05 .15
43 Dick Groat .10 .30
44 Ned Garver .05 .15
45 Richie Ashburn .20 .50
46 Ken Raffensberger .05 .15
47 Ellis Kinder .05 .15
48 Billy Hunter .05 .15
49 Ray Murray .05 .15
50 Yogi Berra .60 1.50
51 Johnny Lindell .05 .15
52 Vic Power .05 .15
53 Jack Dittmer .05 .15
54 Vern Stephens .10 .30
55 Phil Cavarretta MG .10 .30
56 Willie Miranda .05 .15
57 Luis Aloma .05 .15
58 Bob Wilson .05 .15
59 Gene Conley .05 .15
60 Frank Baumholtz .05 .15
61 Bob Cain .05 .15
62 Eddie Robinson .05 .15
63 Johnny Pesky .10 .30
64 Hank Thompson .05 .15
65 Bob Swift .05 .15
66 Ted Lepcio .05 .15
67 Jim Willis .05 .15
68 Sammy Calderone .05 .15
69 Bud Podbielan .05 .15
70 Larry Doby .10 .30
71 Frank Smith .05 .15
72 Preston Ward .05 .15
73 Wayne Terwilliger .05 .15
74 Bill Taylor .05 .15
75 Fred Haney MG .05 .15
76 Bob Scheffing CO .05 .15
77 Ray Boone .05 .15
78 Ted Kazanski .05 .15
79 Andy Pafko .10 .30
80 Jackie Jensen .10 .30
81 Dave Hoskins .05 .15
82 Milt Bolling .05 .15
83 Joe Collins .10 .30
84 Dick Cole .05 .15
85 Bob Turley .10 .30
86 Billy Herman CO .10 .30
87 Roy Face .10 .30
88 Matt Batts .05 .15
89 Howie Pollet .05 .15
90 Willie Mays 2.00 5.00
91 Bob Oldis .05 .15
92 Wally Westlake .05 .15
93 Sid Hudson .05 .15
94 Ernie Banks 1.25 3.00
95 Hal Rice .05 .15
96 Charlie Silvera .10 .30
97 Jerry Lane .05 .15
98 Joe Black .10 .30
99 Bob Hofman .05 .15
100 Bob Keegan .05 .15
101 Gene Woodling .10 .30
102 Gil Hodges .30 .75
103 Jim Lemon .05 .15
104 Mike Sandlock .05 .15
105 Andy Carey .10 .30
106 Dick Kokos .05 .15
107 Duane Pillette .05 .15
108 Thornton Kipper .05 .15
109 Bill Bruton .05 .15
110 Harry Dorish .05 .15
111 Jim Delsing .05 .15
112 Bill Renna .05 .15
113 Bob Boyd .05 .15
114 Dean Stone .05 .15
115 Rip Repulski .05 .15
116 Steve Bilko .05 .15
117 Solly Hemus .05 .15
118 Carl Scheib .05 .15
119 Johnny Antonelli .10 .30
120 Roy McMillan .10 .30
121 Clem Labine .20 .50
122 Johnny Logan .10 .30
123 Bobby Adams .05 .15
124 Marion Fricano .05 .15
125 Harry Perkowski .05 .15
126 Ben Wade .05 .15
127 Steve O'Neill MG .05 .15
128 Henry Aaron 2.50 6.00
129 Forrest Jacobs .05 .15
130 Hank Bauer .10 .30
131 Reno Bertoia .05 .15
132 Tom Lasorda .20 .50
133 Del Baker CO .05 .15
134 Cal Hogue .05 .15
135 Joe Presko .05 .15
136 Connie Ryan .05 .15
137 Wally Moon .10 .30
138 Bob Borkowski .05 .15
139 Ed O'Brien Johnny O'Brien .10 .30
140 Tom Wright .05 .15
141 Joe Jay .05 .15
142 Tom Poholsky .05 .15
143 Rollie Hemsley CO .05 .15
144 Bill Werle .05 .15
145 Elmer Valo .05 .15
146 Don Johnson .05 .15
147 John Riddle CO .05 .15
148 Bob Trice .05 .15
149 Jim Robertson .05 .15
150 Dick Kryhoski .05 .15
151 Alex Grammas .05 .15
152 Mike Blyzka .05 .15
153 Rube Walker .05 .15
154 Mike Fornieles .05 .15
155 Bob Kennedy .05 .15
156 Joe Coleman .05 .15
157 Don Lenhardt .05 .15
158 Peanuts Lowrey .05 .15
159 Dave Philley .05 .15
160 Red Kress CO .05 .15
161 John Hetki .05 .15
162 Herman Wehmeier .05 .15
163 Frank House .05 .15
164 Stu Miller .05 .15
165 Jim Pendleton .05 .15
166 Johnny Podres .10 .30
167 Don Lund .05 .15
168 Morrie Martin .05 .15
169 Jim Hughes .05 .15
170 Dusty Rhodes .05 .15
171 Leo Kiely .05 .15
172 Hal Brown .05 .15
173 Jack Harshman .05 .15
174 Tom Qualters .05 .15
175 Frank Leja .05 .15
176 Bob Keely .05 .15
177 Bob Milliken .05 .15
178 Bill Glynn .05 .15
179 Gair Allie .05 .15
180 Wes Westrum .05 .15
181 Mel Roach .05 .15
182 Chuck Harmon .05 .15
183 Earle Combs CO .30 .75
184 Ed Bailey .05 .15
185 Chuck Stobbs .05 .15
186 Karl Olson .05 .15
187 Heinie Manush CO .30 .75
188 Dave Jolly .05 .15
189 Bob Ross .05 .15
190 Ray Herbert .05 .15
191 Dick Schofield .05 .15
192 Cot Deal CO .05 .15
193 Johnny Hopp CO .05 .15
194 Bill Sarni .05 .15
195 Bill Consolo .05 .15
196 Stan Jok .05 .15
197 Schoolboy Rowe CO .10 .30
198 Carl Sawatski .05 .15
199 Rocky Nelson .05 .15
200 Larry Jansen .05 .15
201 Al Kaline 1.25 3.00
202 Bob Purkey .05 .15
203 Harry Brecheen CO .05 .15
204 Angel Scull .05 .15
205 Johnny Sain .10 .30
206 Ray Crone .05 .15
207 Tom Oliver CO .05 .15

208 Grady Hatton .05 .15
209 Charlie Thompson .05 .15
210 Bob Buhl .05 .15
211 Don Hoak .05 .15
212 Mickey Micelotta .05 .15
213 John Fitzpatrick CO .05 .15
214 Arnold Portocarrero .05 .15
215 Ed McGhee .05 .15
216 Al Sima .05 .15
217 Paul Schreiber CO .05 .15
218 Fred Marsh .05 .15
219 Charlie Kress .05 .15
220 Ruben Gomez .05 .15
221 Dick Brodowski .05 .15
222 Bill Wilson .05 .15
223 Joe Haynes CO .05 .15
224 Dick Weik .05 .15
225 Don Liddle .05 .15
226 Jehosie Heard .05 .15
227 Buster Mills CO .05 .15
228 Gene Hermanski .05 .15
229 Bob Talbot .05 .15
230 Bob Kuzava .05 .15
231 Roy Smalley .05 .15
232 Lou Limmer .05 .15
233 Augie Galan .05 .15
234 Jerry Lynch .05 .15
235 Vern Law .05 .15
236 Paul Penson .05 .15
237 Mike Ryba .05 .15
238 Al Aber .05 .15
239 Bill Skowron .20 .50
240 Sam Mele .05 .15
241 Bob Miller .05 .15
242 Curt Roberts .05 .15
243 Ray Blades CO .05 .15
244 Leroy Wheat .05 .15
245 Roy Sievers .10 .30
246 Howie Fox .05 .15
247 Eddie Mayo CO .05 .15
248 Al Smith .05 .15
249 Wilmer Mizell .10 .30
250 Not Issued
251 Roberto Clemente 4.00 10.00
252 Bob Grim .05 .15
253 Elston Howard .20 .50
254 Harmon Killebrew .30 .75
255 Camilo Pascual .05 .15
256 Herb Score .10 .30
257 Bill Virdon .10 .30
258 Don Zimmer .10 .30
NNO Hank Aaron AU 75.00 150.00
NNO Gold Redemption Card Exp.

1994 Topps Archives '54 Gold

COMPLETE SET (256) 75.00 150.00
*STARS: 1.5X TO 4X BASIC CARDS
RANDOM INSERTS IN PACKS

1995 Topps Archives Brooklyn Dodgers

This 165-card set measures the standard size and is a single series release. The set honors the Brooklyn Dodger teams of 1952-1956 and consists of 127 reprints of Topps and Bowman cards produced during that time. The cards "that never were" have been created for the players not featured on Topps and Bowman cards and replicate the design of the card for the year the player would have been pictured. Cards numbered 117-120 commemorate the four games the Dodgers won for the 1955 World Series Championship. Though the cards are numbered as they were originally issued, Topps renumbered them as a complete set and they are checklisted accordingly. Some dealers believe that cards numbered from 111 through 165 were printed in shorter supply than other cards in this set. A very limited amount of signed Sandy Koufax cards (number 102 and number 146) were signed and randomly inserted into packs.

COMPLETE SET (165) 30.00 80.00
KOUFAX AU'S RANDOM INSERTS IN PACKS
NO KOUFAX AU PRICING DUE TO SCARCITY
1 Andy Pafko .20 .50
2 Wayne Terwilliger .08 .25
3 Billy Loes .20 .50
4 Gil Hodges .75 2.00
5 Duke Snider .40 1.00
6 Jim Russell .08 .25
7 Chris Van Cuyk .08 .25
8 Preacher Roe .20 .50
9 Johnny Schmitz .08 .25
10 Bud Podbielan .08 .25
11 Phil Haugstad .08 .25
12 Clyde King .08 .25
13 Billy Cox .20 .50
14 Rocky Bridges .08 .25
15 Carl Erskine .40 1.00
16 Erv Palica .08 .25
17 Ralph Branca .20 .50
18 Jackie Robinson .75 2.00
19 Roy Campanella .75 2.00
20 Rube Walker .08 .25
21 Johnny Rutherford .08 .25
22 Joe Black .20 .50
23 George Shuba .08 .25
24 Pee Wee Reese .75 2.00
25 Clem Labine .40 1.00
26 Bobby Morgan .08 .25
27 Cookie Lavagetto CO .08 .25
28 Chuck Dressen MG .08 .25
29 Ben Wade .08 .25
30 Rocky Nelson .08 .25
31 Billy Herman CO .20 .50
32 Jake Pitler CO .08 .25
33 Dick Williams .20 .50
34 Cal Abrams .08 .25
35 Carl Furillo .40 1.00
36 Don Newcombe .20 .50
37 Jackie Robinson .75 2.00
38 Ben Wade .08 .25
39 Clem Labine .40 1.00
40 Roy Campanella .75 2.00
41 George Shuba .08 .25
42 Chuck Dressen MG .08 .25
43 Pee Wee Reese .75 2.00
44 Joe Black .20 .50
45 Bobby Morgan .08 .25
46 Dick Williams .20 .50
47 Rube Walker .08 .25
48 Johnny Rutherford .08 .25
49 Billy Loes .20 .50
50 Don Hoak .08 .25
51 Jim Hughes .08 .25
52 Bob Milliken .08 .25
53 Preacher Roe .20 .50
54 Dixie Howell .08 .25
55 Junior Gilliam .40 1.00
56 Johnny Podres .20 .50
57 Bill Antonello .08 .25
58 Ralph Branca .20 .50
59 Gil Hodges .75 2.00
60 Carl Furillo .40 1.00
61 Carl Erskine .40 1.00
62 Don Newcombe .20 .50
63 Duke Snider .40 1.00
64 Billy Cox .20 .50
65 Russ Meyer .08 .25
66 Jackie Robinson .75 2.00
67 Preacher Roe .20 .50
68 Duke Snider .40 1.00
69 Junior Gilliam .40 1.00
70 Billy Herman CO .20 .50
71 Joe Black .20 .50
72 Gil Hodges .75 2.00
73 Clem Labine .40 1.00
74 Ben Wade .08 .25
75 Tom Lasorda .40 1.00
76 Rube Walker .08 .25
77 Johnny Podres .20 .50
78 Jim Hughes .08 .25
79 Bob Milliken .08 .25
80 Charlie Thompson .08 .25
81 Don Hoak .08 .25
82 Roberto Clemente 1.50 4.00
83 Don Zimmer .20 .50
84 Roy Campanella .75 2.00
85 Billy Cox .20 .50
86 Carl Erskine .40 1.00
87 Carl Furillo .40 1.00
88 Don Newcombe .20 .50
89 Pee Wee Reese .75 2.00
90 George Shuba .08 .25
91 Junior Gilliam .40 1.00
92 Billy Herman CO .20 .50
93 Johnny Podres .20 .50
94 Don Hoak .08 .25
95 Jackie Robinson .75 2.00
96 Jim Hughes .08 .25
97 Bob Borkowski .20 .50
98 Sandy Amoros .08 .25
99 Karl Spooner .20 .50
100 Don Zimmer .08 .25
101 Rube Walker .08 .25
102 Bob Milliken 1.50 4.00
103 Sandy Koufax .75 2.00
104 Joe Black .40 1.00
105 Clem Labine .75 2.00
106 Gil Hodges .08 .25
107 Ed Roebuck .08 .25
108 Bert Hamrik .40 1.00
109 Duke Snider .40 1.00
110 Bob Borkowski .08 .25
111 Roger Craig .20 .50
112 Don Drysdale .40 1.00
113 Dixie Howell .08 .25
114 Frank Kellert .08 .25
115 Tom Lasorda .40 1.00
116 Chuck Templeton .08 .25
117 World Series .40 1.00
118 World Series .75 2.00
119 World Series .40 1.00
120 World Series .75 2.00
121 Don Hoak .08 .25
122 Roy Campanella .75 2.00
123 Pee Wee Reese .75 2.00
124 Bob Darnell .08 .25
125 Don Zimmer .20 .50
126 George Shuba .08 .25
127 Johnny Podres .20 .50
128 Junior Gilliam .40 1.00
129 Don Newcombe .20 .50
130 Jim Hughes .08 .25
131 Gil Hodges .75 2.00
132 Carl Furillo .40 1.00
133 Carl Erskine .40 1.00
134 Erv Palica .08 .25
135 Russ Meyer .08 .25
136 Billy Loes .20 .50
137 Walt Moryn .08 .25
138 Chico Fernandez .08 .25
139 Charlie Neal .08 .25
140 Ken Lehman .08 .25
141 Walter Alston MG .40 1.00
142 Jackie Robinson .75 2.00
143 Sandy Amoros .20 .50
144 Ed Roebuck .08 .25
145 Roger Craig .20 .50
146 Sandy Koufax .75 2.00
147 Karl Spooner .08 .25
148 Don Zimmer .20 .50
149 Roy Campanella .75 2.00
150 Gil Hodges .75 2.00
151 Duke Snider .40 1.00
152 Team Card .40 1.00
153 Johnny Podres .20 .50
154 Don Bessent .08 .25
155 Carl Furillo .40 1.00
156 Randy Jackson .08 .25
157 Carl Erskine .40 1.00
158 Don Newcombe .20 .50
159 Pee Wee Reese .75 2.00
160 Billy Loes .20 .50
161 Junior Gilliam .40 1.00
162 Clem Labine .40 1.00
163 Charlie Neal .08 .25
164 Rube Walker .08 .25
165 Checklist .08 .25
AU103 Sandy Koufax 103 AU
AU146 Sandy Koufax 146 AU

2001 Topps Archives

COMPLETE SET (450) 75.00 150.00
COMPLETE SERIES 1 (225) 40.00 80.00
COMPLETE SERIES 2 (225) 40.00 80.00
1 Johnny Antonelli 52 .40 1.00
2 Yogi Berra 52 1.00 2.50
3 Dom DiMaggio 52 .40 1.00
4 Carl Erskine 52 .40 1.00
5 Larry Doby 52 .40 1.00
6 Monte Irvin 52 .40 1.00
7 Vernon Law 52 .40 1.00
8 Eddie Mathews 52 1.00 2.50
9 Willie Mays 52 2.00 5.00
10 Gil McDougald 52 .40 1.00
11 Andy Pafko 52 .60 1.50
12 Phil Rizzuto 52 1.00 2.50
13 Preacher Roe 52 .40 1.00
14 Hank Sauer 52 .40 1.00
15 Bobby Shantz 52 .40 1.00
16 Enos Slaughter 52 .40 1.00
17 Warren Spahn 52 .60 1.50
18 Mickey Vernon 52 .40 1.00
19 Early Wynn 52 .40 1.00
20 Gaylord Perry 62 .40 1.00
21 Johnny Podres 53 .40 1.00
22 Ernie Banks 54 1.00 2.50
23 Moose Skowron 54 .40 1.00
24 Harmon Killebrew 55 1.00 2.50
25 Ted Williams 54 2.00 5.00
26 Jimmy Piersall 56 .40 1.00
27 Frank Thomas 56 .40 1.00
28 Bill Mazeroski 57 1.00 2.50
29 Bobby Richardson 57 .40 1.00
30 Frank Robinson 57 .60 1.50
31 Stan Musial 58 1.50 4.00
32 Johnny Callison 59 .40 1.00
33 Bob Gibson 59 .60 1.50
34 Frank Howard 60 .40 1.00
35 Willie McCovey 60 .40 1.00
36 Carl Yastrzemski 60 1.50 4.00
37 Jim Maloney 61 .40 1.00
38 Ron Santo 61 .60 1.50
39 Lou Brock 62 .60 1.50
40 Tim McCarver 62 .40 1.00
41 Joe Pepitone 62 .20 .50
42 Boog Powell 62 .60 1.50
43 Bill Freehan 63 .40 1.00
44 Dick Allen 64 .40 1.00
45 Willie Horton 64 .20 .50
46 Mickey Lolich 64 .40 1.00
47 Wilbur Wood 64 .20 .50
48 Bert Campaneris 65 .40 1.00
49 Rod Carew 67 .60 1.50
50 Luis Aparicio 56 .40 1.00
51 Joe Morgan 65 .40 1.00
52 Luis Tiant 65 .40 1.00
53 Bobby Murcer 66 .40 1.00
54 Don Sutton 66 .40 1.00
55 Ken Holtzman 67 .20 .50
56 Reggie Smith 67 .40 1.00
57 Hal McRae 68 .40 1.00
58 Roy White 68 .40 1.00
59 Reggie Jackson 69 .60 1.50
60 Graig Nettles 69 .40 1.00
61 Joe Rudi 69 .40 1.00
62 Vida Blue 70 .40 1.00
63 Darrell Evans 70 .40 1.00
64 David Concepcion 71 .40 1.00
65 Bobby Grich 71 .40 1.00
66 Greg Luzinski 71 .40 1.00
67 Ron Cey 72 .40 1.00
68 George Hendrick 72 .20 .50
69 Dwight Evans 73 .60 1.50
70 Gary Matthews 73 .20 .50
71 Mike Schmidt 73 3.00 8.00
72 Jim Kaat 60 .40 1.00
73 Dave Winfield 74 .40 1.00
74 Gary Carter 75 .60 1.50
75 Dennis Eckersley 76 .40 1.00
76 Kent Tekulve 76 .40 1.00
77 Andre Dawson 77 .60 1.50
78 Denny Martinez 77 .40 1.00
79 Bruce Sutter 77 .40 1.00
80 Jack Morris 78 .40 1.00
81 Ozzie Smith 80 2.00 5.00
82 Lee Smith 82 .40 1.00
83 Don Mattingly 84 3.00 8.00
84 Joe Carter 85 .40 1.00
85 Kirby Puckett 85 1.00 2.50
86 Joe Adcock 52 .40 1.00
87 Gus Bell 52 .20 .50
88 Roy Campanella 52 1.00 2.50
89 Jackie Jensen 52 .40 1.00
90 Johnny Mize 52 .60 1.50
91 Allie Reynolds 52 .40 1.00
92 Al Rosen 52 .40 1.00
93 Hal Newhouser 53 .40 1.00
94 Harvey Kuenn 54 .40 1.00
95 Nellie Fox 56 1.00 2.50
96 Elston Howard 56 .60 1.50
97 Sal Maglie 57 .40 1.00
98 Roger Maris 58 1.00 2.50
99 Norm Cash 60 .40 1.00
100 Thurman Munson 70 1.00 2.50
101 Roy Campanella 57 1.00 2.50
102 Larry Doby 59 .40 1.00
103 Dom Dimaggio 53 .40 1.00
104 Johnny Mize 53 .40 1.00
105 Allie Reynolds 53 .40 1.00
106 Preacher Roe 54 .40 1.00
107 Hal Newhouser 55 .20 .50
108 Monte Irvin 56 .40 1.00
109 Carl Erskine 59 .40 1.00
110 Enos Slaughter 59 .40 1.00
111 Gil McDougald 60 .40 1.00
112 Andy Pafko 59 .40 1.00
113 Sal Maglie 59 .20 .50
114 Johnny Antonelli 61 .20 .50
115 Phil Rizzuto 61 .60 1.50
116 Yogi Berra 62 1.00 2.50
117 Jim Wynn 77 .20 .50
118 Mickey Vernon 63 .20 .50
119 Gus Bell 64 .20 .50
120 Ted Williams 58 1.25 3.00
121 Frank Thomas 65 .20 .50
122 Bobby Richardson 66 .40 1.00
123 Gaylord Perry 83 .40 1.00
124 Vernon Law 67 .20 .50
125 Jimmy Piersall 67 .20 .50
126 Moose Skowron 67 .40 1.00
127 Joe Adcock 63 .20 .50
128 Johnny Podres 69 .40 1.00
129 Ernie Banks 71 1.00 2.50
130 Jim Maloney 72 .20 .50
131 Johnny Callison 73 .20 .50
132 Eddie Mathews 68 .60 1.50
133 Joe Pepitone 73 .20 .50
134 Warren Spahn 65 .60 1.50
135 Bill Mazeroski 72 .60 1.50
136 Norm Cash 74 .40 1.00
137 Bob Gibson 75 .60 1.50
138 Harmon Killebrew 75 1.00 2.50
139 Frank Robinson 75 .60 1.50
140 Ron Santo 75 .40 1.00
141 Hank Sauer 59 .20 .50
142 Bobby Shantz 64 .20 .50
143 Nellie Fox 65 .60 1.50
144 Elston Howard 68 .60 1.50
145 Jackie Jensen 61 .40 1.00
146 Al Rosen 56 .40 1.00
147 Dick Allen 76 .20 .50
148 Bill Freehan 77 .40 1.00
149 Boog Powell 77 .40 1.00
150 Lou Brock 79 .60 1.50
151 Rod Carew 86 .60 1.50
152 Wilbur Wood 79 .20 .50
153 Thurman Munson 79 1.00 2.50
154 Ken Holtzman 80 .20 .50
155 Willie Horton 80 .20 .50
156 Mickey Lolich 80 .20 .50
157 Tim McCarver 80 .20 .50
158 Willie McCovey 80 .40 1.00
159 Roy White 80 .20 .50
160 Bobby Murcer 83 .40 1.00
161 Joe Rudi 83 .20 .50
162 Reggie Smith 83 .20 .50
163 Luis Tiant 83 .20 .50
164 Bert Campaneris 84 .20 .50
165 Frank Howard 73 .20 .50
166 Harvey Kuenn 66 .20 .50
167 Greg Luzinski 85 .20 .50
168 Luis Aparicio 74 .40 1.00
169 Willie Mays 73 1.25 3.00
170 Roger Maris 68 1.00 2.50
171 Vida Blue 87 .20 .50
172 Bobby Grich 87 .20 .50
173 Reggie Jackson 87 .60 1.50
174 Hal McRae 87 .20 .50
175 Carl Yastrzemski 83 1.00 2.50
176 David Concepcion 88 .20 .50
177 Ron Cey 87 .20 .50
178 George Hendrick 88 .20 .50
179 Gary Matthews 88 .20 .50
180 Stan Musial 63 1.00 2.50
181 Graig Nettles 88 .20 .50
182 Don Sutton 88 .40 1.00
183 Kent Tekulve 88 .20 .50
184 Bruce Sutter 89 .40 1.00
185 Darrell Evans 90 .20 .50
186 Mike Schmidt 89 1.50 4.00
187 Jim Kaat 83 .20 .50
188 Dwight Evans 92 .60 1.50
189 Gary Carter 93 .40 1.00
190 Jack Morris 94 .20 .50
191 Joe Morgan 85 .40 1.00
192 Dave Winfield 95 .40 1.00
193 Andre Dawson 96 .40 1.00
194 Lee Smith 96 .20 .50
195 Ozzie Smith 96 1.50 4.00
196 Denny Martinez 97 .20 .50
197 Don Mattingly 96 1.50 4.00
198 Joe Carter 98 .40 1.00
199 Dennis Eckersley 98 .40 1.00
200 Kirby Puckett 96 1.00 2.50
201 Walter Alston MG 56 .40 1.00
202 Casey Stengel MG 60 .40 1.00
203 Sparky Anderson MG 71 .40 1.00
204 Tommy Lasorda MG 88 .40 1.00
205 Whitey Herzog MG 88 .20 .50
206 AL HR Leaders 70 .40 1.00
207 NL HR Leaders 68 .40 1.00
208 AL HR Leaders 67 1.00 2.50
209 AL Batting Leaders 65 .40 1.00
210 NL HR Leaders 64 .40 1.00
211 NL HR Leaders 63 .40 1.00
212 AL HR Leaders 68 1.00 2.50
213 Ernie Banks 59 Thrill 1.00 2.50
214 Hank Aaron 59 Thrill 1.25 3.00
215 Willie Mays 59 Thrill 1.25 3.00
216 Al Kaline 59 Thrill 1.00 2.50
217 Stan Musial 59 Thrill 1.00 2.50
218 Duke Snider 59 Thrill .60 1.50
219 The Champs 67 .60 1.50
220 Pride of the NL 63 1.00 2.50
221 Whitey Ford WS 63 .60 1.50
222 Jerry Koosman WS 70 .20 .50
223 Bob Gibson WS 65 .60 1.50
224 Gil Hodges WS 60 .60 1.50
225 Reggie Jackson WS 78 .60 1.50
226 Hank Bauer 52 .40 1.00
227 Ralph Branca 52 .40 1.00
228 Joe Garagiola 52 .40 1.00
229 Bob Feller 52 .40 1.00
230 Dick Groat 52 .40 1.00
231 George Kell 52 .40 1.00
232 Bob Boone 73 .40 1.00
233 Minnie Minoso 52 .40 1.00
234 Billy Pierce 52 .40 1.00
235 Robin Roberts 52 .40 1.00
236 Johnny Sain 52 .40 1.00
237 Red Schoendienst 52 .40 1.00
238 Curt Simmons 52 .40 1.00
239 Duke Snider 52 .60 1.50
240 Bobby Thomson 52 .60 1.50
241 Hoyt Wilhelm 52 .60 1.50
242 Roy Face 53 .40 1.00
243 Ralph Kiner 53 .40 1.00
244 Hank Aaron 54 2.50 6.00
245 Al Kaline 54 1.00 2.50
246 Don Larsen 56 .40 1.00
247 Tug McGraw 65 .40 1.00
248 Don Newcombe 56 .60 1.50
249 Herb Score 56 .40 1.00
250 Clete Boyer 57 .40 1.00
251 Lindy McDaniel 57 .20 .50
252 Brooks Robinson 57 .60 1.50
253 Orlando Cepeda 58 .40 1.00
254 Larry Bowa 70 .40 1.00
255 Mike Cuellar 59 .40 1.00
256 Jim Perry 59 .40 1.00
257 Dave Parker 74 .40 1.00
258 Maury Wills 60 .40 1.00
259 Willie Davis 61 .20 .50
260 Juan Marichal 61 .40 1.00
261 Jim Bouton 62 .40 1.00
262 Dean Chance 62 .40 1.00
263 Sam McDowell 62 .40 1.00
264 Whitey Ford 53 .60 1.50
265 Bob Uecker 62 .60 1.50
266 Willie Stargell 63 .60 1.50
267 Rico Carty 64 .40 1.00
268 Tommy John 64 .40 1.00
269 Phil Niekro 64 .40 1.00
270 Paul Blair 65 .40 1.00
271 Steve Carlton 65 1.25 3.00
272 Jim Lonborg 65 .40 1.00
273 Tony Perez 65 .40 1.00
274 Ron Swoboda 65 .40 1.00
275 Fergie Jenkins 66 .40 1.00
276 Jim Palmer 66 .40 1.00
277 Sal Bando 67 .40 1.00
278 Tom Seaver 67 1.50 4.00
279 Johnny Bench 68 1.50 4.00
280 Nolan Ryan 68 2.50 6.00
281 Rollie Fingers 69 .40 1.00
282 Sparky Lyle 69 .40 1.00
283 Al Oliver 69 .40 1.00
284 Bob Watson 69 .40 1.00
285 Bill Buckner 70 .40 1.00
286 Bert Blyleven 71 .60 1.50
287 George Foster 71 .40 1.00
288 Al Hrabosky 71 .20 .50
289 Cecil Cooper 72 .40 1.00
290 Carlton Fisk 72 .60 1.50
291 Mickey Rivers 72 .40 1.00
292 Goose Gossage 73 .40 1.00
293 Rick Reuschel 73 .40 1.00
294 Bucky Dent 74 .40 1.00
295 Frank Tanana 74 .40 1.00
296 George Brett 75 3.00 8.00
297 Keith Hernandez 75 .40 1.00
298 Fred Lynn 75 .40 1.00
299 Robin Yount 75 1.00 2.50
300 Ron Guidry 76 .40 1.00
301 Jack Clark 77 .40 1.00
302 Mark Fidrych 77 .40 1.00
303 Dale Murphy 77 .60 1.50
304 Willie Hernandez 78 .20 .50
305 Lou Whitaker 78 .40 1.00
306 Kirk Gibson 81 .40 1.00
307 Wade Boggs 83 .60 1.50
308 Ryne Sandberg 83 2.50 6.00
309 Orel Hershiser 85 .40 1.00
310 Jimmy Key 85 .40 1.00
311 Richie Ashburn 52 .60 1.50
312 Smoky Burgess 52 .40 1.00
313 Gil Hodges 52 1.00 2.50
314 Ted Kluszewski 52 .60 1.50
315 Pee Wee Reese 52 1.00 2.50
316 Jackie Robinson 52 1.00 2.50
317 Jim Wynn 64 .20 .50
318 Satchel Paige 53 1.00 2.50
319 Roberto Clemente 55 2.50 6.00
320 Carl Furillo 56 .40 1.00
321 Don Drysdale 57 .60 1.50
322 Curt Flood 58 .40 1.00
323 Bob Allison 59 .40 1.00
324 Tony Conigliaro 64 .40 1.00
325 Dan Quisenberry 80 .40 1.00
326 Ralph Branca 52 .20 .50
327 Bob Feller 53 .40 1.00
328 Satchel Paige 53 1.00 2.50
329 George Kell 58 .40 1.00
330 Pee Wee Reese 58 .60 1.50
331 Bobby Thomson 60 .40 1.00
332 Carl Furillo 60 .20 .50
333 Hank Bauer 61 .20 .50
334 Herb Score 62 .40 1.00
335 Richie Ashburn 63 .60 1.50
336 Billy Pierce 64 .20 .50
337 Duke Snider 64 .60 1.50
338 Early Wynn 62 .20 .50
339 Robin Roberts 66 .40 1.00
340 Dick Groat 67 .40 1.00
341 Curt Simmons 67 .20 .50
342 Bob Uecker 67 .60 1.50
343 Smoky Burgess 67 .20 .50
344 Jim Bouton 68 .20 .50
345 Roy Face 69 .20 .50
346 Don Drysdale 69 .60 1.50
347 Bob Allison 70 .20 .50
348 Clete Boyer 71 .20 .50
349 Dean Chance 71 .20 .50
350 Tony Conigliaro 71 .20 .50
351 Curt Flood 71 .20 .50
352 Hoyt Wilhelm 72 .40 1.00
353 Ron Swoboda 73 .20 .50
354 Roberto Clemente 73 1.50 4.00
355 Tug McGraw 85 .20 .50
356 Orlando Cepeda 74 .40 1.00
357 Joe Garagiola 52 .20 .50
358 Juan Marichal 74 .40 1.00
359 Sam McDowell 74 .20 .50
360 Johnny Sain 55 .20 .50
361 Ted Kluszewski 61 .40 1.00
362 Al Kaline 74 1.00 2.50
363 Lindy McDaniel 75 .20 .50
364 Don Newcombe 60 .40 1.00
365 Jim Perry 75 .20 .50
366 Hank Aaron 76 1.50 4.00
367 Don Larsen 65 .40 1.00
368 Mike Cuellar 77 .20 .50
369 Willie Davis 77 .20 .50
370 Ralph Kiner 53 .40 1.00
371 Minnie Minoso 64 .40 1.00
372 Larry Bowa 85 .20 .50
373 Brooks Robinson 77 .60 1.50
374 Bob Boone 90 .20 .50
375 Jim Lonborg 79 .20 .50
376 Paul Blair 80 .20 .50
377 Rico Carty 80 .20 .50
378 Sal Bando 81 .20 .50
379 Mark Fidrych 81 .20 .50
380 Al Hrabosky 82 .20 .50
381 Willie Stargell 82 .60 1.50
382 Johnny Bench 83 1.00 2.50
383 Dave Parker 91 .20 .50
384 Sparky Lyle 83 .20 .50
385 Fergie Jenkins 84 .40 1.00
386 Jim Palmer 84 .40 1.00
387 Whitey Ford 67 .60 1.50
388 Tony Perez 86 .40 1.00
389 Mickey Rivers 85 .20 .50
390 Bob Watson 85 .20 .50
391 Rollie Fingers 86 .40 1.00
392 George Foster 86 .20 .50
393 Al Oliver 86 .20 .50
394 Tom Seaver 87 .60 1.50
395 Maury Wills 72 .20 .50
396 Steve Carlton 87T .40 1.00
397 Cecil Cooper 88 .20 .50
398 Bill Buckner 88 .20 .50
399 Phil Niekro 87 .40 1.00
400 Red Schoendienst 62 .40 1.00
401 Ron Guidry 89 .20 .50
402 Willie Hernandez 89 .20 .50
403 Tommy John 89 .20 .50
404 Gil Hodges 63 1.00 2.50
405 Bucky Dent 84 .20 .50
406 Keith Hernandez 90 .40 1.00
407 Dan Quisenberry 90 .20 .50
408 Fred Lynn 91 .20 .50
409 Rick Reuschel 91 .20 .50
410 Jackie Robinson 56 1.00 2.50
411 Goose Gossage 92 .20 .50
412 Bert Blyleven 93 .40 1.00
413 Jack Clark 93 .20 .50
414 Carlton Fisk 93 .60 1.50
415 Dale Murphy 93 .60 1.50
416 Frank Tanana 93 .20 .50
417 George Brett 94 1.50 4.00
418 Robin Yount 94 1.00 2.50
419 Kirk Gibson 95 .40 1.00
420 Lou Whitaker 95 .20 .50
421 Ryne Sandberg 97 2.00 5.00
422 Jimmy Key 98 .40 1.00
423 Nolan Ryan 94 1.50 4.00
424 Wade Boggs 00 .40 1.00
425 Orel Hershiser 00 .20 .50
426 Billy Martin MG 84 .60 1.50
427 Ralph Houk MG 62 .40 1.00
428 Chuck Tanner MG 72 .20 .50
429 Earl Weaver MG 71 .40 1.00
430 Leo Durocher MG 52 .40 1.00
431 AL HR Leaders 66 .40 1.00
432 NL HR Leaders 60 1.00 2.50
433 AL Batting Leaders 62 .40 1.00
434 Leading Firemen 79 .20 .50
435 Strikeout Leaders 77 .60 1.50
436 HR Leaders 74 .40 1.00
437 RBI Leaders 73 .60 1.50
438 Roger Maris Blasts 62 1.00 2.50
439 Carl Yastrzemski WS2 68 1.00 2.50
440 Nolan Ryan RB 78 1.50 4.00
441 Baltimore Orioles 70 .40 1.00
442 Tony Perez RB 86 .20 .50
443 Steve Carlton RB 84 .20 .50
444 Wade Boggs RB 89 .40 1.00
445 Andre Dawson RB 89 .40 1.00
446 Whitey Ford WS 62 .60 1.50
447 Hank Aaron WS 59 1.50 4.00
448 Bob Gibson WS 69 .60 1.50
449 Roberto Clemente WS 72 1.50 4.00
450 Orioles .40 1.00
B.Robinson WS 71

2001 Topps Archives Autographs

SER.1 GROUP A ODDS 1:3049
SER.2 GROUP A ODDS 1:2904
SER.1 GROUP B ODDS 1:872
SER.2 GROUP B ODDS 1:480
SER.1 GROUP C ODDS 1:697
SER.2 GROUP C ODDS 1:4782
SER.1 GROUP D ODDS 1:122
SER.2 GROUP D ODDS 1:662
SER.1 GROUP E ODDS 1:26
SER.2 GROUP E ODDS 1:209
SER.1 GROUP F ODDS 1:6097
SER.2 GROUP F ODDS 1:1455
SER.2 GROUP G ODDS 1:320
SER.2 GROUP H ODDS 1:412
SER.2 GROUP I ODDS 1:192
SER.2 GROUP J ODDS 1:38
SER.2 GROUP K ODDS 1:329
SER.1 OVERALL ODDS 1:20
SER.2 OVERALL ODDS 1:20
A1-A2 STATED PRINT RUN 50 SETS
A1-A2/B2 ARE NOT SERIAL-NUMBERED
A1-A2/B2 PRINT RUNS PROVIDED BY TOPPS
SER.1 EXCH.DEADLINE 4/30/02
SER.2 EXCH.DEADLINE 4/30/03
TAA1 Johnny Antonelli E1 6.00 15.00
TAA2 Hank Bauer E1 8.00 20.00
TAA3 Yogi Berra A2 SP/50 *
TAA4 Ralph Branca E1 6.00 15.00
TAA5 Dom DiMaggio E1 25.00 60.00
TAA6 Joe Garagiola E1 25.00 60.00
TAA7 Carl Erskine D1 12.00 30.00
TAA8 Bob Feller E1 12.00 30.00
TAA10 Dick Groat D1 8.00 20.00
TAA11 Monte Irvin E1 6.00 15.00
TAA12 George Kell E1 6.00 15.00
TAA13 Vernon Law E1 8.00 20.00
TAA14 Bob Boone E1 8.00 20.00
TAA16 Willie Mays A2 SP/50 *
TAA17 Gil McDougald E1 6.00 15.00
TAA18 Minnie Minoso E1 12.00 30.00
TAA19 Andy Pafko D2 6.00 15.00
TAA20 Billy Pierce E2 6.00 15.00
TAA21 Phil Rizzuto B2 SP/200 * 50.00 120.00
TAA22 Robin Roberts C1 12.00 30.00
TAA23 Preacher Roe E1 12.50 30.00
TAA24 Johnny Sain E1 6.00 15.00
TAA25 Hank Sauer E1 12.50 30.00
TAA26 Red Schoendienst E1 15.00 40.00
TAA27 Bobby Shantz E1 8.00 20.00
TAA28 Curt Simmons E1 8.00 20.00
TAA29 Enos Slaughter E2 10.00 25.00
TAA30 Duke Snider B1 20.00 50.00
TAA31 Warren Spahn C2 25.00 60.00
TAA32 Bobby Thomson E1 6.00 15.00
TAA33 Mickey Vernon B2 6.00 15.00
TAA34 Hoyt Wilhelm D1 20.00 50.00
TAA35 Jim Wynn E2 6.00 15.00
TAA36 Roy Face E1 6.00 15.00
TAA37 Gaylord Perry C2 6.00 15.00
TAA38 Ralph Kiner B1 25.00 60.00
TAA39 Johnny Podres E2 10.00 25.00
TAA40 Hank Aaron A2 SP/50 *
TAA41 Ernie Banks A2 SP/50 *
TAA42 Al Kaline B1 50.00 120.00
TAA43 Moose Skowron E1 6.00 15.00
TAA44 Don Larsen A1 SP/50 * 200.00 300.00
TAA45 Harmon Killebrew B1 75.00 150.00
TAA46 Tug McGraw E1 12.50 30.00
TAA48 Don Newcombe E1 15.00 40.00
TAA49 Jim Piersall E2 6.00 15.00
TAA50 Herb Score E1 6.00 15.00
TAA51 Frank Thomas E1 8.00 20.00
TAA52 Clete Boyer D1 6.00 15.00
TAA53 Bill Mazeroski C2 30.00 80.00
TAA54 Lindy McDaniel E1 10.00 25.00
TAA55 Bobby Richardson E2 6.00 15.00
TAA56 B.Robinson A1 SP/50 * 250.00 500.00
TAA57 Frank Robinson B1 40.00 80.00
TAA58 Orlando Cepeda B1 30.00 80.00
TAA59 Stan Musial A1 SP/50 * 400.00 600.00
TAA60 Larry Bowa D1 6.00 15.00
TAA61 Johnny Callison E2 6.00 15.00
TAA62 Mike Cuellar D1 10.00 25.00
TAA63 Bob Gibson A1 SP/50 * 200.00 300.00
TAA64 Jim Perry E2 6.00 15.00
TAA65 Frank Howard E1 6.00 15.00
TAA66 Dave Parker E1 10.00 25.00
TAA67 Willie McCovey D2 50.00 120.00
TAA68 Maury Wills E1 8.00 20.00
TAA69 Carl Yastrzemski F1 50.00 100.00
TAA70 Willie Davis E1 6.00 15.00
TAA71 Jim Maloney E2 10.00 25.00
TAA73 Ron Santo E2 25.00 60.00
TAA74 Jim Bouton D1 8.00 20.00
TAA75 Lou Brock A2 SP/50 *
TAA76 Dean Chance E1 6.00 15.00
TAA77 T.McCarver B2 SP/200 * 40.00 80.00
TAA78 Sam McDowell D1 12.00 30.00
TAA79 Joe Pepitone E1 10.00 25.00
TAA80 Whitey Ford F1 20.00 50.00
TAA81 Boog Powell E2 6.00 15.00
TAA83 Bill Freehan D2 6.00 15.00
TAA85 Dick Allen B2 30.00 60.00
TAA86 Rico Carty E1 6.00 15.00
TAA87 Willie Horton E2 12.00 30.00
TAA88 Tommy John E1 6.00 15.00
TAA89 Mickey Lolich E2 8.00 20.00
TAA90 Phil Niekro D1 15.00 40.00
TAA91 Wilbur Wood E1 8.00 20.00
TAA92 Paul Blair E1 6.00 15.00
TAA93 Bert Campaneris E2 6.00 15.00
TAA94 Steve Carlton D1 30.00 80.00
TAA96 Jim Lonborg E1 6.00 15.00
TAA97 Luis Aparicio B1 12.00 30.00
TAA98 Tony Perez D1 30.00 80.00
TAA99 Joe Morgan B2 SP/200 * 20.00 50.00
TAA100 Ron Swoboda D1 8.00 20.00
TAA101 Luis Tiant E2 6.00 15.00
TAA102 Fergie Jenkins D1 15.00 40.00
TAA103 Bobby Murcer D2 12.00 30.00
TAA104 Jim Palmer B1 50.00 100.00
TAA106 Sal Bando E2 6.00 15.00
TAA107 Ken Holtzman B1 30.00 80.00
TAA108 T.Seaver A2 SP/50 *
TAA110 J.Bench A1 SP/50 *
TAA111 Hal McRae E2 6.00 15.00
TAA112 Nolan Ryan A2 SP/50 *
TAA113 Roy White D2 6.00 15.00
TAA114 Rollie Fingers C1 10.00 25.00
TAA115 R.Jackson A2 SP/50 *
TAA116 Sparky Lyle E1 12.00 30.00
TAA117 Graig Nettles D2 6.00 15.00
TAA118 Al Oliver E1 6.00 15.00
TAA119 Joe Rudi B2 6.00 15.00
TAA120 Bob Watson E1 8.00 20.00
TAA121 Vida Blue E2 6.00 15.00
TAA122 Bill Buckner E1 20.00 50.00
TAA123 Darrell Evans E1 6.00 15.00
TAA124 Bert Blyleven D1 20.00 50.00
TAA125 Dave Concepcion D2 30.00 60.00
TAA126 George Foster E1 8.00 20.00
TAA127 Bobby Grich E1 6.00 15.00
TAA128 Al Hrabosky E1 6.00 15.00
TAA129 Greg Luzinski D1 6.00 15.00
TAA130 Cecil Cooper E1 8.00 20.00
TAA131 Ron Cey E2 6.00 15.00
TAA132 Carlton Fisk B1 60.00 120.00
TAA133 George Hendrick E2 6.00 15.00
TAA134 Mickey Rivers E1 6.00 15.00
TAA135 Dwight Evans D2 20.00 50.00
TAA136 Rich Gossage E1 6.00 15.00
TAA137 Gary Matthews B2 6.00 15.00
TAA138 Rick Reuschel E1 6.00 15.00
TAA139 M.Schmidt A1 SP/50 * 300.00 800.00
TAA140 Bucky Dent D1 10.00 25.00
TAA141 Jim Kaat B2 8.00 20.00
TAA142 Frank Tanana E1 6.00 15.00
TAA143 D.Winfield B2 SP/200 * 60.00 120.00
TAA144 G.Brett A1 SP/50 * 400.00 800.00
TAA145 G.Carter B2 SP/200 * 30.00 60.00
TAA147 Fred Lynn C1 20.00 50.00
TAA148 R.Yount B2 SP/200 * 100.00 175.00
TAA149 D.Eckersley B2 SP/200 * 40.00 80.00
TAA150 Ron Guidry E2 10.00 25.00
TAA151 Kent Tekulve D1 6.00 15.00
TAA152 Jack Clark E1 6.00 15.00
TAA153 A.Dawson B2 SP/200 * 50.00 100.00
TAA154 Mark Fidrych E1 20.00 50.00
TAA155 D.Martinez B2 SP/200 * 30.00 60.00
TAA156 Dale Murphy C1 30.00 60.00

TAA157 Bruce Sutter D2 8.00 20.00
TAA158 Willie Hernandez D2 6.00 15.00
TAA160 Lou Whitaker D2 20.00 50.00
TAA162 Kirk Gibson E1 25.00 60.00
TAA163 Lee Smith D2 8.00 20.00
TAA164 Wade Boggs B1 100.00 200.00
TAA165 R.Sandberg B2 SP/200 * 150.00 300.00
TAA166 Don Mattingly D1 40.00 80.00
TAA167 Joe Carter B2 SP/200 * 60.00 120.00
TAA168 Orel Hershiser D2 20.00 50.00
TAA169 Kirby Puckett A2 SP/50 *
TAA170 Jimmy Key C1 20.00 50.00

2001 Topps Archives AutoProofs

SER.1 STATED ODDS 1:2444
SER.2 STATED ODDS 1:2391
STATED PRINT RUN 100 SERIAL #'d SETS
SER.1 EXCH.DEADLINE 04/30/02
SER.2 EXCH.DEADLINE 04/30/03
1 Wade Boggs 99 S1 40.00 80.00
2 Carlton Fisk 93 S2 50.00 100.00
3 Willie Mays 73 S1 100.00 200.00
4 Willie McCovey 80 S1 40.00 80.00
5 Jim Palmer 82/84 S1 30.00 60.00
6 Robin Roberts 66 S2 40.00 80.00
7 Duke Snider 64 S2 40.00 80.00
8 Warren Spahn 65 S2 40.00 80.00
9 Hoyt Wilhelm 63 S2 15.00 40.00
10 Carl Yastrzemski 83 S1 75.00 150.00

2001 Topps Archives Bucks

ONE DOLLAR SER.1 ODDS 1:83
ONE DOLLAR SER.2 ODDS 1:80
FIVE DOLLAR SER.1 ODDS 1:1242
FIVE DOLLAR SER.2 ODDS 1:1203
TEN DOLLAR SER.1 ODDS 1:2483
TEN DOLLAR SER.2 ODDS 1:2406
TB1 Willie Mays $1 4.00 10.00
TB2 Roberto Clemente $5 10.00 25.00
TB3 Jackie Robinson $10 10.00 25.00

2001 Topps Archives Future Rookie Reprints

COMPLETE SET (20) 25.00 50.00
FIVE PER SEALED TOPPS FACT.SET
FIVE PER SEALED TOPPS HTA FACT.SET
1 Barry Bonds 87 3.00 8.00
2 Chipper Jones 91 1.25 3.00
3 Cal Ripken 82 4.00 10.00
4 Shawn Green 92 .50 1.25
5 Frank Thomas 90 1.25 3.00
6 Derek Jeter 93 3.00 8.00
7 Geoff Jenkins 96 .50 1.25
8 Jim Edmonds 93 .50 1.25
9 Bernie Williams 90 .75 2.00
10 Sammy Sosa 90 1.25 3.00
11 Rickey Henderson 80 1.25 3.00
12 Tony Gwynn 83 .50 1.25
13 Randy Johnson 89 1.25 3.00
14 Juan Gonzalez 90 .50 1.25
15 Gary Sheffield 89 .50 1.25
16 Manny Ramirez 92 .75 2.00
17 Pokey Reese 92 .50 1.25
18 Preston Wilson 93 .50 1.25
19 Jay Payton 95 .50 1.25
20 Rafael Palmeiro 87 .75 2.00

2001 Topps Archives Rookie Reprint Bat Relics

SER.1 STATED ODDS 1:1356
SER.2 STATED ODDS 1:1307
TARR1 Johnny Bench 12.00 30.00
TARR2 George Brett 8.00 20.00
TARR3 Fred Lynn 6.00 15.00
TARR4 Reggie Jackson 8.00 20.00
TARR5 Mike Schmidt 8.00 20.00
TARR6 Willie Stargell 8.00 20.00

2002 Topps Archives

COMPLETE SET (200) 20.00 50.00
1 Willie Mays 62 2.00 5.00
2 Dale Murphy 83 .60 1.50
3 Dave Winfield 79 .40 1.00
4 Roger Maris 61 1.00 2.50
5 Ron Cey 77 .40 1.00
6 Lee Smith 91 .40 1.00
7 Len Dykstra 93 .40 1.00
8 Ray Fosse 70 .40 1.00
9 Warren Spahn 57 .60 1.50
10 Herb Score 56 .40 1.00
11 Jim Wynn 74 .40 1.00
12 Sam McDowell 70 .40 1.00
13 Fred Lynn 79 .40 1.00
14 Yogi Berra 54 1.00 2.50
15 Ron Santo 64 .60 1.50
16 Alvin Dark 53 .40 1.00
17 Bill Buckner 85 .40 1.00
18 Rollie Fingers 81 .40 1.00
19 Tony Gwynn 97 1.25 3.00
20 Red Schoendienst 53 .40 1.00
21 Gaylord Perry 72 .40 1.00
22 Jose Cruz 83 .40 1.00
23 Dennis Martinez 91 .40 1.00
24 Dave McNally 68 .40 1.00
25 Norm Cash 61 .40 1.00
26 Ted Kluszewski 54 .60 1.50
27 Rick Reuschel 77 .40 1.00
28 Bruce Sutter 77 .40 1.00
29 Don Larsen 56 .40 1.00
30 Claudell Washington 82 .40 1.00
31 Luis Aparicio 60 .40 1.00
32 Clete Boyer 62 .40 1.00
33 Goose Gossage 77 .40 1.00
34 Ray Knight 79 .40 1.00
35 Roy Campanella 53 1.00 2.50
36 Tug McGraw 71 .40 1.00
37 Bob Lemon 52 .40 1.00
38 Willie Stargell 71 .60 1.50
39 Roberto Clemente 66 2.00 5.00
40 Jim Fregosi 70 .40 1.00
41 Reggie Smith 77 .40 1.00
42 Dave Parker 78 .40 1.00
43 Darrell Evans 73 .40 1.00
44 Ryne Sandberg 90 1.50 4.00
45 Manny Mota 72 .40 1.00
46 Dennis Eckersley 92 .40 1.00
47 Nellie Fox 59 .60 1.50
48 Gil Hodges 54 1.00 2.50
49 Reggie Jackson 69 .60 1.50
50 Bobby Shantz 52 .40 1.00
51 Cecil Cooper 80 .40 1.00
52 Jim Kaat 66 .40 1.00
53 George Hendrick 80 .40 1.00
54 Johnny Podres 61 .40 1.00
55 Bob Gibson 68 .60 1.50
56 Vern Law 60 .40 1.00
57 Joe Adcock 56 .40 1.00
58 Jack Clark 87 .40 1.00
59 Bill Mazeroski 60 .60 1.50
60 Carl Yastrzemski 67 1.50 4.00
61 Bobby Murcer 71 .40 1.00
62 Davey Johnson 73 .40 1.00
63 Jim Palmer 75 .40 1.00
64 Roy Face 59 .40 1.00
65 Dean Chance 64 .40 1.00
66 Moose Skowron 60 .60 1.50
67 Dwight Evans 87 .60 1.50
68 Kirk Gibson 88 .40 1.00
69 Sal Bando 69 .40 1.00
70 Mike Schmidt 80 2.00 5.00
71 Bo Jackson 89 1.00 2.50
72 Chris Chambliss 76 .40 1.00
73 Fergie Jenkins 71 .40 1.00
74 Brooks Robinson 64 .60 1.50
75 Bobby Richardson 62 .40 1.00
76 Duke Snider 54 .60 1.50
77 Allie Reynolds 52 .40 1.00
78 Harmon Killebrew 66 1.00 2.50
79 Steve Carlton 72 .40 1.00
80 Bert Blyleven 73 .40 1.00
81 Phil Niekro 69 .40 1.00
82 Lew Burdette 56 .40 1.00
83 Hoyt Wilhelm 64 .40 1.00
84 Curt Flood 65 .40 1.00
85 Willie Hernandez 84 .40 1.00
86 Robin Yount 82 1.00 2.50
87 Robin Roberts 52 .40 1.00
88 Whitey Ford 61 .60 1.50
89 Tony Oliva 64 .40 1.00
90 Don Newcombe 56 .40 1.00
91 Al Oliver 82 .40 1.00
92 Mike Cuellar 69 .40 1.00
93 Mike Scott 86 .40 1.00
94 Dick Allen 66 .40 1.00
95 Jimmy Piersall 56 .40 1.00
96 Bill Freehan 68 .40 1.00
97 Willie Horton 65 .40 1.00
98 Bob Friend 60 .40 1.00
99 Ken Holtzman 73 .40 1.00
100 Rico Carty 70 .40 1.00
101 Gil McDougald 56 .40 1.00
102 Lee May 69 .40 1.00
103 Joe Pepitone 64 .40 1.00
104 Gene Tenace 75 .40 1.00
105 Gary Carter 85 .40 1.00
106 Tim McCarver 67 .40 1.00
107 Ernie Banks 58 1.00 2.50
108 George Foster 77 .40 1.00
109 Lou Brock 74 .60 1.50
110 Dick Groat 60 .40 1.00
111 Graig Nettles 77 .40 1.00
112 Boog Powell 69 .60 1.50
113 Joe Carter 86 .40 1.00
114 Juan Marichal 66 .40 1.00
115 Larry Doby 54 .40 1.00
116 Fernando Valenzuela 86 .40 1.00
117 Luis Tiant 68 .40 1.00
118 Early Wynn 59 .40 1.00
119 Bill Madlock 75 .40 1.00
120 Eddie Mathews 53 1.00 2.50
121 George Brett 80 2.00 5.00
122 Al Kaline 55 1.00 2.50
123 Frank Howard 69 .40 1.00
124 Mickey Lolich 71 .40 1.00
125 Kirby Puckett 88 1.00 2.50
126 Bob Cerv 58 .40 1.00
127 Will Clark 89 .60 1.50
128 Vida Blue 71 .40 1.00
129 Kevin Mitchell 89 .40 1.00
130 Bucky Dent 80 .40 1.00
131 Tom Seaver 69 .60 1.50
132 Jerry Koosman 76 .40 1.00
133 Orlando Cepeda 61 .40 1.00
134 Nolan Ryan 73 2.50 6.00
135 Tony Kubek 60 .60 1.50
136 Don Drysdale 62 .60 1.50
137 Paul Blair 69 .40 1.00
138 Elston Howard 63 .60 1.50
139 Joe Rudi 74 .40 1.00
140 Tommie Agee 70 .40 1.00
141 Richie Ashburn 58 .60 1.50
142 Jim Bunning 65 .40 1.00
143 Hank Sauer 52 .40 1.00
144 Greg Luzinski 77 .40 1.00
145 Ron Guidry 78 .40 1.00
146 Rod Carew 77 .60 1.50
147 Andre Dawson 87 .40 1.00
148 Keith Hernandez 79 .40 1.00
149 Carlton Fisk 77 .60 1.50
150 Cleon Jones 69 .40 1.00
151 Don Mattingly 85 2.00 5.00
152 Vada Pinson 63 .40 1.00
153 Ozzie Smith 87 1.50 4.00
154 Dave Concepcion 79 .40 1.00
155 Al Rosen 53 .40 1.00
156 Tommy John 68 .40 1.00
157 Bob Ojeda 86 .40 1.00
158 Frank Robinson 66 .60 1.50
159 Darryl Strawberry 87 .40 1.00
160 Bobby Bonds 73 .40 1.00
161 Bert Campaneris 70 .40 1.00
162 Catfish Hunter 74 .60 1.50
163 Bud Harrelson 70 .40 1.00
164 Dwight Gooden 85 .40 1.00
165 Wade Boggs 87 .60 1.50
166 Joe Morgan 76 .40 1.00
167 Ron Swoboda 67 .40 1.00
168 Hank Aaron 57 2.00 5.00
169 Steve Garvey 77 .40 1.00
170 Mickey Rivers 77 .40 1.00
171 Johnny Bench 70 1.00 2.50
172 Ralph Terry 62 .40 1.00
173 Billy Pierce 56 .40 1.00
174 Thurman Munson 76 1.00 2.50
175 Don Sutton 72 .40 1.00
176 Sparky Anderson 84 MG .40 1.00
177 Gil Hodges 69 MG 1.00 2.50
178 Davey Johnson 86 MG .40 1.00
179 Frank Robinson 89 MG .60 1.50
180 Red Schoendienst 67 MG .40 1.00
181 Roger Maris 61 AS 1.00 2.50
182 Willie Mays 62 AS 2.00 5.00
183 Luis Aparicio 60 AS .40 1.00
184 Nellie Fox 59 AS .60 1.50
185 Ernie Banks 58 AS 1.00 2.50
186 Orlando Cepeda 62 AS .40 1.00
187 Whitey Ford 61 AS .60 1.50
188 Bob Gibson 69 AS .60 1.50
189 Bill Mazeroski 59 AS .60 1.50
190 Hank Aaron 58 AS 2.00 5.00
191 1971 AL Home Run Ldrs .40 1.00
192 1962 NL Home Run Ldrs .60 1.50
193 1967 NL RBI Ldrs 1.00 2.50
194 1970 NL Win Ldrs .40 1.00
195 1976 AL ERA Ldrs .40 1.00
196 Hank Aaron 76 HL 2.00 5.00
197 Brooks Robinson 78 HL .60 1.50
198 Tom Seaver 70 HL .40 1.00
199 Jim Palmer 71 HL .40 1.00
200 Lou Brock 75 HL .60 1.50

2002 Topps Archives Autographs

GROUP A ODDS 1:19,803 HOB, 1:20,040 RET
GROUP B ODDS 1:12,872 HOB, 1:13,360 RET
GROUP C ODDS 1:11,193 HOB, 1:11,451 RET
GROUP D ODDS 1:8045 HOB, 1:8016 RET
GROUP E ODDS 1:753 HOB, 1:756 RET
GROUP F ODDS 1:3387 HOB, 1:3340 RET
GROUP G ODDS 1:1355 HOB, 1:1359 RET
GROUP H ODDS 1:1129 HOB, 1:1129 RET
GROUP I ODDS 1:847 HOB, 1:844 RET
GROUP J ODDS 1:59 HOB, 1:59 RET
GROUP K ODDS 1:748 HOB, 1:749 RET
GROUP L ODDS 1:45 HOB, 1:45 RET
OVERALL STATED ODDS 1:22 HOB/RET
TAAAD Alvin Dark 53 J 6.00 15.00
TAAAK Al Kaline 55 E 25.00 50.00
TAABB Bobby Bonds 73 J 8.00 20.00
TAABC Bert Campaneris 70 L 6.00 15.00
TAABD Bucky Dent 80 J 6.00 15.00
TAABH Bud Harrelson 70 L 6.00 15.00
TAABJ Bo Jackson 89 F 30.00 80.00
TAABP Billy Pierce 56 J 6.00 15.00
TAABPO Boog Powell 69 J 10.00 25.00
TAABRO B.Robinson 64 E 20.00 50.00
TAABS Bruce Sutter 77 J 15.00 40.00
TAACC Chris Chambliss 76 J 10.00 25.00
TAADA Dick Allen 66 J 10.00 25.00
TAADEV Darrell Evans 73 J 6.00 15.00
TAADG Dwight Gooden 85 G 30.00 80.00
TAADGR Dick Groat 60 L 6.00 15.00
TAADM Dave McNally 68 L 20.00 50.00
TAADN Don Newcombe 56 I 15.00 40.00
TAADP Dave Parker 78 H 15.00 40.00
TAADS Duke Snider 54 E 25.00 60.00
TAADW Dave Winfield 79 D 30.00 80.00
TAAEB Ernie Banks 58 E 60.00 150.00
TAAFJ Fergie Jenkins 71 J 6.00 15.00
TAAFL Fred Lynn 79 J 15.00 40.00
TAAGB George Brett 80 E 100.00 250.00
TAAGC Gary Carter 85 E 20.00 50.00
TAAGF George Foster 77 L 12.00 30.00
TAAGL Greg Luzinski 77 J 6.00 15.00
TAAGP Gaylord Perry 72 J 10.00 25.00
TAAHA Hank Aaron 57 E 200.00 400.00
TAAHK Harmon Killebrew 69 E 25.00 60.00
TAAHW Hoyt Wilhelm 64 L 6.00 15.00
TAAJBU Jim Bunning 65 L 6.00 15.00
TAAJCR Jose Cruz 83 K 6.00 15.00
TAAJF Jim Fregosi 70 I 6.00 15.00
TAAJK Jim Kaat 66 J 6.00 15.00
TAAJKO Jerry Koosman 76 G 20.00 50.00
TAAJP Jim Palmer 75 E 10.00 25.00
TAAJPI Jimmy Piersall 56 J 6.00 15.00
TAAJPO Johnny Podres 61 J 6.00 15.00
TAAJR Joe Rudi 74 J 6.00 15.00
TAAKH Keith Hernandez 79 J 10.00 28.00
TAAKM Kevin Mitchell 89 J 8.00 20.00
TAAKP Kirby Puckett 88 A 150.00 400.00
TAALB Lew Burdette 56 L 10.00 25.00
TAALD Len Dykstra 94 J 6.00 15.00
TAALS Lee Smith 91 H 6.00 15.00
TAAMR Mickey Rivers 77 L 6.00 15.00
TAAMS Mike Schmidt 80 B 25.00 60.00
TAARCE Ron Cey 77 L 6.00 15.00
TAARS Ron Santo 64 L 20.00 50.00
TAARSM Reggie Smith 77 L 10.00 25.00
TAART Ralph Terry 62 J 6.00 15.00
TAARY Robin Yount 82 C 30.00 80.00
TAASB Sal Bando 69 L 6.00 15.00
TAASG Steve Garvey 77 J 10.00 25.00
TAATJ Tommy John 68 L 6.00 15.00
TAATO Tony Oliva 64 J 12.00 30.00
TAAWH Willie Hernandez 84 L 6.00 15.00

2002 Topps Archives Bat Relics

GROUP A ODDS 1:106 HOB/RET
GROUP B ODDS 1:282 HOB/RET
TBRAD Andre Dawson 87 A 6.00 15.00
TBRBF Bill Freehan 68 A 4.00 10.00
TBRBR Brooks Robinson 64 A 6.00 15.00
TBRCY Carl Yastrzemski 67 B 15.00 40.00
TBRDE Dwight Evans 87 A 4.00 10.00
TBRDM Don Mattingly 85 A 10.00 25.00
TBRDP Dave Parker 78 A 4.00 10.00
TBRGB George Brett 80 A 10.00 25.00
TBRGC Gary Carter 85 A 6.00 15.00
TBRJB Johnny Bench 70 A 10.00 25.00
TBRJC Joe Carter 86 A 4.00 10.00
TBRJM Joe Morgan 76 B 6.00 15.00
TBRNC Norm Cash 61 A 4.00 10.00
TBRRJ Reggie Jackson 69 A 6.00 15.00
TBRRM Roger Maris 61 A 10.00 25.00
TBRRS Ron Santo 64 A 6.00 15.00
TBRRY Robin Yount 82 B 10.00 25.00
TBRWH Willie Horton 65 A 4.00 10.00
TBRWS Willie Stargell 71 A 6.00 15.00

2002 Topps Archives Reprints

COMPLETE SET (10) 10.00 25.00
FIVE PER SEALED TOPPS FACTORY SET
1 Alex Rodriguez 98 1.00 2.50
2 Jason Giambi 94 .75 2.00
3 Pedro Martinez 93 .75 2.00
4 Ichiro Suzuki 01 1.50 4.00
5 Jeff Bagwell 91 .75 2.00
6 Ivan Rodriguez 91 .75 2.00
7 Mike Piazza 93 1.25 3.00
8 Nomar Garciaparra 95 1.25 3.00
9 Ken Griffey Jr. 89 1.50 4.00
10 Albert Pujols 01 1.50 4.00

2002 Topps Archives Seat Relics

GROUP A ODDS 1:1629 HOB, 1:1636 RET
GROUP B ODDS 1:80 HOB, 1:80 RET
GROUP C ODDS 1:1160 HOB, 1:1162 RET
TSRBL Bob Lemon 52 B 6.00 15.00
TSRDP Dave Parker 78 B 6.00 15.00
TSRDS Duke Snider 54 B 8.00 20.00
TSREB Ernie Banks 58 B 10.00 25.00
TSREM Eddie Mathews 53 B 10.00 25.00
TSRHS Herb Score 56 B 6.00 15.00
TSRJB Jim Bunning 65 B 6.00 15.00
TSRJC Joe Carter 86 B 6.00 15.00
TSRJP Jim Palmer 75 B 6.00 15.00
TSRML Mickey Lolich 71 B 6.00 15.00
TSRNF Nellie Fox 59 B 8.00 20.00
TSRRA Richie Ashburn 58 B 8.00 20.00
TSRRC Rod Carew 77 B 8.00 20.00
TSRRG Ron Guidry 78 C 6.00 15.00
TSRSA Sparky Anderson 84 B 6.00 15.00
TSRSM Sam McDowell 70 B 6.00 15.00
TSRTK Ted Kluszewski 54 B 8.00 20.00
TSRWS Warren Spahn 57 B 10.00 25.00
TSRYB Yogi Berra 54 A 10.00 25.00

2002 Topps Archives Uniform Relics

STATED ODDS 1:28 HOB/RET
TURBB Bobby Bonds 73 2.00 5.00
TURDC Dave Concepcion 79 2.00 5.00
TURDE Dennis Eckersley 92 3.00 8.00
TURDM Dale Murphy 83 5.00 12.00
TURDS Don Sutton 72 3.00 8.00
TURDW Dave Winfield 79 3.00 8.00
TURFL Fred Lynn 79 2.00 5.00
TURFR Frank Robinson 66 3.00 8.00
TURGB George Brett 80 10.00 25.00
TURGP Gaylord Perry 72 3.00 8.00
TURKP Kirby Puckett 88 5.00 12.00
TURNR Nolan Ryan 73 15.00 40.00
TUROC Orlando Cepeda 61 3.00 8.00
TUROS Ozzie Smith 87 3.00 8.00
TURPN Phil Niekro 69 3.00 8.00
TURRS Ryne Sandberg 90 10.00 25.00
TURSA Sparky Anderson 84 3.00 8.00
TURSG Steve Garvey 77 2.00 5.00
TURWB Wade Boggs 87 3.00 8.00
TURWC Will Clark 89 3.00 8.00

2001 Topps Archives Reserve

COMPLETE SET (100) 30.00 60.00
1 Joe Adcock 52 .60 1.50
2 Brooks Robinson 57 1.00 2.50
3 Luis Aparicio 74 .60 1.50
4 Richie Ashburn 52 1.00 2.50
5 Hank Bauer 52 .60 1.50
6 Johnny Bench 68 2.50 6.00
7 Wade Boggs 83 1.00 2.50
8 Moose Skowron 54 .60 1.50
9 George Brett 75 4.00 10.00
10 Lou Brock 62 1.00 2.50
11 Roy Campanella 52 1.50 4.00
12 Willie Hernandez 78 .60 1.50
13 Steve Carlton 65 2.00 5.00
14 Gary Carter 75 .60 1.50
15 Hoyt Wilhelm 52 1.00 2.50
16 Orlando Cepeda 58 .60 1.50
17 Roberto Clemente 55 4.00 8.00
18 Dale Murphy 77 1.00 2.50
19 Dave Concepcion 71 .60 1.50
20 Dom DiMaggio 52 .60 1.50
21 Larry Doby 52 .60 1.50
22 Don Drysdale 57 1.00 2.50
23 Dennis Eckersley 76 .60 1.50
24 Bob Feller 52 2.00 5.00
25 Rollie Fingers 69 .60 1.50
26 Carlton Fisk 72 1.00 2.50
27 Nellie Fox 56 .60 1.50
28 Mickey Rivers 72 .60 1.50
29 Tommy John 64 .60 1.50
30 Johnny Sain 52 .60 1.50
31 Keith Hernandez 75 .60 1.50
32 Gil Hodges 52 1.50 4.00
33 Elston Howard 56 1.00 2.50
34 Frank Howard 60 .60 1.50
35 Bob Gibson 59 1.00 2.50
36 Fergie Jenkins 66 .60 1.50
37 Jackie Jensen 52 .60 1.50
38 Al Kaline 54 1.50 4.00
39 Harmon Killebrew 55 1.50 4.00
40 Ralph Kiner 53 .60 1.50
41 Dick Groat 52 .60 1.50
42 Don Larsen 56 .60 1.50
43 Ralph Branca 52 .60 1.50
44 Mickey Lolich 64 .60 1.50
45 Juan Marichal 61 .60 1.50
46 Roger Maris 58 1.50 4.00
47 Bobby Thomson 52 1.00 2.50
48 Eddie Mathews 52 1.50 4.00
49 Don Mattingly 84 4.00 10.00
50 Willie McCovey 60 .60 1.50
51 Gil McDougald 52 .60 1.50
52 Tug McGraw 65 .60 1.50
53 Billy Pierce 52 .60 1.50
54 Minnie Minoso 52 .60 1.50
55 Johnny Mize 52 1.00 2.50
56 Roy Face 53 .60 1.50
57 Joe Morgan 65 .60 1.50
58 Thurman Munson 70 1.50 4.00
59 Stan Musial 58 2.00 5.00
60 Phil Niekro 64 .60 1.50
61 Paul Blair 65 .60 1.50
62 Andy Pafko 52 1.00 2.50
63 Satchel Paige 53 1.50 4.00
64 Tony Perez 65 .60 1.50
65 Sal Bando 67 .60 1.50
66 Jimmy Piersall 56 .60 1.50
67 Kirby Puckett 85 1.50 4.00
68 Phil Rizzuto 52 1.50 4.00
69 Robin Roberts 52 .60 1.50
70 Jackie Robinson 52 1.50 4.00
71 Ryne Sandberg 83 6.00 12.00
72 Mike Schmidt 73 4.00 10.00
73 Red Schoendienst 52 .60 1.50
74 Herb Score 56 .60 1.50
75 Enos Slaughter 52 .60 1.50
76 Ozzie Smith 80 3.00 8.00
77 Warren Spahn 52 1.00 2.50
78 Don Sutton 66 .60 1.50
79 Luis Tiant 65 .60 1.50
80 Ted Kluszewski 52 1.00 2.50
81 Whitey Ford 53 1.00 2.50
82 Maury Wills 60 .60 1.50
83 Dave Winfield 74 .60 1.50
84 Early Wynn 52 .60 1.50
85 Carl Yastrzemski 60 2.00 5.00
86 Robin Yount 75 1.50 4.00
87 Bob Allison 59 .60 1.50
88 Clete Boyer 57 .60 1.50
89 Reggie Jackson 69 1.00 2.50
90 Yogi Berra 52 1.50 4.00
91 Willie Mays 52 4.00 8.00
92 Jim Palmer 66 .60 1.50
93 Pee Wee Reese 52 1.50 4.00
94 Frank Robinson 57 1.00 2.50
95 Boog Powell 62 1.00 2.50
96 Willie Stargell 63 1.00 2.50
97 Nolan Ryan 68 4.00 10.00
98 Tom Seaver 67 2.50 6.00
99 Duke Snider 52 1.00 2.50
100 Bill Mazeroski 57 1.50 4.00

2001 Topps Archives Reserve Autographed Baseballs

STATED ODDS ONE PER BOX
STATED PRINT RUNS LISTED BELOW
1 Johnny Bench/100 * 50.00 100.00
2 Paul Blair/1000 * 10.00 25.00
3 Clete Boyer/1000 * 10.00 25.00
4 Ralph Branca/400 * 15.00 40.00
5 Roy Face/1000 * 10.00 25.00
6 Bob Feller/1000 * 25.00 60.00
7 Whitey Ford/100 * 30.00 80.00
8 Bob Gibson/1000 * 20.00 50.00
9 Dick Groat/1000 * 10.00 25.00
10 Frank Howard/1000 * 10.00 25.00
11 Reggie Jackson/100 * 50.00 100.00
12 Don Larsen/1000 * 15.00 40.00
13 Mickey Lolich/500 * 10.00 25.00
14 Willie Mays/100 * 100.00 250.00
15 Gil McDougald/1000 * 15.00 40.00
16 Tug McGraw/1000 * 10.00 25.00
17 Minnie Minoso/1000 * 15.00 40.00
18 Andy Pafko/500 * 15.00 40.00
19 Joe Pepitone/1000 * 10.00 25.00
20 Robin Roberts/1000 * 10.00 25.00
21 Frank Robinson/100 * 30.00 60.00
22 Nolan Ryan/100 * 75.00 150.00
23 Herb Score/500 * 10.00 25.00
24 Tom Seaver/100 * 25.00 60.00
25 Moose Skowron/1000 * 10.00 25.00
26 Warren Spahn/100 * 50.00 100.00
27 Bobby Thomson/400 * 15.00 40.00
28 Luis Tiant/500 * 10.00 25.00
29 Carl Yastrzemski/100 * 75.00 150.00
30 Maury Wills/1000 * 10.00 25.00

2001 Topps Archives Reserve Future Rookie Reprints

COMPLETE SET (20) 60.00 120.00
FIVE PER TOPPS LTD. FACTORY SET
1 Barry Bonds 67 6.00 15.00
2 Chipper Jones 91 2.50 6.00
3 Cal Ripken 82 10.00 25.00
4 Shawn Green 92 1.00 2.50
5 Frank Thomas 90 2.50 6.00
6 Derek Jeter 93 8.00 20.00
7 Geoff Jenkins 96 1.00 2.50
8 Jim Edmonds 93 1.00 2.50
9 Bernie Williams 90 1.50 4.00
10 Sammy Sosa 90 2.50 6.00
11 Rickey Henderson 80 2.50 6.00
12 Tony Gwynn 83 3.00 8.00
13 Randy Johnson 89 2.50 6.00
14 Juan Gonzalez 90 1.00 2.50
15 Gary Sheffield 89 1.00 2.50
16 Manny Ramirez 92 1.50 4.00
17 Pokey Reese 92 1.00 2.50
18 Preston Wilson 93 1.00 2.50
19 Jay Payton 95 1.00 2.50
20 Rafael Palmeiro 87 1.50 4.00

2001 Topps Archives Reserve Rookie Reprint Autographs

STATED OVERALL ODDS 1:10
SKIP-NUMBERED SET
ARA1 Willie Mays C 150.00 400.00
ARA2 Whitey Ford B 20.00 50.00
ARA3 Nolan Ryan A 60.00 120.00
ARA4 Carl Yastrzemski B 50.00 100.00
ARA5 Frank Robinson B 20.00 50.00
ARA6 Tom Seaver A 30.00 80.00
ARA7 Warren Spahn A 20.00 50.00
ARA8 Johnny Bench A 60.00 120.00
ARA9 Reggie Jackson A 60.00 120.00
ARA10 Bob Gibson B 25.00 60.00
ARA11 Bob Feller D 12.00 30.00
ARA12 Gil McDougald A 10.00 25.00
ARA13 Luis Tiant A 6.00 15.00
ARA14 Minnie Minoso D 12.00 30.00
ARA16 Herb Score B 6.00 15.00
ARA17 Moose Skowron C 6.00 15.00
ARA18 Maury Wills D 6.00 15.00
ARA19 Clete Boyer A 8.00 20.00
ARA21 Don Larsen A 6.00 15.00
ARA23 Tug McGraw C 12.00 30.00
ARA25 Robin Roberts C 12.00 30.00
ARA26 Frank Howard A 12.00 30.00
ARA27 Mickey Lolich D 6.00 15.00
ARA29 Tommy John C 6.00 15.00
ARA32 Dick Groat D 6.00 15.00
ARA33 Roy Face D 8.00 20.00
ARA34 Paul Blair D 6.00 15.00

2001 Topps Archives Reserve Rookie Reprint Relics

STATED ODDS 1:10
ARR1 Brooks Robinson Jsy 8.00 20.00
ARR2 Tony Conigliaro Jsy 10.00 25.00
ARR3 Frank Howard Jsy 2.50 6.00
ARR4 Don Sutton Jsy 4.00 10.00
ARR5 Ferguson Jenkins Jsy 4.00 10.00
ARR6 Frank Robinson Jsy 10.00 25.00
ARR7 Don Mattingly Jsy 12.00 30.00
ARR8 Willie Stargell Jsy 4.00 10.00
ARR9 Moose Skowron Jsy 8.00 20.00
ARR10 Fred Lynn Jsy 2.50 6.00
ARR11 George Brett Jsy 10.00 25.00
ARR12 Nolan Ryan Jsy 20.00 50.00
ARR13 Orlando Cepeda Jsy 6.00 15.00
ARR14 Reggie Jackson Jsy 5.00 12.00
ARR15 Steve Carlton Jsy 4.00 10.00
ARR16 Tom Seaver Jsy 4.00 10.00
ARR17 Thurman Munson Jsy 12.00 30.00
ARR18 Yogi Berra Jsy 6.00 15.00
ARR19 Willie McCovey Jsy 8.00 20.00
ARR20 Robin Yount Jsy 10.00 25.00
ARR21 Al Kaline Bat 8.00 20.00
ARR22 Carl Yastrzemski Bat 10.00 25.00
ARR23 Carlton Fisk Bat 6.00 15.00
ARR24 Dale Murphy Bat 10.00 25.00
ARR25 Dave Winfield Bat 4.00 10.00
ARR26 Dick Groat Bat 2.50 6.00
ARR27 Dom DiMaggio Bat 10.00 25.00
ARR28 Don Mattingly Bat 12.00 30.00
ARR29 Gary Carter Bat 6.00 15.00
ARR30 George Kell Bat 8.00 20.00
ARR31 Harmon Killebrew Bat 12.00 30.00
ARR32 Jackie Jensen Bat 15.00 40.00
ARR33 Jackie Robinson Bat 25.00 60.00
ARR34 Jim Piersall Bat 2.50 6.00
ARR35 Joe Adcock Bat 2.50 6.00
ARR36 Joe Carter Bat 4.00 10.00
ARR37 Johnny Mize Bat 8.00 20.00
ARR38 Kirk Gibson Bat 2.50 6.00
ARR39 Mickey Vernon Bat 6.00 15.00
ARR40 Mike Schmidt Bat 8.00
ARR41 Ryne Sandberg Bat 12.00 30.00
ARR42 Ozzie Smith Bat 12.00 30.00
ARR43 Ted Kluszewski Bat 8.00 20.00
ARR44 Wade Boggs Bat 6.00 15.00
ARR45 Willie Mays Bat 25.00 60.00
ARR46 Duke Snider Bat 4.00 10.00
ARR47 Harvey Kuenn Bat 6.00 15.00
ARR48 Robin Yount Bat 6.00 15.00
ARR49 Red Schoendienst Bat 4.00 10.00
ARR50 Elston Howard Bat 8.00 20.00
ARR51 Bob Allison Bat 6.00 15.00

2002 Topps Archives Reserve

COMPLETE SET (100) 40.00 80.00
1 Lee Smith 91 .60 1.50
2 Gaylord Perry 72 .60 1.50
3 Al Oliver 82 .60 1.50
4 Goose Gossage 77 .60 1.50
5 Bill Madlock 75 .60 1.50
6 Rod Carew 77 1.00 2.50
7 Fred Lynn 79 .60 1.50
8 Frank Robinson 66 1.00 2.50
9 Al Kaline 55 1.50 4.00
10 Len Dykstra 93 .60 1.50
11 Carlton Fisk 77 1.00 2.50
12 Nellie Fox 59 1.00 2.50
13 Reggie Jackson 69 1.00 2.50
14 Bob Gibson 68 1.00 2.50
15 Bill Buckner 85 .60 1.50
16 Harmon Killebrew 69 1.50 4.00
17 Gary Carter 85 .60 1.50
18 Dave Winfield 79 .60 1.50
19 Ozzie Smith 87 2.50 6.00
20 Dwight Evans 87 1.00 2.50
21 Dave Concepcion 79 .60 1.50
22 Joe Morgan 76 .60 1.50
23 Clete Boyer 62 .60 1.50
24 Will Clark 89 1.00 2.50
25 Lee May 69 .60 1.50
26 Kevin Mitchell 89 .60 1.50
27 Roger Maris 61 1.50 4.00
28 Mickey Lolich 71 .60 1.50
29 Luis Aparicio 60 .60 1.50
30 George Foster 77 .60 1.50
31 Don Mattingly 85 3.00 8.00
32 Fernando Valenzuela 86 .60 1.50
33 Bobby Bonds 73 .60 1.50
34 Jim Palmer 75 .60 1.50
35 Dennis Eckersley 92 .60 1.50
36 Kirby Puckett 88 1.50 4.00
37 Jose Cruz 83 .60 1.50
38 Richie Ashburn 58 1.00 2.50
39 Whitey Ford 61 1.00 2.50
40 Robin Roberts 52 .60 1.50
41 Don Newcombe 56 .60 1.50
42 Roy Campanella 53 1.50 4.00
43 Dennis Martinez 91 .60 1.50
44 Larry Doby 54 .60 1.50
45 Steve Garvey 77 .60 1.50
46 Thurman Munson 76 1.50 4.00
47 Dale Murphy 83 1.00 2.50
48 Moose Skowron 60 .60 1.50
49 Tom Seaver 69 1.00 2.50
50 Orlando Cepeda 61 .60 1.50
51 Graig Nettles 77 .60 1.50
52 Willie Stargell 71 1.00 2.50
53 Yogi Berra 54 1.50 4.00
54 Steve Carlton 72 .60 1.50
55 Don Sutton 72 .60 1.50
56 Brooks Robinson 64 1.00 2.50
57 Vida Blue 71 .60 1.50
58 Rollie Fingers 81 .60 1.50
59 Jim Bunning 65 .60 1.50
60 Nolan Ryan 73 4.00 10.00
61 Hank Aaron 57 3.00 8.00
62 Fergie Jenkins 71 .60 1.50
63 Andre Dawson 87 .60 1.50
64 Ernie Banks 58 1.50 4.00
65 Early Wynn 59 .60 1.50
66 Duke Snider 54 .60 1.50
67 Red Schoendienst 53 .60 1.50
68 Don Drysdale 62 1.00 2.50
69 Catfish Hunter 74 1.00 2.50
70 George Brett 80 3.00 8.00
71 Elston Howard 63 1.00 2.50
72 Wade Boggs 87 1.00 2.50
73 Keith Hernandez 79 .60 1.50
74 Billy Pierce 56 .60 1.50
75 Ted Kluszewski 54 1.00 2.50
76 Carl Yastrzemski 67 2.50 6.00
77 Bert Blyleven 73 .60 1.50
78 Tony Oliva 64 .60 1.50
79 Joe Carter 86 .60 1.50
80 Johnny Bench 70 1.50 4.00
81 Tony Gwynn 97 2.00 5.00
82 Mike Schmidt 80 3.00 8.00
83 Phil Niekro 69 .60 1.50
84 Juan Marichal 66 .60 1.50
85 Eddie Mathews 53 1.50 4.00
86 Boog Powell 69 1.00 2.50
87 Dwight Gooden 85 .60 1.50
88 Darryl Strawberry 87 .60 1.50
89 Roberto Clemente 66 4.00 10.00
90 Ryne Sandberg 90 3.00 8.00
91 Jack Clark 87 .60 1.50
92 Willie Mays 62 3.00 8.00
93 Ron Guidry 78 .60 1.50
94 Kirk Gibson 88 .60 1.50
95 Lou Brock 74 1.00 2.50
96 Robin Yount 82 1.50 4.00
97 Bill Mazeroski 60 1.00 2.50
98 Dave Parker 78 .60 1.50
99 Hoyt Wilhelm 64 .60 1.50
100 Warren Spahn 57 1.00 2.50

2002 Topps Archives Reserve Autographed Baseballs

ONE AUTO BALL PER BOX
STATED PRINT RUNS LISTED BELOW
EXCHANGE CARD ODDS 1:219 RETAIL
EXCHANGE DEADLINE 05/27/04
1 Luis Aparicio/1600 10.00 25.00
3 Yogi Berra/100 60.00 150.00
4 Lou Brock/400 20.00 50.00
5 Jim Bunning/500 30.00 60.00
6 Gary Carter/500 12.50 30.00
7 Goose Gossage/500 12.50 30.00
8 Fergie Jenkins/1000 10.00 25.00
9 Al Kaline/250 50.00 120.00
10 Harmon Killebrew/250 30.00 60.00
12 Joe Morgan/250 20.00 50.00
13 Graig Nettles/1600 10.00 25.00
14 Jim Palmer/400 12.50 30.00
15 Gaylord Perry/500 12.50 30.00
16 Brooks Robinson/500 20.00 50.00
17 Mike Schmidt/250 60.00 120.00
18 Duke Snider/100 50.00 100.00
19 Dave Winfield/1650 15.00 40.00
20 Robin Yount/250 50.00 100.00

2002 Topps Archives Reserve Autographs

COMMON CARD D-E 6.00 15.00
COMMON CARD B-C 6.00 15.00
GROUP A ODDS 1:1077 RET
GROUP B ODDS 1:1421 RET
GROUP C ODDS 1:947 RET
GROUP D ODDS 1:1421 RET
GROUP E ODDS 1:718 RET
OVERALL ODDS 1:15 HOBBY, 1:203 RETAIL
TRAAK Al Kaline 55 C 30.00 80.00
TRABR Brooks Robinson 64 B 15.00 40.00
TRADS Duke Snider 54 A 15.00 40.00
TRAEB Ernie Banks 58 A 50.00 100.00
TRAFJ Fergie Jenkins 71 E 6.00 15.00
TRAGC Gary Carter 85 B 25.00 60.00
TRAGN Graig Nettles 77 D 6.00 15.00
TRAGP Gaylord Perry 72 C 6.00 15.00
TRAHK H.Killebrew 69 C 30.00 60.00
TRAJM Joe Morgan 76 B 20.00 50.00
TRALA Luis Aparicio 60 D 10.00 25.00
TRALB Lou Brock 74 B 20.00 50.00
TRALS Lee Smith 91 E 6.00 15.00
TRAMS Mike Schmidt 80 A 50.00 100.00
TRARY Robin Yount 82 A 30.00 80.00
TRAWM Willie Mays 62 A 75.00 150.00
TRAYB Yogi Berra 54 A 60.00 150.00

2002 Topps Archives Reserve Bat Relics

OVERALL STATED ODDS 1:22 HOBBY
TRRCF Carlton Fisk 77 B 6.00 15.00
TRRDW Dave Winfield 79 C 6.00 15.00
TRROC Orlando Cepeda 61 B 6.00 15.00
TRRRM Roger Maris 61 A 15.00 40.00
TRRTM Thurman Munson 76 B 20.00 50.00
TRRCYB Carl Yastrzemski 67 B 15.00 40.00
TRRDMB Don Mattingly 85 B 10.00 25.00
TRREMB Eddie Mathews 53 B 8.00 20.00
TRRGBB George Brett 80 B 10.00 25.00
TRRHAB Hank Aaron 57 B 12.00 30.00

2002 Topps Archives Reserve Uniform Relics

OVERALL STATED ODDS 1:7 HOBBY
BR Brooks Robinson 64 Uni D 6.00 15.00
EB Ernie Banks 58 Uni C 6.00 15.00
GC Gary Carter 85 Jsy C 8.00 20.00
JB Johnny Bench 70 Uni D 8.00 20.00
JM Juan Marichal 66 Jsy A 8.00 20.00
KP Kirby Puckett 88 Jsy D 6.00 15.00
NF Nellie Fox 59 Uni C 8.00 20.00
NR Nolan Ryan 73 Jsy D 10.00 25.00
RS Red Schoendienst 53 Jsy B 6.00 15.00
RY Robin Yount 82 Uni D 6.00 15.00
TG Tony Gwynn 97 Jsy D 6.00 15.00
WB Wade Boggs 87 Jsy D 6.00 15.00
WC Will Clark 89 Jsy C 8.00 20.00
WM Willie Mays 62 Uni C 12.50 30.00
WS Willie Stargell 71 Uni D 6.00 15.00

2012 Topps Archives

COMP.SET W/O HARPER (240) 60.00 120.00
COMP.SET W/O SP's (200) 12.50 30.00
COMMON CARD (1-200) .15 .40
COMMON RC (1-200) .25 .60
COMMON SP (201-240) .75 2.00
SP 201-240 ODDS 1:4 HOBBY
PRINTING PLATE ODDS 1:777 HOBBY
PLATE PRINT RUN 1 SET PER COLOR
BLACK-CYAN-MAGENTA-YELLOW ISSUED
NO PLATE PRICING DUE TO SCARCITY
1 Matt Kemp .30 .75
2 Nick Swisher .30 .75
3 Jered Weaver .30 .75
4 Matt Garza .25 .60
5 Freddie Freeman .50 1.25
6 Paul Goldschmidt .40 1.00
7 Cole Hamels .30 .75
8 Matt Moore RC .60 1.50
9 Brett Gardner .30 .75
10 Ryan Braun .25 .60
11 Curtis Granderson .30 .75
12 Pablo Sandoval .30 .75
13 Mark Teixeira .30 .75
14 Yadier Molina .50 1.25
15 Madison Bumgarner .30 .75
16 Yunel Escobar .25 .60
17 Mat Latos .30 .75
18 Tom Seaver .25 .60
19 Brandon Beachy .25 .60
20 Robinson Cano .30 .75
21 Jeremy Hellickson .25 .60
22 Mickey Mantle 1.25 3.00
23 Chris Young .25 .60
24 Lance Berkman .30 .75
25 Dan Haren .25 .60
26 Paul Konerko .25 .60
27 Carl Crawford .30 .75
28 Melky Cabrera .25 .60
29 B.J. Upton .30 .75
30 Jacoby Ellsbury .30 .75
31 Joe Morgan .25 .60
32 Adam Jones .30 .75
33 Jon Lester .25 .60
34 Jaime Garcia .30 .75
35 Zack Greinke .40 1.00
36 Martin Prado .25 .60
37 Jose Valverde .30 .75
38 Billy Butler .25 .60
39 Jackie Robinson .40 1.00
40 Nelson Cruz .40 1.00
41 Corey Hart .25 .60
42 Aroldis Chapman .40 1.00
43 Wade Boggs .25 .60
44 Cal Ripken Jr. 1.25 3.00
45 Carlos Ruiz .25 .60
46 John Danks .25 .60
47 Drew Pomeranz RC .40 1.00
48 Grady Sizemore .30 .75
49 Mike Moustakas .30 .75
50 Albert Pujols .50 1.25
51 Roy Halladay .30 .75
52 Geovany Soto .30 .75
53 Adam Wainwright .30 .75
54 Jemile Weeks RC .40 1.00
55 Jesus Montero RC .40 1.00
56 Alex Rodriguez .50 1.25
57 Josh Beckett .25 .60
58 Tommy Hanson .25 .60
59 Hunter Pence .30 .75
60 Mariano Rivera .50 1.25
61 Brian McCann .30 .75
62 Hanley Ramirez .30 .75
63 Tim Hudson .30 .75
64 Derek Holland .25 .60
65 Jordan Zimmermann .30 .75
66 Andrew McCutchen .40 1.00
67 Justin Verlander .40 1.00
68 Drew Storen .25 .60
69 Ryan Zimmerman .30 .75
70 Joey Votto .40 1.00
71 Jimmy Rollins .30 .75
72 Ian Kinsler .30 .75
73 Shaun Marcum .25 .60
74 Ty Cobb .60 1.50
75 Reggie Jackson .25 .60
76 Victor Martinez .30 .75
77 Chipper Jones .40 1.00
78 Miguel Montero .25 .60
79 Ervin Santana .25 .60
80 Troy Tulowitzki .40 1.00
81 Adrian Beltre .40 1.00
82 Jose Reyes .25 .60
83 Craig Kimbrel .30 .75
84 Nyjer Morgan .25 .60
85 Matt Holliday .40 1.00
86 Trevor Cahill .25 .60
87 Clay Buchholz .25 .60
88 Mike Schmidt .60 1.50
89 Lou Gehrig .75 2.00
90 Joe Mauer .30 .75
91 Ted Lilly .25 .60
92 Jordan Walden .25 .60
93 Matt Harrison .25 .60
94 Anibal Sanchez .25 .60
95 Yoenis Cespedes RC 1.00 2.50
96 Phil Rizzuto .25 .60
97 Brett Lawrie RC .50 1.25
98 Johan Santana .30 .75
99 Brandon Belt .30 .75
100 Miguel Cabrera .40 1.00
101 Adrian Gonzalez .30 .75
102 Dee Gordon .25 .60
103 Ricky Romero .25 .60
104 Yovani Gallardo .30 .75
105 Torii Hunter .30 .75
106 Alex Gordon .30 .75
107 Josh Johnson .30 .75
108 Cliff Lee .30 .75
109 Catfish Hunter .25 .60
110 Jose Bautista .30 .75
111 John Axford .25 .60
112 Todd Helton .30 .75
113 Ryan Howard .30 .75
114 Jason Motte .25 .60
115 Gio Gonzalez .30 .75
116 Alex Avila .25 .60
117 George Brett .75 2.00
118 Desmond Jennings .30 .75
119 Yu Darvish RC 1.00 2.50
120 Tim Lincecum .30 .75
121 Heath Bell .25 .60
122 Dustin Pedroia .40 1.00
123 Ryan Vogelsong .25 .60
124 Brandon Phillips .25 .60
125 David Freese .25 .60
126 Rickie Weeks .25 .60
127 Evan Longoria .30 .75
128 Shin-Soo Choo .30 .75
129 Darryl Strawberry .15 .40
130 Mike Stanton .40 1.00
131 Elvis Andrus .30 .75
132 Ben Zobrist .30 .75
133 Mark Trumbo .25 .60
134 Chris Carpenter .30 .75
135 Mike Napoli .25 .60
136 David Ortiz .40 1.00
137 Jason Heyward .30 .75
138 Joe DiMaggio .75 2.00
139 Ivan Nova .30 .75
140 Buster Posey .50 1.25
141 J.P. Arencibia .25 .60
142 Ozzie Smith .50 1.25
143 Marco Scutaro .30 .75
144 Ike Davis .25 .60
145 Howie Kendrick .25 .60
146 Jarrod Parker RC .50 1.25
147 Justin Masterson .25 .60
148 R.A. Dickey .30 .75
149 Dustin Ackley .25 .60
150 Clayton Kershaw .60 1.50
151 Stephen Strasburg .40 1.00
152 Johnny Cueto .30 .75
153 Felix Hernandez .30 .75
154 Starlin Castro .30 .75
155 Ichiro Suzuki .50 1.25
156 Ubaldo Jimenez .25 .60
157 Carlos Gonzalez .30 .75
158 Michael Young .25 .60
159 David Price .30 .75
160 Prince Fielder .30 .75
161 Chase Utley .30 .75
162 Jayson Werth .30 .75
163 Aramis Ramirez .25 .60
164 Kevin Youkilis .40 1.00
165 Jay Bruce .30 .75
166 CC Sabathia .30 .75
167 Michael Pineda .25 .60
168 Carlos Santana .30 .75
169 Michael Morse .25 .60
170 Justin Upton .30 .75
171 Lucas Duda .30 .75
172 James Shields .25 .60
173 Daniel Hudson .25 .60
174 Asdrubal Cabrera .30 .75
175 Justin Morneau .30 .75
176 Eric Hosmer .30 .75
177 Shane Victorino .30 .75
178 Adam Lind .30 .75
179 Michael Bourn .25 .60
180 David Wright .30 .75
181 Matt Cain .30 .75
182 Ian Kennedy .25 .60
183 Dan Uggla .30 .75
184 Jim Rice .25 .60
185 Roberto Clemente 1.00 2.50
186 Brian Wilson .40 1.00
187 Nolan Ryan 1.25 3.00
188 Vance Worley .30 .75
189 Babe Ruth 1.00 2.50
190 Josh Hamilton .30 .75
191 Yogi Berra .40 1.00
192 Brad Peacock RC .40 1.00
193 Lonnie Chisenhall .25 .60
194 Gary Carter .25 .60
195 Brandon Morrow .25 .60
196 Andrew Bailey .25 .60
197 Allen Craig .30 .75
198 Casey Kotchman .25 .60
199 Mark Reynolds .25 .60
200 Derek Jeter 1.00 2.50
201 Don Mattingly SP 2.00 5.00
202 Mike Scott SP .75 2.00
203 Willie Mays SP 2.00 5.00
204 Ken Singleton SP .75 2.00
205 Bill Buckner SP .75 2.00
206 Dave Kingman SP .75 2.00
207 Vida Blue SP .75 2.00
208 Frank Howard SP .75 2.00
209 Will Clark SP 1.25 3.00
210 Sandy Koufax SP 2.00 5.00
211 Wally Joyner SP .75 2.00
212 Andy Van Slyke SP .75 2.00
213 Bill Madlock SP .75 2.00
214 Mitch Williams SP .75 2.00
215 Brett Butler SP .75 2.00
216 Bake McBride SP .75 2.00
217 Luis Tiant SP .75 2.00
218 Dave Righetti SP .75 2.00
219 Cecil Cooper SP .75 2.00
220 Ken Griffey Jr. SP 2.00 5.00
221 Jim Abbott SP .75 2.00
222 John Kruk SP .75 2.00
223 Cecil Fielder SP .75 2.00
224 Terry Pendleton SP .75 2.00
225 Ken Griffey SP .75 2.00
226 Jay Buhner SP .75 2.00
227 John Olerud SP .75 2.00
228 Ron Gant SP .75 2.00
229 Roger McDowell SP .75 2.00
230 Lance Parrish SP .75 2.00
231 Jack Clark SP .75 2.00
232 George Bell SP .75 2.00
233 Oscar Gamble SP .75 2.00
234 Shawon Dunston SP .75 2.00
235 Ed Kranepool SP .75 2.00
236 Chili Davis SP .75 2.00
237 Robin Ventura SP .75 2.00
238 Jose Oquendo SP .75 2.00
239 Von Hayes SP .75 2.00
240 Sid Bream SP .75 2.00
241 Bryce Harper SP RC 300.00 600.00

2012 Topps Archives Gold Foil

*GOLD 1-200 VET: 2.5X TO 6X BASIC
*GOLD 1-200 RC: 1.5X TO 4X BASIC RC
STATED ODDS 1:12 HOBBY

2012 Topps Archives 3-D

COMPLETE SET (15) 15.00 40.00
STATED ODDS 1:8 HOBBY
PRINTING PLATE ODDS 1:1196 HOBBY
PLATE PRINT RUN 1 SET PER COLOR
BLACK-CYAN-MAGENTA-YELLOW ISSUED
NO PLATE PRICING DUE TO SCARCITY
AK Al Kaline 1.00 2.50
BR Babe Ruth 2.50 6.00
CS CC Sabathia .75 2.00
CU Chase Utley .75 2.00
DP Dustin Pedroia 1.00 2.50
FH Felix Hernandez .75 2.00
JU Justin Upton .75 2.00
JV Joey Votto 1.00 2.50
MC Miguel Cabrera 1.00 2.50
MK Matt Kemp .75 2.00
MM Mickey Mantle 3.00 8.00
NC Nelson Cruz 1.00 2.50
RC Robinson Cano .75 2.00
WM Willie Mays 2.00 5.00
RCL Roberto Clemente 2.50 6.00

2012 Topps Archives Autographs

GROUP A ODDS 1:368 HOBBY
GROUP B ODDS 1:21 HOBBY
GROUP C ODDS 1:32 HOBBY
G.CARTER ODDS 1:12,440 HOBBY
Y.DARVISH ODDS 1:1685 HOBBY
EXCHANGE DEADLINE 04/30/2015
AO Al Oliver 6.00 15.00
AOT Amos Otis 5.00 12.00
AVS Andy Van Slyke 6.00 15.00
BB Bob Boone 5.00 12.00
BBE Buddy Bell 5.00 12.00
BBU Bill Buckner 8.00 20.00
BG Bobby Grich 6.00 15.00
BH Bud Harrelson 5.00 12.00
BHA Bryce Harper 200.00 500.00
BL Bill Lee 5.00 12.00
BM Bake McBride 6.00 15.00
BMA Bill Madlock 6.00 15.00
BOG Ben Oglivie 5.00 12.00
BP Boog Powell 8.00 20.00
BR Bobby Richardson 5.00 12.00
BRB Brett Butler 5.00 12.00
BT Bobby Thigpen 5.00 12.00
CC Cecil Cooper 5.00 12.00
CD Chili Davis 6.00 15.00
CF Cecil Fielder 8.00 20.00
CJ Cleon Jones 6.00 15.00
CL Carney Lansford 5.00 12.00
DD Doug DeCinces 5.00 12.00
DDR Doug Drabek 6.00 15.00
DG Dick Groat 6.00 15.00
DK Dave Kingman 6.00 15.00
DM Don Mattingly 40.00 80.00
DMA Dennis Martinez 6.00 15.00
DR Dave Righetti 6.00 15.00
EK Ed Kranepool 5.00 12.00
FH Frank Howard 6.00 15.00
GB George Bell 5.00 12.00
GC Gary Carter 50.00 120.00
GF George Foster 6.00 15.00
GL Greg Luzinski 6.00 15.00
HA Hank Aaron 250.00 500.00
JA Jim Abbott 6.00 15.00
JB Jay Buhner 6.00 15.00
JC Joe Charboneau 6.00 15.00
JCL Jack Clark 5.00 12.00
JKE Jimmy Key 5.00 12.00
JKR John Kruk 8.00 20.00
JMC Jack McDowell 5.00 12.00
JO John Olerud 5.00 12.00
JOQ Jose Oquendo 12.50 30.00
JW Jim Wynn 5.00 12.00
KG Ken Griffey Sr. 10.00 25.00
KGJ Ken Griffey Jr. 200.00 600.00
KS Ken Singleton 6.00 15.00
LP Lance Parrish 5.00 12.00
LT Luis Tiant 5.00 12.00
ML Mickey Lolich 6.00 15.00
MSC Mike Scott 5.00 12.00
MW Maury Wills 6.00 15.00
MWI Mitch Williams 10.00 25.00
OG Oscar Gamble 5.00 12.00
RG Ron Gant 6.00 15.00
RK Ron Kittle 5.00 12.00
RL Ray Lankford 5.00 12.00
RM Roger McDowell 6.00 15.00
RV Robin Ventura 5.00 12.00
SB Steve Balboni 5.00 12.00
SBR Sid Bream 6.00 15.00
SD Shawon Dunston 5.00 12.00
SK Sandy Koufax EXCH 300.00 600.00
SR Steve Rogers 5.00 12.00
TH Tom Herr 5.00 12.00
TP Terry Pendleton 8.00 20.00
VB Vida Blue 5.00 12.00
VH Von Hayes 5.00 12.00
WB Wally Backman 5.00 12.00
WC Will Clark 15.00 40.00
WJ Wally Joyner 6.00 15.00
WM Willie Mays 500.00 800.00
WW Willie Wilson 5.00 12.00
YD Yu Darvish 40.00 100.00
128 Hank Aaron/25

2012 Topps Archives Box Topper Autographs

KK1 Martin Kove 6.00 15.00
KK2 Billy Zabka 10.00 25.00

2012 Topps Archives Cloth Stickers

COMPLETE SET (25) 15.00 40.00
STATED ODDS 1:6 HOBBY
PRINTING PLATE ODDS 1:1196 HOBBY
PLATE PRINT RUN 1 SET PER COLOR
BLACK-CYAN-MAGENTA-YELLOW ISSUED
NO PLATE PRICING DUE TO SCARCITY
AM Andrew McCutchen 1.00 2.50
CC Chris Carpenter .75 2.00
CG Curtis Granderson .75 2.00
CH Catfish Hunter .60 1.50
CL Cliff Lee .75 2.00
DJ Derek Jeter 2.50 6.00
EH Eric Hosmer .75 2.00
GB George Brett 2.00 5.00
GC Gary Carter .60 1.50
JB Johnny Bench 1.00 2.50
JE Jacoby Ellsbury .75 2.00
JH Josh Hamilton .75 2.00
JM Joe Morgan .60 1.50
JR Jim Rice .60 1.50
JV Justin Verlander 1.00 2.50
KY Kevin Youkilis 1.00 2.50
MS Giancarlo Stanton 1.00 2.50
RB Ryan Braun .60 1.50
RC Rod Carew .60 1.50
RH Roy Halladay .75 2.00
RJ Reggie Jackson .60 1.50
RY Robin Yount 1.00 2.50
SC Steve Carlton .60 1.50
WS Willie Stargell .60 1.50
SCA Starlin Castro .75 2.00

2012 Topps Archives Combos

STATED ODDS 1:32 RETAIL
BH G.Brett/E.Hosmer 5.00 12.00
CK M.Cabrera/A.Kaline 2.50 6.00
KK C.Kershaw/S.Koufax 5.00 12.00
KR Matt Kemp 2.50 6.00
Jackie Robinson
LM T.Lincecum/W.Mays 5.00 12.00
SC R.Sandberg/S.Castro 5.00 12.00
SF CC Sabathia 2.00 5.00
Whitey Ford
SH M.Schmidt/R.Halladay 4.00 10.00
VB Joey Votto 2.50 6.00
Johnny Bench
YE Yastrzemski/J.Ellsbury 4.00 10.00

2012 Topps Archives Deckle Edge

COMPLETE SET (15) 12.50 30.00
STATED ODDS 1:12 HOBBY
PRINTING PLATE ODDS 1:1196 HOBBY
PLATE PRINT RUN 1 SET PER COLOR
BLACK-CYAN-MAGENTA-YELLOW ISSUED
NO PLATE PRICING DUE TO SCARCITY
1 Roy Halladay .75 2.00
2 Evan Longoria .75 2.00
3 Jose Bautista .75 2.00
4 Mike Napoli .60 1.50
5 David Freese .60 1.50
6 Ichiro Suzuki 1.25 3.00
7 Joe Mauer .75 2.00
8 Bob Gibson .60 1.50
9 Juan Marichal .60 1.50
10 Orlando Cepeda .60 1.50
11 Carl Yastrzemski 1.50 4.00
12 Roberto Clemente 2.50 6.00
13 Willie Mays 2.00 5.00
14 Harmon Killebrew 1.00 2.50
15 Joe Morgan .60 1.50

2012 Topps Archives In Action

STATED ODDS 1:32 RETAIL
I Ichiro Suzuki 2.00 5.00
CR Cal Ripken Jr. 5.00 12.00
JE Jacoby Ellsbury 1.25 3.00
JH Josh Hamilton 1.25 3.00
JK John Kruk .60 1.50
KG Ken Griffey Jr. 3.00 8.00
MN Mike Napoli 1.00 2.50
RC Roberto Clemente 6.00 15.00
TG Tony Gwynn 1.50 4.00
TT Troy Tulowitzki 1.50 4.00

2012 Topps Archives Relics

STATED ODDS 1:120 HOBBY
I Ichiro Suzuki 8.00 20.00
AA Alex Avila 5.00 12.00
AE Andre Ethier 5.00 12.00
AJ Adam Jones 5.00 12.00
AP Andy Pettitte 6.00 15.00
BB Billy Butler 3.00 8.00
BP Brandon Phillips 4.00 10.00
BU B.J. Upton 3.00 8.00
BW Brian Wilson 6.00 15.00
CB Clay Buchholz 3.00 8.00
CC Cecil Cooper 4.00 10.00
CG Carlos Gonzalez 3.00 8.00
DH Dan Haren 3.00 8.00
DM Don Mattingly 12.50 30.00
DO David Ortiz 4.00 10.00
DP Dustin Pedroia 5.00 12.00
DPR David Price 3.00 8.00
DU Dan Uggla 5.00 12.00
DW David Wright 5.00 12.00
EL Evan Longoria 3.00 8.00
FT Frank Thomas 10.00 25.00
GB George Bell 4.00 10.00
JC Johnny Cueto 3.00 8.00
JG Jaime Garcia 5.00 12.00
JH Jeremy Hellickson 4.00 10.00
JHY Jason Heyward 4.00 10.00
JM Jason Motte 5.00 12.00
JR Jimmy Rollins 4.00 10.00
JS James Shields 3.00 8.00
LB Lance Berkman 6.00 15.00
MB Madison Bumgarner 8.00 20.00
MC Miguel Cabrera 6.00 15.00
MM Mike Morse 4.00 10.00
MMO Matt Moore 4.00 10.00
MR Mariano Rivera 6.00 15.00
MT Mark Trumbo 4.00 10.00
MY Michael Young 3.00 8.00
NC Nelson Cruz 3.00 8.00
NS Nick Swisher 5.00 12.00
OC Orlando Cepeda 5.00 12.00
PN Phil Niekro 5.00 12.00
PS Pablo Sandoval 4.00 10.00
RC Roberto Clemente 75.00 150.00
RC Rod Carew 4.00 10.00
RR Ricky Romero 3.00 8.00
RZ Ryan Zimmerman 4.00 10.00
SC Starlin Castro 8.00 20.00
SCA Steve Carlton 10.00 25.00
TH Tommy Hanson 3.00 8.00
THD Tim Hudson 3.00 8.00
THE Todd Helton 3.00 8.00
THU Torii Hunter 3.00 8.00
TL Tim Lincecum 6.00 15.00
WS Willie Stargell 10.00 25.00
YG Yovani Gallardo 3.00 8.00
ZG Zack Greinke 4.00 10.00

2012 Topps Archives Reprints

COMPLETE SET (50) 40.00 80.00
STATED ODDS 1:4 HOBBY
PRINTING PLATE ODDS 1:1196 HOBBY
PLATE PRINT RUN 1 SET PER COLOR
BLACK-CYAN-MAGENTA-YELLOW ISSUED
NO PLATE PRICING DUE TO SCARCITY
8 Don Mattingly 1.50 4.00
19 George Brett 1.50 4.00
28 Brooks Robinson .50 1.25
62 Monte Irvin .50 1.25
70 Harmon Killebrew .75 2.00
80 Darryl Strawberry .30 .75
80 Rod Carew .50 1.25
81 Jim Palmer .50 1.25
88 Bob Feller .50 1.25
95 Johnny Bench .75 2.00
110 Yogi Berra .75 2.00
116 Ozzie Smith 1.00 2.50
130 Reggie Jackson .50 1.25
150 Duke Snider .50 1.25
160 Whitey Ford .50 1.25
160 Eddie Murray .50 1.25
164 Roberto Clemente 2.00 5.00
164 Harmon Killebrew .75 2.00
176 Willie McCovey .50 1.25
191 Yogi Berra .75 2.00
191 Ralph Kiner .50 1.25
220 Tom Seaver .50 1.25
223 Robin Yount .75 2.00
228 George Brett 1.50 4.00
230 Joe Morgan .50 1.25
243 Larry Doby .50 1.25
244 Willie Mays 1.50 4.00
260 Reggie Jackson .50 1.25
287 Carl Yastrzemski 1.25 3.00
295 Gary Carter .50 1.25
300 Tom Seaver .50 1.25
325 Juan Marichal .50 1.25
333 Fergie Jenkins .50 1.25
337 Joe Morgan .50 1.25
338 Sparky Anderson .50 1.25
380 Willie Stargell .50 1.25
385 Jim Hunter .50 1.25
420 Juan Marichal .50 1.25
440 Willie McCovey .50 1.25
440 Roberto Clemente 2.00 5.00
490 Cal Ripken Jr. 2.50 6.00
498 Wade Boggs .50 1.25
500 Duke Snider .50 1.25
530 Dave Winfield .50 1.25
550 Brooks Robinson .50 1.25
575 Jim Palmer .50 1.25
635 Robin Yount .75 2.00
640 Eddie Murray .50 1.25
660 Tony Gwynn .75 2.00
712 Nolan Ryan 2.50 6.00

2012 Topps Archives Stickers

COMPLETE SET (25) 12.50 30.00
STATED ODDS 1:8 HOBBY
PRINTING PLATE ODDS 1:1196 HOBBY
PLATE PRINT RUN 1 SET PER COLOR
BLACK-CYAN-MAGENTA-YELLOW ISSUED
NO PLATE PRICING DUE TO SCARCITY
I Ichiro Suzuki 1.25 3.00
AG Adrian Gonzalez .75 2.00
CG Carlos Gonzalez .75 2.00
CK Clayton Kershaw 1.50 4.00
CY Carl Yastrzemski 1.50 4.00
DJ Derek Jeter 2.50 6.00
IK Ian Kennedy .60 1.50
JB Jose Bautista .75 2.00
JH Josh Hamilton .75 2.00
JM Joe Mauer .75 2.00
JP Jim Palmer .60 1.50
JV Justin Verlander 1.00 2.50
MC Miguel Cabrera 1.00 2.50
MM Mickey Mantle 3.00 8.00
MR Mariano Rivera 1.25 3.00
MT Mark Teixeira .75 2.00
PS Pablo Sandoval .75 2.00
RB Ryan Braun .60 1.50
RH Ryan Howard .75 2.00
RM Roger Maris 1.00 2.50
TL Tim Lincecum .75 2.00
TS Tom Seaver .60 1.50
TT Troy Tulowitzki 1.00 2.50
WM Willie Mays 2.00 5.00
RHA Roy Halladay .75 2.00

2013 Topps Archives

COMP.SET W/O ERRORS (245) 60.00 120.00
COMP.SET W/O SP's (200) 12.50 30.00
SP 201-245 ODDS 1:4 HOBBY
ERROR VARIATION ODDS 1:1717 HOBBY
PRINTING PLATE ODDS 1:536 HOBBY
1 Babe Ruth .60 1.50
2 Gary Carter .20 .50
3 Carlos Beltran .20 .50
4 Marco Scutaro .20 .50
5 Allen Craig .20 .50
6 Adrian Gonzalez .20 .50
7 Jon Jay .15 .40
8 Roy Halladay .20 .50
9 Ryan Braun .20 .50
10 Matt Kemp .20 .50
11 Joe Nathan .15 .40
12 Jarrod Parker .15 .40
13 Ryan Zimmerman .20 .50
14 Yoenis Cespedes .25 .60
15 Mike Morse .15 .40
16 Cal Ripken Jr. .75 2.00
17 Hanley Ramirez .20 .50
18 Jon Lester .20 .50
19 Tyler Skaggs RC .40 1.00
20A Albert Pujols .30 .75
20B Jason Heyward SP 40.00 80.00
21 Adrian Beltre .25 .60
22 Alex Rios .20 .50
23 Jordan Zimmermann .20 .50
24 Ben Zobrist .20 .50
25 Dexter Fowler .20 .50
26 Jayson Werth .20 .50
27 Manny Machado RC 1.50 4.00
28 Mike Schmidt .40 1.00
29 Angel Pagan .15 .40
30 Yu Darvish .25 .60
31 Brock Holt RC .30 .75
32 Wade Boggs .20 .50
33 Corey Hart .15 .40
34 Dwight Gooden .15 .40
35 Adam Dunn .20 .50
36 Wade Miley .15 .40
37 Elvis Andrus .20 .50
38 Derek Jeter .60 1.50
39 Lance Lynn .15 .40
40 Prince Fielder .20 .50
41 Doug Fister .15 .40
42 Mariano Rivera .30 .75
43 Starling Marte .20 .50
44 Chris Davis .20 .50
45 Chase Headley .15 .40
46 Justin Morneau .20 .50
47 Ryan Howard .20 .50
48 Ryne Sandberg .50 1.25
49 Alcides Escobar .20 .50
50 Miguel Cabrera .25 .60
51 Carlos Gonzalez .20 .50
52 Desmond Jennings .20 .50
53 Brandon Phillips .15 .40
54 Cliff Lee .20 .50
55 CC Sabathia .20 .50
56 Josh Reddick .15 .40
57 Todd Frazier .15 .40
58 Cole Hamels .20 .50
59 Joe Morgan .20 .50
60 Robinson Cano .20 .50
61 Shelby Miller RC .60 1.50
62 Jacoby Ellsbury .20 .50
63 David Freese .15 .40
64 Asdrubal Cabrera .20 .50
65 Paul Konerko .20 .50
66 Tim Hudson .20 .50
67 Rickie Weeks .15 .40
68 Matt Harrison .15 .40
69 Eddie Mathews .25 .60
70 Ozzie Smith .30 .75
71 Darwin Barney .15 .40
72 Harmon Killebrew .25 .60
73 Aroldis Chapman .25 .60
74 Miguel Montero .15 .40
75 C.J. Wilson .15 .40
76 Fernando Rodney .15 .40
77 Tony Cingrani RC .50 1.25
78 Johan Santana .20 .50
79 Josh Willingham .20 .50
80 Jered Weaver .20 .50
81 Will Middlebrooks .15 .40
82 Tom Seaver .20 .50
83 Jim Johnson .15 .40
84 Coco Crisp .15 .40
85 Tony Perez .20 .50
86 Jackie Robinson .25 .60
87 A.J. Burnett .15 .40
88 Derek Holland .15 .40
89 Barry Zito .20 .50
90 Matt Cain .20 .50
91 Brandon Beachy .15 .40
92 Ken Griffey Jr. .50 1.25
93 Ian Desmond .15 .40
94 Curtis Granderson .20 .50
95 Reggie Jackson .20 .50
96 Edwin Encarnacion .25 .60
97 David Wright .20 .50
98 Jesus Montero .15 .40
99 Joey Votto .25 .60
100 Bryce Harper .40 1.00
101 Andrew McCutchen .25 .60
102 Matt Moore .20 .50
103 Mike Minor .15 .40
104 Gio Gonzalez .20 .50
105 Mike Moustakas .20 .50
106 Tim Lincecum .20 .50
107 Kendrys Morales .15 .40
108 Austin Jackson .15 .40
109 Sergio Romo .15 .40
110 Josh Hamilton .20 .50
111 Brandon Morrow .15 .40
112 Kris Medlen .20 .50
113 Jake Peavy .15 .40
114 Robin Yount .25 .60
115 Paul Goldschmidt .25 .60
116 Billy Butler .15 .40
117 Carlos Santana .20 .50
118 Brandon Belt .20 .50
119 Ian Kinsler .20 .50
120 Ted Williams .50 1.25
121 Ian Kennedy .15 .40
122 R.A. Dickey .20 .50
123 Jean Segura .20 .50
124 George Brett .50 1.25
125 Kyle Lohse .15 .40
126 Aaron Hill .15 .40
127 David Price .20 .50
128 Mark Trumbo .15 .40
129 Madison Bumgarner .20 .50
130 Clayton Kershaw .40 1.00
131 Salvador Perez .20 .50
132 Bronson Arroyo .15 .40
133 Jurickson Profar RC .30 .75
134 Wei-Yin Chen .15 .40
135 Adam Wainwright .20 .50
136 Nelson Cruz .25 .60
137 Brian McCann .20 .50
138 David Murphy .15 .40
139 Matt Holliday .25 .60
140 Dylan Bundy RC .60 1.50
141 Adam Jones .20 .50
142 Willie Stargell .20 .50
143 Jake Odorizzi RC .30 .75
144 Paul Molitor .25 .60
145 Alfonso Soriano .20 .50
146 Eddie Murray .20 .50
147 Hiroki Kuroda .15 .40
148 Dustin Pedroia .25 .60
149 Hisashi Iwakuma .20 .50
150 Jose Bautista .20 .50
151 Jason Motte .15 .40
152 Craig Kimbrel .20 .50
153 David Ortiz .25 .60
154 Yovani Gallardo .15 .40
155 Wilin Rosario .15 .40
156 Goose Gossage .20 .50
157 Evan Longoria .20 .50
158 Mike Olt RC .30 .75
159 Troy Tulowitzki .25 .60
160 Felix Hernandez .20 .50
161 Anthony Rizzo .30 .75
162 Carlos Ruiz .15 .40
163 Hyun-Jin Ryu RC .60 1.50
164 Dan Uggla .15 .40
165 Stephen Strasburg .25 .60
166 Ryan Vogelsong .15 .40
167 Rod Carew .20 .50
168 Pablo Sandoval .20 .50
169 Pedro Alvarez .15 .40
170 Joe Mauer .20 .50
171 Jay Bruce .20 .50
172 Freddie Freeman .30 .75
173 Jason Kipnis .20 .50
174 Ike Davis .15 .40
175 Yogi Berra .25 .60
176 Jose Altuve .20 .50
177 Starlin Castro .15 .40
178 Giancarlo Stanton .25 .60
179 Tommy Milone .15 .40
180 Buster Posey .30 .75
181 Avisail Garcia RC .30 .75
182 Andre Ethier .20 .50
183 Scott Diamond .15 .40
184 Kyle Seager .15 .40
185 Stan Musial .40 1.00
186 Brett Lawrie .20 .50
187 Alex Gordon .20 .50
188 Mat Latos .20 .50
189 Homer Bailey .15 .40
190 Tony Gwynn .25 .60
191 Mark Teixeira .20 .50
192 Adam Eaton RC .40 1.00
193 Jim Palmer .20 .50
194 Yadier Molina .30 .75
195 Dave Winfield .20 .50
196 Johnny Cueto .20 .50
197 Chris Sale .25 .60
198 Jason Heyward .20 .50
199 Eric Hosmer .20 .50
200 Mike Trout 2.00 5.00
201 John Mayberry SP 1.25 3.00
202 Mike Greenwell SP 1.25 3.00
203 Denny McLain SP 1.25 3.00
204 Charlie Hough SP 1.25 3.00
205 Ruben Sierra SP 1.25 3.00
206 Tim Salmon SP 1.25 3.00
207 Lee May SP 1.25 3.00
208 Keith Miller SP 1.25 3.00
209 Dwight Evans SP 1.25 3.00
210 Bob Tewksbury SP 1.25 3.00
211 Tom Brunansky SP 1.25 3.00
212 Otis Nixon SP 1.25 3.00
213 Juan Samuel SP 1.25 3.00
214 Fred McGriff SP 1.50 4.00
215 Bob Welch SP 1.25 3.00
216 Jesse Barfield SP 1.25 3.00
217 Mookie Wilson SP 1.25 3.00
218 Darrell Evans SP 1.25 3.00
219 Dave Lopes SP 1.25 3.00
220 Ellis Burks SP 1.25 3.00
221 Hal Morris SP 1.25 3.00
222 Howard Johnson SP 1.25 3.00
223 Matt Williams SP 1.25 3.00
224 Paul Blair SP 1.25 3.00
225 Kent Hrbek SP 1.25 3.00
226 Larry Bowa SP 1.25 3.00
227 Mickey Rivers SP 1.25 3.00
228 Delino DeShields SP 1.25 3.00
229 Hubie Brooks SP 1.25 3.00
230 Ray Knight SP 1.25 3.00
231 Kevin McReynolds SP 1.25 3.00
232 Travis Fryman SP 1.25 3.00
233 Vince Coleman SP 1.25 3.00
234 Don Baylor SP 1.25 3.00
235 Gregg Jefferies SP 1.25 3.00
236 Jesse Orosco SP 1.25 3.00
237 Sid Fernandez SP 1.25 3.00
238 Frank White SP 1.25 3.00
239 Dave Parker SP 1.25 3.00
240 Darren Daulton SP 1.25 3.00
241 Fred Lynn SP 1.25 3.00
242 Kevin Mitchell SP 1.25 3.00
243 Lloyd Moseby SP 1.25 3.00
244 Eric Davis SP 1.25 3.00
245 Leon Durham SP 1.25 3.00
400 Joey Votto SP 20.00 50.00
414 Chris Sale SP 30.00 60.00
497 Dylan Bundy SP 50.00 100.00
USA1 George W. Bush

2013 Topps Archives Day Glow

*DAY GLOW: 1.5X TO 4X BASIC
*DAY GLOW RC: 1X TO 2.5X BASIC RC
38 Derek Jeter 8.00 20.00

2013 Topps Archives Gold

*GOLD: 2.5X TO 6X BASIC
*GOLD RC: 1.5X TO 4X BASIC RC
STATED ODDS 1:13 HOBBY
STATED PRINT RUN 199 SER.#'d SETS
38 Derek Jeter 20.00 50.00
100 Bryce Harper 15.00 40.00

2013 Topps Archives '72 Basketball Design

COMPLETE SET (20) 50.00 *100.00
STATED ODDS 1:24 HOBBY
PRINTING PLATE ODDS 1:1020 HOBBY
PLATE PRINT RUN 1 SET PER COLOR
BLACK-CYAN-MAGENTA-YELLOW ISSUED
NO PLATE PRICING DUE TO SCARCITY
AM Andrew McCutchen 2.00 5.00
CC CC Sabathia 1.50 4.00
DW Dave Winfield 1.50 4.00
GS Giancarlo Stanton 2.00 5.00
JB Johnny Bench 2.00 5.00
JH Jason Heyward 1.50 4.00
JM Joe Morgan
KG Ken Griffey Jr. 4.00 10.00
LB Lou Brock 1.50 4.00
MK Matt Kemp 1.50 4.00
OS Ozzie Smith 2.50 6.00
PF Prince Fielder 1.50 4.00
RC Rod Carew 1.50 4.00
RJ Reggie Jackson 1.50 4.00
TG Tony Gwynn 2.00 5.00
TS Tom Seaver 1.50 4.00
TW Ted Williams 4.00 10.00
WM Willie McCovey 1.50 4.00

WS Willie Stargell 1.50 4.00
YD Yu Darvish 2.00 5.00

2013 Topps Archives '83 All-Stars

COMPLETE SET (30) 12.50 30.00
STATED ODDS 1:4 HOBBY
PRINTING PLATE ODDS 1:1020 HOBBY
PLATE PRINT RUN 1 SET PER COLOR
BLACK-CYAN-MAGENTA-YELLOW ISSUED
NO PLATE PRICING DUE TO SCARCITY
AD Andre Dawson .50 1.25
AM Andrew McCutchen .60 1.50
AP Albert Pujols .75 2.00
BH Bryce Harper 1.00 2.50
BP Buster Posey .75 2.00
CF Carlton Fisk .50 1.25
CR Cal Ripken Jr. 2.00 5.00
DE Darrell Evans .40 1.00
DJ Derek Jeter 1.50 4.00
DS Darryl Strawberry .40 1.00
DW Dave Winfield .50 1.25
FL Fred Lynn .40 1.00
GB George Brett 1.25 3.00
GC Gary Carter .50 1.25
GS Giancarlo Stanton .60 1.50
JB Johnny Bench .60 1.50
JR Jim Rice .50 1.25
JV Justin Verlander .60 1.50
LD Leon Durham .40 1.00
MC Miguel Cabrera .60 1.50
MS Mike Schmidt 1.00 2.50
MT Mike Trout 5.00 12.00
NR Nolan Ryan 2.00 5.00
PG Pedro Guerrero .25 .60
PM Paul Molitor .60 1.50
RC Robinson Cano .50 1.25
RH Rickey Henderson .60 1.50
RS Ryne Sandberg 1.25 3.00
SS Stephen Strasburg .60 1.50
TG Tony Gwynn .60 1.50

2013 Topps Archives '89 All-Stars Retail

AP Albert Pujols 20.00 50.00
AR Anthony Rizzo 10.00 25.00
BH Bryce Harper 50.00 100.00
CK Clayton Kershaw 20.00 50.00
CS Chris Sale ·10.00 25.00
DF David Freese 8.00 20.00
DJ Derek Jeter 20.00 50.00
GG Gio Gonzalez 10.00 25.00
JP Jurickson Profar 10.00 25.00
JV Justin Verlander 20.00 50.00
MC Matt Cain 10.00 25.00
MCA Miguel Cabrera 15.00 40.00
MM Manny Machado 60.00 120.00
MT Mike Trout 50.00 100.00
RA R.A. Dickey 8.00 20.00
RB Ryan Braun 8.00 20.00
RC Robinson Cano 12.50 30.00
WM Will Middlebrooks 8.00 20.00
YC Yoenis Cespedes 15.00 40.00
YD Yu Darvish 10.00 25.00

2013 Topps Archives Dual Fan Favorites

BG Dante Bichette .75 2.00
Carlos Gonzalez
DC Rob Dibble 1.00 2.50
Aroldis Chapman
DP Eric Davis .60 1.50
Brandon Phillips
DR Darren Daulton .60 1.50
Carlos Ruiz
EP Dwight Evans 1.00 2.50
Dustin Pedroia
FW Chuck Finley .75 2.00
Jered Weaver
GJ Kirk Gibson .60 1.50
Austin Jackson
LE Fred Lynn .75 2.00
Jacoby Ellsbury
MB John Mayberry .60 1.50
Billy Butler
MS Kevin Mitchell .75 2.00
Pablo Sandoval
NU Otis Nixon .75 2.00
B.J. Upton
PM D.Parker/A.McCutchen 1.00 2.50
SC Ruben Sierra 1.00 2.50
Nelson Cruz
SR Juan Samuel .75 2.00
Jimmy Rollins
WP M.Williams/B.Posey 1.25 3.00

2013 Topps Archives Fan Favorites Autographs

STATED ODDS 1:153 HOBBY
PELE ODDS 1:41,000 HOBBY
EXCHANGE DEADLINE 5/31/2016
AH Al Hrabosky 6.00 15.00
BS Bret Saberhagen 8.00 20.00
BSA Benito Santiago 5.00 12.00
BT Bob Tewksbury 5.00 12.00
BW Bob Welch 10.00 25.00
CF Chuck Finley 5.00 12.00
CH Charlie Hough 5.00 12.00
DB Don Baylor 6.00 15.00
DBO Dennis Boyd 5.00 12.00
DC Dave Concepcion EXCH 12.00 30.00
DD Delino DeShields 5.00 12.00
DDA Darren Daulton 8.00 20.00
DE Darrell Evans 5.00 12.00
DG Dan Gladden 6.00 15.00
DL Dave Lopes 6.00 15.00
DM Denny McLain 8.00 20.00
DP Dave Parker 10.00 25.00
EB Ellis Burks 5.00 12.00
ED Eric Davis 6.00 15.00
FL Fred Lynn 10.00 25.00
FM Fred McGriff 8.00 20.00
FW Frank White 5.00 12.00
GG Gary Gaetti 5.00 12.00
GJ Gregg Jefferies 6.00 15.00
GN Graig Nettles 6.00 15.00
HB Hubie Brooks 5.00 12.00
HJ Howard Johnson 8.00 20.00
HM Hal Morris 5.00 12.00
JB Jesse Barfield 5.00 12.00
JD Jody Davis 5.00 12.00
JM John Mayberry 6.00 15.00
JO Jesse Orosco 5.00 12.00
JS Juan Samuel 5.00 12.00
KH Kent Hrbek 5.00 12.00
KM Kevin McReynolds 6.00 15.00
KMI Keith Miller 5.00 12.00
KML Kevin Mitchell 6.00 15.00
LB Larry Bowa 6.00 15.00
LD Leon Durham 5.00 12.00
LM Lee May 6.00 15.00
LMO Lloyd Moseby 5.00 12.00
LS Lee Smith 6.00 15.00
MG Mike Greenwell 8.00 20.00
MR Mickey Rivers 6.00 15.00
MT Mickey Tettleton 5.00 12.00
MW Mookie Wilson 8.00 20.00
MWI Matt Williams 5.00 12.00
ON Otis Nixon 6.00 15.00
PB Paul Blair 5.00 12.00
RD Ron Darling 8.00 20.00
RK Ray Knight 5.00 12.00
RR Rick Reuschel 5.00 12.00
RSI Ruben Sierra 5.00 12.00
SF Sid Fernandez 5.00 12.00
TB Tom Brunansky 5.00 12.00
TF Travis Fryman 6.00 15.00
TS Tim Salmon 5.00 12.00
VC Vince Coleman 8.00 20.00
75-P Pele

2013 Topps Archives Four-In-One

COMPLETE SET (15) 12.50 30.00
STATED ODDS 1:8 HOBBY
BBMP Berra/Bench/Mauer/Posey .75 2.00
BPDS Don Baylor/Dave Parker/Eric Davis/Darryl Strawberry .40 1.00
CHNL Vince Coleman/Rickey Henderson/Otis Nixon/Kenny Lofton .60 1.50
CMGT Cobb/Mays/Griffey/Trout 5.00 12.00
FSRV Fel/Seav/Ryan/Verland 2.00 5.00
GBRS Gwynn/Boggs/Ripken/Sand 2.00 5.00
MCWP McCov/Clark/Will/Posey .75 2.00
OPJR O'Neill/Pett/Jeter/Rivera 1.50 4.00
PDCP Posey/Dickey/Cab/Price .75 2.00
RGBJ Ruth/Gehrig/Berra/Reggie 1.50 4.00
RJMJ Ruth/Reg/Matting/Jeter 1.50 4.00
SKCK Spahn/Koufax/Carlton/Kersh 1.25 3.00
SWGJ Darryl Strawberry/Mookie Wilson/Dwight Gooden/Howard Johnson .40 1.00
THBK Trout/Harper/Braun/Kemp 5.00 12.00
WRYC Will/Robin/Yaz/Cab 1.25 3.00

2013 Topps Archives Gallery Of Heroes

STATED ODDS 1:31 HOBBY
AP Albert Pujols 2.50 6.00
BP Buster Posey 2.50 6.00
BR Babe Ruth 5.00 12.00
CR Cal Ripken Jr. 6.00 15.00
DJ Derek Jeter 5.00 12.00
JR Jackie Robinson 2.00 5.00
LG Lou Gehrig 4.00 10.00
MC Miguel Cabrera 4.00 10.00
MR Mariano Rivera 2.50 6.00
MT Mike Trout 8.00 20.00
RC Roberto Clemente 5.00 12.00
SK Sandy Koufax 4.00 10.00
TW Ted Williams 4.00 10.00
WM Willie Mays 4.00 10.00
YB Yogi Berra 2.00 5.00

2013 Topps Archives Greatest Moments Box Toppers

STATED ODDS 1:8 HOBBY BOXES
STATED PRINT RUN 99 SER.#'d SETS
1 Jim Rice 12.50 30.00
2 Ryan Braun 6.00 15.00
3 Juan Marichal 12.50 30.00
4 Bob Gibson 10.00 25.00
5 David Freese 8.00 20.00
6 Jim Palmer 8.00 20.00
7 Mike Schmidt 15.00 40.00
8 R.A. Dickey 10.00 25.00
9 Dave Concepcion 12.50 30.00
10 Kirk Gibson 10.00 25.00
11 Manny Machado 30.00 60.00
12 Ken Griffey Jr. 20.00 50.00
13 Will Clark 12.50 30.00
14 Miguel Cabrera 15.00 40.00
15 Bryce Harper 40.00 80.00
16 Mike Trout 40.00 80.00
17 Yu Darvish 6.00 15.00
18 Yoenis Cespedes 12.50 30.00
19 Robinson Cano 15.00 40.00
20 Tom Seaver 15.00 40.00
21 Lou Brock 12.50 30.00
22 Harmon Killebrew 12.50 30.00
23 Vida Blue 6.00 15.00
24 Fergie Jenkins 6.00 15.00
25 Willie Stargell 10.00 25.00

2013 Topps Archives Heavy Metal Autographs

STATED ODDS 1:153 HOBBY
EXCHANGE DEADLINE 5/31/2016
AR Axl Rose 300.00 500.00
BB Bobbie Brown 12.50 30.00
DS Dee Snider 10.00 25.00
KW Kip Winger 6.00 15.00
LF Lita Ford 12.50 30.00
RB Reb Beach 8.00 20.00
SB Sebastian Bach 10.00 25.00
SI Scott Ian 15.00 40.00
SP Stephen Pearcy 10.00 25.00
TL Tommy Lee 20.00 50.00

2013 Topps Archives Mini Tall Boys

COMPLETE SET (40) 20.00 50.00
STATED ODDS 1:5 HOBBY
PRINTING PLATE ODDS 1:1020 HOBBY
PLATE PRINT RUN 1 SET PER COLOR
BLACK-CYAN-MAGENTA-YELLOW ISSUED
NO PLATE PRICING DUE TO SCARCITY
AB Albert Pujols .75 2.00
AK Al Kaline .60 1.50
AR Anthony Rizzo .75 2.00
BH Bryce Harper 1.00 2.50
BP Buster Posey .75 2.00
CK Clayton Kershaw 1.00 2.50
CR Cal Ripken Jr. 2.00 5.00
CS Chris Sale .60 1.50
DB Dante Bichette .40 1.00
DBU Dylan Bundy 1.00 2.50
DC Dave Concepcion .40 1.00
DE Dwight Evans .40 1.00
DF David Freese .40 1.00
DJ Derek Jeter 1.50 4.00
DM Denny McLain .40 1.00
DP Dave Parker .40 1.00
DS Dave Stewart .40 1.00
DW David Wright .50 1.25
EB Ellis Burks .40 1.00
ED Eric Davis .40 1.00
FL Fred Lynn .40 1.00
FM Fred McGriff .50 1.25
FW Frank White .40 1.00
GG Gio Gonzalez .50 1.25
KG Kirk Gibson .25 .60
KM Kevin Mitchell .40 1.00
MC Miguel Cabrera .60 1.50
MG Mike Greenwell .40 1.00
MS Mike Schmidt 1.00 2.50
MT Mike Trout 5.00 12.00
MW Matt Williams .40 1.00
ON Otis Nixon .40 1.00
RB Ryan Braun .50 1.25
RC Robinson Cano .50 1.25
RCL Roberto Clemente 1.50 4.00
RD Rob Dibble .40 1.00
SS Stephen Strasburg .60 1.50
WC Will Clark .50 1.25
WM Will Middlebrooks .40 1.00
YC Yoenis Cespedes .60 1.50

2013 Topps Archives Relics

STATED ODDS 1:216 HOBBY
AB Adrian Beltre 4.00 10.00
AD Adam Dunn 4.00 10.00
AE Andre Ethier 3.00 8.00
AJ Austin Jackson 5.00 12.00
AM Andrew McCutchen 5.00 12.00
AW Adam Wainwright 4.00 10.00
BB Billy Butler 3.00 8.00
BG Brett Gardner 4.00 10.00
BH Bryce Harper 12.50 30.00
BM Brandon Morrow 3.00 8.00
BP Brandon Phillips 4.00 10.00
BR Ben Revere 3.00 8.00
CF Cecil Fielder 10.00 25.00
CS Carlos Santana 3.00 8.00
DB Domonic Brown 5.00 12.00
DG Dwight Gooden 6.00 15.00
EA Elvis Andrus 3.00 8.00
EL Evan Longoria 4.00 10.00
GS Gary Sheffield 4.00 10.00
HR Hanley Ramirez 3.00 8.00
ID Ike Davis 4.00 10.00
IDE Ian Desmond 3.00 8.00
IK Ian Kinsler 4.00 10.00
JB Johnny Bench 12.50 30.00
JBR Jay Bruce 6.00 15.00
JK Jason Kubel 3.00 8.00
JM Jesus Montero 3.00 8.00
JV Justin Verlander 6.00 15.00
JZ Jordan Zimmermann 3.00 8.00
KG Ken Griffey Sr. 6.00 15.00
LT Luis Tiant 8.00 20.00
MB Madison Bumgarner 6.00 15.00
MC Matt Cain 5.00 12.00
MH Matt Harvey 8.00 20.00
MM Matt Moore 3.00 8.00
MMO Miguel Montero 3.00 8.00
MMS Mike Moustakas 3.00 8.00
MT Mike Trout 20.00 50.00
NC Nelson Cruz 3.00 8.00
NM1 Nick Markakis Jsy 5.00 12.00
NM2 Nick Markakis Bat 10.00 25.00
PA Pedro Alvarez 4.00 10.00
PF Prince Fielder 6.00 15.00
PG Paul Goldschmidt 4.00 10.00
PK Paul Konerko 3.00 8.00
PO Paul O'Neill 10.00 25.00
RH Ryan Howard 5.00 12.00
RZ Ryan Zimmerman 4.00 10.00
SC Starlin Castro 4.00 10.00
SSC Shin-Soo Choo 5.00 12.00
TC Trevor Cahill 3.00 8.00
VM Victor Martinez 5.00 12.00
WB Wade Boggs 12.50 30.00
YA Yonder Alonso 3.00 8.00

2013 Topps Archives Triumvirate

STATED ODDS 1:24 HOBBY
1A Mike Trout 12.00 30.00
1B Albert Pujols 2.00 5.00
1C Josh Hamilton 1.25 3.00
2A Albert Belle 1.00 2.50
2B Robin Ventura 1.00 2.50
2C Frank Thomas 1.50 4.00
3A Cole Hamels 1.25 3.00
3B Cliff Lee 1.25 3.00
3C Roy Halladay 1.25 3.00
4A Edgar Martinez 1.00 2.50
4B Ken Griffey Jr. 3.00 8.00
4C Alex Rodriguez 2.00 5.00
5A Mariano Rivera 2.00 5.00
5B Derek Jeter 4.00 10.00
5C Andy Pettitte 1.25 3.00
6A Dylan Bundy 2.50 6.00
6B Adam Jones 1.25 3.00
6C Manny Machado 6.00 15.00
7A Miguel Cabrera 1.50 4.00
7B Justin Verlander 1.50 4.00
7C Prince Fielder 1.25 3.00

2014 Topps Archives

COMP.SET w/o SP's (200) 12.00 30.00
SP ODDS 1:4 HOBBY
PRINTING PLATE ODDS 1:151 HOBBY
PLATE PRINT RUN 1 SET PER COLOR
BLACK-CYAN-MAGENTA-YELLOW ISSUED
NO PLATE PRICING DUE TO SCARCITY
1 Yu Darvish .25 .60
2 Bruce Sutter .15 .40
3 Freddie Freeman .30 .75
4 Andrew Lambo RC .25 .60
5 Carl Crawford .20 .50
6 Marcus Semien RC 1.25 3.00
7 Dustin Pedroia .25 .60
8 Zack Greinke .25 .60
9 Josh Donaldson .20 .50
10 Juan Gonzalez .15 .40
11 Adam Wainwright .20 .50
12 James Shields .15 .40
13 Jarred Cosart .15 .40
14 Dennis Eckersley .20 .50
15 Ralph Kiner .20 .50
16 Matt Harvey .20 .50
17 Joey Votto .25 .60
18 Rickey Henderson .25 .60
19 Nolan Arenado .40 1.00
20 Will Middlebrooks .15 .40
21 Ty Cobb .40 1.00
22 Jake Marisnick RC .25 .60
23 Chris Carter .15 .40
24 Michael Cuddyer .15 .40
25 Jim Palmer .20 .50
26 Juan Marichal .20 .50
27 Tom Seaver .20 .50
28 Joe Kelly .15 .40
29 Carlos Gomez .15 .40
30 Alex Gordon .20 .50
31 Steve Carlton .20 .50
32 Frank Robinson .20 .50
33 Kyuji Fujikawa .20 .50
34 Enny Romero RC .25 .60
35 Patrick Corbin .20 .50
36 Carlos Beltran .20 .50
37 Wilmer Flores RC .30 .75
38 Jason Grilli .15 .40
39 Chris Sale .25 .60
40 Christian Yelich .30 .75
41 Catfish Hunter .20 .50
42 Junior Lake .15 .40
43 Josmil Pinto RC .25 .60
44 Ernie Banks .25 .60
45 Lou Brock .20 .50
46 Cole Hamels .20 .50
47 Tim Lincecum .20 .50
48 CC Sabathia .20 .50
49 Jonny Gomes .15 .40
50 Derek Jeter .60 1.50
51 Lou Gehrig .50 1.25
52 Michael Wacha .20 .50
53 James Paxton RC .40 1.00
54 Marco Scutaro .20 .50
55 Jay Bruce .20 .50
56 Jon Jay .15 .40
57 Tom Glavine .20 .50
58 Brett Lawrie .20 .50
59 Nick Swisher .20 .50
60 Ozzie Smith .30 .75
61 Matt Davidson RC .30 .75
62 Matt Moore .20 .50
63 Austin Jackson .15 .40
64 Hisashi Iwakuma .20 .50
65 Starling Marte .20 .50
66 Craig Biggio .20 .50
67 Jonathan Villar .15 .40
68 Eddie Mathews .25 .60
69 Mark McGwire .50 1.25
70 Giancarlo Stanton .25 .60
71 Nick Franklin .15 .40
72 Evan Longoria .20 .50
73 Erik Johnson RC .25 .60
74 Jon Lester .20 .50
75 Ken Griffey Jr. .50 1.25
76 Josh Hamilton .20 .50
77 Joe Morgan .20 .50
78 Dylan Bundy .20 .50
79 Duke Snider .20 .50
80 Hiroki Kuroda .15 .40
81 Todd Frazier .15 .40
82 Matt Cain .20 .50
83 Billy Butler .15 .40
84 Tony Perez .20 .50
85 Kevin Pillar RC .25 .60
86 Shelby Miller .20 .50
87 Eric Davis .15 .40
88 Evan Gattis .15 .40
89 R.A. Dickey .20 .50
90 George Brett .50 1.25
91 Roberto Clemente .60 1.50
92 Aroldis Chapman .25 .60
93 Xander Bogaerts RC .75 2.00
94 Mike Napoli .15 .40
95 Matt Carpenter .25 .60
96 Robin Yount .25 .60
97 Ivan Rodriguez .20 .50
98 Chris Owings RC .25 .60
99 Salvador Perez .20 .50
100 Bryce Harper .40 1.00
101 Ted Williams .50 1.25
102 Goose Gossage .20 .50
103 Orlando Hernandez .15 .40
104 Jordan Zimmermann .20 .50
105 Tony Gwynn .25 .60
106 Cliff Lee .20 .50
107 Michael Choice RC .25 .60
108 Carlos Santana .20 .50
109 Jose Reyes .20 .50
110 Yoenis Cespedes .25 .60
111 Jason Heyward .20 .50
112 Ethan Martin RC .25 .60
113 Cal Ripken Jr. .75 2.00
114 Brian McCann .20 .50
115 Manny Machado .25 .60
116 Alex Guerrero RC .30 .75
117 Mike Mussina .20 .50
118 Eddie Murray .20 .50
119 Andrelton Simmons .15 .40
120 Yadier Molina .30 .75
121 Kevin Siegrist (RC) .25 .60
122 Larry Doby .20 .50
123 Jarrod Parker .15 .40
124 Trevor Rosenthal .20 .50
125 Jose Fernandez .25 .60
126 Yordano Ventura RC .30 .75
127 Christian Bethancourt RC .25 .60
128 Avisail Garcia .20 .50
129 Phil Niekro .20 .50
130 Matt Holliday .25 .60
131 Ian Kinsler .20 .50
132 Felix Hernandez .20 .50
133 Yovani Gallardo .15 .40
134 Gio Gonzalez .20 .50
135 Jimmy Nelson RC .25 .60
136 Whitey Ford .20 .50
137 Pedro Alvarez .15 .40
138 Warren Spahn .20 .50
139 Bob Feller .20 .50
140 Tony Cingrani .20 .50
141 Pablo Sandoval .20 .50
142 Joe Mauer .20 .50
143 Mike Schmidt .40 1.00
144 Adrian Beltre .25 .60
146 Starlin Castro .15 .40
147 Jose Bautista .20 .50
148 Anthony Rendon .25 .60
149 Madison Bumgarner .20 .50
150 Miguel Cabrera .25 .60
151 Joe DiMaggio .50 1.25
152 Anthony Rizzo .30 .75
153 Fergie Jenkins .20 .50
154 Harmon Killebrew .25 .60
155 Lou Boudreau .20 .50
156 Phil Rizzuto .20 .50
157 Rod Carew .20 .50
158 Willie Stargell .20 .50
159 Bob Gibson .20 .50
160 Don Mattingly .50 1.25
161 Johnny Bench .25 .60
162 Paul O'Neill .20 .50
163 Randy Johnson .25 .60
164 Stan Musial .40 1.00
165 Willie McCovey .20 .50
166 David Holmberg RC .25 .60
167 John Ryan Murphy RC .25 .60
168 Jonathan Schoop RC .25 .60
169 Kolten Wong RC .30 .75
170 Travis d'Arnaud RC .30 .75
171 Adam Eaton .15 .40
172 Albert Pujols .30 .75
173 Allen Craig .20 .50
174 Andre Rienzo RC .25 .60
175 Yogi Berra .25 .60
176 Adrian Gonzalez .20 .50
177 Carlos Gonzalez .20 .50
178 Carlos Martinez .20 .50
179 Chris Davis .15 .40
180 Chris Archer .15 .40
181 Craig Kimbrel .20 .50
182 Curtis Granderson .20 .50
183 David Wright .20 .50
184 Domonic Brown .20 .50
185 Doug Fister .15 .40
186 Gerrit Cole .25 .60
187 Hanley Ramirez .20 .50
188 Jered Weaver .20 .50
189 Jose Altuve .20 .50
190 Julio Teheran .20 .50
191 Justin Upton .20 .50
192 Khris Davis .25 .60
193 Matt Kemp .20 .50
194 Max Scherzer .25 .60
195 Mike Zunino .15 .40
196 Prince Fielder .20 .50
197 Ryan Zimmerman .20 .50
198 Shin-Soo Choo .20 .50
199 Sonny Gray .20 .50
200 Buster Posey .30 .75
201 Babe Ruth SP 3.00 8.00
202 Luis Gonzalez SP .75 2.00
203 Zack Wheeler SP 1.00 2.50
204 Manny Ramirez SP 1.25 3.00
205 Mike Trout SP 6.00 15.00
206 David Freese SP .75 2.00
207 Jorge Posada SP 1.00 2.50
208 Andrew McCutchen SP 1.25 3.00
209 Greg Maddux SP 1.50 4.00
210 Clayton Kershaw SP 2.00 5.00
211 Bo Jackson SP 1.25 3.00
212 Jose Canseco SP 1.00 2.50
213 Mookie Wilson SP .75 2.00
214 Fernando Valenzuela SP .75 2.00
215 Reggie Jackson SP 1.00 2.50
216 Robinson Cano SP 1.00 2.50
217 Jose Abreu SP RC 8.00 20.00
218 Nomar Garciaparra SP 1.00 2.50
219 John Smoltz SP 1.25 3.00
220 Sandy Koufax SP 2.50 6.00
221 Hyun-Jin Ryu SP 1.00 2.50
222 Edgar Martinez SP 1.00 2.50
223 Andy Van Slyke SP .75 2.00
224 Troy Tulowitzki SP 1.25 3.00
225 Wil Myers SP .75 2.00
226 Adam Jones SP 1.00 2.50
227 Nick Castellanos SP RC 3.00 8.00
228 Brandon Phillips SP .75 2.00
229 Wade Boggs SP 1.00 2.50
230 Billy Hamilton SP RC 1.25 3.00
231 Paul Goldschmidt SP 1.25 3.00
232 Nolan Ryan SP 4.00 10.00
233 Graig Nettles SP .75 2.00
234 Don Zimmer SP .75 2.00
235 Darren Daulton SP .75 2.00
236 David Price SP 1.00 2.50
237 Dusty Baker SP .75 2.00
238 David Ortiz SP 1.25 3.00
239 Taijuan Walker SP RC 1.00 2.50
240 Mariano Rivera SP 1.50 4.00
241 Masahiro Tanaka SP RC 3.00 8.00
242 Deion Sanders SP 1.00 2.50
243 Willie Mays SP 2.50 6.00
244 Jacoby Ellsbury SP 1.00 2.50
245 John Olerud SP .75 2.00
246 Justin Verlander SP 1.25 3.00
247 Stephen Strasburg SP 1.25 3.00
248 Jurickson Profar SP 1.00 2.50
249 Pedro Martinez SP 1.00 2.50
250 Yasiel Puig SP 1.25 3.00

2014 Topps Archives Gold

*GOLD: 3X TO 8X BASIC
*GOLD RC: 2X TO 5X BASIC RC
STATED ODDS 1:7 HOBBY
STATED PRINT RUN 199 SER.#'d SETS
50 Derek Jeter 10.00 25.00
93 Xander Bogaerts 8.00 20.00

2014 Topps Archives Silver

*SILVER: 4X TO 10X BASIC
*SILVER RC: 2.5X TO 6X BASIC RC
STATED ODDS 1:14 HOBBY
STATED PRINT RUN 99 SER.#'d SETS
50 Derek Jeter 20.00 50.00
75 Ken Griffey Jr. 10.00 25.00
93 Xander Bogaerts 15.00 40.00

2014 Topps Archives '69 Deckle Minis

COMPLETE SET (40) 30.00 80.00
STATED ODDS 1:5 HOBBY
AM Andrew McCutchen 1.25 3.00
AVS Andy Van Slyke .75 2.00
BH Bryce Harper 2.00 5.00
BP Buster Posey 1.50 4.00
CB Carlos Baerga .75 2.00
CK Clayton Kershaw 2.00 5.00
CR Cal Ripken Jr. 4.00 10.00
DD Darren Daulton .75 2.00
DE David Eckstein .75 2.00
DJ Derek Jeter 3.00 8.00
DP Dave Parker .75 2.00
DW David Wright 1.00 2.50
GN Graig Nettles .75 2.00
HJ Howard Johnson .75 2.00
HJR Hyun-Jin Ryu 1.00 2.50
IR Ivan Rodriguez 1.00 2.50
JAB Jose Abreu 4.00 10.00
JC Jose Canseco 1.00 2.50
JF Jose Fernandez 1.25 3.00
JK Joe Kelly .75 2.00
JO John Olerud .75 2.00
JV Justin Verlander 1.25 3.00
JVO Joey Votto 1.25 3.00
MC Miguel Cabrera 1.25 3.00
ML Mark Lemke .75 2.00
MM Mike Matheny .75 2.00
MMA Manny Machado 1.25 3.00
MS Mel Stottlemyre .75 2.00
MSC Max Scherzer 1.25 3.00
MT Mike Trout 6.00 15.00
MTK Masahiro Tanaka 4.00 10.00
MW Michael Wacha 1.00 2.50
OH Orlando Hernandez .75 2.00
RG Ron Gant .75 2.00
RW Rondell White .75 2.00
TT Troy Tulowitzki 1.25 3.00
WM Wil Myers .75 2.00
YD Yu Darvish 1.25 3.00
YM Yadier Molina 1.50 4.00
YP Yasiel Puig 1.25 3.00

2014 Topps Archives '69 Deckle Minis Autographs

STATED ODDS 1:570 HOBBY
STATED PRINT RUN 25 SER.#'d SETS
EXCHANGE DEADLINE 5/31/2017
AVSA Andy Van Slyke 15.00 40.00
CBA Carlos Baerga 20.00 50.00
DPA Dave Parker 20.00 50.00
GNA Graig Nettles 15.00 40.00
IRA Ivan Rodriguez 12.00 30.00
JCA Jose Canseco 10.00 25.00
JKA Joe Kelly 20.00 50.00
MLA Mark Lemke 15.00 40.00
OHA Orlando Hernandez 50.00 120.00
RGA Ron Gant 15.00 25.00
RWA Rondell White 20.00 50.00
WMA Wil Myers 30.00 80.00

2014 Topps Archives '71-72 Hockey

STATED ODDS 1:24 HOBBY
PRINTING PLATE ODDS 1:151 HOBBY
PLATE PRINT RUN 1 SET PER COLOR
BLACK-CYAN-MAGENTA-YELLOW ISSUED
NO PLATE PRICING DUE TO SCARCITY
71HBH Bryce Harper 3.00 8.00
71HBP Brandon Phillips 1.25 3.00
71HCS Chris Sabo 1.25 3.00
71HED Eric Davis 1.25 3.00
71HFF Freddie Freeman 2.50 6.00
71HGN Graig Nettles 1.25 3.00
71HJA Jose Abreu 8.00 20.00
71HJK Joe Kelly 1.25 3.00
71HJV Joey Votto 2.00 5.00
71HMC Miguel Cabrera 2.00 5.00
71HMT Mike Trout 10.00 25.00
71HMTA Masahiro Tanaka 8.00 20.00
71HPG Paul Goldschmidt 2.00 5.00
71HRC Roberto Clemente 5.00 12.00
71HSM Shelby Miller 1.50 4.00
71HTS Tom Seaver 1.50 4.00
71HWM Wil Myers 1.25 3.00
71HWS Willie Stargell 1.50 4.00
71HYP Yasiel Puig 2.00 5.00

2014 Topps Archives '71-72 Hockey Autographs

STATED ODDS 1:1710 HOBBY
STATED PRINT RUN 25 SER.#'d SETS
EXCHANGE DEADLINE 5/31/2017
71HABP Brandon Phillips 15.00 40.00
71HAED Eric Davis 30.00 80.00
71HAPG Paul Goldschmidt 40.00 100.00
71HASM Shelby Miller 15.00 40.00
71HAWM Wil Myers 40.00 100.00

2014 Topps Archives '81 Mini Autographs

STATED ODDS 1:296 HOBBY
STATED PRINT RUN 25 SER.#'d SETS
EXCHANGE DEADLINE 5/31/2017
81MABP Brandon Phillips 15.00 40.00
81MACB Carlos Baerga 20.00 50.00
81MADP Dave Parker 20.00 50.00
81MADW David Wright 40.00 80.00
81MAED Eric Davis 30.00 80.00
81MAFF Freddie Freeman 25.00 60.00
81MAGN Graig Nettles 15.00 40.00
81MAJC Jose Canseco 30.00 80.00
81MAJK Joe Kelly 20.00 50.00
81MAMW Mookie Wilson 20.00 50.00
81MAOH Orlando Hernandez 30.00 80.00
81MAPG Paul Goldschmidt 40.00 100.00
81MAPN Phil Niekro 20.00 50.00
81MARG Ron Gant 20.00 50.00
81MARW Rondell White 20.00 50.00
81MASC Sean Casey 15.00 40.00
81MATT Troy Tulowitzki EXCH 40.00 100.00
81MAWM Wil Myers 30.00 80.00
81MADEC David Eckstein 15.00 40.00

2014 Topps Archives '87 All-Stars

STATED ODDS 1:4 HOBBY
PRINTING PLATE ODDS 1:151 HOBBY
PLATE PRINT RUN 1 SET PER COLOR
BLACK-CYAN-MAGENTA-YELLOW ISSUED
NO PLATE PRICING DUE TO SCARCITY
87BB Billy Butler .60 1.50
87BH Bryce Harper 1.50 4.00
87CD Chris Davis .60 1.50
87CK Clayton Kershaw 1.50 4.00
87DG Dwight Gooden .60 1.50
87DO David Ortiz 1.00 2.50
87FF Freddie Freeman 1.25 3.00
87FH Felix Hernandez .75 2.00
87FJ Fergie Jenkins .75 2.00
87GC Gary Carter .75 2.00
87GG Goose Gossage .75 2.00
87GN Graig Nettles .60 1.50
87HJ Howard Johnson .60 1.50
87JB Jose Bautista .75 2.00
87JF Jose Fernandez 1.00 2.50
87JG Jason Grilli .60 1.50
87JV Justin Verlander 1.00 2.50
87MC Miguel Cabrera 1.00 2.50
87MH Matt Harvey .75 2.00
87MM Manny Machado 1.00 2.50
87MR Mariano Rivera 1.25 3.00
87MT Mike Trout 5.00 12.00
87OS Ozzie Smith 1.25 3.00
87PG Paul Goldschmidt 1.00 2.50
87RZ Ryan Zimmerman .75 2.00
87SK Sandy Koufax 2.00 5.00
87TF Travis Fryman .60 1.50
87VC Vince Coleman .60 1.50
87WB Wade Boggs .75 2.00
87YD Yu Darvish 1.00 2.50

2014 Topps Archives Fan Favorites Autographs

STATED ODDS 1:17 HOBBY
EXCHANGE DEADLINE 5/31/2017
PRINTING PLATE ODDS 1:1400 HOBBY
PLATE PRINT RUN 1 SET PER COLOR
BLACK-CYAN-MAGENTA-YELLOW ISSUED
NO PLATE PRICING DUE TO SCARCITY
FFAAVS Andy Van Slyke 5.00 12.00
FFABH Bob Horner 4.00 10.00
FFABR Bill Russell 5.00 12.00
FFABRO Bip Roberts 4.00 10.00
FFACB Carlos Baerga 4.00 10.00
FFACS Chris Sabo 6.00 15.00
FFADBA Dusty Baker 6.00 15.00
FFADD Darren Daulton 8.00 20.00
FFADEC David Eckstein 4.00 10.00
FFADPA Dave Parker 8.00 20.00
FFADZ Don Zimmer 10.00 25.00
FFAED Eric Davis 6.00 15.00
FFAGN Graig Nettles 6.00 15.00
FFAGV Greg Vaughn 4.00 10.00
FFAHJ Howard Johnson 4.00 10.00
FFAIR Ivan Rodriguez 15.00 40.00
FFAJA Jose Abreu 200.00 300.00
FFAJB Jeromy Burnitz 4.00 10.00
FFAJC Jose Canseco 30.00 60.00
FFAJO John Olerud 4.00 10.00
FFALD Lenny Dykstra 4.00 10.00
FFALH Lenny Harris 4.00 10.00
FFAMG Mike Greenwell 10.00 25.00
FFAML Mark Lemke 4.00 10.00
FFAMMC Mark McGwire 200.00 300.00
FFAMS Mel Stottlemyre 6.00 15.00
FFAMT Mickey Tettleton 4.00 10.00
FFAMW Mookie Wilson 5.00 12.00
FFAOH Orlando Hernandez 15.00 40.00
FFAPGO Paul Goldschmidt 15.00 40.00
FFAPN Phil Niekro 8.00 20.00
FFARD Rob Dibble 8.00 20.00
FFARG Ron Gant 5.00 12.00
FFARH Rickey Henderson 200.00 300.00
FFARW Rondell White 4.00 10.00
FFASC Sean Casey 4.00 10.00
FFATP Terry Pendleton 5.00 12.00

2014 Topps Archives Fan Favorites Autographs Gold

*GOLD: .75X TO 2X BASIC
STATED PRINT RUN 50 SER.#'d SETS
EXCHANGE DEADLINE 5/31/2017

2014 Topps Archives Fan Favorites Autographs Silver

*SILVER: .75X TO 2X BASIC
STATED ODDS 1:211 HOBBY
STATED PRINT RUN 25 SER.#'d SETS
EXCHANGE DEADLINE 5/31/2017
FFAJC Jose Canseco 50.00 100.00

2014 Topps Archives Future Stars

87FED Eric Davis 2.50 6.00
87FHJ Howard Johnson 2.50 6.00
87FHJR Hyun-Jin Ryu 3.00 8.00
87FJA Jose Abreu 10.00 25.00
87FJF Jose Fernandez 4.00 10.00
87FJK Joe Kelly 2.50 6.00
87FMM Manny Machado 4.00 10.00
87FMT Masahiro Tanaka 12.00 30.00
87FPG Paul Goldschmidt 4.00 10.00
87FRG Ron Gant 2.50 6.00
87FRH Rickey Henderson 4.00 10.00
87FSM Shelby Miller 3.00 8.00
87FWM Wil Myers 2.50 6.00
87FYP Yasiel Puig 4.00 10.00

2014 Topps Archives Future Stars Autographs

STATED PRINT RUN 25 SER.#'d SETS
EXCHANGE DEADLINE 5/31/2017
87FASM Shelby Miller 30.00 80.00
87FAWM Wil Myers 20.00 50.00

2014 Topps Archives Major League

COMPLETE SET (4) 8.00 20.00
STATED ODDS 1:12 HOBBY
PRINTING PLATE ODDS 1:151 HOBBY
PLATE PRINT RUN 1 SET PER COLOR
BLACK-CYAN-MAGENTA-YELLOW ISSUED
NO PLATE PRICING DUE TO SCARCITY
MLCEH Eddie Harris 2.00 5.00

MLCJT Jake Taylor 2.00 5.00
MLCRD Roger Dorn 2.00 5.00
MLCRV Ricky Vaughn 3.00 8.00

2014 Topps Archives Major League Gold

*GOLD: 2.5X TO 6X BASIC
STATED ODDS 1:2700 HOBBY
STATED PRINT RUN 25 SER.#'d SETS

2014 Topps Archives Major League Orange

*ORANGE: 2X TO 5X BASIC
STATED PRINT RUN 50 SER.#'d SETS
MLCRV Ricky Vaughn 30.00 60.00

2014 Topps Archives Major League Autographs

STATED ODDS 1:213 HOBBY
EXCHANGE DEADLINE 5/31/2017
MLAEH Ross/Harris 20.00 50.00
MLAJT Berenger/Taylor 40.00 100.00
MLARD Bernsen/Dorn 25.00 60.00
MLARP Whitton/Phelps 25.00 60.00
MLARV Sheen/Vaughn 500.00 700.00

2014 Topps Archives Relics

STATED ODDS 1:215 HOBBY
68TRAB Adrian Beltre 4.00 10.00
68TRAC Asdrubal Cabrera 3.00 8.00
68TRACH Aroldis Chapman 4.00 10.00
68TRAG Alex Gordon 3.00 8.00
68TRBL Brett Lawrie 3.00 8.00
68TRCA Chris Archer 2.50 6.00
68TRDJ Desmond Jennings 3.00 8.00
68TRDM Devin Mesoraco 2.50 6.00
68TRJB Jose Bautista 3.00 8.00
68TRJBR Jay Bruce 3.00 8.00
68TRJM Joe Mauer 3.00 8.00
68TRMM Mike Minor 2.50 6.00
68TRPC Patrick Corbin 3.00 8.00
68TRPG Paul Goldschmidt 4.00 10.00
68TRPS Pablo Sandoval 3.00 8.00
68TRSC Starlin Castro 2.50 6.00
68TRSM Starling Marte 3.00 8.00
68TRSP Salvador Perez 3.00 8.00
68TRTL Tim Lincecum 6.00 15.00
68TRWM Wade Miley 2.50 6.00

2014 Topps Archives Retail

RCBH Bryce Harper 10.00 25.00
RCDW David Wright 12.00 30.00
RCJB Jose Bautista 5.00 12.00
RCJV Justin Verlander 6.00 15.00
RCMC Miguel Cabrera 6.00 15.00
RCMT Mike Trout 30.00 80.00
RCPG Paul Goldschmidt 10.00 25.00
RCRZ Ryan Zimmerman 5.00 12.00
RCTT Troy Tulowitzki 6.00 15.00
RCYD Yu Darvish 6.00 15.00

2014 Topps Archives Stadium Club Firebrand

COMPLETE SET (10) 12.00 30.00
STATED ODDS 1:24 HOBBY
FBCB Carlos Baerga 1.25 3.00
FBED Eric Davis 1.25 3.00
FBGN Graig Nettles 1.25 3.00
FBIR Ivan Rodriguez 1.50 4.00
FBJC Jose Canseco 1.50 4.00
FBPG Pedro Guerrero 1.25 3.00
FBRG Ron Gant 1.25 3.00
FBRW Rondell White 1.25 3.00
FBWM Wil Myers 1.25 3.00
FBYP Yasiel Puig 2.00 5.00

2014 Topps Archives Stadium Club Firebrand Autographs

STATED ODDS 1:822 HOBBY
STATED PRINT RUN 25 SER.#'d SETS
EXCHANGE DEADLINE 5/31/2017
FBAED Eric Davis 20.00 50.00
FBAGN Graig Nettles 15.00 40.00
FBCB Carlos Baerga 20.00 50.00
FBIR Ivan Rodriguez 30.00 60.00
FBJC Jose Canseco 30.00 80.00
FBRG Ron Gant 20.00 50.00
FBRW Rondell White 15.00 40.00
FBWM Wil Myers 40.00 100.00

2014 Topps Archives The Winners Celebrate Box Topper

67WCAJ Adam Jones 4.00 10.00
67WCAW Adam Wainwright 4.00 10.00
67WCBH Bryce Harper 8.00 20.00
67WCBM Bill Mazeroski 4.00 10.00
67WCBP Brandon Phillips 3.00 8.00
67WCBPO Buster Posey 6.00 15.00
67WCCB Craig Biggio 4.00 10.00
67WCCD Chris Davis 3.00 8.00
67WCCF Carlton Fisk 4.00 10.00
67WCDJ Derek Jeter 12.00 30.00
67WCDO David Ortiz 5.00 12.00
67WCDS Darryl Strawberry 3.00 8.00
67WCJB Jose Bautista 4.00 10.00
67WCJBR Jay Bruce 4.00 10.00
67WCJU Justin Upton 4.00 10.00
67WCMA Matt Adams 3.00 8.00
67WCMC Miguel Cabrera 5.00 12.00
67WCMT Mike Trout 25.00 60.00
67WCPG Paul Goldschmidt 5.00 12.00
67WCSK Sandy Koufax 10.00 25.00
67WCSP Salvador Perez 4.00 10.00
67WCWM Wil Myers 3.00 8.00
67WCYC Yoenis Cespedes 5.00 12.00
67WCYP Yasiel Puig 5.00 12.00

2014 Topps Archives Triple Autographs

STATED ODDS 1:2137 HOBBY
EXCHANGE DEADLINE 5/31/2017
ATACMA Adms/Crg/Mrtnz 60.00 120.00
ATACMJ Jns/Cspds/Mrs 75.00 150.00
ATADMR Mth/d'Arn/IRD EXCH 50.00 100.00
ATAGHA Gssge/Hrnn/Abbtt 75.00 150.00
ATAGPS Plmr/Sttn/Gbsn 75.00 150.00
ATAMWW Mrsnck/Wng/Wlkr 75.00 150.00
ATAWJS Strwbrry/HoJo/Wlsn 75.00 150.00

2015 Topps Archives

COMP.SET w/o SP's (300) 20.00 50.00
SP ODDS 1:70 HOBBY
PRINTING PLATE ODDS 1:865 HOBBY
PLATE PRINT RUN 1 SET PER COLOR
BLACK-CYAN-MAGENTA-YELLOW ISSUED
NO PLATE PRICING DUE TO SCARCITY
1 Clayton Kershaw .40 1.00
2 Chris Sale .25 .60
3 Jon Singleton .20 .50
4 Julio Teheran .20 .50
5 Craig Kimbrel .20 .50
6 Alexei Ramirez .20 .50
7 Michael Pineda .15 .40
8 Jayson Werth .20 .50
9 Chris Carter .15 .40
10 Alex Wood .15 .40
11 Bo Jackson .25 .60
12 Brock Holt .15 .40
13 Joe Mauer .20 .50
14 Wade Boggs .20 .50
15 Jason Rogers RC .40 1.00
16 Javier Baez RC 3.00 8.00
17 Buck Farmer RC .40 1.00
18 Homer Bailey .15 .40
19 Hisashi Iwakuma .20 .50
20 Josh Hamilton .20 .50
21 Billy Hamilton .20 .50
22 Josh Donaldson .20 .50
23 Madison Bumgarner .20 .50
24 Cal Ripken Jr. .75 2.00
25 Yasiel Puig .25 .60
26 Curtis Granderson .20 .50
27 Lorenzo Cain .15 .40
28 Elvis Andrus .20 .50
29 Freddie Freeman .30 .75
30 Carlton Fisk .20 .50
31 Christian Yelich .30 .75
32 Robin Yount .25 .60
33 Oswaldo Arcia .15 .40
34 Jeff Samardzija .15 .40
35 Eddie Murray .20 .50
36 Dylan Bundy .20 .50
37 Jhonny Peralta .15 .40
38 Carlos Gonzalez .20 .50
39 Goose Gossage .20 .50
40 Fernando Rodney .15 .40
41 Matt Adams .15 .40
42 Juan Lagares .15 .40
43 Alcides Escobar .20 .50
44 Jonathan Lucroy .20 .50
45 Ryan Howard .20 .50
46 Tyson Ross .15 .40
47 Henderson Alvarez .15 .40
48 Victor Martinez .20 .50
49 Willie Stargell .20 .50
50 Ken Griffey Jr. .50 1.25
51 Yan Gomes .15 .40
52 Dilson Herrera RC .50 1.25
53 Roberto Alomar .20 .50
54 Ozzie Smith .30 .75
55 Trevor May RC .40 1.00
56 Sonny Gray .20 .50
57 Jorge Posada .20 .50
58 Bruce Sutter .20 .50
59 Yadier Molina .30 .75
60 Anthony Ranaudo RC .40 1.00
61 Tanner Roark .15 .40
62 Robin Roberts .20 .50
63 Rod Carew .20 .50
64 Shin-Soo Choo .20 .50
65 Carlos Martinez .20 .50
66 Dalton Pompey RC .50 1.25
67 Jose Altuve .20 .50
68 Aaron Sanchez .20 .50
69 Nomar Garciaparra .20 .50
70 Jake Arrieta .20 .50
71 Matt Holliday .25 .60
72 Chipper Jones .25 .60
73 Anthony Rendon .25 .60
74 Devin Mesoraco .15 .40
75 George Brett .50 1.25
76 R.A. Dickey .20 .50
77 David Eckstein .15 .40
78 Gary Carter .20 .50
79 Albert Pujols .30 .75
80 J.J. Hardy .15 .40
81 Kevin Gausman .25 .60
82 Buster Posey .30 .75
83 Don Sutton .20 .50
84 Vladimir Guerrero .20 .50
85 Maikel Franco RC .50 1.25
86 Mookie Betts .50 1.25
87 Kennys Vargas .15 .40
88 Lenny Dykstra .15 .40
89 C.J. Wilson .15 .40
90 Ian Kinsler .20 .50
91 Kevin Kiermaier .20 .50
92 Mookie Wilson .15 .40
93 Todd Frazier .15 .40
94 Dellin Betances .20 .50
95 Pablo Sandoval .20 .50
96 Matt Cain .20 .50
97 Juan Gonzalez .15 .40
98 Brett Gardner .20 .50
99 Robinson Cano .20 .50
100 Miguel Cabrera .25 .60
101 Mariano Rivera .30 .75
102 Ken Giles .15 .40
103 Adam LaRoche .15 .40
104 Kolten Wong .20 .50
105 Joe DiMaggio .50 1.25
106 Brandon Finnegan RC .40 1.00
107 Willie McCovey .20 .50
108 Matt Carpenter .25 .60
109 Steven Moya RC .50 1.25
110 Jacob deGrom .50 1.25
111 Starling Marte .20 .50
112 Jesse Hahn .15 .40
113 Salvador Perez .20 .50
114 Doug Fister .15 .40
115 Barry Larkin .20 .50
116 Carlos Carrasco .15 .40
117 Jose Fernandez .25 .60
118 Ryan Braun .20 .50
119 Lonnie Chisenhall .15 .40
120 Felix Hernandez .20 .50
121 Ian Kennedy .15 .40
122 Lance Lynn .15 .40
123 Anibal Sanchez .15 .40
124 Phil Rizzuto .20 .50
125 Babe Ruth .60 1.50
126 Matt Moore .20 .50
127 Adam Eaton .15 .40
128 Ralph Kiner .20 .50
129 Drew Smyly .15 .40
130 Aramis Ramirez .15 .40
131 Charlie Blackmon .25 .60
132 Stephen Strasburg .25 .60
133 Dennis Eckersley .20 .50
134 Duke Snider .20 .50
135 Michael Taylor RC .40 1.00
136 Luis Gonzalez .15 .40
137 Brian McCann .20 .50
138 Paul Goldschmidt .25 .60
139 Michael Wacha .20 .50
140 Austin Jackson .15 .40
141 Jose Quintana .15 .40
142 Khris Davis UER .25 .60
Carlos Gomez pictured
143 Dee Gordon .15 .40
144 Yordano Ventura .20 .50
145 Daniel Murphy .20 .50
146 Danny Salazar .20 .50
147 Evan Longoria .20 .50
148 Hyun-Jin Ryu .20 .50
149 Hunter Pence .20 .50
150 Sandy Koufax .50 1.25
151 David Wright .20 .50
152 Eddie Mathews .25 .60
153 Frank Thomas .25 .60
154 Bob Feller .20 .50
155 Brian Dozier .20 .50
156 Travis d'Arnaud .20 .50
157 Nick Tropeano RC .40 1.00
158 Kole Calhoun .15 .40
159 Johnny Cueto .20 .50
160 Gerrit Cole .25 .60
161 Xander Bogaerts .25 .60
162 Nolan Arenado .40 1.00
163 Deion Sanders .20 .50
164 Aroldis Chapman .25 .60
165 Ty Cobb .40 1.00
166 Max Scherzer .25 .60
167 George Springer .20 .50
168 Mark McGwire .40 1.00
169 Jon Lester .20 .50
170 Warren Spahn .20 .50
171 Ian Desmond .15 .40
172 Corey Dickerson .15 .40
173 Ryan Zimmerman .20 .50
174 Trevor Bauer .30 .75
175 Masahiro Tanaka .20 .50
176 Zack Wheeler .20 .50
177 Rickey Henderson .25 .60
178 Lou Boudreau .20 .50
179 Frank Robinson .20 .50
180 Chase Headley .15 .40
181 Harmon Killebrew .25 .60
182 Christian Walker RC .75 2.00
183 Matt Shoemaker .20 .50
184 Al Kaline .25 .60
185 Zack Greinke .25 .60
186 Brad Ziegler .15 .40
187 Matt Harvey .20 .50
188 Yoenis Cespedes .20 .50
189 Roberto Clemente .60 1.50
190 Daniel Norris RC .40 1.00
191 Prince Fielder .20 .50
192 Matt Barnes RC .40 1.00
193 Billy Williams .20 .50
194 Yusmeiro Petit .15 .40
195 Adrian Beltre .25 .60
196 Corey Kluber .20 .50
197 Bob Lemon .20 .50
198 Michael Brantley .20 .50
199 Joey Votto .25 .60
200 Jose Abreu .25 .60
201 Tony Gwynn .25 .60
202 Johnny Bench .25 .60
203 Yu Darvish .25 .60
204 Wily Peralta .15 .40
205 Chris Davis .15 .40
206 Alex Gordon .20 .50
207 Fergie Jenkins .20 .50
208 Cory Spangenberg RC .40 1.00
209 Tom Seaver .20 .50
210 Carlos Santana .20 .50
211 Kenley Jansen .20 .50
212 Bryce Brentz RC .40 1.00
213 Brooks Robinson .20 .50
214 Orlando Cepeda .20 .50
215 Mark Teixeira .20 .50
216 Wil Myers .20 .50
217 Lou Gehrig .50 1.25
218 Jim Bunning .20 .50
219 Kurt Suzuki .15 .40
220 Jay Bruce .20 .50
221 Marcell Ozuna .25 .60
222 Roenis Elias .15 .40
223 Justin Upton .20 .50
224 Paul Molitor .25 .60
225 Bryce Harper .40 1.00
226 Carlos Beltran .20 .50
227 Reggie Jackson .20 .50
228 Jered Weaver .20 .50
229 Justin Verlander .25 .60
230 Shelby Miller .20 .50
231 Taijuan Walker .15 .40
232 Carlos Gomez .15 .40
233 Greg Holland .20 .50
234 Jacoby Ellsbury .20 .50
235 Giancarlo Stanton .25 .60
236 James Shields .15 .40
237 Jim Rice .20 .50
238 Troy Tulowitzki .25 .60
239 Brandon Belt .20 .50
240 Matt Kemp .20 .50
241 Mike Napoli .15 .40
242 Manny Machado .25 .60
243 Phil Hughes .15 .40
244 Cole Hamels .20 .50
245 Garrett Richards .20 .50
246 Dustin Pedroia .25 .60
247 Eric Hosmer .20 .50
248 Catfish Hunter .20 .50
249 Jake Odorizzi .15 .40
250 Mike Trout 1.25 3.00
251 Omar Vizquel .20 .50
252 Luis Aparicio .20 .50
253 Whitey Ford .20 .50
254 Sean Doolittle .15 .40
255 David Price .20 .50
256 Jason Heyward .20 .50
257 Andrew McCutchen .25 .60
258 Jake Lamb RC .60 1.50
259 J.D. Martinez .25 .60
260 Andrelton Simmons .15 .40
261 Gary Brown RC .40 1.00
262 Chase Utley .20 .50
263 Adam Wainwright .20 .50
264 Joe Morgan .20 .50
265 Starlin Castro .15 .40
266 Gio Gonzalez .20 .50
267 Nick Castellanos .25 .60
268 Kyle Seager .15 .40
269 Jordan Zimmermann .20 .50
270 Nelson Cruz .25 .60
271 Lou Brock .20 .50
272 Adrian Gonzalez .20 .50
273 Orlando Hernandez .15 .40
274 Jose Reyes .20 .50
275 Ted Williams .50 1.25
276 Don Mattingly .50 1.25
277 Edwin Encarnacion .25 .60
278 Alex Cobb .15 .40
279 Joc Pederson RC 1.50 4.00
280 Brandon Phillips .15 .40
281 Hanley Ramirez .20 .50
282 Mike Zunino .15 .40
283 Mike Schmidt .40 1.00
284 Jim Palmer .20 .50
285 Tony Perez .20 .50
286 Danny Santana .15 .40
287 Justin Morneau .20 .50
288 Gregory Polanco .20 .50
289 Bill Mazeroski .20 .50
290 Jason Kipnis .20 .50
291 Jose Bautista .20 .50
292 David Ortiz .25 .60
293 Josh Harrison .15 .40
294 Chris Archer .15 .40
295 Cliff Lee .20 .50
296 Mike Foltynewicz RC .40 1.00
297 Juan Marichal .20 .50
298 Trevor Rosenthal .20 .50
299 Mark Trumbo .15 .40
300 Willie Mays .50 1.25
301 Nolan Ryan SP 12.00 30.00
302 Rick Ferrell SP 6.00 15.00
303 John Smoltz SP 10.00 25.00
304 John Olerud SP 6.00 15.00
305 Andre Dawson SP 8.00 20.00
306 Ryne Sandberg SP 10.00 25.00
307 Jorge Soler SP RC 10.00 25.00
308 Gary Sheffield SP 6.00 15.00
309 Rob Dibble SP 6.00 15.00
310 Adam Jones SP 8.00 20.00
311 Honus Wagner SP 10.00 25.00
312 Rusney Castillo SP RC 8.00 20.00
313 Devon White SP 6.00 15.00
314 Kris Bryant SP RC 300.00 600.00
315 Anthony Rizzo SP 12.00 30.00
316 Larry Doby SP 8.00 20.00
317 Jose Cruz SP 6.00 15.00
318 Vinny Castilla SP 6.00 15.00
319 Sparky Lyle SP 6.00 15.00
320 Satchel Paige SP 10.00 25.00
321 Jose Vidro SP 6.00 15.00
322 Monte Irvin SP 8.00 20.00
323 Hal Newhouser SP 8.00 20.00
324 Red Schoendienst SP 8.00 20.00
325 Enos Slaughter SP 8.00 20.00
326 George Kell SP 8.00 20.00
327 Early Wynn SP 8.00 20.00
328 Hoyt Wilhelm SP 8.00 20.00
329 Bobby Doerr SP 8.00 20.00
330 Jackie Robinson SP 15.00 40.00

2015 Topps Archives Gold

*GOLD: 8X TO 20X BASIC
*GOLD RC: 3X TO 8X BASIC RC
STATED ODDS 1:70 HOBBY
STATED PRINT RUN 50 SER.#'d SETS
201 Tony Gwynn 12.00 30.00
225 Bryce Harper 12.00 30.00
250 Mike Trout 30.00 80.00
279 Joc Pederson 25.00 60.00

2015 Topps Archives Silver

*SILVER: 4X TO 10X BASIC
*SILVER RC: 1.5X TO 4X BASIC RC
STATED ODDS 1:18 HOBBY
STATED PRINT RUN 199 SER.#'d SETS
279 Joc Pederson 12.00 30.00

2015 Topps Archives '68 Topps Game Inserts

COMPLETE SET (33) 25.00 60.00
STATED ODDS 1:6 HOBBY
1 Yasiel Puig 1.25 3.00
2 Mike Trout 6.00 15.00
3 Jose Abreu 1.25 3.00
4 Ian Kinsler 1.00 2.50
5 Joe Mauer 1.00 2.50
6 Adam Jones 1.00 2.50
7 Robinson Cano 1.00 2.50
8 Buster Posey 1.50 4.00
9 Javier Baez 6.00 15.00
10 David Wright 1.00 2.50
11 Justin Upton 1.00 2.50
12 Edwin Encarnacion 1.25 3.00
13 Manny Machado 1.25 3.00
14 Dustin Pedroia 1.25 3.00
15 Ryan Braun 1.00 2.50
16 David Ortiz 1.25 3.00
17 Anthony Rendon 1.25 3.00
18 Freddie Freeman 1.50 4.00
19 Miguel Cabrera 1.25 3.00
20 Paul Goldschmidt 1.25 3.00
21 Jose Bautista 1.00 2.50
22 Jonathan Lucroy 1.00 2.50
23 Bryce Harper 2.00 5.00
24 Christian Yelich 1.50 4.00
25 Andrew McCutchen 1.25 3.00
26 Jacoby Ellsbury 1.00 2.50
27 Yadier Molina 1.50 4.00
28 Evan Longoria 1.00 2.50
29 Carlos Gomez .75 2.00
30 Jose Altuve 1.00 2.50
31 Billy Hamilton 1.00 2.50
32 Anthony Rizzo 1.50 4.00
33 Giancarlo Stanton 1.25 3.00

2015 Topps Archives '90 Topps #1 Draft Picks

COMPLETE SET (15) 10.00 25.00
STATED ODDS 1:8 HOBBY
*GOLD/50: 2.5X TO 6X BASIC
*NNOF: 10X TO 25X BASIC
90DPIAG Adrian Gonzalez .75 2.00
90DPIBH Bryce Harper 1.50 4.00
90DPIBP Buster Posey 1.25 3.00
90DPICK Clayton Kershaw 1.50 4.00
90DPICS Chris Sale 1.00 2.50
90DPIJB Jay Bruce .75 2.00
90DPIJF Jose Fernandez 1.00 2.50
90DPIJM Joe Mauer .75 2.00
90DPIKW Kolten Wong .75 2.00
90DPIMB Madison Bumgarner .75 2.00
90DPIMS Max Scherzer 1.00 2.50
90DPIMT Mike Trout 5.00 12.00
90DPIRB Ryan Braun .75 2.00
90DPISG Sonny Gray .75 2.00
90DPIMAT Mark Teixeira .75 2.00

2015 Topps Archives '90 Topps #1 Draft Picks No Name On Front

*NNOF: 10X TO 25X BASIC
STATED ODDS 1:1008 HOBBY
90DPIMT Mike Trout 150.00 300.00

2015 Topps Archives '90 Topps #1 Draft Picks Autographs

STATED ODDS 1:619 HOBBY
STATED PRINT RUN 199 SER.#'d SETS
EXCHANGE DEADLINE 5/31/2018
PRINTING PLATE ODDS 1:9247 HOBBY
PLATE PRINT RUN 1 SET PER COLOR
NO PLATE PRICING DUE TO SCARCITY
90DPKW Kolten Wong 12.00 30.00
90DPRB Ryan Braun 12.00 30.00
90DPSG Sonny Gray 10.00 25.00

2015 Topps Archives '90 Topps #1 Draft Picks Autographs Gold

*GOLD: .6X TO 1.5X BASIC
STATED ODDS 1:739 HOBBY
STATED PRINT RUN 50 SER.#'d SETS
EXCHANGE DEADLINE 5/31/2018
90DPAG Adrian Gonzalez 25.00 60.00
90DPCK Clayton Kershaw EXCH 100.00 200.00
90DPCS Chris Sale 40.00 100.00
90DPJF Jose Fernandez 25.00 60.00
90DPMT Mike Trout 250.00 350.00

2015 Topps Archives '90 Topps All Star Rookies

COMPLETE SET (20) 15.00 40.00
STATED ODDS 1:12 HOBBY
PRINTING PLATE ODDS 1:8196 HOBBY
PLATE PRINT RUN 1 SET PER COLOR
NO PLATE PRICING DUE TO SCARCITY
*GOLD/50: 2.5X TO 6X BASIC
90ASIAR Anthony Ranaudo .60 1.50
90ASIBF Brandon Finnegan .60 1.50
90ASIBUF Buck Farmer .60 1.50
90ASICS Cory Spangenberg .60 1.50
90ASICW Christian Walker 1.25 3.00
90ASIDH Dilson Herrera .75 2.00
90ASIDN Daniel Norris .60 1.50
90ASIDP Dalton Pompey .75 2.00
90ASIGB Gary Brown .60 1.50
90ASIJB Javier Baez 5.00 12.00
90ASIJL Jake Lamb 1.00 2.50
90ASIJP Joc Pederson 2.50 6.00
90ASIJS Jorge Soler 1.00 2.50
90ASIMB Matt Barnes .60 1.50
90ASIMF Maikel Franco .75 2.00
90ASIMIF Mike Foltynewicz .60 1.50
90ASIMT Michael Taylor .60 1.50
90ASIRC Rusney Castillo .75 2.00
90ASIRL Rymer Liriano .60 1.50
90ASITM Trevor May .60 1.50

2015 Topps Archives '90 Topps All Star Rookies Autographs

STATED ODDS 1:243 HOBBY
STATED PRINT RUN 199 SER.#'d SETS
EXCHANGE DEADLINE 5/31/2018
PRINTING PLATE ODDS 1:13,870 HOBBY
PLATE PRINT RUN 1 SET PER COLOR
NO PLATE PRICING DUE TO SCARCITY
90ASBF Brandon Finnegan 6.00 15.00
90ASDH Dilson Herrera 8.00 20.00
90ASDN Daniel Norris 6.00 15.00
90ASDP Dalton Pompey 8.00 20.00
90ASJP Joc Pederson 50.00 120.00
90ASJS Jorge Soler 15.00 40.00
90ASMF Maikel Franco 20.00 50.00
90ASMT Michael Taylor 6.00 15.00
90ASYT Yasmany Tomas 8.00 20.00

2015 Topps Archives '90 Topps All Star Rookies Autographs Gold

*GOLD: .75X TO 2X BASIC
STATED ODDS 1:927 HOBBY
STATED PRINT RUN 50 SER.#'d SETS
EXCHANGE DEADLINE 5/31/2018
90ASJP Joc Pederson 75.00 200.00

2015 Topps Archives Fan Favorites Autographs

STATED ODDS 1:18 HOBBY
EXCHANGE DEADLINE 5/31/2018
FFAAJ Andruw Jones 8.00 20.00
FFAAL Al Leiter 10.00 25.00
FFAARU Addison Russell EXCH 200.00 300.00
FFABA Brady Anderson 6.00 15.00
FFABB Bret Boone 4.00 10.00
FFABD Bucky Dent 4.00 10.00
FFABW Bernie Williams 40.00 100.00
FFADOW Dontrelle Willis 4.00 10.00
FFADW Devon White 4.00 10.00
FFAEA Edgardo Alfonzo 4.00 10.00
FFAEK Eric Karros 4.00 10.00
FFAFV Frank Viola 6.00 15.00
FFAFVI Fernando Vina 4.00 10.00
FFAGP Gaylord Perry 10.00 25.00
FFAGS Giancarlo Stanton EXCH 100.00 250.00
FFAHB Harold Baines 5.00 12.00
FFAJC Jose Cruz 4.00 10.00
FFAJCJ Jose Cruz Jr. 4.00 10.00
FFAJCO Jeff Conine 4.00 10.00
FFAJD Jacob deGrom 50.00 120.00
FFAJF John Franco 4.00 10.00
FFAJKE Jason Kendall 4.00 10.00
FFAJO Joe Oliver 4.00 10.00
FFAJR Jose Rijo 4.00 10.00
FFAJS J.T. Snow 4.00 10.00
FFAJV Jose Vidro 4.00 10.00
FFAKB Kris Bryant 250.00 400.00
FFAKT Kent Tekulve 6.00 15.00
FFAMB Mike Bordick 4.00 10.00
FFAMG Marquis Grissom 4.00 10.00
FFAMGR Mark Grace 12.00 30.00
FFAMP Mark Prior 5.00 12.00
FFANR Nolan Ryan 300.00 500.00
FFAOG Oscar Gamble 4.00 10.00
FFAPI Pete Incaviglia 4.00 10.00
FFARJ Reggie Jackson 300.00 500.00
FFARK Ryan Klesko 4.00 10.00
FFASB Sid Bream 4.00 10.00
FFASG Shawn Green 4.00 10.00
FFASH Scott Hatteberg 4.00 10.00
FFASL Sparky Lyle 4.00 10.00
FFATF Tony Fernandez 4.00 10.00
FFAVC Vinny Castilla 4.00 10.00

2015 Topps Archives Fan Favorites Autographs Gold

*GOLD: 1X TO 2.5X BASIC
STATED ODDS 1:190 HOBBY
STATED PRINT RUN 50 SER.#'d SETS
EXCHANGE DEADLINE 5/31/2018
FFAJD Jacob deGrom 75.00 200.00
FFARCU Rusney Castillo 30.00 80.00

2015 Topps Archives Fan Favorites Autographs Silver

*SILVER: .6X TO 1.5X BASIC
STATED ODDS 1:83 HOBBY
STATED PRINT RUN 199 SER.#'d SETS
EXCHANGE DEADLINE 5/31/2018
FFAJD Jacob deGrom 50.00 120.00

2015 Topps Archives Presidential Chronicles

COMPLETE SET (10) 4.00 10.00
STATED ODDS 1:12 HOBBY
PCAL Abraham Lincoln .60 1.50
PCBO Barack Obama .60 1.50
PCGF Gerald Ford .60 1.50
PCHH Herbert Hoover .60 1.50
PCJC Jimmy Carter .60 1.50
PCRN Richard Nixon .60 1.50
PCGHW George H. W. Bush .60 1.50
PCGWB George W. Bush .60 1.50
PCHST Harry S. Truman .60 1.50
PCJFK John F. Kennedy .60 1.50

2015 Topps Archives Will Ferrell

COMPLETE SET (10) 30.00 80.00
STATED ODDS 1:24 HOBBY
WF1 Will Ferrell 4.00 10.00
WF2 Will Ferrell 4.00 10.00
WF3 Will Ferrell 4.00 10.00
WF4 Will Ferrell 4.00 10.00
WF5 Will Ferrell 4.00 10.00
WF6 Will Ferrell 4.00 10.00
WF7 Will Ferrell 4.00 10.00
WF8 Will Ferrell 4.00 10.00
WF9 Will Ferrell 4.00 10.00
WF10 Will Ferrell 4.00 10.00

2016 Topps Archives

COMP.SET w/o SP's (300) 20.00 50.00
SP ODDS 1:41 HOBBY
PRINTING PLATE ODDS 1:682 HOBBY
PLATE PRINT RUN 1 SET PER COLOR
BLACK-CYAN-MAGENTA-YELLOW ISSUED
NO PLATE PRICING DUE TO SCARCITY
1 Albert Pujols .30 .75
2 Carlos Carrasco .15 .40
3 Doc Gooden .15 .40
4 Bret Boone .15 .40
5 Richie Shaffer RC .25 .60
6 Kendrys Morales .15 .40
7 Ketel Marte RC .50 1.25
8 Justin Morneau .20 .50
9 Prince Fielder .20 .50
10 Billy Hamilton .20 .50
11 Matt Reynolds RC .25 .60
12 Robin Yount .25 .60
13 Jason Heyward .20 .50
14 Monte Irvin .20 .50
15 George Springer .20 .50
16 Tony Fernandez .15 .40
17 Elvis Andrus .20 .50
18 Chris Sale .25 .60
19 Don Sutton .20 .50
20 Juan Marichal .20 .50
21 Travis d'Arnaud .20 .50
22 Michael Wacha .20 .50
23 Bernie Williams .20 .50
24 Bert Blyleven .20 .50
25 Kyle Schwarber RC .75 2.00
26 Rafael Palmeiro .20 .50
27 Jim Abbott .15 .40
28 Miguel Almonte RC .25 .60
29 Russell Martin .15 .40
30 Manny Machado .25 .60
31 Henry Owens RC .30 .75
32 Kevin Pillar .15 .40
33 Bucky Dent .15 .40
34 Shin-Soo Choo .20 .50
35 Jim Rice .20 .50
36 Hal Newhouser .20 .50
37 Mac Williamson RC .25 .60
38 Danny Salazar .20 .50
39 David Price .20 .50
40 Jacoby Ellsbury .20 .50
41 Ryne Sandberg .50 1.25
42 J.D. Martinez .25 .60
43 David Wright .20 .50
44 Marcus Stroman .20 .50
45 John Smoltz .25 .60
46 Gio Gonzalez .20 .50
47 Jorge Lopez RC .25 .60
48 Brooks Robinson .20 .50
49 Paul O'Neill .20 .50
50 Max Scherzer .25 .60
51 Tony Perez .20 .50
52 Mark McGwire .40 1.00
53 Greg Bird RC .30 .75
54 Phil Niekro .20 .50
55 Fergie Jenkins .20 .50
56 Brian Johnson RC .25 .60
57 Charlie Blackmon .25 .60
58 Glen Perkins .15 .40
59 Robinson Cano .20 .50
60 Stephen Strasburg .25 .60
61 Kolten Wong .20 .50
62 George Brett .50 1.25
63 Nelson Cruz .25 .60
64 Brad Ziegler .15 .40
65 Justin Upton .20 .50
66 Shelby Miller .20 .50
67 Lorenzo Cain .15 .40
68 Trea Turner RC .75 2.00
69 Collin McHugh .15 .40
70 David Robertson .15 .40
71 Byron Buxton .25 .60
72 Dennis Eckersley .20 .50
73 Kyle Seager .15 .40
74 Dustin Pedroia .25 .60
75 Jon Lester .20 .50
76 Stephen Piscotty RC .40 1.00
77 Jason Kipnis .20 .50
78 Eddie Murray .20 .50
79 John Olerud .15 .40
80 Jose Altuve .20 .50
81 Ralph Kiner .20 .50
82 Justin Bour .20 .50
83 Satchel Paige .25 .60
84 Gregory Polanco .20 .50
85 Joe Mauer .20 .50
86 Alex Rodriguez .30 .75
87 Noah Syndergaard .20 .50
88 A.J. Pollock .15 .40
89 Hanley Ramirez .20 .50
90 Carl Yastrzemski .40 1.00
91 Josh Harrison .15 .40
92 Bartolo Colon .15 .40
93 Zach Lee RC .25 .60
94 Darin Ruf .15 .40
95 Jim Bunning .20 .50
96 Duke Snider .20 .50
97 Randal Grichuk .15 .40
98 Jose Quintana .15 .40
99 Masahiro Tanaka .20 .50
100 Buster Posey .30 .75
101 Babe Ruth .60 1.50
102 Jonathan Lucroy .20 .50
103 Randy Johnson .25 .60
104 Evan Longoria .20 .50
105 Max Kepler RC .40 1.00
106 Oscar Gamble .15 .40
107 Corey Kluber .20 .50
108 Socrates Brito RC .25 .60
109 Eric Hosmer .20 .50
110 Jose Canseco .20 .50
111 Sonny Gray .20 .50
112 Roberto Alomar .20 .50
113 Frankie Montas RC .30 .75
114 Jose Reyes .20 .50
115 Early Wynn .20 .50
116 Stephen Vogt .20 .50
117 Craig Biggio .20 .50
118 Bill Mazeroski .20 .50
119 Madison Bumgarner .20 .50
120 Juan Gonzalez .15 .40
121 Jay Bruce .20 .50
122 Carlton Fisk .20 .50
123 Luis Severino RC .30 .75
124 Chris Archer .15 .40
125 David Ortiz .25 .60
126 Yu Darvish .25 .60
127 Paul Molitor .25 .60
128 Ken Griffey Jr. .50 1.25
129 Mike Trout 1.25 3.00
130 Tom Seaver .20 .50
131 Jim Palmer .20 .50
132 Carlos Santana .20 .50
133 Yordano Ventura .20 .50
134 Carlos Rodon .25 .60
135 Ryan Howard .20 .50
136 Troy Tulowitzki .25 .60
137 Zach Britton .20 .50
138 Curtis Granderson .20 .50
139 Carlos Beltran .20 .50
140 Jung Ho Kang .15 .40
141 Stan Musial .40 1.00
142 Dellin Betances .20 .50
143 DJ LeMahieu .25 .60
144 Tyson Ross .15 .40
145 Felix Hernandez .20 .50
146 Mookie Betts .50 1.25
147 Travis Jankowski RC .25 .60
148 Zack Greinke .25 .60
149 Brian Dozier .20 .50
150 Kris Bryant .30 .75
151 Frank Thomas .25 .60
152 Ian Kinsler .20 .50
153 Honus Wagner .25 .60
154 Jon Gray RC .25 .60
155 Jeurys Familia .20 .50
156 Yasiel Puig .25 .60
157 Jose Abreu .25 .60
158 Gary Sheffield .15 .40
159 Raul Mondesi RC .50 1.25
160 Joc Pederson .20 .50
161 Jose Fernandez .25 .60
162 Gary Sanchez RC .75 2.00
163 Bob Feller .20 .50
164 Jacob deGrom .50 1.25
165 Yasmany Tomas .15 .40
166 Hank Aaron .50 1.25
167 Ryan Klesko .15 .40
168 Matt Carpenter .25 .60
169 Jorge Soler .25 .60
170 Brandon Belt .20 .50
171 George Kell .20 .50
172 Joey Votto .25 .60
173 Billy Williams .20 .50
174 Tom Murphy RC .25 .60
175 Andrelton Simmons .15 .40
176 Willie McCovey .20 .50

177 Bruce Sutter .20 .50
178 Richie Ashburn .20 .50
179 Brandon Drury RC .40 1.00
180 Ozzie Smith .30 .75
181 Evan Gattis .15 .40
182 Joe Morgan .20 .50
183 Salvador Perez .20 .50
184 Carlos Martinez .20 .50
185 Wade Boggs .20 .50
186 Peter O'Brien RC .25 .60
187 Kole Calhoun .15 .40
188 Brandon Crawford .20 .50
189 Whitey Ford .20 .50
190 Lou Gehrig .50 1.25
191 Andres Galarraga .20 .50
192 Vladimir Guerrero .20 .50
193 Aaron Nola RC .50 1.25
194 Garrett Richards .20 .50
195 Mark Melancon .15 .40
196 Trevor Plouffe .15 .40
197 Reggie Jackson .20 .50
198 Adam Wainwright .20 .50
199 Enos Slaughter .20 .50
200 Bryce Harper .40 1.00
201 Jackie Robinson .25 .60
202 Yadier Molina .30 .75
203 Johnny Bench .25 .60
204 Miguel Cabrera .25 .60
205 Jose Peraza RC .30 .75
206 Hoyt Wilhelm .20 .50
207 Chris Davis .15 .40
208 Matt Harvey .20 .50
209 Phil Rizzuto .20 .50
210 Orlando Cepeda .20 .50
211 Kevin Kiermaier .20 .50
212 Gaylord Perry .20 .50
213 Aroldis Chapman .25 .60
214 Adam Jones .20 .50
215 Yoenis Cespedes .25 .60
216 Rougned Odor .20 .50
217 Hector Olivera RC .30 .75
218 John Franco .15 .40
219 Kelby Tomlinson RC .25 .60
220 Larry Doby .20 .50
221 Cole Hamels .20 .50
222 Matt Kemp .20 .50
223 Goose Gossage .20 .50
224 Hunter Pence .20 .50
225 Clayton Kershaw .40 1.00
226 Ryan Braun .20 .50
227 Freddie Freeman .30 .75
228 Roberto Clemente .60 1.50
229 Billy Butler .15 .40
230 James Shields .15 .40
231 Paul Goldschmidt .25 .60
232 David Peralta .15 .40
233 Edwin Encarnacion .25 .60
234 Jake Arrieta .20 .50
235 Lou Boudreau .20 .50
236 Roger Maris .25 .60
237 Miguel Sano RC .40 1.00
238 Rod Carew .20 .50
239 Xander Bogaerts .25 .60
240 John Kruk .15 .40
241 Rob Refsnyder RC .30 .75
242 Harmon Killebrew .25 .60
243 Cal Ripken Jr. .75 2.00
244 Trevor Rosenthal .20 .50
245 Adam Eaton .15 .40
246 Gary Carter .20 .50
247 Zack Godley RC .25 .60
248 Anthony Rizzo .30 .75
249 Jose Bautista .20 .50
250 Carlos Correa .25 .60
251 Bobby Doerr .20 .50
252 Trayce Thompson RC .40 1.00
253 Robin Roberts .20 .50
254 Colin Rea RC .25 .60
255 Brandon Phillips .15 .40
256 Chipper Jones .25 .60
257 Giancarlo Stanton .25 .60
258 Odubel Herrera .20 .50
259 Willie Stargell .20 .50
260 Dallas Keuchel .20 .50
261 Joe Mauer .20 .50
262 Andre Dawson .20 .50
263 Eddie Mathews .25 .60
264 Luke Jackson RC .25 .60
265 Warren Spahn .20 .50
266 Hisashi Iwakuma .20 .50
267 Carlos Gonzalez .20 .50
268 Carl Edwards Jr. RC .30 .75
269 Adrian Gonzalez .20 .50
270 Brian McCann .20 .50
271 Ted Williams .50 1.25
272 Taijuan Walker .15 .40
273 Nolan Ryan .75 2.00
274 Michael Brantley .20 .50
275 Corey Seager RC 2.50 6.00
276 Nolan Arenado .40 1.00
277 Ichiro Suzuki .30 .75
278 Lucas Duda .20 .50
279 Josh Donaldson .20 .50
280 Josh Reddick .15 .40
281 Francisco Lindor .25 .60
282 Lou Brock .20 .50
283 Michael Conforto RC .30 .75
284 Catfish Hunter .20 .50
285 Maikel Franco .20 .50
286 Willie Mays .50 1.25
287 Adrian Beltre .25 .60
288 Nomar Garciaparra .20 .50
289 Wade Davis .15 .40
290 Anthony Rendon .25 .60
291 Kaleb Cowart RC .25 .60
292 Andrew Miller .20 .50
293 Craig Kimbrel .20 .50
294 Andrew McCutchen .25 .60
295 Todd Frazier .15 .40
296 Edgar Martinez .20 .50
297 Justin Verlander .25 .60
298 Kyle Waldrop RC .30 .75
299 Hector Rondon .15 .40
300 Sandy Koufax .50 1.25
301 Kenta Maeda SP RC 6.00 15.00
302 Randy Jones SP 3.00 8.00
303 Tom Gordon SP 3.00 8.00
304 Al Kaline SP 6.00 15.00
305 Steve Garvey SP 4.00 10.00
306 Tito Francona SP 3.00 8.00
307 Phil Nevin SP 3.00 8.00
308 Charlie Hayes SP 3.00 8.00
309 Kris Benson SP 3.00 8.00
310 Sandy Koufax SP 12.00 30.00

2016 Topps Archives Blue

*BLUE: 3X TO 8X BASIC
*BLUE RC: 2 TO 5X BASIC RC
STATED ODDS 1:14 HOBBY
STATED PRINT RUN 199 SER.#'d SETS
275 Corey Seager 10.00 25.00

2016 Topps Archives Red

*RED: 8X TO 20X BASIC
*RED RC: 5X TO 12X BASIC RC
STATED ODDS 1:55 HOBBY
STATED PRINT RUN 50 SER.#'d SETS
275 Corey Seager 30.00 80.00

2016 Topps Archives '69 Topps Super

COMPLETE SET (30) 30.00 80.00
STATED ODDS 1:6 HOBBY
PRINTING PLATE ODDS 1:6808 HOBBY
PLATE PRINT RUN 1 SET PER COLOR
NO PLATE PRICING DUE TO SCARCITY
*RED/50: 3X TO 8X BASIC
69TSAG Alex Gordon .60 1.50
69TSAM Andrew Miller .60 1.50
69TSAMU Andrew McCutchen .75 2.00
69TSAN Aaron Nola 1.00 2.50
69TSAP A.J. Pollock .50 1.25
69TSBC Brandon Crawford .60 1.50
69TSBH Bryce Harper 1.25 3.00
69TSBP Buster Posey 1.00 2.50
69TSCH Cole Hamels .60 1.50
69TSCS Chris Sale .75 2.00
69TSDG Dee Gordon .50 1.25
69TSDO David Ortiz .75 2.00
69TSEE Edwin Encarnacion .75 2.00
69TSFF Freddie Freeman 1.00 2.50
69TSFL Francisco Lindor .75 2.00
69TSJA Jose Altuve .60 1.50
69TSJAR Jake Arrieta .60 1.50
69TSJD Josh Donaldson .60 1.50
69TSJP Joc Pederson .60 1.50
69TSKB Kris Bryant 1.00 2.50
69TSKS Kyle Schwarber 1.50 4.00
69TSLS Luis Severino .60 1.50
69TSMH Matt Harvey .60 1.50
69TSMM Manny Machado .75 2.00
69TSMS Miguel Sano .75 2.00
69TSMT Mike Trout 4.00 10.00
69TSPG Paul Goldschmidt .75 2.00
69TSSG Sonny Gray .60 1.50
69TSSP Stephen Piscotty .75 2.00
69TSTR Tyson Ross .50 1.25

2016 Topps Archives '69 Topps Super Autographs

STATED ODDS 1:314 HOBBY
PRINT RUNS B/WN 20-99 COPIES PER
EXCHANGE DEADLINE 5/31/2018
69TSAAG Alex Gordon/75 12.00 30.00
69TSAAN Aaron Nola/99 20.00 50.00
69TSAAP A.J. Pollock/99 8.00 20.00
69TSABH Bryce Harper/99 250.00 500.00
69TSACS Chris Sale/75 15.00 40.00
69TSADG Dee Gordon/99 8.00 20.00
69TSADO David Ortiz/25 125.00 250.00
69TSAEE Edwin Encarnacion/75 12.00 30.00
69TSAFL Francisco Lindor/99 12.00 30.00
69TSAJA Jose Altuve/75 25.00 60.00
69TSAJP Joc Pederson/99 10.00 25.00
69TSAKB Kris Bryant/75 125.00 250.00
69TSAKS Kyle Schwarber/99 25.00 60.00
69TSALS Luis Severino/75 10.00 25.00
69TSAMM Manny Machado/50 50.00 120.00
69TSAMS Miguel Sano/99 12.00 30.00
69TSAMT Mike Trout/20 200.00 300.00
69TSASG Sonny Gray/99 10.00 25.00
69TSASP Stephen Piscotty/99 12.00 30.00

2016 Topps Archives '69 Topps Super Autographs Red

*RED: .5X TO 1.2X BASIC
STATED ODDS 1:622 HOBBY
STATED PRINT RUN 50 SER.#'d SETS
EXCHANGE DEADLINE 5/31/2018

2016 Topps Archives '85 Father Son

COMPLETE SET (7) 3.00 8.00
STATED ODDS 1:12 HOBBY
FSAAL S.Alomar Sr./R.Alomar .75 2.00
FSAL S.Alomar Jr./S.Alomar Sr. .60 1.50
FSBB B.Boone/B.Boone .60 1.50
FSFF T.Francona/T.Francona .75 2.00
FSGG K.Griffey Jr./K.Griffey Sr. 2.00 5.00
FSGGO T.Gordon/D.Gordon .60 1.50
FSPP E.Perez/T.Perez .75 2.00

2016 Topps Archives '85 Topps #1 Draft Pick

COMPLETE SET (18) 6.00 15.00
STATED ODDS 1:8 HOBBY
PRINTING PLATE ODDS 1:10,294 HOBBY
PLATE PRINT RUN 1 SET PER COLOR
NO PLATE PRICING DUE TO SCARCITY
*RED/50: 3X TO 8X BASIC
85DPAB Andy Benes .50 1.25
85DPAG Adrian Gonzalez .60 1.50
85DPAR Alex Rodriguez 1.00 2.50
85DPBH Bryce Harper 1.25 3.00
85DPBS B.J. Surhoff .50 1.25
85DPCC Carlos Correa .75 2.00
85DPCJ Chipper Jones .75 2.00
85DPDP David Price .60 1.50
85DPDS Darryl Strawberry .50 1.25
85DPGC Gerrit Cole .75 2.00
85DPHB Harold Baines .60 1.50
85DPJB Jeff Burroughs .50 1.25
85DPJH Josh Hamilton .60 1.50
85DPJM Joe Mauer .60 1.50
85DPKG Ken Griffey Jr. 1.50 4.00
85DPRB Ron Blomberg .50 1.25
85DPRM Rick Monday .50 1.25
85DPSS Stephen Strasburg .75 2.00

2016 Topps Archives '85 Topps #1 Draft Pick Autographs

STATED ODDS 1:1446 HOBBY
PRINT RUNS B/WN 10-50 COPIES PER
NO PRICING ON QTY 10 OR LESS
EXCHANGE DEADLINE 5/31/2018
85DPAG Adrian Gonzalez/25 60.00 150.00
85DPBS B.J. Surhoff/50 10.00 25.00
85DPCC Carlos Correa/25 200.00 400.00
85DPCJ Chipper Jones/20 300.00 500.00
85DPDS Darryl Strawberry/50 40.00 100.00
85DPHB Harold Baines/50 20.00 50.00
85DPJB Jeff Burroughs/50 10.00 25.00
85DPKB Kris Benson/50 10.00 25.00
85DPKG Ken Griffey Jr./15 1000.00 1500.00
85DPRM Rick Monday/50 10.00 25.00

2016 Topps Archives Bull Durham

COMPLETE SET (7) 4.00 10.00
STATED ODDS 1:12 HOBBY
PRINTING PLATE ODDS 1:28,136 HOBBY
PLATE PRINT RUN 1 SET PER COLOR
NO PLATE PRICING DUE TO SCARCITY
*RED/50: 2X TO 5X BASIC
BDB Bobby 1.00 2.50
BDJ Jimmy 1.00 2.50
BDM Millie 1.00 2.50
BDT Tony 1.00 2.50
BDLH Larry 1.00 2.50
BDNL Nuke LaLoosh 1.00 2.50
BDRS Ron Shelton 1.00 2.50

2016 Topps Archives Bull Durham Autographs

STATED ODDS 1:498 HOBBY
PRINT RUNS B/WN 145-695 COPIES PER
ANNIE,CRASH,NUKE NOT NUMBERED
EXCHANGE DEADLINE 5/31/2018
BDAB Bobby/595 6.00 15.00
BDAJ Jimmy/595 6.00 15.00
BDAM Millie/695 6.00 15.00
BDAT Tony/595 6.00 15.00
BDAAS Annie Savoy 175.00 350.00
BDACD Crash Davis 150.00 300.00
BDALH Larry Hockett/145 25.00 60.00
BDANL Nuke LaLoosh/295 40.00 100.00
BDARS Ron Shelton/345 6.00 15.00

2016 Topps Archives Bull Durham Autographs Red

*RED: 1X TO 2.5X BASIC
STATED ODDS 1:2001 HOBBY
STATED PRINT RUN 50 SER.#'d SETS
EXCHANGE DEADLINE 5/31/2018
BDALH Larry Hockett 40.00 100.00
Robert Wuhl

2016 Topps Archives Fan Favorites Autographs

STATED ODDS 1:19 HOBBY
EXCHANGE DEADLINE 5/31/2018
FFAAB Andy Benes 3.00 8.00
FFAAK Al Kaline 20.00 50.00
FFAAN Aaron Nola 10.00 25.00
FFABB Bob Boone 3.00 8.00
FFABC Bert Campaneris 4.00 10.00
FFABH Bryce Harper 200.00 400.00
FFABS B.J. Surhoff 3.00 8.00
FFABW Billy Wagner 4.00 10.00
FFACC Carlos Correa 75.00 200.00
FFACE Carl Everett 4.00 10.00
FFACH Charlie Hayes 3.00 8.00
FFADG Doc Gooden 8.00 20.00
FFADS Darryl Strawberry 10.00 25.00
FFAEP Eduardo Perez 3.00 8.00
FFAFH Frank Howard 6.00 15.00
FFAFT Fernando Tatis 3.00 8.00
FFAI Ichiro Suzuki 500.00 700.00
FFAJB Jeff Burroughs 3.00 8.00
FFAJK Jim Kaat 5.00 12.00
FFAJL Javy Lopez 5.00 12.00
FFAJN Jeff Nelson 3.00 8.00
FFAJR J.R. Richard 4.00 10.00
FFAJV Jose Vizcaino 3.00 8.00
FFAKBE Kris Benson 3.00 8.00
FFAKM Kenta Maeda 30.00 80.00
FFAKS Kyle Schwarber 15.00 40.00
FFAMA Moises Alou 4.00 10.00
FFAMS Miguel Sano 8.00 20.00
FFAMT Mike Trout 250.00 500.00
FFAPH Pat Hentgen 3.00 8.00
FFAPN Phil Nevin 3.00 8.00
FFARB Ron Blomberg 3.00 8.00
FFARF Rollie Fingers 12.00 30.00
FFARJ Randy Jones 3.00 8.00
FFARM Rick Monday 3.00 8.00
FFASA Sandy Alomar Jr. 5.00 12.00
FFASAJ Sandy Alomar Sr. 5.00 12.00
FFASG Steve Garvey 12.00 30.00
FFASK Sandy Koufax
FFATF Terry Francona 4.00 10.00
FFATG Tom Gordon 6.00 15.00
FFATH Teddy Higuera 3.00 8.00
FFATIF Tito Francona 3.00 8.00
FFAVL Vern Law 3.00 8.00

2016 Topps Archives Fan Favorites Autographs Blue

*BLUE: .5X TO 1.2X BASIC
STATED ODDS 1:63 HOBBY
STATED PRINT RUN 199 SER.#'d SETS
EXCHANGE DEADLINE 5/31/2018
FFADEC Dennis Eckersley 12.00 30.00

2016 Topps Archives Fan Favorites Autographs Red

*RED: .6X TO 1.5X BASIC
STATED ODDS 1:237 HOBBY
STATED PRINT RUN 50 SER.#'d SETS
EXCHANGE DEADLINE 5/31/2018
FFADEC Dennis Eckersley 15.00 40.00

2017 Topps Archives

COMP.SET w/o SP's (300) 20.00 50.00
SP ODDS 1:55 HOBBY
1A Mike Trout 1.25 3.00
1B Trt SP Bat on shldr 8.00 20.00
2A Buster Posey .30 .75
2B Posey SP Wht Jrsy 4.00 10.00
3 Earl Weaver .20 .50
4 Goose Gossage .20 .50
5 Tony Perez .20 .50
6 Ryan Braun .20 .50
7 Billy Hamilton .20 .50
8 DJ LeMahieu .25 .60
9 Mark Trumbo .15 .40
10 Rio Ruiz RC .25 .60
11 Nolan Ryan .75 2.00
12 Andres Galarraga .20 .50
13 Jorge Alfaro RC .30 .75
14 Marcell Ozuna .25 .60
15 Brandon Belt .20 .50
16 Jay Bruce .20 .50
17 Melky Cabrera .15 .40
18 Sean Manaea .15 .40
19 Russell Martin .15 .40
20 Jonathan Lucroy .20 .50
21 Jose Ramirez .20 .50
22 Raimel Tapia RC .30 .75
23 Honus Wagner .25 .60
24 Willie McCovey .20 .50
25A David Dahl RC .30 .75
25B Dahl SP Helmet 2.50 6.00
26 Yoenis Cespedes .25 .60
27 Jonathan Schoop .15 .40
28 Evan Longoria .20 .50
29 Josh Donaldson .20 .50
30 Khris Davis .25 .60
31 David Price .20 .50
32 Juan Gonzalez .25 .60
33 Miguel Sano .20 .50
34 Carl Yastrzemski .40 1.00
35 Brooks Robinson .20 .50
36 Yu Darvish .25 .60
37 Jon Gray .15 .40
38 Luis Aparicio .20 .50
39 Rob Segedin RC .25 .60
40 Joc Pederson .20 .50
41 Justin Bour .20 .50
42 David Cone .15 .40
43 Duke Snider .20 .50
44 Julio Teheran .20 .50
45 Javier Baez .30 .75
46 Aaron Sanchez .20 .50
47 Jeff Hoffman RC .25 .60
48 Jim Palmer .20 .50
49 Brian Dozier .25 .60
50A Hank Aaron .50 1.25
50B Aaron SP Bttng stnce 5.00 12.00
51 Robert Gsellman RC .25 .60
52 Bo Jackson .25 .60
53 Freddie Freeman .30 .75
54 Chris Archer .15 .40
55 Fernando Valenzuela .15 .40
56 Eric Hosmer .20 .50
57 Albert Pujols .30 .75
58 Odubel Herrera .20 .50
59 Rollie Fingers .20 .50
60 Catfish Hunter .20 .50
61 Gary Carter .20 .50
62 Aaron Judge RC 10.00 25.00
63 Ryon Healy RC .30 .75
64 Noah Syndergaard .20 .50
65 Stephen Strasburg .25 .60
66 Adrian Beltre .25 .60
67 Edwin Diaz .20 .50
68 Lorenzo Cain .15 .40
69 Jason Heyward .20 .50
70 Ichiro .30 .75
71 German Marquez RC .40 1.00
72 Edgar Martinez .20 .50
73 Bobby Doerr .20 .50
74 Corey Kluber .20 .50
75A Ty Cobb .40 1.00
75B Cobb SP w/Bat 5.00 12.00
76 Curtis Granderson .20 .50
77 Nomar Mazara .15 .40
78 Nolan Arenado .40 1.00
79 Brandon Crawford .20 .50
80 Max Scherzer .25 .60
81 Tyler Glasnow RC 1.00 2.50
82A Mike Piazza .25 .60
82B Piazza SP Swinging 3.00 8.00
83 Joe Morgan .20 .50
84 Carson Fulmer RC .25 .60
85 Jon Lester .20 .50
86 Drew Smyly .15 .40
87 Dellin Betances .20 .50
88 Salvador Perez .20 .50
89 Adam Duvall .20 .50
90 Kenley Jansen .20 .50
91 Adam Jones .20 .50
92 Masahiro Tanaka .20 .50
93 Matt Kemp .20 .50
94 Manny Margot RC .25 .60
95 Don Mattingly .50 1.25
96 Bruce Sutter .20 .50
97 Johnny Damon .20 .50
98 Jake Lamb .20 .50
99 Lou Gehrig .50 1.25
100A Corey Seager .25 .60
100B Seager SP Swinging 3.00 8.00
101A Dansby Swanson RC .60 1.50
101B Swnsn SP Blue jrsy 6.00 15.00
102A Carlos Correa .25 .60
102B Correa SP Glove 3.00 8.00
103 Alex Reyes RC .30 .75
104 Bert Blyleven .20 .50
105 Jake Odorizzi .15 .40
106 Fergie Jenkins .20 .50
107 Carlos Gonzalez .20 .50
108 Steven Matz .15 .40
109 Gavin Cecchini RC .25 .60
110 Billy Williams .20 .50
111 Danny Salazar .20 .50
112 Francisco Lindor .25 .60
113 Elvis Andrus .20 .50
114 Jose De Leon RC .25 .60
115 Andy Pettitte .20 .50
116 Curt Schilling .20 .50
117 Dee Gordon .15 .40
118 Drew Pomeranz .20 .50
119 Yulieski Gurriel RC .40 1.00
120 Dexter Fowler .20 .50
121 Marcus Stroman .20 .50
122 Willie Stargell .20 .50
123 Gary Sanchez .25 .60
124 Randal Grichuk .15 .40
125A Jackie Robinson .25 .60
125B Rbnsn SP Kneeling 3.00 8.00
126 Jacoby Ellsbury .20 .50
127 Troy Tulowitzki .25 .60
128 Roberto Alomar .20 .50
129 Yasiel Puig .25 .60
130 Robinson Cano .20 .50
131 Jackie Bradley Jr. .25 .60
132 Andrew Benintendi RC .75 2.00
133 Jake Thompson RC .25 .60
134A Whitey Ford .20 .50
134B Ford SP Pitching 2.50 6.00
135 Sonny Gray .20 .50
136 Rob Manfred .15 .40
137 Kyle Hendricks .25 .60
138A Clayton Kershaw .40 1.00
138B Krshw SP Back of jrsy 5.00 12.00
139 Phil Rizzuto .20 .50
140 Lou Brock .20 .50
141 Dallas Keuchel .20 .50
142 Carlos Asuaje RC .25 .60
143 Willson Contreras .25 .60
144 Ken Giles .15 .40
145 Hisashi Iwakuma .20 .50
146 Michael Fulmer .15 .40
147 Jose Bautista .20 .50
148 Harmon Killebrew .25 .60
149 J.D. Martinez .25 .60
150 Jose Quintana .15 .40
151 Jharel Cotton RC .25 .60
152 Victor Martinez .20 .50
153 Frank Thomas .25 .60
154 Roman Quinn RC .25 .60
155 Cole Hamels .20 .50
156 Maikel Franco .20 .50
157 Aledmys Diaz .20 .50
158 Hunter Renfroe RC .30 .75
159 Pedro Martinez .20 .50
160 Roy Oswalt .20 .50
161 Anthony Rizzo .30 .75
162 Roger Maris .25 .60
163 John Smoltz .25 .60
164 Larry Doby .20 .50
165 Wade Davis .15 .40
166 Zach Britton .20 .50
167 Dennis Eckersley .20 .50
168 Orlando Arcia RC .40 1.00
169 Starlin Castro .15 .40
170 Nelson Cruz .25 .60
171 Kevin Pillar .15 .40
172 Rich Hill .15 .40
173 Carlos Martinez .20 .50
174 Jonathan Villar .15 .40
175A Sandy Koufax .50 1.25
175B Koufax SP Pitching 6.00 15.00
176 Stephen Piscotty .20 .50
177 Nomar Garciaparra .20 .50
178 Edwin Encarnacion .25 .60
179 Early Wynn .20 .50
180 Danny Duffy .15 .40
181 Eddie Murray .20 .50
182 Justin Turner .25 .60
183 Anthony Rendon .25 .60
184 Teoscar Hernandez RC 1.00 2.50
185 Ivan Rodriguez .20 .50
186 Monte Irvin .20 .50
187 Jason Kipnis .20 .50
188 Ozzie Smith .30 .75
189 Jeurys Familia .20 .50
190 Zack Greinke .25 .60
191 Sparky Anderson .20 .50
192 Ryne Sandberg .50 1.25
193 Tony Clark .15 .40
194 Xander Bogaerts .25 .60
195 Craig Kimbrel .20 .50
196 Chris Davis .15 .40
197 Jimmie Foxx .25 .60
198 Ben Zobrist .20 .50
199 Carlos Santana .20 .50
200A Kris Bryant .30 .75
200B Brnt SP Gray jrsy 6.00 15.00
201A Roberto Clemente .60 1.50
201B Clmnte SP w/Bat 6.00 15.00
202 Felix Hernandez .20 .50
203 Yasmani Grandal .15 .40
204 Warren Spahn .20 .50
205 Trea Turner .20 .50
206 John Lackey .20 .50
207 Juan Marichal .20 .50
208 Todd Frazier .15 .40
209 George Springer .20 .50
210 Mookie Betts .50 1.25
211 Starling Marte .20 .50
212 Jacob deGrom .50 1.25
213 Paul Konerko .20 .50
214 Seung-Hwan Oh .30 .75
215 Tyler Austin RC .30 .75
216 Christian Yelich .30 .75
217 Kole Calhoun .15 .40
218 Aaron Boone .15 .40
219 Jim Bunning .20 .50
220 Kenta Maeda .20 .50
221 JaCoby Jones RC .30 .75
222 Matt Carpenter .25 .60
223 Jose Abreu .25 .60
224 Bobby Abreu .15 .40
225A Babe Ruth .60 1.50
225B Ruth SP Jacket 6.00 15.00
226 Hanley Ramirez .20 .50
227A Manny Machado .25 .60
227B Mchdo SP Ornge Jrsy 3.00 8.00
228 Bob Lemon .20 .50
229 Gerrit Cole .25 .60
230 Omar Vizquel .20 .50
231 Mark McGwire .40 1.00
232 Lou Boudreau .20 .50
233 A.J. Pollock .15 .40
234 Ian Kinsler .20 .50
235 Chris Sale .25 .60
236 Braden Shipley RC .25 .60
237 Joe Musgrove RC .75 2.00
238 Gregory Polanco .20 .50
239 Kelvin Herrera .15 .40
240 Rick Porcello .20 .50
241 Justin Verlander .25 .60
242 Matt Olson RC 1.25 3.00
243 David Ortiz .25 .60
244 Trevor Story .25 .60
245 Johnny Cueto .20 .50
246 Wil Myers .20 .50
247 Matt Harvey .20 .50
248 Andre Dawson .20 .50
249 Tom Glavine .20 .50
250A Bryce Harper .40 1.00
250B Harper SP Red slve 8.00 20.00
251 Jeff Samardzija .15 .40
252 Evan Gattis .15 .40
253 Jean Segura .20 .50
254 George Brett .50 1.25
255 Reggie Jackson .20 .50
256 Ian Desmond .15 .40
257 T.J. Rivera RC .40 1.00
258 Dustin Pedroia .25 .60
259 Tony La Russa .20 .50
260 Bob Feller .20 .50
261 Rob Zastryzny RC .25 .60
262 Eddie Mathews .25 .60
263 Roberto Osuna .15 .40
264 Kyle Schwarber .25 .60
265 Randy Johnson .25 .60
266 Daniel Murphy .20 .50
267 Seth Lugo RC .25 .60
268 Andrew McCutchen .25 .60
269 Reynaldo Lopez RC .25 .60
270 Mark Melancon .15 .40
271 Justin Upton .20 .50
272 Jose Canseco .20 .50
273 Ted Williams .50 1.25
274 Andrew Miller .20 .50
275A Alex Bregman RC 1.25 3.00
275B Brgmn SP Running 5.00 12.00
276 Giancarlo Stanton .25 .60
277 Yoan Moncada RC .75 2.00
278 Tom Seaver .20 .50
279 Kyle Seager .15 .40
280 Robin Roberts .20 .50
281 Charlie Blackmon .25 .60
282 David Robertson .15 .40
283 Adam Eaton .25 .60
284 Jake Arrieta .20 .50
285 Michael Brantley .20 .50
286 Rougned Odor .20 .50
287 Paul Goldschmidt .25 .60
288 Matt Strahm RC .25 .60
289 Aroldis Chapman .25 .60
290 Kevin Gausman .25 .60
291 Hunter Dozier RC .25 .60
292 Adam Wainwright .20 .50
293 Jose Altuve .20 .50
294 Joey Votto .25 .60
295 Whitey Herzog .15 .40
296 Carlos Carrasco .15 .40
297 Miguel Cabrera .25 .60
298 Addison Russell .25 .60
299 Luis Gonzalez .15 .40
300A Derek Jeter .60 1.50
300B Jeter SP Fldng 6.00 15.00

2017 Topps Archives Blackless No Signature

*BLACKLESS: 6X TO 15X BASIC
*BLACKLESS RC: 4X TO 10X BASIC RC
STATED ODDS 1:110 HOBBY

2017 Topps Archives Blue

*BLUE: 5X TO 12X BASIC
*BLUE RC: 3X TO 8X BASIC RC
STATED ODDS 1:37 HOBBY
STATED PRINT RUN 75 SER.#'d SETS
300 Derek Jeter 8.00 20.00

2017 Topps Archives Gold Winner

*GOLD WINNER: 6X TO 15X BASIC
*GOLD WINNER RC: 4X TO 10X BASIC RC
STATED ODDS 1:110 HOBBY
210 Mookie Betts 10.00 25.00
254 George Brett 20.00 50.00
255 Reggie Jackson 12.00 30.00
258 Dustin Pedroia 8.00 20.00
277 Yoan Moncada 20.00 50.00
297 Miguel Cabrera 10.00 25.00
300 Derek Jeter 10.00 25.00

2017 Topps Archives Gray Back

*GRAY BACK: 6X TO 15X BASIC
*GRAY BACK RC: 4X TO 10X BASIC RC
STATED ODDS 1:110 HOBBY
1 Mike Trout 15.00 40.00
95 Don Mattingly 12.00 30.00

2017 Topps Archives Peach

*PEACH: 4X TO 10X BASIC
*PEACH RC: 2.5X TO 6X BASIC RC
STATED ODDS 1:14 HOBBY
STATED PRINT RUN 199 SER.#'d SETS
300 Derek Jeter 6.00 15.00

2017 Topps Archives Red

*RED: 12X TO 30X BASIC
*RED RC: 8X TO 20X BASIC RC
STATED ODDS 1:110 HOBBY
STATED PRINT RUN 25 SER.#'d SETS
300 Derek Jeter 20.00 50.00

2017 Topps Archives '16 Retro Original

COMPLETE SET (20) 15.00 40.00
STATED ODDS 1:12 HOBBY
RO1 Kris Bryant .75 2.00
RO2 Bryce Harper 1.00 2.50
RO3 Yoenis Cespedes .60 1.50
RO4 Anthony Rizzo .75 2.00
RO5 Gary Sanchez .60 1.50
RO6 Buster Posey .75 2.00
RO7 Jake Arrieta .50 1.25
RO8 Justin Verlander .60 1.50
RO9 Giancarlo Stanton .60 1.50
RO10 Carlos Correa .60 1.50
RO11 Manny Machado .60 1.50
RO12 Clayton Kershaw 1.00 2.50
RO13 Francisco Lindor .60 1.50
RO14 Mike Trout 3.00 8.00
RO15 Mookie Betts 1.25 3.00
RO16 Josh Donaldson .50 1.25
RO17 Max Scherzer .60 1.50
RO18 Miguel Cabrera .60 1.50
RO19 Nolan Arenado 1.00 2.50
RO20 Noah Syndergaard .50 1.25

2017 Topps Archives '59 Bazooka

COMPLETE SET (20) 15.00 40.00
STATED ODDS 1:6 HOBBY
*BLUE/75: 2X TO 5X BASIC
*RED/25: 4X TO 10X BASIC
59B1 Carlos Correa .60 1.50
59B2 Ivan Rodriguez .50 1.25
59B3 Stephen Piscotty .50 1.25
59B4 Yulieski Gurriel .60 1.50
59B5 Bryce Harper 1.00 2.50
59B6 Ozzie Smith .75 2.00
59B7 Aaron Judge 8.00 20.00
59B8 Tom Glavine .50 1.25
59B9 Francisco Lindor .60 1.50
59B10 Alex Bregman 2.00 5.00
59B11 Nolan Ryan 2.00 5.00
59B12 Paul Konerko .50 1.25
59B13 Al Kaline .60 1.50
59B14 Corey Seager .60 1.50
59B15 Kris Bryant .75 2.00
59B16 Omar Vizquel .50 1.25
59B17 Sandy Koufax 1.25 3.00
59B18 Yoan Moncada 1.25 3.00
59B19 Dustin Pedroia .60 1.50
59B20 Mike Trout 3.00 8.00

2017 Topps Archives '59 Bazooka Autographs

STATED ODDS 1:309 HOBBY
PRINT RUNS B/WN 35-99 COPIES PER
EXCHANGE DEADLINE 5/31/2019
59BAAB Alex Bregman/99 20.00 50.00
59BAAJ Aaron Judge/99 60.00 150.00
59BAAK Al Kaline/99 25.00 50.00
59BABH Bryce Harper
59BACC Carlos Correa/99 30.00 80.00
59BACS Corey Seager/99 30.00 80.00
59BADP Dustin Pedroia/99 20.00 50.00
59BAFL Francisco Lindor/99 20.00 50.00
59BAKB Kris Bryant/99 100.00 250.00
59BAMT Mike Trout
59BANR Nolan Ryan/35 150.00 300.00
59BAOS Ozzie Smith/99 20.00 50.00
59BAOV Omar Vizquel/99 5.00 12.00
59BAPK Paul Konerko/99 8.00 20.00
59BASP Stephen Piscotty/99 5.00 12.00
59BATG Tom Glavine/99 15.00 40.00
59BAYG Yulieski Gurriel/99 10.00 25.00
59BAYM Yoan Moncada/99 30.00 80.00

2017 Topps Archives '59 Bazooka Autographs Red

*RED: .6X TO 1.5X BASIC
STATED ODDS 1:961 HOBBY
STATED PRINT RUN 25 SER.#'d SETS
EXCHANGE DEADLINE 5/31/2019
59BAMT Mike Trout 400.00 600.00
59BANR Nolan Ryan 200.00 400.00

2017 Topps Archives '60 Rookie Stars

COMPLETE SET (10) 12.00 30.00
STATED ODDS 1:12 HOBBY
*BLUE/75: .75X TO 2X BASIC
*RED/25: 3X TO 8X BASIC
RS1 Yoan Moncada 1.25 3.00
RS2 Orlando Arcia .60 1.50
RS3 Andrew Benintendi 1.25 3.00
RS4 Dansby Swanson 1.00 2.50
RS5 David Dahl .50 1.25
RS6 Alex Reyes .50 1.25
RS7 Yulieski Gurriel .60 1.50
RS8 Tyler Glasnow 1.50 4.00
RS9 Aaron Judge 8.00 20.00
RS10 Alex Bregman 2.00 5.00

2017 Topps Archives '60 Rookie Stars Autographs

STATED ODDS 1:700 HOBBY
STATED PRINT RUN 150 SER.#'d SETS
EXCHANGE DEADLINE 5/31/2019
RSAAB Alex Bregman 20.00 50.00
RSAABE Andrew Benintendi 60.00 150.00
RSAAJ Aaron Judge 200.00 400.00
RSADD David Dahl 8.00 20.00
RSADS Dansby Swanson
RSAYG Yulieski Gurriel
RSAYM Yoan Moncada

2017 Topps Archives '60 Rookie Stars Autographs Blue

*BLUE: .5X TO 1.2X BASIC
STATED ODDS 1:1401 HOBBY
STATED PRINT RUN 75 SER.#'d SETS
EXCHANGE DEADLINE 5/31/2019
RSADS Dansby Swanson 30.00 80.00
RSAYG Yulieski Gurriel 12.00 30.00
RSAYM Yoan Moncada 50.00 120.00

2017 Topps Archives '60 Rookie Stars Autographs Red

*RED: .6X TO 1.5X BASIC
STATED ODDS 1:4188 HOBBY
STATED PRINT RUN 25 SER.#'d SETS
EXCHANGE DEADLINE 5/31/2019
RSADS Dansby Swanson 40.00 100.00
RSAYG Yulieski Gurriel 15.00 40.00
RSAYM Yoan Moncada 60.00 150.00

2017 Topps Archives Coins

INSERTED IN RETAIL PACKS
*BLUE: 1X TO 2.5X BASIC
C1 Kris Bryant 1.25 3.00
C2 Carlos Correa 1.00 2.50
C3 Gary Sanchez 1.00 2.50
C4 Mookie Betts 2.00 5.00
C5 Yoenis Cespedes 1.00 2.50
C6 Orlando Arcia 1.00 2.50
C7 Noah Syndergaard .75 2.00
C8 Anthony Rizzo 1.25 3.00
C9 David Dahl .75 2.00
C10 Justin Verlander 1.00 2.50
C11 Francisco Lindor 1.00 2.50
C12 Dansby Swanson 1.50 4.00
C13 Nolan Arenado 1.50 4.00
C14 Josh Donaldson .75 2.00
C15 Aaron Judge 8.00 20.00
C16 Yoan Moncada 2.00 5.00
C17 Andrew Benintendi 2.00 5.00
C18 Yulieski Gurriel 1.00 2.50

C19 Mike Trout 5.00 12.00
C20 Bryce Harper 1.50 4.00
C21 Manny Machado 1.00 2.50
C22 Clayton Kershaw 1.50 4.00
C23 Giancarlo Stanton 1.00 2.50
C24 Max Scherzer 1.00 2.50
C25 Alex Bregman 3.00 8.00

2017 Topps Archives Derek Jeter Retrospective

COMP.SET w/o SP's (20) 25.00 60.00
STATED ODDS 1:12 HOBBY
STATED SP ODDS 1:240 HOBBY
*BLUE/150: 1X TO 2.5X BASIC
GREEN/99: 1.2X TO 3X BASIC
GREEN SP/99: .6X TO 1.5X BASIC
*GOLD/50: 3X TO 8X BASIC
*GOLD SP/50: 1.5X TO 4X BASIC
DJ1 Jeter SP '93 Topps 12.00 30.00
DJ2 Derek Jeter '94 Topps 1.50 4.00
DJ3 Derek Jeter '95 Topps 1.50 4.00
DJ4 Derek Jeter '96 Topps 1.50 4.00
DJ5 Derek Jeter '97 Topps 1.50 4.00
DJ6 Derek Jeter '98 Topps 1.50 4.00
DJ7 Derek Jeter '99 Topps 1.50 4.00
DJ8 Derek Jeter '00 Topps 1.50 4.00
DJ9 Derek Jeter '01 Topps 1.50 4.00
DJ10 Derek Jeter '02 Topps 1.50 4.00
DJ11 Derek Jeter '03 Topps 1.50 4.00
DJ12 Derek Jeter '04 Topps 1.50 4.00
DJ13 Derek Jeter '05 Topps 1.50 4.00
DJ14 Derek Jeter '06 Topps 1.50 4.00
DJ16 Derek Jeter '08 Topps 1.50 4.00
DJ17 Derek Jeter '09 Topps 1.50 4.00
DJ18 Derek Jeter '10 Topps 1.50 4.00
DJ19 Derek Jeter '11 Topps 1.50 4.00
DJ20 Derek Jeter '12 Topps 1.50 4.00
DJ21 Derek Jeter '13 Topps 1.50 4.00
DJ22 Derek Jeter '14 Topps 1.50 4.00
DJ23 Jeter SP '15 Topps 12.00 30.00

2017 Topps Archives Fan Favorites Autographs

STATED ODDS 1:19 HOBBY
EXCHANGE DEADLINE 5/31/2019
FFAAB Aaron Boone 10.00 25.00
FFAABE Andrew Benintendi 60.00 150.00
FFAABR Alex Bregman 40.00 100.00
FFAAJ Aaron Judge 100.00 250.00
FFAAR Anthony Rizzo 25.00 60.00
FFABB Billy Bean 3.00 8.00
FFABJ Brian Jordan 3.00 8.00
FFABL Bill "Spaceman" Lee 6.00 15.00
FFABT Bobby Thigpen 3.00 8.00
FFABV Bald Vinny 8.00 20.00
FFACC Carlos Correa 40.00 100.00
FFACJ Cleon Jones 6.00 15.00
FFACK Clayton Kershaw 100.00 250.00
FFADD David Dahl 6.00 15.00
FFADJ Derek Jeter 300.00 600.00
FFADMA Dave Magadan 4.00 10.00
FFADS Dave Stieb 6.00 12.00
FFAER Edgar Renteria 3.00 8.00
FFAGB George Bell EXCH 4.00 10.00
FFAGC Gary Cohen 12.00 30.00
FFAHA Hank Aaron
FFAJC Joe Castiglione 20.00 50.00
FFAJE Jim Edmonds 15.00 40.00
FFAJH John Hirschbeck
FFAJJ Jim Joyce 8.00 20.00
FFAJMC Joe McEwing 3.00 8.00
FFAJS John Smiley 4.00 10.00
FFAJST John Sterling 15.00 40.00
FFAKB Kris Bryant 75.00 200.00
FFAKM Kevin Maas 4.00 10.00
FFAKR Ken Rosenthal 8.00 20.00
FFAKS Kevin Seitzer 4.00 10.00
FFALG Lourdes Gourriel Sr. 3.00 8.00
FFALR Lenny Randle 4.00 10.00
FFAMB Marty Brennaman 15.00 40.00
FFAML Mark Langston 3.00 8.00
FFAMM Manny Mota 4.00 10.00
FFAMMU Mark Mulder 3.00 8.00
FFAMS Mike Scott 3.00 8.00
FFAMT Masahiro Tanaka 150.00 300.00
FFAMT Mike Trout 500.00 800.00
FFAOA Orlando Arcia 4.00 10.00
FFAPG Peter Gammons 15.00 40.00
FFARA Rick Ankiel EXCH 15.00 40.00
FFARCE Ron Cey 6.00 15.00
FFARK Rusty Kuntz 4.00 10.00
FFARM Rob Manfred EXCH 30.00 80.00
FFARO Roy Oswalt 6.00 15.00
FFASA Steve Avery 5.00 12.00
FFASBA Skip Bayless
FFASK Sandy Koufax 1200.00 1600.00
FFATE Theo Epstein
FFATL Tommy Lasorda 60.00 150.00
FFATM Terry Mulholland 3.00 8.00
FFATOC Tony Clark 3.00 8.00
FFATP Tony Pena 5.00 12.00
FFATT Tim Teufel 4.00 10.00
FFATW Tim Wakefield 15.00 40.00
FFATWA Tim Wallach 3.00 8.00
FFATWE Turk Wendell 3.00 8.00
FFATWO Tony Womack 3.00 8.00
FFAWM Wally Moon 5.00 12.00
FFAZH Zack Hample 6.00 15.00

2017 Topps Archives Fan Favorites Autographs Blue

*BLUE: .6X TO 1.5X BASIC
STATED ODDS 1:146 HOBBY
STATED PRINT RUN 75 SER.#'d SETS
EXCHANGE DEADLINE 5/31/2019
FFAAR Anthony Rizzo 30.00 80.00
FFAJC Joe Castiglione 25.00 60.00
FFAJH John Hirschbeck 10.00 25.00
FFAKR Ken Rosenthal 12.00 30.00
FFAPG Peter Gammons 20.00 50.00
FFARA Rick Ankiel EXCH 25.00 60.00
FFASBA Skip Bayless 10.00 25.00
FFATE Theo Epstein 150.00 300.00
FFATW Tim Wakefield 20.00 50.00

2017 Topps Archives Fan Favorites Autographs Peach

*PEACH: .5X TO 1.2X BASIC
STATED ODDS 1:73 HOBBY
STATED PRINT RUN 150 SER.#'d SETS
EXCHANGE DEADLINE 5/31/2019
FFAJH John Hirschbeck 8.00 20.00
FFASBA Skip Bayless 8.00 20.00

2017 Topps Archives Fan Favorites Autographs Red

*RED: .75X TO 2X BASIC
STATED ODDS 1:437 HOBBY
STATED PRINT RUN 25 SER.#'d SETS
EXCHANGE DEADLINE 5/31/2019
FFAAR Anthony Rizzo 40.00 100.00
FFACK Clayton Kershaw 125.00 300.00
FFAJC Joe Castiglione 30.00 80.00
FFAJH John Hirschbeck 12.00 30.00
FFAKR Ken Rosenthal 15.00 40.00
FFAPG Peter Gammons 25.00 60.00
FFARA Rick Ankiel EXCH 30.00 80.00
FFASBA Skip Bayless 12.00 30.00
FFATE Theo Epstein 175.00 350.00
FFATL Tommy Lasorda 125.00 300.00
FFATW Tim Wakefield 25.00 60.00

2017 Topps Archives Originals Autographs

STATED ODDS 1:1753 HOBBY
PRINT RUNS B/WN 5-20 COPIES PER
NO PRICING ON QTY 5
EXCHANGE DEADLINE 5/31/2019
30 Jim Rice 40.00 100.00
97 Curt Schilling 40.00 100.00
JC Jose Canseco
148 Edgar Martinez 20.00 50.00
378 Andy Pettitte 25.00 60.00
382 John Smoltz 60.00 150.00
400 Cal Ripken Jr. 60.00 150.00
414 Frank Thomas 75.00 200.00
500 Chipper Jones 75.00 200.00
551 Carl Yastrzemski 60.00 150.00
586 Rollie Fingers 60.00 150.00
630 Fernando Valenzuela 40.00 100.00
FFAK Al Kaline

2018 Topps Archives

COMP.SET w/o SP's (300) 30.00 80.00
301-320 ODDS 1:8 HOBBY
1 Hank Aaron .50 1.25
2 Noah Syndergaard .20 .50
3 Tom Seaver .20 .50
4 Jack Flaherty RC 1.00 2.50
5 Andrew McCutchen .25 .60
6 Yasiel Puig .25 .60
7 Orlando Cepeda .20 .50
8 Nomar Garciaparra .20 .50
9 Nicky Delmonico RC .25 .60
10 Lucas Giolito .20 .50
11 Scott Kingery RC .40 1.00
12 Corey Seager .25 .60
13 Larry Doby .20 .50
14 Andrew Benintendi .25 .60
15 Ryne Sandberg .50 1.25
16 Harrison Bader RC .40 1.00
17 Sean Manaea .15 .40
18 Ozzie Albies RC .75 2.00
19 Austin Meadows RC .60 1.50
20 Cal Ripken Jr. .75 2.00
21 Dallas Keuchel .20 .50
22 Jordan Hicks RC .50 1.25
23 Don Mattingly .50 1.25
24 Josh Donaldson .20 .50
25 Sandy Koufax .50 1.25
26 Jorge Polanco .20 .50
27 Max Fried RC 1.00 2.50
28 Jackie Bradley Jr. .25 .60
29 Dansby Swanson .25 .60
30 Honus Wagner .25 .60
31 Aaron Judge .60 1.50
32 Miguel Cabrera .25 .60
33 Justin Upton .20 .50
34 Anthony Rendon .25 .60
35 Greg Maddux .30 .75
36 Adam Jones .20 .50
37 Hoyt Wilhelm .20 .50
38 Marcus Stroman .20 .50
39 Adrian Beltre .25 .60
40 Rafael Devers RC .75 2.00
41 Paul Goldschmidt .25 .60
42 Brian Dozier .20 .50
43 Luke Weaver .20 .50
44 Luis Severino .20 .50
45 Joey Gallo .20 .50
46 Warren Spahn .20 .50
47 Carlton Fisk .20 .50
48 Jose Urena .15 .40
49 Bobby Doerr .20 .50
50 Shohei Ohtani RC 3.00 8.00
51 Mike Piazza .25 .60
52 Avisail Garcia .20 .50
53 Edwin Encarnacion .25 .60
54 Odubel Herrera .20 .50
55 Duke Snider .20 .50
56 Aaron Nola .20 .50
57 Mike Zunino .15 .40
58 Whit Merrifield .25 .60
59 Adam Duvall .20 .50
60 Jim Thome .20 .50
61 Manny Machado .25 .60
62 Addison Russell .20 .50
63 Blake Snell .20 .50
64 Evan Longoria .20 .50
65 Brian Anderson RC .30 .75
66 Wade Davis .15 .40
67 Charlie Blackmon .25 .60
68 Will Clark .20 .50
69 Gary Carter .20 .50
70 Tyler Wade RC .30 .75
71 Jake Odorizzi .15 .40
72 Tyler Glasnow .25 .60
73 Juan Soto RC 12.00 30.00
74 Anthony Banda RC .25 .60
75 Giancarlo Stanton .25 .60
76 Michael Conforto .20 .50
77 Jameson Taillon .20 .50
78 Red Schoendienst .20 .50
79 Luis Castillo .20 .50
80 Danny Duffy .15 .40
81 Goose Gossage .20 .50
82 A.J. Pollock .15 .40
83 Jordan Zimmermann .20 .50
84 Bernie Williams .20 .50
85 Bert Blyleven .20 .50
86 Christian Yelich .30 .75
87 Manny Margot .15 .40
88 Paul DeJong .25 .60
89 Julio Teheran .20 .50
90 Andrew Miller .20 .50
91 Garrett Cooper RC .25 .60
92 Albert Pujols .30 .75
93 Justin Verlander .25 .60
94 Lorenzo Cain .15 .40
95 Willy Adames RC .30 .75
96 Eddie Murray .20 .50
97 Dee Gordon .15 .40
98 Ryan Zimmerman .20 .50
99 Khris Davis .25 .60
100 Kris Bryant .30 .75
101 Francisco Lindor .25 .60
102 Daniel Murphy .20 .50
103 Mike Moustakas .20 .50
104 Chris Davis .15 .40
105 Mookie Betts .50 1.25
106 Francisco Mejia RC .30 .75
107 Richie Ashburn .20 .50
108 Amed Rosario RC .30 .75
109 Justin Turner .25 .60
110 Matt Olson .25 .60
111 Kyle Schwarber .25 .60
112 Early Wynn .20 .50
113 Robin Yount .25 .60
114 Didi Gregorius .20 .50
115 Orlando Arcia .15 .40
116 Raisel Iglesias .20 .50
117 Bob Feller .20 .50
118 Jacob deGrom .50 1.25
119 Jim Bunning .20 .50
120 Johnny Bench .25 .60
121 Bruce Sutter .20 .50
122 Nick Markakis .20 .50
123 Joey Lucchesi RC .25 .60
124 Nolan Arenado .40 1.00
125 Justin Bour .15 .40
126 Don Sutton .20 .50
127 Yasmany Tomas .15 .40
128 Rickey Henderson .25 .60
129 DJ LeMahieu .25 .60
130 Brandon Belt .20 .50
131 Byron Buxton .25 .60
132 Chris Archer .15 .40
133 Nomar Mazara .15 .40
134 Stephen Strasburg .25 .60
135 Nelson Cruz .25 .60
136 Marcell Ozuna .25 .60
137 Alex Verdugo RC .40 1.00
138 Brooks Robinson .20 .50
139 Jose Berrios .20 .50
140 Pedro Martinez .20 .50
141 George Springer .20 .50
142 Josh Bell .20 .50
143 Carson Fulmer .15 .40
144 Clint Frazier RC .50 1.25
145 Willie McCovey .20 .50
146 Nick Williams RC .30 .75
147 Enos Slaughter .20 .50
148 Phil Rizzuto .20 .50
149 Zack Cozart .15 .40
150 Clayton Kershaw .40 1.00
151 Carlos Santana .20 .50
152 Billy Hamilton .20 .50
153 Roger Clemens .30 .75
154 Andrew Stevenson RC .25 .60
155 Hunter Pence .20 .50
156 Jimmie Foxx .25 .60
157 Alcides Escobar .20 .50
158 Travis d'Arnaud .20 .50
159 Tim Beckham .20 .50
160 Chris Sale .25 .60
161 Justin Smoak .15 .40
162 Felix Hernandez .20 .50
163 Tommy Pham .15 .40
164 Gleyber Torres RC 2.50 6.00
165 Whitey Ford .20 .50
166 Nicholas Castellanos .25 .60
167 Cole Hamels .20 .50
168 Tommy Lasorda .20 .50
169 George Brett .50 1.25
170 Austin Hedges .15 .40
171 Ozzie Smith .30 .75
172 James McCann .20 .50
173 Carlos Correa .25 .60
174 Anthony Rizzo .30 .75
175 Ryan McMahon RC .60 1.50
176 David Ortiz .25 .60
177 Tim Anderson .25 .60
178 Satchel Paige .25 .60
179 Wil Myers .20 .50
180 Dave Winfield .20 .50
181 Masahiro Tanaka .20 .50
182 Lou Boudreau .20 .50
183 Jake Lamb .20 .50
184 Teoscar Hernandez .25 .60
185 Brad Ziegler .15 .40
186 Austin Hays RC .40 1.00
187 Kevin Kiermaier .20 .50
188 Tyler O'Neill RC .40 1.00
189 Hal Newhouser .20 .50
190 Carlos Carrasco .15 .40
191 Andrelton Simmons .15 .40
192 Barry Larkin .20 .50
193 Tyler Mahle RC .30 .75
194 Jack Morris .20 .50
195 Stephen Piscotty .15 .40
196 Felipe Vazquez .20 .50
197 Ender Inciarte .15 .40
198 Walker Buehler RC 1.25 3.00
199 Corey Knebel .15 .40
200 Derek Jeter .60 1.50
201 Roberto Clemente .60 1.50
202 Ernie Banks .25 .60
203 Yoan Moncada .25 .60
204 Bob Gibson .20 .50
205 Buster Posey .30 .75
206 Robinson Cano .20 .50
207 Luiz Gohara RC .25 .60
208 Starling Marte .20 .50
209 Starlin Castro .15 .40
210 Jonathan Schoop .15 .40
211 Chance Sisco RC .30 .75
212 Ronald Acuna Jr. RC 15.00 40.00
213 Trevor Story .25 .60
214 Kenley Jansen .20 .50
215 Jon Gray .15 .40
216 Michael Fulmer .15 .40
217 Rhys Hoskins RC 1.00 2.50
218 Zack Greinke .25 .60
219 Freddie Freeman .30 .75
220 Yoenis Cespedes .25 .60
221 Tom Glavine .20 .50
222 Jose Ramirez .20 .50
223 Jon Lester .20 .50
224 John Smoltz .25 .60
225 Kyle Seager .15 .40
226 George Kell .20 .50
227 Harmon Killebrew .25 .60
228 Johnny Cueto .20 .50
229 Chipper Jones .25 .60
230 Alex Gordon .20 .50
231 Ichiro .30 .75
232 Joe Morgan .20 .50
233 Trea Turner .20 .50
234 Yadier Molina .30 .75
235 Maikel Franco .20 .50
236 Dustin Pedroia .25 .60
237 Ryan Braun .20 .50
238 Daniel Mengden .15 .40
239 Tony Perez .20 .50
240 Eric Thames .20 .50
241 Edgar Martinez .20 .50
242 Alex Bregman .25 .60
243 Matt Duffy .15 .40
244 Rougned Odor .20 .50
245 Monte Irvin .20 .50
246 Scott Schebler .20 .50
247 Lucas Sims RC .25 .60
248 Wade Boggs .20 .50
249 Alex Rodriguez .30 .75
250 Cody Bellinger .50 1.25
251 Catfish Hunter .20 .50
252 Ervin Santana .15 .40
253 Russell Martin .15 .40
254 Rod Carew .20 .50
255 Randy Johnson .25 .60
256 Jesse Biddle RC .30 .75
257 Hunter Renfroe .15 .40
258 Eddie Mathews .25 .60
259 Patrick Corbin .20 .50
260 Elvis Andrus .20 .50
261 Matt Chapman .25 .60
262 Ralph Kiner .20 .50
263 Fergie Jenkins .20 .50
264 Frank Thomas .25 .60
265 Victor Robles RC .60 1.50
266 Ian Kinsler .20 .50
267 Max Kepler .20 .50
268 Nolan Ryan .75 2.00
269 Dustin Fowler RC .25 .60
270 Reggie Jackson .20 .50
271 Trey Mancini .20 .50
272 Jose Altuve .20 .50
273 Yangervis Solarte .15 .40
274 Tomas Nido RC .25 .60
275 Mark McGwire .40 1.00
276 Aaron Altherr .15 .40
277 Max Scherzer .25 .60
278 Sean Newcomb .20 .50
279 Yu Darvish .25 .60
280 J.P. Crawford RC .25 .60
281 Xander Bogaerts .25 .60
282 Miguel Andujar RC 1.00 2.50
283 Salvador Perez .20 .50
284 Corey Kluber .20 .50
285 Brandon Woodruff RC .75 2.00
286 Dominic Smith RC .30 .75
287 Mike Soroka RC .75 2.00
288 Joey Votto .25 .60
289 Gary Sanchez .25 .60
290 Kevin Pillar .15 .40
291 Matt Carpenter .25 .60
292 Robin Roberts .20 .50
293 Steven Matz .15 .40
294 Adeiny Hechavarria .15 .40
295 Bob Lemon .20 .50
296 Gregory Polanco .20 .50
297 Willie Stargell .20 .50
298 Jose Abreu .25 .60
299 Mike Trout 1.25 3.00
300 Bryce Harper .40 1.00
301 Benintendi/Betts 1.25 3.00
302 Bryant/Rizzo .75 2.00
303 Ohtani/Trout 10.00 25.00
304 Judge/Stanton 1.50 4.00
305 Abreu/Moncada .60 1.50
306 Rosario/Berrios .60 1.50
307 McCutchen/Posey .75 2.00
308 Ichiro/Gordon .75 2.00
309 Pederson/Kemp/Puig .60 1.50
310 Bregman/Altuve/Correa .60 1.50
311 Ichiro TBTC .75 2.00
312 Randy Johnson TBTC .60 1.50
313 Albert Pujols TBTC .75 2.00
314 Mark McGwire TBTC 1.00 2.50
315 Mike Piazza TBTC .60 1.50
316 Jose Canseco TBTC .50 1.25
317 Nolan Ryan TBTC 2.00 5.00
318 Willie McCovey TBTC .50 1.25
319 Hank Aaron TBTC 1.25 3.00
320 Bob Gibson TBTC .50 1.25

2018 Topps Archives Blackless No Signature

*BLACKLESS: 6X TO 15X BASIC
*BLACKLESS RC: 4X TO 10X BASIC RC
STATED ODDS 1:108 HOBBY

2018 Topps Archives Blue

*BLUE: 6X TO 15X BASIC
*BLUE RC: 4X TO 10X BASIC RC
STATED ODDS 1:76 HOBBY
STATED PRINT RUN 25 SER.#'d SETS
23 Don Mattingly 40.00 100.00
31 Aaron Judge 30.00 80.00
169 George Brett 20.00 50.00
198 Walker Buehler 25.00 60.00
200 Derek Jeter 30.00 80.00
268 Nolan Ryan 25.00 60.00

2018 Topps Archives Logo Swap

*LOGO SWAP: 8X TO 20X BASIC
*LOGO SWAP RC: 5X TO 12X BASIC RC
STATED ODDS 1:215 HOBBY

2018 Topps Archives Purple

*PURPLE: 4X TO 10X BASIC
*PURPLE RC: 2.5X TO 6X BASIC RC
STATED ODDS 1:31 HOBBY
STATED PRINT RUN 175 SER.#'d SETS

2018 Topps Archives Silver

*SILVER: 4X TO 10X BASIC
*SILVER RC: 2.5X TO 6X BASIC RC
STATED ODDS 1:55 HOBBY
STATED PRINT RUN 99 SER.#'d SETS

2018 Topps Archives Venezuelan Gray Back

*GRAY BACK: 6X TO 15X BASIC
*GRAY BACK RC: 4X TO 10X BASIC RC
STATED ODDS 1:108 HOBBY

2018 Topps Archives '59 Photo Variations

STATED ODDS 1:239 HOBBY
31 Judge Swing 10.00 25.00
50 Ohtani Swing 15.00 40.00
100 Bryant Fldng 4.00 10.00

2018 Topps Archives '77 Photo Variations

STATED ODDS 1:239 HOBBY
108 Rosario At bat 5.00 12.00
150 Kershaw Ptchng 6.00 15.00
200 Jeter Pnstrp Jrsy 10.00 25.00

2018 Topps Archives '81 Future Stars

COMPLETE SET (10) 6.00 15.00
STATED ODDS 1:8 HOBBY
FSBAL Sisco/Hays/Scott .40 1.00
FSBRA Albies/Acuna/Gohara 8.00 20.00
FSLAA Bridwell/Scribner/Ohtani 6.00 15.00
FSLAD Farmer/Verdugo/Buehler 1.25 3.00
FSMIA Alcantara/Anderson/Cooper .30 .75
FSNYM Smith/Nido/Rosario .30 .75
FSPHI Hoskins/Williams/Crawford 1.00 2.50
FSSTL Mejia/Flaherty/Bader 1.00 2.50
FSWAS Robles/Stevenson/Fedde .60 1.50
FSYAN Frazier/Torres/Andujar 2.50 6.00

2018 Topps Archives '81 Photo Variations

STATED ODDS 1:239 HOBBY
201 Clemente Running 8.00 20.00
202 Banks Pnstp Jrsy 3.00 8.00
300 Harper Wht Jrsy 5.00 12.00

2018 Topps Archives '93 All Stars Dual Autographs

STATED ODDS 1:2149 HOBBY
STATED PRINT RUN 25 SER.#'d SETS
EXCHANGE DEADLINE 7/31/2020
DAAS Altuve/Springer 50.00 120.00
DABT Trout/Bryant EXCH 400.00 800.00
DAHW Hoskins/Williams EXCH 40.00 100.00
DAPK Percival/Kimbrel EXCH 20.00 50.00
DARP Palmer/Robinson EXCH 60.00 150.00
DARS Smith/Rosario 25.00 60.00
DASG Glavine/Smoltz 60.00 150.00
DAWJ Winfield/Judge EXCH 150.00 400.00

2018 Topps Archives Coins

COMPLETE SET (25) 15.00 40.00
INSERTED IN RETAIL PACKS
*SKY BLUE: 3X TO 8X BASIC
C1 Aaron Judge 1.25 3.00
C2 Benny Rodriguez 1.25 3.00
C3 Kris Bryant .60 1.50
C4 Scotty Smalls 1.25 3.00
C5 Squints 1.25 3.00
C6 Carlos Correa .50 1.25
C7 Amed Rosario .40 1.00
C8 Hercules 1.25 3.00
C9 Manny Machado .50 1.25
C10 Rafael Devers 1.00 2.50
C11 Andrew McCutchen .50 1.25
C12 Ozzie Albies 1.00 2.50
C13 Max Scherzer .50 1.25
C14 Victor Robles .75 2.00
C15 Noah Syndergaard .40 1.00
C16 Josh Donaldson .40 1.00
C17 Mike Trout 2.50 6.00
C18 Clint Frazier .60 1.50
C19 Francisco Lindor .50 1.25
C20 Ham 1.25 3.00
C21 Buster Posey .60 1.50
C22 Rhys Hoskins 1.25 3.00
C23 Cody Bellinger 1.00 2.50
C24 Andrew Benintendi .50 1.25
C25 Shohei Ohtani 8.00 20.00

2018 Topps Archives Coming Attraction

COMPLETE SET (20) 10.00 25.00
STATED ODDS 1:6 HOBBY
CA1 Shohei Ohtani 6.00 15.00
CA2 Walker Buehler 1.25 3.00
CA3 Clint Frazier .50 1.25
CA4 Ozzie Albies .75 2.00
CA5 Miguel Andujar 1.00 2.50
CA6 Alex Verdugo .40 1.00
CA7 Victor Robles .60 1.50
CA8 Austin Hays .40 1.00
CA9 J.P. Crawford .25 .60
CA10 Amed Rosario .30 .75
CA11 Gleyber Torres 2.50 6.00
CA12 Ronald Acuna Jr. 8.00 20.00
CA13 Dustin Fowler .25 .60
CA14 Nick Williams .30 .75
CA15 Francisco Mejia .30 .75
CA16 Rhys Hoskins 1.00 2.50
CA17 Dominic Smith .30 .75
CA18 Harrison Bader .40 1.00
CA19 Jack Flaherty 1.00 2.50
CA20 Rafael Devers .75 2.00

2018 Topps Archives Coming Attraction Autographs

STATED ODDS 1:536 HOBBY
PRINT RUNS B/WN 40-99 COPIES PER
EXCHANGE DEADLINE 7/31/2020
*BLUE/25: .6X TO 1.5X BASIC
CAAH Austin Hays/99 10.00 25.00
CAAR Amed Rosario
CAAV Alex Verdugo/99 12.00 30.00
CACF Clint Frazier/50 12.00 30.00
CADF Dustin Fowler/99 6.00 15.00
CADS Dominic Smith
CAFM Francisco Mejia EXCH 8.00 20.00
CAGT Gleyber Torres/99 30.00 80.00
CAHB Harrison Bader/99 10.00 25.00
CAJC J.P. Crawford EXCH 6.00 15.00
CAJF Jack Flaherty/99 25.00 60.00
CAND Nicky Delmonico EXCH 6.00 15.00
CANW Nick Williams/70 8.00 20.00
CAOA Ozzie Albies/80 20.00 50.00
CARA Ronald Acuna/99 150.00 400.00
CARD Rafael Devers/40 20.00 50.00
CARH Rhys Hoskins/50 25.00 60.00
CASO Shohei Ohtani
CAVR Victor Robles/50 25.00 60.00
CAWB Walker Buehler EXCH 25.00 60.00

2018 Topps Archives Fan Favorites Autographs

STATED ODDS 1:20 HOBBY
EXCHANGE DEADLINE 7/31/2020
*PURPLE/150: .5X TO 1.2X BASE
*SILVER/99: .6X TO 1.5X BASE
*BLUE/25: .75X TO 2X BASE
FFAAH A.J. Hinch 12.00 30.00
FFAAJ Aaron Judge 150.00 400.00
FFAAK Adam Kennedy 4.00 10.00
FFAAR Amed Rosario 8.00 20.00
FFABA Brad Ausmus 4.00 10.00
FFABEB Bert Blyleven 12.00 30.00
FFABF Bob Friend 6.00 15.00
FFABH Bryce Harper
FFABJ Bill James 8.00 20.00
FFABM Bill Madlock 8.00 20.00
FFABR Brad Radke 4.00 10.00
FFABV Bobby Valentine 8.00 20.00
FFACC Chris Chambliss 8.00 20.00
FFACJ Charles Johnson 5.00 12.00
FFACN Charles Nagy 4.00 10.00
FFADJ David Justice 10.00 25.00
FFADJ Derek Jeter 500.00 800.00
FFADK Don Kessinger 4.00 10.00
FFADL Derek Lowe 10.00 25.00
FFADR Dave Roberts 15.00 40.00
FFADW Dave Winfield 75.00 200.00
FFAFL Francisco Lindor 20.00 50.00
FFAFM Felix Millan 5.00 12.00
FFAGM Gary Matthews 3.00 8.00
FFAGP Gary Pettis 3.00 8.00
FFAHA Hank Aaron 300.00 500.00
FFAHB Homer Bush 3.00 8.00
FFAHL Hector Lopez 5.00 12.00
FFAJA Jose Altuve 30.00 80.00
FFAJB Jim Bouton 8.00 20.00
FFAJCO Joey Cora 8.00 20.00
FFAJLE Jim Leyland 12.00 30.00
FFAJM Jose Mesa 5.00 12.00
FFAJP Jim Perry 8.00 20.00
FFAJT John Thorn 3.00 8.00
FFAJTO Joe Torre 25.00 60.00
FFAKA Kevin Appier 3.00 8.00
FFAKB Kris Bryant 40.00 100.00
FFAKF Keith Foulke 6.00 15.00
FFALC Luis Castillo 3.00 8.00
FFAMB Marty Barrett 3.00 8.00
FFAMK Michael Kay 12.00 30.00
FFAML Michael Lewis 4.00 10.00
FFAMS Matt Stairs 4.00 10.00
FFAMST Mike Stanton 6.00 15.00
FFAMT Mike Trout 500.00 800.00
FFAMTI Mike Timlin 4.00 10.00
FFAOM Orlando Merced 3.00 8.00
FFAPG Phil Garner 6.00 15.00
FFAPN Pat Neshek 3.00 8.00
FFARA Rich Aurilia 3.00 8.00
FFARD Rafael Devers 25.00 60.00
FFARF Roy Face EXCH 6.00 15.00
FFARH Rhys Hoskins 15.00 40.00
FFARN Robb Nen 3.00 8.00
FFARP Rico Petrocelli 8.00 20.00
FFASK Sandy Koufax 300.00 600.00
FFASO Shohei Ohtani 150.00 400.00
FFASS Shannon Stewart 3.00 8.00
FFATB Tom Browning 3.00 8.00
FFATL Tony La Russa 12.00 30.00
FFATP Troy Percival 5.00 12.00
FFATS Ted Simmons 40.00 100.00
FFATS Terry Steinbach 3.00 8.00
FFAVR Victor Robles 25.00 60.00
FFAWB Wally Backman 10.00 25.00
FFAWW Willie Wilson 6.00 15.00

2018 Topps Archives Rookie History

STATED ODDS 1:12 HOBBY
SP STATED ODDS 1:240 HOBBY
*PURPLE/150: 1.2X TO 3X BASE
*PURPLE SP/150: .4X TO 1X BASE SP
*GREEN/99: 1.5X TO 4X BASE
*GREEN SP/99: .4X TO 1X BASE SP
*BLUE/50: 5X TO 12X BASE
*BLUE SP/50: .5X TO 1.2X BASE SP
8 Don Mattingly 1.00 2.50
4T Jeff Bagwell .40 1.00
98 Derek Jeter SP 20.00 50.00
116 Ozzie Smith .60 1.50
123 Sandy Koufax SP 10.00 25.00
126 Jim Palmer .40 1.00
128 Hank Aaron SP 10.00 25.00
164 Roberto Clemente SP 12.00 30.00
170 Bo Jackson .50 1.25
201 Al Kaline .50 1.25
223 Robin Yount .50 1.25
24T Mike Piazza .50 1.25
260 Reggie Jackson .40 1.00
316 Willie McCovey .40 1.00
333 Chipper Jones .50 1.25
382 John Smoltz .50 1.25
414 Frank Thomas .50 1.25
456 Dave Winfield .40 1.00
557 Pedro Martinez .40 1.00
661 Bryce Harper .75 2.00
726 Ichiro SP 8.00 20.00
779 Tom Glavine .40 1.00
98T Cal Ripken Jr. 1.50 4.00
UH240 Clayton Kershaw .75 2.00
US175 Mike Trout 2.50 6.00

2018 Topps Archives Rookie History Autographs

STATED ODDS 1:268 HOBBY
PRINT RUNS B/WN 20-150 COPIES PER
EXCHANGE DEADLINE 7/31/2020
RHAAK Al Kaline/125 50.00 120.00
RHABJ Bo Jackson/99 50.00 120.00
RHABR Brooks Robinson
RHACB Craig Biggio/99 25.00 60.00
RHACJ Chipper Jones/25 125.00 300.00
RHACRJ Cal Ripken Jr./30 75.00 200.00
RHADE Dennis Eckersley/99 10.00 25.00
RHADG Dwight Gooden/150 20.00 50.00
RHADJ Derek Jeter
RHADM Don Mattingly/150 40.00 100.00
RHADW Dave Winfield/99 25.00 60.00
RHAFT Frank Thomas/99 40.00 100.00
RHAGS Gary Sheffield/150 10.00 25.00
RHAHA Hank Aaron
RHAI Ichiro/20 200.00 500.00
RHAJB Jeff Bagwell/99 30.00 80.00
RHAJD Johnny Damon/150 10.00 25.00
RHAJP Jim Palmer EXCH 20.00 50.00
RHAJS John Smoltz/150 10.00 25.00
RHAMP Mike Piazza/20 60.00 150.00
RHAMT Mike Trout
RHAOS Ozzie Smith/99 25.00 60.00
RHAPM Pedro Martinez
RHARA Roberto Alomar/99 25.00 60.00
RHARJ Reggie Jackson/30 75.00 200.00
RHARY Robin Yount/99 40.00 100.00
RHASK Sandy Koufax
RHATG Tom Glavine/150 12.00 30.00
RHATR Tim Raines/125 20.00 50.00

2018 Topps Archives The Sandlot

COMPLETE SET (11) 10.00 25.00
STATED ODDS 1:8 HOBBY
*GREEN/99: .75X TO 2X BASIC
*BLUE/25: 1.5X TO 4X BASIC
SLH Hercules 1.25 3.00
SLAM Yeah-Yeah McClennan 1.25 3.00
SLBJR Benny Rodriguez 1.25 3.00
SLBW Grover Weeks 1.25 3.00
SLHP Ham Porter 1.25 3.00
SLKD Kenny DeNunez 1.25 3.00
SLMP Squints Palledorous 1.25 3.00
SLSS Scotty Smalls 1.25 3.00
SLTIM Timmy Timmons 1.25 3.00
SLTOM Tommy Timmons 1.25 3.00
SLWP Wendy Peffercorn 1.25 3.00

2018 Topps Archives The Sandlot Autographs

STATED ODDS 1:152 HOBBY
EXCHANGE DEADLINE 7/31/2020
*SILVER/99: .5X TO 1.2X BASIC
*BLUE/25: .75X TO 2X BASIC
SLABW Grant Gelt 12.00 30.00
Bertram Grover Weeks
SLAKD Brandon Adams 15.00 40.00
Kenny DeNunez
SLAMS Mrs. Smalls 60.00 150.00
SLASS Scotty Smalls 30.00 80.00
SLAWP Wendy Peffercorn 40.00 100.00
SLAAYYM Marty York 15.00 40.00
Alan Yeah-Yeah McClennan
SLADME David Mickey Evans 20.00 50.00
SLAHHP Ham Porter 50.00 120.00
SLAMSP Squints Palledorous 25.00 60.00
SLATIM Victor DiMattia 12.00 30.00
Timmy Timmons
SLATOM Shane Obedzinski 12.00 30.00
Tommy Timmons

2019 Topps Archives

COMP.SET w/o SP's (300) 30.00 80.00
1 Derek Jeter .60 1.50
2 Patrick Corbin .20 .50
3 Max Scherzer .25 .60
4 Michael Chavis RC .40 1.00
5 Anthony Rizzo .30 .75
6 Rhys Hoskins .30 .75
7 Roberto Alomar .20 .50
8 Elvis Andrus .20 .50
9 Chance Adams RC .25 .60
10 Matt Duffy .15 .40
11 Nicholas Castellanos .25 .60
12 Hunter Renfroe .15 .40
13 Austin Riley RC 1.25 3.00
14 Vladimir Guerrero Jr. RC 1.50 4.00
15 Carlton Fisk .20 .50
16 Taijuan Walker .15 .40
17 Ozzie Albies .25 .60
18 Freddie Freeman .30 .75
19 Corey Kluber .20 .50
20 Duke Snider .20 .50
21 Kevin Kramer RC .30 .75
22 Starling Marte .20 .50
23 Bob Lemon .20 .50
24 Ted Williams .50 1.25
25 Yusei Kikuchi RC .40 1.00
26 Justin Verlander .25 .60
27 Cavan Biggio RC 1.25 3.00
28 Reggie Jackson .20 .50
29 Vladimir Guerrero .20 .50
30 Robinson Cano .20 .50
31 Ramon Laureano RC .50 1.25
32 Jose Urena .15 .40

33 Max Muncy .20 .50
34 Rowdy Tellez RC .40 1.00
35 Bo Jackson .25 .60
36 Justin Smoak .15 .40
37 Bruce Sutter .20 .50
38 Gregory Polanco .20 .50
39 Pee Wee Reese .20 .50
40 Raisel Iglesias .15 .40
41 Trey Mancini .20 .50
42 Ian Desmond .15 .40
43 Gary Carter .20 .50
44 Jackie Robinson .25 .60
45 Orlando Cepeda .20 .50
46 Jose Berrios .20 .50
47 Carlos Correa .25 .60
48 Kyle Schwarber .25 .60
49 Hunter Dozier .15 .40
50 Mookie Betts .50 1.25
51 Clayton Kershaw .40 1.00
52 Red Schoendienst .20 .50
53 Keston Hiura RC .75 2.00
54 Kyle Seager .15 .40
55 Buster Posey .30 .75
56 Luis Urias RC .40 1.00
57 Trevor Bauer .30 .75
58 Ryan Borucki RC .25 .60
59 Albert Pujols .30 .75
60 Eddie Murray .20 .50
61 Jim Thome .20 .50
62 Lefty Grove .20 .50
63 Eugenio Suarez .20 .50
64 Don Larsen .15 .40
65 Wil Myers .20 .50
66 Rod Carew .20 .50
67 Goose Gossage .20 .50
68 Edwin Diaz .20 .50
69 Yadier Molina .30 .75
70 Jeimer Candelario .15 .40
71 Harrison Bader .20 .50
72 Alex Avila .20 .50
73 Andrew McCutchen .25 .60
74 Byron Buxton .25 .60
75 Fernando Tatis Jr. RC 10.00 25.00
76 Larry Doby .20 .50
77 Josh Hader .20 .50
78 Hank Aaron .50 1.25
79 Starlin Castro .15 .40
80 Ronald Guzman .15 .40
81 Dylan Bundy .20 .50
82 Dee Gordon .15 .40
83 Mike Trout 1.25 3.00
84 Gleyber Torres .50 1.25
85 Jorge Posada .20 .50
86 Sean Manaea .15 .40
87 Randy Johnson .25 .60
88 Chipper Jones .25 .60
89 Whitey Ford .20 .50
90 Alex Rodriguez .30 .75
91 Kyle Wright RC .40 1.00
92 Blake Treinen .15 .40
93 Cole Tucker RC .40 1.00
94 Johnny Bench .25 .60
95 Hoyt Wilhelm .20 .50
96 Lucas Giolito .20 .50
97 Bob Gibson .20 .50
98 Jake Bauers RC .40 1.00
99 Jake Cave RC .30 .75
100 Ronald Acuna Jr. 1.25 3.00
101 Shohei Ohtani .40 1.00
102 Mel Ott .25 .60
103 Scooter Gennett .20 .50
104 Paul Goldschmidt .25 .60
105 Matt Olson .25 .60
106 Lou Boudreau .20 .50
107 Bernie Williams .20 .50
108 Catfish Hunter .20 .50
109 Andy Pettitte .20 .50
110 Jon Duplantier RC .25 .60
111 Brandon Lowe RC .40 1.00
112 Maikel Franco .20 .50
113 Max Kepler .20 .50
114 Early Wynn .20 .50
115 Lorenzo Cain .15 .40
116 Matt Boyd .15 .40
117 Francisco Arcia RC .40 1.00
118 Roger Maris .25 .60
119 Juan Soto .75 2.00
120 David Peralta .15 .40
121 Tony Gwynn .25 .60
122 Sandy Koufax .50 1.25
123 Evan Longoria .20 .50
124 Eddie Rosario .20 .50
125 Mariano Rivera .30 .75
126 Chris Shaw RC .25 .60
127 Jim Bunning .20 .50
128 Ken Griffey Jr. .50 1.25
129 Joey Gallo .20 .50
130 Nolan Ryan .75 2.00
131 Adalberto Mondesi .20 .50
132 Jesse Winker .25 .60
133 Nick Senzel RC .75 2.00
134 Brandon Belt .20 .50
135 Kevin Pillar .15 .40
136 Ty Cobb .40 1.00
137 Marcus Stroman .20 .50
138 Lewis Brinson .15 .40
139 Joey Rickard .15 .40
140 Carter Kieboom RC .40 1.00
141 Touki Toussaint RC .30 .75
142 Deion Sanders .20 .50
143 Rougned Odor .20 .50
144 Gil Hodges .20 .50
145 Hideki Matsui .25 .60
146 Kyle Hendricks .25 .60
147 Rafael Devers .30 .75
148 Chris Sale .25 .60
149 Frank Thomas .25 .60
150 Ichiro .30 .75
151 Al Kaline .25 .60
152 Walker Buehler .30 .75
153 Jeff Bagwell .20 .50
154 Stephen Piscotty .15 .40
155 Michael Kopech RC .75 2.00
156 Blake Snell .20 .50
157 Charlie Blackmon .25 .60
158 Richie Ashburn .20 .50
159 Brad Keller RC .25 .60
160 Josh James RC .40 1.00
161 Andrelton Simmons .15 .40
162 Mitch Haniger .20 .50
163 Shane Greene .15 .40
164 Ivan Rodriguez .20 .50
165 Christy Mathewson .20 .50
166 Willie Stargell .20 .50
167 Tommy Pham .15 .40
168 Luis Severino .20 .50
169 Zack Greinke .25 .60
170 Edwin Encarnacion .25 .60
171 Eloy Jimenez RC 1.00 2.50
172 Steven Duggar RC .30 .75
173 Ryne Sandberg .50 1.25
174 George Springer .20 .50
175 Todd Helton .20 .50
176 Bob Feller .20 .50
177 Josh Donaldson .20 .50
178 Thurman Munson .25 .60
179 Nolan Arenado .40 1.00
180 Manny Margot .15 .40
181 Aaron Judge .60 1.50
182 Enos Slaughter .20 .50
183 Tim Anderson .25 .60
184 Danny Jansen RC .25 .60
185 Jameson Taillon .20 .50
186 George Kell .20 .50
187 Enyel De Los Santos RC .25 .60
188 Cody Bellinger .50 1.25
189 Phil Rizzuto .20 .50
190 Hal Newhouser .20 .50
191 Eric Hosmer .20 .50
192 DJ Stewart RC .30 .75
193 Javier Baez .30 .75
194 Christian Yelich .30 .75
195 Tony Perez .20 .50
196 Salvador Perez .20 .50
197 Andrew Benintendi .25 .60
198 Colin Moran .15 .40
199 Jacob deGrom .50 1.25
200 Bryce Harper .40 1.00
201 Babe Ruth .60 1.50
202 Kolby Allard RC .40 1.00
203 Ryan O'Hearn RC .25 .60
204 Jeff McNeil RC .60 1.50
205 Yonder Alonso .15 .40
206 Carl Yastrzemski .40 1.00
207 Trea Turner .20 .50
208 Aaron Sanchez .20 .50
209 Manny Machado .25 .60
210 George Brett .50 1.25
211 J.D. Martinez .25 .60
212 Robin Roberts .20 .50
213 Cal Quantrill RC .25 .60
214 Whit Merrifield .25 .60
215 Tris Speaker .20 .50
216 Nate Lowe RC 1.25 3.00
217 Xander Bogaerts .25 .60
218 Ernie Banks .25 .60
219 Don Sutton .20 .50
220 Tim Raines .20 .50
221 Justus Sheffield RC .40 1.00
222 Pete Alonso RC 2.00 5.00
223 Jesus Aguilar .20 .50
224 Gary Sanchez .25 .60
225 Kris Bryant .30 .75
226 Steve Carlton .20 .50
227 Rickey Henderson .25 .60
228 Trevor Story .25 .60
229 Brian Anderson .15 .40
230 J.P. Crawford .15 .40
231 Ralph Kiner .20 .50
232 Victor Robles .30 .75
233 Dizzy Dean .25 .60
234 Monte Irvin .20 .50
235 Rogers Hornsby .20 .50
236 Miguel Cabrera .25 .60
237 Fergie Jenkins .20 .50
238 Joey Votto .25 .60
239 Willie McCovey .20 .50
240 Christin Stewart RC .30 .75
241 Dansby Swanson .25 .60
242 Zack Cozart .15 .40
243 Juan Marichal .20 .50
244 Dakota Hudson RC .30 .75
245 Miguel Andujar .25 .60
246 Franmil Reyes .15 .40
247 Bobby Doerr .20 .50
248 Jose Altuve .20 .50
249 Johnny Mize .20 .50
250 Roberto Clemente .60 1.50
251 Williams Astudillo RC .25 .60
252 Carlos Santana .20 .50
253 Aaron Nola .20 .50
254 Kevin Kiermaier .20 .50
255 Eddie Mathews .25 .60
256 Lourdes Gurriel Jr. .20 .50
257 Carlos Martinez .20 .50
258 John Smoltz .25 .60
259 David Dahl .15 .40
260 Josh Bell .20 .50
261 Chris Davis .15 .40
262 Honus Wagner .20 .50
263 Willy Adames .15 .40
264 Don Mattingly .50 1.25
265 Sandy Alcantara .15 .40
266 Harmon Killebrew .25 .60
267 Corey Seager .25 .60
268 Jorge Polanco .20 .50
269 Bryse Wilson RC .30 .75
270 Brandon Nimmo .20 .50
271 Jose Abreu .25 .60
272 Mike Piazza .25 .60
273 Corbin Burnes RC 2.00 5.00
274 Ozzie Smith .30 .75
275 Joe Morgan .20 .50
276 Alex Bregman .25 .60
277 Warren Spahn .20 .50
278 Jake Lamb .20 .50
279 Orlando Arcia .15 .40
280 Nick Markakis .20 .50
281 Lou Gehrig .50 1.25
282 Kyle Tucker RC .60 1.50
283 Brandon Crawford .20 .50
284 Nomar Mazara .15 .40
285 David Ortiz .25 .60
286 Matt Chapman .25 .60
287 Paul DeJong .25 .60
288 Justin Upton .20 .50
289 Sammy Sosa .25 .60
290 Cedric Mullins RC .50 1.25
291 Nomar Garciaparra .20 .50
292 Griffin Canning RC .40 1.00
293 Noah Syndergaard .20 .50
294 Billy Hamilton .20 .50
295 Robin Yount .25 .60
296 Joe Panik .20 .50
297 Roger Clemens .30 .75
298 Jose Ramirez .20 .50
299 Mychal Givens .15 .40
300 Francisco Lindor .25 .60
301 Aaron Judge AS 1.50 4.00
302 Francisco Lindor AS .60 1.50
303 Javier Baez AS .75 2.00
304 Jacob deGrom AS 1.25 3.00
305 Chris Sale AS .60 1.50
306 Christian Yelich AS .75 2.00
307 Nolan Arenado AS 1.00 2.50
308 Mookie Betts AS 1.25 3.00
309 Freddie Freeman AS .75 2.00
310 Mike Trout AS 3.00 8.00
311 Derek Jeter HL 1.50 4.00
312 Miguel Cabrera HL .60 1.50
313 Josh Hader HL .50 1.25
314 Juan Soto HL 2.00 5.00
315 Ichiro HL .75 2.00
316 Shohei Ohtani HL 1.00 2.50
317 Mariano Rivera HL .75 2.00
318 Kris Bryant HL .75 2.00
319 Francisco Lindor HL .60 1.50
320 Ronald Acuna Jr. HL 3.00 8.00
321 Eloy Jimenez 1.50 4.00
322 Michael Kopech 1.25 3.00
323 Rowdy Tellez .60 1.50
324 Vladimir Guerrero Jr. 2.50 6.00
325 Luis Urias .60 1.50
326 Justus Sheffield .60 1.50
327 Jake Bauers .60 1.50
328 Yusei Kikuchi .60 1.50
329 Kyle Wright .60 1.50
330 Pete Alonso 3.00 8.00

2019 Topps Archives Blue

*BLUE: 6X TO 15X BASIC
*BLUE RC: 4X TO 10X BASIC RC
STATED ODDS 1:78 HOBBY
STATED PRINT RUN 25 SER.#'d SETS

2019 Topps Archives Purple

*PURPLE: 4X TO 10X BASIC
*PURPLE RC: 2.5X TO 6X BASIC RC
STATED ODDS 1:30 HOBBY
STATED PRINT RUN 175 SER.#'d SETS

2019 Topps Archives Silver

*SILVER: 5X TO 12X BASIC
*SILVER RC: 3X TO 8X BASIC RC
STATED ODDS 1:53 HOBBY
STATED PRINT RUN 99 SER.#'d SETS

2019 Topps Archives '58 Photo Variations

STATED ODDS 1:207 HOBBY
1 Derek Jeter 12.00 30.00
14 Vladimir Guerrero Jr. 12.00 30.00
50 Mookie Betts 6.00 15.00
100 Ronald Acuna Jr. 15.00 40.00

2019 Topps Archives '75 Photo Variations

STATED ODDS 1:207 HOBBY
101 Shohei Ohtani 10.00 25.00
119 Juan Soto 12.00 30.00
200 Bryce Harper 10.00 25.00

2019 Topps Archives '93 Photo Variations

STATED ODDS 1:207 HOBBY
201 Babe Ruth 8.00 20.00
225 Kris Bryant 10.00 25.00
300 Francisco Lindor 8.00 20.00

2019 Topps Archives '75 Minis

STATED ODDS 1:78 HOBBY
75M1 Shohei Ohtani 5.00 12.00
75M2 Ichiro 4.00 10.00
75M3 Nolan Arenado 5.00 12.00
75M4 Enyel De Los Santos 2.00 5.00
75M5 Javier Baez 4.00 10.00
75M6 Jim Bunning 2.50 6.00
75M7 Chris Shaw 2.00 5.00
75M8 Matt Olson 3.00 8.00
75M9 George Kell 2.50 6.00
75M10 Catfish Hunter 2.50 6.00
75M11 Max Kepler 2.50 6.00
75M12 Mel Ott 3.00 8.00
75M13 David Peralta 2.00 5.00
75M14 Lorenzo Cain 2.00 5.00
75M15 Sandy Koufax 6.00 15.00
75M16 Deion Sanders 2.50 6.00
75M17 Eddie Rosario 2.50 6.00
75M18 Walker Buehler 4.00 10.00
75M19 Maikel Franco 2.50 6.00
75M20 Eric Hosmer 2.50 6.00
75M21 Jesse Winker 3.00 8.00
75M22 Matt Boyd 2.00 5.00
75M23 Brandon Lowe 3.00 8.00
75M24 Tommy Pham 2.00 5.00
75M25 Jacob deGrom 6.00 15.00
75M26 Kyle Hendricks 3.00 8.00
75M27 Christian Yelich 4.00 10.00
75M28 Richie Ashburn 2.50 6.00
75M29 Eloy Jimenez 8.00 20.00
75M30 Hal Newhouser 2.50 6.00
75M31 Willie Stargell 2.50 6.00
75M32 Charlie Blackmon 3.00 8.00
75M33 Bernie Williams 2.50 6.00
75M34 Zack Greinke 3.00 8.00
75M35 Aaron Judge 8.00 20.00
75M36 Tony Gwynn 3.00 8.00
75M37 Roger Maris 3.00 8.00
75M38 Tony Perez 2.50 6.00
75M39 Christy Mathewson 3.00 8.00
75M40 Salvador Perez 2.50 6.00
75M41 Cody Bellinger 6.00 15.00
75M42 Joey Gallo 2.50 6.00
75M43 Early Wynn 2.50 6.00
75M44 Danny Jansen 2.00 5.00
75M45 Lewis Brinson 2.00 5.00
75M46 Scooter Gennett 2.50 6.00
75M47 Adalberto Mondesi 2.50 6.00
75M48 George Springer 2.50 6.00
75M49 Ty Cobb 5.00 12.00
75M50 Bryce Harper 5.00 12.00
75M51 Thurman Munson 3.00 8.00
75M52 Edwin Encarnacion 3.00 8.00
75M53 Nolan Ryan 10.00 25.00
75M54 Rougned Odor 2.50 6.00
75M55 Brandon Belt 2.50 6.00
75M56 Nick Senzel 6.00 15.00
75M57 Brad Keller 2.00 5.00
75M58 Steven Duggar 2.50 6.00
75M59 Paul Goldschmidt 3.00 8.00
75M60 Colin Moran 2.00 5.00
75M61 Stephen Piscotty 2.00 5.00
75M62 Francisco Arcia 3.00 8.00
75M63 DJ Stewart 2.50 6.00
75M64 Kevin Pillar 2.00 5.00
75M65 Enos Slaughter 2.50 6.00
75M66 Shane Greene 2.00 5.00
75M67 Al Kaline 3.00 8.00
75M68 Ivan Rodriguez 2.50 6.00
75M69 Manny Margot 2.00 5.00
75M70 Todd Helton 2.50 6.00
75M71 Gil Hodges 2.50 6.00
75M72 Ryne Sandberg 6.00 15.00
75M73 Rafael Devers 4.00 10.00
75M74 Phil Rizzuto 2.50 6.00
75M75 Jameson Taillon 2.50 6.00
75M76 Chris Sale 3.00 8.00
75M77 Frank Thomas 3.00 8.00
75M78 Blake Snell 2.50 6.00
75M79 Josh Donaldson 2.50 6.00
75M80 Marcus Stroman 2.50 6.00
75M81 Andy Pettitte 2.50 6.00
75M82 Michael Kopech 6.00 15.00
75M83 Hideki Matsui 3.00 8.00
75M84 Carter Kieboom 3.00 8.00
75M85 Touki Toussaint 2.50 6.00
75M86 Luis Severino 2.50 6.00
75M87 Jeff Bagwell 2.50 6.00
75M88 Mitch Haniger 2.50 6.00
75M89 Josh James 3.00 8.00
75M90 Ken Griffey Jr. 6.00 15.00
75M91 Lou Boudreau 2.50 6.00
75M92 Evan Longoria 2.50 6.00
75M93 Tim Anderson 3.00 8.00
75M94 Mariano Rivera 4.00 10.00
75M95 Andrew Benintendi 3.00 8.00
75M96 Andrelton Simmons 2.00 5.00
75M97 Bob Feller 2.50 6.00
75M98 Jon Duplantier 2.00 5.00
75M99 Joey Rickard 2.00 5.00
75M100 Juan Soto 10.00 25.00

2019 Topps Archives '75 Topps Signature Omission

*NO SIG: 8X TO 20X BASIC
*NO SIG RC: 5X TO 12X BASIC RC
STATED ODDS 1:207 HOBBY

2019 Topps Archives '78 Record Breakers Autographs

STATED ODDS 1:10,729 HOBBY
STATED PRINT RUN 25 SER.#'d SETS
EXCHANGE DEADLINE 7/31/2021
RBAFL Francisco Lindor 20.00 50.00
RBAJS Juan Soto 100.00 250.00
RBARAJ Ronald Acuna Jr. 125.00 300.00

2019 Topps Archives '93 Topps Gold

*NO SIG: 8X TO 20X BASIC
*NO SIG RC: 5X TO 12X BASIC RC
STATED ODDS 1:207 HOBBY

2019 Topps Archives '94 Future Stars

COMPLETE SET (25) 20.00 50.00
STATED ODDS 1:12 HOBBY
94FS1 Derek Jeter 1.50 4.00
94FS2 Juan Soto 2.00 5.00
94FS3 Vladimir Guerrero Jr. 2.50 6.00
94FS4 Justus Sheffield .60 1.50
94FS5 Miles Mikolas .60 1.50
94FS6 Pete Alonso 3.00 8.00
94FS7 Alex Rodriguez .75 2.00
94FS8 Shohei Ohtani 1.00 2.50
94FS9 Mike Piazza .60 1.50
94FS10 Yusei Kikuchi .60 1.50
94FS11 Carter Kieboom .60 1.50
94FS12 Lourdes Gurriel Jr. .50 1.25
94FS13 Willy Adames .40 1.00
94FS14 Christin Stewart .50 1.25
94FS15 Ronald Acuna Jr. 3.00 8.00
94FS16 Austin Meadows .60 1.50
94FS17 Luis Urias .60 1.50
94FS18 Kyle Tucker 1.00 2.50
94FS19 Scott Kingery .50 1.25
94FS20 Kyle Wright .60 1.50
94FS21 Rowdy Tellez .60 1.50
94FS22 Amed Rosario .50 1.25
94FS23 Michael Kopech 1.25 3.00
94FS24 Nick Senzel 1.25 3.00
94FS25 Eloy Jimenez 1.50 4.00

2019 Topps Archives '94 Future Stars Autographs

STATED ODDS 1:539 HOBBY
PRINT RUNS B/WN 50-99 COPIES PER
EXCHANGE DEADLINE 7/31/2021
*BLUE/25: .5X TO 1.2X BASIC
94FSAAM Austin Meadows/99 10.00 25.00
94FSAAR Alex Rodriguez
94FSADR Dereck Rodriguez/99 6.00 15.00
94FSAJS Juan Soto/50 40.00 100.00
94FSAJSH Justus Sheffield/99 8.00 20.00
94FSAKW Kyle Wright/99 8.00 20.00
94FSALGJ Lourdes Gurriel Jr./99 10.00 25.00
94FSALU Luis Urias/99 8.00 20.00
94FSAMK Michael Kopech/99 15.00 40.00
94FSAMM Miles Mikolas/99 8.00 20.00
94FSANS Nick Senzel/99 20.00 50.00
94FSARAJ Ronald Acuna Jr./50 100.00 250.00
94FSART Rowdy Tellez/99 8.00 20.00
94FSASK Scott Kingery/99 6.00 15.00
94FSASO Shohei Ohtani
94FSAWA Willy Adames/99 5.00 12.00

2019 Topps Archives 50th Anniversary of the Montreal Expos

STATED ODDS 1:24 HOBBY
*BLUE/150: .5X TO 1.2X BASIC
*GREEN/99: .5X TO 1.2X BASIC
*GOLD/50: 1.2X TO 3X BASIC
MTLAD Andre Dawson 1.25 3.00
MTLAG Andres Galarraga 1.25 3.00
MTLBC Bartolo Colon 1.00 2.50
MTLBG Bill Gullickson 1.00 2.50
MTLCF Cliff Floyd 1.00 2.50
MTLCL Coco Laboy 1.00 2.50
MTLDM Dennis Martinez 1.00 2.50
MTLJF Jeff Fassero 1.00 2.50
MTLJR Jeff Reardon 1.00 2.50
MTLJV Javier Vazquez 1.00 2.50
MTLJVI Jose Vidro 1.00 2.50
MTLKH Ken Hill 1.00 2.50
MTLMA Moises Alou 1.00 2.50
MTLMG Marquis Grissom 1.00 2.50
MTLMW Maury Wills 1.00 2.50
MTLPM Pedro Martinez 1.25 3.00
MTLRJ Randy Johnson 1.50 4.00
MTLRW Rondell White 1.00 2.50
MTLSR Steve Rogers 1.00 2.50
MTLTB Tim Burke 1.00 2.50
MTLTR Tim Raines 1.25 3.00
MTLTW Tim Wallach 1.00 2.50
MTLVG Vladimir Guerrero 6.00 15.00

2019 Topps Archives 50th Anniversary of the Montreal Expos Autographs

STATED ODDS 1:54 HOBBY
EXCHANGE DEADLINE 7/31/2021
*GREEN/99: .5X TO 1.2X BASIC
*GOLD/50: .6X TO 1.5X BASIC
MTLAAD Andre Dawson 20.00 50.00
MTLAAG Andres Galarraga 8.00 20.00
MTLABC Bartolo Colon 8.00 20.00
MTLABG Bill Gullickson 5.00 12.00
MTLACF Cliff Floyd 5.00 12.00
MTLACL Coco Laboy 6.00 15.00
MTLADM Dennis Martinez 8.00 20.00
MTLAJF Jeff Fassero 3.00 8.00
MTLAJR Jeff Reardon 3.00 8.00
MTLAJVI Jose Vidro 3.00 8.00
MTLAKH Ken Hill 3.00 8.00
MTLAMG Marquis Grissom 4.00 10.00
MTLAMW Maury Wills 10.00 25.00
MTLAPM Pedro Martinez 60.00 150.00
MTLARJ Randy Johnson 300.00 500.00
MTLARW Rondell White 4.00 10.00
MTLASR Steve Rogers 3.00 8.00
MTLATB Tim Burke 3.00 8.00
MTLATR Tim Raines 20.00 50.00
MTLATW Tim Wallach 5.00 12.00
MTLAVG Vladimir Guerrero 25.00 60.00

2019 Topps Archives Coins

INSERTED IN RETAIL PACKS
*SKY BLUE: 4X TO 10X BASIC
C1 Shohei Ohtani .75 2.00
C2 Francisco Lindor .50 1.25
C3 Kolby Allard .50 1.25
C4 Juan Soto 1.50 4.00
C5 Luis Urias .50 1.25
C6 George Springer .40 1.00
C7 Aaron Judge 1.25 3.00
C8 Rowdy Tellez .50 1.25
C9 Jose Ramirez .40 1.00
C10 Mike Trout 2.50 6.00
C11 Clayton Kershaw .75 2.00
C12 Mookie Betts 1.00 2.50
C13 Justus Sheffield .50 1.25
C14 J.D. Martinez .50 1.25
C15 Christian Yelich .60 1.50
C16 Kris Bryant .60 1.50
C17 Kyle Tucker .75 2.00
C18 Max Scherzer .50 1.25
C19 Ozzie Albies .50 1.25
C20 Rhys Hoskins .60 1.50
C21 Carlos Correa .60 1.50
C22 Michael Kopech 1.00 2.50
C23 Gleyber Torres 1.00 2.50
C24 Jacob deGrom 1.00 2.50
C25 Ronald Acuna Jr. 2.50 6.00

2019 Topps Archives Fan Favorites Autographs

STATED ODDS 1:25 HOBBY
EXCHANGE DEADLINE 7/31/2021
*PURPLE/150: .5X TO 1.2X BASIC
*SILVER/99: .6X TO 1.5X BASE
*BLUE/25: .75X TO 2X BASE
FFAAC Alex Cora 15.00 40.00
FFABS Bud Selig 30.00 80.00
FFABVW Brodie Van Wagenen GM 10.00 25.00
FFACK Carter Kieboom 5.00 12.00
FFACR Cookie Rojas 4.00 10.00
FFADJA Dr. James Andrews 12.00 30.00
FFADO David Ortiz 30.00 80.00
FFAEG Eric Gagne 8.00 20.00
FFAEJ Eloy Jimenez 25.00 60.00
FFAFF Freddie Freeman 15.00 40.00
FFAFL Francisco Lindor 12.00 30.00
FFAFS Fred Stanley 4.00 10.00
FFAGT Gorman Thomas 4.00 10.00
FFAHA Hank Aaron 300.00 500.00
FFAJD Jermaine Dye 6.00 15.00
FFAJDA Jody Davis 4.00 10.00
FFAJG Jonny Gomes 8.00 20.00
FFAJI Jeff Idelson 4.00 10.00
FFAJL Jerry Layne 3.00 8.00
FFAJM Jessica Mendoza 12.00 30.00
FFAJMC Jack McKeon 8.00 20.00
FFAJP Joe Pepitone 6.00 15.00
FFAJPO Jorge Posada EXCH 25.00 60.00
FFAJR Jerry Remy 10.00 25.00
FFAJRE Jeff Reardon 3.00 8.00
FFAJS Juan Soto 40.00 100.00
FFAKB Ken Burns 15.00 40.00
FFAKG Kelly Gruber 5.00 12.00
FFAKGJ Ken Griffey Jr. 300.00 600.00
FFAKT Kevin Tapani 3.00 8.00
FFALD Laz Diaz 3.00 8.00
FFALDI Larry Dierker 3.00 8.00
FFAML Mike Lieberthal 4.00 10.00
FFAMM Mario Mendoza 5.00 12.00
FFAMS Mike Sweeney 3.00 8.00
FFAMT Mike Trout 400.00 800.00
FFANS Nick Senzel 15.00 40.00
FFAPH Pat Hughes ANNC 8.00 20.00
FFARAJ Ronald Acuna Jr. 100.00 250.00
FFARH Rick Honeycutt 3.00 8.00
FFARO Rey Ordonez 3.00 8.00
FFASK Sandy Koufax
FFASS Steve Stone 6.00 15.00
FFASSA Steve Sax 8.00 20.00
FFATM Tino Martinez 12.00 30.00
FFATO Tony Oliva 20.00 50.00
FFATP Tony Perez 20.00 50.00
FFAVGJ Vladimir Guerrero Jr. 30.00 80.00
FFAVGS Vladimir Guerrero 30.00 80.00
FFAVW Vernon Wells 3.00 8.00
FFAWM Whit Merrifield 8.00 20.00

2019 Topps Archives Ichiro Retrospective

STATED ODDS 1:12 HOBBY
SP STATED ODDS 1:240 HOBBY
*BLUE/150: 1.5X TO 4X BASE
*GREEN/99: 2X TO 5X BASE
*GREEN SP/99: .5X TO 1.2X BASE SP
*GOLD/50: 5X TO 12X BASE
*GOLD SP/50: .5X TO 1.2X BASE SP
I1 Ichiro Suzuki SP 4.00 10.00
I2 Ichiro SP 4.00 10.00
I3 Ichiro .40 1.00
I4 Ichiro .40 1.00
I5 Ichiro .40 1.00
I6 Ichiro .40 1.00
I7 Ichiro .40 1.00
I8 Ichiro .40 1.00
I9 Ichiro .40 1.00
I10 Ichiro .40 1.00
I11 Ichiro .40 1.00
I12 Ichiro .40 1.00
I13 Ichiro .40 1.00
I14 Ichiro .40 1.00
I15 Ichiro .40 1.00
I16 Ichiro SP 4.00 10.00

2019 Topps Archives Ichiro Retrospective Autographs

COMMON ICHIRO 500.00 1000.00
STATED ODDS 1:9963 HOBBY
STATED PRINT RUN 5 SER.#'d SETS
EXCHANGE DEADLINE 7/31/2021

2019 Topps Archives Topps Magazine

COMPLETE SET (20) 10.00 25.00
STATED ODDS 1:6 HOBBY
TM1 Mike Trout 2.00 5.00
TM2 Jacob deGrom .75 2.00
TM3 Kris Bryant .50 1.25
TM4 Ozzie Smith .50 1.25
TM5 Ken Griffey Jr. .75 2.00
TM6 Ronald Acuna Jr. 2.00 5.00
TM7 Francisco Lindor .40 1.00
TM8 Cal Ripken Jr. 1.25 3.00
TM9 Juan Soto 1.25 3.00
TM10 Shohei Ohtani .60 1.50
TM11 Jose Ramirez .30 .75
TM12 Anthony Rizzo .50 1.25
TM13 Pedro Martinez .30 .75
TM14 Derek Jeter 1.00 2.50
TM15 Rhys Hoskins .50 1.25
TM16 George Springer .30 .75
TM17 Barry Larkin .30 .75
TM18 Bryce Harper .60 1.50
TM19 Jose Altuve .30 .75
TM20 Aaron Judge 1.00 2.50

2019 Topps Archives Topps Magazine Autographs

STATED ODDS 1:255 HOBBY
PRINT RUNS B/WN 20-150 COPIES PER
EXCHANGE DEADLINE 7/31/2021
*BLUE/25: .5X TO 1.2X BASIC
TMAAJ Aaron Judge/30 100.00 250.00
TMAAR Anthony Rizzo/60 30.00 80.00
TMABL Barry Larkin/70 20.00 50.00
TMACF Carlton Fisk/85 15.00 40.00
TMACK Corey Kluber/150 6.00 15.00
TMACRJ Cal Ripken Jr./50 75.00 200.00
TMACS Chris Sale/85 12.00 30.00
TMADJ Derek Jeter EXCH
TMAFL Francisco Lindor/150 12.00 30.00
TMAGS George Springer/85 15.00 40.00
TMAJA Jose Altuve/70 20.00 50.00
TMAJD Jacob deGrom/150 25.00 60.00
TMAJR Jose Ramirez/150 6.00 15.00
TMAJS Juan Soto/150 40.00 100.00
TMAKB Kris Bryant/60 25.00 60.00
TMAKGJ Ken Griffey Jr./35 200.00 400.00
TMALS Luis Severino/150 6.00 15.00
TMAMM Mark McGwire/50 30.00 80.00
TMAMT Mike Trout/20 500.00 1000.00
TMANS Noah Syndergaard/150 10.00 25.00
TMAOA Ozzie Albies/150 15.00 40.00
TMAOS Ozzie Smith/85 20.00 50.00
TMAPM Pedro Martinez/40 30.00 80.00
TMARA Roberto Alomar/85 10.00 25.00
TMARAJ Ronald Acuna Jr./85 75.00 200.00
TMARH Rhys Hoskins/150 15.00 40.00
TMASO Shohei Ohtani/20 125.00 300.00

2020 Topps Archives

301-325 ODDS 1:8 HOBBY
1 Babe Ruth .60 1.50
2 Paul Goldschmidt .25 .60
3 Charlie Blackmon .25 .60
4 Nick Senzel .25 .60
5 Steve Carlton .20 .50
6 Aristides Aquino RC .60 1.50
7 Shohei Ohtani .40 1.00
8 Kyle Schwarber .25 .60
9 Joey Gallo .20 .50
10 Mariano Rivera .30 .75
11 Rickey Henderson .25 .60
12 Marcus Stroman .20 .50
13 Seth Brown RC .25 .60
14 Harmon Killebrew .25 .60
15 Albert Pujols .30 .75
16 Willi Castro RC .40 1.00
17 Jorge Soler .25 .60
18 Dylan Cease RC .40 1.00
19 Pete Alonso .60 1.50
20 Whit Merrifield .25 .60
21 Gary Sanchez .25 .60
22 Marcus Semien .25 .60
23 Francisco Lindor .25 .60
24 Xander Bogaerts .25 .60
25 Jackie Robinson .25 .60
26 Keston Hiura .30 .75
27 Mookie Betts .50 1.25
28 Aaron Hicks .20 .50
29 Robin Yount .25 .60
30 George Brett .50 1.25
31 Alex Bregman .25 .60
32 Al Kaline .25 .60
33 Will Smith .25 .60
34 Brusdar Graterol RC .40 1.00
35 Tim Lincecum .20 .50
36 Shane Bieber .25 .60
37 Kyle Lewis RC 2.00 5.00
38 Jose Altuve .20 .50
39 Michael Brantley .20 .50
40 Sam Hilliard RC .40 1.00
41 Deion Sanders .20 .50
42 Jeff McNeil .20 .50
43 Aaron Civale RC .50 1.25
44 Lucas Giolito .20 .50
45 Bo Bichette RC 2.00 5.00
46 Gary Carter .20 .50
47 Goose Gossage .20 .50
48 J.D. Martinez .25 .60
49 George Kell .20 .50
50 Mike Trout 1.25 3.00
51 Brock Burke RC .25 .60
52 Catfish Hunter .20 .50
53 Lou Boudreau .20 .50
54 Max Muncy .20 .50
55 Jose Berrios .20 .50
56 Vladimir Guerrero Jr. .40 1.00
57 Ozzie Albies .25 .60
58 Tim Anderson .25 .60
59 Will Clark .20 .50
60 Carl Yastrzemski .40 1.00
61 Alex Young RC .25 .60
62 Nomar Garciaparra .20 .50
63 Bryan Reynolds .20 .50
64 Joey Votto .25 .60
65 Sean Murphy RC .40 1.00
66 J.T. Realmuto .25 .60
67 Kenta Maeda .20 .50
68 Jack Flaherty .25 .60
69 Trevor Bauer .30 .75
70 Jim Thome .20 .50
71 Zack Greinke .25 .60
72 Isan Diaz RC .40 1.00
73 Ryne Sandberg .50 1.25
74 Ralph Kiner .20 .50
75 Mike Mussina .20 .50
76 Larry Doby .20 .50
77 Paul DeJong .25 .60
78 Gavin Lux RC 1.25 3.00
79 Matt Chapman .25 .60
80 Ramon Laureano .25 .60
81 Corey Seager .25 .60
82 Luis Aparicio .20 .50
83 Tom Glavine .20 .50
84 Amed Rosario .20 .50
85 Jake Fraley RC .30 .75
86 Raisel Iglesias .15 .40
87 Juan Soto .75 2.00
88 Derek Jeter .60 1.50
89 Nolan Arenado .40 1.00
90 Nolan Ryan .75 2.00
91 Jordan Yamamoto RC .25 .60
92 Matt Carpenter .25 .60
93 Mallex Smith .15 .40
94 Charlie Morton .25 .60
95 A.J. Puk RC
96 DJ LeMahieu .25 .60
97 Monte Irvin .20 .50
98 Wade Boggs .20 .50
99 Shin-Soo Choo .20 .50
100 Hank Aaron .50 1.25
101 Ted Williams .50 1.25
102 Bob Gibson .20 .50
103 Mike Clevinger .20 .50
104 Christian Walker .20 .50
105 Chris Paddack .25 .60
106 Tony Gwynn .25 .60
107 Kerry Wood .15 .40
108 Mike Piazza .25 .60
109 Randy Johnson .25 .60
110 Abraham Toro RC .30 .75
111 Nick Solak RC 1.00 2.50
112 Stephen Piscotty .15 .40
113 Hunter Dozier .15 .40
114 Bob Feller .20 .50
115 Mike Moustakas .20 .50
116 Jacob deGrom .50 1.25
117 Shogo Akiyama RC .40 1.00
118 Ernie Banks .25 .60
119 Eloy Jimenez .50 1.25
120 Carlos Correa .25 .60
121 Frank Robinson .20 .50
122 Sandy Koufax .50 1.25
123 Jason Heyward .20 .50
124 Trevor Story .25 .60
125 Mike Schmidt .40 1.00
126 Bobby Bradley RC .25 .60
127 Roberto Alomar .20 .50
128 Fred McGriff .20 .50
129 DJ LeMahieu .25 .60
130 Larry Walker .20 .50
131 Eric Hosmer .20 .50
132 Buster Posey .30 .75
133 Tony Gonsolin RC 1.00 2.50
134 Jon Lester .20 .50
135 Yoshi Tsutsugo RC .60 1.50
136 Ty Cobb .40 1.00
137 Eduardo Escobar .15 .40
138 Blake Snell .20 .50
139 Mike Soroka .25 .60
140 Zack Collins RC .30 .75
141 Dustin May RC .75 2.00
142 Cal Ripken Jr. .75 2.00
143 Brandon Crawford .20 .50
144 Bo Jackson .25 .60
145 Paul Molitor .25 .60
146 Ketel Marte .20 .50

147 Jesus Luzardo RC .50 1.25
148 Josh Hader .20 .50
149 Roberto Clemente .60 1.50
150 Mo Vaughn .15 .40
151 Jeff Bagwell .20 .50
152 Corey Kluber .20 .50
153 Ken Griffey Jr. .50 1.25
154 George Springer .20 .50
155 Justin Dunn RC .30 .75
156 Clayton Kershaw .40 1.00
157 Daniel Vogelbach .15 .40
158 Brooks Robinson .20 .50
159 Luis Robert RC 4.00 10.00
160 Mauricio Dubon RC .30 .75
161 Justin Upton .20 .50
162 Javier Baez .30 .75
163 Max Scherzer .25 .60
164 David Ortiz .25 .60
165 John Smoltz .25 .60
166 Dave Winfield .20 .50
167 Justin Turner .25 .60
168 Nelson Cruz .25 .60
169 Khris Davis .25 .60
170 Rowdy Tellez .20 .50
171 Adbert Alzolay RC .30 .75
172 Zac Gallen RC .60 1.50
173 Lou Brock .20 .50
174 Trey Mancini .25 .60
175 Sammy Sosa .25 .60
176 Duke Snider .20 .50
177 Hyun-Jin Ryu .20 .50
178 Thurman Munson .25 .60
179 Sandy Alcantara .15 .40
180 Gleyber Torres .50 1.25
181 Matthew Boyd .15 .40
182 Willie Stargell .20 .50
183 Walker Buehler .30 .75
184 Trent Grisham RC 1.00 2.50
185 Fernando Tatis Jr. 1.25 3.00
186 Willie McCovey .20 .50
187 Sheldon Neuse RC .30 .75
188 Josh Bell .20 .50
189 Ivan Rodriguez .20 .50
190 Billy Williams .20 .50
191 Andrew Benintendi .25 .60
192 Shun Yamaguchi RC .30 .75
193 Anthony Rizzo .30 .75
194 Victor Robles .30 .75
195 Tom Seaver .20 .50
196 Rhys Hoskins .30 .75
197 Danny Jansen .15 .40
198 Dansby Swanson .25 .60
199 Giancarlo Stanton .25 .60
200 Marco Gonzales .15 .40
201 Manny Machado .25 .60
202 Anthony Kay RC .25 .60
203 Anthony Rendon .25 .60
204 Michel Baez RC .25 .60
205 Kyle Seager .15 .40
206 Juan Gonzalez .15 .40
207 Carter Kieboom .20 .50
208 Chris Sale .25 .60
209 Kenley Jansen .20 .50
210 Ralph Kiner .20 .50
211 Starling Marte .20 .50
212 Orlando Cepeda .20 .50
213 Randy Arozarena RC 2.00 5.00
214 Austin Meadows .25 .60
215 Frank Thomas .25 .60
216 Robel Garcia RC .25 .60
217 Cody Bellinger .50 1.25
218 Reggie Jackson .20 .50
219 Rollie Fingers .20 .50
220 Chipper Jones .25 .60
221 John Means .25 .60
222 Yordan Alvarez RC 2.50 6.00
223 Brad Keller .15 .40
224 Andrelton Simmons .15 .40
225 Evan Longoria .20 .50
226 David Wright .20 .50
227 Ryan Howard .20 .50
228 Gerrit Cole .40 1.00
229 Eugenio Suarez .20 .50
230 Michael Chavis .20 .50
231 Whitey Ford .20 .50
232 Willson Contreras .25 .60
233 Rod Carew .20 .50
234 Yadier Molina .30 .75
235 Ichiro .30 .75
236 Bryce Harper .40 1.00
237 Trevor Hoffman .20 .50
238 Jorge Alfaro .15 .40
239 Alan Trammell .20 .50
240 Nico Hoerner RC 1.00 2.50
241 Ronald Acuna Jr. 1.00 2.50
242 Matt Olson .25 .60
243 Edgar Martinez .20 .50
244 Brendan McKay RC .40 1.00
245 Yuli Gurriel .20 .50
246 Kole Calhoun .15 .40
247 Craig Biggio .20 .50
248 Christian Yelich .30 .75
249 Vladimir Guerrero .20 .50
250 Carlton Fisk .20 .50
251 Logan Allen RC .25 .60
252 Noah Syndergaard .20 .50
253 Aaron Nola .20 .50
254 Rougned Odor .20 .50
255 Dennis Eckersley .20 .50
256 Jorge Polanco .20 .50
257 Aroldis Chapman .25 .60
258 Roger Clemens .30 .75
259 Anthony Santander .15 .40
260 Yu Darvish .25 .60
261 Harrison Bader .20 .50
262 Honus Wagner .25 .60
263 Michael Conforto .20 .50
264 Alex Rodriguez .30 .75
265 Ryan McMahon .25 .60
266 Barry Larkin .20 .50
267 Rafael Devers .30 .75
268 Eddie Rosario .20 .50
269 Andres Munoz RC .40 1.00
270 Jose Abreu .25 .60
271 Jose Ramirez .20 .50
272 Tim Hudson .20 .50
273 Adrian Morejon RC .25 .60
274 Johnny Bench .25 .60
275 Juan Marichal .20 .50
276 Kevin Newman .25 .60
277 Joe Morgan .20 .50
278 Lourdes Gurriel Jr. .20 .50
279 Miguel Cabrera .25 .60
280 Ryan Braun .20 .50
281 Lou Gehrig .50 1.25
282 Brandon Woodruff .25 .60
283 Johnny Cueto .20 .50
284 Wil Myers .20 .50
285 Andruw Jones .15 .40
286 Cavan Biggio .30 .75
287 Jonathan Villar .15 .40
288 Justin Verlander .25 .60
289 Pedro Martinez .20 .50
290 Jose Urquidy RC .30 .75
291 Andy Pettitte .20 .50
292 Yu Chang RC .40 1.00
293 Aaron Judge .60 1.50
294 Elvis Andrus .20 .50
295 Andre Dawson .20 .50
296 Carlos Santana .20 .50
297 Willie Mays .50 1.25
298 Stephen Strasburg .25 .60
299 Kris Bryant .30 .75
300 Freddie Freeman .30 .75
301 Pete Alonso SP 1.25 3.00
302 Aaron Judge SP 1.25 3.00
303 Mike Trout SP 2.50 6.00
304 Francisco Lindor SP .50 1.25
305 Yordan Alvarez SP 3.00 8.00
306 Shohei Ohtani SP .75 2.00
307 Chris Sale SP .50 1.25
308 David Ortiz SP .50 1.25
309 Noah Syndergaard SP .40 1.00
310 Ernie Banks SP .50 1.25
311 Hank Aaron SP 1.00 2.50
312 Mariano Rivera SP .60 1.50
313 Javier Baez SP .60 1.50
315 Duke Snider SP .40 1.00
316 Randy Johnson SP .50 1.25
317 Pedro Martinez SP .40 1.00
318 Miguel Cabrera SP .50 1.25
319 Ryne Sandberg SP 1.00 2.50
320 CC Sabathia SP .40 1.00
321 Jeff Bagwell SP .40 1.00
322 Roberto Alomar SP .40 1.00
323 John Smoltz SP .50 1.25
324 Steve Carlton SP .40 1.00
325 Mark Teixeira SP .40 1.00

2020 Topps Archives Blue

*BLUE: 6X TO 15X BASIC
*BLUE RC: 4X TO 10X BASIC RC
STATED ODDS 1:83 HOBBY
STATED PRINT RUN 25 SER.#'d SETS
27 Mookie Betts 15.00 40.00
88 Derek Jeter 20.00 50.00
149 Roberto Clemente 15.00 40.00
153 Ken Griffey Jr. 30.00 80.00
159 Luis Robert 100.00 250.00
185 Fernando Tatis Jr. 40.00 100.00

2020 Topps Archives Orange Foil

*ORNGE FOIL: 4X TO 10X BASIC
*ORNGE FOIL RC: 2.5X TO 6X BASIC RC
STATED ODDS 1:265 HOBBY
STATED PRINT RUN 75 SER.#'d SETS

2020 Topps Archives Purple

*PURPLE: 3X TO 8X BASIC
*PURPLE RC: 2X TO 5X BASIC RC
STATED ODDS 1:39 HOBBY
STATED PRINT RUN 175 SER.#'d SETS
27 Mookie Betts 8.00 20.00
153 Ken Griffey Jr. 6.00 15.00
159 Luis Robert 20.00 50.00
185 Fernando Tatis Jr. 12.00 30.00

2020 Topps Archives Red

*RED: 4X TO 10X BASIC
*RED RC: 2.5X TO 6X BASIC RC
STATED ODDS 1:89 HOBBY
STATED PRINT RUN 75 SER.#'d SETS
27 Mookie Betts 10.00 25.00
149 Roberto Clemente 10.00 25.00
153 Ken Griffey Jr. 8.00 20.00
159 Luis Robert 30.00 80.00
185 Fernando Tatis Jr. 25.00 60.00

2020 Topps Archives Silver

*SILVER: 4X TO 10X BASIC
*SILVER RC: 2.5X TO 6X BASIC RC
STATED ODDS 1:67 HOBBY
STATED PRINT RUN 99 SER.#'d SETS
27 Mookie Betts 10.00 25.00
149 Roberto Clemente 10.00 25.00
153 Ken Griffey Jr. 8.00 20.00
159 Luis Robert 30.00 80.00
185 Fernando Tatis Jr. 25.00 60.00

2020 Topps Archives Mega Box Foil

*MEGA FOIL: 5X TO 12X BASIC
*MEGA FOIL RC: 3X TO 8X BASIC RC
INSERTED IN MEGA BOXES
27 Mookie Betts 12.00 30.00
149 Roberto Clemente 12.00 30.00
153 Ken Griffey Jr. 25.00 60.00
159 Luis Robert 75.00 200.00
185 Fernando Tatis Jr. 30.00 80.00

2020 Topps Archives '02 Topps Variations

STATED ODDS 1:265 HOBBY
234 Yadier Molina 6.00 15.00

2020 Topps Archives '55 Topps Black and White Variations

STATED ODDS 1:265 HOBBY
6 Aristides Aquino 4.00 10.00
7 Shohei Ohtani 4.00 10.00
56 Vladimir Guerrero Jr. 4.00 10.00
78 Gavin Lux 6.00 15.00
100 Hank Aaron 5.00 12.00

2020 Topps Archives '55 Topps Image Variations

STATED ODDS 1:100 HOBBY
1 Babe Ruth 8.00 20.00
2 Paul Goldschmidt 3.00 8.00
3 Charlie Blackmon 3.00 8.00
4 Nick Senzel 3.00 8.00
5 Steve Carlton 2.50 6.00
6 Aristides Aquino 5.00 12.00
7 Shohei Ohtani 5.00 12.00
8 Kyle Schwarber 3.00 8.00
9 Joey Gallo 3.00 8.00
10 Mariano Rivera 4.00 10.00
11 Rickey Henderson 3.00 8.00
12 Marcus Stroman 2.50 6.00
13 Seth Brown 2.00 5.00
14 Harmon Killebrew 3.00 8.00
15 Albert Pujols 4.00 10.00
16 Willi Castro 3.00 8.00
17 Jorge Soler 3.00 8.00
18 Dylan Cease 3.00 8.00
19 Pete Alonso 8.00 20.00
20 Whit Merrifield 3.00 8.00
21 Gary Sanchez 3.00 8.00
22 Marcus Semien 3.00 8.00
23 Francisco Lindor 3.00 8.00
24 Xander Bogaerts 3.00 8.00
25 Jackie Robinson 3.00 8.00
26 Keston Hiura 4.00 10.00
27 Mookie Betts 6.00 15.00
28 Aaron Hicks 2.50 6.00
29 Robin Yount 3.00 8.00
30 George Brett 6.00 15.00
31 Alex Bregman 3.00 8.00
32 Al Kaline 3.00 8.00
33 Will Smith 3.00 8.00
34 Brusdar Graterol 3.00 8.00
35 Tim Lincecum 2.50 6.00
36 Shane Bieber 3.00 8.00
37 Kyle Lewis 15.00 40.00
38 Jose Altuve 2.50 6.00
39 Michael Brantley 2.50 6.00
40 Sam Hilliard 3.00 8.00
41 Deion Sanders 2.50 6.00
42 Jeff McNeil 2.50 6.00
43 Aaron Civale 4.00 10.00
44 Lucas Giolito 2.50 6.00
45 Bo Bichette 15.00 40.00
46 Gary Carter 2.50 6.00
47 Goose Gossage 2.50 6.00
48 J.D. Martinez 3.00 8.00
49 George Kell 2.50 6.00
50 Mike Trout 30.00 80.00
51 Brock Burke 2.00 5.00
52 Catfish Hunter 2.50 6.00
53 Lou Boudreau 2.50 6.00
54 Max Muncy 2.50 6.00
55 Jose Berrios 2.50 6.00
56 Vladimir Guerrero Jr. 5.00 12.00
57 Ozzie Albies 3.00 8.00
58 Tim Anderson 3.00 8.00
59 Will Clark 2.50 6.00
60 Carl Yastrzemski 5.00 12.00
61 Alex Young 2.00 5.00
62 Nomar Garciaparra 2.50 6.00
63 Bryan Reynolds 2.50 6.00
64 Joey Votto 3.00 8.00
65 Sean Murphy 3.00 8.00
66 J.T. Realmuto 3.00 8.00
67 Kenta Maeda 2.50 6.00
68 Jack Flaherty 3.00 8.00
69 Trevor Bauer 4.00 10.00
70 Jim Thome 2.50 6.00
71 Zack Greinke 3.00 8.00
72 Isan Diaz 3.00 8.00
73 Ryne Sandberg 6.00 15.00
74 Ralph Kiner 2.50 6.00
75 Mike Mussina 2.50 6.00
76 Larry Doby 2.50 6.00
77 Paul DeJong 3.00 8.00
78 Gavin Lux 10.00 25.00
79 Matt Chapman 3.00 8.00
80 Ramon Laureano 2.50 6.00
81 Corey Seager 3.00 8.00
82 Luis Aparicio 2.50 6.00
83 Tom Glavine 2.50 6.00
84 Amed Rosario 2.50 6.00
85 Jake Fraley 2.50 6.00
86 Raisel Iglesias 2.00 5.00
87 Juan Soto 10.00 25.00
88 Derek Jeter 25.00 60.00
89 Nolan Arenado 5.00 12.00
90 Nolan Ryan 10.00 25.00
91 Jordan Yamamoto 2.00 5.00
92 Matt Carpenter 3.00 8.00
93 Mallex Smith 2.00 5.00
94 Charlie Morton 3.00 8.00
95 A.J. Puk 3.00 8.00
96 DJ LeMahieu 3.00 8.00
97 Monte Irvin 2.50 6.00
98 Wade Boggs 2.50 6.00
99 Shin-Soo Choo 2.50 6.00
100 Hank Aaron 6.00 15.00

2020 Topps Archives '74 Topps Variations

STATED ODDS 1:265 HOBBY
105 Chris Paddack 5.00 12.00
163 Max Scherzer 5.00 12.00
185 Fernando Tatis Jr. 25.00 60.00
194 Victor Robles 6.00 15.00

2020 Topps Archives '55 Bowman Archives

STATED ODDS 1:8 HOBBY
B551 Gavin Lux 1.25 3.00
B552 Tony Gonsolin 1.00 2.50
B553 Jesus Luzardo .50 1.25
B554 Jordan Yamamoto .25 .60
B555 Dylan Cease .40 1.00
B556 Adbert Alzolay .30 .75
B557 Justin Dunn .30 .75
B558 A.J. Puk .40 1.00
B559 Bo Bichette 2.00 5.00
B5510 Brusdar Graterol .40 1.00
B5511 Aristides Aquino .60 1.50
B5512 Kyle Lewis 2.00 5.00
B5513 Isan Diaz .40 1.00
B5514 Sean Murphy .40 1.00
B5515 Dustin May .75 2.00
B5516 Bobby Bradley .25 .60
B5517 Shun Yamaguchi .30 .75
B5518 Shogo Akiyama .40 1.00
B5519 Zac Gallen .60 1.50
B5520 Luis Robert 6.00 15.00
B5521 Trent Grisham 1.00 2.50
B5522 Nico Hoerner 1.00 2.50
B5523 Logan Allen .25 .60
B5524 Yoshi Tsutsugo .60 1.50
B5525 Adrian Morejon .25 .60
B5526 Brendan McKay .40 1.00
B5527 Zack Collins .30 .75
B5528 Nick Solak 1.00 2.50
B5529 Mauricio Dubon .30 .75
B5530 Yordan Alvarez 2.50 6.00

2020 Topps Archives '55 Bowman Archives Black

*BLACK: 1.5X TO 4X BASIC
STATED ODDS 1:668 HOBBY
STATED PRINT RUN 99 SER.#'d SETS
B5520 Luis Robert 40.00 100.00

2020 Topps Archives '55 Bowman Archives Red

*RED: 6X TO 15X BASIC
STATED ODDS 1:2645 HOBBY
STATED PRINT RUN 25 SER.#'d SETS
B5520 Luis Robert 150.00 400.00

2020 Topps Archives '55 Topps Mini

STATED ODDS 1:100 HOBBY
55M1 Babe Ruth 5.00 12.00
55M2 Paul Goldschmidt 2.00 5.00
55M3 Charlie Blackmon 2.00 5.00
55M4 Nick Senzel 2.00 5.00
55M5 Steve Carlton 1.50 4.00
55M6 Aristides Aquino 3.00 8.00
55M7 Shohei Ohtani 3.00 8.00
55M8 Kyle Schwarber 2.00 5.00
55M9 Joey Gallo 2.00 5.00
55M10 Mariano Rivera 2.50 6.00
55M11 Rickey Henderson 2.00 5.00
55M12 Marcus Stroman 1.50 4.00
55M13 Seth Brown 1.25 3.00
55M14 Harmon Killebrew 2.00 5.00
55M15 Albert Pujols 2.50 6.00
55M16 Willi Castro 2.00 5.00
55M17 Jorge Soler 2.00 5.00
55M18 Dylan Cease 2.00 5.00
55M19 Pete Alonso 5.00 12.00
55M20 Whit Merrifield 2.00 5.00
55M21 Gary Sanchez 2.00 5.00
55M22 Marcus Semien 2.00 5.00
55M23 Francisco Lindor 2.00 5.00
55M24 Xander Bogaerts 2.00 5.00
55M25 Jackie Robinson 2.00 5.00
55M26 Keston Hiura 2.50 6.00
55M27 Mookie Betts 4.00 10.00
55M28 Aaron Hicks 1.50 4.00
55M29 Robin Yount 2.00 5.00
55M30 George Brett 4.00 10.00
55M31 Alex Bregman 2.00 5.00
55M32 Al Kaline 2.00 5.00
55M33 Will Smith 2.00 5.00
55M34 Brusdar Graterol 2.00 5.00
55M35 Tim Lincecum 1.50 4.00
55M36 Shane Bieber 2.00 5.00
55M37 Kyle Lewis 10.00 25.00
55M38 Jose Altuve 1.50 4.00
55M39 Michael Brantley 1.50 4.00
55M40 Sam Hilliard 2.00 5.00
55M41 Deion Sanders 1.50 4.00
55M42 Jeff McNeil 1.50 4.00
55M43 Aaron Civale 2.50 6.00
55M44 Lucas Giolito 1.50 4.00
55M45 Bo Bichette 10.00 25.00
55M46 Gary Carter 1.50 4.00
55M47 Goose Gossage 1.50 4.00
55M48 J.D. Martinez 2.00 5.00
55M49 George Kell 1.50 4.00
55M50 Mike Trout 20.00 50.00
55M51 Brock Burke 1.25 3.00
55M52 Catfish Hunter 1.50 4.00
55M53 Lou Boudreau 1.50 4.00
55M54 Max Muncy 1.50 4.00
55M55 Jose Berrios 1.50 4.00
55M56 Vladimir Guerrero Jr. 3.00 8.00
55M57 Ozzie Albies 2.00 5.00
55M58 Tim Anderson 2.00 5.00
55M59 Will Clark 1.50 4.00
55M60 Carl Yastrzemski 3.00 8.00
55M61 Alex Young 1.25 3.00
55M62 Nomar Garciaparra 1.50 4.00
55M63 Bryan Reynolds 1.50 4.00
55M64 Joey Votto 2.00 5.00
55M65 Sean Murphy 2.00 5.00
55M66 J.T. Realmuto 2.00 5.00
55M67 Kenta Maeda 1.50 4.00
55M68 Jack Flaherty 2.00 5.00
55M69 Trevor Bauer 2.50 6.00
55M70 Jim Thome 1.50 4.00
55M71 Zack Greinke 2.00 5.00
55M72 Isan Diaz 2.00 5.00
55M73 Ryne Sandberg 4.00 10.00
55M74 Ralph Kiner 1.50 4.00
55M75 Mike Mussina 1.50 4.00
55M76 Larry Doby 1.50 4.00
55M77 Paul DeJong 2.00 5.00
55M78 Gavin Lux 6.00 15.00
55M79 Matt Chapman 2.00 5.00
55M80 Ramon Laureano 1.50 4.00
55M81 Corey Seager 2.00 5.00
55M82 Luis Aparicio 1.50 4.00
55M83 Tom Glavine 1.50 4.00
55M84 Amed Rosario 1.50 4.00
55M85 Jake Fraley 1.50 4.00
55M86 Raisel Iglesias 1.25 3.00
55M87 Juan Soto 6.00 15.00
55M88 Derek Jeter 5.00 12.00
55M89 Nolan Arenado 3.00 8.00
55M90 Nolan Ryan 6.00 15.00
55M91 Jordan Yamamoto 1.25 3.00
55M92 Matt Carpenter 2.00 5.00
55M93 Mallex Smith 1.25 3.00
55M94 Charlie Morton 2.00 5.00
55M95 A.J. Puk 2.00 5.00
55M96 DJ LeMahieu 2.00 5.00
55M97 Monte Irvin 1.50 4.00
55M98 Wade Boggs 1.50 4.00
55M99 Shin-Soo Choo 1.50 4.00
55M100 Hank Aaron 4.00 10.00

2020 Topps Archives '55 Topps Mini Autographs

STATED ODDS 1:941 HOBBY
STATED PRINT RUN 20 SER.#'d SETS
EXCHANGE DEADLINE 7/31/2022
55M2 Paul Goldschmidt 25.00 60.00
55M5 Steve Carlton 40.00 100.00
55M6 Aristides Aquino 75.00 200.00
55M7 Shohei Ohtani
55M10 Mariano Rivera 100.00 250.00
55M11 Rickey Henderson 125.00 300.00
55M13 Seth Brown 100.00 250.00
55M16 W.Castro Not #'d 10.00 25.00
55M17 Jorge Soler
55M18 Dylan Cease 30.00 80.00
55M19 Pete Alonso 50.00 120.00
55M24 Xander Bogaerts 40.00 100.00
55M26 Keston Hiura 40.00 100.00
55M29 Robin Yount 75.00 200.00
55M35 Tim Lincecum 75.00 200.00
55M37 Kyle Lewis 100.00 250.00
55M38 Jose Altuve 40.00 100.00
55M42 Jeff McNeil 25.00 60.00
55M43 Aaron Civale
55M44 Lucas Giolito 30.00 80.00
55M50 Mike Trout
55M51 Brock Burke 20.00 50.00
55M59 Will Clark 60.00 150.00
55M60 Carl Yastrzemski 250.00 600.00
55M61 Alex Young 50.00 120.00
55M62 Nomar Garciaparra 100.00 250.00
55M65 Sean Murphy 40.00 100.00
55M70 Jim Thome 150.00 400.00
55M73 Ryne Sandberg 75.00 200.00
55M75 Mike Mussina
55M77 Paul DeJong 30.00 80.00
55M80 Ramon Laureano 25.00 60.00
55M81 Corey Seager EXCH 60.00 150.00
55M83 Tom Glavine 25.00 60.00
55M85 Jake Fraley 40.00 100.00
55M87 Juan Soto 150.00 400.00
55M88 Don Mattingly 75.00 200.00
55M90 Nolan Ryan 125.00 300.00
55M91 Jordan Yamamoto

2020 Topps Archives '60 Topps All-Star Rookie Autographs

STATED ODDS 1:550 HOBBY
PRINT RUNS B/WN 50-150 COPIES PER
EXCHANGE DEADLINE 7/31/2022
*SILVER/99: .5X TO 1.2X BASIC
*BLUE/25: .6X TO 1.5X BASIC
60ARABR Bryan Reynolds/150 6.00 15.00
60ARAEJ Eloy Jimenez EXCH 30.00 80.00
60ARAFTJ Fernando Tatis Jr. EXCH 125.00 300.00
60ARAJM John Means EXCH 60.00 150.00
60ARAKH Keston Hiura/150 12.00 30.00
60ARAPA Pete Alonso/50 50.00 120.00
60ARAVGJ Vladimir Guerrero Jr. EXCH 20.00 50.00
60ARAVR Victor Robles EXCH 12.00 30.00
60ARAWS Will Smith/150 8.00 20.00

2020 Topps Archives '60 Topps All-Star Rookies

STATED ODDS 1:6 HOBBY
60AREJ Eloy Jimenez .75 2.00
60ARFTJ Fernando Tatis Jr. 2.50 6.00
60ARGT Gleyber Torres .75 2.00
60ARJA Jorge Alfaro .25 .60
60ARJM John Means .40 1.00
60ARJS Juan Soto 1.25 3.00
60ARKH Keston Hiura .50 1.25
60ARMA Miguel Andujar .40 1.00
60ARPA Pete Alonso 1.00 2.50
60ARRA Ronald Acuna Jr. 1.50 4.00
60ARRO Ryan O'Hearn .25 .60
60ARSO Shohei Ohtani .60 1.50
60ARVGJ Vladimir Guerrero Jr. .60 1.50
60ARVR Victor Robles .50 1.25
60ARWA Willy Adames .25 .60
60ARWB Walker Buehler .50 1.25
60ARWS Will Smith .40 1.00
60ARYA Yordan Alvarez 2.50 6.00

2020 Topps Archives '60 Topps All-Star Rookies Black

*BLACK: 1.5X TO 4X BASIC
STATED ODDS 1:2849 HOBBY
STATED PRINT RUN 99 SER.#'d SETS

2020 Topps Archives '60 Topps All-Star Rookies Red Foil

*RED: 4X TO 10X BASIC
STATED ODDS 1:4389 HOBBY
STATED PRINT RUN 25 SER.#'d SETS
60ARFTJ Fernando Tatis Jr. 40.00 100.00
60ARGT Gleyber Torres 20.00 50.00

2020 Topps Archives '60 Topps All-Star Rookies Silver Foil

*SILVER: 2X TO 5X BASIC
STATED ODDS 1:2203 HOBBY
STATED PRINT RUN 50 SER.#'d SETS
60ARFTJ Fernando Tatis Jr. 20.00 50.00
60ARGT Gleyber Torres 10.00 25.00

2020 Topps Archives '60 Topps Combo Cards

STATED ODDS 1:6 HOBBY
*BLACK/99: 1.5X TO 4X BASIC
*SILVER/50: 2X TO 5X BASIC
*RED/25: 4X TO 10X BASIC
60CCAA Alvarez/Altuve 2.00 5.00
60CCGB Guerrero Jr./Bichette 1.50 4.00
60CCHH Hoskins/Harper .50 1.25
60CCJT Judge/Torres .75 2.00
60CCSM Smith/Muncy .30 .75
60CCTO Trout/Ohtani 1.50 4.00
60CCYH Hiura/Yelich .40 1.00

2020 Topps Archives '60 Topps Combo Cards Dual Autographs

STATED ODDS 1:1560 HOBBY
EXCHANGE DEADLINE 7/31/2022
60CCAAA Altuve/Alvarez EXCH 40.00 100.00
60CCAHH Harper/Hoskins EXCH 125.00 300.00
60CCAJT Judge/Torres EXCH
60CCASM Muncy/Smith/150 15.00 40.00
60CCATO Trout/Ohtani EXCH
60CCAYH Hiura/Yelich EXCH 75.00 200.00

2020 Topps Archives '60 Topps Combo Cards Dual Autographs Blue

*BLUE: .75X TO 2X BASIC
STATED ODDS 1:6173 HOBBY
STATED PRINT RUN 25 SER.#'d SETS
EXCHANGE DEADLINE 7/31/2022
60CCAJT Judge/Torres EXCH 200.00 500.00
60CCATO Trout/Ohtani EXCH 500.00 1200.00

2020 Topps Archives '64 Topps Giants

ONE PER BLASTER
*BLUE: X TO X BASIC
64OAA Aristides Aquino 1.50 4.00
64OAJ Aaron Judge 2.50 6.00
64OBB Bo Bichette 5.00 12.00
64OBH Bryce Harper 1.50 4.00
64OBM Brendan McKay 1.00 2.50
64OCJ Chipper Jones 1.00 2.50
64OCK Clayton Kershaw 1.50 4.00
64OCRJ Cal Ripken Jr. 3.00 8.00
64OCY Christian Yelich 1.25 3.00
64ODS Deion Sanders .75 2.00
64OEJ Eloy Jimenez 2.00 5.00
64OFL Francisco Lindor 1.00 2.50
64OFTJ Fernando Tatis Jr. 5.00 12.00
64OGB George Brett 2.00 5.00
64OGL Gavin Lux 3.00 8.00
64OJA Jose Altuve .75 2.00
64OJR Jackie Robinson 1.00 2.50
64OJS Juan Soto 3.00 8.00
64OKH Keston Hiura 1.25 3.00
64OMB Mookie Betts 2.00 5.00
64OMT Mike Trout 5.00 12.00
64ONA Nolan Arenado 1.50 4.00
64ONH Nico Hoerner 2.50 6.00
64ONR Nolan Ryan 3.00 8.00
64OPA Pete Alonso 2.50 6.00
64ORH Rhys Hoskins 1.25 3.00
64ORJ Reggie Jackson .75 2.00
64OTM Thurman Munson 1.00 2.50
64OVGJ Vladimir Guerrero Jr. 1.50 4.00
64OYA Yordan Alvarez 6.00 15.00

2020 Topps Archives '64 Topps Giants Autographs

STATED ODDS 1:1001 BLASTERS
EXCHANGE DEADLINE 7/31/2022
64OAA Aristides Aquino 15.00 40.00
64OBM Brendan McKay EXCH 10.00 25.00
64OCJ Chipper Jones 50.00 120.00
64OCRJ Cal Ripken Jr. 100.00 250.00
64OJA Jose Altuve 25.00 60.00
64OJS Juan Soto 100.00 250.00
64OKH Keston Hiura 12.00 30.00
64OMT Mike Trout 300.00 800.00
64ONH Nico Hoerner 25.00 60.00
64ONR Nolan Ryan 100.00 250.00
64OPA Pete Alonso 40.00 100.00
64ORH Rhys Hoskins 25.00 60.00
64ORJ Reggie Jackson 50.00 120.00

2020 Topps Archives '76 Topps Traded Autographs

STATED ODDS 1:3238 HOBBY
EXCHANGE DEADLINE 7/31/2022
*SILVER/99: .5X TO 1.2X BASIC
*BLUE/50: .6X TO 1.5X BASIC
76TACCS CC Sabathia EXCH 20.00 50.00
76TAJB Jeff Bagwell 25.00 60.00
76TAJS John Smoltz 25.00 60.00
76TAMC Miguel Cabrera 75.00 200.00
76TAMT Mark Teixeira 20.00 50.00
76TAPM Pedro Martinez 20.00 50.00
76TARS Ryne Sandberg 50.00 120.00
76TASC Steve Carlton 25.00 60.00

2020 Topps Archives '89 Topps Corn Field Autographs

STATED ODDS 1:334 HOBBY
EXCHANGE DEADLINE 7/31/2022
*PINSTRIPE/27: .75X TO 2X BASIC
89CFAAJ Aaron Judge EXCH 100.00 250.00
89CFADC Dylan Cease 12.00 30.00
89CFADJ DJ LeMahieu 30.00 80.00
89CFAGT Gleyber Torres 40.00 100.00
89CFAGU Gio Urshela 12.00 30.00
89CFALG Lucas Giolito 20.00 50.00
89CFALR Luis Robert EXCH 300.00 800.00
89CFALV Luke Voit 30.00 80.00
89CFAMA Miguel Andujar 6.00 15.00
89CFATA Tim Anderson 20.00 50.00
89CFAYM Yoan Moncada 25.00 60.00

2020 Topps Archives '90 Topps Rookies

STATED ODDS 1:24 HOBBY
90RAA Aristides Aquino 1.25 3.00
90RAJP A.J. Puk .75 2.00
90RBB Bo Bichette 4.00 10.00
90RBG Brusdar Graterol .75 2.00
90RBM Brendan McKay .75 2.00
90RDC Dylan Cease .75 2.00
90RDM Dustin May 1.50 4.00
90RGL Gavin Lux 2.50 6.00
90RJL Jesus Luzardo 1.00 2.50
90RKL Kyle Lewis 4.00 10.00
90RNH Nico Hoerner 2.00 5.00
90RSB Seth Brown .40 1.00
90RSM Sean Murphy .75 2.00
90RSN Sheldon Neuse .60 1.50
90RYA Yordan Alvarez 5.00 12.00

2020 Topps Archives '90 Topps Rookies Autographs

STATED ODDS 1:742 HOBBY
EXCHANGE DEADLINE 7/31/2022
*BLUE/25: .75X TO 2X BASIC
90RAAA Aristides Aquino 15.00 40.00
90RABM Brendan McKay 6.00 15.00
90RADC Dylan Cease 6.00 15.00
90RADM Dustin May 25.00 60.00
90RAJL Jesus Luzardo 15.00 40.00
90RAKL Kyle Lewis 60.00 150.00
90RASB Seth Brown 4.00 10.00
90RASM Sean Murphy 15.00 40.00

2020 Topps Archives Fan Favorites Autographs

STATED ODDS 1:19 HOBBY
EXCHANGE DEADLINE 7/31/2022
*PURPLE/150: .5X TO 1.2X BASE
*SILVER/99: .6X TO 1.5X BASE
*BLUE/25: .75X TO 2X BASE
FFAAA Andy Ashby 3.00 8.00
FFAAAQ Aristides Aquino 12.00 30.00
FFABB Bruce Bochy 15.00 40.00
FFABC Bernie Carbo 3.00 8.00
FFABL Brad Lidge 3.00 8.00
FFABMO Blue Moon Odom 5.00 12.00
FFABS Buck Showalter 5.00 12.00
FFABSA Benito Santiago 6.00 15.00
FFABW Bob Wickman 3.00 8.00
FFABWA Bob Walk 4.00 10.00
FFACM Charlie Manuel 12.00 30.00
FFADB Dante Bichette 10.00 25.00
FFADE Darin Erstad 5.00 12.00
FFADM Dave Martinez 10.00 25.00
FFADT Danny Tartabull 6.00 15.00
FFAFJ Felix Jose 3.00 8.00
FFAGA Garret Anderson 3.00 8.00
FFAGS Gary Sheffield 10.00 25.00
FFAJG Jerry Grote 6.00 15.00
FFAJGI Joe Girardi 10.00 25.00
FFAJO Jose Offerman 4.00 10.00
FFAJS John Stearns 5.00 12.00
FFAKB Kevin Bass 3.00 8.00
FFAKM Kevin Millar 6.00 15.00
FFALM Lloyd McClendon 3.00 8.00
FFALMA Lee Mazzilli 5.00 12.00
FFALS Lonnie Smith 4.00 10.00
FFAMB Mark Buehrle 12.00 30.00
FFAMG Mark Grudzielanek 4.00 10.00
FFAMP Mike Pagliarulo 5.00 12.00
FFAMS Manny Sanguillen 10.00 25.00
FFAMW Mark Wohlers 4.00 10.00
FFAPH Phil Hughes 10.00 25.00
FFAPHA Pete Harnisch 4.00 10.00
FFAPP Placido Polanco 4.00 10.00
FFAPW Preston Wilson 3.00 8.00
FFARD Ray Durham 10.00 25.00
FFARF Rafael Furcal 5.00 12.00
FFARG Ralph Garr 5.00 12.00
FFARGE Rich Gedman 6.00 15.00
FFARK Roberto Kelly 4.00 10.00
FFARS Reggie Sanders 5.00 12.00
FFASF Steve Finley 4.00 10.00
FFASG Shawn Green 8.00 20.00
FFASS Shane Spencer 5.00 12.00
FFATHE Tom Henke 4.00 10.00
FFATP Tom Pagnozzi 3.00 8.00
FFATW Todd Worrell 4.00 10.00
FFAVL Vern Law 6.00 15.00

2020 Topps Archives Fan Favorites Autographs Premium

STATED ODDS 1:1753 HOBBY
PRINT RUNS B/WN 25-50 COPIES PER
EXCHANGE DEADLINE 7/31/2022
FFPAJ Aaron Judge EXCH 200.00 500.00
FFPBH Bryce Harper/25 250.00 600.00
FFPCJ Chipper Jones/50 125.00 300.00
FFPCRJ Cal Ripken Jr./50 150.00 400.00
FFPDJ Derek Jeter
FFPFTJ Fernando Tatis Jr. EXCH 300.00 800.00
FFPHA Hank Aaron/25 250.00 600.00
FFPMR Mariano Rivera/25 200.00 500.00
FFPMS Mike Schmidt/50 200.00 500.00
FFPMT Mike Trout/25 600.00 1500.00
FFPRAJ Ronald Acuna Jr./50 200.00 500.00
FFPVGJ Vladimir Guerrero Jr./50 60.00 150.00

2020 Topps Archives Hobby Nickname Poster Autographs

INSERTED IN HOBBY BOXES
EXCHANGE DEADLINE 7/31/2022
HNPAJ Aaron Judge
HNPBS Blake Snell
HNPHA Hank Aaron
HNPMT Mike Trout
HNPPA Pete Alonso 75.00 200.00

2020 Topps Archives Hobby Nickname Posters

ONE PER HOBBY BOX
HNPAJ Aaron Judge 2.50 6.00
HNPBS Blake Snell .75 2.00
HNPCS Chris Sale 1.00 2.50
HNPDF Duke Snider .75 2.00
HNPDO David Ortiz 1.00 2.50
HNPEB Ernie Banks 1.00 2.50
HNPFL Francisco Lindor 1.00 2.50
HNPHA Hank Aaron 2.00 5.00
HNPJB Javier Baez 1.25 3.00
HNPMR Mariano Rivera 1.25 3.00
HNPMT Mike Trout 5.00 12.00
HNPNS Noah Syndergaard .75 2.00
HNPPA Pete Alonso 2.50 6.00
HNPSO Shohei Ohtani 1.50 4.00
HNPYA Yordan Alvarez 6.00 15.00

2020 Topps Archives Originals Autographs

STATED ODDS 1:6238 HOBBY
PRINT RUNS B/WN 11-20 COPIES PER
NO PRICING ON QTY 17 OR LESS
EXCHANGE DEADLINE 7/31/2022
214 Shawn Green/20 15.00 40.00

2016 Topps Archives 65th Anniversary

COMP.SET w/o SP's (65) 20.00 50.00
SP ODDS 1:21 PACKS
A65I Ichiro .50 1.25
A65AB Andy Benes .25 .60
A65AG Andres Galarraga .30 .75
A65AP A.J. Pollock .25 .60
A65BD Bucky Dent .25 .60
A65BH Bryce Harper .60 1.50
A65BM Bill Mazeroski .30 .75
A65BP Buster Posey .50 1.25
A65BW Billy Williams .30 .75
A65CH Charlie Hayes .25 .60
A65CJ Chipper Jones .40 1.00
A65CK Clayton Kershaw .60 1.50
A65CR Cal Ripken Jr. 1.25 3.00
A65CS Curt Simmons .25 .60
A65CSE Corey Seager 2.50 6.00
A65CY Carl Yastrzemski .60 1.50
A65DM Don Mattingly .75 2.00
A65DW Dontrelle Willis .25 .60

A65DWR David Wright .30 .75
A65EM Eddie Mathews .40 1.00
A65FH Frank Howard .25 .60
A65FT Frank Thomas .40 1.00
A65FTA Fernando Tatis .25 .60
A65FV Fernando Valenzuela .25 .60
A65FVI Fernando Vina .25 .60
A65HA Hank Aaron .75 2.00
A65HB Harold Baines .30 .75
A65JB Johnny Bench .40 1.00
A65JBU Jeff Burroughs .25 .60
A65JC Jose Cruz .25 .60
A65JCA Jose Canseco .30 .75
A65JCO Jeff Conine .25 .60
A65JCR Jose Cruz Jr. .25 .60
A65JM Joe Morgan .30 .75
A65JR Jackie Robinson .40 1.00
A65JRI Jose Rijo .25 .60
A65JV Jose Vidro .25 .60
A65KB Kris Bryant .50 1.25
A65KG Ken Griffey Jr. .75 2.00
A65KT Kent Tekulve .25 .60
A65MB Mike Bordick .25 .60
A65MT Mike Trout 2.00 5.00
A65MTA Masahiro Tanaka .30 .75
A65NR Nolan Ryan 1.25 3.00
A65OS Ozzie Smith .50 1.25
A65OV Omar Vizquel .30 .75
A65RC Roberto Clemente 1.00 2.50
A65RCA Rod Carew .30 .75
A65RCL Roger Clemens .50 1.25
A65RF Rollie Fingers .30 .75
A65RJ Randy Jones .25 .60
A65RK Ryan Klesko .25 .60
A65RM Roger Maris .40 1.00
A65SAJ Sandy Alomar Jr. .25 .60
A65SAS Sandy Alomar Sr. .25 .60
A65SC Steve Carlton .30 .75
A65SH Scott Hatteberg .25 .60
A65SK Sandy Koufax .75 2.00
A65SL Sparky Lyle .25 .60
A65TF Tito Francona .30 .75
A65TFE Tony Fernandez .25 .60
A65TH Teddy Higuera .25 .60
A65TW Ted Williams .75 2.00
A65VL Vern Law .25 .60
A65WM Willie Mays .75 2.00
A65SCY Carl Yastrzemski SP 10.00 25.00
A65SHA Hank Aaron SP 15.00 40.00
A65SJB Johnny Bench SP 10.00 25.00
A65SJR Jackie Robinson SP 10.00 25.00
A65SRC Roger Clemens SP 10.00 25.00
A65SSK Sandy Koufax SP 12.00 30.00
A65STW Ted Williams SP 12.00 30.00
A65SWM Willie Mays SP 12.00 30.00
A65SKGJ Ken Griffey Jr. SP 12.00 30.00
A65SRCL Roberto Clemente SP 15.00 40.00

2016 Topps Archives 65th Anniversary Green Back

*GREEN BACK: 2.5X TO 6X BASIC
STATED ODDS 1:5 PACKS
STATED PRINT RUN 150 SER.#'d SETS

2016 Topps Archives 65th Anniversary Autographs

OVERALL ONE AUTO PER BOX
PRINTING PLATE ODDS 1:352 PACKS
PLATE PRINT RUN 1 SET PER COLOR
NO PLATE PRICING DUE TO SCARCITY
*GREEN BACK/99: .5X TO 1.2X BASIC
*RED BACK/25: .75X TO 2X BASIC
A65AG Andres Galarraga
A65BD Bucky Dent 4.00 10.00
A65BP Buster Posey
A65CH Charlie Hayes 2.50 6.00
A65CR Cal Ripken Jr.
A65CS Curt Simmons 3.00 8.00
A65DW Dontrelle Willis 5.00 12.00
A65FTA Fernando Tatis 2.50 6.00
A65HB Harold Baines 4.00 10.00
A65JB Johnny Bench
A65JC Jose Cruz 2.50 6.00
A65JCA Jose Canseco 3.00 8.00
A65JCO Jeff Conine 2.50 6.00
A65JCR Jose Cruz Jr. 2.50 6.00
A65JRI Jose Rijo 3.00 8.00
A65JV Jose Vidro 2.50 6.00
A65KG Ken Griffey Jr.
A65KT Kent Tekulve 3.00 8.00
A65MT Mike Trout
A65MTA Masahiro Tanaka 300.00 500.00
A65OV Omar Vizquel
A65RF Rollie Fingers
A65RK Ryan Klesko 2.50 6.00
A65SAJ Sandy Alomar Jr. 2.50 6.00
A65SAS Sandy Alomar Sr. 2.50 6.00
A65SH Scott Hatteberg 3.00 8.00
A65SL Sparky Lyle 3.00 8.00
A65TFE Tony Fernandez 2.50 6.00
A65VL Vern Law 3.00 8.00

2016 Topps Archives 65th Anniversary Red Back

*RED BACK: 6X TO 15X BASIC
STATED ODDS 1:13 PACKS
STATED PRINT RUN 50 SER.#'d SETS

2016 Topps Archives 65th Anniversary Rookie Autographs

STATED ODDS 1:36 PACKS
A65RAAN Aaron Nola 8.00 20.00
A65RABS Blake Snell 15.00 40.00
A65RAKM Kenta Maeda 25.00 60.00
A65RAKS Kyle Schwarber 75.00 200.00
A65RALS Luis Severino 20.00 50.00
A65RAMS Miguel Sano 12.00 30.00

2016 Topps Archives 65th Anniversary Rookie Variations

STATED ODDS 1:42 PACKS
A65RAN Aaron Nola 8.00 20.00
A65RBS Blake Snell 15.00 40.00
A65RCS Corey Seager 150.00 400.00
A65RKM Kenta Maeda 10.00 25.00
A65RKS Kyle Schwarber 75.00 200.00
A65RLS Luis Severino 12.00 30.00
A65RMC Michael Conforto 25.00 60.00
A65RMS Miguel Sano 30.00 80.00
A65RSP Stephen Piscotty 25.00 60.00
A65RBHP Byung Ho Park 12.00 30.00

2017 Topps Archives Snapshots

ASAB Alex Bregman RC 4.00 10.00
ASABE Andrew Benintendi RC 2.50 6.00
ASAG Andres Galarraga 1.00 2.50
ASAJ Aaron Judge RC 6.00 15.00
ASARI Anthony Rizzo 1.50 4.00
ASBA Bobby Abreu .75 2.00
ASBH Bryce Harper 2.00 5.00
ASCB Carlos Baerga .75 2.00
ASCC Carlos Correa 1.25 3.00
ASCJ Cleon Jones .75 2.00
ASCS Corey Seager 1.25 3.00
ASDD Danny Duffy .75 2.00
ASDJ Derek Jeter 4.00 10.00
ASDS Dansby Swanson RC 2.00 5.00
ASER Edgar Renteria .75 2.00
ASFL Francisco Lindor 1.25 3.00
ASHA Hank Aaron 2.50 6.00
ASHK Harmon Killebrew 1.25 3.00
ASHR Hunter Renfroe RC 1.00 2.50
ASJA Jose Altuve 1.00 2.50
ASJC Jose Canseco 1.00 2.50
ASJCO Jharel Cotton RC .75 2.00
ASJE Jim Edmonds .75 2.00
ASKB Kris Bryant 1.50 4.00
ASKS Kyle Schwarber 1.25 3.00
ASLT Luis Tiant .75 2.00
ASMB Mookie Betts 2.50 6.00
ASML Mark Langston .75 2.00
ASMM Mark Mulder .75 2.00
ASMMA Manny Machado 1.25 3.00
ASMS Matt Strahm RC .75 2.00
ASMT Mike Trout 6.00 15.00
ASNG Nomar Garciaparra 1.00 2.50
ASNS Noah Syndergaard 1.00 2.50
ASOA Orlando Arcia RC 1.25 3.00
ASOG Ozzie Guillen .75 2.00
ASPK Paul Konerko 1.00 2.50
ASPM Pedro Martinez 1.00 2.50
ASRC Ron Cey .75 2.00
ASRG Robert Gsellman RC .75 2.00
ASRH Ryon Healy RC 1.00 2.50
ASRJ Randy Johnson 1.25 3.00
ASSK Sandy Koufax 2.50 6.00
ASTA Tyler Austin RC 1.00 2.50
ASTG Tyler Glasnow RC 3.00 8.00
ASTT Trea Turner 1.00 2.50
ASTW Tim Wakefield 1.00 2.50
ASWM Wally Moon .75 2.00
ASYG Yulieski Gurriel RC 1.25 3.00
ASYM Yoan Moncada RC 2.50 6.00

2017 Topps Archives Snapshots Black and White

*B/W: .6X TO 1.5X BASIC
*B/W RC: .6X TO 1.5X BASIC RC
OVERALL ODDS ONE PARALLEL PER BOX

2017 Topps Archives Snapshots Autographs

OVERALL ODDS ONE AUTO PER BOX
PRINT RUNS B/WN 4-350 COPIES PER
NO PRICING ON QTY 14 OR LESS
EXCHANGE DEADLINE 10/31/2019
ASAB Alex Bregman/20 40.00 100.00
ASABE Andrew Benintendi/60 60.00 150.00
ASAG Andres Galarraga/60 5.00 12.00
ASAJ Aaron Judge/80
ASARI Anthony Rizzo
ASCB Carlos Baerga/350 3.00 8.00
ASCJ Cleon Jones/350 3.00 8.00
ASER Edgar Renteria/60 6.00 15.00
ASFL Francisco Lindor/20 60.00 150.00
ASHR Hunter Renfroe/350 4.00 10.00
ASJA Jose Altuve/20
ASJC Jose Canseco/350 6.00 15.00
ASJCO Jharel Cotton/349 3.00 8.00
ASJE Jim Edmonds/60 10.00 25.00
ASKS Kyle Schwarber/20 15.00 40.00
ASLT Luis Tiant/60 8.00 20.00
ASML Mark Langston/346 4.00 10.00
ASMM Mark Mulder/265 3.00 8.00
ASNS Noah Syndergaard/20 25.00 60.00
ASOG Ozzie Guillen/80 4.00 10.00
ASPK Paul Konerko/20 12.00 30.00
ASRC Ron Cey/263 5.00 12.00
ASRG Robert Gsellman/344 3.00 8.00
ASRH Ryon Healy/350 4.00 10.00
ASTA Tyler Austin/348 4.00 10.00
ASTW Tim Wakefield/60 20.00 50.00
ASWM Wally Moon/350 3.00 8.00
ASYG Yulieski Gurriel/350 5.00 12.00

2017 Topps Archives Snapshots Autographs Black and White

*B/W: .5X TO 1.2X BASIC
OVERALL ODDS ONE AUTO PER BOX
STATED PRINT RUN 25 SER.#'d SETS
EXCHANGE DEADLINE 10/31/2019
ASAJ Aaron Judge 300.00 600.00
ASARI Anthony Rizzo 25.00 60.00

2018 Topps Archives Snapshots

ASAJ Andruw Jones .40 1.00
ASAJU Aaron Judge 1.50 4.00
ASAR Amed Rosario RC .50 1.25
ASAS Andrew Stevenson RC .40 1.00
ASAV Alex Verdugo RC .60 1.50
ASBD Brian Dozier .50 1.25
ASBP Buster Posey .75 2.00
ASCB Charlie Blackmon .60 1.50
ASCC Carlos Correa .60 1.50
ASCH Charlie Hough .40 1.00
ASCJ Chipper Jones .60 1.50
ASCK Clayton Kershaw 1.00 2.50
ASCR Cal Ripken Jr. 2.00 5.00
ASCS Chance Sisco RC .50 1.25
ASDE David Eckstein .40 1.00
ASDG Didi Gregorius .50 1.25
ASEM Edgar Martinez .50 1.25
ASFL Francisco Lindor .60 1.50
ASFM Francisco Mejia RC .50 1.25
ASFV Frank Viola .40 1.00
ASGA Greg Allen RC .40 1.00
ASGS Giancarlo Stanton .60 1.50
ASGT Gleyber Torres RC 4.00 10.00
ASJA Jose Altuve .50 1.25
ASJB Jim Bouton .40 1.00
ASJC Jose Canseco .50 1.25
ASJO John Olerud .40 1.00
ASJT Jim Thome .50 1.25
ASJTO Joe Torre .50 1.25
ASKB Kris Bryant .75 2.00
ASKD Khris Davis .60 1.50
ASMF Max Fried RC 1.50 4.00
ASMO Matt Olson .60 1.50
ASMP Mike Piazza .60 1.50
ASMT Mike Trout 3.00 8.00
ASNR Nolan Ryan 2.00 5.00
ASOA Ozzie Albies RC 1.25 3.00
ASPD Paul DeJong .60 1.50
ASRA Rick Ankiel .40 1.00
ASRAC Ronald Acuna Jr. RC 12.00 30.00
ASRD Rafael Devers RC 1.25 3.00
ASRM Ryan McMahon RC 1.00 2.50
ASRR Raudy Read RC .40 1.00
ASSA Sandy Alcantara RC .40 1.00
ASSO Shohei Ohtani RC 10.00 25.00
ASTL Tzu-Wei Lin .50 1.25
ASTM Tyler Mahle RC .50 1.25
ASTP Tommy Pham .40 1.00
ASWB Walker Buehler RC 2.00 5.00
ASYM Yadier Molina .75 2.00

2018 Topps Archives Snapshots Black and White

*B/W: .6X TO 1.5X BASIC
*B/W RC: .6X TO 1.5X BASIC RC
OVERALL ODDS ONE PARALLEL PER BOX

2018 Topps Archives Snapshots Blue

*BLUE 2X TO 5X BASIC
*BLUE RC: 2X TO 5X BASIC RC
OVERALL ODDS ONE PARALLEL PER BOX
STATED PRINT RUN 50 SER.#'d SETS

2018 Topps Archives Snapshots Autographs

OVERALL ODDS ONE AUTO PER BOX
EXCHANGE DEADLINE 9/30/2020
ASAJ Andruw Jones 5.00 12.00
ASAJU Aaron Judge
ASAR Amed Rosario 6.00 15.00
ASAS Andrew Stevenson 3.00 8.00
ASAV Alex Verdugo 6.00 15.00
ASCB Charlie Blackmon 5.00 12.00
ASCH Charlie Hough 3.00 8.00
ASCJ Chipper Jones
ASCS Chance Sisco 4.00 10.00
ASDE David Eckstein 3.00 8.00
ASDG Didi Gregorius EXCH 10.00 25.00
ASFL Francisco Lindor 20.00 50.00
ASFV Frank Viola 3.00 8.00
ASGT Gleyber Torres 25.00 60.00
ASJA Jose Altuve 12.00 30.00
ASJB Jim Bouton 6.00 15.00
ASJC Jose Canseco 10.00 25.00
ASJO John Olerud 8.00 20.00
ASJT Joe Torre 20.00 50.00
ASKB Kris Bryant
ASKD Khris Davis 8.00 20.00
ASMO Matt Olson 6.00 15.00
ASMT Mike Trout 300.00 500.00
ASOA Ozzie Albies 10.00 25.00
ASPD Paul DeJong 5.00 12.00
ASRA Rick Ankiel 3.00 8.00
ASRAC Ronald Acuna Jr. 75.00 200.00
ASRD Rafael Devers 20.00 50.00
ASRM Ryan McMahon 8.00 20.00
ASRR Raudy Read 3.00 8.00
ASSA Sandy Alcantara 3.00 8.00
ASSO Shohei Ohtani 200.00 400.00
ASTL Tzu-Wei Lin 4.00 10.00
ASTM Tyler Mahle 4.00 10.00
ASTP Tommy Pham 3.00 8.00
ASWB Walker Buehler EXCH

2018 Topps Archives Snapshots Autographs Black and White

*B/W: .6X TO 1.5X BASIC
OVERALL ODDS ONE AUTO PER BOX
STATED PRINT RUN 25 SER.#'d SETS
EXCHANGE DEADLINE 9/30/2020
ASTL Tzu-Wei Lin 12.00 30.00
ASWB Walker Buehler EXCH 50.00 120.00

2018 Topps Archives Snapshots Autographs Blue

*BLUE: .5X TO 1.2X BASIC
OVERALL ODDS ONE AUTO PER BOX
STATED PRINT RUN 50 SER.#'d SETS
EXCHANGE DEADLINE 9/30/2020
ASTL Tzu-Wei Lin 10.00 25.00
ASWB Walker Buehler EXCH 40.00 100.00

2019 Topps Archives Snapshots

ASAB Alex Bregman .50 1.25
ASBK Brad Keller RC .50 1.25
ASBN Brandon Nimmo .40 1.00
ASBT Blake Treinen .30 .75
ASCY Christian Yelich .60 1.50
ASDB David Bote .40 1.00
ASDC Dylan Cozens RC .50 1.25
ASDH Dakota Hudson RC .60 1.50
ASDS DJ Stewart RC .60 1.50
ASEG Eric Gagne .30 .75
ASEJ Eloy Jimenez RC 2.00 5.00
ASFL Francisco Lindor .50 1.25
ASFV Framber Valdez RC .50 1.25
ASGT Gleyber Torres 1.00 2.50
ASHB Harold Baines .40 1.00
ASI Ichiro .60 1.50
ASJB Javier Baez .60 1.50
ASJd Jacob deGrom 1.00 2.50
ASJH Josh Hader .40 1.00
ASJJ Josh James RC .75 2.00
ASJR Jose Ramirez .40 1.00
ASJS Juan Soto 1.50 4.00
ASKB Kris Bryant .60 1.50
ASKG Ken Griffey Jr. 1.00 2.50
ASKS Kohl Stewart RC .60 1.50
ASKT Kyle Tucker RC 1.25 3.00
ASLU Luis Urias RC .75 2.00
ASMA Miguel Andujar .50 1.25
ASMB Mookie Betts 1.00 2.50
ASMC Matt Chapman .50 1.25
ASMG Mark Grace .40 1.00
ASMM Manny Machado .50 1.25
ASMMU Max Muncy .40 1.00
ASMT Mike Trout 2.50 6.00
ASOA Ozzie Albies .50 1.25
ASPA Pete Alonso RC 3.00 8.00
ASPC Patrick Corbin .40 1.00
ASPG Paul Goldschmidt .50 1.25
ASRA Ronald Acuna Jr. 2.50 6.00
ASRH Rhys Hoskins .60 1.50
ASRL Ramon Laureano RC 1.00 2.50
ASSO Shohei Ohtani .75 2.00
ASSS Steve Sax .30 .75
ASSSO Sammy Sosa .50 1.25
ASST Stephen Tarpley RC .60 1.50
ASTM Tino Martinez .40 1.00
ASTT Touki Toussaint RC .60 1.50
ASVG Vladimir Guerrero Jr. RC 3.00 8.00
ASVW Vernon Wells .30 .75
ASYK Yusei Kikuchi RC .75 2.00

2019 Topps Archives Snapshots Black and White

*BLK WHT: .75X TO 2X BASIC
*BLK WHT RC: .5X TO 1.2X BASIC RC
RANDOM INSERTS IN PACKS

2019 Topps Archives Snapshots Blue

*BLUE: 3X TO 8X BASIC
*BLUE RC: 2X TO 5X BASIC RC
RANDOM INSERTS IN PACKS
STATED PRINT RUN 50 SER.#'d SETS

2019 Topps Archives Snapshots Autographs

OVERALL AUTO ODDS ONE PER BOX
EXCHANGE DEADLINE 8/31/2021
*BLUE/50: .5X TO 1.2X BASIC
*BLK WHT/25: .6X TO 1.5X BASIC
ASBK Brad Keller 2.50 6.00
ASBN Brandon Nimmo 3.00 8.00
ASBT Blake Treinen 2.50 6.00
ASDB David Bote 3.00 8.00
ASDC Dylan Cozens 2.50 6.00
ASDH Dakota Hudson 3.00 8.00
ASDP Enyel de los Santos 2.50 6.00
ASEG Eric Gagne 2.50 6.00
ASEJ Eloy Jimenez 20.00 50.00
ASFL Francisco Lindor 12.00 30.00
ASFV Framber Valdez 2.50 6.00
ASHB Harold Baines 6.00 15.00
ASJD Jacob deGrom
ASJH Josh Hader 4.00 10.00
ASJJ Josh James 4.00 10.00
ASJR Jose Ramirez 3.00 8.00
ASJS Juan Soto 30.00 80.00
ASKB Kris Bryant
ASKG Ken Griffey Jr.
ASKS Kohl Stewart 3.00 8.00
ASKT Kyle Tucker 10.00 25.00
ASMC Matt Chapman 8.00 20.00
ASMG Mark Grace 8.00 20.00
ASMMU Max Muncy 5.00 12.00
ASMT Mike Trout
ASOA Ozzie Albies 10.00 25.00
ASPA Pete Alonso 60.00 150.00
ASPC Patrick Corbin 3.00 8.00
ASRH Rhys Hoskins 15.00 40.00
ASRL Ramon Laureano 6.00 15.00
ASSS Steve Sax 2.50 6.00
ASSSO Sammy Sosa EXCH
ASTM Tino Martinez 8.00 20.00
ASTW Taylor Ward 2.50 6.00
ASVG Vladimir Guerrero Jr. 50.00 120.00
ASVW Vernon Wells 2.50 6.00

2019 Topps Archives Snapshots Captured in the Moment

RANDOM INSERTS IN PACKS
*BLK WHT/25: 2.5X TO 6X BASIC
CITMAJ Andruw Jones .75 2.00
CITMAJU Aaron Judge 3.00 8.00
CITMBG Bob Gibson 1.00 2.50
CITMCF Carlton Fisk 1.00 2.50
CITMCR Cal Ripken Jr. 4.00 10.00
CITMCY Christian Yelich 1.50 4.00
CITMDB David Bote 1.00 2.50
CITMDG Dwight Gooden .75 2.00
CITMDJ Derek Jeter 3.00 8.00
CITMEG Eric Gagne .75 2.00
CITMHA Hank Aaron 2.50 6.00
CITMI Ichiro 1.50 4.00
CITMJC Jose Canseco 1.00 2.50
CITMJV Jason Varitek 1.25 3.00
CITMLG Luis Gonzalez .75 2.00
CITMMC Miguel Cabrera 1.25 3.00
CITMMM Max Muncy 1.00 2.50
CITMNR Nolan Ryan 4.00 10.00
CITMRH Rickey Henderson 1.25 3.00
CITMRJ Reggie Jackson 1.00 2.50
CITMRJO Randy Johnson 1.25 3.00
CITMSA Sandy Alomar Jr. .75 2.00
CITMSG Scooter Gennett 1.00 2.50
CITMSM Sean Manaea .75 2.00
CITMSP Steve Pearce 1.25 3.00

2019 Topps Archives Snapshots Captured in the Moment Autographs

OVERALL AUTO ODDS ONE PER BOX
PRINT RUNS B/WN 5-40 COPIES PER
NO PRICING ON QTY 15 OR LESS
EXCHANGE DEADLINE 8/31/2021
*BLK WHT/25: .5X TO 1.2X BASIC
CITMAJ Andruw Jones/40 5.00 12.00
CITMBG Bob Gibson EXCH
CITMDB David Bote/40 6.00 15.00
CITMEG Eric Gagne/40 5.00 12.00
CITMJC Jose Canseco/40 10.00 25.00
CITMMM Max Muncy/40 6.00 15.00
CITMSA Sandy Alomar Jr./40 10.00 25.00
CITMSM Sean Manaea

2020 Topps Archives Snapshots

ASAA Adbert Alzolay RC .60 1.50
ASAJ Aaron Judge 1.25 3.00
ASAO Al Oliver .30 .75
ASBA Bryan Abreu RC .50 1.25
ASBB Bo Bichette RC 4.00 10.00
ASBH Bryce Harper .75 2.00
ASBZ Barry Zito .40 1.00
ASCR Cal Ripken Jr. 1.50 4.00
ASDM Dustin May RC 1.50 4.00
ASEK Ed Kranepool .30 .75
ASFT Fernando Tatis Jr. 2.50 6.00
ASGL Gavin Lux RC 2.50 6.00
ASGT Gleyber Torres 1.00 2.50
ASHH Hunter Harvey RC .75 2.00
ASID Isan Diaz RC .75 2.00
ASJA Jim Abbott .30 .75
ASJB Jay Buhner 1.00 2.50
ASJK James Karinchak RC .75 2.00
ASJL Jesus Luzardo RC 1.00 2.50
ASJM Jeff McNeil .40 1.00
ASJS Juan Soto 1.50 4.00
ASJU Jose Urquidy RC .60 1.50
ASKL Kyle Lewis RC 4.00 10.00
ASLA Luis Arraez RC 1.00 2.50
ASLR Luis Robert RC 4.00 10.00
ASMB Mookie Betts 1.00 2.50
ASMD Mauricio Dubon RC .60 1.50
ASMS Mike Schmidt .75 2.00
ASMT Mike Trout 2.50 6.00
ASNH Nico Hoerner RC 2.00 5.00
ASNR Nolan Ryan 2.00 5.00
ASOM Oscar Mercado .50 1.25
ASPA Pete Alonso 1.25 3.00
ASRA Ronald Acuna Jr. 2.00 5.00
ASRJ Randy Johnson 1.00 2.50
ASRS Ruben Sierra .80 2.00
ASSN Sheldon Neuse RC .60 1.50
ASSO Shohei Ohtani .75 2.00
ASSR Steve Rogers .30 .75
ASTE Tommy Edman .50 1.25
ASTG Tony Gonsolin RC 2.00 5.00
ASTL Tim Lincecum 1.00 2.50
ASTZ T.J. Zeuch RC .50 1.25
ASVG Vladimir Guerrero Jr. .75 2.00
ASWM Willie Mays 1.00 2.50
ASYA Yordan Alvarez RC 5.00 12.00
ASAAQ Aristides Aquino RC 1.25 3.00
ASBBR Bobby Bradley RC .50 1.25
ASMBE Matt Beaty .40 1.00
ASTGR Trent Grisham RC 2.00 5.00

2020 Topps Archives Snapshots Black and White

*BLK WHT: .75X TO 2X BASIC
*BLK WHT RC: .5X TO 1.2X BASIC RC
STATED ODDS 1 PER HOBBY
ASCR Cal Ripken Jr. 5.00 12.00
ASWM Willie Mays 3.00 8.00

2020 Topps Archives Snapshots Blue

*BLUE: 3X TO 8X BASIC
*BLUE RC: 2X TO 5X BASIC RC
STATED ODDS 1:5 HOBBY
STATED PRINT RUN 50 SER.#'d SETS
ASAJ Aaron Judge 8.00 20.00
ASCR Cal Ripken Jr. 12.00 30.00
ASJB Jay Buhner 6.00 15.00
ASMB Mookie Betts 6.00 15.00
ASMT Mike Trout 15.00 40.00
ASWM Willie Mays 8.00 20.00

2020 Topps Archives Snapshots Autographs

OVERALL AUTO ODDS ONE PER BOX
EXCHANGE DEADLINE 8/31/2022
ASAA Adbert Alzolay 5.00 12.00
ASAO Al Oliver 2.50 6.00
ASBA Bryan Abreu 2.50 6.00
ASBB Bo Bichette EXCH 60.00 150.00
ASBZ Barry Zito 3.00 8.00
ASDM Dustin May 8.00 20.00
ASEK Ed Kranepool 5.00 12.00
ASGT Gleyber Torres 25.00 60.00
ASHH Hunter Harvey 4.00 10.00
ASJA Jim Abbott 8.00 20.00
ASJB Jay Buhner 8.00 20.00
ASJK James Karinchak 6.00 15.00
ASJL Jesus Luzardo 8.00 20.00
ASJM Jeff McNeil 10.00 25.00
ASJS Juan Soto 50.00 120.00
ASJU Jose Urquidy 3.00 8.00
ASKL Kyle Lewis 25.00 60.00
ASLA Luis Arraez 5.00 12.00
ASLR Luis Robert EXCH 100.00 250.00
ASMD Mauricio Dubon 3.00 8.00
ASMT Mike Trout EXCH 400.00 800.00
ASNH Nico Hoerner 10.00 25.00
ASNR Nolan Ryan 75.00 200.00
ASOM Oscar Mercado 4.00 10.00
ASPA Pete Alonso 30.00 80.00
ASRA Ronald Acuna Jr. 60.00 150.00
ASRS Ruben Sierra 8.00 20.00
ASSO Shohei Ohtani
ASSR Steve Rogers 2.50 6.00
ASTE Tommy Edman 6.00 15.00
ASTG Tony Gonsolin 10.00 25.00
ASTL Tim Lincecum 20.00 50.00
ASTZ T.J. Zeuch 2.50 6.00
ASYA Yordan Alvarez 20.00 50.00
ASAAQ Aristides Aquino 6.00 15.00
ASBBR Bobby Bradley 2.50 6.00
ASMBE Matt Beaty 3.00 8.00
ASTGR Trent Grisham EXCH 15.00 40.00

2020 Topps Archives Snapshots Autographs Black and White Image

*BLK WHT/25: .8X TO 2X BASIC
STATED ODDS 1:15 HOBBY
STATED PRINT RUN 25 SER.#'d SETS
EXCHANGE DEADLINE 8/31/2022
ASAA Adbert Alzolay 15.00 40.00
ASBZ Barry Zito 8.00 20.00
ASEK Ed Kranepool 20.00 50.00
ASJA Jim Abbott 20.00 50.00
ASJK James Karinchak 20.00 50.00
ASJL Jesus Luzardo 20.00 50.00
ASRS Ruben Sierra 25.00 60.00

2020 Topps Archives Snapshots Autographs Blue

*BLUE/50: .5X TO 1.2X BASIC
STATED ODDS 1:8 HOBBY
STATED PRINT RUN 50 SER.#'d SETS
EXCHANGE DEADLINE 8/31/2022
ASJA Jim Abbott 12.00 30.00
ASJK James Karinchak 10.00 25.00
ASJL Jesus Luzardo 12.00 30.00
ASRS Ruben Sierra 15.00 40.00

2020 Topps Archives Snapshots Walk-Off Wires

STATED ODDS 1:2 HOBBY
WWI Ichiro 1.00 2.50
WWBB Bo Bichette 4.00 10.00
WWBH Bryce Harper 1.25 3.00
WWBP Buster Posey 2.00 5.00
WWBW Bernie Williams .60 1.50
WWDL DJ LeMahieu .75 2.00
WWDO David Ortiz .75 2.00
WWDW David Wright 1.50 4.00
WWGB George Brett 6.00 15.00
WWHA Hank Aaron 3.00 8.00
WWJB Johnny Bench 2.50 6.00
WWJC Jose Canseco .60 1.50
WWKH Keston Hiura 1.00 2.50
WWKS Kurt Suzuki 2.00 5.00
WWMK Max Kepler .60 1.50
WWMM Mark McGwire 2.00 5.00
WWMT Mark Teixeira .60 1.50
WWMV Mo Vaughn .50 1.25
WWMY Mike Yastrzemski 1.25 3.00
WWPA Pete Alonso 2.00 5.00
WWRA Ronald Acuna Jr. 3.00 8.00
WWRO Ryan O'Hearn .50 1.25
WWWM Willie Mays 3.00 8.00
WWWS Will Smith 1.50 4.00
WWMTE Miguel Tejada .50 1.25

2020 Topps Archives Snapshots Walk-Off Wires Color Image

*COLOR/25: 3X TO 8X BASIC
STATED ODDS 1:17 HOBBY
STATED PRINT RUN 25 SER.#'d SETS
WWBH Bryce Harper 10.00 25.00
WWBP Buster Posey 6.00 15.00
WWDW David Wright 10.00 25.00
WWGB George Brett 25.00 60.00
WWHA Hank Aaron 20.00 50.00
WWKH Keston Hiura 10.00 25.00
WWKS Kurt Suzuki 10.00 25.00
WWMM Mark McGwire 12.00 30.00
WWPA Pete Alonso 8.00 20.00
WWWM Willie Mays 15.00 40.00

2020 Topps Archives Snapshots Walk-Off Wires Autographs

STATED ODDS 1:17 HOBBY
PRINT RUNS B/WN 5-50 COPIES PER
NO PRICING ON QTY 15 OR LESS
EXCHANGE DEADLINE 8/31/2022
*COLOR/25: .5X TO 1.2X p/r 50
WWBW Bernie Williams 20.00 50.00
WWDL DJ LeMahieu 25.00 60.00
WWDW David Wright 20.00 50.00
WWKH Keston Hiura 15.00 40.00
WWMK Max Kepler 8.00 20.00
WWMV Mo Vaughn 40.00 100.00
WWRA Ronald Acuna Jr. 60.00 150.00
WWWS Will Smith 20.00 50.00
WWMTE Miguel Tejada 12.00 30.00

2009 Topps Attax

COMPLETE SET (220) 12.50 30.00
COMMON CARD .10 .25
1 Bobby Abreu .10 .25
2 Garret Anderson .10 .25
3 Rick Ankiel .10 .25
4 Mike Aviles .10 .25
5 Rocco Baldelli .10 .25
6 Jason Bay .15 .40
7 Josh Beckett .10 .25
8 Erik Bedard .10 .25
9 Ronnie Belliard .10 .25
10 Carlos Beltran .15 .40
11 Adrian Beltre .25 .60
12 Yuniesky Betancourt .10 .25
13 Chad Billingsley .15 .40
14 Casey Blake .10 .25
15 Hank Blalock .10 .25
16 Milton Bradley .10 .25
17 Ryan Braun .15 .40
18 Mark Buehrle .15 .40
19 A.J. Burnett .10 .25
20 Pat Burrell .10 .25
21 Billy Butler .10 .25
22 Eric Byrnes .10 .25
23 Orlando Cabrera .10 .25
24 Daniel Cabrera .10 .25
25 Mike Cameron .10 .25
26 Jorge Cantu .10 .25
27 Fausto Carmona .10 .25
28 Joba Chamberlain .10 .25
29 Eric Chavez .10 .25
30 Ryan Church .10 .25
31 Carl Crawford .15 .40
32 Joe Crede .15 .40
33 Bobby Crosby .10 .25
34 Johnny Cueto .15 .40
35 Johnny Damon .15 .40
36 Chris Davis .15 .40
37 David DeJesus .10 .25
38 Carlos Delgado .10 .25
39 Ryan Dempster .10 .25
40 Mark DeRosa .15 .40
41 Matt Diaz .10 .25
42 Ryan Doumit .10 .25
43 Stephen Drew .10 .25
44 J.D. Drew .10 .25
45 Adam Dunn .15 .40
46 Jermaine Dye .10 .25
47 Jim Edmonds .15 .40
48 Jacoby Ellsbury .20 .50
49 Edwin Encarnacion .25 .60
50 Yunel Escobar .10 .25
51 Andre Ethier .15 .40
52 Pedro Feliz .10 .25
53 Chone Figgins .10 .25
54 Jeff Francoeur .15 .40
55 Kosuke Fukudome .15 .40
56 Rafael Furcal .10 .25
57 Ryan Garko .10 .25
58 Jon Garland .10 .25
59 Matt Garza .10 .25
60 Jason Giambi .10 .25
61 Brian Giles .10 .25
62 Troy Glaus .10 .25
63 Carlos Gomez .10 .25
64 Adrian Gonzalez .20 .50
65 Curtis Granderson .20 .50
66 Ken Griffey Jr. .50 1.25
67 Vladimir Guerrero .15 .40
68 Carlos Guillen .10 .25
69 Jose Guillen .10 .25
70 Cristian Guzman .10 .25
71 Travis Hafner .10 .25
72 Bill Hall .10 .25
73 Cole Hamels .20 .50
74 Rich Harden .10 .25
75 J.J. Hardy .10 .25
76 Dan Haren .10 .25
77 Brendan Harris .10 .25
78 Corey Hart .10 .25
79 Brad Hawpe .10 .25
80 Todd Helton .15 .40
81 Jeremy Hermida .10 .25
82 Ramon Hernandez .10 .25
83 Felix Hernandez .15 .40
84 Trevor Hoffman .15 .40
85 Orlando Hudson .10 .25
86 Tim Hudson .15 .40
87 Aubrey Huff .10 .25
88 Torii Hunter .10 .25
89 Chris Iannetta .10 .25
90 Raul Ibanez .15 .40
91 Akinori Iwamura .10 .25
92 Conor Jackson .10 .25
93 Bobby Jenks .10 .25
94 Derek Jeter .60 1.50
95 Ubaldo Jimenez .10 .25
96 Kenji Johjima .15 .40
97 Kelly Johnson .10 .25
98 Randy Johnson .25 .60
99 Adam Jones .15 .40
100 Scott Kazmir .10 .25
101 Matt Kemp .20 .50
102 Howie Kendrick .10 .25
103 Jeff Kent .10 .25
104 Clayton Kershaw .40 1.00
105 Ian Kinsler .15 .40
106 Paul Konerko .15 .40
107 Casey Kotchman .10 .25
108 Kevin Kouzmanoff .10 .25
109 Hiroki Kuroda .10 .25
110 Adam LaRoche .10 .25
111 Derrek Lee .10 .25
112 Carlos Lee .10 .25
113 Jon Lester .15 .40
114 Fred Lewis .10 .25
115 Brad Lidge .10 .25
116 Francisco Liriano .10 .25
117 James Loney .10 .25
118 Jose Lopez .10 .25
119 Derek Lowe .10 .25
120 Mike Lowell .10 .25
121 Jed Lowrie .10 .25
122 Ryan Ludwick .15 .40
123 John Maine .10 .25
124 Victor Martinez .15 .40
125 Pedro Martinez .15 .40
126 Justin Masterson .10 .25
127 Kaz Matsui .10 .25
128 Hideki Matsui .25 .60
129 Gary Matthews .10 .25
130 Joe Mauer .20 .50
131 Cameron Maybin .10 .25
132 Brian McCann .15 .40
133 Lastings Milledge .10 .25
134 Bengie Molina .10 .25
135 Yadier Molina .30 .75
136 Melvin Mora .10 .25
137 David Murphy .10 .25
138 Brett Myers .10 .25
139 Xavier Nady .10 .25
140 Joe Nathan .10 .25
141 Magglio Ordonez .15 .40
142 David Ortiz .25 .60
143 Roy Oswalt .15 .40
144 Lyle Overbay .10 .25
145 Jonathan Papelbon .15 .40
146 Dustin Pedroia .25 .60
147 Mike Pelfrey .10 .25
148 Carlos Pena .15 .40
149 Hunter Pence .15 .40
150 Jhonny Peralta .10 .25
151 Andy Pettitte .15 .40
152 Brandon Phillips .10 .25
153 Juan Pierre .10 .25
154 A.J. Pierzynski .10 .25
155 Placido Polanco .10 .25
156 Jorge Posada .15 .40
157 David Price .20 .50
158 J.J. Putz .10 .25
159 Aramis Ramirez .10 .25
160 Manny Ramirez .25 .60
161 Edgar Renteria .10 .25
162 Jose Reyes .15 .40
163 Mark Reynolds .10 .25
164 Alex Rios .10 .25
165 Mariano Rivera .30 .75
166 Brian Roberts .10 .25
167 Francisco Rodriguez .15 .40
168 Ivan Rodriguez .15 .40
169 Scott Rolen .15 .40
170 Jimmy Rollins .15 .40
171 Aaron Rowand .10 .25
172 CC Sabathia .15 .40
173 Jarrod Saltalamacchia .10 .25
174 Jeff Samardzija .15 .40
175 Freddy Sanchez .10 .25
176 Max Scherzer .25 .60
177 Brian Schneider .10 .25
178 Luke Scott .10 .25
179 Ben Sheets .10 .25
180 Gary Sheffield .10 .25
181 James Shields .10 .25
182 Grady Sizemore .15 .40
183 Travis Snider .15 .40
184 Chris Snyder .10 .25
185 Geovany Soto .15 .40
186 Denard Span .10 .25
187 Kurt Suzuki .10 .25
188 Mark Teahen .10 .25
189 Mark Teixeira .15 .40
190 Miguel Tejada .15 .40
191 Ryan Theriot .10 .25
192 Jim Thome .15 .40

193 Troy Tulowitzki .25 .60
194 Dan Uggla .10 .25
195 Justin Upton .15 .40
196 B.J. Upton .15 .40
197 Chase Utley .15 .40
198 Jose Valverde .10 .25
199 Jason Varitek .25 .60
200 Javier Vazquez .10 .25
201 Justin Verlander .25 .60
202 Shane Victorino .10 .25
203 Edinson Volquez .10 .25
204 Joey Votto .25 .60
205 Tim Wakefield .15 .40
206 Chien-Ming Wang .20 .50
207 Jered Weaver .15 .40
208 Rickie Weeks .10 .25
209 Vernon Wells .10 .25
210 Jayson Werth .15 .40
211 Ty Wigginton .15 .40
212 Josh Willingham .15 .40
213 Dontrelle Willis .10 .25
214 Randy Winn .10 .25
215 David Wright .20 .50
216 Kevin Youkilis .10 .25
217 Chris Young .10 .25
218 Delmon Young .15 .40
219 Michael Young .10 .25
220 Carlos Zambrano .15 .40

2009 Topps Attax Code Cards

1 Garrett Atkins .40 1.00
2 Lance Berkman .60 1.50
3 Jay Bruce .60 1.50
4 Miguel Cabrera 1.00 2.50
5 Prince Fielder .60 1.50
6 Alex Gordon .60 1.50
7 Roy Halladay .60 1.50
8 Josh Hamilton .60 1.50
9 Matt Holliday 1.00 2.50
10 Ryan Howard .75 2.00
11 Chipper Jones 1.00 2.50
12 John Lackey .60 1.50
13 Cliff Lee .60 1.50
14 Tim Lincecum .60 1.50
15 Evan Longoria .60 1.50
16 Nick Markakis .75 2.00
17 Russell Martin .40 1.00
18 Daisuke Matsuzaka .60 1.50
19 Nate McLouth .40 1.00
20 Justin Morneau .60 1.50
21 Jake Peavy .40 1.00
22 Albert Pujols 1.25 3.00
23 Carlos Quentin .40 1.00
24 Hanley Ramirez .60 1.50
25 Alex Rodriguez 1.25 3.00
26 Johan Santana .60 1.50
27 Alfonso Soriano .60 1.50
28 Ichiro Suzuki 1.25 3.00
29 Brandon Webb .60 1.50
30 Ryan Zimmerman .60 1.50

2009 Topps Attax Gold

1 Garrett Atkins .60 1.50
2 Lance Berkman 1.00 2.50
3 Jay Bruce 1.00 2.50
4 Miguel Cabrera 1.50 4.00
5 Prince Fielder 1.00 2.50
6 Alex Gordon 1.00 2.50
7 Roy Halladay 1.00 2.50
8 Josh Hamilton 1.00 2.50
9 Matt Holliday 1.50 4.00
10 Ryan Howard 1.25 3.00
11 Chipper Jones 1.50 4.00
12 John Lackey 1.00 2.50
13 Cliff Lee 1.00 2.50
14 Tim Lincecum 1.00 2.50
15 Evan Longoria 1.00 2.50
16 Nick Markakis 1.25 3.00
17 Russell Martin .60 1.50
18 Daisuke Matsuzaka 1.00 2.50
19 Nate McLouth .60 1.50
20 Justin Morneau 1.00 2.50
21 Barack Obama 2.00 5.00
22 Jake Peavy .60 1.50
23 Albert Pujols 2.00 5.00
24 Carlos Quentin .60 1.50
25 Hanley Ramirez 1.00 2.50
26 Alex Rodriguez 2.00 5.00
27 Johan Santana 1.00 2.50
28 Alfonso Soriano 1.00 2.50
29 Ichiro Suzuki 2.00 5.00
30 Brandon Webb 1.00 2.50
31 Ryan Zimmerman 1.00 2.50

2009 Topps Attax Gold Starter Pack Exclusives

1 Ty Cobb 10.00 25.00
2 Lou Gehrig 6.00 15.00
3 Greg Maddux 8.00 20.00
4 Mickey Mantle 8.00 20.00
5 Jackie Robinson 6.00 15.00
6 Babe Ruth 15.00 40.00
7 Nolan Ryan 8.00 20.00
8 Honus Wagner 4.00 10.00
9 Cy Young 6.00 15.00

2009 Topps Attax Silver Foil

1 Bobby Abreu .40 1.00
2 Rick Ankiel .40 1.00
3 Jason Bay .60 1.50
4 Josh Beckett .40 1.00
5 Carlos Beltran .60 1.50
6 Ryan Braun .60 1.50
7 Pat Burrell .40 1.00
8 Joba Chamberlain .40 1.00
9 Eric Chavez .40 1.00
10 Carlos Delgado .40 1.00
11 Adam Dunn .60 1.50
12 Adrian Gonzalez .75 2.00
13 Curtis Granderson .75 2.00
14 Vladimir Guerrero .60 1.50
15 Cole Hamels .75 2.00
16 Rich Harden .40 1.00
17 Dan Haren .40 1.00
18 Brad Hawpe .40 1.00
19 Felix Hernandez .60 1.50
20 Torii Hunter .40 1.00
21 Raul Ibanez .60 1.50
22 Derek Jeter 2.50 6.00
23 Scott Kazmir .40 1.00
24 Ian Kinsler .60 1.50
25 Carlos Lee .40 1.00
26 Jon Lester .60 1.50
27 Brad Lidge .40 1.00
28 Derek Lowe .40 1.00
29 Victor Martinez .60 1.50
30 Hideki Matsui 1.00 2.50
31 Joe Mauer .75 2.00
32 Brian McCann .60 1.50
33 Magglio Ordonez .60 1.50
34 David Ortiz 1.00 2.50
35 Roy Oswalt .60 1.50
36 Dustin Pedroia 1.00 2.50
37 Carlos Pena .60 1.50
38 Hunter Pence .60 1.50
39 Brandon Phillips .40 1.00
40 Aramis Ramirez .40 1.00
41 Manny Ramirez 1.00 2.50
42 Jose Reyes .60 1.50
43 Alex Rios .40 1.00
44 Francisco Rodriguez .60 1.50
45 Jimmy Rollins .60 1.50
46 Aaron Rowand .40 1.00
47 CC Sabathia .60 1.50
48 James Shields .40 1.00
49 Grady Sizemore .60 1.50
50 Geovany Soto .60 1.50
51 Mark Teixeira .60 1.50
52 Miguel Tejada .60 1.50
53 Jim Thome .60 1.50
54 Dan Uggla .40 1.00
55 B.J. Upton .60 1.50
56 Chase Utley .60 1.50
57 David Wright .75 2.00
58 Kevin Youkilis .40 1.00
59 Michael Young .40 1.00
60 Carlos Zambrano .60 1.50

2010 Topps Attax

COMPLETE SET (220) 12.50 30.00
COMMON CARD .10 .25
1 Bobby Abreu .10 .25
2 Brett Anderson .10 .25
3 Elvis Andrus .15 .40
4 Andrew Bailey .10 .25
5 Clint Barmes .10 .25
6 Jason Bartlett .10 .25
7 Jason Bay .15 .40
8 Josh Beckett .10 .25
9 Gordon Beckham .10 .25
10 Erik Bedard .10 .25
11 Heath Bell .10 .25
12 Carlos Beltran .15 .40
13 Adrian Beltre .25 .60
14 Lance Berkman .15 .40
15 Casey Blake .10 .25
16 Hank Blalock .10 .25
17 Ryan Braun .15 .40
18 Jonathan Broxton .10 .25
19 Jay Bruce .15 .40
20 Mark Buehrle .15 .40
21 A.J. Burnett .10 .25
22 Billy Butler .10 .25
23 Eric Byrnes .10 .25
24 Asdrubal Cabrera .15 .40
25 Everth Cabrera .10 .25
26 Miguel Cabrera .25 .60
27 Orlando Cabrera .10 .25
28 Matt Cain .15 .40
29 Alberto Callaspo .10 .25
30 Mike Cameron .10 .25
31 Robinson Cano .15 .40
32 Jorge Cantu .10 .25
33 Chris Carpenter .15 .40
34 Luis Castillo .10 .25
35 Joba Chamberlain .10 .25
36 Shin-Soo Choo .15 .40
37 Ryan Church .10 .25
38 Chris Coghlan .10 .25
39 Carl Crawford .15 .40
40 Joe Crede .10 .25
41 Nelson Cruz .25 .60
42 Mike Cuddyer .10 .25
43 Johnny Cueto .15 .40
44 Johnny Damon .15 .40
45 David DeJesus .10 .25
46 Ryan Dempster .10 .25
47 Mark DeRosa .10 .25
48 Matt Diaz .10 .25
49 J.D. Drew .10 .25
50 Stephen Drew .10 .25
51 Adam Dunn .15 .40
52 Jermaine Dye .10 .25
53 Jacoby Ellsbury .20 .50
54 Yunel Escobar .10 .25
55 Andre Ethier .15 .40
56 Scott Feldman .10 .25
57 Neftali Feliz .10 .25
58 Prince Fielder .15 .40
59 Chone Figgins .10 .25
60 Mike Fontenot .10 .25
61 Dexter Fowler .15 .40
62 Jeff Francoeur .15 .40
63 Kosuke Fukudome .15 .40
64 Rafael Furcal .10 .25
65 Yovani Gallardo .10 .25
66 Matt Garza .10 .25
67 Adrian Gonzalez .20 .50
68 Curtis Granderson .20 .50
69 Zack Greinke .25 .60
70 Ken Griffey Jr. .50 1.25
71 Vladimir Guerrero .15 .40
72 Cristian Guzman .10 .25
73 Travis Hafner .10 .25
74 Roy Halladay .15 .40
75 Cole Hamels .20 .50
76 Josh Hamilton .15 .40
77 Tommy Hanson .10 .25
78 J.A. Happ .15 .40
79 Dan Haren .10 .25
80 Corey Hart .10 .25
81 Brad Hawpe .10 .25
82 Todd Helton .15 .40
83 Felix Hernandez .15 .40
84 Ramon Hernandez .10 .25
85 Aaron Hill .10 .25
86 Matt Holliday .25 .60
87 Ryan Howard .20 .50
88 Orlando Hudson .10 .25
89 Torii Hunter .10 .25
90 Raul Ibanez .15 .40
91 Brandon Inge .15 .40
92 Bobby Jenks .10 .25
93 Derek Jeter .60 1.50
94 Ubaldo Jimenez .10 .25
95 Josh Johnson .15 .40
96 Kelly Johnson .10 .25
97 Adam Jones .15 .40
98 Chipper Jones .25 .60
99 Garrett Jones .10 .25
100 Scott Kazmir .10 .25
101 Matt Kemp .20 .50
102 Howie Kendrick .10 .25
103 Adam Kennedy .10 .25
104 Clayton Kershaw .40 1.00
105 Ian Kinsler .15 .40
106 Paul Konerko .15 .40
107 Kevin Kouzmanoff .10 .25
108 Adam LaRoche .10 .25
109 Carlos Lee .10 .25
110 Cliff Lee .15 .40
111 Derrek Lee .10 .25
112 Jon Lester .15 .40
113 Brad Lidge .10 .25
114 Tim Lincecum .15 .40
115 Adam Lind .15 .40
116 James Loney .10 .25
117 Evan Longoria .15 .40
118 Felipe Lopez .10 .25
119 Jose Lopez .10 .25
120 Mike Lowell .10 .25
121 Ryan Ludwick .10 .25
122 Nick Markakis .20 .50
123 Jason Marquis .10 .25
124 Victor Martinez .15 .40
125 Justin Masterson .10 .25
126 Joe Mauer .20 .50
127 Brian McCann .15 .40
128 Nate McLouth .10 .25
129 Andrew McCutchen .25 .60
130 Bengie Molina .10 .25
131 Yadier Molina .30 .75
132 Miguel Montero .10 .25
133 Melvin Mora .10 .25
134 Kendry Morales .10 .25
135 Justin Morneau .15 .40
136 Joe Nathan .10 .25
137 Dioner Navarro .10 .25
138 Magglio Ordonez .15 .40
139 David Ortiz .25 .60
140 Roy Oswalt .15 .40
141 Jonathan Papelbon .15 .40
142 Gerardo Parra .10 .25
143 Jake Peavy .10 .25
144 Dustin Pedroia .25 .60
145 Carlos Pena .15 .40
146 Hunter Pence .15 .40
147 Jhonny Peralta .10 .25
148 Andy Pettitte .15 .40
149 Brandon Phillips .10 .25
150 A.J. Pierzynski .10 .25
151 Placido Polanco .10 .25
152 Rick Porcello .15 .40
153 Jorge Posada .15 .40
154 David Price .20 .50
155 Albert Pujols .30 .75
156 Carlos Quentin .10 .25
157 Alexei Ramirez .15 .40
158 Aramis Ramirez .10 .25
159 Hanley Ramirez .15 .40
160 Manny Ramirez .25 .60
161 Colby Rasmus .15 .40
162 Nolan Reimold .10 .25
163 Edgar Renteria .10 .25
164 Jose Reyes .15 .40
165 Mark Reynolds .10 .25
166 Alex Rios .10 .25
167 Mariano Rivera .30 .75
168 Brian Roberts .15 .40
169 Ryan Roberts .10 .25
170 Alex Rodriguez .30 .75
171 Francisco Rodriguez .15 .40
172 Wandy Rodriguez .10 .25
173 Scott Rolen .15 .40
174 Jimmy Rollins .15 .40
175 Cody Ross .10 .25
176 Aaron Rowand .10 .25
177 CC Sabathia .15 .40
178 Freddy Sanchez .10 .25
179 Pablo Sandoval .15 .40
180 Johan Santana .15 .40
181 Skip Schumaker .10 .25
182 Luke Scott .10 .25
183 Grady Sizemore .15 .40
184 Travis Snider .10 .25
185 Alfonso Soriano .15 .40
186 Geovany Soto .15 .40
187 Denard Span .10 .25
188 Ian Stewart .10 .25
189 Huston Street .10 .25
190 Ichiro Suzuki .30 .75
191 Kurt Suzuki .10 .25
192 Willy Taveras .10 .25
193 Mark Teahen .10 .25
194 Mark Teixeira .15 .40
195 Miguel Tejada .15 .40
196 Ryan Theriot .10 .25
197 Troy Tulowitzki .25 .60
198 Dan Uggla .10 .25
199 B.J. Upton .15 .40
200 Justin Upton .15 .40
201 Chase Utley .15 .40
202 Jose Valverde .10 .25
203 Javier Vazquez .10 .25
204 Justin Verlander .25 .60
205 Shane Victorino .15 .40
206 Joey Votto .25 .60
207 Adam Wainwright .15 .40
208 Jered Weaver .15 .40
209 Vernon Wells .10 .25
210 Jayson Werth .15 .40
211 Josh Willingham .15 .40
212 Randy Winn .10 .25
213 Kerry Wood .10 .25
214 David Wright .20 .50
215 Kevin Youkilis .10 .25
216 Chris Young .10 .25
217 Michael Young .10 .25
218 Carlos Zambrano .15 .40
219 Ryan Zimmerman .15 .40
220 Ben Zobrist .15 .40

2010 Topps Attax Code Cards

1 Lance Berkman .60 1.50
2 Ryan Braun .60 1.50
3 Chris Carpenter .60 1.50
4 Jacoby Ellsbury .75 2.00
5 Prince Fielder .60 1.50
6 Adrian Gonzalez .75 2.00
7 Curtis Granderson .75 2.00
8 Zack Greinke 1.00 2.50
9 Dan Haren .40 1.00
10 Felix Hernandez .60 1.50
11 Ryan Howard .75 2.00
12 Derek Jeter 2.50 6.00
13 Matt Kemp .75 2.00
14 Jon Lester .60 1.50
15 Tim Lincecum .60 1.50
16 Evan Longoria .60 1.50
17 Joe Mauer .75 2.00
18 Albert Pujols 1.25 3.00
19 Hanley Ramirez .60 1.50
20 Manny Ramirez 1.00 2.50
21 Alex Rodriguez 1.25 3.00
22 CC Sabathia .60 1.50
23 Pablo Sandoval .60 1.50
24 Grady Sizemore .60 1.50
25 Ichiro Suzuki 1.25 3.00
26 Mark Teixeira .60 1.50
27 Troy Tulowitzki 1.00 2.50
28 Justin Verlander 1.00 2.50
29 Joey Votto 1.00 2.50
30 David Wright .75 2.00

2010 Topps Attax Gold Foil

1 Lance Berkman 1.00 2.50
2 Ryan Braun 1.00 2.50
3 Chris Carpenter 1.00 2.50
4 Jacoby Ellsbury 1.25 3.00
5 Prince Fielder 1.00 2.50
6 Adrian Gonzalez 1.25 3.00
7 Curtis Granderson 1.25 3.00
8 Zack Greinke 1.50 4.00
9 Dan Haren .60 1.50
10 Felix Hernandez 1.00 2.50
11 Ryan Howard 1.25 3.00
12 Derek Jeter 4.00 10.00
13 Matt Kemp 1.25 3.00
14 Jon Lester 1.00 2.50
15 Tim Lincecum 1.00 2.50
16 Evan Longoria 1.00 2.50
17 Joe Mauer 1.25 3.00
18 Albert Pujols 2.00 5.00
19 Hanley Ramirez 1.00 2.50
20 Manny Ramirez 1.50 4.00
21 Alex Rodriguez 2.00 5.00
22 CC Sabathia 1.00 2.50
23 Pablo Sandoval 1.00 2.50
24 Grady Sizemore 1.00 2.50
25 Ichiro Suzuki 2.00 5.00
26 Mark Teixeira 1.00 2.50
27 Troy Tulowitzki 1.50 4.00
28 Justin Verlander 1.50 4.00
29 Joey Votto 1.50 4.00
30 David Wright 1.25 3.00

2010 Topps Attax Legends

1 Ty Cobb 4.00 10.00
2 Bob Gibson 1.50 4.00
3 Rickey Henderson 2.50 6.00
4 Reggie Jackson 1.25 3.00
5 Mickey Mantle 8.00 20.00
6 Jackie Robinson 2.50 6.00
7 Babe Ruth 6.00 15.00
8 Nolan Ryan 8.00 20.00
9 Mike Schmidt 4.00 10.00
10 Cy Young 2.50 6.00

2010 Topps Attax Silver Foil

1 Elvis Andrus .60 1.50
2 Jason Bay .60 1.50
3 Josh Beckett .40 1.00
4 Gordon Beckham .40 1.00
5 Carlos Beltran .60 1.50
6 Billy Butler .40 1.00
7 Miguel Cabrera 1.00 2.50
8 Matt Cain .60 1.50
9 Robinson Cano .60 1.50
10 Shin-Soo Choo .60 1.50
11 Chris Coghlan .40 1.00
12 Carl Crawford .60 1.50
13 Johnny Cueto .60 1.50
14 Johnny Damon .60 1.50
15 Adam Dunn .60 1.50
16 Yunel Escobar .40 1.00
17 Andre Ethier .60 1.50
18 Scott Feldman .40 1.00
19 Dexter Fowler .60 1.50
20 Yovani Gallardo .40 1.00
21 Roy Halladay .60 1.50
22 Cole Hamels .75 2.00
23 Josh Hamilton .60 1.50
24 Todd Helton .60 1.50
25 Aaron Hill .40 1.00
26 Matt Holliday 1.00 2.50
27 Torii Hunter .40 1.00
28 Ubaldo Jimenez .40 1.00
29 Josh Johnson .60 1.50
30 Howie Kendrick .40 1.00
31 Clayton Kershaw 1.50 4.00
32 Ian Kinsler .60 1.50
33 Carlos Lee .40 1.00
34 Derrek Lee .40 1.00
35 Adam Lind .60 1.50
36 Jose Lopez .40 1.00
37 Nick Markakis .75 2.00
38 Jason Marquis .40 1.00
39 Victor Martinez .60 1.50
40 Andrew McCutchen 1.00 2.50
41 Kendry Morales .40 1.00
42 Justin Morneau .60 1.50
43 David Ortiz 1.00 2.50
44 Dustin Pedroia 1.00 2.50
45 Carlos Pena .60 1.50
46 Hunter Pence .60 1.50
47 Aramis Ramirez .40 1.00
48 Nolan Reimold .40 1.00
49 Mark Reynolds .40 1.00
50 Mariano Rivera 1.25 3.00
51 Brian Roberts .60 1.50
52 Jimmy Rollins .60 1.50
53 Miguel Tejada .60 1.50
54 Dan Uggla .40 1.00
55 Chase Utley .60 1.50
56 Javier Vazquez .40 1.00
57 Adam Wainwright .60 1.50
58 Jered Weaver .60 1.50
59 Jayson Werth .60 1.50
60 Ryan Zimmerman .60 1.50

2010 Topps Attax Battle of the Ages

1 Ty Cobb .50 1.25
2 Prince Fielder .20 .50
3 Bob Gibson .20 .50
4 Zack Greinke .30 .75
5 Rickey Henderson .30 .75
6 Ryan Howard .25 .60
7 Reggie Jackson .20 .50
8 Bo Jackson .30 .75
9 Derek Jeter .75 2.00
10 Jon Lester .20 .50
11 Tim Lincecum .20 .50
12 Evan Longoria .20 .50
13 Mickey Mantle 1.00 2.50
14 Joe Mauer .25 .60
15 Stan Musial .50 1.25
16 Jim Palmer .20 .50
17 Albert Pujols .40 1.00
18 Manny Ramirez .30 .75
19 Cal Ripken Jr. 1.00 2.50
20 Jackie Robinson .30 .75
21 Alex Rodriguez .40 1.00
22 Babe Ruth .75 2.00
23 Nolan Ryan 1.00 2.50
24 CC Sabathia .20 .50
25 Mike Schmidt .50 1.25
26 Tom Seaver .20 .50
27 Ichiro Suzuki .40 1.00
28 Justin Verlander .30 .75
29 David Wright .25 .60
30 Cy Young .30 .75

2010 Topps Attax Battle of the Ages Foil

*FOIL: 2X TO 5X BASIC
1 Ty Cobb 2.50 6.00
2 Prince Fielder 1.00 2.50
3 Bob Gibson 1.00 2.50
4 Zack Greinke 1.50 4.00
5 Rickey Henderson 1.50 4.00
6 Ryan Howard 1.25 3.00
7 Reggie Jackson 1.00 2.50
8 Bo Jackson 1.50 4.00
9 Derek Jeter 4.00 10.00
10 Jon Lester 1.00 2.50
11 Tim Lincecum 1.00 2.50
12 Evan Longoria 1.00 2.50
13 Mickey Mantle 5.00 12.00
14 Joe Mauer 1.25 3.00
15 Stan Musial 2.50 6.00
16 Jim Palmer 1.00 2.50
17 Albert Pujols 2.00 5.00
18 Manny Ramirez 1.50 4.00
19 Cal Ripken Jr. 5.00 12.00
20 Jackie Robinson 1.50 4.00
21 Alex Rodriguez 2.00 5.00
22 Babe Ruth 4.00 10.00
23 Nolan Ryan 5.00 12.00
24 CC Sabathia 1.00 2.50
25 Mike Schmidt 2.50 6.00
26 Tom Seaver 1.00 2.50
27 Ichiro Suzuki 2.00 5.00
28 Justin Verlander 1.50 4.00
29 David Wright 1.25 3.00
30 Cy Young 1.50 4.00

2011 Topps Attax

COMMON CARD (1-206) .10 .25
COMMON MASCOT (207-231) .60 1.50
COMMON STADIUM (232-260) .60 1.50
1 Adam Dunn .15 .40
2 Adam Jones .15 .40
3 Adam LaRoche .10 .25
4 Adam Lind .15 .40
5 Adam Wainwright .15 .40
6 Adrian Beltre .25 .60
7 Adrian Gonzalez .20 .50
8 Albert Pujols .30 .75
9 Alex Rios .10 .25
10 Alex Rodriguez .30 .75
11 Alexei Ramirez .15 .40
12 Alfonso Soriano .15 .40
13 Andre Ethier .15 .40
14 Andres Torres .10 .25
15 Andrew Bailey .10 .25
16 Andrew McCutchen .25 .60
17 Angel Pagan .10 .25
18 Aramis Ramirez .10 .25
19 Aroldis Chapman .30 .75
20 Aubrey Huff .10 .25
21 Austin Jackson .10 .25
22 B.J. Upton .15 .40
23 Ben Zobrist .15 .40
24 Billy Butler .10 .25
25 Bobby Abreu .10 .25
26 Brandon Morrow .10 .25
27 Brandon Phillips .10 .25
28 Brennan Boesch .15 .40
29 Brett Anderson .10 .25
30 Brett Gardner .15 .40
31 Brett Wallace .10 .25
32 Brian Matusz .10 .25
33A B.McCann One hand bat .15 .40
34 Brian Roberts .10 .25
35 Brian Wilson .25 .60
36 Buster Posey .30 .75
37 Carl Crawford .15 .40
38 Carlos Gonzalez .15 .40
39 Carlos Lee .10 .25
40 Carlos Marmol .15 .40
41 Carlos Pena .15 .40
42 Carlos Quentin .10 .25
43 Carlos Santana .25 .60
44 Carlos Zambrano .15 .40
45 Casey McGehee .10 .25
46 CC Sabathia .15 .40
47 Chase Headley .10 .25
48 Chase Utley .15 .40
49 Chipper Jones .25 .60
50 Chone Figgins .10 .25
51 Chris Carpenter .15 .40
52 Chris Coghlan .10 .25
53 Chris Johnson .10 .25
54 Chris Young .10 .25
55 Clay Buchholz .10 .25
56 Clayton Kershaw .40 1.00
57 Cliff Lee .15 .40
58 Coco Crisp .10 .25
59 Colby Rasmus .15 .40
60 Cole Hamels .20 .50
61 Corey Hart .10 .25
62 Curtis Granderson .20 .50
63 Dan Haren .10 .25
64 Dan Uggla .10 .25
65 Danny Valencia .15 .40
66 David Ortiz .25 .60
67 David Price .20 .50
68 Bronson Arroyo .10 .25
69 David Wright .20 .50
70 Delmon Young .15 .40
71 Denard Span .10 .25
72 Derek Jeter .60 1.50
73 Derrek Lee .10 .25
74 Dexter Fowler .15 .40
75 Domonic Brown .20 .50
76 Drew Stubbs .10 .25
77 Dustin Pedroia .25 .60
78 Edinson Volquez .10 .25
79 Elvis Andrus .15 .40
80 Erick Aybar .10 .25
81 Evan Longoria .15 .40
82 Fausto Carmona .10 .25
83 Felix Hernandez .15 .40
84 Francisco Liriano .10 .25
85 Franklin Gutierrez .10 .25
86 Freddy Sanchez .10 .25
87 Gaby Sanchez .10 .25
88 Garrett Jones .10 .25
89 Geovany Soto .15 .40
90 Gordon Beckham .10 .25
91 Grady Sizemore .15 .40
92 Hanley Ramirez .15 .40
93 Heath Bell .10 .25
94 Hideki Matsui .25 .60
95 Howie Kendrick .10 .25
96 Hunter Pence .15 .40
97 Ian Desmond .10 .25
98 Ian Kinsler .15 .40
99 Ian Stewart .10 .25
100 Ichiro Suzuki .30 .75
101 Ike Davis .10 .25
102 Jacoby Ellsbury .20 .50
103 James Loney .10 .25
104 Jason Bay .15 .40
105 Jason Heyward .20 .50
106 Jason Kubel .10 .25
107 Jay Bruce .15 .40
108 Jayson Werth .15 .40
109 Jered Weaver .15 .40
110 Jim Thome .15 .40
111 Joakim Soria .10 .25
112 Joe Mauer .20 .50
113 Joey Votto .25 .60
114 Johan Santana .15 .40
115 John Danks .10 .25
116 Jon Lester .15 .40
117 Jonathan Papelbon .15 .40
118 Jorge Posada .15 .40
119 Jose Bautista .15 .40
120 Jose Reyes .15 .40
121 Jose Tabata .10 .25
122 Jose Valverde .10 .25
123 Josh Beckett .10 .25
124 Josh Hamilton .15 .40
125 Josh Johnson .15 .40
126 Josh Willingham .15 .40
127 Juan Pierre .10 .25
128 Juan Uribe .10 .25
129 Justin Morneau .15 .40
130 Justin Upton .15 .40
131 Justin Verlander .25 .60
132 Kelly Johnson .10 .25
133 Kendry Morales .10 .25
134 Kevin Youkilis .10 .25
135 Koji Uehara .10 .25
136 Kosuke Fukudome .15 .40
137 Kurt Suzuki .10 .25
138 Lance Berkman .15 .40
139 Logan Morrison .10 .25
140 Luke Scott .10 .25
141 Magglio Ordonez .15 .40
142 Manny Ramirez .25 .60
143 Mariano Rivera .30 .75
144 Mark Reynolds .10 .25
145 Mark Teixeira .15 .40
146 Marlon Byrd .10 .25
147 Martin Prado .10 .25
148 Mat Latos .15 .40
149 Matt Cain .15 .40
150 Matt Garza .10 .25
151 Matt Holliday .25 .60
152 Matt Kemp .20 .50
153 Max Scherzer .25 .60
154A M.Bourn Jsy #21 .10 .25
155 Michael Cuddyer .10 .25
156 Michael Young .10 .25
157 Miguel Cabrera .25 .60
158 Miguel Montero .10 .25
159 Miguel Tejada .15 .40
160 Mike Napoli .10 .25
161 Mike Stanton .25 .60
162 Neftali Feliz .10 .25
163 Neil Walker .15 .40
164 Nelson Cruz .25 .60
165 Nick Markakis .20 .50
166 Nick Swisher .15 .40
167 Omar Infante .10 .25
168 Pablo Sandoval .15 .40
169 Paul Konerko .15 .40
170 Phil Hughes .10 .25
171 Placido Polanco .10 .25
172 Prince Fielder .15 .40
173 Rafael Furcal .10 .25
174 Raul Ibanez .15 .40
175 Rickie Weeks .10 .25
176 Ricky Nolasco .10 .25
177 Ricky Romero .10 .25
178 Robinson Cano .15 .40
179 Roy Halladay .15 .40
180 Roy Oswalt .15 .40
181 Ryan Braun .15 .40
182 Ryan Howard .20 .50
183 Ryan Zimmerman .15 .40
184 Scott Rolen .15 .40
185 Shane Victorino .15 .40
186 Shin-Soo Choo .15 .40
187 Starlin Castro .15 .40
188 Stephen Drew .10 .25
189 Stephen Strasburg .25 .60
190 Tim Hudson .15 .40
191 Tim Lincecum .15 .40
192 Todd Helton .15 .40
193 Tommy Hanson .10 .25
194 Torii Hunter .10 .25
195 Travis Hafner .10 .25
196 Trevor Cahill .10 .25
197 Troy Tulowitzki .25 .60
198 Tyler Colvin .10 .25
199 Ubaldo Jimenez .10 .25
200 Vernon Wells .10 .25
201 Victor Martinez .15 .40
202 Vladimir Guerrero .15 .40
203 Wandy Rodriguez .10 .25
204 Yadier Molina .30 .75
205 Yovani Gallardo .10 .25
206 Zack Greinke .25 .60
207 A's Mascot .60 1.50
208 Bernie Brewer .60 1.50
209 Billy the Marlin .60 1.50
210 Blue Jays Mascot .60 1.50
211 Braves Mascot .60 1.50
212 Diamondbacks Mascot .60 1.50
213 Dinger .60 1.50
214 Fredbird .60 1.50
215 Gapper .60 1.50
216 Junction Jack .60 1.50
217 Mariner Moose .60 1.50
218 Mr. Met .75 2.00
219 Orioles Mascot .60 1.50
220 Paws .60 1.50
221 Phillie Phanatic .75 2.00
222 Pirate Parrot .60 1.50
223 Rangers Captain .60 1.50
224 Raymond .60 1.50
225 Royals Mascot .60 1.50
226 Screech .60 1.50
227 Slider .60 1.50
228 Swinging Friar .60 1.50
229 TC .60 1.50
230 Wally the Green Monster .75 2.00
231 White Sox Mascot .60 1.50
240 Fenway Park .75 2.00
257 Wrigley Field .75 2.00
258 Yankee Stadium 1.25 3.00

2011 Topps Attax Foil

*1-206: 1X TO 2.5X BASIC
*207-258: .5X TO 1.2X BASIC

2011 Topps Attax Legends

A1 Mickey Mantle 8.00 20.00
A2 Babe Ruth 10.00 25.00

2005 Topps Barry Bonds Fan Giveaway

COMPLETE SET (1) 2.50 6.00
BB4 Barry Bonds 1.50 4.00

2018 Topps Big League

COMP.SET w/o EXCH (400) 25.00 60.00
NOW EXCH ODDS 1:10,093 HOBBY
NOW EXCH DEADLINE 11/5/2019
1 Aaron Judge .50 1.25
2 Luis Severino .15 .40
3 J.P. Crawford RC .25 .60
4 Jon Lester .15 .40
5 Jeurys Familia .15 .40
6 Zach Davies .12 .30
7 C.J. Cron .12 .30
8 Felix Hernandez .15 .40
9 Ender Inciarte .12 .30
10 Odubel Herrera .15 .40
11 Corey Dickerson .12 .30
12 Whit Merrifield .20 .50
13 Chris Archer .12 .30
14 Dinelson Lamet .12 .30
15 Cody Bellinger .40 1.00
16 Blake Snell .15 .40
17 Eric Thames .15 .40
18 Manny Margot .12 .30
19 Matt Olson .20 .50
20 Alex Gordon .15 .40
21 Rick Porcello .15 .40
22 Mark Reynolds .12 .30
23 Brian Dozier .15 .40
24 Daniel Mengden .12 .30
25 Bryce Harper .30 .75
26 Max Kepler .15 .40
27 Patrick Corbin .15 .40
28 Joey Votto .20 .50
29 Christian Yelich .25 .60
30 Andrew Miller .15 .40
31 Hunter Renfroe .12 .30
32 Marcus Semien .20 .50
33 Scooter Gennett .15 .40
34 Dominic Smith RC .30 .75
35 Gregory Polanco .15 .40
36 Yasiel Puig .20 .50
37 J.D. Martinez .20 .50
38 Byron Buxton .20 .50
39 Dansby Swanson .20 .50

40 Yoan Moncada .20 .50
41 Jason Vargas .12 .30
42 Hector Neris .12 .30
43 Jordy Mercer .12 .30
44 Trey Mancini .15 .40
45 Travis d'Arnaud .15 .40
46 Trevor Story .20 .50
47 Jeff Samardzija .12 .30
48 Ozzie Albies RC .75 2.00
49 Sean Newcomb .15 .40
50 Clayton Kershaw .30 .75
51 Ian Kinsler .15 .40
52 Jason Heyward .15 .40
53 Brandon Drury .12 .30
54 Mitch Haniger .15 .40
55 Kevin Pillar .12 .30
56 Wil Myers .15 .40
57 Carlos Martinez .15 .40
58 Khris Davis .20 .50
59 Jameson Taillon .15 .40
60 Gerrit Cole .20 .50
61 Scott Schebler .15 .40
62 Robinson Cano .15 .40
63 Amed Rosario RC .30 .75
64 Alex Colome .12 .30
65 Matt Harvey .15 .40
66 Jose Urena .12 .30
67 Andrew Stevenson RC .25 .60
68 Edwin Encarnacion .20 .50
69 Nolan Arenado .30 .75
70 Francisco Lindor .20 .50
71 Tim Anderson .20 .50
72 Raisel Iglesias .15 .40
73 Jose Quintana .12 .30
74 Jake Lamb .15 .40
75 Garrett Richards .15 .40
76 Aroldis Chapman .20 .50
77 Austin Hays RC .40 1.00
78 Brad Ziegler .12 .30
79 Jonathan Villar .12 .30
80 Corey Seager .20 .50
81 Jonathan Schoop .12 .30
82 Ryan Braun .15 .40
83 Chris Sale .20 .50
84 Rio Ruiz .12 .30
85 Jose Ramirez .15 .40
86 Ken Giles .12 .30
87 Avisail Garcia .15 .40
88 Russell Martin .12 .30
89 Evan Longoria .15 .40
90 Didi Gregorius .15 .40
91 Anthony Rizzo .25 .60
92 Eric Hosmer .15 .40
93 Andrew Cashner .12 .30
94 Jean Segura .12 .30
95 Trevor Bauer .25 .60
96 Salvador Perez .15 .40
97 Zack Granite RC .25 .60
98 Nicky Delmonico RC .25 .60
99 Jose Abreu .20 .50
100 Eddie Rosario .20 .50
101 Aaron Nola .15 .40
102 Felix Jorge RC .25 .60
103 Paul Blackburn RC .25 .60
104 Jose Altuve .15 .40
105 Manny Machado .20 .50
106 Jake Arrieta .15 .40
107 Tommy Pham .12 .30
108 Jed Lowrie .12 .30
109 Yoenis Cespedes .20 .50
110 Richard Urena RC .25 .60
111 Paul Goldschmidt .20 .50
112 Clint Frazier RC .50 1.25
113 Rhys Hoskins RC 1.00 2.50
114 Marcell Ozuna .20 .50
115 Dexter Fowler .15 .40
116 Walker Buehler RC 1.25 3.00
117 Charlie Blackmon .20 .50
118 Lance McCullers Jr. .12 .30
119 Julio Teheran .15 .40
120 Justin Upton .15 .40
121 DJ LeMahieu .20 .50
122 Martin Perez .15 .40
123 Jorge Polanco .15 .40
124 Brandon Nimmo .15 .40
125 Alex Wood .12 .30
126 Roberto Osuna .12 .30
127 Willson Contreras .20 .50
128 Danny Duffy .12 .30
129 Starlin Castro .12 .30
130 Craig Kimbrel .15 .40
131 Josh Donaldson .15 .40
132 Kevin Kiermaier .15 .40
133 Nick Markakis .15 .40
134 Xander Bogaerts .20 .50
135 Freddie Freeman .25 .60
136 Brandon Woodruff RC .75 2.00
137 James Paxton .15 .40
138 Johnny Cueto .15 .40
139 Ryan Zimmerman .15 .40
140 Joey Gallo .15 .40
141 Shohei Ohtani RC 6.00 15.00
142 Hunter Pence .15 .40
143 Josh Bell .15 .40
144 Nelson Cruz .20 .50
145 Carlos Carrasco .12 .30
146 Corey Knebel .12 .30
147 Ty Blach .12 .30
148 Dustin Pedroia .20 .50
149 David Peralta .12 .30
150 Mike Trout 1.00 2.50
151 Brandon Belt .15 .40
152 Anibal Sanchez .12 .30
153 Andrew McCutchen .20 .50
154 Matt Chapman .20 .50
155 Steven Souza Jr. .15 .40
156 Mike Leake .12 .30
157 Jake Odorizzi .12 .30
158 Chris Davis .12 .30
159 Mookie Betts .40 1.00
160 Juan Lagares .12 .30
161 Tzu-Wei Lin .15 .40
162 Gary Sanchez .20 .50
163 Logan Morrison .12 .30
164 Carson Fulmer .12 .30
165 Chance Sisco RC .30 .75
166 Miguel Andujar RC 1.00 2.50
167 Jack Flaherty RC 1.00 2.50
168 Nomar Mazara .12 .30
169 Anthony Rendon .20 .50
170 Daniel Murphy .15 .40
171 Giancarlo Stanton .20 .50
172 Dee Gordon .12 .30
173 Tucker Barnhart .12 .30
174 Michael Fulmer .12 .30
175 Ervin Santana .12 .30
176 Lucas Duda .15 .40
177 Luke Weaver .15 .40
178 Albert Pujols .25 .60
179 Reynaldo Lopez .15 .40
180 Francisco Mejia RC .30 .75
181 Travis Shaw .12 .30
182 Trea Turner .15 .40
183 Carlos Santana .15 .40
184 Lorenzo Cain .12 .30
185 Shin-Soo Choo .15 .40
186 Josh Reddick .12 .30
187 Matt Kemp .15 .40
188 Orlando Arcia .12 .30
189 Tyler Saladino .12 .30
190 Sandy Alcantara RC .25 .60
191 Erick Fedde RC .25 .60
192 Javier Baez .25 .60
193 Maikel Franco .15 .40
194 Brandon Crawford .15 .40
195 Yolmer Sanchez .12 .30
196 Dallas Keuchel .15 .40
197 Kyle Schwarber .20 .50
198 Miguel Sano .15 .40
199 Paul DeJong .20 .50
200 Carlos Correa .20 .50
201 Cole Hamels .15 .40
202 Addison Russell .15 .40
203 Buster Posey .25 .60
204 A.J. Pollock .12 .30
205 Chris Taylor .15 .40
206 Kole Calhoun .12 .30
207 Tyler Glasnow .20 .50
208 Yangervis Solarte .12 .30
209 Andrelton Simmons .12 .30
210 Billy Hamilton .15 .40
211 Kendrys Morales .12 .30
212 Elvis Andrus .15 .40
213 Victor Robles RC .60 1.50
214 Dillon Peters RC .25 .60
215 Adam Jones .15 .40
216 Sean Manaea .12 .30
217 Zach Britton .12 .30
218 Gerardo Parra .12 .30
219 Jacob deGrom .40 1.00
220 Adam Duvall .15 .40
221 Travis Jankowski .12 .30
222 Joe Panik .15 .40
223 Mike Zunino .12 .30
224 Jordan Zimmermann .15 .40
225 Miguel Gomez RC .25 .60
226 Ichiro .25 .60
227 Vince Velasquez .12 .30
228 Masahiro Tanaka .15 .40
229 Ricky Nolasco .12 .30
230 Adrian Beltre .20 .50
231 Marcus Stroman .15 .40
232 Marco Estrada .12 .30
233 Matt Boyd .12 .30
234 Ivan Nova .15 .40
235 Bartolo Colon .12 .30
236 Luis Castillo .15 .40
237 Ben Gamel .15 .40
238 Miguel Cabrera .20 .50
239 Jon Gray .12 .30
240 Max Scherzer .20 .50
241 Justin Turner .20 .50
242 Nicholas Castellanos .20 .50
243 Keon Broxton .12 .30
244 J.A. Happ .15 .40
245 Luis Perdomo .12 .30
246 Alcides Escobar .15 .40
247 Parker Bridwell RC .25 .60
248 Brad Miller .15 .40
249 Austin Hedges .12 .30
250 Rafael Devers RC .75 2.00
251 Stephen Strasburg .20 .50
252 George Springer .15 .40
253 Chad Bettis .12 .30
254 Yadier Molina .25 .60
255 Justin Smoak .12 .30
256 Kenley Jansen .15 .40
257 Clayton Richard .12 .30
258 Felipe Vazquez .15 .40
259 Tim Beckham .15 .40
260 Luiz Gohara RC .25 .60
261 Domingo Santana .15 .40
262 Jharel Cotton .12 .30
263 Sonny Gray .15 .40
264 Justin Bour .12 .30
265 Stephen Piscotty .12 .30
266 Ryon Healy .12 .30
267 Kevin Gausman .20 .50
268 Mikie Mahtook .12 .30
269 Justin Verlander .20 .50
270 Jose Iglesias .15 .40
271 James McCann .15 .40
272 Brad Hand .12 .30
273 Starling Marte .15 .40
274 Aaron Altherr .12 .30
275 Mike Moustakas .15 .40
276 Andrew Benintendi .20 .50
277 Kyle Seager .12 .30
278 Matt Carpenter .20 .50
279 Greg Allen RC .25 .60
280 Jackie Bradley Jr. .20 .50
281 Ketel Marte .15 .40
282 Noah Syndergaard .15 .40
283 Yasmany Tomas .12 .30
284 Lucas Giolito .15 .40
285 Jorge Alfaro .12 .30
286 Yuli Gurriel .15 .40
287 Alex Bregman .20 .50
288 Logan Forsythe .12 .30
289 Rougned Odor .15 .40
290 Corey Kluber .15 .40
291 Brian Anderson RC .30 .75
292 Jose Berrios .15 .40
293 Carlos Gonzalez .15 .40
294 Matt Moore .15 .40
295 Zack Cozart .12 .30
296 German Marquez .12 .30
297 Nick Williams RC .30 .75
298 Homer Bailey .12 .30
299 Zack Greinke .20 .50
300 Kris Bryant .25 .60
301 Arndo/Bllngr/Gllo .40 1.00
302 Gllo/Dvs/Jdge .50 1.25
303 Gldschmdt/Stntn/Blckmn .20 .50
304 Sprngr/Altve/Jdge .50 1.25
305 Inciarte/Gordon/Blackmon .20 .50
306 Andrs/Hsmr/Altve .15 .40
307 Herrera/Murphy/Arenado .30 .75
308 Btts/Rmrz/Lwre .40 1.00
309 Arndo/Ozna/Stntn .30 .75
310 Dvs/Jdge/Cruz .50 1.25
311 Crpntr/Brnt/Vtto .25 .60
312 Trt/Encrncn/Jdge 1.00 2.50
313 Turner/Hamilton/Gordon .15 .40
314 Altve/Mybn/Mrrfeld .20 .50
315 Murphy/Turner/Blackmon .20 .50
316 Hsmr/Grca/Altve .15 .40
317 Frmn/Blckmn/Stntn .25 .60
318 Rmrz/Jdge/Trt 1.00 2.50
319 Strsbrg/Schrzr/Krshw .30 .75
320 Severino/Sale/Kluber .20 .50
321 Grnke/Dvs/Krshw .30 .75
322 Vargas/Kluber/Carrasco .15 .40
323 Ray/Scherzer/deGrom .40 1.00
324 Archer/Kluber/Sale .20 .50
325 Knebel/Jansen/Holland .15 .40
326 Kimbrel/Osuna/Colome .15 .40
327 Cole/Samardzija/Martinez .20 .50
328 Verlander/Santana/Sale .20 .50
329 Strsbrg/Schrzr/Krshw .30 .75
330 Severino/Kluber/Sale .20 .50
331 Hank Aaron .40 1.00
332 Roger Clemens .25 .60
333 Whitey Ford .15 .40
334 Ernie Banks .20 .50
335 John Smoltz .20 .50
336 Cal Ripken Jr. .60 1.50
337 George Brett .40 1.00
338 Ted Williams .40 1.00
339 Bo Jackson .20 .50
340 Jim Palmer .15 .40
341 Honus Wagner .20 .50
342 Pedro Martinez .15 .40
343 Alex Rodriguez .25 .60
344 Frank Thomas .20 .50
345 Jeff Bagwell .15 .40
346 Rickey Henderson .20 .50
347 Johnny Bench .20 .50
348 Nolan Ryan .60 1.50
349 Mariano Rivera .25 .60
350 Sandy Koufax .40 1.00
351 Bricks Ivy .12 .30
352 Fountains .12 .30
353 Frank Thomas Statue .20 .50
354 Home Run Apple .12 .30
355 Minnie and Paul .12 .30
356 Swimming Pool .12 .30
357 Ernie Banks Statue .20 .50
358 Green Monster .12 .30
359 Touch Tank .12 .30
360 McCovey Cove .12 .30
361 Honus Wagner Statue .20 .50
362 Stan Musial Statue .30 .75
363 Bernie's Dugout .12 .30
364 B&O Warehouse .12 .30
365 Monument Park .12 .30
366 Jordan Hicks RC .50 1.25
367 Tyler O'Neill RC .40 1.00
368 Gleyber Torres RC 2.50 6.00
369 Ronald Acuna Jr. RC 8.00 20.00
370 Lourdes Gurriel Jr. RC .50 1.25
371 Christian Villanueva RC .25 .60
372 Scott Kingery RC .40 1.00
373 Harrison Bader RC .40 1.00
374 Ronald Guzman RC .25 .60
375 Franchy Cordero RC .25 .60
376 Edwin Diaz .15 .40
377 Keynan Middleton .12 .30
378 Jose Martinez .12 .30
379 Todd Frazier .12 .30
380 Dylan Bundy .15 .40
381 Dixon Machado .12 .30
382 Adeiny Hechavarria .12 .30
383 Tyler Austin .20 .50
384 Brett Gardner .15 .40
385 Pedro Alvarez .12 .30
386 Cesar Hernandez .12 .30
387 J.T. Realmuto .20 .50
388 Ben Zobrist .15 .40
389 Yan Gomes .20 .50
390 Jedd Gyorko .12 .30
391 Jason Kipnis .15 .40
392 Chase Utley .15 .40
393 Albert Almora Jr. .15 .40
394 Michael Taylor .12 .30
395 Mitch Moreland .12 .30
396 Jurickson Profar .15 .40
397 Robert Gsellman .12 .30
398 Andrew Triggs .12 .30
399 Chad Kuhl .12 .30
400 Eduardo Rodriguez .12 .30
NNO Topps Now Instant Win 25.00 60.00

2018 Topps Big League Black and White

*BLCK WHTE: 5X TO 12X BASIC
*BLCK WHTE RC: 2.5X TO 6X BASIC RC
STATED ODDS 1:60 HOBBY
STATED PRINT RUN 50 SER.#'d SETS

2018 Topps Big League Blue

*BLUE: 1.5X TO 4X BASIC
*BLUE RC: .75X TO 2X BASIC RC
INSERTED IN RETAIL PACKS

2018 Topps Big League Error Variations

STATED ODDS 1:507 HOBBY
1 Judge Reverse 15.00 40.00
15 Bellinger Reverse 20.00 50.00
25 Harper Blue band 10.00 25.00
50 Kershaw Reverse 10.00 25.00
63 Rosario Flipped 20.00 50.00
70 Lindor Flipped 15.00 40.00
104 Altuve Flipped 12.00 30.00
150 Trout Flipped 30.00 80.00
171 Stanton Grey jsy 20.00 50.00
300 Bryant Reverse 20.00 50.00

2018 Topps Big League Gold

*GOLD: 1.2X TO 3X BASIC
*GOLD RC: .6X TO 1.5X BASIC RC
STATED ODDS 1:1 HOBBY

2018 Topps Big League Players Weekend Photo Variations

STATED ODDS 1:3 HOBBY
1 Aaron Judge 1.50 4.00
19 Matt Olson .60 1.50
28 Joey Votto .60 1.50
38 Byron Buxton .60 1.50
48 Ozzie Albies 1.25 3.00
62 Robinson Cano .50 1.25
63 Amed Rosario .50 1.25
70 Francisco Lindor .60 1.50
80 Corey Seager .60 1.50
91 Anthony Rizzo .75 2.00
96 Salvador Perez .50 1.25
99 Jose Abreu .60 1.50
104 Jose Altuve .50 1.25
105 Manny Machado .60 1.50
111 Paul Goldschmidt .60 1.50
113 Rhys Hoskins 1.50 4.00
117 Charlie Blackmon .60 1.50
131 Josh Donaldson .50 1.25
150 Mike Trout 3.00 8.00
159 Mookie Betts 1.25 3.00
162 Gary Sanchez .60 1.50
203 Buster Posey .75 2.00
219 Jacob deGrom 1.25 3.00
230 Adrian Beltre .60 1.50
250 Rafael Devers 1.25 3.00
254 Yadier Molina .75 2.00
256 Kenley Jansen .50 1.25
276 Andrew Benintendi .60 1.50
287 Alex Bregman .60 1.50
300 Kris Bryant .75 2.00

2018 Topps Big League Rainbow Foil

*RAINBOW: 4X TO 10X BASIC
*RAINBOW RC: 2X TO 5X BASIC RC
STATED ODDS 1:30 HOBBY
STATED PRINT RUN 100 SER.#'d SETS

2018 Topps Big League Autographs

STATED ODDS 1:114 HOBBY
EXCHANGE DEADLINE 6/30/2020
*GOLD/99: .5X TO 1.2X BASIC
*BLCK/WHTE/25: .75X TO 2X BASIC
BLAAA Aaron Altherr 5.00 12.00
BLAAD Adam Duvall 5.00 12.00
BLAAG Avisail Garcia 3.00 8.00
BLABG Ben Gamel 4.00 10.00
BLABP Brandon Belt
BLACSP Cory Spangenberg 2.50 6.00
BLADJ Derek Jeter
BLADS Darryl Strawberry 10.00 25.00
BLAFT Frank Thomas 30.00 80.00
BLAGS Gary Sanchez 12.00 30.00
BLAGW Washington Mascot 12.00 30.00
BLAJA Jose Altuve 20.00 50.00
BLAJB Justin Bour 2.50 6.00
BLAJG Joey Gallo 6.00 15.00
BLAJH Josh Harrison 2.50 6.00
BLAJL Jake Lamb 3.00 8.00
BLAJR Jose Ramirez 12.00 30.00
BLAJS Justin Smoak 6.00 15.00
BLAJT Justin Turner
BLAKB Kris Bryant EXCH 30.00 80.00
BLAKBR Keon Broxton 2.50 6.00
BLAMC Matt Chapman 4.00 10.00
BLAMK Max Kepler 3.00 8.00
BLAMM Mikie Mahtook 2.50 6.00
BLAMO Matt Olson 4.00 10.00
BLAMT Mike Trout 200.00 400.00
BLANS Noah Syndergaard
BLAPP Phillie Phanatic 15.00 40.00
BLART Ronald Torreyes 6.00 15.00
BLASD Sean Doolittle 6.00 15.00
BLASS Steven Souza Jr. 3.00 8.00
BLATB Tim Beckham 8.00 20.00
BLATR Roosevelt Mascot
BLAWM Whit Merrifield 6.00 15.00

2018 Topps Big League Blaster Box Bottoms

HAND CUT FROM BLASTER BOXES
B1 Mike Trout 2.00 5.00
B2 Bryce Harper .60 1.50
B3 Shohei Ohtani 6.00 15.00
B4 Aaron Judge 1.00 2.50

2018 Topps Big League Ministers of Mash

STATED ODDS 1:12 HOBBY
MI1 Aaron Judge 1.25 3.00
MI2 Khris Davis .50 1.25
MI3 Cody Bellinger 1.00 2.50
MI4 Miguel Sano .40 1.00
MI5 Rhys Hoskins 1.25 3.00
MI6 Bryce Harper .75 2.00
MI7 Nelson Cruz .50 1.25
MI8 Giancarlo Stanton .50 1.25
MI9 Kris Bryant .60 1.50
MI10 Mike Trout 2.50 6.00

2018 Topps Big League Rookie Republic Autographs

STATED ODDS 1:102 HOBBY
EXCHANGE DEADLINE 6/30/2020
RRAM A.J. Minter 5.00 12.00
RRAR Amed Rosario 8.00 20.00
RRBA Brian Anderson 4.00 10.00
RRBW Brandon Woodruff 8.00 20.00
RRCF Clint Frazier 12.00 30.00
RRFM Francisco Mejia 4.00 10.00
RRGT Gleyber Torres 50.00 120.00
RRJC J.P. Crawford
RRJD J.D. Davis 4.00 10.00
RRJF Jack Flaherty 10.00 25.00
RRMA Miguel Andujar 15.00 40.00
RRND Nicky Delmonico 2.50 6.00
RROA Ozzie Albies 20.00 50.00
RRRA Ronald Acuna Jr. 60.00 150.00
RRRD Rafael Devers
RRRH Rhys Hoskins 20.00 50.00
RRRU Richard Urena 2.50 6.00
RRSA Sandy Alcantara 2.50 6.00
RRSO Shohei Ohtani 150.00 400.00
RRTN Tomas Nido 5.00 12.00
RRTW Tyler Wade 3.00 8.00
RRVR Victor Robles 15.00 40.00
RRWB Walker Buehler 10.00 25.00

2018 Topps Big League Rookie Republic Autographs Black and White

STATED ODDS 1:1988 HOBBY
STATED PRINT RUN 25 SER.#'d SETS
EXCHANGE DEADLINE 6/30/2020
RRJC J.P. Crawford 8.00 20.00

2018 Topps Big League Rookie Republic Autographs Gold

STATED ODDS 1:716 HOBBY
STATED PRINT RUN 99 SER.#'d SETS
EXCHANGE DEADLINE 6/30/2020
RRJC J.P. Crawford 5.00 12.00

2018 Topps Big League Star Caricature Reproductions

STATED ODDS 1:8 HOBBY
SCRAB Adrian Beltre .50 1.25
SCRAJ Aaron Judge 1.25 3.00
SCRAM Andrew McCutchen .50 1.25
SCRBB Byron Buxton .50 1.25
SCRBH Bryce Harper .75 2.00
SCRBP Buster Posey .60 1.50
SCRCC Carlos Correa .50 1.25
SCRCK Clayton Kershaw .75 2.00
SCREL Evan Longoria .40 1.00
SCRFF Freddie Freeman .60 1.50
SCRFL Francisco Lindor .50 1.25
SCRGS Giancarlo Stanton .50 1.25
SCRJA Jose Abreu .50 1.25
SCRJV Joey Votto .50 1.25
SCRKB Kris Bryant .60 1.50
SCRKD Khris Davis .50 1.25
SCRMB Mookie Betts 1.00 2.50
SCRMC Miguel Cabrera .50 1.25
SCRMM Manny Machado .50 1.25
SCRMS Marcus Stroman .40 1.00
SCRMT Mike Trout 2.50 6.00
SCRNA Nolan Arenado .75 2.00
SCRNS Noah Syndergaard .40 1.00
SCRPG Paul Goldschmidt .50 1.25
SCRRB Ryan Braun .40 1.00
SCRRC Robinson Cano .40 1.00
SCRRH Rhys Hoskins 1.25 3.00
SCRSP Salvador Perez .40 1.00
SCRWM Wil Myers .40 1.00
SCRYM Yadier Molina .60 1.50

2019 Topps Big League

COMP.SET w/o EXCH (400) 20.00 50.00
1 Brad Keller RC .25 .60
2 Max Muncy .15 .40
3 Austin Hedges .12 .30
4 Yasiel Puig .20 .50
5 Josh Bell .15 .40
6A Kevin Gausman .20 .50
6B Fernando Tatis Jr. SP 3.00 8.00
7 Anthony Rizzo .25 .60
8 Adam Eaton .20 .50
9 Jake Cave RC .30 .75
10 David Fletcher .40 1.00
11 C.J. Cron .12 .30
12 Adam Engel .12 .30
13 Rougned Odor .15 .40
14 Jason Kipnis .15 .40
15 Ryon Healy .12 .30
16 Todd Frazier .12 .30
17 Shohei Ohtani .30 .75
18 Andrew Benintendi .20 .50
19 DJ LeMahieu .20 .50
20A Matt Carpenter .20 .50
20B Pete Alonso SP 6.00 15.00
21 Tyler Glasnow .20 .50
22 Ryan McMahon .20 .50
23 Austin Meadows .20 .50
24 Stephen Piscotty .12 .30
25 Chris Archer .12 .30
26 Kenley Jansen .15 .40
27 Zack Godley .12 .30
28 Marcus Stroman .15 .40
29 Eduardo Escobar .12 .30
30 Steven Souza Jr. .15 .40
31 Miguel Sano .15 .40
32 Aaron Judge .50 1.25
33 Jon Lester .15 .40
34 Justin Upton .15 .40
35 Corey Seager .20 .50
36 Marcus Semien .20 .50
37 Derek Dietrich .15 .40
38 Kyle Gibson .15 .40
39 Justin Bour .12 .30
40 Blake Snell .15 .40
41 Kevin Kiermaier .15 .40
42 Joey Gallo .15 .40
43 Ryan Braun .15 .40
44 Albert Almora Jr. .15 .40
45 Xander Bogaerts .20 .50
46 Didi Gregorius .15 .40
47 Danny Duffy .12 .30
48 Raisel Iglesias .12 .30
49 Billy Hamilton .15 .40
50 Ronald Acuna Jr. 1.00 2.50
51 Ronald Guzman .12 .30
52 Justin Smoak .12 .30
53 Josh Reddick .12 .30
54 Sean Manaea .12 .30
55 Steven Duggar RC .30 .75
56 Mark Trumbo .12 .30
57 DJ Stewart RC .30 .75
58 Alex Gordon .15 .40
59 Lucas Giolito .15 .40
60 Jhoulys Chacin .12 .30
61 Kyle Seager .12 .30
62 Wade Davis .12 .30
63 Ben Zobrist .15 .40
64 Stephen Strasburg .20 .50
65 Matt Kemp .15 .40
66 David Bote .15 .40
67 Touki Toussaint RC .30 .75
68 Shane Greene .12 .30
69 Brad Boxberger .12 .30
70 Jose Briceno RC .25 .60
71 Gorkys Hernandez .12 .30
72 Adalberto Mondesi .15 .40
73 Andrelton Simmons .12 .30
74A Buster Posey .25 .60
74B Eloy Jimenez SP 3.00 8.00
75 Trevor Bauer .25 .60
76 Nick Williams .12 .30
77 Paul Goldschmidt .20 .50
78 Lourdes Gurriel Jr. .15 .40
79 Eric Thames .12 .30
80 Magneuris Sierra .20 .50
81 Andrew Heaney .12 .30
82 Justus Sheffield .20 .50
83 Niko Goodrum .15 .40
84 Patrick Corbin .15 .40
85 Mike Zunino .12 .30
86 German Marquez .12 .30
87 Jose Ramirez .15 .40
88 Jake Arrieta .15 .40
89 Brandon Nimmo .15 .40
90 Brandon Belt .15 .40
91 Carlos Correa .20 .50
92 Colin Moran .12 .30
93 Salvador Perez .15 .40
94 Leonys Martin .12 .30
95 Kevin Newman RC .40 1.00
96 J.T. Realmuto .20 .50
97 Aaron Hicks .15 .40
98 Michael Fulmer .12 .30
99 Nicky Delmonico .12 .30
100 Jose Altuve .15 .40
101 Travis Jankowski .12 .30
102 Christin Stewart RC .30 .75
103 Jorge Alfaro .12 .30
104 Jose Abreu .20 .50
105 Felix Hernandez .15 .40
106 Orlando Arcia .12 .30
107 Ender Inciarte .12 .30
108 Corey Kluber .15 .40
109 Jameson Taillon .15 .40
110 Ehire Adrianza .12 .30
111 Joey Lucchesi .12 .30
112 Marcell Ozuna .20 .50
113 James McCann .15 .40
114 Yolmer Sanchez .12 .30
115 Mitch Garver .12 .30
116 Jeff McNeil RC .60 1.50
117 Scott Kingery .15 .40
118 Felipe Vazquez .12 .30
119 Mallex Smith .12 .30
120 Hunter Dozier .12 .30
121 Nicholas Castellanos .20 .50
122 Amed Rosario .15 .40
123 Gregory Polanco .15 .40
124 Dawel Lugo RC .40 1.00
125 Juan Soto .60 1.50
126 Jaime Barria .12 .30
127 Delino DeShields .12 .30
128 Yoan Moncada .20 .50
129 Max Scherzer .20 .50
130 Jorge Bonifacio .12 .30
131 Jonathan Schoop .12 .30
132 Yairo Munoz .12 .30
133 J.D. Martinez .20 .50
134 Trea Turner .15 .40
135 Trevor Richards .12 .30
136 Joey Votto .20 .50
137 Nick Ahmed .12 .30
138 Brett Phillips .12 .30
139 Welington Castillo .12 .30
140 Starling Marte .15 .40
141 Joc Pederson .15 .40
142 Chris Iannetta .12 .30
143 David Dahl .12 .30
144 Jose Peraza .15 .40
145 Ryan O'Hearn RC .25 .60
146 Trey Mancini .15 .40
147 Willy Adames .12 .30
148 Kyle Schwarber .20 .50
149 Dee Gordon .12 .30
150 Albert Pujols .25 .60
151 Rick Porcello .15 .40
152 Charlie Blackmon .20 .50
153 Dylan Bundy .15 .40
154 Jose Berrios .15 .40
155 Jean Segura .20 .50
156 Daniel Palka .12 .30
157 Masahiro Tanaka .15 .40
158 Dominic Smith .12 .30
159 Justin Verlander .20 .50
160 Kris Bryant .25 .60
161 Yoenis Cespedes .20 .50
162 Zack Greinke .20 .50
163 Danny Jansen RC .25 .60
164 Luis Severino .15 .40
165 JaCoby Jones .15 .40
166 Matt Chapman .20 .50
167 Adam Duvall .20 .50
168 Manny Machado .20 .50
169 Adam Frazier .12 .30
170 Mike Trout 1.00 2.50
171 Mitch Haniger .15 .40
172 Travis Shaw .12 .30
173 Miguel Rojas .12 .30
174 George Springer .15 .40
175 Greg Allen .15 .40
176 Hunter Renfroe .12 .30
177 Wilmer Difo .12 .30
178 Tim Beckham .15 .40
179 Chris Taylor .15 .40
180 Jonathan Villar .12 .30
181 Michael Conforto .15 .40
182 Miguel Andujar .20 .50
183 Victor Robles .25 .60
184 Alex Bregman .20 .50
185 Eduardo Nunez .12 .30
186 Jon Gray .12 .30
187 Jake Lamb .15 .40
188 Ben Gamel .15 .40
189 Miles Mikolas .20 .50
190 Edwin Encarnacion .20 .50
191 Robbie Ray .12 .30
192 Nolan Arenado .30 .75
193 Kole Calhoun .12 .30
194 Franmil Reyes .12 .30
195 Freddie Freeman .25 .60
196 Jose Martinez .12 .30
197 Mike Foltynewicz .20 .50
198 Clayton Kershaw .30 .75
199 Joe Panik .15 .40
200 Mookie Betts .40 1.00
201 Isiah Kiner-Falefa .15 .40
202 Paul DeJong .20 .50
203 Tommy Pham .12 .30
204 Cedric Mullins RC .50 1.25
205 Matt Boyd .12 .30
206 Johnny Cueto .15 .40
207 Jackie Bradley Jr. .20 .50
208 Ozzie Albies .20 .50
209 Ian Desmond .12 .30
210 Mitch Moreland .12 .30
211 Miguel Cabrera .20 .50
212 Carlos Martinez .15 .40
213 Andrew Cashner .12 .30
214 David Price .15 .40
215 Javier Baez .25 .60
216 Pablo Sandoval .15 .40
217 Wil Myers .15 .40
218 Francisco Cervelli .12 .30
219 Chance Sisco .12 .30
220 Josh James RC .40 1.00
221 Avisail Garcia .15 .40
222 Rowdy Tellez RC .40 1.00
223 Nomar Mazara .12 .30
224 Gary Sanchez .20 .50
225 Jay Bruce .15 .40
226 Dereck Rodriguez .12 .30
227 Jorge Soler .20 .50
228 Rhys Hoskins .25 .60
229 Maikel Franco .15 .40
230 Ketel Marte .15 .40
231 Scooter Gennett .15 .40
232 Cesar Hernandez .12 .30
233 Evan Longoria .15 .40
234 Teoscar Hernandez .20 .50
235 James Paxton .15 .40
236 Giancarlo Stanton .20 .50
237 Ken Giles .12 .30
238 Ramon Laureano RC .50 1.25
239 Aaron Nola .15 .40
240 Trevor Story .20 .50
241 Anthony Rendon .20 .50
242 Whit Merrifield .20 .50
243 Pat Neshek .12 .30
244 Lorenzo Cain .12 .30
245 Taylor Ward RC .25 .60
246 Starlin Castro .12 .30
247 Willians Astudillo RC .25 .60
248 Robinson Cano .15 .40
249 Franklin Barreto .12 .30
250 Jacob deGrom .40 1.00
251 Tyler O'Neill .15 .40
252 Dansby Swanson .20 .50
253 Josh Donaldson .15 .40
254 Yu Darvish .20 .50
255 Tim Anderson .20 .50
256 Brandon Crawford .15 .40
257 Matt Duffy .12 .30
258 Johan Camargo .12 .30
259 Sean Newcomb .12 .30
260 Kevin Pillar .12 .30
261 Lewis Brinson .12 .30
262 Eugenio Suarez .15 .40
263 Joey Rickard .12 .30
264 Sandy Alcantara .12 .30
265 Andrew McCutchen .20 .50
266 Michael Kopech RC .75 2.00
267 Francisco Lindor .20 .50
268 Ryan Zimmerman .15 .40
269 Caleb Joseph .12 .30
270 Luke Voit .30 .75
271 Willson Contreras .15 .40
272 Tanner Roark .12 .30
273 Eddie Rosario .15 .40
274 Yonder Alonso .12 .30
275 David Peralta .12 .30
276 Jeimer Candelario .12 .30
277 Sean Doolittle .12 .30
278 Odubel Herrera .15 .40
279 Edwin Diaz .15 .40
280 Corey Dickerson .12 .30
281 Nick Martini RC .25 .60
282 Justin Turner .20 .50
283 Shane Bieber .20 .50
284 Luis Urias RC .40 1.00
285 Cole Hamels .15 .40
286 Zack Wheeler .15 .40
287 Jesus Aguilar .15 .40
288 Yan Gomes .20 .50
289 Austin Dean RC .25 .60
290 Collin McHugh .12 .30
291 Jurickson Profar .15 .40
292 Corbin Burnes RC 2.00 5.00
293 Josh Hader .15 .40
294 Kyle Tucker RC .60 1.50
295 Jack Flaherty .20 .50
296 Tyler Naquin .15 .40
297 Luis Castillo .15 .40
298 Walker Buehler .25 .60
299 Roberto Osuna .12 .30
300 Christian Yelich .25 .60
301 Harrison Bader .15 .40
302 Kyle Freeland .15 .40
303 Shin-Soo Choo .15 .40
304 Alen Hanson .15 .40
305 Scott Schebler .15 .40
306 Mike Minor .12 .30
307 Carlos Santana .15 .40
308 Tucker Barnhart .12 .30
309 Joey Wendle .15 .40
310 Rafael Devers .25 .60
311 Aledmys Diaz .12 .30
312 Khris Davis .20 .50
313 Jesse Winker .20 .50
314 Kendrys Morales .12 .30
315 Jorge Polanco .15 .40
316 Dustin Pedroia .20 .50
317 Brian Anderson .12 .30
318 Yuli Gurriel .15 .40
319 Gleyber Torres .40 1.00
320 Bryce Harper .30 .75
321 Eric Hosmer .15 .40
322 Manny Margot .12 .30
323 Max Kepler .15 .40
324 Howie Kendrick .12 .30

325 Gerrit Cole .20 .50
326 Ian Happ .15 .40
327 Cody Bellinger .40 1.00
328 Brandon Lowe RC .40 1.00
329 Blake Treinen .12 .30
330 Mike Fiers .12 .30
331 Brock Holt .12 .30
332 Ian Kinsler .15 .40
333 Kirby Yates .15 .40
334 Matt Olson .20 .50
335 Jose Leclerc .12 .30
336 Tyler Austin .20 .50
337 Chris Sale .20 .50
338 Yadier Molina .25 .60
339 Tyler Mahle .12 .30
340 Randal Grichuk .12 .30
341 Jose Urena .12 .30
342 Noah Syndergaard .15 .40
343 Elvis Andrus .15 .40
344 Nolan Arenado .30 .75
Matt Carpenter/Trevor Story
345 Gallo/Martinez/Davis .20 .50
346 Carpenter/Yelich/Blackmon .25 .60
347 Martinez/Lindor/Betts .40 1.00
348 Markakis/Yelich/Freeman .25 .60
349 Castellanos/Martinez/Merrifield .20 .50
350 Markakis/Bregman/Freeman .25 .60
351 Betts/Bregman/Anduar .40 1.00
352 Arenado/Yelich/Baez .30 .75
353 Encarnacion/Davis/Martinez .20 .50
354 Santana/Votto/Harper .30 .75
355 Bregman/Ramirez/Trout 1.00 2.50
356 Starling Marte .15 .40
Billy Hamilton/Trea Turner
357 Jose Ramirez .20 .50
Mallex Smith/Whit Merrifield
358 Gennett/Freeman/Yelich .25 .60
359 Altuve/Martinez/Betts .40 1.00
360 Arenado/Story/Yelich .30 .75
361 Trout/Martinez/Betts 1.00 2.50
362 Max Scherzer .40 1.00
Aaron Nola/Jacob deGrom
363 Justin Verlander .25 .60
Trevor Bauer/Blake Snell
364 Max Scherzer .20 .50
Miles Mikolas/Jon Lester
365 Luis Severino .15 .40
Corey Kluber/Blake Snell
366 Patrick Corbin .40 1.00
Max Scherzer/Jacob deGrom
367 Sale/Cole/Verlander .20 .50
368 Felipe Vazquez .15 .40
Kenley Jansen/Wade Davis
369 Blake Treinen .15 .40
Craig Kimbrel/Edwin Diaz
370 Aaron Nola .40 1.00
Max Scherzer/Jacob deGrom
371 Dallas Keuchel .20 .50
Justin Verlander/Corey Kluber
372 Aaron Nola .40 1.00
Max Scherzer/Jacob deGrom
373 Corey Kluber .20 .50
Justin Verlander/Blake Snell
374 J.D. Martinez .20 .50
375 Christian Yelich .25 .60
376 Yadier Molina .25 .60
377 Edwin Diaz .15 .40
378 Josh Hader .15 .40
379 Blake Snell .15 .40
380 Shohei Ohtani .30 .75
381 Ronald Acuna Jr. 1.00 2.50
382 Blake Snell .15 .40
383 Jacob deGrom .40 1.00
384 Mookie Betts .40 1.00
385 Christian Yelich .25 .60
386 George Springer .15 .40
387 Adrian Beltre .20 .50
388 Sean Manaea .12 .30
389 Mookie Betts .40 1.00
390 Albert Pujols .25 .60
391 Walker Buehler .25 .60
392 James Paxton .15 .40
393 Gleyber Torres .40 1.00
394 Edwin Diaz .15 .40
395 Rowdy Tellez .20 .50
396 Shohei Ohtani .30 .75
397 Juan Soto .60 1.50
398 Christian Yelich .25 .60
399 Max Scherzer .20 .50
400 Brock Holt .12 .30

2019 Topps Big League Artist Rendition Black and White

*BLCK WHTE: 5X TO 12X BASIC
*BLCK WHTE RC: 2.5X TO 6X BASIC RC
STATED ODDS 1:XXX
STATED PRINT RUN 50 SER.#'d SETS

2019 Topps Big League Blue

*BLUE: 1.5X TO 4X BASIC
*BLUE RC: .75X TO 2X BASIC RC
STATED ODDS 1:XXX

2019 Topps Big League Gold

*GOLD: 1.2X TO 3X BASIC
*GOLD RC: .6X TO 1.5X BASIC RC
STATED ODDS 1:XXX

2019 Topps Big League Rainbow Foil

*RAINBOW: 4X TO 10X BASIC
*RAINBOW RC: 2X TO 5X BASIC RC
STATED ODDS 1:XXX
STATED PRINT RUN 100 SER.#'d SETS

2019 Topps Big League Autographs

STATED ODDS 1:XXX HOBBY
EXCHANGE DEADLINE 4/31/2021
*GOLD/99: .5X TO 1.2X BASIC
*BLCK/WHTE/25: .75X TO 2X BASIC
BLAO Orbit
BLAAB Alex Bregman EXCH 15.00 40.00
BLAAJ Aaron Judge EXCH 60.00 150.00
BLABN Brandon Nimmo 3.00 8.00
BLABS Blake Snell 3.00 8.00
BLACR Cal Ripken Jr. 50.00 120.00
BLACT Chris Taylor 3.00 8.00
BLADR Dereck Rodriguez 8.00 20.00
BLAER Eddie Rosario 8.00 20.00
BLAFR Franmil Reyes 2.50 6.00
BLAHB Harrison Bader 3.00 8.00
BLAJB Jose Berrios 6.00 15.00
BLAJD Jacob deGrom 30.00 80.00
BLAJH Josh Hader 3.00 8.00
BLAJM Jose Martinez 3.00 8.00
BLAJS Jean Segura 6.00 15.00
BLAJSO Juan Soto 50.00 120.00
BLAKB Kris Bryant 50.00 120.00
BLAKF Kyle Freeland 3.00 8.00
BLALV Luke Voit 25.00 60.00
BLAMC Matt Chapman 6.00 15.00
BLAMH Mitch Haniger 6.00 15.00
BLAMMU Max Muncy 3.00 8.00
BLAMT Mike Trout 200.00 500.00
BLANR Nolan Ryan 60.00 150.00
BLAPN Pat Neshek 5.00 12.00
BLARA Ronald Acuna Jr. 40.00 100.00
BLARY Ryan Yarbrough 2.50 6.00
BLASB Shane Bieber 4.00 10.00
BLASM Sean Manaea 2.50 6.00
BLASO Shohei Ohtani
BLASP Steve Pearce 5.00 12.00
BLATS Trevor Story 6.00 15.00
BLAWA Willy Adames 2.50 6.00
BLAWC Willson Contreras 10.00 25.00

2019 Topps Big League Ballpark Oddities

STATED ODDS 1:XXX
BP01 Christian Yelich 12.00 30.00
BP02 Jose Reyes 8.00 20.00
BP03 Shohei Ohtani 15.00 40.00
BP04 Francisco Arcia 10.00 25.00
BP05 Joe Panik 8.00 20.00
BP06 Edwin Jackson 6.00 15.00
BP07 Ryan Yarbrough 6.00 15.00
BP08 Jordan Hicks 8.00 20.00
BP09 Michael Lorenzen 6.00 15.00
BP010 Russell Martin 6.00 15.00

2019 Topps Big League Blast Off

STATED ODDS 1:XXX
B01 Mike Trout 2.50 6.00
B02 Shohei Ohtani .75 2.00
B03 J.D. Martinez .50 1.25
B04 Javier Baez .60 1.50
B05 Avisail Garcia .40 1.00
B06 Trevor Story .50 1.25
B07 Christian Yelich .60 1.50
B08 Aaron Judge 1.25 3.00
B09 Gary Sanchez .50 1.25
B010 Giancarlo Stanton .50 1.25
B011 Matt Olson .50 1.25
B012 Khris Davis .50 1.25
B013 Marcell Ozuna .50 1.25
B014 Joey Gallo .40 1.00
B015 Bryce Harper .75 2.00

2019 Topps Big League Players Weekend Nicknames

STATED ODDS 1:XXX
PW1 Shohei Ohtani .75 2.00
PW2 Jose Altuve .40 1.00
PW3 Matt Chapman .50 1.25
PW4 Ronald Acuna Jr. 2.50 6.00
PW5 Christian Yelich .60 1.50
PW6 Matt Carpenter .50 1.25
PW7 Javier Baez .60 1.50
PW8 Eduardo Escobar .30 .75
PW9 Walker Buehler .60 1.50
PW10 Brandon Crawford .40 1.00
PW11 Francisco Lindor .50 1.25
PW12 Mitch Haniger .40 1.00
PW13 Todd Frazier .30 .75
PW14 Juan Soto 1.50 4.00
PW15 Jonathan Villar .30 .75
PW16 Eric Hosmer .40 1.00
PW17 Maikel Franco .40 1.00
PW18 Starling Marte .40 1.00
PW19 Nomar Mazara .30 .75
PW20 Blake Snell .40 1.00
PW21 Mookie Betts 1.00 2.50
PW22 Mitch Moreland .30 .75
PW23 Nolan Arenado .75 2.00
PW24 Salvador Perez .40 1.00
PW25 Nicholas Castellanos .50 1.25
PW26 Jose Berrios .40 1.00
PW27 Tim Anderson .50 1.25
PW28 Miguel Andujar .50 1.25
PW29 Jason Heyward .40 1.00
PW30 Brian Anderson .30 .75

2019 Topps Big League Rookie Republic Autographs

STATED ODDS 1:XXX HOBBY
EXCHANGE DEADLINE 4/31/2021
*GOLD/99: .5X TO 1.2X BASIC
*BLCK/WHTE/25: .75X TO 2X BASIC
RRABK Brad Keller 4.00 10.00
RRACA Chance Adams 2.50 6.00
RRADL Dawel Lugo 6.00 15.00
RRAEJ Eloy Jimenez 20.00 50.00
RRAFT Fernando Tatis Jr. 50.00 120.00
RRAJM Jeff McNeil 12.00 30.00
RRAJS Justus Sheffield 6.00 15.00
RRAKA Kolby Allard 4.00 10.00
RRAKN Kevin Newman 4.00 10.00
RRAKT Kyle Tucker 10.00 25.00
RRALU Luis Urias 4.00 10.00
RRAMK Michael Kopech 8.00 20.00
RRARO Ryan O'Hearn 5.00 12.00
RRART Rowdy Tellez 4.00 10.00
RRASR Sean Reid-Foley 2.50 6.00
RRATW Taylor Ward 5.00 12.00
RRAVG Vladimir Guerrero Jr.
RRAWA Willians Astudillo 10.00 25.00

2019 Topps Big League Star Caricature Reproductions

STATED ODDS 1:XXX
SCRAB Andrew Benintendi .50 1.25
SCRAG Alex Gordon .40 1.00
SCRAN Aaron Nola .40 1.00
SCRAR Anthony Rizzo .60 1.50
SCRBC Brandon Crawford .40 1.00
SCRBH Billy Hamilton .40 1.00
SCRBS Blake Snell .40 1.00
SCRCA Chris Archer .30 .75
SCRCB Charlie Blackmon .50 1.25
SCRCD Chris Davis .30 .75
SCRCK Corey Kluber .40 1.00
SCRCS Corey Seager .50 1.25
SCRCY Christian Yelich .60 1.50
SCRDG Dee Gordon .30 .75
SCREH Eric Hosmer .40 1.00
SCRGT Gleyber Torres 1.00 2.50
SCRJA Jose Altuve .40 1.00
SCRJB Jose Berrios .40 1.00
SCRLG Lourdes Gurriel Jr. .40 1.00
SCRMC Matt Carpenter .50 1.25
SCRMS Max Scherzer .50 1.25
SCRNC Nicholas Castellanos .50 1.25
SCRNM Nomar Mazara .30 .75
SCRRA Ronald Acuna Jr. 2.50 6.00
SCRSC Starlin Castro .30 .75
SCRSO Shohei Ohtani .75 2.00
SCRSP Stephen Piscotty .30 .75
SCRYM Yoan Moncada .50 1.25
SCRZG Zack Greinke .50 1.25
SCRARO Amed Rosario .40 1.00

2019 Topps Big League Wall Climbers

STATED ODDS 1:XXX
WC1 Kevin Pillar .30 .75
WC2 Ronald Acuna Jr. 2.50 6.00
WC3 Max Kepler .40 1.00
WC4 Christian Yelich .60 1.50
WC5 Odubel Herrera .40 1.00
WC6 Billy Hamilton .40 1.00
WC7 Adam Engel .30 .75
WC8 Corey Dickerson .30 .75
WC9 Mookie Betts 1.00 2.50
WC10 Mike Trout 2.50 6.00

2020 Topps Big League

COMPLETE SET (300) 15.00 40.00
1 Salvador Perez .15 .40
2 Elvis Andrus .15 .40
3 Patrick Corbin .15 .40
4 Nelson Cruz .20 .50
5 George Springer .15 .40
6 Eric Hosmer .15 .40
7 Jonathan Schoop .12 .30
8 Jose Urquidy RC .15 .40
9 Willson Contreras .20 .50
10 DJ LeMahieu .20 .50
11 Mike Moustakas .15 .40
12 Tommy La Stella .12 .30
13 Dee Gordon .12 .30
14 Joey Votto .20 .50
15 Miguel Sano .15 .40
16 Yusei Kikuchi .15 .40
17 Roberto Perez .12 .30
18 Niko Goodrum .15 .40
19 Lorenzo Cain .12 .30
20 Griffin Canning .20 .50
21 Cole Hamels .15 .40
22 Eduardo Escobar .12 .30
23 Walker Buehler .25 .60
24 Alex Young RC .12 .30
25 Brian Anderson .12 .30
26 Matthew Boyd .12 .30
27 Bryan Reynolds .15 .40
28 Shohei Ohtani .30 .75
29 Pete Alonso .50 1.25
30 Kole Calhoun .12 .30
31 Bryce Harper .30 .75
32 Jorge Soler .20 .50
33 Tommy Edman .20 .50
34 Zack Collins RC .15 .40
35 Joey Lucchesi .12 .30
36 Noah Syndergaard .15 .40
37 Jesus Aguilar .15 .40
38 Ryan McMahon .20 .50
39 Nolan Arenado .30 .75
40 Nomar Mazara .12 .30
41 Michael Chavis .15 .40
42 Jeff McNeil .15 .40
43 Cody Bellinger .40 1.00
44 C.J. Cron .12 .30
45 Whit Merrifield .20 .50
46 Nick Senzel .20 .50
47 Aaron Nola .15 .40
48 Keston Hiura .25 .60
49 David Price .15 .40
50 Austin Riley .25 .60
51 Ramon Laureano .15 .40
52 J.T. Realmuto .20 .50
53 Marcus Stroman .15 .40
54 Ozzie Albies .20 .50
55 Sonny Gray .15 .40
56 Sean Murphy RC .20 .50
57 Christian Yelich .25 .60
58 A.J. Puk RC .20 .50
59 Kolten Wong .15 .40
60 Dustin May RC .40 1.00
61 Jesus Luzardo RC .25 .60
62 Hunter Harvey RC .20 .50
63 Max Kepler .15 .40
64 Evan Longoria .15 .40
65 Blake Snell .15 .40
66 Luis Castillo .15 .40
67 Aaron Civale RC .25 .60
68 Mike Trout 1.00 2.50
69 Eloy Jimenez .40 1.00
70 Adalberto Mondesi .15 .40
71 Aroldis Chapman .20 .50
72 Anthony Rizzo .25 .60
73 Charlie Morton .20 .50
74 Amed Rosario .15 .40
75 Jon Lester .15 .40
76 Mike Minor .12 .30
77 Charlie Blackmon .20 .50
78 Alex Bregman .20 .50
79 Jordan Yamamoto RC .12 .30
80 Ian Desmond .12 .30
81 Yasmani Grandal .12 .30
82 Ronald Acuna Jr. .75 2.00
83 Trent Grisham RC .50 1.25
84 Gerrit Cole .30 .75
85 Rafael Devers .25 .60
86 Trea Turner .15 .40
87 Willy Adames .12 .30
88 Dallas Keuchel .15 .40
89 Paul Goldschmidt .20 .50
90 Xander Bogaerts .20 .50
91 Shin-Soo Choo .15 .40
92 Gleyber Torres .40 1.00
93 Javier Baez .25 .60
94 Stephen Strasburg .20 .50
95 Robinson Cano .15 .40
96 Hunter Dozier .12 .30
97 Trevor Story .20 .50
98 Max Fried .20 .50
99 Nicky Lopez .12 .30
100 Michael Conforto .15 .40
101 Joe Musgrove .20 .50
102 Fernando Tatis Jr. 1.00 2.50
103 Eugenio Suarez .15 .40
104 Mitch Keller .20 .50
105 Miguel Cabrera .20 .50
106 Starling Marte .15 .40
107 Aristides Aquino RC .30 .75
108 Bo Bichette RC 1.00 2.50
109 Matt Olson .20 .50
110 Andres Munoz RC .20 .50
111 Juan Soto .60 1.50
112 Buster Posey .25 .60
113 Albert Pujols .25 .60
114 Jorge Polanco .15 .40
115 Ryan Braun .15 .40
116 Freddie Freeman .25 .60
117 Austin Meadows .20 .50
118 Jorge Alfaro .12 .30
119 Andrew Benintendi .20 .50
120 Jean Segura .15 .40
121 Jacob deGrom .40 1.00
122 Brendan McKay RC .20 .50
123 Yordan Alvarez RC 1.25 3.00
124 Wil Myers .15 .40
125 Luis Arraez .25 .60
126 Jack Flaherty .20 .50
127 Yadier Molina .25 .60
128 Lourdes Gurriel Jr. .15 .40
129 Dansby Swanson .20 .50
130 Andrelton Simmons .12 .30
131 German Marquez .20 .50
132 Jeff Samardzija .12 .30
133 Trey Mancini .20 .50
134 Max Scherzer .20 .50
135 Jordan Montgomery .12 .30
136 David Peralta .12 .30
137 Chris Archer .12 .30
138 Brandon Crawford .15 .40
139 Nico Hoerner RC .50 1.25
140 Kevin Newman .20 .50
141 Vladimir Guerrero Jr. .30 .75
142 Eddie Rosario .15 .40
143 Harold Ramirez .12 .30
144 Will Smith .20 .50
145 Marcus Semien .20 .50
146 Danny Santana .12 .30
147 John Means .20 .50
148 Maikel Franco .15 .40
149 Chris Sale .20 .50
150 Hyun-Jin Ryu .15 .40
151 Michel Baez RC .12 .30
152 Christian Walker .15 .40
153 Gary Sanchez .20 .50
154 Shane Bieber .20 .50
155 Mitch Garver .12 .30
156 Nick Solak RC .50 1.25
157 Brandon Lowe .15 .40
158 Gavin Lux RC .60 1.50
159 Paul DeJong .20 .50
160 Kris Bryant .25 .60
161 Jose Berrios .15 .40
162 Carter Kieboom .15 .40
163 Mitch Haniger .15 .40
164 Orlando Arcia .12 .30
165 Daniel Murphy .15 .40
166 Giancarlo Stanton .20 .50
167 Josh Donaldson .15 .40
168 Brendan Rodgers .20 .50
169 Isan Diaz RC .20 .50
170 Eduardo Rodriguez .12 .30
171 Corey Kluber .15 .40
172 Chris Paddack .20 .50
173 Hanser Alberto .12 .30
174 Victor Robles .25 .60
175 Dawel Lugo .12 .30
176 Mallex Smith .12 .30
177 Mike Clevinger .15 .40
178 Lucas Giolito .15 .40
179 Jose Abreu .20 .50
180 Kyle Lewis RC 1.00 2.50
181 Chance Sisco .12 .30
182 Jose Ramirez .15 .40
183 Zack Wheeler .15 .40
184 Manny Machado .20 .50
185 Randal Grichuk .12 .30
186 Mike Yastrzemski .30 .75
187 Howie Kendrick .12 .30
188 Rhys Hoskins .25 .60
189 Carlos Correa .20 .50
190 Brandon Woodruff .20 .50
191 Gio Urshela .20 .50
192 Jonathan Villar .12 .30
193 Cavan Biggio .25 .60
194 Josh Hader .15 .40
195 Andrew McCutchen .20 .50
196 J.D. Martinez .20 .50
197 Kyle Seager .12 .30
198 Corey Seager .20 .50
199 Jake Rogers RC .12 .30
200 Renato Nunez .15 .40
201 Trevor Bauer .25 .60
202 Carlos Santana .15 .40
203 Aaron Judge .50 1.25
204 Josh Bell .15 .40
205 Matt Chapman .20 .50
206 Khris Davis .20 .50
207 Mike Soroka .20 .50
208 Robbie Ray .12 .30
209 Daniel Vogelbach .12 .30
210 Ketel Marte .15 .40
211 Tim Anderson .20 .50
212 Kyle Schwarber .20 .50
213 Rowdy Tellez .15 .40
214 Anthony Rendon .20 .50
215 Francisco Lindor .20 .50
216 Joey Gallo .20 .50
217 Zack Greinke .20 .50
218 Max Muncy .15 .40
219 Oscar Mercado .20 .50
220 Jose Altuve .15 .40
221 Didi Gregorius .15 .40
222 Joc Pederson .15 .40
223 Hunter Renfroe .12 .30
224 Gregory Polanco .15 .40
225 Yoan Moncada .20 .50
226 Brandon Belt .15 .40
227 Dakota Hudson .15 .40
228 Kevin Kiermaier .15 .40
229 Zac Gallen RC .30 .75
230 Clayton Kershaw .30 .75
231 Freddy Galvis .12 .30
232 Luis Robert RC 1.00 2.50
233 Mookie Betts .40 1.00
234 Scott Kingery .15 .40
235 Justin Verlander .20 .50
236 Alnso/Bllngr/Srz LL .50 1.25
237 Brgmn/Trt/Slr LL 1.00 2.50
238 Rndn/Bllngr/Acna Jr. LL .75 2.00
239 Semien/Devers/Betts LL .40 1.00
240 Arenado/Marte/Albies LL .30 .75
241 LeMahieu/Devers/Merrifield LL .25 .60
242 Albies/Seager/Rendon LL .20 .50
243 Semien/Devers/Bogaerts LL .25 .60
244 Frmn/Alnso/Rndn LL .50 1.25
245 Soler/Bogaerts/Abreu LL .20 .50
246 Grndl/Soto/Hskns LL .60 1.50
247 Sntna/Trt/Brgmn LL 1.00 2.50
248 Ylch/Trnr/Acna Jr. LL .75 2.00
249 Villar/Mondesi/Smith LL .15 .40
250 Marte/Rendon/Yelich LL .25 .60
251 Moncada/LeMahieu/Anderson LL .20 .50
252 Rndn/Bllngr/Ylch LL .40 1.00
253 Brgmn/Cruz/Trt LL 1.00 2.50
254 Soroka/deGrom/Ryu LL .40 1.00
255 Morton/Verlander/Cole LL .30 .75
256 Kershaw/Fried/Strasburg LL .30 .75
257 Rodriguez/Cole/Verlander LL .30 .75
258 Scherzer/deGrom/Strasburg LL .40 1.00
259 Bieber/Verlander/Cole LL .30 .75
260 Smith/Hader/Yates LL .15 .40
261 Hand/Chapman/Osuna LL .20 .50
262 Nola/Strasburg/deGrom LL .40 1.00
263 Cole/Bieber/Verlander LL .30 .75
264 Ryu/Flaherty/deGrom LL .40 1.00
265 Bieber/Verlander/Cole LL .30 .75
266 Mike Trout AW 1.00 2.50
267 Cody Bellinger AW .40 1.00
268 Justin Verlander AW .20 .50
269 Jacob deGrom AW .40 1.00
270 Yordan Alvarez AW 1.25 3.00
271 Pete Alonso AW .50 1.25
272 Stephen Strasburg AW .20 .50
273 Shane Bieber AW .20 .50
274 Mike Trout AW 1.00 2.50
275 Christian Yelich AW .25 .60
276 Carlos Carrasco AW .12 .30
277 Josh Donaldson AW .15 .40
278 Aroldis Chapman AW .20 .50
279 Josh Hader AW .15 .40
280 Nelson Cruz AW .20 .50
281 Carlos Carrasco AW .12 .30
282 Curtis Granderson AW .15 .40
283 Mike Trout AW 1.00 2.50
284 Anthony Rendon AW .20 .50
285 Mike Trout AW 1.00 2.50
286 Ichiro HL .25 .60
287 Pete Alonso HL .50 1.25
288 CC Sabathia HL .15 .40
289 Albert Pujols HL .25 .60
290 Bryce Harper HL .30 .75
291 Justin Verlander HL .20 .50
292 Bo Bichette HL 1.00 2.50
293 Mike Trout HL 1.00 2.50
294 Shohei Ohtani HL .30 .75
295 Vladimir Guerrero Jr. HL .30 .75
296 Yordan Alvarez HL 1.25 3.00
297 Mike Fiers HL .12 .30
298 Aristides Aquino HL .30 .75
299 Los Angeles Angels HL .12 .30
300 Ronald Acuna Jr. HL .75 2.00

2020 Topps Big League Black and White

*BLACK WHITE: 5X TO 12X BASIC
*BLACK WHITE RC: 2.5X TO 6X BASIC RC
STATED ODDS 1:75 HOBBY
STATED PRINT RUN 50 SER.#'d SETS

2020 Topps Big League Blue

*BLUE: 1.2X TO 3X BASIC
*BLUE RC: .6X TO 1.5X BASIC RC
FIVE PER BLASTER

2020 Topps Big League Orange

*ORANGE: 1.2X TO 3X BASIC
*ORANGE RC: .6X TO 1.5X BASIC RC
THREE PER FAT PACK

2020 Topps Big League Purple Blaster Box Cut Out

CUT FROM RETAIL BLASTER BOXES
B1 Mike Trout 3.00 8.00
B2 Bryce Harper 1.00 2.50
B3 Miguel Cabrera .60 1.50
B4 Aristides Aquino 1.00 2.50

2020 Topps Big League Rainbow Foil

*RAINBOW: 4X TO 10X BASIC
*RAINBOW RC: 2X TO 5X BASIC RC
STATED ODDS 1:38 HOBBY
STATED PRINT RUN 100 SER.#'d SETS

2020 Topps Big League Autographs

STATED ODDS 1:78 HOBBY
*ORANGE/99: .5X TO 1.2X BASIC
BLAAJ Andruw Jones 8.00 20.00
BLAAO Adam Ottavino 8.00 20.00
BLABL Brandon Lowe 6.00 15.00
BLABR Bryan Reynolds 8.00 20.00
BLABW Brandon Woodruff 4.00 10.00
BLACB Cavan Biggio 8.00 20.00
BLACK Carter Kieboom 6.00 15.00
BLACP Chris Paddack 8.00 20.00
BLADL DJ LeMahieu 15.00 40.00
BLADV Daniel Vogelbach 2.50 6.00
BLAJA Jim Abbott 20.00 50.00
BLAJC Jose Canseco 10.00 25.00
BLAJF Jack Flaherty 8.00 20.00
BLAJM John Means 30.00 80.00
BLAJP Jorge Polanco 3.00 8.00
BLAKH Keston Hiura 10.00 25.00
BLAKM Ketel Marte 3.00 8.00
BLAKT Kyle Tucker 6.00 15.00
BLAKY Kirby Yates 2.50 6.00
BLALG Lourdes Gurriel Jr. 5.00 12.00
BLAMB Matt Beaty 3.00 8.00
BLAMC Matt Chapman 6.00 15.00
BLAMCH Michael Chavis 6.00 15.00
BLAMG Mitch Garver 2.50 6.00
BLAMK Max Kepler 6.00 15.00
BLAMS Mike Soroka 15.00 40.00
BLAMT Mike Trout 150.00 400.00
BLAMY Mike Yastrzemski 8.00 20.00
BLAOM Oscar Mercado 4.00 10.00
BLARN Renato Nunez 3.00 8.00
BLASA Sandy Alomar Jr. 8.00 20.00
BLASN Sheldon Neuse 3.00 8.00
BLATL Tommy La Stella 2.50 6.00
BLAWA Willians Astudillo 2.50 6.00
BLAWS Will Smith 4.00 10.00

2020 Topps Big League Ballpark Oddities

STATED ODDS 1:554 HOBBY
BP01 Jon Duplantier 5.00 12.00
BP02 Joey Gallo 8.00 20.00
BP03 Edwin Jackson 5.00 12.00
BP04 Stevie Wilkerson 8.00 20.00
BP05 Vince Velasquez 5.00 12.00
BP06 Minnesota Twins 8.00 20.00
BP07 Mookie Betts 15.00 40.00
BP08 Michael Lorenzen 12.00 30.00
BP09 Colin Moran 5.00 12.00
BP010 Jonathan Schoop 5.00 12.00

2020 Topps Big League Defensive Wizards

COMPLETE SET (15) 5.00 12.00
STATED ODDS 1:4 HOBBY
DW1 Javier Baez .40 1.00
DW2 Didi Gregorius .25 .60
DW3 Matt Chapman .30 .75
DW4 Scott Kingery .25 .60
DW5 DJ LeMahieu .30 .75
DW6 Fernando Tatis Jr. 1.50 4.00
DW7 George Springer .25 .60
DW8 David Peralta .20 .50
DW9 Gio Urshela .30 .75
DW10 Charlie Blackmon .30 .75
DW11 Paul DeJong .30 .75
DW12 Bryce Harper .50 1.25
DW13 Carlos Correa .30 .75
DW14 Mike Trout 1.50 4.00
DW15 Nolan Arenado .50 1.25

2020 Topps Big League Defensive Wizards Autographs

STATED ODDS 1:2818 HOBBY
STATED PRINT RUN 25 SER.#'d SETS
DWACB Charlie Blackmon
DWADG Didi Gregorius
DWADL DJ LeMahieu 20.00 50.00
DWADP David Peralta 8.00 20.00
DWAFT Fernando Tatis Jr. 60.00 150.00
DWAGS George Springer
DWAGU Gio Urshela 15.00 40.00
DWAMC Matt Chapman 12.00 30.00
DWAPD Paul DeJong 12.00 30.00
DWASK Scott Kingery

2020 Topps Big League Flipping Out

COMPLETE SET (15) 5.00 12.00
STATED ODDS 1:4 HOBBY
FO1 Tim Anderson .30 .75
FO2 Ronald Acuna Jr. 1.25 3.00
FO3 Eugenio Suarez .25 .60
FO4 Aaron Hicks .25 .60
FO5 Aristides Aquino .50 1.25
FO6 Pete Alonso .75 2.00
FO7 Jorge Soler .30 .75
FO8 Max Kepler .25 .60
FO9 Fernando Tatis Jr. 1.50 4.00
FO10 Max Muncy .25 .60
FO11 Aaron Judge .75 2.00
FO12 Rafael Devers .40 1.00
FO13 Bryce Harper .50 1.25
FO14 Vladimir Guerrero Jr. .50 1.25
FO15 Willson Contreras .30 .75

2020 Topps Big League Flipping Out Autographs

STATED ODDS 1:3862 HOBBY
STATED PRINT RUN 25 SER.#'d SETS
FOAA Aristides Aquino 25.00 60.00
FOFT Fernando Tatis Jr. 60.00 150.00
FOJS Jorge Soler 12.00 30.00
FOMK Max Kepler 25.00 60.00
FOMM Max Muncy 15.00 40.00
FORA Ronald Acuna Jr. 60.00 150.00

2020 Topps Big League Opening Act Autographs

STATED ODDS 1:181 HOBBY
*ORANGE/99: .5X TO 1.2X BASIC
OAAAA Adbert Alzolay 3.00 8.00
OAAAAQ Aristides Aquino 6.00 15.00
OAAAK Anthony Kay 2.50 6.00
OAAAP A.J. Puk 4.00 10.00
OAABB Bo Bichette
OAABBR Bobby Bradley 5.00 12.00
OAADM Dustin May 15.00 40.00
OAAHH Hunter Harvey 4.00 10.00
OAAID Isan Diaz 4.00 10.00
OAAJD Justin Dunn 3.00 8.00
OAAJK James Karinchak 12.00 30.00
OAAJU Jose Urquidy 3.00 8.00
OAAKL Kyle Lewis 8.00 20.00
OAAMD Mauricio Dubon 6.00 15.00
OAANH Nico Hoerner 10.00 25.00
OAANS Nick Solak 5.00 12.00
OAASB Seth Brown 2.50 6.00
OAASH Sam Hilliard 4.00 10.00
OAASM Sean Murphy 4.00 10.00
OAATG Trent Grisham 10.00 25.00
OAAYA Yordan Alvarez 25.00 60.00

2020 Topps Big League Roll Call

COMPLETE SET (30) 10.00 25.00
STATED ODDS 1:4 HOBBY
RC1 Ronald Acuna Jr. 1.25 3.00
RC2 Aristides Aquino .50 1.25
RC3 Gavin Lux 1.00 2.50
RC4 Yordan Alvarez 2.00 5.00
RC5 Pete Alonso .75 2.00
RC6 Victor Robles .40 1.00
RC7 Andrew Benintendi .30 .75
RC8 Christian Yelich .40 1.00
RC9 Keston Hiura .40 1.00
RC10 Vladimir Guerrero Jr. .50 1.25
RC11 Max Kepler .25 .60
RC12 Nick Senzel .30 .75
RC13 Matt Chapman .30 .75
RC14 Max Muncy .25 .60
RC15 Tim Anderson .30 .75
RC16 Jacob deGrom .60 1.50
RC17 Bryce Harper .50 1.25
RC18 Manny Machado .30 .75
RC19 Mike Trout 1.50 4.00
RC20 Mookie Betts .60 1.50
RC21 Eloy Jimenez .60 1.50
RC22 Juan Soto 1.00 2.50
RC23 Gerrit Cole .50 1.25
RC24 Max Scherzer .30 .75
RC25 Shohei Ohtani .50 1.25
RC26 Cody Bellinger .60 1.50
RC27 Gleyber Torres .60 1.50
RC28 Bo Bichette 1.50 4.00
RC29 Aaron Judge .75 2.00
RC30 Nolan Arenado .50 1.25

2020 Topps Big League Roll Call Autographs

STATED ODDS 1:1938 HOBBY
STATED PRINT RUN 25 SER.#'d SETS
RCAA Aristides Aquino 25.00 60.00
RCAB Andrew Benintendi
RCAJ Aaron Judge 75.00 200.00
RCGC Gerrit Cole 40.00 100.00
RCGL Gavin Lux 40.00 100.00
RCKH Keston Hiura 15.00 40.00
RCMC Matt Chapman 12.00 30.00
RCMK Max Kepler 25.00 60.00
RCMMU Max Muncy 15.00 40.00
RCMS Max Scherzer 25.00 60.00
RCNS Nick Senzel 12.00 30.00
RCRA Ronald Acuna Jr. 60.00 150.00
RCTA Tim Anderson 15.00 40.00
RCVR Victor Robles 25.00 60.00
RCYA Yordan Alvarez 75.00 200.00

2020 Topps Big League Star Caricature Reproductions

STATED ODDS 1:4 HOBBY
SCOAA Aristides Aquino .50 1.25
SCOAM Austin Meadows .30 .75
SCOBA Brian Anderson .20 .50
SCOBH Bryce Harper .50 1.25
SCOCB Cody Bellinger .60 1.50
SCOCY Christian Yelich .40 1.00
SCODL DJ LeMahieu .30 .75
SCODV Daniel Vogelbach .20 .50
SCOEJ Eloy Jimenez .60 1.50
SCOEL Evan Longoria .25 .60
SCOFL Francisco Lindor .30 .75
SCOFT Fernando Tatis Jr. 1.50 4.00
SCOJB Javier Baez .40 1.00
SCOJBE Josh Bell .25 .60
SCOJG Joey Gallo .30 .75
SCOJS Juan Soto 1.00 2.50
SCOKM Ketel Marte .25 .60
SCOMC Miguel Cabrera .30 .75
SCOMCH Matt Chapman .30 .75
SCOMK Max Kepler .25 .60
SCOMT Mike Trout 1.50 4.00
SCOPA Pete Alonso .75 2.00
SCOPG Paul Goldschmidt .30 .75
SCORA Ronald Acuna Jr. 1.25 3.00
SCORD Rafael Devers .40 1.00
SCOTM Trey Mancini .30 .75
SCOTS Trevor Story .30 .75
SCOVG Vladimir Guerrero Jr. .50 1.25
SCOWM Whit Merrifield .30 .75
SCOYA Yordan Alvarez 2.00 5.00

2020 Topps Big League Veteran and Rookie Autographs

INSERTED IN RETAIL PACKS
12 Tommy LaStella 3.00 8.00
20 Griffin Canning 5.00 12.00
22 Eduardo Escobar 3.00 8.00
24 Alex Young 3.00 8.00
28 Shohei Ohtani 75.00 200.00
31 Bryce Harper
33 Tommy Edman 12.00 30.00
38 Ryan McMahon 5.00 12.00
41 Michael Chavis 8.00 20.00
42 Jeff McNeil 8.00 20.00
45 Whit Merrifield 10.00 25.00
46 Nick Senzel
51 Ramon Laureano 10.00 25.00
56 Sean Murphy 5.00 12.00
58 A.J. Puk 5.00 12.00
61 Jesus Luzardo
62 Hunter Harvey 5.00 12.00
73 Charlie Morton
79 Jordan Yamamoto 3.00 8.00
107 Aristides Aquino 8.00 20.00
110 Andres Munoz 5.00 12.00
118 Jorge Alfaro 3.00 8.00
121 Jacob deGrom
123 Yordan Alvarez 25.00 60.00
126 Jack Flaherty 10.00 25.00
134 Max Scherzer
139 Nico Hoerner 12.00 30.00
140 Kevin Newman 5.00 12.00
147 John Means 40.00 100.00
151 Michel Baez 3.00 8.00
158 Gavin Lux
169 Isan Diaz 5.00 12.00
170 Eduardo Rodriguez 6.00 15.00
172 Chris Paddack 10.00 25.00
177 Mike Clevinger
180 Kyle Lewis 10.00 25.00
186 Mike Yastrzemski 10.00 25.00
190 Brandon Woodruff 5.00 12.00
193 Cavan Biggio 10.00 25.00
200 Renato Nunez 4.00 10.00
203 Aaron Judge
210 Ketel Marte 4.00 10.00
218 Max Muncy 6.00 15.00

219 Oscar Mercado 5.00 12.00
227 Dakota Hudson 8.00 20.00

2008 Topps Big Stix

COMPLETE SET (100) 60.00 150.00
CARDS LISTED ALPHABETICALLY
1 Jason Bay .75 2.00
2 Josh Beckett .50 1.25
3 Erik Bedard .50 1.25
4 Carlos Beltran .75 2.00
5 Adrian Beltre 1.25 3.00
6 Lance Berkman .75 2.00
7 Hank Blalock .50 1.25
8 Ryan Braun .75 2.00
9 Jay Bruce 1.50 4.00
10 Billy Butler .50 1.25
11 Eric Byrnes .50 1.25
12 Miguel Cabrera 1.25 3.00
13 Matt Cain .75 2.00
14 Robinson Cano .75 2.00
15 Joba Chamberlain .50 1.25
16 Eric Chavez .50 1.25
17 Carl Crawford .75 2.00
18 Bobby Crosby .50 1.25
19 Adam Dunn .75 2.00
20 Jacoby Ellsbury 1.00 2.50
21 Prince Fielder .75 2.00
22 Troy Glaus .75 2.00
23 Jonny Gomes .50 1.25
24 Adrian Gonzalez .75 2.00
25 Alex Gordon .75 2.00
26 Curtis Granderson .75 2.00
27 Ken Griffey Jr. 2.50 6.00
28 Vladimir Guerrero .75 2.00
29 Travis Hafner .50 1.25
30 Roy Halladay .75 2.00
31 Cole Hamels 1.00 2.50
32 J.J. Hardy .50 1.25
33 Todd Helton .75 2.00
34 Felix Hernandez .75 2.00
35 Luke Hochevar .75 2.00
36 Matt Holliday 1.25 3.00
37 Ryan Howard .75 2.00
38 Torii Hunter .50 1.25
39 Derek Jeter 3.00 8.00
40 Kenji Johjima .50 1.25
41 Chipper Jones 1.25 3.00
42 Andruw Jones .50 1.25
43 Paul Konerko .75 2.00
44 Hiroki Kuroda 1.25 3.00
45 Derrek Lee .50 1.25
46 Carlos Lee .50 1.25
47 Tim Lincecum .75 2.00
48 Evan Longoria 2.50 6.00
49 Nick Markakis 1.00 2.50
50 Russ Martin .50 1.25
51 Victor Martinez .75 2.00
52 Pedro Martinez .75 2.00
53 Hideki Matsui 1.25 3.00
54 Daisuke Matsuzaka .75 2.00
55 Joe Mauer 1.00 2.50
56 Brian McCann .75 2.00
57 Justin Morneau .75 2.00
58 Magglio Ordonez .75 2.00
59 David Ortiz 1.25 3.00
60 Jonathan Papelbon .75 2.00
61 Jake Peavy .50 1.25
62 Carlos Pena .75 2.00
63 Hunter Pence .75 2.00
64 Jorge Posada .75 2.00
65 Albert Pujols 1.50 4.00
66 Manny Ramirez 1.25 3.00
67 Hanley Ramirez .75 2.00
68 Jose Reyes .75 2.00
69 Alex Rios .50 1.25
70 Brian Roberts .50 1.25
71 Ivan Rodriguez .75 2.00
72 Alex Rodriguez 1.50 4.00
73 Jimmy Rollins .75 2.00
74 C.C. Sabathia .75 2.00
75 Johan Santana .75 2.00
76 Grady Sizemore .75 2.00
77 John Smoltz 1.25 3.00
78 Alfonso Soriano .75 2.00
79 Ichiro Suzuki 1.50 4.00
80 Nick Swisher .75 2.00
81 Mark Teixeira .75 2.00
82 Miguel Tejada .75 2.00
83 Troy Tulowitzki 1.25 3.00
84 Dan Uggla .50 1.25
85 Justin Upton .75 2.00
86 B.J. Upton .75 2.00
87 Chase Utley .75 2.00
88 Justin Verlander 1.25 3.00
89 Joey Votto 4.00 10.00
90 Chien-Ming Wang .75 2.00
91 Brandon Webb .75 2.00
92 Vernon Wells .50 1.25
93 Dontrelle Willis .50 1.25
94 David Wright .75 2.00
95 Chris Young .50 1.25
96 Delmon Young .75 2.00
97 Michael Young .50 1.25
98 Carlos Zambrano .75 2.00
99 Ryan Zimmerman .75 2.00
100 Barry Zito .75 2.00

2018 Topps Bowman Holiday

COMPLETE SET (100) 20.00 50.00
THAB Alex Bregman .40 1.00
THAF Alex Faedo .40 1.00
THAG Andres Gimenez .60 1.50
THAH Adam Haseley .40 1.00
THAJ Aaron Judge 1.00 2.50
THAM Austin Meadows .60 1.50
THAMC Andrew McCutchen .40 1.00
THAR Austin Riley .75 2.00
THARO Amed Rosario .30 .75
THAV Alex Verdugo .40 1.00
THBA Brian Anderson .30 .75
THBB Braden Bishop .25 .60
THBBI Bo Bichette 1.00 2.50
THBH Bryce Harper .60 1.50
THBM Brandon Marsh .40 1.00
THBMC Brendan McKay .40 1.00
THBR Brendan Rodgers .30 .75
THBW Brandon Woodruff .75 2.00
THCB Charcer Burks .25 .60
THCBI Cavan Biggio .50 1.25
THCE Christmas Elf .40 1.00
THCF Clint Frazier .50 1.25
THCK Clayton Kershaw .60 1.50
THCP Cristian Pache 1.25 3.00
THCW Colton Welker .25 .60
THDG Didi Gregorius .30 .75
THDV Daulton Varsho .30 .75
THDW Drew Waters .60 1.50
THEDLS Enyel De Los Santos .30 .75
THEDLS Edwin Diaz .30 .75
THEF Estevan Florial .40 1.00
THEJ Eloy Jimenez 1.00 2.50
THER Eddie Rosario .40 1.00
THFL Francisco Lindor .40 1.00
THFTJ Fernando Tatis Jr. 2.50 6.00
THFW Forrest Whitley .40 1.00
THGS Gregory Soto .25 .60
THGT Gleyber Torres 2.50 6.00
THHC Hans Crouse .40 1.00
THHG Hunter Greene .75 2.00
THJA Jo Adell 1.00 2.50
THJAL Jose Altuve .30 .75
THJC J.P. Crawford .25 .60
THJD Jeter Downs .40 1.00
THJDE Jacob deGrom .75 2.00
THJF Jack Flaherty 1.00 2.50
THJL Jesus Luzardo .40 1.00
THJR Jose Ramirez .30 .75
THJS Jesus Sanchez .40 1.00
THJSE Jean Segura .25 .60
THJSF Justus Sheffield .30 .75
THJSH Jordan Sheffield .25 .60
THJSO Juan Soto 6.00 15.00
THJV Joey Votto .40 1.00
THKB Kris Bryant .50 1.25
THKD Khris Davis .40 1.00
THKM Kevin Maitan .30 .75
THKS Kyle Seager .25 .60
THKT Kyle Tucker .60 1.50
THLS Luis Severino .30 .75
THLU Luis Urias .50 1.25
THMA Miguel Andujar 1.00 2.50
THMBE Mookie Betts .75 2.00
THMC Matt Chapman .40 1.00
THMG MacKenzie Gore .50 1.25
THMH Mitch Haniger .30 .75
THMK Matt Kemp .30 .75
THMK Mitch Keller .30 .75
THMKO Michael Kopech 1.00 2.50
THMS Mike Soroka .75 2.00
THMT Mike Trout 2.00 5.00
THNA Nick Allen .25 .60
THNAR Nolan Arenado .60 1.50
THNL Nicky Lopez .40 1.00
THNS Nick Senzel .75 2.00
THOA Ozzie Albies .75 2.00
THPA Pedro Avila .25 .60
THPG Paul Goldschmidt .40 1.00
THRAJ Ronald Acuna Jr. 10.00 25.00
THRD Rafael Devers .75 2.00
THRH Ryan Helsley .30 .75
THRHO Rhys Hoskins 1.00 2.50
THRL Royce Lewis 1.00 2.50
THSC Sam Carlson .30 .75
THSCL Santa Claus .40 1.00
THSK Scott Kingery .40 1.00
THSO Shohei Ohtani 6.00 15.00
THSS Sixto Sanchez .75 2.00
THTS Trevor Stephan .25 .60
THTSH Travis Shaw .25 .60
THTT Trea Turner .30 .75
THTT Taylor Trammell .40 1.00
THT Turkey .40 1.00
THVGJ Vladimir Guerrero Jr. 2.50 6.00
THVR Victor Robles .60 1.50
THWA Willy Adames .30 .75
THWB Walker Buehler 1.25 3.00
THYM Yadier Molina .50 1.25
THYMO Yoan Moncada .40 1.00
THZB Zack Burdi .25 .60

2018 Topps Bowman Holiday Green Festive

*GREEN: 1.5X TO 4X BASIC
RANDOM INSERTS IN PACKS
STATED PRINT RUN 99 SER.#'d SETS
THCE Christmas Elf 3.00 8.00
THJSO Juan Soto 15.00 40.00
THSCL Santa Claus 8.00 20.00
THSO Shohei Ohtani 20.00 50.00

2018 Topps Bowman Holiday Turkey

*TURKEY: 3X TO 8X BASIC
RANDOM INSERTS IN PACKS
STATED PRINT RUN 35 SER.#'d SETS
THCE Christmas Elf 15.00 40.00
THJSO Juan Soto 30.00 80.00
THSCL Santa Claus 15.00 40.00
THSO Shohei Ohtani 40.00 100.00

2018 Topps Bowman Holiday White Snow

*WHITE SNOW: 2X TO 5X BASIC
RANDOM INSERTS IN PACKS
STATED PRINT RUN 50 SER.#'d SETS
THCE Christmas Elf 10.00 25.00
THJSO Juan Soto 20.00 50.00
THSCL Santa Claus 10.00 25.00
THSO Shohei Ohtani 25.00 60.00

2018 Topps Bowman Holiday Autographs

RANDOM INSERTS IN PACKS
PRINT RUNS B/WN 5-99 COPIES PER
NO PRICING ON QTY 10 OR LESS
*TURKEY/35: .5X TO 1.2X BASIC
THAF Alex Faedo/70 5.00 12.00
THAG Andres Gimenez/35 20.00 50.00
THAH Adam Haseley/99 5.00 12.00
THARO Amed Rosario/50 12.00 30.00
THBB Braden Bishop/99 3.00 8.00
THBM Brandon Marsh/99 8.00 20.00
THBW Brandon Woodruff/99 5.00 12.00
THCB Charcer Burks/99 3.00 8.00
THCBI Cavan Biggio/99 8.00 20.00
THCP Cristian Pache/99 25.00 60.00
THCW Colton Welker/99 3.00 8.00
THDV Daulton Varsho/99 4.00 10.00
THDW Drew Waters/99 10.00 25.00
THEDLS Enyel De Los Santos/99 4.00 10.00
THEDLS Edwin Diaz/99 8.00 20.00
THER Eddie Rosario/30 5.00 12.00
THGS Gregory Soto/99 3.00 8.00
THHC Hans Crouse/99 5.00 12.00
THJA Jo Adell/40 40.00 100.00
THJD Jeter Downs/99 5.00 12.00
THJDE Jacob deGrom/30 40.00 100.00
THJF Jack Flaherty/99 12.00 30.00
THJR Jose Ramirez/50 10.00 25.00
THJS Jesus Sanchez/99 10.00 25.00
THJSE Jean Segura/99 6.00 15.00
THJSH Jordan Sheffield/99 3.00 8.00
THKM Kevin Maitan/99 4.00 10.00
THMC Matt Chapman/30 15.00 40.00
THMH Mitch Haniger/99 4.00 10.00
THMK Mitch Keller/99 4.00 10.00
THMKO Michael Kopech/99 12.00 30.00
THNA Nick Allen/99 3.00 8.00
THNL Nicky Lopez/99 5.00 12.00
THPA Pedro Avila/99 3.00 8.00
THRH Ryan Helsley/99 4.00 10.00
THRHO Rhys Hoskins/50 20.00 50.00
THSC Sam Carlson/99 4.00 10.00
THTS Trevor Stephan/99 3.00 8.00
THTSH Travis Shaw/99 3.00 8.00
THWB Walker Buehler/99 20.00 50.00
THZB Zack Burdi/99 3.00 8.00

2016 Topps Bunt

COMPLETE SET (200) 10.00 25.00
PRINTING PLATE ODDS 1:385 HOBBY
PLATE PRINT RUN 1 SET PER COLOR
NO PLATE PRICING DUE TO SCARCITY
1 Mike Trout 1.00 2.50
2 Juan Gonzalez .12 .30
3 Ryan Braun .15 .40
4 Jose Bautista .15 .40
5 Adam Jones .15 .40
6 Jon Lester .15 .40
7 Dustin Pedroia .20 .50
8 Alex Gordon .15 .40
9 Evan Gattis .12 .30
10 Kris Bryant .25 .60
11 Aledmys Diaz RC .30 .75
12 Troy Tulowitzki .20 .50
13 Jay Bruce .15 .40
14 Wil Myers .15 .40
15 Corey Seager RC 2.00 5.00
16 Mark Teixeira .15 .40
17 Christian Yelich .25 .60
18 Ichiro Suzuki .25 .60
19 Blake Snell RC .25 .60
20 Trea Turner RC .60 1.50
21 Hanley Ramirez .15 .40
22 Dallas Keuchel .15 .40
23 Xander Bogaerts .20 .50
24 Roberto Clemente .50 1.25
25 Bryce Harper .30 .75
26 Babe Ruth .50 1.25
27 Brian Dozier .15 .40
28 Brandon Crawford .15 .40
29 Mike Piazza .20 .50
30 Tyson Ross .12 .30
31 Henry Owens RC .25 .60
32 Joe Morgan .15 .40
33 James Shields .12 .30
34 Carlos Gomez .12 .30
35 Wade Boggs .15 .40
36 Mark Trumbo .12 .30
37 Jacob deGrom .40 1.00
38 Felix Hernandez .15 .40
39 Robinson Cano .15 .40
40 Ben Zobrist .15 .40
41 Don Mattingly .40 1.00
42 Sean Doolittle .12 .30
43 Craig Kimbrel .15 .40
44 Chris Davis .12 .30
45 Steven Matz .12 .30
46 Josh Donaldson .15 .40
47 Andrew McCutchen .20 .50
48 Dwight Gooden .12 .30
49 Marcus Stroman .15 .40
50 Willie McCovey .15 .40
51 Vladimir Guerrero .15 .40
52 Starling Marte .15 .40
53 Stephen Strasburg
54 Aaron Nola RC .40 1.00
55 Johnny Cueto .15 .40
56 Manny Machado .20 .50
57 Curtis Granderson .15 .40
58 Jose Abreu .20 .50
59 Trevor Story RC 1.00 2.50
60 Adam Wainwright .15 .40
61 Jackie Robinson .20 .50
62 Starlin Castro .12 .30
63 Aroldis Chapman .20 .50
64 Adrian Beltre .20 .50
65 Paul Goldschmidt .20 .50
66 Mark McGwire .30 .75
67 Noah Syndergaard .15 .40
68 Prince Fielder .15 .40
69 Matt Harvey .15 .40
70 Gregory Polanco .15 .40
71 Jason Heyward .15 .40
72 Buster Posey .25 .60
73 Chris Archer .12 .30
74 Zack Greinke .20 .50
75 Jose Berrios RC .30 .75
76 Rod Carew .15 .40
77 Russell Martin .12 .30
78 Brandon Belt .15 .40
79 Sonny Gray .15 .40
80 Michael Brantley .15 .40
81 Shin-Soo Choo .15 .40
82 Matt Kemp .15 .40
83 Roger Clemens .25 .60
84 Clayton Kershaw .30 .75
85 Ian Kinsler .15 .40
86 Jose Altuve .15 .40
87 Miguel Cabrera .20 .50
88 Cole Hamels .15 .40
89 J.D. Martinez .20 .50
90 Carlton Fisk .15 .40
91 Kyle Schwarber RC .60 1.50
92 Adrian Gonzalez .15 .40
93 Elvis Andrus .15 .40
94 Jonathan Lucroy .15 .40
95 Darryl Strawberry .12 .30
96 Miguel Sano RC .30 .75
97 Mike Moustakas .15 .40
98 Dee Gordon .12 .30
99 Jason Kipnis .15 .40
100 Joey Votto .20 .50
101 Eric Hosmer .15 .40
102 Luis Severino RC .25 .60
103 George Brett .40 1.00
104 Masahiro Tanaka .15 .40
105 Willie Mays .40 1.00
106 Anthony Rizzo .25 .60
107 Michael Wacha .15 .40
108 Brian McCann .15 .40
109 Maikel Franco .15 .40
110 Yordano Ventura .15 .40
111 Carlos Gonzalez .15 .40
112 Alex Rodriguez .25 .60
113 Justin Verlander .20 .50
114 Brooks Robinson .15 .40
115 Giancarlo Stanton .20 .50
116 Nolan Arenado .30 .75
117 Nolan Ryan .60 1.50
118 Reggie Jackson .15 .40
119 Nelson Cruz .20 .50
120 Julio Urias RC .60 1.50
121 Josh Reddick .12 .30
122 Gerrit Cole .20 .50
123 Ryne Sandberg .40 1.00
124 Todd Frazier .12 .30
125 Hunter Pence .15 .40
126 Max Scherzer .20 .50
127 Brandon Phillips .12 .30
128 David Price .15 .40
129 Ted Williams .40 1.00
130 Charlie Blackmon .20 .50
131 Salvador Perez .15 .40
132 George Springer .15 .40
133 Stephen Piscotty RC .30 .75
134 Peter O'Brien RC .20 .50
135 Randy Johnson .20 .50
136 Albert Pujols .25 .60
137 Danny Salazar .15 .40
138 Nomar Garciaparra .15 .40
139 Stan Musial .30 .75
140 DJ LeMahieu .20 .50
141 Jon Gray RC .20 .50
142 Kolten Wong .15 .40
143 Michael Conforto RC .25 .60
144 Yasiel Puig .20 .50
145 Joc Pederson .15 .40
146 John Smoltz .20 .50
147 Carlos Rodon .20 .50
148 Bo Jackson .20 .50
149 Rougned Odor .15 .40
150 Jeremy Hazelbaker RC .25 .60
151 Jose Reyes .15 .40
152 Ryan Zimmerman .15 .40
153 Yoenis Cespedes .20 .50
154 Byung-Ho Park RC .25 .60
155 Jung Ho Kang .12 .30
156 Addison Russell .20 .50
157 Carlos Correa .20 .50
158 Billy Hamilton .15 .40
159 Yu Darvish .20 .50
160 Corey Kluber .15 .40
161 Carlos Carrasco .12 .30
162 Cal Ripken Jr. .60 1.50
163 Chris Sale .20 .50
164 Michael Pineda .12 .30
165 Jose Fernandez .20 .50
166 Carl Yastrzemski .30 .75
167 Byron Buxton .20 .50
168 Kyle Seager .12 .30
169 Greg Maddux .25 .60
170 Matt Carpenter .20 .50
171 Jose Peraza RC .25 .60
172 Edwin Encarnacion .20 .50
173 Jacoby Ellsbury .15 .40
174 Barry Larkin .15 .40
175 Sandy Koufax .40 1.00
176 Kenta Maeda RC .40 1.00
177 David Ortiz .20 .50
178 David Wright .15 .40
179 Jose Canseco .15 .40
180 Robin Yount .20 .50
181 Matt Duffy .12 .30
182 Chipper Jones .20 .50
183 Nomar Mazara RC .30 .75
184 Frank Thomas .20 .50
185 Johnny Bench .20 .50
186 Freddie Freeman .25 .60
187 Ozzie Smith .25 .60
188 Ivan Rodriguez .15 .40
189 Lorenzo Cain .12 .30
190 Justin Upton .15 .40
191 Anthony Rendon .20 .50
192 Hank Aaron .40 1.00
193 Mookie Betts .40 1.00
194 Andre Dawson .15 .40
195 Ken Griffey Jr. .40 1.00
196 Jean Segura .15 .40
197 Evan Longoria .15 .40
198 Madison Bumgarner .15 .40
199 Francisco Lindor .20 .50
200 Jake Arrieta .15 .40

2016 Topps Bunt Platinum

*PLTNM VET: 5X TO 12X BASIC VET
*PLTNM RC: 3X TO 8X BASIC RC
STATED ODDS 1:53 HOBBY
STATED PRINT RUN 99 SER.#'d SETS

2016 Topps Bunt Topaz

*TOPAZ VET: 6X TO 15X BASIC VET
*TOPAZ RC: 4X TO 10X BASIC RC
STATED ODDS 1:53 HOBBY
STATED PRINT RUN 50 SER.#'d SETS

2016 Topps Bunt Future of the Franchise

COMPLETE SET (15) 5.00 12.00
STATED ODDS 1:14 HOBBY
FF1 Kenta Maeda .40 1.00
FF2 Byung-Ho Park .40 1.00
FF3 Stephen Piscotty .50 1.25
FF4 Trea Turner 1.00 2.50
FF5 Kyle Schwarber 1.00 2.50
FF6 Miguel Sano .50 1.25
FF7 Luis Severino .40 1.00
FF8 Michael Conforto .40 1.00
FF9 Corey Seager 3.00 8.00
FF10 Ketel Marte .60 1.50
FF11 Jon Gray .30 .75
FF12 Peter O'Brien .30 .75
FF13 Aaron Nola .60 1.50
FF14 Hector Olivera .40 1.00
FF15 Jose Peraza .40 1.00

2016 Topps Bunt Light Force

COMPLETE SET (25) 4.00 10.00
STATED ODDS 1:8 HOBBY
LF1 Jose Altuve .25 .60
LF2 Jake Arrieta .25 .60
LF3 Johnny Bench .30 .75
LF4 Dellin Betances .25 .60
LF5 George Brett .60 1.50
LF6 Kris Bryant .40 1.00
LF7 Lorenzo Cain .20 .50
LF8 Luis Gonzalez .25 .60
LF9 Dwight Gooden .20 .50
LF10 Alex Gordon .25 .60
LF11 Matt Harvey .25 .60
LF12 Rickey Henderson .30 .75
LF13 Eric Hosmer .25 .60
LF14 Bo Jackson .30 .75
LF15 Randy Johnson .30 .75
LF16 Sandy Koufax .60 1.50
LF17 Edgar Martinez .25 .60
LF18 Don Mattingly .60 1.50
LF19 Buster Posey .40 1.00
LF20 Anthony Rizzo .40 1.00
LF21 Jackie Robinson .30 .75
LF22 Nolan Ryan 1.00 2.50
LF23 Willie Stargell .25 .60
LF24 Noah Syndergaard .25 .60
LF25 Bernie Williams .25 .60

2016 Topps Bunt Moon Shots

STATED ODDS 1:837 HOBBY
STATED PRINT RUN 50 SER.#'d SETS
MS1 Reggie Jackson 8.00 20.00
MS2 Hank Aaron 12.00 30.00
MS3 Frank Thomas 10.00 25.00
MS4 Edwin Encarnacion 10.00 25.00
MS5 Alex Rodriguez 12.00 30.00
MS6 Manny Machado 10.00 25.00
MS7 David Ortiz 10.00 25.00
MS8 Jayson Werth 8.00 20.00
MS9 Jay Bruce 8.00 20.00
MS10 Miguel Cabrera 10.00 25.00
MS11 Anthony Rizzo 12.00 30.00
MS12 Willie Stargell 8.00 20.00
MS13 Ken Griffey Jr. 12.00 30.00
MS14 Nolan Arenado 15.00 40.00
MS15 Carlos Gonzalez 8.00 20.00
MS16 Joc Pederson 8.00 20.00
MS17 Ryan Howard 12.00 30.00
MS18 Jose Abreu 10.00 25.00
MS19 J.D. Martinez 10.00 25.00
MS20 Yoenis Cespedes 10.00 25.00
MS21 Juan Gonzalez 6.00 15.00
MS22 Mark McGwire 12.00 30.00
MS23 Harmon Killebrew 10.00 25.00
MS24 Vladimir Guerrero 8.00 20.00
MS25 Eddie Murray 10.00 25.00

2016 Topps Bunt Programs

COMPLETE SET (30) 4.00 10.00
STATED ODDS 1:7 HOBBY
P1 Eric Hosmer .25 .60
P2 Jonathan Lucroy .25 .60
P3 Chris Davis .20 .50
P4 Yoenis Cespedes .30 .75
P5 Alex Rodriguez .40 1.00
P6 Andrew McCutchen .30 .75
P7 Kris Bryant .40 1.00
P8 Robinson Cano .25 .60
P9 Yu Darvish .30 .75
P10 Albert Pujols .40 1.00
P11 Jose Altuve .25 .60
P12 David Ortiz .30 .75
P13 Sonny Gray .25 .60
P14 Kevin Kiermaier .25 .60
P15 Marcus Stroman .25 .60
P16 Adam Wainwright .25 .60
P17 Clayton Kershaw .50 1.25
P18 Buster Posey .40 1.00
P19 Justin Verlander .30 .75
P20 Freddie Freeman .40 1.00
P21 Ryan Howard .25 .60
P22 Chris Sale .30 .75
P23 Joey Votto .30 .75
P24 James Shields .20 .50
P25 Joe Mauer .25 .60
P26 Giancarlo Stanton .30 .75
P27 Bryce Harper .50 1.25
P28 Paul Goldschmidt .30 .75
P29 Corey Kluber .25 .60
P30 Carlos Gonzalez .25 .60

2016 Topps Bunt Stadium Heritage

STATED ODDS 1:2798 HOBBY
STATED PRINT RUN 25 SER.#'d SETS
SH1 Tom Seaver 20.00 50.00
SH2 Cal Ripken Jr. 25.00 60.00
SH3 Carl Yastrzemski 20.00 50.00
SH4 Johnny Bench 12.00 30.00
SH5 Jackie Robinson 12.00 30.00
SH6 Lou Gehrig 25.00 60.00
SH7 Nolan Ryan 25.00 60.00
SH8 Roberto Clemente 25.00 60.00
SH9 Ozzie Smith 15.00 40.00
SH10 Fergie Jenkins 10.00 25.00
SH11 Enos Slaughter 10.00 25.00
SH12 Ralph Kiner 10.00 25.00
SH13 Gary Carter 10.00 25.00
SH14 Brooks Robinson 10.00 25.00
SH15 Roberto Alomar 10.00 25.00

2016 Topps Bunt Title Town

STATED ODDS 1:1399 HOBBY
STATED PRINT RUN 75 SER.#'d SETS
*AMBER/50: .4X TO 1X BASIC
TT1 Ruth/Williams/Ford 25.00 60.00
TT2 Pujols/Slaughter/Smith 15.00 40.00
TT3 McGwre/Jcksn/Fngrs 20.00 50.00
TT4 Bmgrnr/Posey/Irvin 20.00 50.00
TT5 Schilling/Ortiz/Ruth 25.00 60.00
TT6 Koufax/Garvey/Snider 20.00 50.00
TT7 Larkin/Bench/Perez 15.00 40.00
TT8 Strgll/Clmnte/Mzrski 20.00 50.00
TT9 Klne/Andrsn/Nwhsr 20.00 50.00
TT10 Rpkn Jr./Rbnsn/Plmr 25.00 60.00

2016 Topps Bunt Unique Unis

COMPLETE SET (10) 2.00 5.00
STATED ODDS 1:7 HOBBY
UU1 Nomar Garciaparra .25 .60
UU2 Randy Johnson .30 .75
UU3 Shin-Soo Choo .25 .60
UU4 Carlos Rodon .30 .75
UU5 Ken Griffey Jr. .60 1.50
UU6 Alex Gordon .25 .60
UU7 J.D. Martinez .30 .75
UU8 Marcell Ozuna .30 .75
UU9 Robinson Cano .25 .60
UU10 Mike Trout 1.50 4.00

2017 Topps Bunt

COMPLETE SET (200) 10.00 25.00
PLATE PRINT RUN 1 SET PER COLOR
NO PLATE PRICING DUE TO SCARCITY
1 Clayton Kershaw .30 .75
2 Mike Trout 1.00 2.50
3 Andrew McCutchen .20 .50
4 Alex Bregman RC 1.00 2.50
5 Yoan Moncada RC .60 1.50
6 Dansby Swanson RC .50 1.25
7 Tyler Glasnow RC .75 2.00
8 Jake Thompson RC .20 .50
9 Orlando Arcia RC .30 .75
10 Joe Musgrove RC .60 1.50
11 Andrew Benintendi RC .60 1.50
12 Matt Strahm RC .20 .50
12 Raimel Tapia RC .25 .60
13 David Dahl RC .25 .60
14 Braden Shipley RC .20 .50
15 Reynaldo Lopez RC .20 .50
16 Carson Fulmer RC .20 .50
17 Ryon Healy RC .25 .60
18 Teoscar Hernandez RC .75 2.00
19 Luke Weaver RC .25 .60
20 Aaron Judge RC 2.50 6.00
21 Tyler Austin RC .25 .60
22 Jeff Hoffman RC .20 .50
23 Yulieski Gurriel RC .30 .75
24 Robert Gsellman RC .20 .50
25 JaCoby Jones RC .25 .60
27 Bryce Harper .30 .75
28 Giancarlo Stanton .20 .50
29 Corey Seager .20 .50
30 Kris Bryant .25 .60
31 Paul Goldschmidt .20 .50
32 Freddie Freeman .25 .60
33 Chris Davis .12 .30
34 Zach Britton .15 .40
35 Mookie Betts .40 1.00
36 Xander Bogaerts .20 .50
37 Craig Kimbrel .15 .40
38 Dustin Pedroia .20 .50
39 Jackie Bradley Jr. .20 .50
40 Kyle Schwarber .20 .50
41 Jason Heyward .15 .40
42 Ben Zobrist .15 .40
43 Addison Russell .20 .50
44 Chris Sale .20 .50
45 Joey Votto .20 .50
46 Danny Salazar .15 .40
47 Francisco Lindor .20 .50
48 Manny Margot RC .20 .50
49 Trevor Story .20 .50
50 Charlie Blackmon .20 .50
51 Chris Archer .12 .30
52 Miguel Cabrera .20 .50
53 Justin Upton .15 .40
54 Dallas Keuchel .15 .40
55 Lance McCullers .12 .30
56 Lorenzo Cain .12 .30
57 Kendrys Morales .12 .30
58 Adrian Gonzalez .15 .40
59 Justin Turner .20 .50
60 Marcell Ozuna .20 .50
61 Ryan Braun .15 .40
62 Jonathan Villar .12 .30
63 Miguel Sano .15 .40
64 Byron Buxton .20 .50
65 Jacob deGrom .40 1.00
66 Matt Harvey .15 .40
67 David Wright .15 .40
68 Jacoby Ellsbury .15 .40
69 Masahiro Tanaka .15 .40
70 Brian McCann .15 .40
71 Dellin Betances .15 .40
72 Sonny Gray .15 .40
73 Sean Doolittle .12 .30
74 Aaron Nola .15 .40
75 Starling Marte .15 .40
76 Gregory Polanco .15 .40
77 Jameson Taillon .15 .40
78 Nelson Cruz .20 .50
79 Felix Hernandez .15 .40
80 Jon Gray .12 .30
81 Johnny Cueto .15 .40
82 Brandon Belt .15 .40
83 Brandon Crawford .15 .40
84 Matt Moore .15 .40
85 Aledmys Diaz .15 .40
86 Adam Wainwright .15 .40
87 Randal Grichuk .12 .30
88 Stephen Piscotty .15 .40
89 Drew Smyly .12 .30
90 Adrian Beltre .20 .50
91 Jonathan Lucroy .15 .40
92 Tanner Roark .12 .30
93 Nomar Mazara .12 .30
94 Jose Bautista .15 .40
95 Troy Tulowitzki .20 .50
96 Marcus Stroman .15 .40
97 Stephen Strasburg .20 .50
98 Daniel Murphy .15 .40
99 Ryan Zimmerman .15 .40
100 David Ortiz .20 .50
101 Gary Sanchez .20 .50
102 Jake Lamb .15 .40
103 Jean Segura .15 .40
104 Adam Duvall .15 .40
105 Rick Porcello .15 .40
106 Albert Pujols .25 .60
107 A.J. Pollock .12 .30
108 Robbie Ray .12 .30
109 Zack Greinke .20 .50
110 Matt Kemp .15 .40
111 Adam Jones .15 .40
112 Manny Machado .20 .50
113 Mark Trumbo .12 .30
114 David Price .15 .40
115 Hanley Ramirez .15 .40
116 Anthony Rizzo .25 .60
117 Aroldis Chapman .20 .50
118 Dexter Fowler .15 .40
119 Jake Arrieta .15 .40
120 Javier Baez .25 .60
121 Jon Lester .15 .40
122 Kyle Hendricks .20 .50
123 Willson Contreras .20 .50
124 James Shields .12 .30
125 Jose Abreu .20 .50
126 Todd Frazier .12 .30
127 Billy Hamilton .15 .40
128 Brandon Phillips .12 .30
129 Andrew Miller .15 .40
130 Corey Kluber .15 .40
131 Jason Kipnis .15 .40
132 Carlos Gonzalez .15 .40
133 Nolan Arenado .30 .75
134 Ian Kinsler .15 .40
135 J.D. Martinez .20 .50
136 Justin Verlander .20 .50
137 Michael Fulmer .12 .30
138 Victor Martinez .15 .40
139 George Springer .15 .40
140 Jose Altuve .15 .40
141 Alex Gordon .15 .40
142 Danny Duffy .12 .30
143 Eric Hosmer .15 .40
144 Salvador Perez .15 .40
145 Julio Urias .20 .50
146 Kenley Jansen .15 .40
147 Kenta Maeda .15 .40
148 Christian Yelich .25 .60
149 Dee Gordon .12 .30
150 Ichiro .25 .60
151 Brian Dozier .20 .50
152 Joe Mauer .15 .40
153 Bartolo Colon .12 .30
154 Curtis Granderson .15 .40
155 Noah Syndergaard .15 .40
156 Yoenis Cespedes .20 .50
157 Jay Bruce .15 .40
158 Jose Reyes .15 .40
159 Brett Gardner .15 .40
160 Khris Davis .20 .50
161 Maikel Franco .15 .40
162 Tommy Joseph .20 .50
163 Gerrit Cole .20 .50
164 Ryan Schimpf .12 .30
165 Wil Myers .15 .40
166 Buster Posey .25 .60
167 Hunter Pence .15 .40
168 Kyle Seager .12 .30
169 Robinson Cano .15 .40
170 Carlos Martinez .15 .40
171 Yadier Molina .25 .60
172 Matt Carpenter .20 .50
173 Seung-Hwan Oh RC .40 1.00
174 Evan Longoria .15 .40
175 Cole Hamels .15 .40
176 Ian Desmond .12 .30
177 Rougned Odor .15 .40
178 Yu Darvish .20 .50
179 Aaron Sanchez .15 .40
180 Edwin Encarnacion .20 .50
181 Josh Donaldson .15 .40
182 Lucas Giolito .15 .40
183 Max Scherzer .20 .50
184 Trea Turner .15 .40
185 Carlos Rodon .20 .50
186 Tim Anderson .20 .50
187 Adam Eaton .20 .50
188 Anthony DeSclafani .12 .30
189 Brandon Finnegan .12 .30
190 Carlos Carrasco .12 .30
191 Carlos Santana .15 .40
192 Cameron Maybin .12 .30
193 Carlos Correa .20 .50
194 Mike Moustakas .15 .40
195 Jorge Alfaro RC .25 .60
196 Gavin Cecchini RC .20 .50
197 Sean Manaea .12 .30
198 Josh Bell RC .50 1.25
199 Jharel Cotton RC .20 .50
200 Alex Reyes RC .25 .60

2017 Topps Bunt Green

*GREEN: 3X TO 8X BASIC
*GREEN RC: 2X TO 5X BASIC RC
STATED PRINT RUN 99 SER.#'d SETS
20 Aaron Judge 10.00 25.00

2017 Topps Bunt Orange

*ORANGE: 5X TO 12X BASIC
*ORANGE RC: 3X TO 8X BASIC RC
STATED PRINT RUN 50 SER.#'d SETS
20 Aaron Judge 15.00 40.00

2017 Topps Bunt Purple

*PURPLE: 8X TO 20X BASIC
*PURPLE RC: 5X TO 12X BASIC RC
STATED PRINT RUN 25 SER.#'d SETS
20 Aaron Judge 25.00 60.00

2017 Topps Bunt Black

*BLACK: 3X TO 8X BASIC
*BLACK RC: 2X TO 5X BASIC RC
2 Mike Trout 8.00 20.00
30 Kris Bryant 8.00 20.00

2017 Topps Bunt Blue

COMPLETE SET (200) 20.00 50.00
*BLUE: 1X TO 2.5X BASIC
*BLUE RC: .6X TO 1.5X BASIC RC

2017 Topps Bunt Autographs

PRINT RUNS B/WN 5-30 COPIES PER
NO PRICING ON QTY 10 OR LESS
AUAB Andrew Benintendi/25 150.00 300.00
AUAD Aledmys Diaz/30 15.00 40.00
AUAJU Aaron Judge/30 100.00 250.00
AUAR Alex Reyes/30 12.00 30.00
AUCC Carlos Correa/15 60.00 150.00
AUDB Dellin Betances/30 12.00 30.00
AUDS Dansby Swanson/25 25.00 60.00
AUGS George Springer/20 20.00 50.00
AUJA Jose Altuve/20 30.00 80.00
AUSMA Steven Matz/30 12.00 30.00
AUTG Tyler Glasnow/30 15.00 40.00
AUTT Trea Turner/30 30.00 80.00
AUYG Yulieski Gurriel/25 20.00 50.00

2017 Topps Bunt Galaxy

STATED PRINT RUN 99 SER.#'d SETS
*ORANGE/50: .5X TO 1.2X BASIC
*BLUE/25: 1.2X TO 3X BASIC
GBH Bryce Harper 10.00 25.00
GEA Elvis Andrus 5.00 12.00
GGC Gerrit Cole 6.00 15.00
GJA Jose Abreu 6.00 15.00
GJAL Jose Altuve 5.00 12.00
GJAR Jake Arrieta 5.00 12.00
GJC Johnny Cueto 5.00 12.00
GJS Jean Segura 5.00 12.00
GJV Justin Verlander 6.00 15.00
GME Marco Estrada 4.00 10.00
GRB Ryan Braun 5.00 12.00
GRC Roberto Clemente 15.00 40.00
GRM Roger Maris 6.00 15.00
GYM Yoan Moncada 12.00 30.00
GYMO Yadier Molina 8.00 20.00

2017 Topps Bunt Infinite

COMPLETE SET (30) 5.00 12.00
PLATE PRINT RUN 1 SET PER COLOR
NO PLATE PRICING DUE TO SCARCITY
*GREEN/99: 2X TO 5X BASIC
*ORANGE/50: 2.5X TO 6X BASIC
*PURPLE/25: 5X TO 12X BASIC
IAM Andrew McCutchen .40 1.00
IAMI Andrew Miller .30 .75
IAR Anthony Rizzo .50 1.25
ICK Clayton Kershaw .60 1.50
IDG Dwight Gooden .25 .60
IDK Dallas Keuchel .30 .75
IDM Daniel Murphy .30 .75
IDP Drew Pomeranz .30 .75
IGG Goose Gossage .30 .75
IGS George Springer .30 .75
IJA Jose Abreu .40 1.00
IJAL Jose Altuve .30 .75
IJD Jacob deGrom .75 2.00
IJH J.A. Happ .30 .75
IJR Jose Ramirez .30 .75
IJRE J.T. Realmuto .40 1.00
IKB Kris Bryant .50 1.25
IKM Kenta Maeda .30 .75
IMB Mookie Betts .75 2.00
IMF Michael Fulmer .25 .60
IMT Mike Trout 2.00 5.00
INC Nelson Cruz .40 1.00
INS Noah Syndergaard .30 .75
IOH Odubel Herrera .30 .75
IRC Robinson Cano .30 .75
ISM Starling Marte .30 .75
ITF Todd Frazier .25 .60
ITT Trea Turner .30 .75
ITTU Troy Tulowitzki .40 1.00
IWF Whitey Ford .30 .75

2017 Topps Bunt Perspectives

COMPLETE SET (20) 5.00 12.00
PLATE PRINT RUN 1 SET PER COLOR
NO PLATE PRICING DUE TO SCARCITY
*GREEN/99: 2X TO 5X BASIC
*ORANGE/50: 2.5X TO 6X BASIC
*PURPLE/25: 5X TO 12X BASIC
PCA Chris Archer .25 .60
PCC Carlos Correa .40 1.00
PCR Cal Ripken Jr. 1.25 3.00
PCS Corey Seager .40 1.00
PED Edwin Diaz .30 .75
PGG Gary Carter .30 .75
PJL John Lackey .30 .75
PJLE Jon Lester .30 .75
PJQ Jose Quintana .25 .60
PMC Miguel Cabrera .40 1.00
PMP Martin Prado .25 .60
PMS Max Scherzer .40 1.00
PMT Mike Trout 2.00 5.00
PNS Noah Syndergaard .30 .75
PRC Robinson Cano .30 .75
PRK Ralph Kiner .30 .75
PRY Robin Yount .40 1.00
PTW Ted Williams .75 2.00
PXB Xander Bogaerts .40 1.00
PYC Yoenis Cespedes .40 1.00

2017 Topps Bunt Programs

COMPLETE SET (30) 6.00 15.00
PLATE PRINT RUN 1 SET PER COLOR
NO PLATE PRICING DUE TO SCARCITY
*GREEN/99: 2X TO 5X BASIC
*ORANGE/50: 2.5X TO 6X BASIC
*PURPLE/25: 5X TO 12X BASIC
PRAC Aroldis Chapman .40 1.00
PRAD Aledmys Diaz .30 .75
PRADU Adam Duvall .30 .75
PRAW Adam Wainwright .30 .75
PRBB Brandon Belt .30 .75
PRBC Bartolo Colon .25 .60
PRCC Carlos Correa .40 1.00
PRCK Clayton Kershaw .60 1.50
PRCY Christian Yelich .50 1.25
PRGB George Brett .75 2.00
PRGG Goose Gossage .30 .75
PRIK Ian Kinsler .30 .75
PRJB Jackie Bradley Jr. .40 1.00
PRJC Johnny Cueto .30 .75
PRJD Josh Donaldson .30 .75
PRJK Jason Kipnis .30 .75
PRJR Jackie Robinson .40 1.00
PRJT Julio Teheran .30 .75
PRJV Jonathan Villar .25 .60
PRKB Kris Bryant .50 1.25
PRKH Kyle Hendricks .40 1.00
PRKJ Kenley Jansen .30 .75
PRMO Marcell Ozuna .40 1.00
PRMS Marcus Stroman .30 .75
PRMW Matt Wieters .40 1.00
PROS Ozzie Smith .50 1.25
PRPN Phil Niekro .30 .75
PRRP Rick Porcello .30 .75
PRRS Ryan Schimpf .25 .60
PRTT Troy Tulowitzki .40 1.00

2017 Topps Bunt Splatter Art

STATED PRINT RUN 99 SER.#'d SETS
PLATE PRINT RUN 1 SET PER COLOR
NO PLATE PRICING DUE TO SCARCITY
*ORANGE/50: .5X TO 1.2X BASIC
*PURPLE/25: 1.2X TO 3X BASIC
SPAB Adrian Beltre 6.00 15.00
SPAS Aaron Sanchez 5.00 12.00
SPCB Charlie Blackmon 6.00 15.00
SPCK Corey Kluber 5.00 12.00
SPDG Dee Gordon 4.00 10.00
SPDK Dallas Keuchel 5.00 12.00
SPJB Javier Baez 8.00 20.00
SPJM J.D. Martinez 6.00 15.00
SPJMA Joe Mauer 5.00 12.00
SPJP Joc Pederson 5.00 12.00
SPJT Julio Teheran 5.00 12.00
SPLC Lorenzo Cain 4.00 10.00
SPMB Mookie Betts 12.00 30.00
SPMH Matt Harvey 5.00 12.00
SPMM Manny Machado 6.00 15.00
SPRH Rickey Henderson 6.00 15.00
SPSG Sonny Gray 5.00 12.00
SPTR Tanner Roark 4.00 10.00
SPYE Yunel Escobar 4.00 10.00
SPZG Zack Greinke 6.00 15.00

2017 Topps Bunt Vapor

STATED PRINT RUN 99 SER.#'d SETS
*ORANGE/50: .5X TO 1.2X BASIC
*BLUE/25: 1X TO 2.5X BASIC
VCD Chris Davis 5.00 12.00
VCG Carlos Gonzalez 6.00 15.00
VCS Chris Sale 8.00 20.00
VDP Dustin Pedroia 8.00 20.00
VGS Giancarlo Stanton 8.00 20.00
VJB Jose Bautista 6.00 15.00
VJBE Johnny Bench 8.00 20.00
VJU Justin Upton 6.00 15.00
VKB Kris Bryant 10.00 25.00
VMP Mike Piazza 8.00 20.00
VMT Masahiro Tanaka 6.00 15.00
VNG Nomar Garciaparra 6.00 15.00
VRJ Randy Johnson 8.00 20.00
VWF Whitey Ford 6.00 15.00
VWR Wilson Ramos 5.00 12.00

2013 Topps Chipz

AB Andrew Bailey .50 1.25
ABE Adrian Beltre .75 2.00
AC Aroldis Chapman .75 2.00
AD Adam Dunn .60 1.50
AJ Austin Jackson .50 1.25
AJO Adam Jones .60 1.50
AM Andrew McCutchen .75 2.00
AP Angel Pagan .50 1.25
APU Albert Pujols 1.00 2.50
AR Alexei Ramirez .60 1.50
ARO Alex Rodriguez 1.00 2.50
BB Billy Butler .50 1.25
BH Bryce Harper 1.25 3.00
BL Brett Lawrie .60 1.50
BM Brian McCann .60 1.50
BP Brandon Phillips .50 1.25
BPO Buster Posey 1.00 2.50
BU B.J. Upton .60 1.50
BZ Ben Zobrist .60 1.50
CB Carlos Beltran .60 1.50
CBU Clay Buchholz .50 1.25
CG Carlos Gonzalez .60 1.50
CGR Curtis Granderson .60 1.50
CH Cole Hamels .60 1.50
CJ Chipper Jones .75 2.00
CK Clayton Kershaw 1.25 3.00
CKI Craig Kimbrel .60 1.50
CL Cliff Lee .60 1.50
CR Colby Rasmus .60 1.50
CS CC Sabathia .60 1.50
DF David Freese .50 1.25
DJ Derek Jeter 2.00 5.00
DO David Ortiz .75 2.00
DP Dustin Pedroia .75 2.00
DPR David Price .60 1.50
DU Dan Uggla .50 1.25
DW David Wright .60 1.50
EA Elvis Andrus .60 1.50
EH Eric Hosmer .60 1.50
EL Evan Longoria .60 1.50
FH Felix Hernandez .60 1.50
GG Gio Gonzalez .60 1.50
GS Giancarlo Stanton .75 2.00
HS Huston Street .50 1.25
IK Ian Kinsler .60 1.50
JA J.P. Arencibia .50 1.25
JAX John Axford .50 1.25
JB Jose Bautista .60 1.50
JBR Jay Bruce .60 1.50
JD John Danks .50 1.25
JE Jacoby Ellsbury .60 1.50
JH Josh Hamilton .60 1.50
JHA Joel Hanrahan .50 1.25
JHR J.J. Hardy .50 1.25
JK Jason Kipnis .60 1.50
JL Jon Lester .60 1.50
JM Joe Mauer .60 1.50
JMO Jason Motte .50 1.25
JP Jonathan Papelbon .60 1.50
JR Josh Reddick .50 1.25
JRE Jose Reyes .60 1.50
JRO Jimmy Rollins .60 1.50
JS Johan Santana .60 1.50
JSH James Shields .50 1.25
JU Justin Upton .60 1.50
JV Justin Verlander .75 2.00
JVO Joey Votto .75 2.00
JW Jered Weaver .60 1.50
MB Michael Bourn .50 1.25
MBU Madison Bumgarner .60 1.50
MC Miguel Cabrera .75 2.00
MCA Melky Cabrera .50 1.25
MCI Matt Cain .60 1.50
MK Matt Kemp .60 1.50
MM Michael Morse .50 1.25
MN Mike Napoli .50 1.25
MT Mark Teixeira .60 1.50
MTR Mike Trout 6.00 15.00
MTU Mark Trumbo .50 1.25
MY Michael Young .50 1.25
NC Nelson Cruz .75 2.00
NF Neftali Feliz .50 1.25
NS Nick Swisher .60 1.50
PA Pedro Alvarez .50 1.25
PF Prince Fielder .60 1.50
PG Paul Goldschmidt .75 2.00
PK Paul Konerko .60 1.50
PS Pablo Sandoval .60 1.50
RB Ryan Braun .60 1.50
RC Robinson Cano .60 1.50
RD R.A. Dickey .60 1.50
RH Roy Halladay .60 1.50
RW Rickie Weeks .50 1.25
RZ Ryan Zimmerman .60 1.50
SC Starlin Castro .50 1.25
SS Stephen Strasburg .75 2.00
TL Tim Lincecum .60 1.50
YC Yoenis Cespedes .75 2.00
YD Yu Darvish .75 2.00
YM Yadier Molina 1.00 2.50

2013 Topps Chipz Glow in the Dark

*GLOW: .5X TO 1.2X BASIC

2013 Topps Chipz Magnets

*MAGNETS: .5X TO 1.2X BASIC

2013 Topps Chipz Gold

*GOLD: .75X TO 2X BASIC

2013 Topps Chipz Silver

*SILVER: .6X TO 1.5X BASIC

2013 Topps Chipz Autographs

STATED PRINT RUN 25 SER.#'d SETS
NO PRICING ON MOST DUE TO LACK OF INFO
BP Buster Posey
DF David Freese
DP Dustin Pedroia
DW David Wright 60.00 120.00
JB Jose Bautista
MT Mark Trumbo
PF Prince Fielder
PG Paul Goldschmidt 40.00 80.00
RD R.A. Dickey 30.00 60.00
SM Starling Marte

2013 Topps Chipz Relics

STATED PRINT RUN 50 SER.#'d SETS
NO PRICING ON MOST DUE TO LACK OF INFO
AJ Adam Jones 30.00 60.00
BR Brooks Robinson
DU Dan Uggla
EA Elvis Andrus
EL Evan Longoria
IK Ian Kinsler
JB Jay Bruce
MK Matt Kemp
PS Pablo Sandoval 20.00 50.00
TG Tony Gwynn 30.00 60.00

2014 Topps Chipz

COMPLETE SET (102)
1 Yonder Alonso .40 1.00
2 Jose Altuve .50 1.25
3 Pedro Alvarez .40 1.00
4 Madison Bumgarner .50 1.25
5 Jose Bautista .50 1.25
6 Adrian Beltre .60 1.50
7 Xander Bogaerts 1.25 3.00
8 Ryan Braun .50 1.25
9 Domonic Brown .50 1.25
10 Clay Buchholz .40 1.00
11 Miguel Cabrera .60 1.50
12 Matt Cain .50 1.25
13 Robinson Cano .50 1.25
14 Matt Carpenter .60 1.50
15 Jason Castro .40 1.00
16 Yoenis Cespedes .60 1.50
17 Aroldis Chapman .60 1.50
18 Gerrit Cole .60 1.50
19 Bartolo Colon .40 1.00
20 Patrick Corbin .50 1.25
21 Allen Craig .50 1.25
22 Travis d'Arnaud .50 1.25
23 Yu Darvish .60 1.50
24 Chris Davis .40 1.00
25 Edwin Encarnacion .60 1.50
26 Jose Fernandez .60 1.50
27 Prince Fielder .50 1.25
28 David Freese .40 1.00
29 Evan Gattis .40 1.00
30 Paul Goldschmidt .60 1.50
31 Carlos Gomez .40 1.00
32 Carlos Gonzalez .50 1.25
33 Adrian Gonzalez .50 1.25
34 Alex Gordon .50 1.25
35 Zack Greinke .60 1.50
36 Jason Grilli .40 1.00
37 Roy Halladay .50 1.25
38 Cole Hamels .50 1.25
39 Josh Hamilton .50 1.25
40 J.J. Hardy .40 1.00
41 Bryce Harper 1.00 2.50
42 Matt Harvey .50 1.25
43 Felix Hernandez .50 1.25
44 Eric Hosmer .50 1.25
45 Ryan Howard .50 1.25
46 Torii Hunter .40 1.00
47 Hisashi Iwakuma .50 1.25
48 Derek Jeter 1.50 4.00
49 Adam Jones .50 1.25
50 Matt Kemp .50 1.25
51 Clayton Kershaw 1.00 2.50
52 Craig Kimbrel .50 1.25
53 Ian Kinsler .50 1.25
54 Jason Kipnis .50 1.25
55 Mat Latos .50 1.25
56 Cliff Lee .50 1.25
57 Evan Longoria .50 1.25
58 Manny Machado .60 1.50
59 Justin Masterson .40 1.00
60 Joe Mauer .50 1.25
61 Andrew McCutchen .60 1.50
62 Shelby Miller .50 1.25
63 Yadier Molina .75 2.00
64 Matt Moore .50 1.25
65 Wil Myers .40 1.00
66 David Ortiz .60 1.50
67 Jake Peavy .40 1.00
68 Dustin Pedroia .60 1.50
69 Salvador Perez .50 1.25
70 Andy Pettitte .50 1.25
71 Brandon Phillips .40 1.00
72 Buster Posey .75 2.00
73 David Price .50 1.25
74 Jurickson Profar .50 1.25
75 Yasiel Puig .60 1.50
76 Albert Pujols .75 2.00
77 Hanley Ramirez .50 1.25
78 Jose Reyes .50 1.25
79 Mariano Rivera .75 2.00
80 Anthony Rizzo .75 2.00
81 Hyun-Jin Ryu .50 1.25
82 CC Sabathia .50 1.25
83 Chris Sale .60 1.50
84 Pablo Sandoval .50 1.25
85 Max Scherzer .60 1.50
86 Marco Scutaro .50 1.25
87 Jean Segura .50 1.25
88 Giancarlo Stanton .60 1.50
89 Stephen Strasburg .60 1.50
90 Nick Swisher .50 1.25
91 Mike Trout 3.00 8.00
92 Troy Tulowitzki .60 1.50
93 Justin Upton .50 1.25
94 Chase Utley .50 1.25
95 Justin Verlander .60 1.50
96 Joey Votto .60 1.50
97 Michael Wacha .50 1.25
98 Adam Wainwright .50 1.25
99 Zack Wheeler .50 1.25
100 David Wright .50 1.25
101 Jordan Zimmermann .50 1.25
102 Jacoby Ellsbury .50 1.25

2014 Topps Chipz Black

*BLACK: .6X TO 1.5X BASIC

2014 Topps Chipz Blue

*BLUE: .5X TO 1.2X BASIC

2014 Topps Chipz Glow in the Dark

*GLOW: .4X TO 1X BASIC
48 Derek Jeter 2.50 6.00

2014 Topps Chipz Glow in the Dark Blue

*BLUE GLOW: .5X TO 1.2X BASIC

2014 Topps Chipz Glow in the Dark Red

*RED GLOW: .5X TO 1.2X BASIC

2014 Topps Chipz Glow in the Dark Silver

*SILVER GLOW: .6X TO 1.5X BASIC

2014 Topps Chipz Gold Foil

*GOLD FOIL: .6X TO 1.5X BASIC

2014 Topps Chipz Magnets

*MAGNET: .4X TO 1X BASIC
48 Derek Jeter 2.50 6.00

2014 Topps Chipz Red

*RED: .5X TO 1.2X BASIC

2014 Topps Chipz Silver

*SILVER: .6X TO 1.5X BASIC

2014 Topps Chipz Mascots

1 Baxter the Bobcat 1.00 2.50
2 Braves Mascot 1.00 2.50
3 Oriole 1.00 2.50
4 Wally the Green Monster 1.25 3.00
5 Chicago White Sox Mascot 1.00 2.50
6 Gapper 1.00 2.50
7 Slider 1.00 2.50
8 Dinger 1.00 2.50
9 Paws 1.00 2.50
10 Orbit 1.00 2.50
11 Lion 1.00 2.50
12 Billy the Marlin 1.00 2.50
13 Bernie Brewer 1.00 2.50
14 TC Bear 1.00 2.50
15 Mr. Met 1.00 2.50
16 Elephant 1.00 2.50
17 Phillie Phanatic 1.25 3.00
18 Pirate Parrot 1.00 2.50
19 Swingin Friar 1.00 2.50
20 Mariner Moose 1.00 2.50
21 Fredbird 1.00 2.50
22 Raymond 1.00 2.50
23 Rangers Captain 1.00 2.50
24 Blue Jay 1.00 2.50
25 Screech 1.00 2.50

2014 Topps Chipz Mascots Black

*BLACK: .5X TO 1.2X BASIC

2014 Topps Chipz Mascots Blue

*BLUE: .5X TO 1.2X BASIC

2014 Topps Chipz Mascots Red

*RED: .5X TO 1.2X BASIC

2014 Topps Chipz Relics

STATED PRINT RUN 50 SER.#'d SETS
*BLUE: .4X TO 1X BASIC
*RED: .4X TO 1X BASIC
1 Miguel Cabrera 12.00 30.00
2 Josh Hamilton 10.00 25.00
3 Derek Jeter 50.00 100.00
4 Adam Jones
5 Matt Kemp 10.00 25.00
6 Evan Longoria 10.00 25.00
7 Wil Myers 8.00 20.00
8 Albert Pujols 15.00 40.00
9 Joey Votto
10 David Wright

2014 Topps Chipz Relics Blue

*BLUE: .4X TO 1X BASIC

2014 Topps Chipz Relics Red

*RED: .4X TO 1X BASIC

1996 Topps Chrome

The 1996 Topps Chrome set was issued in one series totalling 165 cards and features a selection of players from the 1996 Topps regular set. The four-card packs retailed for $3.00 each. Each chromium card is a replica of its regular version with the exception of the Topps Chrome logo replacing the traditional logo. Included in the set is a Mickey Mantle number 7 Commemorative card and a Cal Ripken Tribute card.

COMPLETE SET (165) 20.00 50.00
1 Tony Gwynn STP .50 1.25
2 Mike Piazza STP .75 2.00
3 Greg Maddux STP .75 2.00
4 Jeff Bagwell STP .30 .75
5 Larry Walker STP .30 .75
6 Barry Larkin STP .30 .75
7 Mickey Mantle COMM 4.00 10.00
8 Tom Glavine STP .30 .75
9 Craig Biggio STP .30 .75
10 Barry Bonds STP 1.00 2.50
11 Heathcliff Slocumb STP .30 .75
12 Matt Williams STP .30 .75
13 Todd Helton 1.50 4.00
14 Paul Molitor .30 .75
15 Glenallen Hill .30 .75
16 Troy Percival .30 .75
17 Albert Belle .30 .75
18 Mark Wohlers .30 .75
19 Kirby Puckett .75 2.00
20 Mark Grace .50 1.25
21 J.T. Snow .30 .75
22 David Justice .30 .75
23 Mike Mussina .50 1.25
24 Bernie Williams .50 1.25
25 Ron Gant .30 .75
26 Carlos Baerga .30 .75
27 Gary Sheffield .30 .75
28 Cal Ripken 2131 2.50 6.00
29 Frank Thomas .75 2.00
30 Kevin Seitzer .30 .75
31 Joe Carter .30 .75
32 Jeff King .30 .75
33 David Cone .30 .75
34 Eddie Murray .75 2.00
35 Brian Jordan .30 .75
36 Garret Anderson .30 .75
37 Hideo Nomo .75 2.00
38 Steve Finley .30 .75
39 Ivan Rodriguez .50 1.25
40 Quilvio Veras .30 .75
41 Mark McGwire 2.00 5.00
42 Greg Vaughn .30 .75
43 Randy Johnson .75 2.00
44 David Segui .30 .75
45 Derek Bell .30 .75
46 John Valentin .30 .75
47 Steve Avery .30 .75
48 Tino Martinez .50 1.25
49 Shane Reynolds .30 .75
50 Jim Edmonds .30 .75
51 Raul Mondesi .30 .75
52 Chipper Jones .75 2.00
53 Gregg Jefferies .30 .75
54 Ken Caminiti .30 .75
55 Brian McRae .30 .75
56 Don Mattingly 2.00 5.00
57 Marty Cordova .30 .75
58 Vinny Castilla .30 .75
59 John Smoltz .50 1.25
60 Travis Fryman .30 .75
61 Ryan Klesko .30 .75
62 Alex Fernandez .30 .75
63 Dante Bichette .30 .75
64 Eric Karros .30 .75
65 Roger Clemens 1.50 4.00
66 Randy Myers .30 .75
67 Cal Ripken 2.50 6.00
68 Rod Beck .30 .75
69 Jack McDowell .30 .75
70 Ken Griffey Jr. 1.50 4.00
71 Ramon Martinez .30 .75
72 Jason Giambi .30 .75
73 Nomar Garciaparra 1.25 3.00
74 Billy Wagner .30 .75
75 Todd Greene .30 .75
76 Paul Wilson .30 .75
77 Johnny Damon .50 1.25
78 Alan Benes .30 .75
79 Karim Garcia .30 .75
80 Derek Jeter 2.00 5.00
81 Kirby Puckett STP .50 1.25
82 Cal Ripken STP 1.25 3.00
83 Albert Belle STP .30 .75
84 Randy Johnson STP .50 1.25
85 Wade Boggs STP .30 .75
86 Carlos Baerga STP .30 .75
87 Ivan Rodriguez STP .30 .75
88 Mike Mussina STP .30 .75
89 Frank Thomas STP .50 1.25
90 Ken Griffey Jr. STP 1.00 2.50
91 Jose Mesa STP .30 .75
92 Matt Morris RC 2.00 5.00
93 Mike Piazza 1.25 3.00
94 Edgar Martinez .50 1.25
95 Chuck Knoblauch .30 .75
96 Andres Galarraga .30 .75
97 Tony Gwynn 1.00 2.50
98 Lee Smith .30 .75
99 Sammy Sosa .75 2.00
100 Jim Thome .50 1.25
101 Bernard Gilkey .30 .75
102 Brady Anderson .30 .75
103 Rico Brogna .30 .75
104 Len Dykstra .30 .75
105 Tom Glavine .50 1.25
106 John Olerud .30 .75
107 Terry Steinbach .30 .75
108 Brian Hunter .30 .75
109 Jay Buhner .30 .75
110 Mo Vaughn .30 .75
111 Jose Mesa .30 .75
112 Brett Butler .30 .75
113 Chili Davis .30 .75
114 Paul O'Neill .50 1.25
115 Roberto Alomar .50 1.25
116 Barry Larkin .50 1.25
117 Marquis Grissom .30 .75
118 Will Clark .50 1.25
119 Barry Bonds 2.00 5.00
120 Ozzie Smith 1.25 3.00
121 Pedro Martinez .50 1.25
122 Craig Biggio .50 1.25
123 Moises Alou .30 .75
124 Robin Ventura .30 .75
125 Greg Maddux 1.25 3.00
126 Tim Salmon .50 1.25
127 Wade Boggs .50 1.25
128 Ismael Valdes .30 .75
129 Juan Gonzalez .30 .75
130 Ray Lankford .30 .75
131 Bobby Bonilla .30 .75
132 Reggie Sanders .30 .75
133 Alex Ochoa .30 .75
134 Mark Loretta .30 .75
135 Jason Kendall .30 .75
136 Brooks Kieschnick .30 .75
137 Chris Snopek .30 .75
138 Ruben Rivera .30 .75
139 Jeff Suppan .30 .75
140 John Wasdin .30 .75
141 Jay Payton .30 .75
142 Rick Krivda .30 .75
143 Jimmy Haynes .30 .75
144 Ryne Sandberg 1.25 3.00
145 Matt Williams .30 .75
146 Jose Canseco .50 1.25
147 Larry Walker .30 .75
148 Kevin Appier .30 .75
149 Javy Lopez .30 .75
150 Dennis Eckersley .30 .75
151 Jason Isringhausen .30 .75
152 Dean Palmer .30 .75
153 Jeff Bagwell .50 1.25
154 Rondell White .30 .75
155 Wally Joyner .30 .75
156 Fred McGriff .50 1.25
157 Cecil Fielder .30 .75
158 Rafael Palmeiro .50 1.25
159 Rickey Henderson .75 2.00
160 Shawon Dunston .30 .75
161 Manny Ramirez .50 1.25
162 Alex Gonzalez .30 .75
163 Shawn Green .30 .75
164 Kenny Lofton .30 .75
165 Jeff Conine .30 .75

1996 Topps Chrome Refractors

COMPLETE SET (165) 1000.00 2000.00
*STARS: 2.5X TO 6X BASIC CARDS
*ROOKIES: 1.5X TO 4X BASIC CARDS
STATED ODDS 1:12 HOBBY
CARDS 111-165 CONDITION SENSITIVE

1996 Topps Chrome Masters of the Game

COMPLETE SET (20) 15.00 40.00
STATED ODDS 1:12 HOBBY
*REF: 1X TO 2.5X BASIC
REF.STATED ODDS 1:36 HOBBY
1 Dennis Eckersley .75 2.00
2 Denny Martinez .50 1.25
3 Eddie Murray .75 2.00
4 Paul Molitor 1.25 3.00
5 Ozzie Smith 1.50 4.00
6 Rickey Henderson 1.25 3.00
7 Tim Raines .75 2.00
8 Lee Smith .50 1.25
9 Cal Ripken 4.00 10.00
10 Chili Davis .50 1.25
11 Wade Boggs .75 2.00
12 Tony Gwynn 1.25 3.00
13 Don Mattingly 2.50 6.00
14 Bret Saberhagen .50 1.25
15 Kirby Puckett 1.25 3.00
16 Joe Carter .50 1.25
17 Roger Clemens 1.50 4.00
18 Barry Bonds 2.00 5.00
19 Greg Maddux 2.00 5.00
20 Frank Thomas 1.25 3.00

1996 Topps Chrome Wrecking Crew

COMPLETE SET (15) 12.50 30.00
STATED ODDS 1:24 HOBBY
*REF: 1.5X TO 4X BASIC CHR.WRECKING
REF.STATED ODDS 1:72 HOBBY
WC1 Jeff Bagwell 1.00 2.50
WC2 Albert Belle .60 1.50
WC3 Barry Bonds 2.50 6.00
WC4 Jose Canseco 1.00 2.50
WC5 Joe Carter .60 1.50
WC6 Cecil Fielder .60 1.50
WC7 Ron Gant .60 1.50
WC8 Juan Gonzalez .60 1.50
WC9 Ken Griffey Jr. 3.00 8.00
WC10 Fred McGriff 1.00 2.50
WC11 Mark McGwire 2.50 6.00
WC12 Mike Piazza 1.50 4.00
WC13 Frank Thomas 1.50 4.00
WC14 Mo Vaughn .60 1.50
WC15 Matt Williams .60 1.50

1997 Topps Chrome

The 1997 Topps Chrome set was issued in one series totalling 165 cards and was distributed in four-card packs with a suggested retail price of $3.00. Using Chromium technology to highlight the cards, this set features a metalized version of the cards of some of the best players from the 1997 regular Topps Series one and two. An attractive 8 1/2" by 11" chrome promo sheet was sent to dealers advertising this set.

COMPLETE SET (165) 20.00 50.00
1 Barry Bonds 2.00 5.00
2 Jose Valentin .30 .75
3 Brady Anderson .30 .75
4 Wade Boggs .50 1.25
5 Andres Galarraga .30 .75
6 Rusty Greer .30 .75
7 Derek Jeter 2.00 5.00
8 Ricky Bottalico .30 .75
9 Mike Piazza 1.25 3.00
10 Garret Anderson .30 .75
11 Jeff King .30 .75
12 Kevin Appier .30 .75
13 Mark Grace .50 1.25
14 Jeff D'Amico .30 .75
15 Jay Buhner .30 .75
16 Hal Morris .30 .75
17 Harold Baines .30 .75
18 Jeff Cirillo .30 .75
19 Tom Glavine .50 1.25
20 Andy Pettitte .50 1.25
21 Mark McGwire 2.00 5.00
22 Chuck Knoblauch .30 .75
23 Raul Mondesi .30 .75
24 Albert Belle .30 .75
25 Trevor Hoffman .30 .75
26 Eric Young .30 .75
27 Brian McRae .30 .75
28 Jim Edmonds .30 .75
29 Robb Nen .30 .75
30 Reggie Sanders .30 .75
31 Mike Lansing .30 .75
32 Craig Biggio .50 1.25
33 Ray Lankford .30 .75
34 Charles Nagy .30 .75
35 Paul Wilson .30 .75
36 John Wetteland .30 .75
37 Derek Bell .30 .75
38 Edgar Martinez .50 1.25
39 Rickey Henderson .75 2.00
40 Jim Thome .50 1.25
41 Frank Thomas .75 2.00
42 Jackie Robinson .75 2.00
43 Terry Steinbach .30 .75
44 Kevin Brown .30 .75
45 Joey Hamilton .30 .75
46 Travis Fryman .30 .75
47 Juan Gonzalez .30 .75
48 Ron Gant .30 .75
49 Greg Maddux 1.25 3.00
50 Wally Joyner .30 .75
51 John Valentin .30 .75
52 Bret Boone .30.753 Paul
Molitor .30 .75
54 Rafael Palmeiro .50 1.25
55 Todd Hundley .30 .75
56 Ellis Burks .30 .75
57 Bernie Williams .50 1.25
58 Roberto Alomar .50 1.25
59 Jose Mesa .30 .75
60 Troy Percival .30 .75
61 John Smoltz .50 1.25
62 Jeff Conine .30 .75
63 Bernard Gilkey .30 .75
64 Mickey Tettleton .30 .75
65 Justin Thompson .30 .75
66 Tony Phillips .30 .75
67 Ryne Sandberg 1.25 3.00
68 Geronimo Berroa .30 .75
69 Todd Hollandsworth .30 .75
70 Rey Ordonez .30 .75
71 Marquis Grissom .30 .75
72 Tino Martinez .50 1.25
73 Steve Finley .30 .75
74 Andy Benes .30 .75
75 Jason Kendall .30 .75
76 Johnny Damon .50 1.25
77 Jason Giambi .30 .75
78 Henry Rodriguez .30 .75
79 Edgar Renteria .30 .75
80 Ray Durham .30 .75
81 Gregg Jefferies .30 .75
82 Roberto Hernandez .30 .75
83 Joe Carter .30 .75
84 Jermaine Dye .30 .75
85 Julio Franco .30 .75
86 David Justice .30 .75
87 Jose Canseco .50 1.25
88 Paul O'Neill .50 1.25
89 Mariano Rivera .75 2.00
90 Bobby Higginson .30 .75
91 Mark Grudzielanek .30 .75
92 Lance Johnson .30 .75
93 Ken Caminiti .30 .75
94 Gary Sheffield .30 .75
95 Luis Castillo .30 .75
96 Scott Rolen .50 1.25
97 Chipper Jones .75 2.00
98 Darryl Strawberry .30 .75
99 Nomar Garciaparra 1.25 3.00
100 Jeff Bagwell .50 1.25
101 Ken Griffey Jr. 1.50 4.00
102 Sammy Sosa .75 2.00
103 Jack McDowell .30 .75
104 James Baldwin .30 .75
105 Rocky Coppinger .30 .75
106 Manny Ramirez .50 1.25
107 Tim Salmon .50 1.25
108 Eric Karros .30 .75
109 Brett Butler .30 .75
110 Randy Johnson .75 2.00
111 Pat Hentgen .30 .75
112 Rondell White .30 .75
113 Eddie Murray .75 2.00
114 Ivan Rodriguez .50 1.25
115 Jermaine Allensworth .30 .75
116 Ed Sprague .30 .75
117 Kenny Lofton .30 .75
118 Alan Benes .30 .75
119 Fred McGriff .50 1.25
120 Alex Fernandez .30 .75
121 Al Martin .30 .75
122 Devon White .30 .75
123 David Cone .30 .75
124 Karim Garcia .30 .75
125 Chili Davis .30 .75
126 Roger Clemens 1.50 4.00
127 Bobby Bonilla .30 .75
128 Mike Mussina .50 1.25
129 Todd Walker .30 .75
130 Dante Bichette .30 .75
131 Carlos Baerga .30 .75
132 Matt Williams .30 .75
133 Will Clark .50 1.25
134 Dennis Eckersley .30 .75
135 Ryan Klesko .30 .75
136 Dean Palmer .30 .75
137 Javy Lopez .30 .75
138 Greg Vaughn .30 .75
139 Vinny Castilla .30 .75

140 Cal Ripken 2.50 6.00
141 Ruben Rivera .30 .75
142 Mark Wohlers .30 .75
143 Tony Clark .30 .75
144 Jose Rosado .30 .75
145 Tony Gwynn 1.00 2.50
146 Cecil Fielder .30 .75
147 Brian Jordan .30 .75
148 Bob Abreu .50 1.25
149 Barry Larkin .50 1.25
150 Robin Ventura .30 .75
151 John Olerud .30 .75
152 Rod Beck .30 .75
153 Vladimir Guerrero .75 2.00
154 Marty Cordova .30 .75
155 Todd Stottlemyre .30 .75
156 Hideo Nomo .75 2.00
157 Denny Neagle .30 .75
158 John Jaha .30 .75
159 Mo Vaughn .30 .75
160 Andruw Jones .50 1.25
161 Moises Alou .30 .75
162 Larry Walker .30 .75
163 Eddie Murray SH .50 1.25
164 Paul Molitor SH .30 .75
165 Checklist .30 .75

1997 Topps Chrome Refractors

*STARS: 2.5X TO 6X BASIC CARDS
STATED ODDS 1:12
CONDITION SENSITIVE SET

1997 Topps Chrome All-Stars

COMPLETE SET (22) 40.00 100.00
STATED ODDS 1:24
*REF: 1X TO 2.5X BASIC CHROME AS
REFRACTOR STATED ODDS 1:72
AS1 Ivan Rodriguez 1.50 4.00
AS2 Todd Hundley 1.00 2.50
AS3 Frank Thomas 2.50 6.00
AS4 Andres Galarraga 1.00 2.50
AS5 Chuck Knoblauch 1.00 2.50
AS6 Eric Young 1.00 2.50
AS7 Jim Thome 1.50 4.00
AS8 Chipper Jones 2.50 6.00
AS9 Cal Ripken 8.00 20.00
AS10 Barry Larkin 1.50 4.00
AS11 Albert Belle 1.00 2.50
AS12 Barry Bonds 6.00 15.00
AS13 Ken Griffey Jr. 5.00 12.00
AS14 Ellis Burks 1.00 2.50
AS15 Juan Gonzalez 1.00 2.50
AS16 Gary Sheffield 1.00 2.50
AS17 Andy Pettitte 1.50 4.00
AS18 Tom Glavine 1.50 4.00
AS19 Pat Hentgen 1.00 2.50
AS20 John Smoltz 1.50 4.00
AS21 Roberto Hernandez 1.00 2.50
AS22 Mark Wohlers 1.00 2.50

1997 Topps Chrome Diamond Duos

COMPLETE SET (10) 12.50 30.00
STATED ODDS 1:36
*REF.: 1X TO 2.5X BASIC DIAM.DUOS
REFRACTOR STATED ODDS 1:108
DD1 C.Jones 1.50 4.00
A.Jones
DD2 D.Jeter/B.Williams 4.00 10.00
DD3 K.Griffey Jr./J.Buhner 3.00 8.00
DD4 K.Lofton/M.Ramirez 1.00 2.50
DD5 J.Bagwell/C.Biggio 1.00 2.50
DD6 J.Gonzalez/I.Rodriguez 1.00 2.50
DD7 C.Ripken/B.Anderson 5.00 12.00
DD8 M.Piazza/H.Nomo 1.50 4.00
DD9 A.Galarraga/D.Bichette 1.00 2.50
DD10 F.Thomas/A.Belle 1.50 4.00

1997 Topps Chrome Season's Best

COMPLETE SET (25) 25.00 60.00
STATED ODDS 1:18
*REF: 1X TO 2.5X BASIC SEAS.BEST
REFRACTOR STATED ODDS 1:54
1 Tony Gwynn 2.50 6.00
2 Frank Thomas 2.00 5.00
3 Ellis Burks .75 2.00
4 Paul Molitor .75 2.00
5 Chuck Knoblauch .75 2.00
6 Mark McGwire 5.00 12.00
7 Brady Anderson .75 2.00
8 Ken Griffey Jr. 4.00 10.00
9 Albert Belle .75 2.00
10 Andres Galarraga .75 2.00
11 Andres Galarraga .75 2.00
12 Albert Belle .75 2.00
13 Juan Gonzalez .75 2.00
14 Mo Vaughn .75 2.00
15 Rafael Palmeiro 1.25 3.00
16 John Smoltz 1.25 3.00
17 Andy Pettitte 1.25 3.00
18 Pat Hentgen .75 2.00
19 Mike Mussina 1.25 3.00
20 Andy Benes .75 2.00
21 Kenny Lofton .75 2.00
22 Tom Goodwin .75 2.00
23 Otis Nixon .75 2.00
24 Eric Young .75 2.00
25 Lance Johnson .75 2.00

1997 Topps Chrome Jumbos

This six-card set contains jumbo versions of the six featured players' regular Topps Chrome cards and measures approximately 3 3/4" by 5 1/4". One of these cards was found in a special box with five Topps Chrome packs issued through Wal-Mart. The cards are numbered according to their corresponding number in the regular set.

COMPLETE SET (6) 6.00 15.00
9 Mike Piazza 1.25 3.00
94 Gary Sheffield .50 1.25
97 Chipper Jones 1.00 2.50
101 Ken Griffey Jr. 1.25 3.00
102 Sammy Sosa .60 1.50
140 Cal Ripken Jr. 2.00 5.00

1998 Topps Chrome

The 1998 Topps Chrome set was issued in two separate series of 282 and 221 cards respectively with design and content paralleling the base 1998 Topps set. Four-card packs carried a suggested retail price of $3 each. Card fronts feature color action player photos printed with Chromium technology on metalized cards. The backs carry player information. As is tradition with Topps sets since 1996, card number seven was excluded from the set in honor of Mickey Mantle. Subsets are as follows: Prospects/Draft Picks (245-264/484-501), Season Highlights (265-269/474-478), Inter-League (270-274/479-483), Checklists (275-276/502-503) and World Series (277-283). After four years of being excluded from Topps products, superstar Alex Rodriguez finally made his Topps debut as card number 504. Notable Rookie Cards include Ryan Anderson, Michael Cuddyer, Jack Cust and Troy Glaus.

COMPLETE SET (503) 75.00 150.00
COMPLETE SERIES 1 (282) 30.00 80.00
COMPLETE SERIES 2 (221) 30.00 80.00
REF.STATED ODDS 1:12
CARD NUMBER 7 DOES NOT EXIST
1 Tony Gwynn 1.00 2.50
2 Larry Walker .30 .75
3 Billy Wagner .30 .75
4 Denny Neagle .30 .75
5 Vladimir Guerrero .75 2.00
6 Kevin Brown .50 1.25
8 Mariano Rivera .75 2.00
9 Tony Clark .30 .75
10 Deion Sanders .50 1.25
11 Francisco Cordova .30 .75
12 Matt Williams .30 .75
13 Carlos Baerga .30 .75
14 Mo Vaughn .30 .75
15 Bobby Witt .30 .75
16 Matt Stairs .30 .75
17 Chan Ho Park .30 .75
18 Mike Bordick .30 .75
19 Michael Tucker .30 .75
20 Frank Thomas .75 2.00
21 Roberto Clemente 2.00 5.00
22 Dmitri Young .30 .75
23 Steve Trachsel .30 .75
24 Jeff Kent .30 .75
25 Scott Rolen .50 1.25
26 John Thomson .30 .75
27 Joe Vitiello .30 .75
28 Eddie Guardado .30 .75
29 Charlie Hayes .30 .75
30 Juan Gonzalez .30 .75
31 Garret Anderson .30 .75
32 John Jaha .30 .75
33 Omar Vizquel .50 1.25
34 Brian Hunter .30 .75
35 Jeff Bagwell .50 1.25
36 Mark Lemke .30 .75
37 Doug Glanville .30 .75
38 Dan Wilson .30 .75
39 Steve Cooke .30 .75
40 Chili Davis .30 .75
41 Mike Cameron .30 .75
42 F.P. Santangelo .30 .75
43 Brad Ausmus .30 .75
44 Gary DiSarcina .30 .75
45 Pat Hentgen .30 .75
46 Wilton Guerrero .30 .75
47 Devon White .30 .75
48 Danny Patterson .30 .75
49 Pat Meares .30 .75
50 Rafael Palmeiro .50 1.25
51 Mark Gardner .30 .75
52 Jeff Blauser .30 .75
53 Dave Hollins .30 .75
54 Carlos Garcia .30 .75
55 Ben McDonald .30 .75
56 John Mabry .30 .75
57 Trevor Hoffman .30 .75
58 Tony Fernandez .30 .75
59 Rich Loiselle RC .30 .75
60 Mark Leiter .30 .75
61 Pat Kelly .30 .75
62 John Flaherty .30 .75
63 Roger Bailey .30 .75
64 Tom Gordon .30 .75
65 Ryan Klesko .30 .75
66 Darryl Hamilton .30 .75
67 Jim Eisenreich .30 .75
68 Butch Huskey .30 .75
69 Mark Grudzielanek .30 .75
70 Marquis Grissom .30 .75
71 Mark McLemore .30 .75
72 Gary Gaetti .30 .75
73 Greg Gagne .30 .75
74 Lyle Mouton .30 .75
75 Jim Edmonds .30 .75
76 Shawn Green .30 .75
77 Greg Vaughn .30 .75
78 Terry Adams .30 .75
79 Kevin Polcovich .30 .75
80 Troy O'Leary .30 .75
81 Jeff Shaw .30 .75
82 Rich Becker .30 .75
83 David Wells .30 .75
84 Steve Karsay .30 .75
85 Charles Nagy .30 .75
86 B.J. Surhoff .30 .75
87 Jamey Wright .30 .75
88 James Baldwin .30 .75
89 Edgardo Alfonzo .30 .75
90 Jay Buhner .30 .75
91 Brady Anderson .30 .75
92 Scott Servais .30 .75
93 Edgar Renteria .30 .75
94 Mike Lieberthal .30 .75
95 Rick Aguilera .30 .75
96 Walt Weiss .30 .75
97 Deivi Cruz .30 .75
98 Kurt Abbott .30 .75
99 Henry Rodriguez .30 .75
100 Mike Piazza 1.25 3.00
101 Billy Taylor .30 .75
102 Todd Zeile .30 .75
103 Rey Ordonez .30 .75
104 Willie Greene .30 .75
105 Tony Womack .30 .75
106 Mike Sweeney .30 .75
107 Jeffrey Hammonds .30 .75
108 Kevin Orie .30 .75
109 Alex Gonzalez .30 .75
110 Jose Canseco .50 1.25
111 Paul Sorrento .30 .75
112 Joey Hamilton .30 .75
113 Brad Radke .30 .75
114 Steve Avery .30 .75
115 Esteban Loaiza .30 .75
116 Stan Javier .30 .75
117 Chris Gomez .30 .75
118 Royce Clayton .30 .75
119 Orlando Merced .30 .75
120 Kevin Appier .30 .75
121 Mel Nieves .30 .75
122 Joe Girardi .30 .75
123 Rico Brogna .30 .75
124 Kent Mercker .30 .75
125 Manny Ramirez .50 1.25
126 Jeromy Burnitz .30 .75
127 Kevin Foster .30 .75
128 Matt Morris .30 .75
129 Jason Dickson .30 .75
130 Tom Glavine .50 1.25
131 Wally Joyner .30 .75
132 Rick Reed .30 .75
133 Todd Jones .30 .75
134 Dave Martinez .30 .75
135 Sandy Alomar Jr. .30 .75
136 Mike Lansing .30 .75
137 Sean Berry .30 .75
138 Doug Jones .30 .75
139 Todd Stottlemyre .30 .75
140 Jay Bell .30 .75
141 Jaime Navarro .30 .75
142 Chris Hoiles .30 .75
143 Joey Cora .30 .75
144 Scott Spiezio .30 .75
145 Joe Carter .30 .75
146 Jose Guillen .30 .75
147 Damion Easley .30 .75
148 Lee Stevens .30 .75
149 Alex Fernandez .30 .75
150 Randy Johnson .75 2.00
151 J.T. Snow .30 .75
152 Chuck Finley .30 .75
153 Bernard Gilkey .30 .75
154 David Segui .30 .75
155 Dante Bichette .30 .75
156 Kevin Stocker .30 .75
157 Carl Everett .30 .75
158 Jose Valentin .30 .75
159 Pokey Reese .30 .75
160 Derek Jeter 2.00 5.00
161 Roger Pavlik .30 .75
162 Mark Wohlers .30 .75
163 Ricky Bottalico .30 .75
164 Ozzie Guillen .30 .75
165 Mike Mussina .50 1.25
166 Gary Sheffield .30 .75
167 Hideo Nomo .75 2.00
168 Mark Grace .50 1.25
169 Aaron Sele .30 .75
170 Darryl Kile .30 .75
171 Shawn Estes .30 .75
172 Vinny Castilla .30 .75
173 Ron Coomer .30 .75
174 Jose Rosado .30 .75
175 Kenny Lofton .30 .75
176 Jason Giambi .30 .75
177 Hal Morris .30 .75
178 Darren Bragg .30 .75
179 Orel Hershiser .30 .75
180 Ray Lankford .30 .75
181 Hideki Irabu .30 .75
182 Kevin Young .30 .75
183 Javy Lopez .30 .75
184 Jeff Montgomery .30 .75
185 Mike Holtz .30 .75
186 George Williams .30 .75
187 Cal Eldred .30 .75
188 Tom Candiotti .30 .75
189 Glenallen Hill .30 .75
190 Brian Giles .30 .75
191 Dave Mlicki .30 .75
192 Garrett Stephenson .30 .75
193 Jeff Frye .30 .75
194 Joe Oliver .30 .75
195 Bob Hamelin .30 .75
196 Luis Sojo .30 .75
197 LaTroy Hawkins .30 .75
198 Kevin Elster .30 .75
199 Jeff Reed .30 .75
200 Dennis Eckersley .30 .75
201 Bill Mueller .30 .75
202 Russ Davis .30 .75
203 Armando Benitez .30 .75
204 Quilvio Veras .30 .75
205 Tim Naehring .30 .75
206 Quinton McCracken .30 .75
207 Raul Casanova .30 .75
208 Matt Lawton .30 .75
209 Luis Alicea .30 .75
210 Luis Gonzalez .30 .75
211 Allen Watson .30 .75
212 Gerald Williams .30 .75
213 David Bell .30 .75
214 Todd Hollandsworth .30 .75
215 Wade Boggs .50 1.25
216 Jose Mesa .30 .75
217 Jamie Moyer .30 .75
218 Darren Daulton .30 .75
219 Mickey Morandini .30 .75
220 Rusty Greer .30 .75
221 Jim Bullinger .30 .75
222 Jose Offerman .30 .75
223 Matt Karchner .30 .75
224 Woody Williams .30 .75
225 Mark Loretta .30 .75
226 Mike Hampton .30 .75
227 Willie Adams .30 .75
228 Scott Hatteberg .30 .75
229 Rich Amaral .30 .75
230 Terry Steinbach .30 .75
231 Glendon Rusch .30 .75
232 Bret Boone .30 .75
233 Robert Person .30 .75
234 Jose Hernandez .30 .75
235 Doug Drabek .30 .75
236 Jason McDonald .30 .75
237 Chris Widger .30 .75
238 Tom Martin .30 .75
239 Dave Burba .30 .75
240 Pete Rose Jr. RC .30 .75
241 Bobby Ayala .30 .75
242 Tim Wakefield .30 .75
243 Dennis Springer .30 .75
244 Tim Belcher .30 .75
245 J.Garland .40 1.00
G.Goetz
246 L.Berkman .40 1.00
G.Davis
247 V.Wells .40 1.00
A.Akin
248 A.Kennedy .40 1.00
J.Romano
249 J.Dellaero .40 1.00
T.Cameron
250 J.Sandberg .40 1.00
A.Sanchez
251 P.Ortega .40 1.00
J.Manias
252 Mike Stoner RC .40 1.00
253 J.Patterson .40 1.00
L.Rodriguez
254 R.Minor RC .40 1.00
A.Beltre
255 B.Grieve .40 1.00
D.Brown
256 Wood .40 1.00
Pavano/Meche
257 D.Ortiz 2.00 5.00
Sexson/Ward
258 J.Encarnacion .40 1.00
Winn/Vess
259 Bens .40 1.00
T.Smith RC/C.Dunc RC
260 Warren Morris RC .40 1.00
261 B.Davis .40 1.00
Marrero/R.Hern.
262 E.Chavez .40 1.00
R.Branyan
263 Ryan Jackson RC .40 1.00
264 B.Fuentes RC 2.00 5.00
Clement/Halladay
265 Randy Johnson SH .50 1.25
266 Kevin Brown SH .30 .75
267 Ricardo Rincon SH .30 .75
268 Nomar Garciaparra SH .75 2.00
269 Tino Martinez SH .30 .75
270 Chuck Knoblauch IL .30 .75
271 Pedro Martinez IL .50 1.25
272 Denny Neagle IL .30 .75
273 Juan Gonzalez IL .30 .75
274 Andres Galarraga IL .30 .75
275 Checklist .30 .75
276 Checklist .30 .75
277 Moises Alou WS .30 .75
278 Sandy Alomar Jr. WS .30 .75
279 Gary Sheffield WS .30 .75
280 Matt Williams WS .30 .75
281 Livan Hernandez WS .30 .75
282 Chad Ogea WS .30 .75
283 Marlins Champs .30 .75
284 Tino Martinez .50 1.25
285 Roberto Alomar .50 1.25
286 Jeff King .30 .75
287 Brian Jordan .30 .75
288 Darin Erstad .30 .75
289 Ken Caminiti .30 .75
290 Jim Thome .50 1.25
291 Paul Molitor .30 .75
292 Ivan Rodriguez .50 1.25
293 Bernie Williams .50 1.25
294 Todd Hundley .30 .75
295 Andres Galarraga .30 .75
296 Greg Maddux 1.25 3.00
297 Edgar Martinez .50 1.25
298 Ron Gant .30 .75
299 Derek Bell .30 .75
300 Roger Clemens 1.50 4.00
301 Rondell White .30 .75
302 Barry Larkin .50 1.25
303 Robin Ventura .30 .75
304 Jason Kendall .30 .75
305 Chipper Jones .75 2.00
306 John Franco .30 .75
307 Sammy Sosa .75 2.00
308 Troy Percival .30 .75
309 Chuck Knoblauch .30 .75
310 Ellis Burks .30 .75
311 Al Martin .30 .75
312 Tim Salmon .50 1.25
313 Moises Alou .30 .75
314 Lance Johnson .30 .75
315 Justin Thompson .30 .75
316 Will Clark .50 1.25
317 Barry Bonds 2.00 5.00
318 Craig Biggio .50 1.25
319 John Smoltz .50 1.25
320 Cal Ripken 2.50 6.00
321 Ken Griffey Jr. 1.50 4.00
322 Paul O'Neill .50 1.25
323 Todd Helton .50 1.25
324 John Olerud .30 .75
325 Mark McGwire 2.00 5.00
326 Jose Cruz Jr. .30 .75
327 Jeff Cirillo .30 .75
328 Dean Palmer .30 .75
329 John Wetteland .30 .75
330 Steve Finley .30 .75
331 Albert Belle .30 .75
332 Curt Schilling .30 .75
333 Raul Mondesi .30 .75
334 Andruw Jones .50 1.25
335 Nomar Garciaparra 1.25 3.00
336 David Justice .30 .75
337 Andy Pettitte .50 1.25
338 Pedro Martinez .50 1.25
339 Travis Miller .30 .75
340 Chris Stynes .30 .75
341 Gregg Jefferies .30 .75
342 Jeff Fassero .30 .75
343 Craig Counsell .30 .75
344 Wilson Alvarez .30 .75
345 Bip Roberts .30 .75
346 Kelvim Escobar .30 .75
347 Mark Bellhorn .30 .75
348 Cory Lidle RC 3.00 8.00
349 Fred McGriff .50 1.25
350 Chuck Carr .30 .75
351 Bob Abreu .30 .75
352 Juan Guzman .30 .75
353 Fernando Vina .30 .75
354 Andy Benes .30 .75
355 Dave Nilsson .30 .75
356 Bobby Bonilla .30 .75
357 Ismael Valdes .30 .75
358 Carlos Perez .30 .75
359 Kirk Rueter .30 .75
360 Bartolo Colon .30 .75
361 Mel Rojas .30 .75
362 Johnny Damon .50 1.25
363 Geronimo Berroa .30 .75
364 Reggie Sanders .30 .75
365 Jermaine Allensworth .30 .75
366 Orlando Cabrera .30 .75
367 Jorge Fabregas .30 .75
368 Scott Stahoviak .30 .75
369 Ken Cloude .30 .75
370 Donovan Osborne .30 .75
371 Roger Cedeno .30 .75
372 Neifi Perez .30 .75
373 Chris Holt .30 .75
374 Cecil Fielder .30 .75
375 Marty Cordova .30 .75
376 Tom Goodwin .30 .75
377 Jeff Suppan .30 .75
378 Jeff Brantley .30 .75
379 Mark Langston .30 .75
380 Shane Reynolds .30 .75
381 Mike Fetters .30 .75
382 Todd Greene .30 .75
383 Ray Durham .30 .75
384 Carlos Delgado .30 .75
385 Jeff D'Amico .30 .75
386 Brian McRae .30 .75
387 Alan Benes .30 .75
388 Heathcliff Slocumb .30 .75
389 Eric Young .30 .75
390 Travis Fryman .30 .75
391 David Cone .30 .75
392 Otis Nixon .30 .75
393 Jeremi Gonzalez .30 .75
394 Jeff Juden .30 .75
395 Jose Vizcaino .30 .75
396 Ugueth Urbina .30 .75
397 Ramon Martinez .30 .75
398 Robb Nen .30 .75
399 Harold Baines .30 .75
400 Delino DeShields .30 .75
401 John Burkett .30 .75
402 Sterling Hitchcock .30 .75
403 Mark Clark .30 .75
404 Terrell Wade .30 .75
405 Scott Brosius .30 .75
406 Chad Curtis .30 .75
407 Brian Johnson .30 .75
408 Roberto Kelly .30 .75
409 Dave Dellucci RC .50 1.25
410 Michael Tucker .30 .75
411 Mark Kotsay .30 .75
412 Mark Lewis .30 .75
413 Ryan McGuire .30 .75
414 Shawon Dunston .30 .75
415 Brad Rigby .30 .75
416 Scott Erickson .30 .75
417 Bobby Jones .30 .75
418 Darren Oliver .30 .75
419 John Smiley .30 .75
420 T.J. Mathews .30 .75
421 Dustin Hermanson .30 .75
422 Mike Timlin .30 .75
423 Willie Blair .30 .75
424 Manny Alexander .30 .75
425 Bob Tewksbury .30 .75
426 Pete Schourek .30 .75
427 Reggie Jefferson .30 .75
428 Ed Sprague .30 .75
429 Jeff Conine .30 .75
430 Roberto Hernandez .30 .75
431 Tom Pagnozzi .30 .75
432 Jaret Wright .30 .75
433 Livan Hernandez .30 .75
434 Andy Ashby .30 .75
435 Todd Dunn .30 .75
436 Bobby Higginson .30 .75
437 Rod Beck .30 .75
438 Jim Leyritz .30 .75
439 Matt Williams .30 .75
440 Brett Tomko .30 .75
441 Joe Randa .30 .75
442 Chris Carpenter .30 .75
443 Dennis Reyes .30 .75
444 Al Leiter .30 .75
445 Jason Schmidt .30 .75
446 Ken Hill .30 .75
447 Shannon Stewart .30 .75
448 Enrique Wilson .30 .75
449 Fernando Tatis .30 .75
450 Jimmy Key .30 .75
451 Darrin Fletcher .30 .75
452 John Valentin .30 .75
453 Kevin Tapani .30 .75
454 Eric Karros .30 .75
455 Jay Bell .30 .75
456 Walt Weiss .30 .75
457 Devon White .30 .75
458 Carl Pavano .30 .75
459 Mike Lansing .30 .75
460 John Flaherty .30 .75
461 Richard Hidalgo .30 .75
462 Quinton McCracken .30 .75
463 Karim Garcia .30 .75
464 Miguel Cairo .30 .75
465 Edwin Diaz .30 .75
466 Bobby Smith .30 .75
467 Yamil Benitez .30 .75
468 Rich Butler RC .30 .75
469 Ben Ford RC .30 .75
470 Bubba Trammell .30 .75
471 Brent Brede .30 .75
472 Brooks Kieschnick .30 .75
473 Carlos Castillo .30 .75
474 Brad Radke SH .30 .75
475 Roger Clemens SH .75 2.00
476 Curt Schilling SH .30 .75
477 John Olerud SH .30 .75
478 Mark McGwire SH 1.00 2.50
479 M.Piazza 1.00 2.50
K.Griffey Jr. IL
480 J.Bagwell .50 1.25
F.Thomas IL
481 C.Jones .50 1.25
N.Garciaparra IL
482 L.Walker .30 .75
J.Gonzalez IL
483 G.Sheffield .30 .75
T.Martinez IL
484 D.Gib .40 1.00
M.Colem/Hutchins
485 B.Rose .40 1.00
Looper/Polite
486 E.Milton .40 1.00
Marquis/C.Lee
487 Rob Fick RC .40 1.00
488 A.Ramirez .40 1.00
A.Gonz/Casey
489 D.Bridges .40 1.00
T.Drew RC
490 D.McDonald .40 1.00
N.Ndungidi RC
491 Ryan Anderson RC .40 1.00
492 Troy Glaus RC 2.00 5.00
493 Dan Reichert RC .40 1.00
494 Michael Cuddyer RC 1.00 2.50
495 Jack Cust RC .75 2.00
496 Brian Anderson .40 1.00
497 Tony Saunders .40 1.00
498 J.Sandoval .40 1.00
V.Nunez
499 B.Penny .40 1.00
N.Bierbrodt
500 D.Carr .40 1.00
L.Cruz RC
501 C.Bowers .40 1.00
M.McCain
502 Checklist .30 .75
503 Checklist .30 .75
504 Alex Rodriguez 1.50 4.00

1998 Topps Chrome Refractors

*STARS: 2.5X TO 6X BASIC CARDS
*ROOKIES: 1.25X TO 3X BASIC
STATED ODDS 1:12
CARD NUMBER 7 DOES NOT EXIST

1998 Topps Chrome Baby Boomers

COMPLETE SET (15) 10.00 25.00
SER.1 STATED ODDS 1:24
*REF.: .75X TO 2X BASIC CHR.BOOMERS
REFRACTOR SER.1 STATED ODDS 1:72
BB1 Derek Jeter 4.00 10.00
BB2 Scott Rolen 1.00 2.50
BB3 Nomar Garciaparra 1.00 2.50
BB4 Jose Cruz Jr. .60 1.50
BB5 Darin Erstad .60 1.50
BB6 Todd Helton 1.00 2.50
BB7 Tony Clark .60 1.50
BB8 Jose Guillen .60 1.50
BB9 Andruw Jones .60 1.50
BB10 Vladimir Guerrero 1.00 2.50
BB11 Mark Kotsay .60 1.50
BB12 Todd Greene .60 1.50
BB13 Andy Pettitte 1.00 2.50
BB14 Justin Thompson .60 1.50
BB15 Alan Benes .60 1.50

1998 Topps Chrome Clout Nine

COMPLETE SET (9) 25.00 60.00
SER.2 STATED ODDS 1:24
*REF.: .75X TO 2X BASIC CHR.CLOUT
REFRACTOR SER.2 STATED ODDS 1:72
C1 Edgar Martinez 1.50 4.00
C2 Mike Piazza 4.00 10.00
C3 Frank Thomas 2.50 6.00
C4 Craig Biggio 1.50 4.00
C5 Vinny Castilla 1.00 2.50
C6 Jeff Blauser 1.00 2.50
C7 Barry Bonds 6.00 15.00
C8 Ken Griffey Jr. 5.00 12.00
C9 Larry Walker 1.00 2.50

1998 Topps Chrome Flashback

COMPLETE SET (10) 30.00 80.00
SER.1 STATED ODDS 1:24
*REF.: .75X TO 2X BASIC CHR.FLASHBACK
REFRACTOR SER.1 STATED ODDS 1:72
FB1 Barry Bonds 6.00 15.00
FB2 Ken Griffey Jr. 5.00 12.00
FB3 Paul Molitor 1.00 2.50
FB4 Randy Johnson 2.50 6.00
FB5 Cal Ripken 8.00 20.00
FB6 Tony Gwynn 3.00 8.00
FB7 Kenny Lofton 1.00 2.50
FB8 Gary Sheffield 1.00 2.50
FB9 Deion Sanders 1.50 4.00
FB10 Brady Anderson 1.00 2.50

1998 Topps Chrome HallBound

COMPLETE SET (15) 75.00 150.00
SER.1 STATED ODDS 1:24
*REF.: .75X TO 2X BASIC HALLBOUND
REFRACTOR SER.1 STATED ODDS 1:72
HB1 Paul Molitor 1.25 3.00
HB2 Tony Gwynn 4.00 10.00
HB3 Wade Boggs 2.00 5.00
HB4 Roger Clemens 6.00 15.00
HB5 Dennis Eckersley 1.25 3.00
HB6 Cal Ripken 10.00 25.00
HB7 Greg Maddux 5.00 12.00
HB8 Rickey Henderson 2.00 5.00
HB9 Ken Griffey Jr. 6.00 15.00
HB10 Frank Thomas 3.00 8.00
HB11 Mark McGwire 8.00 20.00
HB12 Barry Bonds 8.00 20.00
HB13 Mike Piazza 5.00 12.00
HB14 Juan Gonzalez 1.25 3.00
HB15 Randy Johnson 3.00 8.00

1998 Topps Chrome Milestones

COMPLETE SET (10) 60.00 120.00
SER.2 STATED ODDS 1:24
*REF.: .75X TO 2X BASIC CHR.MILE
REFRACTOR SER.2 STATED ODDS 1:72
MS1 Barry Bonds 5.00 12.00
MS2 Roger Clemens 4.00 10.00
MS3 Dennis Eckersley .75 2.00
MS4 Juan Gonzalez .75 2.00
MS5 Ken Griffey Jr. 4.00 10.00
MS6 Tony Gwynn 2.50 6.00
MS7 Greg Maddux 3.00 8.00
MS8 Mark McGwire 5.00 12.00
MS9 Cal Ripken 6.00 15.00
MS10 Frank Thomas 2.00 5.00

1998 Topps Chrome Rookie Class

COMPLETE SET (10) 8.00 20.00
SER.2 STATED ODDS 1:12
*REF.: .75X TO 2X BASIC CHR.RK.CLASS
REFRACTOR SER.2 STATED ODDS 1:24
R1 Travis Lee .75 2.00
R2 Richard Hidalgo .75 2.00
R3 Todd Helton 1.25 3.00
R4 Paul Konerko .75 2.00
R5 Mark Kotsay .75 2.00
R6 Derrek Lee .75 2.00
R7 Eli Marrero .75 2.00
R8 Fernando Tatis .75 2.00
R9 Juan Encarnacion .75 2.00
R10 Ben Grieve .75 2.00

1999 Topps Chrome

The 1999 Topps Chrome set totaled 462 cards (though is numbered 1-463 - card number 7 was never issued in honor of Mickey Mantle). The product was distributed in first and second series four-card packs each carrying a suggested retail price of $3. The first series cards were 1-6/8-242, second series cards 243-463. The card fronts feature action color player photos. The backs carry player information. The set contains the following subsets: Season Highlights (200-204), Prospects (205-212/425-437), Draft Picks (213-219/438-444), League Leaders (221-232), World Series (233-240), Strikeout Kings (445-449), All-Topps (450-460) and four Checklist Cards (241-242/462-463). The Mark McGwire Home Run Record Breaker card (220) was released in 70 different variations highlighting every home run that he hit in 1998. The Sammy Sosa Home Run Parade card (461) was issued in 66 different variations. A 462 card set of 1999 Topps Chrome is considered complete with any version of the McGwire 220 and Sosa 461. Rookie Cards of note include Pat Burrell and Alex Escobar.

COMPLETE SET (462) 60.00 120.00
COMPLETE SERIES 1 (241) 25.00 60.00
COMPLETE SERIES 2 (221) 25.00 60.00
COMMON CARD (1-6/8-463) .20 .50
COMMON (205-212/425-437) .40 1.00
CARD NUMBER 7 DOES NOT EXIST
SER.1 SET INCLUDES 1 CARD 220 VARIATION
SER.2 SET INCLUDES 1 CARD 461 VARIATION
1 Roger Clemens 1.50 4.00
2 Andres Galarraga .30 .75
3 Scott Brosius .30 .75
4 John Flaherty .20 .50
5 Jim Leyritz .20 .50
6 Ray Durham .20 .50
8 Jose Vizcaino .20 .50
9 Will Clark .50 1.25
10 David Wells .30 .75
11 Jose Guillen .30 .75
12 Scott Hatteberg .20 .50
13 Edgardo Alfonzo .20 .50
14 Mike Bordick .20 .50
15 Manny Ramirez .50 1.25
16 Greg Maddux 1.25 3.00
17 David Segui .20 .50
18 Darryl Strawberry .30 .75
19 Brad Radke .30 .75
20 Kerry Wood .30 .75
21 Matt Anderson .20 .50
22 Derrek Lee .50 1.25
23 Mickey Morandini .20 .50
24 Paul Konerko .20 .50
25 Travis Lee .20 .50
26 Ken Hill .20 .50
27 Kenny Rogers .30 .75
28 Paul Sorrento .20 .50
29 Quilvio Veras .20 .50
30 Todd Walker .20 .50
31 Ryan Jackson .20 .50
32 John Olerud .30 .75
33 Doug Glanville .20 .50
34 Nolan Ryan 2.50 6.00
35 Ray Lankford .30 .75
36 Mark Loretta .20 .50
37 Jason Dickson .20 .50
38 Sean Bergman .20 .50
39 Quinton McCracken .20 .50
40 Bartolo Colon .30 .75
41 Brady Anderson .30 .75
42 Chris Stynes .20 .50
43 Jorge Posada .50 1.25
44 Justin Thompson .20 .50
45 Johnny Damon .50 1.25
46 Armando Benitez .20 .50
47 Brant Brown .20 .50
48 Charlie Hayes .20 .50
49 Darren Dreifort .20 .50
50 Juan Gonzalez .30 .75
51 Chuck Knoblauch .30 .75

Card	Low	High
52 Todd Helton	.50	1.25
53 Rick Reed	.20	.50
54 Chris Gomez	.20	.50
55 Gary Sheffield	.30	.75
56 Rod Beck	.20	.50
57 Rey Sanchez	.20	.50
58 Garret Anderson	.30	.75
59 Jimmy Haynes	.20	.50
60 Steve Woodard	.20	.50
61 Rondell White	.30	.75
62 Vladimir Guerrero	.75	2.00
63 Eric Karros	.30	.75
64 Russ Davis	.20	.50
65 Mo Vaughn	.30	.75
66 Sammy Sosa	.75	2.00
67 Troy Percival	.30	.75
68 Kenny Lofton	.30	.75
69 Bill Taylor	.20	.50
70 Mark McGwire	2.00	5.00
71 Roger Cedeno	.20	.50
72 Javy Lopez	.30	.75
73 Damion Easley	.20	.50
74 Andy Pettitte	.50	1.25
75 Tony Gwynn	1.00	2.50
76 Ricardo Rincon	.20	.50
77 F.P. Santangelo	.20	.50
78 Jay Bell	.30	.75
79 Scott Servais	.20	.50
80 Jose Canseco	.50	1.25
81 Roberto Hernandez	.20	.50
82 Todd Dunwoody	.20	.50
83 John Wetteland	.30	.75
84 Mike Caruso	.20	.50
85 Derek Jeter	2.00	5.00
86 Aaron Sele	.20	.50
87 Jose Lima	.20	.50
88 Ryan Christenson	.20	.50
89 Jeff Cirillo	.20	.50
90 Jose Hernandez	.20	.50
91 Mark Kotsay	.30	.75
92 Darren Bragg	.20	.50
93 Albert Belle	.30	.75
94 Matt Lawton	.20	.50
95 Pedro Martinez	.50	1.25
96 Greg Vaughn	.20	.50
97 Neifi Perez	.20	.50
98 Gerald Williams	.20	.50
99 Derek Bell	.20	.50
100 Ken Griffey Jr.	1.50	4.00
101 David Cone	.30	.75
102 Brian Johnson	.20	.50
103 Dean Palmer	.30	.75
104 Javier Valentin	.20	.50
105 Trevor Hoffman	.30	.75
106 Butch Huskey	.20	.50
107 Dave Martinez	.20	.50
108 Billy Wagner	.30	.75
109 Shawn Green	.30	.75
110 Ben Grieve	.20	.50
111 Tom Goodwin	.20	.50
112 Jaret Wright	.20	.50
113 Aramis Ramirez	.30	.75
114 Dmitri Young	.30	.75
115 Hideki Irabu	.20	.50
116 Roberto Kelly	.20	.50
117 Jeff Fassero	.20	.50
118 Mark Clark	.20	.50
119 Jason McDonald	.20	.50
120 Matt Williams	.30	.75
121 Dave Burba	.20	.50
122 Bret Saberhagen	.30	.75
123 Deivi Cruz	.20	.50
124 Chad Curtis	.20	.50
125 Scott Rolen	.50	1.25
126 Lee Stevens	.20	.50
127 J.T. Snow	.30	.75
128 Rusty Greer	.30	.75
129 Brian Meadows	.20	.50
130 Jim Edmonds	.30	.75
131 Ron Gant	.30	.75
132 A.J. Hinch	.20	.50
133 Shannon Stewart	.30	.75
134 Brad Fullmer	.20	.50
135 Cal Eldred	.20	.50
136 Matt Walbeck	.20	.50
137 Carl Everett	.30	.75
138 Walt Weiss	.20	.50
139 Fred McGriff	.50	1.25
140 Darin Erstad	.30	.75
141 Dave Nilsson	.20	.50
142 Eric Young	.20	.50
143 Dan Wilson	.20	.50
144 Jeff Reed	.20	.50
145 Brett Tomko	.20	.50
146 Terry Steinbach	.20	.50
147 Seth Greisinger	.20	.50
148 Pat Meares	.20	.50
149 Livan Hernandez	.30	.75
150 Jeff Bagwell	.50	1.25
151 Bob Wickman	.20	.50
152 Omar Vizquel	.50	1.25
153 Eric Davis	.30	.75
154 Larry Sutton	.20	.50
155 Magglio Ordonez	.30	.75
156 Eric Milton	.20	.50
157 Darren Lewis	.20	.50
158 Rick Aguilera	.20	.50
159 Mike Lieberthal	.30	.75
160 Robb Nen	.30	.75
161 Brian Giles	.30	.75
162 Jeff Brantley	.20	.50
163 Gary DiSarcina	.20	.50
164 John Valentin	.20	.50
165 Dave Dellucci	.20	.50
166 Chan Ho Park	.30	.75
167 Masato Yoshii	.20	.50
168 Jason Schmidt	.30	.75
169 LaTroy Hawkins	.20	.50
170 Bret Boone	.30	.75
171 Jerry DiPoto	.20	.50
172 Mariano Rivera	.75	2.00
173 Mike Cameron	.20	.50
174 Scott Erickson	.20	.50
175 Charles Johnson	.30	.75
176 Bobby Jones	.20	.50
177 Francisco Cordova	.20	.50
178 Todd Jones	.20	.50
179 Jeff Montgomery	.20	.50
180 Mike Mussina	.50	1.25
181 Bob Abreu	.30	.75
182 Ismael Valdes	.20	.50
183 Andy Fox	.20	.50
184 Woody Williams	.20	.50
185 Denny Neagle	.20	.50
186 Jose Valentin	.20	.50
187 Darrin Fletcher	.20	.50
188 Gabe Alvarez	.20	.50
189 Eddie Taubensee	.20	.50
190 Edgar Martinez	.50	1.25
191 Jason Kendall	.30	.75
192 Darryl Kile	.30	.75
193 Jeff King	.20	.50
194 Rey Ordonez	.20	.50
195 Andruw Jones	.50	1.25
196 Tony Fernandez	.20	.50
197 Jamey Wright	.20	.50
198 B.J. Surhoff	.30	.75
199 Vinny Castilla	.30	.75
200 David Wells HL	.20	.50
201 Mark McGwire HL	1.00	2.50
202 Sammy Sosa HL	.50	1.25
203 Roger Clemens HL	.75	2.00
204 Kerry Wood HL	.20	.50
205 L.Berkman	.40	1.00
G.Kapler		
206 Alex Escobar RC	.40	1.00
207 Peter Bergeron RC	.40	1.00
208 M.Barrett	.40	1.00
B.Davis/R.Fick		
209 J.Werth	.40	1.00
Hernandez/Cline		
210 R.Anderson	.40	1.00
Chen/Enochs		
211 B.Penny	.40	1.00
Dotel/Lincoln		
212 Chuck Abbott RC	.40	1.00
213 C.Jones	.40	1.00
J.Urban RC		
214 T.Torcato	.40	1.00
A.McDowell RC		
215 J.Tyner	.40	1.00
J.McKinley RC		
216 M.Burch	.40	1.00
S.Etherton RC		
217 R.Elder	.40	1.00
M.Tucker RC		
218 J.M.Gold	.40	1.00
R.Mills RC		
219 A.Brown	.40	1.00
C.Freeman RC		
220A Mark McGwire HR 1	20.00	50.00
220B Mark McGwire HR 2	12.50	30.00
220C Mark McGwire HR 3	12.50	30.00
220D Mark McGwire HR 4	12.50	30.00
220E Mark McGwire HR 5	12.50	30.00
220F Mark McGwire HR 6	12.50	30.00
220G Mark McGwire HR 7	12.50	30.00
220H Mark McGwire HR 8	12.50	30.00
220I Mark McGwire HR 9	12.50	30.00
220J Mark McGwire HR 10	12.50	30.00
220K Mark McGwire HR 11	12.50	30.00
220L Mark McGwire HR 12	12.50	30.00
220M Mark McGwire HR 13	12.50	30.00
220N Mark McGwire HR 14	12.50	30.00
220O Mark McGwire HR 15	12.50	30.00
220P Mark McGwire HR 16	12.50	30.00
220Q Mark McGwire HR 17	12.50	30.00
220R Mark McGwire HR 18	12.50	30.00
220S Mark McGwire HR 19	12.50	30.00
220T Mark McGwire HR 20	12.50	30.00
220U Mark McGwire HR 21	12.50	30.00
220V Mark McGwire HR 22	12.50	30.00
220W Mark McGwire HR 23	12.50	30.00
220X Mark McGwire HR 24	12.50	30.00
220Y Mark McGwire HR 25	12.50	30.00
220Z Mark McGwire HR 26	12.50	30.00
220AA Mark McGwire HR 27	12.50	30.00
220AB Mark McGwire HR 28	12.50	30.00
220AC Mark McGwire HR 29	12.50	30.00
220AD Mark McGwire HR 30	12.50	30.00
220AE Mark McGwire HR 31	12.50	30.00
220AF Mark McGwire HR 32	12.50	30.00
220AG Mark McGwire HR 33	12.50	30.00
220AH Mark McGwire HR 34	12.50	30.00
220AI Mark McGwire HR 35	12.50	30.00
220AJ Mark McGwire HR 36	12.50	30.00
220AK Mark McGwire HR 37	12.50	30.00
220AL Mark McGwire HR 38	12.50	30.00
220AM Mark McGwire HR 39	12.50	30.00
220AN Mark McGwire HR 40	12.50	30.00
220AO Mark McGwire HR 41	12.50	30.00
220AP Mark McGwire HR 42	12.50	30.00
220AQ Mark McGwire HR 43	12.50	30.00
220AR Mark McGwire HR 44	12.50	30.00
220AS Mark McGwire HR 45	12.50	30.00
220AT Mark McGwire HR 46	12.50	30.00
220AU Mark McGwire HR 47	12.50	30.00
220AV Mark McGwire HR 48	12.50	30.00
220AW Mark McGwire HR 49	12.50	30.00
220AX Mark McGwire HR 50	12.50	30.00
220AY Mark McGwire HR 51	12.50	30.00
220AZ Mark McGwire HR 52	12.50	30.00
220BB Mark McGwire HR 53	12.50	30.00
220CC Mark McGwire HR 54	12.50	30.00
220DD Mark McGwire HR 55	12.50	30.00
220EE Mark McGwire HR 56	12.50	30.00
220FF Mark McGwire HR 57	12.50	30.00
220GG Mark McGwire HR 58	12.50	30.00
220HH Mark McGwire HR 59	12.50	30.00
220II Mark McGwire HR 60	12.50	30.00
220JJ Mark McGwire HR 61	20.00	50.00
220KK Mark McGwire HR 62	40.00	80.00
220LL Mark McGwire HR 63	20.00	50.00
220MM Mark McGwire HR 64	20.00	50.00
220NN Mark McGwire HR 65	20.00	50.00
220OO Mark McGwire HR 66	20.00	50.00
220PP Mark McGwire HR 67	20.00	50.00
220QQ Mark McGwire HR 68	20.00	50.00
220RR Mark McGwire HR 69	20.00	50.00
220SS Mark McGwire HR 70	60.00	120.00
221 Larry Walker LL	.20	.50
222 Bernie Williams LL	.30	.75
223 Mark McGwire LL	1.00	2.50
224 Ken Griffey Jr. LL	1.00	2.50
225 Sammy Sosa LL	.50	1.25
226 Juan Gonzalez LL	.20	.50
227 Dante Bichette LL	.20	.50
228 Alex Rodriguez LL	.75	2.00
229 Sammy Sosa LL	.50	1.25
230 Derek Jeter LL	1.00	2.50
231 Greg Maddux LL	.75	2.00
232 Roger Clemens LL	.75	2.00
233 Ricky Ledee WS	.20	.50
234 Chuck Knoblauch WS	.20	.50
235 Bernie Williams WS	.30	.75
236 Tino Martinez WS	.30	.75
237 Orlando Hernandez WS	.20	.50
238 Scott Brosius WS	.20	.50
239 Andy Pettitte WS	.30	.75
240 Mariano Rivera WS	.50	1.25
241 Checklist	.20	.50
242 Checklist	.20	.50
243 Tom Glavine	.50	1.25
244 Andy Benes	.20	.50
245 Sandy Alomar Jr.	.20	.50
246 Wilton Guerrero	.20	.50
247 Alex Gonzalez	.20	.50
248 Roberto Alomar	.50	1.25
249 Ruben Rivera	.20	.50
250 Eric Chavez	.20	.50
251 Ellis Burks	.30	.75
252 Richie Sexson	.30	.75
253 Steve Finley	.30	.75
254 Dwight Gooden	.30	.75
255 Dustin Hermanson	.20	.50
256 Kirk Rueter	.20	.50
257 Steve Trachsel	.20	.50
258 Gregg Jefferies	.20	.50
259 Matt Stairs	.20	.50
260 Shane Reynolds	.20	.50
261 Gregg Olson	.20	.50
262 Kevin Tapani	.20	.50
263 Matt Morris	.30	.75
264 Carl Pavano	.20	.50
265 Nomar Garciaparra	1.25	3.00
266 Kevin Young	.30	.75
267 Rick Helling	.20	.50
268 Matt Franco	.20	.50
269 Brian McRae	.20	.50
270 Cal Ripken	2.50	6.00
271 Jeff Abbott	.20	.50
272 Tony Batista	.20	.50
273 Bill Simas	.20	.50
274 Brian Hunter	.20	.50
275 John Franco	.30	.75
276 Devon White	.30	.75
277 Rickey Henderson	.75	2.00
278 Chuck Finley	.30	.75
279 Mike Blowers	.20	.50
280 Mark Grace	.50	1.25
281 Randy Winn	.20	.50
282 Bobby Bonilla	.30	.75
283 David Justice	.30	.75
284 Shane Monahan	.20	.50
285 Kevin Brown	.50	1.25
286 Todd Zeile	.30	.75
287 Al Martin	.20	.50
288 Troy O'Leary	.20	.50
289 Darryl Hamilton	.20	.50
290 Tino Martinez	.50	1.25
291 David Ortiz	.75	2.00
292 Tony Clark	.20	.50
293 Ryan Minor	.20	.50
294 Mark Leiter	.20	.50
295 Wally Joyner	.30	.75
296 Cliff Floyd	.30	.75
297 Shawn Estes	.30	.75
298 Pat Hentgen	.20	.50
299 Scott Elarton	.20	.50
300 Alex Rodriguez	1.25	3.00
301 Ozzie Guillen	.20	.50
302 Hideo Nomo	.75	2.00
303 Ryan McGuire	.20	.50
304 Brad Ausmus	.30	.75
305 Alex Gonzalez	.20	.50
306 Brian Jordan	.20	.50
307 John Jaha	.20	.50
308 Mark Grudzielanek	.20	.50
309 Juan Guzman	.20	.50
310 Tony Womack	.20	.50
311 Dennis Reyes	.20	.50
312 Marty Cordova	.20	.50
313 Ramiro Mendoza	.20	.50
314 Robin Ventura	.30	.75
315 Rafael Palmeiro	.50	1.25
316 Ramon Martinez	.20	.50
317 Pedro Astacio	.20	.50
318 Dave Hollins	.20	.50
319 Tom Candiotti	.20	.50
320 Al Leiter	.30	.75
321 Rico Brogna	.20	.50
322 Reggie Jefferson	.20	.50
323 Bernard Gilkey	.20	.50
324 Jason Giambi	.30	.75
325 Craig Biggio	.50	1.25
326 Troy Glaus	.50	1.25
327 Delino DeShields	.20	.50
328 Fernando Vina	.20	.50
329 John Smoltz	.50	1.25
330 Jeff Kent	.30	.75
331 Roy Halladay	.75	2.00
332 Andy Ashby	.20	.50
333 Tim Wakefield	.30	.75
334 Roger Clemens	1.50	4.00
335 Bernie Williams	.50	1.25
336 Desi Relaford	.20	.50
337 John Burkett	.20	.50
338 Mike Hampton	.30	.75
339 Royce Clayton	.20	.50
340 Mike Piazza	1.25	3.00
341 Jeremi Gonzalez	.20	.50
342 Mike Lansing	.20	.50
343 Jamie Moyer	.30	.75
344 Ron Coomer	.20	.50
345 Barry Larkin	.50	1.25
346 Fernando Tatis	.20	.50
347 Chili Davis	.30	.75
348 Bobby Higginson	.30	.75
349 Hal Morris	.20	.50
350 Larry Walker	.30	.75
351 Carlos Guillen	.30	.75
352 Miguel Tejada	.30	.75
353 Travis Fryman	.30	.75
354 Jarrod Washburn	.20	.50
355 Chipper Jones	.75	2.00
356 Todd Stottlemyre	.20	.50
357 Henry Rodriguez	.20	.50
358 Eli Marrero	.20	.50
359 Alan Benes	.20	.50
360 Tim Salmon	.50	1.25
361 Luis Gonzalez	.30	.75
362 Scott Spiezio	.20	.50
363 Chris Carpenter	.30	.75
364 Bobby Howry	.20	.50
365 Raul Mondesi	.30	.75
366 Ugueth Urbina	.20	.50
367 Tom Evans	.20	.50
368 Kerry Ligtenberg RC	.30	.75
369 Adrian Beltre	.30	.75
370 Ryan Klesko	.30	.75
371 Wilson Alvarez	.20	.50
372 John Thomson	.20	.50
373 Tony Saunders	.20	.50
374 Dave Mlicki	.20	.50
375 Ken Caminiti	.30	.75
376 Jay Buhner	.30	.75
377 Bill Mueller	.20	.50
378 Jeff Blauser	.20	.50
379 Edgar Renteria	.30	.75
380 Jim Thome	.50	1.25
381 Joey Hamilton	.20	.50
382 Calvin Pickering	.20	.50
383 Marquis Grissom	.30	.75
384 Omar Daal	.20	.50
385 Curt Schilling	.30	.75
386 Jose Cruz Jr.	.20	.50
387 Chris Widger	.20	.50
388 Pete Harnisch	.20	.50
389 Charles Nagy	.20	.50
390 Tom Gordon	.20	.50
391 Bobby Smith	.20	.50
392 Derrick Gibson	.20	.50
393 Jeff Conine	.30	.75
394 Carlos Perez	.20	.50
395 Barry Bonds	2.00	5.00
396 Mark McLemore	.20	.50
397 Juan Encarnacion	.20	.50
398 Wade Boggs	.50	1.25
399 Ivan Rodriguez	.50	1.25
400 Moises Alou	.30	.75
401 Jeromy Burnitz	.30	.75
402 Sean Casey	.30	.75
403 Jose Offerman	.20	.50
404 Joe Fontenot	.20	.50
405 Kevin Millwood	.30	.75
406 Lance Johnson	.20	.50
407 Richard Hidalgo	.20	.50
408 Mike Jackson	.20	.50
409 Brian Anderson	.20	.50
410 Jeff Shaw	.20	.50
411 Preston Wilson	.30	.75
412 Todd Hundley	.20	.50
413 Jim Parque	.20	.50
414 Justin Baughman	.20	.50
415 Dante Bichette	.30	.75
416 Paul O'Neill	.50	1.25
417 Miguel Cairo	.20	.50
418 Randy Johnson	.75	2.00
419 Jesus Sanchez	.20	.50
420 Carlos Delgado	.30	.75
421 Ricky Ledee	.20	.50
422 Orlando Hernandez	.30	.75
423 Frank Thomas	.75	2.00
424 Pokey Reese	.20	.50
425 C.Lee	.40	1.00
M.Lowell		
426 M.Cuddyer	.40	1.00
DeRosa/Hairston		
427 M.Anderson	.40	1.00
Belliard/Cabrera		
428 M.Bowie	.40	1.00
P.Norton RC/Wolf		
429 J.Cressend RC	.40	1.00
Rocker		
430 R.Mateo	.40	1.00
M.Zywica RC		
431 J.LaRue	.40	1.00
LeCroy/Meluskey		
432 Gabe Kapler	.40	1.00
433 A.Kennedy	.40	1.00
M.Lopez RC		
434 Jose Fernandez RC	.40	1.00
C.Truby		
435 Doug Mientkiewicz RC	.60	1.50
436 R.Brown RC	.40	1.00
V.Wells		
437 A.J. Burnett RC	.75	2.00
438 M.Belisle	.40	1.00
M.Roney RC		
439 A.Kearns	1.50	4.00
C.George RC		
440 N.Cornejo	.40	1.00
N.Bump RC		
441 B.Lidge	1.50	4.00
M.Nannini RC		
442 M.Holliday	3.00	8.00
J.Winchester RC		
443 A.Everett	.60	1.50
C.Ambres RC		
444 P.Burrell	1.50	4.00
E.Valent RC		
445 Roger Clemens SK	.75	2.00
446 Kerry Wood SK	.20	.50
447 Curt Schilling SK	.20	.50
448 Randy Johnson SK	.50	1.25
449 Pedro Martinez SK	.50	1.25
450 Bagwell	.75	2.00
Galar/McGwire AT		
451 Olerud	.30	.75
Thome/Martinez AT		
452 ARod	1.00	2.50
Nomar/Jeter AT		
453 Castilla	.50	1.25
Jones/Rolen AT		
454 Sosa	1.00	2.50
Griffey/Gonzalez AT		
455 Bonds	1.00	2.50
Ramirez/Walker AT		
456 Thomas	.75	2.00
Salmon/Justice AT		
457 Lee	.30	.75
Helton/Grieve AT		
458 Guerrero	.30	.75
Vaughn/B.Will AT		
459 Piazza	.75	2.00
IRod/Kendall AT		
460 Clemens	.75	2.00
Wood/Maddux AT		
461A Sammy Sosa HR 1	8.00	20.00
461B Sammy Sosa HR 2	5.00	12.00
461C Sammy Sosa HR 3	5.00	12.00
461D Sammy Sosa HR 4	5.00	12.00
461E Sammy Sosa HR 5	5.00	12.00
461F Sammy Sosa HR 6	5.00	12.00
461G Sammy Sosa HR 7	5.00	12.00
461H Sammy Sosa HR 8	5.00	12.00
461I Sammy Sosa HR 9	5.00	12.00
461J Sammy Sosa HR 10	5.00	12.00
461K Sammy Sosa HR 11	5.00	12.00
461L Sammy Sosa HR 12	5.00	12.00
461M Sammy Sosa HR 13	5.00	12.00
461N Sammy Sosa HR 14	5.00	12.00
461O Sammy Sosa HR 15	5.00	12.00
461P Sammy Sosa HR 16	5.00	12.00
461Q Sammy Sosa HR 17	5.00	12.00
461R Sammy Sosa HR 18	5.00	12.00
461S Sammy Sosa HR 19	5.00	12.00
461T Sammy Sosa HR 20	5.00	12.00
461U Sammy Sosa HR 21	5.00	12.00
461V Sammy Sosa HR 22	5.00	12.00
461W Sammy Sosa HR 23	5.00	12.00
461X Sammy Sosa HR 24	5.00	12.00
461Y Sammy Sosa HR 25	5.00	12.00
461Z Sammy Sosa HR 26	5.00	12.00
461AA Sammy Sosa HR 27	5.00	12.00
461AB Sammy Sosa HR 28	5.00	12.00
461AC Sammy Sosa HR 29	5.00	12.00
461AD Sammy Sosa HR 30	5.00	12.00
461AE Sammy Sosa HR 31	5.00	12.00
461AF Sammy Sosa HR 32	5.00	12.00
461AG Sammy Sosa HR 33	5.00	12.00
461AH Sammy Sosa HR 34	5.00	12.00
461AI Sammy Sosa HR 35	5.00	12.00
461AJ Sammy Sosa HR 36	5.00	12.00
461AK Sammy Sosa HR 37	5.00	12.00
461AL Sammy Sosa HR 38	5.00	12.00
461AM Sammy Sosa HR 39	5.00	12.00
461AN Sammy Sosa HR 40	5.00	12.00
461AO Sammy Sosa HR 41	5.00	12.00
461AP Sammy Sosa HR 42	5.00	12.00
461AR Sammy Sosa HR 43	5.00	12.00
461AS Sammy Sosa HR 44	5.00	12.00
461AT Sammy Sosa HR 45	5.00	12.00
461AU Sammy Sosa HR 46	5.00	12.00
461AV Sammy Sosa HR 47	5.00	12.00
461AW Sammy Sosa HR 48	5.00	12.00
461AX Sammy Sosa HR 49	5.00	12.00
461AY Sammy Sosa HR 50	5.00	12.00
461AZ Sammy Sosa HR 51	5.00	12.00
461BB Sammy Sosa HR 52	5.00	12.00
461CC Sammy Sosa HR 53	5.00	12.00
461DD Sammy Sosa HR 54	5.00	12.00
461EE Sammy Sosa HR 55	5.00	12.00
461FF Sammy Sosa HR 56	5.00	12.00
461GG Sammy Sosa HR 57	5.00	12.00
461HH Sammy Sosa HR 58	5.00	12.00
461II Sammy Sosa HR 59	5.00	12.00
461JJ Sammy Sosa HR 60	5.00	12.00
461KK Sammy Sosa HR 61	8.00	20.00
461LL Sammy Sosa HR 62	12.50	30.00
461MM Sammy Sosa HR 63	8.00	20.00
461NN Sammy Sosa HR 64	8.00	20.00
461OO Sammy Sosa HR 65	8.00	20.00
461PP Sammy Sosa HR 66	30.00	60.00
462 Checklist	.20	.50
463 Checklist	.20	.50

1999 Topps Chrome Refractors

Card	Low	High
*STARS: 2.5X TO 6X BASIC CARDS		
*ROOKIES: 1.25X TO 3X BASIC CARDS		
MCGWIRE 220 HR 1	125.00	250.00
MCGWIRE 220 HR 2-60	60.00	120.00
MCGWIRE 220 HR 61	100.00	200.00
MCGWIRE 220 HR 62	150.00	300.00
MCGWIRE 220 HR 63-69	60.00	120.00
MCGWIRE 220 HR 70	200.00	400.00
SOSA 461 HR 1	30.00	60.00
SOSA 461 HR 2-60	10.00	25.00
SOSA 461 HR 61	20.00	50.00
SOSA 461 HR 62	40.00	80.00
SOSA 461 HR 63-65	10.00	25.00
SOSA 461 HR 66	60.00	120.00
REFRACTOR STATED ODDS 1:12		
CARD NUMBER 7 DOES NOT EXIST		
442 M.Holliday	15.00	40.00
J.Winchester		

1999 Topps Chrome All-Etch

Card	Low	High
COMPLETE SET (30)	40.00	100.00
SER.2 STATED ODDS 1:6		
*REFRACTORS: .75X TO 2X BASIC ALL-ETCH		
SER.2 REFRACTOR ODDS 1:24		
AE1 Mark McGwire	5.00	12.00
AE2 Sammy Sosa	2.00	5.00
AE3 Ken Griffey Jr.	4.00	10.00
AE4 Greg Vaughn	.50	1.25
AE5 Albert Belle	.75	2.00
AE6 Vinny Castilla	.75	2.00
AE7 Jose Canseco	1.25	3.00
AE8 Juan Gonzalez	.75	2.00
AE9 Manny Ramirez	1.25	3.00
AE10 Andres Galarraga	.75	2.00
AE11 Rafael Palmeiro	1.25	3.00
AE12 Alex Rodriguez	3.00	8.00
AE13 Mo Vaughn	.75	2.00
AE14 Eric Chavez	.75	2.00
AE15 Gabe Kapler	1.00	2.50
AE16 Calvin Pickering	.50	1.25
AE17 Ruben Mateo	1.00	2.50
AE18 Roy Halladay	2.00	5.00
AE19 Jeremy Giambi	.50	1.25
AE20 Alex Gonzalez	.50	1.25
AE21 Ron Belliard	1.00	2.50
AE22 Marlon Anderson	1.00	2.50
AE23 Carlos Lee	1.00	2.50
AE24 Kerry Wood	.75	2.00
AE25 Roger Clemens	4.00	10.00
AE26 Curt Schilling	.75	2.00
AE27 Kevin Brown	1.25	3.00
AE28 Randy Johnson	2.00	5.00
AE29 Pedro Martinez	1.25	3.00
AE30 Orlando Hernandez	.75	2.00

1999 Topps Chrome Early Road to the Hall

Card	Low	High
COMPLETE SET (10)	10.00	25.00
SER.1 STATED ODDS 1:12		
*REFRACTORS: 3X TO 8X BASIC ROAD		
SER.1 REFRACTOR ODDS 1:944 HOBBY		
REF.PRINT RUN 100 SERIAL #'d SETS		
ER1 Nomar Garciaparra	.75	2.00
ER2 Derek Jeter	3.00	8.00
ER3 Alex Rodriguez	1.50	4.00
ER4 Juan Gonzalez	.50	1.25
ER5 Ken Griffey Jr.	2.50	6.00
ER6 Chipper Jones	1.25	3.00
ER7 Vladimir Guerrero	.75	2.00
ER8 Jeff Bagwell	.75	2.00
ER9 Ivan Rodriguez	.75	2.00
ER10 Frank Thomas	1.25	3.00

1999 Topps Chrome Fortune 15

Card	Low	High
COMPLETE SET (15)	40.00	100.00
SER.2 STATED ODDS 1:12		
*REFRACTORS: 4X TO 8X BASIC FORT.15		
SER.2 REFRACTOR ODDS 1:627		
REF.PRINT RUN 100 SERIAL #'d SETS		
FF1 Alex Rodriguez	3.00	8.00
FF2 Nomar Garciaparra	3.00	8.00
FF3 Derek Jeter	5.00	12.00
FF4 Troy Glaus	1.25	3.00
FF5 Ken Griffey Jr.	4.00	10.00
FF6 Vladimir Guerrero	2.00	5.00
FF7 Kerry Wood	.75	2.00
FF8 Eric Chavez	.75	2.00
FF9 Greg Maddux	3.00	8.00
FF10 Mike Piazza	3.00	8.00
FF11 Sammy Sosa	2.00	5.00
FF12 Mark McGwire	5.00	12.00
FF13 Ben Grieve	.50	1.25
FF14 Chipper Jones	2.00	5.00
FF15 Manny Ramirez	1.25	3.00

1999 Topps Chrome Lords of the Diamond

Card	Low	High
COMPLETE SET (15)	20.00	50.00
SER.1 STATED ODDS 1:8		
*REFRACTORS: .6X TO 1.5X BASIC LORDS		
SER.1 REFRACTOR ODDS 1:24		
LD1 Ken Griffey Jr.	2.00	5.00
LD2 Chipper Jones	1.00	2.50
LD3 Sammy Sosa	1.00	2.50
LD4 Frank Thomas	1.00	2.50
LD5 Mark McGwire	2.50	6.00
LD6 Jeff Bagwell	.60	1.50
LD7 Alex Rodriguez	1.50	4.00
LD8 Juan Gonzalez	.40	1.00
LD9 Barry Bonds	2.50	6.00
LD10 Nomar Garciaparra	1.50	4.00
LD11 Darin Erstad	.40	1.00
LD12 Tony Gwynn	1.25	3.00
LD13 Andres Galarraga	.40	1.00
LD14 Mike Piazza	1.50	4.00
LD15 Greg Maddux	1.50	4.00

1999 Topps Chrome New Breed

Card	Low	High
COMPLETE SET (15)	40.00	100.00
SER.1 STATED ODDS 1:24		
*REFRACTORS: .6X TO 1.5X BASIC BREED		
SER.1 REFRACTOR ODDS 1:72		
NB1 Darin Erstad	1.25	3.00
NB2 Brad Fullmer	.75	2.00
NB3 Kerry Wood	1.25	3.00
NB4 Nomar Garciaparra	5.00	12.00
NB5 Travis Lee	.75	2.00
NB6 Scott Rolen	2.00	5.00
NB7 Todd Helton	2.00	5.00
NB8 Vladimir Guerrero	3.00	8.00
NB9 Derek Jeter	8.00	20.00
NB10 Alex Rodriguez	5.00	12.00
NB11 Ben Grieve	.75	2.00
NB12 Andruw Jones	2.00	5.00
NB13 Paul Konerko	1.25	3.00
NB14 Aramis Ramirez	1.25	3.00
NB15 Adrian Beltre	1.25	3.00

1999 Topps Chrome Record Numbers

Card	Low	High
COMPLETE SET (10)	15.00	40.00
SER.2 STATED ODDS 1:36		
*REFRACTORS: .75X TO 2X BASIC REC.NUM.		
SER.2 REFRACTOR ODDS 1:144		
RN1 Mark McGwire	2.50	6.00
RN2 Mike Piazza	1.50	4.00
RN3 Curt Schilling	.60	1.50
RN4 Ken Griffey Jr.	3.00	8.00
RN5 Sammy Sosa	1.50	4.00
RN6 Nomar Garciaparra	1.00	2.50
RN7 Kerry Wood	.60	1.50
RN8 Roger Clemens	2.00	5.00
RN9 Cal Ripken	5.00	12.00
RN10 Mark McGwire	2.50	6.00

1999 Topps Chrome Traded

This 121-card set features color photos on Chromium cards of 46 of the most notable transactions of the 1999 season and 75 newcomers accented with the Topps "Rookie Card" logo. The set was distributed only in factory boxes. Due to a very late ship date (January, 2000) this set caused some commotion in the hobby as to its status as a 1999 or 2000 product. Notable Rookie Cards include Carl Crawford, Adam Dunn, Josh Hamilton, Corey Patterson and Alfonso Soriano.

Card	Low	High
COMP.FACT SET (121)	30.00	60.00
DISTRIBUTED ONLY IN FACTORY SET FORM		
CONDITION SENSITIVE SET		
T1 Seth Etherton	.15	.40
T2 Mark Harriger RC	.20	.50
T3 Matt Wise RC	.20	.50
T4 Carlos Eduardo Hernandez RC	.30	.75
T5 Julio Lugo RC	.50	1.25
T6 Mike Nannini	.15	.40
T7 Justin Bowles RC	.20	.50
T8 Mark Mulder RC	1.25	3.00
T9 Roberto Vaz RC	.20	.50
T10 Felipe Lopez RC	1.25	3.00
T11 Matt Belisle	.15	.40
T12 Micah Bowie	.15	.40
T13 Ruben Quevedo RC	.20	.50
T14 Jose Garcia RC	.20	.50
T15 David Kelton RC	.20	.50
T16 Phil Norton	.15	.40
T17 Corey Patterson RC	.75	2.00
T18 Ron Walker RC	.20	.50
T19 Paul Hoover RC	.20	.50
T20 Ryan Rupe RC	.20	.50
T21 J.D. Closser RC	.30	.75
T22 Rob Ryan RC	.20	.50
T23 Steve Colyer RC	.20	.50
T24 Bubba Crosby RC	.50	1.25
T25 Luke Prokopec RC	.20	.50
T26 Matt Blank RC	.20	.50
T27 Josh McKinley	.15	.40
T28 Nate Bump	.20	.50
T29 Giuseppe Chiaramonte RC	.20	.50
T30 Arturo McDowell	.15	.40
T31 Tony Torcato	.15	.40
T32 Dave Roberts RC	.50	1.25
T33 C.C. Sabathia RC	4.00	10.00
T34 Sean Spencer RC	.20	.50
T35 Chip Ambres	.15	.40
T36 A.J. Burnett	.75	2.00
T37 Mo Bruce RC	.20	.50
T38 Jason Tyner	.15	.40
T39 Mamon Tucker	.15	.40
T40 Sean Burroughs RC	.50	1.25
T41 Kevin Eberwein RC	.20	.50
T42 Junior Herndon RC	.20	.50
T43 Bryan Wolff RC	.20	.50
T44 Pat Burrell	1.25	3.00
T45 Eric Valent	.30	.75
T46 Carlos Pena RC	.40	1.00
T47 Mike Zywica	.15	.40
T48 Adam Everett	.40	1.00
T49 Juan Pena RC	.20	.50
T50 Adam Dunn RC	3.00	8.00
T51 Austin Kearns	1.25	3.00
T52 Jacobo Sequea RC	.20	.50
T53 Choo Freeman	.25	.60
T54 Jeff Winchester	.15	.40
T55 Matt Burch	.20	.50
T56 Chris George	.15	.40
T57 Scott Mullen RC	.20	.50
T58 Kit Pellow	.20	.50
T59 Mark Quinn RC	.20	.50
T60 Nate Cornejo	.20	.50
T61 Ryan Mills	.15	.40
T62 Kevin Beirne RC	.20	.50
T63 Kip Wells RC	.30	.75
T64 Juan Rivera RC	.75	2.00
T65 Alfonso Soriano RC	4.00	10.00
T66 Josh Hamilton RC	5.00	12.00
T67 Josh Girdley RC	.20	.50
T68 Kyle Snyder RC	.20	.50
T69 Mike Paradis RC	.20	.50
T70 Jason Jennings RC	.50	1.25
T71 David Walling RC	.20	.50
T72 Omar Ortiz RC	.20	.50
T73 Jay Gehrke RC	.20	.50
T74 Casey Burns RC	.20	.50
T75 Carl Crawford RC	3.00	8.00
T76 Reggie Sanders	.25	.60
T77 Will Clark	.40	1.00
T78 David Wells	.25	.60
T79 Paul Konerko	.25	.60
T80 Armando Benitez	.15	.40
T81 Brant Brown	.15	.40
T82 Mo Vaughn	.25	.60
T83 Jose Canseco	.40	1.00
T84 Albert Belle	.25	.60
T85 Dean Palmer	.25	.60
T86 Greg Vaughn	.15	.40
T87 Mark Clark	.15	.40
T88 Pat Meares	.15	.40
T89 Eric Davis	.25	.60
T90 Brian Giles	.25	.60
T91 Jeff Brantley	.15	.40
T92 Bret Boone	.25	.60
T93 Ron Gant	.25	.60
T94 Mike Cameron	.15	.40
T95 Charles Johnson	.25	.60
T96 Denny Neagle	.15	.40
T97 Brian Hunter	.15	.40
T98 Jose Hernandez	.15	.40
T99 Rick Aguilera	.15	.40
T100 Tony Batista	.15	.40
T101 Roger Cedeno	.15	.40
T102 Creighton Gubanich RC	.20	.50
T103 Tim Belcher	.15	.40
T104 Bruce Aven	.15	.40
T105 Brian Daubach RC	.30	.75
T106 Ed Sprague	.15	.40
T107 Michael Tucker	.15	.40
T108 Homer Bush	.15	.40
T109 Armando Reynoso	.15	.40
T110 Brook Fordyce	.15	.40
T111 Matt Mantei	.15	.40
T112 Dave Mlicki	.15	.40
T113 Kenny Rogers	.25	.60
T114 Livan Hernandez	.25	.60
T115 Butch Huskey	.15	.40
T116 David Segui	.15	.40
T117 Darryl Hamilton	.15	.40
T118 Terry Mulholland	.15	.40
T119 Randy Velarde	.15	.40
T120 Bill Taylor	.15	.40
T121 Kevin Appier	.25	.60

2000 Topps Chrome

Card	Low	High
COMPLETE SET (478)	30.00	60.00
COMPLETE SERIES 1 (239)	12.50	30.00
COMPLETE SERIES 2 (240)	12.50	30.00
COMMON CARD (1-6/8-479)	.30	.75
COMMON RC	.40	1.00
MCGWIRE MM SET (5)	12.50	30.00
MCGWIRE MM (236A-236E)	4.00	10.00
AARON MM SET (5)	12.50	30.00

AARON MM (237A-237E) 4.00 10.00
RIPKEN MM SET (5) 25.00 60.00
RIPKEN MM (238A-238E) 8.00 20.00
BOGGS MM SET (5) 4.00 10.00
BOGGS MM (239A-239E) 1.25 3.00
GWYNN MM SET (5) 6.00 15.00
GWYNN MM (240A-240E) 2.00 5.00
GRIFFEY MM SET (5) 10.00 25.00
GRIFFEY MM (475A-475E) 3.00 8.00
BONDS MM SET (5) 12.50 30.00
BONDS MM (476A-476E) 4.00 10.00
SOSA MM SET (5) 6.00 15.00
SOSA MM (477A-477E) 2.00 5.00
JETER MM SET (5) 15.00 40.00
JETER MM (478A-478E) 5.00 12.00
A.ROD MM SET (5) 10.00 25.00
A.ROD MM (479A-479E) 3.00 8.00
CARD NUMBER 7 DOES NOT EXIST
SER.1 HAS ONLY 1 VERSION OF 236-240
SER.2 HAS ONLY 1 VERSION OF 475-479
MCGWIRE '85 ODDS 1:32
1 Mark McGwire 1.25 3.00
2 Tony Gwynn .75 2.00
3 Wade Boggs .50 1.25
4 Cal Ripken 2.50 6.00
5 Matt Williams .30 .75
6 Jay Buhner .30 .75
8 Jeff Conine .30 .75
9 Todd Greene .30 .75
10 Mike Lieberthal .30 .75
11 Steve Avery .30 .75
12 Bret Saberhagen .30 .75
13 Magglio Ordonez .50 1.25
14 Brad Radke .30 .75
15 Derek Jeter 2.00 5.00
16 Javy Lopez .30 .75
17 Russ Davis .30 .75
18 Armando Benitez .30 .75
19 B.J. Surhoff .30 .75
20 Darryl Kile .30 .75
21 Mark Lewis .30 .75
22 Mike Williams .30 .75
23 Mark McLemore .30 .75
24 Sterling Hitchcock .30 .75
25 Darin Erstad .30 .75
26 Ricky Gutierrez .30 .75
27 John Jaha .30 .75
28 Homer Bush .30 .75
29 Darrin Fletcher .30 .75
30 Mark Grace .50 1.25
31 Fred McGriff .50 1.25
32 Omar Daal .30 .75
33 Eric Karros .30 .75
34 Orlando Cabrera .30 .75
35 J.T. Snow .30 .75
36 Luis Castillo .30 .75
37 Rey Ordonez .30 .75
38 Bob Abreu .30 .75
39 Warren Morris .30 .75
40 Juan Gonzalez .30 .75
41 Mike Lansing .30 .75
42 Chili Davis .30 .75
43 Dean Palmer .30 .75
44 Hank Aaron 1.50 4.00
45 Jeff Bagwell .50 1.25
46 Jose Valentin .30 .75
47 Shannon Stewart .30 .75
48 Kent Bottenfield .30 .75
49 Jeff Shaw .30 .75
50 Sammy Sosa .75 2.00
51 Randy Johnson .75 2.00
52 Benny Agbayani .30 .75
53 Dante Bichette .30 .75
54 Pete Harnisch .30 .75
55 Frank Thomas .75 2.00
56 Jorge Posada .50 1.25
57 Todd Walker .30 .75
58 Juan Encarnacion .30 .75
59 Mike Sweeney .30 .75
60 Pedro Martinez .50 1.25
61 Lee Stevens .30 .75
62 Brian Giles .30 .75
63 Chad Ogea .30 .75
64 Ivan Rodriguez .50 1.25
65 Roger Cedeno .30 .75
66 David Justice .30 .75
67 Steve Trachsel .30 .75
68 Eli Marrero .30 .75
69 Dave Nilsson .30 .75
70 Ken Caminiti .30 .75
71 Tim Raines .50 1.25
72 Brian Jordan .30 .75
73 Jeff Blauser .30 .75
74 Bernard Gilkey .30 .75
75 John Flaherty .30 .75
76 Brent Mayne .30 .75
77 Jose Vidro .30 .75
78 David Bell .30 .75
79 Bruce Aven .30 .75
80 John Olerud .30 .75
81 Pokey Reese .30 .75
82 Woody Williams .30 .75
83 Ed Sprague .30 .75
84 Joe Girardi .50 1.25
85 Barry Larkin .50 1.25
86 Mike Caruso .30 .75
87 Bobby Higginson .30 .75
88 Roberto Kelly .30 .75
89 Edgar Martinez .50 1.25
90 Mark Kotsay .30 .75
91 Paul Sorrento .30 .75
92 Eric Young .30 .75
93 Carlos Delgado .30 .75
94 Troy Glaus .30 .75
95 Ben Grieve .30 .75
96 Jose Lima .30 .75
97 Garret Anderson .30 .75
98 Luis Gonzalez .30 .75
99 Carl Pavano .30 .75
100 Alex Rodriguez 1.00 2.50
101 Preston Wilson .30 .75
102 Ron Gant .30 .75
103 Brady Anderson .30 .75
104 Rickey Henderson .75 2.00
105 Gary Sheffield .30 .75
106 Mickey Morandini .30 .75
107 Jim Edmonds .30 .75
108 Kris Benson .30 .75
109 Adrian Beltre .75 2.00
110 Alex Fernandez .30 .75
111 Dan Wilson .30 .75
112 Mark Clark .30 .75
113 Greg Vaughn .30 .75
114 Neifi Perez .30 .75
115 Paul O'Neill .50 1.25
116 Jermaine Dye .30 .75
117 Todd Jones .30 .75
118 Terry Steinbach .30 .75
119 Greg Norton .30 .75
120 Curt Schilling .50 1.25
121 Todd Zeile .30 .75
122 Edgardo Alfonzo .30 .75
123 Ryan McGuire .30 .75
124 Rich Aurilia .30 .75
125 John Smoltz .75 2.00
126 Bob Wickman .30 .75
127 Richard Hidalgo .30 .75
128 Chuck Finley .30 .75
129 Billy Wagner .30 .75
130 Todd Hundley .30 .75
131 Dwight Gooden .30 .75
132 Russ Ortiz .30 .75
133 Mike Lowell .30 .75
134 Reggie Sanders .30 .75
135 John Valentin .30 .75
136 Brad Ausmus .30 .75
137 Chad Kreuter .30 .75
138 David Cone .30 .75
139 Brook Fordyce .30 .75
140 Roberto Alomar .50 1.25
141 Charles Nagy .30 .75
142 Brian Hunter .30 .75
143 Mike Mussina .50 1.25
144 Robin Ventura .30 .75
145 Kevin Brown .30 .75
146 Pat Hentgen .30 .75
147 Ryan Klesko .30 .75
148 Derek Bell .30 .75
149 Andy Sheets .30 .75
150 Larry Walker .50 1.25
151 Scott Williamson .30 .75
152 Jose Offerman .30 .75
153 Doug Mientkiewicz .30 .75
154 John Snyder RC .40 1.00
155 Sandy Alomar Jr. .30 .75
156 Joe Nathan .30 .75
157 Lance Johnson .30 .75
158 Odalis Perez .30 .75
159 Hideo Nomo .75 2.00
160 Steve Finley .30 .75
161 Dave Martinez .30 .75
162 Matt Walbeck .30 .75
163 Bill Spiers .30 .75
164 Fernando Tatis .30 .75
165 Kenny Lofton .30 .75
166 Paul Byrd .30 .75
167 Aaron Sele .30 .75
168 Eddie Taubensee .30 .75
169 Reggie Jefferson .30 .75
170 Roger Clemens 1.00 2.50
171 Francisco Cordova .30 .75
172 Mike Bordick .30 .75
173 Wally Joyner .30 .75
174 Marvin Benard .30 .75
175 Jason Kendall .30 .75
176 Mike Stanley .30 .75
177 Chad Allen .30 .75
178 Carlos Beltran .50 1.25
179 Deivi Cruz .30 .75
180 Chipper Jones .75 2.00
181 Vladimir Guerrero .50 1.25
182 Dave Burba .30 .75
183 Tom Goodwin .30 .75
184 Brian Daubach .30 .75
185 Jay Bell .30 .75
186 Roy Halladay .50 1.25
187 Miguel Tejada .50 1.25
188 Armando Rios .30 .75
189 Fernando Vina .30 .75
190 Eric Davis .30 .75
191 Henry Rodriguez .30 .75
192 Joe McEwing .30 .75
193 Jeff Kent .30 .75
194 Mike Jackson .30 .75
195 Mike Morgan .30 .75
196 Jeff Montgomery .30 .75
197 Jeff Zimmerman .30 .75
198 Tony Fernandez .30 .75
199 Jason Giambi .30 .75
200 Jose Canseco .50 1.25
201 Alex Gonzalez .30 .75
202 J.Cust .30 .75
M.Colangelo/D.Brown
203 A.Soriano .75 2.00
F.Lopez
204 Durazo .30 .75
Burrell/Johnson
205 John Sneed RC .40 1.00
K.Wells
206 J.Kalinowski .40 1.00
M.Tejera/C.Mears
207 L.Berkman .50 1.25
C.Patterson/R.Brown
208 K.Pellow .30 .75
K.Barker/R.Branyan
209 B.Garbe .40 1.00
L.Bigbie
210 B.Bradley .40 1.00
E.Munson
211 J.Girdley .30 .75
K.Snyder
212 C.Caple .40 1.00
J.Jennings
213 B.Myers 1.25 3.00
R.Christianson
214 J.Stumm .40 1.00
R.Purvis RC
215 D.Walling .30 .75
M.Paradis
216 O.Ortiz .30 .75
J.Gehrke
217 David Cone HL .30 .75
218 Jose Jimenez HL .30 .75
219 Chris Singleton HL .30 .75
220 Fernando Tatis HL .30 .75
221 Todd Helton HL .50 1.25
222 Kevin Millwood DIV .30 .75
223 Todd Pratt DIV .30 .75
224 Orlando Hernandez DIV .30 .75
225 Pedro Martinez DIV .50 1.25
226 Tom Glavine LCS .50 1.25
227 Bernie Williams LCS .50 1.25
228 Mariano Rivera WS 1.00 2.50
229 Tony Gwynn 20CB .75 2.00
230 Wade Boggs 20CB .50 1.25
231 Lance Johnson CB .30 .75
232 Mark McGwire 20CB 1.25 3.00
233 Rickey Henderson 20CB .75 2.00
234 Rickey Henderson 20CB .75 2.00
235 Roger Clemens 20CB 1.00 2.50
236A M.McGwire MM 1st HR 3.00 8.00
236B M.McGwire MM 1987 ROY 3.00 8.00
236C M.McGwire MM 62nd HR 3.00 8.00
236D M.McGwire MM 70th HR 3.00 8.00
236E M.McGwire MM 500th HR 3.00 8.00
237A H.Aaron MM 1st Career HR 4.00 10.00
237B H.Aaron MM 1957 MVP 4.00 10.00
237C H.Aaron MM 3000th Hit 4.00 10.00
237D H.Aaron MM 715th HR 4.00 10.00
237E H.Aaron MM 755th HR 4.00 10.00
238A C.Ripken MM 1982 ROY 6.00 15.00
238B C.Ripken MM 1991 MVP 6.00 15.00
238C C.Ripken MM 2131 Game 6.00 15.00
238D C.Ripken MM Streak Ends 6.00 15.00
238E C.Ripken MM 400th HR 6.00 15.00
239A W.Boggs MM 1983 Batting 1.25 3.00
239B W.Boggs MM 1988 Batting 1.25 3.00
239C W.Boggs MM 2000th Hit 1.25 3.00
239D W.Boggs MM 1996 Champs 1.25 3.00
239E W.Boggs MM 3000th Hit 1.25 3.00
240A T.Gwynn MM 1984 Batting 2.00 5.00
240B T.Gwynn MM 1984 NLCS 2.00 5.00
240C T.Gwynn MM 1995 Batting 2.00 5.00
240D T.Gwynn MM 1998 NLCS 2.00 5.00
240E T.Gwynn MM 3000th Hit 2.00 5.00
241 Tom Glavine .50 1.25
242 David Wells .30 .75
243 Kevin Appier .30 .75
244 Troy Percival .30 .75
245 Ray Lankford .30 .75
246 Marquis Grissom .30 .75
247 Randy Winn .30 .75
248 Miguel Batista .30 .75
249 Darren Dreifort .30 .75
250 Barry Bonds 1.25 3.00
251 Harold Baines .50 1.25
252 Cliff Floyd .30 .75
253 Freddy Garcia .30 .75
254 Kenny Rogers .30 .75
255 Ben Davis .30 .75
256 Charles Johnson .30 .75
257 Bubba Trammell .30 .75
258 Desi Relaford .30 .75
259 Al Martin .30 .75
260 Andy Pettitte .50 1.25
261 Carlos Lee .30 .75
262 Matt Lawton .30 .75
263 Andy Fox .30 .75
264 Chan Ho Park .50 1.25
265 Billy Koch .30 .75
266 Dave Roberts .50 1.25
267 Carl Everett .30 .75
268 Orel Hershiser .30 .75
269 Trot Nixon .30 .75
270 Rusty Greer .30 .75
271 Will Clark .50 1.25
272 Quilvio Veras .30 .75
273 Rico Brogna .30 .75
274 Devon White .30 .75
275 Tim Hudson .50 1.25
276 Mike Hampton .30 .75
277 Miguel Cairo .30 .75
278 Darren Oliver .30 .75
279 Jeff Cirillo .30 .75
280 Al Leiter .30 .75
281 Shane Andrews .30 .75
282 Carlos Febles .30 .75
283 Pedro Astacio .30 .75
284 Juan Guzman .30 .75
285 Orlando Hernandez .30 .75
286 Paul Konerko .30 .75
287 Tony Clark .30 .75
288 Aaron Boone .30 .75
289 Ismael Valdes .30 .75
290 Moises Alou .30 .75
291 Kevin Tapani .30 .75
292 John Franco .30 .75
293 Todd Zeile .30 .75
294 Jason Schmidt .30 .75
295 Johnny Damon .50 1.25
296 Scott Brosius .30 .75
297 Travis Fryman .30 .75
298 Jose Vizcaino .30 .75
299 Eric Chavez .30 .75
300 Mike Piazza .75 2.00
301 Matt Clement .30 .75
302 Cristian Guzman .30 .75
303 C.J. Nitkowski .30 .75
304 Michael Tucker .30 .75
305 Brett Tomko .30 .75
306 Mike Lansing .30 .75
307 Eric Owens .30 .75
308 Livan Hernandez .30 .75
309 Rondell White .30 .75
310 Todd Stottlemyre .30 .75
311 Chris Carpenter .50 1.25
312 Ken Hill .30 .75
313 Mark Loretta .30 .75
314 John Rocker .30 .75
315 Richie Sexson .30 .75
316 Ruben Mateo .30 .75
317 Joe Randa .30 .75
318 Mike Sirotka .30 .75
319 Jose Rosado .30 .75
320 Matt Mantei .30 .75
321 Kevin Millwood .30 .75
322 Gary Disarcina .30 .75
323 Dustin Hermanson .30 .75
324 Mike Stanton .30 .75
325 Kirk Rueter .30 .75
326 Damian Miller RC .40 1.00
327 Doug Glanville .30 .75
328 Scott Rolen .50 1.25
329 Ray Durham .30 .75
330 Butch Huskey .30 .75
331 Mariano Rivera 1.00 2.50
332 Darren Lewis .30 .75
333 Mike Timlin .30 .75
334 Mark Grudzielanek .30 .75
335 Mike Cameron .30 .75
336 Kelvim Escobar .30 .75
337 Bret Boone .30 .75
338 Mo Vaughn .30 .75
339 Craig Biggio .50 1.25
340 Michael Barrett .30 .75
341 Marlon Anderson .30 .75
342 Bobby Jones .30 .75
343 John Halama .30 .75
344 Todd Ritchie .30 .75
345 Chuck Knoblauch .30 .75
346 Rick Reed .30 .75
347 Kelly Stinnett .30 .75
348 Tim Salmon .30 .75
349 A.J. Hinch .30 .75
350 Jose Cruz Jr. .30 .75
351 Roberto Hernandez .30 .75
352 Edgar Renteria .30 .75
353 Jose Hernandez .30 .75
354 Brad Fullmer .30 .75
355 Trevor Hoffman .50 1.25
356 Troy O'Leary .30 .75
357 Justin Thompson .30 .75
358 Kevin Young .30 .75
359 Hideki Irabu .30 .75
360 Jim Thome .50 1.25
361 Steve Karsay .30 .75
362 Octavio Dotel .30 .75
363 Omar Vizquel .50 1.25
364 Raul Mondesi .30 .75
365 Shane Reynolds .30 .75
366 Bartolo Colon .30 .75
367 Chris Widger .30 .75
368 Gabe Kapler .30 .75
369 Bill Simas .30 .75
370 Tino Martinez .30 .75
371 John Thomson .30 .75
372 Delino Deshields .30 .75
373 Carlos Perez .30 .75
374 Eddie Perez .30 .75
375 Jeromy Burnitz .30 .75
376 Jimmy Haynes .30 .75
377 Travis Lee .30 .75
378 Darryl Hamilton .30 .75
379 Jamie Moyer .30 .75
380 Alex Gonzalez .30 .75
381 John Wetteland .30 .75
382 Vinny Castilla .30 .75
383 Jeff Suppan .30 .75
384 Jim Leyritz .30 .75
385 Robb Nen .30 .75
386 Wilson Alvarez .30 .75
387 Andres Galarraga .50 1.25
388 Mike Remlinger .30 .75
389 Geoff Jenkins .30 .75
390 Matt Stairs .30 .75
391 Bill Mueller .30 .75
392 Mike Lowell .30 .75
393 Andy Ashby .30 .75
394 Ruben Rivera .30 .75
395 Todd Helton .50 1.25
396 Bernie Williams .50 1.25
397 Royce Clayton .30 .75
398 Manny Ramirez .75 2.00
399 Kerry Wood .30 .75
400 Ken Griffey Jr. 1.50 4.00
401 Enrique Wilson .30 .75
402 Joey Hamilton .30 .75
403 Shawn Estes .30 .75
404 Ugueth Urbina .30 .75
405 Albert Belle .30 .75
406 Rick Helling .30 .75
407 Steve Parris .30 .75
408 Eric Milton .30 .75
409 Dave Mlicki .30 .75
410 Shawn Green .30 .75
411 Jaret Wright .30 .75
412 Tony Womack .30 .75
413 Vernon Wells .30 .75
414 Ron Belliard .30 .75
415 Ellis Burks .30 .75
416 Scott Erickson .30 .75
417 Rafael Palmeiro .50 1.25
418 Damion Easley .30 .75
419 Jamey Wright .30 .75
420 Corey Koskie .30 .75
421 Bobby Howry .30 .75
422 Ricky Ledee .30 .75
423 Dmitri Young .30 .75
424 Sidney Ponson .30 .75
425 Greg Maddux 1.00 2.50
426 Jose Guillen .30 .75
427 Jon Lieber .30 .75
428 Andy Benes .30 .75
429 Randy Velarde .30 .75
430 Sean Casey .30 .75
431 Torii Hunter .30 .75
432 Ryan Rupe .30 .75
433 David Segui .30 .75
434 Todd Pratt .30 .75
435 Nomar Garciaparra .50 1.25
436 Denny Neagle .30 .75
437 Ron Coomer .30 .75
438 Chris Singleton .30 .75
439 Tony Batista .30 .75
440 Andruw Jones .30 .75
441 A.Huff .30 .75
S.Burroughs/A.Piatt
442 Furcal .50 1.25
Dawkins/Dellaero
443 M.Lamb RC .40 1.00
J.Crede/W.Veras
444 J.Zuleta .40 1.00
J.Toca/D.Stenson
445 G.Maddox Jr. .40 1.00
G.Matthews Jr./T.Raines Jr.
446 M.Mulder .50 1.25
C.Sabathia/M.Riley
447 S.Downs .40 1.00
C.George/M.Belisle
448 D.Mirabelli .50 1.25
B.Petrick/J.Werth
449 J.Hamilton 1.25 3.00
C.Meyers
450 B.Christensen .40 1.00
R.Stahl
451 B.Zito 3.00 8.00
B.Sheets RC
452 K.Ainsworth .40 1.00
T.Howington
453 R.Asadoorian .40 1.00
V.Faison
454 K.Reed .40 1.00
J.Heaverlo
455 M.MacDougal .60 1.50
B.Baker
456 Mark McGwire SH 1.25 3.00
457 Cal Ripken SH 2.50 6.00
458 Wade Boggs SH .50 1.25
459 Tony Gwynn SH .75 2.00
460 Jesse Orosco SH .30 .75
461 L.Walker .50 1.25
N.Garciaparra LL
462 K.Griffey Jr. 1.50 4.00
M.McGwire LL
463 M.Ramirez 1.25 3.00
M.McGwire LL
464 P.Martinez .75 2.00
R.Johnson LL
465 P.Martinez .75 2.00
R.Johnson LL
466 D.Jeter 2.00 5.00
L.Gonzalez LL
467 L.Walker .75 2.00
M.Ramirez LL
468 Tony Gwynn 20CB .75 2.00
469 Mark McGwire 20CB 1.25 3.00
470 Frank Thomas 20CB .75 2.00
471 Harold Baines 20CB .50 1.25
472 Roger Clemens 20CB 1.00 2.50
473 John Franco 20CB .30 .75
474 John Franco 20CB .30 .75
475A K.Griffey Jr. MM 350th HR 4.00 10.00
475B K.Griffey Jr. MM 1997 MVP 4.00 10.00
475C K.Griffey Jr. MM HR Dad 4.00 10.00
475D K.Griffey Jr. MM 1992 AS MVP 4.00 10.00
475E K.Griffey Jr. MM 50 HR 1997 4.00 10.00
476A B.Bonds MM 400HR/400SB 3.00 8.00
476B B.Bonds MM 40HR/40SB 3.00 8.00
476C B.Bonds MM 1993 MVP 3.00 8.00
476D B.Bonds MM 1990 MVP 3.00 8.00
476E B.Bonds MM 1992 MVP 3.00 8.00
477A S.Sosa MM 20 HR June 2.00 5.00
477B S.Sosa MM 66 HR 1998 2.00 5.00
477C S.Sosa MM 60 HR 1999 2.00 5.00
477D S.Sosa MM 1998 MVP 2.00 5.00
477E S.Sosa MM HR's 61/62 2.00 5.00
478A D.Jeter MM 1996 ROY 5.00 12.00
478B D.Jeter MM Wins 1999 WS 5.00 12.00
478C D.Jeter MM Wins 1998 WS 5.00 12.00
478D D.Jeter MM Wins 1996 WS 5.00 12.00
478E D.Jeter MM 17 GM Hit Streak 5.00 12.00
479A A.Rodriguez MM 40HR/40SB 2.50 6.00
479B A.Rodriguez MM 100th HR 2.50 6.00
479C A.Rodriguez MM 1996 POY 2.50 6.00
479D A.Rodriguez MM Wins 1 Million 2.50 6.00
479E A.Rodriguez MM 1996
Batting Leader 2.50 6.00
NNO M.McGwire 85 Reprint 3.00 8.00

2000 Topps Chrome Refractors

*REF: 2.5X TO 6X BASIC
*REF MM: 4X TO 10X BASIC
*REF RC 1-474: 2X TO 5X BASIC
CARD NUMBER 7 DOES NOT EXIST
SER.1 HAS ONLY 1 VERSION OF 236-240
SER.2 HAS ONLY 1 VERSION OF 475-479
STATED ODDS 1:12
MCGWIRE '85 ODDS 1:12,116
MCGWIRE '85 PR.RUN 70 SERIAL #'d CARDS
MM McGwire 85 Reprint/70 50.00 125.00

2000 Topps Chrome 21st Century

COMPLETE SET (10) 6.00 15.00
SER.1 STATED ODDS 1:16
*REF: 1X TO 2.5X BASIC 21ST CENT.
SER.1 REFRACTOR ODDS 1:80
C1 Ben Grieve .40 1.00
C2 Alex Gonzalez .40 1.00
C3 Derek Jeter 2.50 6.00
C4 Sean Casey .40 1.00
C5 Nomar Garciaparra .60 1.50
C6 Alex Rodriguez 1.25 3.00
C7 Scott Rolen .60 1.50
C8 Andruw Jones .40 1.00
C9 Vladimir Guerrero .60 1.50
C10 Todd Helton .60 1.50

2000 Topps Chrome All-Star Rookie Team

COMPLETE SET (10) 8.00 20.00
SER.2 STATED ODDS 1:16
*REF: 1X TO 2.5X BASIC ASR TEAM
REFRACTOR STATED ODDS 1:80
RT1 Mark McGwire 1.50 4.00
RT2 Chuck Knoblauch .40 1.00
RT3 Chipper Jones 1.00 2.50
RT4 Cal Ripken 3.00 8.00
RT5 Manny Ramirez 1.00 2.50
RT6 Jose Canseco .60 1.50
RT7 Ken Griffey Jr. 2.00 5.00
RT8 Mike Piazza 1.00 2.50
RT9 Dwight Gooden .40 1.00
RT10 Billy Wagner .40 1.00

2000 Topps Chrome All-Topps

COMPLETE SET (20) 15.00 40.00
COMPLETE N.L.TEAM (10) 8.00 20.00
COMPLETE A.L.TEAM (10) 8.00 20.00
STATED ODDS 1:32
*REF: 1X TO 2.5X BASIC ALL TOPPS
REFRACTOR ODDS 1:160
N.L. CARDS DISTRIBUTED IN SERIES 1
A.L. CARDS DISTRIBUTED IN SERIES 2
AT1 Greg Maddux 1.25 3.00
AT2 Mike Piazza 1.00 2.50
AT3 Mark McGwire 1.50 4.00
AT4 Craig Biggio .60 1.50
AT5 Chipper Jones 1.00 2.50
AT6 Barry Larkin .60 1.50
AT7 Barry Bonds 1.50 4.00
AT8 Andruw Jones .40 1.00
AT9 Sammy Sosa 1.00 2.50
AT10 Larry Walker .60 1.50
AT11 Pedro Martinez .60 1.50
AT12 Ivan Rodriguez .60 1.50
AT13 Rafael Palmeiro .60 1.50
AT14 Roberto Alomar .60 1.50
AT15 Cal Ripken 3.00 8.00
AT16 Derek Jeter 2.50 6.00
AT17 Albert Belle .40 1.00
AT18 Ken Griffey Jr. 2.00 5.00
AT19 Manny Ramirez 1.00 2.50
AT20 Jose Canseco .60 1.50

2000 Topps Chrome Allegiance

COMPLETE SET (20) 15.00 40.00
SER.1 STATED ODDS 1:16
*REF: 4X TO 10X BASIC ALLEGIANCE
SER.1 REFRACTOR ODDS 1:424 HOBBY
REFRACTOR PRINT RUN 100 SERIAL #'d SETS
TA1 Derek Jeter 2.50 6.00
TA2 Ivan Rodriguez .60 1.50
TA3 Alex Rodriguez 1.25 3.00
TA4 Cal Ripken 3.00 8.00
TA5 Mark Grace .60 1.50
TA6 Tony Gwynn 1.00 2.50
TA7 Tom Glavine .60 1.50
TA8 Frank Thomas 1.00 2.50
TA9 Manny Ramirez 1.00 2.50
TA10 Barry Larkin .60 1.50
TA11 Bernie Williams .60 1.50
TA12 Eric Karros .40 1.00
TA13 Vladimir Guerrero .60 1.50
TA14 Craig Biggio .60 1.50
TA15 Nomar Garciaparra .60 1.50
TA16 Andruw Jones .40 1.00
TA17 Jim Thome .60 1.50
TA18 Scott Rolen .60 1.50
TA19 Chipper Jones 1.00 2.50
TA20 Ken Griffey Jr. 2.00 5.00

2000 Topps Chrome Combos

COMPLETE SET (10) 12.50 30.00
SER.2 STATED ODDS 1:16
*REFRACTORS: 1X TO 2.5X BASIC COMBO
REFRACTOR ODDS 1:80
TC1 Tribe-unal 1.00 2.50
TC2 Batter Baffler's 1.25 3.00
TC3 Torre's Terrors 2.50 6.00
TC4 All-Star Backstops 1.00 2.50
TC5 Three of a Kind 2.50 6.00
TC6 Home Run Kings 1.50 4.00
TC7 Strikeout Kings 1.00 2.50
TC8 Executive Producers 2.00 5.00
TC9 MVP's 1.00 2.50
TC10 3000 Hit Brigade 3.00 8.00

2000 Topps Chrome Kings

COMPLETE SET (10) 8.00 20.00
SER.2 STATED ODDS 1:32
CK1 Mark McGwire 1.50 4.00
CK2 Sammy Sosa 1.00 2.50
CK3 Ken Griffey Jr. 2.00 5.00
CK4 Mike Piazza 1.00 2.50
CK5 Alex Rodriguez 1.25 3.00
CK6 Manny Ramirez 1.00 2.50
CK7 Barry Bonds 1.50 4.00
CK8 Nomar Garciaparra .60 1.50
CK9 Chipper Jones 1.00 2.50
CK10 Vladimir Guerrero .60 1.50

2000 Topps Chrome Kings Refractors

COMPLETE SET (10) 50.00 100.00
SER.2 STATED ODDS 1:514
PRINT RUNS B/WN 92-522 COPIES PER
CK1 Mark McGwire/522 8.00 20.00
CK2 Sammy Sosa/366 5.00 12.00
CK3 Ken Griffey Jr./398 10.00 25.00
CK4 Mike Piazza/240 5.00 12.00
CK5 Alex Rodriguez/148 6.00 15.00
CK6 Manny Ramirez/198 5.00 12.00
CK7 Barry Bonds/445 8.00 20.00
CK8 Nomar Garciaparra/96 3.00 8.00
CK9 Chipper Jones/153 5.00 12.00
CK10 Vladimir Guerrero/92 3.00 8.00

2000 Topps Chrome New Millennium Stars

COMPLETE SET (10) 6.00 15.00
SER.2 STATED ODDS 1:32
*REFRACTORS: 1X TO 2.5X BASIC MILL.
SER.2 REFRACTOR ODDS 1:160
NMS1 Nomar Garciaparra 1.00 2.50
NMS2 Vladimir Guerrero 1.00 2.50
NMS3 Sean Casey .60 1.50
NMS4 Richie Sexson .60 1.50
NMS5 Todd Helton 1.00 2.50
NMS6 Carlos Beltran 1.00 2.50
NMS7 Kevin Millwood .60 1.50
NMS8 Ruben Mateo .60 1.50
NMS9 Pat Burrell .60 1.50
NMS10 Alfonso Soriano 1.50 4.00

2000 Topps Chrome Own the Game

COMPLETE SET (30) 20.00 50.00
SER.2 STATED ODDS 1:11
*REFRACTORS: 1X TO 2.5X BASIC OWN
SER.2 REFRACTOR ODDS 1:55
OTG1 Derek Jeter 2.50 6.00
OTG2 B.J. Surhoff .40 1.00
OTG3 Luis Gonzalez .40 1.00
OTG4 Manny Ramirez 1.00 2.50
OTG5 Rafael Palmeiro .60 1.50
OTG6 Mark McGwire 1.50 4.00
OTG7 Mark McGwire 1.50 4.00
OTG8 Sammy Sosa 1.00 2.50
OTG9 Ken Griffey Jr. 2.00 5.00
OTG10 Larry Walker .60 1.50
OTG11 Nomar Garciaparra .60 1.50
OTG12 Derek Jeter 2.50 6.00
OTG13 Larry Walker .60 1.50
OTG14 Mark McGwire 1.50 4.00
OTG15 Manny Ramirez 1.00 2.50
OTG16 Pedro Martinez .60 1.50
OTG17 Randy Johnson 1.00 2.50
OTG18 Kevin Millwood .40 1.00
OTG19 Randy Johnson 1.00 2.50
OTG20 Pedro Martinez .60 1.50
OTG21 Kevin Brown .40 1.00
OTG22 Chipper Jones 1.00 2.50
OTG23 Ivan Rodriguez .60 1.50
OTG24 Mariano Rivera 1.25 3.00
OTG25 Scott Williamson .40 1.00
OTG26 Carlos Beltran .60 1.50
OTG27 Randy Johnson 1.00 2.50
OTG28 Pedro Martinez .60 1.50
OTG29 Sammy Sosa 1.00 2.50
OTG30 Manny Ramirez 1.00 2.50

2000 Topps Chrome Power Players

COMPLETE SET (20) 12.50 30.00
SER.1 STATED ODDS 1:8
*REFRACTORS: 1X TO 2.5X BASIC POWER
SER.1 REFRACTOR ODDS 1:40
P1 Juan Gonzalez .40 1.00
P2 Ken Griffey Jr. 2.00 5.00
P3 Mark McGwire 1.50 4.00
P4 Nomar Garciaparra .60 1.50
P5 Barry Bonds 1.50 4.00
P6 Mo Vaughn .40 1.00
P7 Larry Walker .60 1.50
P8 Alex Rodriguez 1.25 3.00
P9 Jose Canseco .60 1.50
P10 Jeff Bagwell .60 1.50
P11 Manny Ramirez 1.00 2.50
P12 Albert Belle .40 1.00
P13 Frank Thomas 1.00 2.50
P14 Mike Piazza 1.00 2.50
P15 Chipper Jones 1.00 2.50
P16 Sammy Sosa 1.00 2.50
P17 Vladimir Guerrero .60 1.50
P18 Scott Rolen .60 1.50
P19 Raul Mondesi .40 1.00
P20 Derek Jeter 2.50 6.00

2000 Topps Chrome Traded

COMP.FACT.SET (135) 90.00 150.00
COMMON CARD (T1-T135) .15 .40
COMMON RC .30 .75
T1 Mike MacDougal .25 .60
T2 Andy Tracy RC .30 .75
T3 Brandon Phillips RC 1.25 3.00
T4 Brandon Inge RC 2.00 5.00
T5 Robbie Morrison RC .30 .75
T6 Josh Pressley RC .30 .75
T7 Todd Moser RC .30 .75
T8 Rob Purvis .15 .40
T9 Chance Caple .15 .40
T10 Ben Sheets .40 1.00
T11 Russ Jacobson RC .30 .75
T12 Brian Cole RC .30 .75
T13 Brad Baker .15 .40
T14 Alex Cintron RC .30 .75
T15 Lyle Overbay RC .50 1.25
T16 Mike Edwards RC .30 .75
T17 Sean McGowan RC .30 .75
T18 Jose Molina .15 .40
T19 Marcos Castillo RC .30 .75
T20 Josue Espada RC .30 .75
T21 Alex Gordon RC .30 .75
T22 Rob Pugmire RC .30 .75
T23 Jason Stumm .15 .40
T24 Ty Howington .15 .40
T25 Brett Myers .50 1.25
T26 Maicer Izturis RC .50 1.25
T27 John McDonald .15 .40
T28 Wilfredo Rodriguez RC .30 .75
T29 Carlos Zambrano RC 2.00 5.00
T30 Alejandro Diaz RC .30 .75
T31 Geraldo Guzman RC .30 .75
T32 J.R. House RC .30 .75
T33 Elvin Nina RC .30 .75
T34 Juan Pierre RC 1.50 4.00
T35 Ben Johnson RC .30 .75
T36 Jeff Bailey RC .30 .75
T37 Miguel Olivo RC .50 1.25
T38 Francisco Rodriguez RC 2.00 5.00
T39 Tony Pena Jr. RC .30 .75
T40 Miguel Cabrera RC 125.00 300.00
T41 Asdrubal Oropeza RC .30 .75
T42 Junior Zamora RC .30 .75
T43 Jovanny Cedeno RC .30 .75
T44 John Sneed .15 .40
T45 Josh Kalinowski .15 .40
T46 Mike Young RC 3.00 8.00
T47 Rico Washington RC .30 .75
T48 Chad Durbin RC .30 .75
T49 Junior Brignac RC .30 .75
T50 Carlos Hernandez RC .30 .75
T51 Cesar Izturis RC .30 .75
T52 Oscar Salazar RC .30 .75
T53 Pat Strange RC .30 .75
T54 Rick Asadoorian .15 .40
T55 Keith Reed .15 .40
T56 Leo Estrella RC .30 .75
T57 Wascar Serrano RC .30 .75
T58 Richard Gomez RC .30 .75
T59 Ramon Santiago RC .30 .75
T60 Jovanny Sosa RC .30 .75
T61 Aaron Rowand RC 1.50 4.00
T62 Junior Guerrero RC .30 .75
T63 Luis Terrero RC .30 .75
T64 Brian Sanches RC .30 .75
T65 Scott Sobkowiak RC .30 .75
T66 Gary Majewski RC .30 .75
T67 Barry Zito 1.25 3.00
T68 Ryan Christianson .15 .40
T69 Cristian Guerrero RC .30 .75
T70 Tomas De La Rosa RC .30 .75
T71 Andrew Beinbrink RC .30 .75
T72 Ryan Knox RC .30 .75
T73 Alex Graman RC .30 .75
T74 Juan Guzman RC .30 .75
T75 Ruben Salazar RC .30 .75
T76 Luis Matos RC .30 .75
T77 Tony Mota RC .30 .75

T78 Doug Davis .15 .40
T79 Ben Christensen .15 .40
T80 Mike Lamb .15 .40
T81 Adrian Gonzalez RC 4.00 10.00
T82 Mike Stodolka RC .30 .75
T83 Adam Johnson RC .30 .75
T84 Matt Wheatland RC .30 .75
T85 Corey Smith RC .30 .75
T86 Rocco Baldelli RC .75 2.00
T87 Keith Bucktrot RC .30 .75
T88 Adam Wainwright RC 3.00 8.00
T89 Scott Thorman RC .50 1.25
T90 Tripper Johnson RC .30 .75
T91 Jim Edmonds Cards .15 .40
T92 Masato Yoshii .15 .40
T93 Adam Kennedy .15 .40
T94 Darryl Kile .15 .40
T95 Mark McLemore .15 .40
T96 Ricky Gutierrez .15 .40
T97 Juan Gonzalez .15 .40
T98 Melvin Mora .15 .40
T99 Dante Bichette .15 .40
T100 Lee Stevens .15 .40
T101 Roger Cedeno .15 .40
T102 John Olerud .15 .40
T103 Eric Young .15 .40
T104 Mickey Morandini .15 .40
T105 Travis Lee .15 .40
T106 Greg Vaughn .15 .40
T107 Todd Zeile .15 .40
T108 Chuck Finley .15 .40
T109 Ismael Valdes .15 .40
T110 Reggie Sanders .15 .40
T111 Pat Hentgen .15 .40
T112 Ryan Klesko .15 .40
T113 Derek Bell .15 .40
T114 Hideo Nomo .40 1.00
T115 Aaron Sele .15 .40
T116 Fernando Vina .15 .40
T117 Wally Joyner .15 .40
T118 Brian Hunter .15 .40
T119 Joe Girardi .25 .60
T120 Omar Daal .15 .40
T121 Brook Fordyce .15 .40
T122 Jose Valentin .15 .40
T123 Curt Schilling .25 .60
T124 B.J. Surhoff .15 .40
T125 Henry Rodriguez .15 .40
T126 Mike Bordick .15 .40
T127 David Justice .15 .40
T128 Charles Johnson .15 .40
T129 Will Clark .25 .60
T130 Dwight Gooden .15 .40
T131 David Segui .15 .40
T132 Denny Neagle .15 .40
T133 Jose Canseco .25 .60
T134 Bruce Chen .15 .40
T135 Jason Bere .15 .40

2001 Topps Chrome

COMPLETE SET (661) 150.00 300.00
COMPLETE SERIES 1 (331) 75.00 150.00
COMPLETE SERIES 2 (330) 75.00 150.00
CARDS NO.7 AND 465 DO NOT EXIST
1 Cal Ripken 2.50 6.00
2 Chipper Jones .75 2.00
3 Roger Cedeno .20 .50
4 Garret Anderson .30 .75
5 Robin Ventura .30 .75
6 Daryle Ward .20 .50
8 Phil Nevin .30 .75
9 Jermaine Dye .30 .75
10 Chris Singleton .20 .50
11 Mike Redmond .20 .50
12 Jim Thome .50 1.25
13 Brian Jordan .30 .75
14 Dustin Hermanson .20 .50
15 Shawn Green .30 .75
16 Todd Stottlemyre .20 .50
17 Dan Wilson .20 .50
18 Derek Lowe .30 .75
19 Juan Gonzalez .30 .75
20 Pat Meares .20 .50
21 Paul O'Neill .50 1.25
22 Jeffrey Hammonds .20 .50
23 Pokey Reese .20 .50
24 Mike Mussina .50 1.25
25 Rico Brogna .20 .50
26 Jay Buhner .30 .75
27 Steve Cox .20 .50
28 Quilvio Veras .20 .50
29 Marquis Grissom .30 .75
30 Shigetoshi Hasegawa .30 .75
31 Shane Reynolds .20 .50
32 Adam Piatt .20 .50
33 Preston Wilson .30 .75
34 Ellis Burks .30 .75
35 Armando Rios .20 .50
36 Chuck Finley .30 .75
37 Shannon Stewart .30 .75
38 Mark McGwire 2.00 5.00
39 Gerald Williams .20 .50
40 Eric Young .20 .50
41 Peter Bergeron .20 .50
42 Arthur Rhodes .20 .50
43 Bobby Jones .20 .50
44 Matt Clement .30 .75
45 Pedro Martinez .50 1.25
46 Jose Canseco .50 1.25
47 Matt Anderson .20 .50
48 Torii Hunter .30 .75
49 Carlos Lee .30 .75
50 Eric Chavez .30 .75
51 Rick Helling .20 .50
52 John Franco .30 .75
53 Mike Bordick .30 .75
54 Andres Galarraga .30 .75
55 Jose Cruz Jr. .20 .50
56 Mike Matheny .20 .50
57 Randy Johnson .75 2.00
58 Richie Sexson .30 .75
59 Vladimir Nunez .20 .50
60 Aaron Boone .30 .75
61 Darin Erstad .30 .75
62 Alex Gonzalez .20 .50
63 Gil Heredia .20 .50
64 Shane Andrews .20 .50
65 Todd Hundley .20 .50
66 Bill Mueller .30 .75
67 Mark McLemore .20 .50
68 Scott Spiezio .20 .50
69 Kevin McGlinchy .20 .50
70 Manny Ramirez .50 1.25
71 Mike Lamb .20 .50
72 Brian Buchanan .20 .50
73 Mike Sweeney .30 .75
74 John Wetteland .30 .75
75 Rob Bell .20 .50
76 John Burkett .20 .50
77 Derek Jeter 2.00 5.00
78 J.D. Drew .30 .75
79 Jose Offerman .20 .50
80 Rick Reed .20 .50
81 Will Clark .50 1.25
82 Rickey Henderson .75 2.00
83 Kirk Rueter .20 .50
84 Lee Stevens .20 .50
85 Jay Bell .30 .75
86 Fred McGriff .50 1.25
87 Julio Zuleta .20 .50
88 Brian Anderson .20 .50
89 Orlando Cabrera .30 .75
90 Alex Fernandez .20 .50
91 Derek Bell .20 .50
92 Eric Owens .20 .50
93 Dennys Reyes .20 .50
94 Mike Stanley .20 .50
95 Jorge Posada .50 1.25
96 Paul Konerko .30 .75
97 Mike Remlinger .20 .50
98 Travis Lee .20 .50
99 Ken Caminiti .30 .75
100 Kevin Barker .20 .50
101 Ozzie Guillen .30 .75
102 Randy Wolf .20 .50
103 Michael Tucker .20 .50
104 Darren Lewis .20 .50
105 Joe Randa .30 .75
106 Jeff Cirillo .20 .50
107 David Ortiz .75 2.00
108 Herb Perry .20 .50
109 Jeff Nelson .20 .50
110 Chris Stynes .20 .50
111 Johnny Damon .50 1.25
112 Jason Schmidt .30 .75
113 Charles Johnson .20 .50
114 Pat Burrell .30 .75
115 Gary Sheffield .30 .75
116 Tom Glavine .50 1.25
117 Jason Isringhausen .30 .75
118 Chris Carpenter .30 .75
119 Jeff Suppan .20 .50
120 Ivan Rodriguez .50 1.25
121 Luis Sojo .20 .50
122 Ron Villone .20 .50
123 Mike Sirotka .20 .50
124 Chuck Knoblauch .30 .75
125 Jason Kendall .30 .75
126 Bobby Estalella .20 .50
127 Jose Guillen .30 .75
128 Carlos Delgado .30 .75
129 Benji Gil .20 .50
130 Einar Diaz .20 .50
131 Andy Benes .20 .50
132 Adrian Beltre .30 .75
133 Roger Clemens 1.50 4.00
134 Scott Williamson .20 .50
135 Brad Penny .20 .50
136 Troy Glaus .30 .75
137 Kevin Appier .30 .75
138 Walt Weiss .20 .50
139 Michael Barrett .20 .50
140 Mike Hampton .30 .75
141 Francisco Cordova .20 .50
142 David Segui .20 .50
143 Carlos Febles .20 .50
144 Roy Halladay .30 .75
145 Seth Etherton .20 .50
146 Fernando Tatis .20 .50
147 Livan Hernandez .30 .75
148 B.J. Surhoff .30 .75
149 Barry Larkin .50 1.25
150 Bobby Howry .20 .50
151 Dmitri Young .30 .75
152 Brian Hunter .20 .50
153 Alex Rodriguez 1.00 2.50
154 Hideo Nomo .75 2.00
155 Warren Morris .20 .50
156 Antonio Alfonseca .20 .50
157 Edgardo Alfonzo .20 .50
158 Mark Grudzielanek .20 .50
159 Fernando Vina .20 .50
160 Homer Bush .20 .50
161 Jason Giambi .30 .75
162 Steve Karsay .20 .50
163 Matt Lawton .20 .50
164 Rusty Greer .30 .75
165 Billy Koch .20 .50
166 Todd Hollandsworth .20 .50
167 Raul Ibanez .20 .50
168 Tony Gwynn 1.00 2.50
169 Carl Everett .30 .75
170 Hector Carrasco .20 .50
171 Jose Valentin .20 .50
172 Deivi Cruz .20 .50
173 Bret Boone .30 .75
174 Melvin Mora .30 .75
175 Danny Graves .20 .50
176 Jose Jimenez .20 .50
177 James Baldwin .20 .50
178 C.J. Nitkowski .20 .50
179 Jeff Zimmerman .20 .50
180 Mike Lowell .30 .75
181 Hideki Irabu .20 .50
182 Greg Vaughn .20 .50
183 Omar Daal .20 .50
184 Darren Dreifort .20 .50
185 Gil Meche .20 .50
186 Damian Jackson .20 .50
187 Frank Thomas .75 2.00
188 Luis Castillo .20 .50
189 Bartolo Colon .30 .75
190 Craig Biggio .50 1.25
191 Scott Schoeneweis .20 .50
192 Dave Veres .20 .50
193 Ramon Martinez .20 .50
194 Jose Vidro .20 .50
195 Todd Helton .50 1.25
196 Greg Norton .20 .50
197 Jacque Jones .30 .75
198 Jason Grimsley .20 .50
199 Dan Reichert .20 .50
200 Robb Nen .30 .75
201 Scott Hatteberg .20 .50
202 Terry Shumpert .20 .50
203 Kevin Millar .30 .75
204 Ismael Valdes .20 .50
205 Richard Hidalgo .20 .50
206 Randy Velarde .20 .50
207 Bengie Molina .20 .50
208 Tony Womack .20 .50
209 Enrique Wilson .20 .50
210 Jeff Brantley .20 .50
211 Rick Ankiel .20 .50
212 Terry Mulholland .20 .50
213 Ron Belliard .20 .50
214 Terrence Long .20 .50
215 Alberto Castillo .20 .50
216 Royce Clayton .20 .50
217 Joe McEwing .20 .50
218 Jason McDonald .20 .50
219 Ricky Bottalico .20 .50
220 Keith Foulke .30 .75
221 Brad Radke .30 .75
222 Gabe Kapler .30 .75
223 Pedro Astacio .20 .50
224 Armando Reynoso .20 .50
225 Darryl Kile .30 .75
226 Reggie Sanders .30 .75
227 Esteban Yan .20 .50
228 Joe Nathan .30 .75
229 Jay Payton .20 .50
230 Francisco Cordero .20 .50
231 Gregg Jefferies .20 .50
232 LaTroy Hawkins .20 .50
233 Jacob Cruz .20 .50
234 Chris Holt .20 .50
235 Vladimir Guerrero .75 2.00
236 Marvin Benard .20 .50
237 Alex Ramirez .20 .50
238 Mike Williams .20 .50
239 Sean Bergman .20 .50
240 Juan Encarnacion .20 .50
241 Russ Davis .20 .50
242 Ramon Hernandez .20 .50
243 Sandy Alomar Jr. .20 .50
244 Eddie Guardado .20 .50
245 Shane Halter .20 .50
246 Geoff Jenkins .20 .50
247 Brian Meadows .20 .50
248 Damian Miller .20 .50
249 Darrin Fletcher .20 .50
250 Rafael Furcal .30 .75
251 Mark Grace .50 1.25
252 Mark Mulder .30 .75
253 Joe Torre MG .50 1.25
254 Bobby Cox MG .20 .50
255 Mike Scioscia MG .20 .50
256 Mike Hargrove MG .20 .50
257 Jimy Williams MG .20 .50
258 Jerry Manuel MG .20 .50
259 Charlie Manuel MG .20 .50
260 Don Baylor MG .30 .75
261 Phil Garner MG .30 .75
262 Tony Muser MG .20 .50
263 Buddy Bell MG .30 .75
264 Tom Kelly MG .20 .50
265 John Boles MG .20 .50
266 Art Howe MG .20 .50
267 Larry Dierker MG .20 .50
268 Lou Piniella MG .30 .75
269 Larry Rothschild MG .20 .50
270 Davey Lopes MG .30 .75
271 Johnny Oates MG .20 .50
272 Felipe Alou MG .20 .50
273 Bobby Valentine MG .20 .50
274 Tony LaRussa MG .20 .50
275 Bruce Bochy MG .20 .50
276 Dusty Baker MG .30 .75
277 A.Gonzalez 2.50 6.00
A.Johnson
278 M.Wheatland .40 1.00
B.Digby
279 T.Johnson .40 1.00
S.Thorman
280 P.Dumatrait .75 2.00
A.Wainwright
281 David Parrish RC .40 1.00
282 M.Folsom RC .60 1.50
R.Baldelli
283 Dominic Rich RC .40 1.00
284 M.Stodolka .40 1.00
S.Burnett
285 D.Thompson .40 1.00
C.Smith
286 D.Borrell RC .40 1.00
J.Bourgeois RC
287 Josh Hamilton .75 2.00
288 B.Zito .75 2.00
C.Sabathia
289 Ben Sheets .75 2.00
290 Howington .40 1.00
Kalinowski/Girdley
291 Hee Seop Choi RC .75 2.00
292 Bradley .60 1.50
Ainsworth/Tsao
293 Glendenning .40 1.00
Kelly/Silvestre
294 J.R. House .40 1.00
295 Rafael Soriano RC .60 1.50
296 T.Hafner RC 4.00 10.00
B.Jacobsen
297 Conti .40 1.00
Wakeland/Cole
298 Seabol/Huff/Crede 1.00 2.50
299 Everett .40 1.00
Ortiz/Ginter
300 Hernandez .40 1.00
Guzman/Eaton
301 Kielty .60 1.50
Bradley/J.Rivera
302 Mark McGwire GM 1.00 2.50
303 Don Larsen GM .30 .75
304 Bobby Thomson GM .30 .75
305 Bill Mazeroski GM .30 .75
306 Reggie Jackson GM .50 1.25
307 Kirk Gibson GM .30 .75
308 Roger Maris GM .50 1.25
309 Cal Ripken GM 1.25 3.00
310 Hank Aaron GM .75 2.00
311 Joe Carter GM .30 .75
312 Cal Ripken SH 1.25 3.00
313 Randy Johnson SH .50 1.25
314 Ken Griffey Jr. SH 1.00 2.50
315 Troy Glaus SH .30 .75
316 Kazuhiro Sasaki SH .30 .75
317 S.Sosa .50 1.25
T.Glaus LL
318 T.Helton .30 .75
E.Martinez LL
319 T.Helton .75 2.00
N.Garicaparra LL
320 B.Bonds .75 2.00
J.Giambi LL
321 T.Helton .30 .75
M.Ramirez LL
322 T.Helton .30 .75
D.Erstad LL
323 K.Brown .50 1.25
P.Martinez LL
324 R.Johnson .50 1.25
P.Martinez LL
325 Will Clark HL .50 1.25
326 New York Mets HL .75 2.00
327 New York Yankees HL 1.25 3.00
328 Seattle Mariners HL .30 .75
329 Mike Hampton HL .30 .75
330 New York Yankees HL 1.50 4.00
331 New York Yankees Champs 3.00 8.00
332 Jeff Bagwell .50 1.25
333 Andy Pettitte .50 1.25
334 Tony Armas Jr. .20 .50
335 Jeromy Burnitz .30 .75
336 Javier Vazquez .30 .75
337 Eric Karros .30 .75
338 Brian Giles .30 .75
339 Scott Rolen .50 1.25
340 David Justice .30 .75
341 Ray Durham .30 .75
342 Todd Zeile .30 .75
343 Cliff Floyd .30 .75
344 Barry Bonds 2.00 5.00
345 Matt Williams .30 .75
346 Steve Finley .30 .75
347 Scott Elarton .20 .50
348 Bernie Williams .50 1.25
349 David Wells .30 .75
350 J.T. Snow .30 .75
351 Al Leiter .30 .75
352 Magglio Ordonez .30 .75
353 Raul Mondesi .30 .75
354 Tim Salmon .50 1.25
355 Jeff Kent .30 .75
356 Mariano Rivera .75 2.00
357 John Olerud .30 .75
358 Javy Lopez .30 .75
359 Ben Grieve .20 .50
360 Ray Lankford .30 .75
361 Ken Griffey Jr. 1.50 4.00
362 Rich Aurilia .20 .50
363 Andruw Jones .50 1.25
364 Ryan Klesko .30 .75
365 Roberto Alomar .50 1.25
366 Miguel Tejada .30 .75
367 Mo Vaughn .30 .75
368 Albert Belle .30 .75
369 Jose Canseco .50 1.25
370 Kevin Brown .30 .75
371 Rafael Palmeiro .50 1.25
372 Mark Redman .20 .50
373 Larry Walker .30 .75
374 Greg Maddux 1.25 3.00
375 Nomar Garciaparra 1.25 3.00
376 Kevin Millwood .30 .75
377 Edgar Martinez .50 1.25
378 Sammy Sosa .75 2.00
379 Tim Hudson .30 .75
380 Jim Edmonds .30 .75
381 Mike Piazza 1.25 3.00
382 Brant Brown .20 .50
383 Brad Fullmer .20 .50
384 Alan Benes .20 .50
385 Mickey Morandini .20 .50
386 Troy Percival .30 .75
387 Eddie Perez .20 .50
388 Vernon Wells .30 .75
389 Ricky Gutierrez .20 .50
390 Rondell White .30 .75
391 Kelvim Escobar .20 .50
392 Tony Batista .20 .50
393 Jimmy Haynes .20 .50
394 Billy Wagner .30 .75
395 A.J. Hinch .20 .50
396 Matt Morris .30 .75
397 Lance Berkman .30 .75
398 Jeff D'Amico .20 .50
399 Octavio Dotel .20 .50
400 Olmedo Saenz .20 .50
401 Esteban Loaiza .20 .50
402 Adam Kennedy .20 .50
403 Moises Alou .30 .75
404 Orlando Palmeiro .20 .50
405 Kevin Young .20 .50
406 Tom Goodwin .20 .50
407 Mac Suzuki .30 .75
408 Pat Hentgen .20 .50
409 Kevin Stocker .20 .50
410 Mark Sweeney .20 .50
411 Tony Eusebio .20 .50
412 Edgar Renteria .30 .75
413 John Rocker .30 .75
414 Jose Lima .20 .50
415 Kerry Wood .30 .75
416 Mike Timlin .20 .50
417 Jose Hernandez .20 .50
418 Jeremy Giambi .20 .50
419 Luis Lopez .20 .50
420 Mitch Meluskey .20 .50
421 Garrett Stephenson .20 .50
422 Jamey Wright .20 .50
423 John Jaha .20 .50
424 Placido Polanco .20 .50
425 Marty Cordova .20 .50
426 Joey Hamilton .20 .50
427 Travis Fryman .30 .75
428 Mike Cameron .20 .50
429 Matt Mantei .20 .50
430 Chan Ho Park .30 .75
431 Shawn Estes .20 .50
432 Danny Bautista .20 .50
433 Wilson Alvarez .20 .50
434 Kenny Lofton .30 .75
435 Russ Ortiz .20 .50
436 Dave Burba .20 .50
437 Felix Martinez .20 .50
438 Jeff Shaw .20 .50
439 Mike DiFelice .20 .50
440 Roberto Hernandez .20 .50
441 Bryan Rekar .20 .50
442 Ugueth Urbina .20 .50
443 Vinny Castilla .30 .75
444 Carlos Perez .20 .50
445 Juan Guzman .20 .50
446 Ryan Rupe .20 .50
447 Mike Mordecai .20 .50
448 Ricardo Rincon .20 .50
449 Curt Schilling .30 .75
450 Alex Cora .20 .50
451 Turner Ward .20 .50
452 Omar Vizquel .50 1.25
453 Russ Branyan .20 .50
454 Russ Johnson .20 .50
455 Greg Colbrunn .20 .50
456 Charles Nagy .20 .50
457 Wil Cordero .20 .50
458 Jason Tyner .20 .50
459 Devon White .30 .75
460 Kelly Stinnett .20 .50
461 Wilton Guerrero .20 .50
462 Jason Bere .20 .50
463 Calvin Murray .20 .50
464 Miguel Batista .20 .50
466 Luis Gonzalez .30 .75
467 Jaret Wright .20 .50
468 Chad Kreuter .20 .50
469 Armando Benitez .20 .50
470 Erubiel Durazo .20 .50
470 Sidney Ponson .20 .50
471 Adrian Brown .20 .50
472 Sterling Hitchcock .20 .50
473 Timo Perez .20 .50
474 Jamie Moyer .30 .75
475 Delino DeShields .20 .50
476 Glendon Rusch .20 .50
477 Chris Gomez .20 .50
478 Adam Eaton .20 .50
479 Pablo Ozuna .20 .50
480 Bob Abreu .30 .75
481 Kris Benson .20 .50
482 Keith Osik .20 .50
483 Darryl Hamilton .20 .50
484 Marlon Anderson .20 .50
485 Jimmy Anderson .20 .50
486 John Halama .20 .50
487 Nelson Figueroa .20 .50
488 Alex Gonzalez .20 .50
489 Benny Agbayani .20 .50
490 Ed Sprague .20 .50
491 Scott Erickson .20 .50
492 Doug Glanville .20 .50
493 Jesus Sanchez .20 .50
494 Mike Lieberthal .30 .75
495 Aaron Sele .20 .50
496 Pat Mahomes .20 .50
497 Ruben Rivera .20 .50
498 Wayne Gomes .20 .50
499 Freddy Garcia .30 .75
500 Al Martin .20 .50
501 Woody Williams .20 .50
502 Paul Byrd .20 .50
503 Rick White .20 .50
504 Trevor Hoffman .30 .75
505 Brady Anderson .30 .75
506 Robert Person .20 .50
507 Jeff Conine .30 .75
508 Chris Truby .20 .50
509 Emil Brown .20 .50
510 Ryan Dempster .20 .50
511 Ruben Mateo .20 .50
512 Alex Ochoa .20 .50
513 Jose Rosado .20 .50
514 Masato Yoshii .20 .50
515 Brian Daubach .20 .50
516 Jeff D'Amico .20 .50
517 Brent Mayne .20 .50
518 John Thomson .20 .50
519 Todd Ritchie .20 .50
520 John VanderWal .20 .50
521 Neifi Perez .20 .50
522 Chad Curtis .20 .50
523 Kenny Rogers .30 .75
524 Trot Nixon .30 .75
525 Sean Casey .30 .75
526 Wilton Veras .20 .50
527 Troy O'Leary .20 .50
528 Dante Bichette .30 .75
529 Jose Silva .20 .50
530 Darren Oliver .20 .50
531 Steve Parris .20 .50
532 David McCarty .20 .50
533 Todd Walker .20 .50
534 Brian Rose .20 .50
535 Pete Schourek .20 .50
536 Ricky Ledee .20 .50
537 Justin Thompson .20 .50
538 Benito Santiago .30 .75
539 Carlos Beltran .30 .75
540 Gabe White .20 .50
541 Bret Saberhagen .30 .75
542 Ramon Martinez .20 .50
543 John Valentin .20 .50
544 Frank Catalanotto .20 .50
545 Tim Wakefield .30 .75
546 Michael Tucker .20 .50
547 Juan Pierre .30 .75
548 Rich Garces .20 .50
549 Luis Ordaz .20 .50
550 Jerry Spradlin .20 .50
551 Corey Koskie .20 .50
552 Cal Eldred .20 .50
553 Alfonso Soriano .50 1.25
554 Kip Wells .20 .50
555 Orlando Hernandez .30 .75
556 Bill Simas .20 .50
557 Jim Parque .20 .50
558 Joe Mays .20 .50
559 Tim Belcher .20 .50
560 Shane Spencer .20 .50
561 Glenallen Hill .20 .50
562 Matt LeCroy .20 .50
563 Tino Martinez .50 1.25
564 Eric Milton .20 .50
565 Ron Coomer .20 .50
566 Cristian Guzman .20 .50
567 Kazuhiro Sasaki .30 .75
568 Mark Quinn .20 .50
569 Eric Gagne .30 .75
570 Kerry Ligtenberg .20 .50
571 Rolando Arrojo .20 .50
572 Jon Lieber .20 .50
573 Jose Vizcaino .20 .50
574 Jeff Abbott .20 .50
575 Carlos Hernandez .20 .50
576 Scott Sullivan .20 .50
577 Matt Stairs .20 .50
578 Tom Lampkin .20 .50
579 Donnie Sadler .20 .50
580 Desi Relaford .20 .50
581 Scott Downs .20 .50
582 Mike Mussina .50 1.25
583 Ramon Ortiz .20 .50
584 Mike Myers .20 .50
585 Frank Castillo .20 .50
586 Manny Ramirez Sox .50 1.25
587 Alex Rodriguez 1.00 2.50
588 Andy Ashby .20 .50
589 Felipe Crespo .20 .50
590 Bobby Bonilla .30 .75
591 Denny Neagle .20 .50
592 Dave Martinez .20 .50
593 Mike Hampton .30 .75
594 Gary DiSarcina .20 .50
595 Tsuyoshi Shinjo RC .75 2.00
596 Albert Pujols RC 125.00 300.00
597 Oswalt 1.00 2.50
Strange/Rauch
598 Jake Peavy RC 2.00 5.00
599 S.Smyth RC .40 1.00
Bynum/Haynes
600 Cuddyer .40 1.00
Lawrence/Freeman
601 C.Pena .40 1.00
Barnes/Wise
602 E.Almonte RC .40 1.00
F.Lopez
603 Escobar .40 1.00
Valent/Wilkerson
604 Hall .40 1.00
Barajas/Goldbach
605 Romano .60 1.50
Giles/Ozuna
606 D.Brown .40 1.00
Cust/V.Wells
607 L.Montanez RC .40 1.00
D.Espinosa
608 J.Wayne RC .40 1.00
A.Pluta RC
609 J.Axelson RC .40 1.00
C.Cali RC
610 S.Boyd RC .40 1.00
C.Morris RC
611 T.Arko RC .40 1.00
D.Moylan RC
612 L.Cotto RC .40 1.00
L.Escobar
613 B.Mims RC .40 1.00
B.Williams RC
614 C.Russ RC .40 1.00
B.Edwards
615 J.Torres .40 1.00
B.Diggins
616 Edwin Encarnacion RC 3.00 8.00
617 B.Bass RC .40 1.00
O.Ayala RC
618 M.Matthews RC .40 1.00
J.Kanooi
619 S.McFarland RC .40 1.00
A.Sterrett RC
620 D.Krynzel 2.00 5.00
G.Sizemore
621 K.Bucktrot .40 1.00
D.Sardinha
622 Anaheim Angels TC .30 .75
623 Arizona Diamondbacks TC .30 .75
624 Atlanta Braves TC .30 .75
625 Baltimore Orioles TC .30 .75
626 Boston Red Sox TC .30 .75
627 Chicago Cubs TC .30 .75
628 Chicago White Sox TC .30 .75
629 Cincinnati Reds TC .30 .75
630 Cleveland Indians TC .30 .75
631 Colorado Rockies TC .30 .75
632 Detroit Tigers TC .30 .75
633 Florida Marlins TC .30 .75
634 Houston Astros TC .30 .75
635 Kansas City Royals TC .30 .75
636 Los Angeles Dodgers TC .30 .75
637 Milwaukee Brewers TC .30 .75
638 Minnesota Twins TC .30 .75
639 Montreal Expos TC .30 .75
640 New York Mets TC .30 .75
641 New York Yankees TC 1.50 4.00
642 Oakland Athletics TC .30 .75
643 Philadelphia Phillies TC .30 .75
644 Pittsburgh Pirates TC .30 .75
645 San Diego Padres TC .30 .75
646 San Francisco Giants TC .30 .75
647 Seattle Mariners TC .30 .75
648 St. Louis Cardinals TC .30 .75
649 Tampa Bay Devil Rays TC .30 .75
650 Texas Rangers TC .30 .75
651 Toronto Blue Jays TC .30 .75
652 Bucky Dent GM .20 .50
653 Jackie Robinson GM .75 2.00
654 Roberto Clemente GM 1.00 2.50
655 Nolan Ryan GM 1.25 3.00
656 Kerry Wood GM .30 .75
657 Rickey Henderson GM .75 2.00
658 Lou Brock GM .50 1.25
659 David Wells GM .20 .50
660 Andruw Jones GM .30 .75
661 Carlton Fisk GM .30 .75

2001 Topps Chrome Retrofractors

*STARS: 2.5X TO 6X BASIC CARDS
*PROSPECTS 277-301/595-621: 2X TO 5X
*ROOKIES 277-301/595-621: 2X TO 5X
STATED ODDS 1:12
CARD NO.7 DOES NOT EXIST
596 Albert Pujols 2000.00 5000.00
598 Jake Peavy 12.00 30.00
616 Edwin Encarnacion 20.00 50.00

2001 Topps Chrome Before There Was Topps

COMPLETE SET (10) 30.00 80.00
SER.2 STATED ODDS 1:20 HOBBY/RETAIL
*REFRACTORS: 1.25X TO 3X BASIC BEFORE
SER.2 REFRACTOR ODDS 1:200 HOB/RET
BT1 Lou Gehrig 5.00 12.00
BT2 Babe Ruth 8.00 20.00
BT3 Cy Young 2.50 6.00
BT4 Walter Johnson 2.50 6.00
BT5 Ty Cobb 4.00 10.00
BT6 Rogers Hornsby 2.50 6.00
BT7 Honus Wagner 2.50 6.00
BT8 Christy Mathewson 2.50 6.00
BT9 Grover Alexander 2.50 6.00
BT10 Joe DiMaggio 5.00 12.00

2001 Topps Chrome Combos

COMPLETE SET (20) 20.00 50.00
COMPLETE SERIES 1 (10) 10.00 25.00
COMPLETE SERIES 2 (10) 10.00 25.00
STATED ODDS 1:12 HOBBY/RETAIL, 1:4 HTA
*REFRACTORS: 1.5X TO 4X BASIC COMBO
REFRACTOR ODDS 1:120 H/R
TC1 Decades of Excellence 2.50 6.00
TC2 Power Corner 1.50 4.00
TC3 Glove Birds 3.00 8.00
TC4 Mound Marksmen .60 1.50
TC5 Tools of Success 1.00 2.50
TC6 Shortstop Supremacy 1.25 3.00
TC7 Big Red Machine 2.00 5.00
TC8 Latin Heat 2.50 6.00
TC9 Home Run Royalty 2.00 5.00
TC10 New York State of Mind .60 1.50
TC11 Dodger Blue 2.00 5.00
TC12 60 Home Run Club 2.50 6.00
TC13 Heroes of Fenway 2.00 5.00
TC14 Mound Masters 1.50 4.00
TC15 Sweetness 2.00 5.00
TC16 Ironmen 3.00 8.00
TC17 Southpaw Greatness 2.00 5.00
TC18 Best There Is 1.00 2.50
Was
TC19 All in the Family 2.00 5.00
TC20 Barrier Breakers 1.00 2.50

2001 Topps Chrome Golden Anniversary

COMPLETE SET (50) 150.00 300.00
SER.1 STATED ODDS 1:10
*REFRACTORS: 1.5X TO 4X BASIC ANNV.
SER.1 REFRACTOR ODDS 1:100
GA1 Hank Aaron 4.00 10.00
GA2 Ernie Banks 2.00 5.00
GA3 Mike Schmidt 4.00 10.00
GA4 Willie Mays 4.00 10.00
GA5 Johnny Bench 2.00 5.00
GA6 Tom Seaver 1.25 3.00
GA7 Frank Robinson 1.25 3.00
GA8 Sandy Koufax 6.00 15.00
GA9 Bob Gibson 1.25 3.00
GA10 Ted Williams 4.00 10.00
GA11 Cal Ripken 6.00 15.00
GA12 Tony Gwynn 2.50 6.00
GA13 Mark McGwire 5.00 12.00
GA14 Ken Griffey Jr. 4.00 10.00
GA15 Greg Maddux 3.00 8.00
GA16 Roger Clemens 4.00 10.00
GA17 Barry Bonds 5.00 12.00
GA18 Rickey Henderson 2.00 5.00
GA19 Mike Piazza 3.00 8.00
GA20 Jose Canseco 1.25 3.00
GA21 Derek Jeter 5.00 12.00
GA22 Nomar Garciaparra 3.00 8.00
GA23 Alex Rodriguez 2.50 6.00
GA24 Sammy Sosa 2.00 5.00
GA25 Ivan Rodriguez 1.25 3.00
GA26 Vladimir Guerrero 2.00 5.00
GA27 Chipper Jones 2.00 5.00
GA28 Jeff Bagwell 1.25 3.00
GA29 Pedro Martinez 1.25 3.00
GA30 Randy Johnson 2.00 5.00
GA31 Pat Burrell .75 2.00
GA32 Josh Hamilton 1.50 4.00
GA33 Ryan Anderson .75 2.00
GA34 Corey Patterson .75 2.00
GA35 Eric Munson .75 2.00
GA36 Sean Burroughs .75 2.00
GA37 C.C. Sabathia .75 2.00
GA38 Chin-Feng Chen .75 2.00
GA39 Barry Zito 1.25 3.00
GA40 Adrian Gonzalez 5.00 12.00
GA41 Mark McGwire 5.00 12.00
GA42 Nomar Garciaparra 3.00 8.00
GA43 Todd Helton 1.25 3.00
GA44 Matt Williams .75 2.00
GA45 Troy Glaus .75 2.00
GA46 Geoff Jenkins .75 2.00
GA47 Frank Thomas 2.00 5.00
GA48 Mo Vaughn .75 2.00
GA49 Barry Larkin 1.25 3.00
GA50 J.D. Drew .75 2.00

2001 Topps Chrome King Of Kings

SER.1 ODDS 1:5175 HOB., 1:5209 RET.
SER.2 GROUP A ODDS 1:11,347 H, 1:11,520 R
SER.2 GROUP B ODDS 1:15,348 H, 1:15,648 R
SER.2 OVERALL ODDS 1:6383 H, 1:6520 R
KKGE SER.1 ODDS 1:59,220 HOBBY
KKR1 Hank Aaron 60.00 120.00
KKR2 Nolan Ryan Rangers 50.00 100.00
KKR3 Rickey Henderson 15.00 40.00
KKR5 Bob Gibson 15.00 40.00
KKR6 Nolan Ryan Angels 50.00 100.00

2001 Topps Chrome King Of Kings Refractors

KKR1-3 SER.1 ODDS 1:16,920 HOBBY
KKR5-6 SER.2 ODDS 1:23,022 HOBBY
KKGE SER.1 ODDS 1:212,160 HOBBY
KKR1-KKR6 PRINT RUN 10 SERIAL #'d SETS
KKGE PRINT RUN 5 SERIAL #'d CARDS
CARD NUMBER 4 DOES NOT EXIST
NO PRICING DUE TO SCARCITY

2001 Topps Chrome Originals

SER.1 ODDS 1:1783 HOBBY, 1:1788 RETAIL
SER.2 GROUP A ODDS 1:4863 H, 1:4943 R
SER.2 GROUP B ODDS 1:7855 H, 1:8229 R
SER.2 GROUP C ODDS 1:6588 H, 1:6803 R
SER.2 GROUP D ODDS 1:46,044 H, 1:57,600 R
SER.2 GROUP E ODDS 1:6588 H, 1:6797 R
SER.2 OVERALL ODDS 1:1513 H, 1:1545 R
REFRACT.1-5 SER.1 ODDS 1:9644 HOBBY
REFRACT.6-10 SER.2 ODDS 1:8372 HOBBY
REFRACTOR PRINT RUN 10 #'d SETS
NO REFRACTOR PRICE DUE TO SCARCITY

Card	Low	High
1 Roberto Clemente	175.00	300.00
2 Carl Yastrzemski	125.00	200.00
3 Mike Schmidt	20.00	50.00
4 Wade Boggs	30.00	60.00
5 Chipper Jones	30.00	60.00
6 Willie Mays	175.00	300.00
7 Lou Brock	15.00	40.00
8 Dave Parker	15.00	40.00
9 Barry Bonds	75.00	150.00
10 Alex Rodriguez	30.00	60.00

2001 Topps Chrome Past to Present

Card	Low	High
COMPLETE SET (10)	30.00	60.00
SER.1 STATED ODDS 1:18		
*REFRACTORS: 1.5X TO 4X BASIC PAST		
SER.1 REFRACTOR ODDS 1:180		
PTP1 P.Rizzuto D.Jeter	5.00	12.00
PTP2 W.Spahn G.Maddux	3.00	8.00
PTP3 Y.Berra J.Posada	4.00	10.00
PTP4 W.Mays B.Bonds	8.00	20.00
PTP5 R.Schoendienst F.Vina	1.50	4.00
PTP6 D.Snider S.Green	1.50	4.00
PTP7 B.Feller B.Colon	1.50	4.00
PTP8 J.Mize T.Martinez	1.50	4.00
PTP9 L.Doby M.Ramirez	1.50	4.00
PTP10 E.Mathews C.Jones	2.00	5.00

2001 Topps Chrome Through the Years Reprints

Card	Low	High
COMPLETE SET (50)	150.00	300.00
SER.1 STATED ODDS 1:10		
*REFRACTORS: 1.5X TO 4X BASIC THROUGH		
SER.1 REFRACTOR ODDS 1:100		
1 Yogi Berra 57	2.50	6.00
2 Roy Campanella 56	2.50	6.00
3 Willie Mays 53	4.00	10.00
4 Andy Pafko 52	2.50	6.00
5 Jackie Robinson 52	2.50	6.00
6 Stan Musial 59	3.00	8.00
7 Duke Snider 56	2.00	5.00
8 Warren Spahn 56	2.00	5.00
9 Ted Williams 54	6.00	15.00
10 Eddie Mathews 55	2.50	6.00
11 Willie McCovey 60	2.00	5.00
12 Frank Robinson 69	2.00	5.00
13 Ernie Banks 66	2.50	6.00
14 Hank Aaron 65	4.00	10.00
15 Sandy Koufax 61	5.00	12.00
16 Bob Gibson 68	2.00	5.00
17 Harmon Killebrew 67	2.50	6.00
18 Whitey Ford 64	2.00	5.00
19 Roberto Clemente 63	6.00	15.00
20 Juan Marichal 61	2.00	5.00
21 Johnny Bench 70	2.50	6.00
22 Willie Stargell 73	2.00	5.00
23 Joe Morgan 74	2.00	5.00
24 Carl Yastrzemski 71	3.00	8.00
25 Reggie Jackson 76	2.00	5.00
26 Tom Seaver 78	2.00	5.00
27 Steve Carlton 77	2.00	5.00
28 Jim Palmer 79	2.00	5.00
29 Rod Carew 72	2.00	5.00
30 George Brett 75	6.00	15.00
31 Roger Clemens 85	5.00	12.00
32 Don Mattingly 84	6.00	15.00
33 Ryne Sandberg 89	4.00	10.00
34 Mike Schmidt 81	4.00	10.00
35 Cal Ripken 82	8.00	20.00
36 Tony Gwynn 83	3.00	8.00
37 Ozzie Smith 87	4.00	10.00
38 Wade Boggs 88	2.00	5.00
39 Nolan Ryan 80	6.00	15.00
40 Robin Yount 86	2.50	6.00
41 Mark McGwire 99	5.00	12.00
42 Ken Griffey Jr. 92	4.00	10.00
43 Sammy Sosa 90	2.50	6.00
44 Alex Rodriguez 98	2.50	6.00
45 Barry Bonds 94	5.00	12.00
46 Mike Piazza 95	3.00	8.00
47 Chipper Jones 91	2.50	6.00
48 Greg Maddux 96	3.00	8.00
49 Nomar Garciaparra 97	3.00	8.00
50 Derek Jeter 93	6.00	15.00

2001 Topps Chrome What Could Have Been

Card	Low	High
COMPLETE SET (10)	15.00	40.00
SER.2 STATED ODDS 1:30 HOBBY/RETAIL		
*REFRACTORS: 1.5X TO 4X BASIC WHAT		
SER.2 REFRACTOR ODDS 1:300 HOB/RET		
WCB1 Josh Gibson	4.00	10.00
WCB2 Satchel Paige	1.50	4.00
WCB3 Buck Leonard	1.50	4.00
WCB4 James Bell	1.50	4.00
WCB5 Rube Foster	1.50	4.00
WCB6 Martin DiHigo	1.50	4.00
WCB7 William Johnson	1.50	4.00
WCB8 Mule Suttles	1.50	4.00
WCB9 Ray Dandridge	1.50	4.00
WCB10 John Lloyd	1.50	4.00

2001 Topps Chrome Traded

Card	Low	High
COMPLETE SET (266)	75.00	150.00
COMMON CARD (1-99/145-266)	.30	.75
COMMON REPRINT (100-144)	.50	1.25
T1 Sandy Alomar Jr.	.30	.75
T2 Kevin Appier	.50	1.25
T3 Brad Ausmus	.50	1.25
T4 Derek Bell	.30	.75
T5 Bret Boone	.50	1.25
T6 Rico Brogna	.30	.75
T7 Ellis Burks	.50	1.25
T8 Ken Caminiti	.50	1.25
T9 Roger Cedeno	.30	.75
T10 Royce Clayton	.30	.75
T11 Enrique Wilson	.30	.75
T12 Rheal Cormier	.30	.75
T13 Eric Davis	.50	1.25
T14 Shawon Dunston	.30	.75
T15 Andres Galarraga	.50	1.25
T16 Tom Gordon	.30	.75
T17 Mark Grace	.75	2.00
T18 Jeffrey Hammonds	.30	.75
T19 Dustin Hermanson	.30	.75
T20 Quinton McCracken	.30	.75
T21 Todd Hundley	.30	.75
T22 Charles Johnson	.50	1.25
T23 Marquis Grissom	.50	1.25
T24 Jose Mesa	.30	.75
T25 Brian Boehringer	.30	.75
T26 John Rocker	.50	1.25
T27 Jeff Frye	.30	.75
T28 Reggie Sanders	.50	1.25
T29 David Segui	.30	.75
T30 Mike Sirotka	.30	.75
T31 Fernando Tatis	.30	.75
T32 Steve Trachsel	.30	.75
T33 Ismael Valdes	.30	.75
T34 Randy Velarde	.30	.75
T35 Ryan Kohlmeier	.30	.75
T36 Mike Bordick	.50	1.25
T37 Kent Bottenfield	.30	.75
T38 Pat Rapp	.30	.75
T39 Jeff Nelson	.30	.75
T40 Ricky Bottalico	.30	.75
T41 Luke Prokopec	.30	.75
T42 Hideo Nomo	1.25	3.00
T43 Bill Mueller	.50	1.25
T44 Roberto Kelly	.30	.75
T45 Chris Holt	.30	.75
T46 Mike Jackson	.30	.75
T47 Devon White	.50	1.25
T48 Gerald Williams	.30	.75
T49 Eddie Taubensee	.30	.75
T50 Brian Hunter	.30	.75
T51 Nelson Cruz	.30	.75
T52 Jeff Fassero	.30	.75
T53 Bubba Trammell	.30	.75
T54 Bo Porter	.30	.75
T55 Greg Norton	.30	.75
T56 Benito Santiago	.50	1.25
T57 Ruben Rivera	.30	.75
T58 Dee Brown	.30	.75
T59 Jose Canseco	.75	2.00
T60 Chris Michalak	.30	.75
T61 Tim Worrell	.30	.75
T62 Matt Clement	.50	1.25
T63 Bill Pulsipher	.30	.75
T64 Troy Brohawn RC	.40	1.00
T65 Mark Kotsay	.50	1.25
T66 Jimmy Rollins	.50	1.25
T67 Shea Hillenbrand	.50	1.25
T68 Ted Lilly	.30	.75
T69 Jermaine Dye	.50	1.25
T70 Jerry Hairston Jr.	.30	.75
T71 John Mabry	.30	.75
T72 Kurt Abbott	.30	.75
T73 Eric Owens	.30	.75
T74 Jeff Brantley	.30	.75
T75 Roy Oswalt	1.25	3.00
T76 Doug Mientkiewicz	.50	1.25
T77 Rickey Henderson	1.25	3.00
T78 Jason Grimsley	.30	.75
T79 Christian Parker RC	.40	1.00
T80 Donne Wall	.30	.75
T81 Alex Arias	.30	.75
T82 Willis Roberts	.30	.75
T83 Ryan Minor	.30	.75
T84 Jason LaRue	.30	.75
T85 Ruben Sierra	.50	1.25
T86 Johnny Damon	.75	2.00
T87 Juan Gonzalez	.50	1.25
T88 C.C. Sabathia	.50	1.25
T89 Tony Batista	.30	.75
T90 Jay Witasick	.30	.75
T91 Brent Abernathy	.30	.75
T92 Paul LoDuca	.50	1.25
T93 Wes Helms	.30	.75
T94 Mark Wohlers	.30	.75
T95 Rob Bell	.30	.75
T96 Tim Redding	.30	.75
T97 Bud Smith RC	.40	1.00
T98 Adam Dunn	.75	2.00
T99 I.Suzuki A.Pujols ROY	200.00	500.00
T100 Carlton Fisk 81	.75	2.00
T101 Tim Raines 81	.50	1.25
T102 Juan Marichal 74	.50	1.25
T103 Dave Winfield 81	.50	1.25
T104 Reggie Jackson 82	.75	2.00
T105 Cal Ripken 82	4.00	10.00
T106 Ozzie Smith 82	2.00	5.00
T107 Tom Seaver 83	.75	2.00
T108 Lou Piniella 74	.50	1.25
T109 Dwight Gooden 84	.50	1.25
T110 Bret Saberhagen 84	.50	1.25
T111 Gary Carter 85	.50	1.25
T112 Jack Clark 85	.50	1.25
T113 Rickey Henderson 85	1.25	3.00
T114 Barry Bonds 86	3.00	8.00
T115 Bobby Bonilla 86	.50	1.25
T116 Jose Canseco 86	.75	2.00
T117 Will Clark 86	.75	2.00
T118 Andres Galarraga 86	.50	1.25
T119 Bo Jackson 86	1.25	3.00
T120 Wally Joyner 86	.50	1.25
T121 Ellis Burks 87	.50	1.25
T122 David Cone 87	.50	1.25
T123 Greg Maddux 87	2.00	5.00
T124 Willie Randolph 76	.50	1.25
T125 Dennis Eckersley 87	.50	1.25
T126 Matt Williams 87	.50	1.25
T127 Joe Morgan 81	.50	1.25
T128 Fred McGriff 87	.75	2.00
T129 Roberto Alomar 88	.75	2.00
T130 Lee Smith 88	.50	1.25
T131 David Wells 88	.50	1.25
T132 Ken Griffey Jr. 89	2.50	6.00
T133 Deion Sanders 89	.75	2.00
T134 Nolan Ryan 89	3.00	8.00
T135 David Justice 90	.50	1.25
T136 Joe Carter 91	.50	1.25
T137 Jack Morris 92	.50	1.25
T138 Mike Piazza 93	2.00	5.00
T139 Barry Bonds 93	3.00	8.00
T140 Terrence Long 94	.50	1.25
T141 Ben Grieve 94	.50	1.25
T142 Richie Sexson 95	.50	1.25
T143 Sean Burroughs 99	.50	1.25
T144 Alfonso Soriano 99	.75	2.00
T145 Bob Boone MG	.50	1.25
T146 Larry Bowa MG	.50	1.25
T147 Bob Brenly MG	.30	.75
T148 Buck Martinez MG	.30	.75
T149 Lloyd McClendon MG	.30	.75
T150 Jim Tracy MG	.30	.75
T151 Jared Abruzzo RC	.40	1.00
T152 Kurt Ainsworth	.30	.75
T153 Willie Bloomquist	.50	1.25
T154 Ben Broussard	.30	.75
T155 Bobby Bradley	.30	.75
T156 Mike Bynum	.30	.75
T157 A.J. Hinch	.30	.75
T158 Ryan Christianson	.30	.75
T159 Carlos Silva	.30	.75
T160 Joe Crede	1.25	3.00
T161 Jack Cust	.30	.75
T162 Ben Diggins	.30	.75
T163 Phil Dumatrait	.30	.75
T164 Alex Escobar	.30	.75
T165 Miguel Olivo	.30	.75
T166 Chris George	.30	.75
T167 Marcus Giles	.50	1.25
T168 Keith Ginter	.30	.75
T169 Josh Girdley	.30	.75
T170 Tony Alvarez	.30	.75
T171 Scott Seabol	.30	.75
T172 Josh Hamilton	.60	1.50
T173 Jason Hart	.30	.75
T174 Israel Alcantara	.30	.75
T175 Jake Peavy	1.50	4.00
T176 Stubby Clapp RC	.40	1.00
T177 D'Angelo Jimenez	.30	.75
T178 Nick Johnson	.50	1.25
T179 Ben Johnson	.50	1.25
T180 Larry Bigbie	.30	.75
T181 Allen Levrault	.30	.75
T182 Felipe Lopez	.50	1.25
T183 Sean Burnett	.30	.75
T184 Nick Neugebauer	.30	.75
T185 Austin Kearns	.50	1.25
T186 Corey Patterson	.30	.75
T187 Carlos Pena	.30	.75
T188 Ricardo Rodriguez RC	.40	1.00
T189 Juan Rivera	.30	.75
T190 Grant Roberts	.30	.75
T191 Adam Pettyjohn RC	.40	1.00
T192 Jared Sandberg	.30	.75
T193 Xavier Nady	.30	.75
T194 Dane Sardinha	.30	.75
T195 Shawn Sonnier	.30	.75
T196 Rafael Soriano	.40	1.00
T197 Brian Specht RC	.40	1.00
T198 Aaron Myette	.30	.75
T199 Juan Uribe RC	.50	1.25
T200 Jayson Werth	.30	.75
T201 Brad Wilkerson	.30	.75
T202 Horacio Estrada	.30	.75
T203 Joel Pineiro	.50	1.25
T204 Matt LeCroy	.30	.75
T205 Michael Coleman	.30	.75
T206 Ben Sheets	.75	2.00
T207 Eric Byrnes	.30	.75
T208 Sean Burroughs	.30	.75
T209 Ken Harvey	.30	.75
T210 Travis Hafner	3.00	8.00
T211 Erick Almonte	.40	1.00
T212 Jason Belcher RC	.40	1.00
T213 Wilson Betemit RC	1.50	4.00
T214 Hank Blalock RC	2.50	6.00
T215 Danny Borrell	.40	1.00
T216 John Buck RC	.50	1.25
T217 Freddie Bynum RC	.40	1.00
T218 Noel Devarez RC	.40	1.00
T219 Juan Diaz RC	.40	1.00
T220 Felix Diaz RC	.40	1.00
T221 Josh Fogg RC	.40	1.00
T222 Matt Ford RC	.40	1.00
T223 Scott Heard	.30	.75
T224 Ben Hendrickson RC	.40	1.00
T225 Cody Ross RC	1.50	4.00
T226 Adrian Hernandez RC	.40	1.00
T227 Alfredo Amezaga RC	.40	1.00
T228 Bob Keppel RC	.40	1.00
T229 Ryan Madson RC	.75	2.00
T230 Octavio Martinez RC	.40	1.00
T231 Hee Seop Choi	.50	1.25
T232 Thomas Mitchell	.30	.75
T233 Luis Montanez	.40	1.00
T234 Andy Morales RC	.40	1.00
T235 Justin Morneau RC	4.00	10.00
T236 Toe Nash RC	.40	1.00
T237 Valentino Pascucci RC	.40	1.00
T238 Roy Smith RC	.40	1.00
T239 Antonio Perez RC	.50	1.25
T240 Chad Petty RC	.40	1.00
T241 Steve Smyth	.40	1.00
T242 Jose Reyes RC	3.00	8.00
T243 Eric Reynolds RC	.40	1.00
T244 Dominic Rich	.40	1.00
T245 Jason Richardson RC	.40	1.00
T246 Ed Rogers RC	.40	1.00
T247 Albert Pujols	125.00	300.00
T248 Esix Snead RC	.40	1.00
T249 Luis Torres RC	.40	1.00
T250 Matt White RC	.40	1.00
T251 Blake Williams	.40	1.00
T252 Chris Russ	.40	1.00
T253 Joe Kennedy RC	.50	1.25
T254 Jeff Randazzo RC	.40	1.00
T255 Beau Hale RC	.40	1.00
T256 Brad Hennessey RC	.75	2.00
T257 Jake Gautreau RC	.40	1.00
T258 Jeff Mathis RC	.50	1.25
T259 Aaron Heilman RC	.50	1.25
T260 Bronson Sardinha RC	.40	1.00
T261 Irvin Guzman RC	3.00	8.00
T262 Gabe Gross RC	.50	1.25
T263 J.D. Martin RC	.40	1.00
T264 Chris Smith RC	.40	1.00
T265 Kenny Baugh RC	.40	1.00
T266 Ichiro Suzuki RC	150.00	400.00

2001 Topps Chrome Traded Retrofractors

Card	Low	High
*STARS: 1.5X TO 4X BASIC CARDS		
*REPRINTS: 1X TO 2.5X BASIC		
*ROOKIES: 2.5X TO 6X BASIC		
STATED ODDS 1:12 TOPPS TRADED		
T99 I.Suzuki A.Pujols ROY	1250.00	3000.00
T210 Travis Hafner	20.00	50.00
T235 Justin Morneau	15.00	40.00
T242 Jose Reyes	6.00	15.00
T247 Albert Pujols	750.00	2000.00
T261 Irvin Guzman	50.00	100.00
T266 Ichiro Suzuki	1250.00	3000.00

2002 Topps Chrome

Card	Low	High
COMPLETE SET (660)	100.00	250.00
COMPLETE SERIES 1 (330)	50.00	125.00
COMPLETE SERIES 2 (330)	50.00	125.00
COMMON (1-331/366-695)	.20	.50
COMMON (307-326/671-690)	.60	1.50
COMMON (327-331/691-695)	.60	1.50
VINTAGE TOPPS CARD SER.1 ODDS 1:110		
VINTAGE TOPPS CARD SER.2 ODDS 1:70		
1 Pedro Martinez	.60	1.50
2 Mike Stanton	.20	.50
3 Brad Penny	.20	.50
4 Mike Matheny	.20	.50
5 Johnny Damon	.60	1.50
6 Bret Boone	.40	1.00
8 Chris Truby	.20	.50
9 B.J. Surhoff	.40	1.00
10 Mike Hampton	.40	1.00
11 Juan Pierre	.40	1.00
12 Mark Buehrle	.40	1.00
13 Bob Abreu	.40	1.00
14 David Cone	.40	1.00
15 Aaron Sele	.20	.50
16 Fernando Tatis	.20	.50
17 Bobby Jones	.20	.50
18 Rick Helling	.20	.50
19 Dmitri Young	.40	1.00
20 Mike Mussina	.60	1.50
21 Mike Sweeney	.40	1.00
22 Cristian Guzman	.20	.50
23 Ryan Kohlmeier	.20	.50
24 Adam Kennedy	.20	.50
25 Larry Walker	.40	1.00
26 Eric Davis	.40	1.00
27 Jason Tyner	.20	.50
28 Eric Young	.20	.50
29 Jason Marquis	.20	.50
30 Luis Gonzalez	.40	1.00
31 Kevin Tapani	.20	.50
32 Orlando Cabrera	.40	1.00
33 Marty Cordova	.20	.50
34 Brad Ausmus	.40	1.00
35 Livan Hernandez	.40	1.00
36 Alex Gonzalez	.20	.50
37 Edgar Renteria	.40	1.00
38 Bengie Molina	.20	.50
39 Frank Menechino	.20	.50
40 Rafael Palmeiro	.60	1.50
41 Brad Fullmer	.20	.50
42 Julio Zuleta	.20	.50
43 Darren Dreifort	.20	.50
44 Trot Nixon	.40	1.00
45 Trevor Hoffman	.40	1.00
46 Vladimir Nunez	.20	.50
47 Mark Kotsay	.40	1.00
48 Kenny Rogers	.40	1.00
49 Ben Petrick	.20	.50
50 Jeff Bagwell	.60	1.50
51 Juan Encarnacion	.20	.50
52 Ramiro Mendoza	.20	.50
53 Brian Meadows	.20	.50
54 Chad Curtis	.20	.50
55 Aramis Ramirez	.40	1.00
56 Mark McLemore	.20	.50
57 Dante Bichette	.40	1.00
58 Scott Schoeneweis	.20	.50
59 Jose Cruz Jr.	.20	.50
60 Roger Clemens	2.00	5.00
61 Jose Guillen	.40	1.00
62 Darren Oliver	.20	.50
63 Chris Reitsma	.20	.50
64 Jeff Abbott	.20	.50
65 Robin Ventura	.40	1.00
66 Denny Neagle	.20	.50
67 Al Martin	.20	.50
68 Benito Santiago	.40	1.00
69 Roy Oswalt	.40	1.00
70 Juan Gonzalez	.40	1.00
71 Garret Anderson	.40	1.00
72 Bobby Bonilla	.40	1.00
73 Danny Bautista	.20	.50
74 J.T. Snow	.40	1.00
75 Derek Jeter	2.50	6.00
76 John Olerud	.40	1.00
77 Kevin Appier	.40	1.00
78 Phil Nevin	.40	1.00
79 Sean Casey	.40	1.00
80 Troy Glaus	.40	1.00
81 Joe Randa	.40	1.00
82 Jose Valentin	.20	.50
83 Ricky Bottalico	.20	.50
84 Todd Zeile	.40	1.00
85 Barry Larkin	.60	1.50
86 Bob Wickman	.20	.50
87 Jeff Shaw	.20	.50
88 Greg Vaughn	.20	.50
89 Fernando Vina	.20	.50
90 Mark Mulder	.40	1.00
91 Paul Bako	.20	.50
92 Aaron Boone	.40	1.00
93 Esteban Loaiza	.20	.50
94 Richie Sexson	.40	1.00
95 Alfonso Soriano	.40	1.00
96 Tony Womack	.20	.50
97 Paul Shuey	.20	.50
98 Melvin Mora	.40	1.00
99 Tony Gwynn	1.25	3.00
100 Vladimir Guerrero	1.00	2.50
101 Keith Osik	.20	.50
102 Bud Smith	.20	.50
103 Scott Williamson	.20	.50
104 Daryle Ward	.20	.50
105 Doug Mientkiewicz	.40	1.00
106 Stan Javier	.20	.50
107 Russ Ortiz	.20	.50
108 Wade Miller	.20	.50
109 Luke Prokopec	.20	.50
110 Andruw Jones	.60	1.50
111 Ron Coomer	.20	.50
112 Dan Wilson	.20	.50
113 Luis Castillo	.20	.50
114 Derek Bell	.20	.50
115 Gary Sheffield	.40	1.00
116 Ruben Rivera	.20	.50
117 Paul O'Neill	.60	1.50
118 Craig Paquette	.20	.50
119 Kelvim Escobar	.20	.50
120 Brad Radke	.40	1.00
121 Jorge Fabregas	.20	.50
122 Randy Winn	.20	.50
123 Tom Goodwin	.20	.50
124 Jaret Wright	.20	.50
125 Barry Bonds HR 73	5.00	12.00
126 Al Leiter	.20	.50
127 Ben Davis	.20	.50
128 Frank Catalanotto	.20	.50
129 Jose Cabrera	.20	.50
130 Magglio Ordonez	.40	1.00
131 Jose Macias	.20	.50
132 Ted Lilly	.20	.50
133 Chris Holt	.20	.50
134 Eric Milton	.20	.50
135 Shannon Stewart	.40	1.00
136 Omar Olivares	.20	.50
137 David Segui	.20	.50
138 Jeff Nelson	.20	.50
139 Matt Williams	.40	1.00
140 Ellis Burks	.40	1.00
141 Jason Bere	.20	.50
142 Jimmy Haynes	.20	.50
143 Ramon Hernandez	.20	.50
144 Craig Counsell	.20	.50
145 John Smoltz	.60	1.50
146 Homer Bush	.20	.50
147 Quilvio Veras	.20	.50
148 Esteban Yan	.20	.50
149 Ramon Ortiz	.20	.50
150 Carlos Delgado	.40	1.00
151 Lee Stevens	.20	.50
152 Wil Cordero	.20	.50
153 Mike Bordick	.40	1.00
154 John Flaherty	.20	.50
155 Omar Daal	.20	.50
156 Todd Ritchie	.20	.50
157 Carl Everett	.40	1.00
158 Scott Sullivan	.20	.50
159 Deivi Cruz	.20	.50
160 Albert Pujols	2.00	5.00
161 Royce Clayton	.20	.50
162 Jeff Suppan	.20	.50
163 C.C. Sabathia	.40	1.00
164 Jimmy Rollins	.40	1.00
165 Rickey Henderson	1.00	2.50
166 Rey Ordonez	.20	.50
167 Shawn Estes	.20	.50
168 Reggie Sanders	.40	1.00
169 Jon Lieber	.20	.50
170 Armando Benitez	.20	.50
171 Mike Remlinger	.20	.50
172 Billy Wagner	.40	1.00
173 Troy Percival	.40	1.00
174 Devon White	.40	1.00
175 Ivan Rodriguez	.60	1.50
176 Dustin Hermanson	.20	.50
177 Brian Anderson	.20	.50
178 Graeme Lloyd	.20	.50
179 Russell Branyan	.20	.50
180 Bobby Higginson	.40	1.00
181 Alex Gonzalez	.20	.50
182 John Franco	.40	1.00
183 Sidney Ponson	.20	.50
184 Jose Mesa	.20	.50
185 Todd Hollandsworth	.20	.50
186 Kevin Young	.20	.50
187 Tim Wakefield	.40	1.00
188 Craig Biggio	.60	1.50
189 Jason Isringhausen	.40	1.00
190 Mark Quinn	.20	.50
191 Glendon Rusch	.20	.50
192 Damian Miller	.20	.50
193 Sandy Alomar Jr.	.20	.50
194 Scott Brosius	.40	1.00
195 Dave Martinez	.20	.50
196 Danny Graves	.20	.50
197 Shea Hillenbrand	.40	1.00
198 Jimmy Anderson	.20	.50
199 Travis Lee	.20	.50
200 Randy Johnson	1.00	2.50
201 Carlos Beltran	.40	1.00
202 Jerry Hairston	.20	.50
203 Jesus Sanchez	.20	.50
204 Eddie Taubensee	.20	.50
205 David Wells	.40	1.00
206 Russ Davis	.20	.50
207 Michael Barrett	.20	.50
208 Marquis Grissom	.40	1.00
209 Byung-Hyun Kim	.40	1.00
210 Hideo Nomo	1.00	2.50
211 Ryan Rupe	.20	.50
212 Ricky Gutierrez	.20	.50
213 Darryl Kile	.40	1.00
214 Rico Brogna	.20	.50
215 Terrence Long	.20	.50
216 Mike Jackson	.20	.50
217 Jamey Wright	.20	.50
218 Adrian Beltre	.40	1.00
219 Benny Agbayani	.20	.50
220 Chuck Knoblauch	.40	1.00
221 Randy Wolf	.20	.50
222 Andy Ashby	.20	.50
223 Corey Koskie	.20	.50
224 Roger Cedeno	.20	.50
225 Ichiro Suzuki	2.00	5.00
226 Keith Foulke	.40	1.00
227 Ryan Minor	.20	.50
228 Shawon Dunston	.20	.50
229 Alex Cora	.20	.50
230 Jeromy Burnitz	.40	1.00
231 Mark Grace	.60	1.50
232 Aubrey Huff	.40	1.00
233 Jeffrey Hammonds	.20	.50
234 Olmedo Saenz	.20	.50
235 Brian Jordan	.40	1.00
236 Jeremy Giambi	.20	.50
237 Joe Girardi	.20	.50
238 Eric Gagne	.40	1.00
239 Masato Yoshii	.20	.50
240 Greg Maddux	1.50	4.00
241 Bryan Rekar	.20	.50
242 Ray Durham	.40	1.00
243 Torii Hunter	.40	1.00
244 Derrek Lee	.60	1.50
245 Jim Edmonds	.40	1.00
246 Einar Diaz	.20	.50
247 Brian Bohanon	.20	.50
248 Ron Belliard	.20	.50
249 Mike Lowell	.40	1.00
250 Sammy Sosa	1.00	2.50
251 Richard Hidalgo	.20	.50
252 Bartolo Colon	.40	1.00
253 Jorge Posada	.60	1.50
254 Latroy Hawkins	.20	.50
255 Paul LoDuca	.40	1.00
256 Carlos Febles	.20	.50
257 Nelson Cruz	.20	.50
258 Edgardo Alfonzo	.20	.50
259 Joey Hamilton	.20	.50
260 Cliff Floyd	.40	1.00
261 Wes Helms	.20	.50
262 Jay Bell	.40	1.00
263 Mike Cameron	.20	.50
264 Paul Konerko	.40	1.00
265 Jeff Kent	.40	1.00
266 Robert Fick	.20	.50
267 Allen Levrault	.20	.50
268 Placido Polanco	.20	.50
269 Marlon Anderson	.20	.50
270 Mariano Rivera	1.00	2.50
271 Chan Ho Park	.40	1.00
272 Jose Vizcaino	.20	.50
273 Jeff D'Amico	.20	.50
274 Mark Gardner	.20	.50
275 Travis Fryman	.40	1.00
276 Darren Lewis	.20	.50
277 Bruce Bochy MG	.20	.50
278 Jerry Manuel MG	.20	.50
279 Bob Brenly MG	.20	.50
280 Don Baylor MG	.40	1.00
281 Davey Lopes MG	.40	1.00
282 Jerry Narron MG	.20	.50
283 Tony Muser MG	.20	.50
284 Hal McRae MG	.40	1.00
285 Bobby Cox MG	.20	.50
286 Larry Dierker MG	.20	.50
287 Phil Garner MG	.40	1.00
288 Joe Kerrigan MG	.20	.50
289 Bobby Valentine MG	.20	.50
290 Dusty Baker MG	.40	1.00
291 Lloyd McClendon MG	.20	.50
292 Mike Scioscia MG	.20	.50
293 Buck Martinez MG	.20	.50
294 Larry Bowa MG	.40	1.00
295 Tony LaRussa MG	.40	1.00
296 Jeff Torborg MG	.20	.50
297 Tom Kelly MG	.20	.50
298 Mike Hargrove MG	.20	.50
299 Art Howe MG	.20	.50
300 Lou Piniella MG	.40	1.00
301 Charlie Manuel MG	.20	.50
302 Buddy Bell MG	.40	1.00
303 Tony Perez MG	.40	1.00
304 Bob Boone MG	.40	1.00
305 Joe Torre MG	.60	1.50
306 Jim Tracy MG	.20	.50
307 Jason Lane PROS	.60	1.50
308 Chris George PROS	.60	1.50
309 Hank Blalock PROS	1.00	2.50
310 Joe Borchard PROS	.60	1.50
311 Marlon Byrd PROS	.60	1.50
312 Raymond Cabrera PROS RC	.60	1.50
313 Freddy Sanchez PROS RC	2.50	6.00
314 Scott Wiggins PROS RC	.60	1.50
315 Jason Maule PROS RC	.60	1.50
316 Dionys Cesar PROS RC	.60	1.50
317 Boof Bonser PROS	.60	1.50
318 Juan Tolentino PROS RC	.60	1.50
319 Earl Snyder PROS RC	.60	1.50
320 Travis Wade PROS RC	.60	1.50
321 Napolean Calzado PROS RC	.60	1.50
322 Eric Glaser PROS RC	.60	1.50
323 Craig Kuzmic PROS RC	.60	1.50
324 Nic Jackson PROS RC	.60	1.50
325 Mike Rivera PROS	.60	1.50
326 Jason Bay PROS RC	3.00	8.00
327 Chris Smith DP	.60	1.50
328 Jake Gautreau DP	.60	1.50
329 Gabe Gross DP	.60	1.50
330 Kenny Baugh DP	.60	1.50
331 J.D. Martin DP	.60	1.50
366 Pat Meares	.20	.50
367 Mike Lieberthal	.40	1.00
368 Larry Bigbie	.20	.50
369 Ron Gant	.40	1.00
370 Moises Alou	.40	1.00
371 Chad Kreuter	.20	.50
372 Willis Roberts	.20	.50
373 Toby Hall	.20	.50
374 Miguel Batista	.20	.50
375 John Burkett	.20	.50
376 Cory Lidle	.20	.50
377 Nick Neugebauer	.20	.50
378 Jay Payton	.20	.50
379 Steve Karsay	.20	.50
380 Eric Chavez	.40	1.00
381 Kelly Stinnett	.20	.50
382 Jarrod Washburn	.20	.50
383 Rick White	.20	.50
384 Jeff Conine	.40	1.00
385 Fred McGriff	.60	1.50
386 Marvin Benard	.20	.50
387 Joe Crede	.40	1.00
388 Dennis Cook	.20	.50
389 Rick Reed	.20	.50
390 Tom Glavine	.60	1.50
391 Rondell White	.40	1.00
392 Matt Morris	.40	1.00
393 Pat Rapp	.20	.50
394 Robert Person	.20	.50
395 Omar Vizquel	.60	1.50
396 Jeff Cirillo	.20	.50
397 Dave Mlicki	.20	.50
398 Jose Ortiz	.20	.50
399 Ryan Dempster	.20	.50
400 Curt Schilling	.40	1.00
401 Peter Bergeron	.20	.50
402 Kyle Lohse	.20	.50
403 Craig Wilson	.20	.50
404 David Justice	.40	1.00
405 Darin Erstad	.40	1.00
406 Jose Mercedes	.20	.50
407 Carl Pavano	.40	1.00
408 Albie Lopez	.20	.50
409 Alex Ochoa	.20	.50
410 Chipper Jones	1.00	2.50
411 Tyler Houston	.20	.50
412 Dean Palmer	.40	1.00
413 Damian Jackson	.20	.50
414 Josh Towers	.20	.50
415 Rafael Furcal	.40	1.00
416 Mike Morgan	.20	.50
417 Herb Perry	.20	.50
418 Mike Sirotka	.20	.50
419 Mark Wohlers	.20	.50
420 Nomar Garciaparra	1.50	4.00
421 Felipe Lopez	.20	.50
422 Joe McEwing	.20	.50
423 Jacque Jones	.40	1.00
424 Julio Franco	.40	1.00
425 Frank Thomas	1.00	2.50
426 So Taguchi RC	1.00	2.50
427 Kazuhisa Ishii RC	1.00	2.50
428 D'Angelo Jimenez	.20	.50
429 Chris Stynes	.20	.50
430 Kerry Wood	.40	1.00
431 Chris Singleton	.20	.50
432 Erubiel Durazo	.20	.50
433 Matt Lawton	.20	.50
434 Bill Mueller	.40	1.00
435 Jose Canseco	.60	1.50
436 Ben Grieve	.20	.50
437 Terry Mulholland	.20	.50
438 David Bell	.20	.50
439 A.J. Pierzynski	.40	1.00
440 Adam Dunn	.40	1.00
441 Jon Garland	.40	1.00
442 Jeff Fassero	.20	.50
443 Julio Lugo	.20	.50
444 Carlos Guillen	.40	1.00
445 Orlando Hernandez	.40	1.00
446 Mark Loretta	.20	.50
447 Scott Spiezio	.20	.50
448 Kevin Millwood	.40	1.00
449 Jamie Moyer	.40	1.00
450 Todd Helton	.60	1.50
451 Todd Walker	.20	.50
452 Jose Lima	.20	.50
453 Brook Fordyce	.20	.50
454 Aaron Rowand	.40	1.00
455 Barry Zito	.40	1.00
456 Eric Owens	.20	.50
457 Charles Nagy	.20	.50
458 Raul Ibanez	.20	.50
459 Joe Mays	.20	.50
460 Jim Thome	.60	1.50
461 Adam Eaton	.20	.50
462 Felix Martinez	.20	.50
463 Vernon Wells	.40	1.00
464 Donnie Sadler	.20	.50
465 Tony Clark	.20	.50
466 Jose Hernandez	.20	.50
467 Ramon Martinez	.20	.50
468 Rusty Greer	.40	1.00
469 Rod Barajas	.20	.50
470 Lance Berkman	.40	1.00
471 Brady Anderson	.40	1.00
472 Pedro Astacio	.20	.50
473 Shane Halter	.20	.50
474 Bret Prinz	.20	.50
475 Edgar Martinez	.60	1.50
476 Steve Trachsel	.20	.50
477 Gary Matthews Jr.	.20	.50
478 Ismael Valdes	.20	.50
479 Juan Uribe	.20	.50

480 Shawn Green .40 1.00
481 Kirk Rueter .20 .50
482 Damion Easley .20 .50
483 Chris Carpenter .40 1.00
484 Kris Benson .20 .50
485 Antonio Alfonseca .20 .50
486 Kyle Farnsworth .20 .50
487 Brandon Lyon .20 .50
488 Hideki Irabu .20 .50
489 David Ortiz 1.00 2.50
490 Mike Piazza 1.50 4.00
491 Derek Lowe .40 1.00
492 Chris Gomez .20 .50
493 Mark Johnson .20 .50
494 John Rocker .40 1.00
495 Eric Karros .40 1.00
496 Bill Haselman .20 .50
497 Dave Veres .20 .50
498 Pete Harnisch .20 .50
499 Tomokazu Ohka .20 .50
500 Barry Bonds 2.50 6.00
501 David Dellucci .20 .50
502 Wendell Magee .20 .50
503 Tom Gordon .20 .50
504 Javier Vazquez .40 1.00
505 Ben Sheets .40 1.00
506 Wilton Guerrero .20 .50
507 John Halama .20 .50
508 Mark Redman .20 .50
509 Jack Wilson .20 .50
510 Bernie Williams .60 1.50
511 Miguel Cairo .20 .50
512 Denny Hocking .20 .50
513 Tony Batista .20 .50
514 Mark Grudzielanek .20 .50
515 Jose Vidro .20 .50
516 Sterling Hitchcock .20 .50
517 Billy Koch .20 .50
518 Matt Clement .40 1.00
519 Bruce Chen .20 .50
520 Roberto Alomar .60 1.50
521 Orlando Palmeiro .20 .50
522 Steve Finley .40 1.00
523 Danny Patterson .20 .50
524 Terry Adams .20 .50
525 Tino Martinez .60 1.50
526 Tony Armas Jr. .20 .50
527 Geoff Jenkins .20 .50
528 Kerry Robinson .20 .50
529 Corey Patterson .20 .50
530 Brian Giles .40 1.00
531 Jose Jimenez .20 .50
532 Joe Kennedy .20 .50
533 Armando Rios .20 .50
534 Osvaldo Fernandez .20 .50
535 Ruben Sierra .40 1.00
536 Octavio Dotel .20 .50
537 Luis Sojo .20 .50
538 Brent Butler .20 .50
539 Pablo Ozuna .20 .50
540 Freddy Garcia .40 1.00
541 Chad Durbin .20 .50
542 Orlando Merced .20 .50
543 Michael Tucker .20 .50
544 Roberto Hernandez .20 .50
545 Pat Burrell .40 1.00
546 A.J. Burnett .40 1.00
547 Bubba Trammell .20 .50
548 Scott Elarton .20 .50
549 Mike Darr .20 .50
550 Ken Griffey Jr. 2.00 5.00
551 Ugueth Urbina .20 .50
552 Todd Jones .20 .50
553 Delino Deshields .20 .50
554 Adam Piatt .20 .50
555 Jason Kendall .40 1.00
556 Hector Ortiz .20 .50
557 Turk Wendell .20 .50
558 Rob Bell .20 .50
559 Sun Woo Kim .20 .50
560 Raul Mondesi .40 1.00
561 Brent Abernathy .20 .50
562 Seth Etherton .20 .50
563 Shawn Wooten .20 .50
564 Jay Buhner .40 1.00
565 Andres Galarraga .40 1.00
566 Shane Reynolds .20 .50
567 Rod Beck .20 .50
568 Dee Brown .20 .50
569 Pedro Feliz .20 .50
570 Ryan Klesko .40 1.00
571 John Vander Wal .20 .50
572 Nick Bierbrodt .20 .50
573 Joe Nathan .40 1.00
574 James Baldwin .20 .50
575 J.D. Drew .40 1.00
576 Greg Colbrunn .20 .50
577 Doug Glanville .20 .50
578 Brandon Duckworth .20 .50
579 Shawn Chacon .20 .50
580 Rich Aurilia .20 .50
581 Chuck Finley .40 1.00
582 Abraham Nunez .20 .50
583 Kenny Lofton .40 1.00
584 Brian Daubach .20 .50
585 Miguel Tejada .40 1.00
586 Nate Cornejo .20 .50
587 Kazuhiro Sasaki .40 1.00
588 Chris Richard .20 .50
589 Armando Reynoso .20 .50
590 Tim Hudson .40 1.00
591 Neifi Perez .20 .50
592 Steve Cox .20 .50
593 Henry Blanco .20 .50
594 Ricky Ledee .20 .50
595 Tim Salmon .60 1.50
596 Luis Rivas .20 .50
597 Jeff Zimmerman .20 .50
598 Matt Stairs .20 .50
599 Preston Wilson .40 1.00
600 Mark McGwire 2.50 6.00
601 Timo Perez .20 .50
602 Matt Anderson .20 .50
603 Todd Hundley .20 .50
604 Rick Ankiel .20 .50
605 Tsuyoshi Shinjo .40 1.00
606 Woody Williams .20 .50
607 Jason LaRue .20 .50
608 Carlos Lee .40 1.00
609 Russ Johnson .20 .50
610 Scott Rolen .60 1.50
611 Brent Mayne .20 .50
612 Darrin Fletcher .20 .50
613 Ray Lankford .40 1.00
614 Troy O'Leary .20 .50
615 Javier Lopez .40 1.00
616 Randy Velarde .20 .50
617 Vinny Castilla .40 1.00
618 Milton Bradley .40 1.00
619 Ruben Mateo .20 .50
620 Jason Giambi Yankees .40 1.00
621 Andy Benes .20 .50
622 Joe Mauer RC 8.00 20.00
623 Andy Pettitte .60 1.50
624 Jose Offerman .20 .50
625 Mo Vaughn .40 1.00
626 Steve Sparks .20 .50
627 Mike Matthews .20 .50
628 Robb Nen .40 1.00
629 Kip Wells .20 .50
630 Kevin Brown .40 1.00
631 Arthur Rhodes .20 .50
632 Gabe Kapler .40 1.00
633 Jermaine Dye .40 1.00
634 Josh Beckett .40 1.00
635 Pokey Reese .20 .50
636 Benji Gil .20 .50
637 Marcus Giles .40 1.00
638 Julian Tavarez .20 .50
639 Jason Schmidt .40 1.00
640 Alex Rodriguez 1.25 3.00
641 Anaheim Angels TC .40 1.00
642 Arizona Diamondbacks TC .60 1.50
643 Atlanta Braves TC .40 1.00
644 Baltimore Orioles TC .40 1.00
645 Boston Red Sox TC .40 1.00
646 Chicago Cubs TC .40 1.00
647 Chicago White Sox TC .40 1.00
648 Cincinnati Reds TC .40 1.00
649 Cleveland Indians TC .40 1.00
650 Colorado Rockies TC .40 1.00
651 Detroit Tigers TC .40 1.00
652 Florida Marlins TC .40 1.00
653 Houston Astros TC .40 1.00
654 Kansas City Royals TC .40 1.00
655 Los Angeles Dodgers TC .40 1.00
656 Milwaukee Brewers TC .40 1.00
657 Minnesota Twins TC .40 1.00
658 Montreal Expos TC .40 1.00
659 New York Mets TC .40 1.00
660 New York Yankees TC 1.00 2.50
661 Oakland Athletics TC .40 1.00
662 Philadelphia Phillies TC .40 1.00
663 Pittsburgh Pirates TC .40 1.00
664 San Diego Padres TC .40 1.00
665 San Francisco Giants TC .40 1.00
666 Seattle Mariners TC .60 1.50
667 St. Louis Cardinals TC .40 1.00
668 Tampa Bay Devil Rays TC .40 1.00
669 Texas Rangers TC .40 1.00
670 Toronto Blue Jays TC .40 1.00
671 Juan Cruz PROS .60 1.50
672 Kevin Cash PROS RC .60 1.50
673 Jimmy Gobble PROS RC .60 1.50
674 Mike Hill PROS RC .60 1.50
675 Taylor Buchholz PROS RC .60 1.50
676 Bill Hall PROS .60 1.50
677 Brett Roneberg PROS RC .60 1.50
678 Royce Huffman PROS RC .60 1.50
679 Chris Tritle PROS RC .60 1.50
680 Nate Espy PROS .60 1.50
681 Nick Alvarez PROS RC .60 1.50
682 Jason Botts PROS RC .60 1.50
683 Ryan Gripp PROS RC .60 1.50
684 Dan Phillips PROS RC .60 1.50
685 Pablo Arias PROS RC .60 1.50
686 John Rodriguez PROS RC 1.00 2.50
687 Rich Harden PROS RC 3.00 8.00
688 Neal Frendling PROS RC .60 1.50
689 Rich Thompson PROS RC .60 1.50
690 Greg Montalbano PROS RC .60 1.50
691 Len Dinardo DP RC .60 1.50
692 Ryan Raburn DP RC 1.25 3.00
693 Josh Barfield DP RC 2.00 5.00
694 David Bacani DP RC .60 1.50
695 Dan Johnson DP RC 1.00 2.50

2002 Topps Chrome Black Refractors

*BLACK: 6X TO 15X BASIC CARDS
*BLACK 307-331/671-695: 5X TO 12X BASIC
SER.2 STATED ODDS 1:21 HOBBY
STATED PRINT RUN 50 SERIAL #'d SETS
125 Barry Bonds HR 73 175.00 300.00

2002 Topps Chrome Gold Refractors

*GOLD: 2X TO 5X BASIC
*GOLD 307-331/671-695: 1.25X TO 3X BASIC
SER.1 AND 2 STATED ODDS 1:4

2002 Topps Chrome '52 Reprints

COMPLETE SET (19) 20.00 50.00
COMPLETE SERIES 1 (9) 10.00 25.00
COMPLETE SERIES 2 (10) 10.00 25.00
SER.1 AND 2 STATED ODDS 1:8
*REF: .75X TO 2X BASIC 52 REPRINTS
SER.1 AND 2 REFRACTOR ODDS 1:24
52R1 Roy Campanella 2.00 5.00
52R2 Duke Snider 1.50 4.00
52R3 Carl Erskine 1.50 4.00
52R4 Andy Pafko 1.50 4.00
52R5 Johnny Mize 1.50 4.00
52R6 Billy Martin 1.50 4.00
52R7 Phil Rizzuto 2.00 5.00
52R8 Gil McDougald 1.50 4.00
52R9 Allie Reynolds 1.50 4.00
52R10 Jackie Robinson 2.00 5.00
52R11 Preacher Roe 1.50 4.00
52R12 Gil Hodges 2.00 5.00
52R13 Billy Cox 1.50 4.00
52R14 Yogi Berra 2.00 5.00
52R15 Gene Woodling 1.50 4.00
52R16 Johnny Sain 1.50 4.00
52R17 Ralph Houk 1.50 4.00
52R18 Joe Collins 1.50 4.00
52R19 Hank Bauer 1.50 4.00

2002 Topps Chrome 5-Card Stud Aces Relics

SER.2 STATED ODDS 1:140
5AAL Al Leiter Jsy 6.00 15.00
5ABZ Barry Zito Jsy 6.00 15.00
5ACS Curt Schilling Jsy 6.00 15.00
5AKB Kevin Brown Jsy 6.00 15.00
5ATH Tim Hudson Jsy 6.00 15.00

2002 Topps Chrome 5-Card Stud Deuces are Wild Relics

SER.2 BAT ODDS 1:1098
SER.2 UNIFORM ODDS 1:704
SER.2 OVERALL ODDS 1:428
5DBT Bernie Bat/Tino Bat 15.00 40.00
5DCA Chipper Bat/Andruw Bat 20.00 50.00
5DRC Dempster Uni/Floyd Uni 6.00 15.00

2002 Topps Chrome 5-Card Stud Jack of all Trades Relics

SER.2 BAT ODDS 1:1098
SER.2 JERSEY ODDS 1:704
SER.2 OVERALL ODDS 1:428
5JCJ Chipper Jones Jsy 10.00 25.00
5JMO Magglio Ordonez Bat 6.00 15.00

2002 Topps Chrome 5-Card Stud Kings of the Clubhouse Relics

SER.2 BAT ODDS 1:2204
SER.2 JERSEY ODDS 1:704
SER.2 UNIFORM ODDS 1:704
SER.2 OVERALL ODDS 1:303
5KJB Jeff Bagwell Uniform 8.00 20.00
5KTG Tony Gwynn Jsy 12.50 30.00

2002 Topps Chrome 5-Card Stud Three of a Kind Relics

SER.2 STATED ODDS 1:689
B ='s Bat, J ='s Jsy, U ='s Uniform
5TAIR A.Rod B/I.Rod J/Raffy U 12.00 30.00
5TBEJ Boone B/Edgar B/Olerud B 12.00 30.00
5TJCL Bag U/Biggio B/Berk B 40.00 80.00

2002 Topps Chrome Summer School Like Father Like Son Relics

SER.1 STATED ODDS 1:790
FSCWI P.Wilson U/M.Wilson J 6.00 15.00

2002 Topps Chrome Summer School Battery Mates Relics

SER.1 GROUP A ODDS 1:716
SER.1 GROUP B ODDS 1:681
SER.1 OVERALL STATED ODDS 1:349
BMCGL T.Glavine J/J.Lopez J B 10.00 25.00
BMCHP M.Hampton J/B.Petrick J A 6.00 15.00

2002 Topps Chrome Summer School Top of the Order Relics

SER.1 BAT GROUP A ODDS 1:1383
SER.1 BAT GROUP B ODDS 1:1538
SER.1 BAT GROUP C ODDS 1:3170
SER.1 BAT GROUP D ODDS 1:2902
SER.1 BAT GROUP E ODDS 1:2544
SER.1 JSY GROUP A ODDS 1:790
SER.1 JSY GROUP B ODDS 1:659
SER.1 UNI GROUP A ODDS 1:920
SER.1 UNI GROUP B ODDS 1:651
SER.1 UNI GROUP C ODDS 1:614
SER.1 OVERALL STATED ODDS 1:106
TOCBA Benny Agbayani Uni C 6.00 15.00
TOCCB Craig Biggio Uni A 10.00 25.00
TOCCK Chuck Knoblauch Bat E 6.00 15.00
TOCJD Johnny Damon Bat B 10.00 25.00
TOCJK Jason Kendall Bat D 6.00 15.00
TOCJP Juan Pierre Bat A 6.00 15.00
TOCKL Kenny Lofton Uni B 6.00 15.00
TOCPB Peter Bergeron Jsy A 6.00 15.00
TOCPL Paul LoDuca Bat A 6.00 15.00
TOCRF Rafael Furcal Bat C 6.00 15.00
TOCRH Rickey Henderson Bat B 10.00 25.00
TOCSS Shannon Stewart Jsy B 6.00 15.00

2002 Topps Chrome Traded

COMPLETE SET (275) 30.00 60.00
2 PER 2002 TOPPS TRADED HOBBY PACK
7 PER 2002 TOPPS TRADED HTA PACK
2 PER 2002 TOPPS TRADED RETAIL PACK
T1 Jeff Weaver .20 .50
T2 Jay Powell .20 .50
T3 Alex Gonzalez .20 .50
T4 Jason Isringhausen .30 .75
T5 Tyler Houston .20 .50
T6 Ben Broussard .20 .50
T7 Chuck Knoblauch .30 .75
T8 Brian L. Hunter .20 .50
T9 Dustan Mohr .20 .50
T10 Eric Hinske .20 .50
T11 Roger Cedeno .20 .50
T12 Eddie Perez .20 .50
T13 Jeromy Burnitz .30 .75
T14 Bartolo Colon .30 .75
T15 Rick Helling .20 .50
T16 Dan Plesac .20 .50
T17 Scott Strickland .20 .50
T18 Antonio Alfonseca .20 .50
T19 Ricky Gutierrez .20 .50
T20 John Valentin .20 .50
T21 Raul Mondesi .30 .75
T22 Ben Davis .20 .50
T23 Nelson Figueroa .20 .50
T24 Earl Snyder .20 .50
T25 Robin Ventura .30 .75
T26 Jimmy Haynes .20 .50
T27 Kenny Kelly .20 .50
T28 Morgan Ensberg .30 .75
T29 Reggie Sanders .30 .75
T30 Shigetoshi Hasegawa .30 .75
T31 Mike Timlin .20 .50
T32 Russell Branyan .20 .50
T33 Alan Embree .20 .50
T34 D'Angelo Jimenez .20 .50
T35 Kent Mercker .20 .50
T36 Jesse Orosco .20 .50
T37 Gregg Zaun .20 .50
T38 Reggie Taylor .20 .50
T39 Andres Galarraga .30 .75
T40 Chris Truby .20 .50
T41 Bruce Chen .20 .50
T42 Darren Lewis .20 .50
T43 Ryan Kohlmeier .20 .50
T44 John McDonald .20 .50
T45 Omar Daal .20 .50
T46 Matt Clement .30 .75
T47 Glendon Rusch .20 .50
T48 Chan Ho Park .30 .75
T49 Benny Agbayani .20 .50
T50 Juan Gonzalez .30 .75
T51 Carlos Baerga .20 .50
T52 Tim Raines .30 .75
T53 Kevin Appier .30 .75
T54 Marty Cordova .20 .50
T55 Jeff D'Amico .20 .50
T56 Dmitri Young .30 .75
T57 Roosevelt Brown .20 .50
T58 Dustin Hermanson .20 .50
T59 Jose Rijo .20 .50
T60 Todd Ritchie .20 .50
T61 Lee Stevens .20 .50
T62 Placido Polanco .20 .50
T63 Eric Young .20 .50
T64 Chuck Finley .30 .75
T65 Dicky Gonzalez .20 .50
T66 Jose Macias .20 .50
T67 Gabe Kapler .30 .75
T68 Sandy Alomar Jr. .20 .50
T69 Henry Blanco .20 .50
T70 Julian Tavarez .20 .50
T71 Paul Bako .20 .50
T72 Scott Rolen .50 1.25
T73 Brian Jordan .30 .75
T74 Rickey Henderson .75 2.00
T75 Kevin Mench .20 .50
T76 Hideo Nomo .75 2.00
T77 Jeremy Giambi .20 .50
T78 Brad Fullmer .20 .50
T79 Carl Everett .30 .75
T80 David Wells .30 .75
T81 Aaron Sele .20 .50
T82 Todd Hollandsworth .20 .50
T83 Vicente Padilla .20 .50
T84 Kenny Lofton .30 .75
T85 Corky Miller .20 .50
T86 Josh Fogg .20 .50
T87 Cliff Floyd .30 .75
T88 Craig Paquette .20 .50
T89 Jay Payton .20 .50
T90 Carlos Pena .20 .50
T91 Juan Encarnacion .20 .50
T92 Rey Sanchez .20 .50
T93 Ryan Dempster .20 .50
T94 Mario Encarnacion .20 .50
T95 Jorge Julio .20 .50
T96 John Mabry .20 .50
T97 Todd Zeile .30 .75
T98 Johnny Damon .50 1.25
T99 Deivi Cruz .20 .50
T100 Gary Sheffield .30 .75
T101 Ted Lilly .20 .50
T102 Todd Van Poppel .20 .50
T103 Shawn Estes .20 .50
T104 Cesar Izturis .20 .50
T105 Ron Coomer .20 .50
T106 Grady Little MG RC .20 .50
T107 Jimy Williams MGR .20 .50
T108 Tony Pena MGR .20 .50
T109 Frank Robinson MGR .50 1.25
T110 Ron Gardenhire MGR .20 .50
T111 Dennis Tankersley .20 .50
T112 Alejandro Cadena RC .40 1.00
T113 Justin Reid RC .40 1.00
T114 Nate Field RC .40 1.00
T115 Rene Reyes RC .40 1.00
T116 Nelson Castro RC .40 1.00
T117 Miguel Olivo .20 .50
T118 David Espinosa .20 .50
T119 Chris Bootcheck RC .40 1.00
T120 Rob Henkel RC .40 1.00
T121 Steve Bechler RC .40 1.00
T122 Mark Outlaw RC .40 1.00
T123 Henry Pichardo RC .40 1.00
T124 Michael Floyd RC .40 1.00
T125 Richard Lane RC .40 1.00
T126 Pete Zamora RC .40 1.00
T127 Javier Colina .20 .50
T128 Greg Sain RC .40 1.00
T129 Ronnie Merrill .20 .50
T130 Gavin Floyd RC 1.00 2.50
T131 Josh Bonifay RC .40 1.00
T132 Tommy Marx RC .40 1.00
T133 Gary Cates Jr. RC .40 1.00
T134 Neal Cotts RC 1.00 2.50
T135 Angel Berroa .20 .50
T136 Elio Serrano RC .40 1.00
T137 J.J. Putz RC .50 1.25
T138 Ruben Gotay RC .50 1.25
T139 Eddie Rogers .20 .50
T140 Wily Mo Pena .30 .75
T141 Tyler Yates RC .40 1.00
T142 Colin Young RC .30 .75
T143 Chance Caple .20 .50
T144 Ben Howard RC .40 1.00
T145 Ryan Bukvich RC .40 1.00
T146 Cliff Bartosh RC .40 1.00
T147 Brandon Claussen .20 .50
T148 Cristian Guerrero .20 .50
T149 Derrick Lewis .20 .50
T150 Eric Miller RC .40 1.00
T151 Justin Huber RC .75 2.00
T152 Adrian Gonzalez .20 .50
T153 Brian West RC .40 1.00
T154 Chris Baker RC .40 1.00
T155 Drew Henson .20 .50
T156 Scott Hairston RC .50 1.25
T157 Jason Simontacchi RC .40 1.00
T158 Jason Arnold RC .40 1.00
T159 Brandon Phillips .20 .50
T160 Adam Roller RC .40 1.00

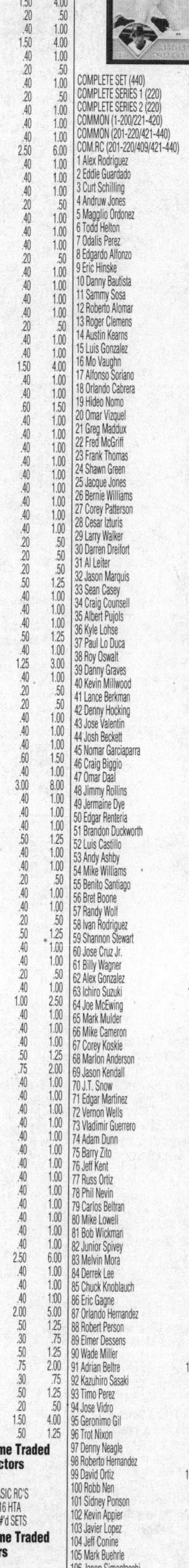

T161 Scotty Layfield RC .40 1.00
T162 Freddie Money RC .40 1.00
T163 Noochie Varner RC .40 1.00
T164 Terrance Hill RC .40 1.00
T165 Jeremy Hill RC .40 1.00
T166 Carlos Cabrera RC .40 1.00
T167 Jose Morban RC .40 1.00
T168 Kevin Frederick RC .40 1.00
T169 Mark Teixeira 1.50 4.00
T170 Brian Rogers .20 .50
T171 Anastacio Martinez RC .40 1.00
T172 Bobby Jenks RC 1.50 4.00
T173 David Gil RC .40 1.00
T174 Andres Torres .20 .50
T175 James Barrett RC .40 1.00
T176 Jimmy Journell .20 .50
T177 Brett Kay RC .40 1.00
T178 Jason Young RC .40 1.00
T179 Mark Hamilton RC .40 1.00
T180 Jose Bautista RC 2.50 6.00
T181 Blake McGinley RC .40 1.00
T182 Ryan Mottl RC .40 1.00
T183 Jeff Austin RC .40 1.00
T184 Xavier Nady .20 .50
T185 Kyle Kane RC .40 1.00
T186 Travis Foley RC .40 1.00
T187 Nathan Kaup RC .40 1.00
T188 Eric Cyr .20 .50
T189 Josh Cisneros RC .40 1.00
T190 Brad Nelson RC .40 1.00
T191 Clint Weibl RC .40 1.00
T192 Ron Calloway RC .40 1.00
T193 Jung Bong .20 .50
T194 Rolando Viera RC .40 1.00
T195 Jason Bulger RC .40 1.00
T196 Chone Figgins RC 1.50 4.00
T197 Jimmy Alvarez RC .40 1.00
T198 Joel Crump RC .40 1.00
T199 Ryan Doumit RC .60 1.50
T200 Demetrius Heath RC .40 1.00
T201 John Ennis RC .40 1.00
T202 Doug Sessions RC .40 1.00
T203 Clinton Hosford RC .40 1.00
T204 Chris Narveson RC .40 1.00
T205 Ross Peeples RC .40 1.00
T206 Alex Requena RC .40 1.00
T207 Matt Erickson RC .40 1.00
T208 Brian Forystek RC .40 1.00
T209 Dewon Brazelton .20 .50
T210 Nathan Haynes .20 .50
T211 Jack Cust .20 .50
T212 Jesse Foppert RC .50 1.25
T213 Jesus Cota RC .40 1.00
T214 Juan M. Gonzalez RC .40 1.00
T215 Tim Kalita RC .40 1.00
T216 Manny Delcarmen RC .50 1.25
T217 Jim Kavourias RC .40 1.00
T218 C.J. Wilson RC 1.25 3.00
T219 Edwin Yan RC .40 1.00
T220 Andy Van Hekken .20 .50
T221 Michael Cuddyer .20 .50
T222 Jeff Verplancke RC .40 1.00
T223 Mike Wilson RC .40 1.00
T224 Corwin Malone RC .40 1.00
T225 Chris Snelling RC .60 1.50
T226 Joe Rogers RC .40 1.00
T227 Jason Bay 3.00 8.00
T228 Ezequiel Astacio RC .40 1.00
T229 Joey Hammond RC .40 1.00
T230 Chris Duffy RC .40 1.00
T231 Mark Prior .50 1.25
T232 Hansel Izquierdo RC .40 1.00
T233 Franklyn German RC .40 1.00
T234 Alexis Gomez .20 .50
T235 Jorge Padilla RC .40 1.00
T236 Ryan Snare RC .40 1.00
T237 Deivis Santos .20 .50
T238 Taggert Bozied RC .50 1.25
T239 Mike Peeples RC .40 1.00
T240 Ronald Acuna RC .40 1.00
T241 Koyie Hill .20 .50
T242 Garrett Guzman RC .40 1.00
T243 Ryan Church RC 1.00 2.50
T244 Tony Fontana RC .40 1.00
T245 Keto Anderson RC .40 1.00
T246 Brad Bouras RC .40 1.00
T247 Jason Dubois RC .50 1.25
T248 Angel Guzman RC .75 2.00
T249 Joel Hanrahan RC .40 1.00
T250 Joe Jiannetti RC .40 1.00
T251 Sean Pierce RC .40 1.00
T252 Jake Mauer RC .40 1.00
T253 Marshall McDougall RC .40 1.00
T254 Edwin Almonte RC .40 1.00
T255 Shawn Riggans RC .40 1.00
T256 Steven Shell RC .40 1.00
T257 Kevin Hooper RC .40 1.00
T258 Michael Frick RC .40 1.00
T259 Travis Chapman RC .40 1.00
T260 Tim Hummel RC .40 1.00
T261 Adam Morrissey RC .40 1.00
T262 Dontrelle Willis RC 2.50 6.00
T263 Justin Sherrod RC .40 1.00
T264 Gerald Smiley RC .40 1.00
T265 Tony Miller RC .40 1.00
T266 Nolan Ryan WW 2.00 5.00
T267 Reggie Jackson WW .50 1.25
T268 Steve Garvey WW .30 .75
T269 Wade Boggs WW .50 1.25
T270 Sammy Sosa WW .75 2.00
T271 Curt Schilling WW .30 .75
T272 Mark Grace WW .50 1.25
T273 Jason Giambi WW .20 .50
T274 Ken Griffey Jr. WW 1.50 4.00
T275 Roberto Alomar WW .50 1.25

2002 Topps Chrome Traded Black Refractors

*BLACK REF: 4X TO 10X BASIC
*BLACK REF RC'S: 4X TO 10X BASIC RC'S
STATED ODDS 1:56 HOB/RET, 1:16 HTA
STATED PRINT RUN 100 SERIAL #'d SETS

2002 Topps Chrome Traded Refractors

*REF: 2X TO 5X BASIC
*REF RC'S: 1.5X TO 4X BASIC RC'S
STATED ODDS 1:12 HOB/RET, 1:12 HTA

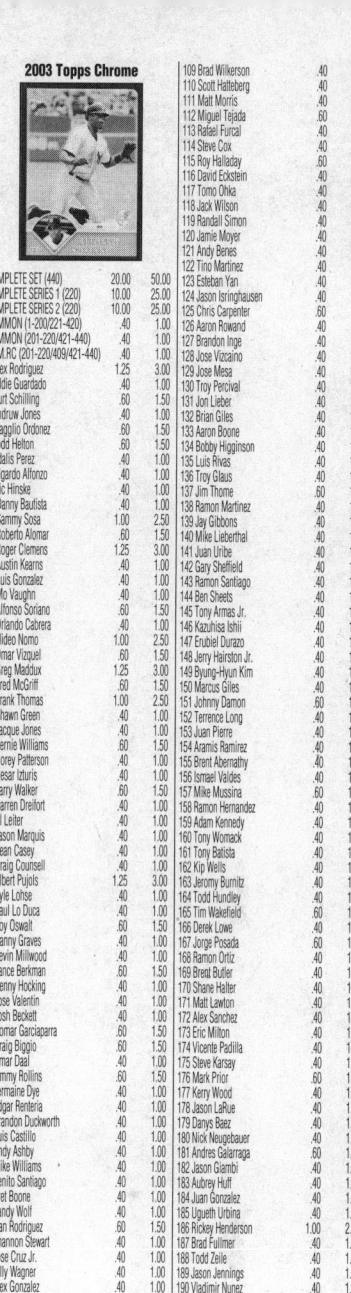

2003 Topps Chrome

COMPLETE SET (440) 20.00 50.00
COMPLETE SERIES 1 (220) 10.00 25.00
COMPLETE SERIES 2 (220) 10.00 25.00
COMMON (1-200/221-420) .40 1.00
COMMON (201-220/421-440) .40 1.00
COM.RC (201-220/409/421-440) .40 1.00
1 Alex Rodriguez 1.25 3.00
2 Eddie Guardado .40 1.00
3 Curt Schilling .60 1.50
4 Andruw Jones .40 1.00
5 Magglio Ordonez .60 1.50
6 Todd Helton .60 1.50
7 Odalis Perez .40 1.00
8 Edgardo Alfonzo .40 1.00
9 Eric Hinske .40 1.00
10 Danny Bautista .40 1.00
11 Sammy Sosa 1.00 2.50
12 Roberto Alomar .60 1.50
13 Roger Clemens 1.25 3.00
14 Austin Kearns .40 1.00
15 Luis Gonzalez .40 1.00
16 Mo Vaughn .40 1.00
17 Alfonso Soriano .60 1.50
18 Orlando Cabrera .40 1.00
19 Hideo Nomo 1.00 2.50
20 Omar Vizquel .60 1.50
21 Greg Maddux 1.25 3.00
22 Fred McGriff .60 1.50
23 Frank Thomas 1.00 2.50
24 Shawn Green .40 1.00
25 Jacque Jones .40 1.00
26 Bernie Williams .60 1.50
27 Corey Patterson .40 1.00
28 Cesar Izturis .40 1.00
29 Larry Walker .60 1.50
30 Darren Dreifort .40 1.00
31 Al Leiter .40 1.00
32 Jason Marquis .40 1.00
33 Sean Casey .40 1.00
34 Craig Counsell .40 1.00
35 Albert Pujols 1.25 3.00
36 Kyle Lohse .40 1.00
37 Paul Lo Duca .40 1.00
38 Roy Oswalt .60 1.50
39 Danny Graves .40 1.00
40 Kevin Millwood .40 1.00
41 Lance Berkman .60 1.50
42 Denny Hocking .40 1.00
43 Jose Valentin .40 1.00
44 Josh Beckett .40 1.00
45 Nomar Garciaparra .60 1.50
46 Craig Biggio .60 1.50
47 Omar Daal .40 1.00
48 Jimmy Rollins .60 1.50
49 Jermaine Dye .40 1.00
50 Edgar Renteria .40 1.00
51 Brandon Duckworth .40 1.00
52 Luis Castillo .40 1.00
53 Andy Ashby .40 1.00
54 Mike Williams .40 1.00
55 Benito Santiago .40 1.00
56 Bret Boone .40 1.00
57 Randy Wolf .40 1.00
58 Ivan Rodriguez .60 1.50
59 Shannon Stewart .40 1.00
60 Jose Cruz Jr. .40 1.00
61 Billy Wagner .40 1.00
62 Alex Gonzalez .40 1.00
63 Ichiro Suzuki 1.25 3.00
64 Joe McEwing .40 1.00
65 Mark Mulder .40 1.00
66 Mike Cameron .40 1.00
67 Corey Koskie .40 1.00
68 Marlon Anderson .40 1.00
69 Jason Kendall .40 1.00
70 J.T. Snow .40 1.00
71 Edgar Martinez .60 1.50
72 Vernon Wells .40 1.00
73 Vladimir Guerrero .60 1.50
74 Adam Dunn .60 1.50
75 Barry Zito .60 1.50
76 Jeff Kent .40 1.00
77 Russ Ortiz .40 1.00
78 Phil Nevin .40 1.00
79 Carlos Beltran .60 1.50
80 Mike Lowell .40 1.00
81 Bob Wickman .40 1.00
82 Junior Spivey .40 1.00
83 Melvin Mora .40 1.00
84 Derrek Lee .40 1.00
85 Chuck Knoblauch .40 1.00
86 Eric Gagne .40 1.00
87 Orlando Hernandez .40 1.00
88 Robert Person .40 1.00
89 Elmer Dessens .40 1.00
90 Wade Miller .40 1.00
91 Adrian Beltre 1.00 2.50
92 Kazuhiro Sasaki .40 1.00
93 Timo Perez .40 1.00
94 Jose Vidro .40 1.00
95 Geronimo Gil .40 1.00
96 Trot Nixon .40 1.00
97 Denny Neagle .40 1.00
98 Roberto Hernandez .40 1.00
99 David Ortiz 1.00 2.50
100 Robb Nen .40 1.00
101 Sidney Ponson .40 1.00
102 Kevin Appier .40 1.00
103 Javier Lopez .40 1.00
104 Jeff Conine .40 1.00
105 Mark Buehrle .60 1.50
106 Jason Simontacchi .40 1.00
107 Jose Jimenez .40 1.00
108 Brian Jordan .40 1.00
109 Brad Wilkerson .40 1.00
110 Scott Hatteberg .40 1.00
111 Matt Morris .40 1.00
112 Miguel Tejada .60 1.50
113 Rafael Furcal .40 1.00
114 Steve Cox .40 1.00
115 Roy Halladay .60 1.50
116 David Eckstein .40 1.00
117 Tomo Ohka .40 1.00
118 Jack Wilson .40 1.00
119 Randall Simon .40 1.00
120 Jamie Moyer .40 1.00
121 Andy Benes .40 1.00
122 Tino Martinez .40 1.00
123 Esteban Yan .40 1.00
124 Jason Isringhausen .40 1.00
125 Chris Carpenter .60 1.50
126 Aaron Rowand .40 1.00
127 Brandon Inge .40 1.00
128 Jose Vizcaino .40 1.00
129 Jose Mesa .40 1.00
130 Troy Percival .40 1.00
131 Jon Lieber .40 1.00
132 Brian Giles .40 1.00
133 Aaron Boone .40 1.00
134 Bobby Higginson .40 1.00
135 Luis Rivas .40 1.00
136 Troy Glaus .40 1.00
137 Jim Thome .60 1.50
138 Ramon Martinez .40 1.00
139 Jay Gibbons .40 1.00
140 Mike Lieberthal .40 1.00
141 Juan Uribe .40 1.00
142 Gary Sheffield .40 1.00
143 Ramon Santiago .40 1.00
144 Ben Sheets .40 1.00
145 Tony Armas Jr. .40 1.00
146 Kazuhisa Ishii .40 1.00
147 Erubiel Durazo .40 1.00
148 Jerry Hairston Jr. .40 1.00
149 Byung-Hyun Kim .40 1.00
150 Marcus Giles .40 1.00
151 Johnny Damon .60 1.50
152 Terrence Long .40 1.00
153 Juan Pierre .40 1.00
154 Aramis Ramirez .40 1.00
155 Brent Abernathy .40 1.00
156 Ismael Valdes .40 1.00
157 Mike Mussina .60 1.50
158 Ramon Hernandez .40 1.00
159 Adam Kennedy .40 1.00
160 Tony Womack .40 1.00
161 Tony Batista .40 1.00
162 Kip Wells .40 1.00
163 Jeromy Burnitz .40 1.00
164 Todd Hundley .40 1.00
165 Tim Wakefield .60 1.50
166 Derek Lowe .40 1.00
167 Jorge Posada .60 1.50
168 Ramon Ortiz .40 1.00
169 Brent Butler .40 1.00
170 Shane Halter .40 1.00
171 Matt Lawton .40 1.00
172 Alex Sanchez .40 1.00
173 Eric Milton .40 1.00
174 Vicente Padilla .40 1.00
175 Steve Karsay .40 1.00
176 Mark Prior .60 1.50
177 Kerry Wood .40 1.00
178 Jason LaRue .40 1.00
179 Danys Baez .40 1.00
180 Nick Neugebauer .40 1.00
181 Andres Galarraga .60 1.50
182 Jason Giambi .40 1.00
183 Aubrey Huff .40 1.00
184 Juan Gonzalez .40 1.00
185 Ugueth Urbina .40 1.00
186 Rickey Henderson 1.00 2.50
187 Brad Fullmer .40 1.00
188 Todd Zeile .40 1.00
189 Jason Jennings .40 1.00
190 Vladimir Nunez .40 1.00
191 David Justice .40 1.00
192 Brian Lawrence .40 1.00
193 Pat Burrell .40 1.00
194 Pokey Reese .40 1.00
195 Robert Fick .40 1.00
196 C.C. Sabathia .60 1.50
197 Fernando Vina .40 1.00
198 Sean Burroughs .40 1.00
199 Ellis Burks .40 1.00
200 Joe Randa .40 1.00
201 Chris Duncan FY RC 1.25 3.00
202 Franklin Gutierrez FY RC 1.00 2.50
203 Adam LaRoche FY .40 1.00
204 Manuel Ramirez FY RC .40 1.00
205 Il Kim FY RC .40 1.00
206 Daryl Clark FY RC .40 1.00
207 Sean Pierce FY .40 1.00
208 Andy Marte FY RC .40 1.00
209 Bernie Castro FY RC .40 1.00
210 Jason Perry FY RC .40 1.00
211 Jaime Bubela FY RC .40 1.00
212 Alexis Rios FY .40 1.00
213 Brendan Harris FY RC .40 1.00
214 Ramon Nivar-Martinez FY RC .40 1.00
215 Terry Tiffee FY RC .40 1.00
216 Kevin Youkilis FY RC 2.50 6.00
217 Derell McCall FY RC .40 1.00
218 Scott Tyler FY RC .40 1.00
219 Craig Brazell FY RC .40 1.00
220 Walter Young FY .40 1.00
221 Francisco Rodriguez .60 1.50
222 Chipper Jones 1.00 2.50
223 Chris Singleton .40 1.00
224 Cliff Floyd .40 1.00
225 Bobby Hill .40 1.00
226 Antonio Osuna .40 1.00
227 Barry Larkin .60 1.50
228 Dean Palmer .40 1.00
229 Eric Owens .40 1.00
230 Randy Johnson 1.00 2.50
231 Jeff Suppan .40 1.00
232 Eric Karros .40 1.00
233 Johan Santana .60 1.50
234 Javier Vazquez .40 1.00
235 John Thomson .40 1.00
236 Nick Johnson .40 1.00

237 Mark Ellis .40 1.00
238 Doug Glanville .40 1.00
239 Ken Griffey Jr. 2.00 5.00
240 Bubba Trammell .40 1.00
241 Livan Hernandez .40 1.00
242 Desi Relaford .40 1.00
243 Eli Marrero .40 1.00
244 Jared Sandberg .40 1.00
245 Barry Bonds 1.50 4.00
246 Aaron Sele .40 1.00
247 Derek Jeter 2.50 6.00
248 Eric Byrnes .40 1.00
249 Rich Aurilia .40 1.00
250 Joel Pineiro .40 1.00
251 Chuck Finley .40 1.00
252 Bengie Molina .40 1.00
253 Steve Finley .40 1.00
254 Marty Cordova .40 1.00
255 Shea Hillenbrand .40 1.00
256 Milton Bradley .40 1.00
257 Carlos Pena .60 1.50
258 Brad Ausmus .40 1.00
259 Carlos Delgado .40 1.00
260 Kevin Mench .40 1.00
261 Joe Kennedy .40 1.00
262 Mark McLemore .40 1.00
263 Bill Mueller .40 1.00
264 Ricky Ledee .40 1.00
265 Ted Lilly .40 1.00
266 Sterling Hitchcock .40 1.00
267 Scott Strickland .40 1.00
268 Damion Easley .40 1.00
269 Torii Hunter .40 1.00
270 Brad Radke .40 1.00
271 Geoff Jenkins .40 1.00
272 Paul Byrd .40 1.00
273 Morgan Ensberg .40 1.00
274 Mike Maroth .40 1.00
275 Mike Hampton .40 1.00
276 Flash Gordon .40 1.00
277 John Burkett .40 1.00
278 Rodrigo Lopez .40 1.00
279 Tim Spooneybarger .40 1.00
280 Quinton McCracken .40 1.00
281 Tim Salmon .40 1.00
282 Jarrod Washburn .40 1.00
283 Pedro Martinez .60 1.50
284 Julio Lugo .40 1.00
285 Armando Benitez .40 1.00
286 Raul Mondesi .40 1.00
287 Robin Ventura .40 1.00
288 Bobby Abreu .40 1.00
289 Josh Fogg .40 1.00
290 Ryan Klesko .40 1.00
291 Tsuyoshi Shinjo .40 1.00
292 Jim Edmonds .60 1.50
293 Chan Ho Park .60 1.50
294 John Mabry .40 1.00
295 Woody Williams .40 1.00
296 Scott Schoeneweis .40 1.00
297 Brian Anderson .40 1.00
298 Brett Tomko .40 1.00
299 Scott Erickson .40 1.00
300 Kevin Millar Sox .40 1.00
301 Danny Wright .40 1.00
302 Jason Schmidt .40 1.00
303 Scott Williamson .40 1.00
304 Einar Diaz .40 1.00
305 Jay Payton .40 1.00
306 Juan Acevedo .40 1.00
307 Ben Grieve .40 1.00
308 Raul Ibanez .60 1.50
309 Richie Sexson .40 1.00
310 Rick Reed .40 1.00
311 Pedro Astacio .40 1.00
312 Bud Smith .40 1.00
313 Tomas Perez .40 1.00
314 Rafael Palmeiro .60 1.50
315 Jason Tyner .40 1.00
316 Scott Rolen .60 1.50
317 Randy Winn .40 1.00
318 Ryan Jensen .40 1.00
319 Trevor Hoffman .60 1.50
320 Craig Wilson .40 1.00
321 Jeremy Giambi .40 1.00
322 Andy Pettitte .60 1.50
323 John Franco .40 1.00
324 Felipe Lopez .40 1.00
325 Mike Piazza 1.00 2.50
326 Cristian Guzman .40 1.00
327 Jose Hernandez .40 1.00
328 Octavio Dotel .40 1.00
329 Brad Penny .40 1.00
330 Dave Veres .40 1.00
331 Ryan Dempster .40 1.00
332 Joe Crede .40 1.00
333 Chad Hermansen .40 1.00
334 Gary Matthews Jr. .40 1.00
335 Frank Catalanotto .40 1.00
336 Darin Erstad .40 1.00
337 Matt Williams .40 1.00
338 B.J. Surhoff .40 1.00
339 Kerry Ligtenberg .40 1.00
340 Mike Bordick .40 1.00
341 Joe Girardi .60 1.50
342 D'Angelo Jimenez .40 1.00
343 Paul Konerko .60 1.50
344 Joe Mays .40 1.00
345 Marquis Grissom .40 1.00
346 Neifi Perez .40 1.00
347 Preston Wilson .40 1.00
348 Jeff Weaver .40 1.00
349 Eric Chavez .40 1.00
350 Placido Polanco .40 1.00
351 Matt Mantei .40 1.00
352 James Baldwin .40 1.00
353 Toby Hall .40 1.00
354 Benji Gil .40 1.00
355 Damian Moss .40 1.00
356 Jorge Julio .40 1.00
357 Matt Clement .40 1.00
358 Lee Stevens .40 1.00
359 Dave Roberts .60 1.50
360 J.C. Romero .40 1.00
361 Bartolo Colon .40 1.00
362 Roger Cedeno .40 1.00
363 Mariano Rivera 1.25 3.00
364 Billy Koch .40 1.00
365 Manny Ramirez 1.00 2.50
366 Travis Lee .40 1.00
367 Oliver Perez .40 1.00
368 Tim Worrell .40 1.00
369 Damian Miller .40 1.00
370 John Smoltz 1.00 2.50
371 Willis Roberts .40 1.00
372 Tim Hudson .60 1.50
373 Moises Alou .40 1.00
374 Corky Miller .40 1.00
375 Ben Broussard .40 1.00
376 Gabe Kapler .40 1.00
377 Chris Woodward .40 1.00
378 Todd Hollandsworth .40 1.00
379 So Taguchi .40 1.00
380 John Olerud .40 1.00
381 Reggie Sanders .40 1.00
382 Jake Peavy .40 1.00
383 Kris Benson .40 1.00
384 Ray Durham .40 1.00
385 Boomer Wells .40 1.00
386 Tom Glavine .60 1.50
387 Antonio Alfonseca .40 1.00
388 Keith Foulke .40 1.00
389 Shawn Estes .40 1.00
390 Mark Grace .60 1.50
391 Dmitri Young .40 1.00
392 A.J. Burnett .40 1.00
393 Richard Hidalgo .40 1.00
394 Mike Sweeney .40 1.00
395 Doug Mientkiewicz .40 1.00
396 Cory Lidle .40 1.00
397 Jeff Bagwell .60 1.50
398 Steve Sparks .40 1.00
399 Sandy Alomar Jr. .40 1.00
400 John Lackey .60 1.50
401 Rick Helling .40 1.00
402 Carlos Lee .40 1.00
403 Garret Anderson .40 1.00
404 Vinny Castilla .40 1.00
405 David Bell .40 1.00
406 Freddy Garcia .40 1.00
407 Scott Spiezio .40 1.00
408 Russell Branyan .40 1.00
409 Jose Contreras RC 1.00 2.50
410 Kevin Brown .40 1.00
411 Tyler Houston .40 1.00
412 A.J. Pierzynski .40 1.00
413 Peter Bergeron .40 1.00
414 Brett Myers .40 1.00
415 Kenny Lofton .40 1.00
416 Ben Davis .40 1.00
417 J.D. Drew .40 1.00
418 Ricky Gutierrez .40 1.00
419 Mark Redman .40 1.00
420 Juan Encarnacion .40 1.00
421 Bryan Bullington DP RC .40 1.00
422 Jeremy Guthrie DP .40 1.00
423 Joey Gomes DP RC .40 1.00
424 Evel Bastida-Martinez DP RC .40 1.00
425 Brian Wright DP RC .40 1.00
426 B.J. Upton DP .60 1.50
427 Jeff Francis DP .40 1.00
428 Jeremy Hermida DP .60 1.50
429 Khalil Greene DP .60 1.50
430 Darrell Rasner DP RC .40 1.00
431 B.Phillips .60 1.50
V.Martinez
432 H.Choi .40 1.00
N.Jackson
433 D.Willis .40 1.00
J.Stokes
434 C.Tracy .40 1.00
L.Overbay
435 J.Borchard .40 1.00
C.Malone
436 J.Mauer 1.00 2.50
J.Morneau
437 D.Henson .40 1.00
B.Claussen
438 C.Utley .60 1.50
G.Floyd
439 T.Bozied .40 1.00
X.Nady
440 A.Heilman 1.00 2.50
J.Reyes

2003 Topps Chrome Black Refractors

*BLACK 1-200/221-420: 2X TO 5X
*BLACK 201-220/409/421-440: 2X TO 5X
SERIES 1 STATED ODDS 1:20 HOB/RET
SERIES 2 STATED ODDS 1:17 HOB/RET
STATED PRINT RUN 199 SERIAL #'d SETS

2003 Topps Chrome Gold Refractors

*GOLD 1-200/221-420: 2.5X TO 6X
*GOLD 201-220/409/421-440: 2.5X TO 6X
SERIES 1 STATED ODDS 1:8 HOB/RET
SERIES 2 STATED ODDS 2:8 HOB/RET
STATED PRINT RUN 449 SERIAL #'d SETS

2003 Topps Chrome Refractors

*REF 1-200/201-420: 1.2X TO 2.5X
*REF 201-220/409/421-440: 1.2X TO 2.5X
SERIES 1 STATED ODDS 1:5 HOB/RET
SERIES 2 STATED ODDS 1:5 HOB/RET
STATED PRINT RUN 699 SERIAL #'d SETS

2003 Topps Chrome Silver Refractors

*SILVER REF 221-420: 1.25X TO 3X BASIC
*SILVER REF 421-440: 1.25X TO 3X BASIC
ONE PER SER.2 RETAIL EXCH.CARD
CARDS WERE ONLY PRODUCED FOR SER.2

2003 Topps Chrome Uncirculated X-Fractors

*X-FRACT 1-200/221-420: 4X TO 10X
*X-FRACT 201-220/409/421-440: 4X TO 10X
ONE CARD PER SEALED HOBBY BOX
1-220 PRINT RUN 50 SERIAL #'d SETS
221-440 PRINT RUN 57 SERIAL #'d SETS

2003 Topps Chrome Blue Backs Relics

BAT ODDS 1:236 HOB/RET
UNI GROUP A ODDS 1:69 HOB/RET
UNI GROUP B ODDS 1:662 HOB/RET
AD Adam Dunn Uni B 6.00 15.00
AP Albert Pujols Uni A 10.00 25.00
AR Alex Rodriguez Bat 10.00 25.00
AS Alfonso Soriano Bat 6.00 15.00
BW Bernie Williams Bat 6.00 15.00
EC Eric Chavez Uni A 4.00 10.00
FT Frank Thomas Uni A 6.00 15.00
JB Josh Beckett Uni A 4.00 10.00
JBA Jeff Bagwell Uni A 4.00 10.00
JR Jimmy Rollins Uni A 4.00 10.00
KW Kerry Wood Uni A 4.00 10.00
LB Lance Berkman Bat 6.00 15.00
MO Magglio Ordonez Uni A 4.00 10.00
MP Mike Piazza Uni A 8.00 20.00
NG Nomar Garciaparra Jsy 10.00 25.00
NJ Nick Johnson Bat 6.00 15.00
PK Paul Konerko Uni A 4.00 10.00
RA Roberto Alomar Bat 6.00 15.00
SG Shawn Green Uni A 4.00 10.00
TS Tsuyoshi Shinjo Bat 6.00 15.00

2003 Topps Chrome Record Breakers Relics

BAT 1 ODDS 1:364 HOB/RET
BAT 2 ODDS 1:131 HOB/RET
UNI GROUP A1 ODDS 1:413 HOB/RET
UNI GROUP B1 ODDS 1:50 HOB/RET
UNI GROUP A2 ODDS 1:1707 HOB/RET
UNI GROUP B2 ODDS 1:127 HOB/RET
AR1 Alex Rodriguez Uni B1 5.00 12.00
AR2 Alex Rodriguez Bat 2 5.00 12.00
BB Barry Bonds Walks Uni B2 6.00 15.00
BB2 Barry Bonds Slg Uni B2 6.00 15.00
BB3 Barry Bonds Bat 2 6.00 15.00
CB Craig Biggio Uni B1 2.50 6.00
CD Carlos Delgado Uni B1 1.50 4.00
CF Cliff Floyd Bat 1 1.50 4.00
DE Darin Erstad Bat 2 1.50 4.00
DLE Dennis Eckersley Uni A2 2.50 6.00
DM Don Mattingly Bat 2 8.00 20.00
FT Frank Thomas Uni B1 4.00 10.00
HK Harmon Killebrew Uni B1 4.00 10.00
HR Harold Reynolds Bat 2 1.50 4.00
JB1 Jeff Bagwell Slg Uni B1 2.50 6.00
JB2 Jeff Bagwell RBI Uni B2 2.50 6.00
JC Jose Canseco Bat 2 2.50 6.00
JG Juan Gonzalez Uni B1 1.50 4.00
JM Joe Morgan Bat 1 2.50 6.00
JS John Smoltz Uni B2 4.00 10.00
KS Kazuhiro Sasaki Uni B1 1.50 4.00
LB Lou Brock Bat 1 2.50 6.00
LG1 Luis Gonzalez RBI Bat 1 1.50 4.00
LG2 Luis Gonzalez Avg Bat 2 1.50 4.00
LW Larry Walker Bat 1 2.50 6.00
MP Mike Piazza Uni B1 4.00 10.00
MR Manny Ramirez Bat 2 4.00 10.00
MS Mike Schmidt Uni A1 6.00 15.00
PM Paul Molitor Bat 2 4.00 10.00
RC Rod Carew Avg Bat 2 2.50 6.00
RC2 Rod Carew Hits Bat 2 2.50 6.00
RH1 R.Henderson A's Bat 1 4.00 10.00
RH2 R.Henderson Yanks Bat 2 20.00 50.00
RJ1 Randy Johnson ERA Uni B1 4.00 10.00
RJ2 Randy Johnson Wins Uni B2 4.00 10.00
RY Robin Yount Uni B1 4.00 10.00
SM Stan Musial Uni A1 12.00 30.00
SS Sammy Sosa Bat 2 4.00 10.00
TH Todd Helton Bat 1 2.50 6.00
TS Tom Seaver Uni B2 2.50 6.00

2003 Topps Chrome Red Backs Relics

SERIES 2 BAT A ODDS 1:342 HOB/RET
SERIES 2 BAT B ODDS 1:383 HOB/RET
SERIES 2 JERSEY ODDS 1:49 HOB/RET
AD Adam Dunn Jsy 2.50 6.00
AJ Andruw Jones Jsy 1.50 4.00
AP Albert Pujols Bat B 5.00 12.00
AR Alex Rodriguez Jsy 5.00 12.00
AS Alfonso Soriano Bat A 2.50 6.00
CJ Chipper Jones Jsy 4.00 10.00
CS Curt Schilling Jsy 2.50 6.00
GA Garrett Anderson Bat A 4.00 10.00
JB Jeff Bagwell Jsy 2.50 6.00
MP Mike Piazza Jsy 4.00 10.00
MR Manny Ramirez Bat B 4.00 10.00
MS Mike Sweeney Jsy 1.50 4.00
NG Nomar Garciaparra Bat A 6.00 15.00
PB Pat Burrell Bat A 4.00 10.00
PM Pedro Martinez Jsy 2.50 6.00
RA Roberto Alomar Jsy 2.50 6.00
RJ Randy Johnson Jsy 4.00 10.00
SR Scott Rolen Bat A 6.00 15.00
TH Todd Helton Jsy 2.50 6.00
TKH Torii Hunter Jsy 2.50 6.00

2003 Topps Chrome Traded

COMPLETE SET (275) 30.00 60.00
COMMON CARD (T1-T120) .40 1.00
COMMON CARD (121-165) .40 1.00
COMMON CARD (166-275) .40 1.00
2 PER 2003 TOPPS TRADED HOBBY PACK
2 PER 2003 TOPPS TRADED HTA PACK
2 PER 2003 TOPPS TRADED RETAIL PACK
T1 Juan Pierre .40 1.00
T2 Mark Grudzielanek .40 1.00
T3 Tanyon Sturtze .40 1.00
T4 Greg Vaughn .40 1.00
T5 Greg Myers .40 1.00
T6 Randall Simon .40 1.00
T7 Todd Hundley .40 1.00
T8 Marlon Anderson .40 1.00
T9 Jeff Reboulet .40 1.00
T10 Alex Sanchez .40 1.00
T11 Mike Rivera .40 1.00
T12 Todd Walker .40 1.00
T13 Ray King .40 1.00
T14 Shawn Estes .40 1.00
T15 Gary Matthews Jr. .40 1.00
T16 Jaret Wright .40 1.00
T17 Edgardo Alfonzo .40 1.00
T18 Omar Daal .40 1.00
T19 Ryan Rupe .40 1.00
T20 Tony Clark .40 1.00
T21 Jeff Suppan .40 1.00
T22 Mike Stanton .40 1.00
T23 Ramon Martinez .40 1.00
T24 Armando Rios .40 1.00
T25 Johnny Estrada .40 1.00
T26 Joe Girardi .60 1.50
T27 Ivan Rodriguez .60 1.50
T28 Robert Fick .40 1.00
T29 Rick White .40 1.00
T30 Robert Person .40 1.00
T31 Alan Benes .40 1.00
T32 Chris Carpenter .60 1.50
T33 Chris Widger .40 1.00
T34 Travis Hafner .40 1.00
T35 Mike Venafro .40 1.00
T36 Jon Lieber .40 1.00
T37 Orlando Hernandez .40 1.00
T38 Aaron Myette .40 1.00
T39 Paul Bako .40 1.00
T40 Erubiel Durazo .40 1.00
T41 Mark Guthrie .40 1.00
T42 Steve Avery .40 1.00
T43 Damian Jackson .40 1.00
T44 Rey Ordonez .40 1.00
T45 John Flaherty .40 1.00
T46 Byung-Hyun Kim .40 1.00
T47 Tom Goodwin .40 1.00
T48 Elmer Dessens .40 1.00
T49 Al Martin .40 1.00
T50 Gene Kingsale .40 1.00
T51 Lenny Harris .40 1.00
T52 David Ortiz Sox 1.00 2.50
T53 Jose Lima .40 1.00
T54 Mike Difelice .40 1.00
T55 Jose Hernandez .40 1.00
T56 Todd Zeile .40 1.00
T57 Roberto Hernandez .40 1.00
T58 Albie Lopez .40 1.00
T59 Roberto Alomar .60 1.50
T60 Russ Ortiz .40 1.00
T61 Brian Daubach .40 1.00
T62 Carl Everett .40 1.00
T63 Jeromy Burnitz .40 1.00
T64 Mark Bellhorn .40 1.00
T65 Ruben Sierra .40 1.00
T66 Mike Fetters .40 1.00
T67 Armando Benitez .40 1.00
T68 Deivi Cruz .40 1.00
T69 Jose Cruz Jr. .40 1.00
T70 Jeremy Fikac .40 1.00
T71 Jeff Kent .40 1.00
T72 Andres Galarraga .60 1.50
T73 Rickey Henderson 1.00 2.50
T74 Royce Clayton .40 1.00
T75 Troy O'Leary .40 1.00
T76 Ron Coomer .40 1.00
T77 Greg Colbrunn .40 1.00
T78 Wes Helms .40 1.00
T79 Kevin Millwood .40 1.00
T80 Damion Easley .40 1.00
T81 Bobby Kielty .40 1.00
T82 Keith Osik .40 1.00
T83 Ramiro Mendoza .40 1.00
T84 Shea Hillenbrand .40 1.00
T85 Shannon Stewart .40 1.00
T86 Eddie Perez .40 1.00
T87 Ugueth Urbina .40 1.00
T88 Orlando Palmeiro .40 1.00
T89 Graeme Lloyd .40 1.00
T90 John Vander Wal .40 1.00
T91 Gary Bennett .40 1.00
T92 Shane Reynolds .40 1.00
T93 Steve Parris .40 1.00
T94 Julio Lugo .40 1.00
T95 John Halama .40 1.00
T96 Carlos Baerga .40 1.00
T97 Jim Parque .40 1.00
T98 Mike Williams .40 1.00
T99 Fred McGriff .60 1.50
T100 Kenny Rogers .40 1.00
T101 Matt Herges .40 1.00
T102 Jay Bell .40 1.00
T103 Esteban Yan .40 1.00
T104 Eric Owens .40 1.00
T105 Aaron Fultz .40 1.00
T106 Rey Sanchez .40 1.00
T107 Jim Thome .60 1.50
T108 Aaron Boone .40 1.00
T109 Raul Mondesi .40 1.00
T110 Kenny Lofton .40 1.00
T111 Jose Guillen .40 1.00
T112 Aramis Ramirez .40 1.00
T113 Sidney Ponson .40 1.00
T114 Scott Williamson .40 1.00
T115 Robin Ventura .40 1.00
T116 Dusty Baker MG .40 1.00
T117 Felipe Alou MG .40 1.00
T118 Buck Showalter MG .40 1.00
T119 Jack McKeon MG .40 1.00
T120 Art Howe MG .40 1.00
T121 Bobby Crosby PROS .40 1.00
T122 Adrian Gonzalez PROS .75 2.00
T123 Kevin Cash PROS .40 1.00
T124 Shin-Soo Choo PROS .60 1.50
T125 Chin-Feng Chen PROS .40 1.00
T126 Miguel Cabrera PROS 5.00 12.00
T127 Jason Young PROS .40 1.00
T128 Alex Herrera PROS .40 1.00
T129 Jason Dubois PROS .40 1.00
T130 Jeff Mathis PROS .40 1.00
T131 Casey Kotchman PROS .40 1.00
T132 Ed Rogers PROS .40 1.00
T133 Wilson Betemit PROS .40 1.00
T134 Jim Kavourias PROS .40 1.00
T135 Taylor Buchholz PROS .40 1.00
T136 Adam LaRoche PROS .40 1.00
T137 Dallas McPherson PROS .40 1.00
T138 Jesus Cota PROS .40 1.00
T139 Clint Nageotte PROS .40 1.00
T140 Boof Bonser PROS .40 1.00
T141 Walter Young PROS .40 1.00
T142 Joe Crede PROS .40 1.00
T143 Denny Bautista PROS .40 1.00
T144 Victor Diaz PROS .40 1.00
T145 Chris Narveson PROS .40 1.00
T146 Gabe Gross PROS .40 1.00
T147 Jimmy Journell PROS .40 1.00
T148 Rafael Soriano PROS .40 1.00
T149 Jerome Williams PROS .40 1.00
T150 Aaron Cook PROS .40 1.00
T151 Anastacio Martinez PROS .40 1.00
T152 Scott Hairston PROS .40 1.00
T153 John Buck PROS .40 1.00
T154 Ryan Ludwick PROS .40 1.00
T155 Chris Bootcheck PROS .40 1.00
T156 John Rheinecker PROS .40 1.00
T157 Jason Lane PROS .40 1.00
T158 Shelley Duncan PROS .40 1.00
T159 Adam Wainwright PROS .60 1.50
T160 Jason Arnold PROS .40 1.00
T161 Jonny Gomes PROS .40 1.00
T162 James Loney PROS .60 1.50
T163 Mike Fontenot PROS .40 1.00
T164 Khalil Greene PROS .60 1.50
T165 Sean Burnett PROS .40 1.00
T166 David Martinez FY RC .40 1.00
T167 Felix Pie FY RC .60 1.50
T168 Joe Valentine FY RC .40 1.00
T169 Brandon Webb FY RC 1.25 3.00
T170 Matt Diaz FY RC .60 1.50
T171 Lew Ford FY RC .40 1.00
T172 Jeremy Griffiths FY RC .40 1.00
T173 Matt Hensley FY RC .40 1.00
T174 Charlie Manning FY RC .40 1.00
T175 Elizardo Ramirez FY RC .40 1.00
T176 Greg Aquino FY RC .40 1.00
T177 Felix Sanchez FY RC .40 1.00
T178 Kelly Shoppach FY RC .60 1.50
T179 Bubba Nelson FY RC .40 1.00
T180 Mike O'Keefe FY RC .40 1.00
T181 Hanley Ramirez FY RC 3.00 8.00
T182 Todd Wellemeyer FY RC .40 1.00
T183 Dustin Moseley FY RC .40 1.00
T184 Eric Crozier FY RC .40 1.00
T185 Ryan Shealy FY RC .40 1.00
T186 Jeremy Bonderman FY RC 1.50 4.00
T187 T.Story-Harden FY RC .40 1.00
T188 Dusty Brown FY RC .40 1.00
T189 Rob Hammock FY RC .40 1.00
T190 Jorge Piedra FY RC .40 1.00
T191 Chris De La Cruz FY RC .40 1.00
T192 Eli Whiteside FY RC .40 1.00
T193 Jason Kubel FY RC 1.25 3.00
T194 Jon Schuerholz FY RC .40 1.00
T195 Stephen Randolph FY RC .40 1.00
T196 Andy Sisco FY RC .40 1.00
T197 Sean Smith FY RC .40 1.00
T198 Jon-Mark Sprowl FY RC .40 1.00
T199 Matt Kata FY RC .40 1.00
T200 Robinson Cano FY RC 6.00 15.00
T201 Nook Logan FY RC .40 1.00
T202 Ben Francisco FY RC .40 1.00
T203 Arnie Munoz FY RC .40 1.00
T204 Ozzie Chavez FY RC .40 1.00
T205 Eric Riggs FY RC .40 1.00
T206 Beau Kemp FY RC .40 1.00
T207 Travis Wong FY RC .40 1.00
T208 Dustin Yount FY RC .40 1.00
T209 Brian McCann FY RC 3.00 8.00
T210 Wilton Reynolds FY RC .40 1.00
T211 Matt Bruback FY RC .40 1.00
T212 Andrew Brown FY RC .40 1.00
T213 Edgar Gonzalez FY RC .40 1.00
T214 Eider Torres FY RC .40 1.00
T215 Aquilino Lopez FY RC .40 1.00
T216 Bobby Basham FY RC .40 1.00
T217 Tim Olson FY RC .40 1.00
T218 Nathan Panther FY RC .40 1.00
T219 Bryan Grace FY RC .40 1.00
T220 Dusty Gomon FY RC .40 1.00
T221 Wil Ledezma FY RC .40 1.00
T222 Josh Willingham FY RC 1.25 3.00
T223 David Cash FY RC .40 1.00
T224 Oscar Villarreal FY RC .40 1.00
T225 Jeff Duncan FY RC .40 1.00
T226 Kade Johnson FY RC .40 1.00
T227 Luke Steidlmayer FY RC .40 1.00
T228 Brandon Watson FY RC .40 1.00
T229 Jose Morales FY RC .40 1.00
T230 Mike Gallo FY RC .40 1.00
T231 Tyler Adamczyk FY RC .40 1.00
T232 Adam Stern FY RC .40 1.00
T233 Brennan King FY RC .40 1.00
T234 Dan Haren FY RC 2.00 5.00
T235 Michel Hernandez FY RC .40 1.00
T236 Ben Fritz FY RC .40 1.00
T237 Clay Hensley FY RC .40 1.00
T238 Tyler Johnson FY RC .40 1.00
T239 Pete LaForest FY RC .40 1.00
T240 Tyler Martin FY RC .40 1.00
T241 J.D. Durbin FY RC .40 1.00
T242 Shane Victorino FY RC 1.25 3.00
T243 Rajai Davis FY RC .40 1.00
T244 Ismael Castro FY RC .40 1.00
T245 Chien-Ming Wang FY RC 1.50 4.00
T246 Travis Ishikawa FY RC 1.00 2.50
T247 Corey Shafer FY RC .40 1.00
T248 Gary Schneidmiller FY RC .40 1.00
T249 Dave Pember FY RC .40 1.00
T250 Keith Stamler FY RC .40 1.00
T251 Tyson Graham FY RC .40 1.00
T252 Ryan Cameron FY RC .40 1.00
T253 Eric Eckenstahler FY .40 1.00
T254 Matthew Peterson FY RC .40 1.00
T255 Dustin McGowan FY RC .40 1.00
T256 Prentice Redman FY RC .40 1.00
T257 Haj Turay FY RC .40 1.00
T258 Carlos Guzman FY RC .40 1.00
T259 Matt DeMarco FY RC .40 1.00
T260 Derek Michaelis FY RC .40 1.00
T261 Brian Burgamy FY RC .40 1.00
T262 Jay Sitzman FY RC .40 1.00
T263 Chris Fallon FY RC .40 1.00
T264 Mike Adams FY RC .60 1.50
T265 Clint Barmes FY RC 1.00 2.50
T266 Eric Reed FY RC .40 1.00
T267 Willie Eyre FY RC .40 1.00
T268 Carlos Duran FY RC .40 1.00
T269 Nick Trzesniak FY RC .40 1.00
T270 Ferdin Tejeda FY RC .40 1.00
T271 Michael Garciaparra FY RC .40 1.00
T272 Michael Hinckley FY RC .40 1.00
T273 Branden Florence FY RC .40 1.00
T274 Trent Oeltjen FY RC .40 1.00
T275 Mike Neu FY RC .40 1.00

2003 Topps Chrome Traded Refractors

*REF 1-120: 2X TO 5X BASIC
*REF 121-165: 1.5X TO 4X BASIC
*REF 166-275: 1.5X TO 4X BASIC
STATED ODDS 1:12 HOB/RET, 1:4 HTA

2004 Topps Chrome

COMP.SERIES 1 w/o SP's (220) 40.00 80.00
COMP.SERIES 2 w/o SP's (220) 40.00 80.00
COMMON (1-210/257-466) .40 1.00
COMMON (211-220/247-256) .50 1.25
COMMON AU (221-246) 4.00 10.00
221-233 SERIES 1 ODDS 1:21 H, 1:33 R
234-246 SERIES 2 ODDS 1:22 H, 1:35 R
345 SULLIVAN ERR SHOULD BE NO.234
1 IN EVERY 5 SULLIVAN'S ARE ERR 345
4 IN EVERY 5 SULLIVAN'S ARE COR 234
SULLIVAN INFO PROVIDED BY TOPPS
1 Jim Thome .60 1.50
2 Reggie Sanders .40 1.00
3 Mark Kotsay .40 1.00
4 Edgardo Alfonzo .40 1.00
5 Tim Wakefield .60 1.50
6 Moises Alou .40 1.00
7 Jorge Julio .40 1.00
8 Bartolo Colon .40 1.00
9 Chan Ho Park .60 1.50
10 Ichiro Suzuki 1.25 3.00
11 Kevin Millwood .40 1.00
12 Preston Wilson .40 1.00
13 Tom Glavine .60 1.50
14 Junior Spivey .40 1.00
15 Marcus Giles .40 1.00
16 David Segui .40 1.00
17 Kevin Millar .40 1.00
18 Corey Patterson .40 1.00
19 Aaron Rowand .40 1.00
20 Derek Jeter 2.50 6.00
21 Luis Castillo .40 1.00
22 Manny Ramirez 1.00 2.50
23 Jay Payton .40 1.00
24 Bobby Higginson .40 1.00
25 Lance Berkman .60 1.50
26 Juan Pierre .40 1.00
27 Mike Mussina .60 1.50
28 Fred McGriff .40 1.00
29 Richie Sexson .40 1.00
30 Tim Hudson .60 1.50
31 Mike Piazza 1.00 2.50
32 Brad Radke .40 1.00
33 Jeff Weaver .40 1.00
34 Ramon Hernandez .40 1.00
35 David Bell .40 1.00
36 Randy Wolf .40 1.00
37 Jake Peavy .40 1.00
38 Tim Worrell .40 1.00
39 Gil Meche .40 1.00
40 Albert Pujols 1.25 3.00
41 Michael Young .40 1.00
42 Josh Phelps .40 1.00
43 Brendan Donnelly .40 1.00
44 Steve Finley .40 1.00
45 John Smoltz 1.00 2.50
46 Jay Gibbons .40 1.00
47 Trot Nixon .40 1.00
48 Carl Pavano .40 1.00
49 Frank Thomas 1.00 2.50
50 Mark Prior .60 1.50
51 Danny Graves .40 1.00
52 Milton Bradley .40 1.00
53 Kris Benson .40 1.00
54 Ryan Klesko .40 1.00
55 Mike Lowell .40 1.00
56 Geoff Blum .40 1.00
57 Michael Tucker .40 1.00
58 Paul Lo Duca .40 1.00
59 Vicente Padilla .40 1.00
60 Jacque Jones .40 1.00
61 Fernando Tatis .40 1.00
62 Ty Wigginton .40 1.00
63 Rich Aurilia .40 1.00
64 Andy Pettitte .60 1.50
65 Terrence Long .40 1.00
66 Cliff Floyd .40 1.00
67 Mariano Rivera 1.25 3.00
68 Kelvim Escobar .40 1.00
69 Marlon Byrd .40 1.00
70 Mark Mulder .40 1.00
71 Francisco Cordero .40 1.00
72 Carlos Guillen .40 1.00
73 Fernando Vina .40 1.00
74 Lance Carter .40 1.00
75 Hank Blalock .40 1.00
76 Jimmy Rollins .60 1.50
77 Francisco Rodriguez .60 1.50
78 Javy Lopez .40 1.00
79 Jerry Hairston Jr. .40 1.00
80 Andruw Jones .40 1.00
81 Rodrigo Lopez .40 1.00
82 Johnny Damon .60 1.50
83 Hee Seop Choi .40 1.00
84 Kazuhiro Sasaki .40 1.00
85 Danny Bautista .40 1.00
86 Matt Lawton .40 1.00
87 Juan Uribe .40 1.00
88 Rafael Furcal .40 1.00
89 Kyle Farnsworth .40 1.00
90 Jose Vidro .40 1.00
91 Luis Rivas .40 1.00
92 Hideo Nomo 1.00 2.50
93 Javier Vazquez .40 1.00
94 Al Leiter .40 1.00
95 Jose Valentin .40 1.00
96 Alex Cintron .40 1.00
97 Zach Day .40 1.00
98 Jorge Posada .60 1.50
99 C.C. Sabathia .60 1.50
100 Alex Rodriguez 1.25 3.00
101 Brad Penny .40 1.00
102 Brad Ausmus .40 1.00
103 Raul Ibanez .60 1.50
104 Mike Hampton .40 1.00
105 Adrian Beltre 1.00 2.50
106 Ramiro Mendoza .40 1.00
107 Rocco Baldelli .40 1.00
108 Esteban Loaiza .40 1.00
109 Russell Branyan .40 1.00
110 Todd Helton .60 1.50
111 Braden Looper .40 1.00
112 Octavio Dotel .40 1.00
113 Mike MacDougal .40 1.00
114 Cesar Izturis .40 1.00
115 Johan Santana .60 1.50
116 Jose Contreras .40 1.00
117 Placido Polanco .40 1.00
118 Jason Phillips .40 1.00
119 Orlando Hudson .40 1.00
120 Vernon Wells .40 1.00
121 Ben Grieve .40 1.00
122 Dave Roberts .60 1.50
123 Ismael Valdes .40 1.00
124 Eric Owens .40 1.00
125 Curt Schilling .60 1.50
126 Russ Ortiz .40 1.00
127 Mark Buehrle .60 1.50
128 Doug Mientkiewicz .40 1.00
129 Dmitri Young .40 1.00
130 Kazuhisa Ishii .40 1.00
131 A.J. Pierzynski .40 1.00
132 Brad Wilkerson .40 1.00
133 Joe McEwing .40 1.00
134 Alex Cora .60 1.50
135 Jose Cruz Jr. .40 1.00
136 Carlos Zambrano .60 1.50
137 Jeff Kent .40 1.00
138 Shigetoshi Hasegawa .40 1.00
139 Jarrod Washburn .40 1.00
140 Greg Maddux 1.25 3.00
141 Josh Beckett .40 1.00
142 Miguel Batista .40 1.00
143 Omar Vizquel .60 1.50
144 Alex Gonzalez .40 1.00
145 Billy Wagner .40 1.00
146 Brian Jordan .40 1.00
147 Wes Helms .40 1.00
148 Deivi Cruz .40 1.00
149 Alex Gonzalez .40 1.00
150 Jason Giambi .40 1.00
151 Erubiel Durazo .40 1.00
152 Mike Lieberthal .40 1.00
153 Jason Kendall .40 1.00
154 Xavier Nady .40 1.00
155 Kirk Rueter .40 1.00
156 Mike Cameron .40 1.00
157 Miguel Cairo .40 1.00
158 Woody Williams .40 1.00
159 Toby Hall .40 1.00
160 Bernie Williams .60 1.50
161 Darin Erstad .40 1.00
162 Matt Mantei .40 1.00
163 Shawn Chacon .40 1.00
164 Bill Mueller .40 1.00
165 Damian Miller .40 1.00
166 Tony Graffanino .40 1.00
167 Sean Casey .40 1.00
168 Brandon Phillips .40 1.00
169 Runelvys Hernandez .40 1.00
170 Adam Dunn .60 1.50
171 Carlos Lee .40 1.00
172 Juan Encarnacion .40 1.00
173 Angel Berroa .40 1.00
174 Desi Relaford .40 1.00
175 Joe Mays .40 1.00
176 Ben Sheets .40 1.00
177 Eddie Guardado .40 1.00
178 Rocky Biddle .40 1.00
179 Eric Gagne .40 1.00
180 Eric Chavez .40 1.00
181 Jason Michaels .40 1.00
182 Dustan Mohr .40 1.00
183 Kip Wells .40 1.00
184 Brian Lawrence .40 1.00
185 Bret Boone .40 1.00
186 Tino Martinez .60 1.50
187 Aubrey Huff .40 1.00
188 Kevin Mench .40 1.00
189 Tim Salmon .40 1.00
190 Carlos Delgado .40 1.00
191 John Lackey .60 1.50
192 Eric Byrnes .40 1.00
193 Luis Matos .40 1.00
194 Derek Lowe .40 1.00
195 Mark Grudzielanek .40 1.00
196 Tom Gordon .40 1.00
197 Matt Clement .40 1.00
198 Byung-Hyun Kim .40 1.00
199 Brandon Inge .40 1.00
200 Nomar Garciaparra .60 1.50
201 Frank Catalanotto .40 1.00
202 Cristian Guzman .40 1.00
203 Bo Hart .40 1.00
204 Jack Wilson .40 1.00
205 Ray Durham .40 1.00
206 Freddy Garcia .40 1.00
207 J.D. Drew .40 1.00
208 Orlando Cabrera .40 1.00
209 Roy Halladay .60 1.50
210 David Eckstein .40 1.00
211 Omar Falcon FY RC .50 1.25
212 Todd Self FY RC .50 1.25
213 David Murphy FY RC .75 2.00
214 Dioner Navarro FY RC .75 2.00
215 Marcus McBeth FY RC .50 1.25
216 Chris O'Riordan FY RC .50 1.25
217 Rodney Choy Foo FY RC .50 1.25
218 Tim Frend FY RC .50 1.25
219 Yadier Molina FY RC 100.00 250.00
220 Zach Duke FY RC .75 2.00
221 Anthony Lerew FY AU RC 6.00 15.00
222 B.Hawksworth FY AU RC 6.00 15.00
223 Bryan Pena FY AU RC 4.00 10.00
224 Craig Ansman FY AU RC 4.00 10.00
225 Jon Knott FY AU RC 4.00 10.00
226 Josh Labandeira FY AU RC 4.00 10.00
227 Khalid Ballouli FY AU RC 4.00 10.00
228 Kyle Davies FY AU RC 10.00 25.00
229 Matt Creighton FY AU RC 4.00 10.00
230 Mike Gosling FY AU RC 4.00 10.00
231 Nic Ungs FY AU RC 4.00 10.00

232 Zach Miner FY AU RC 10.00 25.00
233 Donald Levinski FY AU RC 4.00 10.00
234A Bradley Sullivan FY AU RC 6.00 15.00
234B B.Sullivan FY AU ERR 345 10.00 25.00
235 Carlos Quentin FY AU RC 6.00 15.00
236 Conor Jackson FY AU RC 6.00 15.00
237 Estee Harris FY AU RC 6.00 15.00
238 Jeffrey Allison FY AU RC 4.00 10.00
239 Kyle Sleeth FY AU RC 6.00 15.00
240 Matthew Moses FY AU RC 6.00 15.00
241 Tim Stauffer FY AU RC 4.00 10.00
242 Brad Snyder FY AU RC 5.00 12.00
243 Jason Hirsh FY AU RC 10.00 25.00
244 L.Milledge FY AU RC 5.00 12.00
245 Logan Kensing FY AU RC 4.00 10.00
246 Kory Casto FY AU RC 6.00 15.00
247 David Aardsma FY RC .50 1.25
248 Omar Quintanilla FY RC .50 1.25
249 Ervin Santana FY RC 1.25 3.00
250 Merkin Valdez FY RC .50 1.25
251 Vito Chiaravalloti FY RC .50 1.25
252 Travis Blackley FY RC .50 1.25
253 Chris Shelton FY RC .50 1.25
254 Rudy Guillen FY RC .50 1.25
255 Bobby Brownlie FY RC .50 1.25
256 Paul Maholm FY RC .75 2.00
257 Roger Clemens 1.25 3.00
258 Laynce Nix .40 1.00
259 Eric Hinske .40 1.00
260 Ivan Rodriguez .60 1.50
261 Brandon Webb .40 1.00
262 Jhonny Peralta .40 1.00
263 Adam Kennedy .40 1.00
264 Tony Batista .40 1.00
265 Jeff Suppan .40 1.00
266 Kenny Lofton .40 1.00
267 Scott Sullivan .40 1.00
268 Ken Griffey Jr. 2.00 5.00
269 Juan Rivera .40 1.00
270 Larry Walker .60 1.50
271 Todd Hollandsworth .40 1.00
272 Carlos Beltran .60 1.50
273 Carl Crawford .60 1.50
274 Karim Garcia .40 1.00
275 Jose Reyes .60 1.50
276 Brandon Duckworth .40 1.00
277 Brian Giles .40 1.00
278 J.T. Snow .40 1.00
279 Jamie Moyer .40 1.00
280 Julio Lugo .40 1.00
281 Mark Teixeira .60 1.50
282 Cory Lidle .40 1.00
283 Lyle Overbay .40 1.00
284 Troy Percival .40 1.00
285 Robby Hammock .40 1.00
286 Jason Johnson .40 1.00
287 Damian Rolls .40 1.00
288 Antonio Alfonseca .40 1.00
289 Tom Goodwin .40 1.00
290 Paul Konerko .60 1.50
291 D'Angelo Jimenez .40 1.00
292 Ben Broussard .40 1.00
293 Magglio Ordonez .60 1.50
294 Carlos Pena .60 1.50
295 Chad Fox .40 1.00
296 Jerome Robertson .40 1.00
297 Travis Hafner .40 1.00
298 Joe Randa .40 1.00
299 Brady Clark .40 1.00
300 Barry Zito .60 1.50
301 Ruben Sierra .40 1.00
302 Brett Myers .40 1.00
303 Oliver Perez .40 1.00
304 Benito Santiago .40 1.00
305 David Ross .40 1.00
306 Joe Nathan .40 1.00
307 Jim Edmonds .60 1.50
308 Matt Kata .40 1.00
309 Vinny Castilla .40 1.00
310 Marty Cordova .40 1.00
311 Aramis Ramirez .40 1.00
312 Carl Everett .40 1.00
313 Ryan Freel .40 1.00
314 Mark Bellhorn Sox .40 1.00
315 Joe Mauer .75 2.00
316 Tim Redding .40 1.00
317 Jeromy Burnitz .40 1.00
318 Miguel Cabrera 1.00 2.50
319 Ramon Nivar .40 1.00
320 Casey Blake .40 1.00
321 Adam LaRoche .40 1.00
322 Jermaine Dye .40 1.00
323 Jerome Williams .40 1.00
324 John Olerud .40 1.00
325 Scott Rolen .60 1.50
326 Bobby Kielty .40 1.00
327 Travis Lee .40 1.00
328 Jeff Cirillo .40 1.00
329 Scott Spiezio .40 1.00
330 Melvin Mora .40 1.00
331 Mike Timlin .40 1.00
332 Kerry Wood .40 1.00
333 Tony Womack .40 1.00
334 Jody Gerut .40 1.00
335 Morgan Ensberg .40 1.00
336 Odalis Perez .40 1.00
337 Michael Cuddyer .40 1.00
338 Jose Hernandez .40 1.00
339 LaTroy Hawkins .40 1.00
340 Marquis Grissom .40 1.00
341 Matt Morris .40 1.00
342 Juan Gonzalez .40 1.00
343 Jose Valverde .40 1.00
344 Joe Borowski .40 1.00
345 Josh Bard .40 1.00
346 Austin Kearns .40 1.00
347 Chin-Hui Tsao .40 1.00
348 Wil Ledezma .40 1.00
349 Aaron Guiel .40 1.00
350 Alfonso Soriano .60 1.50
351 Ted Lilly .40 1.00
352 Sean Burroughs .40 1.00
353 Rafael Palmeiro .60 1.50
354 Quinton McCracken .40 1.00
355 David Ortiz 1.00 2.50
356 Randall Simon .40 1.00
357 Wily Mo Pena .40 1.00
358 Brian Anderson .40 1.00
359 Corey Koskie .40 1.00
360 Keith Foulke Sox .40 1.00
361 Sidney Ponson .40 1.00
362 Gary Matthews Jr. .40 1.00
363 Herbert Perry .40 1.00
364 Shea Hillenbrand .40 1.00
365 Craig Biggio .60 1.50
366 Barry Larkin .60 1.50
367 Arthur Rhodes .40 1.00
368 Sammy Sosa 1.00 2.50
369 Joe Crede .40 1.00
370 Gary Sheffield .40 1.00
371 Coco Crisp .40 1.00
372 Torii Hunter .40 1.00
373 Derrek Lee .40 1.00
374 Adam Everett .40 1.00
375 Miguel Tejada .60 1.50
376 Jeremy Affeldt .40 1.00
377 Robin Ventura .40 1.00
378 Scott Podsednik .40 1.00
379 Matthew LeCroy .40 1.00
380 Vladimir Guerrero .60 1.50
381 Steve Karsay .40 1.00
382 Jeff Nelson .40 1.00
383 Chase Utley .60 1.50
384 Bobby Abreu .40 1.00
385 Josh Fogg .40 1.00
386 Trevor Hoffman .60 1.50
387 Matt Stairs .40 1.00
388 Edgar Martinez .60 1.50
389 Edgar Renteria .40 1.00
390 Chipper Jones 1.00 2.50
391 Eric Munson .40 1.00
392 Dewon Brazelton .40 1.00
393 John Thomson .40 1.00
394 Chris Woodward .40 1.00
395 Joe Kennedy .40 1.00
396 Reed Johnson .40 1.00
397 Johnny Estrada .40 1.00
398 Damian Moss .40 1.00
399 Victor Zambrano .40 1.00
400 Dontrelle Willis .40 1.00
401 Troy Glaus .40 1.00
402 Raul Mondesi .40 1.00
403 Jeff Davanon .40 1.00
404 Kurt Ainsworth .40 1.00
405 Pedro Martinez .60 1.50
406 Eric Karros .40 1.00
407 Billy Koch .40 1.00
408 Luis Gonzalez .40 1.00
409 Jack Cust .40 1.00
410 Mike Sweeney .40 1.00
411 Jason Bay .60 1.50
412 Mark Redman .40 1.00
413 Jason Jennings .40 1.00
414 Rondell White .40 1.00
415 Todd Hundley .40 1.00
416 Shannon Stewart .40 1.00
417 Jae Weong Seo .40 1.00
418 Livan Hernandez .40 1.00
419 Mark Ellis .40 1.00
420 Pat Burrell .40 1.00
421 Mark Loretta .40 1.00
422 Robb Nen .40 1.00
423 Joel Pineiro .40 1.00
424 Todd Walker .40 1.00
425 Jeremy Bonderman .40 1.00
426 A.J. Burnett .40 1.00
427 Greg Myers .40 1.00
428 Roy Oswalt .60 1.50
429 Carlos Baerga .40 1.00
430 Garret Anderson .40 1.00
431 Horacio Ramirez .40 1.00
432 Brian Roberts .40 1.00
433 Kevin Brown .40 1.00
434 Eric Milton .40 1.00
435 Ramon Vazquez .40 1.00
436 Alex Escobar .40 1.00
437 Alex Sanchez .40 1.00
438 Jeff Bagwell .60 1.50
439 Claudio Vargas .40 1.00
440 Shawn Green .40 1.00
441 Geoff Jenkins .40 1.00
442 David Wells .40 1.00
443 Nick Johnson .40 1.00
444 Jose Guillen .40 1.00
445 Scott Hatteberg .40 1.00
446 Phil Nevin .40 1.00
447 Jason Schmidt .40 1.00
448 Ricky Ledee .40 1.00
449 So Taguchi .40 1.00
450 Randy Johnson 1.00 2.50
451 Eric Young .40 1.00
452 Chone Figgins .40 1.00
453 Larry Bigbie .40 1.00
454 Scott Williamson .40 1.00
455 Ramon Martinez .40 1.00
456 Roberto Alomar .60 1.50
457 Ryan Dempster .40 1.00
458 Ryan Ludwick .40 1.00
459 Ramon Santiago .40 1.00
460 Jeff Conine .40 1.00
461 Brad Lidge .40 1.00
462 Ken Harvey .40 1.00
463 Guillermo Mota .40 1.00
464 Rick Reed .40 1.00
465 Armando Benitez .40 1.00
466 Wade Miller .40 1.00

2004 Topps Chrome Black Refractors

*BLACK 1-210/257-466: 1.5X TO 4X BASIC
*BLACK 211-220/247-256: 1.2X TO 3X BASIC
1-220 SERIES 1 ODDS 1:10 H, 1:20 R
247-466 SERIES 2 ODDS 1:9 H, 1:20 R
221-233 SERIES 1 ODDS 1:1527 H, 1:2480 R
234-246 SERIES 2 ODDS 1:1579 H, 1:2549 R
221-246 PRINT RUN 25 SERIAL #'d SETS
221-246 NO PRICING DUE TO SCARCITY

2004 Topps Chrome Gold Refractors

*GOLD 1-210/257-466: 1.25X TO 3X BASIC
*GOLD 211-220/247-256: 1X TO 2.5X BASIC
1-220 SERIES 1 ODDS 1:5 H, 1:10 R
247-466 SERIES 2 ODDS 1:9 H, 1:10 R
*GOLD AU 221-246: 2X TO 4X BASIC AU
221-233 SERIES 1 ODDS 1:759 H, 1:1208 R
234-246 SERIES 2 ODDS 1:790 H, 1:1324 R
221-246 PRINT RUN 50 SERIAL #'d SETS

2004 Topps Chrome Red X-Fractors

*RED XF 1-210/257-466: 3X TO 8X BASIC
*RED XF 211-220/247-256: 3X TO 8X BASIC
1-220 ONE PER SER.1 PARALLEL HOT PACK
247-466 1 PER SER.2 PARALLEL HOT PACK
ONE HOT PACK PER SEALED HOBBY BOX
1-220 STATED PRINT RUN 63 SETS
247-466 STATED PRINT RUN 61 SETS
1-220/247-466 ARE NOT SERIAL #'d
1-220/247-466 PRINT RUN GIVEN BY TOPPS
221-233 SERIES 1 ODDS 1:21,371 HOBBY
234-246 SERIES 2 ODDS 1:20,800 HOBBY
221-246 PRINT RUN 1 SERIAL #'d SET
221-246 NO PRICING DUE TO SCARCITY

2004 Topps Chrome Refractors

*REF 1-210/257-466: 1X TO 2.5X BASIC
*REF 211-220/247-256: .75X TO 2X BASIC
1-220 SERIES 1 ODDS 1:4 H/R
247-466 SERIES 2 ODDS 1:4 H/R
*REF AU 221-246: 1X TO 2.5X BASIC AU
221-233 SERIES 1 ODDS 1:380 H, 1:597 R
234-246 SERIES 2 ODDS 1:375 H, 1:680 R
221-246 PRINT RUN 100 SERIAL #'d SETS
232 Zach Miner FY AU 30.00 60.00

2004 Topps Chrome Fashionably Great Relics

ONE RELIC PER SER.1 GU HOBBY PACK
GROUP A 1:59 SER.1 RETAIL
GROUP B 1:107 SER.1 RETAIL
AD Adam Dunn Jsy A 3.00 8.00
AJ Andruw Jones Uni A 4.00 10.00
AP Albert Pujols Jsy A 10.00 25.00
AR Alex Rodriguez Uni A 6.00 15.00
BM Brett Myers Jsy A 3.00 8.00
BW Billy Wagner Jsy B 3.00 8.00
CB Craig Biggio Uni A 4.00 10.00
CD Carlos Delgado Jsy A 3.00 8.00
CF Cliff Floyd Jsy A 3.00 8.00
CJ Chipper Jones Uni A 4.00 10.00
CS Curt Schilling Jsy A 3.00 8.00
DL Derek Lowe Uni B 3.00 8.00
EC Eric Chavez Uni B 3.00 8.00
FG Freddy Garcia Jsy A 3.00 8.00
FM Fred McGriff Jsy A 4.00 10.00
FT Frank Thomas Uni A 4.00 10.00
HB Hank Blalock Jsy A 3.00 8.00
IR Ivan Rodriguez Uni B 4.00 10.00
JB Jeff Bagwell Uni A 4.00 10.00
JBO Joe Borchard Jsy A 3.00 8.00
JO John Olerud Jsy A 3.00 8.00
JR Juan Rivera Jsy A 3.00 8.00
JS John Smoltz Uni A 4.00 10.00
JV Jose Vidro Jsy A 3.00 8.00
KB Kevin Brown Jsy B 3.00 8.00
MM Mark Mulder Uni A 3.00 8.00
MP Mike Piazza Uni A 6.00 15.00
MR Manny Ramirez Uni A 4.00 10.00
MS Mike Sweeney Uni A 3.00 8.00
NG Nomar Garciaparra Uni B 6.00 15.00
PM Pedro Martinez Jsy A 4.00 10.00
RP Rafael Palmeiro Jsy A 4.00 10.00
SS Sammy Sosa Jsy A 4.00 10.00
TH Tim Hudson Uni B 3.00 8.00
THO Trevor Hoffman Uni A 3.00 8.00
VW Vernon Wells Jsy B 3.00 8.00
WP Wily Mo Pena Jsy A 3.00 8.00

2004 Topps Chrome Presidential First Pitch Seat Relics

SERIES 2 ODDS 1:15 BOX-LOADER HOBBY
SERIES 2 ODDS 1:633 HOBBY
STATED PRINT RUN 100 SETS
CARDS ARE NOT SERIAL-NUMBERED
PRINT RUN INFO PROVIDED BY TOPPS
BC Bill Clinton 20.00 50.00
CC Calvin Coolidge 10.00 25.00
DE Dwight Eisenhower 10.00 25.00
FR Franklin D. Roosevelt 15.00 40.00
GB George W. Bush 20.00 50.00
GF Gerald Ford 15.00 40.00
GHB George H.W. Bush 15.00 40.00
HH Herbert Hoover 10.00 25.00
HT Harry Truman 10.00 25.00
JK John F. Kennedy 20.00 50.00
LJ Lyndon B. Johnson 10.00 25.00
RN Richard Nixon 20.00 50.00
RR Ronald Reagan 30.00 60.00
WH Warren Harding 10.00 25.00
WT William Taft 10.00 25.00
WW Woodrow Wilson 10.00 25.00

2004 Topps Chrome Presidential Pastime Refractors

COMPLETE SET (42) 60.00 120.00
SERIES 2 ODDS 1:9 HOBBY
*X-FRACTOR p/r 26-43: 2X TO 5X BASIC
X-FRACTOR SER.2 ODDS 1:400 H, 1:791 R
X-F PRINT RUNS B/WN 1-43 COPIES PER
NO X-F PRICING ON QTY OF 25 OR LESS
PP1 George Washington 2.50 6.00
PP2 John Adams 1.50 4.00
PP3 Thomas Jefferson 2.50 6.00
PP4 James Madison 1.50 4.00
PP5 James Monroe 1.50 4.00
PP6 John Quincy Adams 1.50 4.00
PP7 Andrew Jackson 1.50 4.00
PP8 Martin Van Buren 1.50 4.00
PP9 William Harrison 1.50 4.00
PP10 John Tyler 1.50 4.00
PP11 James Polk 1.50 4.00
PP12 Zachary Taylor 1.50 4.00
PP13 Millard Fillmore 1.50 4.00
PP14 Franklin Pierce 1.50 4.00
PP15 James Buchanan 1.50 4.00
PP16 Abraham Lincoln 2.50 6.00
PP17 Andrew Johnson 1.50 4.00
PP18 Ulysses S. Grant 2.00 5.00
PP19 Rutherford B. Hayes 1.50 4.00
PP20 James Garfield 1.50 4.00
PP21 Chester Arthur 1.50 4.00
PP22 Grover Cleveland 1.50 4.00
PP23 Benjamin Harrison 1.50 4.00
PP24 William McKinley 1.50 4.00
PP25 Theodore Roosevelt 2.00 5.00
PP26 William Taft 1.50 4.00
PP27 Woodrow Wilson 1.50 4.00
PP28 Warren Harding 1.50 4.00
PP29 Calvin Coolidge 1.50 4.00
PP30 Herbert Hoover 1.50 4.00
PP31 Franklin D. Roosevelt 2.00 5.00
PP32 Harry Truman 1.50 4.00
PP33 Dwight Eisenhower 1.50 4.00
PP34 John F. Kennedy 2.00 5.00
PP35 Lyndon B. Johnson 1.50 4.00
PP36 Richard Nixon 2.00 5.00
PP37 Gerald Ford 2.00 5.00
PP38 Jimmy Carter 1.50 4.00
PP39 Ronald Reagan 5.00 12.00
PP40 George H.W. Bush 2.00 5.00
PP41 Bill Clinton 2.50 6.00
PP42 George W. Bush 2.50 6.00

2004 Topps Chrome Town Heroes Relics

SER.2 ODDS 1 PER HOBBY BOX-LOADER
SER.2 ODDS 1:48 RETAIL
AP Albert Pujols Bat 6.00 15.00
AR Alex Rodriguez Bat 6.00 15.00
BZ Barry Zito Uni 3.00 8.00
CJ Chipper Jones Jsy 4.00 10.00
EC Eric Chavez Uni 3.00 8.00
FT Frank Thomas Jsy 4.00 10.00
HN Hideo Nomo Jsy 4.00 10.00
JG Jason Giambi Uni 3.00 8.00
JR Jose Reyes Bat 3.00 8.00
KW Kerry Wood Jsy 3.00 8.00
LB Lance Berkman Jsy 3.00 8.00
MM Mark Mulder Uni 3.00 8.00
MP Mark Prior Bat 4.00 10.00
MR Manny Ramirez Bat 4.00 10.00
MT Miguel Tejada Bat 3.00 8.00
NG Nomar Garciaparra Bat 4.00 10.00
RH Rich Harden Uni 3.00 8.00
RP Rafael Palmeiro Jsy 4.00 10.00
SS Sammy Sosa Jsy 4.00 10.00
SST Shannon Stewart Jsy 3.00 8.00
TH Tim Hudson Uni 3.00 8.00

2004 Topps Chrome Trade

COMPLETE SET (220) 30.00 60.00
COMMON CARD (1-70) .30 .75
COMMON CARD (71-90) .40 1.00
COMMON CARD (91-110) .40 1.00
COMMON CARD (111-220) .40 1.00
2 PER 2004 TOPPS TRADED HOBBY PACK
2 PER 2004 TOPPS TRADED HTA PACK
2 PER 2004 TOPPS TRADED RETAIL PACK
PLATE ODDS 1:1151 H, 1:1173 R, 1:327 HTA
PLATE PRINT RUN 1 SET PER COLOR
BLACK-CYAN-MAGENTA-YELLOW ISSUED
NO PLATE PRICING DUE TO SCARCITY
T1 Pokey Reese .30 .75
T2 Tony Womack .30 .75
T3 Richard Hidalgo .30 .75
T4 Juan Uribe .30 .75
T5 J.D. Drew .30 .75
T6 Alex Gonzalez .30 .75
T7 Carlos Guillen .30 .75
T8 Doug Mientkiewicz .30 .75
T9 Fernando Vina .30 .75
T10 Milton Bradley .30 .75
T11 Kelvim Escobar .30 .75
T12 Ben Grieve .30 .75
T13 Brian Jordan .30 .75
T14 A.J. Pierzynski .30 .75
T15 Billy Wagner .30 .75
T16 Terrence Long .30 .75
T17 Carlos Beltran .50 1.25
T18 Carl Everett .30 .75
T19 Reggie Sanders .30 .75
T20 Javy Lopez .30 .75
T21 Jay Payton .30 .75
T22 Octavio Dotel .30 .75
T23 Eddie Guardado .30 .75
T24 Andy Pettitte .50 1.25
T25 Richie Sexson .30 .75
T26 Ronnie Belliard .30 .75
T27 Michael Tucker .30 .75
T28 Brad Fullmer .30 .75
T29 Freddy Garcia .30 .75
T30 Bartolo Colon .30 .75
T31 Larry Walker Cards .50 1.25
T32 Mark Kotsay .30 .75
T33 Jason Marquis .30 .75
T34 Dustan Mohr .30 .75
T35 Javier Vazquez .30 .75
T36 Nomar Garciaparra .50 1.25
T37 Tino Martinez .50 1.25
T38 Hee Seop Choi .30 .75
T39 Damian Miller .30 .75
T40 Jose Lima .30 .75
T41 Ty Wigginton .30 .75
T42 Raul Ibanez .50 1.25
T43 Danys Baez .30 .75
T44 Tony Clark .30 .75
T45 Greg Maddux 1.00 2.50
T46 Victor Zambrano .30 .75
T47 Orlando Cabrera Sox .30 .75
T48 Jose Cruz Jr. .30 .75
T49 Kris Benson .30 .75
T50 Alex Rodriguez 1.00 2.50
T51 Steve Finley .30 .75
T52 Ramon Hernandez .30 .75
T53 Esteban Loaiza .30 .75
T54 Ugueth Urbina .30 .75
T55 Jeff Weaver .30 .75
T56 Flash Gordon .30 .75
T57 Jose Contreras .30 .75
T58 Paul Lo Duca .30 .75
T59 Junior Spivey .30 .75
T60 Curt Schilling .50 1.25
T61 Brad Penny .30 .75
T62 Braden Looper .30 .75
T63 Miguel Cairo .30 .75
T64 Juan Encarnacion .30 .75
T65 Miguel Batista .30 .75
T66 Terry Francona MG .30 .75
T67 Lee Mazzilli MG .30 .75
T68 Al Pedrique MG .30 .75
T69 Ozzie Guillen MG .30 .75
T70 Phil Garner MG .30 .75
T71 Matt Bush DP RC .60 1.50
T72 Homer Bailey DP RC .60 1.50
T73 Greg Golson DP RC .40 1.00
T74 Kyle Waldrop DP RC .40 1.00
T75 Richie Robnett DP RC .40 1.00
T76 Jay Rainville DP RC .40 1.00
T77 Bill Bray DP RC .40 1.00
T78 Philip Hughes DP RC 1.00 2.50
T79 Scott Elbert DP RC .40 1.00
T80 Josh Fields DP RC .60 1.50
T81 Justin Orenduff DP RC .60 1.50
T82 Dan Putnam DP RC .40 1.00
T83 Chris Nelson DP RC .40 1.00
T84 Blake DeWitt DP RC .60 1.50
T85 J.P. Howell DP RC .40 1.00
T86 Huston Street DP RC .60 1.50
T87 Kurt Suzuki DP RC .60 1.50
T88 Erick San Pedro DP RC .40 1.00
T89 Matt Tuiasosopo DP RC 1.00 2.50
T90 Matt Macri DP RC .60 1.50
T91 Chad Tracy PROS .40 1.00
T92 Scott Hairston PROS .40 1.00
T93 Jonny Gomes PROS .40 1.00
T94 Chin-Feng Chen PROS .40 1.00
T95 Chien-Ming Wang PROS 1.50 4.00
T96 Dustin McGowan PROS .40 1.00
T97 Chris Burke PROS .40 1.00
T98 Denny Bautista PROS .40 1.00
T99 Preston Larrison PROS .40 1.00
T100 Kevin Youkilis PROS .40 1.00
T101 John Maine PROS .40 1.00
T102 Guillermo Quiroz PROS .40 1.00
T103 Dave Krynzel PROS .40 1.00
T104 David Kelton PROS .40 1.00
T105 Edwin Encarnacion PROS 1.00 2.50
T106 Chad Gaudin PROS .40 1.00
T107 Sergio Mitre PROS .40 1.00
T108 Laynce Nix PROS .40 1.00
T109 David Parrish PROS .40 1.00
T110 Brandon Claussen PROS .40 1.00
T111 Frank Francisco FY RC .40 1.00
T112 Brian Dallimore FY RC .40 1.00
T113 Jim Crowell FY RC .40 1.00
T114 Andres Blanco FY RC .40 1.00
T115 Eduardo Villacis FY RC .40 1.00
T116 Kazuhito Tadano FY RC .40 1.00
T117 Aarom Baldiris FY RC .40 1.00
T118 Justin Germano FY RC .40 1.00
T119 Joey Gathright FY RC .40 1.00
T120 Franklyn Gracesqui FY RC .40 1.00
T121 Chin-Lung Hu FY RC .40 1.00
T122 Scott Olsen FY RC .40 1.00
T123 Tyler Davidson FY RC .40 1.00
T124 Fausto Carmona FY RC .60 1.50
T125 Tim Hutting FY RC .40 1.00
T126 Ryan Meaux FY RC .40 1.00
T127 Jon Connolly FY RC .40 1.00
T128 Hector Made FY RC .40 1.00
T129 Jamie Brown FY RC .40 1.00
T130 Paul McAnulty FY RC .40 1.00
T131 Chris Saenz FY RC .40 1.00
T132 Marland Williams FY RC .40 1.00
T133 Mike Huggins FY RC .40 1.00
T134 Jesse Crain FY RC .60 1.50
T135 Chad Bentz FY RC .40 1.00
T136 Kazuo Matsui FY RC .60 1.50
T137 Paul Maholm FY .60 1.50
T138 Brock Jacobsen FY RC .40 1.00
T139 Casey Daigle FY RC .40 1.00
T140 Nyjer Morgan FY RC .40 1.00
T141 Tom Mastny FY RC .40 1.00
T142 Kody Kirkland FY RC .40 1.00
T143 Jose Capellan FY RC .40 1.00
T144 Felix Hernandez FY RC 6.00 15.00
T145 Shawn Hill FY RC .40 1.00
T146 Danny Gonzalez FY RC .40 1.00
T147 Scott Dohmann FY RC .40 1.00
T148 Tommy Murphy FY RC .40 1.00
T149 Akinori Otsuka FY RC .40 1.00
T150 Miguel Perez FY RC .40 1.00
T151 Mike Rouse FY RC .40 1.00
T152 Ramon Ramirez FY RC .40 1.00
T153 Luke Hughes FY RC 1.00 2.50
T154 Howie Kendrick FY RC 2.00 5.00
T155 Ryan Budde FY RC .40 1.00
T156 Charlie Zink FY RC .40 1.00
T157 Warner Madrigal FY RC .40 1.00
T158 Jason Szuminski FY RC .40 1.00
T159 Chad Chop FY RC .40 1.00
T160 Shingo Takatsu FY RC .40 1.00
T161 Matt Lemanczyk FY RC .40 1.00
T162 Wardell Starling FY RC .40 1.00
T163 Nick Gorneault FY RC .40 1.00
T164 Scott Proctor FY RC .40 1.00
T165 Brooks Conrad FY RC .40 1.00
T166 Hector Gimenez FY RC .40 1.00
T167 Kevin Howard FY RC .40 1.00
T168 Vince Perkins FY RC .40 1.00
T169 Brock Peterson FY RC .40 1.00
T170 Chris Shelton FY .40 1.00
T171 Erick Aybar FY RC 1.00 2.50
T172 Paul Bacot FY RC .40 1.00
T173 Matt Capps FY RC .40 1.00
T174 Kory Casto FY .40 1.00
T175 Juan Cedeno FY RC .40 1.00
T176 Vito Chiaravalloti FY .40 1.00
T177 Alec Zumwalt FY RC .40 1.00
T178 J.J. Furmaniak FY RC .40 1.00
T179 Lee Gwaltney FY RC .40 1.00
T180 Donald Kelly FY RC .60 1.50
T181 Benji DeQuin FY RC .40 1.00
T182 Brant Colamarino FY RC .40 1.00
T183 Juan Gutierrez FY RC .40 1.00
T184 Carl Loadenthal FY RC .40 1.00
T185 Ricky Nolasco FY RC .60 1.50
T186 Jeff Salazar FY RC .40 1.00
T187 Rob Tejeda FY RC .40 1.00
T188 Alex Romero FY RC .40 1.00
T189 Yoann Torrealba FY RC .40 1.00
T190 Carlos Sosa FY RC .40 1.00
T191 Tim Bittner FY RC .40 1.00
T192 Chris Aguila FY RC .40 1.00
T193 Jason Frasor FY RC .40 1.00
T194 Reid Gorecki FY RC .40 1.00
T195 Dustin Nippert FY RC .40 1.00
T196 Javier Guzman FY RC .40 1.00
T197 Harvey Garcia FY RC .40 1.00
T198 Ivan Ochoa FY RC .40 1.00
T199 David Murphy FY RC .40 1.00
T200 Joel Zumaya FY RC 1.50 4.00
T201 Casey Kopitzke FY RC .40 1.00
T202 Lincoln Holdzkom FY RC .40 1.00
T203 Chad Santos FY RC .40 1.00
T204 Brian Pilkington FY RC .40 1.00
T205 Terry Jones FY RC .40 1.00
T206 Jerome Gamble FY RC .40 1.00
T207 Brad Eldred FY RC .40 1.00
T208 David Pauley FY RC .60 1.50
T209 Kevin Davidson FY RC .40 1.00
T210 Damaso Espino FY RC .40 1.00
T211 Tom Farmer FY RC .40 1.00
T212 Michael Mooney FY RC .40 1.00
T213 James Tomlin FY RC .40 1.00
T214 Greg Thissen FY RC .40 1.00
T215 Calvin Hayes FY RC .40 1.00
T216 Fernando Cortez FY RC .40 1.00
T217 Sergio Silva FY RC .40 1.00
T218 Jon de Vries FY RC .40 1.00
T219 Don Sutton FY RC .40 1.00
T220 Leo Nunez FY RC .40 1.00

2004 Topps Chrome Traded Refractors

*REF 1-70: 2X TO 5X BASIC
*REF 71-90: 1.5X TO 4X BASIC
*REF 91-110: 1.5X TO 4X BASIC
*REF 111-220: 1.5X TO 4X BASIC
STATED ODDS 1:12 HOB/RET, 1:4 HTA
STATED PRINT RUN 355 SETS
CARDS ARE NOT SERIAL-NUMBERED
PRINT RUN INFO PROVIDED BY TOPPS

2004 Topps Chrome Traded X-Fractors

*XF 1-70: 8X TO 20X BASIC
*XF 91-110: 6X TO 15X BASIC
ONE XF PACK PER SEALED HTA BOX
ONE XF CARD PER XF PACK
STATED PRINT RUN 20 SERIAL #'d SETS
NO PRICING ON 71-90 DUE TO SCARCITY
NO PRICING ON 91-110 DUE TO SCARCITY

2005 Topps Chrome

COMP.SET w/o AU'S (440) 80.00 160.00
COMP.SERIES 1 w/o AU'S (220) 40.00 80.00
COMP.SERIES 2 w/o AU'S (220) 40.00 80.00
COMMON (1-210/253-467) .40 1.00
COMMON (211-220/468-472) .75 2.00
COMMON AU (221-252) 4.00 10.00
221-234 SER.1 ODDS 1:28 H, 1:33 R
235-252 SER.2 ODDS 1:2 MINI BOX, 1:55 R
221-252 STATED PRINT RUN 1770 SETS
221-252 ARE NOT SERIAL-NUMBERED
221-252 PRINT RUN PROVIDED BY TOPPS
EXCHANGE DEADLINE 05/31/07
1-234 PLATE ODDS 1:310 SER.1 HOBBY
235-252 PLATE ODDS 1:350 SER.2 MINI BOX
253-472 PLATE ODDS 1:29 SER.2 MINI BOX
PLATE PRINT RUN 1 SET PER COLOR
BLACK-CYAN-MAGENTA-YELLOW ISSUED
NO PLATE PRICING DUE TO SCARCITY
1 Alex Rodriguez 1.25 3.00
2 Placido Polanco .40 1.00
3 Torii Hunter .40 1.00
4 Lyle Overbay .40 1.00
5 Johnny Damon .60 1.50
6 Johnny Estrada .40 1.00
7 Rich Harden .40 1.00
8 Francisco Rodriguez .60 1.50
9 Jarrod Washburn .40 1.00
10 Sammy Sosa 1.00 2.50
11 Randy Wolf .40 1.00
12 Jason Bay .40 1.00
13 Tom Glavine .60 1.50
14 Michael Tucker .40 1.00
15 Brian Giles .40 1.00
16 Chad Tracy .40 1.00
17 Jim Edmonds .60 1.50
18 John Smoltz 1.00 2.50
19 Roy Halladay .60 1.50
20 Hank Blalock .40 1.00
21 Darin Erstad .40 1.00
22 Todd Walker .40 1.00
23 Mike Hampton .40 1.00
24 Mark Bellhorn .40 1.00
25 Jim Thome .60 1.50
26 Shingo Takatsu .40 1.00
27 Jody Gerut .40 1.00
28 Vinny Castilla .40 1.00
29 Luis Castillo .40 1.00
30 Ivan Rodriguez .60 1.50
31 Craig Biggio .60 1.50
32 Joe Randa .40 1.00
33 Adrian Beltre 1.00 2.50
34 Scott Podsednik .40 1.00
35 Cliff Floyd .40 1.00
36 Livan Hernandez .40 1.00
37 Eric Byrnes .40 1.00
38 Jose Acevedo .40 1.00
39 Jack Wilson .40 1.00
40 Gary Sheffield .40 1.00
41 Chan Ho Park .60 1.50
42 Carl Crawford .60 1.50
43 Shawn Estes .40 1.00
44 David Bell .40 1.00
45 Jeff DaVanon .40 1.00
46 Brandon Webb .60 1.50
47 Lance Berkman .60 1.50
48 Melvin Mora .40 1.00
49 David Ortiz 1.00 2.50
50 Andruw Jones .40 1.00
51 Chone Figgins .40 1.00
52 Danny Graves .40 1.00
53 Preston Wilson .40 1.00
54 Jeremy Bonderman .40 1.00
55 Carlos Guillen .40 1.00
56 Cesar Izturis .40 1.00
57 Kazuo Matsui .40 1.00
58 Jason Schmidt .40 1.00
59 Jason Marquis .40 1.00
60 Jose Vidro .40 1.00
61 Al Leiter .40 1.00
62 Javier Vazquez .40 1.00
63 Erubiel Durazo .40 1.00
64 Scott Spiezio .40 1.00
65 Scott Shields .40 1.00
66 Edgardo Alfonzo .40 1.00
67 Miguel Tejada .60 1.50
68 Francisco Cordero .40 1.00
69 Brett Myers .40 1.00
70 Curt Schilling .60 1.50
71 Matt Kata .40 1.00
72 Bartolo Colon .40 1.00
73 Rodrigo Lopez .40 1.00
74 Tim Wakefield .60 1.50
75 Frank Thomas 1.00 2.50
76 Jimmy Rollins .60 1.50
77 Barry Zito .60 1.50
78 Hideo Nomo 1.00 2.50
79 Brad Wilkerson .40 1.00
80 Adam Dunn .60 1.50
81 Derrek Lee .40 1.00
82 Joe Crede .40 1.00
83 Nate Robertson .40 1.00
84 John Thomson .40 1.00
85 Mike Sweeney .40 1.00
86 Kip Wells .40 1.00
87 Eric Gagne .40 1.00
88 Zach Day .40 1.00
89 Alex Sanchez .40 1.00
90 Bret Boone .40 1.00
91 Mark Loretta .40 1.00
92 Miguel Cabrera 1.00 2.50
93 Randy Winn .40 1.00
94 Adam Everett .40 1.00
95 Aubrey Huff .40 1.00
96 Kevin Mench .40 1.00
97 Frank Catalanotto .40 1.00
98 Flash Gordon .40 1.00
99 Scott Hatteberg .40 1.00
100 Albert Pujols 1.25 3.00
101 J.Molina .40 1.00
B.Molina
102 Jason Johnson
103 Jay Gibbons .40 1.00
104 Byung-Hyun Kim .40 1.00
105 Joe Borowski .40 1.00
106 Mark Grudzielanek .40 1.00
107 Mark Buehrle .60 1.50
108 Paul Wilson .40 1.00
109 Ronnie Belliard .40 1.00
110 Reggie Sanders .40 1.00
111 Tim Redding .40 1.00
112 Brian Lawrence .40 1.00
113 Travis Hafner .40 1.00
114 Jose Hernandez .40 1.00
115 Ben Sheets .40 1.00
116 Johan Santana .60 1.50
117 Billy Wagner .40 1.00
118 Mariano Rivera 1.25 3.00
119 Steve Trachsel .40 1.00
120 Akinori Otsuka .40 1.00
121 Jose Valentin .40 1.00
122 Orlando Hernandez .40 1.00
123 Raul Ibanez .60 1.50
124 Mike Matheny .40 1.00
125 Vernon Wells .40 1.00
126 Jason Isringhausen .40 1.00
127 Jose Guillen .40 1.00
128 Danny Bautista .40 1.00
129 Marcus Giles .40 1.00
130 Javy Lopez .40 1.00
131 Kevin Millar .40 1.00
132 Kyle Farnsworth .40 1.00
133 Carl Pavano .40 1.00
134 Rafael Furcal .40 1.00
135 Casey Blake .40 1.00
136 Matt Holliday 1.00 2.50
137 Bobby Higginson .40 1.00
138 Adam Kennedy .40 1.00
139 Alex Gonzalez .40 1.00
140 Jeff Kent .40 1.00
141 Aaron Guiel .40 1.00
142 Shawn Green .40 1.00
143 Bill Hall .40 1.00
144 Shannon Stewart .40 1.00
145 Juan Rivera .40 1.00
146 Coco Crisp .40 1.00
147 Mike Mussina .60 1.50
148 Eric Chavez .40 1.00
149 Jon Lieber .40 1.00
150 Vladimir Guerrero .60 1.50
151 Alex Cintron .40 1.00
152 Luis Matos .40 1.00
153 Sidney Ponson .40 1.00
154 Trot Nixon .40 1.00
155 Greg Maddux 1.25 3.00
156 Edgar Renteria .40 1.00
157 Ryan Freel .40 1.00
158 Matt Lawton .40 1.00
159 Mark Prior .60 1.50
160 Josh Beckett .40 1.00
161 Ken Harvey .40 1.00
162 Angel Berroa .40 1.00
163 Juan Encarnacion .40 1.00
164 Wes Helms .40 1.00
165 Brad Radke .40 1.00
166 Phil Nevin .40 1.00
167 Mike Cameron .40 1.00
168 Billy Koch .40 1.00
169 Bobby Crosby .40 1.00
170 Mike Lieberthal .40 1.00
171 Rob Mackowiak .40 1.00
172 Sean Burroughs .40 1.00
173 J.T. Snow .40 1.00
174 Paul Konerko .60 1.50
175 Luis Gonzalez .40 1.00
176 John Lackey .60 1.50
177 Oliver Perez .40 1.00
178 Brian Roberts .40 1.00
179 Bill Mueller .40 1.00
180 Carlos Lee .40 1.00
181 Corey Patterson .40 1.00
182 Sean Casey .40 1.00
183 Cliff Lee .60 1.50
184 Jason Jennings .40 1.00
185 Dmitri Young .40 1.00
186 Juan Uribe .40 1.00
187 Andy Pettitte .60 1.50
188 Juan Gonzalez .40 1.00
189 Orlando Hudson .40 1.00
190 Jason Phillips .40 1.00
191 Braden Looper .40 1.00
192 Lew Ford .40 1.00
193 Mark Mulder .40 1.00
194 Bobby Abreu .40 1.00
195 Jason Kendall .40 1.00
196 Khalil Greene .40 1.00

197 A.J. Pierzynski .40 1.00
198 Tim Worrell .40 1.00
199 So Taguchi .40 1.00
200 Jason Giambi .40 1.00
201 Tony Batista .40 1.00
202 Carlos Zambrano .60 1.50
203 Trevor Hoffman .60 1.50
204 Odalis Perez .40 1.00
205 Jose Cruz Jr. .40 1.00
206 Michael Barrett .40 1.00
207 Chris Carpenter .60 1.50
208 Michael Young UER .40 1.00
209 Toby Hall .40 1.00
210 Woody Williams .40 1.00
211 Chris Denorfia FY RC .40 1.00
212 Darren Fenster FY RC .40 1.00
213 Elvys Quezada FY RC .40 1.00
214 Ian Kinsler FY RC 2.00 5.00
215 Matthew Lindstrom FY RC .40 1.00
216 Ryan Goleski FY RC .40 1.00
217 Ryan Sweeney FY RC .60 1.50
218 Sean Marshall FY RC 1.00 2.50
219 Steve Doetsch FY RC .40 1.00
220 Wade Robinson FY RC .40 1.00
221 Andre Ethier FY AU RC 4.00 10.00
222 Brandon Moss FY AU RC 4.00 10.00
223 Chadd Blasko FY AU RC 4.00 10.00
224 Chris Roberson FY AU RC 4.00 10.00
225 Chris Seddon FY AU RC 4.00 10.00
226 Ian Bladergroen FY AU RC 4.00 10.00
227 Jake Dittler FY AU 4.00 10.00
228 Jose Vaquedano FY AU RC 4.00 10.00
229 Jeremy West FY AU RC 4.00 10.00
230 Kole Strayhorn FY AU RC 4.00 10.00
231 Kevin West FY AU RC 4.00 10.00
232 Luis Ramirez FY AU RC 4.00 10.00
233 Melky Cabrera FY AU RC 4.00 10.00
234 Nate Schierholtz FY AU 4.00 10.00
235 Billy Butler FY AU RC 4.00 10.00
236 Brandon Szymanski FY AU 4.00 10.00
237 Chad Orvella FY AU RC 4.00 10.00
238 Chip Cannon FY AU RC 4.00 10.00
239 Eric Nielsen FY AU RC 4.00 10.00
240 Erik Cordier FY AU RC 4.00 10.00
241 Glen Perkins FY AU RC 4.00 10.00
242 Justin Verlander FY AU RC 150.00 400.00
243 Kevin Melillo FY AU RC 6.00 15.00
244 Landon Powell FY AU RC 4.00 10.00
245 Matt Campbell FY AU RC 4.00 10.00
246 Michael Rogers FY AU RC 4.00 10.00
247 Nate McLouth FY AU RC 4.00 10.00
248 Scott Mathieson FY AU RC 4.00 10.00
249 Shane Costa FY AU RC 4.00 10.00
250 Tony Giarratano FY AU RC 4.00 10.00
251 Tyler Pelland FY AU RC 4.00 10.00
252 Wes Swackhamer FY AU RC 4.00 10.00
253 Garret Anderson .40 1.00
254 Randy Johnson 1.00 2.50
255 Charles Thomas .40 1.00
256 Rafael Palmeiro .60 1.50
257 Kevin Youkilis .40 1.00
258 Freddy Garcia .40 1.00
259 Magglio Ordonez .60 1.50
260 Aaron Harang .40 1.00
261 Grady Sizemore .60 1.50
262 Chin-hui Tsao .40 1.00
263 Eric Munson .40 1.00
264 Juan Pierre .40 1.00
265 Brad Lidge .40 1.00
266 Brian Anderson .40 1.00
267 Todd Helton .60 1.50
268 Chad Cordero .40 1.00
269 Kris Benson .40 1.00
270 Brad Halsey .40 1.00
271 Jermaine Dye .40 1.00
272 Manny Ramirez 1.00 2.50
273 Adam Eaton .40 1.00
274 Brett Tomko .40 1.00
275 Bucky Jacobsen .40 1.00
276 Dontrelle Willis .40 1.00
277 B.J. Upton .60 1.50
278 Rocco Baldelli .40 1.00
279 Ryan Drese .40 1.00
280 Ichiro Suzuki 1.25 3.00
281 Brandon Lyon .40 1.00
282 Nick Green .40 1.00
283 Jerry Hairston Jr. .40 1.00
284 Mike Lowell .40 1.00
285 Kerry Wood .40 1.00
286 Omar Vizquel .60 1.50
287 Carlos Beltran .60 1.50
288 Carlos Pena .60 1.50
289 Jeff Weaver .40 1.00
290 Chad Moeller .40 1.00
291 Joe Mays .40 1.00
292 Termel Sledge .40 1.00
293 Richard Hidalgo .40 1.00
294 Justin Duchscherer .40 1.00
295 Eric Milton .40 1.00
296 Ramon Hernandez .40 1.00
297 Jose Reyes .60 1.50
298 Joel Pineiro .40 1.00
299 Matt Morris .40 1.00
300 John Halama .40 1.00
301 Gary Matthews Jr. .40 1.00
302 Ryan Madson .40 1.00
303 Mark Kotsay .40 1.00
304 Carlos Delgado .40 1.00
305 Casey Kotchman .40 1.00
306 Greg Aquino .40 1.00
307 LaTroy Hawkins .40 1.00
308 Jose Contreras .40 1.00
309 Ken Griffey Jr. 2.00 5.00
310 C.C. Sabathia .60 1.50
311 Brandon Inge .40 1.00
312 John Buck .40 1.00
313 Hee Seop Choi .40 1.00
314 Chris Capuano .40 1.00
315 Jesse Crain .40 1.00
316 Geoff Jenkins .40 1.00
317 Mike Piazza 1.00 2.50
318 Jorge Posada .60 1.50
319 Nick Swisher .60 1.50
320 Kevin Millwood .40 1.00
321 Mike Gonzalez .40 1.00
322 Jake Peavy .40 1.00
323 Dustin Hermanson .40 1.00
324 Jeremy Reed .40 1.00
325 Alfonso Soriano .60 1.50
326 Alexis Rios .40 1.00
327 David Eckstein .40 1.00
328 Shea Hillenbrand .40 1.00
329 Russ Ortiz .40 1.00
330 Kurt Ainsworth .40 1.00
331 Orlando Cabrera .40 1.00
332 Carlos Silva .40 1.00
333 Ross Gload .40 1.00
334 Josh Phelps .40 1.00
335 Mike Maroth .40 1.00
336 Guillermo Mota .40 1.00
337 Chris Burke .40 1.00
338 David DeJesus .40 1.00
339 Jose Lima .40 1.00
340 Cristian Guzman .40 1.00
341 Nick Johnson .40 1.00
342 Victor Zambrano .40 1.00
343 Rod Barajas .40 1.00
344 Damian Miller .40 1.00
345 Chase Utley .60 1.50
346 Sean Burnett .40 1.00
347 David Wells .40 1.00
348 Dustan Mohr .40 1.00
349 Bobby Madritsch .40 1.00
350 Reed Johnson .40 1.00
351 R.A. Dickey .60 1.50
352 Scott Kazmir 1.00 2.50
353 Tony Womack .40 1.00
354 Tomas Perez .40 1.00
355 Esteban Loaiza .40 1.00
356 Tomokazu Ohka .40 1.00
357 Ramon Ortiz .40 1.00
358 Richie Sexson .40 1.00
359 J.D. Drew .40 1.00
360 Barry Bonds 1.50 4.00
361 Aramis Ramirez .40 1.00
362 Wily Mo Pena .40 1.00
363 Jeromy Burnitz .40 1.00
364 Nomar Garciaparra .60 1.50
365 Brandon Backe .40 1.00
366 Derek Lowe .40 1.00
367 Doug Davis .40 1.00
368 Joe Mauer .75 2.00
369 Endy Chavez .40 1.00
370 Bernie Williams .60 1.50
371 Jason Michaels .40 1.00
372 Craig Wilson .40 1.00
373 Ryan Klesko .40 1.00
374 Ray Durham .40 1.00
375 Jose Lopez .40 1.00
376 Jeff Suppan .40 1.00
377 David Bush .40 1.00
378 Marlon Byrd .40 1.00
379 Roy Oswalt .60 1.50
380 Rondell White .40 1.00
381 Troy Glaus .40 1.00
382 Scott Hairston .40 1.00
383 Chipper Jones 1.00 2.50
384 Daniel Cabrera .40 1.00
385 Jon Garland .40 1.00
386 Austin Kearns .40 1.00
387 Jake Westbrook .40 1.00
388 Aaron Miles .40 1.00
389 Omar Infante .40 1.00
390 Paul Lo Duca .40 1.00
391 Morgan Ensberg .40 1.00
392 Tony Graffanino .40 1.00
393 Milton Bradley .40 1.00
394 Keith Ginter .40 1.00
395 Justin Morneau .60 1.50
396 Tony Armas Jr. .40 1.00
397 Kevin Brown .40 1.00
398 Marco Scutaro .60 1.50
399 Tim Hudson .60 1.50
400 Pat Burrell .40 1.00
401 Jeff Cirillo .40 1.00
402 Larry Walker .60 1.50
403 Dewon Brazelton .40 1.00
404 Shigetoshi Hasegawa .40 1.00
405 Octavio Dotel .40 1.00
406 Michael Cuddyer .40 1.00
407 Junior Spivey .40 1.00
408 Zack Greinke 1.25 3.00
409 Roger Clemens 1.25 3.00
410 Chris Shelton .40 1.00
411 Ugueth Urbina .40 1.00
412 Rafael Betancourt .40 1.00
413 Willie Harris .40 1.00
414 Keith Foulke .40 1.00
415 Larry Bigbie .40 1.00
416 Paul Byrd .40 1.00
417 Troy Percival .40 1.00
418 Pedro Martinez .60 1.50
419 Matt Clement .40 1.00
420 Ryan Wagner .40 1.00
421 Jeff Francis .40 1.00
422 Jeff Conine .40 1.00
423 Wade Miller .40 1.00
424 Gavin Floyd .40 1.00
425 Kazuhisa Ishii .40 1.00
426 Victor Santos .40 1.00
427 Jacque Jones .40 1.00
428 Hideki Matsui 1.50 4.00
429 Cory Lidle .40 1.00
430 Jose Castillo .40 1.00
431 Alex Gonzalez .40 1.00
432 Kirk Rueter .40 1.00
433 Jolbert Cabrera .40 1.00
434 Erik Bedard .40 1.00
435 Ricky Ledee .40 1.00
436 Mark Hendrickson .40 1.00
437 Laynce Nix .40 1.00
438 Jason Frasor .40 1.00
439 Kevin Gregg .40 1.00
440 Derek Jeter 2.50 6.00
441 Jaret Wright .40 1.00
442 Edwin Jackson .40 1.00
443 Moises Alou .40 1.00
444 Aaron Rowand .40 1.00
445 Kazuhito Tadano .40 1.00
446 Luis Gonzalez .40 1.00
447 A.J. Burnett .40 1.00
448 Jeff Bagwell .60 1.50
449 Brad Penny .40 1.00
450 Corey Koskie .40 1.00
451 Mark Ellis .40 1.00
452 Hector Luna .40 1.00
453 Miguel Olivo .40 1.00
454 Scott Rolen .60 1.50
455 Ricardo Rodriguez .40 1.00
456 Eric Hinske .40 1.00
457 Tim Salmon .40 1.00
458 Adam LaRoche .40 1.00
459 B.J. Ryan .40 1.00
460 Steve Finley .40 1.00
461 Joe Nathan .40 1.00
462 Vicente Padilla .40 1.00
463 Yadier Molina 20.00 50.00
464 Tino Martinez .60 1.50
465 Mark Teixeira .60 1.50
466 Kelvim Escobar .40 1.00
467 Pedro Feliz .40 1.00
468 Ryan Garko FY RC .40 1.00
469 Bobby Livingston FY RC .40 1.00
470 Yorman Bazardo FY RC .40 1.00
471 Mike Bourn FY RC 1.00 2.50
472 Andy LaRoche FY RC .40 1.00

2005 Topps Chrome Black Refractors

*BLACK 1-210/253-467: 1.5X TO 4X BASIC
*BLACK 211-220/468-472: 1.5X TO 4X BASIC
1-220 SER.1 ODDS 1:10 H, 1:20 R
253-472 SER.2 ODDS 1:1 MINI BOX, 1:36 R
1-220/253-472 PRINT RUN 225 #'d SETS
*BLACK AU 221-252: 1X TO 2.5X BASIC AU
221-234 SER.1 ODDS 1:250 H, 1:291 R
235-252 SER.2 ODDS 1:12 MINI BOX, 1:508 R
221-252 PRINT RUN 200 SERIAL #'d SETS

2005 Topps Chrome Red X-Fractors

*RED XF 1-210/253-467: 6X TO 15X BASIC
1-220 SER.1 ODDS 1:50 HOBBY
221-234 SER.1 AU ODDS 1:779 HOBBY
235-252 SER.2 AU ODDS 1:91 MINI BOX
235-252 SER.2 AU ODDS 1:4042 RETAIL
253-472 SER.2 ODDS 1:3 BOX LOADER
STATED PRINT RUN 25 SERIAL #'d SETS
211-252/468-472 NO PRICING AVAILABLE
360 Barry Bonds 25.00 60.00

2005 Topps Chrome Refractors

*REF 1-210/253-467: 1X TO 2.5X BASIC
*REF 211-220/468-472: 1X TO 2.5X BASIC
1-220 SER.1 ODDS 1:6 H, 1:4 R
253-472 SER.2 ODDS 2 PER MINI BOX, 1:5 R
*REF AU 221-252: .5X TO 1.2X BASIC AU
221-234 SER.1 AU ODDS 1:100 H, 1:118 R
235-252 SER.2 AU ODDS 1:5 MINI BOXES
235-252 SER.2 AU ODDS 1:199 RETAIL
221-252 PRINT RUN 500 SERIAL #'d SETS

2005 Topps Chrome A-Rod Throwbacks

COMPLETE SET (4) 3.00 8.00
COMMON CARD (1-4) 1.25 3.00
SER.2 ODDS 2 PER MINI BOX, 1:5 R
*BLACK REF: 2X TO 5X BASIC
BLACK REF SER.2 ODDS 1:14 BOX LOADER
BLACK REF PRINT RUN 225 #'d SETS
GOLD SUPER SER.2 ODDS 1:2968 BOX LDR
GOLD SUPER PRINT RUN 1 #'d SET
NO GOLD SUPER PRICING AVAILABLE
*RED XF: 6X TO 15X BASIC
RED XF SER.2 ODDS 1:124 BOX LOADER
RED XF PRINT RUN 25 #'d SETS
*REFRACTOR: 1X TO 2.5X BASIC
REFRACTOR SER.2 ODDS 1:3 BOX LOADER
1 Alex Rodriguez 1994 1.00 2.50
2 Alex Rodriguez 1995 1.00 2.50
3 Alex Rodriguez 1996 1.00 2.50
4 Alex Rodriguez 1997 1.00 2.50

2005 Topps Chrome Dem Bums Autograph

SERIES 1 ODDS 1:1816 H, 1:7270 R
STATED PRINT RUN 50 SETS
CARDS ARE NOT SERIAL-NUMBERED
PRINT RUN INFO PROVIDED BY TOPPS
CE Carl Erskine 10.00 25.00
CL Clem Labine 30.00 60.00
DS Duke Snider 40.00 80.00
DZ Don Zimmer 30.00 60.00
JP Johnny Podres 10.00 25.00

2005 Topps Chrome the Game Relics

SER.1 GROUP A ODDS 1:15 BOX-LOADER
SER.1 GROUP B ODDS 1:2 BOX-LOADER
AR Alex Rodriguez Bat A 6.00 15.00
AS Alfonso Soriano Uni B 3.00 8.00
JB Jeff Bagwell Uni B 4.00 10.00
JP Jorge Posada Uni B 4.00 10.00
JS John Smoltz Uni B 4.00 10.00
MP Mark Prior Jsy B 4.00 10.00
MPI Mike Piazza Jsy B 4.00 10.00
MY Michael Young Bat A 3.00 8.00
SS Sammy Sosa Jsy B 4.00 10.00
TH Torii Hunter Jsy B 3.00 8.00
WB Wade Boggs Uni B 4.00 10.00

2005 Topps Chrome the Game Patch Relics

*3-COLOR ADD: ADD 20% PREMIUM
SER.1 ODDS 1:8 BOX-LOADER
STATED PRINT RUN 70 SETS
CARDS ARE NOT SERIAL-NUMBERED
PRINT RUN INFO PROVIDED BY TOPPS
AD1 Adam Dunn Pose 6.00 15.00
AD2 Adam Dunn Fielding 6.00 15.00
AP Albert Pujols 20.00 50.00
AR Alex Rodriguez 15.00 40.00
BB Bret Boone 6.00 15.00
CJ Chipper Jones 10.00 25.00
CS C.C. Sabathia 6.00 15.00
DW Dontrelle Willis 6.00 15.00
FT Frank Thomas 10.00 25.00
HN Hideo Nomo 10.00 25.00
JB Jeff Bagwell 10.00 25.00
JBE Josh Beckett 6.00 15.00
KI Kazuhisa Ishii 6.00 15.00
KW Kerry Wood 6.00 15.00
LB Lance Berkman 6.00 15.00
ML Mike Lowell 6.00 15.00
MO Maggio Ordonez 6.00 15.00
MPI Mike Piazza 10.00 25.00
MT Mark Teixeira 10.00 25.00
PL Paul Lo Duca 6.00 15.00
PM Pedro Martinez 10.00 25.00
SS Sammy Sosa 10.00 25.00
TG Troy Glaus 6.00 15.00
TH Todd Helton 10.00 25.00

2005 Topps Chrome Update

COMPLETE SET (237) 200.00 300.00
COMP.SET w/o SP's (220) 40.00 80.00
COM (1-85/216-220) .30 .75
COMMON (86-105) .30 .75
COM (14/65/106-215) .30 .75
COMMON (196-215) .75 2.00
SEMIS 196-215 1.25 3.00
UNLISTED 196-215 2.00 5.00
COMMON AU (221-237) 4.00 10.00
221-237 GROUP A ODDS 1:25 H, 1:49 R
221-237 GROUP B ODDS 1:29 H, 1:57 R
1-220 PLATE ODDS 1:347 H
221-237 PLATE AU ODDS 1:4857 H
PLATE PRINT RUN 1 SET PER COLOR
BLACK-CYAN-MAGENTA-YELLOW ISSUED
NO PLATE PRICING DUE TO SCARCITY
1 Sammy Sosa .75 2.00
2 Jeff Francoeur .75 2.00
3 Tony Clark .30 .75
4 Michael Tucker .30 .75
5 Mike Matheny .30 .75
6 Eric Young .30 .75
7 Jose Valentin .30 .75
8 Matt Lawton .30 .75
9 Juan Rivera .30 .75
10 Shawn Green .30 .75
11 Aaron Boone .30 .75
12 Woody Williams .30 .75
13 Brad Wilkerson .30 .75
14 Anthony Reyes RC .50 1.25
15 Gustavo Chacin .30 .75
16 Michael Restovich .30 .75
17 Humberto Quintero .30 .75
18 Matt Ginter .30 .75
19 Scott Podsednik .30 .75
20 Byung-Hyun Kim .30 .75
21 Orlando Hernandez .30 .75
22 Mark Grudzielanek .30 .75
23 Jody Gerut .30 .75
24 Adrian Beltre .75 2.00
25 Scott Schoeneweis .30 .75
26 Marlon Anderson .30 .75
27 Jason Vargas .30 .75
28 Claudio Vargas .30 .75
29 Jason Kendall .30 .75
30 Aaron Small .30 .75
31 Juan Cruz .30 .75
32 Placido Polanco .30 .75
33 Jorge Sosa .30 .75
34 John Olerud .30 .75
35 Ryan Langerhans .30 .75
36 Randy Winn .30 .75
37 Zach Duke .30 .75
38 Garrett Atkins .30 .75
39 Al Leiter .30 .75
40 Shawn Chacon .30 .75
41 Mark DeRosa .30 .75
42 Miguel Ojeda .30 .75
43 A.J. Pierzynski .30 .75
44 Carlos Lee .30 .75
45 LaTroy Hawkins .30 .75
46 Nick Green .30 .75
47 Shawn Estes .30 .75
48 Eli Marrero .30 .75
49 Jeff Kent .30 .75
50 Joe Randa .30 .75
51 Jose Hernandez .30 .75
52 Joe Blanton .30 .75
53 Huston Street .30 .75
54 Marlon Byrd .30 .75
55 Alex Sanchez .30 .75
56 Livan Hernandez .30 .75
57 Chris Young .50 1.25
58 Brad Eldred .30 .75
59 Terrence Long .30 .75
60 Phil Nevin .30 .75
61 Kyle Farnsworth .30 .75
62 Jon Lieber .30 .75
63 Antonio Alfonseca .30 .75
64 Tony Graffanino .30 .75
65 Tadahito Iguchi RC .50 1.25
66 Brad Thompson .30 .75
67 Jose Vidro .30 .75
68 Jason Phillips .30 .75
69 Carl Pavano .30 .75
70 Pokey Reese .30 .75
71 Jerome Williams .30 .75
72 Kazuhisa Ishii .30 .75
73 Felix Hernandez 1.00 2.50
74 Edgar Renteria .30 .75
75 Mike Myers .30 .75
76 Jeff Cirillo .30 .75
77 Endy Chavez .30 .75
78 Jose Guillen .30 .75
79 Ugueth Urbina .30 .75
80 Zach Day .30 .75
81 Javier Vazquez .30 .75
82 Willy Taveras .30 .75
83 Mark Mulder .30 .75
84 Vinny Castilla .30 .75
85 Russ Adams .30 .75
86 Homer Bailey PROS .30 .75
87 Ervin Santana PROS .30 .75
88 Bill Bray PROS .30 .75
89 Thomas Diamond PROS .30 .75
90 Trevor Plouffe PROS .75 2.00
91 James Houser PROS .30 .75
92 Jake Stevens PROS .30 .75
93 Anthony Whittington PROS .30 .75
94 Philip Hughes PROS .75 2.00
95 Greg Golson PROS .30 .75
96 Paul Maholm PROS .30 .75
97 Carlos Quentin PROS .50 1.25
98 Dan Johnson PROS .30 .75
99 Mark Rogers PROS .30 .75
100 Neil Walker PROS .50 1.25
101 Omar Quintanilla PROS .30 .75
102 Blake DeWitt PROS .50 1.25
103 Taylor Tankersley PROS .30 .75
104 David Murphy PROS .50 1.25
105 Chris Lambert PROS .30 .75
106 Drew Anderson FY RC .30 .75
107 Luis Hernandez FY RC .30 .75
108 Jim Burt FY RC .30 .75
109 Mike Morse FY RC 1.00 2.50
110 Elliot Johnson FY RC .30 .75
111 C.J. Smith FY RC .30 .75
112 Casey McGehee FY RC .50 1.25
113 Brian Miller FY RC .30 .75
114 Chris Vines FY RC .30 .75
115 D.J. Houlton FY RC .30 .75
116 Chuck Tiffany FY RC .75 2.00
117 Humberto Sanchez FY RC .50 1.25
118 Baltazar Lopez FY RC .30 .75
119 Russ Martin FY RC 1.00 2.50
120 Dana Eveland FY RC .30 .75
121 Johan Silva FY RC .30 .75
122 Adam Harben FY RC .30 .75
123 Brian Bannister FY RC .50 1.25
124 Adam Boeve FY RC .30 .75
125 Thomas Oldham FY RC .30 .75
126 Cody Haerther FY RC .30 .75
127 Dan Santin FY RC .30 .75
128 Daniel Haigwood FY RC .30 .75
129 Craig Tatum FY RC .30 .75
130 Martin Prado FY RC 2.00 5.00
131 Errol Simonitsch FY RC .30 .75
132 Lorenzo Scott FY RC .30 .75
133 Hayden Penn FY RC .30 .75
134 Heath Totten FY RC .30 .75
135 Nick Masset FY RC .30 .75
136 Pedro Lopez FY RC .30 .75
137 Ben Harrison FY .30 .75
138 Mike Spidale FY RC .30 .75
139 Jeremy Harts FY RC .30 .75
140 Danny Zell FY RC .30 .75
141 Kevin Collins FY RC .30 .75
142 Tony Arnerich FY RC .30 .75
143 Matt Albers FY RC .30 .75
144 Ricky Barrett FY RC .30 .75
145 Hernan Iribarren FY RC .30 .75
146 Sean Tracey FY RC .30 .75
147 Jerry Owens FY RC .30 .75
148 Steve Nelson FY RC .30 .75
149 Brandon McCarthy FY RC .50 1.25
150 David Shepard FY RC .30 .75
151 Steven Bondurant FY RC .30 .75
152 Billy Sadler FY RC .30 .75
153 Ryan Feierabend FY RC .30 .75
154 Stuart Pomeranz FY RC .30 .75
155 Shaun Marcum FY .75 2.00
156 Erik Schindewolf FY RC .30 .75
157 Stefan Bailie FY RC .30 .75
158 Mike Esposito FY RC .30 .75
159 Buck Coats FY RC .30 .75
160 Andy Sides FY RC .30 .75
161 Micah Schnurstein FY RC .30 .75
162 Jesse Gutierrez FY RC .30 .75
163 Jake Postlewait FY RC .30 .75
164 Willy Mota FY RC .30 .75
165 Ryan Speier FY RC .30 .75
166 Frank Mata FY RC .30 .75
167 Jair Jurrjens FY RC 1.50 4.00
168 Nick Touchstone FY RC .30 .75
169 Matthew Kemp FY RC 1.50 4.00
170 Vinny Rottino FY RC .30 .75
171 J.B. Thurmond FY RC .30 .75
172 Kelvin Pichardo FY RC .30 .75
173 Scott Mitchinson FY RC .30 .75
174 Darwinson Salazar FY RC .30 .75
175 George Kottaras FY RC .50 1.25
176 Kenny Durost FY RC .30 .75
177 Jonathan Sanchez FY RC 1.25 3.00
178 Brandon Moorhead FY RC .30 .75
179 Kennard Bibbs FY RC .30 .75
180 David Gassner FY RC .30 .75
181 Micah Furtado FY RC .30 .75
182 Ismael Ramirez FY RC .30 .75
183 Carlos Gonzalez FY RC 2.50 6.00
184 Brandon Sing FY RC .30 .75
185 Jason Motte FY RC .50 1.25
186 Chuck James FY RC .75 2.00
187 Andy Santana FY RC .30 .75
188 Manny Parra FY RC .75 2.00
189 Chris B.Young FY RC 1.00 2.50
190 Juan Senreiso FY RC .30 .75
191 Franklin Morales FY RC .50 1.25
192 Jared Gothreaux FY RC .30 .75
193 Jayce Tingler FY RC .30 .75
194 Matt Brown FY RC .30 .75
195 Frank Diaz FY RC .30 .75
196 Stephen Drew FY RC 2.50 6.00
197 Jered Weaver FY RC 4.00 10.00
198 Ryan Braun FY RC 6.00 15.00
199 John Mayberry Jr. FY RC 2.00 5.00
200 Aaron Thompson FY RC 1.25 3.00
201 Ben Copeland FY RC .75 2.00
202 Jacoby Ellsbury FY RC 6.00 15.00
203 Garrett Olson FY RC .75 2.00
204 Cliff Pennington FY RC .75 2.00
205 Colby Rasmus FY RC 2.00 5.00
206 Chris Volstad FY RC 2.00 5.00
207 Ricky Romero FY RC 1.25 3.00
208 Ryan Zimmerman FY RC 4.00 10.00
209 C.J. Henry FY RC 1.25 3.00
210 Nelson Cruz FY RC 10.00 25.00
211 Josh Wall FY RC 1.25 3.00
212 Nick Webber FY RC .75 2.00
213 Paul Kelly FY RC .75 2.00
214 Kyle Winters FY RC .75 2.00
215 Mitch Boggs FY RC .75 2.00
216 Craig Biggio HL .50 1.25
217 Greg Maddux HL 1.00 2.50
218 Bobby Abreu HL .30 .75
219 Alex Rodriguez HL 1.00 2.50
220 Trevor Hoffman HL .50 1.25
221 Trevor Bell FY AU A RC 4.00 10.00
222 Jay Bruce FY AU A RC 10.00 25.00
223 Travis Buck FY AU B RC 4.00 10.00
224 Cesar Carrillo FY AU B RC 4.00 10.00
225 Mike Costanzo FY AU A RC 4.00 10.00
226 Brent Cox FY AU A RC 4.00 10.00
227 Matt Garza FY AU A RC 5.00 12.00
228 Josh Geer FY AU A RC 4.00 10.00
229 Tyler Greene FY AU A RC 4.00 10.00
230 Eli Iorg FY AU A RC 4.00 10.00
231 Craig Italiano FY AU B RC 4.00 10.00
232 Beau Jones FY AU A RC 4.00 10.00
233 M.McCormick FY AU B RC 4.00 10.00
234 A.McCutchen FY AU B RC 30.00 80.00
235 Micah Owings FY AU B RC 5.00 12.00
236 Cesar Ramos FY AU B RC 4.00 10.00
237 Chaz Roe FY AU A RC 4.00 10.00

2005 Topps Chrome Update Refractors

*REF 1-85: 1.25X TO 3X BASIC
*REF 86-105: 1.25X TO 3X BASIC
*REF 14/65/106-215: 1X TO 2.5X BASIC
*REF 216-220: 2X TO 5X BASIC
1-220 ODDS 1:5 HOBBY, 1:5 RETAIL
*REF AU 221-237: .6X TO 1.5X BASIC AU
221-237 AU ODDS 1:53 H, 1:115 R
221-237 AU PRINT RUN 500 #'d SETS

2005 Topps Chrome Update Black Refractors

*BLACK 1-85: 2X TO 5X BASIC
*BLACK 86-105: 2X TO 5X BASIC
*BLACK 14/65/106-215: 1.5X TO 4X BASIC
*BLACK 216-220: 2.5X TO 6X BASIC
1-220 ODDS 1:10 HOBBY, 1:19 RETAIL
1-220 PRINT RUN 250 #'d SETS
*BLACK AU 221-237: 1X TO 2.5X BASIC AU
221-237 AU ODDS 1:140 H, 1:279 R
221-237 AU PRINT RUN 200 #'d SETS
222 Jay Bruce FY AU 50.00 120.00

2005 Topps Chrome Update Red X-Fractors

*RED 1-85: 4X TO 10X BASIC
*RED 86-105: 4X TO 10X BASIC
*RED 14/65/106-215: 5X TO 12X BASIC
*RED 216-220: 5X TO 12X BASIC
1-220 ODDS 1:5 HOBBY
1-220 PRINT RUN 65 #'d SETS
221-237 AU ODDS 1:766 HOBBY
221-237 AU PRINT RUN 25 #'d SETS
221-237 NO PRICING DUE TO SCARCITY
183 Carlos Gonzalez FY 100.00 175.00
198 Ryan Braun FY 40.00 100.00

2005 Topps Chrome Update Barry Bonds Home Run History

COMPLETE SET (29) 20.00 50.00
COMPLETE SERIES 1 (15) 12.50 30.00
COMPLETE SERIES 2 (14) 8.00 20.00
COMMON CARD 1.25 3.00
1-350 ODDS 1:12 HOBBY, 1:23 RETAIL
375-700 ODDS 1:6 HOBBY, 1:23 RETAIL
1-350 PLATE ODDS 1:347 H
375-700 PLATE ODDS 1:300 BOX LDR
PLATE PRINT RUN 1 SET PER COLOR
BLACK-CYAN-MAGENTA-YELLOW ISSUED
*REF: 1.25X TO 3X BASIC
1-350 REF ODDS 1:71 H, 1:141 R
375-700 REF ODDS 1:70 H, 1:350 R
375-700 REF PRINT RUN 500 #'d SETS
*BLACK REF: 2X TO 5X BASIC
1-350 BLACK REF.ODDS 1:178 H, 1:365 R
375-700 BLACK REF.ODDS 1:175 H, 1:950 R
BLACK REF.PRINT RUN 200 #'d SETS
*BLUE: 4X TO 10X BASIC
375-700 BLUE REF ODDS 1:300 RETAIL
BLUE REF.PRINT RUN 100 #'d SETS
1-350 GOLD SUPER ODDS 1:22,548 H
375-700 GOLD SUP.ODDS 1:1234 BOX LDR
GOLD SUPER PRINT RUN 1 #'d SET
NO GOLD SUP.PRICING DUE TO SCARCITY
*RED X-F: 6X TO 15X BASIC
1-350 RED X-F ODDS 1:872 H
375-700 RED X-F ODDS 1:48 BOX LDR
RED X-F PRINT RUN 25 #'d SETS
1-350 ISSUED IN '05 CHROME UPDATE
375-700 ISSUED IN '06 CHROME

2006 Topps Chrome

AU 331-354 ODDS 1:15 HOBBY
JOHJIMA AU ODDS 1:1650 HOBBY
1-330 PLATES 1:25 HOBBY BOX LDR
331-354 AU PLATES 1:324 HOBBY BOX LDR
PLATE PRINT RUN 1 SET PER COLOR
BLACK-CYAN-MAGENTA-YELLOW ISSUED
NO PLATE PRICING DUE TO SCARCITY
1 Alex Rodriguez .75 2.00
2 Garrett Atkins .25 .60
3 Carl Crawford .40 1.00
4 Clint Barmes .25 .60
5 Tadahito Iguchi .25 .60
6 Brian Roberts .25 .60
7 Mickey Mantle 2.00 5.00
8 David Wright .50 1.25
9 Jeremy Reed .25 .60
10 Bobby Abreu .25 .60
11 Lance Berkman .40 1.00
12 Jonny Gomes .25 .60
13 Jason Marquis .25 .60
14 Chipper Jones .60 1.50
15 Jon Garland .25 .60
16 Brad Wilkerson .25 .60
17 Rickie Weeks .25 .60
18 Jorge Posada .40 1.00
19 Greg Maddux .75 2.00
20 Jeff Francis .25 .60
21 Felipe Lopez .25 .60
22 Dan Johnson .25 .60
23 Manny Ramirez .60 1.50
24 Joe Mauer .40 1.00
25 Randy Winn .25 .60
26 Pedro Feliz .25 .60
27 Kenny Rogers .25 .60
28 Rocco Baldelli .25 .60
29 Nomar Garciaparra .40 1.00
30 Carlos Lee .25 .60
31 Tom Glavine .40 1.00
32 Craig Biggio .40 1.00
33 Steve Finley .25 .60
34 Eric Gagne .25 .60
35 Dallas McPherson .25 .60
36 Mark Kotsay .25 .60
37 Kerry Wood .25 .60
38 Huston Street .25 .60
39 Hank Blalock .25 .60
40 Brad Radke .25 .60
41 Chien-Ming Wang .40 1.00
42 Mark Buehrle .40 1.00
43 Andy Pettitte .40 1.00
44 Bernie Williams .40 1.00
45 Victor Martinez .40 1.00
46 Darin Erstad .25 .60
47 Gustavo Chacin .25 .60
48 Carlos Guillen .25 .60
49 Lyle Overbay .25 .60
50 Barry Bonds 1.00 2.50
51 Nook Logan .25 .60
52 Mark Teahen .25 .60
53 Mike Lamb .25 .60
54 Jayson Werth .40 1.00
55 Mariano Rivera .75 2.00
56 Julio Lugo .25 .60
57 Adam Dunn .40 1.00
58 Troy Percival .25 .60
59 Chad Tracy .25 .60
60 Edgar Renteria .25 .60
61 Jason Giambi .25 .60
62 Justin Morneau .40 1.00
63 Carlos Delgado .25 .60
64 John Buck .25 .60
65 Shannon Stewart .25 .60
66 Mike Cameron .25 .60
67 Richie Sexson .25 .60
68 Russ Adams .25 .60
69 Josh Beckett .25 .60
70 Ryan Freel .25 .60
71 Victor Zambrano .25 .60
72 Ronnie Belliard .25 .60
73 Brian Giles .25 .60
74 Randy Wolf .25 .60
75 Robinson Cano .40 1.00
76 Joe Blanton .25 .60
77 Esteban Loaiza .25 .60
78 Troy Glaus .25 .60
79 Matt Clement .25 .60
80 Geoff Jenkins .25 .60
81 Roy Oswalt .40 1.00
82 A.J. Pierzynski .25 .60
83 Pedro Martinez .40 1.00
84 Roger Clemens .75 2.00
85 Jack Wilson .25 .60
86 Mike Piazza .60 1.50
87 Paul Lo Duca .25 .60
88 Jeff Bagwell .40 1.00
89 Carlos Zambrano .40 1.00
90 Brandon Claussen .25 .60
91 Travis Hafner .25 .60
92 Chris Shelton .25 .60
93 Rafael Furcal .25 .60
94 Frank Thomas .60 1.50
95 Noah Lowry .25 .60
96 Jhonny Peralta .25 .60
97 Vernon Wells .25 .60
98 Jorge Cantu .25 .60
99 Willy Taveras .25 .60
100 Ivan Rodriguez .40 1.00
101 Jose Reyes .40 1.00
102 Barry Zito .40 1.00
103 Mark Teixeira .40 1.00
104 Chone Figgins .25 .60
105 Todd Helton .40 1.00
106 Tim Wakefield .40 1.00
107 Mike Maroth .25 .60
108 Johnny Damon .40 1.00
109 David DeJesus .25 .60
110 Ryan Klesko .25 .60
111 Nick Johnson .25 .60
112 Freddy Garcia .25 .60
113 Torii Hunter .25 .60
114 Mike Sweeney .25 .60
115 Scott Rolen .40 1.00
116 Jim Thome .40 1.00
117 Adam Kennedy .25 .60
118 Albert Pujols .75 2.00
119 Kazuo Matsui .25 .60
120 Zack Greinke .60 1.50
121 Jimmy Rollins .40 1.00
122 Edgardo Alfonzo .25 .60
123 Billy Wagner .25 .60
124 B.J. Ryan .25 .60
125 Orlando Hudson .25 .60
126 Preston Wilson .25 .60
127 Melvin Mora .25 .60
128 Alfonso Soriano .40 1.00
129 Javy Lopez .25 .60
130 Wilson Betemit .25 .60
131 Garret Anderson .25 .60
132 Jason Bay .25 .60
133 Adam LaRoche .25 .60
134 C.C. Sabathia .40 1.00
135 Bartolo Colon .25 .60
136 Ichiro Suzuki .75 2.00
137 Jim Edmonds .40 1.00
138 David Eckstein .25 .60
139 Cristian Guzman .25 .60
140 Jeff Kent .25 .60
141 Chris Capuano .25 .60
142 Cliff Floyd .25 .60
143 Zach Duke .25 .60
144 Matt Morris .25 .60
145 Jose Vidro .25 .60
146 David Wells .25 .60
147 John Smoltz .60 1.50
148 Felix Hernandez .40 1.00
149 Orlando Cabrera .25 .60
150 Mark Prior .40 1.00

151 Ted Lilly .25 .60
152 Michael Young .25 .60
153 Livan Hernandez .25 .60
154 Yadier Molina .75 2.00
155 Eric Chavez .25 .60
156 Miguel Batista .25 .60
157 Ben Sheets .25 .60
158 Oliver Perez .25 .60
159 Doug Davis .25 .60
160 Andruw Jones .25 .60
161 Hideki Matsui .60 1.50
162 Reggie Sanders .25 .60
163 Joe Nathan .25 .60
164 John Lackey .40 1.00
165 Matt Murton .25 .60
166 Grady Sizemore .40 1.00
167 Brad Thompson .25 .60
168 Kevin Millwood .25 .60
169 Orlando Hernandez .25 .60
170 Mark Mulder .25 .60
171 Chase Utley .40 1.00
172 Moises Alou .25 .60
173 Wily Mo Pena .25 .60
174 Brian McCann .25 .60
175 Jermaine Dye .25 .60
176 Ryan Madson .25 .60
177 Aramis Ramirez .25 .60
178 Khalil Greene .25 .60
179 Mike Hampton .25 .60
180 Mike Mussina .40 1.00
181 Rich Harden .25 .60
182 Woody Williams .25 .60
183 Chris Carpenter .40 1.00
184 Brady Clark .25 .60
185 Luis Gonzalez .25 .60
186 Raul Ibanez .40 1.00
187 Magglio Ordonez .40 1.00
188 Adrian Beltre .60 1.50
189 Marcus Giles .25 .60
190 Odalis Perez .25 .60
191 Derek Jeter 1.50 4.00
192 Jason Schmidt .25 .60
193 Toby Hall .25 .60
194 Danny Haren .25 .60
195 Tim Hudson .40 1.00
196 Jake Peavy .25 .60
197 Casey Blake .25 .60
198 J.D. Drew .25 .60
199 Ervin Santana .25 .60
200 J.J. Hardy .25 .60
201 Austin Kearns .25 .60
202 Pat Burrell .25 .60
203 Jason Vargas .25 .60
204 Ryan Howard .50 1.25
205 Joe Crede .25 .60
206 Vladimir Guerrero .40 1.00
207 Roy Halladay .40 1.00
208 David Dellucci .25 .60
209 Brandon Webb .40 1.00
210 Ryan Church .25 .60
211 Miguel Tejada .40 1.00
212 Mark Loretta .25 .60
213 Kevin Youkilis .25 .60
214 Jon Lieber .25 .60
215 Miguel Cabrera .60 1.50
216 A.J. Burnett .25 .60
217 David Bell .25 .60
218 Eric Byrnes .25 .60
219 Lance Niekro .25 .60
220 Shawn Green .25 .60
221 Ken Griffey Jr. 1.25 3.00
222 Johnny Estrada .25 .60
223 Omar Vizquel .40 1.00
224 Gary Sheffield .25 .60
225 Brad Halsey .25 .60
226 Aaron Cook .25 .60
227 David Ortiz .60 1.50
228 Scott Kazmir .40 1.00
229 Dustin McGowan .25 .60
230 Gregg Zaun .25 .60
231 Carlos Beltran .40 1.00
232 Bob Wickman .25 .60
233 Brett Myers .25 .60
234 Casey Kotchman .25 .60
235 Jeff Francoeur .60 1.50
236 Paul Konerko .40 1.00
237 Juan Rivera .25 .60
238 Bobby Crosby .25 .60
239 Derrek Lee .25 .60
240 Curt Schilling .40 1.00
241 Jake Westbrook .25 .60
242 Dontrelle Willis .25 .60
243 Brad Lidge .25 .60
244 Randy Johnson .60 1.50
245 Nick Swisher .40 1.00
246 Johan Santana .40 1.00
247 Jeremy Bonderman .25 .60
248 Ramon Hernandez .25 .60
249 Mike Lowell .25 .60
250 Javier Vazquez .25 .60
251 Jose Contreras .25 .60
252 Aubrey Huff .25 .60
253 Kenny Rogers AW .25 .60
254 Mark Teixeira AW .40 1.00
255 Orlando Hudson AW .25 .60
256 Derek Jeter AW 1.50 4.00
257 Eric Chavez AW .25 .60
258 Torii Hunter AW .25 .60
259 Vernon Wells AW .25 .60
260 Ichiro Suzuki AW .75 2.00
261 Greg Maddux AW .75 2.00
262 Mike Matheny AW .25 .60
263 Derrek Lee AW .25 .60
264 Luis Castillo AW .25 .60
265 Omar Vizquel AW .40 1.00
266 Mike Lowell AW .25 .60
267 Andruw Jones AW .25 .60
268 Jim Edmonds AW .40 1.00
269 Bobby Abreu AW .25 .60
270 Bartolo Colon AW .25 .60
271 Chris Carpenter AW .40 1.00
272 Alex Rodriguez AW .75 2.00
273 Albert Pujols AW .75 2.00
274 Huston Street AW .25 .60
275 Ryan Howard AW .50 1.25
276 Chris Denorfia (RC) .40 1.00
277 John Van Benschoten (RC) .40 1.00
278 Russ Martin (RC) .60 1.50
279 Fausto Carmona (RC) .40 1.00
280 Freddie Bynum (RC) .40 1.00
281 Kelly Shoppach (RC) .40 1.00
282 Chris Demaria RC .40 1.00
283 Jordan Tata RC .40 1.00
284 Ryan Zimmerman (RC) 1.25 3.00
285a Kenji Johjima RC 1.00 2.50
285b Kenji Johjima AU 5.00 12.00
286 Ruddy Lugo (RC) .40 1.00
287 Tommy Murphy (RC) .40 1.00
288 Bobby Livingston (RC) .40 1.00
289 Anderson Hernandez (RC) .40 1.00
290 Brian Slocum (RC) .40 1.00
291 Sendy Rleal RC .40 1.00
292 Ryan Spilborghs (RC) .40 1.00
293 Brandon Fahey RC .40 1.00
294 Jason Kubel (RC) .40 1.00
295 James Loney (RC) .60 1.50
296 Jeremy Accardo RC .40 1.00
297 Fabio Castro RC .40 1.00
298 Matt Capps (RC) .40 1.00
299 Casey Janssen RC .40 1.00
300 Martin Prado (RC) .60 1.50
301 Ronny Paulino (RC) .40 1.00
302 Josh Barfield (RC) .40 1.00
303 Joel Zumaya (RC) 1.00 2.50
304 Matt Cain (RC) 2.50 6.00
305 Conor Jackson (RC) .60 1.50
306 Brian Anderson (RC) .40 1.00
307 Prince Fielder (RC) 2.00 5.00
308 Jeremy Hermida (RC) .40 1.00
309 Justin Verlander (RC) 3.00 8.00
310 Brian Bannister (RC) .40 1.00
311 Josh Willingham (RC) .60 1.50
312 John Rheinecker (RC) .40 1.00
313 Nick Markakis (RC) .75 2.00
314 Jonathan Papelbon (RC) 2.00 5.00
315 Mike Jacobs (RC) .40 1.00
316 Jose Capellan (RC) .40 1.00
317 Mike Napoli RC .60 1.50
318 Ricky Nolasco (RC) .40 1.00
319 Ben Johnson (RC) .40 1.00
320 Paul Maholm (RC) .40 1.00
321 Drew Meyer (RC) .40 1.00
322 Jeff Mathis (RC) .40 1.00
323 Fernando Nieve (RC) .40 1.00
324 John Koronka (RC) .40 1.00
325 Wil Nieves (RC) .40 1.00
326 Nate McLouth (RC) .40 1.00
327 Howie Kendrick (RC) .75 2.00
328 Sean Marshall (RC) .40 1.00
329 Brandon Watson (RC) .40 1.00
330 Skip Schumaker (RC) .40 1.00
331 Ryan Garko AU (RC) 4.00 10.00
332 Jason Bergmann AU RC 4.00 10.00
333 Chuck James AU (RC) 6.00 15.00
334 Adam Wainwright AU (RC) 10.00 25.00
335 Dan Ortmeier AU (RC) 4.00 10.00
336 Francisco Liriano AU (RC) 6.00 15.00
337 Craig Breslow AU RC 4.00 10.00
338 Darrell Rasner AU (RC) 4.00 10.00
339 Jason Botts AU (RC) 4.00 10.00
340 Ian Kinsler AU (RC) 8.00 20.00
341 Joey Devine AU RC 4.00 10.00
342 Miguel Perez AU (RC) 4.00 10.00
343 Scott Olsen AU (RC) 4.00 10.00
344 Tyler Johnson AU (RC) 4.00 10.00
345 Anthony Lerew AU (RC) 4.00 10.00
346 Nelson Cruz AU (RC) 40.00 100.00
347 Willie Eyre AU (RC) 4.00 10.00
348 Josh Johnson AU (RC) 6.00 15.00
349 Shaun Marcum AU (RC) 4.00 10.00
350 Dustin Nippert AU (RC) 4.00 10.00
351 Josh Wilson AU (RC) 4.00 10.00
352 Hanley Ramirez AU (RC) 5.00 12.00
353 Reggie Abercrombie AU (RC) 4.00 10.00
354 Dan Uggla AU (RC) 6.00 15.00

2006 Topps Chrome Refractors

*REF 1-275: .6X TO 1.5X BASIC
*REF 276-330: .6X TO 1.5X BASIC RC
1-330 STATED ODDS 1:4 H, 1:4 R
*REF AU 331-354: .5X TO 1.2X BASIC AU
331-354 AU ODDS 1:65 HOBBY
331-354 PRINT RUN 500 SERIAL #'d SETS
354 Dan Uggla AU 10.00 25.00

2006 Topps Chrome Black Refractors

*BLACK REF 1-275: 1.25X TO 3X BASIC
*BLACK REF 276-330: 1.25X TO 3X BASIC RC
1-330 STATED ODDS 1:6 H, 1:19 R
1-330 PRINT RUN 549 SERIAL #'d SETS
*BLK REF AU 331-354: .6X TO 1.5X BASIC AU
331-354 AU ODDS 1:162 HOBBY
331-354 PRINT RUN 200 SERIAL #'d SETS
354 Dan Uggla AU 12.50 30.00

2006 Topps Chrome Blue Refractors

*BLUE REF 1-275: 2X TO 5X BASIC
*BLUE REF 276-330: 2X TO 5X BASIC RC
STATED ODDS 1:8 RETAIL

2006 Topps Chrome Red Refractors

*RED REF 1-275: 4X TO 10X BASIC
*RED REF 276-330: 3X TO 8X BASIC RC
1-330 ODDS 1:2 HOBBY BOX LOADER
1-330 PRINT RUN 90 SERIAL #'d SETS
331-354 AU ODDS 1:52 HOBBY BOX LOADER
331-354 AU PRINT RUN 25 SERIAL #'d SETS
NO AU PRICING DUE TO SCARCITY

2006 Topps Chrome X-Fractors

*X-FRAC: 1-275: 1.5X TO 4X BASIC
*X-FRAC: 276-330: 1.5X TO 4X BASIC RC
STATED ODDS 1:6 RETAIL

2006 Topps Chrome Declaration of Independence

COMPLETE SET (56) 60.00 120.00
STATED ODDS 1:7 H, 1:7 R
*REF: .5X TO 1.2X BASIC
REF ODDS 1:11 HOBBY, 1:44 RETAIL
AC Abraham Clark 1.25 3.00
AM Arthur Middleton 1.25 3.00
BF Benjamin Franklin 2.00 5.00
BG Button Gwinnett 1.25 3.00
BH Benjamin Harrison 1.25 3.00
BR Benjamin Rush 1.25 3.00
CB Carter Braxton 1.25 3.00
CC Charles Carroll 1.25 3.00
CR Caesar Rodney 1.25 3.00
EG Elbridge Gerry 1.25 3.00
ER Edward Rutledge 1.25 3.00
FH Francis Hopkinson 1.25 3.00
FL Francis Lewis 1.25 3.00
FLL Francis Lightfoot Lee 1.25 3.00
GC George Clymer 1.25 3.00
GR George Ross 1.25 3.00
GRE George Read 1.25 3.00
GT George Taylor 1.25 3.00
GW George Walton 1.25 3.00
GWY George Wythe 1.25 3.00
JA John Adams 1.25 3.00
JB Josiah Bartlett 1.25 3.00
JH John Hancock 1.25 3.00
JHA John Hart 1.25 3.00
JHE Joseph Hewes 1.25 3.00
JM John Morton 1.25 3.00
JP John Penn 1.25 3.00
JS James Smith 1.25 3.00
JW James Wilson 1.25 3.00
JWI John Witherspoon 1.25 3.00
LH Lyman Hall 1.25 3.00
LM Lewis Morris 1.25 3.00
MT Matthew Thornton 1.25 3.00
OW Oliver Wolcott 1.25 3.00
PL Philip Livingston 1.25 3.00
RHL Richard Henry Lee 1.25 3.00
RM Robert Morris 1.25 3.00
RS Roger Sherman 1.25 3.00
RST Richard Stockton 1.25 3.00
RTP Robert Treat Paine 1.25 3.00
SA Samuel Adams 1.25 3.00
SC Samuel Chase 1.25 3.00
SH Stephen Hopkins 1.25 3.00
SHU Samuel Huntington 1.25 3.00
TH Thomas Heyward Jr. 1.25 3.00
TJ Thomas Jefferson 2.00 5.00
TL Thomas Lynch Jr. 1.25 3.00
TM Thomas McKean 1.25 3.00
TN Thomas Nelson Jr. 1.25 3.00
TS Thomas Stone 1.25 3.00
WE William Ellery 1.25 3.00
WF William Floyd 1.25 3.00
WH William Hooper 1.25 3.00
WP William Paca 1.25 3.00
WW William Whipple 1.25 3.00
WWI William Williams 1.25 3.00
HDR1 Header Card 1 1.25 3.00

2006 Topps Chrome Mantle Home Run History

COMPLETE SET (59) 40.00 80.00
COMP.07TCH SET (13) 8.00 20.00
COMP.07TCH SET (29) 15.00 40.00
COMP.08TCH SET (17) 8.00 20.00
COMMON CARD (1-59) 1.00 2.50
STATED 06 ODDS 1:6 HOBBY, 1:23 RETAIL
STATED 07 ODDS 1:8 HOBBY, 1:24 RETAIL
06 PLATE ODDS 1:300 HOBBY BOX LOADER
07 PLATE ODDS 1:116 HOBBY BOX LOADER
08 PLATE ODDS 1:1971 HOBBY
PLATE PRINT RUN 1 SET PER COLOR
BLACK-CYAN-MAGENTA-YELLOW ISSUED
NO PLATE PRICING DUE TO SCARCITY
*REF: .75X TO 2X BASIC
06 REF ODDS 1:70 HOBBY, 1:350 RETAIL
07 REF ODDS 1:27 HOBBY, 1:71 RETAIL
08 REF ODDS 1:31 HOBBY
REF PRINT RUN 500 SERIAL #'d SETS
08 REF PRINT RUN 400 SER.#'d SETS
*BLACK REF: 2.5X TO 6X BASIC
BLACK ODDS 1:175 HOBBY, 1:950 RETAIL
BLACK PRINT RUN 200 SERIAL #'d SETS
*06-07 BLUE REF: 3X TO 8X BASIC
*08 BLUE REF: 2.5X TO 6X BASIC
06 BLUE ODDS 1:300 RETAIL
07 BLUE ODDS 1:72 RETAIL
06-07 BLUE PRINT RUN 100 SERIAL #'d SETS
08 BLUE PRINT RUN 200 SERIAL #'d SETS
*COPPER REF: 3X TO 8X BASIC
COPPER ODDS 1:117 HOBBY
STATED PRINT RUN 100 SERIAL #'d SETS
06 GOLD SF ODDS 1:1234 HOBBY BOX LDR
07 GOLD SF ODDS
08 GOLD SF ODDS 1:7885 HOBBY
GOLD SF PRINT RUN 1 SERIAL #'d SET
NO GOLD SF PRICING DUE TO SCARCITY
*07 RED REF: 3X TO 8X BASIC
*08 RED REF: 12X TO 30X BASIC
07 RED REF ODDS
08 RED REF ODDS 1:315 HOBBY
07 RED REF PRINT RUN 99 SER.#'d SETS
08 RED REF PRINT RUN 25 SER.#'d SETS
*RED XF: 12X TO 30X BASIC
RED XF ODDS 1:48 HOBBY BOX LOADER
RED XF PRINT RUN 25 SERIAL #'d SETS
*WHITE REF: 2.5X TO 6X BASIC
07 WHITE REF ODDS 1:67 HOBBY, 1:185 RETAIL
WHITE REF PRINT RUN 200 SER.#'d SETS

2006 Topps Chrome Rookie Logos

ONE PER UPDATE HOB.BOX LOADER
STATED PRINT RUN 599 SER.#'d SETS
1 Ben Zobrist 6.00 15.00
2 Shane Komine 2.00 5.00
3 Casey Janssen 1.25 3.00
4 Kevin Frandsen 1.25 3.00
5 John Rheinecker 1.25 3.00
6 Matt Kemp 3.00 8.00
7 Scott Mathieson 1.25 3.00
8 Jered Weaver 4.00 10.00
9 Joel Guzman 1.25 3.00
10 Anibal Sanchez 1.25 3.00
11 Melky Cabrera 2.00 5.00
12 Howie Kendrick 2.50 6.00
13 Cole Hamels 4.00 10.00
14 Willy Aybar 1.25 3.00
15 James Shields 4.00 10.00
16 Kevin Thompson 1.25 3.00
17 Jon Lester 5.00 12.00
18 Stephen Drew 2.50 6.00
19 Andre Ethier 4.00 10.00
20 Jordan Tata 1.25 3.00
21 Mike Napoli 2.00 5.00
22 Kason Gabbard 1.25 3.00
23 Lastings Milledge 1.25 3.00
24 Erick Aybar 1.25 3.00
25 Fausto Carmona 1.25 3.00
26 Russ Martin 2.00 5.00
27 David Pauley 1.25 3.00
28 Andy Marte 1.25 3.00
29 Carlos Quentin 2.00 5.00
30 Franklin Gutierrez 1.25 3.00
31 Taylor Buchholz 1.25 3.00
32 Josh Johnson 3.00 8.00
33 Chad Billingsley 2.00 5.00
34 Kendry Morales 3.00 8.00
35 Adam Loewen 1.25 3.00
36 Yusmeiro Petit 1.25 3.00
37 Matt Albers 1.25 3.00
38 John Maine 2.00 5.00
39 Josh Willingham 2.00 5.00
40 Taylor Tankersley 1.25 3.00
41 Pat Neshek 12.00 30.00
42 Francisco Rosario 1.25 3.00
43 Matt Smith 2.00 5.00
44 Jonathan Sanchez 3.00 8.00
45 Chris Demaria 1.25 3.00
46 Manuel Corpas 1.25 3.00
47 Kevin Reese 1.25 3.00
48 Brent Clevlen 2.00 5.00
49 Anderson Hernandez 1.25 3.00
50 Chris Roberson 1.25 3.00

2006 Topps Chrome United States Constitution

COMPLETE SET (42) 30.00 60.00
STATED ODDS 1:15 H, 1:15 R
*REF: .5X TO 1.2X BASIC
REF ODDS 1:9 HOBBY, 1:36 RETAIL
AB Abraham Baldwin .75 2.00
AH Alexander Hamilton .75 2.00
BF Benjamin Franklin 1.25 3.00
CCP Charles Cotesworth Pinckney .75 2.00
CP Charles Pinckney .75 2.00
DB David Brearly .75 2.00
DC Daniel Carroll .75 2.00
DJ Daniel of St. Thomas Jenifer .75 2.00
GB Gunning Bedford Jr. .75 2.00
GC George Clymer .75 2.00
GM Gouverneur Morris .75 2.00
GR George Read .75 2.00
GW George Washington 1.25 3.00
HW Hugh Williamson .75 2.00
JB John Blair .75 2.00
JBR Jacob Broom .75 2.00
JD Jonathan Dayton .75 2.00
JDI John Dickinson .75 2.00
JI Jared Ingersoll .75 2.00
JL John Langdon .75 2.00
JM James Madison .75 2.00
JMC James McHenry .75 2.00
JR John Rutledge .75 2.00
JW James Wilson .75 2.00
NG Nicholas Gilman .75 2.00
NGO Nathaniel Gorham .75 2.00
PB Pierce Butler .75 2.00
RB Richard Bassett .75 2.00
RDS Richard Dobbs Spaight .75 2.00
RK Rufus King .75 2.00
RM Robert Morris .75 2.00
RS Roger Sherman .75 2.00
TF Thomas Fitzsimons .75 2.00
TM Thomas Mifflin .75 2.00
WB William Blount .75 2.00
WF William Few .75 2.00
WJ William Samuel Johnson .75 2.00
WL William Livingston .75 2.00
WP William Paterson .75 2.00
HDR1 Header Card 1 .75 2.00
HDR2 Header Card 2 .75 2.00
HDR3 Header Card 3 .75 2.00

2007 Topps Chrome

COMP.SET w/o AU's (330) 40.00 80.00
COMMON CARD .20 .50
COMMON ROOKIE .40 1.00
JAPANESE VARIATION UNLISTED 2.00 5.00
JAPANESE VARIATION ODDS 1:82 H
COMMON AUTO 3.00 8.00
AUTO ODDS 1:16 HOBBY, 1:122 RETAIL
PRINT.PLATE ODDS 1:36 HOBBY BOX LDR
VAR.PLATES 1:1943 HOBBY BOX LDR
AU PLATES 1:343 HOBBY BOX LDR
PLATE PRINT RUN 1 SET PER COLOR
BLACK-CYAN-MAGENTA-YELLOW ISSUED
NO PLATE PRICING DUE TO SCARCITY
EXCHANGE DEADLINE 07/31/09
1 Nick Swisher .30 .75
2 Bobby Abreu .20 .50
3 Edgar Renteria .20 .50
4 Mickey Mantle 1.50 4.00
5 Preston Wilson .20 .50
6 C.C. Sabathia .30 .75
7 Julio Lugo .20 .50
8 J.D. Drew .20 .50
9 Jason Varitek .50 1.25
10 Orlando Hernandez .20 .50
11 Corey Patterson .20 .50
12 Josh Bard .20 .50
13 Gary Matthews .20 .50
14 Jason Jennings .20 .50
15 Bronson Arroyo .20 .50
16 Andy Pettitte .30 .75
17 Ervin Santana .20 .50
18 Paul Konerko .30 .75
19 Adam LaRoche .20 .50
20 Jim Edmonds .30 .75
21 Derek Jeter 1.25 3.00
22 Aubrey Huff .20 .50
23 Andre Ethier .30 .75
24 Jeremy Sowers .20 .50
25 Miguel Cabrera .50 1.25
26 Carlos Lee .20 .50
27 Mike Piazza .50 1.25
28 Cole Hamels .40 1.00
29 Mark Loretta .20 .50
30 John Smoltz .50 1.25
31 Dan Uggla .20 .50
32 Lyle Overbay .20 .50
33 Michael Barrett .20 .50
34 Ivan Rodriguez .30 .75
35 Jake Westbrook .20 .50
36 Moises Alou .20 .50
37 Jered Weaver .30 .75
38 Lastings Milledge .30 .75
39 Austin Kearns .20 .50
40 Adam Loewen .20 .50
41 Josh Barfield .20 .50
42 Johan Santana .30 .75
43 Ian Kinsler .30 .75
44 Mike Lowell .20 .50
45 Scott Rolen .30 .75
46 Chipper Jones .50 1.25
47 Joe Crede .20 .50
48 Rafael Furcal .20 .50
49 Dave Bush .20 .50
50 Marcus Giles .20 .50
51 Joe Blanton .20 .50
52 Dontrelle Willis .20 .50
53 Scott Kazmir .30 .75
54 Jeff Kent .20 .50
55 Travis Hafner .20 .50
56 Ryan Garko .20 .50
57 Nick Markakis .40 1.00
58 Michael Cuddyer .20 .50
59 Jason Giambi .20 .50
60 Chone Figgins .20 .50
61 Carlos Delgado .20 .50
62 Aramis Ramirez .20 .50
63 Albert Pujols .60 1.50
64 Gary Sheffield .20 .50
65 Adrian Gonzalez .40 1.00
66 Prince Fielder .30 .75
67 Freddy Sanchez .20 .50
68 Jack Wilson .20 .50
69 Jake Peavy .20 .50
70 Javier Vazquez .20 .50
71 Todd Helton .30 .75
72 Bill Hall .20 .50
73 Jeremy Bonderman .20 .50
74 Rocco Baldelli .20 .50
75 Noah Lowry .20 .50
76 Justin Verlander .50 1.25
77 Mark Buehrle .30 .75
78 Hank Blalock .20 .50
79 Mark Teahen .20 .50
80 Chien-Ming Wang .30 .75
81 Roy Halladay .30 .75
82 Melvin Mora .20 .50
83 Grady Sizemore .30 .75
84 Matt Cain .30 .75
85 Carl Crawford .30 .75
86 Johnny Damon .30 .75
87 Freddy Garcia .20 .50
88 Ryan Shealy .20 .50
89 Carlos Beltran .30 .75
90 Chuck James .20 .50
91 Ben Sheets .20 .50
92 Mark Mulder .20 .50
93 Carlos Quentin .20 .50
94 Richie Sexson .20 .50
95 Brian Schneider .20 .50
96a Hideki Matsui .50 1.25
96b H.Matsui Japanese 2.00 5.00
97 Robinson Tejeda .20 .50
98 Scott Hatteberg .20 .50
99 Jeff Francis .20 .50
100 Robinson Cano .30 .75
101 Barry Zito .30 .75
102 Reed Johnson .20 .50
103 Chris Carpenter .30 .75
104 Chad Tracy .20 .50
105 Anibal Sanchez .20 .50
106 Brad Penny .20 .50
107 David Wright .40 1.00
108 Jimmy Rollins .30 .75
109 Alfonso Soriano .30 .75
110 Greg Maddux .60 1.50
111 Curt Schilling .30 .75
112 Stephen Drew .20 .50
113 Matt Holliday .50 1.25
114 Jorge Posada .30 .75
115 Vladimir Guerrero .30 .75
116 Frank Thomas .50 1.25
117 Jonathan Papelbon .50 1.25
118 Manny Ramirez .50 1.25
119 Magglio Ordonez .30 .75
120 Joe Mauer .40 1.00
121 Ryan Howard .40 1.00
122 Chris Young .20 .50
123 A.J. Burnett .20 .50
124 Brian McCann .20 .50
125 Juan Pierre .20 .50
126 Jonny Gomes .20 .50
127 Roger Clemens .60 1.50
128 Chad Billingsley .30 .75
129a Kenji Johjima .50 1.25
129b Kenji Johjima Japanese 2.00 5.00
130 Brian Giles .20 .50
131 Chase Utley .30 .75
132 Carl Pavano .20 .50
133 Curtis Granderson .40 1.00
134 Sean Casey .20 .50
135 Jon Garland .20 .50
136 David Ortiz .50 1.25
137 Bobby Crosby .20 .50
138 Conor Jackson .20 .50
139 Tim Hudson .30 .75
140 Rickie Weeks .20 .50
141 Mark Prior .30 .75
142 Ben Zobrist .30 .75
143 Troy Glaus .20 .50
144 Cliff Lee .30 .75
145 Adrian Beltre .50 1.25
146 Endy Chavez .20 .50
147 Ramon Hernandez .20 .50
148 Chris Young .20 .50
149 Jason Schmidt .20 .50
150 Kevin Millwood .20 .50
151 Placido Polanco .20 .50
152 Torii Hunter .20 .50
153 Roy Oswalt .30 .75
154 Kelvim Escobar .20 .50
155 Milton Bradley .20 .50
156 Chris Capuano .20 .50
157 Juan Encarnacion .20 .50
158a Ichiro Suzuki .60 1.50
158b Ichiro Suzuki Japanese 3.00 8.00
159 Matt Kemp .40 1.00
160 Matt Morris .20 .50
161 Casey Blake .20 .50
162 Josh Willingham .30 .75
163 Nick Johnson .20 .50
164 Khalil Greene .20 .50
165 Tom Glavine .30 .75
166 Jason Bay .30 .75
167 Brandon Phillips .20 .50
168 Jorge Cantu .20 .50
169 Jeff Weaver .20 .50
170 Melky Cabrera .20 .50
171 Dan Haren .20 .50
172 Jeff Francoeur .50 1.25
173 Randy Wolf .20 .50
174 Carlos Zambrano .30 .75
175 Justin Morneau .30 .75
176 Takashi Saito .20 .50
177 Victor Martinez .30 .75
178 Felix Hernandez .30 .75
179 Paul LoDuca .20 .50
180 Miguel Tejada .30 .75
181 Mark Teixeira .30 .75
182 Pat Burrell .20 .50
183 Mike Cameron .20 .50
184 Josh Beckett .20 .50
185 Francisco Liriano .20 .50
186 Ken Griffey Jr. 1.00 2.50
187 Mike Mussina .30 .75
188 Howie Kendrick .20 .50
189 Ted Lilly .20 .50
190 Mike Hampton .20 .50
191 Jeff Suppan .20 .50
192 Jose Reyes .30 .75
193 Russell Martin .20 .50
194 Jhonny Peralta .20 .50
195 Raul Ibanez .30 .75
196 Hanley Ramirez .30 .75
197 Kerry Wood .20 .50
198 Gary Sheffield .20 .50
199 David Dellucci .20 .50
200 Xavier Nady .20 .50
201 Michael Young .20 .50
202 Kevin Youkilis .20 .50
203 Aaron Harang .20 .50
204 Matt Garza .20 .50
205 Jim Thome .30 .75
206 Jose Contreras .20 .50
207 Tadahito Iguchi .20 .50
208 Eric Chavez .20 .50
209 Vernon Wells .20 .50
210 Doug Davis .20 .50
211 Andruw Jones .20 .50
212 David Eckstein .20 .50
213 J.J. Hardy .20 .50
214 Orlando Hudson .20 .50
215 Pedro Martinez .30 .75
216 Brian Roberts .20 .50
217 Brett Myers .20 .50
218 Alex Rodriguez .60 1.50
219 Kenny Rogers .20 .50
220 Jason Kubel .20 .50
221 Jermaine Dye .20 .50
222 Bartolo Colon .20 .50
223 Craig Biggio .30 .75
224 Alex Rios .20 .50
225 Adam Dunn .30 .75
226 Anthony Reyes .20 .50
227 Derrek Lee .20 .50
228 Jeremy Hermida .20 .50
229 Derek Lowe .20 .50
230 Randy Winn .20 .50
231 Brandon Webb .30 .75
232 Jose Vidro .20 .50
233 Erik Bedard .20 .50
234 Jon Lieber .20 .50
235 Wily Mo Pena .20 .50
236 Kelly Johnson .20 .50
237 David DeJesus .20 .50
238 Andy Marte .20 .50
239 Scott Olsen .20 .50
240 Randy Johnson .50 1.25
241 Nelson Cruz .50 1.25
242 Carlos Guillen .20 .50
243 Brandon McCarthy .20 .50
244 Garret Anderson .20 .50
245 Mike Sweeney .20 .50
246 Brian Bannister .20 .50
247 Jose Guillen .20 .50
248 Brad Wilkerson .20 .50
249 Lance Berkman .30 .75
250 Ryan Zimmerman .30 .75
251 Garrett Atkins .20 .50
252 Johan Santana .30 .75
253 Brandon Webb .30 .75
254 Justin Verlander .50 1.25
255 Hanley Ramirez .30 .75
256 Justin Morneau .30 .75
257 Ryan Howard .40 1.00
258 Eric Chavez .20 .50
259 Scott Rolen .30 .75
260 Derek Jeter 1.25 3.00
261 Omar Vizquel .30 .75
262 Mark Grudzielanek .20 .50
263 Orlando Hudson .20 .50
264 Mark Teixeira .30 .75
265 Albert Pujols .60 1.50
266 Ivan Rodriguez .30 .75
267 Brad Ausmus .20 .50
268 Torii Hunter .20 .50
269 Mike Cameron .20 .50
270 Ichiro Suzuki .60 1.50
271 Carlos Beltran .30 .75
272 Vernon Wells .20 .50
273 Andruw Jones .20 .50
274 Kenny Rogers .20 .50
275 Greg Maddux .60 1.50
276 Danny Putnam (RC) .40 1.00
277 Chase Wright RC 1.00 2.50
278 Zach McClellan RC .40 1.00
279 Jamie Vermilyea RC .40 1.00
280 Felix Pie (RC) .40 1.00
281 Phil Hughes (RC) 1.00 2.50
282 Jon Knott (RC) .40 1.00
283 Micah Owings (RC) .40 1.00
284 Devern Hansack RC .40 1.00
285 Andy Cannizaro RC .40 1.00
286 Lee Gardner (RC) .40 1.00
287 Josh Hamilton (RC) 1.25 3.00
288a Angel Sanchez RC .40 1.00
288b Angel Sanchez AU 3.00 8.00
289 J.D. Durbin (RC) .40 1.00
290 Jaime Burke (RC) .40 1.00
291 Joe Bisenius RC .40 1.00
292 Rick Vanden Hurk RC .40 1.00
293 Brian Barden RC .40 1.00
294 Levale Speigner RC .40 1.00
295 Kevin Cameron RC .40 1.00
296 Don Kelly (RC) .40 1.00
297a Hideki Okajima RC 2.00 5.00
297b Hideki Okajima Japanese 3.00 8.00
298 Andrew Miller RC 1.50 4.00
299 Delmon Young (RC) .60 1.50
300 Vinny Rottino (RC) .40 1.00
301 Philip Humber (RC) .40 1.00
302 Drew Anderson RC .40 1.00
303 Jerry Owens (RC) .40 1.00
304 Jose Garcia RC .40 1.00
305 Shane Youman RC .40 1.00
306 Ryan Feierabend (RC) .40 1.00
307 Mike Rabelo RC .40 1.00
308 Josh Fields (RC) .40 1.00
309 Jon Coutlangus (RC) .40 1.00
310 Travis Buck (RC) .40 1.00
311 Doug Slaten RC .40 1.00
312 Ryan Z. Braun RC .40 1.00
313 Juan Salas (RC) .40 1.00
314 Matt Lindstrom (RC) .40 1.00
315 Cesar Jimenez RC .40 1.00
316 Jay Marshall RC .40 1.00
317 Jared Burton RC .40 1.00
318 Juan Perez RC .40 1.00
319 Elijah Dukes RC .60 1.50
320 Juan Lara RC .40 1.00
321 Justin Hampson (RC) .40 1.00
322a Kei Igawa RC 1.00 2.50
322b Kei Igawa Japanese 2.00 5.00
323 Zack Segovia (RC) .40 1.00
324 Alejandro De Aza RC .60 1.50
325 Brandon Morrow RC 2.00 5.00
326 Gustavo Molina RC .40 1.00
327 Joe Smith RC .40 1.00
328 Jesus Flores RC .40 1.00
329 Jeff Baker (RC) .40 1.00
330a Daisuke Matsuzaka RC 4.00 10.00
330b Daisuke Matsuzaka Japanese 4.00 10.00
331 Troy Tulowitzki AU (RC) 6.00 15.00
332 John Danks AU RC 3.00 8.00
333 Kevin Kouzmanoff AU (RC) 3.00 8.00
334 David Murphy AU (RC) 3.00 8.00
335 Ryan Sweeney AU (RC) 3.00 8.00
336 Fred Lewis AU (RC) 3.00 8.00
337 Delwyn Young AU (RC) 3.00 8.00
338 Matt Chico AU (RC) 3.00 8.00
339 Miguel Montero AU (RC) 3.00 8.00
340 Shawn Riggans AU (RC) 3.00 8.00
341 Brian Stokes AU (RC) 3.00 8.00
342 Scott Moore AU (RC) 3.00 8.00
343 Adam Lind AU (RC) 3.00 8.00
344 Chris Narveson AU (RC) 3.00 8.00
345 Alex Gordon AU RC 8.00 20.00
346 Joaquin Arias AU (RC) 3.00 8.00
347 Brian Burres AU (RC) 3.00 8.00
348 Glen Perkins AU (RC) 3.00 8.00
349 Ubaldo Jimenez AU (RC) 3.00 8.00
350 Chris Stewart AU RC 3.00 8.00
351 Beltran Perez AU (RC) 3.00 8.00
352 Dennis Sarfate AU (RC) 3.00 8.00
353 Carlos Maldonado AU (RC) 3.00 8.00
354 Mitch Maier AU RC 3.00 8.00
355 Kory Casto AU (RC) 3.00 8.00
356 Juan Morillo AU (RC) 3.00 8.00
357 Hector Gimenez AU (RC) 3.00 8.00
358 Alexi Casilla AU RC 3.00 8.00
359 Michael Bourn AU (RC) 4.00 10.00
360 Sean Henn AU (RC) 3.00 8.00
361 Tim Gradoville AU RC 3.00 8.00
363 Oswaldo Navarro AU RC 3.00 8.00

2007 Topps Chrome Refractors

*REF: 1.2X TO 3X BASIC
REF ODDS 1:3 HOB,1:2 RET
*REF RC: .6X TO 1.5X BASIC RC
REF RC ODDS 1:3 HOB, 1:2 RET
*REF VAR: .5X TO 1.2X BASIC VARIATION
REF VAR ODDS 1:73 HOBBY
REF VAR PRINT RUN 500 SER.#'d SETS
*REF AU: .5X TO 1.2X BASIC AUTO
REF AU ODDS 1:71 HOB, 1:570 RET
REF AU PRINT RUN 500 SER.#'d SETS
EXCHANGE DEADLINE 07/31/09

2007 Topps Chrome Blue Refractors

*BLUE: 4X TO 10X BASIC
*BLUE RC: 2.5X TO 6X BASIC RC
STATED ODDS 1:6 RETAIL

2007 Topps Chrome Red Refractors

*RED REF: 4X TO 10X BASIC
*RED REF RC: 2.5X TO 6X BASIC RC
STATED ODDS 1:2 HOB.BOX LDR
STATED PRINT RUN 99 SER.#'d SETS
STATED VAR.ODDS 1:311 HOB.BOX LDR
STATED VAR.PRINT RUN 25 SER.#'d SETS
NO VARIATION PRICING AVAILABLE
STATED AU ODDS 1:55 HOB.BOX LDR
STATED AU PRINT RUN 25 SER.#'d SETS
NO AU PRICING AVAILABLE
EXCHANGE DEADLINE 07/31/09

2007 Topps Chrome White Refractors

*WHITE REF: 1.5X TO 4X BASIC
WHITE REF ODDS 1:6 HOB,1:23 RET
WHITE REF PRINT RUN 660 SER.#'d SETS
*WHITE REF RC: .75X TO 2X BASIC RC
WHITE REF RC ODDS 1:6 HOB, 1:23 RET

WHITE REF RC PRINT RUN 660 SER.#'d SETS
*WHITE REF VAR: .6X TO 1.5X BASIC VAR
WHITE REF VAR ODDS 1:932 HOBBY
WHITE REF VAR PRINT RUN 200 SER.#'d SETS
*WHITE REF AU: .75X TO 2X BASIC AUTO
WHITE REF AU ODDS 1:177 HOB, 1:1475 RET
WHITE REF AU PRINT RUN 200 SER.#'d SETS
EXCHANGE DEADLINE 07/31/09
297b Hideki Okajima Japanese 15.00 40.00
330b Daisuke Matsuzaka Japanese 15.00 40.00

2007 Topps Chrome X-Fractors

*X-F: 1.5X TO 4X BASIC
*X-F RC: 1.5X TO 4X BASIC RC
STATED ODDS 1:3 RETAIL

2007 Topps Chrome Generation Now

COMPLETE SET (41) 10.00 25.00
COMMON A.ETHIER .75 2.00
COMMON R.HOWARD 1.25 3.00
COMMON N.MARKAKIS .50 1.25
COMMON R.MARTIN .30 .75
COMMON J.MORNEAU .50 1.25
COMMON M.NAPOLI .30 .75
COMMON H.RAMIREZ .50 1.25
COMMON N.SWISHER .30 .75
COMMON C.UTLEY .75 2.00
COMMON J.VERLANDER .75 2.00
COMMON C.WANG .75 2.00
COMMON JER.WEAVER .50 1.25
COMMON D.YOUNG .50 1.25
COMMON R.ZIMMERMAN .75 2.00
STATED ODDS 1:5 HOBBY,1:17 RETAIL
PLATE ODDS 1:116 HOB.BOXLOADER
PLATE PRINT RUN 1 SET PER COLOR
BLACK-CYAN-MAGENTA-YELLOW ISSUED
NO PLATE PRICING DUE TO SCARCITY
REF ODDS 1:27 H, 1:71 R
REF PRINT RUN 500 SERIAL #'d SETS
BLUE REF ODDS 1:72 RETAIL
RED REF PRINT RUN 99 SER.#'d SETS
WHITE REF.ODDS 1:67 HOBBY,1:185 RETAIL
SUPERFRAC.PRINT RUN 1 SER.#'d SET
NO SUPERFRAC.PRICING DUE TO SCARCITY

2007 Topps Chrome Generation Now Refractors

*REF: 1X TO 2.5X BASIC
STATED ODDS 1:27 H, 1:71 R
STATED PRINT RUN 500 SER.#'d SETS

2007 Topps Chrome Generation Now Blue Refractors

*BLUE REF: 2.5X TO 6X BASIC
STATED ODDS 1:72 RETAIL
STATED PRINT RUN 100 SER.#'d SETS

2007 Topps Chrome Generation Now Red Refractors

*RED REF: 2.5X TO 6X BASIC
STATED ODDS
STATED PRINT RUN 99 SER.#'d SETS

2007 Topps Chrome Generation Now White Refractors

*WHITE REF: 1.25X TO 3X BASIC
STATED ODDS 1:67 HOBBY,1:185 RETAIL
STATED PRINT RUN 200 SER.#'d SETS

2007 Topps Chrome Mickey Mantle Story

COMMON MANTLE (1-40) .75 2.00
1-30 STATED ODDS 1:7 H, :23 R
46-55 STATED ODDS 1:20 HOBBY
1-30 PLATE ODDS 1:116 HOB.BOXLDR
46-55 PLATE ODDS 1:1971 HOBBY
PLATE PRINT RUN 1 SET PER COLOR
BLACK-CYAN-MAGENTA-YELLOW ISSUED
NO PLATE PRICING DUE TO SCARCITY
*REF: 1X TO 2.5X BASIC
1-30 REF.ODDS 1:27 H, 1:71 R
46-55 REF.ODDS 1:31 HOBBY
1-30 REF PRINT RUN 500 SER.#'d SETS
46-55 REF PRINT RUN 400 SER.#'d SETS
*07 BLUE REF: 2.5X TO 6X BASIC
*08 BLUE REF: 1.2X TO 3X BASIC
07 BLUE REF ODDS 1:72 RETAIL
08 BLUE REF ODDS
07 BLUE REF PRINT RUN 100 SER.#'d SETS
08 BLUE REF PRINT RUN 200 SER.#'d SETS
*COPPER: 2.5X TO 6X BASIC
STATED ODDS 1:117 HOBBY
STATED PRINT RUN 100 SER.#'d SETS
*1-30 RED REF: 2.5X TO 6X BASIC
46-55 RED REF ODDS 1:315 HOBBY
1-30 RED REF 99 SER.#'d SETS
46-55 RED REF 25 SER.#'d SETS
NO 46-55 RED PRICING AVAILABLE
*WHITE REF: 1.2X TO 3X BASIC
WHITE REF.ODDS 1:67 HOBBY,1:185 RETAIL
WHITE REF PRINT RUN 200 SER.#'d SETS
46-55 SUP.FRAC. ODDS 1:7685
SUPERFRAC.PRINT RUN 1 SER.#'d SET
NO SUPERFRAC.PRICING DUE TO SCARCITY
1-30 ISSUED IN 07 TOPPS CHROME
46-55 ISSUED IN 08 TOPPS CHROME

2008 Topps Chrome

COMP.SET w/o AU's (220) 30.00 60.00
COMMON CARD .20 .50
COMMON ROOKIE .60 1.50
COMMON AUTO 4.00 10.00
AUTO ODDS 1:15 HOBBY
PRINT.PLATE ODDS 1:1896 HOBBY
AU PLATES 1:10,961 HOBBY
PLATE PRINT RUN 1 SET PER COLOR
BLACK-CYAN-MAGENTA-YELLOW ISSUED
NO PLATE PRICING DUE TO SCARCITY
EXCHANGE DEADLINE 6/30/2010
1 Alex Rodriguez .60 1.50
2 Barry Zito .30 .75
3 Scott Kazmir .30 .75
4 Stephen Drew .20 .50
5 Miguel Cabrera .50 1.25
6 Daisuke Matsuzaka .30 .75
7 Mickey Mantle 1.50 4.00
8 Jimmy Rollins .30 .75
9 Joe Mauer .40 1.00
10 Cole Hamels .40 1.00
11 Yovani Gallardo .20 .50
12 Miguel Tejada .30 .75
13 Dontrelle Willis .20 .50
14 Orlando Cabrera .30 .75
15 Jake Peavy .20 .50
16 Erik Bedard .20 .50
17 Victor Martinez .30 .75
18 Chris Young .20 .50
19 Jose Reyes .30 .75
20 Mike Lowell .20 .50
21 Dan Uggla .20 .50
22 Garrett Atkins .20 .50
23 Felix Hernandez .30 .75
24 Ivan Rodriguez .30 .75
25 Alex Rios .20 .50
26 Jason Bay .30 .75
27 Vladimir Guerrero .30 .75
28 John Lackey .30 .75
29 Ryan Howard .30 .75
30 Kevin Youkilis .20 .50
31 Justin Morneau .30 .75
32 Johan Santana .30 .75
33 Jeremy Hermida .20 .50
34 Andruw Jones .20 .50
35 Mike Cameron .20 .50
36 Jason Varitek .50 1.25
37 Tim Hudson .30 .75
38 Justin Upton .30 .75
39 Brad Penny .20 .50
40 Robinson Cano .30 .75
41 Brandon Webb .30 .75
42 Magglio Ordonez .30 .75
43 Aaron Hill .20 .50
44 Alfonso Soriano .30 .75
45 Carlos Zambrano .30 .75
46 Ben Sheets .20 .50
47 Tim Lincecum .30 .75
48 Phil Hughes .20 .50
49 Scott Rolen .30 .75
50 John Maine .20 .50
51 Delmon Young .30 .75
52 Tadahito Iguchi .20 .50
53 Yunel Escobar .20 .50
54 Russell Martin .20 .50
55 Orlando Hudson .20 .50
56 Jim Edmonds .30 .75
57 Todd Helton .30 .75
58 Melky Cabrera .20 .50
59 Adrian Beltre .50 1.25
60 Manny Ramirez .50 1.25
61 Gil Meche .20 .50
62 David DeJesus .20 .50
63 Roy Oswalt .30 .75
64 Mark Buehrle .30 .75
65 Hunter Pence .30 .75
66 Dustin Pedroia .50 1.25
67 Roy Halladay .30 .75
68 Rich Harden .20 .50
69 Jim Thome .30 .75
70 Akinori Iwamura .20 .50
71 Dan Haren .20 .50
72 Brandon Phillips .20 .50
73 Brett Myers .20 .50
74 James Loney .20 .50
75 C.C. Sabathia .30 .75
76 Jermaine Dye .20 .50
77 Carlos Ruiz .20 .50
78 Brian McCann .30 .75
79 Paul Konerko .30 .75
80 Jorge Posada .30 .75
81 Chien-Ming Wang .30 .75
82 Carlos Delgado .20 .50
83 Ichiro Suzuki .60 1.50
84 Elijah Dukes .20 .50
85 David Wright .30 .75
86 Carl Crawford .30 .75
87 Mark Teixeira .30 .75
88 Bobby Crosby .20 .50
89 Brian Roberts .20 .50
90 David Ortiz .50 1.25
91 Derrek Lee .20 .50
92 Adam Dunn .30 .75
93 Fausto Carmona .20 .50
94 Grady Sizemore .30 .75
95 Jeff Francoeur .30 .75
96 Jered Weaver .30 .75
97 Troy Tulowitzki .50 1.25
98 Troy Glaus .30 .75
99 Nick Markakis .40 1.00
100 Lance Berkman .30 .75
101 Randy Johnson .50 1.25
102 Kenji Johjima .20 .50
103 Jarrod Saltalamacchia .20 .50
104 Matt Holliday .50 1.25
105 Travis Hafner .20 .50
106 Johnny Damon .30 .75
107 Alex Gordon .30 .75
108 Derek Lowe .20 .50
109 Nick Swisher .30 .75
110 Aaron Harang .20 .50
111 Hanley Ramirez .30 .75
112 Carlos Guillen .20 .50
113 Ryan Braun .30 .75
114 Torii Hunter .20 .50
115 Joe Blanton .20 .50
116 Josh Hamilton .30 .75
117 Pedro Martinez .30 .75
118 Hideki Matsui .50 1.25
119 Cameron Maybin .20 .50
120 Prince Fielder .30 .75
121 Derek Jeter 1.25 3.00
122 Chone Figgins .20 .50
123 Chase Utley .30 .75
124 Jacoby Ellsbury .40 1.00
125 Freddy Sanchez .20 .50
126 Rocco Baldelli .20 .50
127 Tom Gorzelanny .20 .50
128 Adrian Gonzalez .30 .75
129 Geovany Soto .50 1.25
130 Bobby Abreu .20 .50
131 Albert Pujols .60 1.50
132 Chipper Jones .50 1.25
133 Jeremy Bonderman .20 .50
134 B.J. Upton .30 .75
135 Justin Verlander .50 1.25
136 Jeff Francis .20 .50
137 A.J. Burnett .20 .50
138 Travis Buck .30 .75
139 Vernon Wells .20 .50
140 Raul Ibanez .30 .75
141 Ryan Zimmerman .30 .75
142 John Smoltz .50 1.25
143 Carlos Lee .20 .50
144 Chris Young .20 .50
145 Francisco Liriano .20 .50
146 Curt Schilling .30 .75
147 Josh Beckett .20 .50
148 Aramis Ramirez .20 .50
149 Ronnie Belliard .20 .50
150 Homer Bailey .30 .75
151 Curtis Granderson .30 .75
152 Ken Griffey Jr. 1.00 2.50
153 Kazuo Matsui .20 .50
154 Brian Bannister .20 .50
155 Joba Chamberlain .20 .50
156 Tom Glavine .30 .75
157 Carlos Beltran .30 .75
158 Kelly Johnson .20 .50
159 Rich Hill .20 .50
160 Pat Burrell .20 .50
161 Asdrubal Cabrera .30 .75
162 Gary Sheffield .20 .50
163 Greg Maddux .60 1.50
164 Eric Chavez .20 .50
165 Chris Carpenter .30 .75
166 Michael Young .20 .50
167 Carlos Pena .30 .75
168 Frank Thomas .50 1.25
169 Aaron Rowand .20 .50
170 Yadier Molina .60 1.50
171 Luis Castillo .20 .50
172 Ryan Theriot .20 .50
173 Andre Ethier .30 .75
174 Casey Kotchman .20 .50
175 Rickie Weeks .20 .50
176 Milton Bradley .20 .50
177 Daniel Cabrera .20 .50
178 Jo-Jo Reyes .20 .50
179 Livan Hernandez .20 .50
180 Hideki Okajima .20 .50
181 Matt Kemp .40 1.00
182 Jonny Gomes .20 .50
183 Billy Butler .20 .50
184 Adam LaRoche .20 .50
185 Brad Hawpe .20 .50
186 Paul Maholm .20 .50
187 Placido Polanco .20 .50
188 Noah Lowry .20 .50
189 Gregg Zaun .20 .50
190 Nate McLouth .20 .50
191 Edinson Volquez .20 .50
192 Jeff Niemann (RC) .60 1.50
193 Evan Longoria RC 3.00 8.00
194 Adam Jones .30 .75
195 Eugenio Velez RC .60 1.50
196 Joey Votto (RC) 15.00 40.00
197 Nick Blackburn RC 1.00 2.50
198 Harvey Garcia (RC) .60 1.50
199 Hiroki Kuroda RC 1.50 4.00
200 Elliot Johnson (RC) .60 1.50
201 Luis Mendoza (RC) .60 1.50
202 Alex Romero (RC) 1.00 2.50
203 Gregor Blanco (RC) .60 1.50
204 Rico Washington (RC) .60 1.50
205 Brian Bocock RC .60 1.50
206 Evan Meek RC .60 1.50
207 Stephen Holm RC .60 1.50
208 Matt Tupman RC .60 1.50
209 Fernando Hernandez RC .60 1.50
210 Randor Bierd RC .60 1.50
211 Blake DeWitt (RC) 1.00 2.50
212 Randy Wells RC 1.00 2.50
213 Wesley Wright RC .60 1.50
214 Clete Thomas RC 1.00 2.50
215 Kyle McClellan RC .60 1.50
216 Brian Bixler (RC) .60 1.50
217 Kazuo Fukumori RC 1.00 2.50
218 Burke Badenhop RC 1.00 2.50
219 Denard Span (RC) 1.00 2.50
220 Brian Bass (RC) .60 1.50
221 J.R. Towles AU RC 4.00 10.00
222 Felipe Paulino AU RC 4.00 10.00
223 Sam Fuld AU RC 4.00 10.00
224 Kevin Hart AU (RC) 4.00 10.00
225 Nyjer Morgan AU (RC) 4.00 10.00
226 Daric Barton AU (RC) 4.00 10.00
227 Armando Galarraga AU RC 4.00 10.00
228 Chin-Lung Hu AU (RC) 4.00 10.00
229 Buchholz AU (RC) EXCH 4.00 10.00
230 Rich Thompson AU RC 4.00 10.00
231 Brian Barton AU RC 5.00 12.00
232 Ross Ohlendorf AU RC 4.00 10.00
233 Masahide Kobayashi AU RC 4.00 10.00
234 Callix Crabbe AU (RC) 4.00 10.00
235 Matt Tolbert AU RC 4.00 10.00
236 Jayson Nix AU (RC) 4.00 10.00
237 Johnny Cueto AU RC 6.00 15.00
238 Evan Meek AU RC 4.00 10.00
239 Randy Wells AU (RC) 4.00 10.00

2008 Topps Chrome Refractors

*REF: 1.2X TO 3X BASIC
REF ODDS 1:3 HOBBY
*REF RC: .6X TO 1.5X BASIC RC
REF RC ODDS 1:3 HOBBY
*REF AU: .5X TO 1.2X BASIC AUTO
REF AU ODDS 1:95 HOBBY
REF AU PRINT RUN 500 SER.#'d SETS
EXCHANGE DEADLINE 6/30/2010

2008 Topps Chrome Blue Refractors

*BLUE REF: 4X TO 10X BASIC
REF ODDS
*BLUE REF RC: 1.2X TO 3X BASIC RC
REF RC ODDS
*BLUE REF AU: .6X TO 1.5X BASIC AUTO
BLUE REF AU ODDS 1:230 HOBBY
BLUE REF AU PRINT RUN 200 SER.#'d SETS
EXCHANGE DEADLINE 6/30/2010

2008 Topps Chrome Copper Refractors

*COPPER REF: 2X TO 5X BASIC
COPPER.REF ODDS 1:12 HOBBY
*COPPER REF RC: 1X TO 2.5X BASIC RC
REF RC ODDS 1:12 HOBBY
COPPER REF PRINT RUN 599 SER.#'d SETS
*COPPER REF AU: 1X TO 2.5X BASIC AUTO
COPPER REF AU ODDS 1:980 HOBBY
COPPER REF AU PRINT RUN 100 SER.#'d SETS
EXCHANGE DEADLINE 6/30/2010

2008 Topps Chrome Red Refractors

RED 1-220 ODDS 1:143 HOBBY
RED AU 221-239 ODDS 1:2185 HOBBY
STATED PRINT RUN 25 SER.#'d SETS
NO PRICING DUE TO SCARCITY

2008 Topps Chrome National Convention

*NATIONAL 1-200: .5X TO 1.2X BASIC
*NATIONAL 201-220: .5X TO 1.2X BASIC

2008 Topps Chrome 50th Anniversary All Rookie Team

COMPLETE SET (23) 12.50 30.00
STATED ODDS 1:9 HOBBY
PRINTING PLATE ODDS 1:1971 HOBBY
PLATE PRINT RUN 1 SET PER COLOR
BLACK-CYAN-MAGENTA-YELLOW ISSUED
NO PLATE PRICING DUE TO SCARCITY
*REF: .75X TO 2X BASIC
REF ODDS 1:31 HOBBY
REF.PRINT RUN 400 SER.#'d SETS
*BLUE REF: 1.2X TO 3X BASIC
BLUE REF PRINT RUN 200 SER.#'d SETS
*COP.REF: 1X TO 2.5X BASIC
COP.REF ODDS 1:117 HOBBY
COP.REF PRINT RUN 100 SER.#'d SETS
RED.REF ODDS 1:315 HOBBY
RED PRINT RUN 25 SER.#'d SETS
NO RED PRICING DUE TO SCARCITY
SUPFRAC.ODDS 1:7885 HOBBY
SUPFRAC.PRINT RUN 1 SER.#'d SET
NO SUPFRAC.PRICING DUE TO SCARCITY
ARC1 Gary Sheffield .40 1.00
ARC2 Ivan Rodriguez .60 1.50
ARC3 Mike Piazza 1.00 2.50
ARC4 Manny Ramirez 1.00 2.50
ARC5 Chipper Jones 1.00 2.50
ARC6 Derek Jeter 2.50 6.00
ARC7 Andruw Jones .40 1.00
ARC8 Alfonso Soriano .60 1.50
ARC9 Jimmy Rollins .60 1.50
ARC10 Albert Pujols 1.25 3.00
ARC11 Ichiro Suzuki 1.25 3.00
ARC12 Mark Teixeira .60 1.50
ARC13 Matt Holliday 1.00 2.50
ARC14 Joe Mauer .75 2.00
ARC15 Prince Fielder .60 1.50
ARC16 Hideki Okajima .40 1.00
ARC17 Roy Oswalt .60 1.50
ARC18 Hunter Pence .60 1.50
ARC19 Nick Markakis .75 2.00
ARC20 Ryan Zimmerman .60 1.50
ARC21 Ryan Braun .60 1.50
ARC22 C.C. Sabathia .60 1.50
ARC23 Dustin Pedroia 1.00 2.50

2008 Topps Chrome Dick Perez

EXCLUSIVE TO WALMART PACKS
REF: .5X TO 1.2X
WMDPC1 Manny Ramirez 2.00 5.00
WMDPC2 Cameron Maybin .75 2.00
WMDPC3 Ryan Howard 1.25 3.00
WMDPC4 David Ortiz 2.00 5.00
WMDPC5 Tim Lincecum 1.25 3.00
WMDPC6 David Wright 1.25 3.00
WMDPC7 Mickey Mantle 3.00 8.00
WMDPC8 Joba Chamberlain .75 2.00
WMDPC9 Ichiro Suzuki 2.50 6.00
WMDPC10 Prince Fielder 1.25 3.00
WMDPC11 Jacoby Ellsbury 1.50 4.00
WMDPC12 Jake Peavy .75 2.00
WMDPC13 Miguel Cabrera 2.00 5.00
WMDPC14 Josh Beckett .75 2.00
WMDPC15 Jimmy Rollins 1.25 3.00
WMDPC16 Torii Hunter .75 2.00
WMDPC17 Alfonso Soriano 1.25 3.00
WMDPC18 Jose Reyes 1.25 3.00
WMDPC19 C.C. Sabathia 1.25 3.00
WMDPC20 Alex Rodriguez 2.50 6.00

2008 Topps Chrome T205

EXCLUSIVE TO TARGET PACKS
*REF: .5X TO 1.2X BASIC
TCCP1 Albert Pujols 2.50 6.00
TCCP2 Clay Buchholz 1.25 3.00
TCCP3 Matt Holliday 2.00 5.00
TCCP4 Luke Hochevar 1.25 3.00
TCCP5 Alex Rodriguez 2.50 6.00
TCCP6 Joey Votto 6.00 15.00
TCCP7 Chin-Lung Hu .75 2.00
TCCP8 Ryan Braun 1.25 3.00
TCCP9 Joba Chamberlain .75 2.00
TCCP10 Ryan Howard 1.25 3.00
TCCP11 Ichiro Suzuki 2.50 6.00
TCCP12 Steve Pearce 4.00 10.00
TCCP13 Vladimir Guerrero 1.25 3.00
TCCP14 Wladimir Balentien .75 2.00
TCCP15 David Ortiz 2.00 5.00
TCCP16 Jacoby Ellsbury 1.50 4.00
TCCP17 David Wright 1.25 3.00
TCCP18 Chase Utley 1.25 3.00
TCCP19 Manny Ramirez 2.00 5.00
TCCP20 Dan Haren .75 2.00
TCCP21 Nick Markakis 1.50 4.00
TCCP22 Grady Sizemore 1.25 3.00
TCCP23 Hanley Ramirez 1.25 3.00
TCCP24 Daisuke Matsuzaka 1.25 3.00
TCCP25 Troy Tulowitzki 2.00 5.00
TCCP26 Jose Reyes 1.25 3.00
TCCP27 Tim Lincecum 1.25 3.00
TCCP28 Prince Fielder 1.25 3.00
TCCP29 Alfonso Soriano 1.25 3.00
TCCP30 Andrew Miller 1.25 3.00

2008 Topps Chrome Trading Card History

COMPLETE SET (50) 12.50 30.00
STATED ODDS 1:9 HOBBY
PRINTING PLATE ODDS 1:1971 HOBBY
PLATE PRINT RUN 1 SET PER COLOR
BLACK-CYAN-MAGENTA-YELLOW ISSUED
NO PLATE PRICING DUE TO SCARCITY
*REF: .75X TO 2X BASIC
REF ODDS 1:31 HOBBY
REF.PRINT RUN 400 SER.#'d SETS
BLUE REF PRINT RUN 200 SER.#'d SETS
COP.REF ODDS 1:117 HOBBY
COP.REF PRINT RUN 100 SER.#'d SETS
RED.REF ODDS 1:315 HOBBY
RED PRINT RUN 25 SER.#'d SETS
NO RED PRICING DUE TO SCARCITY
SUPFRAC.ODDS 1:7885 HOBBY
SUPFRAC.PRINT RUN 1 SER.#'d SET
NO SUPFRAC.PRICING DUE TO SCARCITY
TCHC1 Jacoby Ellsbury .75 2.00
TCHC2 Joba Chamberlain .40 1.00
TCHC3 Daisuke Matsuzaka .60 1.50
TCHC4 Prince Fielder .60 1.50
TCHC5 Alex Rodriguez 1.25 3.00
TCHC6 Mickey Mantle 2.50 6.00
TCHC7 Ryan Braun .60 1.50
TCHC8 Albert Pujols 1.25 3.00
TCHC9 Joe Mauer .75 2.00
TCHC10 Jose Reyes .60 1.50
TCHC11 Johan Santana .60 1.50
TCHC12 Hunter Pence .60 1.50
TCHC13 Hideki Okajima .40 1.00
TCHC14 Cameron Maybin .40 1.00
TCHC15 Tim Lincecum .60 1.50
TCHC16 Mark Teixeira/Jeff Francoeur .60 1.50
TCHC17 Justin Upton .60 1.50
TCHC18 Alfonso Soriano .60 1.50
TCHC19 Ichiro Suzuki 1.25 3.00
TCHC20 Grady Sizemore .60 1.50
TCHC21 Ryan Howard .60 1.50
TCHC22 David Wright .60 1.50
TCHC23 Jimmy Rollins .60 1.50
TCHC24 Ken Griffey Jr 2.00 5.00
TCHC25 Chipper Jones 1.00 2.50
TCHC26 Justin Verlander 1.00 2.50
TCHC27 Manny Ramirez 1.00 2.50
TCHC28 Chase Utley .60 1.50
TCHC29 Ivan Rodriguez .60 1.50
TCHC30 Josh Beckett .40 1.00
TCHC31 Vladimir Guerrero .60 1.50
TCHC32 Lance Berkman .60 1.50
TCHC33 Gary Sheffield .40 1.00
TCHC34 David Ortiz 1.00 2.50
TCHC35 Andruw Jones .40 1.00
TCHC36 Hideki Matsui 1.00 2.50
TCHC37 C.C. Sabathia .60 1.50
TCHC38 Magglio Ordonez .60 1.50
TCHC39 Pedro Martinez .60 1.50
TCHC40 Derek Jeter 2.50 6.00
TCHC41 Hanley Ramirez .60 1.50
TCHC42 Jake Peavy .40 1.00
TCHC43 Brandon Webb .60 1.50
TCHC44 Matt Holliday 1.00 2.50
TCHC45 Carlos Beltran .60 1.50
TCHC46 Troy Tulowitzki 1.00 2.50
TCHC47 Justin Morneau .60 1.50
TCHC48 Phil Hughes .40 1.00
TCHC49 Torii Hunter .40 1.00
TCHC50 Brad Hawpe .40 1.00

2008 Topps Chrome Trading Card History Blue Refractors

*BLUE REF: 1.2X TO 3X BASIC
STATED PRINT RUN 200 SER.#'d SETS
TCHC1 Jacoby Ellsbury 30.00 60.00

2008 Topps Chrome Trading Card History Copper Refractors

*COP.REF: 1X TO 2.5X BASIC
STATED ODDS 1:117 HOBBY
STATED PRINT RUN 100 SER.#'d SETS
TCHC1 Jacoby Ellsbury* 20.00 50.00

2009 Topps Chrome

COMP.SET w/o AU's (220) 30.00 60.00
COMMON CARD .20 .50
COMMON ROOKIE .60 1.50
COMMON AUTO 4.00 10.00
AUTO ODDS 1:20 HOBBY
PRINT.PLATE ODDS 1:383 HOBBY
AU PLATES 1:5330 HOBBY
PLATE PRINT RUN 1 SET PER COLOR
BLACK-CYAN-MAGENTA-YELLOW ISSUED
NO PLATE PRICING DUE TO SCARCITY
1 Alex Rodriguez .60 1.50
2 Kerry Wood .20 .50
3 Dan Uggla .20 .50
4 Nate McLouth .20 .50
5 Brad Lidge .20 .50
6 Jon Lester .30 .75
7 Mickey Mantle 1.50 4.00
8 Jason Giambi .20 .50
9 Mike Lowell .20 .50
10 Ken Griffey Jr. 1.00 2.50
11 Erick Aybar .20 .50
12 Stephen Drew .20 .50
13 Geoff Jenkins .20 .50
14 Aubrey Huff .20 .50
15 Kazuo Matsui .20 .50
16 David Ortiz .50 1.25
17 Mariano Rivera .60 1.50
18 Jermaine Dye .20 .50
19 Rich Harden .20 .50
20 Brian McCann .30 .75
21 Brad Hawpe .20 .50
22 Justin Morneau .30 .75
23 Akinori Iwamura .20 .50
24 David Wright .40 1.00
25 Garrett Atkins .20 .50
26 David DeJesus .20 .50
27 Francisco Liriano .20 .50
28 George Sherrill .20 .50
29 Hideki Matsui .50 1.25
30 Chris Young .20 .50
31 Kevin Youkilis .20 .50
32 Mark Teixeira .30 .75
33 Roy Oswalt .30 .75
34 Orlando Hudson .20 .50
35 Vladimir Guerrero .30 .75
36 Juan Pierre .20 .50
37 Carlos Delgado .20 .50
38 Tim Hudson .30 .75
39 Brandon Webb .30 .75
40 Alex Gordon .30 .75
41 Glen Perkins .20 .50
42 Kosuke Fukudome .30 .75
43 Ian Stewart .20 .50
44a A.J. Pierzynski .20 .50
44b Barack Obama SP 6.00 15.00
45 Roy Halladay .30 .75
46 Carlos Pena .30 .75
47 Evan Longoria .30 .75
48 Matt Kemp .40 1.00
49 CC Sabathia .30 .75
50 Yadier Molina .60 1.50
51 James Shields .20 .50
52 Jeff Samardzija .30 .75
53 Rafael Furcal .20 .50
54 Cliff Lee .30 .75
55 Daniel Murphy RC 2.50 6.00
56 Randy Johnson .50 1.25
57 Jon Garland .20 .50
58 Chien-Ming Wang .30 .75
59 Zack Greinke .50 1.25
60 Tim Lincecum .30 .75
61 Conor Jackson .20 .50
62 Chase Utley .30 .75
63 Andy Sonnanstine .20 .50
64 Miguel Tejada .30 .75
65 Geovany Soto .30 .75
66 Jeremy Sowers .20 .50
67 Ian Kinsler .30 .75
68 Jay Bruce .30 .75
69 Max Scherzer .50 1.25
70 Scott Rolen .30 .75
71 Justin Upton .30 .75
72 Xavier Nady .20 .50
73 Erik Bedard .20 .50
74 Chad Billingsley .30 .75
75 Ryan Braun .30 .75
76 Pat Burrell .20 .50
77 Edgar Renteria .20 .50
78 Joe Crede .30 .75
79 Manny Ramirez .50 1.25
80 Carlos Zambrano .30 .75
81 Hunter Pence .30 .75
82 Grady Sizemore .30 .75
83 Brian Roberts .20 .50
84 Alex Rios .20 .50
85 Joe Saunders .20 .50
86 Albert Pujols .60 1.50
87 Derrek Lee .20 .50
88 Ichiro Suzuki .60 1.50
89 Javier Vazquez .20 .50
90 Johan Santana .30 .75
91 Miguel Cabrera .50 1.25
92 Daisuke Matsuzaka .30 .75
93 Chris Young .20 .50
94 Joe Mauer .40 1.00
95 Stephen Drew .20 .50
96 Justin Masterson .20 .50
97 Dustin Pedroia .50 1.25
98 Derek Jeter 1.25 3.00
99 John Smoltz .50 1.25
100 Jason Varitek .50 1.25
101 Jorge Posada .30 .75
102 Mark Buehrle .30 .75
103 Bobby Abreu .20 .50
104 Victor Martinez .30 .75
105 Jeff Francis .20 .50
106 Rickie Weeks .20 .50
107 Carlos Quentin .20 .50
108 Howie Kendrick .20 .50
109 Aramis Ramirez .20 .50
110 Jonathan Papelbon .30 .75
111 Dan Haren .20 .50
112 Barry Zito .30 .75
113 Magglio Ordonez .30 .75
114 Alfonso Soriano .30 .75
115 Todd Helton .30 .75
116 Troy Tulowitzki .50 1.25
117 Josh Beckett .20 .50
118 Andy Pettitte .30 .75
119 Hank Blalock .20 .50
120 Curtis Granderson .40 1.00
121 Francisco Rodriguez .30 .75
122 Carlos Lee .20 .50
123 Gavin Floyd .20 .50
124 Joe Nathan .20 .50
125 Matt Holliday .50 1.25
126 Hanley Ramirez .30 .75
127 Javier Valentin .20 .50
128 John Maine .20 .50
129 Jeremy Bonderman .20 .50
130 Nick Markakis .40 1.00
131 Troy Glaus .20 .50
132 Derek Lowe .20 .50
133 Lance Berkman .30 .75
134 Jered Weaver .30 .75
135 Chipper Jones .50 1.25
136 Prince Fielder .30 .75
137 Travis Hafner .20 .50
138 Joba Chamberlain .20 .50
139 Ryan Howard .40 1.00
140 Paul Konerko .30 .75
141 Kenji Johjima .30 .75
142 Yovani Gallardo .20 .50
143 Adrian Gonzalez .40 1.00
144 Jimmy Rollins .30 .75
145 Nick Swisher .30 .75
146 Felix Hernandez .30 .75
147 Garret Anderson .20 .50
148 Russell Martin .20 .50
149 Jason Bay .30 .75
150 Fausto Carmona .20 .50
151 Matt Garza .20 .50
152 Matt Cain .30 .75
153 Ryan Freel .20 .50
154 Rocco Baldelli .20 .50
155 Scott Kazmir .20 .50
156 Alexei Ramirez .30 .75
157 Adam Dunn .30 .75
158 Johnny Damon .30 .75
159 Jake Peavy .20 .50
160 Jose Reyes .30 .75
161 Rick Ankiel .20 .50
162 Michael Young .20 .50
163 Robinson Cano .30 .75
164 Ryan Zimmerman .30 .75
165 Jim Thome .30 .75
166 A.J. Burnett .20 .50
167 Joakim Soria .20 .50
168 J.D. Drew .20 .50
169 Cole Hamels .40 1.00
170 Jacoby Ellsbury .40 1.00
171 Travis Snider RC 1.00 2.50
172 Josh Outman RC 1.00 2.50
173 Dexter Fowler (RC) 1.00 2.50
174 Matt Tuiasosopo (RC) .60 1.50
175 Bobby Parnell RC 1.00 2.50
176 Jason Motte (RC) 1.00 2.50
177 James McDonald RC 1.50 4.00
178 Scott Lewis (RC) .60 1.50
179 George Kottaras (RC) .60 1.50
180 Phil Coke RC 1.00 2.50
181 Jordan Schafer (RC) 1.00 2.50
182 Joe Martinez RC 1.00 2.50
183 Trevor Crowe RC .60 1.50
184 Shairon Martis RC 1.00 2.50
185 Everth Cabrera RC 1.00 2.50
186 Trevor Cahill RC 1.50 4.00
187 Jesse Chavez RC .60 1.50
188 Josh Whitesell RC 1.00 2.50
189 Brian Duensing RC 1.00 2.50
190 Andrew Bailey RC 1.50 4.00
191 Ryan Perry RC 1.50 4.00
192 Brett Anderson RC 1.00 2.50
193 Ricky Romero (RC) 1.00 2.50
194 Elvis Andrus RC 1.50 4.00
195 Kenshin Kawakami RC 1.00 2.50
196 Colby Rasmus (RC) 1.00 2.50
197 David Patton RC 1.00 2.50
198 David Hernandez RC .60 1.50
199 David Freese RC 2.00 5.00
200 Rick Porcello RC 2.00 5.00
201 Fernando Martinez RC 1.50 4.00
202 Edwin Moreno (RC) .60 1.50
203 Koji Uehara RC 1.50 4.00
204 Jason Jaramillo (RC) .60 1.50
205 Ramiro Pena RC 1.00 2.50
206 Brad Nelson (RC) .60 1.50
207 Michael Hinckley (RC) .60 1.50
208 Ronald Belisario (RC) .60 1.50
209 Chris Jakubauskas RC 1.00 2.50
210 Hunter Jones RC 1.00 2.50
211 Walter Silva RC 1.00 2.50
212 Jordan Zimmermann RC 1.50 4.00
213 Andrew McCutchen (RC) 3.00 8.00
214 Gordon Beckham RC 5.00 12.00
215 Anthony Claggett RC 1.00 2.50
216 Mark Melancon (RC) .60 1.50
217 Brett Cecil RC .60 1.50
218 Derek Holland RC 1.00 2.50
219 Greg Golson (RC) .60 1.50
220 Bobby Scales RC 1.00 2.50
221 Jordan Schafer AU 5.00 12.00
222 Trevor Crowe AU 4.00 10.00
223 Ramiro Pena AU 4.00 10.00
224 Trevor Cahill AU 6.00 15.00
225 Ryan Perry AU 5.00 12.00
226 Brett Anderson AU 4.00 10.00
227 Elvis Andrus AU 15.00 40.00
229 Michael Bowden AU (RC) 4.00 10.00
230 David Freese AU 12.50 30.00
231 Nolan Reimold AU (RC) 4.00 10.00
233 Jason Jaramillo AU 4.00 10.00
234 Ricky Romero AU 5.00 12.00
235 Jordan Zimmermann AU 6.00 15.00
236 Derek Holland AU 5.00 12.00
237 George Kottaras AU 3.00 8.00
239 Sergio Escalona AU RC 3.00 8.00
240 Brian Duensing AU 5.00 12.00
241 Everth Cabrera AU 6.00 15.00
242 Andrew Bailey AU 6.00 15.00
243 Chris Jakubauskas AU 4.00 10.00
CL1 Checklist Card .20 .50
CL2 Checklist Card .20 .50
CL3 Checklist Card .20 .50
NNO1 Tommy Hanson AU RC 6.00 15.00
NNO2 Mark Melancon AU 6.00 15.00
NNO3 Will Venable AU RC 4.00 10.00

2009 Topps Chrome Refractors

*REF: 1X TO 2.5X BASIC
REF ODDS 1:3 HOBBY
*REF RC: .6X TO 1.5X BASIC RC
REF RC ODDS 1:3 HOBBY
*REF AU: .5X TO 1.2X BASIC AUTO
REF AU ODDS 1:47 HOBBY
REF AU PRINT RUN 499 SER.#'d SETS
44b Barack Obama 8.00 20.00

2009 Topps Chrome Blue Refractors

*BLUE REF: 2.5X TO 6X BASIC
BLUE REF ODDS 1:13 HOBBY
*BLUE REF RC: 1.2X TO 3X BASIC RC
BLUE REF RC ODDS 1:13 HOBBY
*BLUE REF AU: .6X TO 1.5X BASIC AU
BLUE REF AU ODDS 1:120 HOBBY
BLUE REF.PRINT RUN 199 SER.#'d SETS
44b Barack Obama 12.50 30.00
214 Gordon Beckham 30.00 60.00

2009 Topps Chrome Gold Refractors

*GOLD REF: 4X TO 10X BASIC
GOLD REF ODDS 1:50 HOBBY
*GOLD REF RC: 2X TO 5X BASIC RC
GOLD REF RC ODDS 1:50 HOBBY
GOLD AUTO ODDS 1:473 HOBBY
GOLD REF.PRINT RUN 50 SER.#'d SETS
44b Barack Obama 40.00 80.00
214 Gordon Beckham 60.00 120.00
222 Trevor Crowe AU 12.50 30.00
223 Ramiro Pena AU 8.00 20.00
224 Trevor Cahill AU 40.00 80.00
225 Ryan Perry AU 12.50 30.00
226 Brett Anderson AU 12.50 30.00
227 Elvis Andrus AU 40.00 100.00
229 Michael Bowden AU 12.50 30.00
230 David Freese AU 50.00 120.00
231 Nolan Reimold AU 12.50 30.00
233 Jason Jaramillo AU 12.50 30.00
234 Ricky Romero AU 15.00 40.00
235 Jordan Zimmermann AU 15.00 40.00
236 Derek Holland AU 15.00 40.00
237 George Kottaras AU 10.00 25.00
239 Sergio Escalona AU 10.00 25.00
240 Brian Duensing AU 15.00 40.00
241 Everth Cabrera AU 20.00 50.00
242 Andrew Bailey AU 15.00 40.00
243 Chris Jakubauskas AU 12.50 30.00
NNO3 Will Venable AU 12.50 30.00

2009 Topps Chrome Red Refractors

RED 1-220 ODDS 1:100 HOBBY
RED AU ODDS 1:924 HOBBY

STATED PRINT RUN 25 SER.#'d SETS
NO PRICING DUE TO SCARCITY

2009 Topps Chrome X-Fractors

*X-F: 1.5X TO 4X BASIC
*X-F RC: .75X TO 2X BASIC RC
RANDOM INSERTS IN RETAIL PACKS

2009 Topps Chrome World Baseball Classic

STATED ODDS 1:4 HOBBY
PRINT.PLATE ODDS 1:383 HOBBY
PLATE PRINT RUN 1 SET PER COLOR
BLACK-CYAN-MAGENTA-YELLOW ISSUED
NO PLATE PRICING DUE TO SCARCITY
*REF: 1X TO 2.5X BASIC
REF ODDS 1:16 HOBBY
REF PRINT RUN 500 SER.#'d SETS
*BLUE REF: 1.5X TO 4X BASIC
BLUE REF ODDS 1:13 HOBBY
BLUE REF PRINT RUN 199 SER.#'d SETS
*GOLD REF: 2.5X TO 6X BASIC
GOLD REF ODDS 1:50 HOBBY
GOLD REF PRINT RUN 50 SER.#'d SETS
RED REF ODDS 1:100 HOBBY
RED REF PRINT RUN 25 SER.#'d SETS
NO RED REF PRICING AVAILABLE
SUPERFRAC ODDS 1:1532 HOBBY
SUPERFRAC PRINT RUN 1 SER.#'d SET
NO SUPERFRAC PRICING AVAILABLE
W1 Yu Darvish 1.50 4.00
W2 Yulieski Gourriel 1.25 3.00
W3 Yi-Chuan Lin .60 1.50
W4 Ichiro Suzuki 1.25 3.00
W5 Hung-Wen Chen .40 1.00
W6 Yuneski Maya .40 1.00
W7 Chih-Hsien Chiang 1.00 2.50
W8 Kenji Johjima .60 1.50
W9 Hanley Ramirez .60 1.50
W10 Chenhao Li .40 1.00
W11 Yoennis Cespedes 1.50 4.00
W12 Dae Ho Lee .40 1.00
W13 Alex Rodriguez 1.25 3.00
W14 Luis Durango .40 1.00
W15 Chipper Jones 1.00 2.50
W16 Dennis Neuman .40 1.00
W17 Carlos Lee .40 1.00
W18 Tae Kyun Kim .40 1.00
W19 Adrian Gonzalez .75 2.00
W20 Michel Enriquez .40 1.00
W21 Miguel Cabrera 1.00 2.50
W22 Hisashi Iwakuma 1.25 3.00
W23 Aroldis Chapman 2.00 5.00
W24 Daisuke Matsuzaka .60 1.50
W25 Chris Denorfia .40 1.00
W26 David Wright .75 2.00
W27 Alex Rios .40 1.00
W28 Michihiro Ogasawara .60 1.50
W29 Frederich Cepeda .60 1.50
W30 Chen-Chang Lee .60 1.50
W31 Shunsuke Watanabe .60 1.50
W32 Luca Panerati .40 1.00
W33 David Ortiz 1.00 2.50
W34 Tetsuya Yamaguchi .60 1.50
W35 Jin Young Lee .40 1.00
W36 Tom Stuifbergen .40 1.00
W37 Masahiro Tanaka 2.00 5.00
W38 Cheng-Ming Peng .60 1.50
W39 Yoshiyuki Ishihara .60 1.50
W40 Manuel Corpas .40 1.00
W41 Yi-Feng Kuo .40 1.00
W42 Ruben Tejada .40 1.00
W43 Kenley Jansen 1.25 3.00
W44 Shinnosuke Abe .60 1.50
W45 Shuichi Murata .60 1.50
W46 Yolexis Ulacia .40 1.00
W47 Yueh-Ping Lin .60 1.50
W48 James Beresford .40 1.00
W49 Justin Morneau .60 1.50
W50 Brad Harman .40 1.00
W51 Juan Carlos Sulbaran .40 1.00
W52 Ubaldo Jimenez .40 1.00
W53 Joel Naughton .40 1.00
W54 Rafael Diaz .40 1.00
W55 Russell Martin .40 1.00
W56 Concepcion Rodriguez .40 1.00
W57 Po Yu Lin .40 1.00
W58 Chih-Kang Kao .40 1.00
W59 Gregor Blanco .40 1.00
W60 Justin Erasmus .40 1.00
W61 Kosuke Fukudome .60 1.50
W62 Hiroyuki Nakajima .60 1.50
W63 Luke Hughes .40 1.00
W64 Sidney de Jong .40 1.00
W65 Greg Halman .60 1.50
W66 Seiichi Uchikawa .60 1.50
W67 Tao Bu .40 1.00
W68 Pedro Martinez .60 1.50
W69 Jingchao Wang .60 1.50
W70 Arquimedes Nieto .40 1.00
W71 Yang Yang .40 1.00
W72 Alex Liddi .60 1.50
W73 Fei Feng .40 1.00
W74 Pedro Lazo .40 1.00
W75 Magglio Ordonez .60 1.50
W76 Bryan Engelhardt .40 1.00
W77 Yen-Wen Kuo .40 1.00
W78 Norichika Aoki .60 1.50
W79 Jose Reyes .60 1.50
W80 Kangan Xia .40 1.00
W81 Shin-Soo Choo .60 1.50
W82 Frank Catalanotto .40 1.00
W83 Ray Chang .40 1.00
W84 Nelson Cruz 1.00 2.50
W85 Fu-Te Ni .60 1.50
W86 Hein Robb .40 1.00
W87 Hyun-Soo Kim .40 1.00
W88 Tai-Chi Kuo .40 1.00
W89 Akinori Iwamura .40 1.00
W90 Chi-Hung Cheng .40 1.00
W91 Fujia Chu .40 1.00
W92 Gift Ngoepe .40 1.00
W93 Zhenwang Zhang .40 1.00
W94 Bernie Williams .60 1.50
W95 Dustin Pedroia 1.00 2.50
W96 Dylan Lindsay .60 1.50
W97 Max Ramirez .40 1.00
W98 Yadier Molina 1.25 3.00
W99 Phillippe Aumont .60 1.50
W100 Derek Jeter 2.50 6.00

2010 Topps Chrome

COMPLETE SET (220) 20.00 50.00
COMMON CARD (1-170) .20 .50
COMMON RC (171-220) .40 1.00
PRINTING PLATE ODDS 1:1592 HOBBY
1 Prince Fielder .30 .75
2 Derrek Lee .20 .50
3 Clayton Kershaw .75 2.00
4 Bobby Abreu .20 .50
5 Johnny Cueto .30 .75
6 Dexter Fowler .30 .75
7 Mickey Mantle 1.50 4.00
8 Tommy Hanson .20 .50
9 Shane Victorino .30 .75
10 Adam Jones .30 .75
11 Zach Duke .20 .50
12 Victor Martinez .30 .75
13 Rick Porcello .30 .75
14 Josh Johnson .30 .75
15 Marco Scutaro .30 .75
16 Howie Kendrick .20 .50
17 Joey Votto .50 1.25
18 Zack Greinke .50 1.25
19 John Lackey .30 .75
20 Manny Ramirez .50 1.25
21 CC Sabathia .30 .75
22 David Wright .40 1.00
23 Nick Swisher .30 .75
24 Cole Hamels .40 1.00
25 Adrian Gonzalez .40 1.00
26 Joe Saunders .20 .50
27 Tim Lincecum .30 .75
28 Ken Griffey Jr. 1.00 2.50
29 J.A. Happ .30 .75
30 Ian Kinsler .30 .75
31 Carl Crawford .30 .75
32 Albert Pujols .60 1.50
33 Daniel Murphy .40 1.00
34 Erick Aybar .20 .50
35 Andrew McCutchen .50 1.25
36 Gordon Beckham .20 .50
37 Jorge Posada .30 .75
38 Ichiro Suzuki .60 1.50
39 Vladimir Guerrero .30 .75
40 Cliff Lee .30 .75
41 Freddy Sanchez .20 .50
42 Ryan Dempster .20 .50
43 Adam Wainwright .30 .75
44 Matt Holliday .50 1.25
45 Chone Figgins .20 .50
46 Tim Hudson .30 .75
47 Rich Harden .20 .50
48 Justin Upton .30 .75
49 Yunel Escobar .20 .50
50 Joe Mauer .40 1.00
51 Vernon Wells .20 .50
52 Miguel Tejada .30 .75
53 Denard Span .20 .50
54 Brandon Phillips .20 .50
55 Jason Bay .30 .75
56 Kendry Morales .20 .50
57 Josh Hamilton .30 .75
58 Yovani Gallardo .20 .50
59 Adam Lind .30 .75
60 Nick Johnson .20 .50
61 Hideki Matsui .50 1.25
62 Pablo Sandoval .30 .75
63 James Shields .20 .50
64 Roy Halladay .30 .75
65 Chris Coghlan .20 .50
66 Alexei Ramirez .30 .75
67 Josh Beckett .20 .50
68 Magglio Ordonez .30 .75
69 Matt Kemp .40 1.00
70 Max Scherzer .50 1.25
71 Curtis Granderson .40 1.00
72 David Price .40 1.00
73 Lance Berkman .30 .75
74 Andre Ethier .30 .75
75 Mark Teixeira .30 .75
76 Edwin Jackson .20 .50
77 Akinori Iwamura .20 .50
78 Placido Polanco .20 .50
79 Jair Jurrjens .20 .50
80 Stephen Drew .20 .50
81 Javier Vazquez .20 .50
82 Lyle Overbay .20 .50
83 Orlando Hudson .20 .50
84 Adam Dunn .30 .75
85 Kevin Youkilis .20 .50
86 Chase Utley .30 .75
87 Elvis Andrus .30 .75
88 Scott Kazmir .20 .50
89 Brian McCann .30 .75
90 Alex Rios .20 .50
91 Wandy Rodriguez .20 .50
92 Felix Hernandez .30 .75
93 Carlos Gonzalez .30 .75
94 Kosuke Fukudome .30 .75
95 A.J. Burnett .20 .50
96 Nelson Cruz .50 1.25
97 Luke Hochevar .20 .50
98 Francisco Liriano .20 .50
99 Chris Carpenter .30 .75
100 Russell Martin .20 .50
101 Carlos Pena .30 .75
102 Jake Peavy .20 .50
103 Jose Lopez .20 .50
104 Todd Helton .30 .75
105 Mike Pelfrey .20 .50
106 Jacoby Ellsbury .40 1.00
107 Edinson Volquez .20 .50
108 Michael Young .20 .50
109 Dustin Pedroia .50 1.25
110 Chipper Jones .50 1.25
111 Brad Hawpe .20 .50
112 Justin Morneau .30 .75
113 Hiroki Kuroda .20 .50
114 Robinson Cano .30 .75
115 Torii Hunter .20 .50
116 Jimmy Rollins .30 .75
117 Delmon Young .30 .75
118 Matt Cain .30 .75
119 Ryan Zimmerman .30 .75
120 Johan Santana .30 .75
121 Roy Oswalt .30 .75
122 Jay Bruce .30 .75
123 Ubaldo Jimenez .20 .50
124 Geovany Soto .30 .75
125 Jon Lester .30 .75
126 Ryan Howard .40 1.00
127 Jayson Werth .30 .75
128 David Ortiz .50 1.25
129 Dan Haren .20 .50
130 Daisuke Matsuzaka .30 .75
131 Michael Bourn .20 .50
132 Michael Cuddyer .20 .50
133 Carlos Quentin .20 .50
134 Justin Verlander .50 1.25
135 Carlos Beltran .30 .75
136 Alfonso Soriano .30 .75
137 Ryan Braun .30 .75
138 Carlos Zambrano .30 .75
139 Jose Reyes .30 .75
140 Koji Uehara .20 .50
141 Evan Longoria .30 .75
142 Mark Buehrle .30 .75
143 Troy Tulowitzki .50 1.25
144 Alex Rodriguez .60 1.50
145 Chad Billingsley .30 .75
146 Shin-Soo Choo .30 .75
147 Mark Reynolds .20 .50
148 Jered Weaver .30 .75
149 Carlos Lee .20 .50
150 B.J. Upton .30 .75
151 Aaron Hill .20 .50
152 Nick Markakis .40 1.00
153 Hanley Ramirez .30 .75
154 Alex Gordon .30 .75
155 Mike Napoli .20 .50
156 Miguel Cabrera .50 1.25
157 Grady Sizemore .30 .75
158 Aramis Ramirez .20 .50
159 Brandon Webb .30 .75
160 Gavin Floyd .20 .50
161 Yadier Molina .60 1.50
162 Nate McLouth .20 .50
163 Dan Uggla .20 .50
164 Hunter Pence .30 .75
165 Derek Jeter 1.25 3.00
166 Brian Roberts .20 .50
167 Franklin Gutierrez .20 .50
168 Glen Perkins .20 .50
169 Matt Garza .20 .50
170 Raul Ibanez .30 .75
171 Eric Young Jr. (RC) .40 1.00
172 Bryan Anderson (RC) .40 1.00
173 Jon Link RC .40 1.00
174 Jason Heyward RC 1.50 4.00
175 Scott Sizemore RC .60 1.50
176 Mike Leake RC 1.25 3.00
177 Austin Jackson RC .60 1.50
178 Jon Jay RC .60 1.50
179 John Ely RC .40 1.00
180 Jason Donald RC .40 1.00
181 Tyler Colvin RC .60 1.50
182 Brennan Boesch RC 1.00 2.50
183 Esmil Rogers RC .40 1.00
184 Ike Davis RC .75 2.00
185 Andrew Cashner RC .40 1.00
186 Cole Gillespie RC .40 1.00
187 Luke Hughes (RC) .40 1.00
188 Alex Burnett RC .40 1.00
189 Wilson Ramos RC 1.00 2.50
190 Mike Stanton RC 10.00 25.00
191 Josh Donaldson RC 2.00 5.00
192 Chris Heisey RC .60 1.50
193 Lance Zawadzki RC .40 1.00
194 Cesar Valdez RC .40 1.00
195 Starlin Castro RC 1.00 2.50
196 Kevin Russo RC .40 1.00
197 Brandon Hicks RC .60 1.50
198 Carlos Santana RC 1.25 3.00
199 Allen Craig RC 1.00 2.50
200 Jenrry Mejia RC .60 1.50
201 Ruben Tejada RC .60 1.50
202 Drew Butera (RC) .40 1.00
203 Jesse English (RC) .40 1.00
204 Tyson Ross RC .40 1.00
205 Ian Desmond (RC) .60 1.50
206 Mike McCoy RC .40 1.00
207 Tommy Manzella (RC) .40 1.00
208 Kanekoa Texeira RC .40 1.00
209 Daniel McCutchen RC .60 1.50
210 Brian Matusz RC 1.00 2.50
211 Sergio Santos (RC) .40 1.00
212 Stephen Strasburg RC 3.00 8.00
213 Jake Arrieta RC 1.00 2.50
214 Ivan Nova RC 2.00 5.00
215 Kila Ka'aihue (RC) .60 1.50
216 Drew Storen RC .60 1.50
217 Hisanori Takahashi RC .60 1.50
218 Andy Oliver RC .40 1.00
219 Drew Stubbs RC 1.00 2.50
220 Wade Davis (RC) .60 1.50

2010 Topps Chrome Refractors

*REF VET: 1X TO 2.5X BASIC
*REF RC: 1X TO 2.5X BASIC RC
STATED ODDS 1:3 HOBBY

2010 Topps Chrome Blue Refractors

*BLUE VET: 3X TO 8X BASIC
*BLUE RC: 1.5X TO 4X BASIC RC
STATED ODDS 1:58 HOBBY
STATED PRINT RUN 199 SER.#'d SETS

2010 Topps Chrome Gold Refractors

*GOLD VET: 6X TO 15X BASIC
*GOLD RC: 3X TO 8X BASIC RC
STATED ODDS 1:224 HOBBY
STATED PRINT RUN 50 SER.#'d SETS

2010 Topps Chrome Orange Refractors

*ORANGE VET: 1.5X TO 4X BASIC
*ORANGE RC: 1.2X TO 3X BASIC RC
RANDOM INSERTS IN RETAIL PACKS

2010 Topps Chrome Purple Refractors

*PURPLE VET: 2.5X TO 6X BASIC
*PURPLE RC: 1.25X TO 3X BASIC RC
RANDOM INSERTS IN PACKS
STATED PRINT RUN 599 SER.#'d SETS

2010 Topps Chrome X-Fractors

*X-F VET: 1.5X TO 4X BASIC
*X-F RC: 1.2X TO 3X BASIC RC
RANDOM INSERTS IN RETAIL PACKS

2010 Topps Chrome Rookie Autographs

STATED ODDS 1:20 HOBBY
PRINTING PLATE ODDS 1:11,078 HOBBY
171 Eric Young Jr. 3.00 8.00
172 Bryan Anderson 3.00 8.00
173 Jon Link 3.00 8.00
174 Jason Heyward 4.00 10.00
175 Scott Sizemore 3.00 8.00
176 Mike Leake 3.00 8.00
177 Austin Jackson 3.00 8.00
178 Jon Jay 5.00 12.00
179 John Ely 3.00 8.00
181 Tyler Colvin 4.00 10.00
182 Brennan Boesch 5.00 12.00
183 Esmil Rogers 3.00 8.00
184 Ike Davis 4.00 10.00
186 Cole Gillespie 3.00 8.00
187 Luke Hughes 3.00 8.00
188 Alex Burnett 3.00 8.00
189 Wilson Ramos 6.00 15.00
190 Mike Stanton 50.00 120.00
191 Josh Donaldson 10.00 25.00
192 Chris Heisey 3.00 8.00
193 Lance Zawadzki 3.00 8.00
194 Cesar Valdez 3.00 8.00
195 Starlin Castro 6.00 15.00
196 Kevin Russo 3.00 8.00
197 Brandon Hicks 3.00 8.00
198 Carlos Santana 6.00 15.00
199 Allen Craig 3.00 8.00
200 Jenrry Mejia 4.00 10.00
201 Ruben Tejada 3.00 8.00
202 Drew Butera 3.00 8.00
203 Jesse English 3.00 8.00
204 Tyson Ross 3.00 8.00
205 Ian Desmond 5.00 12.00
206 Mike McCoy 3.00 8.00
207 Tommy Manzella 3.00 8.00
208 Kanekoa Texeira 3.00 8.00
209 Daniel McCutchen 3.00 8.00
210 Brian Matusz 3.00 8.00
211 Sergio Santos 3.00 8.00
212 Stephen Strasburg 30.00 80.00
214 Ivan Nova 3.00 8.00
215 Kila Ka'aihue 3.00 8.00
216 Drew Storen 3.00 8.00
217 Hisanori Takahashi 3.00 8.00
219 Drew Stubbs 3.00 8.00
220 Wade Davis 5.00 12.00

2010 Topps Chrome Rookie Autographs Refractors

*REF: .5X TO 1.2X BASIC
STATED ODDS 1:95 HOBBY
STATED PRINT RUN 499 SER.#'d SETS

2010 Topps Chrome Rookie Autographs Blue Refractors

*BLUE: .75X TO 2X BASIC
STATED ODDS 1:238 HOBBY
STATED PRINT RUN 199 SER.#'d SETS

2010 Topps Chrome Rookie Autographs Gold Refractors

*GOLD: 1.25X TO 3X BASIC
STATED ODDS 1:941 HOBBY
STATED PRINT RUN 50 SER.#'d SETS
200 Jenrry Mejia 20.00 50.00

2010 Topps Chrome 206 Chrome

STATED ODDS 1:25 HOBBY
STATED PRINT RUN 999 SER.#'d SETS
*BLUE: .75X TO 2X BASIC
BLUE ODDS 1:125 HOBBY
BLUE PRINT RUN 199 SER.#'d SETS
*GOLD: 2.5X TO 6X BASIC
GOLD ODDS 1:497 HOBBY
GOLD PRINT RUN 50 SER.#'d SETS
PRINTING PLATE ODDS 1:1595 HOBBY
RED ODDS 1:814 HOBBY
RED PRINT RUN 25 SER.#'d SETS
*REF: .5X TO 1.2X BASIC
REF.ODDS 1:50 HOBBY
REF.PRINT RUN 499 HOBBY
SUPERFRAC.ODDS 1:20,384 HOBBY
SUPERFRAC.PRINT RUN 1 SER.#'d SET
TC1 Matt Holliday 1.50 4.00
TC2 Shane Victorino 1.00 2.50
TC3 Zack Greinke 1.50 4.00
TC4 Mike Leake 2.00 5.00
TC5 Justin Upton 1.00 2.50
TC6 Gordon Beckham .60 1.50
TC7 Yovani Gallardo .60 1.50
TC8 Martin Prado .60 1.50
TC9 Adrian Gonzalez 1.25 3.00
TC10 Justin Verlander 1.50 4.00
TC11 Pablo Sandoval 1.00 2.50
TC12 Josh Beckett .60 1.50
TC13 Matt Kemp 1.25 3.00
TC14 Mickey Mantle 5.00 12.00
TC15 Jorge Posada 1.00 2.50
TC16 Evan Longoria 1.00 2.50
TC17 Howie Kendrick .60 1.50
TC18 Joey Votto 1.50 4.00
TC19 Mark Teixeira 1.00 2.50
TC20 Alex Rodriguez 2.00 5.00
TC21 B.J. Upton 1.00 2.50
TC22 Troy Tulowitzki 1.50 4.00
TC23 Ian Kinsler 1.00 2.50
TC24 Brett Anderson .60 1.50
TC25 Roy Halladay 1.00 2.50
TC26 Cliff Lee 1.00 2.50
TC27 Ryan Braun 1.00 2.50
TC28 Jake Peavy .60 1.50
TC29 Neftali Feliz .60 1.50
TC30 Derek Jeter 4.00 10.00
TC31 Austin Jackson 1.00 2.50
TC32 Stephen Strasburg 5.00 12.00
TC33 Dan Haren .60 1.50
TC34 Hanley Ramirez 1.00 2.50
TC35 Victor Martinez 1.00 2.50
TC36 Stephen Drew .60 1.50
TC37 Adam Jones 1.00 2.50
TC38 Vladimir Guerrero 1.00 2.50
TC39 Jacoby Ellsbury 1.25 3.00
TC40 Joe Mauer 1.25 3.00
TC41 Rick Porcello 1.00 2.50
TC42 Albert Pujols 2.00 5.00
TC43 Francisco Liriano .60 1.50
TC44 Dan Uggla .60 1.50
TC45 Hideki Matsui 1.50 4.00
TC46 Tim Lincecum 1.00 2.50
TC47 Ryan Howard 1.25 3.00
TC48 Carl Crawford 1.00 2.50
TC49 Andrew McCutchen 1.50 4.00
TC50 Alfonso Soriano 1.00 2.50

2010 Topps Chrome National Chicle

STATED ODDS 1:25 HOBBY
STATED PRINT RUN 999 SER.#'d SETS
*BLUE: .75X TO 2X BASIC
BLUE ODDS 1:125 HOBBY
BLUE PRINT RUN 199 SER.#'d SETS
*GOLD: 2.5X TO 6X BASIC
GOLD ODDS 1:497 HOBBY
GOLD PRINT RUN 50 SER.#'d SETS
PRINTING PLATE ODDS 1:1595 HOBBY
RED ODDS 1:814 HOBBY
RED PRINT RUN 25 SER.#'d SETS
*REF: .5X TO 1.2X BASIC
REF.ODDS 1:50 HOBBY
REF.PRINT RUN 499 HOBBY
SUPERFRAC.ODDS 1:20,384 HOBBY
SUPERFRAC.PRINT RUN 1 SER.#'d SET
CC1 Albert Pujols 2.00 5.00
CC2 Grady Sizemore 1.00 2.50
CC3 Ichiro Suzuki 2.00 5.00
CC4 Daisuke Matsuzaka 1.00 2.50
CC5 James Loney .60 1.50
CC6 Tim Wakefield 1.00 2.50
CC7 Shane Victorino 1.00 2.50
CC8 Jacoby Ellsbury 1.25 3.00
CC9 Hunter Pence 1.00 2.50
CC10 Andy Pettitte 1.00 2.50
CC11 David Wright 1.25 3.00
CC12 Derek Jeter 4.00 10.00
CC13 Ryan Howard 1.25 3.00
CC14 Russell Martin .60 1.50
CC15 Michael Young .60 1.50
CC16 Johnny Damon 1.00 2.50
CC17 Robinson Cano 1.00 2.50
CC18 Adrian Gonzalez 1.25 3.00
CC19 Gordon Beckham .60 1.50
CC20 Aramis Ramirez .60 1.50
CC21 Alex Rodriguez 2.00 5.00
CC22 Johan Santana 1.00 2.50
CC23 Vladimir Guerrero 1.00 2.50
CC24 Nick Markakis 1.25 3.00
CC25 Justin Verlander 1.50 4.00
CC26 Adam Jones 1.00 2.50
CC27 Chone Figgins .60 1.50
CC28 Cole Hamels 1.25 3.00
CC29 Roy Oswalt 1.00 2.50
CC30 Ryan Braun 1.00 2.50
CC31 Alexei Ramirez 1.00 2.50
CC32 Adam Dunn 1.00 2.50
CC33 Pablo Sandoval 1.00 2.50
CC34 Todd Helton 1.00 2.50
CC35 Carlos Beltran 1.00 2.50
CC36 Ubaldo Jimenez .60 1.50
CC37 Tommy Hanson .60 1.50
CC38 Zack Greinke 1.50 4.00
CC39 Chris Coghlan .60 1.50
CC40 Chris Young .60 1.50
CC41 Jake Peavy .60 1.50
CC42 Dexter Fowler 1.00 2.50
CC43 Phil Hughes .60 1.50
CC44 Chase Utley 1.00 2.50
CC45 Ian Stewart .60 1.50
CC46 John Danks .60 1.50
CC47 Ichiro Suzuki 2.00 5.00
CC48 Lance Berkman 1.00 2.50
CC49 Ryan Zimmerman 1.00 2.50
CC50 Albert Pujols 2.00 5.00

2010 Topps Chrome Target Exclusive Refractors

COMPLETE SET (5) 6.00 15.00
BC1 Stephen Strasburg 2.50 6.00
BC2 Starlin Castro .75 2.00
BC3 Jason Heyward 1.25 3.00
BC4 Mickey Mantle 2.50 6.00
BC5 Jackie Robinson .75 2.00

2010 Topps Chrome USA Baseball Autographs

STATED ODDS 1:287 HOBBY
USA1 Tyler Anderson 8.00 20.00
USA2 Matt Barnes 5.00 12.00
USA3 Jackie Bradley Jr. 10.00 25.00
USA4 Gerrit Cole 15.00 40.00
USA5 Alex Dickerson 5.00 12.00
USA6 Nolan Fontana 5.00 12.00
USA7 Sean Gilmartin 6.00 15.00
USA8 Sonny Gray 12.00 30.00
USA9 Brian Johnson 8.00 20.00
USA10 Andrew Maggi 8.00 20.00
USA11 Mike Mahtook 10.00 25.00
USA12 Scott McGough 5.00 12.00
USA13 Brad Miller 8.00 20.00
USA14 Brett Mooneyham 8.00 20.00
USA15 Peter O'Brien 8.00 20.00
USA16 Nick Ramirez 8.00 20.00
USA17 Noe Ramriez 8.00 20.00
USA19 Steve Rodriguez 8.00 20.00
USA20 George Springer 25.00 60.00
USA21 Kyle Winkler 8.00 20.00
USA22 Ryan Wright 5.00 12.00

2010 Topps Chrome Wal-Mart Exclusive Refractors

COMPLETE SET (3) 6.00 15.00
WME1 Babe Ruth 2.00 5.00
WME2 Cal Ripken Jr. 2.50 6.00
WME3 Stephen Strasburg 2.50 6.00

2010 Topps Chrome Wrapper Redemption Autographs

STATED PRINT RUN 90 SER.#'d SETS
174 Jason Heyward 100.00 200.00
221 Buster Posey 300.00 500.00

2010 Topps Chrome Wrapper Redemption Refractors

COMPLETE SET (15) 10.00 25.00
*GREEN RC: .5X TO 1.2X BASIC
*GREEN VET: .5X TO 1.2X BASIC
GREEN PRINT RUN 599 SER.#'d SETS
174 Jason Heyward 3.00 8.00
176 Mike Leake 2.50 6.00
177 Austin Jackson 1.25 3.00
181 Tyler Colvin 1.25 3.00
184 Ike Davis 1.50 4.00
190 Mike Stanton 25.00 60.00
195 Starlin Castro 2.00 5.00
198 Carlos Santana 2.50 6.00
212 Stephen Strasburg 6.00 15.00
221 Buster Posey 10.00 25.00
222 Babe Ruth 5.00 12.00
223 Lou Gehrig 4.00 10.00
224 Jackie Robinson 2.00 5.00
225 Ty Cobb 3.00 8.00
226 Mickey Mantle 6.00 15.00

2011 Topps Chrome

COMPLETE SET (220) 20.00 50.00
COMMON CARD (1-169) .20 .50
COMMON RC (1-220) .40 1.00
PRINTING PLATE ODDS 1:718 HOBBY
PLATE PRINT RUN 1 SET PER COLOR
BLACK-CYAN-MAGENTA-YELLOW ISSUED
NO PLATE PRICING DUE TO SCARCITY
1 Buster Posey .60 1.50
2 Chipper Jones .50 1.25
3 Carl Crawford .30 .75
4 Andre Ethier .30 .75
5 David Wright .40 1.00
6 Zack Greinke .50 1.25
7 Mickey Mantle 1.50 4.00
8 Andrew McCutchen .50 1.25
9 Prince Fielder .30 .75
10 Hanley Ramirez .30 .75
11 Ryan Zimmerman .30 .75
12 David Ortiz .50 1.25
13 Evan Longoria .30 .75
14 Adam Dunn .30 .75
15 Tim Lincecum .30 .75
16 Jason Heyward .40 1.00
17 Starlin Castro .30 .75
18 Ian Kinsler .30 .75
19 Joey Votto .50 1.25
20 Derek Jeter 1.25 3.00
21 Carlos Ruiz .20 .50
22 Nick Markakis .40 1.00
23 Russ Martin .20 .50
24 Matt Kemp .40 1.00
25 Adrian Gonzalez .40 1.00
26 Dan Uggla .20 .50
27 Orlando Hudson .20 .50
28 Austin Jackson .20 .50
29 Phil Hughes .20 .50
30 Miguel Cabrera .50 1.25
31 Tommy Hunter .20 .50
32 Yadier Molina .60 1.50
33 Danny Espinosa RC .40 1.00
34 Josh Beckett .20 .50
35 Chase Utley .30 .75
36 Rafael Soriano .20 .50
37 Mike Leake .30 .75
38 Justin Upton .30 .75
39 Travis Wood .20 .50
40 Cliff Lee .30 .75
41 Danny Valencia .30 .75
42 Mariano Rivera .60 1.50
43 Josh Johnson .30 .75
44 David Price .40 1.00
45 Ryan Howard .40 1.00
46 Billy Butler .20 .50
47 James Loney .20 .50
48 Jay Bruce .30 .75
49 Jonathan Papelbon .30 .75
50 Ichiro Suzuki .60 1.50
51 Gordon Beckham .20 .50
52 CC Sabathia .30 .75
53 Carlos Santana .50 1.25
54 Ryan Braun .30 .75
55 Jon Lester .30 .75
56 Gio Gonzalez .30 .75
57 John Jaso .20 .50
58 Jason Bay .30 .75
59 Joe Nathan .20 .50
60 Josh Hamilton .30 .75
61 Yovani Gallardo .20 .50
62 Brian Wilson .50 1.25
63 Neil Walker .30 .75
64 Vernon Wells .20 .50
65 Jason Bartlett .20 .50
66 Neftali Feliz .20 .50
67 Aaron Hill .20 .50
68 Aroldis Chapman RC 1.25 3.00
69 Michael Young .20 .50
70 Robinson Cano .30 .75
71 Colby Rasmus .30 .75
72 Brian McCann .30 .75
73 James Shields .20 .50
74 Nelson Cruz .50 1.25
75 Roy Halladay .30 .75
76 Jose Bautista .30 .75
77 David DeJesus .20 .50
78 Sean Rodriguez .20 .50
79 Jonathan Sanchez .20 .50
80 Joe Mauer .40 1.00
81 Mat Latos .30 .75
82 Franklin Gutierrez .20 .50
83 Adam Jones .30 .75
84 Jorge Posada .30 .75
85 Mike Stanton .50 1.25
86 Drew Stubbs .20 .50
87 Todd Helton .30 .75
88 Joakim Soria .20 .50
89 Gaby Sanchez .20 .50
90 Kevin Youkilis .20 .50
91 Alfonso Soriano .30 .75
92 Jake Peavy .20 .50
93 Pablo Sandoval .30 .75
94 Shane Victorino .30 .75
95 Cameron Maybin .20 .50
96 Hunter Pence .30 .75
97 Ubaldo Jimenez .20 .50
98 Heath Bell .20 .50
99 Kendry Morales .20 .50
100 Alex Rodriguez .60 1.50
101 Tim Hudson .30 .75
102 Jordan Zimmerman .30 .75
103 Shin-Soo Choo .30 .75
104 Matt Garza .20 .50
105 Felix Hernandez .30 .75
106 Ike Davis .20 .50
107 Clayton Kershaw .75 2.00
108 Mike Morse .20 .50
109 Ricky Romero .20 .50
110 Carlos Gonzalez .30 .75
111 Marlon Byrd .20 .50
112 Carlos Pena .30 .75
113 Jayson Werth .30 .75
114 Carlos Beltran .30 .75
115 Justin Verlander .50 1.25
116 Clay Buchholz .20 .50
117 Jimmy Rollins .30 .75
118 Francisco Liriano .20 .50
119 Ryan Ludwick .20 .50
120 Stephen Strasburg .50 1.25
121 Chris Carpenter .30 .75
122 Adam Lind .30 .75
123 B.J. Upton .30 .75
124 Jacoby Ellsbury .40 1.00
125 Roy Oswalt .30 .75
126 Johan Santana .30 .75
127 Madison Bumgarner .40 1.00
128 Matt Joyce .20 .50
129 Mark Reynolds .20 .50
130 Matt Holliday .50 1.25
131 Tyler Colvin .20 .50
132 Matt Cain .30 .75
133 Drew Storen .20 .50
134 Grady Sizemore .30 .75
135 Martin Prado .20 .50
136 C.J. Wilson .20 .50
137 Chris Young .20 .50
138 Jose Reyes .30 .75
139 Clayton Richard .20 .50
140 Mark Teixeira .30 .75
141 Lance Berkman .30 .75
142 John Buck .20 .50
143 Brett Anderson .20 .50
144 Johnny Damon .30 .75
145 Rickie Weeks .20 .50
146 Brett Myers .20 .50
147 Chone Figgins .20 .50
148 Derrek Lee .20 .50
149 Ian Desmond .20 .50
150 Albert Pujols .60 1.50
151 Pedro Alvarez .75 2.00
152 Josh Thole .20 .50
153 Jonathan Broxton .20 .50
154 Justin Morneau .30 .75
155 Tommy Hanson .20 .50
156 Cole Hamels .40 1.00
157 Angel Pagan .20 .50
158 Curtis Granderson .40 1.00
159 Paul Konerko .30 .75
160 Troy Tulowitzki .50 1.25
161 Dustin Pedroia .50 1.25
162 Elvis Andrus .30 .75
163 Logan Morrison .20 .50
164 Jered Weaver .30 .75
165 Adrian Beltre .50 1.25
166 Victor Martinez .30 .75
167 Chad Billingsley .30 .75
168 J.A. Happ .30 .75
169 Rafael Furcal .20 .50
170 Eric Hosmer RC 2.50 6.00
171 Tsuyoshi Nishioka RC 1.25 3.00
172 Brandon Belt RC 1.00 2.50
173 Freddie Freeman RC 6.00 15.00
174 Michael Pineda RC 1.00 2.50
175 Ben Revere RC .60 1.50
176 Brandon Beachy RC 1.00 2.50
177 Aneury Rodriguez RC .40 1.00
178 Mark Trumbo (RC) 1.00 2.50
179 Marcos Mateo RC .60 1.50
180 Hank Conger RC .60 1.50
181 Jake McGee (RC) .75 2.00
182 J.P. Arencibia (RC) .40 1.00
183 Jordan Walden RC .40 1.00
184 Eric Sogard RC .40 1.00
185 Matt Young RC .40 1.00
186 Domonic Brown (RC) .75 2.00
187 Scott Cousins RC .40 1.00
188 Alexi Ogando RC 1.00 2.50
189 Mike Nickeas (RC) .40 1.00
190 Ivan DeJesus RC .40 1.00
191 Andrew Cashner (RC) .40 1.00
192 Josh Lueke RC .40 1.00
193 Darwin Barney RC 1.25 3.00
194 Mason Tobin RC .40 1.00
195 Craig Kimbrel RC 1.00 2.50
196 Lance Pendleton RC .40 1.00
197 Julio Teheran RC .60 1.50
198 Eduardo Nunez RC 1.00 2.50
199 Pedro Beato RC .40 1.00
200 Jeremy Hellickson RC 1.00 2.50
201 Vinnie Pestano RC .40 1.00
202 Tom Wilhelmsen RC .40 1.00
203 Brett Wallace (RC) .40 1.00
204 Chris Pettit (RC) .40 1.00
205 Chris Sale RC 3.00 8.00
206 Brandon Kintzler RC .40 1.00
207 Alex Cobb RC .40 1.00
208 Michael Kohn RC .40 1.00
209 Cory Luebke RC .40 1.00
210 Pedro Strop (RC) .40 1.00
211 Jerry Sands RC 1.00 2.50
212 Dee Gordon RC .60 1.50
213 Joe Paterson RC .60 1.50
214 Brent Morel RC .40 1.00

215 Kyle Drabek RC .60 1.50
216 Zach Britton RC 1.00 2.50
217 Mike Minor (RC) .40 1.00
218 Hector Noesi RC .60 1.50
219 Carlos Peguero RC .60 1.50
220 Aaron Crow RC .60 1.50

2011 Topps Chrome Refractors

*REF VET: 1X TO 2.5X BASIC
*REF RC: .6X TO 1.5X BASIC RC
STATED ODDS 1:3 HOBBY

2011 Topps Chrome Atomic Refractors

*ATOMIC VET: 2X TO 5X BASIC
*ATOMIC RC: 1X TO 2.5X BASIC RC
STATED ODDS 1:19 HOBBY
STATED PRINT RUN 225 SER.#'d SETS
170 Eric Hosmer 30.00 60.00

2011 Topps Chrome Black Refractors

*BLACK VET: 4X TO 10X BASIC
*BLACK RC: 2X TO 5X BASIC RC
STATED ODDS 1:84 HOBBY
STATED PRINT RUN 100 SER.#'d SETS

2011 Topps Chrome Blue Refractors

*BLUE VET: 4X TO 10X BASIC
*BLUE RC: 2X TO 5X BASIC RC
STATED ODDS 1:57 HOBBY
STATED PRINT RUN 99 SER.#'d SETS

2011 Topps Chrome Gold Refractors

*GOLD VET: 5X TO 12X BASIC
*GOLD RC: 2.5X TO 6X BASIC RC
STATED ODDS 1:111 HOBBY
STATED PRINT RUN 50 SER.#'d SETS

2011 Topps Chrome Orange Refractors

*ORANGE VET: 1.5X TO 4X BASIC
*ORANGE RC: .75X TO 2X BASIC RC

2011 Topps Chrome Purple Refractors

*PURPLE VET: 2X TO 5X BASIC
*PURPLE RC: 1X TO 2.5X BASIC RC
STATED PRINT RUN 499 SER.#'d SETS
170 Eric Hosmer 12.50 30.00

2011 Topps Chrome Sepia Refractors

*SEPIA VET: 4X TO 10X BASIC
*SEPIA RC: 2X TO 5X BASIC RC
STATED ODDS 1:43 HOBBY
STATED PRINT RUN 99 SER.#'d SETS

2011 Topps Chrome X-Fractors

*X-FRAC.VET: 1.5X TO 4X BASIC
*X-FRAC.RC: .75X TO 2X BASIC RC

2011 Topps Chrome Rookie Autographs

STATED ODDS 1:12 HOBBY
PRINTING PLATE ODDS 1:8217 HOBBY
PLATE PRINT RUN 1 SET PER COLOR
BLACK-CYAN-MAGENTA-YELLOW ISSUED
NO PLATE PRICING DUE TO SCARCITY
EXCHANGE DEADLINE 8/31/2014
33 Danny Espinosa 3.00 8.00
170 Eric Hosmer EXCH 40.00 100.00
171 Tsuyoshi Nishioka EXCH 50.00 100.00
172 Brandon Belt 5.00 12.00
173 Freddie Freeman 100.00 250.00
174 Michael Pineda 5.00 12.00
175 Ben Revere 3.00 8.00
176 Brandon Beachy 3.00 8.00
178 Mark Trumbo 6.00 15.00
181 Jake McGee 3.00 8.00
182 J.P. Arencibia 3.00 8.00
183 Jordan Walden 4.00 10.00
184 Eric Sogard 3.00 8.00
188 Alexi Ogando 3.00 8.00
190 Ivan DeJesus Jr. 3.00 8.00
191 Andrew Cashner 3.00 8.00
193 Darwin Barney 3.00 8.00
195 Craig Kimbrel 15.00 40.00
197 Julio Teheran 4.00 10.00
198 Eduardo Nunez 4.00 10.00
205 Chris Sale 20.00 50.00
207 Alex Cobb 3.00 8.00
214 Brent Morel 3.00 8.00
215 Kyle Drabek 3.00 8.00
216 Zach Britton 5.00 12.00
217 Mike Minor 5.00 12.00
218 Hector Noesi 3.00 8.00
219 Carlos Peguero 3.00 8.00
220 Aaron Crow 3.00 8.00

2011 Topps Chrome Rookie Autographs Refractors

*REF: .5X TO 1.2X BASIC
STATED ODDS 1:72 HOBBY
STATED PRINT RUN 499 SER.#'d SETS
EXCHANGE DEADLINE 8/31/2014

2011 Topps Chrome Rookie Autographs Black Refractors

*BLACK REF: 1X TO 2.5X BASIC
STATED ODDS 1:328 HOBBY
STATED PRINT RUN 100 SER.#'d SETS
EXCHANGE DEADLINE 8/31/2014

2011 Topps Chrome Rookie Autographs Blue Refractors

*BLUE REF: .75X TO 2X BASIC
STATED ODDS 1:181 HOBBY
STATED PRINT RUN 199 SER.#'d SETS
EXCHANGE DEADLINE 8/31/2014

2011 Topps Chrome Rookie Autographs Gold Refractors

*GOLD REF: 1.2X TO 3X BASIC
STATED ODDS 1:694 HOBBY
STATED PRINT RUN 50 SER.#'d SETS
EXCHANGE DEADLINE 8/31/2014
171 Tsuyoshi Nishioka EXCH 125.00 300.00

2011 Topps Chrome Rookie Autographs Sepia Refractors

*SEPIA REF: 1X TO 2.5X BASIC
STATED ODDS 1:350 HOBBY
STATED PRINT RUN 99 SER.#'d SETS
EXCHANGE DEADLINE 8/31/2014

2011 Topps Chrome USA Baseball Autographs

EXCHANGE CARD ODDS 1:824 HOBBY
EXCHANGE DEADLINE 9/6/2012
PRINTING PLATE ODDS 1:230,000 HOBBY
PLATE PRINT RUN 1 SET PER COLOR
BLACK-CYAN-MAGENTA-YELLOW ISSUED
NO PLATE PRICING DUE TO SCARCITY
USABB1 Mark Appel 10.00 25.00
USABB2 DJ Baxendale 4.00 10.00
USABB3 Josh Elander 4.00 10.00
USABB4 Chris Elder 4.00 10.00
USABB5 Dominic Ficociello 4.00 10.00
USABB6 Nolan Fontana 4.00 10.00
USABB7 Kevin Gausman 6.00 15.00
USABB8 Brian Johnson 4.00 10.00
USABB9 Branden Kline 4.00 10.00
USABB10 Corey Knebel 5.00 12.00
USABB11 Michael Lorenzen 4.00 10.00
USABB12 David Lyon 4.00 10.00
USABB13 Deven Marrero 4.00 10.00
USABB14 Hoby Milner 4.00 10.00
USABB15 Andrew Mitchell 4.00 10.00
USABB16 Tom Murphy 4.00 10.00
USABB17 Tyler Naquin 15.00 40.00
USABB18 Matt Reynolds 4.00 10.00
USABB19 Brady Rodgers 4.00 10.00
USABB20 Marcus Stroman 8.00 20.00
USABB21 Michael Wacha 25.00 60.00
USABB22 Erich Weiss 4.00 10.00
NNO Exchange Card 30.00 60.00

2011 Topps Chrome USA Baseball Autographs Refractors

*REF: .5X TO 1.2X BASIC
EXCHANGE ODDS 1:1173 HOBBY
STATED PRINT RUN 199 SER.#'d SETS
EXCHANGE DEADLINE 9/6/2012
NNO Exchange Card 40.00 80.00

2011 Topps Chrome USA Baseball Autographs Blue Refractors

*BLUE REF: .75X TO 2X BASIC
EXCHANGE ODDS 1:2397 HOBBY
STATED PRINT RUN 99 SER.#'d SETS
EXCHANGE DEADLINE 9/6/2012
NNO Exchange Card 60.00 120.00

2011 Topps Chrome USA Baseball Autographs Gold Refractors

*GOLD REF: 1.25X TO 3X BASIC
EXCHANGE ODDS 1:4900 HOBBY
STATED PRINT RUN 50 SER.#'d SETS
EXCHANGE DEADLINE 9/6/2012
NNO Exchange Card 100.00 200.00

2011 Topps Chrome USA Baseball Refractors

EXCHANGE CARD ODDS 1:964 HOBBY
STATED PRINT RUN 999 SER.#'d SETS
EXCHANGE DEADLINE 9/6/2012
PRINTING PLATE ODDS 1:230,000 HOBBY
PLATE PRINT RUN 1 SET PER COLOR
BLACK-CYAN-MAGENTA-YELLOW ISSUED
NO PLATE PRICING DUE TO SCARCITY
USABB1 Mark Appel 1.50 4.00
USABB2 DJ Baxendale 1.00 2.50
USABB3 Josh Elander .60 1.50
USABB4 Chris Elder .60 1.50
USABB5 Dominic Ficociello .60 1.50
USABB6 Nolan Fontana .60 1.50
USABB7 Kevin Gausman 3.00 8.00
USABB8 Brian Johnson .60 1.50
USABB9 Branden Kline .60 1.50
USABB10 Corey Knebel .60 1.50
USABB11 Michael Lorenzen .60 1.50
USABB12 David Lyon .60 1.50
USABB13 Deven Marrero 1.50 4.00
USABB14 Hoby Milner .60 1.50
USABB15 Andrew Mitchell .60 1.50
USABB16 Tom Murphy .60 1.50
USABB17 Tyler Naquin 1.50 4.00
USABB18 Matt Reynolds 1.00 2.50
USABB19 Brady Rodgers .60 1.50
USABB20 Marcus Stroman 1.50 4.00
USABB21 Michael Wacha 2.00 5.00
USABB22 Erich Weiss .60 1.50

2011 Topps Chrome USA Baseball Blue Refractors

*BLUE: .6X TO 1.5X BASIC
EXCHANGE ODDS 1:2025 HOBBY
STATED PRINT RUN 499 SER.#'d SETS
EXCHANGE DEADLINE 9/6/2012

2011 Topps Chrome USA Baseball Gold Refractors

*GOLD: 1.5X TO 4X BASIC
EXCHANGE ODDS 1:18,400 HOBBY
STATED PRINT RUN 50 SER.#'d SETS
EXCHANGE DEADLINE 9/6/2012

2011 Topps Chrome Vintage Chrome

COMPLETE SET (50) 20.00 50.00
STATED ODDS 1:6 HOBBY
VC1 Buster Posey 1.00 2.50
VC2 Chipper Jones .75 2.00
VC3 Carl Crawford .50 1.25
VC4 David Wright .60 1.50
VC5 Prince Fielder .50 1.25
VC6 Hanley Ramirez .50 1.25
VC7 Ryan Zimmerman .50 1.25
VC8 David Ortiz .75 2.00
VC9 Evan Longoria .50 1.25
VC10 Tim Lincecum .50 1.25
VC11 Jason Heyward .60 1.50
VC12 Joey Votto .75 2.00
VC13 Derek Jeter 2.00 5.00
VC14 Matt Kemp .60 1.50
VC15 Adrian Gonzlez .60 1.50
VC16 Dan Uggla .30 .75
VC17 Austin Jackson .30 .75
VC18 Starlin Castro .50 1.25
VC19 Chase Utley .50 1.25
VC20 David Price .60 1.50
VC21 Ryan Howard .60 1.50
VC22 Ichiro Suzuki 1.00 2.50
VC23 CC Sabathia .50 1.25
VC24 Ryan Braun .50 1.25
VC25 Josh Hamilton .50 1.25
VC26 Robinson Cano .50 1.25
VC27 Brian McCann .50 1.25
VC28 Nelson Cruz .75 2.00
VC29 Roy Halladay .50 1.25
VC30 Jose Bautista .50 1.25
VC31 Joe Mauer .60 1.50
VC32 Mike Stanton .75 2.00
VC33 Troy Tulowitzki .75 2.00
VC34 Kevin Youkilis .30 .75
VC35 Miguel Cabrera .75 2.00
VC36 Alex Rodriguez 1.00 2.50
VC37 Felix Hernandez .50 1.25
VC38 Stephen Strasburg .75 2.00
VC39 Mark Teixeira .60 1.50
VC40 Albert Pujols 1.00 2.50
VC41 Carlos Gonzalez .50 1.25
VC42 Dustin Pedroia .75 2.00
VC43 Tsuyoshi Nishioka 1.00 2.50
VC44 Brandon Belt .75 2.00
VC45 Freddie Freeman 5.00 12.00
VC46 J.P. Arencibia .30 .75
VC47 Domonic Brown .60 1.50
VC48 Aroldis Chapman 1.00 2.50
VC49 Jeremy Hellickson .75 2.00
VC50 Kyle Drabek .50 1.25

2012 Topps Chrome

COMP.SET w/o VAR (220) 20.00 50.00
PHOTO VAR ODDS 1:918 HOBBY
VARIATIONS ARE REFRACTORS
NO VARIATION PRICING AVAILABLE
PRINTING PLATE ODDS 1:958 HOBBY
PLATE PRINT RUN 1 SET PER COLOR
NO PLATE PRICING DUE TO SCARCITY
1A Tim Lincecum Follow Through .40 1.00
1B Lincecum Arm Back SP 12.50 30.00
2 Craig Kimbrel .40 1.00
3 Shane Victorino .40 1.00
4 David Ortiz .50 1.25
5 Ryan Lavarnway .30 .75
6 Jon Lester .30 .75
7 Michael Pineda .30 .75
8 C.J. Wilson .30 .75
9 Brian McCann .40 1.00
10A Justin Upton Swinging .40 1.00
10B J.Upton Bubble SP 10.00 25.00
11 Ian Kennedy .30 .75
12 Jason Heyward .40 1.00
13 Ian Kinsler .40 1.00
14 CC Sabathia .40 1.00
15 Jimmy Rollins .40 1.00
16 Jose Valverde .40 1.00
17 Chris Carpenter .40 1.00
18 Cameron Maybin .30 .75
19 Freddie Freeman .60 1.50
20 Adrian Gonzalez .40 1.00
21 Dustin Pedroia .50 1.25
22 Shin-Soo Choo .40 1.00
23 Clay Buchholz .30 .75
24 Buster Posey .60 1.50
25 Chase Utley .40 1.00
26 Prince Fielder .40 1.00
27 Mark Reynolds .30 .75
28A Roy Halladay .40 1.00
29 Carl Crawford .40 1.00
30A Josh Hamilton .40 1.00
30B J.Hamilton SP 30.00 60.00
31 Ben Zobrist .40 1.00
32 Giancarlo Stanton .50 1.25
33 Tommy Hanson .30 .75
34 Aroldis Chapman .50 1.25
35 Paul Goldschmidt .50 1.25
36 Cole Hamels .40 1.00
37 Jeremy Hellickson .30 .75
38 Andrew McCutchen .50 1.25
39 Jacob Turner .40 1.00
40 Joey Votto .50 1.25
41 David Wright .40 1.00
42 Zack Cozart .30 .75
43 Desmond Jennings .40 1.00
44 Jhoulys Chacin .30 .75
45 Alex Gordon .40 1.00
46 Dan Uggla .40 1.00
47 Billy Butler .30 .75
48 Matt Cain .40 1.00
49A Alex Rodriguez .60 1.50
49B A.Rod Throwing SP 15.00 40.00
50 Joe Mauer .40 1.00
51 Torii Hunter .40 1.00
52 Jered Weaver .40 1.00
53 Gio Gonzalez .40 1.00
54 Ike Davis .30 .75
55 Paul Konerko .30 .75
56 Mike Napoli .30 .75
57 Nelson Cruz .50 1.25
58 Shaun Marcum .30 .75
59 James Shields .30 .75
60 Curtis Granderson .40 1.00
61 Eric Hosmer .40 1.00
62 Michael Morse .30 .75
63 Josh Johnson .40 1.00
64 Lucas Duda .40 1.00
65 Ubaldo Jimenez .30 .75
66 Mat Latos .40 1.00
67 Daniel Hudson .30 .75
68 Michael Young .30 .75
69 Lance Berkman .40 1.00
70A Stephen Strasburg Arm Back .50 1.25
70B Strasburg Leg Up SP 50.00 100.00
71 Ryan Howard .40 1.00
72 Anibal Sanchez .30 .75
73 Mark Teixeira .40 1.00
74 Hanley Ramirez .40 1.00
75A Jose Reyes .30 .75
75B J.Reyes No Bat SP 15.00 40.00
76 Zack Greinke .50 1.25
77 Tim Hudson .40 1.00
78 Jayson Werth .40 1.00
79 Brandon Phillips .30 .75
80A Albert Pujols .60 1.50
80B Pujols Facing Right SP 12.50 30.00
81 Kyle Blanks .30 .75
82 Hunter Pence .40 1.00
83 Mark Trumbo .30 .75
84A Derek Jeter Jumping 1.25 3.00
84B Jeter Standing SP 50.00 100.00
85 Carlos Gonzalez .40 1.00
86 Ricky Romero .30 .75
87A Jacoby Ellsbury Sliding .40 1.00
87B Ellsbury Running SP 30.00 60.00
88 Jason Motte .30 .75
89 Mike Moustakas .40 1.00
90 Evan Longoria .40 1.00
91 Allen Craig .40 1.00
92 Derek Holland .30 .75
93A Justin Verlander .50 1.25
93B Verlander Arm Up SP 20.00 50.00
94 Justin Morneau .40 1.00
95 Matt Garza .30 .75
96 Chipper Jones .50 1.25
97 Yadier Molina .60 1.50
98 Brian Wilson .50 1.25
99 Jemile Weeks RC .30 .75
100A Ichiro Suzuki .60 1.50
101 Yonder Alonso .30 .75
102 Madison Bumgarner .40 1.00
103 Cliff Lee .40 1.00
104 David Freese .30 .75
105 Adam Lind .40 1.00
106 Adam Jones .40 1.00
107 Dustin Ackley .30 .75
108 Nick Swisher .40 1.00
109 Kevin Youkilis .50 1.25
110A Troy Tulowitzki .50 1.25
111 Miguel Montero .30 .75
112 Clayton Kershaw .75 2.00
113 Michael Bourn .30 .75
114 Carlos Santana .40 1.00
115 Josh Beckett .30 .75
116 Felix Hernandez .40 1.00
117 Ryan Braun .30 .75
118 Ryan Zimmerman .40 1.00
119 Jaime Garcia .40 1.00
120A Matt Kemp .40 1.00
120B Kemp Batting SP 30.00 60.00
121 Nyjer Morgan .30 .75
122 Brandon Beachy .30 .75
123 Brandon Belt .40 1.00
124 Salvador Perez .40 1.00
125 Matt Holliday .50 1.25
126 Dan Haren .30 .75
127 Starlin Castro .40 1.00
128 Asdrubal Cabrera .40 1.00
129 Ivan Nova .40 1.00
130 Miguel Cabrera .50 1.25
131 Alex Avila .30 .75
132 Adrian Beltre .50 1.25
133 David Price .40 1.00
134 Melky Cabrera .30 .75
135 Drew Stubbs .30 .75
136 Dee Gordon .30 .75
137 B.J. Upton .40 1.00
138 Ryan Vogelsong .30 .75
139 Pablo Sandoval .40 1.00
140 Jose Bautista .40 1.00
141 Jay Bruce .40 1.00
142 Yovani Gallardo .40 1.00
143 Robinson Cano .40 1.00
144 Mike Trout 40.00 100.00
145 Chris Young .30 .75
146 Aramis Ramirez .30 .75
147 Rickie Weeks .30 .75
148 Johnny Cueto .40 1.00
149 Elvis Andrus .40 1.00
150 Mariano Rivera .60 1.50
151A Yu Darvish Arm Back RC 1.50 4.00
151B Darvish Arm Down SP 20.00 50.00
152 Alex Liddi RC .60 1.50
153 Adron Chambers RC 1.00 2.50
154 Liam Hendriks RC .60 1.50
155 Drew Pomeranz RC .60 1.50
156 Austin Romine RC .60 1.50
157 Tim Federowicz RC .60 1.50
158 Joe Benson RC .60 1.50
159 Matt Dominguez RC .75 2.00
160A Matt Moore Grey Jsy RC 1.00 2.50
160B Moore Lt.Blue Jsy SP 12.50 30.00
161 Jordan Pacheco RC .60 1.50
162 Chris Parmelee RC .60 1.50
163 Brad Peacock RC .60 1.50
164 Brett Pill RC 1.00 2.50
165 Wilin Rosario RC .60 1.50
166 Addison Reed RC .60 1.50
167 Dellin Betances RC 1.00 2.50
168 Kelvin Herrera RC .60 1.50
169 Tom Milone RC .60 1.50
170A Jesus Montero Teal Jsy RC .60 1.50
170B Montero White Jsy SP 10.00 25.00
171 Michael Taylor RC .60 1.50
172 Devin Mesoraco RC .60 1.50
173A Brett Lawrie RC .75 2.00
173B Lawrie One Hand on Bat SP 30.00 60.00
174 James Darnell RC .60 1.50
175 Leonys Martin RC .60 1.50
176 Jeff Locke RC 1.00 2.50
177 Jarrod Parker RC .75 2.00
178 Collin Cowgill RC .60 1.50
179 Taylor Green RC .60 1.50
180A Cespedes Grn Jsy RC 1.50 4.00
180B Cespedes Wht Jsy SP 20.00 50.00
181 Eric Surkamp RC 1.00 2.50
182 Andrelton Simmons RC 1.00 2.50
183 Tyler Pastornicky RC .60 1.50
184 Norichika Aoki RC .75 2.00
185 Tsuyoshi Wada RC .60 1.50
186 Hisashi Iwakuma RC 1.25 3.00
187 Adrian Cardenas RC .60 1.50
188 Wei-Yin Chen RC 1.50 4.00
189 Xavier Avery RC .60 1.50
190 Matt Hague RC .60 1.50
191 Drew Smyly RC .60 1.50
192 Kirk Nieuwenhuis RC .60 1.50
193 Drew Hutchison RC .75 2.00
194 Wily Peralta RC .60 1.50
195 Jordany Valdespin RC .75 2.00
196A Bryce Harper Hitting RC 10.00 25.00
196B B.Harper Sliding SP 75.00 150.00
197 Will Middlebrooks RC .75 2.00
198 Brian Dozier RC 2.00 5.00
199 Matt Adams RC .75 2.00
200 Irving Falu RC .60 1.50
201 Howie Kendrick .30 .75
202 Chris Davis .30 .75
203 Alcides Escobar .40 1.00
204 A.J. Pierzynski .30 .75
205 Edwin Encarnacion .50 1.25
206 Adam Dunn .40 1.00
207 Mike Aviles .30 .75
208 Jason Kipnis .40 1.00
209 Andre Ethier .40 1.00
210 Carlos Beltran .40 1.00
211 Adam LaRoche .30 .75
212 Carlos Ruiz .30 .75
213 Jake Peavy .30 .75
214 Chris Sale .50 1.25
215 R.A. Dickey .40 1.00
216 Mark Buehrle .40 1.00
217 Derek Lowe .30 .75
218 Jason Vargas .30 .75
219 Kyle Seager .30 .75
220 Omar Infante .30 .75

2012 Topps Chrome Refractors

*REF: 1X TO 2.5X BASIC
*REF RC: .5X TO 1.2X BASIC RC
STATED ODDS 1:3 HOBBY

2012 Topps Chrome Black Refractors

*BLACK REF: 4X TO 10X BASIC
*BLACK RC: 2X TO 5X BASIC RC
STATED ODDS 1:41 HOBBY
STATED PRINT RUN 100 SER.#'d SETS
196 Bryce Harper 40.00 80.00

2012 Topps Chrome Blue Refractors

*BLUE REF: 1.5X TO 4X BASIC
*BLUE RC: 1X TO 2.5X BASIC RC
STATED ODDS 1:21 HOBBY
STATED PRINT RUN 199 SER.#'d SETS
188 Wei-Yin Chen 8.00 20.00
196 Bryce Harper 20.00 50.00

2012 Topps Chrome Gold Refractors

*GOLD REF: 6X TO 15X BASIC
*GOLD RC: 3X TO 8X BASIC
STATED ODDS 1:82 HOBBY
STATED PRINT RUN 50 SER.#'d SETS
188 Wei-Yin Chen 50.00 100.00
196 Bryce Harper 50.00 100.00

2012 Topps Chrome Orange Refractors

*ORANGE REF: 1.5X TO 4X BASIC
*ORANGE RC: .75X TO 2X BASIC RC
196 Bryce Harper 15.00 40.00

2012 Topps Chrome Purple Refractors

*PURPLE: 1.5X TO 4X BASIC
*PURPLE RC: .75X TO 2X BASIC RC
196 Bryce Harper 12.50 30.00

2012 Topps Chrome Sepia Refractors

*SEPIA REF: 5X TO 12X BASIC
*SEPIA RC: 2.5X TO 6X BASIC
STATED ODDS 1:55 HOBBY
STATED PRINT RUN 75 SER.#'d SETS
196 Bryce Harper 40.00 80.00

2012 Topps Chrome X-Fractors

*XFRAC: 1.2X TO 3X BASIC
*XFRAC RC: .6X TO 1.5X BASIC
STATED ODDS 1:6 HOBBY
196 Bryce Harper 12.50 30.00

2012 Topps Chrome Dynamic Die Cuts

STATED ODDS 1:24 HOBBY
AC Aroldis Chapman 1.50 4.00
AG Adrian Gonzalez 1.25 3.00
AJ Adam Jones 1.25 3.00
AL Adam Lind 1.25 3.00
AM Andrew McCutchen 1.50 4.00
AP Albert Pujols 2.00 5.00
BG Brett Gardner 1.25 3.00
BL Brett Lawrie 1.25 3.00
BP Buster Posey 2.00 5.00
CG Curtis Granderson 1.25 3.00
CK Clayton Kershaw 2.50 6.00
CL Cliff Lee 1.25 3.00
CS CC Sabathia 1.25 3.00
DA Dustin Ackley 1.00 2.50
DJ Derek Jeter 4.00 10.00
DO David Ortiz 1.50 4.00
DPA Dustin Pedroia 1.50 4.00
EA Elvis Andrus 1.25 3.00
EH Eric Hosmer 1.25 3.00
FH Felix Hernandez 1.25 3.00
GS Giancarlo Stanton 1.50 4.00
IK Ian Kinsler 1.25 3.00
IN Ivan Nova 1.25 3.00
I Ichiro Suzuki 2.00 5.00
JB Jose Bautista 1.25 3.00
JBR Jay Bruce 1.25 3.00
JE Jacoby Ellsbury 1.25 3.00
JH Josh Hamilton 1.25 3.00
JM Jesus Montero 1.00 2.50
JR Jose Reyes 1.00 2.50
JU Justin Upton 1.25 3.00
JV Justin Verlander 1.50 4.00
JVO Joey Votto 1.50 4.00
MK Matt Kemp 1.25 3.00
MM Matt Moore 1.50 4.00
MMO Michael Morse 1.00 2.50
MP Michael Pineda 1.00 2.50
MT Mike Trout 40.00 100.00
NC Nelson Cruz 1.50 4.00
PF Prince Fielder 1.25 3.00
PG Paul Goldschmidt 1.50 4.00
PS Pablo Sandoval 1.25 3.00
RB Ryan Braun 1.00 2.50
RC Robinson Cano 1.25 3.00
RH Roy Halladay 1.25 3.00
SC Starlin Castro 1.25 3.00
SS Stephen Strasburg 1.50 4.00
TL Tim Lincecum 1.25 3.00
TT Troy Tulowitzki 1.50 4.00
YD Yu Darvish 2.50 6.00

2012 Topps Chrome Rookie Autographs

STATED ODDS 1:19 HOBBY
PRINTING PLATE ODDS 1:6587 HOBBY
PLATE PRINT RUN 1 SET PER COLOR
NO PLATE PRICING DUE TO SCARCITY
EXCHANGE DEADLINE 07/31/2015
5 Ryan Lavarnway 3.00 8.00
39 Jacob Turner 4.00 10.00
42 Zack Cozart 4.00 10.00
BH Bryce Harper 250.00 400.00
TB Trevor Bauer 30.00 80.00
WP Wily Peralta 3.00 8.00
101 Yonder Alonso 3.00 8.00
151 Yu Darvish 20.00 50.00
154 Liam Hendriks 3.00 8.00
155 Drew Pomeranz 3.00 8.00
156 Austin Romine 3.00 8.00
159 Matt Dominguez 3.00 8.00
160 Matt Moore 4.00 10.00
161 Jordan Pacheco 3.00 8.00
162 Chris Parmelee 3.00 8.00
163 Brad Peacock 3.00 8.00
166 Addison Reed 6.00 15.00
167 Dellin Betances 6.00 15.00
169 Tom Milone 3.00 8.00
170 Jesus Montero 5.00 12.00
172 Devin Mesoraco 3.00 8.00
173 Brett Lawrie 6.00 15.00
177 Jarrod Parker 3.00 8.00
178 Collin Cowgill 3.00 8.00
180 Yoenis Cespedes 20.00 50.00
181 Eric Surkamp 3.00 8.00
183 Tyler Pastornicky 3.00 8.00
185 Tsuyoshi Wada 5.00 12.00
190 Matt Hague 3.00 8.00
191 Drew Smyly 3.00 8.00
192 Kirk Nieuwenhuis 3.00 8.00
193 Drew Hutchison 3.00 8.00

2012 Topps Chrome Rookie Autographs Refractors

*REF: .5X TO 1.2X BASIC
STATED ODDS 1:73 HOBBY
STATED PRINT RUN 499 SER.#'d SETS
EXCHANGE DEADLINE 07/31/2015

2012 Topps Chrome Rookie Autographs Black Refractors

*BLACK REF: 1X TO 2.5X BASIC
STATED ODDS 1:296 HOBBY
STATED PRINT RUN 100 SER.#'d SETS
EXCHANGE DEADLINE 07/31/2015
BH Bryce Harper 300.00 500.00

2012 Topps Chrome Rookie Autographs Blue Refractors

*BLUE REF: .75X TO 2X BASIC
STATED ODDS 1:149 HOBBY
STATED PRINT RUN 199 SER.#'d SETS
EXCHANGE DEADLINE 07/31/2015
BH Bryce Harper 300.00 500.00

2012 Topps Chrome Rookie Autographs Gold Refractors

*GOLD REF: 1.2X TO 3X BASIC
STATED ODDS 1:588 HOBBY
STATED PRINT RUN 50 SER.#'d SETS
EXCHANGE DEADLINE 07/31/2015
BH Bryce Harper 400.00 600.00
185 Tsuyoshi Wada 20.00 50.00
193 Drew Hutchison 15.00 40.00

2012 Topps Chrome Rookie Autographs Sepia Refractors

*SEPIA REF: 1X TO 2.5X BASIC
STATED ODDS 1:395 HOBBY
STATED PRINT RUN 75 SER.#'d SETS
EXCHANGE DEADLINE 07/31/2015
BH Bryce Harper 300.00 500.00

2013 Topps Chrome

COMP.SET w/o VAR (220) 20.00 50.00
PHOTO VAR ODDS 1:968 HOBBY
PRINTING PLATE ODDS 1:1265 HOBBY
PLATE PRINT RUN 1 SET PER COLOR
BLACK-CYAN-MAGENTA-YELLOW ISSUED
NO PLATE PRICING DUE TO SCARCITY
1A Mike Trout 2.50 6.00
1B Trout Holding Award 40.00 80.00
2 Hunter Pence .25 .60
3 Jesus Montero .20 .50
4 Jon Jay .20 .50
5 Lucas Duda .25 .60
6 Jason Heyward .25 .60
7 Lance Lynn .20 .50
8 Matt Cain .25 .60
9 Trevor Bauer .40 1.00
10 Derek Jeter .75 2.00
11 Evan Longoria .25 .60
12 Manny Machado RC 2.50 6.00
13 Yovani Gallardo .20 .50
14 Josh Rutledge .20 .50
15 Melky Cabrera .20 .50
16 Wil Myers RC .60 1.50
17 Fernando Rodney .20 .50
18 Kris Medlen .25 .60
19 Adrian Gonzalez .25 .60
20A Matt Kemp .25 .60
20B Kemp VAR w/glv 20.00 50.00
21 Carlos Santana .25 .60
22 Khristopher Davis RC 1.25 3.00
23 Julio Teheran .25 .60
24 Nick Maronde RC .50 1.25
25A Hyun-Jin Ryu RC 1.00 2.50
25B Ryu VAR w/glasses 10.00 25.00
26 Carlos Ruiz .20 .50
27 Rob Brantly .20 .50
28 Hiroki Kuroda .20 .50
29 Shane Victorino .25 .60
30 Adam Warren RC .40 1.00
31 Chase Headley .20 .50
32 Jose Fernandez RC 1.00 2.50
33 Marcell Ozuna RC 1.00 2.50
34A Felix Hernandez .25 .60
34B Hernan VAR w/glasses 10.00 25.00
35 Jose Altuve .25 .60
36 Jim Johnson .20 .50
37 Madison Bumgarner .25 .60
38A Joe Mauer .25 .60
38B Mauer VAR w/glv 15.00 40.00
39 Mike Zunino RC .60 1.50
40 Max Scherzer .30 .75
41 Jayson Werth .25 .60
42 J.P. Arencibia .20 .50
43 Adam Wainwright .25 .60
44 Billy Butler .20 .50
45 Salvador Perez .25 .60
46 Mike Napoli .20 .50
47 Jake Peavy .20 .50
48 Andre Ethier .25 .60
49A Andrew McCutchen .30 .75
49B McCutchen VAR w/glv 20.00 50.00
50 Stephen Strasburg .30 .75
51 Sergio Romo .20 .50
52 Troy Tulowitzki .30 .75
53 Derek Holland .20 .50
54 Brett Lawrie .25 .60
55 Mike Olt RC .50 1.25
56 Carl Crawford .25 .60
57 Jurickson Profar RC .50 1.25
58 Asdrubal Cabrera .25 .60
59 Jeurys Familia RC .60 1.50
60 Jonathon Niese .20 .50
61 Jonathan Papelbon .25 .60
62 R.A. Dickey .25 .60
63 Alex Colome RC .40 1.00
64 Tim Lincecum .25 .60
65 Didi Gregorius RC 1.50 4.00
66 Avisail Garcia RC .50 1.25
67 Ryan Vogelsong .20 .50
68 Paul Konerko .25 .60
69 Brad Ziegler .20 .50
70 Josh Hamilton .25 .60
71 Ryan Wheeler RC .40 1.00
72 Victor Martinez .25 .60
73 Trevor Rosenthal (RC) .75 2.00
74 Michael Bourn .20 .50
75 Robinson Cano .25 .60
76 Cole Hamels .25 .60
77 Josh Johnson .25 .60
78 Nolan Arenado RC 20.00 50.00
79A David Ortiz .30 .75
79B Ortiz VAR w/flag 30.00 60.00
80 Shelby Miller RC 1.00 2.50
81 Starling Marte .25 .60
82 Robbie Grossman RC .40 1.00
83 Shin-Soo Choo .25 .60
84A Starlin Castro .20 .50
84B Castro VAR Helmet off 20.00 50.00
85 Bruce Rondon RC .40 1.00
86 Angel Pagan .20 .50
87 Kyle Gibson RC .60 1.50
88 Tyler Skaggs RC .60 1.50
89 Russell Martin .20 .50
90A Ben Revere .20 .50
90B Revere VAR Hat/glv 12.50 30.00
91A Josh Reddick .20 .50
91B Reddick VAR w/glasses 12.50 30.00
92 Dustin Pedroia .30 .75
93 Brandon Barnes .20 .50
94 Jose Bautista .25 .60
95 Austin Jackson .20 .50
96A Yoenis Cespedes .30 .75
96B Cesped VAR w/glasses 12.50 30.00
97 Nate Freiman RC .40 1.00
98 Johnny Cueto .25 .60
99 Craig Kimbrel .25 .60
100A Miguel Cabrera .30 .75
100B Cabrera VAR w/glasses 12.00 30.00
101 Eury Perez RC .50 1.25
102 Brandon Maurer RC .50 1.25
103 Chase Utley .25 .60
104 Roy Halladay .25 .60
105 Casey Kelly RC .50 1.25
106 Jered Weaver .25 .60
107 Carlos Martinez RC .60 1.50
108 Rickie Weeks .20 .50
109 Jay Bruce .25 .60
110 Matt Magill RC .40 1.00
111 Jon Lester .25 .60
112 Allen Webster RC .50 1.25
113 Brian McCann .25 .60
114 Mark Trumbo .20 .50
115 Edwin Encarnacion .30 .75
116 Adeiny Hechavarria (RC) .50 1.25
117 Matt Harvey .25 .60
118A Mariano Rivera .40 1.00
118B Rivera VAR Shaking hands 20.00 50.00
119 Michael Wacha RC .50 1.25
120 Jason Kipnis .25 .60
121 Allen Craig .25 .60
122 Adrian Beltre .30 .75
123 Todd Frazier .20 .50
124 Aroldis Chapman .30 .75
125 Dylan Bundy RC 1.00 2.50
126 Jonathan Pettibone RC .60 1.50
127A David Price .25 .60
127B Price VAR w/dog 12.50 30.00
128 Anthony Rendon RC 2.50 6.00
129 Jason Kubel .20 .50
130 Kyuji Fujikawa RC .60 1.50
131 Carlos Gonzalez .25 .60
132 Ricky Nolasco .20 .50
133 Will Middlebrooks .20 .50
134 Kendrys Morales .20 .50
135 David Freese .20 .50
136A Albert Pujols .40 1.00
136B Pujols VAR Horizontal 12.50 30.00
137 Mat Latos .25 .60
138A Yasiel Puig RC 1.50 4.00
138B Puig VAR High five 50.00 100.00
139 Wade Miley .20 .50
140 Alex Gordon .25 .60
141 Neftali Feliz .20 .50
142A David Wright .25 .60
142B Wright VAR w/glv 20.00 50.00
143A Justin Upton .25 .60
143B Upton VAR w/glasses 15.00 40.00
144 Alex Rios .25 .60
145 Jose Reyes .25 .60

146 Yadier Molina .40 1.00
147 Sean Doolittle RC .40 1.00
148 Evan Gattis RC .75 2.00
149 Yonder Alonso .20 .50
150 Justin Verlander .30 .75
151 Justin Wilson RC .40 1.00
152 Adam Jones .25 .60
153 Dan Straily .20 .50
154 Nick Franklin RC .50 1.25
155 Adam Eaton RC .60 1.50
156 Mike Kickham RC .40 1.00
157 Melky Mesa RC .50 1.25
158 Anthony Rizzo .40 1.00
159 Chris Johnson .20 .50
160 Ian Kinsler .25 .60
161 Zack Greinke .30 .75
162 Donald Lutz RC .40 1.00
163 Ryan Braun .25 .60
164 Alex Wood RC .50 1.25
165 Ryan Howard .25 .60
166 Jackie Bradley Jr. RC 1.00 2.50
167 Brandon Phillips .20 .50
168 Alex Rodriguez .40 1.00
169 A.J. Pierzynski .20 .50
170 Carter Capps RC .40 1.00
171 Tony Cingrani RC .75 2.00
172 Mark Teixeira .25 .60
173 Paul Goldschmidt .30 .75
174 CC Sabathia .25 .60
175A Clayton Kershaw .50 1.25
175B Kershaw VAR w/helmet 15.00 40.00
176 Wilin Rosario .20 .50
177 Mike Moustakas .25 .60
178 Jedd Gyorko RC .75 2.00
179 Aaron Hicks RC .60 1.50
180 Zack Wheeler RC 1.25 3.00
181 Ian Desmond .20 .50
182 Paco Rodriguez RC .60 1.50
183 Matt Holliday .30 .75
184A Prince Fielder .25 .60
184B Fielder VAR Head of hair 20.00 50.00
185 Kevin Youkilis .20 .50
186 Oswaldo Arcia RC .40 1.00
187 Chris Sale .30 .75
188 Martin Prado .20 .50
189 Alfredo Marte RC .60 1.50
190 Adam LaRoche .20 .50
191 Dexter Fowler .25 .60
192 Jake Odorizzi RC .75 2.00
193 Nelson Cruz .30 .75
194 Kevin Gausman RC 1.25 3.00
195 Curtis Granderson .25 .60
196 Jarrod Parker .20 .50
197 Giancarlo Stanton .30 .75
198 Tommy Milone .20 .50
199A Yu Darvish .30 .75
199B Darvish VAR w/glasses 15.00 40.00
200A Buster Posey .40 1.00
200B Posey VAR Shaking hands 40.00 80.00
201 Adam Dunn .25 .60
202 James Shields .20 .50
203 Desmond Jennings .25 .60
204 Jacoby Ellsbury .25 .60
205 Ben Zobrist .25 .60
206 Joey Votto .30 .75
207 Miguel Montero .20 .50
208 Cliff Lee .25 .60
209 Jeremy Hellickson .20 .50
210A Gerrit Cole RC 4.00 10.00
210B Cole VAR Walk to dugout 20.00 50.00
211 Carlos Beltran .25 .60
212 Ryan Zimmerman .25 .60
213 Gio Gonzalez .25 .60
214 Eric Hosmer .25 .60
215 Domonic Brown .25 .60
216 Pablo Sandoval .25 .60
217 Justin Morneau .25 .60
218 B.J. Upton .25 .60
219A Freddie Freeman .40 1.00
219B Freeman VAR over rail 20.00 50.00
220A Bryce Harper .50 1.25
220B Harper VAR w/award 40.00 80.00

2013 Topps Chrome Black Refractors

*BLACK REF: 3X TO 8X BASIC
*BLACK REF RC: 1.5X TO 4X BASIC RC
STATED ODDS 1:55 HOBBY
STATED PRINT RUN 100 SER.#'d SETS
10 Derek Jeter 15.00 40.00
12 Manny Machado 15.00 40.00

2013 Topps Chrome Blue Refractors

*BLUE REF: 2X TO 5X BASIC
*BLUE REF RC: 1X TO 2.5X BASIC RC
STATED ODDS 1:30 HOBBY
STATED PRINT RUN 199 SER.#'d SETS

2013 Topps Chrome Gold Refractors

*GOLD REF: 6X TO 15X BASIC
*GOLD REF RC: 3X TO 8X BASIC RC
STATED ODDS 1:112 HOBBY
STATED PRINT RUN 50 SER.#'d SETS
10 Derek Jeter 40.00 80.00
12 Manny Machado 40.00 80.00

2013 Topps Chrome Orange Refractors

*ORANGE REF: 1.5X TO 4X BASIC
*ORANGE REF RC: .75X TO 2X BASIC RC

2013 Topps Chrome Purple Refractors

*PURPLE REF: 1.5X TO 4X BASIC
*PURPLE REF RC: .75X TO 2X BASIC RC

2013 Topps Chrome Red Refractors

*RED REF: 8X TO 20X BASIC
*RED REF RC: 4X TO 10X BASIC RC
STATED ODDS 1:223 HOBBY
STATED PRINT RUN 25 SER.#'d SETS
10 Derek Jeter 50.00 120.00
12 Manny Machado 40.00 100.00
118 Mariano Rivera 30.00 60.00
130 Kyuji Fujikawa 20.00 50.00
220 Bryce Harper 30.00 80.00

2013 Topps Chrome Refractors

*REF: 1X TO 2.5X BASIC
*REF RC: .5X TO 1.2X BASIC RC
STATED ODDS 1:3 HOBBY
UNCUT SHEET ODDS 1:55,700 HOBBY
SHEET EXCHANGE 9/30/2016
NNO Uncut Sheet EXCH 75.00 150.00

2013 Topps Chrome Sepia Refractors

*SEPIA REF: 4X TO 10X BASIC
*SEPIA REF RC: 2X TO 5X BASIC RC
STATED ODDS 1:75 HOBBY
STATED PRINT RUN 75 SER.#'d SETS
1 Mike Trout 20.00 50.00
10 Derek Jeter 20.00 50.00
12 Manny Machado 20.00 50.00
138 Yasiel Puig 60.00 120.00
220 Bryce Harper 15.00 40.00

2013 Topps Chrome X-Fractors

*X-F: 1.2X TO 3X BASIC
*X-F RC: .6X TO 1.5X BASIC RC
STATED ODDS 1:6 HOBBY
UNCUT SHEET ODDS 1:74,300 HOBBY
SHEET EXCHANGE 9/30/2016
NNO Uncut Sheet EXCH 150.00 250.00

2013 Topps Chrome '72 Chrome

STATED ODDS 1:12 HOBBY
72CAM Andrew McCutchen 1.00 2.50
72CAP Albert Pujols 1.25 3.00
72CBH Bryce Harper 1.50 4.00
72CCK Clayton Kershaw 1.50 4.00
72CDB Dylan Bundy 1.50 4.00
72CDJ Derek Jeter 2.50 6.00
72CGS Giancarlo Stanton 1.00 2.50
72CJH Josh Hamilton .75 2.00
72CJM Joe Mauer .75 2.00
72CJP Jurickson Profar .75 2.00
72CJU Justin Upton .75 2.00
72CJV Justin Verlander 1.00 2.50
72CMC Miguel Cabrera 1.00 2.50
72CMM Manny Machado 4.00 10.00
72CRB Ryan Braun .75 2.00
72CRC Robinson Cano .75 2.00
72CSS Stephen Strasburg 1.00 2.50
72CTS Tyler Skaggs 1.00 2.50
72CWM Wil Myers 1.00 2.50
72CYC Yoenis Cespedes 1.00 2.50
72CYD Yu Darvish 1.00 2.50
72CYP Yasiel Puig 6.00 15.00
72CCKR Craig Kimbrel .75 2.00
72CHJR Hyun-Jin Ryu 1.50 4.00
72CJHE Jason Heyward .75 2.00

2013 Topps Chrome '72 Chrome Autographs

STATED ODDS 1:10,000 HOBBY
STATED PRINT RUN 25 SER.#'d SETS
EXCHANGE DEADLINE 9/30/2016
72CAJP Jurickson Profar 60.00 150.00
72CAMM Manny Machado EXCH 125.00 250.00
72CATS Tyler Skaggs 30.00 60.00
72CAWM Wil Myers
72CARHJ Hyun-Jin Ryu

2013 Topps Chrome Chrome Connections Die Cuts

STATED ODDS 1:12 HOBBY
CCAB Adrian Beltre 1.00 2.50
CCAG Adrian Gonzalez .75 2.00
CCBH Bryce Harper 1.50 4.00
CCBP Buster Posey 1.25 3.00
CCBU B.J. Upton .75 2.00
CCCG Carlos Gonzalez .75 2.00
CCDF David Freese .60 1.50
CCDJ Derek Jeter 2.50 6.00
CCDO David Ortiz 1.00 2.50
CCDP David Price .75 2.00
CCDW David Wright .75 2.00
CCEL Evan Longoria .75 2.00
CCJB Jose Bautista .75 2.00
CCJH Josh Hamilton .75 2.00
CCJR Jose Reyes .75 2.00
CCJU Justin Upton .75 2.00
CCJV Justin Verlander 1.00 2.50
CCMC Miguel Cabrera 1.00 2.50
CCMH Matt Harvey .75 2.00
CCMK Matt Kemp .75 2.00
CCMT Mike Trout 8.00 20.00
CCPF Prince Fielder .75 2.00
CCRC Robinson Cano .75 2.00
CCSS Stephen Strasburg 1.00 2.50
CCTL Tim Lincecum .75 2.00
CCTT Troy Tulowitzki 1.00 2.50
CCYD Yu Darvish 1.00 2.50
CCDPE Dustin Pedroia 1.00 2.50
CCJHE Jason Heyward .75 2.00
CCMHO Matt Holliday 1.00 2.50

2013 Topps Chrome Chrome Connections Die Cuts Autographs

STATED ODDS 1:10,000 HOBBY
STATED PRINT RUN 25 SER.#'d SETS
EXCHANGE DEADLINE 9/30/2016
CCBP Buster Posey 100.00 175.00
CCJH Josh Hamilton 20.00 50.00
CCMC Miguel Cabrera 60.00 120.00
CCMT Mike Trout 175.00 350.00
CCPF Prince Fielder EXCH 30.00 60.00

2013 Topps Chrome Chrome Connections Die Cuts Relics

STATED ODDS 1:10,220 HOBBY
STATED PRINT RUN 25 SER.#'d SETS
EXCHANGE DEADLINE 9/30/2016
CCRBH Bryce Harper 20.00 50.00
CCRDJ Derek Jeter 20.00 50.00
CCRJV Justin Verlander 20.00 50.00
CCRRC Robinson Cano 12.50 30.00
CCRSS Stephen Strasburg 10.00 25.00

2013 Topps Chrome Dynamic Die Cuts

STATED ODDS 1:24 HOBBY
DYAC Aroldis Chapman 1.00 2.50
DYAJ Adam Jones .75 2.00
DYAM Andrew McCutchen 1.00 2.50
DYAP Albert Pujols 1.25 3.00
DYAW Adam Wainwright .75 2.00
DYBH Bryce Harper 1.50 4.00
DYCC CC Sabathia .75 2.00
DYCG Carlos Gonzalez .75 2.00
DYCH Cole Hamels .75 2.00
DYCK Clayton Kershaw 1.50 4.00
DYCM Carlos Martinez 1.00 2.50
DYCS Carlos Santana .75 2.00
DYDB Domonic Brown .75 2.00
DYDF David Freese .60 1.50
DYDJ Derek Jeter 2.50 6.00
DYDW David Wright .75 2.00
DYEL Evan Longoria .75 2.00
DYFH Felix Hernandez .75 2.00
DYGS Giancarlo Stanton 1.00 2.50
DYHR Hanley Ramirez .75 2.00
DYJB Jay Bruce .75 2.00
DYJC Johnny Cueto .75 2.00
DYJH Josh Hamilton .75 2.00
DYJP Jarrod Parker .60 1.50
DYJR Jose Reyes .75 2.00
DYJT Julio Teheran .75 2.00
DYJV Joey Votto 1.00 2.50
DYJW Jered Weaver .75 2.00
DYMC Miguel Cabrera 1.00 2.50
DYMK Matt Kemp .75 2.00
DYMM Manny Machado 4.00 10.00
DYMN Mike Napoli .60 1.50
DYMT Mike Trout 8.00 20.00
DYPG Paul Goldschmidt 1.00 2.50
DYRB Ryan Braun
DYRC Robinson Cano .75 2.00
DYSP Salvador Perez .75 2.00
DYSS Stephen Strasburg 1.00 2.50
DYTB Trevor Bauer 1.25 3.00
DYWR Wilin Rosario .60 1.50
DYYC Yoenis Cespedes 1.00 2.50
DYYD Yu Darvish 1.00 2.50
DYYP Yasiel Puig 2.50 6.00
DYCKR Craig Kimbrel .75 2.00
DYCSA Chris Sale 1.00 2.50
DYDBU Dylan Bundy 1.50 4.00
DYHJR Hyun-Jin Ryu 1.50 4.00
DYJBA Jose Bautista .75 2.00
DYJPR Jurickson Profar .75 2.00
DYJVE Justin Verlander 1.00 2.50

2013 Topps Chrome Dynamic Die Cuts Autographs

STATED ODDS 1:2450 HOBBY 20.00 50.00
STATED PRINT RUN 25 SER.#'d SETS
EXCHANGE DEADLINE 9/30/2016
DYCM Carlos Martinez 12.00 30.00
DYCS Chris Sale 20.00 50.00
DYDB Domonic Brown 12.50 30.00
DYEL Evan Longoria 20.00 50.00
DYFH Felix Hernandez 20.00 50.00
DYJB Jose Bautista 12.50 30.00
DYJB Jay Bruce 20.00 50.00
DYJT Julio Teheran 20.00 50.00
DYJW Jered Weaver 12.00 30.00
DYMC Miguel Cabrera 90.00 150.00
DYMM Manny Machado 100.00 175.00
DYMN Mike Napoli 12.00 30.00
DYMT Mike Trout 150.00 400.00
DYPG Paul Goldschmidt 30.00 60.00
DYSP Salvador Perez 15.00 40.00
DYTB Trevor Bauer 12.50 30.00
DYYD Yu Darvish EXCH 60.00 120.00
DYCSA Carlos Santana 12.50 30.00
DYHJR Hyun-Jin Ryu EXCH 50.00 100.00
DYJPR Jurickson Profar 90.00 150.00

2013 Topps Chrome Red Hot Rookies Autographs

STATED ODDS 1:4945 HOBBY
STATED PRINT RUN 25 SER.#'d SETS
EXCHANGE DEADLINE 9/30/2016
RHRAE Adam Eaton EXCH 10.00 25.00
RHRDB Dylan Bundy 30.00 60.00
RHRGC Gerrit Cole 60.00 120.00
RHRJP Jurickson Profar
RHRMM Manny Machado 150.00 250.00
RHRMO Mike Olt
RHRTS Tyler Skaggs 40.00 80.00
RHRWM Wil Myers 60.00 120.00
RHRZW Zack Wheeler 40.00 80.00
RHRRHJ Hyun-Jin Ryu 40.00 80.00

2013 Topps Chrome Rookie Autographs

STATED ODDS 1:19 HOBBY
PRINTING PLATE ODDS 1:6965 HOBBY
PLATE PRINT RUN 1 SET PER COLOR
BLACK-CYAN-MAGENTA-YELLOW ISSUED
NO PLATE PRICING DUE TO SCARCITY
EXCHANGE DEADLINE 9/30/2016
CY Christian Yelich 100.00 250.00
GC Gerrit Cole 40.00 100.00
KG Kyle Gibson EXCH 3.00 8.00
MZ Mike Zunino 3.00 8.00
NF Nick Franklin 3.00 8.00
WM Wil Myers 8.00 20.00
YP Yasiel Puig 25.00 60.00
ZW Zack Wheeler 4.00 10.00
12 Manny Machado 60.00 150.00
16 Darin Ruf 3.00 8.00
24 Nick Maronde 3.00 8.00
25 Hyun-Jin Ryu 40.00 100.00
27 Rob Brantly 3.00 8.00
32 Jose Fernandez 12.00 30.00
57 Jurickson Profar 3.00 8.00
59 Jeurys Familia 3.00 8.00
65 Didi Gregorius 6.00 15.00
66 Avisail Garcia 3.00 8.00
78 Nolan Arenado 100.00 250.00
80 Shelby Miller 3.00 8.00
85 Bruce Rondon 3.00 8.00
88 Tyler Skaggs 3.00 8.00
102 Brandon Maurer 3.00 8.00
105 Casey Kelly 3.00 8.00
107 Carlos Martinez 4.00 10.00
112 Allen Webster 3.00 8.00
116 Adeiny Hechavarria 3.00 8.00
125 Dylan Bundy 5.00 12.00
128 Anthony Rendon 30.00 80.00
130 Kyuji Fujikawa 3.00 8.00
148 Evan Gattis 3.00 8.00
154 L.J. Hoes 3.00 8.00
155 Adam Eaton 5.00 12.00
157 Melky Mesa 3.00 8.00
171 Tony Cingrani 3.00 8.00
178 Jedd Gyorko 3.00 8.00
182 Paco Rodriguez 3.00 8.00
186 Oswaldo Arcia EXCH 3.00 8.00
189 Alfredo Marte 3.00 8.00
192 Jake Odorizzi 3.00 8.00

2013 Topps Chrome Rookie Autographs Black Refractors

*BLACK REF: .75X TO 2X BASIC
STATED ODDS 1:301 HOBBY
STATED PRINT RUN 100 SER.#'d SETS
EXCHANGE DEADLINE 9/30/2016

2013 Topps Chrome Rookie Autographs Blue Refractors

*BLUE REF: .6X TO 1.5X BASIC
STATED ODDS 1:152 HOBBY
STATED PRINT RUN 199 SER.#'d SETS
EXCHANGE DEADLINE 9/30/2016

2013 Topps Chrome Rookie Autographs Gold Refractors

*GOLD REF: 1.2X TO 3X BASIC
STATED ODDS 1:605 HOBBY
STATED PRINT RUN 50 SER.#'d SETS
EXCHANGE DEADLINE 9/30/2016

2013 Topps Chrome Rookie Autographs Red Refractors

*RED REF: 1.5X TO 4X BASIC
STATED ODDS 1:1210 HOBBY
STATED PRINT RUN 25 SER.#'d SETS
EXCHANGE DEADLINE 9/30/2016
192 Jake Odorizzi 15.00 40.00

2013 Topps Chrome Rookie Autographs Refractors

*REF: .5X TO 1.2X BASIC
STATED ODDS 1:83 HOBBY
STATED PRINT RUN 499 SER.#'d SETS
EXCHANGE DEADLINE 9/30/2016

2013 Topps Chrome Rookie Autographs Sepia Refractors

*SEPIA REF: .75X TO 2X BASIC
STATED ODDS 1:403 HOBBY
STATED PRINT RUN 75 SER.#'d SETS
EXCHANGE DEADLINE 9/30/2016

2013 Topps Chrome Rookie Autographs Silver Ink Black Refractors

*SILVER INK REF: 1.5X TO 4X BASIC
STATED ODDS 1:1210 HOBBY
STATED PRINT RUN 25 SER.#'d SETS
EXCHANGE DEADLINE 9/30/2016

2013 Topps Chrome Update

COMPLETE SET (55) 60.00 120.00
MB1 Robinson Cano .60 1.50
MB2 Miguel Cabrera .75 2.00
MB3 Matt Harvey .60 1.50
MB4 Jose Fernandez RC 1.25 3.00
MB5 Anthony Rendon RC 3.00 8.00
MB6 Yoenis Cespedes .75 2.00
MB7 Justin Verlander .75 2.00
MB8 Clayton Kershaw 1.25 3.00
MB9 Mike Trout 6.00 15.00
MB10 Chris Archer .50 1.25
MB11 Carlos Martinez RC .75 2.00
MB12 Nick Franklin RC .60 1.50
MB13 Allen Craig .60 1.50
MB14 Joey Votto .75 2.00
MB15 Michael Cuddyer .50 1.25
MB16 Justin Upton .60 1.50
MB17 Kevin Gausman RC 1.50 4.00
MB18 Bud Norris .50 1.25
MB19 Mike Zunino RC .75 2.00
MB20 Gerrit Cole RC 3.00 8.00
MB21 Yu Darvish .75 2.00
MB22 Ian Kennedy .50 1.25
MB23 Dan Haren .50 1.25
MB24 Pedro Alvarez .50 1.25
MB25 Michael Young .50 1.25
MB26 Jake Peavy .50 1.25
MB27 Bryce Harper 1.25 3.00
MB28 Rafael Soriano .50 1.25
MB29 David Wright .60 1.50
MB30 Bryce Harper 1.25 3.00
MB31 James Shields .50 1.25
MB32 Zach Wheeler RC 1.00 2.50
MB33 Alfonso Soriano .60 1.50
MB34 Brian Wilson .75 2.00
MB35 Marcell Ozuna RC 1.25 3.00
MB36 Prince Fielder .60 1.50
MB37 Jose Fernandez 1.25 3.00
MB38 Kyle Gibson RC .75 2.00
MB39 Nolan Arenado RC 40.00 100.00
MB40 Oswaldo Arcia RC .50 1.25
MB41 Yasiel Puig RD 2.00 5.00
MB42 Wil Myers RC .75 2.00
MB43 Mariano Rivera 1.00 2.50
MB44 Shelby Miller RC 1.25 3.00
MB45 David Wright .60 1.50
MB46 Buster Posey 1.00 2.50
MB47 Christian Yelich RC 60.00 150.00
MB48 Adam Wainwright .60 1.50
MB49 Matt Garza .50 1.25
MB50 Francisco Liriano .50 1.25
MB51 Hyun-Jin Ryu 1.25 3.00
MB52 Evan Gattis RC 1.00 2.50
MB53 Yasiel Puig RC 2.00 5.00
MB54 Chris Davis .60 1.50
MB55 Jurickson Profar RC .60 1.50

2013 Topps Chrome Update Black Refractors

*BLACK: 2.5X TO 6X BASIC
STATED PRINT RUN 99 SER.#'d SETS
MB47 Christian Yelich 250.00 500.00

2013 Topps Chrome Update Gold Refractors

*GOLD: 2X TO 5X BASIC
STATED PRINT RUN 250 SER.#'d SETS
MB47 Christian Yelich 200.00 400.00

2014 Topps Chrome

COMP.SET w/o VAR (220) 15.00 40.00
PHOTO VAR ODDS 1:1400 HOBBY
PRINTING PLATE ODDS 1:1480 HOBBY
PLATE PRINT RUN 1 SET PER COLOR
BLACK-CYAN-MAGENTA-YELLOW ISSUED
NO PLATE PRICING DUE TO SCARCITY
1A Mike Trout 1.50 4.00
1B Trout Hi-Five VAR 30.00 60.00
2 Alex Gordon .25 .60
3 Enny Romero RC .40 1.00
4 Nick Castellanos RC 1.25 3.00
5 Ryan Braun .25 .60
6 Matt Carpenter .30 .75
7 Matt Cain .25 .60
8 Yoenis Cespedes .30 .75
9 Curtis Granderson .25 .60
10A Masahiro Tanaka RC 1.25 3.00
10B Tanaka Dugout VAR 40.00 80.00
10C Tanaka Japanese 40.00 100.00
11 Norichika Aoki .20 .50
12 Abraham Almonte RC .40 1.00
13 Jean Segura .25 .60
14 Alex Guerrero RC .50 1.25
15 David Robertson .20 .50
16 Yadier Molina .40 1.00
17 Stephen Strasburg .30 .75
18 Corey Kluber .25 .60
19 Oscar Taveras RC .50 1.25
20 Hanley Ramirez .25 .60
21 James Paxton RC .60 1.50
22 Taijuan Walker RC .40 1.00
23 Stefen Romero RC .40 1.00
24 Josmil Pinto RC .40 1.00
25A Xander Bogaerts RC 1.25 3.00
26 Erisbel Arruebarrena RC .40 1.00
27 Hiroki Kuroda .20 .50
28 Joey Votto .30 .75
29 Victor Martinez .25 .60
30 Mike Napoli .20 .50
31A Clay Buchholz .20 .50
31B Buchholz Guitar VAR 12.00 30.00
32 CC Sabathia .25 .60
33 Jonathan Schoop RC .40 1.00
34 Adam Jones .25 .60
35 Edwin Encarnacion .30 .75
36 Josh Hamilton .25 .60
37 Cliff Lee .25 .60
38 Carlos Gomez .20 .50
39 Mike Moustakas .25 .60
40 Wilin Rosario .20 .50
41 Jedd Gyorko .20 .50
42 Shane Victorino .25 .60
43 Marcus Semien RC 2.00 5.00
44 Adam Wainwright .25 .60
45 Jose Ramirez RC 3.00 8.00
46 Gerrit Cole .30 .75
47 Will Middlebrooks .20 .50
48 Alex Cobb .20 .50
50 Adrian Beltre .30 .75
51 Matt Adams .20 .50
52 Jose Altuve .25 .60
53 Chase Headley .20 .50
54 Carlos Martinez .25 .60
55 Jon Singleton RC .50 1.25
56A Derek Jeter .75 2.00
56B Jeter w/crowd VAR 75.00 200.00
57 Jordan Zimmermann .25 .60
58 Anthony Rizzo .40 1.00
59 Rafael Montero RC .40 1.00
60 Jayson Werth .25 .60
61A Felix Hernandez .25 .60
61B King Felix Pointing VAR 20.00 50.00
62 Zach Walters RC .40 1.00
63 David Price .25 .60
64 Brandon Phillips .20 .50
65 Nick Martinez RC .40 1.00
66 Yordano Ventura RC .50 1.25
67 Wilmer Flores RC .50 1.25
68 Billy Butler .20 .50
69 John Ryan Murphy RC .40 1.00
70 Allen Craig .25 .60
71 Prince Fielder .25 .60
72 Mat Latos .25 .60
73 Jered Weaver .25 .60
74 Dexter Fowler .25 .60
75A Billy Hamilton RC .50 1.25
75B Hamilton Fldng VAR 50.00 120.00
76 Marcus Stroman RC .60 1.50
77 Robbie Erlin RC .40 1.00
78 Kenley Jansen .25 .60
79 Mike Minor .20 .50
80A Wil Myers .20 .50
80B Myers Waving VAR 20.00 50.00
81 Kevin Siegrist (RC) .40 1.00
82 Brad Miller .25 .60
83 Jon Lester .25 .60
84 Chris Colabello .20 .50
85 James Shields .20 .50
86 Brian McCann .25 .60
87 Zack Wheeler .25 .60
88 Michael Choice RC .40 1.00
89 Hisashi Iwakuma .25 .60
90A Yasiel Puig .30 .75
90B Puig w/crowd VAR 60.00 150.00
91 Christian Bethancourt RC .40 1.00
92 Matt den Dekker RC .50 1.25
93A Justin Upton .25 .60
93B Upton Throwback VAR 40.00 100.00
94 Alexei Ramirez .25 .60
95 Cole Hamels .25 .60
96 Tony Cingrani .25 .60
97 Ian Desmond .20 .50
98 Erik Johnson RC .40 1.00
99 Evan Longoria .25 .60
100 Clayton Kershaw .50 1.25
101 Ben Zobrist .25 .60
102 Matt Moore .25 .60
103A Jose Fernandez .30 .75
103B J.Fern w/Phanatic VAR 20.00 50.00
104 R.A. Dickey .25 .60
105A Andrew McCutchen .30 .75
105B MCutch On deck VAR 30.00 60.00
106 Kyle Seager .20 .50
107A Hyun-Jin Ryu .25 .60
107B Ryu w/Puig VAR 40.00 80.00
108 Jake Marisnick RC .40 1.00
109 Pedro Alvarez .20 .50
110 Brandon Belt .25 .60
111 Tim Beckham RC .60 1.50
112 Troy Tulowitzki .30 .75
113 Everth Cabrera .20 .50
114 Sonny Gray .25 .60
115 Francisco Liriano .20 .50
116A Robinson Cano .25 .60
116B Cano Gum VAR 12.00 30.00
117 Aroldis Chapman .30 .75
118 Homer Bailey .20 .50
119 Jacoby Ellsbury .25 .60
120 Jeff Samardzija .20 .50
121 Koji Uehara .20 .50
122 Shin-Soo Choo .25 .60
123 Jose Bautista .25 .60
124 Travis d'Arnaud RC .50 1.25
125A Paul Goldschmidt .30 .75
125B Paul Goldschmidt VAR 20.00 50.00
126 Yangervis Solarte RC .40 1.00
127 Tanner Roark RC .40 1.00
128 Ethan Martin RC .40 1.00
129 Johnny Cueto .25 .60
130 Albert Pujols .40 1.00
131 Desmond Jennings .25 .60
132 Chris Davis .20 .50
133 Onelki Garcia RC .40 1.00
134 David Holmberg RC .40 1.00
135 Martin Prado .20 .50
136 Matt Davidson RC .50 1.25
137 Ivan Nova .25 .60
138 George Springer RC 1.50 4.00
139 Matt Holliday .30 .75
140 Justin Verlander .30 .75
141 Trevor Rosenthal .25 .60
142 Grady Sizemore .25 .60
143 Shelby Miller .25 .60
144 Joe Mauer .25 .60
145 J.J. Hardy .20 .50
146 Freddie Freeman .40 1.00
147 Austin Jackson .20 .50
148 Avisail Garcia .25 .60
149 Jose Reyes .25 .60
150A Bryce Harper .50 1.25
150B Harper Drk helmet VAR 75.00 150.00
151 C.J. Cron RC .40 1.00
152 Buster Posey .40 1.00
153 Domonic Brown .25 .60
154 Salvador Perez .25 .60
155 Craig Kimbrel .25 .60
156 Evan Gattis .20 .50
157 Michael Cuddyer .20 .50
158 Aramis Ramirez .20 .50
159 Eric Hosmer .25 .60
160 Nelson Cruz .30 .75
161 Chris Owings RC .40 1.00
162 Zack Greinke .30 .75
163 Greg Holland .20 .50
164 Jay Bruce .25 .60
165A Starlin Castro .20 .50
166 Hunter Pence .25 .60
167 Pablo Sandoval .25 .60
168 Manny Machado .30 .75
169 Kole Calhoun .20 .50
170A David Wright .25 .60
170B Wright Hi-Five VAR 30.00 80.00
171 Andrelton Simmons .20 .50
172 Starling Marte .25 .60
173 Giancarlo Stanton .30 .75
174 Chase Utley .25 .60
175 Yu Darvish .30 .75
176 Ryan Howard .25 .60
177 Sergio Romo .20 .50
178 Danny Salazar .25 .60
179 Carlos Beltran .25 .60
180 Alex Rios .25 .60
181 Chris Sale .30 .75
182 Mark Trumbo .20 .50
183 Brandon Moss .20 .50
184 Jonathan Lucroy .25 .60
185 Ian Kinsler .25 .60
186 Brett Gardner .25 .60
187 Elvis Andrus .25 .60
188 Kolten Wong RC .50 1.25
189A Madison Bumgarner .25 .60
189B Bumgarn Batting VAR 30.00 60.00
190 Carlos Gonzalez .25 .60
191 Joe Nathan .20 .50
192 Carl Crawford .25 .60
193A Josh Donaldson .25 .60
193B J.Donald Water VAR 20.00 50.00
194 Julio Teheran .25 .60
195 Gio Gonzalez .25 .60
196 Jason Kipnis .25 .60
197 Andrew Cashner .20 .50
198 Tommy Medica RC .40 1.00
199A Jose Abreu RC 3.00 8.00
200 Asdrubal Cabrera .25 .60
201A David Ortiz .30 .75
201B Ortiz w/rings VAR 30.00 80.00
202 Matt Kemp .25 .60
203 Jimmy Nelson RC .40 1.00
204A Dustin Pedroia .30 .75
204B Pedroia Flding VAR 60.00 150.00
205 Ryan Zimmerman .25 .60
206 Andre Rienzo RC .40 1.00
207 Anibal Sanchez .20 .50
208 Jason Grilli .20 .50
209 Andrew Lambo RC .40 1.00
210 Carlos Santana .25 .60
211 Jurickson Profar .25 .60
212 Dean Anna RC .40 1.00
213 Rougned Odor RC 1.00 2.50
214 Jason Heyward .25 .60
215 Christian Yelich .40 1.00
216 Nolan Arenado 2.50 6.00
217 Aaron Hill .20 .50
218 Max Scherzer .30 .75
219 Brett Lawrie .25 .60
220A Miguel Cabrera .30 .75
220B Cabrera Hi-Five VAR 30.00 80.00

2014 Topps Chrome Black Refractors

*BLACK REF: 4X TO 10X BASIC
*BLACK REF RC: 2X TO 5X BASIC RC
STATED ODDS 1:80 HOBBY
STATED PRINT RUN 100 SER.#'d SETS
56 Derek Jeter 25.00 60.00

2014 Topps Chrome Blue Refractors

*BLUE REF: 2.5X TO 6X BASIC
*BLUE REF RC: 1.2X TO 3X BASIC RC
STATED ODDS 1:40 HOBBY
STATED PRINT RUN 199 SER.#'d SETS
1 Mike Trout 8.00 20.00
56 Derek Jeter 8.00 20.00

2014 Topps Chrome Gold Refractors

*GOLD REF: 8X TO 20X BASIC
*GOLD REF RC: 4X TO 10X BASIC RC
STATED ODDS 1:160 HOBBY
STATED PRINT RUN 50 SER.#'d SETS
1 Mike Trout 50.00 120.00
19 Oscar Taveras 20.00 50.00
100 Clayton Kershaw 15.00 40.00
138 George Springer 20.00 50.00
150 Bryce Harper 15.00 40.00
199 Jose Abreu 60.00 150.00

2014 Topps Chrome Orange Refractors

*ORANGE REF: 2X TO 5X BASIC
*ORANGE REF RC: 1X TO 2.5X BASIC RC
RANDOM INSERTS IN PACKS
1 Mike Trout 6.00 15.00
56 Derek Jeter 6.00 15.00

2014 Topps Chrome Purple Refractors

*PURPLE REF: 2X TO 5X BASIC
*PURPLE REF RC: 1X TO 2.5X BASIC RC
RANDOM INSERTS IN PACKS
1 Mike Trout 6.00 15.00
56 Derek Jeter 6.00 15.00

2014 Topps Chrome Red Refractors

*RED REF: 10X TO 25X BASIC
*RED REF RC: 5X TO 12X BASIC RC
STATED ODDS 1:320 HOBBY
STATED PRINT RUN 25 SER.#'d SETS
1 Mike Trout 60.00 150.00
19 Oscar Taveras 25.00 60.00
56 Derek Jeter 60.00 150.00
100 Clayton Kershaw 20.00 50.00
138 George Springer 25.00 60.00
150 Bryce Harper 20.00 50.00
199 Jose Abreu 75.00 200.00

2014 Topps Chrome Refractors

*REFRACTOR: 1X TO 2.5X BASIC
*REFRACTOR RC: .5X TO 1.2X BASIC RC
STATED ODDS 1:3 HOBBY

2014 Topps Chrome Sepia Refractors

*SEPIA REF: 5X TO 12X BASIC
*SEPIA REF RC: 2.5X TO 6X BASIC RC
STATED ODDS 1:105 HOBBY
STATED PRINT RUN 75 SER.#'d SETS

2014 Topps Chrome X-Fractors

*X-FRACTOR: 1.5X TO 4X BASIC
*X-FRACTOR RC: .75X TO 2X BASIC RC
STATED ODDS 1:6 HOBBY

2014 Topps Chrome '89 Chrome Refractors

COMPLETE SET (25) 20.00 50.00
STATED ODDS 1:12 HOBBY
89TCAM Andrew McCutchen 1.00 2.50
89TCAP Albert Pujols 1.25 3.00
89TCBH Billy Hamilton .75 2.00
89TCBHA Bryce Harper 1.50 4.00
89TCBP Buster Posey 1.25 3.00
89TCCG Carlos Gonzalez .75 2.00
89TCCK Clayton Kershaw 1.50 4.00
89TCDO David Ortiz 1.00 2.50
89TCDP Dustin Pedroia 1.00 2.50
89TCDW David Wright .75 2.00
89TCJA Jose Abreu 4.00 10.00
89TCJE Jacoby Ellsbury .75 2.00
89TCKGJ Ken Griffey Jr. 2.00 5.00
89TCMC Miguel Cabrera 1.00 2.50
89TCMT Mike Trout 5.00 12.00
89TCMTA Masahiro Tanaka 3.00 8.00
89TCNC Nick Castellanos 2.00 5.00
89TCPF Prince Fielder .75 2.00
89TCPG Paul Goldschmidt 1.00 2.50
89TCRB Ryan Braun .75 2.00
89TCRC Robinson Cano .75 2.00
89TCTT Troy Tulowitzki 1.00 2.50
89TCTW Taijuan Walker .60 1.50
89TCYD Yu Darvish 1.00 2.50
89TCYP Yasiel Puig 1.00 2.50

2014 Topps Chrome All Time Rookies

STATED ODDS 1:280 HOBBY
2 Buster Posey 12.00 30.00
8 Don Mattingly 10.00 25.00
35 Frank Robinson 6.00 15.00
36 Eddie Murray 6.00 15.00
94 Ernie Banks 8.00 20.00
98 Derek Jeter 20.00 50.00
116 Ozzie Smith 10.00 25.00
123 Sandy Koufax 15.00 40.00
164 Roberto Clemente 8.00 20.00
223 Robin Yount 8.00 20.00
228 George Brett 10.00 25.00
260 Reggie Jackson 6.00 15.00
261 Willie Mays 8.00 20.00
312 Jackie Robinson 8.00 20.00
316 Willie McCovey 6.00 15.00
328 Brooks Robinson 20.00 50.00
41T Ken Griffey Jr. 15.00 40.00
482 Rickey Henderson 12.00 30.00
482 Tony Gwynn 8.00 20.00
498 Wade Boggs 6.00 15.00
514 Bob Gibson 6.00 15.00
661 Bryce Harper 10.00 25.00
98T Cal Ripken Jr. 10.00 25.00
T40 Miguel Cabrera 8.00 20.00
US175 Mike Trout 15.00 40.00

2014 Topps Chrome Chrome Connections Die Cuts

COMPLETE SET (30) 20.00 50.00
STATED ODDS 1:12 HOBBY
CCAB Adrian Beltre 1.00 2.50
CCAJ Adam Jones .75 2.00
CCAM Andrew McCutchen 1.00 2.50
CCAP Albert Pujols 1.25 3.00
CCBH Bryce Harper 1.50 4.00
CCCD Chris Davis .60 1.50
CCCG Carlos Gonzalez .75 2.00
CCCK Clayton Kershaw 1.50 4.00
CCDJ Derek Jeter 2.50 6.00

CCDP Dustin Pedroia 1.00 2.50
CCDW David Wright .75 2.00
CCFH Felix Hernandez .75 2.00
CCHR Hanley Ramirez .75 2.00
CCIK Ian Kinsler .75 2.00
CCJE Jacoby Ellsbury .75 2.00
CCJF Jose Fernandez 1.00 2.50
CCJK Jason Kipnis .75 2.00
CCJV Justin Verlander 1.00 2.50
CCMC Miguel Cabrera 1.00 2.50
CCMK Matt Kemp .75 2.00
CCMT Mike Trout 5.00 12.00
CCMTA Masahiro Tanaka 3.00 8.00
CCPF Prince Fielder .75 2.00
CCPG Paul Goldschmidt 1.00 2.50
CCRB Ryan Braun .75 2.00
CCRC Robinson Cano .75 2.00
CCSS Stephen Strasburg 1.00 2.50
CCTT Troy Tulowitzki 1.00 2.50
CCYD Yu Darvish 1.00 2.50
CCYP Yasiel Puig 1.00 2.50

2014 Topps Chrome Chrome Connections Die Cuts Autographs

STATED ODDS 1:14,200 HOBBY
STATED PRINT RUN 25 SER.#'d SETS
EXCHANGE DEADLINE 8/31/2017
CCAAJ Adam Jones 12.00 30.00
CCAMC Miguel Cabrera 100.00 200.00
CCARB Ryan Braun 15.00 40.00
CCARC Robinson Cano 50.00 100.00

2014 Topps Chrome Chrome Connections Die Cuts Relics

STATED ODDS 1:14,000 HOBBY
STATED PRINT RUN 25 SER.#'d SETS
CCRAM Andrew McCutchen 20.00 50.00
CCRCD Chris Davis 15.00 40.00
CCRDJ Derek Jeter 50.00 120.00

2014 Topps Chrome Rookie Autographs

STATED ODDS 1:15 HOBBY
PRINTING PLATE ODDS 1:12,400 HOBBY
PLATE PRINT RUN 1 SET PER COLOR
BLACK-CYAN-MAGENTA-YELLOW ISSUED
NO PLATE PRICING DUE TO SCARCITY
EXCHANGE DEADLINE 8/31/2017
4 Nick Castellanos 8.00 20.00
12 Abraham Almonte 3.00 8.00
22 Taijuan Walker 3.00 8.00
23 Stefen Romero 3.00 8.00
24 Josmil Pinto 3.00 8.00
33 Jonathan Schoop 3.00 8.00
45 Jose Ramirez 40.00 100.00
59 Tyler Collins 3.00 8.00
62 Zach Walters 3.00 8.00
66 Yordano Ventura 4.00 10.00
67 Wilmer Flores 4.00 10.00
69 J.R. Murphy 3.00 8.00
76 Jeff Kobernus 3.00 8.00
81 Kevin Siegrist 3.00 8.00
98 Erik Johnson 3.00 8.00
108 Jake Marisnick 3.00 8.00
126 Yangervis Solarte 3.00 8.00
128 Ethan Martin 3.00 8.00
133 Onelki Garcia 3.00 8.00
134 David Holmberg 3.00 8.00
136 Matt Davidson 4.00 10.00
161 Chris Owings 3.00 8.00
188 Kolten Wong 4.00 10.00
198 Tommy Medica 3.00 8.00
203 Jimmy Nelson 3.00 8.00
209 Andrew Lambo 3.00 8.00
212 Dean Anna 3.00 8.00
AH Andrew Heaney 3.00 8.00
AS Aaron Sanchez 3.00 8.00
EB Eddie Butler 3.00 8.00
ER Enny Romero 3.00 8.00
GP Gregory Polanco 5.00 12.00
GS George Springer 15.00 40.00
JA Jose Abreu 60.00 150.00
MC Michael Choice 3.00 8.00
MST Marcus Stroman 5.00 12.00
NM Nick Martinez 3.00 8.00
OT Oscar Taveras 4.00 10.00
RE Roenis Elias 3.00 8.00

2014 Topps Chrome Rookie Autographs Black Refractors

*BLACK REF: .75X TO 2X BASIC
STATED ODDS 1:610 HOBBY
STATED PRINT RUN 100 SER.#'d SETS
EXCHANGE DEADLINE 8/31/2017
25 Xander Bogaerts 75.00 200.00
124 Travis d'Arnaud 8.00 20.00
AG Alexander Guerrero 15.00 40.00
EA Erisbel Arruebarrena 6.00 15.00
RO Rougned Odor 15.00 40.00

2014 Topps Chrome Rookie Autographs Blue Refractors

*BLUE REF: .6X TO 1.5X BASIC
STATED ODDS 1:306 HOBBY
STATED PRINT RUN 199 SER.#'d SETS
EXCHANGE DEADLINE 8/31/2017
25 Xander Bogaerts 60.00 150.00
AG Alexander Guerrero 12.00 30.00
EA Erisbel Arruebarrena 5.00 12.00
RO Rougned Odor 12.00 30.00

2014 Topps Chrome Rookie Autographs Gold Refractors

*GOLD REF: 1.2X TO 3X BASIC
STATED ODDS 1:1210 HOBBY
STATED PRINT RUN 50 SER.#'d SETS
EXCHANGE DEADLINE 8/31/2017
25 Xander Bogaerts 125.00 300.00
124 Travis d'Arnaud 12.00 30.00
AG Alexander Guerrero 40.00 100.00
EA Erisbel Arruebarrena 10.00 25.00
RO Rougned Odor 25.00 60.00

2014 Topps Chrome Rookie Autographs Red Refractors

*RED REF: 1.5X TO 4X BASIC
STATED ODDS 1:2450 HOBBY
STATED PRINT RUN 25 SER.#'d SETS
EXCHANGE DEADLINE 8/31/2017
25 Xander Bogaerts 125.00 300.00
124 Travis d'Arnaud 20.00 50.00
GS George Springer 150.00 400.00

2014 Topps Chrome Rookie Autographs Refractors

*REF: .5X TO 1.2X BASIC
STATED ODDS 1:128 HOBBY
STATED PRINT RUN 499 SER.#'d SETS
EXCHANGE DEADLINE 8/31/2017
AG Alexander Guerrero 10.00 25.00
EA Erisbel Arruebarrena 4.00 10.00
RO Rougned Odor 10.00 25.00

2014 Topps Chrome Rookie Autographs Sepia Refractors

*SEPIA REF: .75X TO 2X BASIC
STATED ODDS 1:810 HOBBY
STATED PRINT RUN 75 SER.#'d SETS
EXCHANGE DEADLINE 8/31/2017
25 Xander Bogaerts 75.00 200.00
124 Travis d'Arnaud 8.00 20.00
AG Alexander Guerrero 15.00 40.00
EA Erisbel Arruebarrena 6.00 15.00
RO Rougned Odor 15.00 40.00

2014 Topps Chrome Rookie Autographs Silver Ink Black Refractors

*SLVR/BLACK REF: 1.5X TO 4X BASIC
STATED ODDS 1:2450 HOBBY
STATED PRINT RUN 25 SER.#'d SETS
EXCHANGE DEADLINE 8/31/2017
25 Xander Bogaerts 150.00 400.00
EA Erisbel Arruebarrena 12.00 30.00
RO Rougned Odor 30.00 80.00
124 Travis d'Arnaud 15.00 40.00

2014 Topps Chrome Topps of the Class Autographs

STATED ODDS 1:7100 HOBBY
STATED PRINT RUN 25 SER.#'d SETS
EXCHANGE DEADLINE 8/31/2017
TOCBH Billy Hamilton EXCH 60.00 120.00
TOCJA Jose Abreu EXCH 200.00 300.00
TOCKW Kolten Wong 30.00 60.00
TOCMD Matt Davidson 8.00 20.00
TOCTD Travis d'Arnaud 8.00 20.00
TOCYV Yordano Ventura 20.00 50.00

2014 Topps Chrome Topps Shelf Refractors

STATED ODDS 1:24 HOBBY
TSAG Adrian Gonzalez 1.00 2.50
TSAJ Adam Jones 1.00 2.50
TSAM Andrew McCutchen 1.25 3.00
TSAP Albert Pujols 1.50 4.00
TSAW Adam Wainwright 1.00 2.50
TSBH Bryce Harper 2.00 5.00
TSBP Buster Posey 1.50 4.00
TSCD Chris Davis .75 2.00
TSCG Carlos Gonzalez 1.00 2.50
TSCK Clayton Kershaw 2.00 5.00
TSCKI Craig Kimbrel 1.00 2.50
TSCL Cliff Lee 1.00 2.50
TSDJ Derek Jeter 3.00 8.00
TSDO David Ortiz 1.25 3.00
TSDP Dustin Pedroia 1.25 3.00
TSDPR David Price 1.00 2.50
TSDW David Wright 1.00 2.50
TSEL Evan Longoria 1.00 2.50
TSFF Freddie Freeman 1.50 4.00
TSFH Felix Hernandez 1.00 2.50
TSGS Giancarlo Stanton 1.25 3.00
TSGSP George Springer 3.00 8.00
TSHR Hanley Ramirez 1.00 2.50
TSJA Jose Abreu 5.00 12.00
TSJB Jose Bautista 1.00 2.50
TSJBR Jay Bruce 1.00 2.50
TSJE Jacoby Ellsbury 1.00 2.50
TSJF Jose Fernandez 1.25 3.00
TSJH Josh Hamilton 1.00 2.50
TSJK Jason Kipnis 1.00 2.50
TSJR Jose Reyes 1.00 2.50
TSJU Justin Upton 1.00 2.50
TSJV Joey Votto 1.25 3.00
TSJVE Justin Verlander 1.25 3.00
TSMC Miguel Cabrera 1.25 3.00
TSMS Max Scherzer 1.25 3.00
TSMT Mike Trout 6.00 15.00
TSMTA Masahiro Tanaka 4.00 10.00
TSPF Prince Fielder 1.00 2.50
TSPG Paul Goldschmidt 1.25 3.00
TSRB Ryan Braun 1.00 2.50
TSRC Robinson Cano 1.00 2.50
TSSS Stephen Strasburg 1.25 3.00
TSSSC Shin-Soo Choo 1.00 2.50
TSTT Troy Tulowitzki 1.25 3.00
TSWM Wil Myers .75 2.00
TSYC Yoenis Cespedes 1.25 3.00
TSYD Yu Darvish 1.25 3.00
TSYM Yadier Molina 1.50 4.00
TSYP Yasiel Puig 1.25 3.00

2014 Topps Chrome Topps Shelf Autographs

STATED ODDS 1:3560 HOBBY
STATED PRINT RUN 25 SER.#'d SETS
EXCHANGE DEADLINE 8/31/2017
TSAJ Adam Jones 12.00 30.00
TSBH Bryce Harper 75.00 150.00
TSBP Buster Posey 100.00 200.00
TSDP Dustin Pedroia 75.00 150.00
TSDW David Wright 15.00 40.00
TSEL Evan Longoria 15.00 40.00
TSFF Freddie Freeman 30.00 60.00
TSJB Jose Bautista 15.00 40.00
TSJBR Jay Bruce 15.00 40.00
TSJV Joey Votto 75.00 150.00
TSMT Mike Trout 250.00 350.00
TSPG Paul Goldschmidt 30.00 60.00
TSRB Ryan Braun 15.00 40.00
TSRC Robinson Cano 20.00 50.00
TSWM Wil Myers EXCH 15.00 40.00
TSYC Yoenis Cespedes 30.00 60.00

2014 Topps Chrome Update

COMPLETE SET (55) 50.00 100.00
RANDOM INSERTS IN HOLIDAY MEGA BOXES
*GOLD/250: 1.5X TO 4X BASIC
*BLACK/99: 2X TO 5X BASIC
MB1 Brian McCann .60 1.50
MB2 Shin-Soo Choo .60 1.50
MB3 David Freese .50 1.25
MB4 George Springer RC 2.00 5.00
MB5 Ubaldo Jimenez .50 1.25
MB6 Grady Sizemore .60 1.50
MB7 Justin Morneau .60 1.50
MB8 Chris Young .50 1.25
MB9 Daisuke Matsuzaka .60 1.50
MB10 Yangervis Solarte RC .50 1.25
MB11 Michael Choice RC .50 1.25
MB12 Daniel Webb RC .50 1.25
MB13 Stefen Romero RC .50 1.25
MB14 Tommy La Stella RC .50 1.25
MB15 George Springer RD 2.00 5.00
MB16 Adrian Nieto RC .50 1.25
MB17 Robbie Ray RC .50 1.25
MB18 Rafael Montero RC .50 1.25
MB19 Jacob deGrom RC 125.00 300.00
MB20 Mookie Betts RC 50.00 120.00
MB21 James Jones RC .50 1.25
MB22 Jhonny Peralta .50 1.25
MB23 Rougned Odor RC 1.25 3.00
MB24 Nick Tepesch RC .50 1.25
MB25 Tony Sanchez RC .50 1.25
MB26 Bronson Arroyo .50 1.25
MB27 Mark Trumbo .50 1.25
MB28 Raul Ibanez .60 1.50
MB29 Chase Anderson RC .50 1.25
MB30 Erisbel Arruebarrena RC .50 1.25
MB31 Delmon Young .60 1.50
MB32 Jason Giambi .50 1.25
MB33 Rajai Davis .50 1.25
MB34 C.J. Cron RC .50 1.25
MB35 Drew Pomeranz .60 1.50
MB36 Masahiro Tanaka RC 1.50 4.00
MB37 Miguel Cabrera .75 2.00
MB38 Albert Pujols 1.00 2.50
MB39 Jose Abreu RC 4.00 10.00
MB40 Yu Darvish .75 2.00
MB41 Jose Abreu RD 4.00 10.00
MB42 Oscar Taveras RC .60 1.50
MB43 Masahiro Tanaka RD 1.50 4.00
MB44 Jon Singleton RC .60 1.50
MB45 Gregory Polanco RC .75 2.00
MB46 Mookie Betts RD 30.00 80.00
MB47 Andrew Heaney RC .50 1.25
MB48 Gregory Polanco RD .75 2.00
MB49 Oscar Taveras RD .60 1.50
MB50 Jon Singleton RD .60 1.50
MB51 Andrew Heaney RD .50 1.25
MB52 Cam Bedrosian RC .50 1.25
MB53 Marcus Stroman RC .75 2.00
MB54 Jacob deGrom RD 50.00 120.00
MB55 Brandon McCarthy .50 1.25

2014 Topps Chrome Update All-Star Stitches

RANDOM INSERTS IN HOLIDAY MEGA BOXES
ASCRAJ Adam Jones 2.50 6.00
ASCRAM Andrew McCutchen 3.00 8.00
ASCRAR Anthony Rizzo 4.00 10.00
ASCRAW Adam Wainwright 2.50 6.00
ASCRCB Charlie Blackmon 3.00 8.00
ASCRCKL Clayton Kershaw 5.00 12.00
ASCRCU Chase Utley 2.50 6.00
ASCRDJ Derek Jeter 30.00 60.00
ASCRFF Freddie Freeman 4.00 10.00
ASCRFH Felix Hernandez 2.50 6.00
ASCRGS Giancarlo Stanton 3.00 8.00
ASCRJA Jose Abreu 10.00 25.00
ASCRJB Jose Bautista 2.50 6.00
ASCRJL Jonathan Lucroy 2.50 6.00
ASCRKU Koji Uehara 2.00 5.00
ASCRMT Mike Trout 15.00 40.00
ASCRPG Paul Goldschmidt 3.00 8.00
ASCRRC Robinson Cano 2.50 6.00
ASCRTT Troy Tulowitzki 3.00 8.00
ASCRYC Yoenis Cespedes 3.00 8.00
ASCRYD Yu Darvish 3.00 8.00
ASCRYP Yasiel Puig 3.00 8.00

2014 Topps Chrome Update All-Star Stitches Autographs

RANDOM INSERTS IN HOLIDAY MEGA BOXES
STATED PRINT RUN 25 SER.#'d SETS
ASCARGP Glen Perkins 25.00 60.00
ASCARJH Josh Harrison 50.00 120.00
ASCARNC Nelson Cruz 25.00 60.00

2014 Topps Chrome Update World Series Heroes

RANDOM INSERTS IN HOLIDAY MEGA BOXES
WSC1 David Ortiz 1.00 2.50
WSC2 Albert Pujols 1.25 3.00
WSC3 Pedro Martinez .75 2.00
WSC4 Manny Ramirez 1.00 2.50
WSC5 Josh Beckett .60 1.50
WSC6 Randy Johnson 1.00 2.50
WSC7 Derek Jeter 2.50 6.00
WSC8 Mariano Rivera 1.25 3.00
WSC9 Tom Glavine .75 2.00
WSC10 Greg Maddux 1.25 3.00
WSC11 John Smoltz 1.00 2.50
WSC12 Rickey Henderson 1.00 2.50
WSC13 Mookie Wilson .60 1.50
WSC14 George Brett 2.00 5.00
WSC15 Mike Schmidt 1.50 4.00
WSC16 Reggie Jackson .75 2.00
WSC17 Roberto Clemente 2.50 6.00
WSC18 Sandy Koufax 2.00 5.00
WSC19 Hank Aaron 2.00 5.00
WSC20 Brooks Robinson .75 2.00

2015 Topps Chrome

COMP.SET w/o SPs (200) 15.00 40.00
VAR ODDS 1:1:765 H,1:235 J,1:766 R
PLATE ODDS 1:2388 HOB,1:737 JUM,1:2395 RET
PLATE PRINT RUN 1 SET PER COLOR
BLACK-CYAN-MAGENTA-YELLOW ISSUED
NO PLATE PRICING DUE TO SCARCITY
1 Derek Jeter 2.00 5.00
2 Ryan Rua RC .40 1.00
3 Scooter Gennett .25 .60
4 Joe Mauer .25 .60
5 Starling Marte .25 .60
6 Brandon Phillips .20 .50
7 Adam Jones .25 .60
8 Denard Span .20 .50
9 Andrelton Simmons .20 .50
10 Matt Adams .20 .50
11 Carlos Gonzalez .25 .60
12 Prince Fielder .25 .60
13 Jonathan Lucroy .25 .60
14 Paul Konerko .25 .60
15 Anthony Ranaudo RC .40 1.00
16 Tommy La Stella .20 .50
17 Mike Foltynewicz RC .40 1.00
18 Dalton Pompey RC .50 1.25
19 Kendall Graveman RC .40 1.00
20 Roenis Elias .20 .50
21 Matt Barnes RC .40 1.00
22 Nick Tropeano RC .40 1.00
23A Stephen Strasburg .30 .75
23B Strsbrg SP Goggles 8.00 20.00
24 Addison Russell RC 1.25 3.00
25 Yadier Molina .40 1.00
26 Madison Bumgarner .25 .60
27A Joe Panik .25 .60
27B Panik SP Black shirt 15.00 40.00
28 Adeiny Hechavarria .20 .50
29 Yorman Rodriguez RC .40 1.00
30 Alex Gordon .25 .60
31 Jon Lester .25 .60
32 Jonathan Schoop .20 .50
33 Alex Cobb .20 .50
34 Austin Jackson .20 .50
35 Matt Kemp .25 .60
36 Brad Ziegler .20 .50
37 Chris Owings .20 .50
38 Pablo Sandoval .25 .60
39 Hunter Strickland RC .40 1.00
40 Jon Singleton .25 .60
41 Sean Doolittle .20 .50
42 Manny Machado .30 .75
43 Michael Taylor RC .40 1.00
44 Jason Rogers RC .40 1.00
45 David Peralta .20 .50
46 James McCann RC .60 1.50
47 Brandon Belt .25 .60
48 Christian Yelich .40 1.00
49A Jacoby Ellsbury .25 .60
49B Ellsbury SP Hldng hlmt 12.00 30.00
50 Kolten Wong .25 .60
51A Mike Trout 1.50 4.00
51B Trout SP Celebrate 60.00 150.00
52 Yasiel Puig .30 .75
53 Wil Myers .25 .60
54 George Springer .25 .60
55 Clayton Kershaw .50 1.25
56 Ian Desmond .20 .50
57 Chris Sale .30 .75
58 Justin Morneau .25 .60
59 Kevin Kiermaier .25 .60
60 Eric Hosmer .25 .60
61 Russell Martin .20 .50
62 Anthony Rendon .30 .75
63 Nick Castellanos .30 .75
64 Lisalverto Bonilla RC .40 1.00
65 Giancarlo Stanton .30 .75
66 Nolan Arenado .50 1.25
67 Mookie Betts .60 1.50
68 Masahiro Tanaka .25 .60
69 Bryce Brentz RC .40 1.00
70 Dioner Navarro .20 .50
71 Melvin Mercedes RC .40 1.00
72 Todd Frazier .20 .50
73 Carlos Gomez .20 .50
74 Carlos Martinez .25 .60
75 Matt Shoemaker .25 .60
76 Andrew McCutchen .30 .75
77 Charlie Blackmon .30 .75
78 Corey Kluber .25 .60
79 Jordan Zimmermann .25 .60
80 Dilson Herrera RC .50 1.25
81 Bryce Harper .50 1.25
82 Adam Wainwright .25 .60
83 Hunter Pence .25 .60
84 Aroldis Chapman .30 .75
85 Michael Wacha .25 .60
86 Mitch Moreland .20 .50
87 Daniel Norris RC .40 1.00
88 Brett Gardner .25 .60
89 Javier Baez RC 12.00 30.00
90 Carlos Rodon RC 1.00 2.50
91 Michael Brantley .25 .60
92 Ken Giles .20 .50
93 Ian Kinsler .25 .60
94 Ryan Howard .25 .60
95 Adam Eaton .20 .50
96 Archie Bradley RC .40 1.00
97 Carlos Santana .25 .60
98 Max Scherzer .30 .75
99 Doug Fister .20 .50
100 Chase Utley .25 .60
101 Maikel Franco RC .50 1.25
102 David Wright .25 .60
103 Billy Hamilton .25 .60
104 Johnny Cueto .25 .60
105 Freddie Freeman .40 1.00
106 Paul Goldschmidt .30 .75
107 Steven Souza Jr. .25 .60
108 Rafael Ynoa RC .40 1.00
109 Torii Hunter .20 .50
110 Nelson Cruz .30 .75
111 Brandon Crawford .25 .60
112 Kris Bryant RC 12.00 30.00
113 Albert Pujols .40 1.00
114 Victor Martinez .25 .60
115 Matt Harvey .25 .60
116 Rymer Liriano RC .40 1.00
117 Zack Wheeler .25 .60
118 Trevor May RC .40 1.00
119 Travis d'Arnaud .25 .60
120 R.J. Alvarez RC .40 1.00
121 Anthony Rizzo .40 1.00
122 Guilder Rodriguez RC .40 1.00
123 Yimi Garcia RC .40 1.00
124A David Ortiz .30 .75
124B Ortiz SP w/Teammate 12.00 30.00
125A Troy Tulowitzki .30 .75
126 Gregory Polanco .25 .60
127 Melky Cabrera .20 .50
128 John Holdzkom RC .40 1.00
129A Joc Pederson RC 1.50 4.00
129B Pdrsn SP w/Teammate 20.00 50.00
130 Terrance Gore RC .40 1.00
131 Miguel Alfredo Gonzalez RC .40 1.00
132 Cory Spangenberg RC .40 1.00
133 Sonny Gray .25 .60
134 Edwin Encarnacion .30 .75
135 Brandon Moss .20 .50
136 Yordano Ventura .25 .60
137 Jose Bautista .25 .60
138 Adrian Gonzalez .25 .60
139 Starlin Castro .20 .50
140 Josh Harrison .20 .50
141 Jose Fernandez .30 .75
142 David Price .25 .60
143 CC Sabathia .25 .60
144 Dallas Keuchel .25 .60
145 Erik Cordier RC .40 1.00
146 J.J. Hardy .20 .50
147 Jonathan Papelbon .25 .60
148 Jake Lamb RC .60 1.50
149 Evan Gattis .20 .50
150 Mike Napoli .20 .50
151A Jose Altuve .25 .60
151B Altuve SP White jsy 12.00 30.00
152 Chris Archer .20 .50
153 Micah Johnson RC .40 1.00
154A Jorge Soler RC .60 1.50
154B Soler SP w/Teammate 8.00 20.00
155 James Shields .20 .50
156 Kennys Vargas .20 .50
157 Aramis Ramirez .20 .50
158 Nick Swisher .25 .60
159 Kyle Lobstein RC .40 1.00
160 Rusney Castillo RC .50 1.25
161 Jose Pirela RC .40 1.00
162 Miguel Cabrera .30 .75
163 Craig Kimbrel .25 .60
164 Mike Moustakas .25 .60
165 Rougned Odor .25 .60
166 Xavier Scruggs RC .40 1.00
167 Danny Santana .20 .50
168 Edwin Escobar RC .40 1.00
169 Salvador Perez .25 .60
170 Ender Inciarte RC .40 1.00
171 Buck Farmer RC .40 1.00
172 Dustin Pedroia .30 .75
173 Robinson Cano .25 .60
174 Samuel Tuivailala RC .40 1.00
175 Josh Reddick .20 .50
176 Lorenzo Cain .20 .50
177 Steven Moya RC .50 1.25
178 Evan Longoria .25 .60
179 Buster Posey .40 1.00
180 Jose Abreu .30 .75
181 Felix Hernandez .25 .60
182 Marcell Ozuna .30 .75
183 Jacob deGrom .60 1.50
184 Devon Travis RC .40 1.00
185 Phil Hughes .20 .50
186 Mark Teixeira .25 .60
187 Yu Darvish .30 .75
188 Kyle Seager .20 .50
189 Yasmany Tomas RC .50 1.25
190 Michael Cuddyer .20 .50
191 Justin Verlander .30 .75
192 Christian Walker RC .75 2.00
193 Adrian Beltre .30 .75
194 Dellin Betances .25 .60
195A Brandon Finnegan RC .40 1.00
195B Finnegan SP Gatorade 10.00 25.00
196 Kevin Gausman .30 .75
197 Mike Minor .20 .50
198 Garrett Richards .25 .60
199 Hanley Ramirez .25 .60
200 Ryan Braun .25 .60
201 Noah Syndergaard SP RC 6.00 15.00
202 Francisco Lindor SP RC 125.00 300.00
203 Byron Buxton SP RC 20.00 50.00
204 Joey Gallo SP RC 20.00 50.00
205 Carlos Correa SP RC 20.00 50.00

2015 Topps Chrome Blue Refractors

*BLUE REF: 4X TO 10X BASIC
*BLUE REF RC: 2X TO 5X BASIC RC
STATED ODDS 1:64 H,1:20 J,1:64 R
STATED PRINT RUN 150 SER.#'d SETS
51 Mike Trout 20.00 50.00

2015 Topps Chrome Gold Refractors

*GOLD REF: 6X TO 15X BASIC
*GOLD REF RC: 3X TO 8X BASIC RC
*GOLD REF 201-205: 1.5X TO 4X BASE
STATED ODDS 1:191 H,1:59 J,1:191 R
STATED PRINT RUN 50 SER.#'d SETS
51 Mike Trout 60.00 150.00
55 Clayton Kershaw 12.00 30.00
81 Bryce Harper 20.00 50.00

2015 Topps Chrome Green Refractors

*GREEN REF: 5X TO 12X BASIC
*GREEN REF RC: 2.5X TO 6X BASIC RC
*GREEN REF 201-205: .75X TO 2X BASIC
STATED ODDS 1:97 H,1:30 J,1:97 R
STATED PRINT RUN 99 SER.#'d SETS
51 Mike Trout 20.00 50.00

2015 Topps Chrome Orange Refractors

*ORANGE REF: 10X TO 25X BASIC
*ORANGE REF RC: 5X TO 12X BASIC RC
STATED ODDS 1:382 H,1:118 J,1:383 R
STATED PRINT RUN 25 SER.#'d SETS
26 Madison Bumgarner 20.00 50.00
51 Mike Trout 75.00 200.00
55 Clayton Kershaw 15.00 40.00
81 Bryce Harper 25.00 60.00

2015 Topps Chrome Pink Refractors

*PINK REF: 3X TO 8X BASIC
*PINK REF RC: 1.5X TO 4X BASIC RC
THREE PER RETAIL VALUE PACK

2015 Topps Chrome Prism Refractors

*PRISM REF: 1.5X TO 4X BASIC
*PRISM REF RC: .75X TO 2X BASIC RC
STATED ODDS 1:6 H,1:2 J,1:6 R

2015 Topps Chrome Purple Refractors

*PURPLE REF: 3X TO 8X BASIC
*PURPLE REF RC: 1.5X TO 4X BASIC RC
STATED ODDS 1:38 H,1:12 J,1:38 R
STATED PRINT RUN 250 SER.#'d SETS
51 Mike Trout 10.00 25.00

2015 Topps Chrome Refractors

*REF: 1X TO 2.5X BASIC
*REF RC: .5X TO 1.2X BASIC RC
STATED ODDS 1:3 H,1:1 J,1:3 R

2015 Topps Chrome Sepia Refractors

*SEPIA REF: 2.5X TO 6X BASIC
*SEPIA REF RC: 1.2X TO 3X BASIC RC
FOUR PER RETAIL BLASTER

2015 Topps Chrome Commencements

STATED ODDS 1:48 H,1:12 J
COM1 Jacob deGrom 2.00 5.00
COM2 Masahiro Tanaka .75 2.00
COM3 Yordano Ventura .75 2.00
COM4 Jose Abreu .60 1.50
COM5 Kolten Wong .75 2.00
COM6 Xander Bogaerts 1.00 2.50
COM7 Matt Shoemaker .75 2.00
COM8 Mookie Betts 2.00 5.00
COM9 Arismendy Alcantara .60 1.50
COM10 Kennys Vargas .60 1.50
COM11 Anthony Rendon 1.00 2.50
COM12 Christian Yelich 1.25 3.00
COM13 Jose Fernandez 1.00 2.50
COM14 Gregory Polanco .75 2.00
COM15 Dellin Betances .75 2.00
COM16 Wil Myers .75 2.00
COM17 Billy Hamilton .75 2.00
COM18 Joe Panik .75 2.00
COM19 Yasiel Puig 1.00 2.50
COM20 Julio Teheran .75 2.00

2015 Topps Chrome Culminations

STATED ODDS 1:288 HOBBY
CULAB Adrian Beltre 8.00 20.00
CULAG Adrian Gonzalez 6.00 15.00
CULAP Albert Pujols 10.00 25.00
CULCB Carlos Beltran 6.00 15.00
CULCK Clayton Kershaw 12.00 30.00
CULCS CC Sabathia 6.00 15.00
CULDJ Derek Jeter 40.00 80.00
CULDO David Ortiz 8.00 20.00
CULDP Dustin Pedroia 8.00 20.00
CULDW David Wright 6.00 15.00
CULHR Hanley Ramirez 6.00 15.00
CULJH Josh Hamilton 6.00 15.00
CULJL Jon Lester 6.00 15.00
CULJM Joe Mauer 10.00 25.00
CULMC Miguel Cabrera 10.00 25.00
CULMT Mark Teixeira 10.00 25.00
CULPS Pablo Sandoval 6.00 15.00
CULRB Ryan Braun 6.00 15.00
CULRC Robinson Cano 6.00 15.00
CULYM Yadier Molina 10.00 25.00

2015 Topps Chrome Culminations Autographs

STATED ODDS 1:3785 H,1:770 J,1:13,174 R
STATED PRINT RUN 50 SER.#'d SETS
EXCHANGE DEADLINE 8/31/2018
CULCK Clayton Kershaw 75.00 150.00
CULDP Dustin Pedroia 25.00 60.00
CULHR Hanley Ramirez 6.00 15.00
CULJL Jon Lester 12.00 30.00
CULJM Joe Mauer 20.00 50.00
CULMT Mark Teixeira 12.00 30.00
CULPS Pablo Sandoval 10.00 25.00
CULRC Robinson Cano 12.00 30.00

2015 Topps Chrome Future Stars

STATED ODDS 1:12 H,1:4 J,1:12 R
*GOLD/50: 4X TO 10X BASIC
*ORANGE: 5X TO 12X BASIC
FSC01 Joc Pederson 1.50 4.00
FSC02 Rusney Castillo .50 1.25
FSC03 Jorge Soler .60 1.50
FSC04 Javier Baez 3.00 8.00
FSC05 Trevor May .40 1.00
FSC06 Dalton Pompey .50 1.25
FSC07 Michael Taylor .40 1.00
FSC08 Steven Moya .50 1.25
FSC09 Matt Barnes .40 1.00
FSC10 Anthony Ranaudo .40 1.00
FSC11 Maikel Franco .50 1.25
FSC12 Christian Walker .75 2.00
FSC13 Jake Lamb .60 1.50
FSC14 Cory Spangenberg .40 1.00
FSC15 Mike Foltynewicz .40 1.00
FSC16 Dilson Herrera .50 1.25
FSC17 Daniel Norris .40 1.00
FSC18 Brandon Finnegan .40 1.00
FSC19 Rafael Ynoa .40 1.00
FSC20 Samuel Tuivailala .40 1.00

2015 Topps Chrome Gallery of Greats

STATED ODDS 1:24 H,1:8 J,1:24 R
GGR01 Clayton Kershaw 1.25 3.00
GGR02 Derek Jeter 2.00 5.00
GGR03 Miguel Cabrera .75 2.00
GGR04 Yasiel Puig .60 1.50
GGR05 Freddie Freeman 1.00 2.50
GGR06 Albert Pujols 1.00 2.50
GGR07 Bryce Harper 1.25 3.00
GGR08 Mike Trout 4.00 10.00
GGR09 Josh Donaldson .60 1.50
GGR10 Corey Kluber .60 1.50
GGR11 Adrian Beltre .75 2.00
GGR12 Felix Hernandez .60 1.50
GGR13 Yu Darvish .75 2.00
GGR14 Chris Sale .75 2.00
GGR15 Alex Gordon .60 1.50
GGR16 Jose Altuve .60 1.50
GGR17 Troy Tulowitzki .75 2.00
GGR18 Jose Abreu .75 2.00
GGR19 Robinson Cano .60 1.50
GGR20 Andrew McCutchen .75 2.00
GGR21 Buster Posey 1.00 2.50
GGR22 Giancarlo Stanton .75 2.00
GGR23 Jose Bautista .60 1.50
GGR24 David Ortiz .75 2.00
GGR25 Anthony Rizzo 1.00 2.50
GGR26 Evan Longoria .60 1.50
GGR27 Paul Goldschmidt .75 2.00
GGR28 Adam Jones .60 1.50
GGR29 Cole Hamels .60 1.50
GGR30 Johnny Cueto .60 1.50

2015 Topps Chrome Gallery of Greats Gold Refractors

*GOLD: 4X TO 10X BASIC
STATED ODDS 1:525 H,1:1031 J
STATED PRINT RUN 50 SER.#'d SETS
GGR02 Derek Jeter 30.00 80.00

2015 Topps Chrome Gallery of Greats Orange Refractors

*ORANGE: 6X TO 15X BASIC
STATED ODDS 1:1091 H,1:677 J
STATED PRINT RUN 25 SER.#'d SETS
GGR02 Derek Jeter 60.00 150.00

2015 Topps Chrome Illustrious Autographs

STATED ODDS 1:1512 H,1:308 J,1:5270 R
STATED PRINT RUN 50 SER.#'d SETS
EXCHANGE DEADLINE 8/31/2018
PLATE ODDS 1:5646 RETAIL
PLATE PRINT RUN 1 SET PER COLOR
NO PLATE PRICING DUE TO SCARCITY
IAAR Anthony Rizzo 20.00 50.00
IACKR Corey Kluber 12.00 30.00
IACS Chris Sale 15.00 40.00
IACY Christian Yelich 12.00 30.00
IAJA Jose Abreu 20.00 50.00
IAJP Joc Pederson 12.00 30.00
IAPG Paul Goldschmidt 20.00 50.00

2015 Topps Chrome Illustrious Autographs Orange Refractors

*ORANGE: .6X TO 1.5X BASIC
STATED ODDS 1:1082 HOBBY
STATED PRINT RUN 25 SER.#'d SETS
EXCHANGE DEADLINE 8/31/2018
IABP Buster Posey 125.00 250.00
IAMT Mike Trout 250.00 350.00

2015 Topps Chrome Rookie Autographs

STATED ODDS 1:21 H,1:3 J,1:137 R
PRINTING PLATE ODDS 1:2955 RETAIL
PLATE PRINT RUN 1 SET PER COLOR
NO PLATE PRICING DUE TO SCARCITY
EXCHANGE DEADLINE 8/31/2018
ARAB Archie Bradley 4.00 10.00
ARAC A.J. Cole 2.50 6.00
ARARU Addison Russell EXCH 100.00 250.00
ARBB Bryce Brentz 2.50 6.00
ARBBN Byron Buxton 75.00 200.00
ARBFN Brandon Finnegan 3.00 8.00
ARBFR Buck Farmer 2.50 6.00
ARBM Bryan Mitchell 2.50 6.00
ARBST Blake Swihart 3.00 8.00
ARCC Carlos Correa 30.00 80.00
ARCS Cory Spangenberg 2.50 6.00
ARCW Christian Walker 5.00 12.00
ARDC Daniel Corcino 2.50 6.00
ARDH Dilson Herrera 3.00 8.00
ARDN Daniel Norris 2.50 6.00
ARDP Dalton Pompey 3.00 8.00
ARDT Devon Travis 2.50 6.00
AREC Erik Cordier 2.50 6.00
AREE Edwin Escobar 2.50 6.00
ARFL Francisco Lindor 125.00 300.00
ARGB Gary Brown 2.50 6.00
ARHS Hunter Strickland 2.50 6.00
ARJB Javier Baez 25.00 60.00
ARJH John Holdzkom 2.50 6.00
ARJK Jung-ho Kang 15.00 40.00
ARJL Jake Lamb 5.00 12.00
ARJLN Jacob Lindgren 3.00 8.00
ARJPA Jose Pirela 3.00 8.00
ARJPN Joc Pederson 12.00 30.00
ARJR Jason Rogers 2.50 6.00
ARJS Jorge Soler 4.00 10.00
ARKB Kris Bryant 100.00 250.00
ARKG Kendall Graveman 2.50 6.00
ARKL Kyle Lobstein 2.50 6.00
ARKP Kevin Plawecki 2.50 6.00
ARMB Matt Barnes 2.50 6.00
ARMC Matt Clark 2.50 6.00
ARMFO Maikel Franco 8.00 20.00
ARMJ Micah Johnson 2.50 6.00
ARMT Michael Taylor 4.00 10.00
ARNT Nick Tropeano 2.50 6.00
ARRAZ R.J. Alvarez 2.50 6.00
ARRC Rusney Castillo 3.00 8.00
ARRI Raisel Iglesias 3.00 8.00
ARRL Rymer Liriano 2.50 6.00
ARRR Ryan Rua 2.50 6.00
ARSM Steven Moya 3.00 8.00
ARST Samuel Tuivailala 2.50 6.00
ARTG Terrance Gore 2.50 6.00
ARTM Trevor May 2.50 6.00
ARXS Xavier Scruggs 3.00 8.00
ARYG Yimi Garcia 2.50 6.00
ARYR Yorman Rodriguez 2.50 6.00

2015 Topps Chrome Rookie Autographs Blue Refractors

*BLUE REF: .6X TO 1.5X BASIC
STATED ODDS 1:280 H,1:57 J,1:982 R
STATED PRINT RUN 150 SER.#'d SETS
EXCHANGE DEADLINE 8/31/2018
ARNS Noah Syndergaard 25.00 60.00
ARYT Yasmany Tomas 5.00 12.00

2015 Topps Chrome Rookie Autographs Gold Refractors

*GOLD REF: 1.5X TO 4X BASIC
STATED ODDS 1:234 R
STATED PRINT RUN 50 SER.#'d SETS
EXCHANGE DEADLINE 8/31/2018
ARBBN Byron Buxton 300.00 600.00
ARNS Noah Syndergaard 60.00 150.00
ARYT Yasmany Tomas 12.00 30.00

2015 Topps Chrome Rookie Autographs Green Refractors

*GREEN REF: .75X TO 2X BASIC
STATED ODDS 1:424 H,1:86 J,1:1484 R
STATED PRINT RUN 99 SER.#'d SETS
EXCHANGE DEADLINE 8/31/2018
ARNS Noah Syndergaard 30.00 80.00
ARYT Yasmany Tomas 6.00 15.00

2015 Topps Chrome Rookie Autographs Orange Refractors
*ORANGE REF: 2X TO 5X BASIC
STATED ODDS 1:602 H
STATED PRINT RUN 25 SER.#'d SETS
EXCHANGE DEADLINE 8/31/2018
ARAB Archie Bradley 20.00 50.00
ARBBN Byron Buxton 400.00 800.00
ARKB Kris Bryant 400.00 800.00
ARNS Noah Syndergaard 75.00 200.00

2015 Topps Chrome Rookie Autographs Purple Refractors
*PURPLE REF: .6X TO 1.5X BASIC
STATED ODDS 1:168 H,1:34 J,1:589 R
STATED PRINT RUN 250 SER.#'d SETS
EXCHANGE DEADLINE 8/31/2018
ARCR Carlos Rodon 10.00 25.00
ARNS Noah Syndergaard 25.00 60.00
ARYT Yasmany Tomas 5.00 12.00

2015 Topps Chrome Rookie Autographs Refractors
*REF: .5X TO 1.2X BASIC
STATED ODDS 1:54 H,1:29 J,1:211 R
STATED PRINT RUN 499 SER.#'d SETS
EXCHANGE DEADLINE 8/31/2018

2015 Topps Chrome Thrill of the Chase Die Cut Autographs
STATED ODDS 1:3595 H,1:731 J,1:12,647 R
STATED PRINT RUN 35 SER.#'d SETS
EXCHANGE DEADLINE 8/31/2018
PLATE ODDS 1:8783 RETAIL
PLATE PRINT RUN 1 SET PER COLOR
NO PLATE PRICING DUE TO SCARCITY
TCCK Clayton Kershaw 60.00 150.00
TCFF Freddie Freeman 25.00 60.00
TCJH Jason Heyward 30.00 80.00
TCJL Jon Lester 30.00 80.00
TCPG Paul Goldschmidt 20.00 50.00
TCRC Robinson Cano EXCH 15.00 40.00

2016 Topps Chrome
COMP.SET w/o SPs (200) 15.00 40.00
VAR ODDS 1:464 HOBBY
ALL VARIATIONS ARE REFRACTORS
PLATE ODDS 1:2900 HOBBY
PLATE PRINT RUN 1 SET PER COLOR
BLACK-CYAN-MAGENTA-YELLOW ISSUED
NO PLATE PRICING DUE TO SCARCITY
1A Mike Trout 1.50 4.00
1B Trt SP REF w/Fans 40.00 100.00
2 Lorenzo Cain .20 .50
3A Francisco Lindor .30 .75
3B Lndr SP REF Slide 8.00 20.00
4 J.D. Martinez .30 .75
5 Masahiro Tanaka .25 .60
6 Salvador Perez .25 .60
7 Addison Russell .30 .75
8 Jon Gray RC .40 1.00
9 Nolan Arenado .50 1.25
10 Freddie Freeman .40 1.00
11 Gerrit Cole .30 .75
12 Adam Jones .25 .60
13 Byung-Ho Park RC .50 1.25
14 Tyler Naquin RC .60 1.50
15 Charlie Blackmon .30 .75
16 Max Scherzer .30 .75
17 Prince Fielder .25 .60
18 Justin Verlander .30 .75
19 Brandon Drury RC .60 1.50
20 Yu Darvish .30 .75
21 Alex Gordon .25 .60
22 Brian McCann .25 .60
23 Jacoby Ellsbury .25 .60
24 Rob Refsnyder RC .50 1.25
25 Jake Arrieta .25 .60
26 Adrian Gonzalez .25 .60
27 Jose Altuve .25 .60
28 Raul Mondesi RC .75 2.00
29 Richie Shaffer RC .40 1.00
30 Manny Machado .30 .75
31 Curtis Granderson .25 .60
32 Trea Turner RC 1.25 3.00
33A Luis Severino RC .50 1.25
33B Luis Severino SP REF Gray jersey 6.00 15.00
34 Michael Brantley .25 .60
35 George Springer .25 .60
36 Joey Gallo .25 .60
37 DJ LeMahieu .30 .75
38 Zack Greinke .30 .75
39 Madison Bumgarner .25 .60
40 Stephen Strasburg .30 .75
41 Joey Rickard RC .40 1.00
42 Robinson Cano .25 .60
43 Jay Bruce .25 .60
44 Nelson Cruz .30 .75
45 Trevor Story RC 2.00 5.00
46 Albert Pujols .40 1.00
47 Chris Davis .20 .50
48 Adrian Beltre .30 .75
49 Patrick Corbin .25 .60
50A Kris Bryant .40 1.00
50B Brnt SP REF w/Fans 30.00 80.00
51 Carlos Gonzalez .25 .60
52 Michael Conforto RC .50 1.25
53A Giancarlo Stanton .30 .75
53B Giancarlo Stanton SP REF Fist bump 8.00 20.00
54 Dee Gordon .20 .50
55 John Lackey .25 .60
56 Yordano Ventura .25 .60
57 Jeurys Familia .25 .60
58 Joc Pederson .25 .60
59 Tom Murphy RC .40 1.00
60 Carlos Martinez .25 .60
61 Hisashi Iwakuma .25 .60
62 Billy Hamilton .25 .60
63 Jose Abreu .30 .75
64 Maikel Franco .25 .60
65 Jung Ho Kang .20 .50
66 Dallas Keuchel .25 .60
67 Adam Wainwright .25 .60
68 Matt Reynolds .20 .50
69 Eric Hosmer .25 .60
70 Tyler White RC .40 1.00
71 Carlos Ruiz .20 .50
72 Ryan Howard .25 .60
73 Noah Syndergaard .25 .60
74 Matt Kemp .25 .60
75A Carlos Correa .30 .75
75B Crra SP REF w/Fans 8.00 20.00
76 Nick Markakis .25 .60
77 Todd Frazier .20 .50
78 Dustin Pedroia .30 .75
79 Michael Wacha .25 .60
80 Brad Ziegler .20 .50
81 Edwin Encarnacion .30 .75
82 Joe Mauer .25 .60
83 Byron Buxton .30 .75
84 Evan Longoria .25 .60
85 Carl Edwards Jr. RC .50 1.25
86 Rougned Odor .25 .60
87 Anthony Rizzo .40 1.00
88 Mark Melancon .20 .50
89 Hector Olivera RC .50 1.25
90 Josh Reddick .20 .50
91 James Shields .20 .50
92A Kenta Maeda RC .75 2.00
92B Mda SP REF Bttng 10.00 25.00
93 Ross Stripling RC .40 1.00
94 Jorge Lopez RC .40 1.00
95 Tyson Ross .20 .50
96 Jackie Bradley Jr. .30 .75
97 Matt Harvey .25 .60
98 Seung-Hwan Oh RC 1.00 2.50
99 Jose Berrios RC .60 1.50
100 Josh Donaldson .25 .60
101 Andrew Heaney .20 .50
102 Kevin Pillar .20 .50
103 Jason Heyward .25 .60
104 Miguel Sano RC .60 1.50
105 Kevin Kiermaier .25 .60
106 Melky Cabrera .20 .50
107 David Price .25 .60
108 Mallex Smith RC .40 1.00
109 Miguel Cabrera .30 .75
110 Jeremy Hazelbaker RC .50 1.25
111 Marcus Stroman .25 .60
112 Sean Doolittle .20 .50
113 Mark Teixeira .25 .60
114 Aaron Nola RC .75 2.00
115 Starling Marte .25 .60
116 Ichiro .40 1.00
117 Alcides Escobar .25 .60
118 Carlos Gomez .20 .50
119 Craig Kimbrel .25 .60
120 Ben Zobrist .25 .60
121 Ketel Marte RC .75 2.00
122 Jake Odorizzi .20 .50
123 Brett Gardner .25 .60
124 Luke Jackson RC .40 1.00
125 Buster Posey .40 1.00
126 Miguel Almonte RC .40 1.00
127 Rusney Castillo .20 .50
128 Greg Bird RC .50 1.25
129 Odubel Herrera .25 .60
130 Frankie Montas RC .50 1.25
131 Trayce Thompson RC .60 1.50
132 Stephen Piscotty RC .60 1.50
133 Henry Owens RC .50 1.25
134 David Wright .25 .60
135 Russell Martin .20 .50
136 Jeff Samardzija .20 .50
137 Brian Johnson RC .40 1.00
138 Max Kepler RC .60 1.50
139 Chris Sale .30 .75
140 Justin Upton .25 .60
141 Aroldis Chapman .30 .75
142 Cole Hamels .25 .60
143 Gary Sanchez RC 4.00 10.00
144 Jacob deGrom .60 1.50
145A Clayton Kershaw .50 1.25
145B Krshw SP REF Run 10.00 25.00
146 Alex Rodriguez .40 1.00
147 Johnny Cueto .25 .60
148 Robert Stephenson RC .40 1.00
149 Yasiel Puig .30 .75
150 Corey Seager RC 20.00 50.00
151 Trevor Rosenthal .25 .60
152 Yadier Molina .40 1.00
153 David Ortiz .30 .75
154 Matt Garza .20 .50
155 Zach Britton .25 .60
156 Stephen Vogt .25 .60
157 Matt Carpenter .30 .75
158 Carlos Carrasco .20 .50
159 A.J. Pollock .20 .50
160 Taylor Jungmann .20 .50
161 Mookie Betts .60 1.50
162 Paul Goldschmidt .30 .75
163 Ian Kinsler .25 .60
164 Nomar Mazara RC .60 1.50
165 Ryan Braun .25 .60
166A Kyle Schwarber RC 1.25 3.00
166B Schwrbr SP REF Wave 15.00 40.00
167 Hunter Pence .25 .60
168 Dellin Betances .25 .60
169 Yoenis Cespedes .30 .75
170 Garrett Richards .25 .60
171 Zach Lee RC .40 1.00
172 Kyle Seager .20 .50
173 Wei-Yin Chen .20 .50
174 Ben Paulsen .20 .50
175 Andrew McCutchen .30 .75
176 Andrew Miller .25 .60
177 Jose Peraza RC .50 1.25
178 Francisco Liriano .20 .50
179 Dae-Ho Lee RC .60 1.50
180 Hanley Ramirez .25 .60
181 Blake Snell RC .50 1.25
182 Corey Kluber .25 .60
183 Brian Dozier .25 .60
184 Jason Kipnis .25 .60
185 Joey Votto .30 .75
186 Mike Foltynewicz .20 .50
187 Christian Yelich .40 1.00
188 Sonny Gray .25 .60
189 Wade Davis .20 .50
190 Brandon Phillips .20 .50
191 Jose Bautista .25 .60
192 Felix Hernandez .25 .60
193 Julio Teheran .25 .60
194 Troy Tulowitzki .30 .75
195 Steven Matz .20 .50
196 Aaron Blair RC .40 1.00
197 Jose Fernandez .30 .75
198 Daniel Murphy .25 .60
199 Peter O'Brien RC .40 1.00
200A Bryce Harper .50 1.25
200B Hrpr SP REF w/Fans 12.00 30.00

2016 Topps Chrome Black Refractors
*BLACK REF: 3X TO 8X BASIC
*BLACK REF RC: 1.5X TO 4X BASIC RC
HOBBY HOT BOX EXCLUSIVE

2016 Topps Chrome Blue Refractors
*BLUE REF: 4X TO 10X BASIC
*BLUE REF RC: 2X TO 5X BASIC
STATED ODDS 1:78 HOBBY
STATED PRINT RUN 150 SER.#'d SETS

2016 Topps Chrome Gold Refractors
*GOLD REF: 10X TO 25X BASIC
*GOLD REF RC: 5X TO 12X BASIC RC
STATED ODDS 1:232 HOBBY
STATED PRINT RUN 50 SER.#'d SETS
50 Kris Bryant 20.00 50.00

2016 Topps Chrome Green Refractors
*GREEN REF: 8X TO 20X BASIC
*GREEN SP REF: .3X TO .8X BASIC
*GREEN REF RC: 4X TO 10X BASIC RC
STATED ODDS 1:117 HOBBY
STATED SP ODDS 1:2337 HOBBY
STATED PRINT RUN 99 SER.#'d SETS
50A Kris Bryant 20.00 50.00
50B Brnt SP REF w/Fans 20.00 50.00

2016 Topps Chrome Orange Refractors
*ORANGE REF: 12X TO 30X BASIC
*ORANGE REF RC: 6X TO 15X BASIC RC
STATED ODDS 1:149 HOBBY
STATED SP ODDS 1:9225 HOBBY
STATED PRINT RUN 25 SER.#'d SETS
50A Kris Bryant 25.00 60.00
50B Brnt SP REF w/Fans 25.00 60.00

2016 Topps Chrome Pink Refractors
*PINK REF: 2X TO 5X BASIC
*PINK REF RC: 1X TO 2.5X BASIC RC

2016 Topps Chrome Prism Refractors
*PRISM REF: 1.5X TO 4X BASIC
*PRISM REF RC: .75X TO 2X BASIC RC
STATED ODDS 1:6 HOBBY

2016 Topps Chrome Purple Refractors
*PURPLE REF: 4X TO 10X BASIC
*PURPLE REF RC: 2X TO 5X BASIC RC
STATED ODDS 1:43 HOBBY
STATED PRINT RUN 275 SER.#'d SETS

2016 Topps Chrome Refractors
*REF: 1.2X TO 3X BASIC
*REF RC: .6X TO 1.5X BASIC RC
STATED ODDS 1:3 HOBBY

2016 Topps Chrome Sepia Refractors
*SEPIA REF: 2.5X TO 6X BASIC
*SEPIA REF RC: 1.2X TO 3X BASIC RC

2016 Topps Chrome Dual Autographs
STATED ODDS 1:8769 HOBBY
STATED PRINT RUN 25 SER.#'d SETS
PRINTING PLATE ODDS 1:54,636 HOBBY
PLATE PRINT RUN 1 SET PER COLOR
NO PLATE PRICING DUE TO SCARCITY
EXCHANGE DEADLINE 7/31/2018
DABS Bryant/Schwarber 200.00 400.00
DACL Correa/Lindor 60.00 150.00
DADM Darvish/Maeda 150.00 300.00
DAGE Gordon/Escobar 25.00 60.00
DAHT Harper/Trout 600.00 900.00
DAIG Ichiro/Gordon 150.00 300.00
DASG Gray/Severino 15.00 40.00
DASR Rendon/Scherzer 60.00 150.00
DAST Seager/Turner 250.00 400.00
DAWC Wright/Conforto 40.00 100.00

2016 Topps Chrome First Pitch
COMPLETE SET (20) 20.00 50.00
STATED ODDS 1:24 HOBBY
FPC1 Don Cherry 1.00 2.50
FPC2 Mo'ne Davis 1.00 2.50
FPC3 Evelyn Jones 1.00 2.50
FPC4 Bree Morse 1.00 2.50
FPC5 Jordan Spieth 20.00 50.00
FPC6 Kristaps Porzingis 1.00 2.50
FPC7 James Taylor 1.00 2.50
FPC8 LeVar Burton 1.00 2.50
FPC9 Tony Hawk 1.00 2.50
FPC10 Johnny Knoxville 1.00 2.50
FPC11 Steve Aoki 1.00 2.50
FPC12 Tim McGraw 1.00 2.50
FPC13 Jimmy Kimmel 1.00 2.50
FPC14 Billy Joe Armstrong 1.00 2.50
FPC15 Nina Agdal 1.00 2.50
FPC16 Jim Harbaugh 1.25 3.00
FPC17 Miguel Cotto 1.00 2.50
FPC18 Tom Watson 1.00 2.50
FPC19 George H. W. Bush 1.00 2.50
FPC20 Kendrick Lamar 1.00 2.50

2016 Topps Chrome First Pitch Green Refractors
*GREEN: 1.2X TO 3X BASIC
RANDOM INSERTS IN PACKS
STATED PRINT RUN 99 SER.#'d SETS

2016 Topps Chrome First Pitch Orange Refractors
*ORANGE: 1.5X TO 4X BASIC
STATED ODDS 1:4643 HOBBY
STATED PRINT RUN 25 SER.#'d SETS

2016 Topps Chrome Future Stars
STATED ODDS 1:8 HOBBY
*GREEN/99: 2X TO 5X BASIC
*ORANGE/25: 5X TO 12X BASIC
FS1 Kris Bryant .75 2.00
FS2 Francisco Lindor .60 1.50
FS3 Joc Pederson .50 1.25
FS4 Jose Abreu .60 1.50
FS5 Jacob deGrom 1.25 3.00
FS6 Dellin Betances .50 1.25
FS7 Addison Russell .60 1.50
FS8 Joe Panik .50 1.25
FS9 Roberto Osuna .40 1.00
FS10 Noah Syndergaard .50 1.25
FS11 Byron Buxton .60 1.50
FS12 Steven Matz .40 1.00
FS13 Blake Swihart .50 1.25
FS14 Mookie Betts 1.25 3.00
FS15 Maikel Franco .50 1.25
FS16 Kevin Kiermaier .50 1.25
FS17 George Springer .50 1.25
FS18 Jorge Soler .60 1.50
FS19 Jung Ho Kang .40 1.00
FS20 Carlos Correa .60 1.50

2016 Topps Chrome MLB Debut Autographs
STATED ODDS 1:4305 HOBBY
STATED PRINT RUN 50 SER.#'d SETS
PRINTING PLATE ODDS 1:32,285 HOBBY
PLATE PRINT RUN 1 SET PER COLOR
NO PLATE PRICING DUE TO SCARCITY
EXCHANGE DEADLINE 7/31/2018
MLBAAGO Adrian Gonzalez 10.00 25.00
MLBAAJ Adam Jones 12.00 30.00
MLBAALG Alex Gordon 12.00 30.00
MLBACK Clayton Kershaw 30.00 80.00
MLBACS Chris Sale 15.00 40.00
MLBADG Dee Gordon 8.00 20.00
MLBADK Dallas Keuchel 6.00 15.00
MLBADP Dustin Pedroia 20.00 50.00
MLBAFF Freddie Freeman 15.00 40.00
MLBAFL Francisco Lindor 30.00 80.00
MLBAJA Jose Altuve 50.00 120.00
MLBAJS James Shields 5.00 12.00
MLBAKB Kris Bryant 100.00 250.00
MLBASM Starling Marte 10.00 25.00
MLBAYG Yasmani Grandal 5.00 12.00

2016 Topps Chrome MLB Debut Autographs Orange Refractors
*ORANGE: .5X TO 1.2X BASIC
STATED ODDS 1:5185 HOBBY
STATED PRINT RUN 25 SER.#'d SETS
EXCHANGE DEADLINE 7/31/2018
MLBABH Bryce Harper 150.00 300.00
MLBACC Carlos Correa 100.00 250.00
MLBADW David Wright 15.00 40.00
MLBAMT Mike Trout

2016 Topps Chrome Perspectives
COMPLETE SET (20) 6.00 15.00
STATED ODDS 1:6 HOBBY
*GREEN/99: 3X TO 8X BASIC
*ORANGE/25: 6X TO 15X BASIC
PC1 Andrew McCutchen .50 1.25
PC2 Adrian Gonzalez .40 1.00
PC3 Robinson Cano .40 1.00
PC4 Bryce Harper .75 2.00
PC5 Yasiel Puig .50 1.25
PC6 Troy Tulowitzki .50 1.25
PC7 Kris Bryant .60 1.50
PC8 David Ortiz .50 1.25
PC9 Ichiro .60 1.50
PC10 Byron Buxton .50 1.25
PC11 Yadier Molina .60 1.50
PC12 Evan Longoria .40 1.00
PC13 Mark Teixeira .40 1.00
PC14 Billy Hamilton .40 1.00
PC15 Ryan Braun .40 1.00
PC16 Mike Trout 2.50 6.00
PC17 Miguel Sano .50 1.25
PC18 Corey Seager 3.00 8.00
PC19 Michael Conforto .40 1.00
PC20 Kyle Schwarber 1.00 2.50

2016 Topps Chrome Rookie Autographs
STATED ODDS 1:19 HOBBY
PRINTING PLATE ODDS 1:8879 HOBBY
PLATE PRINT RUN 1 SET PER COLOR
NO PLATE PRICING DUE TO SCARCITY
EXCHANGE DEADLINE 7/31/2018
RAAB Aaron Blair 2.50 6.00
RAAH Alen Hanson 3.00 8.00
RAAJR A.J. Reed 2.50 6.00
RAALA Albert Almora 10.00 25.00
RAAN Aaron Nola 15.00 40.00
RABD Brandon Drury 4.00 10.00
RABE Brian Ellington 2.50 6.00
RABJ Brian Johnson 2.50 6.00
RABP Byung-Ho Park 3.00 8.00
RABS Blake Snell 20.00 50.00
RACE Carl Edwards Jr. 3.00 8.00
RACR Colin Rea 2.50 6.00
RACS Corey Seager 100.00 250.00
RADA Dariel Alvarez 2.50 6.00
RADL Dae-Ho Lee 4.00 10.00
RADS Darnell Sweeney 2.50 6.00
RAFM Frankie Montas 3.00 8.00
RAGB Greg Bird 3.00 8.00
RAHOL Hector Olivera 3.00 8.00
RAHOW Henry Owens 3.00 8.00
RAJE Jerad Eickhoff 4.00 10.00
RAJG Jon Gray 2.50 6.00
RAJHA Jeremy Hazelbaker 3.00 8.00
RAJOS Jose Berrios 10.00 25.00
RAJPA James Pazos 3.00 8.00
RAJPE Jose Peraza 3.00 8.00
RAJR Joey Rickard 2.50 6.00
RAJTA Jameson Taillon 8.00 20.00
RAJU Julio Urias 25.00 60.00
RAKC Kaleb Cowart 2.50 6.00
RAKM Ketel Marte 20.00 50.00
RAKMA Kenta Maeda 15.00 40.00
RAKSA Keyvius Sampson 2.50 6.00
RAKSC Kyle Schwarber 15.00 40.00
RAKT Kelby Tomlinson 2.50 6.00
RAKW Kyle Waldrop 3.00 8.00
RALG Lucas Giolito 15.00 40.00
RALJ Luke Jackson 2.50 6.00
RALS Luis Severino 15.00 40.00
RAMAL Miguel Almonte 2.50 6.00
RAMAR Matt Reynolds 2.50 6.00
RAMC Michael Conforto 30.00 80.00
RAMD Matt Duffy 2.50 6.00
RAMIR Michael Reed 2.50 6.00
RAMK Max Kepler 12.00 30.00
RAMS Miguel Sano 4.00 10.00
RAMSM Mallex Smith 2.50 6.00
RAMW Mac Williamson 2.50 6.00
RANM Nomar Mazara 4.00 10.00
RAPO Peter O'Brien 2.50 6.00
RARD Ryan Dull 2.50 6.00
RARM Raul Mondesi 15.00 40.00
RAROS Robert Stephenson 2.50 6.00
RARR Rob Refsnyder 3.00 8.00
RARS Ross Stripling 2.50 6.00
RARSH Richie Shaffer 2.50 6.00
RASOB Socrates Brito 2.50 6.00
RASP Stephen Piscotty 4.00 10.00
RATA Tim Anderson 60.00 150.00
RATB Trevor Brown 3.00 8.00
RATD Tyler Duffey 2.50 6.00
RATJ Travis Jankowski 2.50 6.00
RATM Tom Murphy 2.50 6.00
RATN Tyler Naquin 4.00 10.00
RATS Trevor Story 50.00 120.00
RATTH Trayce Thompson 4.00 10.00
RATTU Trea Turner 25.00 60.00
RATW Tyler White 2.50 6.00
RATZ Tony Zych 2.50 6.00
RAZG Zack Godley 2.50 6.00
RAZL Zach Lee 2.50 6.00

2016 Topps Chrome Rookie Autographs Blue Refractors
*BLUE REF: .6X TO 1.5X BASIC
STATED ODDS 1:237 HOBBY
STATED PRINT RUN 150 SER.#'d SETS
EXCHANGE DEADLINE 7/31/2018

2016 Topps Chrome Rookie Autographs Gold Refractors
*GOLD REF: 1.5X TO 4X BASIC
STATED ODDS 1:709 HOBBY
STATED PRINT RUN 50 SER.#'d SETS
EXCHANGE DEADLINE 7/31/2018

2016 Topps Chrome Rookie Autographs Green Refractors
*GREEN REF: .75X TO 2X BASIC
RANDOM INSERTS IN PACKS
STATED PRINT RUN 99 SER.#'d SETS
EXCHANGE DEADLINE 7/31/2018

2016 Topps Chrome Rookie Autographs Purple Refractors
*PURPLE REF: .6X TO 1.5X BASIC
STATED ODDS 1:142 HOBBY
STATED PRINT RUN 250 SER.#'d SETS
EXCHANGE DEADLINE 7/31/2018

2016 Topps Chrome Rookie Autographs Refractors
*REF: .5X TO 1.2X BASIC
STATED ODDS 1:82 HOBBY
STATED PRINT RUN 499 SER.#'d SETS
EXCHANGE DEADLINE 7/31/2018

2016 Topps Chrome ROY Chronicles
STATED ODDS 1:288 HOBBY
*GREEN/99: .6X TO 1.5X BASIC
*ORANGE/25: 1.2X TO 3X BASIC
ROYI Ichiro 3.00 8.00
ROYBH Bryce Harper 4.00 10.00
ROYBP Buster Posey 3.00 8.00
ROYCC Carlos Correa 2.50 6.00
ROYDP Dustin Pedroia 2.50 6.00
ROYEL Evan Longoria 2.00 5.00
ROYHR Hanley Ramirez 2.00 5.00
ROYJA Jose Abreu 2.50 6.00
ROYJD Jacob deGrom 5.00 12.00
ROYJF Jose Fernandez 2.50 6.00
ROYJV Justin Verlander 2.50 6.00
ROYKB Kris Bryant 12.00 30.00
ROYMT Mike Trout 12.00 30.00
ROYRB Ryan Braun 2.00 5.00
ROYWM Wil Myers 2.00 5.00

2016 Topps Chrome ROY Chronicles Autographs
STATED ODDS 1:11,098 HOBBY
STATED PRINT RUN 50 SER.#'d SETS
PRINTING PLATE ODDS 1:59,189 HOBBY
PLATE PRINT RUN 1 SET PER COLOR
NO PLATE PRICING DUE TO SCARCITY
EXCHANGE DEADLINE 7/31/2018
ROYADP Dustin Pedroia 20.00 50.00
ROYAHR Hanley Ramirez 6.00 15.00
ROYAJD Jacob deGrom 30.00 80.00
ROYAKB Kris Bryant 200.00 400.00
ROYARB Ryan Braun 12.00 30.00
ROYAWM Wil Myers 6.00 15.00

2016 Topps Chrome ROY Chronicles Autographs Orange Refractors
*ORANGE: .5X TO 1.2X BASIC
STATED ODDS 1:9865 HOBBY
STATED PRINT RUN 25 SER.#'d SETS
EXCHANGE DEADLINE 7/31/2018
ROYAI Ichiro 300.00 500.00
ROYABH Bryce Harper 150.00 300.00
ROYABP Buster Posey
ROYACC Carlos Correa 100.00 250.00
ROYAEL Evan Longoria
ROYAMT Mike Trout 150.00 400.00

2016 Topps Chrome Team Logo Autographs
STATED ODDS 1:5301 HOBBY
PRINT RUNS B/WN 7-99 COPIES PER
NO PRICING ON QTY 7
PRINTING PLATE ODDS 1:41,780 HOBBY
PLATE PRINT RUN 1 SET PER COLOR
NO PLATE PRICING DUE TO SCARCITY
EXCHANGE DEADLINE 7/31/2018
TLACS Chris Sale/75 6.00 15.00
TLADW David Wright/30 20.00 50.00
TLAFF Freddie Freeman/30 20.00 50.00
TLAFL Francisco Lindor/99 20.00 50.00
TLAJF Jose Fernandez/27 30.00 80.00
TLAKB Kris Bryant/30 200.00 400.00
TLASG Sonny Gray/99 5.00 12.00

2016 Topps Chrome Team Logo Autographs Orange Refractors
*ORANGE: .5X TO 1.2X BASIC
STATED ODDS 1:7981 HOBBY
STATED PRINT RUN 25 SER.#'d SETS
EXCHANGE DEADLINE 7/31/2018
TLABH Bryce Harper 150.00 300.00
TLACC Carlos Correa 100.00 250.00
TLAEL Evan Longoria 20.00 50.00
TLAJB Jose Bautista
TLAMT Mike Trout 150.00 400.00

2016 Topps Chrome Youth Impact
COMPLETE SET (20) 6.00 15.00
STATED ODDS 1:12 HOBBY
*GREEN/99: 2X TO 5X BASIC
*ORANGE/25: 5X TO 12X BASIC
YI1 Corey Seager 4.00 10.00
YI2 Byung-Ho Park .50 1.25
YI3 Luis Severino .50 1.25
YI4 Michael Conforto .50 1.25
YI5 Jon Gray .40 1.00
YI6 Miguel Sano .60 1.50
YI7 Kyle Schwarber 1.25 3.00
YI8 Trea Turner 1.25 3.00
YI9 Henry Owens .50 1.25
YI10 Trevor Story 2.00 5.00
YI11 Robert Stephenson .40 1.00
YI12 Aaron Nola .75 2.00
YI13 Nomar Mazara .60 1.50
YI14 Stephen Piscotty .60 1.50
YI15 Carl Edwards Jr. .50 1.25
YI16 Raul Mondesi .75 2.00
YI17 Blake Snell .50 1.25
YI18 Aaron Blair .40 1.00
YI19 Jose Berrios .60 1.50
YI20 Kenta Maeda .75 2.00

2016 Topps Chrome Youth Impact Autographs
STATED ODDS 1:977 HOBBY
PRINT RUNS B/WN 75-150 COPIES PER
PRINTING PLATE ODDS 1:35,513 HOBBY
PLATE PRINT RUN 1 SET PER COLOR
NO PLATE PRICING DUE TO SCARCITY
EXCHANGE DEADLINE 7/31/2018
YIAAN Aaron Nola/150 6.00 15.00
YIACE Carl Edwards Jr./150 10.00 25.00
YIACS Corey Seager/75
YIAFM Frankie Montas/150 5.00 12.00
YIAGB Greg Bird/150 5.00 12.00
YIAHOL Hector Olivera/150 5.00 12.00
YIAHOW Henry Owens/75 5.00 12.00
YIAJG Jon Gray/75 4.00 10.00
YIAJP Jose Peraza/150 5.00 12.00
YIAKM Ketel Marte/150 8.00 20.00
YIAKS Kyle Schwarber/75 30.00 80.00
YIALS Luis Severino/75 10.00 25.00
YIAMC Michael Conforto/75 15.00 40.00
YIAMS Miguel Sano/75 6.00 15.00
YIARM Raul Mondesi/150 8.00 20.00
YIASP Stephen Piscotty/150 12.00 30.00
YIATTH Trayce Thompson/150 6.00 15.00
YIATTU Trea Turner/75 30.00 80.00

2016 Topps Chrome Youth Impact Autographs Orange Refractors
*ORANGE: .75X TO 2X BASE p/r 150
*ORANGE: .5X TO 1.2X BASE p/r 75
STATED ODDS 1:5870 HOBBY
STATED PRINT RUN 25 SER.#'d SETS
EXCHANGE DEADLINE 7/31/2018

2017 Topps Chrome
COMP.SET w/o SPs (200) 25.00 60.00
SP ODDS 1:143 HOBBY
ALL VARIATIONS ARE REFRACTORS
PRINTING PLATE ODDS 1:3779 HOBBY
PLATE PRINT RUN 1 SET PER COLOR
BLACK-CYAN-MAGENTA-YELLOW ISSUED
NO PLATE PRICING DUE TO SCARCITY
1A Kris Bryant .40 1.00
1B Brynt SP REF No hat 5.00 12.00
2 JaCoby Jones RC .50 1.25
3 Matt Holliday .30 .75
4 Michael Fulmer .20 .50
5 Corey Kluber .25 .60
6 Ben Zobrist .25 .60
7 Jake Thompson RC .40 1.00
8A Dansby Swanson RC 1.00 2.50
8B Swnsn SP REF No hlmt 6.00 15.00
9A Alex Bregman RC 2.00 5.00
9B Brgmn SP REF Bttng cage 12.00 30.00
10 Aroldis Chapman .30 .75
11 Zack Greinke .30 .75
12 Carson Fulmer RC .40 1.00
13 Johnny Cueto .25 .60
14 Kenta Maeda .25 .60
15 Jorge Alfaro RC .50 1.25
16 Matt Carpenter .30 .75
17 Kyle Schwarber .30 .75
18A Hunter Renfroe RC .50 1.25
18B Rnfre SP REF Fist bump 3.00 8.00
19 Kyle Hendricks .30 .75
20 Felix Hernandez .25 .60
21A Yoenis Cespedes .30 .75
21B Cspds SP REF Hrzntl 4.00 10.00
22 Edwin Encarnacion .30 .75
23 Mark Trumbo .20 .50
24 Jordan Montgomery RC .60 1.50
25A Clayton Kershaw .50 1.25
25B Krshw SP REF No hat 6.00 15.00
26 Ryan Braun .25 .60
27 Ian Desmond .20 .50
28 Brett Gardner .25 .60
29 Mitch Haniger RC .60 1.50
30 Jose Quintana .20 .50
31 Ender Inciarte .20 .50
32 Yadier Molina .40 1.00
33 Bartolo Colon .20 .50
34 Andrew Toles RC .40 1.00
35 Starling Marte .25 .60
36 Addison Russell .30 .75
37 Jose Altuve .25 .60
38 Brandon Drury .20 .50
39 Marcus Stroman .25 .60
40 Manny Machado .30 .75
41 Dee Gordon .20 .50
42 German Marquez RC .60 1.50
43 Robert Gsellman RC .40 1.00
44 Aaron Sanchez .25 .60
45 Xander Bogaerts .30 .75
46 Carlos Martinez .25 .60
47A Trey Mancini RC .75 2.00
47B Mncni SP REF Wht jrsy 5.00 12.00
48A Bryce Harper .50 1.25
48B Harper SP REF Red jrsy 10.00 25.00
49 Max Kepler .25 .60
50 Corey Seager .30 .75
51 Braden Shipley RC .40 1.00
52 A.J. Pollock .20 .50
53 Jake Arrieta .25 .60
54 Joe Mauer .25 .60
55 Willson Contreras .30 .75
56 Stephen Piscotty .25 .60
57 Andrew McCutchen .30 .75
58 Chris Owings .20 .50
59 Kyle Freeland RC .50 1.25
60 Julio Urias .30 .75
61 Luke Weaver RC .50 1.25
62 Gregory Polanco .25 .60
63 J.D. Martinez .30 .75
64 Jackie Bradley Jr. .30 .75
65 Albert Pujols .40 1.00
66 Alex Reyes RC .50 1.25
67 Ryon Healy RC .50 1.25
68 Nick Castellanos .30 .75
69 Starlin Castro .20 .50
70 Jeff Hoffman RC .40 1.00
71 Anthony Rendon .30 .75
72 Christian Yelich .40 1.00
73A Orlando Arcia RC .60 1.50
73B Arcia SP REF Thrwng 4.00 10.00
74 Jesse Winker RC 1.50 4.00
75A Yoan Moncada RC 3.00 8.00
75B Mncda SP REF Bag 10.00 25.00
76 Carlos Gonzalez .25 .60
77 Jose De Leon RC .40 1.00
78 Tyler Austin RC .50 1.25
79 Cody Bellinger RC 10.00 25.00
80 Jharel Cotton RC .40 1.00
81 Cole Hamels .25 .60
82 Nomar Mazara .20 .50
83 Amir Garrett RC .40 1.00
84 Rick Porcello .25 .60
85 Todd Frazier .20 .50
86 Dan Vogelbach RC .60 1.50
87 Dustin Pedroia .30 .75
88 Aledmys Diaz .25 .60
89 Rob Zastryzny RC .40 1.00
90 Robinson Cano .25 .60
91 Kenley Jansen .25 .60
92 Trevor Story .30 .75
93A Justin Verlander .30 .75
93B Vrlndr SP REF Running 4.00 10.00
94 Joey Votto .30 .75
95 Jameson Taillon .25 .60
96 Gavin Cecchini RC .40 1.00
97 Matt Strahm RC .40 1.00
98 Matt Olson RC 2.00 5.00
99 Renato Nunez RC .75 2.00
100A Andrew Benintendi RC 1.25 3.00
100B Bnntndi SP REF Warm up 20.00 50.00
101 Hunter Dozier RC .40 1.00
102A Nolan Arenado .50 1.25
102B Arndo SP REF Prple jrsy 6.00 15.00
103A Noah Syndergaard .25 .60
103B Syndrgrd SP REF ATV 3.00 8.00
104 Lucas Giolito .25 .60
105 Adrian Gonzalez .25 .60
106 Mark Melancon .20 .50
107 Yu Darvish .30 .75
108 Kevin Kiermaier .25 .60
109 Jay Bruce .25 .60
110 Steven Matz .20 .50
111 Brandon Crawford .25 .60
112A Carlos Correa .30 .75
112B Crra SP REF Signing 4.00 10.00
113 Adam Wainwright .25 .60
114 Javier Baez .40 1.00
115 Jason Heyward .25 .60
116 Teoscar Hernandez RC 1.50 4.00
117 Odubel Herrera .25 .60
118 Kyle Seager .20 .50
119 Maikel Franco .25 .60
120 Joe Musgrove RC 1.25 3.00
121 Carlos Santana .25 .60
122 Gary Sanchez .30 .75
123 Wil Myers .25 .60
124 Yulieski Gurriel RC .60 1.50
125 Ian Kinsler .25 .60
126A Francisco Lindor .30 .75
126B Lndr SP REF w/Trophies 4.00 10.00
127 Matt Kemp .25 .60
128 Hunter Pence .25 .60
129 George Springer .25 .60
130 Adrian Beltre .30 .75
131 Lorenzo Cain .20 .50
132 Miguel Cabrera .30 .75
133 Nelson Cruz .30 .75
134 Paul Goldschmidt .30 .75
135 Roman Quinn RC .40 1.00
136 Gerrit Cole .30 .75
137 Antonio Senzatela RC .40 1.00
138 Tyler Naquin .30 .75
139 Seth Lugo RC .40 1.00
140 Joc Pederson .25 .60
141 Chad Pinder RC .40 1.00
142 Jon Lester .25 .60
143 Dellin Betances .25 .60
144 Billy Hamilton .25 .60
145A Buster Posey .40 1.00
145B Posey SP REF In gear 8.00 20.00
146 Freddie Freeman .40 1.00
147 David Price .25 .60
148 Josh Donaldson .25 .60
149A Khris Davis .30 .75
149B Davis SP REF Yllw jrsy 4.00 10.00
150 David Ortiz .30 .75
151 Rougned Odor .25 .60
152 Zach Britton .25 .60
153 Eric Hosmer .25 .60
154 Justin Upton .25 .60
155A Giancarlo Stanton .30 .75
155B Stntn SP REF Running 4.00 10.00
156 Ivan Nova .25 .60
157 Masahiro Tanaka .25 .60
158 Josh Bell RC 1.00 2.50
159A Max Scherzer .30 .75
159B Schrzr SP REF Dugout 4.00 10.00

160 Chris Sale .30 .75
161 Evan Longoria .25 .60
162 Salvador Perez .25 .60
163 Reynaldo Lopez RC .40 1.00
164 Jason Kipnis .25 .60
165 Michael Brantley .25 .60
166 Melky Cabrera .20 .50
167 Jake Odorizzi .20 .50
168 Jose Abreu .30 .75
169A Aaron Judge RC 12.00 30.00
169B Judge SP REF Running 50.00 120.00
170 Adam Jones .25 .60
171 Jose Bautista .25 .60
172 Yasiel Puig .30 .75
173A Anthony Rizzo .40 1.00
173B Rizzo SP REF No helmey 5.00 12.00
174 Adam Duvall .25 .60
175 Andrew Miller .25 .60
176 Brandon Belt .25 .60
177 Chris Archer .20 .50
178 DJ LeMahieu .30 .75
179 Dexter Fowler .25 .60
180 Christian Arroyo RC .60 1.50
181 Justin Bour .25 .60
182 Chris Davis .20 .50
183 Eugenio Suarez .25 .60
184 Jacob deGrom .60 1.50
185 Eduardo Rodriguez .20 .50
186 David Dahl RC .50 1.25
187 Ryan Schimpf .20 .50
188 Craig Kimbrel .25 .60
189 Tyler Glasnow RC 1.50 4.00
190 Brian Dozier .30 .75
191 J.T. Realmuto .30 .75
192 Joe Jimenez RC .50 1.25
193 Brad Ziegler .20 .50
194A Trea Turner .25 .60
194B Trnr SP REF Spring hat 3.00 8.00
195 Edwin Diaz .25 .60
196 Pat Neshek .20 .50
197 Manny Margot RC .40 1.00
198 Troy Tulowitzki .30 .75
199A Mookie Betts .60 1.50
199B Betts SP REF Pointing 8.00 20.00
200A Mike Trout 1.50 4.00
200B Trout SP REF Podium 20.00 50.00

2017 Topps Chrome Blue Refractors

*BLUE REF: 5X TO 12X BASIC
*BLUE REF RC: 2.5X TO 6X BASIC
STATED ODDS 1:101 HOBBY
STATED PRINT RUN 150 SER.#'d SETS
100 Andrew Benintendi 30.00 80.00

2017 Topps Chrome Blue Wave Refractors

*BLUE WAVE REF: 6X TO 15X BASIC
*BLUE WAVE REF RC: 3X TO 8X BASIC
STATED ODDS 1:135 HOBBY
STATED PRINT RUN 75 SER.#'d SETS
100 Andrew Benintendi 40.00 100.00
200 Mike Trout 20.00 50.00

2017 Topps Chrome Gold Refractors

*GOLD REF: 8X TO 20X BASIC
*GOLD REF RC: 4X TO 10X BASIC RC
STATED ODDS 1:303 HOBBY
STATED PRINT RUN 50 SER.#'d SETS
48 Bryce Harper 25.00 60.00
100 Andrew Benintendi 50.00 120.00
169 Aaron Judge 125.00 300.00
200 Mike Trout 40.00 100.00

2017 Topps Chrome Gold Wave Refractors

*GOLD WAVE REF: 8X TO 20X BASIC
*GOLD WAVE REF RC: 4X TO 10X BASIC RC
STATED ODDS 1:202 HOBBY
STATED PRINT RUN 50 SER.#'d SETS
48 Bryce Harper 25.00 60.00
100 Andrew Benintendi 50.00 120.00
169 Aaron Judge 125.00 300.00
200 Mike Trout 40.00 100.00

2017 Topps Chrome Green Refractors

*GREEN REF: 6X TO 15X BASIC
*GREEN SP REF: .5X TO 1.2X BASIC
*GREEN REF RC: 3X TO 8X BASIC RC
STATED ODDS 1:153 HOBBY
STATED SP ODDS 1:1221 HOBBY
STATED PRINT RUN 99 SER.#'d SETS
75B Mncda SP REF Bag 25.00 60.00
100A Andrew Benintendi 40.00 100.00
100B Bnntndi SP REF Warm up 40.00 100.00
169B Judge SP REF Running 60.00 150.00
200A Mike Trout 20.00 50.00
200B Trout SP REF Podium 20.00 50.00

2017 Topps Chrome Negative Refractors

*SEPIA REF: 3X TO 8X BASIC
*SEPIA REF RC: 1.5X TO 4X BASIC RC
STATED ODDS 1:38 HOBBY
100 Andrew Benintendi 20.00 50.00
200 Mike Trout 10.00 25.00

2017 Topps Chrome Orange Refractors

*ORANGE REF: 10X TO 25X BASIC
*ORANGE SP REF: .75X TO 2X BASIC
*ORANGE REF RC: 5X TO 12X BASIC RC
STATED ODDS 1:190 HOBBY
STATED SP ODDS 1:4825 HOBBY
STATED PRINT RUN 25 SER.#'d SETS
48A Bryce Harper 30.00 80.00
48B Harper SP REF Red jrsy 20.00 50.00
75B Mncda SP REF Bag 40.00 100.00
100A Andrew Benintendi 60.00 150.00
100B Bnntndi SP REF Warm up 60.00 150.00
169A Aaron Judge 150.00 400.00
169B Judge SP REF Running 100.00 250.00
200A Mike Trout 60.00 150.00
200B Trout SP REF Podium 60.00 150.00

2017 Topps Chrome Pink Refractors

*PINK REF: 1.5X TO 4X BASIC
*PINK REF RC: .75X TO 2X BASIC RC
THREE PER RETAIL VALUE BOX
100 Andrew Benintendi 10.00 25.00

2017 Topps Chrome Prism Refractors

*PRISM REF:1.5X TO 4X BASIC
*PRISM REF RC:.75X TO 2X BASIC RC
STATED ODDS 1:6 HOBBY
100 Andrew Benintendi 10.00 25.00

2017 Topps Chrome Purple Refractors

*PURPLE REF: 2.5X TO 6X BASIC
*PURPLE REF RC: 1.2X TO 3X BASIC RC
STATED ODDS 1:51 HOBBY
STATED PRINT RUN 299 SER.#'d SETS
100 Andrew Benintendi 15.00 40.00
200 Mike Trout 8.00 20.00

2017 Topps Chrome Refractors

*REF:1.2X TO 3X BASIC
*REF RC:.6X TO 1.5X BASIC RC
STATED ODDS 1:3 HOBBY
100 Andrew Benintendi 8.00 20.00

2017 Topps Chrome Sepia Refractors

*SEPIA REF: 1.5X TO 4X BASIC
*SEPIA REF RC: .75X TO 2X BASIC RC
FIVE PER RETAIL BLASTER
100 Andrew Benintendi 10.00 25.00

2017 Topps Chrome X-Fractors

*XFRACTOR: 1.5X TO 4X BASIC
*XFRACTOR RC: .75X TO 2X BASIC RC
TEN PER WALMART MEGA BOX
100 Andrew Benintendi 10.00 25.00

2017 Topps Chrome '87 Topps

COMPLETE SET (25) 20.00 50.00
STATED ODDS 1:6 HOBBY
87T1 Kris Bryant .75 2.00
87T2 Dansby Swanson 1.00 2.50
87T3 Orlando Arcia .60 1.50
87T4 Manny Machado .60 1.50
87T5 Alex Bregman 2.00 5.00
87T6 Buster Posey .75 2.00
87T7 Corey Seager .60 1.50
87T8 Aaron Judge 6.00 15.00
87T9 Noah Syndergaard .50 1.25
87T10 Carlos Correa .60 1.50
87T11 Francisco Lindor .60 1.50
87T12 George Springer .50 1.25
87T13 Luke Weaver .50 1.25
87T14 Masahiro Tanaka .50 1.25
87T15 Nolan Arenado 1.00 2.50
87T16 Stephen Piscotty .50 1.25
87T17 Addison Russell .60 1.50
87T18 Jake Arrieta .50 1.25
87T19 Danny Duffy .40 1.00
87T20 Yoan Moncada 1.25 3.00
87T21 Jacob deGrom 1.25 3.00
87T22 Anthony Rizzo .75 2.00
87T23 Yulieski Gurriel .60 1.50
87T24 David Dahl .50 1.25
87T25 Andrew Benintendi 1.25 3.00

2017 Topps Chrome '87 Topps Orange Refractors

*ORANGE: 6X TO 15X BASIC
STATED ODDS 1:4825 HOBBY
STATED PRINT RUN 25 SER.#'d SETS
87T8 Aaron Judge 50.00 120.00

2017 Topps Chrome '87 Topps Autographs

STATED ODDS 1:2817 HOBBY
STATED PRINT RUN 50 SER.#'d SETS
EXCHANGE DEADLINE 6/30/2019
*ORANGE/25: .6X TO 1.5X BASIC
PRINTING PLATE ODDS 1:34,884 HOBBY
PLATE PRINT RUN 1 SET PER COLOR
BLACK-CYAN-MAGENTA-YELLOW ISSUED
NO PLATE PRICING DUE TO SCARCITY
87TAAB Alex Bregman 50.00 120.00
87TAABE Andrew Benintendi 75.00 200.00
87TAAJ Aaron Judge 250.00 500.00
87TAAR Anthony Rizzo 30.00 80.00
87TAARU Addison Russell 15.00 40.00
87TABP Buster Posey
87TACC Carlos Correa
87TADD David Dahl 12.00 30.00
87TADDU Danny Duffy 10.00 25.00
87TAFL Francisco Lindor EXCH 30.00 80.00
87TAGS George Springer 12.00 30.00
87TAJD Jacob deGrom
87TAKB Kris Bryant
87TAMT Masahiro Tanaka
87TANS Noah Syndergaard 25.00 60.00
87TAOA Orlando Arcia 15.00 40.00
87TASP Stephen Piscotty 8.00 20.00
87TAYG Yulieski Gurriel
87TAYM Yoan Moncada

2017 Topps Chrome Bowman Then and Now

COMPLETE SET (20) 20.00 50.00
STATED ODDS 1:24 HOBBY
*GREEN/99: 1.5X TO 4X BASIC
*ORANGE/25: 3X TO 8X BASIC
BTN1 Kris Bryant 1.00 2.50
BTN3 Nomar Mazara .50 1.25
BTN4 Trevor Story .75 2.00
BTN5 Ryan Braun .60 1.50
BTN6 Jacob deGrom 1.50 4.00
BTN7 Noah Syndergaard .60 1.50
BTN8 Corey Seager .60 1.50
BTN9 Kyle Seager .50 1.25
BTN10 Bryce Harper 1.25 3.00
BTN11 Manny Machado .75 2.00
BTN12 Francisco Lindor .75 2.00
BTN13 Joe Panik .60 1.50
BTN14 Robinson Cano .60 1.50
BTN15 Jose Altuve .60 1.50
BTN16 Carlos Correa .75 2.00
BTN17 Buster Posey 1.00 2.50
BTN18 Nolan Arenado 1.25 3.00
BTN19 Matt Carpenter .75 2.00
BTN20 Mike Trout 4.00 10.00
BTN20 Addison Russell .75 2.00

2017 Topps Chrome Bowman Then and Now Autographs

STATED ODDS 1:3748 HOBBY
STATED PRINT RUN 50 SER.#'d SETS
EXCHANGE DEADLINE 6/30/2019
PRINTING PLATE ODDS 1:45,348 HOBBY
PLATE PRINT RUN 1 SET PER COLOR
BLACK-CYAN-MAGENTA-YELLOW ISSUED
NO PLATE PRICING DUE TO SCARCITY
BTNAAR Addison Russell 20.00 50.00
BTNABH Bryce Harper
BTNABP Buster Posey 50.00 120.00
BTNACC Carlos Correa 40.00 100.00
BTNACS Corey Seager 40.00 100.00
BTNAFL Francisco Lindor EXCH 30.00 80.00
BTNAJA Jose Altuve 25.00 60.00
BTNAJP Joe Panik 12.00 30.00
BTNAKB Kris Bryant 75.00 200.00
BTNAKS Kyle Seager 12.00 30.00
BTNAMC Matt Carpenter 8.00 20.00
BTNAMT Mike Trout
BTNANM Nomar Mazara 10.00 25.00
BTNANS Noah Syndergaard 20.00 50.00
BTNARB Ryan Braun 12.00 30.00
BTNATS Trevor Story 10.00 25.00

2017 Topps Chrome Bowman Then and Now Autographs Orange Refractors

*ORANGE: .5X TO 1.2X BASIC
STATED ODDS 1:7496 HOBBY
STATED PRINT RUN 25 SER.#'d SETS
EXCHANGE DEADLINE 6/30/2019
BTNAMT Mike Trout 350.00 700.00

2017 Topps Chrome Freshman Flash

COMPLETE SET (20) 15.00 40.00
STATED ODDS 1:12 HOBBY
*GREEN/99: 2X TO 5X BASIC
*ORANGE/25: 4X TO 10X BASIC
FF1 Yoan Moncada 1.25 3.00
FF2 Hunter Renfroe .50 1.25
FF3 Christian Arroyo .60 1.50
FF4 David Dahl .50 1.25
FF5 Cody Bellinger 6.00 15.00
FF6 Orlando Arcia .60 1.50
FF7 Jorge Alfaro .50 1.25
FF8 Tyler Austin .50 1.25
FF9 Jose De Leon .40 1.00
FF10 Alex Bregman 2.00 5.00
FF11 Aaron Judge 5.00 12.00
FF12 Tyler Glasnow 1.50 4.00
FF13 Jharel Cotton .40 1.00
FF14 Manny Margot .40 1.00
FF15 Carson Fulmer .40 1.00
FF16 Luke Weaver .50 1.25
FF17 Alex Reyes .50 1.25
FF18 Dansby Swanson 1.00 2.50
FF19 Yulieski Gurriel .60 1.50
FF20 Andrew Benintendi 1.25 3.00

2017 Topps Chrome Freshman Flash Autographs

STATED ODDS 1:1894 HOBBY
STATED PRINT RUN 99 SER.#'d SETS
EXCHANGE DEADLINE 6/30/2019
*ORANGE/25: .5X TO 1.2X BASIC
PRINTING PLATE ODDS 1:45,348 HOBBY
PLATE PRINT RUN 1 SET PER COLOR
BLACK-CYAN-MAGENTA-YELLOW ISSUED
NO PLATE PRICING DUE TO SCARCITY
FFAAB Alex Bregman 20.00 50.00
FFAABE Andrew Benintendi 40.00 100.00
FFAAJ Aaron Judge 125.00 300.00
FFAAR Alex Reyes 6.00 15.00
FFADD David Dahl 8.00 20.00
FFAHR Hunter Renfroe 8.00 20.00
FFAJA Jorge Alfaro 5.00 12.00
FFAJC Jharel Cotton 4.00 10.00
FFAJDL Jose De Leon 4.00 10.00
FFALW Luke Weaver 10.00 25.00
FFAMM Manny Margot 6.00 15.00
FFAOA Orlando Arcia 10.00 25.00
FFATA Tyler Austin 8.00 20.00
FFATG Tyler Glasnow 12.00 30.00
FFAYG Yulieski Gurriel 6.00 15.00
FFAYM Yoan Moncada 25.00 60.00

2017 Topps Chrome Future Stars

COMPLETE SET (15) 5.00 12.00
STATED ODDS 1:8 HOBBY
*GREEN/99: 2X TO 5X BASIC
*ORANGE/25: 4X TO 10X BASIC
FS1 Gary Sanchez .60 1.50
FS2 Willson Contreras .60 1.50
FS3 Steven Matz .40 1.00
FS4 Tyler Naquin .60 1.50
FS5 Noah Syndergaard .50 1.25
FS6 Michael Fulmer .40 1.00
FS7 Julio Urias .60 1.50
FS8 Nomar Mazara .40 1.00
FS9 Trea Turner .50 1.25
FS10 Francisco Lindor .60 1.50
FS11 Kenta Maeda .50 1.25
FS12 Addison Russell .60 1.50
FS13 Lucas Giolito .50 1.25
FS14 Trevor Story .60 1.50
FS15 Corey Seager .60 1.50

2017 Topps Chrome MLB Award Winners

STATED ODDS 1:288 HOBBY
*GREEN/99: .75X TO 2X BASIC
*ORANGE/25: 1.2X TO 3X BASIC
MAW1 Sandy Koufax 6.00 15.00
MAW2 Mike Piazza 4.00 10.00
MAW3 Mike Trout 12.00 30.00
MAW4 Carlos Correa 3.00 8.00
MAW5 Ichiro 4.00 10.00
MAW6 Clayton Kershaw 5.00 12.00
MAW7 Josh Donaldson 5.00 12.00
MAW8 Frank Thomas 5.00 12.00
MAW9 Ken Griffey Jr. 10.00 25.00
MAW10 Hank Aaron 10.00 25.00
MAW11 Bryce Harper 5.00 12.00
MAW12 Buster Posey 8.00 20.00
MAW13 Derek Jeter 10.00 25.00
MAW14 David Price 2.50 6.00
MAW15 Kris Bryant 4.00 10.00

2017 Topps Chrome MLB Award Winners Autographs

STATED ODDS 1:6573 HOBBY
PRINT RUNS B/WN 15-50 COPIES PER
NO PRICING ON QTY 15
EXCHANGE DEADLINE 6/30/2019
*ORANGE/25: .5X TO 1.2X BASIC
PRINTING PLATE ODDS 1:50,387 HOBBY
PLATE PRINT RUN 1 SET PER COLOR
BLACK-CYAN-MAGENTA-YELLOW ISSUED
NO PLATE PRICING DUE TO SCARCITY
MAWABH Bryce Harper/30 125.00 300.00
MAWACC Carlos Correa/40 30.00 80.00
MAWADP David Price/50 10.00 25.00
MAWAFT Frank Thomas/50 25.00 60.00
MAWAKB Kris Bryant/30 100.00 250.00
MAWAMT Mike Trout/25 300.00 600.00

2017 Topps Chrome Rookie Autographs

STATED ODDS 1:18 HOBBY
PRINTING PLATE ODDS 1:12,775 HOBBY
PLATE PRINT RUN 1 SET PER COLOR
BLACK-CYAN-MAGENTA-YELLOW ISSUED
NO PLATE PRICING DUE TO SCARCITY
EXCHANGE DEADLINE 6/30/2019
RAAB Alex Bregman 60.00 150.00
RAABE Andrew Benintendi 15.00 40.00
RAAG Amir Garrett 2.50 6.00
RAAJ Aaron Judge 150.00 400.00
RAAR Alex Reyes 3.00 8.00
RAAT Andrew Toles 2.50 6.00
RABM Bruce Maxwell 2.50 6.00
RABP Brett Phillips 3.00 8.00
RABS Braden Shipley 2.50 6.00
RABZ Bradley Zimmer 3.00 8.00
RACA Christian Arroyo 4.00 10.00
RACAS Carlos Asuaje 2.50 6.00
RACB Cody Bellinger 125.00 300.00
RACFU Carson Fulmer 4.00 10.00
RACP Chad Pinder 2.50 6.00
RADD David Dahl 3.00 8.00
RADH Donnie Hart 3.00 8.00
RADP David Paulino 3.00 8.00
RADS Dansby Swanson
RADV Dan Vogelbach 4.00 10.00
RAEG Eddie Gamboa 2.50 6.00
RAFB Franklin Barreto 2.50 6.00
RAGM German Marquez 6.00 15.00
RAHD Hunter Dozier 2.50 6.00
RAHR Hunter Renfroe 3.00 8.00
RAIH Ian Happ 12.00 30.00
RAJA Jorge Alfaro 3.00 8.00
RAJC Jharel Cotton 2.50 6.00
RAJDL Jose De Leon 2.50 6.00
RAJH Jeff Hoffman 2.50 6.00
RAJHA Josh Hader 10.00 25.00
RAJHU Jason Hursh 2.50 6.00
RAJJ Joe Jimenez 3.00 8.00
RAJJO JaCoby Jones 3.00 8.00
RAJM Joe Musgrove 20.00 50.00
RAJS Josh Smoker 2.50 6.00
RAJT Jake Thompson 2.50 6.00
RAJW Jesse Winker 25.00 60.00
RALB Lewis Brinson 4.00 10.00
RALW Luke Weaver 3.00 8.00
RAMH Mitch Haniger 15.00 40.00
RAMM Manny Margot 2.50 6.00
RAMO Matt Olson 15.00 40.00
RAMS Matt Strahm 2.50 6.00
RAPV Pat Valaika 3.00 8.00
RARG Robert Gsellman 2.50 6.00
RARH Ryon Healy 3.00 8.00
RARL Reynaldo Lopez 2.50 6.00
RARN Renato Nunez 5.00 12.00
RARQ Roman Quinn 2.50 6.00
RARS Rob Segedin 2.50 6.00
RART Raimel Tapia 6.00 15.00
RARZ Rob Zastryzny 2.50 6.00
RASL Seth Lugo 2.50 6.00
RASN Sean Newcomb 3.00 8.00
RATA Tyler Austin 3.00 8.00
RATBL Ty Blach 3.00 8.00
RATG Tyler Glasnow 25.00 60.00
RATH Teoscar Hernandez 15.00 40.00
RATM Trey Mancini 8.00 20.00
RATR T.J. Rivera 4.00 10.00
RAYG Yulieski Gurriel 10.00 25.00
RAYM Yoan Moncada 40.00 100.00

2017 Topps Chrome Rookie Autographs Blue Refractors

*BLUE REF: .75X TO 2X BASIC
STATED ODDS 1:341 HOBBY
STATED PRINT RUN 150 SER.#'d SETS
EXCHANGE DEADLINE 6/30/2019

2017 Topps Chrome Rookie Autographs Blue Wave Refractors

*BLUE WAVE REF: 1X TO 2.5X BASIC
STATED ODDS 1:479 HOBBY
STATED PRINT RUN 75 SER.#'d SETS
EXCHANGE DEADLINE 6/30/2019
RADS Dansby Swanson 40.00 100.00

2017 Topps Chrome Rookie Autographs Gold Refractors

*GOLD REF: 1.5X TO 4X BASIC
STATED ODDS 1:1023 HOBBY
STATED PRINT RUN 50 SER.#'d SETS
EXCHANGE DEADLINE 6/30/2019
RADS Dansby Swanson 60.00 150.00

2017 Topps Chrome Rookie Autographs Green Refractors

*GREEN REF: 1X TO 2.5X BASIC
STATED ODDS 1:182 RETAIL
STATED PRINT RUN 99 SER.#'d SETS
EXCHANGE DEADLINE 6/30/2019
RADS Dansby Swanson 40.00 100.00

2017 Topps Chrome Rookie Autographs Orange Refractors

*ORANGE REF: 3X TO 8X BASIC
STATED ODDS 1:677 HOBBY
STATED PRINT RUN 25 SER.#'d SETS
EXCHANGE DEADLINE 6/30/2019
RADS Dansby Swanson 125.00 300.00

2017 Topps Chrome Rookie Autographs Purple Refractors

*PURPLE REF: .6X TO 1.5X BASIC
STATED ODDS 1:205 HOBBY
STATED PRINT RUN 250 SER.#'d SETS
EXCHANGE DEADLINE 6/30/2019

2017 Topps Chrome Rookie Autographs Refractors

*REF: .5X TO 1.2X BASIC
STATED ODDS 1:103 HOBBY
STATED PRINT RUN 499 SER.#'d SETS
EXCHANGE DEADLINE 6/30/2019

2017 Topps Chrome Rookie Autographs X-Fractors

*XFRACTOR: 3X TO 8X BASIC
RANDOM INSERTS IN PACKS
STATED PRINT RUN 20 SER.#'d SETS
EXCHANGE DEADLINE 6/30/2019
RADS Dansby Swanson 125.00 300.00

2017 Topps Chrome Sophomore Stat Lines Autographs

COMPLETE SET (13)
STATED ODDS 1:2835 HOBBY
STATED PRINT RUN 99 SER.#'d SETS
EXCHANGE DEADLINE 6/30/2019
*ORANGE/25: .5X TO 1.2X BASIC
PRINTING PLATE ODDS 1:69,767 HOBBY
PLATE PRINT RUN 1 SET PER COLOR
BLACK-CYAN-MAGENTA-YELLOW ISSUED
NO PLATE PRICING DUE TO SCARCITY
SSLAAD Aledmys Diaz 5.00 12.00
SSLABS Blake Snell 5.00 12.00
SSLACS Corey Seager 30.00 80.00
SSLAJT Jameson Taillon 5.00 12.00
SSLAJU Julio Urias 10.00 25.00
SSLAKM Kenta Maeda 10.00 25.00
SSLALG Lucas Giolito 8.00 20.00
SSLAMF Michael Fulmer 4.00 10.00
SSLANM Nomar Mazara
SSLASP Stephen Piscotty 10.00 25.00
SSLATS Trevor Story 10.00 25.00
SSLATT Trea Turner 12.00 30.00
SSLAWC Willson Contreras 15.00 40.00

2017 Topps Chrome Update

COMPLETE SET (100) 15.00 40.00
PRINTING PLATE ODDS 1:1375 PACKS
PLATE PRINT RUN 1 SET PER COLOR
BLACK-CYAN-MAGENTA-YELLOW ISSUED
NO PLATE PRICING DUE TO SCARCITY
HMT1 Bryce Harper AS .50 1.25
HMT2 Luis Severino AS .25 .60
HMT3 Trey Mancini RD .40 1.00
HMT4 Kyle Freeland RC .50 1.25
HMT5 Josh Reddick .20 .50
HMT6 Antonio Senzatela RC .40 1.00
HMT7 Bradley Zimmer RC .50 1.25
HMT8 Salvador Perez AS .25 .60
HMT9 Paul Goldschmidt AS .30 .75
HMT10 Cody Bellinger RC 20.00 50.00
HMT11 Derek Fisher RD .25 .60
HMT12 Nolan Arenado AS .50 1.25
HMT13 Yandy Diaz RC .75 2.00
HMT14 Jose De Leon RC .40 1.00
HMT15 Domingo German RC 1.25 3.00
HMT16 Miguel Sano AS .25 .60
HMT17 Joey Votto AS .30 .75
HMT18 Gary Sanchez AS .30 .75
HMT19 Sam Travis RC .50 1.25
HMT20 Buster Posey AS .40 1.00
HMT21 Wade Davis .20 .50
HMT22 Derek Fisher RC .50 1.25
HMT23 Lewis Brinson RC .60 1.50
HMT24 Jorge Bonifacio RC .40 1.00
HMT25 Clayton Kershaw AS .50 1.25
HMT26 Mookie Betts AS .60 1.50
HMT27 Giancarlo Stanton AS .30 .75
HMT28 Yulieski Gurriel RD .30 .75
HMT29 Tyler Austin RD .25 .60
HMT30 Corey Seager AS .30 .75
HMT31 Jesse Winker RC 1.50 4.00
HMT32 Christian Arroyo RC .60 1.50
HMT33 Alex Reyes RD .25 .60
HMT34 Reynaldo Lopez RC .40 1.00
HMT35 Andrew Benintendi RD .60 1.50
HMT36 Luke Voit RC 10.00 25.00
HMT37 Dinelson Lamet RC .40 1.00
HMT38 Kendrys Morales .20 .50
HMT39 Carlos Correa AS .30 .75
HMT40 Aaron Judge AS 2.50 6.00
HMT41 Yoan Moncada RD .60 1.50
HMT42 Paul DeJong RC 1.25 3.00
HMT43 Ryan Zimmerman AS .25 .60
HMT44 Michael Conforto AS .25 .60
HMT45 Jose Altuve AS .25 .60
HMT46 Jose Quintana .20 .50
HMT47 Carlos Beltran .25 .60
HMT48 Gift Ngoepe RC .40 1.00
HMT49 Tyler Glasnow RD .75 2.00
HMT50 Aaron Judge RD 2.50 6.00
HMT51 Ian Happ RD .40 1.00
HMT52 Orlando Arcia RD .30 .75
HMT53 Matt Chapman RC 1.25 3.00
HMT54 Josh Hader RC .50 1.25
HMT55 Franklin Barreto RC .40 1.00
HMT56 Brian McCann .25 .60
HMT57 Yadier Molina AS .40 1.00
HMT58 Jordan Montgomery RC .60 1.50
HMT59 Jose Ramirez .25 .60
HMT60 Alex Bregman RD 1.00 2.50
HMT61 Jacob Faria RC .40 1.00
HMT62 Jaycob Brugman RC .40 1.00
HMT63 Luis Castillo RC 1.25 3.00
HMT64 Sean Newcomb RC .50 1.25
HMT65 Max Scherzer AS .30 .75
HMT66 Ian Happ RC .75 2.00
HMT67 Francisco Lindor AS .30 .75
HMT68 Daniel Murphy AS .25 .60
HMT69 Charlie Blackmon AS .30 .75
HMT70 Chris Sale .30 .75
HMT71 Christian Arroyo RD .30 .75
HMT72 Magneuris Sierra RC .40 1.00
HMT73 Michael Fulmer AS .20 .50
HMT74 Dellin Betances AS .25 .60
HMT75 Dansby Swanson RD .50 1.25
HMT76 Jeff Hoffman RD .20 .50
HMT77 Brett Phillips RC .50 1.25
HMT78 Amir Garrett RD .20 .50
HMT79 Daniel Robertson RC .40 1.00
HMT80 Chris Sale AS .30 .75
HMT81 Cody Bellinger AS 3.00 8.00
HMT82 Cameron Maybin .20 .50
HMT83 Robinson Cano AS .25 .60
HMT84 Ryon Healy RD .25 .60
HMT85 George Springer AS .25 .60
HMT86 Yu Darvish AS .30 .75
HMT87 Corey Kluber AS .25 .60
HMT88 Justin Upton AS .25 .60
HMT89 Hunter Renfroe RD .25 .60
HMT90 Jean Segura .25 .60
HMT91 Franklin Barreto RD .20 .50
HMT92 Stephen Strasburg AS .30 .75
HMT93 Anthony Alford RC .40 1.00
HMT94 Matt Adams .20 .50
HMT95 Adam Eaton .30 .75
HMT96 Bradley Zimmer RD .25 .60
HMT97 Craig Kimbrel AS .25 .60
HMT98 Yoan Moncada RC 1.25 3.00
HMT99 Cody Bellinger RD 3.00 8.00
HMT100 David Dahl RD .25 .60

2017 Topps Chrome Update Gold Refractors

*GOLD REFRACTORS: 5X TO 12X BASIC
*GOLD REFRACTORS: 2.5X TO 6X BASIC
STATED ODDS 1:110 PACKS
STATED PRINT RUN 50 SER.#'d SETS
HMT40 Aaron Judge AS 50.00 120.00
HMT50 Aaron Judge RD 50.00 120.00

2017 Topps Chrome Update Red Refractors

*RED REFRACTORS: 6X TO 15X BASIC
*RED REFRACTORS RC: 3X TO 8X BASIC
STATED ODDS 1:220 PACKS
STATED PRINT RUN 25 SER.#'d SETS
HMT40 Aaron Judge AS 150.00 400.00
HMT50 Aaron Judge RD 150.00 400.00

2017 Topps Chrome Update Refractors

*REFRACTORS: 1.2X TO 3X BASIC
*REFRACTORS RC: .6X TO 1.5X BASIC
STATED ODDS 1:22 PACKS
STATED PRINT RUN 250 SER.#'d SETS
HMT40 Aaron Judge AS 20.00 50.00
HMT50 Aaron Judge RD 20.00 50.00

2017 Topps Chrome Update X-Fractors

*X-FRACTORS: 1.5X TO 4X BASIC
*X-FRACTORS RC: .75X TO 2X BASIC
STATED ODDS 1:56 PACKS
STATED PRINT RUN 99 SER.#'d SETS
HMT40 Aaron Judge AS 25.00 60.00
HMT50 Aaron Judge RD 25.00 60.00

2017 Topps Chrome Update All Rookie Cup

COMPLETE SET (20) 12.00 30.00
STATED ODDS 1:2 PACKS
TARC1 Bryce Harper 1.25 3.00
TARC2 Carlton Fisk .60 1.50
TARC3 Rod Carew .60 1.50
TARC4 Mark McGwire 1.25 3.00
TARC5 Ichiro 1.00 2.50
TARC6 Buster Posey 1.00 2.50
TARC7 Mike Trout 4.00 10.00
TARC8 Chipper Jones .75 2.00
TARC9 Johnny Bench .75 2.00
TARC10 Noah Syndergaard .60 1.50
TARC11 Eddie Murray .60 1.50
TARC12 Tom Seaver .60 1.50
TARC13 Joe Morgan .60 1.50
TARC14 Derek Jeter 2.00 5.00
TARC15 Kris Bryant 1.00 2.50
TARC16 Ken Griffey Jr. 1.50 4.00
TARC17 Carlos Correa .75 2.00
TARC18 Cal Ripken Jr. 2.50 6.00
TARC19 Joey Votto .75 2.00
TARC20 Willie McCovey .60 1.50

2017 Topps Chrome Update Autographs

STATED ODDS 1:56 PACKS
PRINTING PLATE ODDS 1:2501 PACKS
PLATE PRINT RUN 1 SET PER COLOR
BLACK-CYAN-MAGENTA-YELLOW ISSUED
NO PLATE PRICING DUE TO SCARCITY
EXCHANGE DEADLINE 10/31/2019
HMT1 Bryce Harper 60.00 150.00
HMT2 Luis Severino 8.00 20.00
HMT3 Trey Mancini 6.00 15.00
HMT4 Kyle Freeland 4.00 10.00
HMT5 Josh Reddick
HMT6 Antonio Senzatela 3.00 8.00
HMT9 Paul Goldschmidt 15.00 40.00
HMT10 Cody Bellinger 75.00 200.00
HMT14 Jose De Leon
HMT15 Domingo German 15.00 40.00
HMT17 Joey Votto 20.00 50.00
HMT19 Sam Travis 4.00 10.00
HMT20 Buster Posey EXCH 40.00 100.00
HMT22 Derek Fisher 6.00 15.00
HMT23 Lewis Brinson 5.00 12.00
HMT25 Clayton Kershaw 60.00 150.00
HMT28 Yulieski Gurriel 6.00 15.00
HMT29 Tyler Austin 4.00 10.00
HMT30 Corey Seager EXCH 25.00 60.00
HMT31 Jesse Winker 30.00 80.00
HMT32 Christian Arroyo 5.00 12.00
HMT33 Alex Reyes 6.00 15.00
HMT34 Reynaldo Lopez 3.00 8.00
HMT35 Andrew Benintendi 25.00 60.00
HMT37 Dinelson Lamet 3.00 8.00
HMT38 Kendrys Morales 3.00 8.00
HMT39 Carlos Correa 30.00 80.00
HMT40 Aaron Judge 75.00 200.00
HMT42 Paul DeJong 20.00 50.00
HMT45 Jose Altuve 15.00 40.00
HMT50 Aaron Judge 75.00 200.00
HMT51 Ian Happ 6.00 15.00
HMT54 Josh Hader 6.00 15.00
HMT55 Franklin Barreto 5.00 12.00
HMT56 Brian McCann
HMT58 Jordan Montgomery 10.00 25.00
HMT60 Alex Bregman 20.00 50.00
HMT61 Jacob Faria 3.00 8.00
HMT63 Luis Castillo 15.00 40.00
HMT64 Sean Newcomb 4.00 10.00
HMT66 Ian Happ 6.00 15.00
HMT69 Charlie Blackmon 5.00 12.00
HMT71 Christian Arroyo 5.00 12.00
HMT72 Magneuris Sierra 8.00 20.00
HMT73 Michael Fulmer 3.00 8.00
HMT75 Dansby Swanson 15.00 40.00
HMT77 Brett Phillips 4.00 10.00
HMT79 Daniel Robertson 3.00 8.00
HMT80 Chris Sale 10.00 25.00
HMT81 Cody Bellinger 75.00 200.00
HMT85 George Springer 12.00 30.00
HMT87 Corey Kluber 30.00 80.00
HMT89 Hunter Renfroe 6.00 15.00
HMT90 Jean Segura 4.00 10.00
HMT93 Anthony Alford 3.00 8.00
HMT94 Matt Adams 3.00 8.00
HMT96 Bradley Zimmer
HMT97 Craig Kimbrel
HMT98 Yoan Moncada 25.00 60.00
HMT99 Cody Bellinger 75.00 200.00
HMT100 David Dahl 5.00 12.00

2017 Topps Chrome Update Autographs Gold Refractors

*GOLD REF: .75X TO 2X BASIC
STATED ODDS 1:240 PACKS
STATED PRINT RUN 50 SER.#'d SETS
EXCHANGE DEADLINE 10/31/2019

2017 Topps Chrome Update Autographs Red Refractors

*RED REF: 1X TO 2.5X BASIC
STATED ODDS 1:449 PACKS
STATED PRINT RUN 25 SER.#'d SETS
EXCHANGE DEADLINE 10/31/2019
HMT5 Josh Reddick 12.00 30.00
HMT96 Bradley Zimmer 30.00 80.00

2017 Topps Chrome Update Autographs X-Fractors

*X-FRACTORS: .5X TO 1.2X BASIC
STATED ODDS 1:165 PACKS
STATED PRINT RUN 99 SER.#'d SETS
EXCHANGE DEADLINE 10/31/2019

2018 Topps Chrome

PRINTING PLATE ODDS 1:5397 HOBBY
PLATE PRINT RUN 1 SET PER COLOR
BLACK-CYAN-MAGENTA-YELLOW ISSUED
NO PLATE PRICING DUE TO SCARCITY
1 Aaron Judge .75 2.00
2 Marcus Stroman .25 .60
3 Tim Beckham .25 .60
4 Jack Flaherty RC 1.50 4.00
5 Alex Reyes .25 .60
6 Didi Gregorius .25 .60
7 Eric Thames .25 .60
8 Josh Donaldson .25 .60
9 Victor Arano RC .40 1.00
10 Masahiro Tanaka .25 .60
11 Kevin Pillar .20 .50
12 Tyler Mahle RC .50 1.25
13 Miguel Gomez RC .40 1.00
14 Miguel Andujar RC 1.50 4.00
15 Billy Hamilton .25 .60
16 Chris Davis .20 .50
17 George Springer .25 .60
18 Wil Myers .25 .60
19 Taijuan Walker .20 .50
20 Corey Kluber .25 .60
21 Ryan McMahon RC 1.00 2.50
22 Brian Anderson RC .50 1.25
23 Freddie Freeman .40 1.00
24 Yadier Molina .40 1.00
25 Rafael Devers RC 8.00 20.00
26 Miguel Cabrera .30 .75
27 Max Kepler .25 .60
28 Gregory Polanco .25 .60
29 Buster Posey .40 1.00
30 Alex Colome .20 .50
31 Gleyber Torres RC 8.00 20.00
32 Tyler Wade RC .50 1.25
33 Matt Carpenter .30 .75
34 Luis Castillo .25 .60
35 Tyler O'Neill RC .60 1.50
36 Justin Turner .30 .75
37 Paul Goldschmidt .30 .75
38 Marwin Gonzalez .20 .50
39 Alex Wood .20 .50
40 Harrison Bader RC .60 1.50
41 Eugenio Suarez .25 .60
42 Lucas Sims RC .40 1.00
43 Richard Urena RC .40 1.00
44 Tim Anderson .30 .75
45 Albert Pujols .40 1.00
46 Odubel Herrera .25 .60
47 Byron Buxton .30 .75
48 Jose Quintana .20 .50
49 Anthony Rizzo .40 1.00
50 Kris Bryant .40 1.00
51 Ian Happ .25 .60
52 Robinson Cano .25 .60
53 Craig Kimbrel .25 .60
54 Anthony Banda RC .40 1.00
55 Trevor Bauer .40 1.00
56 Kyle Schwarber .30 .75
57 Jacob Faria .20 .50
58 Ender Inciarte .20 .50
59 Hanley Ramirez .25 .60
60 Amed Rosario RC .50 1.25
61 J.P. Crawford RC .40 1.00
62 Manny Margot .20 .50
63 Lucas Giolito .25 .60
64 Matt Olson .30 .75
65 Luis Severino .25 .60
66 Max Fried RC 1.50 4.00
67 Khris Davis .30 .75
68 Justin Bour .20 .50
69 Chris Sale .30 .75
70 Rhys Hoskins RC 1.50 4.00
71 Walker Buehler RC 3.00 8.00
72 Ozzie Albies RC 1.25 3.00
73 Francisco Lindor .30 .75
74 Andrew McCutchen .30 .75
75 Jameson Taillon .25 .60
76 Erick Fedde RC .40 1.00
77 Parker Bridwell RC .40 1.00
78 Josh Bell .25 .60
79 Paul DeJong .30 .75
80 German Marquez .20 .50
81 Rougned Odor .25 .60
82 Raisel Iglesias .25 .60
83 Chris Taylor .25 .60
84 Greg Allen RC .40 1.00
85 Kendrys Morales .20 .50
86 Addison Russell .25 .60

87 Austin Hays RC .60 1.50
88 Luke Weaver .25 .60
89 Ryan Braun .25 .60
90 Nicky Delmonico RC .40 1.00
91 Kenley Jansen .25 .60
92 Francisco Mejia RC .50 1.25
93 Domingo Santana .25 .60
94 Manny Machado .30 .75
95 Evan Longoria .25 .60
96 Justin Verlander .30 .75
97 Andrelton Simmons .20 .50
98 Jonathan Schoop .20 .50
99 Noah Syndergaard .25 .60
100 Mike Trout 1.50 4.00
101 Jen-Ho Tseng RC .40 1.00
102 Chris Archer .20 .50
103 Carlos Correa .30 .75
104 Nicholas Castellanos .30 .75
105 Travis Shaw .20 .50
106 Jake Lamb .25 .60
107 Salvador Perez .25 .60
108 Joey Gallo .25 .60
109 Brett Gardner .25 .60
110 Jackson Stephens RC .40 1.00
111 Brandon Crawford .25 .60
112 David Robertson .20 .50
113 Willie Calhoun RC .60 1.50
114 Nelson Cruz .30 .75
115 Jackie Bradley Jr. .30 .75
116 Maikel Franco .25 .60
117 Andrew Miller .25 .60
118 Tommy Pham .20 .50
119 Yoenis Cespedes .30 .75
120 Raudy Read RC .40 1.00
121 Clayton Kershaw .50 1.25
122 Dillon Peters RC .40 1.00
123 Joey Votto .30 .75
124 Lewis Brinson .20 .50
125 Luiz Gohara RC .40 1.00
126 Scott Kingery RC .60 1.50
127 Felix Jorge RC .40 1.00
128 Sandy Alcantara RC .40 1.00
129 Robbie Ray .20 .50
130 Elvis Andrus .25 .60
131 Adrian Beltre .30 .75
132 Cody Bellinger .60 1.50
133 Chance Sisco RC .50 1.25
134 Cole Hamels .25 .60
135 Orlando Arcia .20 .50
136 Michael Conforto .25 .60
137 Sean Doolittle .20 .50
138 Adam Jones .25 .60
139 Bryce Harper .50 1.25
140 Brian Dozier .25 .60
141 Starlin Castro .20 .50
142 Trey Mancini .25 .60
143 Jacob deGrom .60 1.50
144 Whit Merrifield .30 .75
145 Max Scherzer .30 .75
146 Trea Turner .25 .60
147 Nick Williams RC .50 1.25
148 Clint Frazier RC .75 2.00
149 Marcell Ozuna .30 .75
150 Shohei Ohtani RC 25.00 60.00
151 Andrew Benintendi .30 .75
152 Tomas Nido RC .40 1.00
153 Ervin Santana .20 .50
154 Zack Granite RC .40 1.00
155 Edwin Diaz .25 .60
156 Zack Greinke .30 .75
157 Dustin Fowler RC .40 1.00
158 Paul Blackburn RC .40 1.00
159 Kyle Seager .20 .50
160 Yoan Moncada .30 .75
161 Cody Allen .20 .50
162 Dominic Smith RC .50 1.25
163 Nolan Arenado .50 1.25
164 Troy Scribner RC .40 1.00
165 Anthony Rendon .30 .75
166 Dallas Keuchel .25 .60
167 Alex Verdugo RC .60 1.50
168 Yuli Gurriel .25 .60
169 Jose Abreu .30 .75
170 Aaron Altherr .20 .50
171 Jon Gray .20 .50
172 Jay Bruce .25 .60
173 Carlos Carrasco .20 .50
174 Greg Bird .25 .60
175 Victor Robles RC 1.00 2.50
176 Michael Fulmer .20 .50
177 J.D. Davis RC .50 1.25
178 Nomar Mazara .20 .50
179 Brandon Woodruff RC 1.25 3.00
180 A.J. Minter RC .50 1.25
181 Kenta Maeda .25 .60
182 Gary Sanchez .30 .75
183 Mookie Betts .60 1.50
184 Hunter Renfroe .20 .50
185 Stephen Strasburg .30 .75
186 Giancarlo Stanton .30 .75
187 Jose Berrios .25 .60
188 Garrett Cooper RC .40 1.00
189 Jose Ramirez .25 .60
190 Matt Chapman .30 .75
191 Jon Lester .25 .60
192 Corey Seager .30 .75
193 Ronald Acuna RC 60.00 150.00
194 Charlie Blackmon .30 .75
195 Alex Bregman .30 .75
196 Daniel Murphy .25 .60
197 Willson Contreras .30 .75
198 Andrew Stevenson RC .40 1.00
199 Edwin Encarnacion .30 .75
200 Jose Altuve .25 .60

2018 Topps Chrome Black and White Negative Refractors

*SEPIA REF: 3X TO 8X BASIC
*SEPIA REF RC: 1.5X TO 4X BASIC RC
STATED ODDS 1:53 HOBBY
14 Miguel Andujar 10.00 25.00
25 Rafael Devers 15.00 40.00
31 Gleyber Torres 30.00 80.00
70 Rhys Hoskins 10.00 25.00

2018 Topps Chrome Blue Refractors

*BLUE REF: 5X TO 12X BASIC
*BLUE REF RC: 2.5X TO 6X BASIC
STATED ODDS 1:141 HOBBY
STATED PRINT RUN 150 SER.#'d SETS
14 Miguel Andujar 15.00 40.00
70 Rhys Hoskins 15.00 40.00

2018 Topps Chrome Blue Wave Refractors

*BLUE WAVE REF: 6X TO 15X BASIC
*BLUE WAVE REF RC: 3X TO 8X BASIC
STATED ODDS 1:164 HOBBY
STATED PRINT RUN 75 SER.#'d SETS
14 Miguel Andujar 20.00 50.00
70 Rhys Hoskins 20.00 50.00

2018 Topps Chrome Gold Refractors

*GOLD REF: 8X TO 20X BASIC
*GOLD REF RC: 4X TO 10X BASIC RC
STATED ODDS 1:422 HOBBY
STATED PRINT RUN 50 SER.#'d SETS
1 Aaron Judge 40.00 100.00
14 Miguel Andujar 25.00 60.00
70 Rhys Hoskins 25.00 60.00
100 Mike Trout 50.00 120.00
175 Victor Robles 15.00 40.00

2018 Topps Chrome Gold Wave Refractors

*GOLD REF: 8X TO 20X BASIC
*GOLD REF.RC: 4X TO 10X BASIC RC
STATED ODDS 1:246 HOBBY
STATED PRINT RUN 50 SER.#'d SETS
1 Aaron Judge 40.00 100.00
14 Miguel Andujar 25.00 60.00
70 Rhys Hoskins 25.00 60.00
100 Mike Trout 50.00 120.00
175 Victor Robles 15.00 40.00

2018 Topps Chrome Green Refractors

*GREEN REF: 6X TO 15X BASIC
*GREEN REF RC: 3X TO 8X BASIC RC
STATED ODDS 1:213 HOBBY
STATED PRINT RUN 99 SER.#'d SETS
14 Miguel Andujar 20.00 50.00

2018 Topps Chrome Green Wave Refractors

*GREEN WAVE REF: 6X TO 15X BASIC
*GREEN WAVE REF RC: 3X TO 8X BASIC RC
STATED ODDS 1:124 HOBBY
STATED PRINT RUN 99 SER.#'d SETS
14 Miguel Andujar 20.00 50.00
70 Rhys Hoskins 20.00 50.00

2018 Topps Chrome Orange Refractors

*ORANGE REF: 10X TO 25X BASIC
*ORANGE REF RC: 5X TO 12X BASIC RC
STATED ODDS 1:229 HOBBY
STATED PRINT RUN 25 SER.#'d SETS
1 Aaron Judge 50.00 120.00
14 Miguel Andujar 30.00 80.00
70 Rhys Hoskins 30.00 80.00
100 Mike Trout 60.00 150.00
175 Victor Robles 20.00 50.00

2018 Topps Chrome Pink Refractors

*PINK REF: 1.2X TO 3X BASIC
*PINK REF RC: .6X TO 1.5X BASIC RC
STATED ODDS 1:XXX
14 Miguel Andujar 4.00 10.00
70 Rhys Hoskins 4.00 10.00

2018 Topps Chrome Prism Refractors

*PRISM REF:1.2X TO 3X BASIC
*PRISM REF RC:.6X TO 1.5X BASIC RC
STATED ODDS 1:6 HOBBY
14 Miguel Andujar 4.00 10.00
70 Rhys Hoskins 4.00 10.00

2018 Topps Chrome Purple Refractors

*PURPLE REF: 2.5X TO 6X BASIC
*PURPLE REF RC: 1.2X TO 3X BASIC RC
STATED ODDS 1:71 HOBBY
STATED PRINT RUN 299 SER.#'d SETS
14 Miguel Andujar 8.00 20.00
70 Rhys Hoskins 8.00 20.00

2018 Topps Chrome Refractors

*REF: 1X TO 2.5X BASIC
*REF RC:.5X TO 1.2X BASIC RC
STATED ODDS 1:3 HOBBY
14 Miguel Andujar 3.00 8.00
70 Rhys Hoskins 3.00 8.00

2018 Topps Chrome Sepia Refractors

*SEPIA REF: 1.2X TO 3X BASIC
*SEPIA REF RC: .6X TO 1.5X BASIC RC
STATED ODDS 1:XXX
14 Miguel Andujar 4.00 10.00
70 Rhys Hoskins 4.00 10.00

2018 Topps Chrome X-Fractors

*XFRACTOR: 2X TO 5X BASIC
*XFRACTOR RC: 1X TO 2.5X BASIC RC
STATED ODDS 1:XXX
14 Miguel Andujar 6.00 15.00
70 Rhys Hoskins 6.00 15.00

2018 Topps Chrome Base Set Variation Refractors

STATED ODDS 1:1999 HOBBY
*GREEN/99: 1X TO 2.5X BASIC
*ORANGE/25: 2X TO 5X BASIC
1 Judge Hoodie 10.00 25.00
8 Donaldson Spryng bat 3.00 8.00
25 Devers Dugout 8.00 20.00
29 Posey Hat 5.00 12.00
49 Rizzo Pullover 5.00 12.00
50 Bryant Signing 5.00 12.00
52 Cano Blue jrsy 3.00 8.00
60 Rosario Holding pen 3.00 8.00
70 Hoskins Fence 10.00 25.00
72 Albies Headset 8.00 20.00
73 Lindor Dugout 4.00 10.00
94 Machado In cage 4.00 10.00
99 Syndergaard Beanie 3.00 8.00
100 Trout Signing 20.00 50.00
121 Kershaw Bubble 6.00 15.00
139 Harper Dugout 6.00 15.00
147 Williams Red jrsy 3.00 8.00
148 Frazier No hat 5.00 12.00
150 Ohtani Running 125.00 300.00
151 Benintendi No hat 4.00 10.00
162 Smith Orange hat 3.00 8.00
167 Verdugo Fence 4.00 10.00
175 Robles Sliding 6.00 15.00
186 Stanton Looking at bat 4.00 10.00
200 Altuve Holding hat 3.00 8.00

2018 Topps Chrome '83 Topps Autographs

STATED ODDS 1:3601 HOBBY
STATED PRINT RUN 50 SER.#'d SETS
PRINTING PLATE ODDS 1:45,458 HOBBY
PLATE PRINT RUN 1 SET PER COLOR
BLACK-CYAN-MAGENTA-YELLOW ISSUED
NO PLATE PRICING DUE TO SCARCITY
EXCHANGE DEADLINE 6/30/2020
*ORANGE/25: .5X TO 1.2X BASIC
83TAAR Amed Rosario 12.00 30.00
83TACS Chris Sale/50 20.00 50.00
83TADG Didi Gregorius/50 40.00 100.00
83TAGT Gleyber Torres 75.00 200.00
83TAIH Ian Happ/50 12.00 30.00
83TAMO Matt Olson/50 10.00 25.00
83TANS Noah Syndergaard 12.00 30.00
83TAPD Paul DeJong 10.00 25.00
83TAPG Paul Goldschmidt 15.00 40.00
83TARA Ronald Acuna 100.00 250.00
83TARH Rhys Hoskins/50 75.00 200.00

2018 Topps Chrome '83 Topps Refractors

COMPLETE SET (25) 12.00 30.00
STATED ODDS 1:6 HOBBY
*GREEN/99: 4X TO 10X BASIC
*ORANGE/25: 10X TO 25X BASIC
83T1 Aaron Judge 1.00 2.50
83T2 Amed Rosario .30 .75
83T3 Ian Happ .30 .75
83T4 Mookie Betts .75 2.00
83T5 Carlos Correa .40 1.00
83T6 Shohei Ohtani 6.00 15.00
83T7 Didi Gregorius .30 .75
83T8 Victor Robles .60 1.50
83T9 Manny Machado .40 1.00
83T10 Kris Bryant .50 1.25
83T11 Matt Olson .40 1.00
83T12 Mike Trout 2.00 5.00
83T13 Jake Lamb .30 .75
83T14 Noah Syndergaard .30 .75
83T15 Justin Turner .40 1.00
83T16 Dominic Smith .30 .75
83T17 Clint Frazier .50 1.25
83T18 Rafael Devers .75 2.00
83T19 Paul Goldschmidt .40 1.00
83T20 Nick Williams .30 .75
83T21 Rhys Hoskins 1.00 2.50
83T22 Paul DeJong .40 1.00
83T23 Giancarlo Stanton .40 1.00
83T24 Clayton Kershaw .60 1.50
83T25 Bryce Harper .60 1.50

2018 Topps Chrome Dual Rookie Autographs

STATED ODDS 1:28,711 HOBBY
STATED PRINT RUN 25 SER.#'d SETS
EXCHANGE DEADLINE 6/30/2020
DRAAA Albies/Acuna EXCH 400.00 800.00
DRAAS Sims/Albies
DRAHW Williams/Hoskins
DRARS Smith/Rosario

2018 Topps Chrome Freshman Flash Autographs

STATED ODDS 1:1816 HOBBY
STATED PRINT RUN 99 SER.#'d SETS
EXCHANGE DEADLINE 6/30/2020
PRINTING PLATE ODDS 1:45,458 HOBBY
PLATE PRINT RUN 1 SET PER COLOR
BLACK-CYAN-MAGENTA-YELLOW ISSUED
NO PLATE PRICING DUE TO SCARCITY
EXCHANGE DEADLINE 6/30/2020
*ORANGE/25: .5X TO 1.2X BASIC
FFAAH Austin Hays/99 10.00 25.00
FFAAR Amed Rosario/99 8.00 20.00
FFAAV Alex Verdugo/99 10.00 25.00
FFADF Dustin Fowler/99 6.00 15.00
FFADS Dominic Smith/99 10.00 25.00
FFAFM Francisco Mejia/99 8.00 20.00
FFAGT Gleyber Torres/99 75.00 200.00
FFAJC J.P. Crawford/99 6.00 15.00
FFAJF Jack Flaherty/99 25.00 60.00
FFAMA Miguel Andujar/99 25.00 60.00
FFAND Nicky Delmonico/99 6.00 15.00
FFAOA Ozzie Albies/99 60.00 150.00
FFARA Ronald Acuna/99 75.00 200.00
FFARH Rhys Hoskins/99 12.00 30.00
FFASA Sandy Alcantara/99 6.00 15.00
FFASO Shohei Ohtani EXCH
FFAWB Walker Buehler/99 30.00 80.00

2018 Topps Chrome Freshman Flash Refractors

COMPLETE SET (15) 8.00 20.00
STATED ODDS 1:12 HOBBY
*GREEN/99: 4X TO 10X BASIC
*ORANGE/25: 10X TO 25X BASIC
FF1 Shohei Ohtani 6.00 15.00
FF2 Rhys Hoskins 1.00 2.50
FF3 Dominic Smith .30 .75
FF4 J.P. Crawford .25 .60
FF5 Francisco Mejia .30 .75
FF6 Austin Hays .40 1.00
FF7 Clint Frazier .50 1.25
FF8 Ozzie Albies .75 2.00
FF9 Amed Rosario .30 .75
FF10 Alex Verdugo .40 1.00
FF11 Victor Robles .60 1.50
FF12 Nick Williams .30 .75
FF13 Willie Calhoun .40 1.00
FF14 Harrison Bader .40 1.00
FF15 Rafael Devers .75 2.00

2018 Topps Chrome Future Stars Autographs

STATED ODDS 1:3421 HOBBY
PRINT RUNS B/WN 15-99 COPIES PER
NO PRICING ON QTY 15
PRINTING PLATE ODDS 1:60,611 HOBBY
PLATE PRINT RUN 1 SET PER COLOR
BLACK-CYAN-MAGENTA-YELLOW ISSUED
NO PLATE PRICING DUE TO SCARCITY
EXCHANGE DEADLINE 6/30/2020
*ORANGE/25: .6X TO 1.5X BASIC
FSAABR Alex Bregman/40 20.00 50.00
FSABZ Bradley Zimmer/99 5.00 12.00
FSAFB Franklin Barreto/99 5.00 12.00
FSAGS Gary Sanchez/40 20.00 50.00
FSAIH Ian Happ/99 6.00 15.00
FSAKB Keon Broxton/99 5.00 12.00
FSALW Luke Weaver EXCH 6.00 15.00
FSAMO Matt Olson/99 8.00 20.00
FSAPD Paul DeJong/99 8.00 20.00
FSATM Trey Mancini/99 10.00 25.00

2018 Topps Chrome Future Stars Refractors

COMPLETE SET (20) 6.00 15.00
STATED ODDS 1:8 HOBBY
*GREEN/99: 2.5X TO 6X BASIC
*ORANGE/25: 6X TO 15X BASIC
FS1 Aaron Judge 1.00 2.50
F2 Matt Olson .40 1.00
FS3 Gary Sanchez .40 1.00
FS4 Sean Newcomb .30 .75
FS5 Bradley Zimmer .25 .60
FS6 Lucas Giolito .30 .75
FS7 Jordan Montgomery .25 .60
FS8 Franklin Barreto .25 .60
FS9 Alex Bregman .40 1.00
FS10 Christian Arroyo .25 .60
FS11 Jacob Faria .25 .60
FS12 Ian Happ .30 .75
FS13 Andrew Benintendi .40 1.00
FS14 Joe Jimenez .25 .60
FS15 Luke Weaver .30 .75
FS16 Trey Mancini .30 .75
FS17 Paul DeJong .40 1.00
FS18 Keon Broxton .25 .60
FS19 Lewis Brinson .25 .60
FS20 Cody Bellinger .75 2.00

2018 Topps Chrome Rookie Autographs

STATED ODDS 1:17 HOBBY
UPD.ODDS 1:1451 PACKS
PRINTING PLATE ODDS 1:16,284 HOBBY
UPD.PLATE ODDS 1:53,562 PACKS
PLATE PRINT RUN 1 SET PER COLOR
BLACK-CYAN-MAGENTA-YELLOW ISSUED
NO PLATE PRICING DUE TO SCARCITY
EXCHANGE DEADLINE 6/30/2020
UPD.EXCH.DEADLINE 9/30/2020
RAAB Anthony Banda 2.50 6.00
RAAH Austin Hays 6.00 15.00
RAAM A.J. Minter 3.00 8.00
RAAME Alex Mejia 2.50 6.00
RAANS Anthony Santander 8.00 20.00
RAAR Amed Rosario 6.00 15.00
RAAS Andrew Stevenson 2.50 6.00
RAASA Adrian Sanchez 2.50 6.00
RAAUM Austin Meadows 20.00 50.00
RAAV Alex Verdugo 15.00 40.00
RABA Brian Anderson 5.00 12.00
RABV Breyvic Valera 2.50 6.00
RABW Brandon Woodruff 12.00 30.00
RACF Clint Frazier 12.00 30.00
RACS Chance Sisco 3.00 8.00
RACST Chris Stratton 2.50 6.00
RADF Dustin Fowler 2.50 6.00
RADP Dillon Peters 2.50 6.00
RADS Dominic Smith 4.00 10.00
RAFJ Felix Jorge 2.50 6.00
RAFM Francisco Mejia 3.00 8.00
RAFR Fernando Romero 2.50 6.00
RAGA Greg Allen 2.50 6.00
RAGC Garrett Cooper 2.50 6.00
RAGG Giovanny Gallegos 2.50 6.00
RAGT Gleyber Torres 100.00 250.00
RAHB Harrison Bader 8.00 20.00
RAHW Hunter Wood 2.50 6.00
RAJBA Jacob Barnes 2.50 6.00
RAJC J.P. Crawford 4.00 10.00
RAJD J.D. Davis 3.00 8.00
RAJF Jack Flaherty 25.00 60.00
RAJL Jordan Luplow 2.50 6.00
RAJM Juan Minaya UPD 2.50 6.00
RAJS Jackson Stephens 2.50 6.00
RAKF Kyle Farmer 2.50 6.00
RAKM Keury Mella 2.50 6.00
RAKM Kyle Martin UPD 2.50 6.00
RALS Lucas Sims 2.50 6.00
RAMA Miguel Andujar 15.00 40.00
RAMF Max Fried 20.00 50.00
RAMG Miguel Gomez 2.50 6.00
RAMS Mike Soroka 25.00 60.00
RAND Nicky Delmonico 2.50 6.00
RANW Nick Williams 3.00 8.00
RAOA Ozzie Albies 30.00 80.00
RAPB Paul Blackburn 2.50 6.00
RAPBR Parker Bridwell 2.50 6.00
RARA Ronald Acuna 500.00 1200.00
RARD Rafael Devers 75.00 200.00
RARH Rhys Hoskins 20.00 50.00
RARHE Ronald Herrera 3.00 8.00
RARJ Ryder Jones 2.50 6.00
RARM Ryan McMahon 6.00 15.00
RARMO Reyes Moronta 2.50 6.00
RARR Raudy Read 2.50 6.00
RARU Richard Urena 2.50 6.00
RASA Sandy Alcantara 5.00 12.00
RASK Scott Kingery 4.00 10.00
RASO Shohei Ohtani 300.00 800.00
RATD Tyler Danish UPD 2.50 6.00
RATG Tayron Guerrero 2.50 6.00
RATM Tyler Mahle 3.00 8.00
RATN Tomas Nido 2.50 6.00
RATS Troy Scribner 2.50 6.00
RATSC Tanner Scott 2.50 6.00
RATT Travis Taijeron UPD 3.00 8.00
RATV Thyago Vieira 2.50 6.00
RATW Tyler Wade 3.00 8.00
RATWI Trevor Williams 2.50 6.00
RAVA Victor Arano 2.50 6.00
RAVC Victor Caratini 3.00 8.00
RAVR Victor Robles 15.00 40.00
RAWA Willy Adames 8.00 20.00
RAWB Walker Buehler 50.00 120.00
RAZG Zack Granite 2.50 6.00

2018 Topps Chrome Rookie Autographs Blue Refractors

*BLUE REF: .75X TO 2X BASIC
STATED ODDS 1:434 HOBBY
UPD.ODDS 1:2065 PACKS
STATED PRINT RUN 150 SER.#'d SETS
EXCHANGE DEADLINE 6/30/2020
UPD.EXCH.DEADLINE 9/30/2020
RASO Shohei Ohtani 600.00 1500.00

2018 Topps Chrome Rookie Autographs Blue Wave Refractors

*BLUE WAVE REF: .75X TO 2X BASIC
STATED ODDS 1:434 HOBBY
UPD.ODDS 1:1950 PACKS
STATED PRINT RUN 150 SER.#'d SETS
EXCHANGE DEADLINE 6/30/2020
UPD.EXCH.DEADLINE 9/30/2020
RASO Shohei Ohtani 600.00 1500.00

2018 Topps Chrome Rookie Autographs Gold Refractors

*GOLD REF: 1.2X TO 3X BASIC
STATED ODDS 1:1307 HOBBY
UPD.ODDS 1:5994 PACKS
STATED PRINT RUN 50 SER.#'d SETS
EXCHANGE DEADLINE 6/30/2020
UPD.EXCH.DEADLINE 9/30/2020
RASO Shohei Ohtani 1000.00 2500.00

2018 Topps Chrome Rookie Autographs Gold Wave Refractors

*GOLD WAVE REF: 1.2X TO 3X BASIC
STATED ODDS 1:874 HOBBY
UPD.ODDS 1:5963 PACKS
STATED PRINT RUN 50 SER.#'d SETS
EXCHANGE DEADLINE 6/30/2020
UPD.EXCH.DEADLINE 9/30/2020
RASO Shohei Ohtani 1000.00 2500.00

2018 Topps Chrome Rookie Autographs Green Refractors

*GREEN REF: 1X TO 2.5X BASIC
STATED ODDS 1:XXX
UPD.ODDS 1:3157 PACKS
STATED PRINT RUN 99 SER.#'d SETS
EXCHANGE DEADLINE 6/30/2020
UPD.EXCH.DEADLINE 9/30/2020
RASO Shohei Ohtani 750.00 2000.00

2018 Topps Chrome Rookie Autographs Orange Refractors

*ORANGE REF: 1.5X TO 4X BASIC
STATED ODDS 1:813 HOBBY
UPD.ODDS 1:13,416 PACKS
STATED PRINT RUN 25 SER.#'d SETS
EXCHANGE DEADLINE 6/30/2020
UPD.EXCH.DEADLINE 9/30/2020
RASO Shohei Ohtani 1250.00 3000.00

2018 Topps Chrome Rookie Autographs Purple Refractors

*PURPLE REF: .6X TO 1.5X BASIC
STATED ODDS 1:260 HOBBY
STATED PRINT RUN 250 SER.#'d SETS
EXCHANGE DEADLINE 6/30/2020
RASO Shohei Ohtani 500.00 1200.00

2018 Topps Chrome Rookie Autographs Refractors

*REF: .5X TO 1.2X BASIC
STATED ODDS 1:131 HOBBY
STATED PRINT RUN 499 SER.#'d SETS
EXCHANGE DEADLINE 6/30/2020

2018 Topps Chrome Rookie Debut Medal Autographs

STATED ODDS 1:2668 HOBBY
PRINT RUNS B/WN 10-99 COPIES PER
NO PRICING ON QTY 10
EXCHANGE DEADLINE 6/30/2020
RDMAB Adrian Beltre/40 40.00 100.00
RDMAJ Aaron Judge 40.00 100.00
RDMAR Amed Rosario/99 30.00 80.00
RDMBH Bryce Harper/20 150.00 400.00
RDMJC J.P. Crawford/99 10.00 25.00
RDMKB Kris Bryant EXCH 20.00 50.00
RDMMT Mike Trout
RDMOA Ozzie Albies 50.00 120.00
RDMRD Rafael Devers EXCH 40.00 100.00
RDMRH Rhys Hoskins/99 75.00 200.00
RDMVR Victor Robles/99 25.00 60.00

2018 Topps Chrome Rookie Debut Medal Refractors

STATED ODDS 1:466 HOBBY
*GREEN/99: .5X TO 1.2X BASIC
*ORANGE/25: 75X TO 2X BASIC
RDMAB Adrian Beltre 4.00 10.00
RDMAJ Aaron Judge 15.00 40.00
RDMAR Amed Rosario 3.00 8.00
RDMAV Alex Verdugo 4.00 10.00
RDMBH Bryce Harper 6.00 15.00
RDMCB Cody Bellinger 8.00 20.00
RDMCC Carlos Correa 4.00 10.00
RDMCF Clint Frazier 5.00 12.00
RDMCK Corey Kluber 3.00 8.00
RDMDS Dominic Smith 4.00 10.00
RDMFL Francisco Lindor 4.00 10.00
RDMGS Giancarlo Stanton 4.00 10.00
RDMI Ichiro 8.00 20.00
RDMJA Jose Altuve 3.00 8.00
RDMJC J.P. Crawford 2.50 6.00
RDMKB Kris Bryant 5.00 12.00
RDMMT Mike Trout 20.00 50.00
RDMNA Nolan Arenado 6.00 15.00
RDMNS Noah Syndergaard 3.00 8.00
RDMNW Nick Williams 3.00 8.00
RDMOA Ozzie Albies 10.00 25.00
RDMRC Robinson Cano 3.00 8.00
RDMRD Rafael Devers 8.00 20.00
RDMRH Rhys Hoskins 10.00 25.00
RDMVR Victor Robles 6.00 15.00

2018 Topps Chrome Superstar Sensations Autographs

STATED ODDS 1:4786 HOBBY
PRINT RUNS B/WN 15-99 COPIES PER
NO PRICING ON QTY 15
PRINTING PLATE ODDS 1:60,611 HOBBY
PLATE PRINT RUN 1 SET PER COLOR
BLACK-CYAN-MAGENTA-YELLOW ISSUED
NO PLATE PRICING DUE TO SCARCITY
EXCHANGE DEADLINE 6/30/2020
*ORANGE/25: .5X TO 1.2X BASIC
SSAAB Adrian Beltre/30 40.00 100.00
SSAAR Anthony Rizzo/20 30.00 80.00
SSACK Craig Kimbrel/70 10.00 25.00
SSACSA Chris Sale/60 10.00 25.00
SSAFL Francisco Lindor EXCH 25.00 60.00
SSAGS George Springer/60 12.00 30.00
SSAJB Jose Berrios/99 8.00 20.00
SSAKB Kris Bryant/20 50.00 120.00
SSAKS Kyle Schwarber/70 10.00 25.00
SSALS Luis Severino/70 15.00 40.00
SSAMM Manny Machado/30 20.00 50.00
SSANS Noah Syndergaard/40 12.00 30.00
SSAYC Yoenis Cespedes/30 15.00 40.00

2018 Topps Chrome Superstar Sensations Refractors

STATED ODDS 1:24 HOBBY
*GREEN/99: 1.5X TO 4X BASIC
*ORANGE/25: 4X TO 10X BASIC
SS1 Aaron Judge 1.00 2.50
SS2 Manny Machado .40 1.00
SS3 George Springer .30 .75
SS4 Bryce Harper .60 1.50
SS5 Corey Seager .40 1.00
SS6 Mike Trout 2.00 5.00
SS7 Cody Bellinger .75 2.00
SS8 Francisco Lindor .40 1.00
SS9 Anthony Rizzo .50 1.25
SS10 Kyle Schwarber .40 1.00
SS11 Yoenis Cespedes .40 1.00
SS12 Carlos Correa .40 1.00
SS13 Giancarlo Stanton .40 1.00
SS14 Noah Syndergaard .30 .75
SS15 Kris Bryant .50 1.25

2018 Topps Chrome Update

COMPLETE SET (100)
PRINTING PLATE ODDS 1:2981 HOBBY
PLATE PRINT RUN 1 SET PER COLOR
BLACK-CYAN-MAGENTA-YELLOW ISSUED
NO PLATE PRICING DUE TO SCARCITY
HMT1 Shohei Ohtani RC 15.00 40.00
HMT2 Jordan Hicks RC .75 2.00
HMT3 Joey Lucchesi RC .40 1.00
HMT4 Tyler Beede RC .40 1.00
HMT5 Chris Stratton RC .40 1.00
HMT6 Daniel Mengden RC .40 1.00
HMT7 Miles Mikolas RC .50 1.25
HMT8 Tyler O'Neill RC .60 1.50
HMT9 Gleyber Torres RC 4.00 10.00
HMT10 Jesse Biddle RC .50 1.25
HMT11 Lourdes Gurriel Jr. RC .75 2.00
HMT12 Isiah Kiner-Falefa RC .60 1.50
HMT13 Dustin Fowler RC .40 1.00
HMT14 Nick Kingham RC .40 1.00
HMT15 David Bote RC 1.00 2.50
HMT16 Michael Soroka RC 1.25 3.00
HMT17 Fernando Romero RC .40 1.00
HMT18 Jack Flaherty RC 1.50 4.00
HMT19 Walker Buehler RC 2.00 5.00
HMT20 Miguel Andujar RC 1.50 4.00
HMT21 Clint Frazier RC .75 2.00
HMT22 Victor Robles RC 1.00 2.50
HMT23 Rafael Devers RC 1.25 3.00
HMT24 Scott Kingery RC .60 1.50
HMT25 Ronald Acuna Jr. RC 40.00 100.00
HMT26 Gleyber Torres RC 4.00 10.00
HMT27 Ozzie Albies RC 1.25 3.00
HMT28 Rhys Hoskins RC 1.50 4.00
HMT29 Amed Rosario RC .50 1.25
HMT30 Scott Kingery RD .30 .75
HMT31 Ronald Acuna Jr. RD 15.00 40.00
HMT32 Shohei Ohtani RD 15.00 40.00
HMT33 Gleyber Torres RD 2.00 5.00
HMT34 Jordan Hicks RD .40 1.00
HMT35 Michael Soroka RD .60 1.50
HMT36 Nick Kingham RD .20 .50
HMT37 Andrew McCutchen .30 .75
HMT38 Giancarlo Stanton .30 .75
HMT39 Eric Hosmer .25 .60
HMT40 J.D. Martinez .30 .75
HMT41 Matt Kemp .25 .60
HMT42 Zack Cozart .20 .50
HMT43 Carlos Santana .25 .60
HMT44 Ian Kinsler .25 .60
HMT45 Ichiro .40 1.00
HMT46 Marcell Ozuna .30 .75
HMT47 Christian Yelich .40 1.00
HMT48 Matt Harvey .25 .60
HMT49 Todd Frazier .20 .50
HMT50 Randal Grichuk .20 .50
HMT51 Jose Bautista .25 .60
HMT52 Stephen Piscotty .20 .50
HMT53 Evan Longoria .25 .60
HMT54 Austin Meadows RC 3.00 8.00
HMT55 Juan Soto RC 75.00 200.00
HMT56 Willy Adames RC .50 1.25
HMT57 Dylan Cozens RC .40 1.00
HMT58 Felipe Vazquez .25 .60
HMT59 Shane Bieber RC 10.00 25.00
HMT60 Jose Abreu .30 .75
HMT61 Freddie Freeman .40 1.00
HMT62 Jose Altuve .25 .60
HMT63 Javier Baez .40 1.00
HMT64 Jose Ramirez .25 .60
HMT65 Nolan Arenado .50 1.25
HMT66 Manny Machado .30 .75
HMT67 Brandon Crawford .25 .60
HMT68 Mookie Betts .60 1.50
HMT69 Mike Trout 1.50 4.00
HMT70 Aaron Judge .75 2.00
HMT71 Nick Markakis .25 .60
HMT72 Matt Kemp .25 .60
HMT73 Bryce Harper .50 1.25
HMT74 Willson Contreras .30 .75
HMT75 J.D. Martinez .30 .75
HMT76 Ozzie Albies .60 1.50
HMT77 Max Scherzer .30 .75
HMT78 Jacob deGrom .60 1.50
HMT79 Josh Hader .25 .60
HMT80 Gleyber Torres 2.00 5.00
HMT81 Francisco Lindor .30 .75
HMT82 Alex Bregman .30 .75
HMT83 Chris Sale .30 .75
HMT84 Luis Severino .25 .60
HMT85 Corey Kluber .25 .60
HMT86 Lorenzo Cain .20 .50
HMT87 Yadier Molina .40 1.00
HMT88 Mitch Haniger .25 .60
HMT89 Joey Votto .30 .75
HMT90 Gerrit Cole .30 .75
HMT91 Scooter Gennett .25 .60
HMT92 Kenley Jansen .25 .60
HMT93 Freddy Peralta RC .40 1.00
HMT94 Yairo Munoz RC .40 1.00
HMT95 Trevor Story .30 .75
HMT96 Charlie Blackmon .30 .75
HMT97 Manny Machado .30 .75
HMT98 Juan Soto RD 5.00 12.00
HMT99 Austin Meadows RD .50 1.25
HMT100 Willy Adames RD .25 .60

2018 Topps Chrome Update Gold Refractors

*GOLD: 6X TO 15X BASIC
*GOLD RC: 3X TO 8X BASIC RC
STATED ODDS 1:236 PACKS
STATED PRINT RUN 50 SER.#'d SETS
HMT20 Miguel Andujar 30.00 80.00
HMT22 Victor Robles 15.00 40.00
HMT23 Rafael Devers 20.00 50.00
HMT25 Ronald Acuna Jr. 300.00 800.00
HMT27 Ozzie Albies 15.00 40.00
HMT55 Juan Soto 600.00 1500.00
HMT68 Mookie Betts 20.00 50.00
HMT69 Mike Trout 40.00 100.00
HMT98 Juan Soto 75.00 200.00

2018 Topps Chrome Update Pink Refractors

*PINK: 1.2X TO 3X BASIC
*PINK RC: .6X TO 1.5X BASIC RC
RANDOM INSERTS IN PACKS
HMT25 Ronald Acuna Jr. 60.00 150.00
HMT55 Juan Soto 100.00 250.00

2018 Topps Chrome Update Red Refractors

*RED: 8X TO 20X BASIC
*RED RC: 4X TO 10X BASIC RC
STATED ODDS 1:472 PACKS
STATED PRINT RUN 25 SER.#'d SETS
HMT18 Jack Flaherty 25.00 60.00
HMT20 Miguel Andujar 40.00 100.00
HMT22 Victor Robles 20.00 50.00
HMT23 Rafael Devers 25.00 60.00
HMT25 Ronald Acuna Jr. 400.00 1000.00
HMT27 Ozzie Albies 20.00 50.00
HMT28 Rhys Hoskins 30.00 80.00
HMT38 Giancarlo Stanton 50.00 120.00
HMT47 Christian Yelich 30.00 80.00
HMT55 Juan Soto 750.00 2000.00
HMT68 Mookie Betts 40.00 100.00
HMT69 Mike Trout 50.00 120.00
HMT98 Juan Soto 100.00 250.00

2018 Topps Chrome Update Refractors

*REF: 1.5X TO 4X BASIC
*REF RC: 2.5X TO 6X BASIC RC
STATED ODDS 1:48 PACKS
STATED PRINT RUN 250 SER.#'d SETS
HMT20 Miguel Andujar 8.00 20.00
HMT23 Rafael Devers 5.00 12.00
HMT25 Ronald Acuna Jr. 75.00 200.00
HMT27 Ozzie Albies 4.00 10.00
HMT55 Juan Soto 300.00 800.00
HMT98 Juan Soto 20.00 50.00

2018 Topps Chrome Update X-fractors

*X-FRAC: 3X TO 8X BASIC
*X-FRAC RC: 1.5X TO 4X BASIC RC
STATED ODDS 1:119 PACKS
STATED PRINT RUN 99 SER.#'d SETS
HMT20 Miguel Andujar 15.00 40.00
HMT23 Rafael Devers 10.00 25.00
HMT25 Ronald Acuna Jr. 150.00 400.00
HMT27 Ozzie Albies 8.00 20.00
HMT55 Juan Soto 400.00 1000.00
HMT98 Juan Soto 40.00 100.00

2018 Topps Chrome Update An International Affair

COMPLETE SET (20) 8.00 20.00
STATED ODDS 1:2 PACKS
IAI Ichiro .50 1.25
IAAJ Aaron Judge 1.00 2.50
IACC Carlos Correa .40 1.00
IADG Didi Gregorius .30 .75
IAFF Freddie Freeman .50 1.25
IAFL Francisco Lindor .40 1.00
IAGS Gary Sanchez .50 1.25
IAGT Gleyber Torres 2.50 6.00
IAJA Jose Altuve .30 .75
IAJB Javier Baez .50 1.25
IAJV Joey Votto .40 1.00
IAKD Khris Davis .40 1.00
IAMM Manny Machado .40 1.00
IAMT Mike Trout 2.00 5.00
IAOA Ozzie Albies .75 2.00
IARA Ronald Acuna Jr. 8.00 20.00
IARD Rafael Devers .75 2.00
IASO Shohei Ohtani 6.00 15.00
IAYC Yoenis Cespedes .40 1.00
IAYM Yoan Moncada .40 1.00

2018 Topps Chrome Update Autograph Refractors

STATED ODDS 1:49 PACKS
EXCHANGE DEADLINE 9/30/2020
HMT1 Shohei Ohtani 200.00 500.00
HMT2 Jordan Hicks 8.00 20.00
HMT4 Tyler Beede 3.00 8.00
HMT5 Chris Stratton 3.00 8.00
HMT6 Daniel Mengden 3.00 8.00
HMT7 Miles Mikolas 4.00 10.00
HMT9 Gleyber Torres 60.00 150.00
HMT10 Jesse Biddle 4.00 10.00
HMT11 Lourdes Gurriel Jr. 10.00 25.00
HMT12 Isiah Kiner-Falefa 5.00 12.00
HMT13 Dustin Fowler 3.00 8.00
HMT14 Nick Kingham 3.00 8.00
HMT15 David Bote 10.00 25.00
HMT16 Michael Soroka 25.00 60.00
HMT17 Fernando Romero 3.00 8.00
HMT18 Jack Flaherty 20.00 50.00

HMT19 Walker Buehler 50.00 120.00
HMT21 Clint Frazier 12.00 30.00
HMT22 Victor Robles 15.00 40.00
HMT23 Rafael Devers 15.00 40.00
HMT24 Scott Kingery 10.00 25.00
HMT25 Ronald Acuna Jr. 300.00 800.00
HMT27 Ozzie Albies 40.00 100.00
HMT28 Rhys Hoskins 20.00 50.00
HMT29 Amed Rosario 4.00 10.00
HMT37 Andrew McCutchen 20.00 50.00
HMT42 Zack Cozart 3.00 8.00
HMT43 Carlos Santana 4.00 10.00
HMT44 Ian Kinsler 4.00 10.00
HMT45 Ichiro 100.00 250.00
HMT46 Marcell Ozuna 5.00 12.00
HMT47 Christian Yelich 25.00 60.00
HMT53 Evan Longoria 4.00 10.00
HMT54 Austin Meadows 30.00 80.00
HMT55 Juan Soto 1500.00 4000.00
HMT56 Willy Adames EXCH 4.00 10.00
HMT57 Dylan Cozens EXCH 3.00 8.00
HMT58 Felipe Vazquez 4.00 10.00
HMT59 Shane Bieber 75.00 200.00
HMT79 Josh Hader EXCH 4.00 10.00
HMT88 Mitch Haniger 6.00 15.00
HMT93 Freddy Peralta 3.00 8.00
ACBUFM Francisco Mejia 4.00 10.00

2018 Topps Chrome Update Autograph Gold Refractors
*GOLD: .75X TO 2X BASIC
STATED ODDS 1:514 PACKS
STATED PRINT RUN 50 SER.#'d SETS
EXCHANGE DEADLINE 9/30/2020
HMT56 Willy Adames EXCH 20.00 50.00

2018 Topps Chrome Update Autograph Orange Refractors
*ORANGE: 1X TO 2.5X BASIC
STATED ODDS 1:1032 PACKS
STATED PRINT RUN 25 SER.#'d SETS
EXCHANGE DEADLINE 9/30/2020
HMT1 Shohei Ohtani 300.00 800.00
HMT45 Ichiro 150.00 400.00
HMT56 Willy Adames EXCH 25.00 60.00

2018 Topps Chrome Update Autograph X-fractors
*XF: .6X TO 1.5X BASIC
STATED ODDS 1:206 PACKS
STATED PRINT RUN 125 SER.#'d SETS
EXCHANGE DEADLINE 9/30/2020

2019 Topps Chrome
PRINTING PLATE ODDS 1:6540 HOBBY
PLATE PRINT RUN 1 SET PER COLOR
BLACK-CYAN-MAGENTA-YELLOW ISSUED
NO PLATE PRICING DUE TO SCARCITY
1 Shohei Ohtani .50 1.25
2 Rowdy Tellez RC .60 1.50
3 Hunter Renfroe .20 .50
4 Andrelton Simmons .20 .50
5 Dylan Bundy .25 .60
6 Reese McGuire RC .60 1.50
7 Maikel Franco .25 .60
8 Brandon Nimmo .25 .60
9 David Peralta .20 .50
10 Jesus Aguilar .25 .60
11 Whit Merrifield .30 .75
12 Brian Anderson .20 .50
13 Harrison Bader .25 .60
14 Joe Panik .25 .60
15 J.P. Crawford .20 .50
16 Christian Yelich .40 1.00
17 Michael Kopech RC 1.25 3.00
18 Starling Marte .25 .60
19 Alex Bregman .30 .75
20 Jose Altuve .25 .60
21 Shane Greene .20 .50
22 Gary Sanchez .30 .75
23 Zack Greinke .30 .75
24 Josh Hader .25 .60
25 Kris Bryant .40 1.00
26 Nomar Mazara .20 .50
27 Albert Pujols .40 1.00
28 Justin Verlander .30 .75
29 Lorenzo Cain .20 .50
30 Francisco Arcia RC .60 1.50
31 Joey Votto .30 .75
32 Max Muncy .25 .60
33 Victor Robles .40 1.00
34 Alex Avila .25 .60
35 Danny Jansen RC .40 1.00
36 Paul DeJong .30 .75
37 Willians Astudillo RC .40 1.00
38 Joey Gallo .25 .60
39 Kyle Tucker RC 1.00 2.50
40 Ronald Guzman .20 .50
41 Chris Davis .20 .50
42 George Springer .25 .60
43 Zack Cozart .20 .50
44 Carlos Santana .25 .60
45 Tommy Pham .20 .50
46 Matt Chapman .30 .75
47 Trey Mancini .25 .60
48 Javier Baez .40 1.00
49 Mychal Givens .20 .50
50 Mookie Betts .60 1.50
51 Yadier Molina .40 1.00
52 Cedric Mullins RC .75 2.00
53 Ryan O'Hearn RC .40 1.00
54 Brad Keller RC .40 1.00
55 Josh James RC .60 1.50
56 Bryse Wilson RC .50 1.25
57 Ozzie Albies .30 .75
58 Scooter Gennett .25 .60
59 Jacob deGrom .60 1.50
60 Joey Rickard .20 .50
61 Jesse Winker .30 .75
62 Cionel Perez RC .40 1.00
63 Jeimer Candelario .20 .50
64 Carlos Correa .30 .75
65 Colin Moran .20 .50
66 Matt Olson .30 .75
67 Max Kepler .25 .60
68 Francisco Lindor .30 .75
69 Christin Stewart RC .50 1.25
70 Lucas Giolito .25 .60
71 Jake Bauers RC .60 1.50
72 Justin Upton .25 .60
73 Yusei Kikuchi RC .60 1.50
74 Edwin Diaz .25 .60
75 Daniel Ponce de Leon RC .60 1.50
76 Blake Snell .25 .60
77 Andrew McCutchen .30 .75
78 Taylor Ward RC .40 1.00
79 Dean Deetz RC .40 1.00
80 Eugenio Suarez .25 .60
81 Jorge Polanco .25 .60
82 Buster Posey .40 1.00
83 Matt Boyd .20 .50
84 Corbin Burnes RC 3.00 8.00
85 Josh Donaldson .25 .60
86 Gleyber Torres .60 1.50
87 Freddie Freeman .40 1.00
88 Kevin Kramer RC .50 1.25
89 Jose Abreu .30 .75
90 Walker Buehler .40 1.00
91 David Dahl .20 .50
92 Franmil Reyes .20 .50
93 Trevor Richards RC .40 1.00
94 Evan Longoria .25 .60
95 Nicholas Castellanos .30 .75
96 Xander Bogaerts .30 .75
97 Heath Fillmyer RC .40 1.00
98 Luis Severino .25 .60
99 Kolby Allard RC .60 1.50
100 Aaron Judge .75 2.00
101 Edwin Encarnacion .30 .75
102 Yonder Alonso .20 .50
103 Odubel Herrera .25 .60
104 Matt Duffy .20 .50
105 Enyel De Los Santos RC .40 1.00
106 Corey Seager .30 .75
107 Trevor Bauer .40 1.00
108 Miguel Andujar .30 .75
109 Chance Adams RC .40 1.00
110 Justus Sheffield RC .60 1.50
111 Kyle Schwarber .30 .75
112 Clayton Kershaw .50 1.25
113 Ian Desmond .20 .50
114 Byron Buxton .30 .75
115 Miguel Cabrera .30 .75
116 Jake Lamb .25 .60
117 Ronald Acuna Jr. 1.50 4.00
118 Lourdes Gurriel Jr. .25 .60
119 Sandy Alcantara .20 .50
120 Kyle Wright RC .60 1.50
121 Josh Rogers RC .40 1.00
122 Lewis Brinson .20 .50
123 Jose Berrios .25 .60
124 Nolan Arenado .50 1.25
125 Brandon Belt .25 .60
126 Nick Burdi RC .40 1.00
127 Jose Ramirez .25 .60
128 Marcus Stroman .25 .60
129 Aramis Garcia RC .40 1.00
130 Anthony Rizzo .40 1.00
131 Noah Syndergaard .25 .60
132 Aaron Sanchez .25 .60
133 J.D. Martinez .30 .75
134 Kevin Newman RC .60 1.50
135 DJ Stewart RC .50 1.25
136 Sean Reid-Foley RC .40 1.00
137 Kevin Pillar .20 .50
138 Mitch Haniger .25 .60
139 Paul Goldschmidt .30 .75
140 Max Scherzer .30 .75
141 Luis Urias RC .60 1.50
142 Billy Hamilton .25 .60
143 Taijuan Walker .20 .50
144 Blake Treinen .20 .50
145 Nick Markakis .25 .60
146 Patrick Wisdom RC .40 1.00
147 Eddie Rosario .25 .60
148 Dakota Hudson RC .50 1.25
149 Carlos Martinez .25 .60
150 Steven Duggar RC .50 1.25
151 Brandon Lowe RC .60 1.50
152 Jeff McNeil RC 1.00 2.50
153 Wil Myers .25 .60
154 Manny Margot .20 .50
155 Juan Soto 1.00 2.50
156 Kyle Seager .20 .50
157 Elvis Andrus .25 .60
158 Cody Bellinger .60 1.50
159 Gregory Polanco .25 .60
160 Charlie Blackmon .30 .75
161 Jake Cave RC .50 1.25
162 Josh Bell .25 .60
163 Patrick Corbin .25 .60
164 Adalberto Mondesi .25 .60
165 Chris Sale .30 .75
166 Hunter Dozier .20 .50
167 Stephen Piscotty .20 .50
168 Jonathan Loaisiga RC .50 1.25
169 Dansby Swanson .30 .75
170 Sean Manaea .20 .50
171 Starlin Castro .20 .50
172 Dawel Lugo RC .60 1.50
173 Chris Shaw RC .40 1.00
174 Eric Hosmer .25 .60
175 Trea Turner .25 .60
176 Aaron Nola .25 .60
177 Justin Smoak .20 .50
178 Ramon Laureano RC .75 2.00
179 Willy Adames .25 .60
180 Kevin Kiermaier .25 .60
181 David Fletcher RC 1.25 3.00
182 Jacob Nix RC .50 1.25
183 Trevor Story .30 .75
184 Rafael Devers .40 1.00
185 Kyle Hendricks .30 .75
186 Tim Anderson .30 .75
187 Ryan Borucki RC .40 1.00
188 Corey Kluber .25 .60
189 Orlando Arcia .20 .50
190 Brandon Crawford .25 .60
191 Rougned Odor .25 .60
192 Raisel Iglesias .20 .50
193 Robinson Cano .25 .60
194 Jameson Taillon .25 .60
195 Rhys Hoskins .40 1.00
196 Dee Gordon .20 .50
197 Touki Toussaint RC .50 1.25
198 Salvador Perez .25 .60
199 Jose Urena .20 .50
200 Mike Trout 1.50 4.00
201 Vladimir Guerrero Jr. RC 25.00 60.00
202 Eloy Jimenez RC 10.00 25.00
203 Fernando Tatis Jr. RC 75.00 200.00
204 Pete Alonso RC 3.00 8.00

2019 Topps Chrome Blue Refractors
*BLUE REF: 5X TO 12X BASIC
*BLUE REF RC: 2.5X TO 6X BASIC
STATED ODDS 1:175 HOBBY
STATED PRINT RUN 150 SER.#'d SETS
203 Fernando Tatis Jr. 750.00 2000.00

2019 Topps Chrome Blue Wave Refractors
*BLUE WAVE REF: 6X TO 15X BASIC
*BLUE WAVE REF RC: 3X TO 8X BASIC
STATED ODDS 1:176 HOBBY
STATED PRINT RUN 75 SER.#'d SETS
200 Mike Trout 30.00 80.00
203 Fernando Tatis Jr. 1000.00 2500.00

2019 Topps Chrome Gold Refractors
*GOLD REF: 8X TO 20X BASIC
*GOLD REF RC: 4X TO 10X BASIC RC
STATED ODDS 1:525 HOBBY
STATED PRINT RUN 50 SER.#'d SETS
39 Kyle Tucker 20.00 50.00
117 Ronald Acuna Jr. 60.00 150.00
200 Mike Trout 75.00 200.00
203 Fernando Tatis Jr. 1250.00 3000.00

2019 Topps Chrome Gold Wave Refractors
*GOLD WAVE REF: 8X TO 20X BASIC
*GOLD WAVE REF RC: 4X TO 10X BASIC RC
STATED ODDS 1:264 HOBBY
STATED PRINT RUN 50 SER.#'d SETS
39 Kyle Tucker 20.00 50.00
117 Ronald Acuna Jr. 60.00 150.00
200 Mike Trout 75.00 200.00
203 Fernando Tatis Jr. 1250.00 3000.00

2019 Topps Chrome Green Refractors
*GREEN REF: 6X TO 15X BASIC
*GREEN REF RC: 3X TO 8X BASIC RC
STATED ODDS 1:265 HOBBY
STATED PRINT RUN 99 SER.#'d SETS
200 Mike Trout 30.00 80.00
203 Fernando Tatis Jr. 1000.00 2500.00

2019 Topps Chrome Green Wave Refractors
*GREEN WAVE REF: 6X TO 15X BASIC
*GREEN WAVE REF RC: 3X TO 8X BASIC RC
STATED ODDS 1:134 HOBBY
STATED PRINT RUN 99 SER.#'d SETS
200 Mike Trout 30.00 80.00
203 Fernando Tatis Jr. 1000.00 2500.00

2019 Topps Chrome Negative Refractors
*SEPIA REF: 3X TO 8X BASIC
*SEPIA REF RC: 1.5X TO 4X BASIC RC
STATED ODDS 1:66 HOBBY
203 Fernando Tatis Jr. 500.00 1200.00

2019 Topps Chrome Orange Refractors
*ORANGE REF: 10X TO 25X BASIC
*ORANGE REF RC: 6X TO 15X BASIC RC
STATED ODDS 1:255 HOBBY
STATED PRINT RUN 25 SER.#'d SETS
39 Kyle Tucker 25.00 60.00
117 Ronald Acuna Jr. 75.00 200.00
200 Mike Trout 100.00 250.00
203 Fernando Tatis Jr. 1500.00 4000.00

2019 Topps Chrome Orange Wave Refractors
*ORNGE WAVE REF: 10X TO 25X BASIC
*ORNGE WAVE REF RC: 5X TO 12X BASIC RC
STATED ODDS 1:528 HOBBY
STATED PRINT RUN 25 SER.#'d SETS
39 Kyle Tucker 25.00 60.00
117 Ronald Acuna Jr. 75.00 200.00
200 Mike Trout 100.00 250.00
203 Fernando Tatis Jr. 1500.00 4000.00

2019 Topps Chrome Pink Refractors
*PINK REF: 1.2X TO 3X BASIC
*PINK REF RC: .6X TO 1.5X BASIC RC
THREE PER VALUE PACK
203 Fernando Tatis Jr. 200.00 500.00

2019 Topps Chrome Prism Refractors
*PRISM REF: 1.2X TO 3X BASIC
*PRISM REF RC: .6X TO 1.5X BASIC RC
STATED ODDS 1:6 HOBBY
203 Fernando Tatis Jr. 200.00 500.00

2019 Topps Chrome Purple Refractors
*PURPLE REF: 2.5X TO 6X BASIC
*PURPLE REF RC: 1.2X TO 3X BASIC RC
STATED ODDS 1:68 HOBBY
STATED PRINT RUN 299 SER.#'d SETS
203 Fernando Tatis Jr. 400.00 1000.00

2019 Topps Chrome Refractors
*REF: 1X TO 2.5X BASIC
*REF RC: .5X TO 1.2X BASIC RC
STATED ODDS 1:3 HOBBY
203 Fernando Tatis Jr. 150.00 400.00

2019 Topps Chrome Sepia Refractors
*SEPIA REF: 1.2X TO 3X BASIC
*SEPIA REF RC: .6X TO 1.5X BASIC RC
RANDOM INSERTS IN PACKS
203 Fernando Tatis Jr. 200.00 500.00

2019 Topps Chrome X-Fractors
*XFRACTOR: 2X TO 5X BASIC
*XFRACTOR RC: 1X TO 2.5X BASIC RC
TEN PER MEGA BOX
203 Fernando Tatis Jr. 300.00 800.00

2019 Topps Chrome Photo Variation Refractors
STATED ODDS 1:247 HOBBY
*GREEN/99: .6X TO 1.5X BASIC
*GOLD/50: 1X TO 2.5X BASIC
*ORANGE/25: 1.2X TO 3X BASIC
1 Ohtain w/Ichiro 6.00 15.00
2 Rowdy Tellez 4.00 10.00
Fielding
16 Yelich Thrwbck 5.00 12.00
17 Kopech Workout 8.00 20.00
25 Bryant Bttng 5.00 12.00
31 Joey Votto 4.00 10.00
Tossing ball
39 Tucker Hldng Hlmt 6.00 15.00
48 Baez Bttng 5.00 12.00
50 Betts Workout 8.00 20.00
57 Ozzie Albies 4.00 10.00
Fielding
59 Jacob deGrom 8.00 20.00
Dugout
64 Carlos Correa 4.00 10.00
Jacket
69 Christin Stewart 3.00 8.00
Kneeling
71 Jake Bauers 4.00 10.00
Blue jersey
73 Kikuchi w/Ichiro 5.00 12.00
100 Judge Bat Shldr 10.00 25.00
110 Justus Sheffield 4.00 10.00
Blue jersey
112 Kershaw Fence 6.00 15.00
117 Acuna Knees 40.00 100.00
124 Nolan Arenado 6.00 15.00
Press conference
141 Urias Blue jrsy 4.00 10.00
155 Soto Sldng 30.00 80.00
195 Hoskins At wall 5.00 12.00
197 Touki Toussaint 3.00 8.00
Batting
200 Trout Dugout 50.00 120.00

2019 Topps Chrome '84 Topps
STATED ODDS 1:6 HOBBY
*GREEN/99: 4X TO 10X BASIC
*GOLD/50: 6X TO 15X BASIC
*ORANGE/25: 8X TO 20X BASIC
84TC1 Aaron Judge 1.00 2.50
84TC2 Juan Soto 1.25 3.00
84TC3 Michael Kopech .75 2.00
84TC4 Cedric Mullins .50 1.25
84TC5 Gleyber Torres .75 2.00
84TC6 Jacob deGrom .75 2.00
84TC7 Joey Votto .40 1.00
84TC8 Matt Chapman .40 1.00
84TC9 Anthony Rizzo .50 1.25
84TC10 Justin Upton .30 .75
84TC11 Luis Urias .40 1.00
84TC12 Noah Syndergaard .30 .75
84TC13 Giancarlo Stanton .40 1.00
84TC14 Ichiro .50 1.25
84TC15 Whit Merrifield .40 1.00
84TC16 Francisco Lindor .40 1.00
84TC17 Mike Trout 3.00 8.00
84TC18 Kyle Tucker .60 1.50
84TC19 Yusei Kikuchi .40 1.00
84TC20 Mookie Betts .75 2.00
84TC21 Jake Bauers .40 1.00
84TC22 Kolby Allard .40 1.00
84TC23 Justus Sheffield .40 1.00
84TC24 Ronald Acuna Jr. 2.00 5.00
84TC25 Shohei Ohtani .60 1.50

2019 Topps Chrome '84 Topps Autographs
STATED ODDS 1:4360 HOBBY
PRINT RUNS B/WN 20-50 COPIES PER
EXCHANGE DEADLINE 6/30/2021
84TCAAJ Aaron Judge
84TCAAR Anthony Rizzo/30 25.00 60.00
84TCACM Cedric Mullins/50 15.00 40.00
84TCAEJ Eloy Jimenez EXCH 75.00 200.00
84TCAFTJ Fernando Tatis Jr./50 500.00 1000.00
84TCAI Ichiro/20 125.00 300.00
84TCAJB Jake Bauers/50 8.00 20.00
84TCAJD Jacob deGrom/50 25.00 60.00
84TCAJS Justus Sheffield/50 8.00 20.00
84TCAJSO Juan Soto/50 50.00 120.00
84TCAJU Justin Upton/50 8.00 20.00
84TCAKA Kolby Allard/50 8.00 20.00
84TCAKT Kyle Tucker/50 20.00 50.00
84TCAMK Michael Kopech/50 15.00 40.00
84TCAMT Mike Trout/20 400.00 800.00
84TCANS Noah Syndergaard/50 20.00 50.00
84TCARAJ Ronald Acuna Jr./50 125.00 300.00
84TCASO Shohei Ohtani/20 125.00 300.00
84TCAVGJ Vladimir Guerrero Jr./50 200.00 500.00
84TCAWM Whit Merrifield/50 10.00 25.00

2019 Topps Chrome '84 Topps Autographs Orange Refractors
*ORANGE/25: .6X TO 1.5X p/r 50
*ORANGE/25: .5X TO 1.2X p/r 30
STATED ODDS 1:9503 HOBBY
STATED PRINT RUN 25 SER.#'d SETS
84TCAJSO Juan Soto 100.00 250.00

2019 Topps Chrome '99 Chrome Autographs
STATED ODDS 1:4439 HOBBY
PRINT RUNS B/WN 15-99 COPIES PER
NO PRICING ON QTY 15
EXCHANGE DEADLINE 6/30/2021
*ORANGE/25: .6X TO 1.5X p/r 75-99
*ORANGE/25: .5X TO 1.2X p/r 30-55
99TCAAB Adrian Beltre/30 25.00 60.00
99TCABW Bernie Williams/45 25.00 60.00
99TCAFTJ Fernando Tatis Jr./99 150.00 400.00
99TCAJA Jose Altuve/30 25.00 60.00
99TCAJS Justus Sheffield/99 8.00 20.00
99TCAJSO Juan Soto/75 40.00 100.00
99TCAKA Kolby Allard/99 8.00 20.00
99TCAKB Kris Bryant/40 40.00 100.00
99TCAMK Michael Kopech/99 10.00 25.00
99TCAMM Mark McGwire/30 75.00 200.00
99TCAPG Paul Goldschmidt/45 20.00 50.00
99TCAPM Pedro Martinez 50.00 120.00
99TCARAJ Ronald Acuna Jr./75 60.00 150.00
99TCAVGJ Vladimir Guerrero Jr./99 150.00 400.00
99TCAYM Yadier Molina/55 30.00 80.00

2019 Topps Chrome Debut Gear
STATED ODDS 1:554 HOBBY
*GREEN/99: .5X TO 1.2X BASIC
*ORANGE/25: 1X TO 2.5X BASIC
DGAB Adrian Beltre 4.00 10.00
DGAC Aroldis Chapman 4.00 10.00
DGAM Andrew McCutchen 4.00 10.00
DGAP Albert Pujols 5.00 12.00
DGAR Alex Rodriguez 5.00 12.00
DGBD Brian Dozier 3.00 8.00
DGCF Carlton Fisk 6.00 15.00
DGCK Craig Kimbrel 3.00 8.00
DGCS Chris Sale 4.00 10.00
DGDG Didi Gregorius 3.00 8.00
DGDM Daniel Murphy 3.00 8.00
DGEL Mike Piazza 4.00 10.00
DGGM Greg Maddux 5.00 12.00
DGGS Giancarlo Stanton 4.00 10.00
DGIK Ian Kinsler 3.00 8.00
DGIR Ivan Rodriguez 3.00 8.00
DGI Ichiro
DGJD Josh Donaldson 3.00 8.00
DGJH Jason Heyward 3.00 8.00
DGJM J.D. Martinez 4.00 10.00
DGJS Jean Segura 4.00 10.00
DGJSC Jonathan Schoop 2.50 6.00
DGJV Justin Verlander 4.00 10.00
DGMM Manny Machado 4.00 10.00
DGMMC Mark McGwire 6.00 15.00
DGMMO Mike Moustakas 3.00 8.00
DGMO Marcell Ozuna 4.00 10.00
DGMS Max Scherzer 4.00 10.00
DGNC Nelson Cruz 4.00 10.00
DGNG Nomar Garciaparra 3.00 8.00
DGRC Robinson Cano 3.00 8.00
DGRCL Roger Clemens 5.00 12.00
DGRH Rickey Henderson 6.00 15.00
DGVGS Vladimir Guerrero 3.00 8.00
DGWM Wil Myers 3.00 8.00
DGYD Yu Darvish 4.00 10.00
DGYM Yoan Moncada 4.00 10.00

2019 Topps Chrome Debut Gear Autographs
STATED ODDS 1:2349 HOBBY
STATED PRINT RUN 50 SER.#'d SETS
EXCHANGE DEADLINE 6/30/2021
DGAB Adrian Beltre 20.00 50.00
DGAM Andrew McCutchen 40.00 100.00
DGAP Albert Pujols 75.00 200.00
DGAR Alex Rodriguez 60.00 510.00
DGCF Carlton Fisk
DGCS Chris Sale 12.00 30.00
DGDG Didi Gregorius 12.00 30.00
DGEL Mike Piazza 40.00 100.00
DGIK Ian Kinsler
DGIR Ivan Rodriguez 20.00 50.00
DGI Ichiro 125.00 300.00
DGJS Jean Segura 8.00 20.00
DGMMC Mark McGwire 25.00 60.00
DGMO Marcell Ozuna 12.00 30.00
DGRCL Roger Clemens 20.00 50.00
DGRH Rickey Henderson 40.00 100.00
DGTP Tommy Pham 5.00 12.00
DGVGS Vladimir Guerrero Sr. 30.00 80.00
DGWC Will Clark

2019 Topps Chrome Dual Rookie Autographs
STATED ODDS 1:25,339 HOBBY
STATED PRINT RUN 25 SER.#'d SETS
EXCHANGE DEADLINE 6/30/2021
DRAAW Allard/Wright 15.00 40.00
DRAFA Arcia/Fletcher 20.00 50.00
DRAGJ Guerrero Jr./Jimenez 125.00 300.00
DRAJT Tellez/ Jansen 15.00 40.00
DRAKO O'Hearn/Keller 30.00 80.00
DRALB Lowe/Bauers 25.00 60.00
DRAPH Hudson/Ponce de Leon 50.00 120.00
DRATU Urias/Tatis Jr. EXCH 400.00 1000.00

2019 Topps Chrome Freshman Flash
STATED ODDS 1:12 HOBBY
*GREEN/99: 4X TO 10X BASIC
*GOLD/50: 6X TO 15X BASIC
*ORANGE/25: 8X TO 20X BASIC
FF1 Kyle Tucker .60 1.50
FF2 Christin Stewart .30 .75
FF3 Chance Adams .25 .60
FF4 Kyle Wright .40 1.00
FF5 Jake Bauers .40 1.00
FF6 Cedric Mullins .50 1.25
FF7 Rowdy Tellez .40 1.00
FF8 Yusei Kikuchi .40 1.00
FF9 Ramon Laureano .50 1.25
FF10 Kolby Allard .40 1.00
FF11 Chris Shaw .25 .60
FF12 Justus Sheffield .40 1.00
FF13 Ryan O'Hearn .25 .60
FF14 Michael Kopech .75 2.00
FF15 Luis Urias .40 1.00

2019 Topps Chrome Freshman Flash Autographs
STATED ODDS 1:2883 HOBBY
STATED PRINT RUN 99 SER.#'d SETS
EXCHANGE DEADLINE 6/30/2021
*ORANGE/25: .6X TO 1.5X BASIC
FFABK Brad Keller 6.00 15.00
FFABL Brandon Lowe 12.00 30.00
FFACA Chance Adams 5.00 12.00
FFACM Cedric Mullins 15.00 40.00
FFACS Chris Shaw 8.00 20.00
FFACST Christin Stewart 6.00 15.00
FFADF David Fletcher 15.00 40.00
FFADH Dakota Hudson 6.00 15.00
FFADJ Danny Jansen 5.00 12.00
FFAFA Francisco Arcia 8.00 20.00
FFAFTJ Fernando Tatis Jr. 200.00 500.00
FFAJB Jake Bauers 8.00 20.00
FFAJS Justus Sheffield 8.00 20.00
FFAKA Kolby Allard 8.00 20.00
FFAKT Kyle Tucker 15.00 40.00
FFAKW Kyle Wright 8.00 20.00
FFAMK Michael Kopech 15.00 40.00
FFARL Ramon Laureano 20.00 50.00
FFAROH Ryan O'Hearn 5.00 12.00
FFART Rowdy Tellez 8.00 20.00
FFAVGJ Vladimir Guerrero Jr. 100.00 250.00

2019 Topps Chrome Future Stars
STATED ODDS 1:8 HOBBY
*GREEN/99: 4X TO 10X BASIC
*GOLD/50: 6X TO 15X BASIC
*ORANGE/25: 8X TO 20X BASIC
FS1 Shohei Ohtani .60 1.50
FS2 Willy Adames .25 .60
FS3 Miles Mikolas .40 1.00
FS4 David Bote .30 .75
FS5 Lourdes Gurriel Jr. .30 .75
FS6 Nick Kingham .25 .60
FS7 Freddy Peralta .40 1.00
FS8 Dereck Rodriguez .25 .60
FS9 Austin Meadows .40 1.00
FS10 Juan Soto 1.25 3.00
FS11 Sandy Alcantara .25 .60
FS12 Franmil Reyes .25 .60
FS13 Dylan Cozens .25 .60
FS14 Gleyber Torres .75 2.00
FS15 Isiah Kiner-Falefa .30 .75
FS16 Brian Anderson .25 .60
FS17 Scott Kingery .30 .75
FS18 Amed Rosario .30 .75
FS19 Carson Kelly .25 .60
FS20 Ronald Acuna Jr. 2.00 5.00

2019 Topps Chrome Future Stars Autographs
STATED ODDS 1:2883 HOBBY
PRINT RUNS B/WN 30-99
EXCHANGE DEADLINE 6/30/2021
*ORANGE/25: .6X TO 1.5X p/r 99
*ORANGE/25: .5X TO 1.2X p/r 30
FSAAM Austin Meadows 8.00 20.00
FSACK Carson Kelly 5.00 12.00
FSADB David Bote 8.00 20.00
FSADC Dylan Cozens 5.00 12.00
FSADR Dereck Rodriguez
FSAFR Franmil Reyes 8.00 20.00
FSAJS Juan Soto 40.00 100.00
FSALGJ Lourdes Gurriel Jr. 6.00 15.00
FSAMM Miles Mikolas 8.00 20.00
FSARAJ Ronald Acuna Jr. 60.00 150.00
FSASK Scott Kingery 6.00 15.00
FSASO Shohei Ohtani/30 75.00 200.00
FSAWA Willy Adames 5.00 12.00

2019 Topps Chrome Greatness Returns
STATED ODDS 1:24 HOBBY
*GREEN/99: 4X TO 10X BASIC
*GOLD/50: 6X TO 15X BASIC
*ORANGE/25: 8X TO 20X BASIC
GRE1 Benintendi/Yaz .60 1.50
GRE2 Ryan/Verlander 1.25 3.00
GRE3 Ryan/Ohtani 1.25 3.00
GRE4 Gibson/Scherzer .40 1.00
GRE5 Alomar/Lindor .40 1.00
GRE6 Judge/ Jeter 1.00 2.50
GRE7 Cobb/Harper .60 1.50
GRE8 Hank/Trout 2.00 5.00
GRE9 Yount/ Yelich .50 1.25
GRE10 Acuna Jr./ Trout 2.00 5.00
GRE11 Torres/Jeter 1.00 2.50
GRE12 Williams/Betts .75 2.00
GRE13 Stanton/ Jackson .40 1.00
GRE14 Baez/Banks .50 1.25
GRE15 Koufax/Kershaw .75 2.00

2019 Topps Chrome Rookie Autographs
STATED ODDS 1:17 HOBBY
PRINTING PLATE ODDS 1:15,594 HOBBY
PLATE PRINT RUN 1 SET PER COLOR
BLACK-CYAN-MAGENTA-YELLOW ISSUED
NO PLATE PRICING DUE TO SCARCITY
EXCHANGE DEADLINE 6/30/2021
RAAC Adam Cimber 2.50 6.00
RAAD Austin Dean 2.50 6.00
RAAG Adolis Garcia 30.00 80.00
RAAGA Aramis Garcia 2.50 6.00
RAAR Austin Riley 40.00 100.00
RABK Brad Keller 2.50 6.00
RABL Brandon Lowe 12.00 30.00
RABR Brendan Rodgers 8.00 20.00
RABW Bryse Wilson 6.00 15.00
RACA Chance Adams 2.50 6.00
RACB Corbin Burnes 8.00 20.00
RACM Cedric Mullins 8.00 20.00
RACP Cionel Perez 2.50 6.00
RACPA Chris Paddack 20.00 50.00
RACS Chris Shaw 2.50 6.00
RACST Christin Stewart 3.00 8.00
RADF David Fletcher 8.00 20.00
RADH Dakota Hudson 6.00 15.00
RADJ Danny Jansen EXCH 10.00 25.00
RADL Dawel Lugo 4.00 10.00
RADP Daniel Poncedeleon 4.00 10.00
RADS DJ Stewart 3.00 8.00
RADSA Dennis Santana EXCH 6.00 15.00
RAEDL Enyel De Los Santos 2.50 6.00
RAEJ Eloy Jimenez 30.00 80.00
RAFA Francisco Arcia 4.00 10.00
RAFT Fernando Tatis Jr. 400.00 1000.00
RAFV Framber Valdez 6.00 15.00
RAGC Griffin Canning 5.00 12.00
RAHF Heath Fillmyer 2.50 6.00
RAIG Isaac Galloway 2.50 6.00
RAJB Jake Bauers 4.00 10.00
RAJBE Jalen Beeks 2.50 6.00
RAJC Jake Cave 5.00 12.00
RAJD Jon Duplantier 2.50 6.00
RAJJ Josh James 4.00 10.00
RAJM Jeff McNeil 15.00 40.00
RAJN Jacob Nix 3.00 8.00
RAJR Josh Rogers 2.50 6.00
RAJS Jeffrey Springs 2.50 6.00
RAJSH Justus Sheffield 4.00 10.00
RAKA Kolby Allard 4.00 10.00
RAKH Keston Hiura 30.00 80.00
RAKK Kevin Kramer 3.00 8.00
RAKN Kevin Newman 4.00 10.00
RAKT Kyle Tucker 15.00 40.00
RAKW Kyle Wright 10.00 25.00
RAMK Michael Kopech 25.00 60.00
RAMKE Mitch Keller 3.00 8.00
RAMS Myles Straw 4.00 10.00
RANB Nick Burdi 2.50 6.00
RANC Nicholas Ciuffo 2.50 6.00
RANS Nick Senzel 12.00 30.00
RAPA Peter Alonso 60.00 150.00
RAPL Pablo Lopez 5.00 12.00
RAPW Patrick Wisdom 2.50 6.00
RARB Ray Black 2.50 6.00
RARBO Ryan Borucki 2.50 6.00
RARL Ramon Laureano 10.00 25.00
RARM Reese McGuire 4.00 10.00
RAROH Ryan O'Hearn 2.50 6.00
RART Rowdy Tellez 4.00 10.00
RASD Steven Duggar 3.00 8.00
RASG Stephen Gonsalves 2.50 6.00
RASRF Sean Reid-Foley 2.50 6.00
RATB Ty Buttrey 2.50 6.00
RATP Thomas Pannone 4.00 10.00
RATR Trevor Richards 2.50 6.00
RATT Touki Toussaint EXCH 4.00 10.00
RATW Taylor Ward 2.50 6.00
RAVGJ Vladimir Guerrero Jr. 200.00 500.00
RAWA Willians Astudillo 2.50 6.00
RAWS Will Smith 25.00 60.00
RAYK Yusei Kikuchi 8.00 20.00

2019 Topps Chrome Rookie Autographs Blue Refractors
*BLUE REF: .75X TO 2X BASIC
STATED ODDS 1:409 HOBBY
STATED PRINT RUN 150 SER.#'d SETS
EXCHANGE DEADLINE 6/30/2021
RAJL Jonathan Loaisiga 10.00 25.00
RALU Luis Urias 20.00 50.00

2019 Topps Chrome Rookie Autographs Blue Wave Refractors
*BLUE WAVE REF: .75X TO 2X BASIC
STATED ODDS 1:409 HOBBY
STATED PRINT RUN 150 SER.#'d SETS
EXCHANGE DEADLINE 6/30/2021
RAJL Jonathan Loaisiga 10.00 25.00
RALU Luis Urias 20.00 50.00

2019 Topps Chrome Rookie Autographs Gold Refractors
*GOLD REF: 1.2X TO 3X BASIC
STATED ODDS 1:1227 HOBBY
STATED PRINT RUN 50 SER.#'d SETS
EXCHANGE DEADLINE 6/30/2021
RABR Brendan Rodgers 30.00 80.00
RAJL Jonathan Loaisiga 15.00 40.00
RAJM Jeff McNeil 60.00 150.00
RAKH Keston Hiura 150.00 400.00
RALU Luis Urias 60.00 150.00

2019 Topps Chrome Rookie Autographs Gold Wave Refractors
*GOLD WAVE REF: 1.2X TO 3X BASIC
STATED ODDS 1:834 HOBBY
STATED PRINT RUN 50 SER.#'d SETS
EXCHANGE DEADLINE 6/30/2021
RABR Brendan Rodgers 30.00 80.00
RAJL Jonathan Loaisiga 15.00 40.00
RAJM Jeff McNeil 60.00 150.00
RAKH Keston Hiura 150.00 400.00
RALU Luis Urias 60.00 150.00

2019 Topps Chrome Rookie Autographs Green Refractors
*GREEN REF: 1X TO 2.5X BASIC
STATED ODDS 1:416 BLASTER
STATED PRINT RUN 99 SER.#'d SETS
EXCHANGE DEADLINE 6/30/2021
RAJL Jonathan Loaisiga 12.00 30.00
RALU Luis Urias 25.00 60.00

2019 Topps Chrome Rookie Autographs Orange Refractors
*ORANGE REF: 1.5X TO 4X BASIC
STATED ODDS 1:793 HOBBY
STATED PRINT RUN 25 SER.#'d SETS
EXCHANGE DEADLINE 6/30/2021
RABR Brendan Rodgers 40.00 100.00
RAJL Jonathan Loaisiga 20.00 50.00
RAJM Jeff McNeil 75.00 200.00
RAKH Keston Hiura 200.00 500.00
RALU Luis Urias 75.00 200.00

2019 Topps Chrome Rookie Autographs Orange Wave Refractors
*ORANGE WAVE REF: 1.5X TO 4X BASIC
STATED ODDS 1:1667 HOBBY
STATED PRINT RUN 25 SER.#'d SETS
EXCHANGE DEADLINE 6/30/2021
RABR Brendan Rodgers 40.00 100.00
RAJL Jonathan Loaisiga 20.00 50.00
RAJM Jeff McNeil 75.00 200.00
RAKH Keston Hiura 200.00 500.00
RALU Luis Urias 75.00 200.00

2019 Topps Chrome Rookie Autographs Purple Refractors
*PURPLE REF: .6X TO 1.5X BASIC
STATED ODDS 1:246 HOBBY
STATED PRINT RUN 250 SER.#'d SETS
EXCHANGE DEADLINE 6/30/2021
RAJL Jonathan Loaisiga 5.00 12.00
RALU Luis Urias 15.00 40.00

2019 Topps Chrome Rookie Autographs Refractors
*REF: .5X TO 1.2X BASIC
STATED ODDS 1:123 HOBBY
STATED PRINT RUN 499 SER.#'d SETS
EXCHANGE DEADLINE 6/30/2021
RALU Luis Urias 12.00 30.00

2019 Topps Chrome Update
PRINTING PLATE ODDS 1:4576 PACKS
PLATE PRINT RUN 1 SET PER COLOR
BLACK-CYAN-MAGENTA-YELLOW ISSUED
NO PLATE PRICING DUE TO SCARCITY
1 Paul Goldschmidt .30 .75
2 Josh Donaldson .25 .60
3 Yasiel Puig .30 .75
4 Adam Ottavino .20 .50
5 DJ LeMahieu .30 .75
6 Dallas Keuchel .25 .60
7 Charlie Morton .30 .75
8 Zack Britton .20 .50
9 C.J. Cron .20 .50
10 Jonathan Schoop .20 .50
11 Robinson Cano .25 .60
12 Edwin Encarnacion .30 .75
13 Domingo Santana .25 .60
14 J.T. Realmuto .30 .75

15 Hunter Pence .25 .60
16 Edwin Diaz .25 .60
17 Yasmani Grandal .20 .50
18 Chris Paddack RC .75 2.00
19 Jon Duplantier RC .40 1.00
20 Nick Anderson RC .40 1.00
21 Vladimir Guerrero Jr. RC 2.50 6.00
22 Carter Kieboom RC .60 1.50
23 Nate Lowe RC 2.00 5.00
24 Pedro Avila RC .40 1.00
25 Ryan Helsley RC .50 1.25
26 Lane Thomas RC .60 1.50
27 Michael Chavis RC .60 1.50
28 Thairo Estrada RC .60 1.50
29 Bryan Reynolds RC 1.25 3.00
30 Darwinzon Hernandez RC .40 1.00
31 Griffin Canning RC .60 1.50
32 Nick Senzel RC 1.25 3.00
33 Cal Quantrill RC .40 1.00
34 Matthew Beaty RC .75 2.00
35 Spencer Turnbull RC .60 1.50
36 Corbin Martin RC .60 1.50
37 Austin Riley RC 2.00 5.00
38 Keston Hiura RC 1.25 3.00
39 Nicky Lopez RC .60 1.50
40 Oscar Mercado RC 1.00 2.50
41 Harold Ramirez RC .60 1.50
42 Cavan Biggio RC 2.00 5.00
43 Kevin Cron RC 1.25 3.00
44 Josh Naylor RC .50 1.25
45 Luis Arraez RC 1.50 4.00
46 Shaun Anderson RC .40 1.00
47 Will Smith RC 1.00 2.50
48 Mitch Keller RC .50 1.25
49 Mike Yastrzemski RC 3.00 8.00
50 Craig Kimbrel .25 .60
51 Yusei Kikuchi RD .30 .75
52 Pete Alonso RD 1.50 4.00
53 Eloy Jimenez RD .75 2.00
54 Fernando Tatis Jr. RD 20.00 50.00
55 Chris Paddack RD .40 1.00
56 Nick Senzel RD .60 1.50
57 Michael Chavis RD .30 .75
58 Vladimir Guerrero Jr. RD 1.25 3.00
59 Carter Kieboom RD .30 .75
60 Corbin Martin RD .30 .75
61 Austin Riley RD 1.00 2.50
62 Keston Hiura RD .60 1.50
63 Brendan Rodgers RD .30 .75
64 Cavan Biggio RD 1.00 2.50
65 Griffin Canning RD .30 .75
66 Gary Sanchez AS .30 .75
67 Willson Contreras AS .25 .60
68 Carlos Santana AS .25 .60
69 Freddie Freeman AS .40 1.00
70 DJ LeMahieu AS .30 .75
71 Ketel Marte AS .25 .60
72 Alex Bregman AS .30 .75
73 Nolan Arenado AS .50 1.25
74 Jorge Polanco AS .25 .60
75 Javier Baez AS .40 1.00
76 Mike Trout AS 1.50 4.00
77 Christian Yelich AS .40 1.00
78 George Springer AS .25 .60
79 Cody Bellinger AS .60 1.50
80 Michael Brantley AS .25 .60
81 Ronald Acuna Jr. AS 1.50 4.00
82 Francisco Lindor AS .30 .75
83 Mookie Betts AS .60 1.50
84 Lucas Giolito AS .25 .60
85 Justin Verlander AS .30 .75
86 Pete Alonso AS 1.50 4.00
87 Josh Bell AS .25 .60
88 Kris Bryant AS .40 1.00
89 Walker Buehler AS .40 1.00
90 Trevor Story AS .30 .75
91 Clayton Kershaw AS .50 1.25
92 Jake Odorizzi AS .20 .50
93 Luis Castillo AS .25 .60
94 Matt Chapman AS .30 .75
95 Joey Gallo AS .25 .60
96 Austin Meadows AS .30 .75
97 Charlie Blackmon AS .30 .75
98 Whit Merrifield AS .30 .75
99 David Dahl AS .20 .50
100 Shane Bieber AS .30 .75

2019 Topps Chrome Update Blue Refractors

*BLUE REF: 3X TO 8X BASIC
*BLUE REF RC: 1.5X TO 4X BASIC RC
STATED ODDS 1:123 PACKS
STATED PRINT RUN 150 SER.#'d SETS
18 Chris Paddack 12.00 30.00
21 Vladimir Guerrero Jr. 50.00 120.00
22 Carter Kieboom 20.00 50.00
23 Nate Lowe 5.00 12.00
27 Michael Chavis 8.00 20.00
28 Thairo Estrada 8.00 20.00
29 Bryan Reynolds 10.00 25.00
32 Nick Senzel 20.00 50.00
38 Keston Hiura 30.00 80.00
40 Oscar Mercado 10.00 25.00
45 Luis Arraez 25.00 60.00
47 Will Smith 15.00 40.00
48 Mitch Keller 5.00 12.00
52 Pete Alonso 30.00 80.00
53 Eloy Jimenez 8.00 20.00
58 Vladimir Guerrero Jr. 25.00 60.00
62 Keston Hiura 12.00 30.00
86 Pete Alonso AS 20.00 50.00

2019 Topps Chrome Update Gold Refractors

*GOLD REF: 6X TO 15X BASIC
*GOLD REF RC: 3X TO 8X BASIC RC
STATED ODDS 1:367 PACKS
STATED PRINT RUN 50 SER.#'d SETS
18 Chris Paddack 25.00 60.00
21 Vladimir Guerrero Jr. 100.00 250.00
22 Carter Kieboom 40.00 100.00
23 Nate Lowe 10.00 25.00
27 Michael Chavis 15.00 40.00
28 Thairo Estrada 15.00 40.00
29 Bryan Reynolds 20.00 50.00
32 Nick Senzel 40.00 100.00
37 Austin Riley 30.00 80.00
38 Keston Hiura 60.00 150.00
40 Oscar Mercado 20.00 50.00
45 Luis Arraez 50.00 120.00
47 Will Smith 30.00 80.00
48 Mitch Keller 10.00 25.00
52 Pete Alonso 60.00 150.00
53 Eloy Jimenez 15.00 40.00
58 Vladimir Guerrero Jr. 50.00 120.00
62 Keston Hiura 25.00 60.00
86 Pete Alonso AS 40.00 100.00

2019 Topps Chrome Update Green Refractors

*GREEN REF: 4X TO 10X BASIC
*GREEN REF RC: 2X TO 5X BASIC RC
STATED ODDS 1:186 PACKS
STATED PRINT RUN 99 SER.#'d SETS
18 Chris Paddack 15.00 40.00
21 Vladimir Guerrero Jr. 60.00 150.00
22 Carter Kieboom 25.00 60.00
23 Nate Lowe 6.00 15.00
27 Michael Chavis 10.00 25.00
28 Thairo Estrada 10.00 25.00
29 Bryan Reynolds 12.00 30.00
32 Nick Senzel 25.00 60.00
38 Keston Hiura 40.00 100.00
40 Oscar Mercado 12.00 30.00
45 Luis Arraez 30.00 80.00
47 Will Smith 20.00 50.00
48 Mitch Keller 6.00 15.00
52 Pete Alonso 40.00 100.00
53 Eloy Jimenez 10.00 25.00
58 Vladimir Guerrero Jr. 30.00 80.00
62 Keston Hiura 15.00 40.00
86 Pete Alonso AS 25.00 60.00

2019 Topps Chrome Update Orange Refractors

*ORANGE REF: 8X TO 20X BASIC
*ORANGE REF RC: 4X TO 10X BASIC RC
STATED ODDS 1:734 PACKS
STATED PRINT RUN 25 SER.#'d SETS
18 Chris Paddack 30.00 80.00
21 Vladimir Guerrero Jr. 125.00 300.00
22 Carter Kieboom 50.00 120.00
23 Nate Lowe 12.00 30.00
27 Michael Chavis 20.00 50.00
28 Thairo Estrada 20.00 50.00
29 Bryan Reynolds 25.00 60.00
32 Nick Senzel 50.00 120.00
37 Austin Riley 40.00 100.00
38 Keston Hiura 75.00 200.00
40 Oscar Mercado 25.00 60.00
45 Luis Arraez 60.00 150.00
47 Will Smith 40.00 100.00
48 Mitch Keller 12.00 30.00
52 Pete Alonso 75.00 200.00
53 Eloy Jimenez 20.00 50.00
58 Vladimir Guerrero Jr. 60.00 150.00
62 Keston Hiura 30.00 80.00
86 Pete Alonso AS 60.00 150.00

2019 Topps Chrome Update Pink Refractors

*PINK REF: 2X TO 5X BASIC
*PINK REF RC: 1X TO 2.5X BASIC RC
TWO PER HANGER PACK

2019 Topps Chrome Update Purple Refractors

*PURPLE REF: 2.5X TO 6X BASIC
*PURPLE REF RC: 1.2X TO 3X BASIC RC
STATED ODDS 1:105 PACKS
STATED PRINT RUN 175 SER.#'d SETS
18 Chris Paddack 10.00 25.00
21 Vladimir Guerrero Jr. 40.00 100.00
22 Carter Kieboom 15.00 40.00
23 Nate Lowe 4.00 10.00
27 Michael Chavis 6.00 15.00
28 Thairo Estrada 6.00 15.00
29 Bryan Reynolds 8.00 20.00
32 Nick Senzel 15.00 40.00
38 Keston Hiura 25.00 60.00
40 Oscar Mercado 8.00 20.00
45 Luis Arraez 20.00 50.00
47 Will Smith 12.00 30.00
48 Mitch Keller 4.00 10.00
52 Pete Alonso 25.00 60.00
53 Eloy Jimenez 6.00 15.00
58 Vladimir Guerrero Jr. 20.00 50.00
62 Keston Hiura 10.00 25.00
86 Pete Alonso AS 15.00 40.00

2019 Topps Chrome Update Refractors

*REF: 1.5X TO 4X BASIC
*REF RC: .75X TO 2X BASIC RC
STATED ODDS 1:74 PACKS
STATED PRINT RUN 250 SER.#'d SETS
18 Chris Paddack 6.00 15.00
21 Vladimir Guerrero Jr. 25.00 60.00
22 Carter Kieboom 10.00 25.00
23 Nate Lowe 2.50 6.00
27 Michael Chavis 4.00 10.00
28 Thairo Estrada 4.00 10.00
29 Bryan Reynolds 5.00 12.00
32 Nick Senzel 10.00 25.00
38 Keston Hiura 15.00 40.00
40 Oscar Mercado 5.00 12.00
45 Luis Arraez 12.00 30.00
47 Will Smith 8.00 20.00
48 Mitch Keller 2.50 6.00
52 Pete Alonso 15.00 40.00
53 Eloy Jimenez 4.00 10.00
58 Vladimir Guerrero Jr. 12.00 30.00
62 Keston Hiura 6.00 15.00
86 Pete Alonso AS 10.00 25.00

2019 Topps Chrome Update X-Fractors

*X-FRAC: 2.5X TO 6X BASIC
*X-FRAC RC: 1.2X TO 3X BASIC RC
STATED ODDS 1:93 PACKS
STATED PRINT RUN 199 SER.#'d SETS
18 Chris Paddack 10.00 25.00
21 Vladimir Guerrero Jr. 40.00 100.00
22 Carter Kieboom 15.00 40.00
23 Nate Lowe 4.00 10.00
27 Michael Chavis 6.00 15.00
28 Thairo Estrada 6.00 15.00
29 Bryan Reynolds 8.00 20.00
32 Nick Senzel 15.00 40.00
38 Keston Hiura 25.00 60.00
40 Oscar Mercado 8.00 20.00
45 Luis Arraez 20.00 50.00
47 Will Smith 12.00 30.00
48 Mitch Keller 4.00 10.00
52 Pete Alonso 25.00 60.00
53 Eloy Jimenez 6.00 15.00
58 Vladimir Guerrero Jr. 20.00 50.00
62 Keston Hiura 10.00 25.00
86 Pete Alonso AS 15.00 40.00

2019 Topps Chrome Update 150 Years of Professional Baseball

STATED ODDS 1:4 PACKS
150C1 Nolan Ryan 1.25 3.00
150C2 David Ortiz .40 1.00
150C3 Ichiro .50 1.25
150C4 Rickey Henderson .40 1.00
150C5 Carl Yastrzemski .60 1.50
150C6 Justin Verlander .40 1.00
150C7 Ozzie Smith .50 1.25
150C8 Steve Carlton .30 .75
150C9 Mark McGwire .60 1.50
150C10 Mike Trout 2.00 5.00
150C11 Babe Ruth 1.00 2.50
150C12 Ted Williams .75 2.00
150C13 Cal Ripken Jr. 1.25 3.00
150C14 Ken Griffey Jr. .75 2.00
150C15 Roberto Clemente 1.00 2.50
150C16 Sandy Koufax .75 2.00
150C17 Jackie Robinson .40 1.00
150C18 Frank Robinson .30 .75
150C19 Johnny Bench .40 1.00
150C20 Frank Thomas .40 1.00
150C21 Clayton Kershaw .60 1.50
150C22 Hank Aaron .75 2.00
150C23 Derek Jeter 1.00 2.50
150C24 Tony Gwynn .40 1.00
150C25 George Brett .75 2.00

2019 Topps Chrome Update Autograph Refractors

STATED ODDS 1:40 PACKS
EXCHANGE DEADLINE 9/30/2021
CUAAB Andrew Benintendi 15.00 40.00
CUAAH Adam Haseley 4.00 10.00
CUAAK Andrew Knizner 4.00 10.00
CUAAN Aaron Nola 6.00 15.00
CUAAR Austin Riley 12.00 30.00
CUABL Brandon Lowe 20.00 50.00
CUABRE Bryan Reynolds 8.00 20.00
CUABW Brandon Woodruff 4.00 10.00
CUACA Chance Adams 2.50 6.00
CUACF Clint Frazier 4.00 10.00
CUACP Chris Paddack 10.00 25.00
CUACT Cole Tucker 4.00 10.00
CUADH Darwinzon Hernandez 2.50 6.00
CUADSW Dansby Swanson 10.00 25.00
CUAEL Elvis Luciano 4.00 10.00
CUAGU Gio Urshela 15.00 40.00
CUAHR Harold Ramirez 4.00 10.00
CUAJA Jorge Alfaro 2.50 6.00
CUAJB Jalen Beeks 2.50 6.00
CUAJD Jon Duplantier 2.50 6.00
CUAJH JD Hammer 3.00 8.00
CUAJMA Jason Martin 3.00 8.00
CUAJN Josh Naylor 10.00 25.00
CUAJS Jean Segura 4.00 10.00
CUALA Luis Arraez 25.00 60.00
CUALT Lane Thomas 10.00 25.00
CUALV Luke Voit 50.00 120.00
CUAMKE Merrill Kelly 2.50 6.00
CUAMM Manny Machado 25.00 60.00
CUAMY Mike Yastrzemski 40.00 100.00
CUANL Nicky Lopez 4.00 10.00
CUANLO Nate Lowe 6.00 15.00
CUAPA Pedro Avila 2.50 6.00
CUAPC Patrick Corbin 3.00 8.00
CUARH Ryan Helsley 3.00 8.00
CUARHO Rhys Hoskins 8.00 20.00
CUARL Richard Lovelady 2.50 6.00
CUASA Shaun Anderson 2.50 6.00
CUASO Shohei Ohtani 75.00 200.00
CUATB Trevor Bauer 15.00 40.00
CUATE Thairo Estrada 10.00 25.00
CUATT Trent Thornton 2.50 6.00
CUAVR Victor Robles 6.00 15.00
CUAWS Will Smith 15.00 40.00
CUAZP Zach Plesac 25.00 60.00

2019 Topps Chrome Update Autograph Gold Refractors

*GOLD REF: 1.2X TO 3X BASIC
STATED ODDS 1:715 PACKS
STATED PRINT RUN 50 SER.#'d STES
EXCHANGE DEADLINE 9/30/2021

2019 Topps Chrome Update Autograph Orange Refractors

*ORANGE REF: 1.5X TO 4X BASIC
STATED ODDS 1:1404 PACKS
STATED PRINT RUN 25 SER.#'d STES
EXCHANGE DEADLINE 9/30/2021
CUASO Shohei Ohtani 125.00 300.00

2019 Topps Chrome Update Autograph X-Fractors

*X-FRAC: .6X TO 1.5X BASIC
STATED ODDS 1:292 PACKS
STATED PRINT RUN 125 SER.#'d STES
EXCHANGE DEADLINE 9/30/2021

2019 Topps Chrome Update Rookie Autograph Refractors

STATED ODDS 1:40 PACKS
EXCHANGE DEADLINE 9/30/2021
*X-FRAC/125: .6X TO 1.5X
*GOLD REF/50: 1.2X TO 3X
*ORANGE REF/25: 1.5X TO 4X
RDACK Carter Kieboom 12.00 30.00
RDAEJ Eloy Jimenez 25.00 60.00
RDAFT Fernando Tatis Jr. 100.00 250.00
RDAKH Keston Hiura 20.00 50.00
RDAMC Michael Chavis 12.00 30.00
RDAPA Pete Alonso 75.00 200.00
RDAVG Vladimir Guerrero Jr. 60.00 150.00

2019 Topps Chrome Update The Family Business

STATED ODDS 1:4 PACKS
FBC1 Ken Griffey Jr. .75 2.00
FBC2 Cal Ripken Jr. 1.25 3.00
FBC3 Roberto Alomar .30 .75
FBC4 Vladimir Guerrero .30 .75
FBC5 Ivan Rodriguez .30 .75
FBC6 Roger Clemens .50 1.25
FBC7 Yadier Molina .50 1.25
FBC8 Ronald Acuna Jr. 2.00 5.00
FBC9 Cecil Fielder .25 .60
FBC10 Mariano Rivera .50 1.25
FBC11 Hank Aaron .75 2.00
FBC12 Tim Raines .30 .75
FBC13 Jose Canseco .30 .75
FBC14 Bryce Harper .60 1.50
FBC15 Fernando Tatis Jr. 4.00 10.00
FBC16 Tony Gwynn .40 1.00
FBC17 Corey Seager .40 1.00
FBC18 Nolan Arenado .60 1.50
FBC19 Vladimir Guerrero Jr. 1.50 4.00
FBC20 Robinson Cano .30 .75
FBC21 Cody Bellinger .75 2.00
FBC22 Pedro Martinez .30 .75
FBC23 Manny Machado .40 1.00
FBC24 Dee Gordon .25 .60
FBC25 Reggie Jackson .30 .75

2016 Topps Chrome Holiday Mega Box

HMT1 Trevor Story 3.00 8.00
HMT2 Seung-Hwan Oh 1.50 4.00
HMT3 Ian Kennedy .60 1.50
HMT4 Miguel Sano 1.00 2.50
HMT5 Pedro Alvarez .60 1.50
HMT6 Joey Rickard .60 1.50
HMT7 Kenta Maeda 1.25 3.00
HMT8 Hyun-Soo Kim 1.00 2.50
HMT9 Robert Stephenson .60 1.50
HMT10 Todd Frazier .60 1.50
HMT11 Doug Fister .60 1.50
HMT12 Asdrubal Cabrera .75 2.00
HMT13 Zack Greinke 1.00 2.50
HMT14 Cameron Maybin .60 1.50
HMT15 Byung-Ho Park .75 2.00
HMT16 Denard Span .60 1.50
HMT17 Yonder Alonso .60 1.50
HMT18 Trayce Thompson 1.00 2.50
HMT19 Nomar Mazara 1.00 2.50
HMT20 Jeremy Hazelbaker .75 2.00
HMT21 Ross Stripling .60 1.50
HMT22 Jameson Taillon .75 2.00
HMT23 Mallex Smith .60 1.50
HMT24 Vince Velasquez .60 1.50
HMT25 Tyler Naquin 1.00 2.50
HMT26 Blake Snell .75 2.00
HMT27 Julio Urias 2.00 5.00
HMT28 Ian Desmond .60 1.50
HMT29 Neil Walker .60 1.50
HMT30 Jeremy Hellickson .60 1.50
HMT31 Craig Kimbrel .75 2.00
HMT32 Albert Almora .75 2.00
HMT33 Aledmys Diaz 1.00 2.50
HMT34 Shelby Miller .75 2.00
HMT35 Starlin Castro .60 1.50
HMT36 Matt Wieters 1.00 2.50
HMT37 Jose Berrios 1.00 2.50
HMT38 Dexter Fowler .75 2.00
HMT39 James Shields .60 1.50
HMT40 Jed Lowrie .60 1.50
HMT41 Corey Seager 6.00 15.00
HMT42 Michael Fulmer 1.00 2.50
HMT43 Michael Conforto .75 2.00
HMT44 Luis Severino .75 2.00
HMT45 Francisco Rodriguez .75 2.00
HMT46 Stephen Piscotty 1.00 2.50
HMT47 Matt Joyce .60 1.50
HMT48 Aaron Nola 1.25 3.00
HMT49 Kyle Schwarber 2.00 5.00
HMT50 Ben Revere .60 1.50

2016 Topps Chrome Holiday Mega Box Gold Refractors

*GOLD REF: 3X TO 8X BASIC
STATED PRINT RUN 50 SER.#'d SETS

2016 Topps Chrome Holiday Mega Box Refractors

*REF: .75X TO 2X BASIC
STATED PRINT RUN 250 SER.#'d SETS

2016 Topps Chrome Holiday Mega Box X-Fractors

*X-FRACTOR: 1X TO 2.5X BASIC
STATED PRINT RUN 99 SER.#'d SETS

2016 Topps Chrome Holiday Mega Box 3000 Hits Club

3000C1 Carl Yastrzemski 1.50 4.00
3000C2 Ty Cobb 1.50 4.00
3000C3 Hank Aaron 2.00 5.00
3000C4 Stan Musial 1.50 4.00
3000C5 Honus Wagner 1.00 2.50
3000C6 Paul Molitor 1.00 2.50
3000C7 Willie Mays 2.00 5.00
3000C8 Eddie Murray .75 2.00
3000C9 Cal Ripken Jr. 3.00 8.00
3000C10 George Brett 2.00 5.00
3000C11 Robin Yount 1.00 2.50
3000C12 Tony Gwynn 1.00 2.50
3000C13 Ichiro Suzuki 1.25 3.00
3000C14 Craig Biggio .75 2.00
3000C15 Rickey Henderson 1.00 2.50
3000C16 Rod Carew .75 2.00
3000C17 Lou Brock .75 2.00
3000C18 Wade Boggs .75 2.00
3000C19 Roberto Clemente 2.50 6.00
3000C20 Al Kaline 1.00 2.50

2016 Topps Chrome Holiday Mega Box All Star Stitches

ASRCAR Addison Russell 6.00 15.00
ASRCARI Anthony Rizzo 8.00 20.00
ASRCBH Bryce Harper 10.00 25.00
ASRCBP Buster Posey 8.00 20.00
ASRCCK Clayton Kershaw 10.00 25.00
ASRCCS Corey Seager 40.00 100.00
ASRCDO David Ortiz 6.00 15.00
ASRCEE Edwin Encarnacion 6.00 15.00
ASRCEH Eric Hosmer 5.00 12.00
ASRCFL Francisco Lindor 6.00 15.00
ASRCJA Jake Arrieta 5.00 12.00
ASRCJD Josh Donaldson 5.00 12.00
ASRCKB Kris Bryant 8.00 20.00
ASRCMB Mookie Betts 12.00 30.00
ASRCMBU Madison Bumgarner 5.00 12.00
ASRCMC Miguel Cabrera 6.00 15.00
ASRCMMA Manny Machado 6.00 15.00
ASRCMS Max Scherzer 6.00 15.00
ASRCMT Mike Trout 30.00 80.00
ASRCNS Noah Syndergaard 5.00 12.00
ASRCRC Robinson Cano 5.00 12.00
ASRCSP Salvador Perez 5.00 12.00
ASRCSS Stephen Strasburg 6.00 15.00
ASRCXB Xander Bogaerts 6.00 15.00

2017 Topps Chrome Sapphire Edition

1 Kris Bryant
2 Jason Hammel 1.50 4.00
3 Chris Capuano 1.25 3.00
4 Mark Reynolds 1.25 3.00
5 Corey Seager 2.00 5.00
6 Kevin Pillar 1.25 3.00
7 Gary Sanchez 2.00 5.00
8 Jose Berrios 1.50 4.00
9 Chris Sale 2.00 5.00
10 Steven Souza Jr. 1.50 4.00
11 Jake Smolinski 1.25 3.00
12 Jerad Eickhoff 1.25 3.00
13 Adeiny Hechavarria 1.25 3.00
14 Travis d'Arnaud 1.50 4.00
15 Braden Shipley 1.25 3.00
16 Lance McCullers 1.25 3.00
17 Daniel Descalso 1.25 3.00
18 Jake Arrieta WS HL 1.50 4.00
19 David Wright 1.50 4.00
20 Mike Trout 100.00 250.00
21 Robert Gsellman 1.25 3.00
22 Keone Kela 1.25 3.00
23 Marcell Ozuna 2.00 5.00
24 Christian Friedrich 1.25 3.00
25 Giancarlo Stanton 2.00 5.00
26 David Peralta 1.25 3.00
27 Kurt Suzuki 1.25 3.00
28 Rick Porcello LL 1.50 4.00
29 Marco Estrada 1.25 3.00
30 Josh Bell 15.00 40.00
31 Carlos Carrasco 1.25 3.00
32 Thor and the Dark Knight 1.50 4.00
Matt Harvey/Noah Syndergaard
33 Carson Fulmer 1.25 3.00
34 Bryce Harper 6.00 15.00
35 Nolan Arenado LL 3.00 8.00
36 B'more Boppers 2.00 5.00
Mark Trumbo/Adam Jones/Manny Machado/Chris Davis
37 Toronto Blue Jays 1.25 3.00
38 Stephen Strasburg 2.00 5.00
39 Aroldis Chapman WS HL 2.00 5.00
40 Jordan Zimmermann 1.50 4.00
41 Paulo Orlando 1.25 3.00
42 Trevor Story 2.00 5.00
43 Tyler Austin 1.50 4.00
44 Paul Goldschmidt 2.00 5.00
45 Joakim Soria 1.25 3.00
46 Will Middlebrooks 1.25 3.00
47 Gregor Blanco 1.25 3.00
48 Brian McCann 1.50 4.00
49 Scooter Gennett 1.50 4.00
50 Clayton Kershaw 3.00 8.00
51 Jake Barrett 1.25 3.00
52 Neftali Feliz 1.25 3.00
53 Ryon Healy 1.50 4.00
54 Dellin Betances 1.50 4.00
55 Mark Trumbo LL 1.25 3.00
56 Danny Salazar 1.50 4.00
57 C.J. Cron 1.25 3.00
58 Starling Marte 1.50 4.00
59 Carlos Rodon 2.00 5.00
60 Jose Bautista 1.50 4.00
61 Xander Bogaerts 2.00 5.00
62 Daniel Murphy 1.50 4.00
63 Mike Moustakas 1.50 4.00
64 Adam Eaton 2.00 5.00
65 Madison Bumgarner 1.50 4.00
66 Aaron Altherr 1.25 3.00
67 Teoscar Hernandez 5.00 12.00
68 Zach Britton 1.50 4.00
69 Henry Owens 1.25 3.00
70 Wily Peralta 1.25 3.00
71 Matt Shoemaker 1.50 4.00
72 Chicago Cubs 1.25 3.00
73 Kyle Schwarber 2.00 5.00
74 Brett Lawrie 1.50 4.00
75 Carlos Correa 2.00 5.00
76 Andre Ethier 1.50 4.00
77 Austin Jackson 1.25 3.00
78 Addison Russell WS HL 2.00 5.00
79 Gabriel Ynoa 1.25 3.00
80 Ivan Nova 1.50 4.00
81 DJ LeMahieu LL 2.00 5.00
82 Aaron Sanchez LL 1.50 4.00
83 Anibal Sanchez 1.25 3.00
84 Daniel Murphy LL 1.50 4.00
85 Brandon Finnegan 1.25 3.00
86 Asdrubal Cabrera 1.50 4.00
87 Dansby Swanson 3.00 8.00
88 Freddy Galvis 1.25 3.00
89 Brandon Moss 1.25 3.00
90 Jason Grilli 1.25 3.00
91 Troy Tulowitzki 2.00 5.00
92 Derek Norris 1.25 3.00
93 Matt Joyce 1.25 3.00
94 Kyle Barraclough 1.25 3.00
95 Chris Davis 1.25 3.00
96 Jose Quintana 1.25 3.00
97 Marcus Semien 2.00 5.00
98 Junior Guerra 1.25 3.00
99 Michael Wacha 1.50 4.00
100 Nate Jones 1.25 3.00
101 Pedro Alvarez 1.25 3.00
102 Cameron Maybin 1.25 3.00
103 Alex Reyes 1.50 4.00
104 Dioner Navarro 1.25 3.00
105 Francisco Rodriguez 1.50 4.00
106 Brandon Crawford 1.50 4.00
107 Howie Kendrick 1.25 3.00
108 Nick Hundley 1.25 3.00
109 Nelson Cruz 2.00 5.00
110 Joey Votto LL 2.00 5.00
111 Edinson Volquez 1.25 3.00
112 Angel Pagan 1.25 3.00
113 Kyle Hendricks LL 2.00 5.00
114 Colin Rea 1.25 3.00
115 Joaquin Benoit 1.25 3.00
116 Archie Bradley 1.25 3.00
117 Adrian Gonzalez 1.50 4.00
118 Billy Butler 1.25 3.00
119 Francisco Lindor 2.00 5.00
120 Reynaldo Lopez 1.25 3.00
121 Carlos Santana 1.50 4.00
122 Cleveland Indians 1.25 3.00
123 Jean Segura 1.50 4.00
124 Travis Jankowski 1.25 3.00
125 Yangervis Solarte 1.25 3.00
126 Miguel Sano 1.50 4.00
127 Michael Bourn 1.25 3.00
128 Adam Duvall 1.50 4.00
129 Adonis Garcia 1.25 3.00
130 Dustin Pedroia 2.00 5.00
131 J.A. Happ LL 1.50 4.00
132 Randal Grichuk 1.25 3.00
133 Jace Peterson 1.25 3.00
134 Chase Utley 1.50 4.00
135 Jered Weaver 1.50 4.00
136 Matt Reynolds 1.25 3.00
137 Yan Gomes 2.00 5.00
138 Tyson Ross 1.25 3.00
139 JaCoby Jones 1.50 4.00
140 Jesse Hahn 1.25 3.00
141 Baltimore Orioles 1.25 3.00
142 Carlos Ruiz 1.25 3.00
143 Nick Noonan 1.25 3.00
144 Jon Lester LL 1.50 4.00
145 Max Scherzer LL 2.00 5.00
146 Chad Pinder 1.25 3.00
147 Marcus Stroman 1.50 4.00
148 Tim Anderson 2.00 5.00
149 Gregory Polanco 1.50 4.00
150 Miguel Cabrera 2.00 5.00
151 Jonathan Villar 1.25 3.00
152 Nolan Arenado LL 3.00 8.00
153 Nori Aoki 1.25 3.00
154 Kevin Kiermaier 1.50 4.00
155 Jacob deGrom 4.00 10.00
156 Alex Colome 1.25 3.00
157 Sean Doolittle 1.25 3.00
158 Tommy Pham 1.25 3.00
159 Justin Verlander LL 2.00 5.00
160 Evan Gattis 1.25 3.00
161 Mookie Betts 4.00 10.00
162 Jon Lester LL 1.50 4.00
163 Adam Conley 1.25 3.00
164 Matt Harvey 1.50 4.00
165 Corey Dickerson 1.25 3.00
166 Jorge Soler 2.00 5.00
167 Lorenzo Cain 1.25 3.00
168 Ryan Zimmerman 1.50 4.00
169 Steve Pearce 2.00 5.00
170 Chris Carter LL 1.25 3.00
171 Seth Smith 1.25 3.00
172 Wilmer Flores 1.50 4.00
173 Chicago White Sox 1.25 3.00
174 Philadelphia Phillies 1.25 3.00
175 Houston Astros 1.25 3.00
176 Jaime Garcia 1.25 3.00
177 Sonny Gray 1.50 4.00
178 Rick Porcello 1.50 4.00
179 Matt Moore 1.50 4.00
180 Jake McGee 1.50 4.00
181 Aaron Hicks 1.50 4.00
182 Keon Broxton 1.25 3.00
183 Wade Miley 1.25 3.00
184 Oswaldo Arcia 1.25 3.00
185 Raisel Iglesias 1.50 4.00
186 Andrew Cashner 1.25 3.00
187 Sean Manaea 1.25 3.00
188 Caleb Cotham 1.25 3.00
189 Los Angeles Angels 1.25 3.00
190 Blake Snell 1.50 4.00
191 Wilson Ramos 1.25 3.00
192 San Diego Padres 1.25 3.00
193 Jimmy Nelson 1.25 3.00
194 A.J. Ramos 1.25 3.00
195 Edwin Encarnacion LL 2.00 5.00
196 Colby Rasmus 1.50 4.00
197 Jacoby Ellsbury 1.50 4.00
198 Francisco Cervelli 1.25 3.00
199 Johnny Cueto 1.50 4.00
200 Homer Bailey 1.25 3.00
201 Eddie Rosario 1.50 4.00
202 Masahiro Tanaka LL 1.50 4.00
203 Tyler Naquin 2.00 5.00
204 Anthony Rizzo LL 2.50 6.00
205 Kendrys Morales 1.25 3.00
206 Chicago Cubs WS HL 1.25 3.00
207 Justin Upton 1.50 4.00
208 Masahiro Tanaka 1.50 4.00
209 Jon Gray 1.25 3.00
210 Yoan Moncada 40.00 100.00
211 Noah Syndergaard LL 1.50 4.00
212 Tanner Roark 1.25 3.00
213 Alex Wood 1.25 3.00
214 Jose Altuve LL 1.50 4.00
215 Johnny Giavotella 1.25 3.00
216 Denard Span 1.25 3.00
217 Miami Marlins 1.25 3.00
218 Michael Saunders 1.50 4.00
219 Joe Musgrove 4.00 10.00
220 Ryan Braun 1.50 4.00
221 Adam Wainwright 1.50 4.00
222 Cesar Hernandez 1.25 3.00
223 Jason Heyward 1.50 4.00
224 Hector Rondon 1.25 3.00
225 Wade Davis 1.25 3.00
226 Logan Morrison 1.25 3.00
227 Byron Buxton 2.00 5.00
228 Mike Foltynewicz 1.25 3.00
229 David Ortiz LL 2.00 5.00
230 Northern (High)lights 2.00 5.00
Josh Donaldson/Troy Tulowitzki
231 Rubby De La Rosa 1.25 3.00
232 Geovany Soto 1.25 3.00
233 Nomar Mazara 1.25 3.00
234 Luke Weaver 1.50 4.00
235 San Francisco Giants 1.25 3.00
236 Lucas Duda UER 1.50 4.00
Eric Campbell pictured
237 Joey Gallo 1.50 4.00
238 Ben Zobrist 1.50 4.00
239 Rajai Davis 1.25 3.00
240 Mike Aviles 1.25 3.00
241 Chris Young 1.25 3.00
242 Mookie Betts LL 4.00 10.00
243 Felix Hernandez 1.50 4.00
244 Freddie Freeman 2.50 6.00
245 Jackie Bradley Jr. 2.00 5.00
246 Hunter Strickland 1.25 3.00
247 Hector Neris 1.25 3.00
248 Yasmany Tomas 1.25 3.00
249 New York Yankees 1.25 3.00
250 Sean Rodriguez 1.25 3.00
251 Justin Turner 2.00 5.00
252 Clint Robinson 1.25 3.00
253 Tucker Barnhart 1.25 3.00
254 Wade LeBlanc 1.25 3.00
255 Orlando Arcia 2.00 5.00
256 Tony Watson 1.25 3.00
257 Corey Kluber LL 1.50 4.00
258 Matt Adams 1.25 3.00
259 Taijuan Walker 1.25 3.00
260 Stephen Piscotty 1.50 4.00
261 Nathan Eovaldi 1.50 4.00
262 Liam Hendriks 1.25 3.00
263 Addison Russell 2.00 5.00
264 Cory Spangenberg 1.25 3.00
265 Charlie Blackmon 2.00 5.00
266 Tampa Bay Rays 1.25 3.00
267 Clay Buchholz 1.25 3.00
268 Anthony Gose 1.25 3.00
269 Jose De Leon 1.25 3.00
270 Jake Arrieta LL 1.50 4.00
271 Nelson Cruz LL 2.00 5.00
272 Pat Neshek 1.25 3.00
273 A.J. Reed 1.25 3.00
274 Matt Strahm 1.25 3.00
275 Dallas Keuchel 1.50 4.00
276 Big Fish 2.50 6.00
Marcell Ozuna/Giancarlo Stanton/Christian Yelich
277 Kris Bryant LL 2.50 6.00
278 Julio Teheran 1.50 4.00
279 Leonys Martin 1.25 3.00
280 Adrian Beltre 2.00 5.00
281 Coco Crisp 1.25 3.00
282 Tyler Flowers 1.25 3.00
283 Andrew Benintendi 20.00 50.00
284 Elvis Andrus 1.50 4.00
285 Tyler White 1.25 3.00
286 Drew Pomeranz 1.50 4.00
287 Aaron Judge 125.00 300.00
288 Joey Votto 2.00 5.00
289 Brian Goodwin 1.25 3.00
290 Shin-Soo Choo 1.50 4.00
291 Khris Davis LL 2.00 5.00
292 Fernando Rodney 1.25 3.00
293 Aledmys Diaz 1.50 4.00
294 Kole Calhoun 1.25 3.00
295 Matt Kemp LL 1.50 4.00
296 Tyler Clippard 1.25 3.00
297 Anthony DeSclafani 1.25 3.00
298 New Blake Street Bombers 3.00 8.00
Trevor Story/Nolan Arenado
299 Yulieski Gurriel 2.00 5.00
300 Arodys Vizcaino 1.25 3.00
301 Jeurys Familia 1.50 4.00
302 David Freese 1.25 3.00
303 Pedro Strop 1.25 3.00
304 Minnesota Twins 1.25 3.00
305 Tyler Duffey 1.25 3.00
306 David Dahl 1.50 4.00
307 Zach Duke 1.25 3.00
308 Yovani Gallardo 1.25 3.00
309 Craig Kimbrel 1.50 4.00
310 Scott Schebler 1.50 4.00
311 Tyler Chatwood 1.25 3.00
312 Brandon Guyer 1.25 3.00
313 Robbie Grossman 1.25 3.00
314 Ryan Flaherty 1.25 3.00
315 Carlos Beltran 1.50 4.00
316 Justin Smoak 1.25 3.00
317 Mitch Moreland 1.25 3.00
318 Matt Carasiti 1.25 3.00
319 Seth Lugo 1.25 3.00
320 Arizona Diamondbacks 1.25 3.00
321 Dustin Pedroia LL 2.00 5.00
322 Albert Pujols LL 2.50 6.00
323 Jameson Taillon 1.50 4.00
324 Ben Revere 1.25 3.00
325 Chris Hatcher 1.25 3.00
326 Chris Archer 1.25 3.00
327 Danny Espinosa 1.25 3.00
328 Adam Lind 1.50 4.00
329 Josh Reddick 1.25 3.00
330 Doug Fister 1.25 3.00
331 Jake Lamb 1.50 4.00
332 Huston Street 1.25 3.00
333 Jarred Cosart 1.25 3.00
334 Drew Smyly 1.25 3.00
335 Jeff Hoffman 1.25 3.00
336 Hector Santiago 1.25 3.00
337 Scott Van Slyke 1.25 3.00
338 Alcides Escobar 1.50 4.00
339 Daniel Norris 1.25 3.00
340 Aaron Nola 1.50 4.00
341 Alex Bregman 60.00 150.00
342 Josh Tomlin 1.25 3.00
343 Mike Zunino 1.25 3.00
344 Jake Thompson 1.25 3.00
345 Kevin Gausman 2.00 5.00
346 Jonathan Lucroy 1.50 4.00
347 Brandon Belt 1.50 4.00
348 Jeremy Hellickson 1.25 3.00
349 Tyler Glasnow 5.00 12.00
350 David Ortiz 2.00 5.00
351 German Marquez 2.00 5.00
352 Cameron Rupp 1.25 3.00
353 Felipe Rivero 1.50 4.00
354 Nick Tropeano 1.25 3.00
355 Shelby Miller 1.50 4.00
356 Brad Miller 1.50 4.00
357 Kelvin Herrera 1.25 3.00
358 Brad Boxberger 1.25 3.00
359 Matt Carpenter 2.00 5.00
360 Jon Lester 1.50 4.00
361 Dylan Bundy 1.50 4.00
362 John Lackey 1.50 4.00
363 Yunel Escobar 1.25 3.00
364 Koda Glover 1.25 3.00
365 Jorge De La Rosa 1.25 3.00
366 Jayson Werth 1.50 4.00

367 Jurickson Profar 1.50 4.00
368 Jhonny Peralta 1.25 3.00
369 Mark Canha 1.25 3.00
370 St. Louis Cardinals 1.25 3.00
371 Chad Bettis 1.25 3.00
372 Ryan Schimpf 1.25 3.00
373 Yadier Molina 2.50 6.00
374 Jim Johnson 1.25 3.00
375 Yasiel Puig 2.00 5.00
376 Chase Anderson 1.25 3.00
377 Adam Rosales 1.25 3.00
378 They Got Hops! 2.00 5.00
Francisco Lindor/Tyler Naquin
379 Phil Hughes 1.25 3.00
380 Albert Pujols 2.50 6.00
381 Hunter Renfroe 1.50 4.00
382 Josh Harrison 1.25 3.00
383 Adam Frazier 1.25 3.00
384 Welington Castillo 1.25 3.00
385 DJ LeMahieu 2.00 5.00
386 Michael Lorenzen 1.25 3.00
387 Zack Godley 1.25 3.00
388 Yasmani Grandal 1.25 3.00
389 George Springer 1.50 4.00
390 Evan Longoria 1.50 4.00
391 Jonathan Schoop 1.25 3.00
392 Pablo Sandoval 1.50 4.00
393 Koji Uehara 1.25 3.00
394 Detroit Tigers 1.25 3.00
395 Drew Storen 1.25 3.00
396 J.T. Realmuto 2.00 5.00
397 Stephen Cardullo 1.25 3.00
398 Blake Treinen 2.00 5.00
399 Ender Inciarte 1.25 3.00
400 Nolan Arenado 3.00 8.00
401 Manny Margot 1.25 3.00
402 Logan Forsythe 1.25 3.00
403 John Axford 1.25 3.00
404 Joe Mauer 1.50 4.00
405 Max Kepler 1.50 4.00
406 Stephen Vogt 1.50 4.00
407 Eduardo Escobar 1.25 3.00
408 Michael Conforto 1.50 4.00
409 R.A. Dickey 1.50 4.00
410 Jarrett Parker 1.25 3.00
411 Maikel Franco 1.50 4.00
412 Chris Iannetta 1.25 3.00
413 Rob Segedin 1.25 3.00
414 Zack Cozart 1.25 3.00
415 Pat Valaika 1.50 4.00
416 Neil Walker 1.25 3.00
417 Darren O'Day 1.25 3.00
418 James McCann 1.50 4.00
419 Roberto Perez 1.25 3.00
420 Matt Wisler 1.25 3.00
421 Santiago Casilla 1.25 3.00
422 Andrew Miller 1.50 4.00
423 Sergio Romo 1.25 3.00
424 Derek Dietrich 1.50 4.00
425 Carlos Gonzalez 1.50 4.00
426 New York Mets 1.25 3.00
427 Carlos Gomez 1.25 3.00
428 Jay Bruce 1.50 4.00
429 Mark Melancon 1.25 3.00
430 Texas Rangers 1.25 3.00
431 Tommy Joseph 2.00 5.00
432 Lucas Giolito 1.50 4.00
433 Mitch Haniger 2.00 5.00
434 Tyler Saladino 1.25 3.00
435 Robbie Ray 1.25 3.00
436 Cody Allen 1.25 3.00
437 Trevor Rosenthal 1.25 3.00
438 Chris Carter 1.25 3.00
439 Salvador Perez 1.50 4.00
440 Eduardo Rodriguez 1.25 3.00
441 Jose Iglesias 1.50 4.00
442 Javier Baez 2.50 6.00
443 Dee Gordon 1.25 3.00
444 Andrew Heaney 1.25 3.00
445 Alex Gordon 1.50 4.00
446 Dexter Fowler 1.50 4.00
447 Scott Kazmir 1.25 3.00
448 Jose Martinez 2.00 5.00
449 Ian Kennedy 1.25 3.00
450 Justin Verlander 2.00 5.00
451 Jharel Cotton 1.25 3.00
452 Travis Shaw 1.25 3.00
453 Danny Santana 1.25 3.00
454 Andrew Toles 1.25 3.00
455 Mauricio Cabrera 1.25 3.00
456 Steve Cishek 1.25 3.00
457 Brett Gardner 1.50 4.00
458 Hernan Perez 1.25 3.00
459 Wil Myers 1.50 4.00
460 Alejandro De Aza 1.25 3.00
461 Bruce Maxwell 1.25 3.00
462 Rich Hill 1.25 3.00
463 Jeff Samardzija 1.25 3.00
464 Hisashi Iwakuma 1.50 4.00
465 CC Sabathia 1.50 4.00
466 David Robertson 1.25 3.00
467 Adam Ottavino 1.25 3.00
468 Kyle Hendricks 2.00 5.00
469 Francisco Liriano 1.25 3.00
470 Brandon Drury 1.25 3.00
471 Nick Franklin 1.25 3.00
472 Pittsburgh Pirates 1.25 3.00
473 Eugenio Suarez 1.50 4.00
474 Michael Pineda 1.25 3.00
475 Peter O'Brien 1.25 3.00
476 Matt Olson 6.00 15.00
477 Zach Davies 1.25 3.00
478 Rob Zastryzny 1.25 3.00
479 Ryan Madson 1.25 3.00
480 Jason Kipnis 1.50 4.00
481 Kansas City Royals 1.25 3.00
482 Didi Gregorius 1.50 4.00
483 Anthony Rendon 2.00 5.00
484 Yonder Alonso 1.25 3.00
485 Greg Bird 1.50 4.00
486 Aroldis Chapman 2.00 5.00
487 Jose Ramirez 1.50 4.00
488 Jake Odorizzi 1.25 3.00
489 Jarrod Dyson 1.25 3.00
490 Joc Pederson 1.50 4.00
491 Ryan Vogelsong 1.25 3.00
492 Avisail Garcia 1.50 4.00
493 Hunter Dozier 1.25 3.00
494 Tom Murphy 1.25 3.00
495 Adam Jones 1.50 4.00
496 Mike Fiers 1.25 3.00
497 Boston Red Sox 1.25 3.00
498 Roman Quinn 1.25 3.00
499 Danny Valencia 1.50 4.00
500 Anthony Rizzo 2.50 6.00
501 Ian Kinsler 1.50 4.00
502 Willson Contreras 2.00 5.00
503 Jesus Aguilar 3.00 8.00
504 Austin Hedges 1.25 3.00
505 Seung-Hwan Oh 2.50 6.00
506 Jose Peraza 1.50 4.00
507 Matt Garza 1.25 3.00
508 Hanley Ramirez 1.50 4.00
509 Miguel Rojas 1.25 3.00
510 Kelby Tomlinson 1.25 3.00
511 Devin Mesoraco 1.25 3.00
512 Mallex Smith 1.25 3.00
513 Tony Kemp 1.25 3.00
514 Jeremy Jeffress 1.25 3.00
515 Nick Castellanos 2.00 5.00
516 Tony Wolters 1.25 3.00
517 Kolten Wong 1.50 4.00
518 Christian Yelich 2.50 6.00
519 Dan Vogelbach 2.00 5.00
520 Andrelton Simmons 1.25 3.00
521 Brandon Phillips 1.25 3.00
522 Edwin Diaz 1.50 4.00
523 Carlos Martinez 1.50 4.00
524 James Loney 1.25 3.00
525 Curtis Granderson 1.50 4.00
526 Jake Marisnick 1.25 3.00
527 Gio Gonzalez 1.50 4.00
528 Jake Arrieta 1.50 4.00
529 J.J. Hardy 1.25 3.00
530 Jabari Blash 1.25 3.00
531 Nick Markakis 1.50 4.00
532 Eduardo Nunez 1.25 3.00
533 Trevor Bauer 2.50 6.00
534 Cody Asche 1.25 3.00
535 Lonnie Chisenhall 1.25 3.00
536 Trey Mancini 2.50 6.00
537 Gerardo Parra 1.25 3.00
538 Brad Ziegler 1.25 3.00
539 Amir Garrett 1.25 3.00
540 Billy Hamilton 1.50 4.00
541 Shawn Kelley 1.25 3.00
542 Trevor Plouffe 1.25 3.00
543 Brian Dozier 2.00 5.00
544 Luis Severino 1.50 4.00
545 Martin Perez 1.50 4.00
546 Addison Reed 1.25 3.00
547 Vince Velasquez 1.25 3.00
548 David Price 1.50 4.00
549 Miguel Gonzalez 1.25 3.00
550 Mikie Mahtook 1.25 3.00
551 Matt Duffy 1.25 3.00
552 Tom Koehler 1.25 3.00
553 T.J. Rivera 2.00 5.00
554 Jason Castro 1.25 3.00
555 Noah Syndergaard 1.50 4.00
556 Starlin Castro 1.25 3.00
557 Milwaukee Brewers 1.25 3.00
558 Oakland Athletics 1.25 3.00
559 Jason Motte 1.25 3.00
560 Zack Greinke 2.00 5.00
561 Ricky Nolasco 1.25 3.00
562 Nick Ahmed 1.25 3.00
563 Marwin Gonzalez 1.25 3.00
564 Washington Nationals 1.25 3.00
565 J.D. Martinez 2.00 5.00
566 Heart of Texas 1.50 4.00
Elvis Andrus/Rougned Odor
567 Devon Travis 1.25 3.00
568 Ryan Pressly 1.25 3.00
569 Jorge Alfaro 1.50 4.00
570 Josh Donaldson 1.50 4.00
571 J.C. Ramirez 1.25 3.00
572 Atlanta Braves 1.25 3.00
573 Bartolo Colon 1.25 3.00
574 Trayce Thompson 1.50 4.00
575 Chris Owings 1.25 3.00
576 Russell Martin 1.25 3.00
577 Chris Tillman 1.25 3.00
578 Jed Lowrie 1.25 3.00
579 Taylor Jungmann 1.25 3.00
580 Matt Holliday 2.00 5.00
581 Brock Holt 1.25 3.00
582 Julio Urias 2.00 5.00
583 Colorado Rockies 1.25 3.00
584 Tater Triumph 3.00 8.00
Jayson Werth/Bryce Harper
585 Collin McHugh 1.25 3.00
586 Aaron Sanchez 1.50 4.00
587 Gerrit Cole 2.00 5.00
588 Kirk Nieuwenhuis 1.25 3.00
589 Ian Desmond 1.25 3.00
590 Triplet of Twins 2.00 5.00
Miguel Sano/Byron Buxton/Eduardo Escobar
591 Matt Bush 1.50 4.00
592 Kendall Graveman 1.25 3.00
593 Jose Abreu 2.00 5.00
594 Justin Bour 1.50 4.00
595 Max Scherzer 2.00 5.00
596 Ken Giles 1.25 3.00
597 Kenta Maeda 1.50 4.00
598 Michael Taylor 1.25 3.00
599 Cincinnati Reds 1.25 3.00
600 Yoenis Cespedes 2.00 5.00
601 Khris Davis 2.00 5.00
602 Alex Dickerson 1.25 3.00
603 Eric Thames 1.50 4.00
604 Gavin Cecchini 1.25 3.00
605 Michael Brantley 1.50 4.00
606 Glen Perkins 1.25 3.00
607 Tyler Thornburg 1.25 3.00
608 Los Angeles Dodgers 1.25 3.00
609 Adalberto Mejia 1.25 3.00
610 Ryan Buchter 1.25 3.00
611 Victor Martinez 1.50 4.00
612 Odubel Herrera 1.50 4.00
613 Jonathan Broxton 1.25 3.00
614 Shawn O'Malley 1.25 3.00
615 John Jaso 1.25 3.00
616 Mark Trumbo 1.25 3.00
617 A.J. Pollock 1.25 3.00
618 Kenley Jansen 1.50 4.00
619 Brad Brach 1.25 3.00
620 Sam Dyson 1.25 3.00
621 Chase Headley 1.25 3.00
622 Steven Wright 1.25 3.00
623 Melvin Upton Jr. 1.50 4.00
624 Brandon Maurer 1.25 3.00
625 Ty Blach 1.25 3.00
626 Roberto Osuna 1.25 3.00
627 Zach Putnam 1.25 3.00
628 Domingo Santana 1.50 4.00
629 Jordy Mercer 1.25 3.00
630 Edwin Encarnacion 2.00 5.00
631 Zack Wheeler 1.50 4.00
632 Steven Matz 1.25 3.00
633 Hunter Pence 1.50 4.00
634 Danny Duffy 1.25 3.00
635 Michael Fulmer 1.25 3.00
636 Allegheny Armada 2.00 5.00
Andrew McCutchen/John Jaso
637 Ryan Rua 1.25 3.00
638 Luis Valbuena 1.25 3.00
639 Matt Kemp 1.50 4.00
640 Cole Hamels 1.50 4.00
641 Robinson Cano 1.50 4.00
642 Renato Nunez 2.50 6.00
643 Wei-Yin Chen 1.25 3.00
644 Jose Altuve 1.50 4.00
645 Trea Turner 1.50 4.00
646 Corey Knebel 1.25 3.00
647 Jose Reyes 1.50 4.00
648 Seattle Mariners 1.25 3.00
649 Manny Machado 2.00 5.00
650 Andrew McCutchen 2.00 5.00
651 Jose Lobaton 1.25 3.00
652 Kyle Seager 1.25 3.00
653 Cam Bedrosian 1.25 3.00
654 Chris Young 1.25 3.00
655 Garrett Richards 1.50 4.00
656 Todd Frazier 1.25 3.00
657 Kevin Quackenbush 1.25 3.00
658 James Paxton 1.50 4.00
659 Melky Cabrera 1.25 3.00
660 Jeanmar Gomez 1.25 3.00
661 Peter Bourjos 1.25 3.00
662 J.A. Happ 1.50 4.00
663 Ketel Marte 1.50 4.00
664 Blake Swihart 1.50 4.00
665 Yu Darvish 2.00 5.00
666 Rougned Odor 1.50 4.00
667 Alex Cobb 1.25 3.00
668 Jedd Gyorko 1.25 3.00
669 Corey Kluber 1.50 4.00
670 Martin Maldonado 1.25 3.00
671 Joe Ross 1.25 3.00
672 Luke Maile 1.25 3.00
673 Joe Panik 1.50 4.00
674 Martin Prado 1.25 3.00
675 Buster Posey 2.50 6.00
676 Eric Hosmer 1.50 4.00
677 Cheslor Cuthbert 1.25 3.00
678 Ervin Santana 1.25 3.00
679 Jung Ho Kang 1.25 3.00
680 Mike Pelfrey 1.25 3.00
681 Mike Napoli 1.25 3.00
682 James Shields 1.25 3.00
683 Mac Williamson 1.25 3.00
684 Jorge Polanco 1.50 4.00
685 Enrique Hernandez 2.00 5.00
686 Luis Sardinas 1.25 3.00
687 Tyler Collins 1.25 3.00
688 Mike Clevinger 1.50 4.00
689 Jason Vargas 1.25 3.00
690 Andres Blanco 1.25 3.00
691 Richard Bleier 1.25 3.00
692 Rob Refsnyder 1.25 3.00
693 Matt Cain 1.50 4.00
694 Matt Wieters 2.00 5.00
695 Jon Jay 1.25 3.00
696 Jeff Mathis 1.50 4.00
697 Christian Bethancourt 1.50 4.00
698 Tony Cingrani 1.50 4.00
699 Ichiro 2.50 6.00
700 Ryan Goins 1.25 3.00

2018 Topps Chrome Sapphire Edition

1 Aaron Judge 5.00 12.00
2 Clayton Kershaw LL 3.00 8.00
3 Dylan Bundy 1.50 4.00
4 Kevin Pillar 1.25 3.00
5 Chris Tillman 1.25 3.00
6 Dominic Smith 1.50 4.00
7 Clint Frazier 2.50 6.00
8 Detroit Tigers 1.25 3.00
9 Jon Gray 1.25 3.00
10 Francisco Lindor 2.00 5.00
11 Aaron Nola 1.50 4.00
12 Joey Gallo LL 1.50 4.00
13 Jay Bruce 1.50 4.00
14 Amir Garrett 1.25 3.00
15 Andrelton Simmons 1.25 3.00
16 Daniel Coulombe 2.00 5.00
17 Robbie Ray 1.25 3.00
18 Rafael Devers 125.00 300.00
19 Garrett Richards 1.50 4.00
20 Chris Sale 2.00 5.00
21 Harrison Bader 2.00 5.00
22 Edinson Volquez 1.25 3.00
23 Jordy Mercer 1.25 3.00
24 Martin Maldonado 1.25 3.00
25 Manny Machado 2.00 5.00
26 Cesar Hernandez 1.25 3.00
27 Josh Tomlin 1.25 3.00
28 Jayson Werth 1.50 4.00
29 Hunter Renfroe 1.50 4.00
30 Carlos Correa 2.00 5.00
31 Corey Kluber LL 1.50 4.00
32 Jose Iglesias 1.50 4.00
33 Dexter Fowler 1.50 4.00
34 Luis Severino LL 1.50 4.00
35 Logan Forsythe 1.25 3.00
36 Anthony Rendon 2.00 5.00
37 Corey Kluber LL 1.50 4.00
38 Danny Salazar 1.25 3.00
39 Alex Bregman WS HL 2.00 5.00
40 Carlos Santana 1.50 4.00
41 Daniel Norris 1.25 3.00
42 Cody Bellinger 40.00 100.00
43 Eduardo Rodriguez 1.25 3.00
44 Trea Turner 1.50 4.00
45 Giancarlo Stanton LL 2.00 5.00
46 Cam Bedrosian 1.25 3.00
47 Hunter Pence 1.50 4.00
48 Boston Red Sox 1.25 3.00
49 Ervin Santana 1.25 3.00
50 Anthony Rizzo 2.50 6.00
51 Michael Wacha 1.50 4.00
52 Brad Hand 1.25 3.00
53 Alex Avila 1.50 4.00
54 Chase Anderson 1.25 3.00
55 Raisel Iglesias 1.50 4.00
56 Rougned Odor 1.50 4.00
57 Scott Feldman 1.25 3.00
58 Ryan Zimmerman 1.50 4.00
59 Clayton Kershaw LL 3.00 8.00
60 Starling Marte 1.50 4.00
61 Keon Broxton 1.25 3.00
62 Austin Hays 2.00 5.00
63 Amed Rosario 1.50 4.00
64 Giancarlo Stanton LL 2.00 5.00
65 Alex Wood 1.25 3.00
66 Ian Kennedy 1.25 3.00
67 Aledmys Diaz 1.50 4.00
68 Billy Hamilton 1.50 4.00
69 Jed Lowrie 1.25 3.00
70 Johnny Cueto 1.50 4.00
71 Mike Foltynewicz 1.25 3.00
72 Cheslor Cuthbert 1.25 3.00
73 Miami Marlins 1.25 3.00
74 Roberto Osuna 1.25 3.00
75 Andrew Miller 1.50 4.00
76 Eduardo Nunez 1.25 3.00
77 Martin Prado 1.25 3.00
78 Carlos Carrasco LL 1.25 3.00
79 J.T. Realmuto 2.00 5.00
80 Dellin Betances 1.50 4.00
81 Adam Wainwright 1.50 4.00
82 Justin Smoak 1.25 3.00
83 Howie Kendrick 1.25 3.00
84 Todd Frazier 1.25 3.00
85 Antonio Senzatela 1.25 3.00
86 Eric Hosmer 1.50 4.00
87 Brandon Phillips 1.25 3.00
88 Michael Conforto 1.50 4.00
89 Yasiel Puig 2.00 5.00
90 Miguel Cabrera 2.00 5.00
91 Travis d'Arnaud 1.25 3.00
92 Charlie Blackmon LL 2.00 5.00
93 Jack Flaherty 5.00 12.00
94 Robbie Grossman 1.25 3.00
95 Tyler Mahle 1.50 4.00
96 David Dahl 1.25 3.00
97 Dinelson Lamet 1.25 3.00
98 Chicago White Sox 1.25 3.00
99 Greg Allen 1.25 3.00
100 Giancarlo Stanton 2.00 5.00
101 Avisail Garcia 1.50 4.00
102 Wil Myers 1.50 4.00
103 Christian Vazquez 1.50 4.00
104 Mitch Moreland 1.25 3.00
105 Daniel Murphy 1.50 4.00
106 Jharel Cotton 1.25 3.00
107 Jorge Polanco 1.50 4.00
108 Justin Turner LL 2.00 5.00
109 Starlin Castro 1.25 3.00
110 Carlos Gonzalez 1.50 4.00
111 Aaron Judge LL 5.00 12.00
112 Pat Valaika 1.25 3.00
113 Gio Gonzalez 1.50 4.00
114 Cody Bellinger LL 4.00 10.00
115 Zack Granite 1.25 3.00
116 Ariel Miranda 2.00 5.00
117 Kendrys Morales 1.25 3.00
118 Ian Happ 1.50 4.00
119 Los Angeles Angels 1.25 3.00
120 Carlos Carrasco 1.25 3.00
121 Rich Hill 1.25 3.00
122 Chris Owings 1.25 3.00
123 A.J. Ramos 1.25 3.00
124 Julio Urias 2.00 5.00
125 Yoenis Cespedes 2.00 5.00
126 A.Rizzo/B.Harper 3.00 8.00
127 Byron Buxton 2.00 5.00
128 Jake Marisnick 1.25 3.00
129 Chris Sale LL 2.00 5.00
130 Brian Dozier 1.50 4.00
131 Jonathan Schoop 1.25 3.00
132 Marcell Ozuna 2.00 5.00
133 Nomar Mazara 1.25 3.00
134 Lance Lynn 1.25 3.00
135 Atlanta Braves 1.25 3.00
136 Raudy Read 1.25 3.00
137 Michael Lorenzen 1.25 3.00
138 Luiz Gohara 1.25 3.00
139 Zach Davies LL 1.25 3.00
140 Mookie Betts 4.00 10.00
141 Brandon Drury 1.25 3.00
142 Adam Jones 1.50 4.00
143 James Paxton 1.50 4.00
144 Jean Segura 1.50 4.00
145 Michael Fulmer 1.25 3.00
146 Zack Greinke LL 2.00 5.00
147 Randal Grichuk 1.25 3.00
148 Richard Urena 1.25 3.00
149 John Jaso 1.25 3.00
150 Nolan Arenado 3.00 8.00
151 Ryan McMahon 3.00 8.00
152 Matt Barnes 1.25 3.00
153 Scooter Gennett 1.50 4.00
154 George Springer WS HL 1.50 4.00
155 Matt Joyce 1.25 3.00
156 Milwaukee Brewers 1.25 3.00
157 Ichiro 2.50 6.00
158 Stephen Piscotty 1.25 3.00
159 Joc Pederson 1.50 4.00
160 Masahiro Tanaka 1.50 4.00
161 Matt Moore 1.50 4.00
162 Matt Shoemaker 1.50 4.00
163 Mike Leake 1.25 3.00
164 Adeiny Hechavarria 1.25 3.00
165 Ty Blach 1.25 3.00
166 Victor Robles 3.00 8.00
167 Dansby Swanson 2.00 5.00
168 Ricky Nolasco 1.25 3.00
169 Khris Davis LL 2.00 5.00
170 Christian Yelich 2.50 6.00
171 John Lackey 1.50 4.00
172 Willson Contreras 2.00 5.00
173 Mike Moustakas 1.50 4.00
174 Jimmie Sherfy 1.25 3.00
175 Jose Quintana 1.25 3.00
176 Seattle Mariners 1.25 3.00
177 Walker Buehler 50.00 120.00
178 Matt Adams 1.25 3.00
179 Brandon Woodruff 4.00 10.00
180 Ryan Braun 1.50 4.00
181 Garrett Cooper 1.25 3.00
182 Alex Bregman 2.00 5.00
183 Matt Kemp 1.50 4.00
184 Mike Fiers 1.25 3.00
185 Chance Sisco 1.50 4.00
186 Luis Perdomo 1.25 3.00
187 Chad Kuhl 1.25 3.00
188 Matt Harvey 1.50 4.00
189 Jedd Gyorko 1.25 3.00
190 Justin Upton 1.50 4.00
191 Chris Archer 1.25 3.00
192 Nolan Arenado LL 3.00 8.00
193 Aaron Judge LL 5.00 12.00
194 Lonnie Chisenhall 1.25 3.00
195 Avisail Garcia LL 1.50 4.00
196 Orlando Arcia 1.25 3.00
197 Maikel Franco 1.50 4.00
198 Marcus Semien 2.00 5.00
199 Shin-Soo Choo 1.50 4.00
200 Andrew McCutchen 2.00 5.00
201 Gregory Polanco 1.50 4.00
202 Brett Phillips 1.25 3.00
203 Odubel Herrera 1.50 4.00
204 Brett Gardner 1.50 4.00
205 Seattle Slayers 1.50 4.00
Robinson Cano/Kyle Seager
206 Nick Markakis 1.50 4.00
207 Jackson Stephens 1.25 3.00
208 Andrew Cashner 1.25 3.00
209 Eugenio Suarez 1.50 4.00
210 Brandon Belt 1.50 4.00
211 Betts/Bradley/Benintendi 4.00 10.00
212 Lance McCullers WS HL 1.25 3.00
213 J.A. Happ 1.50 4.00
214 Corey Knebel 1.25 3.00
215 Marwin Gonzalez 1.25 3.00
216 A.J. Pollock 1.25 3.00
217 Erick Fedde 1.25 3.00
218 Khris Davis LL 2.00 5.00
219 J.P. Crawford 1.25 3.00
220 Nelson Cruz 2.00 5.00
221 Steven Matz 1.25 3.00
222 Ivan Nova 1.50 4.00
223 Evan Longoria 1.50 4.00
224 Dillon Peters 1.25 3.00
225 Kyle Schwarber 2.00 5.00
226 Nick Williams 1.50 4.00
227 Corey Dickerson 1.25 3.00
228 Zack Wheeler 1.50 4.00
229 Texas Rangers 1.25 3.00
230 Trevor Story 2.00 5.00
231 Joe Mauer 1.50 4.00
232 Nate Jones 1.25 3.00
233 Stephen Strasburg 2.00 5.00
234 Brian Anderson 1.50 4.00
235 Mark Reynolds 1.25 3.00
236 CC Sabathia 1.50 4.00
237 Mike Clevinger 1.50 4.00
238 Jose Bautista 1.50 4.00
239 Cleveland Indians 1.25 3.00
240 Robinson Cano 1.50 4.00
241 Nick Pivetta 1.25 3.00
242 Craig Kimbrel 1.50 4.00
243 James McCann 1.50 4.00
244 Francisco Mejia 1.50 4.00
245 Willie Calhoun 2.00 5.00
246 Yangervis Solarte 1.25 3.00
247 Anthony Banda 1.25 3.00
248 Jake Lamb 1.50 4.00
249 Christian Arroyo 1.25 3.00
250 Buster Posey 2.50 6.00
251 Aaron Sanchez 1.50 4.00
252 Tim Anderson 2.00 5.00
253 Nelson Cruz LL 2.00 5.00
254 Adrian Beltre 2.00 5.00
255 Zach Davies 1.25 3.00
256 Eric Hosmer LL 1.50 4.00
257 J.D. Martinez 2.00 5.00
258 Tyler Saladino 1.25 3.00
259 Rhys Hoskins 30.00 80.00
260 Rick Porcello 1.50 4.00
261 Andrew Stevenson 1.25 3.00
262 Potent Pair 1.50 4.00
Eric Hosmer/Miguel Sano
263 Chase Utley 1.50 4.00
264 Carlos Rodon 2.00 5.00
265 Javier Baez 2.50 6.00
266 Jon Lester 1.50 4.00
267 Yoan Moncada 2.00 5.00
268 Neil Walker 1.25 3.00
269 Greg Holland 1.25 3.00
270 Jackie Bradley Jr. 2.00 5.00
271 Cam Gallagher 1.25 3.00
272 Paul Blackburn 1.25 3.00
273 Charlie Blackmon LL 2.00 5.00
274 Jeff Samardzija 1.25 3.00
275 George Springer 1.50 4.00
276 Ozzie Albies 40.00 100.00
277 Aaron Slegers 2.00 5.00
278 Lucas Sims 1.25 3.00
279 Jordan Zimmermann 1.50 4.00
280 Jose Abreu 2.00 5.00
281 Alex Verdugo 2.00 5.00
282 Ender Inciarte 1.25 3.00
283 Koji Uehara 1.25 3.00
284 Jose Pirela 1.25 3.00
285 Trey Mancini 1.50 4.00
286 New York Yankees 1.25 3.00
287 Mark Trumbo 1.25 3.00
288 Miguel Sano 1.50 4.00
289 Jonathan Villar 1.25 3.00
290 Salvador Perez 1.50 4.00
291 Marcell Ozuna LL 2.00 5.00
292 Baltimore Orioles 1.25 3.00
293 Felipe Rivero 1.50 4.00
294 Jose Altuve LL 1.50 4.00
295 Zack Godley 1.25 3.00
296 Lewis Brinson 1.25 3.00
297 Kevin Kiermaier 1.50 4.00
298 All Smiles 1.50 4.00
Yulieski Gurriel/Jake Marisnick
299 Luis Santos 2.00 5.00
300 Mike Trout 75.00 200.00
301 Brandon Finnegan 1.25 3.00
302 Troy Tulowitzki 2.00 5.00
303 Luis Severino 1.50 4.00
304 Whit Merrifield 2.00 5.00
305 Miguel Andujar 10.00 25.00
306 Nicky Delmonico 1.25 3.00
307 Daniel Murphy LL 1.50 4.00
308 Cameron Rupp 1.25 3.00
309 Josh Reddick 1.25 3.00
310 Jason Kipnis 1.50 4.00
311 Yulieski Gurriel 1.50 4.00
312 Carlos Asuaje 1.25 3.00
313 Raimel Tapia 1.25 3.00
314 Colorado Rockies 1.25 3.00
315 Chris Rowley 2.00 5.00
316 Max Fried 5.00 12.00
317 Chase Headley 1.25 3.00
318 Danny Duffy 1.25 3.00
319 David Peralta 1.25 3.00
320 Yasmani Grandal 1.25 3.00
321 Edwin Diaz 1.50 4.00
322 Parker Bridwell 1.25 3.00
323 Elvis Andrus 1.50 4.00
324 Jake Odorizzi 1.25 3.00
325 Khris Davis 2.00 5.00
326 Joey Gallo 1.50 4.00
327 Jason Vargas LL 1.25 3.00
328 Tyler Flowers 1.25 3.00
329 George Springer WS HL 1.50 4.00
330 Ian Kinsler 1.50 4.00
331 Zack Cozart 1.25 3.00
332 Alex Colome 1.25 3.00
333 Joe Musgrove 2.00 5.00
334 Eddie Rosario 1.50 4.00
335 Stephen Strasburg LL 2.00 5.00
336 Bruce Maxwell 1.25 3.00
337 Nick Ahmed 1.25 3.00
338 Brandon McCarthy 1.25 3.00
339 Philadelphia Phillies 1.25 3.00
340 Gary Sanchez 2.00 5.00
341 J.D. Davis 1.50 4.00
342 Sean Manaea 1.25 3.00
343 Kevin Gausman 2.00 5.00
344 Wilmer Flores 1.50 4.00
345 Jose Reyes 1.50 4.00
346 Max Scherzer LL 2.00 5.00
347 Kolten Wong 1.50 4.00
348 Hisashi Iwakuma 1.50 4.00
349 Washington Nationals 1.25 3.00
350 Clayton Kershaw 3.00 8.00
351 Bryce Harper 3.00 8.00
352 Cincinnati Reds 1.25 3.00
353 Yan Gomes 2.00 5.00
354 Robert Stephenson 1.25 3.00
355 Joe Ross 1.25 3.00
356 Jeff Hoffman 1.25 3.00
357 Josh Hader 1.50 4.00
358 Brad Brach 1.25 3.00
359 Wade Miley 1.25 3.00
360 Taijuan Walker 1.25 3.00
361 C.Correa/J.Altuve 2.00 5.00
362 Miguel Rojas 1.25 3.00
363 Bryan Shaw 1.25 3.00
364 Y.Puig/C.Bellinger 4.00 10.00
365 Mallex Smith 1.25 3.00
366 Tyler Glasnow FS 2.00 5.00
367 Liam Hendriks 1.25 3.00
368 Matt Strahm 1.25 3.00
369 Chris Taylor 1.50 4.00
370 Steven Wright 1.25 3.00
371 Cole Hamels 1.50 4.00
372 Nick Tropeano 1.25 3.00
373 Jorge Bonifacio 1.25 3.00
374 Bradley Zimmer FS 1.25 3.00
375 Evan Gattis 1.25 3.00
376 Kyle McGrath 1.25 3.00
377 Domingo Santana 1.50 4.00
378 Aaron Wilkerson 1.25 3.00
379 Ryan Zimmerman 1.50 4.00
Jayson Werth/Power Up
380 Kelby Tomlinson 1.25 3.00
381 Kole Calhoun 1.25 3.00
382 Brandon Guyer 1.25 3.00
383 JaCoby Jones 1.25 3.00
384 Addison Russell 1.50 4.00
385 Jason Hammel 1.25 3.00
386 James Shields 1.25 3.00
387 Julio Teheran 1.50 4.00
388 Taylor Motter 1.25 3.00
389 G.Stanton/A.Judge 5.00 12.00
390 Jesse Chavez 1.25 3.00
391 Ben Zobrist 1.50 4.00
392 Marcus Stroman 1.50 4.00
393 Corey Kluber 1.50 4.00
394 Chad Pinder 1.25 3.00
395 Martin Perez 1.50 4.00
396 Matt Olson 2.00 5.00
397 Dallas Keuchel 1.50 4.00
398 Sam Dyson 1.25 3.00
399 Chicago Cubs 1.25 3.00
400 Jose Altuve 1.50 4.00
401 Michael Brantley 1.50 4.00
402 Adam Warren 1.25 3.00
403 Luis Torrens 2.00 5.00
404 Alex Claudio 1.25 3.00
405 T.J. Rivera 1.25 3.00
406 Kelvin Herrera 1.25 3.00
407 Pat Neshek 1.25 3.00
408 Mikie Mahtook 1.25 3.00
409 Scott Kingery 2.00 5.00
410 Felix Jorge 1.25 3.00
411 David Price 1.50 4.00
412 Mike Minor 1.25 3.00
413 Trevor Bauer 2.50 6.00
414 Danny Valencia 1.50 4.00
415 Jace Peterson 1.25 3.00
416 Derek Fisher FS 1.25 3.00
417 Yolmer Sanchez 1.25 3.00
418 Jose Ramirez 1.50 4.00
419 Fernando Rodney 1.25 3.00
420 Alex Cobb 1.25 3.00
421 Lorenzo Cain 1.25 3.00
422 Victor Caratini 1.50 4.00
423 Houston Astros 1.25 3.00
424 Matt Wieters 2.00 5.00
425 Shelby Miller 1.50 4.00
426 Jacob Faria 1.25 3.00
427 Jordan Montgomery 1.25 3.00
428 Jakob Junis 1.25 3.00
429 Victor Martinez 1.50 4.00
430 Manny Margot FS 1.25 3.00
431 Charlie Blackmon 2.00 5.00
432 Albert Almora 1.50 4.00
433 Anthony Santander 1.25 3.00
434 Miguel Montero 1.25 3.00
435 Matt Holliday 2.00 5.00
436 Yu Darvish 2.00 5.00
437 J.J. Hardy 1.25 3.00
438 Stephen Vogt 1.50 4.00
439 Dustin Pedroia 2.00 5.00
440 Troy Scribner 1.25 3.00
441 Danny Santana 1.25 3.00
442 Jesus Aguilar 1.50 4.00
443 Gerrit Cole 2.00 5.00
444 Aaron Altherr 1.25 3.00
445 Trevor Cahill 1.25 3.00
446 Lucas Duda 1.50 4.00
447 Carlos Gomez 1.25 3.00
448 Max Kepler 1.50 4.00
449 DJ LeMahieu 2.00 5.00
450 Joey Votto 2.00 5.00
451 Ubaldo Jimenez 1.25 3.00
452 Tucker Barnhart 1.25 3.00
453 Devon Travis 1.25 3.00
454 Kyle Seager 1.25 3.00
455 Hernan Perez 1.25 3.00
456 Jimmy Nelson 1.25 3.00
457 Hanley Ramirez 1.50 4.00
458 Yovani Gallardo 1.25 3.00
459 Breyvic Valera 1.25 3.00
460 Robert Gsellman 1.25 3.00
461 Michael Taylor 1.25 3.00
462 Paul DeJong FS 2.00 5.00
463 Cory Spangenberg 1.25 3.00
464 Travis Jankowski 1.25 3.00
465 San Diego Padres 1.25 3.00
466 Tim Locastro 1.25 3.00
467 Carlos Ramirez 1.25 3.00
468 Tampa Bay Rays 1.25 3.00
469 Sonny Gray 1.50 4.00
470 Alex Mejia 1.25 3.00
471 Josh Harrison 1.25 3.00
472 Matt Garza 1.25 3.00
473 Wilmer Difo 1.25 3.00
474 Jeff Mathis 1.50 4.00
475 Aroldis Chapman 2.00 5.00
476 Wilson Ramos 1.25 3.00
477 Logan Morrison 1.25 3.00
478 Brad Miller 1.50 4.00
479 Daniel Descalso 1.25 3.00
480 Aaron Hicks 1.50 4.00
481 Ronald Torreyes 1.25 3.00
482 Delino DeShields 1.25 3.00
483 Drew Pomeranz 1.25 3.00
484 Kenta Maeda 1.50 4.00
485 Kyle Farmer 1.25 3.00
486 Tomas Nido 1.25 3.00
487 Carl Edwards Jr. 1.25 3.00
488 Joe Panik 1.50 4.00
489 Blake Snell 1.50 4.00
490 Jarrod Dyson 1.25 3.00
491 Andrew Heaney 1.25 3.00
492 Jon Jay 1.25 3.00
493 Kyle Gibson 1.50 4.00
494 Adalberto Mejia 1.25 3.00
495 Aaron Bummer 1.25 3.00
496 Leury Garcia 1.25 3.00
497 Chasen Shreve 1.25 3.00
498 Jen-Ho Tseng 1.25 3.00
499 Justin Bour 1.25 3.00
500 Kris Bryant 2.50 6.00
501 Clayton Richard 1.25 3.00
502 Xander Bogaerts 2.00 5.00
503 Josh Donaldson 1.50 4.00
504 Scott Schebler 1.50 4.00
505 Taylor Williams 1.50 4.00
506 Jose Berrios 1.50 4.00
507 Zack Greinke 2.00 5.00
508 Ryon Healy 1.25 3.00
509 Santiago Casilla 1.25 3.00
510 Freddie Freeman 2.50 6.00
511 Wade Davis 1.25 3.00
512 Mike Napoli 1.25 3.00
513 Mike Zunino 1.25 3.00
514 A.J. Minter 1.50 4.00
515 Greg Bird 1.50 4.00
516 Ken Giles 1.25 3.00
517 Phillip Evans 1.25 3.00
518 Andrew Toles 1.25 3.00
519 Reyes Moronta 1.25 3.00
520 Jim Johnson 1.25 3.00
521 Jose Osuna 1.25 3.00
522 Guillermo Heredia 1.25 3.00
523 Matt Bush 1.25 3.00
524 Steve Pearce 2.00 5.00
525 Johan Camargo 1.50 4.00
526 Tanner Roark 1.25 3.00
527 Francisco Cervelli 1.25 3.00
528 Marco Estrada 1.25 3.00
529 K.Bryant/K.Schwarber 2.50 6.00
530 Jason Vargas 1.25 3.00
531 Chris O'Grady 1.25 3.00
532 Tim Beckham 1.50 4.00
533 Kennys Vargas 1.25 3.00
534 German Marquez 1.25 3.00
535 Jhoulys Chacin 1.25 3.00
536 San Francisco Giants 1.25 3.00
537 Phil Hughes 1.25 3.00
538 Jason Castro 1.25 3.00
539 Lance McCullers 1.50 4.00
540 Mitch Garver 1.25 3.00
541 Dwight Smith Jr. 1.50 4.00
542 Pittsburgh Pirates 1.25 3.00
543 Luis Castillo 1.50 4.00
544 Yadier Molina 2.50 6.00
545 Nicholas Castellanos 2.00 5.00
546 Jordan Luplow 1.50 4.00
547 Travis Wood 1.25 3.00
548 Alex Meyer 1.25 3.00
549 Alex Gordon 1.50 4.00
550 Corey Seager 2.00 5.00
551 Yacksel Rios 1.25 3.00

552 Kyle Hendricks 2.00 5.00
553 Denard Span 1.25 3.00
554 Yonder Alonso 1.25 3.00
555 Jacob deGrom 4.00 10.00
556 Andrew Benintendi FS 2.00 5.00
557 Jacoby Ellsbury 1.50 4.00
558 Ben Gamel 1.50 4.00
559 Ian Desmond 1.25 3.00
560 Mark Melancon 1.25 3.00
561 Dan Straily 1.25 3.00
562 Brian McCann 1.50 4.00
563 Hector Neris 1.25 3.00
564 Joey Rickard 1.25 3.00
564 New York Mets 1.25 3.00
566 Yasmany Tomas 1.25 3.00
567 Felix Hernandez 1.50 4.00
568 J.C. Ramirez 1.25 3.00
569 Keone Kela 1.25 3.00
570 Trevor Williams 1.25 3.00
571 C.J. Cron 1.25 3.00
572 Dillon Maples 1.25 3.00
573 Mark Leiter Jr. 1.50 4.00
574 Jared Hughes 1.25 3.00
575 Adrian Gonzalez 1.50 4.00
576 Didi Gregorius 1.50 4.00
577 Yunel Escobar 1.25 3.00
578 Melky Cabrera 1.25 3.00
579 Carson Fulmer 1.25 3.00
580 Oakland Athletics 1.25 3.00
581 Jesse Winker 2.00 5.00
582 Albert Pujols 2.50 6.00
583 Tommy Joseph 2.00 5.00
584 Toronto Blue Jays 1.25 3.00
585 Brandon Crawford 1.50 4.00
586 Kyle Freeland 1.50 4.00
587 Chris Davis 1.25 3.00
588 David Wright 1.50 4.00
589 Adam Duvall 1.50 4.00
590 Dee Gordon 1.25 3.00
591 Daniel Nava 1.25 3.00
592 Gorkys Hernandez 1.25 3.00
593 Luke Weaver FS 1.50 4.00
594 Sandy Alcantara 1.25 3.00
595 Addison Reed 1.25 3.00
596 Keury Mella 1.25 3.00
597 Caleb Joseph 1.25 3.00
598 David Robertson 1.25 3.00
599 Justin Turner 2.00 5.00
600 Noah Syndergaard 1.50 4.00
601 Jose Peraza 1.50 4.00
602 Michael Pineda 1.25 3.00
603 Zach Britton 1.25 3.00
604 Gerardo Parra 1.25 3.00
605 Lucas Giolito 1.50 4.00
606 Jake Arrieta 1.50 4.00
607 Sean Newcomb FS 1.50 4.00
608 Kurt Suzuki 1.25 3.00
609 Austin Hedges 1.25 3.00
610 Scott Kazmir 1.25 3.00
611 Josh Bell FS 1.50 4.00
612 Steven Souza Jr. 1.50 4.00
613 Cory Gearrin 1.25 3.00
614 Minnesota Twins 1.25 3.00
615 Eric Thames 1.50 4.00
616 Greg Garcia 1.25 3.00
617 Doug Fister 1.25 3.00
618 Paul Goldschmidt 2.00 5.00
619 Jeremy Hellickson 1.25 3.00
620 Chris Young 1.25 3.00
621 Jerad Eickhoff 1.25 3.00
622 Ryan Rua 1.25 3.00
623 Josh Fields 1.25 3.00
624 Franklin Barreto 1.25 3.00
625 Los Angeles Dodgers 1.25 3.00
626 Brandon Maurer 1.25 3.00
627 Matthew Boyd 1.25 3.00
628 Vince Velasquez 1.25 3.00
629 Max Scherzer 2.00 5.00
630 Alcides Escobar 1.50 4.00
631 David Freese 1.25 3.00
632 Edwin Encarnacion 2.00 5.00
633 Jameson Taillon 1.50 4.00
634 Carlos Martinez 1.50 4.00
635 Cody Allen 1.25 3.00
636 Freddy Galvis 1.25 3.00
637 Manny Pina 1.25 3.00
638 Travis Shaw 1.25 3.00
639 Niko Goodrum 2.00 5.00
640 Seth Lugo 1.25 3.00
641 Cameron Maybin 1.25 3.00
642 Ben Revere 1.25 3.00
643 Justin Wilson 1.25 3.00
644 Carlos Perez 1.25 3.00
645 Welington Castillo 1.25 3.00
646 Jose de Leon 1.25 3.00
647 Jose Urena 1.25 3.00
648 Derek Holland 1.25 3.00
649 Curtis Granderson 1.50 4.00
650 Justin Verlander 2.00 5.00
651 JT Riddle 1.25 3.00
652 Matt Carpenter 2.00 5.00
653 Jorge Soler 2.00 5.00
654 Trayce Thompson 1.50 4.00
655 Andre Ethier 1.50 4.00
656 Brian Goodwin 1.25 3.00
657 Derek Dietrich 1.50 4.00
658 Tom Koehler 1.25 3.00
659 Arizona Diamondbacks 1.25 3.00
660 Mitch Haniger FS 1.50 4.00
661 Christian Villanueva 1.25 3.00
662 Patrick Corbin 1.50 4.00
663 Seth Smith 1.25 3.00
664 Gregor Blanco 1.25 3.00
665 Tommy Pham 1.25 3.00
666 Eric Sogard 1.25 3.00
667 Jonathan Lucroy 1.50 4.00
668 Tyler Anderson 1.25 3.00
669 Matt Chapman 2.00 5.00
670 Asdrubal Cabrera 1.50 4.00
671 Tyler Clippard 1.25 3.00
672 Brandon Nimmo 1.50 4.00
673 Adam Frazier 1.25 3.00
674 Jose Martinez 1.25 3.00
675 Victor Arano 1.25 3.00
676 Chad Green 1.25 3.00
677 Brandon Moss 1.25 3.00
678 Chad Bettis 1.25 3.00
679 Tyson Ross 1.25 3.00
680 Enrique Hernandez 2.00 5.00
681 Ehire Adrianza 1.25 3.00
682 Kansas City Royals 1.25 3.00
683 Adam Eaton 2.00 5.00
684 Hunter Strickland 1.25 3.00
685 Russell Martin 1.25 3.00
686 Bud Norris 1.25 3.00
687 Blake Treinen 1.25 3.00
688 Tony Wolters 1.25 3.00
689 Jeurys Familia 1.50 4.00
690 St. Louis Cardinals 1.25 3.00
691 Jason Heyward 1.50 4.00
692 Tony Watson 1.25 3.00
693 Brandon Kintzler 1.25 3.00
694 Anthony DeSclafani 1.25 3.00
695 Matt Davidson 1.50 4.00
696 Kenley Jansen 1.50 4.00
697 Eduardo Escobar 1.25 3.00
698 Ryan Sherriff 1.25 3.00
699 Drew Smyly 1.25 3.00
700 Shohei Ohtani 200.00 500.00

2018 Topps Chrome Sapphire Edition Photo Variations

698 Ronald Acuna Jr. 1500.00 2500.00
699 Gleyber Torres 20.00 50.00

2018 Topps Chrome Sapphire Edition Autographs

OVERALL AUTO ODDS THREE PER BOX
EXCHANGE DEADLINE 9/30/2020
ACAV Alex Verdugo 10.00 25.00
ACCF Clint Frazier 10.00 25.00
ACDF Dustin Fowler 3.00 8.00
ACFM Francisco Mejia 10.00 25.00
ACGT Gleyber Torres EXCH 250.00 600.00
ACHB Harrison Bader 5.00 12.00
ACJF Jack Flaherty 12.00 30.00
ACMA Miguel Andujar 40.00 100.00
ACND Nicky Delmonico 3.00 8.00
ACOA Ozzie Albies 75.00 200.00
ACRA Ronald Acuna 300.00 600.00
ACRD Rafael Devers 100.00 250.00
ACRM Ryan McMahon 8.00 20.00
ACSA Sandy Alcantara 3.00 8.00
ACSO Shohei Ohtani 300.00 600.00
ACVR Victor Robles 40.00 100.00

2018 Topps Chrome Sapphire Edition Autographs Green

*GREEN: .75X TO 2X BASIC
OVERALL AUTO ODDS THREE PER BOX
STATED PRINT RUN 50 SER.#'d SETS
EXCHANGE DEADLINE 9/30/2020
ACDS Dominic Smith 8.00 20.00
ACJC J.P. Crawford 10.00 25.00
ACRH Rhys Hoskins 50.00 120.00

2018 Topps Chrome Sapphire Edition Autographs Orange

*ORANGE: 1.2X TO 3X BASIC
OVERALL AUTO ODDS THREE PER BOX
STATED PRINT RUN 25 SER.#'d SETS
EXCHANGE DEADLINE 9/30/2020
ACDS Dominic Smith 12.00 30.00
ACJC J.P. Crawford 15.00 40.00
ACRH Rhys Hoskins 75.00 200.00
ACSO Shohei Ohtani 800.00 1200.00

2019 Topps Chrome Sapphire

1 Ronald Acuna Jr. 40.00 100.00
2 Tyler Anderson 1.25 3.00
3 Eduardo Nunez 1.25 3.00
4 Dereck Rodriguez 1.25 3.00
5 Chase Anderson 1.25 3.00
6 Max Scherzer 2.00 5.00
7 Gleyber Torres 8.00 20.00
8 Adam Jones 1.50 4.00
9 Ben Zobrist 1.50 4.00
10 Clayton Kershaw 3.00 8.00
11 Mike Zunino 1.25 3.00
12 Rizzo/Perez 2.50 6.00
13 David Price 1.50 4.00
14 Judge/Gregorius 3.00 8.00
15 J.P. Crawford 1.25 3.00
16 Charlie Blackmon 2.00 5.00
17 Caleb Joseph 1.25 3.00
18 Blake Parker 1.25 3.00
19 Jacob deGrom 4.00 10.00
20 Jose Urena 1.25 3.00
21 Jean Segura 2.00 5.00
22 Adalberto Mondesi 1.50 4.00
23 J.D. Martinez 2.00 5.00
24 Blake Snell 1.50 4.00
25 Chad Green 1.25 3.00
26 Angel Stadium 1.25 3.00
27 Mike Leake 1.25 3.00
28 Betts/Benintendi 4.00 10.00
29 Eugenio Suarez 1.50 4.00
30 Josh Hader 1.50 4.00
31 Busch Stadium 1.25 3.00
32 Carlos Correa 2.00 5.00
33 Jacob Nix RC 1.50 4.00
34 Josh Donaldson 1.50 4.00
35 Joey Rickard 1.25 3.00
36 Paul Blackburn 1.25 3.00
37 Marcus Stroman 1.50 4.00
38 Kolby Allard RC 2.00 5.00
39 Richard Urena 1.25 3.00
40 Jon Lester 1.50 4.00
41 Corey Seager 2.00 5.00
42 Edwin Encarnacion 2.00 5.00
43 Nick Burdi RC 1.25 3.00
44 Jay Bruce 1.50 4.00
45 Nick Pivetta 1.25 3.00
46 Jose Abreu 2.00 5.00
47 Yankee Stadium 1.25 3.00
48 PNC Park 1.25 3.00
49 Michael Kopech RC 20.00 50.00
50 Mookie Betts 4.00 10.00
51 Michael Brantley 1.50 4.00
52 J.T. Realmuto 2.00 5.00
53 Brandon Crawford 1.50 4.00
54 Rick Porcello 1.50 4.00
55 Yuli Gurriel 1.50 4.00
56 Christian Villanueva 1.25 3.00
57 Justin Verlander 2.00 5.00
58 Carlos Martinez 1.50 4.00
59 Zack Godley 1.25 3.00
60 Kyle Tucker RC 25.00 60.00
61 Touki Toussaint RC 1.50 4.00
62 Elvis Andrus 1.50 4.00
63 Jake Odorizzi 1.25 3.00
64 Ramon Laureano RC 15.00 40.00
65 Derek Dietrich 1.50 4.00
66 Stephen Piscotty 1.25 3.00
67 Danny Jansen RC 1.25 3.00
68 Nick Ahmed 1.25 3.00
69 Jorge Polanco 1.50 4.00
70 Nolan Arenado 3.00 8.00
71 SunTrust Park 1.25 3.00
72 Chris Taylor 1.50 4.00
73 Jon Gray 1.25 3.00
74 Chad Bettis 1.25 3.00
75 Safeco Field 1.25 3.00
76 J.D. Martinez 2.00 5.00
77 J.D. Martinez 2.00 5.00
78 Francisco Arcia RC 2.00 5.00
79 Miller Park 1.25 3.00
80 Tim Anderson 2.00 5.00
81 Wade Davis 1.25 3.00
82 Lourdes Gurriel Jr. 1.50 4.00
83 Lou Trivino 1.25 3.00
84 Matt Carpenter 2.00 5.00
85 Garrett Hampson RC 2.00 5.00
86 David Bote 1.50 4.00
87 Danny Duffy 1.25 3.00
88 Jonathan Villar 1.25 3.00
89 Corey Dickerson 1.25 3.00
90 Javier Baez 2.50 6.00
91 Hector Rondon 1.25 3.00
92 Clayton Richard 1.25 3.00
93 Matthew Boyd 1.25 3.00
94 Corbin Burnes RC 10.00 25.00
95 Dennis Santana RC 1.25 3.00
96 Trevor Williams 1.25 3.00
97 Harrison Bader 1.50 4.00
98 Chance Adams RC 1.25 3.00
99 Aroldis Chapman 2.00 5.00
100 Mike Trout 20.00 50.00
101 Michael Taylor 1.25 3.00
102 Shin-Soo Choo 1.50 4.00
103 Sean Manaea 1.25 3.00
104 Joe Musgrove 2.00 5.00
105 Jose Quintana 1.25 3.00
106 Adam Ottavino 1.25 3.00
107 Scooter Gennett 1.50 4.00
108 Ian Kennedy 1.25 3.00
109 Michael Conforto 1.50 4.00
110 Trevor Bauer 2.50 6.00
111 Reynaldo Lopez 1.50 4.00
112 Joey Gallo 1.50 4.00
113 Willie Calhoun 1.25 3.00
114 Brandon Lowe RC 5.00 12.00
115 Tyler Glasnow 2.00 5.00
116 Miguel Sano 1.50 4.00
117 Enrique Hernandez 2.00 5.00
118 Julio Teheran 1.50 4.00
119 Willson Contreras 1.50 4.00
120 Robert Gsellman 1.25 3.00
121 Joey Wendle 1.50 4.00
122 Zach Davies 1.25 3.00
123 Jose Martinez 1.25 3.00
124 Jason Kipnis 1.50 4.00
125 Paul DeJong 2.00 5.00
126 Oakland Coliseum 1.25 3.00
127 Seranthony Dominguez 1.25 3.00
128 Yoenis Cespedes 2.00 5.00
129 Kenley Jansen 1.50 4.00
130 Blake Snell 1.50 4.00
131 Mark Trumbo 1.25 3.00
132 Miguel Andujar 2.00 5.00
133 Ryan Zimmerman 1.50 4.00
134 Sean Reid-Foley RC 1.25 3.00
135 Wade LeBlanc 1.25 3.00
136 Brad Peacock 1.25 3.00
137 Carlos Rodon 2.00 5.00
138 Kyle Barraclough 1.25 3.00
139 Mitch Haniger 1.50 4.00
140 Daniel Ponce de Leon RC 2.00 5.00
141 Ryon Healy 1.25 3.00
142 Pedro Strop 1.25 3.00
143 Yan Gomes 2.00 5.00
144 Jake Arrieta 1.50 4.00
145 Harper/ Gennett 3.00 8.00
146 Jesse Winker 2.00 5.00
147 Blake Treinen 1.25 3.00
148 Brandon Belt 1.50 4.00
149 Khris Davis 2.00 5.00
150 Aaron Judge 5.00 12.00
151 Pablo Lopez RC 1.25 3.00
152 Teoscar Hernandez 2.00 5.00
153 Hunter Strickland 1.25 3.00
154 Johnny Cueto 1.50 4.00
155 James McCann 1.50 4.00
156 Luis Castillo 1.50 4.00
157 Buster Posey 2.50 6.00
158 Byron Buxton 2.00 5.00
159 Minute Maid Park 1.25 3.00
160 Fenway Park 1.25 3.00
161 Eric Hosmer 1.50 4.00
162 Yasiel Puig 2.00 5.00
163 Aaron Nola 1.50 4.00
164 Billy Hamilton 1.50 4.00
165 Robbie Ray 1.25 3.00
166 Matt Chapman 2.00 5.00
167 Xander Bogaerts 2.00 5.00
168 Salvador Perez 1.50 4.00
169 Charlie Morton 2.00 5.00
170 Manny Margot 1.25 3.00
171 Kyle Hendricks 2.00 5.00
172 Brandon Nimmo 1.50 4.00
173 Michael Fulmer 1.25 3.00
174 Jose Leclerc 1.25 3.00
175 Tommy Pham 1.25 3.00
176 Trea Turner 1.50 4.00
177 Kohl Stewart RC 1.50 4.00
178 Jose Altuve 1.50 4.00
179 Jackie Bradley Jr. 2.00 5.00
180 Justin Turner 2.00 5.00
181 Antonio Senzatela 1.25 3.00
182 Archie Bradley 1.25 3.00
183 Freddie Freeman 2.50 6.00
184 Ken Giles 1.25 3.00
185 Matt Duffy 1.25 3.00
186 Franmil Reyes 1.25 3.00
187 Citizens Bank Park 1.25 3.00
188 Matt Davidson 1.50 4.00
189 Khris Davis 2.00 5.00
190 Steven Duggar RC 1.50 4.00
191 Dansby Swanson 2.00 5.00
192 Luis Urias RC 12.00 30.00
193 Addison Reed 1.25 3.00
194 Felipe Vazquez 1.25 3.00
195 Brett Phillips 1.25 3.00
196 Adam Engel 1.25 3.00
197 Wrigley Field 1.25 3.00
198 Gregory Polanco 1.50 4.00
199 Mike Clevinger 1.50 4.00
200 Jacob deGrom 4.00 10.00
201 Marcus Semien 2.00 5.00
202 Muncy/Bellinger 2.00 5.00
203 Will Smith 1.25 3.00
204 Zack Cozart 1.25 3.00
205 Todd Frazier 1.25 3.00
206 Jaime Barria 1.25 3.00
207 Richard Bleier 1.25 3.00
208 Josh Bell 1.50 4.00
209 Nicholas Castellanos 2.00 5.00
210 Kris Bryant 2.50 6.00
211 Jeimer Candelario 1.25 3.00
212 Brian Anderson 1.25 3.00
213 Juan Soto 20.00 50.00
214 Colin Moran 1.25 3.00
215 Didi Gregorius 1.50 4.00
216 Arenado/Baez 3.00 8.00
217 Joe Jimenez 1.25 3.00
218 Scott Schebler 1.50 4.00
219 Martin Perez 1.50 4.00
220 Alex Colome 1.25 3.00
221 Luis Severino 1.50 4.00
222 Zack Greinke 2.00 5.00
223 Jose Ramirez 1.50 4.00
224 Odubel Herrera 1.50 4.00
225 Yadier Molina 2.50 6.00
226 Albert Almora 1.50 4.00
227 Adolis Garcia RC 20.00 50.00
228 Rafael Devers 2.50 6.00
229 Shane Greene 1.25 3.00
230 Miguel Cabrera 2.00 5.00
231 Joc Pederson 1.50 4.00
232 Kyle Seager 1.25 3.00
233 Dylan Bundy 1.50 4.00
234 Austin Hedges 1.25 3.00
235 Luke Weaver 1.25 3.00
236 Sean Doolittle 1.25 3.00
237 Seth Lugo 1.25 3.00
238 Whit Merrifield 2.00 5.00
239 Christian Yelich 4.00 10.00
240 Trey Mancini 1.50 4.00
241 James Paxton 1.50 4.00
242 Anthony Rendon 2.00 5.00
243 Jonathan Loaisiga RC 1.50 4.00
244 Tyler Flowers 1.25 3.00
245 Rogers Centre 1.25 3.00
246 Ryan Borucki RC 1.25 3.00
247 Sam Tuivailala 1.25 3.00
248 Justin Bour 1.25 3.00
249 Jordan Zimmermann 1.50 4.00
250 Shohei Ohtani 3.00 8.00
251 Niko Goodrum 1.50 4.00
252 Jakob Junis 1.25 3.00
253 Starling Marte 1.50 4.00
254 Dodger Stadium 1.25 3.00
255 Andrelton Simmons 1.25 3.00
256 Cody Allen 1.25 3.00
257 Andrew Heaney 1.25 3.00
258 Eddie Rosario 1.50 4.00
259 Jonathan Schoop 1.25 3.00
260 Aaron Hicks 1.50 4.00
261 Jedd Gyorko 1.25 3.00
262 Mitch Moreland 1.25 3.00
263 Gray/Gregorius 1.50 4.00
264 Avisail Garcia 1.50 4.00
265 Joey Lucchesi 1.25 3.00
266 Ohtani/Bregman 3.00 8.00
267 Ross Stripling 1.25 3.00
268 Blake Snell 1.50 4.00
269 Francisco Lindor 2.00 5.00
270 Brad Keller RC 1.25 3.00
271 Shane Bieber 2.00 5.00
272 Orlando Arcia 1.25 3.00
273 Kole Calhoun 1.25 3.00
274 Francisco Cervelli 1.25 3.00
275 Steve Pearce 2.00 5.00
276 Nolan Arenado 3.00 8.00
277 Mitch Garver 1.25 3.00
278 Mike Minor 1.25 3.00
279 Rhys Hoskins 2.50 6.00
280 Miles Mikolas 2.00 5.00
281 Jeff McNeil RC 15.00 40.00
282 Tim Beckham 1.50 4.00
283 Rich Hill 1.25 3.00
284 Joey Votto 2.00 5.00
285 Sonny Gray 1.50 4.00
286 Taijuan Walker 1.25 3.00
287 Jesus Aguilar 1.50 4.00
288 Joe Panik 1.50 4.00
289 Matt Olson 2.00 5.00
290 Steven Souza Jr. 1.50 4.00
291 Enyel De Los Santos RC 1.25 3.00
292 Dee Gordon 1.25 3.00
293 Andrew Miller 1.50 4.00
294 Correa/Altuve 2.00 5.00
295 Pujols/Betts 2.00 5.00
296 Lewis Brinson 1.25 3.00
297 Paul Goldschmidt 2.00 5.00
298 Devon Travis 1.25 3.00
299 Edwin Diaz 1.50 4.00
300 Christian Yelich 4.00 10.00
301 Tanner Roark 1.25 3.00
302 Jose Berrios 1.50 4.00
303 Ranger Suarez RC 1.25 3.00
304 Michael Lorenzen 1.25 3.00
305 Brad Boxberger 1.25 3.00
306 Justus Sheffield RC 2.00 5.00
307 Jorge Soler 2.00 5.00
308 Yolmer Sanchez 1.25 3.00
309 Randal Grichuk 1.25 3.00
310 Javier Baez 2.50 6.00
311 Jake Bauers RC 2.00 5.00
312 Mookie Betts 4.00 10.00
313 Robinson Cano 1.50 4.00
314 David Price 1.50 4.00
315 Duane Underwood Jr. RC 1.25 3.00
316 Adam Eaton 2.00 5.00
317 Kevin Gausman 2.00 5.00
318 Cedric Mullins RC 2.50 6.00
319 Alex Gordon 1.50 4.00
320 Ronald Guzman 1.25 3.00
321 Jack Flaherty 2.00 5.00
322 Brian McCann 1.50 4.00
323 George Springer 1.50 4.00
324 Logan Morrison 1.25 3.00
325 Dan Straily 1.25 3.00
326 Heath Fillmyer RC 1.25 3.00
327 Maikel Franco 1.50 4.00
328 Yonder Alonso 1.25 3.00
329 Jordan Hicks 1.50 4.00
330 Lorenzo Cain 1.25 3.00
331 Cesar Hernandez 1.25 3.00
332 Ryan O'Hearn RC 1.25 3.00
333 Ray Black RC 1.25 3.00
334 Jake Lamb 1.50 4.00
335 Ervin Santana 1.25 3.00
336 Corey Kluber 1.50 4.00
337 Mychal Givens 1.25 3.00
338 Andrew Cashner 1.25 3.00
339 Josh Harrison 1.25 3.00
340 Vladimir Guerrero Jr. RC 250.00 600.00
341 Nationals Park 1.25 3.00
342 Wilmer Difo 1.25 3.00
343 Sal Romano 1.25 3.00
344 Max Scherzer 2.00 5.00
345 Justin Upton 1.50 4.00
346 Chris Iannetta 1.25 3.00
347 Kirby Yates 1.50 4.00
348 Russell Martin 1.25 3.00
349 Kyle Schwarber 2.00 5.00
350 Nick Markakis 1.50 4.00
351 Jarrod Dyson 1.25 3.00
352 David Peralta 1.25 3.00
353 Gary Sanchez 2.00 5.00
354 Nomar Mazara 1.25 3.00
355 Stephen Gonsalves RC 1.25 3.00
356 Stephen Strasburg 2.00 5.00
357 Chris Martin 1.25 3.00
358 Leonys Martin 1.25 3.00
359 Noah Syndergaard 1.50 4.00
360 Mark Melancon 1.25 3.00
361 Taylor Davis 1.25 3.00
362 Jeremy Jeffress 1.25 3.00
363 Max Stassi 1.25 3.00
364 Kenta Maeda 1.50 4.00
365 Ketel Marte 1.50 4.00
366 Isiah Kiner-Falefa 1.50 4.00
367 Ohtani/Trout 6.00 15.00
368 Brad Hand 1.25 3.00
369 Charlie Culberson 1.25 3.00
370 Jacoby Ellsbury 1.50 4.00
371 Zack Wheeler 1.50 4.00
372 Yu Darvish 2.00 5.00
373 Christian Vazquez 1.50 4.00
374 Alex Blandino 1.25 3.00
375 Cody Reed 1.25 3.00
376 Framber Valdez RC 1.25 3.00
377 Yoan Moncada 2.00 5.00
378 Brandon Workman 1.25 3.00
379 Carter Kieboom RC 2.00 5.00
380 Chris Archer 1.25 3.00
381 Juan Lagares 1.25 3.00
382 Daniel Norris 1.25 3.00
383 Adalberto Mejia 1.25 3.00
384 Dominic Leone 1.25 3.00
385 Ender Inciarte 1.25 3.00
386 Ryan Pressly 1.25 3.00
387 Mike Foltynewicz 2.00 5.00
388 Dominic Smith 1.25 3.00
389 Victor Caratini 1.25 3.00
390 Evan Longoria 1.50 4.00
391 Jung Ho Kang 1.25 3.00
392 Cionel Perez RC 1.25 3.00
393 Hunter Renfroe 1.25 3.00
394 Miguel Rojas 1.25 3.00
395 Andrew McCutchen 2.00 5.00
396 Masahiro Tanaka 1.50 4.00
397 Lance McCullers Jr. 1.25 3.00
398 Erick Fedde 1.25 3.00
399 Tyler Mahle 1.25 3.00
400 Bryce Harper 3.00 8.00
401 Tony Kemp 1.25 3.00
402 Victor Robles 2.50 6.00
403 Ivan Nova 1.50 4.00
404 Jace Peterson 1.25 3.00
405 Chaz Roe 1.25 3.00
406 Jason Castro 1.25 3.00
407 Eduardo Nunez 1.25 3.00
408 Sean Newcomb 1.25 3.00
409 Nate Jones 1.25 3.00
410 Fernando Tatis Jr. RC 600.00 1500.00
411 Magneuris Sierra 2.00 5.00
412 Clint Frazier 1.50 4.00
413 Mike Fiers 1.25 3.00
414 Michael Soroka 2.00 5.00
415 Bryan Shaw 1.25 3.00
416 Keon Broxton 1.25 3.00
417 Noel Cuevas RC 1.25 3.00
418 Jason Vargas 1.25 3.00
419 Sandy Leon 1.25 3.00
420 Kevin Kiermaier 1.50 4.00
421 Yoshihisa Hirano 1.25 3.00
422 Matt Barnes 1.25 3.00
423 Ji-Man Choi 1.25 3.00
424 Target Field 1.25 3.00
425 Steel City Slammers 1.25 3.00
Corey Dickerson
426 Austin Romine 1.25 3.00
427 Jorge Bonifacio 1.25 3.00
428 Pablo Sandoval 1.50 4.00
429 Wilmer Font 1.25 3.00
430 Roman Quinn 1.25 3.00
431 Lonnie Chisenhall 1.25 3.00
432 Ryan Yarbrough 1.25 3.00
433 Pedro Baez 1.25 3.00
434 Roberto Osuna 1.25 3.00
435 Steven Brault 1.25 3.00
436 Kendrys Morales 1.25 3.00
437 Albert Pujols 2.50 6.00
438 Max Kepler 1.50 4.00
439 Ryan McMahon 2.00 5.00
440 Dustin Pedroia 2.00 5.00
441 Oriole Park at Camden 1.25 3.00
442 Reese McGuire RC 2.00 5.00
443 Steven Matz 1.25 3.00
444 Powerful Pair 3.00 8.00
Aaron Judge/Giancarlo Stanton
445 Walker Buehler 6.00 15.00
446 Francisco Mejia 1.50 4.00
447 Altuve/Springer 1.50 4.00
448 Willians Astudillo RC 1.25 3.00
449 Matt Moore 1.50 4.00
450 Greg Garcia 1.25 3.00
451 Jorge Alfaro 1.25 3.00
452 Chris Paddack RC 25.00 60.00
453 Taylor Rogers 1.25 3.00
454 Matt Kemp 1.50 4.00
455 Zach Eflin 1.25 3.00
456 Austin Barnes 1.25 3.00
457 Nick Ciuffo RC 1.25 3.00
458 Alex Avila 1.50 4.00
459 Trevor Hildenberger 1.25 3.00
460 Trevor Story 2.00 5.00
461 Eduardo Rodriguez 1.25 3.00
462 Luke Voit 3.00 8.00
463 Wily Peralta 1.25 3.00
464 Alex Wood 1.25 3.00
465 Raisel Iglesias 1.25 3.00
466 Yairo Munoz 1.25 3.00
467 A.J. Minter 1.50 4.00
468 Anthony DeSclafani 1.25 3.00
469 Brandon Morrow 1.25 3.00
470 Peter O'Brien 1.25 3.00
471 Kevin Newman RC 2.00 5.00
472 Scott Kingery 1.50 4.00
473 Kyle Wright RC 2.00 5.00
474 Carson Kelly 1.25 3.00
475 Pete Alonso RC 125.00 300.00
476 Arodys Vizcaino 1.25 3.00
477 Mikie Mahtook 1.25 3.00
478 Alen Hanson 1.50 4.00
479 Wei-Yin Chen 1.25 3.00
480 Vince Velasquez 1.25 3.00
481 J.A. Happ 1.50 4.00
482 Starlin Castro 1.25 3.00
483 Alex Cobb 1.25 3.00
484 Andrew Chafin 1.25 3.00
485 Wil Myers 1.50 4.00
486 CC Sabathia 1.50 4.00
487 Renfroe/Hosmer 1.50 4.00
488 Dexter Fowler 1.50 4.00
489 Joe Ross 1.25 3.00
490 Matt Harvey 1.50 4.00
491 Comerica Park 1.25 3.00
492 Adam Plutko 1.25 3.00
493 JaCoby Jones 1.50 4.00
494 Ian Desmond 1.25 3.00
495 Progressive Field 1.25 3.00
496 Buck Farmer 1.25 3.00
497 Citi Field 1.25 3.00
498 Pablo Reyes RC 1.25 3.00
499 Daniel Murphy 1.50 4.00
500 Manny Machado 2.00 5.00
501 Carlos Carrasco 1.25 3.00
502 Mike Montgomery 1.25 3.00
503 Marcell Ozuna 2.00 5.00
504 Stephen Tarpley RC 1.50 4.00
505 Dellin Betances 1.50 4.00
506 Ben Gamel 1.50 4.00
507 Cody Bellinger 4.00 10.00
508 Albies/Acuna Jr. 10.00 25.00
509 Globe Life Park in Arlington 1.25 3.00
510 Patrick Corbin 1.50 4.00
511 Rougned Odor 1.50 4.00
512 Franklin Barreto 1.25 3.00
513 Brett Gardner 1.50 4.00
514 Greg Allen 1.50 4.00
515 Hyun-Jin Ryu 1.50 4.00
516 Keone Kela 1.25 3.00
517 Shawn Armstrong 1.25 3.00
518 Steven Wright 1.25 3.00
519 Julio Urias 2.00 5.00
520 David Fletcher RC 4.00 10.00
521 Chase Field 1.25 3.00
522 Brian Johnson 1.25 3.00
523 Marco Gonzales 1.25 3.00
524 Chad Pinder 1.25 3.00
525 Ian Kinsler 1.50 4.00
526 Sandy Alcantara 1.25 3.00
527 Guaranteed Rate Field 1.25 3.00
528 Jon Edwards 1.25 3.00
529 Chance Sisco 1.25 3.00
530 Ian Happ 1.50 4.00
531 Josh Reddick 1.25 3.00
532 Lance Lynn 1.25 3.00
533 Matt Shoemaker 1.50 4.00
534 Aaron Altherr 1.25 3.00
535 Tyler Naquin 1.50 4.00
536 Molina/Ozuna 2.50 6.00
537 Ronald Torreyes 1.25 3.00
538 Seung-Hwan Oh 1.50 4.00
539 Franchy Cordero 1.25 3.00
540 Cole Hamels 1.50 4.00
541 Michael Wacha 1.50 4.00
542 Chris Davis 1.25 3.00
543 Nick Williams 1.25 3.00
544 Jake Marisnick 1.25 3.00
545 Tyler White 1.25 3.00
546 Brock Holt 1.25 3.00
547 Trevor Richards RC 1.25 3.00
548 Chris Owings 1.25 3.00
549 Sale/Vazquez 2.00 5.00
550 Adam Cimber RC 1.25 3.00
551 Kolten Wong 1.50 4.00
552 David Hess 1.25 3.00
553 Daniel Mengden 1.25 3.00
554 Corey Knebel 1.25 3.00
555 Marlins Park 1.25 3.00
556 Rowdy Tellez RC 2.00 5.00
557 Adam Duvall 2.00 5.00
558 Phillip Ervin 1.25 3.00
559 Ildemaro Vargas 1.25 3.00
560 Victor Reyes RC 1.25 3.00
561 Ozzie Albies 2.00 5.00
562 Willy Adames 1.25 3.00
563 Keynan Middleton 1.25 3.00
564 Austin Meadows 2.00 5.00
565 Andrew Triggs 1.25 3.00
566 Tropicana Field 1.25 3.00
567 Josh Rogers RC 1.25 3.00
568 Giancarlo Stanton 2.00 5.00
569 Carl Edwards Jr. 1.25 3.00
570 Eduardo Escobar 1.25 3.00
571 Bobby Poyner RC 1.50 4.00
572 Gerrit Cole 2.00 5.00
573 Tucker Barnhart 1.25 3.00
574 Jeff Samardzija 1.25 3.00
575 Jimmy Yacabonis 1.25 3.00
576 Jake Cave RC 1.50 4.00
577 Nicky Delmonico 1.25 3.00
578 Patrick Wisdom RC 1.25 3.00
579 Andrew Benintendi 2.00 5.00
580 DJ Stewart RC 1.50 4.00
581 Travis Jankowski 1.25 3.00
582 Austin Wynns RC 1.25 3.00
583 Nick Senzel RC 20.00 50.00
584 Josh James RC 2.00 5.00
585 Carlos Santana 1.50 4.00
586 Drew VerHagen 1.25 3.00
587 Johan Camargo 1.25 3.00
588 Taylor Ward RC 1.25 3.00
589 Jeurys Familia 1.50 4.00
590 Jose Peraza 1.50 4.00
591 Wilson Ramos 1.25 3.00
592 Eric Lauer 1.25 3.00
593 John Hicks 1.25 3.00
594 Austin Slater 1.25 3.00
595 Yandy Diaz 1.50 4.00
596 Anthony Rizzo 2.50 6.00
597 Kyle Gibson 1.50 4.00
598 Chris Devenski 1.25 3.00
599 Daniel Palka 1.25 3.00
600 Shohei Ohtani 3.00 8.00
601 David Dahl 1.25 3.00
602 German Marquez 1.25 3.00
603 J.D. Davis 1.25 3.00
604 Coors Field 1.25 3.00
605 Jeffrey Springs RC 1.25 3.00
606 Johnny Field RC 1.50 4.00
607 J.T. Riddle 1.25 3.00
608 Ehire Adrianza 1.25 3.00
609 Kauffman Stadium 1.25 3.00
610 Howie Kendrick 1.25 3.00
611 Chris Shaw RC 1.25 3.00
612 Mark Canha 1.25 3.00
613 Welington Castillo 1.25 3.00
614 Ryan Braun 1.50 4.00
615 Nick Tropeano 1.25 3.00
616 Oracle Park 1.25 3.00
617 Hernan Perez 1.25 3.00
618 Nick Martini RC 1.25 3.00
619 Tommy Hunter 1.25 3.00
620 Jared Hughes 1.25 3.00
621 Pat Valaika 1.25 3.00
622 Troy Tulowitzki 2.00 5.00
623 Kevin Pillar 1.25 3.00
624 Amed Rosario 1.50 4.00
625 Yelich/Arcia 2.50 6.00
626 Robbie Erlin 1.25 3.00
627 Freddy Peralta 2.00 5.00
628 Roenis Elias 1.25 3.00
629 Myles Straw RC 2.00 5.00
630 Dustin Fowler 1.25 3.00
631 Tyler Austin 2.00 5.00
632 Yusei Kikuchi RC 2.00 5.00
633 Addison Russell 1.50 4.00
634 John Gant 1.25 3.00
635 Adam Frazier 1.25 3.00
636 Jace Fry 1.25 3.00
637 Yusmeiro Petit 1.25 3.00
638 Kristopher Negron 1.25 3.00
639 Roberto Perez 1.25 3.00
640 Brian Goodwin 1.25 3.00
641 Bryse Wilson RC 1.50 4.00
642 Jhoulys Chacin 1.25 3.00
643 Chris Sale 2.00 5.00
644 Delino DeShields 1.25 3.00
645 Steve Cishek 1.25 3.00
646 Jason Heyward 1.50 4.00
647 Kyle Freeland 1.50 4.00
648 Kevin Kramer RC 1.50 4.00
649 Carlos Tocci RC 1.25 3.00
650 Austin Riley RC 25.00 60.00
651 Jorge Lopez 1.25 3.00
652 Rosell Herrera RC 1.25 3.00
653 Greg Bird 1.50 4.00
654 Kurt Suzuki 1.25 3.00
655 Tyler O'Neill 1.50 4.00
656 Jacob Faria 1.25 3.00
657 JC Ramirez 1.25 3.00
658 Max Muncy 1.50 4.00
659 Aramis Garcia RC 1.25 3.00
660 Dawel Lugo RC 2.00 5.00
661 Zack Greinke 2.00 5.00
662 Jameson Taillon 1.50 4.00
663 Adam Conley 1.25 3.00
664 Lucas Giolito 1.50 4.00
665 David Freese 1.25 3.00
666 Cam Gallagher 1.25 3.00
667 Ronny Rodriguez RC 1.25 3.00
668 Pat Neshek 1.25 3.00
669 Mallex Smith 1.25 3.00
670 Eloy Jimenez RC 75.00 200.00
671 Alex Verdugo 1.50 4.00
672 Christin Stewart RC 1.50 4.00
673 Danny Salazar 1.50 4.00
674 Collin McHugh 1.25 3.00
675 Nelson Cruz 2.00 5.00
676 Travis Shaw 1.25 3.00
677 Aaron Sanchez 1.50 4.00
678 Brendan Rodgers RC 12.00 30.00
679 Adam Wainwright 1.50 4.00
680 Justin Smoak 1.25 3.00
681 Jeff Mathis 1.50 4.00
682 Petco Park 1.25 3.00
683 Isaac Galloway RC 1.25 3.00
684 Keston Hiura RC 125.00 300.00
685 Billy McKinney 1.25 3.00
686 Brandon Drury 1.25 3.00
687 Brandon Woodruff 2.00 5.00
688 Jalen Beeks RC 1.25 3.00
689 Jose Briceno RC 1.25 3.00
690 Hunter Dozier 1.25 3.00
691 Great American Ball Park 1.25 3.00
692 Fernando Rodney 1.25 3.00
693 Ryan Brasier 1.25 3.00
694 Steve Pearce 2.00 5.00
695 Eric Thames 1.25 3.00
696 Sam Dyson 1.25 3.00
697 Dakota Hudson RC 1.50 4.00
698 Baez/Contreras 2.00 5.00

699 Felix Hernandez 1.50 4.00
700 Alex Bregman 2.00 5.00

2019 Topps Chrome Sapphire Orange

STATED ODDS 1:11 HOBBY
STATED PRINT RUN 25 SER.#'d SETS
EXCHANGE DEADLINE 8/31/2021
*ORANGE: 1X TO 2.5X BASIC
1 Ronald Acuna Jr. 75.00 200.00
7 Gleyber Torres 125.00 300.00
10 Clayton Kershaw 12.00 30.00
28 Boston's Boys 12.00 30.00
Mookie Betts/Andrew Benintendi
64 Ramon Laureano 40.00 100.00
100 Mike Trout 150.00 400.00
150 Aaron Judge 75.00 200.00
157 Buster Posey 15.00 40.00
178 Jose Altuve 12.00 30.00
213 Juan Soto 125.00 300.00
216 Bring It In 12.00 30.00
Nolan Arenado/Javier Baez
250 Shohei Ohtani 60.00 150.00
367 Ohtani Gets Hot 25.00 60.00
Shohei Ohtani/Mike Trout
475 Pete Alonso 1000.00 1500.00
507 Cody Bellinger 15.00 40.00
561 Ozzie Albies 12.00 30.00
600 Shohei Ohtani 60.00 150.00
650 Austin Riley 100.00 250.00

2019 Topps Chrome Sapphire Rookie Autographs

CSAAR Austin Riley 50.00 120.00
CSABK Brad Keller 8.00 20.00
CSABL Brandon Lowe 40.00 100.00
CSABW Bryse Wilson 8.00 20.00
CSACK Carter Kieboom 40.00 100.00
CSACM Cedric Mullins 10.00 25.00
CSACS Chris Shaw 10.00 25.00
CSADH Dakota Hudson 10.00 25.00
CSADL Dawel Lugo 5.00 12.00
CSADP Daniel Ponce de Leon 5.00 12.00
CSADS DJ Stewart 4.00 10.00
CSAEJ Eloy Jimenez 100.00 250.00
CSAJC Jake Cave 4.00 10.00
CSAJJ Josh James 5.00 12.00
CSAJN Jacob Nix 4.00 10.00
CSAJS Justus Sheffield 15.00 40.00
CSAKA Kolby Allard 5.00 12.00
CSAKK Kevin Kramer 6.00 15.00
CSAKN Kevin Newman 10.00 25.00
CSAKS Kohl Stewart 4.00 10.00
CSAKT Kyle Tucker 75.00 200.00
CSAKW Kyle Wright 6.00 15.00
CSAMS Myles Straw 5.00 12.00
CSANC Nick Ciuffo 8.00 20.00
CSAPA Pete Alonso 600.00 1000.00
CSARB Ray Black 3.00 8.00
CSARM Reese McGuire 10.00 25.00
CSARR Ronny Rodriguez 3.00 8.00
CSART Rowdy Tellez 6.00 15.00
CSASD Steven Duggar 4.00 10.00
CSASG Stephen Gonsalves 3.00 8.00
CSATB Ty Buttrey 3.00 8.00
CSATT Touki Toussaint 8.00 20.00
CSATW Taylor Ward 8.00 20.00
CSAWA Willians Astudillo 3.00 8.00
CSAYK Yusei Kikuchi 15.00 40.00
CSAFTJ Fernando Tatis Jr. EXCH 750.00 2000.00
CSAMKE Mitch Keller 12.00 30.00
CSAVGJ Vladimir Guerrero Jr. 300.00 600.00

2019 Topps Chrome Sapphire Rookie Autographs Green

CSAAR Austin Riley
CSACK Carter Kieboom
CSAEJ Eloy Jimenez
CSAKW Kyle Wright 20.00 50.00
CSAPA Pete Alonso
CSAFTJ Fernando Tatis Jr. EXCH

2019 Topps Chrome Sapphire Rookie Autographs Orange

CSAAR Austin Riley
CSACK Carter Kieboom
CSAEJ Eloy Jimenez
CSAKW Kyle Wright 30.00 80.00
CSAPA Pete Alonso
CSAFTJ Fernando Tatis Jr. EXCH

2020 Topps Chrome

PRINTING PLATE ODDS 1:8634 HOBBY
PLATE PRINT RUN 1 SET PER COLOR
BLACK-CYAN-MAGENTA-YELLOW ISSUED
NO PLATE PRICING DUE TO SCARCITY
1 Mike Trout 1.50 4.00
2 Liam Hendriks .20 .50
3 Bobby Bradley RC .40 1.00
4 Rogelio Armenteros RC .50 1.25
5 Jesus Luzardo RC .75 2.00
6 Miguel Cabrera .30 .75
7 Trea Turner .25 .60
8 Brendan McKay RC .60 1.50
9 Joey Votto .30 .75
10 Domingo Leyba RC .50 1.25
11 Austin Nola RC .60 1.50
12 Juan Soto 1.00 2.50
13 Max Muncy .25 .60
14 Archie Bradley .20 .50
15 David Peralta .20 .50
16 Luis Castillo .25 .60
17 Bryan Reynolds .25 .60
18 Michael Fulmer .20 .50
19 Jeimer Candelario .20 .50
20 Jorge Soler .30 .75
21 Shohei Ohtani .50 1.25
22 Cavan Biggio .40 1.00
23 Seth Brown RC .40 1.00
24 Nick Senzel .30 .75
25 Keston Hiura .40 1.00
26 Travis Demeritte RC .60 1.50
27 Christian Walker .25 .60
28 Andrew Heaney .20 .50
29 Carlos Correa .30 .75
30 Dan Vogelbach .20 .50
31 Adalberto Mondesi .25 .60
32 Sean Murphy RC .60 1.50
33 Nick Solak RC 1.50 4.00
34 Gio Urshela .30 .75
35 Michael Conforto .25 .60
36 Ian Desmond .20 .50
37 Mitch Haniger .25 .60
38 Jean Segura .25 .60
39 Chris Paddack .30 .75
40 Josh Hader .25 .60
41 Corey Kluber .25 .60
42 Jose Altuve .25 .60
43 Dylan Cease RC .60 1.50
44 German Marquez .30 .75
45 Gleyber Torres .60 1.50
46 Lucas Giolito .25 .60
47 Jake Rogers RC .40 1.00
48 Yusei Kikuchi .25 .60
49 Randy Arozarena RC 5.00 12.00
50 Aaron Judge .75 2.00
51 Danny Jansen .20 .50
52 Kyle Seager .20 .50
53 Kris Bryant .40 1.00
54 Chris Archer .20 .50
55 DJ LeMahieu .30 .75
56 Abraham Toro RC .50 1.25
57 Andrew Benintendi .30 .75
58 Noah Syndergaard .25 .60
59 Trevor Story .30 .75
60 Luis Robert RC 15.00 40.00
61 Sheldon Neuse RC .50 1.25
62 Ozzie Albies .30 .75
63 Hunter Dozier .20 .50
64 Scott Kingery .25 .60
65 Dansby Swanson .30 .75
66 Jose Abreu .30 .75
67 Sam Hilliard RC .60 1.50
68 Blake Snell .25 .60
69 Nelson Cruz .30 .75
70 Jeff McNeil .25 .60
71 Anthony Rizzo .40 1.00
72 Andrelton Simmons .20 .50
73 Charlie Blackmon .30 .75
74 Matthew Boyd .20 .50
75 Jonathan Villar .20 .50
76 Manny Machado .30 .75
77 Cody Bellinger .60 1.50
78 Eddie Rosario .25 .60
79 Hanser Alberto .20 .50
80 Pete Alonso .75 2.00
81 Jacob deGrom .60 1.50
82 Jordan Yamamoto RC .40 1.00
83 Matt Thaiss RC .50 1.25
84 Fernando Tatis Jr. 1.50 4.00
85 Kyle Schwarber .30 .75
86 Adrian Morejon RC .40 1.00
87 Zack Collins RC .50 1.25
88 Brandon Crawford .25 .60
89 Paul Goldschmidt .30 .75
90 Tim Anderson .30 .75
91 Brusdar Graterol RC .60 1.50
92 Nicky Lopez .20 .50
93 Rafael Devers .40 1.00
94 Tommy Edman .30 .75
95 Edwin Rios RC 1.00 2.50
96 Mike Soroka .30 .75
97 Bryce Harper .50 1.25
98 Kevin Newman .30 .75
99 Colin Moran .20 .50
100 Mookie Betts .60 1.50
101 Trent Grisham RC 1.50 4.00
102 Alex Bregman .30 .75
103 Mike Yastrzemski .50 1.25
104 Walker Buehler .40 1.00
105 Miguel Rojas .20 .50
106 Harold Ramirez .20 .50
107 Dee Gordon .20 .50
108 Eric Hosmer .25 .60
109 Nomar Mazara .20 .50
110 Adbert Alzolay RC .50 1.25
111 Aristides Aquino RC 1.00 2.50
112 Ronald Acuna Jr. 1.25 3.00
113 Austin Meadows .30 .75
114 Tony Gonsolin RC 1.50 4.00
115 Alex Young RC .40 1.00
116 A.J. Puk RC .60 1.50
117 Logan Webb RC .60 1.50
118 Tyler Glasnow .30 .75
119 Brandon Lowe .25 .60
120 Anthony Kay RC .40 1.00
121 John Means .30 .75
122 Clayton Kershaw .50 1.25
123 Jon Lester .25 .60
124 Max Kepler .25 .60
125 Jose Berrios .25 .60
126 Victor Reyes .20 .50
127 Albert Pujols .40 1.00
128 Eugenio Suarez .25 .60
129 Ronald Guzman .20 .50
130 Anthony Santander .20 .50
131 Freddie Freeman .40 1.00
132 Zac Gallen RC 1.00 2.50
133 Vladimir Guerrero Jr. .50 1.25
134 Eloy Jimenez .60 1.50
135 Jack Flaherty .30 .75
136 Justin Dunn RC .50 1.25
137 Xander Bogaerts .30 .75
138 Christian Yelich .40 1.00
139 Max Scherzer .30 .75
140 Orlando Arcia .20 .50
141 Rowdy Tellez .25 .60
142 Jose Urquidy RC .50 1.25
143 Aaron Civale RC .75 2.00
144 Marcus Semien .30 .75
145 Yoan Moncada .30 .75
146 Brian Anderson .20 .50
147 Brandon Belt .25 .60
148 Gavin Lux RC 3.00 8.00
149 Andres Munoz RC .60 1.50
150 Bo Bichette RC 10.00 25.00
151 Ketel Marte .25 .60
152 Pablo Lopez .20 .50
153 Lorenzo Cain .20 .50
154 Whit Merrifield .30 .75
155 Logan Allen RC .40 1.00
156 Francisco Lindor .30 .75
157 Buster Posey .40 1.00
158 Elvis Andrus .25 .60
159 Brock Burke RC .40 1.00
160 Ramon Laureano .25 .60
161 Nico Hoerner RC 1.50 4.00
162 Junior Fernandez RC .40 1.00
163 Trevor Williams .20 .50
164 Justin Verlander .30 .75
165 Carlos Santana .25 .60
166 Masahiro Tanaka .30 .75
167 Lourdes Gurriel Jr. .25 .60
168 Mauricio Dubon RC .50 1.25
169 Luis Urias .25 .60
170 Isan Diaz RC .60 1.50
171 Carter Kieboom .25 .60
172 Luis Arraez .40 1.00
173 Yu Chang RC .60 1.50
174 Nolan Arenado .50 1.25
175 Raisel Iglesias .20 .50
176 Dustin May RC 3.00 8.00
177 Shin-Soo Choo .25 .60
178 Paul DeJong .30 .75
179 Willy Adames .20 .50
180 Miles Mikolas .20 .50
181 Robel Garcia RC .40 1.00
182 Oscar Mercado .30 .75
183 Matt Olson .30 .75
184 Rhys Hoskins .40 1.00
185 Jose Urena .20 .50
186 Kyle Lewis RC 5.00 12.00
187 Michel Baez RC .40 1.00
188 Trey Mancini .30 .75
189 J.D. Martinez .30 .75
190 Jose Ramirez .25 .60
191 Joey Gallo .30 .75
192 Robbie Ray .20 .50
193 Matt Chapman .30 .75
194 George Springer .25 .60
195 Patrick Corbin .25 .60
196 Corey Seager .30 .75
197 Jeff Samardzija .20 .50
198 Javier Baez .40 1.00
199 Aaron Nola .25 .60
200 Yordan Alvarez RC 8.00 20.00

2020 Topps Chrome Blue Refractors

*BLUE REF: 5X TO 12X BASIC
*BLUE REF RC: 2.5X TO 6X BASIC RC
STATED ODDS 1:230 HOBBY
STATED PRINT RUN 150 SER.#'d SETS
1 Mike Trout 50.00 120.00
12 Juan Soto 25.00 60.00
49 Randy Arozarena 40.00 100.00
60 Luis Robert 250.00 600.00
62 Ozzie Albies 8.00 20.00
84 Fernando Tatis Jr. 60.00 150.00
100 Mookie Betts 30.00 80.00
101 Trent Grisham 25.00 60.00
112 Ronald Acuna Jr. 25.00 60.00
132 Zac Gallen 15.00 40.00
134 Eloy Jimenez 15.00 40.00
148 Gavin Lux 50.00 120.00
150 Bo Bichette 200.00 500.00
160 Ramon Laureano 10.00 25.00
161 Nico Hoerner 25.00 60.00
186 Kyle Lewis 75.00 200.00

2020 Topps Chrome Blue Wave Refractors

*BLUE REF: 6X TO 15X BASIC
*BLUE REF RC: 3X TO 8X BASIC RC
STATED ODDS 1:187 HOBBY
STATED PRINT RUN 75 SER.#'d SETS
1 Mike Trout 60.00 150.00
12 Juan Soto 30.00 80.00
49 Randy Arozarena 50.00 120.00
55 DJ LeMahieu 8.00 20.00
60 Luis Robert 300.00 800.00
62 Ozzie Albies 10.00 25.00
84 Fernando Tatis Jr. 75.00 200.00
100 Mookie Betts 40.00 100.00
101 Trent Grisham 30.00 80.00
112 Ronald Acuna Jr. 30.00 80.00
132 Zac Gallen 20.00 50.00
134 Eloy Jimenez 20.00 50.00
148 Gavin Lux 60.00 150.00
150 Bo Bichette 250.00 600.00
156 Francisco Lindor 15.00 40.00
160 Ramon Laureano 12.00 30.00
161 Nico Hoerner 30.00 80.00
186 Kyle Lewis 100.00 250.00

2020 Topps Chrome Gold Refractors

*GOLD REF: 8X TO 20X BASIC
*GOLD REF RC: 4X TO 10X BASIC RC
STATED ODDS 1:690 HOBBY
STATED PRINT RUN 50 SER.#'d SETS
1 Mike Trout 125.00 300.00
5 Jesus Luzardo 25.00 60.00
12 Juan Soto 40.00 100.00
21 Shohei Ohtani 20.00 50.00
45 Gleyber Torres 25.00 60.00
49 Randy Arozarena 60.00 150.00
50 Aaron Judge 40.00 100.00
55 DJ LeMahieu 10.00 25.00
57 Andrew Benintendi 12.00 30.00
60 Luis Robert 400.00 1000.00
62 Ozzie Albies 12.00 30.00
77 Cody Bellinger 20.00 50.00
80 Pete Alonso 20.00 50.00
84 Fernando Tatis Jr. 200.00 500.00
90 Tim Anderson 15.00 40.00
91 Brusdar Graterol 15.00 40.00
96 Mike Soroka 15.00 40.00
97 Bryce Harper 30.00 80.00
100 Mookie Betts 75.00 200.00
101 Trent Grisham 75.00 200.00
111 Aristides Aquino 20.00 50.00
112 Ronald Acuna Jr. 40.00 100.00
114 Tony Gonsolin 20.00 50.00
122 Clayton Kershaw 20.00 50.00
131 Freddie Freeman 15.00 40.00
132 Zac Gallen 25.00 60.00
133 Vladimir Guerrero Jr. 25.00 60.00
134 Eloy Jimenez 25.00 60.00
137 Xander Bogaerts 12.00 30.00
143 Aaron Civale 20.00 50.00
148 Gavin Lux 75.00 200.00
150 Bo Bichette 300.00 800.00
156 Francisco Lindor 20.00 50.00
160 Ramon Laureano 15.00 40.00
161 Nico Hoerner 50.00 120.00
170 Isan Diaz 15.00 40.00
173 Yu Chang 10.00 25.00
186 Kyle Lewis 125.00 300.00
191 Joey Gallo 15.00 40.00
198 Javier Baez 20.00 50.00
199 Aaron Nola 10.00 25.00
200 Yordan Alvarez 125.00 300.00

2020 Topps Chrome Gold Wave Refractors

*GOLD WAVE REF: 8X TO 20X BASIC
*GOLD WAVE REF RC: 4X TO 10X BASIC RC
STATED ODDS 1:280 HOBBY
STATED PRINT RUN 50 SER.#'d SETS
1 Mike Trout 125.00 300.00
5 Jesus Luzardo 25.00 60.00
12 Juan Soto 40.00 100.00
21 Shohei Ohtani 20.00 50.00
45 Gleyber Torres 25.00 60.00
49 Randy Arozarena 60.00 150.00
50 Aaron Judge 40.00 100.00
55 DJ LeMahieu 10.00 25.00
57 Andrew Benintendi 12.00 30.00
60 Luis Robert 400.00 1000.00
62 Ozzie Albies 12.00 30.00
77 Cody Bellinger 20.00 50.00
80 Pete Alonso 20.00 50.00
84 Fernando Tatis Jr. 200.00 500.00
90 Tim Anderson 15.00 40.00
91 Brusdar Graterol 15.00 40.00
96 Mike Soroka 15.00 40.00
97 Bryce Harper 30.00 80.00
100 Mookie Betts 75.00 200.00
101 Trent Grisham 75.00 200.00
111 Aristides Aquino 20.00 50.00
112 Ronald Acuna Jr. 40.00 100.00
114 Tony Gonsolin 20.00 50.00
122 Clayton Kershaw 20.00 50.00
131 Freddie Freeman 15.00 40.00
132 Zac Gallen 25.00 60.00
133 Vladimir Guerrero Jr. 25.00 60.00
134 Eloy Jimenez 25.00 60.00
137 Xander Bogaerts 12.00 30.00
143 Aaron Civale 20.00 50.00
148 Gavin Lux 75.00 200.00
150 Bo Bichette 300.00 800.00
156 Francisco Lindor 20.00 50.00
160 Ramon Laureano 15.00 40.00
161 Nico Hoerner 50.00 120.00
170 Isan Diaz 15.00 40.00
173 Yu Chang 10.00 25.00
186 Kyle Lewis 125.00 300.00
191 Joey Gallo 15.00 40.00
198 Javier Baez 20.00 50.00
199 Aaron Nola 10.00 25.00
200 Yordan Alvarez 125.00 300.00

2020 Topps Chrome Green Refractors

*GREEN REF: 6X TO 15X BASIC
*GREEN REF RC: 3X TO 8X BASIC RC
STATED ODDS 1:349 HOBBY
STATED PRINT RUN 99 SER.#'d SETS
1 Mike Trout 60.00 150.00
12 Juan Soto 30.00 80.00
49 Randy Arozarena 50.00 120.00
55 DJ LeMahieu 8.00 20.00
60 Luis Robert 300.00 800.00
62 Ozzie Albies 10.00 25.00
84 Fernando Tatis Jr. 75.00 200.00
100 Mookie Betts 40.00 100.00
101 Trent Grisham 30.00 80.00
112 Ronald Acuna Jr. 30.00 80.00
132 Zac Gallen 20.00 50.00
134 Eloy Jimenez 20.00 50.00
148 Gavin Lux 60.00 150.00
150 Bo Bichette 250.00 600.00
156 Francisco Lindor 15.00 40.00
160 Ramon Laureano 12.00 30.00
161 Nico Hoerner 30.00 80.00
186 Kyle Lewis 100.00 250.00

2020 Topps Chrome Green Wave Refractors

*GREEN WAVE REF: 6X TO 15X BASIC
*GREEN WAVE REF RC: 3X TO 8X BASIC RC
STATED ODDS 1:142 HOBBY
STATED PRINT RUN 99 SER.#'d SETS
1 Mike Trout 60.00 150.00
12 Juan Soto 30.00 80.00
49 Randy Arozarena 50.00 120.00
55 DJ LeMahieu 8.00 20.00
60 Luis Robert 300.00 800.00
62 Ozzie Albies 10.00 25.00
84 Fernando Tatis Jr. 75.00 200.00
100 Mookie Betts 40.00 100.00
101 Trent Grisham 30.00 80.00
112 Ronald Acuna Jr. 30.00 80.00
132 Zac Gallen 20.00 50.00
134 Eloy Jimenez 20.00 50.00
148 Gavin Lux 60.00 150.00
150 Bo Bichette 250.00 600.00
156 Francisco Lindor 15.00 40.00
160 Ramon Laureano 12.00 30.00
161 Nico Hoerner 30.00 80.00
186 Kyle Lewis 100.00 250.00

2020 Topps Chrome Negative Refractors

*NEG REF: 4X TO 10X BASIC
*NEG REF RC: 2X TO 5X BASIC RC
STATED ODDS 1:87 HOBBY
1 Mike Trout 40.00 100.00
12 Juan Soto 20.00 50.00
49 Randy Arozarena 30.00 80.00
60 Luis Robert 200.00 500.00
62 Ozzie Albies 6.00 15.00
84 Fernando Tatis Jr. 50.00 120.00
100 Mookie Betts 25.00 60.00
101 Trent Grisham 20.00 50.00
112 Ronald Acuna Jr. 20.00 50.00
132 Zac Gallen 12.00 30.00
134 Eloy Jimenez 12.00 30.00
148 Gavin Lux 40.00 100.00
150 Bo Bichette 150.00 400.00
161 Nico Hoerner 20.00 50.00
186 Kyle Lewis 60.00 150.00

2020 Topps Chrome Orange Refractors

*ORANGE REF: 10X TO 25X BASIC
*ORANGE REF RC: 5X TO 12X BASIC RC
STATED ODDS 1:273 HOBBY
STATED PRINT RUN 25 SER.#'d SETS
1 Mike Trout 150.00 400.00
5 Jesus Luzardo 40.00 100.00
12 Juan Soto 50.00 120.00
21 Shohei Ohtani 25.00 60.00
45 Gleyber Torres 30.00 80.00
49 Randy Arozarena 75.00 200.00
50 Aaron Judge 50.00 120.00
55 DJ LeMahieu 12.00 30.00
57 Andrew Benintendi 15.00 40.00
60 Luis Robert 500.00 1200.00
62 Ozzie Albies 15.00 40.00
77 Cody Bellinger 25.00 60.00
80 Pete Alonso 25.00 60.00
84 Fernando Tatis Jr. 250.00 600.00
90 Tim Anderson 20.00 50.00
91 Brusdar Graterol 20.00 50.00
96 Mike Soroka 20.00 50.00
97 Bryce Harper 40.00 100.00
100 Mookie Betts 100.00 250.00
101 Trent Grisham 100.00 250.00
111 Aristides Aquino 25.00 60.00
112 Ronald Acuna Jr. 50.00 120.00
114 Tony Gonsolin 25.00 60.00
122 Clayton Kershaw 25.00 60.00
131 Freddie Freeman 20.00 50.00
132 Zac Gallen 30.00 80.00
133 Vladimir Guerrero Jr. 30.00 80.00
134 Eloy Jimenez 30.00 80.00
137 Xander Bogaerts 15.00 40.00
143 Aaron Civale 25.00 60.00
148 Gavin Lux 100.00 250.00
150 Bo Bichette 400.00 1000.00
156 Francisco Lindor 25.00 60.00
160 Ramon Laureano 20.00 50.00
161 Nico Hoerner 60.00 150.00
170 Isan Diaz 20.00 50.00
173 Yu Chang 12.00 30.00
186 Kyle Lewis 150.00 400.00
191 Joey Gallo 20.00 50.00
198 Javier Baez 25.00 60.00
199 Aaron Nola 12.00 30.00
200 Yordan Alvarez 150.00 400.00

2020 Topps Chrome Orange Wave Refractors

*ORANGE WAVE REF: 10X TO 25X BASIC
*ORANGE WAVE REF RC: 5X TO 12X BASIC RC
STATED ODDS 1:560 HOBBY
STATED PRINT RUN 25 SER.#'d SETS
1 Mike Trout 150.00 400.00
5 Jesus Luzardo 40.00 100.00
12 Juan Soto 50.00 120.00
21 Shohei Ohtani 25.00 60.00
45 Gleyber Torres 30.00 80.00
49 Randy Arozarena 75.00 200.00
50 Aaron Judge 50.00 60.00
55 DJ LeMahieu 12.00 30.00
57 Andrew Benintendi 15.00 40.00
60 Luis Robert 500.00 1200.00
62 Ozzie Albies 15.00 40.00
77 Cody Bellinger 25.00 60.00
80 Pete Alonso 25.00 60.00
84 Fernando Tatis Jr. 250.00 600.00
90 Tim Anderson 20.00 50.00
91 Brusdar Graterol 20.00 50.00
96 Mike Soroka 20.00 50.00
97 Bryce Harper 40.00 100.00
100 Mookie Betts 100.00 250.00
101 Trent Grisham 100.00 250.00
111 Aristides Aquino 25.00 60.00
112 Ronald Acuna Jr. 50.00 120.00
114 Tony Gonsolin 25.00 60.00
122 Clayton Kershaw 25.00 60.00
131 Freddie Freeman 20.00 50.00
132 Zac Gallen 30.00 80.00
133 Vladimir Guerrero Jr. 30.00 80.00
134 Eloy Jimenez 30.00 80.00
137 Xander Bogaerts 15.00 40.00
143 Aaron Civale 25.00 60.00
148 Gavin Lux 100.00 250.00
150 Bo Bichette 400.00 1000.00
156 Francisco Lindor 25.00 60.00
160 Ramon Laureano 20.00 50.00
161 Nico Hoerner 60.00 150.00
170 Isan Diaz 20.00 50.00
173 Yu Chang 12.00 30.00
186 Kyle Lewis 150.00 400.00
191 Joey Gallo 20.00 50.00
198 Javier Baez 25.00 60.00
199 Aaron Nola 12.00 30.00
200 Yordan Alvarez 150.00 400.00

2020 Topps Chrome Pink Refractors

*PINK REF: 1.2X TO 3X BASIC
*PINK REF RC:.6X TO 1.5X BASIC RC
FIVE PER VALUE PACK
49 Randy Arozarena 10.00 25.00
60 Luis Robert 60.00 150.00
84 Fernando Tatis Jr. 15.00 40.00
148 Gavin Lux 12.00 30.00
150 Bo Bichette 50.00 120.00
186 Kyle Lewis 10.00 25.00

2020 Topps Chrome Prism Refractors

*PRISM REF: 1.5X TO 4X BASIC
*PRISM REF RC:.75X TO 2X BASIC RC
STATED ODDS 1:6 HOBBY
49 Randy Arozarena 12.00 30.00
60 Luis Robert 75.00 200.00
84 Fernando Tatis Jr. 20.00 50.00
148 Gavin Lux 15.00 40.00
150 Bo Bichette 60.00 150.00
186 Kyle Lewis 20.00 50.00

2020 Topps Chrome Purple Refractors

*PURPLE REF: 2.5X TO 6X BASIC
*PURPLE REF RC:1.2X TO 3X BASIC RC
STATED ODDS 1:116 HOBBY
STATED PRINT RUN 250 SER.#'d SETS
1 Mike Trout 25.00 60.00
49 Randy Arozarena 20.00 50.00
60 Luis Robert 125.00 300.00
62 Ozzie Albies 4.00 10.00
84 Fernando Tatis Jr. 30.00 40.00
100 Mookie Betts 15.00 40.00
101 Trent Grisham 12.00 30.00
112 Ronald Acuna Jr. 12.00 30.00
132 Zac Gallen 8.00 20.00
134 Eloy Jimenez 8.00 20.00
148 Gavin Lux 25.00 60.00
150 Bo Bichette 100.00 250.00
161 Nico Hoerner 12.00 30.00
186 Kyle Lewis 40.00 100.00

2020 Topps Chrome Refractors

*REF: 1X TO 2.5X BASIC
*REF RC:.5X TO 1.2X BASIC RC
STATED ODDS 1:3 HOBBY
49 Randy Arozarena 8.00 20.00
84 Fernando Tatis Jr. 12.00 30.00
148 Gavin Lux 10.00 25.00
150 Bo Bichette 40.00 100.00
186 Kyle Lewis 8.00 20.00

2020 Topps Chrome X-Fractors

*XFRACTOR: 2X TO 5X BASIC
*XFRACTOR RC: 1X TO 2.5X BASIC RC
49 Randy Arozarena 15.00 40.00
60 Luis Robert 60.00 150.00
84 Fernando Tatis Jr. 20.00 50.00
132 Zac Gallen 6.00 15.00
148 Gavin Lux 20.00 50.00
150 Bo Bichette 30.00 80.00
186 Kyle Lewis 15.00 40.00

2020 Topps Chrome Photo Variation Refractors

STATED ODDS 1:406 HOBBY
*GREEN/99: .6X TO 1.5X BASIC
*GOLD/50: 1X TO 2.5X BASIC
*ORANGE/25: 1.2X TO 3X BASIC
1A Trout Horizontal 75.00 200.00
1B Mike Trout
Backwards cap
12 Soto Running 30.00 80.00
50A Judge Catching 15.00 40.00
50B Derek Jeter
60A Robert Throwing 100.00 250.00
60B Luis Robert
T-Shirt
77A Bellinger Horizontal 10.00 25.00
77B Jackie Robinson
80 Alonso Horizontal 10.00 25.00
81 deGrom Blue jrsy 6.00 15.00
84 Tatis Jr. Horizontal 60.00 150.00
97 Harper Horizontal 8.00 20.00
111 Aquino Horizontal 8.00 20.00
112 Acuna Jr. Horizontal 20.00 50.00
125 Jose Berrios 4.00 10.00
Horizontal
138 Yelich Blue jrsy 5.00 12.00
148 Lux Horizontal 8.00 20.00
150 Bichette Blue shirt 60.00 150.00
157 Willie Mays
161 Hoerner Pinstripe jrsy 20.00 50.00
174 Arenado Horizontal 6.00 15.00
186 Lewis Blue jrsy 60.00 150.00
198 Baez Horizontal 10.00 25.00
200 Alvarez Horizontal 50.00 120.00

2020 Topps Chrome Super Short Prints

STATED ODDS 1:13,868 HOBBY
1 Mike Trout 250.00 600.00
50 Derek Jeter 125.00 300.00
60 Luis Robert 1000.00 2000.00
77 Jackie Robinson 40.00 100.00
157 Willie Mays 100.00 250.00

2020 Topps Chrome '85 Topps

STATED ODDS 1:6 HOBBY
*GREEN/99: 4X TO 10X BASIC
85TC1 Mike Trout 2.00 5.00
85TC2 Bo Bichette 2.00 5.00
85TC3 Juan Soto 1.25 3.00
85TC4 Yordan Alvarez 2.50 6.00
85TC5 Gavin Lux 1.25 3.00
85TC6 Vladimir Guerrero Jr. .60 1.50
85TC7 Shohei Ohtani .60 1.50
85TC8 Rafael Devers .50 1.25
85TC9 Kris Bryant .50 1.25
85TC10 Jesus Luzardo .50 1.25
85TC11 Eloy Jimenez .75 2.00
85TC12 Nico Hoerner 1.00 2.50
85TC13 Brendan McKay .40 1.00
85TC14 A.J. Puk .40 1.00
85TC15 Christian Yelich .50 1.25
85TC16 Keston Hiura .50 1.25
85TC17 Luis Robert 8.00 20.00
85TC18 Pete Alonso 1.00 2.50
85TC19 Jose Altuve .30 .75
85TC20 Rhys Hoskins .50 1.25
85TC21 Aristides Aquino .60 1.50
85TC22 Kyle Lewis 3.00 8.00
85TC23 Austin Riley .50 1.25
85TC24 Nolan Arenado .60 1.50
85TC25 Ronald Acuna Jr. 1.50 4.00

2020 Topps Chrome '85 Topps Gold Refractors

*GOLD: 6X TO 15X BASIC
STATED ODDS 1:5524 HOBBY
STATED PRINT RUN 50 SER.#'d SETS
85TC1 Mike Trout 125.00 300.00

2020 Topps Chrome '85 Topps Orange Refractors

*ORANGE: 8X TO 20X BASIC
STATED ODDS 1:11,048 HOBBY
STATED PRINT RUN 25 SER.#'d SETS
85TC1 Mike Trout 150.00 400.00

2020 Topps Chrome '85 Topps Autographs

STATED ODDS 1:5669 HOBBY
STATED PRINT RUN 99 SER.#'d SETS
EXCHANGE DEADLINE 6/30/2022
*ORANGE/25: .5X TO 1.2X p/r 50
*ORANGE/25: .4X TO 1X p/r 20-40
85TCAAA Aristides Aquino/50 30.00 80.00
85TCAAR Austin Riley/40 15.00 40.00
85TCABB Bo Bichette EXCH
85TCAGL Gavin Lux/50 75.00 200.00
85TCAJA Jose Altuve/30 20.00 50.00
85TCAJL Jesus Luzardo/50 40.00 100.00
85TCAJS Juan Soto/40 125.00 300.00
85TCAKB Kris Bryant/25 60.00 150.00
85TCAKH Keston Hiura/50 25.00 60.00
85TCAKL Kyle Lewis/50 125.00 300.00
85TCAMT Mike Trout/20 300.00 800.00
85TCANH Nico Hoerner/50 100.00 250.00
85TCAPA Pete Alonso/40 60.00 150.00
85TCARAJ Ronald Acuna Jr./40 75.00 200.00
85TCARH Rhys Hoskins/40 25.00 60.00
85TCASO Shohei Ohtani/20 100.00 250.00
85TCAYA Yordan Alvarez/50 50.00 120.00

2020 Topps Chrome All Time Rookie Cup Team Autographs

STATED ODDS 1:12,537 HOBBY
PRINT RUNS B/WN 15-40 COPIES PER
EXCHANGE DEADLINE 6/30/2022
*ORANGE/25: .6X TO 1.5X p/r 40
*ORANGE/25: .4X TO 1X p/r 25-30
RCTAAJ Aaron Judge/20 125.00 300.00
RCTAAR Anthony Rizzo/25 40.00 100.00
RCTACJ Chipper Jones/30 75.00 200.00
RCTACRJ Cal Ripken Jr./30 50.00 120.00
RCTAJB Johnny Bench/30 100.00 250.00
RCTAKB Kris Bryant/30 75.00 200.00
RCTAMM Mark McGwire/30 50.00 120.00
RCTAMTE Mark Teixeira/40 15.00 40.00
RCTAOS Ozzie Smith/40 30.00 80.00
RCTARAJ Ronald Acuna Jr./40 100.00 250.00
RCTARS Ryne Sandberg/25 100.00 250.00

2020 Topps Chrome Decade of Dominance Die Cut

STATED ODDS 1:24 HOBBY
*GREEN/99: 4X TO 10X BASIC
*GOLD/50: 6X TO 15X BASIC
*ORANGE/25: 8X TO 20X BASIC
DOD1 Mike Trout 3.00 8.00
DOD2 Mariano Rivera .50 1.25
DOD3 Rickey Henderson .40 1.00
DOD4 Hank Aaron .75 2.00
DOD5 Ted Williams .75 2.00
DOD6 Johnny Bench .40 1.00
DOD7 Willie Mays .75 2.00
DOD8 Sandy Koufax .75 2.00
DOD9 Randy Johnson .40 1.00
DOD10 Nolan Ryan 1.25 3.00
DOD11 Honus Wagner .40 1.00
DOD12 Mark McGwire .60 1.50
DOD13 Alex Rodriguez .50 1.25
DOD14 Ichiro .50 1.25
DOD15 Babe Ruth 1.00 2.50

2020 Topps Chrome Dual Rookie Autographs

STATED ODDS 1:30:321 HOBBY
STATED PRINT RUN 25 SER.#'d SETS
EXCHANGE DEADLINE 6/30/2022
DRAAT Y.Alvarez/A.Toro 125.00 300.00
DRAHG R.Garcia/N.Hoerner 125.00 300.00
DRALD J.Dunn/K.Lewis 75.00 200.00
DRAML D.May/G.Lux 125.00 300.00
DRANM S.Neuse/S.Murphy 60.00 150.00

2020 Topps Chrome Freshman Flash

STATED ODDS 1:12 HOBBY
*GREEN/99: 4X TO 10X BASIC
*GOLD/50: 5X TO 12X BASIC
*ORANGE/25: 6X TO 15X BASIC
FF1 Bo Bichette 2.00 5.00
FF2 Aristides Aquino .60 1.50
FF3 Dylan Cease .40 1.00
FF4 Dustin May .75 2.00
FF5 Luis Robert 5.00 12.00
FF6 Brendan McKay .40 1.00
FF7 Sheldon Neuse .30 .75
FF8 Jesus Luzardo .50 1.25
FF9 A.J. Puk .40 1.00
FF10 Nico Hoerner 1.00 2.50
FF11 Sean Murphy .40 1.00
FF12 Gavin Lux 1.25 3.00
FF13 Kyle Lewis 2.00 5.00
FF14 Isan Diaz .40 1.00
FF15 Yordan Alvarez 2.50 6.00

2020 Topps Chrome Freshman Flash Autographs

STATED ODDS 1:2362 HOBBY
STATED PRINT RUN 99 SER.#'d SETS
EXCHANGE DEADLINE 6/30/2022
*ORANGE/25: .6X TO 1.5X BASIC
FFAAA Aristides Aquino 12.00 30.00
FFAAAL Adbert Alzolay 6.00 15.00
FFAAT Abraham Toro 6.00 15.00
FFABB Bo Bichette EXCH 75.00 200.00
FFABM Brendan McKay 8.00 20.00
FFADC Dylan Cease 8.00 20.00
FFADM Dustin May 25.00 60.00
FFAGL Gavin Lux 60.00 150.00
FFAID Isan Diaz 8.00 20.00
FFAJL Jesus Luzardo 10.00 25.00
FFAJY Jordan Yamamoto 5.00 12.00
FFAKL Kyle Lewis 100.00 250.00
FFAMD Mauricio Dubon 6.00 15.00
FFANH Nico Hoerner 20.00 50.00
FFASB Seth Brown 5.00 12.00
FFASM Sean Murphy 8.00 20.00
FFASN Sheldon Neuse 6.00 15.00
FFAYA Yordan Alvarez 50.00 120.00

2020 Topps Chrome Future Stars

STATED ODDS 1:8 HOBBY
*GREEN/99: 4X TO 10X BASIC
*GOLD/50: 6X TO 15X BASIC
*ORANGE/25: 8X TO 20X BASIC
FS1 Pete Alonso 1.00 2.50
FS2 Will Smith .40 1.00
FS3 Eloy Jimenez .75 2.00
FS4 Michael Chavis .30 .75
FS5 Mike Yastrzemski .60 1.50
FS6 Carter Kieboom .30 .75
FS7 Victor Robles .50 1.25
FS8 Chris Paddack .40 1.00
FS9 Bryan Reynolds .30 .75
FS10 Mitch Keller .40 1.00
FS11 Fernando Tatis Jr. 2.00 5.00
FS12 Brendan Rodgers .40 1.00
FS13 Cavan Biggio .50 1.25
FS14 Ramon Laureano .30 .75
FS15 Keston Hiura .50 1.25
FS16 Austin Riley .50 1.25
FS17 Willians Astudillo .25 .60
FS18 John Means .40 1.00

FS19 Mike Tauchman .40 1.00
FS20 Vladimir Guerrero Jr. .60 1.50

2020 Topps Chrome Future Stars Autographs

STATED ODDS 1:3141 HOBBY
STATED PRINT RUN 99 SER.#'d SETS
EXCHANGE DEADLINE 6/30/2022
*ORANGE/25: .6X TO 1.5X BASIC
FSAAR Austin Riley 10.00 25.00
FSABR Bryan Reynolds 6.00 15.00
FSABRE Brendan Rodgers 12.00 30.00
FSACB Cavan Biggio 12.00 30.00
FSACK Carter Kieboom 6.00 15.00
FSACP Chris Paddack 8.00 20.00
FSAEJ Eloy Jimenez 20.00 50.00
FSAFTJ Fernando Tatis Jr. 150.00 400.00
FSAJM John Means 30.00 80.00
FSAKH Keston Hiura 20.00 50.00
FSAMC Michael Chavis 6.00 15.00
FSAMK Mitch Keller 8.00 20.00
FSAMT Mike Tauchman 12.00 30.00
FSAMY Mike Yastrzemski 25.00 60.00
FSAPA Pete Alonso 40.00 100.00
FSARL Ramon Laureano 20.00 50.00
FSAVR Victor Robles 10.00 25.00
FSAWS Will Smith 15.00 40.00

2020 Topps Chrome Retro Rookie Chrome Relic Autographs

STATED ODDS 1:2366 HOBBY
PRINT RUNS B/WN 25-99 COPIES PER
EXCHANGE DEADLINE 6/30/2022
ARRCRAJ Aaron Judge/30 125.00 300.00
ARRCRBH Bryce Harper/25 150.00 400.00
ARRCRCJ Chipper Jones/40 125.00 300.00
ARRCRCRJ Cal Ripken Jr./50 100.00 250.00
ARRCRCY Carl Yastrzemski/50 75.00 200.00
ARRCRDM Don Mattingly/75 60.00 150.00
ARRCRFT Frank Thomas/75 75.00 200.00
ARRCRGT Gleyber Torres/99 100.00 250.00
ARRCRI Ichiro/25 400.00 1000.00
ARRCRJA Jose Altuve/75 30.00 80.00
ARRCRJS Juan Soto/99 200.00 500.00
ARRCRKB Kris Bryant/60 50.00 120.00
ARRCRKGJ Ken Griffey Jr./35 500.00 1200.00
ARRCRMT Mark Teixeira/99 15.00 40.00
ARRCRMTR Mike Trout/25 1250.00 3000.00
ARRCRRAJ Ronald Acuna Jr./99 200.00 500.00
ARRCRRH Rickey Henderson
ARRCRRJ Reggie Jackson/50 100.00 250.00

2020 Topps Chrome Retro Rookie Chrome Relics

STATED ODDS 1:517 HOBBY
*GREEN REF/99: .5X TO 1.2X BASIC
*ORANGE REF/25: .75X TO 2X BASIC
RRCRAB Alex Bregman 5.00 12.00
RRCRAJ Aaron Judge 10.00 25.00
RRCRAP Albert Pujols 20.00 50.00
RRCRAR Anthony Rizzo 10.00 25.00
RRCRBH Bryce Harper 10.00 25.00
RRCRBP Buster Posey 10.00 25.00
RRCRCB Cody Bellinger 10.00 25.00
RRCRCJ Chipper Jones 12.00 30.00
RRCRCK Clayton Kershaw 15.00 40.00
RRCRCRJ Cal Ripken Jr. 15.00 40.00
RRCRCY Carl Yastrzemski 12.00 30.00
RRCRDM Don Mattingly 15.00 40.00
RRCREM Eddie Mathews 10.00 25.00
RRCRFT Frank Thomas 15.00 40.00
RRCRGB George Brett 15.00 40.00
RRCRGT Gleyber Torres 10.00 25.00
RRCRI Ichiro 15.00 40.00
RRCRJA Jose Altuve 6.00 15.00
RRCRJB Johnny Bench 12.00 30.00
RRCRJBA Javier Baez 8.00 20.00
RRCRJV Justin Verlander 12.00 30.00
RRCRJVO Joey Votto 10.00 25.00
RRCRKB Kris Bryant 10.00 25.00
RRCRKGJ Ken Griffey Jr. 50.00 120.00
RRCRMB Mookie Betts 15.00 40.00
RRCRMT Mark Teixeira 4.00 10.00
RRCRMTA Masahiro Tanaka 5.00 12.00
RRCRMTR Mike Trout 60.00 150.00
RRCROS Ozzie Smith 12.00 30.00
RRCRRAJ Ronald Acuna Jr. 30.00 80.00
RRCRRC Roberto Clemente 60.00 150.00
RRCRRH Rickey Henderson 30.00 80.00
RRCRRJ Reggie Jackson 10.00 25.00
RRCRTG Tony Gwynn 12.00 30.00
RRCRTW Ted Williams 25.00 60.00

2020 Topps Chrome Rookie Autographs

STATED ODDS 1:17 HOBBY
PRINTING PLATE ODDS 1:15,900 HOBBY
PLATE PRINT RUN 1 SET PER COLOR
BLACK-CYAN-MAGENTA-YELLOW ISSUED
NO PLATE PRICING DUE TO SCARCITY
EXCHANGE DEADLINE 6/30/2022
RAAA Adbert Alzolay 5.00 12.00
RAAAQ Aristides Aquino 15.00 40.00
RAAC Aaron Civale 8.00 20.00
RAAJP A.J. Puk EXCH 12.00 30.00
RAAK Anthony Kay 2.50 6.00
RAAMU Andres Munoz 4.00 10.00
RAAN Austin Nola 6.00 15.00
RAAT Abraham Toro 3.00 8.00
RAAY Alex Young 2.50 6.00
RABA Bryan Abreu 2.50 6.00
RABB Bobby Bradley 8.00 20.00
RABBI Bo Bichette 250.00 600.00
RABBU Brock Burke 2.50 6.00
RABG Brusdar Graterol 6.00 15.00
RABM Brendan McKay 8.00 20.00
RACPO Colin Poche 2.50 6.00
RADA Dario Agrazal 3.00 8.00
RADCE Dylan Cease 10.00 25.00
RADL Domingo Leyba 5.00 12.00
RADM Dustin May 25.00 60.00
RADME Danny Mendick 3.00 8.00
RADN Dom Nunez 3.00 8.00
RAEC Emmanuel Clase 4.00 10.00
RAGL Gavin Lux 40.00 100.00
RAHH Hunter Harvey 4.00 10.00
RAID Isan Diaz 4.00 10.00
RAJD Justin Dunn 3.00 8.00
RAJDA Jaylin Davis 4.00 10.00
RAJF Jake Fraley 3.00 8.00
RAJFE Junior Fernandez 2.50 6.00
RAJH Jonathan Hernandez 2.50 6.00
RAJL Jesus Luzardo 10.00 25.00
RAJMA James Marvel 2.50 6.00
RAJPO Joe Palumbo 2.50 6.00
RAJR Jake Rogers 2.50 6.00
RAJRO Jose Rodriguez 2.50 6.00
RAJS Josh Staumont 8.00 20.00
RAJT Jesus Tinoco 2.50 6.00
RAJU Jose Urquidy 3.00 8.00
RAJW Jacob Waguespack 3.00 8.00
RAJY Jordan Yamamoto 2.50 6.00
RAKG Kyle Garlick 6.00 15.00
RAKL Kyle Lewis 40.00 100.00
RAKW Kean Wong 4.00 10.00
RALA Logan Allen 2.50 6.00
RALR Luis Robert 200.00 500.00
RALT Lewis Thorpe 2.50 6.00
RALW Logan Webb 4.00 10.00
RAMB Michel Baez 2.50 6.00
RAMBR Michael Brosseau 5.00 12.00
RAMD Mauricio Dubon 5.00 12.00
RAMK Mike King 4.00 10.00
RAMT Matt Thaiss 3.00 8.00
RANH Nico Hoerner 15.00 40.00
RANS Nick Solak 10.00 25.00
RARA Rogelio Armenteros 3.00 8.00
RARAR Randy Arozarena 100.00 250.00
RARD Robert Dugger 2.50 6.00
RARG Robel Garcia 2.50 6.00
RARR Rangel Ravelo 3.00 8.00
RASA Shogo Akiyama 10.00 25.00
RASB Seth Brown 2.50 6.00
RASH Sam Hilliard 4.00 10.00
RASM Sean Murphy 8.00 20.00
RASN Sheldon Neuse 3.00 8.00
RATA Tyler Alexander 4.00 10.00
RATD Travis Demeritte 4.00 10.00
RATE Tom Eshelman 5.00 12.00
RATG Tony Gonsolin 6.00 15.00
RATGR Trent Grisham 30.00 80.00
RATL Tim Lopes 3.00 8.00
RATLA Travis Lakins 2.50 6.00
RATZ T.J. Zeuch 2.50 6.00
RAWC Willi Castro 20.00 50.00
RAYA Yordan Alvarez 75.00 200.00
RAZC Zack Collins 3.00 8.00
RAZG Zac Gallen 20.00 50.00

2020 Topps Chrome Rookie Autographs Blue Refractors

*BLUE REF: .75X TO 2X BASIC
STATED ODDS 1:426 HOBBY
STATED PRINT RUN 150 SER.#'d SETS
EXCHANGE DEADLINE 6/30/2022

2020 Topps Chrome Rookie Autographs Blue Wave Refractors

*BLUE WAVE REF: .75X TO 2X BASIC
STATED ODDS 1:426 HOBBY
STATED PRINT RUN 150 SER.#'d SETS
EXCHANGE DEADLINE 6/30/2022

2020 Topps Chrome Rookie Autographs Gold Refractors

*GOLD REF: 1.2X TO 3X BASIC
STATED ODDS 1:1278 HOBBY
STATED PRINT RUN 50 SER.#'d SETS
EXCHANGE DEADLINE 6/30/2022

2020 Topps Chrome Rookie Autographs Gold Wave Refractors

*GOLD WAVE REF: 1.2X TO 3X BASIC
STATED ODDS 1:755 HOBBY
STATED PRINT RUN 50 SER.#'d SETS
EXCHANGE DEADLINE 6/30/2022

2020 Topps Chrome Rookie Autographs Orange Refractors

*ORANGE REF: 2X TO 5X BASIC
STATED ODDS 1:736 HOBBY
STATED PRINT RUN 25 SER.#'d SETS
EXCHANGE DEADLINE 6/30/2022

2020 Topps Chrome Rookie Autographs Orange Wave Refractors

*ORANGE WAVE REF: 2X TO 5X BASIC
STATED ODDS 1:1509 HOBBY
STATED PRINT RUN 25 SER.#'d SETS
EXCHANGE DEADLINE 6/30/2022

2020 Topps Chrome Rookie Autographs Purple Refractors

*PURPLE REF: .6X TO 1.5X BASIC
STATED ODDS 1:256 HOBBY
STATED PRINT RUN 250 SER.#'d SETS
EXCHANGE DEADLINE 6/30/2022

2020 Topps Chrome Rookie Autographs Refractors

*REF: .5X TO 1.2X BASIC
STATED ODDS 1:130 HOBBY
STATED PRINT RUN 499 SER.#'d SETS
EXCHANGE DEADLINE 6/30/2022

2020 Topps Chrome Topps Fire Preview

COMPLETE SET (9) 10.00 25.00
FIVE PER TARGET HANGER
FP1 Aaron Judge 1.25 3.00
FP2 Mike Trout 2.50 6.00
FP3 Ken Griffey Jr. 1.00 2.50
FP4 Luis Robert 2.50 6.00
FP5 Fernando Tatis Jr. 2.50 6.00
FP6 Juan Soto 1.50 4.00
FP7 Bryce Harper .75 2.00
FP8 David Ortiz .50 1.25
FP9 Pete Alonso 1.25 3.00

2020 Topps Chrome Topps Gallery Preview

COMPLETE SET (10) 8.00 20.00
FIVE PER WALMART HANGER
GP1 Mike Trout 2.00 5.00
GP2 Ronald Acuna Jr. 1.50 4.00
GP3 Fernando Tatis Jr. 2.00 5.00
GP4 Aaron Judge 1.00 2.50
GP5 Christian Yelich .50 1.25
GP6 Bryce Harper .60 1.50
GP7 Juan Soto 1.25 3.00
GP8 Pete Alonso 1.00 2.50
GP9 Yordan Alvarez 2.50 6.00
GP10 Cody Bellinger .75 2.00

2020 Topps Chrome Topps Update Preview

COMPLETE SET (8) 8.00 20.00
UP1 Bo Bichette 3.00 8.00
UP2 Brendan McKay .50 1.25
UP3 Yordan Alvarez 3.00 8.00
UP4 Gavin Lux 1.50 4.00
UP5 Kyle Lewis 2.50 6.00
UP6 Nico Hoerner 1.25 3.00
UP7 Jesus Luzardo .60 1.50
UP8 Aristides Aquino .75 2.00

2020 Topps Chrome Update

U1 Anthony Rendon .40 1.00
U2 David Price .30 .75
U3 Starling Marte .30 .75
U4 Kole Calhoun .25 .60
U5 Alex Verdugo .30 .75
U6 Jason Kipnis .30 .75
U7 Alec Mills RC .50 1.25
U8 Edwin Encarnacion .40 1.00
U9 Yasmani Grandal .25 .60
U10 Mike Moustakas .30 .75
U11 Cameron Maybin .25 .60
U12 C.J. Cron .25 .60
U13 Jonathan Villar .25 .60
U14 Jesus Aguilar .30 .75
U15 Logan Morrison .25 .60
U16 Kenta Maeda .30 .75
U17 Rich Hill .25 .60
U18 Johnny Davis RC .50 1.25
U19 Neil Walker .25 .60
U20 Zack Wheeler .30 .75
U21 Tommy Pham .25 .60
U22 Zach Davies .25 .60
U23 Nik Turley RC .50 1.25
U24 Hunter Pence .30 .75
U25 Todd Frazier .25 .60
U26 Yoshi Tsutsugo RC 1.25 3.00
U27 Josh Taylor RC .75 2.00
U28 Ian Miller RC .50 1.25
U29 Phillip Diehl RC .60 1.50
U30 Dario Agrazal RC .60 1.50
U31 Jesus Tinoco RC .50 1.25
U32 Cody Stashak RC .50 1.25
U33 Mike King RC .75 2.00
U34 Trent Grisham RC 4.00 10.00
U35 Randy Arozarena RC 4.00 10.00
U36 Tyler Heineman RC .50 1.25
U37 Nestor Cortes RC .50 1.25
U38 Wilmer Flores .30 .75
U39 Deivy Grullon RC .50 1.25
U40 Erick Mejia RC .75 2.00
U41 Zach Green RC .50 1.25
U42 Starlin Castro .25 .60
U43 Eric Thames .25 .60
U44 Jarrod Dyson .25 .60
U45 Brock Holt .25 .60
U46 Cesar Hernandez .25 .60
U47 Domingo Santana .30 .75
U48 Kevin Pillar .25 .60
U49 Gabe Speier RC .50 1.25
U50 Cy Sneed RC .50 1.25
U51 Bo Bichette RC 4.00 10.00
U52 Brendan McKay RC .75 2.00
U53 Yordan Alvarez RC 6.00 15.00
U54 Gavin Lux RC 4.00 10.00
U55 Nico Hoerner RC 2.50 6.00
U56 Jesus Luzardo RC 1.00 2.50
U57 Aristides Aquino RC 2.50 6.00
U58 Luis Robert RC 5.00 12.00
U59 Kyle Lewis RC 3.00 8.00
U60 Nick Solak RC 2.00 5.00
U61 Pedro Martinez AS .30 .75
U62 Kris Bryant AS .50 1.25
U63 Ken Griffey Jr. AS 1.50 4.00
U64 Ichiro AS .50 1.25
U65 Aaron Judge AS 1.00 2.50
U66 Bryce Harper AS .60 1.50
U67 Derek Jeter AS 2.00 5.00
U68 Buster Posey AS .50 1.25
U69 Mike Trout AS 2.00 5.00
U70 Cal Ripken Jr. AS 1.50 4.00
U71 Alex Bregman AS .40 1.00
U72 Mariano Rivera AS .50 1.25
U73 Andrew McCutchen AS .40 1.00
U74 Clayton Kershaw AS .60 1.50
U75 Ronald Acuna Jr. AS 1.50 4.00
U76 Gleyber Torres AS .75 2.00
U77 Javier Baez AS .50 1.25
U78 Albert Pujols AS .50 1.25
U79 Jose Altuve AS .30 .75
U80 Joey Votto AS .40 1.00
U81 Jacob deGrom AS .75 2.00
U82 David Ortiz AS .40 1.00
U83 Yadier Molina AS .50 1.25
U84 Pete Alonso AS 1.00 2.50
U85 Anthony Rizzo AS .50 1.25
U86 Pete Alonso HRD 1.00 2.50
U87 Ken Griffey Jr. HRD 1.50 4.00
U88 Tino Martinez HRD .30 .75
U89 Bryce Harper HRD .60 1.50
U90 Aaron Judge HRD 1.00 2.50
U91 Giancarlo Stanton HRD .40 1.00
U92 Mark McGwire HRD 1.50 4.00
U93 Ryan Howard HRD .30 .75
U94 David Ortiz HRD .40 1.00
U95 Mark McGwire HRD 1.50 4.00
U96 Todd Frazier HRD .25 .60
U97 Robinson Cano HRD .30 .75
U98 Yoenis Cespedes HRD .40 1.00
U99 Cal Ripken Jr. HRD 1.50 4.00
U100 Eric Davis HRD .25 .60

2020 Topps Chrome Update Gold Refractors

*GOLD: 6X TO 15X BASIC
*GOLD RC: 2X TO 5X BASIC RC
STATED ODDS 1:510 MEGA
STATED PRINT RUN 50 SER.#'d SETS
U34 Trent Grisham 40.00 100.00
U35 Randy Arozarena 300.00 800.00
U51 Bo Bichette 125.00 300.00
U54 Gavin Lux 30.00 80.00
U58 Luis Robert 300.00 800.00
U59 Kyle Lewis 75.00 200.00
U63 Ken Griffey Jr. AS 40.00 100.00
U64 Ichiro AS 50.00 120.00
U67 Derek Jeter AS 40.00 100.00
U69 Mike Trout AS 75.00 200.00
U87 Ken Griffey Jr. HRD 40.00 100.00

2020 Topps Chrome Update Pink Refractors

*PINK: 1.2X TO 3X BASIC
*PINK RC: .6X TO 1.5X BASIC RC
STATED ODDS 2 PER VALUE
U35 Randy Arozarena 75.00 200.00
U51 Bo Bichette 8.00 20.00
U58 Luis Robert 50.00 120.00
U59 Kyle Lewis 12.00 30.00
U63 Ken Griffey Jr. AS 10.00 25.00
U87 Ken Griffey Jr. HRD 10.00 25.00

2020 Topps Chrome Update Pink Wave Refractors

*PINK WAVE: 1.2X TO 3X BASIC
*PINK WAVE RC: .6X TO 1.5X BASIC RC
STATED ODDS 2 PER HANGER
U35 Randy Arozarena 20.00 50.00
U51 Bo Bichette 15.00 40.00
U58 Luis Robert 50.00 120.00
U59 Kyle Lewis 15.00 40.00
U63 Ken Griffey Jr. AS 10.00 25.00
U67 Derek Jeter AS 15.00 40.00
U87 Ken Griffey Jr. HRD 10.00 25.00

2020 Topps Chrome Update Red Refractors

*RED: 8X TO 20X BASIC
*RED RC: 2.5X TO 6X BASIC RC
STATED ODDS 1:1020 MEGA
STATED PRINT RUN 25 SER.#'d SETS
U34 Trent Grisham 50.00 120.00
U35 Randy Arozarena 200.00 500.00
U51 Bo Bichette 150.00 400.00
U54 Gavin Lux 75.00 200.00
U57 Aristides Aquino 20.00 50.00
U58 Luis Robert 1500.00 3000.00
U59 Kyle Lewis 100.00 250.00
U63 Ken Griffey Jr. AS 50.00 120.00
U64 Ichiro AS 60.00 150.00
U67 Derek Jeter AS 125.00 300.00
U69 Mike Trout AS 100.00 250.00
U70 Cal Ripken Jr. AS 75.00 200.00
U87 Ken Griffey Jr. HRD 50.00 120.00
U99 Cal Ripken Jr. HRD 75.00 200.00

2020 Topps Chrome Update Refractors

*REF.: 1.5X TO 4X BASIC
*REF. RC: .8X TO 2X BASIC RC
STATED ODDS 1:102 MEGA
STATED PRINT RUN 250 SER.#'d SETS
U35 Randy Arozarena 100.00 250.00
U51 Bo Bichette 40.00 100.00
U54 Gavin Lux 10.00 25.00
U58 Luis Robert 100.00 250.00
U59 Kyle Lewis 20.00 50.00
U63 Ken Griffey Jr. AS 12.00 30.00
U64 Ichiro AS 15.00 40.00
U67 Derek Jeter AS 12.00 30.00
U69 Mike Trout AS 25.00 60.00
U87 Ken Griffey Jr. HRD 12.00 30.00

2020 Topps Chrome Update X-Fractors

*XFRACTOR.: 3X TO 8X BASIC
*XFRACTOR RC: 1X TO 2.5X BASIC RC
STATED ODDS 1:258 MEGA
STATED PRINT RUN 99 SER.#'d SETS
U34 Trent Grisham 25.00 60.00
U35 Randy Arozarena 200.00 500.00
U51 Bo Bichette 75.00 200.00
U54 Gavin Lux 20.00 50.00
U58 Luis Robert 200.00 500.00
U59 Kyle Lewis 40.00 100.00
U63 Ken Griffey Jr. AS 25.00 60.00
U64 Ichiro AS 30.00 80.00
U67 Derek Jeter AS 25.00 60.00
U69 Mike Trout AS 50.00 120.00
U87 Ken Griffey Jr. HRD 25.00 60.00

2020 Topps Chrome Update A Numbers Game

STATED ODDS 1:4 HOBBY
NGC1 Roberto Alomar .50 1.25
NGC2 Ryne Sandberg 1.25 3.00
NGC3 Roberto Clemente 1.50 4.00
NGC4 Randy Johnson .60 1.50
NGC5 Rickey Henderson .60 1.50
NGC6 Nolan Ryan 2.00 5.00
NGC7 Jackie Robinson .60 1.50
NGC8 Jeff Bagwell .50 1.25
NGC9 Chipper Jones .60 1.50
NGC10 Ken Griffey Jr. 1.25 3.00
NGC11 Stan Musial 1.00 2.50
NGC12 Robin Yount .60 1.50
NGC13 Mariano Rivera .75 2.00
NGC14 Ted Williams 1.25 3.00
NGC15 Tony Gwynn .60 1.50
NGC16 Cal Ripken Jr. 1.25 3.00
NGC17 Mike Piazza .60 1.50
NGC18 Willie Mays 1.25 3.00
NGC19 Ernie Banks .60 1.50
NGC20 Sandy Koufax 1.25 3.00
NGC21 Ozzie Smith .75 2.00
NGC22 Derek Jeter 1.50 4.00
NGC23 Mike Schmidt 1.00 2.50
NGC24 Johnny Bench .60 1.50
NGC25 Hank Aaron 1.25 3.00

2020 Topps Chrome Update Autograph Refractors

STATED ODDS 1:41 PACKS
EXCHANGE DEADLINE 10/31/22
USAAH Aaron Hicks 10.00 25.00
USAAM Austin Meadows 8.00 20.00
USAAN Aaron Nola 10.00 25.00
USAAO Adam Ottavino 4.00 10.00
USAAR Anthony Rendon 12.00 30.00
USABH Bryce Harper
USABO Brian O'Grady 3.00 8.00
USACB Cody Bellinger
USACK Carter Kieboom 6.00 15.00
USACP Colin Poche 3.00 8.00
USACT Cole Tucker 5.00 12.00
USACW Chad Wallach 6.00 15.00
USADB David Bednar 3.00 8.00
USADP Daniel Ponce de Leon 3.00 8.00
USAEH Eric Hosmer 10.00 25.00
USAET Eric Thames 3.00 8.00
USAFB Franklin Barreto 3.00 8.00
USAGC Gerrit Cole 40.00 100.00
USAGS Garrett Stubbs 3.00 8.00
USAHP Hunter Pence 8.00 20.00
USAHR Hyun-Jin Ryu
USAIH Ian Happ 8.00 20.00
USAJB Jon Berti 8.00 20.00
USAJM Jack Mayfield 3.00 8.00
USAJP Jorge Polanco 4.00 10.00
USAJR J.T. Realmuto 12.00 30.00
USAJS Juan Soto 300.00 600.00
USAJT Jesus Tinoco 3.00 8.00
USAJV Josh VanMeter 5.00 12.00
USAKG Kyle Garlick 5.00 12.00
USAKH Kyle Hendricks 15.00 40.00
USAKK Kwang-Hyun Kim 12.00 30.00
USAKM Kenta Maeda 15.00 40.00
USAKS Kyle Schwarber 15.00 40.00
USAKW Kean Wong 10.00 25.00
USALW LaMonte Wade Jr. 5.00 12.00
USAMB Matthew Boyd 8.00 20.00
USAMK Mike King 6.00 15.00
USAMM Mike Moustakas 10.00 25.00
USAMT Mike Trout 300.00 600.00
USAMY Mike Yastrzemski 10.00 25.00
USANC Nick Castellanos 12.00 30.00
USANM Nick Martini 3.00 8.00
USAOM Oscar Mercado 5.00 12.00
USAPA Pete Alonso
USAPC Patrick Corbin 6.00 15.00
USARD Randy Dobnak 10.00 25.00
USARI Raisel Iglesias 3.00 8.00
USARL Ramon Laureano 12.00 30.00
USARM Ryan McBroom 4.00 10.00
USARR Rangel Ravelo 4.00 10.00
USASB Shane Bieber 30.00 80.00
USASC Shin-Soo Choo 10.00 25.00
USASH Scott Heineman UER 3.00 8.00
last name mispelled Heinenman
USASM Seth Mejias-Brean 3.00 8.00
USASS Steven Souza Jr.
USASY Shun Yamaguchi 4.00 10.00
USATE Tommy Edman 40.00 100.00
USATL Tommy La Stella 3.00 8.00
USATT Tyrone Taylor 6.00 15.00
USATW Trey Wingenter 3.00 8.00
USAWM Whit Merrifield 10.00 25.00
USAXB Xander Bogaerts 25.00 60.00
USAYD Yonathan Daza 4.00 10.00
USAYM Yadier Molina 40.00 100.00
USAZG Zac Gallen 15.00 40.00
USAZW Zack Wheeler 4.00 10.00
USACBI Cavan Biggio 10.00 25.00
USAGSP George Springer 10.00 25.00
USAJKA James Karinchak 12.00 30.00
USAJPA Joe Palumbo 3.00 8.00
USAJSM Justin Smoak
USAKGI Kevin Ginkel 6.00 15.00
USAKWO Kolten Wong 6.00 15.00
USAMMA Manny Machado 30.00 80.00
USANCI Nick Ciuffo 3.00 8.00
USARRO Ronny Rodriguez 3.00 8.00
USASMA Sean Manaea 3.00 8.00
USATLA Travis Lakins Sr. 6.00 15.00

2020 Topps Chrome Update Autograph Gold Refractors

*GOLD: 1X TO 2.5X BASIC
STATED ODDS 1:603 PACKS
STATED PRINT RUN 50 SER.#'d SETS
EXCHANGE DEADLINE 10/31/22
USAHR Hyun-Jin Ryu 50.00 120.00
USAMK Mike King 25.00 60.00
USAPA Pete Alonso 50.00 120.00

2020 Topps Chrome Update Autograph Orange Refractors

*ORANGE: 1.2X TO 3X BASIC
STATED ODDS 1:1151 PACKS
STATED PRINT RUN 25 SER.#'d SETS
EXCHANGE DEADLINE 10/31/22
USAHR Hyun-Jin Ryu 60.00 150.00
USAMK Mike King 30.00 80.00
USAPA Pete Alonso 60.00 150.00

2020 Topps Chrome Update Autograph X-Fractors

*XFRACTOR: .6X TO 1.5X BASIC
STATED ODDS 1:258 PACKS
PRINT RUNS B/WN 100-125 COPIES PER
EXCHANGE DEADLINE 10/31/22
USAHR Hyun-Jin Ryu/100 30.00 80.00
USAMK Mike King/125 15.00 40.00

2020 Topps Chrome Update Decade's Next

STATED ODDS 1:4 HOBBY
DNC1 Vladimir Guerrero Jr. 1.00 2.50
DNC2 Luis Robert 3.00 8.00
DNC3 Fernando Tatis Jr. 3.00 8.00
DNC4 Yordan Alvarez 4.00 10.00
DNC5 Ronald Acuna Jr. 2.50 6.00
DNC6 Gleyber Torres 1.25 3.00
DNC7 Brendan Rodgers .60 1.50
DNC8 Eloy Jimenez 1.25 3.00
DNC9 Pete Alonso 1.50 4.00
DNC10 Juan Soto 2.00 5.00
DNC11 Bo Bichette 3.00 8.00
DNC12 Nick Senzel .60 1.50
DNC13 Ozzie Albies .60 1.50
DNC14 Walker Buehler .75 2.00
DNC15 Rafael Devers .75 2.00
DNC16 Cody Bellinger 1.25 3.00
DNC17 Victor Robles .75 2.00
DNC18 Shohei Ohtani 1.00 2.50
DNC19 Kyle Lewis 3.00 8.00
DNC20 Chris Paddack .60 1.50
DNC21 Brendan McKay .60 1.50
DNC22 Jesus Luzardo .75 2.00
DNC23 Shogo Akiyama .60 1.50
DNC24 Nico Hoerner 1.50 4.00
DNC25 Gavin Lux 2.00 5.00

2020 Topps Chrome Update Rookie Debut Autograph Refractors

RANDOM INSERTS IN PACKS
EXCHANGE DEADLINE 10/31/22
*XFRACTOR./125: .6X TO 1.5X BASIC
RDUSAAA Aristides Aquino 10.00 25.00
RDUSABB Bo Bichette EXCH
RDUSABM Brendan McKay 5.00 12.00
RDUSAKL Kyle Lewis 75.00 200.00
RDUSALR Luis Robert EXCH 200.00 500.00
RDUSANH Nico Hoerner 15.00 40.00
RDUSANS Nick Solak 10.00 25.00
RDUSAYA Yordan Alvarez 60.00 150.00

2020 Topps Chrome Update Rookie Debut Autograph Gold Refractors

*GOLD: 1X TO 2.5X BASIC
RANDOM INSERTS IN PACKS
STATED PRINT RUN 50 SER.#'d SETS
EXCHANGE DEADLINE 10/31/22
RDUSALR Luis Robert EXCH 1000.00 2000.00

2020 Topps Chrome Update Rookie Debut Autograph Orange Refractors

*ORANGE: 1.2X TO 3X BASIC
RANDOM INSERTS IN PACKS
STATED PRINT RUN 25 SER.#'d SETS
EXCHANGE DEADLINE 10/31/22
RDUSALR Luis Robert EXCH 1200.00 2500.00

2020 Topps Chrome Update Sapphire

U1 Bo Bichette 60.00 150.00
U2 Adam Engel 1.25 3.00
U3 Trea Turner 1.50 4.00
Wilmer Difo
U4 Mike Trout AS 15.00 40.00
U5 Starlin Castro 1.25 3.00
U6 Mike Moustakas 1.50 4.00
U7 Alex Bregman 4.00 10.00
Yordan Alvarez
U8 Buster Posey AS 2.50 6.00
U9 Ken Griffey Jr. HRD 20.00 50.00
U10 Anthony Alford 1.25 3.00
U11 Chris Owings 1.25 3.00
U12 Aaron Bummer 1.25 3.00
U13 Jose Martinez 1.25 3.00
U14 Giancarlo Stanton HRD 2.00 5.00
U15 Aaron Judge AS 8.00 20.00
U16 Phillip Diehl RC 1.50 4.00
U17 Josh Fuentes 1.25 3.00
U18 Felix Pena 1.25 3.00
U19 Yasmani Grandal 1.25 3.00
U20 Francisco Cervelli 1.25 3.00
U21 Kyle Lewis 25.00 60.00
U22 Cody Stashak RC 1.25 3.00
U23 Cheslor Cuthbert 1.25 3.00
U24 Buck Farmer 1.25 3.00
U25 Josh Taylor RC 2.00 5.00
U26 Kyle Gibson 1.25 3.00
U27 Kyle Ryan 1.25 3.00
U28 Eduardo Nunez 1.25 3.00
U29 Aristides Aquino 6.00 15.00
U30 Yasmany Tomas 1.25 3.00
U31 Curt Casali 1.25 3.00
U32 Drew Pomeranz 1.25 3.00
U33 Alex Verdugo 1.50 4.00
U34 Justin Verlander 2.00 5.00
U35 Kyle Farmer 1.25 3.00
U36 Robinson Cano HRD 1.50 4.00
U37 Yoenis Cespedes HRD 2.00 5.00
U38 Albert Pujols 2.50 6.00
U39 Kevin Plawecki 1.25 3.00
U40 Antonio Senzatela 1.25 3.00
U41 Josh Lindblom 1.25 3.00
U42 Kris Bryant AS 4.00 10.00
U43 Alex Blandino 1.25 3.00
U44 Jorge Alcala RC 1.25 3.00
U45 Zack Wheeler 1.50 4.00
U46 Jose Suarez 1.25 3.00
U47 Jose Peraza 1.50 4.00
U48 Sandy Leon 1.25 3.00
U49 Jared Walsh 8.00 20.00
U50 Nolan Arenado AS 3.00 8.00
U51 Matt Davidson 1.50 4.00
U52 Kyle Higashioka 2.00 5.00
U53 Brad Miller 1.25 3.00
U54 Alex Avila 1.25 3.00
U55 Miguel Cabrera AS 2.00 5.00
U56 Lane Thomas 1.50 4.00
U57 Yoan Lopez 1.25 3.00
U58 Erick Mejia RC 2.00 5.00
U59 Ryan Howard HRD 1.50 4.00
U60 Brendan McKay 2.00 5.00
U61 Jedd Gyorko 1.25 3.00
U62 David Ortiz HRD 2.00 5.00
U63 Terrance Gore 1.25 3.00
U64 Alex Bregman AS 2.00 5.00
U65 Yoshi Tsutsugo RC 3.00 8.00
U66 Max Scherzer 2.00 5.00
U67 Michael Fulmer 1.25 3.00
U68 Greg Garcia 1.25 3.00
U69 Derek Holland 1.25 3.00
U70 Skye Bolt 1.25 3.00
U71 Jesus Aguilar 1.50 4.00
U72 Drew Butera 1.25 3.00
U73 Todd Frazier 1.25 3.00
U74 Bryce Harper 3.00 8.00
Jean Segura
U75 Pedro Martinez AS 1.50 4.00
U76 Edwin Encarnacion 2.00 5.00
U77 Jalen Beeks 1.25 3.00
U78 Joe Jimenez 1.25 3.00
U79 Sean Poppen RC 2.00 5.00
U80 Cody Bellinger AS 5.00 12.00
U81 Junior Guerra 1.25 3.00
U82 Kenley Jansen 1.50 4.00
U83 Trent Grisham RC 25.00 60.00
U84 Yusmeiro Petit 1.25 3.00
U85 Felix Hernandez AS 1.50 4.00
U86 Josh Harrison 1.25 3.00
U87 Zack Greinke 2.00 5.00
U88 Craig Kimbrel 1.50 4.00
U89 Brian Johnson 1.25 3.00
U90 Clayton Kershaw 3.00 8.00
U91 Julio Teheran 1.50 4.00
U92 Jacob deGrom 4.00 10.00
U93 Tyler White 1.25 3.00
U94 Jesus Luzardo 2.50 6.00
U95 Domingo Santana 1.50 4.00
U96 Logan Morrison 1.25 3.00
U97 Donovan Solano 2.00 5.00
U98 Jose Iglesias 1.50 4.00
U99 Cesar Hernandez 1.25 3.00
U100 David Price 1.50 4.00
U101 Nick Dini RC 1.50 4.00
U102 Kevin Ginkel RC 1.25 3.00
U103 Michael Hermosillo 1.25 3.00
U104 Grayson Greiner 1.25 3.00
U105 Jake Newberry RC 1.25 3.00
U106 Meibrys Viloria 1.25 3.00
U107 Eric Thames 1.25 3.00
U108 Taylor Ward 2.00 5.00
U109 Pedro Strop 1.25 3.00
U110 Mark McGwire HRD 6.00 15.00
U111 Rich Hill 1.25 3.00
U112 Nik Turley RC 1.25 3.00
U113 Devin Williams RC 3.00 8.00
U114 Josh Phegley 1.25 3.00
U115 Brad Peacock 1.25 3.00
U116 Robinson Chirinos 1.25 3.00
U117 Cameron Maybin 1.25 3.00
U118 Frank Schwindel RC 2.00 5.00
U119 Mike Trout 15.00 40.00
U120 Stevie Wilkerson 2.00 5.00
U121 Ichiro AS 10.00 25.00
U122 Tino Martinez HRD 1.50 4.00
U123 Neil Walker 1.25 3.00
U124 David Ortiz AS 2.00 5.00
U125 Chris Martin 1.25 3.00
U126 Jhoulys Chacin 1.25 3.00
U127 Ryan Weber 1.25 3.00
U128 Jonathan Davis 1.50 4.00
U129 Hunter Pence 1.50 4.00
U130 Richie Martin 1.25 3.00
U131 Alex Reyes 1.50 4.00
U132 Daniel Descalso 1.25 3.00
U133 Chris Iannetta 1.25 3.00
U134 Gleyber Torres AS 8.00 20.00
U135 Brandon Dixon 1.25 3.00
U136 David McKay 1.25 3.00
U137 Touki Toussaint 1.50 4.00
U138 Tommy Pham 1.25 3.00
U139 Greg Allen 1.50 4.00
U140 Clayton Kershaw 3.00 8.00
U141 Jonathan Villar 1.25 3.00
U142 Albert Pujols 2.50 6.00
U143 Francisco Lindor AS 2.00 5.00
U144 Mookie Betts 4.00 10.00
Gleyber Torres
U145 Ronald Acuna Jr. AS 12.00 30.00
U146 Andrew Knizner 1.25 3.00
U147 Robinson Cano 1.50 4.00
U148 Pete Alonso HRD 6.00 15.00
U149 Nick Solak 5.00 12.00
U150 Ken Griffey Jr. HRD 20.00 50.00
U151 Jairo Diaz 1.25 3.00
U152 Sam Haggerty RC 2.00 5.00
U153 Robert Stephenson 1.25 3.00
U154 Mariano Rivera AS 2.50 6.00
U155 Zach Davies 1.25 3.00
U156 Wilmer Flores 1.50 4.00
U157 Deivy Grullon RC 1.25 3.00
U158 Jason Kipnis 1.50 4.00
U159 Steven Souza Jr. 1.25 3.00
U160 Richard Bleier 1.25 3.00
U161 Jake Marisnick 1.25 3.00
U162 Giovanny Gallegos 1.25 3.00
U163 JT Riddle 1.25 3.00
U164 Sam Travis 1.25 3.00
U165 Kyle Wright 2.00 5.00
U166 Adolis Garcia 10.00 25.00
U167 Yoshi Hirano 1.25 3.00
U168 Keynan Middleton 1.25 3.00
U169 Yadier Molina AS 2.50 6.00
U170 Travis Shaw 1.25 3.00
U171 Bryse Wilson 1.50 4.00
U172 Tyler Wade 1.25 3.00
U173 Edwin Encarnacion 2.00 5.00
U174 Logan Forsythe 1.25 3.00
U175 Diego Castillo 1.25 3.00
U176 Brock Holt 1.25 3.00
U177 Andy Burns RC 1.25 3.00
U178 Jarrod Dyson 1.25 3.00
U179 Jeff Hoffman 1.25 3.00
U180 C.J. Cron 1.25 3.00
U181 Mitch Moreland 1.25 3.00
U182 Josh Tomlin 1.25 3.00
U183 Steve Cishek 1.25 3.00
U184 Miguel Cabrera 2.00 5.00
U185 Max Scherzer AS 2.00 5.00
U186 Rowdy Tellez 1.50 4.00
U187 Pete Alonso AS 6.00 15.00
U188 Luis Severino 1.50 4.00
U189 Johnny Davis RC 1.25 3.00
U190 Ken Griffey Jr. AS 20.00 50.00
U191 Zack Greinke 2.00 5.00
U192 Ian Miller RC 1.25 3.00
U193 Miguel Cabrera 2.00 5.00
U194 Justin Verlander AS 2.00 5.00
U195 Daniel Hudson 1.25 3.00
U196 Nestor Cortes RC 1.25 3.00
U197 Zach Green RC 1.25 3.00
U198 Hunter Renfroe 1.25 3.00
U199 Adeiny Hechavarria 1.25 3.00
U200 Anthony Rendon 2.00 5.00
U201 Anthony Rizzo AS 2.50 6.00
U202 Asdrubal Cabrera 1.50 4.00
U203 Austin Pruitt 1.25 3.00
U204 Eric Davis HRD 1.25 3.00
U205 Kenta Maeda 1.50 4.00
U206 Asher Wojciechowski 1.25 3.00
U207 Jorge Lopez 1.25 3.00
U208 Randy Arozarena RC 100.00 250.00
U209 Cal Ripken Jr. AS 8.00 20.00
U210 Gabe Speier RC 1.25 3.00
U211 Drew Smyly 1.25 3.00
U212 Jordan Lyles 1.25 3.00
U213 Keury Mella 1.25 3.00
U214 Kendall Graveman 1.25 3.00
U215 Joey Votto 2.00 5.00
U216 Luis Robert 100.00 250.00
U217 Andrew Suarez 1.25 3.00

U218 Matt Chapman 2.00 5.00
Matt Olson
U219 Zack Greinke 2.00 5.00
U220 Alec Mills RC 1.25 3.00
U221 Joe Panik 1.50 4.00
U222 Scott Barlow 1.25 3.00
U223 Chris Devenski 1.25 3.00
U224 Cy Sneed RC 1.25 3.00
U225 Jharel Cotton 1.25 3.00
U226 Franchy Cordero 1.25 3.00
U227 Garrett Richards 1.50 4.00
U228 Starling Marte 1.50 4.00
U229 Giancarlo Stanton AS 2.00 5.00
U230 Cal Ripken Jr. HRD 8.00 20.00
U231 Jordy Mercer 1.25 3.00
U232 Jason Castro 1.25 3.00
U233 Mike Montgomery 1.25 3.00
U234 Gavin Lux 20.00 50.00
U235 Javier Baez AS 2.50 6.00
U236 Bartolo Colon 1.25 3.00
U237 Clayton Kershaw AS 3.00 8.00
U238 Tim Locastro 1.25 3.00
U239 Jefry Rodriguez 1.25 3.00
U240 Justin Verlander 2.00 5.00
U241 Tyler Heineman RC 1.25 3.00
U242 Ty France 2.00 5.00
U243 Mike Trout 15.00 40.00
U244 Wade LeBlanc 1.25 3.00
U245 Justin Verlander 2.00 5.00
U246 Greg Holland 1.25 3.00
U247 Kole Calhoun 1.25 3.00
U248 Miguel Cabrera 2.00 5.00
U249 Aroldis Chapman 2.00 5.00
U250 Omar Narvaez 1.25 3.00
U251 Nico Hoerner 15.00 40.00
U252 Alex Wood 1.25 3.00
U253 Peter Lambert 1.50 4.00
U254 Taijuan Walker 1.25 3.00
U255 Bryce Harper HRD 4.00 10.00
U256 Jose Ramirez 2.00 5.00
Francisco Lindor
U257 Derek Jeter AS 10.00 25.00
U258 Todd Frazier HRD 1.25 3.00
U259 Albert Pujols 2.50 6.00
U260 Kyle Crick 1.25 3.00
U261 Mike Trout 6.00 15.00
Justin Upton
U262 Ty Buttrey 1.25 3.00
U263 Miguel Cabrera 2.00 5.00
U264 Aaron Judge HRD 8.00 20.00
U265 Dario Agrazal RC 1.50 4.00
U266 Andrew McCutchen AS 2.00 5.00
U267 Albert Pujols AS 2.50 6.00
U268 Mookie Betts AS 8.00 20.00
U269 Christian Yelich AS 2.50 6.00
U270 Dustin Garneau 1.25 3.00
U271 Kevin Pillar 1.25 3.00
U272 Joey Votto AS 2.00 5.00
U273 Rafael Devers 2.50 6.00
Xander Bogaerts
U274 Jordan Montgomery 1.25 3.00
U275 Brett Anderson 1.25 3.00
U276 Joe Kelly 1.25 3.00
U277 Jose Altuve AS 1.50 4.00
U278 Austin Allen 1.50 4.00
U279 Bryce Harper AS 4.00 10.00
U280 Albert Pujols 2.50 6.00
U281 Joel Kuhnel RC 1.25 3.00
U282 Christian Arroyo 1.25 3.00
U283 Tomas Nido 1.25 3.00
U284 Walker Buehler 2.50 6.00
Russell Martin
U285 Billy Hamilton 1.50 4.00
U286 Chase Anderson 1.25 3.00
U287 Chris Sale AS 2.00 5.00
U288 Giancarlo Stanton 2.00 5.00
U289 Myles Straw 1.50 4.00
U290 Pete Alonso 5.00 12.00
Jeff McNeil
U291 Trayce Thompson 1.25 3.00
U292 Mike Trout 15.00 40.00
U293 Mike King RC 2.00 5.00
U294 Adam Plutko 1.25 3.00
U295 Chris Sale 2.00 5.00
U296 Mark McGwire HRD 6.00 15.00
U297 Jesus Tinoco RC 1.25 3.00
U298 Magneuris Sierra 1.25 3.00
U299 Jacob deGrom AS 4.00 10.00
U300 Yordan Alvarez 25.00 60.00

2020 Topps Chrome Update Sapphire Green Refractors

*GREEN: .6X TO 1.5X BASIC
STATED ODDS 1:16 HOBBY
STATED PRINT RUN 45 SER.#'d SETS
U4 Mike Trout AS 50.00 120.00
U9 Ken Griffey Jr. HRD 100.00 250.00
U15 Aaron Judge AS 20.00 50.00
U29 Aristides Aquino 12.00 30.00
U119 Mike Trout 50.00 120.00
U150 Ken Griffey Jr. HRD 100.00 250.00
U190 Ken Griffey Jr. AS 100.00 250.00
U243 Mike Trout 50.00 120.00
U264 Aaron Judge HRD 20.00 50.00
U268 Mookie Betts AS 30.00 80.00
U292 Mike Trout 50.00 120.00

2020 Topps Chrome Update Sapphire Orange Refractors

*ORANGE: 1X TO 2.5X BASIC
STATED ODDS 1:27 HOBBY
STATED PRINT RUN 25 SER.#'d SETS
U1 Bo Bichette 400.00 1000.00
U4 Mike Trout AS 150.00 400.00
U9 Ken Griffey Jr. HRD 150.00 400.00
U15 Aaron Judge AS 30.00 80.00
U29 Aristides Aquino 20.00 50.00
U42 Kris Bryant AS 20.00 50.00
U80 Cody Bellinger AS 20.00 50.00
U119 Mike Trout 150.00 400.00
U150 Ken Griffey Jr. HRD 150.00 400.00
U190 Ken Griffey Jr. AS 150.00 400.00
U216 Luis Robert 1000.00 2000.00
U243 Mike Trout 150.00 400.00
U255 Bryce Harper HRD 20.00 50.00
U264 Aaron Judge HRD 30.00 80.00
U268 Mookie Betts AS 50.00 120.00
U279 Bryce Harper AS 20.00 50.00
U292 Mike Trout 150.00 400.00
U300 Yordan Alvarez 100.00 250.00

2020 Topps Chrome Update Sapphire Autographs

RANDOM INSERTS IN PACKS
EXCHANGE DEADLINE 11/30/22
AAJ Aaron Judge 100.00 250.00
AAR Anthony Rendon 25.00 60.00
ABH Bryce Harper
AEA Elvis Andrus 8.00 20.00
AGC Gerrit Cole 50.00 120.00
AGS George Springer 25.00 60.00
AJG Joey Gallo 12.00 30.00
AMM Manny Machado 50.00 120.00
AMT Mike Trout
ARH Rhys Hoskins 25.00 60.00
AKHI Keston Hiura

2020 Topps Chrome Update Sapphire Autographs Green Refractors

*GREEN: .6X TO 1.5X BASIC
STATED ODDS 1:116 HOBBY
STATED PRINT RUN 50 SER.#'d SETS
EXCHANGE DEADLINE 11/30/22
ABH Bryce Harper 100.00 250.00

2020 Topps Chrome Update Sapphire Autographs Orange Refractors

*ORANGE: 1X TO 2.5X BASIC
STATED ODDS 1:232 HOBBY
STATED PRINT RUN 25 SER.#'d SETS
EXCHANGE DEADLINE 11/30/22
ABH Bryce Harper 150.00 400.00

2020 Topps Chrome Update Sapphire Rookie Autographs

RANDOM INSERTS IN PACKS
EXCHANGE DEADLINE 11/30/22
RAAA Aristides Aquino 25.00 60.00
RAAT Abraham Toro 6.00 15.00
RABB Bo Bichette EXCH
RABM Brendan McKay 25.00 60.00
RABO Brian O'Grady 3.00 8.00
RADM Dustin May 40.00 100.00
RAGL Gavin Lux EXCH 100.00 250.00
RAJD Justin Dunn 10.00 25.00
RAJF Jake Fraley 10.00 25.00
RAJL Jesus Luzardo 30.00 80.00
RAJM James Marvel 6.00 15.00
RAJT Jesus Tinoco 3.00 8.00
RAJY Jordan Yamamoto 6.00 15.00
RAKG Kyle Garlick 5.00 12.00
RAKH Kwang-Hyun Kim 20.00 50.00
RAKL Kyle Lewis 125.00 300.00
RALR Luis Robert EXCH
RAMD Mauricio Dubon 12.00 30.00
RANH Nico Hoerner 40.00 100.00
RANS Nick Solak 20.00 50.00
RAPL Peter Lambert 4.00 10.00
RARA Randy Arozarena 200.00 500.00
RARD Randy Dobnak 10.00 25.00
RASA Shogo Akiyama 12.00 30.00
RASY Shun Yamaguchi 4.00 10.00
RATL Travis Lakins 3.00 8.00
RATT Tyrone Taylor 10.00 25.00
RAYA Yordan Alvarez 150.00 400.00
RAZG Zac Gallen 40.00 100.00
RAWCA Willi Castro 60.00 150.00

2020 Topps Chrome Update Sapphire Rookie Autographs Green Refractors

*GREEN: .6X TO 1.5X BASIC
STATED ODDS 1:116 HOBBY
STATED PRINT RUN 50 SER.#'d SETS
EXCHANGE DEADLINE 11/30/22
RAMD Mauricio Dubon 30.00 80.00

2020 Topps Chrome Update Sapphire Rookie Autographs Orange Refractors

*ORANGE: 1X TO 2.5X BASIC
RAMD Mauricio Dubon 50.00 120.00

2020 Topps Chrome Ben Baller

1 Mike Trout 15.00 40.00
2 Liam Hendriks .40 1.00
3 Bobby Bradley RC .60 1.50
4 Rogelio Armenteros RC .75 2.00
5 Jesus Luzardo RC 1.25 3.00
6 Miguel Cabrera .60 1.50
7 Trea Turner .50 1.25
8 Brendan McKay RC 1.00 2.50
9 Joey Votto .60 1.50
10 Domingo Leyba RC .75 2.00
11 Austin Nola RC 1.00 2.50
12 Juan Soto 6.00 15.00
13 Max Muncy .50 1.25
14 Archie Bradley .40 1.00
15 David Peralta .40 1.00
16 Luis Castillo .50 1.25
17 Bryan Reynolds .50 1.25
18 Michael Fulmer .40 1.00
19 Jeimer Candelario .40 1.00
20 Jorge Soler .60 1.50
21 Shohei Ohtani 1.00 2.50
22 Cavan Biggio .75 2.00
23 Seth Brown RC .60 1.50
24 Nick Senzel .60 1.50
25 Keston Hiura .75 2.00
26 Travis Demeritte RC 4.00 10.00
27 Christian Walker .50 1.25
28 Andrew Heaney .40 1.00
29 Carlos Correa .60 1.50
30 Dan Vogelbach .40 1.00
31 Adalberto Mondesi .50 1.25
32 Sean Murphy RC 1.00 2.50
33 Nick Solak RC 8.00 20.00
34 Gio Urshela .60 1.50
35 Michael Conforto .50 1.25
36 Ian Desmond .40 1.00
37 Mitch Haniger .50 1.25
38 Jean Segura .50 1.25
39 Chris Paddack .60 1.50
40 Josh Hader .50 1.25
41 Corey Kluber .50 1.25
42 Jose Altuve 2.00 5.00
43 Dylan Cease RC 1.00 2.50
44 German Marquez .60 1.50
45 Gleyber Torres 3.00 8.00
46 Lucas Giolito .50 1.25
47 Jake Rogers RC .60 1.50
48 Yusei Kikuchi .50 1.25
49 Randy Arozarena RC 15.00 40.00
50 Aaron Judge 5.00 12.00
51 Danny Jansen .40 1.00
52 Kyle Seager 3.00 8.00
53 Kris Bryant 4.00 10.00
54 Chris Archer .40 1.00
55 DJ LeMahieu .60 1.50
56 Abraham Toro RC .75 2.00
57 Andrew Benintendi .60 1.50
58 Noah Syndergaard .50 1.25
59 Trevor Story .60 1.50
60 Luis Robert RC 40.00 100.00
61 Sheldon Neuse RC .75 2.00
62 Ozzie Albies .60 1.50
63 Hunter Dozier .40 1.00
64 Scott Kingery .50 1.25
65 Dansby Swanson .60 1.50
66 Jose Abreu 2.00 5.00
67 Sam Hilliard RC 1.00 2.50
68 Blake Snell .50 1.25
69 Nelson Cruz .60 1.50
70 Jeff McNeil .50 1.25
71 Anthony Rizzo .75 2.00
72 Andrelton Simmons .40 1.00
73 Charlie Blackmon .60 1.50
74 Matthew Boyd .40 1.00
75 Jonathan Villar .40 1.00
76 Manny Machado .60 1.50
77 Cody Bellinger 4.00 10.00
78 Eddie Rosario .50 1.25
79 Hanser Alberto .40 1.00
80 Pete Alonso 1.50 4.00
81 Jacob deGrom 1.25 3.00
82 Jordan Yamamoto RC .60 1.50
83 Matt Thaiss RC .75 2.00
84 Fernando Tatis Jr. 8.00 20.00
85 Kyle Schwarber .60 1.50
86 Adrian Morejon RC 2.00 5.00
87 Zack Collins RC .75 2.00
88 Brandon Crawford .50 1.25
89 Paul Goldschmidt .60 1.50
90 Tim Anderson 1.50 4.00
91 Brusdar Graterol RC 1.00 2.50
92 Nicky Lopez .40 1.00
93 Rafael Devers 3.00 8.00
94 Tommy Edman .60 1.50
95 Edwin Rios RC 1.50 4.00
96 Mike Soroka .60 1.50
97 Bryce Harper 4.00 10.00
98 Kevin Newman .60 1.50
99 Colin Moran .40 1.00
100 Mookie Betts 6.00 15.00
101 Trent Grisham RC 8.00 20.00
102 Alex Bregman .60 1.50
103 Mike Yastrzemski 1.00 2.50
104 Walker Buehler 4.00 10.00
105 Miguel Rojas .40 1.00
106 Harold Ramirez .40 1.00
107 Dee Gordon .40 1.00
108 Eric Hosmer 1.25 3.00
109 Nomar Mazara .40 1.00
110 Adbert Alzolay RC 4.00 10.00
111 Aristides Aquino RC 5.00 12.00
112 Ronald Acuna Jr. 8.00 20.00
113 Austin Meadows .60 1.50
114 Tony Gonsolin RC 2.50 6.00
115 Alex Young RC .60 1.50
116 A.J. Puk RC 1.00 2.50
117 Logan Webb RC 1.00 2.50
118 Tyler Glasnow .60 1.50
119 Brandon Lowe .50 1.25
120 Anthony Kay RC .60 1.50
121 John Means .60 1.50
122 Clayton Kershaw 3.00 8.00
123 Jon Lester .50 1.25
124 Max Kepler .50 1.25
125 Jose Berrios .50 1.25
126 Victor Reyes .40 1.00
127 Albert Pujols .75 2.00
128 Eugenio Suarez .50 1.25
129 Ronald Guzman .40 1.00
130 Anthony Santander .40 1.00
131 Freddie Freeman .75 2.00
132 Zac Gallen RC 1.50 4.00
133 Vladimir Guerrero Jr. 4.00 10.00
134 Eloy Jimenez 1.25 3.00
135 Jack Flaherty .60 1.50
136 Justin Dunn RC .75 2.00
137 Xander Bogaerts .60 1.50
138 Christian Yelich .75 2.00
139 Max Scherzer .60 1.50
140 Orlando Arcia .40 1.00
141 Rowdy Tellez .50 1.25
142 Jose Urquidy RC .75 2.00
143 Aaron Civale RC 1.25 3.00
144 Marcus Semien .60 1.50
145 Yoan Moncada .60 1.50
146 Brian Anderson .40 1.00
147 Brandon Belt .50 1.25
148 Gavin Lux RC 8.00 20.00
149 Andres Munoz RC 1.00 2.50
150 Bo Bichette RC 40.00 100.00
151 Ketel Marte .50 1.25
152 Pablo Lopez .40 1.00
153 Lorenzo Cain .40 1.00
154 Whit Merrifield .60 1.50
155 Logan Allen RC .60 1.50
156 Francisco Lindor .60 1.50
157 Buster Posey .75 2.00
158 Elvis Andrus .50 1.25
159 Brock Burke RC .60 1.50
160 Ramon Laureano .50 1.25
161 Nico Hoerner RC 6.00 15.00
162 Junior Fernandez RC .60 1.50
163 Trevor Williams .40 1.00
164 Justin Verlander .60 1.50
165 Carlos Santana .50 1.25
166 Masahiro Tanaka .60 1.50
167 Lourdes Gurriel Jr. .50 1.25
168 Mauricio Dubon RC 4.00 10.00
169 Luis Urias .50 1.25
170 Isan Diaz RC 2.00 5.00
171 Carter Kieboom .50 1.25
172 Luis Arraez .75 2.00
173 Yu Chang RC 1.00 2.50
174 Nolan Arenado 1.00 2.50
175 Raisel Iglesias .40 1.00
176 Dustin May RC 5.00 12.00
177 Shin-Soo Choo .50 1.25
178 Paul DeJong .60 1.50
179 Willy Adames .40 1.00
180 Miles Mikolas .40 1.00
181 Robel Garcia RC .60 1.50
182 Oscar Mercado .60 1.50
183 Matt Olson .60 1.50
184 Rhys Hoskins .75 2.00
185 Jose Urena .40 1.00
186 Kyle Lewis RC 25.00 60.00
187 Michel Baez RC .60 1.50
188 Trey Mancini .60 1.50
189 J.D. Martinez .60 1.50
190 Jose Ramirez .50 1.25
191 Joey Gallo .60 1.50
192 Robbie Ray .40 1.00
193 Matt Chapman .60 1.50
194 George Springer .50 1.25
195 Patrick Corbin .50 1.25
196 Corey Seager .60 1.50
197 Jeff Samardzija .40 1.00
198 Javier Baez .75 2.00
199 Aaron Nola .50 1.25
200 Yordan Alvarez RC 12.00 30.00

2020 Topps Chrome Ben Baller Blue Refractors

*BLUE: 1.2X TO 3X BASIC
*BLUE RC: .8X TO 2X BASIC RC
RANDOM INSERTS IN PACKS
STATED PRINT RUN 75 SER.#'d SETS
1 Mike Trout 40.00 100.00
7 Trea Turner 4.00 10.00
11 Austin Nola 12.00 30.00
21 Shohei Ohtani 8.00 20.00
29 Carlos Correa 5.00 12.00
42 Jose Altuve 6.00 15.00
43 Dylan Cease 5.00 12.00
48 Yusei Kikuchi 10.00 25.00
50 Aaron Judge 25.00 60.00
52 Kyle Seager 12.00 30.00
57 Andrew Benintendi 8.00 20.00
60 Luis Robert 100.00 250.00
81 Jacob deGrom 10.00 25.00
84 Fernando Tatis Jr. 50.00 120.00
100 Mookie Betts 50.00 120.00
111 Aristides Aquino 12.00 30.00
112 Ronald Acuna Jr. 25.00 60.00
127 Albert Pujols 10.00 25.00
156 Francisco Lindor 15.00 40.00
176 Dustin May 12.00 30.00

2020 Topps Chrome Ben Baller Gold Refractors

*GOLD: 2X TO 5X BASIC
*GOLD RC: 1.2X TO 3X BASIC RC
RANDOM INSERTS IN PACKS
STATED PRINT RUN 50 SER.#'d SETS
1 Mike Trout 40.00 100.00
6 Miguel Cabrera 30.00 80.00
7 Trea Turner 6.00 15.00
11 Austin Nola 20.00 50.00
12 Juan Soto 60.00 150.00
21 Shohei Ohtani 12.00 30.00
29 Carlos Correa 8.00 20.00
42 Jose Altuve 10.00 25.00
43 Dylan Cease 8.00 20.00
48 Yusei Kikuchi 15.00 40.00
50 Aaron Judge 40.00 100.00
52 Kyle Seager 25.00 60.00
57 Andrew Benintendi 12.00 30.00
60 Luis Robert 200.00 500.00
66 Jose Abreu 12.00 30.00
81 Jacob deGrom 20.00 50.00
84 Fernando Tatis Jr. 75.00 200.00
100 Mookie Betts 75.00 200.00
111 Aristides Aquino 20.00 50.00
112 Ronald Acuna Jr. 50.00 120.00
127 Albert Pujols 15.00 40.00
156 Francisco Lindor 25.00 60.00
170 Isan Diaz 10.00 25.00
176 Dustin May 20.00 50.00
186 Kyle Lewis 200.00 500.00

2020 Topps Chrome Ben Baller Green Refractors

*GREEN: 1.2X TO 3X BASIC
*GREEN RC: .8X TO 2X BASIC RC
RANDOM INSERTS IN PACKS
STATED PRINT RUN 99 SER.#'d SETS
1 Mike Trout 40.00 100.00
7 Trea Turner 4.00 10.00
11 Austin Nola 12.00 30.00
21 Shohei Ohtani 8.00 20.00
29 Carlos Correa 5.00 12.00
42 Jose Altuve 6.00 15.00
43 Dylan Cease 5.00 12.00
48 Yusei Kikuchi 10.00 25.00
52 Kyle Seager 12.00 30.00
57 Andrew Benintendi 8.00 20.00
60 Luis Robert 100.00 250.00
81 Jacob deGrom 10.00 25.00
84 Fernando Tatis Jr. 50.00 120.00
100 Mookie Betts 50.00 120.00
111 Aristides Aquino 12.00 30.00
112 Ronald Acuna Jr. 25.00 60.00
127 Albert Pujols 10.00 25.00
156 Francisco Lindor 15.00 40.00
176 Dustin May 12.00 30.00

2020 Topps Chrome Ben Baller Orange Refractors

*ORANGE: 3X TO 8X BASIC
*ORANGE RC: 2X TO 5X BASIC RC
RANDOM INSERTS IN PACKS
STATED PRINT RUN 25 SER.#'d SETS
1 Mike Trout 150.00 400.00
6 Miguel Cabrera 50.00 120.00
7 Trea Turner 12.00 30.00
11 Austin Nola 30.00 80.00
12 Juan Soto 125.00 300.00
21 Shohei Ohtani 20.00 50.00
29 Carlos Correa 12.00 30.00
42 Jose Altuve 15.00 40.00
43 Dylan Cease 8.00 20.00
48 Yusei Kikuchi 25.00 60.00
50 Aaron Judge 60.00 150.00
52 Kyle Seager 40.00 100.00
57 Andrew Benintendi 20.00 50.00
60 Luis Robert 300.00 800.00
66 Jose Abreu 20.00 50.00
80 Pete Alonso 20.00 50.00
81 Jacob deGrom 30.00 80.00
84 Fernando Tatis Jr. 125.00 300.00
100 Mookie Betts 125.00 300.00
111 Aristides Aquino 30.00 80.00
112 Ronald Acuna Jr. 75.00 200.00
127 Albert Pujols 25.00 60.00
156 Francisco Lindor 40.00 100.00
170 Isan Diaz 20.00 50.00
176 Dustin May 30.00 80.00
186 Kyle Lewis 300.00 800.00

2020 Topps Chrome Ben Baller '85 Topps

STATED ODDS 1:12 PACKS
85TC1 Mike Trout 25.00 60.00
85TC2 Bo Bichette 25.00 60.00
85TC3 Juan Soto 6.00 15.00
85TC4 Yordan Alvarez 6.00 15.00
85TC5 Gavin Lux 10.00 25.00
85TC6 Vladimir Guerrero Jr. 3.00 8.00
85TC7 Shohei Ohtani 1.50 4.00
85TC8 Rafael Devers 1.25 3.00
85TC9 Kris Bryant 1.25 3.00
85TC10 Jesus Luzardo 1.25 3.00
85TC11 Eloy Jimenez 2.00 5.00
85TC12 Nico Hoerner 2.50 6.00
85TC13 Brendan McKay 1.00 2.50
85TC14 A.J. Puk 1.00 2.50
85TC15 Christian Yelich 1.25 3.00
85TC16 Keston Hiura 4.00 10.00
85TC17 Luis Robert 40.00 100.00
85TC18 Pete Alonso 2.50 6.00
85TC19 Jose Altuve .75 2.00
85TC20 Rhys Hoskins 1.25 3.00
85TC21 Aristides Aquino 4.00 10.00
85TC22 Kyle Lewis 20.00 50.00
85TC23 Austin Riley 4.00 10.00
85TC24 Nolan Arenado 1.50 4.00
85TC25 Ronald Acuna Jr. 8.00 20.00

2020 Topps Chrome Ben Baller '85 Topps Gold Refractors

*GOLD: 1X TO 2.5X BASIC
STATED ODDS 1:21 PACKS
STATED PRINT RUN 50 SER.#'d SETS
85TC1 Mike Trout 100.00 250.00
85TC3 Juan Soto 40.00 100.00
85TC6 Vladimir Guerrero Jr. 20.00 50.00
85TC17 Luis Robert 125.00 300.00
85TC22 Kyle Lewis 75.00 200.00

2020 Topps Chrome Ben Baller '85 Topps Orange Refractors

*ORANGE: 1.5X TO 4X BASIC
STATED ODDS 1:41 PACKS
STATED PRINT RUN 25 SER.#'d SETS
85TC1 Mike Trout 150.00 400.00
85TC3 Juan Soto 60.00 150.00
85TC6 Vladimir Guerrero Jr. 30.00 80.00
85TC17 Luis Robert 200.00 500.00
85TC22 Kyle Lewis 125.00 300.00
85TC23 Austin Riley 20.00 50.00

2020 Topps Chrome Ben Baller Autographs Gold Refractors

STATED ODDS 1:403 PACKS
STATED PRINT RUN 50 SER.#'d SETS
BBAAA Aristides Aquino 50.00 120.00
BBAEJ Eloy Jimenez 40.00 100.00
BBAJA Jose Altuve 40.00 100.00
BBAMT Mike Trout 600.00 1500.00
BBANH Nico Hoerner
BBAPA Pete Alonso 100.00 250.00
BBAPG Paul Goldschmidt 40.00 100.00
BBARA Ronald Acuna Jr. 200.00 500.00
BBARH Rhys Hoskins 20.00 50.00
BBASO Shohei Ohtani 75.00 200.00
BBAWB Walker Buehler 125.00 300.00

2020 Topps Chrome Ben Baller Autographs Orange Refractors

*ORANGE: .6X TO 1.5X BASIC
STATED ODDS 1:804 PACKS
STATED PRINT RUN 25 SER.#'d SETS
BBAMT Mike Trout 800.00 2000.00
BBARH Rhys Hoskins 40.00 100.00

2020 Topps Chrome Ben Baller Diamond Die Cuts

STATED ODDS 1:24 PACKS
BDC1 Mike Trout 40.00 100.00
BDC2 Cody Bellinger 12.00 30.00
BDC3 Shohei Ohtani 8.00 20.00
BDC4 Fernando Tatis Jr. 20.00 50.00
BDC5 Ronald Acuna Jr. 15.00 40.00
BDC6 Christian Yelich 5.00 12.00
BDC7 Bryce Harper 15.00 40.00
BDC8 Pete Alonso 10.00 25.00
BDC9 Juan Soto 20.00 50.00
BDC10 Vladimir Guerrero Jr. 8.00 20.00
BDC11 Aristides Aquino 8.00 20.00
BDC12 Bo Bichette 30.00 80.00
BDC13 Yordan Alvarez 20.00 50.00
BDC14 Gavin Lux 20.00 50.00
BDC15 Luis Robert 40.00 100.00

2020 Topps Chrome Ben Baller Diamond Die Cuts Gold Refractors

*GOLD: .6X TO 1.5X BASIC
STATED ODDS 1:269 PACKS
STATED PRINT RUN 50 SER.#'d SETS
BDC2 Cody Bellinger 30.00 80.00
BDC3 Shohei Ohtani 40.00 100.00
BDC4 Fernando Tatis Jr. 50.00 120.00
BDC5 Ronald Acuna Jr. 60.00 150.00
BDC8 Pete Alonso 25.00 60.00
BDC9 Juan Soto 50.00 120.00
BDC10 Vladimir Guerrero Jr. 30.00 80.00
BDC13 Yordan Alvarez 40.00 100.00
BDC15 Luis Robert 125.00 300.00

2020 Topps Chrome Ben Baller Diamond Die Cuts Orange Refractors

*ORANGE: 1.2X TO 3X BASIC
STATED ODDS 1:537 PACKS
STATED PRINT RUN 25 SER.#'d SETS
BDC1 Mike Trout 300.00 800.00
BDC2 Cody Bellinger 75.00 200.00
BDC3 Shohei Ohtani 75.00 200.00
BDC4 Fernando Tatis Jr. 100.00 250.00
BDC5 Ronald Acuna Jr. 100.00 250.00
BDC8 Pete Alonso 50.00 120.00
BDC9 Juan Soto 100.00 250.00
BDC10 Vladimir Guerrero Jr. 60.00 150.00
BDC13 Yordan Alvarez 75.00 200.00
BDC15 Luis Robert 300.00 800.00

2020 Topps Chrome Black

1 Cody Bellinger 4.00 10.00
2 Jose Urquidy RC .75 2.00
3 Manny Machado .60 1.50
4 Ketel Marte .50 1.25
5 Eloy Jimenez 1.25 3.00
6 Nico Hoerner RC 8.00 20.00
7 Domingo Leyba RC .75 2.00
8 Chris Paddack .60 1.50
9 Brendan McKay RC 1.00 2.50
10 Nolan Arenado 2.50 6.00
11 Jack Flaherty .60 1.50
12 Trent Grisham RC 5.00 12.00
13 Luis Robert RC 50.00 120.00
14 Shohei Ohtani 8.00 20.00
15 Pete Alonso 4.00 10.00
16 Keston Hiura 1.50 4.00
17 Gary Sanchez .60 1.50
18 Michel Baez RC .60 1.50
19 Max Scherzer .60 1.50
20 Mookie Betts 8.00 20.00
21 Tommy Edman .60 1.50
22 A.J. Puk RC 1.00 2.50
23 Xander Bogaerts .60 1.50
24 Yu Chang RC 1.00 2.50
25 Fernando Tatis Jr. 20.00 50.00
26 Alex Bregman .60 1.50
27 Isan Diaz RC 1.00 2.50
28 Nick Castellanos .60 1.50
29 Danny Mendick RC .75 2.00
30 Aaron Judge 5.00 12.00
31 Rhys Hoskins 2.00 5.00
32 Gleyber Torres 6.00 15.00
33 Shogo Akiyama RC 1.00 2.50
34 Paul Goldschmidt .60 1.50
35 Javier Baez 1.50 4.00
36 Travis Demeritte RC 1.00 2.50
37 Aristides Aquino RC 6.00 15.00
38 Kris Bryant 2.00 5.00
39 Chad Wallach RC .60 1.50
40 Bryce Harper 3.00 8.00
41 Trevor Story .60 1.50
42 Freddie Freeman 2.00 5.00
43 Jake Rogers RC .60 1.50
44 Whit Merrifield .60 1.50
45 Joey Gallo .60 1.50
46 Austin Meadows .60 1.50
47 Bobby Bradley RC .60 1.50
48 Willson Contreras .60 1.50
49 Marcus Semien .60 1.50
50 Vladimir Guerrero Jr. 4.00 10.00
51 Gavin Lux RC 8.00 20.00
52 Luis Castillo .50 1.25
53 Zac Gallen RC 6.00 15.00
54 Jorge Soler .60 1.50
55 Kwang-Hyun Kim RC 1.25 3.00
56 Josh Bell .50 1.25
57 Walker Buehler 1.25 3.00
58 Mitch Garver .40 1.00
59 Jake Fraley RC .75 2.00
60 Juan Soto 20.00 50.00
61 Jaylin Davis RC 1.00 2.50
62 Trevor Bauer .75 2.00
63 Tony Gonsolin RC 2.50 6.00
64 Logan Allen RC .60 1.50
65 Justin Dunn RC .75 2.00
66 Stephen Strasburg .60 1.50
67 Tim Anderson .60 1.50
68 Jesus Luzardo RC 4.00 10.00
69 Luis Arraez .75 2.00
70 Gerrit Cole 1.50 4.00
71 Sean Murphy RC 1.00 2.50
72 Seth Brown RC .60 1.50
73 Zack Collins RC .75 2.00
74 Josh Donaldson .50 1.25
75 Ronald Acuna Jr. 30.00 80.00
76 Carter Kieboom .50 1.25
77 Justin Verlander .60 1.50
78 Nick Solak RC 2.50 6.00
79 John Means .60 1.50
80 Francisco Lindor .60 1.50
81 Bo Bichette RC 40.00 100.00
82 Hyun-Jin Ryu .50 1.25
83 Corey Kluber .50 1.25
84 Trey Mancini .60 1.50
85 Dylan Cease RC 1.00 2.50
86 Jacob deGrom 1.25 3.00
87 Rafael Devers 2.00 5.00
88 Shun Yamaguchi .50 1.25
89 Dustin May RC 6.00 15.00
90 Anthony Rendon .60 1.50
91 Brusdar Graterol RC 1.00 2.50
92 James Karinchak RC 1.00 2.50
93 Christian Yelich 4.00 10.00
94 Mauricio Dubon RC .75 2.00
95 Matt Chapman .60 1.50
96 Yordan Alvarez RC 20.00 50.00
97 Jeff McNeil .50 1.25
98 Kyle Lewis RC 25.00 60.00
99 Clayton Kershaw 6.00 15.00
100 Mike Trout 40.00 100.00

2020 Topps Chrome Black Blue Refractors

*BLUE REF.: 2X TO 5X BASIC
*BLUE REF. RC: 1.2X TO 3X BASIC
STATED ODDS 1:XX HOBBY
STATED PRINT RUN 75 SER.#'d SETS
13 Luis Robert 150.00 400.00
20 Mookie Betts 50.00 120.00
33 Shogo Akiyama 5.00 12.00
35 Javier Baez 15.00 40.00
38 Kris Bryant 12.00 30.00
42 Freddie Freeman 12.00 30.00
68 Jesus Luzardo 15.00 40.00
81 Bo Bichette 150.00 400.00
82 Hyun-Jin Ryu 10.00 25.00
87 Rafael Devers 12.00 30.00

2020 Topps Chrome Black Gold Refractors

*GOLD REF.: 2.5X TO 6X BASIC
*GOLD REF. RC: 1.5X TO 4X BASIC
STATED ODDS 1:XX HOBBY
STATED PRINT RUN 50 SER.#'d SETS
1 Cody Bellinger 30.00 80.00
13 Luis Robert 200.00 500.00
16 Keston Hiura 12.00 30.00
20 Mookie Betts 60.00 150.00
33 Shogo Akiyama 10.00 25.00
35 Javier Baez 20.00 50.00
38 Kris Bryant 20.00 50.00
40 Bryce Harper 25.00 60.00
42 Freddie Freeman 15.00 40.00
55 Kwang-Hyun Kim 10.00 25.00
57 Walker Buehler 12.00 30.00
68 Jesus Luzardo 20.00 50.00
81 Bo Bichette 200.00 500.00
82 Hyun-Jin Ryu 12.00 30.00
85 Dylan Cease 8.00 20.00
87 Rafael Devers 15.00 40.00

2020 Topps Chrome Black Green Refractors

*GRN REF.: 1.5X TO 4X BASIC
*GRN REF. RC: 1X TO 2.5X BASIC
STATED ODDS 1:XX HOBBY
STATED PRINT RUN 99 SER.#'d SETS
13 Luis Robert 125.00 300.00
20 Mookie Betts 40.00 100.00
33 Shogo Akiyama 4.00 10.00
35 Javier Baez 12.00 30.00
38 Kris Bryant 10.00 25.00
81 Bo Bichette 125.00 300.00
82 Hyun-Jin Ryu 6.00 15.00

2020 Topps Chrome Black Orange Refractors

*ORNG REF.: 3X TO 8X BASIC
*ORNG REF. RC: 2X TO 5X BASIC
STATED ODDS 1:XX HOBBY
STATED PRINT RUN 25 SER.#'d SETS
1 Cody Bellinger 40.00 100.00
13 Luis Robert 250.00 600.00
16 Keston Hiura 15.00 40.00
20 Mookie Betts 75.00 200.00
22 A.J. Puk 15.00 40.00
30 Aaron Judge 50.00 120.00
33 Shogo Akiyama 12.00 30.00
35 Javier Baez 25.00 60.00
38 Kris Bryant 25.00 60.00
40 Bryce Harper 30.00 80.00
42 Freddie Freeman 25.00 60.00
55 Kwang-Hyun Kim 30.00 80.00
57 Walker Buehler 15.00 40.00
68 Jesus Luzardo 25.00 60.00
70 Gerrit Cole 15.00 40.00
81 Bo Bichette 250.00 600.00
82 Hyun-Jin Ryu 15.00 40.00
85 Dylan Cease 10.00 25.00
87 Rafael Devers 20.00 50.00

2020 Topps Chrome Black Refractors

*REF.: 1X TO 2.5X BASIC
*REF. RC: .6X TO 1.5X BASIC
STATED ODDS 1:XX HOBBY
STATED PRINT RUN 199 SER.#'d SETS
13 Luis Robert 100.00 250.00
20 Mookie Betts 25.00 60.00
81 Bo Bichette 75.00 200.00

2020 Topps Chrome Black Autographs

STATED ODDS 1:XX HOBBY
EXCHANGE DEADLINE 10/31/22
*REF./150: .5X TO 1.2X BASIC
*GRN REF./99: .6X TO 1.5X BASIC
CBAAR Anthony Rendon 20.00 50.00
CBAARD Alex Rodriguez 50.00 120.00
CBAAV Alex Verdugo 20.00 50.00
CBABL Adrian Beltre 25.00 60.00
CBABR Bryan Reynolds 8.00 20.00
CBABRG Alex Bregman 25.00 60.00
CBACB Miguel Cabrera 40.00 100.00
CBACDY Cody Bellinger 75.00 200.00
CBACF Carlton Fisk 12.00 30.00
CBACJ Chipper Jones 75.00 200.00
CBACKL Corey Kluber 8.00 20.00
CBACLK Will Clark 20.00 50.00
CBACR Cal Ripken Jr. 60.00 150.00
CBACS Corey Seager 30.00 80.00
CBADE Dennis Eckersley 20.00 50.00
CBADJ Derek Jeter 200.00 500.00
CBADLY Domingo Leyba 3.00 8.00
CBADM Dustin May 25.00 60.00
CBADMT Don Mattingly 50.00 120.00
CBADST Darryl Strawberry 15.00 40.00
CBADWT David Wright 30.00 80.00
CBADYL Dylan Cease 12.00 30.00
CBAED Edgar Martinez 20.00 50.00
CBAFT Frank Thomas 40.00 100.00
CBAGC Gerrit Cole 40.00 100.00
CBAGRY Sonny Gray 12.00 30.00
CBAGS Gary Sheffield 15.00 40.00
CBAGSP George Springer 20.00 50.00
CBAGT Gleyber Torres 40.00 100.00
CBAHA Hank Aaron 150.00 400.00
CBAHR Hyun-Jin Ryu 40.00 100.00
CBAIR Ivan Rodriguez 20.00 50.00
CBAIS Ichiro 150.00 400.00
CBAJD J.D. Martinez 12.00 30.00
CBAJM Jeff McNeil 12.00 30.00
CBAJO Joe Mauer 20.00 50.00
CBAJR J.T. Realmuto 15.00 40.00
CBAJS Juan Soto 100.00 250.00
CBAJYG Joey Gallo 15.00 40.00
CBAKM Ketel Marte 8.00 20.00
CBALA Luis Arraez 12.00 30.00
CBALC Luis Castillo 3.00 8.00
CBALFT Kenny Lofton 15.00 40.00
CBALG Lucas Giolito 15.00 40.00
CBALR Luis Robert EXCH 400.00 800.00
CBALV Luke Voit 12.00 30.00
CBALW Larry Walker 25.00 60.00
CBAMA Miguel Andujar 10.00 25.00
CBAMAX Max Kepler 10.00 25.00
CBAMB Michael Brantley 10.00 25.00
CBAMC Matt Carpenter 8.00 20.00

CBAMMC Mark McGwire 50.00 120.00
CBAMO Matt Olson 12.00 30.00
CBAMR Mariano Rivera 75.00 200.00
CBAMS Mike Schmidt 60.00 150.00
CBAMT Mike Trout 500.00 1000.00
CBAMY Mike Yastrzemski 20.00 50.00
CBANC Nick Castellanos 10.00 25.00
CBANG Nomar Garciaparra 25.00 60.00
CBANH Nico Hoerner 20.00 50.00
CBANS Nick Solak 20.00 50.00
CBAPA Pete Alonso 30.00 80.00
CBAPC Patrick Corbin 3.00 8.00
CBAPD Paul DeJong 10.00 25.00
CBAPG Paul Goldschmidt 25.00 60.00
CBAPM Pedro Martinez 50.00 120.00
CBARA Ronald Acuna Jr. 125.00 300.00
CBARC Rod Carew 20.00 50.00
CBARD Rafael Devers 20.00 50.00
CBARH Rhys Hoskins 15.00 40.00
CBASA Shogo Akiyama 12.00 30.00
CBASC Shin-Soo Choo 15.00 40.00
CBASK Sandy Koufax 150.00 400.00
CBASOL Jorge Soler 10.00 25.00
CBASOR Mike Soroka 15.00 40.00
CBASY Shun Yamaguchi 6.00 15.00
CBATE Tommy Edman 15.00 40.00
CBATEJ Miguel Tejada 8.00 20.00
CBATG Tom Glavine 20.00 50.00
CBATP Tony Perez 30.00 80.00
CBAVG Vladimir Guerrero 20.00 50.00
CBAVGJ Vladimir Guerrero Jr. 50.00 120.00
CBAVR Victor Robles 10.00 25.00
CBAWB Walker Buehler 30.00 80.00
CBAWC Willson Contreras 12.00 30.00
CBAWM Whit Merrifield 8.00 20.00
CBAXB Xander Bogaerts 25.00 60.00
CBAYA Yordan Alvarez 75.00 200.00
CBAYG Yuli Gurriel 8.00 20.00
CBAZG Zac Gallen 20.00 50.00

2020 Topps Chrome Black Autographs Gold Refractors

*GOLD REF.: .8X TO 2X BASIC
STATED ODDS 1:XX HOBBY
STATED PRINT RUN 50 SER.#'d SETS
EXCHANGE DEADLINE 10/31/22
CBACS Corey Seager 75.00 200.00
CBADM Dustin May 60.00 150.00
CBALR Luis Robert EXCH 1000.00 2000.00
CBAMT Mike Trout 800.00 1500.00

2020 Topps Chrome Black Autographs Orange Refractors

*ORNG REF.: 1X TO 2.5X BASIC
STATED ODDS 1:XX HOBBY
STATED PRINT RUN 25 SER.#'d SETS
EXCHANGE DEADLINE 10/31/22
CBACS Corey Seager 100.00 250.00
CBADM Dustin May 75.00 200.00
CBAJS Juan Soto 400.00 1000.00
CBALR Luis Robert EXCH 1500.00 3000.00
CBAMT Mike Trout 1000.00 2000.00

2020 Topps Chrome Black Super Futures Autographs

STATED ODDS 1:XX HOBBY
STATED PRINT RUN 99 SER.#'d SETS
EXCHANGE DEADLINE 10/31/22
SFAAM Austin Meadows 25.00 60.00
SFAJS Juan Soto 125.00 300.00
SFAKM Ketel Marte 10.00 25.00
SFAKN Kevin Newman 12.00 30.00
SFANH Nico Hoerner 20.00 50.00
SFAOM Oscar Mercado 10.00 25.00
SFAPA Pete Alonso 40.00 100.00
SFARA Ronald Acuna Jr. 150.00 400.00
SFARD Rafael Devers 30.00 80.00
SFARH Rhys Hoskins 12.00 30.00
SFATE Tommy Edman 15.00 40.00
SFAVG Vladimir Guerrero Jr. 40.00 100.00
SFAVR Victor Robles 15.00 40.00
SFAWB Walker Buehler 30.00 80.00
SFAYA Yordan Alvarez 100.00 250.00

2020 Topps Chrome Black Super Futures Autographs Gold Refractors

*GOLD REF.: .5X TO 1.2X BASIC
STATED ODDS 1:XX HOBBY
STATED PRINT RUN 50 SER.#'d SETS
EXCHANGE DEADLINE 10/31/22
SFAPA Pete Alonso 60.00 150.00

2020 Topps Chrome Black Super Futures Autographs Orange Refractors

*ORNG REF.: .6X TO 1.5X BASIC
STATED ODDS 1:XX HOBBY
STATED PRINT RUN 25 SER.#'d SETS
EXCHANGE DEADLINE 10/31/22
SFAPA Pete Alonso 75.00 200.00
SFARH Rhys Hoskins 40.00 100.00

2020 Topps Chrome Sapphire

1 Mike Trout 75.00 200.00
2 Gerrit Cole 3.00 8.00
3 Nicky Lopez 1.25 3.00
4 Robinson Cano 1.50 4.00
5 JaCoby Jones 1.50 4.00
6 Juan Soto 25.00 60.00
7 Aaron Judge 8.00 20.00
8 Jonathan Villar 1.25 3.00
9 Trent Grisham RC 40.00 100.00
10 Austin Meadows 2.00 5.00
11 Anthony Rendon 2.00 5.00
12 Sam Hilliard RC 2.00 5.00
13 Miles Mikolas 1.25 3.00
14 Anthony Rendon 2.00 5.00
15 Fernando Tatis Jr. 10.00 25.00
Manny Machado CL
16 Gleyber Torres 8.00 20.00
17 Franmil Reyes 1.25 3.00
18 Mitch Garver 2.00 5.00
Nelson Cruz CL
19 Los Angeles Angels 1.25 3.00
20 Aristides Aquino RC 12.00 30.00
21 Shane Greene 1.25 3.00
22 Emilio Pagan 1.25 3.00
23 Christin Stewart 1.25 3.00
24 Kenley Jansen 1.50 4.00
25 Kirby Yates 1.25 3.00
26 Kyle Hendricks 2.00 5.00
27 Milwaukee Brewers 1.25 3.00
28 Tim Anderson 2.00 5.00
29 Starlin Castro 1.25 3.00
30 Josh VanMeter 2.00 5.00
31 Niko Goodrum CL 1.50 4.00
32 Brandon Woodruff 2.00 5.00
33 Houston Astros 1.25 3.00
34 Ian Kinsler 1.50 4.00
35 Adalberto Mondesi 1.50 4.00
36 Sean Doolittle 1.25 3.00
37 Albert Almora 1.50 4.00
38 Austin Nola RC 2.00 5.00
39 Tyler O'neill 1.50 4.00
40 Bobby Bradley RC 1.25 3.00
41 Brian Anderson 1.25 3.00
42 Lewis Brinson 1.25 3.00
43 Leury Garcia 1.25 3.00
44 Tommy Edman 2.00 5.00
45 Mitch Haniger 1.50 4.00
46 Gary Sanchez 2.00 5.00
47 Dansby Swanson 2.00 5.00
48 Jeff McNeil 1.50 4.00
49 Eloy Jimenez 12.00 30.00
50 Cody Bellinger 5.00 12.00
51 Anthony Rizzo 2.50 6.00
52 Yasmani Grandal 1.25 3.00
53 Pete Alonso 6.00 15.00
54 Hunter Dozier 1.25 3.00
55 Jose Martinez 1.25 3.00
56 Andres Munoz RC 2.00 5.00
57 Travis Demeritte RC 2.00 5.00
58 Jesse Winker 2.00 5.00
59 Chris Archer 1.25 3.00
60 Matt Barnes 1.25 3.00
61 Cavan Biggio 10.00 25.00
Bo Bichette CL
62 Chase Anderson 1.25 3.00
63 Christian Vazquez 1.50 4.00
64 Kyle Lewis RC 100.00 250.00
65 Cleveland Indians 1.25 3.00
66 Andrew Heaney 1.25 3.00
67 Tyler Beede 1.25 3.00
68 James Paxton 1.50 4.00
69 Brendan McKay RC 2.00 5.00
70 Nico Hoerner RC 25.00 60.00
71 Sandy Alcantara 1.25 3.00
72 Keston Hiura 2.50 6.00
Ben Gamel CL
73 Oakland Athletics 1.25 3.00
74 Bubba Starling RC 2.50 6.00
75 Michael Conforto 1.50 4.00
76 Stephen Strasburg 2.00 5.00
77 Charlie Culberson 1.25 3.00
78 Bo Bichette RC 500.00 1000.00
79 Brad Keller 1.25 3.00
80 Austin Barnes 1.25 3.00
81 Ryan Yarbrough 1.25 3.00
82 Jorge Polanco 1.50 4.00
83 New York Yankees 1.25 3.00
84 Ken Giles 1.25 3.00
85 Tim Anderson 2.00 5.00
Yolmer Sanchez CL
86 Hyun-Jin Ryu 1.50 4.00
87 St. Louis Cardinals 1.25 3.00
88 Jorge Alfaro 1.25 3.00
89 Kurt Suzuki 1.25 3.00
90 Brock Holt 1.25 3.00
91 Yolmer Sanchez 1.25 3.00
92 Blake Treinen 1.25 3.00
93 Alex Colome 1.25 3.00
94 Marwin Gonzalez 1.25 3.00
95 Ian Kennedy 1.25 3.00
96 Jose Abreu 2.00 5.00
97 Lewis Thorpe RC 1.25 3.00
98 Jesus Aguilar 1.50 4.00
99 Dan Vogelbach 1.25 3.00
100 Alex Bregman 2.00 5.00
101 Brad Hand 1.25 3.00
102 Josh Phegley 1.25 3.00
103 Danny Hultzen RC 1.50 4.00
104 Marco Gonzales 1.25 3.00
105 Niko Goodrum 1.50 4.00
106 Rogelio Armenteros RC 1.50 4.00
107 Luis Castillo 1.50 4.00
108 Josh Rojas RC 1.25 3.00
109 Reese McGuire 1.50 4.00
110 Jesus Luzardo RC 2.50 6.00
111 Buster Posey 2.50 6.00
112 Max Stassi 1.25 3.00
113 Matt Carpenter 2.00 5.00
114 Ildemaro Vargas 1.25 3.00
115 Matt Thaiss RC 1.50 4.00
116 Daniel Murphy 1.50 4.00
117 Max Kepler 1.50 4.00
118 Clayton Kershaw 3.00 8.00
119 Kyle Schwarber 2.00 5.00
120 Kenta Maeda 1.50 4.00
121 DJ LeMahieu 2.00 5.00
122 Caleb Smith 1.25 3.00
123 Seth Brown RC 1.25 3.00
124 Jose Berrios 1.50 4.00
125 Shohei Ohtani 3.00 8.00
126 German Marquez 2.00 5.00
127 Matt Chapman 2.00 5.00
128 Steven Matz 1.25 3.00
129 Yoan Moncada 2.00 5.00
130 Michael Chavis 1.50 4.00
131 Ketel Marte 1.50 4.00
132 Jay Bruce 1.50 4.00
133 Michael Brosseau RC 2.50 6.00
134 David Fletcher 2.00 5.00
135 Enrique Hernandez 2.00 5.00
136 Amed Rosario 1.50 4.00
137 Merrill Kelly 1.25 3.00
138 Jackie Bradley Jr. 2.00 5.00
139 Jose Quintana 1.25 3.00
140 Trevor Bauer 2.50 6.00
141 Roberto Osuna 1.25 3.00
142 Tyler Flowers 1.25 3.00
143 Christian Yelich 2.50 6.00
144 Jake Arrieta 1.50 4.00
145 Paul Goldschmidt 2.00 5.00
146 Dwight Smith Jr. 1.25 3.00
147 Jake Rogers RC 1.25 3.00
148 Willy Adames 1.25 3.00
149 Orlando Arcia 1.25 3.00
150 Ronald Acuna Jr. 20.00 50.00
151 Tommy La Stella 1.25 3.00
152 Zack Wheeler 1.50 4.00
153 Andrew Cashner 1.25 3.00
154 C.J. Cron 1.25 3.00
155 Jack Flaherty 2.00 5.00
156 Nick Markakis 1.50 4.00
157 Gleyber Torres CL 8.00 20.00
158 Jake Lamb 1.50 4.00
159 Jorge Soler 2.00 5.00
160 Christian Yelich 3.00 8.00
Nolan Arenado CL
161 Aroldis Chapman 2.00 5.00
162 Michel Baez RC 1.25 3.00
163 Ryan Pressly 1.25 3.00
164 Matt Strahm 1.25 3.00
165 Matthew Boyd 1.25 3.00
166 Nick Solak RC 5.00 12.00
167 Anthony Kay RC 1.25 3.00
168 Fernando Tatis Jr. 100.00 250.00
169 Jacob Waguespack 1.50 4.00
170 Gregory Polanco 1.50 4.00
171 Kole Calhoun 1.25 3.00
172 Sonny Gray 1.50 4.00
173 Yadier Molina 2.50 6.00
174 Alex Verdugo 1.50 4.00
175 Lucas Giolito 1.50 4.00
176 Brandon Belt 1.50 4.00
177 Craig Kimbrel 1.50 4.00
178 Mauricio Dubon RC 1.50 4.00
179 Ramon Laureano 1.50 4.00
180 Max Scherzer 2.00 5.00
181 Stephen Strasburg 2.00 5.00
182 Vladimir Guerrero Jr. 20.00 50.00
183 Starling Marte 1.50 4.00
184 Mychal Givens 1.25 3.00
185 Johnny Cueto 1.50 4.00
186 Roberto Perez 1.25 3.00
187 Chance Sisco 1.25 3.00
188 Manny Machado 2.00 5.00
189 Mike Moustakas 1.50 4.00
190 Aaron Nola 1.50 4.00
191 Jeremy Jeffress 1.25 3.00
192 Yusei Kikuchi 1.50 4.00
193 Anibal Sanchez 1.50 4.00
194 Liam Hendriks 1.25 3.00
195 Julio Teheran 1.50 4.00
196 Andrew Benintendi 2.00 5.00
197 Raisel Iglesias 1.25 3.00
198 Erick Fedde 1.25 3.00
199 Domingo Santana 1.50 4.00
200 Christian Yelich 2.50 6.00
201 Francisco Lindor 2.00 5.00
202 New York Mets 1.25 3.00
203 Joc Pederson 1.50 4.00
204 Hector Neris 1.25 3.00
205 Patrick Sandoval RC 2.00 5.00
206 Tommy Pham 1.25 3.00
207 Zac Gallen RC 3.00 8.00
208 Zack Collins RC 1.50 4.00
209 Derek Dietrich 1.50 4.00
210 Mitch Garver 1.25 3.00
211 Trevor Richards 1.25 3.00
212 Mike Fiers 1.25 3.00
213 Minnesota Twins 1.25 3.00
214 Trea Turner 1.50 4.00
215 Luke Jackson 1.25 3.00
216 Scott Kingery 1.50 4.00
217 Amir Garrett 1.25 3.00
218 Atlanta Braves 1.25 3.00
219 Jean Segura 1.50 4.00
220 J.T. Realmuto 2.00 5.00
221 Nick Pivetta 1.25 3.00
222 Andrew Chafin 1.25 3.00
223 Aaron Civale RC 2.50 6.00
224 Juan Soto 25.00 60.00
225 Oscar Mercado 2.00 5.00
226 Trent Thornton 1.25 3.00
227 David Peralta 1.25 3.00
228 Logan Allen RC 1.25 3.00
229 Randy Arozarena RC 125.00 300.00
230 Nolan Arenado 3.00 8.00
231 Randal Grichuk 1.25 3.00
232 Justin Verlander 2.00 5.00
233 David Dahl 1.25 3.00
234 Cesar Hernandez 1.25 3.00
235 Dustin May RC 5.00 12.00
236 Brandon Crawford 1.50 4.00
237 Luis Garcia 1.25 3.00
238 Freddy Peralta 1.25 3.00
239 Anthony Rendon 2.00 5.00
240 Jameson Taillon 1.50 4.00
241 Mike Clevinger 1.50 4.00
242 Alex Young RC 1.25 3.00
243 Jeimer Candelario 1.25 3.00
244 Chris Paddack 2.00 5.00
245 Los Angeles Dodgers 1.25 3.00
246 Philadelphia Phillies 1.25 3.00
247 Garrett Cooper 1.25 3.00
248 Hunter Renfroe 1.25 3.00
249 Jordan Yamamoto RC 1.25 3.00
250 Bryce Harper 10.00 25.00
251 A.J. Puk RC 2.00 5.00
252 Aaron Hicks 1.50 4.00
253 Brandon Drury 1.25 3.00
254 Andrew Miller 1.50 4.00
255 Max Muncy 1.50 4.00
256 Roman Quinn 1.25 3.00
257 Joey Lucchesi 1.25 3.00
258 Max Scherzer 2.00 5.00
259 Jaylin Davis RC 2.00 5.00
260 Zack Greinke 2.00 5.00
261 Daniel Mengden 1.25 3.00
262 Anthony Santander 1.25 3.00
263 J.P. Crawford 1.25 3.00
264 Abraham Toro RC 1.50 4.00
265 Patrick Corbin 1.50 4.00
266 Austin Riley 2.50 6.00
267 Joey Votto 2.00 5.00
268 Ian Desmond 1.25 3.00
269 J.D. Martinez 2.00 5.00
270 Jose Urena 1.25 3.00
271 Josh Bell 1.50 4.00
272 Carlos Santana 1.50 4.00
273 Bryan Abreu RC 1.25 3.00
274 Boston Red Sox 1.25 3.00
275 JT Riddle 1.25 3.00
276 Yordan Alvarez 150.00 400.00
277 Dominic Smith 1.25 3.00
278 Isan Diaz RC 2.00 5.00
279 Masahiro Tanaka 2.00 5.00
280 Tony Gonsolin RC 8.00 20.00
281 Nelson Cruz 2.00 5.00
282 Jake Marisnick 1.25 3.00
283 Robel Garcia RC 1.25 3.00
284 Jason Kipnis 1.50 4.00
285 Tyler Alexander RC 2.00 5.00
286 Blake Parker 1.25 3.00
287 Jose Peraza 1.50 4.00
288 Jon Gray 1.25 3.00
289 Yuli Gurriel 1.50 4.00
290 Nick Senzel 2.00 5.00
291 Tyler Naquin 1.50 4.00
292 Gavin Lux RC 75.00 200.00
293 Wade Davis 1.25 3.00
294 Jordan Zimmermann 1.50 4.00
295 Jeff Samardzija 1.25 3.00
296 Whit Merrifield 2.00 5.00
297 Mike Yastrzemski 3.00 8.00
298 Cody Bellinger 4.00 10.00
Alex Verdugo
299 David Price 1.50 4.00
300 Javier Baez 2.50 6.00
301 Mike Tauchman 2.00 5.00
302 Tim Anderson 2.00 5.00
303 Mallex Smith 1.25 3.00
304 Shane Bieber 2.00 5.00
305 Tyler Glasnow 2.00 5.00
306 Jon Lester 1.50 4.00
307 Daniel Palka 1.25 3.00
308 Carlos Rodon 2.00 5.00
309 Robbie Grossman 1.25 3.00
310 Jose Urquidy RC 1.50 4.00
311 David Bote 1.50 4.00
312 Billy Hamilton 1.50 4.00
313 Melky Cabrera 1.25 3.00
314 Rafael Devers 2.50 6.00
315 Adam Frazier 1.25 3.00
316 Justin Turner 2.00 5.00
317 Sean Murphy RC 2.00 5.00
318 Omar Narvaez 1.25 3.00
319 Matt Olson 2.00 5.00
320 Austin Hedges 1.25 3.00
321 Eduardo Rodriguez 1.25 3.00
322 Dario Agrazal RC 1.50 4.00
323 Tyler White 1.25 3.00
324 Mike Soroka 2.00 5.00
325 Kyle Schwarber CL 2.00 5.00
326 Dylan Cease RC 2.00 5.00
327 Cavan Biggio 2.50 6.00
328 Chris Davis 1.25 3.00
329 Washington Nationals 1.25 3.00
330 George Springer 1.50 4.00
331 Kevin McCarthy 1.25 3.00
332 Jacob deGrom 4.00 10.00
333 Evan Longoria 1.50 4.00
334 Kevin Pillar 1.25 3.00
335 Luke Voit 2.50 6.00
336 Miguel Cabrera 2.00 5.00
337 Michael Pineda 1.25 3.00
338 Chicago Cubs 1.25 3.00
339 Hansel Robles 1.25 3.00
340 Adbert Alzolay RC 1.50 4.00
341 Hanser Alberto 1.25 3.00
342 Taylor Rogers 1.25 3.00
343 Carson Kelly 1.25 3.00
344 Ben Gamel 1.50 4.00
345 Justin Verlander 2.00 5.00
346 Lourdes Gurriel Jr. 1.50 4.00
347 Ryan Braun 1.50 4.00
348 Adrian Morejon RC 1.25 3.00
349 Carlos Correa 2.00 5.00
350 Pete Alonso 12.00 30.00
351 Gerrit Cole 5.00 12.00
352 Tanner Roark 1.25 3.00
353 DJ Stewart 1.25 3.00
354 Luke Weaver 1.25 3.00
355 Max Fried 2.00 5.00
356 Franklin Barreto 1.25 3.00
357 Homer Bailey 1.25 3.00
358 Rio Ruiz 1.25 3.00
359 Domingo Leyba RC 1.50 4.00
360 Luis Rengifo 1.25 3.00
361 Zach Eflin 1.25 3.00
362 Chris Shaw 1.25 3.00
363 Shed Long 1.50 4.00
364 Hunter Harvey RC 2.00 5.00
365 Joey Gallo 2.00 5.00
Willie Calhoun/Elvis Andrus CL
366 Marcus Semien 2.00 5.00
367 Giancarlo Stanton 2.00 5.00
368 Wade Miley 1.25 3.00
369 Kolten Wong 1.50 4.00
370 Seth Mejias-Brean RC 1.25 3.00
371 Victor Caratini 1.25 3.00
372 Josh Donaldson 1.50 4.00
373 Kevin Cron 2.00 5.00
374 Jose Ramirez 1.50 4.00
375 Jose Osuna 1.25 3.00
376 Shogo Akiyama RC 2.00 5.00
377 Phillip Ervin 1.25 3.00
378 Nathan Eovaldi 1.50 4.00
379 Ivan Nova 1.50 4.00
380 James Karinchak RC 2.00 5.00
381 Kyle Garlick RC 2.00 5.00
382 Archie Bradley 1.25 3.00
383 Steven Brault 1.25 3.00
384 Carlos Carrasco 1.25 3.00
385 Ryan Zimmerman 1.50 4.00
386 Dakota Hudson 1.50 4.00
387 Tony Wolters 1.25 3.00
388 Dustin Pedroia 2.00 5.00
389 Ryan O'Hearn 1.25 3.00
390 Emmanuel Clase RC 2.00 5.00
391 Justin Upton 1.50 4.00
392 Luis Robert RC 600.00 1200.00
393 Dereck Rodriguez 1.25 3.00
394 Keone Kela 1.25 3.00
395 Scott Oberg 1.25 3.00
396 Miami Marlins 1.25 3.00
397 Charlie Blackmon 2.00 5.00
398 Miguel Andujar 2.00 5.00
399 Adrian Houser 1.25 3.00
400 Hyun-Jin Ryu 1.50 4.00
401 Jake Fraley RC 1.50 4.00
402 Vince Velazquez 1.25 3.00
403 Jose Trevino 1.25 3.00
404 Raimel Tapia 1.25 3.00
405 San Francisco Giants 1.25 3.00
406 Charlie Morton 2.00 5.00
407 T.J. Zeuch RC 1.25 3.00
408 Brendan Rodgers 2.00 5.00
409 Jake Odorizzi 1.25 3.00
410 Luis Urias 1.50 4.00
411 Mark Melancon 1.25 3.00
412 Nelson Cruz 2.00 5.00
Miguel Sano CL
413 Rich Hill 1.25 3.00
414 Gio Gonzalez 1.50 4.00
415 Joey Gallo 2.00 5.00
416 Chris Taylor 1.50 4.00
417 Colorado Rockies 1.25 3.00
418 Alex Dickerson 1.25 3.00
419 J.A. Happ 1.50 4.00
420 Mookie Betts 30.00 80.00
421 Garrett Stubbs RC 1.25 3.00
422 Will Smith 1.25 3.00
423 Andrelton Simmons 1.25 3.00
424 Miguel Sano 1.50 4.00
425 Mike Foltynewicz 1.25 3.00
426 Yoenis Cespedes 2.00 5.00
427 Edwin Diaz 1.50 4.00
428 Jaime Barria 1.25 3.00
429 Joe Musgrove 2.00 5.00
430 Darwinzon Hernandez 1.25 3.00
431 Cincinnati Reds 1.25 3.00
432 Walker Buehler 2.50 6.00
433 Noah Syndergaard 1.50 4.00
434 Brusdar Graterol RC 2.00 5.00
435 Mitch Keller 2.00 5.00
436 Travis d'Arnaud 1.50 4.00
437 Scott Heineman RC 1.25 3.00
438 Danny Duffy 1.25 3.00
439 Dee Gordon 1.25 3.00
440 Carter Kieboom 1.50 4.00
441 Nick Wittgren 2.00 5.00
442 Tom Eshelman RC 1.50 4.00
443 Johan Camargo 1.25 3.00
444 Martin Perez 1.50 4.00
445 Spencer Turnbull 1.25 3.00
446 Bryce Harper 3.00 8.00
Rhys Hoskins CL
447 Griffin Canning 2.00 5.00
448 Ian Happ 1.50 4.00
449 Shun Yamaguchi RC 1.50 4.00
450 Jorge Soler 2.00 5.00
451 Justus Sheffield 2.00 5.00
452 Joe Jimenez 1.25 3.00
453 Miguel Rojas 1.25 3.00
454 Austin Voth 1.25 3.00
455 Kris Bryant 4.00 10.00
456 Dom Nunez RC 1.50 4.00
457 Kevin Gausman 2.00 5.00
458 Trey Mancini 2.00 5.00
459 Kwang-Hyun Kim RC 2.50 6.00
460 Tyler Mahle 1.25 3.00
461 Harrison Bader 1.50 4.00
462 Tony Kemp 1.25 3.00
463 Frankie Montas 1.25 3.00
464 Randy Dobnak RC 2.50 6.00
465 Eugenio Suarez 1.50 4.00
466 Garrett Hampson 1.25 3.00
467 Andrew McCutchen 2.00 5.00
468 Chad Green 1.25 3.00
469 Kris Bryant CL 4.00 10.00
470 Yan Gomes 2.00 5.00
471 Lorenzo Cain 1.25 3.00
472 Steven Duggar 1.25 3.00
473 Lance McCullers Jr. 1.25 3.00
474 Mark Canha 1.25 3.00
475 Robert Dugger RC 1.25 3.00
476 James Marvel RC 1.25 3.00
477 Brent Suter 1.25 3.00
478 Cole Tucker 2.00 5.00
479 Dexter Fowler 1.50 4.00
480 Ozzie Albies 2.00 5.00
481 Victor Reyes 1.25 3.00
482 Adam Duvall 1.50 4.00
483 Eddie Rosario 1.50 4.00
484 Brian Goodwin 1.25 3.00
485 Jack Mayfield RC 1.25 3.00
486 Dawel Lugo 1.25 3.00
487 Yandy Diaz 1.50 4.00
488 Reynaldo Lopez 1.50 4.00
489 Colin Moran 1.25 3.00
490 Austin Slater 1.25 3.00
491 Will Smith 2.00 5.00
492 Paul DeJong 2.00 5.00
493 Christian Walker 1.50 4.00
494 Rowan Wick 1.25 3.00
495 LaMonte WADE Jr. RC 2.00 5.00
496 Lucas Sims 1.25 3.00
497 Albert Pujols 2.50 6.00
498 Brandon Workman 1.25 3.00
499 Sam Tuivailala 1.25 3.00
500 Nick Anderson 1.25 3.00
501 Tampa Bay Rays 1.25 3.00
502 Willians Astudillo 1.25 3.00
503 Dylan Bundy 1.50 4.00
504 Pablo Lopez 1.25 3.00
505 Billy McKinney 1.25 3.00
506 Delino DeShields 1.25 3.00
507 Blake Snell 1.50 4.00
508 Carlos Martinez 1.50 4.00
509 Willi Castro RC 2.00 5.00
510 Michael Lorenzen 1.25 3.00
511 Jordan Hicks 1.50 4.00
512 Josh James 1.25 3.00
513 Michael Brantley 1.50 4.00
514 Logan Webb RC 2.00 5.00
515 Maikel Franco 1.50 4.00
516 Texas Rangers 1.25 3.00
517 Dylan Moore 1.25 3.00
518 Shin-Soo Choo 1.50 4.00
519 Didi Gregorius 1.50 4.00
520 Justin Smoak 1.25 3.00
521 Felix Hernandez 1.50 4.00
522 J.D. Davis 1.25 3.00
523 Corey Kluber 1.50 4.00
524 Jurickson Profar 1.50 4.00
525 Jake Cave 1.50 4.00
526 Byron Buxton 2.00 5.00
527 Khris Davis 2.00 5.00
528 Harold Ramirez 1.25 3.00
529 Ender Inciarte 1.25 3.00
530 Xander Bogaerts 2.00 5.00
531 David Bednar RC 1.25 3.00
532 Robbie Ray 1.25 3.00
533 Nick Castellanos 2.00 5.00
534 Michael Wacha 1.50 4.00
535 Avisail Garcia 1.50 4.00
536 Elvis Luciano 1.25 3.00
537 Marcell Ozuna 2.00 5.00
538 Ozzie Albies 10.00 25.00
Ronald Acuna Jr. CL
539 Tyrone Taylor RC 1.25 3.00
540 Kean Wong RC 2.00 5.00
541 Danny Mendick RC 1.50 4.00
542 Tom Murphy 1.25 3.00
543 Harold Castro 1.50 4.00
544 Wil Myers 1.50 4.00
545 Kevin Kiermaier 1.50 4.00
546 Ross Stripling 1.25 3.00
547 Victor Robles 2.50 6.00
548 Brian O'Grady RC 1.25 3.00
549 Freddie Freeman 8.00 20.00
550 John Means 2.00 5.00
551 Clint Frazier 1.50 4.00
552 Yu Darvish 2.00 5.00
553 Salvador Perez 1.50 4.00
554 Mike Zunino 1.25 3.00
555 Marcus Stroman 1.50 4.00
556 Josh Naylor 1.25 3.00
557 Adam Ottavino 1.50 4.00
558 Sean Manaea 1.25 3.00
559 Josh Hader 1.50 4.00
560 Chad Pinder 1.25 3.00
561 Trevor Williams 1.25 3.00
562 Gio Urshela 2.00 5.00
563 Danny Jansen 1.25 3.00
564 Matt Beaty 1.50 4.00
565 Jordan Luplow 1.25 3.00
566 Seattle Mariners 1.25 3.00
567 Yonathan Daza RC 1.50 4.00
568 Adam Eaton 2.00 5.00
569 Eloy Jimenez 4.00 10.00
Tim Anderson CL
570 Manny Pina 1.25 3.00
571 Keston Hiura 2.50 6.00
572 Manuel Margot 1.25 3.00
573 Jason Heyward 1.50 4.00
574 Brandon Lowe 1.50 4.00
575 Kyle Seager 1.25 3.00
576 Sergio Romo 1.25 3.00
577 Elvis Andrus 1.50 4.00
578 Chris Bassitt 1.25 3.00
579 Kevin Kramer 1.25 3.00
580 Dellin Betances 1.50 4.00
581 Michael Taylor 1.25 3.00
582 Willie Calhoun 1.25 3.00
583 Josh Staumont RC 1.25 3.00
584 Michael Kopech 2.50 6.00
585 Kyle Tucker 2.00 5.00
586 Stevie Wilkerson 2.00 5.00
587 Lou Trivino 1.25 3.00
588 Tommy Kahnle 1.25 3.00
589 Eric Lauer 1.25 3.00
590 Yu Chang RC 2.00 5.00
591 Aaron Judge 3.00 8.00
Gary Sanchez CL
592 Corey Dickerson 1.50 4.00
593 Stephen Piscotty 1.25 3.00
594 Pittsburgh Pirates 1.25 3.00
595 Eduardo Escobar 1.25 3.00
596 Daniel Norris 1.25 3.00
597 Jonathan Hernandez RC 1.25 3.00
598 Jacob Stallings 1.50 4.00
599 Ryan McMahon 2.00 5.00
600 Drew Steckenrider 1.25 3.00
601 Tucker Barnhart 1.25 3.00
602 Jose Altuve 1.50 4.00
603 Dinelson Lamet 1.25 3.00
604 Derek Fisher 1.25 3.00
605 Stephen Vogt 1.50 4.00
606 Martin Maldonado 1.25 3.00
607 Cal Quantrill 1.25 3.00
608 Sam Gaviglio 1.25 3.00
609 Ronald Guzman 1.25 3.00
610 Cole Hamels 1.50 4.00
611 Ryan Braun 2.50 6.00
Lorenzo Cain/Christian Yelich CL
612 Luis Arraez 2.50 6.00
613 Isiah Kiner-Falefa 1.50 4.00
614 Brett Gardner 1.50 4.00
615 Junior Fernandez RC 1.25 3.00
616 Cam Gallagher 1.25 3.00
617 Bryan Reynolds 1.50 4.00
618 Joey Wendle 1.50 4.00
619 Rick Porcello 1.50 4.00
620 Corey Seager 2.00 5.00
621 Dallas Keuchel 1.50 4.00
622 Brett Phillips 1.25 3.00
623 Mike Ford 2.00 5.00
624 Renato Nunez 1.50 4.00
625 Detroit Tigers 1.25 3.00
626 Nate Lowe 3.00 8.00
627 Eric Hosmer 1.50 4.00
628 Julio Urias 2.00 5.00
629 Toronto Blue Jays 1.25 3.00
630 Francisco Mejia 1.50 4.00
631 Stephen Strasburg 2.00 5.00
632 Austin Hays 2.00 5.00
633 Lance Lynn 1.25 3.00
634 San Diego Padres 1.25 3.00
635 Sean Newcomb 1.25 3.00
636 Jake Bauers 1.50 4.00
637 Trevor Story 2.00 5.00
638 Nomar Mazara 1.25 3.00
639 Kolby Allard 1.25 3.00
640 Adam Eaton 2.00 5.00
Howie Kendrick CL
641 A.J. Pollock 1.25 3.00
642 Ryan Borucki 1.25 3.00
643 Wilson Ramos 1.25 3.00
644 Teoscar Hernandez 2.00 5.00
645 Jeff Mathis 1.50 4.00
646 Kevin Newman 2.00 5.00
647 Joe Ross 1.25 3.00
648 Mike Leake 1.25 3.00
649 Jed Lowrie 1.25 3.00
650 Kelvin Herrera 1.25 3.00
651 Arizona Diamondbacks 1.25 3.00
652 Pedro Severino 1.25 3.00
653 Zach Plesac 2.00 5.00
654 Tim Lopes RC 1.50 4.00
655 Howie Kendrick 1.25 3.00
656 Alex Cobb 1.25 3.00
657 Rougned Odor 1.50 4.00
658 Chad Wallach RC 1.25 3.00
659 Aledmys Diaz 1.25 3.00
660 Brandon Nimmo 1.50 4.00
661 Justin Dunn RC 1.50 4.00
662 Andrew Knapp 1.25 3.00
663 Chicago White Sox 1.25 3.00
664 Yonny Chirinos 1.25 3.00
665 Willson Contreras 2.00 5.00
666 Kyle Freeland 1.50 4.00
667 Adam Haseley 1.50 4.00
668 Kansas City Royals 1.25 3.00
669 Luis Severino 1.50 4.00
670 Aaron Barrett 1.25 3.00
671 Ryan McBroom RC 1.50 4.00
672 Chris Sale 2.00 5.00
673 Anthony DeSclafani 1.25 3.00
674 Jose Abreu 2.00 5.00
675 David Robertson 1.25 3.00
676 Rangel Ravelo RC 1.50 4.00
677 Ji-Man Choi 1.25 3.00
678 Jose Rodriguez RC 1.25 3.00
679 Glenn Sparkman 1.25 3.00
680 Nick Ahmed 1.25 3.00
681 Edwin Rios RC 3.00 8.00
682 Ronny Rodriguez 1.25 3.00
683 Jakob Junis 1.25 3.00
684 Mike Minor 1.25 3.00
685 Freddy Galvis 1.25 3.00
686 Josh Reddick 1.25 3.00
687 Rhys Hoskins 2.50 6.00
688 Austin Romine 1.25 3.00
689 James McCann 1.50 4.00
690 Ehire Adrianza 1.25 3.00
691 Brock Burke RC 1.25 3.00
692 Jonathan Schoop 1.25 3.00
693 Jon Berti RC 1.25 3.00
694 Baltimore Orioles 1.25 3.00
695 Danny Santana 1.25 3.00
696 Gleyber Torres 8.00 20.00
Francisco Lindor CL
697 Eric Sogard 1.25 3.00
698 Tyler Chatwood 1.25 3.00
699 Sheldon Neuse RC 1.50 4.00
700 Adam Wainwright 1.50 4.00

2020 Topps Chrome Sapphire Orange Refractors

*ORANGE: 1X TO 2.5X BASIC
STATED ODDS 1:11 HOBBY
STATED PRINT RUN 25 SER.#'d SETS
7 Aaron Judge 30.00 80.00
9 Trent Grisham 200.00 500.00
49 Eloy Jimenez 50.00 120.00
50 Cody Bellinger 20.00 50.00
64 Kyle Lewis 400.00 1000.00
250 Bryce Harper 60.00 150.00
392 Luis Robert 1500.00 3000.00
455 Kris Bryant 20.00 50.00
469 Kris Bryant 20.00 50.00
696 Gleyber Torres 25.00 60.00
Francisco Lindor

2020 Topps Chrome Sapphire Autographs

RANDOM INSERTS IN PACKS
EXCHANGE DEADLINE 7/6/22
CSAAA Aristides Aquino 40.00 100.00
CSAAC Aaron Civale 15.00 40.00
CSAAK Anthony Kay 3.00 8.00
CSAAM Andres Munoz 10.00 25.00
CSAAT Abraham Toro 6.00 15.00
CSABB Bo Bichette
CSABM Brendan McKay 25.00 60.00
CSADC Dylan Cease 20.00 50.00
CSADM Dustin May 40.00 100.00
CSAGL Gavin Lux 20.00 50.00
CSAJD Justin Dunn 10.00 25.00
CSAJL Jesus Luzardo 30.00 80.00
CSAJR Jake Rogers 8.00 20.00
CSAJS Josh Staumont 10.00 25.00
CSAJU Jose Urquidy 10.00 25.00
CSAJY Jordan Yamamoto 6.00 15.00
CSALA Logan Allen 3.00 8.00
CSALR Luis Robert 1000.00 2500.00
CSALW Logan Webb 5.00 12.00
CSAMD Mauricio Dubon 12.00 30.00
CSANH Nico Hoerner 40.00 100.00
CSANS Nick Solak 20.00 50.00
CSASB Seth Brown 6.00 15.00
CSASM Sean Murphy 20.00 50.00
CSATD Travis Demeritte 8.00 20.00
CSATG Trent Grisham 200.00 500.00
CSAYA Yordan Alvarez 150.00 400.00
CSAYC Yu Chang 15.00 40.00
CSAZC Zack Collins 10.00 25.00
CSABBU Brock Burke 3.00 8.00

2020 Topps Chrome Sapphire Autographs Green Refractors

*GREEN: .6X TO 1.5X BASIC
STATED ODDS 1:124 HOBBY
STATED PRINT RUN 50 SER.#'d SETS
EXCHANGE DEADLINE 7/6/22
CSAMD Mauricio Dubon 30.00 80.00
CSAZC Zack Collins 25.00 60.00

2020 Topps Chrome Sapphire Autographs Orange Refractors

*ORANGE: 1X TO 2.5X BASIC
STATED ODDS 1:249 HOBBY
STATED PRINT RUN 25 SER.#'d SETS
EXCHANGE DEADLINE 7/6/22
CSALW Logan Webb 15.00 40.00
CSAMD Mauricio Dubon 50.00 120.00
CSASM Sean Murphy 100.00 250.00
CSAZC Zack Collins 40.00 100.00

2017 Topps Clearly Authentic Autographs

OVERALL AUTO ODDS 1:1 HOBBY
EXCHANGE DEADLINE 6/30/2019
CAAUAB Andrew Benintendi RC 20.00 50.00
CAAUABR Alex Bregman RC 20.00 50.00
CAAUAD Aledmys Diaz 5.00 12.00
CAAUAJ Aaron Judge RC 125.00 300.00
CAAUAJO Adam Jones 10.00 25.00

CAAUAJU Aaron Judge RC 125.00 300.00
CAAUALB Alex Bregman RC 20.00 50.00
CAAUAN Aaron Nola 5.00 12.00
CAAUANB Andrew Benintendi RC 40.00 100.00
CAAUAR Alex Reyes RC 6.00 15.00
CAAUARE Alex Reyes RC 6.00 15.00
CAAUARI Anthony Rizzo 15.00 40.00
CAAUARU Addison Russell 10.00 25.00
CAAUAT Andrew Toles RC 4.00 10.00
CAAUBH Bryce Harper 100.00 250.00
CAAUBP Buster Posey 40.00 100.00
CAAUCF Carson Fulmer RC 4.00 10.00
CAAUCK Clayton Kershaw 50.00 120.00
CAAUCKL Corey Kluber 12.00 30.00
CAAUCS Chris Sale 20.00 50.00
CAAUCSE Corey Seager 25.00 60.00
CAAUDB Dellin Betances 5.00 12.00
CAAUDD David Dahl RC 5.00 12.00
CAAUDDU Danny Duffy 5.00 12.00
CAAUDO David Ortiz 40.00 100.00
CAAUDSW Dansby Swanson RC 25.00 60.00
CAAUDV Dan Vogelbach RC 6.00 15.00
CAAUFF Freddie Freeman 15.00 40.00
CAAUGS George Springer 5.00 12.00
CAAUHD Hunter Dozier RC 5.00 12.00
CAAUHR Hunter Renfroe RC 6.00 15.00
CAAUHRE Hunter Renfroe RC 6.00 15.00
CAAUI Ichiro 150.00 400.00
CAAUJA Jorge Alfaro RC 6.00 15.00
CAAUJAL Jose Altuve 25.00 60.00
CAAUJB Javier Baez 12.00 30.00
CAAUJC Jharel Cotton RC 4.00 10.00
CAAUJD Jose De Leon RC 5.00 12.00
CAAUJDE Jacob deGrom 25.00 60.00
CAAUJH Jeff Hoffman RC 4.00 10.00
CAAUJJ JaCoby Jones RC 6.00 15.00
CAAUJMU Joe Musgrove RC 12.00 30.00
CAAUJP Joe Panik 5.00 12.00
CAAUJT Jake Thompson RC 4.00 10.00
CAAUJTA Jameson Taillon 5.00 12.00
CAAUJU Julio Urias 8.00 20.00
CAAUJV Joey Votto 30.00 80.00
CAAUKB Kris Bryant 100.00 250.00
CAAUKM Kenta Maeda 12.00 30.00
CAAUKSE Kyle Seager 6.00 15.00
CAAULG Lucas Giolito 15.00 40.00
CAAULW Luke Weaver RC 10.00 25.00
CAAULWE Luke Weaver RC 10.00 25.00
CAAUMF Maikel Franco 5.00 12.00
CAAUMFU Michael Fulmer 8.00 20.00
CAAUMM Manny Machado 30.00 80.00
CAAUMMA Manny Margot RC 10.00 25.00
CAAUMO Matt Olson RC 8.00 20.00
CAAUMT Masahiro Tanaka 50.00 120.00
CAAUMTR Mike Trout 175.00 350.00
CAAUNS Noah Syndergaard 10.00 25.00
CAAURB Ryan Braun
CAAURG Randal Grichuk 4.00 10.00
CAAURGS Robert Gsellman RC 5.00 12.00
CAAURH Ryon Healy RC 5.00 12.00
CAAURL Reynaldo Lopez RC 6.00 15.00
CAAURQ Roman Quinn RC 6.00 15.00
CAAURT Raimel Tapia RC 5.00 12.00
CAAUSL Seth Lugo RC 6.00 15.00
CAAUSMA Steven Matz
CAAUTA Tyler Austin RC 6.00 15.00
CAAUTB Ty Blach RC 4.00 10.00
CAAUTG Tyler Glasnow RC 12.00 30.00
CAAUTGL Tyler Glasnow RC 12.00 30.00
CAAUTH Teoscar Hernandez RC 8.00 20.00
CAAUTM Trey Mancini RC 5.00 12.00
CAAUTN Tyler Naquin 6.00 15.00
CAAUTS Trevor Story 8.00 20.00
CAAUWC Willson Contreras 12.00 30.00
CAAUYG Yulieski Gurriel RC 10.00 25.00
CAAUYGU Yulieski Gurriel RC 10.00 25.00
CAAUYM Yoan Moncada RC

2017 Topps Clearly Authentic Autographs Blue

BLUE: .75X TO 2X BASIC
STATED ODDS ODDS 1:17 HOBBY
STATED PRINT RUN 25 SER.#'d SETS
EXCHANGE DEADLINE 6/30/2019
CAAUAJ Aaron Judge 500.00 1000.00
CAAUAJU Aaron Judge 500.00 1000.00
CAAUDSW Dansby Swanson 50.00 120.00
CAAUI Ichiro 250.00 500.00
CAAUKB Kris Bryant 150.00 400.00
CAAUMT Masahiro Tanaka 100.00 250.00
CAAUMTR Mike Trout 250.00 500.00
CAAURB Ryan Braun 12.00 30.00
CAAUSMA Steven Matz 15.00 40.00
CAAUYM Yoan Moncada 60.00 150.00

2017 Topps Clearly Authentic Autographs Green

GREEN: .5X TO 1.2X BASIC
OVERALL AUTO ODDS 1:1 HOBBY
STATED PRINT RUN 99 SER.#'d SETS
EXCHANGE DEADLINE 6/30/2019

2017 Topps Clearly Authentic Autographs Red

RED: .6X TO 1.5X BASIC
STATED ODDS ODDS 1:10 HOBBY
STATED PRINT RUN 50 SER.#'d SETS
EXCHANGE DEADLINE 6/30/2019
CAAUDSW Dansby Swanson 40.00 100.00
CAAUKB Kris Bryant 125.00 300.00
CAAURB Ryan Braun 10.00 25.00
CAAUSMA Steven Matz 12.00 30.00
CAAUYM Yoan Moncada 50.00 120.00

2017 Topps Clearly Authentic Reprint Autographs

STATED ODDS 1:10 HOBBY
PRINT RUNS B/WN 30-135 COPIES PER
EXCHANGE DEADLINE 6/30/2019
CARAUAG Andres Galarraga/135 12.00 30.00
CARAUAKA Al Kaline/110 50.00 120.00
CARAUAR Addison Russell/135 15.00 40.00
CARAUBJ Bo Jackson/40 150.00 400.00
CARAUBJA Bo Jackson/70 150.00 400.00
CARAUBP Buster Posey/45 100.00 250.00
CARAUCJ Chipper Jones/110 75.00 200.00
CARAUCR Cal Ripken Jr./45 150.00 400.00
CARAUCY Carl Yastrzemski/45 60.00 150.00
CARAUDJ Derek Jeter/30 400.00 800.00
CARAUDM Don Mattingly/110 75.00 200.00
CARAUFL Francisco Lindor/135 25.00 60.00
CARAUFR Frank Robinson/110 50.00 120.00
CARAUFT Frank Thomas/135 50.00 120.00
CARAUGM Greg Maddux/40 75.00 200.00
CARAUHA Hank Aaron/30 300.00 600.00
CARAUI Ichiro/30 350.00 700.00
CARAUJB Johnny Bench/45 100.00 250.00
CARAUJC Jose Canseco/135 30.00 80.00
CARAUJD Jacob DeGrom/135 25.00 60.00
CARAUJV Joey Votto/135 50.00 120.00
CARAUKB Kris Bryant/70 150.00 400.00
CARAULB Lou Brock/135 40.00 100.00
CARAUMMC Mark McGwire/70 100.00 250.00
CARAUMT Mike Trout/40 1000.00 1500.00
CARAUNR Nolan Ryan/45 200.00 400.00
CARAUNRY Nolan Ryan/40 200.00 400.00
CARAUNS Noah Syndergaard/135 25.00 60.00
CARAUOC Orlando Cepeda/135 25.00 60.00
CARAUOS Ozzie Smith/135 30.00 80.00
CARAUOV Omar Vizquel/135 20.00 50.00
CARAURC Rod Carew/110 30.00 80.00
CARAURH Rickey Henderson/55 60.00 150.00
CARAURJ Reggie Jackson/45 125.00 300.00
CARAURJO Randy Johnson/40 75.00 200.00
CARAURS Ryne Sandberg/110 60.00 150.00
CARAUSC Steve Carlton/110 30.00 80.00
CARAUSK Sandy Koufax/30 250.00 600.00
CARAUWB Wade Boggs/135 40.00 100.00

2018 Topps Clearly Authentic Autographs

OVERALL AUTO ODDS 1:1 HOBBY
EXCHANGE DEADLINE 6/30/2020
CAAAB Anthony Banda RC 3.00 8.00
CAAAH Austin Hays RC 8.00 20.00
CAAAJ Aaron Judge 150.00 300.00
CAAAME Austin Meadows RC 8.00 20.00
CAAAN Aaron Nola 6.00 15.00
CAAAR Amed Rosario RC 5.00 12.00
CAAAV Alex Verdugo RC 15.00 40.00
CAACF Clint Frazier RC 6.00 15.00
CAACT Chris Taylor 4.00 10.00
CAACV Christian Villanueva RC 6.00 15.00
CAADF Dustin Fowler RC 3.00 8.00
CAADM Dillon Maples RC 3.00 8.00
CAAFM Francisco Mejia RC EXCH 4.00 10.00
CAAGA Greg Allen RC 6.00 15.00
CAAGT Gleyber Torres RC 60.00 150.00
CAAJA Jose Altuve 12.00 30.00
CAAJB Justin Bour 3.00 8.00
CAAJS Jackson Stephens RC 3.00 8.00
CAAJSH Jimmie Sherfy RC 3.00 8.00
CAAJV Joey Votto 25.00 60.00
CAAKB Kris Bryant 75.00 200.00
CAAKS Kyle Schwarber 10.00 25.00
CAALC Luis Castillo 4.00 10.00
CAAMA Miguel Andujar RC 12.00 30.00
CAAMF Max Fried RC 25.00 60.00
CAAMG Miguel Gomez RC 3.00 8.00
CAAMM Manny Machado EXCH 12.00 30.00
CAAMO Matt Olson 5.00 12.00
CAAMT Mike Trout 200.00 400.00
CAANG Niko Goodrum RC 8.00 20.00
CAANSY Noah Syndergaard EXCH 10.00 25.00
CAAOA Ozzie Albies RC 12.00 30.00
CAAPB Paul Blackburn RC 3.00 8.00
CAAPD Paul DeJong 5.00 12.00
CAARA Ronald Acuna RC 125.00 300.00
CAARD Rafael Devers RC 20.00 50.00
CAARH Rhys Hoskins RC 10.00 25.00
CAARR Raudy Read RC 3.00 8.00
CAARU Richard Urena RC 3.00 8.00
CAASA Sandy Alcantara RC 3.00 8.00
CAASO Shohei Ohtani RC 125.00 300.00
CAATLO Tim Locastro RC 3.00 8.00
CAATN Tomas Nido RC 3.00 8.00
CAATP Tommy Pham 3.00 8.00
CAATS Travis Shaw 3.00 8.00
CAATSC Troy Scribner RC 3.00 8.00
CAAVA Victor Arano RC 3.00 8.00
CAAVR Victor Robles RC 8.00 20.00
CAAWB Walker Buehler RC 25.00 60.00
CAAWM Whit Merrifield 8.00 20.00

2018 Topps Clearly Authentic Autographs Black

*BLACK: .5X TO 1.2X BASIC
OVERALL AUTO ODDS 1:15 HOBBY
STATED PRINT RUN 75 SER.#'d SETS
EXCHANGE DEADLINE 6/30/2020
CAAAA Aaron Altherr 4.00 10.00
CAADS Dominic Smith 8.00 20.00

2018 Topps Clearly Authentic Autographs Blue

*BLUE: .75X TO 2X BASIC
STATED ODDS ODDS 1:41 HOBBY
STATED PRINT RUN 25 SER.#'d SETS
EXCHANGE DEADLINE 6/30/2020
CAAAA Aaron Altherr 6.00 15.00
CAADS Dominic Smith 12.00 30.00
CAAMT Mike Trout 250.00 500.00

2018 Topps Clearly Authentic Autographs Green

*GREEN: .5X TO 1.2X BASIC
OVERALL AUTO ODDS 1:14 HOBBY
STATED PRINT RUN 99 SER.#'d SETS
EXCHANGE DEADLINE 6/30/2020
CAAAA Aaron Altherr 4.00 10.00
CAADS Dominic Smith 8.00 20.00

2018 Topps Clearly Authentic Autographs Red

*RED: .5X TO 1.2X BASIC
STATED ODDS ODDS 1:22 HOBBY
STATED PRINT RUN 50 SER.#'d SETS
EXCHANGE DEADLINE 6/30/2020
CAAAA Aaron Altherr 4.00 10.00
CAADS Dominic Smith 8.00 20.00

2018 Topps Clearly Authentic '93 Finest Stars Autographs

STATED ODDS 1:14 HOBBY
PRINT RUNS B/WN 10-99 COPIES PER
NO PRICING ON 15 OR LESS
EXCHANGE DEADLINE 6/30/2020
93FSAABR Alex Bregman EXCH 30.00 80.00
93FSAAR Anthony Rizzo/30 75.00 200.00
93FSAARO Amed Rosario/199 10.00 25.00
93FSABJ Bo Jackson/30 75.00 200.00
93FSACF Clint Frazier EXCH 10.00 25.00
93FSACJ Chipper Jones/30 125.00 300.00
93FSACR Cal Ripken Jr. EXCH 100.00 250.00
93FSADM Don Mattingly/50 75.00 200.00
93FSAFL Francisco Lindor/99 20.00 50.00
93FSAFM Francisco Mejia/199 10.00 25.00
93FSAFT Frank Thomas/50 60.00 150.00
93FSAJC Jose Canseco/99 20.00 50.00
93FSAJP Joc Pederson/99 10.00 25.00
93FSAJSM John Smoltz/50 50.00 120.00
93FSAKB Kris Bryant EXCH 100.00 250.00
93FSAKS Kyle Schwarber/99 15.00 40.00
93FSAMM Manny Machado EXCH 30.00 80.00
93FSAMMC Mark McGwire/30 60.00 150.00
93FSANR Nolan Ryan/30 125.00 300.00
93FSANS Noah Syndergaard EXCH
93FSAOA Ozzie Albies EXCH 40.00 100.00
93FSARD Rafael Devers/199 15.00 40.00
93FSASG Sonny Gray/99 10.00 25.00
93FSATG Tom Glavine/50 40.00 100.00
93FSATM Trey Mancini/99 12.00 30.00
93FSAVR Victor Robles/199 20.00 50.00
93FSAWCO Willson Contreras/99 12.00 30.00

2018 Topps Clearly Authentic Legendary Autographs

STATED ODDS 1:227 HOBBY
PRINT RUNS B/WN 10-25 COPIES PER
NO PRICING ON 10 OR LESS
EXCHANGE DEADLINE 6/30/2020
CLAAK Al Kaline/25 30.00 80.00
CLABJ Bo Jackson/25
CLACJ Chipper Jones/25 75.00 200.00
CLADJ Derek Jeter
CLADM Don Mattingly/25 60.00 150.00
CLADO David Ortiz/25 40.00 100.00
CLAFT Frank Thomas/25
CLAHA Hank Aaron
CLAMM Mark McGwire
CLANR Nolan Ryan/25 100.00 250.00
CLAOS Ozzie Smith/25 30.00 80.00

2018 Topps Clearly Authentic MLB Awards Autographs

OVERALL AUTO ODDS 1:17 HOBBY
EXCHANGE DEADLINE 6/30/2020
MLBAABB Byron Buxton 5.00 12.00
MLBAACBL Charlie Blackmon 10.00 25.00
MLBAACK Craig Kimbrel 10.00 25.00
MLBAAGSP George Springer 12.00 30.00
MLBAAJA Jose Altuve 20.00 50.00
MLBAAJR Jose Ramirez EXCH 12.00 30.00

2018 Topps Clearly Authentic MLB Awards Autographs Black

*BLACK: .5X TO 1.2X BASIC
OVERALL AUTO ODDS 1:50 HOBBY
STATED PRINT RUN 75 SER.#'d SETS
EXCHANGE DEADLINE 6/30/2020
MLBAACKL Corey Kluber 15.00 40.00
MLBAAFL Francisco Lindor 20.00 50.00
MLBAAGS Gary Sanchez 20.00 50.00
MLBAAPG Paul Goldschmidt 15.00 40.00
MLBAAPGO Paul Goldschmidt 15.00 40.00

2018 Topps Clearly Authentic MLB Awards Autographs Blue

*BLUE: .75X TO 2X BASIC
STATED ODDS ODDS 1:117 HOBBY
STATED PRINT RUN 25 SER.#'d SETS
EXCHANGE DEADLINE 6/30/2020
MLBAAAR Anthony Rizzo 50.00 120.00
MLBAACKL Corey Kluber 25.00 60.00
MLBAAFL Francisco Lindor 30.00 80.00
MLBAAGS Gary Sanchez 30.00 80.00
MLBAAPG Paul Goldschmidt 25.00 60.00
MLBAAPGO Paul Goldschmidt 25.00 60.00

2018 Topps Clearly Authentic MLB Awards Autographs Green

*GREEN: .5X TO 1.2X BASIC
OVERALL AUTO ODDS 1:52 HOBBY
STATED PRINT RUN 99 SER.#'d SETS
EXCHANGE DEADLINE 6/30/2020
MLBAABD Brian Dozier 5.00 12.00
MLBAAPG Paul Goldschmidt 15.00 40.00
MLBAAPGO Paul Goldschmidt 15.00 40.00

2018 Topps Clearly Authentic MLB Awards Autographs Red

*RED: .5X TO 1.2X BASIC
STATED ODDS ODDS 1:59 HOBBY
STATED PRINT RUN 50 SER.#'d SETS
EXCHANGE DEADLINE 6/30/2020
MLBAAAR Anthony Rizzo 30.00 80.00
MLBAAFL Francisco Lindor 20.00 50.00
MLBAAGS Gary Sanchez 20.00 50.00
MLBAAPG Paul Goldschmidt 15.00 40.00
MLBAAPGO Paul Goldschmidt 15.00 40.00

2018 Topps Clearly Authentic Reprint Autographs

STATED ODDS 1:22 HOBBY
PRINT RUNS B/WN 15-199 COPIES PER
NO PRICING ON 15 OR LESS
EXCHANGE DEADLINE 6/30/2020
CARAK Al Kaline/99 50.00 120.00
CARAKA Al Kaline/99 50.00 120.00
CARBH Bryce Harper/15 150.00 400.00
CARBJ Bo Jackson/50 100.00 250.00
CARBL Barry Larkin/99 40.00 100.00
CARCR Cal Ripken Jr./30 100.00 250.00
CARDG Dwight Gooden/99 40.00 100.00
CARDM Don Mattingly/50 75.00 200.00
CARDS Darryl Strawberry/99 25.00 60.00
CARFT Frank Thomas/99 40.00 100.00
CARIR Ivan Rodriguez/99 30.00 80.00
CARJC Jose Canseco/99 40.00 100.00
CARJCA Jose Canseco/199 25.00 60.00
CARJP Jim Palmer/99 20.00 50.00
CARLB Lou Brock/99 25.00 60.00
CARNR Nolan Ryan/30 200.00 400.00
CAROS Ozzie Smith/99 50.00 120.00
CARRA Roberto Alomar/150 15.00 40.00
CARRH Rickey Henderson/30 100.00 250.00
CARRJ Reggie Jackson/30 150.00 400.00
CARRY Robin Yount/99 30.00 80.00
CARWB Wade Boggs/50 40.00 100.00

2018 Topps Clearly Authentic Salute Autographs

OVERALL AUTO ODDS 1:9 HOBBY
EXCHANGE DEADLINE 6/30/2020
CASABG Ben Gamel 4.00 10.00
CASADB Dellin Betances 4.00 10.00
CASADG Didi Gregorius EXCH 10.00 25.00
CASADS Domingo Santana 4.00 10.00
CASAET Eric Thames 4.00 10.00
CASAHR Hunter Renfroe 4.00 10.00
CASAIH Ian Happ 8.00 20.00
CASAJBE Jose Berrios 4.00 10.00
CASAKB Keon Broxton 3.00 8.00
CASAKD Khris Davis 10.00 25.00

2018 Topps Clearly Authentic Salute Autographs Black

*BLACK: .5X TO 1.2X BASIC
OVERALL AUTO ODDS 1:37 HOBBY
STATED PRINT RUN 75 SER.#'d SETS
EXCHANGE DEADLINE 6/30/2020
CASACS Chris Sale EXCH 12.00 30.00
CASAJS Jean Segura 4.00 10.00
CASAPG Paul Goldschmidt 15.00 40.00

2018 Topps Clearly Authentic Salute Autographs Blue

*BLUE: .75X TO 2X BASIC
STATED ODDS ODDS 1:103 HOBBY
STATED PRINT RUN 25 SER.#'d SETS
EXCHANGE DEADLINE 6/30/2020
CASACS Chris Sale EXCH 20.00 50.00
CASAJS Jean Segura 6.00 15.00
CASAPG Paul Goldschmidt 25.00 60.00

2018 Topps Clearly Authentic Salute Autographs Green

*GREEN: .5X TO 1.2X BASIC
OVERALL AUTO ODDS 1:28 HOBBY
STATED PRINT RUN 99 SER.#'d SETS
EXCHANGE DEADLINE 6/30/2020
CASACS Chris Sale EXCH 12.00 30.00
CASAJS Jean Segura 4.00 10.00
CASAPG Paul Goldschmidt 15.00 40.00

2018 Topps Clearly Authentic Salute Autographs Red

*RED: .5X TO 1.2X BASIC
STATED ODDS ODDS 1:37 HOBBY
STATED PRINT RUN 50 SER.#'d SETS
EXCHANGE DEADLINE 6/30/2020
CASACS Chris Sale EXCH 12.00 30.00
CASAJS Jean Segura 4.00 10.00
CASAPG Paul Goldschmidt 15.00 40.00

2019 Topps Clearly Authentic Autographs

RANDOM INSERTS IN PACKS
*GREEN/99: .5X TO 1.2X BASIC
*BLACK/75: .5X TO 1.2X BASIC
*RED/50: .5X TO 1.2X BASIC
*BLUE/25: .75X TO 2X BASIC
CAABL Brandon Lowe RC 15.00 40.00
CAACB Corbin Burnes RC 10.00 25.00
CAACH Christin Stewart RC 4.00 10.00
CAACK Carter Kieboom RC 10.00 25.00
CAACM Cedric Mullins RC 10.00 25.00
CAACS Chris Sale 8.00 20.00
CAACT Cole Tucker RC 10.00 25.00
CAADJ Danny Jansen RC 3.00 8.00
CAADP Daniel Ponce de Leon RC 5.00 12.00
CAADR Dereck Rodriguez 4.00 10.00
CAAEJ Eloy Jimenez RC 30.00 80.00
CAAFF Freddie Freeman 15.00 40.00
CAAFL Francisco Lindor 12.00 30.00
CAAFT Fernando Tatis Jr. RC 150.00 400.00
CAAGS George Springer 12.00 30.00
CAAJA Jesus Aguilar 4.00 10.00
CAAJE Jean Segura 5.00 12.00
CAAJO Jose Martinez 3.00 8.00
CAAJS Justus Sheffield RC 8.00 20.00
CAAJU Juan Soto 50.00 120.00
CAAKB Kris Bryant 30.00 80.00
CAAKK Kevin Kramer RC 4.00 10.00
CAAKT Kyle Tucker RC 15.00 40.00
CAAKW Kyle Wright RC 5.00 12.00
CAALT Lane Thomas RC 8.00 20.00
CAAMC Michael Chavis RC 12.00 30.00
CAAMK Michael Kopech RC 10.00 25.00
CAAMM Max Muncy 8.00 20.00
CAAMT Mike Trout
CAAPA Peter Alonso RC 60.00 150.00
CAAPG Paul Goldschmidt 20.00 50.00
CAARA Ronald Acuna Jr. 50.00 120.00
CAARH Rhys Hoskins 10.00 25.00
CAART Rowdy Tellez RC 5.00 12.00
CAASB Shane Bieber 20.00 50.00
CAASM Sean Manaea 3.00 8.00
CAASO Shohei Ohtani 75.00 200.00
CAASP Salvador Perez 8.00 20.00
CAASR Sean Reid-Foley RC 3.00 8.00
CAATA Tim Anderson 10.00 25.00
CAATE Thairo Estrada RC 10.00 25.00
CAATT Touki Toussaint RC 4.00 10.00
CAAVG Vladimir Guerrero Jr. RC 125.00 300.00
CAAYK Yusei Kikuchi RC 5.00 12.00

2019 Topps Clearly Authentic '52 Reimagining Autographs

STATED ODDS 1:25 HOBBY
PRINT RUNS B/WN 5-50 COPIES PER
NO PRICING ON QTY 15 OR LESS
RAAD Andre Dawson/50 25.00 60.00
RAAM Andrew McCutchen/50 50.00 120.00
RAAP Andy Pettitte/50 25.00 60.00
RAAT Anthony Rizzo/50 40.00 100.00
RABG Bob Gibson/50 40.00 100.00
RABJ Bo Jackson/25 75.00 200.00
RACK Clayton Kershaw/50 40.00 100.00
RACR Cal Ripken Jr./25 75.00 200.00
RACS Chris Sale/50 15.00 40.00
RACY Carl Yastrzemski/25 60.00 150.00
RADJ Derek Jeter
RADM Dale Murphy/50 30.00 80.00
RAFL Francisco Lindor/50 20.00 50.00
RAFT Frank Thomas/50
RAHM Hideki Matsui/25 40.00 100.00
RAJA Jose Altuve/50 40.00 100.00
RAJB Javier Baez/50 20.00 50.00
RAJE Jeff Bagwell/50 30.00 80.00
RAJF Jack Flaherty/50 25.00 60.00
RAJK Jason Varitek/50 20.00 50.00
RAJO Johnny Bench/25 75.00 200.00
RAJP Jorge Posada/50 25.00 60.00
RAJV Joey Votto/50 30.00 80.00
RAKB Kris Bryant/25 75.00 200.00
RAMA Miguel Andujar/50 20.00 50.00
RAMM Mark McGwire/25 50.00 120.00
RANR Nolan Ryan/25 75.00 200.00
RANS Noah Syndergaard/50 20.00 50.00
RAOS Ozzie Smith/50 30.00 80.00
RAPG Paul Goldschmidt/50 25.00 60.00
RARA2 Roberto Alomar/50 20.00 50.00
RARAJ Ronald Acuna Jr./50 75.00 200.00
RARH Rhys Hoskins/50 25.00 60.00
RARJ Reggie Jackson/25 50.00 120.00
RAVG Vladimir Guerrero/50 50.00 120.00
RAWC Willson Contreras/50 30.00 80.00
RAWI Will Clark/50 50.00 120.00

2019 Topps Clearly Authentic '84 Topps Autographs

STATED ODDS 1:8 HOBBY
*GREEN/99: .5X TO 1.2X BASIC
*BLACK/75: .5X TO 1.2X BASIC
*RED/50: .5X TO 1.2X BASIC
*BLUE/25: .75X TO 2X BASIC
TBABM Brandon Nimmo 6.00 15.00
TBABS Blake Snell 6.00 15.00
TBACY Christian Yelich 30.00 80.00
TBADM Don Mattingly 50.00 120.00
TBADS Darryl Strawberry 10.00 25.00
TBAJB Jose Berrios 6.00 15.00
TBAJC Jose Canseco 8.00 20.00
TBAJD Jacob deGrom 30.00 80.00
TBAKS Kyle Schwarber 20.00 50.00
TBAMH Mitch Haniger 6.00 15.00
TBAMM Miles Mikolas 5.00 12.00
TBAMO Matt Olson 6.00 15.00
TBAOA Ozzie Albies 20.00 50.00
TBAPD Paul DeJong 5.00 12.00
TBATM Trey Mancini 6.00 15.00
TBAVR Victor Robles 12.00 30.00
TBAWM Whit Merrifield 6.00 15.00

2019 Topps Clearly Authentic 150 Years of Professional Baseball Autographs

STATED ODDS 1:20 HOBBY
*GREEN/99: .5X TO 1.2X BASIC
*BLACK/75: .5X TO 1.2X BASIC
*RED/50: .5X TO 1.2X BASIC
*BLUE/25: .75X TO 2X BASIC
YPBCF Carlton Fisk 12.00 30.00
YBPAK Al Kaline 20.00 50.00
YBPBB Bert Blyleven 8.00 20.00
YBPDE Dennis Eckersley 10.00 25.00
YBPDG Dwight Gooden 10.00 25.00
YBPDS Don Sutton 6.00 15.00
YBPIR Ivan Rodriguez 15.00 40.00
YBPJE Jim Rice 8.00 20.00
YBPJG Juan Gonzalez 10.00 25.00
YBPJM Juan Marichal 12.00 30.00
YBPJO Johnny Damon 6.00 15.00
YBPRC Rod Carew 15.00 40.00
YBPSC Steve Carlton 10.00 25.00

2019 Topps Clearly Authentic T206 Autographs

STATED ODDS 1:19 HOBBY
PRINT RUNS B/WN 15-99 COPIES PER
NO PRICING ON QTY 15
*BLUE/25: .75X TO 2X p/r 50-99
*BLUE/25: .4X TO 1X p/r 30
TAAB Adrian Beltre/30 30.00 80.00
TAAK Al Kaline/50 40.00 100.00
TAAT Alan Trammell/99 15.00 40.00
TABL Barry Larkin/30 25.00 60.00
TACF Carlton Fisk/50 25.00 60.00
TACJ Chipper Jones/30 50.00 120.00
TACY Christian Yelich/50 50.00 120.00
TADM Don Mattingly/50 50.00 120.00
TADS Darryl Strawberry/99 15.00 40.00
TAEJ Eloy Jimenez/99 25.00 60.00
TAFF Freddie Freeman/99 30.00 80.00
TAFT Fernando Tatis Jr./50 125.00 300.00
TAGS George Springer/50 30.00 80.00
TAJC Jose Canseco/99 15.00 40.00
TAJR Jose Ramirez/99 12.00 30.00
TAJS Juan Soto/99 60.00 150.00
TAJU Justin Smoak/50 4.00 10.00
TAKS Kyle Schwarber/99 10.00 25.00
TAKW Kerry Wood/50 12.00 30.00
TALB Lou Brock/99 25.00 60.00
TANG Nomar Garciaparra/30 20.00 50.00
TAOA Ozzie Albies/99 12.00 30.00
TARA Rick Ankiel/50 8.00 20.00
TARD Rafael Devers/99 20.00 50.00
TARO Rod Carew/50 20.00 50.00
TARS Ryne Sandberg/30 30.00 80.00
TASC Steve Carlton/50 15.00 40.00
TATG Tom Glavine/30 20.00 50.00
TATS Trevor Story/99 12.00 30.00
TAWB Wade Boggs/99 25.00 60.00

2020 Topps Clearly Authentic Autographs

RANDOM INSERTS IN PACKS
EXCHANGE DEADLINE 5/31/2022
CCAAA Adbert Alzolay 8.00 20.00
CCAAC Aaron Civale 8.00 20.00
CCAAK Anthony Kay 6.00 15.00
CCAAT Abraham Toro 8.00 20.00
CCAAY Alex Young 3.00 8.00
CCABB Bobby Bradley 8.00 20.00
CCABM Brendan McKay 5.00 12.00
CCABO Bo Bichette EXCH 125.00 300.00
CCADC Dylan Cease 10.00 25.00
CCAGL Gavin Lux 40.00 100.00
CCAHH Hunter Harvey 5.00 12.00
CCAJD Justin Dunn 8.00 20.00
CCAJF Junior Fernandez 3.00 8.00
CCAJL Jesus Luzardo 12.00 30.00
CCAJR Jake Rogers 3.00 8.00
CCAJY Jordan Yamamoto 8.00 20.00
CCAKL Kyle Lewis 60.00 150.00
CCALA Logan Allen 3.00 8.00
CCALR Luis Robert 150.00 400.00
CCALW Logan Webb 6.00 15.00
CCAMD Mauricio Dubon 10.00 25.00
CCAMT Matt Thaiss 8.00 20.00
CCANH Nico Hoerner 25.00 60.00
CCANS Nick Solak 10.00 25.00
CCARA Randy Arozarena 40.00 100.00
CCASB Seth Brown 3.00 8.00
CCASH Sam Hilliard 8.00 20.00
CCASM Sean Murphy 8.00 20.00
CCATG Trent Grisham 20.00 50.00
CCAYA Yordan Alvarez 40.00 100.00
CCAZC Zack Collins 10.00 25.00
CCAAAQ Aristides Aquino 15.00 40.00
CCAJDA Jaylin Davis 5.00 12.00
CCAJFR Jake Fraley 8.00 20.00
CCAJRO Josh Rojas 3.00 8.00
CCAJUR Jose Urquidy 4.00 10.00

2020 Topps Clearly Authentic Autographs Black

*BLACK: .5X TO 1.2X BASIC
STATED ODDS 1:17 HOBBY
STATED PRINT RUN 75 SER.#'d SETS
EXCHANGE DEADLINE 5/31/2022
CCAGL Gavin Lux 60.00 150.00
CCAJL Jesus Luzardo 20.00 50.00
CCAJY Jordan Yamamoto 15.00 40.00
CCASH Sam Hilliard 15.00 40.00
CCAYA Yordan Alvarez 60.00 150.00

2020 Topps Clearly Authentic Autographs Blue

*BLUE: .8X TO 2X BASIC
STATED ODDS 1:51 HOBBY
STATED PRINT RUN 25 SER.#'d SETS
EXCHANGE DEADLINE 5/31/2022
CCADC Dylan Cease 30.00 80.00
CCAGL Gavin Lux 100.00 250.00
CCAJL Jesus Luzardo 30.00 80.00
CCAJY Jordan Yamamoto 25.00 60.00
CCAMT Matt Thaiss 25.00 60.00
CCASH Sam Hilliard 25.00 60.00
CCASM Sean Murphy 25.00 60.00
CCAYA Yordan Alvarez 125.00 300.00
CCAAAQ Aristides Aquino 50.00 120.00

2020 Topps Clearly Authentic Autographs Green

*GREEN: .5X TO 1.2X BASIC
STATED ODDS 1:13 HOBBY
STATED PRINT RUN 99 SER.#'d SETS
EXCHANGE DEADLINE 5/31/2022
CCAGL Gavin Lux 60.00 150.00
CCAJL Jesus Luzardo 20.00 50.00
CCASH Sam Hilliard 12.00 30.00

2020 Topps Clearly Authentic Autographs Red

*RED: .5X TO 1.2X BASIC
STATED ODDS 1:26 HOBBY
STATED PRINT RUN 50 SER.#'d SETS
EXCHANGE DEADLINE 5/31/2022
CCADC Dylan Cease 20.00 50.00
CCAGL Gavin Lux 60.00 150.00
CCAJL Jesus Luzardo 20.00 50.00
CCAJY Jordan Yamamoto 15.00 40.00
CCAMT Matt Thaiss 15.00 40.00
CCASH Sam Hilliard 15.00 40.00
CCASM Sean Murphy 15.00 40.00
CCAYA Yordan Alvarez 75.00 200.00
CCAAAQ Aristides Aquino 30.00 80.00

2020 Topps Clearly Authentic '51 Red Blue Backs Autographs

STATED ODDS 1:26 HOBBY
PRINT RUNS B/WN 15-99 COPIES PER
NO PRICING ON QTY 15 OR LESS
EXCHANGE DEADLINE 5/31/2022
*BLUE: .6X TO 1.5X p/r 50-99
*BLUE: .4X TO 2X p/r 25-30
51AI Ichiro 125.00 300.00
51AAA Aristides Aquino 20.00 50.00
51ABH Bryce Harper 125.00 300.00
51ABL Barry Larkin 20.00 50.00
51ABP Buster Posey 75.00 200.00
51ACF Carlton Fisk 30.00 80.00
51ACY Christian Yelich 50.00 120.00
51ADM Don Mattingly 60.00 150.00
51ADO David Ortiz 50.00 120.00
51AEJ Eloy Jimenez 25.00 60.00
51AFT Fernando Tatis Jr. 50.00 120.00
51AGS George Springer 20.00 50.00
51AJC Jose Canseco 25.00 60.00
51AJS Juan Soto 50.00 120.00
51AKB Kris Bryant 75.00 200.00
51ALB Rhys Hoskins 20.00 50.00
51AMM Mike Mussina 25.00 60.00
51ARD Rafael Devers 30.00 80.00
51ARO Rod Carew 20.00 50.00
51ARS Ryne Sandberg 40.00 100.00
51ASC Jacob deGrom 60.00 150.00
51ASO Shohei Ohtani 75.00 200.00
51ATG Tom Glavine 25.00 60.00
51ATH Rickey Henderson 75.00 200.00
51AVG Vladimir Guerrero Jr. EXCH 40.00 100.00
51ADMA Dustin May 20.00 50.00
51AJLU Jesus Luzardo 15.00 40.00
51AKWO Kerry Wood 30.00 80.00
51ALWE Kyle Lewis 50.00 120.00
51APAL Pete Alonso 60.00 150.00

2020 Topps Clearly Authentic '53 Topps Reimagining Autographs

STATED ODDS 1:19 HOBBY
PRINT RUNS B/WN 10-99 COPIES PER
NO PRICING ON QTY 15 OR LESS
EXCHANGE DEADLINE 5/31/2022
RAAD Andre Dawson 30.00 80.00
RAAJ Aaron Judge 30.00 80.00
RAAP Andy Pettitte 15.00 40.00
RAAT Anthony Rizzo 40.00 100.00
RABB Bo Bichette EXCH 60.00 150.00
RABG Bob Gibson 50.00 120.00
RACK Clayton Kershaw 75.00 200.00
RACR Cal Ripken Jr. 100.00 250.00
RACS Chris Sale 15.00 40.00
RADJ Derek Jeter EXCH
RADM Dale Murphy 20.00 50.00
RAFM Fred McGriff 20.00 50.00
RAFT Frank Thomas 40.00 100.00
RAGL Gavin Lux 100.00 250.00
RAGT Gleyber Torres 60.00 150.00
RAHM Hideki Matsui 40.00 100.00
RAJA Jose Altuve 20.00 50.00
RAJF Jack Flaherty 30.00 80.00
RAJK Jason Varitek 20.00 50.00
RAJO Johnny Bench 60.00 150.00
RAJS John Smoltz 25.00 60.00
RAJV Joey Votto 30.00 80.00
RAMM Mark McGwire 60.00 150.00
RAMT Mike Trout 400.00 1000.00
RANH Nico Hoerner 40.00 100.00
RANR Nolan Ryan 75.00 200.00
RAOS Ozzie Smith 30.00 80.00
RAPG Paul Goldschmidt 20.00 50.00
RARH Rhys Hoskins 25.00 60.00
RARJ Reggie Jackson 30.00 80.00
RASO Shohei Ohtani 15.00 40.00
RAWC Willson Contreras 15.00 40.00
RAWI Will Clark 100.00 250.00
RAYA Yordan Alvarez 50.00 120.00
RAFTJ Fernando Tatis Jr. 60.00 150.00
RAKGJ Ken Griffey Jr. 250.00 600.00
RARAJ Ronald Acuna Jr. 100.00 250.00

2020 Topps Clearly Authentic '85 Topps Autographs

STATED ODDS 1:7 HOBBY
EXCHANGE DEADLINE 5/31/2022
TBAAJ Aaron Judge 100.00 250.00
TBAAR Austin Riley 15.00 40.00
TBADW David Wright 20.00 50.00
TBAED Eric Davis 25.00 60.00
TBAEJ Eloy Jimenez 25.00 60.00
TBAFT Fernando Tatis Jr. 100.00 250.00
TBAJA Jose Altuve 15.00 40.00
TBAJF Jack Flaherty 15.00 40.00
TBAJS Juan Soto 50.00 120.00
TBAKH Kyle Hendricks 15.00 40.00
TBALV Luke Voit 20.00 50.00
TBAMK Max Kepler 8.00 20.00
TBAMS Mike Soroka 12.00 30.00
TBAMT Mike Trout 400.00 800.00
TBAPA Pete Alonso 60.00 150.00
TBAPC Patrick Corbin 6.00 15.00
TBARH Rhys Hoskins 6.00 15.00
TBATE Tommy Edman 15.00 40.00
TBAVR Victor Robles 12.00 30.00
TBAWC Will Clark 30.00 80.00
TBAECK Dennis Eckersley 15.00 40.00
TBAJCA Jose Canseco 20.00 50.00
TBAJSO Jorge Soler 10.00 25.00
TBAJTR J.T. Realmuto 20.00 50.00
TBAKHI Keston Hiura 12.00 30.00
TBAMMC Mark McGwire 60.00 150.00
TBAMMU Max Muncy 10.00 25.00
TBAOSM Ozzie Smith 25.00 60.00
TBATAN Tim Anderson 15.00 40.00
TBATLI Tim Lincecum 20.00 50.00
TBAWCO Willson Contreras 12.00 30.00
TBAWSM Will Smith 12.00 30.00
TBARYNO Ryne Sandberg 40.00 100.00

2020 Topps Clearly Authentic '85 Topps Autographs Black

*BLACK: .5X TO 1.2X BASIC
STATED ODDS 1:21 HOBBY
STATED PRINT RUN 75 SER.#'d SETS
EXCHANGE DEADLINE 5/31/2022
TBAJF Jack Flaherty 25.00 60.00
TBARH Rhys Hoskins 12.00 30.00
TBATE Tommy Edman 25.00 60.00
TBAJSO Jorge Soler 25.00 60.00

2020 Topps Clearly Authentic '85 Topps Autographs Blue

*BLUE: .8X TO 2X BASIC
STATED ODDS 1:50 HOBBY
STATED PRINT RUN 25 SER.#'d SETS
EXCHANGE DEADLINE 5/31/2022
TBAJF Jack Flaherty 50.00 120.00
TBAJS Juan Soto 125.00 300.00
TBARH Rhys Hoskins 40.00 100.00
TBATE Tommy Edman 40.00 100.00
TBAJSO Jorge Soler 40.00 100.00
TBAJTR J.T. Realmuto 50.00 120.00
TBAOSM Ozzie Smith 60.00 150.00

2020 Topps Clearly Authentic '85 Topps Autographs Green

*GREEN: .5X TO 1.2X BASIC
STATED ODDS 1:16 HOBBY
STATED PRINT RUN 99 SER.#'d SETS
EXCHANGE DEADLINE 5/31/2022
TBARH Rhys Hoskins 12.00 30.00
TBAJSO Jorge Soler 25.00 60.00

2020 Topps Clearly Authentic '85 Topps Autographs Red

*RED: .5X TO 1.2X BASIC
STATED ODDS 1:29 HOBBY
STATED PRINT RUN 50 SER.#'d SETS
EXCHANGE DEADLINE 5/31/2022
TBAJF Jack Flaherty 30.00 80.00
TBAJS Juan Soto 75.00 200.00
TBARH Rhys Hoskins 25.00 60.00
TBATE Tommy Edman 25.00 60.00
TBAJSO Jorge Soler 25.00 60.00
TBAJTR J.T. Realmuto 30.00 80.00
TBAOSM Ozzie Smith 40.00 100.00

2020 Topps Clearly Authentic Decades Best Autographs

STATED ODDS 1:35 HOBBY
EXCHANGE DEADLINE 5/31/2022
DBABB Bert Blyleven 8.00 20.00
DBABG Bob Gibson 25.00 60.00
DBABL Barry Larkin 20.00 50.00
DBACJ Chipper Jones 50.00 120.00
DBADM Don Mattingly 40.00 100.00
DBADO David Ortiz 25.00 60.00
DBADS Darryl Strawberry 15.00 40.00
DBAFT Frank Thomas 30.00 80.00
DBAJR Jim Rice 10.00 25.00
DBAMT Mike Trout 300.00 600.00
DBARA Roberto Alomar 15.00 40.00
DBARC Rod Carew 20.00 50.00
DBASC Steve Carlton 15.00 40.00
DBATH Todd Helton 12.00 30.00
DBAVG Vladimir Guerrero 20.00 50.00
DBADMU Dale Murphy 20.00 50.00
DBAJBE Johnny Bench 40.00 100.00
DBAJVO Joey Votto 20.00 50.00
DBAMCA Miguel Cabrera 50.00 120.00

2020 Topps Clearly Authentic Decades Best Autographs Blue

*BLUE: .8X TO 2X BASIC

STATED ODDS 1:84 HOBBY
STATED PRINT RUN 25 SER.#'d SETS
EXCHANGE DEADLINE 5/31/2022
DBABB Bert Blyleven 25.00 60.00
DBAMT Mike Trout 400.00 800.00
DBAMCA Miguel Cabrera 125.00 300.00

2020 Topps Clearly Authentic Decades Best Autographs Red

*RED: .5X TO 1.2X BASIC
STATED ODDS 1:50 HOBBY
STATED PRINT RUN 50 SER.#'d SETS
EXCHANGE DEADLINE 5/31/2022
DBABB Bert Blyleven 15.00 40.00
DBAMCA Miguel Cabrera 75.00 200.00

2004 Topps Clubhouse Relics

TWO RELICS PER PACK
GROUP A CARDS NOT SERIAL-NUMBERED
GROUP A PRINT RUNS PROVIDED BY TOPPS
AB Armando Benitez Jsy C 1.50 4.00
AD Adam Dunn Jsy C 2.50 6.00
AG Adrian Gonzalez Jsy C 3.00 8.00
AJ Andruw Jones Jsy C 1.50 4.00
AK Al Kaline Jsy E 6.00 15.00
AL Al Leiter Jsy C 1.50 4.00
AP Albert Pujols Jsy C 5.00 12.00
AR Alex Rodriguez Bat C 8.00 20.00
ARA Aramis Ramirez Bat B 1.50 4.00
AS Alfonso Soriano Bat D 2.50 6.00
BA Bobby Abreu Jsy D 1.50 4.00
BB Bret Boone Jsy E 1.50 4.00
BF Brad Fullmer Bat A/200 2.00 5.00
BL Barry Larkin Bat A/200 3.00 8.00
BM Brett Myers Jsy D 1.50 4.00
BW Bernie Williams Uni C 2.50 6.00
BWA Billy Wagner Jsy C 1.50 4.00
BZ Barry Zito Jsy A/230 3.00 8.00
CCR Carl Crawford Bat B 2.50 6.00
CD Carlos Delgado Jsy A/200 2.00 5.00
CE Carl Everett Bat C 1.50 4.00
CFC Chin-Feng Chen Jsy E 5.00 12.00
CFL Cliff Floyd Uni B 1.50 4.00
CG Cristian Guzman Jsy B 1.50 4.00
CJ Chipper Jones Jsy E 4.00 10.00
CL Chris Lubanski Jsy A/209 2.00 5.00
CP Chan Ho Park Jsy E 2.50 6.00
CPA Corey Patterson Jsy A/267 2.00 5.00
CR Cal Ripken Jsy E 6.00 15.00
CS C.C. Sabathia Jsy E 2.50 6.00
CSC Curt Schilling Jsy C 2.50 6.00
CST Casey Stengel Uni A/217 3.00 8.00
CY Carl Yastrzemski Jsy E 4.00 10.00
DC Dave Concepcion Bat D 1.50 4.00
DE Dennis Eckersley Uni E 2.50 6.00
DJ Derek Jeter Bat C 10.00 25.00
DL Derek Lowe Jsy A/200 2.00 5.00
DP Dave Parker Bat A/292 2.00 5.00
DS Duke Snider Bat C 2.50 6.00
EA Edgardo Alfonzo Bat A/286 2.00 5.00
EC Eric Chavez Uni E 1.50 4.00
EG Eric Gagne Uni E 1.50 4.00
EH Estee Harris Jsy A/206 2.00 5.00
EL Esteban Loaiza Jsy B 1.50 4.00
EM Eddie Mathews Jsy A/174 5.00 12.00
EMA Edgar Martinez Bat A/200 3.00 8.00
EMU Eddie Murray Bat B 2.50 6.00
FM Fred McGriff Bat E 1.50 4.00
FR Frank Robinson Uni B 2.50 6.00
FT Frank Thomas Bat C 4.00 10.00
FV Fern Valenzuela Bat A/288 2.00 5.00
GB George Brett Uni E 8.00 20.00
GC Gary Carter Jkt A/221 3.00 8.00
GM Greg Maddux Jsy B 5.00 12.00
GS Gary Sheffield Jsy D 1.50 4.00
HA Hank Aaron Bat A/113 12.00 30.00
HB Hank Bauer Bat B 1.50 4.00
HBL Hank Blalock Jsy E 1.50 4.00
HN Hideo Nomo Bat A/207 5.00 12.00
IR Ivan Rodriguez Jsy D 2.50 6.00
JB Jeff Bagwell Jsy A/200 3.00 8.00
JBE Johnny Bench Uni E 4.00 10.00
JBU Jeromy Burnitz Bat A/208 2.00 5.00
JC Jeff Cirillo Bat B 1.50 4.00
JCA Joe Carter Jsy A/259 2.00 5.00
JF Jonathan Fulton Jsy A/200 2.00 5.00
JG Jason Giambi Uni E 1.50 4.00
JGO Juan Gonzalez Bat B 1.50 4.00
JH James Houser Jsy A/182 2.00 5.00
JKE Jeff Kent Jsy A/200 2.00 5.00
JL Javy Lopez Jsy D 1.50 4.00
JO John Olerud Jsy B 1.50 4.00
JP Jorge Posada Jsy A/264 3.00 8.00
JPB Josh Beckett Jsy A/195 2.00 5.00
JR Jackie Robinson Bat A/262 12.00 30.00
JRE Jose Reyes Jsy E 2.50 6.00
JRO Jimmy Rollins Jsy E 2.50 6.00
JS Jay Sborz Jsy A/176 2.00 5.00
JSM John Smoltz Jsy E 4.00 10.00
JT Jim Thome Jsy C 2.50 6.00
JV Javier Vazquez Jsy A/283 2.00 5.00
JVI Jose Vidro Jsy A/275 2.00 5.00
KB Kevin Brown Uni A/168 2.00 5.00
KG Ken Griffey Jr. Jsy A/200 10.00 25.00
KI Kazuhisa Ishii Jsy C 1.50 4.00
KM Kevin Millwood Jsy E 1.50 4.00
LB Lance Berkman Jsy B 2.50 6.00
LG Luis Gonzalez Jsy B 1.50 4.00
LW Larry Walker Jsy C 2.50 6.00
MB Marlon Byrd Jsy B 1.50 4.00
MC Miguel Cabrera Jsy B 4.00 10.00
MDG Marquis Grissom Bat B 1.50 4.00
MG Mark Grace Jsy E 2.50 6.00
MH Mickey Hall Jsy A/217 2.00 5.00
MM Mark Mulder Uni E 1.50 4.00
MO Magglio Ordonez Bat B 2.50 6.00
MP Mike Piazza Jsy B 4.00 10.00
MR Manny Ramirez Jsy A/207 5.00 12.00
MRI Mariano Rivera Uni A/239 6.00 15.00
MS Mike Schmidt Jsy D 6.00 15.00
MSW Mike Sweeney Jsy E 1.50 4.00
MT Mark Teixeira Jsy D 2.50 6.00
MTE Miguel Tejada Uni B 2.50 6.00
NG Nomar Garciaparra Bat B 2.50 6.00
NR Nolan Ryan Uni E 4.00 10.00
OC Orlando Cepeda Bat B 2.50 6.00
OH Orel Hershiser Jsy E 1.50 4.00
OHU Orlando Hudson Jsy A/200 2.00 5.00
OS Ozzie Smith Jsy D 5.00 12.00
PB Pat Burrell Jsy E 1.50 4.00
PK Paul Konerko Bat B 2.50 6.00
PL Paul Lo Duca Uni B 1.50 4.00
PM Pedro Martinez Jsy A/200 3.00 8.00
PW Preston Wilson Jsy B 1.50 4.00
RA Roberto Alomar Uni E 2.50 6.00
RB Rocco Baldelli Jsy E 1.50 4.00
RC Roberto Clemente Bat B 15.00 40.00
RCE Ron Cey Bat B 1.50 4.00
RF Rafael Furcal Jsy E 1.50 4.00
RH Ramon Hernandez Jsy E 1.50 4.00
RHE Rickey Henderson Uni E 4.00 10.00
RJ Reggie Jackson Jsy D 2.50 6.00
RLC Roger Cedeno Bat B 1.50 4.00
RP Rafael Palmeiro Uni A/200 3.00 8.00
RS Richie Sexson Bat A/200 2.00 5.00
RSA Ryne Sandberg Bat E 8.00 20.00
RSI Ruben Sierra Bat B 1.50 4.00
RY Robin Yount Bat B 4.00 10.00
SF Steve Finley Jsy C 1.50 4.00
SG Shawn Green Jsy C 1.50 4.00
SL Steve Lerud Jsy A/213 2.00 5.00
SR Scott Rolen Bat B 2.50 6.00
SS Sammy Sosa Jsy E 4.00 10.00
TA Tony Armas Jr. Jsy C 1.50 4.00
TB Tony Batista Jsy E 1.50 4.00
TG Tom Glavine Jsy B 2.50 6.00
TGL Troy Glaus Jsy E 1.50 4.00
TGW Tony Gwynn Bat E 4.00 10.00
TH Tim Hudson Uni E 2.50 6.00
THE Todd Helton Bat C 2.50 6.00
THU Torii Hunter Jsy E 1.50 4.00
TM Tino Martinez Uni E 2.50 6.00
TP Tony Perez Uni B 2.50 6.00
TPE Troy Percival Uni B 1.50 4.00
TS Tim Salmon Uni C 1.50 4.00
VG Vladimir Guerrero Jsy E 2.50 6.00
VW Vernon Wells Bat A/200 2.00 5.00
WB Wade Boggs Jsy A/250 3.00 8.00
WC Will Clark Jsy E 2.50 6.00
WF Whitey Ford Uni A/296 3.00 8.00
WM Willie Mays Jsy D 8.00 20.00
WP Wily Mo Pena Jsy B 1.50 4.00
WS Willie Stargell Uni A/200 3.00 8.00
YB Yogi Berra Uni B 4.00 10.00

2004 Topps Clubhouse Black Relics

*BLACK: 1.25X TO 3X ACTIVE GROUP C-E
*BLACK: 1X TO 2.5X RETIRED GROUP C-E
*BLACK: 1.25X TO 3X ACTIVE GROUP B
*BLACK: .75X TO 2X RETIRED GROUP B
*BLACK: .75X TO 2X ACTIVE GROUP A
*BLACK: .6X TO 1.5X RETIRED GROUP A
STATED ODDS 1:16
STATED PRINT RUN 25 SERIAL #'d SETS
NO RC YR PRICING DUE TO SCARCITY

2004 Topps Clubhouse Copper Relics

*COPPER: .5X TO 1.2X ACTIVE C-E
*COPPER: .6X TO 1.5X RETIRED C-E
*COPPER: .5X TO 1.2X ACTIVE B
*COPPER: .5X TO 1.2X RETIRED B
*COPPER: .4X TO 1X ACTIVE A
*COPPER: .4X TO 1X RETIRED A
STATED ODDS 1:4
STATED PRINT RUN 99 SERIAL #'d SETS

2004 Topps Clubhouse All-Star Appeal Relics Base

*BASE: .5X TO 1.2X ON-DECK CIRCLE
STATED ODDS 1:36
STATED PRINT RUN 65 SERIAL #'d SETS
ER Edgar Renteria 4.00 10.00
RF Rafael Furcal 4.00 10.00

2004 Topps Clubhouse All-Star Appeal Relics On-Deck Circle

STATED ODDS 1:26
STATED PRINT RUN 90 SERIAL #'d SETS
BALL STATED ODDS 1:237
BALL PRINT RUN 10 SERIAL #'d SETS
NO BALL PRICING DUE TO SCARCITY
AJ Andruw Jones 4.00 10.00
AP Albert Pujols 8.00 20.00
AR Alex Rodriguez 6.00 15.00
AS Alfonso Soriano 3.00 8.00
BB Bret Boone 3.00 8.00
CD Carlos Delgado 3.00 8.00
EM Edgar Martinez 4.00 10.00
GA Garret Anderson 3.00 8.00
GS Gary Sheffield 3.00 8.00
HB Hank Blalock 3.00 8.00
JE Jim Edmonds 3.00 8.00
JG Jason Giambi 3.00 8.00
JL Javy Lopez 3.00 8.00
JP Jorge Posada 4.00 10.00
JV Jose Vidro 3.00 8.00
LC Luis Castillo 3.00 8.00
LG Luis Gonzalez 3.00 8.00
ML Mike Lowell 3.00 8.00
MO Magglio Ordonez 3.00 8.00
NG Nomar Garciaparra 6.00 15.00
PW Preston Wilson 3.00 8.00
RS Richie Sexson 3.00 8.00
SR Scott Rolen 4.00 10.00
TG Troy Glaus 3.00 8.00
TH Todd Helton 4.00 10.00
VW Vernon Wells 3.00 8.00

2004 Topps Clubhouse All-Star Appeal Relics Autographs Ball

STATED ODDS 1:510
STATED PRINT RUN 30 SERIAL #'d SETS
GA Garret Anderson 12.00 30.00
GS Gary Sheffield 20.00 50.00
HB Hank Blalock 12.00 30.00
JP Jorge Posada 30.00 80.00

2004 Topps Clubhouse All-Star Appeal Relics Autographs Base

STATED ODDS 1:308
STATED PRINT RUN 50 SERIAL #'d SETS
GA Garret Anderson 10.00 25.00
GS Gary Sheffield 15.00 40.00
HB Hank Blalock 10.00 25.00
JP Jorge Posada 60.00 120.00

2004 Topps Clubhouse All-Star Appeal Relics Autographs On-Deck Circle

GROUP A ODDS 1:363
GROUP B ODDS 1:192
GROUP C ODDS 1:146
GROUP D ODDS 1:67
PRINT RUNS B/WN 170-920 COPIES PER
GA Garret Anderson B/320 6.00 15.00
GS Gary Sheffield A/170 6.00 15.00
HB Hank Blalock D/920 4.00 10.00
JP Jorge Posada C/420 12.00 30.00

2004 Topps Clubhouse Career Legends Relics

STATED ODDS 1:46
PRINT RUNS B/WN 11-184 COPIES PER
NO PRICING ON QTY OF 12 OR LESS
BR1 Babe Ruth HR Bat/60 100.00 200.00
BR2 Babe Ruth RBI Bat/171 60.00 120.00
BR3 Babe Ruth 2B Bat/45 100.00 200.00
BR4 Babe Ruth 3B Bat/16 150.00 250.00
BR5 Babe Ruth SN Bat/22 150.00 250.00
EB1 Ernie Banks RBI Uni/143 8.00 20.00
EB2 Ernie Banks 2B Uni/34 12.50 30.00
EB3 Ernie Banks HR Jkt/47 10.00 25.00
EB5 Ernie Banks SN Jkt/19 20.00 50.00
EB6 Ernie Banks BB Jkt/71 10.00 25.00
LG1 Lou Gehrig HR Bat/49 60.00 120.00
LG2 Lou Gehrig RBI Bat/184 60.00 120.00
LG3 Lou Gehrig 2B Bat/52 60.00 120.00
LG4 Lou Gehrig 3B Bat/20 60.00 120.00
LG5 Lou Gehrig SN Bat/17 60.00 120.00
TC1 Ty Cobb SN Bat/24 75.00 150.00
TC3 Ty Cobb 2B Uni/47 75.00 150.00
TC4 Ty Cobb 3B Uni/24 100.00 200.00
WM1 Willie Mays HR Jsy/52 15.00 40.00
WM2 Willie Mays RBI Jsy/141 15.00 40.00
WM3 Willie Mays 2B Jsy/43 15.00 40.00
WM4 Willie Mays 3B Jsy/20 15.00 40.00
WM5 Willie Mays SN Jsy/22 15.00 40.00

2004 Topps Clubhouse Double Play Relics

STATED ODDS 1:165
STATED PRINT RUN 75 SERIAL #'d SETS
B ='S BAT, J ='S JSY, U ='S UNI
CLE Phillips J/Vizquel J/Hafner B 10.00 25.00
NYM Reyes J/Wiggin U/Piazza B 10.00 25.00
NYY Jeter B/A.Rod B/Giambi B 20.00 50.00
PHI Rollins J/Bell B/Thome B 10.00 25.00
SDP Greene J/Burr B/Nevin J 10.00 25.00

2004 Topps Clubhouse Frozen Ropes Relics

STATED ODDS 1:26
STATED PRINT RUN 50 SERIAL #'d SETS
AD Adam Dunn Jsy 4.00 10.00
ADA Andre Dawson Bat 4.00 10.00
AH Aubrey Huff Jsy 4.00 10.00
AP Albert Pujols Jsy 10.00 25.00
AR Alex Rodriguez Bat 15.00 40.00
AS Alfonso Soriano Bat 4.00 10.00
BA Bobby Abreu Jsy 4.00 10.00
BR Brooks Robinson Bat 6.00 15.00
BW Bernie Williams Uni 6.00 15.00
CB Craig Biggio Bat 6.00 15.00
CE Carl Everett Bat 4.00 10.00
CJ Chipper Jones Jsy 6.00 15.00
CY Carl Yastrzemski Jsy 12.50 30.00
DM Don Mattingly Jsy 15.00 40.00
DMU Dale Murphy Bat 6.00 15.00
DS Duke Snider Bat 6.00 15.00
EC Eric Chavez Jsy 4.00 10.00
EM Edgar Martinez Bat 6.00 15.00
GC Gary Carter Jkt 4.00 10.00
GS Gary Sheffield Jsy 4.00 10.00
HB Hank Blalock Jsy 4.00 10.00
IR Ivan Rodriguez Jsy 6.00 15.00
JB Jeff Bagwell Jsy 6.00 15.00
JBE Johnny Bench Uni 10.00 25.00
JG Jason Giambi Uni 4.00 10.00
JR Jose Reyes Jsy 6.00 15.00
JT Jim Thome Jsy 6.00 15.00
KP Kirby Puckett Uni 10.00 25.00
LB Lance Berkman Jsy 4.00 10.00
LG Luis Gonzalez Jsy 4.00 10.00
MO Magglio Ordonez Bat 4.00 10.00
MP Mike Piazza Jsy 8.00 20.00
MR Manny Ramirez Jsy 6.00 15.00
MS Mike Schmidt Jsy 15.00 40.00
MT Miguel Tejada Uni 4.00 10.00
OS Ozzie Smith Jsy 12.50 30.00
PK Paul Konerko Bat 4.00 10.00
PW Preston Wilson Jsy 4.00 10.00
RB Rocco Baldelli Jsy 4.00 10.00
RF Rafael Furcal Jsy 4.00 10.00
RP Rafael Palmeiro Jsy 6.00 15.00
RS Ryne Sandberg Bat 15.00 40.00
SG Shawn Green Jsy 4.00 10.00
SS Sammy Sosa Jsy 6.00 15.00
TH Todd Helton Bat 6.00 15.00
VG Vladimir Guerrero Jsy 6.00 15.00
WB Wade Boggs Jsy 6.00 15.00

2004 Topps Clubhouse Heart of the Lineup Relics

STATED ODDS 1:52
STATED PRINT RUN 100 SERIAL #'d SETS
B ='S BAT, J ='S JSY, U ='S UNI
ARI Finley J/Sexson J/L.Gonz J 6.00 15.00
CHC Sosa J/Alou U/Aramis B 10.00 25.00
CHW Magglio J/Thomas J/C.Lee B 10.00 25.00
CIN Griffey Jr. J/Kearns J/Dunn J 15.00 40.00
COL Helton J/Walker J/Wilson J 10.00 25.00
HOU Bagwell J/Kent B/Berkman B 10.00 25.00
NYY A.Rod B/Giambi U/Sheff J 15.00 40.00
PHI Thome J/Burrell J/Abreu J 10.00 25.00
SEA Edgar J/Boone J/Olerud J 10.00 25.00
STL Pujols J/Edmonds J/Rolen B 12.50 30.00
TEX Soriano B/Teix J/Blalock J 10.00 25.00
TOR Wells J/Delgado J/Hinske B 6.00 15.00

2004 Topps Clubhouse Patch Place Relics

STATED ODDS 1:50
STATED PRINT RUN 25 SERIAL #'d SETS
AD Adam Dunn 6.00 15.00
ADA Andre Dawson 10.00 25.00
AP Albert Pujols 30.00 60.00
AR Alex Rodriguez 20.00 50.00
CB Craig Biggio 10.00 25.00
CD Carlos Delgado 6.00 15.00
CS Curt Schilling 6.00 15.00
CY Carl Yastrzemski 40.00 80.00
DE Darin Erstad 6.00 15.00
DM Dale Murphy 15.00 40.00
EG Eric Gagne 6.00 15.00
EM Eddie Mathews 40.00 80.00
FR Frank Robinson 10.00 25.00
GB George Brett 30.00 60.00
GC Gary Carter 10.00 25.00
HB Hank Blalock 6.00 15.00
IR Ivan Rodriguez 10.00 25.00
JB Jeff Bagwell 10.00 25.00
JBE Josh Beckett 6.00 15.00
JE Jim Edmonds 6.00 15.00
KI Kazuhisa Ishii 6.00 15.00
LB Lance Berkman 6.00 15.00
LBR Lou Brock 15.00 40.00
LG Luis Gonzalez 6.00 15.00
MM Mark Mulder 6.00 15.00
MP Mike Piazza 20.00 50.00
MR Manny Ramirez 10.00 25.00
MS Mike Schmidt 40.00 80.00
MT Mark Teixeira 10.00 25.00
MTE Miguel Tejada 6.00 15.00
NG Nomar Garciaparra 20.00 50.00
NR Nolan Ryan 40.00 80.00
PM Pedro Martinez 10.00 25.00
RB Rocco Baldelli 6.00 15.00
RH Rickey Henderson 15.00 40.00
RJ Randy Johnson 15.00 40.00
RJA Reggie Jackson 15.00 40.00
RP Rafael Palmeiro 10.00 25.00
RY Robin Yount 15.00 40.00
SG Shawn Green 6.00 15.00
SR Scott Rolen 10.00 25.00
SS Sammy Sosa 15.00 40.00
TG Tony Gwynn 20.00 50.00
TH Todd Helton 10.00 25.00
THU Torii Hunter 6.00 15.00
TS Tom Seaver 15.00 40.00
VG Vladimir Guerrero 15.00 40.00
WB Wade Boggs 15.00 40.00
WM Willie Mays 60.00 120.00

2004 Topps Clubhouse Power Pieces Relics

STATED ODDS 1:62
PRINT RUNS B/WN 2-75 COPIES PER
NO PRICING ON QTY OF 14 OR LESS
AJ Andruw Jones Jsy/25 8.00 20.00
BM Brett Myers Jsy/39 3.00 8.00
BP Brad Penny Jsy/31 5.00 12.00
BZ Barry Zito Uni/75 3.00 8.00
CD Carlos Delgado Jsy/25 5.00 12.00
CP Corey Patterson Jsy/20 5.00 12.00
CS Curt Schilling Jsy/38 3.00 8.00
FR Frank Robinson Uni/20 10.00 25.00
JB Josh Beckett Jsy/61 3.00 8.00
JG Jason Giambi Uni/25 5.00 12.00
JP Jorge Posada Jsy/20 5.00 12.00
JT Jim Thome Jsy/25 8.00 20.00
KI Kazuhisa Ishii Jsy/17 6.00 15.00
KS Kazuhiro Sasaki Jsy/22 10.00 25.00
MC Miguel Cabrera Jsy/24 8.00 20.00
MM Mark Mulder Uni/20 5.00 12.00
MP Mike Piazza Jsy/31 15.00 40.00
MS Mike Schmidt Jsy/20 40.00 80.00
MT Mark Teixeira Jsy/25 8.00 20.00
NR Nolan Ryan Uni/34 40.00 80.00
PM Pedro Martinez Jsy/45 5.00 12.00
RJ Reggie Jackson Jsy/44 10.00 25.00
SR Scott Rolen Bat/27 8.00 20.00
SS Sammy Sosa Jsy/21 4.00 10.00
TG Troy Glaus Jsy/25 5.00 12.00
TH Tim Hudson Uni/15 6.00 15.00
THE Todd Helton Bat/17 10.00 25.00
THU Torii Hunter Jsy/48 3.00 8.00
WM Willie Mays Jsy/24 40.00 80.00

2006 Topps Co-Signers

COMP.SET w/o AU's (100) 15.00 40.00
COMMON CARD (1-100) .30 .75
101-120 GROUP A ODDS 1:2025
101-120 GROUP B ODDS 1:1625
101-120 GROUP C ODDS 1:920
101-120 GROUP D ODDS 1:81
101-120 GROUP E ODDS 1:270
101-120 GROUP F ODDS 1:68
101-120 GROUP G ODDS 1:12
101-120 GROUP A PRINT RUN 200 CARDS
101-120 GROUP B PRINT RUN 250 CARDS
101-120 GROUP C PRINT RUN 440 CARDS
A-C CARDS ARE NOT SERIAL NUMBERED
A-C PRINT RUNS PROVIDED BY TOPPS
1 Albert Pujols 1.00 2.50
2 Roger Clemens 1.00 2.50
3 Paul Konerko .50 1.25
4 Jeff Francoeur .75 2.00
5 Miguel Tejada .50 1.25
6 Curt Schilling .50 1.25
7 Mickey Mantle 2.50 6.00
8 Miguel Cabrera .75 2.00
9 Derrek Lee .30 .75
10 Jeff Kent .30 .75
11 Gary Sheffield .30 .75
12 Rich Harden .30 .75
13 Scott Rolen .50 1.25
14 David Wright .60 1.50
15 Troy Glaus .30 .75
16 Torii Hunter .30 .75
17 Nolan Ryan 2.50 6.00
18 Alfonso Soriano .50 1.25
19 Hank Blalock .30 .75
20 Chase Utley .50 1.25
21 Ryan Howard .60 1.50
22 Robinson Cano .50 1.25
23 Derek Jeter 2.00 5.00
24 Huston Street .30 .75
25 Jason Giambi .30 .75
26 Rafael Furcal .30 .75
27 Rickie Weeks .30 .75
28 Ivan Rodriguez .50 1.25
29 Travis Hafner .30 .75
30 Greg Maddux 1.00 2.50
31 Andruw Jones .30 .75
32 Andy Pettitte .50 1.25
33 Scott Podsednik .30 .75
34 Francisco Rodriguez .50 1.25
35 Josh Beckett .30 .75
36 Lance Berkman .50 1.25
37 Roy Oswalt .50 1.25
38 Pedro Martinez .50 1.25
39 Jimmy Rollins .50 1.25
40 Johan Santana .50 1.25
41 Randy Johnson .75 2.00
42 Mariano Rivera 1.00 2.50
43 Nick Johnson .30 .75
44 Josh Gibson .75 2.00
45 Shawn Green .30 .75
46 Adrian Beltre .75 2.00
47 Johnny Damon .50 1.25
48 Joe Mauer .50 1.25
49 Todd Helton .50 1.25
50 Alex Rodriguez 1.00 2.50
51 Jake Peavy .30 .75
52 David Ortiz .75 2.00
53 Mark Buehrle .50 1.25
54 Eric Gagne .30 .75
55 Hideki Matsui .75 2.00
56 Bobby Abreu .30 .75
57 Victor Martinez .50 1.25
58 Brian Roberts .30 .75
59 Chipper Jones .75 2.00
60 Carlos Beltran .50 1.25
61 Tim Hudson .50 1.25
62 Carlos Lee .30 .75
63 Barry Zito .50 1.25
64 Moises Alou .30 .75
65 Mark Teixeira .50 1.25
66 Lyle Overbay .30 .75
67 Kerry Wood .30 .75
68 B.J. Ryan .30 .75
69 Jim Edmonds .50 1.25
70 Carlos Delgado .30 .75
71 Magglio Ordonez .50 1.25
72 Juan Pierre .30 .75
73 Manny Ramirez .75 2.00
74 Dontrelle Willis .30 .75
75 Ichiro Suzuki 1.00 2.50
76 Nomar Garciaparra .50 1.25
77 Zach Duke .30 .75
78 Chris Carpenter .50 1.25
79 A.J. Burnett .30 .75
80 Scott Kazmir .50 1.25
81 Carl Crawford .50 1.25
82 Mark Prior .50 1.25
83 Adam Dunn .50 1.25
84 Justin Morneau .50 1.25
85 Morgan Ensberg .30 .75
86 Pat Burrell .30 .75
87 Paul Lo Duca .30 .75
88 Jason Bay .30 .75
89 Aubrey Huff .30 .75
90 Kevin Millwood .30 .75
91 Vernon Wells .30 .75
92 Javy Lopez .30 .75
93 Michael Young .30 .75
94 Felix Hernandez .50 1.25
95 Ken Griffey Jr. 1.50 4.00
96 Bartolo Colon .30 .75
97 Billy Wagner .30 .75
98 Vladimir Guerrero .50 1.25
99 Jose Reyes .50 1.25
100 Barry Bonds 1.25 3.00
101 Anthony LeRew AU G (RC) 4.00 10.00
102 R.Zimm AU C/440 (RC) * 6.00 15.00
103 C.Hansen AU B/250 RC * 20.00 50.00
104 F.Liriano AU G (RC) 3.00 8.00
105 Jason Botts AU G (RC) 3.00 8.00
106 Josh Johnson AU G (RC) 3.00 8.00
107 Hanley Ramirez AU G (RC) 6.00 15.00
108 A.Wainwright AU G (RC) 12.00 30.00
109 K.Johjima AU A/200 RC * 10.00 25.00
110 Dan Ortmeier AU G (RC) 4.00 10.00
111 Darrell Rasner AU G (RC) 4.00 10.00
112 Chuck James AU F (RC) 6.00 15.00
113 Nelson Cruz AU F (RC) 10.00 25.00
114 Hong-Chih Kuo AU E (RC) 6.00 15.00
115 Ryan Garko AU G (RC) 4.00 10.00
116 R.Abercrombie AU D (RC) 4.00 10.00
117 Ian Kinsler AU D (RC) 6.00 15.00
118 Joel Zumaya AU D (RC) 5.00 12.00
119 Willie Eyre AU D (RC) 4.00 10.00
120 Dan Uggla AU D (RC) 6.00 15.00

2006 Topps Co-Signers Changing Faces Blue

*BLUE: .75X TO 2X BASIC
STATED ODDS 1:11
STATED PRINT RUN 125 SERIAL #'d SETS

2006 Topps Co-Signers Changing Faces Bronze

*BRONZE: .75X TO 2X BASIC
STATED ODDS 1:9
STATED PRINT RUN 150 SERIAL #'d SETS

2006 Topps Co-Signers Changing Faces Gold

*GOLD: .75X TO 2X BASIC
STATED ODDS 1:12
STATED PRINT RUN 115 SERIAL #'d SETS

2006 Topps Co-Signers Changing Faces Red

*RED: .75X TO 2X BASIC
STATED ODDS 1:9
STATED PRINT RUN 150 SERIAL #'d SETS

2006 Topps Co-Signers Changing Faces Silver Blue

*SILVER BLUE: 1X TO 2.5X BASIC
STATED ODDS 1:18
STATED PRINT RUN 75 SERIAL #'d SETS

2006 Topps Co-Signers Changing Faces Silver Bronze

*SILVER BRONZE: .75X TO 2X BASIC
STATED ODDS 1:11
STATED PRINT RUN 125 SERIAL #'d SETS

2006 Topps Co-Signers Changing Faces Silver Gold

*SILVER GOLD: 1.25X TO 3X BASIC
STATED ODDS 1:27
STATED PRINT RUN 50 SERIAL #'d SETS

2006 Topps Co-Signers Changing Faces Silver Red

*SILVER RED: .75X TO 2X BASIC
STATED ODDS 1:14
STATED PRINT RUN 100 SERIAL #'d SETS

2006 Topps Co-Signers Changing Faces HyperSilver Bronze

*HYPER BRONZE: 1X TO 2.5X BASIC
STATED ODDS 1:18
STATED PRINT RUN 75 SERIAL #'d SETS

2006 Topps Co-Signers Changing Faces HyperSilver Red

*HYPER RED: 2X TO 5X BASIC
STATED ODDS 1:54
STATED PRINT RUN 25 SERIAL #'d SETS
NO BONDS PRICING DUE TO VOLATILITY

2006 Topps Co-Signers Dual Autographs

GROUP A ODDS 1:11,375
GROUP B ODDS 1:20,350
GROUP C ODDS 1:522
GROUP D ODDS 1:1013
GROUP E ODDS 1:2705
GROUP F ODDS 1:580
GROUP G ODDS 1:3223
GROUP H ODDS 1:2025
GROUP I ODDS 1:540
GROUP J ODDS 1:1352
GROUP K ODDS 1:1158
GROUP L ODDS 1:950
GROUP M ODDS 1:902
GROUP N ODDS 1:162
GROUP O ODDS 1:624
GROUP P ODDS 1:270
GROUP Q ODDS 1:68
GROUP R ODDS 1:90
GROUP S ODDS 1:29
GROUP A PRINT RUN 18 SETS
GROUP B PRINT RUN 20 SETS
GROUP C PRINT RUN 25 SETS
GROUP D PRINT RUN 50 SETS
GROUP E PRINT RUN 75 SETS
GROUP F PRINT RUN 100 SETS
GROUP G PRINT RUN 125 SETS
GROUP H PRINT RUN 200 SETS
GROUP I PRINT RUN 250 SETS
AROD/BONDS PRINT RUN 25 SERIAL #'d SETS
CARDS ARE NOT SERIAL NUMBERED
PRINT RUN INFO PROVIDED BY TOPPS
NO GROUP A-C PRICING DUE TO SCARCITY
CS15 P.Fielder/R.Zimm I/250 * 12.50 30.00
CS22 R.Howard/D.Lee E/75 * 12.50 30.00
CS23 J.Mathis/C.Snyder S 4.00 10.00
CS25 R.Knight/K.Hern F/100 * 12.50 30.00
CS27 B.Wagner/P.Lo Duca D/50 * 8.00 20.00
CS30 D.Gooden/D.Straw D/50 * 20.00 50.00
CS31 R.Howard/H.Street N 6.00 15.00
CS33 P.Fielder/R.Howard D/50 * 12.50 30.00
CS34 R.Cano/Chase Utley E/75 * 40.00 80.00
CS37 D.Wright/J.Reyes D/50 * 30.00 60.00
CS38 J.Mathis/R.Garko S 10.00 25.00
CS39 B.McCarthy/P.Lopez S 4.00 10.00
CS40 D.Just/D.Murphy F/100 * 30.00 60.00
CS42 J.Mauer/F.Liriano Q 10.00 25.00
CS44 R.Zimm/D.Wright F/100 * 15.00 40.00
CS45 R.Rhoden/D.Parker F/100 * 10.00 25.00
CS46 J.Papelbon/C.Breslow R 6.00 15.00
CS48 D.John/P.Fielder F/100 * 8.00 20.00
CS49 V.Martinez/R.Garko N 8.00 20.00
CS50 B.Hendrickson/A.Reyes Q 6.00 15.00
CS51 N.Cruz/P.Fielder F/100 * 10.00 25.00
CS52 J.Papelbon/A.Reyes R 10.00 25.00
CS53 B.Hendrickson/R.Hill Q 6.00 15.00
CS55 F.Liriano/J.Sant F/100 * 10.00 25.00
CS56 B.McCarthy/Z.Duke S 6.00 15.00
CS57 J.Johnson/S.Olsen S 6.00 15.00
CS58 T.John/B.Welch K 10.00 25.00
CS59 R.White/J.Pepitone N 8.00 20.00
CS60 C.Fielder/P.Fielder N 30.00 60.00
CS62 C.Jackson/R.Howard Q 6.00 15.00
CS63 D.Willis/Z.Duke D/50 * 5.00 12.00
CS65 H.Kuo/S.Choo Q 12.50 30.00
CS66 J.Leyritz/C.Field G/125 * 12.50 30.00
CS67 S.Kazmir/F.Liriano P 6.00 15.00
CS68 S.Kazmir/R.Osw D/50 * 6.00 15.00
CS69 C.James/A.LeRew S 6.00 15.00
CS70 C.Field/R.How I/250 * 15.00 40.00
CS72 S.Choo/C.Wang D/50 * 60.00 120.00
CS73 N.Cruz/J.Botts Q 6.00 15.00
CS74 F.Liriano/E.Santana S 6.00 15.00
CS75 A.Wainwright/A.Reyes S 8.00 20.00
CS76 S.Kaz/E.Sant H/200 * 6.00 15.00
CS77 R.Cano/G.Shef I/250 * 20.00 50.00
CS78 D.Wright/M.Cab D/50 * 75.00 150.00
CS79 D.Johnson/C.Jackson P 6.00 15.00
CS80 F.Tanana/M.Tettleton R 6.00 15.00
CS81 A.Jones/C.Jones J 40.00 80.00
CS82 M.Ensberg/R.Oswalt M 4.00 10.00
CS83 M.Young/O.Smith O 12.00 30.00
CS84 G.Sizemore/N.Swisher L 8.00 20.00
CS85 G.Atkins/C.Barmes N 5.00 12.00

2006 Topps Co-Signers Dual Cut Signatures

GROUP A ODDS 1:30,000
GROUP B ODDS 1:6800
GROUP C ODDS 1:43,000
GROUP D ODDS 1:21,000
GROUP E ODDS 1:1125
GROUP F ODDS 1:4450
GROUP G ODDS 1:875
GROUP H ODDS 1:3650
GROUP I ODDS 1:5150
GROUP J ODDS 1:1980
GROUP A PRINT RUN 1 SERIAL #'d SET
NO A-F PRICING DUE TO SCARCITY
GWTJ A.B.Chandler/B.Herman H 60.00 120.00
ABCWH A.Chand/W.Harr G 30.00 60.00
BLJH B.Lemon/J.Hunter G 40.00 80.00
BLJJ B.Leonard/J.Johnson J 50.00 100.00
BLLB B.Lemon/L.Boudreau I 30.00 60.00
BLRF B.Lemon/R.Ferrell G 40.00 80.00
CGRF C.Gehringer/R.Ferrell G 75.00 150.00
CHBH C.Gehringer/B.Herman G 75.00 150.00
EALB E.Averill/L.Boudreau F 30.00 60.00
FCGW F.Crosetti/G.Wood G 30.00 60.00
HKCG H.Kuenn/C.Gehringer J 30.00 60.00
JSLA J.Sewell/L.Appling G 100.00 175.00
JSLB J.Sewell/L.Boudreau G 60.00 120.00
LWCG L.Waner/C.Gehringer G 40.00 80.00

2006 Topps Co-Signers Solo Sigs

GROUP A ODDS 1:2528
GROUP B ODDS 1:1790
GROUP C ODDS 1:2025
GROUP D ODDS 1:2700
GROUP E ODDS 1:2025
GROUP F ODDS 1:2025
GROUP G ODDS 1:540
GROUP H ODDS 1:135
GROUP I ODDS 1:600
GROUP J ODDS 1:108
GROUP K ODDS 1:45
GROUP A PRINT RUN 20 SETS
GROUP B PRINT RUN 25 SETS
GROUP C PRINT RUN 50 SETS
GROUP D PRINT RUN 75 SETS
GROUP E PRINT RUN 100 SETS
GROUP F-G PRINT RUN 250 SETS
CARDS ARE NOT SERIAL NUMBERED
PRINT RUN INFO PROVIDED BY TOPPS
NO A-B PRICING DUE TO SCARCITY
AD Andre Dawson H 8.00 20.00
AK Al Kaline E/100 * 20.00 50.00
ARE Anthony Reyes K 6.00 15.00
CB Clint Barmes J 4.00 10.00
CBR Craig Breslow K 6.00 15.00
CF Cecil Fielder J 6.00 15.00
CM Craig Monroe K 4.00 10.00
CS Chris Snyder K 4.00 10.00
DJ Dan Johnson F/250 * 4.00 10.00
DL Don Larsen H 10.00 25.00
DLE Derrek Lee C/50 * 20.00 50.00
DM Don Mattingly C/50 * 20.00 50.00
DS Darryl Strawberry J 6.00 15.00
DW David Wright D/75 * 40.00 80.00
DWI Dontrelle Willis H 4.00 10.00
ES Ervin Santana G/250 * 4.00 10.00
GC Gustavo Chacin K 4.00 10.00
HS Huston Street G/250 * 4.00 10.00
JC Jack Clark H 4.00 10.00
JM Jeff Mathis K 4.00 10.00
JMA Joe Mauer D/75 * 30.00 60.00
JP Jonathan Papelbon H 6.00 15.00
JS Johan Santana C/50 * 10.00 25.00
PF Prince Fielder G/250 * 8.00 20.00
RC Robinson Cano J 10.00 25.00
RH Ryan Howard E/100 * 12.00 30.00
RHI Rich Hill K 4.00 10.00
RR Rick Rhoden J 5.00 12.00
SK Scott Kazmir H 4.00 10.00
SO Scott Olsen K 4.00 10.00
SSC Shin-Soo Choo K 10.00 25.00
VM Victor Martinez C/50 * 4.00 10.00
ZD Zach Duke I 4.00 10.00

2007 Topps Co-Signers

COMP.SET w/o AU's (100) 12.50 30.00
COMMON CARD (1-92) .25 .60
COMMON ROOKIE (93-100) .30 .75
COMMON ROOKIE AU (96-121) 3.00 8.00
ROOKIE AUTO ODDS 1:28
ROOKIE AUTO VARIATION ODDS 1:198
PRINTING PLATE ODDS 1:705
PRINTING PLATE AUTO ODDS 1:21,168
PLATE PRINT RUN 1 SET PER COLOR
BLACK-CYAN-MAGENTA-SPOT-YELLOW ISSUED
NO PLATE PRICING DUE TO SCARCITY
1 Ryan Howard .50 1.25
2 Jered Weaver .40 1.00
3 Brian McCann .25 .60
4 Garrett Atkins .25 .60
5 Travis Hafner .25 .60
6 Jason Schmidt .25 .60
7 Curtis Granderson .50 1.25
8 Ben Sheets .25 .60
9 Chien-Ming Wang .40 1.00
10 Francisco Liriano .25 .60
11 Freddy Sanchez .25 .60
12 Roy Oswalt .40 1.00
13 Jim Edmonds .40 1.00
14 Matt Cain .40 1.00
15 Jake Peavy .25 .60
16 Ryan Zimmerman .40 1.00
17 Troy Glaus .25 .60
18 Kenji Johjima .60 1.50
19 Curt Schilling .40 1.00
20 Alfonso Soriano .40 1.00
21 Adam Dunn .40 1.00
22 Hanley Ramirez .40 1.00
23 Mark Teahen .25 .60
24 Todd Helton .40 1.00
25 Alex Rodriguez .75 2.00
26 Mike Mussina .40 1.00
27 Jason Bay .40 1.00
28 Carl Crawford .40 1.00
29 Vernon Wells .25 .60
30 Rich Harden .25 .60
31 Justin Morneau .40 1.00
32 Andre Ethier .40 1.00

33 Ramon Hernandez .25 .60
34 Erik Bedard .25 .60
35 Vladimir Guerrero .40 1.00
36 Stephen Drew .25 .60
37 Felix Hernandez .40 1.00
38 C.C. Sabathia .40 1.00
39 Adrian Gonzalez .50 1.25
40 Prince Fielder .40 1.00
41 Carlos Delgado .25 .60
42 Jimmy Rollins .40 1.00
43 Raul Ibanez .40 1.00
44 Jorge Cantu .25 .60
45 Michael Young .25 .60
46 Austin Kearns .25 .60
47 Ivan Rodriguez .40 1.00
48 Mark Teixeira .40 1.00
49 David Ortiz .60 1.50
50 David Wright .50 1.25
51 Justin Verlander .60 1.50
52 Nick Markakis .50 1.25
53 Miguel Cabrera .60 1.50
54 Lance Berkman .40 1.00
55 Robinson Cano .40 1.00
56 Jon Lieber .25 .60
57 Andruw Jones .25 .60
58 Dan Haren .25 .60
59 Grady Sizemore .40 1.00
60 Gary Sheffield .25 .60
61 Paul Lo Duca .25 .60
62 Cole Hamels .50 1.25
63 Richie Sexson .25 .60
64 David Eckstein .25 .60
65 Carlos Zambrano .40 1.00
66 Scott Kazmir .40 1.00
67 Anthony Reyes .25 .60
68 Mark Kotsay .25 .60
69 Miguel Tejada .40 1.00
70 Pedro Martinez .40 1.00
71 Jack Wilson .25 .60
72 Joe Mauer .50 1.25
73 Brian Giles .25 .60
74 Jonathan Papelbon .60 1.50
75 Albert Pujols .75 2.00
76 Nick Swisher .40 1.00
77 Bill Hall .25 .60
78 Jose Contreras .25 .60
79 David DeJesus .25 .60
80 Bobby Abreu .25 .60
81 John Smoltz .60 1.50
82 Chipper Jones .60 1.50
83 Mark Buehrle .40 1.00
84 Josh Barfield .25 .60
85 Derrek Lee .25 .60
86 Jim Thome .40 1.00
87 Kenny Rogers .25 .60
88 Jeremy Sowers .25 .60
89 Brandon Webb .40 1.00
90 Roy Halladay .40 1.00
91 Tadahito Iguchi .25 .60
92 Jeff Kent .25 .60
93 Johnny Damon .40 1.00
94 Daisuke Matsuzaka RC 1.25 3.00
95 Kei Igawa RC .75 2.00
96a Delmon Young (RC) .50 1.25
96b Delmon Young AU 8.00 20.00
97a Jeff Baker (RC) .30 .75
97b Jeff Baker AU 3.00 8.00
98a Michael Bourn (RC) .50 1.25
98b Michael Bourn AU 4.00 10.00
99a Ubaldo Jimenez (RC) 1.00 2.50
99b Ubaldo Jimenez AU 10.00 25.00
100a Andrew Miller RC 1.25 3.00
100b Andrew Miller AU 10.00 25.00
101 Angel Sanchez AU RC 3.00 8.00
102 Troy Tulowitzki AU (RC) 6.00 15.00
103 Joaquin Arias AU (RC) 3.00 8.00
104 Beltran Perez AU (RC) 3.00 8.00
105 Josh Fields AU (RC) 4.00 10.00
106 Hector Gimenez AU (RC) 3.00 8.00
107 Kevin Kouzmanoff AU (RC) 4.00 10.00
108 Miguel Montero AU (RC) 3.00 8.00
109 Philip Humber AU (RC) 4.00 10.00
110 Jerry Owens AU (RC) 3.00 8.00
111 Shawn Riggans AU (RC) 3.00 8.00
112 Brian Stokes AU (RC) 3.00 8.00
113 Scott Moore AU (RC) 3.00 8.00
114 David Murphy AU (RC) 3.00 8.00
115 Mitch Maier AU RC 3.00 8.00
116 Adam Lind AU (RC) 4.00 10.00
117 Glen Perkins AU (RC) 4.00 10.00
118 Dennis Sarfate AU (RC) 3.00 8.00
119 Elijah Dukes AU RC 3.00 8.00
120 Josh Hamilton AU (RC) 4.00 10.00
121 Alex Gordon AU RC 8.00 20.00
122 Barry Bonds 3.00 8.00

2007 Topps Co-Signers Blue

*BLUE: .75X TO 2X BASIC
*BLUE RC: .5X TO 1.2X BASIC
*BLUE AUTO: .4X TO 1X BASIC
BASE/ROOKIE CARD ODDS 1:10
ROOKIE AUTO ODDS 1:104
BASE/RC PRINT RUN 250 SER.#'d SETS
RC AUTO PRINT RUN 225 SER.#'d SETS

2007 Topps Co-Signers Bronze

*BRONZE: .75X TO 2X BASIC
*BRONZE RC: .5X TO 1.2X BASIC
*BRONZE AUTO: .4X TO 1X BASIC
BASE/ROOKIE CARD ODDS 1:9
ROOKIE AUTO ODDS 1:94
BASE/RC PRINT RUN 275 SER.#'d SETS
RC AUTO PRINT RUN 250 SER.#'d SETS

2007 Topps Co-Signers Gold

*GOLD: .75X TO 2X BASIC
*GOLD RC: .5X TO 1.2X BASIC
*GOLD AUTO: .4X TO 1X BASIC
BASE/ROOKIE CARD ODDS 1:11
ROOKIE AUTO ODDS 1:117
BASE/RC PRINT RUN 225 SER.#'d SETS
RC AUTO PRINT RUN 200 SER.#'d SETS

2007 Topps Co-Signers Red

*RED: .75X TO 2X BASIC
*RED RC: .5X TO 1.2X BASIC
*RED AUTO: .4X TO 1X BASIC
BASE/ROOKIE CARD ODDS 1:9
ROOKIE AUTO ODDS 1:85
BASE/RC PRINT RUN 299 SER.#'d SETS
RC AUTO PRINT RUN 275 SER.#'d SETS

2007 Topps Co-Signers Hyper Silver Bronze

*HS BRONZE: 1.2X TO 3X BASIC
*HS BRONZE RC: 1.2X TO 3X BASIC
*HS BRONZE AUTO: .6X TO 1.5X BASIC
BASE/ROOKIE CARD ODDS 1:49
ROOKIE AUTO ODDS 1:468
STATED PRINT RUN 50 SER.#'d SETS

2007 Topps Co-Signers Hyper Silver Red

*HS RED: 1X TO 2.5X BASIC
*HS RED RC: .75X TO 2X BASIC
*HS RED AUTO: .6X TO 1.5X BASIC
BASE/ROOKIE CARD ODDS 1:33
ROOKIE AUTO ODDS 1:312
STATED PRINT RUN 75 SER.#'d SETS

2007 Topps Co-Signers Silver Blue

*SIL BLUE: .75X TO 2X BASIC
*SIL BLUE RC: .5X TO 1.2X BASIC
*SIL BLUE AUTO: .5X TO 1.2X BASIC
BASE/ROOKIE CARD ODDS 1:17
ROOKIE AUTO ODDS 1:187
BASE/RC PRINT RUN 150 SER.#'d SETS
RC AUTO PRINT RUN 125 SER.#'d SETS

2007 Topps Co-Signers Silver Bronze

*SIL BRONZE: .75X TO 2X BASIC
*SIL BRONZE RC: .5X TO 1.2X BASIC
*SIL BRONZE AUTO: .5X TO 1.2X BASIC
BASE/ROOKIE CARD ODDS 1:14
ROOKIE AUTO ODDS 1:156
BASE/RC PRINT RUN 175 SER.#'d SETS
RC AUTO PRINT RUN 150 SER.#'d SETS

2007 Topps Co-Signers Silver Gold

*SIL GOLD: 1X TO 2.5X BASIC
*SIL GOLD RC: .75X TO 2X BASIC
*SIL GOLD AUTO: .5X TO 1.2X BASIC
BASE/ROOKIE CARD ODDS 1:20
ROOKIE AUTO ODDS 1:234
BASE/RC PRINT RUN 125 SER.#'d SETS
RC AUTO PRINT RUN 100 SER.#'d SETS

2007 Topps Co-Signers Silver Red

*SIL RED: .75X TO 2X BASIC
*SIL RED RC: .5X TO 1.2X BASIC
*SIL RED AUTO: .5X TO 1.2X BASIC
BASE/ROOKIE CARD ODDS 1:13
ROOKIE AUTO ODDS 1:134
BASE/RC PRINT RUN 199 SER.#'d SETS
RC AUTO PRINT RUN 175 SER.#'d SETS

2007 Topps Co-Signers Dual Autographs

GROUP A ODDS 1:17
GROUP B ODDS 1:49
GROUP C ODDS 1:1646
GROUP D ODDS 1:2464
GROUP E ODDS 1:328
AH G.Atkins/M.Holliday B 6.00 15.00
AI M.Albers/C.Iannetta A 4.00 10.00
AS M.Albers/B.Slocum A 4.00 10.00
BB B.Bannister/F.Bannister A 4.00 10.00
BDE E.Bedard/Z.Duke A 6.00 15.00
BG J.Bonderman/C.Granderson B 6.00 15.00
BS J.Baker/J.Salazar B 4.00 10.00
BV J.Bonderman/J.Verlander E 10.00 25.00
CC Mel.Cabrera/R.Cano E 25.00 60.00
CJ C.Carpenter/T.Johnson E 10.00 25.00
CK R.Cano/C.Knoblach E 10.00 25.00
CM F.Castro/S.Mathieson A 4.00 10.00
CW Mig.Cabrera/D.Willis B 20.00 50.00
CY A.Callaspo/C.Young B 5.00 12.00
CZ A.Callaspo/B.Zobrist A 8.00 20.00
GB G.Atkins/C.Barmes B 4.00 10.00
GC C.Granderson/M.Cabrera A 4.00 10.00
GM H.Gimenez/M.Montero A 4.00 10.00
GS D.Gooden/D.Strawberry E 15.00 40.00
HH B.Hall/J.Hardy A 4.00 10.00
HO R.Howard/D.Ortiz E 15.00 40.00
IK C.Iannetta/M.Kemp A 4.00 10.00
IM C.Iannetta/M.Montero A 6.00 15.00
JJ A.Jones/D.Justice E 10.00 25.00
JS U.Jimenez/D.Sarfate A 10.00 25.00
JY C.Jackson/C.Young D 6.00 15.00
KA H.Kendrick/E.Aybar A 6.00 15.00
KF K.Kouzmanoff/J.Fields B 6.00 15.00
KG M.Kemp/F.Gutierrez A 6.00 15.00
KM J.Kinney/T.Mastny A 4.00 10.00
KMA J.Karstens/S.Mathieson A 4.00 10.00
KZ A.Kearns/R.Zimmerman A 6.00 15.00
LG A.LaRoche/T.Gorzelanny A 4.00 10.00
LK F.Liriano/J.Kaat B 6.00 15.00
LL T.Larussa/J.Leyland E 12.00 30.00
LP F.Liriano/J.Papelbon C 6.00 15.00
LV F.Liriano/J.Verlander B 10.00 25.00
LY A.Lind/D.Young A 6.00 15.00
MB N.Markakis/B.Roberts B 12.50 30.00
MC O.Minaya/B.Cashman E 15.00 40.00
MCA N.Markakis/M.Cabrera B 8.00 20.00
MG C.Monroe/C.Granderson A 6.00 15.00
MH J.Maine/P.Humber B 12.00 30.00
MM L.Milledge /J.Maine B 12.00 30.00
MMA D.Murphy/M.Maier A 4.00 10.00
MP A.Miller/G.Perkins B 6.00 15.00
MQ N.Markakis/C.Quetin B 6.00 15.00
MS J.Morneau/N.Swisher B 6.00 15.00
MSL T.Mastny/B.Slocum A 4.00 10.00
MW L.Milledge/D.Wright E 10.00 25.00
OB J.Owens/M.Bourn B 4.00 10.00
PC A.Pagan/B.Coats A 4.00 10.00
PS Y.Petit/A.Sanchez A 5.00 12.00
PV J.Papelbon/J.Verlander B 20.00 50.00
SH J.Sanchez/B.Hennessey A 8.00 20.00
SM F.Sanchez/J.Mauer E 8.00 20.00
SMA C.Stewart/C.Maldonado A 4.00 10.00
SR B.Stokes/S.Riggans A 4.00 10.00
VF J.Verlander/M.Fidrych B 30.00 80.00
VM Van Benschoten/S.Mathieson A 4.00 10.00
VP J.Varitek/J.Posada E 40.00 100.00
WC D.Wright/R.Cano E 40.00 100.00
WS D.Willis/A.Sanchez E 6.00 15.00
YL C.Young/N.Logan B 6.00 15.00
YU D.Young/B.Upton E 20.00 50.00
ZG B.Zobrist/J.Guzman A 6.00 15.00

2007 Topps Co-Signers Moon Shots Autographs

STATED ODDS 1:339
AW Alfred Worden 50.00 100.00
BA Buzz Aldrin 125.00 250.00
CD Charles Duke 50.00 100.00
EM Edgar Mitchell 50.00 100.00
FH Fred Haise 60.00 120.00
RC Robert Crippen 60.00 120.00
RG Richard Gordon 50.00 100.00
SC Scott Carpenter 60.00 120.00
WC Walt Cunningham 50.00 100.00
WS Wally Schirra 75.00 150.00

2007 Topps Co-Signers Solo Sigs

GROUP A ODDS 1:25
GROUP B ODDS 1:164
GROUP C ODDS 1:2464
GROUP D ODDS 1:9908
AH Aaron Hill A 5.00 12.00
AL Anthony Lerew B 4.00 10.00
AS Anibal Sanchez A 4.00 10.00
BB Boof Bonser A 4.00 10.00
CB Clint Barmes A 4.00 10.00
CH Cole Hamels A 8.00 20.00
CJ Chuck James A 4.00 10.00
CQ Carlos Quentin A 5.00 12.00
DH Dave Henderson A 4.00 10.00
DU Dan Uggla A 4.00 10.00
ES Ervin Santana B 4.00 10.00
FL Francisco Liriano A 4.00 10.00
FS Freddy Sanchez A 4.00 10.00
GA Garrett Atkins A 4.00 10.00
HK Howie Kendrick B 6.00 15.00
HM Hideki Matsui D 100.00 200.00
HR Hanley Ramirez A 6.00 15.00
JM Justin Morneau B 10.00 25.00
JS Jeremy Sowers A 4.00 10.00
MC Matt Cain A 6.00 15.00
MH Matt Holliday A 8.00 20.00
NM Nick Markakis A 4.00 10.00
RC Robinson Cano A 10.00 40.00
RG Ryan Garko A 4.00 10.00
RH Ryan Howard B 4.00 10.00
RR Rick Rhoden A 4.00 10.00
VG Vladimir Guerrero C 15.00 40.00
RCE Ronny Cedeno B 4.00 10.00

2007 Topps Co-Signers Tri-Signers

STATED ODDS 1:264
ANS Arias/Navar/Sanchez 10.00 25.00
CPC Cabrera/Pena/Cabrera 15.00 40.00
HLC Henne/Sanchez/Cain 6.00 15.00
JGK C.Jackson/Garko/Kendrick 6.00 15.00
JHS James/Hamels/Sowers 12.50 30.00
LNB Liriano/Nathan/Bonser 20.00 50.00
MAR Morneau/Atkins/Roberts 10.00 25.00
MLM Morneau/Liriano/Garza 10.00 25.00
MLP Morneau/Liriano/Perkins 10.00 25.00
MSG Morneau/Swisher/A.Gonz 20.00 50.00
MYT A.Miller/Delmon/Tulo 10.00 25.00
OPV Ortiz/Papelbon/Varitek 20.00 50.00
OWH Ortiz/Wright/Howard 60.00 120.00
QJY Quentin/Jackson/Young 15.00 40.00
RCC A.Rod/Cabrera/Cano 40.00 80.00
RWH A.Rod/Wright/Howard 20.00 50.00
SHH Street/Harden/Haren 20.00 50.00
TPW Tankersley/Petit/Willis 10.00 25.00
URW Uggla/Hanley/Willis 10.00 25.00

2008 Topps Co-Signers

COMP.SET w/o AU's (100) 12.50 30.00
COMMON CARD (1-95) .25 .60
COMMON RC (96-100) .60 1.50
AU RC VAR ODDS 1:315 HOBBY
COMMON AU RC 3.00 8.00
AU RC ODDS 1:22 HOBBY
PRINTING PLATE VET/RC ODDS 1:445
PRINTING PLATE AU RC VAR ODDS 1:29,736
PRINTING PLATE AU RC ODDS 1:5216
PLATE PRINT RUN 1 SET PER COLOR
5TH-BLACK-CYAN-MAGENTA-YELLOW ISSUED
NO PLATE PRICING DUE TO SCARCITY
1 Jacoby Ellsbury .50 1.25
2 Michael Young .25 .60
3 Cameron Maybin .25 .60
4 Dmitri Young .25 .60
5 Grady Sizemore .40 1.00
6 Brandon Webb .40 1.00
7 Derrek Lee .25 .60
8 Jeff Francis .25 .60
9 Aaron Harang .25 .60
10 John Smoltz .60 1.50
11 Nick Markakis .50 1.25
12 Tom Gorzelanny .25 .60
13 Miguel Cabrera .60 1.50
14 Josh Beckett .25 .60
15 Magglio Ordonez .40 1.00
16 Joe Mauer .50 1.25
17 Carl Crawford .40 1.00
18 Barry Zito .40 1.00
19 Brad Penny .25 .60
20 C.C. Sabathia .40 1.00
21 Mark Buehrle .40 1.00
22 Carlos Lee .25 .60
23 Chipper Jones .60 1.50
24 Chase Utley .40 1.00
25 David Ortiz .60 1.50
26 Justin Morneau .40 1.00
27 Erik Bedard .25 .60
28 Greg Maddux .75 2.00
29 Joba Chamberlain .25 .60
30 Vernon Wells .25 .60
31 Orlando Hudson .25 .60
32 Kevin Youkilis .25 .60
33 Curtis Granderson .40 1.00
34 Chone Figgins .25 .60
35 Jorge Posada .40 1.00
36 Ken Griffey Jr. 1.25 3.00
37 Tim Hudson .40 1.00
38 Nick Swisher .40 1.00
39 Carlos Beltran .40 1.00
40 Alex Gordon .40 1.00
41 Andre Ethier .40 1.00
42 Todd Helton .40 1.00
43 Miguel Tejada .40 1.00
44 Yadier Molina .75 2.00
45 Hanley Ramirez .40 1.00
46 Justin Verlander .60 1.50
47 Adam Dunn .40 1.00
48 Raul Ibanez .40 1.00
49 Scott Rolen .40 1.00
50 Alex Rodriguez .75 2.00
51 Garret Anderson .25 .60
52 Andruw Jones .25 .60
53 Matt Cain .40 1.00
54 Daisuke Matsuzaka .40 1.00
55 Ichiro Suzuki .75 2.00
56 Scott Kazmir .40 1.00
57 Jeff Kent .25 .60
58 Aubrey Huff .25 .60
59 Justin Upton .40 1.00
60 Prince Fielder .40 1.00
61 Alex Rios .25 .60
62 Alfonso Soriano .40 1.00
63 Paul Konerko .40 1.00
64 Matt Holliday .60 1.50
65 Felix Hernandez .40 1.00
66 Ivan Rodriguez .40 1.00
67 John Maine .25 .60
68 Roy Oswalt .40 1.00
69 Brian McCann .40 1.00
70 Albert Pujols .75 2.00
71 John Lackey .40 1.00
72 Travis Hafner .25 .60
73 Gil Meche .25 .60
74 Ben Sheets .25 .60
75 Ryan Howard .40 1.00
76 Hideki Matsui .60 1.50
77 Mike Lowell .25 .60
78 Dan Haren .25 .60
79 Adrian Gonzalez .40 1.00
80 David Wright .40 1.00
81 Jason Bay .40 1.00
82 Carlos Zambrano .40 1.00
83 Johan Santana .40 1.00
84 David DeJesus .25 .60
85 Ryan Zimmerman .40 1.00
86 Bobby Abreu .25 .60
87 Richie Sexson .25 .60
88 Eric Chavez .25 .60
89 Derek Lowe .25 .60
90 Jake Peavy .25 .60
91 Joe Blanton .25 .60
92 Jermaine Dye .25 .60
93 Pedro Martinez .40 1.00
94 B.J. Upton .40 1.00
95 Vladimir Guerrero .40 1.00
96 Ross Ohlendorf RC 1.00 2.50
97 J.R. Towles RC 1.00 2.50
98 Jonathan Meloan RC 1.00 2.50
99a Chin-Lung Hu (RC) .60 1.50
99b Chin-Lung Hu AU 10.00 25.00
100a Clay Buchholz (RC) 1.00 2.50
100b Clay Buchholz AU 4.00 10.00
101 Willie Collazo AU RC 3.00 8.00
102 David Davidson AU RC 3.00 8.00
103 Joe Koshansky AU (RC) 3.00 8.00
104 Sam Fuld AU RC 6.00 15.00
105 Nyjer Morgan AU (RC) 3.00 8.00
106 Clint Sammons AU (RC) 3.00 8.00
107 Josh Anderson AU (RC) 3.00 8.00
108 Bronson Sardinha AU (RC) 3.00 8.00
109 Wladimir Balentien AU (RC) 3.00 8.00
110 Kevin Hart AU (RC) 3.00 8.00
111 Felipe Paulino AU RC 3.00 8.00
112 Rob Johnson AU (RC) 3.00 8.00

2008 Topps Co-Signers Hyper Plaid Blue

*HS BLUE VET: 1.2X TO 3X BASIC
STATED VET ODDS 1:32 HOBBY
VET PRINT RUN 50 SER.#'D SETS
*HS BLUE RC: 1.5X TO 4X BASIC
STATED RC ODDS 1:32 HOBBY
RC PRINT RUN 50 SER.#'D SETS
*HS BLUE AU: .5X TO 1.2X BASIC AU RC
STATED AU RC ODDS 1:540 HOBBY
AU PRINT RUN 50 SER.#'d SETS

2008 Topps Co-Signers Hyper Plaid Bronze

*HS BRONZE VET: 1X TO 2.5X BASIC
STATED VET ODDS 1:21 HOBBY
VET PRINT RUN 75 SER.#'D SETS
*HS BRONZE RC: 1X TO 2.5X BASIC
STATED RC ODDS 1:21 HOBBY
RC PRINT RUN 100 SER.#'D SETS
*HS BRONZE AU: .5X TO 1.2X BASIC AU RC
STATED AU RC ODDS 1:355 HOBBY
AU PRINT RUN 75 SER.#'d SETS

2008 Topps Co-Signers Hyper Plaid Red

*HS RED VET: 1X TO 2.5X BASIC
STATED VET ODDS 1:16 HOBBY
VET PRINT RUN 100 SER.#'D SETS
*HS RED RC: 1X TO 2.5X BASIC
STATED RC ODDS 1:16 HOBBY
RC PRINT RUN 100 SER.#'D SETS
*HS RED AU: .4X TO 1X BASIC AU RC
STATED AU RC ODDS 1:264 HOBBY
AU PRINT RUN 100 SER.#'d SETS

2008 Topps Co-Signers Silver Blue

*BLUE VET: .6X TO 1.5X BASIC
STATED VET ODDS 1:7 HOBBY
VET PRINT RUN 250 SER.#'D SETS
*BLUE RC: .6X TO 1.5X BASIC
STATED RC ODDS 1:7 HOBBY
RC PRINT RUN 250 SER.#'D SETS
*BLUE AU: .4X TO 1X BASIC AU RC
STATED AU RC ODDS 1:87 HOBBY
AU PRINT RUN 300 SER.#'d SETS

2008 Topps Co-Signers Silver Bronze

*BRONZE VET: .6X TO 1.5X BASIC
STATED VET ODDS 1:6 HOBBY
VET PRINT RUN 300 SER.#'D SETS
*BRONZE RC: .6X TO 1.5X BASIC
STATED RC ODDS 1:6 HOBBY
RC PRINT RUN 300 SER.#'D SETS
*BRONZE AU: .4X TO 1X BASIC AU RC
STATED AU RC ODDS 1:65 HOBBY
AU PRINT RUN 400 SER.#'d SETS

2008 Topps Co-Signers Silver Gold

*GOLD VET: .75X TO 2X BASIC
STATED VET ODDS 1:11 HOBBY
VET PRINT RUN 150 SER.#'D SETS
*GOLD RC: .75X TO 2X BASIC
STATED RC ODDS 1:11 HOBBY
RC PRINT RUN 150 SER.#'D SETS
*GOLD AU: .4X TO 1X BASIC AU RC
STATED AU RC ODDS 1:175 HOBBY
AU PRINT RUN 150 SER.#'d SETS

2008 Topps Co-Signers Silver Green

*GREEN VET: .75X TO 2X BASIC
STATED VET ODDS 1:8 HOBBY
VET PRINT RUN 200 SER.#'D SETS
*GREEN RC: .75X TO 2X BASIC
STATED RC ODDS 1:8 HOBBY
RC PRINT RUN 200 SER.#'D SETS
*GREEN AU: .4X TO 1X BASIC AU RC
STATED AU RC ODDS 1:131 HOBBY
AU PRINT RUN 200 SER.#'d SETS

2008 Topps Co-Signers Silver Red

*RED VET: .6X TO 1.5X BASIC
STATED VET ODDS 1:4 HOBBY
VET PRINT RUN 400 SER.#'d SETS
*RED RC: .6X TO 1.5X BASIC
STATED RC ODDS 1:4 HOBBY
RC PRINT RUN 400 SER.#'d SETS
*RED AU: .4X TO 1X BASIC AU RC
STATED AU RC ODDS 1:52 HOBBY
AU PRINT RUN 500 SER.#'d SETS

2008 Topps Co-Signers Dual Autographs

GROUP A ODDS 1:23 HOBBY
GROUP B ODDS 1:39 HOBBY
GROUP C ODDS 1:101 HOBBY
GROUP D ODDS 1:443 HOBBY
GROUP E ODDS 1:3912 HOBBY
AC J.Arce/I.Calderon C 6.00 15.00
BA Josh Banks 4.00 10.00
Jeremy Accardo A
BB D.Barton/C.Buchholz A 10.00 25.00
BJ E.Bedard/A.Jones B 6.00 15.00
BM B.Buck/C.Maybin B 4.00 10.00
BMP R.Mancini/K.Pavlik E 75.00 150.00
BZ Jason Bartlett/Ben Zobrist A 6.00 15.00
CB Steve Cunningham 4.00 10.00
Shannon Briggs C
CC R.Cano/A.Cabrera A 12.00 30.00
CCC M.Castillo/J.Chavez C 12.50 30.00
CE Jack Cust 4.00 10.00
Mark Ellis A
CG J.Cochran/C.Granderson B 6.00 15.00
CLC J.Casamayor/J.Castillo C 6.00 15.00
DB C.Dawson/A.Berto C 5.00 12.00
DD J.Diaz/J.Diaz C 6.00 15.00
DG Vic Darchinyan 4.00 10.00
Danny Green C
DR C.Duncan/B.Ryan A 10.00 25.00
EH B.Engle/F.Hernandez B 10.00 25.00
FC C.Figgins/C.Crawford D 6.00 15.00
FH Jeff Francis 4.00 10.00
Jason Hirsh A
FHO P.Fielder/R.Howard D 40.00 80.00
FJ J.Francis/U.Jimenez B 4.00 10.00
FP Sam Fuld 4.00 10.00
Felix Pie A
GS Tom Gorzelanny 4.00 10.00
Freddy Sanchez A
HC F.Hernandez/Joba A 10.00 25.00
HCA Josue Herrera 4.00 10.00
Fausto Carmona B
JA Brandon Jones 4.00 10.00
Josh Anderson A
JM D.Jennings/N.Markakis B 6.00 15.00
KA R.Karmazin/A.Abraham C 6.00 15.00
KC T.Kelly/J.Chamberlain B 6.00 15.00
LG Don Lyle 4.00 10.00
Ryan Garko B
LH A.LaRoche/C.Hu B 10.00 25.00
MB Edison Miranda 4.00 10.00
O'Neil Bell C EXCH
MD Lastings Milledge 4.00 10.00
Elijah Dukes B
MM A.Miller/C.Maybin A 4.00 10.00
MMJ J.Marquez/C.John C 10.00 25.00
MP J.Mason/J.Papelbon B 6.00 15.00
MS C.Marmol/G.Soto A 5.00 12.00
MV R.Marquez/I.Vasquez C 20.00 50.00
OB Garrett Olsen 4.00 10.00
Brian Burres A
OBA Dan Ontiveros 4.00 10.00
Daric Barton B
PG Ponce de Leon/Guzman C 10.00 25.00
PKS Glen Perkins 4.00 10.00
Kevin Slowey A
PO J.Papelbon/H.Okajima D 10.00 25.00
PP S.Peter/A.Pryor C 12.50 30.00
PS Steve Pearce 6.00 15.00
Freddy Sanchez A
RM A.Rios/N.Markakis B 5.00 12.00
RO E.Ramirez/R.Ohlendorf A 6.00 15.00
RR J.Rollins/J.Reyes D 10.00 25.00
RW J.Reyes/D.Wright D 20.00 50.00
SC B.Schneider/R.Castro A 6.00 15.00
SE A.Shorin/M.Eisner E 30.00 60.00
SG Andy Sonnanstine/Matt Garza A 4.00 10.00
SP G.Soto/F.Pie A 6.00 15.00
SZ A.Smith/R.Zimmerman B 6.00 15.00
VC J.Votto/D.Barton B 15.00 40.00
WB D.Wright/R.Braun D 15.00 40.00
WF D.Willis/M.Fidrych D 6.00 15.00

2008 Topps Co-Signers Solo Sigs

STATED ODDS 1:21 HOBBY
EXCHANGE DEADLINE 4/30/10
AA Arthur Abraham 4.00 10.00
AB Andre Berto 6.00 15.00
AP Aaron Pryor 6.00 15.00
AW Andre Ward 6.00 15.00
BS Bert Sugar EXCH 8.00 20.00
CD Chad Dawson 5.00 12.00
CJ Chris John 4.00 10.00
DP Daniel Ponce de Leon 5.00 12.00
EM Edison Miranda 6.00 15.00
FM Fernando Montiel 4.00 10.00
IC Ivan Calderon 6.00 15.00
IV Israel Vasquez 8.00 20.00
JA Jorge Arce 6.00 15.00
JC Joel Casamayor 6.00 15.00
JD Juan Diaz 6.00 15.00
JF Jeff Fenech 4.00 10.00
JG Joan Guzman 4.00 10.00
JM Juan Manuel Marquez 8.00 20.00
KP Kelly Pavlik 12.50 30.00
MC Martin Castillo 4.00 10.00
OB O'Neil Bell EXCH 4.00 10.00
RK Roman Karmazin 4.00 10.00
RM Rafael Marquez 6.00 15.00
SB Shannon Briggs 5.00 12.00
SC Steve Cunningham 4.00 10.00
SP Samuel Peter 6.00 15.00
TA Teddy Atlas 8.00 20.00
VD Vic Darchinyan 4.00 10.00
DAG Danny Green EXCH 4.00 10.00
JCC J.Cesar Chavez Jr. EXCH 8.00 20.00
JLC Jose Luis Castillo 5.00 12.00
JUD Julio Diaz 4.00 10.00
RBBM Ray Mancini 30.00 60.00

2008 Topps Co-Signers Tri Signers

STATED ODDS 1:317 HOBBY
EXCHANGE DEADLINE 4/30/10
BHH Buchholz/Hughes/F.Hernandez 12.50 30.00
CEC A.Cabrera/Y.Escobar/Cano 12.50 30.00
CHC Joba/Hughes/Melky 10.00 25.00
GFH Gorzelanny/Francis/Hamels 10.00 25.00
HSY Hamilton/Salty/M.Young 30.00 60.00
MGY Maybin/Granderson/C.Young 10.00 25.00
MHR Markakis/Holliday/Rios 20.00 50.00
MRH Maybin/Hanley/Hermida EXCH 10.00 25.00
PBG Parra/Braun/Gallardo EXCH 50.00 100.00
WZB Wright/Zim/Braun EXCH 60.00 120.00

2004 Topps Cracker Jack

COMPLETE SET (250) 40.00 80.00
COMP.SET w/o SP's (200) 6.00 15.00
COMMON CARD .15 .40
COMMON RC .15 .40
COMMON SP 1.50 4.00
COMMON SP RC 1.50 4.00
SP STATED ODDS 1:3
SP CL: 1/3B/13/17/20/25B/35/50-51/60/80A
SP CL: 80B/87/95B/100/104B/108-109/126
SP CL: 140B/145/163/165-167/172/175/179
SP CL: 182/184/186/192-193/195-196/198
SP CL: 200/206/209-211214/216/220/224B
SP CL: 226/229B/232/236A-236B
VINT.BUYBACK ODDS 1:2598 H, 1:3084 R
550 TOTAL BUYBACKS SEEDED IN PACKS
BUYBACK PRINT RUN INFO FROM TOPPS
1 Jose Reyes SP 1.50 4.00
2 Edgar Renteria .15 .40
3A Albert Pujols Portrait .50 1.25
3B Albert Pujols Swinging SP 3.00 8.00
4 Garret Anderson .15 .40
5 Bobby Abreu .15 .40
6 Andruw Jones .15 .40
7 Jeff Kent .15 .40
8 Magglio Ordonez .25 .60
9 Kris Benson .15 .40
10 Luis Gonzalez .15 .40
11 Corey Patterson .15 .40
12 Connie Mack MG .15 .40
13 Vernon Wells SP 1.50 4.00
14 Jim Edmonds .25 .60
15 Bret Boone .15 .40
16 Travis Lee .15 .40
17 Alex Rodriguez Yanks SP 3.00 8.00
18 Erubiel Durazo .15 .40
19 Brett Myers .15 .40
20 Scott Rolen SP 2.00 5.00
21 Paul Lo Duca .15 .40
22 Geoff Jenkins .15 .40
23 Charles Comiskey .15 .40
24 Cliff Floyd .15 .40
25A Jim Thome Batting .25 .60
25B Jim Thome Fielding SP 2.00 5.00
26 Russ Ortiz .15 .40
27 Bill Mueller .15 .40
28 Kenny Lofton .15 .40
29 Jay Gibbons .15 .40
30 Ken Griffey Jr. .75 2.00
31 Jeff Bagwell .25 .60
32 Jose Lima .15 .40
33 Brad Radke .15 .40
34 Ramon Hernandez .15 .40
35 Brian Giles SP 1.50 4.00
36 Jeremy Bonderman .15 .40
37 Jerome Williams .15 .40
38 Rafael Palmeiro .25 .60
39 Scott Podsednik .15 .40
40 Rafael Furcal .15 .40
41 Roy Oswalt .25 .60
42 Orlando Hudson .15 .40
43 Todd Helton .25 .60
44 Kerry Wood .15 .40
45 Tom Glavine .25 .60
46 David Eckstein .15 .40
47 Trot Nixon .15 .40
48 Preston Wilson .15 .40
49 Bernie Williams .25 .60
50 Eric Gagne SP 1.50 4.00
51 Ichiro Suzuki SP 3.00 8.00
52 Juan Gonzalez .15 .40
53 Torii Hunter .15 .40
54 Bartolo Colon .15 .40
55A Dick Hoblitzel ERR .15 .40
55B Dick Hoblitzell COR .15 .40
56 Al Leiter .15 .40
57 Johnny Damon .25 .60
58 Larry Walker .25 .60
59 Brian Jordan .15 .40
60 Richie Sexson SP 1.50 4.00
61 Orlando Cabrera .15 .40
62 Jason Phillips .15 .40
63 Phil Nevin .15 .40
64 John Olerud .15 .40
65 Miguel Tejada .25 .60
66A Nap La Joie ERR .40 1.00
66B Nap Lajoie COR .40 1.00
67 C.C. Sabathia .25 .60
68 Ty Wigginton .15 .40
69 Troy Glaus .15 .40
70 Mike Piazza .40 1.00
71 Craig Biggio .25 .60
72 Cristian Guzman .15 .40
73 Dmitri Young .15 .40
74 Roger Clemens .50 1.25
75 Runelvys Hernandez .15 .40
76 Nomar Garciaparra .25 .60
77 Mark Mulder .15 .40
78 Derek Lowe .15 .40
79 Paul Konerko .25 .60
80A Sammy Sosa SP 2.00 5.00
80B Felix Pie SP 2.00 5.00
81 Vladimir Guerrero .25 .60
82 Xavier Nady .15 .40
83 Joel Pineiro .15 .40
84 Chipper Jones .40 1.00
85 Manny Ramirez .40 1.00
86A Burt Shotten ERR .15 .40
86B Burt Shotton COR .15 .40
87 Raul Ibanez SP 1.50 4.00
88 Eric Chavez .15 .40
89 Frank Catalanotto .15 .40
90 Dontrelle Willis .15 .40
91 Roy Halladay .25 .60
92 Jermaine Dye .15 .40
93 Jason Kendall .15 .40
94 Jacque Jones .15 .40
95A Gary Sheffield Braves .15 .40
95B Gary Sheffield Yanks SP 2.00 5.00
96 Mike Lieberthal .15 .40
97 Adam Dunn .25 .60
98 Carl Crawford .25 .60
99 Reggie Sanders .15 .40
100 Mark Prior SP 2.00 5.00
101 Luis Matos .15 .40
102 Barry Zito .25 .60
103 Randy Johnson .40 1.00
104A Kevin Brown .15 .40
104B Edwin Jackson SP 1.50 4.00
105 Pat Burrell .15 .40
106 Steve Finley .15 .40
107 Moises Alou .15 .40
108 David Ortiz SP 2.50 6.00
109 Austin Kearns SP 1.50 4.00
110 Carlos Beltran .25 .60
111 Shawn Green .15 .40
112 Javier Vazquez .15 .40
113 Hideo Nomo .40 1.00
114 Kazuhisa Ishii .15 .40
115 Corey Koskie .15 .40
116 Kevin Millwood .15 .40
117 Randy Wolf .15 .40
118 Darin Erstad .15 .40
119 Fernando Vina .15 .40
120 Pedro Martinez .25 .60
121 Melvin Mora .15 .40
122 Carl Everett .15 .40
123 Matt Morris .15 .40
124 Greg Maddux .50 1.25
125 Jason Schmidt .15 .40
126 Mark Teixeira SP 2.00 5.00
127 Randy Winn .15 .40
128 Rich Aurilia .15 .40
129 Vicente Padilla .15 .40
130 Tim Hudson .25 .60
131 Marlon Byrd .15 .40
132 Jae Weong Seo .15 .40
133 Branch Rickey MG .15 .40
134 A.J. Pierzynski .15 .40
135 Ryan Klesko .15 .40
136 Eric Hinske .15 .40
137 Mike Cameron .15 .40
138 Roberto Alomar .25 .60
139 Jarrod Washburn .15 .40
140A Curt Schilling D'backs .25 .60
140B Curt Schilling Sox SP 2.00 5.00
141 Omar Vizquel .25 .60
142 Mike Sweeney .15 .40
143 Wade Miller .15 .40
144 Jose Vidro .15 .40
145 Rich Harden SP 1.50 4.00
146 Eric Munson .15 .40
147 Lance Berkman .25 .60
148 Mark Buehrle .25 .60
149 Carlos Delgado .15 .40
150 Sean Burroughs .15 .40
151 Kevin Millar .15 .40
152 Frank Thomas .40 1.00
153 Adrian Beltre .40 1.00
154 Shannon Stewart .15 .40
155 Johan Santana .25 .60
156 Edgardo Alfonzo .15 .40
157 Jose Cruz Jr. .15 .40
158 Sidney Ponson .15 .40
159 Edgar Martinez .25 .60
160 Jamie Moyer .15 .40
161 Tony Batista .15 .40
162 Wes Helms .15 .40
163 Brandon Webb SP 1.50 4.00
164 Gil Meche .15 .40
165 Marcus Giles SP 1.50 4.00
166 Angel Berroa SP 1.50 4.00
167 Rocco Baldelli SP 1.50 4.00
168 Michael Young .15 .40
169 Esteban Loaiza .15 .40
170 Casey Blake .15 .40
171 Jody Gerut .15 .40
172 Bo Hart SP 1.50 4.00
173 Kelvim Escobar .15 .40
174 Aaron Guiel .15 .40
175 Javy Lopez SP 1.50 4.00
176 Aubrey Huff .15 .40
177 Hank Blalock .15 .40
178 Edwin Jackson .15 .40

179 Delmon Young SP 2.00 5.00
180 Bobby Jenks .15 .40
181 Felix Pie .15 .40
182 Jeremy Reed SP 1.50 4.00
183 Aaron Hill .15 .40
184 Casey Kotchman SP 1.50 4.00
185 Grady Sizemore .25 .60
186 Joe Mauer SP 2.00 5.00
187 Ryan Harvey .15 .40
188 Neal Cotts .15 .40
189 Victor Martinez .25 .60
190 Rene Reyes .15 .40
191 Eric Duncan .15 .40
192 B.J. Upton SP 2.00 5.00
193 Khalil Greene SP 2.00 5.00
194 Bobby Crosby .15 .40
195 Rickie Weeks SP 1.50 4.00
196 Zack Greinke SP 1.50 4.00
197 Laynce Nix .15 .40
198 Vito Chiaravalloti SP RC 1.50 4.00
199 Estee Harris RC .15 .40
200 Jon Knott SP RC 1.50 4.00
201 Dioner Navarro RC .25 .60
202 Craig Ansman RC .15 .40
203 Travis Blackley RC .15 .40
204 Yadier Molina RC 12.00 30.00
205 Rodney Choy Foo RC .15 .40
206 Kyle Sleeth SP RC 2.00 5.00
207 Jeff Allison RC .15 .40
208 Josh Labandeira RC .15 .40
209 Lastings Milledge SP RC 3.00 8.00
210 Rudy Guillen SP RC 2.00 5.00
211 Blake Hawksworth SP RC 2.00 5.00
212 David Aardsma RC .15 .40
213 Shawn Hill RC .15 .40
214 Erick Aybar SP RC 2.00 5.00
215 Ervin Santana RC .40 1.00
216 Tim Stauffer SP RC 2.00 5.00
217 Merkin Valdez RC .15 .40
218 Jack McKeon MG .15 .40
219 Jeff Conine .15 .40
220 Josh Beckett SP 1.50 4.00
221 Luis Castillo .15 .40
222 Mike Lowell .15 .40
223 Juan Pierre .15 .40
224A Ivan Rodriguez Marlins .25 .60
224B Ivan Rodriguez Tigers SP 2.00 5.00
225 A.J. Burnett .15 .40
226 Miguel Cabrera SP 2.00 5.00
227 Jeffrey Loria .15 .40
228 Joe Torre MG .25 .60
229A Jason Giambi Portrait .15 .40
229B Jason Giambi Fielding SP 1.50 4.00
230 Aaron Boone .15 .40
231 Jose Contreras .15 .40
232 Derek Jeter SP 3.00 8.00
233 Ruben Sierra .15 .40
234 Mike Mussina .25 .60
235 Mariano Rivera .50 1.25
236A Jorge Posada SP 2.00 5.00
236B Dioner Navarro SP 2.00 5.00
237 Alfonso Soriano .25 .60
NNO Alex Rodriguez Yanks 1.00 2.50
VB Vintage Buyback

2004 Topps Cracker Jack Mini

COMP.SET w/o SP's (200) 40.00 80.00
*MINI: .75X TO 2X BASIC
*MINI: .75X TO 2X BASIC RC
*MINI SP: .6X TO 1.5X BASIC SP
*MINI SP: .5X TO 1.2X BASIC SP RC
MINI STATED ODDS ONE PER PACK
MINI SP STATED ODDS 1:20
SP'S ARE SAME AS IN BASIC SET

2004 Topps Cracker Jack Mini Autographs

STATED ODDS 1:258 HOBBY/RETAIL
SHEFFIELD PRINT RUN 50 CARDS
SHEFFIELD IS NOT SERIAL NUMBERED
SHEFFIELD INFO PROVIDED BY TOPPS
EXCHANGE DEADLINE 03/31/06
112 Javier Vazquez 15.00 40.00
163 Brandon Webb 6.00 15.00
165 Marcus Giles 8.00 20.00
221 Luis Castillo 4.00 10.00
226 Miguel Cabrera 20.00 50.00

2004 Topps Cracker Jack Mini Blue

*BLUE: 4X TO 10X BASIC
*BLUE: 4X TO 10X BASIC RC
*BLUE SP: 1.25X TO 3X BASIC SP
*BLUE SP: 1X TO 2.5X BASIC SP RC
BLUE STATED ODDS 1:10
BLUE SP STATED ODDS 1:60
SP'S ARE SAME AS IN BASIC SET

2004 Topps Cracker Jack Mini Stickers

*STICKERS: .75X TO 2X BASIC
*STICKERS: .75X TO 2X BASIC RC
*SP STICKERS: .4X TO 1X BASIC SP
*SP STICKERS: .4X TO 1X BASIC SP RC
ONE PER SURPRISE PACK
SP ODDS 1:10 SURPRISE PACKS
SP'S ARE SAME AS IN BASIC SET

2004 Topps Cracker Jack 1-2-3 Strikes You're Out Relics

GROUP A 1:5045 H, 1:5310 R SURPRISE
GROUP B 1:103 H, 1:109 R SURPRISE
GROUP C 1:177 H, 1:202 R SURPRISE
GROUP D 1:157 H, 1:191 R SURPRISE
BM Brett Myers Jsy C 3.00 8.00
BW Billy Wagner Jsy B 3.00 8.00
BZ Barry Zito Jsy B 3.00 8.00
CCS C.C. Sabathia Jsy C 3.00 8.00
CS Curt Schilling Jsy A 6.00 15.00
DL Derek Lowe Jsy B 3.00 8.00
EG Eric Gagne Jsy C 3.00 8.00
HN Hideo Nomo Jsy B 4.00 10.00
JB Josh Beckett Uni B 3.00 8.00
JS John Smoltz Jsy D 4.00 10.00
KB Kevin Brown Uni B 3.00 8.00
KM Kevin Millwood Jsy D 3.00 8.00
KW Kerry Wood Jsy C 3.00 8.00
MAM Mark Mulder Uni D 3.00 8.00
MM Mike Mussina Uni A 8.00 20.00
PM Pedro Martinez Jsy B 4.00 10.00
RH Rich Harden Jsy B 3.00 8.00
RJ Randy Johnson Jsy B 4.00 10.00

2004 Topps Cracker Jack Secret Surprise Signatures

GROUP A 1:1448 H, 1:1657 R SURPRISE
GROUP B 1:451 H, 1:524 R SURPRISE
GROUP C 1:323 H, 1:368 R SURPRISE
GROUP D 1:372 H, 1:404 R SURPRISE
EXCHANGE DEADLINE 03/31/06
AH Aubrey Huff B 6.00 15.00
BG Brian Giles D 6.00 15.00
CF Cliff Floyd B 6.00 15.00
DM Dustin McGowan B 4.00 10.00
DW Dontrelle Willis A 10.00 25.00
FP Felix Pie C 4.00 10.00
JW Jerome Williams A 4.00 10.00
ML Mike Lamb C 4.00 10.00
MV Merkin Valdez B 6.00 15.00
SP Scott Podsednik D 10.00 25.00
SR Scott Rolen C 6.00 15.00

2004 Topps Cracker Jack Take Me Out to the Ballgame Relics

GROUP A 1:654 H, 1:765 R SURPRISE
GROUP B 1:645 H, 1:645 R SURPRISE
GROUP C 1:152 H, 1:194 R SURPRISE
GROUP D 1:131 H, 1:223 R SURPRISE
GROUP E 1:99 H, 1:125 R SURPRISE
GROUP F 1:201 H, 1:264 R SURPRISE
GROUP G 1:211 H, 1:297 R SURPRISE
GROUP H 1:190 H, 1:226 R SURPRISE
GROUP I 1:126 H, 1:154 R SURPRISE
GROUP J 1:149 H, 1:189 R SURPRISE
GROUP K 1:89 H, 1:93 R SURPRISE
AB Angel Berroa Bat I 3.00 8.00
AD Adam Dunn Jsy C 3.00 8.00
AP Albert Pujols Uni G 6.00 15.00
AP2 Albert Pujols Bat C 6.00 15.00
AR Alex Rodriguez Jsy H 4.00 10.00
AR2 A.Rodriguez Yanks Bat C 8.00 20.00
AS Alfonso Soriano Uni G 3.00 8.00
AS2 Alfonso Soriano Bat A 4.00 10.00
BA Bob Abreu Jsy E 3.00 8.00
BB1 Bret Boone Bat C 3.00 8.00
BB2 Bret Boone Jsy K 3.00 8.00
CB Craig Biggio Jsy E 4.00 10.00
CJ Chipper Jones Jsy K 4.00 10.00
EC Eric Chavez Uni F 3.00 8.00
GA Garrett Anderson Bat B 4.00 10.00
HB Hank Blalock Bat C 3.00 8.00
IR Ivan Rodriguez Bat D 4.00 10.00
JB Jeff Bagwell Uni E 4.00 10.00
JE Jim Edmonds Jsy E 3.00 8.00
JGA Jason Giambi Jsy C 3.00 8.00
JGH Jason Giambi Uni F 3.00 8.00
JL Javy Lopez Jsy E 3.00 8.00
JL2 Javy Lopez Bat A 4.00 10.00
JR Jose Reyes Jsy D 3.00 8.00
JRO Jimmy Rollins Jsy E 3.00 8.00
JT Jim Thome Jsy I 4.00 10.00
KW Kerry Wood Jsy G 3.00 8.00
LB Lance Berkman Bat F 3.00 8.00
LB2 Lance Berkman Jsy K 3.00 8.00
LG Luis Gonzalez Jsy B 4.00 10.00
LW Larry Walker Jsy J 3.00 8.00
MA Moises Alou Jsy J 3.00 8.00
MC Miguel Cabrera Bat H 4.00 10.00
MCT Mark Teixeira Jsy I 4.00 10.00
MG Marcus Giles Jsy E 3.00 8.00
MP Mike Piazza Jsy F 4.00 10.00
MR Manny Ramirez Uni C 4.00 10.00
MS Mike Sweeney Jsy A 4.00 10.00
MT Miguel Tejada Bat K 3.00 8.00
MY Michael Young Jsy D 3.00 8.00
NG Nomar Garciaparra Jsy B 6.00 15.00
NG2 Nomar Garciaparra Bat A 6.00 15.00
PB Pat Burrell Jsy E 3.00 8.00
PL Paul Lo Duca Uni D 3.00 8.00
RB Rocco Baldelli Bat H 3.00 8.00
RF Rafael Furcal Jsy J 3.00 8.00
SG Shawn Green Uni D 3.00 8.00
SG2 Shawn Green Bat C 3.00 8.00
SS Sammy Sosa Bat D 4.00 10.00
SS2 Sammy Sosa Jsy E 4.00 10.00
TG Troy Glaus Jsy I 3.00 8.00
TH Todd Helton Jsy K 4.00 10.00
TKH Torii Hunter Jsy B 4.00 10.00
VW Vernon Wells Jsy D 3.00 8.00

2005 Topps Cracker Jack

COMPLETE SET (250) 50.00 100.00
COMP.SET w/o SP'S (200) 15.00 40.00
COMMON CARD .15 .40
COMMON RC .15 .40
COMMON SP .75 2.00
COMMON SP RC .75 2.00
SP STATED ODDS 1:3 HOBBY/RETAIL
SP CL: 1/3B/4/6/11/13/21/26/30/31/41/51
SP CL: 56/60B/71/75A/75B/84/85B/106/110
SP CL: 111/112/126/135A/135B/146/151/156
SP CL: 164B/166/176/181/186/191/196/201
SP CL: 211/216/221A/221B/225/226/228B
SP CL: 231/235/236A/236B
1 David Wright SP 1.50 4.00
2 Rafael Furcal .15 .40
3A Alex Rodriguez Portrait .50 1.25
3B Alex Rodriguez Fielding SP 2.50 6.00
4 Victor Martinez SP 1.25 3.00
5 Ken Griffey Jr. .75 2.00
6 Bobby Crosby SP .75 2.00
7 Ivan Rodriguez .25 .60
8 Darin Erstad .15 .40
9 Javy Lopez .15 .40
10 Brian Giles .15 .40
11 Aaron Rowand SP .75 2.00
12 Joe Torre MG .25 .60
13 Zack Greinke SP 2.50 6.00
14 Shannon Stewart .15 .40
15 Jack Wilson .15 .40
16 Jose Vidro .15 .40
17 Josh Beckett .15 .40
18 Barry Zito .25 .60
19 Bret Boone .15 .40
20 Greg Maddux .50 1.25
21 Carl Crawford SP 1.25 3.00
22 Mark Teixeira .25 .60
23 Jason Schmidt .15 .40
24 Kazuhisa Ishii .15 .40
25 Mike Piazza .40 1.00
26 Daniel Cabrera SP .75 2.00
27 Mike Lieberthal .15 .40
28 Gil Meche .15 .40
29 Phil Nevin .15 .40
30 Adrian Beltre SP 2.00 5.00
31 Chipper Jones SP 2.00 5.00
32 Zach Day .15 .40
33 Ben Sheets .15 .40
34 Carlos Zambrano .25 .60
35 Melvin Mora .15 .40
36 Joe Mauer .30 .75
37 Ken Harvey .15 .40
38 Bernie Williams .25 .60
39 Mike Maroth .15 .40
40 Eric Chavez .15 .40
41 Matt Lawton SP .75 2.00
42 Ray Durham .15 .40
43 Vernon Wells .15 .40
44 Mike Lowell .15 .40
45 Jim Thome .25 .60
46 Joel Pineiro .15 .40
47 Lance Berkman .25 .60
48 Ryan Klesko .15 .40
49 Adam Dunn .25 .60
50 Vladimir Guerrero .25 .60
51 Eric Gagne SP .75 2.00
52 Richie Sexson .15 .40
53 Javier Vazquez .15 .40
54 Roy Oswalt .25 .60
55 Carlos Delgado .15 .40
56 John Buck SP .75 2.00
57 Kenny Rogers .15 .40
58 Sidney Ponson .15 .40
59 Vicente Padilla .15 .40
60A Mark Prior Leg Up .25 .60
60B Mark Prior Portrait SP 1.25 3.00
61 A.J. Pierzynski .15 .40
62 Aubrey Huff .15 .40
63 Shea Hillenbrand .15 .40
64 Carlos Guillen .15 .40
65 Lyle Overbay .15 .40
66 Al Leiter .15 .40
67 Eric Hinske .15 .40
68 Laynce Nix .15 .40
69 Scott Hairston .15 .40
70 Roger Clemens .50 1.25
71 Cesar Izturis SP .75 2.00
72 Shawn Green .15 .40
73 Marcus Giles .15 .40
74 Rafael Palmeiro .25 .60
75A Gary Sheffield SP .75 2.00
75B Melky Cabrera SP 2.50 6.00
76 Juan Pierre .15 .40
77 Pat Burrell .15 .40
78 Sean Burroughs .15 .40
79 Frank Thomas .40 1.00
80 Andruw Jones .15 .40
81 C.C. Sabathia .25 .60
82 Jeff Bagwell .25 .60
83 Tom Glavine .25 .60
84 Craig Wilson SP .75 2.00
85A Johan Santana Throwing .25 .60
85B Johan Santana Portrait SP 1.25 3.00
86 Raul Ibanez .25 .60
87 Sean Casey .15 .40
88 Bucky Jacobsen .15 .40
89 B.J. Upton .25 .60
90 Bobby Abreu .15 .40
91 Geoff Jenkins .15 .40
92 Troy Glaus .15 .40
93 Dontrelle Willis .15 .40
94 Jose Lima .15 .40
95 Rocco Baldelli .15 .40
96 Aramis Ramirez .15 .40
97 Paul Lo Duca .15 .40
98 Torii Hunter .15 .40
99 Jay Payton .15 .40
100 Carlos Beltran .25 .60
101 Jaret Wright .15 .40
102 Jason Bay .15 .40
103 Cliff Floyd .15 .40
104 Mike Sweeney .15 .40
105 Sammy Sosa .40 1.00
106 Khalil Greene SP .75 2.00
107 David DeJesus .15 .40
108 Jermaine Dye .15 .40
109 Miguel Cabrera .40 1.00
110 Miguel Tejada SP 1.25 3.00
111 Johnny Estrada SP .75 2.00
112 Ronnie Belliard SP .75 2.00
113 Austin Kearns .15 .40
114 Erubiel Durazo .15 .40
115 Preston Wilson .15 .40
116 Hideo Nomo .40 1.00
117 Dmitri Young .15 .40
118 Jon Lieber .15 .40
119 Derrek Lee .15 .40
120 Todd Helton .25 .60
121 Omar Vizquel .25 .60
122 Wily Mo Pena .15 .40
123 J.D. Drew .15 .40
124 Matt Holliday .40 1.00
125 Ichiro Suzuki .50 1.25
126 Mark Buehrle SP 1.25 3.00
127 Barry Bonds .60 1.50
128 Jeff Kent .15 .40
129 Kerry Wood .15 .40
130 Mariano Rivera .50 1.25
131 Nick Johnson .15 .40
132 Randy Winn .15 .40
133 Phil Garner MG .15 .40
134 Jose Reyes .25 .60
135A Michael Young SP .75 2.00
135B Ian Kinsler SP 4.00 10.00
136 Jose Contreras .15 .40
137 Oliver Perez .15 .40
138 Roy Halladay .25 .60
139 Kevin Millwood .15 .40
140 Jorge Posada .25 .60
141 Mike Cameron .15 .40
142 Edgardo Alfonzo .15 .40
143 Chris Shelton .15 .40
144 Luis Castillo .15 .40
145 Alfonso Soriano .25 .60
146 Ryan Drese SP .75 2.00
147 Mark Mulder .15 .40
148 Jason Giambi .15 .40
149 Travis Hafner .15 .40
150 Randy Johnson .40 1.00
151 Paul Konerko SP 1.25 3.00
152 Mike Mussina .25 .60
153 Brad Wilkerson .15 .40
154 Tim Hudson .25 .60
155 Garret Anderson .15 .40
156 Chase Utley SP 1.25 3.00
157 Jamie Moyer .15 .40
158 Scott Kazmir .40 1.00
159 Brett Myers .15 .40
160 Kazuo Matsui .15 .40
161 Orlando Hudson .15 .40
162 Luis Gonzalez .15 .40
163 Kevin Youkilis .15 .40
164A Jason Kendall .15 .40
164B Landon Powell SP .75 2.00
165 Hank Blalock .15 .40
166 Mark Loretta SP .75 2.00
167 Miguel Cairo .15 .40
168 Corey Patterson .15 .40
169 Victor Zambrano .15 .40
170 Magglio Ordonez .25 .60
171 J.T. Snow .15 .40
172 Randy Wolf .15 .40
173 Rich Harden .15 .40
174 Bartolo Colon .15 .40
175 Derek Jeter 1.00 2.50
176 Casey Kotchman SP .75 2.00
177 Val Majewski .15 .40
178 Grady Sizemore .25 .60
179 Rickie Weeks .15 .40
180 Robinson Cano .50 1.25
181 Nick Swisher SP 1.25 3.00
182 Ryan Howard .30 .75
183 John Van Benschoten .15 .40
184 Delmon Young .40 1.00
185 Aaron Hill .25 .60
186 Chris Burke SP .75 2.00
187 Merkin Valdez .15 .40
188 Jeremy Reed .15 .40
189 Conor Jackson .25 .60
190 Mark Teahen .15 .40
191 Joey Gathright SP .75 2.00
192 Gavin Floyd .15 .40
193 Joe Blanton .15 .40
194 Jason Kubel .15 .40
195 Jeff Francis .15 .40
196 Angel Guzman SP .75 2.00
197 Dallas McPherson .15 .40
198 Melky Cabrera RC .50 1.25
199 Jake Dittler .15 .40
200 Elvys Quezada RC .15 .40
201 Ian Kinsler SP RC 4.00 10.00
202 Nate McLouth RC .25 .60
203 Chris Seddon RC .15 .40
204 Chad Orvella RC .15 .40
205 Ian Bladergroen RC .15 .40
206 James Jurries SP RC .75 2.00
207 Landon Powell RC .15 .40
208 Eric Nielsen RC .15 .40
209 Chris Roberson RC .15 .40
210 Andre Ethier RC 1.25 3.00
211 Chris Denorfia SP RC .75 2.00
212 Darren Fenster RC .15 .40
213 Jeremy West RC .15 .40
214 Sean Marshall RC .40 1.00
215 Ryan Sweeney RC .25 .60
216 Steve Doetsch SP RC .75 2.00
217 Kevin Melillo RC .15 .40
218 Chip Cannon RC .15 .40
219 Tony La Russa MG .25 .60
220 Chris Carpenter .25 .60
221A Edgar Renteria Sox SP .75 2.00
221B Edgar Renteria Cards SP .75 2.00
222 Albert Pujols .50 1.25
223 Jim Edmonds .25 .60
224 Jason Marquis .15 .40
225 Scott Rolen SP 1.25 3.00
226 Larry Walker SP 1.25 3.00
227 Matt Morris .15 .40
228A Mike Matheny Giants .15 .40
228B Mike Matheny Cards SP .75 2.00
229 Jeromy Burnitz .15 .40
230 Terry Francona MG .25 .60
231 Johnny Damon SP 1.25 3.00
232 Keith Foulke .15 .40
233 Trot Nixon .15 .40
234 Manny Ramirez .40 1.00
235 David Ortiz SP 2.00 5.00
236A Pedro Martinez Sox SP 1.25 3.00
236B Pedro Martinez Mets SP 1.25 3.00
237 Curt Schilling .25 .60
238 Kevin Millar .15 .40
239 Bill Mueller .15 .40
240 Mark Bellhorn .15 .40
NNO Josh Beckett NNO SP .75 2.00

2005 Topps Cracker Jack Mini Blue

*BLUE: 8X TO 20X BASIC
*BLUE: 5X TO 12X BASIC RC
STATED ODDS 1:75 HOBBY/RETAIL
STATED PRINT RUN 50 SERIAL #'d SETS
1 David Wright 6.00 15.00
3B Alex Rodriguez Fielding 10.00 25.00
4 Victor Martinez 5.00 12.00
6 Bobby Crosby 3.00 8.00
11 Aaron Rowand 3.00 8.00
13 Zack Greinke 10.00 25.00
21 Carl Crawford 5.00 12.00
26 Daniel Cabrera 3.00 8.00
30 Adrian Beltre 8.00 20.00
31 Chipper Jones 8.00 20.00
41 Matt Lawton 3.00 8.00
51 Eric Gagne 3.00 8.00
56 John Buck 3.00 8.00
60A Mark Prior Leg Up 5.00 12.00
60B Mark Prior Portrait 5.00 12.00
71 Cesar Izturis 3.00 8.00
75A Gary Sheffield 3.00 8.00
75B Melky Cabrera 10.00 25.00
84 Craig Wilson 3.00 8.00
85B Johan Santana Portrait 5.00 12.00
106 Khalil Greene 3.00 8.00
110 Miguel Tejada 5.00 12.00
111 Johnny Estrada 3.00 8.00
112 Ronnie Belliard 3.00 8.00
126 Mark Buehrle 5.00 12.00
135A Michael Young 3.00 8.00
135B Ian Kinsler 15.00 40.00
146 Ryan Drese 3.00 8.00
151 Paul Konerko 5.00 12.00
156 Chase Utley 5.00 12.00
164B Landon Powell 3.00 8.00
166 Mark Loretta 3.00 8.00
176 Casey Kotchman 3.00 8.00
181 Nick Swisher 5.00 12.00
186 Chris Burke 3.00 8.00
191 Joey Gathright 3.00 8.00
196 Angel Guzman 3.00 8.00
201 Ian Kinsler 15.00 40.00
206 James Jurries 3.00 8.00
216 Steve Doetsch 3.00 8.00
221A Edgar Renteria Sox 3.00 8.00
221B Edgar Renteria Cards 3.00 8.00
225 Scott Rolen 5.00 12.00
226 Larry Walker 5.00 12.00
228B Mike Matheny Cards 3.00 8.00
231 Johnny Damon 5.00 12.00
235 David Ortiz 8.00 20.00
236A Pedro Martinez Sox 5.00 12.00
236B Pedro Martinez Mets 5.00 12.00
NNO Josh Beckett NNO 3.00 8.00

2005 Topps Cracker Jack Mini Red

COMP.SET w/o SP'S (200) 40.00 80.00
*RED: .75X TO 2X BASIC
*RED: .75X TO 2X BASIC RC
ONE PER PACK
*RED SP: .6X TO 1.5X BASIC SP
*RED SP: .5X TO 1.2X BASIC SP RC
SP STATED ODDS 1:20 HOBBY/RETAIL

2005 Topps Cracker Jack Mini Stickers

COMP.SET w/o SP'S (200) 40.00 80.00
*STICKER: .75X TO 2X BASIC
*STICKER: .75X TO 2X BASIC RC
ONE PER PACK
*STICKER SP: .6X TO 1.5X BASIC SP
*STICKER SP: .5X TO 1.2X BASIC SP RC
SP STATED ODDS 1:20 HOBBY/RETAIL

2005 Topps Cracker Jack 1-2-3 Strikes You're Out Mini Relics

STATED ODDS 1:204 HOBBY/RETAIL
BR Brad Radke Jsy 3.00 8.00
CS Curt Schilling Jsy 6.00 15.00
JB Josh Beckett Uni 3.00 8.00
JW Jaret Wright Jsy 3.00 8.00
RD Ryan Drese Jsy 3.00 8.00
RO Russ Ortiz Jsy 3.00 8.00

2005 Topps Cracker Jack Autographs

GROUP A ODDS 1:38,675 HOBBY/RETAIL
GROUP B ODDS 1:1864 HOBBY/RETAIL
GROUP A PRINT RUN 25 SERIAL #'d SETS
GROUP B PRINT RUN 50 SERIAL #'d SETS
NO GROUP A PRICING DUE TO SCARCITY
AR Alex Rodriguez B/50 150.00 250.00
CC Carl Crawford B/50 12.50 30.00
CS C.C. Sabathia B/50 12.50 30.00
CW Craig Wilson B/50 15.00 40.00
DW David Wright B/50 10.00 25.00
EC Eric Chavez B/50 30.00 60.00
EG Eric Gagne B/50 40.00 80.00
GA Garret Anderson B/50 30.00 60.00
JS Johan Santana B/50 30.00 60.00

2005 Topps Cracker Jack Secret Surprise Mini Autographs

GROUP A ODDS 1:2328 HOBBY/RETAIL
GROUP B ODDS 1:517 HOBBY/RETAIL
GROUP C ODDS 1:1864 HOBBY/RETAIL
GROUP D ODDS 1:163 HOBBY/RETAIL
GROUP E ODDS 1:930 HOBBY/RETAIL
GROUP F ODDS 1:155 HOBBY/RETAIL
GROUP A PRINT RUN 100 COPIES PER
GROUP A ARE NOT SERIAL-NUMBERED
GROUP A PRINT RUN PROVIDED BY TOPPS
AG Angel Guzman F 4.00 10.00
AR Alex Rodriguez A/100 * 75.00 200.00
CC Carl Crawford D 6.00 15.00
CN Chris Nelson F 8.00 20.00
CS C.C. Sabathia D 6.00 15.00
CT Curtis Thigpen B 6.00 15.00
CW Craig Wilson D 4.00 10.00
DM Dallas McPherson A/100 * 10.00 25.00
DW David Wright D 12.50 30.00
EC Eric Chavez B 10.00 25.00
EG Eric Gagne D 6.00 15.00
GA Garret Anderson B 10.00 25.00
HB Hank Blalock D 6.00 15.00
JS Johan Santana B 6.00 15.00
KM Kevin Millar F 6.00 15.00
MK Mark Kotsay A/100 * 10.00 25.00
ML Mark Loretta A/100 * 10.00 25.00
MM Melvin Mora E 6.00 15.00
RR Richie Robnett F 6.00 15.00
SK Scott Kazmir C 10.00 25.00

2005 Topps Cracker Jack Take Me Out to the Ballgame Mini Relics

STATED ODDS 1:16 HOBBY/RETAIL
AB Adrian Beltre Bat 3.00 8.00
AB1 Angel Berroa Bat 3.00 8.00
AB2 Angel Berroa Uni 3.00 8.00
AD Adam Dunn Bat 3.00 8.00
AL Adam LaRoche Bat 3.00 8.00
AP Albert Pujols Jsy 8.00 20.00
AR Alex Rodriguez Bat 6.00 15.00
ARA Aramis Ramirez Bat 3.00 8.00
AS Alfonso Soriano Bat 3.00 8.00
BB Barry Bonds Uni 12.50 30.00
BC Bobby Cox Uni 3.00 8.00
BCR Bobby Crosby Bat 3.00 8.00
BK Bobby Kielty Bat 3.00 8.00
BS Benito Santiago Bat 4.00 10.00
BW Bernie Williams Uni 4.00 10.00
CB Carlos Beltran Bat 3.00 8.00
CBI Craig Biggio Uni 4.00 10.00
CC Coco Crisp Bat 3.00 8.00
CG Cristian Guzman Bat 3.00 8.00
CP Corey Patterson Bat 3.00 8.00
CT Charles Thomas Bat 3.00 8.00
DE Darin Erstad Bat 3.00 8.00
DM Doug Mientkiewicz Bat 3.00 8.00
DO David Ortiz Bat 4.00 10.00
DW Dontrelle Willis Bat 3.00 8.00
EC1 Eric Chavez Bat 3.00 8.00
EC2 Eric Chavez Uni 3.00 8.00
GS Gary Sheffield Bat 3.00 8.00
HB1 Hank Blalock Bat 3.00 8.00
HB2 Hank Blalock Uni 3.00 8.00
HB3 Hank Blalock Jsy 3.00 8.00
IR1 Ivan Rodriguez Bat 4.00 10.00
IR2 Ivan Rodriguez Jsy 4.00 10.00
JB Jeff Bagwell Uni 4.00 10.00
JE Johnny Estrada Jsy 3.00 8.00
JE1 Jim Edmonds Bat 3.00 8.00
JE2 Jim Edmonds Jsy 3.00 8.00
JG Jody Gerut Bat 3.00 8.00
JGI Jay Gibbons Bat 3.00 8.00
JGU Jose Guillen Bat 3.00 8.00
JJ Jacque Jones Bat 3.00 8.00
JK Jason Kendall Bat 3.00 8.00
JP1 Jorge Posada Bat 4.00 10.00
JP2 Jorge Posada Jsy 4.00 10.00
JR Jeremy Reed Bat 3.00 8.00
JT Jim Thome Bat 4.00 10.00
JTO Joe Torre Uni 6.00 15.00
KM Kevin Millar Bat 4.00 10.00
KME Kevin Mench Jsy 3.00 8.00
LB1 Lance Berkman Bat 3.00 8.00
LB2 Lance Berkman Jsy 3.00 8.00
LG Luis Gonzalez Bat 3.00 8.00
LN Laynce Nix Jsy 3.00 8.00
MC Miguel Cabrera Bat 4.00 10.00
MG Marcus Giles Bat 3.00 8.00
MK Mark Kotsay Bat 3.00 8.00
MM Melvin Mora Bat 3.00 8.00
MO Magglio Ordonez Bat 3.00 8.00
MP Mike Piazza Uni 4.00 10.00
MR Manny Ramirez Bat 4.00 10.00
MRE Mike Restovich Bat 3.00 8.00
MTE1 Miguel Tejada Uni 3.00 8.00
MTE2 Miguel Tejada Bat 3.00 8.00
MT1 Mark Teixeira Uni 4.00 10.00
MT2 Mark Teixeira Jsy 4.00 10.00
MT3 Mark Teixeira Bat 4.00 10.00
MY Michael Young Jsy 3.00 8.00
NG Nick Green Jsy 3.00 8.00
OV Omar Vizquel Bat 4.00 10.00
PK Paul Konerko Bat 3.00 8.00
PN Phil Nevin Bat 3.00 8.00
RB Ron Belliard Bat 3.00 8.00
RF Rafael Furcal Jsy 3.00 8.00
RK Ryan Klesko Jsy 3.00 8.00
RP Rafael Palmeiro Bat 4.00 10.00
RS Reggie Sanders Bat 3.00 8.00
SB Sean Burroughs Bat 3.00 8.00
SG Shawn Green Bat 3.00 8.00
TG Troy Glaus Bat 3.00 8.00
TH Todd Helton Bat 4.00 10.00
THU Torii Hunter Bat 3.00 8.00
VC Vinny Castilla Bat 3.00 8.00
VG Vladimir Guerrero Bat 4.00 10.00
VM Victor Martinez Bat 3.00 8.00

1995 Topps D3

Manufactured by Topps, this set consists of 59 three-dimension standard-size cards of better players. Utilizing uncluttered fronts, the player's name is at the top with the set logo toward bottom right. The backs offer a small photo with statistical breakdowns in areas such as Home, Away, Day, Night, etc. A second series was planned for this issue but was never issued due to lack of consumer interest. Promo cards featuring Greg Gagne and Tim Bogar were distributed to dealers and hobby media to preview the set.

COMPLETE SET (59) 6.00 15.00
1 David Justice .10 .30
2 Cal Ripken 1.00 2.50
3 Ruben Sierra .10 .30
4 Roberto Alomar .20 .50
5 Denny Martinez .10 .30
6 Todd Zeile .10 .30
7 Albert Belle .10 .30
8 Chuck Knoblauch .10 .30
9 Roger Clemens .60 1.50
10 Cal Eldred .05 .15
11 Dennis Eckersley .10 .30
12 Andy Benes .05 .15
13 Moises Alou .10 .30
14 Andres Galarraga .10 .30
15 Jim Thome .20 .50
16 Tim Salmon .20 .50
17 Carlos Garcia .05 .15
18 Scott Leius .05 .15
19 Jeff Montgomery .05 .15
20 Brian Anderson .05 .15
21 Will Clark .20 .50
22 Bobby Bonilla .10 .30
23 Mike Stanley .05 .15
24 Barry Bonds .75 2.00
25 Jeff Conine .10 .30
26 Paul O'Neill .20 .50
27 Mike Piazza .50 1.25
28 Tom Glavine .20 .50
29 Jim Edmonds .20 .50
30 Lou Whitaker .10 .30
31 Jeff Frye .05 .15
32 Ivan Rodriguez .20 .50
33 Bret Boone .10 .30
34 Mike Greenwell .05 .15
35 Mark Grace .20 .50
36 Darren Lewis .05 .15
37 Don Mattingly .75 2.00
38 Jose Rijo .05 .15
39 Robin Ventura .10 .30
40 Bob Hamelin .05 .15
41 Tim Wallach .05 .15
42 Tony Gwynn .40 1.00
43 Ken Griffey Jr. .60 1.50
44 Doug Drabek .05 .15
45 Rafael Palmeiro .20 .50
46 Dean Palmer .10 .30
47 Bip Roberts .05 .15
48 Barry Larkin .20 .50
49 Dave Nilsson .05 .15
50 Wil Cordero .05 .15
51 Travis Fryman .10 .30
52 Chuck Carr .05 .15
53 Rey Sanchez .05 .15
54 Walt Weiss .05 .15
55 Joe Carter .10 .30
56 Len Dykstra .10 .30
57 Orlando Merced .05 .15
58 Ozzie Smith .50 1.25
59 Chris Gomez .05 .15
PB1 Greg Gagne Baseball Promo .40 1.00
TB1 Tim Bogar Baseball Promo .40 1.00

1995 Topps D3 Zone

COMPLETE SET (6) 2.00 5.00
RANDOM INSERTS IN PACKS
DIIIZ PREFIX ON CARD NUMBERS
1 Frank Thomas .40 1.00
2 Kirby Puckett .40 1.00
3 Jeff Bagwell .40 1.00
4 Fred McGriff .40 1.00
5 Raul Mondesi .40 1.00
6 Kenny Lofton .40 1.00

2017 Topps Definitive Collection Autograph Relics

RANDOM INSERTS IN PACKS
PRINT RUNS B/WN 5-50 COPIES PER
NO PRICING ON QTY 15 OR LESS
EXCHANGE DEADLINE 6/30/2019
ARCAB Andrew Benintendi/50 RC 50.00 120.00
ARCABR Alex Bregman/50 RC 30.00 80.00
ARCAD Aledmys Diaz/50 6.00 15.00
ARCAJ Adam Jones/30 10.00 25.00
ARCAJU Aaron Judge/50 RC 200.00 400.00
ARCAR Alex Reyes/20 RC 10.00 25.00
ARCBH Bryce Harper EXCH
ARCCK Clayton Kershaw/30 60.00 150.00
ARCCKL Corey Kluber/50 12.00 30.00
ARCCSE Corey Seager/50 20.00 50.00
ARCDD David Dahl/50 RC 8.00 20.00
ARCDP Dustin Pedroia/50 20.00 50.00
ARCDPR David Price/50 12.00 30.00
ARCDS Dansby Swanson RC
ARCFF Freddie Freeman/30 15.00 40.00
ARCFL Francisco Lindor EXCH 12.00 30.00
ARCGSP George Springer/50 12.00 30.00
ARCI Ichiro EXCH
ARCJA Jose Altuve EXCH 25.00 60.00
ARCJB Javier Baez/50 25.00 60.00
ARCJD Jacob deGrom/50 30.00 80.00
ARCJP Joe Panik
ARCJPE Joc Pederson
ARCJU Julio Urias EXCH 12.00 30.00
ARCKM Kenta Maeda/50 8.00 20.00
ARCKS Kyle Schwarber EXCH 12.00 30.00
ARCKSE Kyle Seager/35 10.00 25.00
ARCMCA Matt Carpenter/50 10.00 25.00
ARCMF Maikel Franco/50 8.00 20.00
ARCMS Miguel Sano
ARCNM Nomar Mazara/50 6.00 15.00
ARCNS Noah Syndergaard/50 20.00 50.00
ARCRB Ryan Braun/50 12.00 30.00
ARCSM Starling Marte/50 12.00 30.00
ARCSMA Steven Matz/50 6.00 15.00
ARCSP Stephen Piscotty/50 8.00 20.00
ARCTS Trevor Story/50 10.00 25.00
ARCWC Willson Contreras/50 20.00 50.00

2017 Topps Definitive Collection Autograph Relics Green

*GREEN: .75X TO 2X BASIC
RANDOM INSERTS IN PACKS
PRINT RUNS B/WN 10-25 COPIES PER
NO PRICING DUE TO SCARICTY
NO PRICING ON QTY 10
ARCJP Joe Panik/25 20.00 50.00
ARCJPE Joc Pederson/25 12.00 30.00
ARCMS Miguel Sano/25 25.00 60.00

2017 Topps Definitive Collection Autographs

RANDOM INSERTS IN PACKS
PRINT RUNS B/WN 5-50 COPIES PER
NO PRICING ON QTY 15 OR LESS
EXCHANGE DEADLINE 6/30/2019
DCAIAB Andrew Benintendi/35 150.00 400.00
DCAIABR Alex Bregman/35 30.00 80.00
DCAIAG Andres Galarraga/35 12.00 30.00
DCAIAJ Aaron Judge/35 350.00 800.00
DCAIAR Anthony Rizzo/35 40.00 100.00
DCAIBH Bryce Harper/5
DCAICK Clayton Kershaw/25 100.00 250.00
DCAICR Cal Ripken Jr.
DCAICS Corey Seager/35 25.00 60.00
DCAIDM Don Mattingly/25 50.00 120.00
DCAIDS Dansby Swanson/35 15.00 40.00
DCAIFL Francisco Lindor/35 50.00 120.00
DCAIFT Frank Thomas/25 40.00 100.00
DCAIJS John Smoltz/35 25.00 60.00
DCAIJU Julio Urias/35 20.00 50.00
DCAIKM Kenta Maeda/35 20.00 50.00
DCAIMM Manny Machado/35 60.00 150.00
DCAIMMC Mark McGwire/5
DCAINR Nolan Ryan

DCAINS Noah Syndergaard/35 25.00 60.00
DCAIOS Ozzie Smith/35 25.00 60.00
DCAIOV Omar Vizquel/35 12.00 30.00
DCAIPM Pedro Martinez/25 150.00 300.00
DCAIWB Wade Boggs/35 60.00 150.00
DCAIYM Yoan Moncada/35 40.00 100.00

2017 Topps Definitive Collection Definitive Autograph Relics

RANDOM INSERTS IN PACKS
PRINT RUNS B/WN 5-40 COPIES PER
NO PRICING ON QTY 15 OR LESS
EXCHANGE DEADLINE 6/30/2019
DCARAD Andre Dawson/40 20.00 50.00
DCARAG Andres Galarraga/40 8.00 20.00
DCARAP Andy Pettitte/40 20.00 50.00
DCARBH Bryce Harper EXCH
DCARBL Barry Larkin/40 20.00 50.00
DCARCB Craig Biggio/40 12.00 30.00
DCARCC Carlos Correa/20 50.00 120.00
DCARCJ Chipper Jones/25 50.00 120.00
DCARCK Clayton Kershaw/40 60.00 150.00
DCARCR Cal Ripken Jr./25 75.00 200.00
DCARCS Corey Seager/40 30.00 80.00
DCARDM Don Mattingly/40 40.00 100.00
DCARDP Dustin Pedroia/30 25.00 60.00
DCARFF Freddie Freeman/40 20.00 50.00
DCARFL Francisco Lindor EXCH 30.00 80.00
DCARFT Frank Thomas/40 30.00 80.00
DCARHA Hank Aaron/15
DCARIR Ivan Rodriguez/40 20.00 50.00
DCARJC Jose Canseco/40 20.00 50.00
DCARJD Johnny Damon/40 15.00 40.00
DCARJS John Smoltz/40 30.00 80.00
DCARJV Joey Votto/40 40.00 100.00
DCARKB Kris Bryant/40 100.00 250.00
DCARKS Kyle Schwarber EXCH 30.00 80.00
DCARMM Manny Machado/40 40.00 100.00
DCARMMC Mark McGwire/25 60.00 150.00
DCARMP Mike Piazza
DCARMTR Mike Trout
DCARNS Noah Syndergaard/40 25.00 60.00
DCAROS Ozzie Smith/40 25.00 60.00
DCAROSM Ozzie Smith/40 25.00 60.00
DCARRA Roberto Alomar/40 20.00 50.00
DCARRC Rod Carew/40 20.00 50.00
DCARRCL Roger Clemens
DCARRH Rickey Henderson/30 40.00 100.00
DCARRY Robin Yount/25 25.00 60.00
DCARSC Steve Carlton/40 15.00 40.00
DCARTG Tom Glavine/40 15.00 40.00
DCARTS Trevor Story/40 10.00 25.00
DCARWB Wade Boggs/25 25.00 60.00

2017 Topps Definitive Collection Dual Autograph Relics

RANDOM INSERTS IN PACKS
PRINT RUNS B/WN 10-35 COPIES PER
NO PRICING ON QTY 15 OR LESS
EXCHANGE DEADLINE 6/30/2019
DARCBA Biggio/Altuve/35 75.00 200.00
DARCBC Bregman/Correa/35 75.00 200.00
DARCCA Altuve/Correa/25 125.00 250.00
DARCCD Diaz/Carpenter/35 15.00 40.00
DARCCP Piscotty/Carpenter/25 15.00 40.00
DARCFS Swnsn/Frmn EXCH 50.00 120.00
DARCGR Gonzalez/Rodriguez/25 25.00 60.00
DARCKL Klbr/Lindor EXCH 15.00 40.00
DARCKS Seager/Kershaw/25 125.00 300.00
DARCMU Maeda/Urias EXCH 25.00 60.00
DARCOD Ortiz/Damon/25 50.00 120.00
DARCOP Ortiz/Pedroia/25 75.00 200.00
DARCPO Pettitte/O'Neill/35
DARCPP Price/Pedroia/20 30.00 80.00
DARCRC Carew/Ryan/25 100.00 250.00
DARCRUB Baez/Russell/35 50.00 120.00
DARCRYS Syndrgrd/Ryan/25 100.00 250.00
DARCSG Smoltz/Glavine/25 50.00 120.00
DARCSD Syndrgrd/dGrm EXCH 125.00 300.00
DARCSU Urias/Seager/35 30.00 80.00
DARCTK Trout/Kershaw EXCH

2017 Topps Definitive Collection Dual Autographs

RANDOM INSERTS IN PACKS
PRINT RUNS B/WN 10-35 COPIES PER
NO PRICING ON QTY 15 OR LESS
EXCHANGE DEADLINE 6/30/2019
DCDABA Altuve/Biggio EX 40.00 100.00
DCDABC Bregman/Correa/35 50.00 120.00
DCDABR Rizzo/Bryant EX 125.00 300.00
DCDABT Bryant/Trout/10
DCDACA Correa/Altuve/35 75.00 200.00
DCDACD Carpenter/Diaz/35 15.00 40.00
DCDAFS Swanson/Freeman/35 20.00 50.00
DCDAGA Abreu/Galarraga/35 10.00 25.00
DCDAGR Gonzalez/Rodriguez/35 30.00 80.00
DCDAGV Galarraga/Vizquel/35 20.00 50.00
DCDAJS Smoltz/Jones/25 60.00 150.00
DCDAKL Lindor/Kluber EX 60.00 150.00
DCDAKS Seager/Kershaw/35 100.00 250.00
DCDAMU Maeda/Urias/35 15.00 40.00
DCDAOD Ortiz/Damon/25 60.00 150.00
DCDAPO O'Neill/Pettitte/35 30.00 80.00
DCDARC Carew/Ryan/20 100.00 250.00
DCDARYS Syndergaard/Ryan/25
DCDASB Sandberg/Bryant/25 125.00 300.00
DCDASD deGrom/Syndrgrd/35 100.00 250.00
DCDASG Smoltz/Glavine/35 50.00 120.00
DCDASU Seager/Urias/35 30.00 80.00
DCDATH Trout/Harper EX 800.00 1200.00
DCDAVD Damon/Varitek/35 30.00 80.00
DCDAVL Lindor/Vizquel EX 50.00 120.00
DCDAVU Urias/Valenzuela/35 40.00 100.00

2017 Topps Definitive Collection Framed Autograph Patches

RANDOM INSERTS IN PACKS
PRINT RUNS B/WN 5-30 COPIES PER
NO PRICING ON QTY 15 OR LESS
EXCHANGE DEADLINE 6/30/2019
DFAPAB Andrew Benintendi/30 100.00 250.00
DFAPABR Alex Bregman/30 75.00 200.00
DFAPAJ Adam Jones/30 20.00 50.00
DFAPAJU Aaron Judge
DFAPBH Bryce Harper
DFAPBP Buster Posey
DFAPCSE Corey Seager/30 100.00 250.00
DFAPDP Dustin Pedroia/25 40.00 100.00
DFAPFF Freddie Freeman/20 30.00 80.00
DFAPFL Francisco Lindor/20 75.00 200.00
DFAPJA Jose Altuve/30 75.00 200.00
DFAPJB Javier Baez/30 60.00 150.00
DFAPJD Jacob deGrom/30 50.00 120.00
DFAPJU Julio Urias/25 25.00 60.00
DFAPKM Kenta Maeda/20 30.00 80.00
DFAPKSE Kyle Seager/30 20.00 50.00
DFAPMCA Matt Carpenter/30 25.00 60.00
DFAPMM Manny Machado/25 30.00 80.00
DFAPNS Noah Syndergaard/30 40.00 100.00
DFAPSM Starling Marte/20 40.00 100.00
DFAPSP Stephen Piscotty/30 12.00 30.00
DFAPTS Trevor Story/30 25.00 60.00

2017 Topps Definitive Collection Framed Autographs

RANDOM INSERTS IN PACKS
PRINT RUNS B/WN 5-30 COPIES PER
NO PRICING ON QTY 15 OR LESS
EXCHANGE DEADLINE 6/30/2019
DCFAAB Andrew Benintendi/30 75.00 200.00
DCFAABR Alex Bregman/30 40.00 100.00
DCFAAG Andres Galarraga/30 12.00 30.00
DCFAAJ Aaron Judge/30 250.00 500.00
DCFAAR Anthony Rizzo/30 60.00 150.00
DCFABH Bryce Harper/5
DCFABJ Bo Jackson EXCH 100.00 250.00
DCFABL Barry Larkin/25 30.00 80.00
DCFACC Carlos Correa/25 60.00 150.00
DCFACJ Chipper Jones/25 60.00 150.00
DCFACK Clayton Kershaw/25 75.00 200.00
DCFACR Cal Ripken Jr.
DCFACS Corey Seager/30 40.00 100.00
DCFACY Carl Yastrzemski/30 50.00 120.00
DCFADM Don Mattingly/25 40.00 100.00
DCFAFL Francisco Lindor/30 30.00 80.00
DCFAGM Greg Maddux/30 75.00 200.00
DCFAHA Hank Aaron EXCH
DCFAJB Johnny Bench/30 50.00 120.00
DCFAJS John Smoltz/25 25.00 60.00
DCFAJU Julio Urias/30 15.00 40.00
DCFAKB Kris Bryant/25 125.00 300.00
DCFAMM Manny Machado/30 40.00 100.00
DCFANR Nolan Ryan/30 75.00 200.00
DCFANS Noah Syndergaard/30 30.00 80.00
DCFAOS Ozzie Smith/25 30.00 80.00
DCFAOV Omar Vizquel/30 12.00 30.00
DCFAPM Pedro Martinez/30 50.00 120.00
DCFARH Rickey Henderson/30 40.00 100.00
DCFARJO Randy Johnson EXCH 60.00 150.00
DCFARS Ryne Sandberg/30 40.00 100.00
DCFAYM Yoan Moncada/25 40.00 100.00

2017 Topps Definitive Collection Helmets

RANDOM INSERTS IN PACKS
PRINT RUNS B/WN 25-50 COPIES PER
EXCHANGE DEADLINE 6/30/2019
DHCAB Alex Bregman/50 20.00 50.00
DHCAR Anthony Rizzo/50 30.00 80.00
DHCGS George Springer/25 15.00 40.00
DHCJB Javier Baez/50 25.00 60.00
DHCJH Jason Heyward/25 15.00 40.00
DHCJM J.D. Martinez/25 25.00 60.00
DHCJU Justin Upton/25 15.00 40.00
DHCMM Manny Machado/50 40.00 100.00
DHCSP Stephen Piscotty/50 15.00 40.00
DHCVM Victor Martinez/25 30.00 80.00

2017 Topps Definitive Collection Jumbo Relics

RANDOM INSERTS IN PACKS
STATED PRINT RUN 50 SER.#'d SETS
*BLUE/30: .4X TO 1X BASIC
DJRCAM Andrew McCutchen 30.00 80.00
DJRCAMC Andrew McCutchen 30.00 80.00
DJRCAP Albert Pujols 15.00 40.00
DJRCBP Brandon Phillips 4.00 10.00
DJRCCA Chris Archer 4.00 10.00
DJRCCB Carlos Beltran 6.00 15.00
DJRCCC Carlos Correa 6.00 15.00
DJRCCG Carlos Gonzalez 5.00 12.00
DJRCCGO Carlos Gonzalez 5.00 12.00
DJRCCGR Curtis Granderson 5.00 12.00
DJRCCH Cole Hamels 6.00 15.00
DJRCCK Corey Kluber 5.00 12.00
DJRCCS Carlos Santana 8.00 20.00
DJRCCY Christian Yelich 8.00 20.00
DJRCCYE Christian Yelich 8.00 20.00
DJRCDB Dellin Betances 8.00 20.00
DJRCEL Evan Longoria 6.00 15.00
DJRCELON Evan Longoria 6.00 15.00
DJRCFH Felix Hernandez 10.00 25.00
DJRCGP Gregory Polanco 12.00 30.00
DJRCGPO Gregory Polanco 12.00 30.00
DJRCJB Jose Bautista 6.00 15.00
DJRCJD Jacob deGrom 8.00 20.00
DJRCJDO Josh Donaldson 6.00 15.00
DJRCJL Jon Lester 5.00 12.00
DJRCJP Joe Panik 8.00 20.00
DJRCJV Justin Verlander 10.00 25.00
DJRCKS Kyle Seager 10.00 25.00
DJRCMC Michael Conforto 8.00 20.00
DJRCMH Matt Harvey 5.00 12.00
DJRCMS Miguel Sano 8.00 20.00
DJRCMTE Mark Teixeira 6.00 15.00
DJRCNC Nelson Cruz 8.00 20.00
DJRCNM Nomar Mazara 8.00 20.00
DJRCRB Ryan Braun 8.00 20.00
DJRCSM Starling Marte 15.00 40.00
DJRCSMA Steven Matz 4.00 10.00
DJRCTT Troy Tulowitzki 6.00 15.00
DJRCYC Yoenis Cespedes 8.00 20.00
DJRCZG Zack Greinke 8.00 20.00

2017 Topps Definitive Collection Legendary Autographs

RANDOM INSERTS IN PACKS
PRINT RUNS B/WN 5-50 COPIES PER
NO PRICING ON QTY 15 OR LESS
EXCHANGE DEADLINE 6/30/2019
DCLAAD Andre Dawson/35 20.00 50.00
DCLAAG Andres Galarraga/35 12.00 30.00
DCLAAK Al Kaline/35 25.00 50.00
DCLAAR Alex Rodriguez/25 75.00 200.00
DCLABL Barry Larkin/25 30.00 80.00
DCLACB Craig Biggio/50 12.00 30.00
DCLACJ Chipper Jones/25 60.00 150.00
DCLACY Carl Yastrzemski/25 50.00 120.00
DCLADM Don Mattingly/25 40.00 100.00
DCLAHA Hank Aaron EXCH
DCLAIR Ivan Rodriguez/35 20.00 50.00
DCLAJB Johnny Bench/25 50.00 120.00
DCLAJD Johnny Damon/50 20.00 50.00
DCLAJS John Smoltz/35 20.00 50.00
DCLALB Lou Brock/35 25.00 60.00
DCLANR Nolan Ryan/25 75.00 200.00
DCLAOS Ozzie Smith/35 40.00 100.00
DCLAOV Omar Vizquel/35 12.00 30.00
DCLARA Roberto Alomar/35 20.00 50.00
DCLARC Rod Carew/35 20.00 50.00
DCLARH Rickey Henderson/25 40.00 100.00
DCLASC Steve Carlton/35
DCLATG Tom Glavine/50 12.00 30.00
DCLAWB Wade Boggs/25 30.00 80.00

2017 Topps Definitive Collection Rookie Autographs

RANDOM INSERTS IN PACKS
PRINT RUNS B/WN 30-50 COPIES PER
EXCHANGE DEADLINE 6/30/2019
*GREEN/25: .5X TO 1.2X BASIC
DCRAAB Andrew Benintendi/50 50.00 120.00
DCRAABE Andrew Benintendi/50 50.00 120.00
DCRAABR Alex Bregman/50 30.00 80.00
DCRAABRE Alex Bregman/50 30.00 80.00
DCRAAJ Aaron Judge/50 150.00 300.00
DCRAAJU Aaron Judge/50 150.00 300.00
DCRAAR Alex Reyes/50 10.00 25.00
DCRAARE Alex Reyes/50 10.00 25.00
DCRACF Carson Fulmer/50 6.00 15.00
DCRADD David Dahl/50 8.00 20.00
DCRADS Dansby Swanson/50 20.00 50.00
DCRADSW Dansby Swanson/50 20.00 50.00
DCRADV Dan Vogelbach/30 10.00 25.00
DCRAGC Gavin Cecchini/30 8.00 20.00
DCRAHD Hunter Dozier/50 6.00 15.00
DCRAHR Hunter Renfroe/50 10.00 25.00
DCRAHRE Hunter Renfroe/50 10.00 25.00
DCRAJA Jorge Alfaro/50 10.00 25.00
DCRAJC Jharel Cotton/30 6.00 15.00
DCRAJD Jose De Leon/50 6.00 15.00
DCRAJH Jeff Hoffman/30 6.00 15.00
DCRAJJ JaCoby Jones/30 8.00 20.00
DCRAJM Joe Musgrove/30 20.00 50.00
DCRAJTH Jake Thompson/50 6.00 15.00
DCRALW Luke Weaver/50 10.00 25.00
DCRALWE Luke Weaver/50 10.00 25.00
DCRAMM Manny Margot/40 8.00 20.00
DCRARH Ryon Healy/30 8.00 20.00
DCRARL Reynaldo Lopez/30 6.00 15.00
DCRATG Tyler Glasnow/50 20.00 50.00
DCRATGL Tyler Glasnow/50 20.00 50.00
DCRATM Trey Mancini/30 15.00 40.00
DCRAYG Yulieski Gurriel/50 12.00 30.00
DCRAYGU Yulieski Gurriel/50 12.00 30.00
DCRAYMO Yoan Moncada/50 30.00 80.00

2018 Topps Definitive Collection Autograph Relics

RANDOM INSERTS IN PACKS
PRINT RUNS B/WN 5-30 COPIES PER
NO PRICING ON QTY 15 OR LESS
EXCHANGE DEADLINE 6/30/2020
ARCABE Andrew Benintendi EXCH
ARCABR Alex Bregman/30 30.00 80.00
ARCAJ Adam Jones/30 12.00 30.00
ARCARO Amed Rosario/30 RC 12.00 30.00
ARCARU Addison Russell/30 12.00 30.00
ARCAV Alex Verdugo/30 RC 10.00 25.00
ARCCF Clint Frazier/30 RC 12.00 30.00
ARCCS Chris Sale/30 15.00 40.00
ARCCSE Corey Seager/30 20.00 50.00
ARCDG Didi Gregorius/30 15.00 40.00
ARCDP Dustin Pedroia/30 20.00 50.00
ARCDS Dominic Smith/30 RC 8.00 20.00
ARCET Eric Thames/30 8.00 20.00
ARCFF Freddie Freeman
ARCFM Francisco Mejia/30 RC 12.00 30.00
ARCGSP George Springer/30 20.00 50.00
ARCIH Ian Happ/30 15.00 40.00
ARCJA Jose Altuve/30 15.00 40.00
ARCJB Javier Baez/30 40.00 100.00
ARCJC J.P. Crawford/30 RC 20.00 50.00
ARCJD Jacob deGrom
ARCKB Kris Bryant/5
ARCKS Kyle Schwarber/30 15.00 40.00
ARCLS Luis Severino/30 20.00 50.00
ARCMS Miguel Sano/30 8.00 20.00
ARCNS Noah Syndergaard/30 20.00 50.00
ARCPD Paul DeJong/30 10.00 25.00
ARCPG Paul Goldschmidt/30 30.00 80.00
ARCRD Rafael Devers/30 RC 20.00 50.00
ARCRH Rhys Hoskins/30 RC 15.00 40.00
ARCRM Ryan McMahon/30 RC 15.00 40.00
ARCSG Sonny Gray/30 10.00 25.00
ARCTM Trey Mancini/30 12.00 30.00
ARCVR Victor Robles/30 RC 25.00 60.00
ARCWCO Willson Contreras/30 20.00 50.00
ARCYC Yoenis Cespedes/20 8.00 20.00

2018 Topps Definitive Collection Autograph Relics Green

*GREEN/25: .4X TO 1X BASIC
RANDOM INSERTS IN PACKS
PRINT RUNS B/WN 10-25 COPIES PER
NO PRICING ON QTY 15 OR LESS
EXCHANGE DEADLINE 6/30/2020

2018 Topps Definitive Collection Autographs

RANDOM INSERTS IN PACKS
PRINT RUNS B/WN 5-35 COPIES PER
EXCHANGE DEADLINE 6/30/2020
DCAAR Anthony Rizzo/25 40.00 100.00
DCAARO Amed Rosario/35 15.00 40.00
DCABJ Bo Jackson/25 50.00 120.00
DCABL Barry Larkin/35 25.00 60.00
DCABP Buster Posey
DCACF Clint Frazier/35 30.00 80.00
DCACJ Chipper Jones/25 75.00 200.00
DCACK Clayton Kershaw/25 50.00 120.00
DCACSA Chris Sale/35 12.00 30.00
DCADM Don Mattingly/25 75.00 200.00
DCAFL Francisco Lindor/25 25.00 60.00
DCAFT Frank Thomas/35 30.00 80.00
DCAGS Gary Sanchez/25 50.00 120.00
DCAGSP George Springer/35 12.00 30.00
DCAIABR Alex Bregman/35 50.00 120.00
DCAIAP Andy Pettitte/35 15.00 40.00
DCAIBW Bernie Williams/25 40.00 100.00
DCAIEM Edgar Martinez/25 25.00 60.00
DCAIJA Jose Altuve/25 150.00 300.00
DCAIJD Johnny Damon/25 25.00 60.00
DCAING Nomar Garciaparra/35 30.00 80.00
DCAIOC Orlando Cepeda/35 10.00 25.00
DCAITGL Tom Glavine/35 25.00 40.00
DCAJS John Smoltz/35 25.00 60.00
DCAKB Kris Bryant EXCH 125.00 300.00
DCAMM Manny Machado/25 40.00 100.00
DCAMS Miguel Sano/35 10.00 25.00
DCANR Nolan Ryan
DCANS Noah Syndergaard/25 25.00 60.00
DCAOS Ozzie Smith/35 25.00 60.00
DCARA Roberto Alomar/25 30.00 80.00
DCARD Rafael Devers/35 40.00 100.00
DCARHO Rhys Hoskins/35 30.00 80.00
DCARS Ryne Sandberg/25 75.00 200.00
DCARY Robin Yount/25 40.00 100.00
DCAWB Wade Boggs/25

2018 Topps Definitive Collection Definitive Autograph Relics

RANDOM INSERTS IN PACKS
PRINT RUNS B/WN 5-40 COPIES PER
NO PRICING ON QTY 15 OR LESS
EXCHANGE DEADLINE 6/30/2020
DCARAD Andre Dawson/40 20.00 50.00
DCARAK Al Kaline/40 30.00 80.00
DCARAP Andy Pettitte/40 20.00 50.00
DCARAR Anthony Rizzo/35 25.00 60.00
DCARAROS Amed Rosario/40 20.00 50.00
DCARBJ Bo Jackson/35 40.00 100.00
DCARBL Barry Larkin/35 20.00 50.00
DCARCF Clint Frazier/40 12.00 30.00
DCARCJ Chipper Jones/35 40.00 100.00
DCARCK Clayton Kershaw/35 60.00 150.00
DCARCS Corey Seager/40 20.00 50.00
DCARDM Don Mattingly/35 30.00 80.00
DCARDP Dustin Pedroia/40 12.00 30.00
DCARFF Freddie Freeman/35 25.00 60.00
DCARFT Frank Thomas/40 30.00 80.00
DCARGS Gary Sanchez/40 30.00 80.00
DCARHA Hank Aaron
DCARIR Ivan Rodriguez/40 15.00 40.00
DCARJB Johnny Bench
DCARJC Jose Canseco/40 20.00 50.00
DCARJS John Smoltz/40 25.00 60.00
DCARJV Joey Votto/35 30.00 80.00
DCARKB Kris Bryant EXCH
DCARKS Kyle Schwarber/40 15.00 40.00
DCARMM Manny Machado/35 30.00 80.00
DCARMTR Mike Trout
DCARNG Nomar Garciaparra/40 10.00 25.00
DCARNS Noah Syndergaard/40 15.00 40.00
DCAROS Ozzie Smith/40 20.00 50.00
DCARRA Roberto Alomar/40 25.00 60.00
DCARRC Rod Carew/40 15.00 40.00
DCARRD Rafael Devers/40 20.00 50.00
DCARRS Ryne Sandberg/35 30.00 80.00
DCARRY Robin Yount/35 30.00 80.00
DCARSC Steve Carlton/40 15.00 40.00
DCARTG Tom Glavine/40 15.00 40.00
DCARWB Wade Boggs/35 15.00 40.00

2018 Topps Definitive Collection Dual Autograph Relics

RANDOM INSERTS IN PACKS
PRINT RUNS B/WN 10-35 COPIES PER
NO PRICING ON QTY 15 OR LESS
EXCHANGE DEADLINE 6/30/2020
DARCBA Altuve/Biggio EXCH 75.00 200.00
DARCBR Bryant/Rizzo EXCH 100.00 250.00
DARCBRO Beltre/IRod/25 50.00 120.00
DARCBT Thames/Braun/35 20.00 50.00
DARCBTR Bryant/Trout EXCH
DARCCB Contreras/Baez/35 40.00 100.00
DARCGRS Sancez/Gregorius EXCH 40.00 100.00
DARCGS Severino/Gray/35 10.00 25.00
DARCJM Mancini/Jones/35 30.00 80.00
DARCJSM Smoltz/Chipper/35 75.00 200.00
DARCPW Williams/Pettitte/35 40.00 100.00
DARCRS Rizzo/Schwarber EXCH 40.00 100.00
DARCRSM Amed Rosario Dominic Smith/35 12.00 30.00
DARCRUB Russell/Baez EXCH 40.00 100.00
DARCSAL Altuve/Springer/35 60.00 150.00
DARCSB Sandberg/Bryant EXCH
DARCSBU Byron Buxton Miguel Sano/35 15.00 40.00
DARCSD deGrom/Syndergaard/35 60.00 150.00
DARCSG Glavine/Smoltz/35 75.00 200.00
DARCSK Sale/Kimbrel/35 40.00 100.00
DARCSR Rosario/Sybdergaard/35 30.00 80.00
DARCSS Sanchez/Severino EXCH 40.00 100.00

2018 Topps Definitive Collection Dual Autographs

RANDOM INSERTS IN PACKS
PRINT RUNS B/WN 10-35 COPIES PER
NO PRICING ON QTY 15 OR LESS
EXCHANGE DEADLINE 6/30/2020
DACAL Lindor/Alomar/35 40.00 100.00
DACBB Biggio/Bagwell/35 60.00 150.00
DACBD Benintendi/Devers EXCH 25.00 60.00
DACBT Bryant/Trout EXCH
DACCB Buxton/Carew/25 25.00 60.00
DACCBA Baez/Contreras/35 75.00 200.00
DACFE Eckersley/Fingers/35 12.00 30.00
DACGS Severino/Gray/35 20.00 50.00
DACGSA Sanchez/Gregorius/35 15.00 40.00
DACHN Hoskins/Nola/35 60.00 150.00
DACJJ Jeter/Judge
DACJR Rivera/Jeter
DACJS Chipper/Smoltz/25 75.00 200.00
DACJUS Sanchez/Judge/35 200.00 400.00
DACKK Koufax/Kershaw
DACKL Kluber/Lindor/35 40.00 100.00
DACLV Larkin/Votto/30 50.00 120.00
DACPW Williams/Pettitte/35 15.00 40.00
DACRS Rizzo/Schwarber/35 25.00 60.00
DACRYS Ryan/Syndergaard/25 60.00 150.00
DACSA Altuve/Springer/35 30.00 80.00
DACSB Miguel Sano Byron Buxton/35 15.00 40.00
DACSBE Benintendi/Sale EXCH 50.00 120.00
DACSC Strawberry/Cespedes/35 25.00 60.00
DACSG Smoltz/Glavine/35 75.00 200.00
DACSGO Strawberry/Gooden/35 12.00 30.00
DACSR Syndergaard/Rosario/35 30.00 80.00
DACSS Sanchez/Severino EXCH 40.00 100.00
DACTH Harper/Trout
DACTKL Kluber/Thome EXCH 60.00 150.00

2018 Topps Definitive Collection Framed Autograph Patches

RANDOM INSERTS IN PACKS
PRINT RUNS B/WN 10-30 COPIES PER
NO PRICING ON QTY 15 OR LESS
EXCHANGE DEADLINE 6/30/2020
DFAPAJ Adam Jones/30 30.00 80.00
DFAPARO Amed Rosario/30 30.00 80.00
DFAPBB Byron Buxton/30 40.00 100.00
DFAPCF Clint Frazier/30 50.00 125.00
DFAPCS Chris Sale/30 25.00 60.00
DFAPCSE Corey Seager/30 50.00 120.00
DFAPDGR Didi Gregorius/30 30.00 80.00
DFAPFF Freddie Freeman/30 60.00 150.00
DFAPGSP George Springer/30 30.00 80.00
DFAPJA Jose Altuve/30 40.00 100.00
DFAPJB Javier Baez/20 75.00 200.00
DFAPJD Jacob deGrom/30 100.00 250.00
DFAPKB Kris Bryant EXCH
DFAPKS Kyle Schwarber/30 40.00 100.00
DFAPLS Luis Severino/30 30.00 80.00
DFAPMM Manny Machado/30 60.00 150.00
DFAPMS Miguel Sano/30 30.00 80.00
DFAPMT Masahiro Tanaka
DFAPNS Noah Syndergaard/30 30.00 80.00
DFAPPG Paul Goldschmidt/30 30.00 80.00
DFAPRD Rafael Devers/30 50.00 120.00
DFAPTMA Trey Mancini/30 30.00 80.00
DFAPWC Willson Contreras/30 60.00 150.00
DFAPYC Yoenis Cespedes 10.00 25.00

2018 Topps Definitive Collection Framed Autographs

RANDOM INSERTS IN PACKS
PRINT RUNS B/WN 5-30 COPIES PER
EXCHANGE DEADLINE 6/30/2020
DCFAAP Andy Pettitte/30 20.00 50.00
DCFAAR Anthony Rizzo/30 30.00 80.00
DCFAARO Amed Rosario/30 20.00 50.00
DCFABB Byron Buxton/30 12.00 30.00
DCFABJ Bo Jackson/25 50.00 210.00
DCFABL Barry Larkin/30 25.00 60.00
DCFACF Clint Frazier/30 15.00 40.00
DCFACK Clayton Kershaw/25
DCFACKL Corey Kluber/30 15.00 40.00
DCFACS Corey Seager/30 25.00 60.00
DCFADE Dennis Eckersley/30
DCFADM Don Mattingly/30 30.00 80.00
DCFAEM Edgar Martinez/30 20.00 50.00
DCFAFL Francisco Lindor/30 30.00 80.00
DCFAFT Frank Thomas/30 50.00 120.00
DCFAJA Jose Altuve/30 25.00 60.00
DCFAJBA Javier Baez/30 40.00 100.00
DCFAJC Jose Canseco/30 30.00 80.00
DCFAJD Josh Donaldson/25 20.00 50.00
DCFAJDA Johnny Damon/30 10.00 25.00
DCFAJS John Smoltz/30 25.00 60.00
DCFAJT Jim Thome/25 25.00 120.00
DCFAJV Joey Votto/25 20.00 50.00
DCFAMM Manny Machado/25 40.00 100.00
DCFANS Noah Syndergaard/30 20.00 50.00
DCFAOS Ozzie Smith/30 40.00 100.00
DCFAPG Paul Goldschmidt/30 25.00 60.00
DCFARA Roberto Alomar/30 20.00 50.00
DCFARD Rafael Devers/30 25.00 60.00
DCFARHO Rhys Hoskins/30 40.00 100.00
DCFASO Shohei Ohtani/30 150.00 400.00
DCFATG Tom Glavine/30 15.00 40.00
DCFAVR Victor Robles/30 30.00 80.00

2018 Topps Definitive Collection Helmet Collection

RANDOM INSERTS IN PACKS
PRINT RUNS B/WN 45-50 COPIES PER
DHCBB Byron Buxton/50 12.00 30.00
DHCBC Brandon Crawford/50 12.00 30.00
DHCBG Brett Gardner/50 20.00 50.00
DHCJP Joc Pederson/50 20.00 50.00
DHCMM Manny Machado/50 20.00 50.00
DHCNS Noah Syndergaard/50 15.00 40.00
DHCRB Ryan Braun/45 12.00 30.00

2018 Topps Definitive Collection Jumbo Relics

RANDOM INSERTS IN PACKS
PRINT RUNS B/WN 20-50 COPIES PER
*BLUE/20-25: .6X TO 1.5X p/r 40-50
*BLUE/20-25: .5X TO 1.2X p/r 30
*BLUE/20-25: .4X TO 1X p/r 20-25
DJRCAB Andrew Benintendi/40 12.00 30.00
DJRCABE Andrew Benintendi/40 12.00 30.00
DJRCAM Andrew McCutchen/50 12.00 30.00
DJRCAN Aaron Nola/30 15.00 40.00
DJRCAP Albert Pujols/30 10.00 25.00
DJRCAPU Albert Pujols/50 8.00 20.00
DJRCAR Amed Rosario/30 6.00 15.00
DJRCAW Adam Wainwright/30 8.00 20.00
DJRCAWA Adam Wainwright/50 6.00 15.00
DJRCBG Brett Gardner/25 12.00 30.00
DJRCBP Buster Posey/30 12.00 30.00
DJRCCB Charlie Blackmon/45 6.00 15.00
DJRCCC Carlos Correa/30 8.00 20.00
DJRCCK Clayton Kershaw/30 10.00 25.00
DJRCCKI Craig Kimbrel/30 12.00 30.00
DJRCCM Carlos Martinez/40 5.00 12.00
DJRCCS Corey Seager/30 8.00 20.00
DJRCCY Christian Yelich/30 10.00 25.00
DJRCDB Dellin Betances/30 6.00 15.00
DJRCDGR Didi Gregorius/25 8.00 20.00
DJRCDK Dallas Keuchel/25 8.00 20.00
DJRCDP Dustin Pedroia/30 8.00 20.00
DJRCEH Eric Hosmer/50 5.00 12.00
DJRCEI Ender Inciarte/50 4.00 10.00
DJRCET Eric Thames/20 10.00 25.00
DJRCHR Hanley Ramirez/20 8.00 20.00
DJRCHRY Hyun-Jin Ryu/50 5.00 12.00
DJRCJA Jose Altuve/50 5.00 12.00
DJRCJB Josh Bell/50 12.00 30.00
DJRCJBR Jackie Bradley Jr./30 8.00 20.00
DJRCJH Josh Harrison/30 8.00 20.00
DJRCJHA Josh Harrison/50 6.00 15.00
DJRCJHE Jason Heyward/30 12.00 30.00
DJRCJV Joey Votto/50 10.00 25.00
DJRCKD Khris Davis/20 10.00 25.00
DJRCKS Kyle Schwarber/20 15.00 40.00
DJRCMC Miguel Cabrera/50 6.00 15.00
DJRCMCA Miguel Cabrera/50 6.00 15.00
DJRCMCO Michael Conforto/50 5.00 12.00
DJRCMM Manny Machado/50 15.00 40.00
DJRCMT Masahiro Tanaka/20 12.00 30.00
DJRCNC Nelson Cruz/50 6.00 15.00
DJRCNS Noah Syndergaard/50 5.00 12.00
DJRCRB Ryan Braun/20 8.00 20.00
DJRCRC Robinson Cano/50 5.00 12.00
DJRCRZ Ryan Zimmerman/50 5.00 12.00
DJRCSST Stephen Strasburg/30 12.00 30.00
DJRCTS Trevor Story/25 15.00 40.00
DJRCTT Trea Turner/30 8.00 20.00
DJRCYG Yuli Gurriel/50 5.00 12.00
DJRCYM Yadier Molina/40 12.00 30.00

2018 Topps Definitive Collection Legendary Autographs

RANDOM INSERTS IN PACKS
PRINT RUNS B/WN 5-35 COPIES PER
NO PRICING ON QTY 15 OR LESS
EXCHANGE DEADLINE 6/30/2020
DCLAAD Andre Dawson/35 12.00 30.00
DCLAAK Al Kaline/35 25.00 50.00
DCLAAP Andy Pettitte/35 20.00 50.00
DCLAAR Alex Rodriguez
DCLABJ Bo Jackson/25 40.00 100.00
DCLABL Barry Larkin/35 20.00 50.00
DCLABW Bernie Williams/35 40.00 100.00
DCLACJ Chipper Jones/25 40.00 100.00
DCLADE Dennis Eckersley/35 12.00 30.00
DCLADM Don Mattingly/35 30.00 80.00
DCLAEM Edgar Martinez/35 12.00 30.00
DCLAFT Frank Thomas/35 30.00 80.00
DCLAGM Greg Maddux
DCLAI Ichiro
DCLAJD Johnny Damon/35 12.00 30.00
DCLAJP Jim Palmer/35 12.00 30.00
DCLAJS John Smoltz/35 20.00 50.00
DCLALB Lou Brock/35 15.00 40.00
DCLANG Nomar Garciaparra/35 12.00 30.00
DCLAOC Orlando Cepeda/30 12.00 30.00
DCLAOS Ozzie Smith/35 25.00 60.00
DCLARA Roberto Alomar/35 15.00 40.00
DCLARC Rod Carew/35 15.00 40.00
DCLARH Rickey Henderson/25 50.00 120.00
DCLARS Ryne Sandberg/25 50.00 120.00
DCLARY Robin Yount/25 40.00 100.00
DCLASC Steve Carlton/35 20.00 50.00
DCLATG Tom Glavine/35 12.00 30.00
DCLAWB Wade Boggs/25 25.00 60.00

2018 Topps Definitive Collection Rookie Autographs

RANDOM INSERTS IN PACKS
PRINT RUNS B/WN 30-50 COPIES PER
EXCHANGE DEADLINE 6/30/2020
*GREEN/25: .5X TO 1.2X BASIC
DRAAB Anthony Banda/50 4.00 10.00
DRAAH Austin Hays/50 6.00 15.00
DRAAHA Austin Hays/50 6.00 15.00
DRAAR Amed Rosario/50 5.00 12.00
DRAARO Amed Rosario/50 5.00 12.00
DRAAV Alex Verdugo/50 12.00 30.00
DRAAVE Alex Verdugo/50 12.00 30.00
DRABW Brandon Woodruff/50 12.00 30.00
DRACF Clint Frazier/50 12.00 30.00
DRACFR Clint Frazier/50 12.00 30.00
DRACS Chance Sisco/50 5.00 12.00
DRADF Dustin Fowler/50 6.00 15.00
DRADS Dominic Smith/30 5.00 12.00
DRADSM Dominic Smith/30 5.00 12.00
DRAFM Francisco Mejia/50 12.00 30.00
DRAFME Francisco Mejia/50 12.00 30.00
DRAHB Harrison Bader/50 6.00 15.00
DRAHBA Harrison Bader/50 6.00 15.00
DRAJCR J.P. Crawford/50 6.00 15.00
DRAJD J.D. Davis/50 5.00 12.00
DRAJF Jack Flaherty/50 15.00 40.00
DRAJFL Jack Flaherty/50 15.00 40.00
DRAJPC J.P. Crawford/50 6.00 15.00
DRALS Lucas Sims/50 4.00 10.00
DRAMA Miguel Andujar/50 40.00 100.00
DRAND Nicky Delmonico/50 4.00 10.00
DRAOA Ozzie Albies/50 30.00 80.00
DRAOAL Ozzie Albies/50 30.00 80.00
DRARD Rafael Devers/50 20.00 50.00
DRARDE Rafael Devers/50 20.00 50.00
DRARH Rhys Hoskins/50 40.00 100.00
DRARHO Rhys Hoskins/50 40.00 100.00
DRARM Ryan McMahon/50 10.00 25.00
DRARMC Ryan McMahon/50 10.00 25.00
DRASO Shohei Ohtani/50 400.00 800.00
DRATM Tyler Mahle/50 6.00 15.00
DRATMA Tyler Mahle/50 6.00 15.00
DRAVR Victor Robles/50 20.00 50.00
DRAVRO Victor Robles/50 20.00 50.00
DRAWB Walker Buehler/50 25.00 60.00
DRAWBU Walker Buehler/50 25.00 60.00
DRAZG Zack Granite/50 4.00 10.00

2019 Topps Definitive Collection Autograph Relics

RANDOM INSERTS IN PACKS
PRINT RUNS B/WN 5-50 COPIES PER
NO PRICING ON QTY 15 OR LESS
EXCHANGE DEADLINE 5/31/2021
ARCALB Alex Bregman/50 20.00 50.00
ARCAR Anthony Rizzo/35 40.00 100.00
ARCCS Chris Sale/50 20.00 50.00
ARCDG Didi Gregorius/50 15.00 40.00
ARCDP Dustin Pedroia/50 10.00 25.00
ARCFF Freddie Freeman/50 30.00 80.00
ARCFL Francisco Lindor/50 20.00 50.00
ARCGS George Springer/50 15.00 40.00
ARCGSA Gary Sanchez/35 25.00 60.00
ARCGT Gleyber Torres/50 40.00 100.00
ARCJA Jose Altuve/35 30.00 80.00
ARCJBA Javier Baez/50 40.00 100.00
ARCJD Jacob deGrom/50 25.00 60.00
ARCJS Juan Soto/50 30.00 80.00
ARCJU Justin Upton/50 10.00 25.00
ARCJUS Justus Sheffield RC/50 10.00 25.00
ARCJV Joey Votto/35 20.00 50.00
ARCKS Kyle Schwarber/50 15.00 40.00
ARCKT Kyle Tucker RC/50 15.00 40.00
ARCLS Luis Severino/50 12.00 30.00
ARCMAN Miguel Andujar/50 10.00 25.00
ARCMCH Matt Chapman/50 12.00 30.00
ARCMMI Miles Mikolas/35 10.00 25.00
ARCNS Noah Syndergaard/50 12.00 30.00
ARCOA Ozzie Albies/50 15.00 40.00
ARCPG Paul Goldschmidt/50 15.00 40.00
ARCRA Ronald Acuna Jr./50 60.00 150.00
ARCRD Rafael Devers/35 15.00 40.00
ARCRH Rhys Hoskins/50 20.00 50.00
ARCSP Salvador Perez/50 10.00 25.00
ARCWC Willson Contreras/50 8.00 20.00
ARCYM Yadier Molina/50 30.00 80.00

2019 Topps Definitive Collection Autograph Relics Green

*GREEN/25: .5X TO 1.2X BASIC
RANDOM INSERTS IN PACKS
PRINT RUNS B/WN 10-25 COPIES PER
NO PRICING ON QTY 15 OR LESS
EXCHANGE DEADLINE 5/31/2021
ARCBSN Blake Snell/25 20.00 50.00
ARCIH Ian Happ/25 10.00 25.00
ARCKD Khris Davis/25 15.00 40.00
ARCMAT Matt Carpenter/25 12.00 30.00
ARCMH Mitch Haniger/25 20.00 50.00
ARCMO Marcell Ozuna/25 12.00 30.00

2019 Topps Definitive Collection Autographs

RANDOM INSERTS IN PACKS
PRINT RUNS B/WN 5-25 COPIES PER
NO PRICING ON QTY 10 OR LESS
EXCHANGE DEADLINE 5/31/2021
DCAABR Alex Bregman/25 30.00 80.00
DCAAP Andy Pettitte/25 15.00 40.00
DCAAR Anthony Rizzo/25 75.00 200.00
DCABG Bob Gibson/25 25.00 60.00
DCABL Barry Larkin/25 40.00 100.00
DCACR Cal Ripken Jr.
DCADE Dennis Eckersley/25 15.00 40.00
DCADM Don Mattingly/25 30.00 80.00
DCAEJ Eloy Jimenez/25 40.00 100.00
DCAFF Freddie Freeman/25 60.00 150.00
DCAFL Francisco Lindor/25 20.00 50.00
DCAFT Frank Thomas/25 40.00 100.00
DCAJA Jose Altuve/25 25.00 60.00
DCAJR Jose Ramirez/25 12.00 30.00
DCAJS Juan Soto/25 75.00 200.00
DCAJSM John Smoltz/25 30.00 80.00
DCAJV Joey Votto
DCAMMA Manny Machado EXCH
DCANS Noah Syndergaard/25 8.00 20.00
DCAOA Ozzie Albies/25 75.00 200.00
DCAOS Ozzie Smith/25 30.00 80.00
DCAPG Paul Goldschmidt/25 25.00 60.00
DCARA Roberto Alomar/25 25.00 60.00
DCARAJ Ronald Acuna Jr./25 60.00 150.00
DCARH Rhys Hoskins/25 60.00 150.00
DCARJO Randy Johnson
DCAVG Vladimir Guerrero/25 40.00 100.00
DCAVGJ Vladimir Guerrero Jr./25 300.00 600.00
DCAWC Will Clark/25 30.00 80.00
DCAYM Yadier Molina/25 30.00 80.00

2019 Topps Definitive Collection Defining Moments Autographs

RANDOM INSERTS IN PACKS
PRINT RUNS B/WN 5-30 COPIES PER
NO PRICING ON QTY 19 OR LESS
EXCHANGE DEADLINE 5/31/2021
DMACBW Bernie Williams/22 30.00 80.00
DMACDO David Ortiz/20 30.00 80.00
DMACDS Darryl Strawberry/25 20.00 50.00
DMACNG Nomar Garciaparra/30 20.00 50.00
DMACRA Roberto Alomar/30 20.00 50.00
DMACWC Will Clark/29 20.00 50.00

2019 Topps Definitive Collection Definitive Autograph Relics

RANDOM INSERTS IN PACKS
PRINT RUNS B/WN 10-50 COPIES PER
NO PRICING ON QTY 10 OR LESS
EXCHANGE DEADLINE 5/31/2021
DARCAD Andre Dawson/50 20.00 50.00
DARCAK Al Kaline/50 30.00 80.00
DARCAP Andy Pettitte/50 20.00 50.00
DARCBGI Bob Gibson/50 40.00 100.00
DARCBL Barry Larkin/50 25.00 60.00
DARCBO Bo Jackson/25 40.00 100.00
DARCBW Bernie Williams/50 20.00 50.00
DARCCF Carlton Fisk/50 20.00 50.00
DARCCJ Chipper Jones/50 60.00 150.00
DARCCR Cal Ripken Jr./25 40.00 100.00
DARCCY Carl Yastrzemski/25 50.00 120.00
DARCDM Dale Murphy/50 15.00 40.00
DARCDMA Don Mattingly/50 40.00 100.00
DARCDO David Ortiz/25 25.00 60.00
DARCFM Fred McGriff/50 20.00 50.00
DARCFT Frank Thomas/50 25.00 60.00
DARCHM Hideki Matsui/25 75.00 200.00
DARCICH Ichiro
DARCIR Ivan Rodriguez/50 15.00 40.00
DARCJB Johnny Bench/25 50.00 120.00
DARCJC Jose Canseco/50 25.00 60.00
DARCJD Johnny Damon/50 15.00 40.00
DARCJMA Juan Marichal/50 25.00 60.00
DARCJP Jorge Posada/50 25.00 60.00
DARCJS John Smoltz/50 20.00 50.00
DARCKB Kris Bryant/50 40.00 100.00
DARCMM Mark McGwire/25 30.00 80.00
DARCMP Mike Piazza/10 40.00 100.00
DARCNG Nomar Garciaparra/50 20.00 50.00
DARCNR Nolan Ryan/25 75.00 200.00
DARCOS Ozzie Smith/50 30.00 80.00
DARCRA Roberto Alomar/50 15.00 40.00
DARCRCA Rod Carew/50 20.00 50.00
DARCRH Rickey Henderson/25 40.00 100.00
DARCRJ Reggie Jackson/25 40.00 100.00
DARCRS Ryne Sandberg/50 30.00 80.00
DARCRY Robin Yount/50 25.00 60.00
DARCSC Steve Carlton/50 25.00 60.00
DARCTG Tom Glavine/50 15.00 40.00

DARCTR Tim Raines/50 15.00 40.00
DARCWB Wade Boggs/50 20.00 50.00
DARCWC Will Clark/50 25.00 60.00

2019 Topps Definitive Collection Dual Autograph Relics

RANDOM INSERTS IN PACKS
PRINT RUNS B/WN 10-35 COPIES PER
NO PRICING ON QTY 15 OR LESS
EXCHANGE DEADLINE 5/31/2021
DARAA Acuna Jr./Albies/35 125.00 300.00
DARAP Pettitte/Posada/35 40.00 100.00
DARAR Rodriguez/Beltre EXCH 25.00 60.00
DARBA Altuve/Bregman EXCH 60.00 150.00
DARBR Rizzo/Bryant EXCH 100.00 250.00
DARCH Hunter/Carew/35 30.00 80.00
DARGB Springer/Bregman/35 50.00 120.00
DARGS Smith/Gibson/35 75.00 200.00
DARHU Hunter/Upton/35 30.00 80.00
DARIM Rodriguez/Molina/35 60.00 150.00
DARJA Acuna Jr./Jones/35 100.00 250.00
DARLR Lindor/Ramirez/35 25.00 60.00
DARMS Murphy/Smoltz/35 30.00 80.00
DAROM Molina/Smith/35 75.00 200.00
DARPS Pedroia/Sale/35 15.00 40.00
DARRC Hoskins/Carlton/35 40.00 100.00
DARRS Schwarber/Rizzo/35 30.00 80.00
DARSD deGrom/Syndergaard/35 125.00 300.00
DARSM McGriff/Smoltz/35 40.00 100.00
DARSR Soto/Robles/35 60.00 150.00
DARTF Yastrzemski/Fisk/35 75.00 200.00
DARTS Pedroia/Sale/35 40.00 100.00

2019 Topps Definitive Collection Dual Autographs

RANDOM INSERTS IN PACKS
PRINT RUNS B/WN 10-35 COPIES PER
NO PRICING ON QTY 15 OR LESS
EXCHANGE DEADLINE 5/31/2021
DACAA Albies/Acuna Jr./35 100.00 250.00
DACBR Bryant/Rizzo EXCH 75.00 200.00
DACBS Baez/Schwarber/35 40.00 100.00
DACCG Guerrero/Carew/25 40.00 100.00
DACCM McGwire/Clark/35 75.00 200.00
DACDG Guerrero/Dawson/35 40.00 100.00
DACGB Brock/Gibson/35 75.00 200.00
DACGG Guerrero Jr./Guerrero/35 150.00 400.00
DACGR Rodriguez/Molina/35 50.00 120.00
DACHC Henderson/Canseco/35 60.00 150.00
DACJA Jones/Albies/35 50.00 120.00
DACJG Jones/Glavine/25 75.00 200.00
DACJT Torres/Judge/25 125.00 300.00
DACKM Kershaw/Machado EXCH
DACLR Lindor/Ramirez/35 25.00 60.00
DACMJ Jones/Murphy/35 75.00 200.00
DACMS Martinez/Sale/25 40.00 100.00
DACPS Sale/Pedroia/35 30.00 80.00
DACRA Altuve/Ryan/25 60.00 150.00
DACRG Gonzalez/Rodriguez/25 30.00 80.00
DACSB Bregman/Springer/35 40.00 100.00
DACSD Syndergaard/deGrom/35 60.00 15.00
DACSM Smith/Molina EXCH 75.00 200.00
DACSR Soto/Robles/35 50.00 120.00
DACTS Severino/Torres/35 40.00 100.00
DACWP Williams/Posada/35 50.00 120.00
DACYF Fisk/Yastrzemski/25 75.00 200.00

2019 Topps Definitive Collection Framed Autograph Patches

RANDOM INSERTS IN PACKS
PRINT RUNS B/WN 5-30 COPIES PER
NO PRICING ON QTY 15 OR LESS
EXCHANGE DEADLINE 5/31/2021
FACAJ Aaron Judge
FACDP Dustin Pedroia/30 20.00 50.00
FACFF Freddie Freeman/30 50.00 125.00
FACFL Francisco Lindor
FACGSP George Springer/30 25.00 60.00
FACJA Jose Altuve/30 50.00 125.00
FACJD Jacob deGrom/30 50.00 120.00
FACJV Joey Votto/30 40.00 100.00
FACKD Khris Davis/30 15.00 40.00
FACKS Kyle Schwarber/30 25.00 60.00
FACLS Luis Severino/30 12.00 30.00
FACMC Matt Carpenter/30 15.00 40.00
FACNS Noah Syndergaard/30
FACSP Salvador Perez/30 12.00 30.00
FACWC Willson Contreras/30 30.00 80.00

2019 Topps Definitive Collection Framed Autographs

RANDOM INSERTS IN PACKS
PRINT RUNS B/WN 5-30 COPIES PER
NO PRICING ON QTY 15 OR LESS
EXCHANGE DEADLINE 5/31/2021
DCFAABR Alex Bregman/25 30.00 80.00
DCFAAR Anthony Rizzo/25 75.00 200.00
DCFABG Bob Gibson/25 25.00 60.00
DCFABL Barry Larkin/30 20.00 50.00
DCFADE Dennis Eckersley/30 15.00 40.00
DCFADM Don Mattingly/25 40.00 100.00
DCFAEJ Eloy Jimenez/25 40.00 100.00
DCFAFL Francisco Lindor/25 20.00 50.00
DCFAFT Frank Thomas/25 40.00 100.00
DCFAGT Gleyber Torres/30 50.00 120.00
DCFAJA Jose Altuve/25 25.00 60.00
DCFAJBE Johnny Bench/30 40.00 100.00
DCFAJR Jose Ramirez/25 12.00 30.00
DCFAJS Juan Soto/30 60.00 150.00
DCFAJV Joey Votto/25 25.00 60.00
DCFAMM Manny Machado EXCH 30.00 80.00
DCFAOS Ozzie Smith/30 30.00 80.00
DCFAPG Paul Goldschmidt/30 25.00 60.00
DCFARA Roberto Alomar/30 20.00 50.00
DCFARAJ Ronald Acuna Jr./30 60.00 150.00
DCFARH Rhys Hoskins/30 40.00 100.00
DCFARS Ryne Sandberg/30 40.00 100.00
DCFAVG Vladimir Guerrero/25 40.00 100.00
DCFAVGJ Vladimir Guerrero Jr. EXCH 300.00 600.00
DCFAWC Will Clark/30 30.00 80.00
DCFAYK Yusei Kikuchi EXCH 25.00 60.00
DCFAYM Yadier Molina/30 30.00 80.00

2019 Topps Definitive Collection Helmets

RANDOM INSERTS IN PACKS
PRINT RUNS B/WN 25-35 COPIES PER
EXCHANGE DEADLINE 5/31/2021
DHCFL Francisco Lindor/25
DHCGS Gary Sanchez/25 30.00 80.00
DHCJA Jose Altuve/25 25.00 60.00
DHCJD Jacob deGrom/35 15.00 40.00
DHCKD Khris Davis/25
DHCMC Matt Chapman/25 20.00 50.00
DHCMCA Matt Carpenter/25 15.00 40.00
DHCRH Rhys Hoskins/35 25.00 60.00
DHCWC Willson Contreras/35 20.00 50.00
DHCYM Yadier Molina/35 40.00 100.00

2019 Topps Definitive Collection Jumbo Relics

RANDOM INSERTS IN PACKS
PRINT RUNS B/WN 20-50 COPIES PER
*BLUE/20: .6X TO 1.5X p/r 35-50
*BLUE/20: .4X TO 1X p/r 20
DJRCAB Andrew Benintendi/50 6.00 15.00
DJRCAM Andrew McCutchen/35 12.00 30.00
DJRCBP Buster Posey/35 10.00 25.00
DJRCCB Cody Bellinger/50 20.00 50.00
DJRCCBL Charlie Blackmon/35 6.00 15.00
DJRCCC Carlos Correa/50 10.00 25.00
DJRCDB Dellin Betances/35 5.00 12.00
DJRCDG Dee Gordon/35 8.00 20.00
DJRCDK Dallas Keuchel/35 5.00 12.00
DJRCDO David Ortiz/50 10.00 25.00
DJRCDP Dustin Pedroia/35 6.00 15.00
DJRCDPR David Price/35 5.00 12.00
DJRCDS Dansby Swanson/35 20.00 50.00
DJRCEE Edwin Encarnacion/35 6.00 15.00
DJRCEH Eric Hosmer/35 8.00 20.00
DJRCEL Evan Longoria/35 10.00 25.00
DJRCFFR Freddie Freeman/50 25.00 60.00
DJRCFFRE Freddie Freeman/35 25.00 60.00
DJRCFL Francisco Lindor/35 10.00 25.00
DJRCGSP George Springer/50 10.00 25.00
DJRCJAB Jose Abreu/20 15.00 40.00
DJRCJH Jason Heyward/35 5.00 12.00
DJRCJM J.D. Martinez/50 6.00 15.00
DJRCJP Joc Pederson/35 10.00 25.00
DJRCJR Jose Ramirez/35 5.00 12.00
DJRCJT Jameson Taillon/35 5.00 12.00
DJRCJV Joey Votto/35 10.00 25.00
DJRCKB Kris Bryant/50 12.00 30.00
DJRCKD Khris Davis/35 6.00 15.00
DJRCKS Kyle Schwarber/35 8.00 20.00
DJRCLS Luis Severino/35 5.00 12.00
DJRCMB Mookie Betts/50 12.00 30.00
DJRCMCA Miguel Cabrera/35 20.00 50.00
DJRCMCH Matt Chapman/35 6.00 15.00
DJRCMCO Michael Conforto/35 5.00 12.00
DJRCMO Marcell Ozuna/50 6.00 15.00
DJRCMS Max Scherzer/35 12.00 30.00
DJRCNA Nolan Arenado/50 12.00 30.00
DJRCNAR Nolan Arenado/35 12.00 30.00
DJRCNC Nicholas Castellanos/35 6.00 15.00
DJRCNM Nomar Mazara/35 4.00 10.00
DJRCPD Paul DeJong/50 6.00 15.00
DJRCPG Paul Goldschmidt/50 10.00 25.00
DJRCRB Ryan Braun/35 10.00 25.00
DJRCRD Rafael Devers/50 8.00 20.00
DJRCRH Rhys Hoskins/50 8.00 20.00
DJRCRZ Ryan Zimmerman/35 5.00 12.00
DJRCSG Scooter Gennett/35 10.00 25.00
DJRCTM Trey Mancini/35 8.00 20.00
DJRCTS Trevor Story/35 8.00 20.00
DJRCTT Trea Turner/35 5.00 12.00
DJRCWC Willson Contreras/35 15.00 40.00
DJRCWM Whit Merrifield/35 15.00 40.00
DJRCXB Xander Bogaerts/35 12.00 30.00
DJRCYM Yoan Moncada/35 6.00 15.00
DJRCYMO Yadier Molina/35 10.00 25.00
DJRCZG Zack Greinke/35 8.00 20.00

2019 Topps Definitive Collection Legendary Autographs

RANDOM INSERTS IN PACKS
PRINT RUNS B/WN 5-25 COPIES PER
NO PRICING ON QTY 10 OR LESS
EXCHANGE DEADLINE 5/31/2021
LACAD Andre Dawson/25 12.00 30.00
LACAK Al Kaline/25 50.00 120.00
LACAP Andy Pettitte/25 15.00 40.00
LACBG Bob Gibson/25 25.00 60.00
LACBJA Bo Jackson/25 40.00 100.00
LACCJ Chipper Jones/25 60.00 150.00
LACCR Cal Ripken Jr./25 50.00 120.00
LACDE Dennis Eckersley/25 15.00 40.00
LACDM Dale Murphy/25 40.00 100.00
LACDMA Don Mattingly/25 40.00 100.00
LACDO David Ortiz/25 40.00 100.00
LACFM Fred McGriff/25 20.00 50.00
LACFT Frank Thomas/25 40.00 100.00
LACHM Hideki Matsui/25 60.00 150.00
LACJB Johnny Bench/25 30.00 80.00
LACJM Juan Marichal/25 20.00 50.00
LACLB Lou Brock/25 20.00 50.00
LACMMC Mark McGwire/25 40.00 100.00
LACNR Nolan Ryan/25 50.00 120.00
LACOS Ozzie Smith/25 25.00 60.00
LACRA Roberto Alomar/25 15.00 40.00
LACRC Rod Carew/25 20.00 50.00
LACRH Rickey Henderson/25 30.00 80.00
LACRJA Reggie Jackson/25 25.00 60.00
LACRS Ryne Sandberg/25 25.00 60.00
LACRY Robin Yount/25 20.00 50.00
LACSC Steve Carlton/25 15.00 40.00
LACWB Wade Boggs/25 25.00 60.00
LACWC Will Clark/25 25.00 60.00

2019 Topps Definitive Collection Rookie Autographs

RANDOM INSERTS IN PACKS
STATED PRINT RUN 50 SER.#'d SETS
EXCHANGE DEADLINE 5/31/2021
*GREEN/25: .5X TO 1.2X BASIC
DRABL Brandon Lowe 10.00 25.00
DRACA Chance Adams 8.00 20.00
DRACAD Chance Adams 8.00 20.00
DRACBU Corbin Burnes 12.00 30.00
DRACM Cedric Mullins 6.00 15.00
DRACMU Cedric Mullins 6.00 15.00
DRACS Christin Stewart 12.00 30.00
DRACST Christin Stewart 12.00 30.00
DRADJ Danny Jansen 8.00 20.00
DRADJA Danny Jansen 8.00 20.00
DRAELJ Eloy Jimenez 30.00 80.00
DRAFTJ Fernando Tatis Jr. EXCH 125.00 300.00
DRAJB Jake Bauers 6.00 15.00
DRAJM Jeff McNeil 12.00 30.00
DRAJMC Jeff McNeil 12.00 30.00
DRAJS Justus Sheffield 8.00 20.00
DRAJUS Justus Sheffield 8.00 20.00
DRAKA Kolby Allard 6.00 15.00
DRAKOA Kolby Allard 6.00 15.00
DRAKT Kyle Tucker 20.00 50.00
DRAKW Kyle Wright 6.00 15.00
DRAKWR Kyle Wright 6.00 15.00
DRAKYT Kyle Tucker 20.00 50.00
DRALU Luis Urias 30.00 80.00
DRALUR Luis Urias 30.00 80.00
DRAMIK Michael Kopech 15.00 40.00
DRAMK Michael Kopech 15.00 40.00
DRAPA Peter Alonso EXCH 75.00 200.00
DRARL Ramon Laureano 20.00 50.00
DRARO Ryan O'Hearn 4.00 10.00
DRASD Steven Duggar 10.00 25.00
DRATT Touki Toussaint 5.00 12.00
DRATTO Touki Toussaint 5.00 12.00
DRAVGJ Vladimir Guerrero Jr. 200.00 400.00
DRAYK Yusei Kikuchi EXCH 30.00 80.00

2020 Topps Definitive Collection Autograph Relics

RANDOM INSERTS IN PACKS
PRINT RUN BTW 15-50 COPIES PER
NO PRICING QTY 15 OR LESS
EXCHANGE DEADLINE 3/31/2022
ARCAN Aaron Nola/30 20.00 50.00
ARCBB Bo Bichette/50 RC 50.00 125.00
ARCBM Brendan McKay/30 RC 15.00 40.00
ARCCS CC Sabathia/30 25.00 60.00
ARCCY Christian Yelich/30 60.00 150.00
ARCDS Dansby Swanson/30 15.00 40.00
ARCGS George Springer/30 20.00 50.00
ARCGT Gleyber Torres/30 75.00 200.00
ARCJA Jose Altuve/30 20.00 50.00
ARCJD Jacob deGrom/30 50.00 120.00
ARCJS Juan Soto/50 50.00 120.00
ARCKH Keston Hiura/30 25.00 60.00
ARCNS Nick Senzel/30 15.00 40.00
ARCPA Pete Alonso/50 50.00 120.00
ARCPC Patrick Corbin/30 12.00 30.00
ARCPG Paul Goldschmidt/30 20.00 50.00
ARCRA Ronald Acuna Jr./30 150.00 400.00
ARCRD Rafael Devers/50 20.00 50.00
ARCRH Rhys Hoskins/30 40.00 100.00
ARCWB Walker Buehler/30 25.00 60.00
ARCWC Willson Contreras/30 20.00 50.00
ARCWM Whit Merrifield/30 12.00 30.00
ARCXB Xander Bogaerts/30 25.00 60.00
ARCYA Yordan Alvarez/50 RC 60.00 150.00
ARCCKI Carter Kieboom/30 15.00 40.00
ARCCSA Chris Sale/30 12.00 30.00
ARCFTJ Fernando Tatis Jr./50 75.00 200.00
ARCJDM J.D. Martinez/30 20.00 50.00
ARCMCA Miguel Cabrera/30 100.00 250.00
ARCMKE Max Kepler/30 25.00 60.00
ARCMTA Masahiro Tanaka EXCH/50 50.00 120.00
ARCMTE Mark Teixeira/30 30.00 80.00

2020 Topps Definitive Collection Autograph Relics Green

*GREEN: .5X TO 1.2X p/r 30-50
RANDOM INSERTS IN PACKS
STATED PRINT RUN 25 SER. #'d SETS
EXCHANGE DEADLINE 3/31/2022
ARCAN Aaron Nola 30.00 80.00
ARCDS Dansby Swanson 25.00 60.00
ARCGC Gerrit Cole 40.00 100.00
ARCPd Paul deJong
ARCRD Rafael Devers 30.00 80.00
ARCMKE Max Kepler 40.00 100.00

2020 Topps Definitive Collection Autograph Ultra Patches

DAUPPG Paul Goldschmidt/12
DAUPCCJ Chipper Jones/14
DAUPCCY Christian Yelich/10
DAUPCDO David Ortiz
DAUPCJS John Smoltz/13
DAUPCKH Keston Hiura/8
DAUPCMT Mike Trout/12
DAUPCRH Rhys Hoskins/12
DAUPCWB Walker Buehler/9
DAUPCXB Xander Bogaerts/14

2020 Topps Definitive Collection Autographs

RANDOM INSERTS IN PACKS
PRINT RUN BTW 5-50 COPIES PER
NO PRICING QTY 15 OR LESS
EXCHANGE DEADLINE 3/31/2022
DCAAP Andy Pettitte/25 40.00 100.00
DCAAR Anthony Rizzo/25 50.00 120.00
DCABB Bo Bichette/35 125.00 300.00
DCABL Barry Larkin/25 30.00 80.00
DCACC CC Sabathia/25 40.00 100.00
DCADE Dennis Eckersley/25 20.00 50.00
DCADM Dale Murphy/50 40.00 100.00
DCAEJ Pete Alonso/35 75.00 200.00
DCAFL Francisco Lindor/25 75.00 200.00
DCAFT Frank Thomas/35 50.00 120.00
DCAGS Fernando Tatis Jr./35 125.00 300.00
DCAJA Jose Altuve/25 40.00 100.00
DCAJS Juan Soto/35 150.00 400.00
DCAJT Jim Thome/50 30.00 80.00
DCALS Luis Severino/50 15.00 40.00
DCAOS Ozzie Smith/25 50.00 120.00
DCARA Roberto Alomar/25 30.00 80.00
DCARD Rafael Devers/35 25.00 60.00
DCARH Rhys Hoskins/25 50.00 120.00
DCARJ Reggie Jackson/25 40.00 100.00
DCASK Sandy Koufax
DCATG Tom Glavine/50 30.00 80.00
DCAVG Vladimir Guerrero/35 40.00 100.00
DCAWC Will Clark/35 30.00 80.00
DCAXB Xander Bogaerts/50 60.00 150.00
DCAABR Yordan Alvarez 75.00 200.00
DCACKL Christian Yelich/25 60.00 150.00
DCADMA Don Mattingly/35 60.00 150.00
DCAICH Ichiro/5
DCAJDE Jacob deGrom/50 200.00 500.00
DCAJSM John Smoltz/50 25.00 60.00
DCAMCA Miguel Cabrera/35 75.00 200.00
DCARAJ Ronald Acuna Jr./35 150.00 400.00

2020 Topps Definitive Collection Definitive Autograph Relics

RANDOM INSERTS IN PACKS
PRINT RUN BTW 5-50 COPIES PER
NO PRICING QTY 15 OR LESS
EXCHANGE DEADLINE 3/31/2022
DARCAN Andy Pettitte/50 30.00 80.00
DARCAP Andy Pettitte/50 30.00 80.00
DARCBL Barry Larkin/50 36.00 60.00
DARCBW Bernie Williams/50 30.00 80.00
DARCCF Carlton Fisk/25 30.00 80.00
DARCCJ Chipper Jones/25 75.00 200.00
DARCCR Cal Ripken Jr./25 50.00 120.00
DARCCY Carl Yastrzemski/25 40.00 100.00
DARCDM Don Mattingly/50 75.00 200.00
DARCDS Darryl Strawberry/50 25.00 60.00
DARCFM Fred McGriff/50 30.00 80.00
DARCFT Frank Thomas/50 40.00 100.00
DARCHM Hideki Matsui/25 40.00 100.00
DARCJB Johnny Bench/25 50.00 120.00
DARCJC Jose Canseco/50 30.00 80.00
DARCJP Jorge Posada/50 25.00 60.00
DARCJS John Smoltz/50 20.00 50.00
DARCJT Jim Thome/50 30.00 80.00
DARCMM Mark McGwire/25 50.00 120.00
DARCNG Nomar Garciaparra/50 25.00 60.00
DARCNR Nolan Ryan/25 100.00 250.00
DARCOS Ozzie Smith/50 30.00 80.00
DARCPM Pedro Martinez/25 50.00 120.00
DARCRA Roberto Alomar/50 20.00 50.00
DARCRH Rickey Henderson/25 50.00 120.00
DARCRJ Randy Johnson/25 50.00 120.00
DARCRS Ryne Sandberg/25 40.00 100.00
DARCRY Robin Yount/50 50.00 120.00
DARCSC Steve Carlton/50 25.00 60.00
DARCTG Tom Glavine/50 25.00 60.00
DARCTR Tim Raines/50 20.00 50.00
DARCVG Vladimir Guerrero/50 30.00 80.00
DARCWB Wade Boggs/25 30.00 80.00
DARCWC Will Clark/50 30.00 80.00
DARCCFI Carlton Fisk/50 25.00 60.00
DARCDMU Dale Murphy/50 25.00 60.00
DARCJBA Jeff Bagwell/50 30.00 80.00
DARCJTH Jim Thome/50 30.00 80.00
DARCNRY Nolan Ryan/25 100.00 250.00
DARCRCA Rod Carew/50 20.00 50.00
DARCRJA Reggie Jackson/25 40.00 100.00
DARCWBO Wade Boggs/25 30.00 80.00
DARCRCAR Rod Carew/50 20.00 50.00
DARCRJAC Reggie Jackson/25 40.00 100.00

2020 Topps Definitive Collection Dual Autograph Relics

RANDOM INSERTS IN PACKS
PRINT RUN BTW 10-35 COPIES PER
NO PRICING QTY 15 OR LESS
EXCHANGE DEADLINE 3/31/2022
DARAC G.Cole/J.Altuve 40.00 100.00
DARAR N.Arenado/B.Rodgers 60.00 150.00
DARAS G.Springer/J.Altuve 40.00 100.00
DARBB X.Bogaerts/A.Benintendi 75.00 200.00
DARDA P.Alonso/J.deGrom 200.00 500.00
DARDB R.Devers/X.Bogaerts 75.00 200.00
DARDF J.Flaherty/P.DeJong 30.00 80.00
DARDR A.Riley/D.Swanson 30.00 80.00
DARGB B.Bichette/V.Guerrero Jr. 300.00 600.00
DARGT K.Griffey Jr./M.Trout
DARHN R.Hoskins/A.Nola 50.00 120.00
DARHY K.Hiura/C.Yelich 100.00 250.00
DARJY Y.Alvarez/J.Altuve 60.00 150.00
DARNA N.Senzel/A.Aquino 60.00 150.00
DAROD R.Devers/D.Ortiz 75.00 200.00
DARSA G.Springer/Y.Alvarez 50.00 120.00
DARSM B.Snell/B.McKay 30.00 80.00
DARTP F.Tatis Jr./C.Paddack 150.00 400.00
DARTS M.Teixeira/C.Sabathia 50.00 120.00
DARVS J.Votto/N.Senzel 60.00 150.00
DARYH R.Yount/K.Hiura 60.00 150.00

2020 Topps Definitive Collection Dual Autographs

RANDOM INSERTS IN PACKS
PRINT RUN BTW 5-50 COPIES PER
NO PRICING QTY 15 OR LESS
EXCHANGE DEADLINE 3/31/2022
DACAL R.Alomar/F.Lindor 75.00 200.00
DACAS J.Soto/R.Acuna Jr. 400.00 800.00
DACBA J.Bagwell/J.Altuve
DACBD R.Devers/X.Bogaerts 60.00 150.00
DACBR A.Rizzo/K.Bryant 75.00 200.00
DACCE D.Eckersley/J.Canseco 40.00 100.00
DACCN A.Nola/S.Carlton 60.00 150.00
DACDA J.deGrom/P.Alonso 200.00 500.00
DACFV J.Varitek/C.Fisk 60.00 150.00
DACGB V.Guerrero Jr./B.Bichette 150.00 400.00
DACJY J.Altuve/Y.Alvarez 75.00 200.00
DACKC M.Cabrera/A.Kaline 150.00 400.00
DACMC M.McGwire/W.Clark 75.00 200.00
DACMJ C.Jones/D.Murphy 125.00 300.00
DACML G.Lux/M.Muncy 60.00 150.00
DACMS C.Sale/J.Martinez 30.00 80.00
DACMT D.Mattingly/G.Torres 200.00 500.00
DACNR N.Ryan/R.Carew 100.00 250.00
DACPC W.Clark/B.Posey 100.00 250.00
DACPM M.Mussina/A.Pettitte 60.00 150.00
DACRC G.Cole/N.Ryan 125.00 300.00
DACSA P.Alonso/D.Strawberry 100.00 250.00
DACSG P.Goldschmidt/O.Smith 60.00 150.00
DACSR R.Sandberg/A.Rizzo 75.00 200.00
DACTJ F.Thomas/E.Jimenez 100.00 250.00
DACVA A.Aquino/J.Votto 60.00 150.00
DACVF V.Guerrero Jr./F.Tatis Jr. 400.00 1000.00
DACYY R.Yount/C.Yelich 100.00 250.00

2020 Topps Definitive Collection Framed Autograph Patches

RANDOM INSERTS IN PACKS
PRINT RUN BTW 10-25 COPIES PER
NO PRICING QTY 15 OR LESS
EXCHANGE DEADLINE 3/31/2022
FACAB Andrew Benintendi/25
FACGC Gerrit Cole/25 40.00 100.00
FACKH Keston Hiura/25 60.00 150.00
FACNA Nolan Arenado EXCH/30 60.00 150.00
FACWB Walker Buehler/25 60.00 150.00

2020 Topps Definitive Collection Framed Autographs

RANDOM INSERTS IN PACKS
PRINT RUN BTW 5-50 COPIES PER
NO PRICING QTY 15 OR LESS
EXCHANGE DEADLINE 3/31/2022
DCFAAA Aristides Aquino/30 40.00 100.00
DCFABB Bo Bichette/30 125.00 300.00
DCFACJ Chipper Jones/30 60.00 150.00
DCFACS Chris Sale/30 20.00 50.00
DCFACY Christian Yelich/30 60.00 150.00
DCFADM Don Mattingly/30 60.00 150.00
DCFAFL Francisco Lindor/30 40.00 100.00
DCFAFT Frank Thomas/30 50.00 120.00
DCFAGL Gavin Lux/30 100.00 250.00
DCFAGT Gleyber Torres/30 100.00 250.00
DCFAHM Hideki Matsui/30 50.00 120.00
DCFAJA Jose Altuve/30 20.00 50.00
DCFAJB Jeff Bagwell/30 40.00 100.00
DCFAJD Jacob deGrom/30 60.00 150.00
DCFAJS Juan Soto/30 75.00 200.00
DCFAMM Mark McGwire/30 50.00 120.00
DCFANR Nolan Ryan/30 75.00 200.00
DCFAOS Ozzie Smith/30 30.00 80.00
DCFAPA Pete Alonso/30 100.00 250.00
DCFAPG Paul Goldschmidt/30 25.00 60.00
DCFARD Rafael Devers/30 25.00 60.00
DCFARH Rickey Henderson/30 40.00 100.00
DCFARS Ryne Sandberg/30 50.00 120.00
DCFAWC Will Clark/30 30.00 80.00
DCFAYA Yordan Alvarez/30 100.00 250.00
DCFAARI Anthony Rizzo/30 40.00 100.00
DCFACRJ Cal Ripken Jr./30 60.00 150.00
DCFACYA Carl Yastrzemski/30 50.00 120.00
DCFAFTJ Fernando Tatis Jr./30 200.00 500.00
DCFARAJ Ronald Acuna Jr./30 125.00 300.00
DCFARHO Rhys Hoskins/30 25.00 60.00
DCFARJA Reggie Jackson/25 40.00 100.00

2020 Topps Definitive Collection Rookie Autographs

RANDOM INSERTS IN PACKS
STATED PRINT RUN 50 SER. #'d SETS
EXCHANGE DEADLINE 3/31/2022
DRAAA Aristides Aquino 40.00 100.00
DRAAP A.J. Puk 8.00 20.00
DRABB Bo Bichette 75.00 200.00
DRABM Brendan McKay 12.00 30.00
DRADC Dylan Cease 15.00 40.00
DRADM Dustin May 25.00 60.00
DRAGL Gavin Lux 75.00 200.00
DRAJL Jesus Luzardo 10.00 25.00
DRAJY Jordan Yamamoto 5.00 12.00
DRAKL Kyle Lewis 15.00 40.00
DRALR Luis Robert EXCH 150.00 400.00
DRANH Nico Hoerner 30.00 80.00
DRASM Sean Murphy 8.00 20.00
DRATG Trent Grisham 20.00 50.00
DRAYA Yordan Alvarez 75.00 200.00
DRAAAQ Aristides Aquino 40.00 100.00
DRAAPU A.J. Puk 8.00 20.00
DRABBI Bo Bichette 75.00 200.00
DRABMC Brendan McKay 12.00 30.00
DRABOB Bo Bichette 75.00 200.00
DRABRM Brendan McKay 12.00 30.00
DRADCE Dylan Cease 15.00 40.00
DRADMA Dustin May 25.00 60.00
DRAGLU Gavin Lux 75.00 200.00
DRAJLU Jesus Luzardo 10.00 25.00
DRAJOY Jordan Yamamoto 5.00 12.00
DRAKLE Kyle Lewis 15.00 40.00
DRALRO Luis Robert EXCH 150.00 400.00
DRALUZ Jesus Luzardo 10.00 25.00
DRANHO Nico Hoerner 30.00 80.00
DRANHR Nico Hoerner 30.00 80.00
DRASMU Sean Murphy 8.00 20.00
DRATGR Trent Grisham 20.00 50.00
DRAYAL Yordan Alvarez 75.00 200.00
DRAYOA Yordan Alvarez 75.00 200.00
DRAAAQU Aristides Aquino 40.00 100.00
DRAGLUX Gavin Lux 75.00 200.00

2020 Topps Definitive Collection Rookie Autographs Green

*GREEN: .5X TO 1.2X BASIC
RANDOM INSERTS IN PACKS
STATED PRINT RUN 25 SER. #'d SETS
EXCHANGE DEADLINE 3/31/2022
DRABB Bo Bichette 150.00 400.00
DRABBI Bo Bichette 150.00 400.00
DRABOB Bo Bichette 150.00 400.00

2020 Topps Definitive Collection Helmets

RANDOM INSERTS IN PACKS
STATED PRINT RUN 35 COPIES PER
DHCAR Anthony Rizzo 30.00 80.00
DHCEJ Eloy Jimenez 20.00 50.00
DHCFF Freddie Freeman 25.00 60.00
DHCFL Francisco Lindor 20.00 50.00
DHCGS George Springer 15.00 40.00
DHCJS Juan Soto 30.00 80.00
DHCKH Keston Hiura 20.00 50.00
DHCOA Ozzie Albies 20.00 50.00
DHCRH Rhys Hoskins 20.00 50.00
DHCTS Trevor Story 15.00 40.00

2020 Topps Definitive Collection Jumbo Relics

RANDOM INSERTS IN PACKS
PRINT RUN BTW 35-50 COPIES PER
DJRCAA Aristides Aquino/50 10.00 25.00
DJRCAB Alex Bregman/50 8.00 20.00
DJRCAE Adam Eaton/35 15.00 40.00
DJRCAM Adalberto Mondesi/35 8.00 20.00
DJRCAR Amed Rosario/35 5.00 12.00
DJRCBC Brandon Crawford/35 5.00 12.00
DJRCCS Chris Sale/50 8.00 20.00
DJRCDD David Dahl/50 4.00 10.00
DJRCDP Dustin Pedroia/35 8.00 20.00
DJRCEA Elvis Andrus/50 5.00 12.00
DJRCEE Eduardo Escobar/35 4.00 10.00
DJRCEL Evan Longoria/35 5.00 12.00
DJRCHD Hunter Dozier/35 4.00 10.00
DJRCHR Hunter Renfroe/35 4.00 10.00
DJRCJA Jose Altuve/50 8.00 20.00
DJRCJG Joey Gallo/45 6.00 15.00
DJRCJH Josh Hader/35 5.00 12.00
DJRCJM Jeff McNeil/35 5.00 12.00
DJRCJP Joc Pederson/50 5.00 12.00
DJRCJR Jose Ramirez/35 5.00 12.00
DJRCJS Jorge Soler/35 6.00 15.00
DJRCJT Julio Teheran/35 5.00 12.00
DJRCJV Joey Votto/50 12.00 30.00
DJRCKD Khris Davis/50 6.00 15.00
DJRCKK Kevin Kiermaier/35 5.00 12.00
DJRCKW Kolten Wong/35 5.00 12.00
DJRCLC Lorenzo Cain/35 4.00 10.00
DJRCLG Lucas Giolito/45 5.00 12.00
DJRCMC Michael Chavis/35 5.00 12.00
DJRCMK Max Kepler/50 5.00 12.00
DJRCMS Marcus Semien/35 6.00 15.00
DJRCMT Mike Trout/50 50.00 120.00
DJRCNS Nick Senzel/50 6.00 15.00
DJRCRB Ryan Braun/35 5.00 12.00
DJRCRC Robinson Cano/35 5.00 12.00
DJRCRD Rafael Devers/50 12.00 30.00
DJRCRZ Ryan Zimmerman/35 5.00 12.00
DJRCSP Stephen Piscotty/35 4.00 10.00
DJRCSS Stephen Strasburg/50 8.00 20.00
DJRCTP Tommy Pham/35 4.00 10.00
DJRCTS Trevor Story/50 6.00 15.00
DJRCTT Trea Turner/50 5.00 12.00
DJRCXB Xander Bogaerts/50 6.00 15.00
DJRCYG Yuli Gurriel/35 5.00 12.00
DJRCAMC Andrew McCutchen/50 15.00 40.00
DJRCDDO David Ortiz/50 12.00 30.00
DJRCJPA James Paxton/35 5.00 12.00
DJRCJTR J.T. Realmuto/50 10.00 25.00
DJRCLGR Lourdes Gurriel Jr./35 5.00 12.00
DJRCMCO Michael Conforto/50 5.00 12.00
DJRCMSA Miguel Sano/50 5.00 12.00
DJRCMTE Mark Teixeira/35 5.00 12.00
DJRCYGR Yasmani Grandal 4.00 10.00

2020 Topps Definitive Collection Jumbo Relics Blue

*BLUE/29-30: .4X TO 1X BASIC
*BLUE/20: .5X TO 1.2X BASIC
RANDOM INSERTS IN PACKS
PRINT RUN BTW 20-30 COPIES PER
EXCHANGE DEADLINE 3/31/2022
DJRCAM Adalberto Mondesi/30 10.00 25.00
DJRCMT Mike Trout/30 125.00 300.00
DJRCAMC Andrew McCutchen/30 25.00 60.00
DJRCDDO David Ortiz/30 20.00 50.00

2020 Topps Definitive Collection Legendary Autographs

RANDOM INSERTS IN PACKS
PRINT RUN BTW 5-50 COPIES PER
NO PRICING QTY 15 OR LESS
EXCHANGE DEADLINE 3/31/2022
LACAD Andre Dawson/35 20.00 50.00
LACAK Al Kaline/35 40.00 100.00
LACAP Andy Pettitte/35 25.00 60.00
LACAR Alex Rodriguez
LACBL Barry Larkin/25 30.00 80.00
LACBW Bernie Williams/50 25.00 60.00
LACCF Carlton Fisk/35 20.00 50.00
LACCJ Chipper Jones/25 75.00 200.00
LACCR Cal Ripken Jr./25 75.00 200.00
LACCY Carl Yastrzemski/25 60.00 150.00
LACDE Dennis Eckersley/35 15.00 40.00
LACDM Dale Murphy/35 40.00 100.00
LACFM Fred McGriff/50 25.00 60.00
LACFT Frank Thomas/35 50.00 120.00
LACJB Johnny Bench/25 50.00 120.00
LACJM Juan Marichal/50 30.00 80.00
LACJS John Smoltz/50 25.00 60.00
LACJT Jim Thome/35 30.00 80.00
LACLB Lou Brock/35 25.00 60.00
LACMM Mike Mussina/35 30.00 80.00
LACNG Nomar Garciaparra/50 25.00 60.00
LACNR Nolan Ryan/25 100.00 250.00
LACOS Ozzie Smith/35 30.00 80.00
LACRA Roberto Alomar/35 25.00 60.00
LACRC Rod Carew/35 30.00 80.00
LACRS Ryne Sandberg/25 50.00 120.00
LACRY Robin Yount/25 40.00 100.00
LACSC Steve Carlton/35 20.00 50.00
LACTG Tom Glavine/50 30.00 80.00
LACWB Wade Boggs/25 30.00 80.00
LACWC Will Clark/35 30.00 80.00
LACDMA Don Mattingly/35 60.00 150.00
LACDST Darryl Strawberry/50 25.00 60.00
LACICH Ichiro
LACJBA Jeff Bagwell/50 40.00 100.00
LACMMC Mark McGwire/25 50.00 120.00
LACRJA Reggie Jackson/25 40.00 100.00

2017 Topps Diamond Icons Autographs

STATED PRINT RUN 25 SER.#'d SETS
EXCHANGE DEADLINE 9/30/2019
AUAB Andrew Benintendi RC 30.00 80.00
AUABE Adrian Beltre 60.00 150.00
AUABR Alex Bregman RC 25.00 60.00
AUAG Andres Galarraga 8.00 20.00
AUAJU Aaron Judge RC 250.00 500.00
AUAK Al Kaline 25.00 50.00
AUAP Andy Pettitte 20.00 50.00
AUAPU Albert Pujols
AUAR Alex Reyes RC 12.00 30.00
AUARI Anthony Rizzo 30.00 80.00
AUARO Alex Rodriguez
AUBA Bobby Abreu 10.00 25.00
AUBB Barry Bonds 75.00 200.00
AUBH Bryce Harper
AUBJ Bo Jackson 40.00 100.00
AUBL Barry Larkin 20.00 50.00
AUBP Buster Posey
AUCB Craig Biggio 12.00 30.00
AUCBE Cody Bellinger RC 60.00 150.00
AUCC Carlos Correa 40.00 100.00
AUCJ Chipper Jones 40.00 100.00
AUCK Clayton Kershaw 60.00 150.00
AUCR Cal Ripken Jr.
AUCS Chris Sale 20.00 50.00
AUCSC Curt Schilling 20.00 50.00
AUCSE Corey Seager 25.00 60.00
AUCY Carl Yastrzemski
AUDD David Dahl RC 10.00 25.00
AUDJ Derek Jeter
AUDM Don Mattingly 40.00 100.00
AUDO David Ortiz 30.00 80.00
AUDP Dustin Pedroia 12.00 30.00
AUDPR David Price 8.00 20.00
AUDSW Dansby Swanson RC 15.00 40.00
AUDW David Wright 15.00 40.00
AUFB Franklin Barreto RC 6.00 15.00
AUFL Francisco Lindor 20.00 50.00
AUFR Frank Robinson 15.00 40.00
AUFT Frank Thomas 30.00 80.00
AUGM Greg Maddux
AUGS George Springer 12.00 30.00
AUHA Hank Aaron
AUHM Hideki Matsui 75.00 200.00
AUIH Ian Happ RC 25.00 60.00
AUIR Ivan Rodriguez 15.00 40.00
AUI Ichiro
AUJAU Jose Altuve 30.00 80.00
AUJB Jeff Bagwell 20.00 50.00
AUJBE Johnny Bench
AUJD Jacob deGrom 25.00 60.00
AUJDO Josh Donaldson 25.00 60.00
AUJH Jason Heyward 25.00 60.00
AUJS John Smoltz 12.00 30.00
AUJT Jim Thome 60.00 150.00
AUJU Julio Urias 10.00 25.00
AUJV Jason Varitek 20.00 50.00
AUKB Kris Bryant 75.00 200.00
AUKM Kenta Maeda 12.00 30.00
AUKS Kyle Schwarber 10.00 25.00
AULG Lucas Giolito 8.00 20.00
AULW Luke Weaver RC 15.00 40.00
AUMF Michael Fulmer 6.00 15.00
AUMM Manny Machado 15.00 40.00
AUMMC Mark McGwire 50.00 120.00
AUMP Mike Piazza
AUMT Masahiro Tanaka
AUMTR Mike Trout 400.00 800.00
AUNM Nomar Mazara 6.00 15.00
AUNR Nolan Ryan 75.00 200.00
AUNS Noah Syndergaard 15.00 40.00
AUOS Ozzie Smith 20.00 50.00
AUOV Omar Vizquel 8.00 20.00
AUPG Paul Goldschmidt 25.00 60.00
AURCL Roger Clemens
AURCR Rod Carew 25.00 60.00
AURH Rickey Henderson
AURJ Reggie Jackson
AURJO Randy Johnson
AURS Ryne Sandberg 20.00 50.00
AUSC Steve Carlton 12.00 30.00
AUSK Sandy Koufax
AUTG Tom Glavine 12.00 30.00
AUTR Tim Raines 12.00 30.00
AUTS Trevor Story 10.00 25.00
AUWB Wade Boggs
AUYG Yulieski Gurriel RC 12.00 30.00
AUYMO Yoan Moncada RC 60.00 150.00

2017 Topps Diamond Icons Authenticated Jumbo Patch Autographs

STATED PRINT RUN 25 SER.#'d SETS
EXCHANGE DEADLINE 9/30/2019
JPAAB Andrew Benintendi
JPAABR Alex Bregman
JPAAJ Adam Jones 25.00 60.00
JPAAP Andy Pettitte
JPAAPU Albert Pujols
JPAARI Anthony Rizzo
JPABH Bryce Harper
JPABP Buster Posey 100.00 250.00
JPACC Carlos Correa 100.00 250.00
JPACJ Chipper Jones 75.00 200.00
JPACK Clayton Kershaw
JPACSE Corey Seager
JPADJ Derek Jeter
JPADO David Ortiz 75.00 200.00
JPADP Dustin Pedroia 30.00 80.00
JPADPR David Price
JPAFL Francisco Lindor
JPAFT Frank Thomas 75.00 200.00
JPAIR Ivan Rodriguez 25.00 60.00
JPAI Ichiro 250.00 400.00
JPAJA Jose Altuve
JPAJB Jeff Bagwell
JPAJD Josh Donaldson
JPAJd Jacob deGrom 50.00 120.00
JPAJS John Smoltz
JPAJT Jim Thome
JPAKB Kris Bryant
JPAKM Kenta Maeda
JPAMP Mike Piazza
JPAMT Masahiro Tanaka 100.00 250.00
JPAMTR Mike Trout
JPANS Noah Syndergaard
JPAPM Pedro Martinez
JPATG Tom Glavine
JPATR Tim Raines
JPATS Trevor Story

2017 Topps Diamond Icons Diamond Autographs

STATED PRINT RUN 25 SER.#'d SETS
EXCHANGE DEADLINE 9/30/2019
DAAB Alex Bregman 40.00 100.00
DAABE Andrew Benintendi 60.00 150.00
DAAG Andres Galarraga 8.00 20.00
DAAJ Aaron Judge 350.00 700.00
DAAP Andy Pettitte 20.00 50.00
DAARE Alex Reyes 12.00 30.00
DAARI Anthony Rizzo 30.00 80.00
DABA Bobby Abreu 10.00 25.00
DACB Craig Biggio
DACC Carlos Correa 30.00 80.00
DACK Clayton Kershaw 60.00 510.00
DACS Chris Sale 20.00 50.00
DACSC Curt Schilling 20.00 50.00
DACSE Corey Seager 60.00 150.00
DADJ Derek Jeter
DADM Don Mattingly 40.00 100.00
DADO David Ortiz 50.00 120.00
DADP David Price 8.00 20.00
DADS Dansby Swanson 25.00 60.00
DAFL Francisco Lindor 40.00 100.00
DAIR Ivan Rodriguez 15.00 40.00
DAJBA Jeff Bagwell 30.00 80.00
DAJD Jacob deGrom 25.00 60.00
DAJS John Smoltz 20.00 50.00
DAJU Julio Urias 10.00 25.00
DAJV Jason Varitek 50.00 120.00
DAKB Kris Bryant
DAKM Kenta Maeda 12.00 30.00

DAKS Kyle Schwarber 20.00 50.00
DAMM Mark McGwire 50.00 120.00
DAMT Mike Trout 250.00 500.00
DANR Nolan Ryan 75.00 200.00
DANS Noah Syndergaard 15.00 40.00
DAOS Ozzie Smith 20.00 50.00
DAOV Omar Vizquel 12.00 30.00
DATG Tom Glavine 20.00 50.00
DATS Trevor Story 10.00 25.00
DAYG Yulieski Gurriel 12.00 30.00
DAYM Yoan Moncada 60.00 150.00

2017 Topps Diamond Icons Red Ink Autographs

STATED PRINT RUN 25 SER.#'d SETS
EXCHANGE DEADLINE 9/30/2019
RAAB Andrew Benintendi 25.00 60.00
RAABE Adrian Beltre 50.00 120.00
RAABR Alex Bregman 40.00 100.00
RAAG Andres Galarraga 8.00 20.00
RAAJU Aaron Judge 350.00 700.00
RAAK Al Kaline 25.00 50.00
RAAP Andy Pettitte 20.00 50.00
RAAPU Albert Pujols
RAAR Alex Reyes 12.00 30.00
RAARI Anthony Rizzo 30.00 80.00
RAARO Alex Rodriguez
RABA Bobby Abreu 10.00 25.00
RABH Bryce Harper
RABJ Bo Jackson 30.00 80.00
RABL Barry Larkin 20.00 50.00
RABP Buster Posey
RACB Craig Biggio 20.00 50.00
RACBE Cody Bellinger
RACC Carlos Correa 30.00 80.00
RACJ Chipper Jones 40.00 100.00
RACK Clayton Kershaw 60.00 150.00
RACR Cal Ripken Jr.
RACS Chris Sale 20.00 50.00
RACSC Curt Schilling 10.00 25.00
RACSE Corey Seager 40.00 100.00
RACY Carl Yastrzemski
RADD David Dahl 10.00 25.00
RADJ Derek Jeter
RADM Don Mattingly 40.00 100.00
RADO David Ortiz 20.00 50.00
RADP Dustin Pedroia 12.00 30.00
RADPO David Price 8.00 20.00
RADSW Dansby Swanson 15.00 40.00
RADW David Wright 8.00 20.00
RAFB Franklin Barreto 6.00 15.00
RAFL Francisco Lindor 40.00 100.00
RAFR Frank Robinson
RAFT Frank Thomas 30.00 80.00
RAGM Greg Maddux
RAGS George Springer 12.00 30.00
RAHA Hank Aaron
RAHM Hideki Matsui 75.00 200.00
RAIR Ivan Rodriguez 15.00 40.00
RAI Ichiro
RAJA Jose Altuve 30.00 80.00
RAJB Jeff Bagwell 15.00 40.00
RAJBE Johnny Bench
RAJD Jacob deGrom 25.00 60.00
RAJDO Josh Donaldson 25.00 60.00
RAJH Jason Heyward
RAJS John Smoltz 20.00 50.00
RAJT Jim Thome 40.00 100.00
RAJU Julio Urias 10.00 25.00
RAJV Jason Varitek 20.00 50.00
RAKB Kris Bryant
RAKM Kenta Maeda 12.00 30.00
RAKS Kyle Schwarber 10.00 25.00
RALG Lucas Giolito 8.00 20.00
RALW Luke Weaver 15.00 40.00
RAMF Michael Fulmer 15.00 40.00
RAMM Manny Machado 15.00 40.00
RAMMC Mark McGwire 50.00 120.00
RAMP Mike Piazza
RAMT Masahiro Tanaka
RAMTR Mike Trout 250.00 500.00
RANM Nomar Mazara
RANR Nolan Ryan 75.00 200.00
RANS Noah Syndergaard 30.00 80.00
RAOS Ozzie Smith 20.00 50.00
RAOV Omar Vizquel 8.00 20.00
RAPG Paul Goldschmidt 25.00 60.00
RARCL Roger Clemens
RARCR Rod Carew 25.00 60.00
RARH Rickey Henderson
RARJ Reggie Jackson
RARJO Randy Johnson
RARS Ryne Sandberg 20.00 50.00
RASC Steve Carlton 12.00 30.00
RASK Sandy Koufax
RATG Tom Glavine 10.00 25.00
RATR Tim Raines 12.00 30.00
RATS Trevor Story 10.00 25.00
RAWB Wade Boggs
RAYG Yulieski Gurriel 12.00 30.00
RAYMN Yoan Moncada 30.00 80.00

2018 Topps Diamond Icons Autographs

RANDOM INSERTS IN PACKS
STATED PRINT RUN 25 SER.#'d SETS
EXCHANGE DEADLINE 7/31/2020
ACAB Alex Bregman 25.00 60.00
ACAD Andre Dawson 20.00 50.00
ACAJU Aaron Judge 125.00 300.00
ACAK Al Kaline 40.00 100.00
ACAP Andy Pettitte 15.00 40.00
ACAR Addison Russell 8.00 20.00
ACARI Anthony Rizzo 30.00 80.00
ACARO Alex Rodriguez 100.00 250.00
ACARS Amed Rosario RC 10.00 25.00
ACBH Bryce Harper
ACBJ Bo Jackson 40.00 100.00
ACBL Barry Larkin 20.00 50.00
ACBP Buster Posey 40.00 100.00
ACBW Bernie Williams 15.00 40.00
ACCBI Craig Biggio 15.00 40.00
ACCF Clint Frazier RC 20.00 50.00
ACCJ Chipper Jones 40.00 100.00
ACCK Corey Kluber 12.00 30.00
ACCKE Clayton Kershaw 50.00 120.00
ACCKI Craig Kimbrel 12.00 30.00
ACCS Chris Sale 20.00 50.00
ACDE Dennis Eckersley 15.00 40.00
ACDMA Don Mattingly 40.00 100.00
ACDO David Ortiz 30.00 80.00
ACDS Dominic Smith RC 8.00 20.00
ACDW Dave Winfield 12.00 30.00
ACEM Edgar Martinez 25.00 60.00
ACFF Freddie Freeman 30.00 80.00
ACFL Francisco Lindor 25.00 60.00
ACFT Frank Thomas 30.00 60.00
ACGM Greg Maddux 50.00 120.00
ACGS Gary Sanchez 15.00 40.00
ACGT Gleyber Torres RC 125.00 300.00
ACHA Hank Aaron 150.00 400.00
ACHM Hideki Matsui 60.00 150.00
ACIH Ian Happ 8.00 20.00
ACI Ichiro 200.00 400.00
ACJA Jose Altuve 25.00 60.00
ACJB Javier Baez 50.00 120.00
ACJBA Jeff Bagwell 20.00 50.00
ACJBE Johnny Bench 40.00 100.00
ACJC Jose Canseco 12.00 30.00
ACJD Jacob deGrom 30.00 80.00
ACJDA Johnny Damon
ACJP Jim Palmer 15.00 40.00
ACJR Jose Ramirez 20.00 50.00
ACJS John Smoltz 25.00 60.00
ACJV Joey Votto 30.00 80.00
ACKS Kyle Schwarber 10.00 25.00
ACLB Lou Brock 15.00 40.00
ACLS Luis Severino 15.00 40.00
ACMM Manny Machado 25.00 60.00
ACMMC Mark McGwire 40.00 100.00
ACMR Mariano Rivera
ACNG Nomar Garciaparra
ACNR Nolan Ryan 75.00 200.00
ACNS Noah Syndergaard 15.00 40.00
ACOA Ozzie Albies RC 30.00 80.00
ACOC Orlando Cepeda 12.00 30.00
ACOS Ozzie Smith 25.00 60.00
ACPG Paul Goldschmidt 20.00 50.00
ACPM Pedro Martinez 50.00 120.00
ACRA Ronald Acuna RC 150.00 400.00
ACRAL Roberto Alomar 12.00 30.00
ACRC Rod Carew 30.00 80.00
ACRD Rafael Devers RC 20.00 50.00
ACRH Rickey Henderson 40.00 100.00
ACRHO Rhys Hoskins RC 40.00 100.00
ACRJ Reggie Jackson 30.00 80.00
ACRJO Randy Johnson
ACRS Ryne Sandberg 25.00 60.00
ACRY Robin Yount 25.00 60.00
ACSC Steve Carlton 15.00 40.00
ACSK Sandy Koufax
ACSO Shohei Ohtani RC 400.00 800.00
ACTG Tom Glavine 15.00 40.00
ACTS Tom Seaver 50.00 120.00
ACVR Victor Robles RC 20.00 50.00
ACWB Wade Boggs 20.00 50.00
ACWC Willson Contreras 10.00 25.00

2018 Topps Diamond Icons Diamond Autographs

RANDOM INSERTS IN PACKS
STATED PRINT RUN 25 SER.#'d SETS
EXCHANGE DEADLINE 7/31/2020
DAAJ Aaron Judge 125.00 300.00
DAAK Al Kaline 40.00 100.00
DAAR Amed Rosario 12.00 30.00
DAARI Anthony Rizzo 30.00 80.00
DABJ Bo Jackson 40.00 100.00
DABL Barry Larkin 20.00 50.00
DACF Clint Frazier 20.00 50.00
DACJ Chipper Jones 50.00 120.00
DACR Cal Ripken Jr. 50.00 120.00
DACS Chris Sale 15.00 40.00
DADJ Derek Jeter
DADM Don Mattingly 50.00 120.00
DADO David Ortiz 30.00 80.00
DAFF Freddie Freeman 30.00 80.00
DAFL Francisco Lindor 25.00 60.00
DAFT Frank Thomas 40.00 100.00
DAGSA Gary Sanchez 25.00 60.00
DAGT Gleyber Torres 125.00 300.00
DAHA Hank Aaron 150.00 400.00
DAI Ichiro 200.00 400.00
DAJA Jose Altuve 25.00 60.00
DAJC Jose Canseco 25.00 60.00
DAJS John Smoltz 25.00 60.00
DAJV Joey Votto 30.00 80.00
DAKB Kris Bryant 75.00 200.00
DAKS Kyle Schwarber 20.00 50.00
DALS Luis Severino 15.00 40.00
DAMG Mark McGwire 40.00 100.00
DAMM Manny Machado 25.00 60.00
DAMT Mike Trout
DANR Nolan Ryan 75.00 200.00
DANS Noah Syndergaard 25.00 60.00
DAOA Ozzie Albies 30.00 80.00
DAOS Ozzie Smith 25.00 60.00
DAPG Paul Goldschmidt 20.00 50.00
DARA Ronald Acuna 150.00 400.00
DARD Rafael Devers 20.00 50.00
DARH Rhys Hoskins 40.00 100.00
DASO Shohei Ohtani 400.00 800.00
DASOH Shohei Ohtani 400.00 800.00
DAVR Victor Robles 20.00 50.00

2018 Topps Diamond Icons Jumbo Patch Autographs

RANDOM INSERTS IN PACKS
STATED PRINT RUN 25 SER.#'d SETS
EXCHANGE DEADLINE 7/31/2020
AJPAAB Alex Bregman 50.00 120.00
AJPAAJ Adam Jones 30.00 80.00
AJPAAP Albert Pujols
AJPAAR Addison Russell 25.00 60.00
AJPAARI Anthony Rizzo 75.00 200.00
AJPAARO Amed Rosario
AJPABB Byron Buxton 30.00 80.00
AJPABH Bryce Harper
AJPABP Buster Posey 50.00 120.00
AJPACK Craig Kimbrel 25.00 60.00
AJPACKE Clayton Kershaw 75.00 200.00
AJPACKL Corey Kluber 40.00 100.00
AJPACS Chris Sale
AJPADG Didi Gregorius 25.00 60.00
AJPAFF Freddie Freeman 40.00 100.00
AJPAGS George Springer 25.00 60.00
AJPAGSA Gary Sanchez 30.00 80.00
AJPAIH Ian Happ 25.00 60.00
AJPAJA Jose Altuve 50.00 120.00
AJPAJB Javier Baez 75.00 200.00
AJPAJD Jacob deGrom 75.00 200.00
AJPAJDO Josh Donaldson 25.00 60.00
AJPAJV Joey Votto 50.00 120.00
AJPAKB Kris Bryant 125.00 300.00
AJPAKS Kyle Schwarber 40.00 100.00
AJPALS Luis Severino 25.00 60.00
AJPAMM Manny Machado 50.00 120.00
AJPAMT Mike Trout
AJPANS Noah Syndergaard 25.00 60.00
AJPAOA Ozzie Albies
AJPAPG Paul Goldschmidt 30.00 80.00
AJPARD Rafael Devers
AJPASM Starling Marte 25.00 60.00
AJPAVR Victor Robles
AJPAWC Willson Contreras
AJPAYMO Yadier Molina

2018 Topps Diamond Icons Red Ink Autographs

RANDOM INSERTS IN PACKS
STATED PRINT RUN 25 SER.#'d SETS
EXCHANGE DEADLINE 7/31/2020
RIAAB Alex Bregman 25.00 60.00
RIAAD Andre Dawson 10.00 25.00
RIAAK Al Kaline 40.00 100.00
RIAAP Andy Pettitte 15.00 40.00
RIAAR Addison Russell 8.00 20.00
RIAARI Anthony Rizzo 25.00 60.00
RIAARO Alex Rodriguez 60.00 150.00
RIAARS Amed Rosario 12.00 30.00
RIABG Bob Gibson 25.00 60.00
RIABH Bryce Harper
RIABJ Bo Jackson 40.00 100.00
RIABL Barry Larkin 20.00 50.00
RIABP Buster Posey 40.00 100.00
RIABR Brooks Robinson
RIABW Bernie Williams 15.00 40.00
RIACBI Craig Biggio 15.00 40.00
RIACF Clint Frazier 20.00 50.00
RIACJ Chipper Jones 50.00 120.00
RIACK Craig Kimbrel 15.00 40.00
RIACKE Clayton Kershaw 50.00 120.00
RIACKL Corey Kluber 12.00 30.00
RIACR Cal Ripken Jr. 50.00 120.00
RIACS Chris Sale 15.00 40.00
RIADE Dennis Eckersley 15.00 40.00
RIADG Didi Gregorius 20.00 50.00
RIADMA Don Mattingly 50.00 120.00
RIADO David Ortiz 30.00 80.00
RIADW Dave Winfield 12.00 30.00
RIAEM Edgar Martinez 12.00 30.00
RIAFF Freddie Freeman 30.00 80.00
RIAFL Francisco Lindor 25.00 60.00
RIAFT Frank Thomas 40.00 100.00
RIAGM Greg Maddux 50.00 120.00
RIAGSA Gary Sanchez 25.00 60.00
RIAGT Gleyber Torres 125.00 300.00
RIAHM Hideki Matsui 60.00 150.00
RIAIH Ian Happ 8.00 20.00
RIAI Ichiro 200.00 400.00
RIAJA Jose Altuve 25.00 60.00
RIAJB Jeff Bagwell 15.00 40.00
RIAJBE Johnny Bench 40.00 100.00
RIAJBU Javier Baez 50.00 120.00
RIAJC Jose Canseco 15.00 40.00
RIAJD Jacob deGrom 30.00 80.00
RIAJP Jim Palmer 15.00 40.00
RIAJS John Smoltz 15.00 40.00
RIAJU Justin Upton 10.00 25.00
RIAJV Joey Votto 30.00 80.00
RIAKB Kris Bryant 50.00 120.00
RIAKS Kyle Schwarber 20.00 50.00
RIALB Lou Brock 25.00 60.00
RIALS Luis Severino 15.00 40.00
RIAMM Manny Machado 25.00 60.00
RIAMMA Mark McGwire 40.00 100.00
RIANG Nomar Garciaparra
RIANR Nolan Ryan 75.00 200.00
RIANS Noah Syndergaard 12.00 30.00
RIAOA Ozzie Albies 30.00 80.00
RIAOC Orlando Cepeda 12.00 30.00
RIAOS Ozzie Smith 10.00 25.00
RIAPG Paul Goldschmidt 20.00 50.00
RIAPM Pedro Martinez 50.00 120.00
RIARA Ronald Acuna 150.00 400.00
RIARAL Roberto Alomar 10.00 25.00
RIARC Rod Carew 15.00 80.00
RIARD Rafael Devers 20.00 50.00
RIARH Rhys Hoskins 40.00 100.00
RIARHE Rickey Henderson 40.00 100.00
RIARJ Reggie Jackson 30.00 80.00
RIARS Ryne Sandberg 25.00 60.00
RIARY Robin Yount 25.00 60.00
RIASC Steve Carlton 15.00 40.00
RIASO Shohei Ohtani 400.00 800.00
RIATG Tom Glavine 12.00 30.00
RIATS Tom Seaver 50.00 120.00
RIAVR Victor Robles 20.00 50.00
RIAWB Wade Boggs 25.00 60.00
RIAWCL Will Clark 40.00 100.00
RIAWCO Willson Contreras 8.00 20.00
RIAYM Yadier Molina 50.00 120.00

2019 Topps Diamond Icons Autographs

RANDOM INSERTS IN PACKS
STATED PRINT RUN 25 SER.#'d SETS
EXCHANGE DEADLINE 6/30/2021
ACAD Andre Dawson 12.00 30.00
ACAJU Aaron Judge 100.00 250.00
ACAK Al Kaline 30.00 80.00
ACAP Andy Pettitte 12.00 30.00
ACARI Anthony Rizzo 30.00 80.00
ACARO Alex Rodriguez 50.00 120.00
ACBG Bob Gibson 15.00 40.00
ACBJ Bo Jackson 40.00 100.00
ACBL Barry Larkin 20.00 50.00
ACCF Carlton Fisk 30.00 80.00
ACCJ Chipper Jones 40.00 100.00
ACCK Corey Kluber 8.00 20.00
ACCKE Clayton Kershaw EXCH 60.00 150.00
ACCR Cal Ripken Jr. 50.00 120.00
ACCS Chris Sale 10.00 25.00
ACDE Dennis Eckersley 12.00 30.00
ACDMA Don Mattingly 40.00 100.00
ACDMU Dale Murphy 60.00 150.00
ACDO David Ortiz 25.00 60.00
ACDP Dustin Pedroia
ACEJ Eloy Jimenez RC 75.00 200.00
ACEM Edgar Martinez 25.00 60.00
ACFF Freddie Freeman 30.00 80.00
ACFL Francisco Lindor 25.00 60.00
ACFM Fred McGriff 15.00 40.00
ACFT Frank Thomas 30.00 80.00
ACFTJ Fernando Tatis Jr. RC 250.00 600.00
ACGSP George Springer 8.00 20.00
ACHA Hank Aaron
ACHM Hideki Matsui 50.00 120.00
ACI Ichiro 150.00 400.00
ACJA Jose Altuve 15.00 40.00
ACJBA Jeff Bagwell 15.00 40.00
ACJBE Johnny Bench 30.00 80.00
ACJC Jose Canseco 25.00 60.00
ACJD Jacob deGrom 25.00 60.00
ACJDA Johnny Damon 8.00 20.00
ACJM Juan Marichal 12.00 30.00
ACJP Jorge Posada 15.00 40.00
ACJS John Smoltz 20.00 50.00
ACJSO Juan Soto 40.00 100.00
ACJV Joey Votto 20.00 50.00
ACJVA Jason Varitek 20.00 50.00
ACKB Kris Bryant 60.00 150.00
ACKS Kyle Schwarber 12.00 30.00
ACKT Kyle Tucker RC 15.00 40.00
ACLB Lou Brock 20.00 50.00
ACLS Luis Severino 8.00 20.00
ACMA Miguel Andujar 15.00 40.00
ACMC Miguel Cabrera 50.00 120.00
ACMCA Matt Carpenter 10.00 25.00
ACMMC Mark McGwire 40.00 100.00
ACMP Mike Piazza 40.00 100.00
ACMT Mike Trout 300.00 500.00
ACMTA Masahiro Tanaka 40.00 100.00
ACNG Nomar Garciaparra 15.00 40.00
ACNR Nolan Ryan 60.00 150.00
ACNS Noah Syndergaard 15.00 40.00
ACOA Ozzie Albies 20.00 50.00
ACOS Ozzie Smith 25.00 60.00
ACPA Peter Alonso RC
ACPG Paul Goldschmidt 25.00 60.00
ACPM Pedro Martinez 30.00 80.00
ACRA Ronald Acuna Jr. 60.00 150.00
ACRAL Roberto Alomar 15.00 40.00
ACRC Rod Carew 20.00 50.00
ACRH Rickey Henderson 40.00 100.00
ACRHO Rhys Hoskins 25.00 60.00
ACRJ Reggie Jackson 25.00 60.00
ACRS Ryne Sandberg 30.00 80.00
ACRY Robin Yount 25.00 60.00
ACSC Steve Carlton 8.00 20.00
ACSK Sandy Koufax
ACSO Shohei Ohtani 150.00 400.00
ACTG Tom Glavine 15.00 40.00
ACVG Vladimir Guerrero 25.00 60.00
ACVGJ Vladimir Guerrero Jr. RC 250.00 500.00
ACVR Victor Robles 12.00 30.00
ACWB Wade Boggs 30.00 80.00
ACWC Willson Contreras 10.00 25.00
ACWCL Will Clark 25.00 60.00

2019 Topps Diamond Icons Diamond Icons Autographs

RANDOM INSERTS IN PACKS
STATED PRINT RUN 25 SER.#'d SETS
EXCHANGE DEADLINE 6/30/2021
DIAAJ Aaron Judge 100.00 250.00
DIAAK Al Kaline 30.00 80.00
DIAAZ Anthony Rizzo 30.00 80.00
DIABG Bob Gibson 30.00 80.00
DIABL Barry Larkin 20.00 50.00
DIABP Buster Posey 40.00 100.00
DIACJ Chipper Jones 40.00 100.00
DIACRJ Cal Ripken Jr. 50.00 120.00
DIACS Chris Sale 10.00 25.00
DIADJ Derek Jeter
DIADM Don Mattingly 40.00 100.00
DIAEJ Eloy Jimenez 75.00 200.00
DIAEM Edgar Martinez 25.00 60.00
DIAFF Freddie Freeman 30.00 80.00
DIAFL Francisco Lindor 25.00 60.00
DIAFT Frank Thomas 40.00 100.00
DIAFTJ Fernando Tatis Jr. 250.00 600.00
DIAHA Hank Aaron
DIAHM Hideki Matsui 50.00 120.00
DIAIS Ichiro 150.00 400.00
DIAJA Jose Altuve 15.00 40.00
DIAJB Johnny Bench 30.00 80.00
DIAJD Jacob deGrom 25.00 60.00
DIAJR Jose Ramirez 8.00 20.00
DIAJS Juan Soto 30.00 80.00
DIAJV Joey Votto 30.00 80.00
DIAKB Kris Bryant 60.00 150.00
DIAKS Kyle Schwarber 12.00 30.00
DIALB Lou Brock 15.00 40.00
DIAMT Mike Trout 300.00 500.00
DIANR Nolan Ryan 60.00 150.00
DIAOS Ozzie Smith 25.00 60.00
DIAPG Paul Goldschmidt 25.00 60.00
DIARAJ Ronald Acuna Jr. 60.00 150.00
DIARC Rod Carew 20.00 50.00
DIARH Rickey Henderson 40.00 100.00
DIARJ Reggie Jackson 25.00 60.00
DIARS Ryne Sandberg 30.00 80.00
DIARY Rhys Hoskins 25.00 60.00
DIASK Sandy Koufax
DIASO Shohei Ohtani 150.00 400.00
DIAVG Vladimir Guerrero Jr. 250.00 500.00
DIAWB Wade Boggs 30.00 80.00
DIAWI Will Clark 25.00 60.00

2019 Topps Diamond Icons Jumbo Patch Autographs

RANDOM INSERTS IN PACKS
STATED PRINT RUN 25 SER.#'d SETS
EXCHANGE DEADLINE 6/30/2021
AJPAD Adrian Beltre 30.00 80.00
AJPAJ Aaron Judge
AJPAN Aaron Nola EXCH 30.00 80.00
AJPAR Anthony Rizzo 40.00 100.00
AJPBP Buster Posey 60.00 150.00
AJPCB Charlie Blackmon 20.00 50.00
AJPCL Clayton Kershaw EXCH 60.00 150.00
AJPCS Chris Sale 20.00 50.00
AJPDP Dustin Pedroia
AJPFF Freddie Freeman 40.00 100.00
AJPFL Francisco Lindor 25.00 60.00
AJPGS George Springer 30.00 80.00
AJPJA Jose Altuve 40.00 100.00
AJPJD Jacob deGrom 60.00 150.00
AJPJR Jose Ramirez 20.00 50.00
AJPJS Juan Soto 75.00 200.00
AJPJU Justin Upton 20.00 50.00
AJPJV Joey Votto 40.00 100.00
AJPKB Kris Bryant 125.00 300.00
AJPKD Khris Davis EXCH 15.00 40.00
AJPKS Kyle Schwarber 30.00 80.00
AJPLS Luis Severino 20.00 50.00
AJPMA Matt Carpenter 25.00 60.00
AJPMC Miguel Cabrera 75.00 200.00
AJPMH Masahiro Tanaka
AJPMJ Miguel Andujar 15.00 40.00
AJPMP Matt Chapman EXCH 30.00 80.00
AJPMT Mike Trout 400.00 800.00
AJPNS Noah Syndergaard 15.00 40.00
AJPOA Ozzie Albies
AJPPG Paul Goldschmidt 40.00 100.00
AJPRY Rhys Hoskins
AJPSO Shohei Ohtani
AJPSP Salvador Perez 20.00 50.00
AJPTM Trey Mancini 20.00 50.00
AJPWC Willson Contreras 40.00 100.00
AJPWM Whit Merrifield 30.00 80.00
AJPYM Yadier Molina 40.00 100.00

2019 Topps Diamond Icons Red Ink Autographs

RANDOM INSERTS IN PACKS
STATED PRINT RUN 25 SER.#'d SETS
EXCHANGE DEADLINE 6/30/2021
RIAJ Aaron Judge 100.00 250.00
RIAK Al Kaline 30.00 80.00
RIAN Anthony Rizzo 30.00 80.00
RIAP Andy Pettitte 12.00 30.00
RIBG Bob Gibson 30.00 80.00
RIBL Barry Larkin 20.00 50.00
RIBP Buster Posey 40.00 100.00
RICF Carlton Fisk 30.00 80.00
RICJ Chipper Jones 40.00 100.00
RICR Cal Ripken Jr. 50.00 120.00
RICS Chris Sale 10.00 25.00
RIDE Dennis Eckersley 12.00 30.00
RIDJ Derek Jeter
RIDM Don Mattingly 40.00 100.00
RIDO David Ortiz 30.00 80.00
RIEM Edgar Martinez 25.00 60.00
RIFF Freddie Freeman 30.00 80.00
RIFL Francisco Lindor 25.00 60.00
RIFT Frank Thomas 40.00 100.00
RIGS George Springer 8.00 20.00
RIHM Hideki Matsui 50.00 120.00
RIIS Ichiro 150.00 400.00
RIJA Jose Altuve 15.00 40.00
RIJB Johnny Bench 30.00 80.00
RIJC Jose Canseco 25.00 60.00
RIJD Jacob deGrom 25.00 60.00
RIJM Juan Marichal 20.00 50.00
RIJO Johnny Damon 8.00 20.00
RIJS Jason Varitek 20.00 50.00
RIJU Juan Soto 30.00 80.00
RIJV Joey Votto 30.00 80.00
RIKB Kris Bryant 60.00 150.00
RIKS Kyle Schwarber 12.00 30.00
RILB Lou Brock 15.00 40.00
RILS Luis Severino 8.00 20.00
RIMM Mark McGwire 40.00 100.00
RIMP Mike Piazza 40.00 100.00
RIMR Mariano Rivera 125.00 300.00
RIMS Masahiro Tanaka 40.00 100.00
RING Nomar Garciaparra 15.00 40.00
RINR Nolan Ryan 60.00 150.00
RINS Noah Syndergaard 15.00 40.00
RIOA Ozzie Albies 20.00 50.00
RIOS Ozzie Smith 25.00 60.00
RIPG Paul Goldschmidt 15.00 40.00
RIPM Pedro Martinez 30.00 80.00
RIRA Ronald Acuna Jr. 60.00 150.00
RIRC Rod Carew 20.00 50.00
RIRH Rickey Henderson 40.00 100.00
RIRJ Reggie Jackson 25.00 60.00
RIRS Ryne Sandberg 30.00 80.00
RIRY Rhys Hoskins 25.00 60.00
RISO Shohei Ohtani 150.00 400.00
RITG Tom Glavine 15.00 40.00
RIWB Wade Boggs 15.00 40.00
RIWC Willson Contreras 20.00 50.00
RIWI Will Clark 25.00 60.00

2019 Topps Diamond Icons Silver Ink Autographs

RANDOM INSERTS IN PACKS
STATED PRINT RUN 25 SER.#'d SETS
EXCHANGE DEADLINE 6/30/2021
SIAK Al Kaline 30.00 80.00
SIAR Anthony Rizzo 30.00 80.00
SIBJ Bo Jackson 40.00 100.00
SIBL Barry Larkin 20.00 50.00
SIDM Don Mattingly 40.00 100.00
SIDO David Ortiz 25.00 60.00
SIEJ Eloy Jimenez 75.00 200.00
SIEM Edgar Martinez 25.00 60.00
SIFT Frank Thomas 40.00 100.00
SIHM Hideki Matsui 50.00 120.00
SIJD Jacob deGrom 25.00 60.00
SIJM Juan Marichal 20.00 50.00
SIJS Juan Soto 30.00 80.00
SIJV Jason Varitek 20.00 50.00
SIKB Kris Bryant 60.00 150.00
SIMA Miguel Andujar 15.00 40.00
SIMC Miguel Cabrera 50.00 120.00
SIMI Mike Trout 400.00 800.00
SIMT Masahiro Tanaka 40.00 100.00
SINR Nolan Ryan 60.00 150.00
SIOS Ozzie Smith 25.00 60.00
SIRA Roberto Alomar 15.00 40.00
SIRAJ Ronald Acuna Jr. 60.00 150.00
SIRC Rod Carew 20.00 50.00
SIRH Rhys Hoskins 25.00 60.00
SIRI Rickey Henderson 40.00 100.00
SIRS Ryne Sandberg 30.00 80.00
SIVG Vladimir Guerrero 25.00 60.00
SIVGJ Vladimir Guerrero Jr. 250.00 500.00

2020 Topps Diamond Icons Autographs

RANDOM INSERTS IN PACKS
PRINT RUN BTW 15-25 COPIES PER
NO PRICING QTY 15 OR LESS
EXCHANGE DEADLINE 5/31/2022
ACI Ichiro
ACAD Andre Dawson 25.00 60.00
ACAK Al Kaline 40.00 100.00
ACAP Andy Pettitte 25.00 60.00
ACBG Bob Gibson 30.00 80.00
ACBL Barry Larkin 25.00 60.00
ACCF Carlton Fisk 20.00 50.00
ACCJ Chipper Jones 50.00 120.00
ACCR Cal Ripken Jr. 60.00 150.00
ACCS Chris Sale 20.00 50.00
ACDE Dennis Eckersley 12.00 30.00
ACDO David Ortiz 50.00 120.00
ACEJ Eloy Jimenez 30.00 80.00
ACEM Edgar Martinez 15.00 40.00
ACFM Fred McGriff 20.00 50.00
ACFT Frank Thomas 40.00 100.00
ACGT Gleyber Torres 60.00 150.00
ACHA Hank Aaron
ACHM Hideki Matsui 40.00 100.00
ACJA Jose Altuve 15.00 40.00
ACJC Jose Canseco 20.00 50.00
ACJD Jacob deGrom 75.00 200.00
ACJM Juan Marichal 25.00 60.00
ACJS John Smoltz 25.00 60.00
ACJV Joey Votto 20.00 50.00
ACKB Kris Bryant 50.00 120.00
ACKH Christian Yelich 40.00 100.00
ACKS Kyle Schwarber 15.00 40.00
ACLB Lou Brock 20.00 50.00
ACLS DJ LeMahieu 30.00 80.00
ACMC Miguel Cabrera 60.00 150.00
ACMT Mike Trout
ACNG Nomar Garciaparra 25.00 60.00
ACNH Nico Hoerner RC 40.00 100.00
ACNR Nolan Ryan 75.00 200.00
ACOS Ozzie Smith 30.00 80.00
ACPA Pete Alonso 60.00 150.00
ACPG Paul Goldschmidt 20.00 50.00
ACRA Ronald Acuna Jr. 75.00 200.00
ACRC Rod Carew 25.00 60.00
ACRH Rickey Henderson 40.00 100.00
ACRJ Reggie Jackson 25.00 60.00
ACRS Ryne Sandberg 30.00 80.00
ACRY Robin Yount 40.00 100.00
ACSC Steve Carlton 25.00 60.00
ACSK Sandy Koufax
ACSO Shohei Ohtani
ACTG Tom Glavine 30.00 80.00
ACVG Vladimir Guerrero 30.00 80.00
ACWB Wade Boggs 30.00 80.00
ACWC Willson Contreras 20.00 50.00
ACYA Yordan Alvarez RC 75.00 200.00
ACAAQ Aristides Aquino RC 40.00 100.00
ACAJU Aaron Judge
ACARI Anthony Rizzo 30.00 80.00
ACARO Alex Rodriguez
ACBIC Bo Bichette RC EXCH 100.00 250.00
ACCKE Clayton Kershaw
ACDMA Don Mattingly 60.00 150.00
ACDMU Dale Murphy 30.00 80.00
ACDWR David Wright 30.00 80.00
ACFTJ Fernando Tatis Jr. 75.00 200.00
ACGCO Gerrit Cole 75.00 200.00
ACGLU Gavin Lux RC 75.00 200.00
ACGSP George Springer 15.00 40.00
ACJBA Jeff Bagwell 30.00 80.00
ACJBE Johnny Bench 30.00 80.00
ACJDA Johnny Damon 8.00 20.00
ACJLU Jesus Luzardo RC 12.00 30.00
ACJSO Juan Soto 60.00 150.00
ACJTH Jim Thome 30.00 80.00
ACJVA Jason Varitek 30.00 80.00
ACKGJ Ken Griffey Jr.
ACLRO Luis Robert RC 150.00 400.00
ACLUX Gavin Lux RC 75.00 200.00
ACMMC Mark McGwire 50.00 120.00
ACMSC Mike Schmidt 100.00 250.00
ACMTA Masahiro Tanaka
ACRAL Roberto Alomar 25.00 60.00
ACRCL Roger Clemens
ACRDE Rafael Devers 25.00 60.00
ACRHO Rhys Hoskins 40.00 100.00
ACRJO Randy Johnson
ACSBI Shane Bieber 20.00 50.00
ACSCH Max Scherzer 50.00 120.00
ACWBU Walker Buehler 30.00 80.00
ACWCL Will Clark 25.00 60.00
ACYAL Yordan Alvarez RC 75.00 200.00

2020 Topps Diamond Icons Diamond Icons Autographs

RANDOM INSERTS IN PACKS
STATED PRINT RUN 25 COPIES PER
EXCHANGE DEADLINE 5/31/2022
DIAAJ Aaron Judge 100.00 250.00
DIAAR Alex Rodriguez
DIABH Bryce Harper 125.00 300.00
DIABL Barry Larkin 25.00 60.00
DIACC CC Sabathia 30.00 80.00
DIACY Christian Yelich 40.00 100.00
DIADM Don Mattingly 60.00 150.00
DIADO David Ortiz 50.00 120.00
DIADS Darryl Strawberry 25.00 60.00
DIADW David Wright 30.00 80.00
DIAEJ Eloy Jimenez 30.00 80.00
DIAFT Frank Thomas 40.00 100.00
DIAGT Gleyber Torres 60.00 150.00
DIAHM Hideki Matsui 40.00 100.00
DIAIS Ichiro
DIAJF Jack Flaherty 25.00 60.00
DIAJS Juan Soto 60.00 150.00
DIAKH Keston Hiura 25.00 60.00
DIALR Luis Robert 150.00 400.00
DIAMM Mark McGwire 50.00 120.00
DIAMS Max Scherzer 50.00 120.00
DIAMT Mike Trout
DIANR Nolan Ryan 75.00 200.00
DIAOS Ozzie Smith 30.00 80.00
DIAPA Pete Alonso 60.00 150.00
DIARC Roger Clemens 30.00 80.00
DIARH Rickey Henderson 40.00 100.00
DIARY Robin Yount 40.00 100.00
DIASK Sandy Koufax
DIASO Shohei Ohtani
DIATL Tim Lincecum 75.00 200.00
DIAWB Walker Buehler 30.00 80.00
DIAAAQ Aristides Aquino 40.00 100.00
DIAANO Aaron Nola 30.00 80.00
DIABBI Bo Bichette EXCH 100.00 250.00
DIACRJ Cal Ripken Jr. 60.00 150.00
DIAFTJ Fernando Tatis Jr. 125.00 300.00
DIAGCO Gerrit Cole 75.00 200.00
DIAGLU Gavin Lux 75.00 200.00
DIAJBA Jeff Bagwell 30.00 80.00
DIAJTH Jim Thome 30.00 80.00
DIAKGJ Ken Griffey Jr. 150.00 400.00
DIAMSC Mike Schmidt 100.00 250.00
DIARAJ Ronald Acuna Jr. 125.00 300.00
DIASCA Steve Carlton 25.00 60.00
DIAYAL Yordan Alvarez 75.00 200.00

2020 Topps Diamond Icons Jumbo Patch Autographs

RANDOM INSERTS IN PACKS
PRINT RUN BTW 15-25 COPIES PER
NO PRICING QTY 15 OR LESS
EXCHANGE DEADLINE 5/31/2022
AJPAJ Aaron Judge
AJPAN Aaron Nola 40.00 100.00
AJPAR Anthony Rizzo 50.00 120.00
AJPBH Bryce Harper
AJPBP Buster Posey 60.00 150.00
AJPCL Clayton Kershaw EXCH 75.00 200.00
AJPCP Chris Paddack 25.00 60.00
AJPCY Christian Yelich
AJPDO David Ortiz 60.00 150.00
AJPGS George Springer 20.00 50.00
AJPGT Gleyber Torres
AJPJA Jose Altuve 20.00 50.00
AJPJR Jose Ramirez 20.00 50.00
AJPJV Joey Votto 40.00 100.00
AJPKS Kyle Schwarber 25.00 60.00
AJPMC Miguel Cabrera 75.00 200.00
AJPMH Masahiro Tanaka
AJPMT Mike Trout
AJPPG Paul Goldschmidt 25.00 60.00
AJPSO Shohei Ohtani
AJPTL Tim Lincecum 100.00 250.00
AJPWB Walker Buehler 75.00 200.00
AJPWC Willson Contreras 25.00 60.00
AJPWM Whit Merrifield 25.00 60.00
AJPXB Xander Bogaerts 30.00 80.00
AJPYA Yordan Alvarez 150.00 400.00
AJPABE Andrew Benintendi 40.00 100.00
AJPEMA Edgar Martinez 40.00 100.00
AJPFTJ Fernando Tatis Jr.
AJPJFL Jack Flaherty 40.00 100.00
AJPKGJ Ken Griffey Jr.
AJPKHI Keston Hiura 60.00 150.00
AJPMAX Max Scherzer 50.00 120.00
AJPMTE Mark Teixeira 20.00 50.00
AJPRAJ Ronald Acuna Jr.
AJPRAL Roberto Alomar
AJPRHE Rickey Henderson
AJPRHO Rhys Hoskins 50.00 120.00
AJPSBI Shane Bieber 25.00 60.00
AJPWBO Wade Boggs 25.00 60.00

2020 Topps Diamond Icons Red Ink Autographs

RANDOM INSERTS IN PACKS
PRINT RUN BTW 15-25 COPIES PER
NO PRICING QTY 15 OR LESS
EXCHANGE DEADLINE 5/31/2022
RIAA Aristides Aquino 40.00 100.00
RIAP Andy Pettitte 25.00 60.00
RIBG Bob Gibson 30.00 80.00
RIBH Bryce Harper
RIBL Barry Larkin 25.00 60.00
RIBP Buster Posey 40.00 100.00
RICF Carlton Fisk 20.00 50.00
RICJ Chipper Jones 50.00 120.00
RICR Cal Ripken Jr.
RICS Chris Sale 20.00 50.00
RIDE Dennis Eckersley 12.00 30.00
RIFE Fernando Tatis Jr. 125.00 300.00
RIGL Gavin Lux 75.00 200.00
RIGS George Springer 15.00 40.00
RIGT Gleyber Torres 60.00 150.00
RIHM Hideki Matsui
RIJA Jose Altuve 15.00 40.00
RIJB Johnny Bench
RIJD Jacob deGrom 75.00 200.00
RIJS Juan Soto 60.00 150.00
RIJV Joey Votto 40.00 100.00
RILB Lou Brock 20.00 50.00
RIMC Miguel Cabrera 60.00 150.00
RIMM Mark McGwire
RIMT Masahiro Tanaka
RING Nomar Garciaparra 25.00 60.00
RIPG Paul Goldschmidt 20.00 50.00
RIRD Rafael Devers 25.00 60.00
RIRH Rhys Hoskins 40.00 100.00
RIRJ Reggie Jackson 25.00 60.00
RISO Shohei Ohtani
RITG Tom Glavine 30.00 80.00
RITL Tim Lincecum 75.00 200.00
RIVG Vladimir Guerrero 30.00 80.00
RIWB Wade Boggs 30.00 80.00
RIWI Will Clark 25.00 60.00
RIYA Yordan Alvarez 75.00 200.00
RIAJU Aaron Judge 100.00 250.00
RIAKA Al Kaline 40.00 100.00
RIARI Anthony Rizzo 30.00 80.00
RIDMA Don Mattingly 60.00 150.00
RIDOR David Ortiz 50.00 120.00
RIEJI Eloy Jimenez 30.00 80.00
RIEMA Edgar Martinez 20.00 50.00
RIFTH Frank Thomas 40.00 100.00
RIICH Ichiro
RIJMA Juan Marichal 25.00 60.00
RIKBR Kris Bryant 50.00 120.00
RIKGJ Ken Griffey Jr.
RILRO Luis Robert 150.00 400.00
RIMMU Mike Mussina 30.00 80.00
RIMTR Mike Trout
RINHO Nico Hoerner 40.00 100.00
RINRY Nolan Ryan 75.00 200.00
RIOZM Ozzie Smith 30.00 80.00
RIRAJ Ronald Acuna Jr. 125.00 300.00
RIRAL Roberto Alomar 25.00 60.00
RIRCA Rod Carew 25.00 60.00
RIRHE Rickey Henderson
RIRJO Randy Johnson
RIRSA Ryne Sandberg 30.00 80.00
RIWBU Walker Buehler 30.00 80.00

2020 Topps Diamond Icons Silver Ink Autographs

RANDOM INSERTS IN PACKS
STATED PRINT RUN 25 COPIES PER
EXCHANGE DEADLINE 5/31/2022

Card	Low	High
SIAR Anthony Rizzo	30.00	80.00
SIBL Barry Larkin	25.00	60.00
SIBS Blake Snell	15.00	40.00
SIDM Don Mattingly	60.00	150.00
SIDS Darryl Strawberry	25.00	60.00
SIGL Gavin Lux	75.00	200.00
SIGT Gleyber Torres	60.00	150.00
SIHM Hideki Matsui	40.00	100.00
SIJD Jacob deGrom	75.00	200.00
SIJM Juan Marichal	25.00	60.00
SIJS Juan Soto	60.00	150.00
SIKB Kris Bryant	50.00	120.00
SIKG Ken Griffey Jr.		
SIKH Keston Hiura	25.00	60.00
SILR Luis Robert	150.00	400.00
SIMS Max Scherzer	50.00	120.00
SIMT Masahiro Tanaka		
SINR Nolan Ryan	75.00	200.00
SIOZ Ozzie Smith	30.00	80.00
SIPA Pete Alonso	60.00	150.00
SIRC Rod Carew	25.00	60.00
SIRD Rafael Devers	25.00	60.00
SIRH Rickey Henderson	40.00	100.00
SIRS Ryne Sandberg	30.00	80.00
SIVG Vladimir Guerrero	30.00	80.00
SIXB Xander Bogaerts	30.00	80.00
SIYA Yordan Alvarez	75.00	200.00
SIAJU Aaron Judge		
SIAKA Al Kaline	40.00	100.00
SIDOR David Ortiz		
SIFTH Frank Thomas	40.00	100.00
SIFTJ Fernando Tatis Jr.	125.00	300.00
SIICH Ichiro		
SIRAJ Ronald Acuna Jr.	125.00	300.00
SIRHO Rhys Hoskins	40.00	100.00

2014 Topps Dynasty Autograph Patches

OVERALL AUTO ODDS 1:1
STATED PRINT RUN 10 SER.#'d SETS
ALL VERSION EQUALLY PRICED
EXCHANGE DEADLINE 12/31/2017

Card	Low	High
APAG1 Adrian Gonzalez	50.00	125.00
APAG2 Adrian Gonzalez	50.00	125.00
APAG3 Adrian Gonzalez	50.00	125.00
APAG4 Adrian Gonzalez	50.00	125.00
APAG5 Adrian Gonzalez	50.00	125.00
APAG6 Adrian Gonzalez	50.00	125.00
APAP1 Albert Pujols	200.00	300.00
APAP2 Albert Pujols	200.00	300.00
APAP3 Albert Pujols	200.00	300.00
APAP4 Albert Pujols	200.00	300.00
APBH1 Bryce Harper	300.00	600.00
APBH2 Bryce Harper	300.00	600.00
APBH3 Bryce Harper	300.00	600.00
APBH4 Bryce Harper	300.00	600.00
APBH5 Bryce Harper	300.00	600.00
APBH6 Bryce Harper	300.00	600.00
APBH7 Bryce Harper	300.00	600.00
APBH8 Bryce Harper	300.00	600.00
APBH9 Bryce Harper	300.00	600.00
APBH10 Bryce Harper	300.00	600.00
APBH11 Bryce Harper	300.00	600.00
APBJ1 Bo Jackson	150.00	300.00
APBJ2 Bo Jackson	150.00	300.00
APBJ3 Bo Jackson	150.00	300.00
APBJ4 Bo Jackson	150.00	300.00
APBJ5 Bo Jackson	150.00	300.00
APBJ6 Bo Jackson	150.00	300.00
APBJ7 Bo Jackson	150.00	300.00
APBJ8 Bo Jackson	150.00	300.00
APBP1 Buster Posey	200.00	300.00
APBP2 Buster Posey	200.00	300.00
APBP3 Buster Posey	200.00	300.00
APBP4 Buster Posey	80.00	200.00
APBP5 Buster Posey	80.00	200.00
APCB1 Craig Biggio	50.00	125.00
APCB2 Craig Biggio	50.00	125.00
APCB3 Craig Biggio	50.00	125.00
APCB4 Craig Biggio	50.00	125.00
APCB5 Craig Biggio	50.00	125.00
APCB6 Craig Biggio	50.00	125.00
APCB7 Craig Biggio	50.00	125.00
APCB8 Craig Biggio	50.00	125.00
APCF1 Carlton Fisk	100.00	200.00
APCF2 Carlton Fisk	100.00	200.00
APCF3 Carlton Fisk	100.00	200.00
APCF4 Carlton Fisk	100.00	200.00
APCF5 Carlton Fisk	100.00	200.00
APCF6 Carlton Fisk	100.00	200.00
APCJ1 Chipper Jones	150.00	300.00
APCJ10 Chipper Jones	60.00	150.00
APCJ11 Chipper Jones	60.00	150.00
APCJ2 Chipper Jones	150.00	300.00
APCJ3 Chipper Jones	150.00	300.00
APCJ4 Chipper Jones	150.00	300.00
APCJ5 Chipper Jones	150.00	300.00
APCJ6 Chipper Jones	150.00	300.00
APCJ7 Chipper Jones	150.00	300.00
APCJ8 Chipper Jones	150.00	300.00
APCJ9 Chipper Jones	150.00	300.00
APCK1 Clayton Kershaw	250.00	400.00
APCK2 Clayton Kershaw	250.00	400.00
APCK3 Clayton Kershaw	250.00	400.00
APCK4 Clayton Kershaw	250.00	400.00
APCK5 Clayton Kershaw	250.00	400.00
APCR1 Cal Ripken Jr.	200.00	300.00
APCR2 Cal Ripken Jr.	200.00	300.00
APCR3 Cal Ripken Jr.	200.00	300.00
APCR4 Cal Ripken Jr.	200.00	300.00
APCR5 Cal Ripken Jr.	200.00	300.00
APCR6 Cal Ripken Jr.	200.00	300.00
APCR7 Cal Ripken Jr.	200.00	300.00
APCR8 Cal Ripken Jr.	200.00	300.00
APDM1 Daisuke Matsuzaka	100.00	200.00
APDM2 Daisuke Matsuzaka	100.00	200.00
APDM3 Daisuke Matsuzaka	100.00	200.00
APDM4 Daisuke Matsuzaka	100.00	200.00
APDM5 Daisuke Matsuzaka	100.00	200.00
APDM6 Daisuke Matsuzaka	100.00	200.00
APDM7 Daisuke Matsuzaka	100.00	200.00
APDM8 Daisuke Matsuzaka	100.00	200.00
APDMT1 Don Mattingly	125.00	300.00
APDMT2 Don Mattingly	125.00	300.00
APDMT3 Don Mattingly	125.00	300.00
APDMT4 Don Mattingly	125.00	300.00
APDMT5 Don Mattingly	125.00	300.00
APDMT6 Don Mattingly	125.00	300.00
APDMT7 Don Mattingly	125.00	300.00
APDMT8 Don Mattingly	125.00	300.00
APDO1 David Ortiz	150.00	300.00
APDO2 David Ortiz	150.00	300.00
APDO3 David Ortiz	150.00	300.00
APDO4 David Ortiz	150.00	300.00
APDO5 David Ortiz	150.00	300.00
APDO6 David Ortiz	150.00	300.00
APDP1 Dustin Pedroia	100.00	250.00
APDP2 Dustin Pedroia	100.00	250.00
APDP3 Dustin Pedroia	100.00	250.00
APDP4 Dustin Pedroia	100.00	250.00
APDP5 Dustin Pedroia	100.00	250.00
APDP6 Dustin Pedroia	100.00	250.00
APDW1 David Wright	100.00	200.00
APDW2 David Wright	100.00	200.00
APDW3 David Wright	100.00	200.00
APDW4 David Wright	100.00	200.00
APDW5 David Wright	100.00	200.00
APDW6 David Wright	100.00	200.00
APEL1 Evan Longoria	50.00	125.00
APEL2 Evan Longoria	50.00	125.00
APEL3 Evan Longoria	50.00	125.00
APEL4 Evan Longoria	50.00	125.00
APEL5 Evan Longoria	50.00	125.00
APEL6 Evan Longoria	50.00	125.00
APEL7 Evan Longoria	50.00	125.00
APEL8 Evan Longoria	50.00	125.00
APEL9 Evan Longoria	50.00	125.00
APEL10 Evan Longoria	50.00	125.00
APEL11 Evan Longoria	50.00	125.00
APFF1 Freddie Freeman	80.00	200.00
APFF2 Freddie Freeman	80.00	200.00
APFF3 Freddie Freeman	80.00	200.00
APFF4 Freddie Freeman	80.00	200.00
APFF5 Freddie Freeman	80.00	200.00
APFF6 Freddie Freeman	80.00	200.00
APFF7 Freddie Freeman	80.00	200.00
APFF8 Freddie Freeman	80.00	200.00
APFF9 Freddie Freeman	80.00	200.00
APFF10 Freddie Freeman	80.00	200.00
APFF11 Freddie Freeman	80.00	200.00
APFT1 Frank Thomas	200.00	300.00
APFT2 Frank Thomas	200.00	300.00
APFT3 Frank Thomas	200.00	300.00
APFT4 Frank Thomas	200.00	300.00
APFT5 Frank Thomas	200.00	300.00
APFT6 Frank Thomas	200.00	300.00
APFT7 Frank Thomas	200.00	300.00
APFT8 Frank Thomas	200.00	300.00
APGM1 Greg Maddux EXCH	200.00	300.00
APGP1 Gregory Polanco RC	60.00	150.00
APGP2 Gregory Polanco RC	60.00	150.00
APGP3 Gregory Polanco RC	60.00	150.00
APGP4 Gregory Polanco RC	60.00	150.00
APGP5 Gregory Polanco RC	60.00	150.00
APGP6 Gregory Polanco RC	60.00	150.00
APGP7 Gregory Polanco RC	60.00	150.00
APGP8 Gregory Polanco RC	60.00	150.00
APGS1 Giancarlo Stanton	150.00	300.00
APGS2 Giancarlo Stanton	150.00	300.00
APGS3 Giancarlo Stanton	150.00	300.00
APGS4 Giancarlo Stanton	150.00	300.00
APGS5 Giancarlo Stanton	150.00	300.00
APGS6 Giancarlo Stanton	150.00	300.00
APGSP1 George Springer RC	150.00	400.00
APGSP2 George Springer RC	150.00	400.00
APGSP3 George Springer RC	150.00	400.00
APHI1 Hisashi Iwakuma	100.00	200.00
APHI2 Hisashi Iwakuma	100.00	200.00
APHI3 Hisashi Iwakuma	100.00	200.00
APHI4 Hisashi Iwakuma	100.00	200.00
APHI5 Hisashi Iwakuma	100.00	200.00
APHI6 Hisashi Iwakuma	100.00	200.00
APHI7 Hisashi Iwakuma	100.00	200.00
APHI8 Hisashi Iwakuma	100.00	200.00
APHR1 Hanley Ramirez	50.00	125.00
APHR2 Hanley Ramirez	50.00	125.00
APHR3 Hanley Ramirez	50.00	125.00
APHR4 Hanley Ramirez	50.00	125.00
APHR5 Hanley Ramirez	50.00	125.00
APHR6 Hanley Ramirez	50.00	125.00
APHR7 Hanley Ramirez	50.00	125.00
APHR8 Hanley Ramirez	50.00	125.00
APJA1 Jose Abreu RC	250.00	400.00
APJA2 Jose Abreu RC	250.00	400.00
APJA3 Jose Abreu RC	250.00	400.00
APJA4 Jose Abreu RC	250.00	400.00
APJA5 Jose Abreu RC	250.00	400.00
APJA6 Jose Abreu RC	250.00	400.00
APJA7 Jose Abreu RC	250.00	400.00
APJA8 Jose Abreu RC	250.00	400.00
APJF1 Jose Fernandez	100.00	200.00
APJF2 Jose Fernandez	100.00	200.00
APJF3 Jose Fernandez	100.00	200.00
APJF4 Jose Fernandez	100.00	200.00
APJF5 Jose Fernandez	100.00	200.00
APJF6 Jose Fernandez	100.00	200.00
APJF7 Jose Fernandez	100.00	200.00
APJF8 Jose Fernandez	100.00	200.00
APJH1 Josh Hamilton	50.00	125.00
APJH2 Josh Hamilton	50.00	125.00
APJH3 Josh Hamilton	50.00	125.00
APJH4 Josh Hamilton	50.00	125.00
APJH5 Josh Hamilton	50.00	125.00
APJH6 Josh Hamilton	50.00	125.00
APJH7 Josh Hamilton	50.00	125.00
APJHE1 Jason Heyward	50.00	125.00
APJHE2 Jason Heyward	50.00	125.00
APJHE3 Jason Heyward	50.00	125.00
APJHE4 Jason Heyward	50.00	125.00
APJHE5 Jason Heyward	50.00	125.00
APJHE6 Jason Heyward	50.00	125.00
APJHE7 Jason Heyward	50.00	125.00
APJM1 Joe Mauer	125.00	250.00
APJM2 Joe Mauer	125.00	250.00
APJM3 Joe Mauer	125.00	250.00
APJM4 Joe Mauer	125.00	250.00
APJM5 Joe Mauer	125.00	250.00
APJM6 Joe Mauer	125.00	250.00
APJS1 John Smoltz	125.00	250.00
APJS2 John Smoltz	125.00	250.00
APJS3 John Smoltz	125.00	250.00
APJS4 John Smoltz	125.00	250.00
APJS5 John Smoltz	125.00	250.00
APJS6 John Smoltz	125.00	250.00
APJS7 John Smoltz	125.00	250.00
APJV1 Joey Votto	60.00	150.00
APJV2 Joey Votto	60.00	150.00
APJV3 Joey Votto	60.00	150.00
APJV4 Joey Votto	60.00	150.00
APJV5 Joey Votto	60.00	150.00
APJV6 Joey Votto	60.00	150.00
APJV7 Joey Votto	60.00	150.00
APJV8 Joey Votto	60.00	150.00
APKG1 Ken Griffey Jr.	200.00	400.00
Cincinnati Reds		
APKG2 Ken Griffey Jr.	200.00	400.00
Cincinnati Reds		
APKG3 Ken Griffey Jr.	200.00	400.00
Cincinnati Reds		
APKG4 Ken Griffey Jr.	200.00	400.00
Cincinnati Reds		
APKG5 Ken Griffey Jr.	200.00	400.00
Cincinnati Reds		
APKG6 Ken Griffey Jr.	200.00	400.00
Cincinnati Reds		
APKG7 Ken Griffey Jr.	200.00	400.00
Cincinnati Reds		
APKG8 Ken Griffey Jr.	200.00	400.00
Cincinnati Reds		
APKG9 Ken Griffey Jr.	200.00	400.00
Seattle Mariners		
APKG10 Ken Griffey Jr.	200.00	400.00
Seattle Mariners		
APKG11 Ken Griffey Jr.	200.00	400.00
Seattle Mariners		
APKG12 Ken Griffey Jr.	200.00	400.00
Seattle Mariners		
APKG13 Ken Griffey Jr.	200.00	400.00
Seattle Mariners		
APKG14 Ken Griffey Jr.	200.00	400.00
Seattle Mariners		
APKG15 Ken Griffey Jr.	200.00	400.00
Seattle Mariners		
APKG16 Ken Griffey Jr.	200.00	400.00
Seattle Mariners		
APMC1 Miguel Cabrera	250.00	400.00
APMC2 Miguel Cabrera	250.00	400.00
APMC3 Miguel Cabrera	250.00	400.00
APMC4 Miguel Cabrera	250.00	400.00
APMC5 Miguel Cabrera	250.00	400.00
APMC6 Miguel Cabrera	250.00	400.00
APMC7 Miguel Cabrera	250.00	400.00
APMC8 Miguel Cabrera	250.00	400.00
APMM1 Mark McGwire	125.00	300.00
APMM2 Mark McGwire	125.00	300.00
APMM3 Mark McGwire	125.00	300.00
APMM4 Mark McGwire	125.00	300.00
APMM5 Mark McGwire	125.00	300.00
APMM6 Mark McGwire	125.00	300.00
APMM7 Mark McGwire	125.00	300.00
APMM8 Mark McGwire	125.00	300.00
APMMA1 Manny Machado	100.00	200.00
APMMA2 Manny Machado	100.00	200.00
APMMA3 Manny Machado	100.00	200.00
APMMA4 Manny Machado	100.00	200.00
APMMA5 Manny Machado	100.00	200.00
APMMA6 Manny Machado	100.00	200.00
APMMA7 Manny Machado	100.00	200.00
APMMA8 Manny Machado	100.00	200.00
APMP1 Mike Piazza	125.00	250.00
New York Mets		
APMP2 Mike Piazza	125.00	250.00
New York Mets		
APMP3 Mike Piazza	125.00	250.00
New York Mets		
APMP4 Mike Piazza	125.00	250.00
New York Mets		
APMP5 Mike Piazza	125.00	250.00
New York Mets		
APMP6 Mike Piazza	125.00	250.00
New York Mets		
APMP7 Mike Piazza	125.00	250.00
New York Mets		
APMP8 Mike Piazza	125.00	250.00
New York Mets		
APMP9 Mike Piazza	125.00	250.00
Los Angeles Dodgers		
APMP10 Mike Piazza	125.00	250.00
Los Angeles Dodgers		
APMP11 Mike Piazza	125.00	250.00
Los Angeles Dodgers		
APMP12 Mike Piazza	125.00	250.00
Los Angeles Dodgers		
APMP13 Mike Piazza	125.00	250.00
Los Angeles Dodgers		
APMP14 Mike Piazza	125.00	250.00
Los Angeles Dodgers		
APMP15 Mike Piazza	125.00	250.00
Los Angeles Dodgers		
APMP16 Mike Piazza	125.00	250.00
Los Angeles Dodgers		
APMR1 Mariano Rivera	300.00	500.00
APMR2 Mariano Rivera	300.00	500.00
APMR3 Mariano Rivera	300.00	500.00
APMR4 Mariano Rivera	300.00	500.00
APMR5 Mariano Rivera	300.00	500.00
APMR6 Mariano Rivera	300.00	500.00
APMR7 Mariano Rivera	300.00	500.00
APMT1 Mike Trout	400.00	600.00
APMT2 Mike Trout	400.00	600.00
APMT3 Mike Trout	400.00	600.00
APMT4 Mike Trout	400.00	600.00
APMT5 Mike Trout	400.00	600.00
APMT6 Mike Trout	400.00	600.00
APMT7 Mike Trout	400.00	600.00
APMT8 Mike Trout	400.00	600.00
APMW1 Michael Wacha	50.00	125.00
APMW2 Michael Wacha	50.00	125.00
APMW3 Michael Wacha	50.00	125.00
APMW4 Michael Wacha	50.00	125.00
APMW5 Michael Wacha	50.00	125.00
APMW6 Michael Wacha	50.00	125.00
APMW7 Michael Wacha	50.00	125.00
APNC1 Nick Castellanos RC	50.00	120.00
APNC2 Nick Castellanos RC	50.00	120.00
APNC3 Nick Castellanos RC	50.00	120.00
APNC4 Nick Castellanos RC	50.00	120.00
APNC5 Nick Castellanos RC	50.00	120.00
APNC6 Nick Castellanos RC	50.00	120.00
APNR1 Nolan Ryan	150.00	250.00
Houston Astros		
APNR2 Nolan Ryan	150.00	250.00
Houston Astros		
APNR3 Nolan Ryan	150.00	250.00
Houston Astros		
APNR4 Nolan Ryan	150.00	250.00
Houston Astros		
APNR5 Nolan Ryan	150.00	250.00
Houston Astros		
APNR6 Nolan Ryan	150.00	250.00
Houston Astros		
APNR7 Nolan Ryan	150.00	250.00
Houston Astros		
APNR8 Nolan Ryan	150.00	250.00
Houston Astros		
APNR9 Nolan Ryan	150.00	250.00
Texas Rangers		
APNR10 Nolan Ryan	150.00	250.00
Texas Rangers		
APNR11 Nolan Ryan	150.00	250.00
Texas Rangers		
APNR12 Nolan Ryan	150.00	250.00
Texas Rangers		
APNR13 Nolan Ryan	150.00	250.00
Texas Rangers		
APNR14 Nolan Ryan	150.00	250.00
Texas Rangers		
APNR15 Nolan Ryan	150.00	250.00
Texas Rangers		
APNR16 Nolan Ryan	150.00	250.00
Texas Rangers		
APOT1 Oscar Taveras RC	50.00	120.00
APOT2 Oscar Taveras RC	50.00	120.00
APOT3 Oscar Taveras RC	50.00	120.00
APOT4 Oscar Taveras RC	50.00	120.00
APOT5 Oscar Taveras RC	50.00	120.00
APOT6 Oscar Taveras RC	50.00	120.00
APOT7 Oscar Taveras RC	50.00	120.00
APPG1 Paul Goldschmidt	60.00	150.00
APPG2 Paul Goldschmidt	60.00	150.00
APPG3 Paul Goldschmidt	60.00	150.00
APPG4 Paul Goldschmidt	60.00	150.00
APPG5 Paul Goldschmidt	60.00	150.00
APPG6 Paul Goldschmidt	60.00	150.00
APPG7 Paul Goldschmidt	60.00	150.00
APPG8 Paul Goldschmidt	60.00	150.00
APPG9 Paul Goldschmidt	60.00	150.00
APPM1 Pedro Martinez	100.00	200.00
APPM2 Pedro Martinez	100.00	200.00
APPM3 Pedro Martinez	100.00	200.00
APPM4 Pedro Martinez	100.00	200.00
APPM5 Pedro Martinez	100.00	200.00
APPM6 Pedro Martinez	100.00	200.00
APPM7 Pedro Martinez	100.00	200.00
APRA1 Roberto Alomar	100.00	200.00
APRA2 Roberto Alomar	100.00	200.00
APRA3 Roberto Alomar	100.00	200.00
APRA4 Roberto Alomar	100.00	200.00
APRA5 Roberto Alomar	100.00	200.00
APRA6 Roberto Alomar	100.00	200.00
APRA7 Roberto Alomar	100.00	200.00
APRB1 Ryan Braun	50.00	125.00
APRB2 Ryan Braun	50.00	125.00
APRB3 Ryan Braun	50.00	125.00
APRB4 Ryan Braun	50.00	125.00
APRB5 Ryan Braun	50.00	125.00
APRB6 Ryan Braun	50.00	125.00
APRB7 Ryan Braun	50.00	125.00
APRB8 Ryan Braun	50.00	125.00
APRB9 Ryan Braun	50.00	125.00
APRB10 Ryan Braun	50.00	125.00
APRB11 Ryan Braun	50.00	125.00
APRCL1 Roger Clemens	125.00	250.00
APRCL2 Roger Clemens	125.00	250.00
APRCL3 Roger Clemens	125.00	250.00
APRCL4 Roger Clemens	125.00	250.00
APRCL5 Roger Clemens	125.00	250.00
APRCL6 Roger Clemens	125.00	250.00
APRCL7 Roger Clemens	125.00	250.00
APRH1 Rickey Henderson EXCH	100.00	200.00
New York Mets		
APRH10 Rickey Henderson	100.00	200.00
(Oakland Athletics		
APRJ1 Reggie Jackson	60.00	150.00
APRJ2 Reggie Jackson	60.00	150.00
APRJ3 Reggie Jackson	60.00	150.00
APRJ4 Reggie Jackson	60.00	150.00
APRJ5 Reggie Jackson	60.00	150.00
APRJ6 Reggie Jackson	60.00	150.00
APRJ7 Reggie Jackson	60.00	150.00
APRJO1 Randy Johnson	150.00	300.00
APRJO2 Randy Johnson	150.00	300.00
APRJO3 Randy Johnson	150.00	300.00
APRJO4 Randy Johnson	150.00	300.00
APRJO5 Randy Johnson	150.00	300.00
APRJO6 Randy Johnson	150.00	300.00
APRJO7 Randy Johnson	150.00	300.00
APRJO8 Randy Johnson	150.00	300.00
APRS1 Ryne Sandberg	125.00	250.00
APRS2 Ryne Sandberg	125.00	250.00
APRS3 Ryne Sandberg	125.00	250.00
APRS4 Ryne Sandberg	125.00	250.00
APRY1 Robin Yount	60.00	150.00
APRY2 Robin Yount	60.00	150.00
APRY3 Robin Yount	60.00	150.00
APRY4 Robin Yount	60.00	150.00
APRY5 Robin Yount	60.00	150.00
APRY6 Robin Yount	60.00	150.00
APSC1 Steve Carlton	60.00	150.00
APSC2 Steve Carlton	60.00	150.00
APSC3 Steve Carlton	60.00	150.00
APSC4 Steve Carlton	60.00	150.00
APSC5 Steve Carlton	60.00	150.00
APSC6 Steve Carlton	60.00	150.00
APSC7 Steve Carlton	60.00	150.00
APSG1 Sonny Gray	50.00	120.00
APSG2 Sonny Gray	50.00	120.00
APSG3 Sonny Gray	50.00	120.00
APSG4 Sonny Gray	50.00	120.00
APSG5 Sonny Gray	50.00	120.00
APSG6 Sonny Gray	50.00	120.00
APSM1 Shelby Miller	50.00	125.00
APSM2 Shelby Miller	50.00	125.00
APSM3 Shelby Miller	50.00	125.00
APSM4 Shelby Miller	50.00	125.00
APSM5 Shelby Miller	50.00	125.00
APTGL1 Tom Glavine	100.00	200.00
APTGL2 Tom Glavine	100.00	200.00
APTGL3 Tom Glavine	100.00	200.00
APTGL4 Tom Glavine	100.00	200.00
APTGL5 Tom Glavine	100.00	200.00
APTT1 Troy Tulowitzki	60.00	150.00
APTT2 Troy Tulowitzki	60.00	150.00
APTT3 Troy Tulowitzki	60.00	150.00
APTT4 Troy Tulowitzki	60.00	150.00
APTT5 Troy Tulowitzki	60.00	150.00
APTT6 Troy Tulowitzki	60.00	150.00
APTT7 Troy Tulowitzki	60.00	150.00
APTT8 Troy Tulowitzki	60.00	150.00
APTW1 Taijuan Walker RC	40.00	100.00
APTW2 Taijuan Walker RC	40.00	100.00
APTW3 Taijuan Walker RC	40.00	100.00
APTW4 Taijuan Walker RC	40.00	100.00
APTW5 Taijuan Walker RC	40.00	100.00
APTW6 Taijuan Walker RC	40.00	100.00
APTW7 Taijuan Walker RC	40.00	100.00
APVG1 Vladimir Guerrero	60.00	150.00
Los Angeles Angels		
APVG2 Vladimir Guerrero	60.00	150.00
Los Angeles Angels		
APVG3 Vladimir Guerrero	60.00	150.00
Los Angeles Angels		
APVG4 Vladimir Guerrero	60.00	150.00
Los Angeles Angels		
APVG5 Vladimir Guerrero	60.00	150.00
Los Angeles Angels		
APVG6 Vladimir Guerrero	60.00	150.00
Los Angeles Angels		
APVG7 Vladimir Guerrero	60.00	150.00
Los Angeles Angels		
APVG8 Vladimir Guerrero	60.00	150.00
Los Angeles Angels		
APVGE1 Vladimir Guerrero	60.00	150.00
Montreal Expos		
APVGE2 Vladimir Guerrero	60.00	150.00
Montreal Expos		
APVGE3 Vladimir Guerrero	60.00	150.00
Montreal Expos		
APVGE4 Vladimir Guerrero	60.00	150.00
Montreal Expos		
APVGE5 Vladimir Guerrero	60.00	150.00
Montreal Expos		
APVGE6 Vladimir Guerrero	60.00	150.00
Montreal Expos		
APVGE7 Vladimir Guerrero	60.00	150.00
Montreal Expos		
APVGE8 Vladimir Guerrero	60.00	150.00
Montreal Expos		
APWB1 Wade Boggs	50.00	125.00
New York Yankees		
APWB2 Wade Boggs	50.00	125.00
New York Yankees		
APWB3 Wade Boggs	50.00	125.00
New York Yankees		
APWB4 Wade Boggs	50.00	125.00
New York Yankees		
APWB5 Wade Boggs	50.00	125.00
New York Yankees		
APWB6 Wade Boggs	100.00	200.00
New York Yankees		
APWB7 Wade Boggs	100.00	200.00
New York Yankees		
APWB8 Wade Boggs	100.00	200.00
New York Yankees		
APWB9 Wade Boggs	100.00	200.00
Boston Red Sox		
APWB10 Wade Boggs	100.00	200.00
Boston Red Sox		
APWB11 Wade Boggs	100.00	200.00
Boston Red Sox		
APWB12 Wade Boggs	100.00	200.00
Boston Red Sox		
APWB13 Wade Boggs	100.00	200.00
Boston Red Sox		
APWB14 Wade Boggs	100.00	200.00
Boston Red Sox		
APWB15 Wade Boggs	100.00	200.00
Boston Red Sox		
APWB16 Wade Boggs	100.00	200.00
Boston Red Sox		
APWM1 Wil Myers	40.00	100.00
APWM2 Wil Myers	40.00	100.00
APWM3 Wil Myers	40.00	100.00
APWM4 Wil Myers	40.00	100.00
APWM5 Wil Myers	40.00	100.00
APWM6 Wil Myers	40.00	100.00
APWM7 Wil Myers	40.00	100.00
APWM8 Wil Myers	40.00	100.00
APWMA1 Willie Mays EXCH	400.00	600.00
APYC1 Yoenis Cespedes	60.00	150.00
APYC2 Yoenis Cespedes	60.00	150.00
APYC3 Yoenis Cespedes	60.00	150.00
APYC4 Yoenis Cespedes	60.00	150.00
APYC5 Yoenis Cespedes	60.00	150.00
APYD1 Yu Darvish	125.00	250.00
APYD2 Yu Darvish	125.00	250.00
APYM1 Yadier Molina	150.00	300.00
APYM2 Yadier Molina	150.00	300.00
APYM3 Yadier Molina	150.00	300.00
APYM4 Yadier Molina	150.00	300.00
APYM5 Yadier Molina	150.00	300.00
APYM6 Yadier Molina	150.00	300.00
APYM7 Yadier Molina	150.00	300.00
APYP1 Yasiel Puig	200.00	400.00
APYP2 Yasiel Puig	200.00	400.00
APYP3 Yasiel Puig	200.00	400.00
APYP4 Yasiel Puig	200.00	400.00
APYP5 Yasiel Puig	200.00	400.00
APYP6 Yasiel Puig	200.00	400.00
APYP7 Yasiel Puig	200.00	400.00
APYP8 Yasiel Puig	200.00	400.00

2014 Topps Dynasty Dual Relic Autographs

OVERALL AUTO ODDS 1:1
STATED PRINT RUN 5 SER.#'d SETS
ALL VERSION EQUALLY PRICED
NO MAYS OR KOUFAX PRICING AVAILABLE
EXCHANGE DEADLINE 12/31/2017

Card	Low	High
DRGDM1 Don Mattingly	100.00	200.00
DRGDM2 Don Mattingly	100.00	200.00
DRGDM3 Don Mattingly	100.00	200.00
DRGDM4 Don Mattingly	100.00	200.00
DRGDM5 Don Mattingly	100.00	200.00
DRGEB1 Ernie Banks	150.00	300.00
DRGEB2 Ernie Banks	150.00	300.00
DRGEB3 Ernie Banks	150.00	300.00
DRGEB4 Ernie Banks	150.00	300.00
DRGEB5 Ernie Banks	150.00	300.00
DRGHA1 Hank Aaron	300.00	500.00
DRGHA2 Hank Aaron	300.00	500.00
DRGHA3 Hank Aaron	300.00	500.00
DRGHA4 Hank Aaron	300.00	500.00
DRGHA5 Hank Aaron	300.00	500.00
DRGJB1 Johnny Bench	100.00	250.00
DRGJB2 Johnny Bench	100.00	250.00
DRGJB3 Johnny Bench	100.00	250.00
DRGJB4 Johnny Bench	100.00	250.00
DRGJB5 Johnny Bench	100.00	250.00
DRGJB6 Johnny Bench	100.00	250.00

2015 Topps Dynasty Autograph Patches

OVERALL AUTO ODDS 1:1
STATED PRINT RUN 10 SER.#'d SETS
ALL VERSIONS EQUALLY PRICED
EXCHANGE DEADLINE 12/31/2017

Card	Low	High
APAGA1 Andres Galarraga	300.00	600.00
APAGA2 Andres Galarraga	300.00	600.00
APAGA3 Andres Galarraga	300.00	600.00
APAGA4 Andres Galarraga	300.00	600.00
APAGA5 Andres Galarraga	300.00	600.00
APAGA6 Andres Galarraga	300.00	600.00
APAGA7 Andres Galarraga	300.00	600.00
APAGA8 Andres Galarraga	300.00	600.00
APAP1 Albert Pujols	150.00	300.00
APAP2 Albert Pujols	150.00	300.00
APAP3 Albert Pujols	150.00	300.00
APAP4 Albert Pujols	150.00	300.00
APAP5 Albert Pujols	150.00	300.00
APAR1 Anthony Rizzo	125.00	250.00
APAR2 Anthony Rizzo	125.00	250.00
APAR3 Anthony Rizzo	125.00	250.00
APAR4 Anthony Rizzo	125.00	250.00
APAR5 Anthony Rizzo	125.00	250.00
APAR6 Anthony Rizzo	125.00	250.00
APBBU1 Byron Buxton RC	100.00	200.00
APBBU2 Byron Buxton RC	100.00	200.00
APBBU3 Byron Buxton RC	100.00	200.00
APBBU4 Byron Buxton RC	100.00	200.00
APBH1 Bryce Harper	300.00	500.00
APBH2 Bryce Harper	300.00	500.00
APBH3 Bryce Harper	300.00	500.00
APBH4 Bryce Harper	300.00	500.00
APBH5 Bryce Harper	300.00	500.00
APBH6 Bryce Harper	300.00	500.00
APBJA1 Bo Jackson	100.00	200.00
APBJA2 Bo Jackson	100.00	200.00
APBJA3 Bo Jackson	100.00	200.00
APBJA4 Bo Jackson	100.00	200.00
APBJA5 Bo Jackson	100.00	200.00
APBJA6 Bo Jackson	100.00	200.00
APBP1 Buster Posey	150.00	300.00
APBP2 Buster Posey	150.00	300.00
APBP3 Buster Posey	150.00	300.00
APBP4 Buster Posey	150.00	300.00
APBP5 Buster Posey	150.00	300.00
APBP6 Buster Posey	150.00	300.00
APBP7 Buster Posey	150.00	300.00
APBP8 Buster Posey	150.00	300.00
APBP9 Buster Posey	150.00	300.00
APCB1 Craig Biggio	75.00	150.00
APCB2 Craig Biggio	75.00	150.00
APCB3 Craig Biggio	75.00	150.00
APCB4 Craig Biggio	75.00	150.00
APCB5 Craig Biggio	75.00	150.00
APCF1 Carlton Fisk	100.00	200.00
APCF2 Carlton Fisk	100.00	200.00
APCF3 Carlton Fisk	100.00	200.00
APCF4 Carlton Fisk	100.00	200.00
APCH1 Cole Hamels	60.00	120.00
APCH2 Cole Hamels	60.00	120.00
APCH3 Cole Hamels	60.00	120.00
APCH4 Cole Hamels	60.00	120.00
APCH5 Cole Hamels	60.00	120.00
APCJ1 Chipper Jones	125.00	250.00
APCJ2 Chipper Jones	125.00	250.00
APCJ3 Chipper Jones	125.00	250.00
APCJ4 Chipper Jones	125.00	250.00
APCJ5 Chipper Jones	125.00	250.00
APCK1 Clayton Kershaw	150.00	300.00
APCK2 Clayton Kershaw	150.00	300.00
APCK3 Clayton Kershaw	150.00	300.00
APCK4 Clayton Kershaw	150.00	300.00
APCK5 Clayton Kershaw	150.00	300.00
APCKL1 Corey Kluber	50.00	100.00
APCKL2 Corey Kluber	50.00	100.00
APCKL3 Corey Kluber	50.00	100.00
APCKL4 Corey Kluber	50.00	100.00
APCKL5 Corey Kluber	50.00	100.00
APCRJ1 Cal Ripken Jr.	200.00	400.00
APCRJ2 Cal Ripken Jr.	200.00	400.00
APCRJ3 Cal Ripken Jr.	200.00	400.00
APCRJ4 Cal Ripken Jr.	200.00	400.00
APCRJ5 Cal Ripken Jr.	200.00	400.00
APCRJ6 Cal Ripken Jr.	200.00	400.00
APCRJ7 Cal Ripken Jr.	200.00	400.00
APDE1 Dennis Eckersley	50.00	100.00
APDE2 Dennis Eckersley	50.00	100.00
APDE3 Dennis Eckersley	50.00	100.00
APDE4 Dennis Eckersley	50.00	100.00
APDE5 Dennis Eckersley	50.00	100.00
APDM1 Dan Marino	250.00	400.00
APDM2 Dan Marino	250.00	400.00
APDO1 David Ortiz	125.00	250.00
APDO2 David Ortiz	125.00	250.00
APDO3 David Ortiz	125.00	250.00
APDO4 David Ortiz	125.00	250.00
APDO5 David Ortiz	125.00	250.00
APDO6 David Ortiz	125.00	250.00
APDP1 Dustin Pedroia	75.00	150.00
APDP2 Dustin Pedroia	75.00	150.00
APDP3 Dustin Pedroia	75.00	150.00
APDP4 Dustin Pedroia	75.00	150.00
APDP5 Dustin Pedroia	75.00	150.00
APDP6 Dustin Pedroia	75.00	150.00
APDS1 Deion Sanders	100.00	200.00
APDS2 Deion Sanders	100.00	200.00
APDS3 Deion Sanders	100.00	200.00
APDS4 Deion Sanders	100.00	200.00
APDS5 Deion Sanders	100.00	200.00
APDW1 David Wright	60.00	120.00
APDW2 David Wright	60.00	120.00
APDW3 David Wright	60.00	120.00
APDW4 David Wright	60.00	120.00
APDW5 David Wright	60.00	120.00
APEL1 Evan Longoria	50.00	100.00
APEL2 Evan Longoria	50.00	100.00
APEL3 Evan Longoria	50.00	100.00
APEL4 Evan Longoria	50.00	100.00
APEL5 Evan Longoria	50.00	100.00
APFF1 Freddie Freeman	60.00	120.00
APFF2 Freddie Freeman	60.00	120.00
APFF3 Freddie Freeman	60.00	120.00
APFF4 Freddie Freeman	60.00	120.00
APFF5 Freddie Freeman	60.00	120.00
APFF6 Freddie Freeman	60.00	120.00
APFH1 Felix Hernandez	100.00	200.00
APFH2 Felix Hernandez	100.00	200.00
APFH3 Felix Hernandez	100.00	200.00
APFH4 Felix Hernandez	100.00	200.00
APFH5 Felix Hernandez	100.00	200.00
APFL1 Francisco Lindor RC	100.00	200.00
APFL2 Francisco Lindor RC	100.00	200.00
APFL3 Francisco Lindor RC	100.00	200.00
APFL4 Francisco Lindor RC	100.00	200.00
APFL5 Francisco Lindor RC	100.00	200.00
APFM1 Fred McGriff	50.00	100.00
APFM2 Fred McGriff	50.00	100.00
APFM3 Fred McGriff	50.00	100.00
APFM4 Fred McGriff	50.00	100.00
APFM5 Fred McGriff	50.00	100.00
APFT1 Frank Thomas	150.00	300.00
APFT2 Frank Thomas	150.00	300.00
APFT3 Frank Thomas	150.00	300.00
APFT4 Frank Thomas	150.00	300.00
APFT5 Frank Thomas	150.00	300.00
APGM1 Greg Maddux EXCH	150.00	300.00
APGM2 Greg Maddux EXCH	150.00	300.00
APGM3 Greg Maddux EXCH	150.00	300.00
APGM4 Greg Maddux EXCH	150.00	300.00
APGM5 Greg Maddux EXCH	150.00	300.00
APHR1 Hanley Ramirez	50.00	100.00
APHR2 Hanley Ramirez	50.00	100.00
APHR3 Hanley Ramirez	50.00	100.00
APHR4 Hanley Ramirez	50.00	100.00
APHR5 Hanley Ramirez	50.00	100.00
APHR6 Hanley Ramirez	50.00	100.00
API1 Ichiro Suzuki	400.00	600.00
API2 Ichiro Suzuki	400.00	600.00
API3 Ichiro Suzuki	400.00	600.00
API4 Ichiro Suzuki	400.00	600.00
API5 Ichiro Suzuki	400.00	600.00
API6 Ichiro Suzuki	400.00	600.00
API7 Ichiro Suzuki	400.00	600.00
API8 Ichiro Suzuki	400.00	600.00
API9 Ichiro Suzuki	400.00	600.00
API10 Ichiro Suzuki	400.00	600.00
APJA1 Jose Abreu	75.00	150.00
APJA2 Jose Abreu	75.00	150.00
APJA3 Jose Abreu	75.00	150.00
APJA4 Jose Abreu	75.00	150.00
APJA5 Jose Abreu	75.00	150.00
APJA6 Jose Abreu	75.00	150.00
APJB1 Jeff Bagwell	100.00	200.00
APJB2 Jeff Bagwell	100.00	200.00
APJB3 Jeff Bagwell	100.00	200.00
APJB4 Jeff Bagwell	100.00	200.00
APJC1 Jose Canseco	125.00	250.00
APJC2 Jose Canseco	125.00	250.00
APJC3 Jose Canseco	125.00	250.00
APJC4 Jose Canseco	125.00	250.00
APJC5 Jose Canseco	125.00	250.00
APJD1 Jacob deGrom	250.00	600.00
APJD2 Jacob deGrom	250.00	600.00
APJD3 Jacob deGrom	250.00	600.00
APJD4 Jacob deGrom	250.00	600.00
APJD5 Jacob deGrom	250.00	600.00
APJD6 Jacob deGrom	250.00	600.00
APJE1 John Elway	250.00	400.00
APJE2 John Elway	250.00	400.00
APJF1 Jose Fernandez	75.00	150.00
APJF2 Jose Fernandez	75.00	150.00
APJF3 Jose Fernandez	75.00	150.00
APJF4 Jose Fernandez	75.00	150.00
APJF5 Jose Fernandez	75.00	150.00
APJF6 Jose Fernandez	75.00	150.00
APJG1 Joey Gallo RC	100.00	200.00
APJG2 Joey Gallo RC	100.00	200.00
APJG3 Joey Gallo RC	100.00	200.00
APJG4 Joey Gallo RC	100.00	200.00
APJG5 Joey Gallo RC	100.00	200.00
APJH1 Jason Heyward	75.00	150.00
APJH2 Jason Heyward	75.00	150.00
APJH3 Jason Heyward	75.00	150.00
APJH4 Jason Heyward	75.00	150.00
APJH5 Jason Heyward	75.00	150.00
APJHK1 Jung Ho Kang RC EXCH	200.00	400.00
APJHK2 Jung Ho Kang EXCH	200.00	400.00
APJHK3 Jung Ho Kang EXCH	200.00	400.00
APJHK4 Jung Ho Kang EXCH	200.00	400.00
APJL1 Jon Lester	75.00	150.00
APJL2 Jon Lester	75.00	150.00
APJL3 Jon Lester	75.00	150.00
APJL4 Jon Lester	75.00	150.00
APJL5 Jon Lester	75.00	150.00
APJM1 Joe Mauer	100.00	200.00
APJM2 Joe Mauer	100.00	200.00
APJM3 Joe Mauer	100.00	200.00
APJM4 Joe Mauer	100.00	200.00
APJM5 Joe Mauer	100.00	200.00
APJM6 Joe Mauer	100.00	200.00
APJP1 Joc Pederson RC	100.00	200.00
APJP2 Joc Pederson RC	100.00	200.00
APJP3 Joc Pederson RC	100.00	200.00
APJS1 John Smoltz	75.00	150.00
APJS2 John Smoltz	75.00	150.00
APJS3 John Smoltz	75.00	150.00
APJS4 John Smoltz	75.00	150.00
APJV1 Joey Votto	60.00	120.00
APJV2 Joey Votto	60.00	120.00
APJV3 Joey Votto	60.00	120.00
APJV4 Joey Votto	60.00	120.00
APJV5 Joey Votto	60.00	120.00
APKB1 Kris Bryant RC	600.00	900.00
APKB2 Kris Bryant RC	600.00	900.00
APKB3 Kris Bryant RC	600.00	900.00
APKB4 Kris Bryant RC	600.00	900.00
APKB5 Kris Bryant RC	600.00	900.00
APKG1 Ken Griffey Jr.	250.00	500.00
APKG2 Ken Griffey Jr.	250.00	500.00
APKG3 Ken Griffey Jr.	250.00	500.00
APKG4 Ken Griffey Jr.	250.00	500.00

APKG5 Ken Griffey Jr. 250.00 500.00
APKG6 Ken Griffey Jr. 250.00 500.00
APKG7 Ken Griffey Jr. 250.00 500.00
APKG8 Ken Griffey Jr. 250.00 500.00
APKG9 Ken Griffey Jr. 250.00 500.00
APKS1 Kyle Seager 60.00 120.00
APKS2 Kyle Seager 60.00 120.00
APKS3 Kyle Seager 60.00 120.00
APKS4 Kyle Seager 60.00 120.00
APKS5 Kyle Seager 60.00 120.00
APMC1 Matt Carpenter 60.00 120.00
APMC2 Matt Carpenter 60.00 120.00
APMC3 Matt Carpenter 60.00 120.00
APMC4 Matt Carpenter 60.00 120.00
APMC5 Matt Carpenter 60.00 120.00
APMH1 Matt Harvey EXCH 100.00 200.00
APMH2 Matt Harvey EXCH 100.00 200.00
APMH3 Matt Harvey EXCH 100.00 200.00
APMH4 Matt Harvey EXCH 100.00 200.00
APMH5 Matt Harvey EXCH 100.00 200.00
APMH6 Matt Harvey EXCH 100.00 200.00
APMM1 Manny Machado 150.00 300.00
APMM2 Manny Machado 150.00 300.00
APMM3 Manny Machado 150.00 300.00
APMM4 Manny Machado 150.00 300.00
APMM5 Manny Machado 150.00 300.00
APMMC1 Mark McGwire 150.00 300.00
APMMC2 Mark McGwire 150.00 300.00
APMMC3 Mark McGwire 150.00 300.00
APMMC4 Mark McGwire 150.00 300.00
APMMC5 Mark McGwire 150.00 300.00
APMMC6 Mark McGwire 150.00 300.00
APMMC7 Mark McGwire 150.00 300.00
APMMC8 Mark McGwire 150.00 300.00
APMMC9 Mark McGwire 150.00 300.00
APMP1 Mike Piazza 150.00 300.00
APMP2 Mike Piazza 150.00 300.00
APMP3 Mike Piazza 150.00 300.00
APMP4 Mike Piazza 150.00 300.00
APMP5 Mike Piazza 150.00 300.00
APMR1 Mariano Rivera 200.00 400.00
APMR2 Mariano Rivera 200.00 400.00
APMR3 Mariano Rivera 200.00 400.00
APMR4 Mariano Rivera 200.00 400.00
APMR5 Mariano Rivera 200.00 400.00
APMS1 Max Scherzer 100.00 250.00
APMS2 Max Scherzer 100.00 250.00
APMS3 Max Scherzer 100.00 250.00
APMS4 Max Scherzer 100.00 250.00
APMS5 Max Scherzer 100.00 250.00
APMT1 Mike Trout 300.00 600.00
APMT2 Mike Trout 300.00 600.00
APMT3 Mike Trout 300.00 600.00
APMT4 Mike Trout 300.00 600.00
APMT5 Mike Trout 300.00 600.00
APMT6 Mike Trout 300.00 600.00
APMT7 Mike Trout 300.00 600.00
APMT8 Mike Trout 300.00 600.00
APMT9 Mike Trout 300.00 600.00
APMW1 Michael Wacha 75.00 150.00
APMW2 Michael Wacha 75.00 150.00
APMW3 Michael Wacha 75.00 150.00
APMW4 Michael Wacha 75.00 150.00
APMW5 Michael Wacha 75.00 150.00
APNG1 Nomar Garciaparra 75.00 150.00
APNG2 Nomar Garciaparra 75.00 150.00
APNG3 Nomar Garciaparra 75.00 150.00
APNG4 Nomar Garciaparra 75.00 150.00
APNG5 Nomar Garciaparra 75.00 150.00
APNG6 Nomar Garciaparra 75.00 150.00
APNS1 Noah Syndergaard RC 150.00 300.00
APNS2 Noah Syndergaard RC 150.00 300.00
APNS3 Noah Syndergaard RC 150.00 300.00
APNS4 Noah Syndergaard RC 150.00 300.00
APNS5 Noah Syndergaard RC 150.00 300.00
APNS6 Noah Syndergaard RC 150.00 300.00
APPF1 Prince Fielder 60.00 120.00
APPF2 Prince Fielder 60.00 120.00
APPF3 Prince Fielder 60.00 120.00
APPF4 Prince Fielder 60.00 120.00
APPF5 Prince Fielder 60.00 120.00
APPG1 Paul Goldschmidt 100.00 200.00
APPG2 Paul Goldschmidt 100.00 200.00
APPG3 Paul Goldschmidt 100.00 200.00
APPG4 Paul Goldschmidt 100.00 200.00
APPG5 Paul Goldschmidt 100.00 200.00
APPS1 Pablo Sandoval 50.00 100.00
APPS2 Pablo Sandoval 50.00 100.00
APPS3 Pablo Sandoval 50.00 100.00
APPS4 Pablo Sandoval 50.00 100.00
APPS5 Pablo Sandoval 50.00 100.00
APPS6 Pablo Sandoval 50.00 100.00
APRA1 Roberto Alomar 60.00 120.00
APRA2 Roberto Alomar 60.00 120.00
APRA3 Roberto Alomar 60.00 120.00
APRA4 Roberto Alomar 60.00 120.00
APRA5 Roberto Alomar 60.00 120.00
APRC1 Robinson Cano 75.00 150.00
APRC2 Robinson Cano 75.00 150.00
APRC3 Robinson Cano 75.00 150.00
APRC4 Robinson Cano 75.00 150.00
APRC5 Robinson Cano 75.00 150.00
APRC6 Robinson Cano 75.00 150.00
APRC7 Robinson Cano 75.00 150.00
APRCL1 Roger Clemens 100.00 200.00
APRCL2 Roger Clemens 100.00 200.00
APRCL3 Roger Clemens 100.00 200.00
APRCL4 Roger Clemens 100.00 200.00
APRCL5 Roger Clemens 100.00 200.00
APRCL6 Roger Clemens 100.00 200.00
APRCL7 Roger Clemens 100.00 200.00
APRCL8 Roger Clemens 100.00 200.00
APRCL9 Roger Clemens 100.00 200.00
APRCS1 Rusney Castillo RC 60.00 120.00
APRCS2 Rusney Castillo RC 60.00 120.00
APRCS3 Rusney Castillo RC 60.00 120.00
APRCS4 Rusney Castillo RC 60.00 120.00
APRCS5 Rusney Castillo RC 60.00 120.00
APRH1 Rickey Henderson 100.00 200.00
APRH2 Rickey Henderson 100.00 200.00
APRH3 Rickey Henderson 100.00 200.00
APRH4 Rickey Henderson 100.00 200.00
APRH5 Rickey Henderson 100.00 200.00
APRH6 Rickey Henderson 100.00 200.00
APRH7 Rickey Henderson 100.00 200.00
APRH8 Rickey Henderson 100.00 200.00
APRH9 Rickey Henderson 100.00 200.00
APRJA1 Reggie Jackson 75.00 150.00
APRJA2 Reggie Jackson 75.00 150.00
APRJA3 Reggie Jackson 75.00 150.00
APRJA4 Reggie Jackson 75.00 150.00
APRJA5 Reggie Jackson 75.00 150.00
APRJA6 Reggie Jackson 75.00 150.00
APRJA7 Reggie Jackson 75.00 150.00
APRJN1 Randy Johnson 125.00 250.00
APRJN2 Randy Johnson 125.00 250.00
APRJN3 Randy Johnson 125.00 250.00
APRJN4 Randy Johnson 125.00 250.00
APRJN5 Randy Johnson 125.00 250.00
APRJN6 Randy Johnson 125.00 250.00
APRJN7 Randy Johnson 125.00 250.00
APRJN8 Randy Johnson 125.00 250.00
APRJN9 Randy Johnson 125.00 250.00
APRJO1 Reggie Jackson 75.00 150.00
APRJO2 Reggie Jackson 75.00 150.00
APRJO3 Reggie Jackson 75.00 150.00
APRJO4 Reggie Jackson 75.00 150.00
APRJO5 Reggie Jackson 75.00 150.00
APRJO6 Reggie Jackson 75.00 150.00
APRW1 Russell Wilson 250.00 400.00
APRW2 Russell Wilson 250.00 400.00
APSC1 Steve Carlton 75.00 150.00
APSG1 Sonny Gray 60.00 120.00
APSG2 Sonny Gray 60.00 120.00
APSG3 Sonny Gray 60.00 120.00
APSG4 Sonny Gray 60.00 120.00
APSG5 Sonny Gray 60.00 120.00
APSM1 Steven Matz RC 125.00 250.00
APSM2 Steven Matz RC 125.00 250.00
APSM3 Steven Matz RC 125.00 250.00
APSM4 Steven Matz RC 125.00 250.00
APSM5 Steven Matz RC 125.00 250.00
APTG1 Tom Glavine 75.00 150.00
APTG2 Tom Glavine 75.00 150.00
APTG3 Tom Glavine 75.00 150.00
APTG4 Tom Glavine 75.00 150.00
APTG5 Tom Glavine 75.00 150.00
APTG6 Tom Glavine 75.00 150.00
APTL1 Tim Lincecum 150.00 300.00
APTL2 Tim Lincecum 150.00 300.00
APTL3 Tim Lincecum 150.00 300.00
APTL4 Tim Lincecum 150.00 300.00
APTL5 Tim Lincecum 150.00 300.00
APVG1 Vladimir Guerrero 50.00 100.00
APVG2 Vladimir Guerrero 50.00 100.00
APVG3 Vladimir Guerrero 50.00 100.00
APVG4 Vladimir Guerrero 50.00 100.00
APVG5 Vladimir Guerrero 50.00 100.00
APVG6 Vladimir Guerrero 50.00 100.00
APVG7 Vladimir Guerrero 50.00 100.00
APWFA1 Will Ferrell 300.00 500.00
APWFA2 Will Ferrell 300.00 500.00
APWFA3 Will Ferrell 300.00 500.00
APWFA4 Will Ferrell 300.00 500.00
APWFA5 Will Ferrell 300.00 500.00
APWFD1 Will Ferrell 300.00 500.00
APWFD2 Will Ferrell 300.00 500.00
APWFD3 Will Ferrell 300.00 500.00
APWFD4 Will Ferrell 300.00 500.00
APWFD5 Will Ferrell 300.00 500.00
APYC1 Yoenis Cespedes EXCH 60.00 120.00
APYC2 Yoenis Cespedes EXCH 60.00 120.00
APYC3 Yoenis Cespedes EXCH 60.00 120.00
APYC4 Yoenis Cespedes EXCH 60.00 120.00
APYC5 Yoenis Cespedes EXCH 60.00 120.00
APYC6 Yoenis Cespedes EXCH 60.00 120.00
APYD1 Yu Darvish 60.00 120.00
APYD2 Yu Darvish 60.00 120.00
APYD3 Yu Darvish 60.00 120.00
APYD4 Yu Darvish 60.00 120.00
APYD5 Yu Darvish 60.00 120.00
APYD6 Yu Darvish 60.00 120.00
APYP1 Yasiel Puig 100.00 200.00
APYP2 Yasiel Puig 100.00 200.00
APYP3 Yasiel Puig 100.00 200.00
APYP4 Yasiel Puig 100.00 200.00
APYP5 Yasiel Puig 100.00 200.00
APYT1 Yasmany Tomas RC 50.00 100.00
APYT2 Yasmany Tomas RC 50.00 100.00
APYT3 Yasmany Tomas RC 50.00 100.00
APYT4 Yasmany Tomas RC 50.00 100.00
APYT5 Yasmany Tomas RC 50.00 100.00

2015 Topps Dynasty Autograph Patches Emerald

*EMERALD: .6X TO 1.5X BASIC
RANDOM INSERTS IN PACKS
STATED PRINT RUN 5 SER.#'d SETS
EXCHANGE DEADLINE 12/31/2017

2015 Topps Dynasty Dual Relic Greats Autographs

STATED ODDS 1:38 PACKS
STATED PRINT RUN 5 SER.#'d SETS
ALL VERSIONS EQUALLY PRICED
EXCHANGE DEADLINE 12/31/2017
ADRGDM1 Don Mattingly 100.00 250.00
ADRGDM2 Don Mattingly 100.00 250.00
ADRGDM3 Don Mattingly 100.00 250.00
ADRGDM4 Don Mattingly 100.00 250.00
ADRGDM5 Don Mattingly 100.00 250.00
ADRGFR1 Frank Robinson 75.00 150.00
ADRGFR2 Frank Robinson 75.00 150.00
ADRGFR3 Frank Robinson 75.00 150.00
ADRGFR4 Frank Robinson 75.00 150.00
ADRGFR5 Frank Robinson 75.00 150.00
ADRGHA1 Hank Aaron 250.00 500.00
ADRGHA2 Hank Aaron 250.00 500.00
ADRGHA3 Hank Aaron 250.00 500.00
ADRGHA4 Hank Aaron 250.00 500.00
ADRGHA5 Hank Aaron 250.00 500.00
ADRGJB1 Johnny Bench 150.00 300.00
ADRGJB2 Johnny Bench 150.00 300.00
ADRGJB3 Johnny Bench 150.00 300.00
ADRGJB4 Johnny Bench 150.00 300.00
ADRGJB5 Johnny Bench 150.00 300.00
ADRGOS1 Ozzie Smith 75.00 150.00
ADRGOS2 Ozzie Smith 75.00 150.00
ADRGOS3 Ozzie Smith 75.00 150.00
ADRGOS4 Ozzie Smith 75.00 150.00
ADRGOS5 Ozzie Smith 75.00 150.00
ADRGSC1 Steve Carlton 60.00 120.00
ADRGSC2 Steve Carlton 60.00 120.00
ADRGSC3 Steve Carlton 60.00 120.00
ADRGSC4 Steve Carlton 60.00 120.00
ADRGSC5 Steve Carlton 60.00 120.00
ADRGSK1 Sandy Koufax 600.00 800.00
ADRGSK2 Sandy Koufax 600.00 800.00
ADRGSK3 Sandy Koufax 600.00 800.00
ADRGSK4 Sandy Koufax 600.00 800.00
ADRGSK5 Sandy Koufax 600.00 800.00

2016 Topps Dynasty Autograph Patches

OVERALL AUTO ODDS 1:1
STATED PRINT RUN 10 SER.#'d SETS
ALL VERSIONS EQUALLY PRICED
EXCHANGE DEADLINE 11/30/2018
LOGO/TAG PATCHES MAY SELL FOR PREMIUM
API1 Ichiro Suzuki 300.00 600.00
API2 Ichiro Suzuki 300.00 600.00
API3 Ichiro Suzuki 300.00 600.00
API4 Ichiro Suzuki 300.00 600.00
API5 Ichiro Suzuki 300.00 600.00
API6 Ichiro Suzuki 300.00 600.00
API7 Ichiro Suzuki 300.00 600.00
API8 Ichiro Suzuki 300.00 600.00
API9 Ichiro Suzuki 300.00 600.00
API10 Ichiro Suzuki 300.00 600.00
APP1 Pele 250.00 400.00
APP2 Pele 250.00 400.00
APP3 Pele 250.00 400.00
APP4 Pele 250.00 400.00
APP5 Pele 250.00 400.00
APP6 Pele 250.00 400.00
APAG1 Adrian Gonzalez 40.00 100.00
APAG2 Adrian Gonzalez 40.00 100.00
APAG3 Adrian Gonzalez 40.00 100.00
APAG4 Adrian Gonzalez 40.00 100.00
APAG5 Adrian Gonzalez 40.00 100.00
APAG6 Adrian Gonzalez 40.00 100.00
APAG7 Adrian Gonzalez 40.00 100.00
APAG8 Adrian Gonzalez 40.00 100.00
APAGO1 Alex Gordon 40.00 100.00
APAGO2 Alex Gordon 40.00 100.00
APAGO3 Alex Gordon 40.00 100.00
APAGO4 Alex Gordon 40.00 100.00
APAJ1 Adam Jones 60.00 150.00
APAJ2 Adam Jones 60.00 150.00
APAJ3 Adam Jones 60.00 150.00
APAJ4 Adam Jones 60.00 150.00
APAJ5 Adam Jones 60.00 150.00
APAJ6 Adam Jones 60.00 150.00
APAP1 Andy Pettitte 50.00 120.00
APAP2 Andy Pettitte 50.00 120.00
APAP3 Andy Pettitte 50.00 120.00
APAP4 Andy Pettitte 50.00 120.00
APAP5 Andy Pettitte 50.00 120.00
APAP6 Andy Pettitte 50.00 120.00
APAP7 Andy Pettitte 50.00 120.00
APAPT1 Andy Pettitte 50.00 120.00
APAPT2 Andy Pettitte 50.00 120.00
APAPT3 Andy Pettitte 50.00 120.00
APAPT4 Andy Pettitte 50.00 120.00
APAPT5 Andy Pettitte 50.00 120.00
APAPU1 Albert Pujols 150.00 300.00
APAPU2 Albert Pujols 150.00 300.00
APAPU3 Albert Pujols 150.00 300.00
APAPU4 Albert Pujols 150.00 300.00
APAPU5 Albert Pujols 150.00 300.00
APAPU6 Albert Pujols 150.00 300.00
APAR1 Anthony Rizzo 100.00 250.00
APAR2 Anthony Rizzo 100.00 250.00
APAR3 Anthony Rizzo 100.00 250.00
APAR4 Anthony Rizzo 100.00 250.00
APAR5 Anthony Rizzo 100.00 250.00
APAR6 Anthony Rizzo 100.00 250.00
APAR7 Anthony Rizzo 100.00 250.00
APARD1 Alex Rodriguez 125.00 300.00
APARD2 Alex Rodriguez 125.00 300.00
APARD3 Alex Rodriguez 125.00 300.00
APARD4 Alex Rodriguez 125.00 300.00
APARU1 Addison Russell 75.00 200.00
APARU2 Addison Russell 75.00 200.00
APARU3 Addison Russell 75.00 200.00
APARU4 Addison Russell 75.00 200.00
APARU5 Addison Russell 75.00 200.00
APARU6 Addison Russell 75.00 200.00
APBA8 Bobby Abreu 40.00 100.00
APBA9 Bobby Abreu 40.00 100.00
APBA10 Bobby Abreu 40.00 100.00
APBA11 Bobby Abreu 40.00 100.00
APBA12 Bobby Abreu 40.00 100.00
APBA13 Bobby Abreu 40.00 100.00
APBH1 Bryce Harper 200.00 400.00
APBH2 Bryce Harper 200.00 400.00
APBH3 Bryce Harper 200.00 400.00
APBH4 Bryce Harper 200.00 400.00
APBH5 Bryce Harper 200.00 400.00
APBH6 Bryce Harper 200.00 400.00
APBH7 Bryce Harper 200.00 400.00
APBH8 Bryce Harper 200.00 400.00
APBL1 Barry Larkin 60.00 150.00
APBL2 Barry Larkin 60.00 150.00
APBL3 Barry Larkin 60.00 150.00
APBL4 Barry Larkin 60.00 150.00
APBL5 Barry Larkin 60.00 150.00
APBL6 Barry Larkin 60.00 150.00
APBP1 Buster Posey 100.00 250.00
APBP2 Buster Posey 100.00 250.00
APBP3 Buster Posey 100.00 250.00
APBP4 Buster Posey 100.00 250.00
APBP5 Buster Posey 100.00 250.00
APBP6 Buster Posey 100.00 250.00
APBP7 Buster Posey 100.00 250.00
APCB1 Craig Biggio 40.00 100.00
APCB2 Craig Biggio 40.00 100.00
APCB3 Craig Biggio 40.00 100.00
APCB4 Craig Biggio 40.00 100.00
APCB5 Craig Biggio 40.00 100.00
APCB6 Craig Biggio 40.00 100.00
APCC1 Carlos Correa 125.00 300.00
APCC2 Carlos Correa 125.00 300.00
APCC3 Carlos Correa 125.00 300.00
APCC4 Carlos Correa 125.00 300.00
APCC5 Carlos Correa 125.00 300.00
APCC6 Carlos Correa 125.00 300.00
APCC7 Carlos Correa 125.00 300.00
APCC8 Carlos Correa 125.00 300.00
APCF1 Carlton Fisk 50.00 120.00
APCF2 Carlton Fisk 50.00 120.00
APCF3 Carlton Fisk 50.00 120.00
APCF4 Carlton Fisk 50.00 120.00
APCF5 Carlton Fisk 50.00 120.00
APCH1 Cole Hamels 30.00 80.00
APCH2 Cole Hamels 30.00 80.00
APCH3 Cole Hamels 30.00 80.00
APCH4 Cole Hamels 30.00 80.00
APCH6 Cole Hamels 30.00 80.00
APCJ1 Chipper Jones 125.00 300.00
APCJ2 Chipper Jones 125.00 300.00
APCJ3 Chipper Jones 125.00 300.00
APCJ4 Chipper Jones 125.00 300.00
APCJ5 Chipper Jones 125.00 300.00
APCJ6 Chipper Jones 125.00 300.00
APCJ7 Chipper Jones 125.00 300.00
APCJ8 Chipper Jones 125.00 300.00
APCK1 Clayton Kershaw 125.00 250.00
APCK2 Clayton Kershaw 125.00 250.00
APCK3 Clayton Kershaw 125.00 250.00
APCK4 Clayton Kershaw 125.00 250.00
APCK6 Clayton Kershaw 125.00 250.00
APCK7 Clayton Kershaw 125.00 250.00
APCS1 Corey Seager RC 500.00 700.00
APCS2 Corey Seager RC 500.00 700.00
APCS3 Corey Seager RC 500.00 700.00
APCS4 Corey Seager RC 500.00 700.00
APCS5 Corey Seager RC 500.00 700.00
APCS6 Corey Seager RC 500.00 700.00
APCS7 Corey Seager RC 500.00 700.00
APCSL1 Chris Sale 50.00 120.00
APCSL2 Chris Sale 50.00 120.00
APCSL3 Chris Sale 50.00 120.00
APCSL4 Chris Sale 50.00 120.00
APCSL5 Chris Sale 50.00 120.00
APCSL6 Chris Sale 50.00 120.00
APDJ1 Derek Jeter 800.00 1200.00
APDJ2 Derek Jeter 800.00 1200.00
APDJ3 Derek Jeter 800.00 1200.00
APDJ4 Derek Jeter 800.00 1200.00
APDJ5 Derek Jeter 800.00 1200.00
APDMU1 Dale Murphy 75.00 200.00
APDMU2 Dale Murphy 75.00 200.00
APDMU3 Dale Murphy 75.00 200.00
APDMU4 Dale Murphy 75.00 200.00
APDO1 David Ortiz 150.00 300.00
APDO2 David Ortiz 150.00 300.00
APDO3 David Ortiz 150.00 300.00
APDO4 David Ortiz 150.00 300.00
APDO5 David Ortiz 150.00 300.00
APDO6 David Ortiz 150.00 300.00
APDO7 David Ortiz 150.00 300.00
APDP1 Dustin Pedroia 60.00 150.00
APDP2 Dustin Pedroia 60.00 150.00
APDP3 Dustin Pedroia 60.00 150.00
APDP4 Dustin Pedroia 60.00 150.00
APDP5 Dustin Pedroia 60.00 150.00
APDP6 Dustin Pedroia 60.00 150.00
APDP7 Dustin Pedroia 60.00 150.00
APDP8 Dustin Pedroia 60.00 150.00
APDPR1 David Price 50.00 120.00
APDPR2 David Price 50.00 120.00
APDPR3 David Price 50.00 120.00
APDPR4 David Price 50.00 120.00
APDPR5 David Price 50.00 120.00
APDPR6 David Price 50.00 120.00
APDSA1 Deion Sanders 40.00 100.00
APDSA2 Deion Sanders 40.00 100.00
APDSA3 Deion Sanders 40.00 100.00
APDSA4 Deion Sanders 40.00 100.00
APDSA5 Deion Sanders 40.00 100.00
APDW1 David Wright 60.00 150.00
APDW2 David Wright 60.00 150.00
APDW3 David Wright 60.00 150.00
APDW4 David Wright 60.00 150.00
APDW5 David Wright 60.00 150.00
APDW6 David Wright 60.00 150.00
APDW7 David Wright 60.00 150.00
APDW8 David Wright 60.00 150.00
APFF1 Freddie Freeman 50.00 120.00
APFF2 Freddie Freeman 50.00 120.00
APFF3 Freddie Freeman 50.00 120.00
APFF4 Freddie Freeman 50.00 120.00
APFF5 Freddie Freeman 50.00 120.00
APFF6 Freddie Freeman 50.00 120.00
APFF7 Freddie Freeman 50.00 120.00
APFF8 Freddie Freeman 50.00 120.00
APFH1 Felix Hernandez 40.00 100.00
APFH2 Felix Hernandez 40.00 100.00
APFH3 Felix Hernandez 40.00 100.00
APFH4 Felix Hernandez 40.00 100.00
APFH5 Felix Hernandez 40.00 100.00
APFH6 Felix Hernandez 40.00 100.00
APFL1 Francisco Lindor 75.00 200.00
APFL2 Francisco Lindor 75.00 200.00
APFL3 Francisco Lindor 75.00 200.00
APFL4 Francisco Lindor 75.00 200.00
APFL5 Francisco Lindor 75.00 200.00
APFL6 Francisco Lindor 75.00 200.00
APFT1 Frank Thomas 75.00 200.00
APFT2 Frank Thomas 75.00 200.00
APFT3 Frank Thomas 75.00 200.00
APFT4 Frank Thomas 75.00 200.00
APFT5 Frank Thomas 75.00 200.00
APGS1 George Springer 40.00 100.00
APGS2 George Springer 40.00 100.00
APGS3 George Springer 40.00 100.00
APGS4 George Springer 40.00 100.00
APGS5 George Springer 40.00 100.00
APGS6 George Springer 40.00 100.00
APJA1 Jose Altuve 75.00 200.00
APJA2 Jose Altuve 75.00 200.00
APJA3 Jose Altuve 75.00 200.00
APJA4 Jose Altuve 75.00 200.00
APJA5 Jose Altuve 75.00 200.00
APJA6 Jose Altuve 75.00 200.00
APJA7 Jose Altuve 75.00 200.00
APJAR1 Jake Arrieta EXCH 150.00 300.00
APJAR2 Jake Arrieta EXCH 150.00 300.00
APJAR3 Jake Arrieta EXCH 150.00 300.00
APJAR4 Jake Arrieta EXCH 150.00 300.00
APJAR5 Jake Arrieta EXCH 150.00 300.00
APJAR6 Jake Arrieta EXCH 150.00 300.00
APJD1 Jacob deGrom 100.00 250.00
APJD2 Jacob deGrom 100.00 250.00
APJD3 Jacob deGrom 100.00 250.00
APJD4 Jacob deGrom 100.00 250.00
APJD5 Jacob deGrom 100.00 250.00
APJD6 Jacob deGrom 100.00 250.00
APJD7 Jacob deGrom 100.00 250.00
APJH1 Jason Heyward 50.00 120.00
APJH2 Jason Heyward 50.00 120.00
APJH3 Jason Heyward 50.00 120.00
APJH4 Jason Heyward 50.00 120.00
APJH5 Jason Heyward 50.00 120.00
APJP1 Joc Pederson 50.00 120.00
APJP2 Joc Pederson 50.00 120.00
APJP3 Joc Pederson 50.00 120.00
APJP4 Joc Pederson 50.00 120.00
APJP5 Joc Pederson 50.00 120.00
APJP6 Joc Pederson 50.00 120.00
APJP7 Joc Pederson 50.00 120.00
APJS1 John Smoltz 60.00 150.00
APJS2 John Smoltz 60.00 150.00
APJS3 John Smoltz 60.00 150.00
APJS4 John Smoltz 60.00 150.00
APJS5 John Smoltz 60.00 150.00
APJS6 John Smoltz 60.00 150.00
APJS7 John Smoltz 60.00 150.00
APJS8 John Smoltz 60.00 150.00
APJU1 Julio Urias RC 50.00 120.00
APJU2 Julio Urias RC 50.00 120.00
APJU3 Julio Urias RC 50.00 120.00
APJU4 Julio Urias RC 50.00 120.00
APJU5 Julio Urias RC 50.00 120.00
APJVO1 Joey Votto 40.00 100.00
APJVO2 Joey Votto 40.00 100.00
APJVO3 Joey Votto 40.00 100.00
APJVO4 Joey Votto 40.00 100.00
APJVO5 Joey Votto 40.00 100.00
APJVO6 Joey Votto 40.00 100.00
APJVO7 Joey Votto 40.00 100.00
APJVO8 Joey Votto 40.00 100.00
APKB1 Kris Bryant 500.00 800.00
APKB2 Kris Bryant 500.00 800.00
APKB3 Kris Bryant 500.00 800.00
APKB4 Kris Bryant 500.00 800.00
APKB5 Kris Bryant 500.00 800.00
APKB6 Kris Bryant 500.00 800.00
APKB7 Kris Bryant 500.00 800.00
APKG1 Ken Griffey Jr. 400.00 800.00
APKG5 Ken Griffey Jr. 400.00 800.00
APKG6 Ken Griffey Jr. 400.00 800.00
APKG7 Ken Griffey Jr. 400.00 800.00
APKG8 Ken Griffey Jr. 400.00 800.00
APKG9 Ken Griffey Jr. 400.00 800.00
APKM1 Kenta Maeda RC 50.00 120.00
APKM2 Kenta Maeda RC 50.00 120.00
APKM3 Kenta Maeda RC 50.00 120.00
APKM4 Kenta Maeda RC 50.00 120.00
APKM5 Kenta Maeda RC 50.00 120.00
APKM6 Kenta Maeda RC 50.00 120.00
APKM7 Kenta Maeda RC 50.00 120.00
APKS1 Kyle Schwarber RC 125.00 300.00
APKS2 Kyle Schwarber RC 125.00 300.00
APKS3 Kyle Schwarber RC 125.00 300.00
APKS4 Kyle Schwarber RC 125.00 300.00
APKS5 Kyle Schwarber RC 125.00 300.00
APKS6 Kyle Schwarber RC 125.00 300.00
APKS7 Kyle Schwarber RC 125.00 300.00
APLG1 Lucas Giolito RC 30.00 80.00
APLG2 Lucas Giolito RC 30.00 80.00
APLG3 Lucas Giolito RC 30.00 80.00
APLG4 Lucas Giolito RC 30.00 80.00
APLG5 Lucas Giolito RC 30.00 80.00
APLS1 Luis Severino RC 30.00 80.00
APLS2 Luis Severino RC 30.00 80.00
APLS3 Luis Severino RC 30.00 80.00
APLS4 Luis Severino RC 30.00 80.00
APLS5 Luis Severino RC 30.00 80.00
APLS6 Luis Severino RC 30.00 80.00
APLS7 Luis Severino RC 30.00 80.00
APMM1 Mark McGwire 75.00 200.00
APMM10 Mark McGwire 75.00 200.00
APMM2 Mark McGwire 75.00 200.00
APMM3 Mark McGwire 75.00 200.00
APMM4 Mark McGwire 75.00 200.00
APMM5 Mark McGwire 75.00 200.00
APMM6 Mark McGwire 75.00 200.00
APMM7 Mark McGwire 75.00 200.00
APMM8 Mark McGwire 75.00 200.00
APMM9 Mark McGwire 75.00 200.00
APMMA1 Manny Machado 100.00 250.00
APMMA2 Manny Machado 100.00 250.00
APMMA3 Manny Machado 100.00 250.00
APMMA4 Manny Machado 100.00 250.00
APMMA5 Manny Machado 100.00 250.00
APMMA6 Manny Machado 100.00 250.00
APMMA7 Manny Machado 100.00 250.00
APMMA8 Manny Machado 100.00 250.00
APMP1 Mike Piazza 100.00 250.00
APMP10 Mike Piazza 100.00 250.00
APMP2 Mike Piazza 100.00 250.00
APMP3 Mike Piazza 100.00 250.00
APMP4 Mike Piazza 100.00 250.00
APMP5 Mike Piazza 100.00 250.00
APMP6 Mike Piazza 100.00 250.00
APMP7 Mike Piazza 100.00 250.00
APMP8 Mike Piazza 100.00 250.00
APMP9 Mike Piazza 100.00 250.00
APMS1 Miguel Sano RC 30.00 80.00
APMS2 Miguel Sano RC 30.00 80.00
APMS3 Miguel Sano RC 30.00 80.00
APMS4 Miguel Sano RC 30.00 80.00
APMS5 Miguel Sano RC 30.00 80.00
APMS6 Miguel Sano RC 30.00 80.00
APMS7 Miguel Sano RC 30.00 80.00
APMT1 Mike Trout 300.00 600.00
APMT2 Mike Trout 300.00 600.00
APMT3 Mike Trout 300.00 600.00
APMT4 Mike Trout 300.00 600.00
APMT5 Mike Trout 300.00 600.00
APMT6 Mike Trout 300.00 600.00
APMT7 Mike Trout 300.00 600.00
APMT8 Mike Trout 300.00 600.00
APMW1 Michael Wacha 30.00 80.00
APMW2 Michael Wacha 30.00 80.00
APMW3 Michael Wacha 30.00 80.00
APMW4 Michael Wacha 30.00 80.00
APMW5 Michael Wacha 30.00 80.00
APNA1 Nolan Arenado 75.00 200.00
APNA2 Nolan Arenado 75.00 200.00
APNA3 Nolan Arenado 75.00 200.00
APNA4 Nolan Arenado 75.00 200.00
APNA5 Nolan Arenado 75.00 200.00
APNA6 Nolan Arenado 75.00 200.00
APNR1 Nolan Ryan 150.00 300.00
APNR2 Nolan Ryan 150.00 300.00
APNR3 Nolan Ryan 150.00 300.00
APNR4 Nolan Ryan 150.00 300.00
APNR5 Nolan Ryan 150.00 300.00
APNR6 Nolan Ryan 150.00 300.00
APNR7 Nolan Ryan 150.00 300.00
APNR8 Nolan Ryan 150.00 300.00
APNR9 Nolan Ryan 150.00 300.00
APNS1 Noah Syndergaard 75.00 200.00
APNS2 Noah Syndergaard 75.00 200.00
APNS3 Noah Syndergaard 75.00 200.00
APNS4 Noah Syndergaard 75.00 200.00
APNS5 Noah Syndergaard 75.00 200.00
APNS6 Noah Syndergaard 75.00 200.00
APNS7 Noah Syndergaard 75.00 200.00
APNS8 Noah Syndergaard 75.00 200.00
APPF1 Prince Fielder 30.00 80.00
APPF2 Prince Fielder 30.00 80.00
APPF3 Prince Fielder 30.00 80.00
APPF4 Prince Fielder 30.00 80.00
APPF5 Prince Fielder 30.00 80.00
APPF6 Prince Fielder 30.00 80.00
APPMA1 Pedro Martinez 60.00 150.00
APPMA10 Pedro Martinez 60.00 150.00
APPMA11 Pedro Martinez 60.00 150.00
APPMA12 Pedro Martinez 60.00 150.00
APPMA13 Pedro Martinez 60.00 150.00
APPMA14 Pedro Martinez 60.00 150.00
APPMA15 Pedro Martinez 60.00 150.00
APPMA16 Pedro Martinez 60.00 150.00
APPMA17 Pedro Martinez 60.00 150.00
APPMA2 Pedro Martinez 60.00 150.00
APPMA3 Pedro Martinez 60.00 150.00
APPMA4 Pedro Martinez 60.00 150.00
APPMA5 Pedro Martinez 60.00 150.00
APPMA6 Pedro Martinez 60.00 150.00
APPMA7 Pedro Martinez 60.00 150.00
APPMA8 Pedro Martinez 60.00 150.00
APPMA9 Pedro Martinez 60.00 150.00
APRC1 Roger Clemens 60.00 150.00
APRC2 Roger Clemens 60.00 150.00
APRC3 Roger Clemens 60.00 150.00
APRC4 Roger Clemens 60.00 150.00
APRC5 Roger Clemens 60.00 150.00
APRCA1 Robinson Cano 50.00 120.00
APRCA2 Robinson Cano 50.00 120.00
APRCA3 Robinson Cano 50.00 120.00
APRCA4 Robinson Cano 50.00 120.00
APRCA5 Robinson Cano 50.00 120.00
APRCA6 Robinson Cano 50.00 120.00
APRCR1 Rod Carew 50.00 120.00
APRCR2 Rod Carew 50.00 120.00
APRCR3 Rod Carew 50.00 120.00
APRCR4 Rod Carew 50.00 120.00
APRCR5 Rod Carew 50.00 120.00
APRH1 Rickey Henderson 75.00 200.00
APRH2 Rickey Henderson 75.00 200.00
APRH3 Rickey Henderson 75.00 200.00
APRH4 Rickey Henderson 75.00 200.00
APRH5 Rickey Henderson 75.00 200.00
APRH6 Rickey Henderson 75.00 200.00
APRH7 Rickey Henderson 75.00 200.00
APRJ1 Reggie Jackson 50.00 120.00
APRJ2 Reggie Jackson 50.00 120.00
APRJ3 Reggie Jackson 50.00 120.00
APRJ4 Reggie Jackson 50.00 120.00
APRJ5 Reggie Jackson 50.00 120.00
APRJ6 Reggie Jackson 50.00 120.00
APRY1 Robin Yount 75.00 200.00
APRY2 Robin Yount 75.00 200.00
APRY3 Robin Yount 75.00 200.00
APRY4 Robin Yount 75.00 200.00
APSC1 Steve Carlton 50.00 120.00
APSC2 Steve Carlton 50.00 120.00
APSC2 Steve Carlton 50.00 120.00
APSG1 Sonny Gray 30.00 80.00
APSG2 Sonny Gray 30.00 80.00
APSG3 Sonny Gray 30.00 80.00
APSG4 Sonny Gray 30.00 80.00
APSG5 Sonny Gray 30.00 80.00
APSG6 Sonny Gray 30.00 80.00
APSM2 Steven Matz 50.00 120.00
APSM3 Steven Matz 50.00 120.00
APSM4 Steven Matz 50.00 120.00
APSM5 Steven Matz 50.00 120.00
APSM6 Steven Matz 50.00 120.00
APTGL1 Tom Glavine 50.00 120.00
APTGL2 Tom Glavine 50.00 120.00
APTGL3 Tom Glavine 50.00 120.00
APTGL4 Tom Glavine 50.00 120.00
APTGL5 Tom Glavine 50.00 120.00
APTGL6 Tom Glavine 50.00 120.00
APTS1 Trevor Story RC 60.00 150.00
APTS2 Trevor Story RC 60.00 150.00
APTS3 Trevor Story RC 60.00 150.00
APTS4 Trevor Story RC 60.00 150.00
APTS5 Trevor Story RC 60.00 150.00
APTS6 Trevor Story RC 60.00 150.00
APTT1 Troy Tulowitzki 40.00 100.00
APTT2 Troy Tulowitzki 40.00 100.00
APTT3 Troy Tulowitzki 40.00 100.00
APTT4 Troy Tulowitzki 40.00 100.00
APTT5 Troy Tulowitzki 40.00 100.00
APTT6 Troy Tulowitzki 40.00 100.00
APVG1 Vladimir Guerrero 40.00 100.00
APVG2 Vladimir Guerrero 40.00 100.00
APVG3 Vladimir Guerrero 40.00 100.00
APVG4 Vladimir Guerrero 40.00 100.00
APVG5 Vladimir Guerrero 40.00 100.00
APVG6 Vladimir Guerrero 40.00 100.00
APWB1 Wade Boggs 50.00 120.00
APWB2 Wade Boggs 50.00 120.00
APWB3 Wade Boggs 50.00 120.00
APWB5 Wade Boggs 50.00 120.00
APWBO2 Wade Boggs 50.00 120.00
APWBO3 Wade Boggs 50.00 120.00
APWBO4 Wade Boggs 50.00 120.00
APWBO5 Wade Boggs 50.00 120.00
APWBO1 Wade Boggs 50.00 120.00

2016 Topps Dynasty Autograph Patches 5

*EMERALD: .5X TO 1.2X BASIC
RANDOM INSERTS IN PACKS
STATED PRINT RUN 5 SER.#'d SETS
EXCHANGE DEADLINE 11/30/2018
LOGO/TAG PATCHES MAY SELL FOR PREMIUM

2016 Topps Dynasty Dual Relic Greats Autographs

STATED ODDS 1:28
STATED PRINT RUN 5 SER.#'d SETS
ALL VERSIONS EQUALLY PRICED
EXCHANGE DEADLINE 11/30/2018
ADRGAD1 Andre Dawson 40.00 100.00
ADRGAD2 Andre Dawson 40.00 100.00
ADRGAD3 Andre Dawson 40.00 100.00
ADRGAD4 Andre Dawson 40.00 100.00
ADRGAD5 Andre Dawson 40.00 100.00
ADRGAK1 Al Kaline 75.00 200.00
ADRGAK2 Al Kaline 75.00 200.00
ADRGAK3 Al Kaline 75.00 200.00
ADRGAK4 Al Kaline 75.00 200.00
ADRGAK5 Al Kaline 75.00 200.00
ADRGCY1 Carl Yastrzemski 60.00 150.00
ADRGCY2 Carl Yastrzemski 60.00 150.00
ADRGCY3 Carl Yastrzemski 60.00 150.00
ADRGCY4 Carl Yastrzemski 60.00 150.00
ADRGCY5 Carl Yastrzemski 60.00 150.00
ADRGDM1 Don Mattingly 100.00 250.00
ADRGDM2 Don Mattingly 100.00 250.00
ADRGDM3 Don Mattingly 100.00 250.00
ADRGDM4 Don Mattingly 100.00 250.00
ADRGDM5 Don Mattingly 100.00 250.00
ADRGFR1 Frank Robinson 50.00 120.00
ADRGFR2 Frank Robinson 50.00 120.00
ADRGFR3 Frank Robinson 50.00 120.00
ADRGFR4 Frank Robinson 50.00 120.00
ADRGFR5 Frank Robinson 50.00 120.00
ADRGHA1 Hank Aaron 200.00 400.00
ADRGHA2 Hank Aaron 200.00 400.00
ADRGHA3 Hank Aaron 200.00 400.00
ADRGHA4 Hank Aaron 200.00 400.00
ADRGHA5 Hank Aaron 200.00 400.00
ADRGJB1 Johnny Bench 75.00 200.00
ADRGJB2 Johnny Bench 75.00 200.00
ADRGJB3 Johnny Bench 75.00 200.00
ADRGJB4 Johnny Bench 75.00 200.00
ADRGJB5 Johnny Bench 75.00 200.00
ADRGLB1 Lou Brock 50.00 120.00
ADRGLB2 Lou Brock 50.00 120.00
ADRGLB3 Lou Brock 50.00 120.00
ADRGLB4 Lou Brock 50.00 120.00
ADRGLB5 Lou Brock 50.00 120.00
ADRGOS1 Ozzie Smith 60.00 150.00
ADRGOS2 Ozzie Smith 60.00 150.00
ADRGOS3 Ozzie Smith 60.00 150.00
ADRGOS4 Ozzie Smith 60.00 150.00
ADRGOS5 Ozzie Smith 60.00 150.00
ADRGOV1 Omar Vizquel 75.00 200.00
ADRGOV2 Omar Vizquel 75.00 200.00
ADRGOV3 Omar Vizquel 75.00 200.00
ADRGOV4 Omar Vizquel 75.00 200.00
ADRGRS1 Ryne Sandberg 60.00 150.00
ADRGRS2 Ryne Sandberg 60.00 150.00
ADRGRS3 Ryne Sandberg 60.00 150.00
ADRGRS4 Ryne Sandberg 60.00 150.00
ADRGRS5 Ryne Sandberg 60.00 150.00
ADRGSC1 Steve Carlton 40.00 100.00
ADRGSC2 Steve Carlton 40.00 100.00

2017 Topps Dynasty Autograph Patches

OVERALL AUTO ODDS 1:1
STATED PRINT RUN 10 SER.#'d SETS
ALL VERSIONS EQUALLY PRICED
LOGO/TAG PATCHES MAY SELL FOR PREMIUM
EXCHANGE DEADLINE 10/31/2019
APAA1 Aaron Judge RC 600.00 1000.00
APAA2 Aaron Judge RC 600.00 1000.00
APAA3 Aaron Judge RC 600.00 1000.00
APAB1 Alex Bregman RC 75.00 200.00
APAB2 Alex Bregman RC 75.00 150.00
APAB3 Alex Bregman RC 75.00 150.00
APAB4 Alex Bregman RC 75.00 150.00
APAB5 Alex Bregman RC 75.00 150.00
APAB6 Alex Bregman RC 75.00 150.00
APAB7 Alex Bregman RC 75.00 150.00
APAB8 Alex Bregman RC 75.00 150.00
APADB1 Adrian Beltre 60.00 150.00
APADB2 Adrian Beltre 60.00 150.00
APADB3 Adrian Beltre 60.00 150.00
APADB4 Adrian Beltre 60.00 150.00
APADB5 Adrian Beltre 60.00 150.00
APADB6 Adrian Beltre 60.00 150.00
APADB7 Adrian Beltre 60.00 150.00
APADB8 Adrian Beltre 60.00 150.00
APADR1 Addison Russell 40.00 100.00
APADR2 Addison Russell 40.00 100.00
APADR3 Addison Russell 40.00 100.00
APADR4 Addison Russell 40.00 100.00
APADR5 Addison Russell 40.00 100.00
APADR6 Addison Russell 40.00 100.00
APADR7 Addison Russell 40.00 100.00
APADR8 Addison Russell 40.00 100.00
APAJ1 Adam Jones 30.00 80.00
APAJ2 Adam Jones 30.00 80.00
APAJ3 Adam Jones 30.00 80.00
APAJ4 Adam Jones 30.00 80.00
APAJ5 Adam Jones 30.00 80.00
APAJ6 Adam Jones 30.00 80.00
APAJ7 Adam Jones 30.00 80.00
APAJ8 Adam Jones 30.00 80.00
APALB1 Andrew Benintendi RC 100.00 250.00
APALB2 Andrew Benintendi RC 100.00 250.00
APALB3 Andrew Benintendi RC 100.00 250.00
APALB4 Andrew Benintendi RC 100.00 250.00
APALB5 Andrew Benintendi RC 100.00 250.00
APALB6 Andrew Benintendi RC 100.00 250.00
APALB7 Andrew Benintendi RC 100.00 250.00
APALB8 Andrew Benintendi RC 100.00 250.00
APAO1 Alex Rodriguez 100.00 250.00
APAO2 Alex Rodriguez 100.00 250.00
APAO3 Alex Rodriguez 100.00 250.00
APAO4 Alex Rodriguez 100.00 250.00
APAO5 Alex Rodriguez 100.00 250.00
APAO6 Alex Rodriguez 100.00 250.00
APAP1 Albert Pujols 100.00 250.00
APAP2 Albert Pujols 100.00 250.00
APAP3 Albert Pujols 100.00 250.00
APAP4 Albert Pujols 100.00 250.00
APAP5 Albert Pujols 100.00 250.00
APAP6 Albert Pujols 100.00 250.00
APAPT1 Andy Pettitte 30.00 80.00
APAPT4 Andy Pettitte 30.00 80.00
APAPT5 Andy Pettitte 30.00 80.00
APAPT6 Andy Pettitte 30.00 80.00
APAZ1 Anthony Rizzo 75.00 200.00
APAZ2 Anthony Rizzo 75.00 200.00
APAZ3 Anthony Rizzo 75.00 200.00
APAZ4 Anthony Rizzo 75.00 200.00
APAZ5 Anthony Rizzo 75.00 200.00
APAZ6 Anthony Rizzo 75.00 200.00

APBH3 Bryce Harper 150.00 400.00
APBH4 Bryce Harper 150.00 400.00
APBH5 Bryce Harper 150.00 400.00
APBH6 Bryce Harper 150.00 400.00
APBH7 Bryce Harper 150.00 400.00
APBH8 Bryce Harper 150.00 400.00
APBL1 Barry Larkin 30.00 80.00
APBL2 Barry Larkin 30.00 80.00
APBL3 Barry Larkin 30.00 80.00
APBL4 Barry Larkin 30.00 80.00
APBL5 Barry Larkin 30.00 80.00
APBL6 Barry Larkin 30.00 80.00
APBP1 Buster Posey 75.00 200.00
APBP2 Buster Posey 75.00 200.00
APBP3 Buster Posey 75.00 200.00
APBP4 Buster Posey 75.00 200.00
APBP5 Buster Posey 75.00 200.00
APBP6 Buster Posey 75.00 200.00
APBR1 Bryce Harper 150.00 400.00
APBR2 Bryce Harper 150.00 400.00
APCB1 Cody Bellinger RC 200.00 500.00
APCB2 Cody Bellinger RC 200.00 500.00
APCB3 Cody Bellinger RC 200.00 500.00
APCB4 Cody Bellinger RC 200.00 500.00
APCB5 Cody Bellinger RC 200.00 500.00
APCB6 Cody Bellinger RC 200.00 500.00
APCC1 Carlos Correa 100.00 250.00
APCC10 Carlos Correa 100.00 250.00
APCC11 Carlos Correa 100.00 250.00
APCC12 Carlos Correa 100.00 250.00
APCC13 Carlos Correa 100.00 250.00
APCC2 Carlos Correa 100.00 250.00
APCC3 Carlos Correa 100.00 250.00
APCC4 Carlos Correa 100.00 250.00
APCC5 Carlos Correa 100.00 250.00
APCC6 Carlos Correa 100.00 250.00
APCC7 Carlos Correa 100.00 250.00
APCC8 Carlos Correa 100.00 250.00
APCC9 Carlos Correa 100.00 250.00
APCE1 Clayton Kershaw EXCH 100.00 250.00
APCE2 Clayton Kershaw EXCH 100.00 250.00
APCE3 Clayton Kershaw EXCH 100.00 250.00
APCE4 Clayton Kershaw EXCH 100.00 250.00
APCE5 Clayton Kershaw EXCH 100.00 250.00
APCE6 Clayton Kershaw EXCH 100.00 250.00
APCI1 Craig Biggio 30.00 80.00
APCI2 Craig Biggio 30.00 80.00
APCI3 Craig Biggio 30.00 80.00
APCI4 Craig Biggio 30.00 80.00
APCI5 Craig Biggio 30.00 80.00
APCI6 Craig Biggio 30.00 80.00
APCJ1 Chipper Jones 75.00 200.00
APCJ2 Chipper Jones 75.00 200.00
APCJ3 Chipper Jones 75.00 200.00
APCJ4 Chipper Jones 75.00 200.00
APCJ5 Chipper Jones 75.00 200.00
APCJ6 Chipper Jones 75.00 200.00
APCJ7 Chipper Jones 75.00 200.00
APCJ8 Chipper Jones 75.00 200.00
APCOS1 Corey Seager 75.00 200.00
APCOS2 Corey Seager 75.00 200.00
APCOS3 Corey Seager 75.00 200.00
APCOS4 Corey Seager 75.00 200.00
APCOS5 Corey Seager 75.00 200.00
APCOS6 Corey Seager 75.00 200.00
APCOS7 Corey Seager 75.00 200.00
APCOS8 Corey Seager 75.00 200.00
APCR1 Cal Ripken Jr. 100.00 250.00
APCR2 Cal Ripken Jr. 100.00 250.00
APCR3 Cal Ripken Jr. 100.00 250.00
APCR4 Cal Ripken Jr. 100.00 250.00
APCR5 Cal Ripken Jr. 100.00 250.00
APCS1 Chris Sale 30.00 80.00
APCS2 Chris Sale 30.00 80.00
APCS3 Chris Sale 30.00 80.00
APCS4 Chris Sale 30.00 80.00
APCS5 Chris Sale 30.00 80.00
APCS6 Chris Sale 30.00 80.00
APCS7 Chris Sale 30.00 80.00
APCS8 Chris Sale 30.00 80.00
APDJ1 Derek Jeter 400.00 800.00
APDJ2 Derek Jeter 400.00 800.00
APDJ3 Derek Jeter 400.00 800.00
APDJ4 Derek Jeter 400.00 800.00
APDJ5 Derek Jeter 400.00 800.00
APDJ6 Derek Jeter 400.00 800.00
APDO1 David Ortiz 75.00 200.00
APDO2 David Ortiz 75.00 200.00
APDO3 David Ortiz 75.00 200.00
APDO4 David Ortiz 75.00 200.00
APDO5 David Ortiz 75.00 200.00
APDO6 David Ortiz 75.00 200.00
APDO7 David Ortiz 75.00 200.00
APDO8 David Ortiz 75.00 200.00
APDP1 David Price 25.00 60.00
APDP2 David Price 25.00 60.00
APDP3 David Price 25.00 60.00
APDP4 David Price 25.00 60.00
APDP5 David Price 25.00 60.00
APDP6 David Price 25.00 60.00
APDS2 Dansby Swanson RC 50.00 120.00
APDS3 Dansby Swanson RC 50.00 120.00
APDS4 Dansby Swanson RC 50.00 120.00
APDS5 Dansby Swanson RC 50.00 120.00
APDS6 Dansby Swanson RC 50.00 120.00
APDS7 Dansby Swanson RC 50.00 120.00
APDS8 Dansby Swanson RC 50.00 120.00
APDUP1 Dustin Pedroia 40.00 100.00
APDUP2 Dustin Pedroia 40.00 100.00
APDUP3 Dustin Pedroia 40.00 100.00
APDUP4 Dustin Pedroia 40.00 100.00
APDUP5 Dustin Pedroia 40.00 100.00
APDUP6 Dustin Pedroia 40.00 100.00
APDW1 Dave Winfield 40.00 100.00
APDW2 Dave Winfield 40.00 100.00
APDW3 Dave Winfield 40.00 100.00
APDW4 Dave Winfield 40.00 100.00
APDW5 Dave Winfield 40.00 100.00
APDW6 Dave Winfield 40.00 100.00
APDW7 Dave Winfield 40.00 100.00
APEE1 Edwin Encarnacion EXCH 40.00 100.00
APEE2 Edwin Encarnacion EXCH 40.00 100.00
APEE3 Edwin Encarnacion EXCH 40.00 100.00
APFF1 Freddie Freeman 50.00 120.00
APFF2 Freddie Freeman 50.00 120.00
APFF3 Freddie Freeman 50.00 120.00
APFF4 Freddie Freeman 50.00 120.00
APFF5 Freddie Freeman 50.00 120.00
APFF6 Freddie Freeman 50.00 120.00
APFF7 Freddie Freeman 50.00 120.00
APFF8 Freddie Freeman 50.00 120.00
APFL1 Francisco Lindor 60.00 150.00
APFL2 Francisco Lindor 60.00 150.00
APFL3 Francisco Lindor 60.00 150.00
APFL4 Francisco Lindor 60.00 150.00
APFL5 Francisco Lindor 60.00 150.00
APFL6 Francisco Lindor 60.00 150.00
APFM1 Floyd Mayweather Jr. 200.00 500.00
APFM2 Floyd Mayweather Jr. 200.00 500.00
APFM3 Floyd Mayweather Jr. 200.00 500.00
APFM4 Floyd Mayweather Jr. 200.00 500.00
APFM5 Floyd Mayweather Jr. 200.00 500.00
APFT1 Frank Thomas 75.00 200.00
APFT2 Frank Thomas 75.00 200.00
APFT3 Frank Thomas 75.00 200.00
APFT4 Frank Thomas 75.00 200.00
APFT5 Frank Thomas 75.00 200.00
APFT6 Frank Thomas 75.00 200.00
APGA1 Gary Sheffield
APGA2 Gary Sheffield
APGA3 Gary Sheffield
APGA4 Gary Sheffield
APGA5 Gary Sheffield
APGA6 Gary Sheffield
APGA7 Gary Sheffield
APGM1 Greg Maddux 75.00 200.00
APGM2 Greg Maddux 75.00 200.00
APGM3 Greg Maddux 75.00 200.00
APGM4 Greg Maddux 75.00 200.00
APGM5 Greg Maddux 75.00 200.00
APGS1 George Springer 50.00 120.00
APGS2 George Springer 50.00 120.00
APGS3 George Springer 50.00 120.00
APGS4 George Springer 50.00 120.00
APGS5 George Springer 50.00 120.00
APGS6 George Springer 50.00 120.00
APGS7 George Springer 50.00 120.00
APGS8 George Springer 50.00 120.00
APGY1 Gary Sanchez 60.00 150.00
APGY2 Gary Sanchez 60.00 150.00
APGY3 Gary Sanchez 60.00 150.00
APGY4 Gary Sanchez 60.00 150.00
APGY5 Gary Sanchez 60.00 150.00
APGY6 Gary Sanchez 60.00 150.00
APIR1 Ivan Rodriguez 50.00 120.00
APIR2 Ivan Rodriguez 50.00 120.00
APIR3 Ivan Rodriguez 50.00 120.00
APIR4 Ivan Rodriguez 50.00 120.00
APIR5 Ivan Rodriguez 50.00 120.00
API1 Ichiro 300.00 600.00
API2 Ichiro 300.00 600.00
API5 Ichiro 300.00 600.00
API6 Ichiro 300.00 600.00
API7 Ichiro 300.00 600.00
API8 Ichiro 300.00 600.00
API9 Ichiro 300.00 600.00
API10 Ichiro 300.00 600.00
APJA1 Jose Altuve 75.00 200.00
APJA2 Jose Altuve 75.00 200.00
APJA3 Jose Altuve 75.00 200.00
APJA4 Jose Altuve 75.00 200.00
APJA5 Jose Altuve 75.00 200.00
APJA6 Jose Altuve 75.00 200.00
APJA7 Jose Altuve 75.00 200.00
APJA8 Jose Altuve 75.00 200.00
APJB1 Javier Baez
APJB2 Javier Baez
APJB3 Javier Baez
APJB4 Javier Baez
APJB5 Javier Baez
APJB6 Javier Baez
APJB7 Javier Baez
APJB8 Javier Baez
APJD1 Jacob deGrom 75.00 200.00
APJD2 Jacob deGrom 75.00 200.00
APJD3 Jacob deGrom 75.00 200.00
APJD4 Jacob deGrom 75.00 200.00
APJD5 Jacob deGrom 75.00 200.00
APJD6 Jacob deGrom 75.00 200.00
APJE1 Jeff Bagwell 75.00 200.00
APJE2 Jeff Bagwell 75.00 200.00
APJE3 Jeff Bagwell 75.00 200.00
APJE4 Jeff Bagwell 75.00 200.00
APJE5 Jeff Bagwell 75.00 200.00
APJE6 Jeff Bagwell 75.00 200.00
APJH1 Jason Heyward EXCH 25.00 60.00
APJH2 Jason Heyward EXCH 25.00 60.00
APJH3 Jason Heyward EXCH 25.00 60.00
APJH4 Jason Heyward EXCH 25.00 60.00
APJH5 Jason Heyward EXCH 25.00 60.00
APJH6 Jason Heyward EXCH 25.00 60.00
APJO1 Josh Donaldson 30.00 80.00
APJO2 Josh Donaldson 30.00 80.00
APJO3 Josh Donaldson 30.00 80.00
APJO4 Josh Donaldson 30.00 80.00
APJO5 Josh Donaldson 30.00 80.00
APJO6 Josh Donaldson 30.00 80.00
APJS1 John Smoltz 40.00 100.00
APJS2 John Smoltz 40.00 100.00
APJS3 John Smoltz 40.00 100.00
APJS4 John Smoltz 40.00 100.00
APJS5 John Smoltz 40.00 100.00
APJS6 John Smoltz 40.00 100.00
APJS7 John Smoltz 40.00 100.00
APJS8 John Smoltz 40.00 100.00
APJT1 Jim Thome 60.00 150.00
APJT2 Jim Thome 60.00 150.00
APJT3 Jim Thome 60.00 150.00
APJT4 Jim Thome 60.00 150.00
APJT5 Jim Thome 60.00 150.00
APJT6 Jim Thome 60.00 150.00
APJV1 Joey Votto 60.00 150.00
APJV2 Joey Votto 60.00 150.00
APJV3 Joey Votto 60.00 150.00
APJV4 Joey Votto 60.00 150.00
APJV5 Joey Votto 60.00 150.00
APJV6 Joey Votto 60.00 150.00
APKB1 Kris Bryant 150.00 400.00
APKB2 Kris Bryant 150.00 400.00
APKB3 Kris Bryant 150.00 400.00
APKB4 Kris Bryant 150.00 400.00
APKB5 Kris Bryant 150.00 400.00
APKB6 Kris Bryant 150.00 400.00
APKB7 Kris Bryant 150.00 400.00
APKM1 Kenta Maeda 25.00 60.00
APKM2 Kenta Maeda 25.00 60.00
APKM3 Kenta Maeda 25.00 60.00
APKM4 Kenta Maeda 25.00 60.00
APKM5 Kenta Maeda 25.00 60.00
APKM6 Kenta Maeda 25.00 60.00
APKS1 Kyle Schwarber 40.00 100.00
APKS2 Kyle Schwarber 40.00 100.00
APKS3 Kyle Schwarber 40.00 100.00
APKS4 Kyle Schwarber 40.00 100.00
APKS5 Kyle Schwarber 40.00 100.00
APKS6 Kyle Schwarber 40.00 100.00
APKS7 Kyle Schwarber 40.00 100.00
APKS8 Kyle Schwarber 40.00 100.00
APMF2 Michael Fulmer 25.00 60.00
APMF3 Michael Fulmer 25.00 60.00
APMF4 Michael Fulmer 25.00 60.00
APMF5 Michael Fulmer 25.00 60.00
APMF6 Michael Fulmer 25.00 60.00
APMF7 Michael Fulmer 25.00 60.00
APMF8 Michael Fulmer 25.00 60.00
APMM1 Mark McGwire 60.00 150.00
APMM2 Mark McGwire 60.00 150.00
APMM3 Mark McGwire 60.00 150.00
APMM4 Mark McGwire 60.00 150.00
APMM5 Mark McGwire 60.00 150.00
APMM6 Mark McGwire 60.00 150.00
APMM7 Mark McGwire 60.00 150.00
APMM8 Mark McGwire 60.00 150.00
APMMA1 Manny Machado 60.00 150.00
APMMA2 Manny Machado 60.00 150.00
APMMA3 Manny Machado 60.00 150.00
APMMA4 Manny Machado 60.00 150.00
APMMA5 Manny Machado 60.00 150.00
APMMA6 Manny Machado 60.00 150.00
APMO1 Mike Trout 150.00 400.00
APMO2 Mike Trout 150.00 400.00
APMP1 Mike Piazza 60.00 150.00
APMP2 Mike Piazza 60.00 150.00
APMP3 Mike Piazza 60.00 150.00
APMP4 Mike Piazza 60.00 150.00
APMP5 Mike Piazza 60.00 150.00
APMP6 Mike Piazza 60.00 150.00
APMP7 Mike Piazza 60.00 150.00
APMP8 Mike Piazza 60.00 150.00
APMT3 Mike Trout 150.00 400.00
APMT4 Mike Trout 150.00 400.00
APMT5 Mike Trout 150.00 400.00
APMT6 Mike Trout 150.00 400.00
APMT7 Mike Trout 150.00 400.00
APMT8 Mike Trout 150.00 400.00
APMTA1 Masahiro Tanaka 75.00 200.00
APMTA2 Masahiro Tanaka 75.00 200.00
APMTA3 Masahiro Tanaka 75.00 200.00
APMTA4 Masahiro Tanaka 75.00 200.00
APMTA5 Masahiro Tanaka 75.00 200.00
APMTA6 Masahiro Tanaka 75.00 200.00
APMTA7 Masahiro Tanaka 75.00 200.00
APNR5 Nolan Ryan 125.00 300.00
APNR6 Nolan Ryan 125.00 300.00
APNR7 Nolan Ryan 125.00 300.00
APNR8 Nolan Ryan 125.00 300.00
APNR9 Nolan Ryan 125.00 300.00
APNS1 Noah Syndergaard 40.00 100.00
APNS2 Noah Syndergaard 40.00 100.00
APNS3 Noah Syndergaard 40.00 100.00
APNS4 Noah Syndergaard 40.00 100.00
APNS5 Noah Syndergaard 40.00 100.00
APNS6 Noah Syndergaard 40.00 100.00
APNS7 Noah Syndergaard 40.00 100.00
APNS8 Noah Syndergaard 40.00 100.00
APPG1 Paul Goldschmidt 50.00 120.00
APPG2 Paul Goldschmidt 50.00 120.00
APPG3 Paul Goldschmidt 50.00 120.00
APPG4 Paul Goldschmidt 50.00 120.00
APPG5 Paul Goldschmidt 50.00 120.00
APPG6 Paul Goldschmidt 50.00 120.00
APPM1 Pedro Martinez 50.00 120.00
APPM2 Pedro Martinez 50.00 120.00
APPM3 Pedro Martinez 50.00 120.00
APPM4 Pedro Martinez 50.00 120.00
APPM5 Pedro Martinez 50.00 120.00
APPM6 Pedro Martinez 50.00 120.00
APPM7 Pedro Martinez 50.00 120.00
APPM8 Pedro Martinez 50.00 120.00
APPM9 Pedro Martinez 50.00 120.00
APRB1 Ryan Braun 25.00 60.00
APRB2 Ryan Braun 25.00 60.00
APRB3 Ryan Braun 25.00 60.00
APRB4 Ryan Braun 25.00 60.00
APRB5 Ryan Braun 25.00 60.00
APRB6 Ryan Braun 25.00 60.00
APRB7 Ryan Braun 25.00 60.00
APRB8 Ryan Braun 25.00 60.00
APRC1 Rod Carew 30.00 80.00
APRC2 Rod Carew 30.00 80.00
APRE1 Rickey Henderson 60.00 150.00
APRE2 Rickey Henderson 60.00 150.00
APRE3 Rickey Henderson 60.00 150.00
APRE4 Rickey Henderson 60.00 150.00
APRE5 Rickey Henderson 60.00 150.00
APRH1 Roy Halladay 100.00 250.00
APRH2 Roy Halladay 100.00 250.00
APRH3 Roy Halladay 100.00 250.00
APRH4 Roy Halladay 100.00 250.00
APRH5 Roy Halladay 100.00 250.00
APRH6 Roy Halladay 100.00 250.00
APRJ1 Reggie Jackson 50.00 120.00
APRJ2 Reggie Jackson 50.00 120.00
APRJ3 Reggie Jackson 50.00 120.00
APRJ4 Reggie Jackson 50.00 120.00
APRJ5 Reggie Jackson 50.00 120.00
APRL1 Roger Clemens 75.00 200.00
APRL2 Roger Clemens 75.00 200.00
APRL3 Roger Clemens 75.00 200.00
APRL4 Roger Clemens 75.00 200.00
APRL5 Roger Clemens 75.00 200.00
APRO1 Robinson Cano 40.00 100.00
APRO2 Robinson Cano 40.00 100.00
APRO3 Robinson Cano 40.00 100.00
APRO4 Robinson Cano 40.00 100.00
APRO5 Robinson Cano 40.00 100.00
APRO6 Robinson Cano 40.00 100.00
APRR1 Randy Johnson 60.00 150.00
APRR2 Randy Johnson 60.00 150.00
APRS1 Ryne Sandberg 125.00 300.00
APRS2 Ryne Sandberg 125.00 300.00
APRS3 Ryne Sandberg 125.00 300.00
APSP4 Stephen Piscotty 25.00 60.00
APSP5 Stephen Piscotty 25.00 60.00
APSP6 Stephen Piscotty 25.00 60.00
APSP7 Stephen Piscotty 25.00 60.00
APSP8 Stephen Piscotty 25.00 60.00
APTE1 Theo Epstein 75.00 200.00
APTE2 Theo Epstein 75.00 200.00
APTE3 Theo Epstein 75.00 200.00
APTL1 Tom Glavine 40.00 100.00
APTL2 Tom Glavine 40.00 100.00
APTL3 Tom Glavine 40.00 100.00
APTL4 Tom Glavine 40.00 100.00
APTL5 Tom Glavine 40.00 100.00
APTS1 Trevor Story 25.00 60.00
APTS2 Trevor Story 25.00 60.00
APTS3 Trevor Story 25.00 60.00
APTS4 Trevor Story 25.00 60.00
APTS5 Trevor Story 25.00 60.00
APTS6 Trevor Story 25.00 60.00
APTS7 Trevor Story 25.00 60.00
APTS8 Trevor Story 25.00 60.00
APTT1 Trea Turner
APTT2 Trea Turner
APTT3 Trea Turner
APTT4 Trea Turner
APTT5 Trea Turner
APTT6 Trea Turner
APTT7 Trea Turner
APTT8 Trea Turner
APYC1 Yoenis Cespedes 30.00 80.00
APYC2 Yoenis Cespedes 30.00 80.00
APYC3 Yoenis Cespedes 30.00 80.00
APYC4 Yoenis Cespedes 30.00 80.00
APYC5 Yoenis Cespedes 30.00 80.00
APYC6 Yoenis Cespedes 30.00 80.00
APYG1 Yulieski Gurriel RC 30.00 80.00
APYG2 Yulieski Gurriel RC 30.00 80.00
APYG3 Yulieski Gurriel RC 30.00 80.00
APYG4 Yulieski Gurriel RC 30.00 80.00
APYG5 Yulieski Gurriel RC 30.00 80.00
APYG6 Yulieski Gurriel RC 30.00 80.00
APYG7 Yulieski Gurriel RC 30.00 80.00
APYM1 Yoan Moncada RC 60.00 150.00
APYM2 Yoan Moncada RC 60.00 150.00
APYM3 Yoan Moncada RC 60.00 150.00
APYM4 Yoan Moncada RC 60.00 150.00
APYM5 Yoan Moncada RC 60.00 150.00
APYM6 Yoan Moncada RC 60.00 150.00

2017 Topps Dynasty Autograph Patches Gold

*GOLD: .5X TO 1.2X BASIC
RANDOM INSERTS IN PACKS
STATED PRINT RUN 5 SER.#'d SETS
ALL VERSIONS EQUALLY PRICED
LOGO/TAG PATCHES MAY SELL FOR PREMIUM
EXCHANGE DEADLINE 10/31/2019
APFM1 Floyd Mayweather Jr. 400.00 800.00
APJB1 Javier Baez 125.00 300.00

2017 Topps Dynasty Dual Relic Autographs

STATED ODDS 1:63 BOXES
STATED PRINT RUN 5 SER.#'d SETS
MOST NOT PRICED DUE TO SCARCITY
ALL VERSIONS EQUALLY PRICED
ADRDM1 Don Mattingly 60.00 150.00
ADRDM2 Don Mattingly 60.00 150.00
ADRDM3 Don Mattingly 60.00 150.00
ADRJB1 Johnny Bench 100.00 250.00
ADRJB2 Johnny Bench 100.00 250.00
ADRJB3 Johnny Bench 100.00 250.00

2018 Topps Dynasty Autograph Patches

OVERALL AUTO ODDS 1:1
STATED PRINT RUN 10 SER.#'d SETS
ALL VERSIONS EQUALLY PRICED
LOGO/TAG PATCHES MAY SELL FOR PREMIUM
EXCHANGE DEADLINE 10/31/2020
APAB1 Alex Bregman 60.00 150.00
APAB2 Alex Bregman 60.00 150.00
APAB3 Alex Bregman 60.00 150.00
APAB4 Alex Bregman 60.00 150.00
APAB5 Alex Bregman 60.00 150.00
APAB6 Alex Bregman 60.00 150.00
APAB7 Alex Bregman 60.00 150.00
APAB8 Alex Bregman 60.00 150.00
APABL1 Adrian Beltre 50.00 120.00
APABL2 Adrian Beltre 50.00 120.00
APABL3 Adrian Beltre 50.00 120.00
APABL4 Adrian Beltre 50.00 120.00
APABL5 Adrian Beltre 50.00 120.00
APABL6 Adrian Beltre 50.00 120.00
APABL7 Adrian Beltre 50.00 120.00
APABL8 Adrian Beltre 50.00 120.00
APABN1 Andrew Benintendi 60.00 150.00
APABN2 Andrew Benintendi 60.00 150.00
APABN3 Andrew Benintendi 60.00 150.00
APABN4 Andrew Benintendi 60.00 150.00
APABN5 Andrew Benintendi 60.00 150.00
APABN6 Andrew Benintendi 60.00 150.00
APABN7 Andrew Benintendi 60.00 150.00
APABN8 Andrew Benintendi 60.00 150.00
APAJ1 Adam Jones 30.00 80.00
APAJ2 Adam Jones 30.00 80.00
APAJ3 Adam Jones 30.00 80.00
APAJ4 Adam Jones 30.00 80.00
APAJ5 Adam Jones 30.00 80.00
APALO1 Roberto Alomar 50.00 120.00
APALO2 Roberto Alomar 50.00 120.00
APALO3 Roberto Alomar 50.00 120.00
APAM1 Andrew McCutchen 75.00 200.00
APAM2 Andrew McCutchen 75.00 200.00
APAM3 Andrew McCutchen 75.00 200.00
APAM4 Andrew McCutchen 75.00 200.00
APAM5 Andrew McCutchen 75.00 200.00
APAMR1 Amed Rosario RC 25.00 60.00
APAMR2 Amed Rosario RC 25.00 60.00
APAMR3 Amed Rosario RC 25.00 60.00
APAMR4 Amed Rosario RC 25.00 60.00
APAMR5 Amed Rosario RC 25.00 60.00
APAMR6 Amed Rosario RC 25.00 60.00
APAMR7 Amed Rosario RC 25.00 60.00
APAMR8 Amed Rosario RC 25.00 60.00
APAP1 Albert Pujols 100.00 250.00
APAP2 Albert Pujols 100.00 250.00
APAPT4 Andy Pettitte 40.00 100.00
APAPT5 Andy Pettitte 40.00 100.00
APAPT6 Andy Pettitte 40.00 100.00
APAR1 Alex Rodriguez 100.00 250.00
APAR2 Alex Rodriguez 100.00 250.00
APAR3 Alex Rodriguez 100.00 250.00
APAR4 Alex Rodriguez 100.00 250.00
APAR5 Alex Rodriguez 100.00 250.00
APARJ1 Aaron Judge 250.00 500.00
APARJ2 Aaron Judge 250.00 500.00
APARJ3 Aaron Judge 250.00 500.00
APARJ4 Aaron Judge 250.00 500.00
APAZ1 Anthony Rizzo 50.00 120.00
APAZ2 Anthony Rizzo 50.00 120.00
APAZ3 Anthony Rizzo 50.00 120.00
APAZ4 Anthony Rizzo 50.00 120.00
APAZ5 Anthony Rizzo 50.00 120.00
APAZ6 Anthony Rizzo 50.00 120.00
APBH1 Bryce Harper 125.00 300.00
APBH2 Bryce Harper 125.00 300.00
APBH3 Bryce Harper 125.00 300.00
APBH4 Bryce Harper 125.00 300.00
APBH5 Bryce Harper 125.00 300.00
APBL1 Barry Larkin 40.00 100.00
APBL2 Barry Larkin 40.00 100.00
APBL3 Barry Larkin 40.00 100.00
APBL4 Barry Larkin 40.00 100.00
APBL5 Barry Larkin 40.00 100.00
APBL6 Barry Larkin 40.00 100.00
APBP1 Buster Posey 60.00 150.00
APBP2 Buster Posey 60.00 150.00
APBP3 Buster Posey 60.00 150.00
APBP4 Buster Posey 60.00 150.00
APBP5 Buster Posey 60.00 150.00
APBP6 Buster Posey 60.00 150.00
APCBG1 Craig Biggio 40.00 100.00
APCBG2 Craig Biggio 40.00 100.00
APCBG3 Craig Biggio 40.00 100.00
APCBG4 Craig Biggio 40.00 100.00
APCBL1 Charlie Blackmon 40.00 100.00
APCBL2 Charlie Blackmon 40.00 100.00
APCBL3 Charlie Blackmon 40.00 100.00
APCBL4 Charlie Blackmon 40.00 100.00
APCBL5 Charlie Blackmon 40.00 100.00
APCBL6 Charlie Blackmon 40.00 100.00
APCBL7 Charlie Blackmon 40.00 100.00
APCF1 Clint Frazier RC 30.00 80.00
APCF2 Clint Frazier RC 30.00 80.00
APCF3 Clint Frazier RC 30.00 80.00
APCF4 Clint Frazier RC 30.00 80.00
APCF5 Clint Frazier RC 30.00 80.00
APCF6 Clint Frazier RC 30.00 80.00
APCJ1 Chipper Jones 75.00 200.00
APCJ2 Chipper Jones 75.00 200.00
APCJ3 Chipper Jones 75.00 200.00
APCJ4 Chipper Jones 75.00 200.00
APCJ5 Chipper Jones 75.00 200.00
APCJ6 Chipper Jones 75.00 200.00
APCK1 Clayton Kershaw 75.00 200.00
APCK2 Clayton Kershaw 75.00 200.00
APCK3 Clayton Kershaw 75.00 200.00
APCK4 Clayton Kershaw 75.00 200.00
APCK5 Clayton Kershaw 75.00 200.00
APCK6 Clayton Kershaw 75.00 200.00
APCR1 Cal Ripken Jr. 100.00 250.00
APCR2 Cal Ripken Jr. 100.00 250.00
APCR3 Cal Ripken Jr. 100.00 250.00
APCR4 Cal Ripken Jr. 100.00 250.00
APCR5 Cal Ripken Jr. 100.00 250.00
APCSL1 Chris Sale 40.00 100.00
APCSL2 Chris Sale 40.00 100.00
APCSL3 Chris Sale 40.00 100.00
APCSL4 Chris Sale 40.00 100.00
APCSL5 Chris Sale 40.00 100.00
APCSL6 Chris Sale 40.00 100.00
APCSL7 Chris Sale 40.00 100.00
APCSL8 Chris Sale 40.00 100.00
APCY1 Christian Yelich 50.00 120.00
APCY2 Christian Yelich 50.00 120.00
APCY3 Christian Yelich 50.00 120.00
APDG1 Didi Gregorius 40.00 100.00
APDG2 Didi Gregorius 40.00 100.00
APDG3 Didi Gregorius 40.00 100.00
APDG4 Didi Gregorius 40.00 100.00
APDG5 Didi Gregorius 40.00 100.00
APDJ1 Derek Jeter 400.00 800.00
APDJ2 Derek Jeter 400.00 800.00
APDO1 David Ortiz 60.00 150.00
APDO2 David Ortiz 60.00 150.00
APDO3 David Ortiz 60.00 150.00
APDO4 David Ortiz 60.00 150.00
APDO5 David Ortiz 60.00 150.00
APDO6 David Ortiz 60.00 150.00
APDO7 David Ortiz 60.00 150.00
APDO8 David Ortiz 60.00 150.00
APDP1 Dustin Pedroia 40.00 100.00
APDP2 Dustin Pedroia 40.00 100.00
APDP3 Dustin Pedroia 40.00 100.00
APDP4 Dustin Pedroia 40.00 100.00
APDP5 Dustin Pedroia 40.00 100.00
APDP6 Dustin Pedroia 40.00 100.00
APDP7 Dustin Pedroia 40.00 100.00
APDP8 Dustin Pedroia 40.00 100.00
APFF1 Freddie Freeman 50.00
APFF2 Freddie Freeman 50.00 120.00
APFF3 Freddie Freeman 50.00 120.00
APFF4 Freddie Freeman 50.00 120.00
APFF5 Freddie Freeman 50.00 120.00
APFF6 Freddie Freeman 50.00 120.00
APFF7 Freddie Freeman 50.00 120.00
APFF8 Freddie Freeman 50.00 120.00
APFL1 Francisco Lindor 50.00 120.00
APFL2 Francisco Lindor 50.00 120.00
APFL3 Francisco Lindor 50.00 120.00
APFL4 Francisco Lindor 50.00 120.00
APFL5 Francisco Lindor 50.00 120.00
APFL6 Francisco Lindor 50.00 120.00
APFL7 Francisco Lindor 50.00 120.00
APFL8 Francisco Lindor 50.00 120.00
APFT1 Frank Thomas 60.00 150.00
APFT2 Frank Thomas 60.00 150.00
APFT3 Frank Thomas 60.00 150.00
APFT4 Frank Thomas 60.00 150.00
APFT5 Frank Thomas 60.00 150.00
APFT6 Frank Thomas 60.00 150.00
APGS1 Gary Sanchez 30.00 80.00
APGS2 Gary Sanchez 30.00 80.00
APGS3 Gary Sanchez 30.00 80.00
APGS4 Gary Sanchez 30.00 80.00
APGS5 Gary Sanchez 30.00 80.00
APGS6 Gary Sanchez 30.00 80.00
APGSP1 George Springer 40.00 100.00
APGSP2 George Springer 40.00 100.00
APGSP3 George Springer 40.00 100.00
APGSP4 George Springer 40.00 100.00
APGSP5 George Springer 40.00 100.00
APGSP6 George Springer 40.00 100.00
APGSP7 George Springer 40.00 100.00
APGSP8 George Springer 40.00 100.00
APGT1 Gleyber Torres RC 125.00 300.00
APGT2 Gleyber Torres RC 125.00 300.00
APGT3 Gleyber Torres RC 125.00 300.00
APIR1 Ivan Rodriguez 40.00 100.00
APIR2 Ivan Rodriguez 40.00 100.00
APIR3 Ivan Rodriguez 40.00 100.00
APIR4 Ivan Rodriguez 40.00 100.00
APIR5 Ivan Rodriguez 40.00 100.00
API3 Ichiro 300.00 600.00
API4 Ichiro 300.00 600.00
APJA1 Jose Altuve 50.00 120.00
APJA2 Jose Altuve 50.00 120.00
APJA3 Jose Altuve 50.00 120.00
APJA4 Jose Altuve 50.00 120.00
APJA5 Jose Altuve 50.00 120.00
APJA6 Jose Altuve 50.00 120.00
APJA7 Jose Altuve 50.00 120.00
APJA8 Jose Altuve 50.00 120.00
APJB1 Jeff Bagwell 75.00 200.00
APJB2 Jeff Bagwell 75.00 200.00
APJB3 Jeff Bagwell 75.00 200.00
APJB4 Jeff Bagwell 75.00 200.00
APJBZ1 Javier Baez 75.00 200.00
APJBZ2 Javier Baez 75.00 200.00
APJBZ3 Javier Baez 75.00 200.00
APJBZ4 Javier Baez 75.00 200.00
APJBZ5 Javier Baez 75.00 200.00
APJBZ6 Javier Baez 75.00 200.00
APJBZ7 Javier Baez 75.00 200.00
APJBZ8 Javier Baez 75.00 200.00
APJDG1 Jacob deGrom 60.00 150.00
APJDG2 Jacob deGrom 60.00 120.00
APJDG3 Jacob deGrom 60.00 120.00
APJDG4 Jacob deGrom 60.00 120.00
APJDG5 Jacob deGrom 60.00 120.00
APJDG6 Jacob deGrom 60.00 120.00
APJDG7 Jacob deGrom 60.00 120.00
APJDG8 Jacob deGrom 60.00 120.00
APJRM1 Jose Ramirez 40.00 100.00
APJRM2 Jose Ramirez 40.00 100.00
APJRM3 Jose Ramirez 40.00 100.00
APJRM4 Jose Ramirez 40.00 100.00
APJSM1 John Smoltz 40.00 100.00
APJSM2 John Smoltz 40.00 100.00
APJSM3 John Smoltz 40.00 100.00
APJSM4 John Smoltz 40.00 100.00
APJSM5 John Smoltz 40.00 100.00
APJSM6 John Smoltz 40.00 100.00
APJSO1 Juan Soto RC 500.00 1000.00
APJSO2 Juan Soto RC 500.00 1000.00
APJSO3 Juan Soto RC 500.00 1000.00
APJU1 Justin Upton 25.00 60.00
APJU2 Justin Upton 25.00 60.00
APJU3 Justin Upton 25.00 60.00
APJV1 Joey Votto 50.00 120.00
APJV2 Joey Votto 50.00 120.00
APJV3 Joey Votto 50.00 120.00
APJV4 Joey Votto 50.00 120.00
APJV5 Joey Votto 50.00 120.00
APJV6 Joey Votto 50.00 120.00
APKB1 Kris Bryant EXCH 100.00 250.00
APKB2 Kris Bryant EXCH 100.00 250.00
APKB3 Kris Bryant EXCH 100.00 250.00
APKB4 Kris Bryant EXCH 100.00 250.00
APKB5 Kris Bryant EXCH 100.00 250.00
APKS1 Kyle Schwarber 30.00 80.00
APKS2 Kyle Schwarber 30.00 80.00
APKS3 Kyle Schwarber 30.00 80.00
APKS4 Kyle Schwarber 30.00 80.00
APKS5 Kyle Schwarber 30.00 80.00
APKS6 Kyle Schwarber 30.00 80.00
APKS7 Kyle Schwarber 30.00 80.00
APKS8 Kyle Schwarber 30.00 80.00
APLS1 Luis Severino 40.00 100.00
APLS2 Luis Severino 40.00 100.00
APLS3 Luis Severino 40.00 100.00
APLS4 Luis Severino 40.00 100.00
APLS5 Luis Severino 40.00 100.00
APLS6 Luis Severino 40.00 100.00
APLS7 Luis Severino 40.00 100.00
APLS8 Luis Severino 40.00 100.00
APMCG1 Mark McGwire 60.00 150.00
APMCG2 Mark McGwire 60.00 150.00
APMCG3 Mark McGwire 60.00 150.00
APMCG4 Mark McGwire 60.00 150.00
APMK1 Masahiro Tanaka 60.00 150.00
APMK2 Masahiro Tanaka 60.00 150.00
APMK3 Masahiro Tanaka 60.00 150.00
APMK4 Masahiro Tanaka 60.00 150.00
APMM1 Manny Machado 100.00 250.00
APMM2 Manny Machado 100.00 250.00
APMM3 Manny Machado 100.00 250.00
APMM4 Manny Machado 100.00 250.00
APMM5 Manny Machado 100.00 250.00
APMM6 Manny Machado 100.00 250.00
APMP1 Mike Piazza 60.00 150.00
APMP2 Mike Piazza 60.00 150.00
APMP3 Mike Piazza 60.00 150.00
APMP4 Mike Piazza 60.00 150.00
APMP5 Mike Piazza 60.00 150.00
APMP6 Mike Piazza 60.00 150.00
APMR1 Mariano Rivera 100.00 250.00
APMR2 Mariano Rivera 100.00 250.00
APMR3 Mariano Rivera 100.00 250.00
APMT1 Mike Trout 400.00 800.00
APMT2 Mike Trout 400.00 800.00
APMT3 Mike Trout 400.00 800.00
APMT4 Mike Trout 400.00 800.00
APMT5 Mike Trout 400.00 800.00
APMT6 Mike Trout 400.00 800.00
APNG1 Nomar Garciaparra 40.00 100.00
APNG2 Nomar Garciaparra 40.00 100.00
APNG3 Nomar Garciaparra 40.00 100.00
APNG4 Nomar Garciaparra 40.00 100.00
APNS1 Noah Syndergaard 30.00 80.00
APNS2 Noah Syndergaard 30.00 80.00
APNS3 Noah Syndergaard 30.00 80.00
APNS4 Noah Syndergaard 30.00 80.00
APNS5 Noah Syndergaard 30.00 80.00
APNS6 Noah Syndergaard 30.00 80.00
APOA1 Ozzie Albies RC 50.00 120.00
APOA2 Ozzie Albies RC 50.00 120.00
APOA3 Ozzie Albies RC 50.00 120.00
APOA4 Ozzie Albies RC 50.00 120.00
APOA5 Ozzie Albies RC 50.00 120.00
APOA6 Ozzie Albies RC 50.00 120.00
APOA7 Ozzie Albies RC 50.00 120.00
APOA8 Ozzie Albies RC 50.00 120.00
APPG1 Paul Goldschmidt 40.00 100.00
APPG2 Paul Goldschmidt 40.00 100.00
APPG3 Paul Goldschmidt 40.00 100.00
APPG4 Paul Goldschmidt 40.00 100.00
APPG5 Paul Goldschmidt 40.00 100.00
APPG6 Paul Goldschmidt 40.00 100.00
APPG7 Paul Goldschmidt 40.00 100.00
APPG8 Paul Goldschmidt 40.00 100.00
APPM1 Pedro Martinez 40.00 100.00
APPM2 Pedro Martinez 40.00 100.00
APPM3 Pedro Martinez 40.00 100.00
APPM4 Pedro Martinez 40.00 100.00
APPM6 Pedro Martinez 40.00 100.00
APPM7 Pedro Martinez 40.00 100.00
APPM8 Pedro Martinez 40.00 100.00
APRAC1 Ronald Acuna Jr. RC 300.00 600.00
APRAC2 Ronald Acuna Jr. RC 300.00 600.00
APRAC3 Ronald Acuna Jr. RC 300.00 600.00
APRAC4 Ronald Acuna Jr. RC 300.00 600.00
APRAC5 Ronald Acuna Jr. RC 300.00 600.00
APRAC6 Ronald Acuna Jr. RC 300.00 600.00
APRC1 Roger Clemens 60.00 150.00
APRC2 Roger Clemens 60.00 150.00
APRC3 Roger Clemens 60.00 150.00
APRC4 Roger Clemens 60.00 150.00
APRC5 Roger Clemens 60.00 150.00
APRD1 Rafael Devers RC EXCH 60.00 150.00
APRD2 Rafael Devers RC EXCH 60.00 150.00
APRD3 Rafael Devers RC EXCH 60.00 150.00
APRD4 Rafael Devers RC EXCH 60.00 150.00
APRD5 Rafael Devers RC EXCH 60.00 150.00
APRD6 Rafael Devers RC EXCH 60.00 150.00
APRD7 Rafael Devers RC EXCH 60.00 150.00
APRH1 Rickey Henderson 60.00 150.00
APRH2 Rickey Henderson 60.00 150.00
APRH3 Rickey Henderson 60.00 150.00
APRH4 Rickey Henderson 60.00 150.00
APRH5 Rickey Henderson 60.00 150.00
APRHY1 Rhys Hoskins RC 75.00 200.00
APRHY2 Rhys Hoskins RC 75.00 200.00
APRHY3 Rhys Hoskins RC 75.00 200.00
APRHY4 Rhys Hoskins RC 75.00 200.00
APRHY5 Rhys Hoskins RC 75.00 200.00
APRHY6 Rhys Hoskins RC 75.00 200.00
APRHY7 Rhys Hoskins RC 75.00 200.00
APRJX1 Reggie Jackson 40.00 100.00
APRJX2 Reggie Jackson 40.00 100.00
APRJX3 Reggie Jackson 40.00 100.00
APRJX4 Reggie Jackson 40.00 100.00
APRJX5 Reggie Jackson 40.00 100.00
APRW1 Russell Wilson 125.00 300.00
APRW2 Russell Wilson 125.00 300.00
APRW3 Russell Wilson 125.00 300.00
APRW4 Russell Wilson 125.00 300.00
APRW5 Russell Wilson 125.00 300.00
APRY1 Robin Yount 60.00 150.00
APRY2 Robin Yount 60.00 150.00
APSO1 Shohei Ohtani RC 600.00 1200.00
APSO2 Shohei Ohtani RC 600.00 1200.00
APSO3 Shohei Ohtani RC 600.00 1200.00
APSO4 Shohei Ohtani RC 600.00 1200.00
APSO5 Shohei Ohtani RC 600.00 1200.00
APSO6 Shohei Ohtani RC 600.00 1200.00
APSO7 Shohei Ohtani RC 600.00 1200.00
APTG1 Tom Glavine 30.00 80.00
APTG2 Tom Glavine 30.00 80.00
APTG3 Tom Glavine 30.00 80.00
APVG1 Vladimir Guerrero 50.00 120.00
APVG2 Vladimir Guerrero 50.00 120.00
APVG3 Vladimir Guerrero 50.00 120.00
APVG4 Vladimir Guerrero 50.00 120.00
APWC1 Willson Contreras 40.00 100.00
APWC2 Willson Contreras 40.00 100.00
APWC3 Willson Contreras 40.00 100.00
APWC4 Willson Contreras 40.00 100.00
APWC5 Willson Contreras 40.00 100.00
APWC6 Willson Contreras 40.00 100.00
APWC7 Willson Contreras 40.00 100.00
APWCL1 Will Clark 60.00 150.00
APWCL2 Will Clark 60.00 150.00
APWCL3 Will Clark 60.00 150.00
APWCL4 Will Clark 60.00 150.00
APWCL5 Will Clark 60.00 150.00
APWCL6 Will Clark 60.00 150.00
APYML1 Yadier Molina EXCH 75.00 200.00
APYML2 Yadier Molina EXCH 75.00 200.00
APYML3 Yadier Molina EXCH 75.00 200.00
APYML4 Yadier Molina EXCH 75.00 200.00
APYML5 Yadier Molina EXCH 75.00 200.00
APYML6 Yadier Molina EXCH 75.00 200.00
APYML7 Yadier Molina EXCH 75.00 200.00
APYML8 Yadier Molina EXCH 75.00 200.00

2018 Topps Dynasty Autograph Patches Blue

*GOLD: .5X TO 1.2X BASIC
RANDOM INSERTS IN PACKS
STATED PRINT RUN 5 SER.#'d SETS
ALL VERSIONS EQUALLY PRICED
LOGO/TAG PATCHES MAY SELL FOR PREMIUM
EXCHANGE DEADLINE 10/31/2020

2019 Topps Dynasty Autograph Patches

OVERALL AUTO ODDS 1:1
STATED PRINT RUN 10 SER.#'d SETS
SOME NOT PRICED DUE TO SCARCITY
ALL VERSIONS EQUALLY PRICED
LOGO/TAG PATCHES MAY SELL FOR PREMIUM
EXCHANGE DEADLINE 10/31/2021
DAPAB1 Alex Bregman 40.00 100.00
DAPAB2 Alex Bregman 40.00 100.00
DAPAB3 Alex Bregman 40.00 100.00
DAPAB4 Alex Bregman 40.00 100.00
DAPAB5 Alex Bregman 40.00 100.00
DAPAB6 Alex Bregman 40.00 100.00
DAPAB7 Alex Bregman 40.00 100.00
DAPAB8 Alex Bregman 40.00 100.00
DAPABE1 Adrian Beltre 40.00 100.00
DAPABE2 Adrian Beltre 40.00 100.00
DAPABE4 Adrian Beltre 40.00 100.00
DAPABE5 Adrian Beltre 40.00 100.00
DAPABE6 Adrian Beltre 40.00 100.00

DAPABE7 Adrian Beltre 40.00 100.00
DAPABN1 Andrew Benintendi 50.00 120.00
DAPABN2 Andrew Benintendi 50.00 120.00
DAPABN3 Andrew Benintendi 50.00 120.00
DAPABN4 Andrew Benintendi 50.00 120.00
DAPABN5 Andrew Benintendi 50.00 120.00
DAPABN6 Andrew Benintendi 50.00 120.00
DAPABN7 Andrew Benintendi 50.00 120.00
DAPABN8 Andrew Benintendi 50.00 120.00
DAPAJ1 Aaron Judge 100.00 250.00
DAPAJ2 Aaron Judge 100.00 250.00
DAPAJ3 Aaron Judge 100.00 250.00
DAPAJ4 Aaron Judge 100.00 250.00
DAPAJ5 Aaron Judge 100.00 250.00
DAPAJ6 Aaron Judge 100.00 250.00
DAPAN1 Aaron Nola 50.00 120.00
DAPAN2 Aaron Nola 50.00 120.00
DAPAN3 Aaron Nola 50.00 120.00
DAPAN4 Aaron Nola 50.00 120.00
DAPAN5 Aaron Nola 50.00 120.00
DAPAP1 Andy Pettitte 40.00 100.00
DAPAP2 Andy Pettitte 40.00 100.00
DAPAR1 Alex Rodriguez 75.00 200.00
DAPAR1 Austin Riley RC 60.00 150.00
DAPAR2 Austin Riley RC 60.00 150.00
DAPAR2 Alex Rodriguez 75.00 200.00
DAPAR3 Alex Rodriguez 75.00 200.00
DAPAR3 Austin Riley RC 60.00 150.00
DAPAR4 Alex Rodriguez 75.00 200.00
DAPARZ1 Anthony Rizzo 40.00 100.00
DAPARZ2 Anthony Rizzo 40.00 100.00
DAPARZ3 Anthony Rizzo 40.00 100.00
DAPARZ4 Anthony Rizzo 40.00 100.00
DAPARZ5 Anthony Rizzo 40.00 100.00
DAPARZ6 Anthony Rizzo 40.00 100.00
DAPBH1 Bryce Harper 150.00 400.00
DAPBH2 Bryce Harper 150.00 400.00
DAPBH3 Bryce Harper 150.00 400.00
DAPBL1 Barry Larkin 40.00 100.00
DAPBL2 Barry Larkin 40.00 100.00
DAPBL3 Barry Larkin 40.00 100.00
DAPBL4 Barry Larkin 40.00 100.00
DAPBP1 Buster Posey 40.00 100.00
DAPBP2 Buster Posey 40.00 100.00
DAPBP3 Buster Posey 40.00 100.00
DAPBP4 Buster Posey 40.00 100.00
DAPBP5 Buster Posey 40.00 100.00
DAPBP6 Buster Posey 40.00 100.00
DAPBR1 Brendan Rodgers RC 30.00 80.00
DAPBR2 Brendan Rodgers RC 30.00 80.00
DAPBR3 Brendan Rodgers RC 30.00 80.00
DAPBR4 Brendan Rodgers RC 30.00 80.00
DAPBR5 Brendan Rodgers RC 30.00 80.00
DAPBR6 Brendan Rodgers RC 30.00 80.00
DAPBS1 Blake Snell 25.00 60.00
DAPBS2 Blake Snell 25.00 60.00
DAPBS3 Blake Snell 25.00 60.00
DAPBS4 Blake Snell 25.00 60.00
DAPBS5 Blake Snell 25.00 60.00
DAPCBL1 Charlie Blackmon 40.00 100.00
DAPCBL2 Charlie Blackmon 40.00 100.00
DAPCBL3 Charlie Blackmon 40.00 100.00
DAPCC1 CC Sabathia 50.00 120.00
DAPCC2 CC Sabathia 50.00 120.00
DAPCC3 CC Sabathia 50.00 120.00
DAPCC4 CC Sabathia 50.00 120.00
DAPCC5 CC Sabathia 50.00 120.00
DAPCC6 CC Sabathia 50.00 120.00
DAPCJ1 Chipper Jones 60.00 150.00
DAPCJ2 Chipper Jones 60.00 150.00
DAPCJ3 Chipper Jones 60.00 150.00
DAPCJ4 Chipper Jones 60.00 150.00
DAPCJ5 Chipper Jones 60.00 150.00
DAPCJ6 Chipper Jones 60.00 150.00
DAPCK1 Clayton Kershaw 60.00 150.00
DAPCK2 Clayton Kershaw 60.00 150.00
DAPCP1 Chris Paddack RC 40.00 100.00
DAPCP2 Chris Paddack RC 40.00 100.00
DAPCP3 Chris Paddack RC 40.00 100.00
DAPCP4 Chris Paddack RC 40.00 100.00
DAPCSA1 Chris Sale 40.00 100.00
DAPCSA2 Chris Sale 40.00 100.00
DAPCSA3 Chris Sale 40.00 100.00
DAPCSA4 Chris Sale 40.00 100.00
DAPCSA5 Chris Sale 40.00 100.00
DAPCSA6 Chris Sale 40.00 100.00
DAPCSA7 Chris Sale 40.00 100.00
DAPCSA8 Chris Sale 40.00 100.00
DAPCY1 Christian Yelich 75.00 200.00
DAPCY2 Christian Yelich 75.00 200.00
DAPCY3 Christian Yelich 75.00 200.00
DAPCY4 Christian Yelich 75.00 200.00
DAPDJ1 Derek Jeter 250.00 600.00
DAPDJ2 Derek Jeter 250.00 600.00
DAPDO1 David Ortiz 50.00 120.00
DAPDO2 David Ortiz 50.00 120.00
DAPDO3 David Ortiz 50.00 120.00
DAPDO4 David Ortiz 50.00 120.00
DAPDO5 David Ortiz 50.00 120.00
DAPDO6 David Ortiz 50.00 120.00
DAPDP1 David Price 25.00 60.00
DAPDP1 Dustin Pedroia 30.00 80.00
DAPDP2 Dustin Pedroia 30.00 80.00
DAPDP2 David Price 25.00 60.00
DAPDP3 Dustin Pedroia 30.00 80.00
DAPDP4 Dustin Pedroia 30.00 80.00
DAPDP5 Dustin Pedroia 30.00 80.00
DAPDP6 Dustin Pedroia 30.00 80.00
DAPDPR1 David Price 25.00 60.00
DAPDPR2 David Price 25.00 60.00
DAPFF1 Freddie Freeman 50.00 125.00
DAPFF2 Freddie Freeman 50.00 125.00
DAPFF3 Freddie Freeman 50.00 125.00
DAPFF4 Freddie Freeman 50.00 125.00
DAPFF5 Freddie Freeman 50.00 125.00
DAPFF6 Freddie Freeman 50.00 125.00
DAPFF7 Freddie Freeman 50.00 125.00
DAPFF8 Freddie Freeman 50.00 125.00
DAPFL1 Francisco Lindor 50.00 120.00
DAPFL2 Francisco Lindor 50.00 120.00
DAPFL3 Francisco Lindor 50.00 120.00
DAPFL4 Francisco Lindor 50.00 120.00
DAPFL5 Francisco Lindor 50.00 120.00
DAPFL6 Francisco Lindor 50.00 120.00
DAPFL7 Francisco Lindor 50.00 120.00
DAPFM1 Fred McGriff 50.00 120.00
DAPFM2 Fred McGriff 50.00 120.00
DAPFT1 Frank Thomas 75.00 200.00
DAPFT2 Frank Thomas 75.00 200.00
DAPFT3 Frank Thomas 75.00 200.00
DAPFTJ1 Fernando Tatis Jr. RC 400.00 1000.00
DAPFTJ2 Fernando Tatis Jr. RC 400.00 1000.00
DAPFTJ3 Fernando Tatis Jr. RC 400.00 1000.00
DAPFTJ4 Fernando Tatis Jr. RC 400.00 1000.00
DAPFTJ5 Fernando Tatis Jr. RC 400.00 1000.00
DAPFTJ6 Fernando Tatis Jr. RC 400.00 1000.00
DAPFTJ7 Fernando Tatis Jr. RC 400.00 1000.00
DAPFTJ8 Fernando Tatis Jr. RC 400.00 1000.00
DAPGC1 Gerrit Cole 50.00 120.00
DAPGC2 Gerrit Cole 50.00 120.00
DAPGC3 Gerrit Cole 50.00 120.00
DAPGC4 Gerrit Cole 50.00 120.00
DAPGC5 Gerrit Cole 50.00 120.00
DAPGC6 Gerrit Cole 50.00 120.00
DAPGSP1 George Springer 30.00 80.00
DAPGSP2 George Springer 30.00 80.00
DAPGSP3 George Springer 30.00 80.00
DAPGSP4 George Springer 30.00 80.00
DAPGSP5 George Springer 30.00 80.00
DAPGSP6 George Springer 30.00 80.00
DAPGSP7 George Springer 30.00 80.00
DAPGSP8 George Springer 30.00 80.00
DAPIR1 Ivan Rodriguez 40.00 100.00
DAPIR2 Ivan Rodriguez 40.00 100.00
DAPIR3 Ivan Rodriguez 40.00 100.00
DAPIR4 Ivan Rodriguez 40.00 100.00
DAPI1 Ichiro 150.00 400.00
DAPI2 Ichiro 150.00 400.00
DAPJA1 Jose Altuve 60.00 150.00
DAPJA2 Jose Altuve 60.00 150.00
DAPJA3 Jose Altuve 60.00 150.00
DAPJA4 Jose Altuve 60.00 150.00
DAPJA5 Jose Altuve 60.00 150.00
DAPJA6 Jose Altuve 60.00 150.00
DAPJA7 Jose Altuve 60.00 150.00
DAPJA8 Jose Altuve 60.00 150.00
DAPJB1 Jeff Bagwell 100.00 250.00
DAPJB2 Jeff Bagwell 100.00 250.00
DAPJB3 Jeff Bagwell 100.00 250.00
DAPJB4 Jeff Bagwell 100.00 250.00
DAPJdG1 Jacob deGrom 100.00 250.00
DAPJdG2 Jacob deGrom 75.00 200.00
DAPJdG3 Jacob deGrom 60.00 200.00
DAPJdG4 Jacob deGrom 75.00 200.00
DAPJdG5 Jacob deGrom 75.00 200.00
DAPJdG6 Jacob deGrom 75.00 200.00
DAPJdG7 Jacob deGrom 75.00 200.00
DAPJdG8 Jacob deGrom 75.00 200.00
DAPJDM1 J.D. Martinez 30.00 80.00
DAPJDM2 J.D. Martinez 30.00 80.00
DAPJDM3 J.D. Martinez 30.00 80.00
DAPJDM4 J.D. Martinez 30.00 80.00
DAPJDM5 J.D. Martinez 30.00 80.00
DAPJDM6 J.D. Martinez 30.00 80.00
DAPJDM7 J.D. Martinez 30.00 80.00
DAPJDM8 J.D. Martinez 30.00 80.00
DAPJR1 Jose Ramirez 30.00 80.00
DAPJR2 Jose Ramirez 30.00 80.00
DAPJR3 Jose Ramirez 30.00 80.00
DAPJR4 Jose Ramirez 30.00 80.00
DAPJR5 Jose Ramirez 30.00 80.00
DAPJR6 Jose Ramirez 30.00 80.00
DAPJR7 Jose Ramirez 30.00 80.00
DAPJR8 Jose Ramirez 30.00 80.00
DAPJS1 Juan Soto 100.00 250.00
DAPJS1 John Smoltz 50.00 120.00
DAPJS2 John Smoltz 50.00 120.00
DAPJS2 Juan Soto 100.00 250.00
DAPJS3 Juan Soto 100.00 250.00
DAPJS3 John Smoltz 50.00 120.00
DAPJS4 John Smoltz 50.00 120.00
DAPJS4 Juan Soto 100.00 250.00
DAPJS5 Juan Soto 100.00 250.00
DAPJS6 Juan Soto 100.00 250.00
DAPJS7 Juan Soto 100.00 250.00
DAPJS8 Juan Soto 100.00 250.00
DAPJT1 Jim Thome 40.00 100.00
DAPJT2 Jim Thome 40.00 100.00
DAPJT3 Jim Thome 40.00 100.00
DAPJV1 Joey Votto 40.00 100.00
DAPJV2 Joey Votto 40.00 100.00
DAPJV3 Joey Votto 40.00 100.00
DAPJV4 Joey Votto 40.00 100.00
DAPJV5 Joey Votto 40.00 100.00
DAPJV6 Joey Votto 40.00 100.00
DAPKB1 Kris Bryant 60.00 150.00
DAPKB2 Kris Bryant 60.00 150.00
DAPKB3 Kris Bryant 60.00 150.00
DAPKB4 Kris Bryant 60.00 150.00
DAPKB5 Kris Bryant 60.00 150.00
DAPKB6 Kris Bryant 60.00 150.00
DAPKG1 Ken Griffey Jr. 400.00 1000.00
DAPKG2 Ken Griffey Jr. 400.00 1000.00
DAPKG3 Ken Griffey Jr. 400.00 1000.00
DAPKG4 Ken Griffey Jr. 400.00 1000.00
DAPKG5 Ken Griffey Jr. 400.00 1000.00
DAPKG6 Ken Griffey Jr. 400.00 1000.00
DAPKG7 Ken Griffey Jr. 400.00 1000.00
DAPKH1 Keston Hiura RC 100.00 250.00
DAPKH2 Keston Hiura RC 100.00 250.00
DAPKH3 Keston Hiura RC 100.00 250.00
DAPKH4 Keston Hiura RC 100.00 250.00
DAPKH5 Keston Hiura RC 100.00 250.00
DAPKIE1 Carter Kieboom RC 50.00 120.00
DAPKIE2 Carter Kieboom RC 50.00 120.00
DAPKIE3 Carter Kieboom RC 50.00 120.00
DAPKIE4 Carter Kieboom RC 50.00 120.00
DAPKIE5 Carter Kieboom RC 50.00 120.00
DAPKS1 Kyle Schwarber 40.00 100.00
DAPKS2 Kyle Schwarber 40.00 100.00
DAPKS3 Kyle Schwarber 40.00 100.00
DAPKS4 Kyle Schwarber 40.00 100.00
DAPLS1 Luis Severino 30.00 80.00
DAPLS2 Luis Severino 30.00 80.00
DAPLS3 Luis Severino 30.00 80.00
DAPLS4 Luis Severino 30.00 80.00
DAPLS5 Luis Severino 30.00 80.00
DAPLS6 Luis Severino 30.00 80.00
DAPLS7 Luis Severino 30.00 80.00
DAPMC1 Miguel Cabrera 75.00 200.00
DAPMC2 Miguel Cabrera 75.00 200.00
DAPMC3 Miguel Cabrera 75.00 200.00
DAPMC4 Miguel Cabrera 75.00 200.00
DAPMC5 Miguel Cabrera 75.00 200.00
DAPMC6 Miguel Cabrera 75.00 200.00
DAPMC7 Miguel Cabrera 75.00 200.00
DAPMC8 Miguel Cabrera 75.00 200.00
DAPMCA1 Matt Chapman 50.00 120.00
DAPMCA2 Matt Chapman 50.00 120.00
DAPMCA3 Matt Chapman 50.00 120.00
DAPMCH1 Michael Chavis RC 40.00 100.00
DAPMCH2 Michael Chavis RC 40.00 100.00
DAPMCH3 Michael Chavis RC 40.00 100.00
DAPMCH4 Michael Chavis RC 40.00 100.00
DAPMCH5 Michael Chavis RC 40.00 100.00
DAPMMC1 Mark McGwire 50.00 120.00
DAPMMC2 Mark McGwire 50.00 120.00
DAPMMC3 Mark McGwire 50.00 120.00
DAPMMC4 Mark McGwire 50.00 120.00
DAPMMC5 Mark McGwire 50.00 120.00
DAPMR1 Mariano Rivera 125.00 300.00
DAPMR2 Mariano Rivera 125.00 300.00
DAPMR3 Mariano Rivera 125.00 300.00
DAPMT1 Masahiro Tanaka 50.00 120.00
DAPMT2 Masahiro Tanaka 50.00 120.00
DAPMT3 Masahiro Tanaka 50.00 120.00
DAPMTR1 Mike Trout 250.00 600.00
DAPMTR2 Mike Trout 250.00 600.00
DAPMTR3 Mike Trout 250.00 600.00
DAPMTR4 Mike Trout 250.00 600.00
DAPMTR5 Mike Trout 250.00 600.00
DAPMTR6 Mike Trout 250.00 600.00
DAPNA1 Nolan Arenado 100.00 250.00
DAPNA2 Nolan Arenado 100.00 250.00
DAPNA3 Nolan Arenado 100.00 250.00
DAPNA4 Nolan Arenado 100.00 250.00
DAPNA5 Nolan Arenado 100.00 250.00
DAPNA6 Nolan Arenado 100.00 250.00
DAPNA7 Nolan Arenado 100.00 250.00
DAPNA8 Nolan Arenado 100.00 250.00
DAPNS1 Noah Syndergaard 25.00 60.00
DAPNS2 Noah Syndergaard 25.00 60.00
DAPNS3 Noah Syndergaard 25.00 60.00
DAPNS4 Noah Syndergaard 25.00 60.00
DAPNS5 Noah Syndergaard 25.00 60.00
DAPNS6 Noah Syndergaard 25.00 60.00
DAPNS7 Noah Syndergaard 25.00 60.00
DAPNS8 Noah Syndergaard 25.00 60.00
DAPOA1 Ozzie Albies 40.00 100.00
DAPOA2 Ozzie Albies 40.00 100.00
DAPOA3 Ozzie Albies 40.00 100.00
DAPOA4 Ozzie Albies 40.00 100.00
DAPOA5 Ozzie Albies 40.00 100.00
DAPOA6 Ozzie Albies 40.00 100.00
DAPPA1 Pete Alonso RC 200.00 500.00
DAPPA2 Pete Alonso RC 200.00 500.00
DAPPA3 Pete Alonso RC 200.00 500.00
DAPPA4 Pete Alonso RC 200.00 500.00
DAPPG1 Paul Goldschmidt 50.00 120.00
DAPPG2 Paul Goldschmidt 50.00 120.00
DAPPG3 Paul Goldschmidt 50.00 120.00
DAPPG4 Paul Goldschmidt 50.00 120.00
DAPPG5 Paul Goldschmidt 50.00 120.00
DAPPG6 Paul Goldschmidt 50.00 120.00
DAPPG7 Paul Goldschmidt 50.00 120.00
DAPPG8 Paul Goldschmidt 50.00 120.00
DAPPM3 Pedro Martinez 50.00 120.00
DAPPM4 Pedro Martinez 50.00 120.00
DAPPM5 Pedro Martinez 50.00 120.00
DAPPM7 Pedro Martinez 50.00 120.00
DAPRA1 Roberto Alomar 60.00 150.00
DAPRA1 Ronald Acuna Jr. 150.00 400.00
DAPRA2 Ronald Acuna Jr. 150.00 400.00
DAPRA2 Roberto Alomar 60.00 150.00
DAPRA3 Roberto Alomar 60.00 150.00
DAPRA3 Ronald Acuna Jr. 150.00 400.00
DAPRA4 Ronald Acuna Jr. 150.00 400.00
DAPRA4 Roberto Alomar 60.00 150.00
DAPRA5 Roberto Alomar 60.00 150.00
DAPRA5 Ronald Acuna Jr. 150.00 400.00
DAPRA6 Ronald Acuna Jr. 150.00 400.00
DAPRA6 Roberto Alomar 60.00 150.00
DAPRA7 Ronald Acuna Jr. 150.00 400.00
DAPRD1 Rafael Devers 50.00 125.00
DAPRD2 Rafael Devers 50.00 125.00
DAPRD3 Rafael Devers 50.00 125.00
DAPRD4 Rafael Devers 50.00 125.00
DAPRH1 Rickey Henderson 60.00 150.00
DAPRH2 Rickey Henderson 60.00 150.00
DAPRH3 Rickey Henderson 60.00 150.00
DAPRH5 Rickey Henderson 60.00 150.00
DAPRHO1 Rhys Hoskins 50.00 125.00
DAPRHO2 Rhys Hoskins 50.00 125.00
DAPRHO3 Rhys Hoskins 50.00 125.00
DAPRHO4 Rhys Hoskins 50.00 125.00
DAPRHO5 Rhys Hoskins 50.00 125.00
DAPRHO6 Rhys Hoskins 50.00 125.00
DAPRHO7 Rhys Hoskins 50.00 125.00
DAPRHO8 Rhys Hoskins 50.00 125.00
DAPRJ1 Randy Johnson 75.00 200.00
DAPRJ2 Randy Johnson 75.00 200.00
DAPRJ3 Randy Johnson 75.00 200.00
DAPRJ4 Randy Johnson 75.00 200.00
DAPRY1 Robin Yount 50.00 120.00
DAPRY2 Robin Yount 50.00 120.00
DAPRY3 Robin Yount 50.00 120.00
DAPSO1 Shohei Ohtani 125.00 300.00
DAPSO2 Shohei Ohtani 125.00 300.00
DAPSO3 Shohei Ohtani 125.00 300.00
DAPSO4 Shohei Ohtani 125.00 300.00
DAPTBA1 Trevor Bauer 50.00 125.00
DAPTBA2 Trevor Bauer 50.00 125.00
DAPTBA3 Trevor Bauer 50.00 125.00
DAPTBA4 Trevor Bauer 50.00 125.00
DAPTBA5 Trevor Bauer 50.00 125.00
DAPTBA6 Trevor Bauer 50.00 125.00
DAPTG1 Tom Glavine 40.00 100.00
DAPTG2 Tom Glavine 40.00 100.00
DAPVGJ1 Vladimir Guerrero Jr. RC 250.00 600.00
DAPVGJ2 Vladimir Guerrero Jr. RC 250.00 600.00
DAPVGJ3 Vladimir Guerrero Jr. RC 250.00 600.00
DAPVGJ4 Vladimir Guerrero Jr. RC 250.00 600.00
DAPVGJ5 Vladimir Guerrero Jr. RC 250.00 600.00
DAPVR1 Victor Robles 40.00 100.00
DAPVR2 Victor Robles 40.00 100.00
DAPVR3 Victor Robles 40.00 100.00
DAPVR4 Victor Robles 40.00 100.00
DAPVR5 Victor Robles 40.00 100.00
DAPVR6 Victor Robles 40.00 100.00
DAPWB1 Walker Buehler 75.00 200.00
DAPWB1 Wade Boggs 40.00 100.00
DAPWB2 Wade Boggs 40.00 100.00
DAPWB2 Walker Buehler 75.00 200.00
DAPWB3 Walker Buehler 75.00 200.00
DAPWC1 Willson Contreras 30.00 80.00
DAPWC2 Willson Contreras 30.00 80.00
DAPWC3 Willson Contreras 30.00 80.00
DAPWC4 Willson Contreras 30.00 80.00
DAPWC5 Willson Contreras 30.00 80.00
DAPXB1 Xander Bogaerts 75.00 200.00
DAPXB2 Xander Bogaerts 75.00 200.00
DAPXB3 Xander Bogaerts 75.00 200.00
DAPXB4 Xander Bogaerts 75.00 200.00
DAPXB5 Xander Bogaerts 75.00 200.00
DAPXB6 Xander Bogaerts 75.00 200.00
DAPYK1 Yusei Kikuchi RC 40.00 100.00
DAPYK2 Yusei Kikuchi RC 40.00 100.00
DAPYM1 Yadier Molina 75.00 200.00
DAPYM2 Yadier Molina 75.00 200.00
DAPYM3 Yadier Molina 75.00 200.00
DAPYM4 Yadier Molina 75.00 200.00
DAPYM5 Yadier Molina 75.00 200.00
DAPYM6 Yadier Molina 75.00 200.00
DAPYM7 Yadier Molina 75.00 200.00

2019 Topps Dynasty Autograph Patches Silver

*GOLD: .5X TO 1.2X BASIC
RANDOM INSERTS IN PACKS
STATED PRINT RUN 5 SER.#'d SETS
SOME NOT PRICED DUE TO SCARCITY
ALL VERSIONS EQUALLY PRICED
LOGO/TAG PATCHES MAY SELL FOR PREMIUM
EXCHANGE DEADLINE 10/31/2021

2020 Topps Dynasty Autograph Patches

OVERALL AUTO ODDS 1:1
STATED PRINT RUN 10 SER.#'d SETS
SOME NOT PRICED DUE TO SCARCITY
ALL VERSIONS EQUALLY PRICED
LOGO/TAG PATCHES MAY SELL FOR PREMIUM
EXCHANGE DEADLINE 10/31/2022

DAPAA1 Aristides Aquino RC 60.00 150.00
DAPAA2 Aristides Aquino RC 60.00 150.00
DAPAA3 Aristides Aquino RC 60.00 150.00
DAPAA4 Aristides Aquino RC 60.00 150.00
DAPAA5 Aristides Aquino RC 60.00 150.00
DAPAB1 Alex Bregman 60.00 150.00
DAPAB2 Alex Bregman 60.00 150.00
DAPAB3 Alex Bregman 60.00 150.00
DAPAB4 Alex Bregman 60.00 150.00
DAPAB5 Alex Bregman 60.00 150.00
DAPAB6 Alex Bregman 60.00 150.00
DAPAB7 Alex Bregman 60.00 150.00
DAPAB8 Alex Bregman 60.00 150.00
DAPABE1 Adrian Beltre 60.00 150.00
DAPABE2 Adrian Beltre 60.00 150.00
DAPABE3 Adrian Beltre 60.00 150.00
DAPABE4 Adrian Beltre 60.00 150.00
DAPABN1 Andrew Benintendi 40.00 100.00
DAPABN2 Andrew Benintendi 40.00 100.00
DAPABN3 Andrew Benintendi 40.00 100.00
DAPABN4 Andrew Benintendi 40.00 100.00
DAPABN5 Andrew Benintendi 40.00 100.00
DAPABN6 Andrew Benintendi 40.00 100.00
DAPABN7 Andrew Benintendi 40.00 100.00
DAPABN8 Andrew Benintendi 40.00 100.00
DAPAJ1 Aaron Judge 125.00 300.00
DAPAJ2 Aaron Judge 125.00 300.00
DAPAJ3 Aaron Judge 125.00 300.00
DAPAJ4 Aaron Judge 125.00 300.00
DAPAJP A.J. Puk RC 40.00 100.00
DAPAJP2 A.J. Puk RC 40.00 100.00
DAPAM1 Austin Meadows 50.00 120.00
DAPAM2 Austin Meadows 50.00 120.00
DAPAM3 Austin Meadows 50.00 120.00
DAPAM4 Austin Meadows 50.00 120.00
DAPAM5 Austin Meadows 50.00 120.00
DAPAM6 Austin Meadows 50.00 120.00
DAPAN1 Aaron Nola 50.00 120.00
DAPAN2 Aaron Nola 50.00 120.00
DAPAN3 Aaron Nola 50.00 120.00
DAPAN4 Aaron Nola 50.00 120.00
DAPAN5 Aaron Nola 50.00 120.00
DAPAN6 Aaron Nola 50.00 120.00
DAPAP1 Albert Pujols 250.00 600.00
DAPAP1 Andy Pettitte 40.00 100.00
DAPAP2 Andy Pettitte 40.00 100.00
DAPAP2 Albert Pujols 250.00 600.00
DAPAP3 Andy Pettitte 40.00 100.00
DAPAP4 Andy Pettitte 40.00 100.00
DAPAP5 Andy Pettitte 40.00 100.00
DAPARZ1 Anthony Rizzo 75.00 200.00
DAPARZ2 Anthony Rizzo 75.00 200.00
DAPARZ3 Anthony Rizzo 75.00 200.00
DAPARZ4 Anthony Rizzo 75.00 200.00
DAPARZ5 Anthony Rizzo 75.00 200.00
DAPARZ6 Anthony Rizzo 75.00 200.00
DAPARZ7 Anthony Rizzo 75.00 200.00
DAPARZ8 Anthony Rizzo 75.00 200.00
DAPBB1 Bo Bichette RC EXCH 200.00 500.00
DAPBB2 Bo Bichette RC EXCH 200.00 500.00
DAPBB3 Bo Bichette RC EXCH 200.00 500.00
DAPBH1 Bryce Harper 150.00 400.00
DAPBH2 Bryce Harper 150.00 400.00
DAPBH3 Bryce Harper 150.00 400.00
DAPBH4 Bryce Harper 150.00 400.00
DAPBL1 Barry Larkin 30.00 80.00
DAPBL2 Barry Larkin 30.00 80.00
DAPBL3 Barry Larkin 30.00 80.00
DAPBP1 Buster Posey 75.00 200.00
DAPBP2 Buster Posey 75.00 200.00
DAPBP3 Buster Posey 75.00 200.00
DAPBP4 Buster Posey 75.00 200.00
DAPBP5 Buster Posey 75.00 200.00
DAPBP6 Buster Posey 75.00 200.00
DAPBS1 Blake Snell 50.00 120.00
DAPBS2 Blake Snell 50.00 120.00
DAPBS3 Blake Snell 50.00 120.00
DAPCB1 Cody Bellinger 125.00 300.00
DAPCB2 Cody Bellinger 125.00 300.00
DAPCB3 Cody Bellinger 125.00 300.00
DAPCB4 Cody Bellinger 125.00 300.00
DAPCB5 Cody Bellinger 125.00 300.00
DAPCB6 Cody Bellinger 125.00 300.00
DAPCB7 Cody Bellinger 125.00 300.00
DAPCB8 Cody Bellinger 125.00 300.00
DAPCC1 CC Sabathia 50.00 120.00
DAPCC2 CC Sabathia 50.00 120.00
DAPCC3 CC Sabathia 50.00 120.00
DAPCC4 CC Sabathia 50.00 120.00
DAPCC5 CC Sabathia 50.00 120.00
DAPCC6 CC Sabathia 50.00 120.00
DAPCF1 Carlton Fisk 50.00 120.00
DAPCF2 Carlton Fisk 50.00 120.00
DAPCF3 Carlton Fisk 50.00 120.00
DAPCJ1 Chipper Jones 100.00 250.00
DAPCJ2 Chipper Jones 100.00 250.00
DAPCJ3 Chipper Jones 100.00 250.00
DAPCJ4 Chipper Jones 100.00 250.00
DAPCJ5 Chipper Jones 100.00 250.00
DAPCJ6 Chipper Jones 100.00 250.00
DAPCS1 Corey Seager 75.00 200.00
DAPCS2 Corey Seager 75.00 200.00
DAPCS3 Corey Seager 75.00 200.00
DAPCS4 Corey Seager 75.00 200.00
DAPCS5 Corey Seager 75.00 200.00
DAPCS6 Corey Seager 75.00 200.00
DAPCSA1 Chris Sale 40.00 100.00
DAPCSA2 Chris Sale 40.00 100.00
DAPCSA3 Chris Sale 40.00 100.00
DAPCY1 Christian Yelich 75.00 200.00
DAPCY2 Christian Yelich 75.00 200.00
DAPCY3 Christian Yelich 75.00 200.00
DAPCY4 Christian Yelich 75.00 200.00
DAPCY5 Christian Yelich 75.00 200.00
DAPCY6 Christian Yelich 75.00 200.00
DAPCY7 Christian Yelich 75.00 200.00
DAPCY8 Christian Yelich 75.00 200.00
DAPDJ1 Derek Jeter 300.00 800.00
DAPDJ2 Derek Jeter 300.00 800.00
DAPDJL1 DJ LeMahieu 75.00 200.00
DAPDJL2 DJ LeMahieu 75.00 200.00
DAPDJL3 DJ LeMahieu 75.00 200.00
DAPDJL4 DJ LeMahieu 75.00 200.00
DAPDJL5 DJ LeMahieu 75.00 200.00
DAPDJL6 DJ LeMahieu 75.00 200.00
DAPDO1 David Ortiz 75.00 200.00
DAPDO2 David Ortiz 75.00 200.00
DAPDO3 David Ortiz 75.00 200.00
DAPDO4 David Ortiz 75.00 200.00
DAPDO5 David Ortiz 75.00 200.00
DAPDO6 David Ortiz 75.00 200.00
DAPDO7 David Ortiz 75.00 200.00
DAPDSA1 Deion Sanders 75.00 200.00
DAPDSA2 Deion Sanders 75.00 200.00
DAPDW1 David Wright 60.00 150.00
DAPDW2 David Wright 60.00 150.00
DAPDW3 David Wright 60.00 150.00
DAPEA1 Elvis Andrus 40.00 100.00
DAPEA2 Elvis Andrus 40.00 100.00
DAPEA3 Elvis Andrus 40.00 100.00
DAPFF1 Freddie Freeman 100.00 250.00
DAPFF2 Freddie Freeman 100.00 250.00
DAPFF3 Freddie Freeman 100.00 250.00
DAPFF4 Freddie Freeman 100.00 250.00
DAPFF5 Freddie Freeman 100.00 250.00
DAPFF6 Freddie Freeman 100.00 250.00
DAPFF7 Freddie Freeman 100.00 250.00
DAPFF8 Freddie Freeman 100.00 250.00
DAPFT1 Frank Thomas 75.00 200.00
DAPFT2 Frank Thomas 75.00 200.00
DAPFT3 Frank Thomas 75.00 200.00
DAPFTJ1 Fernando Tatis Jr. EXCH 250.00 600.00
DAPFTJ2 Fernando Tatis Jr. EXCH 250.00 600.00
DAPFTJ3 Fernando Tatis Jr. EXCH 250.00 600.00
DAPFTJ4 Fernando Tatis Jr. EXCH 250.00 600.00
DAPFTJ5 Fernando Tatis Jr. EXCH 250.00 600.00
DAPFTJ6 Fernando Tatis Jr. EXCH 250.00 600.00
DAPFTJ7 Fernando Tatis Jr. EXCH 250.00 600.00
DAPFTJ8 Fernando Tatis Jr. EXCH 250.00 600.00
DAPGM1 Greg Maddux 125.00 300.00
DAPGM2 Greg Maddux 125.00 300.00
DAPGM3 Greg Maddux 125.00 300.00
DAPGSP1 George Springer 50.00 120.00
DAPGSP2 George Springer 50.00 120.00
DAPGSP3 George Springer 50.00 120.00
DAPGSP4 George Springer 50.00 120.00
DAPGSP5 George Springer 50.00 120.00
DAPGSP6 George Springer 50.00 120.00
DAPGSP7 George Springer 50.00 120.00
DAPGSP8 George Springer 50.00 120.00
DAPGT1 Gleyber Torres 80.00 200.00
DAPGT2 Gleyber Torres 80.00 200.00
DAPGT3 Gleyber Torres 80.00 200.00
DAPGT4 Gleyber Torres 80.00 200.00
DAPGT5 Gleyber Torres 80.00 200.00
DAPGT6 Gleyber Torres 80.00 200.00
DAPGT7 Gleyber Torres 80.00 200.00
DAPGT8 Gleyber Torres 80.00 200.00
DAPI1 Ichiro 250.00 600.00
DAPI3 Ichiro 250.00 600.00
DAPJA1 Jose Altuve 40.00 100.00
DAPJA2 Jose Altuve 40.00 100.00
DAPJA3 Jose Altuve 40.00 100.00
DAPJA4 Jose Altuve 40.00 100.00
DAPJA5 Jose Altuve 40.00 100.00
DAPJA6 Jose Altuve 40.00 100.00
DAPJA7 Jose Altuve 40.00 100.00
DAPJA8 Jose Altuve 40.00 100.00
DAPJB1 Jeff Bagwell 125.00 300.00
DAPJB2 Jeff Bagwell 125.00 300.00
DAPJdG1 Jacob deGrom 150.00 400.00
DAPJdG2 Jacob deGrom 150.00 400.00
DAPJdG3 Jacob deGrom 150.00 400.00
DAPJdG4 Jacob deGrom 15.00 400.00
DAPJdG5 Jacob deGrom 150.00 400.00
DAPJdG6 Jacob deGrom 150.00 400.00
DAPJF1 Jack Flaherty 60.00 150.00
DAPJF2 Jack Flaherty 60.00 150.00
DAPJF3 Jack Flaherty 60.00 150.00
DAPJL1 Jesus Luzardo RC 60.00 150.00
DAPJL2 Jesus Luzardo RC 60.00 150.00
DAPJL3 Jesus Luzardo RC 60.00 150.00
DAPJL4 Jesus Luzardo RC 60.00 150.00
DAPJS1 John Smoltz 50.00 120.00
DAPJS1 Juan Soto 150.00 400.00
DAPJS2 John Smoltz 50.00 120.00
DAPJS2 Juan Soto 150.00 400.00
DAPJS3 John Smoltz 50.00 120.00
DAPJS3 Juan Soto 150.00 400.00
DAPJS4 John Smoltz 50.00 120.00
DAPJS5 John Smoltz 50.00 120.00
DAPJS6 John Smoltz 50.00 120.00
DAPJT1 Jim Thome 40.00 100.00
DAPJT2 Jim Thome 40.00 100.00
DAPJTR1 J.T. Realmuto 60.00 150.00
DAPJTR2 J.T. Realmuto 60.00 150.00
DAPJTR3 J.T. Realmuto 60.00 150.00
DAPJV1 Joey Votto 60.00 150.00
DAPJV2 Joey Votto 60.00 150.00
DAPJV3 Joey Votto 60.00 150.00
DAPJV4 Joey Votto 60.00 150.00
DAPJV5 Joey Votto 60.00 150.00
DAPJV6 Joey Votto 60.00 150.00
DAPJV7 Joey Votto 60.00 150.00
DAPJV8 Joey Votto 60.00 150.00
DAPKG1 Ken Griffey Jr. 250.00 600.00
DAPKG2 Ken Griffey Jr. 250.00 600.00
DAPKG5 Ken Griffey Jr. 250.00 600.00
DAPKG6 Ken Griffey Jr. 250.00 600.00
DAPKH1 Keston Hiura 50.00 125.00
DAPKH2 Keston Hiura 50.00 125.00
DAPKH3 Keston Hiura 50.00 125.00
DAPKH4 Keston Hiura 50.00 125.00
DAPKH5 Keston Hiura 50.00 125.00
DAPKH6 Keston Hiura 50.00 125.00
DAPKL1 Kyle Lewis RC 125.00 300.00
DAPKL2 Kyle Lewis RC 125.00 300.00
DAPKL3 Kyle Lewis RC 125.00 300.00
DAPKS1 Kyle Schwarber 40.00 100.00
DAPKS2 Kyle Schwarber 40.00 100.00
DAPKS3 Kyle Schwarber 40.00 100.00
DAPLW1 Larry Walker 60.00 150.00
DAPLW2 Larry Walker 60.00 150.00
DAPLW3 Larry Walker 60.00 150.00
DAPLW4 Larry Walker 60.00 150.00
DAPMC1 Miguel Cabrera 100.00 250.00
DAPMC2 Miguel Cabrera 100.00 250.00
DAPMC3 Miguel Cabrera 100.00 250.00
DAPMC4 Miguel Cabrera 100.00 250.00
DAPMC5 Miguel Cabrera 100.00 250.00
DAPMC6 Miguel Cabrera 100.00 250.00
DAPMC7 Miguel Cabrera 100.00 250.00
DAPMC8 Miguel Cabrera 100.00 250.00
DAPMCA1 Matt Chapman 60.00 150.00
DAPMCA2 Matt Chapman 60.00 150.00
DAPMCA3 Matt Chapman 60.00 150.00
DAPMCA4 Matt Chapman 60.00 150.00
DAPMCA5 Matt Chapman 60.00 150.00
DAPMMC1 Mark McGwire 100.00 250.00
DAPMMC2 Mark McGwire 100.00 250.00
DAPMMC3 Mark McGwire 100.00 250.00
DAPMMC4 Mark McGwire 100.00 250.00
DAPMMU1 Max Muncy 40.00 100.00
DAPMMU2 Max Muncy 40.00 100.00
DAPMMU3 Max Muncy 40.00 100.00
DAPMMU4 Max Muncy 40.00 100.00
DAPMMU5 Max Muncy 40.00 100.00
DAPMR1 Mariano Rivera 150.00 400.00
DAPMR2 Mariano Rivera 150.00 400.00
DAPMR3 Mariano Rivera 150.00 400.00
DAPMS1 Mike Soroka 60.00 150.00
DAPMS2 Mike Soroka 60.00 150.00
DAPMS3 Mike Soroka 60.00 150.00
DAPMS4 Mike Soroka 60.00 150.00
DAPMS5 Mike Soroka 60.00 150.00
DAPMS6 Mike Soroka 60.00 150.00
DAPMT1 Masahiro Tanaka 60.00 150.00
DAPMT2 Masahiro Tanaka 60.00 150.00
DAPMT3 Masahiro Tanaka 60.00 150.00
DAPMT4 Masahiro Tanaka 60.00 150.00
DAPMT5 Masahiro Tanaka 60.00 150.00
DAPMT6 Masahiro Tanaka 60.00 150.00
DAPMTR1 Mike Trout 600.00 1500.00
DAPMTR2 Mike Trout 600.00 1500.00
DAPMTR3 Mike Trout 600.00 1500.00
DAPMTR4 Mike Trout 600.00 1500.00
DAPMTR5 Mike Trout 600.00 1500.00
DAPMTR6 Mike Trout 600.00 1500.00
DAPMTR7 Mike Trout 600.00 1500.00
DAPNA1 Nolan Arenado 60.00 150.00
DAPNA2 Nolan Arenado 60.00 150.00
DAPNA3 Nolan Arenado 60.00 150.00
DAPNA4 Nolan Arenado 60.00 150.00
DAPNA5 Nolan Arenado 60.00 150.00
DAPNA6 Nolan Arenado 60.00 150.00
DAPNA7 Nolan Arenado 60.00 150.00
DAPNA8 Nolan Arenado 60.00 150.00
DAPPA1 Pete Alonso 100.00 250.00
DAPPA2 Pete Alonso 100.00 250.00
DAPPA3 Pete Alonso 100.00 250.00
DAPPM1 Pedro Martinez 75.00 200.00
DAPPM2 Pedro Martinez 75.00 200.00
DAPPM3 Pedro Martinez 75.00 200.00
DAPPM4 Pedro Martinez 75.00 80.00
DAPRA1 Ronald Acuna Jr. 200.00 500.00
DAPRA1 Roberto Alomar 50.00 120.00
DAPRA2 Ronald Acuna Jr. 200.00 500.00
DAPRA2 Roberto Alomar 50.00 120.00
DAPRA3 Ronald Acuna Jr. 200.00 500.00
DAPRA4 Ronald Acuna Jr. 200.00 500.00
DAPRA4 Roberto Alomar 50.00 120.00
DAPRA5 Ronald Acuna Jr. 200.00 500.00
DAPRA6 Ronald Acuna Jr. 200.00 500.00
DAPRA6 Roberto Alomar 50.00 120.00
DAPRA7 Ronald Acuna Jr. 200.00 500.00
DAPRA8 Ronald Acuna Jr. 200.00 500.00
DAPRC1 Rod Carew 40.00 100.00
DAPRC2 Rod Carew 40.00 100.00
DAPRC2 Roger Clemens 75.00 200.00
DAPRC3 Rod Carew 40.00 100.00
DAPRC3 Roger Clemens 75.00 200.00
DAPRC4 Roger Clemens 75.00 200.00
DAPRC5 Roger Clemens 75.00 200.00
DAPRD1 Rafael Devers 50.00 125.00
DAPRD2 Rafael Devers 50.00 125.00
DAPRD3 Rafael Devers 50.00 125.00
DAPRD4 Rafael Devers 50.00 125.00
DAPRD5 Rafael Devers 50.00 125.00
DAPRD6 Rafael Devers 50.00 125.00
DAPRD7 Rafael Devers 50.00 125.00
DAPRD8 Rafael Devers 50.00 125.00
DAPRH1 Rickey Henderson 100.00 250.00
DAPRH2 Rickey Henderson 100.00 250.00
DAPRH3 Rickey Henderson 100.00 250.00
DAPRH5 Rickey Henderson 100.00 250.00
DAPRH6 Rickey Henderson 100.00 250.00
DAPRHO1 Rhys Hoskins 50.00 125.00
DAPRHO2 Rhys Hoskins 50.00 125.00
DAPRHO3 Rhys Hoskins 50.00 125.00
DAPRHO4 Rhys Hoskins 50.00 125.00
DAPRHO5 Rhys Hoskins 50.00 125.00
DAPRHO6 Rhys Hoskins 50.00 125.00
DAPRHO7 Rhys Hoskins 50.00 125.00
DAPRHO8 Rhys Hoskins 50.00 125.00
DAPRJA1 Reggie Jackson 60.00 150.00
DAPRJA2 Reggie Jackson 60.00 150.00
DAPRJA3 Reggie Jackson 60.00 150.00
DAPRJA4 Reggie Jackson 60.00 150.00
DAPRY1 Robin Yount 60.00 150.00
DAPRY2 Robin Yount 60.00 150.00
DAPRY3 Robin Yount 60.00 150.00
DAPRY4 Robin Yount 60.00 150.00
DAPRY5 Robin Yount 60.00 150.00
DAPSC1 Steve Carlton 50.00 120.00
DAPSC2 Steve Carlton 50.00 120.00
DAPSG1 Sonny Gray 40.00 100.00
DAPSG2 Sonny Gray 40.00 100.00
DAPSG3 Sonny Gray 40.00 100.00
DAPSO1 Shohei Ohtani 125.00 300.00
DAPSO2 Shohei Ohtani 125.00 300.00
DAPSO3 Shohei Ohtani 125.00 300.00
DAPSTR1 Stephen Strasburg 75.00 200.00
DAPSTR2 Stephen Strasburg 75.00 200.00
DAPSTR3 Stephen Strasburg 75.00 200.00
DAPSTR4 Stephen Strasburg 75.00 200.00
DAPSTR5 Stephen Strasburg 75.00 200.00
DAPSTR6 Stephen Strasburg 75.00 200.00
DAPTBA1 Trevor Bauer 75.00 200.00
DAPTBA2 Trevor Bauer 75.00 200.00
DAPTBA3 Trevor Bauer 75.00 200.00
DAPTG1 Tom Glavine 50.00 120.00
DAPTG2 Tom Glavine 50.00 120.00
DAPTG3 Tom Glavine 50.00 120.00
DAPTS1 Trevor Story 40.00 100.00
DAPTS2 Trevor Story 40.00 100.00
DAPTS3 Trevor Story 40.00 100.00
DAPTS4 Trevor Story 40.00 100.00
DAPTS5 Trevor Story 40.00 100.00
DAPTS6 Trevor Story 40.00 100.00
DAPVR1 Victor Robles 50.00 125.00
DAPVR2 Victor Robles 50.00 125.00
DAPVR3 Victor Robles 50.00 125.00
DAPVR4 Victor Robles 50.00 125.00
DAPVR5 Victor Robles 50.00 125.00
DAPVR6 Victor Robles 50.00 125.00
DAPWB1 Walker Buehler 75.00 200.00
DAPWB1 Wade Boggs 75.00 200.00
DAPWB2 Walker Buehler 75.00 200.00
DAPWB2 Wade Boggs 75.00 200.00
DAPWB3 Walker Buehler 75.00 200.00
DAPWB3 Wade Boggs 75.00 200.00
DAPWB4 Walker Buehler 75.00 200.00
DAPWB4 Wade Boggs 75.00 200.00
DAPWB5 Walker Buehler 75.00 200.00
DAPWB6 Walker Buehler 75.00 200.00
DAPWB7 Walker Buehler 75.00 200.00
DAPWB8 Walker Buehler 75.00 200.00
DAPWC1 Willson Contreras 50.00 120.00
DAPWC1 Will Clark 60.00 150.00
DAPWC2 Willson Contreras 50.00 120.00
DAPWC2 Will Clark 60.00 150.00
DAPWC3 Willson Contreras 50.00 120.00
DAPWC4 Willson Contreras 50.00 120.00
DAPWC5 Willson Contreras 50.00 120.00
DAPWC6 Willson Contreras 50.00 120.00
DAPWM1 Whit Merrifield 50.00 120.00
DAPWM2 Whit Merrifield 50.00 120.00
DAPWM3 Whit Merrifield 50.00 120.00
DAPXB1 Xander Bogaerts 50.00 120.00
DAPXB2 Xander Bogaerts 50.00 120.00
DAPXB3 Xander Bogaerts 50.00 120.00
DAPXB4 Xander Bogaerts 50.00 120.00
DAPXB5 Xander Bogaerts 50.00 120.00
DAPXB6 Xander Bogaerts 50.00 120.00
DAPXB7 Xander Bogaerts 50.00 120.00
DAPXB8 Xander Bogaerts 50.00 120.00
DAPYA1 Yordan Alvarez RC 250.00 600.00
DAPYA2 Yordan Alvarez RC 250.00 600.00
DAPYA3 Yordan Alvarez RC 250.00 600.00
DAPYA4 Yordan Alvarez RC 250.00 600.00
DAPYA5 Yordan Alvarez RC 250.00 600.00
DAPYA6 Yordan Alvarez RC 250.00 600.00
DAPYA7 Yordan Alvarez RC 250.00 600.00
DAPYA8 Yordan Alvarez RC 250.00 600.00
DAPZG1 Zac Gallen RC 60.00 150.00
DAPZG2 Zac Gallen RC 60.00 150.00

2020 Topps Dynasty Autograph Patches Silver

*GOLD: .5X TO 1.2X BASIC
RANDOM INSERTS IN PACKS
STATED PRINT RUN 5 SER.#'d SETS
SOME NOT PRICED DUE TO SCARCITY
ALL VERSIONS EQUALLY PRICED
LOGO/TAG PATCHES MAY SELL FOR PREMIUM
EXCHANGE DEADLINE 10/31/2022

1995 Topps Embossed

This 140-card standard-size set was issued by Topps. The cards were issued in six-card packs with five regular cards and one parallel Golden Idols card in each pack. The suggested retail price of the packs was $3 with 24 packs per box. Each case contained four boxes. Cards 97-120 are a subset dedicated to active players who have won major awards. The cards are embossed on both sides. The fronts have an embossed player photo surrounded by a gray border. In addition, the TMB (Topps Embossed) logo is in an upper corner and the player's name at the bottom. The horizontal backs have an embossed player photo on the left, while vital statistics, seasonal and career statistics and some interesting facts about the player are on the right.

COMPLETE SET (140) 10.00 25.00
1 Kenny Lofton .10 .30
2 Gary Sheffield .10 .30
3 Hal Morris .05 .15
4 Cliff Floyd .10 .30
5 Pat Hentgen .05 .15
6 Tony Gwynn .40 1.00
7 Jose Valentin .05 .15
8 Jason Bere .05 .15
9 Jeff Kent .10 .30
10 John Valentin .05 .15

11 Brian Anderson .05 .15
12 Deion Sanders .20 .50
13 Ryan Thompson .05 .15
14 Ruben Sierra .10 .30
15 Jay Bell .10 .30
16 Chuck Carr .05 .15
17 Brent Gates .05 .15
18 Bret Boone .10 .30
19 Paul Molitor .10 .30
20 Chili Davis .10 .30
21 Ryan Klesko .10 .30
22 Will Clark .20 .50
23 Greg Vaughn .05 .15
24 Moises Alou .10 .30
25 Ray Lankford .10 .30
26 Jose Rijo .05 .15
27 Bobby Jones .05 .15
28 Rick Wilkins .05 .15
29 Cal Eldred .05 .15
30 Juan Gonzalez .10 .30
31 Royce Clayton .05 .15
32 Bryan Harvey .05 .15
33 Dave Nilsson .05 .15
34 Chris Hoiles .05 .15
35 David Nied .05 .15
36 Javier Lopez .10 .30
37 Tim Wallach .05 .15
38 Bobby Bonilla .10 .30
39 Danny Tartabull .05 .15
40 Andy Benes .05 .15
41 Dean Palmer .10 .30
42 Chris Gomez .05 .15
43 Kevin Appier .10 .30
44 Brady Anderson .10 .30
45 Alex Fernandez .05 .15
46 Roberto Kelly .05 .15
47 Dave Hollins .05 .15
48 Chuck Finley .10 .30
49 Wade Boggs .20 .50
50 Travis Fryman .10 .30
51 Ken Griffey Jr. .60 1.50
52 John Olerud .10 .30
53 Delino DeShields .05 .15
54 Ivan Rodriguez .20 .50
55 Tommy Greene .05 .15
56 Tom Pagnozzi .05 .15
57 Bip Roberts .05 .15
58 Luis Gonzalez .10 .30
59 Rey Sanchez .05 .15
60 Ken Ryan .05 .15
61 Darren Daulton .10 .30
62 Rick Aguilera .10 .30
63 Wally Joyner .10 .30
64 Mike Greenwell .05 .15
65 Jay Buhner .10 .30
66 Craig Biggio .20 .50
67 Charles Nagy .05 .15
68 Devon White .10 .30
69 Randy Johnson .30 .75
70 Shawon Dunston .05 .15
71 Kirby Puckett .30 .75
72 Paul O'Neill .20 .50
73 Tino Martinez .20 .50
74 Carlos Garcia .05 .15
75 Ozzie Smith .50 1.25
76 Cecil Fielder .10 .30
77 Mike Stanley .05 .15
78 Lance Johnson .05 .15
79 Tony Phillips .05 .15
80 Bobby Munoz .05 .15
81 Kevin Tapani .05 .15
82 William VanLandingham .05 .15
83 Dante Bichette .10 .30
84 Tom Candiotti .05 .15
85 Wil Cordero .05 .15
86 Jeff Conine .10 .30
87 Joey Hamilton .05 .15
88 Mark Whiten .05 .15
89 Jeff Montgomery .05 .15
90 Andres Galarraga .10 .30
91 Roberto Alomar .20 .50
92 Orlando Merced .05 .15
93 Mike Mussina .20 .50
94 Pedro Martinez .20 .50
95 Carlos Baerga .05 .15
96 Steve Trachsel .05 .15
97 Lou Whitaker .10 .30
98 David Cone .10 .30
99 Chuck Knoblauch .10 .30
100 Frank Thomas .30 .75
101 David Justice .10 .30
102 Raul Mondesi .10 .30
103 Rickey Henderson .30 .75
104 Doug Drabek .05 .15
105 Sandy Alomar Jr. .05 .15
106 Roger Clemens .60 1.50
107 Mark McGwire .75 2.00
108 Tim Salmon .20 .50
109 Greg Maddux .50 1.25
110 Mike Piazza .50 1.25
111 Tom Glavine .20 .50
112 Walt Weiss .05 .15
113 Cal Ripken 1.00 2.50
114 Eddie Murray .30 .75
115 Don Mattingly .75 2.00
116 Ozzie Guillen .10 .30
117 Bob Hamelin .05 .15
118 Jeff Bagwell .20 .50
119 Eric Karros .10 .30
120 Barry Bonds .75 2.00
121 Mickey Tettleton .05 .15
122 Mark Langston .05 .15
123 Robin Ventura .10 .30
124 Bret Saberhagen .10 .30
125 Albert Belle .10 .30
126 Rafael Palmeiro .20 .50
127 Fred McGriff .20 .50
128 Jimmy Key .10 .30
129 Barry Larkin .20 .50
130 Tim Raines .10 .30
131 Len Dykstra .10 .30
132 Todd Zeile .10 .30
133 Joe Carter .10 .30
134 Matt Williams .10 .30
135 Terry Steinbach .05 .15
136 Manny Ramirez .20 .50
137 John Wetteland .10 .30
138 Rod Beck .05 .15
139 Mo Vaughn .10 .30
140 Darren Lewis .05 .15

1995 Topps Embossed Golden Idols

COMPLETE SET (140) 60.00 120.00
*STARS: 1.5X TO 4X BASIC CARDS
ONE PER PACK

2017 Topps Fire

COMPLETE SET (200) 30.00 80.00
1 Kris Bryant .40 1.00
2 A.J. Pollock .20 .50
3 Matt Olson RC 1.50 4.00
4 Randy Johnson .30 .75
5 Evan Longoria .25 .60
6 Freddie Freeman .40 1.00
7 Sean Newcomb RC .40 1.00
8 Aledmys Diaz .25 .60
9 Seth Lugo RC .30 .75
10 Chris Sale .30 .75
11 Gary Carter .25 .60
12 Willie Stargell .25 .60
13 Mark Melancon .20 .50
14 Cal Ripken Jr. 1.00 2.50
15 Adam Jones .25 .60
16 Paul Konerko .25 .60
17 Nomar Garciaparra .25 .60
18 Andy Pettitte .25 .60
19 Justin Verlander .30 .75
20 Andrew Miller .25 .60
21 Phil Niekro .25 .60
22 Mark McGwire .50 1.25
23 Daniel Murphy .25 .60
24 Greg Maddux .40 1.00
25 Sandy Koufax .60 1.50
26 Corey Kluber .25 .60
27 Jon Lester .25 .60
28 Johnny Cueto .25 .60
29 Curt Schilling .25 .60
30 Lorenzo Cain .20 .50
31 Javier Baez .40 1.00
32 Michael Fulmer .20 .50
33 Harmon Killebrew .30 .75
34 Tom Glavine .25 .60
35 David Ortiz .30 .75
36 Ender Inciarte .20 .50
37 Eric Hosmer .25 .60
38 Jonathan Villar .20 .50
39 Paul Goldschmidt .30 .75
40 Rob Zastryzny RC .30 .75
41 Joe Musgrove RC 1.00 2.50
42 George Brett .60 1.50
43 Eddie Mathews .30 .75
44 Frank Thomas .30 .75
45 Pedro Martinez .25 .60
46 Gary Sanchez .30 .75
47 Lou Brock .25 .60
48 Masahiro Tanaka .25 .60
49 Bo Jackson .30 .75
50 Mike Trout 1.50 4.00
51 Billy Hamilton .25 .60
52 Jacob deGrom .60 1.50
53 Johnny Damon .25 .60
54 Lou Gehrig .60 1.50
55 Jim Edmonds .20 .50
56 Nelson Cruz .30 .75
57 Warren Spahn .25 .60
58 Jeff Hoffman RC .30 .75
59 Jeurys Familia .25 .60
60 Matt Carpenter .30 .75
61 Mookie Betts .60 1.50
62 Aaron Judge RC 4.00 10.00
63 Reynaldo Lopez RC .30 .75
64 Steven Wright .20 .50
65 Andrew Benintendi RC 1.00 2.50
66 Kyle Hendricks .30 .75
67 Tony Perez .25 .60
68 Ian Kinsler .25 .60
69 Yu Darvish .30 .75
70 Dennis Eckersley .25 .60
71 Aaron Boone .20 .50
72 Roberto Clemente .75 2.00
73 George Springer .25 .60
74 Fergie Jenkins .25 .60
75 Derek Jeter .75 2.00
76 Bryce Harper .50 1.25
77 Kenta Maeda .25 .60
78 David Dahl RC .40 1.00
79 Robinson Cano .25 .60
80 Raimel Tapia RC .40 1.00
81 Jharel Cotton RC .30 .75
82 Dan Vogelbach RC .50 1.25
83 Ken Griffey Jr. .60 1.50
84 Lewis Brinson RC .50 1.25
85 Wade Davis .20 .50
86 Andre Dawson .25 .60
87 Wil Myers .25 .60
88 Rickey Henderson .30 .75
89 Aroldis Chapman .30 .75
90 Dellin Betances .25 .60
91 Ted Williams .60 1.50
92 Edwin Encarnacion .30 .75
93 Stephen Strasburg .30 .75
94 Ryon Healy RC .40 1.00
95 Jose Canseco .25 .60
96 Ian Happ RC .60 1.50
97 Edgar Renteria .20 .50
98 Maikel Franco .25 .60
99 Adrian Beltre .30 .75
100 Yoan Moncada RC 1.00 2.50
101 Jackie Robinson .30 .75
102 Yoenis Cespedes .30 .75
103 Addison Russell .30 .75
104 Stephen Piscotty .25 .60
105 Renato Nunez RC .60 1.50
106 Yulieski Gurriel RC .50 1.25
107 Julio Urias .30 .75
108 Noah Syndergaard .25 .60
109 Christian Yelich .40 1.00
110 Miguel Cabrera .30 .75
111 Tyler Glasnow RC 1.25 3.00
112 Didi Gregorius .25 .60
113 Chris Davis .20 .50
114 Ryne Sandberg .60 1.50
115 Trea Turner .25 .60
116 Carlos Martinez .25 .60
117 Aaron Sanchez .25 .60
118 Jason Heyward .25 .60
119 Brian Dozier .30 .75
120 Clayton Kershaw .50 1.25
121 Cody Bellinger RC 5.00 12.00
122 Jose De Leon RC .30 .75
123 Jose Altuve .25 .60
124 Anthony Rizzo .40 1.00
125 Steven Matz .20 .50
126 Alex Bregman RC 1.50 4.00
127 Ichiro .40 1.00
128 Carlos Correa .30 .75
129 Ivan Rodriguez .25 .60
130 JaCoby Jones RC .40 1.00
131 Larry Doby .25 .60
132 Andrew McCutchen .30 .75
133 Carl Yastrzemski .50 1.25
134 Manny Machado .30 .75
135 Hunter Renfroe RC .40 1.00
136 Max Scherzer .30 .75
137 Brooks Robinson .25 .60
138 Danny Duffy .20 .50
139 Ernie Banks .30 .75
140 Adam Duvall .25 .60
141 Albert Pujols .40 1.00
142 Gavin Cecchini RC .30 .75
143 Jorge Alfaro RC .40 1.00
144 Hunter Dozier RC .30 .75
145 Chipper Jones .30 .75
146 Seung-Hwan Oh .40 1.00
147 Yasmani Grandal .20 .50
148 Kyle Seager .20 .50
149 Joey Votto .30 .75
150 Corey Seager .30 .75
151 Gregory Polanco .25 .60
152 Kyle Schwarber .30 .75
153 Orlando Arcia RC .50 1.25
154 Luke Weaver RC .40 1.00
155 Trey Mancini RC .60 1.50
156 Dave Winfield .25 .60
157 Drew Pomeranz .25 .60
158 Jose Bautista .25 .60
159 Chris Archer .20 .50
160 Willie McCovey .25 .60
161 Josh Bell RC .75 2.00
162 Dansby Swanson RC .75 2.00
163 Hank Aaron .60 1.50
164 Braden Shipley RC .30 .75
165 Jackie Bradley Jr. .30 .75
166 Steve Carlton .25 .60
167 Willson Contreras .30 .75
168 Giancarlo Stanton .30 .75
169 Dexter Fowler .25 .60
170 Dustin Pedroia .30 .75
171 Xander Bogaerts .30 .75
172 Roberto Osuna .20 .50
173 Zach Britton .25 .60
174 Alex Reyes RC .40 1.00
175 Nolan Arenado .50 1.25
176 Ryan Braun .25 .60
177 Carson Fulmer RC .30 .75
178 Jose Abreu .30 .75
179 Justin Upton .25 .60
180 Nolan Ryan 1.00 2.50
181 David Price .25 .60
182 Reggie Jackson .25 .60
183 Tyler Austin RC .40 1.00
184 Lucas Giolito .25 .60
185 Manny Margot RC .30 .75
186 Odubel Herrera .25 .60
187 Trevor Story .30 .75
188 Robert Gsellman RC .30 .75
189 Luis Severino .25 .60
190 Josh Donaldson .25 .60
191 Omar Vizquel .25 .60
192 Mike Piazza .30 .75
193 Jake Arrieta .25 .60
194 Henry Owens .20 .50
195 Jake Thompson RC .30 .75
196 Francisco Lindor .30 .75
197 Jacoby Ellsbury .25 .60
198 Carlos Gonzalez .25 .60
199 Rougned Odor .25 .60
200 Babe Ruth .75 2.00

2017 Topps Fire Blue Chip

*BLUE CHIP: 1.2X TO 3X BASIC
*BLUE CHIP RC: .75X TO 2X BASIC RC
121 Cody Bellinger 6.00 15.00
180 Nolan Ryan 5.00 12.00

2017 Topps Fire Flame

*FLAME: 1.2X TO 3X BASIC
*FLAME RC: .75X TO 2X BASIC RC
STATED ODDS 1:4 RETAIL
121 Cody Bellinger 6.00 15.00
180 Nolan Ryan 5.00 12.00

2017 Topps Fire Gold Minted

*GOLD MINTED: 1.2X TO 3X BASIC
*GOLD MINTED RC: .75X TO 2X BASIC RC
121 Cody Bellinger 6.00 15.00
180 Nolan Ryan 5.00 12.00

2017 Topps Fire Green

*GREEN: 2X TO 5X BASIC
*GREEN RC: 1.2X TO 3X BASIC RC
STATED ODDS 1:14 RETAIL
STATED PRINT RUN 199 SER.#'d SETS
14 Cal Ripken Jr. 8.00 20.00
42 George Brett 10.00 25.00
62 Aaron Judge 15.00 40.00
72 Roberto Clemente 8.00 20.00
83 Ken Griffey Jr. 5.00 12.00
91 Ted Williams 8.00 20.00
121 Cody Bellinger 10.00 25.00
180 Nolan Ryan 8.00 20.00

2017 Topps Fire Magenta

*MAGENTA: 4X TO 10X BASIC
*MAGENTA RC: 2.5X TO 6X BASIC RC
STATED ODDS 1:108 RETAIL
STATED PRINT RUN 25 SER.#'d SETS
14 Cal Ripken Jr. 15.00 40.00
42 George Brett 20.00 50.00
49 Bo Jackson 12.00 30.00
62 Aaron Judge 30.00 80.00
72 Roberto Clemente 15.00 40.00
75 Derek Jeter 20.00 50.00
83 Ken Griffey Jr. 10.00 25.00
91 Ted Williams 15.00 40.00
121 Cody Bellinger 20.00 50.00
180 Nolan Ryan 15.00 40.00

2017 Topps Fire Orange

*ORANGE: 1.5X TO 4X BASIC
*ORANGE RC: 1X TO 2.5X BASIC RC
STATED ODDS 1:10 RETAIL
STATED PRINT RUN 299 SER.#'d SETS
14 Cal Ripken Jr. 6.00 15.00
42 George Brett 8.00 20.00
83 Ken Griffey Jr. 4.00 10.00
91 Ted Williams 6.00 15.00
121 Cody Bellinger 8.00 20.00
180 Nolan Ryan 6.00 15.00

2017 Topps Fire Purple

*PURPLE: 2.5X TO 6X BASIC
*PURPLE RC: 1.5X TO 4X BASIC RC
STATED ODDS 1:128 RETAIL
STATED PRINT RUN 99 SER.#'d SETS
14 Cal Ripken Jr. 10.00 25.00
42 George Brett 12.00 30.00
49 Bo Jackson 8.00 20.00
62 Aaron Judge 20.00 50.00
72 Roberto Clemente 10.00 25.00
83 Ken Griffey Jr. 6.00 15.00
91 Ted Williams 10.00 25.00
121 Cody Bellinger 12.00 30.00
180 Nolan Ryan 10.00 25.00

2017 Topps Fire Autograph Patches

STATED ODDS 1:303 RETAIL
STATED PRINT RUN 25 SER.#'d SETS
EXCHANGE DEADLINE 8/31/2019
FAPAB Alex Bregman 30.00 80.00
FAPAD Aledmys Diaz
FAPAJ Aaron Judge
FAPAN Aaron Nola 20.00 50.00
FAPARE Alex Reyes 8.00 20.00
FAPBS Blake Snell 8.00 20.00
FAPCC Carlos Correa
FAPCF Carson Fulmer
FAPCS Corey Seager
FAPDD David Dahl
FAPFL Francisco Lindor EXCH 25.00 60.00
FAPHR Hunter Renfroe
FAPJC Jharel Cotton
FAPJT Jameson Taillon
FAPKB Kris Bryant 75.00 200.00
FAPLG Lucas Giolito
FAPLS Luis Severino
FAPLW Luke Weaver
FAPMF Michael Fulmer
FAPMM Manny Machado
FAPMT Mike Trout 125.00 300.00
FAPNS Noah Syndergaard 8.00 20.00
FAPRG Robert Gsellman 6.00 15.00
FAPRH Ryon Healy
FAPRT Raimel Tapia
FAPSM Steven Matz
FAPSP Stephen Piscotty
FAPTA Tim Anderson 10.00 25.00
FAPTAU Tyler Austin 8.00 20.00
FAPTT Trea Turner
FAPWC Willson Contreras 25.00 60.00
FAPYG Yulieski Gurriel 20.00 50.00
FAPYM Yoan Moncada 30.00 80.00

2017 Topps Fire Autographs

STATED ODDS 1:29 RETAIL
PRINT RUNS B/WN 40-500 COPIES PER
EXCHANGE DEADLINE 8/31/2019
FAAJ Aaron Judge/250 75.00 200.00
FAAR Anthony Rizzo/40 10.00 25.00
FAARE Alex Reyes/420 4.00 10.00
FACC Carlos Correa/40 20.00 50.00
FADG Didi Gregorius/490 6.00 15.00
FADV Dan Vogelbach/486 4.00 10.00
FAEI Ender Inciarte/500 2.50 6.00
FAFJ Fergie Jenkins/250 6.00 15.00
FAFT Frank Thomas/40 25.00 60.00
FAHA Hank Aaron
FAHO Henry Owens/466 2.50 6.00
FAHR Hunter Renfroe/500 3.00 8.00
FAIH Ian Happ/200 15.00 40.00
FAJA Jorge Alfaro/500 3.00 8.00
FAJC Jharel Cotton/500 2.50 6.00
FAJJ JaCoby Jones/500 3.00 8.00
FAJT Jake Thompson/120 2.50 6.00
FALS Luis Severino/350 10.00 25.00
FALW Luke Weaver/500 3.00 8.00
FAMF Michael Fulmer/325 2.50 6.00
FAMM Manny Machado/40 25.00 60.00
FAMO Matt Olson/500 6.00 15.00
FARL Reynaldo Lopez/500 2.50 6.00
FARO Roberto Osuna/230 5.00 12.00
FART Raimel Tapia/500 3.00 8.00
FASK Sandy Koufax
FASL Seth Lugo/500 2.50 6.00
FASM Steven Matz/200 4.00 10.00
FATA Tyler Austin/500 3.00 8.00
FATT Trea Turner/65 3.00 8.00
FAWD Wade Davis/490 2.50 6.00
FAYG Yasmani Grandal/490 2.50 6.00
FAYM Yoan Moncada/40 40.00 100.00

2017 Topps Fire Autographs Green

*GREEN: .5X TO 1.2X BASIC
STATED ODDS 1:76 RETAIL
STATED PRINT RUN 75 SER.#'d SETS
EXCHANGE DEADLINE 8/31/2019
FAAB Alex Bregman EXCH 12.00 30.00
FAAP A.J. Pollock 3.00 8.00
FACB Cody Bellinger EXCH 75.00 200.00
FANS Noah Syndergaard 8.00 20.00
FAPN Phil Niekro

2017 Topps Fire Autographs Magenta

*MAGENTA: .75X TO 2X BASIC
STATED ODDS 1:226 RETAIL
STATED PRINT RUN 25 SER.#'d SETS
EXCHANGE DEADLINE 8/31/2019
FAAB Alex Bregman EXCH 20.00 50.00
FAABE Andrew Benintendi 50.00 120.00
FAAP A.J. Pollock 5.00 12.00
FABH Bryce Harper EXCH 75.00 200.00
FACB Cody Bellinger EXCH 125.00 300.00
FACD Chris Davis 20.00 50.00
FACS Corey Seager EXCH 60.00 150.00
FAEB Ernie Banks 30.00 80.00
FAFL Francisco Lindor EXCH 40.00 100.00
FAGM Greg Maddux 40.00 100.00
FAKB Kris Bryant 75.00 200.00
FAKGJ Ken Griffey Jr. 75.00 200.00
FALG Lucas Giolito 8.00 20.00
FAMS Max Scherzer 30.00 80.00
FAMT Mike Trout 125.00 300.00
FANS Noah Syndergaard 12.00 30.00
FAPM Pedro Martinez 40.00 100.00
FAPN Phil Niekro 20.00 50.00
FARH Ryon Healy EXCH 10.00 25.00

2017 Topps Fire Autographs Purple

*PURPLE: .6X TO 1.5X BASIC
STATED ODDS 1:114 RETAIL
STATED PRINT RUN 50 SER.#'d SETS
EXCHANGE DEADLINE 8/31/2019
FAAB Alex Bregman EXCH 15.00 40.00
FAABE Andrew Benintendi 40.00 100.00
FAAP A.J. Pollock 4.00 10.00
FACB Cody Bellinger EXCH 100.00 250.00
FACD Chris Davis 15.00 40.00
FACS Corey Seager EXCH
FAFL Francisco Lindor EXCH 30.00 80.00
FALG Lucas Giolito 6.00 15.00
FAMS Max Scherzer 25.00 60.00
FANS Noah Syndergaard 10.00 25.00
FAPN Phil Niekro

2017 Topps Fire Fired Up

STATED ODDS 1:20 RETAIL
*BLUE: .6X TO 1.5X BASIC
*GOLD: .75X TO 2X BASIC
F1 Kris Bryant .75 2.00
F2 Clayton Kershaw 1.00 2.50
F3 Yasiel Puig .60 1.50
F4 Noah Syndergaard .50 1.25
F5 Mike Trout 3.00 8.00
F6 Jose Bautista .50 1.25
F7 Marcus Stroman .50 1.25
F8 Carlos Correa .60 1.50
F9 Max Scherzer .60 1.50
F10 Bryce Harper 1.00 2.50

2017 Topps Fire Flame Throwers

STATED ODDS 1:14 RETAIL
*BLUE: .6X TO 1.5X BASIC
*GOLD: .75X TO 2X BASIC
FT1 Aroldis Chapman .60 1.50
FT2 Chris Archer .40 1.00
FT3 Carlos Martinez .50 1.25
FT4 Edwin Diaz .50 1.25
FT5 Stephen Strasburg .60 1.50
FT6 Dellin Betances .50 1.25
FT7 Chris Sale .60 1.50
FT8 Noah Syndergaard .50 1.25
FT9 Justin Verlander .60 1.50
FT10 Andrew Miller .50 1.25
FT11 Kelvin Herrera .40 1.00
FT12 Max Scherzer .60 1.50
FT13 Craig Kimbrel .50 1.25
FT14 Felix Hernandez .50 1.25
FT15 Clayton Kershaw 1.00 2.50

2017 Topps Fire Golden Grabs

STATED ODDS 1:10 RETAIL
*BLUE: .6X TO 1.5X BASIC
*GOLD: .75X TO 2X BASIC
GG1 Anthony Rizzo .75 2.00
GG2 Manny Machado .60 1.50
GG3 Kole Calhoun .40 1.00
GG4 Mookie Betts 1.25 3.00
GG5 Melky Cabrera .40 1.00
GG6 Ryan Braun .50 1.25
GG7 Kevin Kiermaier .50 1.25
GG8 George Springer .50 1.25
GG9 Kevin Kiermaier .50 1.25
GG10 Andrew Benintendi 1.25 3.00
GG11 Curtis Granderson .50 1.25
GG12 Travis Jankowski .40 1.00
GG13 Xander Bogaerts .60 1.50
GG14 Joey Votto .60 1.50
GG15 Billy Hamilton .50 1.25
GG16 Nolan Arenado 1.00 2.50
GG17 Byron Buxton .60 1.50
GG18 George Springer .50 1.25
GG19 Kevin Pillar .40 1.00
GG20 Mike Trout 3.00 8.00

2017 Topps Fire Monikers

STATED ODDS 1:5 RETAIL
*BLUE: .5X TO 1.2X BASIC
*GOLD: .6X TO 1.5X BASIC
M1 Babe Ruth 2.50 6.00
M2 Cal Ripken Jr. 3.00 8.00
M3 Felix Hernandez .75 2.00
M4 Rickey Henderson 1.00 2.50
M5 Roger Clemens 1.25 3.00
M6 David Ortiz 1.00 2.50
M7 Brooks Robinson .75 2.00
M8 Nelson Cruz 1.00 2.50
M9 Miguel Cabrera 1.00 2.50
M10 Jose Bautista .75 2.00
M11 Jose Altuve .75 2.00
M12 Frank Thomas 1.00 2.50
M13 Bob Feller .75 2.00
M14 Cecil Fielder .60 1.50
M15 Ryne Sandberg 2.00 5.00
M16 Wade Boggs .75 2.00
M17 Reggie Jackson .75 2.00
M18 Mike Moustakas .75 2.00
M19 Mark McGwire 1.50 4.00
M20 Bill Lee .60 1.50
M21 Bryce Harper 1.50 4.00
M22 Duke Snider .75 2.00
M23 Ozzie Smith 1.25 3.00
M24 Aaron Judge 8.00 20.00
M25 Chris Davis .60 1.50
M26 Noah Syndergaard .75 2.00
M27 Matt Harvey .75 2.00
M28 Brandon Belt .75 2.00
M29 Whitey Ford .75 2.00
M30 Phil Rizzuto .75 2.00
M31 Carl Yastrzemski 1.50 4.00
M32 Randy Johnson 1.00 2.50
M33 Gary Carter .75 2.00
M34 Mike Trout 5.00 12.00
M35 Jacob deGrom 2.00 5.00
M36 Jim Hunter .75 2.00
M37 Rich Gossage .75 2.00
M38 Nolan Ryan 3.00 8.00
M39 Don Mattingly 2.00 5.00
M40 Derek Jeter 2.50 6.00

2017 Topps Fire Relics

STATED ODDS 1:71 RETAIL
STATED PRINT RUN 110 SER.#'d SETS
*GREEN/75: .4X TO 1X BASIC
*PURPLE/50: .5X TO 1.2X BASIC
MAGENTA/25: .6X TO 1.5X BASIC
FRAB Andrew Benintendi 8.00 20.00
FRAD Aledmys Diaz 3.00 8.00
FRAG Alex Bregman 5.00 12.00
FRAJ Aaron Judge 30.00 80.00
FRAR Alex Reyes 3.00 8.00
FRCC Carlos Correa 4.00 10.00
FRCF Carson Fulmer 2.50 6.00
FRCS Corey Seager 4.00 10.00
FRDD David Dahl 3.00 8.00
FRDS Dansby Swanson 6.00 15.00
FRFL Francisco Lindor 4.00 10.00
FRHR Hunter Renfroe 3.00 8.00
FRJC Jharel Cotton 2.50 6.00
FRJT Jameson Taillon 3.00 8.00
FRJU Julio Urias 4.00 10.00
FRKB Kris Bryant 5.00 12.00
FRKS Kyle Schwarber 4.00 10.00
FRLG Lucas Giolito 3.00 8.00
FRLS Luis Severino 3.00 8.00
FRLW Luke Weaver 3.00 8.00
FRMF Michael Fulmer 2.50 6.00
FRMM Manny Machado 4.00 10.00
FRMS Miguel Sano 3.00 8.00
FRMT Mike Trout 20.00 50.00
FRNS Noah Syndergaard 3.00 8.00
FRRH Ryon Healy 3.00 8.00
FRSM Steven Matz 2.50 6.00
FRSP Stephen Piscotty 3.00 8.00
FRTAU Tyler Austin 3.00 8.00
FRTG Tyler Glasnow 10.00 25.00
FRTS Trevor Story 4.00 10.00
FRTT Trea Turner 3.00 8.00
FRWC Willson Contreras 4.00 10.00
FRYG Yulieski Gurriel 4.00 10.00
FRYM Yoan Moncada 5.00 12.00

2017 Topps Fire Walk It Off

STATED ODDS 1:14 RETAIL
*BLUE: .6X TO 1.5X BASIC
*GOLD: .75X TO 2X BASIC
WO1 Kris Bryant .75 2.00
WO2 George Springer .50 1.25
WO3 Edwin Encarnacion .60 1.50
WO4 Khris Davis .60 1.50
WO5 Albert Pujols .75 2.00
WO6 Justin Upton .50 1.25
WO7 Freddie Freeman .75 2.00
WO8 Josh Donaldson .50 1.25
WO9 Adrian Beltre .60 1.50
WO10 Carlos Correa .60 1.50
WO11 Mark Trumbo .40 1.00
WO12 Brian Dozier .60 1.50
WO13 Tyler Naquin .60 1.50
WO14 Joey Votto .60 1.50
WO15 Bryce Harper 1.00 2.50

2018 Topps Fire

COMPLETE SET (200) 30.00 80.00
1 Aaron Judge .75 2.00
2 Derek Jeter .75 2.00
3 Dwight Gooden .20 .50
4 Adam Duvall .25 .60
5 Dustin Fowler RC .30 .75
6 Xander Bogaerts .30 .75
7 Ian Kinsler .25 .60
8 Pedro Martinez .25 .60
9 Eric Hosmer .25 .60
10 Ryne Sandberg .60 1.50
11 Alex Verdugo RC .50 1.25
12 Stephen Piscotty .20 .50
13 Joe Mauer .25 .60
14 Luke Weaver .25 .60
15 Josh Bell .25 .60
16 Goose Gossage .25 .60
17 Justin Smoak .20 .50
18 Bob Feller .25 .60
19 Orlando Arcia .20 .50
20 Satchel Paige .30 .75
21 Jake Lamb .25 .60
22 Scott Kingery RC .50 1.25
23 Justin Verlander .30 .75
24 Corey Knebel .20 .50
25 Victor Robles RC .75 2.00
26 Kevin Kiermaier .25 .60
27 Josh Donaldson .25 .60
28 Max Fried RC 1.25 3.00
29 Ozzie Albies RC 1.00 2.50
30 Greg Bird .25 .60
31 Joey Gallo .25 .60
32 Ryan McMahon RC .75 2.00
33 Khris Davis .30 .75
34 Salvador Perez .25 .60
35 Jonathan Schoop .20 .50
36 Anthony Banda RC .30 .75
37 Rickey Henderson .30 .75
38 Willie McCovey .25 .60
39 Ian Happ .25 .60
40 David Ortiz .30 .75
41 Chance Sisco RC .40 1.00
42 Carson Kelly .20 .50
43 Gary Sanchez .30 .75
44 Hunter Pence .25 .60
45 Paul Goldschmidt
46 Alex Rodriguez .40 1.00
47 Luis Severino .25 .60
48 Byron Buxton .30 .75
49 Duke Snider .25 .60
50 Rhys Hoskins RC 1.25 3.00
51 Andrew Stevenson RC .30 .75
52 Chris Archer .20 .50
53 Bryce Harper .50 1.25
54 Trevor Story .30 .75
55 Maikel Franco .25 .60
56 Zack Greinke .30 .75
57 Wade Boggs .25 .60
58 Billy Hamilton .25 .60
59 Sean Doolittle .20 .50
60 Max Scherzer .30 .75
61 Corey Kluber .25 .60
62 Lucas Giolito .25 .60
63 Amed Rosario RC .40 1.00
64 Marcell Ozuna .30 .75
65 Dansby Swanson .30 .75
66 Don Mattingly .60 1.50
67 Garrett Richards .25 .60
68 Adrian Beltre .30 .75
69 Paul DeJong .30 .75
70 Miguel Gomez RC .30 .75
71 Phil Rizzuto .25 .60
72 Anthony Rizzo .40 1.00
73 Ernie Banks .30 .75
74 Javier Baez .40 1.00
75 Matt Chapman .30 .75
76 Scooter Gennett .25 .60
77 Justin Bour .20 .50
78 Carlos Correa .30 .75
79 Manny Machado .30 .75
80 Clayton Kershaw .50 1.25
81 Jose Abreu .30 .75
82 Trey Mancini .25 .60
83 Eddie Mathews .30 .75
84 Mike Piazza .30 .75
85 Evan Longoria .25 .60
86 J.D. Davis RC .40 1.00
87 Yu Darvish .30 .75
88 George Springer .25 .60
89 Nicholas Castellanos .30 .75
90 Lorenzo Cain .20 .50
91 Chris Sale .30 .75
92 Lewis Brinson .20 .50
93 Austin Hays RC .50 1.25
94 Jacob deGrom .60 1.50
95 Michael Fulmer .20 .50
96 Victor Arano RC .30 .75
97 Kris Bryant .40 1.00
98 Hunter Renfroe .20 .50
99 Stephen Strasburg .30 .75
100 Mike Trout 1.50 4.00
101 Whit Merrifield .30 .75
102 Paul Blackburn RC .30 .75
103 Clint Frazier RC .60 1.50
104 Christian Yelich .40 1.00
105 Jose Altuve .25 .60
106 Starlin Castro .20 .50
107 Miguel Andujar RC 1.25 3.00
108 Robinson Cano .25 .60
109 Ronald Acuna Jr. RC 10.00 25.00
110 Tyler Mahle RC .40 1.00
111 A.J. Pollock .20 .50
112 Nolan Ryan 1.00 2.50
113 Francisco Lindor .30 .75
114 Cody Bellinger .60 1.50
115 Aaron Altherr .20 .50
116 Carlos Martinez .25 .60
117 Chris Davis .20 .50
118 Rafael Devers RC 1.00 2.50
119 Gleyber Torres RC 3.00 8.00
120 Josh Harrison .20 .50
121 Gregory Polanco .25 .60
122 Ronald Torreyes .20 .50
123 Franklin Barreto .20 .50
124 Lou Boudreau .25 .60
125 Giancarlo Stanton .30 .75
126 Randy Johnson .30 .75
127 Travis Shaw .20 .50
128 Tyler O'Neill RC .50 1.25
129 Ichiro .40 1.00
130 Tom Seaver .25 .60
131 Justin Upton .25 .60
132 Greg Maddux .40 1.00
133 Sandy Alcantara RC .30 .75
134 Frank Thomas .30 .75
135 Andrelton Simmons .20 .50
136 Cal Ripken Jr. 1.00 2.50
137 Noah Syndergaard .25 .60
138 Jose Ramirez .25 .60
139 Walker Buehler RC 1.50 4.00
140 Tyler Wade RC .40 1.00
141 Zack Granite RC .30 .75
142 Miguel Cabrera .30 .75
143 Nolan Arenado .50 1.25
144 Andrew McCutchen .30 .75
145 Reynaldo Lopez .25 .60
146 Whitey Ford .25 .60
147 Brian Anderson RC .40 1.00
148 Lucas Sims RC .30 .75
149 Max Kepler .25 .60
150 Shohei Ohtani RC 8.00 20.00
151 Freddie Freeman .40 1.00
152 Blake Snell .25 .60
153 Bert Blyleven .25 .60
154 Wil Myers .25 .60
155 Brandon Woodruff RC 1.00 2.50
156 Jed Lowrie .20 .50
157 Mike Moustakas .25 .60
158 Garrett Cooper RC .30 .75
159 Yoan Moncada .30 .75
160 Raisel Iglesias .25 .60
161 Chris Taylor .25 .60
162 Tomas Nido RC .30 .75
163 Harrison Bader RC .50 1.25
164 Charlie Blackmon .30 .75
165 Kyle Schwarber .30 .75
166 Francisco Mejia RC .40 1.00
167 Jake Arrieta .25 .60
168 Alex Gordon .25 .60
169 Andrew Benintendi .30 .75
170 Joey Votto .30 .75
171 Fernando Romero RC .30 .75
172 Matt Olson .30 .75
173 Martin Maldonado .20 .50
174 Zack Godley .20 .50
175 Jack Flaherty RC 1.25 3.00
176 George Brett .60 1.50
177 Jose Canseco .25 .60
178 Jose Berrios .25 .60
179 Joe Morgan .25 .60
180 Felix Hernandez .25 .60
181 Juan Soto RC 8.00 20.00
182 Justin Turner .30 .75
183 Reggie Jackson .25 .60
184 Chipper Jones .30 .75
185 Tommy Pham .20 .50
186 Willy Adames RC .40 1.00
187 Zack Cozart .20 .50
188 Johnny Bench .30 .75
189 Ralph Kiner .25 .60
190 Mark McGwire .50 1.25

191 Nicky Delmonico RC .30 .75
192 Yadier Molina .40 1.00
193 Dominic Smith RC .40 1.00
194 Jordan Hicks RC .60 1.50
195 Yoenis Cespedes .30 .75
196 Dave Winfield .25 .60
197 Willson Contreras .30 .75
198 Roger Clemens .40 1.00
199 Tim Beckham .25 .60
200 Sandy Koufax .60 1.50

2018 Topps Fire Blue

*BLUE: .75X TO 2X BASIC
*BLUE RC: .5X TO 1.2X BASIC RC
RANDOM INSERTS IN PACKS
109 Ronald Acuna Jr. 8.00 20.00
112 Nolan Ryan 4.00 10.00
136 Cal Ripken Jr. 5.00 12.00
150 Shohei Ohtani 6.00 15.00
176 George Brett 4.00 10.00

2018 Topps Fire Flame

*FLAME: .75X TO 2X BASIC
*FLAME RC: .5X TO 1.2X BASIC RC
STATED ODDS 1:4 RETAIL
109 Ronald Acuna Jr. 8.00 20.00
112 Nolan Ryan 4.00 10.00
136 Cal Ripken Jr. 5.00 12.00
150 Shohei Ohtani 6.00 15.00
176 George Brett 4.00 10.00

2018 Topps Fire Gold

*GOLD: .75X TO 2X BASIC
*GOLD RC: .5X TO 1.2X BASIC RC
RANDOM INSERTS IN PACKS
109 Ronald Acuna Jr. 8.00 20.00
112 Nolan Ryan 4.00 10.00
136 Cal Ripken Jr. 5.00 12.00
150 Shohei Ohtani 6.00 15.00
176 George Brett 4.00 10.00

2018 Topps Fire Green

*GREEN: 1.2X TO 3X BASIC
*GREEN RC: .75X TO 2X BASIC RC
STATED ODDS 1:19 RETAIL
STATED PRINT RUN 199 SER.#'d SETS
109 Ronald Acuna Jr. 12.00 30.00
112 Nolan Ryan 6.00 15.00
136 Cal Ripken Jr. 8.00 20.00
150 Shohei Ohtani 10.00 25.00
176 George Brett 6.00 15.00

2018 Topps Fire Magenta

*MAGENTA: 3X TO 8X BASIC
*MAGENTA RC: 2X TO 5X BASIC RC
STATED ODDS 1:152 RETAIL
STATED PRINT RUN 25 SER.#'d SETS
109 Ronald Acuna Jr. 30.00 80.00
112 Nolan Ryan 15.00 40.00
136 Cal Ripken Jr. 20.00 50.00
150 Shohei Ohtani 25.00 60.00
176 George Brett 15.00 40.00

2018 Topps Fire Orange

*ORANGE: 1.2X TO 3X BASIC
*ORANGE RC: .75X TO 2X BASIC RC
STATED ODDS 1:13 RETAIL
STATED PRINT RUN 299 SER.#'d SETS
109 Ronald Acuna Jr. 12.00 30.00
112 Nolan Ryan 6.00 15.00
136 Cal Ripken Jr. 8.00 20.00
150 Shohei Ohtani 10.00 25.00
176 George Brett 6.00 15.00

2018 Topps Fire Purple

*PURPLE: 1.5X TO 4X BASIC
*PURPLE RC: 1X TO 2.5X BASIC RC
STATED ODDS 1:39 RETAIL
STATED PRINT RUN 99 SER.#'d SETS
109 Ronald Acuna Jr. 15.00 40.00
112 Nolan Ryan 8.00 20.00
136 Cal Ripken Jr. 10.00 25.00
150 Shohei Ohtani 12.00 30.00
176 George Brett 8.00 20.00

2018 Topps Fire Autograph Patches

STATED ODDS 1:518 RETAIL
STATED PRINT RUN 25 SER.#'d SETS
EXCHANGE DEADLINE 7/31/2020
FAPAC Alex Colome/25
FAPAJ Aaron Judge/25
FAPAS Andrew Stevenson/25
FAPBA Brian Anderson/25
FAPBD Brian Dozier/25
FAPCF Carson Fulmer/25 8.00 20.00
FAPCK Corey Kluber/25
FAPDF Dustin Fowler/25
FAPDS Dominic Smith/25
FAPDV Dan Vogelbach/25
FAPFL Francisco Lindor/25
FAPFM Francisco Mejia/25
FAPGC Garrett Cooper/25 8.00 20.00
FAPHB Harrison Bader/25
FAPHD Hunter Dozier/25
FAPJA Jorge Alfaro/25
FAPJK Jason Kipnis/25
FAPJM Joe Musgrove/25 12.00 30.00
FAPKB Kris Bryant/25 75.00
FAPKH Kelvin Herrera/25
FAPKS Kyle Schwarber/25
FAPLS Lucas Sims/25 8.00 20.00
FAPLW Luke Weaver/25
FAPMA Miguel Andujar/25 75.00 200.00
FAPMG Miguel Gomez/25 20.00 50.00
FAPMM Manny Machado/25
FAPND Nicky Delmonico/25
FAPNS Noah Syndergaard/25 20.00 50.00
FAPOA Ozzie Albies/25
FAPRG Robert Gsellman/25
FAPRH Rhys Hoskins/25 30.00 80.00
FAPRQ Roman Quinn/25
FAPRS Robert Stephenson/22
FAPRT Raimel Tapia/25 8.00 20.00
FAPSM Steven Matz/25
FAPSO Shohei Ohtani/25
FAPSP Salvador Perez/25 20.00 50.00
FAPTM Trey Mancini/25 20.00 50.00
FAPTMA Tyler Mahle/20
FAPTN Tyler Naquin/25
FAPVR Victor Robles/25
FAPWC Willson Contreras/25 30.00 80.00
FAPYG Yuli Gurriel/25

2018 Topps Fire Autographs

STATED ODDS 1:29 RETAIL
EXCHANGE DEADLINE 7/31/2020
*GREEN/75: .5X TO 1.2X BASE
*PURPLE/50: .6X TO 1.5X BASE
*MAGENTA/25: .75X TO 2X BASE
FAAB Anthony Banda 2.50 6.00
FAAD Adam Duvall 5.00 12.00
FAAH Austin Hays 8.00 20.00
FAAJ Aaron Judge 60.00 150.00
FAAR Anthony Rizzo
FAARO Amed Rosario 8.00 20.00
FAAV Alex Verdugo 4.00 10.00
FABA Brian Anderson 3.00 8.00
FABS Blake Snell 6.00 15.00
FABW Brandon Woodruff 8.00 20.00
FACF Clint Frazier
FACK Carson Kelly 2.50 6.00
FACRJ Cal Ripken Jr. 40.00 100.00
FACT Chris Taylor 5.00 12.00
FACY Christian Yelich 20.00 50.00
FADG Dwight Gooden 12.00 30.00
FADJ Derek Jeter
FADO David Ortiz
FAGB Greg Bird 3.00 8.00
FAGT Gleyber Torres 25.00 60.00
FAHB Harrison Bader 4.00 10.00
FAIH Ian Happ 6.00 15.00
FAJA Jose Altuve 30.00 80.00
FAJB Jose Berrios 3.00 8.00
FAJC Jose Canseco 12.00 30.00
FAJD J.D. Davis 3.00 8.00
FAJL Jake Lamb 3.00 8.00
FAKB Kris Bryant 40.00 100.00
FAKD Khris Davis 6.00 15.00
FALG Lucas Giolito 3.00 8.00
FALW Luke Weaver 3.00 8.00
FAMAM Martin Maldonado 2.50 6.00
FAMC Matt Chapman 8.00 20.00
FAMF Max Fried 4.00 10.00
FAMG Miguel Gomez 2.50 6.00
FAMK Max Kepler 3.00 8.00
FAMM Mark McGwire 30.00 80.00
FAMMA Manny Machado 12.00 30.00
FAMO Matt Olson 5.00 12.00
FAMP Mike Piazza 40.00 100.00
FAMT Mike Trout
FAND Nicky Delmonico 2.50 6.00
FAOA Ozzie Albies 12.00 30.00
FAPB Paul Blackburn 2.50 6.00
FAPD Paul DeJong
FARAJ Ronald Acuna Jr. 75.00 200.00
FARC Roger Clemens 40.00 100.00
FARD Rafael Devers 12.00 30.00
FARH Rhys Hoskins 20.00 50.00
FARHE Rickey Henderson
FARI Raisel Iglesias 3.00 8.00
FARJ Randy Johnson
FARL Reynaldo Lopez 3.00 8.00
FARM Ryan McMahon 6.00 15.00
FARO Ronald Torreyes 5.00 12.00
FASA Sandy Alcantara 2.50 6.00
FASD Sean Doolittle 2.50 6.00
FASO Shohei Ohtani
FASP Salvador Perez 8.00 20.00
FATM Trey Mancini 20.00 50.00
FATN Tomas Nido 2.50 6.00
FAVA Victor Arano 2.50 6.00
FAVR Victor Robles 8.00 20.00
FAWB Walker Buehler 20.00 50.00
FAWC Willson Contreras 10.00 25.00
FAWM Whit Merrifield 4.00 10.00
FAYM Yadier Molina 25.00 60.00

2018 Topps Fire Cannons

STATED ODDS 1:14 RETAIL
*BLUE: .6X TO 1.5X BASIC
*GOLD: .75X TO 2X BASIC
C1 Ichiro .75 2.00
C2 Avisail Garcia .50 1.25
C3 Alex Gordon .50 1.25
C4 Yadier Molina .75 2.00
C5 Andrew Benintendi .60 1.50
C6 Tucker Barnhart .40 1.00
C7 Adam Duvall .50 1.25
C8 Nolan Arenado 1.00 2.50
C9 Carlos Correa .60 1.50
C10 Brett Gardner .50 1.25
C11 Gary Sanchez .60 1.50
C12 Billy Hamilton .50 1.25
C13 Manny Machado .60 1.50
C14 Hunter Renfroe .40 1.00
C15 Bryce Harper 1.00 2.50

2018 Topps Fire Dual Autographs

STATED ODDS 1:4559 RETAIL
STATED PRINT RUN 20 SER.#'d SETS
EXCHANGE DEADLINE 7/31/2020
FDAAA Acuna/Albies
FDAAF Albies/Fried 40.00 100.00
FDADC Canseco/Davis 75.00 200.00
FDAGD Delmonico/Giolito
FDAMD Molina/DeJong 50.00 120.00
FDAMH Hays/Mancini 60.00 150.00
FDAOC Chapman/Olson 40.00 100.00
FDAOR Ortiz/Devers
FDAPM Perez/Merrifield
FDAVT Verdugo/Taylor
FDAWK Weaver/Kelly

2018 Topps Fire Fired Up

STATED ODDS 1:14 RETAIL
*BLUE: .6X TO 1.5X BASIC
*GOLD: .75X TO 2X BASIC
F1 Mike Trout 3.00 8.00
F2 Charlie Blackmon .60 1.50
F3 Francisco Lindor .60 1.50
F4 Chris Sale .60 1.50
F5 Cody Bellinger 1.25 3.00
F6 Manny Machado .60 1.50
F7 Carlos Correa .60 1.50
F8 Giancarlo Stanton .60 1.50
F9 Noah Syndergaard .50 1.25
F10 Aaron Judge 1.50 4.00
F11 Jose Altuve .50 1.25
F12 Clayton Kershaw 1.00 2.50
F13 Andrew Benintendi .60 1.50
F14 Max Scherzer .60 1.50
F15 Bryce Harper 1.00 2.50

2018 Topps Fire Flame Throwers

STATED ODDS 1:14 RETAIL
*BLUE: .6X TO 1.5X BASIC
*GOLD: .75X TO 2X BASIC
FT1 Max Scherzer .60 1.50
FT2 Robbie Ray
FT3 Craig Kimbrel .50 1.25
FT4 Zack Greinke .60 1.50
FT5 Noah Syndergaard .50 1.25
FT6 Kenley Jansen .50 1.25
FT7 Luis Severino .50 1.25
FT8 Stephen Strasburg .60 1.50
FT9 Luis Castillo .50 1.25
FT10 Walker Buehler 2.00 5.00
FT11 Justin Verlander .60 1.50
FT12 Carlos Martinez .50 1.25
FT13 Shohei Ohtani 10.00 25.00
FT14 Chris Sale .60 1.50
FT15 Aroldis Chapman .60 1.50

2018 Topps Fire Golden Sledgehammer

STATED ODDS 1:14 RETAIL
*BLUE: .6X TO 1.5X BASIC
*GOLD: .75X TO 2X BASIC
PP1 Joey Gallo .50 1.25
PP2 Giancarlo Stanton .60 1.50
PP3 Kendrys Morales .40 1.00
PP4 Mark Reynolds .40 1.00
PP5 Aaron Judge 1.50 4.00
PP6 J.D. Martinez .60 1.50
PP7 Marcell Ozuna .60 1.50
PP8 Gary Sanchez .60 1.50
PP9 Miguel Sano .50 1.25
PP10 Mike Trout 3.00 8.00
PP11 Charlie Blackmon .60 1.50
PP12 Ryon Healy .40 1.00
PP13 Wil Myers .50 1.25
PP14 Mike Zunino .40 1.00
PP15 Jake Lamb .50 1.25

2018 Topps Fire Hot Starts

STATED ODDS 1:8 RETAIL
*BLUE: .6X TO 1.5X BASIC
*GOLD: .75X TO 2X BASIC
HS1 Shohei Ohtani 10.00 25.00
HS2 Charlie Morton .60 1.50
HS3 Manny Machado .60 1.50
HS4 Khris Davis .60 1.50
HS5 Carlos Correa .60 1.50
HS6 Didi Gregorius .50 1.25
HS7 Patrick Corbin .50 1.25
HS8 Corey Kluber .50 1.25
HS9 Jed Lowrie .40 1.00
HS10 Bryce Harper 1.00 2.50
HS11 Rick Porcello .50 1.25
HS12 Rhys Hoskins 1.50 4.00
HS13 Aaron Judge 1.50 4.00
HS14 Jarlin Garcia .40 1.00
HS15 Javier Baez .75 2.00
HS16 Christian Villanueva .40 1.00
HS17 Mookie Betts 1.25 3.00
HS18 Johnny Cueto .50 1.25
HS19 Charlie Blackmon .60 1.50
HS20 Edwin Diaz .50 1.25
HS21 Gerrit Cole .60 1.50
HS22 Joey Lucchesi .40 1.00
HS23 Mitch Haniger .50 1.25
HS24 A.J. Pollock .40 1.00

2018 Topps Fire Relics

STATED ODDS 1:29 RETAIL
*GREEN/75: .5X TO 1.2X BASIC
*PURPLE/50: .6X TO 1.5X BASIC
MAGENTA/25: .75X TO 2X BASIC
FRAH Austin Hays 3.00 8.00
FRAJ Aaron Judge 8.00 20.00
FRAR Amed Rosario 2.50 6.00
FRAS Andrew Stevenson 2.00 5.00
FRBD Brian Dozier 2.50 6.00
FRCF Clint Frazier 4.00 10.00
FRCK Corey Kluber 2.50 6.00
FRCS Chance Sisco 2.50 6.00
FRDF Dustin Fowler 2.00 5.00
FRDS Dominic Smith 2.50 6.00
FRFL Francisco Lindor 3.00 8.00
FRFM Francisco Mejia 2.50 6.00
FRGC Garrett Cooper 2.00 5.00
FRHB Harrison Bader 3.00 8.00
FRJF Jack Flaherty 4.00 10.00
FRJK Jason Kipnis 2.50 6.00
FRKB Kris Bryant 4.00 10.00
FRKS Kyle Schwarber 3.00 8.00
FRLS Lucas Sims 2.00 5.00
FRLW Luke Weaver 2.50 6.00
FRMA Miguel Andujar 5.00 12.00
FRMG Miguel Gomez 2.00 5.00
FRMM Manny Machado 3.00 8.00
FRND Nicky Delmonico 2.00 5.00
FRNS Noah Syndergaard 2.50 6.00
FROA Ozzie Albies 6.00 15.00
FRRD Rafael Devers 6.00 15.00
FRRH Rhys Hoskins 5.00 12.00
FRRM Ryan McMahon 5.00 12.00
FRSM Steven Matz 2.00 5.00
FRSO Shohei Ohtani 6.00 15.00
FRSP Salvador Perez 2.50 6.00
FRTM Trey Mancini 2.50 6.00
FRTMA Tyler Mahle 2.50 6.00
FRTW Tyler Wade 2.50 6.00
FRVR Victor Robles 4.00 10.00
FRWC Willson Contreras 3.00 8.00
FRYG Yuli Gurriel 2.50 6.00
FRZC Zack Granite 2.00 5.00

2018 Topps Fire Speed Demons

STATED ODDS 1:14 RETAIL
*BLUE: .6X TO 1.5X BASIC
*GOLD: .75X TO 2X BASIC
SD1 Jose Altuve .50 1.25
SD2 Amed Rosario .50 1.25
SD3 Elvis Andrus .50 1.25
SD4 Trea Turner .50 1.25
SD5 Starling Marte .50 1.25
SD6 Brett Gardner .50 1.25
SD7 Mike Trout 3.00 8.00
SD8 Dee Gordon .40 1.00
SD9 Mookie Betts 1.25 3.00
SD10 Whit Merrifield .60 1.50
SD11 A.J. Pollock .40 1.00
SD12 Byron Buxton .60 1.50
SD13 Tommy Pham .40 1.00
SD14 Lorenzo Cain .40 1.00
SD15 Billy Hamilton .50 1.25

2019 Topps Fire

COMPLETE SET (200) 30.00 80.00
1 Shohei Ohtani .50 1.25
2 Chipper Jones .30 .75
3 Heath Fillmyer RC .30 .75
4 Willians Astudillo RC .30 .75
5 Orlando Arcia .20 .50
6 Zack Greinke .30 .75
7 Kolby Allard RC .50 1.25
8 Aramis Garcia RC .30 .75
9 Albert Pujols .40 1.00
10 Willson Contreras .25 .60
11 Steven Duggar RC .40 1.00
12 Nick Markakis .25 .60
13 Kris Bryant .40 1.00
14 Lourdes Gurriel Jr. .25 .60
15 Rowdy Tellez RC .50 1.25
16 Carter Kieboom RC .50 1.25
17 Ozzie Albies .30 .75
18 Christian Yelich .40 1.00
19 Mike Trout 1.50 4.00
20 Jonathan Loaisiga RC .40 1.00
21 Jeff McNeil RC .75 2.00
22 Yadier Molina .40 1.00
23 Mike Fiers .20 .50
24 Justin Verlander .30 .75
25 Danny Jansen RC .30 .75
26 Khris Davis .30 .75
27 Ryan O'Hearn RC .30 .75
28 Freddie Freeman .40 1.00
29 Javier Baez .40 1.00
30 Lorenzo Cain .20 .50
31 Marcus Stroman .25 .60
32 Anthony Rizzo .40 1.00
33 Jake Lamb .25 .60
34 Justin Upton .25 .60
35 Griffin Canning RC .50 1.25
36 Chris Shaw RC .30 .75
37 Ronald Acuna Jr. 1.50 4.00
38 Ken Griffey Jr. .60 1.50
39 Justin Turner .30 .75
40 Christin Stewart RC .40 1.00
41 Mariano Rivera .40 1.00
42 Taylor Ward RC .30 .75
43 Harrison Bader .25 .60
44 Corey Seager .30 .75
45 Mike Foltynewicz .30 .75
46 Jack Flaherty .30 .75
47 Dansby Swanson .30 .75
48 Cal Quantrill RC .30 .75
49 Ryan Borucki RC .30 .75
50 Justus Sheffield RC .50 1.25
51 Dakota Hudson RC .40 1.00
52 Clayton Kershaw .50 1.25
53 Brandon Lowe RC .50 1.25
54 Nick Ahmed .20 .50
55 Ramon Laureano RC .60 1.50
56 Cedric Mullins RC .60 1.50
57 Chance Adams RC .30 .75
58 Michael Kopech RC 1.00 2.50
59 Cody Bellinger .60 1.50
60 Jurickson Profar .25 .60
61 Luis Urias RC .50 1.25
62 Derek Jeter .75 2.00
63 Trevor Hoffman .25 .60
64 Kyle Schwarber .30 .75
65 Josh James RC .50 1.25
66 Paul Goldschmidt .30 .75
67 Matt Chapman .30 .75
68 Corbin Burnes RC 2.50 6.00
69 George Springer .25 .60
70 Kyle Tucker RC .75 2.00
71 DJ Stewart RC .40 1.00
72 Alex Bregman .30 .75
73 Sean Reid-Foley RC .30 .75
74 Blake Treinen .20 .50
75 Enyel De Los Santos RC .30 .75
76 Brad Keller RC .30 .75
77 Jhoulys Chacin .20 .50
78 Alex Rodriguez .40 1.00
79 Touki Toussaint RC .40 1.00
80 Jose Altuve .25 .60
81 Freddy Galvis .20 .50
82 Gerrit Cole .30 .75
83 Kevin Pillar .20 .50
84 Ryan Braun .25 .60
85 Robbie Ray .20 .50
86 Jake Bauers RC .50 1.25
87 David Fletcher RC 1.00 2.50
88 Jake Cave RC .40 1.00
89 Walker Buehler .40 1.00
90 Jim Thome .25 .60
91 Jon Duplantier RC .30 .75
92 Todd Helton .25 .60
93 David Ortiz .30 .75
94 Kevin Kramer RC .40 1.00
95 Jon Lester .25 .60
96 Kevin Newman RC .50 1.25
97 Nick Senzel RC 1.00 2.50
98 Andrelton Simmons .20 .50
99 Jordan Hicks .25 .60
100 Cal Ripken Jr. 1.00 2.50
101 Tim Anderson .30 .75
102 David Price .25 .60
103 Trevor Bauer .40 1.00
104 Nelson Cruz .30 .75
105 Whit Merrifield .30 .75
106 Charlie Blackmon .30 .75
107 Manny Machado .30 .75
108 Brian Anderson .20 .50
109 Grayson Greiner .20 .50
110 Trey Mancini .25 .60
111 Mitch Haniger .25 .60
112 Jose Urena .20 .50
113 Francisco Lindor .30 .75
114 Noah Syndergaard .25 .60
115 Trea Turner .25 .60
116 Shin-Soo Choo .25 .60
117 Adalberto Mondesi .25 .60
118 Chris Archer .20 .50
119 Jordan Zimmermann .25 .60
120 Willy Adames .20 .50
121 Tucker Barnhart .20 .50
122 Aaron Judge .75 2.00
123 Byron Buxton .30 .75
124 Ryan Zimmerman .25 .60
125 Starlin Castro .20 .50
126 Giancarlo Stanton .30 .75
127 Corey Dickerson .20 .50
128 Pete Alonso RC 4.00 10.00
129 Miguel Cabrera .30 .75
130 Nolan Arenado .50 1.25
131 Aaron Nola .25 .60
132 Vladimir Guerrero Jr. RC 4.00 10.00
133 Xander Bogaerts .30 .75
134 Amed Rosario .25 .60
135 Elvis Andrus .25 .60
136 Joey Lucchesi .20 .50
137 Bryce Harper .50 1.25
138 Blake Snell .25 .60
139 Jose Berrios .25 .60
140 Joey Gallo .25 .60
141 Edwin Encarnacion .30 .75
142 Jonathan Villar .20 .50
143 James Paxton .25 .60
144 Andrew Benintendi .30 .75
145 Trevor May .20 .50
146 Lewis Brinson .20 .50
147 Jose Ramirez .25 .60
148 Yonder Alonso .20 .50
149 Nicholas Castellanos .30 .75
150 Juan Soto 1.00 2.50
151 Jose Abreu .30 .75
152 Wil Myers .25 .60
153 Sean Doolittle .20 .50
154 Rougned Odor .25 .60
155 Alex Gordon .25 .60
156 Kevin Kiermaier .25 .60
157 Fernando Tatis Jr. RC 3.00 8.00
158 Jacob deGrom .60 1.50
159 Mike Clevinger .25 .60
160 Corey Kluber .25 .60
161 Sonny Gray .25 .60
162 Scooter Gennett .25 .60
163 Starling Marte .25 .60
164 Chance Sisco .20 .50
165 Brandon Belt .25 .60
166 Alex Cobb .20 .50
167 Josh Bell .25 .60
168 Eloy Jimenez RC 1.25 3.00
169 Eric Hosmer .25 .60
170 Luis Severino .25 .60
171 Kyle Freeland .25 .60
172 Kyle Gibson .25 .60
173 Dee Gordon .20 .50
174 Ryan McMahon .30 .75
175 Yoan Moncada .30 .75
176 Max Scherzer .30 .75
177 Michael Conforto .25 .60
178 Robinson Cano .25 .60
179 Rhys Hoskins .40 1.00
180 Miguel Andujar .30 .75
181 Reynaldo Lopez .25 .60
182 Stephen Strasburg .30 .75
183 Marco Gonzales .20 .50
184 J.D. Martinez .30 .75
185 Ryon Healy .20 .50
186 Mookie Betts .60 1.50
187 Trevor Story .30 .75
188 Brandon Crawford .25 .60
189 Ryan Yarbrough .20 .50
190 J.T. Realmuto .30 .75
191 Buster Posey .40 1.00
192 Chris Sale .30 .75
193 Gleyber Torres .60 1.50
194 Joey Votto .30 .75
195 Austin Hedges .20 .50
196 Evan Longoria .25 .60
197 Jake Arrieta .25 .60
198 Felipe Vazquez .20 .50
199 Hunter Dozier .20 .50
200 Yasiel Puig .30 .75

2019 Topps Fire Blue

*BLUE: 1X TO 2.5X BASIC
*BLUE RC: .6X TO 1.5X BASIC RC
RANDOM INSERTS IN PACKS

2019 Topps Fire Gold Mint

*GOLD: 1X TO 2.5X BASIC
*GOLD RC: .6X TO 1.5X BASIC RC
RANDOM INSERTS IN PACKS

2019 Topps Fire Green

*GREEN: 1.5X TO 4X BASIC
*GREEN RC: 1X TO 2.5X BASIC RC
STATED ODDS 1:17 RETAIL
STATED PRINT RUN 199 SER.#'d SETS

2019 Topps Fire Magenta

*MAGENTA: 6X TO 15X BASIC
*MAGENTA RC: 4X TO 10X BASIC RC
STATED ODDS 1:129 RETAIL
STATED PRINT RUN 25 SER.#'d SETS

2019 Topps Fire Orange

*ORANGE: 1.5X TO 4X BASIC
*ORANGE RC: 1X TO 2.5X BASIC RC
STATED ODDS 1:11 RETAIL
STATED PRINT RUN 299 SER.#'d SETS

2019 Topps Fire Purple

*PURPLE: 2X TO 5X BASIC
*PURPLE RC: 1.2X TO 3X BASIC RC
STATED ODDS 1:33 RETAIL
STATED PRINT RUN 99 SER.#'d SETS

2019 Topps Fire Autograph Patches

STATED ODDS 1:549 RETAIL
STATED PRINT RUN 25 SER.#'d SETS
EXCHANGE DEADLINE 7/31/2021
FAPAJ Aaron Judge
FAPBK Brad Keller
FAPBN Brandon Nimmo 10.00 25.00
FAPBS Blake Snell 10.00 25.00
FAPBT Blake Treinen
FAPCA Chance Adams
FAPCB Corbin Burnes
FAPCM Cedric Mullins
FAPCS Chris Shaw
FAPDH Dakota Hudson
FAPDJ Danny Jansen 8.00 20.00
FAPFL Francisco Lindor 40.00 100.00
FAPJA Jesus Aguilar 10.00 25.00
FAPJC Jake Cave
FAPJH Josh Hader 10.00 25.00
FAPJN Jacob Nix 10.00 25.00
FAPJR Josh Rogers
FAPJS Justus Sheffield 12.00 30.00
FAPKB Kris Bryant
FAPKS Kyle Schwarber 12.00 30.00
FAPKT Kyle Tucker 50.00 120.00
FAPKW Kyle Wright 12.00 30.00
FAPMA Miguel Andujar
FAPMH Mitch Haniger
FAPMT Mike Trout
FAPNC Nick Ciuffo
FAPNS Noah Syndergaard 20.00 50.00
FAPOA Ozzie Albies
FAPRAJ Ronald Acuna Jr. 75.00 200.00
FAPRB Ryan Borucki 8.00 20.00
FAPRH Rhys Hoskins
FAPRL Ramon Laureano 60.00 150.00
FAPRT Rowdy Tellez
FAPSK Scott Kingery
FAPSO Shohei Ohtani
FAPSRF Sean Reid-Foley 8.00 20.00
FAPTW Taylor Ward
FAPVR Victor Robles

2019 Topps Fire Autographs

STATED ODDS 1:29 RETAIL
EXCHANGE DEADLINE 7/31/2021
*GREEN/75: .5X TO 1.2X BASE
*PURPLE/50: .6X TO 1.5X BASE
*MAGENTA/25: .75X TO 2X BASE
FAAR Anthony Rizzo 12.00 30.00
FABK Brad Keller 2.50 6.00
FABP Buster Posey 25.00 60.00
FABS Blake Snell 3.00 8.00
FACG Chad Green 5.00 12.00
FACJ Chipper Jones 20.00 50.00
FACS Christin Stewart
FADO David Ortiz 20.00 50.00
FADP Daniel Ponce de Leon 4.00 10.00
FAEJ Eloy Jimenez 15.00 40.00
FAFL Francisco Lindor 12.00 30.00
FAFT Frank Thomas 20.00 50.00
FAFTJ Fernando Tatis Jr. 60.00 150.00
FAGCA Griffin Canning 4.00 10.00
FAGH Garrett Hampson 4.00 10.00
FAGS George Springer 12.00 30.00
FAHB Harrison Bader 3.00 8.00
FAI Ichiro 100.00 250.00
FAJDU Jon Duplantier
FAJJ Josh James 4.00 10.00
FAJM Jose Martinez 2.50 6.00
FAJN Jacob Nix 3.00 8.00
FAJR Josh Rogers 2.50 6.00
FAJRA Jose Ramirez 15.00 40.00
FAJS Juan Soto 20.00 50.00
FAKB Kris Bryant
FAKK Kevin Kramer 3.00 8.00
FAKN Kevin Newman 4.00 10.00
FALV Luke Voit 10.00 25.00
FAMC Miguel Cabrera
FAMM Max Muncy 6.00 15.00
FAMMA Manny Machado 20.00 50.00
FAMMI Miles Mikolas 4.00 10.00
FAMS Myles Straw 4.00 10.00
FAMT Mike Trout 200.00 400.00
FANC Nick Ciuffo 2.50 6.00
FANSE Nick Senzel
FAPA Pete Alonso 40.00 100.00
FAPC Patrick Corbin 3.00 8.00
FARAJ Ronald Acuna Jr. 50.00 120.00
FARH Rhys Hoskins 12.00 30.00
FARL Ramon Laureano 6.00 15.00
FASO Shohei Ohtani 75.00 200.00
FATB Trevor Bauer 5.00 12.00
FATW Taylor Ward 2.50 6.00
FAVGJ Vladimir Guerrero Jr. 50.00 120.00
FAWA Willians Astudillo 2.50 6.00
FAYK Yusei Kikuchi 10.00 25.00

2019 Topps Fire Dual Autographs

STATED ODDS 1:2005 RETAIL
PRINT RUNS B/WN 10-20 COPIES PER
NO PRICING ON QTY 15 OR LESS
EXCHANGE DEADLINE 7/31/2021
FDABR Bryant/Rizzo/20 75.00 200.00
FDACD Davis/Canseco
FDAHM McCutchen/Hoskins
FDAJA Jones/Acuna/20
FDAMU Urias/Machado
FDANK Newman/Kramer
FDAST Springer/Tucker/20

2019 Topps Fire En Fuego

STATED ODDS 1:8 RETAIL
*BLUE: .6X TO 1.5X BASIC
*GOLD: .75X TO 2X BASIC
EF1 Aaron Judge 1.25 3.00
EF2 Yadier Molina .60 1.50
EF3 Starling Marte .40 1.00
EF4 Max Scherzer .50 1.25
EF5 Corey Kluber .40 1.00
EF6 Yuli Gurriel .40 1.00
EF7 Francisco Lindor .50 1.25
EF8 Ivan Rodriguez .40 1.00
EF9 Shohei Ohtani .75 2.00
EF10 Christian Yelich .60 1.50
EF11 Clayton Kershaw .75 2.00
EF12 Whit Merrifield .50 1.25
EF13 Miguel Cabrera .50 1.25
EF14 Adrian Beltre .50 1.25
EF15 Rickey Henderson .50 1.25
EF16 Trevor Story .50 1.25
EF17 Derek Jeter 1.25 3.00
EF18 Freddie Freeman .60 1.50
EF19 Nolan Arenado .75 2.00
EF20 Kris Bryant .60 1.50
EF21 Matt Chapman .50 1.25
EF22 Khris Davis .50 1.25
EF23 Mariano Rivera .60 1.50
EF24 Anthony Rizzo .60 1.50
EF25 Mike Trout 2.50 6.00

2019 Topps Fire Fired Up

STATED ODDS 1:14 RETAIL
*BLUE: .6X TO 1.5X BASIC
*GOLD: .75X TO 2X BASIC
FIU1 Mike Trout 2.50 6.00
FIU2 Francisco Lindor .50 1.25
FIU3 Javier Baez .60 1.50
FIU4 Chris Sale .50 1.25
FIU5 Josh Hader .40 1.00
FIU6 Bryce Harper .75 2.00
FIU7 Jacob deGrom 1.00 2.50
FIU8 Juan Soto 1.50 4.00
FIU9 George Springer .40 1.00
FIU10 Aaron Judge 1.25 3.00
FIU11 Max Scherzer .50 1.25
FIU12 Ronald Acuna Jr. 2.50 6.00
FIU13 Mookie Betts 1.00 2.50
FIU14 Carlos Correa .50 1.25
FIU15 Shohei Ohtani .75 2.00

2019 Topps Fire Flame

*FLAME: 1X TO 2.5X BASIC
*FLAME RC: .6X TO 1.5X BASIC RC
STATED ODDS 1:4 RETAIL

2019 Topps Fire Flame Throwers

STATED ODDS 1:14 RETAIL
*BLUE: .6X TO 1.5X BASIC
*GOLD: .75X TO 2X BASIC
FT1 Shohei Ohtani .75 2.00
FT2 Aroldis Chapman .50 1.25
FT3 Walker Buehler .60 1.50
FT4 Max Scherzer .50 1.25
FT5 Gerrit Cole .50 1.25
FT6 Trevor Bauer .60 1.50
FT7 Blake Treinen .30 .75
FT8 Luis Severino .40 1.00
FT9 Justin Verlander .50 1.25
FT10 Josh Hader .40 1.00
FT11 Nathan Eovaldi .40 1.00
FT12 Chris Sale .50 1.25
FT13 Edwin Diaz .40 1.00
FT14 Noah Syndergaard .40 1.00
FT15 Jacob deGrom 1.00 2.50

2019 Topps Fire Lasting Legacies

STATED ODDS 1:14 RETAIL
*BLUE: .6X TO 1.5X BASIC
*GOLD: .75X TO 2X BASIC
LL1 Kershaw/Koufax 1.00 2.50
LL2 Ryan/Verlander 1.50 4.00
LL3 Benintendi/Yaz .75 2.00
LL4 Harper/Cobb .75 2.00
LL5 Roberto Alomar .50 1.25
Francisco Lindor
LL6 Acuna/Trout 2.50 6.00
LL7 Betts/Williams 1.00 2.50
LL8 Yount/Yelich .60 1.50
LL9 Bob Gibson .50 1.25
Max Scherzer
LL10 Judge/Jeter 1.25 3.00
LL11 Giancarlo Stanton .50 1.25
Reggie Jackson
LL12 Trout/Aaron 2.50 6.00
LL13 Torres/Jeter 1.25 3.00
LL14 Baez/Banks .60 1.50
LL15 Ohtani/Ryan 1.50 4.00

2019 Topps Fire Maximum Velocity

STATED ODDS 1:14 RETAIL
*BLUE: .6X TO 1.5X BASIC
*GOLD: .75X TO 2X BASIC
MV1 Joey Gallo .40 1.00
MV2 Miguel Cabrera .50 1.25
MV3 David Bote .40 1.00
MV4 Aaron Judge 1.25 3.00
MV5 Nelson Cruz .50 1.25
MV6 Giancarlo Stanton .50 1.25
MV7 Franchy Cordero .30 .75
MV8 Matt Chapman .50 1.25
MV9 Matt Olson .50 1.25
MV10 Mark Trumbo .30 .75
MV11 Derek Fisher .30 .75
MV12 Robinson Cano .40 1.00
MV13 Tommy Pham .30 .75
MV14 Luke Voit .75 2.00
MV15 J.D. Martinez .50 1.25

2019 Topps Fire Relics

STATED ODDS 1:32 RETAIL
*GREEN/75: .5X TO 1.2X BASIC
*PURPLE/50: .6X TO 1.5X BASIC
MAGENTA/25: .75X TO 2X BASIC
FRAB Alex Bregman 2.50 6.00
FRABE Andrew Benintendi 2.50 6.00
FRAJ Aaron Judge 12.00 30.00
FRAV Alex Verdugo 2.00 5.00
FRBK Brad Keller 1.50 4.00
FRBT Blake Treinen 1.50 4.00
FRBW Bryse Wilson 2.00 5.00
FRCA Chance Adams 1.50 4.00
FRCC Carlos Correa 2.50 6.00
FRCF Clint Frazier 2.00 5.00
FRCM Cedric Mullins 3.00 8.00
FRCS Corey Seager 2.50 6.00
FRDJ Danny Jansen 1.50 4.00
FRDL Dawel Lugo 2.50 6.00
FRDR Dereck Rodriguez 1.50 4.00
FRFL Francisco Lindor 2.50 6.00
FRGT Gleyber Torres 5.00 12.00
FRHB Harrison Bader 2.00 5.00
FRIH Ian Happ 2.00 5.00
FRJA Jesus Aguilar 2.00 5.00
FRJB Javier Baez 3.00 8.00
FRJF Jack Flaherty 2.50 6.00
FRJH Josh Hader 2.00 5.00
FRJS Justus Sheffield 2.50 6.00
FRKA Kolby Allard 2.50 6.00
FRKB Kris Bryant 3.00 8.00
FRKS Kyle Schwarber 2.50 6.00
FRKT Kyle Tucker 4.00 10.00
FRKW Kyle Wright 2.50 6.00
FRLU Luis Urias 2.50 6.00
FRLV Luke Voit 4.00 10.00
FRMA Miguel Andujar 2.50 6.00
FRMK Michael Kopech 5.00 12.00
FRMM Miles Mikolas 2.50 6.00
FRMO Matt Olson 2.50 6.00
FRMT Mike Trout 15.00 40.00
FRNS Noah Syndergaard 2.00 5.00
FROA Ozzie Albies 2.50 6.00
FRRAJ Ronald Acuna Jr. 12.00 30.00
FRRD Rafael Devers 3.00 8.00

FRRH Rhys Hoskins 3.00 8.00
FRRL Ramon Laureano 3.00 8.00
FRROH Ryan O'Hearn 1.50 4.00
FRRT Rowdy Tellez 2.50 6.00
FRSK Scott Kingery 2.00 5.00
FRSO Shohei Ohtani 6.00 15.00
FRTS Trevor Story 2.50 6.00
FRTT Trea Turner 2.00 5.00
FRVR Victor Robles 3.00 8.00
FRWC Willson Contreras 2.00 5.00

2019 Topps Fire Smoke and Mirrors

STATED ODDS 1:14 RETAIL
*BLUE: .6X TO 1.5X BASIC
*GOLD: .75X TO 2X BASIC
SM1 Clayton Kershaw .75 2.00
SM2 Carlos Carrasco .30 .75
SM3 Mike Foltynewicz .50 1.25
SM4 Aaron Nola .40 1.00
SM5 Jameson Taillon .40 1.00
SM6 Trevor Bauer .60 1.50
SM7 German Marquez .30 .75
SM8 Jordan Hicks .40 1.00
SM9 Corey Kluber .40 1.00
SM10 Jose Berrios .40 1.00
SM11 Zack Greinke .50 1.25
SM12 Luis Severino .40 1.00
SM13 Gerrit Cole .50 1.25
SM14 Blake Snell .40 1.00
SM15 Aroldis Chapman .50 1.25

2020 Topps Fire

1 Lorenzo Cain .20 .50
2 Chris Sale .30 .75
3 Nico Hoerner RC 1.25 3.00
4 Luis Severino .25 .60
5 Shun Yamaguchi .25 .60
6 Anthony Rizzo .40 1.00
7 Brandon Crawford .25 .60
8 Pete Alonso .75 2.00
9 Blake Snell .25 .60
10 Willson Contreras .30 .75
11 Tim Lincecum .25 .60
12 Eric Hosmer .25 .60
13 Joe Mauer .25 .60
14 Jameson Taillon .25 .60
15 DJ LeMahieu .30 .75
16 Jorge Alfaro .20 .50
17 Jordan Zimmermann .25 .60
18 Ichiro .40 1.00
19 Kyle Freeland .25 .60
20 Javier Baez .40 1.00
21 Nathan Eovaldi .25 .60
22 Trey Mancini .30 .75
23 Danny Hultzen RC .40 1.00
24 Francisco Lindor .30 .75
25 Evan Longoria .25 .60
26 Michael Kopech .40 1.00
27 Clayton Kershaw .50 1.25
28 Ronald Acuna Jr. 1.25 3.00
29 Cedric Mullins .25 .60
30 Jesus Aguilar .25 .60
31 Albert Pujols .40 1.00
32 Carlos Correa .30 .75
33 Aaron Judge .75 2.00
34 Trevor Story .30 .75
35 Matt Olson .30 .75
36 Bubba Starling RC .60 1.50
37 Rafael Devers .40 1.00
38 Gerrit Cole .50 1.25
39 Ozzie Albies .30 .75
40 Danny Mendick RC .40 1.00
41 Marcus Semien .30 .75
42 Max Scherzer .30 .75
43 Matt Kemp .25 .60
44 Nick Senzel .30 .75
45 Trent Grisham RC 1.25 3.00
46 Jeff Bagwell .25 .60
47 Juan Soto 1.00 2.50
48 Jacob deGrom .60 1.50
49 Shohei Ohtani .50 1.25
50 Willy Adames .20 .50
51 Aaron Nola .25 .60
52 Ryan Braun .25 .60
53 Dylan Cease RC .50 1.25
54 John Means .30 .75
55 Jose Berrios .25 .60
56 Mookie Betts .60 1.50
57 Stephen Strasburg .30 .75
58 Joey Gallo .30 .75
59 Eugenio Suarez .25 .60
60 Ronald Guzman .20 .50
61 Cavan Biggio .40 1.00
62 Kolten Wong .25 .60
63 Tim Anderson .30 .75
64 Jose Abreu .30 .75
65 Gleyber Torres .60 1.50
66 Michael Conforto .25 .60
67 Zack Greinke .30 .75
68 Matt Thaiss RC .40 1.00
69 Joey Votto .30 .75
70 Giancarlo Stanton .30 .75
71 Bo Bichette RC 4.00 10.00
72 Josh Bell .25 .60
73 J.T. Realmuto .30 .75
74 Freddie Freeman .40 1.00
75 Gregory Polanco .25 .60
76 Gary Sanchez .30 .75
77 Junior Fernandez RC .30 .75
78 Rhys Hoskins .40 1.00
79 Randy Dobnak RC .60 1.50
80 Cody Bellinger .60 1.50
81 Jake Lamb .25 .60
82 Carlos Carrasco .20 .50
83 Ramon Laureano .25 .60
84 Dallas Keuchel .25 .60
85 Jorge Soler .30 .75
86 Trea Turner .25 .60
87 Trevor Bauer .40 1.00
88 Mike Foltynewicz .20 .50
89 Michael Brosseau RC .60 1.50
90 Byron Buxton .30 .75
91 Jesus Luzardo RC .60 1.50
92 Dee Gordon .20 .50
93 Mariano Rivera .40 1.00
94 Jorge Polanco .25 .60
95 Fernando Tatis Jr. 1.50 4.00
96 Kris Bryant .40 1.00
97 David Ortiz .30 .75
98 Aristides Aquino RC .75 2.00
99 Didi Gregorius .25 .60
100 Luis Castillo .25 .60
101 Matthew Boyd .20 .50
102 Mike Clevinger .25 .60
103 Elvis Andrus .25 .60
104 Alex Verdugo .25 .60
105 Willi Castro RC .50 1.25
106 Brusdar Graterol RC .50 1.25
107 Adbert Alzolay RC .40 1.00
108 Corey Kluber .25 .60
109 Jon Lester .25 .60
110 Dustin May RC 1.00 2.50
111 Brendan McKay RC .50 1.25
112 Austin Nola RC .50 1.25
113 A.J. Puk RC .50 1.25
114 Mauricio Dubon RC .40 1.00
115 Max Muncy .25 .60
116 Andrew McCutchen .30 .75
117 Lewis Thorpe RC .30 .75
118 Jake Fraley RC .40 1.00
119 Robinson Cano .25 .60
120 Yusei Kikuchi .25 .60
121 Nolan Arenado .50 1.25
122 Sammy Sosa .30 .75
123 Kyle Schwarber .30 .75
124 Mallex Smith .20 .50
125 Sandy Alcantara .20 .50
126 George Springer .25 .60
127 Austin Meadows .30 .75
128 Dan Vogelbach .20 .50
129 Anthony Rendon .30 .75
130 Kyle Lewis RC 2.00 5.00
131 Cole Tucker .30 .75
132 Manny Machado .30 .75
133 Robbie Ray .20 .50
134 Salvador Perez .25 .60
135 Nick Solak RC 1.25 3.00
136 Shane Bieber .30 .75
137 Zack Wheeler .25 .60
138 Jose Quintana .20 .50
139 Eloy Jimenez .60 1.50
140 Robel Garcia RC .30 .75
141 Jordan Yamamoto RC .30 .75
142 Walker Buehler .40 1.00
143 Domingo Leyba RC .40 1.00
144 Alex Cobb .20 .50
145 Noah Syndergaard .25 .60
146 Buster Posey .40 1.00
147 Nelson Cruz .30 .75
148 Vladimir Guerrero Jr. .50 1.25
149 Paul DeJong .30 .75
150 Eddie Rosario .25 .60
151 Brandon Belt .25 .60
152 Justin Dunn RC .40 1.00
153 Hyun-Jin Ryu .25 .60
154 Jeimer Candelario .20 .50
155 Luis Robert RC 2.50 6.00
156 Chris Paddack .30 .75
157 Yoan Moncada .30 .75
158 Bryce Harper .50 1.25
159 Ryan Zimmerman .25 .60
160 Kole Calhoun .20 .50
161 Lourdes Gurriel Jr. .25 .60
162 Alex Bregman .30 .75
163 Austin Hedges .20 .50
164 Sean Manaea .20 .50
165 Jackie Bradley Jr. .30 .75
166 Miguel Cabrera .30 .75
167 Edwin Rios RC .75 2.00
168 Miguel Sano .25 .60
169 Seth Brown RC .30 .75
170 Justin Verlander .30 .75
171 Shogo Akiyama .30 .75
172 Jose Altuve .25 .60
173 Andres Munoz RC .50 1.25
174 Whit Merrifield .30 .75
175 Jack Flaherty .30 .75
176 Ken Griffey Jr. .60 1.50
177 Victor Robles .40 1.00
178 Brendan Rodgers .30 .75
179 Brandon Lowe .25 .60
180 Nick Ahmed .20 .50
181 Tony Gwynn .30 .75
182 Gavin Lux RC 1.50 4.00
183 Josh Hader RC .40 1.00
184 Paul Goldschmidt .30 .75
185 Kwang-Hyun Kim .40 1.00
186 Sam Hilliard RC .50 1.25
187 Yoshi Tsutsugo RC .75 2.00
188 Tony Gonsolin RC 1.25 3.00
189 Ketel Marte .25 .60
190 Matt Chapman .30 .75
191 Corey Seager .30 .75
192 Jose Ramirez .25 .60
193 Barry Zito .25 .60
194 Andrew Benintendi .30 .75
195 Yordan Alvarez RC 3.00 8.00
196 Jakob Junis .20 .50
197 Mike Trout 1.50 4.00
198 Christian Yelich .40 1.00
199 Max Kepler .25 .60
200 Patrick Corbin .25 .60

2020 Topps Fire Green

*GREEN: 1.5X TO 4X BASIC
*GREEN RC: 1X TO 2.5X BASIC
STATED ODDS 1:XX HOBBY
STATED PRINT RUN 199 SER.#'d SETS
95 Fernando Tatis Jr. 8.00 20.00
130 Kyle Lewis 10.00 25.00
176 Ken Griffey Jr. 15.00 40.00
182 Gavin Lux 8.00 20.00

2020 Topps Fire Magenta

*MAGENTA: 6X TO 15X BASIC
*MAGENTA RC: 4X TO 10X BASIC
STATED ODDS 1:XX HOBBY
STATED PRINT RUN 25 SER.#'d SETS
65 Gleyber Torres 15.00 40.00
95 Fernando Tatis Jr. 40.00 100.00
130 Kyle Lewis 40.00 100.00
176 Ken Griffey Jr. 75.00 200.00
182 Gavin Lux 30.00 80.00

2020 Topps Fire Orange

*ORANGE: 1.5X TO 4X BASIC
*ORANGE RC: 1X TO 2.5X BASIC
STATED ODDS 1:XX HOBBY
STATED PRINT RUN 299 SER.#'d SETS
95 Fernando Tatis Jr. 8.00 20.00
130 Kyle Lewis 10.00 25.00
176 Ken Griffey Jr. 12.00 30.00
182 Gavin Lux 8.00 20.00

2020 Topps Fire Purple

*PURPLE: 2X TO 5X BASIC
*PURPLE RC: 1.2X TO 3X BASIC
STATED ODDS 1:XX HOBBY
STATED PRINT RUN 99 SER.#'d SETS
95 Fernando Tatis Jr. 12.00 30.00
130 Kyle Lewis 12.00 30.00
176 Ken Griffey Jr. 20.00 50.00
182 Gavin Lux 10.00 25.00

2020 Topps Fire Arms Ablaze

STATED ODDS 1:XX HOBBY
AA1 Aaron Judge 1.25 3.00
AA2 Yasiel Puig .50 1.25
AA3 Trevor Story .50 1.25
AA4 Ronald Acuna Jr. 2.00 5.00
AA5 Andrelton Simmons .30 .75
AA6 Cody Bellinger 1.00 2.50
AA7 Jackie Bradley Jr. .50 1.25
AA8 Nolan Arenado .75 2.00
AA9 Bryce Harper .75 2.00
AA10 Javier Baez .60 1.50
AA11 Mookie Betts 1.00 2.50
AA12 Matt Chapman .50 1.25
AA13 Carlos Correa .50 1.25
AA14 Aaron Hicks .40 1.00
AA15 Trea Turner .40 1.00
AA16 Manny Machado .50 1.25
AA17 Ramon Laureano .40 1.00
AA18 Orlando Arcia .30 .75
AA19 Jason Heyward .40 1.00
AA20 Luis Robert 10.00 25.00

2020 Topps Fire Arms Ablaze Gold Minted

*GOLD: .8X TO 2X BASIC
STATED ODDS 1:XX HOBBY
AA20 Luis Robert 15.00 40.00

2020 Topps Fire Autographs

STATED ODDS 1:XX HOBBY
EXCHANGE DEADLINE 7/31/22
FAAA Adbert Alzolay 3.00 8.00
FAAN Austin Nola 4.00 10.00
FAAP A.J. Puk 4.00 10.00
FABA Bryan Abreu 2.50 6.00
FABM Brendan McKay 4.00 10.00
FABR Brendan Rodgers 4.00 10.00
FACA Chance Adams 2.50 6.00
FACK Carter Kieboom 3.00 8.00
FADC Dylan Cease 4.00 10.00
FADL Domingo Leyba 3.00 8.00
FADN Dom Nunez 3.00 8.00
FAGC Griffin Canning 4.00 10.00
FAGL Gavin Lux 20.00 50.00
FAID Isan Diaz 8.00 20.00
FAJL Jesus Luzardo 5.00 12.00
FAJM Jeff McNeil 3.00 8.00
FAJP Joe Palumbo 2.50 6.00
FAJR Jake Rogers 2.50 6.00
FAJY Jordan Yamamoto 2.50 6.00
FAKH Keston Hiura 6.00 15.00
FAKK Kwang-Hyun Kim 15.00 40.00
FALA Logan Allen 2.50 6.00
FAMB Matt Beaty 3.00 8.00
FAMC Michael Chavis 3.00 8.00
FARG Robel Garcia 2.50 6.00
FARR Rangel Ravelo 3.00 8.00
FASA Shogo Akiyama 4.00 10.00
FASM Sean Murphy 4.00 10.00
FASY Shun Yamaguchi 3.00 8.00
FATG Tony Gonsolin 8.00 20.00
FATL Tim Lopes 3.00 8.00
FAVR Victor Robles 5.00 12.00
FAWM Whit Merrifield 4.00 10.00
FAWS Will Smith 4.00 10.00
FAYA Yordan Alvarez 25.00 60.00
FAYC Yu Chang 4.00 10.00
FAZP Zach Plesac 6.00 15.00
FAAAQ Aristides Aquino 10.00 25.00
FADMA Dustin May 20.00 50.00
FAJBA Jake Bauers 3.00 8.00
FAJLO Jonathan Loaisiga 3.00 8.00
FAJMO Jordan Montgomery 2.50 6.00
FAMBR Michael Brosseau 5.00 12.00
FAMTH Matt Thaiss 3.00 8.00
FANSO Nick Solak 5.00 12.00

2020 Topps Fire Autographs Green

*GREEN/75: .5X TO 1.2X BASIC
STATED ODDS 1:XX HOBBY
STATED PRINT RUN 75 SER.#'d SETS
EXCHANGE DEADLINE 7/31/22
FAGL Gavin Lux 30.00 80.00
FALR Luis Robert 150.00 400.00
FAPA Pete Alonso 40.00 100.00
FAVG Vladimir Guerrero Jr. 25.00 60.00
FAARI Austin Riley 15.00 40.00

2020 Topps Fire Autographs Magenta

*MAGENTA/25: .8X TO 2X BASIC
STATED ODDS 1:XX HOBBY
STATED PRINT RUN 25 SER.#'d SETS
EXCHANGE DEADLINE 7/31/22
FABB Bo Bichette EXCH 100.00 250.00
FACY Christian Yelich 30.00 80.00
FAEJ Eloy Jimenez 50.00 120.00
FAGL Gavin Lux 75.00 200.00
FAGT Gleyber Torres 40.00 100.00
FAJd Jacob deGrom 75.00 200.00
FALR Luis Robert 250.00 600.00
FAMT Mike Trout 200.00 500.00
FAPA Pete Alonso 60.00 150.00
FASO Shohei Ohtani 60.00 150.00
FAVG Vladimir Guerrero Jr. 40.00 100.00
FAARI Austin Riley 25.00 60.00
FAJMA J.D. Martinez 10.00 25.00
FAJSO Juan Soto 60.00 150.00

2020 Topps Fire Autographs Orange

*ORANGE/99: .5X TO 1.2X BASIC
STATED ODDS 1:XX HOBBY
STATED PRINT RUN 99 SER.#'d SETS
EXCHANGE DEADLINE 7/31/22
FAGL Gavin Lux 30.00 80.00
FAPA Pete Alonso 40.00 100.00
FAARI Austin Riley 15.00 40.00

2020 Topps Fire Autographs Purple

*PURPLE/50: .6X TO 1.5X BASIC
STATED ODDS 1:XX HOBBY
STATED PRINT RUN 50 SER.#'d SETS
EXCHANGE DEADLINE 7/31/22
FABB Bo Bichette EXCH 75.00 200.00
FAEJ Eloy Jimenez 40.00 100.00
FAGL Gavin Lux 60.00 150.00
FAJd Jacob deGrom 30.00 80.00
FALR Luis Robert 200.00 500.00
FAPA Pete Alonso 50.00 120.00
FAVG Vladimir Guerrero Jr. 30.00 80.00
FAARI Austin Riley 20.00 50.00
FAJMA J.D. Martinez 8.00 20.00
FAJSO Juan Soto 50.00 120.00

2020 Topps Fire Dual Autographs

STATED ODDS 1:XX HOBBY
STATED PRINT RUN 20 SER.#'d SETS
EXCHANGE DEADLINE 7/31/22
DAAA J.Altuve/Y.Alvarez 100.00 250.00
DAAD J.deGrom/P.Alonso 125.00 300.00
DABM X.Bogaerts/J.Martinez
DAHH R.Hoskins/B.Harper
DALM G.Lux/D.May
DARJ L.Robert/E.Jimenez 250.00 600.00
DASM B.Snell/B.McKay
DAAAL Y.Alvarez/P.Alonso
DAAAQ A.Aquino/N.Senzel
DARAJ A.Riley/R.Acuna Jr. 100.00 250.00

2020 Topps Fire Fired Up

STATED ODDS 1:XX HOBBY
*GOLD: .8X TO 2X BASIC
FIU1 Bryce Harper .75 2.00
FIU2 Bo Bichette 5.00 12.00
FIU3 Aristides Aquino .75 2.00
FIU4 Francisco Lindor .50 1.25
FIU5 Rafael Devers .60 1.50
FIU6 Cody Bellinger 1.00 2.50
FIU7 Javier Baez .60 1.50
FIU8 Justin Verlander .50 1.25
FIU9 Alex Bregman .50 1.25
FIU10 Nolan Arenado .75 2.00
FIU11 Christian Yelich .60 1.50
FIU12 Mookie Betts 1.00 2.50
FIU13 Charlie Blackmon .50 1.25
FIU14 Gleyber Torres 1.00 2.50
FIU15 Manny Machado .50 1.25

2020 Topps Fire Flame Throwers

STATED ODDS 1:XX HOBBY
*GOLD: .8X TO 2X BASIC
FT1 Jacob deGrom 1.00 2.50
FT2 Raisel Iglesias .30 .75
FT3 Josh Hader .40 1.00
FT4 Aroldis Chapman .50 1.25
FT5 Shane Bieber .50 1.25
FT6 Jack Flaherty .50 1.25
FT7 Noah Syndergaard .40 1.00
FT8 Mike Soroka .50 1.25
FT9 Aaron Nola .40 1.00
FT10 Gerrit Cole .75 2.00
FT11 Lucas Giolito .40 1.00
FT12 Brendan McKay .50 1.25
FT13 Stephen Strasburg .50 1.25
FT14 Walker Buehler .60 1.50
FT15 Max Scherzer .50 1.25

2020 Topps Fire Power and Pride

STATED ODDS 1:XX HOBBY
*GOLD: .8X TO 2X BASIC
PP1 Shohei Ohtani .75 2.00
PP2 Ronald Acuna Jr. 2.00 5.00
PP3 Aroldis Chapman .50 1.25
PP4 Francisco Lindor .50 1.25
PP5 Xander Bogaerts .50 1.25
PP6 Eugenio Suarez .40 1.00
PP7 Aristides Aquino .75 2.00
PP8 Juan Soto 1.50 4.00
PP9 Aaron Judge 1.25 3.00
PP10 Jose Berrios .40 1.00
PP11 Cody Bellinger 1.00 2.50
PP12 Javier Baez .60 1.50
PP13 Jose Altuve .40 1.00
PP14 Freddie Freeman .60 1.50
PP15 Raisel Iglesias .30 .75

2020 Topps Fire Shattering Stats

STATED ODDS 1:XX HOBBY
*GOLD: .8X TO 2X BASIC
SS1 Pete Alonso 1.25 3.00
SS2 Ronald Acuna Jr. 2.00 5.00
SS3 Mike Trout 2.50 6.00
SS4 Alex Rodriguez .60 1.50
SS5 Miguel Cabrera .50 1.25
SS6 Rickey Henderson .50 1.25
SS7 Kris Bryant .60 1.50
SS8 Nolan Arenado .75 2.00
SS9 Albert Pujols .60 1.50
SS10 Mariano Rivera .60 1.50
SS11 Jacob deGrom 1.00 2.50
SS12 Cody Bellinger 1.00 2.50
SS13 Shohei Ohtani .75 2.00
SS14 Nelson Cruz .50 1.25
SS15 Aaron Judge 1.25 3.00

2020 Topps Fire Smoke and Mirrors

STATED ODDS 1:XX HOBBY
*GOLD: .8X TO 2X BASIC
SM1 Blake Snell .40 1.00
SM2 Andrew Miller .40 1.00
SM3 Jose Berrios .40 1.00
SM4 Max Scherzer .50 1.25
SM5 Chris Sale .50 1.25
SM6 Jameson Taillon .40 1.00
SM7 Josh Hader .40 1.00
SM8 Clayton Kershaw .75 2.00
SM9 Adam Ottavino .40 1.00
SM10 Joey Lucchesi .30 .75
SM11 Raisel Iglesias .30 .75
SM12 Jacob deGrom 1.00 2.50
SM13 Corey Kluber .40 1.00
SM14 Brendan McKay .50 1.25
SM15 Aroldis Chapman .50 1.25
SM16 Shohei Ohtani 2.50 6.00
SM17 Shun Yamaguchi .40 1.00
SM18 Justin Verlander .50 1.25
SM19 Michael Kopech .60 1.50
SM20 Jake Arrieta .40 1.00

2012 Topps Five Star

STATED PRINT RUN 80 SER.#'d SETS
1 Bryce Harper RC 125.00 250.00
2 Eddie Murray 2.50 6.00
3 Johnny Bench 4.00 10.00
4 Buster Posey 5.00 12.00
5 Ichiro Suzuki 5.00 12.00
6 Stephen Strasburg 4.00 10.00
7 Jered Weaver 3.00 8.00
8 Roy Halladay 3.00 8.00
9 CC Sabathia 3.00 8.00
10 Ryan Braun 2.50 6.00
11 Jacoby Ellsbury 3.00 8.00
12 Don Mattingly 8.00 20.00
13 Harmon Killebrew 4.00 10.00
14 Giancarlo Stanton 4.00 10.00
15 Alex Rodriguez 5.00 12.00
16 David Ortiz 4.00 10.00
17 Andre Ethier 3.00 8.00
18 Curtis Granderson 3.00 8.00
19 Derek Jeter 10.00 25.00
20 Joey Votto 4.00 10.00
21 Willie Mays 8.00 20.00
22 Ralph Kiner 2.50 6.00
23 Cole Hamels 3.00 8.00
24 Robinson Cano 3.00 8.00
25 Mariano Rivera 5.00 12.00
26 Felix Hernandez 3.00 8.00
27 Ian Kinsler 3.00 8.00
28 Joe DiMaggio 8.00 20.00
29 Paul Konerko 2.50 6.00
30 Babe Ruth 10.00 25.00
31 Carlos Gonzalez 3.00 8.00
32 Troy Tulowitzki 4.00 10.00
33 Mike Schmidt 6.00 15.00
34 Tom Seaver 2.50 6.00
35 Albert Pujols 5.00 12.00
36 David Price 3.00 8.00
37 Mike Trout 125.00 300.00
38 Andrew McCutchen 4.00 10.00
39 Adam Jones 3.00 8.00
40 Sandy Koufax 8.00 20.00
41 Joe Mauer 3.00 8.00
42 Jackie Robinson 4.00 10.00
43 George Brett 8.00 20.00
44 Dave Winfield 2.50 6.00
45 Jose Bautista 3.00 8.00
46 David Freese 2.50 6.00
47 Tim Lincecum 3.00 8.00
48 Prince Fielder 3.00 8.00
49 Adrian Gonzalez 3.00 8.00
50 Josh Hamilton 3.00 8.00
51 Roberto Clemente 10.00 25.00
52 Dustin Pedroia 4.00 10.00
53 Carl Yastrzemski 6.00 15.00
54 Nolan Ryan 12.00 30.00
55 Joe Morgan 2.50 6.00
56 Cliff Lee 3.00 8.00
57 Evan Longoria 3.00 8.00
58 David Wright 3.00 8.00
59 Yogi Berra 4.00 10.00
60 Ken Griffey Jr. 8.00 20.00
61 Yu Darvish RC 20.00 50.00
62 Mark Trumbo 2.50 6.00
63 Ty Cobb 6.00 15.00
64 Wade Boggs 2.50 6.00
65 Justin Verlander 4.00 10.00
66 Reggie Jackson 2.50 6.00
67 Cal Ripken Jr. 12.00 30.00
68 Johan Santana 3.00 8.00
69 Starlin Castro 3.00 8.00
70 Clayton Kershaw 6.00 15.00
71 Hanley Ramirez 3.00 8.00
72 Jim Palmer 2.50 6.00
73 Rod Carew 2.50 6.00
74 Justin Upton 3.00 8.00
75 Rickey Henderson 4.00 10.00
76 Matt Kemp 3.00 8.00
77 Mickey Mantle 12.00 30.00
78 Bob Gibson 2.50 6.00
79 Lou Gehrig 8.00 20.00
80 Miguel Cabrera 4.00 10.00

2012 Topps Five Star Active Autographs

PRINT RUNS B/WN 40-150 COPIES PER
EXCHANGE DEADLINE 10/31/2015
AE Andre Ethier/50 10.00 25.00
AG Adrian Gonzalez/150 6.00 15.00
AP Albert Pujols/40 100.00 200.00
AR Anthony Rizzo/150 15.00 40.00
BH Bryce Harper/150 125.00 250.00
BL Brett Lawrie/150 6.00 15.00
BP Buster Posey/150 40.00 80.00
CJ Chipper Jones/150 30.00 80.00
CJW C.J. Wilson/150 6.00 15.00
CK Clayton Kershaw/150 40.00 80.00
DF David Freese/150 6.00 15.00
DP Dustin Pedroia/150 15.00 40.00
DU Dan Uggla/150 6.00 15.00
DW David Wright/150 12.00 30.00
EH Eric Hosmer/150 15.00 40.00
EL Evan Longoria/106 30.00 60.00
GS Giancarlo Stanton/150 20.00 50.00
JBA Jose Bautista/150 12.00 30.00
JBR Jay Bruce/150 10.00 25.00
JHA Josh Hamilton/150 12.00 30.00
JHE Jason Heyward/150 12.00 30.00
JM Joe Mauer/150 15.00 40.00
JMO Jesus Montero/150 6.00 15.00
JW Jered Weaver EXCH 8.00 20.00
MB Madison Bumgarner/113 15.00 40.00
MC Miguel Cabrera/106 60.00 120.00
MK Matt Kemp/150 10.00 25.00
MM Matt Moore/150 6.00 15.00
MN Mike Napoli/113 6.00 15.00
MT Mike Trout/150 300.00 800.00
NC Nelson Cruz/150 6.00 15.00
PF Prince Fielder/150 20.00 50.00
PG Paul Goldschmidt/150 15.00 40.00
PS Pablo Sandoval/150 6.00 15.00
RB Ryan Braun/150 10.00 25.00
RC Robinson Cano 15.00 40.00
RHA Roy Halladay EXCH 25.00 60.00
RZ Ryan Zimmerman/150 6.00 15.00
SC Starlin Castro/150 8.00 20.00
TB Trevor Bauer/150 15.00 40.00
WMB Will Middlebrooks/150 12.00 30.00
YC Yoenis Cespedes/150 10.00 25.00
YD Yu Darvish/150 75.00 200.00

2012 Topps Five Star Jumbo Jersey

PRINT RUNS B/WN 54-92 COPIES PER
I Ichiro Suzuki 15.00 40.00
AB Adrian Beltre 5.00 12.00
AE Andre Ethier 6.00 15.00
AG Adrian Gonzalez 8.00 20.00
AM Andrew McCutchen 8.00 20.00
AP Albert Pujols 12.50 30.00
AR Alex Rodriguez 10.00 25.00
BH Bryce Harper 20.00 50.00
BP Buster Posey 12.50 30.00
CCS CC Sabathia 8.00 20.00
CG Carlos Gonzalez 5.00 12.00
CGA Curtis Granderson 10.00 25.00
CH Cole Hamels 10.00 25.00
CJ Chipper Jones 10.00 25.00
CK Clayton Kershaw 8.00 20.00
CL Cliff Lee 10.00 25.00
CW C.J. Wilson 5.00 12.00
DF David Freese 12.50 30.00
DJ Derek Jeter 30.00 60.00
DO David Ortiz 8.00 20.00
DP Dustin Pedroia 6.00 15.00
DPR David Price 6.00 15.00
DW David Wright 6.00 15.00
EL Evan Longoria 8.00 20.00
FH Felix Hernandez 8.00 20.00
GS Giancarlo Stanton 6.00 15.00
HR Hanley Ramirez 5.00 12.00
IK Ian Kinsler 5.00 12.00
JB Jose Bautista 6.00 15.00
JE Jacoby Ellsbury 10.00 25.00
JH Josh Hamilton 10.00 25.00
JM Joe Mauer 8.00 20.00
JS Johan Santana 6.00 15.00
JU Justin Upton 5.00 12.00
JV Justin Verlander 12.50 30.00
JVO Joey Votto 10.00 25.00
JW Jered Weaver 5.00 12.00
MC Miguel Cabrera 12.50 30.00
MK Matt Kemp 8.00 20.00
MM Matt Moore 5.00 12.00
MR Mariano Rivera 15.00 40.00
MT Mike Trout 125.00 300.00
PF Prince Fielder 6.00 15.00
PK Paul Konerko 10.00 25.00
RB Ryan Braun 8.00 20.00
RH Roy Halladay 10.00 25.00
SC Starlin Castro 8.00 20.00
SS Stephen Strasburg/54 12.50 30.00
TL Tim Lincecum 10.00 25.00
TT Troy Tulowitzki 8.00 20.00
YD Yu Darvish 15.00 40.00

2012 Topps Five Star Jumbo Relic Autograph Books

STATED ODDS 1:30 HOBBY
STATED PRINT RUN 49 SER.#'d SETS
EXCHANGE DEADLINE 10/31/2015
BH Bryce Harper 250.00 350.00
JB Jose Bautista 20.00 50.00
JW Jered Weaver EXCH 20.00 50.00
MH Matt Holliday EXCH 40.00 80.00
SK Sandy Koufax 400.00 600.00

2012 Topps Five Star Legends Relics

STATED ODDS 1:12 HOBBY
STATED PRINT RUN 25 SER.#'d SETS
BR Babe Ruth 100.00 200.00
CY Carl Yastrzemski 20.00 50.00
DW Dave Winfield 10.00 25.00
EB Ernie Banks 20.00 50.00
JB Johnny Bench 20.00 50.00
JD Joe DiMaggio 30.00 60.00
JR Jackie Robinson 40.00 80.00
MM Mickey Mantle 200.00 300.00
MS Mike Schmidt 12.50 30.00
RC Roberto Clemente 125.00 250.00
RH Rickey Henderson 30.00 60.00
RK Ralph Kiner 12.50 30.00
RS Ryne Sandberg 15.00 40.00
SC Steve Carlton 10.00 25.00
SK Sandy Koufax 50.00 100.00
SM Stan Musial 20.00 50.00
TC Ty Cobb 30.00 60.00
TG Tony Gwynn 20.00 50.00
TS Tom Seaver 30.00 60.00
WM Willie Mays 50.00 100.00
WMC Willie McCovey 10.00 25.00

2012 Topps Five Star Quad Relic Autograph Books

STATED ODDS 1:31 HOBBY
PRINT RUNS B/WN 23-49 COPIES PER
EXCHANGE DEADLINE 10/31/2015
EL Evan Longoria/49 50.00 100.00
JV Justin Verlander/49 60.00 120.00
MT Mike Trout/49 300.00 800.00
YD Yu Darvish/49 150.00 250.00

2012 Topps Five Star Relic Autographs

PRINT RUNS B/WN 9-97 COPIES PER
NO PRICING ON QTY 25 OR LESS
EXCHANGE DEADLINE 10/31/2015
AB Albert Belle/97 8.00 20.00
AD Andre Dawson/55 12.50 30.00
AE Andre Ethier/97 8.00 20.00
AG Adrian Gonzalez/97 6.00 15.00
AK Al Kaline/97 20.00 50.00
BL Brett Lawrie/97 6.00 15.00
BP Brandon Phillips/73 5.00 12.00
CF Carlton Fisk/43 20.00 50.00
CG Carlos Gonzalez/97 10.00 25.00
CJ Chipper Jones/97 50.00 120.00
CK Clayton Kershaw/97 40.00 80.00
CW C.J. Wilson/97 10.00 25.00
DF David Freese 15.00 40.00
DM Dale Murphy/97 20.00 50.00
DP Dustin Pedroia/97 15.00 40.00
DU Dan Uggla/97 8.00 20.00
EH Eric Hosmer/97 15.00 40.00
FH Felix Hernandez EXCH 20.00 50.00
FT Frank Thomas/97 25.00 60.00
GG Gio Gonzalez/97 6.00 15.00
GS Giancarlo Stanton/97 20.00 50.00
HA Hank Aaron/97 150.00 300.00
JB Jose Bautista/97 15.00 40.00
JH Josh Hamilton/97 12.50 30.00
JM Jesus Montero/97 10.00 25.00
JU Justin Upton/97 10.00 25.00
MC Miguel Cabrera/97 50.00 100.00
MK Matt Kemp/97 10.00 25.00
MM Matt Moore/97 8.00 20.00
MN Mike Napoli/73 6.00 15.00
MS Mike Schmidt/97 25.00 60.00
PF Prince Fielder/97 30.00 60.00
PM Paul Molitor/97 12.00 30.00
PO Paul O'Neill/97 12.50 30.00
PS Pablo Sandoval/97 6.00 15.00
RB Ryan Braun/97 8.00 20.00
RS Ryne Sandberg/97 25.00 60.00
SC Starlin Castro/97 8.00 20.00
TG Tony Gwynn/68 30.00 80.00
WC Will Clark/97 20.00 50.00
YC Yoenis Cespedes/97 20.00 50.00

2012 Topps Five Star Relic Autographs Gold

*GOLD: .4X TO 1X BASIC
STATED ODDS 1:4
PRINT RUNS B/WN 43-55 COPIES PER
EXCHANGE DEADLINE 10/31/2015

2012 Topps Five Star Retired Autographs

PRINT RUNS B/WN 25-208 COPIES PER
EXCHANGE DEADLINE 10/31/2015
AB Albert Belle/208 6.00 15.00
AD Andre Dawson/106 15.00 40.00
AK Al Kaline/208 20.00 50.00
BB Bill Buckner/208 10.00 25.00
BG Bob Gibson/106 20.00 50.00
BW Billy Williams/208 12.50 30.00
CF Carlton Fisk/106 20.00 50.00
CFI Cecil Fielder/208 10.00 25.00
CR Cal Ripken Jr./40 75.00 150.00
CY Carl Yastrzemski/62 40.00 80.00
DE Dennis Eckersley/208 6.00 15.00
DK Dave Kingman/208 6.00 15.00
DM Dale Murphy/208 6.00 15.00
EB Ernie Banks/62 60.00 150.00
EM Edgar Martinez/208 10.00 25.00
FJ Fergie Jenkins/208 6.00 15.00
FR Frank Robinson/62 30.00 60.00
GB George Bell/208 8.00 20.00
HA Hank Aaron/208 125.00 300.00
JB Johnny Bench/62 25.00 60.00
JK John Kruk/208 6.00 15.00
JMA Juan Marichal/208 12.50 30.00
JS John Smoltz/208 15.00 40.00
KG Ken Griffey Jr./62 75.00 150.00
KGS Ken Griffey Sr./208 8.00 20.00
LT Luis Tiant/208 6.00 15.00
MS Mike Schmidt/106 30.00 60.00
MW Maury Wills/208 12.00 30.00
NR Nolan Ryan/62 40.00 100.00
OC Orlando Cepeda/208 12.00 30.00
PM Paul Molitor/208 12.00 30.00
PO Paul O'Neill/106 10.00 25.00
RH Rickey Henderson/62 40.00 100.00
RJ Reggie Jackson/62 30.00 60.00
RS Ryne Sandberg/106 30.00 60.00
RV Robin Ventura/208 6.00 15.00
SK Sandy Koufax/25 200.00 400.00
SM Stan Musial/62 30.00 80.00
VB Vida Blue/208 4.00 10.00
WC Will Clark/208 12.00 30.00
WM Willie Mays/25 200.00 300.00

2012 Topps Five Star Silver Ink Autographs

PRINT RUNS B/WN 69-99 COPIES PER
EXCHANGE DEADLINE 10/31/2015
AB Albert Belle/99 6.00 15.00
AD Andre Dawson/99 10.00 25.00
AE Andre Ethier/99 6.00 15.00
AJ Adam Jones/99 6.00 15.00
AP Andy Pettitte/99 20.00 50.00
BB Bill Buckner/99 8.00 20.00
BL Brett Lawrie/99 10.00 25.00
BW Billy Williams/99 6.00 15.00
CG Carlos Gonzalez/99 10.00 25.00
CK Clayton Kershaw/99 40.00 100.00
CS Chris Sale/99 10.00 25.00
CW C.J. Wilson/99 8.00 20.00
DE Dennis Eckersley/99 10.00 25.00
DF David Freese/99 15.00 40.00
DK Dave Kingman/99 10.00 25.00
DM Dale Murphy/99 12.50 30.00
DW David Wright/99 15.00 40.00
EM Edgar Martinez/99 12.50 30.00
FF Freddie Freeman/99 10.00 25.00
FJ Fergie Jenkins/99 6.00 15.00
GF George Foster/99 10.00 25.00
GS Giancarlo Stanton/99 30.00 60.00
HR Hanley Ramirez/99 12.50 30.00
JB Jay Bruce/99 10.00 25.00
JH Jeremy Hellickson/99 10.00 25.00
JK John Kruk/99 10.00 25.00
JM Juan Marichal/99 10.00 25.00
JMO Jesus Montero/99 8.00 20.00
JP Jim Palmer/99 10.00 25.00
JR Jim Rice/99 10.00 25.00
KG Ken Griffey Jr./99 75.00 150.00
KGS Ken Griffey Sr./99 10.00 25.00
LT Luis Tiant/99 6.00 15.00
MK Matt Kemp/99 12.50 30.00
MM Matt Moore/99 10.00 25.00
MT Mike Trout/99 300.00 800.00
MW Maury Wills/99 10.00 25.00
NC Nelson Cruz/99 6.00 15.00
PO Paul O'Neill/99 10.00 25.00
RAD R.A. Dickey/99 10.00 25.00
RC Robinson Cano/99 15.00 40.00
RV Robin Ventura/75 10.00 25.00
SC Starlin Castro/99 10.00 25.00

SK Sandy Koufax/69 150.00 250.00
TP Terry Pendleton/99 6.00 15.00
VB Vida Blue/99 6.00 15.00
WC Will Clark/99 15.00 40.00
WM Will Middlebrooks/99 3.00 8.00
YC Yoenis Cespedes/99 10.00 25.00

2012 Topps Five Star Triple Relic Autograph Books

STATED ODDS 1:30 HOBBY
STATED PRINT RUN 49 SER.#'d SETS
EXCHANGE DEADLINE 10/31/2015
DM Don Mattingly 75.00 150.00
DW David Wright 25.00 60.00
MS Mike Schmidt 60.00 120.00
RB Ryan Braun 30.00 60.00
SM Stan Musial 150.00 300.00

2013 Topps Five Star

STATED PRINT RUN 75 SER.#'d SETS
1 Buster Posey 8.00 20.00
2 Zack Wheeler RC 10.00 25.00
3 Yoenis Cespedes 6.00 15.00
4 Whitey Ford 6.00 15.00
5 Willie Stargell 5.00 12.00
6 Giancarlo Stanton 6.00 15.00
7 Troy Tulowitzki 6.00 15.00
8 Adam Jones 5.00 12.00
9 Adrian Beltre 6.00 15.00
10 Shelby Miller RC 12.00 30.00
11 Ryan Braun 5.00 12.00
12 Lou Gehrig 12.00 30.00
13 Babe Ruth 15.00 40.00
14 Wade Boggs 10.00 25.00
15 Adam Wainwright 5.00 12.00
16 Ozzie Smith 8.00 20.00
17 Don Mattingly 12.00 30.00
18 Jose Bautista 5.00 12.00
19 Mike Schmidt 10.00 25.00
20 Roberto Clemente 25.00 60.00
21 Prince Fielder 5.00 12.00
22 Matt Cain 5.00 12.00
23 Derek Jeter 20.00 50.00
24 Ted Williams 12.00 30.00
25 Bo Jackson 6.00 15.00
26 Robinson Cano 5.00 12.00
27 Willie Mays 12.00 30.00
28 Miguel Cabrera 12.00 30.00
29 Josh Hamilton 5.00 12.00
30 Stan Musial 10.00 25.00
31 Bob Gibson 5.00 12.00
32 Andrew McCutchen 6.00 15.00
33 Joey Votto 10.00 25.00
34 Gerrit Cole RC 12.00 30.00
35 CC Sabathia 5.00 12.00
36 Mike Trout 50.00 125.00
37 Monte Irvin 4.00 10.00
38 Wil Myers RC 8.00 20.00
39 Cliff Lee 5.00 12.00
40 Fergie Jenkins 6.00 15.00
41 Clayton Kershaw 12.50 30.00
42 Matt Harvey 5.00 12.00
43 Robin Yount 6.00 15.00
44 John Smoltz 6.00 15.00
45 Mike Zunino RC 8.00 20.00
46 Ken Griffey Jr. 12.00 30.00
47 Al Kaline 6.00 15.00
48 Aroldis Chapman 6.00 15.00
49 Johnny Bench 6.00 15.00
50 Bryce Harper 15.00 40.00
51 Paul Molitor 6.00 15.00
52 Alex Rodriguez 8.00 20.00
53 George Kell 5.00 12.00
54 Yadier Molina 8.00 20.00
55 Juan Marichal 5.00 12.00
56 Ryan Howard 5.00 12.00
57 R.A. Dickey 5.00 12.00
58 Jurickson Profar RC 6.00 15.00
59 Frank Robinson 5.00 12.00
60 Yasiel Puig RC 75.00 150.00
61 Lou Brock 5.00 12.00
62 Evan Longoria 5.00 12.00
63 Bob Feller 10.00 25.00
64 Gary Carter 5.00 12.00
65 Harmon Killebrew 6.00 15.00
66 Carlos Gonzalez 5.00 12.00
67 Anthony Rendon RC 12.00 30.00
68 Stephen Strasburg 6.00 15.00
69 Carlton Fisk 5.00 12.00
70 Paul Goldschmidt 6.00 15.00
71 Andre Dawson 5.00 12.00
72 Mariano Rivera 8.00 20.00
73 Joe Mauer 5.00 12.00
74 Felix Hernandez 8.00 20.00
75 Dylan Bundy RC 12.00 30.00
76 Reggie Jackson 5.00 12.00
77 Manny Machado RC 50.00 100.00
78 Nolan Ryan 12.00 30.00
79 Ernie Banks 6.00 15.00
80 Adrian Gonzalez 5.00 12.00
81 Cal Ripken Jr. 20.00 50.00
82 Larry Doby 4.00 10.00
83 Dustin Pedroia 6.00 15.00
84 Billy Williams 5.00 12.00
85 Cole Hamels 5.00 12.00
86 Frank Thomas 8.00 20.00
87 Albert Pujols 8.00 20.00
88 Chipper Jones 6.00 15.00
89 Rickey Henderson 6.00 15.00
90 Sandy Koufax 15.00 40.00
91 Justin Verlander 6.00 15.00
92 Chris Davis 5.00 12.00
93 David Price 5.00 12.00
94 Chris Sale 6.00 15.00
95 Jacoby Ellsbury 8.00 20.00
96 Ryne Sandberg 12.50 30.00
97 David Wright 12.50 30.00
98 Matt Kemp 5.00 12.00
99 Ty Cobb 10.00 25.00
100 Yu Darvish 10.00 25.00

2013 Topps Five Star Autographs

PRINT RUNS B/WN 50-386 COPIES PER
EXCHANGE DEADLINE 11/30/2016
AD Andre Dawson/386 10.00 25.00
AG Adrian Gonzalez/333 10.00 25.00
AJ Adam Jones/353 12.00 30.00
AK Al Kaline/353 25.00 50.00
AR Anthony Rizzo/386 20.00 50.00
BB Billy Butler/386 4.00 10.00
BG Bob Gibson/50 30.00 60.00
BH Bryce Harper/30 150.00 250.00
BJ Bo Jackson/50 50.00 100.00
BP Buster Posey/50 60.00 120.00
BW Billy Williams/353 8.00 20.00
CB Craig Biggio/333 15.00 40.00
CH Cole Hamels/386 5.00 12.00
CR Cal Ripken Jr./30 75.00 200.00
CS Chris Sale/353 8.00 20.00
DB Dylan Bundy/386 8.00 20.00
DE Dennis Eckersley/353 10.00 25.00
DF David Freese/353 5.00 12.00
DM Don Mattingly/50 50.00 100.00
DMU Dale Murphy/386 15.00 40.00
DP Dustin Pedroia/333 20.00 50.00
DS Dave Stewart/386 5.00 12.00
DW David Wright/50 25.00 60.00
EB Ernie Banks/50 40.00 100.00
ED Eric Davis/386 15.00 40.00
EL Evan Longoria/50 20.00 50.00
EM Edgar Martinez/386 20.00 50.00
FF Freddie Freeman/386 15.00 40.00
FJ Fergie Jenkins/333 6.00 15.00
FL Fred Lynn/353 6.00 15.00
FM Fred McGriff/333 8.00 20.00
FT Frank Thomas/50 60.00 120.00
GC Gerrit Cole/353 15.00 40.00
GS Giancarlo Stanton 40.00 100.00
HA Hank Aaron/30 150.00 300.00
JB Jose Bautista/333 12.00 30.00
JBE Johnny Bench/50 40.00 80.00
JC Johnny Cueto/386 5.00 12.00
JF Jose Fernandez/386 20.00 50.00
JH Josh Hamilton/333 12.50 30.00
JHE Jason Heyward/333 6.00 15.00
JM Juan Marichal/353 10.00 25.00
JP Jurickson Profar/386 5.00 12.00
JPA Jim Palmer/333 10.00 25.00
JR Jim Rice/386 10.00 25.00
JS John Smoltz/333 15.00 40.00
JSH James Shields/386 4.00 10.00
JU Justin Upton/333 5.00 12.00
KGR Ken Griffey Jr./30 150.00 300.00
KL Kenny Lofton/386 20.00 50.00
LS Lee Smith/386 6.00 15.00
MB Madison Bumgarner/386 15.00 40.00
MC Miguel Cabrera/50 60.00 120.00
MM Matt Moore/386 4.00 10.00
MMA Manny Machado 30.00 80.00
MMU Mike Mussina/333 10.00 25.00
MS Mike Schmidt/50 40.00 80.00
MT Mike Trout/50 125.00 250.00
MTR Mark Trumbo/386 4.00 10.00
MW Matt Williams/386 6.00 15.00
NG Nomar Garciaparra/333 15.00 40.00
NR Nolan Ryan/50 75.00 150.00
OC Orlando Cepeda/333 6.00 15.00
PG Paul Goldschmidt/386 12.00 30.00
PM Pedro Martinez/50 60.00 150.00
PMO Paul Molitor/386 10.00 25.00
PO Paul O'Neill/386 12.00 30.00
RB Ryan Braun/333 10.00 25.00
RD R.A. Dickey/333 6.00 15.00
RH Rickey Henderson/50 60.00 120.00
RJ Reggie Jackson/50 40.00 80.00
RS Ryne Sandberg/50 40.00 80.00
RZ Ryan Zimmerman/386 8.00 20.00
SK Sandy Koufax/30 175.00 350.00
SM Shelby Miller/386 4.00 10.00
SP Salvador Perez/386 15.00 40.00
TG Tom Glavine/333 12.00 30.00
TGW Tony Gwynn/50 30.00 60.00
TS Tom Seaver/50 40.00 100.00
WC Will Clark/353 15.00 40.00
WMA Willie Mays/30 200.00 400.00
WMY Wil Myers/386 6.00 15.00
YC Yoenis Cespedes/353 12.00 30.00
YD Yu Darvish 50.00 120.00

2013 Topps Five Star Autographs Rainbow

*RAINBOW: .6X TO 1.5X BASIC p/r 333-386
*RAINBOW: .5X TO 1.2X BASIC p/r 30-50
STATED PRINT RUN 25 SER.#'d SETS
EXCHANGE DEADLINE 11/30/2016
AR Anthony Rizzo 60.00 150.00
HR Hyun-Jin Ryu 50.00 100.00
YP Yasiel Puig 200.00 400.00

2013 Topps Five Star Jumbo Jersey

STATED PRINT RUN 35 SER.#'d SETS
AC Aroldis Chapman 6.00 15.00
AGZ Adrian Gonzalez 5.00 12.00
AP Andy Pettitte 6.00 15.00
APU Albert Pujols 10.00 25.00
AR Alex Rodriguez 15.00 40.00
ARZ Anthony Rizzo 6.00 15.00
BB Billy Butler 4.00 10.00
BH Bryce Harper 12.50 30.00
BH2 Bryce Harper 12.50 30.00
BP Buster Posey 12.50 30.00
CB Craig Biggio 6.00 15.00
CCS CC Sabathia 12.00 30.00
CD Chris Davis 8.00 20.00
CF Carlton Fisk 6.00 15.00
CG Curtis Granderson 4.00 10.00
CGZ Carlos Gonzalez 6.00 15.00
CS Chris Sale 6.00 15.00
DJ Derek Jeter 20.00 50.00
DM Don Mattingly 20.00 50.00
DP Dustin Pedroia 4.00 10.00
DW David Wright 10.00 25.00
EL Evan Longoria 6.00 15.00
FH Felix Hernandez 6.00 15.00
FM Fred McGriff 4.00 10.00
GG Gio Gonzalez 4.00 10.00
GS Giancarlo Stanton 6.00 15.00
JB Jose Bautista 4.00 10.00
JH Josh Hamilton 6.00 15.00
JP Jurickson Profar 6.00 15.00
JR Jose Reyes 6.00 15.00
JRC Jim Rice 6.00 15.00
JU Justin Upton 4.00 10.00
LT Luis Tiant 5.00 12.00
MC Miguel Cabrera 10.00 25.00
MH Matt Harvey 10.00 25.00
MK Matt Kemp 4.00 10.00
MM Matt Moore 5.00 12.00
MR Mariano Rivera 10.00 25.00
MT Mike Trout 25.00 60.00
PF Prince Fielder 5.00 12.00
PN Phil Niekro 12.50 30.00
RAD R.A. Dickey 6.00 15.00
RB Ryan Braun 5.00 12.00
RH Ryan Howard 10.00 25.00
SC Starlin Castro 6.00 15.00
SS Stephen Strasburg 8.00 20.00
TL Tim Lincecum 10.00 25.00
TT Troy Tulowitzki 6.00 15.00
YC Yoenis Cespedes 5.00 12.00
YD Yu Darvish 10.00 25.00
YP Yasiel Puig 30.00 60.00

2013 Topps Five Star Jumbo Jersey Blue

*BLUE: .4X TO 1X BASIC
STATED PRINT RUN 30 SER.#'d SETS
EXCHANGE DEADLINE 11/30/2016

2013 Topps Five Star Jumbo Jersey Red

*RED: .5X TO 1.2X BASIC
STATED PRINT RUN 25 SER.#'d SETS
EXCHANGE DEADLINE 11/30/2016

2013 Topps Five Star Jumbo Relic Autographs Books

STATED PRINT RUN 49 SER.#'d SETS
EXCHANGE DEADLINE 11/30/2016
JB Johnny Bench 60.00 120.00
KG Ken Griffey Jr. 125.00 300.00
RJ Reggie Jackson 60.00 120.00
TG Tony Gwynn 50.00 100.00
WM Willie Mays 175.00 350.00

2013 Topps Five Star Legends Autographs

PRINT RUNS B/WN 49-75 COPIES PER
EXCHANGE DEADLINE 11/30/2016
P Pele 250.00 350.00
BB Bjorn Borg 30.00 60.00
BR Bill Russell 60.00 120.00

2013 Topps Five Star Legends Relics

STATED PRINT RUN 25 SER.#'d SETS
BF Bob Feller 30.00 60.00
BG Bob Gibson 20.00 50.00
CRJ Cal Ripken Jr. 20.00 50.00
EB Ernie Banks 20.00 50.00
EM Eddie Mathews 12.50 30.00
GB George Brett 20.00 50.00
HK Harmon Killebrew 12.50 30.00
JB Johnny Bench 15.00 40.00
JB2 Johnny Bench 15.00 40.00
JF Jimmie Foxx 30.00 60.00
JR Jackie Robinson 40.00 80.00
KGJ Ken Griffey Jr. 50.00 100.00
MS Mike Schmidt 12.50 30.00
NR Nolan Ryan 30.00 60.00
RC Roberto Clemente 75.00 150.00
RC2 Roberto Clemente 75.00 150.00
RH Rickey Henderson 30.00 60.00
RJ Reggie Jackson 10.00 25.00
SM Stan Musial 20.00 50.00
TC Ty Cobb 40.00 80.00
TC2 Ty Cobb 40.00 80.00
TW Ted Williams 30.00 80.00
WM Willie Mays 50.00 100.00
WMC Willie McCovey 20.00 50.00
YB Yogi Berra 15.00 40.00

2013 Topps Five Star Patch Autographs

STATED PRINT RUN 35 SER.#'d SETS
AJ Adam Jones 50.00 100.00
BP Buster Posey 100.00 200.00
CR Cal Ripken Jr. 100.00 200.00
CS Chris Sale 15.00 40.00
DP Dustin Pedroia 40.00 80.00
DW David Wright 40.00 80.00
JC Johnny Cueto EXCH 10.00 25.00
JH Jason Heyward 20.00 50.00
JS John Smoltz 30.00 60.00
MC Miguel Cabrera 125.00 250.00
MM Mike Mussina 20.00 50.00
MS Mike Schmidt 50.00 120.00
MT Mike Trout 175.00 350.00
PS Pablo Sandoval 15.00 40.00
RC Robinson Cano 20.00 50.00

2013 Topps Five Star Quad Relic Autographs Books

STATED PRINT RUN 49 SER.#'d SETS
EXCHANGE DEADLINE 11/30/2016
BH Bryce Harper 75.00 200.00
CB Craig Biggio 40.00 80.00
DW David Wright 60.00 120.00
MC Miguel Cabrera 100.00 250.00
RB Ryan Braun 30.00 60.00

2013 Topps Five Star Silver Signings

STATED PRINT RUN 65 SER.#'d SETS
EXCHANGE DEADLINE 11/30/2016
AD Andre Dawson 10.00 25.00
AG Adrian Gonzalez 12.50 30.00
AK Al Kaline 25.00 50.00
AR Anthony Rizzo 12.50 30.00
CB Craig Biggio 15.00 40.00
CF Carlton Fisk 15.00 40.00
CH Cole Hamels 10.00 25.00
CK Clayton Kershaw 50.00 100.00
CS Chris Sale 12.50 30.00
DB Dylan Bundy 12.50 30.00
DE Dennis Eckersley 10.00 25.00
DF David Freese 10.00 25.00
DM Dale Murphy 10.00 25.00
DS Dave Stewart 8.00 20.00
DSN Deion Sanders 20.00 50.00
DW David Wright 20.00 50.00
ED Eric Davis 6.00 15.00
FF Freddie Freeman 15.00 40.00
FL Fred Lynn 10.00 25.00
FM Fred McGriff 15.00 40.00
HA Hank Aaron 100.00 250.00
HR Hyun-Jin Ryu
JBA Jose Bautista 10.00 25.00
JC Johnny Cueto 8.00 20.00
JF Jose Fernandez 30.00 60.00
JM Juan Marichal 10.00 25.00
JP Jurickson Profar 10.00 25.00
JR Jim Rice 10.00 25.00
JS John Smoltz 20.00 50.00
JSH James Shields 8.00 20.00
JU Justin Upton 10.00 25.00
LS Lee Smith 5.00 12.00
MB Madison Bumgarner 20.00 50.00
MC Matt Cain 10.00 25.00
MM Matt Moore 10.00 25.00
MMA Manny Machado 30.00 60.00
MMU Mike Mussina 10.00 25.00
MTR Mike Trout 100.00 250.00
MW Matt Williams 10.00 25.00
NG Nomar Garciaparra 20.00 50.00
OC Orlando Cepeda 10.00 25.00
PG Paul Goldschmidt 15.00 40.00
PM Paul Molitor 6.00 15.00
PO Paul O'Neill 15.00 40.00
SM Shelby Miller 10.00 25.00
SP Salvador Perez 10.00 25.00
TG Tom Glavine 20.00 50.00
TR Tim Raines 8.00 20.00
WM Wil Myers 12.00 30.00
YC Yoenis Cespedes 20.00 50.00
ZW Zack Wheeler 20.00 50.00

2013 Topps Five Star Silver Signings Blue

*BLUE: .5X TO 1.2X BASIC
STATED PRINT RUN 25 SER.#'d SETS
EXCHANGE DEADLINE 11/30/2016

2013 Topps Five Star Triple Relic Autographs Books

STATED PRINT RUN 49 SER.#'d SETS
EXCHANGE DEADLINE 11/30/2016
CR Cal Ripken Jr. 100.00 200.00
MS Mike Schmidt 60.00 120.00
MT Mike Trout 150.00 300.00
NG Nomar Garciaparra 20.00 50.00
YD Yu Darvish 100.00 200.00

2014 Topps Five Star Autographs

RANDOM INSERTS IN PACKS
PRINT RUNS B/WN 50-499 COPIES PER
EXCHANGE DEADLINE 11/30/2017
FSAAA Arismendy Alcantara/499 3.00 8.00
FSAAC Allen Craig/399 4.00 10.00
FSAAD Andre Dawson/149 10.00 25.00
FSAAG Alex Guerrero/499 4.00 10.00
FSAAGO Adrian Gonzalez/149 8.00 20.00
FSAAS Andrelton Simmons/499 4.00 10.00
FSAASA Aaron Sanchez/499 3.00 8.00
FSABHA Bryce Harper/50 100.00 200.00
FSABJ Bo Jackson/50 50.00 120.00
FSACB Craig Biggio/149 12.00 30.00
FSACF Carlton Fisk/50 20.00 50.00
FSACG Carlos Gonzalez/138 12.00 30.00
FSACJ Chipper Jones/50 60.00 150.00
FSACK Clayton Kershaw/50 75.00 200.00
FSACO Chris Owings/499 3.00 8.00
FSACR Cal Ripken Jr./50 75.00 200.00
FSACS Chris Sabo/499 6.00 15.00
FSACSA Chris Sale/399 8.00 20.00
FSACW C.J. Wilson/399 3.00 8.00
FSADAI Daisuke Matsuzaka/499 12.00 30.00
FSADC David Cone/399 6.00 15.00
FSADE Dennis Eckersley/299 4.00 10.00
FSADM Dale Murphy/299 10.00 25.00
FSADMA Don Mattingly/50 30.00 80.00
FSADPA Dave Parker/499 3.00 8.00
FSADW David Wright/50 15.00 40.00
FSAEBU Eddie Butler/399 3.00 8.00
FSAEL Evan Longoria/50 8.00 20.00
FSAEM Edgar Martinez/399 8.00 20.00
FSAFF Freddie Freeman/199 12.00 30.00
FSAFT Frank Thomas/50 30.00 80.00
FSAFV Fernando Valenzuela/199 10.00 25.00
FSAGP Gregory Polanco/399 4.00 10.00
FSAGS Giancarlo Stanton/136 15.00 40.00
FSAGSP George Springer/499 15.00 40.00
FSAHR Hanley Ramirez/50 10.00 25.00
FSAIR Ivan Rodriguez/149 12.00 30.00
FSAJA Jose Abreu/199 10.00 25.00
FSAJB Jay Bruce/399 4.00 10.00
FSAJBE Johnny Bench/50 30.00 80.00
FSAJC Jose Canseco/399 8.00 20.00
FSAJD Josh Donaldson/399 10.00 25.00
FSAJF Jose Fernandez/299 12.00 30.00
FSAJG Juan Gonzalez/399 3.00 8.00
FSAJH Jason Heyward/199 4.00 10.00
FSAJM Joe Mauer/50 15.00 40.00
FSAJP Jorge Posada/149 20.00 50.00
FSAJR Jim Rice/399 6.00 15.00
FSAJS John Smoltz/149 15.00 40.00
FSAJSC Jonathan Schoop/499 8.00 20.00
FSAJT Julio Teheran/105 4.00 10.00
FSAJTA Junichi Tazawa/499 3.00 8.00
FSAJV Joey Votto/50 25.00 60.00
FSAKG Ken Griffey Jr./50 100.00 200.00
FSAKU Koji Uehara/499 10.00 25.00
FSAKW Kolten Wong/499 4.00 10.00
FSALB Lou Brock/299 12.00 30.00
FSALH Livan Hernandez/499 3.00 8.00
FSAMA Matt Adams/499 3.00 8.00
FSAMB M.Bumgarner/299 25.00 60.00
FSAMBE Mookie Betts/499 100.00 250.00
FSAMC Miguel Cabrera/50 40.00 100.00
FSAMCA Matt Carpenter/499 6.00 15.00
FSAMM Manny Machado/105 12.00 30.00
FSAMMC Mark McGwire/50 75.00 200.00
FSAMP Mike Piazza/50 50.00 120.00
FSAMS Mike Schmidt/50 20.00 50.00
FSAMSC Max Scherzer/299 30.00 80.00
FSAMT Mike Trout/50 150.00 250.00
FSAMW Michael Wacha/399 4.00 10.00
FSANC Nick Castellanos/499 10.00 25.00
FSANG Nomar Garciaparra/50 10.00 25.00
FSANR Nolan Ryan/50 60.00 150.00
FSAOH Orlando Hernandez/499 3.00 8.00
FSAOS Ozzie Smith/50 20.00 50.00
FSAOTA Oscar Taveras/399 4.00 10.00
FSAOV Omar Vizquel/499 6.00 15.00
FSAPG Paul Goldschmidt/399 12.00 30.00
FSAPMO Paul Molitor/50 15.00 40.00
FSAPN Phil Niekro/299 4.00 10.00
FSAPO Paul O'Neill/399 6.00 15.00
FSARA Roberto Alomar/149 15.00 40.00
FSARB Ryan Braun/50 15.00 40.00
FSARC Robinson Cano/50 15.00 40.00
FSARCA Rod Carew/149 15.00 40.00
FSARJ Reggie Jackson/50 30.00 80.00
FSARP Rafael Palmeiro/299 6.00 15.00
FSARY Robin Yount/50 40.00 100.00
FSARZ Ryan Zimmerman/399 4.00 10.00
FSASC Steve Carlton/149 12.00 30.00
FSASM Shelby Miller/499 4.00 10.00
FSATGL Tom Glavine/50 15.00 40.00
FSATT Troy Tulowitzki/50 5.00 12.00
FSATW Taijuan Walker/499 3.00 8.00
FSAVG Vladimir Guerrero/149 15.00 40.00
FSAWM Wil Myers/399 3.00 8.00
FSAYC Yoenis Cespedes/399 5.00 12.00
FSAYM Yadier Molina/149 40.00 100.00
FSAYS Yangervis Solarte/499 3.00 8.00
FSAZW Zack Wheeler/499 4.00 10.00

2014 Topps Five Star Autographs Rainbow

*RAINBOW: .6X TO 1.5X BASE p/r 149-499
*RAINBOW: .5X TO 1.2X BASE p/r 50
STATED PRINT RUN 25 SER.#'d SETS
EXCHANGE DEADLINE 11/30/2017
FSADMO Dan Marino 100.00 250.00
FSASK Sandy Koufax 200.00 400.00
FSAWMA Willie Mays EXCH 150.00 300.00

2014 Topps Five Star Golden Graphs

RANDOM INSERTS IN PACKS
STATED PRINT RUN 50 SER.#'d SETS
EXCHANGE DEADLINE 11/30/2017
*PURPLE/25: .5X TO 1.2X BASIC
FSGGAA Arismendy Alcantara 6.00 15.00
FSGGAG Adrian Gonzalez 8.00 20.00
FSGGCB Craig Biggio 15.00 40.00
FSGGCS CC Sabathia 25.00 60.00
FSGGDC David Cone 12.00 30.00
FSGGDM Don Mattingly 30.00 80.00
FSGGDMA Daisuke Matsuzaka 15.00 40.00
FSGGEL Evan Longoria 15.00 40.00
FSGGEM Edgar Martinez 5.00 12.00
FSGGFF Freddie Freeman 12.00 30.00
FSGGGS George Springer 20.00 50.00
FSGGJB Johnny Bench 30.00 80.00
FSGGJC Jose Canseco 15.00 40.00
FSGGJV Joey Votto 15.00 40.00
FSGGMB Mookie Betts 75.00 200.00
FSGGMR Mariano Rivera 75.00 200.00
FSGGNC Nick Castellanos 20.00 50.00
FSGGNG Nomar Garciaparra 10.00 25.00
FSGGPG Paul Goldschmidt 15.00 40.00
FSGGPO Paul O'Neill 15.00 40.00
FSGGRA Roberto Alomar 15.00 40.00
FSGGRC Rod Carew 15.00 40.00
FSGGTG Tom Glavine 20.00 50.00
FSGGTT Troy Tulowitzki 20.00 50.00
FSGGYC Yoenis Cespedes 10.00 25.00
FSGGZW Zack Wheeler 8.00 20.00

2014 Topps Five Star Jumbo Patch Autographs

RANDOM INSERTS IN PACKS
STATED PRINT RUN 35 SER.#'d SETS
EXCHANGE DEADLINE 11/30/2017
FAJPAG Adrian Gonzalez 20.00 50.00
FAJPBH Billy Hamilton 20.00 50.00
FAJPBP Buster Posey 150.00 250.00
FAJPCG Carlos Gonzalez 20.00 50.00
FAJPDM Daisuke Matsuzaka 40.00 100.00
FAJPDO David Ortiz 60.00 150.00
FAJPDW David Wright 40.00 100.00
FAJPFF Freddie Freeman 40.00 100.00
FAJPGS Giancarlo Stanton 60.00 150.00
FAJPHR Hanley Ramirez 20.00 50.00
FAJPJM Joe Mauer 40.00 100.00
FAJPJP Jorge Posada 25.00 60.00
FAJPJV Joey Votto 30.00 80.00
FAJPPG Paul Goldschmidt 25.00 60.00
FAJPRA Roberto Alomar 25.00 60.00
FAJPRB Ryan Braun 25.00 60.00
FAJPTW Taijuan Walker 15.00 40.00
FAJPYV Yordano Ventura 20.00 50.00

2014 Topps Five Star Jumbo Relic Autographs Books

RANDOM INSERTS IN PACKS
STATED PRINT RUN 50 SER.#'d SETS
EXCHANGE DEADLINE 11/30/2017
FSABDW David Wright 30.00 80.00
FSABMS Mike Schmidt 50.00 120.00
FSABNG Nomar Garciaparra 30.00 80.00
FSABRCL Roger Clemens 60.00 150.00
FSABRS Ryne Sandberg 50.00 120.00
FSABRY Robin Yount 25.00 60.00

2014 Topps Five Star Legends Relics

RANDOM INSERTS IN PACKS
STATED PRINT RUN 25 SER.#'d SETS
FSLRAK Al Kaline 15.00 40.00
FSLRBF Bob Feller 20.00 50.00
FSLRBR Babe Ruth 60.00 150.00
FSLRDJ Derek Jeter 50.00 120.00
FSLRDS Duke Snider 50.00 120.00
FSLREM Eddie Mathews 25.00 60.00
FSLRES Enos Slaughter 20.00 50.00
FSLREW Early Wynn 20.00 50.00
FSLRHA Hank Aaron 40.00 100.00
FSLRHK Harmon Killebrew 25.00 60.00
FSLRJD Joe DiMaggio 40.00 100.00
FSLRJM Joe Morgan 20.00 50.00
FSLRJR Jackie Robinson 30.00 80.00
FSLRLG Lou Gehrig 60.00 150.00
FSLRMT Masahiro Tanaka 30.00 80.00
FSLRRC Roberto Clemente 60.00 150.00
FSLRRF Rick Ferrell 40.00 100.00
FSLRRM Roger Maris 25.00 60.00
FSLRRS Red Schoendienst 20.00 50.00
FSLRTP Tony Perez 20.00 50.00
FSLRWF Whitey Ford 20.00 50.00
FSLRWS Warren Spahn 25.00 60.00
FSLRWST Willie Stargell 20.00 50.00

2014 Topps Five Star Quad Relic Autographs Books

RANDOM INSERTS IN PACKS
STATED PRINT RUN 50 SER.#'d SETS
EXCHANGE DEADLINE 11/30/2017
FSSBBR Brooks Robinson 50.00 120.00
FSSBCR Cal Ripken Jr. 60.00 150.00
FSSBDM Don Mattingly 40.00 100.00
FSSBMM Mark McGwire 100.00 200.00
FSSBMS Max Scherzer 40.00 100.00
FSSBOZ Ozzie Smith 50.00 120.00
FSSBRB Ryan Braun 20.00 50.00
FSSBTGL Tom Glavine 40.00 100.00

2014 Topps Five Star Silver Signatures

RANDOM INSERTS IN PACKS
STATED PRINT RUN 50 SER.#'d SETS
EXCHANGE DEADLINE 11/30/2017
*PURPLE/25: .5X TO 1.2X BASIC
FSSSAA Arismendy Alcantara 8.00 20.00
FSSSAG Adrian Gonzalez 10.00 25.00
FSSSCB Craig Biggio 10.00 25.00
FSSSCS CC Sabathia 20.00 50.00
FSSSDC David Cone 12.00 30.00
FSSSDM Don Mattingly 25.00 60.00
FSSSDMA Daisuke Matsuzaka 30.00 80.00
FSSSEL Evan Longoria 15.00 40.00
FSSSEM Edgar Martinez 12.00 30.00
FSSSFF Freddie Freeman 12.00 30.00
FSSSGS George Springer 25.00 60.00
FSSSIR Ivan Rodriguez 12.00 30.00
FSSSJB Johnny Bench 30.00 80.00
FSSSJC Jose Canseco 10.00 25.00
FSSSJP Jim Palmer 15.00 40.00
FSSSJV Joey Votto 20.00 50.00
FSSSMB Mookie Betts 40.00 100.00
FSSSNC Nick Castellanos 25.00 60.00
FSSSNG Nomar Garciaparra 15.00 40.00
FSSSPG Paul Goldschmidt 15.00 40.00
FSSSPO Paul O'Neill 15.00 40.00
FSSSRA Roberto Alomar 25.00 60.00
FSSSRC Rod Carew 15.00 40.00
FSSSRJ Randy Johnson 40.00 100.00
FSSSTG Tom Glavine 20.00 50.00
FSSSTT Troy Tulowitzki 12.00 30.00
FSSSTW Taijuan Walker 8.00 20.00
FSSSZW Zack Wheeler 10.00 25.00

2015 Topps Five Star Autographs

OVERALL TWO AUTOS PER BOX
EXCHANGE DEADLINE 9/30/2017
FSAAB Archie Bradley RC 5.00 12.00
FSAACO A.J. Cole RC 3.00 8.00
FSAAG Andres Galarraga 6.00 15.00
FSAAGA Andres Galarraga 6.00 15.00
FSAAJ Andruw Jones 3.00 8.00
FSAAL Al Leiter 4.00 10.00
FSAARU Addison Russell RC 8.00 20.00
FSABB Brandon Belt 4.00 10.00
FSABBR Bryce Brentz RC 4.00 10.00
FSABBU Byron Buxton RC 6.00 15.00
FSABF Brandon Finnegan RC 3.00 8.00
FSABS Blake Swihart RC 4.00 10.00
FSABW Bernie Williams 15.00 40.00
FSACB Craig Biggio 12.00 30.00
FSACD Carlos Delgado 5.00 12.00
FSACK Clayton Kershaw 6.00 15.00
FSACKL Corey Kluber 4.00 10.00
FSACRO Carlos Rodon RC 8.00 20.00
FSADE Dennis Eckersley 6.00 15.00
FSADF Doug Fister 3.00 8.00
FSADG Didi Gregorius 10.00 25.00
FSAEE Edwin Encarnacion 5.00 12.00
FSAEI Ender Inciarte 3.00 8.00
FSAEM Edgar Martinez 12.00 30.00
FSAFF Freddie Freeman 6.00 15.00
FSAFL Francisco Lindor RC 20.00 50.00
FSAFV Fernando Valenzuela 20.00 50.00
FSAHR Hanley Ramirez 4.00 10.00
FSAJA Jose Abreu 8.00 20.00
FSAJAL Jose Altuve 10.00 25.00
FSAJBA Javier Baez RC 40.00 100.00
FSAJD Jacob deGrom 50.00 120.00
FSAJH Josh Harrison 3.00 8.00
FSAJHK Jung-Ho Kang RC 10.00 25.00
FSAJL Jon Lester 15.00 40.00
FSAJLI Jacob Lindgren RC 4.00 10.00
FSAJP Joc Pederson RC 6.00 15.00
FSAJPI Jose Pirela RC 3.00 8.00
FSAJS John Smoltz 10.00 25.00
FSAJSH James Shields 3.00 8.00
FSAJSO Jorge Soler RC 10.00 25.00
FSAJUG Juan Gonzalez 8.00 20.00
FSAKB Kris Bryant RC 75.00 200.00
FSAKC Kole Calhoun 3.00 8.00
FSAKP Kevin Plawecki RC 3.00 8.00
FSAMC Matt Carpenter 5.00 12.00
FSAMFR Maikel Franco RC 6.00 15.00
FSAMG Mark Grace 10.00 25.00
FSAMGR Marquis Grissom 3.00 8.00
FSAMJ Micah Johnson RC 3.00 8.00
FSAMTA Michael Taylor RC 3.00 8.00
FSAMW Matt Wisler RC 5.00 12.00
FSAMWA Michael Wacha 5.00 12.00
FSAMZ Mike Zunino 3.00 8.00
FSANS Noah Syndergaard RC 20.00 50.00
FSAOS Ozzie Smith 15.00 40.00
FSAOV Omar Vizquel 5.00 12.00
FSAPO Paul O'Neill 4.00 10.00
FSAPS Pablo Sandoval 8.00 20.00
FSARB Ryan Braun 4.00 10.00
FSARI Raisel Iglesias RC 4.00 10.00
FSARJA Reggie Jackson 20.00 50.00
FSARO Roberto Osuna 3.00 8.00
FSARP Rick Porcello 4.00 10.00
FSARPA Rafael Palmeiro 5.00 12.00
FSARUC Rusney Castillo RC 8.00 20.00
FSASC Steve Carlton 10.00 25.00
FSASG Shawn Green 3.00 8.00
FSASM Starling Marte 5.00 12.00
FSASMA Steven Matz RC 3.00 8.00
FSASS Steven Souza 4.00 10.00
FSATG Tom Glavine 12.00 30.00
FSAVC Vinny Castilla 3.00 8.00
FSAYGO Yan Gomes 3.00 8.00

2015 Topps Five Star Autographs Gold

*GOLD: .5X TO 1.2X BASIC
RANDOM INSERTS IN PACKS
STATED PRINT RUN 50 SER.#'d SETS
EXCHANGE DEADLINE 9/30/2017
FSABL Barry Larkin 20.00 50.00
FSACK Clayton Kershaw 40.00 100.00
FSADM Don Mattingly 20.00 50.00
FSAFR Frank Robinson 20.00 50.00
FSAI Ichiro Suzuki 250.00 350.00
FSANG Nomar Garciaparra 10.00 25.00
FSAPF Prince Fielder 10.00 25.00

2015 Topps Five Star Autographs Rainbow

*RAINBOW: .6X TO 1.5X BASIC
STATED ODDS 1:6 HOBBY
STATED PRINT RUN 25 SER.#'d SETS
EXCHANGE DEADLINE 9/30/2017
FSAAG Andres Galarraga 30.00 80.00
FSAAGA Andres Galarraga 30.00 80.00
FSABJ Bo Jackson 50.00 120.00
FSABL Barry Larkin 25.00 60.00
FSABP Buster Posey 60.00 150.00
FSACK Clayton Kershaw 50.00 120.00
FSACR Cal Ripken Jr. 100.00 200.00
FSADM Don Mattingly 25.00 60.00
FSADO David Ortiz 40.00 100.00
FSAEL Evan Longoria 10.00 25.00
FSAFR Frank Robinson 25.00 60.00
FSAFT Frank Thomas 50.00 120.00
FSAI Ichiro Suzuki 300.00 400.00
FSAMM Mark McGwire 100.00 200.00
FSAMP Mike Piazza 100.00 200.00
FSAMR Mariano Rivera 150.00 250.00
FSAMT Mike Trout 300.00 400.00
FSANG Nomar Garciaparra 12.00 30.00
FSANR Nolan Ryan 75.00 150.00
FSAPF Prince Fielder 12.00 30.00
FSARC Roger Clemens 40.00 100.00
FSARCA Robinson Cano 15.00 40.00
FSARH Rickey Henderson 30.00 80.00
FSARJ Randy Johnson 75.00 150.00
FSARS Ryne Sandberg 25.00 60.00
FSASK Sandy Koufax 200.00 300.00
FSAWB Wade Boggs 30.00 80.00

2015 Topps Five Star Five Tools Autographs

STATED ODDS 1:27 HOBBY
STATED PRINT RUN 25 SER.#'d SETS
EXCHANGE DEADLINE 9/30/2017
FTAAD Andre Dawson 20.00 50.00
FTAAJ Adam Jones 30.00 80.00
FTABB Byron Buxton 50.00 125.00
FTABH Bryce Harper 125.00 250.00
FTABJ Bo Jackson 40.00 100.00
FTACB Craig Biggio 15.00 40.00
FTACJ Chipper Jones 150.00 250.00
FTADP Dustin Pedroia 15.00 40.00
FTADW David Wright 12.00 30.00
FTAHA Hank Aaron 200.00 300.00
FTAHR Hanley Ramirez 12.00 30.00
FTAKB Kris Bryant 200.00 400.00
FTAKG Ken Griffey Jr. 300.00 400.00
FTAMM Manny Machado 60.00 150.00
FTAMT Mike Trout 300.00 400.00
FTANG Nomar Garciaparra 12.00 30.00
FTAPM Paul Molitor 30.00 80.00
FTARB Ryan Braun 12.00 30.00
FTARH Rickey Henderson 30.00 80.00
FTASM Starling Marte 12.00 30.00

2015 Topps Five Star Golden Graphs

STATED ODDS 1:13 HOBBY
STATED PRINT RUN 50 SER.#'d SETS
EXCHANGE DEADLINE 9/30/2017
*BLUE/20: .5X TO 1.2X
*PURPLE/25: .5X TO 1.2X
GGAL Al Leiter 10.00 25.00
GGBL Barry Larkin 20.00 50.00
GGCB Craig Biggio 12.00 30.00
GGCK Corey Kluber 8.00 20.00
GGDE Dennis Eckersley 12.00 30.00
GGDF Doug Fister 6.00 15.00
GGDG Didi Gregorius 10.00 25.00
GGDM Don Mattingly 25.00 60.00
GGEE Edwin Encarnacion 10.00 25.00
GGFF Freddie Freeman 12.00 30.00
GGFV Fernando Valenzuela 10.00 25.00
GGJB Javier Baez 12.00 30.00
GGJD Jacob deGrom 30.00 80.00
GGJH Josh Harrison 6.00 15.00
GGJHK Jung-Ho Kang 6.00 15.00
GGJP Joc Pederson 20.00 50.00
GGJS James Shields 6.00 15.00
GGJSM John Smoltz 15.00 40.00
GGKW Kolten Wong 12.00 30.00
GGMC Matt Carpenter 12.00 30.00
GGMF Maikel Franco 15.00 40.00
GGMG Mark Grace 12.00 30.00
GGOS Ozzie Smith 20.00 50.00
GGPF Prince Fielder 8.00 20.00
GGRCL Roger Clemens 25.00 60.00
GGSG Sonny Gray 8.00 20.00
GGTG Tom Glavine 20.00 50.00

2015 Topps Five Star Jumbo Patch Autographs

STATED ODDS 1:23 HOBBY
STATED PRINT RUN 35 SER.#'d SETS
EXCHANGE DEADLINE 9/30/2017
FSAJAG Adrian Gonzalez 25.00 60.00
FSAJAJ Adam Jones 25.00 60.00
FSAJBB Brandon Belt 25.00 60.00
FSAJBM Brian McCann 25.00 60.00
FSAJCK Clayton Kershaw 75.00 200.00
FSAJDO David Ortiz 60.00 150.00
FSAJDW David Wright 25.00 60.00
FSAJEL Evan Longoria 30.00 80.00
FSAJJA Jose Altuve 60.00 150.00
FSAJJB Javier Baez 50.00 120.00
FSAJKG Ken Griffey Jr. 200.00 300.00
FSAJLD Lucas Duda 50.00 120.00
FSAJMA Matt Adams 20.00 50.00
FSAJMC Matt Carpenter 30.00 80.00
FSAJPG Paul Goldschmidt 30.00 80.00
FSAJRC Rusney Castillo 25.00 60.00
FSAJRCA Robinson Cano 60.00 150.00

2015 Topps Five Star Silver Signatures

STATED ODDS 1:13 HOBBY
STATED PRINT RUN 50 SER.#'d SETS
EXCHANGE DEADLINE 9/30/2017

*BLUE/20: .5X TO 1.2X
*PURPLE/25: .5X TO 1.2X
SSAG Andres Galarraga 15.00 40.00
SSBB Brandon Belt 8.00 20.00
SSBL Barry Larkin 25.00 60.00
SSCB Craig Biggio 12.00 30.00
SSCK Corey Kluber 8.00 20.00
SSCKE Clayton Kershaw 40.00 100.00
SSDF Doug Fister 6.00 15.00
SSDG Didi Gregorius 10.00 25.00
SSDM Don Mattingly 25.00 60.00
SSEE Edwin Encarnacion 10.00 25.00
SSEM Edgar Martinez 8.00 20.00
SSFV Fernando Valenzuela 10.00 25.00
SSGS George Springer 12.00 30.00
SSJA Jose Altuve 25.00 60.00
SSJAB Jose Abreu 10.00 25.00
SSJB Javier Baez 12.00 30.00
SSJHK Jung-Ho Kang 30.00 80.00
SSJP Joc Pederson 20.00 50.00
SSJS Jorge Soler 10.00 25.00
SSMF Maikel Franco 15.00 40.00
SSMG Mark Grace 8.00 20.00
SSOS Ozzie Smith 20.00 50.00
SSOV Omar Vizquel 15.00 40.00
SSPF Prince Fielder 12.00 30.00
SSPO Paul O'Neill 8.00 20.00
SSRC Rusney Castillo 8.00 20.00
SSRCL Roger Clemens 25.00 60.00
SSSM Starling Marte 10.00 25.00
SSTG Tom Glavine 15.00 40.00

2016 Topps Five Star Autographs

EXCHANGE DEADLINE 8/31/2018
FSAADZ Aledmys Diaz RC 4.00 10.00
FSAAGA Andres Galarraga 4.00 10.00
FSAAK Al Kaline 12.00 30.00
FSAAN Aaron Nola RC 5.00 12.00
FSAAP Andy Pettitte 15.00 40.00
FSAARE A.J. Reed RC 3.00 8.00
FSAARI Anthony Rizzo 25.00 60.00
FSAARU Addison Russell 10.00 25.00
FSABBO Barry Bonds
FSABH Bryce Harper
FSABJA Bo Jackson
FSABPO Buster Posey
FSABSN Blake Snell RC 10.00 25.00
FSACB Craig Biggio
FSACC Carlos Correa 12.00 30.00
FSACJ Chipper Jones
FSACRI Cal Ripken Jr.
FSACRO Carlos Rodon 8.00 20.00
FSACSA Chris Sale
FSACSC Curt Schilling
FSACSE Corey Seager RC 30.00 80.00
FSACY Carl Yastrzemski
FSADM Don Mattingly
FSADO David Ortiz 40.00 120.00
FSADW David Wright
FSAFH Felix Hernandez
FSAFL Franciso Lindor
FSAFT Frank Thomas
FSAGM Greg Maddux
FSAGS George Springer 8.00 20.00
FSAHA Hank Aaron
FSAHOL Hector Olivera RC 4.00 10.00
FSAHOW Henry Owens RC 4.00 10.00
FSAI Ichiro Suzuki
FSAIR Ivan Rodriguez
FSAJA Jose Altuve 30.00 80.00
FSAJBE Jose Berrios RC 5.00 12.00
FSAJDA Johnny Damon
FSAJDG Jacob deGrom 10.00 25.00
FSAJGR Jon Gray 3.00 8.00
FSAJPD Joc Pederson 8.00 20.00
FSAJPE Jose Peraza RC 5.00 12.00
FSAJR Jim Rice 8.00 20.00
FSAJSM John Smoltz
FSAJSO Jorge Soler 5.00 12.00
FSAJU Julio Urias RC
FSAJVA Jason Varitek 15.00 40.00
FSAKB Kris Bryant 75.00 200.00
FSAKG Ken Griffey Jr.
FSAKMA Kenta Maeda RC 8.00 20.00
FSAKS Kyle Schwarber RC 10.00 25.00
FSALGI Lucas Giolito RC 5.00 12.00
FSALGO Luis Gonzalez 4.00 10.00
FSALS Luis Severino RC 8.00 20.00
FSAMK Max Kepler RC 5.00 12.00
FSAMMA Manny Machado
FSAMMG Mark McGwire
FSAMP Mike Piazza
FSAMS Mallex Smith RC 3.00 8.00
FSAMSA Miguel Sano RC 5.00 12.00
FSAMTE Mark Teixeira
FSAMTR Mike Trout
FSANA Nolan Arenado 40.00 100.00
FSANM Nomar Mazara RC 10.00 25.00
FSANR Nolan Ryan
FSANS Noah Syndergaard 15.00 40.00
FSAOG Ozzie Guillen 3.00 8.00
FSAOS Ozzie Smith
FSAOV Omar Vizquel 5.00 12.00
FSAP Pele
FSAPOB Peter O'Brien RC 3.00 8.00
FSARCL Roger Clemens
FSARH Rickey Henderson
FSARJA Reggie Jackson
FSARJO Randy Johnson
FSARM Raul Mondesi 5.00 12.00
FSARP Rafael Palmeiro 6.00 15.00
FSARS Ross Stripling 3.00 8.00
FSARSA Ryne Sandberg
FSARST Robert Stephenson RC 3.00 8.00
FSASG Sonny Gray 5.00 12.00
FSASK Sandy Koufax
FSASMA Steven Matz 3.00 8.00
FSASP Stephen Piscotty RC 3.00 8.00
FSATGL Tom Glavine
FSATN Tyler Naquin RC 5.00 12.00
FSATS Trevor Story RC 10.00 25.00
FSATTR Trea Turner RC 10.00 25.00
FSATTU Troy Tulowitzki
FSATW Tyler White RC 5.00 12.00
FSAVS Vin Scully
FSAWC Willson Contreras RC 15.00 40.00

2016 Topps Five Star Autographs Gold

*GOLD: .5X TO 1.2X BASIC
STATED PRINT RUN 50 SER.#'d SETS
EXCHANGE DEADLINE 8/31/2018
FSAAP Andy Pettitte 20.00 50.00
FSACB Craig Biggio 15.00 40.00
FSACJ Chipper Jones 60.00 150.00
FSACRI Cal Ripken Jr. 60.00 150.00
FSACSC Curt Schilling 8.00 20.00
FSACSE Corey Seager 40.00 100.00
FSACY Carl Yastrzemski 50.00 120.00
FSADO David Ortiz 60.00 150.00
FSADW David Wright
FSAFH Felix Hernandez 20.00 50.00
FSAGM Greg Maddux
FSAJDA Johnny Damon 12.00 30.00
FSAJU Julio Urias 25.00 60.00
FSAJVA Jason Varitek 20.00 50.00
FSAMMA Manny Machado 50.00 120.00
FSAMMG Mark McGwire 60.00 150.00
FSAMP Mike Piazza
FSAMTE Mark Teixeira 10.00 25.00
FSANR Nolan Ryan 50.00 120.00
FSARCL Roger Clemens
FSARH Rickey Henderson
FSATGL Tom Glavine 15.00 40.00
FSAVS Vin Scully 300.00 600.00

2016 Topps Five Star Autographs Rainbow

*RAINBOW: .6X TO 1.5X BASIC
STATED ODDS 1:8 HOBBY
STATED PRINT RUN 25 SER.#'d SETS
EXCHANGE DEADLINE 8/31/2018
FSAAP Andy Pettitte 25.00 60.00
FSABBO Barry Bonds 100.00 250.00
FSABH Bryce Harper 100.00 250.00
FSABPO Buster Posey 60.00 150.00
FSACB Craig Biggio 20.00 50.00
FSACJ Chipper Jones 75.00 200.00
FSACRI Cal Ripken Jr. 75.00 200.00
FSACSA Chris Sale 20.00 50.00
FSACSC Curt Schilling 12.00 30.00
FSACSE Corey Seager 50.00 120.00
FSACY Carl Yastrzemski 60.00 150.00
FSADO David Ortiz 75.00 200.00
FSADW David Wright 20.00 50.00
FSAFH Felix Hernandez 25.00 60.00
FSAGM Greg Maddux 75.00 200.00
FSAI Ichiro Suzuki 400.00 600.00
FSAJDA Johnny Damon 15.00 40.00
FSAJU Julio Urias 30.00 80.00
FSAJVA Jason Varitek 25.00 60.00
FSAMMA Manny Machado 60.00 150.00
FSAMMG Mark McGwire 75.00 200.00
FSAMP Mike Piazza 75.00 200.00
FSAMTE Mark Teixeira 121.00 30.00
FSANR Nolan Ryan 60.00 150.00
FSARCL Roger Clemens 60.00 150.00
FSARH Rickey Henderson 60.00 150.00
FSATGL Tom Glavine 20.00 50.00
FSAVS Vin Scully 400.00 800.00

2016 Topps Five Star Golden Graphs

STATED ODDS 1:13 HOBBY
STATED PRINT RUN 50 SER.#'d SETS
EXCHANGE DEADLINE 8/31/2018
*BLUE/20: .5X TO 1.2X
*PURPLE/25: .5X TO 1.2X
FSGCAG Alex Gordon
FSGCAN Aaron Nola 6.00 15.00
FSGCAP Andy Pettitte
FSGCBJ Bo Jackson 30.00 80.00
FSGCBL Barry Larkin 20.00 50.00
FSGCBP Buster Posey 40.00 100.00
FSGCBW Bernie Williams 15.00 40.00
FSGCCB Craig Biggio 10.00 25.00
FSGCCC Carlos Correa 30.00 80.00
FSGCDO David Ortiz 50.00 120.00
FSGCEM Edgar Martinez 12.00 30.00
FSGCFL Francisco Lindor 40.00 100.00
FSGCFV Fernando Valenzuela 10.00 25.00
FSGCHOW Henry Owens
FSGCJA Jose Altuve 30.00 80.00
FSGCJC Jose Canseco 20.00 50.00
FSGCJS Jorge Soler
FSGCJV Jason Varitek 20.00 50.00
FSGCKB Kris Bryant 125.00 250.00
FSGCKM Kenta Maeda 15.00 40.00
FSGCKS Kyle Schwarber 30.00 80.00
FSGCLS Luis Severino 10.00 25.00
FSGCMS Miguel Sano 12.00 30.00
FSGCNG Nomar Garciaparra 15.00 40.00
FSGCNS Noah Syndergaard 12.00 30.00
FSGCOG Ozzie Guillen
FSGCOS Ozzie Smith 20.00 50.00
FSGCPM Paul Molitor 10.00 25.00
FSGCRF Rollie Fingers 8.00 20.00
FSGCRY Robin Yount 20.00 50.00
FSGCSP Stephen Piscotty
FSGCYC Yoenis Cespedes 12.00 30.00

2016 Topps Five Star Heart of a Champion Autographs

STATED PRINT RUN 25 SER.#'d SETS
EXCHANGE DEADLINE 8/31/2018
FSHCAP Andy Pettitte
FSHCBW Bernie Williams 15.00 40.00
FSHCCF Carlton Fisk
FSHCCS Curt Schilling 25.00 60.00
FSHCDE Dennis Eckersley 12.00 30.00
FSHCDO David Ortiz
FSHCEM Edgar Martinez 15.00 40.00
FSHCIR Ivan Rodriguez 20.00 50.00
FSHCJB Johnny Bench 25.00 60.00
FSHCJD Jacob deGrom
FSHCJS John Smoltz
FSHCLG Luis Gonzalez
FSHCLH Livan Hernandez
FSHCMW Michael Wacha
FSHCOS Ozzie Smith
FSHCPM Paul Molitor 15.00 40.00
FSHCRA Roberto Alomar
FSHCRC Roger Clemens 20.00 50.00
FSHCRF Rollie Fingers
FSHCRH Rickey Henderson 30.00 80.00
FSHCRJA Reggie Jackson 20.00 50.00
FSHCRJO Randy Johnson
FSHCSK Sandy Koufax
FSHCTG Tom Glavine 30.00 80.00
FSHCWD Wade Davis

2016 Topps Five Star Jumbo Patch Autographs

STATED ODDS 1:51 HOBBY
STATED PRINT RUN 25 SER.#'d SETS
EXCHANGE DEADLINE 8/31/2018
FAJPAP Andy Pettitte
FAJPBH Bryce Harper 150.00 300.00
FAJPCB Craig Biggio 60.00 150.00
FAJPCR Cal Ripken Jr.
FAJPDW David Wright 40.00 100.00
FAJPFF Freddie Freeman
FAJPFH Felix Hernandez
FAJPJD Jacob deGrom 100.00 250.00
FAJPMM Manny Machado 100.00 250.00
FAJPPM Paul Molitor 60.00 150.00
FAJPSM Steven Matz 100.00 250.00
FAJPVG Vladimir Guerrero

2016 Topps Five Star Silver Signatures

STATED ODDS 1:13 HOBBY
STATED PRINT RUN 50 SER.#'d SETS
EXCHANGE DEADLINE 8/31/2018
*BLUE/20: .5X TO 1.2X
*PURPLE/25: .5X TO 1.2X
FSSSAG Alex Gordon 6.00 15.00
FSSSAN Aaron Nola 12.00 30.00
FSSSAP Andy Pettitte 20.00 50.00
FSSSBJ Bo Jackson 30.00 80.00
FSSSBL Barry Larkin 20.00 50.00
FSSSBP Buster Posey 40.00 100.00
FSSSCB Craig Biggio 6.00 15.00
FSSSCK Clayton Kershaw 40.00 100.00
FSSSCS Chris Sale
FSSSDO David Ortiz 40.00 100.00
FSSSEM Edgar Martinez 12.00 30.00
FSSSFL Francisco Lindor 12.00 30.00
FSSSHOW Henry Owens
FSSSJA Jose Altuve 20.00 50.00
FSSSJC Jose Canseco 15.00 40.00
FSSSJH Jason Heyward 6.00 15.00
FSSSJV Jason Varitek 12.00 30.00
FSSSKB Kris Bryant 100.00 250.00
FSSSKM Kenta Maeda 10.00 25.00
FSSSKS Kyle Schwarber
FSSSLG Luis Gonzalez 8.00 20.00
FSSSLS Luis Severino 10.00 25.00
FSSSMS Miguel Sano 10.00 25.00
FSSSMT Mark Teixeira 20.00 50.00
FSSSNG Nomar Garciaparra 15.00 40.00
FSSSNS Noah Syndergaard 25.00 60.00
FSSSOG Ozzie Guillen 6.00 15.00
FSSSOS Ozzie Smith 10.00 25.00
FSSSRC Rod Carew 10.00 25.00
FSSSSP Stephen Piscotty
FSSSYC Yoenis Cespedes

2017 Topps Five Star Autographs

EXCHANGE DEADLINE 9/30/2019
FSAABE Andrew Benintendi RC 20.00 50.00
FSAABR Alex Bregman RC 25.00 60.00
FSAADI Aledmys Diaz 4.00 10.00
FSAAG Andres Galarraga 4.00 10.00
FSAAJ Aaron Judge RC 60.00 150.00
FSAAK Al Kaline 15.00 40.00
FSAARE Alex Reyes RC 4.00 10.00
FSAARI Anthony Rizzo 15.00 40.00
FSAARU Addison Russell 8.00 20.00
FSAAT Andrew Toles RC 3.00 8.00
FSABH Bryce Harper 75.00 200.00
FSABL Barry Larkin
FSACB Cody Bellinger RC 50.00 120.00
FSACC Carlos Correa
FSACFU Carson Fulmer RC 3.00 8.00
FSACJ Chipper Jones
FSACKE Clayton Kershaw
FSACKL Corey Kluber 6.00 15.00
FSACR Cal Ripken Jr.
FSACSA Chris Sale 10.00 25.00
FSACSE Corey Seager 15.00 40.00
FSADB Dellin Betances 4.00 10.00
FSADJ Derek Jeter
FSADM Don Mattingly
FSADS Dansby Swanson RC 12.00 30.00
FSADV Dan Vogelbach RC 5.00 12.00
FSADW Dave Winfield
FSAEM Edgar Martinez 6.00 15.00
FSAFF Freddie Freeman 10.00 25.00
FSAFL Francisco Lindor 12.00 30.00
FSAGC Gavin Cecchini RC 3.00 8.00
FSAGSP George Springer 8.00 20.00
FSAHA Hank Aaron
FSAHR Hunter Renfroe RC 4.00 10.00
FSAIR Ivan Rodriguez 6.00 15.00
FSAI Ichiro
FSAJAT Jose Altuve 20.00 50.00
FSAJBA Jeff Bagwell 20.00 50.00
FSAJBE Javier Baez 20.00 50.00
FSAJCA Jose Canseco 8.00 20.00
FSAJCO Jharel Cotton RC 3.00 8.00
FSAJDA Johnny Damon 6.00 15.00
FSAJDG Jacob deGrom 12.00 30.00
FSAJDL Jose De Leon RC 3.00 8.00
FSAJDO Josh Donaldson
FSAJG Juan Gonzalez 5.00 12.00
FSAJM Joe Musgrove RC 10.00 25.00
FSAJS John Smoltz
FSAJTH Jake Thompson RC 3.00 8.00
FSAJU Julio Urias 5.00 12.00
FSAKB Kris Bryant
FSAKM Kenta Maeda 6.00 15.00
FSAKSC Kyle Schwarber 5.00 12.00
FSAKSE Kyle Seager 3.00 8.00
FSALG Lucas Giolito 4.00 10.00
FSALW Luke Weaver RC 4.00 10.00
FSAMC Matt Carpenter 5.00 12.00
FSAMMA Manny Machado
FSAMMG Mark McGwire
FSAMMR Manny Margot RC 3.00 8.00
FSAMTA Masahiro Tanaka
FSAMTR Mike Trout
FSANR Nolan Ryan
FSANS Noah Syndergaard 8.00 20.00
FSAOS Ozzie Smith
FSAOV Omar Vizquel 4.00 10.00
FSARGR Randal Grichuk 3.00 8.00
FSARGS Robert Gsellman RC 3.00 8.00
FSARH Ryon Healy RC 4.00 10.00
FSARL Reynaldo Lopez RC 3.00 8.00
FSARO Roy Oswalt 4.00 10.00
FSART Raimel Tapia RC 4.00 10.00
FSASK Sandy Koufax
FSASMR Starling Marte 4.00 10.00
FSASMZ Steven Matz 3.00 8.00
FSATA Tyler Austin RC 4.00 10.00
FSATE Theo Epstein 50.00 120.00
FSATGS Tyler Glasnow RC 10.00 25.00
FSATGV Tom Glavine
FSATM Trey Mancini RC 4.00 10.00
FSATR Tim Raines 5.00 12.00
FSATS Trevor Story 5.00 12.00
FSAYG Yulieski Gurriel RC 8.00 20.00

2017 Topps Five Star Autographs Blue

*BLUE: .6X TO 1.5X BASIC
STATED PRINT RUN 25 SER.#'d SETS
EXCHANGE DEADLINE 9/30/2019
FSABL Barry Larkin 20.00 50.00
FSACC Carlos Correa 40.00 100.00
FSACJ Chipper Jones 50.00 120.00
FSACKE Clayton Kershaw 50.00 120.00
FSACR Cal Ripken Jr. 60.00 150.00
FSADM Don Mattingly 30.00 80.00
FSADW Dave Winfield 20.00 50.00
FSAJDO Josh Donaldson 10.00 25.00
FSAJS John Smoltz 12.00 30.00
FSAKB Kris Bryant 60.00 150.00
FSAMMA Manny Machado 30.00 80.00
FSAMMG Mark McGwire 40.00 100.00
FSANR Nolan Ryan 100.00 250.00
FSAOS Ozzie Smith 20.00 50.00
FSATGV Tom Glavine 12.00 30.00

2017 Topps Five Star Autographs Purple

*PURPLE: .5X TO 1.2X BASIC
STATED PRINT RUN 50 SER.#'d SETS
EXCHANGE DEADLINE 9/30/2019
FSABL Barry Larkin 15.00 40.00
FSACC Carlos Correa 30.00 80.00
FSACKE Clayton Kershaw 40.00 100.00
FSADM Don Mattingly 25.00 60.00
FSADW Dave Winfield 15.00 40.00
FSAJDO Josh Donaldson 8.00 20.00
FSAJS John Smoltz 10.00 25.00
FSAKB Kris Bryant 50.00 120.00
FSAMMA Manny Machado 25.00 60.00
FSAOS Ozzie Smith 15.00 40.00
FSATGV Tom Glavine 10.00 25.00

2017 Topps Five Star Golden Graphs

PRINT RUNS B/WN 30-50 COPIES PER
EXCHANGE DEADLINE 9/30/2019
GGABE Andrew Benintendi/50 25.00 60.00
GGABR Alex Bregman/50 15.00 40.00
GGARE Alex Reyes/50 8.00 20.00
GGCC Carlos Correa
GGCJ Chipper Jones
GGCK Corey Kluber/30 10.00 25.00
GGCSA Chris Sale/30 15.00 40.00
GGDPE Dustin Pedroia
GGDPR David Price
GGDS Dansby Swanson/50 15.00 40.00
GGDW Dave Winfield
GGFF Freddie Freeman/30 12.00 30.00
GGFL Francisco Lindor/50 20.00 50.00
GGGM Greg Maddux
GGJA Jose Altuve EXCH 25.00 60.00
GGJB Jeff Bagwell
GGJD Josh Donaldson
GGJS John Smoltz
GGJV Joey Votto
GGKB Kris Bryant
GGKM Kenta Maeda/30 10.00 25.00
GGKS Kyle Schwarber/50 15.00 40.00
GGMM Manny Machado
GGNS Noah Syndergaard/50 12.00 30.00
GGOV Omar Vizquel/30 6.00 15.00
GGRG Roger Clemens
GGRJ Randy Johnson
GGTG Tyler Glasnow/50 15.00 40.00
GGTR Tim Raines
GGYG Yulieski Gurriel/50 15.00 40.00

2017 Topps Five Star Golden Graphs Blue

*BLUE: .5X TO 1.2X BASIC
STATED PRINT RUN 20 SER.#'d SETS
EXCHANGE DEADLINE 9/30/2019
GGCC Carlos Correa 30.00 80.00
GGDPE Dustin Pedroia 20.00 50.00
GGDPR David Price 8.00 20.00
GGDW Dave Winfield 15.00 40.00
GGJB Jeff Bagwell 15.00 40.00
GGJS John Smoltz 15.00 40.00
GGJV Joey Votto 40.00 100.00
GGKB Kris Bryant 100.00 250.00
GGMM Manny Machado 30.00 80.00
GGTR Tim Raines 15.00 40.00

2017 Topps Five Star Golden Graphs Purple

*PURPLE: .5X TO 1.2X BASIC
STATED PRINT RUN 25 SER.#'d SETS
EXCHANGE DEADLINE 9/30/2019
GGDPE Dustin Pedroia 20.00 50.00
GGDPR David Price 8.00 20.00
GGDW Dave Winfield 15.00 40.00
GGJB Jeff Bagwell 15.00 40.00
GGJS John Smoltz 15.00 40.00
GGJV Joey Votto
GGKB Kris Bryant 100.00 250.00
GGMM Manny Machado 30.00 80.00
GGTR Tim Raines 15.00 40.00

2017 Topps Five Star Heart of a Champion Autographs

PRINT RUNS B/WN 5-35 COPIES PER
NO PRICING ON QTY 15 OR LESS
EXCHANGE DEADLINE 9/30/2019
FSHCAK Al Kaline/35 50.00 120.00
FSHCAP Andy Pettitte/35 15.00 40.00
FSHCARI Anthony Rizzo/35 30.00 80.00
FSHCARO Alex Rodriguez/25 100.00 250.00
FSHCARU Addison Russell/35 20.00 50.00
FSHCBL Barry Larkin/35 25.00 60.00
FSHCBP Buster Posey/25 50.00 120.00
FSHCCJ Chipper Jones/25 60.00 150.00
FSHCCK Corey Kluber/35 15.00 40.00
FSHCDO David Ortiz/25 50.00 120.00
FSHCDP Dustin Pedroia/35 20.00 50.00
FSHCEL Evan Longoria/25 15.00 40.00
FSHCEM Edgar Martinez/35 20.00 50.00
FSHCFR Frank Robinson/35 25.00 60.00
FSHCHA Hank Aaron/5
FSHCJBA Jeff Bagwell/35 20.00 50.00
FSHCJBE Javier Baez/35 30.00 80.00
FSHCJD Johnny Damon/35 12.00 30.00
FSHCJS John Smoltz/35 30.00 80.00
FSHCKB Kris Bryant/25 125.00 300.00
FSHCKS Kyle Schwarber/35 20.00 50.00
FSHCMM Mark McGwire/25 60.00 150.00
FSHCOS Ozzie Smith/35 20.00 50.00
FSHCOV Omar Vizquel/35 12.00 30.00
FSHCPK Paul Konerko/35 25.00 60.00
FSHCPM Pedro Martinez/25 50.00 120.00
FSHCRO Roy Oswalt/35 25.00 60.00
FSHCTG Tom Glavine/35 20.00 50.00

2017 Topps Five Star Jumbo Patch Autographs

PRINT RUNS B/WN 35-50 COPIES PER
EXCHANGE DEADLINE 9/30/2019
FAJPAJ Adam Jones/35 25.00 60.00
FAJPARI Anthony Rizzo
FAJPARU Addison Russell EXCH 15.00 40.00
FAJPBP Buster Posey
FAJPCC Carlos Correa/50 60.00 150.00
FAJPCJ Chipper Jones
FAJPCK Corey Kluber
FAJPDB Dellin Betances/50 12.00 30.00
FAJPDO David Ortiz
FAJPDPE Dustin Pedroia/35 25.00 60.00
FAJPDPR David Price
FAJPEL Evan Longoria/50 20.00 50.00
FAJPFF Freddie Freeman EXCH 20.00 50.00
FAJPGS George Springer/50 30.00 80.00
FAJPI Ichiro
FAJPJA Jose Altuve 40.00 100.00
FAJPJDG Jacob deGrom/50 40.00 100.00
FAJPJS John Smoltz/35 25.00 60.00
FAJPJT Jameson Taillon/35 20.00 50.00
FAJPJV Joey Votto/50 40.00 100.00
FAJPKSE Kyle Seager/35 20.00 50.00
FAJPMC Matt Carpenter/35 15.00 40.00
FAJPMF Michael Fulmer/35 10.00 25.00
FAJPMM Manny Machado
FAJPMS Miguel Sano/35 30.00 80.00
FAJPMT Masahiro Tanaka
FAJPNSY Noah Syndergaard/50 25.00 60.00
FAJPPM Pedro Martinez
FAJPSM Starling Marte/35 12.00 30.00
FAJPSP Stephen Piscotty
FAJPTGS Tyler Glasnow/35 20.00 50.00
FAJPTGV Tom Glavine
FAJPYC Yoenis Cespedes EXCH 25.00 60.00
FAJPYG Yulieski Gurriel

2017 Topps Five Star Jumbo Patch Autographs Gold

*GOLD: .5X TO 1.2X BASIC
STATED PRINT RUN 25 SER.#'d SETS
EXCHANGE DEADLINE 9/30/2019
FAJPCK Corey Kluber 40.00 100.00
FAJPDPR David Price 20.00 50.00
FAJPI Ichiro 400.00 600.00
FAJPMT Masahiro Tanaka 100.00 250.00
FAJPSP Stephen Piscotty 20.00 50.00
FAJPTGV Tom Glavine 40.00 100.00

2017 Topps Five Star Signatures

PRINT RUNS B/WN 5-20 COPIES PER
NO PRICING ON QTY 15 OR LESS
EXCHANGE DEADLINE 9/30/2019
FSIABE Andrew Benintendi/20 75.00 200.00
FSIAG Andres Galarraga/20 5.00 12.00
FSIBH Bryce Harper EXCH
FSICB Craig Biggio
FSICK Clayton Kershaw EXCH
FSICS Corey Seager EXCH
FSIJA Jose Altuve
FSIJC Jose Canseco/20 25.00 60.00
FSIJDO Josh Donaldson EXCH
FSIMMG Mark McGwire
FSIMT Mike Trout
FSIOV Omar Vizquel/20 20.00 50.00
FSIPM Pedro Martinez
FSISK Sandy Koufax

2017 Topps Five Star Silver Signatures

PRINT RUNS B/WN 30-50 COPIES PER
EXCHANGE DEADLINE 9/30/2019
SSABE Andrew Benintendi EXCH 30.00 80.00
SSAD Aledmys Diaz/50 5.00 12.00
SSAG Andres Galarraga/30 5.00 12.00
SSAJ Aaron Judge/50 125.00 300.00
SSAK Al Kaline
SSAP Andy Pettitte
SSARE Alex Reyes/50 6.00 15.00
SSBH Bryce Harper
SSBL Barry Larkin
SSCB Craig Biggio
SSCK Clayton Kershaw
SSCS Corey Seager
SSDM Don Mattingly
SSDS Dansby Swanson
SSEM Edgar Martinez/30 10.00 25.00
SSFT Frank Thomas
SSIR Ivan Rodriguez 10.00 25.00
SSJC Jose Canseco/30 25.00 60.00
SSJD Johnny Damon
SSJDG Jacob deGrom
SSJG Juan Gonzalez/30 12.00 30.00
SSJU Julio Urias/50 6.00 15.00
SSKS Kyle Schwarber/50 12.00 30.00
SSNS Noah Syndergaard/50 20.00 50.00
SSOS Ozzie Smith
SSOV Omar Vizquel/50 6.00 15.00
SSRO Roy Oswalt/30 5.00 12.00
SSYM Yoan Moncada

2017 Topps Five Star Silver Signatures Blue

*BLUE: .5X TO 1.2X BASIC
STATED PRINT RUN 20 SER.#'d SETS
EXCHANGE DEADLINE 9/30/2019
SSAK Al Kaline 25.00 50.00
SSAP Andy Pettitte 15.00 40.00
SSBL Barry Larkin 20.00 50.00
SSCS Corey Seager EXCH 25.00 60.00
SSDM Don Mattingly 30.00 80.00
SSDS Dansby Swanson 15.00 40.00
SSIR Ivan Rodriguez 12.00 30.00
SSJD Johnny Damon 10.00 25.00
SSJDG Jacob deGrom 30.00 80.00
SSOS Ozzie Smith 20.00 50.00

2017 Topps Five Star Silver Signatures Purple

*PURPLE: .5X TO 1.2X BASIC
STATED PRINT RUN 25 SER.#'d SETS
EXCHANGE DEADLINE 9/30/2019
SSAK Al Kaline 25.00 50.00
SSAP Andy Pettitte 15.00 40.00
SSBL Barry Larkin
SSCS Corey Seager EXCH 25.00 60.00
SSDM Don Mattingly 30.00 80.00
SSDS Dansby Swanson 15.00 40.00
SSIR Ivan Rodriguez 12.00 30.00
SSJD Johnny Damon 10.00 25.00
SSJDG Jacob deGrom 30.00 80.00

2018 Topps Five Star Autographs

EXCHANGE DEADLINE 8/31/2020
FSAAB Anthony Banda RC 3.00 8.00
FSAAH Austin Hays RC 5.00 12.00
FSAAI Anthony Rizzo EXCH 15.00 40.00
FSAAJ Aaron Judge 60.00 150.00
FSAAM Austin Meadows RC 10.00 25.00
FSAAN Aaron Nola 6.00 15.00
FSAAR Amed Rosario RC 5.00 12.00
FSAAV Alex Verdugo RC 5.00 12.00
FSAAW Alex Wood 3.00 8.00
FSABA Brian Anderson RC 4.00 10.00
FSABD Brian Dozier 4.00 10.00
FSABH Bryce Harper 75.00 200.00
FSABJ Bo Jackson 50.00 120.00
FSACB Charlie Blackmon 5.00 12.00
FSACF Clint Frazier RC 6.00 15.00
FSACK Corey Kluber 8.00 20.00
FSACR Cal Ripken Jr. 60.00 150.00
FSACS Chance Sisco RC 4.00 10.00
FSACT Chris Taylor EXCH 4.00 10.00
FSADF Dustin Fowler RC 3.00 8.00
FSADJ Derek Jeter 125.00 300.00
FSADM Don Mattingly 25.00 60.00
FSADO Dwight Gooden 10.00 25.00
FSADT Darryl Strawberry 12.00 30.00
FSAFL Francisco Lindor 25.00 60.00
FSAFM Francisco Mejia RC 4.00 10.00
FSAFT Frank Thomas 25.00 60.00
FSAGP George Springer 10.00 25.00
FSAGS Gary Sanchez 10.00 25.00
FSAGT Gleyber Torres RC 40.00 100.00
FSAHA Hank Aaron 175.00 350.00
FSAHB Harrison Bader RC 5.00 12.00
FSAHR Hunter Renfroe 3.00 8.00
FSAIH Ian Happ 4.00 10.00
FSAIK Ian Kinsler 4.00 10.00
FSAJA Jose Altuve 20.00 50.00
FSAJC Jose Canseco 10.00 25.00
FSAJE Jose Berrios 4.00 10.00
FSAJF Jack Flaherty RC 15.00 40.00
FSAJI J.D. Davis RC 4.00 10.00
FSAJL Jake Lamb 4.00 10.00
FSAJR Jose Ramirez 10.00 25.00
FSAJS Justin Smoak 3.00 8.00
FSAJSO Juan Soto RC 75.00 200.00
FSAJU Justin Upton 8.00 20.00
FSAJV Joey Votto EXCH 20.00 50.00
FSAKB Kris Bryant EXCH 50.00 120.00
FSAKD Khris Davis 5.00 12.00
FSAKS Kyle Schwarber 8.00 20.00
FSALS Lucas Sims RC 3.00 8.00
FSAMA Miguel Andujar RC 20.00 50.00
FSAMF Max Fried RC 10.00 25.00
FSAMM Mark McGwire 30.00 80.00
FSAMO Matt Olson 5.00 12.00
FSAMR Manny Margot 3.00 8.00
FSAMT Mike Trout 150.00 400.00
FSANR Nolan Ryan
FSAOA Ozzie Albies RC 12.00 30.00
FSAPD Paul DeJong 5.00 12.00
FSAPG Paul Goldschmidt 10.00 25.00
FSARA Ronald Acuna RC 75.00 200.00
FSARD Rafael Devers RC 20.00 50.00
FSARH Rhys Hoskins RC 20.00 50.00
FSARM Ryan McMahon RC 8.00 20.00
FSASI Scott Kingery RC 12.00 30.00
FSASK Sandy Koufax
FSASM Starling Marte 5.00 12.00
FSASO Shohei Ohtani RC 125.00 300.00
FSATA Tyler Mahle RC 4.00 10.00
FSATM Trey Mancini 4.00 10.00
FSATP Tommy Pham 3.00 8.00
FSATS Travis Shaw 3.00 8.00
FSAVC Victor Caratini RC 4.00 10.00
FSAVR Victor Robles RC 10.00 25.00
FSAWB Walker Buehler RC 40.00 100.00
FSAWC Willson Contreras 8.00 20.00
FSAWM Whit Merrifield 8.00 20.00

2018 Topps Five Star Autographs Blue

*BLUE: .6X TO 1.5X BASIC
STATED ODDS 1:10 HOBBY
STATED PRINT RUN 25 SER.#'d SETS
EXCHANGE DEADLINE 8/31/2020
FSAHA Hank Aaron 200.00 400.00
FSANR Nolan Ryan 50.00 120.00

2018 Topps Five Star Autographs Purple

*PURPLE: .5X TO 1.2X BASIC
RANDOM INSERTS IN PACKS
STATED PRINT RUN 50 SER.#'d SETS
EXCHANGE DEADLINE 8/31/2020

2018 Topps Five Star Career Year Autographs

STATED ODDS 1:18 HOBBY
PRINT RUNS B/WN 5-50 COPIES PER
NO PRICING ON QTY 15 OR LESS
EXCHANGE DEADLINE 8/31/2020
CRAAJ Andruw Jones/50 12.00 30.00
CRAAK Al Kaline/35 25.00 50.00
CRABG Bob Gibson/45 12.00 30.00
CRACJ Chipper Jones/25 60.00 150.00
CRACR Cal Ripken Jr./25 60.00 150.00
CRADE Dennis Eckersley/35 10.00 25.00
CRADM Don Mattingly/45 40.00 100.00
CRADP Dustin Pedroia/45 12.00 30.00
CRADS Darryl Strawberry/45 12.00 30.00
CRAEM Edgar Martinez/35 15.00 40.00
CRAFT Frank Thomas/45 40.00 100.00
CRAJC Jose Canseco/35 15.00 40.00
CRAJP Jim Palmer/35 15.00 40.00
CRAJS John Smoltz/45 20.00 50.00
CRAJV Joey Votto/45 25.00 60.00
CRAKB Kris Bryant/45 50.00 120.00
CRALB Lou Brock/50 12.00 30.00
CRAMM Mark McGwire/25 40.00 100.00
CRAOS Ozzie Smith/45 20.00 50.00
CRARA Roberto Alomar/35 15.00 40.00
CRARS Ryne Sandberg/25 25.00 60.00
CRARY Robin Yount/45 30.00 80.00
CRASC Steve Carlton/45 15.00 40.00
CRATG Tom Glavine/45 20.00 50.00
CRAWB Wade Boggs/25 40.00 100.00
CRAWC Will Clark/45 25.00 60.00

2018 Topps Five Star Golden Graphs

STATED ODDS 1:18 HOBBY
PRINT RUNS B/WN 35-50 COPIES PER
EXCHANGE DEADLINE 8/31/2020
FGGAR Amed Rosario/35 8.00 20.00
FGGAT Alan Trammell/35 25.00 60.00
FGGBG Bob Gibson/35 15.00 40.00
FGGDP Dustin Pedroia/35 12.00 30.00
FGGET Eric Thames/50 5.00 12.00
FGGFF Freddie Freeman/35 20.00 50.00
FGGFL Francisco Lindor/35 25.00 60.00
FGGGS George Springer/35 12.00 30.00
FGGJC Jose Canseco/35 12.00 30.00
FGGJd Jacob deGrom/35 30.00 80.00
FGGJM Jack Morris/35 20.00 50.00
FGGJP Jim Palmer EXCH 12.00 30.00
FGGLB Lou Brock/35 15.00 40.00
FGGNS Noah Syndergaard/35 10.00 25.00
FGGPD Paul DeJong/35 6.00 15.00
FGGPG Paul Goldschmidt/35 12.00 30.00
FGGSM Starling Marte/35 8.00 20.00
FGGTG Tom Glavine/35 12.00 30.00
FGGWC Will Clark/35 30.00 80.00
FGGYM Yadier Molina/35 40.00 100.00

2018 Topps Five Star Golden Graphs Blue

*BLUE: .5X TO 1.2X BASIC
STATED ODDS 1:45 HOBBY
STATED PRINT RUN 20 SER.#'d SETS
EXCHANGE DEADLINE 8/31/2020
FGGAN Aaron Nola 15.00 40.00
FGGCJ Chipper Jones 50.00 120.00
FGGCK Corey Kluber 15.00 40.00
FGGJA Jose Altuve 25.00 60.00
FGGJS John Smoltz 30.00 80.00
FGGKB Kris Bryant EXCH 50.00 120.00
FGGSO Shohei Ohtani 200.00 500.00

2018 Topps Five Star Golden Graphs Purple

*PURPLE: .5X TO 1.2X BASIC
STATED ODDS 1:36 HOBBY
STATED PRINT RUN 25 SER.#'d SETS
EXCHANGE DEADLINE 8/31/2020
FGGCK Corey Kluber 15.00 40.00
FGGSO Shohei Ohtani 200.00 500.00

2018 Topps Five Star Jumbo Patch Autographs

STATED ODDS 1:16 HOBBY
PRINT RUNS B/WN 30-35 COPIES PER
EXCHANGE DEADLINE 8/31/2020
FSJPAB Andrew Benintendi EXCH 50.00 120.00
FSJPCB Charlie Blackmon/30 25.00 60.00
FSJPCI Craig Kimbrel/30 25.00 60.00
FSJPCS Chris Sale/30 30.00 80.00
FSJPDG Didi Gregorius/30 40.00 100.00
FSJPIR Ivan Rodriguez/35 50.00 120.00
FSJPJA Jose Altuve/30 50.00 120.00
FSJPJd Jacob deGrom/30 60.00 150.00
FSJPJH Josh Harrison/30 20.00 50.00
FSJPJM Johnny Damon/30 15.00 40.00
FSJPKD Khris Davis/30 15.00 40.00
FSJPKE Kyle Seager/30 10.00 25.00
FSJPPM Pedro Martinez/35 50.00 120.00
FSJPRA Roberto Alomar/30 40.00 100.00
FSJPRD Rafael Devers/30 40.00 100.00
FSJPRH Rickey Henderson/35 40.00 100.00
FSJPRHE Rickey Henderson/35 40.00 100.00
FSJPTG Tom Glavine/30 20.00 50.00
FSJPWM Whit Merrifield/35 20.00 50.00

2018 Topps Five Star Jumbo Patch Autographs Gold

*GOLD: .5X TO 1.2X BASIC
STATED ODDS 1:28 HOBBY
PRINT RUNS B/WN 5-25 COPIES PER
NO PRICING ON QTY 5
EXCHANGE DEADLINE 8/31/2020
FSJPAG Alex Bregman 50.00 120.00
FSJPAN Aaron Nola 50.00 120.00
FSJPBB Byron Buxton 20.00 50.00
FSJPBP Buster Posey EXCH 60.00 150.00
FSJPCJ Chipper Jones 60.00 150.00
FSJPDO David Ortiz 75.00 200.00
FSJPDP Dustin Pedroia 50.00 120.00
FSJPFF Freddie Freeman 50.00 120.00
FSJPGS Gary Sanchez 30.00 80.00
FSJPI Ichiro 300.00 500.00
FSJPIH Ian Happ 15.00 40.00
FSJPJC J.P. Crawford 12.00 30.00
FSJPJV Joey Votto 40.00 100.00
FSJPKS Kyle Schwarber 15.00 40.00
FSJPOA Ozzie Albies 40.00 100.00
FSJPPG Paul Goldschmidt 30.00 80.00

FSJPSM Starling Marte 40.00 100.00
FSJPTP Tommy Pham 6.00 15.00
FSJPYG Yuli Gurriel 15.00 40.00
FSJPYM Yadier Molina 100.00 250.00

2018 Topps Five Star Signatures

STATED ODDS 1:13 HOBBY
PRINT RUNS B/WN 5-50 COPIES PER
NO PRICING ON QTY 15 OR LESS
EXCHANGE DEADLINE 8/31/2020
FSSAI Anthony Rizzo/35 20.00 50.00
FSSAK Al Kaline/35 25.00 50.00
FSSAP Andy Pettitte/35 25.00 60.00
FSSAR Amed Rosario/45 6.00 15.00
FSSBG Bob Gibson/35 15.00 40.00
FSSBH Bryce Harper EXCH 75.00 200.00
FSSBJ Bo Jackson/25 40.00 100.00
FSSBP Buster Posey EXCH 30.00 80.00
FSSCB Craig Biggio/35 10.00 25.00
FSSCF Clint Frazier/45 10.00 25.00
FSSCJ Chipper Jones/35 50.00 120.00
FSSCR Cal Ripken Jr./25 60.00 150.00
FSSCS Chris Sale/35 15.00 40.00
FSSDM Don Mattingly/35 40.00 100.00
FSSFL Francisco Lindor/35 20.00 50.00
FSSFT Frank Thomas/35 30.00 80.00
FSSGS Gary Sanchez/35 15.00 40.00
FSSGT Gleyber Torres/50 40.00 100.00
FSSJA Jose Altuve/45 20.00 50.00
FSSJB Jeff Bagwell/35 12.00 30.00
FSSJD Johnny Damon/35 8.00 20.00
FSSJN Jose Canseco/35 12.00 30.00
FSSJS John Smoltz/35 20.00 50.00
FSSJU Justin Upton/35 8.00 20.00
FSSJV Joey Votto/35 25.00 60.00
FSSKB Kris Bryant 50.00 120.00
FSSMC Mark McGwire/25 40.00 100.00
FSSMP Mike Piazza/20 40.00 100.00
FSSMR Mariano Rivera/20 125.00 300.00
FSSNR Nolan Ryan/25 75.00 200.00
FSSOA Ozzie Albies/35 15.00 40.00
FSSOS Ozzie Smith/35 20.00 50.00
FSSPM Pedro Martinez/20 50.00 120.00
FSSRA Ronald Acuna/50 75.00 200.00
FSSRC Roger Clemens/20 25.00 60.00
FSSRD Rafael Devers/35 20.00 50.00
FSSRJ Randy Johnson/20 40.00 100.00
FSSSO Shohei Ohtani/25 75.00 200.00
FSSTG Tom Glavine/35 15.00 40.00
FSSTR Tim Raines/35 8.00 20.00
FSSWL Will Clark/45 25.00 60.00
FSSYM Yadier Molina/45 40.00 100.00

2018 Topps Five Star Silver Signatures

STATED ODDS 1:18 HOBBY
PRINT RUNS B/WN 35-50 COPIES PER
EXCHANGE DEADLINE 8/31/2020
FFSSAO Amed Rosario/35 8.00 20.00
FFSSBB Byron Buxton/35 6.00 15.00
FFSSBD Brian Dozier/35 6.00 15.00
FFSSBY Bert Blyleven/35 10.00 25.00
FFSSCA Charlie Blackmon EXCH 6.00 15.00
FFSSCF Clint Frazier/35 10.00 25.00
FFSSCK Craig Kimbrel/35 8.00 20.00
FFSSCS Chris Sale/35 15.00 40.00
FFSSCY Christian Yelich/50 25.00 60.00
FFSSDE Dennis Eckersley/35 10.00 25.00
FFSSJD Johnny Damon/35 8.00 20.00
FFSSOA Ozzie Albies/35 20.00 50.00
FFSSRD Rafael Devers/35 20.00 50.00
FFSSTM Trey Mancini/35 6.00 15.00
FFSSTR Tim Raines/35 8.00 20.00

2018 Topps Five Star Silver Signatures Blue

*BLUE: .5X TO 1.2X BASIC
STATED ODDS 1:45 HOBBY
STATED PRINT RUN 20 SER.#'d SETS
EXCHANGE DEADLINE 8/31/2020
FFSSAB Adrian Beltre 25.00 60.00
FFSSAK Al Kaline 25.00 50.00
FFSSAR Anthony Rizzo EXCH 25.00 60.00
FFSSJU Justin Upton 12.00 30.00
FFSSJV Joey Votto EXCH 20.00 50.00
FFSSLS Luis Severino 15.00 40.00
FFSSRA Roberto Alomar 20.00 50.00
FFSSRC Rod Carew 15.00 40.00
FFSSRS Ryne Sandberg 25.00 60.00
FFSSSO Shohei Ohtani EXCH 200.00 500.00
FFSSVR Victor Robles 20.00 50.00
FFSSWB Wade Boggs 25.00 60.00
FFSSWC Willson Contreras 12.00 30.00

2018 Topps Five Star Silver Signatures Purple

*PURPLE: .5X TO 1.2X BASIC
STATED ODDS 1:36 HOBBY
STATED PRINT RUN 25 SER.#'d SETS
EXCHANGE DEADLINE 8/31/2020
FFSSAK Al Kaline 25.00 50.00
FFSSJU Justin Upton 12.00 30.00
FFSSRA Roberto Alomar 20.00 50.00
FFSSSO Shohei Ohtani EXCH 200.00 500.00
FFSSVR Victor Robles 20.00 50.00
FFSSWC Willson Contreras 12.00 30.00

2019 Topps Five Star Autographs

EXCHANGE DEADLINE 8/31/2021
FSAAA Aaron Judge 75.00 200.00
FSAAN Aaron Nola 6.00 15.00
FSAAR Anthony Rizzo 15.00 40.00
FSABM Brandon Nimmo 4.00 10.00
FSABW Bryse Wilson RC 8.00 20.00
FSACB Corbin Burnes RC 10.00 25.00
FSACM Cedric Mullins RC 10.00 25.00
FSACRJ Cal Ripken Jr. 60.00 150.00
FSADH Dakota Hudson RC 4.00 10.00
FSADJ Danny Jansen RC 3.00 8.00
FSADP Daniel Ponce de Leon RC 5.00 12.00
FSADS Darryl Strawberry 12.00 30.00
FSADST DJ Stewart RC 4.00 10.00
FSAEJ Eloy Jimenez RC 30.00 80.00
FSAFF Freddie Freeman 15.00 40.00
FSAFL Francisco Lindor 30.00 80.00
FSAFT Frank Thomas 30.00 80.00
FSAFTJ Fernando Tatis Jr. RC 150.00 400.00
FSAJA Jose Altuve 15.00 40.00
FSAJB Jake Bauers RC 5.00 12.00
FSAJC Jake Cave RC 4.00 10.00
FSAJCA Jose Canseco 10.00 25.00
FSAJD Jacob deGrom 12.00 30.00
FSAJE Jean Segura 5.00 12.00
FSAJF Jack Flaherty 8.00 20.00
FSAJH Josh Hader 4.00 10.00
FSAJJ Josh James RC 5.00 12.00
FSAJM Jeff McNeil RC 12.00 30.00
FSAJR Jose Ramirez 6.00 15.00
FSAJS Justus Sheffield RC 12.00 30.00
FSAJSM Justin Smoak 3.00 8.00
FSAJSO Juan Soto 40.00 100.00
FSAJV Joey Votto 15.00 40.00
FSAKA Kolby Allard RC 5.00 12.00
FSAKIE Carter Kieboom RC 8.00 20.00
FSAKST Kohl Stewart RC 4.00 10.00
FSAKW Kyle Wright RC 5.00 12.00
FSALS Luis Severino 6.00 15.00
FSALV Luke Voit 30.00 80.00
FSAMA Matt Kemp 4.00 10.00
FSAMCH Matt Chapman 6.00 15.00
FSAMH Mitch Haniger 4.00 10.00
FSAMI Miguel Andujar 5.00 12.00
FSAMK Michael Kopech RC 10.00 25.00
FSAMM Max Muncy 6.00 15.00
FSAMO Matt Olson 5.00 12.00
FSAMR Mark McGwire
FSAMS Myles Straw RC 5.00 12.00
FSAMT Mike Trout
FSANM Nick Martini RC 3.00 8.00
FSANS Nick Senzel RC EXCH 12.00 30.00
FSAPA Pete Alonso RC 50.00 120.00
FSAPC Patrick Corbin 6.00 15.00
FSAPD Paul DeJong 8.00 20.00
FSAPG Paul Goldschmidt 10.00 25.00
FSAPW Patrick Wisdom RC 3.00 8.00
FSARA Ronald Acuna Jr. 60.00 150.00
FSARD Rafael Devers 12.00 30.00
FSARH Rhys Hoskins 10.00 25.00
FSARL Ramon Laureano RC 10.00 25.00
FSARM Reese McGuire RC 5.00 12.00
FSART Rowdy Tellez RC 5.00 12.00
FSASD Steven Duggar RC 4.00 10.00
FSASM Steven Matz 3.00 8.00
FSASO Shohei Ohtani 100.00 250.00
FSATB Trevor Bauer 10.00 25.00
FSATP Tommy Pham 3.00 8.00
FSATRI Trevor Richards RC 3.00 8.00
FSATT Touki Toussaint RC 4.00 10.00
FSAVGJ Vladimir Guerrero Jr. RC 50.00 120.00
FSAVR Victor Robles 8.00 20.00
FSAWA Willians Astudillo RC 3.00 8.00
FSAWM Whit Merrifield 10.00 25.00
FSAYK Yusei Kikuchi RC 6.00 15.00

2019 Topps Five Star Autographs Blue

*BLUE: .6X TO 1.5X BASIC
STATED ODDS 1:11 HOBBY
STATED PRINT RUN 25 SER.#'d SETS
EXCHANGE DEADLINE 8/31/2021
FSABJ Bo Jackson 40.00 100.00
FSAKB Kris Bryant 60.00 150.00
FSAKD Khris Davis 8.00 20.00

2019 Topps Five Star Autographs Purple

*PURPLE: .5X TO 1.2X BASIC
STATED ODDS 1:6 HOBBY
STATED PRINT RUN 50 SER.#'d SETS
EXCHANGE DEADLINE 8/31/2021
FSAKD Khris Davis 6.00 15.00

2019 Topps Five Star Five Tool Phenom Autographs

STATED ODDS 1:24 HOBBY
STATED PRINT RUN 25 SER.#'d SETS
EXCHANGE DEADLINE 8/31/2021
FTPAJ Aaron Judge 100.00 250.00
FTPBB Byron Buxton 8.00 20.00
FTPBM Brandon Nimmo 6.00 15.00
FTPFL Francisco Lindor 15.00 40.00
FTPFTJ Fernando Tatis Jr. 250.00 600.00
FTPJS Juan Soto 75.00 200.00
FTPKB Kris Bryant 60.00 150.00
FTPKS Kyle Schwarber EXCH 12.00 30.00
FTPMA Miguel Andujar 8.00 20.00
FTPMC Matt Chapman 10.00 25.00
FTPMO Matt Olson 10.00 25.00
FTPMT Mike Trout 300.00 500.00
FTPNS Nick Senzel EXCH 50.00 120.00
FTPOA Ozzie Albies EXCH 15.00 40.00
FTPPA Pete Alonso 100.00 250.00
FTPRAC Ronald Acuna Jr. 75.00 200.00
FTPRD Rafael Devers 15.00 40.00
FTPRH Rhys Hoskins 20.00 50.00
FTPSO Shohei Ohtani 100.00 250.00
FTPVGJ Vladimir Guerrero Jr. 100.00 250.00
FTPVR Victor Robles 10.00 25.00
FTPWC Willson Contreras 6.00 15.00

2019 Topps Five Star Golden Graphs

STATED ODDS 1:26 HOBBY
PRINT RUNS B/WN 15-50 COPIES PER
EXCHANGE DEADLINE 8/31/2021
*PURPLE/25: .4X TO 1X p/r 30
*PURPLE/25: .5X TO 1.2X p/r 50
*BLUE/20: .4X TO 1X p/r 25-30
*BLUE/20: .5X TO 1.2X p/r 50
GGTP Tony Perez/30 15.00 40.00
GGAB Adrian Beltre/25 20.00 50.00
GGAK Al Kaline/30 25.00 50.00
GGBB Bert Blyleven/50 8.00 20.00
GGBS Blake Snell/30 6.00 15.00
GGDA Dale Murphy/30 25.00 60.00
GGDP David Price/30 10.00 25.00
GGDM Don Mattingly/25 40.00 100.00
GGFM Fred McGriff/30 15.00 40.00
GGGS George Springer/25 15.00 40.00
GGJC Jose Canseco/30 12.00 30.00
GGJM Juan Marichal/30 12.00 30.00
GGJV Jason Varitek/30 15.00 40.00
GGKB Kris Bryant/25 50.00 120.00
GGKD Khris Davis/30 10.00 25.00
GGKS Kyle Schwarber/30 12.00 30.00
GGMC Matt Carpenter/30 8.00 20.00
GGMK Matt Kemp/50 6.00 15.00
GGMO Marcell Ozuna/50 6.00 15.00
GGNR Nolan Ryan/25 75.00 200.00
GGPA Peter Alonso/50 40.00 100.00
GGPD Paul DeJong/50 8.00 20.00
GGRC Rod Carew/25 15.00 40.00
GGRH Rhys Hoskins/30 30.00 80.00
GGRS Ryne Sandberg/25 40.00 100.00
GGRY Robin Yount/25 20.00 50.00

2019 Topps Five Star Jumbo Patch Autographs

STATED ODDS 1:45 HOBBY
PRINT RUNS B/WN 15-25 COPIES PER
NO PRICING ON QTY 15
EXCHANGE DEADLINE 8/31/2021
AJPAN Aaron Nola
AJPAP Albert Pujols
AJPAR Anthony Rizzo
AJPBN Brandon Nimmo
AJPBS Blake Snell
AJPCF Carlton Fisk
AJPCK Corey Kluber
AJPCRJ Cal Ripken Jr.
AJPDE Dennis Eckersley
AJPDJ Derek Jeter
AJPDP David Price/25 15.00 40.00
AJPFF Freddie Freeman/25 30.00 80.00
AJPIS Ichiro
AJPJF Jack Flaherty
AJPJUS Justin Smoak
AJPJV Joey Votto/25 50.00 120.00
AJPKB Kris Bryant
AJPKD Khris Davis/25 20.00 50.00
AJPKGJ Ken Griffey Jr.
AJPKS Kyle Schwarber
AJPLS Luis Severino
AJPLU Luis Urias
AJPMA Miguel Andujar
AJPMAC Matt Chapman
AJPMAM Max Muncy
AJPMAO Marcell Ozuna
AJPMC Miguel Cabrera/25 75.00 200.00
AJPMO Matt Olson
AJPMP Mike Piazza
AJPMR Mariano Rivera
AJPMT Mike Trout
AJPNS Noah Syndergaard/25 15.00 40.00
AJPOA Ozzie Albies
AJPPD Paul DeJong
AJPRD Rafael Devers/25 40.00 100.00
AJPRH Rhys Hoskins/25 50.00 12.00
AJPSO Shohei Ohtani
AJPSP Salvador Perez
AJPTH Torii Hunter
AJPTT Touki Toussaint
AJPVR Victor Robles
AJPWC Willson Contreras
AJPWM Whit Merrifield

2019 Topps Five Star Pentamerous Penmanship Autographs

STATED ODDS 1:27 HOBBY
PRINT RUN B/WN 15-25 COPIESPER
NO PRICING ON QTY 15
EXCHANGE DEADLINE 8/31/2021
PPAK Al Kaline/25 30.00 80.00
PPBL Barry Larkin/25 20.00 50.00
PPCS Chris Sale/25 10.00 25.00
PPDM Don Mattingly/25 60.00 150.00
PPFL Francisco Lindor/25 15.00 40.00
PPFT Frank Thomas/25 40.00 100.00
PPJA Jose Altuve/25 20.00 50.00
PPJDG Jacob deGrom/25 50.00 120.00
PPJO Juan Soto/25 40.00 100.00
PPKGJ Ken Griffey Jr./25
PPMP Mike Piazza
PPMR Mariano Rivera
PPOS Ozzie Smith/25 10.00 25.00
PPPG Paul Goldschmidt/25 20.00 50.00
PPR Ronald Acuna Jr./25 75.00 200.00
PPRH Rhys Hoskins/25 25.00 60.00
PPRY Robin Yount/25 25.00 60.00
PPSK Sandy Koufax
PPVGJ Vladimir Guerrero Jr./25 100.00 250.00

2019 Topps Five Star Signatures

STATED ODDS 1:27 HOBBY
PRINT RUNS B/WN 5-20 COPIES PER
NO PRICING ON QTY 10 OR LESS
EXCHANGE DEADLINE 8/31/2021
FSAK Al Kaline/20 30.00 80.00
FSAR Anthony Rizzo/20 40.00 100.00
FSBG Bob Gibson/20 15.00 40.00
FSBL Barry Larkin/20 20.00 50.00
FSBP Buster Posey
FSCS Chris Sale/20 15.00 40.00
FSDJ Derek Jeter EXCH
FSDM Dale Murphy/20 50.00 120.00
FSDON Don Mattingly/20 40.00 100.00
FSDS Deion Sanders/20 40.00 100.00
FSFL Francisco Lindor/20 25.00 60.00
FSHA Hank Aaron EXCH
FSHM Hideki Matsui/20 50.00 120.00
FSJA Jose Altuve/20 50.00 120.00
FSJAV Jason Varitek/20 40.00 100.00
FSJDG Jacob deGrom/20 75.00 200.00
FSJM Juan Marichal/20 12.00 30.00
FSJUS Juan Soto/20 75.00 200.00
FSKB Kris Bryant/20 75.00 200.00
FSKGJ Ken Griffey Jr./20 125.00 300.00
FSKS Kyle Schwarber/20 20.00 50.00
FSMM Mark McGwire
FSMP Mike Piazza
FSMT Mike Trout
FSOS Ozzie Smith/20 25.00 60.00
FSPG Paul Goldschmidt/20 20.00 50.00
FSRA Ronald Acuna Jr./20 100.00 250.00
FSSO Shohei Ohtani
FSVGJ Vladimir Guerrero Jr./20 100.00 250.00

2019 Topps Five Star Silver Signatures

COMMON p/r 25-30 5.00 12.00
SEMIS p/r 25-30 6.00 15.00
UNLISTED p/r 25-30 8.00 20.00
STATED ODDS 1:25 HOBBY
PRINT RUNS B/WN 25-50 COPIES PER
EXCHANGE DEADLINE 8/31/2021
*PURPLE/25: .4X TO 1X p/r 30
*PURPLE/25: .5X TO 1.2X p/r 50
*BLUE/20: .4X TO 1X p/r 25-30
*BLUE/20: .5X TO 1.2X p/r 50
SSAD Andre Dawson/30 12.00 30.00
SSAM Andrew McCutchen/30 50.00 120.00
SSBG Bob Gibson/30 20.00 50.00
SSCAF Carlton Fisk/30 15.00 40.00
SSCJ Chipper Jones/25 50.00 120.00
SSCS Chris Sale/30 12.00 30.00
SSDE Dennis Eckersley/30 12.00 30.00
SSDS Darryl Strawberry/50 15.00 40.00
SSEJ Eloy Jimenez/30 50.00 120.00
SSEM Edgar Martinez/30 20.00 50.00
SSIR Ivan Rodriguez/30 20.00 50.00
SSJP Jorge Posada/30 20.00 50.00
SSJS Juan Soto/50 75.00 200.00
SSJSM John Smoltz/30 15.00 40.00
SSLB Lou Brock/30 15.00 40.00
SSMC Miguel Cabrera/25 50.00 120.00
SSMK Michael Kopech/50 12.00 30.00
SSMR Mariano Rivera/25 100.00 250.00
SSRA Roberto Alomar/30 20.00 50.00
SSRP Rafael Palmeiro/50 6.00 15.00
SSSC Steve Carlton/30 15.00 40.00
SSTG Tom Glavine/30 12.00 30.00
SSTH Torii Hunter/30 10.00 25.00
SSTR Tim Raines/30 8.00 20.00
SSVG Vladimir Guerrero/30 25.00 60.00
SSVGJ Vladimir Guerrero Jr./30 100.00 250.00
SSVR Victor Robles/50 10.00 25.00
SSYK Yusei Kikuchi/30 10.00 25.00

2020 Topps Five Star Autographs

STATED ODDS 1:8 HOBBY
EXCHANGE DEADLINE 7/31/2022
FSAAA Aaron Judge EXCH 100.00 250.00
FSAAAZ Aristides Aquino RC 8.00 20.00
FSAAN Aaron Nola 10.00 25.00
FSAAT Abraham Toro RC 4.00 10.00
FSABB Bo Bichette RC EXCH 50.00 120.00
FSABM Brendan McKay RC 5.00 12.00
FSABP Buster Posey
FSACRJ Cal Ripken Jr.
FSADC Dylan Cease RC 5.00 12.00
FSADM Dustin May RC 40.00 100.00
FSAEJ Eloy Jimenez 15.00 40.00
FSAFF Dansby Swanson 12.00 30.00
FSAFT Frank Thomas 40.00 100.00
FSAFTJ Fernando Tatis Jr. EXCH 100.00 250.00
FSAGL Gavin Lux RC EXCH 30.00 80.00
FSAGS George Springer 12.00 30.00
FSAGT Gleyber Torres 30.00 80.00
FSAJA Jose Altuve 12.00 30.00
FSAJCA Jose Canseco 12.00 30.00
FSAJD Jacob deGrom 25.00 60.00
FSAJF Jack Flaherty 10.00 25.00
FSAJL Jesus Luzardo RC 6.00 15.00
FSAJM Jeff McNeil 8.00 20.00
FSAJR J.T. Realmuto 15.00 40.00
FSAJRZ Jake Rogers RC 3.00 8.00
FSAJS Jorge Soler 5.00 12.00
FSAJSO Juan Soto 60.00 150.00
FSAJV Jaylin Davis RC 8.00 20.00
FSAJX Justin Dunn RC 8.00 20.00
FSAJY Jordan Yamamoto RC 3.00 8.00
FSAKH Keston Hiura 8.00 20.00
FSAKHK Kwang-Hyun Kim RC 40.00 100.00
FSAKIE Carter Kieboom 6.00 15.00
FSAKL Kyle Lewis RC 25.00 60.00
FSALR Luis Robert RC 150.00 400.00
FSALW Logan Webb RC 5.00 12.00
FSAMD Mauricio Dubon RC 6.00 15.00
FSAMGZ Mitch Garver 3.00 8.00
FSAMO Matt Olson 10.00 25.00
FSAMR Mark McGwire 40.00 100.00
FSAMSO Mike Soroka 10.00 25.00
FSAMT Mike Trout 250.00 600.00
FSAMW Matt Thaiss RC 4.00 10.00
FSANH Nico Hoerner RC 12.00 30.00
FSANS Nick Senzel 8.00 20.00
FSANX Nick Solak RC 8.00 20.00
FSAPA Pete Alonso 30.00 80.00
FSAPC Patrick Corbin 4.00 10.00
FSAPG Paul Goldschmidt 20.00 50.00
FSARA Ronald Acuna Jr. 75.00 200.00
FSARG Robel Garcia RC 3.00 8.00
FSARH Rhys Hoskins 12.00 30.00
FSARL Ramon Laureano 6.00 15.00
FSARRA Randy Arozarena RC 60.00 150.00
FSASA Shogo Akiyama RC 6.00 15.00
FSASH Sam Hilliard RC 5.00 12.00
FSASM Sean Murphy RC 5.00 12.00
FSASO Shohei Ohtani
FSASY Shun Yamaguchi RC 6.00 15.00
FSATE Tommy Edman 8.00 20.00
FSATG Trent Grisham RC 20.00 50.00
FSAWC Willson Contreras 8.00 20.00
FSAWM Whit Merrifield 10.00 25.00
FSAWS Will Smith 8.00 20.00
FSAYA Yordan Alvarez RC 30.00 80.00
FSAYT Yoshi Tsutsugo RC 40.00 100.00

2020 Topps Five Star Autographs Blue

*BLUE: .6X TO 1.5X BASIC
STATED ODDS 1:14 HOBBY
STATED PRINT RUN 25 SER.#'d SETS
EXCHANGE DEADLINE 7/31/2022

2020 Topps Five Star Autographs Purple

*PURPLE: .5X TO 1.2X BASIC
STATED ODDS 1:8 HOBBY
STATED PRINT RUN 50 SER.#'d SETS
EXCHANGE DEADLINE 7/31/2022

2020 Topps Five Star Five Tool Phenom Autographs

STATED ODDS 1:28 HOBBY
STATED PRINT RUN 25 SER.#'d SETS
EXCHANGE DEADLINE 7/31/2020
FTPAJ Aaron Judge EXCH 125.00 300.00
FTPARI Austin Riley 20.00 50.00
FTPBB Luis Robert 200.00 500.00
FTPBH Bryce Harper 125.00 300.00
FTPBMC Brendan McKay 10.00 25.00
FTPBR Brendan Rodgers
FTPCKI Carter Kieboom 6.00 15.00
FTPCY Christian Yelich EXCH 40.00 100.00
FTPDSW Dansby Swanson 30.00 80.00
FTPFTJ Fernando Tatis Jr. EXCH 100.00 250.00
FTPGT Gleyber Torres 60.00 150.00
FTPJS Juan Soto 75.00 200.00
FTPKHI Keston Hiura 20.00 50.00
FTPMC Nolan Arenado 60.00 150.00
FTPMT Mike Trout 300.00 800.00
FTPNHO Nico Hoerner 30.00 80.00
FTPNS Aristides Aquino 20.00 50.00
FTPNSE Nick Senzel 8.00 20.00
FTPPA Pete Alonso 50.00 120.00
FTPRAC Ronald Acuna Jr.
FTPRD Rafael Devers 20.00 50.00
FTPRH Rhys Hoskins 25.00 60.00
FTPSO Shohei Ohtani 75.00 200.00
FTPVGJ Vladimir Guerrero Jr.
FTPVR Victor Robles 10.00 25.00
FTPWC Willson Contreras 12.00 30.00
FTPYAL Yordan Alvarez

2020 Topps Five Star Golden Graphs

STATED ODDS 1:24 HOBBY
STATED PRINT RUN 40 SER.#'d SETS
EXCHANGE DEADLINE 7/31/2022
*PURPLE/25: .5X TO 1.2X BASIC
*BLUE/20: .5X TO 1.2X BASIC
GGAAQ Aristides Aquino
GGAD Andre Dawson 15.00 40.00
GGEM Edgar Martinez 20.00 50.00
GGBG Bob Gibson 25.00 60.00
GGBLA Barry Larkin 20.00 50.00
GGBMC Brendan McKay
GGCAF Carlton Fisk 20.00 50.00
GGCCS CC Sabathia EXCH 20.00 50.00
GGCFI Cecil Fielder 15.00 40.00
GGCPA Chris Paddack 10.00 25.00
GGCY Christian Yelich
GGDE Dennis Eckersley 10.00 25.00
GGDJ David Justice 15.00 40.00
GGDST Jesus Luzardo
GGFTJ Fernando Tatis Jr. EXCH
GGJAB Jim Abbott 15.00 40.00
GGJBA Jeff Bagwell 25.00 60.00
GGJBE Johnny Bench
GGJLU Darryl Strawberry 12.00 30.00
GGJMA Joe Mauer 30.00 80.00
GGJSM John Smoltz 25.00 60.00
GGJTH Jim Thome EXCH 30.00 80.00
GGJVO Joey Votto
GGLB Lou Brock 30.00 80.00
GGMC Miguel Cabrera
GGMVA Mo Vaughn
GGNGA Nomar Garciaparra 15.00 40.00
GGNRY Nolan Ryan
GGOZZ Ozzie Smith 25.00 60.00
GGRA Roberto Alomar 15.00 40.00
GGRHE Rickey Henderson
GGSC Steve Carlton 10.00 25.00
GGTGL Tom Glavine 15.00 40.00
GGTL Tim Lincecum 30.00 80.00
GGTR Tim Raines 12.00 30.00
GGVG Vladimir Guerrero 20.00 50.00
GGWBO Wade Boggs 20.00 50.00
GGYAL Yordan Alvarez

2020 Topps Five Star Jumbo Patch Autographs

STATED ODDS 1:26 HOBBY
PRINT RUNS B/WN 15-25 COPIESPER
NO PRICING ON QTY 15 OR LESS
EXCHANGE DEADLINE 7/31/2022
AJPAA Aristides Aquino/25 20.00 50.00
AJPAB Andrew Benintendi/25 30.00 80.00
AJPAN Aaron Nola/25 50.00 120.00
AJPBH Bryce Harper
AJPBMC Brendan McKay/25 20.00 50.00
AJPBS Blake Snell EXCH
AJPCCS CC Sabathia/25 30.00 80.00
AJPCY Christian Yelich EXCH
AJPDJL DJ LeMahieu/25 60.00 150.00
AJPEJ Eloy Jimenez
AJPFM Fred McGriff
AJPFTJ Fernando Tatis Jr. EXCH
AJPGS George Springer/25 30.00 80.00
AJPGTO Gleyber Torres/25 75.00 200.00
AJPIROD Ivan Rodriguez
AJPJA Jose Altuve/25
AJPJD Jacob deGrom
AJPJDM J.D. Martinez/25 15.00 40.00
AJPJF Jack Flaherty/25 60.00 150.00
AJPJMA Joe Mauer
AJPJMC Jeff McNeil/25 30.00 80.00
AJPJS Juan Soto
AJPJTR J.T. Realmuto/25 75.00 200.00
AJPJVA Jason Varitek
AJPKHI Keston Hiura/25 60.00 150.00
AJPMA Miguel Andujar/25 25.00 60.00
AJPMC Miguel Cabrera/25 60.00 150.00
AJPMKE Max Kepler/25 25.00 60.00
AJPMT Mike Trout/25 500.00 1200.00
AJPMTA Masahiro Tanaka EXCH
AJPMTE Mark Teixeira/25 30.00 80.00
AJPPCO Patrick Corbin
AJPRD Rafael Devers/25 40.00 100.00
AJPRHO Ryan Howard
AJPSO Shohei Ohtani
AJPTL Tim Lincecum
AJPVGJ Vladimir Guerrero Jr.
AJPWBO Wade Boggs
AJPWC Willson Contreras
AJPWM Whit Merrifield/25 30.00 80.00
AJPXBO Xander Bogaerts/25 40.00 100.00

2020 Topps Five Star Pentamerous Penmanship Autographs

STATED ODDS 1:29 HOBBY
PRINT RUNS B/WN 15-25 COPIES PER
NO PRICING ON QTY 15 OR LESS
EXCHANGE DEADLINE 7/31/2022
PPAJ Aaron Judge EXCH
PPBHA Bryce Harper
PPCRJ Cal Ripken Jr.
PPDM Don Mattingly/25 50.00 120.00
PPDMU Dale Murphy/25 25.00 60.00
PPFTJ Fernando Tatis Jr. EXCH
PPJB Jeff Bagwell/25 20.00 50.00
PPJSO Juan Soto/25 100.00 250.00
PPKGJ Ken Griffey Jr.
PPMM Darryl Strawberry/25 25.00 60.00
PPMSC Mike Schmidt
PPNAR Nolan Arenado/25 100.00 250.00
PPPA Pete Alonso/25 50.00 120.00
PPPG Paul Goldschmidt/25 25.00 60.00
PPRAJ Ronald Acuna Jr.
PPRD Rafael Devers/25 25.00 60.00
PPVGJ Vladimir Guerrero Jr./25
PPWBO Wade Boggs
PPWBU Walker Buehler/25 30.00 80.00
PPWC Will Clark/25 30.00 80.00

2020 Topps Five Star Signatures

STATED ODDS 1:31 HOBBY
PRINT RUNS B/WN 5-25 COPIES PER
NO PRICING ON QTY 10 OR LESS
EXCHANGE DEADLINE 7/31/2022
FSAJ Aaron Judge EXCH
FSBG Yordan Alvarez/20
FSBL Barry Larkin/20 25.00 60.00
FSCFI Carlton Fisk/20 20.00 50.00
FSCY Christian Yelich EXCH
FSDJ Derek Jeter/25 250.00 600.00
FSDM Dale Murphy/20 15.00 40.00
FSDON Don Mattingly/20 40.00 100.00
FSDWR David Wright/20 25.00 60.00
FSEJ Luis Robert/20 200.00 500.00
FSEM Edgar Martinez
FSFT Frank Thomas/20 40.00 100.00
FSFTJ Fernando Tatis Jr.
FSGT Gleyber Torres/20 40.00 100.00
FSHA Hank Aaron/20 200.00 500.00
FSJA Jose Altuve/20 15.00 40.00
FSJB Jeff Bagwell/20 40.00 100.00
FSJDG Jacob deGrom/20 40.00 100.00
FSJMA Joe Mauer/20 40.00 100.00
FSJUS Juan Soto
FSMR Mariano Rivera
FSMS Mike Schmidt
FSMT Mike Trout
FSNAR Nolan Arenado/20 60.00 150.00
FSOS Ozzie Smith/20 30.00 80.00
FSPA Pete Alonso/20 60.00 150.00
FSPG Paul Goldschmidt/20 20.00 50.00
FSRA Ronald Acuna Jr.
FSRC Roger Clemens
FSRD Rafael Devers/20 20.00 50.00
FSRH Rhys Hoskins/20 15.00 40.00
FSTG Tom Glavine/20 20.00 50.00
FSTL Tim Lincecum/20 30.00 80.00
FSVGJ Vladimir Guerrero Jr./20 50.00 120.00
FSWC Will Clark/20 30.00 80.00
FSWIC Willson Contreras

2020 Topps Five Star Silver Signatures

STATED ODDS 1:24 HOBBY
STATED PRINT RUN 40 SER.#'d SETS
EXCHANGE DEADLINE 7/31/2022
*PURPLE/25: .5X TO 1.2X BASIC
*BLUE/20: .5X TO 1.2X BASIC
SSAPE Andy Pettitte 15.00 40.00
SSBB Bert Blyleven 8.00 20.00
SSDM Don Mattingly 40.00 100.00
SSDMU Dale Murphy 25.00 60.00
SSDWR David Wright 20.00 50.00
SSFM Fred McGriff 20.00 50.00
SSIROD Ivan Rodriguez 15.00 40.00
SSJDM J.D. Martinez 12.00 30.00
SSJGO Juan Gonzalez 12.00 30.00
SSJM Juan Marichal 12.00 30.00
SSJV Jason Varitek 20.00 50.00
SSKLE Kyle Lewis 100.00 250.00
SSKWO Kerry Wood 15.00 40.00
SSLRO Luis Robert
SSLT Luis Tiant 8.00 20.00
SSMBR Michael Brantley 10.00 25.00
SSMGR Mark Grace 20.00 50.00
SSMSC Mike Schmidt
SSNHO Nico Hoerner
SSRHO Ryan Howard 25.00 60.00
SSPA Pete Alonso
SSRC Rod Carew 15.00 40.00
SSRF Rollie Fingers 10.00 25.00
SSRS Ryne Sandberg
SSRY Robin Yount 25.00 60.00
SSTHE Todd Helton 15.00 40.00
SSTMA Tino Martinez 15.00 40.00
SSTPE Tony Perez 15.00 40.00
SSWB Walker Buehler 20.00 50.00
SSWC Will Clark 25.00 60.00
SSYTS Yoshi Tsutsugo 50.00 120.00

2012 Topps Five Star Club

STATED PRINT RUN 50 SER.#'d SETS
FSC1 Willie Mays
FSC2 Yu Darvish 25.00 50.00
FSC3 Bryce Harper
FSC4 Mike Trout 75.00 125.00
FSC5 Mickey Mantle 20.00 40.00

2001 Topps Fusion

COMPLETE SET (250) 100.00 200.00
1 Albert Belle BB .20 .50
2 Albert Belle FIN .20 .50
3 Albert Belle GAL .20 .50
4 Nick Bierbrodt GL .15 .40
5 Alex Rodriguez Rangers SC .60 1.50
6 Alex Rodriguez Rangers BB .60 1.50
7 Alex Rodriguez Rangers FIN .60 1.50
8 Alex Rodriguez Rangers GAL .60 1.50
9 Eric Munson GL .15 .40
10 Barry Bonds SC 1.25 3.00
11 Andruw Jones BB .30 .75
12 Antonio Alfonseca FIN .20 .50
13 Andres Galarraga GAL .20 .50
14 Joe Crede GL .50 1.25
15 Barry Larkin SC .30 .75
16 Barry Bonds BB 1.25 3.00
17 Barry Bonds FIN 1.25 3.00
18 Andruw Jones GAL .30 .75
19 C.C. Sabathia GL .20 .50
20 Bobby Higginson SC .20 .50
21 Barry Larkin BB .30 .75
22 Ben Grieve FIN .15 .40
23 Barry Bonds GAL 1.25 3.00
24 Corey Patterson GL .15 .40
25 Carlos Delgado SC .20 .50
26 Bernie Williams BB .30 .75
27 Brian Giles FIN .20 .50
28 Barry Larkin GAL .30 .75
29 Travis Dawkins GL .15 .40
30 Chipper Jones SC .50 1.25
31 Brian Giles BB .20 .50
32 Carlos Delgado FIN .20 .50
33 Ben Grieve GAL .15 .40
34 Geoff Goetz GL .15 .40
35 Cristian Guzman SC .15 .40
36 Cal Ripken BB 1.50 4.00
37 Chipper Jones FIN .50 1.25
38 Bernie Williams GAL .30 .75
39 Pablo Ozuna GL .15 .40
40 Vinny Castilla SC .20 .50
41 Carlos Delgado BB .20 .50
42 Craig Biggio FIN .30 .75
43 Cal Ripken GAL 1.50 4.00
44 Tim Redding GL .15 .40
45 Darin Erstad SC .20 .50
46 Chipper Jones BB .50 1.25
47 Darin Erstad FIN .20 .50
48 Carlos Delgado GAL .20 .50
49 Josh Hamilton .30 .75
50 Derek Jeter SC 1.25 3.00
51 Darin Erstad BB .20 .50
52 Dean Palmer FIN .20 .50
53 Chipper Jones GAL .50 1.25
54 Chin-Feng Chen GL .20 .50
55 Edgar Martinez SC .30 .75
56 Derek Jeter BB 1.25 3.00
57 Derek Jeter FIN 1.25 3.00
58 Craig Biggio GAL .30 .75
59 Keith Ginter GL .15 .40
60 Edgardo Alfonzo SC .15 .40
61 Edgar Martinez BB .30 .75
62 Edgardo Alfonzo FIN .15 .40
63 David Justice GAL .20 .50
64 Roy Oswalt GL .50 1.25
65 Eric Karros SC .20 .50
66 Edgardo Alfonzo BB .15 .40
67 Frank Thomas FIN .60 1.50
68 Dean Palmer GAL .20 .50
69 Alfonso Soriano GL .30 .75
70 Fernando Vina SC .15 .40
71 Frank Thomas BB .60 1.50
72 Garret Anderson FIN .20 .50
73 Derek Jeter GAL 1.25 3.00
74 Bobby Bradley GL .15 .40
75 Frank Thomas SC .60 1.50
76 Gary Sheffield BB .20 .50
77 Geoff Jenkins FIN .15 .40
78 Edgar Martinez GAL .30 .75
79 Nick Johnson GL .20 .50
80 Fred McGriff SC .30 .75
81 Geoff Jenkins BB .15 .40
82 Greg Maddux FIN .75 2.00
83 Edgardo Alfonzo GAL .15 .40
84 Hee Seop Choi GL RC .40 1.00
85 Garret Anderson SC .20 .50
86 Greg Maddux BB .75 2.00
87 Ivan Rodriguez FIN .30 .75
88 Eric Karros GAL .20 .50
89 Scott Seabol GL .15 .40
90 Ivan Rodriguez SC .30 .75
91 Ivan Rodriguez BB .30 .75
92 J.D. Drew FIN .20 .50
93 Frank Thomas GAL .60 1.50
94 Ryan Anderson GL .15 .40
95 Jason Giambi SC .20 .50
96 Jason Giambi BB .20 .50
97 Jason Kendall FIN .20 .50
98 Gary Sheffield GAL .20 .50
99 Milton Bradley GL .20 .50
100 Jason Kendall SC .20 .50
101 Jason Kendall BB .20 .50
102 Jeff Bagwell FIN .30 .75
103 Greg Maddux GAL .75 2.00
104 Sean Burroughs GL .15 .40
105 Jay Bell SC .20 .50
106 Jeff Bagwell BB .30 .75
107 Jeffrey Hammonds FIN .15 .40
108 Ivan Rodriguez GAL .30 .75
109 Ben Petrick GL .15 .40
110 Jeff Bagwell SC .30 .75
111 Jeff Cirillo BB .15 .40
112 Jermaine Dye FIN .20 .50
113 J.T. Snow GAL .20 .50
114 Ben Davis GL .15 .40
115 Jeff Cirillo SC .15 .40
116 Jeff Kent BB .20 .50
117 Jeromy Burnitz FIN .20 .50
118 Jay Bell GAL .20 .50
119 Jason Hart GL .15 .40
120 Jeff Kent SC .20 .50
121 Jermaine Dye BB .20 .50
122 John Olerud FIN .20 .50
123 Jeff Bagwell GAL .30 .75
124 Jeff Segar GL RC .30 .75
125 Jeromy Burnitz SC .20 .50
126 Jeromy Burnitz BB .20 .50
127 Johnny Damon FIN .30 .75
128 Jim Edmonds GAL .20 .50
129 Tim Christman GL RC .30 .75
130 Jim Thome SC .30 .75
131 Jim Edmonds BB .20 .50
132 Jorge Posada FIN .30 .75
133 Jim Thome GAL .30 .75
134 Danny Borrell GL RC .30 .75
135 Johnny Damon SC .30 .75
136 Jim Thome BB .30 .75
137 Jose Vidro FIN .15 .40
138 Ken Griffey Jr. GAL 1.00 2.50
139 Sean Burnett GL .15 .40
140 Larry Walker SC .20 .50
141 Jose Vidro BB .15 .40
142 Ken Griffey Jr. FIN 1.00 2.50
143 Larry Walker GAL .20 .50
144 Robert Keppel GL RC .30 .75
145 Luis Castillo SC .15 .40
146 Ken Griffey Jr. BB 1.00 2.50

147 Kevin Brown FIN .20 .50
148 Manny Ramirez Sox GAL .30 .75
149 David Parrish GL RC .30 .75
150 Manny Ramirez SC .30 .75
151 Kevin Brown BB .20 .50
152 Luis Castillo FIN .15 .40
153 Mark Grace GAL .20 .50
154 Mike Jacobs GL RC 5.00 12.00
155 Mark Grace SC .30 .75
156 Larry Walker BB .30 .75
157 Magglio Ordonez FIN .20 .50
158 Mark McGwire GAL 1.25 3.00
159 Adam Johnson GL .15 .40
160 Mark McGwire SC 1.25 3.00
161 Magglio Ordonez BB .20 .50
162 Mark McGwire FIN 1.25 3.00
163 Matt Williams GAL .20 .50
164 Oscar Ramirez GL RC .30 .75
165 Mike Piazza SC .75 2.00
166 Manny Ramirez Sox BB .30 .75
167 Mike Piazza FIN .75 2.00
168 Mike Mussina GAL .30 .75
169 Odannis Ayala GL RC .30 .75
170 Mike Sweeney SC .20 .50
171 Mark McGwire BB 1.25 3.00
172 Nomar Garciaparra FIN .75 2.00
173 Mike Piazza GAL .75 2.00
174 J.R. House GL .15 .40
175 Neifi Perez SC .15 .40
176 Mike Piazza BB .75 2.00
177 Pedro Martinez FIN .30 .75
178 Mo Vaughn GAL .20 .50
179 Shawn Fagan GL RC .30 .75
180 Nomar Garciaparra SC .75 2.00
181 Mo Vaughn BB .20 .50
182 Rafael Palmeiro FIN .30 .75
183 Nomar Garciaparra GAL .75 2.00
184 Chris Bass GL RC .30 .75
185 Raul Mondesi SC .20 .50
186 Nomar Garciaparra BB .75 2.00
187 Randy Johnson FIN .50 1.25
188 Omar Vizquel GAL .30 .75
189 Erick Almonte GL RC .30 .75
190 Ray Durham SC .20 .50
191 Pedro Martinez BB .30 .75
192 Robb Nen FIN .20 .50
193 Pedro Martinez GAL .30 .75
194 Luis Montanez GL RC .30 .75
195 Ray Lankford SC .20 .50
196 Rafael Palmeiro BB .30 .75
197 Roberto Alomar FIN .30 .75
198 Rafael Palmeiro GAL .30 .75
199 Chad Petty GL RC .30 .75
200 Richard Hidalgo SC .15 .40
201 Randy Johnson BB .50 1.25
202 Robin Ventura FIN .20 .50
203 Randy Johnson GAL .50 1.25
204 Derek Thompson GL .15 .40
205 Sammy Sosa SC .60 1.50
206 Roberto Alomar BB .30 .75
207 Sammy Sosa FIN .60 1.50
208 Raul Mondesi GAL .20 .50
209 Scott Heard GL .15 .40
210 Scott Rolen SC .30 .75
211 Sammy Sosa BB .60 1.50
212 Scott Rolen FIN .30 .75
213 Roberto Alomar GAL .30 .75
214 Dominic Rich GL RC .30 .75
215 Sean Casey SC .20 .50
216 Scott Rolen BB .30 .75
217 Sean Casey FIN .20 .50
218 Robin Ventura GAL .20 .50
219 William Smith GL RC .30 .75
220 Tim Salmon SC .30 .75
221 Sean Casey BB .20 .50
222 Shannon Stewart FIN .20 .50
223 Sammy Sosa GAL .60 1.50
224 Joel Pineiro GL .20 .50
225 Tino Martinez SC .30 .75
226 Shawn Green BB .20 .50
227 Shawn Green FIN .20 .50
228 Scott Rolen GAL .30 .75
229 Greg Morrison GL RC .30 .75
230 Tony Gwynn SC .60 1.50
231 Todd Helton BB .30 .75
232 Steve Finley FIN .20 .50
233 Scott Williamson GAL .15 .40
234 Talmadge Nunnari GL .15 .40
235 Tony Womack SC .15 .40
236 Tony Batista BB .15 .40
237 Tim Salmon FIN .30 .75
238 Shawn Green GAL .20 .50
239 Carlos Villalobos GL RC .30 .75
240 Troy Glaus SC .20 .50
241 Troy Glaus BB .20 .50
242 Todd Helton FIN .30 .75
243 Tim Salmon GAL .30 .75
244 Marcos Scutaro GL RC 6.00 15.00
245 Troy O'Leary SC .15 .40
246 Vladimir Guerrero BB .50 1.25
247 Vladimir Guerrero FIN .50 1.25
248 Vladimir Guerrero GAL .50 1.25
249 Horacio Estrada GL .15 .40
250 Vladimir Guerrero SC .50 1.25

2001 Topps Fusion Autographs

GROUP A ODDS 1:151 HOB/RET
GROUP B ODDS 1:1227 H, 1:1235 R
GROUP C ODDS 1:164 HOB/RET
GROUP D ODDS 1:109 HOB/RET
GROUP E ODDS 1:246 HOB/RET
GROUP F ODDS 1:447 HOB/RET
GROUP G ODDS 1:65 HOB, 1:66 RET
FA1 Rafael Furcal FIN D 6.00 15.00
FA2 Mike Lamb GAL D 4.00 10.00
FA3 Jason Marquis BB D 4.00 10.00
FA4 Milton Bradley SC D 4.00 10.00
FA5 Barry Zito GL D 6.00 15.00
FA6 Derrek Lee SC F 4.00 10.00
FA7 Corey Patterson BB A 4.00 10.00
FA8 Josh Hamilton 6.00 15.00
FA9 Sean Burroughs GL A 4.00 10.00
FA10 Jason Hart FIN A 4.00 10.00
FA11 Luis Montanez GL G 4.00 10.00
FA12 Robert Keppel SC G 4.00 10.00
FA13 Blake Williams FIN G 4.00 10.00
FA14 Phil Wilson BB G 4.00 10.00
FA15 Jake Peavy GAL G 15.00 40.00
FA16 Alex Rodriguez BB C 30.00 60.00
FA17 Ivan Rodriguez GL C 15.00 40.00
FA18 Don Larsen BB E 6.00 15.00
FA19 Todd Helton SC C 10.00 25.00
FA20 Carlos Delgado FIN B 6.00 15.00
FA21 Geoff Jenkins GAL C 4.00 10.00
FA22 Willie Stargell GAL E 40.00 80.00
FA23 Frank Robinson FIN E 8.00 20.00
FA24 Warren Spahn GL E 15.00 40.00
FA25 Harmon Killebrew SC E 30.00 60.00
FA26 Chipper Jones BB C 20.00 50.00
FA27 Chipper Jones FIN C 20.00 50.00
FA28 Chipper Jones GAL C 20.00 50.00
FA29 Chipper Jones GL C 20.00 50.00
FA30 Chipper Jones SC C 20.00 50.00
FA31 Rocco Baldelli GAL G 4.00 10.00
FA32 Keith Ginter GAL G 4.00 10.00
FA33 J.R. House GAL G 4.00 10.00
FA34 Alex Cabrera GAL G 4.00 10.00
FA35 Tony Alvarez GAL G 4.00 10.00
FA36 Pablo Ozuna GAL G 4.00 10.00
FA37 Juan Salas GAL G 4.00 10.00

2001 Topps Fusion Double Feature

BAT-BAT ODDS 1:491 HOBBY, 1:492 RETAIL
JSY-JSY GROUP A 1:1964 H, 1:1998 R
JSY-JSY GROUP B 1:6531 H, 1:6584 R
JSY-JSY GROUP C 1:10068 H, 1:10656 R
DF1 I.Rod/R.Henderson Bat 15.00 40.00
DF2 J.Smoltz/T.Glavine Bat 10.00 25.00
DF3 W.Stargell/F.Thomas Bat 10.00 25.00
DF4 C.Delgado/T.Helton Jsy A 10.00 25.00
DF5 A.Gonzalez/P.Burrell Bat 40.00 25.00
DF6 J.Vidro/R.Alomar Bat 10.00 25.00
DF7 C.Jones/R.Ventura Bat 15.00 40.00
DF8 J.Drew/M.Lawton Bat 6.00 15.00
DF9 J.Hamilton/C.Chen 60.00 120.00
DF10 R.Furcal/M.Tejada Bat 6.00 15.00
DF11 J.Beckett/R.Anderson Jsy C 10.00 25.00

2001 Topps Fusion Feature

BAT STATED ODDS 1:82 HOB/RET
JSY GROUP A ODDS 1:327 HOB/RET
JSY GROUP B ODDS 1:1313 H, 1:1332 R
JSY GROUP C ODDS 1:1405 H, 1:1411 R
JSY GROUP D ODDS 1:4931 H, 1:5328 R
F1 Ivan Rodriguez Bat 6.00 15.00
F2 Rickey Henderson Bat 6.00 15.00
F3 John Smoltz Bat 6.00 15.00
F4 Tom Glavine Bat 6.00 15.00
F5 Willie Stargell Bat 6.00 15.00
F6 Frank Thomas Bat 6.00 15.00
F7 Carlos Delgado Jsy A 4.00 10.00
F8 Todd Helton Jsy A 6.00 15.00
F9 Adrian Gonzalez Bat 4.00 10.00
F10 Pat Burrell Bat 4.00 10.00
F11 Jose Vidro Bat 4.00 10.00
F12 Roberto Alomar Bat 6.00 15.00
F13 Chipper Jones Bat 6.00 15.00
F14 Robin Ventura Bat 4.00 10.00
F15 J.D. Drew Bat 4.00 10.00
F16 Matt Lawton Bat 4.00 10.00
F17 Josh Hamilton 8.00 20.00
F18 Chin-Feng Chen Jsy B 15.00 40.00
F19 Rafael Furcal Bat 4.00 10.00
F20 Miguel Tejada Bat 4.00 10.00
F21 Josh Beckett Jsy C 6.00 15.00
F22 Ryan Anderson Jsy D 4.00 10.00

1996 Topps Gallery

The 1996 Topps Gallery set was issued in one series totalling 180 cards. The eight-card packs retailed for $3.00 each. The set is divided into five themes: Classics (1-90), New Editions (91-108), Modernists (109-126), Futurists (127-144) and Masters (145-180). Each theme features a different design on front, but the bulk of the set has full-bleed, color action shots. A Mickey Mantle Masterpiece was inserted into these packs at a rate of one every 48 packs. It is priced at the bottom of these listings.

COMPLETE SET (180) 15.00 40.00
MANTLE STATED ODDS 1:48
1 Tom Glavine .30 .75
2 Carlos Baerga .20 .50
3 Dante Bichette .20 .50
4 Mark Langston .20 .50
5 Ray Lankford .20 .50
6 Moises Alou .20 .50
7 Marquis Grissom .20 .50
8 Ramon Martinez .20 .50
9 Steve Finley .20 .50
10 Todd Hundley .20 .50
11 Brady Anderson .20 .50
12 John Valentin .20 .50
13 Heathcliff Slocumb .20 .50
14 Ruben Sierra .20 .50
15 Jeff Conine .20 .50
16 Jay Buhner .20 .50
17 Sammy Sosa .50 1.25
18 Doug Drabek .20 .50
19 Jose Mesa .20 .50
20 Jeff King .20 .50
21 Mickey Tettleton .20 .50
22 Jeff Montgomery .20 .50
23 Alex Fernandez .20 .50
24 Greg Vaughn .20 .50
25 Chuck Finley .20 .50
26 Terry Steinbach .20 .50
27 Rod Beck .20 .50
28 Jack McDowell .20 .50
29 Mark Wohlers .20 .50
30 Len Dykstra .20 .50
31 Bernie Williams .30 .75
32 Travis Fryman .20 .50
33 Jose Canseco .30 .75
34 Ken Caminiti .20 .50
35 Devon White .20 .50
36 Bobby Bonilla .20 .50
37 Paul Sorrento .20 .50
38 Ryne Sandberg .75 2.00
39 Derek Bell .20 .50
40 Bobby Jones .20 .50
41 J.T. Snow .20 .50
42 Denny Neagle .20 .50
43 Tim Wakefield .20 .50
44 Andres Galarraga .20 .50
45 David Segui .20 .50
46 Lee Smith .20 .50
47 Mel Rojas .20 .50
48 John Franco .20 .50
49 Pete Schourek .20 .50
50 John Wetteland .20 .50
51 Paul Molitor .20 .50
52 Ivan Rodriguez .30 .75
53 Chris Hoiles .20 .50
54 Mike Greenwell .20 .50
55 Orel Hershiser .20 .50
56 Brian McRae .20 .50
57 Geronimo Berroa .20 .50
58 Craig Biggio .30 .75
59 David Justice .20 .50
60 Lance Johnson .20 .50
61 Andy Ashby .20 .50
62 Randy Myers .20 .50
63 Gregg Jefferies .20 .50
64 Kevin Appier .20 .50
65 Rick Aguilera .20 .50
66 Shane Reynolds .20 .50
67 John Smoltz .30 .75
68 Ron Gant .20 .50
69 Eric Karros .20 .50
70 Jim Thome .30 .75
71 Terry Pendleton .20 .50
72 Kenny Rogers .20 .50
73 Robin Ventura .20 .50
74 Dave Nilsson .20 .50
75 Brian Jordan .20 .50
76 Glenallen Hill .20 .50
77 Greg Colbrunn .20 .50
78 Roberto Alomar .30 .75
79 Rickey Henderson .50 1.25
80 Carlos Garcia .20 .50
81 Dean Palmer .20 .50
82 Mike Stanley .20 .50
83 Hal Morris .20 .50
84 Wade Boggs .30 .75
85 Chad Curtis .20 .50
86 Roberto Hernandez .20 .50
87 John Olerud .20 .50
88 Frank Castillo .20 .50
89 Rafael Palmeiro .30 .75
90 Trevor Hoffman .20 .50
91 Marty Cordova .20 .50
92 Hideo Nomo .50 1.25
93 Johnny Damon .30 .75
94 Bill Pulsipher .20 .50
95 Garret Anderson .20 .50
96 Ray Durham .20 .50
97 Ricky Bottalico .20 .50
98 Carlos Perez .20 .50
99 Troy Percival .20 .50
100 Chipper Jones .50 1.25
101 Esteban Loaiza .20 .50
102 John Mabry .20 .50
103 Jon Nunnally .20 .50
104 Andy Pettitte .30 .75
105 Lyle Mouton .20 .50
106 Jason Isringhausen .20 .50
107 Brian L.Hunter .20 .50
108 Quilvio Veras .20 .50
109 Jim Edmonds .20 .50
110 Ryan Klesko .20 .50
111 Pedro Martinez .30 .75
112 Joey Hamilton .20 .50
113 Vinny Castilla .20 .50
114 Alex Gonzalez .20 .50
115 Raul Mondesi .20 .50
116 Rondell White .20 .50
117 Dan Miceli .20 .50
118 Tom Goodwin .20 .50
119 Bret Boone .20 .50
120 Shawn Green .20 .50
121 Jeff Cirillo .20 .50
122 Rico Brogna .20 .50
123 Chris Gomez .20 .50
124 Ismael Valdes .20 .50
125 Javy Lopez .20 .50
126 Manny Ramirez .30 .75
127 Paul Wilson .20 .50
128 Billy Wagner .20 .50
129 Eric Owens .20 .50
130 Todd Greene .20 .50
131 Karim Garcia .20 .50
132 Jimmy Haynes .20 .50
133 Michael Tucker .20 .50
134 John Wasdin .20 .50
135 Brooks Kieschnick .20 .50
136 Alex Ochoa .20 .50
137 Ariel Prieto .20 .50
138 Tony Clark .20 .50
139 Mark Loretta .20 .50
140 Rey Ordonez .20 .50
141 Chris Snopek .20 .50
142 Roger Cedeno .20 .50
143 Derek Jeter 1.25 3.00
144 Jeff Suppan .20 .50
145 Greg Maddux .75 2.00
146 Ken Griffey Jr. 1.00 2.50
147 Tony Gwynn .60 1.50
148 Darren Daulton .20 .50
149 Will Clark .30 .75
150 Mo Vaughn .20 .50
151 Reggie Sanders .20 .50
152 Kirby Puckett .50 1.25
153 Paul O'Neill .30 .75
154 Tim Salmon .30 .75
155 Mark McGwire 1.25 3.00
156 Barry Bonds 1.25 3.00
157 Albert Belle .20 .50
158 Edgar Martinez .30 .75
159 Mike Mussina .30 .75
160 Cecil Fielder .20 .50
161 Kenny Lofton .20 .50
162 Randy Johnson .50 1.25
163 Juan Gonzalez .20 .50
164 Jeff Bagwell .30 .75
165 Joe Carter .20 .50
166 Mike Piazza .75 2.00
167 Eddie Murray .50 1.25
168 Cal Ripken 1.50 4.00
169 Barry Larkin .30 .75
170 Chuck Knoblauch .20 .50
171 Chili Davis .20 .50
172 Fred McGriff .30 .75
173 Matt Williams .20 .50
174 Roger Clemens 1.00 2.50
175 Frank Thomas .50 1.25
176 Dennis Eckersley .20 .50
177 Gary Sheffield .20 .50
178 David Cone .20 .50
179 Larry Walker .20 .50
180 Mark Grace .30 .75
NNO M.Mantle Masterpiece 8.00 20.00

1996 Topps Gallery Players Private Issue

COMPLETE SET (180) 500.00 800.00
*STARS: 5X TO 12X BASIC CARDS
*ROOKIES: 4X TO 10X BASIC CARDS
STATED ODDS 1:8
STATED PRINT RUN 999 SERIAL #'d SETS
FIRST 100 CARDS SENT TO MLB PLAYERS
TOPPS ALSO DESTROYED 400 SETS

1996 Topps Gallery Expressionists

COMPLETE SET (20) 30.00 80.00
STATED ODDS 1:24
1 Mike Piazza 3.00 8.00
2 J.T. Snow .75 2.00
3 Ken Griffey Jr. 4.00 10.00
4 Kirby Puckett 2.00 5.00
5 Carlos Baerga .75 2.00
6 Chipper Jones 2.00 5.00
7 Hideo Nomo 2.00 5.00
8 Mark McGwire 5.00 12.00
9 Gary Sheffield .75 2.00
10 Randy Johnson 2.00 5.00
11 Ray Lankford .75 2.00
12 Sammy Sosa 2.00 5.00
13 Denny Martinez .75 2.00
14 Jose Canseco 1.25 3.00
15 Tony Gwynn 2.50 6.00
16 Edgar Martinez 1.25 3.00
17 Reggie Sanders .75 2.00
18 Andres Galarraga .75 2.00
19 Albert Belle .75 2.00
20 Barry Larkin 1.25 3.00

1996 Topps Gallery Photo Gallery

COMPLETE SET (15) 30.00 80.00
STATED ODDS 1:30
PG1 Eddie Murray 2.50 6.00
PG2 Randy Johnson 2.50 6.00
PG3 Cal Ripken 8.00 20.00
PG4 Bret Boone 1.00 2.50
PG5 Frank Thomas 2.50 6.00
PG6 Jeff Conine 1.00 2.50
PG7 Johnny Damon 1.50 4.00
PG8 Roger Clemens 5.00 12.00
PG9 Albert Belle 1.00 2.50
PG10 Ken Griffey Jr. 5.00 12.00
PG11 Kirby Puckett 2.50 6.00
PG12 David Justice 1.00 2.50
PG13 Bobby Bonilla 1.00 2.50
PG14 Colorado Rockies 1.00 2.50
PG15 Atlanta Braves 1.00 2.50

1997 Topps Gallery Promos

COMPLETE SET (4) 4.00 10.00
PP1 Andruw Jones 1.25 3.00
PP2 Derek Jeter 2.50 6.00
PP3 Mike Piazza 1.50 4.00
PP4 Craig Biggio .40 1.00

1997 Topps Gallery

The 1997 Topps Gallery set was issued in one series totalling 180 cards. The eight-card packs retailed for $4.00 each. This hobby only set is divided into four themes: Veterans, Prospects, Rising Stars and Young Stars. Printed on 24-point card stock with a high-gloss film and etch stamped with one or more foils, each theme features a different design on front with a variety of informative statistics and revealing player text on the back.

COMPLETE SET (180) 12.50 30.00
1 Paul Molitor .20 .50
2 Devon White .20 .50
3 Andres Galarraga .20 .50
4 Cal Ripken 1.50 4.00
5 Tony Gwynn .60 1.50
6 Mike Stanley .20 .50
7 Orel Hershiser .20 .50
8 Jose Canseco .30 .75
9 Chili Davis .20 .50
10 Harold Baines .20 .50
11 Rickey Henderson .50 1.25
12 Darryl Strawberry .20 .50
13 Todd Worrell .20 .50
14 Cecil Fielder .20 .50
15 Gary Gaetti .20 .50
16 Bobby Bonilla .20 .50
17 Will Clark .30 .75
18 Kevin Brown .20 .50
19 Tom Glavine .30 .75
20 Wade Boggs .30 .75
21 Edgar Martinez .30 .75
22 Lance Johnson .20 .50
23 Gregg Jefferies .20 .50
24 Bip Roberts .20 .50
25 Tony Phillips .20 .50
26 Greg Maddux .75 2.00
27 Mickey Tettleton .20 .50
28 Terry Steinbach .20 .50
29 Ryne Sandberg .75 2.00
30 Wally Joyner .20 .50
31 Joe Carter .20 .50
32 Ellis Burks .20 .50
33 Fred McGriff .30 .75
34 Barry Larkin .30 .75
35 John Franco .20 .50
36 Rafael Palmeiro .30 .75
37 Mark McGwire 1.25 3.00
38 Ken Caminiti .20 .50
39 David Cone .20 .50
40 Julio Franco .20 .50
41 Roger Clemens 1.00 2.50
42 Barry Bonds 1.25 3.00
43 Dennis Eckersley .20 .50
44 Eddie Murray .50 1.25
45 Paul O'Neill .30 .75
46 Craig Biggio .30 .75
47 Roberto Alomar .30 .75
48 Mark Grace .30 .75
49 Matt Williams .20 .50
50 Jay Buhner .20 .50
51 John Smoltz .30 .75
52 Randy Johnson .50 1.25
53 Ramon Martinez .20 .50
54 Curt Schilling .20 .50
55 Gary Sheffield .20 .50
56 Jack McDowell .20 .50
57 Brady Anderson .20 .50
58 Dante Bichette .20 .50
59 Ron Gant .20 .50
60 Alex Fernandez .20 .50
61 Moises Alou .20 .50
62 Travis Fryman .20 .50
63 Dean Palmer .20 .50
64 Todd Hundley .20 .50
65 Jeff Brantley .20 .50
66 Bernard Gilkey .20 .50
67 Geronimo Berroa .20 .50
68 John Wetteland .20 .50
69 Robin Ventura .20 .50
70 Ray Lankford .20 .50
71 Kevin Appier .20 .50
72 Larry Walker .20 .50
73 Juan Gonzalez .20 .50
74 Jeff King .20 .50
75 Greg Vaughn .20 .50
76 Steve Finley .20 .50
77 Brian McRae .20 .50
78 Paul Sorrento .20 .50
79 Ken Griffey Jr. 1.00 2.50
80 Omar Vizquel .30 .75
81 Jose Mesa .20 .50
82 Albert Belle .20 .50
83 Glenallen Hill .20 .50
84 Sammy Sosa .50 1.25
85 Andy Benes .20 .50
86 David Justice .20 .50
87 Marquis Grissom .20 .50
88 John Olerud .20 .50
89 Tino Martinez .30 .75
90 Frank Thomas .50 1.25
91 Raul Mondesi .20 .50
92 Steve Trachsel .20 .50
93 Jim Edmonds .20 .50
94 Rusty Greer .20 .50
95 Joey Hamilton .20 .50
96 Ismael Valdes .20 .50
97 Dave Nilsson .20 .50
98 John Jaha .20 .50
99 Alex Gonzalez .20 .50
100 Javy Lopez .20 .50
101 Ryan Klesko .20 .50
102 Tim Salmon .30 .75
103 Bernie Williams .30 .75
104 Roberto Hernandez .20 .50
105 Chuck Knoblauch .20 .50
106 Mike Lansing .20 .50
107 Vinny Castilla .20 .50
108 Reggie Sanders .20 .50
109 Mo Vaughn .20 .50
110 Rondell White .20 .50
111 Ivan Rodriguez .30 .75
112 Mike Mussina .30 .75
113 Carlos Baerga .20 .50
114 Jeff Conine .20 .50
115 Jim Thome .30 .75
116 Manny Ramirez .30 .75
117 Kenny Lofton .20 .50
118 Wilson Alvarez .20 .50
119 Eric Karros .20 .50
120 Robb Nen .20 .50
121 Mark Wohlers .20 .50
122 Ed Sprague .20 .50
123 Pat Hentgen .20 .50
124 Juan Guzman .20 .50
125 Derek Bell .20 .50
126 Jeff Bagwell .30 .75
127 Eric Young .20 .50
128 John Valentin .20 .50
129 Al Martin UER .20 .50
130 Trevor Hoffman .20 .50
131 Henry Rodriguez .20 .50
132 Pedro Martinez .30 .75
133 Mike Piazza .75 2.00
134 Brian Jordan .20 .50
135 Jose Valentin .20 .50
136 Jeff Cirillo .20 .50
137 Chipper Jones .50 1.25
138 Ricky Bottalico .20 .50
139 Hideo Nomo .50 1.25
140 Troy Percival .20 .50
141 Rey Ordonez .20 .50
142 Edgar Renteria .20 .50
143 Luis Castillo .20 .50
144 Vladimir Guerrero .50 1.25
145 Jeff D'Amico .20 .50
146 Andruw Jones .30 .75
147 Darin Erstad .20 .50
148 Bob Abreu .30 .75
149 Carlos Delgado .20 .50
150 Jamey Wright .20 .50
151 Nomar Garciaparra .75 2.00
152 Jason Kendall .20 .50
153 Jermaine Allensworth .20 .50
154 Scott Rolen .30 .75
155 Rocky Coppinger .20 .50
156 Paul Wilson .20 .50
157 Garret Anderson .20 .50
158 Mariano Rivera .50 1.25
159 Ruben Rivera .20 .50
160 Andy Pettitte .30 .75
161 Derek Jeter 1.25 3.00
162 Neifi Perez .20 .50
163 Ray Durham .20 .50
164 James Baldwin .20 .50
165 Marty Cordova .20 .50
166 Tony Clark .20 .50
167 Michael Tucker .20 .50
168 Mike Sweeney .20 .50
169 Johnny Damon .30 .75
170 Jermaine Dye .20 .50
171 Alex Ochoa .20 .50
172 Jason Isringhausen .20 .50
173 Mark Grudzielanek .20 .50
174 Jose Rosado .20 .50
175 Todd Hollandsworth .20 .50
176 Alan Benes .20 .50
177 Jason Giambi .20 .50
178 Billy Wagner .20 .50
179 Justin Thompson .20 .50
180 Todd Walker .20 .50

1997 Topps Gallery Player's Private Issue

*STARS: 6X TO 15X BASIC CARDS
STATED ODDS 1:12
STATED PRINT RUN 250 SETS

1997 Topps Gallery Gallery of Heroes

COMPLETE SET (10) 25.00 60.00
STATED ODDS 1:36
GH1 Derek Jeter 6.00 15.00
GH2 Chipper Jones 2.50 6.00
GH3 Frank Thomas 2.50 6.00
GH4 Ken Griffey Jr. 5.00 12.00
GH5 Cal Ripken 8.00 20.00
GH6 Mark McGwire 4.00 10.00
GH7 Mike Piazza 2.50 6.00
GH8 Jeff Bagwell 1.50 4.00
GH9 Tony Gwynn 2.50 6.00
GH10 Mo Vaughn 1.00 2.50

1997 Topps Gallery Peter Max Serigraphs

COMPLETE SET (10) 100.00 200.00
STATED ODDS 1:24
*AUTOS: 3X TO 8X BASIC SERIGRAPHS
AUTOS RANDOM INSERTS IN PACKS
AUTOS STATED PRINT RUN 40 SETS
AU'S SIGNED BY MAX BENEATH UV COATING
1 Derek Jeter 20.00 50.00
2 Albert Belle 1.50 4.00
3 Ken Caminiti 1.50 4.00
4 Chipper Jones 4.00 10.00
5 Ken Griffey Jr. 8.00 20.00
6 Frank Thomas 4.00 10.00
7 Cal Ripken 12.00 30.00
8 Mark McGwire 6.00 15.00
9 Barry Bonds 6.00 15.00
10 Mike Piazza 4.00 10.00

1997 Topps Gallery Photo Gallery

COMPLETE SET (16) 40.00 100.00
STATED ODDS 1:24
PG1 John Wetteland 1.00 2.50
PG2 Paul Molitor 1.00 2.50
PG3 Eddie Murray 2.50 6.00
PG4 Ken Griffey Jr. 5.00 12.00
PG5 Chipper Jones 2.50 6.00
PG6 Derek Jeter 6.00 15.00
PG7 Frank Thomas 2.50 6.00
PG8 Mark McGwire 6.00 15.00
PG9 Kenny Lofton 1.00 2.50
PG10 Gary Sheffield 1.00 2.50
PG11 Mike Piazza 4.00 10.00
PG12 Vinny Castilla 1.00 2.50
PG13 Andres Galarraga 1.00 2.50
PG14 Andy Pettitte 1.50 4.00
PG15 Robin Ventura 1.00 2.50
PG16 Barry Larkin 1.50 4.00

1998 Topps Gallery Pre-Production

PP1 Andruw Jones
PP2 Juan Gonzalez
PP3 Barry Bonds
PP4 Derek Jeter 2.50 6.00
PP5 Nomar Garciaparra .60 1.50

1998 Topps Gallery

The 1998 Topps Gallery hobby-only set was issued in one series totalling 150 cards. The six-card packs retailed for $3.00 each. The set is divided by five subset groupings: Expressionists, Exhibitionists, Impressions, Portraits and Permanent Collection. Each theme features a different design with informative stats and text on each player.

COMPLETE SET (150) 12.50 30.00
1 Andruw Jones .30 .75
2 Fred McGriff .30 .75
3 Wade Boggs .30 .75
4 Pedro Martinez .30 .75
5 Matt Williams .20 .50
6 Wilson Alvarez .20 .50
7 Henry Rodriguez .20 .50
8 Jay Bell .20 .50
9 Marquis Grissom .20 .50
10 Darryl Kile .20 .50
11 Chuck Knoblauch .20 .50
12 Kenny Lofton .20 .50
13 Quinton McCracken .20 .50
14 Andres Galarraga .20 .50
15 Brian Jordan .20 .50
16 Mike Lansing .20 .50
17 Travis Fryman .20 .50
18 Tony Saunders .20 .50
19 Moises Alou .20 .50
20 Travis Lee .20 .50
21 Garret Anderson .20 .50
22 Ken Caminiti .20 .50
23 Pedro Astacio .20 .50
24 Ellis Burks .20 .50
25 Albert Belle .20 .50
26 Alan Benes .20 .50
27 Jay Buhner .20 .50
28 Derek Bell .20 .50
29 Jeromy Burnitz .20 .50
30 Kevin Appier .20 .50
31 Jeff Cirillo .20 .50
32 Bernard Gilkey .20 .50
33 David Cone .20 .50
34 Jason Dickson .20 .50
35 Jose Cruz Jr. .20 .50
36 Marty Cordova .20 .50
37 Ray Durham .20 .50
38 Jaret Wright .20 .50
39 Billy Wagner .20 .50
40 Roger Clemens 1.00 2.50
41 Juan Gonzalez .20 .50
42 Jeremi Gonzalez .20 .50
43 Mark Grudzielanek .20 .50
44 Tom Glavine .30 .75
45 Barry Larkin .30 .75
46 Lance Johnson .20 .50
47 Bobby Higginson .20 .50
48 Mike Mussina .30 .75
49 Al Martin .20 .50
50 Mark McGwire 1.25 3.00
51 Todd Hundley .20 .50
52 Ray Lankford .20 .50
53 Jason Kendall .20 .50
54 Javy Lopez .20 .50
55 Ben Grieve .20 .50
56 Randy Johnson .50 1.25
57 Jeff King .20 .50
58 Mark Grace .30 .75
59 Rusty Greer .20 .50
60 Greg Maddux .75 2.00
61 Jeff Kent .20 .50
62 Rey Ordonez .20 .50
63 Hideo Nomo .50 1.25
64 Charles Nagy .20 .50
65 Rondell White .20 .50
66 Todd Helton .30 .75
67 Jim Thome .30 .75
68 Denny Neagle .20 .50
69 Ivan Rodriguez .30 .75
70 Vladimir Guerrero .50 1.25
71 Jorge Posada .30 .75
72 J.T. Snow .20 .50
73 Reggie Sanders .20 .50
74 Scott Rolen .30 .75
75 Robin Ventura .20 .50
76 Mariano Rivera .50 1.25
77 Cal Ripken 1.50 4.00
78 Justin Thompson .20 .50
79 Mike Piazza .75 2.00
80 Kevin Brown .30 .75
81 Sandy Alomar Jr. .20 .50
82 Craig Biggio .30 .75
83 Vinny Castilla .20 .50
84 Eric Young .20 .50
85 Bernie Williams .30 .75
86 Brady Anderson .20 .50
87 Bobby Bonilla .20 .50
88 Tony Clark .20 .50
89 Dan Wilson .20 .50
90 John Wetteland .20 .50
91 Barry Bonds 1.25 3.00
92 Chan Ho Park .20 .50
93 Carlos Delgado .20 .50
94 David Justice .20 .50
95 Chipper Jones .50 1.25
96 Shawn Estes .20 .50
97 Jason Giambi .20 .50
98 Ron Gant .20 .50
99 John Olerud .20 .50
100 Frank Thomas .50 1.25
101 Jose Guillen .20 .50
102 Brad Radke .20 .50
103 Troy Percival .20 .50
104 John Smoltz .30 .75
105 Edgardo Alfonzo .20 .50
106 Dante Bichette .20 .50
107 Larry Walker .20 .50
108 John Valentin .20 .50
109 Roberto Alomar .30 .75
110 Mike Cameron .20 .50
111 Eric Davis .20 .50
112 Johnny Damon .30 .75
113 Darin Erstad .20 .50
114 Omar Vizquel .30 .75
115 Derek Jeter 1.25 3.00
116 Tony Womack .20 .50
117 Edgar Renteria .20 .50
118 Raul Mondesi .20 .50
119 Tony Gwynn .60 1.50
120 Ken Griffey Jr. 1.00 2.50
121 Jim Edmonds .20 .50
122 Brian Hunter .20 .50
123 Neifi Perez .20 .50
124 Dean Palmer .20 .50
125 Alex Rodriguez .75 2.00
126 Tim Salmon .30 .75
127 Curt Schilling .20 .50
128 Kevin Orie .20 .50
129 Andy Pettitte .30 .75
130 Gary Sheffield .20 .50
131 Jose Rosado .20 .50
132 Manny Ramirez .30 .75
133 Rafael Palmeiro .30 .75
134 Sammy Sosa .50 1.25
135 Jeff Bagwell .30 .75
136 Delino DeShields .20 .50
137 Ryan Klesko .20 .50
138 Mo Vaughn .20 .50
139 Steve Finley .20 .50
140 Nomar Garciaparra .75 2.00
141 Paul Molitor .20 .50
142 Pat Hentgen .20 .50
143 Eric Karros .20 .50
144 Bobby Jones .20 .50
145 Tino Martinez .30 .75
146 Matt Morris .20 .50
147 Livan Hernandez .20 .50
148 Edgar Martinez .30 .75
149 Paul O'Neill .30 .75
150 Checklist .20 .50

1998 Topps Gallery Gallery Proofs

*STARS: 10X TO 25X BASIC CARDS
STATED ODDS 1:34 HOBBY
STATED PRINT RUN 125 SERIAL #'d SETS

1998 Topps Gallery Original Printing Plates

STATED ODDS 1:537 HOBBY

1998 Topps Gallery Player's Private Issue

COMPLETE SET (150) 1500.00 3000.00
*STARS: 5X TO 12X BASIC CARDS
STATED ODDS 1:17 HOBBY
STATED PRINT RUN 250 SERIAL #'d SETS

1998 Topps Gallery Player's Private Issue Auction 25 Point

COMPLETE SET (150) 40.00 100.00
*STARS: .75X TO 2X BASIC CARDS
AUCTION RULES ON CARD BACK
AUCTION CLOSED 10/16/98

1998 Topps Gallery Awards Gallery

COMPLETE SET (10) 25.00 60.00
STATED ODDS 1:24 HOBBY
AG1 Ken Griffey Jr. 5.00 12.00
AG2 Larry Walker 1.00 2.50
AG3 Roger Clemens 5.00 12.00
AG4 Pedro Martinez 1.50 4.00
AG5 Nomar Garciaparra 4.00 10.00
AG6 Scott Rolen 1.50 4.00
AG7 Frank Thomas 2.50 6.00
AG8 Tony Gwynn 3.00 8.00
AG9 Mark McGwire 6.00 15.00
AG10 Livan Hernandez 1.00 2.50

1998 Topps Gallery Gallery of Heroes

COMPLETE SET (15) 25.00 60.00
STATED ODDS 1:24 HOBBY
ONE JUMBO PER HOBBY BOX
GH1 Ken Griffey Jr. 4.00 10.00
GH2 Derek Jeter 5.00 12.00
GH3 Barry Bonds 3.00 8.00
GH4 Alex Rodriguez 2.50 6.00
GH5 Frank Thomas 2.00 5.00
GH6 Nomar Garciaparra 1.25 3.00
GH7 Mark McGwire 3.00 8.00
GH8 Mike Piazza 2.00 5.00
GH9 Cal Ripken 6.00 15.00
GH10 Jose Cruz Jr. .75 2.00
GH11 Jeff Bagwell 1.25 3.00
GH12 Chipper Jones 2.00 5.00
GH13 Juan Gonzalez .75 2.00
GH14 Hideo Nomo 2.00 5.00
GH15 Greg Maddux 2.50 6.00

1998 Topps Gallery Photo Gallery

COMPLETE SET (10) 10.00 25.00
STATED ODDS 1:24 HOBBY
PG1 Alex Rodriguez 1.25 3.00
PG2 Frank Thomas 1.00 2.50
PG3 Derek Jeter 2.50 6.00
PG4 Cal Ripken 3.00 8.00
PG5 Ken Griffey Jr. 2.00 5.00
PG6 Mike Piazza 1.00 2.50
PG7 Nomar Garciaparra .60 1.50
PG8 Tim Salmon .40 1.00
PG9 Jeff Bagwell .60 1.50
PG10 Barry Bonds 1.50 4.00

1999 Topps Gallery Previews

This three-card standard-size set was released to preview the 1999 Topps Gallery set. The set features a regular design as well as a couple of the subsets involved in this set.

COMPLETE SET (3) 2.00 5.00
PP1 Scott Rolen 1.00 2.50
PP2 Andres Galarraga MAST .60 1.50
PP3 Brad Fullmer ART .40 1.00

1999 Topps Gallery

The 1999 Topps Gallery set was issued in one series totalling 150 cards and was distributed in six-card packs for a suggested retail price of $3. The set features 100 veteran stars and 50 subset cards finely crafted and printed on 24-pt. stock, with serigraph textured frame, etched foil stamping, and spot UV finish. The set contains the following subsets: Masters (101-115), Artisans (116-127), and Apprentices (128-150). Rookie Cards inlcude Pat Burrell, Nick Johnson and Alfonso Soriano.

COMPLETE SET (150) 20.00 50.00
COMP.SET w/o SP's (100) 10.00 25.00
COMMON CARD (1-100) .10 .30
COMMON CARD (101-150) .30 .75
CARDS 101-150 ONE PER PACK
1 Mark McGwire .75 2.00
2 Jim Thome .20 .50
3 Bernie Williams .20 .50
4 Larry Walker .10 .30
5 Juan Gonzalez .10 .30
6 Ken Griffey Jr. .60 1.50
7 Raul Mondesi .10 .30
8 Sammy Sosa .30 .75
9 Greg Maddux .50 1.25
10 Jeff Bagwell .20 .50
11 Vladimir Guerrero .30 .75
12 Scott Rolen .20 .50
13 Nomar Garciaparra .50 1.25
14 Mike Piazza .50 1.25
15 Travis Lee .10 .30
16 Carlos Delgado .10 .30
17 Darin Erstad .10 .30
18 David Justice .10 .30
19 Cal Ripken 1.00 2.50
20 Derek Jeter .75 2.00
21 Tony Clark .10 .30
22 Barry Larkin .20 .50
23 Greg Vaughn .10 .30
24 Jeff Kent .10 .30
25 Wade Boggs .20 .50
26 Andres Galarraga .10 .30
27 Ken Caminiti .10 .30
28 Jason Kendall .10 .30
29 Todd Helton .20 .50
30 Chuck Knoblauch .10 .30
31 Roger Clemens .60 1.50
32 Jeromy Burnitz .10 .30
33 Javy Lopez .10 .30
34 Roberto Alomar .20 .50
35 Eric Karros .10 .30
36 Ben Grieve .10 .30
37 Eric Davis .10 .30
38 Rondell White .10 .30
39 Dmitri Young .10 .30
40 Ivan Rodriguez .20 .50
41 Paul O'Neill .20 .50
42 Jeff Cirillo .10 .30
43 Kerry Wood .10 .30
44 Albert Belle .10 .30
45 Frank Thomas .30 .75
46 Manny Ramirez .20 .50
47 Tom Glavine .20 .50
48 Mo Vaughn .10 .30
49 Jose Cruz Jr. .10 .30
50 Sandy Alomar Jr. .10 .30
51 Edgar Martinez .20 .50
52 John Olerud .10 .30
53 Todd Walker .10 .30
54 Tim Salmon .20 .50
55 Derek Bell .10 .30
56 Matt Williams .10 .30
57 Alex Rodriguez .50 1.25
58 Rusty Greer .10 .30
59 Vinny Castilla .10 .30
60 Jason Giambi .10 .30
61 Mark Grace .20 .50
62 Jose Canseco .20 .50
63 Gary Sheffield .10 .30
64 Brad Fullmer .10 .30
65 Trevor Hoffman .10 .30
66 Mark Kotsay .10 .30
67 Mike Mussina .20 .50
68 Johnny Damon .20 .50
69 Tino Martinez .20 .50
70 Curt Schilling .10 .30
71 Jay Buhner .10 .30
72 Kenny Lofton .10 .30
73 Randy Johnson .30 .75
74 Kevin Brown .20 .50
75 Brian Jordan .10 .30
76 Craig Biggio .20 .50
77 Barry Bonds .75 2.00
78 Tony Gwynn .40 1.00
79 Jim Edmonds .10 .30
80 Shawn Green .10 .30
81 Todd Hundley .10 .30
82 Cliff Floyd .10 .30
83 Jose Guillen .10 .30
84 Dante Bichette .10 .30
85 Moises Alou .10 .30
86 Chipper Jones .30 .75
87 Ray Lankford .10 .30
88 Fred McGriff .20 .50
89 Rod Beck .10 .30
90 Dean Palmer .10 .30
91 Pedro Martinez .20 .50
92 Andruw Jones .20 .50
93 Robin Ventura .10 .30
94 Ugueth Urbina .10 .30
95 Orlando Hernandez .10 .30
96 Sean Casey .10 .30
97 Denny Neagle .10 .30
98 Troy Glaus .20 .50
99 John Smoltz .20 .50
100 Al Leiter .10 .30
101 Ken Griffey Jr. MAS 1.25 3.00
102 Frank Thomas MAS .60 1.50
103 Mark McGwire MAS 1.50 4.00
104 Sammy Sosa MAS .60 1.50
105 Chipper Jones MAS .60 1.50
106 Alex Rodriguez MAS 1.00 2.50
107 Nomar Garciaparra MAS 1.00 2.50
108 Juan Gonzalez MAS .30 .75
109 Derek Jeter MAS 1.50 4.00
110 Mike Piazza MAS 1.00 2.50
111 Barry Bonds MAS 1.50 4.00
112 Tony Gwynn MAS .75 2.00
113 Cal Ripken MAS 2.00 5.00
114 Greg Maddux MAS 1.00 2.50
115 Roger Clemens MAS 1.25 3.00
116 Brad Fullmer ART .30 .75
117 Kerry Wood ART .30 .75
118 Ben Grieve ART .30 .75
119 Todd Helton ART .40 1.00
120 Kevin Millwood ART .30 .75
121 Sean Casey ART .30 .75
122 Vladimir Guerrero ART .60 1.50
123 Travis Lee ART .30 .75
124 Troy Glaus ART .40 1.00
125 Bartolo Colon ART .30 .75
126 Andruw Jones ART .40 1.00
127 Scott Rolen ART .40 1.00
128 Alfonso Soriano APP RC 2.00 5.00
129 Nick Johnson APP RC .75 2.00
130 Matt Belisle APP RC .30 .75
131 Jorge Toca APP RC .30 .75
132 Masao Kida APP RC .30 .75
133 Carlos Pena APP RC .40 1.00
134 Adrian Beltre APP .30 .75
135 Eric Chavez APP .30 .75
136 Carlos Beltran APP .40 1.00
137 Alex Gonzalez APP .30 .75
138 Ryan Anderson APP .30 .75
139 Ruben Mateo APP .30 .75
140 Bruce Chen APP .30 .75
141 Pat Burrell APP RC 1.25 3.00
142 Michael Barrett APP .30 .75
143 Carlos Lee APP .30 .75
144 Mark Mulder APP RC 1.00 2.50
145 Choo Freeman APP RC .30 .75
146 Gabe Kapler APP .30 .75
147 Juan Encarnacion APP .30 .75
148 Jeremy Giambi APP .30 .75
149 Jason Tyner APP RC .30 .75
150 George Lombard APP .30 .75

1999 Topps Gallery Player's Private Issue

*STARS 1-100: 8X TO 20X BASIC CARDS
*MASTERS 101-115: 4X TO 10X BASIC
*ARTISANS 116-127: 3X TO 8X BASIC
*APPRENTICES 128-150: 3X TO 8X BASIC
*APP.RC'S 128-150: 2X TO 5X BASIC
STATED ODDS 1:17
STATED PRINT RUN 250 SERIAL #'d SETS

1999 Topps Gallery Autographs

COMPLETE SET (3) 30.00 80.00
STATED ODDS 1:209
GA1 Troy Glaus 6.00 15.00
GA2 Adrian Beltre 8.00 20.00
GA3 Eric Chavez 6.00 15.00

1999 Topps Gallery Awards Gallery

COMPLETE SET (10) 12.50 30.00
STATED ODDS 1:12
AG1 Kerry Wood .50 1.25
AG2 Ben Grieve .50 1.25
AG3 Roger Clemens 2.50 6.00
AG4 Tom Glavine .75 2.00
AG5 Juan Gonzalez .50 1.25
AG6 Sammy Sosa 1.25 3.00
AG7 Ken Griffey Jr. 2.50 6.00
AG8 Mark McGwire 3.00 8.00
AG9 Bernie Williams .75 2.00
AG10 Larry Walker .50 1.25

1999 Topps Gallery Exhibitions

COMPLETE SET (20) 100.00 200.00
STATED ODDS 1:48
E1 Sammy Sosa 3.00 8.00
E2 Mark McGwire 8.00 20.00
E3 Greg Maddux 5.00 12.00
E4 Roger Clemens 6.00 15.00
E5 Ben Grieve 1.25 3.00
E6 Kerry Wood 1.25 3.00
E7 Ken Griffey Jr. 6.00 15.00
E8 Tony Gwynn 4.00 10.00
E9 Cal Ripken 10.00 25.00
E10 Frank Thomas 3.00 8.00
E11 Jeff Bagwell 2.00 5.00
E12 Derek Jeter 8.00 20.00
E13 Alex Rodriguez 5.00 12.00
E14 Nomar Garciaparra 5.00 12.00
E15 Manny Ramirez 2.00 5.00
E16 Vladimir Guerrero 3.00 8.00
E17 Darin Erstad 1.25 3.00
E18 Scott Rolen 2.00 5.00
E19 Mike Piazza 5.00 12.00
E20 Andres Galarraga 1.25 3.00

1999 Topps Gallery Gallery of Heroes

COMPLETE SET (10) 30.00 80.00
STATED ODDS 1:24
GH1 Mark McGwire 5.00 12.00
GH2 Sammy Sosa 2.00 5.00
GH3 Ken Griffey Jr. 4.00 10.00
GH4 Mike Piazza 3.00 8.00
GH5 Derek Jeter 5.00 12.00
GH6 Nomar Garciaparra 3.00 8.00
GH7 Kerry Wood .75 2.00
GH8 Ben Grieve .75 2.00
GH9 Chipper Jones 2.00 5.00
GH10 Alex Rodriguez 3.00 8.00

1999 Topps Gallery Heritage

COMPLETE SET (20) 75.00 150.00
STATED ODDS 1:12
*PROOFS: .4X TO 1X BASIC HERITAGE
PROOFS STATED ODDS 1:48
TH1 Hank Aaron 6.00 15.00
TH2 Ben Grieve 1.25 3.00
TH3 Nomar Garciaparra 2.00 5.00
TH4 Roger Clemens 4.00 10.00
TH5 Travis Lee 1.25 3.00
TH6 Tony Gwynn 3.00 8.00
TH7 Alex Rodriguez 4.00 10.00
TH8 Ken Griffey Jr. 6.00 15.00
TH9 Derek Jeter 8.00 20.00
TH10 Sammy Sosa 3.00 8.00
TH11 Scott Rolen 2.00 5.00
TH12 Chipper Jones 3.00 8.00
TH13 Cal Ripken 10.00 25.00
TH14 Kerry Wood 1.25 3.00
TH15 Barry Bonds 5.00 12.00
TH16 Juan Gonzalez 1.25 3.00
TH17 Mike Piazza 3.00 8.00
TH18 Greg Maddux 4.00 10.00
TH19 Frank Thomas 3.00 8.00
TH20 Mark McGwire 5.00 12.00

1999 Topps Gallery Heritage Postcards

This seven-card postcard-sized set was issued by Topps in 1999. The set features superstar players painted by James Fiorentino.

COMPLETE SET (7) 15.00 40.00
1 Mark McGwire 2.00 5.00
2 Sammy Sosa 1.25 3.00
3 Roger Clemens 2.00 5.00
4 Mike Piazza 2.50 6.00
5 Cal Ripken 4.00 10.00
6 Derek Jeter 4.00 10.00
7 Ken Griffey Jr. 2.50 6.00

2000 Topps Gallery Pre-Production

COMPLETE SET (3) 3.00 8.00
PP1 Derek Jeter 2.50 6.00
PP2 Mark McGwire 1.50 4.00
PP3 Josh Hamilton 1.25 3.00

2000 Topps Gallery

COMPLETE SET (150) 12.50 30.00
COMP.SET w/o SP's (100) 4.00 10.00
COMMON CARD (1-100) .12 .30
COMMON CARD (101-150) .40 1.00
CARDS 101-150 ONE PER PACK
1 Nomar Garciaparra .20 .50
2 Kevin Millwood .12 .30
3 Jay Bell .12 .30
4 Rusty Greer .12 .30
5 Bernie Williams .20 .50
6 Barry Larkin .20 .50
7 Carlos Beltran .20 .50
8 Damion Easley .12 .30
9 Magglio Ordonez .20 .50
10 Matt Williams .12 .30
11 Shannon Stewart .12 .30
12 Ray Lankford .12 .30
13 Vinny Castilla .12 .30
14 Miguel Tejada .20 .50
15 Craig Biggio .20 .50
16 Chipper Jones .30 .75
17 Albert Belle .12 .30
18 Doug Glanville .12 .30
19 Brian Giles .12 .30
20 Shawn Green .12 .30
21 Bret Boone .12 .30
22 Luis Gonzalez .12 .30
23 Carlos Delgado .12 .30
24 J.D. Drew .12 .30
25 Ivan Rodriguez .20 .50
26 Tino Martinez .12 .30
27 Erubiel Durazo .12 .30
28 Scott Rolen .20 .50
29 Gary Sheffield .12 .30
30 Manny Ramirez .30 .75
31 Luis Castillo .12 .30
32 Fernando Tatis .12 .30
33 Darin Erstad .12 .30
34 Tim Hudson .20 .50
35 Sammy Sosa .30 .75
36 Jason Kendall .12 .30
37 Todd Walker .12 .30
38 Orlando Hernandez .12 .30
39 Pokey Reese .12 .30
40 Mike Piazza .30 .75
41 B.J. Surhoff .12 .30
42 Tony Gwynn .30 .75
43 Kevin Brown .12 .30
44 Preston Wilson .12 .30
45 Kenny Lofton .12 .30
46 Rondell White .12 .30
47 Frank Thomas .30 .75
48 Neifi Perez .12 .30
49 Edgardo Alfonzo .12 .30
50 Ken Griffey Jr. .60 1.50
51 Barry Bonds .50 1.25
52 Brian Jordan .12 .30
53 Raul Mondesi .12 .30
54 Troy Glaus .12 .30
55 Curt Schilling .20 .50
56 Mike Mussina .20 .50
57 Brian Daubach .12 .30
58 Roger Clemens .40 1.00
59 Carlos Febles .12 .30
60 Todd Helton .20 .50
61 Mark Grace .20 .50
62 Randy Johnson .30 .75
63 Jeff Bagwell .20 .50
64 Tom Glavine .20 .50
65 Adrian Beltre .30 .75
66 Rafael Palmeiro .20 .50
67 Paul O'Neill .20 .50
68 Robin Ventura .12 .30
69 Ray Durham .12 .30
70 Mark McGwire .50 1.25
71 Greg Vaughn .12 .30
72 Javy Lopez .12 .30
73 Ryan Klesko .12 .30
74 Mike Lieberthal .12 .30
75 Cal Ripken 1.00 2.50
76 Juan Gonzalez .12 .30
77 Sean Casey .12 .30
78 Jermaine Dye .12 .30
79 John Olerud .12 .30
80 Jose Canseco .20 .50
81 Eric Karros .12 .30
82 Roberto Alomar .20 .50
83 Ben Grieve .12 .30
84 Greg Maddux .40 1.00
85 Pedro Martinez .20 .50
86 Tony Clark .12 .30
87 Richie Sexson .12 .30
88 Cliff Floyd .12 .30
89 Eric Chavez .12 .30
90 Andruw Jones .12 .30
91 Vladimir Guerrero .20 .50
92 Alex Gonzalez .12 .30
93 Jim Thome .20 .50
94 Bob Abreu .12 .30
95 Derek Jeter .75 2.00
96 Larry Walker .20 .50
97 Mike Hampton .12 .30
98 Mo Vaughn .12 .30
99 Jason Giambi .12 .30
100 Alex Rodriguez .40 1.00
101 Mark McGwire MAS 1.50 4.00
102 Sammy Sosa MAS 1.00 2.50
103 Alex Rodriguez MAS 1.25 3.00
104 Derek Jeter MAS 2.50 6.00
105 Greg Maddux MAS 1.25 3.00
106 Jeff Bagwell MAS .60 1.50
107 Nomar Garciaparra MAS .60 1.50
108 Mike Piazza MAS 1.00 2.50
109 Pedro Martinez MAS .60 1.50
110 Chipper Jones MAS 1.00 2.50
111 Randy Johnson MAS 1.00 2.50
112 Barry Bonds MAS 1.50 4.00
113 Ken Griffey Jr. MAS 2.00 5.00
114 Manny Ramirez MAS 1.00 2.50
115 Ivan Rodriguez MAS .60 1.50
116 Juan Gonzalez MAS .40 1.00
117 Vladimir Guerrero MAS .60 1.50
118 Tony Gwynn MAS 1.00 2.50
119 Larry Walker MAS .60 1.50
120 Cal Ripken MAS 3.00 8.00
121 Josh Hamilton 1.25 3.00
122 Corey Patterson SG .40 1.00
123 Pat Burrell SG .40 1.00
124 Nick Johnson SG .40 1.00
125 Adam Piatt SG .40 1.00
126 Rick Ankiel SG .60 1.50
127 A.J. Burnett SG .40 1.00
128 Ben Petrick SG .40 1.00
129 Rafael Furcal SG .60 1.50
130 Alfonso Soriano SG 1.00 2.50
131 Dee Brown SG .40 1.00
132 Ruben Mateo SG .40 1.00
133 Pablo Ozuna SG .40 1.00
134 Sean Burroughs SG UER .40 1.00
135 Mark Mulder SG .40 1.00
136 Jason Jennings SG .40 1.00
137 Eric Munson SG .40 1.00
138 Vernon Wells SG .40 1.00
139 Brett Myers SG RC 1.25 3.00
140 Ben Christensen SG RC .40 1.00
141 Bobby Bradley SG RC .40 1.00
142 Ruben Salazar SG RC .40 1.00
143 Ryan Christianson SG RC .40 1.00
144 Corey Myers SG RC .40 1.00
145 Aaron Rowand SG RC 2.00 5.00
146 Julio Zuleta SG RC .40 1.00
147 Kurt Ainsworth SG RC .40 1.00
148 Scott Downs SG RC .40 1.00
149 Larry Bigbie SG RC .40 1.00
150 Chance Caple SG RC .40 1.00

2000 Topps Gallery Player's Private Issue

*PRIVATE ISSUE 1-100: 5X TO 12X BASIC
*PRIVATE ISSUE 101-120: 1.5X TO 4X BASIC
STATED ODDS 1:20
STATED PRINT RUN 250 SERIAL #'d SETS

2000 Topps Gallery Autographs

STATED ODD 1:153
BP Ben Petrick 4.00 10.00
CP Corey Patterson 4.00 10.00
RA Rick Ankiel 4.00 10.00
RM Ruben Mateo 4.00 10.00
VW Vernon Wells 6.00 15.00

2000 Topps Gallery Exhibits

COMPLETE SET (30) 100.00 200.00
STATED ODDS 1:18
GE1 Mark McGwire 5.00 12.00
GE2 Jeff Bagwell 2.00 5.00
GE3 Mike Piazza 3.00 8.00
GE4 Alex Rodriguez 4.00 10.00
GE5 Nomar Garciaparra 2.00 5.00
GE6 Ivan Rodriguez 2.00 5.00
GE7 Chipper Jones 3.00 8.00
GE8 Cal Ripken 10.00 25.00
GE9 Tony Gwynn 3.00 8.00
GE10 Jose Canseco 2.00 5.00
GE11 Albert Belle 1.25 3.00
GE12 Greg Maddux 4.00 10.00
GE13 Barry Bonds 5.00 12.00
GE14 Ken Griffey Jr. 6.00 15.00
GE15 Juan Gonzalez 1.25 3.00
GE16 Rickey Henderson 3.00 8.00
GE17 Craig Biggio 2.00 5.00
GE18 Vladimir Guerrero 2.00 5.00
GE19 Rey Ordonez 1.25 3.00
GE20 Roberto Alomar 2.00 5.00
GE21 Derek Jeter 8.00 20.00
GE22 Manny Ramirez 3.00 8.00
GE23 Shawn Green 1.25 3.00
GE24 Sammy Sosa 3.00 8.00
GE25 Larry Walker 2.00 5.00
GE26 Pedro Martinez 2.00 5.00
GE27 Randy Johnson 3.00 8.00
GE28 Pat Burrell 1.25 3.00
GE29 Josh Hamilton 4.00 10.00
GE30 Corey Patterson 1.25 3.00

2000 Topps Gallery Gallery of Heroes

COMPLETE SET (10) 20.00 50.00
STATED ODDS 1:24
GH1 Alex Rodriguez 2.50 6.00
GH2 Chipper Jones 2.00 5.00
GH3 Pedro Martinez 1.25 3.00
GH4 Sammy Sosa 2.00 5.00
GH5 Mark McGwire 3.00 8.00
GH6 Nomar Garciaparra 1.25 3.00
GH7 Vladimir Guerrero 1.25 3.00
GH8 Ken Griffey Jr. 4.00 10.00
GH9 Mike Piazza 2.00 5.00
GH10 Derek Jeter 5.00 12.00

2000 Topps Gallery Heritage

COMPLETE SET (20) 25.00 60.00
STATED ODDS 1:12
*PROOFS: .75X TO 2X BASIC HERITAGE
PROOFS STATED ODDS 1:27
TGH1 Mark McGwire 2.50 6.00
TGH2 Sammy Sosa 1.50 4.00
TGH3 Greg Maddux 2.00 5.00
TGH4 Mike Piazza 1.50 4.00
TGH5 Ivan Rodriguez 1.00 2.50
TGH6 Manny Ramirez 1.50 4.00
TGH7 Jeff Bagwell 1.00 2.50
TGH8 Sean Casey .60 1.50
TGH9 Orlando Hernandez .60 1.50
TGH10 Randy Johnson 1.50 4.00
TGH11 Pedro Martinez 1.00 2.50
TGH12 Vladimir Guerrero 1.00 2.50
TGH13 Shawn Green .60 1.50
TGH14 Ken Griffey Jr. 3.00 8.00
TGH15 Alex Rodriguez 2.00 5.00
TGH16 Nomar Garciaparra 1.00 2.50
TGH17 Derek Jeter 4.00 10.00
TGH18 Tony Gwynn 1.50 4.00
TGH19 Chipper Jones 1.50 4.00
TGH20 Cal Ripken 5.00 12.00

2000 Topps Gallery Proof Positive

COMPLETE SET (10) 15.00 40.00
STATED ODDS 1:48
P1 K.Griffey Jr. / R.Mateo 3.00 8.00
P2 D.Jeter / A.Soriano 4.00 10.00
P3 M.McGwire / P.Burrell 2.50 6.00
P4 P.Martinez / A.J.Burnett 1.00 2.50
P5 A.Rodriguez / R.Furcal 2.00 5.00
P6 S.Sosa / C.Patterson 1.50 4.00
P7 R.Johnson / R.Ankiel 1.50 4.00
P8 C.Jones / A.Piatt 1.50 4.00
P9 N.Garciparra / P.Ozuna 1.00 2.50
P10 M.Piazza / E.Munson 1.50 4.00

2001 Topps Gallery

COMPLETE SET (150) 50.00 80.00
COMP.SET w/o SP's (100) 15.00 40.00
COMMON (1-49/51-101) .20 .50
COMMON CARD (102-150) 1.25 3.00
PROSPECTS 102-141 ODDS 1:2.5
ROOKIES 102-141 ODDS 1:3.5
RETIRED 142-150 ODDS 1:5
150-CARD SET INCLUDES CARD 50 HTA
CARD 50 HTA AVAIL.VIA HTA HOBBY SHOPS
CARD 50 HTA EXCH.DEADLINE 10/24/01
I.SUZUKI EXCH.CARDS RANDOM IN PACKS
I.SUZUKI EXCH.DEADLINE 06/30/03
1 Darin Erstad .20 .50
2 Chipper Jones .50 1.25
3 Nomar Garciaparra .75 2.00
4 Fernando Vina .20 .50
5 Bartolo Colon .20 .50
6 Bobby Higginson .20 .50
7 Antonio Alfonseca .20 .50
8 Mike Sweeney .20 .50
9 Kevin Brown .20 .50
10 Jose Vidro .20 .50
11 Derek Jeter 1.25 3.00
12 Jason Giambi .20 .50
13 Pat Burrell .20 .50
14 Jeff Kent .20 .50
15 Alex Rodriguez .60 1.50
16 Rafael Palmeiro .30 .75
17 Garret Anderson .20 .50
18 Brad Fullmer .20 .50
19 Doug Glanville .20 .50
20 Mark Quinn .20 .50
21 Mo Vaughn .20 .50
22 Andruw Jones .30 .75
23 Pedro Martinez .30 .75
24 Ken Griffey Jr. 1.00 2.50
25 Roberto Alomar .30 .75
26 Dean Palmer .20 .50
27 Jeff Bagwell .30 .75
28 Jermaine Dye .20 .50
29 Chan Ho Park .20 .50
30 Vladimir Guerrero .50 1.25
31 Bernie Williams .30 .75
32 Ben Grieve .20 .50
33 Jason Kendall .20 .50
34 Barry Bonds 1.25 3.00
35 Jim Edmonds .20 .50
36 Ivan Rodriguez .30 .75
37 Javy Lopez .20 .50
38 J.T. Snow .20 .50
39 Erubiel Durazo .20 .50
40 Terrence Long .20 .50
41 Tim Salmon .30 .75
42 Greg Maddux .75 2.00
43 Sammy Sosa .50 1.25
44 Sean Casey .20 .50
45 Jeff Cirillo .20 .50
46 Juan Gonzalez .20 .50
47 Richard Hidalgo .20 .50
48 Shawn Green .20 .50
49 Jeromy Burnitz .20 .50
50 Willie Mays HTA 6.00 15.00
50 Willie Mays RETAIL 15.00 40.00
51 David Justice .20 .50
52 Tim Hudson .20 .50
53 Brian Giles .20 .50
54 Robb Nen .20 .50
55 Fernando Tatis .20 .50
56 Tony Batista .20 .50
57 Pokey Reese .20 .50
58 Ray Durham .20 .50
59 Greg Vaughn .20 .50
60 Kazuhiro Sasaki .20 .50
61 Troy Glaus .20 .50
62 Rafael Furcal .20 .50
63 Magglio Ordonez .20 .50
64 Jim Thome .30 .75
65 Todd Helton .30 .75
66 Preston Wilson .20 .50
67 Moises Alou .20 .50
68 Gary Sheffield .20 .50
69 Geoff Jenkins .20 .50
70 Mike Piazza .75 2.00
71 Jorge Posada .30 .75
72 Bobby Abreu .20 .50
73 Phil Nevin .20 .50
74 John Olerud .20 .50
75 Mark McGwire 1.25 3.00
76 Jose Cruz Jr. .20 .50
77 David Segui .20 .50
78 Neifi Perez .20 .50
79 Omar Vizquel .30 .75
80 Rick Ankiel .20 .50
81 Randy Johnson .50 1.25
82 Albert Belle .20 .50
83 Frank Thomas .50 1.25
84 Manny Ramirez Sox .30 .75
85 Larry Walker .20 .50
86 Luis Castillo .20 .50
87 Johnny Damon .30 .75
88 Adrian Beltre .20 .50
89 Cristian Guzman .20 .50
90 Jay Payton .20 .50
91 Miguel Tejada .20 .50
92 Scott Rolen .30 .75
93 Ryan Klesko .20 .50
94 Edgar Martinez .30 .75
95 Fred McGriff .30 .75
96 Carlos Delgado .20 .50
97 Barry Zito .30 .75
98 Mike Lieberthal .20 .50
99 Trevor Hoffman .20 .50
100 Gabe Kapler .20 .50
101 Edgardo Alfonzo .20 .50
102 Corey Patterson 1.25 3.00
103 Alfonso Soriano 1.25 3.00
104 Keith Ginter 1.25 3.00
105 Keith Reed 1.25 3.00
106 Nick Johnson 1.25 3.00
107 Carlos Pena 1.25 3.00
108 Vernon Wells 1.25 3.00
109 Roy Oswalt 1.50 4.00
110 Alex Escobar 1.25 3.00
111 Adam Everett 1.25 3.00
112 Jimmy Rollins 1.25 3.00
113 Marcus Giles 1.25 3.00
114 Jack Cust 1.25 3.00
115 Chin-Feng Chen 1.25 3.00
116 Pablo Ozuna 1.25 3.00
117 Ben Sheets 1.25 3.00
118 Adrian Gonzalez 8.00 20.00
119 Ben Davis 1.25 3.00
120 Eric Valent 1.25 3.00
121 Scott Heard 1.25 3.00
122 David Parrish RC 1.25 3.00
123 Sean Burnett 1.25 3.00
124 Derek Thompson 1.25 3.00
125 Tim Christman RC 1.25 3.00
126 Mike Jacobs RC 3.00 8.00
127 Luis Montanez RC 1.25 3.00
128 Chris Bass RC 1.25 3.00
129 Will Smith RC 1.25 3.00
130 Justin Wayne RC 1.25 3.00
131 Shawn Fagan RC 1.25 3.00
132 Chad Petty RC 1.25 3.00
133 J.R. House 1.25 3.00
134 Joel Pineiro 1.25 3.00
135 Albert Pujols RC 20.00 50.00
136 Carmen Cali RC 1.25 3.00
137 Steve Smyth RC 1.25 3.00
138 John Lackey 1.25 3.00
139 Bob Keppel RC 1.25 3.00
140 Dominic Rich RC 1.25 3.00
141 Josh Hamilton 2.50 6.00
142 Nolan Ryan 2.50 6.00
143 Tom Seaver 1.50 4.00
144 Reggie Jackson 1.50 4.00
145 Johnny Bench 1.50 4.00
146 Warren Spahn 1.50 4.00
147 Brooks Robinson 1.50 4.00
148 Carl Yastrzemski 2.00 5.00
149 Al Kaline 1.50 4.00
150 Bob Feller 1.25 3.00
151A Ichiro Suzuki English RC 8.00 20.00
151B Ichiro Suzuki Japan RC 8.00 20.00
NNO Checklist .10 .25

2001 Topps Gallery Press Plates

NO PRICING DUE TO SCARCITY

2001 Topps Gallery Autographs

GROUP A STATED ODDS 1:1066
GROUP B STATED ODDS 1:1144
GROUP C STATED ODDS 1:400
OVERALL ODDS 1:232
GAAG Adrian Gonzalez B 6.00 15.00
GAAR Alex Rodriguez A 25.00 60.00
GABB Barry Bonds A 60.00 120.00
GAIR Ivan Rodriguez A 20.00 50.00
GAPB Pat Burrell C 6.00 15.00
GARA Rick Ankiel C 15.00 40.00

2001 Topps Gallery Bucks

STATED ODDS 1:102
1 Johnny Bench $5 2.00 5.00

2001 Topps Gallery Heritage

COMPLETE SET (10) 30.00 60.00
STATED ODDS 1:12
GH1 Todd Helton 1.25 3.00
GH2 Greg Maddux 3.00 8.00
GH3 Pedro Martinez 1.25 3.00
GH4 Orlando Cepeda 1.25 3.00
GH5 Willie McCovey 1.25 3.00
GH6 Ken Griffey Jr. 4.00 10.00
GH7 Alex Rodriguez 2.50 6.00
GH8 Derek Jeter 5.00 12.00
GH9 Mark McGwire 5.00 12.00
GH10 Vladimir Guerrero 2.00 5.00

2001 Topps Gallery Heritage Game Jersey

STATED ODDS 1:133
V.GUERRERO AVAIL.VIA MYSTERY EXCH.
GHRGM Greg Maddux 6.00 15.00
GHROC Orlando Cepeda 3.00 8.00
GHRPM Pedro Martinez 3.00 8.00
GHRVG Vladimir Guerrero 5.00 12.00
GHRWM Willie McCovey 3.00 8.00

2001 Topps Gallery Originals Game Bat

STATED ODDS 1:133
GRAG Adrian Gonzalez 4.00 10.00
GRAJ Andruw Jones 6.00 15.00
GRBW Bernie Williams 6.00 15.00
GRDE Darin Erstad 4.00 10.00
GRJD Jermaine Dye 4.00 10.00
GRJG Jason Giambi 4.00 10.00
GRJK Jason Kendall 4.00 10.00
GRJFK Jeff Kent 4.00 10.00
GRMR1 Mystery Relic .40 1.00
GRMR2 Mystery Relic .40 1.00
GRPR Pokey Reese 4.00 10.00
GRPW Preston Wilson 4.00 10.00
GRRA Roberto Alomar 6.00 15.00
GRRP Rafael Palmeiro 6.00 15.00
GRRV Robin Ventura 4.00 10.00
GRSG Shawn Green 4.00 10.00
GRSS Sammy Sosa 6.00 15.00

2001 Topps Gallery Star Gallery

COMPLETE SET (10) 10.00 25.00
STATED ODDS 1:8
SG1 Vladimir Guerrero 1.00 2.50
SG2 Alex Rodriguez 1.25 3.00
SG3 Derek Jeter 2.50 6.00
SG4 Nomar Garciaparra .60 1.50
SG5 Ken Griffey Jr. 2.00 5.00
SG6 Mark McGwire 1.50 4.00
SG7 Chipper Jones 1.00 2.50
SG8 Sammy Sosa .60 1.50
SG9 Barry Bonds 1.50 4.00
SG10 Mike Piazza 1.00 2.50

2002 Topps Gallery

COMPLETE SET (200) 10.00 25.00
COMMON CARD (1-150) .20 .50
COMMON CARD (151-190) .40 1.00
COMMON CARD (191-200) .75 2.00
1 Jason Giambi .20 .50
2 Mark Grace .30 .75
3 Bret Boone .20 .50
4 Antonio Alfonseca .20 .50
5 Kevin Brown .20 .50
6 Cristian Guzman .20 .50
7 Magglio Ordonez .20 .50
8 Luis Gonzalez .20 .50
9 Jorge Posada .30 .75
10 Roberto Alomar .30 .75
11 Mike Sweeney .20 .50
12 Jeff Kent .20 .50
13 Matt Morris .20 .50
14 Alfonso Soriano .20 .50
15 Adam Dunn .20 .50
16 Neifi Perez .20 .50
17 Todd Walker .20 .50
18 J.D. Drew .20 .50
19 Eric Chavez .20 .50
20 Alex Rodriguez .60 1.50

21 Ray Lankford .20 .50
22 Roger Cedeno .20 .50
23 Chipper Jones .50 1.25
24 Josh Beckett .20 .50
25 Mike Piazza .75 2.00
26 Freddy Garcia .20 .50
27 Todd Helton .30 .75
28 Tino Martinez .30 .75
29 Kazuhiro Sasaki .20 .50
30 Curt Schilling .20 .50
31 Mark Buehrle .20 .50
32 John Olerud .20 .50
33 Brad Radke .20 .50
34 Steve Sparks .20 .50
35 Jason Tyner .20 .50
36 Jeff Shaw .20 .50
37 Mariano Rivera .50 1.25
38 Russ Ortiz .20 .50
39 Richard Hidalgo .20 .50
40 Carl Everett .20 .50
41 John Burkett .20 .50
42 Tim Hudson .20 .50
43 Mike Hampton .20 .50
44 Orlando Cabrera .20 .50
45 Barry Zito .20 .50
46 C.C. Sabathia .20 .50
47 Chan Ho Park .20 .50
48 Tom Glavine .30 .75
49 Aramis Ramirez .20 .50
50 Lance Berkman .20 .50
51 Al Leiter .20 .50
52 Phil Nevin .20 .50
53 Javier Vazquez .20 .50
54 Troy Glaus .20 .50
55 Tsuyoshi Shinjo .20 .50
56 Albert Pujols 1.00 2.50
57 John Smoltz .30 .75
58 Derek Jeter 1.25 3.00
59 Robb Nen .20 .50
60 Jason Kendall .20 .50
61 Eric Gagne .20 .50
62 Vladimir Guerrero .50 1.25
63 Corey Patterson .20 .50
64 Rickey Henderson .50 1.25
65 Jack Wilson .20 .50
66 Jason LaRue .20 .50
67 Sammy Sosa .50 1.25
68 Ken Griffey Jr. 1.00 2.50
69 Randy Johnson .50 1.25
70 Nomar Garciaparra .75 2.00
71 Ivan Rodriguez .30 .75
72 J.T. Snow .20 .50
73 Darryl Kile .20 .50
74 Andruw Jones .30 .75
75 Brian Giles .20 .50
76 Pedro Martinez .30 .75
77 Jeff Bagwell .30 .75
78 Rafael Palmeiro .30 .75
79 Ryan Dempster .20 .50
80 Jeff Cirillo .20 .50
81 Geoff Jenkins .20 .50
82 Brandon Duckworth .20 .50
83 Roger Clemens 1.00 2.50
84 Fred McGriff .30 .75
85 Hideo Nomo .50 1.25
86 Larry Walker .20 .50
87 Sean Casey .20 .50
88 Trevor Hoffman .20 .50
89 Robert Fick .20 .50
90 Armando Benitez .20 .50
91 Jeromy Burnitz .20 .50
92 Bernie Williams .30 .75
93 Carlos Delgado .20 .50
94 Troy Percival .20 .50
95 Nate Cornejo .20 .50
96 Derrek Lee .30 .75
97 Jose Ortiz .20 .50
98 Brian Jordan .20 .50
99 Jose Cruz Jr. .20 .50
100 Ichiro Suzuki 1.00 2.50
101 Jose Mesa .20 .50
102 Tim Salmon .30 .75
103 Bud Smith .20 .50
104 Paul LoDuca .20 .50
105 Juan Pierre .20 .50
106 Ben Grieve .20 .50
107 Russell Branyan .20 .50
108 Bob Abreu .20 .50
109 Moises Alou .20 .50
110 Richie Sexson .20 .50
111 Jerry Hairston Jr. .20 .50
112 Marlon Anderson .20 .50
113 Juan Gonzalez .20 .50
114 Craig Biggio .30 .75
115 Carlos Beltran .20 .50
116 Eric Milton .20 .50
117 Cliff Floyd .20 .50
118 Rich Aurilia .20 .50
119 Adrian Beltre .20 .50
120 Jason Bere .20 .50
121 Darin Erstad .20 .50
122 Ben Sheets .20 .50
123 Johnny Damon Sox .30 .75
124 Jimmy Rollins .20 .50
125 Shawn Green .20 .50
126 Greg Maddux .75 2.00
127 Mark Mulder .20 .50
128 Bartolo Colon .20 .50
129 Shannon Stewart .20 .50
130 Ramon Ortiz .20 .50
131 Kerry Wood .20 .50
132 Ryan Klesko .20 .50
133 Preston Wilson .20 .50
134 Roy Oswalt .20 .50
135 Rafael Furcal .30 .75
136 Eric Karros .20 .50
137 Nick Neugebauer .20 .50
138 Doug Mientkiewicz .20 .50
139 Paul Konerko .20 .50
140 Bobby Higginson .20 .50
141 Garret Anderson .20 .50
142 Wes Helms .20 .50
143 Brent Abernathy .20 .50
144 Scott Rolen .30 .75
145 Dmitri Young .20 .50
146 Jim Thome .30 .75
147 Raul Mondesi .20 .50
148 Pat Burrell .20 .50
149 Gary Sheffield .20 .50
150 Miguel Tejada .20 .50
151 Brandon Inge PROS .40 1.00
152 Carlos Pena PROS .40 1.00
153 Jason Lane PROS .40 1.00
154 Nathan Haynes PROS .40 1.00
155 Hank Blalock PROS .60 1.50
156 Juan Cruz PROS .40 1.00
157 Morgan Ensberg PROS .40 1.00
158 Sean Burroughs PROS .40 1.00
159 Ed Rogers PROS .40 1.00
160 Nick Johnson PROS .40 1.00
161 Orlando Hudson PROS .40 1.00
162 Anastacio Martinez PROS RC .40 1.00
163 Jeremy Affeldt PROS .40 1.00
164 Brandon Claussen PROS .40 1.00
165 Deivis Santos PROS .40 1.00
166 Mike Rivera PROS .40 1.00
167 Carlos Silva PROS .40 1.00
168 Val Pascucci PROS .40 1.00
169 Xavier Nady PROS .40 1.00
170 David Espinosa PROS .40 1.00
171 Dan Phillips FYP RC .40 1.00
172 Tony Fontana FYP RC .40 1.00
173 Juan Silvestre FYP .40 1.00
174 Henry Pichardo FYP RC .40 1.00
175 Pablo Arias FYP RC .40 1.00
176 Brett Roneberg FYP RC .40 1.00
177 Chad Qualls FYP RC .60 1.50
178 Greg Sain FYP RC .40 1.00
179 Rene Reyes FYP RC .40 1.00
180 So Taguchi FYP RC .60 1.50
181 Dan Johnson FYP RC .75 2.00
182 Justin Backsmeyer FYP RC .40 1.00
183 Juan M. Gonzalez FYP RC .40 1.00
184 Jason Ellison FYP RC .60 1.50
185 Kazuhisa Ishii FYP RC .60 1.50
186 Joe Mauer FYP RC 5.00 12.00
187 James Shanks FYP RC .40 1.00
188 Kevin Cash FYP RC .40 1.00
189 J.J. Trujillo FYP RC .40 1.00
190 Jorge Padilla FYP RC .40 1.00
191 Nolan Ryan RET 2.50 6.00
192 George Brett RET 2.00 5.00
193 Ryne Sandberg RET 2.00 5.00
194 Robin Yount RET 1.00 2.50
195 Tom Seaver RET .75 2.00
196 Mike Schmidt RET 2.00 5.00
197 Frank Robinson RET .75 2.00
198 Harmon Killebrew RET 1.00 2.50
199 Kirby Puckett RET 1.00 2.50
200 Don Mattingly RET 2.00 5.00

2002 Topps Gallery Veteran Variation 1

STATED ODDS 1:24 HOB/RET
1 Jason Giambi Solid Blue 1.00 2.50
20 Alex Rodriguez Grey Jsy 3.00 8.00
25 Mike Piazza Black Jsy 4.00 10.00
27 Todd Helton Solid Blue 1.50 4.00
56 Albert Pujols Red Hat 5.00 12.00
58 Derek Jeter Solid Blue 6.00 15.00
67 Sammy Sosa Black Bat 2.50 6.00
71 Ivan Rodriguez Blue Jsy 1.50 4.00
76 Pedro Martinez Red Shirt 1.50 4.00
100 Ichiro Suzuki Empty Dugout 5.00 12.00

2002 Topps Gallery Autographs

GROUP A ODDS 1:815 HOB/RET
GROUP B ODDS 1:1017 HOB, 1:1023 RET
GROUP C ODDS 1:509 HOB/RET
OVERALL ODDS 1:240 HOB/RET
GABBO Bret Boone A 4.00 10.00
GAJD J.D. Drew B 4.00 10.00
GAJL Jason Lane C 4.00 10.00
GAJP Jorge Posada A 20.00 50.00
GAJS Juan Silvestre C 4.00 10.00
GALB Lance Berkman A 12.00 30.00
GALG Luis Gonzalez B 6.00 15.00
GAMO Magglio Ordonez A 10.00 25.00
GASG Shawn Green A 4.00 10.00

2002 Topps Gallery Bucks

STATED ODDS 1:127 HOB/RET
NNO Nolan Ryan $5 3.00 8.00

2002 Topps Gallery Heritage

COMPLETE SET (25) 20.00 50.00
STATED ODDS 1:12 HOB/RET
GHAK Al Kaline 54 1.00 2.50
GHAR Alex Rodriguez 98 1.25 3.00
GHBR Brooks Robinson 57 .60 1.50
GHBBO Bret Boone 93 .40 1.00
GHCJ Chipper Jones 91 1.00 2.50
GHCY Carl Yastrzemski 60 1.50 4.00
GHGM Greg Maddux 87 1.50 4.00
GHJG Jason Giambi 91 .40 1.00
GHKG Ken Griffey Jr. 89 2.00 5.00
GHLG Luis Gonzalez 91 .40 1.00
GHMM Mark McGwire 85 1.50 4.00
GHMP Mike Piazza 93 1.00 2.50
GHMS Mike Schmidt 73 1.50 4.00
GHNR Nolan Ryan 68 3.00 8.00
GHPM Pedro Martinez 93 .60 1.50
GHRA Roberto Alomar 88 .60 1.50
GHRC Roger Clemens 85 1.25 3.00
GHRJ Reggie Jackson 69 .60 1.50
GHRY Robin Yount 75 1.00 2.50
GHSG Shawn Green 92 .40 1.00
GHSM Stan Musial 58 1.50 4.00
GHSS Sammy Sosa 90 1.00 2.50
GHTG Tony Gwynn 83 1.00 2.50
GHTS Tom Seaver 67 .60 1.50
GHTSH Tsuyoshi Shinjo 01 .40 1.00

2002 Topps Gallery Heritage Uniform Relics

GROUP A ODDS 1:106 HOB/RET
GROUP B ODDS 1:424 HOB/RET
OVERALL ODDS 1:85 HOB/RET
GHRAR Alex Rodriguez 98 A 8.00 20.00
GHRCJ Chipper Jones 91 B 6.00 15.00
GHRGM Greg Maddux 87 A 6.00 15.00
GHRLG Luis Gonzalez 91 A 4.00 10.00
GHRMP Mike Piazza 93 A 6.00 15.00
GHRPM Pedro Martinez 93 A 6.00 15.00
GHRTG Tony Gwynn 83 A 6.00 15.00
GHRTS Tsuyoshi Shinjo 01 A 4.00 10.00
GHRBBO Bret Boone 93 A 4.00 10.00

2002 Topps Gallery Original Bat Relics

STATED ODDS 1:169 HOB/RET
GOAJ Andruw Jones 6.00 15.00
GOAP Albert Pujols 6.00 15.00
GOAR Alex Rodriguez 6.00 15.00
GOAS Alfonso Soriano 4.00 10.00
GOBW Bernie Williams 6.00 15.00
GOBBO Bret Boone 4.00 10.00
GOCD Carlos Delgado 4.00 10.00
GOCJ Chipper Jones 6.00 15.00
GOJC Jose Canseco 6.00 15.00
GOJG Juan Gonzalez 4.00 10.00
GOLG Luis Gonzalez 4.00 10.00
GOMP Mike Piazza 6.00 15.00
GOTG Tony Gwynn 8.00 20.00
GOTH Todd Helton 6.00 15.00
GOTM Tino Martinez 6.00 15.00

2003 Topps Gallery

COMP.SET w/o SP's (200) 20.00 50.00
COMMON (1-150/168-190) .20 .50
COMMON CARD (151-167) .25 .60
COMMON VARIATION (1-167) 2.00 5.00
VARIATION STATED ODDS 1:20
COMMON CARD (191-200) .30 .75
1 Jason Giambi .20 .50
1A Jason Giambi Blue Jsy 2.00 5.00
2 Miguel Tejada .30 .75
3 Mike Lieberthal .20 .50
4 Jason Kendall .20 .50
5 Robb Nen .20 .50
6 Freddy Garcia .20 .50
7 Scott Rolen .30 .75
8 Boomer Wells .20 .50
9 Rafael Palmeiro .30 .75
10 Garret Anderson .20 .50
11 Curt Schilling .30 .75
12 Greg Maddux .60 1.50
13 Rodrigo Lopez .20 .50
14 Nomar Garciaparra .30 .75
14A Nomar Garciaparra Btg Glv 3.00 8.00
15 Kerry Wood .20 .50
16 Frank Thomas .50 1.25
17 Ken Griffey Jr. 1.00 2.50
18 Jim Thome .30 .75
19 Todd Helton .30 .75
20 Lance Berkman .30 .75
21 Robert Fick .20 .50
22 Kevin Brown .20 .50
23 Richie Sexson .20 .50
24 Eddie Guardado .20 .50
25 Vladimir Guerrero .30 .75
26 Mike Piazza .50 1.25
27 Bernie Williams .30 .75
28 Eric Chavez .20 .50
29 Jimmy Rollins .30 .75
30 Ichiro Suzuki .60 1.50
30A Ichiro Suzuki Black Sleeve 5.00 12.00
31 J.D. Drew .20 .50
32 Nick Johnson .20 .50
33 Shannon Stewart .20 .50
34 Tim Salmon .20 .50
35 Andruw Jones .20 .50
36 Jay Gibbons .20 .50
37 Johnny Damon .30 .75
38 Fred McGriff .30 .75
39 Carlos Lee .20 .50
40 Adam Dunn .30 .75
40A Adam Dunn Red Sleeve 3.00 8.00
41 Jason Jennings .20 .50
42 Mike Lowell .20 .50
43 Mike Sweeney .20 .50
44 Shawn Green .20 .50
45 Doug Mientkiewicz .20 .50
46 Bartolo Colon .20 .50
47 Edgardo Alfonzo .20 .50
48 Roger Clemens .60 1.50
49 Randy Wolf .20 .50
50 Alex Rodriguez .60 1.50
50A Alex Rodriguez Red Shirt 5.00 12.00
51 Vernon Wells .20 .50
52 Kenny Lofton .20 .50
53 Mariano Rivera .60 1.50
54 Brian Jordan .20 .50
55 Roberto Alomar .30 .75
56 Carlos Pena .30 .75
57 Moises Alou .20 .50
58 John Smoltz .50 1.25
59 Adam Kennedy .20 .50
60 Randy Johnson .50 1.25
61 Mark Buehrle .30 .75
62 C.C. Sabathia .30 .75
63 Craig Biggio .30 .75
64 Eric Karros .20 .50
65 Jose Vidro .20 .50
66 Tim Hudson .30 .75
67 Trevor Hoffman .30 .75
68 Bret Boone .20 .50
69 Carl Crawford .30 .75
70 Derek Jeter 1.25 3.00
71 Troy Percival .20 .50
72 Gary Sheffield .20 .50
73 Rickey Henderson .50 1.25
74 Paul Konerko .30 .75
75 Larry Walker .30 .75
76 Pat Burrell .20 .50
77 Brian Giles .20 .50
78 Jeff Kent .20 .50
79 Kazuhiro Sasaki .20 .50
80 Chipper Jones .50 1.25
81 Darin Erstad .20 .50
82 Sean Casey .20 .50
83 Luis Gonzalez .20 .50
84 Roy Oswalt .30 .75
85 Dustan Mohr .20 .50
86 Al Leiter .20 .50
87 Mike Mussina .30 .75
88 Vicente Padilla .20 .50
89 Rich Aurilia .20 .50
90 Albert Pujols .60 1.50
91 John Olerud .20 .50
92 Ivan Rodriguez .30 .75
93 Eric Hinske .20 .50
94 Phil Nevin .20 .50
95 Barry Zito .30 .75
96 Armando Benitez .20 .50
97 Torii Hunter .20 .50
98 Paul Lo Duca .20 .50
99 Preston Wilson .20 .50
100 Sammy Sosa .50 1.25
100A Sammy Sosa Black Bat 5.00 12.00
101 Jarrod Washburn .20 .50
102 Steve Finley .20 .50
103 Cliff Floyd .20 .50
104 Mark Prior .30 .75
105 Austin Kearns .20 .50
106 Jeff Bagwell .30 .75
107 A.J. Pierzynski .20 .50
108 Pedro Martinez .30 .75
109 Orlando Cabrera .20 .50
110 Raul Mondesi .20 .50
111 Russ Ortiz .20 .50
112 Ruben Sierra .20 .50
113 Tino Martinez .20 .50
114 Manny Ramirez .50 1.25
115 Troy Glaus .20 .50
116 Magglio Ordonez .30 .75
117 Omar Vizquel .30 .75
118 Carlos Beltran .30 .75
119 Jose Hernandez .20 .50
120 Javier Vazquez .20 .50
121 Jorge Posada .30 .75
122 Aramis Ramirez .20 .50
123 Jason Schmidt .20 .50
124 Jamie Moyer .20 .50
125 Jim Edmonds .30 .75
126 Aubrey Huff .20 .50
127 Carlos Delgado .20 .50
128 Junior Spivey .20 .50
129 Tom Glavine .30 .75
130 Marty Cordova .20 .50
131 Derek Lowe .20 .50
132 Ellis Burks .20 .50
133 Barry Bonds .75 2.00
134 Josh Beckett .20 .50
135 Raul Ibanez .30 .75
136 Kazuhisa Ishii .20 .50
137 Geoff Jenkins .20 .50
138 Eric Milton .20 .50
139 Mo Vaughn .20 .50
140 Mark Mulder .20 .50
141 Bobby Abreu .20 .50
142 Ryan Klesko .20 .50
143 Tsuyoshi Shinjo .20 .50
144 Jose Mesa .20 .50
145 Shea Hillenbrand .20 .50
146 Edgar Renteria .20 .50
147 Juan Gonzalez .20 .50
148 Edgar Martinez .30 .75
149 Matt Morris .20 .50
150 Alfonso Soriano .30 .75
150A Alfonso Soriano No Pad 3.00 8.00
151 Bryan Bullington FY RC .25 .60
151A B.Bullington Red Back FY 2.00 5.00
152 Andy Marte FY RC .25 .60
152A Andy Marte No Necklace FY 2.00 5.00
153 Brendan Harris FY RC .25 .60
154 Juan Camacho FY RC .25 .60
155 Byron Gettis FY RC .25 .60
156 Daryl Clark FY RC .25 .60
157 J.D. Durbin FY RC .25 .60
158 Craig Brazell FY RC .25 .60
158A Craig Brazell Black Jsy 2.00 5.00
159 Jason Kubel FY RC .75 2.00
160 Brandon Roberson FY RC .25 .60
161 Jose Contreras FY RC .60 1.50
162 Hanley Ramirez FY RC 2.00 5.00
163 Jaime Bubela FY RC .25 .60
164 Chris Duncan FY RC .75 2.00
165 Tyler Johnson FY RC .25 .60
166 Joey Gomes FY RC .25 .60
167 Ben Francisco FY RC .25 .60
168 Adam LaRoche PROS .20 .50
169 Tommy Whiteman PROS .20 .50
170 Trey Hodges PROS .20 .50
171 Francisco Rodriguez PROS .30 .75
172 Jason Arnold PROS .20 .50
173 Brett Myers PROS .20 .50
174 Rocco Baldelli PROS .20 .50
175 Adrian Gonzalez PROS .40 1.00
176 Dontrelle Willis PROS .20 .50
177 Walter Young PROS .20 .50
178 Marlon Byrd PROS .20 .50
179 Aaron Heilman PROS .20 .50
180 Casey Kotchman PROS .20 .50
181 Miguel Cabrera PROS 2.50 6.00
182 Hee Seop Choi PROS .20 .50
183 Drew Henson PROS .20 .50
184 Jose Reyes PROS .50 1.25
185 Michael Cuddyer PROS .20 .50
186 Brandon Phillips PROS .20 .50
187 Victor Martinez PROS .30 .75
188 Joe Mauer PROS .50 1.25
189 Hank Blalock PROS .20 .50
190 Mark Teixeira PROS .30 .75
191 Willie Mays RET 1.50 4.00
192 George Brett RET 1.50 4.00
193 Tony Gwynn RET .75 2.00
194 Carl Yastrzemski RET 1.25 3.00
195 Nolan Ryan RET 2.50 6.00
196 Reggie Jackson RET .50 1.25
197 Mike Schmidt RET 1.25 3.00
198 Cal Ripken RET 2.50 6.00
199 Don Mattingly RET 1.50 4.00
200 Tom Seaver RET .50 1.25

2003 Topps Gallery Artist's Proofs

*AP 1-150/168-190: .75X TO 2X BASIC
*AP 151-167: .75X TO 2X BASIC
*AP 191-200: 1X TO 2.5X BASIC
ONE PER PACK
AP'S FEATURE SILVER HOLO-FOIL

2003 Topps Gallery Press Plates

STATED PRINT RUN 4 SERIAL #'d SETS
NO PRICING DUE TO SCARCITY

2003 Topps Gallery Bucks

STATED ODDS 1:41
5 Willie Mays $5 2.00 5.00

2003 Topps Gallery Currency Collection Coin Relics

ONE PER SEALED HOBBY BOX
AJ Andruw Jones 1.25 3.00
AP Albert Pujols 4.00 10.00
AS Alfonso Soriano 2.00 5.00
BA Bobby Abreu 1.25 3.00
BC Bartolo Colon 1.25 3.00
ER Edgar Renteria 1.25 3.00
FR Francisco Rodriguez 2.00 5.00
HC Hee Seop Choi 1.25 3.00
HN Hideo Nomo 3.00 8.00
IS Ichiro Suzuki 4.00 10.00
JR Jose Reyes 3.00 8.00
KI Kazuhisa Ishii 1.25 3.00
KS Kazuhiro Sasaki 1.25 3.00
LW Larry Walker 2.00 5.00
MO Magglio Ordonez 2.00 5.00
MR Manny Ramirez 3.00 8.00
MRI Mariano Rivera 4.00 10.00
OC Orlando Cabrera 1.25 3.00
OV Omar Vizquel 2.00 5.00
PM Pedro Martinez 2.00 5.00
RL Rodrigo Lopez 1.25 3.00
RM Raul Mondesi 1.25 3.00
SS Sammy Sosa 3.00 8.00
VG Vladimir Guerrero 2.00 5.00
VP Vicente Padilla 1.25 3.00

2003 Topps Gallery Heritage

STATED ODDS 1:10
AD Adam Dunn 1.25 3.00
AS Alfonso Soriano 1.25 3.00
BW Bernie Williams 1.25 3.00
CY Carl Yastrzemski 3.00 8.00
DJ Derek Jeter 5.00 12.00
DS Duke Snider 1.25 3.00
GB George Brett 4.00 10.00
HK Harmon Killebrew 2.00 5.00
HN Hideo Nomo 2.00 5.00
IR Ivan Rodriguez 1.25 3.00
IS Ichiro Suzuki 2.50 6.00
JC Jose Canseco 1.25 3.00
JT Jim Thome 1.25 3.00
KP Kirby Puckett 2.00 5.00
KR J.Koosman
N.Ryan 6.00 15.00
MJ Miguel Tejada 1.25 3.00
NG Nomar Garciaparra 1.25 3.00
RC Roger Clemens 2.50 6.00
RH Rickey Henderson 2.00 5.00
RJ Randy Johnson 2.00 5.00
SG Shawn Green .75 2.00
TG Tom Glavine 1.25 3.00
TGW Tony Gwynn 2.00 5.00
WB Wade Boggs 1.25 3.00
WM Willie Mays 4.00 10.00

2003 Topps Gallery Heritage Autograph Relics

NO PRICING DUE TO SCARCITY

2003 Topps Gallery Heritage Relics

GROUP A ODDS 1:141
GROUP B ODDS 1:67
GB George Brett Bat A 10.00 25.00
HK Harmon Killebrew Bat A 5.00 12.00
HN Hideo Nomo Jsy A 6.00 15.00
JC Jose Canseco Bat B 4.00 10.00
KP Kirby Puckett Bat A 6.00 15.00
RC Roger Clemens Jsy A 6.00 15.00
RH Rickey Henderson Bat B 4.00 10.00
SG Shawn Green Jsy B 3.00 8.00
TG Tony Gwynn Jsy B 6.00 15.00
WB Wade Boggs Uni B 4.00 10.00

2003 Topps Gallery Originals Bat Relics

GROUP A ODDS 1:131
GROUP B ODDS 1:81
GROUP C ODDS 1:15
AD Adam Dunn C 3.00 8.00
AJ Andruw Jones C 4.00 10.00
AP Albert Pujols B 8.00 20.00
AR Alex Rodriguez C 6.00 15.00
AS Alfonso Soriano B 3.00 8.00
BB Bret Boone C 3.00 8.00
BW Bernie Williams C 4.00 10.00
CJ Chipper Jones C 4.00 10.00
CY Carl Yastrzemski A 8.00 20.00
DH Drew Henson B 3.00 8.00
FT Frank Thomas C 4.00 10.00
GS Gary Sheffield C 3.00 8.00
IR Ivan Rodriguez C 4.00 10.00
JM Joe Mauer A 8.00 20.00
JT Jim Thome C 4.00 10.00
LB Lance Berkman C 3.00 8.00
LG Luis Gonzalez A 4.00 10.00
MA Moises Alou B 3.00 8.00
MJ Miguel Tejada A 4.00 10.00
MO Magglio Ordonez C 3.00 8.00
MP Mike Piazza C 6.00 15.00
MR Manny Ramirez C 4.00 10.00
NG Nomar Garciaparra B 6.00 15.00
RA Roberto Alomar C 4.00 10.00
RH Rickey Henderson C 4.00 10.00
RP Rafael Palmeiro C 4.00 10.00
SG Shawn Green B 3.00 8.00
TG Tony Gwynn C 4.00 10.00
TH Todd Helton C 4.00 10.00
THU Torii Hunter A 4.00 10.00

2005 Topps Gallery

COMP.SET w/o SP'S (150) 30.00 60.00
COMMON CARD (1-150) .30 .75
COMMON CARD (151-170) .60 1.50
COMMON CARD (171-185) .60 1.50
COMMON CARD (186-195) .60 1.50
151-195 ODDS FIVE PER MINI-BOX
COMMON VARIATION 1.25 3.00
VARIATION ODDS 1:8 MINI-BOXES
VARIATION STATED PRINT RUN 517 SETS
VARIATIONS ARE NOT SERIAL-NUMBERED
PRINT RUN INFO PROVIDED BY TOPPS
VAR CL: 1/40/100/154-155/157/165
VAR CL: 167-168/187
SEE BECKETT.COM FOR VARIATION INFO
PLATE ODDS 1:48 MINI-BOXES
PLATE PRINT RUN 1 SET PER COLOR
BLACK-CYAN-MAGENTA-YELLOW ISSUED
NO PLATE PRICING DUE TO SCARCITY
1A A.Rodriguez White Glv 1.00 2.50
1B A.Rodriguez Blk Glv SP 4.00 10.00
2 Eric Chavez .30 .75
3 Mike Piazza .75 2.00
4 Bret Boone .30 .75
5 Albert Pujols 1.00 2.50
6 Vernon Wells .30 .75
7 Andruw Jones .30 .75
8 Miguel Tejada .50 1.25
9 Johnny Damon .50 1.25
10 Nomar Garciaparra .50 1.25
11 Pat Burrell .30 .75
12 Bartolo Colon .30 .75
13 Johnny Estrada .30 .75
14 Luis Gonzalez .30 .75
15 Jay Gibbons .30 .75
16 Curt Schilling .50 1.25
17 Aramis Ramirez .30 .75
18 Frank Thomas .75 2.00
19 Adam Dunn .50 1.25
20 Sammy Sosa .75 2.00
21 Matt Lawton .30 .75
22 Preston Wilson .30 .75
23 Carlos Pena .50 1.25
24 Josh Beckett .30 .75
25 Carlos Beltran .50 1.25
26 Juan Gonzalez .30 .75
27 Adrian Beltre .75 2.00
28 Lyle Overbay .30 .75
29 Justin Morneau .50 1.25
30 Derek Jeter 2.00 5.00
31 Barry Zito .50 1.25
32 Bobby Abreu .30 .75
33 Jason Bay .30 .75
34 Jose Reyes .50 1.25
35 Nick Johnson .30 .75
36 Lew Ford .30 .75
37 Scott Podsednik .30 .75
38 Rocco Baldelli .30 .75
39 Eric Hinske .30 .75
40A Ichiro Black Wall 1.00 2.50
40B Ichiro Writing on Wall SP 4.00 10.00
41 Larry Walker .50 1.25
42 Mark Teixeira .50 1.25
43 Khalil Greene .30 .75
44 Edgardo Alfonzo .30 .75
45 Javier Vazquez .30 .75
46 Cliff Floyd .30 .75
47 Geoff Jenkins .30 .75
48 Ken Griffey Jr. 1.50 4.00
49 Vinny Castilla .30 .75
50 Mark Prior .50 1.25
51 Jose Guillen .30 .75
52 J.D. Drew .30 .75
53 Rafael Palmeiro .50 1.25
54 Kevin Youkilis .30 .75
55 Derrek Lee .30 .75
56 Freddy Garcia .30 .75
57 Wily Mo Pena .30 .75
58 C.C. Sabathia .50 1.25
59 Craig Biggio .50 1.25
60 Ivan Rodriguez .50 1.25
61 Angel Berroa .30 .75
62 Ben Sheets .30 .75
63 Johan Santana .50 1.25
64 Al Leiter .30 .75
65 Bernie Williams .50 1.25
66 Bobby Crosby .30 .75
67 Jack Wilson .30 .75
68 A.J. Pierzynski .30 .75
69 Jimmy Rollins .50 1.25
70 Jason Giambi .30 .75
71 Tom Glavine .50 1.25
72 Kevin Brown .30 .75
73 B.J. Upton .50 1.25
74 Edgar Renteria .30 .75
75 Alfonso Soriano .50 1.25
76 Mike Lieberthal .30 .75
77 Kazuo Matsui .30 .75
78 Phil Nevin .30 .75
79 Shawn Green .30 .75
80 Miguel Cabrera .75 2.00
81 Todd Helton .50 1.25
82 Magglio Ordonez .50 1.25
83 Manny Ramirez .75 2.00
84 Bill Mueller .30 .75
85 Troy Glaus .30 .75
86 Richie Sexson .30 .75
87 Javy Lopez .30 .75
88 David Ortiz .75 2.00
89 Greg Maddux 1.00 2.50
90 Vladimir Guerrero .50 1.25
91 Jeromy Burnitz .30 .75
92 Jeff Kent .30 .75
93 Travis Hafner .30 .75
94 Mark Buehrle .50 1.25
95 Paul Lo Duca .30 .75
96 Roy Oswalt .50 1.25
97 Torii Hunter .30 .75
98 Gary Sheffield .30 .75
99 Erubiel Durazo .30 .75
100A J.Thome Kid's Shirt Blue .50 1.25
100B J.Thome Kid's Shirt Red SP 2.00 5.00
101 Ken Harvey .30 .75
102 Shannon Stewart .30 .75
103 Dmitri Young .30 .75
104 Kevin Millar .30 .75
105 Kerry Wood .30 .75
106 Paul Konerko .50 1.25
107 Ronnie Belliard .30 .75
108 Mike Lowell .30 .75
109 Hee Seop Choi .30 .75
110 Joe Mauer .60 1.50
111 David Wright .60 1.50
112 Jorge Posada .50 1.25
113 Tim Hudson .50 1.25
114 Brian Giles .30 .75
115 Jason Schmidt .30 .75
116 Aubrey Huff .30 .75
117 Hank Blalock .30 .75
118 Jim Edmonds .50 1.25
119 Raul Ibanez .50 1.25
120 Carlos Delgado .30 .75
121 Craig Wilson .30 .75
122 Ryan Klesko .30 .75
123 Mark Mulder .30 .75
124 Jose Vidro .30 .75
125 Mike Sweeney .30 .75
126 Lance Berkman .50 1.25
127 Juan Pierre .30 .75
128 Austin Kearns .30 .75
129 Moises Alou .30 .75
130 Garret Anderson .30 .75
131 Pedro Martinez .50 1.25
132 Melvin Mora .30 .75
133 Marcus Giles .30 .75
134 Corey Patterson .30 .75
135 Carlos Lee .30 .75
136 Sean Casey .30 .75
137 Jody Gerut .30 .75
138 Jose Valentin .30 .75
139 Aaron Miles .30 .75
140 Randy Johnson .75 2.00
141 Carlos Guillen .30 .75
142 Dontrelle Willis .30 .75
143 Jeff Bagwell .50 1.25
144 Jason Kendall .30 .75
145 Mark Loretta .30 .75
146 Scott Rolen .50 1.25
147 Carl Crawford .50 1.25
148 Michael Young .30 .75
149 Jermaine Dye .30 .75
150 Chipper Jones .75 2.00
151 Melky Cabrera FY RC 2.00 5.00
152 Chris Seddon FY RC .60 1.50
153 Nate Schierholtz FY .60 1.50
154A Ian Kinsler FY Green RC 3.00 8.00
154B Ian Kinsler FY Gold SP 6.00 15.00
155A B.Moss FY Black Hat RC 2.50 6.00
155B B.Moss FY Red Hat SP 5.00 12.00
156 Chadd Blasko FY RC 1.00 2.50
157A J.West FY Red Jsy RC .60 1.50
157B J.West FY Navy Jsy SP 1.25 3.00
158 Sean Marshall FY RC 1.50 4.00
159 Ryan Sweeney FY RC 1.00 2.50
160 Matthew Lindstrom FY RC .60 1.50
161 Ryan Goleski FY RC .60 1.50
162 Brett Harper FY RC .60 1.50
163 Chris Roberson FY RC .60 1.50
164 Andre Ethier FY RC 5.00 12.00
165A I.Bladergroen FY Pose RC .60 1.50
165B I.Bladergroen FY Swing SP 1.25 3.00
166 James Jurries FY RC .60 1.50
167A Billy Butler FY Vest RC 3.00 8.00
167B B.Butler FY Black Uni SP 6.00 15.00
168A M.Rogers FY Ball Air RC .60 1.50
168B M.Rogers FY Ball Hand SP 1.25 3.00
169 Tyler Clippard FY RC 4.00 10.00
170 Luis Ramirez FY RC .60 1.50
171 Casey Kotchman PROS .60 1.50
172 Chris Burke PROS .60 1.50
173 Dallas McPherson PROS .60 1.50
174 Edwin Jackson PROS .60 1.50
175 Felix Hernandez PROS 2.00 5.00
176 Gavin Floyd PROS .60 1.50
177 Guillermo Quiroz PROS .60 1.50
178 Jason Kubel PROS .60 1.50
179 Jeff Mathis PROS 1.00 2.50
180 Rickie Weeks PROS .60 1.50
181 Ryan Howard PROS 1.25 3.00
182 Franklin Gutierrez PROS 2.00 5.00
183 Jeremy Reed PROS .60 1.50
184 Carlos Quentin PROS 1.00 2.50
185 Jeff Francis PROS .60 1.50
186 Nolan Ryan RET 5.00 12.00
187A Hank Aaron RET w/o 755 3.00 8.00
187B Hank Aaron RET w/755 SP 6.00 15.00
188 Duke Snider RET 1.00 2.50
189 Mike Schmidt RET 2.50 6.00
190 Ernie Banks RET 1.50 4.00
191 Frank Robinson RET 1.00 2.50
192 Harmon Killebrew RET 1.50 4.00
193 Al Kaline RET 1.50 4.00
194 Rod Carew RET 1.00 2.50
195 Johnny Bench RET 1.50 4.00

2005 Topps Gallery Artist's Proof

*AP 1-150: 1X TO 2.5X BASIC
1-150 ODDS FIVE PER MINI-BOX
*AP 151-195: .75X TO 2X BASIC
151-195 ODDS 1:4 MINI-BOXES
151-195 STATED PRINT RUN 259 SETS
151-195 ARE NOT SERIAL-NUMBERED
*AP VAR: .75X TO 2X BASIC VAR
VARIATION ODDS 1:29 MINI-BOXES
VARIATION STATED PRINT RUN 130 SETS
VARIATIONS ARE NOT SERIAL-NUMBERED
PRINT RUN INFO PROVIDED BY TOPPS

2005 Topps Gallery Gallo's Gallery

STATED ODDS 1:3 MINI-BOXES
AP Albert Pujols 3.00 8.00
AR Alex Rodriguez 3.00 8.00
AS Alfonso Soriano 1.50 4.00
CJ Chipper Jones 2.50 6.00
DJ Derek Jeter 6.00 15.00
HA Hank Aaron 5.00 12.00
HB Hank Blalock 1.00 2.50
IR Ivan Rodriguez 1.50 4.00
IS Ichiro Suzuki 3.00 8.00
JT Jim Thome 1.50 4.00
MP Mark Prior 1.50 4.00
MPI Mike Piazza 2.50 6.00
MS Mike Schmidt 4.00 10.00
MT Miguel Tejada 1.50 4.00
NG Nomar Garciaparra 1.50 4.00
NR Nolan Ryan 8.00 20.00
RJ Randy Johnson 2.50 6.00
SS Sammy Sosa 2.50 6.00
TH Todd Helton 1.50 4.00
VG Vladimir Guerrero 1.50 4.00

2005 Topps Gallery Heritage

STATED ODDS 1:3 MINI-BOXES
AK Al Kaline 59 Thrill 3.00 8.00
AP Albert Pujols 01 TT 4.00 10.00
BG Bob Gibson 59 2.00 5.00
BR Brooks Robinson 72 Boy 2.00 5.00
CB Carlos Beltran 95 DP 2.00 5.00
CS Curt Schilling 90 2.00 5.00
DM Don Mattingly 84 6.00 15.00
DS Darryl Strawberry 84 1.25 3.00
DSN Duke Snider 59 Thrill 2.00 5.00
DW Dontrelle Willis 02 TT 1.25 3.00
EB Ernie Banks 54 3.00 8.00
FR Frank Robinson 57 2.00 5.00
GB George Brett 77 RB 6.00 15.00
HB Hank Blalock 01 1.25 3.00
IR Ivan Rodriguez 04 2.00 5.00
JB Johnny Bench 69 3.00 8.00
JC Jose Canseco 87 2.00 5.00
JP Jim Palmer 73 Boy 2.00 5.00
MS Mike Schmidt 83 SV 5.00 12.00
NR Nolan Ryan 90 HL 10.00 25.00
OS Ozzie Smith 79 4.00 10.00
RJ A.Rod
Jeter Kings of NY 8.00 20.00
RP Rafael Palmeiro 87 2.00 5.00
RR F Rob 2.00 5.00
Brooks 68 Belters
TS Thome 5.00 12.00
Schmidt Sluggers

2005 Topps Gallery Heritage Relics

STATED ODDS 1:8 MINI BOXES
AP Albert Pujols 01 TT Jsy 4.00 10.00
AR Alex Rodriguez 04 Bat 4.00 10.00
DM Don Mattingly 84 Bat 6.00 15.00
DS Darryl Strawberry 84 Bat 1.25 3.00
DW Dontrelle Willis 02 TT Jsy 1.25 3.00
GB George Brett 77 RB Bat 6.00 15.00
IR Ivan Rodriguez 04 Bat 2.00 5.00
JC Jose Canseco 87 Bat 2.00 5.00
NR Nolan Ryan 90 HL Jsy 10.00 25.00
OS Ozzie Smith 79 Bat 4.00 10.00

2005 Topps Gallery Originals Relics

STATED ODDS 1:2 MINI-BOXES
AB Angel Berroa Bat 3.00 8.00
AP Albert Pujols Jsy 8.00 20.00
AR Alex Rodriguez Uni 6.00 15.00
AS Alfonso Soriano Bat 3.00 8.00
BU B.J. Upton Bat 4.00 10.00
BW Bernie Williams Bat 4.00 10.00
CJ Chipper Jones Jsy 4.00 10.00
DO David Ortiz Bat 4.00 10.00
DW Dontrelle Willis Jsy 3.00 8.00
FT Frank Thomas Bat 4.00 10.00
HB Hank Blalock Jsy 3.00 8.00
HBB Hank Blalock Bat 3.00 8.00
IR Ivan Rodriguez Bat 4.00 10.00
JB Jeff Bagwell Uni 4.00 10.00
JBE Josh Beckett Bat 3.00 8.00
JD Johnny Damon Bat 4.00 10.00
JG Jason Giambi Bat 3.00 8.00
JL Javy Lopez Bat 3.00 8.00
JR Jose Reyes Bat 3.00 8.00
KM Kazuo Matsui Bat 4.00 10.00
KW Kerry Wood Jsy 3.00 8.00
LB Lance Berkman Jsy 3.00 8.00
LN Laynce Nix Jsy 3.00 8.00
MC Miguel Cabrera Jsy 4.00 10.00
MG Marcus Giles Jsy 3.00 8.00
ML Mike Lowell Jsy 3.00 8.00
MP Mike Piazza Jsy 4.00 10.00
MPB Mike Piazza Bat 4.00 10.00
MPR Mark Prior Jsy 4.00 10.00
MR Manny Ramirez Bat 4.00 10.00
MT Mark Teixeira Jsy 4.00 10.00
MTE Miguel Tejada Bat 3.00 8.00
MY Michael Young Jsy 3.00 8.00
PM Pedro Martinez Jsy 4.00 10.00
RB Rocco Baldelli Bat 3.00 8.00
RD Ryan Drese Jsy 3.00 8.00
RH Rich Harden Uni 3.00 8.00
SS Sammy Sosa Jsy 4.00 10.00
TH Todd Helton Jsy 4.00 10.00
VG Vladimir Guerrero Bat 4.00 10.00

2005 Topps Gallery Penmanship Autographs

GROUP A ODDS 1:786 MINI-BOXES
GROUP B ODDS 1:132 MINI-BOXES
GROUP C ODDS 1:39 MINI-BOXES
GROUP D ODDS 1:39 MINI-BOXES
GROUP E ODDS 1:5 MINI-BOXES
GROUP A STATED PRINT RUN 25 SETS
GROUP A PRINT RUN PROVIDED BY TOPPS
NO GROUP A PRICING DUE TO SCARCITY
EXCHANGE DEADLINE 01/31/07
AH Aubrey Huff C 4.00 10.00
DM Dallas McPherson E 4.00 10.00
EC Eric Chavez D 6.00 15.00
FH Felix Hernandez E 12.00 30.00
JB Jason Bartlett E 4.00 10.00
JJ Justin Jones B 4.00 10.00
TB Taylor Buchholz E 4.00 10.00
VW Vernon Wells C 6.00 15.00

2017 Topps Gallery

COMP.SET w/o SP's (150) 20.00 50.00
STATED SP ODDS 1:20 PACKS
PRINTING PLATE ODDS 1:1217 HOBBY
PLATE PRINT RUN 1 SET PER COLOR
BLACK-CYAN-MAGENTA-YELLOW ISSUED
NO PLATE PRICING DUE TO SCARCITY
1 Mike Trout 1.50 4.00
2 Yoenis Cespedes .30 .75
3 Andrew McCutchen .30 .75
4 Jose Berrios .25 .60
5 Carlos Rodon .30 .75
6 Archie Bradley
7 Joey Gallo .25 .60
8 Steven Matz .20 .50
9 Amir Garrett RC .30 .75
10 Jose Altuve .25 .60
11 Adam Jones .25 .60
12 Max Kepler .25 .60
13 Carlos Correa .30 .75
14 Tyler Austin RC .40 1.00
15 Yoan Moncada RC 1.00 2.50
16 Trevor Story .30 .75
17 George Springer .25 .60
18 Addison Russell .30 .75
19 Carson Fulmer RC .30 .75
20 Evan Longoria .25 .60
21 Hunter Pence .25 .60
22 Ryon Healy RC .40 1.00
23 Hunter Dozier RC .30 .75
24 Charlie Blackmon .30 .75
25 Bryce Harper .50 1.25
26 Yu Darvish .30 .75
27 Noah Syndergaard .25 .60
28 Sean Newcomb RC .30 .75
29 Taijuan Walker .20 .50
30 Justin Bour .25 .60
31 Francisco Lindor .30 .75
32 Gregory Polanco .25 .60
33 Dansby Swanson RC .75 2.00
34 Jake Arrieta .25 .60
35 Antonio Senzatela RC .30 .75
36 Tim Anderson .30 .75
37 DJ LeMahieu .30 .75
38 Tyler Glasnow RC 1.25 3.00
39 Adrian Beltre .30 .75
40 Josh Donaldson .25 .60
41 Brett Phillips RC .40 1.00
42 Alex Bregman RC 1.50 4.00
43 Matt Carpenter .30 .75
44 Eduardo Rodriguez .20 .50
45 Matt Kemp .25 .60
46 Wil Myers .25 .60
47 Jackie Bradley Jr. .30 .75
48 Dustin Pedroia .30 .75
49 Jharel Cotton RC .30 .75
50 Kris Bryant .40 1.00
51 Javier Baez .40 1.00
52 Paul DeJong RC 1.00 2.50
53 Kenta Maeda .25 .60
54 Jose De Leon RC .30 .75
55 Jose Bautista .25 .60
56 Hunter Renfroe RC .40 1.00
57 Jameson Taillon .25 .60
58 Daniel Murphy .25 .60
59 Khris Davis .30 .75
60 Paul Goldschmidt .30 .75
61 Jacob deGrom .60 1.50
62 Yasmani Grandal .20 .50
63 Kendall Graveman .20 .50
64 German Marquez RC .50 1.25
65 Aaron Nola .25 .60
66 Maikel Franco .25 .60
67 Kyle Seager .20 .50
68 Orlando Arcia RC .50 1.25
69 Blake Snell .25 .60
70 Giancarlo Stanton .30 .75
71 Alex Reyes RC .40 1.00
72 Luis Severino .25 .60
73 Corey Kluber .25 .60
74 Michael Conforto .25 .60
75 Stephen Strasburg .30 .75
76 Stephen Piscotty .25 .60
77 Miguel Sano .25 .60
78 Edwin Encarnacion .30 .75
79 Jake Thompson RC .30 .75
80 Freddie Freeman .40 1.00
81 Magneuris Sierra RC .30 .75
82 Anthony Alford RC .30 .75
83 Aledmys Diaz .25 .60
84 Trey Mancini RC .60 1.50
85 Troy Tulowitzki .30 .75
86 Trea Turner .25 .60
87 Kevin Kiermaier .25 .60
88 Yulieski Gurriel RC .50 1.25
89 Hanley Ramirez .25 .60
90 Eric Thames .25 .60
91 Dinelson Lamet RC .30 .75
92 Mark Trumbo .20 .50
93 Ian Happ RC .60 1.50
94 Jesse Winker RC 1.25 3.00
95 Josh Bell RC .75 2.00
96 Manny Margot RC .30 .75
97 Ketel Marte .25 .60
98 Salvador Perez .25 .60
99 Randal Grichuk .20 .50
100 Clayton Kershaw .50 1.25
101 Cole Hamels .25 .60
102 Chris Davis .20 .50
103 Ty Blach RC .30 .75
104 Reynaldo Lopez RC .30 .75
105 Daniel Norris .20 .50
106 Robert Gsellman RC .30 .75
107 Bradley Zimmer RC .40 1.00
108 Joe Musgrove RC 1.00 2.50
109 Mitch Haniger RC .50 1.25
110 Chris Sale .30 .75
111 Ryan Braun .25 .60
112 Keon Broxton .20 .50
113 Andrew Toles .20 .50
114 David Dahl RC .40 1.00
115 Justin Verlander .30 .75
116 Felix Hernandez .25 .60
117 Aaron Judge RC 4.00 10.00
118 Adrian Gonzalez .25 .60
119 Buster Posey .40 1.00
120 Corey Seager .30 .75
121 Christian Yelich .40 1.00
122 Zack Greinke .30 .75
123 Carlos Gonzalez .25 .60
124 Christian Arroyo RC .50 1.25
125 Manny Machado .30 .75
126 Andrew Benintendi RC 1.00 2.50
127 Rick Porcello .25 .60
128 Greg Bird .25 .60
129 Jordan Montgomery RC .50 1.25
130 Nolan Arenado .50 1.25
131 Matt Harvey .25 .60
132 David Price .25 .60
133 Gary Sanchez .30 .75
134 Matt Duffy .20 .50
135 Kyle Schwarber .30 .75
136 Brian Dozier .30 .75
137 Ichiro .40 1.00
138 Luke Weaver RC .40 1.00
139 Jake Lamb .25 .60
140 Anthony Rizzo .40 1.00
141 Julio Urias .30 .75
142 Michael Fulmer .20 .50
143 Cody Bellinger RC 3.00 8.00
144 J.D. Martinez .30 .75
145 Didi Gregorius .25 .60
146 Gerrit Cole .30 .75
147 Brandon Finnegan .20 .50
148 Lucas Giolito .25 .60
149 Lewis Brinson RC .50 1.25
150 Max Scherzer .30 .75
151 Gary Carter SP 3.00 8.00
152 Jose Abreu SP 4.00 10.00
153 Willson Contreras SP 4.00 10.00
154 Johnny Cueto SP 3.00 8.00
155 Lou Gehrig SP 6.00 15.00
156 Nelson Cruz SP 4.00 10.00
157 Andrew Miller SP 3.00 8.00
158 Eric Hosmer SP 3.00 8.00
159 Todd Frazier SP 2.50 6.00
160 Roberto Clemente SP 10.00 25.00
161 Albert Pujols SP 5.00 12.00
162 Frank Thomas SP 4.00 10.00
163 Joey Votto SP 5.00 12.00
164 Tom Glavine SP 3.00 8.00
165 Ted Williams SP 6.00 15.00
166 Bo Jackson SP 4.00 10.00
167 Ian Kinsler SP 3.00 8.00
168 Jonathan Lucroy SP 3.00 8.00
169 Chipper Jones SP 4.00 10.00
170 Ernie Banks SP 4.00 10.00
171 Miguel Cabrera SP 6.00 15.00
172 Ian Desmond SP 2.50 6.00
173 Jason Kipnis SP 3.00 8.00
174 Chris Archer SP 2.50 6.00
175 Jackie Robinson SP 6.00 15.00
176 Starling Marte SP 3.00 8.00
177 Jose Canseco SP 3.00 8.00
178 Fernando Valenzuela SP 5.00 12.00
179 Xander Bogaerts SP 4.00 10.00
180 Derek Jeter SP 10.00 25.00
181 Dee Gordon SP 5.00 12.00
182 Jon Lester SP 3.00 8.00
183 Rickey Henderson SP 6.00 15.00
184 Rougned Odor SP 3.00 8.00
185 Cal Ripken Jr. SP 8.00 20.00
186 Kole Calhoun SP 2.50 6.00
187 Mark McGwire SP 5.00 12.00
188 John Smoltz SP 6.00 15.00
189 Don Mattingly SP 8.00 20.00
190 Ken Griffey Jr. SP 5.00 12.00
191 Marcell Ozuna SP 4.00 10.00
192 Robinson Cano SP 3.00 8.00
193 Mookie Betts SP 8.00 20.00
194 Ryne Sandberg SP 5.00 12.00
195 Nolan Ryan SP 6.00 15.00
196 Duke Snider SP 3.00 8.00
197 David Ortiz SP 4.00 10.00
198 Masahiro Tanaka SP 3.00 8.00
199 Adam Eaton SP 4.00 10.00
200 Babe Ruth SP 5.00 12.00

2017 Topps Gallery Artist Promo

DB Dan Bergren 1.00 2.50
MS Mayumi Seto 1.00 2.50

2017 Topps Gallery Artist Proof

*ARTIST PROOF: .75X TO 2X BASIC
*ARTIST PROOF RC: 5X TO 1.2X BASIC
FOUR PER VALUE BLASTER

2017 Topps Gallery Blue

*BLUE: 4X TO 10X BASIC
*BLUE RC: 2.5X TO 6X BASIC
STATED ODDS 1:98 PACKS
STATED PRINT RUN 50 SER.#'d SETS

2017 Topps Gallery Canvas

*CANVAS: .1X TO 2.5X BASIC
*CANVAS RC: .6X TO 1.5X BASIC
TWO PER FAT PACK

2017 Topps Gallery Green

*GREEN: 2X TO 5X BASIC
*GREEN RC: 1.2X TO 3X BASIC
STATED ODDS 1:50 PACKS
STATED PRINT RUN 99 SER.#'d SETS

2017 Topps Gallery Orange

*ORANGE: 6X TO 15X BASIC
*ORANGE RC: 4X TO 10X BASIC
STATED ODDS 1:196 PACKS
STATED PRINT RUN 25 SER.#'d SETS

2017 Topps Gallery Private Issue

*PRIVATE: 1.5X TO 4X BASIC
*PRIVATE RC: 1X TO 2.5X BASIC
STATED ODDS 1:8 PACKS
STATED PRINT RUN 250 SER.#'d SETS

2017 Topps Gallery Autographs

STATED ODDS 1:15 PACKS
STATED SP ODDS 1:2115 PACKS
NO SP PRICING DUE TO SCARCITY
EXCHANGE DEADLINE 10/31/2019
1 Mike Trout
5 Carlos Rodon 4.00 10.00
6 Archie Bradley 2.50 6.00
7 Joey Gallo 6.00 15.00
8 Steven Matz 2.50 6.00
9 Amir Garrett 2.50 6.00
10 Jose Altuve 25.00 60.00
11 Adam Jones
13 Carlos Correa
14 Tyler Austin 6.00 15.00
15 Yoan Moncada 25.00 60.00
17 George Springer 8.00 20.00
20 Evan Longoria 6.00 15.00
25 Bryce Harper
27 Noah Syndergaard 10.00 25.00
28 Sean Newcomb 3.00 8.00
29 Taijuan Walker 2.50 6.00
30 Justin Bour
33 Dansby Swanson 10.00 25.00
35 Antonio Senzatela 2.50 6.00
36 Tim Anderson 4.00 10.00
37 DJ LeMahieu
40 Josh Donaldson
41 Brett Phillips 3.00 8.00
42 Alex Bregman 15.00 40.00
44 Eduardo Rodriguez 2.50 6.00
49 Jharel Cotton 2.50 6.00
50 Kris Bryant
52 Paul DeJong 4.00 10.00
56 Hunter Renfroe 4.00 10.00
57 Jameson Taillon
60 Paul Goldschmidt 12.00 30.00
61 Jacob DeGrom 15.00 40.00
63 Kendall Graveman 2.50 6.00
64 German Marquez 4.00 10.00
71 Alex Reyes 5.00 12.00
72 Luis Severino
76 Stephen Piscotty
78 Edwin Encarnacion 10.00 25.00
81 Magneuris Sierra 6.00 15.00
82 Anthony Alford 3.00 8.00
84 Trey Mancini 6.00 15.00
85 Troy Tulowitzki
87 Kevin Kiermaier 3.00 8.00
88 Yulieski Gurriel 5.00 12.00
91 Dinelson Lamet 2.50 6.00
93 Ian Happ 5.00 12.00
94 Jesse Winker 8.00 20.00
96 Manny Margot 2.50 6.00
97 Ketel Marte 3.00 8.00
103 Ty Blach 2.50 6.00
104 Reynaldo Lopez 2.50 6.00
105 Daniel Norris 3.00 8.00
106 Robert Gsellman 2.50 6.00
108 Joe Musgrove 8.00 20.00
109 Mitch Haniger 4.00 10.00
110 Chris Sale
111 Ryan Braun
112 Keon Broxton 3.00 8.00
113 Andrew Toles 2.50 6.00
116 Felix Hernandez
117 Aaron Judge 75.00 200.00
119 Buster Posey
120 Corey Seager
124 Christian Arroyo 4.00 10.00
125 Manny Machado 25.00 60.00
126 Andrew Benintendi 20.00 50.00
128 Greg Bird 3.00 8.00
129 Jordan Montgomery 4.00 10.00
134 Matt Duffy 2.50 6.00
135 Kyle Schwarber 5.00 12.00
137 Ichiro 150.00 400.00
138 Luke Weaver 3.00 8.00
140 Anthony Rizzo
143 Cody Bellinger EXCH 50.00 120.00
147 Brandon Finnegan 2.50 6.00
148 Lucas Giolito 3.00 8.00
149 Lewis Brinson 4.00 10.00

2017 Topps Gallery Autographs Blue

*BLUE: .6X TO 1.5X BASIC
STATED ODDS 1:116 PACKS
PRINT RUNS B/WN 40-50 COPIES PER
EXCHANGE DEADLINE 10/31/2019
10 Jose Altuve/50 40.00 100.00
30 Justin Bour/40 5.00 12.00
57 Jameson Taillon/50 12.00 30.00
72 Luis Severino/50 10.00 25.00
76 Stephen Piscotty/50 10.00 25.00
85 Troy Tulowitzki/50 6.00 15.00

2017 Topps Gallery Autographs Green

*GREEN: .5X TO 1.2X BASIC
STATED ODDS 1:69 PACKS
STATED PRINT RUN 99 SER.#'d SETS
EXCHANGE DEADLINE 10/31/2019
72 Luis Severino 8.00 20.00

2017 Topps Gallery Autographs Orange

*ORANGE: .75X TO 2X BASIC
STATED ODDS 1:195 PACKS
PRINT RUNS B/WN 10-25 COPIES PER
NO PRICING ON QTY 10
EXCHANGE DEADLINE 10/31/2019
10 Jose Altuve/25 50.00 120.00
15 Yoan Moncada/25 30.00 80.00
27 Noah Syndergaard/25 12.00 30.00
30 Justin Bour/25 6.00 15.00
72 Luis Severino/25 12.00 30.00
76 Stephen Piscotty/25 12.00 30.00
110 Chris Sale/25 12.00 30.00
119 Buster Posey/10 40.00 100.00
120 Corey Seager/25 40.00 100.00

2017 Topps Gallery Expressionists

STATED ODDS 1:82 PACKS
E1 Paul Goldschmidt 3.00 8.00
E2 Ichiro 4.00 10.00
E3 Yoenis Cespedes 3.00 8.00
E4 Addison Russell 3.00 8.00
E5 Carlos Santana 2.50 6.00
E6 Jose Altuve 2.50 6.00
E7 Jackie Bradley Jr. 3.00 8.00
E8 Matt Carpenter 3.00 8.00
E9 Mike Trout 12.00 30.00
E10 David Price 2.50 6.00
E11 Kris Bryant 10.00 25.00
E12 Bryce Harper 5.00 12.00
E13 Francisco Lindor 3.00 8.00
E14 Corey Seager 3.00 8.00
E15 Corey Kluber 2.50 6.00
E16 Clayton Kershaw 5.00 12.00
E17 Noah Syndergaard 2.50 6.00
E18 Adrian Beltre 3.00 8.00
E19 Daniel Murphy 2.50 6.00
E20 Justin Verlander 3.00 8.00
E21 Max Scherzer 3.00 8.00
E22 Felix Hernandez 2.50 6.00
E23 Nolan Arenado 5.00 12.00
E24 Giancarlo Stanton 3.00 8.00
E25 Chris Sale 3.00 8.00
E26 Josh Donaldson 2.50 6.00
E27 Carlos Correa 3.00 8.00
E28 Mookie Betts 6.00 15.00
E29 Evan Longoria 2.50 6.00
E30 Buster Posey 4.00 10.00

2017 Topps Gallery Hall of Fame

STATED ODDS 1:5 PACKS
*GREEN/250: 1.2X TO 3X BASIC
*BLUE/99: 2X TO 5X BASIC
*ORAGE/25: 3X TO 8X BASIC
HOF1 Ken Griffey Jr. 1.25 3.00
HOF2 Ted Williams 1.25 3.00
HOF3 Carlton Fisk .50 1.25
HOF4 Bob Feller .50 1.25
HOF5 Craig Biggio .50 1.25
HOF6 Hank Aaron 1.25 3.00
HOF7 Richie Ashburn .50 1.25
HOF8 George Brett 1.50 4.00
HOF9 Tim Raines .50 1.25
HOF10 Roberto Clemente 1.50 4.00
HOF11 Willie McCovey .50 1.25
HOF12 Joe Morgan .50 1.25
HOF13 Harmon Killebrew .60 1.50
HOF14 Dave Winfield .50 1.25
HOF15 Sandy Koufax 1.25 3.00
HOF16 Johnny Bench .60 1.50
HOF17 Lou Gehrig 1.25 3.00
HOF18 Ivan Rodriguez .50 1.25
HOF19 Jim Palmer .50 1.25
HOF20 Randy Johnson .60 1.50
HOF21 Rod Carew .50 1.25
HOF22 Reggie Jackson .50 1.25
HOF23 Wade Boggs .50 1.25
HOF24 Roberto Alomar .50 1.25
HOF25 Cal Ripken Jr. 2.00 5.00
HOF26 Ozzie Smith .75 2.00
HOF27 Ernie Banks .60 1.50
HOF28 Robin Yount .60 1.50
HOF29 Al Kaline .60 1.50
HOF30 Mike Piazza .60 1.50

2017 Topps Gallery Heritage

STATED ODDS 1:10 PACKS
*GREEN/250: 1.2X TO 3X BASIC
*BLUE/99: 2X TO 5X BASIC
*ORAGE/25: 3X TO 8X BASIC
H1 Andrew Benintendi 1.25 3.00
H2 Nolan Arenado 1.00 2.50
H3 Andrew McCutchen .60 1.50
H4 Johnny Cueto .50 1.25
H5 Cody Bellinger 1.50 4.00
H6 Yu Darvish .60 1.50
H7 Carlos Martinez .50 1.25
H8 Aaron Judge 4.00 10.00
H9 Jacob deGrom 1.25 3.00
H10 Freddie Freeman .75 2.00
H11 Manny Machado .60 1.50
H12 Chris Sale .60 1.50
H13 Kris Bryant .75 2.00
H14 Francisco Lindor .60 1.50
H15 Anthony Rizzo .75 2.00
H16 Dansby Swanson 1.00 2.50
H17 Bryce Harper 1.00 2.50
H18 Miguel Sano .50 1.25
H19 Noah Syndergaard .50 1.25
H20 Alex Bregman 2.00 5.00
H21 Jose Abreu .60 1.50
H22 Corey Seager .60 1.50
H23 Buster Posey .75 2.00
H24 Yadier Molina .75 2.00
H25 Robinson Cano .50 1.25
H26 Kyle Seager .40 1.00
H27 Matt Carpenter .60 1.50
H28 Yoenis Cespedes .60 1.50
H29 Corey Kluber .50 1.25
H30 Trevor Story .60 1.50
H31 Evan Longoria .50 1.25
H32 Christian Yelich .75 2.00
H33 Troy Tulowitzki .60 1.50
H34 Clayton Kershaw 1.00 2.50
H35 Jose Altuve .50 1.25
H36 Trea Turner .50 1.25
H37 Javier Baez .75 2.00
H38 Mike Trout 3.00 8.00
H39 Daniel Murphy .50 1.25
H40 Miguel Cabrera .60 1.50

2017 Topps Gallery Masterpieces

STATED ODDS 1:10 PACKS
*GREEN/250: 1.2X TO 3X BASIC
*BLUE/99: 2X TO 5X BASIC
*ORAGE/25: 3X TO 8X BASIC
MP1 Andres Galarraga .50 1.25
MP2 Rickey Henderson .60 1.50
MP3 Carlos Correa .60 1.50
MP4 Joey Votto .60 1.50
MP5 Max Scherzer .60 1.50
MP6 Adrian Beltre .60 1.50
MP7 Omar Vizquel .50 1.25
MP8 Josh Donaldson .50 1.25
MP9 Justin Verlander .60 1.50
MP10 Ichiro .75 2.00
MP11 Mookie Betts 1.25 3.00
MP12 Adam Jones .50 1.25
MP13 Albert Pujols .75 2.00
MP14 Bryce Harper 1.00 2.50
MP15 Wil Myers .50 1.25
MP16 Brian Dozier .60 1.50
MP17 Felix Hernandez .50 1.25
MP18 Bo Jackson .60 1.50
MP19 Giancarlo Stanton .60 1.50
MP20 Mike Trout 3.00 8.00
MP21 Nolan Ryan 2.00 5.00
MP22 Kris Bryant .75 2.00
MP23 Mark McGwire 1.00 2.50
MP24 Derek Jeter 1.50 4.00
MP25 Frank Thomas .60 1.50
MP26 Ken Griffey Jr. 1.25 3.00
MP27 Greg Maddux .75 2.00
MP28 Paul Goldschmidt .60 1.50
MP29 Eric Hosmer .50 1.25
MP30 Don Mattingly 1.50 4.00

2018 Topps Gallery

COMP.SET w/o SP's (150) 30.00 80.00
151-200 STATED ODDS 1:5 PACKS
1 Aaron Judge .75 2.00
2 George Springer .25 .60
3 Sean Doolittle .20 .50
4 Michael Taylor .20 .50
5 Christian Yelich .40 1.00
6 A.J. Minter RC .40 1.00
7 Scott Kingery RC .50 1.25
8 Chris Stratton RC .30 .75
9 Tim Locastro RC .30 .75
10 Alex Verdugo RC .50 1.25
11 Matt Chapman .30 .75
12 Lewis Brinson .20 .50
13 Jake Odorizzi .20 .50
14 Don Mattingly .60 1.50
15 Luke Weaver .25 .60
16 Franmil Reyes RC .50 1.25
17 Javier Baez .40 1.00
18 Yasiel Puig .30 .75
19 Jose Abreu .30 .75
20 Max Fried RC 1.25 3.00
21 Garrett Cooper RC .30 .75
22 Jackson Stephens RC .30 .75
23 Steven Souza Jr. .25 .60
24 Mike Foltynewicz .20 .50
25 Mike Soroka RC 1.00 2.50
26 Lourdes Gurriel Jr. RC .60 1.50
27 Matt Olson .30 .75
28 Greg Bird .25 .60
29 Dustin Pedroia .30 .75
30 Marcell Ozuna .30 .75
31 Jose Berrios .25 .60
32 Avisail Garcia .25 .60
33 Ryon Healy .20 .50
34 Chris Taylor .25 .60
35 Bryce Harper .50 1.25
36 Whit Merrifield .30 .75
37 Zack Greinke .30 .75
38 Victor Robles RC .75 2.00
39 Carlos Correa .30 .75
40 Miles Mikolas RC .40 1.00
41 Kyle Seager .20 .50
42 Troy Scribner .20 .50
43 Mark McGwire .50 1.25
44 Paul Goldschmidt .30 .75
45 Anthony Rizzo .40 1.00
46 Luis Severino .25 .60
47 Parker Bridwell .20 .50
48 Nolan Ryan 1.00 2.50
49 Daniel Mengden .20 .50
50 Giancarlo Stanton .30 .75
51 Andrew McCutchen .30 .75
52 Aaron Altherr .20 .50
53 Brian Anderson RC .40 1.00
54 Christian Arroyo RC .30 .75
55 Will Clark .25 .60
56 Aaron Nola .25 .60
57 Felix Hernandez .25 .60
58 J.D. Davis RC .40 1.00
59 Paul Blackburn .20 .50
60 Trevor Williams .20 .50
61 Brandon Woodruff .60 1.50
62 Buster Posey .40 1.00
63 Justin Verlander .30 .75
64 Christian Villanueva RC .30 .75
65 Justin Upton .25 .60
66 Willy Adames RC .40 1.00
67 Ozzie Albies RC 1.00 2.50
68 Bo Jackson .30 .75
69 Adrian Beltre .30 .75
70 Corey Kluber .25 .60
71 Dominic Smith RC .40 1.00
72 Adam Duvall .25 .60
73 Tyler O'Neill RC .50 1.25
74 Nick Pivetta .20 .50
75 Kris Bryant .40 1.00
76 Blake Snell .25 .60
77 Paul DeJong .30 .75
78 Jose Canseco .25 .60
79 J.D. Martinez .30 .75
80 Martin Maldonado .20 .50
81 Ildemaro Vargas RC .30 .75
82 Jose Urena .20 .50
83 Jack Flaherty RC 1.25 3.00
84 Cal Ripken Jr. 1.00 2.50
85 Clint Frazier RC .60 1.50
86 Anthony Banda RC .30 .75
87 Fernando Romero RC .30 .75
88 Jesse Winker .30 .75
89 Gleyber Torres RC 3.00 8.00
90 Austin Meadows RC .75 2.00
91 David Ortiz .30 .75
92 Joey Votto .30 .75
93 Trea Turner .25 .60
94 Chipper Jones .30 .75
95 Dylan Cozens RC .30 .75
96 Harrison Bader RC .50 1.25
97 Richard Urena RC .30 .75
98 Ian Kinsler .25 .60
99 Austin Hays RC .50 1.25
100 Mike Trout 1.50 4.00
101 Miguel Andujar RC 1.25 3.00
102 Ian Happ .25 .60
103 Ryan McMahon RC .75 2.00
104 Zack Godley .20 .50
105 Amed Rosario RC .40 1.00
106 Tyler Wade RC .40 1.00
107 Nick Williams RC .40 1.00
108 Dillon Peters .20 .50
109 Josh Donaldson .25 .60
110 Evan Longoria .25 .60
111 Kyle Farmer RC .30 .75
112 Frank Thomas .30 .75
113 Adam Jones .25 .60
114 Ryne Sandberg .60 1.50
115 Chad Green .20 .50
116 Shohei Ohtani RC 8.00 20.00
117 Trevor Story .30 .75
118 Freddy Peralta RC .30 .75
119 Albert Pujols .40 1.00
120 Chris Sale .30 .75
121 Trey Mancini .25 .60
122 Raudy Read RC .30 .75
123 Salvador Perez .25 .60
124 Yasmani Grandal .20 .50
125 Jose Altuve .25 .60
126 Juan Soto RC 8.00 20.00
127 Rafael Devers RC 1.00 2.50
128 Freddie Freeman .40 1.00
129 Rickey Henderson .30 .75
130 Drew Smyly .20 .50
131 Nick Kingham RC .30 .75
132 Jacob deGrom .60 1.50
133 Rhys Hoskins RC 1.25 3.00
134 Jordan Hicks RC .60 1.50
135 Miguel Gomez RC .30 .75
136 Victor Arano RC .30 .75
137 Victor Caratini RC .40 1.00
138 Zack Cozart .20 .50
139 Clayton Kershaw .50 1.25
140 Ronald Acuna Jr. RC 10.00 25.00
141 Walker Buehler RC 1.50 4.00
142 Willson Contreras .30 .75
143 Didi Gregorius .25 .60
144 Manny Machado .30 .75
145 John Smoltz .30 .75
146 Charlie Blackmon .30 .75
147 Starling Marte .25 .60
148 Ichiro .40 1.00
149 Cam Gallagher RC .30 .75
150 Babe Ruth .75 2.00
151 Roberto Clemente SP 4.00 10.00
152 Kyle Schwarber SP 1.50 4.00
153 Willie Calhoun SP RC 1.50 4.00
154 Justin Smoak SP 1.00 2.50
155 Max Scherzer SP 1.50 4.00
156 Greg Maddux SP 2.00 5.00
157 Stephen Strasburg SP 1.50 4.00
158 Jon Lester SP 1.25 3.00
159 Eric Hosmer SP 1.25 3.00
160 Mookie Betts SP 3.00 8.00
161 Khris Davis SP 1.50 4.00
162 Francisco Lindor SP 1.50 4.00
163 Ted Williams SP 3.00 8.00
164 George Brett SP 3.00 8.00
165 Hideki Matsui SP 1.50 4.00
166 Xander Bogaerts SP 1.50 4.00
167 Ernie Banks SP 1.50 4.00
168 Yu Darvish SP 1.50 4.00
169 Nelson Cruz SP 1.50 4.00
170 Darryl Strawberry SP 1.00 2.50
171 Gary Sanchez SP 1.50 4.00
172 Rick Ankiel SP 1.00 2.50
173 Masahiro Tanaka SP 1.25 3.00
174 Dustin Fowler SP 1.00 2.50
175 Derek Jeter SP 4.00 10.00
176 Dee Gordon SP 1.00 2.50
177 Randy Johnson SP 1.50 4.00
178 Lou Gehrig SP 3.00 8.00
179 Alex Bregman SP 1.50 4.00
180 Pedro Martinez SP 1.25 3.00
181 Corey Seager SP 1.50 4.00
182 Gerrit Cole SP 1.50 4.00
183 Miguel Cabrera SP 1.50 4.00
184 Carlos Rodon SP 1.50 4.00
185 Yadier Molina SP 2.00 5.00
186 Julio Urias SP 1.50 4.00
187 Max Kepler SP 1.25 3.00
188 Hank Aaron SP 3.00 8.00
189 Dallas Keuchel SP 1.25 3.00
190 Matt Kemp SP 1.25 3.00
191 Michael Conforto SP 1.25 3.00
192 Nolan Arenado SP 2.50 6.00
193 Chance Sisco SP RC 1.25 3.00
194 Andrew Benintendi SP 1.50 4.00
195 Noah Syndergaard SP 1.25 3.00
196 Franklin Barreto SP 1.00 2.50
197 Joc Pederson SP 1.25 3.00
198 Sandy Koufax SP 3.00 8.00
199 Robinson Cano SP 1.25 3.00
200 Jackie Robinson SP 1.50 4.00

2018 Topps Gallery Artists Proof

*AP: 1X TO 2.5X BASIC
*AP RC: .6X TO 1.5X BASIC RC
FOUR PER BLASTER BOX

2018 Topps Gallery Blue

*BLUE: 3X TO 8X BASIC
*BLUE RC: 2X TO 5X BASIC RC
STATED ODDS 1:171 PACKS
STATED PRINT RUN 50 SER.#'d SETS

2018 Topps Gallery Canvas

*CANVAS: 1.2X TO 3X BASIC
*CANVAS RC: .75X TO 2X BASIC RC
TWO PER FAT PACK

2018 Topps Gallery Green

*GREEN: 2.5X TO 6X BASIC
*GREEN RC: 1.5X TO 4X BASIC RC
STATED ODDS 1:86 PACKS
STATED PRINT RUN 99 SER.#'d SETS

2018 Topps Gallery Orange

*ORANGE: 5X TO 12X BASIC
*ORANGE RC: 3X TO 8X BASIC RC
STATED ODDS 1:340 PACKS
STATED PRINT RUN 25 SER.#'d SETS

2018 Topps Gallery Private Issue

*PI: 1.5X TO 4X BASIC
*PI RC: 1X TO 2.5X BASIC RC
STATED ODDS 1:13 PACKS
STATED PRINT RUN 250 SER.#'d SETS

2018 Topps Gallery Autographs

STATED ODDS 1:14 PACKS
SP ODDS 1:4074 PACKS
SP PRINT RUN 10 SER.#'d SETS
NO SP PRICING DUE TO SCARCITY
EXCHANGE DEADLINE 10/31/2020
*GREEN/99: .5X TO 1.2X
*BLUE/50: .6X TO 1.5X
*ORANGE/25: .75X TO 2X
1 Aaron Judge
2 George Springer
3 Sean Doolittle 4.00 10.00
4 Michael Taylor 2.50 6.00
5 Christian Yelich 15.00 40.00
6 A.J. Minter 3.00 8.00
7 Scott Kingery 5.00 12.00
8 Chris Stratton 2.50 6.00
9 Tim Locastro 4.00 10.00
10 Alex Verdugo
11 Matt Chapman 6.00 15.00
12 Lewis Brinson 2.50 6.00
13 Jake Odorizzi 2.50 6.00
15 Luke Weaver 3.00 8.00
16 Franmil Reyes
20 Max Fried 10.00 25.00
21 Garrett Cooper 2.50 6.00
22 Jackson Stephens 2.50 6.00
23 Steven Souza Jr. 3.00 8.00

24 Mike Foltynewicz 2.50 6.00
25 Mike Soroka 10.00 25.00
26 Lourdes Gurriel Jr. 5.00 12.00
27 Matthew Olson 5.00 12.00
28 Greg Bird 3.00 8.00
30 Marcell Ozuna
31 Jose Berrios
32 Avisail Garcia 3.00 8.00
33 Ryon Healy 2.50 6.00
34 Chris Taylor 3.00 8.00
35 Bryce Harper
36 Whit Merrifield 10.00 25.00
38 Victor Robles 10.00 25.00
39 Carlos Correa
40 Miles Mikolas 6.00 15.00
41 Kyle Seager
42 Troy Scribner 2.50 6.00
43 Mark McGwire
45 Anthony Rizzo
46 Luis Severino
47 Parker Bridwell 2.50 6.00
49 Daniel Mengden 2.50 6.00
51 Andrew McCutchen
52 Aaron Altherr 2.50 6.00
54 Christian Arroyo 2.50 6.00
55 Will Clark 30.00 80.00
58 J.D. Davis 3.00 8.00
59 Paul Blackburn 2.50 6.00
60 Trevor Williams 2.50 6.00
61 Brandon Woodruff 8.00 20.00
64 Christian Villanueva
65 Justin Upton
66 Willy Adames
67 Ozzie Albies 12.00 30.00
68 Bo Jackson
69 Adrian Beltre
70 Corey Kluber
71 Dominic Smith
72 Adam Duvall 6.00 15.00
73 Tyler O'Neill 4.00 10.00
74 Nick Pivetta 2.50 6.00
75 Kris Bryant
76 Blake Snell 6.00 15.00
77 Paul DeJong 4.00 10.00
78 Jose Canseco 6.00 15.00
80 Martin Maldonado 2.50 6.00
81 Ildemaro Vargas 2.50 6.00
82 Jose Urena 2.50 6.00
83 Jack Flaherty 10.00 25.00
85 Clint Frazier 6.00 15.00
86 Anthony Banda 2.50 6.00
87 Fernando Romero 2.50 6.00
88 Jesse Winker 4.00 10.00
89 Gleyber Torres EXCH 50.00 120.00
90 Austin Meadows 6.00 15.00
91 David Ortiz
94 Chipper Jones
96 Harrison Bader 4.00 10.00
97 Richard Urena 2.50 6.00
98 Ian Kinsler 3.00 8.00
99 Austin Hays 5.00 12.00
100 Mike Trout 150.00 400.00
101 Miguel Andujar 20.00 50.00
102 Ian Happ 3.00 8.00
103 Ryan Mcmahon 6.00 15.00
104 Zack Godley 2.50 6.00
105 Amed Rosario
106 Tyler Wade
108 Dillon Peters 2.50 6.00
110 Evan Longoria
111 Kyle Farmer 2.50 6.00
115 Chad Green 6.00 15.00
116 Shohei Ohtani 100.00 250.00
118 Freddy Peralta 2.50 6.00
119 Albert Pujols
121 Trey Mancini 6.00 15.00
122 Raudy Read 2.50 6.00
123 Salvador Perez 6.00 15.00
124 Yasmani Grandal 2.50 6.00
125 Jose Altuve 12.00
126 Juan Soto 60.00 150.00
127 Rafael Devers EXCH 10.00 25.00
129 Rickey Henderson
130 Drew Smyly 2.50 6.00
131 Nick Kingham 2.50 6.00
132 Jacob deGrom
133 Rhys Hoskins 15.00 40.00
135 Miguel Gomez 2.50 6.00
136 Victor Arano 2.50 6.00
137 Victor Caratini 3.00 8.00
138 Zack Cozart 2.50 6.00
140 Ronald Acuna Jr. 75.00 200.00
141 Walker Buehler 15.00 40.00
142 Willson Contreras
144 Manny Machado
146 Charlie Blackmon 5.00 12.00
148 Ichiro
149 Cam Gallagher 2.50 6.00

2018 Topps Gallery Boxloader

STATED ODDS 1 PER BOX
OBTAB Adrian Beltre 4.00 10.00
OBTAJ Aaron Judge 10.00 25.00
OBTAM Andrew McCutchen 4.00 10.00
OBTAME Austin Meadows 6.00 15.00
OBTAP Albert Pujols 5.00 12.00
OBTBH Bryce Harper 6.00 15.00
OBTBJ Bo Jackson 4.00 10.00
OBTBP Buster Posey 5.00 12.00
OBTBR Babe Ruth 8.00 20.00
OBTCK Clayton Kershaw 6.00 15.00
OBTCR Cal Ripken Jr. 10.00 25.00
OBTCS Corey Seager 4.00 10.00
OBTDJ Derek Jeter 10.00 25.00
OBTDM Don Mattingly 8.00 20.00
OBTDO David Ortiz 4.00 10.00
OBTDP Dustin Pedroia 4.00 10.00
OBTEB Ernie Banks 4.00 10.00
OBTFL Francisco Lindor 4.00 10.00
OBTFT Frank Thomas 4.00 10.00
OBTGB George Brett 8.00 20.00
OBTGS Giancarlo Stanton 4.00 10.00
OBTGT Gleyber Torres 8.00 20.00
OBTHM Hideki Matsui 4.00 10.00
OBTI Ichiro 5.00 12.00
OBTJA Jose Altuve 3.00 8.00
OBTJB Javier Baez 5.00 12.00
OBTJD Josh Donaldson 3.00 8.00
OBTJR Jackie Robinson 4.00 10.00
OBTJS Juan Soto 12.00 30.00
OBTJV Justin Verlander 4.00 10.00
OBTJVO Joey Votto 4.00 10.00
OBTKB Kris Bryant 5.00 12.00
OBTLG Lou Gehrig 8.00 20.00
OBTMB Mookie Betts 8.00 20.00
OBTMC Michael Conforto 3.00 8.00
OBTMM Manny Machado 4.00 10.00
OBTMS Max Scherzer 4.00 10.00
OBTMT Mike Trout 8.00 20.00
OBTNA Nolan Arenado 6.00 15.00
OBTNR Nolan Ryan 10.00 25.00
OBTNS Noah Syndergaard 3.00 8.00
OBTOA Ozzie Albies 8.00 20.00
OBTRA Ronald Acuna Jr. 10.00 25.00
OBTRC Roberto Clemente 8.00 20.00
OBTRH Rickey Henderson 6.00 15.00
OBTRJ Randy Johnson 4.00 10.00
OBTSK Sandy Koufax 8.00 20.00
OBTSO Shohei Ohtani 10.00 25.00
OBTWC Will Clark 3.00 8.00
OBTYM Yadier Molina 5.00 12.00

2018 Topps Gallery Hall of Fame

STATED ODDS 1:10 PACKS
*GREEN/250: 1.2X TO 3X BASIC
*BLUE/99: 2X TO 5X BASIC
*ORANGE/25: 3X TO 8X BASIC
HOF1 Honus Wagner .60 1.50
HOF2 Ty Cobb 1.00 2.50
HOF3 Jeff Bagwell .50 1.25
HOF4 Bob Gibson .50 1.25
HOF5 Eddie Mathews .60 1.50
HOF6 Reggie Jackson .50 1.25
HOF7 Eddie Murray .50 1.25
HOF8 Jackie Robinson .60 1.50
HOF9 Lou Brock .50 1.25
HOF10 Brooks Robinson .50 1.25
HOF11 Andre Dawson .50 1.25
HOF12 Steve Carlton .50 1.25
HOF13 Ryne Sandberg 1.25 3.00
HOF14 Pedro Martinez .50 1.25
HOF15 Randy Johnson .60 1.50
HOF16 Paul Molitor .60 1.50
HOF17 Trevor Hoffman .50 1.25
HOF18 Frank Thomas .60 1.50
HOF19 Jim Thome .60 1.50
HOF20 Rod Carew .50 1.25
HOF21 Juan Marichal .50 1.25
HOF22 Barry Larkin .50 1.25
HOF23 Tom Seaver .50 1.25
HOF24 Whitey Ford .50 1.25
HOF25 Hank Aaron 1.25 3.00
HOF26 Babe Ruth 1.50 4.00
HOF27 Rickey Henderson .60 1.50
HOF28 Nolan Ryan 2.00 5.00
HOF29 George Brett 1.25 3.00
HOF30 Chipper Jones .60 1.50

2018 Topps Gallery Heritage

STATED ODDS 1:5 PACKS
*GREEN/250: .75X TO 2X BASIC
*BLUE/99: 1.2X TO 3X BASIC
*ORANGE/25: 2X TO 5X BASIC
H1 Max Scherzer .60 1.50
H2 Rafael Devers 1.25 3.00
H3 Miguel Andujar 1.50 4.00
H4 Nolan Arenado 1.00 2.50
H5 Josh Donaldson .50 1.25
H6 Willie Calhoun .60 1.50
H7 Jose Altuve .50 1.25
H8 Victor Robles 1.00 2.50
H9 Yu Darvish .60 1.50
H10 Ichiro .75 2.00
H11 Joey Votto .60 1.50
H12 Rhys Hoskins 1.50 4.00
H13 Clint Frazier .75 2.00
H14 Andrew Benintendi .60 1.50
H15 Cody Bellinger 1.25 3.00
H16 Yadier Molina .75 2.00
H17 Paul Goldschmidt .60 1.50
H18 Ozzie Albies 1.25 3.00
H19 Bryce Harper 1.00 2.50
H20 Francisco Lindor .60 1.50
H21 Amed Rosario .50 1.25
H22 Manny Machado .60 1.50
H23 Carlos Correa .60 1.50
H24 Gary Sanchez .60 1.50
H25 Buster Posey .75 2.00
H26 Shohei Ohtani 10.00 25.00
H27 Corey Seager .60 1.50
H28 Noah Syndergaard .50 1.25
H29 Mookie Betts 1.25 3.00
H30 Trea Turner .50 1.25
H31 Andrew McCutchen .60 1.50
H32 Francisco Mejia .50 1.25
H33 Clayton Kershaw 1.00 2.50
H34 Gleyber Torres 4.00 10.00
H35 Mike Trout 3.00 8.00
H36 Giancarlo Stanton .60 1.50
H37 Anthony Rizzo .75 2.00
H38 Walker Buehler 2.00 5.00
H39 Aaron Judge 1.50 4.00
H40 Ronald Acuna Jr. 12.00 30.00

2018 Topps Gallery Impressionists

STATED ODDS 1:142 PACKS
I1 Clint Frazier 6.00 15.00
I2 Kris Bryant 6.00 15.00
I3 Anthony Rizzo 6.00 15.00
I4 Ichiro 6.00 15.00
I5 Max Scherzer 5.00 12.00
I6 Manny Machado 5.00 12.00
I7 Bryce Harper 8.00 20.00
I8 Ozzie Albies 10.00 25.00
I9 Amed Rosario 4.00 10.00
I10 Shohei Ohtani 25.00 60.00
I11 Carlos Correa 5.00 12.00
I12 Giancarlo Stanton 5.00 12.00
I13 Mookie Betts 10.00 25.00
I14 Paul Goldschmidt 5.00 12.00
I15 Rhys Hoskins 12.00 30.00
I16 Victor Robles 8.00 20.00
I17 Buster Posey 6.00 15.00
I18 Andrew Benintendi 5.00 12.00
I19 Yu Darvish 5.00 12.00
I20 Jose Altuve 4.00 10.00
I21 Andrew McCutchen 5.00 12.00
I22 Rafael Devers 10.00 25.00
I23 Clayton Kershaw 8.00 20.00
I24 Aaron Judge 15.00 40.00
I25 Francisco Lindor 5.00 12.00
I26 Corey Seager 5.00 12.00
I27 Gary Sanchez 5.00 12.00
I28 Yadier Molina 6.00 15.00
I29 Joey Votto 5.00 12.00
I30 Cody Bellinger 10.00 25.00

2018 Topps Gallery Masterpiece

STATED ODDS 1:10 PACKS
*GREEN/250: .75X TO 2X BASIC
*BLUE/99: 1.2X TO 3X BASIC
*ORANGE/25: 2X TO 5X BASIC
M1 Derek Jeter 1.50 4.00
M2 Clint Frazier .75 2.00
M3 Charlie Blackmon .60 1.50
M4 Amed Rosario .50 1.25
M5 Bryce Harper 1.00 2.50
M6 Andrew McCutchen .60 1.50
M7 Andrew Benintendi .60 1.50
M8 Cal Ripken Jr. 2.00 5.00
M9 Rhys Hoskins 1.50 4.00
M10 Mike Trout 3.00 8.00
M11 Cody Bellinger 1.25 3.00
M12 Noah Syndergaard .50 1.25
M13 David Ortiz .60 1.50
M14 Chipper Jones .60 1.50
M15 Aaron Judge 1.50 4.00
M16 Yadier Molina .75 2.00
M17 Rickey Henderson .60 1.50
M18 Victor Robles 1.00 2.50
M19 Randy Johnson .60 1.50
M20 Rafael Devers 1.25 3.00
M21 Roberto Clemente 1.50 4.00
M22 Anthony Rizzo .75 2.00
M23 Clayton Kershaw 1.00 2.50
M24 Gleyber Torres 4.00 10.00
M25 Jose Altuve .50 1.25
M26 Hank Aaron 1.25 3.00
M27 Ronald Acuna Jr. 12.00 30.00
M28 Ichiro .75 2.00
M29 Francisco Lindor .60 1.50
M30 Shohei Ohtani 10.00 25.00

2019 Topps Gallery

151-200 STATED ODDS 1:5 PACKS
1 Williams Astudillo RC .30 .75
2 Nate Lowe RC 1.50 4.00
3 Clayton Kershaw .50 1.25
4 Lance McCullers Jr. .20 .50
5 Austin Riley RC 1.50 4.00
6 Shane Bieber .30 .75
7 Juan Soto 1.00 2.50
8 David Peralta .20 .50
9 George Springer .25 .60
10 Nolan Arenado .50 1.25
11 Ramon Laureano RC .60 1.50
12 Bryan Reynolds RC 1.00 2.50
13 Brendan Rodgers RC .50 1.25
14 Trevor Story .30 .75
15 Javier Baez .40 1.00
16 Harold Ramirez RC .50 1.25
17 Justin Upton .25 .60
18 Rowdy Tellez RC .50 1.25
19 Myles Straw RC .50 1.25
20 Xander Bogaerts .30 .75
21 Jon Duplantier RC .30 .75
22 Jalen Beeks RC .30 .75
23 Jonathan Villar .20 .50
24 Pete Alonso RC 2.50 6.00
25 Shohei Ohtani .50 1.25
26 Michael Kopech RC 1.00 2.50
27 Albert Pujols .40 1.00
28 Austin Meadows .30 .75
29 Kris Bryant .40 1.00
30 Bryce Harper .50 1.25
31 Taylor Ward RC .50 1.25
32 Aaron Judge .75 2.00
33 Carson Kelly .20 .50
34 Daniel Ponce de Leon RC .50 1.25
35 Mitch Keller RC .40 1.00
36 Brad Keller RC .30 .75
37 Mike Foltynewicz .30 .75
38 Nicky Lopez RC .50 1.25
39 Heath Fillmyer RC .30 .75
40 Josh Naylor RC .40 1.00
41 Jake Bauers RC .50 1.25
42 Yu Darvish .30 .75
43 Jon Lester .25 .60
44 Brandon Lowe RC .50 1.25
45 Jeff McNeil RC .75 2.00
46 Kolby Allard RC .50 1.25
47 Matt Chapman .30 .75
48 Pablo Lopez RC .30 .75
49 Justus Sheffield RC .50 1.25
50 Francisco Lindor .30 .75
51 Khris Davis .30 .75
52 Adam Cimber .20 .50
53 Keston Hiura RC 1.00 2.50
54 Pedro Avila RC .30 .75
55 Kevin Newman RC .50 1.25
56 Fernando Tatis Jr. RC 5.00 12.00
57 Nicholas Castellanos .30 .75
58 Dakota Hudson RC .40 1.00
59 Blake Snell .25 .60
60 Michael Chavis RC .50 1.25
61 Max Scherzer .30 .75
62 Christian Yelich .40 1.00
63 Trevor Bauer .40 1.00
64 Zack Greinke .30 .75
65 Jacob Nix RC .40 1.00
66 Chris Paddack RC .60 1.50
67 Joey Votto .30 .75
68 Kohl Stewart RC .40 1.00
69 Corey Kluber .25 .60
70 Lane Thomas RC .50 1.25
71 Jose Berrios .25 .60
72 Gary Sanchez .30 .75
73 Josh James RC .50 1.25
74 Josh Hader .25 .60
75 Touki Toussaint RC .40 1.00
76 Josh Donaldson .25 .60
77 Bryse Wilson RC .40 1.00
78 Ronald Acuna Jr. 1.50 4.00
79 Kyle Freeland .25 .60
80 Christin Stewart RC .40 1.00
81 Justin Verlander .30 .75
82 Dawel Lugo RC .50 1.25
83 Andrew McCutchen .30 .75
84 Whit Merrifield .30 .75
85 Reese McGuire RC .50 1.25
86 Steven Duggar RC .40 1.00
87 Ozzie Albies .30 .75
88 Matt Carpenter .30 .75
89 Sean Reid-Foley RC .30 .75
90 Mike Clevinger .25 .60
91 Alex Bregman .30 .75
92 Willson Contreras .25 .60
93 Noah Syndergaard .25 .60
94 Byron Buxton .30 .75
95 Trey Mancini .25 .60
96 Cedric Mullins RC .60 1.50
97 Kyle Wright RC .50 1.25
98 Vladimir Guerrero Jr. RC 2.00 5.00
99 Jake Cave RC .40 1.00
100 Salvador Perez .25 .60
101 Jacob deGrom .60 1.50
102 Mike Yastrzemski RC 2.00 5.00
103 Will Smith RC .75 2.00
104 Merrill Kelly RC .30 .75
105 Mike Trout 1.50 4.00
106 Rhys Hoskins .40 1.00
107 Max Muncy .30 .75
108 Carter Kieboom RC .50 1.25
109 Shaun Anderson RC .30 .75
110 Anthony Rizzo .40 1.00
111 Chance Adams RC .30 .75
112 Elvis Luciano RC .50 1.25
113 Domingo Santana .25 .60
114 Danny Jansen RC .30 .75
115 Buster Posey .40 1.00
116 Yusei Kikuchi RC .50 1.25
117 Mookie Betts .60 1.50
118 David Fletcher RC 1.00 2.50
119 DJ Stewart RC .40 1.00
120 Dennis Santana RC .30 .75
121 Kyle Tucker RC .75 2.00
122 Ryan Borucki RC .30 .75
123 Luis Severino .25 .60
124 JD Hammer RC .40 1.00
125 Garrett Hampson RC .50 1.25
126 Ryan Helsley RC .40 1.00
127 Aaron Nola .25 .60
128 Cole Tucker RC .50 1.25
129 Jose Altuve .25 .60
130 Kyle Schwarber .30 .75
131 Paul Goldschmidt .30 .75
132 Luke Voit .30 .75
133 Nick Senzel RC 1.00 2.50
134 Trent Thornton RC .30 .75
135 Luis Arraez RC 1.25 3.00
136 Freddie Freeman .40 1.00
137 Jose Ramirez .25 .60
138 Cavan Biggio RC 1.50 4.00
139 Miguel Andujar .30 .75
140 Chris Sale .30 .75
141 Dustin Pedroia .30 .75
142 Patrick Wisdom RC .30 .75
143 Manny Machado .30 .75
144 Framber Valdez RC .30 .75
145 Miguel Cabrera .30 .75
146 Thairo Estrada RC .50 1.25
147 Eloy Jimenez RC 1.25 3.00
148 Rafael Devers .40 1.00
149 Mitch Haniger .25 .60
150 Yadier Molina .40 1.00
151 Ichiro 2.00 5.00
152 Rickey Henderson 1.50 4.00
153 Cal Ripken Jr. 5.00 12.00
154 Mark McGwire 2.50 6.00
155 Frank Thomas 1.50 4.00
156 Chipper Jones 1.50 4.00
157 Nolan Ryan 5.00 12.00
158 Babe Ruth 4.00 10.00
159 Derek Jeter 4.00 10.00
160 Jackie Robinson 1.50 4.00
161 Hank Aaron 3.00 8.00
162 Stan Musial 2.50 6.00
163 Ted Williams 3.00 8.00
164 Lou Gehrig 3.00 8.00
165 Ken Griffey Jr. 3.00 8.00
166 Joey Gallo 1.25 3.00
167 Lorenzo Cain 1.00 2.50
168 Charlie Blackmon 1.50 4.00
169 Starling Marte 1.25 3.00
170 Giancarlo Stanton 1.50 4.00
171 Robinson Cano 1.25 3.00
172 Ernie Banks 1.50 4.00
173 Adrian Beltre 1.50 4.00
174 Felix Hernandez 1.25 3.00
175 Stephen Strasburg 1.50 4.00
176 Evan Longoria 1.25 3.00
177 Eric Hosmer 1.25 3.00
178 J.D. Martinez 1.50 4.00
179 Carlos Correa 1.50 4.00
180 Gerrit Cole 1.50 4.00
181 Cody Bellinger 3.00 8.00
182 Andrew Benintendi 1.50 4.00
183 Josh Bell 1.25 3.00
184 Trea Turner 1.50 4.00
185 Marcus Stroman 1.25 3.00
186 Michael Conforto 1.25 3.00
187 Gleyber Torres 3.00 8.00
188 Chris Archer 1.00 2.50
189 Miguel Sano 1.25 3.00
190 Amed Rosario 1.25 3.00
191 Corey Seager 1.50 4.00
192 Walker Buehler 2.00 5.00
193 Victor Robles 2.00 5.00
194 Yoan Moncada 1.50 4.00
195 J.T. Realmuto 1.50 4.00
196 Willie Mays 3.00 8.00
197 Tony Gwynn 1.50 4.00
198 Roberto Clemente 4.00 10.00
199 George Brett 3.00 8.00
200 Johnny Bench 1.50 4.00

2019 Topps Gallery Artist Proof

*AP: 1X TO 2.5X BASIC
*AP RC: .6X TO 1.5X BASIC RC
STATED ODDS 4 PER BLASTER BOX
24 Pete Alonso 6.00 15.00

2019 Topps Gallery Blue

*BLUE: 3X TO 8X BASIC
*BLUE RC: 2X TO 5X BASIC RC
STATED ODDS 1:174 PACKS
STATED PRINT RUN 50 SER.#'d SETS
24 Pete Alonso 20.00 50.00

2019 Topps Gallery Green

*GREEN: 2.5X TO 5X BASIC
*GREEN RC: 1.5X TO 4X BASIC RC
STATED ODDS 1:68 PACKS
STATED PRINT RUN 99 SER.#'d SETS
24 Pete Alonso 15.00 40.00

2019 Topps Gallery Orange

*ORANGE: 5X TO 12X BASIC
*ORANGE RC: 3X TO 8X BASIC RC
STATED ODDS 1:349 PACKS
STATED PRINT RUN 25 SER.#'d SETS
24 Pete Alonso 30.00 80.00

2019 Topps Gallery Private Issue

*PI: 1.5X TO 4X BASIC
*PI RC: 1X TO 2.5X BASIC RC
STATED ODDS 1:14 PACKS
STATED PRINT RUN 250 SER.#'d SETS
24 Pete Alonso 10.00 25.00

2019 Topps Gallery Autographs

STATED ODDS 1:14 PACKS
EXCHANGE DEADLINE XX/XX/XX
*GREEN/99: .5X TO 1.2X
*BLUE/50: .6X TO 1.5X
*ORANGE/25: .75X TO 2X
1 Williams Astudillo 5.00 12.00
2 Nate Lowe 12.00 30.00
3 Clayton Kershaw
5 Austin Riley 12.00 30.00
6 Shane Bieber 4.00 10.00
7 Juan Soto
8 David Peralta 2.50 6.00
9 George Springer 8.00 20.00
10 Nolan Arenado 25.00 60.00
11 Ramon Laureano 10.00 25.00
12 Bryan Reynolds 6.00 15.00
16 Harold Ramirez 4.00 10.00
17 Justin Upton 3.00 8.00
18 Rowdy Tellez 4.00 10.00
19 Myles Straw 4.00 10.00
21 Jon Duplantier 2.50 6.00
22 Jalen Beeks 2.50 6.00
24 Pete Alonso 50.00 120.00
25 Shohei Ohtani
26 Michael Kopech 8.00 20.00
27 Albert Pujols 125.00 300.00
29 Kris Bryant 25.00 60.00
31 Taylor Ward 2.50 6.00
33 Carson Kelly 2.50 6.00
34 Daniel Ponce de Leon 4.00 10.00
35 Mitch Keller 3.00 8.00
36 Brad Keller 2.50 6.00
37 Mike Foltynewicz 4.00 10.00
38 Nicky Lopez 4.00 10.00
39 Heath Fillmyer 2.50 6.00
40 Josh Naylor 3.00 8.00
41 Jake Bauers 4.00 10.00
44 Brandon Lowe 6.00 15.00
45 Jeff McNeil 12.00 30.00
46 Kolby Allard 4.00 10.00
47 Matt Chapman 8.00 20.00
48 Pablo Lopez 2.50 6.00
49 Justus Sheffield 4.00 10.00
52 Adam Cimber 2.50 6.00
53 Keston Hiura 12.00 30.00
54 Pedro Avila 2.50 6.00
55 Kevin Newman 4.00 10.00
56 Fernando Tatis Jr. 75.00 200.00
58 Dakota Hudson 6.00 15.00
59 Blake Snell 6.00 15.00
60 Michael Chavis 8.00 20.00
61 Max Scherzer 12.00 30.00
62 Christian Yelich 30.00 80.00
63 Trevor Bauer 5.00 12.00
65 Jacob Nix 3.00 8.00
66 Chris Paddack 10.00 25.00
67 Joey Votto 15.00 40.00
68 Kohl Stewart 3.00 8.00
69 Corey Kluber 10.00 25.00
70 Lane Thomas 5.00 12.00
71 Jose Berrios 3.00 8.00
72 Gary Sanchez
74 Josh Hader 3.00 8.00
75 Touki Toussaint 3.00 8.00
77 Bryse Wilson 3.00 8.00
78 Ronald Acuna Jr. 40.00 100.00
80 Christin Stewart 3.00 8.00
82 Dawel Lugo 4.00 10.00
83 Andrew McCutchen 20.00 50.00
84 Whit Merrifield 4.00 10.00
85 Reese McGuire 4.00 10.00
87 Ozzie Albies 10.00 25.00
88 Matt Carpenter 4.00 10.00
89 Sean Reid-Foley 2.50 6.00
90 Mike Clevinger
92 Willson Contreras 3.00 8.00
93 Noah Syndergaard
94 Byron Buxton
95 Trey Mancini 6.00 15.00
96 Cedric Mullins 8.00 20.00
97 Kyle Wright
98 Vladimir Guerrero Jr. 30.00 80.00
99 Jake Cave 3.00 8.00
100 Salvador Perez
101 Jacob deGrom 25.00 60.00
102 Mike Yastrzemski 20.00 50.00
103 Will Smith 8.00 20.00
104 Merrill Kelly 2.50 6.00
105 Mike Trout 125.00 300.00
106 Rhys Hoskins 15.00 40.00
107 Max Muncy 3.00 8.00
108 Carter Kieboom 8.00 20.00
109 Shaun Anderson 5.00 12.00
110 Anthony Rizzo
112 Elvis Luciano 4.00 10.00
113 Domingo Santana 3.00 8.00
114 Danny Jansen 2.50 6.00
115 Buster Posey
116 Yusei Kikuchi 4.00 10.00
118 David Fletcher 8.00 20.00
119 DJ Stewart 4.00 10.00
120 Dennis Santana 2.50 6.00
121 Kyle Tucker 4.00 10.00
123 Luis Severino
124 JD Hammer 3.00 8.00
125 Garrett Hampson 4.00 10.00
126 Ryan Helsley 3.00 8.00
127 Aaron Nola
128 Cole Tucker 4.00 10.00
129 Jose Altuve
130 Kyle Schwarber 6.00 15.00
131 Paul Goldschmidt
135 Luis Arraez 10.00 25.00
137 Jose Ramirez 8.00 20.00
139 Miguel Andujar
140 Chris Sale
141 Dustin Pedroia 15.00 40.00
143 Manny Machado 12.00 30.00
145 Miguel Cabrera 20.00 50.00
146 Thairo Estrada 4.00 10.00
147 Eloy Jimenez
148 Rafael Devers 10.00 25.00
149 Mitch Haniger 3.00 8.00

2019 Topps Gallery Box Toppers

STATED ODDS 1 PER BOX
OBTAB Alex Bregman 4.00 10.00
OBTAJ Aaron Judge 10.00 25.00
OBTAR Anthony Rizzo 5.00 12.00
OBTBB Byron Buxton 4.00 10.00
OBTBH Bryce Harper 6.00 15.00
OBTBP Buster Posey 5.00 12.00
OBTBS Blake Snell 3.00 8.00
OBTCB Cody Bellinger 8.00 20.00
OBTCK Clayton Kershaw 6.00 15.00
OBTCS Chris Sale 4.00 10.00
OBTCY Christian Yelich 5.00 12.00
OBTEJ Eloy Jimenez 10.00 25.00
OBTFL Francisco Lindor 4.00 10.00
OBTGS George Springer 3.00 8.00
OBTJA Jose Altuve 3.00 8.00
OBTJB Javier Baez 5.00 12.00
OBTJD Jacob deGrom 8.00 20.00
OBTJR Jose Ramirez 3.00 8.00
OBTJS Juan Soto 12.00 30.00
OBTJV Justin Verlander 4.00 10.00
OBTKB Kris Bryant 5.00 12.00
OBTKD Khris Davis 4.00 10.00
OBTMB Mookie Betts 8.00 20.00
OBTMC Miguel Cabrera 4.00 10.00
OBTMM Manny Machado 4.00 10.00
OBTMS Max Scherzer 4.00 10.00
OBTMT Mike Trout 20.00 50.00
OBTNA Nolan Arenado 6.00 15.00
OBTNS Noah Syndergaard 3.00 8.00
OBTOA Ozzie Albies 4.00 10.00
OBTPA Pete Alonso 20.00 50.00
OBTPG Paul Goldschmidt 4.00 10.00
OBTRA Ronald Acuna Jr. 20.00 50.00
OBTRD Rafael Devers 5.00 12.00
OBTRH Rhys Hoskins 5.00 12.00
OBTSO Shohei Ohtani 6.00 15.00
OBTTM Trey Mancini 3.00 8.00
OBTWM Whit Merrifield 4.00 10.00
OBTYK Yusei Kikuchi 4.00 10.00
OBTYM Yadier Molina 5.00 12.00
OBTZG Zack Greinke 4.00 10.00
OBTCBI Cavan Biggio 12.00 30.00
OBTFTJ Fernando Tatis Jr. 40.00 100.00
OBTGSA Gary Sanchez 4.00 10.00
OBTJBE Jose Berrios 3.00 8.00
OBTJVO Joey Votto 4.00 10.00
OBTMCH Matt Chapman 4.00 10.00
OBTNSE Nick Senzel 8.00 20.00
OBTVGJ Vladimir Guerrero Jr. 15.00 40.00
OBTWCO Willson Contreras 3.00 8.00

2019 Topps Gallery Hall of Fame

STATED ODDS 1:10 PACKS
*GREEN/250: .75X TO 2X BASIC
*BLUE/99: 1.2X TO 3X BASIC
*ORANGE/25: 2X TO 5X BASIC
HOFG1 Tony Gwynn .60 1.50
HOFG2 Stan Musial 1.00 2.50
HOFG3 Edgar Martinez .50 1.25
HOFG4 Mel Ott .60 1.50
HOFG5 Roy Halladay .50 1.25
HOFG6 Pee Wee Reese .50 1.25
HOFG7 Christy Mathewson .60 1.50
HOFG8 Lou Gehrig 1.25 3.00
HOFG9 Roberto Clemente 1.50 4.00
HOFG10 Rogers Hornsby .50 1.25
HOFG11 Ernie Banks .60 1.50
HOFG12 Ted Williams 1.25 3.00
HOFG13 Hank Aaron 1.25 3.00
HOFG14 Sandy Koufax 1.25 3.00
HOFG15 Willie Mays 1.25 3.00
HOFG16 Robin Yount .60 1.50
HOFG17 Johnny Bench .60 1.50
HOFG18 Ozzie Smith .75 2.00
HOFG19 Ken Griffey Jr. 2.00 5.00
HOFG20 Mariano Rivera .75 2.00

2019 Topps Gallery Hall of Fame Blue

*BLUE/99: 1.2X TO 3X BASIC
STATED ODDS 1:628 PACKS
STATED PRINT RUN 99 SER.#'d SETS
HOFG2 Stan Musial 4.00 10.00
HOFG8 Lou Gehrig 6.00 15.00
HOFG12 Ted Williams 8.00 20.00
HOFG15 Willie Mays 10.00 25.00
HOFG19 Ken Griffey Jr. 15.00 40.00

2019 Topps Gallery Hall of Fame Green

*GREEN/250: .75X TO 2X BASIC
STATED ODDS 1:260 PACKS
STATED PRINT RUN 250 SER.#'d SETS
HOFG12 Ted Williams 4.00 10.00
HOFG15 Willie Mays 6.00 15.00
HOFG19 Ken Griffey Jr. 6.00 15.00

2019 Topps Gallery Hall of Fame Orange

*ORANGE/25: 2X TO 5X BASIC
STATED ODDS 1:2601 PACKS
STATED PRINT RUN 25 SER.#'d SETS
HOFG2 Stan Musial 15.00 40.00
HOFG8 Lou Gehrig 10.00 25.00
HOFG9 Roberto Clemente 15.00 40.00
HOFG12 Ted Williams 12.00 30.00
HOFG15 Willie Mays 15.00 40.00
HOFG19 Ken Griffey Jr. 25.00 60.00

2019 Topps Gallery Heritage

STATED ODDS 1:5 PACKS
*GREEN/250: .75X TO 2X BASIC
*BLUE/99: 1.2X TO 3X BASIC
*ORANGE/25: 2X TO 5X BASIC
HT1 Mike Trout 3.00 8.00
HT2 Shohei Ohtani 1.00 2.50
HT3 Freddie Freeman .75 2.00
HT4 Ronald Acuna Jr. 3.00 8.00
HT5 Mookie Betts 1.25 3.00
HT6 J.D. Martinez .60 1.50
HT7 Javier Baez .75 2.00
HT8 Kris Bryant .75 2.00
HT9 Joey Votto .60 1.50
HT10 Francisco Lindor .60 1.50
HT11 Nolan Arenado 1.00 2.50
HT12 Jose Altuve .50 1.25
HT13 Alex Bregman .60 1.50
HT14 Kyle Tucker 1.00 2.50
HT15 Justin Verlander .60 1.50
HT16 Clayton Kershaw 1.00 2.50
HT17 Christian Yelich .75 2.00
HT18 Jacob deGrom 1.25 3.00
HT19 Noah Syndergaard .50 1.25
HT20 Miguel Andujar .60 1.50
HT21 Gary Sanchez .60 1.50
HT22 Aaron Judge 1.50 4.00
HT23 Giancarlo Stanton .60 1.50
HT24 Khris Davis .60 1.50
HT25 Andrew McCutchen .60 1.50
HT26 Rhys Hoskins .75 2.00
HT27 Manny Machado .60 1.50
HT28 Buster Posey .75 2.00
HT29 Andrew Benintendi .60 1.50
HT30 Ichiro .75 2.00
HT31 Yusei Kikuchi .60 1.50
HT32 Paul Goldschmidt .60 1.50
HT33 Yadier Molina .75 2.00
HT34 Blake Snell .50 1.25
HT35 Bryce Harper 1.00 2.50
HT36 Juan Soto 2.00 5.00
HT37 Trea Turner .50 1.25
HT38 Fernando Tatis Jr. 6.00 15.00
HT39 Vladimir Guerrero Jr. 2.50 6.00
HT40 Eloy Jimenez 1.50 4.00

2019 Topps Gallery Heritage Blue

*BLUE/99: 1.2X TO 3X BASIC
STATED ODDS 1:329 PACKS
STATED PRINT RUN 99 SER.#'d SETS
HT1 Mike Trout 15.00 40.00
HT22 Aaron Judge 15.00 40.00

2019 Topps Gallery Heritage Green

*GREEN/250: .75X TO 2X BASIC
STATED ODDS 1:131 PACKS
STATED PRINT RUN 250 SER.#'d SETS
HT22 Aaron Judge 10.00 25.00

2019 Topps Gallery Heritage Orange

*ORANGE/25: 2X TO 5X BASIC
STATED ODDS 1:1316 PACKS
STATED PRINT RUN 25 SER.#'d SETS
HT1 Mike Trout 25.00 60.00
HT22 Aaron Judge 25.00 60.00
HT35 Bryce Harper 12.00 30.00
HT39 Vladimir Guerrero Jr. 30.00 80.00

2019 Topps Gallery Impressionists

STATED ODDS 1:87 PACKS
IM1 Mike Trout 12.00 30.00
IM2 Shohei Ohtani 4.00 10.00
IM3 Eloy Jimenez 6.00 15.00
IM4 Ronald Acuna Jr. 12.00 30.00
IM5 Mookie Betts 8.00 20.00
IM6 Andrew Benintendi 2.50 6.00
IM7 Javier Baez 3.00 8.00
IM8 Kris Bryant 3.00 8.00
IM9 Joey Votto 2.50 6.00
IM10 Francisco Lindor 2.50 6.00
IM11 Nolan Arenado 4.00 10.00
IM12 Jose Altuve 2.00 5.00
IM13 Alex Bregman 2.50 6.00
IM14 Carlos Correa 2.50 6.00
IM15 Clayton Kershaw 4.00 10.00
IM16 Christian Yelich 3.00 8.00
IM17 Jacob deGrom 5.00 12.00
IM18 Fernando Tatis Jr. 15.00 40.00
IM19 Aaron Judge 6.00 15.00
IM20 Yusei Kikuchi 2.50 6.00
IM21 Khris Davis 2.50 6.00
IM22 Rhys Hoskins 3.00 8.00
IM23 Vladimir Guerrero Jr. 10.00 25.00
IM24 Manny Machado 2.50 6.00
IM25 Buster Posey 3.00 8.00
IM26 Yadier Molina 3.00 8.00
IM27 Paul Goldschmidt 2.50 6.00
IM28 Bryce Harper 8.00 20.00
IM29 Juan Soto 12.00 30.00
IM30 Max Scherzer 2.50 6.00

2019 Topps Gallery Master and Apprentice

STATED ODDS 1:5 PACKS
*GREEN/250: .75X TO 2X BASIC
*BLUE/99: 1.2X TO 3X BASIC
*ORANGE/25: 2X TO 5X BASIC
MAAA Aaron/Acuna Jr. 3.00 8.00
MAGM Tony Gwynn .60 1.50
Manny Machado
MAKK Kershaw/Koufax 1.25 3.00
MAMG Goldschmidt/Musial 1.00 2.50
MARJ Judge/Ruth 1.50 4.00
MATJ Jimenez/Thomas 1.50 4.00
MAWB Williams/Betts 1.25 3.00
MAYY Yelich/Yount .75 2.00
MAGGJ Guerrero/Guerrero Jr. 2.50 6.00
MAMTJ Tatis Jr./Machado 6.00 15.00

2019 Topps Gallery Master and Apprentice Blue

*BLUE/99: 1.2X TO 3X BASIC
STATED ODDS 1:316 PACKS
STATED PRINT RUN 99 SER.#'d SETS

MARJ Aaron Judge 10.00 25.00
Babe Ruth
MAWB Ted Williams 12.00 30.00
Mookie Betts

2019 Topps Gallery Master and Apprentice Green

*GREEN/250: .75X TO 2X BASIC
STATED ODDS 1:523 PACKS
STATED PRINT RUN 250 SER.#'d SETS
MARJ Aaron Judge 6.00 15.00
Babe Ruth
MAWB Ted Williams 8.00 20.00
Mookie Betts

2019 Topps Gallery Master and Apprentice Orange

*ORANGE/25: 2X TO 5X BASIC
STATED ODDS 1:5201 PACKS
STATED PRINT RUN 25 SER.#'d SETS
MAAA Hank Aaron 25.00 60.00
Ronald Acuna Jr.
MARJ Aaron Judge 15.00 40.00
Babe Ruth
MAWB Ted Williams 20.00 50.00
Mookie Betts

2019 Topps Gallery Masterpiece

STATED ODDS 1:10 PACKS
*GREEN/250: .75X TO 2X BASIC
*BLUE/99: 1.2X TO 3X BASIC
*ORANGE/25: 2X TO 5X BASIC
MP1 Mike Trout 3.00 8.00
MP2 Ronald Acuna Jr. 3.00 8.00
MP3 Randy Johnson .60 1.50
MP4 Cal Ripken Jr. 2.00 5.00
MP5 Mookie Betts 1.25 3.00
MP6 Kris Bryant .75 2.00
MP7 Frank Thomas .60 1.50
MP8 Johnny Bench .60 1.50
MP9 Francisco Lindor .60 1.50
MP10 Nolan Arenado 1.00 2.50
MP11 Alex Bregman .60 1.50
MP12 George Brett 1.25 3.00
MP13 Clayton Kershaw 1.00 2.50
MP14 Christian Yelich .75 2.00
MP15 Jacob deGrom 1.25 3.00
MP16 Rod Carew .50 1.25
MP17 Mariano Rivera .75 2.00
MP18 Mark McGwire 1.00 2.50
MP19 Rhys Hoskins .75 2.00
MP20 Roberto Clemente 1.50 4.00
MP21 Tony Gwynn .60 1.50
MP22 Nolan Ryan 2.00 5.00
MP23 Willie Mays 1.25 3.00
MP24 Ken Griffey Jr. 1.25 3.00
MP25 Paul Goldschmidt .60 1.50
MP26 Blake Snell .50 1.25
MP27 Miguel Cabrera .60 1.50
MP28 Javier Baez .75 2.00
MP29 Vladimir Guerrero Jr. 2.50 6.00
MP30 Max Scherzer .60 1.50

2019 Topps Gallery Masterpiece Blue

*BLUE/99: 1.2X TO 3X BASIC
STATED ODDS 1:439 PACKS
STATED PRINT RUN 99 SER.#'d SETS
MP1 Mike Trout 15.00 40.00
MP4 Cal Ripken Jr. 10.00 25.00
MP17 Mariano Rivera 5.00 12.00
MP20 Roberto Clemente 8.00 20.00
MP24 Ken Griffey Jr. 8.00 20.00
MP29 Vladimir Guerrero Jr. 15.00 40.00

2019 Topps Gallery Masterpiece Green

*GREEN/250: .75X TO 2X BASIC
STATED ODDS 1:174 PACKS
STATED PRINT RUN 250 SER.#'d SETS
MP1 Mike Trout 10.00 25.00
MP4 Cal Ripken Jr. 6.00 15.00
MP17 Mariano Rivera 3.00 8.00
MP20 Roberto Clemente 5.00 12.00
MP29 Vladimir Guerrero Jr. 10.00 25.00

2019 Topps Gallery Masterpiece Orange

*ORANGE/25: 2X TO 5X BASIC
STATED ODDS 1:1776 PACKS
STATED PRINT RUN 25 SER.#'d SETS
MP1 Mike Trout 25.00 60.00
MP4 Cal Ripken Jr. 15.00 40.00
MP17 Mariano Rivera 8.00 20.00
MP20 Roberto Clemente 20.00 50.00
MP21 Tony Gwynn 10.00 25.00
MP24 Ken Griffey Jr. 12.00 30.00
MP29 Vladimir Guerrero Jr. 25.00 60.00

2020 Topps Gallery

151-200 STATED ODDS 1:5 PACKS
1 Mike Trout 1.50 4.00
2 Gleyber Torres .60 1.50
3 Aristides Aquino RC .75 2.00
4 Juan Soto 1.00 2.50
5 Matthew Boyd .20 .50
6 Mauricio Dubon RC .40 1.00
7 Marcell Ozuna .30 .75
8 Christian Yelich .40 1.00
9 Kyle Schwarber .30 .75
10 Jose Altuve .25 .60
11 Ryan McMahon .30 .75
12 Mike Clevinger .25 .60
13 Logan Webb RC .50 1.25
14 Andrew McCutchen .30 .75
15 Matt Olson .30 .75
16 Yordan Alvarez RC 3.00 8.00
17 Hyun-Jin Ryu .25 .60
18 Nico Hoerner RC 1.25 3.00
19 Mike Moustakas .25 .60
20 Dereck Rodriguez .20 .50
21 Eloy Jimenez .60 1.50
22 Jesus Tinoco RC .30 .75
23 Paul Goldschmidt .30 .75
24 Xander Bogaerts .30 .75
25 Christian Walker .25 .60
26 Shane Bieber .30 .75
27 Stephen Gonsalves .20 .50
28 DJ Stewart .20 .50
29 Matt Thaiss RC .40 1.00
30 Pablo Lopez .20 .50
31 Nick Solak RC 1.25 3.00
32 Francisco Lindor .30 .75
33 Jesus Luzardo RC .60 1.50
34 Kyle Lewis RC 2.50 6.00
35 Shogo Akiyama .30 .75
36 Gerrit Cole .50 1.25
37 Ryan Yarbrough .20 .50
38 Adam Haseley .25 .60
39 Nolan Arenado .50 1.25
40 Gary Sanchez .30 .75
41 Shohei Ohtani .50 1.25
42 Dario Agrazal RC .40 1.00
43 Luis Severino .25 .60
44 Colin Moran .20 .50
45 Jeff McNeil .25 .60
46 Josh VanMeter .30 .75
47 Corey Kluber .25 .60
48 Mike King RC .50 1.25
49 Lane Thomas .25 .60
50 Hunter Harvey RC .50 1.25
51 Martin Maldonado .20 .50
52 Lewis Thorpe RC .30 .75
53 Cesar Hernandez .20 .50
54 Tommy Edman .30 .75
55 Rafael Devers .40 1.00
56 Aaron Civale RC .60 1.50
57 Jaylin Davis RC .50 1.25
58 Chris Sale .30 .75
59 Miguel Cabrera .30 .75
60 Carter Kieboom .25 .60
61 A.J. Puk RC .50 1.25
62 George Springer .25 .60
63 Jose Berrios .25 .60
64 Anthony Kay RC .30 .75
65 Brendan McKay RC .50 1.25
66 Junior Fernandez RC .30 .75
67 Andres Munoz RC .50 1.25
68 Jordan Luplow .20 .50
69 Shed Long .25 .60
70 Travis Demeritte RC .50 1.25
71 Eric Hosmer .25 .60
72 Sean Murphy RC .50 1.25
73 Yusei Kikuchi .25 .60
74 Alex Young RC .30 .75
75 Matt Chapman .30 .75
76 Robel Garcia RC .30 .75
77 Noah Syndergaard .25 .60
78 J.T. Realmuto .30 .75
79 Seth Brown RC .30 .75
80 Rhys Hoskins .40 1.00
81 Max Muncy .25 .60
82 Bryce Harper .50 1.25
83 Yoshi Tsutsugo .50 1.25
84 Mitch Moreland .20 .50
85 Framber Valdez .20 .50
86 Salvador Perez .25 .60
87 Byron Buxton .30 .75
88 Fernando Tatis Jr. 1.50 4.00
89 Kyle Tucker .30 .75
90 Eric Thames .20 .50
91 Pete Alonso .75 2.00
92 Jake Rogers RC .30 .75
93 Tommy Kahnle .20 .50
94 Whit Merrifield .30 .75
95 Elvis Andrus .25 .60
96 Bryan Abreu RC .30 .75
97 Willson Contreras .30 .75
98 Zac Gallen RC .75 2.00
99 Max Scherzer .30 .75
100 Aaron Judge .75 2.00
101 Albert Pujols .40 1.00
102 Abraham Toro RC .40 1.00
103 Anthony Rizzo .40 1.00
104 Jonathan Villar .20 .50
105 Justin Upton .25 .60
106 Keston Hiura .40 1.00
107 Gavin Lux RC 1.50 4.00
108 Adbert Alzolay RC .40 1.00
109 Lance McCullers Jr. .20 .50
110 James Karinchak RC .50 1.25
111 Marwin Gonzalez .20 .50
112 Jordan Montgomery .20 .50
113 Jorge Soler .30 .75
114 Charlie Blackmon .30 .75
115 Kris Bryant .40 1.00
116 Blake Snell .25 .60
117 Daniel Mengden .20 .50
118 Marcus Stroman .25 .60
119 Dustin May RC 1.00 2.50
120 Patrick Sandoval RC .50 1.25
121 Sheldon Neuse RC .40 1.00
122 Ketel Marte .25 .60
123 Nick Burdi .20 .50
124 Buster Posey .40 1.00
125 Shin-Soo Choo .25 .60
126 Trevor Richards .20 .50
127 Mike Tauchman .30 .75
128 Zack Collins RC .40 1.00
129 Matt Kemp .25 .60
130 Bo Bichette RC 2.50 6.00
131 Manny Machado .30 .75
132 Kyle Freeland .25 .60
133 Zack Littell .20 .50
134 Shun Yamaguchi .25 .60
135 Mike Yastrzemski .50 1.25
136 Trevor Bauer .40 1.00
137 Ozzie Albies .30 .75
138 Dean Deetz .20 .50
139 Walker Buehler .40 1.00
140 Alex Bregman .30 .75
141 Kwang-Hyun Kim .40 1.00
142 Jack Flaherty .30 .75
143 T.J. Zeuch RC .30 .75
144 Luis Robert RC 2.50 6.00
145 Vladimir Guerrero Jr. .50 1.25
146 Sam Hilliard RC .50 1.25
147 Jacob deGrom .60 1.50
148 J.D. Martinez .30 .75
149 Joey Votto .30 .75
150 Ronald Acuna Jr. 1.25 3.00
151 Miguel Andujar SP 1.50 4.00
152 Sandy Koufax SP 3.00 8.00
153 Carlos Correa SP 1.50 4.00
154 Willie Mays SP 3.00 8.00
155 Trea Turner SP 1.25 3.00
156 Jackie Robinson SP 1.50 4.00
157 Cal Ripken Jr. SP 5.00 12.00
158 Mitch Keller SP 1.50 4.00
159 Mookie Betts SP 3.00 8.00
160 Joey Gallo SP 1.50 4.00
161 Anthony Rendon SP 1.50 4.00
162 Yoan Moncada SP 1.50 4.00
163 Clayton Kershaw SP 2.50 6.00
164 Roberto Clemente SP 4.00 10.00
165 Josh Donaldson SP 1.25 3.00
166 Corey Seager SP 1.50 4.00
167 Yadier Molina SP 2.00 5.00
168 Cody Bellinger SP 3.00 8.00
169 Hank Aaron SP 3.00 8.00
170 Rickey Henderson SP 1.50 4.00
171 Frank Thomas SP 1.50 4.00
172 Yu Darvish SP 1.50 4.00
173 Babe Ruth SP 4.00 10.00
174 George Brett SP 3.00 8.00
175 Ichiro SP 2.00 5.00
176 Josh Bell SP 1.25 3.00
177 Tony Gwynn SP 1.50 4.00
178 Javier Baez SP 2.00 5.00
179 Ty Cobb SP 2.50 6.00
180 Mark McGwire SP 2.50 6.00
181 Aaron Nola SP 1.25 3.00
182 Ted Williams SP 3.00 8.00
183 Ken Griffey Jr. SP 5.00 12.00
184 Robinson Cano SP 1.25 3.00
185 Austin Meadows SP 1.50 4.00
186 Trevor Story SP 1.50 4.00
187 Johnny Bench SP 1.50 4.00
188 Ernie Banks SP 1.50 4.00
189 Nolan Ryan SP 5.00 12.00
190 Justin Verlander SP 1.50 4.00
191 Don Mattingly SP 3.00 8.00
192 Andrew Benintendi SP 1.50 4.00
193 Freddie Freeman SP 2.00 5.00
194 Stan Musial SP 2.50 6.00
195 Stephen Strasburg SP 1.50 4.00
196 Nelson Cruz SP 1.50 4.00
197 Michael Conforto SP 1.25 3.00
198 Ramon Laureano SP 1.25 3.00
199 Victor Robles SP 2.00 5.00
200 Derek Jeter SP 4.00 10.00

2020 Topps Gallery Artist Proof

*AP: 1X TO 2.5X BASIC
*AP RC: .6X TO 1.5X BASIC RC
STATED ODDS 4 PER BLASTER BOX
144 Luis Robert 8.00 20.00

2020 Topps Gallery Blue

*BLUE: 3X TO 8X BASIC
*BLUE RC: 2X TO 5X BASIC RC
STATED ODDS 1:175 PACKS
STATED PRINT RUN 50 SER.#'d SETS
16 Yordan Alvarez 10.00 25.00
141 Kwang-Hyun Kim 6.00 15.00
144 Luis Robert 25.00 60.00

2020 Topps Gallery Green

*GREEN: 2.5X TO 5X BASIC
*GREEN RC: 1.5X TO 4X BASIC RC
STATED ODDS 1:89 PACKS
STATED PRINT RUN 99 SER.#'d SETS
16 Yordan Alvarez 8.00 20.00
141 Kwang-Hyun Kim 5.00 12.00
144 Luis Robert 20.00 50.00

2020 Topps Gallery Private Issue

*PI: 1.5X TO 4X BASIC
*PI RC: 1X TO 2.5X BASIC RC
STATED ODDS 1:15 PACKS
STATED PRINT RUN 250 SER.#'d SETS
144 Luis Robert 15.00 40.00

2020 Topps Gallery Rainbow Foil

*RAINBOW: 1X TO 2.5X BASIC
*RAINBOW RC: .6X TO 1.5X BASIC RC
STATED ODDS 1:3 PACKS
144 Luis Robert 8.00 20.00

2020 Topps Gallery Wood

*WOOD: 1.2X TO 3X BASIC
*WOOD RC: .8X TO 2X BASIC RC
STATED ODDS 2 PER HANGER PACK
144 Luis Robert 10.00 25.00

2020 Topps Gallery Autographs

RANDOM INSERTS IN PACKS
1 Mike Trout
2 Gleyber Torres 25.00 60.00
3 Aristides Aquino 6.00 15.00
4 Juan Soto
5 Matthew Boyd 2.50 6.00
6 Mauricio Dubon 3.00 8.00
7 Marcell Ozuna 12.00 30.00
10 Jose Altuve 8.00 20.00
11 Ryan McMahon 4.00 10.00
12 Mike Clevinger 3.00 8.00
13 Logan Webb 4.00 10.00
14 Andrew McCutchen 40.00 100.00
16 Yordan Alvarez
17 Hyun-Jin Ryu 10.00 25.00
18 Nico Hoerner 12.00 30.00
19 Mike Moustakas 8.00 20.00
20 Dereck Rodriguez 2.50 6.00
22 Jesus Tinoco 2.50 6.00
23 Paul Goldschmidt
24 Xander Bogaerts 15.00 40.00
25 Christian Walker 3.00 8.00
26 Shane Bieber 20.00 50.00
27 Stephen Gonsalves 2.50 6.00
28 DJ Stewart 2.50 6.00
29 Matt Thaiss 3.00 8.00
30 Pablo Lopez 2.50 6.00
31 Nick Solak 5.00 12.00
33 Jesus Luzardo 5.00 12.00
34 Kyle Lewis 25.00 60.00
35 Shogo Akiyama 4.00 10.00
36 Gerrit Cole 15.00 40.00
37 Ryan Yarbrough 2.50 6.00
38 Adam Haseley 3.00 8.00
40 Gary Sanchez 10.00 25.00
41 Shohei Ohtani 50.00 120.00
42 Dario Agrazal 3.00 8.00
43 Luis Severino
44 Colin Moran 2.50 6.00
46 Josh VanMeter 4.00 10.00
47 Corey Kluber 3.00 8.00
48 Mike King 4.00 10.00
49 Lane Thomas 3.00 8.00
50 Hunter Harvey 4.00 10.00
51 Martin Maldonado 2.50 6.00
52 Lewis Thorpe 2.50 6.00
53 Cesar Hernandez 2.50 6.00
54 Tommy Edman 4.00 10.00
56 Aaron Civale 5.00 12.00
57 Jaylin Davis 4.00 10.00
58 Chris Sale 10.00 25.00
59 Miguel Cabrera 100.00 250.00
61 A.J. Puk
62 George Springer
63 Jose Berrios 3.00 8.00
64 Anthony Kay 2.50 6.00
65 Brendan McKay 4.00 10.00
66 Junior Fernandez 2.50 6.00
67 Andres Munoz 4.00 10.00
68 Jordan Luplow 2.50 6.00
69 Shed Long 3.00 8.00
70 Travis Demeritte 4.00 10.00
71 Eric Hosmer 8.00 20.00
72 Sean Murphy 4.00 10.00
73 Yusei Kikuchi 3.00 8.00
74 Alex Young 2.50 6.00
76 Robel Garcia 2.50 6.00
77 Noah Syndergaard 8.00 20.00
78 J.T. Realmuto 10.00 25.00
79 Seth Brown 2.50 6.00
80 Rhys Hoskins 15.00 40.00
82 Bryce Harper 60.00 150.00
83 Yoshi Tsutsugo
84 Mitch Moreland 2.50 6.00
85 Framber Valdez 2.50 6.00
86 Salvador Perez
88 Fernando Tatis Jr.
89 Kyle Tucker 8.00 20.00
90 Eric Thames 2.50 6.00
91 Pete Alonso 25.00 60.00
92 Jake Rogers 2.50 6.00
93 Tommy Kahnle 2.50 6.00
95 Elvis Andrus 8.00 20.00
96 Bryan Abreu 2.50 6.00
98 Zac Gallen 15.00 40.00
100 Aaron Judge 30.00 80.00
101 Albert Pujols 40.00 100.00
102 Abraham Toro 3.00 8.00
103 Anthony Rizzo
104 Jonathan Villar 2.50 6.00
105 Justin Upton 3.00 8.00
107 Gavin Lux EXCH 25.00 60.00
108 Adbert Alzolay 3.00 8.00
109 Lance McCullers Jr. 2.50 6.00
110 James Karinchak 6.00 15.00
111 Marwin Gonzalez 2.50 6.00
112 Jordan Montgomery 2.50 6.00
115 Kris Bryant 25.00 60.00
117 Daniel Mengden 2.50 6.00
119 Dustin May
120 Patrick Sandoval 4.00 10.00
121 Sheldon Neuse 3.00 8.00
122 Ketel Marte 5.00 12.00
123 Nick Burdi 2.50 6.00
124 Buster Posey 30.00 80.00
125 Shin-Soo Choo 12.00 30.00
126 Trevor Richards 2.50 6.00
127 Mike Tauchman 6.00 15.00
128 Zack Collins 3.00 8.00
129 Matt Kemp 3.00 8.00
130 Bo Bichette EXCH 30.00 80.00
131 Manny Machado
132 Kyle Freeland 3.00 8.00
133 Zack Littell 2.50 6.00
134 Shun Yamaguchi 3.00 8.00
135 Mike Yastrzemski
136 Trevor Bauer 6.00 15.00
138 Dean Deetz 2.50 6.00
140 Alex Bregman
141 Kwang-Hyun Kim 12.00 30.00
143 T.J. Zeuch 2.50 6.00
144 Luis Robert EXCH 50.00 120.00
145 Vladimir Guerrero Jr.
146 Sam Hilliard 4.00 10.00
147 Jacob deGrom
149 Joey Votto 20.00 50.00
150 Ronald Acuna Jr. 40.00 100.00
152 Sandy Koufax
157 Cal Ripken Jr.
158 Mitch Keller 4.00 10.00
160 Joey Gallo 10.00 25.00
161 Anthony Rendon
163 Clayton Kershaw
166 Corey Seager 20.00 50.00
167 Yadier Molina 40.00 100.00
168 Cody Bellinger 40.00 100.00
170 Rickey Henderson
171 Frank Thomas
175 Ichiro 75.00 200.00
180 Mark McGwire 40.00 100.00
181 Aaron Nola 8.00 20.00
185 Austin Meadows
187 Johnny Bench 40.00 100.00
189 Nolan Ryan
191 Don Mattingly
192 Andrew Benintendi 12.00 30.00
193 Freddie Freeman
195 Stephen Strasburg
198 Ramon Laureano 3.00 8.00
200 Derek Jeter 150.00 400.00

2020 Topps Gallery Autographs Blue

*BLUE/50: .6X TO 1.5X BASIC
STATED ODDS 1:135 HOBBY
STATED PRINT RUN 50 SER.#'d SETS
EXCHANGE DEADLINE 8/31/22
16 Yordan Alvarez 40.00 100.00
34 Kyle Lewis 50.00 120.00
65 Brendan McKay 8.00 20.00
86 Salvador Perez 10.00 25.00
136 Trevor Bauer 12.00 30.00

2020 Topps Gallery Autographs Green

*GREEN/99: .5X TO 1.2X BASIC
STATED ODDS 1:XX HOBBY
STATED PRINT RUN 99 SER.#'d SETS
EXCHANGE DEADLINE 8/31/22
16 Yordan Alvarez 30.00 80.00
34 Kyle Lewis 40.00 100.00
65 Brendan McKay 6.00 15.00
136 Trevor Bauer 10.00 25.00

2020 Topps Gallery Autographs Orange

*ORANGE/25: .8X TO 2X BASIC
STATED ODDS 1:266 HOBBY
STATED PRINT RUN 25 SER.#'d SETS
EXCHANGE DEADLINE 8/31/22
1 Mike Trout 125.00 300.00
16 Yordan Alvarez 50.00 120.00
34 Kyle Lewis 60.00 150.00
43 Luis Severino 8.00 20.00
62 George Springer 20.00 50.00
65 Brendan McKay 10.00 25.00
83 Yoshi Tsutsugo 15.00 40.00
86 Salvador Perez 12.00 30.00
135 Mike Yastrzemski 20.00 50.00
136 Trevor Bauer 15.00 40.00
144 Luis Robert EXCH 200.00 500.00
145 Vladimir Guerrero Jr. 25.00 60.00

2020 Topps Gallery Box Toppers

STATED ODDS 1 PER BOX
OBTI Ichiro 6.00 15.00
OBTAB Alex Bregman 3.00 8.00
OBTAJ Aaron Judge 4.00 10.00
OBTAP Albert Pujols 4.00 10.00
OBTAR Anthony Rizzo 4.00 10.00
OBTBH Bryce Harper 6.00 15.00
OBTBR Babe Ruth 8.00 20.00
OBTCB Cody Bellinger 6.00 15.00
OBTCK Clayton Kershaw 5.00 12.00
OBTCY Christian Yelich 4.00 10.00
OBTDJ Derek Jeter 6.00 15.00
OBTDM Don Mattingly 10.00 25.00
OBTFL Francisco Lindor 3.00 8.00
OBTFT Frank Thomas 8.00 20.00
OBTGB George Brett 6.00 15.00
OBTGC Gerrit Cole 5.00 12.00
OBTGL Gavin Lux 6.00 15.00
OBTHA Hank Aaron 6.00 15.00
OBTJB Javier Baez 4.00 10.00
OBTJD Jacob deGrom 6.00 15.00
OBTJL Jesus Luzardo 4.00 10.00
OBTJR Jackie Robinson 4.00 10.00
OBTJS Juan Soto 6.00 15.00
OBTJV Justin Verlander 3.00 8.00
OBTKB Kris Bryant 4.00 10.00
OBTKL Kyle Lewis 4.00 10.00
OBTLR Luis Robert 8.00 20.00
OBTMB Mookie Betts 6.00 15.00
OBTMS Max Scherzer 3.00 8.00
OBTMT Mike Trout 8.00 20.00
OBTNA Nolan Arenado 5.00 12.00
OBTNC Nelson Cruz 3.00 8.00
OBTNR Nolan Ryan 6.00 15.00
OBTPA Pete Alonso 8.00 20.00
OBTRA Ronald Acuna Jr. 8.00 20.00
OBTRC Roberto Clemente 8.00 20.00
OBTRD Rafael Devers 4.00 10.00
OBTRH Rickey Henderson 5.00 12.00
OBTSK Sandy Koufax 6.00 15.00
OBTSO Shohei Ohtani 6.00 15.00
OBTTG Tony Gwynn 8.00 20.00
OBTWM Willie Mays 6.00 15.00
OBTYA Yordan Alvarez 8.00 20.00
OBTYM Yadier Molina 4.00 10.00
OBTBBI Bo Bichette 8.00 20.00
OBTCRJ Cal Ripken Jr. 8.00 20.00
OBTFTJ Fernando Tatis Jr. 5.00 12.00
OBTJVO Joey Votto 3.00 8.00
OBTKGJ Ken Griffey Jr. 10.00 25.00
OBTVGJ Vladimir Guerrero Jr. 5.00 12.00

2020 Topps Gallery Hall of Fame

STATED ODDS 1:XX HOBBY
HOFG1 Lou Gehrig 1.25 3.00
HOFG2 Derek Jeter 1.50 4.00
HOFG3 Ted Williams 1.25 3.00
HOFG4 George Brett 1.25 3.00
HOFG5 Sandy Koufax 1.25 3.00
HOFG6 Willie Mays 1.25 3.00
HOFG7 Rickey Henderson .60 1.50
HOFG8 Chipper Jones .60 1.50
HOFG9 Jeff Bagwell .50 1.25
HOFG10 Nolan Ryan 2.00 5.00
HOFG11 Randy Johnson .60 1.50
HOFG12 Barry Larkin .50 1.25
HOFG13 Cal Ripken Jr. 2.00 5.00
HOFG14 Ryne Sandberg 1.25 3.00
HOFG15 Roberto Clemente 1.50 4.00
HOFG16 Roberto Alomar .50 1.25
HOFG17 Jackie Robinson .60 1.50
HOFG18 Mike Schmidt 1.00 2.50
HOFG19 Ken Griffey Jr. 1.25 3.00
HOFG20 Mariano Rivera .75 2.00

2020 Topps Gallery Hall of Fame Blue

*BLUE/99: 1.2X TO 3X BASIC
STATED ODDS 1:XX HOBBY
STATED PRINT RUN 99 SER.#'d SETS
HOFG2 Derek Jeter 6.00 15.00
HOFG3 Ted Williams 10.00 25.00
HOFG6 Willie Mays 8.00 20.00
HOFG19 Ken Griffey Jr. 12.00 30.00

2020 Topps Gallery Hall of Fame Green

HOFG6 Willie Mays 4.00 10.00
HOFG19 Ken Griffey Jr. 8.00 20.00

2020 Topps Gallery Hall of Fame Orange

*ORANGE/25: 2X TO 5X BASIC
STATED ODDS 1:2617 HOBBY
STATED PRINT RUN 25 SER.#'d SETS
HOFG2 Derek Jeter 10.00 25.00
HOFG3 Ted Williams 15.00 40.00
HOFG6 Willie Mays 12.00 30.00
HOFG17 Jackie Robinson 10.00 25.00
HOFG19 Ken Griffey Jr. 20.00 50.00

2020 Topps Gallery Heritage

STATED ODDS 1:XX HOBBY
HT1 Mike Trout 3.00 8.00
HT2 Shohei Ohtani 1.00 2.50
HT3 Freddie Freeman .75 2.00
HT4 Ronald Acuna Jr. 2.50 6.00
HT5 Mookie Betts 1.25 3.00
HT6 Rafael Devers .75 2.00
HT7 Javier Baez .75 2.00
HT8 Kris Bryant .75 2.00
HT9 Joey Votto .60 1.50
HT10 Francisco Lindor .60 1.50
HT11 Nolan Arenado 1.00 2.50
HT12 Jose Altuve .50 1.25
HT13 Alex Bregman .60 1.50
HT14 Yordan Alvarez 4.00 10.00
HT15 Justin Verlander .60 1.50
HT16 Clayton Kershaw 1.00 2.50
HT17 Christian Yelich .75 2.00
HT18 Jacob deGrom 1.25 3.00
HT19 Pete Alonso 1.50 4.00
HT20 Gavin Lux 2.00 5.00
HT21 Gleyber Torres 1.25 3.00
HT22 Aaron Judge 1.50 4.00
HT23 Giancarlo Stanton .60 1.50
HT24 Jesus Luzardo .75 2.00
HT25 Bo Bichette 3.00 8.00
HT26 Aristides Aquino 1.00 2.50
HT27 Walker Buehler .75 2.00
HT28 Buster Posey .75 2.00
HT29 Luis Robert 3.00 8.00
HT30 Nico Hoerner 1.50 4.00
HT31 Kyle Lewis 3.00 8.00
HT32 Paul Goldschmidt .60 1.50
HT33 Yadier Molina .75 2.00
HT34 Brendan McKay .60 1.50
HT35 Bryce Harper 1.00 2.50
HT36 Juan Soto 2.00 5.00
HT37 Max Scherzer .60 1.50
HT38 Fernando Tatis Jr. 3.00 8.00
HT39 Vladimir Guerrero Jr. 1.00 2.50
HT40 Eloy Jimenez 1.25 3.00

2020 Topps Gallery Heritage Blue

*BLUE/99: 1.2X TO 3X BASIC
STATED ODDS 1:XX HOBBY
STATED PRINT RUN 99 SER.#'d SETS
HT1 Mike Trout 20.00 50.00
HT38 Fernando Tatis Jr. 10.00 25.00

2020 Topps Gallery Heritage Green

*GREEN/250: .8X TO 2X BASIC
STATED ODDS 1:XX HOBBY
STATED PRINT RUN 250 SER.#'d SETS
HT1 Mike Trout 12.00 30.00

2020 Topps Gallery Heritage Orange

*ORANGE/25: 2X TO 5X BASIC
STATED ODDS 1:1309 HOBBY
STATED PRINT RUN 25 SER.#'d SETS
HT1 Mike Trout 30.00 80.00
HT38 Fernando Tatis Jr. 20.00 50.00

2020 Topps Gallery Impressionists

STATED ODDS 1:88 HOBBY
IM1 Mike Trout 15.00 40.00
IM2 Shohei Ohtani 4.00 10.00
IM3 Luis Robert 12.00 30.00
IM4 Ronald Acuna Jr. 8.00 20.00
IM5 Mookie Betts 8.00 20.00
IM6 Cody Bellinger 6.00 15.00
IM7 Javier Baez 3.00 8.00
IM8 Kris Bryant 3.00 8.00
IM9 Joey Votto 2.50 6.00
IM10 Francisco Lindor 2.50 6.00
IM11 Nolan Arenado 4.00 10.00
IM12 Gavin Lux 8.00 20.00
IM13 Alex Bregman 2.50 6.00
IM14 Pete Alonso 12.00 30.00
IM15 Clayton Kershaw 4.00 10.00
IM16 Christian Yelich 3.00 8.00
IM17 Jacob deGrom 5.00 12.00
IM18 Fernando Tatis Jr. 12.00 30.00
IM19 Aaron Judge 8.00 20.00
IM20 Yordan Alvarez 10.00 25.00
IM21 Jesus Luzardo 3.00 8.00
IM22 Bo Bichette 10.00 25.00
IM23 Vladimir Guerrero Jr. 4.00 10.00
IM24 Gerrit Cole 4.00 10.00
IM25 Buster Posey 3.00 8.00
IM26 Yadier Molina 3.00 8.00
IM27 Paul Goldschmidt 2.50 6.00
IM28 Bryce Harper 4.00 10.00
IM29 Juan Soto 6.00 15.00
IM30 Max Scherzer 2.50 6.00

2020 Topps Gallery Master and Apprentice

STATED ODDS 1:XX HOBBY
MA1 A.Judge/D.Mattingly 1.50 4.00
MA2 R.Devers/D.Ortiz .75 2.00
MA3 Y.Alvarez/J.Bagwell 4.00 10.00
MA4 G.Lux/C.Bellinger 2.00 5.00
MA5 P.Alonso/J.deGrom 1.50 4.00
MA6 L.Robert/F.Thomas 3.00 8.00
MA7 F.Tatis Jr./T.Gwynn 3.00 8.00
MA8 W.Buehler/C.Kershaw 1.00 2.50
MA9 R.Alomar/B.Bichette 3.00 8.00
MA10 K.Bryant/R.Santo .75 2.00

2020 Topps Gallery Master and Apprentice Blue

*BLUE/99: 1.2X TO 3X BASIC
STATED ODDS 1:XX HOBBY
STATED PRINT RUN 99 SER.#'d SETS
MA1 A.Judge/D.Mattingly 15.00 40.00
MA5 P.Alonso/J.deGrom 15.00 40.00
MA7 F.Tatis Jr./T.Gwynn 20.00 50.00
MA8 W.Buehler/C.Kershaw 6.00 15.00

2020 Topps Gallery Master and Apprentice Green

MA1 A.Judge/D.Mattingly 10.00 25.00
MA7 F.Tatis Jr./T.Gwynn 6.00 15.00
MA8 W.Buehler/C.Kershaw 4.00 10.00

2020 Topps Gallery Master and Apprentice Orange

*ORANGE/25: 2X TO 5X BASIC
MA1 A.Judge/D.Mattingly 25.00 60.00
MA3 Y.Alvarez/J.Bagwell 25.00 60.00
MA5 P.Alonso/J.deGrom 25.00 60.00
MA6 L.Robert/F.Thomas 5.00 120.00
MA7 F.Tatis Jr./T.Gwynn 30.00 80.00
MA8 W.Buehler/C.Kershaw 10.00 25.00

2020 Topps Gallery Modern Artists

STATED ODDS 1:XX HOBBY
MP1 Mike Trout 3.00 8.00
MP2 Ronald Acuna Jr. 2.50 6.00
MP3 Vladimir Guerrero Jr. 1.00 2.50
MP4 Juan Soto 2.00 5.00
MP5 Fernando Tatis Jr. 3.00 8.00
MP6 Kris Bryant .75 2.00
MP7 Bo Bichette 3.00 8.00
MP8 Aristides Aquino 1.00 2.50
MP9 Gavin Lux 2.00 5.00
MP10 Gleyber Torres 1.25 3.00
MP11 Alex Bregman .60 1.50
MP12 Nolan Arenado 1.00 2.50
MP13 Yordan Alvarez 4.00 10.00
MP14 Pete Alonso 1.50 4.00
MP15 Ozzie Albies .60 1.50
MP16 Rafael Devers .75 2.00
MP17 Shane Bieber .60 1.50
MP18 Jack Flaherty .60 1.50
MP19 Shohei Ohtani 1.00 2.50
MP20 Walker Buehler .75 2.00
MP21 Francisco Lindor .60 1.50
MP22 Javier Baez .75 2.00
MP23 Eloy Jimenez 1.25 3.00
MP24 Cody Bellinger 1.25 3.00
MP25 Jesus Luzardo .75 2.00
MP26 Mookie Betts 1.25 3.00
MP27 Aaron Judge 1.50 4.00
MP28 Luis Robert 3.00 8.00
MP29 Matt Chapman .60 1.50
MP30 Christian Yelich .75 2.00

2020 Topps Gallery Modern Artists Blue

MP1 Mike Trout 15.00 40.00
MP5 Fernando Tatis Jr. 12.00 30.00
MP28 Luis Robert 15.00 40.00

2020 Topps Gallery Modern Artists Green

*GREEN/250: .8X TO 2X BASIC
STATED ODDS 1:XX HOBBY
STATED PRINT RUN 250 SER.#'d SETS
MP1 Mike Trout 10.00 25.00
MP5 Fernando Tatis Jr. 8.00 20.00
MP28 Luis Robert 10.00 25.00

2020 Topps Gallery Modern Artists Orange

*ORANGE/25: 2X TO 5X BASIC
MP1 Mike Trout 25.00 60.00
MP5 Fernando Tatis Jr. 25.00 60.00
MP28 Luis Robert 25.00 60.00

2003 Topps Gallery HOF

COMPLETE SET (74) 15.00 40.00
COMMON CARD (1-74) .25 .60
COMMON VARIATION (1-74) .40 1.00
VARIATION STATED ODDS 1:1
VARIATIONS LISTED WITH B SUFFIX
1 Willie Mays Bleachers 1.25 3.00
1B Willie Mays Gold 2.00 5.00
2 Al Kaline Stripes .40 1.00
2B Al Kaline No Stripes .60 1.50
3 Hank Aaron Black Hat 1.25 3.00
3B Hank Aaron Blue Hat 2.00 5.00
4 Carl Yastrzemski Black Ltr 1.00 2.50
4B Carl Yastrzemski Red Ltr 1.50 4.00
5 Luis Aparicio Wood Bat .40 1.00
5B Luis Aparicio Black Bat .60 1.50
6 Sam Crawford Grey Uni .40 1.00
6B Sam Crawford Navy Uni .60 1.50
7 Tom Lasorda Trees .40 1.00
7B Tom Lasorda Red .60 1.50
8 John McGraw MG No Logo .40 1.00
8B John McGraw MG NY Logo .60 1.50
9 Edd Roush White C .40 1.00
9B Edd Roush Red C .60 1.50
10 Reggie Jackson Grass .40 1.00
10B Reggie Jackson Red .60 1.50
11 Catfish Hunter Yellow Jsy .40 1.00
11B Catfish Hunter White Jsy .60 1.50
12 Roberto Clemente White Uni 1.50 4.00
12B Roberto Clemente Yellow Uni 2.50 6.00
13 Eddie Collins Grey Uni .40 1.00
13B Eddie Collins Navy Uni .60 1.50
14 Frankie Frisch Olive .40 1.00
14B Frankie Frisch Blue .60 1.50
15 Nolan Ryan Leather Glv 2.00 5.00
15B Nolan Ryan Black Glv 3.00 8.00
16 Brooks Robinson Yellow .40 1.00
16B Brooks Robinson Green .60 1.50
17 Phil Niekro Black Hat .40 1.00
17B Phil Niekro Blue Hat .60 1.50
18 Joe Cronin Blue Sleeve .25 .60
18B Joe Cronin White Sleeve .40 1.00
19 Joe Tinker White Hat .40 1.00
19B Joe Tinker Blue Hat .60 1.50
20 Johnny Bench Day .60 1.50
20B Johnny Bench Night 1.00 2.50
21 Harry Heilmann Day .40 1.00
21B Harry Heilmann Night .60 1.50
22 Ernie Harwell BRD Red Tie .40 1.00
22B Ernie Harwell BRD Blue Tie .60 1.50
23 Warren Spahn Patch .40 1.00
23B Warren Spahn No Patch .60 1.50
24 George Kelly Blue Bill .25 .60
24B George Kelly Red Bill .40 1.00
25 Phil Rizzuto Bleachers .40 1.00
25B Phil Rizzuto Green .60 1.50
26 Robin Roberts Day .40 1.00
26B Robin Roberts Night .60 1.50
27 Ozzie Smith Red Sleeve .75 2.00
27B Ozzie Smith Blue Sleeve 1.25 3.00
28 Jim Palmer White Hat .40 1.00
28B Jim Palmer Black Hat .60 1.50
29 Duke Snider No Patch .40 1.00
29B Duke Snider Flag Patch .60 1.50
30 Bob Feller White Uni .40 1.00
30B Bob Feller Grey Uni .60 1.50
31 Buck Leonard Bleachers .25 .60
31B Buck Leonard Red .40 1.00
32 Kirby Puckett Wood Bat .60 1.50
32B Kirby Puckett Black Bat 1.00 2.50
33 Monte Irvin Black Sleeve .40 1.00
33B Monte Irvin White Sleeve .60 1.50
34 Chuck Klein Black Socks .25 .60
34B Chuck Klein Red Socks .40 1.00

35 Willie Stargell Yellow Uni .40 1.00
35B Willie Stargell White Uni .60 1.50
36 Juan Marichal Ballpark .40 1.00
36B Juan Marichal Gold .60 1.50
37 Lou Brock Day .40 1.00
37B Lou Brock Night .60 1.50
38 Bucky Harris Black W .25 .60
38B Bucky Harris Red W .40 1.00
39 Bobby Doerr Ballpark .40 1.00
39B Bobby Doerr Red .60 1.50
40 Lee MacPhail Blue Tie .25 .60
40B Lee MacPhail Red Tie .40 1.00
41 Heinie Manush Grey Sleeve .25 .60
41B Heinie Manush Navy Sleeve .40 1.00
42 George Brett Patch 1.25 3.00
42B George Brett No Patch 2.00 5.00
43 Harmon Killebrew Blue Hat .60 1.50
43B Harmon Killebrew Red Hat 1.00 2.50
44 Whitey Ford Day .40 1.00
44B Whitey Ford Night .60 1.50
45 Eddie Mathews Day .60 1.50
45B Eddie Mathews Night 1.00 2.50
46 Gaylord Perry Leather Glv .40 1.00
46B Gaylord Perry Black Glv .60 1.50
47 Red Schoendienst Stripes .40 1.00
47B Red Schoendienst No Stripes .60 1.50
48 Earl Weaver MG Day .40 1.00
48B Earl Weaver MG Night .60 1.50
49 Joe Morgan Day .40 1.00
49B Joe Morgan Night .60 1.50
50 Mike Schmidt Grey Uni 1.00 2.50
50B Mike Schmidt White Uni 1.50 4.00
51 Willie McCovey Wood Bat .40 1.00
51B Willie McCovey Black Bat .60 1.50
52 Stan Musial Day 1.00 2.50
52B Stan Musial Night 1.50 4.00
53 Don Sutton Ballpark .40 1.00
53B Don Sutton Gray .60 1.50
54 Hank Greenberg w/Player .60 1.50
54B Hank Greenberg No Player 1.00 2.50
55 Robin Yount w/Player .60 1.50
55B Robin Yount No Player 1.00 2.50
56 Tom Seaver Leather Glv .40 1.00
56B Tom Seaver Black Glv .60 1.50
57 Tony Perez Wood Bat .40 1.00
57B Tony Perez Black Bat .60 1.50
58 George Sisler w/Ad .40 1.00
58B George Sisler No Ad .60 1.50
59 Jim Bottomley White Hat .25 .60
59B Jim Bottomley Red Hat .40 1.00
60 Yogi Berra Leather Chest .60 1.50
60B Yogi Berra Navy Chest 1.00 2.50
61 Fred Lindstrom Blue Bill .25 .60
61B Fred Lindstrom Red Bill .40 1.00
62 Napoleon Lajoie White Uni .60 1.50
62B Napoleon Lajoie Navy Uni 1.00 2.50
63 Frank Robinson Wood Bat .40 1.00
63B Frank Robinson Black Bat .60 1.50
64 Carlton Fisk Red Ltr .40 1.00
64B Carlton Fisk Black Ltr .60 1.50
65 Orlando Cepeda Blue Sky .40 1.00
65B Orlando Cepeda Sunset .60 1.50
66 Fergie Jenkins Leather Glv .40 1.00
66B Fergie Jenkins Black Glv .60 1.50
67 Ernie Banks Day .60 1.50
67B Ernie Banks Night 1.00 2.50
68 Bill Mazeroski No Sleeves .40 1.00
68B Bill Mazeroski w/Sleeves .60 1.50
69 Jim Bunning Grey Uni .40 1.00
69B Jim Bunning White Uni .60 1.50
70 Rollie Fingers Day .40 1.00
70B Rollie Fingers Night .60 1.50
71 Jimmie Foxx Black Sleeve .60 1.50
71B Jimmie Foxx White Sleeve 1.00 2.50
72 Rod Carew Red Btg Glv .40 1.00
72B Rod Carew Blue Btg Glv .60 1.50
73 Sparky Anderson Blue Sky .40 1.00
73B Sparky Anderson Yellow .60 1.50
74 George Kell Red D .40 1.00
74B George Kell White D .60 1.50

2003 Topps Gallery HOF Artist's Proofs

COMPLETE SET (74) 60.00 150.00
*ARTIST'S PROOFS: .75X TO 2X BASIC
STATED ODDS 1:1
*VARIATIONS: 2X TO 5X BASIC VAR
VARIATION STATED ODDS 1:20
AP'S FEATURE SILVER HOLO-FOIL

2003 Topps Gallery HOF Accent Mark Autographs

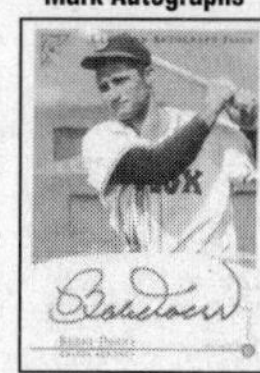

GROUP A ODDS 1:3446
GROUP B ODDS 1:2074
GROUP C ODDS 1:1483
GROUP D ODDS 1:1149
GROUP E ODDS 1:941
GROUP F ODDS 1:545
ARTIST'S PROOFS ODDS 1:1723
ARTIST'S PROOFS PRINT RUN 25 #'d SETS
NO AP PRICING DUE TO SCARCITY
AP'S FEATURE SILVER HOLO-FOIL
BD Bobby Doerr B 12.00 30.00
LM Lee MacPhail D 50.00 100.00
RR Robin Roberts E 15.00 40.00
RS Red Schoendienst C 15.00 40.00
WS Warren Spahn F 15.00 40.00
YB Yogi Berra A 40.00 100.00

2003 Topps Gallery HOF ARTifact Relics

BAT GROUP A ODDS 1:1812
BAT GROUP B ODDS 1:469
BAT GROUP C ODDS 1:242
BAT GROUP D ODDS 1:111
BAT GROUP E ODDS 1:96
BAT GROUP F ODDS 1:28
BAT GROUP G ODDS 1:62
JSY/UNI GROUP A ODDS 1:1812
JSY/UNI GROUP B ODDS 1:2353
JSY/UNI GROUP C ODDS 1:728
JSY/UNI GROUP D ODDS 1:151
JSY/UNI GROUP E ODDS 1:145
ARTIST'S PROOFS BAT ODDS 1:345
ARTIST'S PROOFS JSY/UNI ODDS 1:967
ARTIST'S PROOFS PRINT RUN 25 #'d SETS
NO AP PRICING DUE TO SCARCITY
AP'S FEATURE SILVER HOLO-FOIL
AK Al Kaline Bat F 2.50 6.00
BD Bobby Doerr Jsy D 2.50 6.00
BH Bucky Harris Bat F 6.00 15.00
BR Babe Ruth Bat B 75.00 200.00
BRO Brooks Robinson Bat D 2.50 6.00
CF Carlton Fisk Bat G 2.50 6.00
CK Chuck Klein Bat F 6.00 15.00
CY Carl Yastrzemski Bat F 6.00 15.00
DS Duke Snider Bat F 2.50 6.00
DSU Don Sutton Bat D 2.50 6.00
EB Ernie Banks Uni B 25.00 60.00
EC Eddie Collins Bat B 2.50 6.00
EM Eddie Mathews Jsy A 50.00 120.00
ER Edd Roush Bat B 50.00 120.00
FF Frankie Frisch Bat E 10.00 25.00
FR Frank Robinson Bat G 2.50 6.00
GB George Brett Jsy D 8.00 20.00
GK George Kelly Bat D 6.00 15.00
GP Gaylord Perry Uni E 2.50 6.00
GS George Sisler Bat F 6.00 15.00
HA Hank Aaron Bat F 10.00 25.00
HG Hank Greenberg Bat D 10.00 25.00
HH Harry Heilmann Bat B 2.50 6.00
HK Harmon Killebrew Jsy E 4.00 10.00
HM Heinie Manush Bat B 1.50 4.00
HW Honus Wagner Bat A 200.00 400.00
HWI Hoyt Wilhelm Uni D 2.50 6.00
JB Jim Bottomley Bat E 6.00 15.00
JBE Johnny Bench Bat G 4.00 10.00
JF Jimmie Foxx Bat A 150.00 250.00
JM Joe Morgan Bat E 2.50 6.00
JP Jim Palmer Jsy A 25.00 60.00
JR Jackie Robinson Bat C 12.00 30.00
JT Joe Tinker Bat E 2.50 6.00
KP Kirby Puckett Bat E 4.00 10.00
LA Luis Aparicio Bat A 25.00 60.00
LB Lou Brock Bat A 75.00 200.00
LG Lou Gehrig Bat C 60.00 150.00
MS Mike Schmidt Uni E 8.00 20.00
NR Nolan Ryan Bat C 12.00 30.00
OC Orlando Cepeda Bat F 2.50 6.00
OS Ozzie Smith Bat E 5.00 12.00
PN Phil Niekro Uni D 2.50 6.00
PW Paul Waner Bat C 10.00 25.00
RCA Rod Carew Jsy E 2.50 6.00
RJ Reggie Jackson Bat F 2.50 6.00
RY Robin Yount Bat F 8.00 20.00
SA Sparky Anderson Uni A 12.00 30.00
SC Sam Crawford Bat D 10.00 25.00
SM Stan Musial Bat D 10.00 25.00
TC Ty Cobb Bat C 40.00 100.00
TLA Tom Lasorda Jsy A 60.00 150.00
TP Tony Perez Bat F 2.50 6.00
TS Tom Seaver Bat C 2.50 6.00
WM Willie Mays Jsy C 15.00 40.00
WMC Willie McCovey Bat F 2.50 6.00
WS Willie Stargell Jsy C 2.50 6.00

2003 Topps Gallery HOF ARTifact Relics Autographs

GROUP A ODDS 1:3446
GROUP B ODDS 1:691
GROUP C ODDS 1:691
ARTIST'S PROOFS ODDS 1:941
ARTIST'S PROOFS PRINT RUN 25 #'d SETS
NO AP PRICING DUE TO SCARCITY
AP'S FEATURE SILVER HOLO-FOIL
AK Al Kaline Bat C 25.00 50.00
BD Bobby Doerr Jsy C 20.00 50.00
BRO Brooks Robinson Bat C 40.00 80.00
DS Duke Snider Bat B 40.00 80.00
HK Harmon Killebrew Jsy B 40.00 100.00
JM Joe Morgan Bat B 20.00 50.00

2003 Topps Gallery HOF Currency Connection Coin Relics

STATED ODDS ONE PER BOX
BF B.Feller 1945 Dime B 10.00 25.00
BR B.Ruth 1916 Dime A 20.00 50.00
EB E.Banks 1958 Penny B 12.00 30.00
HG H.Greenberg 1945 Nickel B 10.00 25.00
JR J.Robinson 1946 Dime B 12.00 30.00
LG L.Gehrig 1938 Nickel A 12.00 30.00
OC O.Cepeda 1958 Penny B 8.00 20.00
SM S.Musial 1943 Penny B 12.00 30.00
TC T.Cobb 1909 Penny A 12.00 30.00
WM W.Mays 1958 Penny B 10.00 25.00
WMA W.Mays 1954 Nickel B 10.00 25.00
WMC W.McCovey 1959 Penny B 8.00 20.00

1998 Topps Gold Label Pre-Production

COMPLETE SET (3) 2.50 6.00
PP1 Vinny Castilla .20 .50
PP2 Ken Griffey Jr. 1.25 3.00
PP3 Mike Piazza 1.25 3.00

1998 Topps Gold Label Class 1

This 150 standard-size set was issued in many different confusing versions. The basic Class 1 set is a gold set featuring fielding poses in the background. The SRP of these packs were $3 each and the packs contained three cards wiith 24 packs in a box and 8 boxes in a case. The HTA packs contained five cards and the SRP packs on those packs were $5, keeping both packs at $1 per card.

COMP.GOLD SET (100) 20.00 50.00
1 Kevin Brown .30 .75
2 Greg Maddux .75 2.00
3 Albert Belle .20 .50
4 Andres Galarraga .20 .50
5 Craig Biggio .30 .75
6 Matt Williams .20 .50
7 Derek Jeter 1.25 3.00
8 Randy Johnson .50 1.25
9 Jay Bell .20 .50
10 Jim Thome .30 .75
11 Roberto Alomar .30 .75
12 Tom Glavine .30 .75
13 Reggie Sanders .20 .50
14 Tony Gwynn .60 1.50
15 Mark McGwire 1.25 3.00
16 Jeromy Burnitz .20 .50
17 Andruw Jones .30 .75
18 Jay Buhner .20 .50
19 Robin Ventura .20 .50
20 Jeff Bagwell .30 .75
21 Roger Clemens 1.00 2.50
22 Masato Yoshii RC .25 .60
23 Travis Fryman .20 .50
24 Rafael Palmeiro .30 .75
25 Alex Rodriguez .75 2.00
26 Sandy Alomar Jr. .20 .50
27 Chipper Jones .50 1.25
28 Rusty Greer .20 .50
29 Cal Ripken 1.50 4.00
30 Tony Clark .20 .50
31 Derek Bell .20 .50
32 Fred McGriff .30 .75
33 Paul O'Neill .30 .75
34 Moises Alou .20 .50
35 Henry Rodriguez .20 .50
36 Steve Finley .20 .50
37 Marquis Grissom .20 .50
38 Jason Giambi .20 .50
39 Javy Lopez .20 .50
40 Damion Easley .20 .50
41 Mariano Rivera .50 1.25
42 Mo Vaughn .20 .50
43 Mike Mussina .30 .75
44 Jason Kendall .20 .50
45 Pedro Martinez .30 .75
46 Frank Thomas .50 1.25
47 Jim Edmonds .20 .50
48 Hideki Irabu .20 .50
49 Eric Karros .20 .50
50 Juan Gonzalez .20 .50
51 Ellis Burks .20 .50
52 Dean Palmer .20 .50
53 Scott Rolen .30 .75
54 Raul Mondesi .20 .50
55 Quinton McCracken .20 .50
56 John Olerud .20 .50
57 Ken Caminiti .20 .50
58 Brian Jordan .20 .50
59 Wade Boggs .30 .75
60 Mike Piazza .75 2.00
61 Darin Erstad .20 .50
62 Curt Schilling .20 .50
63 David Justice .20 .50
64 Kenny Lofton .20 .50
65 Barry Bonds 1.25 3.00
66 Ray Lankford .20 .50
67 Brian Hunter .20 .50
68 Chuck Knoblauch .20 .50
69 Vinny Castilla .20 .50
70 Vladimir Guerrero .50 1.25
71 Tim Salmon .30 .75
72 Larry Walker .20 .50
73 Paul Molitor .20 .50
74 Barry Larkin .30 .75
75 Edgar Martinez .30 .75
76 Bernie Williams .30 .75
77 Dante Bichette .20 .50
78 Nomar Garciaparra .75 2.00
79 Ben Grieve .20 .50
80 Ivan Rodriguez .30 .75
81 Todd Helton .30 .75
82 Ryan Klesko .20 .50
83 Sammy Sosa .50 1.25
84 Travis Lee .20 .50
85 Jose Cruz Jr. .20 .50
86 Mark Kotsay .20 .50
87 Richard Hidalgo .20 .50
88 Rondell White .20 .50
89 Greg Vaughn .20 .50
90 Gary Sheffield .20 .50
91 Paul Konerko .20 .50
92 Mark Grace .30 .75
93 Kevin Millwood RC .60 1.50
94 Manny Ramirez .30 .75
95 Tino Martinez .30 .75
96 Brad Fullmer .20 .50
97 Todd Walker .20 .50
98 Carlos Delgado .20 .50
99 Kerry Wood .25 .60
100 Ken Griffey Jr. 1.00 2.50

1998 Topps Gold Label Class 1 Black

*CLASS 1 BLACK: 3X TO 8X C1 GOLD
STATED ODDS 1:8

1998 Topps Gold Label Class 1 Red

*CLASS 1 RED: 12X TO 30X C1 GOLD
*CLASS 1 RED RC'S: 12X TO 30X C1 GOLD
STATED ODDS 1:99
STATED PRINT RUN 100 SERIAL #'d SETS

1998 Topps Gold Label Class 1 One to One

RANDOM INSERTS IN PACKS
STATED PRINT RUN 1 SERIAL #'d SET
BLACK, GOLD AND RED VERSIONS EXIST
NINE VERSIONS OF EACH 1 OF 1 EXIST
NO PRICING DUE TO SCARCITY

1998 Topps Gold Label Class 2

COMP.GOLD SET (100) 75.00 150.00
CLASS 2 GOLD STATED ODDS 1:2
CLASS 2 BLACK STATED ODDS 1:16
CLASS 2 RED STATED ODDS 1:198
CLASS 2 RED PRINT RUN 50 SERIAL #'d SETS
CLASS 2: SPARKLING SILVER TEXT ON FRONT

1998 Topps Gold Label Class 3

COMP.GOLD SET (100) 125.00 250.00
COMMON CARD (1-100) .75 2.00
GOLD STATED ODDS 1:4
CLASS 3 BLACK STATED ODDS 1:32
CLASS 3 RED STATED ODDS 1:396
CLASS 3 RED PRINT RUN 25 SERIAL #'d SETS
CLASS 3: SPARKLING GOLD TEXT ON FRONT

1998 Topps Gold Label Home Run Race

COMPLETE SET (4) 6.00 15.00
STATED ODDS 1:12 HTA
*BLACK HR: 1.25X TO 3X GOLD HR
BLACK HR STATED ODDS 1:48
*RED HR: 4X TO 10X GOLD HR
RED HR STATED ODDS 1:4055 HTA
RED HR STATED PRINT RUN 61 SETS
HR1 Roger Maris 2.00 5.00
HR2 Mark McGwire 3.00 8.00
HR3 Ken Griffey Jr. 4.00 10.00
HR4 Sammy Sosa 2.00 5.00

1999 Topps Gold Label Class 1

This 100-card set was distributed in four-card packs with a suggested retail price of $3.99. The set features color action player photos printed with spectral reflective rainbow technology on 35-point card stock. Three different versions of the cards were produced each having the same foreground player photo but a different background photo. This Class 1 set carried a Fielding background player photo or a Set Position photo for pitchers.

COMP.GOLD SET (100) 15.00 40.00
1 Mike Piazza .75 2.00
2 Andres Galarraga .20 .50
3 Mark Grace .30 .75
4 Tony Clark .20 .50
5 Jim Thome .30 .75
6 Tony Gwynn .60 1.50
7 Kelly Dransfeldt RC .20 .50
8 Eric Chavez .20 .50
9 Brian Jordan .20 .50
10 Todd Hundley .20 .50
11 Rondell White .20 .50
12 Dmitri Young .20 .50
13 Jeff Kent .20 .50
14 Derek Bell .20 .50
15 Todd Helton .30 .75
16 Chipper Jones .50 1.25
17 Albert Belle .20 .50
18 Barry Larkin .30 .75
19 Dante Bichette .20 .50
20 Gary Sheffield .20 .50
21 Cliff Floyd .20 .50
22 Derek Jeter 1.25 3.00
23 Jason Giambi .20 .50
24 Ray Lankford .20 .50
25 Alex Rodriguez .75 2.00
26 Ruben Mateo .20 .50
27 Wade Boggs .30 .75
28 Carlos Delgado .20 .50
29 Tim Salmon .30 .75
30 Alfonso Soriano RC 2.50 6.00
31 Javy Lopez .20 .50
32 Jason Kendall .20 .50
33 Nick Johnson RC .60 1.50
34 A.J. Burnett RC .50 1.25
35 Troy Glaus .30 .75
36 Pat Burrell RC 1.00 2.50
37 Jeff Cirillo .20 .50
38 David Justice .20 .50
39 Ivan Rodriguez .30 .75
40 Bernie Williams .30 .75
41 Jay Buhner .20 .50
42 Mo Vaughn .20 .50
43 Randy Johnson .50 1.25
44 Pedro Martinez .30 .75
45 Larry Walker .20 .50
46 Todd Walker .20 .50
47 Roberto Alomar .30 .75
48 Kevin Brown .30 .75
49 Mike Mussina .30 .75
50 Tom Glavine .30 .75
51 Curt Schilling .20 .50
52 Ken Caminiti .20 .50
53 Brad Fullmer .20 .50
54 Bobby Seay RC .20 .50
55 Orlando Hernandez .20 .50
56 Sean Casey .20 .50
57 Al Leiter .20 .50
58 Sandy Alomar Jr. .20 .50
59 Mark Kotsay .20 .50
60 Matt Williams .20 .50
61 Raul Mondesi .20 .50
62 Joe Crede RC 3.00 8.00
63 Jim Edmonds .20 .50
64 Jose Cruz Jr. .20 .50
65 Juan Gonzalez .20 .50
66 Sammy Sosa .50 1.25
67 Cal Ripken 1.50 4.00
68 Vinny Castilla .20 .50
69 Craig Biggio .30 .75
70 Mark McGwire 1.25 3.00
71 Greg Vaughn .20 .50
72 Greg Maddux .75 2.00
73 Paul O'Neill .30 .75
74 Scott Rolen .30 .75
75 Ben Grieve .20 .50
76 Vladimir Guerrero .50 1.25
77 John Olerud .20 .50
78 Eric Karros .20 .50
79 Jeromy Burnitz .20 .50
80 Jeff Bagwell .30 .75
81 Kenny Lofton .20 .50
82 Manny Ramirez .30 .75
83 Andruw Jones .30 .75
84 Travis Lee .20 .50
85 Darin Erstad .20 .50
86 Nomar Garciaparra .75 2.00
87 Frank Thomas .50 1.25
88 Moises Alou .20 .50
89 Tino Martinez .30 .75
90 Carlos Pena RC .25 .60
91 Shawn Green .20 .50
92 Rusty Greer .20 .50
93 Matt Belisle RC .20 .50
94 Adrian Beltre .20 .50
95 Roger Clemens 1.00 2.50
96 John Smoltz .30 .75
97 Mark Mulder RC .75 2.00
98 Kerry Wood .20 .50
99 Barry Bonds 1.25 3.00
100 Ken Griffey Jr. 1.00 2.50

1999 Topps Gold Label Class 1 Black

*C1 BLACK: 1.5X TO 4X C1 GOLD
*C1 BLACK RC's: 1X TO 2.5X C1 GOLD
STATED ODDS 1:12 RETAIL, 1:8 HTA
62 Joe Crede 4.00 10.00

1999 Topps Gold Label Class 1 Red

*CLASS 1 RED: 8X TO 20X C1 GOLD
*CLASS 1 RED RC'S: 4X TO 10X C1 GOLD
STATED ODDS 1:148 RETAIL, 1:118 HTA
STATED PRINT RUN 100 SERIAL #'d SETS
62 Joe Crede 12.50 30.00

1999 Topps Gold Label Class 2

COMP.GOLD SET (100) 75.00 150.00
*CLASS 2 GOLD: X TO X CLASS 1 GOLD
CLASS 2 GOLD ODDS 1:4 RETAIL, 1:2 HTA

1999 Topps Gold Label Class 2 Black

*C2 BLACK: 1.5X TO 4X C2 GOLD
*C2 BLACK RC'S: 1X TO 2.5X C2 GOLD
STATED ODDS 1:24 RETAIL, 1:16 HTA
62 Joe Crede 6.00 15.00

1999 Topps Gold Label Class 2 Red

*C2 RED: 6X TO 15X C2 GOLD
*C2 RED RC'S: 4X TO 10X C2 GOLD
STATED ODDS 1:296 RETAIL, 1:237 HTA
STATED PRINT RUN 50 SERIAL #'d SETS
62 Joe Crede 20.00 50.00

1999 Topps Gold Label Class 3

COMP.GOLD SET (100) 125.00 250.00
*CLASS 3 GOLD: 1.5X TO 4X CLASS 1 GOLD
GOLD STATED ODDS 1:8 RETAIL, 1:4 HTA

1999 Topps Gold Label Class 3 Black

*C3 BLACK: 1.5X TO 4X C3 GOLD
*C3 BLACK RC'S: .1X TO 2.5X C3 GOLD
STATED ODDS 1:48 RETAIL, 1:32 HTA
62 Joe Crede 10.00 25.00

1999 Topps Gold Label Class 3 Red

*C3 RED: 6X TO 15X C3 GOLD
STATED ODDS 1:591 RETAIL, 1:473 HTA
STATED PRINT RUN 25 SERIAL #'d SETS
NO C3 RED RC PRICING DUE TO SCARCITY

1999 Topps Gold Label Race to Aaron

COMPLETE SET (10) 25.00 60.00
STATED ODDS 1:20 RETAIL, 1:12 HTA
*BLACK: 1X TO 2.5X BASIC RACE TO AARON
BLACK ODDS 1:80 RETAIL, 1:48 HTA
*RED: 8X TO 20X BASIC RACETO AARON
RED ODDS 1:3343 RETAIL, 1:2695 HTA
RED PRINT RUN 44 SERIAL #'d SETS
AARON ONE TO ONE PARALLELS EXIST
1 TO 1'S NOT PRICED DUE TO SCARCITY
RA1 Mark McGwire 4.00 10.00
RA2 Ken Griffey Jr. 3.00 8.00
RA3 Alex Rodriguez 2.50 6.00
RA4 Vladimir Guerrero 1.50 4.00
RA5 Albert Belle .60 1.50
RA6 Nomar Garciaparra 2.50 6.00
RA7 Ken Griffey Jr. 3.00 8.00
RA8 Alex Rodriguez 2.50 6.00
RA9 Juan Gonzalez .60 1.50
RA10 Barry Bonds 4.00 10.00

2000 Topps Gold Label Pre-Production

COMPLETE SET (3) 4.00 10.00
COMMON CARD (PP1-PP3) 1.25 3.00

2000 Topps Gold Label Class 1

COMPLETE SET (100) 25.00 60.00
COMMON CARD (1-100) .20 .50
COMMON RC .20 .50
1 Sammy Sosa .50 1.25
2 Greg Maddux .60 1.50
3 Mark Quinn .20 .50
4 Rondell White .20 .50
5 Fernando Tatis .20 .50
6 Troy Glaus .20 .50
7 Nick Johnson .20 .50
8 Albert Belle .20 .50
9 Scott Rolen .30 .75
10 Rafael Palmeiro .30 .75
11 Tony Gwynn .50 1.25
12 Kevin Brown .20 .50
13 Roberto Alomar .30 .75
14 John Olerud .20 .50
15 Rick Ankiel .30 .75
16 Chipper Jones .50 1.25
17 Craig Biggio .30 .75
18 Mark Mulder .20 .50
19 Carlos Delgado .20 .50
20 Alex Gonzalez .20 .50
21 Gabe Kapler .20 .50
22 Derek Jeter 1.25 3.00
23 Carlos Beltran .30 .75
24 Todd Helton .30 .75
25 Mark McGwire .75 2.00
26 Ben Grieve .20 .50
27 Rafael Furcal .30 .75
28 Vernon Wells .20 .50
29 Greg Vaughn .20 .50
30 Vladimir Guerrero .30 .75
31 Mike Piazza .50 1.25
32 Roger Clemens .60 1.50
33 Barry Larkin .30 .75
34 Pedro Martinez .30 .75
35 Matt Williams .20 .50
36 Mo Vaughn .20 .50
37 Tim Hudson .30 .75
38 Andruw Jones .20 .50
39 Vinny Castilla .20 .50
40 Frank Thomas .50 1.25
41 Pokey Reese .20 .50
42 Corey Patterson .20 .50
43 Jeromy Burnitz .20 .50
44 Preston Wilson .20 .50
45 Juan Gonzalez .20 .50
46 Brian Giles .20 .50
47 Todd Walker .20 .50
48 Magglio Ordonez .30 .75
49 Alfonso Soriano .50 1.25
50 Ken Griffey Jr. 1.00 2.50
51 Michael Barrett .20 .50
52 Shawn Green .20 .50
53 Erubiel Durazo .20 .50
54 Adam Piatt .20 .50
55 Pat Burrell .20 .50
56 Mike Mussina .30 .75
57 Bernie Williams .30 .75
58 Sean Casey .20 .50
59 Randy Johnson .50 1.25
60 Jeff Bagwell .30 .75
61 Eric Chavez .20 .50
62 Josh Hamilton .60 1.50
63 A.J. Burnett .20 .50
64 Jim Thome .30 .75
65 Raul Mondesi .20 .50
66 Jason Kendall .20 .50
67 Mike Lieberthal .20 .50
68 Robin Ventura .20 .50
69 Ivan Rodriguez .30 .75
70 Larry Walker .30 .75
71 Eric Munson .20 .50
72 Brian Jordan .20 .50
73 Edgardo Alfonzo .20 .50
74 Curt Schilling .30 .75
75 Nomar Garciaparra .30 .75
76 Mark Grace .30 .75
77 Shannon Stewart .20 .50
78 J.D. Drew .20 .50
79 Jack Cust .20 .50
80 Cal Ripken 1.50 4.00
81 Bob Abreu .20 .50
82 Ruben Mateo .20 .50
83 Orlando Hernandez .20 .50
84 Kris Benson .20 .50
85 Barry Bonds .75 2.00
86 Manny Ramirez .50 1.25
87 Jose Canseco .30 .75
88 Sean Burroughs .20 .50
89 Kevin Millwood .20 .50
90 Alex Rodriguez .60 1.50
91 Brett Myers RC .60 1.50
92 Rick Asadoorian RC .20 .50
93 Ben Christensen RC .20 .50
94 Bobby Bradley RC .20 .50
95 Chris Wakeland RC .20 .50
96 Brad Baisley RC .20 .50
97 Aaron McNeal RC .20 .50
98 Aaron Rowand RC 1.00 2.50
99 Scott Downs RC .20 .50
100 Michael Tejera RC .20 .50

2000 Topps Gold Label Class 1 Gold

*CLASS 1 GKD: 8X TO 20X BASIC
STATED ODDS 1:68 H/R, 1:101 HTA
STATED PRINT RUN 100 SERIAL #'d SETS

2000 Topps Gold Label Class 2

COMPLETE SET (100) 25.00 60.00
*CLASS 2: .4X TO 1X CLASS 1
CLASS 2 IS SAME QTY AS CLASS 1

2000 Topps Gold Label Class 2 Gold

*CLASS 2 GLD: 8X TO 20X BASIC
STATED ODDS 1:68 H/R, 1:101 HTA
STATED PRINT RUN 100 SERIAL #'d SETS

2000 Topps Gold Label Class 3

COMPLETE SET (100) 25.00 60.00
*CLASS 3: .4X TO 1X CLASS 1
CLASS 3 IS SAME QTY AS CLASS 1

2000 Topps Gold Label Class 3 Gold

*CLASS 3 GLD: 8X TO 20X BASIC
STATED ODDS 1:68 H/R, 1:101 HTA
STATED PRINT RUN 100 SERIAL #'d SETS

2000 Topps Gold Label Bullion

STATED ODDS 1:32
ONE TO ONE PRINT RUN 1 SERIAL #'d SET
ONE TO ONE NO PRICING DUE TO SCARCITY
B1 Thome 2.00 5.00
M.Ramirez/Alomar
B2 Jeter 5.00 12.00
O.Hern/B.Williams
B3 C.Jones 2.50 6.00
A.Jones/Maddux
B4 A.Rod 2.50 6.00
Buhner/Olerud
B5 Garciaparra 1.25 3.00
P.Mart/Daub
B6 McGwire 3.00 8.00
Drew/Ankiel
B7 Sosa 2.00 5.00
Grace/Wood
B8 Griffey Jr. 4.00 10.00
Casey/Larkin
B9 Piazza 2.00 5.00
Alfonzo/Ventura
B10 R.Johnson 2.00 5.00
M.Will/Durazo

2000 Topps Gold Label End of the Rainbow

COMPLETE SET (15) 5.00 12.00
STATED ODDS 1:7
ONE TO ONE PRINT RUN 1 SERIAL #'d SET
ONE TO ONE NO PRICING DUE TO SCARCITY
ER1 Pat Burrell .40 1.00
ER2 Corey Patterson .40 1.00
ER3 Josh Hamilton 1.25 3.00
ER4 Eric Munson .40 1.00
ER5 Sean Burroughs .40 1.00
ER6 Jack Cust .40 1.00
ER7 Rafael Furcal .60 1.50
ER8 Ruben Salazar .40 1.00
ER9 Brett Myers 1.25 3.00
ER10 Bobby Bradley .40 1.00
ER11 Nick Johnson .40 1.00
ER12 Scott Downs .40 1.00
ER13 Choo Freeman .40 1.00
ER14 Brad Baisley .40 1.00
ER15 A.J. Burnett .40 1.00

2000 Topps Gold Label Prospector's Dream

STATED ODDS 1:16
ONE TO ONE PRINT RUN 1 SERIAL #'d SET
ONE TO ONE NO PRICING DUE TO SCARCITY
PD1 Mark McGwire 1.50 4.00
PD2 Alex Rodriguez 1.25 3.00
PD3 Nomar Garciaparra .60 1.50
PD4 Pat Burrell .40 1.00
PD5 Todd Helton .60 1.50
PD6 Derek Jeter 2.50 6.00
PD7 Adam Piatt .40 1.00
PD8 Chipper Jones 1.00 2.50
PD9 Shawn Green .40 1.00
PD10 Josh Hamilton 1.25 3.00

2000 Topps Gold Label The Treasury

STATED ODDS 1:13
ONE TO ONE PRINT RUN 1 SERIAL #'d SET
ONE TO ONE NO PRICING DUE TO SCARCITY
T1 Ken Griffey Jr. 2.00 5.00
T2 Derek Jeter 2.50 6.00
T3 Chipper Jones 1.00 2.50
T4 Manny Ramirez 1.00 2.50
T5 Nomar Garciaparra .60 1.50
T6 Sammy Sosa 1.00 2.50
T7 Cal Ripken 3.00 8.00
T8 Alex Rodriguez 1.25 3.00
T9 Mike Piazza 1.00 2.50
T10 Pedro Martinez .60 1.50
T11 Vladimir Guerrero .60 1.50
T12 Jeff Bagwell .60 1.50
T13 Shawn Green .40 1.00
T14 Greg Maddux 1.25 3.00
T15 Mark McGwire 1.50 4.00
T16 Josh Hamilton 1.25 3.00
T17 Corey Patterson .40 1.00
T18 Dee Brown .40 1.00
T19 Rafael Furcal .60 1.50
T20 Pat Burrell .40 1.00
T21 Alfonso Soriano 1.00 2.50
T22 Adam Piatt .40 1.00
T23 A.J. Burnett .40 1.00
T24 Mark Mulder .40 1.00
T25 Ruben Mateo .40 1.00

2001 Topps Gold Label Class 1

COMPLETE SET (115) 100.00 200.00
COMP.SET w/o SP's (100) 20.00 50.00
COMMON CARD (1-115) .20 .50
COMMON SP 4.00 10.00
SP STATED ODDS 1:87
SP STATED PRINT RUN 999 SERIAL #'d SETS
1 Adrian Beltre .20 .50
2 Danny Borrell SP RC 4.00 10.00
3 Albert Belle .20 .50
4 Jay Buhner .20 .50
5 Alex Rodriguez .60 1.50
6 Andruw Jones .30 .75
7 Antonio Alfonseca .20 .50
8 Barry Bonds 1.25 3.00
9 Barry Larkin .30 .75
10 Ben Grieve .20 .50
11 Ben Molina .20 .50
12 Bernie Williams .30 .75
13 Bobby Abreu .20 .50
14 Bobby Higginson .20 .50
15 Brad Fullmer .20 .50
16 Brian Giles .20 .50
17 Cal Ripken 1.50 4.00
18 Carlos Delgado .20 .50
19 Chad Petty SP RC 4.00 10.00
20 Charles Johnson .20 .50
21 Chipper Jones .50 1.25
22 Cristian Guzman .20 .50
23 Darin Erstad .20 .50
24 David Justice .20 .50
25 David Segui .20 .50
26 Derek Jeter 1.25 3.00
27 Edgar Martinez .30 .75
28 Edgardo Alfonzo .20 .50
29 Fernando Tatis .20 .50
30 Eric Karros .20 .50
31 Eric Munson .20 .50
32 Eric Young .20 .50
33 Frank Thomas .50 1.25
34 Fernando Vina .20 .50
35 Garret Anderson .20 .50
36 Gary Sheffield .20 .50
37 Geoff Jenkins .20 .50
38 Greg Maddux .75 2.00
39 Ivan Rodriguez .30 .75
40 J.D. Drew .20 .50
41 J.R. House SP 4.00 10.00
42 J.T. Snow .20 .50
43 Jason Giambi .20 .50
44 Jason Kendall .20 .50
45 Jay Payton .20 .50
46 Jeff Bagwell .30 .75
47 Jeff Cirillo .20 .50
48 Jeff Kent .20 .50
49 Chan Ho Park .20 .50
50 Jermaine Dye .20 .50
51 Jeromy Burnitz .20 .50
52 Jim Edmonds .20 .50
53 Jim Thome .30 .75
54 John Olerud .20 .50
55 Johnny Damon .30 .75
56 Jorge Posada .30 .75
57 Jose Cruz Jr. .20 .50
58 Jose Vidro .20 .50
59 Josh Hamilton .40 1.00
60 Juan Gonzalez .20 .50
61 Steve Smyth SP RC 4.00 10.00
62 Justin Wayne SP RC 4.00 10.00
63 Kazuhiro Sasaki .20 .50
64 Ken Griffey Jr. 1.00 2.50
65 Kevin Brown .20 .50
66 Kevin Young .20 .50
67 Larry Walker .20 .50
68 Luis Castillo .20 .50
69 Steve Finley .20 .50
70 Magglio Ordonez .20 .50
71 Manny Ramirez Sox .30 .75
72 Mark McGwire 1.25 3.00
73 Mark Quinn .20 .50
74 Miguel Tejada .20 .50
75 Mike Piazza .75 2.00
76 Mike Sweeney .20 .50
77 Mo Vaughn .20 .50
78 Moises Alou .20 .50
79 Nomar Garciaparra .75 2.00
80 Pat Burrell .20 .50
81 Paul Konerko .20 .50
82 Pedro Martinez .30 .75
83 Phil Nevin .20 .50
84 Preston Wilson .20 .50
85 Rafael Furcal .20 .50
86 Todd Zeile .20 .50

87 Randy Johnson .50 1.25
88 Travis Lee .20 .50
89 Carl Everett .20 .50
90 Quilvio Veras .20 .50
91 Rick Ankiel .20 .50
92 Rick Brosseau SP RC 4.00 10.00
93 Robert Keppel SP RC 4.00 10.00
94 Roberto Alomar .30 .75
95 Ryan Klesko .20 .50
96 Sammy Sosa .50 1.25
97 Scott Heard SP 4.00 10.00
98 Scott Rolen .30 .75
99 Sean Casey .20 .50
100 Shawn Green .20 .50
101 Terrence Long .20 .50
102 Tim Salmon .30 .75
103 Todd Helton .30 .75
104 Tom Glavine .30 .75
105 Tony Batista .20 .50
106 Travis Baptist SP RC 4.00 10.00
107 Troy Glaus .20 .50
108 Victor Hall SP RC 4.00 10.00
109 Vladimir Guerrero .50 1.25
110 Tim Hudson .20 .50
111 Brian Roberts SP RC 6.00 15.00
112 Virgil Chevalier SP RC 4.00 10.00
113 Fernando Rodney SP RC 4.00 10.00
114 Paul Phillips SP RC 4.00 10.00
115 Cesar Bolivar SP RC 4.00 10.00

2001 Topps Gold Label Class 1 Gold

*STARS: 2.5X TO 6X BASIC CARDS
STATED ODDS 1:13
STATED PRINT RUN 999 SERIAL #'d SETS
*SP'S: .75X TO 2X BASIC SP'S
SP STATED ODDS 1:883
SP STATED PRINT RUN 99 SERIAL #'d SETS
111 Brian Roberts SP 12.50 30.00

2001 Topps Gold Label Class 2

*STARS: 1.25X TO 3X CLASS 1
STATED ODDS 1:7
*SP'S: .5X TO 1.2X CLASS 1 SP'S
SP STATED ODDS 1:125
SP STATED PRINT RUN 699 SERIAL #'d SETS

2001 Topps Gold Label Class 2 Gold

*STARS: 3X TO 8X BASIC CLASS 1
STATED ODDS 1:19
STATED PRINT RUN 699 SERIAL #'d SETS
*SP'S: 1X TO 2.5X BASIC SP'S
SP STATED ODDS 1:1271
SP STATED PRINT RUN 69 SERIAL #'d SETS
111 Brian Roberts SP 15.00 40.00

2001 Topps Gold Label Class 3

*STARS: 3X TO 8X CLASS 1
STATED ODDS 1:20
*SP'S: .6X TO 1.5X CLASS 1 SP'S
SP STATED ODDS 1:292
SP STATED PRINT RUN 299 SERIAL #'d SETS

2001 Topps Gold Label Class 3 Gold

*STARS: 5X TO 12X BASIC CLASS 1
STATED ODDS 1:44
STATED PRINT RUN 299 SERIAL #'d SETS
*SP'S: 1.25X TO 3X BASIC SP'S
SP STATED ODDS 1:3051
SP STATED PRINT RUN 29 SERIAL #'d SETS
111 Brian Roberts SP 20.00 50.00

2001 Topps Gold Label Gold Fixtures

STATED ODDS 1:374
GF1 Alex Rodriguez 5.00 12.00
GF2 Mark McGwire 6.00 15.00
GF3 Derek Jeter 20.00 50.00
GF4 Nomar Garciaparra 2.50 6.00
GF5 Chipper Jones 4.00 10.00
GF6 Sammy Sosa 2.50 6.00
GF7 Ken Griffey Jr. 8.00 20.00
GF8 Carlos Delgado 1.50 4.00
GF9 Frank Thomas 4.00 10.00
GF10 Barry Bonds 6.00 15.00

2001 Topps Gold Label MLB Award Ceremony Relics

STATED ODDS 1:24
AB1 Albert Belle RBI Bat 1.50 4.00
AB2 Albert Belle HR Bat 1.50 4.00
AG1 Andres Galarraga BTG Bat 2.50 6.00
AG2 Andres Galarraga HR Bat 2.50 6.00
AR Alex Rodriguez BTG Bat 5.00 12.00
BB1 Barry Bonds HR Bat 10.00 25.00
BB2 Barry Bonds MVP Jsy 10.00 25.00
BB3 Barry Bonds RBI Bat 10.00 25.00
BG Ben Grieve ROY Jsy 1.50 4.00
BL Barry Larkin MVP Bat 2.50 6.00
BW Bernie Williams BTG Bat 2.50 6.00
CB Carlos Beltran ROY Bat 1.50 4.00
CJ Chipper Jones MVP Jsy 4.00 10.00
CK Chuck Knoblauch ROY Bat 1.50 4.00
CR1 Cal Ripken ROY Jsy 8.00 20.00
CR2 Cal Ripken MVP Jsy 8.00 20.00
DB1 Dante Bichette HR Bat 1.50 4.00
DB2 Dante Bichette RBI Bat 1.50 4.00
DG Dwight Gooden CY Jsy 1.50 4.00
DJ1 Derek Jeter ROY Bat 12.00 30.00
DJ2 Derek Jeter WS MVP Bat 12.00 30.00
DS1 Darryl Strawberry HR Bat 1.50 4.00
DS2 Darryl Strawberry ROY Jsy 1.50 4.00
EM1 Edgar Martinez BTG Bat 2.50 6.00
EM2 Edgar Martinez RBI Bat 2.50 6.00
FM Fred McGriff HR Bat 2.50 6.00
FT1 Frank Thomas BTG Bat 4.00 10.00
FT2 Frank Thomas MVP Jsy 4.00 10.00
GM Greg Maddux CY Jsy 6.00 15.00
GS Gary Sheffield BTG Bat 1.50 4.00
HN Hideo Nomo ROY Jsy 8.00 20.00
IR Ivan Rodriguez MVP Jsy 2.50 6.00
JB1 Jeff Bagwell ROY Bat 2.50 6.00
JB2 Jeff Bagwell MVP Bat 2.50 6.00
JB3 Jeff Bagwell RBI Bat 2.50 6.00
JC1 Jose Canseco HR Bat 2.50 6.00
JC2 Jose Canseco MVP Bat 2.50 6.00
JC3 Jose Canseco RBI Bat 2.50 6.00
JC4 Jose Canseco ROY Jsy 2.50 6.00
JG Jason Giambi MVP Bat 1.50 4.00
JG1 Juan Gonzalez HR Bat 1.50 4.00
JG2 Juan Gonzalez MVP Jsy 1.50 4.00
JG3 Juan Gonzalez RBI Bat 1.50 4.00
JK Jeff Kent MVP Bat 1.50 4.00
JO John Olerud BTG Bat 1.50 4.00
JS John Smoltz CY Jsy 2.50 6.00
JW John Wetteland WS MVP Jsy 5.00 12.00
KG1 Ken Griffey Jr. HR Bat 10.00 20.00
KG2 Ken Griffey Jr. MVP Jsy 8.00 20.00
KG3 Ken Griffey Jr. RBI Bat 8.00 20.00
KS Kazuhiro Sasaki ROY Jsy 1.50 4.00
LW1 Larry Walker BTG Bat 2.50 6.00
LW2 Larry Walker HR Bat 2.50 6.00
LW3 Larry Walker MVP Jsy 2.50 6.00
MC Marty Cordova ROY Bat 1.50 4.00
MM1 Mark McGwire HR Bat 20.00 50.00
MM2 Mark McGwire ROY Jsy 10.00 25.00
MP Mike Piazza ROY Bat 4.00 10.00
MV1 Mo Vaughn MVP Jsy 1.50 4.00
MV2 Mo Vaughn RBI Bat 1.50 4.00
MW1 Matt Williams HR Bat 1.50 4.00
MW2 Matt Williams RBI Bat 1.50 4.00
NG1 Nomar Garciaparra BTG Bat 2.50 6.00
NG2 Nomar Garciaparra ROY Jsy 2.50 6.00
PM Pedro Martinez CY Jsy 2.50 6.00
PO Paul O'Neill BTG Bat 2.50 6.00
RC1 Roger Clemens CY Jsy 6.00 15.00
RC2 Roger Clemens MVP Jsy 6.00 15.00
RF Rafael Furcal ROY Bat 1.50 4.00
RH Rickey Henderson MVP Jsy 4.00 10.00
RJ Randy Johnson CY Jsy 4.00 10.00
RM Raul Mondesi ROY Bat 1.50 4.00
SA Sandy Alomar Jr. ROY Bat 1.50 4.00
SB Scott Brosius WS MVP Bat 1.50 4.00
SR Scott Rolen ROY Jsy 2.50 6.00
SS1 Sammy Sosa HR Bat 2.50 6.00
SS2 Sammy Sosa MVP Jsy 2.50 6.00
SS3 Sammy Sosa RBI Bat 2.50 6.00
TG Troy Glaus HR Bat 1.50 4.00
TH1 Todd Helton BTG Bat 2.50 6.00
TH2 Todd Helton RBI Bat 2.50 6.00
TS Tim Salmon ROY Jsy 2.50 6.00
WC Will Clark RBI Bat 2.50 6.00
DJU David Justice ROY Jsy 1.50 4.00
TGL1 Tom Glavine CY Jsy 2.50 6.00
TGL2 Tom Glavine WS MVP Jsy 2.50 6.00
TGW Tony Gwynn BTG Bat 4.00 10.00
THO T.Hollandsworth ROY Bat 1.50 4.00

2002 Topps Gold Label

COMPLETE SET (200) 30.00 60.00
1 Alex Rodriguez .60 1.50
2 Derek Jeter 1.25 3.00
3 Luis Gonzalez .20 .50
4 Troy Glaus .20 .50
5 Albert Pujols 1.00 2.50
6 Lance Berkman .20 .50
7 J.D. Drew .20 .50
8 Chipper Jones .50 1.25
9 Miguel Tejada .20 .50
10 Randy Johnson .50 1.25
11 Mike Cameron .20 .50
12 Brian Giles .20 .50
13 Roger Cedeno .20 .50
14 Kerry Wood .20 .50
15 Ken Griffey Jr. 1.00 2.50
16 Carlos Lee .20 .50
17 Todd Helton .30 .75
18 Gary Sheffield .20 .50
19 Richie Sexson .20 .50
20 Vladimir Guerrero .50 1.25
21 Bobby Higginson .20 .50
22 Roger Clemens 1.00 2.50
23 Barry Zito .20 .50
24 Juan Pierre .20 .50
25 Pedro Martinez .30 .75
26 Sean Casey .20 .50
27 David Segui .20 .50
28 Jose Garcia RC .20 .50
29 Curt Schilling .20 .50
30 Bernie Williams .30 .75
31 Ben Grieve .20 .50
32 Hideo Nomo .50 1.25
33 Aramis Ramirez .20 .50
34 Cristian Guzman .20 .50
35 Rich Aurilia .20 .50
36 Greg Maddux .75 2.00
37 Eric Chavez .20 .50
38 Shawn Green .20 .50
39 Luis Rivas .20 .50
40 Magglio Ordonez .20 .50
41 Jose Vidro .20 .50
42 Mariano Rivera .50 1.25
43 Chris Tritle RC .20 .50
44 C.C. Sabathia .20 .50
45 Larry Walker .20 .50
46 Raul Mondesi .20 .50
47 Kevin Brown .20 .50
48 Jeff Bagwell .30 .75
49 Earl Snyder RC .20 .50
50 Jason Giambi .20 .50
51 Ichiro Suzuki 1.00 2.50
52 Andruw Jones .30 .75
53 Ivan Rodriguez .30 .75
54 Jim Edmonds .20 .50
55 Preston Wilson .20 .50
56 Greg Vaughn .20 .50
57 Jon Lieber .20 .50
58 Justin Sherrod RC .20 .50
59 Marcus Giles .20 .50
60 Roberto Alomar .30 .75
61 Pat Burrell .20 .50
62 Doug Mientkiewicz .20 .50
63 Mark Mulder .20 .50
64 Mike Hampton .20 .50
65 Adam Dunn .20 .50
66 Moises Alou .20 .50
67 Jose Cruz Jr. .20 .50
68 Derek Bell .20 .50
69 Sammy Sosa .50 1.25
70 Joe Mays .20 .50
71 Phil Nevin .20 .50
72 Edgardo Alfonzo .20 .50
73 Barry Bonds 1.25 3.00
74 Edgar Martinez .30 .75
75 Juan Encarnacion .20 .50
76 Jason Tyner .20 .50
77 Edgar Renteria .20 .50
78 Bret Boone .20 .50
79 Scott Rolen .30 .75
80 Nomar Garciaparra .75 2.00
81 Frank Thomas .50 1.25
82 Roy Oswalt .20 .50
83 Tsuyoshi Shinjo .20 .50
84 Ben Sheets .20 .50
85 Hank Blalock .30 .75
86 Carlos Delgado .20 .50
87 Tim Hudson .20 .50
88 Alfonso Soriano .20 .50
89 Michael Hill RC .20 .50
90 Jim Thome .30 .75
91 Craig Biggio .30 .75
92 Ryan Klesko .20 .50
93 Geoff Jenkins .20 .50
94 Matt Morris .20 .50
95 Jorge Posada .30 .75
96 Cliff Floyd .20 .50
97 Jimmy Rollins .20 .50
98 Mike Sweeney .20 .50
99 Frank Catalanotto .20 .50
100 Mike Piazza .75 2.00
101 Mark Quinn .20 .50
102 Torii Hunter .20 .50
103 Lee Stevens .20 .50
104 Byung-Hyun Kim .20 .50
105 Freddy Sanchez RC .75 2.00
106 David Cone .20 .50
107 Jerry Hairston Jr. .20 .50
108 Kyle Farnsworth .20 .50
109 Rafael Furcal .20 .50
110 Bartolo Colon .20 .50
111 Juan Rivera .20 .50
112 Kevin Young .20 .50
113 Chris Narveson RC .30 .75
114 Richard Hidalgo .20 .50
115 Andy Pettitte .30 .75
116 Darin Erstad .20 .50
117 Corey Koskie .20 .50
118 So Taguchi RC .30 .75
119 Derrek Lee .30 .75
120 Sean Burroughs .20 .50
121 Paul Konerko .20 .50
122 Ross Peeples RC .20 .50
123 Terrence Long .20 .50
124 John Smoltz .30 .75
125 Brandon Duckworth .20 .50
126 Luis Maza .20 .50
127 Morgan Ensberg .20 .50
128 Eric Valent .20 .50
129 Shannon Stewart .20 .50
130 D'Angelo Jimenez .20 .50
131 Jeff Cirillo .20 .50
132 Jack Cust .20 .50
133 Dmitri Young .20 .50
134 Darryl Kile .20 .50
135 Reggie Sanders .20 .50
136 Marlon Byrd .20 .50
137 Napoleon Calzado RC .20 .50
138 Javy Lopez .20 .50
139 Orlando Cabrera .20 .50
140 Mike Mussina .30 .75
141 Josh Beckett .20 .50
142 Kazuhiro Sasaki .20 .50
143 Jermaine Dye .20 .50
144 Carlos Beltran .20 .50
145 Trevor Hoffman .20 .50
146 Kazuhisa Ishii RC .30 .75
147 Alex Gonzalez .20 .50
148 Marty Cordova .20 .50
149 Kevin Deaton RC .20 .50
150 Toby Hall .20 .50
151 Rafael Palmeiro .30 .75
152 John Olerud .20 .50
153 David Eckstein .20 .50
154 Doug Glanville .20 .50
155 Johnny Damon Sox .30 .75
156 Javier Vazquez .20 .50
157 Jason Bay RC 2.00 5.00
158 Robb Nen .20 .50
159 Rafael Soriano .20 .50
160 Placido Polanco .20 .50
161 Garret Anderson .20 .50
162 Aaron Boone .20 .50
163 Mike Lieberthal .20 .50
164 Joe Mauer RC 10.00 25.00
165 Matt Lawton .20 .50
166 Juan Tolentino RC .20 .50
167 Alex Gonzalez .20 .50
168 Steve Finley .20 .50
169 Troy Percival .20 .50
170 Bud Smith .20 .50
171 Freddy Garcia .20 .50
172 Ray Lankford .20 .50
173 Tim Redding .20 .50
174 Ryan Dempster .20 .50
175 Travis Lee .20 .50
176 Jeff Kent .20 .50
177 Ramon Hernandez .20 .50
178 Carl Everett .20 .50
179 Tom Glavine .30 .75
180 Juan Gonzalez .20 .50
181 Nick Johnson .20 .50
182 Mike Lowell .20 .50
183 Al Leiter .20 .50
184 Jason Maule RC .20 .50
185 Wilson Betemit .20 .50
186 Tino Martinez .30 .75
187 Jason Standridge .20 .50
188 Mike Peeples RC .20 .50
189 Jason Kendall .20 .50
190 Fred McGriff .30 .75
191 John Rodriguez RC .30 .75
192 Brett Roneberg RC .20 .50
193 Marlyn Tisdale RC .20 .50
194 J.T. Snow .20 .50
195 Craig Kuzmic RC .20 .50
196 Cory Lidle .20 .50
197 Alex Cintron .20 .50
198 Fernando Vina .20 .50
199 Austin Kearns .20 .50
200 Paul LoDuca .20 .50

2002 Topps Gold Label Class 1 Gold

*CLASS 1 GOLD: 2.5X TO 6X BASIC
*CLASS 1 GOLD RC'S: 1X TO 2.5X BASIC
STATED ODDS 1:7 HOB, 1:11 RET
STATED PRINT RUN 500 SERIAL #'d SETS

2002 Topps Gold Label Class 2 Platinum

*CLASS 2 PLAT: 4X TO 10X BASIC
*CLASS 2 PLAT RC'S: 1.5X TO 4X BASIC
STATED ODDS 1:13 HOB, 1:28 RET
STATED PRINT RUN 250 SERIAL #'d SETS

2002 Topps Gold Label Class 3 Titanium

*CLASS 3 TITAN: 6X TO 15X BASIC
*CLASS 3 TITAN RC'S: 2.5X TO 6X BASIC
STATED ODDS 1:33 HOB, 1:1:60 RET
STATED PRINT RUN 100 SERIAL #'d SETS

2002 Topps Gold Label Major League Moments Relics Gold

GOLD BAT ODDS 1:245 HOB, 1:678 RET
GOLD JSY ODDS 1:306 HOB, 1:844 RET
*PLATINUM BAT: .6X TO 1.5X BASIC BAT
*PLATINUM JSY: .5X TO 1.2X BASIC JSY
PLATINUM BAT ODDS 1:613 H, 1:1707 R
PLATINUM JSY ODDS 1:460 H, 1:1280: R
*TITANIUM BAT:.1X TO 2.5X BASIC BAT
*TITANIUM JSY: .75X TO 2X BASIC JSY
TITANIUM BAT ODDS 1:1228 H, 1:3435 R
TITANIUM JSY ODDS 1:920 H, 1:2560 R
AR Alex Rodriguez Bat 8.00 20.00
BB1 Bret Boone Bat 4.00 10.00
BB2 Bret Boone Jsy 4.00 10.00
BLB Barry Bonds Jsy 10.00 25.00
CD Carlos Delgado Bat 4.00 10.00
CL Carlos Lee Bat 4.00 10.00
JL Javy Lopez Bat 4.00 10.00
MO Magglio Ordonez Bat 4.00 10.00
RP1 Rafael Palmeiro Bat 6.00 15.00
RP2 Rafael Palmeiro Bat 6.00 15.00
TG Tony Gwynn Jsy 6.00 15.00
TH Toby Hall Bat 4.00 10.00

2002 Topps Gold Label MLB Awards Ceremony Relics Gold

GOLD BAT ODDS 1:32 HOB, 1:84 RET
GOLD JSY ODDS 1:38 HOB, 1:106 RET
*PLATINUM BAT: .6X TO 1.5X GOLD BAT
*PLATINUM JSY: .5X TO 1.2X GOLD JSY
PLATINUM BAT ODDS 1:79 HOB, 1:217 RET
PLATINUM JSY ODDS 1:57 HOB, 1:159 RET
*TITANIUM BAT: 1X TO 2.5X GOLD BAT
*TITANIUM JSY: .75X TO 2X GOLD JSY
TITANIUM BAT ODDS 1:158 HOB, 1:435 RET
TITANIUM JSY ODDS 1:115 HOB, 1:317 RET
AB Al Bumbry ROY Bat 4.00 10.00
AEP Andy Pettitte LC MVP Jsy 6.00 15.00
AO Al Oliver RBI Bat 4.00 10.00
AP Albert Pujols ROY Bat 8.00 20.00
AR Alex Rodriguez HR Bat 6.00 15.00
BB Bill Buckner BTG Jsy 4.00 10.00
BB1 Barry Bonds MVP Uni 10.00 25.00
BB2 Barry Bonds HR Uni 10.00 25.00
BFW B.Williams LC MVP Jsy 6.00 15.00
BLB Bobby Bonds AS MVP Bat 4.00 10.00
BM1 Bill Madlock AS MVP Jsy 4.00 10.00
BM2 Bill Madlock BTG Bat 4.00 10.00
BR Brooks Robinson MVP Bat 6.00 15.00
BRB Bret Boone RBI Bat 4.00 10.00
BRB2 Bret Boone RBI Jsy 4.00 10.00
BS Bret Saberhagen CY Jsy 4.00 10.00
BW Billy Williams ROY Bat 4.00 10.00
CC Craig Counsell LC MVP Bat 4.00 10.00
CF Carlton Fisk ROY Bat 6.00 15.00
CY1 Carl Yastrzemski MVP Bat 15.00 40.00
CY2 Carl Yastrzemski BTG Bat 15.00 40.00
DA Dick Allen ROY Bat 6.00 15.00
DB Don Baylor MVP Bat 4.00 10.00
DC D.Concepcion AS MVP Bat 4.00 10.00
DE Dennis Eckersley CY Jsy 4.00 10.00
DJ David Justice ROY Bat 4.00 10.00
DM Don Mattingly MVP Bat 10.00 25.00
DP1 Dave Parker MVP Bat 6.00 15.00
DP2 Dave Parker RBI Bat 6.00 15.00
DP3 Dave Parker AS MVP Bat 6.00 15.00
DP4 Dave Parker BTG Bat 6.00 15.00
DS1 Darryl Strawberry HR Bat 4.00 10.00
DS2 Darryl Strawberry ROY Bat 4.00 10.00
DW Dave Winfield RBI Bat 4.00 10.00
EB Ernie Banks MVP Jacket 10.00 25.00
EM1 Eddie Murray RBI Uni 6.00 15.00
EM2 Eddie Murray ROY Bat 6.00 15.00
FM Fred McGriff AS MVP Bat 6.00 15.00
FR Frank Robinson MVP Bat 6.00 15.00
FV Fernando Valenzuela ROY Bat 4.00 10.00
FW Frank White LC MVP Jsy 4.00 10.00
GB1 George Brett MVP Bat 15.00 40.00
GB2 George Brett LC MVP Bat 15.00 40.00
GC Gary Carter RBI Bat 4.00 10.00
GF George Foster HR Bat 4.00 10.00
GL Greg Luzinski RBI Bat 4.00 10.00
HS Hank Sauer MVP Bat 4.00 10.00
JB Johnny Bench WS MVP Bat 6.00 15.00
JL Javy Lopez LC MVP Jsy 4.00 10.00
JM Joe Morgan MVP Bat 4.00 10.00
JS John Smoltz CY Jsy 6.00 15.00
JT Joe Torre MVP Uni 6.00 15.00
KG Ken Griffey Sr. AS MVP Bat 4.00 10.00
KH Keith Hernandez MVP Bat 4.00 10.00
KHG Kirk Gibson MVP Bat 4.00 10.00
KM1 Kevin Mitchell MVP Bat 4.00 10.00
KM2 Kevin Mitchell HR Bat 4.00 10.00
KP1 Kirby Puckett LC MVP Jsy 6.00 15.00
KP2 Kirby Puckett AS MVP Bat 6.00 15.00
KP3 Kirby Puckett BTG Bat 6.00 15.00
LP Lou Piniella ROY Bat 4.00 10.00
LW Larry Walker BTG Bat 4.00 10.00
MH Mike Hargrove ROY Bat 4.00 10.00
MP Mike Piazza AS MVP Bat 6.00 15.00
MR M.Rivera WS MVP Jsy 6.00 15.00
MW Maury Wills MVP Jsy 4.00 10.00
NC Norm Cash BTG Bat 10.00 25.00
PM Paul Molitor WS MVP Bat 4.00 10.00
RA Roberto Alomar AS MVP Bat 6.00 15.00
RAC Rico Carty BTG Bat 4.00 10.00
RCC Ron Cey WS MVP Bat 4.00 10.00
RC1 Rod Carew ROY Bat 6.00 15.00
RC2 Rod Carew BTG Bat 6.00 15.00
RH R Henderson LC MVP Jsy 6.00 15.00
RJ Randy Johnson CY Jsy 6.00 15.00
RJ1 Reggie Jackson MVP Bat 6.00 15.00
RJ2 R.Jackson WS MVP Bat 6.00 15.00
RWC Roger Clemens CY Uni 10.00 25.00
RY Robin Yount MVP Bat 6.00 15.00
SA Sandy Alomar AS MVP Bat 4.00 10.00
SG1 Steve Garvey MVP Uni 6.00 15.00
SG2 Steve Garvey AS MVP Bat 4.00 10.00
TG1 Tony Gwynn BTG Bat 6.00 15.00
TG2 Tony Gwynn BTG Jsy 6.00 15.00
TK2 Ted Kluszewski HR Bat 6.00 15.00
TP Tony Perez AS MVP Bat 4.00 10.00
TR Tim Raines AS MVP Bat 4.00 10.00
WB Wade Boggs BTG Bat 6.00 15.00
WC Will Clark LC MVP Bat 6.00 15.00
WS Willie Stargell MVP Bat 6.00 15.00
YB Yogi Berra MVP Jsy 6.00 15.00

2016 Topps Gold Label Class 1

COMPLETE SET (100) 25.00 60.00
1 Mike Trout 2.00 5.00
2 Carlos Gonzalez .30 .75
3 George Springer .30 .75
4 Eric Hosmer .30 .75
5 Johnny Bench .40 1.00
6 Chris Archer .25 .60
7 Jose Altuve .30 .75
8 Cal Ripken Jr. 1.25 3.00
9 Reggie Jackson .30 .75
10 Justin Upton .30 .75
11 Yu Darvish .40 1.00
12 Troy Tulowitzki .40 1.00
13 Albert Pujols .50 1.25
14 Nolan Arenado .60 1.50
15 Craig Kimbrel .30 .75
16 Bo Jackson .40 1.00
17 Kris Bryant .50 1.25
18 Kenta Maeda RC .50 1.25
19 Darryl Strawberry .25 .60
20 Giancarlo Stanton .40 1.00
21 Roberto Clemente 1.00 2.50
22 Clayton Kershaw .60 1.50
23 Don Mattingly .75 2.00
24 Ken Griffey Jr. .75 2.00
25 Jose Fernandez .40 1.00
26 Jose Bautista .30 .75
27 David Wright .30 .75
28 Buster Posey .50 1.25
29 Yoenis Cespedes .40 1.00
30 Chipper Jones .40 1.00
31 Sandy Koufax .75 2.00
32 David Ortiz .40 1.00
33 Ryan Braun .30 .75
34 Bryce Harper .60 1.50
35 Frank Thomas .40 1.00
36 Jose Abreu .40 1.00
37 Stephen Strasburg .40 1.00
38 Mookie Betts .75 2.00
39 Hyun-Soo Kim RC .40 1.00
40 Felix Hernandez .30 .75
41 Aroldis Chapman .40 1.00
42 Nolan Ryan 1.25 3.00
43 Byung-Ho Park RC .30 .75
44 Anthony Rizzo .50 1.25
45 Zack Greinke .40 1.00
46 Lucas Giolito RC .40 1.00
47 Stan Musial .60 1.50
48 Josh Donaldson .30 .75
49 Jacob deGrom .75 2.00
50 Hunter Pence .30 .75
51 Ichiro Suzuki .50 1.25
52 Wade Boggs .30 .75
53 Johnny Cueto .30 .75
54 Sonny Gray .30 .75
55 Jose Berrios RC .40 1.00
56 Edwin Encarnacion .40 1.00
57 Roger Clemens .50 1.25
58 Prince Fielder .30 .75
59 Robinson Cano .30 .75
60 Kyle Schwarber RC .75 2.00
61 David Price .30 .75
62 Julio Urias RC .75 2.00
63 Miguel Sano RC .40 1.00
64 Freddie Freeman .50 1.25
65 Mark McGwire .60 1.50
66 Gerrit Cole .40 1.00
67 Jason Heyward .30 .75
68 Michael Conforto RC .30 .75
69 Luis Severino RC .30 .75
70 Stephen Piscotty RC .40 1.00
71 Andre Dawson .30 .75
72 Jake Arrieta .30 .75
73 Manny Machado .40 1.00
74 Trea Turner RC .75 2.00
75 Corey Seager RC 2.50 6.00
76 Carl Yastrzemski .60 1.50
77 Aaron Nola RC .50 1.25
78 Mike Piazza .40 1.00
79 Chris Sale .40 1.00
80 Blake Snell RC .30 .75
81 Miguel Cabrera .40 1.00
82 Matt Harvey .30 .75
83 Andrew McCutchen .40 1.00
84 Hank Aaron .75 2.00
85 Carlos Correa .40 1.00
86 Paul Goldschmidt .40 1.00
87 Ozzie Smith .50 1.25
88 Greg Maddux .50 1.25
89 Randy Johnson .40 1.00
90 Yasiel Puig .40 1.00
91 Joey Votto .40 1.00
92 Justin Verlander .40 1.00
93 Adrian Gonzalez .30 .75
94 Madison Bumgarner .30 .75
95 Adam Jones .30 .75
96 Todd Frazier .25 .60
97 Matt Kemp .30 .75
98 Noah Syndergaard .30 .75
99 Max Scherzer .40 1.00
100 Willie Mays .75 2.00

2016 Topps Gold Label Class 1 Blue

*CLASS 1 BLUE: .5X TO 1.2X CLASS 1
*CLASS 1 BLUE RC: .5X TO 1.2X CLASS 1 RC
STATED ODDS 1:2 HOBBY

2016 Topps Gold Label Class 1 Red

*CLASS 1 RED: 2.5X TO 6X CLASS 1
*CLASS 1 RED RC: 2.5X TO 6X CLASS 1 RC
STATED ODDS 1:13 HOBBY
STATED PRINT RUN 100 SER.#'d SETS

2016 Topps Gold Label Class 2

COMPLETE SET (100) 60.00 150.00
*CLASS 2: 1X TO 2.5X CLASS 1
*CLASS 2 RC: 1X TO 2.5X CLASS 1 RC

2016 Topps Gold Label Class 2 Blue

*CLASS 2 BLUE: 2X TO 5X CLASS 1
*CLASS 2 BLUE RC: 2X TO 5X CLASS 1 RC
STATED ODDS 1:6 HOBBY

2016 Topps Gold Label Class 2 Red

*CLASS 2 RED: 3X TO 8X CLASS 1
*CLASS 2 RED RC: 3X TO 8X CLASS 1 RC
STATED ODDS 1:25 HOBBY
STATED PRINT RUN 50 SER.#'d SETS

2016 Topps Gold Label Class 3

*CLASS 3: 1.5X TO 4X CLASS 1
*CLASS 3 RC: 1.5X TO 4X CLASS 1 RC

2016 Topps Gold Label Class 3 Blue

*CLASS 3 BLUE: 4X TO 10X CLASS 1
*CLASS 3 BLUE RC: 4X TO 10X CLASS 1 RC
STATED ODDS 1:20 HOBBY

2016 Topps Gold Label Class 3 Red

*CLASS 3 RED: 8X TO 20X CLASS 1
*CLASS 3 RED RC: 8X TO 20X CLASS 1 RC
STATED ODDS 1:50 HOBBY
STATED PRINT RUN 25 SER.#'d SETS

2016 Topps Gold Label Framed Autographs Black Frame

*BLACK/50: .5X TO 1.2X BASIC
*BLACK/25: .75X TO 2X BASIC
STATED ODDS 1:49 HOBBY
PRINT RUNS B/WN 3-50 COPIES PER
NO PRICING ON QTY 15 OR LESS
EXCHANGE DEADLINE 9/30/2018
GLFAMM Mark McGwire/25 75.00 200.00

2016 Topps Gold Label Framed Autographs Gold Frame

STATED ODDS 1:9 HOBBY
EXCHANGE DEADLINE 9/30/2018
GLFAAC Alex Cobb 4.00 10.00
GLFAAG Alex Gordon 10.00 25.00
GLFAAGA Andres Galarraga 5.00 12.00
GLFAAJ Andruw Jones 4.00 10.00
GLFAAN Aaron Nola 10.00 25.00
GLFAAP A.J. Pollock 4.00 10.00
GLFAAR Anthony Rizzo 60.00 150.00
GLFABH Bryce Harper
GLFABJ Bo Jackson 60.00 150.00
GLFABP Byung-Ho Park 8.00 20.00
GLFABS Blake Snell 5.00 12.00
GLFACD Corey Dickerson 4.00 10.00
GLFACE Carl Edwards Jr. 5.00 12.00
GLFACJ Chipper Jones 75.00 200.00
GLFACK Clayton Kershaw 60.00 150.00
GLFACKL Corey Kluber 15.00 40.00
GLFACM Carlos Martinez 6.00 15.00
GLFACR Cal Ripken Jr.
GLFACS Corey Seager
GLFADG Didi Gregorius 6.00 15.00
GLFADM Don Mattingly
GLFAFL Francisco Lindor 25.00 60.00
GLFAFM Frankie Montas 5.00 12.00
GLFAFT Frank Thomas
GLFAGB Greg Bird 5.00 12.00
GLFAGS George Springer 5.00 12.00
GLFAHA Hank Aaron 150.00 250.00
GLFAHO Henry Owens 5.00 12.00
GLFAHOL Hector Olivera 5.00 12.00
GLFAI Ichiro Suzuki 300.00 50.00
GLFAJA Jose Altuve EXCH 40.00 100.00
GLFAJAB Jim Abbott 6.00 15.00
GLFAJC Jose Canseco 10.00 25.00
GLFAJd Jacob deGrom 30.00 80.00
GLFAJE Jerad Eickhoff 6.00 15.00
GLFAJG Juan Gonzalez 8.00 20.00
GLFAJH Jason Heyward 12.00 30.00
GLFAJO John Olerud 12.00 30.00
GLFAJPE Jose Peraza 6.00 15.00
GLFAJR Jim Rice 10.00 25.00
GLFAJSO Jorge Soler 8.00 20.00
GLFAJUR Julio Urias EXCH 12.00 30.00
GLFAKB Kris Bryant 50.00 120.00
GLFAKC Kole Calhoun 4.00 10.00
GLFAKG Ken Griffey Jr. EXCH 200.00 300.00
GLFAKM Kenta Maeda 15.00 40.00
GLFAKMA Ketel Marte 8.00 20.00
GLFAKS Kyle Schwarber 15.00 40.00
GLFALG Lucas Giolito 12.00 30.00
GLFALS Luis Severino 15.00 40.00
GLFAMF Maikel Franco 5.00 12.00
GLFAMM Mark McGwire
GLFAMP Mike Piazza
GLFAMS Miguel Sano 6.00 15.00
GLFAMT Mike Trout
GLFANA Nolan Arenado 40.00 100.00
GLFANS Noah Syndergaard 15.00 40.00
GLFAOV Omar Vizquel 8.00 20.00
GLFAPOB Peter O'Brien 4.00 10.00
GLFARM Raul Mondesi 8.00 20.00
GLFARR Rob Refsnyder 5.00 12.00
GLFASD Sean Doolittle 4.00 10.00
GLFASG Sonny Gray 8.00 20.00
GLFASGR Shawn Green 4.00 10.00
GLFASK Sandy Koufax EXCH 200.00 300.00
GLFASM Starling Marte 5.00 12.00
GLFASMA Steven Matz 4.00 10.00
GLFASP Stephen Piscotty 6.00 15.00
GLFATT Trea Turner 15.00 40.00
GLFATTO Trayce Thompson 4.00 10.00

2017 Topps Gold Label Class 1

COMPLETE SET (100) 30.00 80.00
1 Bryce Harper 1.00 2.50
2 Jose Bautista .50 1.25
3 Trevor Story .60 1.50
4 Felix Hernandez .50 1.25
5 Carl Yastrzemski 1.00 2.50
6 Jake Arrieta .50 1.25
7 Aledmys Diaz .50 1.25
8 Addison Russell .60 1.50
9 Stephen Strasburg .60 1.50
10 Buster Posey .75 2.00
11 Ozzie Smith .75 2.00
12 Giancarlo Stanton .60 1.50
13 Sonny Gray .50 1.25
14 Trea Turner .50 1.25
15 David Dahl RC .50 1.25
16 Robinson Cano .50 1.25
17 Eric Hosmer .50 1.25
18 Evan Longoria .50 1.25
19 Cody Bellinger RC 6.00 15.00
20 Dansby Swanson RC 1.00 2.50
21 Alex Bregman RC 2.00 5.00
22 Yoenis Cespedes .60 1.50
23 Jharel Cotton RC .30 .75
24 Don Mattingly 1.25 3.00
25 Mike Trout 3.00 8.00
26 Roberto Clemente 1.50 4.00
27 Ernie Banks .60 1.50
28 Max Scherzer .60 1.50
29 Matt Kemp .50 1.25
30 Justin Verlander .60 1.50
31 Corey Seager .60 1.50
32 Paul Goldschmidt .60 1.50
33 Julio Urias .60 1.50
34 Mike Piazza .60 1.50
35 Sandy Koufax 1.25 3.00
36 Johnny Bench .60 1.50
37 Freddie Freeman .75 2.00
38 Jake Thompson RC .40 1.00
39 Miguel Sano .50 1.25
40 Anthony Rizzo .75 2.00
41 Tyler Glasnow RC 1.50 4.00
42 Adam Jones .50 1.25
43 Jacob deGrom 1.25 3.00
44 Ian Happ RC .75 2.00
45 Chipper Jones .60 1.50
46 Javier Baez .75 2.00
47 Manny Machado .60 1.50
48 Andrew Benintendi RC 1.25 3.00
49 Josh Bell RC 1.00 2.50
50 Kris Bryant .75 2.00
51 Hunter Pence .50 1.25
52 Frank Thomas .60 1.50
53 Ryan Braun .50 1.25
54 Yulieski Gurriel RC .60 1.50
55 George Brett 1.25 3.00
56 Yoan Moncada RC 1.25 3.00
57 Adrian Gonzalez .50 1.25
58 Trey Mancini RC .75 2.00
59 Alex Reyes RC .50 1.25
60 Brooks Robinson .50 1.25
61 Randy Johnson .60 1.50
62 Luke Weaver RC .50 1.25
63 Andrew McCutchen .60 1.50
64 Johnny Cueto .50 1.25
65 Albert Pujols .75 2.00
66 Joey Votto .60 1.50
67 Yu Darvish .60 1.50
68 Miguel Cabrera .60 1.50
69 Edwin Encarnacion .60 1.50
70 Josh Donaldson .50 1.25
71 Jose Altuve .50 1.25
72 David Ortiz .60 1.50
73 Wil Myers .50 1.25
74 Troy Tulowitzki .60 1.50
75 Mookie Betts 1.25 3.00
76 Mitch Haniger RC .60 1.50
77 Gary Sanchez .60 1.50
78 Jose Abreu .60 1.50
79 Ken Griffey Jr. 1.25 3.00
80 Chris Sale .60 1.50
81 Masahiro Tanaka .50 1.25
82 Nolan Ryan 2.00 5.00
83 Kenta Maeda .50 1.25
84 Bo Jackson .60 1.50
85 Clayton Kershaw 1.00 2.50
86 Aaron Judge RC 5.00 12.00
87 Francisco Lindor .60 1.50
88 Greg Maddux .75 2.00
89 Christian Arroyo RC .60 1.50
90 Carlos Correa .60 1.50
91 Hank Aaron 1.25 3.00
92 Reggie Jackson .50 1.25
93 Nolan Arenado 1.00 2.50
94 Kyle Schwarber .60 1.50
95 Ichiro .75 2.00
96 Noah Syndergaard .50 1.25
97 Cal Ripken Jr. 2.00 5.00
98 Carlos Gonzalez .50 1.25
99 Roger Clemens .75 2.00
100 Mark McGwire 1.00 2.50

2017 Topps Gold Label Class 1 Black

*CLASS 1 BLACK: .5X TO 1.2X CLASS 1
*CLASS 1 BLACK RC: .5X TO 1.2X CLASS 1 RC

2017 Topps Gold Label Class 1 Blue

*CLASS 1 BLUE: 1X TO 2.5X CLASS 1
*CLASS 1 BLUE RC: 1X TO 2.5X CLASS 1 RC
STATED PRINT RUN 150 SER.#'d SETS
86 Aaron Judge 20.00 50.00
97 Cal Ripken Jr. 6.00 15.00

2017 Topps Gold Label Class 1 Red

*CLASS 1 BLUE: 1.2X TO 3X CLASS 1
*CLASS 1 BLUE RC: 1.2X TO 3X CLASS 1 RC
STATED PRINT RUN 75 SER.#'d SETS
86 Aaron Judge 25.00 60.00
97 Cal Ripken Jr. 8.00 20.00

2017 Topps Gold Label Class 2

*CLASS 2: .6X TO 1.5X CLASS 1
*CLASS 2 RC: .6X TO 1.5X CLASS 1 RC

2017 Topps Gold Label Class 2 Black
*CLASS 2 BLACK: .75X TO 2X CLASS 1
*CLASS 2 BLACK RC: .75X TO 2X CLASS 1 RC
86 Aaron Judge 12.00 30.00

2017 Topps Gold Label Class 2 Blue
*CLASS 2 BLUE: 1.2X TO 3X CLASS 1
*CLASS 2 BLUE RC: 1.2X TO 3X CLASS 1 RC
STATED PRINT RUN 99 SER.#'d SETS
86 Aaron Judge 25.00 60.00
97 Cal Ripken Jr. 8.00 20.00

2017 Topps Gold Label Class 2 Red
*CLASS 2 RED: 1.5X TO 4X CLASS 1
*CLASS 2 RED RC: 1.5X TO 4X CLASS 1 RC
STATED PRINT RUN 50 SER.#'d SETS
55 George Brett 10.00 25.00
79 Ken Griffey Jr. 8.00 20.00
82 Nolan Ryan 10.00 25.00
86 Aaron Judge 30.00 80.00
97 Cal Ripken Jr. 10.00 25.00

2017 Topps Gold Label Class 3
*CLASS 3: .75X TO 2X CLASS 1
*CLASS 3 RC: .75X TO 2X CLASS 1 RC
86 Aaron Judge 12.00 30.00

2017 Topps Gold Label Class 3 Black
*CLASS 3 BLACK: 1X TO 2.5X CLASS 1
*CLASS 3 BLACK RC: 1X TO 2.5X CLASS 1 RC
55 George Brett 12.00 30.00
79 Ken Griffey Jr. 10.00 25.00
82 Nolan Ryan 12.00 30.00
86 Aaron Judge 40.00 100.00
97 Cal Ripken Jr. 12.00 30.00

2017 Topps Gold Label Class 3 Blue
*CLASS 3 BLUE: 1.5X TO 4X CLASS 1
*CLASS 3 BLUE RC: 1.5X TO 4X CLASS 1 RC
STATED PRINT RUN 50 SER.#'d SETS
55 George Brett 10.00 25.00
79 Ken Griffey Jr. 8.00 20.00
82 Nolan Ryan 10.00 25.00
86 Aaron Judge 30.00 80.00
97 Cal Ripken Jr. 10.00 25.00

2017 Topps Gold Label Class 3 Red
*CLASS 3 RED: 2.5X TO 6X CLASS 1
*CLASS 3 RED RC: 2.5X TO 6X CLASS 1 RC
STATED PRINT RUN 25 SER.#'d SETS
19 Cody Bellinger 60.00 150.00
24 Don Mattingly 15.00 40.00
25 Mike Trout 20.00 50.00
26 Roberto Clemente 30.00 80.00
49 Josh Bell 12.00 30.00
55 George Brett 15.00 40.00
79 Ken Griffey Jr. 12.00 30.00
82 Nolan Ryan 15.00 40.00
86 Aaron Judge 75.00 200.00
91 Hank Aaron 15.00 40.00
92 Reggie Jackson 10.00 25.00
95 Ichiro 15.00 40.00
97 Cal Ripken Jr. 25.00 60.00
100 Mark McGwire 12.00 30.00

2017 Topps Gold Label Framed Autographs
PRINT RUNS B/WN 50-501 COPIES PER
NOT ALL CARDS SERIAL NUMBERED
EXCHANGE DEADLINE 8/31/2019
*BLACK/75: .5X TO 1.2X BASIC
*BLACK/25: .6X TO 1.5X BASIC
*BLUE/50: .5X TO 1.2X BASIC
*RED/25: .6X TO 1.5X BASIC
FAABE Andrew Benintendi 30.00 80.00
FAABR Alex Bregman 20.00 50.00
FAAD Aledmys Diaz 4.00 10.00
FAAG Andres Galarraga 8.00 20.00
FAAJ Aaron Judge 75.00 200.00
FAAP Andy Pettitte 25.00 60.00
FAARE Alex Reyes 4.00 10.00
FAARI Anthony Rizzo 30.00 80.00
FAARU Addison Russell
FAAT Andrew Toles 3.00 8.00
FABH Bryce Harper EXCH
FABL Barry Larkin 20.00 50.00
FABP Buster Posey
FABZ Bradley Zimmer/492 4.00 10.00
FACB Cody Bellinger/100 60.00 150.00
FACC Carlos Correa 40.00 100.00
FACFU Carson Fulmer 3.00 8.00
FACK Clayton Kershaw
FACS Corey Seager 30.00 80.00
FADB Dellin Betances 4.00 10.00
FADJ Derek Jeter
FADS Dansby Swanson EXCH
FADV Dan Vogelbach 5.00 12.00
FAEM Edgar Martinez/50 15.00 40.00
FAFB Franklin Barreto/491 5.00 12.00
FAFL Francisco Lindor EXCH 25.00 60.00
FAGC Gavin Cecchini 3.00 8.00
FAHA Hank Aaron
FAHD Hunter Dozier/501 3.00 8.00
FAHR Hunter Renfroe 4.00 10.00
FAI Ichiro
FAIR Ivan Rodriguez EXCH 20.00 50.00
FAJAF Jorge Alfaro/486 4.00 10.00
FAJBA Jeff Bagwell 20.00 50.00
FAJBZ Javier Baez 25.00 60.00
FAJCA Jose Canseco 12.00 30.00
FAJCO Jharel Cotton 3.00 8.00
FAJDG Jacob deGrom/50 25.00 60.00
FAJDL Jose De Leon 3.00 8.00
FAJDO Josh Donaldson EXCH 20.00 50.00
FAJJO JaCoby Jones 4.00 10.00
FAJM Joe Musgrove 10.00 25.00
FAJS John Smoltz 20.00 50.00
FAJT Jake Thompson 3.00 8.00
FAJU Julio Urias EXCH 6.00 15.00
FAKB Kris Bryant 150.00 300.00
FAKSE Kyle Seager 10.00 25.00
FALB Lewis Brinson/400 10.00 25.00
FALW Luke Weaver 3.00 8.00
FAMMA Manny Machado 15.00 40.00
FAMMG Mark McGwire
FAMMR Manny Margot 5.00 12.00
FAMTA Masahiro Tanaka
FAMTR Mike Trout
FANS Noah Syndergaard 15.00 40.00
FAOV Omar Vizquel
FARG Robert Gsellman 3.00 8.00
FARH Ryon Healy 4.00 10.00
FARL Reynaldo Lopez 3.00 8.00
FARQ Roman Quinn/300 3.00 8.00
FART Raimel Tapia 4.00 10.00
FASK Sandy Koufax
FASMA Steven Matz 3.00 8.00
FASN Sean Newcomb/400 4.00 10.00
FATA Tyler Austin 8.00 20.00
FATB Ty Blach 5.00 12.00
FATGL Tyler Glasnow 5.00 12.00
FATM Trey Mancini 8.00 20.00
FATS Trevor Story 8.00 20.00
FAYG Yulieski Gurriel 10.00 25.00
FAYM Yoan Moncada 25.00 60.00

2017 Topps Gold Label Legend Relics
PRINT RUNS B/WN 10-75 COPIES PER
NO PRICING ON QTY 10 OR LESS
GLRBJ Bo Jackson/75 12.00 30.00
GLRCJ Chipper Jones/75 8.00 20.00
GLRCR Cal Ripken Jr./75 8.00 20.00
GLRCY Carl Yastrzemski/75 8.00 20.00
GLRDM Don Mattingly/75 10.00 25.00
GLREM Eddie Murray/75 12.00 30.00
GLRGM Greg Maddux/75 6.00 15.00
GLRJB Johnny Bench/75 8.00 20.00
GLRJR Jackie Robinson
GLRKG Ken Griffey Jr./75 10.00 25.00
GLRMM Mark McGwire/75 8.00 20.00
GLRMP Mike Piazza/75 5.00 12.00
GLRNR Nolan Ryan/75 20.00 50.00
GLROS Ozzie Smith/75 8.00 20.00
GLRRCA Rod Carew/75 6.00 15.00
GLRRCL Roberto Clemente/50 30.00 80.00
GLRRH Rickey Henderson/75 8.00 20.00
GLRRJ Reggie Jackson/75 6.00 15.00
GLRTW Ted Williams/50 25.00 60.00

2018 Topps Gold Label Class 1
COMPLETE SET (100) 25.00 60.00
1 Rafael Devers RC 1.25 3.00
2 Aaron Judge 1.50 4.00
3 Bryce Harper 1.00 2.50
4 Jose Altuve .50 1.25
5 Hank Aaron 1.25 3.00
6 Mike Trout 3.00 8.00
7 Greg Maddux .75 2.00
8 Chipper Jones .60 1.50
9 Freddie Freeman .75 2.00
10 Ozzie Albies RC 1.25 3.00
11 Manny Machado .60 1.50
12 Adam Jones .50 1.25
13 Cal Ripken Jr. 2.00 5.00
14 Trey Mancini .50 1.25
15 Austin Hays RC .60 1.50
16 Justin Upton .50 1.25
17 Shohei Ohtani RC 10.00 25.00
18 Paul Goldschmidt .60 1.50
19 Zack Greinke .60 1.50
20 Mookie Betts 1.25 3.00
21 Chris Sale .60 1.50
22 Ted Williams 1.25 3.00
23 David Ortiz .60 1.50
24 Andrew Benintendi .60 1.50
25 Jackie Robinson .60 1.50
26 Kris Bryant .75 2.00
27 Anthony Rizzo .75 2.00
28 Yu Darvish .60 1.50
29 Ernie Banks .60 1.50
30 Ryne Sandberg 1.25 3.00
31 Javier Baez .75 2.00
32 Ian Happ .50 1.25
33 Frank Thomas .60 1.50
34 Yoan Moncada .60 1.50
35 Joey Votto .60 1.50
36 Johnny Bench .60 1.50
37 Barry Larkin .50 1.25
38 Francisco Lindor .60 1.50
39 Corey Kluber .50 1.25
40 Francisco Mejia RC .50 1.25
41 Nolan Arenado 1.00 2.50
42 Charlie Blackmon .60 1.50
43 Ryan McMahon RC 1.00 2.50
44 Miguel Cabrera .60 1.50
45 Justin Verlander .60 1.50
46 Carlos Correa .60 1.50
47 Nolan Ryan 2.00 5.00
48 George Springer .50 1.25
49 Alex Bregman .60 1.50
50 George Brett 1.25 3.00
51 Bo Jackson .60 1.50
52 Clayton Kershaw 1.00 2.50
53 Corey Seager .60 1.50
54 Cody Bellinger 1.25 3.00
55 Sandy Koufax 1.25 3.00
56 Walker Buehler RC 2.00 5.00
57 Alex Verdugo RC .60 1.50
58 Christian Yelich .75 2.00
59 Byron Buxton .60 1.50
60 Miguel Sano .50 1.25
61 Brian Dozier .50 1.25
62 Noah Syndergaard .50 1.25
63 Jacob deGrom 1.25 3.00
64 Yoenis Cespedes .60 1.50
65 Mike Piazza .60 1.50
66 Michael Conforto .50 1.25
67 Giancarlo Stanton .60 1.50
68 Masahiro Tanaka .50 1.25
69 Gary Sanchez .60 1.50
70 Derek Jeter 1.50 4.00
71 Don Mattingly 1.25 3.00
72 Luis Severino .50 1.25
73 Clint Frazier RC .75 2.00
74 Mariano Rivera .75 2.00
75 Miguel Andujar RC 1.50 4.00
76 Khris Davis .60 1.50
77 Matt Olson .60 1.50
78 Rhys Hoskins RC 1.50 4.00
79 J.P. Crawford RC .40 1.00
80 Roberto Clemente 1.50 4.00
81 Eric Hosmer .50 1.25
82 Wil Myers .50 1.25
83 Buster Posey .75 2.00
84 Andrew McCutchen .60 1.50
85 Ichiro .75 2.00
86 Felix Hernandez .50 1.25
87 Robinson Cano .50 1.25
88 Randy Johnson .60 1.50
89 Mark McGwire 1.00 2.50
90 Ozzie Smith .75 2.00
91 Marcell Ozuna .60 1.50
92 Chris Archer .40 1.00
93 Adrian Beltre .60 1.50
94 Josh Donaldson .50 1.25
95 Max Scherzer .60 1.50
96 Stephen Strasburg .60 1.50
97 Victor Robles RC 1.00 2.50
98 Gleyber Torres RC 4.00 10.00
99 Ronald Acuna Jr. RC 12.00 30.00
100 Scott Kingery RC .60 1.50

2018 Topps Gold Label Class 1 Black
*CLASS 1 BLACK: .5X TO 1.2X CLASS 1
*CLASS 1 BLACK RC: .5X TO 1.2X CLASS 1 RC
STATED ODDS 1:2 HOBBY

2018 Topps Gold Label Class 1 Blue
*CLASS 1 BLUE: 1X TO 2.5X CLASS 1
*CLASS 1 BLUE RC: 1X TO 2.5X CLASS 1 RC
STATED ODDS 1:14 HOBBY
STATED PRINT RUN 150 SER.#'d SETS

2018 Topps Gold Label Class 1 Red
*CLASS 1 BLUE: 1.2X TO 3X CLASS 1
*CLASS 1 BLUE RC: 1.2X TO 3X CLASS 1 RC
STATED ODDS 1:28 HOBBY
STATED PRINT RUN 75 SER.#'d SETS
17 Shohei Ohtani 20.00 50.00

2018 Topps Gold Label Class 2
*CLASS 2: .6X TO 1.5X CLASS 1
*CLASS 2 RC: .6X TO 1.5X CLASS 1 RC

2018 Topps Gold Label Class 2 Black
*CLASS 2 BLACK: .75X TO 2X CLASS 1
*CLASS 2 BLACK RC: .75X TO 2X CLASS 1 RC
STATED ODDS 1:6 HOBBY

2018 Topps Gold Label Class 2 Blue
*CLASS 2 BLUE: 1.2X TO 3X CLASS 1
*CLASS 2 BLUE RC: 1.2X TO 3X CLASS 1 RC
STATED ODDS 1:21 HOBBY
STATED PRINT RUN 99 SER.#'d SETS
17 Shohei Ohtani 20.00 50.00

2018 Topps Gold Label Class 2 Red
*CLASS 2 RED: 1.5X TO 4X CLASS 1
*CLASS 2 RED RC: 1.5X TO 4X CLASS 1 RC
STATED ODDS 1:42 HOBBY
STATED PRINT RUN 50 SER.#'d SETS
17 Shohei Ohtani 25.00 60.00
99 Ronald Acuna Jr. 25.00 60.00

2018 Topps Gold Label Class 3
*CLASS 3: .75X TO 2X CLASS 1
*CLASS 3 RC: .75X TO 2X CLASS 1 RC

2018 Topps Gold Label Class 3 Black
*CLASS 3 BLACK: 1X TO 2.5X CLASS 1
*CLASS 3 BLACK RC: 1X TO 2.5X CLASS 1 RC
STATED ODDS 1:20 HOBBY

2018 Topps Gold Label Class 3 Blue
*CLASS 3 BLUE: 1.5X TO 4X CLASS 1
*CLASS 3 BLUE RC: 1.5X TO 4X CLASS 1 RC
STATED ODDS 1:42 HOBBY
STATED PRINT RUN 50 SER.#'d SETS
17 Shohei Ohtani 25.00 60.00
99 Ronald Acuna Jr. 25.00 60.00

2018 Topps Gold Label Class 3 Red
*CLASS 3 RED: 2.5X TO 6X CLASS 1
*CLASS 3 RED RC: 2.5X TO 6X CLASS 1 RC
STATED ODDS 1:83 HOBBY
STATED PRINT RUN 25 SER.#'d SETS
17 Shohei Ohtani 40.00 100.00
99 Ronald Acuna Jr. 40.00 100.00

2018 Topps Gold Label Framed Autographs
STATED ODDS 1:11 HOBBY
EXCHANGE DEADLINE 9/30/2020
FAAB Anthony Banda 3.00 8.00
FAAH Austin Hays 6.00 15.00
FAAI Anthony Rizzo EXCH 25.00 60.00
FAAJ Aaron Judge
FAAM Austin Meadows 10.00 25.00
FAAN Aaron Nola 8.00 20.00
FAAR Amed Rosario 4.00 10.00
FAAV Alex Verdugo 15.00 40.00
FABD Brian Dozier 6.00 15.00
FABY Bryce Harper EXCH
FACF Clint Frazier 12.00 30.00
FACS Chance Sisco 4.00 10.00
FACST Chris Stratton 3.00 8.00
FACT Chris Taylor 4.00 10.00
FACY Christian Yelich 25.00 60.00
FADF Dustin Fowler 3.00 8.00
FADG Dwight Gooden 6.00 15.00
FADR Didi Gregorius EXCH 8.00 20.00
FADS Darryl Strawberry 12.00 30.00
FAEP George Springer 15.00 40.00
FAFM Francisco Mejia 6.00 15.00
FAGC Garrett Cooper 3.00 8.00
FAGT Gleyber Torres 40.00 100.00
FAHB Harrison Bader 5.00 12.00
FAIH Ian Happ 6.00 15.00
FAIK Ian Kinsler 4.00 10.00
FAJA Jose Altuve 20.00 50.00
FAJB Jose Berrios 4.00 10.00
FAJC Jose Canseco 10.00 25.00
FAJD J.D. Davis 4.00 10.00
FAJE Jacob deGrom 20.00 50.00
FAJF Jack Flaherty 15.00 40.00
FAJL Jake Lamb 4.00 10.00
FAJR Jose Ramirez 15.00 40.00
FAJSO Juan Soto EXCH 100.00 250.00
FAJU Justin Upton 8.00 20.00
FAJV Joey Votto 25.00 60.00
FAJW J.P. Crawford 4.00 10.00
FAKB Kris Bryant EXCH 60.00 150.00
FAKD Khris Davis 10.00 25.00
FALB Lewis Brinson EXCH 3.00 8.00
FALC Luis Castillo 4.00 10.00
FALS Lucas Sims 3.00 8.00
FAMA Miguel Andujar 20.00 50.00
FAMF Max Fried 8.00 20.00
FAMO Matt Olson 5.00 12.00
FAND Nicky Delmonico 3.00 8.00
FANY Noah Syndergaard 10.00 25.00
FAOA Ozzie Albies 25.00 60.00
FAPB Paul Blackburn 3.00 8.00
FAPD Paul DeJong 6.00 15.00
FAPG Paul Goldschmidt 15.00 40.00
FAPT Tommy Pham 3.00 8.00
FARA Ronald Acuna Jr. 100.00 250.00
FARD Rafael Devers 30.00 80.00
FARE Trey Mancini 5.00 12.00
FARH Rhys Hoskins 20.00 50.00
FARM Ryan McMahon 8.00 20.00
FARN Rick Ankiel 3.00 8.00
FASKI Scott Kingery 6.00 15.00
FASM Starling Marte 4.00 10.00
FASN Sean Newcomb 4.00 10.00
FASO Shohei Ohtani 300.00 600.00
FASP Salvador Perez 10.00 25.00
FAST Travis Shaw 3.00 8.00
FATM Tyler Mahle 4.00 10.00
FAVC Victor Caratini 4.00 10.00
FAVR Victor Robles 10.00 25.00
FAWB Walker Buehler 25.00 60.00
FAWC Willson Contreras 15.00 40.00
FAWM Whit Merrifield 8.00 20.00

2018 Topps Gold Label Framed Autographs Black
*BLACK/75: .5X TO 1.2X BASIC
STATED ODDS 1:45 HOBBY
PRINT RUNS B/WN 15-75 COPIES PER
NO PRICING ON QTY 15
EXCHANGE DEADLINE 9/30/2020
FAAJ Aaron Judge 125.00 300.00
FACL Charlie Blackmon 6.00 15.00
FADS Darryl Strawberry 6.00 15.00

2018 Topps Gold Label Framed Autographs Blue
*BLUE/50: .5X TO 1.2X BASIC
STATED ODDS 1:67 HOBBY
PRINT RUNS B/WN 10-50 COPIES PER
NO PRICING ON QTY 10
EXCHANGE DEADLINE 9/30/2020
FAAJ Aaron Judge 125.00 300.00
FACL Charlie Blackmon 6.00 15.00
FADS Darryl Strawberry 6.00 15.00

2018 Topps Gold Label Framed Autographs Red
*RED/25: .6X TO 1.5X BASIC
STATED ODDS 1:134 HOBBY
PRINT RUNS B/WN 5-25 COPIES PER
NO PRICING ON QTY 5
EXCHANGE DEADLINE 9/30/2020
FAAJ Aaron Judge 150.00 400.00
FABA Brian Anderson 15.00 40.00
FACL Charlie Blackmon 8.00 20.00
FADS Darryl Strawberry 8.00 20.00

2018 Topps Gold Label Golden Greats Framed Autograph Relics
STATED ODDS 1:611 HOBBY
PRINT RUNS B/WN 10-25 COPIES PER
NO PRICING ON QTY 10
EXCHANGE DEADLINE 9/30/2020
GGARAK Al Kaline/25 40.00 100.00
GGARAP Andy Pettitte/25 20.00 50.00
GGARBJ Bo Jackson/15 50.00 120.00
GGARBL Barry Larkin EXCH 40.00 100.00
GGARCB Craig Biggio
GGARDE Dennis Eckersley/25 10.00 25.00
GGARDM Don Mattingly/25 50.00 120.00
GGARFT Frank Thomas/25 60.00 150.00
GGARGM Greg Maddux
GGARJS John Smoltz/25
GGARMP Mike Piazza
GGARNG Nomar Garciaparra/25
GGAROS Ozzie Smith/25 60.00 150.00
GGARRL Roger Clemens
GGARRO Randy Johnson
GGARRS Ryne Sandberg

2018 Topps Gold Label Legends Relics
STATED ODDS 1:122 HOBBY
PRINT RUNS B/WN 25-50 COPIES PER
LRBL Barry Larkin/75 5.00 12.00
LRCB Craig Biggio/75 5.00 12.00
LRCR Cal Ripken Jr./75 8.00 20.00
LRDJ Derek Jeter/50 20.00 50.00
LRDM Don Mattingly/75 15.00 40.00
LRFT Frank Thomas/75 6.00 15.00
LRGB George Brett/75 15.00 40.00
LRGM Greg Maddux/75 6.00 15.00
LRHA Hank Aaron/50 15.00 40.00
LRJB Johnny Bench/75 6.00 15.00
LRJS John Smoltz/75 6.00 15.00
LRMM Mark McGwire/75 8.00 20.00
LRMP Mike Piazza/75 6.00 15.00
LRNG Nomar Garciaparra/75 5.00 12.00
LRNR Nolan Ryan/75 15.00 40.00
LROS Ozzie Smith/75 10.00 25.00
LRPM Pedro Martinez/75 5.00 12.00
LRRC Roberto Clemente/25 60.00 150.00
LRRH Rickey Henderson/75 6.00 15.00
LRRJ Reggie Jackson/75 6.00 15.00
LRRL Roger Clemens/75 8.00 20.00
LRTG Tom Glavine/75 5.00 12.00
LRTS Tom Seaver/25 10.00 25.00
LRTW Ted Williams/50 20.00 50.00
LRWB Wade Boggs/75 8.00 20.00

2019 Topps Gold Label Class 1
COMPLETE SET (100) 25.00 60.00
1 Mike Trout 3.00 8.00
2 Albert Pujols .75 2.00
3 Shohei Ohtani 1.00 2.50
4 Paul Goldschmidt .60 1.50
5 Freddie Freeman .75 2.00
6 Ozzie Albies .60 1.50
7 Ronald Acuna Jr. 3.00 8.00
8 Mookie Betts 1.25 3.00
9 Chris Sale .60 1.50
10 Andrew Benintendi .60 1.50
11 J.D. Martinez .60 1.50
12 Kris Bryant .75 2.00
13 Anthony Rizzo .75 2.00
14 Javier Baez .75 2.00
15 Michael Kopech RC 1.25 3.00
16 Joey Votto .60 1.50
17 Francisco Lindor .60 1.50
18 Yusei Kikuchi RC .60 1.50
19 Trevor Bauer .75 2.00
20 Jose Ramirez .50 1.25
21 Nolan Arenado 1.00 2.50
22 Charlie Blackmon .60 1.50
23 Trevor Story .60 1.50
24 Miguel Cabrera .60 1.50
25 Justin Verlander .60 1.50
26 Carlos Correa .60 1.50
27 Jose Altuve .50 1.25
28 George Springer .50 1.25
29 Alex Bregman .60 1.50
30 Kyle Tucker RC 1.00 2.50
31 Pete Alonso RC 3.00 8.00
32 Whit Merrifield .60 1.50
33 Manny Machado .60 1.50
34 Clayton Kershaw 1.00 2.50
35 Corey Seager .60 1.50
36 Cody Bellinger 1.25 3.00
37 Christian Yelich .75 2.00
38 Noah Syndergaard .50 1.25
39 Jacob deGrom 1.25 3.00
40 Robinson Cano .50 1.25
41 Giancarlo Stanton .60 1.50
42 Masahiro Tanaka .50 1.25
43 Gary Sanchez .60 1.50
44 Aaron Judge 1.50 4.00
45 Luis Severino .50 1.25
46 Gleyber Torres 1.25 3.00
47 Brendan Rodgers RC .60 1.50
48 Khris Davis .60 1.50
49 Matt Chapman .60 1.50
50 Rhys Hoskins .75 2.00
51 Aaron Nola .50 1.25
52 Carter Kieboom RC .60 1.50
53 Keston Hiura RC 1.25 3.00
54 Buster Posey .75 2.00
55 Ichiro Suzuki .75 2.00
56 Ken Griffey Jr. 1.25 3.00
57 Nick Senzel RC 1.25 3.00
58 Yadier Molina .75 2.00
59 Blake Snell .50 1.25
60 Austin Riley RC 2.00 5.00
61 Joey Gallo .50 1.25
62 Bryce Harper 1.00 2.50
63 Max Scherzer .60 1.50
64 Trea Turner .50 1.25
65 Stephen Strasburg .60 1.50
66 Juan Soto 2.00 5.00
67 Josh Donaldson .50 1.25
68 Roberto Alomar .50 1.25
69 J.T. Realmuto .60 1.50
70 Luis Urias RC .60 1.50
71 Hideki Matsui .60 1.50
72 Rickey Henderson .60 1.50
73 Chipper Jones .60 1.50
74 Cal Ripken Jr. 2.00 5.00
75 Ted Williams 1.25 3.00
76 David Ortiz .60 1.50
77 Mariano Rivera .75 2.00
78 Jackie Robinson .60 1.50
79 Ernie Banks .60 1.50
80 Ryne Sandberg 1.25 3.00
81 Frank Thomas .60 1.50
82 Johnny Bench .60 1.50
83 Barry Larkin .50 1.25
84 Nolan Ryan 2.00 5.00
85 Bo Jackson .60 1.50
86 Sandy Koufax 1.25 3.00
87 Walker Buehler .75 2.00
88 Mike Piazza .60 1.50
89 Derek Jeter 1.50 4.00
90 Don Mattingly 1.25 3.00
91 Roberto Clemente 1.50 4.00
92 Tony Gwynn .60 1.50
93 Mark McGwire 1.00 2.50
94 Ozzie Smith .75 2.00
95 Chris Archer .40 1.00
96 Deion Sanders .50 1.25
97 Roger Clemens .75 2.00
98 Eloy Jimenez RC 1.50 4.00
99 Vladimir Guerrero Jr. RC 2.50 6.00
100 Fernando Tatis Jr. RC 6.00 15.00

2019 Topps Gold Label Class 1 Black
2018 Topps Gold Label Class 1 Black
2018 Topps Gold Label Class 1 Black
2018 Topps Gold Label Class 1 Black

2019 Topps Gold Label Class 1 Blue
*CLASS 1 BLUE: 1X TO 2.5X CLASS 1
*CLASS 1 BLUE RC: 1X TO 2.5X CLASS 1 RC
STATED ODDS 1:15 HOBBY
STATED PRINT RUN 150 SER.#'d SETS
56 Ken Griffey Jr. 8.00 20.00
72 Rickey Henderson 4.00 10.00
84 Nolan Ryan 6.00 15.00
89 Derek Jeter 8.00 20.00
90 Don Mattingly 5.00 12.00

2019 Topps Gold Label Class 1 Red
*CLASS 1 BLUE: 1.2X TO 3X CLASS 1
*CLASS 1 BLUE RC: 1.2X TO 3X CLASS 1 RC
STATED ODDS 1:30 HOBBY
STATED PRINT RUN 75 SER.#'d SETS
56 Ken Griffey Jr. 10.00 25.00
72 Rickey Henderson 5.00 12.00
84 Nolan Ryan 8.00 20.00
89 Derek Jeter 10.00 25.00
90 Don Mattingly 6.00 15.00

2019 Topps Gold Label Class 2
*CLASS 2: .6X TO 1.5X CLASS 1
*CLASS 2 RC: .6X TO 1.5X CLASS 1 RC

2019 Topps Gold Label Class 2 Black
*CLASS 2 BLACK: .75X TO 2X CLASS 1
*CLASS 2 BLACK RC: .75X TO 2X CLASS 1 RC
STATED ODDS 1:6 HOBBY

2019 Topps Gold Label Class 2 Blue
*CLASS 2 BLUE: 1.2X TO 3X CLASS 1
*CLASS 2 BLUE RC: 1.2X TO 3X CLASS 1 RC
STATED ODDS 1:23 HOBBY
STATED PRINT RUN 99 SER.#'d SETS
56 Ken Griffey Jr. 1.00 25.00
72 Rickey Henderson 5.00 12.00
84 Nolan Ryan 8.00 20.00
89 Derek Jeter 10.00 25.00
90 Don Mattingly 6.00 15.00

2019 Topps Gold Label Class 2 Red
*CLASS 2 RED: 1.5X TO 4X CLASS 1
*CLASS 2 RED RC: 1.5X TO 4X CLASS 1 RC
STATED ODDS 1:45 HOBBY
STATED PRINT RUN 50 SER.#'d SETS
56 Ken Griffey Jr. 12.00 30.00
72 Rickey Henderson 6.00 15.00
84 Nolan Ryan 10.00 25.00
89 Derek Jeter 12.00 30.00
90 Don Mattingly 8.00 20.00

2019 Topps Gold Label Class 3
*CLASS 3: .75X TO 2X CLASS 1
*CLASS 3 RC: .75X TO 2X CLASS 1 RC

2019 Topps Gold Label Class 3 Black
*CLASS 3 BLACK: 1X TO 2.5X CLASS 1
*CLASS 3 BLACK RC: 1X TO 2.5X CLASS 1 RC
STATED ODDS 1:20 HOBBY
56 Ken Griffey Jr. 8.00 20.00
72 Rickey Henderson 4.00 10.00
84 Nolan Ryan 6.00 15.00
89 Derek Jeter 8.00 20.00
90 Don Mattingly 5.00 12.00

2019 Topps Gold Label Class 3 Blue
*CLASS 3 BLUE: 1.5X TO 4X CLASS 1
*CLASS 3 BLUE RC: 1.5X TO 4X CLASS 1 RC
STATED ODDS 1:45 HOBBY
STATED PRINT RUN 50 SER.#'d SETS
56 Ken Griffey Jr. 12.00 30.00
72 Rickey Henderson 6.00 15.00
84 Nolan Ryan 10.00 25.00
89 Derek Jeter 12.00 30.00
90 Don Mattingly 8.00 20.00

2019 Topps Gold Label Class 3 Red
*CLASS 3 RED: 2.5X TO 6X CLASS 1
*CLASS 3 RED RC: 2.5X TO 6X CLASS 1 RC
STATED ODDS 1:90 HOBBY
STATED PRINT RUN 25 SER.#'d SETS
56 Ken Griffey Jr. 20.00 50.00
72 Rickey Henderson 10.00 25.00
84 Nolan Ryan 15.00 40.00
89 Derek Jeter 20.00 50.00
90 Don Mattingly 12.00 30.00

2019 Topps Gold Label Framed Autographs
STATED ODDS 1:10 HOBBY
EXCHANGE DEADLINE 8/31/2021
GLAAM Andrew McCutchen 25.00 60.00
GLABK Brad Keller 3.00 8.00
GLABL Brandon Lowe 20.00 50.00
GLABW Bryse Wilson 6.00 15.00
GLACB Corbin Burnes 10.00 25.00
GLACM Cedric Mullins 10.00 25.00
GLACSH Chris Shaw 3.00 8.00
GLADH Dakota Hudson 4.00 10.00
GLADJ Danny Jansen 3.00 8.00
GLADMU Dale Murphy 40.00 100.00
GLADP Daniel Ponce de Leon 5.00 12.00
GLADR Dereck Rodriguez 5.00 12.00
GLADS Darryl Strawberry 12.00 30.00
GLADST DJ Stewart 4.00 10.00
GLAEJ Eloy Jimenez 25.00 60.00
GLAEM Edgar Martinez 25.00 60.00
GLAFL Francisco Lindor 20.00 50.00
GLAFTA Fernando Tatis Jr. 100.00 250.00
GLAJA Jose Altuve 25.00 60.00
GLAJC Jose Canseco 10.00 25.00
GLAJd Jacob deGrom 40.00 100.00
GLAJF Jack Flaherty 10.00 25.00
GLAJH Josh Hader 5.00 12.00
GLAJJ Josh James 5.00 12.00
GLAJM Jeff McNeil 10.00 25.00
GLAJS Juan Soto 30.00 80.00
GLAJSH Justus Sheffield 5.00 12.00
GLAJSM Justin Smoak 3.00 8.00
GLAKA Kolby Allard 4.00 10.00
GLAKK Kevin Kramer 4.00 10.00
GLAKN Kevin Newman 5.00 12.00
GLAKS Kyle Schwarber 10.00 25.00
GLAKST Kohl Stewart 4.00 10.00
GLAKT Kyle Tucker 15.00 40.00
GLAKW Kyle Wright 10.00 25.00
GLALU Luis Urias 8.00 20.00
GLALV Luke Voit 15.00 40.00
GLAMA Miguel Andujar 8.00 20.00
GLAMMU Max Muncy 12.00 30.00
GLAMS Myles Straw 5.00 12.00
GLANM Nick Martini 3.00 8.00
GLANSY Noah Syndergaard 12.00 30.00
GLAPA Pete Alonso 60.00 150.00
GLAPG Paul Goldschmidt 15.00 40.00
GLAPW Patrick Wisdom 3.00 8.00
GLARA Ronald Acuna Jr. 50.00 120.00
GLARD Rafael Devers 15.00 40.00
GLARH Rhys Hoskins 15.00 40.00
GLARL Ramon Laureano 12.00 30.00
GLARM Reese McGuire 5.00 12.00
GLARO Ryan O'Hearn 5.00 12.00
GLART Rowdy Tellez 5.00 12.00
GLASD Steven Duggar 4.00 10.00
GLASK Sandy Koufax
GLASR Sean Reid-Foley 3.00 8.00
GLATB Trevor Bauer 6.00 15.00
GLATT Touki Toussaint 4.00 10.00
GLAVG Vladimir Guerrero Jr. 40.00 100.00
GLAWA Willians Astudillo 3.00 8.00
GLAYK Yusei Kikuchi 8.00 20.00

2019 Topps Gold Label Framed Autographs Black
*BLACK/75: .5X TO 1.2X BASIC
STATED ODDS 1:56 HOBBY
PRINT RUNS B/WN 15-75 COPIES PER
NO PRICING ON QTY 15
EXCHANGE DEADLINE 8/31/2021
GLAMH Mitch Haniger/75 8.00 20.00
GLAMK Michael Kopech/75 12.00 30.00

2019 Topps Gold Label Framed Autographs Blue
*BLUE/50: .5X TO 1.2X BASIC
STATED ODDS 1:83 HOBBY
PRINT RUNS B/WN 10-50 COPIES PER
NO PRICING ON QTY 10
EXCHANGE DEADLINE 8/31/2021
GLACK Carter Kieboom/50 15.00 40.00
GLAMH Mitch Haniger/50 8.00 20.00
GLAMK Michael Kopech/50 12.00 30.00
GLANS Nick Senzel/50 40.00 100.00

2019 Topps Gold Label Framed Autographs Red
*RED/25: .75X TO 2X BASIC
STATED ODDS 1:165 HOBBY
PRINT RUNS B/WN 5-25 COPIES PER
NO PRICING ON QTY 5
EXCHANGE DEADLINE 8/31/2021
GLACK Carter Kieboom/25 25.00 60.00
GLAMH Mitch Haniger/25 12.00 30.00
GLAMK Michael Kopech/25 20.00 50.00
GLANS Nick Senzel/25 60.00 150.00

2019 Topps Gold Label Gold Prospect Relics
STATED ODDS 1:866 HOBBY
STATED PRINT RUN 25 SER.#'d SETS
GPREJ Eloy Jimenez 60.00 150.00
GPRFT Fernando Tatis Jr. 100.00 250.00
GPRGT Gleyber Torres
GPRJS Juan Soto
GPRNS Nick Senzel 75.00 200.00
GPRPA Pete Alonso
GPRRA Ronald Acuna Jr.
GPRSO Shohei Ohtani 125.00 300.00
GPRVG Vladimir Guerrero Jr. 150.00 400.00
GPRVR Victor Robles
GPRWB Walker Buehler
GPRYK Yusei Kikuchi 40.00 100.00

2019 Topps Gold Label Golden Greats Framed Autograph Relics
STATED ODDS 1:572 HOBBY
PRINT RUNS B/WN 10-25 COPIES PER
NO PRICING ON QTY 15 OR LESS
EXCHANGE DEADLINE 8/31/2021
GGARAD Andre Dawson/25 25.00 60.00
GGARAK Al Kaline/25
GGARCF Carlton Fisk/25 15.00 40.00
GGARDE Dennis Eckersley/25
GGARDJ Derek Jeter
GGARHA Hank Aaron
GGARMR Mariano Rivera
GGAROS Ozzie Smith
GGARRC Rod Carew/25
GGARRJ Reggie Jackson
GGARRY Robin Yount/25 30.00 80.00
GGARVG Vladimir Guerrero/25
GGARWC Will Clark/25 50.00 120.00

2019 Topps Gold Label Legends Relics
STATED ODDS 1:151 HOBBY
PRINT RUNS B/WN 10-50 COPIES PER
BLRAK Al Kaline
BLRBF Bob Feller
BLRBG Bob Gibson/50
BLRBL Barry Larkin/50 6.00 15.00
BLRCR Cal Ripken Jr./50 20.00 50.00
BLRDJ Derek Jeter/25 25.00 60.00
BLRDM Don Mattingly/50
BLREM Eddie Mathews/50 10.00 25.00
BLRFT Frank Thomas/50
BLRGB George Brett
BLRHA Hank Aaron/25 20.00 50.00
BLRJB Johnny Bench/25 10.00 25.00
BLRJS John Smoltz/50 10.00 25.00
BLRKG Ken Griffey Jr./50 25.00 60.00
BLRMM Mark McGwire/50 6.00 15.00
BLRMP Mike Piazza/50 6.00 15.00
BLRNG Nomar Garciaparra/50 5.00 12.00
BLRNR Nolan Ryan/50 20.00 50.00
BLROS Ozzie Smith/50 8.00 20.00
BLRPM Pedro Martinez/50 5.00 12.00
BLRPR Pee Wee Reese/50 5.00 12.00
BLRRC Roberto Clemente 15.00 40.00
BLRRH Rickey Henderson
BLRRJ Reggie Jackson/25 10.00 25.00
BLRRS Ryne Sandberg/50 12.00 30.00
BLRRY Robin Yount/50 10.00 25.00
BLRTG Tony Gwynn/50 10.00 25.00
BLRTW Ted Williams/25 25.00 60.00
BLRWB Wade Boggs/50 10.00 25.00
BLRWM Willie McCovey/50 12.00 30.00
BLREMU Eddie Murray/50 5.00 12.00
BLRRCL Roger Clemens 8.00 20.00
BLRRHO Rogers Hornsby/50 12.00 30.00
BLRTGL Tom Glavine/50

2020 Topps Gold Label Class 1
1 Mike Trout 3.00 8.00
2 Albert Pujols .75 2.00
3 Shohei Ohtani 1.00 2.50
4 Anthony Rendon .60 1.50
5 Ketel Marte .50 1.25
6 Freddie Freeman .75 2.00
7 Ozzie Albies .60 1.50
8 Ronald Acuna Jr. 2.50 6.00
9 Chipper Jones .60 1.50
10 Cal Ripken Jr. 2.00 5.00
11 Mookie Betts 1.25 3.00
12 Chris Sale .60 1.50
13 Rafael Devers .75 2.00
14 J.D. Martinez .60 1.50
15 Xander Bogaerts .60 1.50
16 Jackie Robinson .60 1.50
17 Nico Hoerner RC 1.50 4.00
18 Kris Bryant .75 2.00

19 Anthony Rizzo .75 2.00
20 Javier Baez .75 2.00
21 Robel Garcia RC .40 1.00
22 Willson Contreras .60 1.50
23 Frank Thomas .60 1.50
24 Eloy Jimenez 1.25 3.00
25 Tim Anderson .60 1.50
26 Yoan Moncada .60 1.50
27 Joey Votto .60 1.50
28 Nick Castellanos .60 1.50
29 Max Kepler .50 1.25
30 Sonny Gray .50 1.25
31 Aristides Aquino RC 1.00 2.50
32 Francisco Lindor .60 1.50
33 Shane Bieber .60 1.50
34 Mike Clevinger .50 1.25
35 Carlos Santana .50 1.25
36 Nolan Arenado 1.00 2.50
37 Charlie Blackmon .60 1.50
38 Trevor Story .60 1.50
39 Miguel Cabrera .60 1.50
40 Justin Verlander .60 1.50
41 Carlos Correa .60 1.50
42 Jose Altuve .50 1.25
43 George Springer .50 1.25
44 Alex Bregman .60 1.50
45 Yordan Alvarez RC 4.00 10.00
46 Whit Merrifield .60 1.50
47 Jorge Soler .60 1.50
48 Clayton Kershaw 1.00 2.50
49 Cody Bellinger 1.25 3.00
50 Walker Buehler .75 2.00
51 Gavin Lux RC 2.00 5.00
52 Christian Yelich .75 2.00
53 Keston Hiura .75 2.00
54 Robin Yount .60 1.50
55 Noah Syndergaard .50 1.25
56 Jacob deGrom 1.25 3.00
57 Robinson Cano .50 1.25
58 Pete Alonso 1.50 4.00
59 Darryl Strawberry .40 1.00
60 Giancarlo Stanton .60 1.50
61 Masahiro Tanaka .60 1.50
62 Aaron Judge 1.50 4.00
63 Gleyber Torres 1.25 3.00
64 Don Mattingly 1.25 3.00
65 Mariano Rivera .75 2.00
66 Gerrit Cole 1.00 2.50
67 A.J. Puk RC .60 1.50
68 Jesus Luzardo RC .75 2.00
69 Matt Chapman .60 1.50
70 Rickey Henderson .60 1.50
71 Mark McGwire 1.00 2.50
72 Rhys Hoskins .75 2.00
73 Andrew McCutchen .60 1.50
74 J.T. Realmuto .60 1.50
75 Bryce Harper 1.00 2.50
76 Mike Schmidt 1.00 2.50
77 Zac Gallen RC 1.00 2.50
78 Josh Bell .50 1.25
79 Luis Robert RC 3.00 8.00
80 Manny Machado .60 1.50
81 Tony Gwynn .60 1.50
82 Fernando Tatis Jr. 3.00 8.00
83 Buster Posey .75 2.00
84 Willie Mays 1.25 3.00
85 Ichiro .75 2.00
86 Ken Griffey Jr. 1.25 3.00
87 Kyle Lewis RC 3.00 8.00
88 Paul Goldschmidt .60 1.50
89 Yadier Molina .75 2.00
90 Yoshi Tsutsugo 1.00 2.50
91 Brendan McKay RC .60 1.50
92 Blake Snell .50 1.25
93 Nolan Ryan 2.00 5.00
94 Joey Gallo .60 1.50
95 Bo Bichette RC 3.00 8.00
96 Vladimir Guerrero Jr. 1.00 2.50
97 Max Scherzer .60 1.50
98 Trea Turner .50 1.25
99 Stephen Strasburg .60 1.50
100 Juan Soto 2.00 5.00

2020 Topps Gold Label Class 1 Black

*CLASS 1 BLACK: .5X TO 1.2X CLASS 1
*CLASS 1 BLACK RC: .5X TO 1.2X CLASS 1 RC
STATED ODDS 1:2 HOBBY

2020 Topps Gold Label Class 1 Blue

*CLASS 1 BLUE: 1X TO 2.5X CLASS 1
*CLASS 1 BLUE RC: 1X TO 2.5X CLASS 1 RC
STATED ODDS 1:17 HOBBY
STATED PRINT RUN 150 SER.#'d SETS
11 Mookie Betts 5.00 12.00
48 Clayton Kershaw 5.00 12.00
64 Don Mattingly 5.00 12.00
76 Mike Schmidt 4.00 10.00
85 Ichiro 4.00 10.00
86 Ken Griffey Jr. 10.00 25.00
93 Nolan Ryan 8.00 20.00

2020 Topps Gold Label Class 1 Red

*CLASS 1 BLUE: 1.2X TO 3X CLASS 1
*CLASS 1 BLUE RC: 1.2X TO 3X CLASS 1 RC
STATED ODDS 1:34 HOBBY
STATED PRINT RUN 75 SER.#'d SETS
10 Cal Ripken Jr. 8.00 20.00
11 Mookie Betts 6.00 15.00
48 Clayton Kershaw 8.00 20.00
64 Don Mattingly 8.00 20.00
71 Mark McGwire 5.00 12.00
76 Mike Schmidt 8.00 20.00
85 Ichiro 5.00 12.00
86 Ken Griffey Jr. 12.00 30.00
93 Nolan Ryan 10.00 25.00

2020 Topps Gold Label Class 2

*CLASS 2: .6X TO 1.5X CLASS 1
*CLASS 2 RC: .6X TO 1.5X CLASS 1 RC
STATED ODDS 1 PER HOBBY

2020 Topps Gold Label Class 2 Black

*CLASS 2 BLACK: .75X TO 2X CLASS 1
*CLASS 2 BLACK RC: .75X TO 2X CLASS 1 RC
STATED ODDS 1:6 HOBBY

2020 Topps Gold Label Class 2 Blue

*CLASS 2 BLUE: 1.2X TO 3X CLASS 1
*CLASS 2 BLUE RC: 1.2X TO 3X CLASS 1 RC
STATED ODDS 1:26 HOBBY
STATED PRINT RUN 99 SER.#'d SETS
10 Cal Ripken Jr. 8.00 20.00
11 Mookie Betts 6.00 15.00
48 Clayton Kershaw 8.00 20.00
64 Don Mattingly 8.00 20.00
71 Mark McGwire 5.00 12.00
76 Mike Schmidt 8.00 20.00
85 Ichiro 5.00 12.00
86 Ken Griffey Jr. 12.00 30.00
93 Nolan Ryan 10.00 25.00

2020 Topps Gold Label Class 3

*CLASS 3: .75X TO 2X CLASS 1
*CLASS 3 RC: .75X TO 2X CLASS 1 RC
STATED ODDS 1:2 HOBBY

2020 Topps Gold Label Class 3 Black

*CLASS 3 BLACK: 1X TO 2.5X CLASS 1
*CLASS 3 BLACK RC: 1X TO 2.5X CLASS 1 RC
STATED ODDS 1:20 HOBBY
11 Mookie Betts 5.00 12.00
48 Clayton Kershaw 5.00 12.00
64 Don Mattingly 5.00 12.00
76 Mike Schmidt 4.00 10.00
85 Ichiro 4.00 10.00
86 Ken Griffey Jr. 10.00 25.00
93 Nolan Ryan 8.00 20.00

2020 Topps Gold Label Class 3 Blue

*CLASS 3 BLUE: 1.5X TO 4X CLASS 1
*CLASS 3 BLUE RC: 1.5X TO 4X CLASS 1 RC
STATED ODDS 1:50 HOBBY
STATED PRINT RUN 50 SER.#'d SETS
1 Mike Trout 15.00 40.00
10 Cal Ripken Jr. 12.00 30.00
11 Mookie Betts 8.00 20.00
48 Clayton Kershaw 10.00 25.00
64 Don Mattingly 12.00 30.00
65 Mariano Rivera 6.00 15.00
71 Mark McGwire 6.00 15.00
76 Mike Schmidt 12.00 30.00
85 Ichiro 6.00 15.00
86 Ken Griffey Jr. 15.00 40.00
87 Kyle Lewis 15.00 40.00
93 Nolan Ryan 15.00 40.00
95 Bo Bichette 25.00 60.00

2020 Topps Gold Label Class 3 Red

*CLASS 3 RED: 2.5X TO 6X CLASS 1
*CLASS 3 RED RC: 2.5X TO 6X CLASS 1 RC
STATED ODDS 1:100 HOBBY
STATED PRINT RUN 25 SER.#'d SETS
1 Mike Trout 50.00 120.00
10 Cal Ripken Jr. 25.00 60.00
11 Mookie Betts 15.00 40.00
45 Yordan Alvarez 15.00 40.00
48 Clayton Kershaw 15.00 40.00
64 Don Mattingly 25.00 60.00
65 Mariano Rivera 15.00 40.00
71 Mark McGwire 15.00 40.00
76 Mike Schmidt 20.00 50.00
79 Luis Robert 50.00 120.00
85 Ichiro 10.00 25.00
86 Ken Griffey Jr. 25.00 60.00
87 Kyle Lewis 25.00 60.00
93 Nolan Ryan 30.00 80.00
95 Bo Bichette 40.00 100.00

2020 Topps Gold Label Framed Autographs

STATED ODDS 1:10 HOBBY
EXCHANGE DEADLINE 8/31/2022
GLAAA Aristides Aquino 10.00 25.00
GLAAH Aaron Hicks 10.00 25.00
GLAAJ Aaron Judge
GLAAK Anthony Kay 6.00 15.00
GLAAT Abraham Toro 5.00 12.00
GLABA Bryan Abreu 6.00 15.00
GLABB Bo Bichette 75.00 200.00
GLABH Bryce Harper
GLABM Brendan McKay 5.00 12.00
GLACR Cal Ripken Jr.
GLACY Christian Yelich 30.00 80.00
GLADC Dylan Cease 8.00 20.00
GLADJ Derek Jeter
GLADM Dale Murphy 30.00 80.00
GLADS Darryl Strawberry 20.00 50.00
GLADW David Wright 50.00 120.00
GLAEJ Eloy Jimenez 20.00 50.00
GLAEM Edgar Martinez 15.00 40.00
GLAES Eugenio Suarez 20.00 50.00
GLAGL Gavin Lux EXCH 75.00 200.00
GLAHH Hunter Harvey 5.00 12.00
GLAJC Jose Canseco 15.00 40.00
GLAJR Jake Rogers 3.00 8.00
GLAJS Juan Soto
GLAJU Jose Urquidy 4.00 10.00
GLAJY Jordan Yamamoto 3.00 8.00
GLAKH Keston Hiura 10.00 25.00
GLAKK Kwang-Hyun Kim 20.00 50.00
GLAKM Ketel Marte 8.00 20.00
GLALR Luis Robert EXCH 75.00 200.00
GLALW Logan Webb 5.00 12.00
GLAMB Michael Brosseau 10.00 25.00
GLAMD Mauricio Dubon 10.00 25.00
GLAMK Max Kepler 8.00 20.00
GLAMM Mark McGwire
GLAMT Mike Trout
GLANH Nico Hoerner 15.00 40.00
GLANS Nick Solak 8.00 20.00
GLAPA Pete Alonso
GLAPC Patrick Corbin 6.00 15.00
GLAPG Paul Goldschmidt 30.00 80.00
GLARA Ronald Acuna Jr.
GLARD Rafael Devers 15.00 40.00
GLARG Robel Garcia 3.00 8.00
GLARH Rhys Hoskins
GLASA Shogo Akiyama 12.00 30.00
GLASM Sean Murphy 5.00 12.00
GLASO Shohei Ohtani
GLATL Tim Lincecum 30.00 80.00
GLAVG Vladimir Guerrero Jr.
GLAAAL Adbert Alzolay 6.00 15.00
GLABBR Bobby Bradley 3.00 8.00
GLADMA Dustin May 20.00 50.00
GLADMT Don Mattingly 50.00 120.00
GLAJDA Jaylin Davis 5.00 12.00
GLAJDU Justin Dunn 4.00 10.00
GLAJFE Junior Fernandez 3.00 8.00
GLAJRE J.T. Realmuto 20.00 50.00
GLAMKI Mike King 5.00 12.00
GLAMTH Matt Thaiss 6.00 15.00
GLARAR Randy Arozarena 60.00 150.00
GLARHO Ryan Howard 25.00 10.00
GLARRA Rangel Ravelo 4.00 10.00
GLAWCA Willi Castro 15.00 40.00
GLAWCL Will Clark 25.00 60.00

2020 Topps Gold Label Framed Autographs Black

*BLACK/75: .5X TO 1.2X BASIC
STATED ODDS 1:66 HOBBY
PRINT RUNS B/WN 15-75 COPIES PER
NO PRICING ON QTY 15
EXCHANGE DEADLINE 8/31/2022
GLAJS Juan Soto/75 50.00 120.00
GLAKK Kwang-Hyun Kim/75 30.00 80.00
GLALR Luis Robert EXCH/75 125.00 300.00
GLAPA Pete Alonso/75 30.00 80.00
GLARA Ronald Acuna Jr./75 75.00 200.00
GLARH Rhys Hoskins/75 12.00 30.00
GLAVG Vladimir Guerrero Jr./75 30.00 80.00

2020 Topps Gold Label Framed Autographs Blue

*BLUE/50: .5X TO 1.2X BASIC
STATED ODDS 1:97 HOBBY
PRINT RUNS B/WN 10-50 COPIES PER
NO PRICING ON QTY 10
EXCHANGE DEADLINE 8/31/2022
GLAJS Juan Soto/50 50.00 120.00
GLAKH Keston Hiura/50 15.00 40.00
GLAKK Kwang-Hyun Kim/50 30.00 80.00
GLALR Luis Robert EXCH/50 200.00 500.00
GLAPA Pete Alonso/50 30.00 80.00
GLARA Ronald Acuna Jr./50 75.00 200.00
GLARH Rhys Hoskins/50 12.00 30.00
GLAVG Vladimir Guerrero Jr./50 30.00 80.00
GLARAR Randy Arozarena/50 100.00 250.00

2020 Topps Gold Label Framed Autographs Red

*RED/25: .75X TO 2X BASIC
STATED ODDS 1:194 HOBBY
PRINT RUNS B/WN 5-25 COPIES PER
NO PRICING ON QTY 5
EXCHANGE DEADLINE 8/31/2022
GLAJS Juan Soto/25 125.00 300.00
GLAKH Keston Hiura/25 25.00 60.00
GLAKK Kwang-Hyun Kim/25 100.00 250.00
GLALR Luis Robert EXCH/25 300.00 800.00
GLAPA Pete Alonso/25 60.00 150.00
GLARA Ronald Acuna Jr./25 125.00 300.00
GLARH Rhys Hoskins/25 20.00 50.00
GLAVG Vladimir Guerrero Jr./25 50.00 120.00
GLARAR Randy Arozarena/25 150.00 400.00

2020 Topps Gold Label Golden Greats Framed Autograph Relics

STATED ODDS 1:482 HOBBY
PRINT RUNS B/WN 10-25 COPIES PER
NO PRICING ON QTY 15 OR LESS
EXCHANGE DEADLINE 8/31/22
GLRAP Andy Pettitte/25 30.00 80.00
GLRCF Carlton Fisk/25 15.00 40.00
GLRDE Dennis Eckersley/25
GLREM Edgar Martinez/25 30.00 80.00
GLRFT Frank Thomas/25 50.00 120.00
GLRMS Mike Schmidt/25 60.00 150.00
GLROS Ozzie Smith/25 40.00 100.00
GLRRC Rod Carew/25 15.00 40.00
GLRRS Ryne Sandberg/25 50.00 120.00
GLRRY Robin Yount/25 75.00 200.00
GLRSC Steve Carlton/25 30.00 80.00
GLRVG Vladimir Guerrero/25 30.00 80.00
GLRWB Wade Boggs/25 40.00 100.00
GLRWC Will Clark/25 40.00 100.00
GLRJBA Jeff Bagwell/25 50.00 120.00
GLRKGJ Ken Griffey Jr.

2020 Topps Gold Label Legends Relics

STATED ODDS 1:145 HOBBY
PRINT RUNS B/WN 10-50 COPIES PER
NO PRICING ON QTY 15 OR LESS
MLRI Ichiro/25 15.00 40.00
MLRAK Al Kaline/50 6.00 15.00
MLRBL Barry Larkin/50 10.00 25.00
MLRBR Brooks Robinson/50 10.00 25.00
MLRCJ Chipper Jones/50 20.00 50.00
MLRCR Cal Ripken Jr./50 25.00 60.00
MLRCY Carl Yastrzemski/50 12.00 30.00
MLRDM Don Mattingly/50 15.00 40.00
MLREM Eddie Mathews/25 20.00 50.00
MLRFR Frank Robinson/25 30.00 80.00
MLRFT Frank Thomas
MLRGB George Brett/50 20.00 50.00
MLRHA Hank Aaron/25 20.00 50.00
MLRJB Johnny Bench/50 10.00 25.00
MLRJM Joe Morgan/50 10.00 25.00
MLRJS John Smoltz/50 8.00 20.00
MLRKG Ken Griffey Jr./50 25.00 60.00
MLRMM Mark McGwire/50 10.00 25.00
MLRMR Mariano Rivera/50 15.00 40.00
MLRMS Mike Schmidt/50 30.00 80.00
MLRNG Nomar Garciaparra/50 5.00 12.00
MLRNR Nolan Ryan/50 20.00 50.00
MLROS Ozzie Smith/50 15.00 40.00
MLRPM Pedro Martinez/50 5.00 12.00
MLRRH Rickey Henderson/50 20.00 50.00
MLRRJ Reggie Jackson/25 15.00 40.00
MLRRS Ryne Sandberg/50 12.00 30.00
MLRRY Robin Yount/50 6.00 15.00
MLRTG Tony Gwynn/50 15.00 40.00
MLRTW Ted Williams/25 50.00 120.00
MLRWB Wade Boggs/50 10.00 25.00
MLRWM Willie McCovey/50 10.00 25.00
MLREMU Eddie Murray/50 15.00 40.00
MLRRCA Rod Carew/50 12.00 30.00
MLRRCL Roger Clemens/50 10.00 25.00
MLRRJO Randy Johnson/25 30.00 80.00
MLRTGL Tom Glavine/50 5.00 12.00
MLRWMA Willie Mays/25 25.00 60.00

2011 Topps Gypsy Queen

COMPLETE SET (350)
COMP.SET w/o SP's (300) 30.00 60.00
COMMON CARD (1-300) .15 .40
COMMON RC (1-300) .40 1.00
COMMON SP (301-350) 1.50 4.00
PLATE PRINT RUN 1 SET PER COLOR
BLACK-CYAN-MAGENTA-YELLOW ISSUED
NO PLATE PRICING DUE TO SCARCITY
1 Ichiro Suzuki .50 1.25
2 Roy Halladay .25 .60
3 Cole Hamels .30 .75
4 Jackie Robinson .40 1.00
5 Tris Speaker .25 .60
6 Frank Robinson .25 .60
7 Jim Palmer .25 .60
8 Troy Tulowitzki .40 1.00
9 Scott Rolen .25 .60
10 Jason Heyward .30 .75
11 Zack Greinke .40 1.00
12 Ryan Howard .30 .75
13 Joey Votto .40 1.00
14 Brooks Robinson .25 .60
15 Matt Kemp .30 .75
16 Chris Carpenter .25 .60
17 Mark Teixeira .25 .60
18 Christy Mathewson .40 1.00
19 Jon Lester .25 .60
20 Andre Dawson .25 .60
21 David Wright .30 .75
22 Barry Larkin .25 .60
23 Johnny Cueto .25 .60
24 Chipper Jones .40 1.00
25 Mel Ott .40 1.00
26 Adrian Gonzalez .30 .75
27 Roy Oswalt .25 .60
28 Tony Gwynn .40 1.00
29 Ty Cobb .60 1.50
30 Hanley Ramirez .25 .60
31 Joe Mauer .30 .75
32 Carl Crawford .25 .60
33 Ian Kinsler .25 .60
34 Johan Santana .25 .60
35 Pee Wee Reese .25 .60
36 Vladimir Guerrero .25 .60
37 Ryan Braun .25 .60
38 Walter Johnson .40 1.00
39 Johnny Mize .25 .60
40 George Sisler .25 .60
41 Matt Holliday .40 1.00
42 Jose Reyes .25 .60
43 Matt Cain .25 .60
44 Bob Gibson .25 .60
45 Carlos Gonzalez .25 .60
46 Thurman Munson .40 1.00
47 Jimmy Rollins .25 .60
48 Roger Maris .40 1.00
49 Honus Wagner .40 1.00
50 Al Kaline .40 1.00
51 Alex Rodriguez .50 1.25
52 Carlos Santana .40 1.00
53 Jimmie Foxx .40 1.00
54 Frank Thomas .40 1.00
55 Evan Longoria .25 .60
56 Mat Latos .25 .60
57 David Ortiz .40 1.00
58 Dale Murphy .40 1.00
59 Duke Snider .25 .60
60 Rogers Hornsby .25 .60
61 Robin Yount .40 1.00
62 Red Schoendienst .25 .60
63 Jimmie Foxx .40 1.00
64 Josh Hamilton .25 .60
65 Babe Ruth 1.00 2.50
66 Sandy Koufax .75 2.00
67 Dave Winfield .25 .60
68 Gary Carter .25 .60
69 Kevin Youkilis .15 .40
70 Rogers Hornsby .25 .60
71 CC Sabathia .25 .60
72 Justin Morneau .25 .60
73 Carl Yastrzemski .60 1.50
74 Tom Seaver .25 .60
75 Albert Pujols .50 1.25
76 Felix Hernandez .25 .60
77 Hunter Pence .25 .60
78 Ryne Sandberg .75 2.00
79 Andrew McCutchen .40 1.00
80 Stephen Strasburg .40 1.00
81 Nelson Cruz .40 1.00
82 Starlin Castro .25 .60
83 David Price .30 .75
84 Tim Lincecum .25 .60
85 Frank Robinson .25 .60
86 Prince Fielder .25 .60
87 Clayton Kershaw .60 1.50
88 Robinson Cano .25 .60
89 Mickey Mantle 1.25 3.00
90 Derek Jeter 1.00 2.50
91 Josh Johnson .25 .60
92 Mariano Rivera .50 1.25
93 Victor Martinez .25 .60
94 Buster Posey .50 1.25
95 George Sisler .25 .60
96 Ubaldo Jimenez .15 .40
97 Stan Musial .60 1.50
98 Aroldis Chapman RC 1.25 3.00
99 Ozzie Smith .50 1.25
100 Nolan Ryan 1.25 3.00
101 Ricky Nolasco .15 .40
102 Jorge Posada .25 .60
103 Magglio Ordonez .25 .60
104 Lucas Duda RC 1.00 2.50
105 Chris Carter .15 .40
106 Ben Revere RC .60 1.50
107 Brian Wilson .40 1.00
108 Brett Wallace .15 .40
109 Chris Volstad .15 .40
110 Todd Helton .25 .60
111 Jason Bay .25 .60
112 Carlos Zambrano .25 .60
113 Jose Bautista .25 .60
114 Chris Coghlan .15 .40
115 Jeremy Jeffress RC .40 1.00
116 Jake Peavy .15 .40
117 Dallas Braden .15 .40
118 Mike Pelfrey .15 .40
119 Brian Bogusevic (RC) .40 1.00
120 Gaby Sanchez .15 .40
121 Michael Cuddyer .15 .40
122 Derrek Lee .15 .40
123 Ted Lilly .15 .40
124 J.J. Hardy .15 .40
125 Francisco Liriano .15 .40
126 Billy Butler .15 .40
127 Rickie Weeks .15 .40
128 Dan Haren .15 .40
129 Aaron Hill .15 .40
130 Will Venable .15 .40
131 Cody Ross .15 .40
132 David Murphy .15 .40
133 Pablo Sandoval .25 .60
134 Kelly Johnson .15 .40
135 Ryan Dempster .15 .40
136 Brett Myers .15 .40
137 Ricky Romero .15 .40
138 Yovani Gallardo .15 .40
139 Raul Ibanez .25 .60
140 Shaun Marcum .15 .40
141 Brandon Inge .15 .40
142 Max Scherzer .40 1.00
143 Carl Pavano .15 .40
144 Jon Niese .15 .40
145 Jason Bartlett .15 .40
146 Melky Cabrera .15 .40
147 Kurt Suzuki .15 .40
148 Carlos Quentin .15 .40
149 Adam Jones .25 .60
150 Kosuke Fukudome .25 .60
151 Michael Young .15 .40
152 Paul Maholm .15 .40
153 Delmon Young .25 .60
154 Dan Uggla .15 .40
155 R.A. Dickey .25 .60
156 Brennan Boesch .25 .60
157 Ryan Ludwick .15 .40
158 Madison Bumgarner .30 .75
159 Ervin Santana .15 .40
160 Miguel Montero .15 .40
161 Aramis Ramirez .15 .40
162 Cliff Lee .25 .60
163 Russell Martin .15 .40
164 Cy Young .40 1.00
165 Yadier Molina .50 1.25
166 Gordon Beckham .15 .40
167 Cal Ripken Jr. 1.25 3.00
168 Alex Gordon .25 .60
169 Orlando Hudson .15 .40
170 Nick Swisher .25 .60
171 Manny Ramirez .40 1.00
172 Ryan Zimmerman .25 .60
173 Adam Dunn .25 .60
174 Reggie Jackson .25 .60
175 Edwin Jackson .15 .40
176 Kendry Morales .15 .40
177 Bernie Williams .25 .60
178 Chone Figgins .15 .40
179 Neil Walker .25 .60
180 Alexei Ramirez .25 .60
181 Lars Anderson .25 .60
182 Bobby Abreu .15 .40
183 Rafael Furcal .15 .40
184 Gerardo Parra .15 .40
185 Logan Morrison .15 .40
186 Tommy Hunter .15 .40
187 Lance Berkman .25 .60
188 Chris Sale RC 3.00 8.00
189 Mike Aviles .15 .40
190 Jaime Garcia .25 .60
191 Desmond Jennings RC .60 1.50
192 Jair Jurrjens .15 .40
193 Carlos Beltran .25 .60
194 Lorenzo Cain .15 .40
195 Bronson Arroyo .15 .40
196 Pat Burrell .15 .40
197 Colby Rasmus .25 .60
198 Jayson Werth .25 .60
199 James Shields .15 .40
200 John Lackey .25 .60
201 Travis Snider .15 .40
202 Adam Wainwright .25 .60
203 Brian Matusz .15 .40
204 Neftali Feliz .15 .40
205 Chris Johnson .15 .40
206 Torii Hunter .15 .40
207 Kyle Drabek RC .60 1.50
208 Mike Stanton .40 1.00
209 Tim Hudson .25 .60
210 Aaron Rowand .15 .40
211 Rollie Fingers .25 .60
212 Miguel Tejada .25 .60
213 Rick Porcello .25 .60
214 Pedro Alvarez RC .75 2.00
215 Trevor Cahill .15 .40
216 Angel Pagan .15 .40
217 Adrian Beltre .40 1.00
218 Austin Jackson .15 .40
219 Casey McGehee .15 .40
220 Tyler Colvin .15 .40
221 Martin Prado .15 .40
222 Heath Bell .15 .40
223 Ivan Rodriguez .25 .60
224 Drew Stubbs .15 .40
225 Vernon Wells .15 .40
226 Geovany Soto .25 .60
227 Cameron Maybin .15 .40
228 Ryan Kalish .25 .60
229 Alex Gonzalez .15 .40
230 Ian Desmond .15 .40
231 Mark Reynolds .15 .40
232 Jhonny Peralta .15 .40
233 Yunesky Maya RC .40 1.00
234 Sean Rodriguez .15 .40
235 Johnny Bench .40 1.00
236 Alex Rios .15 .40
237 Roy Campanella .40 1.00
238 Brandon Beachy RC 1.00 2.50
239 Josh Willingham .25 .60
240 Fausto Carmona .15 .40
241 Brian Roberts .15 .40
242 Joba Chamberlain .15 .40
243 Jim Thome .25 .60
244 Scott Kazmir .15 .40
245 Hank Conger RC .60 1.50
246 A.J. Burnett .15 .40
247 Matt Garza .15 .40
248 Dustin Pedroia .40 1.00
249 Jacoby Ellsbury .30 .75
250 Joe Saunders .15 .40
251 Mark Buehrle .25 .60
252 David DeJesus .15 .40
253 Carlos Lee .15 .40
254 Brandon Phillips .15 .40
255 Barry Zito .25 .60
256 Wade Davis .15 .40
257 James Loney .15 .40
258 Freddy Sanchez .15 .40
259 Aubrey Huff .15 .40
260 Marlon Byrd .15 .40
261 Daniel Bard .15 .40
262 Marco Scutaro .25 .60
263 Johnny Damon .25 .60
264 Jeremy Hellickson RC 1.00 2.50
265 Stephen Drew .15 .40
266 Daric Barton .15 .40
267 Jake Arrieta .30 .75
268 Wandy Rodriguez .15 .40
269 Curtis Granderson .30 .75
270 Brad Lidge .15 .40
271 John Danks .15 .40
272 Felix Pie .15 .40
273 Chad Billingsley .25 .60
274 Jose Tabata .15 .40
275 Ruben Tejada .15 .40
276 Ian Stewart .15 .40
277 Derek Lowe .15 .40
278 Denard Span .15 .40
279 Josh Thole .15 .40
280 Jonathan Sanchez .15 .40
281 Juan Pierre .15 .40
282 B.J. Upton .25 .60
283 Rick Ankiel .15 .40
284 Jed Lowrie .15 .40
285 Colby Lewis .15 .40
286 Jason Kubel .15 .40
287 Jorge De la Rosa .15 .40
288 C.J. Wilson .15 .40
289 Will Rhymes .15 .40
290 Jake McGee (RC) .75 2.00
291 Chris Young .15 .40
292 Andre Ethier .25 .60
293 Joakim Soria .15 .40
294 Garrett Jones .15 .40
295 Phil Hughes .15 .40
296 Ty Cobb .60 1.50
297 Grady Sizemore .25 .60
298 Tris Speaker .25 .60
299 Andruw Jones .15 .40
300 Franklin Gutierrez .15 .40
301 Alfonso Soriano SP 2.00 5.00
302 Brian McCann SP 2.00 5.00
303 Johnny Mize SP 2.00 5.00
304 Brian Duensing SP 1.50 4.00
305 Mark Ellis SP 1.50 4.00
306 Tommy Hanson SP 2.00 5.00
307 Danny Valencia SP 2.00 5.00
308 Kila Ka'aihue SP 1.50 4.00
309 Clay Buchholz SP 2.00 5.00
310 Jon Garland SP 1.50 4.00
311 Hisanori Takahashi SP 1.50 4.00
312 Justin Verlander SP 2.00 5.00
313 Mike Minor SP 1.50 4.00
314 Yonder Alonso RC SP 2.00 5.00
315 Jered Weaver SP 1.50 4.00
316 Lou Gehrig SP 4.00 10.00
317 Justin Upton SP 1.50 4.00
318 Hank Aaron SP 4.00 10.00
319 Elvis Andrus SP 2.00 5.00
320 Dexter Fowler SP 1.50 4.00
321 Brett Sinkbeil SP 1.50 4.00
322 Ike Davis SP 2.00 5.00
323 Shin-Soo Choo SP 2.50 6.00
324 Jay Bruce SP 2.00 5.00
325 Jason Castro SP 1.50 4.00
326 Chase Utley SP 2.50 6.00
327 Miguel Cabrera SP 2.50 6.00
328 Brett Anderson SP 2.00 5.00
329 Ian Kennedy SP 1.50 4.00
330 Brandon Morrow SP 1.50 4.00
331 Greg Halman RC SP 2.50 6.00
332 Ty Wigginton SP 1.50 4.00
333 Travis Wood SP 1.50 4.00
334 Nick Markakis SP 2.50 6.00
335 Freddie Freeman RC SP 5.00 12.00
336 Domonic Brown SP 2.50 6.00
337 Jason Vargas SP 1.50 4.00
338 Babe Ruth SP 5.00 12.00
339 Omar Infante SP 1.50 4.00
340 Miguel Olivo SP 1.50 4.00
341 Nyjer Morgan SP 1.50 4.00
342 Placido Polanco SP 1.50 4.00
343 Mitch Moreland SP 1.50 4.00
344 Josh Beckett SP 2.00 5.00
345 Erik Bedard SP 1.50 4.00
346 Shane Victorino SP 2.00 5.00
347 Konrad Schmidt RC SP 1.50 4.00
348 J.A. Happ SP 2.00 5.00
349 Xavier Nady SP 1.50 4.00
350 Carlos Pena SP 2.00 5.00

2011 Topps Gypsy Queen Framed Green

*GREEN: 1.2X TO 3X BASIC
*GREEN RC .5X TO 1.2X BASIC RC

2011 Topps Gypsy Queen Framed Paper

*PAPER: 1.5X TO 4X BASIC
*PAPER RC: .6X TO 1.5X BASIC RC
STATED PRINT RUN 999 SER.#'d SETS

2011 Topps Gypsy Queen Mini

*MINI 1-300: 1.2X TO 3X BASIC
*MINI RC 1-300 .5X TO 1.2X BASIC
PLATE PRINT RUN 1 SET PER COLOR
BLACK-CYAN-MAGENTA-YELLOW ISSUED
NO PLATE PRICING DUE TO SCARCITY
1B Suzuki SP Follow Through 5.00 12.00
2B Roy Halladay SP/Facing right 2.50 6.00
3B Cole Hamels SP/Arm back 3.00 8.00
4B Jackie Robinson SP/Glove up 4.00 10.00
5B Tris Speaker SP/Standing 2.50 6.00
6B Frank Robinson SP/Portrait 2.50 6.00
7B Jim Palmer SP/Portrait 2.50 6.00
8B Troy Tulowitzki SP/Swinging 4.00 10.00
9B Scott Rolen SP/Running 2.50 6.00
10B Heyward SP Swing 3.00 8.00
11B Zack Greinke SP/White jersey 4.00 10.00
12B Howard SP Follow Through 3.00 8.00
13B Joey Votto SP/Running 4.00 10.00
14B Brooks Robinson SP/Fielding 2.50 6.00
15B Matt Kemp SP/Front leg up 3.00 8.00
16B Chris Carpenter SP/Pitching 2.50 6.00
17B Mark Teixeira SP/Swinging 2.50 6.00
18B Christy Mathewson SP/With bat 4.00 10.00
19B Jon Lester SP/Front leg up 2.50 6.00
20B Andre Dawson SP/Cubs 2.50 6.00
21B Wright SP Swing 3.00 8.00
22B Barry Larkin SP/Running 2.00 5.00
23B Johnny Cueto SP/Pitching 2.50 6.00
24B Chipper Jones SP/Swinging 4.00 10.00
25B Mel Ott SP/Bat on shoulder 4.00 10.00
26B Adrian Gonzalez SP/Running 3.00 8.00
27B Roy Oswalt SP/Knee up 2.50 6.00
28B Tony Gwynn SP/Pinstripped jersey 4.00 10.00
29B Cobb SP w/Glove 6.00 15.00
30B Hanley Ramirez SP/Swinging 2.50 6.00
31B Joe Mauer SP/Blue jersey 3.00 8.00
32B Carl Crawford SP/Bat on shoulder 2.50 6.00
33B Ian Kinsler SP/Red jersey 2.50 6.00
34B Johan Santana SP/Arm up 2.50 6.00
35B Pee Wee Reese SP/With bat 2.50 6.00
36B Vladimir Guerrero SP/Swinging 2.50 6.00
37B Braun SP Running 2.50 6.00
38B Walter Johnson SP
Pitch follow through 4.00 10.00
39B Johnny Mize SP/Yankees 2.50 6.00
40B George Sisler SP/Bat on shoulder 2.50 6.00
41B Matt Holliday SP/Swinging 4.00 10.00
42B Jose Reyes SP/Swinging 2.50 6.00
43B Matt Cain SP/Portrait 2.50 6.00
44B Bob Gibson SP/Leg up 2.50 6.00
45B Carlos Gonzalez SP/Front leg up 2.50 6.00
46B Thurman Munson SP
Swing follow through 4.00 10.00
47B Jimmy Rollins SP/Facing right 2.50 6.00
48B Roger Maris SP/Cardinals 4.00 10.00
49B Honus Wagner SP/With glove 4.00 10.00
50B Al Kaline SP/With glove 3.00 8.00
51B Rodriguez SP Running 5.00 12.00
52B Carlos Santana SP/With bat 4.00 10.00
53B Jimmie Foxx SP/Bat on left shoulder 4.00 10.00
54B Frank Thomas SP/Facing left 4.00 10.00
55B Longoria SP Running 2.50 6.00
56B Mat Latos SP/Hands together 2.50 6.00
57B David Ortiz SP/Front leg down 4.00 10.00
58B Dale Murphy SP/Red jersey 4.00 10.00
59B Duke Snider SP/Hands together 2.00 5.00
60B Rogers Hornsby SP/Leaning on knee 2.00 5.00
61B Robin Yount SP/Blue jersey 3.00 8.00
62B Red Schoendienst SP/With ball 2.50 6.00
63B Jimmie Foxx SP/Glove up 4.00 10.00
64B Josh Hamilton SP/Blue jersey 2.50 6.00
65B Ruth SP w/Bat 8.00 20.00
66B Koufax SP Hands Together 8.00 20.00
67B Dave Winfield SP
Swing follow through 2.50 6.00
68B Gary Carter SP/Mets 2.50 6.00
69B Kevin Youkilis SP/Facing left 1.50 4.00
70B Rogers Hornsby SP/Giants 2.00 5.00
71B CC Sabathia SP
No crowd in background 2.00 5.00
72B Justin Morneau SP/Blue jersey 2.50 6.00
73B Carl Yastrzemski SP/Bat up 6.00 15.00
74B Tom Seaver SP/Arms up 2.00 5.00
75B Pujols SP w/Bat 5.00 12.00
76B Felix Hernandez SP/White jersey 2.50 6.00
77B Hunter Pence SP/Facing right 2.50 6.00
78B Sandberg SP w/Bat 6.00 15.00
79B McCutchen SP Arms back 4.00 10.00
80B Strasburg SP 37 Showing 4.00 10.00
81B Nelson Cruz SP/Red jersey 4.00 10.00
82B Starlin Castro SP/Blue jersey 2.50 6.00
83B David Price SP/Hands together 3.00 8.00
84B Lincecum SP Blk Jsy 2.50 6.00
85B Frank Robinson SP/Fielding 2.50 6.00
86B Prince Fielder SP/Bat up 2.50 6.00
87B C.Kershaw SP Leg up 6.00 15.00
88B Robinson Cano SP/Swinging 2.50 6.00
89B Mantle SP Bat Up 12.00 30.00
90B Jeter SP w/Bat 40.00 80.00
91B Josh Johnson SP/Leg up 2.00 5.00
92B Mariano Rivera SP 5.00 12.00
93B Victor Martinez SP/Facing right 2.50 6.00
94B Posey SP w/Bat 5.00 12.00
95B George Sisler SP/Both hands on bat 2.50 6.00
96B Ubaldo Jimenez SP/Portrait 1.50 4.00
97B Musial SP Facing Left 5.00 12.00
98B Chapman SP Portrait 5.00 12.00
99B Smith SP w/Bat 5.00 12.00
100B Ryan SP Angels 12.00 30.00
301 Alfonso Soriano 1.00 2.50
302 Brian McCann 1.00 2.50
303 Johnny Mize 1.00 2.50
304 Brian Duensing .60 1.50
305 Mark Ellis .60 1.50
306 Tommy Hanson .60 1.50
307 Danny Valencia 1.00 2.50
308 Kila Ka'aihue .60 1.50
309 Clay Buchholz .60 1.50
310 Jon Garland .60 1.50
311 Hisanori Takahashi .60 1.50
312 Justin Verlander 1.50 4.00
313 Mike Minor .60 1.50
314 Yonder Alonso 1.00 2.50
315 Jered Weaver 1.00 2.50
316 Lou Gehrig 3.00 8.00
317 Justin Upton 1.00 2.50
318 Hank Aaron 3.00 8.00
319 Elvis Andrus 1.00 2.50
320 Dexter Fowler 1.00 2.50
321 Brett Sinkbeil .60 1.50
322 Ike Davis .60 1.50
323 Shin-Soo Choo 1.00 2.50
324 Jay Bruce 1.00 2.50
325 Jason Castro .60 1.50
326 Chase Utley 1.00 2.50
327 Miguel Cabrera 1.50 4.00
328 Brett Anderson .60 1.50
329 Ian Kennedy .60 1.50
330 Brandon Morrow .60 1.50
331 Greg Halman 1.00 2.50
332 Ty Wigginton .60 1.50
333 Travis Wood .60 1.50

334 Nick Markakis 1.25 3.00
335 Freddie Freeman 10.00 25.00
336 Domonic Brown 1.25 3.00
337 Jason Vargas .60 1.50
338 Babe Ruth 4.00 10.00
339 Omar Infante .60 1.50
340 Miguel Olivo .60 1.50
341 Nyjer Morgan .60 1.50
342 Placido Polanco .60 1.50
343 Mitch Moreland .60 1.50
344 Josh Beckett .60 1.50
345 Erik Bedard .60 1.50
346 Shane Victorino 1.00 2.50
347 Konrad Schmidt .60 1.50
348 J.A. Happ 1.00 2.50
349 Xavier Nady .60 1.50
350 Carlos Pena 1.00 2.50

2011 Topps Gypsy Queen Mini Black

*BLACK: 2.5X TO 6X BASIC
*BLACK RC: 1X TO 2.5X BASIC
90 Derek Jeter 20.00 50.00
301 Alfonso Soriano 1.50 4.00
302 Brian McCann 1.50 4.00
303 Johnny Mize 1.50 4.00
304 Brian Duensing 1.00 2.50
305 Mark Ellis 1.00 2.50
306 Tommy Hanson 1.00 2.50
307 Danny Valencia 1.50 4.00
308 Kila Ka'aihue 1.00 2.50
309 Clay Buchholz 1.00 2.50
310 Jon Garland 1.00 2.50
311 Hisanori Takahashi 1.00 2.50
312 Justin Verlander 2.50 6.00
313 Mike Minor 1.00 2.50
314 Yonder Alonso 1.50 4.00
315 Jered Weaver 1.50 4.00
316 Lou Gehrig 5.00 12.00
317 Justin Upton 1.50 4.00
318 Hank Aaron 5.00 12.00
319 Elvis Andrus 1.50 4.00
320 Dexter Fowler 1.50 4.00
321 Brett Sinkbeil 1.00 2.50
322 Ike Davis 1.00 2.50
323 Shin-Soo Choo 1.50 4.00
324 Jay Bruce 1.50 4.00
325 Jason Castro 1.00 2.50
326 Chase Utley 1.50 4.00
327 Miguel Cabrera 2.50 6.00
328 Brett Anderson 1.00 2.50
329 Ian Kennedy 1.00 2.50
330 Brandon Morrow 1.00 2.50
331 Greg Halman 1.50 4.00
332 Ty Wigginton 1.00 2.50
333 Travis Wood 1.00 2.50
334 Nick Markakis 2.00 5.00
335 Freddie Freeman 15.00 40.00
336 Domonic Brown 2.00 5.00
337 Jason Vargas 1.00 2.50
338 Babe Ruth 6.00 15.00
339 Omar Infante 1.00 2.50
340 Miguel Olivo 1.00 2.50
341 Nyjer Morgan 1.00 2.50
342 Placido Polanco 1.00 2.50
343 Mitch Moreland 1.00 2.50
344 Josh Beckett 1.00 2.50
345 Erik Bedard 1.00 2.50
346 Shane Victorino 1.50 4.00
347 Konrad Schmidt 1.00 2.50
348 J.A. Happ 1.50 4.00
349 Xavier Nady 1.00 2.50
350 Carlos Pena 1.50 4.00

2011 Topps Gypsy Queen Mini Red Gypsy Queen Back

*RED: 1.5X TO 4X BASIC
*RED RC: .6X TO 1.5X BASIC
167 Cal Ripken Jr. 15.00 40.00
301 Alfonso Soriano 1.00 2.50
302 Brian McCann 1.00 2.50
303 Johnny Mize 1.00 2.50
304 Brian Duensing .60 1.50
305 Mark Ellis .60 1.50
306 Tommy Hanson .60 1.50
307 Danny Valencia 1.00 2.50
308 Kila Ka'aihue .60 1.50
309 Clay Buchholz .60 1.50
310 Jon Garland .60 1.50
311 Hisanori Takahashi .60 1.50
312 Justin Verlander 1.50 4.00
313 Mike Minor .60 1.50
314 Yonder Alonso 1.00 2.50
315 Jered Weaver 1.00 2.50
316 Lou Gehrig 3.00 8.00
317 Justin Upton 1.00 2.50
318 Hank Aaron 3.00 8.00
319 Elvis Andrus 1.00 2.50
320 Dexter Fowler 1.00 2.50
321 Brett Sinkbeil .60 1.50
322 Ike Davis .60 1.50
323 Shin-Soo Choo 1.00 2.50
324 Jay Bruce 1.00 2.50
325 Jason Castro .60 1.50
326 Chase Utley 1.00 2.50
327 Miguel Cabrera 1.50 4.00
328 Brett Anderson .60 1.50
329 Ian Kennedy .60 1.50
330 Brandon Morrow .60 1.50
331 Greg Halman 1.00 2.50
332 Ty Wigginton .60 1.50
333 Travis Wood .60 1.50
334 Nick Markakis 1.25 3.00
335 Freddie Freeman 10.00 25.00
336 Domonic Brown 1.25 3.00
337 Jason Vargas .60 1.50
338 Babe Ruth 4.00 10.00
339 Omar Infante .60 1.50
340 Miguel Olivo .60 1.50
341 Nyjer Morgan .60 1.50
342 Placido Polanco .60 1.50
343 Mitch Moreland .60 1.50
344 Josh Beckett .60 1.50
345 Erik Bedard .60 1.50
346 Shane Victorino 1.00 2.50
347 Konrad Schmidt .60 1.50
348 J.A. Happ 1.00 2.50
349 Xavier Nady .60 1.50
350 Carlos Pena 1.00 2.50

2011 Topps Gypsy Queen Mini Sepia

*SEPIA: 3X TO 8X BASIC
*SEPIA RC: 1.2X TO 3X BASIC RC
STATED PRINT RUN 99 SER.#'d SETS
1 Ichiro Suzuki 6.00 15.00
29 Ty Cobb 6.00 15.00
78 Ryne Sandberg 8.00 20.00
80 Stephen Strasburg 12.50 30.00
84 Tim Lincecum 6.00 15.00
90 Derek Jeter 20.00 50.00

2011 Topps Gypsy Queen Autographs

EXCHANGE DEADLINE 4/30/2014
AC Andrew Cashner 4.00 10.00
ACH Aroldis Chapman 60.00 120.00
AK Al Kaline 12.00 30.00
AP Angel Pagan 4.00 10.00
AT Andres Torres 4.00 10.00
BC Brett Cecil 4.00 10.00
BR Brooks Robinson 12.00 30.00
CB Clay Buchholz 5.00 12.00
CR Cal Ripken Jr. 30.00 80.00
CS CC Sabathia 20.00 50.00
CSA Chris Sale 10.00 25.00
DB Domonic Brown 4.00 10.00
DD David DeJesus 5.00 12.00
DH Daniel Hudson 4.00 10.00
DO David Ortiz 30.00 60.00
EL Evan Longoria 15.00 40.00
FF Freddie Freeman 10.00 25.00
FR Frank Robinson 10.00 25.00
GB Gordon Beckham 4.00 10.00
GG Gio Gonzalez 5.00 12.00
HA Hank Aaron 150.00 250.00
JB Jose Bautista 6.00 15.00
JC Jason Castro 6.00 15.00
JH Josh Hamilton 5.00 12.00
JHE Jason Heyward 10.00 25.00
JJ Josh Johnson 4.00 10.00
JJA Jon Jay 6.00 15.00
JT Josh Tomlin 5.00 12.00
MB Marlon Byrd 4.00 10.00
MS Mike Stanton 60.00 150.00
NC Nelson Cruz 4.00 10.00
NF Neftali Feliz 6.00 15.00
NM Nick Markakis 6.00 15.00
PS Pablo Sandoval 10.00 25.00
RH Roy Halladay 75.00 150.00
RHA Ryan Howard 30.00 60.00
RN Ricky Nolasco 8.00 10.00
RS Ryne Sandberg 20.00 50.00
RSH Red Schoendienst 10.00 25.00
SK Sandy Koufax 200.00 500.00
SV Shane Victorino 8.00 20.00
TH Tommy Hunter 4.00 10.00
WV Will Venable 4.00 10.00
YA Yonder Alonso 4.00 10.00

2011 Topps Gypsy Queen Framed Mini Relics

BL Barry Larkin 4.00 10.00
BR Babe Ruth 75.00 150.00
CR Cal Ripken Jr. 6.00 15.00
CU Chase Utley 4.00 10.00
DJ Derek Jeter 10.00 25.00
DO David Ortiz 3.00 8.00
DU Dan Uggla 4.00 10.00
DW David Wright 4.00 10.00
EL Evan Longoria 4.00 10.00
FR Frank Robinson 4.00 10.00
JH Josh Hamilton 5.00 12.00
JR Jackie Robinson 15.00 40.00
LG Lou Gehrig 25.00 60.00
MC Miguel Cabrera 3.00 8.00
MH Matt Holliday 5.00 12.00
MK Matt Kemp 3.00 8.00
NR Nolan Ryan 12.50 30.00
OS Ozzie Smith 5.00 12.00
PF Prince Fielder 3.00 8.00
RC Robinson Cano 6.00 15.00
RH Ryan Howard 3.00 8.00
RHE Rickey Henderson 4.00 10.00
SM Stan Musial 10.00 25.00
TM Thurman Munson 12.50 30.00

2011 Topps Gypsy Queen Future Stars

COMPLETE SET (20) 10.00 25.00
PLATE PRINT RUN 1 SET PER COLOR
BLACK-CYAN-MAGENTA-YELLOW ISSUED
NO PLATE PRICING DUE TO SCARCITY
*MINI: .75X TO 2X BASIC
FS1 Brian Matusz .40 1.00
FS2 Kyle Drabek .60 1.50
FS3 Yonder Alonso .60 1.50
FS4 Freddie Freeman 6.00 15.00
FS5 Desmond Jennings .60 1.50
FS6 Trevor Cahill .40 1.00
FS7 Ike Davis .40 1.00
FS8 Jason Heyward .75 2.00
FS9 Starlin Castro .60 1.50
FS10 Phil Hughes .40 1.00
FS11 Buster Posey 1.25 3.00
FS12 Neftali Feliz .40 1.00
FS13 Stephen Strasburg 1.00 2.50
FS14 Mat Latos .60 1.50
FS15 Jose Tabata .40 1.00
FS16 David Price .75 2.00
FS17 Clay Buchholz .40 1.00
FS18 Aroldis Chapman 1.25 3.00
FS19 Gordon Beckham .40 1.00
FS20 Mike Stanton 1.00 2.50

2011 Topps Gypsy Queen Great Ones

COMPLETE SET (30) 20.00 50.00
PLATE PRINT RUN 1 SET PER COLOR
BLACK-CYAN-MAGENTA-YELLOW ISSUED
NO PLATE PRICING DUE TO SCARCITY
*MINI: .75X TO 2X BASIC
GO1 Andre Dawson .60 1.50
GO2 Babe Ruth 2.50 6.00
GO3 Bob Gibson .60 1.50
GO4 Brooks Robinson .60 1.50
GO5 Christy Mathewson 1.00 2.50
GO6 Frank Robinson .60 1.50
GO7 George Sisler .60 1.50
GO8 Jackie Robinson 1.00 2.50
GO9 Jim Palmer .60 1.50
GO10 Jimmie Foxx 1.00 2.50
GO11 Johnny Mize .60 1.50
GO12 Johnny Bench 1.00 2.50
GO13 Lou Gehrig 2.00 5.00
GO14 Mel Ott 1.00 2.50
GO15 Mickey Mantle 3.00 8.00
GO16 Nolan Ryan 3.00 8.00
GO17 Pee Wee Reese .60 1.50
GO18 Robin Yount 1.00 2.50
GO19 Rogers Hornsby .60 1.50
GO20 Rollie Fingers .60 1.50
GO21 Thurman Munson 1.00 2.50
GO22 Tom Seaver .60 1.50
GO23 Tris Speaker .60 1.50
GO24 Ty Cobb 1.50 4.00
GO25 Walter Johnson 1.00 2.50
GO26 Honus Wagner 1.00 2.50
GO27 Cy Young 1.00 2.50
GO28 Babe Ruth 2.50 6.00
GO29 Frank Robinson .60 1.50
GO30 Nolan Ryan 3.00 8.00

2011 Topps Gypsy Queen Gypsy Queens

COMPLETE SET (19) 30.00 60.00
*RED TAROT: .6X TO 1.5X BASIC
GQ1 Zenda 1.50 4.00
GQ2 Oriana 1.50 4.00
GQ3 Halaveni 1.50 4.00
GQ4 Keyseria 1.50 4.00
GQ5 Sonia 1.50 4.00
GQ6 Sheerah 1.50 4.00
GQ7 Kara 1.50 4.00
GQ8 Dianamara 1.50 4.00
GQ9 Kali 1.50 4.00
GQ10 Levitia 1.50 4.00
GQ11 Mahrya 1.50 4.00
GQ12 Adara 1.50 4.00
GQ13 Mirela 1.50 4.00
GQ14 Angelina 1.50 4.00
GQ15 Lavenia 1.50 4.00
GQ16 Stefumari 1.50 4.00
GQ17 Olga 1.50 4.00
GQ18 Hevalia 1.50 4.00
GQ19 Adamina 1.50 4.00

2011 Topps Gypsy Queen Gypsy Queens Autographs

GQA1 Zenda 8.00 20.00
GQA2 Oriana 8.00 20.00
GQA3 Halaveni 8.00 20.00
GQA4 Keyseria 8.00 20.00
GQA5 Sonia 8.00 20.00
GQA6 Sheerah 8.00 20.00
GQA7 Kara 8.00 20.00
GQA8 Dianamara 8.00 20.00
GQA9 Kali 8.00 20.00
GQA10 Levitia 8.00 20.00
GQA11 Mahrya 8.00 20.00
GQA12 Adara 8.00 20.00
GQA13 Mirela 8.00 20.00
GQA14 Angelina 8.00 20.00
GQA15 Lavenia 8.00 20.00
GQA16 Stefumari 8.00 20.00
GQA17 Olga 8.00 20.00
GQA18 Hevalia 8.00 20.00
GQA19 Adamina 8.00 20.00

2011 Topps Gypsy Queen Gypsy Queens Jewel Relics

GQR1 Zenda 12.50 30.00
GQR2 Oriana 12.50 30.00
GQR3 Halaveni 12.50 30.00
GQR4 Keyseria 12.50 30.00
GQR5 Sonia 12.50 30.00
GQR6 Sheerah 12.50 30.00
GQR7 Kara 12.50 30.00
GQR8 Dianamara 12.50 30.00
GQR9 Kali 12.50 30.00
GQR10 Levitia 12.50 30.00
GQR11 Mahrya 12.50 30.00
GQR12 Adara 12.50 30.00
GQR13 Mirela 12.50 30.00
GQR14 Angelina 12.50 30.00
GQR15 Lavenia 12.50 30.00
GQR16 Stefumari 12.50 30.00
GQR17 Olga 12.50 30.00
GQR18 Hevalia 12.50 30.00
GQR19 Adamina 12.50 30.00

2011 Topps Gypsy Queen Home Run Heroes

COMPLETE SET (25) 10.00 25.00
PLATE PRINT RUN 1 SET PER COLOR
BLACK-CYAN-MAGENTA-YELLOW ISSUED
NO PLATE PRICING DUE TO SCARCITY
*MINI: .75X TO 2X BASIC
HH1 Babe Ruth 2.50 6.00
HH2 Albert Pujols 1.25 3.00
HH3 Jose Bautista .60 1.50
HH4 Mark Teixeira .60 1.50
HH5 Carlos Pena .60 1.50
HH6 Ryan Howard .75 2.00
HH7 Miguel Cabrera 1.00 2.50
HH8 Prince Fielder .60 1.50
HH9 Alex Rodriguez 1.25 3.00
HH10 David Ortiz 1.00 2.50
HH11 Andruw Jones .40 1.00
HH12 Adrian Beltre 1.00 2.50
HH13 Manny Ramirez 1.00 2.50
HH14 Jim Thome .60 1.50
HH15 Troy Glaus .40 1.00
HH16 Andre Dawson .60 1.50
HH17 Frank Robinson .60 1.50
HH18 Jimmie Foxx 1.00 2.50
HH19 Johnny Mize .60 1.50
HH20 Johnny Bench 1.00 2.50
HH21 Lou Gehrig 2.00 5.00
HH22 Mel Ott 1.00 2.50
HH23 Mickey Mantle 3.00 8.00
HH24 Rogers Hornsby .60 1.50
HH25 Tris Speaker .60 1.50

2011 Topps Gypsy Queen Relics

AR Alex Rodriguez 5.00 12.00
BG Brett Gardner 3.00 8.00
CR Cal Ripken Jr. 8.00 20.00
DJ Derek Jeter 8.00 20.00
DO David Ortiz 3.00 8.00
DP Dustin Pedroia 4.00 10.00
HR Hanley Ramirez 3.00 8.00
JE Jacoby Ellsbury 3.00 8.00
JJ Josh Johnson 3.00 8.00
JP Jorge Posada 3.00 8.00
KF Kosuke Fukudome 3.00 8.00
KY Kevin Youkilis 3.00 8.00
PF Prince Fielder 3.00 8.00
RB Ryan Braun 4.00 10.00
RC Robinson Cano 5.00 12.00
RH Ryan Howard 4.00 10.00
SC Scott Rolen 3.00 8.00
TH Tommy Hanson 3.00 8.00
YM Yadier Molina 5.00 12.00
JWE Jayson Werth 3.00 8.00

2011 Topps Gypsy Queen Royal Wedding Jewel Relic

PWR Prince William/K.Middleton 100.00 200.00

2011 Topps Gypsy Queen Sticky Fingers

SF1 Derek Jeter 2.50 6.00
SF2 Chase Utley .60 1.50
SF3 David Eckstein .40 1.00
SF4 Starlin Castro .60 1.50
SF5 Elvis Andrus .60 1.50
SF6 Mark Teixeira .60 1.50
SF7 Jose Reyes .60 1.50
SF8 Ivan Rodriguez .60 1.50
SF9 Brandon Phillips .40 1.00
SF10 David Wright .75 2.00
SF11 Hanley Ramirez .60 1.50
SF12 Orlando Hudson .40 1.00
SF13 Kevin Youkilis .40 1.00
SF14 Alcides Escobar .60 1.50
SF15 Jason Bartlett .40 1.00

2011 Topps Gypsy Queen Wall Climbers

WC1 Torii Hunter .40 1.00
WC2 Mike Stanton 1.00 2.50
WC3 Nick Swisher .60 1.50
WC4 Denard Span .40 1.00
WC5 Rajai Davis .40 1.00
WC6 Ichiro Suzuki 1.25 3.00
WC7 Franklin Gutierrez .40 1.00
WC8 Michael Brantley .40 1.00
WC9 Jason Heyward .75 2.00
WC10 David DeJesus .40 1.00

2012 Topps Gypsy Queen

COMP.SET w/o SP's (300) 20.00 50.00
COMMON CARD (1-350) .15 .40
COMMON RC (1-350) .20 .50
COMMON VAR SP (1-350) .75 2.00
PRINTING PLATE ODDS 1:1424 HOBBY
PLATE PRINT RUN 1 SET PER COLOR
BLACK-CYAN-MAGENTA-YELLOW ISSUED
NO PLATE PRICING DUE TO SCARCITY
1A Jesus Montero RC .60 1.50
1B Jesus Montero VAR SP 1.25 3.00
2 Hunter Pence .30 .75
3 Billy Butler .25 .60
4 Nyjer Morgan .25 .60
5 Russell Martin .25 .60
6A Matt Moore RC 1.00 2.50
6B M.Moore VAR SP 2.00 5.00
7 Aroldis Chapman .40 1.00
8 Jordan Zimmermann .30 .75
9 Max Scherzer .40 1.00
10A Roy Halladay .30 .75
10B Roy Halladay VAR SP 1.50 4.00
11 Matt Joyce .25 .60
12 Brennan Boesch .25 .60
13 Anibal Sanchez .25 .60
14 Miguel Montero .25 .60
15 Asdrubal Cabrera .30 .75
16A Eric Hosmer .30 .75
16B Eric Hosmer VAR SP 1.50 4.00
17 Trevor Cahill .25 .60
18 Jackie Robinson .40 1.00
19 Seth Smith .25 .60
20 Chipper Jones .40 1.00
21 Mat Latos .30 .75
22A Kevin Youkilis .25 .60
22B Kevin Youkilis VAR SP 2.00 5.00
23 Phil Hughes .25 .60
24 Matt Cain .30 .75
25 Doug Fister .25 .60
26 Brian Wilson .40 1.00
27 Mark Reynolds .25 .60
28 Michael Morse .25 .60
29 Ryan Roberts .25 .60
30 Cole Hamels .30 .75
31 Ted Lilly .25 .60
32 Michael Pineda .25 .60
33 Ben Zobrist .30 .75
34 Mark Trumbo .25 .60
35 Jon Lester .25 .60
36 Adam Lind .30 .75
37 Drew Storen .25 .60
38 James Loney .25 .60
39 Jaime Garcia .30 .75
40A Ichiro Suzuki .50 1.25
40B Ichiro Suzuki VAR SP 2.50 6.00
41 Yadier Molina .50 1.25
42 Tommy Hanson .25 .60
43 Stephen Drew .25 .60
44A Matt Kemp .30 .75
44B Matt Kemp VAR SP 1.50 4.00
45 Madison Bumgarner .30 .75
46 Chad Billingsley .25 .60
47 Derek Holland .25 .60
48 Jay Bruce .30 .75
49 Adrian Beltre .40 1.00
50A Miguel Cabrera .40 1.00
50B Miguel Cabrera VAR SP 2.00 5.00
51 Ian Desmond .25 .60
52 Colby Lewis .25 .60
53 Angel Pagan .25 .60
54A Mariano Rivera .50 1.25
54B Mariano Rivera VAR SP 2.50 6.00
55 Matt Holliday .40 1.00
56 Edwin Jackson .25 .60
57 Michael Young .25 .60
58 Zack Greinke .40 1.00
59 Clay Buchholz .25 .60
60A Jacoby Ellsbury .30 .75
60B Jacoby Ellsbury VAR SP 1.50 4.00
61 Yunel Escobar .25 .60
62 Jhonny Peralta .25 .60
63 John Axford .25 .60
64 Jason Kipnis .30 .75
65 Alex Avila .25 .60
66 Brandon Belt .30 .75
67A Josh Hamilton .30 .75
67B Josh Hamilton VAR SP 1.50 4.00
68 Alex Rodriguez .50 1.25
69 Troy Tulowitzki .40 1.00
70 David Price .30 .75
71A Ian Kennedy .25 .60
71B Ian Kennedy VAR SP 1.25 3.00
72 Ryan Dempster .25 .60
73 Ben Revere .30 .75
74 Bobby Abreu .25 .60
75 Ivan Nova .30 .75
76A Mike Napoli .25 .60
76B Mike Napoli VAR SP 1.25 3.00
77 J.P. Arencibia .25 .60
78 Sergio Santos .25 .60
79 Melky Cabrera .25 .60
80A Ryan Braun .25 .60
80B Ryan Braun VAR SP 1.25 3.00
81 Alcides Escobar .25 .60
82 David Wright .30 .75
83A Ryan Howard .30 .75
83B Ryan Howard VAR SP 1.50 4.00
84A Freddie Freeman .50 1.25
84B Freddie Freeman VAR SP 2.50 6.00
85 Adam Jones .25 .60
86 Jhoulys Chacin .25 .60
87 Jayson Werth .30 .75
88 Erick Aybar .25 .60
89 Bud Norris .25 .60
90 Mark Teixeira .30 .75
91 Tim Hudson .30 .75
92 Adrian Gonzalez .30 .75
93 Johnny Cueto .30 .75
94 Matt Garza .25 .60
95 Dexter Fowler .30 .75
96 Alexi Ogando .25 .60
97 Ubaldo Jimenez .25 .60
98 Jason Heyward .30 .75
99 Hanley Ramirez .30 .75
100A Derek Jeter 1.00 2.50
100B D.Jeter VAR SP 5.00 12.00
101 Paul Konerko .30 .75
102 Pedro Alvarez .25 .60
103 Shaun Marcum .25 .60
104 Desmond Jennings .30 .75
105 Pablo Sandoval .30 .75
106 John Danks .25 .60
107 Chris Sale .40 1.00
108 Guillermo Moscoso .25 .60
109 Cory Luebke .25 .60
110A Jose Bautista .30 .75
110B Jose Bautista VAR SP 1.50 4.00
111 Jose Tabata .25 .60
112 Neil Walker .25 .60
113 Carlos Ruiz .25 .60
114 Brad Peacock RC .60 1.50
115 Kurt Suzuki .25 .60
116 Josh Reddick .25 .60
117 Marco Scutaro .30 .75
118 Ike Davis .25 .60
119 Justin Morneau .30 .75
120A Mickey Mantle 1.25 3.00
120B M.Mantle VAR SP 6.00 15.00
121 Scott Baker .25 .60
122 Casey McGehee .25 .60
123 Geovany Soto .30 .75
124 Dee Gordon .25 .60
125 David Robertson .25 .60
126 Brett Myers .25 .60
127 Drew Pomeranz RC .60 1.50
128 Grady Sizemore .30 .75
129 Scott Rolen .30 .75
130 Justin Verlander .40 1.00
131 Domonic Brown .30 .75
132 Brandon McCarthy .25 .60
133 Mike Adams .25 .60
134 Juan Nicasio .25 .60
135A Clayton Kershaw .60 1.50
135B Clayton Kershaw VAR SP 3.00 8.00
136 Martin Prado .25 .60
137 Jose Reyes .30 .75
138 Chris Carpenter .30 .75
139 James Shields .25 .60
140 Joe Mauer .30 .75
141A Roy Oswalt .30 .75
141B Roy Oswalt VAR SP 1.50 4.00
142A Carlos Gonzalez .30 .75
142B Carlos Gonzalez VAR SP 1.50 4.00
143A Dustin Pedroia .40 1.00
143B Dustin Pedroia VAR SP 2.00 5.00
144 Andrew McCutchen .40 1.00
145A Ian Kinsler .30 .75
145B Ian Kinsler VAR SP 1.50 4.00
146 Elvis Andrus .30 .75
147A Mike Stanton .40 1.00
147B Mike Stanton VAR SP 2.00 5.00
148 Dan Haren .25 .60
149A Ryan Zimmerman .30 .75
149B Ryan Zimmerman VAR SP 1.50 4.00
150A CC Sabathia .30 .75
150B CC Sabathia VAR SP 1.50 4.00
151 Carl Crawford .30 .75
152 Dan Uggla .25 .60
153 Alex Gordon .30 .75
154 Victor Martinez .30 .75
155 Yovani Gallardo .30 .75
156 Michael Bourn .25 .60
157A Nelson Cruz .40 1.00
157B Nelson Cruz VAR SP 2.00 5.00
158 Rickie Weeks .25 .60
159 Shane Victorino .30 .75
160 Prince Fielder .30 .75
161 Aramis Ramirez .25 .60
162 Shin-Soo Choo .30 .75
163 Brandon Phillips .25 .60
164 Brian McCann .30 .75
165 Drew Stubbs .25 .60
166 Corey Hart .25 .60
167 Brett Gardner .30 .75
168 Ricky Romero .25 .60
169 B.J. Upton .30 .75
170A Cliff Lee .30 .75
170B Cliff Lee VAR SP 1.50 4.00
171 Jimmy Rollins .30 .75
172 Cameron Maybin .25 .60
173 David Ortiz .40 1.00
174 Josh Beckett .25 .60
175 Nick Swisher .30 .75
176 Howie Kendrick .25 .60
177 Nick Markakis .30 .75
178 Jose Valverde .25 .60
179 Paul Goldschmidt .40 1.00
180 Albert Pujols .50 1.25
181 Jeremy Hellickson .25 .60
182 Buster Posey .50 1.25
183 Heath Bell .25 .60
184A Stephen Strasburg .40 1.00
184B S.Strasburg VAR SP 2.00 5.00
185 Lance Berkman .30 .75
186 Josh Johnson .30 .75
187 Brandon Beachy .30 .75
188 J.J. Hardy .25 .60
189 Neftali Feliz .25 .60
190A Robinson Cano .30 .75
190B Robinson Cano VAR SP 1.50 4.00
191 Michael Cuddyer .25 .60
192 Ervin Santana .25 .60
193 Chris Young .25 .60
194 Torii Hunter .30 .75
195 Mike Trout 12.00 30.00
196 Adam Wainwright .30 .75
197A David Freese .30 .75
197B David Freese VAR SP 1.25 3.00
198 Lucas Duda .30 .75
199 Casey Kotchman .25 .60
200A Felix Hernandez .30 .75
200B Felix Hernandez VAR SP 1.50 4.00
201 Allen Craig .30 .75
202 Jason Motte .25 .60
203 Matt Harrison .25 .60
204 Jemile Weeks .60 1.50
205 Devin Mesoraco RC .60 1.50
206 David Murphy .25 .60
207 Matt Dominguez RC .75 2.00
208 Adron Chambers RC 1.00 2.50
209 Dellin Betances RC 1.00 2.50
210A Justin Upton .30 .75
210B Justin Upton VAR SP 1.50 4.00
211 Mike Moustakas .30 .75
212 Salvador Perez .30 .75
213 Ryan Lavarnway .25 .60
214 J.D. Martinez .40 1.00
215 Lonnie Chisenhall .30 .75
216 Jesus Guzman .25 .60
217 Eric Thames .30 .75
218 Colby Rasmus .30 .75
219 Alex Cobb .15 .40
220A Joey Votto .40 1.00
220B Joey Votto VAR SP 2.00 5.00
221 Javier Vazquez .15 .40
222 Ryan Vogelsong .25 .60
223 R.A. Dickey .30 .75
224 Luis Aparicio .25 .60
225 Albert Belle .15 .40
226A Johnny Bench .40 1.00
226B Johnny Bench VAR SP 2.00 5.00
227 Ralph Kiner .25 .60
228 Eddie Mathews .40 1.00
229A Ty Cobb .60 1.50
229B Ty Cobb VAR SP 3.00 8.00
230A Evan Longoria .30 .75
230B Evan Longoria VAR SP 1.50 4.00
231 Andre Dawson .25 .60
232A Joe DiMaggio .75 2.00
232B J.DiMaggio VAR SP 4.00 10.00
233 Duke Snider .25 .60
234 Carlton Fisk .25 .60
235 Orlando Cepeda .25 .60
236A Lou Gehrig .75 2.00
236B L.Gehrig VAR SP 4.00 10.00
237 Bob Gibson .25 .60
238 Rollie Fingers .25 .60
239 Juan Marichal .25 .60
240A Tim Lincecum .30 .75
240B Tim Lincecum VAR SP 1.50 4.00
241 Larry Doby .25 .60
242 Al Kaline .40 1.00
243 Catfish Hunter .25 .60
244 Roger Maris .40 1.00
245 Darryl Strawberry .15 .40
246 Willie McCovey .25 .60
247 Paul Molitor .40 1.00
248A Wade Boggs .25 .60
248B Wade Boggs VAR SP 1.25 3.00
249 Stan Musial .60 1.50
250A Ken Griffey Jr. .75 2.00
250B Ken Griffey Jr. VAR SP 4.00 10.00
251 Gary Carter .25 .60
252A Tony Gwynn .40 1.00
252B Tony Gwynn VAR SP 2.00 5.00
253 Cal Ripken Jr. 1.25 3.00
254 Brooks Robinson .25 .60
255 Frank Robinson .25 .60
256 Nolan Ryan 1.25 3.00
257 Ryne Sandberg .75 2.00
258A Mike Schmidt .60 1.50
258B Mike Schmidt VAR SP 3.00 8.00
259 Dave Winfield .25 .60
260A Curtis Granderson .30 .75
260B Curtis Granderson VAR SP 1.50 4.00
261 John Smoltz .40 1.00
262 Frank Thomas .40 1.00
263 Eddie Murray .25 .60
264 Ernie Banks .40 1.00
265 Warren Spahn .40 1.00
266 Carl Yastrzemski .60 1.50
267 Bob Feller .25 .60
268 Rod Carew .25 .60
269 Willie Stargell .25 .60
270A Roberto Clemente 1.00 2.50
270B R.Clemente VAR SP 5.00 12.00
271A Jered Weaver .30 .75
271B Jered Weaver VAR SP 1.50 4.00
272 Craig Kimbrel .30 .75
273 Starlin Castro .30 .75
274 Justin Masterson .25 .60
275 Mark Melancon .25 .60
276 Ricky Nolasco .25 .60
277 Vance Worley .30 .75
278 Dustin Ackley .25 .60
279 Jeff Niemann .25 .60
280 Willie Mays .75 2.00
281 James McDonald .25 .60
282 Jordan Walden .25 .60
283 Mike Leake .25 .60
284 Todd Helton .30 .75
285 Carlos Santana .30 .75
286 Chase Utley .30 .75
287 Daniel Hudson .25 .60
288A C.J. Wilson .25 .60
288B Yu Darvish VAR SP RC 60.00 200.00
289 Gio Gonzalez .30 .75
290 Sandy Koufax .75 2.00
291 Jarrod Parker RC .75 2.00
292 Delmon Young .25 .60
293 Yogi Berra .40 1.00
294A Reggie Jackson .25 .60
294B Reggie Jackson VAR SP 1.25 3.00
295 Doc Gooden .15 .40
296A Tom Seaver .25 .60
296B Tom Seaver VAR SP 1.25 3.00
297 Lou Brock .25 .60
298 Brandon Morrow .25 .60
299 Mike Carp .25 .60
300 Babe Ruth 1.00 2.50

2012 Topps Gypsy Queen Framed Blue

*FRAMED BLUE VET: 1.2X TO 3X BASIC VET
*FRAMED BLUE RC: .5X TO 1.2X BASIC RC
STATED ODDS 1:15 HOBBY
STATED PRINT RUN 599 SER.#'d SETS

2012 Topps Gypsy Queen Autographs

GROUP A ODDS 1:2310 HOBBY
GROUP B ODDS 1:201 HOBBY
GROUP C ODDS 1:80 HOBBY
GROUP D ODDS 1:16 HOBBY
EXCHANGE DEADLINE 3/31/2015
AB Albert Belle 10.00 25.00
AC Aroldis Chapman 10.00 25.00
ACR Allen Craig 6.00 15.00
AE Alcides Escobar 3.00 8.00
AET Andre Ethier 8.00 20.00
AG Adrian Gonzalez 10.00 25.00
AK Al Kaline 20.00 50.00
AL Adam Lind 3.00 8.00
AP Albert Pujols 100.00 200.00
AR Aramis Ramirez 6.00 15.00
BA Brett Anderson 3.00 8.00
BB Brandon Belt 4.00 10.00
BGI Bob Gibson 20.00 50.00
BL Brett Lawrie 6.00 15.00
BP Brandon Phillips 4.00 10.00
BPK Brad Peacock 3.00 8.00
CC Carl Crawford 4.00 10.00
CF Carlton Fisk 15.00 40.00
CG Carlos Gonzalez 10.00 25.00
CH Chris Heisey 3.00 8.00
CK Clayton Kershaw 60.00 150.00
CR Cal Ripken Jr. 25.00 60.00
CY Chris Young 3.00 8.00
DB Daniel Bard 3.00 8.00
DE Dennis Eckersley 8.00 20.00
DES Danny Espinosa 3.00 8.00
DH Daniel Hudson 3.00 8.00
DM Don Mattingly 30.00 60.00
DP Dustin Pedroia 15.00 40.00
DS Drew Stubbs 4.00 10.00
DU Dan Uggla 6.00 15.00
EA Elvis Andrus 6.00 15.00
EH Eric Hosmer 10.00 25.00
FH Felix Hernandez 20.00 50.00
FR Frank Robinson 15.00 40.00
FT Frank Thomas 30.00 80.00
GS Gaby Sanchez 3.00 8.00
HA Hank Aaron 200.00 300.00
JA J.P. Arencibia 4.00 10.00
JB Jose Bautista 12.00 30.00
JB Joe Benson 3.00 8.00
JC Johnny Cueto 3.00 8.00
JJ Jon Jay 3.00 8.00
JM Jesus Montero 3.00 8.00
JMO Jason Motte 6.00 15.00
JN Jon Niese 3.00 8.00
JP Jhonny Peralta 5.00 12.00
JS John Smoltz 15.00 40.00
JW Jered Weaver 12.50 30.00
JWE Jemile Weeks 3.00 8.00
JZ Jordan Zimmermann 5.00 12.00
KG Ken Griffey Jr. 200.00 300.00
KS Kyle Seager 5.00 12.00
MB Marlon Byrd 3.00 8.00
MC Miguel Cabrera 75.00 150.00
MK Matt Kemp 6.00 15.00
MM Mike Morse 5.00 12.00
MMO Mitch Moreland 6.00 15.00
MMR Matt Moore 4.00 10.00
NC Nelson Cruz 4.00 10.00
NE Nathan Eovaldi 5.00 12.00
NW Neil Walker 3.00 10.00
RC Robinson Cano 20.00 50.00
RD Randall Delgado 4.00 10.00
RS Ryne Sandberg 30.00 60.00
RZ Ryan Zimmerman 3.00 8.00
SC Starlin Castro 4.00 10.00
SK Sandy Koufax 150.00 400.00
SP Salvador Perez 12.00 30.00
TC Trevor Cahill 3.00 8.00
TW Travis Wood 3.00 8.00
YD Yu Darvish 200.00 400.00

2012 Topps Gypsy Queen Framed Mini Relics

GROUP A ODDS 1:227 HOBBY
GROUP B ODDS 1:365 HOBBY
GROUP C ODDS 1:27 HOBBY

AA Alex Avila 3.00 8.00
AJ Adam Jones 3.00 8.00
AM Andrew McCutchen 4.00 10.00
APE Andy Pettitte 3.00 8.00
BM Brian McCann 3.00 8.00
BP Brandon Phillips 4.00 10.00
CF Carlton Fisk 4.00 10.00
DF David Freese 8.00 20.00
DH Dan Haren 3.00 8.00
DHO Derek Holland 4.00 10.00
DO David Ortiz 3.00 8.00
DPR David Price 3.00 8.00
DW David Wright 4.00 10.00
EL Evan Longoria 3.00 8.00
EM Eddie Murray 4.00 10.00
FH Felix Hernandez 4.00 10.00
JB Jose Bautista 5.00 12.00
JD Joe DiMaggio 40.00 80.00
JH Jeremy Hellickson 3.00 8.00
JHE Jason Heyward 3.00 8.00
JL Jon Lester 3.00 8.00
JR Jose Reyes 3.00 8.00
JRO Jimmy Rollins 3.00 8.00
JS James Shields 3.00 8.00
JU Justin Upton 5.00 12.00
KY Kevin Youkilis 3.00 8.00
MB Madison Bumgarner 4.00 10.00
MCA Miguel Cabrera 8.00 20.00
MR Mariano Rivera 5.00 12.00
MT Mark Trumbo 3.00 8.00
NC Nelson Cruz 3.00 8.00
OS Ozzie Smith 6.00 15.00
PF Prince Fielder 3.00 8.00
PN Phil Niekro 10.00 25.00
PS Pablo Sandoval 4.00 10.00
RCL Roberto Clemente 40.00 80.00
RK Ralph Kiner 8.00 20.00
RM Roger Maris 12.00 30.00
RR Ricky Romero 3.00 8.00
RY Robin Yount 8.00 20.00
RZ Ryan Zimmerman 3.00 8.00
SC Steve Carlton 6.00 15.00
SG Steve Garvey 4.00 10.00
TH Tim Hudson 3.00 8.00
THA Tommy Hanson 3.00 8.00
TL Tim Lincecum 5.00 12.00
VM Victor Martinez 3.00 8.00
WB Wade Boggs 4.00 10.00
WS Willie Stargell 5.00 12.00
YG Yovani Gallardo 3.00 8.00
ZG Zack Greinke 3.00 8.00

2012 Topps Gypsy Queen Future Stars

COMPLETE SET (15) 10.00 25.00
PRINTING PLATE ODDS 1:1980 HOBBY
PLATE PRINT RUN 1 SET PER COLOR
BLACK-CYAN-MAGENTA-YELLOW ISSUED
NO PLATE PRICING DUE TO SCARCITY
BB Brandon Beachy .60 1.50
CK Craig Kimbrel .75 2.00
DH Derek Holland .60 1.50
DJ Desmond Jennings .75 2.00
EH Eric Hosmer .75 2.00
FF Freddie Freeman 1.25 3.00
JH Jeremy Hellickson .60 1.50
JM Jesus Montero .60 1.50
JU Justin Upton .75 2.00
MM Matt Moore 1.00 2.50
MP Michael Pineda .60 1.50
MS Mike Stanton 1.00 2.50
MT Mark Trumbo .60 1.50
PG Paul Goldschmidt 1.00 2.50
SC Starlin Castro .75 2.00

2012 Topps Gypsy Queen Glove Stories

COMPLETE SET (10) 5.00 12.00
STATED ODDS 1:6 HOBBY
PRINTING PLATE ODDS 1:1980 HOBBY
PLATE PRINT RUN 1 SET PER COLOR
BLACK-CYAN-MAGENTA-YELLOW ISSUED
NO PLATE PRICING DUE TO SCARCITY
BR Ben Revere .75 2.00
CY Chris Young .60 1.50
DJ Derek Jeter 2.50 6.00
DV Endy Chavez .60 1.50
DW Dewayne Wise .40 1.00
JF Jeff Francoeur .75 2.00
JH Josh Hamilton .75 2.00
KG Ken Griffey Jr. 2.00 5.00
TR Trayvon Robinson .60 1.50
WM Willie Mays 2.00 5.00

2012 Topps Gypsy Queen Glove Stories Mini

COMPLETE SET (10) 6.00 15.00
STATED ODDS 1 PER MINI BOX TOPPER
MINI PLATE ODDS 1:14,850 HOBBY
PLATE PRINT RUN 1 SET PER COLOR
BLACK-CYAN-MAGENTA-YELLOW ISSUED
NO PLATE PRICING DUE TO SCARCITY
BR Ben Revere 1.00 2.50
CY Chris Young .75 2.00
DJ Derek Jeter 3.00 8.00
DV Endy Chavez .75 2.00
DW Dewayne Wise .50 1.25
JF Jeff Francoeur 1.00 2.50
JH Josh Hamilton 1.00 2.50
KG Ken Griffey Jr. 2.50 6.00
TR Trayvon Robinson .75 2.00
WM Willie Mays 2.50 6.00

2012 Topps Gypsy Queen Gypsy King Autographs

STATED ODDS 1:495 HOBBY
1 Drago Koval 6.00 15.00
2 Zoran Marko 6.00 15.00
3 Zorislav Dragon 6.00 15.00
4 Prince Wasso 6.00 15.00
5 King Pavlov 6.00 15.00
6 Felek Horvath 6.00 15.00
7 Adamo the Bold 6.00 15.00
8 Aladar the Cruel 6.00 15.00
9 Damian Dolinski 6.00 15.00
10 Kosta Sarov 6.00 15.00
11 Antoni Stojka 6.00 15.00
12 Savo the Savage 6.00 15.00

2012 Topps Gypsy Queen Gypsy King Relics

STATED ODDS 1:1980 HOBBY
STATED PRINT RUN 25 SER.#'d SETS
1 Drago Koval 8.00 20.00
2 Zoran Marko 8.00 20.00
3 Zorislav Dragon 8.00 20.00
4 Prince Wasso 8.00 20.00
5 King Pavlov 8.00 20.00
6 Felek Horvath 8.00 20.00
7 Adamo the Bold 8.00 20.00
8 Aladar the Cruel 8.00 20.00
9 Damian Dolinski 8.00 20.00
10 Kosta Sarov 8.00 20.00
11 Antoni Stojka 8.00 20.00
12 Savo the Savage 8.00 20.00

2012 Topps Gypsy Queen Gypsy Kings

COMPLETE SET 20.00 50.00
STATED ODDS 1:48 HOBBY
1 Drago Koval 2.00 5.00
2 Zoran Marko 2.00 5.00
3 Zorislav Dragon 2.00 5.00
4 Prince Wasso 2.00 5.00
5 King Pavlov 2.00 5.00
6 Felek Horvath 2.00 5.00
7 Adamo the Bold 2.00 5.00
8 Aladar the Cruel 2.00 5.00
9 Damian Dolinski 2.00 5.00
10 Kosta Sarov 2.00 5.00
11 Antoni Stojka 2.00 5.00
12 Savo the Savage 2.00 5.00

2012 Topps Gypsy Queen Hallmark Heroes

COMPLETE SET (15) 12.50 30.00
PRINTING PLATE ODDS 1:1980 HOBBY
PLATE PRINT RUN 1 SET PER COLOR
BLACK-CYAN-MAGENTA-YELLOW ISSUED
NO PLATE PRICING DUE TO SCARCITY
BG Bob Gibson .40 1.00
CR Cal Ripken Jr. 2.00 5.00
EB Ernie Banks .60 1.50
FR Frank Robinson .40 1.00
JB Johnny Bench .60 1.50
JD Joe DiMaggio 1.25 3.00
JR Jackie Robinson .60 1.50
LG Lou Gehrig 1.25 3.00
MM Mickey Mantle 2.00 5.00
NR Nolan Ryan 2.00 5.00
RC Roberto Clemente 1.50 4.00
SK Sandy Koufax 1.25 3.00
SM Stan Musial 1.00 2.50
TC Ty Cobb 1.00 2.50
WM Willie Mays 1.25 3.00

2012 Topps Gypsy Queen Mini

PRINTING PLATE ODDS 1:336 HOBBY
PLATE PRINT RUN 1 SET PER COLOR
BLACK-CYAN-MAGENTA-YELLOW ISSUED
NO PLATE PRICING DUE TO SCARCITY
1A Jesus Montero .60 1.50
1B Jesus Montero VAR .75 2.00
2A Hunter Pence .75 2.00
2B Hunter Pence VAR 1.00 2.50
3 Billy Butler .60 1.50
4 Nyjer Morgan .60 1.50
5 Russell Martin .60 1.50
6A Matt Moore 1.00 2.50
6B Matt Moore VAR 1.25 3.00
7 Aroldis Chapman 1.00 2.50
8 Jordan Zimmermann .75 2.00
9 Max Scherzer 1.00 2.50
10A Roy Halladay .75 2.00
10B Roy Halladay VAR 1.00 2.50
11 Matt Joyce .60 1.50
12 Brennan Boesch .60 1.50
13 Anibal Sanchez .60 1.50
14 Miguel Montero .60 1.50
15 Asdrubal Cabrera .75 2.00
16A Eric Hosmer .75 2.00
16B Eric Hosmer VAR 1.00 2.50
17 Trevor Cahill .60 1.50
18 Jackie Robinson 1.00 2.50
19 Seth Smith .60 1.50
20 Chipper Jones 1.00 2.50
21 Mat Latos .75 2.00
22A Kevin Youkilis 1.00 2.50
22B Kevin Youkilis VAR 1.25 3.00
23 Phil Hughes .60 1.50
24 Matt Cain .75 2.00
25 Doug Fister .60 1.50
26A Brian Wilson 1.00 2.50
26B Brian Wilson VAR 1.25 3.00
27 Mark Reynolds .60 1.50
28 Michael Morse .60 1.50
29 Ryan Roberts .60 1.50
30A Cole Hamels .75 2.00
30B Cole Hamels VAR 1.00 2.50
31 Ted Lilly .60 1.50
32 Michael Pineda .60 1.50
33 Ben Zobrist .75 2.00
34A Mark Trumbo .60 1.50
34B Mark Trumbo VAR .75 2.00
35A Jon Lester .60 1.50
35B Jon Lester VAR .75 2.00
36 Adam Lind .75 2.00
37 Drew Storen .60 1.50
38 James Loney .60 1.50
39A Jaime Garcia .75 2.00
39B Jaime Garcia VAR 1.00 2.50
40A Ichiro Suzuki 1.25 3.00
40B Ichiro Suzuki VAR 1.50 4.00
41A Yadier Molina 1.25 3.00
41B Yadier Molina VAR 1.50 4.00
42A Tommy Hanson .60 1.50
42B Tommy Hanson VAR .75 2.00
43 Stephen Drew .60 1.50
44A Matt Kemp .75 2.00
44B Matt Kemp VAR 1.00 2.50
45A Madison Bumgarner .75 2.00
45B Madison Bumgarner VAR 1.00 2.50
46 Chad Billingsley .60 1.50
47 Derek Holland .60 1.50
48A Jay Bruce .75 2.00
48B Jay Bruce VAR 1.00 2.50
49 Adrian Beltre 1.00 2.50
50A Miguel Cabrera 1.00 2.50
50B Miguel Cabrera VAR 1.25 3.00
51 Ian Desmond .60 1.50
52 Colby Lewis .60 1.50
53 Angel Pagan .60 1.50
54A Mariano Rivera 1.25 3.00
54B Mariano Rivera VAR 1.50 4.00
55A Matt Holliday 1.00 2.50
55B Matt Holliday VAR 1.25 3.00
56 Edwin Jackson .60 1.50
57 Michael Young .60 1.50
58 Zack Greinke 1.00 2.50
59 Clay Buchholz .60 1.50
60A Jacoby Ellsbury .75 2.00
60B Jacoby Ellsbury VAR 1.00 2.50
61 Yunel Escobar .60 1.50
62 Jhonny Peralta .60 1.50
63 John Axford .60 1.50
64 Jason Kipnis .75 2.00
65A Alex Avila .60 1.50
65B Alex Avila VAR .75 2.00
66 Brandon Belt .75 2.00
67A Josh Hamilton .75 2.00
67B Josh Hamilton VAR 1.00 2.50
68A Alex Rodriguez 1.25 3.00
68B Alex Rodriguez VAR 1.50 4.00
69 Troy Tulowitzki 1.00 2.50
70 David Price .75 2.00
71A Ian Kennedy .60 1.50
71B Ian Kennedy VAR .75 2.00
72 Ryan Dempster .60 1.50
73 Ben Revere .75 2.00
74 Bobby Abreu .60 1.50
75 Ivan Nova .75 2.00
76A Mike Napoli .60 1.50
76B Mike Napoli VAR .75 2.00
77 J.P. Arencibia .60 1.50
78 Sergio Santos .60 1.50
79 Melky Cabrera .60 1.50
80A Ryan Braun .60 1.50
80B Ryan Braun VAR .75 2.00
81 Alcides Escobar .75 2.00
82A David Wright .75 2.00
82B David Wright VAR 1.00 2.50
83A Ryan Howard .75 2.00
83B Ryan Howard VAR 1.00 2.50
84A Freddie Freeman 1.25 3.00
84B Freddie Freeman VAR 1.50 4.00
85A Adam Jones .75 2.00
85B Adam Jones VAR 1.00 2.50
86 Jhoulys Chacin .60 1.50
87 Jayson Werth .60 1.50
88 Erick Aybar .60 1.50
89 Bud Norris .60 1.50
90A Mark Teixeira .75 2.00
90B Mark Teixeira VAR 1.00 2.50
91 Tim Hudson .75 2.00
92 Adrian Gonzalez .75 2.00
93 Johnny Cueto .75 2.00
94 Matt Garza .60 1.50
95 Dexter Fowler .75 2.00
96 Alexi Ogando .60 1.50
97 Ubaldo Jimenez .60 1.50
98A Jason Heyward .75 2.00
98B Jason Heyward VAR 1.00 2.50
99 Hanley Ramirez .75 2.00
100A Derek Jeter 2.50 6.00
100B Derek Jeter VAR 3.00 8.00
101A Paul Konerko .60 1.50
101B Paul Konerko VAR .75 2.00
102 Pedro Alvarez .60 1.50
103 Shaun Marcum .60 1.50
104 Desmond Jennings .75 2.00
105A Pablo Sandoval .75 2.00
105B Pablo Sandoval VAR 1.00 2.50
106 John Danks .60 1.50
107 Chris Sale 1.00 2.50
108 Guillermo Moscoso .75 2.00
109 Cory Luebke .60 1.50
110A Jose Bautista .75 2.00
110B Jose Bautista VAR 1.00 2.50
111 Jose Tabata .60 1.50
112 Neil Walker .60 1.50
113 Carlos Ruiz .60 1.50
114 Brad Peacock .60 1.50
115 Kurt Suzuki .60 1.50
116 Josh Reddick .60 1.50
117 Marco Scutaro .75 2.00
118 Ike Davis .60 1.50
119 Justin Morneau .75 2.00
120A Mickey Mantle 3.00 8.00
120B Mickey Mantle VAR 4.00 10.00
121 Scott Baker .60 1.50
122 Casey McGehee .60 1.50
123 Geovany Soto .75 2.00
124 Dee Gordon .60 1.50
125 David Robertson .60 1.50
126 Brett Myers .60 1.50
127 Drew Pomeranz .60 1.50
128 Grady Sizemore .75 2.00
129 Scott Rolen .60 1.50
130 Justin Verlander 1.00 2.50
131 Domonic Brown .75 2.00
132 Brandon McCarthy .60 1.50
133 Mike Adams .60 1.50
134 Juan Nicasio .60 1.50
135A Clayton Kershaw 1.50 4.00
135B Clayton Kershaw VAR 2.00 5.00
136 Martin Prado .60 1.50
137 Jose Reyes .60 1.50
138A Chris Carpenter .75 2.00
138B Chris Carpenter VAR 1.00 2.50
139A James Shields .60 1.50
139B James Shields VAR .75 2.00
140A Joe Mauer .75 2.00
140B Joe Mauer VAR 1.00 2.50
141A Roy Oswalt .75 2.00
141B Roy Oswalt VAR 1.00 2.50
142A Carlos Gonzalez .75 2.00
142B Carlos Gonzalez VAR 1.00 2.50
143A Dustin Pedroia 1.00 2.50
143B Dustin Pedroia VAR 1.25 3.00
144A Andrew McCutchen 1.00 2.50
144B McCutchen VAR 1.25 3.00
145A Ian Kinsler .75 2.00
145B Ian Kinsler VAR 1.00 2.50
146 Elvis Andrus .75 2.00
147A Mike Stanton 1.00 2.50
147B Mike Stanton VAR 1.25 3.00
148 Dan Haren .60 1.50
149A Ryan Zimmerman .75 2.00
149B Ryan Zimmerman VAR 1.00 2.50
150A CC Sabathia .75 2.00
150B CC Sabathia VAR 1.00 2.50
151 Carl Crawford .60 1.50
152A Dan Uggla .75 2.00
152B Dan Uggla VAR 1.00 2.50
153A Alex Gordon .75 2.00
153B Alex Gordon VAR 1.00 2.50
154A Victor Martinez .75 2.00
154B Victor Martinez VAR 1.00 2.50
155A Yovani Gallardo .75 2.00
155B Yovani Gallardo VAR 1.00 2.50
156 Michael Bourn .60 1.50
157A Nelson Cruz 1.00 2.50
157B Nelson Cruz VAR 1.25 3.00
158 Rickie Weeks .60 1.50
159 Shane Victorino .75 2.00
160 Prince Fielder .75 2.00
161 Aramis Ramirez .60 1.50
162 Shin-Soo Choo .75 2.00
163 Brandon Phillips .60 1.50
164 Brian McCann .75 2.00
165 Drew Stubbs .60 1.50
166 Corey Hart .60 1.50
167 Brett Gardner .75 2.00
168 Ricky Romero .60 1.50
169 B.J. Upton .75 2.00
170A Cliff Lee .75 2.00
170B Cliff Lee VAR 1.00 2.50
171A Jimmy Rollins .75 2.00
171B Jimmy Rollins VAR 1.00 2.50
172 Cameron Maybin .60 1.50
173A David Ortiz 1.00 2.50
173B David Ortiz VAR 1.25 3.00
174 Josh Beckett .60 1.50
175 Nick Swisher .75 2.00
176 Howie Kendrick .60 1.50
177 Nick Markakis .75 2.00
178 Jose Valverde .75 2.00
179A Paul Goldschmidt 1.00 2.50
179B Paul Goldschmidt VAR 1.25 3.00
180 Albert Pujols 1.25 3.00
181A Jeremy Hellickson .60 1.50
181B Jeremy Hellickson VAR .75 2.00
182A Buster Posey 1.25 3.00
182B Buster Posey VAR 1.50 4.00
183 Heath Bell .60 1.50
184A Stephen Strasburg 1.00 2.50
184B Stephen Strasburg VAR 1.25 3.00
185A Lance Berkman .75 2.00
185B Lance Berkman VAR 1.00 2.50
186A Josh Johnson .75 2.00
186B Josh Johnson VAR 1.00 2.50
187A Brandon Beachy .60 1.50
187B Brandon Beachy VAR .75 2.00
188 J.J. Hardy .60 1.50
189 Neftali Feliz .60 1.50
190A Robinson Cano .75 2.00
190B Robinson Cano VAR 1.00 2.50
191 Michael Cuddyer .60 1.50
192 Ervin Santana .60 1.50
193 Chris Young .60 1.50
194 Torii Hunter .75 2.00
195 Mike Trout 30.00 80.00
196 Adam Wainwright .75 2.00
197A David Freese .60 1.50
197B David Freese VAR .75 2.00
198 Lucas Duda .75 2.00
199 Casey Kotchman .60 1.50
200A Felix Hernandez .75 2.00
200B Felix Hernandez VAR 1.00 2.50
201 Allen Craig .75 2.00
202 Jason Motte .60 1.50
203 Matt Harrison .60 1.50
204 Jemile Weeks .60 1.50
205 Devin Mesoraco .60 1.50
206 David Murphy .60 1.50
207 Matt Dominguez .75 2.00
208 Adron Chambers .60 1.50
209 Dellin Betances 1.00 2.50
210A Justin Upton .75 2.00
210B Justin Upton VAR 1.00 2.50
211 Mike Moustakas .75 2.00
212 Salvador Perez .75 2.00
213 Ryan Lavarnway .60 1.50
214 J.D. Martinez 1.00 2.50
215 Lonnie Chisenhall .60 1.50
216 Jesus Guzman .60 1.50
217 Eric Thames .75 2.00
218 Colby Rasmus .75 2.00
219 Alex Cobb .40 1.00
220A Joey Votto 1.00 2.50
220B Joey Votto VAR 1.25 3.00
221 Javier Vazquez .40 1.00
222 Ryan Vogelsong .60 1.50
223 R.A. Dickey .75 2.00
224 Luis Aparicio .60 1.50
225 Albert Belle .40 1.00
226A Johnny Bench 1.00 2.50
226B Johnny Bench VAR 1.25 3.00
227 Ralph Kiner .60 1.50
228 Eddie Mathews 1.00 2.50
229A Ty Cobb 1.50 4.00
229B Ty Cobb VAR 2.00 5.00
230A Evan Longoria .75 2.00
230B Evan Longoria VAR 1.00 2.50
231 Andre Dawson .60 1.50
232A Joe DiMaggio 2.00 5.00
232B Joe DiMaggio VAR 2.50 6.00
233 Duke Snider .60 1.50
234 Carlton Fisk .60 1.50
235 Orlando Cepeda .60 1.50
236A Lou Gehrig 2.00 5.00
236B Lou Gehrig VAR 2.50 6.00
237 Bob Gibson .60 1.50
238 Rollie Fingers .60 1.50
239 Juan Marichal .60 1.50
240A Tim Lincecum .75 2.00
240B Tim Lincecum VAR 1.00 2.50
241 Larry Doby .60 1.50
242 Al Kaline 1.00 2.50
243 Catfish Hunter .60 1.50
244 Roger Maris 1.00 2.50
245 Darryl Strawberry .40 1.00
246 Willie McCovey .60 1.50
247 Paul Molitor 1.00 2.50
248A Wade Boggs .60 1.50
248B Wade Boggs VAR .75 2.00
249 Stan Musial 1.50 4.00
250A Ken Griffey Jr. 2.00 5.00
250B Ken Griffey Jr. VAR 2.50 6.00
251 Gary Carter .60 1.50
252A Tony Gwynn 1.00 2.50
252B Tony Gwynn VAR 1.25 3.00
253 Cal Ripken Jr. 3.00 8.00
254 Brooks Robinson .60 1.50
255 Frank Robinson .60 1.50
256 Nolan Ryan 3.00 8.00
257 Ryne Sandberg 2.00 5.00
258A Mike Schmidt 1.50 4.00
258B Mike Schmidt VAR 2.00 5.00
259 Dave Winfield .60 1.50
260A Curtis Granderson .75 2.00
260B Curtis Granderson VAR 1.00 2.50
261 John Smoltz 1.00 2.50
262 Frank Thomas 1.00 2.50
263 Eddie Murray .60 1.50
264 Ernie Banks 1.00 2.50
265 Warren Spahn .60 1.50
266 Carl Yastrzemski 1.50 4.00
267 Bob Feller .60 1.50
268 Rod Carew .60 1.50
269 Willie Stargell .60 1.50
270A Roberto Clemente 2.50 6.00
270B Roberto Clemente VAR 3.00 8.00
271A Jered Weaver .75 2.00
271B Jered Weaver VAR 1.00 2.50
272A Craig Kimbrel .75 2.00
272B Craig Kimbrel VAR 1.00 2.50
273A Starlin Castro .75 2.00
273B Starlin Castro VAR 1.00 2.50
274 Justin Masterson .60 1.50
275 Mark Melancon .60 1.50
276 Ricky Nolasco .60 1.50
277 Vance Worley .75 2.00
278 Dustin Ackley .60 1.50
279 Jeff Niemann .60 1.50
280 Willie Mays 2.00 5.00
281 James McDonald .60 1.50
282 Jordan Walden .60 1.50
283 Mike Leake .60 1.50
284 Todd Helton .75 2.00
285A Carlos Santana .75 2.00
285B Carlos Santana VAR 1.00 2.50
286A Chase Utley .75 2.00
286B Chase Utley VAR 1.00 2.50
287A Daniel Hudson .60 1.50
287B Daniel Hudson VAR .75 2.00
288 C.J. Wilson .60 1.50
289A Gio Gonzalez .75 2.00
289B Gio Gonzalez VAR 1.00 2.50
290 Sandy Koufax 2.00 5.00
291 Jarrod Parker .75 2.00
292 Delmon Young .60 1.50
293 Yogi Berra 1.00 2.50
294A Reggie Jackson .60 1.50
294B Reggie Jackson VAR .75 2.00
295 Doc Gooden .40 1.00
296A Tom Seaver .60 1.50
296B Tom Seaver VAR .75 2.00
297 Lou Brock .60 1.50
298 Brandon Morrow .60 1.50
299 Mike Carp .60 1.50
300 Babe Ruth 2.50 6.00
301 Billy Butler .75 2.00
302 Anibal Sanchez .75 2.00
303 Asdrubal Cabrera 1.00 2.50
304 Seth Smith .75 2.00
305 Matt Cain 1.00 2.50
306 Mark Reynolds .75 2.00
307 Michael Morse .75 2.00
308 Adrian Beltre 1.25 3.00
309 Michael Young .75 2.00
310 Zack Greinke 1.25 3.00
311 Brandon Belt 1.00 2.50
312 Troy Tulowitzki 1.25 3.00
313 David Price 1.00 2.50
314 Bobby Abreu .75 2.00
315 J.P. Arencibia .75 2.00
316 Jayson Werth 1.00 2.50
317 Tim Hudson 1.00 2.50
318 Johnny Cueto 1.00 2.50
319 Hanley Ramirez 1.00 2.50
320 Justin Verlander 1.25 3.00
321 Jose Reyes 1.00 2.50
322 Elvis Andrus 1.00 2.50
323 Michael Bourn .75 2.00
324 Rickie Weeks .75 2.00
325 Shane Victorino 1.00 2.50
326 Prince Fielder 1.00 2.50
327 Brandon Phillips .75 2.00
328 Drew Stubbs .75 2.00
329 Lou Brock .75 2.00
330 B.J. Upton .75 2.00
331 Josh Beckett .75 2.00
332 Nick Swisher 1.00 2.50
333 Albert Pujols 1.50 4.00
334 Heath Bell .75 2.00
335 Chris Young .75 2.00
336 Mike Trout 40.00 100.00
337 Eric Thames 1.00 2.50
338 Ryan Vogelsong .75 2.00
339 Albert Belle .50 1.25
340 Duke Snider .75 2.00
341 Larry Doby .75 2.00
342 Darryl Strawberry .50 1.25
343 Gary Carter .75 2.00
344 Cal Ripken Jr. 4.00 10.00
345 John Smoltz 1.25 3.00
346 Frank Thomas 1.25 3.00
347 Ernie Banks 1.25 3.00
348 Bob Feller .75 2.00
349 Dustin Ackley .75 2.00
350 Delmon Young 1.00 2.50

2012 Topps Gypsy Queen Mini Black

*BLACK 1-300: .6X TO 1.5X BASIC 1-300
*BLACK 301-350: .5X TO 1.2X BASIC 301-350
STATED ODDS 1:12 HOBBY

2012 Topps Gypsy Queen Mini Green

*GREEN 1-300: .6X TO 1.5X BASIC 1-300
*GREEN 301-350: .5X TO 1.2X BASIC 301-350
STATED ODDS 1:24 HOBBY
100 Derek Jeter 12.00 30.00

2012 Topps Gypsy Queen Mini Gypsy Queen Back

*GQ BACK 1-300: .5X TO 1.2X BASIC 1-300
*GQ BACK 301-350: .4X TO 1X BASIC 301-350
STATED ODDS 1:6 HOBBY

2012 Topps Gypsy Queen Mini Sepia

*SEPIA 1-300: 1.2X TO 3X BASIC 1-300
*SEPIA 301-350: 1X TO 2.5X BASIC 301-350
STATED ODDS 1:20 HOBBY
STATED PRINT RUN 99 SER.#'d SETS
100 Derek Jeter 12.50 30.00

2012 Topps Gypsy Queen Mini Straight Cut Back

*STRAIGHT 1-300: .5X TO 1.2X BASIC 1-300
*STRAIGHT 301-350: .4X TO 1X BASIC 301-350
STATED ODDS 1:6 HOBBY

2012 Topps Gypsy Queen Mini Stadium Seat Relics

STATED ODDS 1:2125 HOBBY
STATED PRINT RUN 100 SER.#'d SETS
SP Sportsman's Park 10.00 25.00
TS Tiger Stadium 15.00 40.00
WF Wrigley Field 12.50 30.00
MCS Milwaukee County Stadium 10.00 25.00
SHP Shibe Park 20.00 50.00

2012 Topps Gypsy Queen Moonshots

COMPLETE SET (20) 6.00 15.00
STATED ODDS 1:3 HOBBY
PRINTING PLATE ODDS 1:1980 HOBBY
PLATE PRINT RUN 1 SET PER COLOR
BLACK-CYAN-MAGENTA-YELLOW ISSUED
NO PLATE PRICING DUE TO SCARCITY
AB Albert Belle .40 1.00
AP Albert Pujols 1.25 3.00
BR Babe Ruth 2.50 6.00
CG Curtis Granderson .75 2.00
EL Evan Longoria .75 2.00
FR Frank Robinson .60 1.50
FT Frank Thomas 1.00 2.50
JB Jose Bautista .75 2.00
JH Josh Hamilton .75 2.00
JT Jim Thome .75 2.00
MM Mickey Mantle 3.00 8.00
MS Mike Stanton 1.00 2.50
NC Nelson Cruz 1.00 2.50
PF Prince Fielder .75 2.00
RH Ryan Howard .75 2.00
RJ Reggie Jackson .60 1.50
RK Ralph Kiner .60 1.50
WM Willie Mays 2.00 5.00
MSC Mike Schmidt 1.50 4.00
WMC Willie McCovey .60 1.50

2012 Topps Gypsy Queen Moonshots Mini

COMPLETE SET (20) 8.00 20.00
STATED ODDS 1 PER MINI BOX TOPPER
MINI PLATE ODDS 1:7425 HOBBY
PLATE PRINT RUN 1 SET PER COLOR
BLACK-CYAN-MAGENTA-YELLOW ISSUED
NO PLATE PRICING DUE TO SCARCITY
AB Albert Belle .50 1.25
AP Albert Pujols 1.50 4.00
BR Babe Ruth 3.00 8.00
CG Curtis Granderson 1.00 2.50
EL Evan Longoria 1.00 2.50
FR Frank Robinson .75 2.00
FT Frank Thomas 1.25 3.00
JB Jose Bautista 1.00 2.50
JH Josh Hamilton 1.00 2.50
JT Jim Thome 1.00 2.50
MM Mickey Mantle 4.00 10.00
MS Mike Stanton 1.25 3.00
NC Nelson Cruz 1.25 3.00
PF Prince Fielder 1.00 2.50
RH Ryan Howard 1.00 2.50
RJ Reggie Jackson .75 2.00
RK Ralph Kiner .75 2.00
WM Willie Mays 2.50 6.00
MSC Mike Schmidt 2.00 5.00
WMC Willie McCovey .75 2.00

2012 Topps Gypsy Queen Relic Autographs

STATED ODDS 1:1420 HOBBY
PRINT RUNS B/WN 5-25 COPIES PER
NO PRICING ON QTY 10 OR LESS
EXCHANGE DEADLINE 03/31/2015
AJ Adam Jones EXCH 25.00 60.00
AK Al Kaline/25 60.00 150.00
AR Aramis Ramirez/25 10.00 25.00
CF Carlton Fisk/25 30.00 80.00
CG Carlos Gonzalez/25 25.00 60.00
DE Danny Espinosa/25 10.00 25.00
DH Daniel Hudson/25 10.00 25.00
DM Don Mattingly/25 60.00 150.00
DU Dan Uggla/25 12.00 30.00
FT Frank Thomas/25
JB Jay Bruce/25 30.00 80.00
JJ Jon Jay EXCH 15.00 40.00
JV Justin Verlander/25 75.00 200.00
MC Miguel Cabrera/25 60.00 150.00
NC Nelson Cruz/25 15.00 40.00
RB Ryan Braun EXCH 40.00 100.00
RJ Reggie Jackson/25 60.00 150.00
SC Starlin Castro/25 12.00 30.00
TH Tommy Hanson/25 10.00 25.00
JMA Joe Mauer EXCH 40.00 100.00

2012 Topps Gypsy Queen Relics

GROUP A ODDS 1:576 HOBBY
GROUP B ODDS 1:313 HOBBY
GROUP C ODDS 1:28 HOBBY
AA Alex Avila 3.00 8.00
AJ Adam Jones 3.00 8.00
AM Andrew McCutchen 4.00 10.00
AP Andy Pettitte 3.00 8.00
BBU Billy Butler 3.00 8.00
BM Brian McCann 3.00 8.00
BP Brandon Phillips 3.00 8.00
CF Carlton Fisk 4.00 10.00
CW C.J. Wilson 3.00 8.00
DF David Freese 5.00 12.00
DH Dan Haren 3.00 8.00
DHO Derek Holland 3.00 8.00
DO David Ortiz 3.00 8.00
DP Dustin Pedroia 5.00 12.00
DPR David Price 3.00 8.00
DW David Wright 3.00 8.00
EL Evan Longoria 4.00 10.00
EM Eddie Murray 3.00 8.00
EMA Eddie Mathews 6.00 15.00
FR Frank Robinson 8.00 20.00
JD Joe DiMaggio 30.00 60.00
JE Jacoby Ellsbury 4.00 10.00
JH Jeremy Hellickson 3.00 8.00
JHE Jason Heyward 3.00 8.00
JL Jon Lester 3.00 8.00
JR Jose Reyes 3.00 8.00
JRO Jimmy Rollins 3.00 8.00
JS James Shields 3.00 8.00
JU Justin Upton 3.00 8.00
JW Jayson Werth 3.00 8.00
KY Kevin Youkilis 3.00 8.00
MB Madison Bumgarner 4.00 10.00
MC Matt Cain 3.00 8.00
MCA Miguel Cabrera 12.50 30.00
MH Matt Holliday 4.00 10.00
MR Mariano Rivera 5.00 12.00
MS Mike Stanton 3.00 8.00
MT Mark Trumbo 3.00 8.00
NC Nelson Cruz 3.00 8.00
OS Ozzie Smith 4.00 10.00
PF Prince Fielder 3.00 8.00
PN Phil Niekro 3.00 8.00
PS Pablo Sandoval 3.00 8.00
RC Rod Carew 3.00 8.00
RCL Roberto Clemente 30.00 60.00
RJ Reggie Jackson 10.00 25.00
RK Ralph Kiner 6.00 15.00
RM Roger Maris 12.50 30.00
RR Ricky Romero 3.00 8.00
RY Robin Yount 8.00 20.00
RZ Ryan Zimmerman 3.00 8.00
SC Steve Carlton 4.00 10.00
SG Steve Garvey 3.00 8.00
TG Tony Gwynn 6.00 15.00
TH Tim Hudson 3.00 8.00
THA Tommy Hanson 3.00 8.00
TL Tim Lincecum 4.00 10.00
VM Victor Martinez 3.00 8.00
WB Wade Boggs 4.00 10.00
WS Willie Stargell 6.00 15.00
YG Yovani Gallardo 3.00 8.00
ZG Zack Greinke 3.00 8.00

2012 Topps Gypsy Queen Sliding Stars

COMPLETE SET (15) 4.00 10.00
STATED ODDS 1:3 HOBBY
PRINTING PLATE ODDS 1:1980 HOBBY
PLATE PRINT RUN 1 SET PER COLOR
BLACK-CYAN-MAGENTA-YELLOW ISSUED
NO PLATE PRICING DUE TO SCARCITY
AM Andrew McCutchen 1.00 2.50
CG Curtis Granderson .75 2.00
DG Dee Gordon .60 1.50
DJ Derek Jeter 2.50 6.00
DP Dustin Pedroia 1.00 2.50
EA Elvis Andrus .75 2.00
IK Ian Kinsler .75 2.00
JE Jacoby Ellsbury .75 2.00
JR Jose Reyes .60 1.50
JW Jemile Weeks .60 1.50
MK Matt Kemp .75 2.00
NM Nyjer Morgan .60 1.50
RB Ryan Braun .60 1.50
SC Starlin Castro .75 2.00
JRO Jimmy Rollins .75 2.00

2012 Topps Gypsy Queen Sliding Stars Mini

COMPLETE SET (15) 5.00 12.00
STATED ODDS 1 PER MINI BOX TOPPER
MINI PLATE ODDS 1:9900 HOBBY
PLATE PRINT RUN 1 SET PER COLOR
BLACK-CYAN-MAGENTA-YELLOW ISSUED
AM Andrew McCutchen 1.25 3.00
CG Curtis Granderson 1.00 2.50
DG Dee Gordon .75 2.00
DJ Derek Jeter 3.00 8.00
DP Dustin Pedroia 1.25 3.00
EA Elvis Andrus 1.00 2.50
IK Ian Kinsler 1.00 2.50
JE Jacoby Ellsbury 1.00 2.50
JR Jose Reyes .75 2.00
JW Jemile Weeks .75 2.00
MK Matt Kemp 1.00 2.50
NM Nyjer Morgan .75 2.00
RB Ryan Braun .75 2.00
SC Starlin Castro 1.00 2.50
JRO Jimmy Rollins 1.00 2.50

2013 Topps Gypsy Queen

COMP.SET w/o SP's (300) 15.00 40.00
SP ODDS 1:24 HOBBY
SP VAR ODDS 1:465 HOBBY
PRINTING PLATE ODDS 1:459 HOBBY
1A Adam Jones .30 .75
1B A.Jones SP VAR 50.00 100.00
2 Joe Nathan .25 .60
3A Adrian Beltre .40 1.00
3B A.Beltre SP VAR 10.00 25.00
4 L.J. Hoes RC .50 1.25
5 Adrian Gonzalez .30 .75
6 Alex Rodriguez .50 1.25
7 Mike Schmidt SP 2.50 6.00
8 Andre Dawson .30 .75
9A Andrew McCutchen .40 1.00
9B A.McCutchen SP VAR 30.00 60.00
10 Al Kaline .40 1.00
11 Anthony Rizzo .50 1.25
12 Aroldis Chapman .40 1.00
13 Wei-Yin Chen .25 .60
14A Mike Trout SP 12.00 30.00
14B M.Trout SP VAR 50.00 100.00
15 Tyler Skaggs RC .60 1.50
16 Brandon Beachy .25 .60
17 Brandon Belt .30 .75
18 Brett Jackson .25 .60
19 Nolan Ryan SP 5.00 12.00
20A Albert Pujols .50 1.25
20B A.Pujols SP VAR 20.00 50.00
21 Ivan Nova .30 .75

22 CC Sabathia .30 .75
23 Cecil Fielder .25 .60
24 Chris Carter .25 .60
25 Chris Sale .40 1.00
26A Clayton Kershaw .60 1.50
26B Clayton Kershaw SP VAR 12.50 30.00
In Dugout
27 Chad Billingsley .30 .75
28 R.A. Dickey SP 1.25 3.00
29 Cole Hamels .30 .75
30 Bert Blyleven .30 .75
31 Josh Willingham .30 .75
32 Darin Ruf RC .75 2.00
33 Rob Brantly RC .40 1.00
34A David Freese .25 .60
34B David Freese SP VAR 12.50 30.00
High-fiving
35A David Price .30 .75
35B David Price SP VAR 12.50 30.00
With Jose Molina
36 Avisail Garcia RC .50 1.25
37 David Wright .30 .75
38 Derek Norris .25 .60
39 Dexter Fowler .30 .75
40 Bill Buckner .25 .60
41 Dylan Bundy RC 1.00 2.50
42 Jose Quintana .25 .60
43 Enos Slaughter .30 .75
44 Evan Longoria .30 .75
45A Felix Hernandez .30 .75
45B Felix Hernandez SP VAR 12.50 30.00
Hugging
46 Frank Thomas .40 1.00
47 Freddie Freeman .50 1.25
48 Gary Carter .30 .75
49 George Kell .30 .75
50 Babe Ruth 1.00 2.50
51 Clay Buchholz .25 .60
52 Hanley Ramirez .30 .75
53 Clayton Richard .25 .60
54 Jacoby Ellsbury .30 .75
55 Nathan Eovaldi .30 .75
56 Jason Heyward .30 .75
57 Jayson Werth .30 .75
58 Jean Segura .30 .75
59 Jered Weaver .30 .75
60 Billy Williams .30 .75
61A Joe Mauer .30 .75
61B Joe Mauer SP VAR 12.50 30.00
With Justin Morneau
62A Ryan Braun SP 1.25 3.00
62B R.Braun SP VAR 20.00 50.00
63 Joe Morgan .30 .75
64A Joey Votto .40 1.00
64B J.Votto SP VAR 20.00 50.00
65 Johan Santana .30 .75
66 John Kruk .25 .60
67 John Smoltz .40 1.00
68 Johnny Cueto .30 .75
69 Jon Jay .25 .60
70 Bob Feller .30 .75
71 Jose Bautista .30 .75
72 Josh Hamilton .30 .75
73 Casey Kelly RC .50 1.25
74 Josh Rutledge .25 .60
75 Juan Marichal .30 .75
76 Jurickson Profar RC .50 1.25
77 Justin Upton .30 .75
78 Kyle Seager .25 .60
79 Ken Griffey Jr. .75 2.00
80 Bob Gibson .30 .75
81 Larry Doby .25 .60
82 Lou Brock .30 .75
83 Lou Gehrig .75 2.00
84 Madison Bumgarner .30 .75
85 Manny Machado RC 2.50 6.00
86 Mariano Rivera .50 1.25
87 Stan Musial SP 2.50 6.00
88 Mark Trumbo .25 .60
89 Matt Adams .25 .60
90 Brooks Robinson .30 .75
91 Matt Holliday .40 1.00
92 Tim Lincecum SP 1.25 3.00
93 Matt Moore .30 .75
94 Melky Cabrera .25 .60
95 Michael Bourn .25 .60
96 Michael Fiers .25 .60
97 Troy Tulowitzki SP 1.50 4.00
98 Jake Odorizzi RC .50 1.25
99A Yu Darvish SP 1.50 4.00
99B Y.Darvish SP VAR 15.00 40.00
100A Bryce Harper .60 1.50
100B B.Harper SP VAR 50.00 100.00
101 Mike Olt RC .50 1.25
102 Tyler Colvin .25 .60
103 Trevor Rosenthal (RC) .75 2.00
104 Paco Rodriguez RC .60 1.50
105 Allen Craig .30 .75
106 Monte Irvin .25 .60
107 Alcides Escobar SP 1.25 3.00
108 Nick Maronde RC .50 1.25
109 Andy Pettitte .30 .75
110A Buster Posey .50 1.25
110B B.Posey SP VAR 10.00 25.00
111 Carlos Ruiz SP 1.00 2.50
112 Paul Goldschmidt .40 1.00
113 Paul Molitor .40 1.00
114 Alex Rios SP 1.25 3.00
115 Pedro Alvarez .25 .60
116 Phil Niekro .30 .75
117A Prince Fielder .30 .75
117B P.Fielder SP VAR 20.00 50.00
118 Ruben Tejada .25 .60
119 Torii Hunter .25 .60
120 Cal Ripken Jr. 1.25 3.00
121 Rickey Henderson .40 1.00
122 Early Wynn SP 1.25 3.00
123 Jon Niese .25 .60
124 Elvis Andrus SP 1.25 3.00
125 Robin Yount .40 1.00
126 Edwin Encarnacion SP 1.50 4.00
127 Rod Carew .30 .75
128 Roger Bernadina .15 .40
129 Roy Halladay .30 .75
130 Carlton Fisk .30 .75
131 Hal Newhouser SP 1.25 3.00
132 Ryan Howard .30 .75
133 Adam Dunn SP 1.25 3.00
134 Ryan Zimmerman .30 .75
135 Ryne Sandberg .75 2.00
136 Salvador Perez .30 .75
137 Sandy Koufax .75 2.00
138 Scott Diamond .25 .60
139 Shaun Marcum .25 .60
140 Catfish Hunter .30 .75
141 Alex Gordon .30 .75
142 Starlin Castro .25 .60
143 Starling Marte .30 .75
144 Red Schoendienst SP 1.25 3.00
145 Ryan Ludwick .25 .60
146 Erick Aybar .25 .60
147 David Ortiz .40 1.00
148 Todd Frazier .25 .60
149 Tom Seaver .30 .75
150A Derek Jeter 1.00 2.50
150B D.Jeter SP VAR 30.00 60.00
151 Travis Snider .25 .60
152 Trevor Bauer .50 1.25
153 Raul Ibanez .30 .75
154 Jim Palmer .30 .75
155 Ty Cobb .60 1.50
156 Cody Ross .25 .60
157 Vida Blue .25 .60
158 Wade Boggs .30 .75
159 Wade Miley .25 .60
160 Don Mattingly .75 2.00
161 Whitey Ford .30 .75
162 Bruce Sutter SP 1.25 3.00
163 Will Clark .30 .75
164 Will Middlebrooks .25 .60
165 Russell Martin .25 .60
166 Austin Jackson .25 .60
167 Willie McCovey .30 .75
168 Willie Stargell .30 .75
169 Wily Peralta .25 .60
170 Don Sutton .25 .60
171 Yasmani Grandal .25 .60
172A Yoenis Cespedes .40 1.00
172B Yoenis Cespedes SP VAR 12.50 30.00
High-fiving
173 Yonder Alonso .25 .60
174 Yovani Gallardo .25 .60
175 Brandon Moss .25 .60
176 Tony Perez .30 .75
177 Michael Brantley .25 .60
178 David Murphy .25 .60
179 Carlos Santana .30 .75
180 Duke Snider .30 .75
181 Nick Swisher SP 1.25 3.00
182 Alejandro de Aza .25 .60
183 Al Lopez SP 1.00 2.50
184 Chris Davis .30 .75
185 Ryan Doumit .25 .60
186 Alexei Ramirez .30 .75
187 Curtis Granderson SP 1.25 3.00
188 Jose Altuve .30 .75
189A Cliff Lee SP 1.25 3.00
189B C.Lee SP VAR 15.00 40.00
190 Eddie Murray .30 .75
191 Jordan Pacheco .25 .60
192 James Shields SP 1.00 2.50
193 Chase Headley .25 .60
194 Brandon Phillips .25 .60
195 Chris Johnson .25 .60
196 Omar Infante .25 .60
197 Garrett Jones .25 .60
198 Ian Kinsler SP 1.25 3.00
199 Carlos Beltran .30 .75
200 Ernie Banks .40 1.00
201 Justin Morneau .30 .75
202 Goose Gossage SP 1.25 3.00
203 Dayan Viciedo .25 .60
204 Andre Ethier SP 1.25 3.00
205 Jay Bruce .30 .75
206 Danny Espinosa .25 .60
207 Zack Cozart .25 .60
208 Gio Gonzalez SP 1.25 3.00
209 Mike Moustakas .30 .75
210 Fergie Jenkins .30 .75
211 Dan Uggla .25 .60
212 Kevin Youkilis .25 .60
213 Rick Ferrell SP 1.00 2.50
214 Jemile Weeks .25 .60
215 Kris Medlen SP 1.25 3.00
216 Colby Rasmus .30 .75
217 Neil Walker .25 .60
218 Adam Wainwright SP 1.25 3.00
219 Jake Peavy .25 .60
220 Frank Robinson .30 .75
221 Jason Kipnis .30 .75
222 A.J. Burnett .25 .60
223 Jeff Samardzija .25 .60
224 C.J. Wilson .25 .60
225 Homer Bailey .25 .60
226 Jon Lester .30 .75
227 Francisco Liriano .25 .60
228 Hiroki Kuroda .25 .60
229 Josh Johnson .30 .75
230 George Brett .75 2.00
231 Edinson Volquez .25 .60
232 Felix Doubront .25 .60
233 Ike Davis .25 .60
234 Corey Hart .25 .60
235 Ben Zobrist .30 .75
236 Kendrys Morales .25 .60
237 Coco Crisp .25 .60
238 Angel Pagan .25 .60
239 Josh Reddick SP 1.00 2.50
240 Harmon Killebrew .40 1.00
241 Chris Capuano .25 .60
242 Asdrubal Cabrera .30 .75
243 Brett Lawrie .30 .75
244 Ian Kennedy .25 .60
245 Derek Holland .25 .60
246 Mike Minor .25 .60
247 Jose Reyes .30 .75
248 Matt Harrison SP 1.00 2.50
249 Dan Haren .25 .60
250 Hank Aaron .75 2.00
251 Doug Fister .25 .60
252 Jason Vargas .25 .60
253 Tommy Milone .25 .60
254 Bronson Arroyo .25 .60
255 Mark Buehrle .30 .75
256 Eric Hosmer .30 .75
257 Craig Kimbrel .30 .75
258 Eddie Mathews SP 1.50 4.00
259A Justin Verlander .40 1.00
259B J.Verlander SP VAR 20.00 50.00
260 Jackie Robinson .40 1.00
261 Vance Worley .30 .75
262 Hisashi Iwakuma .30 .75
263 Brandon Morrow .25 .60
264 Jaime Garcia .30 .75
265 Josh Beckett .25 .60
266 Fernando Rodney .25 .60
267 Hoyt Wilhelm SP 1.25 3.00
268 Jim Johnson .25 .60
269 Ben Revere .25 .60
270 Jim Abbott .25 .60
271 Adam Eaton RC .60 1.50
272 Anthony Gose .25 .60
273 Carlos Gonzalez .30 .75
274 Jonny Gomes .25 .60
275 Dustin Pedroia .40 1.00
276A Giancarlo Stanton .40 1.00
276B G.Stanton SP VAR 15.00 40.00
277 Orlando Cepeda SP 1.25 3.00
278 Jordan Zimmermann .30 .75
279 Lance Lynn .25 .60
280 Jim Rice .30 .75
281 Matt Cain .30 .75
282 Mike Morse .25 .60
283 Daniel Murphy .30 .75
284 Reggie Jackson .30 .75
285 Matt Garza .25 .60
286 Brandon McCarthy .25 .60
287 Tony Gwynn .40 1.00
288 Jim Bunning SP 1.25 3.00
289 Yadier Molina .50 1.25
290 Dwight Gooden .25 .60
291 Howie Kendrick .25 .60
292 Ian Desmond .25 .60
293 Delmon Young .30 .75
294 Rickie Weeks .25 .60
295 Bobby Doerr SP 1.25 3.00
296 Phil Hughes .25 .60
297 Trevor Cahill .25 .60
298 Michael Young .25 .60
299 Barry Zito .30 .75
300 Johnny Bench .40 1.00
301 Tommy Hanson .25 .60
302 Lou Boudreau SP 1.25 3.00
303 Billy Butler .25 .60
304 Ralph Kiner SP 1.00 2.50
305 Brian McCann .30 .75
306 Mike Leake .25 .60
307 Shelby Miller RC 1.00 2.50
308 Mark Teixeira .30 .75
309 Bob Lemon SP 1.25 3.00
310A Miguel Cabrera SP 1.50 4.00
310B M.Cabrera SP VAR 40.00 80.00
311A Matt Kemp .30 .75
311B M.Kemp SP VAR 15.00 40.00
312 Miguel Gonzalez .25 .60
313 Miguel Montero .25 .60
314 Nelson Cruz .40 1.00
315 Ozzie Smith .50 1.25
316 Paul O'Neill .30 .75
317 Alex Cobb .25 .60
318 Robin Roberts SP 1.25 3.00
319 Robin Ventura .25 .60
320 Roberto Clemente SP 4.00 10.00
321A Robinson Cano .30 .75
321B R.Cano SP VAR 30.00 60.00
322 Jason Motte .25 .60
323 Ryan Vogelsong .25 .60
324A Stephen Strasburg .40 1.00
324B S.Strasburg SP VAR 15.00 40.00
325 Wilin Rosario .25 .60
326 Aaron Hill .25 .60
327 A.J. Pierzynski .25 .60
328 Denard Span .25 .60
329 Shin-Soo Choo .30 .75
330 Ted Williams SP 3.00 8.00
331 Darryl Strawberry SP 1.00 2.50
332 Marco Scutaro .30 .75
333 A.J. Ellis .25 .60
334 Bill Mazeroski SP 1.25 3.00
335 Alfonso Soriano .30 .75
336 Hunter Pence .30 .75
337 Desmond Jennings .30 .75
338 Mark Reynolds .25 .60
339 Anibal Sanchez .25 .60
340 Willie Mays SP 3.00 8.00
341 Darwin Barney .25 .60
342 B.J. Upton .30 .75
343 Kyle Lohse .25 .60
344 Tim Hudson .30 .75
345 Grant Balfour .25 .60
346 Phil Rizzuto SP 1.25 3.00
347 Jesus Montero .25 .60
348 Warren Spahn 1.25 3.00
349 Mat Latos .30 .75
350 Yogi Berra SP 1.50 4.00

2013 Topps Gypsy Queen Framed Blue

STATED ODDS 1:21 HOBBY
STATED PRINT RUN 499 SER.#'d SETS
1 Adam Jones .75 2.00
3 Adrian Beltre 1.00 2.50
9 Andrew McCutchen 1.00 2.50
10 Al Kaline 1.00 2.50
13 Wei-Yin Chen .60 1.50
17 Brandon Belt .75 2.00
23 Cecil Fielder .60 1.50
26 Clayton Kershaw 1.50 4.00
29 Cole Hamels .75 2.00
30 Bert Blyleven .75 2.00
31 Josh Willingham .75 2.00
34 David Freese .60 1.50
37 David Wright .75 2.00
39 Dexter Fowler .75 2.00
42 Jose Quintana .60 1.50
48 Gary Carter .75 2.00
54 Jacoby Ellsbury .75 2.00
57 Jayson Werth .75 2.00
63 Joe Morgan .75 2.00
65 Johan Santana .75 2.00
70 Bob Feller .75 2.00
71 Jose Bautista .75 2.00
74 Josh Rutledge .60 1.50
78 Kyle Seager .60 1.50
80 Bob Gibson .75 2.00
81 Larry Doby .60 1.50
86 Mariano Rivera 1.25 3.00
89 Matt Adams .60 1.50
90 Brooks Robinson .75 2.00
93 Matt Moore .75 2.00
95 Michael Bourn .60 1.50
102 Tyler Colvin .60 1.50
105 Allen Craig .75 2.00
109 Andy Pettitte .75 2.00
112 Paul Goldschmidt 1.00 2.50
117 Prince Fielder .75 2.00
120 Cal Ripken Jr. 3.00 8.00
123 Jon Niese .60 1.50
129 Roy Halladay .75 2.00
130 Carlton Fisk .75 2.00
137 Sandy Koufax 2.00 5.00
141 Alex Gordon .75 2.00
145 Ryan Ludwick .60 1.50
148 Todd Frazier .60 1.50
154 Jim Palmer .75 2.00
158 Wade Boggs .75 2.00
161 Whitey Ford .75 2.00
163 Will Clark .75 2.00
166 Austin Jackson .60 1.50
168 Willie Stargell .75 2.00
173 Yonder Alonso .60 1.50
176 Tony Perez .75 2.00
179 Carlos Santana .75 2.00
180 Duke Snider .75 2.00
182 Alejandro de Aza .60 1.50
184 Chris Davis .75 2.00
193 Chase Headley .60 1.50
196 Omar Infante .60 1.50
199 Carlos Beltran .75 2.00
200 Ernie Banks 1.00 2.50
205 Jay Bruce .75 2.00
207 Zack Cozart .60 1.50
211 Dan Uggla .60 1.50
214 Jemile Weeks .60 1.50
220 Frank Robinson .75 2.00
221 Jason Kipnis .75 2.00
224 C.J. Wilson .60 1.50
229 Josh Johnson .75 2.00
233 Ike Davis .60 1.50
237 Coco Crisp .60 1.50
240 Harmon Killebrew 1.00 2.50
241 Chris Capuano .60 1.50
243 Brett Lawrie .75 2.00
245 Derek Holland .60 1.50
247 Jose Reyes .75 2.00
249 Dan Haren .60 1.50
253 Tommy Milone .60 1.50
255 Mark Buehrle .75 2.00
257 Craig Kimbrel .75 2.00
261 Vance Worley .75 2.00
263 Brandon Morrow .60 1.50
265 Josh Beckett .60 1.50
269 Ben Revere .60 1.50
270 Jim Abbott .60 1.50
276 Giancarlo Stanton 1.00 2.50
284 Reggie Jackson .75 2.00
289 Yadier Molina 1.25 3.00
292 Ian Desmond .60 1.50
296 Phil Hughes .60 1.50
300 Johnny Bench 1.00 2.50
301 Tommy Hanson .60 1.50
303 Billy Butler .60 1.50
313 Miguel Montero .60 1.50
321 Robinson Cano .75 2.00
323 Ryan Vogelsong .60 1.50
328 Denard Span .60 1.50
332 Marco Scutaro .75 2.00
335 Alfonso Soriano .75 2.00
337 Desmond Jennings .75 2.00
341 Darwin Barney .60 1.50

2013 Topps Gypsy Queen Framed White

1 Adam Jones .50 1.25
3 Adrian Beltre .60 1.50
9 Andrew McCutchen .60 1.50
10 Al Kaline .60 1.50
13 Wei-Yin Chen .40 1.00
17 Brandon Belt .50 1.25
23 Cecil Fielder .40 1.00
26 Clayton Kershaw 1.00 2.50
29 Cole Hamels .50 1.25
30 Bert Blyleven .50 1.25
31 Josh Willingham .50 1.25
34 David Freese .40 1.00
37 David Wright .50 1.25
39 Dexter Fowler .50 1.25
42 Jose Quintana .40 1.00
48 Gary Carter .50 1.25
54 Jacoby Ellsbury .50 1.25
57 Jayson Werth .50 1.25
63 Joe Morgan .50 1.25
65 Johan Santana .50 1.25
70 Bob Feller .50 1.25
71 Jose Bautista .50 1.25
74 Josh Rutledge .40 1.00
78 Kyle Seager .40 1.00
80 Bob Gibson .50 1.25
81 Larry Doby .40 1.00
86 Mariano Rivera .75 2.00
89 Matt Adams .40 1.00
90 Brooks Robinson .50 1.25
93 Matt Moore .50 1.25
95 Michael Bourn .40 1.00
102 Tyler Colvin .40 1.00
105 Allen Craig .50 1.25
109 Andy Pettitte .50 1.25
112 Paul Goldschmidt .60 1.50
117 Prince Fielder .50 1.25
120 Cal Ripken Jr. 2.00 5.00
123 Jon Niese .40 1.00
129 Roy Halladay .50 1.25
130 Carlton Fisk .50 1.25
137 Sandy Koufax 1.25 3.00
141 Alex Gordon .50 1.25
145 Ryan Ludwick .40 1.00
148 Todd Frazier .40 1.00
154 Jim Palmer .50 1.25
158 Wade Boggs .50 1.25
161 Whitey Ford .50 1.25
163 Will Clark .50 1.25
166 Austin Jackson .40 1.00
168 Willie Stargell .50 1.25
173 Yonder Alonso .40 1.00
176 Tony Perez .50 1.25
179 Carlos Santana .50 1.25
180 Duke Snider .50 1.25
182 Alejandro de Aza .40 1.00
184 Chris Davis .50 1.25
193 Chase Headley .40 1.00
196 Omar Infante .40 1.00
199 Carlos Beltran .50 1.25
200 Ernie Banks .60 1.50
205 Jay Bruce .50 1.25
207 Zack Cozart .40 1.00
211 Dan Uggla .40 1.00
214 Jemile Weeks .40 1.00
220 Frank Robinson .50 1.25
221 Jason Kipnis .50 1.25
224 C.J. Wilson .40 1.00
229 Josh Johnson .50 1.25
233 Ike Davis .40 1.00
237 Coco Crisp .40 1.00
240 Harmon Killebrew .60 1.50
241 Chris Capuano .40 1.00
243 Brett Lawrie .50 1.25
245 Derek Holland .40 1.00
247 Jose Reyes .50 1.25
249 Dan Haren .40 1.00
253 Tommy Milone .40 1.00
255 Mark Buehrle .50 1.25
257 Craig Kimbrel .50 1.25
261 Vance Worley .50 1.25
263 Brandon Morrow .40 1.00
265 Josh Beckett .40 1.00
269 Ben Revere .40 1.00
270 Jim Abbott .40 1.00
276 Giancarlo Stanton .60 1.50
284 Reggie Jackson .50 1.25
289 Yadier Molina .75 2.00
292 Ian Desmond .40 1.00
296 Phil Hughes .40 1.00
300 Johnny Bench .60 1.50
301 Tommy Hanson .40 1.00
303 Billy Butler .40 1.00
313 Miguel Montero .40 1.00
321 Robinson Cano .50 1.25
323 Ryan Vogelsong .40 1.00
328 Denard Span .40 1.00
332 Marco Scutaro .50 1.25
335 Alfonso Soriano .50 1.25
337 Desmond Jennings .50 1.25
341 Darwin Barney .40 1.00

2013 Topps Gypsy Queen Autographs

STATED ODDS 1:13 HOBBY
EXCHANGE DEADLINE 02/28/2016
AE Adam Eaton 4.00 10.00
AG Anthony Gose 4.00 10.00
AR Anthony Rizzo 20.00 50.00
ARA A.J. Ramos 4.00 10.00
BB Billy Butler 6.00 15.00
BH Brock Holt 4.00 10.00
BHA Bryce Harper 100.00 200.00
BJ Brett Jackson 4.00 10.00
BW Billy Williams 10.00 25.00
CA Chris Archer 4.00 10.00
CD Cole De Vries 4.00 10.00
CF Cecil Fielder 10.00 25.00
CR Carlos Ruiz 4.00 10.00
CRJ Cal Ripken Jr. EXCH 50.00 100.00
DB Dylan Bundy 12.00 30.00
DF David Freese 4.00 10.00
DL DJ LeMahieu 10.00 25.00
DR Darin Ruf 4.00 10.00
DS Dave Stewart 5.00 12.00
FF Freddie Freeman 10.00 25.00
GR Garrett Richards 4.00 10.00
JA Jim Abbott 5.00 12.00
JB Jose Bautista 10.00 25.00
JF Jeurys Familia 4.00 10.00
JJ Jon Jay 5.00 12.00
JK John Kruk 4.00 10.00
JM Jesus Montero 4.00 10.00
JP Jurickson Profar 50.00 100.00
JR Josh Rutledge 4.00 10.00
JS Jean Segura 5.00 12.00
JSH James Shields 4.00 10.00
JU Justin Upton 5.00 12.00
JZ Jordan Zimmermann 6.00 15.00
KL Kenny Lofton 6.00 15.00
KN Kirk Nieuwenhuis 4.00 10.00
LL Lance Lynn 6.00 15.00
MA Matt Adams 4.00 10.00
MC Matt Cain 4.00 10.00
MCA Matt Carpenter 8.00 20.00
MF Michael Fiers 4.00 10.00
MM Mike Morse 5.00 12.00
MMA Manny Machado 30.00 80.00
MMO Matt Moore 4.00 10.00
MT Mark Trumbo 4.00 10.00
MTR Mike Trout 125.00 250.00
NC Nelson Cruz 4.00 10.00
NM Nick Maronde 4.00 10.00
NR Nolan Ryan 25.00 60.00
PG Paul Goldschmidt 10.00 25.00
RD R.A. Dickey 4.00 10.00
SD Scott Diamond 4.00 10.00
SM Starling Marte 6.00 15.00
SMA Shaun Marcum 4.00 10.00
TB Trevor Bauer 6.00 15.00
TF Todd Frazier 6.00 15.00
TG Tony Gwynn 40.00 80.00
VB Vida Blue 6.00 15.00
WJ Wally Joyner 6.00 15.00
WM Wade Miley 4.00 10.00
WMA Willie Mays EXCH 125.00 250.00
WP Wily Peralta 4.00 10.00
WR Wilin Rosario 4.00 10.00
YA Yonder Alonso 4.00 10.00
YC Yoenis Cespedes 8.00 20.00
YG Yovani Gallardo 5.00 12.00
YGR Yasmani Grandal 4.00 10.00
ZC Zack Cozart 4.00 10.00

2013 Topps Gypsy Queen Collisions At The Plate

COMPLETE SET (10) 5.00 12.00
STATED ODDS 1:8 HOBBY
PRINTING PLATE ODDS 1:2131 HOBBY
BM Brian McCann .60 1.50
BP Buster Posey 1.00 2.50
CF Carlton Fisk .60 1.50
CR Carlos Ruiz .50 1.25
GC Gary Carter .60 1.50
JB Johnny Bench .75 2.00
MM Miguel Montero .50 1.25
SP Salvador Perez .60 1.50
WR Wilin Rosario .50 1.25
YM Yadier Molina 1.00 2.50

2013 Topps Gypsy Queen Dealing Aces

COMPLETE SET (20)
STATED ODDS 1:4 HOBBY
PRINTING PLATE ODDS 1:2131 HOBBY
AW Adam Wainwright .60 1.50
CC CC Sabathia .60 1.50
CK Clayton Kershaw 1.25 3.00
CL Cliff Lee .60 1.50
CS Chris Sale .75 2.00
DB Dylan Bundy 1.25 3.00
DP David Price .60 1.50
FH Felix Hernandez .60 1.50
GG Gio Gonzalez .60 1.50
JC Johnny Cueto .60 1.50
JV Justin Verlander .75 2.00
JW Jered Weaver .60 1.50
MB Madison Bumgarner .60 1.50
MC Matt Cain .60 1.50
MM Matt Moore .60 1.50
RD R.A. Dickey .60 1.50
RH Roy Halladay .60 1.50
SS Stephen Strasburg .75 2.00
TB Trevor Bauer 1.00 2.50
YD Yu Darvish .75 2.00

2013 Topps Gypsy Queen Framed Mini Relics

STATED ODDS 1:25 HOBBY
AG Alex Gordon 4.00 10.00
AJ Austin Jackson 4.00 10.00
AJO Adam Jones 3.00 8.00
AM Andrew McCutchen 4.00 10.00
AO Alexi Ogando 3.00 8.00
AR Addison Reed 3.00 8.00
BB Brandon Beachy 3.00 8.00
BBE Brandon Belt 4.00 10.00
BBU Billy Butler 3.00 8.00
BM Brian McCann 3.00 8.00
BMO Brandon Morrow 3.00 8.00
BP Brandon Phillips 3.00 8.00
BPO Buster Posey 8.00 20.00
BU B.J. Upton 3.00 8.00
CF Carlton Fisk 4.00 10.00
CH Corey Hart 3.00 8.00
CK Clayton Kershaw 5.00 12.00
CKI Craig Kimbrel 4.00 10.00
CQ Carlos Quentin 3.00 8.00
CS Carlos Santana 3.00 8.00
DH Dan Haren 3.00 8.00
DM Devin Mesoraco 3.00 8.00
DS Drew Stubbs 3.00 8.00
EH Eric Hosmer 3.00 8.00
EL Evan Longoria 4.00 10.00
EM Eddie Murray 5.00 12.00
FF Freddie Freeman 4.00 10.00
FM Fred McGriff 4.00 10.00
IK Ian Kinsler 3.00 8.00
IKE Ian Kennedy 3.00 8.00
JB Jay Bruce 3.00 8.00
JH Jason Heyward 4.00 10.00
JHA Josh Hamilton 4.00 10.00
JHN Joel Hanrahan 3.00 8.00
JJ Jon Jay 3.00 8.00
JM Jason Motte 3.00 8.00
JMO Justin Morneau 3.00 8.00
JP Jordan Pacheco 3.00 8.00
JPE Jake Peavy 3.00 8.00
JPR Jhonny Peralta 3.00 8.00
JR Jimmy Rollins 3.00 8.00
JR Jackie Robinson 40.00 80.00
JV Justin Verlander 6.00 15.00
JZ Jordan Zimmermann 3.00 8.00
KN Kirk Nieuwenhuis 3.00 8.00
MC Melky Cabrera 3.00 8.00
MG Matt Garza 3.00 8.00
MH Matt Harvey 10.00 25.00
MHO Matt Holliday 4.00 10.00
MK Matt Kemp 4.00 10.00
MM Mike Minor 3.00 8.00
MMR Mitch Moreland 3.00 8.00
MN Mike Napoli 3.00 8.00
MR Mark Reynolds 3.00 8.00
NF Neftali Feliz 3.00 8.00
PA Pedro Alvarez 3.00 8.00
PK Paul Konerko 3.00 8.00
PN Phil Niekro 4.00 10.00
RC Rod Carew 4.00 10.00
RH Roy Halladay 4.00 10.00
RHO Ryan Howard 4.00 10.00
RN Ricky Nolasco 3.00 8.00
RR Ricky Romero 3.00 8.00
RY Robin Yount 6.00 15.00
SC Starlin Castro 5.00 12.00
SM Shaun Marcum 3.00 8.00
SR Scott Rolen 3.00 8.00
TC Trevor Cahill 3.00 8.00
TG Tony Gwynn 5.00 12.00
TH Torii Hunter 3.00 8.00
TL Tim Lincecum 6.00 15.00
WR Wilin Rosario 3.00 8.00
YA Yonder Alonso 3.00 8.00
YG Yovani Gallardo 3.00 8.00

2013 Topps Gypsy Queen Glove Stories

COMPLETE SET (10) 6.00 15.00
STATED ODDS 1:6 HOBBY
PRINTING PLATE ODDS 1:2131 HOBBY
BH Bryce Harper 1.25 3.00
CC Coco Crisp .50 1.25
DJ Derek Jeter 2.00 5.00
GB Gregor Blanco .50 1.25
JJ Jon Jay .50 1.25
JW Jayson Werth .60 1.50
MM Manny Machado 3.00 8.00
MT Mike Trout 6.00 15.00
RB Roger Bernadina .30 .75
TS Travis Snider .50 1.25

2013 Topps Gypsy Queen No Hitters

COMPLETE SET (15) 6.00 15.00
STATED ODDS 1:4 HOBBY
PRINTING PLATE ODDS 1:2131 HOBBY
BF Bob Feller .60 1.50
CH Catfish Hunter .60 1.50
FH Felix Hernandez .60 1.50
HB Homer Bailey .50 1.25
JA Jim Abbott .50 1.25
JS Johan Santana .60 1.50
JV Justin Verlander .75 2.00
JW Jered Weaver .60 1.50
KM Kevin Millwood .50 1.25
MC Matt Cain .60 1.50
NR Nolan Ryan 2.50 6.00
PH Philip Humber .50 1.25
RH Roy Halladay .60 1.50
SK Sandy Koufax 1.50 4.00
WS Warren Spahn .60 1.50

2013 Topps Gypsy Queen Relics

STATED ODDS 1:25 HOBBY
AA Alex Avila 3.00 8.00
AB Adrian Beltre 3.00 8.00
AC Asdrubal Cabrera 3.00 8.00
AD Adam Dunn 3.00 8.00
AE Andre Ethier 3.00 8.00
AES Alcides Escobar 3.00 8.00
AG Alex Gordon 4.00 10.00
BB Brandon Beachy 3.00 8.00
BBE Brandon Belt 4.00 10.00
BBU Billy Butler 3.00 8.00
BM Brandon Morrow 3.00 8.00
BP Brandon Phillips 3.00 8.00
BU B.J. Upton 3.00 8.00
CG Carlos Gonzalez 3.00 8.00
CR Colby Rasmus 3.00 8.00
CS Chris Sale 3.00 8.00
CSA Carlos Santana 3.00 8.00
DE Danny Espinosa 3.00 8.00
DG Dee Gordon 3.00 8.00
DH Dan Haren 3.00 8.00
DM Devin Mesoraco 3.00 8.00
DMA Don Mattingly 10.00 25.00
DP David Price 3.00 8.00
DU Dan Uggla 3.00 8.00
EA Elvis Andrus 3.00 8.00
EL Evan Longoria 3.00 8.00
GG Gio Gonzalez 3.00 8.00
HK Harmon Killebrew 10.00 25.00
ID Ian Desmond 3.00 8.00
IK Ian Kinsler 3.00 8.00
JB Jay Bruce 4.00 10.00
JBE Johnny Bench 12.50 30.00
JC Johnny Cueto 3.00 8.00
JG Jaime Garcia 3.00 8.00
JH Jason Heyward 4.00 10.00
JM Jason Motte 3.00 8.00
JP Jake Peavy 3.00 8.00
JPA Jordan Pacheco 3.00 8.00
JPE Jhonny Peralta 3.00 8.00
JR Jim Rice 4.00 10.00
JV Justin Verlander 5.00 12.00
JZ Jordan Zimmermann 3.00 8.00
KN Kirk Nieuwenhuis 3.00 8.00
MB Michael Bourn 3.00 8.00
MBU Madison Bumgarner 6.00 15.00
MC Melky Cabrera 3.00 8.00
MCA Matt Cain 5.00 12.00
MCB Miguel Cabrera 6.00 15.00
MG Matt Garza 3.00 8.00
MM Miguel Montero 3.00 8.00
MMO Mitch Moreland 3.00 8.00
MMR Mike Morse 3.00 8.00
MS Max Scherzer 5.00 12.00
MSC Mike Schmidt 10.00 25.00
NA Norichika Aoki 4.00 10.00
NC Nelson Cruz 3.00 8.00
NG Nomar Garciaparra 5.00 12.00
NM Nick Markakis 3.00 8.00
PA Pedro Alvarez 3.00 8.00
PK Paul Konerko 3.00 8.00
PS Pablo Sandoval 4.00 10.00
SC Shin-Soo Choo 3.00 8.00
SCA Starlin Castro 4.00 10.00
SM Shaun Marcum 3.00 8.00
SR Scott Rolen 3.00 8.00
TC Trevor Cahill 3.00 8.00
TG Tony Gwynn 5.00 12.00
TH Tommy Hanson 3.00 8.00
THU Tim Hudson 3.00 8.00
WB Wade Boggs 4.00 10.00
WR Wilin Rosario 3.00 8.00
YA Yonder Alonso 3.00 8.00
YG Yovani Gallardo 3.00 8.00

2013 Topps Gypsy Queen Sliding Stars

COMPLETE SET (15) 6.00 15.00
STATED ODDS 1:6 HOBBY
PRINTING PLATE ODDS 1:2131 HOBBY
AJ Austin Jackson .50 1.25
AM Andrew McCutchen .75 2.00
BH Bryce Harper 1.25 3.00
CG Carlos Gonzalez .60 1.50
DJ Derek Jeter 2.00 5.00
JH Jason Heyward .60 1.50
JM Joe Morgan .60 1.50
KG Ken Griffey Jr. 1.50 4.00
LB Lou Brock .60 1.50
MT Mike Trout 6.00 15.00
OS Ozzie Smith 1.00 2.50
PF Prince Fielder .60 1.50
RB Ryan Braun .60 1.50
RH Rickey Henderson .75 2.00
AJO Adam Jones .60 1.50

2013 Topps Gypsy Queen Mini

PRINTING PLATE ODDS 1:331 HOBBY
1A Adam Jones .75 2.00
1B Adam Jones SP VAR 1.00 2.50
2 Joe Nathan .60 1.50
3A Adrian Beltre 1.00 2.50
3B Adrian Beltre SP VAR 1.25 3.00
4 L.J. Hoes .75 2.00
5A Adrian Gonzalez .75 2.00
5B Adrian Gonzalez SP VAR 1.00 2.50
6A Alex Rodriguez 1.25 3.00

6B A.Rodriguez SP VAR 1.50 4.00
7A Mike Schmidt 1.50 4.00
7B M.Schmidt SP VAR 2.00 5.00
8 Andre Dawson .75 2.00
9A Andrew McCutchen 1.00 2.50
9B Andrew McCutchen SP VAR 1.25 3.00
10A Al Kaline 1.00 2.50
10B Al Kaline SP VAR 1.25 3.00
11A Anthony Rizzo 1.25 3.00
11B Anthony Rizzo SP VAR 1.50 4.00
12A Aroldis Chapman 1.00 2.50
12B Aroldis Chapman SP VAR 1.25 3.00
13 Wei-Yin Chen .60 1.50
14A Mike Trout 8.00 20.00
14B Mike Trout SP VAR 10.00 25.00
15 Tyler Skaggs 1.00 2.50
16 Brandon Beachy .60 1.50
17 Brandon Belt .75 2.00
18 Brett Jackson .60 1.50
20A Albert Pujols 1.25 3.00
20B Albert Pujols SP VAR 1.50 4.00
21 Ivan Nova .75 2.00
22A CC Sabathia .75 2.00
22B CC Sabathia SP VAR 1.00 2.50
23 Cecil Fielder .60 1.50
24 Chris Carter .60 1.50
25 Chris Sale 1.00 2.50
26A Clayton Kershaw 1.50 4.00
26B Clayton Kershaw SP VAR 2.00 5.00
27 Chad Billingsley .75 2.00
28A R.A. Dickey .75 2.00
28B R.A. Dickey SP VAR 1.00 2.50
29A Cole Hamels .75 2.00
29B Cole Hamels SP VAR 1.00 2.50
30 Bert Blyleven .75 2.00
31 Josh Willingham .75 2.00
32 Darin Ruf 1.25 3.00
33 Rob Brantly .60 1.50
34A David Freese .60 1.50
34B David Freese SP VAR .75 2.00
35A David Price .75 2.00
35B David Price SP VAR 1.00 2.50
36 Avisail Garcia .75 2.00
37A David Wright .75 2.00
37B David Wright SP VAR 1.00 2.50
38 Derek Norris .60 1.50
39 Dexter Fowler .75 2.00
40 Bill Buckner .60 1.50
41A Dylan Bundy 1.50 4.00
41B Dylan Bundy SP VAR 2.00 5.00
42 Jose Quintana .60 1.50
43 Enos Slaughter .75 2.00
44A Evan Longoria .75 2.00
44B Evan Longoria SP VAR 1.00 2.50
45A Felix Hernandez .75 2.00
45B Felix Hernandez SP VAR 1.00 2.50
46A Frank Thomas 1.00 2.50
46B Frank Thomas SP VAR 1.25 3.00
47 Freddie Freeman 1.25 3.00
48 Gary Carter .75 2.00
49A George Kell .75 2.00
49B George Kell SP VAR 1.00 2.50
50A Babe Ruth 2.50 6.00
50B Babe Ruth SP VAR 3.00 8.00
51 Clay Buchholz .60 1.50
52 Hanley Ramirez .75 2.00
53 Clayton Richard .60 1.50
54 Jacoby Ellsbury .75 2.00
55 Nathan Eovaldi .75 2.00
56 Jason Heyward .75 2.00
57 Jayson Werth .75 2.00
58 Jean Segura .75 2.00
59A Jered Weaver .75 2.00
59B Jered Weaver SP VAR 1.00 2.50
60 Billy Williams .75 2.00
61A Joe Mauer .75 2.00
61B Joe Mauer SP VAR 1.00 2.50
62A Ryan Braun .75 2.00
62B Ryan Braun SP VAR 1.00 2.50
63A Joe Morgan .75 2.00
63B Joe Morgan SP VAR 1.00 2.50
64A Joey Votto 1.00 2.50
64B Joey Votto SP VAR 1.25 3.00
65 Johan Santana .75 2.00
66 John Kruk .60 1.50
67A John Smoltz 1.00 2.50
67B John Smoltz SP VAR 1.25 3.00
68A Johnny Cueto .75 2.00
68B Johnny Cueto SP VAR 1.00 2.50
69 Jon Jay .60 1.50
70A Bob Feller .75 2.00
70B Bob Feller SP VAR 1.00 2.50
71A Jose Bautista .75 2.00
71B Jose Bautista SP VAR 1.00 2.50
72A Josh Hamilton .75 2.00
72B Josh Hamilton SP VAR 1.00 2.50
73 Casey Kelly .75 2.00
74 Josh Rutledge .60 1.50
75A Juan Marichal .75 2.00
75B Juan Marichal SP VAR 1.00 2.50
76A Jurickson Profar .75 2.00
76B J.Profar SP VAR 1.00 2.50
77A Justin Upton .75 2.00
77B Justin Upton SP VAR 1.00 2.50
78 Kyle Seager .60 1.50
79A Ken Griffey Jr. 2.00 5.00
79B Ken Griffey Jr. SP VAR 2.50 6.00
80A Bob Gibson .75 2.00
80B Bob Gibson SP VAR 1.00 2.50
81A Larry Doby .60 1.50
81B Larry Doby SP VAR .75 2.00
82A Lou Brock .75 2.00
82B Lou Brock SP VAR 1.00 2.50
83A Lou Gehrig 2.00 5.00
83B Lou Gehrig SP VAR 2.50 6.00
84 Madison Bumgarner .75 2.00
85A Manny Machado 4.00 10.00
85B M.Machado SP VAR 5.00 12.00
86A Mariano Rivera 1.25 3.00
86B Mariano Rivera SP VAR 1.50 4.00
87A Stan Musial 1.50 4.00
87B Stan Musial SP VAR 2.00 5.00
88 Mark Trumbo .60 1.50
89 Matt Adams .60 1.50
90A Brooks Robinson .75 2.00
90B Brooks Robinson SP VAR 1.00 2.50
91 Matt Holliday 1.00 2.50
92 Tim Lincecum .75 2.00
93 Matt Moore .75 2.00
94 Melky Cabrera .60 1.50
95 Michael Bourn .60 1.50
96 Michael Fiers .60 1.50
97A Troy Tulowitzki 1.00 2.50
97B Troy Tulowitzki SP VAR 1.25 3.00
98 Jake Odorizzi .75 2.00
99A Yu Darvish 1.00 2.50
99B Yu Darvish SP VAR 1.25 3.00
100A Bryce Harper 1.50 4.00
100B Bryce Harper SP VAR 2.00 5.00
101 Mike Olt .75 2.00
102 Tyler Colvin .60 1.50
103 Trevor Rosenthal 1.25 3.00
104 Paco Rodriguez 1.00 2.50
105A Allen Craig .75 2.00
105B Allen Craig SP VAR 1.00 2.50
106 Monte Irvin .60 1.50
107 Alcides Escobar .75 2.00
108 Nick Maronde .75 2.00
109 Andy Pettitte .75 2.00
110A Buster Posey 1.25 3.00
110B Buster Posey SP VAR 1.50 4.00
111 Carlos Ruiz .60 1.50
112A Paul Goldschmidt 1.00 2.50
112B Paul Goldschmidt SP VAR 1.25 3.00
113A Paul Molitor 1.00 2.50
113B Paul Molitor SP VAR 1.25 3.00
114 Alex Rios .75 2.00
115 Pedro Alvarez .60 1.50
116 Phil Niekro .75 2.00
117A Prince Fielder .75 2.00
117B Prince Fielder SP VAR 1.00 2.50
118 Ruben Tejada .60 1.50
119 Torii Hunter .60 1.50
120A Cal Ripken Jr. 3.00 8.00
120B C.Ripken Jr. SP VAR 4.00 10.00
121A Rickey Henderson 1.00 2.50
121B Rickey Henderson SP VAR 1.25 3.00
122 Early Wynn .75 2.00
123 Jon Niese .60 1.50
124 Elvis Andrus .75 2.00
125A Robin Yount 1.00 2.50
125B Robin Yount SP VAR 1.25 3.00
126 Edwin Encarnacion 1.00 2.50
127 Rod Carew .75 2.00
128 Roger Bernadina .40 1.00
129A Roy Halladay .75 2.00
129B Roy Halladay SP VAR 1.00 2.50
130 Carlton Fisk .75 2.00
131 Hal Newhouser .75 2.00
132 Ryan Howard .75 2.00
133 Adam Dunn .75 2.00
134 Ryan Zimmerman .75 2.00
135 Ryne Sandberg 2.00 5.00
136 Salvador Perez .75 2.00
137A Sandy Koufax 2.00 5.00
137B Sandy Koufax SP VAR 2.50 6.00
138 Scott Diamond .60 1.50
139 Shaun Marcum .60 1.50
140 Catfish Hunter .75 2.00
141 Alex Gordon .75 2.00
142A Starlin Castro .60 1.50
142B Starlin Castro SP VAR .75 2.00
143 Starling Marte .75 2.00
144 Red Schoendienst .75 2.00
145 Ryan Ludwick .60 1.50
146 Erick Aybar .60 1.50
147 David Ortiz 1.00 2.50
148 Todd Frazier .60 1.50
149A Tom Seaver .75 2.00
149B Tom Seaver SP VAR 1.00 2.50
150A Derek Jeter 2.50 6.00
150B Derek Jeter SP VAR 3.00 8.00
151 Travis Snider .60 1.50
152A Trevor Bauer 1.25 3.00
152B Trevor Bauer SP VAR 1.50 4.00
153 Raul Ibanez .75 2.00
154 Jim Palmer .75 2.00
155A Ty Cobb 1.50 4.00
155B Ty Cobb SP VAR 2.00 5.00
156 Cody Ross .60 1.50
157 Vida Blue .60 1.50
158A Wade Boggs .75 2.00
158B Wade Boggs SP VAR 1.00 2.50
159 Wade Miley .60 1.50
160 Don Mattingly 2.00 5.00
161 Whitey Ford .75 2.00
162 Bruce Sutter .75 2.00
163A Will Clark .75 2.00
163B Will Clark SP VAR 1.00 2.50
164A Will Middlebrooks .60 1.50
164B W.Middlebrooks SP VAR .75 2.00
165 Russell Martin .60 1.50
166 Austin Jackson .60 1.50
167A Willie McCovey .75 2.00
167B Willie McCovey SP VAR 1.00 2.50
168A Willie Stargell .75 2.00
168B Willie Stargell SP VAR 1.00 2.50
169 Wily Peralta .60 1.50
170 Don Sutton .60 1.50
171 Yasmani Grandal .60 1.50
172A Yoenis Cespedes 1.00 2.50
172B Y.Cespedes SP VAR 1.25 3.00
173 Yonder Alonso .60 1.50
174 Yovani Gallardo .60 1.50
175 Brandon Moss .60 1.50
176 Tony Perez .75 2.00
177 Michael Brantley .60 1.50
178 David Murphy .60 1.50
179 Carlos Santana .75 2.00
180A Duke Snider .75 2.00
180B Duke Snider SP VAR 1.00 2.50
181 Nick Swisher .75 2.00
182 Alejandro de Aza .60 1.50
183 Al Lopez .60 1.50
184 Chris Davis .75 2.00
185 Ryan Doumit .60 1.50
186 Alexei Ramirez .75 2.00
187 Curtis Granderson .75 2.00
188 Jose Altuve .75 2.00
189 Cliff Lee .75 2.00
190A Eddie Murray .75 2.00
190B Eddie Murray SP VAR 1.00 2.50
191 Jordan Pacheco .60 1.50
192 James Shields .60 1.50
193 Chase Headley .60 1.50
194 Brandon Phillips .60 1.50
195 Chris Johnson .60 1.50
196 Omar Infante .60 1.50
197 Garrett Jones .60 1.50
198 Ian Kinsler .75 2.00
199 Carlos Beltran .75 2.00
19A Nolan Ryan 3.00 8.00
19B Nolan Ryan SP VAR 4.00 10.00
200A Ernie Banks 1.00 2.50
200B Ernie Banks SP VAR 1.25 3.00
201 Justin Morneau .75 2.00
202 Goose Gossage .75 2.00
203 Dayan Viciedo .60 1.50
204 Andre Ethier .75 2.00
205 Jay Bruce .75 2.00
206 Danny Espinosa .60 1.50
207 Zack Cozart .60 1.50
208A Gio Gonzalez .75 2.00
208B Gio Gonzalez SP VAR 1.00 2.50
209 Mike Moustakas .75 2.00
210 Fergie Jenkins .75 2.00
211 Dan Uggla .60 1.50
212 Kevin Youkilis .60 1.50
213 Rick Ferrell .60 1.50
214 Jemile Weeks .60 1.50
215 Kris Medlen .75 2.00
216 Colby Rasmus .75 2.00
217 Neil Walker .60 1.50
218 Adam Wainwright .75 2.00
219 Jake Peavy .60 1.50
220 Frank Robinson .75 2.00
221 Jason Kipnis .75 2.00
222 A.J. Burnett .60 1.50
223 Jeff Samardzija .60 1.50
224 C.J. Wilson .60 1.50
225 Homer Bailey .60 1.50
226 Jon Lester .75 2.00
227 Francisco Liriano .60 1.50
228 Hiroki Kuroda .60 1.50
229 Josh Johnson .75 2.00
230A George Brett 2.00 5.00
230B George Brett SP VAR 2.50 6.00
231 Edinson Volquez .60 1.50
232 Felix Doubront .60 1.50
233 Ike Davis .60 1.50
234 Corey Hart .60 1.50
235 Ben Zobrist .75 2.00
236 Kendrys Morales .60 1.50
237 Coco Crisp .60 1.50
238 Angel Pagan .60 1.50
239 Josh Reddick .60 1.50
240A Harmon Killebrew 1.00 2.50
240B Harmon Killebrew SP VAR 1.25 3.00
241 Chris Capuano .60 1.50
242 Asdrubal Cabrera .75 2.00
243 Brett Lawrie .75 2.00
244 Ian Kennedy .60 1.50
245 Derek Holland .60 1.50
246 Mike Minor .60 1.50
247 Jose Reyes .75 2.00
248 Matt Harrison .60 1.50
249 Dan Haren .60 1.50
250A Hank Aaron 2.00 5.00
250B Hank Aaron SP VAR 2.50 6.00
251 Doug Fister .60 1.50
252 Jason Vargas .60 1.50
253 Tommy Milone .60 1.50
254 Bronson Arroyo .60 1.50
255 Mark Buehrle .75 2.00
256 Eric Hosmer .75 2.00
257 Craig Kimbrel .75 2.00
258A Eddie Mathews 1.00 2.50
258B Eddie Mathews SP VAR 1.25 3.00
259A Justin Verlander 1.00 2.50
259B Justin Verlander SP VAR 1.25 3.00
260A Jackie Robinson 1.00 2.50
260B Jackie Robinson SP VAR 1.25 3.00
261 Vance Worley .75 2.00
262 Hisashi Iwakuma .75 2.00
263 Brandon Morrow .60 1.50
264 Jaime Garcia .75 2.00
265 Josh Beckett .60 1.50
266 Fernando Rodney .60 1.50
267 Hoyt Wilhelm .75 2.00
268 Jim Johnson .60 1.50
269 Ben Revere .60 1.50
270 Jim Abbott .60 1.50
271 Adam Eaton 1.00 2.50
272 Anthony Gose .60 1.50
273A Carlos Gonzalez .75 2.00
273B Carlos Gonzalez SP VAR 1.00 2.50
274 Jonny Gomes .60 1.50
275A Dustin Pedroia 1.00 2.50
275B Dustin Pedroia SP VAR 1.25 3.00
276A Giancarlo Stanton 1.00 2.50
276B Giancarlo Stanton SP VAR 1.25 3.00
277A Orlando Cepeda .75 2.00
277B Orlando Cepeda SP VAR 1.00 2.50
278 Jordan Zimmermann .75 2.00
279 Lance Lynn .60 1.50
280 Jim Rice .75 2.00
281A Matt Cain .75 2.00
281B Matt Cain SP VAR 1.00 2.50
282 Mike Morse .60 1.50
283 Daniel Murphy .75 2.00
284A Reggie Jackson .75 2.00
284B Reggie Jackson SP VAR 1.00 2.50
285 Matt Garza .60 1.50
286 Brandon McCarthy .60 1.50
287A Tony Gwynn 1.00 2.50
287B Tony Gwynn SP VAR 1.25 3.00
288 Jim Bunning .75 2.00
289A Yadier Molina 1.25 3.00
289B Yadier Molina SP VAR 1.50 4.00
290 Dwight Gooden .60 1.50
291 Howie Kendrick .60 1.50
292 Ian Desmond .60 1.50
293 Delmon Young .75 2.00
294 Rickie Weeks .60 1.50
295 Bobby Doerr .75 2.00
296 Phil Hughes .60 1.50
297 Trevor Cahill .60 1.50
298 Michael Young .60 1.50
299 Barry Zito .75 2.00
300A Johnny Bench 1.00 2.50
300B Johnny Bench SP VAR 1.25 3.00
301 Tommy Hanson .60 1.50
302 Lou Boudreau .75 2.00
303A Billy Butler .60 1.50
303B Billy Butler SP VAR .75 2.00
304A Ralph Kiner .60 1.50
304B Ralph Kiner SP VAR .75 2.00
305 Brian McCann .75 2.00
306 Mike Leake .60 1.50
307 Shelby Miller 1.50 4.00
308 Mark Teixeira .75 2.00
309 Bob Lemon .75 2.00
310A Miguel Cabrera 1.00 2.50
310B Miguel Cabrera SP VAR 1.25 3.00
311A Matt Kemp .75 2.00
311B Matt Kemp SP VAR 1.00 2.50
312 Miguel Gonzalez .60 1.50
313 Miguel Montero .60 1.50
314 Nelson Cruz 1.00 2.50
315A Ozzie Smith 1.25 3.00
315B Ozzie Smith SP VAR 1.50 4.00
316 Paul O'Neill .75 2.00
317 Alex Cobb .60 1.50
318 Robin Roberts .75 2.00
319 Robin Ventura .60 1.50
320 Roberto Clemente 2.50 6.00
321 Robinson Cano .75 2.00
322 Jason Motte .60 1.50
323A Ryan Vogelsong .60 1.50
323B Ryan Vogelsong SP VAR .75 2.00
324A Stephen Strasburg 1.00 2.50
324B S.Strasburg SP VAR 1.25 3.00
325 Wilin Rosario .60 1.50
326 Aaron Hill .60 1.50
327 A.J. Pierzynski .60 1.50
328 Denard Span .60 1.50
329 Shin-Soo Choo .75 2.00
330A Ted Williams 2.00 5.00
330B Ted Williams SP VAR 2.50 6.00
331 Darryl Strawberry .60 1.50
332 Marco Scutaro .75 2.00
333 A.J. Ellis .60 1.50
334 Bill Mazeroski .75 2.00
335 Alfonso Soriano .75 2.00
336 Hunter Pence .75 2.00
337 Desmond Jennings .75 2.00
338 Mark Reynolds .60 1.50
339 Anibal Sanchez .60 1.50
340A Willie Mays 2.00 5.00
340B Willie Mays SP VAR 2.50 6.00
341 Darwin Barney .60 1.50
342 B.J. Upton .75 2.00
343 Kyle Lohse .60 1.50
344 Tim Hudson .75 2.00
345 Grant Balfour .60 1.50
346 Phil Rizzuto .75 2.00
347 Jesus Montero .60 1.50
348 Warren Spahn .75 2.00
349 Mat Latos .75 2.00
350A Yogi Berra 1.00 2.50
350B Yogi Berra SP VAR 1.25 3.00

2013 Topps Gypsy Queen Mini Black

*BLACK: .6X TO 1.5X BASIC MINI
STATED ODDS 1:15 HOBBY
STATED PRINT RUN 199 SER.#'d SETS

2013 Topps Gypsy Queen Mini Green

*GREEN: .75X TO 2X BASIC MINI
STATED ODDS 1:30 HOBBY
STATED PRINT RUN 99 SER.#'d SETS

2013 Topps Gypsy Queen Mini Sepia

*SEPIA: 1X TO 2.5X BASIC MINI
STATED ODDS 1:59 HOBBY
STATED PRINT RUN 50 SER.#'d SETS
19 Nolan Ryan 20.00 50.00
100 Bryce Harper 20.00 50.00
120 Cal Ripken Jr. 20.00 50.00
150 Derek Jeter 20.00 50.00

2012 Topps Gypsy Queen Mini National Convention

1 Bryce Harper 12.50 30.00
2 Yu Darvish 5.00 12.00
3 Yoenis Cespedes 4.00 10.00

2013 Topps Gypsy Queen National Convention

NCCYP Yasiel Puig 10.00 25.00

2014 Topps Gypsy Queen

COMPLETE SET (400)
COMP.SET w/o SP's (300) 12.00 30.00
SP ODDS 1:4 HOBBY
REV NEG SP ODDS 1:118 HOBBY
PRINTING PLATE ODDS 1:292 HOBBY
PLATE PRINT RUN 1 SET PER COLOR
BLACK-CYAN-MAGENTA-YELLOW ISSUED
NO PLATE PRICING DUE TO SCARCITY
1A Miguel Cabrera .30 .75
1B Cabrera Rev Neg SP 12.00 30.00
2 Frank Robinson .25 .60
3 Robin Yount .30 .75
4 Taijuan Walker RC .30 .75
5A CC Sabathia .25 .60
5B CC Sabathia Rev Neg SP 5.00 12.00
6 Nick Swisher .25 .60
7 Freddie Freeman .40 1.00
8 Alex Gordon .25 .60
9 Nolan Arenado .50 1.25
10A Jim Palmer .25 .60
10B Jim Palmer Rev Neg SP 5.00 12.00
11 Domonic Brown .25 .60
12 Kyuji Fujikawa .25 .60
13A Xander Bogaerts RC 1.00 2.50
13B Xander Rev Neg SP 12.00 30.00
14 Shane Victorino .25 .60
15 Kolten Wong RC .40 1.00
16 Jake Marisnick RC .30 .75
17 Adeiny Hechavarria .20 .50
18 Hiroki Kuroda .20 .50
19 Nelson Cruz .30 .75
20 Derek Holland .20 .50
21 Elvis Andrus .25 .60
22 Starlin Castro .20 .50
23 Billy Butler .20 .50
24 John Smoltz .30 .75
25A Derek Jeter .75 2.00
25B Jeter Rev Neg SP 25.00 60.00
26 Chris Owings RC .30 .75
27 Kevin Gausman .30 .75
28 Lou Boudreau .25 .60
29 Ralph Kiner .25 .60
30 Bronson Arroyo .20 .50
31 Jay Bruce .25 .60
32 Christian Bethancourt RC .30 .75
33 Nick Franklin .20 .50
34 Colby Rasmus .25 .60
35 Anibal Sanchez .20 .50
36 Robin Roberts .25 .60
37 Lou Brock .25 .60
38 Julio Teheran .25 .60
39 Salvador Perez .25 .60
40 Fergie Jenkins .25 .60
41 Jered Weaver .25 .60
42A Mariano Rivera SP 1.50 4.00
42B Rivera Rev Neg SP 10.00 25.00
43A Juan Marichal .25 .60
43B Juan Marichal Rev Neg SP 5.00 12.00
44 Trevor Rosenthal .25 .60
45 Evan Gattis .20 .50
46 Mike Zunino .20 .50
47 Mike Leake .20 .50
48 Kevin Pillar RC .30 .75
49A Wil Myers .20 .50
49B Wil Myers Rev Neg SP 8.00 20.00
50 Roberto Clemente .75 2.00
51 Goose Gossage .25 .60
52 Jayson Werth .25 .60
53A Tony Gwynn .30 .75
53B Tony Gwynn Rev Neg SP 6.00 15.00
54 Tim Lincecum .25 .60
55 Jake Peavy .20 .50
56A Yoenis Cespedes .30 .75
56B Yoenis Cespedes Rev Neg SP 6.00 15.00
57 Brandon Beachy .20 .50
58 Shin-Soo Choo .25 .60
59 Wilmer Flores RC .40 1.00
60 Andrelton Simmons .20 .50
61 Tony Cingrani .25 .60
62 Yadier Molina .40 1.00
63 Anthony Rizzo .40 1.00
64 Jarrod Saltalamacchia .20 .50
65 Todd Frazier .20 .50
66 Jonny Gomes .20 .50
67 Hisashi Iwakuma .25 .60
68 Fernando Rodney .20 .50
69 Enny Romero RC .30 .75
70 James Loney .20 .50
71 Nick Markakis .25 .60
72 Marco Estrada .20 .50
73 Ben Zobrist .25 .60
74 Troy Tulowitzki .30 .75
75 Greg Maddux .40 1.00
76 Bruce Sutter .20 .50
77A Reggie Jackson .25 .60
77B Reggie Jackson Rev Neg SP 5.00 12.00
78 Marcus Semien RC 1.50 4.00
79 Yasmani Grandal .20 .50
80 Adam Jones .25 .60
81 Brett Oberholtzer .20 .50
82 Juan Gonzalez .20 .50
83 Ian Desmond .20 .50
84 Joe Kelly .20 .50
85 David Ross .20 .50
86 J.J. Hardy .20 .50
87 Mike Minor .20 .50
88 Jason Grilli .20 .50
89 Craig Biggio .25 .60
90 Juan Uribe .20 .50
91 Marcell Ozuna .30 .75
92 Travis d'Arnaud RC .40 1.00
93 Yordano Ventura RC .40 1.00
94 Matt Cain .25 .60
95 Nick Castellanos RC 1.00 2.50
96 Asdrubal Cabrera .25 .60
97 Khris Davis .30 .75
98 Phil Niekro .25 .60
99 Eric Hosmer .25 .60
100A Bryce Harper .50 1.25
100B Harper Rev Neg SP 15.00 40.00
101 Doug Fister .20 .50
102 A.J. Griffin .20 .50
103 Daniel Murphy .25 .60
104 Andrew Lambo RC .30 .75
105 Hanley Ramirez .25 .60
106 Francisco Liriano .20 .50
107 Edwin Encarnacion .30 .75
108 Lance Lynn .20 .50
109 Adam Lind .25 .60
110 Anthony Rendon .30 .75
111 Ernie Banks .30 .75
112 Matt Holliday .30 .75
113 Michael Choice RC .30 .75
114 Deion Sanders .25 .60
115 Daniel Nava .20 .50
116 Mike Schmidt .50 1.25
117 Matt Garza .20 .50
118 Jose Quintana .20 .50
119 Kyle Lohse .20 .50
120 Jon Jay .20 .50
121 Kevin Siegrist (RC) .30 .75
122 Adrian Gonzalez .25 .60
123 Felix Hernandez .25 .60
124 Jason Kipnis .25 .60
125 Justin Verlander .30 .75
126A Pedro Martinez .25 .60
126B Pedro Martinez Rev Neg SP 5.00 12.00
127 Kyle Gibson .25 .60
128 Ethan Martin RC .30 .75
129 Omar Infante .20 .50
130 Jedd Gyorko .20 .50
131 Jose Iglesias .25 .60
132 Kris Medlen .25 .60
133 Kyle Seager .20 .50
134 Ryan Vogelsong .20 .50
135 Gio Gonzalez .25 .60
136 Willie Stargell .25 .60
137 Jeff Locke .20 .50
138 Curtis Granderson .25 .60
139A Yu Darvish .30 .75
139B Yu Darvish Rev Neg SP 6.00 15.00
140 Craig Kimbrel .25 .60
141 Christian Yelich .40 1.00
142 Gerrit Cole .30 .75
143 Dustin Pedroia .30 .75
144 Eddie Mathews .30 .75
145 Joey Votto .30 .75
146 Kendrys Morales .20 .50
147 A.J. Burnett .20 .50
148 Raul Ibanez .25 .60
149 Russell Martin .20 .50
150 Robinson Cano .25 .60
151A Michael Wacha .25 .60
151B Wacha Rev Neg SP 5.00 12.00
152 J.R. Murphy RC .30 .75
153 Harmon Killebrew .30 .75
154 Jason Castro .20 .50
155 Koji Uehara .20 .50
156A Tom Glavine .25 .60
156B Tom Glavine Rev Neg SP 5.00 12.00
157A Joe Mauer .25 .60
157B Joe Mauer Rev Neg SP 5.00 12.00
158 R.A. Dickey .25 .60
159 Matt Dominguez .20 .50
160 Jonathan Lucroy .25 .60
161 Phil Rizzuto .25 .60
162 Brad Ziegler .20 .50
163 Carlos Gomez .20 .50
164 Ian Kennedy .20 .50
165 Giancarlo Stanton .30 .75
166 A.J. Pierzynski .20 .50
167 Josh Reddick .20 .50
168 Adam Wainwright .25 .60
169 Chase Headley .20 .50
170A Randy Johnson .30 .75
170B Randy Johnson Rev Neg SP 6.00 15.00
171 Mike Moustakas .25 .60
172 Prince Fielder .25 .60
173 Carlos Martinez .25 .60
174 Yovani Gallardo .20 .50
175A Cal Ripken Jr. 1.00 2.50
175B Ripken Rev Neg SP 20.00 50.00
176 Brett Lawrie .25 .60
177 Brad Miller .25 .60
178 Jose Altuve .25 .60
179 Ian Kinsler .25 .60
180 Max Scherzer .30 .75
181 Paul Konerko .25 .60
182 Peter Bourjos .20 .50
183 Jeff Bagwell .25 .60
184 Jeff Samardzija .20 .50
185 George Brett .60 1.50
186 Chris Archer .20 .50
187 Oswaldo Arcia .20 .50
188 Adam Eaton .20 .50
189A Rod Carew .25 .60
189B Rod Carew Rev Neg SP 5.00 12.00
190 Jean Segura .25 .60
191A Mark McGwire .60 1.50
191B McGw Rev Neg SP 12.00 30.00
192 Mark Trumbo .20 .50
193 Miguel Gonzalez .20 .50
194 Aroldis Chapman .30 .75
195 Josmil Pinto RC .30 .75
196 Zack Greinke .30 .75
197 Henderson Alvarez .20 .50
198 Pete Kozma .20 .50
199 Larry Doby .25 .60
200 Rickey Henderson .30 .75
201 Ben Revere .20 .50
202 Ozzie Smith .40 1.00
203 Dan Haren .20 .50
204 Carlos Ruiz .20 .50
205 Joe Nathan .20 .50
206 Carlos Santana .25 .60
207 Carlos Gonzalez .25 .60
208 Adrian Beltre .30 .75
209 Jorge De La Rosa .20 .50
210 Homer Bailey .20 .50
211 Bob Feller .25 .60
212 Allen Craig .25 .60
213 Jordan Zimmermann .25 .60
214 Junior Lake .20 .50
215 Tony Perez .25 .60
216 Andre Rienzo RC .30 .75
217 Willie McCovey .25 .60
218 Jim Bunning .25 .60
219 Brandon Moss .20 .50
220 Brandon Belt .25 .60
221 Matt Davidson RC .40 1.00
222 Desmond Jennings .25 .60
223 Jake Odorizzi .20 .50
224 Wei-Yin Chen .20 .50
225A Nolan Ryan 1.00 2.50
225B Ryan Rev Neg SP 20.00 50.00
226 Neil Walker .20 .50
227A Chris Davis .20 .50
227B Chris Davis Rev Neg SP 4.00 10.00
228 Brandon Phillips .20 .50
229 Jon Lester .25 .60
230 Andrew McCutchen .30 .75
231 Mat Latos .25 .60
232 Pablo Sandoval .25 .60
233 Johnny Cueto .25 .60
234 Jim Johnson .20 .50
235 Ryan Zimmerman .25 .60
236 Miguel Montero .20 .50
237 Pedro Alvarez .20 .50
238 Stan Musial .50 1.25
239 Johnny Bench .30 .75
240 Victor Martinez .25 .60
241 Tommy Milone .20 .50
242 C.J. Wilson .20 .50
243 Matt Kemp .25 .60
244 Carl Crawford .25 .60
245 Wade Miley .20 .50
246 Michael Brantley .25 .60
247 Chris Johnson .20 .50
248 Jarrod Parker .20 .50
249A Bob Gibson .25 .60
249B Bob Gibson Rev Neg SP 5.00 12.00
250A Sandy Koufax .60 1.50
250B Koufax Rev Neg SP 12.00 30.00
251 Erik Johnson RC .30 .75
252 Marco Scutaro .25 .60
253 Andrew Cashner .20 .50
254 Avisail Garcia .25 .60
255 Chase Utley .25 .60
256 Ryan Wheeler .20 .50
257 Coco Crisp .20 .50
258A Steve Carlton .25 .60
258B Steve Carlton Rev Neg SP 5.00 12.00
259 Martin Prado .20 .50
260 Jonathan Schoop RC .30 .75
261 Joe Morgan .25 .60
262 Jhoulys Chacin .20 .50
263 Catfish Hunter .25 .60
264 Jose Reyes .25 .60
265 Tyler Skaggs .20 .50
266A Whitey Ford .25 .60
266B Whitey Ford Rev Neg SP 5.00 12.00
267 Jed Lowrie .20 .50
268 Tim Hudson .25 .60
269 Travis Wood .20 .50
270A Don Mattingly .60 1.50
270B Matting Rev Neg SP 12.00 30.00
271 Ty Cobb .50 1.25
272 Aaron Hill .20 .50
273 Alejandro De Aza .20 .50
274 Alex Cobb .20 .50
275A Buster Posey .40 1.00
275B Posey Rev Neg SP 8.00 20.00
276A Duke Snider .25 .60
276B Duke Snider Rev Neg SP 5.00 12.00
277 Ubaldo Jimenez .20 .50
278 David Freese .20 .50
279 Chris Tillman .20 .50
280A Manny Machado .30 .75
280B Mach Rev Neg SP 6.00 15.00
281 Trevor Bauer .40 1.00
282 Alex Rios .25 .60
283 James Shields .20 .50
284 Austin Jackson .20 .50
285 Bartolo Colon .20 .50
286 John Lackey .25 .60
287 Adam Dunn .25 .60
288 Chris Carter .20 .50
289 Andre Ethier .25 .60
290 David Holmberg RC .30 .75
291 Starling Marte .25 .60
292 Neftali Feliz .20 .50
293 Brian McCann .25 .60
294 Jonathan Villar .20 .50
295 Eddie Murray .25 .60
296 Jimmy Nelson RC .30 .75
297 Cole Hamels .25 .60
298 Patrick Corbin .25 .60
299 Jason Heyward .25 .60
300 Clayton Kershaw .50 1.25
301A Babe Ruth SP 3.00 8.00
301B Ruth Rev Neg SP 10.00 25.00
302A Bo Jackson SP 1.25 3.00
302B Bo Jackson Rev Neg SP 6.00 15.00
303 Mike Napoli SP .75 2.00
304A Ted Williams SP 2.50 6.00
304B Williams Rev Neg SP 10.00 25.00
305A Chris Sale SP 1.25 3.00
305B Sale Rev Neg SP 6.00 15.00
306 Carlos Beltran SP 1.00 2.50
307 Josh Hamilton SP 1.00 2.50
308 Evan Longoria SP 1.00 2.50
309A Matt Harvey SP 1.00 2.50
309B Matt Harvey Rev Neg SP 12.00 30.00
310A Albert Pujols SP 1.50 4.00
310B Pujols Rev Neg SP 8.00 20.00
311A Paul Goldschmidt SP 1.25 3.00
311B Paul Goldschmidt Rev Neg SP 6.00 15.00
312 Joe DiMaggio SP 2.50 6.00
313 Josh Donaldson SP 1.00 2.50
314 Hyun-Jin Ryu SP 1.00 2.50
315 Zack Wheeler SP 1.00 2.50
316 Jacoby Ellsbury SP 1.00 2.50
317 Michael Cuddyer SP .75 2.00
318 Luis Gonzalez SP .75 2.00
319A Jose Fernandez SP 1.25 3.00
319B Jose Fernandez Rev Neg SP 6.00 15.00
320A Jose Abreu RC SP 6.00 15.00
320B Abreu Rev Neg SP 25.00 60.00
321A David Price SP 1.00 2.50
321B David Price Rev Neg SP 5.00 12.00
322A David Wright SP 1.00 2.50
322B David Wright Rev Neg SP 5.00 12.00
323 Cliff Lee SP 1.00 2.50
324 James Paxton SP RC 1.25 3.00
325A Warren Spahn 1.00 2.50
325B Warren Spahn Rev Neg SP 5.00 12.00
326 Madison Bumgarner SP 1.00 2.50
327 Wade Boggs SP 1.00 2.50
328A Willie Mays SP 2.50 6.00
328B Mays Rev Neg SP 8.00 20.00
329A David Ortiz SP 1.25 3.00
329B David Ortiz Rev Neg SP 6.00 15.00
330 Ivan Rodriguez SP 1.00 2.50
331 Eric Davis SP .75 2.00
332 Matt Carpenter SP 1.25 3.00
333 Torii Hunter SP .75 2.00
334A Stephen Strasburg SP 1.25 3.00
334B Stephen Strasburg Rev Neg SP 6.00 15.00
335 Hunter Pence SP 1.00 2.50
336 Ivan Nova SP 1.00 2.50
337 Sonny Gray SP 1.00 2.50
338 Alfonso Soriano SP 1.00 2.50
339 Shelby Miller SP 1.00 2.50
340 Justin Upton SP 1.00 2.50
341 Jose Bautista SP 1.00 2.50
342 Jurickson Profar SP 1.00 2.50
343 Matt Moore SP 1.00 2.50

344 Billy Hamilton SP RC 1.00 2.50
345 Will Middlebrooks SP .75 2.00
346A Masahiro Tanaka SP RC 2.50 6.00
346B Tanaka Rev Neg SP 25.00 60.00
347 Jarred Cosart SP .75 2.00
348A Lou Gehrig SP 2.50 6.00
348B Gehrig Rev Neg SP 12.00 30.00
349A Mike Trout SP 6.00 15.00
349B Trout Rev Neg SP 25.00 60.00
350A Yasiel Puig SP 1.25 3.00
350B Puig Rev Neg SP 6.00 15.00

2014 Topps Gypsy Queen Framed Blue

*BLUE: 1.2X TO 3X BASIC
*BLUE RC: .75X TO 2X BASIC RC
STATED ODDS 1:13 HOBBY
STATED PRINT RUN 499 SER.#'d SETS
25 Derek Jeter 4.00 10.00

2014 Topps Gypsy Queen Framed White

*WHITE VET: .75X TO 2X BASIC
*WHITE RC: .5X TO 1.2X BASIC RC

2014 Topps Gypsy Queen Mini

*MINI VET: 1X TO 2.5X BASIC VET
*MINI RC: .6X TO 1.5X BASIC RC
*MINI SP: .4X TO 1X BASIC SP
MINI SP ODDS 1:24 HOBBY
COMMON VAR (1-350) .60 1.50
VAR SEMIS .75 2.00
VAR UNLISTED 1.00 2.50
PRINTING PLATE ODDS 1:227 HOBBY
PLATE PRINT RUN 1 SET PER COLOR
BLACK-CYAN-MAGENTA-YELLOW ISSUED
NO PLATE PRICING DUE TO SCARCITY
1B Cabrera Bat up 1.00 2.50
4B Walker Ball top .60 1.50
5B Sabathia No ball .75 2.00
7B Freeman Stance 1.25 3.00
13B Bogaerts Running 2.00 5.00
25B Jeter Logo showing 2.50 6.00
42B Rivera Grey jsy 1.25 3.00
49B Myers Running .60 1.50
50B Clemente Ylw helmet 2.50 6.00
54B Lincecum Standing .75 2.00
56B Cespedes Ylw jsy 1.00 2.50
62B Molina Mask up 1.25 3.00
67B Iwakuma Blue jsy .75 2.00
74B Tulo Batting 1.00 2.50
75B Maddux No ball 1.25 3.00
77B Reggie White jsy .75 2.00
80B A.Jones White jsy .75 2.00
100B Harper TB jsy 1.50 4.00
105B Hanley Bat up .75 2.00
116B Schmidt Bat down 1.50 4.00
122B A.Gonz Batting .75 2.00
123B F.Hernan White jsy .75 2.00
125B Verlander White jsy 1.00 2.50
126B Pedro Hands together .75 2.00
136B Stargell Swinging .75 2.00
139B Darvish White jsy 1.00 2.50
140B Kimbrel Pitching .75 2.00
141B Yelich Orange jsy 1.25 3.00
142B G.Cole Arm back 1.00 2.50
143B D.Pedr 1 hand on bat 1.00 2.50
145B Votto White jsy 1.00 2.50
150B Cano Swinging .75 2.00
157B Mauer Pinstripes .75 2.00
165B Stanton Orange jsy 1.00 2.50
168B Wainwright Blue hat .75 2.00
170B Johnson Leg up 1.00 2.50
172B Fielder Glasses .75 2.00
175B Ripken Face left 3.00 8.00
180B Scherz Short sleeve 1.00 2.50
196B Greinke Fist 1.00 2.50
200B R.Henderson Green jsy 1.00 2.50
202B Ozzie Swinging 1.25 3.00
207B C.Gonzalez Batting .75 2.00
208B A.Beltre Blue jsy 1.00 2.50
212B A.Craig Swinging .75 2.00
213B J.Zim Red jsy .75 2.00
225B N.Ryan w/ball 3.00 8.00
227B C.Davis Bat up .60 1.50
228B Phillips Red jsy .60 1.50
230B McCutch Face left 1.00 2.50
232B P.Sandoval Fldng .75 2.00
235B R.Zim Throwback jersey .75 2.00
238B S.Musial w/bat 1.50 4.00
239B Bench Batting 1.00 2.50
249B Gibson Face right .75 2.00
250B Koufax Hand hip 2.00 5.00
255B C.Utley Fielding .75 2.00
266B Ford Throwing .75 2.00
270B Mattingly w/bat 2.00 5.00
271B Cobb D visible 1.50 4.00
275B Posey Batting 1.25 3.00
280B Machado Batting 1.00 2.50
300B Kershaw White jsy 1.50 4.00
301B B.Ruth In jacket 2.50 6.00
302B B.Jackson Fldng 1.00 2.50
303B Napoli Red undershirt .60 1.50
304B Williams Standing 2.00 5.00
305B C.Sale Black hat 1.00 2.50
306B Beltran Running .75 2.00
307B Hamilton Bttng .75 2.00
308B Longoria Running .75 2.00
309B Harvey Pinstripe jsy .75 2.00
310B Pujols Pointing up 1.25 3.00
311B Goldschmidt Fldng 1.00 2.50
312B DiMaggio Bat back 2.00 5.00
313B Donaldson Bttng .75 2.00
314B Ryu Grey jsy .75 2.00
316B Ellsbury Face right .75 2.00
319B Fernandez Orange jsy 1.00 2.50
320B Abreu Facing left 5.00 12.00
321B Price Glasses .75 2.00
322B Wright White jsy .75 2.00
323B C.Lee Red hat .75 2.00
326B Bumgarner Black hat .75 2.00
328B Mays w/bat 2.00 5.00
329B Ortiz White jsy 1.00 2.50
330B I.Rod Batting .75 2.00
332B Carpenter Running 1.00 2.50
333B Hunter Face left .60 1.50
334B Strasburg Brown glv 1.00 2.50
339B Miller Hands together .75 2.00
340B Upton Face right .75 2.00
341B Bautista White jsy .75 2.00
342B Profar Batting .75 2.00
343B M.Moore Arm up .75 2.00
344B Hamilton Running .75 2.00
348B Gehrig Sitting 2.00 5.00
349B Trout Swinging 5.00 12.00
350B Puig Throwing 1.00 2.50

2014 Topps Gypsy Queen Mini Black

*BLK VET: 1.5X TO 4X BASIC VET
*BLK RC: 1X TO 2.5X BASIC RC
*BLK SP: .4X TO 1X BASIC SP
STATED ODDS 1:9 HOBBY
STATED PRINT RUN 199 SER.#'d SETS
25 Derek Jeter 6.00 15.00
42 Mariano Rivera 5.00 12.00
185 George Brett 4.00 10.00
191 Mark McGwire 5.00 12.00
320 Jose Abreu 10.00 25.00
349 Mike Trout 6.00 15.00

2014 Topps Gypsy Queen Mini Red

*RED VET: 5X TO 12X BASIC VET
*RED RC: 3X TO 8X BASIC RC
*RED SP: 1.2X TO 3X BASIC SP
STATED PRINT RUN 99 SER.#'d SETS
25 Derek Jeter 12.00 30.00
42 Mariano Rivera 10.00 25.00
50 Roberto Clemente 8.00 20.00
185 George Brett 10.00 25.00
191 Mark McGwire 8.00 20.00
270 Don Mattingly 6.00 15.00
304 Ted Williams 6.00 15.00
320 Jose Abreu 20.00 50.00
348 Lou Gehrig 6.00 15.00

2014 Topps Gypsy Queen Mini Sepia

*SEPIA VET: 6X TO 15X BASIC VET
*SEPIA RC: 4X TO 10X BASIC RC
*SEPIA SP: 1.5X TO 4X BASIC SP
STATED ODDS 1:32 HOBBY
STATED PRINT RUN 50 SER.#'d SETS
25 Derek Jeter 25.00 60.00
42 Mariano Rivera 12.00 30.00
50 Roberto Clemente 10.00 25.00
185 George Brett 12.00 30.00
191 Mark McGwire 10.00 25.00
270 Don Mattingly 8.00 20.00
304 Ted Williams 8.00 20.00
320 Jose Abreu 20.00 50.00
348 Lou Gehrig 8.00 20.00

2014 Topps Gypsy Queen Around the Horn Autographs

STATED ODDS 1:10.280 HOBBY
STATED PRINT RUN 25 SER.#'d SETS
EXCHANGE DEADLINE 3/31/2017
ATHCB Craig Biggio 25.00 60.00
ATHCS Chris Sale 15.00 40.00
ATHFF Freddie Freeman 40.00 80.00
ATHJB Jose Bautista 40.00 80.00
ATHJU Justin Upton 30.00 60.00
ATHJW Jered Weaver 20.00 50.00
ATHPG Paul Goldschmidt 40.00 80.00
ATHSK Sandy Koufax 150.00 300.00
ATHSM Shelby Miller 75.00 150.00
ATHWM Wil Myers 20.00 50.00

2014 Topps Gypsy Queen Autographs

STATED ODDS 1:15 HOBBY
EXCHANGE DEADLINE 3/31/2017
GQAAE Adam Eaton 2.50 6.00
GQAAH Adeiny Hechavarria 2.50 6.00
GQAAJ Adam Jones 8.00 20.00
GQAAR Anthony Rizzo 12.00 30.00
GQAAW Allen Webster 2.50 6.00
GQAAWO Alex Wood 2.50 6.00
GQABJ Bo Jackson 40.00 80.00
GQABM Brandon Maurer 2.50 6.00
GQABP Brandon Phillips 4.00 10.00
GQABR Ben Revere 5.00 12.00
GQABZ Ben Zobrist 3.00 8.00
GQACM Carlos Martinez 3.00 8.00
GQADG Didi Gregorius 3.00 8.00
GQADH Derek Holland 4.00 10.00
GQADP David Phelps 2.50 6.00
GQADS Dave Stewart 2.50 6.00
GQADW David Wright 20.00 50.00
GQAEB Ernie Banks 25.00 60.00
GQAED Eric Davis 12.00 30.00
GQAEG Evan Gattis 10.00 25.00
GQAFL Fred Lynn 6.00 15.00
GQAFM Fred McGriff 8.00 20.00
GQAGN Graig Nettles 6.00 15.00
GQAHA Hank Aaron 150.00 300.00
GQAJBE Johnny Bench 30.00 60.00
GQAJC Jose Canseco 25.00 60.00
GQAJH Jeremy Hefner 2.50 6.00
GQAJL Jeff Locke 2.50 6.00
GQAJO Jake Odorizzi 2.50 6.00
GQAJP Jonathan Pettibone 2.50 6.00
GQAJPO Jorge Posada 20.00 50.00
GQAJQ Jose Quintana 8.00 20.00
GQAJS Jean Segura 3.00 8.00
GQAJT Julio Teheran 8.00 20.00
GQAKM Kris Medlen 3.00 8.00
GQAKMI Kevin Mitchell 5.00 12.00
GQAKS Kyle Seager 2.50 6.00
GQALM Leonys Martin 2.50 6.00
GQALS Lee Smith 5.00 12.00
GQAMC Miguel Cabrera 75.00 150.00
GQAMK Mike Kickham 2.50 6.00
GQAMM Matt Moore 3.00 8.00
GQAMMA Matt Magill 2.50 6.00
GQAMMC Mark McGwire 100.00 200.00
GQAMMI Mike Minor 5.00 12.00
GQAMW Matt Williams 5.00 12.00
GQAMWA Michael Wacha 10.00 25.00
GQAOCB Oil Can Boyd 6.00 15.00
GQAPC Patrick Corbin 3.00 8.00
GQAPG Paul Goldschmidt 12.00 30.00
GQAPO Paul O'Neill 12.00 30.00
GQARH Rickey Henderson 50.00 100.00
GQARN Ricky Nolasco 2.50 6.00
GQARY Robin Yount 30.00 60.00
GQASD Steve Delabar 2.50 6.00
GQATD Travis d'Arnaud 3.00 8.00
GQATR Tim Raines 8.00 20.00
GQATT Troy Tulowitzki 10.00 25.00
GQAWF Wilmer Flores 3.00 8.00
GQAWM Wil Myers 10.00 25.00
GQAYD Yu Darvish 60.00 120.00
GQAZW Zack Wheeler 8.00 20.00

2014 Topps Gypsy Queen Autographs Gold

*GOLD: .6X TO 1.5X BASIC
STATED PRINT RUN 25 SER.#'d SETS
STATED ODDS 1:266 HOBBY
EXCHANGE DEADLINE 3/31/2017
GQACM Carlos Martinez 15.00 40.00
GQADP David Phelps 6.00 15.00
GQAHA Hank Aaron 150.00 300.00
GQAKS Kyle Seager 8.00 20.00
GQARH Rickey Henderson 60.00 120.00
GQAWF Wilmer Flores 8.00 20.00
GQAYD Yu Darvish 75.00 150.00

2014 Topps Gypsy Queen Autographs Red

*RED: .5X TO 1.2X BASIC
STATED PRINT RUN 49 SER.#'d SETS
STATED ODDS 1:157 HOBBY
EXCHANGE DEADLINE 3/31/2017
GQACM Carlos Martinez 8.00 20.00
GQADP David Phelps 5.00 12.00
GQAKS Kyle Seager 6.00 15.00
GQAWF Wilmer Flores 6.00 15.00

2014 Topps Gypsy Queen Dealing Aces

COMPLETE SET (20) 4.00 10.00
STATED ODDS 1:4 HOBBY
PRINTING PLATE ODDS 1:1460 HOBBY
PLATE PRINT RUN 1 SET PER COLOR
BLACK-CYAN-MAGENTA-YELLOW ISSUED
NO PLATE PRICING DUE TO SCARCITY
DAAW Adam Wainwright .40 1.00
DACC CC Sabathia .40 1.00
DACK Clayton Kershaw .75 2.00
DACL Cliff Lee .40 1.00
DACS Chris Sale .50 1.25
DADP David Price .40 1.00
DAFH Felix Hernandez .40 1.00
DAGC Gerrit Cole .50 1.25
DAGM Greg Maddux .60 1.50
DAHR Hyun-Jin Ryu .40 1.00
DAJF Jose Fernandez .50 1.25
DAJT Julio Teheran .40 1.00
DAJV Justin Verlander .50 1.25
DAMB Madison Bumgarner .40 1.00
DAMS Max Scherzer .50 1.25
DAMW Michael Wacha .40 1.00
DAPM Pedro Martinez .40 1.00
DARJ Randy Johnson .50 1.25
DASS Stephen Strasburg .50 1.25
DAYD Yu Darvish .50 1.25

2014 Topps Gypsy Queen Debut All Stars

COMPLETE SET (15) 4.00 10.00
STATED ODDS 1:6 HOBBY
PRINTING PLATE ODDS 1:1460 HOBBY
PLATE PRINT RUN 1 SET PER COLOR
BLACK-CYAN-MAGENTA-YELLOW ISSUED
NO PLATE PRICING DUE TO SCARCITY
ASBH Bryce Harper .75 2.00
ASCK Clayton Kershaw .75 2.00
ASDO David Ortiz .50 1.25
ASEL Evan Longoria .40 1.00
ASFH Felix Hernandez .40 1.00
ASJF Jose Fernandez .50 1.25
ASJV Justin Verlander .50 1.25
ASMC Miguel Cabrera .50 1.25
ASMH Matt Harvey .40 1.00
ASMM Manny Machado .50 1.25
ASMT Mike Trout 2.50 6.00
ASPF Prince Fielder .40 1.00
ASPG Paul Goldschmidt .50 1.25
ASRC Robinson Cano .40 1.00
ASYD Yu Darvish .50 1.25

2014 Topps Gypsy Queen Framed Mini Relics

STATED ODDS 1:25 HOBBY
GMRAB Adrian Beltre 3.00 8.00
GMRAC Alex Cobb 2.00 5.00
GMRAG Alex Gordon 2.50 6.00
GMRAJ Adam Jones 2.50 6.00
GMRAL Adam Lind 2.50 6.00
GMRAR Anthony Rizzo 4.00 10.00
GMRAS Andrelton Simmons 2.00 5.00
GMRBL Brett Lawrie 2.50 6.00
GMRBM Brian McCann 2.50 6.00
GMRBR Bruce Rondon 2.00 5.00
GMRCA Chris Archer 2.00 5.00
GMRCH Chase Headley 2.00 5.00
GMRCK Craig Kimbrel 2.50 6.00
GMRCR Carlos Ruiz 2.00 5.00
GMRCS CC Sabathia 2.50 6.00
GMRDB Domonic Brown 2.50 6.00
GMRDD Daniel Descalso 2.00 5.00
GMRDG Dillon Gee 2.00 5.00
GMRDH Derek Holland 2.00 5.00
GMRDJ Desmond Jennings 2.50 6.00
GMREA Elvis Andrus 2.50 6.00
GMREE Edwin Encarnacion 3.00 8.00
GMREG Evan Gattis 2.00 5.00
GMREH Eric Hosmer 2.50 6.00
GMRGG Gio Gonzalez 2.50 6.00
GMRJB Jose Bautista 2.50 6.00
GMRJBR Jay Bruce 2.50 6.00
GMRJC Jhoulys Chacin 2.00 5.00
GMRJH Jeremy Hellickson 2.00 5.00
GMRJP Jhonny Peralta 2.00 5.00
GMRJT Julio Teheran 2.50 6.00
GMRJU Justin Upton 2.50 6.00
GMRJV Joey Votto 3.00 8.00
GMRJZ Jordan Zimmermann 2.50 6.00
GMRKS Kyle Seager 2.00 5.00
GMRMA Matt Adams 2.00 5.00
GMRML Mike Leake 2.00 5.00
GMRMM Mike Minor 2.00 5.00
GMRMMO Matt Moore 2.50 6.00
GMRPB Peter Bourjos 2.00 5.00
GMRPC Patrick Corbin 2.50 6.00
GMRRB Ryan Braun 2.50 6.00
GMRRP Rick Porcello 2.50 6.00
GMRRZ Ryan Zimmerman 2.50 6.00
GMRSM Starling Marte 2.50 6.00
GMRSP Salvador Perez 2.50 6.00
GMRTH Todd Helton 2.50 6.00
GMRTT Troy Tulowitzki 3.00 8.00
GMRWM Wade Miley 2.00 5.00
GMRWR Wilin Rosario 2.00 5.00
GMRYM Yadier Molina 5.00 12.00

2014 Topps Gypsy Queen Glove Stories

COMPLETE SET (10) 3.00 8.00
STATED ODDS 1:6 HOBBY
PRINTING PLATE ODDS 1:1460 HOBBY
PLATE PRINT RUN 1 SET PER COLOR
BLACK-CYAN-MAGENTA-YELLOW ISSUED
NO PLATE PRICING DUE TO SCARCITY
GSAR Anthony Rizzo .60 1.50
GSBH Bryce Harper .75 2.00
GSCC Carl Crawford .40 1.00
GSCG Carlos Gomez .30 .75
GSDJ Derek Jeter 1.25 3.00
GSJD Josh Donaldson .40 1.00
GSJI Jose Iglesias .40 1.00
GSMT Mike Trout 2.50 6.00
GSYP Yasiel Puig .50 1.25
GSYP2 Yasiel Puig .50 1.25

2014 Topps Gypsy Queen Jumbo Relics Black

STATED ODDS 1:27 HOBBY
STATED PRINT RUN 25 SER.#'d SETS
GJRAB Adrian Beltre 8.00 20.00
GJRAC Allen Craig 20.00 50.00
GJRAD Andre Dawson 12.00 30.00
GJRAJ Adam Jones 15.00 40.00
GJRAP Andy Pettitte 6.00 15.00
GJRAPU Albert Pujols 10.00 25.00
GJRBH Bryce Harper 12.00 30.00
GJRBP Buster Posey 10.00 25.00
GJRBW Billy Williams 6.00 15.00
GJRCG Carlos Gonzalez 6.00 15.00
GJRCK Clayton Kershaw 12.00 30.00
GJRCKI Craig Kimbrel 20.00 50.00
GJRCS CC Sabathia 6.00 15.00
GJRCSA Chris Sale 8.00 20.00
GJRDJ Derek Jeter 20.00 50.00
GJRDO David Ortiz 12.00 30.00
GJRDP David Price 6.00 15.00
GJREB Ernie Banks 20.00 50.00
GJREH Eric Hosmer 6.00 15.00
GJREL Evan Longoria 6.00 15.00
GJRFF Freddie Freeman 10.00 25.00
GJRFH Felix Hernandez 6.00 15.00
GJRGS Giancarlo Stanton 8.00 20.00
GJRHJR Hyun-Jin Ryu 6.00 15.00
GJRJF Jose Fernandez 8.00 20.00
GJRJM Joe Morgan 15.00 40.00
GJRJU Justin Upton 6.00 15.00
GJRJV Joey Votto 15.00 40.00
GJRJVE Justin Verlander 8.00 20.00
GJRMC Miguel Cabrera 15.00 40.00
GJRMH Matt Harvey 6.00 15.00
GJRMM Manny Machado 20.00 50.00
GJRMMO Matt Moore 6.00 15.00
GJRMR Mariano Rivera 20.00 50.00
GJRMS Max Scherzer 8.00 20.00
GJRMT Mike Trout 40.00 100.00
GJRPF Prince Fielder 6.00 15.00
GJRPG Paul Goldschmidt 8.00 20.00
GJRPN Phil Niekro 15.00 40.00
GJRSM Shelby Miller 15.00 40.00
GJRSS Stephen Strasburg 8.00 20.00
GJRTG Tom Glavine 15.00 40.00
GJRTGW Tony Gwynn 12.00 30.00
GJRTH Torii Hunter 5.00 12.00
GJRTL Tim Lincecum 6.00 15.00
GJRTT Troy Tulowitzki 8.00 20.00
GJRWB Wade Boggs 15.00 40.00
GJRWM Wil Myers 5.00 12.00
GJRYD Yu Darvish 12.00 30.00
GJRYM Yadier Molina 20.00 50.00
GJRYP Yasiel Puig 8.00 20.00

2014 Topps Gypsy Queen N174 Gypsy Queen

COMPLETE SET (15) 6.00 15.00
STATED ODDS 1:4 HOBBY
PRINTING PLATE ODDS 1:1460 HOBBY
PLATE PRINT RUN 1 SET PER COLOR
BLACK-CYAN-MAGENTA-YELLOW ISSUED
NO PLATE PRICING DUE TO SCARCITY
N174BH Bryce Harper .75 2.00
N174BR Babe Ruth 1.25 3.00
N174CK Clayton Kershaw .75 2.00
N174CR Cal Ripken Jr. 1.50 4.00
N174DJ Derek Jeter 1.25 3.00
N174MC Miguel Cabrera .50 1.25
N174MR Mariano Rivera .60 1.50
N174MS Max Scherzer .50 1.25
N174MT Mike Trout 2.50 6.00
N174RH Rickey Henderson .50 1.25
N174RJ Reggie Jackson .40 1.00
N174TS Tom Seaver .40 1.00
N174WB Wade Boggs .40 1.00
N174YB Yogi Berra .50 1.25
N174YP Yasiel Puig .50 1.25

2014 Topps Gypsy Queen Relic Autographs

STATED ODDS 1:892 HOBBY
STATED PRINT RUN 25 SER.#'d SETS
EXCHANGE DEADLINE 3/31/2017
ARAJ Adam Jones 30.00 60.00
ARAR Anthony Rizzo 20.00 50.00
ARBP Brandon Phillips 15.00 40.00
ARBZ Ben Zobrist 15.00 40.00
ARCB Craig Biggio EXCH 20.00 50.00
ARDH Derek Holland 10.00 25.00
ARDW David Wright 20.00 50.00
AREG Evan Gattis 10.00 25.00
ARFF Freddie Freeman 30.00 60.00
ARJG Jedd Gyorko EXCH 10.00 25.00
ARJS Jean Segura 10.00 25.00
ARJT Julio Teheran EXCH 10.00 25.00
ARMM Matt Moore 10.00 25.00
ARMMI Mike Minor 12.00 30.00
ARMT Mike Trout 150.00 250.00
ARPG Paul Goldschmidt 20.00 50.00
ARRH Rickey Henderson EXCH 50.00 100.00
ARTT Troy Tulowitzki 30.00 60.00
ARWM Wil Myers 30.00 60.00
ARZW Zack Wheeler 20.00 50.00

2014 Topps Gypsy Queen Relics

STATED ODDS 1:27 HOBBY
GQRAB Adrian Beltre 3.00 8.00
GQRAC Alex Cobb 2.00 5.00
GQRACR Allen Craig 2.50 6.00
GQRAG Alex Gordon 2.50 6.00
GQRAJ Adam Jones 2.50 6.00
GQRAL Adam Lind 2.50 6.00
GQRAS Andrelton Simmons 2.00 5.00
GQRAW Allen Webster 2.00 5.00
GQRBL Brett Lawrie 2.50 6.00
GQRBM Brian McCann 2.50 6.00
GQRBR Bruce Rondon 2.00 5.00
GQRBZ Ben Zobrist 2.50 6.00
GQRCA Chris Archer 2.00 5.00
GQRCK Craig Kimbrel 2.50 6.00
GQRCT Chris Tillman 2.00 5.00
GQRDB Domonic Brown 2.50 6.00
GQRDJ Desmond Jennings 2.50 6.00
GQRDP David Price 2.50 6.00
GQREE Edwin Encarnacion 3.00 8.00
GQRFF Freddie Freeman 4.00 10.00
GQRFH Felix Hernandez 2.50 6.00
GQRHP Hunter Pence 2.50 6.00
GQRID Ian Desmond 2.00 5.00
GQRJB Jose Bautista 2.50 6.00
GQRJBR Jay Bruce 2.50 6.00
GQRJC Jhoulys Chacin 2.00 5.00
GQRJH Jeremy Hellickson 2.00 5.00
GQRJP Jhonny Peralta 2.00 5.00
GQRJSH James Shields 2.00 5.00
GQRJT Julio Teheran 2.50 6.00
GQRKM Kris Medlen 2.50 6.00
GQRMA Matt Adams 2.00 5.00
GQRMC Matt Cain 2.50 6.00
GQRML Mike Leake 2.00 5.00
GQRMM Mike Minor 2.00 5.00
GQRMP Martin Perez 2.50 6.00
GQRMW Michael Wacha 5.00 12.00
GQRNA Nolan Arenado 5.00 12.00
GQRPA Pedro Alvarez 4.00 10.00
GQRRB Ryan Braun 2.50 6.00
GQRRP Rick Porcello 2.50 6.00
GQRSM Starling Marte 2.50 6.00
GQRSP Salvador Perez 2.50 6.00
GQRTF Todd Frazier 2.00 5.00
GQRTH Torii Hunter 2.00 5.00
GQRTL Tim Lincecum 2.50 6.00
GQRWB Wade Boggs 4.00 10.00
GQRWM Wil Myers 2.00 5.00
GQRWMI Will Middlebrooks 2.00 5.00
GQRZG Zack Greinke 3.00 8.00
GQRZW Zack Wheeler 2.50 6.00

2015 Topps Gypsy Queen

COMP.SET w/o SP's (300) 12.00 30.00
SP ODDS 1:4 HOBBY
SP VAR ODDS 1:165 HOBBY
PRINTING PLATE ODDS 1:281 HOBBY
PLATE PRINT RUN 1 SET PER COLOR
BLACK-CYAN-MAGENTA-YELLOW ISSUED
NO PLATE PRICING DUE TO SCARCITY
1A Mike Trout 1.50 4.00
1B Trout VAR Hands up 60.00 150.00
2 Hank Aaron .60 1.50
3 Joc Pederson RC 1.25 3.00
4 Maikel Franco RC .40 1.00
5A Derek Jeter .75 2.00
5B Jeter VAR Hands up 40.00 100.00
6 David Wright .25 .60
7 Yordano Ventura .25 .60
8 Jose Canseco .25 .60
9 Bo Jackson .30 .75
10 David Price .25 .60
11 Hanley Ramirez .25 .60
12A Jordan Zimmermann .25 .60
12B Jordan Zimmermann VAR 10.00 25.00
Arm Up
13 Zack Greinke .30 .75
14A Jose Altuve .25 .60
14B Altuve Arm Up 10.00 25.00
15 Todd Frazier .20 .50
16 Paul Goldschmidt .30 .75
17 Ty Cobb .50 1.25
18 Tom Glavine .25 .60
19A Yu Darvish .30 .75
19B Yu Darvish VAR 12.00 30.00
Clapping
20 Frank Thomas .30 .75
21 Robin Yount .30 .75
22 Kevin Gausman .30 .75
23A Adam Jones .25 .60
23B Adam Jones VAR 10.00 25.00
Hugging
24 Joey Votto .30 .75
25A Matt Carpenter .30 .75
25B Matt Carpenter VAR 12.00 30.00
Clapping
26A Freddie Freeman .40 1.00
26B Freeman VAR Hug 20.00 50.00
27 John Lackey .25 .60
28 Wil Myers .25 .60
29 Chris Sale .30 .75
30A Jose Bautista .25 .60
30B Jose Bautista VAR 10.00 25.00
Running
31 Mike Mussina .25 .60
32 Hisashi Iwakuma .25 .60
33 Starlin Castro .20 .50
34A Andrew McCutchen .30 .75
34B McCutchen VAR Gry jsy 12.00 30.00
35 Nolan Ryan 1.00 2.50
36 Don Sutton .25 .60
37 Mark McGwire .50 1.25
38 Matt Kemp .25 .60
39 Lou Gehrig .60 1.50
40 Jorge Soler RC .50 1.25
41A Ivan Rodriguez .25 .60
41B Ivan Rodriguez VAR 10.00 25.00
Making fist
42 Kennys Vargas .20 .50
43 Josh Hamilton .25 .60
44 Steve Carlton .25 .60
45A Bryce Harper .50 1.25
45B Harper VAR Yelll 20.00 50.00
46A Adrian Beltre .30 .75
46B Adrian Beltre VAR 12.00 30.00
Celebrating
47 Ozzie Smith .40 1.00
48 Shelby Miller .25 .60
49 Albert Pujols .40 1.00
50A Salvador Perez .25 .60
50B Salvador Perez VAR 10.00 25.00
Making fist
51A Anthony Rendon .30 .75
51B Anthony Rendon VAR 12.00 30.00
Laughing
52 Nelson Cruz .30 .75
53 Prince Fielder .25 .60
54 Brandon Finnegan RC .30 .75
55A Robinson Cano .25 .60
55B Robinson Cano VAR 10.00 25.00
Pointing up
56 Vladimir Guerrero .25 .60
57 Jason Vargas .20 .50
58 Yovani Gallardo .20 .50
59 Adam Wainwright .25 .60
60A Mookie Betts .60 1.50
60B Betts High five 25.00 60.00
61 Derek Holland .20 .50
62A Kenley Jansen .25 .60
62B Kenley Jansen VAR 10.00 25.00
With bat
63 Huston Street .20 .50
64 Tony Perez .25 .60
65 Devin Mesoraco .20 .50
66 Joe Mauer .25 .60
67A Eric Hosmer .25 .60
67B Eric Hosmer VAR 10.00 25.00
Celebrating
68 Alex Wood .20 .50
69 Nick Markakis .25 .60
70 Adam LaRoche .20 .50
71A Aroldis Chapman .30 .75
71B Aroldis Chapman VAR 12.00 30.00
Red jersey
72 Carlos Martinez .25 .60
73 Ben Zobrist .25 .60
74 Julio Teheran .25 .60
75 Mat Latos .25 .60
76 Gio Gonzalez .25 .60
77 Andrew Cashner .20 .50
78 Charlie Blackmon .30 .75
79 Andre Dawson .25 .60
80 Gerrit Cole .30 .75
81 Josh Donaldson .25 .60
82 Mookie Wilson .20 .50
83A Jacoby Ellsbury .25 .60
83B Jacoby Ellsbury VAR 10.00 25.00
Pointing
84 John Smoltz .30 .75
85 Jon Singleton .25 .60
86 Juan Marichal .25 .60
87 Cal Ripken Jr. 1.00 2.50
88 Justin Upton .25 .60
89 Jon Lester .25 .60
90 Carlos Santana .25 .60
91A Javier Baez RC 2.50 6.00
91B Javier Baez VAR 60.00 150.00
Pointing up
92 Matt Harvey .25 .60
93 Max Scherzer .30 .75
94 Evan Longoria .25 .60
95 Corey Kluber .25 .60
96 Edwin Encarnacion .30 .75
97 Anthony Rizzo .40 1.00
98A Jose Reyes .25 .60
98B Jose Reyes VAR 10.00 25.00
Celebrating
99 Roger Maris .30 .75
100 Willie Mays .60 1.50
101 Lucas Duda .25 .60
102 Johnny Cueto .25 .60
103 Taijuan Walker .20 .50
104 Matt Moore .25 .60
105A Billy Hamilton .25 .60
105B Billy Hamilton VAR 10.00 25.00
Running
106 Alex Cobb .20 .50
107 Dalton Pompey RC .40 1.00
108 Yoenis Cespedes .25 .60
109 David Cone .20 .50
110 Justin Verlander .30 .75
111A Adrian Gonzalez .25 .60
111B Adrian Gonzalez VAR 10.00 25.00
Arms up
112 Evan Gattis .20 .50
113 Craig Biggio .25 .60
114A Jose Abreu .30 .75
114B J.Abreu VAR Laugh 12.00 30.00
115 Chipper Jones .30 .75
116 Nolan Arenado .50 1.25
117A Manny Machado .30 .75
117B Manny Machado VAR 12.00 30.00
Glasses
118 Goose Gossage .25 .60
119A Clayton Kershaw .50 1.25
119B Kershaw VAR Celebrat 20.00 50.00
120 Joe DiMaggio .60 1.50
121A Gregory Polanco .25 .60
121B Gregory Polanco VAR 10.00 25.00
With glove
122 Ken Griffey Jr. .60 1.50
123 Yusmeiro Petit .20 .50
124 Mike Piazza .30 .75
125 Roger Clemens .40 1.00
126 Carlos Gonzalez .25 .60
127 Dee Gordon .20 .50
128 Anthony Ranaudo RC .30 .75
129 Drew Smyly .20 .50
130 Tim Hudson .25 .60
131 Zack Wheeler .25 .60
132 Jose Fernandez .30 .75
133 Ernie Banks .30 .75
134 Ralph Kiner .25 .60
135 Craig Kimbrel .25 .60
136A Jonathan Papelbon .25 .60
136B Jonathan Papelbon VAR 10.00 25.00
Making fist
137 Chris Davis .20 .50
138 Greg Maddux .40 1.00
139 Jason Kipnis .25 .60
140 Mark Teixeira .25 .60
141 Nomar Garciaparra .25 .60
142 Larry Doby .25 .60
143A Masahiro Tanaka .25 .60
143B Tanaka VAR Tipping 10.00 25.00
144 Justin Morneau .25 .60
145 Deion Sanders .25 .60
146 Matt Cain .25 .60
147 Jarrod Parker .20 .50
148 Anibal Sanchez .20 .50
149A Miguel Cabrera .30 .75
149B Cabrera VAR Looki left 12.00 30.00
150A Felix Hernandez .25 .60
150B Hernandez VAR Tip cap 20.00 50.00
151 Ryne Sandberg .60 1.50
152 Rod Carew .25 .60
153 Wade Boggs .25 .60
154 Ryan Howard .25 .60
155 Troy Tulowitzki .30 .75
156 Ted Williams .60 1.50
157 Rusney Castillo RC .40 1.00
158 Rymer Liriano RC .30 .75
159 Roberto Alomar .25 .60
160 Hyun-Jin Ryu .25 .60
161 Lorenzo Cain .20 .50
162 Jonathan Lucroy .25 .60
163 Willie McCovey .25 .60
164 Tony Gwynn .30 .75
165 Michael Brantley .25 .60
166 Jeff Samardzija .20 .50
167 Ian Kinsler .25 .60
168A David Ortiz .30 .75
168B Ortiz VAR Hands up 25.00 60.00
169 Ryan Braun .25 .60
170 Christian Yelich .40 1.00
171A Dilson Herrera RC .40 1.00
171B Dilson Herrera VAR 10.00 25.00
Pointing up
172 Phil Hughes .20 .50
173A Jayson Werth .25 .60
173B Jayson Werth VAR 10.00 25.00
Red jersey
174 Chase Utley .25 .60
175 Cole Hamels .25 .60
176A Yasiel Puig .30 .75
176B Puig VAR Making fist 12.00 30.00
177 Martin Prado .20 .50
178 Ryan Zimmerman .25 .60
179A James Shields .20 .50
179B James Shields VAR 8.00 20.00
Arms down
180 Giancarlo Stanton .30 .75
181 Cliff Lee .25 .60
182 Sonny Gray .25 .60
183 George Springer .25 .60
184 Michael Wacha .25 .60
185 Chris Archer .20 .50
186 Stephen Strasburg .30 .75
187A Xander Bogaerts .30 .75
187B Xander Bogaerts VAR 12.00 30.00
Smiling
188A Carlos Gomez .20 .50
188B Carlos Gomez VAR 8.00 20.00
Finger to mouth
189 Daniel Norris RC .30 .75
190 Rickey Henderson .30 .75
191 Pablo Sandoval .25 .60
192 Garrett Richards .25 .60
193 CC Sabathia .25 .60
194A Alex Gordon .25 .60
194B Alex Gordon VAR 10.00 25.00
Making fists
195 Jacob deGrom .60 1.50
196 Travis d'Arnaud .25 .60
197 Matt Adams .20 .50
198 J.J. Hardy .20 .50
199 Mike Zunino .20 .50
200 Mike Napoli .20 .50
201 Marcell Ozuna .30 .75
202 Juan Lagares .20 .50
203 Nick Castellanos .30 .75
204 Jake Odorizzi .20 .50
205 Dylan Bundy .25 .60
206 Roenis Elias .20 .50
207 Jonathon Niese .20 .50
208A Dellin Betances .25 .60
208B Betances VAR Hug 20.00 50.00
209A Sean Doolittle .20 .50
209B Doolittle VAR w/catcher 20.00 50.00
210 David Robertson .25 .60
211 Fernando Rodney .20 .50
212 Mark Melancon .20 .50
213 LaTroy Hawkins .20 .50
214A Daniel Murphy .25 .60
214B Murphy VAR fists 15.00 40.00
215 Kyle Seager .20 .50
216 Scott Kazmir .20 .50
217 Desmond Jennings .25 .60
218 Jake Peavy .20 .50
219 Carlos Carrasco .20 .50
220 Francisco Liriano .20 .50
221 Jean Segura .25 .60
222 Russell Martin .20 .50
223 Ian Desmond .20 .50
224 Patrick Corbin .25 .60
225 Alexei Ramirez .25 .60
226 Melky Cabrera .20 .50
227 Tanner Roark .20 .50
228 Jhonny Peralta .20 .50
229 Coco Crisp .20 .50
230 Howie Kendrick .20 .50
231 Ian Kennedy .20 .50
232 Matt Garza .20 .50
233A Bartolo Colon .20 .50
233B Bartolo Colon VAR 8.00 20.00
Batting
234 Jarred Cosart .20 .50
235 Tyson Ross .20 .50
236 Jake McGee .25 .60
237 Billy Butler .20 .50
238 Carlos Beltran .25 .60
239 Victor Martinez .25 .60
240 Cody Allen .20 .50
241 Curtis Granderson .25 .60
242 Satchel Paige .30 .75
243 Pedro Alvarez .20 .50
244 Nori Aoki .20 .50
245 Andrelton Simmons .20 .50
246 Brian McCann .25 .60
247 Chris Carter .20 .50

248 Jose Quintana .20 .50
249 Brandon Moss .20 .50
250 Aramis Ramirez .20 .50
251 Ervin Santana .20 .50
252 Wily Peralta .20 .50
253 A.J. Burnett .20 .50
254 Andrew Miller .25 .60
255 Zach Britton .25 .60
256 Francisco Rodriguez .25 .60
257 Yan Gomes .20 .50
258A Starling Marte .25 .60
258B Starling Marte VAR 10.00 25.00
Celebrating
259 Mike Foltynewicz RC .30 .75
260 Babe Ruth .75 2.00
261A Hunter Pence .25 .60
261B Pence VAR fists 20.00 50.00
262 Lonnie Chisenhall .20 .50
263 Mark Buehrle .25 .60
264 Alex Rios .25 .60
265 Jason Heyward .25 .60
266 Austin Jackson .20 .50
267 Trevor Bauer .40 1.00
268 Elvis Andrus .25 .60
269 Mike Leake .20 .50
270 Mike Minor .20 .50
271 Lance Lynn .20 .50
272 Josh Harrison .20 .50
273 Allen Craig .20 .50
274 Dan Haren .20 .50
275 Khris Davis .30 .75
276 R.A. Dickey .25 .60
277 Henderson Alvarez .20 .50
278 Nathan Eovaldi .25 .60
279 Jered Weaver .25 .60
280 C.J. Wilson .20 .50
281 Wade Davis .20 .50
282 Greg Holland .20 .50
283 Steve Cishek .20 .50
284 Trevor Rosenthal .25 .60
285A Jenrry Mejia .20 .50
285B Jenrry Mejia VAR 8.00 20.00
Orange jersey
286 Ken Giles .20 .50
287 Brian Dozier .25 .60
288 Wilin Rosario .20 .50
289 Mark Trumbo .20 .50
290 Jay Bruce .25 .60
291A Brett Gardner .25 .60
291B Brett Gardner VAR 10.00 25.00
Arm up
292 Aaron Sanchez .25 .60
293 Danny Salazar .25 .60
294 Brandon Phillips .20 .50
295 Shin-Soo Choo .25 .60
296 Brandon Belt .25 .60
297 Homer Bailey .20 .50
298 Ubaldo Jimenez .20 .50
299A Kolten Wong .25 .60
299B Kolten Wong VAR 10.00 25.00
Yelling
300 Jesse Hahn .20 .50
301 Jackie Robinson SP 1.25 3.00
302 Eddie Mathews SP 1.25 3.00
303 Duke Snider SP 1.00 2.50
304 Bill Mazeroski SP 1.00 2.50
305 Whitey Ford SP 1.00 2.50
306 Sandy Koufax SP 2.50 6.00
307 Lou Brock SP 1.00 2.50
308 Brooks Robinson SP 1.00 2.50
309 Orlando Cepeda SP 1.00 2.50
310 Al Kaline SP 1.25 3.00
311 Tom Seaver SP 1.00 2.50
312 Jim Palmer SP 1.00 2.50
313 Willie Stargell SP 1.00 2.50
314 Catfish Hunter SP 1.00 2.50
315 Hoyt Wilhelm SP 1.00 2.50
316 Phil Rizzuto SP 1.00 2.50
317 Johnny Bench SP 1.25 3.00
318 Joe Morgan SP 1.00 2.50
319 Reggie Jackson SP 1.00 2.50
320 Gary Carter SP 1.00 2.50
321 Dave Parker SP .75 2.00
322 Mike Schmidt SP 2.00 5.00
323 Fernando Valenzuela SP .75 2.00
324 Bruce Sutter SP 1.00 2.50
325 Sparky Anderson SP 1.00 2.50
326 George Brett SP 2.50 6.00
327 Dwight Gooden SP .75 2.00
328 Dennis Eckersley SP 1.00 2.50
329 Eric Davis SP .75 2.00
330 David Cone SP .75 2.00
331 John Olerud SP .75 2.00
332 Fred McGriff SP 1.00 2.50
333 Luis Aparicio SP 1.00 2.50
334 Livan Hernandez SP .75 2.00
335 Orlando Hernandez SP .75 2.00
336 Mariano Rivera SP 1.50 4.00
337 Jorge Posada SP 1.00 2.50
338 Luis Gonzalez SP .75 2.00
339 David Eckstein SP .75 2.00
340 Josh Beckett SP .75 2.00
341 Paul Konerko SP 1.00 2.50
342 Matt Holliday SP 1.25 3.00
343 Dustin Pedroia SP 1.25 3.00
344 Jimmy Rollins SP 1.00 2.50
345 Alex Rodriguez SP 1.50 4.00
346 Tim Lincecum SP 1.00 2.50
347 Yadier Molina SP 1.50 4.00
348 Buster Posey SP 1.50 4.00
349 Koji Uehara SP .75 2.00
350 Madison Bumgarner SP 1.00 2.50

2015 Topps Gypsy Queen Framed Bronze

*FRME BRNZ: 1.5X TO 4X BASIC
*FRME BRNZ RC: 1X TO 2.5X BASIC RC
STATED ODDS 1:17 HOBBY
STATED PRINT RUN 499 SER.#'d SETS
5 Derek Jeter 6.00 15.00

2015 Topps Gypsy Queen Framed White

*FRME WHTE: 1.2X TO 3X BASIC
*FRME WHTE RC: .75X TO 2X BASIC RC
RANDOM INSERTS IN PACKS
5 Derek Jeter 5.00 12.00

2015 Topps Gypsy Queen Mini

*MINI 1-300: 1.2X TO 3X BASIC
*MINI 1-300 RC: .75X TO 2X BASIC
*MINI 301-350: .5X TO 1.2X BASIC
MINI SP ODDS 1:24 HOBBY

2015 Topps Gypsy Queen Mini Box Variations

*MINI BOX VAR: 1.2X TO 3X BASIC
*MINI BOX VAR RC: .75X TO 2X BASIC RC
ONE MINI BOX PER HOBBY BOX
TEN CARDS PER MINI BOX

2015 Topps Gypsy Queen Mini Gold

*GOLD 1-300: 4X TO 10X BASIC
*GOLD 1-300 RC: 2.5X TO 6X BASIC
*GOLD 301-350: 1X TO 2.5X BASIC
RANDOM INSERTS IN PACKS
STATED PRINT RUN 99 SER.#'d SETS
1 Mike Trout 12.00 30.00
3 Joc Pederson 10.00 25.00
5 Derek Jeter 15.00 40.00
20 Frank Thomas 8.00 20.00
34 Andrew McCutchen 6.00 15.00
47 Ozzie Smith 6.00 15.00
87 Cal Ripken Jr. 12.00 30.00
119 Clayton Kershaw 8.00 20.00
122 Ken Griffey Jr. 8.00 20.00
176 Yasiel Puig 8.00 20.00
319 Reggie Jackson SP 6.00 15.00
322 Mike Schmidt SP 8.00 20.00
326 George Brett SP 10.00 25.00
347 Yadier Molina SP 8.00 20.00

2015 Topps Gypsy Queen Mini Red

*RED 1-300: 4X TO 10X BASIC
*RED 1-300 RC: 2.5X TO 6X BASIC
*RED 301-350: 1X TO 2.5X BASIC
STATED ODDS 1:48 PACKS
STATED PRINT RUN 50 SER.#'d SETS
1 Mike Trout 15.00 40.00
3 Joc Pederson 12.00 30.00
5 Derek Jeter 20.00 50.00
20 Frank Thomas 10.00 25.00
34 Andrew McCutchen 8.00 20.00
47 Ozzie Smith 8.00 20.00
87 Cal Ripken Jr. 15.00 40.00
119 Clayton Kershaw 10.00 25.00
122 Ken Griffey Jr. 10.00 25.00
176 Yasiel Puig 10.00 25.00
319 Reggie Jackson SP 8.00 20.00
322 Mike Schmidt SP 10.00 25.00
326 George Brett SP 12.00 30.00
347 Yadier Molina SP 10.00 25.00

2015 Topps Gypsy Queen Mini Silver

*SILVER 1-300: 2.5X TO 6X BASIC
*SILVER 1-300 RC: 1.5X TO 4X BASIC
*SILVER 301-350: .75X TO 2X BASIC
STATED ODDS 1:12 HOBBY
STATED PRINT RUN 199 SER.#'d SETS
1 Mike Trout 8.00 20.00
3 Joc Pederson 6.00 15.00
5 Derek Jeter 10.00 25.00
20 Frank Thomas 5.00 12.00
87 Cal Ripken Jr. 8.00 20.00
319 Reggie Jackson SP 5.00 12.00
322 Mike Schmidt SP 6.00 15.00
326 George Brett SP 8.00 20.00
347 Yadier Molina SP 6.00 15.00

2015 Topps Gypsy Queen Autographs

STATED ODDS 1:14 HOBBY
EXCHANGE DEADLINE 3/31/2018
GQAAA Abraham Almonte 2.50 6.00
GQAAR Anthony Ranaudo 2.50 6.00
GQABC Brandon Crawford 5.00 12.00
GQABF Brandon Finnegan 2.50 6.00
GQABHO Brock Holt 2.50 6.00
GQACA Chris Archer 2.50 6.00
GQACJ Chris Johnson 2.50 6.00
GQACS Cory Spangenberg 2.50 6.00
GQACY Christian Yelich 15.00 40.00
GQADC David Cone 4.00 10.00
GQADN Daniel Norris 2.50 6.00
GQADPO Dalton Pompey 3.00 8.00
GQAEG Evan Gattis 2.50 6.00
GQAGS George Springer 12.00 30.00
GQAJB Javier Baez 30.00 80.00
GQAJC Jose Canseco 10.00 25.00
GQAJD Jacob deGrom 30.00 80.00
GQAJG Juan Gonzalez 4.00 10.00
GQAJL Juan Lagares 2.50 6.00
GQAJP Joc Pederson 5.00 12.00
GQAJS Jorge Soler 4.00 10.00
GQAJW Josh Willingham 2.50 6.00
GQAKG Kevin Gausman 4.00 10.00
GQAKV Kennys Vargas 2.50 6.00
GQAKW Kolten Wong 3.00 8.00
GQAMA Matt Adams 3.00 8.00
GQAMF Maikel Franco 3.00 8.00
GQAMJ Matt Joyce 2.50 6.00
GQAMSH Matt Shoemaker 3.00 8.00
GQAMT Michael Taylor 2.50 6.00
GQARC Rusney Castillo 3.00 8.00
GQASS Scott Sizemore 2.50 6.00
GQAYV Yordano Ventura 5.00 12.00

2015 Topps Gypsy Queen Autographs Gold

*GOLD: .6X TO 1.5X BASIC
STATED ODDS 1:403 HOBBY
STATED PRINT RUN 25 SER.#'d SETS
EXCHANGE DEADLINE 3/31/2018
GQAAD Andre Dawson 25.00 60.00
GQAAJ Adam Jones 5.00 12.00
GQABJ Bo Jackson 50.00 100.00
GQACK Clayton Kershaw 75.00 150.00
GQACR Cal Ripken Jr. EXCH 75.00 150.00
GQADP Dustin Pedroia 25.00 60.00
GQAFF Freddie Freeman 25.00 60.00
GQAFT Frank Thomas 50.00 120.00
GQAGP Gregory Polanco 20.00 50.00
GQAHA Hank Aaron 250.00 350.00
GQAJA Jose Abreu 40.00 100.00
GQAJF Jose Fernandez 20.00 50.00
GQAJSM John Smoltz 40.00 80.00
GQAKGR Ken Griffey Jr. EXCH 200.00 300.00
GQAMTR Mike Trout 200.00 300.00
GQANG Nomar Garciaparra 30.00 80.00
GQAOS Ozzie Smith 30.00 80.00
GQAPG Paul Goldschmidt 15.00 40.00
GQAPN Phil Niekro 12.00 30.00
GQARH Rickey Henderson EXCH 30.00 80.00
GQATG Tom Glavine EXCH 25.00 60.00
GQATT Troy Tulowitzki EXCH 25.00 60.00
GQAYP Yasiel Puig 75.00 150.00

2015 Topps Gypsy Queen Autographs Silver

*SILVER: .5X TO 1.2X BASIC
STATED ODDS 1:199 HOBBY
STATED PRINT RUN 50 SER.#'d SETS
EXCHANGE DEADLINE 3/31/2018
GQAAJ Adam Jones 4.00 10.00
GQACK Clayton Kershaw 60.00 120.00
GQAFF Freddie Freeman 20.00 50.00
GQAGP Gregory Polanco 15.00 40.00
GQAJA Jose Abreu 30.00 80.00
GQAJF Jose Fernandez 15.00 40.00
GQAPG Paul Goldschmidt 12.00 30.00
GQAPN Phil Niekro 10.00 25.00

2015 Topps Gypsy Queen Basics of Base Ball Minis

COMPLETE SET (15) 20.00 50.00
STATED ODDS 1:24 HOBBY
BBMR1 Windup 1.50 4.00
BBMR2 Grip the Bat 1.50 4.00
BBMR3 Sacrifice Fly 1.50 4.00
BBMR4 Head-First Slide 1.50 4.00
BBMR5 Cut-Off 1.50 4.00
BBMR6 Take a Lead 1.50 4.00
BBMR7 Tag Up 1.50 4.00
BBMR8 Infield Shift 1.50 4.00
BBMR9 Pitchout 1.50 4.00
BBMR10 Steal 1.50 4.00
BBMR11 Intentional Walk 1.50 4.00
BBMR12 Squeeze Bunt 1.50 4.00
BBMR13 Rundown 1.50 4.00
BBMR14 Crowd the Plate 1.50 4.00
BBMR15 Knuckleball 1.50 4.00

2015 Topps Gypsy Queen Framed Mini Relics

STATED ODDS 1:28 HOBBY
*GOLD/25: .6X TO 1.5X BASIC
GMRAB Adrian Beltre 3.00 8.00
GMRAC Aroldis Chapman 3.00 8.00
GMRAG Adrian Gonzalez 2.50 6.00
GMRAW Adam Wainwright 2.50 6.00
GMRCA Chris Archer 2.00 5.00
GMRCC Carl Crawford 2.50 6.00
GMRCD Chris Davis 2.00 5.00
GMRCH Cole Hamels 2.50 6.00
GMRCK Clayton Kershaw 5.00 12.00
GMRCS Chris Sale 3.00 8.00
GMRCY Christian Yelich 4.00 10.00
GMRDO David Ortiz 3.00 8.00
GMRDP David Price 2.50 6.00
GMRDW David Wright 2.50 6.00
GMREA Elvis Andrus 2.50 6.00
GMREG Evan Gattis 2.00 5.00
GMREH Eric Hosmer 2.50 6.00
GMRFF Freddie Freeman 4.00 10.00
GMRGB Gary Brown 2.00 5.00
GMRGC Gerrit Cole 3.00 8.00
GMRGG Gio Gonzalez 2.50 6.00
GMRGP Gregory Polanco 2.50 6.00
GMRHI Hisashi Iwakuma 2.50 6.00
GMRHR Hyun-Jin Ryu 2.50 6.00
GMRIK Ian Kinsler 2.50 6.00
GMRJH Jason Heyward 2.50 6.00
GMRJS Jon Singleton 2.50 6.00
GMRJU Justin Upton 2.50 6.00
GMRJV Justin Verlander 5.00 12.00
GMRKW Kolten Wong 2.50 6.00
GMRMA Matt Adams 2.00 5.00
GMRMB Madison Bumgarner 2.50 6.00
GMRMC Miguel Cabrera 3.00 8.00
GMRMH Matt Holliday 3.00 8.00
GMRMMI Mike Minor 2.00 5.00
GMRMT Masahiro Tanaka 2.50 6.00
GMRMTR Mike Trout 10.00 25.00
GMRMW Michael Wacha 2.50 6.00
GMRNC Nick Castellanos 3.00 8.00
GMRPS Pablo Sandoval 2.50 6.00
GMRRB Ryan Braun 2.50 6.00
GMRSC Starlin Castro 2.00 5.00
GMRSCI Steve Cishek 2.00 5.00
GMRSM Shelby Miller 2.50 6.00
GMRSP Salvador Perez 2.50 6.00
GMRSS Stephen Strasburg 3.00 8.00
GMRTD Travis d'Arnaud 2.50 6.00
GMRTW Taijuan Walker 2.00 5.00
GMRVM Victor Martinez 2.50 6.00
GMRWM Wil Myers 2.50 6.00
GMRXB Xander Bogaerts 3.00 8.00
GMRYM Yadier Molina 5.00 12.00
GMRYV Yordano Ventura 2.50 6.00
GMRZG Zack Greinke 3.00 8.00

2015 Topps Gypsy Queen Glove Stories

COMPLETE SET (15) 3.00 8.00
STATED ODDS 1:6 HOBBY
PRINTING PLATE ODDS 1:13,441 HOBBY
PLATE PRINT RUN 1 SET PER COLOR
NO PLATE PRICING DUE TO SCARCITY
GS1 Steven Souza Jr. .40 1.00
GS2 Billy Hamilton .40 1.00
GS3 Adam Eaton .30 .75
GS4 Peter Bourjos .30 .75
GS5 Mike Aviles .30 .75
GS6 Dustin Ackley .30 .75
GS7 Ben Revere .30 .75
GS8 Mookie Betts 1.00 2.50
GS9 Alex Gordon .40 1.00
GS10 Pablo Sandoval .40 1.00
GS11 Norichika Aoki .30 .75
GS12 Hunter Pence .40 1.00
GS13 Carlos Gomez .30 .75
GS14 Aaron Hicks .40 1.00
GS15 Mike Moustakas .40 1.00

2015 Topps Gypsy Queen Jumbo Relics

STATED ODDS 1:651 HOBBY
STATED PRINT RUN 50 SER.#'d SETS
*GOLD/25: .6X TO 1.5X BASIC
GJRAM Andrew McCutchen 15.00 40.00
GJRAR Anthony Rendon 6.00 15.00
GJRAS Andrelton Simmons 12.00 30.00
GJRAW Adam Wainwright 10.00 25.00
GJRBH Billy Hamilton 5.00 12.00
GJRBP Buster Posey 25.00 60.00
GJRCK Clayton Kershaw 10.00 25.00
GJRCS Chris Sale 6.00 15.00
GJRDJ Derek Jeter 50.00 100.00
GJRFH Felix Hernandez 10.00 25.00
GJRGS Giancarlo Stanton 6.00 15.00
GJRHR Hyun-Jin Ryu 5.00 12.00
GJRJB Jose Bautista 12.00 30.00
GJRMC Miguel Cabrera 6.00 15.00
GJRMP Mike Piazza 6.00 15.00
GJRMS Max Scherzer 6.00 15.00
GJRMT Mike Trout 30.00 80.00
GJRMTA Masahiro Tanaka 5.00 12.00
GJRRB Ryan Braun 5.00 12.00
GJRRC Roger Clemens 8.00 20.00
GJRRP Rafael Palmeiro 15.00 40.00
GJRSS Stephen Strasburg 6.00 15.00
GJRVM Victor Martinez 8.00 20.00
GJRYC Yoenis Cespedes 8.00 20.00
GJRYP Yasiel Puig 6.00 15.00

2015 Topps Gypsy Queen Mini Relic Autograph Booklets

STATED ODDS 1:628 MINI BOX
STATED PRINT RUN 25 SER.#'d SETS
EXCHANGE DEADLINE 3/31/2018
MARAD Andre Dawson 40.00 100.00
MARAJ Adam Jones 40.00 100.00
MARBM Brian McCann 50.00 120.00
MARCB Craig Biggio 50.00 120.00
MARCK Clayton Kershaw 100.00 250.00
MARCR Cal Ripken Jr. 150.00 300.00
MARCS Chris Sale 50.00 120.00
MARDP Dustin Pedroia 75.00 200.00
MARFF Freddie Freeman 50.00 120.00
MARGSN Giancarlo Stanton EXCH 50.00 125.00
MARJA Jose Abreu 100.00 250.00
MARJB Javier Baez 250.00 600.00
MARJD Josh Donaldson 40.00 100.00
MARJG Juan Gonzalez 30.00 80.00
MARJM Joe Mauer 50.00 120.00
MARJP Joc Pederson 100.00 250.00
MARKG Ken Griffey Jr. 250.00 400.00
MARMS Max Scherzer 50.00 120.00
MARMT Mike Trout 250.00 400.00
MARRB Ryan Braun 40.00 100.00
MARRC Robinson Cano 60.00 150.00
MARRCA Rusney Castillo 40.00 100.00
MARSG Sonny Gray 40.00 100.00

2015 Topps Gypsy Queen Pillars of the Community

COMPLETE SET (10) 12.00 30.00
STATED ODDS 1:24 HOBBY
PCBH Bryce Harper 2.00 5.00
PCBP Buster Posey 1.50 4.00
PCDO David Ortiz 1.25 3.00
PCDW David Wright 1.00 2.50
PCJA Jose Abreu 1.25 3.00
PCJB Jose Bautista 1.00 2.50
PCMT Masahiro Tanaka 1.00 2.50
PCRC Robinson Cano 1.00 2.50
PCYM Yadier Molina 1.50 4.00
PCYP Yasiel Puig 1.25 3.00

2015 Topps Gypsy Queen Relic Autographs

STATED ODDS 1:815 HOBBY
STATED PRINT RUN 50 SER.#'d SETS
EXCHANGE DEADLINE 3/31/2018
*GOLD/25: .5X TO 1.2X BASIC
ARCG Carlos Gonzalez EXCH 6.00 15.00
ARCK Clayton Kershaw 60.00 150.00
ARCS Chris Sale 10.00 25.00
ARDP Dustin Pedroia 20.00 50.00
ARFF Freddie Freeman 15.00 40.00
ARFT Frank Thomas 20.00 50.00
ARGSN Giancarlo Stanton EXCH 40.00 80.00
ARJA Jose Abreu 30.00 80.00
ARJF Jose Fernandez 30.00 80.00
ARJP Joc Pederson 10.00 25.00
ARJT Julio Teheran 6.00 15.00
ARMA Matt Adams 15.00 40.00
ARMF Maikel Franco 25.00 60.00
ARMS Max Scherzer EXCH 15.00 40.00
ARPG Paul Goldschmidt 20.00 50.00
ARRH Rickey Henderson 25.00 60.00
ARYD Yu Darvish 30.00 80.00
ARYP Yasiel Puig 40.00 100.00
ARYV Yordano Ventura 10.00 25.00

2015 Topps Gypsy Queen Relics

STATED ODDS 1:28 HOBBY
*GOLD/25: .6X TO 1.5X BASIC
GQRAD Andre Dawson 2.50 6.00
GQRAG Adrian Gonzalez 2.50 6.00
GQRAH Adeiny Hechavarria 2.00 5.00
GQRAJ Adam Jones 2.50 6.00
GQRAS Andrelton Simmons 2.00 5.00
GQRAW Adam Wainwright 2.50 6.00
GQRBH Billy Hamilton 2.50 6.00
GQRBP Buster Posey 4.00 10.00
GQRCA Chris Archer 2.00 5.00
GQRCC Carl Crawford 2.50 6.00
GQRCH Cole Hamels 2.50 6.00
GQRCK Clayton Kershaw 5.00 12.00
GQRCKI Craig Kimbrel 2.50 6.00
GQRDJ Derek Jeter 10.00 25.00
GQRDM Don Mattingly 5.00 12.00
GQRDP David Price 2.50 6.00
GQRDW David Wright 2.50 6.00
GQREA Elvis Andrus 2.50 6.00
GQRFF Freddie Freeman 4.00 10.00
GQRFH Felix Hernandez 2.50 6.00
GQRFT Frank Thomas 5.00 12.00
GQRGC Gerrit Cole 3.00 8.00
GQRGG Gio Gonzalez 2.50 6.00
GQRHI Hisashi Iwakuma 2.50 6.00
GQRHR Hyun-Jin Ryu 2.50 6.00
GQRIK Ian Kinsler 2.50 6.00
GQRJB Jose Bautista 2.50 6.00
GQRJH Jason Heyward 2.50 6.00
GQRJM Joe Mauer 2.50 6.00
GQRJS Jon Singleton 2.50 6.00
GQRJV Justin Verlander 3.00 8.00
GQRJVO Joey Votto 3.00 8.00
GQRKW Kolten Wong 2.50 6.00
GQRMA Matt Adams 2.00 5.00
GQRMH Matt Holliday 3.00 8.00
GQRNA Nolan Arenado 5.00 12.00
GQRNC Nick Castellanos 3.00 8.00
GQRPS Pablo Sandoval 2.50 6.00
GQRRC Robinson Cano 2.50 6.00
GQRSC Starlin Castro 2.00 5.00
GQRSM Starling Marte 2.50 6.00
GQRSMI Shelby Miller 2.50 6.00
GQRTD Travis d'Arnaud 2.50 6.00
GQRTW Taijuan Walker 2.00 5.00
GQRVG Vladimir Guerrero 2.50 6.00
GQRVM Victor Martinez 2.50 6.00
GQRXB Xander Bogaerts 3.00 8.00
GQRYC Yoenis Cespedes 2.50 6.00
GQRYM Yadier Molina 5.00 12.00
GQRYP Yasiel Puig 3.00 8.00
GQRYV Yordano Ventura 2.50 6.00
GQRZG Zack Greinke 3.00 8.00

2015 Topps Gypsy Queen Framed Mini Retail Autographs

RANDOM INSERTS IN RETAIL PACKS
RMAAR Anthony Rizzo EXCH 50.00 100.00
RMACK Clayton Kershaw 125.00 250.00
RMACR Cal Ripken Jr. 50.00 120.00
RMADP Dustin Pedroia 75.00 150.00
RMAFF Freddie Freeman 75.00 150.00
RMAFT Frank Thomas 50.00 100.00
RMAGSR George Springer 50.00 100.00
RMAJA Jose Abreu 50.00 120.00
RMAJP Joc Pederson 100.00 200.00
RMAJSR Jorge Soler 150.00 250.00
RMAMF Maikel Franco 75.00 150.00
RMARC Rusney Castillo 30.00 80.00
RMAYV Yordano Ventura 12.00 30.00

2015 Topps Gypsy Queen The Queen's Throwbacks

COMPLETE SET (25) 5.00 12.00
STATED ODDS 1:6 HOBBY
PRINTING PLATE ODDS 1:8182 HOBBY
PLATE PRINT RUN 1 SET PER COLOR
NO PLATE PRICING DUE TO SCARCITY
QT1 Miguel Cabrera .50 1.25
QT2 Andrelton Simmons .30 .75
QT3 Anthony Rizzo .60 1.50
QT4 Michael Morse .30 .75
QT5 Alex Gordon .40 1.00
QT6 James Shields .30 .75
QT7 Nelson Cruz .50 1.25
QT8 Ian Kinsler .40 1.00
QT9 Adrian Beltre .50 1.25
QT10 Rougned Odor .40 1.00
QT11 Jose Altuve .40 1.00
QT12 Miguel Gonzalez .30 .75
QT13 George Springer .40 1.00
QT14 Robinson Cano .40 1.00
QT15 Ryan Braun .40 1.00
QT16 Joe Mauer .40 1.00
QT17 Starlin Castro .30 .75
QT18 Gerrit Cole .50 1.25
QT19 Curtis Granderson .40 1.00
QT20 Manny Machado .50 1.25
QT21 Sonny Gray .40 1.00
QT22 Mike Trout 2.50 6.00
QT23 Jered Weaver .40 1.00
QT24 Julio Teheran .40 1.00
QT25 Jason Kipnis .40 1.00

2015 Topps Gypsy Queen Walk Off Winners

COMPLETE SET (25) 5.00 12.00
STATED ODDS 1:4 HOBBY
PRINTING PLATE ODDS 1:8182 HOBBY
PLATE PRINT RUN 1 SET PER COLOR
NO PLATE PRICING DUE TO SCARCITY
GWO1 Bill Mazeroski .40 1.00
GWO2 Ken Griffey Jr. 1.00 2.50
GWO3 Giancarlo Stanton .50 1.25
GWO4 David Ortiz .50 1.25
GWO5 Derek Jeter 1.25 3.00
GWO6 Derek Jeter 1.25 3.00
GWO7 David Freese .30 .75
GWO8 Carlton Fisk .40 1.00
GWO9 Ozzie Smith .60 1.50
GWO10 Mike Trout 2.50 6.00
GWO11 Raul Ibanez .40 1.00
GWO12 Scott Hatteberg .30 .75
GWO13 Luis Gonzalez .30 .75
GWO14 Salvador Perez .40 1.00
GWO15 Bryce Harper .75 2.00
GWO16 Evan Longoria .40 1.00
GWO17 Lenny Dykstra .30 .75
GWO18 Carlos Gonzalez .40 1.00
GWO19 Travis Ishikawa .30 .75
GWO20 Jason Giambi .30 .75
GWO21 Kolten Wong .40 1.00
GWO22 Jayson Werth .40 1.00
GWO23 Alex Gordon .40 1.00
GWO24 Neil Walker .30 .75
GWO25 Mookie Wilson .30 .75

2016 Topps Gypsy Queen

COMP.SET w/SP (350) 50.00 120.00
COMP.SET w/o SP's (300) 12.00 30.00
SP ODDS 1:4 HOBBY
SP VAR ODDS 1:58 HOBBY
PRINTING PLATE ODDS 1:512 HOBBY
PLATE PRINT RUN 1 SET PER COLOR
BLACK-CYAN-MAGENTA-YELLOW ISSUED
NO PLATE PRICING DUE TO SCARCITY
1A Giancarlo Stanton .30 .75
Batting
1B Giancarlo Stanton SP 5.00 12.00
Fielding
2A Buster Posey .40 1.00
Batting
2B Posey SP Ctchng 10.00 25.00
3A A.J. Pollock .20 .50
Running
3B A.J. Pollock SP 3.00 8.00
Fielding
4 Adam Jones .25 .60
5 Albert Pujols .40 1.00
6 Carlos Gonzalez .25 .60
7A Corey Seager RC 3.00 8.00
Running
7B Seager SP Fldng 15.00 40.00
8A Freeman Gry Jrsy .40 1.00
8B Freeman SP In rain 10.00 25.00
9 Hector Olivera RC .40 1.00
10A Ichiro Suzuki .40 1.00
Throwing
10B Ichiro SP Rnnng 6.00 15.00
11 Jason Heyward .25 .60
12A Jose Bautista .25 .60
Running
12B Jose Bautista SP 4.00 10.00
w/Glove
13A Luis Severino RC .40 1.00
Gray jersey
13B Luis Severino SP 4.00 10.00
Pinstripes
14A Marcus Stroman .25 .60
Blue jersey
14B Marcus Stroman SP 4.00 10.00
White jersey
15 Michael Brantley .25 .60
16A Miguel Sano RC .50 1.25
Batting
16B Sano SP Fldng 5.00 12.00
17A Nolan Arenado .50 1.25
Gray jersey
17B Nolan Arenado SP 8.00 20.00
Purple jersey
18A Robinson Cano .25 .60
Batting
18B Robinson Cano SP 4.00 10.00
Fielding
19A Stephen Strasburg .30 .75
Pitching
19B Stephen Strasburg SP 5.00 12.00
Batting
20 Todd Frazier .20 .50
21A Adam Wainwright .25 .60
Pitching
21B Adam Wainwright SP 4.00 10.00
Red cap
22 Aroldis Chapman .30 .75
23A Bryce Harper .50 1.25
Batting
23B Harper SP w/Glve 15.00 40.00
24 Charlie Blackmon .30 .75
25A Sale Pitching .30 .75
25B Sale Wht Jrsy 5.00 12.00
26 Cole Hamels .25 .60
27 Craig Kimbrel .25 .60
28 David Price .25 .60
29 Eric Hosmer .25 .60
30A Jake Arrieta .25 .60
Pitching
30B Jake Arrieta SP 4.00 10.00
Batting
31 Jason Kipnis .25 .60
32 Johnny Cueto .25 .60
33A Jose Fernandez .30 .75
Arm back
33B Jose Fernandez SP 5.00 12.00
Brown glove
34 Justin Verlander .30 .75
35 Jacoby Ellsbury .25 .60
36 Joe Mauer .25 .60
37 John Lackey .25 .60
38 Justin Upton .25 .60
39 Randal Grichuk .20 .50
40 Carlos Martinez .25 .60
41 Garrett Richards .25 .60
42 Gio Gonzalez .25 .60
43 Henry Owens RC .40 1.00
44 Hyun-Jin Ryu .25 .60
45 J.D. Martinez .30 .75
46 Jordan Zimmermann .25 .60
47 Jung Ho Kang .20 .50
48 Andre Ethier .25 .60
49 David Peralta .20 .50
50 Dexter Fowler .25 .60
51 Frankie Montas .25 .60
52 Jeff Samardzija .20 .50
53 Jonathan Papelbon .25 .60
54 Matt Kemp .25 .60
55 Andrelton Simmons .20 .50
56 Daniel Murphy .25 .60
57 Kolten Wong .25 .60
58 Eduardo Rodriguez .20 .50
59A Madison Bumgarner .25 .60
Pitching
59B Bumgarner SP Bttng 8.00 20.00
60A Matt Carpenter .30 .75
Red cap
60B Matt Carpenter SP 5.00 12.00
Dark cap
61A Michael Conforto RC .40 1.00
Running
61B Conforto SP Blu jsy 20.00 50.00
62A Sonny Gray .25 .60
Ball in glove
62B Sonny Gray SP 4.00 10.00
Ball visable
63 Steven Matz .20 .50
64A Truner RC No Ball 1.00 2.50
64B Truner SP Ball 10.00 25.00
65 Xander Bogaerts .30 .75
66 Zack Greinke .30 .75
67A Addison Russell .30 .75
Batting
67B Addison Russell SP 5.00 12.00
Fielding
68 Anthony Rendon .30 .75
69 Edwin Encarnacion .30 .75
70 Evan Gattis .20 .50
71A Francisco Lindor .30 .75
Batting
71B Lindor SP Fldng 8.00 20.00
72 Gary Sanchez RC 1.00 2.50
73 Greg Bird RC .40 1.00
74 Hisashi Iwakuma .25 .60
75 Jeurys Familia .25 .60
76 Jon Gray RC .30 .75
77 Jorge Soler .30 .75
78A Josh Donaldson .25 .60
Arm forward
78B Josh Donaldson SP 4.00 10.00
Arm back
79A Kris Bryant .40 1.00
White jersey
79B Bryant SP Blu jsy 6.00 15.00
80 Maikel Franco .25 .60
81A Matt Duffy RC .30 .75
Batting
81B Duffy SP Fldng 15.00 40.00
82 Nelson Cruz .30 .75
83 Salvador Perez .25 .60
84 Starlin Castro .20 .50
85 Yu Darvish .30 .75
86 Adrian Beltre .30 .75
87 Alex Gordon .25 .60
88A Andrew McCutchen .30 .75
Batting
88B McCtchn SP w/Glve 10.00 25.00
89A A.Rizzo Bttng .40 1.00
89B Anthony Rizzo SP 6.00 15.00
Fielding
90A Carlos Correa .30 .75
Orange jersey
90B Correa SP Gray jsy 5.00 12.00
91A Chris Archer .20 .50
Pitching
91B Chris Archer SP 3.00 8.00
In dugout
92 Lance McCullers .20 .50
93 Matt Moore .25 .60
94 Rougned Odor .25 .60
95 Aaron Nola RC .60 1.50
96 Alex Cobb .20 .50
97 Carlos Carrasco .20 .50
98 Carlos Rodon .30 .75
99 Daniel Norris .20 .50
100 Mike Moustakas .25 .60
101 Rusney Castillo .20 .50
102 Yadier Molina .40 1.00
103 Zack Wheeler .25 .60
104 Ben Zobrist .25 .60
105 Danny Salazar .25 .60
106 David Wright .25 .60
107A Devin Mesoraco .20 .50
Batting
107B Devin Mesoraco SP 3.00 8.00
Catching
108 Richie Shaffer RC .30 .75
109 Tyson Ross .20 .50
110 Yovani Gallardo .20 .50
111 Brandon Belt .25 .60
112 Brett Gardner .25 .60
113 Joe Ross .20 .50
114 Jose Iglesias .25 .60
115 Michael Pineda .20 .50
116 Brandon Crawford .25 .60
117 Carlos Santana .25 .60
118 Christian Yelich .40 1.00
119 Drew Smyly .20 .50
120 Victor Martinez .25 .60
121 Brian Dozier .25 .60
122 Corey Dickerson .20 .50
123 George Springer .25 .60
124 Jon Lester .25 .60
125 Jose Abreu .30 .75
126A Kyle Schwarber RC 1.00 2.50
Blue jersey
126B Schwrbr SP Gray jsy 10.00 25.00
127 Lorenzo Cain .20 .50
128A Manny Machado .30 .75
Batting
128B Machado SP Blck jsy 8.00 20.00
129 Mark Teixeira .25 .60
130A Matt Harvey .25 .60
Pitching
130B Harvey SP Bttng 8.00 20.00
131A Max Scherzer .30 .75
Pitching
131B Max Scherzer SP 5.00 12.00
Batting
132A Michael Wacha .25 .60
Pitching
132B Michael Wacha SP 4.00 10.00
Batting
133A Mike Trout 1.50 4.00
On base
133B Trout SP w/Glve 25.00 60.00
134A Prince Fielder .25 .60
Batting
134B Prince Fielder SP 4.00 10.00
Throwing
135 Starling Marte .25 .60
136A Wade Davis .20 .50
Blue jersey
136B Wade Davis SP 3.00 8.00
Gray jersey
137A Yasiel Puig .30 .75
White jersey
137B Puig SP Gray jsy 8.00 20.00
138 Adrian Gonzalez .25 .60
139 Alex Rodriguez .40 1.00
140 Andrew Miller .25 .60
141 Byung-Ho Park RC .40 1.00
142 Carlos Gomez .20 .50
143 Chris Davis .20 .50
144A Clayton Kershaw .50 1.25
Pitching
144B Kershaw SP Bttng 8.00 20.00
145 Corey Kluber .25 .60
146A Dallas Keuchel .25 .60
Orange jersey
146B Dallas Keuchel SP 4.00 10.00
Light jersey
147 David Ortiz .30 .75
148 Dee Gordon .20 .50
149 Dustin Pedroia .30 .75
150 Felix Hernandez .25 .60
151A Gerrit Cole .30 .75
Black jersey
151B Gerrit Cole SP 5.00 12.00
White jersey
152 Hanley Ramirez .25 .60
153 Jacob deGrom .60 1.50
154 Joey Votto .30 .75
155 Jose Altuve .25 .60
156 Masahiro Tanaka .25 .60

157A Miguel Cabrera Running .30 .75
157B Cabrera SP Fldng 12.00 30.00
158A Betts Batting .60 1.50
158B Betts SP Fldng 10.00 25.00
159A Noah Syndergaard Pitching .25 .60
159B Syndrgrd SP Bttng 8.00 20.00
160A Paul Goldschmidt Red jersey .30 .75
160B Paul Goldschmidt SP w/Glove 5.00 12.00
161 Ryan Braun .25 .60
162 Shelby Miller .25 .60
163 Stephen Piscotty RC .50 1.25
164A Troy Tulowitzki Running .30 .75
164B Troy Tulowitzki SP Fielding 5.00 12.00
165 Yoenis Cespedes .30 .75
166 Evan Longoria .25 .60
167 Francisco Liriano .20 .50
168 Gregory Polanco .25 .60
169 Jay Bruce .25 .60
170 Joey Gallo .25 .60
171 Taijuan Walker .20 .50
172 Travis d'Arnaud .25 .60
173 Kenley Jansen .25 .60
174 Matt Holliday .30 .75
175 Jose Peraza RC .40 1.00
176 Billy Hamilton .25 .60
177 Ian Kinsler .25 .60
178 James Shields .20 .50
179 Jonathan Lucroy .25 .60
180 Jose Quintana .20 .50
181 Josh Harrison .20 .50
182 Kyle Seager .20 .50
183 Yasmany Tomas .20 .50
184 Wil Myers .25 .60
185 Ian Kennedy .20 .50
186 Jhonny Peralta .20 .50
187 Josh Hamilton .25 .60
188 Scott Kazmir .20 .50
189 Trevor Rosenthal .25 .60
190 Devon Travis .20 .50
191 Joc Pederson .25 .60
192 Justin Turner .30 .75
193 Raisel Iglesias .25 .60
194 Roberto Osuna .20 .50
195 Taylor Jungmann .20 .50
196 Anibal Sanchez .20 .50
197 Arodys Vizcaino .20 .50
198 Blake Swihart .25 .60
199 Brandon Finnegan .20 .50
200 Brian McCann .25 .60
201 Carl Edwards Jr. .25 .60
202 CC Sabathia .25 .60
203 Chris Heston .20 .50
204 Cody Anderson .20 .50
205 R.A. Dickey .25 .60
206 Delino DeShields Jr. .20 .50
207 Eddie Rosario .25 .60
208 Enrique Hernandez .30 .75
209 Hunter Pence .25 .60
210 Jose Reyes .25 .60
211 Julio Teheran .25 .60
212 Ketel Marte RC .60 1.50
213 Koji Uehara .20 .50
214 Lance Lynn .20 .50
215 Matt Adams .20 .50
216 Nathan Eovaldi .25 .60
217 Pedro Alvarez .20 .50
218 Ryan Howard .25 .60
219 Shin-Soo Choo .25 .60
220 Trayce Thompson RC .50 1.25
221 Tyler Duffey RC .30 .75
222 Wilmer Flores .25 .60
223 Yordano Ventura .25 .60
224 Zach Lee .20 .50
225 Aaron Altherr .20 .50
226 Alcides Escobar .25 .60
227 Anthony DeSclafani .20 .50
228 Brad Ziegler .20 .50
229 Brandon Phillips .20 .50
230 Carlos Beltran .25 .60
231 Dellin Betances .25 .60
232 Didi Gregorius .25 .60
233 Francisco Cervelli .20 .50
234 Jerad Eickhoff RC .50 1.25
235 Joe Panik .25 .60
236 Kole Calhoun .20 .50
237 Kevin Gausman .30 .75
238 Mark Canha .20 .50
239 Mike Minor .20 .50
240 Nathan Karns .20 .50
241 Odubel Herrera .25 .60
242 Peter O'Brien RC .30 .75
243 Ryan Zimmerman .25 .60
244 Tom Murphy RC .30 .75
245 Andrew Heaney .20 .50
246 Bartolo Colon .20 .50
247 Chi Chi Gonzalez .20 .50
248 Christian Colon .20 .50
249 Collin McHugh .20 .50
250 Curtis Granderson .25 .60
251 David Robertson .20 .50
252 Derek Holland .20 .50
253 Domingo Santana .25 .60
254 Ian Desmond .20 .50
255 J.J. Hardy .20 .50
256 Jake Odorizzi .20 .50
257 Javier Baez .40 1.00
258 Justin Bour .25 .60
259 Ken Giles .20 .50
260 Kevin Kiermaier .25 .60
261 Logan Forsythe .20 .50
262 Mark Melancon .20 .50
263 Max Kepler RC .50 1.25
264 Pablo Sandoval .25 .60
265 Preston Tucker .20 .50
266 Rob Refsnyder RC .40 1.00
267 Steven Souza Jr. .25 .60
268 Tommy Pham .20 .50
269 Trevor Bauer .40 1.00
270 Aaron Sanchez .25 .60
271 Miguel Almonte RC .30 .75
272 DJ LeMahieu .30 .75
273 Elvis Andrus .25 .60
274 Homer Bailey .20 .50
275 J.T. Realmuto .30 .75
276 James McCann .25 .60
277 Justin Nicolino .20 .50
278 Kendrys Morales .20 .50
279 Kevin Pillar .20 .50
280 Nick Ahmed .20 .50
281 Patrick Corbin .25 .60
282 Robbie Ray .20 .50
283 Russell Martin .20 .50
284 Zach Britton .25 .60
285 Adam Eaton .20 .50
286 Kyle Waldrop RC .40 1.00
287 Brandon Drury RC .50 1.25
288 Brian Johnson RC .30 .75
289 Carson Smith .20 .50
290 Ender Inciarte .20 .50
291 Francisco Rodriguez .25 .60
292 Howie Kendrick .20 .50
293 Jean Segura .25 .60
294 Kevin Plawecki .20 .50
295 Lucas Duda .25 .60
296 Marco Estrada .20 .50
297 Dilson Herrera .25 .60
298 Zach Davies RC .40 1.00
299 Marcell Ozuna .30 .75
300 Nick Castellanos .30 .75
301 Johnny Bench SP 1.00 2.50
302 Bill Mazeroski SP .75 2.00
303 Al Kaline SP 1.00 2.50
304 Don Sutton SP .75 2.00
305 Ralph Kiner SP .75 2.00
306 Larry Doby SP .75 2.00
307 Willie McCovey SP .75 2.00
308 Eddie Mathews SP 1.00 2.50
309 Duke Snider SP .75 2.00
310 Whitey Ford SP .75 2.00
311 Brooks Robinson SP .75 2.00
312 Jim Palmer SP .75 2.00
313 Willie Stargell SP .75 2.00
314 Catfish Hunter SP .75 2.00
315 Joe Morgan SP .75 2.00
316 Bruce Sutter SP .75 2.00
317 George Brett SP 2.00 5.00
318 Phil Rizzuto SP .75 2.00
319 Sparky Anderson SP .75 2.00
320 Gary Carter SP .75 2.00
321 Tony Perez SP .75 2.00
322 Goose Gossage SP .75 2.00
323 Sandy Koufax SP 2.00 5.00
324 Satchel Paige SP 1.00 2.50
325 John Smoltz SP 1.00 2.50
326 Cal Ripken Jr. SP 3.00 8.00
327 Willie Mays SP 2.00 5.00
328 Rod Carew SP .75 2.00
329 Craig Biggio SP .75 2.00
330 Wade Boggs SP .75 2.00
331 Orlando Cepeda SP .75 2.00
332 Dennis Eckersley SP .75 2.00
333 Bo Jackson SP 1.00 2.50
334 Robin Yount SP 1.00 2.50
335 Luis Aparicio SP .75 2.00
336 Babe Ruth SP 2.50 6.00
337 Lou Brock SP .75 2.00
338 Bob Feller SP .75 2.00
339 Fergie Jenkins SP .75 2.00
340 Harmon Killebrew SP 1.00 2.50
341 Juan Marichal SP .75 2.00
342 Eddie Murray SP .75 2.00
343 Kenta Maeda SP RC 6.00 15.00
344 Ozzie Smith SP 1.25 3.00
345 Warren Spahn SP .75 2.00
346 Roberto Alomar SP .75 2.00
347 Torii Hunter SP .60 1.50
348 Roger Clemens SP 1.25 3.00
349 Hank Aaron SP 2.00 5.00
350 Tom Seaver SP .75 2.00

2016 Topps Gypsy Queen Framed Blue

*FRME BLUE: 1.5X TO 4X BASIC
*FRME BLUE RC: 1X TO 2.5X BASIC RC
RANDOM INSERTS IN RETAIL PACKS

2016 Topps Gypsy Queen Framed Green

*FRME GREEN: 3X TO 8X BASIC
*FRME GREEN RC: 2X TO 5X BASIC RC
STATED ODDS 1:73 HOBBY
STATED PRINT RUN 99 SER.#'d SETS
7 Corey Seager 12.00 30.00

2016 Topps Gypsy Queen Framed Purple

*FRME PURPLE: 2X TO 5X BASIC
*FRME PURPLE RC: 1.2X TO 3X BASIC RC
STATED ODDS 1:29 HOBBY
STATED PRINT RUN 250 SER.#'d SETS

2016 Topps Gypsy Queen Mini

*MINI 1-300: 1.2X TO 3X BASIC
*MINI 1-300 RC: .75X TO 2X BASIC
*MINI 301-350: .5X TO 1.2X BASIC
MINI SP ODDS 1:24 HOBBY
PRINTING PLATE ODDS 1:512 HOBBY
PLATE PRINT RUN 1 SET PER COLOR
NO PLATE PRICING DUE TO SCARCITY
343 Kenta Maeda SP 1.50 4.00

2016 Topps Gypsy Queen Mini Foil

*FOIL: .6X TO 1.5X BASIC
RANDOM INSERTS IN PACKS
343 Kenta Maeda 5.00 12.00

2016 Topps Gypsy Queen Mini Gold

*GOLD 1-300: 5X TO 12X BASIC
*GOLD 1-300 RC: 3X TO 8X BASIC
*GOLD 301-350: 1.5X TO 4X BASIC
STATED ODDS 1:41 HOBBY
STATED PRINT RUN 50 SER.#'d SETS
7 Corey Seager 15.00 40.00
90 Carlos Correa 15.00 40.00

2016 Topps Gypsy Queen Mini Green

*GREEN 1-300: 3X TO 8X BASIC
*GREEN 1-300 RC: 2X TO 5X BASIC
*GREEN 301-350: 1X TO 2.5X BASIC
RANDOM INSERTS IN PACKS
STATED PRINT RUN 99 SER.#'d SETS
343 Kenta Maeda 3.00 8.00

2016 Topps Gypsy Queen Mini Purple

*PURPLE 1-300: 2X TO 5X BASIC
*PURPLE 1-300 RC: 1.2X TO 3X BASIC
*PURPLE 301-350: .6X TO 1.5X BASIC
STATED ODDS 1:9 HOBBY
STATED PRINT RUN 250 SER.#'d SETS

2016 Topps Gypsy Queen Mini Variations

*MINI BOX VAR: 1.2X TO 3X BASIC
*MINI BOX VAR RC: .75X TO 2X BASIC RC
ONE MINI BOX PER HOBBY BOX
TEN CARDS PER MINI BOX
343 Kenta Maeda 1.25 3.00

2016 Topps Gypsy Queen Autographs

STATED ODDS 1:17 HOBBY
GQAAE Alcides Escobar 5.00 12.00
GQAAJ Andruw Jones 6.00 15.00
GQAAM Andrew Miller 6.00 15.00
GQAAN Aaron Nola 5.00 12.00
GQAAP A.J. Pollock 2.50 6.00
GQABJ Brian Johnson 2.50 6.00
GQACD Corey Dickerson 2.50 6.00
GQACDE Carlos Delgado 4.00 10.00
GQACE Carl Edwards Jr. 3.00 8.00
GQACK Corey Kluber 4.00 10.00
GQACS Corey Seager 30.00 80.00
GQADG Dee Gordon 10.00 25.00
GQADL DJ LeMahieu 15.00 40.00
GQAER Eduardo Rodriguez 4.00 10.00
GQAGB Greg Bird 3.00 8.00
GQAGH Greg Holland 6.00 15.00
GQAGS George Springer 6.00 15.00
GQAHO Henry Owens 3.00 8.00
GQAHOL Hector Olivera 6.00 15.00
GQAJFA Jeurys Familia 4.00 10.00
GQAJGR Jon Gray 2.50 6.00
GQAJP Jimmy Paredes 2.50 6.00
GQAKM Ketel Marte 5.00 12.00
GQAKMA Kenta Maeda 75.00 200.00
GQAKS Kyle Schwarber 15.00 40.00
GQALS Luis Severino 10.00 25.00
GQAMA Miguel Almonte 2.50 6.00
GQAMF Maikel Franco 3.00 8.00
GQAMK Max Kepler 6.00 15.00
GQAMSA Miguel Sano 6.00 15.00
GQAPO Peter O'Brien 2.50 6.00
GQARO Roberto Osuna 2.50 6.00
GQARR Rob Refsnyder 3.00 8.00
GQASM Steve Matz
GQASP Stephen Piscotty 4.00 10.00
GQATT Trea Turner 8.00 20.00
GQAVC Vinny Castilla 2.50 6.00
GQAWD Wade Davis 2.50 6.00
GQAYG Yasmani Grandal 5.00 12.00
GQAZL Zach Lee 2.50 6.00

2016 Topps Gypsy Queen Autographs Gold

*GOLD: .6X TO 1.5X BASIC
STATED ODDS 1:183 HOBBY
STATED PRINT RUN 50 SER.#'d SETS
GQABBU Byron Buxton 20.00 50.00
GQAJS Jorge Soler 10.00 25.00
GQAMC Michael Conforto 40.00 100.00
GQANS Noah Syndergaard 30.00 80.00
GQASG Sonny Gray 8.00 20.00

2016 Topps Gypsy Queen Autographs Green

*GREEN: .5X TO 1.2X BASIC
STATED ODDS 1:101 HOBBY
STATED PRINT RUN 99 SER.#'d SETS
GQAJPE Joc Pederson 4.00 10.00
GQAJS Jorge Soler 8.00 20.00
GQAMC Michael Conforto 30.00 80.00
GQANS Noah Syndergaard 25.00 60.00
GQASG Sonny Gray 6.00 15.00
GQASM Steven Matz 3.00 8.00

2016 Topps Gypsy Queen Glove Stories

COMPLETE SET (10) 3.00 8.00
STATED ODDS 1:6 HOBBY
PRINTING PLATE ODDS 1:17,589 HOBBY
PLATE PRINT RUN 1 SET PER COLOR
NO PLATE PRICING DUE TO SCARCITY
GS1 Mike Trout 2.50 6.00
GS2 Nolan Arenado .75 2.00
GS3 Kevin Kiermaier .40 1.00
GS4 Juan Perez .30 .75
GS5 Kevin Pillar .30 .75
GS6 Billy Burns .30 .75
GS7 Mookie Betts 1.00 2.50
GS8 George Springer .40 1.00
GS9 Freddy Galvis .30 .75
GS10 Joey Votto .50 1.25

2016 Topps Gypsy Queen Mini Autographs

STATED ODDS 1:22 MINI BOX
STATED PRINT RUN 25 SER.#'d SETS
GMAAN Aaron Nola 20.00 50.00
GMABB Byron Buxton 30.00 80.00
GMABJ Brian Johnson 6.00 15.00
GMACK Corey Kluber 10.00 25.00
GMACS Corey Seager 100.00 200.00
GMADE Dennis Eckersley 20.00 50.00
GMAER Eduardo Rodriguez 6.00 15.00
GMAFF Freddie Freeman 30.00 80.00
GMAHO Henry Owens 12.00 30.00
GMAHOL Hector Olivera 15.00 40.00
GMAJD Jacob deGrom 40.00 100.00
GMAJG Jon Gray
GMAJP Joc Pederson 20.00 50.00
GMAJS Jorge Soler 15.00 40.00
GMAKB Kris Bryant 200.00 300.00
GMAKS Kyle Schwarber 50.00 120.00
GMALS Luis Severino 20.00 50.00
GMAMH Matt Harvey 30.00 80.00
GMAMM Manny Machado 125.00 250.00
GMAMS Miguel Sano 40.00 100.00
GMAMSC Max Scherzer 30.00 80.00
GMANS Noah Syndergaard 50.00 120.00
GMARR Rob Refsnyder 15.00 40.00
GMASM Steven Matz 30.00 80.00
GMASP Stephen Piscotty 25.00 60.00
GMATT Trea Turner 15.00 40.00

2016 Topps Gypsy Queen Mini Patch Autograph Booklets

STATED ODDS 1:27 MINI BOX
PRINT RUNS B/WN 20-30 COPIES PER
MAPAJ Andruw Jones/20 40.00 100.00
MAPBH Bryce Harper/20 250.00 400.00
MAPCK Corey Kluber/30 15.00 40.00
MAPCS Chris Sale/30 30.00 80.00
MAPDP Dustin Pedroia/20 60.00 150.00
MAPFF Freddie Freeman/30 60.00 150.00
MAPFT Frank Thomas/20 100.00 200.00
MAPJP Joc Pederson/20 30.00 80.00
MAPMF Maikel Franco/30 40.00 100.00
MAPMM Manny Machado/30 60.00 150.00
MAPMP Mike Piazza/30 75.00 200.00
MAPMT Mike Trout/20 250.00 400.00
MAPNS Noah Syndergaard/20 150.00 250.00
MAPRC Roger Clemens/20 60.00 150.00
MAPSM Starling Marte/30 40.00 100.00
MAPTW Taijuan Walker/30 25.00 60.00

2016 Topps Gypsy Queen Mini Relics

STATED ODDS 1:31 HOBBY
*GOLD/50: .6X TO 1.5X BASIC
GMRAP Albert Pujols 5.00 12.00
GMRAR Anthony Rizzo 5.00 12.00
GMRBP Buster Posey 5.00 12.00
GMRCB Craig Biggio 3.00 8.00
GMRCE Carl Edwards Jr. 3.00 8.00
GMRCJ Chipper Jones 5.00 12.00
GMRCK Corey Kluber 3.00 8.00
GMRCKE Clayton Kershaw 6.00 15.00
GMRCR Cal Ripken Jr. 10.00 25.00
GMRCSA Chris Sale 4.00 10.00
GMRCSE Corey Seager 8.00 20.00
GMRDO David Ortiz 4.00 10.00
GMREL Evan Longoria 3.00 8.00
GMRFM Frankie Montas 3.00 8.00
GMRFT Frank Thomas 5.00 12.00
GMRGC Gerrit Cole 4.00 10.00
GMRGS Gary Sanchez 8.00 20.00
GMRJBA Javier Baez 5.00 12.00
GMRJD Johnny Damon 3.00 8.00
GMRJDG Jacob deGrom 8.00 20.00
GMRJF Jose Fernandez 4.00 10.00
GMRJS John Smoltz 5.00 12.00
GMRJV Joey Votto 4.00 10.00
GMRKG Ken Griffey Jr. 10.00 25.00
GMRKM Ketel Marte 5.00 12.00
GMRMBE Mookie Betts 8.00 20.00
GMRMCA Miguel Cabrera 4.00 10.00
GMRMMA Manny Machado 5.00 12.00
GMRMMG Mark McGwire 10.00 25.00
GMRMP Mike Piazza 5.00 12.00
GMRMTA Masahiro Tanaka 3.00 8.00
GMRMTR Mike Trout 20.00 50.00
GMROS Ozzie Smith 5.00 12.00
GMRPG Paul Goldschmidt 4.00 10.00
GMRPO Peter O'Brien 2.50 6.00
GMRRCA Robinson Cano 3.00 8.00
GMRRCL Roger Clemens 5.00 12.00
GMRRH Rickey Henderson 4.00 10.00
GMRRJA Reggie Jackson 5.00 12.00
GMRRJO Randy Johnson 4.00 10.00
GMRSM Starling Marte 3.00 8.00
GMRSMI Shelby Miller 3.00 8.00
GMRWM Willie Mays 20.00 50.00
GMRXB Xander Bogaerts 4.00 10.00
GMRYM Yadier Molina 6.00 15.00

2016 Topps Gypsy Queen MVP Minis

COMPLETE SET (25) 8.00 20.00
STATED ODDS 1:8 HOBBY
PRINTING PLATE ODDS 1:7196 HOBBY
PLATE PRINT RUN 1 SET PER COLOR
NO PLATE PRICING DUE TO SCARCITY
MVPMBE Johnny Bench .60 1.50
MVPMBH Bryce Harper 1.00 2.50
MVPMBL Barry Larkin .50 1.25
MVPMBP Buster Posey .75 2.00
MVPMBR Babe Ruth 1.50 4.00
MVPMCJ Chipper Jones .60 1.50
MVPMCK Clayton Kershaw 1.00 2.50
MVPMCR Cal Ripken Jr. 2.00 5.00
MVPMCY Carl Yastrzemski 1.00 2.50
MVPMDE Dennis Eckersley .50 1.25
MVPMDP Dustin Pedroia .60 1.50
MVPMFR Frank Robinson .50 1.25
MVPMFT Frank Thomas .60 1.50
MVPMHA Hank Aaron 1.25 3.00
MVPMJB Jeff Bagwell .50 1.25
MVPMJR Jackie Robinson .60 1.50
MVPMLG Lou Gehrig 1.25 3.00
MVPMMT Mike Trout 3.00 8.00
MVPMRC Roger Clemens .75 2.00
MVPMRJ Reggie Jackson .50 1.25
MVPMSK Sandy Koufax 1.25 3.00
MVPMSM Stan Musial 1.00 2.50
MVPMTC Ty Cobb 1.00 2.50
MVPMTW Ted Williams 1.25 3.00
MVPMWM Willie Mays 1.25 3.00

2016 Topps Gypsy Queen MVP Minis Autographs

STATED ODDS 1:2111 HOBBY
PRINT RUNS B/WN 15-25 COPIES PER
MVPABL Barry Larkin/25 25.00 60.00
MVPABP Buster Posey/15
MVPACJ Chipper Jones/15 125.00 250.00
MVPACK Clayton Kershaw/25 150.00 250.00
MVPACR Cal Ripken Jr./15
MVPADE Dennis Eckersley/25 20.00 50.00
MVPAFR Frank Robinson/25 100.00 200.00
MVPAFT Frank Thomas/25 60.00 150.00
MVPAJB Jeff Bagwell/25 40.00 100.00
MVPAJBE Johnny Bench/15 60.00 150.00
MVPAJR Jim Rice/25 20.00 50.00
MVPAMT Mike Trout/15 300.00 500.00
MVPARB Ryan Braun/25 25.00 60.00
MVPARC Roger Clemens/15 30.00 80.00
MVPARJ Reggie Jackson/15
MVPASK Sandy Koufax/15
MVPAVG Vladimir Guerrero/25 15.00 40.00

2016 Topps Gypsy Queen Power Alley

COMPLETE SET (30) 6.00 15.00
STATED ODDS 1:4 HOBBY
PRINTING PLATE ODDS 1:5974 HOBBY
PLATE PRINT RUN 1 SET PER COLOR
NO PLATE PRICING DUE TO SCARCITY
PA1 Willie Mays 1.00 2.50
PA2 Ted Williams 1.00 2.50
PA3 Jose Canseco .40 1.00
PA4 Frank Thomas .50 1.25
PA5 Carlos Delgado .30 .75
PA6 Chipper Jones .50 1.25
PA7 Dave Winfield .40 1.00
PA8 Alex Rodriguez .60 1.50
PA9 Frank Robinson .40 1.00
PA10 Andre Dawson .40 1.00
PA11 Reggie Jackson .40 1.00
PA12 Willie Stargell .40 1.00
PA13 Stan Musial .75 2.00
PA14 Eddie Mathews .50 1.25
PA15 Fred McGriff .40 1.00
PA16 Lou Gehrig 1.00 2.50
PA17 Babe Ruth 1.25 3.00
PA18 Ken Griffey Jr. 1.00 2.50
PA19 David Ortiz .50 1.25
PA20 Vladimir Guerrero .40 1.00
PA21 Mark McGwire .75 2.00
PA22 Harmon Killebrew .50 1.25
PA23 Willie McCovey .40 1.00
PA24 Rafael Palmeiro .40 1.00
PA25 Eddie Murray .40 1.00
PA26 Albert Pujols .60 1.50
PA27 Hank Aaron 1.00 2.50
PA28 Jeff Bagwell .40 1.00
PA29 Carl Yastrzemski .75 2.00
PA30 Andres Galarraga .40 1.00

2016 Topps Gypsy Queen Relic Autographs

STATED ODDS 1:266 HOBBY
STATED PRINT RUN 50 SER.#'d SETS
GQARBB Brandon Belt 20.00 50.00
GQARBM Brandon Moss 15.00 40.00
GQARBS Blake Swihart 10.00 25.00
GQARCB Craig Biggio 15.00 40.00
GQARCS Chris Sale 12.00 30.00
GQARDG Dee Gordon 8.00 20.00
GQARFL Francisco Lindor 20.00 50.00
GQARGH Greg Holland 8.00 20.00
GQARJA Jose Altuve 25.00 60.00
GQARJC Jose Canseco 20.00 50.00
GQARJH Josh Harrison 8.00 20.00
GQARJPE Joc Pederson 10.00 25.00
GQARJS Jorge Soler 12.00 30.00
GQARKB Kris Bryant 125.00 250.00
GQARKW Kolten Wong 10.00 25.00
GQARMC Matt Carpenter 10.00 25.00
GQARMF Maikel Franco 15.00 40.00
GQARMH Matt Harvey 30.00 80.00
GQARNS Noah Syndergaard 30.00 80.00
GQARRO Roberto Osuna 8.00 20.00
GQARSM Starling Marte 20.00 50.00
GQARTW Taijuan Walker 12.00 30.00
GQARYG Yasmani Grandal 8.00 20.00
GQARZW Zack Wheeler 10.00 25.00

2016 Topps Gypsy Queen Relics

STATED ODDS 1:25 HOBBY
GQRAP Albert Pujols 4.00 10.00
GQRBP Buster Posey 4.00 10.00
GQRCB Craig Biggio 2.50 6.00
GQRCJ Chipper Jones 3.00 8.00
GQRCK Clayton Kershaw 5.00 12.00
GQRCR Cal Ripken Jr. 5.00 12.00
GQRDO David Ortiz 3.00 8.00
GQRDW David Wright 2.50 6.00
GQREL Evan Longoria 2.50 6.00
GQRFT Frank Thomas 3.00 8.00
GQRGC Gerrit Cole 3.00 8.00
GQRGS Gary Sanchez 6.00 15.00
GQRJD Jacob deGrom 6.00 15.00
GQRJG Joey Gallo 2.50 6.00
GQRJK Jason Kipnis 2.50 6.00
GQRJM J.D. Martinez 3.00 8.00
GQRKG Ken Griffey Jr. 5.00 12.00
GQRKM Ketel Marte 4.00 10.00
GQRMH Matt Harvey 2.50 6.00
GQRMP Michael Pineda 2.00 5.00
GQROS Ozzie Smith 4.00 10.00
GQRPG Paul Goldschmidt 3.00 8.00
GQRPO Peter O'Brien 2.00 5.00
GQRRH Rickey Henderson 4.00 10.00
GQRRJ Reggie Jackson 3.00 8.00
GQRSM Steven Matz 2.00 5.00
GQRTH Torii Hunter 2.00 5.00
GQRTW Taijuan Walker 2.00 5.00
GQRXB Xander Bogaerts 3.00 8.00
GQRYP Yasiel Puig 3.00 8.00
GQRARE Anthony Rendon 3.00 8.00
GQRARI Anthony Rizzo 4.00 10.00
GQRCSA Chris Sale 3.00 8.00
GQRCSE Corey Seager 5.00 12.00
GQRJFE Jose Fernandez 3.00 8.00
GQRJHK Jung Ho Kang 2.00 5.00
GQRJSM John Smoltz 3.00 8.00
GQRJSO Jorge Soler 3.00 8.00
GQRMBE Mookie Betts 6.00 15.00
GQRMCA Miguel Cabrera 3.00 8.00
GQRMCR Matt Carpenter 3.00 8.00
GQRMMA Manny Machado 3.00 8.00
GQRMMC Mark McGwire 5.00 12.00
GQRMMO Mike Moustakas 2.50 6.00
GQRMPI Mike Piazza 3.00 8.00
GQRMTA Masahiro Tanaka 2.50 6.00
GQRMTR Mike Trout 8.00 20.00
GQRRCA Robinson Cano 2.50 6.00
GQRRCL Roger Clemens 4.00 10.00
GQRRCS Rusney Castillo 2.00 5.00
GQRRJO Randy Johnson 3.00 8.00

2016 Topps Gypsy Queen Relics Gold

*GOLD: .6X TO 1.5X BASIC
STATED ODDS 1:221 HOBBY
STATED PRINT RUN 50 SER.#'d SETS
GQRCR Cal Ripken Jr. 20.00 50.00
GQRFT Frank Thomas 12.00 30.00
GQRKG Ken Griffey Jr. 20.00 50.00
GQROS Ozzie Smith 12.00 30.00
GQRCSE Corey Seager 12.00 30.00
GQRMCA Miguel Cabrera 10.00 25.00
GQRMMC Mark McGwire 12.00 30.00
GQRMTR Mike Trout 20.00 50.00

2016 Topps Gypsy Queen Walk Off Winners

COMPLETE SET (10) 3.00 8.00
STATED ODDS 1:6 HOBBY
PRINTING PLATE ODDS 1:17,589 HOBBY
PLATE PRINT RUN 1 SET PER COLOR
NO PLATE PRICING DUE TO SCARCITY
GWO1 Eric Hosmer .40 1.00
GWO2 Manny Machado .50 1.25
GWO3 Andruw Jones .30 .75
GWO4 Jackie Robinson .50 1.25
GWO5 Josh Donaldson .40 1.00
GWO6 Starling Marte .40 1.00
GWO7 Wilmer Flores .40 1.00
GWO8 Omar Vizquel .40 1.00
GWO9 Mike Trout 2.50 6.00
GWO10 Kris Bryant .60 1.50

2017 Topps Gypsy Queen

COMP.SET w/SP (320) 75.00 200.00
COMP.SET w/o SP's (300) 20.00 50.00
SP ODDS 1:24 HOBBY
CAPLESS ODDS 1:158 HOBBY
THRWBCK ODDS 1:420 HOBBY
GUM BACK ODDS 1:629 HOBBY
1A Kris Bryant .40 1.00
1B Bryant SP No Cap 6.00 15.00
1C Kris Bryant SP TB 8.00 20.00
1D Kris Bryant SP VAR Gum back
2 Edwin Diaz .25 .60
3 Marcus Semien .30 .75
4 Jorge Alfaro RC .40 1.00
5 Adrian Gonzalez .25 .60
6 Bartolo Colon .20 .50
7 Stephen Strasburg .30 .75
8 Carlos Martinez .25 .60
9 Matt Harvey .25 .60
10A Miguel Cabrera .30 .75
10B Cabrera SP No Cap 5.00 12.00
10C Miguel Cabrera SP GB 5.00 12.00
11 Jordan Zimmermann .25 .60
12 Greg Bird .25 .60
13 Taijuan Walker .20 .50
14 Matt Olson RC 1.50 4.00
15 Danny Valencia .25 .60
16 Trea Turner .25 .60
17 Dexter Fowler .25 .60
18 Kendall Graveman .20 .50
19A David Dahl RC .40 1.00
19B Dahl SP No Cap 4.00 10.00
20 Zack Greinke .30 .75
21 Braden Shipley RC .30 .75
22 Yulieski Gurriel RC .50 1.25
23 Blake Snell .25 .60
24 Adam Ottavino .20 .50
25 Michael Fulmer .20 .50
26 Alex Gordon .25 .60
27 Roberto Osuna .20 .50
28 Odubel Herrera .25 .60
29 JaCoby Jones RC .40 1.00
30 Jonathan Schoop .20 .50
31 Brandon Phillips .20 .50
32 Johnny Cueto .25 .60
33 Tom Murphy .20 .50
34 Rick Porcello .25 .60
35 Jim Johnson .20 .50
36 Hisashi Iwakuma .25 .60
37 Alex Reyes RC .40 1.00
38 David Robertson .20 .50
39 Jacoby Ellsbury .25 .60
40 Nomar Mazara .20 .50
41 A.J. Ramos .20 .50
42 J.D. Martinez .30 .75
43 Manny Margot RC .30 .75
44 Kirk Nieuwenhuis .20 .50
45 Chris Carter .20 .50
46 Brandon Belt .25 .60
47 Yangervis Solarte .20 .50
48 Hunter Renfroe RC .40 1.00
49 Kevin Gausman .30 .75
50A Anthony Rizzo .40 1.00
50B Rizzo SP No Cap 6.00 15.00
51 Kevin Kiermaier .25 .60
52 Jose Bautista .25 .60
53 Jace Peterson .20 .50
54 Starlin Castro .20 .50
55 Corey Dickerson .20 .50
56 Yasmani Grandal .20 .50
57 Jean Segura .25 .60
58 Jung Ho Kang .20 .50
59 Kenley Jansen .25 .60
60 Jameson Taillon .25 .60
61 Kyle Hendricks .30 .75
62 Mark Trumbo .20 .50
63 Madison Bumgarner .25 .60
64 Khris Davis .30 .75
65 Matt Strahm RC .30 .75
66 Justin Upton .25 .60
67 Trevor Story .30 .75
68 Alcides Escobar .25 .60
69 Randal Grichuk .20 .50
70 Leonys Martin .20 .50
71 Huston Street .20 .50
72 Cameron Rupp .20 .50
73 Brett Gardner .25 .60
74A Carlos Correa .30 .75
74B Correa SP No Cap 5.00 12.00
74C Carlos Correa SP GB 5.00 12.00
75A Clayton Kershaw .50 1.25
75B Kershaw SP No Cap 8.00 20.00
75C Clayton Kershaw SP GB 8.00 20.00
76 Scott Kazmir .20 .50
77 Gary Sanchez .30 .75
78 Robert Gsellman RC .30 .75
79 Nelson Cruz .30 .75
80 Scooter Gennett .25 .60
81 Starling Marte .25 .60
82 Brad Ziegler .20 .50
83 Tyler Austin RC .40 1.00
84 Ender Inciarte .20 .50
85 Raimel Tapia RC .40 1.00
86 Chris Archer .20 .50
87 Jake Lamb .25 .60
88 Ian Kennedy .20 .50
89 Yu Darvish .30 .75
90 Justin Turner .30 .75
91A Dansby Swanson RC .75 2.00
91B Swanson SP No Cap 10.00 25.00
92 Vince Velasquez .20 .50
93 Ichiro .40 1.00
94 Ryan Schimpf .20 .50
95 Carlos Rodon .30 .75
96 Daniel Murphy .25 .60
97 Gavin Cecchini RC .30 .75
98 Adam Wainwright .25 .60
99 Brandon Crawford .25 .60
100A Mookie Betts .60 1.50
100B Betts SP No Cap 10.00 25.00
100C Mookie Betts SP TB 12.00 30.00
101 Seth Lugo RC .30 .75
102 Albert Pujols .40 1.00
103 Mitch Moreland .20 .50
104 Jeanmar Gomez .20 .50
105A Andrew McCutchen .30 .75
105B McCutchen SP TB 6.00 15.00
106 Hunter Dozier RC .30 .75
107 Tim Anderson .30 .75
108 Giancarlo Stanton .30 .75
109 Dan Straily .20 .50
110 David Paulino RC .40 1.00
111 Freddie Freeman .40 1.00
112 Paul Goldschmidt .30 .75
113 Edwin Encarnacion .30 .75
114 Carlos Carrasco .20 .50
115 Byron Buxton .30 .75
116 Robbie Ray .20 .50
117 Jonathan Villar .20 .50
118 Wade Davis .20 .50
119 Kendrys Morales .20 .50
120 Jered Weaver .25 .60
121A Jacob deGrom .60 1.50
121B deGrom SP No Cap 8.00 20.00
121C Jacob deGrom SP TB 12.00 30.00
122 Dee Gordon .20 .50
123 Jerad Eickhoff .20 .50
124 Buster Posey .40 1.00
125 Francisco Cervelli .20 .50
126 Justin Verlander .30 .75
127 Yoenis Cespedes .30 .75
128 Reynaldo Lopez RC .30 .75
129 Mike Napoli .20 .50
130 Chris Tillman .20 .50
131 Mark Melancon .20 .50
132 Teoscar Hernandez RC 1.25 3.00
133 Seung-hwan Oh .40 1.00
134 Chad Pinder RC .30 .75
135 Jeurys Familia .25 .60
136 Kyle Seager .20 .50
137 David Price .25 .60
138 Matt Moore .25 .60
139 Curtis Granderson .25 .60
140 Craig Kimbrel .25 .60
141 Adonis Garcia .20 .50
142 Todd Frazier .20 .50
143 Jimmy Nelson .20 .50
144A Francisco Lindor .30 .75
144B Lindor SP No Cap 5.00 12.00
144C Francisco Lindor SP TB 6.00 15.00
144D Francisco Lindor SP GB 5.00 12.00
145 Zack Cozart .20 .50
146 Ricky Nolasco .20 .50
147 Jose Berrios .25 .60
148 Aledmys Diaz .25 .60
149 Matt Holliday .30 .75
150A Corey Seager .30 .75
150B Seager SP No Cap 5.00 12.00
150C Corey Seager SP GB 12.00 30.00
151 Danny Duffy .20 .50
152 Wilson Ramos .20 .50
153 Logan Forsythe .20 .50
154A Manny Machado .30 .75
154B Manny Machado SP Thowback
155 Max Kepler .25 .60
156 Marcus Stroman .25 .60
157 Jason Kipnis .25 .60
158 Hanley Ramirez .25 .60
159 Matt Kemp .25 .60
160 Josh Donaldson .25 .60
161A Wil Myers .25 .60
161B Wil Myers SP TB 5.00 12.00
162 A.J. Pollock .20 .50
163 Renato Nunez RC .60 1.50
164 Ryon Healy RC .40 1.00
165 J.A. Happ .25 .60
166 Joe Mauer .25 .60
167 Jackie Bradley Jr. .30 .75
168A Aaron Judge RC 4.00 10.00
168B Judge SP No Cap 30.00 80.00
169 Stephen Vogt .25 .60
170 Stephen Piscotty .25 .60
171A Bryce Harper .50 1.25
171B Harper SP No Cap 8.00 20.00
171C Bryce Harper SP TB 10.00 25.00
171D Bryce Harper SP GB 15.00 40.00
172 Jon Gray .20 .50
173 Zach Britton .25 .60
174 Evan Longoria .25 .60
175 Gregory Polanco .25 .60
176 Carson Fulmer RC .30 .75
177A Xander Bogaerts .30 .75
177B Bogaerts SP No Cap 8.00 20.00
177C Xander Bogaerts SP TB 6.00 15.00
178 Dallas Keuchel .25 .60
179 Martin Prado .20 .50
180 Tanner Roark .20 .50
181 Sean Manaea .20 .50
182 Sam Dyson .20 .50
183 George Springer .25 .60
184 Austin Hedges .20 .50
185 Francisco Rodriguez .25 .60
186 Matt Wieters .30 .75
187 Kenta Maeda .25 .60
188 Anthony DeSclafani .20 .50
189 Felix Hernandez .25 .60
190 Miguel Sano .25 .60
191 Marcell Ozuna .30 .75
192 Christian Yelich .40 1.00
193 Joe Musgrove RC 1.00 2.50
194A Joey Votto .30 .75

194B Joey Votto SP TB 6.00 15.00
195 Sonny Gray .25 .60
196 Russell Martin .20 .50
197 Luis Perdomo .20 .50
198A Noah Syndergaard .25 .60
198B Syndergaard SP No Cap 4.00 10.00
198C Syndergaard SP TB 5.00 12.00
199 Jose Quintana .20 .50
200A Mike Trout 1.50 4.00
200B Trout SP No Cap 25.00 60.00
200C Mike Trout SP TB 30.00 80.00
200D Mike Trout SP GB 25.00 60.00
201 Ben Zobrist .25 .60
202 Welington Castillo .20 .50
203 Jharel Cotton RC .30 .75
204 Carlos Gonzalez .25 .60
205 Alex Dickerson .20 .50
206 Dustin Pedroia .30 .75
207 Jeremy Hellickson .20 .50
208 Billy Hamilton .25 .60
209 Hunter Pence .25 .60
210 Adam Jones .25 .60
211 Travis Jankowski .20 .50
212 Masahiro Tanaka .25 .60
213 Elvis Andrus .25 .60
214 Corey Kluber .25 .60
215 Bruce Maxwell RC .30 .75
216 Aaron Sanchez .25 .60
217 Josh Harrison .20 .50
218 Ken Giles .20 .50
219A Lorenzo Cain .20 .50
219B Lorenzo Cain SP TB 4.00 10.00
220 Maikel Franco .25 .60
221 Rob Segedin RC .30 .75
222 Evan Gattis .20 .50
223 Troy Tulowitzki .30 .75
224 Matt Carpenter .30 .75
225 Jose De Leon RC .30 .75
226 Eric Hosmer .25 .60
227 Jeff Samardzija .20 .50
228 Andrew Miller .25 .60
229 Julio Teheran .25 .60
230 Aroldis Chapman .30 .75
231 Yadier Molina .40 1.00
232 Justin Bour .25 .60
233 Adam Duvall .25 .60
234 Andrelton Simmons .20 .50
235A Jake Arrieta .25 .60
235B Jake Arrieta SP GB 4.00 10.00
236 Nick Markakis .25 .60
237 Jon Lester .25 .60
238 Tyler Naquin .30 .75
239 Asdrubal Cabrera .25 .60
240A Alex Bregman RC 1.50 4.00
240B Alex Bregman SP GB 15.00 40.00
241 Josh Bell RC .75 2.00
242 Chris Davis .20 .50
243A Chris Sale .30 .75
243B Sale SP No Cap 5.00 12.00
244 Ian Desmond .20 .50
245 DJ LeMahieu .30 .75
246 Kole Calhoun .20 .50
247 Charlie Blackmon .30 .75
248 Gerrit Cole .30 .75
249 Luke Weaver RC .40 1.00
250A Yoan Moncada RC 1.00 2.50
250B Moncada SP No Cap 10.00 25.00
251 Pat Neshek .20 .50
252A Nolan Arenado .50 1.25
252B Arenado SP No Cap 8.00 20.00
253 C.J. Cron .20 .50
254 Danny Salazar .25 .60
255 Matt Wisler .20 .50
256 Cole Hamels .25 .60
257 Addison Russell .30 .75
258 Ervin Santana .20 .50
259 Rougned Odor .25 .60
260 Trey Mancini RC .60 1.50
261 Jose Iglesias .25 .60
262 Robinson Cano .25 .60
263 Colin Rea .20 .50
264A Adrian Beltre .30 .75
264B Adrian Beltre SP TB 6.00 15.00
265 Eugenio Suarez .25 .60
266 Yunel Escobar .20 .50
267 Zach Davies .20 .50
268 Joe Panik .25 .60
269 Brian Dozier .30 .75
270 Tyler Thornburg .20 .50
271 Colby Rasmus .25 .60
272 Robbie Grossman .20 .50
273 Ian Kinsler .25 .60
274 Jake Odorizzi .20 .50
275 Dellin Betances .25 .60
276 Tyler Glasnow RC 1.25 3.00
277 Salvador Perez .25 .60
278 Alex Colome .20 .50
279 Ryan Braun .25 .60
280 Joc Pederson .25 .60
281 Steven Matz .20 .50
282 Andrew Benintendi RC 1.00 2.50
283 Lance McCullers .20 .50
284 Tommy Joseph .30 .75
285 Kirby Yates .25 .60
286 Roman Quinn RC .30 .75
287 Tony Watson .20 .50
288 Jeff Hoffman RC .30 .75
289A Max Scherzer .30 .75
289B Scherzer SP No Cap 5.00 12.00
290 Yonder Alonso .20 .50
291 Didi Gregorius .25 .60
292 Ryan Zimmerman .25 .60
293 Carlos Santana .25 .60
294 Melky Cabrera .20 .50
295 Yasmany Tomas .20 .50
296 Jose Abreu .30 .75
297 Adam Lind .25 .60
298 Jose Altuve .25 .60
299A Orlando Arcia RC .50 1.25
299B Orlando Arcia SP TB 6.00 15.00
300 David Ortiz .30 .75
301 Babe Ruth SP 4.00 10.00
302 Ryne Sandberg SP 3.00 8.00
303 Derek Jeter SP 4.00 10.00
304 Mike Piazza SP 1.50 4.00
305 Whitey Ford SP 1.25 3.00
306 Ken Griffey Jr. SP 3.00 8.00
307 Randy Johnson SP 1.50 4.00
308 Jackie Robinson SP 1.50 4.00
309 Andy Pettitte SP 1.25 3.00
310 Lou Gehrig SP 3.00 8.00
311 Ozzie Smith SP 2.00 5.00
312 Mark McGwire SP 2.50 6.00
313 Ty Cobb SP 2.50 6.00
314 Hank Aaron SP 3.00 8.00
315 Rod Carew SP 1.25 3.00
316 Ivan Rodriguez SP 1.25 3.00
317 Jim Palmer SP 1.25 3.00
318 George Brett SP 3.00 8.00
319 Phil Rizzuto SP 1.25 3.00
320 Sandy Koufax SP 3.00 8.00

2017 Topps Gypsy Queen Black and White

*BLACK WHITE: 5X TO 12X BASIC
*BLACK WHITE RC: 3X TO 8X BASIC RC
STATED ODDS 1:31 HOBBY
STATED PRINT RUN 50 SER.#'d SETS
1A Kris Bryant 20.00 50.00
200 Mike Trout 20.00 50.00

2017 Topps Gypsy Queen Green

*GREEN: 1.5X TO 4X BASIC
*GREEN RC: 1X TO 2.5X BASIC RC
*GREEN SP: .75X TO 2X BASIC SP
*GREEN CL: .5X TO 1.2X BASE CL
*GREEN TB: .3X TO .8X BASE TB
INSERTED IN RETAIL PACKS
SP/CL/TB ALL SERIAL #'d/99

2017 Topps Gypsy Queen Green Back

*GREEN BCK: 5X TO 12X BASIC
*GREEN BCK RC: 3X TO 8X BASIC RC
*GREEN BCK SP: X TO X BASIC SP
STATED ODDS 1:63 HOBBY
SP ODDS 1:943 HOBBY
ANNCD PRINT RUN 50 COPIES PER

2017 Topps Gypsy Queen Missing Blackplate

*NO BLACK: 2X TO 5X BASIC
*NO BLACK RC: 1.2X TO 3X BASIC RC
*NO BLACK SP: X TO X BASIC SP
*NO BLACK CL: X TO X BASE CL
*NO BLACK TB: X TO X BASE TB
*NO BLACK GB: X TO X BASE GB
STATED ODDS 1:9 HOBBY
SP ODDS 1:135 HOBBY
CAPLESS ODDS 1:315 HOBBY
THROWBACK ODDS 1:629 HOBBY
GUM BACK ODDS 1:943 HOBBY
282 Andrew Benintendi 10.00 25.00

2017 Topps Gypsy Queen Missing Nameplate

*NO NAME: 3X TO 8X BASIC
*NO NAME RC: 2X TO 5X BASIC RC
*NO NAME SP: X TO X BASIC SP
STATED ODDS 1:21 HOBBY
SP ODDS 1:315 HOBBY
282 Andrew Benintendi 15.00 40.00

2017 Topps Gypsy Queen Purple

*PURPLE: 2.5X TO 6X BASIC
*PURPLE RC: 1.5X TO 4X BASIC RC
STATED ODDS 1:13 HOBBY
STATED PRINT RUN 250 SER.#'d SETS
282 Andrew Benintendi 12.00 30.00

2017 Topps Gypsy Queen Autograph Garments

STATED ODDS 1:486 HOBBY
STATED PRINT RUN 50 SER.#'d SETS
EXCHANGE DEADLINE 2/28/2019
AGAR Anthony Rizzo 50.00 120.00
AGBH Bryce Harper 100.00 250.00
AGCC Carlos Correa 40.00 100.00
AGCS Chris Sale 10.00 25.00
AGDE Dennis Eckersley 12.00 30.00
AGDG Didi Gregorius 20.00 50.00
AGFL Francisco Lindor 60.00 150.00
AGHO Henry Owens 8.00 20.00
AGJA Jose Altuve 25.00 60.00
AGJC Jose Canseco 25.00 60.00
AGJD Jacob deGrom 30.00 80.00
AGJG Juan Gonzalez 15.00 40.00
AGJM J.D. Martinez 12.00 30.00
AGJP Joe Panik 10.00 25.00
AGJS John Smoltz 25.00 60.00
AGKB Kris Bryant 60.00 150.00
AGKK Kevin Kiermaier 10.00 25.00
AGMS Miguel Sano 12.00 30.00
AGNS Noah Syndergaard 30.00 80.00
AGSMA Steven Matz 15.00 40.00
AGWC Willson Contreras 40.00 100.00

2017 Topps Gypsy Queen Autograph Patch Booklet

STATED ODDS 1:1686 HOBBY
STATED PRINT RUN 20 SER.#'d SETS
EXCHANGE DEADLINE 2/28/2019
APBAR Anthony Rizzo 200.00 400.00
APBCC Carlos Correa 150.00 300.00
APBDG Didi Gregorius 60.00 150.00
APBFL Francisco Lindor 200.00 400.00
APBIR Ivan Rodriguez 60.00 150.00
APBJD Jacob deGrom 150.00 400.00
APBJM J.D. Martinez
APBJP Joe Panik 150.00 250.00
APBJS John Smoltz 75.00 200.00
APBKB Kris Bryant
APBKK Kevin Kiermaier 60.00 150.00
APBMS Miguel Sano 60.00 150.00
APBMST Marcus Stroman 75.00 200.00
APBNS Noah Syndergaard
APBSMA Steven Matz 60.00 150.00

2017 Topps Gypsy Queen Autographs

STATED ODDS 1:19 HOBBY
EXCHANGE DEADLINE 2/28/2019
*PURPLE/150: .5X TO 1.2X BASIC
*BW/99: .6X TO 1.5X BASIC
*NO BLACK: .6X TO 1.5X BASIC
*NO NAME: .75X TO 2X BASIC
GQAAB Alex Bregman 15.00 40.00
GQAABE Andrew Benintendi 25.00 60.00
GQAAC Adam Conley 2.50 6.00
GQAAJ Aaron Judge 100.00 250.00
GQAAR Alex Reyes 3.00 8.00
GQABB Barry Bonds
GQABH Bryce Harper 100.00 250.00
GQABS Blake Snell 6.00 15.00
GQABSH Braden Shipley 2.50 6.00
GQACC Carlos Correa 30.00 80.00
GQACJ Chipper Jones 60.00 150.00
GQACP Chad Pinder 2.50 6.00
GQACR Cal Ripken Jr. 60.00 150.00
GQACRE Cody Reed 2.50 6.00
GQACRO Carlos Rodon 4.00 10.00
GQACSE Corey Seager 25.00 60.00
GQADD David Dahl 5.00 12.00
GQADDU Danny Duffy 4.00 10.00
GQADF Dexter Fowler 8.00 20.00
GQADJ Derek Jeter
GQADS Dansby Swanson 12.00 30.00
GQAFL Francisco Lindor 15.00 40.00
GQAHO Henry Owens 2.50 6.00
GQAIR Ivan Rodriguez 15.00 40.00
GQAJDL Jose De Leon 4.00 10.00
GQAJMU Joe Musgrove 8.00 20.00
GQAJPE Jose Peraza 3.00 8.00
GQAJU Julio Urias 6.00 15.00
GQAKB Kris Bryant 50.00 120.00
GQAKG Ken Giles 2.50 6.00
GQALS Luis Severino 5.00 12.00
GQALV Logan Verrett 2.50 6.00
GQALW Luke Weaver 3.00 8.00
GQAMF Michael Fulmer 8.00 20.00
GQAMP Mike Piazza 40.00 100.00
GQAMST Matt Strahm 4.00 10.00
GQAMT Mike Trout 200.00 400.00
GQAMTA Masahiro Tanaka EXCH 125.00 250.00
GQANE Nathan Eovaldi 3.00 8.00
GQANM Nomar Mazara 8.00 20.00
GQANS Noah Syndergaard 10.00 25.00
GQAOV Omar Vizquel 5.00 12.00
GQAPV Pat Venditte 2.50 6.00
GQARG Robert Gsellman 2.50 6.00
GQARH Ryon Healy 3.00 8.00
GQART Raimel Tapia 3.00 8.00
GQASP Stephen Piscotty 5.00 12.00
GQASW Steven Wright 4.00 10.00
GQATA Tyler Austin 6.00 15.00
GQATGL Tyler Glasnow 5.00 12.00
GQATS Trevor Story 4.00 10.00
GQAYG Yulieski Gurriel 4.00 10.00
GQAYM Yoan Moncada 75.00 200.00

2017 Topps Gypsy Queen Chewing Gum Mini Autographs

STATED ODDS 1:771 HOBBY
EXCHANGE DEADLINE 2/28/2019
*NO BLACK: .5X TO 1.2X BASIC
CGMAAB Alex Bregman 30.00 80.00
CGMAAG Andres Galarraga 10.00 25.00
CGMACC Carlos Correa 40.00 100.00
CGMADF Dexter Fowler 10.00 25.00
CGMAHA Hank Aaron
CGMAJU Julio Urias EXCH 15.00 40.00
CGMANM Nomar Mazara 8.00 20.00
CGMANS Noah Syndergaard 20.00 50.00
CGMAOV Omar Vizquel 10.00 25.00
CGMASK Sandy Koufax 250.00 400.00
CGMASMA Steven Matz 8.00 20.00
CGMASP Stephen Piscotty 10.00 25.00
CGMATS Trevor Story 12.00 30.00
CGMAYG Yulieski Gurriel 10.00 25.00
CGMAYM Yoan Moncada 30.00 80.00

2017 Topps Gypsy Queen Fortune Teller Mini

COMPLETE SET (20) 8.00 20.00
STATED ODDS 1:6 HOBBY
*GREEN/99: 2X TO 5X BASIC
*RED: 5X TO 12X BASIC
FTAB Alex Bregman 1.50 4.00
FTABE Adrian Beltre .50 1.25
FTAG Adrian Gonzalez .40 1.00
FTAJ Aaron Judge 4.00 10.00
FTAP Albert Pujols .60 1.50
FTCH Cole Hamels .40 1.00
FTCK Clayton Kershaw .75 2.00
FTDS Dansby Swanson .75 2.00
FTGS Gary Sanchez .50 1.25
FTIR Ivan Rodriguez .40 1.00
FTJA Jose Altuve .40 1.00
FTJL Jon Lester .40 1.00
FTKB Kris Bryant .60 1.50
FTMB Madison Bumgarner .40 1.00
FTMS Max Scherzer .50 1.25
FTMT Mike Trout 2.50 6.00
FTRB Ryan Braun .40 1.00
FTRC Robinson Cano .40 1.00
FTYG Yulieski Gurriel .50 1.25
FTYM Yoan Moncada 1.00 2.50

2017 Topps Gypsy Queen GlassWorks Box Topper

*PURPLE/150: .6X TO 1.5X BASIC
*RED/25: 1.2X TO 3X BASIC
GWAM Andrew McCutchen 3.00 8.00
GWAR Anthony Rizzo 4.00 10.00
GWBH Bryce Harper 5.00 12.00
GWBP Buster Posey 4.00 10.00
GWCC Carlos Correa 3.00 8.00
GWCK Clayton Kershaw 5.00 12.00
GWCS Chris Sale
GWDP David Price 2.50 6.00
GWFH Felix Hernandez 2.50 6.00
GWFL Francisco Lindor 3.00 8.00
GWJA Jake Arrieta 2.50 6.00
GWJF Jose Fernandez 3.00 8.00
GWKB Kris Bryant 4.00 10.00
GWMB Madison Bumgarner 2.50 6.00
GWMC Miguel Cabrera 3.00 8.00
GWMS Marcus Stroman 2.50 6.00
GWMT Mike Trout 15.00 40.00
GWNA Nolan Arenado 5.00 12.00
GWNM Nomar Mazara 2.00 5.00
GWRC Robinson Cano 2.50 6.00
GWSM Steven Matz 2.00 5.00
GWSP Stephen Piscotty 2.50 6.00
GWTS Trevor Story 3.00 8.00
GWXB Xander Bogaerts 3.00 8.00
GWZG Zack Greinke 3.00 8.00

2017 Topps Gypsy Queen GlassWorks Box Topper Autographs

STATED ODDS 1:50 HOBBY BOXES
STATED PRINT RUN 25 SER.#'d SETS
EXCHANGE DEADLINE 2/28/2019
GWAR Anthony Rizzo 200.00 400.00
GWBH Bryce Harper 300.00 500.00
GWBP Buster Posey 150.00 300.00
GWCC Carlos Correa 100.00 250.00
GWFL Francisco Lindor 100.00 250.00
GWKB Kris Bryant 300.00 500.00
GWMT Mike Trout 300.00 500.00
GWNM Nomar Mazara 30.00 80.00
GWTS Trevor Story 50.00 125.00

2017 Topps Gypsy Queen Gum Back Autographs

STATED ODDS 1:824 HOBBY
EXCHANGE DEADLINE 2/28/2019
CBCAAB Alex Bregman 75.00 200.00
CBCABH Bryce Harper
CBCACC Carlos Correa 60.00 150.00
CBCADF Dexter Fowler 12.00 30.00
CBCAFL Francisco Lindor 40.00 100.00
CBCAGS George Springer 10.00 25.00
CBCAKA Jose Altuve 30.00 80.00
CBCAKB Kris Bryant
CBCANS Noah Syndergaard
CBCASM Steven Matz 8.00 20.00
CBCASP Stephen Piscotty 10.00 25.00
CBCATS Trevor Story 12.00 30.00

2017 Topps Gypsy Queen Hand Drawn Art Reproductions

COMPLETE SET (38) 25.00 60.00
STATED ODDS 1:8 HOBBY
GQARAJ1 Adam Jones .40 1.00
GQARAJ2 Adam Jones .40 1.00
GQARAR1 Anthony Rizzo .60 1.50
GQARAR2 Anthony Rizzo .60 1.50
GQARBH1 Bryce Harper .75 2.00
GQARBH2 Bryce Harper .75 2.00
GQARBL1 Barry Larkin .40 1.00
GQARBL2 Barry Larkin .40 1.00
GQARCC1 Carlos Correa .50 1.25
GQARCC2 Carlos Correa .50 1.25
GQARCH1 Cole Hamels .40 1.00
GQARCH2 Cole Hamels .40 1.00
GQARCS1 Chris Sale .50 1.25
GQARCS2 Chris Sale .50 1.25
GQARGS1 Giancarlo Stanton .50 1.25
GQARGS2 Giancarlo Stanton .50 1.25
GQARI2 Ichiro .60 1.50
GQARI1 Ichiro .60 1.50
GQARKB1 Kris Bryant .60 1.50
GQARKB2 Kris Bryant .60 1.50
GQARMM1 Manny Machado .50 1.25
GQARMM2 Manny Machado .50 1.25
GQARMMC1 Mark McGwire .75 2.00
GQARMMC2 Mark McGwire .75 2.00
GQARMS1 Max Scherzer .50 1.25
GQARMS2 Max Scherzer .50 1.25
GQARMT1 Mike Trout 2.50 6.00
GQARMT2 Mike Trout 2.50 6.00
GQARNS1 Noah Syndergaard .40 1.00
GQARNS2 Noah Syndergaard .40 1.00
GQARRC1 Robinson Cano .40 1.00
GQARRC2 Robinson Cano .40 1.00
GQARRCL1 Roger Clemens .60 1.50
GQARRCL2 Roger Clemens .60 1.50
GQARXB1 Xander Bogaerts .50 1.25
GQARXB2 Xander Bogaerts .50 1.25
GQARZG1 Zack Greinke .50 1.25
GQARZG2 Zack Greinke .50 1.25

2018 Topps Gypsy Queen

COMP.SET w/o SP's (300) 20.00 50.00
SP ODDS 1:24 HOBBY
1 Mike Trout 1.50 4.00
2 Corey Knebel .20 .50
3 Andrew Stevenson RC .30 .75
4 Lucas Giolito .25 .60
5 Andrew Cashner .20 .50
6 Yadier Molina .40 1.00
7 Rick Porcello .25 .60
8 Eric Hosmer .25 .60
9 Kevin Pillar .20 .50
10 Max Kepler .25 .60
11 Zach Davies .20 .50
12 Maikel Franco .25 .60
13 Ivan Nova .25 .60
14 Yoenis Cespedes .30 .75
15 Starling Marte .25 .60
16 Luis Severino .25 .60
17 Jeff Samardzija .20 .50
18 Wil Myers .25 .60
19 Nick Castellanos .30 .75
20 Johnny Cueto .25 .60
21 Juan Lagares .20 .50
22 Amed Rosario RC .40 1.00
23 Francisco Lindor .30 .75
24 Byron Buxton .30 .75
25 Carlos Correa .30 .75
26 Clint Frazier RC .60 1.50
27 Scooter Gennett .25 .60
28 Alex Colome .20 .50
29 Matt Carpenter .30 .75
30 A.J. Jimenez RC .30 .75
31 Felipe Rivero .25 .60
32 Martin Perez UER .25 .60
Nick Martinez Pictured
33 Zack Granite RC .30 .75
34 Matt Boyd .20 .50
35 Ichiro .40 1.00
36 Jack Flaherty RC 1.25 3.00
37 Stephen Strasburg .30 .75
38 David Peralta .20 .50
39 Kendrys Morales .20 .50
40 Zack Greinke .30 .75
41 Mikie Mahtook .20 .50
42 Adam Jones .25 .60
43 Gerardo Parra .20 .50
44 Brad Miller .25 .60
45 Jason Vargas .20 .50
46 Adam Duvall .25 .60
47 Jose Iglesias .25 .60
48 Parker Bridwell RC .30 .75
49 Yolmer Sanchez .20 .50
50 Bryce Harper .50 1.25
51 Sandy Alcantara RC .30 .75
52 Anibal Sanchez .20 .50
53 Rafael Devers RC 1.00 2.50
54 Aroldis Chapman .30 .75
55 Jonathan Villar .20 .50
56 Josh Reddick .20 .50
57 Gary Sanchez .30 .75
58 Ryan Zimmerman .25 .60
59 Steven Souza Jr. .25 .60
60 Stephen Piscotty .20 .50
61 Eddie Rosario .30 .75
62 J.A. Happ .25 .60
63 Alex Gordon .25 .60
64 Cole Hamels .25 .60
65 Trevor Story .30 .75
66 Tucker Barnhart .20 .50
67 Ketel Marte .25 .60
68 Christian Yelich .40 1.00
69 Paul DeJong .30 .75
70 Jose Quintana .20 .50
71 Ken Giles .20 .50
72 Rio Ruiz .20 .50
73 Lorenzo Cain .20 .50
74 Noah Syndergaard .25 .60
75 Shin-Soo Choo .25 .60
76 Chris Taylor .25 .60
77 Ian Kinsler .25 .60
78 Luiz Gohara RC .30 .75
79 Jose Altuve .25 .60
80 Billy Hamilton .25 .60
81 Buster Posey .40 1.00
82 Paul Goldschmidt .30 .75
83 Mark Reynolds .20 .50
84 Josh Bell .25 .60
85 Brandon Drury .20 .50
86 Ervin Santana .20 .50
87 Anthony Rizzo .40 1.00
88 Jose Berrios .25 .60
89 Shohei Ohtani RC 6.00 15.00
90 Luis Perdomo .20 .50
91 Julio Teheran .25 .60
92 Zack Cozart .20 .50
93 Jon Gray .20 .50
94 Nick Markakis .25 .60
95 Jon Lester .25 .60
96 Aaron Nola .25 .60
97 Jonathan Schoop .20 .50
98 Manny Machado .30 .75
99 Tyler Glasnow .30 .75
100 Chris Sale .30 .75
101 Jed Lowrie .20 .50
102 Miguel Gomez RC .30 .75
103 Trea Turner .25 .60
104 Felix Jorge RC .30 .75
105 Brandon Crawford .25 .60
106 Kevin Kiermaier .25 .60
107 Mike Leake .20 .50
108 Garrett Richards .25 .60
109 Jordan Zimmermann .25 .60
110 Patrick Corbin .25 .60
111 Andrelton Simmons .20 .50
112 Logan Forsythe .20 .50
113 Elvis Andrus .25 .60
114 Dominic Smith RC .40 1.00
115 Willson Contreras .30 .75
116 James McCann .25 .60
117 Starlin Castro .20 .50
118 Eric Thames .25 .60
119 Austin Hedges .20 .50
120 Dinelson Lamet .20 .50
121 Austin Hays RC .50 1.25
122 Felix Hernandez .25 .60
123 Alex Bregman .30 .75
124 Matt Harvey .25 .60
125 Corey Seager .30 .75
126 Melky Cabrera .20 .50
127 Scott Schebler .25 .60
128 Matt Chapman .30 .75
129 Ricky Nolasco .20 .50
130 Michael Fulmer .20 .50
131 Gerrit Cole .30 .75
132 Kyle Schwarber .30 .75
133 Lance McCullers Jr. .20 .50
134 Marcell Ozuna .30 .75
135 Addison Russell .25 .60
136 Carlos Santana .25 .60
137 Carlos Gonzalez .25 .60
138 Jose Urena .20 .50
139 Mike Zunino .20 .50
140 Blake Snell .25 .60
141 Russell Martin .20 .50
142 Clayton Richard .20 .50
143 Yoan Moncada .30 .75
144 Odubel Herrera .25 .60
145 Paul Blackburn RC .30 .75
146 Carlos Martinez .25 .60
147 Jason Heyward .25 .60
148 Josh Donaldson .25 .60
149 Anthony Rendon .30 .75
150 Clayton Kershaw .50 1.25
151 Xander Bogaerts .30 .75
152 Chance Sisco RC .40 1.00
153 Justin Upton .25 .60
154 Travis Shaw .20 .50
155 Brandon Nimmo .25 .60
156 Yasiel Puig .30 .75
157 Jharel Cotton .20 .50
158 Gregory Polanco .25 .60
159 Travis Jankowski .20 .50
160 Chad Bettis .20 .50
161 Kenley Jansen .25 .60
162 Francisco Mejia RC .40 1.00
163 Ozzie Albies RC 1.00 2.50
164 Hunter Renfroe .20 .50
165 Justin Turner .30 .75
166 Ben Gamel .25 .60
167 Masahiro Tanaka .25 .60
168 Jorge Polanco .25 .60
169 J.D. Martinez .30 .75
170 Ryon Healy .20 .50
171 Tzu-Wei Lin RC .40 1.00
172 Danny Duffy .20 .50
173 Mike Moustakas .25 .60
174 Dallas Keuchel .25 .60
175 Joe Panik .25 .60
176 Jacob deGrom .60 1.50
177 Jeurys Familia .25 .60
178 Brandon Woodruff RC 1.00 2.50
179 Yasmany Tomas .20 .50
180 Mookie Betts .60 1.50
181 Jarrett Parker .20 .50
182 Brandon Belt .25 .60
183 Zach Britton .20 .50
184 Dansby Swanson .30 .75
185 Jean Segura .20 .50
186 Travis d'Arnaud .25 .60
187 Matt Olson .30 .75
188 Jordy Mercer .20 .50
189 Miguel Cabrera .30 .75
190 Matt Kemp .25 .60
191 Andrew McCutchen .30 .75
192 Joey Gallo .25 .60
193 Erick Fedde RC .30 .75
194 Corey Kluber .25 .60
195 Vince Velasquez .20 .50
196 Nick Williams RC .40 1.00
197 Evan Longoria .25 .60
198 Didi Gregorius .25 .60
199 Rhys Hoskins RC 1.25 3.00
200 Cody Bellinger .60 1.50
201 Chris Archer .20 .50
202 George Springer .25 .60
203 C.J. Cron .20 .50
204 Tommy Pham .20 .50
205 Reynaldo Lopez .25 .60
206 DJ LeMahieu .30 .75
207 Luis Castillo .25 .60
208 Khris Davis .30 .75
209 Kevin Gausman .30 .75
210 Domingo Santana .25 .60
211 Corey Dickerson .20 .50
212 Sonny Gray .25 .60
213 Mitch Haniger .25 .60
214 Manny Margot .20 .50
215 Greg Allen RC .30 .75
216 Marcus Semien .30 .75
217 Joey Votto .30 .75
218 Chris Davis .20 .50
219 Nicky Delmonico RC .30 .75
220 Brian Anderson RC .40 1.00
221 Sean Newcomb .25 .60
222 Walker Buehler RC 1.50 4.00
223 Albert Pujols .40 1.00
224 Giancarlo Stanton .30 .75
225 Kyle Seager .20 .50
226 Yangervis Solarte .20 .50
227 Whit Merrifield .30 .75
228 Brad Ziegler .20 .50
229 Justin Bour .20 .50
230 Logan Morrison .20 .50
231 Miguel Sano .25 .60
232 A.J. Pollock .20 .50
233 Robinson Cano .25 .60
234 Dillon Peters RC .30 .75
235 Avisail Garcia .25 .60
236 J.P. Crawford RC .30 .75
237 Andrew Benintendi .30 .75
238 Marco Estrada .20 .50
239 Carson Fulmer .20 .50
240 Jose Abreu .30 .75
241 Brad Hand .20 .50
242 Daniel Murphy .25 .60
243 Matt Moore .25 .60
244 Jackie Bradley Jr. .30 .75
245 Trevor Bauer .40 1.00
246 Ryan Braun .25 .60
247 Richard Urena RC .30 .75
248 Orlando Arcia .20 .50
249 Jameson Taillon .25 .60
250 Max Scherzer .30 .75
251 Hunter Pence .25 .60
252 Ender Inciarte .20 .50
253 Jose Ramirez .25 .60
254 Victor Robles RC .75 2.00
255 Roberto Osuna .20 .50
256 James Paxton .25 .60
257 Adrian Beltre .30 .75
258 Hector Neris .20 .50
259 Edwin Encarnacion .30 .75
260 Kris Bryant .40 1.00
261 Dexter Fowler .25 .60
262 Justin Smoak .20 .50
263 Sean Manaea .20 .50
264 Freddie Freeman .40 1.00
265 Justin Verlander .30 .75
266 Aaron Altherr .20 .50
267 Dustin Pedroia .30 .75
268 Rougned Odor .25 .60
269 Brian Dozier .25 .60
270 Alex Wood .20 .50
271 Kole Calhoun .20 .50
272 Raisel Iglesias .25 .60
273 Alcides Escobar .25 .60
274 Tim Beckham .25 .60
275 Craig Kimbrel .25 .60
276 Homer Bailey .20 .50
277 Miguel Andujar RC 1.25 3.00
278 Javier Baez .40 1.00
279 Keon Broxton .20 .50
280 Yuli Gurriel .25 .60
281 Andrew Miller .25 .60
282 Tim Anderson .30 .75
283 Luke Weaver .25 .60
284 Jake Odorizzi .20 .50
285 Carlos Carrasco .20 .50
286 Jake Lamb .25 .60
287 Charlie Blackmon .30 .75
288 Jorge Alfaro .20 .50
289 Tyler Saladino .20 .50
290 Jake Arrieta .25 .60
291 Trey Mancini .25 .60
292 Nolan Arenado .50 1.25
293 Daniel Mengden RC .30 .75
294 Nomar Mazara .20 .50
295 Marcus Stroman .25 .60
296 German Marquez .20 .50
297 Nelson Cruz .30 .75
298 Salvador Perez .25 .60
299 Dee Gordon .20 .50
300 Aaron Judge .75 2.00
301 Hank Aaron SP 2.50 6.00
302 Jeff Bagwell SP 1.00 2.50
303 Cal Ripken Jr. SP 4.00 10.00
304 George Brett SP 2.50 6.00
305 Alex Rodriguez SP 1.50 4.00
306 Satchel Paige SP 1.25 3.00
307 Nolan Ryan SP 4.00 10.00
308 Carlton Fisk SP 1.00 2.50
309 Jimmie Foxx SP 1.25 3.00
310 Mariano Rivera SP 1.50 4.00
311 Whitey Ford SP 1.00 2.50
312 Johnny Bench SP 1.25 3.00
313 Frank Thomas SP 1.25 3.00
314 Roger Clemens SP 1.50 4.00
315 Ted Williams SP 2.50 6.00
316 Honus Wagner SP 1.25 3.00
317 Rickey Henderson SP 1.25 3.00
318 Bo Jackson SP 1.25 3.00
319 Pedro Martinez SP 1.00 2.50
320 Sandy Koufax SP 2.50 6.00

2018 Topps Gypsy Queen Bazooka Back

*BAZOOKA: 3X TO 8X BASIC
*BAZOOKA RC: 2X TO 5X BASIC RC
*BAZOOKA SP: 2.5X TO 6X BASIC SP
STATED ODDS 1:43 HOBBY
STATED SP ODDS 1:1263 HOBBY
89 Shohei Ohtani 100.00 250.00

2018 Topps Gypsy Queen Black and White

*BLACK WHITE: 5X TO 12X BASIC
*BLACK WHITE RC: 3X TO 8X BASIC RC
STATED ODDS 1:41 HOBBY
STATED PRINT RUN 50 SER.#'d SETS
89 Shohei Ohtani 150.00 400.00

2018 Topps Gypsy Queen Capless Variations

STATED ODDS 1:121 HOBBY
*SWAP: .6X TO 1.5X BASIC
22 Amed Rosario 3.00 8.00
23 Francisco Lindor 4.00 10.00
35 Ichiro 5.00 12.00
50 Bryce Harper 6.00 15.00
79 Jose Altuve 3.00 8.00
81 Buster Posey 5.00 12.00
98 Manny Machado 4.00 10.00
100 Chris Sale 4.00 10.00
148 Josh Donaldson 3.00 8.00
165 Justin Turner 4.00 10.00
166 Ben Gamel 3.00 8.00
176 Jacob deGrom 8.00 20.00
199 Rhys Hoskins 10.00 25.00
200 Cody Bellinger 8.00 20.00
208 Khris Davis 4.00 10.00
260 Scooter Gennett 3.00 8.00
280 Yuli Gurriel 3.00 8.00
287 Charlie Blackmon 4.00 10.00
297 Nelson Cruz 4.00 10.00
300 Aaron Judge 15.00 40.00

2018 Topps Gypsy Queen GQ Logo Swap

*SWAP: 2.5X TO 6X BASIC
*SWAP RC: 1.5X TO 4X BASIC RC
*SWAP SP: 2X TO 5X BASIC SP
STATED ODDS 1:22 HOBBY
STATED SP ODDS 1:843 HOBBY
89 Shohei Ohtani 40.00 100.00

2018 Topps Gypsy Queen Green

*GREEN: 1.5X TO 4X BASIC
*GREEN RC: 1X TO 2.5X BASIC RC
RANDOM INSERTS IN RETAIL PACKS
89 Shohei Ohtani 25.00 60.00

2018 Topps Gypsy Queen Indigo

*INDIGO: 3X TO 8X BASIC
*INDIGO RC: 2X TO 5X BASIC RC
STATED ODDS 1:17 HOBBY
STATED PRINT RUN 250 SER.#'d SETS
89 Shohei Ohtani 60.00 150.00

2018 Topps Gypsy Queen Jackie Robinson Day Variations

STATED ODDS 1:106 HOBBY
*SWAP: .6X TO 1.5X BASIC
8 Eric Hosmer 3.00 8.00
14 Yoenis Cespedes 4.00 10.00
23 Francisco Lindor 4.00 10.00
25 Carlos Correa 4.00 10.00
35 Ichiro 5.00 12.00
42 Adam Jones 3.00 8.00
50 Bryce Harper 6.00 15.00
65 Trevor Story 4.00 10.00
79 Jose Altuve 3.00 8.00
86 Ervin Santana 2.50 6.00
98 Manny Machado 4.00 10.00
100 Chris Sale 4.00 10.00
118 Eric Thames 3.00 8.00
123 Alex Bregman 4.00 10.00
125 Corey Seager 4.00 10.00
133 Lance McCullers Jr. 2.50 6.00
146 Carlos Martinez 3.00 8.00
156 Yasiel Puig 4.00 10.00
176 Jacob deGrom 8.00 20.00
191 Andrew McCutchen 4.00 10.00
192 Corey Kluber 3.00 8.00
202 George Springer 3.00 8.00
208 Khris Davis
217 Joey Votto 4.00 10.00
242 Daniel Murphy 3.00 8.00
256 James Paxton 3.00 8.00
259 Edwin Encarnacion 4.00 10.00
265 Justin Verlander 4.00 10.00
287 Charlie Blackmon 4.00 10.00
292 Nolan Arenado 6.00 15.00

2018 Topps Gypsy Queen Missing Blackplate

*NO BLACK: 1.2X TO 3X BASIC
*NO BLACK RC: .75X TO 2X BASIC RC
INSERTED IN RETAIL PACKS
89 Shohei Ohtani 20.00 50.00

2018 Topps Gypsy Queen Missing Nameplate

*NO NAME: 1.5X TO 4X BASIC
*NO NAME RC: 1X TO 2.5X BASIC RC
*NO NAME SP: 1.2X TO 3X BASIC SP
STATED ODDS 1:16 HOBBY
STATED SP ODDS 1:422 HOBBY
89 Shohei Ohtani 25.00 60.00

2018 Topps Gypsy Queen Team Swap Variations
STATED ODDS 1:843 HOBBY
1 Mike Trout Dodgers 30.00 80.00
25 Carlos Correa Rangers 8.00 20.00
50 Bryce Harper Orioles 20.00 50.00
53 Rafael Devers Yankees 20.00 50.00
74 Noah Syndergaard Phillies 20.00 50.00
125 Corey Seager Giants 25.00 60.00
163 Albies Mets 15.00 40.00
164 Hunter Renfroe Diamondbacks 5.00 12.00
187 Matt Olson Mariners 8.00 20.00
199 Rhys Hoskins Nationals 30.00 80.00
233 Robinson Cano Athletics 6.00 15.00
253 J.Ramirez DET 6.00 15.00
260 Kris Bryant Cardinals 30.00 80.00
268 Rougned Odor Angels 6.00 15.00
300 Aaron Judge Red Sox 40.00 100.00

2018 Topps Gypsy Queen Autograph Garments
STATED ODDS 1:921 HOBBY
PRINT RUNS B/WN 10-50 COPIES PER
AGAB Andrew Benintendi/50 150.00 400.00
AGAJ Aaron Judge EXCH 300.00 600.00
AGBJ Bo Jackson/25
AGBP Brett Phillips/50 12.00 30.00
AGBZ Bradley Zimmer/50 12.00 30.00
AGCA Christian Arroyo/50 12.00 30.00
AGCF Clint Frazier/50 30.00 80.00
AGCK Craig Kimbrel/50 30.00 80.00
AGCSA Chris Sale/50 30.00 80.00
AGDB Dellin Betances/50 12.00 30.00
AGDM Daniel Murphy EXCH 20.00 50.00
AGDP David Price/50 15.00 40.00
AGFB Franklin Barreto/50 12.00 30.00
AGIH Ian Happ/50 15.00 40.00
AGKB Kris Bryant EXCH 150.00 400.00
AGLS Luis Severino/50 25.00 60.00
AGMT Mike Trout/10
AGNS Noah Syndergaard/50 60.00 150.00

2018 Topps Gypsy Queen Autograph Patch Booklets
STATED ODDS 1:2877 HOBBY
STATED PRINT RUN 20 SER.#'d SETS
EXCHANGE DEADLINE 2/28/2020
GQAPAB Andrew Benintendi EXCH 150.00 400.00
GQAPBJ Bo Jackson 100.00 250.00
GQAPBP Brett Phillips 75.00 200.00
GQAPCF Clint Frazier 100.00 250.00
GQAPDB Dellin Betances 50.00 120.00
GQAPIH Ian Happ 100.00 250.00
GQAPKD Khris Davis 50.00 120.00
GQAPLS Luis Severino 60.00 150.00
GQAPMT Mike Trout
GQAPNS Noah Syndergaard EXCH 75.00 200.00
GQAPRH Rickey Henderson 100.00 250.00

2018 Topps Gypsy Queen Autographs
STATED ODDS 1:19 HOBBY
EXCHANGE DEADLINE 2/28/2020
GQAAB Anthony Banda 3.00 8.00
GQAAD Adam Duvall 4.00 10.00
GQAAJ Aaron Judge EXCH 60.00 150.00
GQAAR Amed Rosario 4.00 10.00
GQAAS Andrew Stevenson 3.00 8.00
GQAAT Andrew Toles 3.00 8.00
GQAAV Alex Verdugo 8.00 20.00
GQABJ Bo Jackson 60.00 150.00
GQABP Brett Phillips 3.00 8.00
GQABS Blake Snell 6.00 15.00
GQABW Brandon Woodruff 10.00 25.00
GQACA Christian Arroyo 3.00 8.00
GQACC Carlos Correa 25.00 60.00
GQACCA Carlos Carrasco 3.00 8.00
GQACF Clint Frazier 12.00 30.00
GQACK Craig Kimbrel 4.00 10.00
GQADF Dustin Fowler 3.00 8.00
GQADJ Derek Jeter 400.00 600.00
GQADR Daniel Robertson 3.00 8.00
GQADSM Dominic Smith 10.00 25.00
GQAFB Franklin Barreto 3.00 8.00
GQAFM Francisco Mejia
GQAGC Garrett Cooper 3.00 8.00
GQAGSA Gary Sanchez 30.00 80.00
GQAHB Harrison Bader 5.00 12.00
GQAHM Hideki Matsui EXCH 75.00 200.00
GQAJB Jose Berrios 4.00 10.00
GQAJC J.P. Crawford 4.00 10.00
GQAJF Jacob Faria 3.00 8.00
GQAJM Jordan Montgomery 3.00 8.00
GQAJT Jim Thome EXCH 25.00 60.00
GQAKB Kris Bryant 100.00 250.00
GQAKD Khris Davis 6.00 15.00
GQAKG Koda Glover 3.00 8.00
GQALB Lewis Brinson 3.00 8.00
GQALG Lucas Giolito 5.00 12.00
GQAMA Miguel Andujar 10.00 25.00
GQAMB Matt Bush 3.00 8.00
GQAMM Manny Machado 25.00 60.00
GQAMT Mike Trout 300.00 500.00
GQAOA Ozzie Albies 20.00 50.00
GQAPB Parker Bridwell 3.00 8.00
GQAPD Paul DeJong 6.00 15.00
GQARD Rafael Devers 20.00 50.00
GQARHO Rhys Hoskins 15.00 40.00
GQARM Ryan McMahon 8.00 20.00
GQASK Sandy Koufax 200.00 400.00
GQASN Sean Newcomb 4.00 10.00
GQASO Shohei Ohtani 250.00 600.00
GQATP Tommy Pham 3.00 8.00
GQAZG Zack Granite 3.00 8.00

2018 Topps Gypsy Queen Autographs Bazooka Back
*BAZOOKA: 1X TO 2.5X BASIC
STATED ODDS 1:668 HOBBY
STATED PRINT RUN BTWN 24-25 SER.#'d SETS
EXCHANGE DEADLINE 2/28/2020
GQABJ Bo Jackson/25 60.00 150.00
GQAFM Francisco Mejia/25 30.00 80.00
GQAGSA Gary Sanchez/25 60.00 150.00
GQAJT Jim Thome EXCH 60.00 150.00
GQAMM Manny Machado/25 40.00 100.00
GQASO Shohei Ohtani/25 600.00 1200.00

2018 Topps Gypsy Queen Autographs Black and White
*BW: .75X TO 2X BASIC
STATED ODDS 1:247 HOBBY
PRINT RUNS B/WN 35-50 COPIES PER
EXCHANGE DEADLINE 2/28/2020
GQAFM Francisco Mejia/50 25.00 60.00
GQAGSA Gary Sanchez/50 50.00 120.00
GQAJT Jim Thome EXCH 50.00 120.00
GQAMM Manny Machado/50 30.00 80.00
GQASO Shohei Ohtani/50 500.00 1000.00

2018 Topps Gypsy Queen Autographs GQ Logo Swap
*SWAP: .6X TO 1.5X BASIC
STATED ODDS 1:169 HOBBY
PRINT RUNS B/WN 80-99 COPIES PER
EXCHANGE DEADLINE 2/28/2020
GQAFM Francisco Mejia/99 20.00 50.00
GQAGSA Gary Sanchez/99 40.00 100.00

2018 Topps Gypsy Queen Autographs Indigo
*INDIGO: .5X TO 1.2X BASIC
STATED ODDS 1:112 HOBBY
PRINT RUNS B/WN 92-150 COPIES PER
EXCHANGE DEADLINE 2/28/2020
GQAFM Francisco Mejia/150 15.00 40.00

2018 Topps Gypsy Queen Autographs Jackie Robinson Day Variations
RANDOMLY INSERTED IN PACKS
PRINT RUNS B/WN 30-99 COPIES PER
EXCHANGE DEADLINE 2/28/2020
*BW/42: .5X TO 1.2X BASIC
25 Carlos Correa/30 60.00 150.00
42 Adam Jones/70 20.00 50.00
79 Jose Altuve EXCH 40.00 100.00
98 Manny Machado/40 40.00 100.00
100 Chris Sale/70 25.00 60.00
118 Eric Thames/99 6.00 15.00
123 Alex Bregman/75 20.00 50.00
194 Corey Kluber/45 20.00 50.00
208 Khris Davis/99 6.00 15.00
217 Joey Votto/30 75.00 200.00
242 Daniel Murphy EXCH 15.00 40.00
259 Edwin Encarnacion EXCH 15.00 40.00

2018 Topps Gypsy Queen Bases Around the League Autographs
STATED ODDS 1:4015 HOBBY
STATED PRINT RUN 20 SER.#'d SETS
EXCHANGE DEADLINE 2/28/2020
BALAB Andrew Benintendi/20 150.00 400.00
BALAJ Aaron Judge/20 400.00 800.00
BALAR Anthony Rizzo/20 150.00 400.00
BALCC Carlos Correa/20 150.00 400.00
BALKB Kris Bryant EXCH 300.00 500.00
BALMM Manny Machado/20 300.00 500.00
BALMT Mike Trout/10
BALPG Paul Goldschmidt/20 150.00 400.00

2018 Topps Gypsy Queen Fortune Teller Mini
STATED ODDS 1:6 HOBBY
*INDIGO/250: 1X TO 2.5X BASIC
*GREEN/99: 2.5X TO 6X BASIC
FTM1 Aaron Judge 1.25 3.00
FTM2 Manny Machado .50 1.25
FTM3 Carlos Carrasco .30 .75
FTM4 J.P. Crawford .30 .75
FTM5 Rafael Devers 1.00 2.50
FTM6 Kris Bryant .60 1.50
FTM7 Khris Davis .50 1.25
FTM8 Corey Seager .50 1.25
FTM9 Daniel Murphy .40 1.00
FTM10 Cody Bellinger 1.00 2.50
FTM11 Carlos Correa .50 1.25
FTM12 Gary Sanchez .50 1.25
FTM13 Bryce Harper .75 2.00
FTM14 Bradley Zimmer .30 .75
FTM15 Noah Syndergaard .40 1.00
FTM16 Amed Rosario .40 1.00
FTM17 Dellin Betances .40 1.00
FTM18 Clint Frazier .60 1.50
FTM19 Trey Mancini .40 1.00
FTM20 Mike Trout 2.50 6.00

2018 Topps Gypsy Queen Fortune Teller Mini Autographs
STATED ODDS 1:1526 HOBBY
PRINT RUNS B/WN 20-50 COPIES PER
EXCHANGE DEADLINE 2/28/2020
GFTAAR Amed Rosario/50 20.00 50.00
GFTABZ Bradley Zimmer/50 6.00 15.00
GFTACC Carlos Correa/20 40.00 100.00
GFTACCA Carlos Carrasco/50 10.00 25.00
GFTACF Clint Frazier/50 12.00 30.00
GFTADB Dellin Betances/50 10.00 25.00
GFTADM Daniel Murphy EXCH 12.00 30.00
GFTAGSA Gary Sanchez/30
GFTAJC J.P. Crawford/50 15.00 40.00
GFTAKB Kris Bryant EXCH 150.00 400.00
GFTAKD Khris Davis/50 10.00 25.00
GFTAMM Manny Machado/20 30.00 80.00
GFTAMT Mike Trout
GFTANS Noah Syndergaard/30 60.00 150.00
GFTARD Rafael Devers/50 12.00 30.00
GFTATM Trey Mancini/50 25.00 60.00

2018 Topps Gypsy Queen Glassworks Box Topper
STATED ODDS 1:1 HOBBY BOXES
*INDIGO/150: .75X TO 2X BASIC
*RED/25: 3X TO 8X BASIC
GWAB Andrew Benintendi 2.50 6.00
GWAJ Aaron Judge 6.00 15.00
GWAR Anthony Rizzo 3.00 8.00
GWBH Bryce Harper 4.00 10.00
GWBP Buster Posey 3.00 8.00
GWCB Cody Bellinger 5.00 12.00
GWCC Carlos Correa 2.50 6.00
GWCK Clayton Kershaw 4.00 10.00
GWCS Corey Seager 2.50 6.00
GWCSA Chris Sale 2.50 6.00
GWFF Freddie Freeman 3.00 8.00
GWFL Francisco Lindor 2.50 6.00
GWGS Giancarlo Stanton 2.50 6.00
GWIH Ian Happ 2.00 5.00
GWJA Jose Altuve 2.00 5.00
GWJD Josh Donaldson 2.00 5.00
GWKB Kris Bryant 8.00 20.00
GWMB Mookie Betts 5.00 12.00
GWMM Manny Machado 2.50 6.00
GWMS Max Scherzer 2.50 6.00
GWMT Mike Trout 10.00 25.00
GWNA Nolan Arenado 4.00 10.00
GWNS Noah Syndergaard 2.00 5.00
GWPG Paul Goldschmidt 2.50 6.00
GWTS Trevor Story 2.50 6.00

2018 Topps Gypsy Queen Glassworks Box Topper Autographs
STATED ODDS 1:1584 HOBBY BOXES
STATED PRINT RUN 25 SER.#'d SETS
EXCHANGE DEADLINE 2/28/2020
GWAB Andrew Benintendi EXCH 100.00 250.00
GWAR Anthony Rizzo 100.00 250.00
GWCC Carlos Correa 60.00 150.00
GWFF Freddie Freeman 75.00 200.00
GWIH Ian Happ 75.00 200.00
GWJA Jose Altuve EXCH 60.00 150.00
GWKB Kris Bryant EXCH 150.00 400.00
GWMT Mike Trout 300.00 600.00
GWPG Paul Goldschmidt 60.00 150.00

2018 Topps Gypsy Queen Mini Rookie Autographs
STATED ODDS 1:809 HOBBY
STATED PRINT RUN 99 SER.#'d SETS
EXCHANGE DEADLINE 2/28/2020
*BW/50: .5X TO 1.2X BASIC
GQRAAR Amed Rosario
GQRAAV Alex Verdugo 15.00 40.00
GQRABW Brandon Woodruff 12.00 30.00
GQRACF Clint Frazier 15.00 40.00
GQRADF Dustin Fowler 4.00 10.00
GQRADS Dominic Smith 5.00 12.00
GQRAFM Francisco Mejia 20.00 50.00
GQRAJC J.P. Crawford 10.00 25.00
GQRAOA Ozzie Albies EXCH 25.00 60.00
GQRAPB Parker Bridwell 4.00 10.00
GQRARD Rafael Devers 60.00 150.00
GQRARH Rhys Hoskins 40.00 100.00

2018 Topps Gypsy Queen Tarot of the Diamond
STATED ODDS 1:8 HOBBY
*INDIGO/250: 1X TO 2.5X BASIC
*GREEN/99: 2X TO 5X BASIC
TOD1 Aaron Judge 1.25 3.00
TOD2 Rafael Devers 1.00 2.50
TOD3 Giancarlo Stanton .50 1.25
TOD4 Chris Sale .50 1.25
TOD5 Cody Bellinger 1.00 2.50
TOD6 Kenley Jansen .40 1.00
TOD7 Francisco Lindor .50 1.25
TOD8 Clayton Kershaw .75 2.00
TOD9 Marcus Stroman .40 1.00
TOD10 Giancarlo Stanton .50 1.25
TOD11 Khris Davis .50 1.25
TOD12 Carlos Correa .50 1.25
TOD13 Aroldis Chapman .50 1.25
TOD14 Aaron Judge 1.25 3.00
TOD15 Chris Sale .50 1.25
TOD16 Kevin Kiermaier .40 1.00
TOD17 Noah Syndergaard .40 1.00
TOD18 Bryce Harper .75 2.00
TOD19 Yasiel Puig .50 1.25
TOD20 Albert Pujols .60 1.50
TOD21 Ichiro .60 1.50
TOD22 Mike Trout 2.50 6.00

2019 Topps Gypsy Queen
SP ODDS 1:24 HOBBY
1 Mike Trout 1.50 4.00
2 Jesus Aguilar .25 .60
3 Khris Davis .30 .75
4 Kyle Schwarber .30 .75
5 Carlos Carrasco .20 .50
6 Yadier Molina .40 1.00
7 JaCoby Jones .25 .60
8 Julio Teheran .25 .60
9 Victor Robles .40 1.00
10 Giancarlo Stanton .30 .75
11 Charlie Blackmon .30 .75
12 Jose Peraza .25 .60
13 Kyle Seager .20 .50
14 Josh Reddick .20 .50
15 Alex Gordon .25 .60
16 Jacob Nix RC .40 1.00
17 Buster Posey .40 1.00
18 Cody Bellinger .60 1.50
19 Mike Fiers .20 .50
20 Aaron Nola .25 .60
21 Matt Davidson .25 .60
22 Ryan Borucki RC .30 .75
23 Xander Bogaerts .30 .75
24 Matt Boyd .20 .50
25 Kolby Allard RC .50 1.25
26 Dee Gordon .20 .50
27 Kevin Kiermaier .25 .60
28 Hunter Renfroe .20 .50
29 Dawel Lugo RC .50 1.25
30 Jean Segura .30 .75
31 Jake Arrieta .25 .60
32 Anthony Rizzo .40 1.00
33 Corey Kluber .25 .60
34 Lewis Brinson .20 .50
35 Starling Marte .25 .60
36 Justin Upton .25 .60
37 Eddie Rosario .25 .60
38 Johan Camargo .20 .50
39 Avisail Garcia .25 .60
40 Mike Zunino .20 .50
41 Mookie Betts .60 1.50
42 Archie Bradley .20 .50
43 Josh Rogers RC .30 .75
44 Jeimer Candelario .20 .50
45 Paul DeJong .30 .75
46 Brandon Belt .25 .60
47 Jalen Beeks RC .30 .75
48 Josh Bell .25 .60
49 Josh Harrison .20 .50
50 Mike Minor .20 .50
51 Kendrys Morales .20 .50
52 Jakob Junis .20 .50
53 Freddie Freeman .40 1.00
54 Michael Brantley .25 .60
55 Shohei Ohtani .50 1.25
56 Elvis Andrus .25 .60
57 Juan Soto 1.00 2.50
58 Addison Reed .20 .50
59 Zack Wheeler .25 .60
60 Mark Trumbo .20 .50
61 Dereck Rodriguez .20 .50
62 Zack Greinke .30 .75
63 Carlos Correa .30 .75
64 Dakota Hudson RC .40 1.00
65 Mike Clevinger .25 .60
66 Miguel Cabrera .30 .75
67 Jake Lamb .25 .60
68 Ian Happ .25 .60
69 Maikel Franco .25 .60
70 Nick Williams .20 .50
71 Miles Mikolas .30 .75
72 Eugenio Suarez .25 .60
73 Carlos Santana .25 .60
74 Max Muncy .25 .60
75 Dustin Pedroia .30 .75
76 Marcus Stroman .25 .60
77 Andrew McCutchen .30 .75
78 Byron Buxton .30 .75
79 Willson Contreras .25 .60
80 Ronald Guzman .20 .50
81 Trevor Bauer .40 1.00
82 Whit Merrifield .30 .75
83 Kyle Hendricks .30 .75
84 Marcell Ozuna .30 .75
85 Ryan McMahon .30 .75
86 C.J. Cron .20 .50
87 Taijuan Walker .20 .50
88 Tyler Mahle .20 .50
89 Ian Desmond .20 .50
90 Brett Phillips .20 .50
91 Albert Almora Jr. .25 .60
92 Gleyber Torres .60 1.50
93 Tyler Glasnow .30 .75
94 Francisco Lindor .30 .75
95 J.T. Realmuto .30 .75
96 Seranthony Dominguez .20 .50
97 Austin Meadows .30 .75
98 Enyel De Los Santos .20 .50
99 Christian Yelich .40 1.00
100 Kris Bryant .40 1.00
101 Blake Snell .25 .60
102 Rhys Hoskins .40 1.00
103 Miguel Andujar .30 .75
104 Ozzie Albies .30 .75
105 Bryce Harper .50 1.25
106 Robinson Chirinos .20 .50
107 Max Kepler .25 .60
108 Steven Duggar RC .40 1.00
109 Gerrit Cole .30 .75
110 Salvador Perez .25 .60
111 Justin Verlander .30 .75
112 Kevin Kramer RC .40 1.00
113 Jorge Polanco .25 .60
114 Chris Davis .20 .50
115 Manny Machado .30 .75
116 Manny Margot .20 .50
117 Francisco Arcia RC .50 1.25
118 Starlin Castro .20 .50
119 Luis Guillorme .20 .50
120 Ramon Laureano RC .60 1.50
121 Joey Votto .30 .75
122 J.D. Martinez .30 .75
123 Daniel Palka .25 .60
124 Joey Gallo .25 .60
125 Tim Anderson .30 .75
126 Wil Myers .25 .60
127 Sean Doolittle .20 .50
128 Rick Porcello .25 .60
129 Joe Panik .25 .60
130 Michael Kopech RC 1.00 2.50
131 JT Riddle .20 .50
132 Blake Treinen .20 .50
133 George Springer .25 .60
134 Yolmer Sanchez .20 .50
135 Wade Davis .20 .50
136 Lorenzo Cain .20 .50
137 Todd Frazier .20 .50
138 Chris Sale .30 .75
139 Taylor Ward RC .30 .75
140 Scott Schebler .25 .60
141 Chance Adams RC .30 .75
142 Dylan Bundy .25 .60
143 Mitch Haniger .25 .60
144 Daniel Poncedeleon RC .50 1.25
145 Ryan O'Hearn RC .30 .75
146 Kyle Freeland .25 .60
147 Rafael Devers .40 1.00
148 Trey Mancini .25 .60
149 Gregory Polanco .25 .60
150 Ronald Acuna Jr. 1.50 4.00
151 Brandon Woodruff .30 .75
152 Willians Astudillo RC .30 .75
153 Trevor Story .30 .75
154 Carlos Rodon .30 .75
155 Javier Baez .40 1.00
156 Jake Cave RC .40 1.00
157 Raisel Iglesias .20 .50
158 Luis Urias RC .50 1.25
159 Dennis Santana RC .30 .75
160 Jackie Bradley Jr. .30 .75
161 Seth Lugo .20 .50
162 Robbie Ray .20 .50
163 Stephen Piscotty .20 .50
164 Jake Odorizzi .20 .50
165 Aramis Garcia RC .30 .75
166 Jose Altuve .25 .60
167 Tim Beckham .25 .60
168 Kevin Pillar .20 .50
169 Travis Shaw .20 .50
170 Lou Trivino .20 .50
171 Clayton Kershaw .50 1.25
172 Ryan Braun .25 .60
173 Scooter Gennett .25 .60
174 Corey Seager .30 .75
175 Jack Flaherty .30 .75
176 Brandon Nimmo .25 .60
177 Zack Godley .20 .50
178 Corey Dickerson .20 .50
179 Adam Eaton .30 .75
180 Tommy Pham .20 .50
181 Niko Goodrum .25 .60
182 Yu Darvish .30 .75
183 Adam Cimber RC .30 .75
184 Yuli Gurriel .25 .60
185 Jose Leclerc .20 .50
186 Brandon Lowe RC .50 1.25
187 Justus Sheffield RC .50 1.25
188 Cory Spangenberg .20 .50
189 Edwin Encarnacion .30 .75
190 Yan Gomes .30 .75
191 Corbin Burnes 1.50 4.00
192 Walker Buehler .40 1.00
193 Johnny Cueto .25 .60
194 Jeremy Jeffress .20 .50
195 Tucker Barnhart .20 .50
196 Yoan Moncada .30 .75
197 Sean Manaea .20 .50
198 Joey Lucchesi .20 .50
199 Austin Dean RC .30 .75
200 Jacob deGrom .60 1.50
201 Marcus Semien .30 .75
202 Kyle Wright RC .50 1.25
203 James Paxton .25 .60
204 Josh Hader .25 .60
205 Andrew Benintendi .30 .75
206 Sandy Alcantara .20 .50
207 Andrelton Simmons .20 .50
208 Dansby Swanson .20 .50
209 Scott Kingery .25 .60
210 Paul Goldschmidt .30 .75
211 Stephen Strasburg .30 .75
212 Christin Stewart RC .40 1.00
213 Nolan Arenado .50 1.25
214 David Peralta .20 .50
215 Chris Archer .20 .50
216 Lourdes Gurriel Jr. .25 .60
217 Framber Valdez RC .30 .75
218 Kevin Newman RC .50 1.25
219 Kole Calhoun .20 .50
220 Heath Fillmyer RC .30 .75
221 Justin Turner .30 .75
222 Ryon Healy .20 .50
223 Tyler Austin .30 .75
224 Masahiro Tanaka .25 .60
225 Kyle Tucker RC .75 2.00
226 Billy Hamilton .25 .60
227 Jose Ramirez .25 .60
228 Trevor Richards RC .30 .75
229 Zack Cozart .20 .50
230 Brad Keller RC .30 .75
231 Tyler Skaggs .20 .50
232 Dylan Bundy .25 .60
233 Harrison Bader .20 .50
234 Anthony Rendon .30 .75
235 Luis Severino .25 .60
236 Justin Smoak .20 .50
237 Luis Castillo .25 .60
238 Jose Berrios .25 .60
239 James McCann .25 .60
240 Jon Gray .20 .50
241 David Dahl .25 .60
242 Felix Hernandez .25 .60
243 Francisco Mejia .25 .60
244 Felipe Vazquez .25 .60
245 Jameson Taillon .25 .60
246 Shane Greene .20 .50
247 Edwin Diaz .25 .60
248 Chris Shaw RC .30 .75
249 Jake Bauers RC .50 1.25
250 Sean Newcomb .20 .50
251 Didi Gregorius .25 .60
252 Orlando Arcia .20 .50
253 Ender Inciarte .20 .50
254 Hunter Dozier .20 .50
255 Jeffrey Springs RC .30 .75
256 Brian Anderson .20 .50
257 Jeff McNeil RC .75 2.00
258 Shin-Soo Choo .25 .60
259 Amed Rosario .25 .60
260 Matt Chapman .30 .75
261 Billy McKinney .20 .50
262 Tanner Roark .20 .50
263 David Price .25 .60
264 Evan Longoria .25 .60
265 Brandon Crawford .25 .60
266 Jose Martinez .20 .50
267 Alex Bregman .30 .75
268 Willy Adames .25 .60
269 Nomar Mazara .20 .50
270 Alex Cobb .20 .50
271 Trea Turner .30 .75
272 Jason Heyward .25 .60
273 Jose Urena .20 .50
274 Nicholas Castellanos .30 .75
275 Antonio Senzatela .20 .50
276 Rowdy Tellez .30 .75
277 Max Scherzer .30 .75
278 Enrique Hernandez .30 .75
279 Patrick Corbin .25 .60
280 Matt Olson .30 .75
281 Ken Giles .20 .50
282 Rougned Odor .30 .75
283 Danny Jansen RC .30 .75
284 Jonathan Villar .20 .50
285 Robinson Cano .25 .60
286 Kenley Jansen .25 .60
287 Cedric Mullins RC .60 1.50
288 Jose Abreu .30 .75
289 Franmil Reyes .20 .50
290 Pablo Lopez RC .30 .75
291 Noah Syndergaard .25 .60
292 Matt Carpenter .25 .60
293 Eric Hosmer .25 .60
294 Reynaldo Lopez .25 .60
295 Eduardo Escobar .20 .50
296 Adalberto Mondesi .25 .60
297 Michael Conforto .25 .60
298 Albert Pujols .40 1.00
299 Odubel Herrera .25 .60
300 Aaron Judge .75 2.00
301 Jackie Robinson SP 1.25 3.00
302 Roberto Alomar SP 1.00 2.50
303 Tommy Lasorda SP 1.00 2.50
304 Reggie Jackson SP 1.00 2.50
305 Vladimir Guerrero SP 1.00 2.50
306 Mark McGwire SP 2.00 5.00
307 Roberto Clemente SP 3.00 8.00
308 Ivan Rodriguez SP 1.00 2.50
309 Roger Maris SP 1.25 3.00
310 Pedro Martinez SP 1.00 2.50
311 Hank Aaron SP 2.50 6.00
312 Gary Carter SP 1.00 2.50
313 Don Mattingly SP 2.50 6.00
314 Derek Jeter SP 3.00 8.00
315 George Brett SP 2.50 6.00
316 Bo Jackson SP 1.25 3.00
317 Lou Gehrig SP 2.50 6.00
318 Ty Cobb SP 2.00 5.00
319 Sandy Koufax SP 2.50 6.00
320 Babe Ruth SP 3.00 8.00

2019 Topps Gypsy Queen Bazooka Back
*BAZOOKA: 4X TO 10X BASIC
*BAZOOKA RC: 2.5X TO 6X BASIC RC
*BAZOOKA SP: 2X TO 5X BASIC SP
STATED ODDS 1:57 HOBBY
STATED SP ODDS 1:1687 HOBBY

2019 Topps Gypsy Queen Black and White
*BLACK WHITE: 6X TO 15X BASIC
*BLACK WHITE RC: 4X TO 10X BASIC RC
STATED ODDS 1:47 HOBBY
STATED PRINT RUN 50 SER.#'d SETS

2019 Topps Gypsy Queen GQ Logo Swap
*SWAP: 2.5X TO 6X BASIC
*SWAP RC: 1.5X TO 4X BASIC RC
*SWAP SP: 1.2X TO 3X BASIC SP
STATED ODDS 1:29 HOBBY
STATED SP ODDS 1:1125 HOBBY

2019 Topps Gypsy Queen Green
*GREEN: 1X TO 2.5X BASIC
*GREEN RC: .6X TO 1.5X BASIC RC
RANDOM INSERTS IN RETAIL PACKS

2019 Topps Gypsy Queen Indigo
*INDIGO: 3X TO 8X BASIC
*INDIGO RC: 2X TO 5X BASIC RC
STATED ODDS 1:23 HOBBY
STATED PRINT RUN 250 SER.#'d SETS

2019 Topps Gypsy Queen Missing Nameplate
*NO NAME: 1.5X TO 4X BASIC
*NO NAME RC: 1X TO 2.5X BASIC RC
*NO NAME SP: 1.2X TO 3X BASIC SP
STATED ODDS 1:21 HOBBY
STATED SP ODDS 1:563 HOBBY

2019 Topps Gypsy Queen Purple
*PURPLE: 1X TO 2.5X BASIC
*PURPLE RC: .6X TO 1.5X BASIC RC
RANDOM INSERTS IN RETAIL PACKS

2019 Topps Gypsy Queen 4th of July Variations
STATED ODDS 1:1125 HOBBY
55 Shohei Ohtani 50.00 120.00
76 Marcus Stroman 10.00 25.00
81 Trevor Bauer 20.00 50.00
92 Gleyber Torres 30.00 80.00
99 Christian Yelich 30.00 80.00
114 Chris Davis 8.00 20.00
132 Blake Treinen 8.00 20.00
147 Rafael Devers 15.00 40.00
150 Ronald Acuna Jr. 125.00 300.00
155 Javier Baez 15.00 40.00
166 Jose Altuve 10.00 25.00
173 Scooter Gennett 10.00 25.00
196 Yoan Moncada 12.00 30.00
233 Harrison Bader 15.00 40.00
299 Odubel Herrera 8.00 20.00

2019 Topps Gypsy Queen Jackie Robinson Day Variations
STATED ODDS 1:141 HOBBY
*SWAP: .6X TO 1.5X BASIC
1 Mike Trout 20.00 50.00
3 Khris Davis 4.00 10.00
6 Yadier Molina 5.00 12.00
10 Giancarlo Stanton 4.00 10.00
11 Charlie Blackmon 4.00 10.00
26 Dee Gordon 2.50 6.00
32 Anthony Rizzo 5.00 12.00
53 Freddie Freeman 5.00 12.00
63 Carlos Correa 4.00 10.00
77 Andrew McCutchen 4.00 10.00
82 Whit Merrifield 4.00 10.00
92 Gleyber Torres 8.00 20.00
94 Francisco Lindor 6.00 15.00
100 Kris Bryant 6.00 15.00
105 Bryce Harper 6.00 15.00
127 Sean Doolittle 2.50 6.00
138 Chris Sale 6.00 15.00
153 Trevor Story 4.00 10.00
155 Javier Baez 5.00 12.00
166 Jose Altuve 3.00 8.00
171 Clayton Kershaw 6.00 15.00
177 Zack Godley 2.50 6.00
198 Joey Lucchesi 2.50 6.00
199 Brandon Nimmo 3.00 8.00
210 Paul Goldschmidt 4.00 10.00
271 Trea Turner 3.00 8.00
291 Noah Syndergaard 3.00 8.00
300 Aaron Judge 20.00 50.00

2019 Topps Gypsy Queen Players Weekend Variations
STATED ODDS 1:139 HOBBY
*SWAP: .6X TO 1.5X BASIC
1 Mike Trout 20.00 50.00
18 Cody Bellinger 8.00 20.00
31 Jake Arrieta 3.00 8.00
32 Anthony Rizzo 5.00 12.00
35 Starling Marte 3.00 8.00
37 Eddie Rosario 3.00 8.00
41 Mookie Betts 8.00 20.00
59 Zack Wheeler 4.00 10.00
77 Giancarlo Stanton 6.00 15.00
94 Francisco Lindor 6.00 15.00
118 Starlin Castro 2.50 6.00
166 Jose Altuve 3.00 8.00
173 Scooter Gennett 4.00 10.00
201 Marcus Semien 4.00 10.00
238 Jose Berrios 3.00 8.00
247 Edwin Diaz 3.00 8.00
274 Nicholas Castellanos 6.00 15.00
289 Franmil Reyes 2.50 6.00
297 Michael Conforto 3.00 8.00
300 Aaron Judge 10.00 25.00

2019 Topps Gypsy Queen Autograph Garments
STATED ODDS 1:1245 HOBBY
PRINT RUNS B/WN 10-50 COPIES PER
NO PRICING ON QTY 10
EXCHANGE DEADLINE 2/28/2020
AGAR Anthony Rizzo/25 40.00 100.00
AGCF Clint Frazier/50 15.00 40.00
AGCY Christian Yelich/50 60.00 150.00
AGDG Didi Gregorius/50 50.00 120.00
AGJA Jose Altuve/30 50.00 120.00
AGJD Jacob deGrom/50 60.00 150.00
AGKB Kris Bryant EXCH 125.00 300.00
AGKD Khris Davis/50 40.00 100.00
AGKT Kyle Tucker/50 30.00 80.00
AGLS Luis Severino/50 30.00 80.00
AGOA Ozzie Albies/50 20.00 50.00
AGRH Rickey Henderson/25 60.00 150.00
AGRI Raisel Iglesias/50 12.00 30.00
AGSK Scott Kingery/50 60.00 510.00
AGTM Trey Mancini/50 40.00 100.00
AGVGS Vladimir Guerrero/30 75.00 200.00
AGYM Yadier Molina/40 60.00 150.00

2019 Topps Gypsy Queen Autograph Patch Booklets
STATED ODDS 1:5463 HOBBY
STATED PRINT RUN 20 SER.#'d SETS
EXCHANGE DEADLINE 2/28/2020
GQAPFT Frank Thomas 150.00 400.00
GQAPGS George Springer 75.00 200.00
GQAPJB Jose Berrios 75.00 200.00
GQAPJD Jacob deGrom 125.00 300.00
GQAPKT Kyle Tucker 125.00 300.00
GQAPLS Luis Severino 75.00 200.00
GQAPMT Mike Trout 400.00 800.00
GQAPWM Whit Merrifield 75.00 200.00

2019 Topps Gypsy Queen Autographs
STATED ODDS 1:16 HOBBY
EXCHANGE DEADLINE 2/28/2020
*INDIGO/150: .5X TO 1.2X BASIC
*SWAP/99: .5X TO 1.2X BASIC
GQAAJ Aaron Judge 100.00 250.00
GQAAM Andrew McCutchen 20.00 50.00
GQAAME Austin Meadows 5.00 12.00
GQABK Brad Keller 3.00 8.00
GQABN Brandon Nimmo 6.00 15.00
GQABW Bryse Wilson 4.00 10.00
GQACA Chance Adams 3.00 8.00
GQACB Corbin Burnes 15.00 40.00
GQACH Cesar Hernandez 3.00 8.00
GQACK Carson Kelly 3.00 8.00
GQACM Colin Moran 3.00 8.00
GQACMU Cedric Mullins 10.00 25.00
GQACS Carlos Santana 4.00 10.00
GQACST Christin Stewart 4.00 10.00
GQACY Christian Yelich 40.00 100.00
GQADB David Bote 4.00 10.00
GQADC Dylan Cozens 3.00 8.00
GQADJ Danny Jansen 8.00 20.00
GQADM Daniel Mengden 3.00 8.00
GQAER Eddie Rosario 6.00 15.00
GQAFA Francisco Arcia 5.00 12.00
GQAFL Francisco Lindor 15.00 40.00
GQAGS George Springer 10.00 25.00
GQAJA Jose Altuve 20.00 50.00
GQAJB Jake Bauers 5.00 12.00
GQAJD Jacob deGrom 20.00 50.00
GQAJM Jose Martinez 4.00 10.00
GQAJS Juan Soto 50.00 120.00
GQAKA Kolby Allard 5.00 12.00
GQAKB Kris Bryant EXCH 75.00 200.00
GQAKD Khris Davis 5.00 12.00
GQAKT Kyle Tucker 12.00 30.00
GQALU Luis Urias 5.00 12.00
GQAMC Matt Chapman 10.00 25.00
GQAMF Mike Foltynewicz 5.00 12.00
GQAMH Mitch Haniger 4.00 10.00
GQAMK Michael Kopech 8.00 20.00
GQAMM Max Muncy 6.00 15.00
GQAMO Matt Olson 5.00 12.00
GQAMR Mariano Rivera 100.00 250.00
GQAMT Mike Trout 300.00 600.00
GQARB Ryan Borucki 3.00 8.00
GQARI Raisel Iglesias 3.00 8.00
GQASD Steven Duggar 4.00 10.00
GQASK Sandy Koufax 150.00 400.00
GQASO Shohei Ohtani 200.00 400.00
GQATH Torii Hunter 10.00 25.00
GQATS Trevor Story 10.00 25.00
GQAVGS Vladimir Guerrero 25.00 60.00
GQAWA Willy Adames 3.00 8.00
GQAWM Whit Merrifield 6.00 15.00
GQAYK Yusei Kikuchi EXCH 12.00 30.00

2019 Topps Gypsy Queen Autographs Bazooka Back
*BAZOOKA: .75X TO 2X BASIC
STATED ODDS 1:826 HOBBY
STATED PRINT RUN 25 SER.#'d SETS
EXCHANGE DEADLINE 2/28/2020
GQAAJ Aaron Judge 125.00 300.00
GQAKB Kris Bryant EXCH 100.00 250.00

2019 Topps Gypsy Queen Autographs Black and White
*BW: .6X TO 1.5X BASIC
STATED ODDS 1:302 HOBBY
STATED PRINT RUN 50 SER.#'d SETS
EXCHANGE DEADLINE 2/28/2020

2019 Topps Gypsy Queen Autographs Jackie Robinson Day Variations
STATED ODDS 1:1281 HOBBY

PRINT RUNS B/WN 10-99 COPIES PER
NO PRICING ON QTY 10
EXCHANGE DEADLINE 2/28/2020
*BW/42: .5X TO 1.2X BASIC
3 Khris Davis/99 15.00 40.00
6 Yadier Molina/50 60.00 150.00
32 Anthony Rizzo/25 60.00 150.00
53 Freddie Freeman/50 50.00 120.00
77 Andrew McCutchen/40 50.00 120.00
82 Whit Merrifield/99 12.00 30.00
94 Francisco Lindor/50 30.00 80.00
100 Kris Bryant EXCH 100.00 250.00
127 Sean Doolittle/99 10.00 25.00
153 Trevor Story/99 10.00 25.00
155 Javier Baez/45 40.00 100.00
166 Jose Altuve/40 25.00 60.00
291 Noah Syndergaard
300 Aaron Judge

2019 Topps Gypsy Queen Bases Around the League Autographs
STATED ODDS 1:6121 HOBBY
STATED PRINT RUN 20 SER.#'d SETS
EXCHANGE DEADLINE 2/28/2020
BALBB Byron Buxton 60.00 150.00
BALCS Carlos Santana 75.00 200.00
BALER Eddie Rosario 75.00 200.00
BALI Ichiro 400.00 800.00
BALJD Jacob deGrom 150.00 400.00

2019 Topps Gypsy Queen Chrome Box Topper Autographs
STATED ODDS 1:75 HOBBY BOXES
STATED PRINT RUN 25 SER.#'d SETS
EXCHANGE DEADLINE 2/28/2020
GQCAAM Andrew McCutchen 50.00 120.00
GQCAAR Anthony Rizzo 50.00 120.00
GQCABH Bryce Harper 150.00 400.00
GQCABN Brandon Nimmo 20.00 50.00
GQCACB Corbin Burnes 50.00 120.00
GQCAFL Francisco Lindor 50.00 120.00
GQCAJA Jose Altuve 50.00 120.00
GQCAJD Jacob deGrom 60.00 150.00
GQCAKB Kris Bryant EXCH 100.00 250.00
GQCAKT Kyle Tucker 75.00 200.00
GQCAMH Mitch Haniger 30.00 80.00
GQCAPD Paul DeJong 25.00 60.00
GQCATH Torii Hunter 30.00 80.00
GQCATS Trevor Story 25.00 60.00
GQCAVGS Vladimir Guerrero 40.00 100.00

2019 Topps Gypsy Queen Chrome Box Toppers
*INDIGO: 1X TO 2.5X BASIC
1 Mike Trout 8.00 20.00
2 Jesus Aguilar 1.25 3.00
3 Khris Davis 1.50 4.00
4 Kyle Schwarber 1.50 4.00
5 Yadier Molina 2.00 5.00
11 Charlie Blackmon 1.50 4.00
18 Cody Bellinger 3.00 8.00
20 Aaron Nola 1.25 3.00
23 Xander Bogaerts 1.50 4.00
29 Dawel Lugo 1.50 4.00
30 Jean Segura 1.50 4.00
32 Anthony Rizzo 2.00 5.00
33 Corey Kluber 1.25 3.00
34 Lewis Brinson 1.00 2.50
36 Justin Upton 1.25 3.00
37 Eddie Rosario 1.25 3.00
41 Mookie Betts 3.00 8.00
45 Paul DeJong 1.50 4.00
48 Josh Bell 1.25 3.00
50 Shohei Ohtani 2.50 6.00
53 Freddie Freeman 2.00 5.00
57 Juan Soto 5.00 12.00
62 Zack Greinke 1.50 4.00
63 Carlos Correa 1.50 4.00
66 Miguel Cabrera 1.50 4.00
69 Maikel Franco 1.25 3.00
72 Eugenio Suarez 1.25 3.00
73 Carlos Santana 1.25 3.00
76 Marcus Stroman 1.25 3.00
80 Ronald Guzman 1.00 2.50
82 Whit Merrifield 1.50 4.00
92 Gleyber Torres 3.00 8.00
94 Francisco Lindor 1.50 4.00
100 Kris Bryant 2.00 5.00
101 Blake Snell 1.25 3.00
102 Rhys Hoskins 2.00 5.00
103 Miguel Andujar 1.50 4.00
104 Ozzie Albies 1.50 4.00
107 Max Kepler 1.25 3.00
110 Salvador Perez 1.25 3.00
111 Justin Verlander 1.50 4.00
118 Starlin Castro 1.00 2.50
120 Ramon Laureano 2.00 5.00
121 Joey Votto 1.50 4.00
122 J.D. Martinez 1.50 4.00
124 Joey Gallo 1.25 3.00
126 Wil Myers 1.25 3.00
130 Michael Kopech 3.00 8.00
133 George Springer 1.25 3.00
136 Lorenzo Cain 1.00 2.50
143 Mitch Haniger 1.25 3.00
145 Ryan O'Hearn 1.00 2.50
147 Rafael Devers 2.00 5.00
148 Trey Mancini 1.25 3.00
149 Gregory Polanco 1.25 3.00
150 Ronald Acuna Jr. 8.00 20.00
155 Javier Baez 2.00 5.00
158 Luis Urias 1.50 4.00
163 Trevor Story 1.50 4.00
166 Jose Altuve 1.25 3.00
168 Kevin Pillar 1.00 2.50
171 Clayton Kershaw 2.50 6.00
176 Brandon Nimmo 1.25 3.00
189 Edwin Encarnacion 1.50 4.00
196 Yoan Moncada 1.50 4.00
200 Jacob deGrom 3.00 8.00
203 James Paxton 1.25 3.00
204 Josh Hader 1.25 3.00
208 Dansby Swanson 1.50 4.00
210 Paul Goldschmidt 1.50 4.00
213 Nolan Arenado 2.50 6.00
214 David Peralta 1.00 2.50
215 Chris Archer 1.00 2.50
221 Justin Turner 1.50 4.00
226 Billy Hamilton 1.25 3.00
227 Jose Ramirez 1.25 3.00
232 Dylan Bundy 1.25 3.00
235 Luis Severino 1.25 3.00
238 Jose Berrios 1.25 3.00
248 Chris Shaw 1.00 2.50
249 Jake Bauers 1.50 4.00
250 Max Scherzer 1.50 4.00
256 Brian Anderson 1.00 2.50
260 Matt Chapman 1.50 4.00
264 Evan Longoria 1.25 3.00
265 Brandon Crawford 1.25 3.00
266 Jose Martinez 1.00 2.50
268 Willy Adames 1.00 2.50
271 Trea Turner 1.25 3.00
274 Nicholas Castellanos 1.50 4.00
280 Matt Olson 1.50 4.00
282 Rougned Odor 1.25 3.00
283 Danny Jansen 1.00 2.50
286 Kenley Jansen 1.25 3.00
287 Cedric Mullins 2.00 5.00
288 Jose Abreu 1.50 4.00
291 Noah Syndergaard 1.25 3.00
292 Matt Carpenter 1.50 4.00
293 Eric Hosmer 1.25 3.00
300 Aaron Judge 4.00 10.00

2019 Topps Gypsy Queen Chrome Box Toppers Gold Refractors
*GOLD: 1.5X TO 4X BASIC
STATED ODDS 1:6 HOBBY BOXES
STATED PRINT RUN 50 SER.#'d SETS
1 Mike Trout 50.00 120.00

2019 Topps Gypsy Queen Fortune Teller Mini
STATED ODDS 1:6 HOBBY
*INDIGO/250: 1X TO 2.5X BASIC
GREEN/99: 2X TO 5X BASIC
FTMAJ Aaron Judge 1.25 3.00
FTMAN Aaron Nola .40 1.00
FTMBS Blake Snell .40 1.00
FTMCY Christian Yelich .60 1.50
FTMED Edwin Diaz .40 1.00
FTMFF Freddie Freeman .60 1.50
FTMGT Gleyber Torres 1.00 2.50
FTMJA Jose Altuve .40 1.00
FTMJB Javier Baez .60 1.50
FTMJD Jacob deGrom 1.00 2.50
FTMJM J.D. Martinez .50 1.25
FTMJS Juan Soto 1.50 4.00
FTMJV Justin Verlander .50 1.25
FTMKB Kris Bryant .60 1.50
FTMKD Khris Davis .50 1.25
FTMKT Kyle Tucker .75 2.00
FTMLU Luis Urias .50 1.25
FTMMS Max Scherzer .50 1.25
FTMNA Nolan Arenado .75 2.00
FTMRAJ Ronald Acuna Jr. 2.50 6.00

2019 Topps Gypsy Queen Fortune Teller Mini Autographs
STATED ODDS 1:1691 HOBBY
PRINT RUNS B/WN 10-50 COPIES PER
NO PRICING ON QTY 10
EXCHANGE DEADLINE 2/28/2020
FTMAAM Andrew McCutchen/20 40.00 100.00
FTMAAME Austin Meadows/50 15.00 40.00
FTMABN Brandon Nimmo/50 12.00 30.00
FTMACS Carlos Santana/50 15.00 40.00
FTMAFL Francisco Lindor/40 30.00 80.00
FTMAGS George Springer/40 20.00 50.00
FTMAJB Jake Bauers/50 15.00 40.00
FTMAJS Juan Soto/50 75.00 200.00
FTMAKB Kris Bryant EXCH 75.00 200.00
FTMAMA Miguel Andujar/50 20.00 50.00
FTMAPD Paul DeJong/50 15.00 40.00
FTMATS Trevor Story/50 15.00 40.00
FTMAWA Willy Adames/50 10.00 25.00

2019 Topps Gypsy Queen Mini Rookie Autographs
STATED ODDS 1:999 HOBBY
STATED PRINT RUN 99 SER.#'d SETS
EXCHANGE DEADLINE 2/28/2020
*BW/50: .5X TO 1.2X BASIC
MRABK Brad Keller 12.00 30.00
MRABW Bryse Wilson 15.00 40.00
MRACA Chance Adams 8.00 20.00
MRACB Corbin Burnes 12.00 30.00
MRACM Cedric Mullins 10.00 25.00
MRADJ Danny Jansen 4.00 10.00
MRAKA Kolby Allard 6.00 15.00
MRAKT Kyle Tucker 25.00 60.00
MRALU Luis Urias 15.00 40.00
MRAMK Michael Kopech 10.00 25.00

2019 Topps Gypsy Queen Mystery Redemption Autographs
RANDOM INSERTS IN PACKS
EXCHANGE DEADLINE 2/28/2020
*INDIGO/150: .5X TO 1.2X BASIC
*SWAP/99: .6X TO 1.5X BASIC
*BW/50: .75X TO 2X BASIC
*BAZOOKA/25: 1X TO 2.5X BASIC
NNO1 Mystery EXCH A 75.00 200.00
NNO2 Mystery EXCH B 60.00 150.00

2019 Topps Gypsy Queen Tarot of the Diamond
STATED ODDS 1:8 HOBBY
*INDIGO/250: 1X TO 2.5X BASIC
*GREEN/99: 2X TO 5X BASIC
1 Shohei Ohtani .75 2.00
2 Edwin Encarnacion .50 1.25
3 Xander Bogaerts .50 1.25
4 Craig Kimbrel .40 1.00
5 Mike Trout 2.50 6.00
6 J.D. Martinez .50 1.25
7 Nolan Arenado .75 2.00
8 Giancarlo Stanton .50 1.25
9 Clayton Kershaw .75 2.00
10 Jacob deGrom 1.00 2.50
11 Yasiel Puig .50 1.25
12 Ozzie Albies .50 1.25
13 Edwin Diaz .40 1.00
14 Bryce Harper .75 2.00
15 Mookie Betts 1.00 2.50
16 Khris Davis .50 1.25
17 Shohei Ohtani .75 2.00
18 Ronald Acuna Jr. 2.50 6.00
19 Jose Altuve .40 1.00
20 Corey Kluber .40 1.00
21 Jesus Aguilar .40 1.00
22 Aaron Judge 1.25 3.00

2020 Topps Gypsy Queen
SP ODDS 1:24 HOBBY
1 Mookie Betts .60 1.50
2 J.T. Realmuto .30 .75
3 Ramon Laureano .25 .60
4 Matt Olson .30 .75
5 Dom Nunez RC .40 1.00
6 Brandon Woodruff .30 .75
7 Zack Greinke .30 .75
8 Garrett Hampson .20 .50
9 Harold Ramirez .20 .50
10 Rangel Ravelo RC .40 1.00
11 Cedric Mullins .25 .60
12 Max Kepler .25 .60
13 Howie Kendrick .20 .50
14 John Means .30 .75
15 Justin Smoak .20 .50
16 Michael Brantley .25 .60
17 Bo Bichette RC 2.50 6.00
18 Asdrubal Cabrera .25 .60
19 Brock Holt .20 .50
20 Yusei Kikuchi .25 .60
21 Clayton Kershaw .50 1.25
22 Victor Robles .40 1.00
23 Trent Grisham RC 1.25 3.00
24 Michael Conforto .25 .60
25 Christian Yelich .40 1.00
26 Adrian Morejon RC .30 .75
27 Joey Votto .30 .75
28 Brock Burke RC .30 .75
29 Willson Contreras .30 .75
30 Carter Kieboom .25 .60
31 Carlos Santana .25 .60
32 Dawel Lugo .20 .50
33 Tom Eshelman RC .40 1.00
34 Adbert Alzolay RC .40 1.00
35 Aristides Aquino RC .75 2.00
36 Hanser Alberto .20 .50
37 Dario Agrazal RC .40 1.00
38 Kris Bryant .40 1.00
39 Yolmer Sanchez .20 .50
40 Danny Jansen .20 .50
41 Blake Snell .25 .60
42 Gio Urshela .30 .75
43 Jacob deGrom .60 1.50
44 Alex Colome .20 .50
45 Didi Gregorius .25 .60
46 Willians Astudillo .20 .50
47 Paul Goldschmidt .30 .75
48 Vladimir Guerrero Jr. .50 1.25
49 Brandon Crawford .25 .60
50 Aaron Judge .75 2.00
51 Austin Dean .20 .50
52 Brendan McKay RC .50 1.25
53 Harrison Bader .25 .60
54 Jeff McNeil .25 .60
55 Trea Turner .25 .60
56 Giancarlo Stanton .30 .75
57 Jose Altuve .25 .60
58 Ty France .30 .75
59 Willie Calhoun .20 .50
60 Joe Jimenez .20 .50
61 Josh Bell .25 .60
62 Dylan Cease RC .50 1.25
63 Austin Nola RC .50 1.25
64 Mitch Haniger .25 .60
65 Pete Alonso .75 2.00
66 Kirby Yates .20 .50
67 David Price .25 .60
68 Randy Arozarena RC 2.50 6.00
69 Max Fried .30 .75
70 Bobby Bradley RC .30 .75
71 Jose Berrios .25 .60
72 Kyle Hendricks .30 .75
73 Jorge Alfaro .20 .50
74 T.J. Zeuch RC .30 .75
75 David Dahl .20 .50
76 Bryce Harper .50 1.25
77 Josh Staumont RC .30 .75
78 A.J. Minter .25 .60
79 Jack Flaherty .30 .75
80 Tim Lopes RC .40 1.00
81 David Peralta .20 .50
82 Matt Thaiss RC .40 1.00
83 Noah Syndergaard .25 .60
84 Eric Hosmer .25 .60
85 Eduardo Rodriguez .20 .50
86 Anthony Rizzo .40 1.00
87 Junior Fernandez RC .30 .75
88 Wilson Ramos .20 .50
89 Jake Arrieta .25 .60
90 Brandon Belt .25 .60
91 Seth Brown RC .30 .75
92 Justin Turner .30 .75
93 Gerrit Cole .50 1.25
94 Eloy Jimenez .60 1.50
95 Jorge Polanco .25 .60
96 Xander Bogaerts .30 .75
97 Kyle Seager .20 .50
98 Nick Solak RC 1.25 3.00
99 Matthew Boyd .20 .50
100 Gleyber Torres .60 1.50
101 Sean Murphy RC .50 1.25
102 Mike Soroka .30 .75
103 Charlie Blackmon .30 .75
104 Fernando Tatis Jr. 1.50 4.00
105 Eugenio Suarez .25 .60
106 Meibrys Viloria .20 .50
107 Nelson Cruz .30 .75
108 Logan Webb RC .50 1.25
109 Andrelton Simmons .20 .50
110 Brian Anderson .20 .50
111 Trevor Story .30 .75
112 Jonathan Hernandez RC .30 .75
113 A.J. Puk RC .50 1.25
114 David Fletcher .30 .75
115 Rhys Hoskins .40 1.00
116 Brendan Rodgers .30 .75
117 Andrew Benintendi .30 .75
118 Ender Inciarte .20 .50
119 Robbie Ray .20 .50
120 Lourdes Gurriel Jr. .25 .60
121 Chance Sisco .20 .50
122 Luis Robert RC 2.50 6.00
123 Logan Allen RC .30 .75
124 Mark Melancon .20 .50
125 Tyler Alexander .30 .75
126 Amed Rosario .25 .60
127 Jose Rodriguez RC .30 .75
128 Zac Gallen RC .75 2.00
129 Tommy Pham .20 .50
130 Kevin Newman .30 .75
131 Colin Moran .20 .50
132 Yoan Moncada .30 .75
133 Kole Calhoun .20 .50
134 Tim Anderson .30 .75
135 Corey Seager .30 .75
136 Rafael Devers .40 1.00
137 Yordan Alvarez RC 3.00 8.00
138 Jose Urena .20 .50
139 Eduardo Escobar .20 .50
140 Eric Thames .20 .50
141 Lorenzo Cain .20 .50
142 Luis Severino .25 .60
143 Robert Dugger RC .30 .75
144 Justin Dunn RC .40 1.00
145 Mitch Garver .20 .50
146 Anthony Santander .20 .50
147 Bubba Starling RC .60 1.50
148 Nomar Mazara .20 .50
149 Shin-Soo Choo .25 .60
150 Cody Bellinger .60 1.50
151 Michael Lorenzen .20 .50
152 Gary Sanchez .30 .75
153 Austin Hays .30 .75
154 Nick Williams .20 .50
155 Dustin May RC 1.00 2.50
156 Rougned Odor .25 .60
157 Yuli Gurriel .25 .60
158 Walker Buehler .40 1.00
159 Carlos Correa .30 .75
160 Mike Minor .20 .50
161 Kean Wong RC .50 1.25
162 Anthony Kay RC .30 .75
163 Patrick Corbin .25 .60
164 Shane Bieber .30 .75
165 Jose Abreu .30 .75
166 Max Scherzer .30 .75
167 Bryan Reynolds .25 .60
168 Jake Fraley RC .40 1.00
169 Adam Ottavino .25 .60
170 Kyle Schwarber .30 .75
171 Yu Chang RC .50 1.25
172 Jon Lester .25 .60
173 Jordan Yamamoto RC .30 .75
174 Gavin Lux RC 1.50 4.00
175 Hyun-Jin Ryu .25 .60
176 Kevin Kiermaier .25 .60
177 James Paxton .25 .60
178 Juan Soto 1.00 2.50
179 Nicky Lopez .20 .50
180 Keston Hiura .40 1.00
181 Jean Segura .25 .60
182 Brandon Dixon .20 .50
183 Yasmani Grandal .20 .50
184 Miles Mikolas .20 .50
185 Jose Iglesias .25 .60
186 Evan Longoria .25 .60
187 Ronald Acuna Jr. 1.25 3.00
188 Matt Chapman .30 .75
189 Tyler Glasnow .30 .75
190 Eddie Rosario .25 .60
191 Victor Reyes .20 .50
192 Ryan O'Hearn .20 .50
193 Trevor Williams .20 .50
194 Jaylin Davis RC .50 1.25
195 J.D. Martinez .30 .75
196 Mitch Keller .30 .75
197 Hunter Harvey RC .50 1.25
198 Alex Young RC .30 .75
199 Adam Haseley .25 .60
200 Alex Bregman .30 .75
201 Nico Hoerner RC 1.25 3.00
202 Max Muncy .25 .60
203 Luis Arraez .40 1.00
204 Albert Pujols .40 1.00
205 Austin Meadows .30 .75
206 Christian Vazquez .25 .60
207 Paul DeJong .30 .75
208 Adalberto Mondesi .25 .60
209 J.D. Davis .20 .50
210 Khris Davis .30 .75
211 Austin Riley .40 1.00
212 Marcus Semien .30 .75
213 Aroldis Chapman .30 .75
214 Danny Duffy .20 .50
215 Anthony Rendon .30 .75
216 Willy Adames .25 .60
217 Sheldon Neuse RC .40 1.00
218 Starling Marte .25 .60
219 Will Smith .30 .75
220 James Marvel RC .30 .75
221 Dansby Swanson .30 .75
222 Michael Chavis .25 .60
223 Cavan Biggio .40 1.00
224 Trey Mancini .30 .75
225 Jake Rogers RC .30 .75
226 Kyle Lewis RC 2.50 6.00
227 Oscar Mercado .30 .75
228 Francisco Lindor .30 .75
229 Emmanuel Clase RC .50 1.25
230 Francisco Mejia .20 .50
231 Aaron Nola .25 .60
232 Aaron Civale RC .60 1.50
233 Javier Baez .40 1.00
234 Michel Baez RC .30 .75
235 Ryan McMahon .20 .50
236 Derek Dietrich .25 .60
237 Sandy Alcantara .20 .50
238 Ozzie Albies .30 .75
239 Nick Senzel .30 .75
240 Scott Kingery .25 .60
241 Ryan Braun .25 .60
242 Hunter Dozier .20 .50
243 Buster Posey .40 1.00
244 Shed Long .25 .60
245 Marcus Stroman .25 .60
246 Brusdar Graterol RC .50 1.25
247 Ronald Guzman .20 .50
248 Steven Matz .20 .50
249 Luis Castillo .25 .60
250 Justin Verlander .30 .75
251 Jose Ramirez .25 .60
252 Will Smith .20 .50
253 Rowdy Tellez .25 .60
254 Chris Archer .20 .50
255 Luke Weaver .20 .50
256 Christian Walker .25 .60
257 Willi Castro RC .30 .75
258 Mike Yastrzemski .50 1.25
259 Starlin Castro .20 .50
260 Zack Collins RC .40 1.00
261 Shohei Ohtani .50 1.25
262 Andres Munoz RC .50 1.25
263 Dwight Smith Jr. .30 .75
264 Trevor Bauer .40 1.00
265 Sam Hilliard RC .50 1.25
266 Miguel Cabrera .30 .75
267 Peter Lambert .25 .60
268 Mauricio Dubon RC .40 1.00
269 Jorge Soler .30 .75
270 Franmil Reyes .20 .50
271 Michael Brosseau RC .60 1.50
272 Raisel Iglesias .20 .50
273 Yadier Molina .40 1.00
274 Andrew Heaney .20 .50
275 Jeff Samardzija .20 .50
276 George Springer .25 .60
277 Lucas Giolito .25 .60
278 DJ LeMahieu .30 .75
279 Randal Grichuk .20 .50
280 Travis d'Arnaud .25 .60
281 Whit Merrifield .30 .75
282 Aaron Nola .25 .60
283 Zach Davies .20 .50
284 Robel Garcia RC .30 .75
285 Stephen Strasburg .30 .75
286 Domingo Leyba RC .40 1.00
287 Jesus Luzardo RC .60 1.50
288 Josh Hader .25 .60
289 Byron Buxton .30 .75
290 Tommy La Stella .20 .50
291 Tommy Edman .30 .75
292 Manny Machado .30 .75
293 Isan Diaz RC .50 1.25
294 Nolan Arenado .50 1.25
295 Ketel Marte .25 .60
296 Archie Bradley .20 .50
297 Travis Demeritte RC .50 1.25
298 Freddie Freeman .40 1.00
299 Sonny Gray .25 .60
300 Mike Trout 1.50 4.00
301 Babe Ruth SP 3.00 8.00
302 Mariano Rivera SP 1.50 4.00
303 Deion Sanders SP 1.00 2.50
304 Reggie Jackson SP 1.00 2.50
305 Tony Gwynn SP 1.25 3.00
306 Carl Yastrzemski SP 2.00 5.00
307 Mike Schmidt SP 2.00 5.00
308 Roberto Clemente SP 3.00 8.00
309 Johnny Bench SP 1.25 3.00
310 Vladimir Guerrero SP 1.00 2.50
311 Chipper Jones SP 1.25 3.00
312 Sammy Sosa SP 1.25 3.00
313 Pedro Martinez SP 1.00 2.50
314 Ted Williams SP 2.50 6.00
315 Sandy Koufax SP 2.50 6.00
316 Rickey Henderson SP 1.25 3.00
317 Cal Ripken Jr. SP 4.00 10.00
318 Ken Griffey Jr. SP 2.50 6.00
319 Honus Wagner SP 1.25 3.00
320 Jackie Robinson SP 1.25 3.00

2020 Topps Gypsy Queen Armed Forces Day Variations
STATED ODDS 1:1210 HOBBY
1 Mookie Betts 30.00 80.00
25 Christian Yelich 25.00 60.00
31 Carlos Santana 10.00 25.00
71 Jose Berrios 15.00 40.00
76 Bryce Harper 30.00 80.00
86 Anthony Rizzo 25.00 60.00
132 Yoan Moncada 12.00 30.00
136 Rafael Devers 25.00 60.00
188 Matt Chapman 20.00 50.00
190 Eddie Rosario 20.00 50.00
200 Alex Bregman 15.00 40.00
238 Ozzie Albies 25.00 60.00
278 DJ LeMahieu 25.00 60.00
294 Nolan Arenado 20.00 50.00
298 Freddie Freeman 25.00 60.00

2020 Topps Gypsy Queen Bazooka Back
*BAZOOKA: 4X TO 10X BASIC
*BAZOOKA RC: 2.5X TO 6X BASIC RC
*BAZOOKA SP: 8X TO 20X BASIC SP
STATED ODDS 1:61 HOBBY
STATED SP ODDS 1:1817 HOBBY
122 Luis Robert 75.00 200.00
300 Mike Trout 50.00 120.00

2020 Topps Gypsy Queen Black and White
*BLACK WHITE: 6X TO 15X BASIC
*BLACK WHITE RC: 4X TO 10X BASIC RC
STATED ODDS 1:50 HOBBY
STATED PRINT RUN 50 SER.#'d SETS
122 Luis Robert 100.00 250.00
300 Mike Trout 60.00 150.00

2020 Topps Gypsy Queen Blue
*BLUE: 5X TO 12X BASIC
*BLUE RC: 3X TO 8X BASIC RC
*BLUE SP: 1.5X TO 4X BASIC RC
STATED ODDS 1:41 HOBBY
STATED PRINT RUN 150 SER.#'d SETS
122 Luis Robert 75.00 200.00

2020 Topps Gypsy Queen GQ Logo Swap
*SWAP: 2.5X TO 6X BASIC
*SWAP RC: 1.5X TO 4X BASIC RC
*SWAP SP: 1.2X TO 3X BASIC SP
STATED ODDS 1:31 HOBBY
STATED SP ODDS 1:1210 HOBBY
122 Luis Robert 50.00 120.00

2020 Topps Gypsy Queen Green
*GREEN: 1X TO 2.5X BASIC
*GREEN RC: .6X TO 1.5X BASIC RC
FIVE PER BLASTER BOX

2020 Topps Gypsy Queen Indigo
*INDIGO: 2.5X TO 6X BASIC
*INDIGO RC: 1.5X TO 4X BASIC RC
STATED ODDS 1:25 HOBBY
STATED PRINT RUN 250 SER.#'d SETS
122 Luis Robert 50.00 120.00

2020 Topps Gypsy Queen Jackie Robinson Day Variations
STATED ODDS 1:152 HOBBY
*SWAP: .75X TO 2X BASIC
21 Clayton Kershaw 5.00 12.00
25 Christian Yelich 4.00 10.00
29 Willson Contreras 3.00 8.00
38 Kris Bryant 4.00 10.00
46 Willians Astudillo 2.00 5.00
65 Pete Alonso 8.00 20.00
83 Noah Syndergaard 2.50 6.00
96 Xander Bogaerts 3.00 8.00
104 Fernando Tatis Jr. 15.00 40.00
115 Rhys Hoskins 4.00 10.00
134 Tim Anderson 3.00 8.00
136 Rafael Devers 4.00 10.00
195 J.D. Martinez 3.00 8.00
200 Alex Bregman 3.00 8.00
202 Max Muncy 2.50 6.00
233 Javier Baez 4.00 10.00
263 Dwight Smith Jr. 2.00 5.00
264 Trevor Bauer 4.00 10.00
282 Aaron Nola 2.50 6.00
292 Manny Machado 3.00 8.00

2020 Topps Gypsy Queen Missing Nameplate
*NO NAME: 1.5X TO 4X BASIC
*NO NAME RC: 1X TO 2.5X BASIC RC
*NO NAME SP: 2X TO 5X BASIC SP
STATED ODDS 1:23 HOBBY
STATED SP ODDS 1:605 HOBBY
122 Luis Robert 30.00 80.00

2020 Topps Gypsy Queen Players Weekend Variations
STATED ODDS 1:150 HOBBY
*SWAP: .75X TO 2X BASIC
9 Harold Ramirez 2.00 5.00
14 John Means 3.00 8.00
21 Clayton Kershaw 5.00 12.00
25 Christian Yelich 4.00 10.00
35 Aristides Aquino 5.00 12.00
38 Kris Bryant 4.00 10.00
43 Jacob deGrom 6.00 15.00
48 Vladimir Guerrero Jr. 5.00 12.00
50 Aaron Judge 12.00 30.00
62 Dylan Cease 3.00 8.00
66 Kirby Yates 2.00 5.00
71 Jose Berrios 2.50 6.00
96 Xander Bogaerts 3.00 8.00
97 Kyle Seager 2.00 5.00
98 Nick Solak 8.00 20.00
103 Charlie Blackmon 3.00 8.00
167 Bryan Reynolds 2.50 6.00
176 Kevin Kiermaier 2.50 6.00
178 Juan Soto 10.00 25.00
187 Ronald Acuna Jr. 12.00 30.00
207 Paul DeJong 3.00 8.00
212 Marcus Semien 3.00 8.00
227 Oscar Mercado 3.00 8.00
242 Hunter Dozier 3.00 8.00
258 Mike Yastrzemski 5.00 12.00
266 Miguel Cabrera 3.00 8.00
276 George Springer 2.50 6.00
282 Aaron Nola 2.50 6.00
295 Ketel Marte 2.50 6.00
300 Mike Trout 30.00 80.00

2020 Topps Gypsy Queen Silver
*SILVER: 1X TO 2.5X BASIC
*SILVER RC: .6X TO 1.5X BASIC RC
TWELVE PER MONSTER BOX

2020 Topps Gypsy Queen Autograph Garments
STATED ODDS 1:1930 HOBBY
PRINT RUNS B/WN 10-50 COPIES PER
NO PRICING ON QTY 10
EXCHANGE DEADLINE 2/29/2022
AGAN Aaron Nola/50 15.00 40.00
AGCA Chance Adams/50 12.00 30.00
AGCP Chris Paddack/50 20.00 50.00
AGCY Christian Yelich/40 50.00 120.00
AGFTJ Fernando Tatis Jr./50 125.00 300.00
AGGT Gleyber Torres/40 75.00 200.00
AGGU Gio Urshela/50 20.00 50.00
AGJD Jon Duplantier/50 12.00 30.00
AGKB Kris Bryant/25 75.00 200.00
AGKH Keston Hiura/50 25.00 60.00
AGMC Michael Chavis/50 15.00 40.00
AGMM Max Muncy/50 15.00 40.00
AGMS Max Scherzer/40 60.00 150.00
AGRAJ Ronald Acuna Jr./40 100.00 250.00
AGRH Rhys Hoskins/50 30.00 80.00
AGSO Shohei Ohtani EXCH 100.00 250.00
AGVGJ Vladimir Guerrero Jr./50 50.00 120.00
AGWC Willson Contreras/50 20.00 50.00
AGYA Yordan Alvarez/50 75.00 200.00

2020 Topps Gypsy Queen Autograph Patch Booklets
STATED ODDS 1:8135 HOBBY
PRINT RUNS B/WN 10-20 COPIES PER
NO PRICING ON QTY 10
EXCHANGE DEADLINE 2/29/2022
GQAPAJ Aaron Judge/10
GQAPFTJ Fernando Tatis Jr./20 300.00 800.00
GQAPGH Garrett Hampson/20 40.00 100.00
GQAPJDM J.D. Martinez/20 60.00 150.00
GQAPJF Jack Flaherty/20 125.00 300.00
GQAPNA Nolan Arenado/20 150.00 400.00
GQAPRH Rickey Henderson
GQAPSO Shohei Ohtani EXCH 250.00 600.00
GQAPWA Willians Astudillo/20 40.00 100.00
GQAPWM Whit Merrifield 80.00 200.00
GQAPYA Yordan Alvarez 250.00 600.00

2020 Topps Gypsy Queen Autographs
STATED ODDS 1:15 HOBBY
EXCHANGE DEADLINE 2/29/2020
GQAAA Adbert Alzolay 3.00 8.00
GQAAAQ Aristides Aquino 20.00 50.00
GQAAC Aaron Civale 5.00 12.00
GQAAJ Aaron Judge 100.00 250.00
GQAAM Austin Meadows 5.00 12.00
GQAAP A.J. Puk 6.00 15.00
GQAAR Austin Riley 15.00 40.00
GQAAY Alex Young 2.50 6.00
GQABB Bobby Bradley 4.00 10.00
GQABBI Bo Bichette 50.00 120.00
GQABM Brendan McKay 10.00 25.00
GQACD Corey Dickerson 3.00 8.00
GQACJ Carter Kieboom 3.00 8.00
GQACM Charlie Morton 4.00 10.00
GQACP Chris Paddack 6.00 15.00
GQACY Christian Yelich 30.00 80.00
GQADC Dylan Cease 5.00 12.00
GQADP David Peralta 3.00 8.00
GQADSJ Dwight Smith Jr. 3.00 8.00
GQAGL Gavin Lux 30.00 80.00
GQAGT Gleyber Torres 50.00 120.00
GQAGU Gio Urshela 12.00 30.00
GQAID Isan Diaz 5.00 12.00
GQAJDM J.D. Martinez 12.00 30.00
GQAJF Jack Flaherty 12.00 30.00
GQAJL Jesus Luzardo 10.00 25.00
GQAJY Jordan Yamamoto 2.50 6.00
GQAKA Kolby Allard 2.50 6.00
GQAKH Keston Hiura 6.00 15.00
GQAKN Kevin Newman 6.00 15.00
GQALA Logan Allen 4.00 10.00
GQALGJ Lourdes Gurriel Jr. 3.00 8.00
GQALMJ Lance McCullers Jr. 4.00 10.00
GQALR Luis Robert 125.00 300.00
GQAMB Michel Baez 2.50 6.00
GQAMBE Matt Beaty 8.00 20.00
GQAMC Miguel Cabrera 30.00 80.00
GQAMCH Michael Chavis 6.00 15.00
GQAMF Mike Foltynewicz 4.00 10.00
GQAMM Mike Mussina 25.00 60.00
GQAMMI Miles Mikolas EXCH 6.00 15.00
GQAMMU Max Muncy 10.00 25.00
GQAMT Mike Trout 400.00 800.00
GQANH Nico Hoerner 10.00 25.00
GQANS Nick Senzel 10.00 25.00
GQAPD Paul DeJong 4.00 10.00
GQARAJ Ronald Acuna Jr. 100.00 250.00
GQARG Robel Garcia 2.50 6.00
GQARH Rickey Henderson 50.00 120.00
GQASL Shed Long 3.00 8.00
GQATE Thairo Estrada 5.00 12.00
GQATG Dustin May 15.00 40.00
GQATW Taylor Ward 4.00 10.00
GQAVGJ Vladimir Guerrero Jr. 40.00 100.00
GQAWA Willians Astudillo 4.00 10.00
GQAWM Whit Merrifield 10.00 25.00
GQAWS Will Smith 10.00 25.00
GQAYA Yordan Alvarez 50.00 120.00
GQAZC Zack Collins 3.00 8.00

2020 Topps Gypsy Queen Autographs Bazooka Back
*BAZOOKA: .75X TO 2X BASIC
STATED ODDS 1:1218 HOBBY
PRINT RUNS B/WN 24-25 COPIES PER
EXCHANGE DEADLINE 2/29/2020
GQAAJ Aaron Judge/25 125.00 300.00
GQABBI Bo Bichette/25 150.00 400.00
GQABR Bryan Reynolds/25 20.00 50.00
GQACA Chance Adams/25 10.00 25.00
GQACY Christian Yelich/25 100.00 250.00
GQAFTJ Fernando Tatis Jr./25 EXCH 150.00 400.00
GQAKH Keston Hiura/25 40.00 100.00
GQAKN Kevin Newman/25 25.00 60.00
GQAMS Max Scherzer/25 EXCH 50.00 120.00
GQAMT Mike Trout/25 500.00 1000.00
GQAPA Pete Alonso/25 60.00 150.00
GQAPD Paul DeJong/25 20.00 50.00
GQARH Rickey Henderson/25 60.00 150.00
GQASO Shohei Ohtani/24 125.00 300.00
GQAWM Whit Merrifield/25 25.00 60.00
GQAWS Will Smith/25 25.00 60.00
GQAYA Yordan Alvarez/25 200.00 500.00

2020 Topps Gypsy Queen Autographs Black and White
*BW: .6X TO 1.5X BASIC
STATED ODDS 1:272 HOBBY
PRINT RUNS B/WN 34-50 COPIES PER
EXCHANGE DEADLINE 2/29/2020
GQABR Bryan Reynolds/50 15.00 40.00
GQACA Chance Adams/50 8.00 20.00
GQAFTJ Fernando Tatis Jr./50 EXCH 125.00 300.00
GQAMS Max Scherzer/50 EXCH 40.00 100.00
GQAPA Pete Alonso/50 50.00 120.00
GQASO Shohei Ohtani/34 100.00 250.00

2020 Topps Gypsy Queen Autographs Blue
*BLUE: .5X TO 1.2X BASIC
STATED ODDS 1:387 HOBBY
STATED PRINT RUN 99 SER.#'d SETS
EXCHANGE DEADLINE 2/29/2020
GQABR Bryan Reynolds 12.00 30.00
GQACA Chance Adams 6.00 15.00
GQAPA Pete Alonso 40.00 100.00

2020 Topps Gypsy Queen Autographs GQ Logo Swap
*GQ LOGO: .5X TO 1.2X BASIC
STATED ODDS 1:343 HOBBY
STATED PRINT RUN 99 SER.#'d SETS
EXCHANGE DEADLINE 2/29/2020
GQABR Bryan Reynolds 12.00 30.00
GQACA Chance Adams 6.00 15.00
GQAFTJ Fernando Tatis Jr. EXCH 100.00 250.00
GQAMS Max Scherzer EXCH 30.00 80.00
GQAPA Pete Alonso 40.00 100.00

2020 Topps Gypsy Queen Autographs Indigo
*INDIGO: .5X TO 1.2X BASIC
STATED ODDS 1:279 HOBBY
STATED PRINT RUN 150 SER.#'d SETS
EXCHANGE DEADLINE 2/29/2020
GQABR Bryan Reynolds 12.00 30.00
GQACA Chance Adams 6.00 15.00
GQAPA Pete Alonso 40.00 100.00

2020 Topps Gypsy Queen Autographs Jackie Robinson Day Variations
STATED ODDS 1:1734 HOBBY

PRINT RUNS B/WN 15-99 COPIES PER
NO PRICING ON QTY 15
EXCHANGE DEADLINE 2/29/2022
*BW/42: .5X TO 1.2X BASIC
25 Christian Yelich/40 60.00 150.00
29 Willson Contreras/40 15.00 40.00
38 Kris Bryant/25 100.00 250.00
46 Willians Astudillo/99 6.00 15.00
115 Rhys Hoskins/70 25.00 60.00
134 Tim Anderson/99 10.00 25.00
136 Rafael Devers/70 25.00 60.00
195 J.D. Martinez/50 20.00 50.00
202 Max Muncy/99 10.00 25.00
263 Dwight Smith Jr./99 10.00 25.00
264 Trevor Bauer/75 12.00 30.00
282 Aaron Nola/75 12.00 30.00

2020 Topps Gypsy Queen Bases Around the League Autographs

STATED ODDS 1:11,185 HOBBY
STATED PRINT RUN 20 SER.#'d SETS
EXCHANGE DEADLINE 2/29/2022
BALBH Bryce Harper 300.00 600.00
BALMY Mike Yastrzemski 100.00 250.00
BALPA Pete Alonso 300.00 600.00
BALPD Paul DeJong 50.00 125.00
BALRH Rhys Hoskins 125.00 300.00
BALRAJ Ronald Acuna Jr. 400.00 800.00

2020 Topps Gypsy Queen Chrome Box Topper Autographs

STATED ODDS 1:87 HOBBY BOXES
STATED PRINT RUN 25 SER.#'d SETS
EXCHANGE DEADLINE 2/29/2022
25 Christian Yelich 125.00 300.00
42 Gio Urshela
48 Vladimir Guerrero Jr. 100.00 250.00
50 Aaron Judge 125.00 300.00
52 Brendan McKay 20.00 50.00
62 Dylan Cease 20.00 50.00
100 Gleyber Torres 125.00 300.00
137 Yordan Alvarez 150.00 400.00
180 Keston Hiura 50.00 120.00
187 Ronald Acuna Jr. 200.00 500.00
202 Max Muncy 30.00 80.00
205 Austin Meadows 30.00 80.00
222 Michael Chavis 15.00 40.00

2020 Topps Gypsy Queen Chrome Box Toppers

INSERTED IN HOBBY BOXES
1 Mookie Betts 2.00 5.00
2 J.T. Realmuto 1.00 2.50
7 Zack Greinke 1.00 2.50
12 Max Kepler .75 2.00
16 Michael Brantley .75 2.00
17 Bo Bichette 5.00 12.00
21 Clayton Kershaw 1.50 4.00
24 Michael Conforto .75 2.00
25 Christian Yelich 1.25 3.00
30 Carter Kieboom .75 2.00
31 Carlos Santana .75 2.00
35 Aristides Aquino 1.50 4.00
38 Kris Bryant 1.25 3.00
42 Gio Urshela 1.00 2.50
43 Jacob deGrom 2.00 5.00
45 Didi Gregorius .75 2.00
46 Willians Astudillo .60 1.50
47 Paul Goldschmidt 1.00 2.50
48 Vladimir Guerrero Jr. 1.50 4.00
50 Aaron Judge 3.00 8.00
52 Brendan McKay 1.00 2.50
54 Jeff McNeil .75 2.00
55 Trea Turner .75 2.00
57 Jose Altuve .75 2.00
61 Josh Bell .75 2.00
62 Dylan Cease 1.00 2.50
65 Pete Alonso 2.50 6.00
66 Kirby Yates .60 1.50
71 Jose Berrios .75 2.00
72 Kyle Hendricks 1.00 2.50
76 Bryce Harper 1.50 4.00
83 Noah Syndergaard .75 2.00
86 Anthony Rizzo 1.25 3.00
91 Seth Brown .60 1.50
92 Justin Turner 1.00 2.50
93 Gerrit Cole 1.50 4.00
95 Jorge Polanco .75 2.00
96 Xander Bogaerts 1.00 2.50
100 Gleyber Torres 2.00 5.00
103 Charlie Blackmon 1.00 2.50
104 Fernando Tatis Jr. 5.00 12.00
105 Eugenio Suarez .75 2.00
107 Nelson Cruz 1.00 2.50
111 Trevor Story 1.00 2.50
113 A.J. Puk 1.00 2.50
115 Rhys Hoskins 1.25 3.00
117 Andrew Benintendi 1.00 2.50
123 Logan Allen .60 1.50
129 Tommy Pham .60 1.50
136 Rafael Devers 1.25 3.00
137 Yordan Alvarez 6.00 15.00
139 Eduardo Escobar .60 1.50
150 Cody Bellinger 2.00 5.00
152 Gary Sanchez 1.00 2.50
157 Yuli Gurriel .75 2.00
158 Walker Buehler 1.25 3.00
163 Patrick Corbin .75 2.00
164 Shane Bieber 1.00 2.50
165 Jose Abreu 1.00 2.50
166 Max Scherzer 1.00 2.50
173 Jordan Yamamoto .60 1.50
174 Gavin Lux 3.00 8.00
177 James Paxton .75 2.00
178 Juan Soto 3.00 8.00
180 Keston Hiura 1.25 3.00
187 Ronald Acuna Jr. 4.00 10.00
188 Matt Chapman 1.00 2.50
190 Eddie Rosario .75 2.00
195 J.D. Martinez 1.00 2.50
200 Alex Bregman 1.00 2.50
202 Max Muncy .75 2.00
205 Austin Meadows 1.00 2.50
207 Paul DeJong 1.00 2.50
208 Adalberto Mondesi .75 2.00
210 Khris Davis 1.00 2.50
212 Marcus Semien 1.00 2.50
213 Aroldis Chapman 1.00 2.50
218 Starling Marte .75 2.00
219 Will Smith 1.00 2.50
222 Michael Chavis .75 2.00
224 Trey Mancini 1.00 2.50
228 Francisco Lindor 1.00 2.50
233 Javier Baez 1.25 3.00
238 Ozzie Albies 1.00 2.50
239 Nick Senzel 1.00 2.50
246 Brusdar Graterol 1.00 2.50
250 Justin Verlander 1.00 2.50
261 Shohei Ohtani 1.50 4.00
270 Franmil Reyes .60 1.50
276 George Springer .75 2.00
277 Lucas Giolito .75 2.00
278 DJ LeMahieu 1.00 2.50
281 Whit Merrifield 1.00 2.50
282 Aaron Nola .75 2.00
285 Stephen Strasburg 1.00 2.50
292 Manny Machado 1.00 2.50
294 Nolan Arenado 1.50 4.00
295 Ketel Marte .75 2.00
298 Freddie Freeman 1.25 3.00
300 Mike Trout 5.00 12.00

2020 Topps Gypsy Queen Chrome Box Toppers Blue Refractors

*BLUE REF: 1.2X TO 3X BASIC
STATED ODDS 1:4 HOBBY BOXES
STATED PRINT RUN 99 SER.#'d SETS
50 Aaron Judge 20.00 50.00
300 Mike Trout 25.00 60.00

2020 Topps Gypsy Queen Chrome Box Toppers Gold Refractors

*GOLD REF: 2.5X TO 6X BASIC
STATED ODDS 1:7 HOBBY BOXES
STATED PRINT RUN 50 SER.#'d SETS
50 Aaron Judge 40.00 100.00
300 Mike Trout 60.00 150.00

2020 Topps Gypsy Queen Chrome Box Toppers Indigo Refractors

*INDIGO: .75X TO 2X BASIC
STATED ODDS 1:3 HOBBY BOXES
STATED PRINT RUN 150 SER.#'d SETS
50 Aaron Judge 12.00 30.00
300 Mike Trout 15.00 40.00

2020 Topps Gypsy Queen Fortune Teller Mini

STATED ODDS 1:6 HOBBY
*INDIGO/250: 1X TO 2.5X BASIC
GREEN/99: 2X TO 5X BASIC
FTM1 Shohei Ohtani .75 2.00
FTM2 Mike Trout 2.50 6.00
FTM3 Luis Robert 2.50 6.00
FTM4 Michael Chavis .40 1.00
FTM5 Yordan Alvarez 3.00 8.00
FTM6 Paul DeJong .50 1.25
FTM7 Brendan McKay .50 1.25
FTM8 Max Scherzer .50 1.25
FTM9 Bo Bichette 2.50 6.00
FTM10 Gleyber Torres 1.00 2.50
FTM11 Vladimir Guerrero Jr. .75 2.00
FTM12 Keston Hiura .60 1.50
FTM13 Christian Yelich .60 1.50
FTM14 Nick Senzel .50 1.25
FTM15 Ronald Acuna Jr. 2.00 5.00
FTM16 Fernando Tatis Jr. 2.50 6.00
FTM17 Dylan Cease .50 1.25
FTM18 Austin Meadows .50 1.25
FTM19 Willians Astudillo .30 .75
FTM20 Aaron Judge 1.25 3.00

2020 Topps Gypsy Queen Fortune Teller Mini Autographs

STATED ODDS 1:3314 HOBBY
PRINT RUNS B/WN 20-50 COPIES PER
EXCHANGE DEADLINE 2/29/2022
FTMAAJ Aaron Judge
FTMAAM Austin Meadows/50 12.00 30.00
FTMABB Bo Bichette/50 75.00 200.00
FTMABM Brendan McKay/40 20.00 50.00
FTMACY Christian Yelich/20 60.00 150.00
FTMADC Dylan Cease 15.00 40.00
FTMAGT Gleyber Torres/20 60.00 150.00
FTMAMC Michael Chavis/50 30.00 80.00
FTMAPD Paul DeJong/50 12.00 30.00
FTMARAJ Ronald Acuna Jr./20 150.00 400.00
FTMAVGJ Vladimir Guerrero Jr./40 60.00 150.00
FTMAWA Willians Astudillo/50 10.00 25.00
FTMAYA Yordan Alvarez/40 60.00 150.00

2020 Topps Gypsy Queen Mini Rookie Autographs

STATED ODDS 1:1135 HOBBY
PRINT RUNS B/WN 15-99 COPIES PER
NO PRICING ON QTY 15
*BW/50: .5X TO 1.2X BASIC
MRAAA Adbert Alzolay 4.00 10.00
MRAAC Aaron Civale 8.00 20.00
MRAAP A.J. Puk 5.00 12.00
MRABB Bobby Bradley 8.00 20.00
MRABBI Bo Bichette 60.00 150.00
MRABM Brendan McKay 10.00 25.00
MRADC Dylan Cease 8.00 20.00
MRAJL Jesus Luzardo 6.00 15.00
MRAJY Jordan Yamamoto 10.00 25.00
MRALA Logan Allen 8.00 20.00
MRARG Robel Garcia 8.00 20.00
MRAYA Yordan Alvarez 60.00 150.00
MRAZC Zack Collins 8.00 20.00

2020 Topps Gypsy Queen Tarot of the Diamond

STATED ODDS 1:8 HOBBY
*INDIGO/250: 1X TO 2.5X BASIC
*GREEN/99: 2X TO 5X BASIC
TOD1 Ronald Acuna Jr. 2.00 5.00
TOD2 Noah Syndergaard .40 1.00
TOD3 Bo Bichette 2.50 6.00
TOD4 Starling Marte .40 1.00
TOD5 Yordan Alvarez 3.00 8.00
TOD6 Trevor Story .50 1.25
TOD7 Walker Buehler .60 1.50
TOD8 Mike Trout 2.50 6.00
TOD9 Pete Alonso 1.25 3.00
TOD10 Christian Yelich .60 1.50
TOD11 Aroldis Chapman .50 1.25
TOD12 Kris Bryant .60 1.50
TOD13 George Springer .40 1.00
TOD14 Freddie Freeman .60 1.50
TOD15 Justin Verlander .50 1.25
TOD16 Alex Bregman .50 1.25
TOD17 Bryce Harper .75 2.00
TOD18 Javier Baez .60 1.50
TOD19 Aaron Judge 1.25 3.00
TOD20 Aaron Nola .40 1.00
TOD21 Rafael Devers .60 1.50
TOD22 Cody Bellinger 1.00 2.50

2000 Topps HD

COMPLETE SET (100) 20.00 50.00
COMMON CARD (1-100) .25 .60
COMMON RC .25 .60
1 Derek Jeter 1.50 4.00
2 Andruw Jones .25 .60
3 Ben Grieve .25 .60
4 Carlos Beltran .40 1.00
5 Randy Johnson .60 1.50
6 Javy Lopez .25 .60
7 Gary Sheffield .25 .60
8 John Olerud .25 .60
9 Vinny Castilla .25 .60
10 Barry Larkin .40 1.00
11 Tony Clark .25 .60
12 Roberto Alomar .40 1.00
13 Brian Jordan .25 .60
14 Wade Boggs .40 1.00
15 Carlos Febles .25 .60
16 Alfonso Soriano .60 1.50
17 A.J. Burnett .25 .60
18 Matt Williams .25 .60
19 Alex Gonzalez .25 .60
20 Larry Walker .40 1.00
21 Jeff Bagwell .40 1.00
22 Al Leiter .25 .60
23 Ken Griffey Jr. 1.25 3.00
24 Ruben Mateo .25 .60
25 Mark Grace .40 1.00
26 Carlos Delgado .25 .60
27 Vladimir Guerrero .40 1.00
28 Kenny Lofton .25 .60
29 Rusty Greer .25 .60
30 Pedro Martinez .40 1.00
31 Todd Helton .40 1.00
32 Ray Lankford .25 .60
33 Jose Canseco .40 1.00
34 Raul Mondesi .25 .60
35 Mo Vaughn .25 .60
36 Eric Chavez .25 .60
37 Manny Ramirez .60 1.50
38 Jason Kendall .25 .60
39 Mike Mussina .40 1.00
40 Dante Bichette .25 .60
41 Troy Glaus .25 .60
42 Rickey Henderson .60 1.50
43 Pablo Ozuna .25 .60
44 Michael Barrett .25 .60
45 Tony Gwynn .60 1.50
46 John Smoltz .60 1.50
47 Rafael Palmeiro .40 1.00
48 Curt Schilling .40 1.00
49 Todd Walker .25 .60
50 Greg Vaughn .25 .60
51 Orlando Hernandez .25 .60
52 Jim Thome .40 1.00
53 Pat Burrell .25 .60
54 Tim Salmon .25 .60
55 Tom Glavine .40 1.00
56 Travis Lee .25 .60
57 Gabe Kapler .25 .60
58 Greg Maddux .75 2.00
59 Scott Rolen .40 1.00
60 Cal Ripken 2.00 5.00
61 Preston Wilson .25 .60
62 Ivan Rodriguez .40 1.00
63 Johnny Damon .40 1.00
64 Bernie Williams .40 1.00
65 Barry Bonds 1.00 2.50
66 Sammy Sosa .60 1.50
67 Robin Ventura .25 .60
68 Tony Fernandez .25 .60
69 Jay Bell .25 .60
70 Mark McGwire 1.00 2.50
71 Jeromy Burnitz .25 .60
72 Chipper Jones .60 1.50
73 Josh Hamilton .75 2.00
74 Darin Erstad .25 .60
75 Alex Rodriguez .75 2.00
76 Sean Casey .25 .60
77 Tino Martinez .25 .60
78 Juan Gonzalez .25 .60
79 Cliff Floyd .25 .60
80 Craig Biggio .40 1.00
81 Shawn Green .25 .60
82 Adrian Beltre .60 1.50
83 Mike Piazza .60 1.50
84 Nomar Garciaparra .40 1.00
85 Kevin Brown .25 .60
86 Roger Clemens .75 2.00
87 Frank Thomas .60 1.50
88 Albert Belle .25 .60
89 Erubiel Durazo .25 .60
90 David Walling .25 .60
91 John Sneed RC .25 .60
92 Larry Bigbie RC .25 .60
93 B.J. Garbe RC .25 .60
94 Bobby Bradley RC .25 .60
95 Ryan Christianson RC .25 .60
96 Jay Gehrke .25 .60
97 Jason Stumm RC .25 .60
98 Brett Myers RC .75 2.00
99 Chance Caple RC .25 .60
100 Corey Myers RC .25 .60

2000 Topps HD Platinum

*PLATINUM: 8X TO 20X BASIC
STATED ODDS 1:44
STATED PRINT RUN 99 SERIAL #'d SETS

2000 Topps HD Autographs

JETER STATED ODDS 1:859
RIPKEN STATED ODDS 1:4386
RIPKEN EXCH.DEADLINE 6/30/00
HDA1 Derek Jeter 100.00 175.00
HDA2 Cal Ripken 100.00 200.00

2000 Topps HD Ballpark Figures

COMPLETE SET (10) 8.00 20.00
STATED ODDS 1:11
BF1 Mark McGwire 1.50 4.00
BF2 Ken Griffey Jr. 2.00 5.00
BF3 Nomar Garciaparra .60 1.50
BF4 Derek Jeter 2.50 6.00
BF5 Sammy Sosa 1.00 2.50
BF6 Mike Piazza 1.00 2.50
BF7 Juan Gonzalez .40 1.00
BF8 Larry Walker .60 1.50
BF9 Ben Grieve .40 1.00
BF10 Barry Bonds 1.50 4.00

2000 Topps HD Clearly Refined

COMPLETE SET (10) 10.00 25.00
STATED ODDS 1:20
CR1 Alfonso Soriano 2.50 6.00
CR2 Ruben Mateo 1.00 2.50
CR3 Josh Hamilton 3.00 8.00
CR4 Chad Hermansen 1.00 2.50
CR5 Ryan Anderson 1.00 2.50
CR6 Nick Johnson 1.00 2.50
CR7 Octavio Dotel 1.00 2.50
CR8 Peter Bergeron 1.00 2.50
CR9 Adam Piatt 1.00 2.50
CR10 Pat Burrell 1.00 2.50

2000 Topps HD Image

COMPLETE SET (10) 40.00 80.00
STATED ODDS 1:44
HDI1 Sammy Sosa 3.00 8.00
HDI2 Mark McGwire 5.00 12.00
HDI3 Derek Jeter 8.00 20.00
HDI4 Albert Belle 1.25 3.00
HDI5 Vladimir Guerrero 2.00 5.00
HDI6 Ken Griffey Jr. 6.00 15.00
HDI7 Mike Piazza 3.00 8.00
HDI8 Alex Rodriguez 4.00 10.00
HDI9 Barry Bonds 5.00 12.00
HDI10 Nomar Garciaparra 2.00 5.00

2000 Topps HD On the Cutting Edge

COMPLETE SET (10) 12.50 30.00
STATED ODDS 1:22
CE1 Andruw Jones .60 1.50
CE2 Nomar Garciaparra 1.00 2.50
CE3 Barry Bonds 2.50 6.00
CE4 Larry Walker 1.00 2.50
CE5 Vladimir Guerrero 1.00 2.50
CE6 Jeff Bagwell 1.00 2.50
CE7 Derek Jeter 4.00 10.00
CE8 Sammy Sosa 1.50 4.00
CE9 Alex Rodriguez 2.00 5.00
CE10 Ken Griffey Jr. 3.00 8.00

2001 Topps HD

COMPLETE SET (120) 100.00 200.00
COMP.SET w/o SP's (100) 15.00 40.00
COMMON CARD (1-100) .25 .60
COMMON CARD (101-120) 1.25 3.00
SS 101-120 STATED ODDS 1:6
1 Derek Jeter 1.50 4.00
2 Magglio Ordonez .25 .60
3 Eric Munson .25 .60
4 Jermaine Dye .25 .60
5 Larry Walker .25 .60
6 Pokey Reese .25 .60
7 Pedro Martinez .40 1.00
8 Rafael Palmeiro .40 1.00
9 Jason Kendall .25 .60
10 Mike Lieberthal .25 .60
11 Ryan Klesko .25 .60
12 Cal Ripken 2.00 5.00
13 Mike Piazza 1.00 2.50
14 Adam Sterrett RC .25 .60
15 John Olerud .25 .60
16 Manny Ramirez .40 1.00
17 Chad Petty RC .25 .60
18 Vladimir Guerrero .60 1.50
19 Kevin Brown .25 .60
20 Luis Cotto RC .25 .60
21 Josh Hamilton .50 1.25
22 Mark Grace .40 1.00
23 Mark McGwire 1.50 4.00
24 Jeromy Burnitz .25 .60
25 Andruw Jones .40 1.00
26 Raul Mondesi .25 .60
27 Stuart McFarland RC .25 .60
28 Craig Biggio .40 1.00
29 Troy Glaus .25 .60
30 Carlos Delgado .25 .60
31 Rafael Furcal .25 .60
32 J.D. Drew .25 .60
33 Corey Patterson .25 .60
34 Gary Sheffield .25 .60
35 Jeff Kent .25 .60
36 Alex Rodriguez .75 2.00
37 Edgardo Alfonzo .25 .60
38 Jeff Segar RC .25 .60
39 Bob Abreu .25 .60
40 Brian Giles .25 .60
41 Jason Smith RC .25 .60
42 Mo Vaughn .25 .60
43 Pat Burrell .25 .60
44 Barry Larkin .40 1.00
45 Carlos Beltran .25 .60
46 Eric Mosley RC .25 .60
47 Alfonso Soriano .40 1.00
48 Tim Salmon .40 1.00
49 Jason Giambi .25 .60
50 Greg Maddux 1.00 2.50
51 Randy Johnson .60 1.50
52 Jose Vidro .25 .60
53 Edgar Martinez .40 1.00
54 Albert Belle .25 .60
55 Ivan Rodriguez .40 1.00
56 Sean Casey .25 .60
57 Jorge Posada .40 1.00
58 Preston Wilson .25 .60
59 Paul Konerko .25 .60
60 Todd Helton .40 1.00
61 Dominic Rich RC .25 .60
62 Tony Gwynn .75 2.00
63 Bernie Williams .40 1.00
64 Anthony Brewer RC .25 .60
65 Shawn Green .25 .60
66 Jeff Bagwell .40 1.00
67 Jose Cruz Jr. .25 .60
68 Darin Erstad .25 .60
69 Jim Edmonds .25 .60
70 Frank Thomas .60 1.50
71 Ryan Anderson .25 .60
72 Scott Rolen .40 1.00
73 Jeff Cirillo .25 .60
74 Chris Bass RC .25 .60
75 William Smith RC .25 .60
76 Trot Nixon .25 .60
77 Bobby Bradley .25 .60
78 Odannis Ayala RC .25 .60
79 Jim Thome .40 1.00
80 Sammy Sosa .60 1.50
81 Geoff Jenkins .25 .60
82 Ben Grieve .25 .60
83 Andres Galarraga .25 .60
84 Rick Ankiel .25 .60
85 Barry Bonds 1.50 4.00
86 Alex Gonzalez .25 .60
87 Sean Burroughs .25 .60
88 Nomar Garciaparra 1.00 2.50
89 Ken Griffey Jr. 1.25 3.00
90 Tim Hudson .25 .60
91 Chipper Jones .60 1.50
92 Matt Williams .25 .60
93 Roberto Alomar .40 1.00
94 Adrian Gonzalez 1.50 4.00
95 Juan Gonzalez .25 .60
96 Brian Bass RC .25 .60
97 Rick Brosseau RC .25 .60
98 Mariano Rivera .60 1.50
99 James Baldwin .25 .60
100 Dean Palmer .25 .60
101 Pedro Martinez SS 1.25 3.00
102 Randy Johnson SS 1.25 3.00
103 Greg Maddux SS 2.50 6.00
104 Sammy Sosa SS 1.25 3.00
105 Mark McGwire SS 4.00 10.00
106 Ivan Rodriguez SS 1.25 3.00
107 Mike Piazza SS 2.50 6.00
108 Chipper Jones SS 1.25 3.00
109 Vladimir Guerrero SS 1.25 3.00
110 Alex Rodriguez SS 2.00 5.00
111 Ken Griffey Jr. SS 3.00 8.00
112 Cal Ripken SS 5.00 12.00
113 Derek Jeter SS 4.00 10.00
114 Barry Bonds SS 4.00 10.00
115 Nomar Garciaparra SS 2.50 6.00
116 Jeff Bagwell SS .40 1.00
117 Todd Helton SS 1.25 3.00
118 Darin Erstad SS 1.25 3.00
119 Shawn Green SS 1.25 3.00
120 Roberto Alomar SS 1.25 3.00

2001 Topps HD Platinum

*STARS 1-100: 4X TO 10X BASIC CARDS
*YNG.STARS 1-100: 4X TO 10X BASIC CARDS
*ROOKIES 1-100: 2X TO 5X BASIC CARDS
*SS 101-120: 1.5X TO 4X BASIC CARDS
STATED ODDS 1:18
STATED PRINT RUN 199 SERIAL #'d SETS

2001 Topps HD 20-20

COMPLETE SET (10) 15.00 30.00
STATED ODDS 1:12
ALUMINUM STATED ODDS 1:36
TW1 Barry Bonds 2.50 6.00
TW2 Chipper Jones 1.00 2.50
TW3 Ken Griffey Jr. 2.00 5.00
TW4 Alex Rodriguez 1.25 3.00
TW5 Ivan Rodriguez .60 1.50
TW6 Sammy Sosa 1.00 2.50
TW7 Roberto Alomar .60 1.50
TW8 Larry Walker .60 1.50
TW9 Shawn Green .60 1.50
TW10 Jeff Bagwell .60 1.50

2001 Topps HD Clear Autographs

STATED ODDS 1:431
HDA1 Todd Helton 10.00 25.00
HDA2 Rick Ankiel 4.00 10.00
HDA3 Mark Quinn 4.00 10.00
HDA4 Adrian Gonzalez 10.00 25.00

2001 Topps HD Clear Jerseys

STATED ODDS 1:108
HDCR1 Grant Roberts 4.00 10.00
HDCR2 Vernon Wells 6.00 15.00
HDCR3 Travis Dawkins 4.00 10.00
HDCR4 Ramon Ortiz 4.00 10.00
HDCR5 Steve Finley 6.00 15.00
HDCR6 Ramon Hernandez 4.00 10.00
HDCR7 Jay Payton 4.00 10.00
HDCR8 Jeromy Burnitz 6.00 15.00

2001 Topps HD Game Defined

COMPLETE SET (10) 12.00 30.00
STATED ODDS 1:24
*ALUMINUM: .75X TO 2X BASIC GAME.DEF
ALUMINUM STATED ODDS 1:72
GD1 Ken Griffey Jr. 3.00 8.00
GD2 Derek Jeter 4.00 10.00
GD3 Sammy Sosa 1.00 2.50
GD4 Mark McGwire 2.50 6.00
GD5 Todd Helton 1.00 2.50
GD6 Mike Piazza 1.50 4.00
GD7 Chipper Jones 1.50 4.00
GD8 Vladimir Guerrero 1.50 4.00
GD9 Alex Rodriguez 2.00 5.00
GD10 Nomar Garciaparra 1.00 2.50

2001 Topps HD Images of Excellence

COMPLETE SET (10) 30.00 60.00
STATED ODDS 1:8
*ALUMINUM: .75X TO 2X BASIC IMAGES
ALUMINUM STATED ODDS 1:24
IE1 Willie Mays 3.00 8.00
IE2 Reggie Jackson 2.00 5.00
IE3 Ernie Banks 2.00 5.00
IE4 Hank Aaron 4.00 10.00
IE5 Ted Williams 4.00 10.00
IE6 Mike Schmidt 4.00 10.00
IE7 Tom Seaver 2.00 5.00
IE8 Johnny Bench 2.00 5.00
IE9 George Brett 4.00 10.00
IE10 Nolan Ryan 5.00 12.00

2001 Topps Heritage Pre-Production

COMPLETE SET (3) 1.60 4.00
PP1 Kevin Brown .40 1.00
PP2 Andres Galarraga .40 1.00
PP3 Roger Clemens 1.00 2.50

2001 Topps Heritage

COMP.MASTER SET (487) 350.00 500.00
COMPLETE SET (407) 200.00 400.00
COMP.BASIC SET (230) 30.00 60.00
COMMON CARD (81-310) .20 .50
FOLLOWING AVAIL.ONLY AS BLACK-BACKS
103/159/171/176/179/188/201/212/224/241
COMMON CARD (1-80) 1.00 2.50
RED-BLACK BACKS: EQUAL QUANTITIES
RED-BLACK BACKS: EQUAL VALUE
COMMON CARD (311-407) 2.00 5.00
311-407 STATED ODDS 1:2
'52 CARD REDEMPTION ODDS 1:3,689
REPLICA HAT-JSY REDEMPTION ODDS 1:9,581
EXCHANGE DEADLINE 2/28/02
RED OR BLACK BACKS OK IN 407-CARD SET
1 Kris Benson 1.00 2.50
1 Kris Benson Black 1.00 2.50
2 Brian Jordan 1.00 2.50
2 Brian Jordan Black 1.00 2.50
3 Fernando Vina 1.00 2.50
3 Fernando Vina Black 1.00 2.50
4 Mike Sweeney 1.00 2.50
4 Mike Sweeney Black 1.00 2.50
5 Rafael Palmeiro 1.00 2.50
5 Rafael Palmeiro Black 1.00 2.50
6 Paul O'Neill 1.00 2.50
6 Paul O'Neill Black 1.00 2.50
7 Todd Helton 1.00 2.50
7 Todd Helton Black 1.00 2.50
8 Ramiro Mendoza 1.00 2.50
8 Ramiro Mendoza Black 1.00 2.50
9 Kevin Millwood 1.00 2.50
9 Kevin Millwood Black 1.00 2.50
10 Chuck Knoblauch 1.00 2.50
10 Chuck Knoblauch Black 1.00 2.50
11 Derek Jeter 4.00 10.00
11 Derek Jeter Black 10.00 25.00
12 Alex Rodriguez Rangers 2.00 5.00
12 A.Rod Black Rangers 2.00 5.00
13 Geoff Jenkins 1.00 2.50
13 Geoff Jenkins Black 1.00 2.50
14 David Justice 1.00 2.50
14 David Justice Black 1.00 2.50
15 David Cone 1.00 2.50
15 David Cone Black 1.00 2.50
16 Andres Galarraga 1.00 2.50
16 Andres Galarraga Black 1.00 2.50
17 Garret Anderson 1.00 2.50
17 Garret Anderson Black 1.00 2.50
18 Roger Cedeno 1.00 2.50
18 Roger Cedeno Black 1.00 2.50
19 Randy Velarde 1.00 2.50
19 Randy Velarde Black 1.00 2.50
20 Carlos Delgado 1.00 2.50
20 Carlos Delgado Black 1.00 2.50
21 Quilvio Veras 1.00 2.50
21 Quilvio Veras Black 1.00 2.50
22 Jose Vidro 1.00 2.50
22 Jose Vidro Black 1.00 2.50
23 Corey Patterson 1.00 2.50
23 Corey Patterson Black 1.00 2.50
24 Jorge Posada 1.00 2.50
24 Jorge Posada Black 1.00 2.50
25 Eddie Perez 1.00 2.50
25 Eddie Perez Black 1.00 2.50
26 Jack Cust 1.00 2.50
26 Jack Cust Black 1.00 2.50
27 Sean Burroughs 1.00 2.50
27 Sean Burroughs Black 1.00 2.50
28 Randy Wolf 1.00 2.50
28 Randy Wolf Black 1.00 2.50
29 Mike Lamb 1.00 2.50
29 Mike Lamb Black 1.00 2.50
30 Rafael Furcal 1.00 2.50
30 Rafael Furcal Black 1.00 2.50
31 Barry Bonds 4.00 10.00
31 Barry Bonds Black 4.00 10.00
32 Tim Hudson 1.00 2.50
32 Tim Hudson Black 1.00 2.50
33 Tom Glavine 1.00 2.50
33 Tom Glavine Black 1.00 2.50
34 Javy Lopez 1.00 2.50
34 Javy Lopez Black 1.00 2.50
35 Aubrey Huff 1.00 2.50
35 Aubrey Huff Black 1.00 2.50
36 Wally Joyner 1.00 2.50
36 Wally Joyner Black 1.00 2.50
37 Magglio Ordonez 1.00 2.50
37 Magglio Ordonez Black 1.00 2.50
38 Matt Lawton 1.00 2.50
38 Matt Lawton Black 1.00 2.50
39 Mariano Rivera 1.50 4.00
39 Mariano Rivera Black 1.50 4.00
40 Andy Ashby 1.00 2.50
40 Andy Ashby Black 1.00 2.50
41 Mark Buehrle 1.00 2.50
41 Mark Buehrle Black 1.00 2.50
42 Esteban Loaiza 1.00 2.50
42 Esteban Loaiza Black 1.00 2.50
43 Mark Redman 1.00 2.50
43 Mark Redman Black 1.00 2.50
44 Mark Quinn 1.00 2.50
44 Mark Quinn Black 1.00 2.50
45 Tino Martinez 1.00 2.50
45 Tino Martinez Black 1.00 2.50
46 Joe Mays 1.00 2.50
46 Joe Mays Black 1.00 2.50
47 Walt Weiss 1.00 2.50
47 Walt Weiss Black 1.00 2.50
48 Roger Clemens 3.00 8.00
48 Roger Clemens Black 3.00 8.00
49 Greg Maddux 2.50 6.00
49 Greg Maddux Black 2.50 6.00
50 Richard Hidalgo 1.00 2.50
50 Richard Hidalgo Black 1.00 2.50
51 Orlando Hernandez 1.00 2.50
51 Orlando Hernandez Black 1.00 2.50
52 Chipper Jones 1.50 4.00
52 Chipper Jones Black 1.50 4.00
53 Ben Grieve 1.00 2.50
53 Ben Grieve Black 1.00 2.50
54 Jimmy Haynes 1.00 2.50
54 Jimmy Haynes Black 1.00 2.50
55 Ken Caminiti 1.00 2.50
55 Ken Caminiti Black 1.00 2.50
56 Tim Salmon 1.00 2.50
56 Tim Salmon Black 1.00 2.50
57 Andy Pettitte 1.00 2.50
57 Andy Pettitte Black 1.00 2.50
58 Darin Erstad 1.00 2.50
58 Darin Erstad Black 1.00 2.50
59 Marquis Grissom 1.00 2.50
59 Marquis Grissom Black 1.00 2.50
60 Raul Mondesi 1.00 2.50
60 Raul Mondesi Black 1.00 2.50
61 Bengie Molina 1.00 2.50
61 Bengie Molina Black 1.00 2.50
62 Miguel Tejada 1.00 2.50
62 Miguel Tejada Black 1.00 2.50
63 Jose Cruz Jr. 1.00 2.50
63 Jose Cruz Jr. Black 1.00 2.50
64 Billy Koch 1.00 2.50
64 Billy Koch Black 1.00 2.50
65 Troy Glaus 1.00 2.50
65 Troy Glaus Black 1.00 2.50
66 Cliff Floyd 1.00 2.50
66 Cliff Floyd Black 1.00 2.50
67 Tony Batista 1.00 2.50
67 Tony Batista Black 1.00 2.50
68 Jeff Bagwell 1.00 2.50
68 Jeff Bagwell Black 1.00 2.50
69 Billy Wagner 1.00 2.50
69 Billy Wagner Black 1.00 2.50
70 Eric Chavez 1.00 2.50
70 Eric Chavez Black 1.00 2.50
71 Troy Percival 1.00 2.50
71 Troy Percival Black 1.00 2.50
72 Andruw Jones 1.00 2.50
72 Andruw Jones Black 1.00 2.50
73 Shane Reynolds 1.00 2.50
73 Shane Reynolds Black 1.00 2.50
74 Barry Zito 1.00 2.50
74 Barry Zito Black 1.00 2.50
75 Roy Halladay 1.00 2.50
75 Roy Halladay Black 1.00 2.50
76 David Wells 1.00 2.50
76 David Wells Black 1.00 2.50
77 Jason Giambi 1.00 2.50
77 Jason Giambi Black 1.00 2.50
78 Scott Elarton 1.00 2.50
78 Scott Elarton Black 1.00 2.50
79 Moises Alou 1.00 2.50
79 Moises Alou Black 1.00 2.50
80 Adam Piatt 1.00 2.50
80 Adam Piatt Black 1.00 2.50
81 Wilton Veras .20 .50
82 Darryl Kile .25 .60
83 Johnny Damon .40 1.00
84 Tony Armas Jr. .20 .50
85 Ellis Burks .25 .60
86 Jamey Wright .20 .50
87 Jose Vizcaino .20 .50
88 Bartolo Colon .25 .60
89 Carmen Cali RC .20 .50
90 Kevin Brown .25 .60
91 Josh Hamilton .40 1.00
92 Jay Buhner .25 .60
93 Scott Pratt RC .25 .60
94 Alex Cora .20 .50
95 Luis Montanez RC .25 .60
96 Dmitri Young .25 .60
97 J.T. Snow .25 .60
98 Damion Easley .20 .50
99 Greg Norton .20 .50
100 Matt Wheatland .20 .50
101 Chin-Feng Chen .25 .60
102 Tony Womack .20 .50
103 Adam Kennedy Black .20 .50
104 J.D. Drew .25 .60
105 Carlos Febles .20 .50
106 Jim Thome .40 1.00
107 Danny Graves .20 .50
108 Dave Mlicki .20 .50
109 Ron Coomer .20 .50
110 James Baldwin .20 .50
111 Shaun Boyd RC .20 .50
112 Brian Bohanon .20 .50
113 Jacque Jones .25 .60
114 Alfonso Soriano .40 1.00
115 Tony Clark .20 .50
116 Terrence Long .20 .50
117 Todd Hundley .20 .50
118 Kazuhiro Sasaki .25 .60
119 Brian Sellier RC .20 .50
120 John Olerud .25 .60
121 Javier Vazquez .25 .60
122 Sean Burnett .20 .50
123 Matt LeCroy .20 .50
124 Erubiel Durazo .20 .50
125 Juan Encarnacion .20 .50
126 Pablo Ozuna .20 .50
127 Russ Ortiz .20 .50
128 David Segui .20 .50
129 Mark McGwire 1.50 4.00
130 Mark Grace .40 1.00
131 Fred McGriff .40 1.00

132 Carl Pavano .25 .60
133 Derek Thompson .20 .50
134 Shawn Green .25 .60
135 B.J. Surhoff .25 .60
136 Michael Tucker .20 .50
137 Jason Isringhausen .25 .60
138 Eric Milton .20 .50
139 Mike Stodolka .20 .50
140 Milton Bradley .25 .60
141 Curt Schilling .25 .60
142 Sandy Alomar Jr. .20 .50
143 Brent Mayne .20 .50
144 Todd Jones .20 .50
145 Charles Johnson .25 .60
146 Dean Palmer .25 .60
147 Masato Yoshii .20 .50
148 Edgar Renteria .25 .60
149 Joe Randa .25 .60
150 Adam Johnson .20 .50
151 Greg Vaughn .20 .50
152 Adrian Beltre .25 .60
153 Glenallen Hill .20 .50
154 David Parrish RC .20 .50
155 Neifi Perez .20 .50
156 Pete Harnisch .20 .50
157 Paul Konerko .25 .60
158 Dennys Reyes .20 .50
159 Jose Lima Black .20 .50
160 Eddie Taubensee .20 .50
161 Miguel Cairo .20 .50
162 Jeff Kent .25 .60
163 Dustin Hermanson .20 .50
164 Alex Gonzalez .20 .50
165 Hideo Nomo .60 1.50
166 Sammy Sosa .60 1.50
167 C.J. Nitkowski .20 .50
168 Cal Eldred .20 .50
169 Jeff Abbott .20 .50
170 Jim Edmonds .25 .60
171 Mark Mulder Black .25 .60
172 Dominic Rich RC .20 .50
173 Ray Lankford .25 .60
174 Danny Borrell RC .20 .50
175 Rick Aguilera .20 .50
176 Shannon Stewart Black .25 .60
177 Steve Finley .25 .60
178 Jim Parque .20 .50
179 Kevin Appier Black .25 .60
180 Adrian Gonzalez 1.25 3.00
181 Tom Goodwin .20 .50
182 Kevin Tapani .20 .50
183 Fernando Tatis .20 .50
184 Mark Grudzielanek .20 .50
185 Ryan Anderson .20 .50
186 Jeffrey Hammonds .20 .50
187 Corey Koskie .20 .50
188 Brad Fullmer Black .20 .50
189 Rey Sanchez .20 .50
190 Michael Barrett .20 .50
191 Rickey Henderson .60 1.50
192 Jermaine Dye .25 .60
193 Scott Brosius .25 .60
194 Matt Anderson .20 .50
195 Brian Buchanan .20 .50
196 Derrek Lee .40 1.00
197 Larry Walker .25 .60
198 Dan Moylan RC .20 .50
199 Vinny Castilla .25 .60
200 Ken Griffey Jr. 1.25 3.00
201 Matt Stairs Black .20 .50
202 Ty Howington .20 .50
203 Andy Benes .20 .50
204 Luis Gonzalez .25 .60
205 Brian Moehler .20 .50
206 Harold Baines .25 .60
207 Pedro Astacio .20 .50
208 Cristian Guzman .20 .50
209 Kip Wells .20 .50
210 Frank Thomas .60 1.50
211 Jose Rosado .20 .50
212 Vernon Wells Black .25 .60
213 Bobby Higginson .25 .60
214 Juan Gonzalez .25 .60
215 Omar Vizquel .40 1.00
216 Bernie Williams .40 1.00
217 Aaron Sele .20 .50
218 Shawn Estes .20 .50
219 Roberto Alomar .40 1.00
220 Rick Ankiel .20 .50
221 Josh Kalinowski .20 .50
222 David Bell .20 .50
223 Keith Foulke .25 .60
224 Craig Biggio Black .40 1.00
225 Josh Axelson RC .20 .50
226 Scott Williamson .20 .50
227 Ron Belliard .20 .50
228 Chris Singleton .20 .50
229 Alex Serrano RC .20 .50
230 Deivi Cruz .20 .50
231 Eric Munson .20 .50
232 Luis Castillo .20 .50
233 Edgar Martinez .40 1.00
234 Jeff Shaw .20 .50
235 Jeromy Burnitz .25 .60
236 Richie Sexson .25 .60
237 Will Clark .40 1.00
238 Ron Villone .20 .50
239 Kerry Wood .25 .60
240 Rich Aurilia .20 .50
241 Mo Vaughn Black .25 .60
242 Travis Fryman .25 .60
243 Manny Ramirez Sox .40 1.00
244 Chris Stynes .20 .50
245 Ray Durham .25 .60
246 Juan Uribe RC .40 1.00
247 Juan Guzman .20 .50
248 Lee Stevens .20 .50
249 Devon White .25 .60
250 Kyle Lohse RC .40 1.00
251 Bryan Wolff .20 .50
252 Matt Galante RC .25 .60
253 Eric Young .20 .50
254 Freddy Garcia .25 .60
255 Jay Bell .25 .60
256 Steve Cox .20 .50
257 Torii Hunter .25 .60
258 Jose Canseco .40 1.00
259 Brad Ausmus .25 .60
260 Jeff Cirillo .20 .50
261 Brad Penny .20 .50
262 Antonio Alfonseca .20 .50
263 Russ Branyan .20 .50
264 Chris Morris RC .20 .50
265 John Lackey .20 .50
266 Justin Wayne RC .25 .60
267 Brad Radke .25 .60
268 Todd Stottlemyre .20 .50
269 Mark Loretta .20 .50
270 Matt Williams .25 .60
271 Kenny Lofton .25 .60
272 Jeff D'Amico .20 .50
273 Jamie Moyer .25 .60
274 Darren Dreifort .20 .50
275 Denny Neagle .20 .50
276 Orlando Cabrera .25 .60
277 Chuck Finley .25 .60
278 Miguel Batista .25 .60
279 Carlos Beltran .25 .60
280 Eric Karros .25 .60
281 Mark Kotsay .25 .60
282 Ryan Dempster .20 .50
283 Barry Larkin .40 1.00
284 Jeff Suppan .20 .50
285 Gary Sheffield .25 .60
286 Jose Valentin .20 .50
287 Robb Nen .25 .60
288 Chan Ho Park .25 .60
289 John Halama .20 .50
290 Steve Smyth RC .25 .60
291 Gerald Williams .20 .50
292 Preston Wilson .25 .60
293 Victor Hall RC .25 .60
294 Ben Sheets .40 1.00
295 Eric Davis .25 .60
296 Kirk Rueter .20 .50
297 Chad Petty RC .20 .50
298 Kevin Millar .25 .60
299 Marvin Benard .20 .50
300 Vladimir Guerrero .60 1.50
301 Livan Hernandez .25 .60
302 Travis Baptist RC .20 .50
303 Bill Mueller .25 .60
304 Mike Cameron .20 .50
305 Randy Johnson .60 1.50
306 Alan Mahaffey RC .20 .50
307 Timo Perez UER .20 .50
308 Pokey Reese .20 .50
309 Ryan Rupe .20 .50
310 Carlos Lee .25 .60
311 Doug Glanville SP 2.00 5.00
312 Jay Payton SP 2.00 5.00
313 Troy O'Leary SP 2.00 5.00
314 Francisco Cordero SP 2.00 5.00
315 Rusty Greer SP 2.00 5.00
316 Cal Ripken SP 10.00 25.00
317 Ricky Ledee SP 2.00 5.00
318 Brian Daubach SP 2.00 5.00
319 Robin Ventura SP 2.00 5.00
320 Todd Zeile SP 2.00 5.00
321 Francisco Cordova SP 2.00 5.00
322 Henry Rodriguez SP 2.00 5.00
323 Pat Meares SP 2.00 5.00
324 Glendon Rusch SP 2.00 5.00
325 Keith Osik SP 2.00 5.00
326 Robert Keppel SP RC 2.00 5.00
327 Bobby Jones SP 2.00 5.00
328 Alex Ramirez SP 2.00 5.00
329 Robert Person SP 2.00 5.00
330 Ruben Mateo SP 2.00 5.00
331 Rob Bell SP 2.00 5.00
332 Carl Everett SP 2.00 5.00
333 Jason Schmidt SP 2.00 5.00
334 Scott Rolen SP 3.00 8.00
335 Jimmy Anderson SP 2.00 5.00
336 Bret Boone SP 2.00 5.00
337 Delino DeShields SP 2.00 5.00
338 Trevor Hoffman SP 2.00 5.00
339 Bob Abreu SP 2.00 5.00
340 Mike Williams SP 2.00 5.00
341 Mike Hampton SP 2.00 5.00
342 John Wetteland SP 2.00 5.00
343 Scott Erickson SP 2.00 5.00
344 Enrique Wilson SP 2.00 5.00
345 Tim Wakefield SP 2.00 5.00
346 Mike Lowell SP 2.00 5.00
347 Todd Pratt SP 2.00 5.00
348 Brook Fordyce SP 2.00 5.00
349 Benny Agbayani SP 2.00 5.00
350 Gabe Kapler SP 2.00 5.00
351 Sean Casey SP 2.00 5.00
352 Darren Oliver SP 2.00 5.00
353 Todd Ritchie SP 2.00 5.00
354 Kenny Rogers SP 2.00 5.00
355 Jason Kendall SP 2.00 5.00
356 John Vander Wal SP 2.00 5.00
357 Ramon Martinez SP 2.00 5.00
358 Edgardo Alfonzo SP 2.00 5.00
359 Phil Nevin SP 2.00 5.00
360 Albert Belle SP 2.00 5.00
361 Ruben Rivera SP 2.00 5.00
362 Pedro Martinez SP 3.00 8.00
363 Derek Lowe SP 2.00 5.00
364 Pat Burrell SP 2.00 5.00
365 Mike Mussina SP 3.00 8.00
366 Brady Anderson SP 2.00 5.00
367 Darren Lewis SP 2.00 5.00
368 Sidney Ponson SP 2.00 5.00
369 Adam Eaton SP 2.00 5.00
370 Eric Owens SP 2.00 5.00
371 Aaron Boone SP 2.00 5.00
372 Matt Clement SP 2.00 5.00
373 Derek Bell SP 2.00 5.00
374 Trot Nixon SP 2.00 5.00
375 Travis Lee SP 2.00 5.00
376 Mike Benjamin SP 2.00 5.00
377 Jeff Zimmerman SP 2.00 5.00
378 Mike Lieberthal SP 2.00 5.00
379 Rick Reed SP 2.00 5.00
380 Nomar Garciaparra SP 5.00 12.00
381 Omar Daal SP 2.00 5.00
382 Ryan Klesko SP 2.00 5.00
383 Rey Ordonez SP 2.00 5.00
384 Kevin Young SP 2.00 5.00
385 Rick Helling SP 2.00 5.00
386 Brian Giles SP 2.00 5.00
387 Tony Gwynn SP 4.00 10.00
388 Ed Sprague SP 2.00 5.00
389 J.R. House SP 2.00 5.00
390 Scott Hatteberg SP 2.00 5.00
391 John Valentin SP 2.00 5.00
392 Melvin Mora SP 2.00 5.00
393 Royce Clayton SP 2.00 5.00
394 Jeff Fassero SP 2.00 5.00
395 Manny Alexander SP 2.00 5.00
396 John Franco SP 2.00 5.00
397 Luis Alicea SP 2.00 5.00
398 Ivan Rodriguez SP 3.00 8.00
399 Kevin Jordan SP 2.00 5.00
400 Jose Offerman SP 2.00 5.00
401 Jeff Conine SP 2.00 5.00
402 Seth Etherton SP 2.00 5.00
403 Mike Bordick SP 2.00 5.00
404 Al Leiter SP 2.00 5.00
405 Mike Piazza SP 5.00 12.00
406 Armando Benitez SP 2.00 5.00
407 Warren Morris SP 2.00 5.00
CL1 Checklist 1 .10 .25
CL2 Checklist 2 .10 .25

2001 Topps Heritage Chrome

STATED ODDS 1:25 HOB/RET
STATED PRINT RUN 552 SERIAL #'d SETS
CP1 Cal Ripken 50.00 120.00
CP2 Jim Thome 12.00 30.00
CP3 Derek Jeter 60.00 150.00
CP4 Andres Galarraga 5.00 12.00
CP5 Carlos Delgado 3.00 8.00
CP6 Roberto Alomar 5.00 12.00
CP7 Tom Glavine 5.00 12.00
CP8 Gary Sheffield 3.00 8.00
CP9 Mo Vaughn 3.00 8.00
CP10 Preston Wilson 3.00 8.00
CP11 Mike Mussina 5.00 12.00
CP12 Greg Maddux 20.00 50.00
CP13 Ivan Rodriguez 5.00 12.00
CP14 Al Leiter 3.00 8.00
CP15 Seth Etherton 3.00 8.00
CP16 Edgardo Alfonzo 3.00 8.00
CP17 Richie Sexson 3.00 8.00
CP18 Andruw Jones 5.00 12.00
CP19 Bartolo Colon 3.00 8.00
CP20 Darin Erstad 3.00 8.00
CP21 Kevin Brown 3.00 8.00
CP22 Mike Sweeney 3.00 8.00
CP23 Mike Piazza 15.00 40.00
CP24 Rafael Palmeiro 5.00 12.00
CP25 Terrence Long 3.00 8.00
CP26 Kazuhiro Sasaki 3.00 8.00
CP27 John Olerud 3.00 8.00
CP28 Mark McGwire 25.00 60.00
CP29 Fred McGriff 5.00 12.00
CP30 Todd Helton 5.00 12.00
CP31 Curt Schilling 3.00 8.00
CP32 Alex Rodriguez 20.00 50.00
CP33 Jeff Kent 3.00 8.00
CP34 Pat Burrell 3.00 8.00
CP35 Jim Edmonds 5.00 12.00
CP36 Mark Mulder 3.00 8.00
CP37 Troy Glaus 3.00 8.00
CP38 Jay Payton 3.00 8.00
CP39 Jermaine Dye 3.00 8.00
CP40 Larry Walker 5.00 12.00
CP41 Ken Griffey Jr. 30.00 80.00
CP42 Jeff Bagwell 5.00 12.00
CP43 Rick Ankiel 3.00 8.00
CP44 Mark Redman 3.00 8.00
CP45 Edgar Martinez 5.00 12.00
CP46 Mike Hampton 3.00 8.00
CP47 Manny Ramirez Sox 8.00 20.00
CP48 Ray Durham 3.00 8.00
CP49 Rafael Furcal 3.00 8.00
CP50 Sean Casey 3.00 8.00
CP51 Jose Canseco 5.00 12.00
CP52 Barry Bonds 15.00 40.00
CP53 Tim Hudson 3.00 8.00
CP54 Barry Zito 5.00 12.00
CP55 Chuck Finley 3.00 8.00
CP56 Maggio Ordonez 3.00 8.00
CP57 David Wells 3.00 8.00
CP58 Jason Giambi 3.00 8.00
CP59 Tony Gwynn 10.00 25.00
CP60 Vladimir Guerrero 12.00 30.00
CP61 Randy Johnson 10.00 25.00
CP62 Bernie Williams 5.00 12.00
CP63 Craig Biggio 5.00 12.00
CP64 Jason Kendall 3.00 8.00
CP65 Pedro Martinez 5.00 12.00
CP66 Mark Quinn 3.00 8.00
CP67 Frank Thomas 30.00 80.00
CP68 Nomar Garciaparra 15.00 40.00
CP69 Brian Giles 3.00 8.00
CP70 Shawn Green 3.00 8.00
CP71 Roger Clemens 20.00 50.00
CP72 Sammy Sosa 5.00 12.00
CP73 Juan Gonzalez 3.00 8.00
CP74 Orlando Hernandez 3.00 8.00
CP75 Chipper Jones 12.00 30.00
CP76 Josh Hamilton 5.00 12.00
CP77 Adam Johnson 3.00 8.00
CP78 Shaun Boyd 3.00 8.00
CP79 Alfonso Soriano 5.00 12.00
CP80 Derek Thompson 3.00 8.00
CP81 Adrian Gonzalez 10.00 25.00
CP82 Ryan Anderson 3.00 8.00
CP83 Corey Patterson 3.00 8.00
CP84 J.R. House 3.00 8.00
CP85 Sean Burroughs 3.00 8.00
CP86 Bryan Wolff 3.00 8.00
CP87 John Lackey 5.00 12.00
CP88 Ben Sheets 3.00 8.00
CP89 Timo Perez 3.00 8.00
CP90 Robert Keppel 3.00 8.00
CP91 Luis Montanez 3.00 8.00
CP92 Sean Burnett 3.00 8.00
CP93 Justin Wayne 3.00 8.00
CP94 Eric Munson 3.00 8.00
CP95 Steve Smyth 3.00 8.00
CP96 Matt Galante 3.00 8.00
CP97 Carmen Cali 3.00 8.00
CP98 Brian Sellier 3.00 8.00
CP99 David Parrish 3.00 8.00
CP100 Danny Borrell 3.00 8.00
CP101 Chad Petty 3.00 8.00
CP102 Dominic Rich 3.00 8.00
CP103 Josh Axelson 3.00 8.00
CP104 Alex Serrano 3.00 8.00
CP105 Juan Uribe 3.00 8.00
CP106 Travis Baptist 3.00 8.00
CP107 Alan Mahaffey 3.00 8.00
CP108 Kyle Lohse 3.00 8.00
CP109 Victor Hall 3.00 8.00
CP110 Scott Pratt 3.00 8.00

2001 Topps Heritage Autographs

STATED ODDS 1:142 HOB/RET
*RED INK: .75X TO 1.5X BASIC AU
RED INK ODDS 1:545 HOB, 1:546 RET
RED INK PRINT RUN 52 SERIAL #'d SETS
THAAH Aubrey Huff 10.00 25.00
THAAP Andy Pafko 50.00 100.00
THAAR Alex Rodriguez 75.00 150.00
THABB Barry Bonds 150.00 400.00
THABS Bobby Shantz 10.00 25.00
THABT Bobby Thomson 15.00 40.00
THACD Carlos Delgado 15.00 40.00
THACF Cliff Floyd 10.00 25.00
THACJ Chipper Jones 100.00 250.00
THACP Corey Patterson 12.50 30.00
THACS Curt Simmons 20.00 50.00
THADD Dom DiMaggio 30.00 80.00
THADG Dick Groat 25.00 60.00
THADS Duke Snider 40.00 100.00
THAES Enos Slaughter 60.00 150.00
THAFV Fernando Vina 10.00 25.00
THAGJ Geoff Jenkins 10.00 25.00
THAGM Gil McDougald 25.00 60.00
THAHB Hank Bauer 20.00 50.00
THAHS Hank Sauer 30.00 60.00
THAHW Hoyt Wilhelm 25.00 60.00
THAJG Joe Garagiola 25.00 60.00
THAJM Joe Mays 10.00 25.00
THAJS Johnny Sain 25.00 60.00
THAJV Jose Vidro 10.00 25.00
THAKB Kris Benson 10.00 25.00
THAMB Mark Buehrle 25.00 60.00
THAMI Monte Irvin 20.00 50.00
THAML Mike Lamb 12.00 30.00
THAML Matt Lawton 10.00 25.00
THAMM Minnie Minoso 25.00 60.00
THAMO Maggio Ordonez 10.00 25.00
THAMQ Mark Quinn 20.00 50.00
THAMR Mark Redman 10.00 25.00
THAMS Mike Sweeney 10.00 25.00
THAMV Mickey Vernon 15.00 40.00
THANG Nomar Garciaparra 60.00 150.00
THAPR Preacher Roe 20.00 50.00
THAPFR Phil Rizzuto 75.00 200.00
THARH Richard Hidalgo 10.00 25.00
THARR Robin Roberts 25.00 60.00
THARS Red Schoendienst 30.00 80.00
THARW Randy Wolf 10.00 25.00
THASPB Sean Burroughs 10.00 25.00
THATG Tom Glavine 40.00 100.00
THATH Todd Helton 15.00 40.00
THATL Terrence Long 10.00 25.00
THAVL Vernon Law 20.00 50.00
THAWM Willie Mays 150.00 400.00
THAWS Warren Spahn 60.00 150.00

2001 Topps Heritage Autographs Red Ink

STATED ODDS 1:545 HOBBY, 1:546 RETAIL
STATED PRINT RUN 52 SERIAL #'d SETS

2001 Topps Heritage AutoProofs

NO PRICING DUE TO SCARCITY
AUTOPROOF IS A REAL '52 TOPPS CARD

2001 Topps Heritage Classic Renditions

COMPLETE SET (10) 8.00 20.00
STATED ODDS 1:5 HOBBY, 1:9 RETAIL
CR1 Mark McGwire 1.50 4.00
CR2 Nomar Garciaparra 1.00 2.50
CR3 Barry Bonds 1.50 4.00
CR4 Sammy Sosa .60 1.50
CR5 Chipper Jones .60 1.50
CR6 Pat Burrell .40 1.00
CR7 Frank Thomas .60 1.50
CR8 Manny Ramirez .40 1.00
CR9 Derek Jeter 1.50 4.00
CR10 Ken Griffey Jr. 1.25 3.00

2001 Topps Heritage Clubhouse Collection

BAT ODDS 1:590 HOB/RET
JERSEY ODDS 1:798 HOB, 1:799 RET
DUAL BAT ODDS 1:5701 HOB, 1:5772 RET
DUAL JERSEY ODDS 1:28,744 H, 1:29820 R
AU BAT ODDS 1:19,710 HOB, 1:20,928 RET
AU JERSEY ODDS 1:62,714 H, 1:83,712 R
NO PRICING ON QTY OF 25 OR LESS
BB Barry Bonds Bat 40.00 80.00
CJ Chipper Jones Bat 20.00 50.00
DS Duke Snider Bat 12.00 30.00
EM Eddie Mathews Bat 12.00 30.00
FT Frank Thomas Jsy 15.00 40.00
FV Fernando Vina Bat 15.00 40.00
MM Minnie Minoso Jsy 15.00 40.00
RA Richie Ashburn Bat 20.00 50.00
RS Red Schoendienst Bat 15.00 40.00
SG Shawn Green Bat 15.00 40.00
SR Scott Rolen Bat 20.00 50.00
WM Willie Mays Bat 30.00 60.00
DSSG Snider/Green Bat/52 60.00 150.00
EMCJ Mathews/Jones Bat/52 100.00 200.00
MMFT Minoso/Thomas Jsy/52 60.00 150.00
RASR Ashburn/Rolen Bat/52 100.00 250.00
RSFV Schoen/Vina Bat/52 125.00 200.00
WMBB Mays/Bonds Bat/52 200.00 350.00

2001 Topps Heritage Grandstand Glory

STATED ODDS 1:211 HOB/RET
JR Jackie Robinson 10.00 25.00
NF Nellie Fox 10.00 25.00
PR Phil Rizzuto 15.00 40.00
RA Richie Ashburn 10.00 25.00
RR Robin Roberts 10.00 25.00
WM Willie Mays 20.00 50.00
YB Yogi Berra 15.00 40.00

2001 Topps Heritage New Age Performers

COMPLETE SET (15) 20.00 50.00
STATED ODDS 1:8 HOBBY, 1:15 RETAIL
NAP1 Mike Piazza 1.50 4.00
NAP2 Sammy Sosa 1.00 2.50
NAP3 Alex Rodriguez 1.25 3.00
NAP4 Barry Bonds 2.50 6.00
NAP5 Ken Griffey Jr. 2.00 5.00
NAP6 Chipper Jones 1.00 2.50
NAP7 Randy Johnson 1.00 2.50
NAP8 Derek Jeter 2.50 6.00
NAP9 Nomar Garciaparra 1.50 4.00
NAP10 Mark McGwire 2.50 6.00
NAP11 Jeff Bagwell 1.00 2.50
NAP12 Pedro Martinez 1.00 2.50
NAP13 Todd Helton 1.00 2.50
NAP14 Vladimir Guerrero 1.00 2.50
NAP15 Greg Maddux 1.50 4.00

2001 Topps Heritage Then and Now

COMPLETE SET (10) 15.00 30.00
STATED ODDS 1:8 HOBBY, 1:15 RETAIL
TH1 Y.Berra M.Piazza 1.25 3.00
TH2 D.Snider S.Sosa .75 2.00
TH3 W.Mays K.Griffey Jr. 2.00 5.00
TH4 P.Rizzuto D.Jeter 2.00 5.00
TH5 P.Reese N.Garciaparra 1.25 3.00
TH6 J.Robinson A.Rodriguez 1.00 2.50
TH7 J.Mize M.McGwire 2.00 5.00
TH8 B.Feller P.Martinez .75 2.00
TH9 R.Roberts G.Maddux 1.25 3.00
TH10 W.Spahn R.Johnson .75 2.00

2001 Topps Heritage Time Capsule

STATED ODDS 1:369 HOB/RET
COMBO ODDS 1:28744 HOB, 1:29820 RET
DN Don Newcombe 10.00 25.00
TW Ted Williams 40.00 80.00
WF Whitey Ford 10.00 25.00
WM Willie Mays 20.00 50.00
WMTW Mays/Williams/52 125.00 200.00

2002 Topps Heritage

COMPLETE SET (450) 200.00 400.00
COMP.SET w/o SP's (350) 40.00 80.00
COMMON CARD (1-363) .20 .50
COMMON SP (364-446) 2.00 5.00
SP STATED ODDS 1:2
LOW SERIES SP'S: 1/37/53/82/104/220/244
253/261/267/268/271/275 DO NOT EXIST
1953 REPURCHASED EXCH.ODDS 1:1163
1 Ichiro Suzuki SP 6.00 15.00
2 Darin Erstad .25 .60
3 Rod Beck .25 .60
4 Doug Mientkiewicz .25 .60
5 Mike Sweeney .25 .60
6 Roger Clemens 1.25 3.00
7 Jason Tyner .20 .50
8 Alex Gonzalez .20 .50
9 Eric Young .20 .50
10 Randy Johnson .60 1.50
10N Randy Johnson Night SP 3.00 8.00
11 Aaron Sele .20 .50
12 Tony Clark .20 .50
13 C.C. Sabathia .25 .60
14 Melvin Mora .25 .60
15 Tim Hudson .25 .60
16 Ben Petrick .20 .50
17 Tom Glavine .40 1.00
18 Jason Lane .25 .60
19 Larry Walker .25 .60
20 Mark Mulder .25 .60
21 Steve Finley .25 .60
22 Bengie Molina .20 .50
23 Rob Bell .20 .50
24 Nathan Haynes .20 .50
25 Rafael Furcal .25 .60
25N Rafael Furcal Night SP 2.00 5.00
26 Mike Mussina .40 1.00
27 Paul LoDuca .25 .60
28 Torii Hunter .25 .60
29 Carlos Lee .25 .60
30 Jimmy Rollins .25 .60
31 Arthur Rhodes .20 .50
32 Ivan Rodriguez .40 1.00
33 Wes Helms .20 .50
34 Cliff Floyd .25 .60
35 Julian Tavarez .20 .50
36 Mark McGwire 1.50 4.00
37 Chipper Jones SP 3.00 8.00
38 Denny Neagle .20 .50
39 Odalis Perez .20 .50
40 Antonio Alfonseca .20 .50
41 Edgar Renteria .25 .60
42 Troy Glaus .25 .60
43 Scott Brosius .25 .60
44 Abraham Nunez .20 .50
45 Jamey Wright .20 .50
46 Bobby Bonilla .25 .60
47 Ismael Valdes .20 .50
48 Chris Reitsma .20 .50
49 Neifi Perez .20 .50
50 Juan Cruz .20 .50
51 Kevin Brown .25 .60
52 Ben Grieve .20 .50
53 Alex Rodriguez SP 4.00 10.00
54 Charles Nagy .20 .50
55 Reggie Sanders .25 .60
56 Nelson Figueroa .20 .50
57 Felipe Lopez .20 .50
58 Bill Ortega .20 .50
59 Jeffrey Hammonds .25 .60
60 Johnny Estrada .20 .50
61 Bob Wickman .20 .50
62 Doug Glanville .20 .50
63 Jeff Cirillo .20 .50
63N Jeff Cirillo Night SP 2.00 5.00
64 Corey Patterson .20 .50
65 Aaron Myette .20 .50
66 Maggio Ordonez .25 .60
67 Ellis Burks .25 .60
68 Miguel Tejada .25 .60
69 John Olerud .25 .60
69N John Olerud Night SP 2.00 5.00
70 Greg Vaughn .20 .50
71 Andy Pettitte .40 1.00
72 Mike Matheny .20 .50
73 Brandon Duckworth .20 .50
74 Scott Schoeneweis .20 .50
75 Mike Lowell .25 .60
76 Einar Diaz .20 .50
77 Tino Martinez .40 1.00
78 Matt Williams .25 .60
79 Jason Young RC .40 1.00
80 Nate Cornejo .20 .50
81 Andres Galarraga .25 .60
82 Bernie Williams SP 3.00 8.00
83 Ryan Klesko .25 .60
84 Dan Wilson .20 .50
85 Henry Pichardo RC .40 1.00
86 Ray Durham .25 .60
87 Omar Daal .20 .50
88 Derrek Lee .40 1.00
89 Al Leiter .25 .60
90 Darrin Fletcher .20 .50
91 Josh Beckett .25 .60
92 Johnny Damon .40 1.00
92N Johnny Damon Night SP 3.00 8.00
93 Abraham Nunez .20 .50
94 Ricky Ledee .20 .50
95 Richie Sexson .25 .60
96 Adam Kennedy .20 .50
97 Raul Mondesi .25 .60
98 John Burkett .25 .60
99 Ben Sheets .25 .60
99N Ben Sheets Night SP 2.00 5.00
100 Preston Wilson .25 .60
100N Preston Wilson Night SP 2.00 5.00
101 Boof Bonser .20 .50
102 Shigetoshi Hasegawa .25 .60
103 Carlos Febles .20 .50
104 Jorge Posada SP 3.00 8.00
105 Michael Tucker .20 .50
106 Roberto Hernandez .25 .60
107 John Rodriguez RC .40 1.00
108 Danny Graves .20 .50
109 Rich Aurilia .20 .50
110 Jon Lieber .20 .50
111 Tim Hummel RC .40 1.00
112 J.T. Snow .25 .60
113 Kris Benson .20 .50
114 Derek Jeter 1.50 4.00
115 John Franco .25 .60
116 Matt Stairs .20 .50
117 Ben Davis .20 .50
118 Darryl Kile .25 .60
119 Mike Peeples RC .40 1.00
120 Kevin Tapani .20 .50
121 Armando Benitez .20 .50
122 Damian Miller .20 .50
123 Jose Jimenez .20 .50
124 Pedro Astacio .20 .50
125 Marlyn Tisdale RC .40 1.00
126 Deivi Cruz .20 .50
127 Paul O'Neill .40 1.00
128 Jermaine Dye .25 .60
129 Marcus Giles .25 .60
130 Mark Loretta .20 .50
131 Garret Anderson .25 .60
132 Todd Ritchie .20 .50
133 Joe Crede .25 .60
134 Kevin Millwood .25 .60
135 Shane Reynolds .20 .50
136 Mark Grace .40 1.00
137 Shannon Stewart .25 .60
138 Nick Neugebauer .20 .50
139 Nic Jackson RC .40 1.00
140 Robb Nen UER .25 .60
141 Dmitri Young .25 .60
142 Kevin Appier .25 .60
143 Jack Cust .20 .50
144 Andres Torres .20 .50
145 Frank Thomas .60 1.50
146 Jason Kendall .25 .60
147 Greg Maddux 1.00 2.50
148 David Justice .25 .60
149 Hideo Nomo .60 1.50
150 Bret Boone .25 .60
151 Wade Miller .20 .50
152 Jeff Kent .25 .60
153 Scott Williamson .20 .50
154 Julio Lugo .20 .50
155 Bobby Higginson .25 .60
156 Geoff Jenkins .20 .50
157 Darren Dreifort .20 .50
158 Freddy Sanchez RC 1.25 3.00
159 Bud Smith .20 .50
160 Phil Nevin .25 .60
161 Cesar Izturis .20 .50
162 Sean Casey .25 .60
163 Jose Ortiz .20 .50
164 Brent Abernathy .20 .50
165 Kevin Young .20 .50
166 Daryle Ward .20 .50
167 Trevor Hoffman .25 .60
168 Rondell White .25 .60
169 Kip Wells .20 .50
170 John Vander Wal .20 .50
171 Jose Lima .20 .50
172 Wilton Guerrero .20 .50
173 Aaron Dean RC .40 1.00
174 Rick Helling .20 .50
175 Juan Pierre .25 .60
176 Jay Bell .25 .60
177 Craig House .20 .50
178 David Bell .20 .50
179 Pat Burrell .25 .60
180 Eric Gagne .25 .60
181 Adam Pettyjohn .20 .50
182 Ugueth Urbina .20 .50
183 Peter Bergeron .20 .50
184 Adrian Gonzalez .20 .50
184N Adrian Gonzalez Night SP 2.00 5.00
185 Damion Easley .20 .50
186 Gookie Dawkins .20 .50
187 Matt Lawton .20 .50
188 Frank Catalanotto .20 .50
189 David Wells .25 .60
190 Roger Cedeno .20 .50
191 Brian Giles .25 .60
192 Julio Zuleta .20 .50
193 Timo Perez .20 .50
194 Billy Wagner .25 .60
195 Craig Counsell .20 .50
196 Bart Miadich .20 .50
197 Gary Sheffield .25 .60
198 Richard Hidalgo .20 .50
199 Juan Uribe .20 .50
200 Curt Schilling .25 .60
201 Javy Lopez .25 .60
202 Jimmy Haynes .20 .50
203 Jim Edmonds .25 .60
204 Pokey Reese .20 .50
204N Pokey Reese Night SP 2.00 5.00
205 Matt Clement .25 .60
206 Dean Palmer .25 .60
207 Nick Johnson .25 .60
208 Nate Espy RC .40 1.00
209 Pedro Feliz .20 .50
210 Aaron Rowand .25 .60
211 Masato Yoshii .20 .50
212 Jose Cruz Jr. .20 .50
213 Paul Byrd .20 .50
214 Mark Phillips RC .40 1.00
215 Benny Agbayani .20 .50
216 Frank Menechino .20 .50
217 John Flaherty .20 .50
218 Brian Boehringer .20 .50
219 Todd Hollandsworth .20 .50
220 Sammy Sosa SP 3.00 8.00
221 Steve Sparks .20 .50
222 Homer Bush .20 .50
223 Mike Hampton .25 .60
224 Bobby Abreu .25 .60
225 Barry Larkin .40 1.00
226 Ryan Rupe .20 .50
227 Bubba Trammell .20 .50
228 Todd Zeile .25 .60
229 Jeff Shaw .20 .50
230 Alex Ochoa .20 .50
231 Orlando Cabrera .25 .60
232 Jeremy Giambi .20 .50
233 Tomo Ohka .20 .50
234 Luis Castillo .20 .50
235 Chris Holt .20 .50
236 Shawn Green .25 .60
237 Sidney Ponson .20 .50
238 Lee Stevens .20 .50
239 Hank Blalock .40 1.00
240 Randy Winn .20 .50
241 Pedro Martinez .40 1.00
242 Vinny Castilla .25 .60
243 Steve Karsay .20 .50
244 Barry Bonds SP 8.00 20.00
245 Jason Bere .20 .50
246 Scott Rolen .40 1.00
246N Scott Rolen Night SP 3.00 8.00
247 Ryan Kohlmeier .20 .50
248 Kerry Wood .25 .60
249 Aramis Ramirez .25 .60
250 Lance Berkman .25 .60
251 Omar Vizquel .40 1.00
252 Juan Encarnacion .20 .50
254 David Segui .20 .50
255 Brian Anderson .20 .50
256 Jay Payton .20 .50
257 Mark Grudzielanek .20 .50
258 Jimmy Anderson .20 .50
259 Eric Valent .20 .50
260 Chad Durbin .20 .50
262 Alex Gonzalez .20 .50
263 Scott Dunn .20 .50
264 Scott Elarton .20 .50
265 Tom Gordon .20 .50
266 Moises Alou .25 .60
269 Mark Buehrle .25 .60
270 Jerry Hairston .20 .50
272 Luke Prokopec .20 .50
273 Graeme Lloyd .20 .50
274 Bret Prinz .20 .50
276 Chris Carpenter .40 1.00
277 Ryan Minor .20 .50
278 Jeff D'Amico .20 .50
279 Raul Ibanez .20 .50
280 Joe Mays .20 .50
281 Livan Hernandez .25 .60
282 Robin Ventura .25 .60
283 Gabe Kapler .25 .60
284 Tony Batista .20 .50
285 Ramon Hernandez .20 .50
286 Craig Paquette .20 .50
287 Mark Kotsay .25 .60
288 Mike Lieberthal .25 .60
289 Joe Borchard .20 .50
290 Cristian Guzman .20 .50
291 Craig Biggio .40 1.00
292 Joaquin Benoit .20 .50
293 Ken Caminiti .25 .60
294 Sean Burroughs .20 .50
295 Eric Karros .25 .60
296 Eric Chavez .25 .60
297 LaTroy Hawkins .20 .50
298 Alfonso Soriano .25 .60
299 John Smoltz .40 1.00
300 Adam Dunn .25 .60
301 Ryan Dempster .20 .50
302 Travis Hafner .25 .60
303 Russell Branyan .20 .50
304 Dustin Hermanson .20 .50
305 Jim Thome .40 1.00

Card	Low	High
306 Carlos Beltran	.25	.60
307 Jason Botts RC	.25	.60
308 David Cone	.25	.60
309 Ivanon Coffie	.20	.50
310 Brian Jordan	.25	.60
311 Todd Walker	.20	.50
312 Jeromy Burnitz	.25	.60
313 Tony Armas Jr.	.20	.50
314 Jeff Conine	.25	.60
315 Todd Jones	.20	.50
316 Roy Oswalt	.25	.60
317 Aubrey Huff	.25	.60
318 Josh Fogg	.20	.50
319 Jose Vidro	.20	.50
320 Jace Brewer	.20	.50
321 Mike Redmond	.20	.50
322 Noochie Varner RC	.40	1.00
323 Russ Ortiz	.20	.50
324 Edgardo Alfonzo	.20	.50
325 Ruben Sierra	.25	.60
326 Calvin Murray	.20	.50
327 Marlon Anderson	.20	.50
328 Albie Lopez	.20	.50
329 Chris Gomez	.20	.50
330 Fernando Tatis	.20	.50
331 Stubby Clapp	.20	.50
332 Rickey Henderson	.60	1.50
333 Brad Radke	.25	.60
334 Brent Mayne	.20	.50
335 Cory Lidle	.20	.50
336 Edgar Martinez	.40	1.00
337 Aaron Boone	.25	.60
338 Jay Witasick	.20	.50
339 Benito Santiago	.25	.60
340 Jose Mercedes	.20	.50
341 Fernando Vina	.20	.50
342 A.J. Pierzynski	.25	.60
343 Jeff Bagwell	.40	1.00
344 Brian Bohanon	.20	.50
345 Adrian Beltre	.25	.60
346 Troy Percival	.25	.60
347 Napoleon Calzado RC	.40	1.00
348 Ruben Rivera	.20	.50
349 Rafael Soriano	.20	.50
350 Damian Jackson	.20	.50
351 Joe Randa	.25	.60
352 Chan Ho Park	.25	.60
353 Dante Bichette	.25	.60
354 Bartolo Colon	.25	.60
355 Jason Bay RC	2.00	5.00
356 Shea Hillenbrand	.25	.60
357 Matt Morris	.25	.60
358 Brad Penny	.20	.50
359 Mark Quinn	.20	.50
360 Marquis Grissom	.25	.60
361 Henry Blanco	.20	.50
362 Billy Koch	.20	.50
363 Mike Cameron	.20	.50
364 Albert Pujols SP	6.00	15.00
365 Paul Konerko SP	2.00	5.00
366 Eric Milton SP	2.00	5.00
367 Nick Bierbrodt SP	2.00	5.00
368 Rafael Palmeiro SP	3.00	8.00
369 Jorge Padilla SP RC	2.00	5.00
370 Jason Giambi Yankees SP	2.00	5.00
371 Mike Piazza SP	5.00	12.00
372 Alex Cora SP	2.00	5.00
373 Todd Helton SP	3.00	8.00
374 Juan Gonzalez SP	2.00	5.00
375 Mariano Rivera SP	10.00	25.00
376 Jason LaRue SP	2.00	5.00
377 Tony Gwynn SP	4.00	10.00
378 Wilson Betemit SP	2.00	5.00
379 J.J. Trujillo SP RC	2.00	5.00
380 Brad Ausmus SP	2.00	5.00
381 Chris George SP	2.00	5.00
382 Jose Canseco SP	3.00	8.00
383 Ramon Ortiz SP	2.00	5.00
384 John Rocker SP	2.00	5.00
385 Rey Ordonez SP	2.00	5.00
386 Ken Griffey Jr. SP	6.00	15.00
387 Juan Pena SP	2.00	5.00
388 Michael Barrett SP	2.00	5.00
389 J.D. Drew SP	2.00	5.00
390 Corey Koskie SP	2.00	5.00
391 Vernon Wells SP	2.00	5.00
392 Juan Tolentino SP RC	2.00	5.00
393 Luis Gonzalez SP	2.00	5.00
394 Terrence Long SP	2.00	5.00
395 Travis Lee SP	2.00	5.00
396 Earl Snyder SP RC	2.00	5.00
397 Nomar Garciaparra SP	5.00	12.00
398 Jason Schmidt SP	2.00	5.00
399 David Espinosa SP	2.00	5.00
400 Steve Green SP	2.00	5.00
401 Jack Wilson SP	2.00	5.00
402 Chris Tritle SP RC	2.00	5.00
403 Angel Berroa SP	2.00	5.00
404 Josh Towers SP	2.00	5.00
405 Andruw Jones SP	3.00	8.00
406 Brent Butler SP	2.00	5.00
407 Craig Kuzmic SP	2.00	5.00
408 Derek Bell SP	2.00	5.00
409 Eric Glaser SP RC	2.00	5.00
410 Joel Pineiro SP	2.00	5.00
411 Alexis Gomez SP	2.00	5.00
412 Mike Rivera SP	2.00	5.00
413 Shawn Estes SP	2.00	5.00
414 Milton Bradley SP	2.00	5.00
415 Carl Everett SP	2.00	5.00
416 Kazuhiro Sasaki SP	2.00	5.00
417 Tony Fontana SP RC	2.00	5.00
418 Josh Pearce SP	2.00	5.00
419 Gary Matthews Jr. SP	2.00	5.00
420 Raymond Cabrera SP RC	2.00	5.00
421 Joe Kennedy SP	2.00	5.00
422 Jason Maule SP RC	2.00	5.00
423 Casey Fossum SP	2.00	5.00
424 Christian Parker SP	2.00	5.00
425 Laynce Nix SP RC	4.00	10.00
426 Byung-Hyun Kim SP	2.00	5.00
427 Freddy Garcia SP	2.00	5.00
428 Herbert Perry SP	2.00	5.00
429 Jason Marquis SP	2.00	5.00
430 Sandy Alomar Jr. SP	2.00	5.00
431 Roberto Alomar SP	3.00	8.00
432 Tsuyoshi Shinjo SP	2.00	5.00
433 Tim Wakefield SP	2.00	5.00
434 Robert Fick SP	2.00	5.00
435 Vladimir Guerrero SP	3.00	8.00
436 Jose Mesa SP	2.00	5.00
437 Scott Spiezio SP	2.00	5.00
438 Jose Hernandez SP	2.00	5.00
439 Jose Acevedo SP	2.00	5.00
440 Brian West SP RC	2.00	5.00
441 Barry Zito SP	2.00	5.00
442 Luis Maza SP	2.00	5.00
443 Marlon Byrd SP	2.00	5.00
444 A.J. Burnett SP	2.00	5.00
445 Dee Brown SP	2.00	5.00
446 Carlos Delgado SP	2.00	5.00
CL1 Checklist 1	.20	.50
CL2 Checklist 2	.20	.50

2002 Topps Heritage Chrome

STATED ODDS 1:29
STATED PRINT RUN 553 SERIAL #'d SETS

Card	Low	High
THC1 Darin Erstad	5.00	12.00
THC2 Doug Mientkiewicz	5.00	12.00
THC3 Mike Sweeney	5.00	12.00
THC4 Roger Clemens	15.00	40.00
THC5 C.C. Sabathia	5.00	12.00
THC6 Tim Hudson	5.00	12.00
THC7 Jason Lane	5.00	12.00
THC8 Larry Walker	5.00	12.00
THC9 Mark Mulder	5.00	12.00
THC10 Mike Mussina	5.00	12.00
THC11 Paul LoDuca	5.00	12.00
THC12 Jimmy Rollins	5.00	12.00
THC13 Ivan Rodriguez	5.00	12.00
THC14 Mark McGwire	20.00	50.00
THC15 Edgar Renteria	5.00	12.00
THC16 Scott Brosius	5.00	12.00
THC17 Juan Cruz	5.00	12.00
THC18 Kevin Brown	5.00	12.00
THC19 Charles Nagy	5.00	12.00
THC20 Bill Ortega	5.00	12.00
THC21 Corey Patterson	5.00	12.00
THC22 Magglio Ordonez	5.00	12.00
THC23 Brandon Duckworth	5.00	12.00
THC24 Scott Schoeneweis	5.00	12.00
THC25 Tino Martinez	5.00	12.00
THC26 Jason Young	5.00	12.00
THC27 Nate Cornejo	5.00	12.00
THC28 Ryan Klesko	5.00	12.00
THC29 Omar Daal	5.00	12.00
THC30 Raul Mondesi	5.00	12.00
THC31 Boof Bonser	5.00	12.00
THC32 Rich Aurilia	5.00	12.00
THC33 Jon Lieber	5.00	12.00
THC34 Tim Hummel	5.00	12.00
THC35 J.T. Snow	5.00	12.00
THC36 Derek Jeter	30.00	80.00
THC37 Darryl Kile	5.00	12.00
THC38 Armando Benitez	5.00	12.00
THC39 Marlyn Tisdale	5.00	12.00
THC40 Shannon Stewart	5.00	12.00
THC41 Nic Jackson	5.00	12.00
THC42 Robb Nen UER	5.00	12.00
THC43 Dmitri Young	5.00	12.00
THC44 Greg Maddux	12.50	30.00
THC45 Hideo Nomo	8.00	20.00
THC46 Bret Boone	5.00	12.00
THC47 Wade Miller	5.00	12.00
THC48 Jeff Kent	5.00	12.00
THC49 Freddy Sanchez	8.00	20.00
THC50 Bud Smith	5.00	12.00
THC51 Sean Casey	5.00	12.00
THC52 Brent Abernathy	5.00	12.00
THC53 Trevor Hoffman	5.00	12.00
THC54 Aaron Dean	5.00	12.00
THC55 Juan Pierre	5.00	12.00
THC56 Pat Burrell	5.00	12.00
THC57 Gookie Dawkins	5.00	12.00
THC58 Roger Cedeno	5.00	12.00
THC59 Brian Giles	5.00	12.00
THC60 Jim Edmonds	5.00	12.00
THC61 Dean Palmer	5.00	12.00
THC62 Nick Johnson	5.00	12.00
THC63 Nate Espy	5.00	12.00
THC64 Aaron Rowand	5.00	12.00
THC65 Mark Phillips	5.00	12.00
THC66 Mike Hampton	5.00	12.00
THC67 Bobby Abreu	5.00	12.00
THC68 Alex Ochoa	5.00	12.00
THC69 Shawn Green	5.00	12.00
THC70 Hank Blalock	5.00	12.00
THC71 Pedro Martinez	5.00	12.00
THC72 Ryan Kohlmeier	5.00	12.00
THC73 Kerry Wood	5.00	12.00
THC74 Aramis Ramirez	5.00	12.00
THC75 Lance Berkman	5.00	12.00
THC76 Scott Dunn	5.00	12.00
THC77 Moises Alou	5.00	12.00
THC78 Mark Buehrle	5.00	12.00
THC79 Jerry Hairston	5.00	12.00
THC80 Joe Borchard	5.00	12.00
THC81 Cristian Guzman	5.00	12.00
THC82 Sean Burroughs	5.00	12.00
THC83 Alfonso Soriano	5.00	12.00
THC84 Adam Dunn	5.00	12.00
THC85 Jim Thome	5.00	12.00
THC86 Jason Botts	5.00	12.00
THC87 Jeromy Burnitz	5.00	12.00
THC88 Roy Oswalt	5.00	12.00
THC89 Russ Ortiz	5.00	12.00
THC90 Marlon Anderson	5.00	12.00
THC91 Stubby Clapp	5.00	12.00
THC92 Rickey Henderson	8.00	20.00
THC93 Brad Radke	5.00	12.00
THC94 Jeff Bagwell	5.00	12.00
THC95 Troy Percival	5.00	12.00
THC96 Napoleon Calzado	5.00	12.00
THC97 Joe Randa	5.00	12.00
THC98 Chan Ho Park	5.00	12.00
THC99 Jason Bay	10.00	25.00
THC100 Mark Quinn	5.00	12.00

2002 Topps Heritage Classic Renditions

Card	Low	High
COMPLETE SET (10)	8.00	20.00
STATED ODDS 1:12		
CR1 Kerry Wood	.75	2.00
CR2 Brian Giles	.75	2.00
CR3 Roger Cedeno	.75	2.00
CR4 Jason Giambi	.75	2.00
CR5 Albert Pujols	2.00	5.00
CR6 Mark Buehrle	.75	2.00
CR7 Cristian Guzman	.75	2.00
CR8 Jimmy Rollins	.75	2.00
CR9 Jim Thome	.75	2.00
CR10 Shawn Green	.75	2.00

2002 Topps Heritage Clubhouse Collection

BAT STATED ODDS 1:498
JERSEY STATED ODDS 1:332

Card	Low	High
CCAD Alvin Dark Bat	10.00	25.00
CCBB Barry Bonds Bat	12.50	30.00
CCCP Corey Patterson Bat	10.00	25.00
CCEM Eddie Mathews Jsy	15.00	40.00
CCGK George Kell Jsy	15.00	40.00
CCGM Greg Maddux Jsy	15.00	40.00
CCHS Hank Sauer Bat	10.00	25.00
CCJP Jorge Posada Bat	10.00	25.00
CCNG Nomar Garciaparra Bat	10.00	25.00
CCRA Rich Aurilia Bat	10.00	25.00
CCWM Willie Mays Bat	15.00	40.00
CCYB Yogi Berra Jsy	10.00	25.00

2002 Topps Heritage Clubhouse Collection Duos

STATED ODDS 1:5016
STATED PRINT RUN 53 SERIAL #'d SETS
NO PRICING DUE TO SCARCITY

Card	Low	High
CC2BP Y.Berra/J.Posada	40.00	80.00
CC2DA A.Dark/R.Aurilia	40.00	80.00
CC2KR G.Kell/N.Garciaparra	40.00	80.00
CC2MB W.Mays/B.Bonds	150.00	250.00
CC2SM E.Mathews/G.Maddux	40.00	80.00
CC2SP H.Sauer/C.Patterson	30.00	60.00

2002 Topps Heritage Grandstand Glory

GROUP A STATED ODDS 1:4115
GROUP B STATED ODDS 1:531
GROUP C STATED ODDS 1:1576
GROUP D STATED ODDS 1:370
GROUP E STATED ODDS 1:483

Card	Low	High
GGBF Bob Feller E	10.00	25.00
GGBM Billy Martin B	10.00	25.00
GGBP Billy Pierce B	8.00	20.00
GGBS Bobby Shantz D	8.00	20.00
GGEW Early Wynn E	10.00	25.00
GGHN Hal Newhouser B	10.00	25.00
GGHS Hank Sauer C	8.00	20.00
GGRC Roy Campanella D	15.00	40.00
GGSP Satchel Paige A	12.50	30.00
GGTK Ted Kluszewski E	15.00	40.00
GGWF Whitey Ford D	10.00	25.00
GGWS Warren Spahn D	15.00	40.00

2002 Topps Heritage New Age Performers

Card	Low	High
COMPLETE SET (15)	10.00	25.00
STATED ODDS 1:15		
NA1 Luis Gonzalez	.40	1.00
NA2 Mark McGwire	1.50	4.00
NA3 Barry Bonds	1.50	4.00
NA4 Ken Griffey Jr.	2.00	5.00
NA5 Ichiro Suzuki	1.25	3.00
NA6 Sammy Sosa	1.00	2.50
NA7 Andruw Jones	.40	1.00
NA8 Derek Jeter	2.50	6.00
NA9 Todd Helton	.60	1.50
NA10 Alex Rodriguez	1.25	3.00
NA11 Jason Giambi Yankees	.40	1.00
NA12 Bret Boone	.40	1.00
NA13 Roberto Alomar	.60	1.50
NA14 Albert Pujols	2.00	5.00
NA15 Vladimir Guerrero	.60	1.50

2002 Topps Heritage Real One Autographs

GROUP 1 STATED ODDS 1:346
GROUP 2 STATED ODDS 1:6363
GROUP 3 STATED ODDS 1:4908
GROUP 4 STATED ODDS 1:3196
GROUP 5 STATED ODDS 1:498
*RED INK: .75X TO 1.5X BASIC AUTO'S
RED INK ODDS 1:306
RED INK PRINT RUN 53 SERIAL #'d SETS

Card	Low	High
ROAC Andy Carey 1	30.00	60.00
ROAD Alvin Dark 1	10.00	25.00
ROAR Al Rosen 1	20.00	50.00
ROARO Alex Rodriguez 2	30.00	80.00
ROASC Al Schoendienst 1	30.00	60.00
ROBF Bob Feller 1	50.00	100.00
ROBG Brian Giles 5	10.00	25.00
ROBS Bobby Shantz 1	20.00	50.00
ROCG Cristian Guzman 5	6.00	15.00
RODD Dom DiMaggio 1	25.00	60.00
ROES Enos Slaughter 1	30.00	60.00
ROGK George Kell 1	20.00	50.00
ROGM Gil McDougald 1	15.00	40.00
ROHW Hoyt Wilhelm 1	50.00	100.00
ROJB Joe Black 1	30.00	60.00
ROJE Jim Edmonds 4	15.00	40.00
ROJP John Podres 1	15.00	40.00
ROMI Monte Irvin 1	20.00	50.00
ROOM Minnie Minoso 1	30.00	60.00
ROPR Phil Rizzuto 1	50.00	100.00
ROPRO Preacher Roe 1	30.00	60.00
RORB Ray Boone 1	50.00	100.00
RORF Roy Face 1	10.00	25.00
RORCL Roger Clemens 3	30.00	80.00
ROWF Whitey Ford 1	40.00	100.00
ROWM Willie Mays 1	150.00	400.00
ROWS Warren Spahn 1	25.00	60.00
ROYB Yogi Berra 1	40.00	100.00

2002 Topps Heritage Then and Now

Card	Low	High
COMPLETE SET (10)	12.50	30.00
STATED ODDS 1:15		
TN1 E.Mathews / B.Bonds	2.50	6.00
TN2 A.Rosen / A.Rodriguez	1.25	3.00
TN3 C.Furillo / L.Walker	.75	2.00
TN4 M.Minoso / I.Suzuki	2.00	5.00
TN5 R.Ashburn / R.Aurilia	.75	2.00
TN6 A.Rosen / B.Boone	.75	2.00
TN7 D.Snider / S.Sosa	1.00	2.50
TN8 A.Rosen / A.Rodriguez	1.25	3.00
TN9 R.Roberts / R.Johnson	1.00	2.50
TN10 B.Pierce / H.Nomo	1.00	2.50

2003 Topps Heritage

Card	Low	High
COMPLETE SET (453)	125.00	250.00
COMP.SET w/o SP's (353)	30.00	60.00
COMMON CARD	.20	.50
COMMON RC	.40	1.00
COMMON SP	2.00	5.00
COMMON SP RC	2.00	5.00

SP STATED ODDS 1:2
BASIC SP: 3/25/85/94/128/132/141/170
BASIC SP: 175/200/201/239/250/364-430
BLACK SP: 1/7/18/20/50/80/139/150
BLACK SP: 260/340
OLD LOGO SP: 6/10/11/27/30/100/156/190
OLD LOGO SP: 302/325

Card	Low	High
1A Alex Rodriguez Red	.60	1.50
1B Alex Rodriguez Black SP	5.00	12.00
2 Jose Cruz Jr.	.20	.50
3 Ichiro Suzuki SP	6.00	15.00
4 Rich Aurilia	.20	.50
5 Trevor Hoffman	.30	.75
6A Brian Giles New Logo	.20	.50
6B Brian Giles Old Logo SP	2.00	5.00
7A Albert Pujols Orange	.60	1.50
7B Albert Pujols Black SP	6.00	15.00
8 Vicente Padilla	.20	.50
9 Bobby Crosby	.20	.50
10A Derek Jeter New Logo	1.25	3.00
10B Derek Jeter Old Logo SP	6.00	15.00
11A Pat Burrell New Logo	.20	.50
11B Pat Burrell Old Logo SP	2.00	5.00
12 Armando Benitez	.20	.50
13 Javier Vazquez	.20	.50
14 Justin Morneau	.30	.75
15 Doug Mientkiewicz	.20	.50
16 Kevin Brown	.20	.50
17 Alexis Gomez	.20	.50
18A Lance Berkman Blue	.30	.75
18B Lance Berkman Black SP	3.00	8.00
19 Adrian Gonzalez	.40	1.00
20A Todd Helton Green	.30	.75
20B Todd Helton Black SP	3.00	8.00
21 Carlos Pena	.30	.75
22 Matt Lawton	.20	.50
23 Elmer Dessens	.20	.50
24 Hee Seop Choi	.20	.50
25 Chris Duncan SP RC	5.00	12.00
26 Ugueth Urbina	.20	.50
27A Rodrigo Lopez New Logo	.20	.50
27B Rodrigo Lopez Old Logo SP	2.00	5.00
28 Damian Moss	.20	.50
29 Steve Finley	.20	.50
30A Sammy Sosa New Logo	.50	1.25
30B Sammy Sosa Old Logo SP	5.00	12.00
31 Kevin Cash	.20	.50
32 Kenny Rogers	.20	.50
33 Ben Grieve	.20	.50
34 Jason Simontacchi	.20	.50
35 Shin-Soo Choo	.30	.75
36 Freddy Garcia	.20	.50
37 Jesse Foppert	.20	.50
38 Tony LaRussa MG	.30	.75
39 Mark Kotsay	.20	.50
40 Barry Zito	.30	.75
41 Josh Fogg	.20	.50
42 Marlon Byrd	.20	.50
43 Marcus Thames	.20	.50
44 Al Leiter	.20	.50
45 Michael Barrett	.20	.50
46 Jake Peavy	.20	.50
47 Dustan Mohr	.20	.50
48 Alex Sanchez	.20	.50
49 Chin-Feng Chen	.20	.50
50A Kazuhisa Ishii Blue	.20	.50
50B Kazuhisa Ishii Black SP	2.00	5.00
51 Carlos Beltran	.30	.75
52 Franklin Gutierrez RC	1.00	2.50
53 Miguel Cabrera	2.50	6.00
54 Roger Clemens	.60	1.50
55 Juan Cruz	.20	.50
56 Jason Young	.20	.50
57 Alex Herrera	.20	.50
58 Aaron Boone	.20	.50
59 Mark Buehrle	.30	.75
60 Larry Walker	.30	.75
61 Morgan Ensberg	.20	.50
62 Barry Larkin	.30	.75
63 Joe Borchard	.20	.50
64 Jason Dubois	.20	.50
65 Shea Hillenbrand	.20	.50
66 Jay Gibbons	.20	.50
67 Vinny Castilla	.20	.50
68 Jeff Mathis	.20	.50
69 Curt Schilling	.30	.75
70 Garret Anderson	.20	.50
71 Josh Phelps	.20	.50
72 Chan Ho Park	.30	.75
73 Edgar Renteria	.20	.50
74 Kazuhiro Sasaki	.20	.50
75 Lloyd McClendon MG	.20	.50
76 Jon Lieber	.20	.50
77 Rolando Viera	.20	.50
78 Jeff Conine	.20	.50
79 Kevin Millwood	.20	.50
80A Randy Johnson Green	.50	1.25
80B Randy Johnson Black SP	5.00	12.00
81 Troy Percival	.20	.50
82 Cliff Floyd	.20	.50
83 Tony Graffanino	.20	.50
84 Austin Kearns	.20	.50
85 Manuel Ramirez SP RC	2.00	5.00
86 Jim Tracy MG	.20	.50
87 Rondell White	.20	.50
88 Trot Nixon	.20	.50
89 Carlos Lee	.20	.50
90 Mike Lowell	.20	.50
91 Raul Ibanez	.30	.75
92 Ricardo Rodriguez	.20	.50
93 Ben Sheets	.20	.50
94 Jason Perry SP RC	2.00	5.00
95 Mark Teixeira	.30	.75
96 Brad Fullmer	.20	.50
97 Casey Kotchman	.20	.50
98 Craig Counsell	.20	.50
99 Jason Marquis	.20	.50
100A N.Garciaparra New Logo	.30	.75
100B N.Garciaparra Old Logo SP	3.00	8.00
101 Ed Rogers	.20	.50
102 Wilson Betemit	.20	.50
103 Wayne Lydon RC	.40	1.00
104 Jack Cust	.20	.50
105 Derrek Lee	.20	.50
106 Jim Kavourias	.20	.50
107 Joe Randa	.20	.50
108 Taylor Buchholz	.20	.50
109 Gabe Kapler	.20	.50
110 Preston Wilson	.20	.50
111 Craig Biggio	.30	.75
112 Paul Lo Duca	.20	.50
113 Eddie Guardado	.20	.50
114 Andres Galarraga	.30	.75
115 Edgardo Alfonzo	.20	.50
116 Robin Ventura	.20	.50
117 Jeremy Giambi	.20	.50
118 Ray Durham	.20	.50
119 Mariano Rivera	.60	1.50
120 Jimmy Rollins	.30	.75
121 Dennis Tankersley	.20	.50
122 Jason Schmidt	.20	.50
123 Bret Boone	.20	.50
124 Josh Hamilton	.30	.75
125 Scott Rolen	.30	.75
126 Steve Cox	.20	.50
127 Larry Bowa MG	.20	.50
128 Adam LaRoche SP	2.00	5.00
129 Ryan Klesko	.20	.50
130 Tim Hudson	.30	.75
131 Brandon Claussen	.20	.50
132 Craig Brazell SP RC	2.00	5.00
133 Grady Little MG	.20	.50
134 Jarrod Washburn	.20	.50
135 Lyle Overbay	.20	.50
136 John Burkett	.20	.50
137 Daryl Clark RC	.40	1.00
138 Kirk Rueter	.20	.50
139A Mauer Brothers Green	.50	1.25
139B Mauer Brothers Black SP	5.00	12.00
140 Troy Glaus	.20	.50
141 Trey Hodges SP	2.00	5.00
142 Dallas McPherson	.20	.50
143 Art Howe MG	.20	.50
144 Jesus Cota	.20	.50
145 J.R. House	.20	.50
146 Reggie Sanders	.20	.50
147 Clint Nageotte	.20	.50
148 Jim Edmonds	.30	.75
149 Carl Crawford	.30	.75
150A Mike Piazza Blue	.50	1.25
150B Mike Piazza Black SP	5.00	12.00
151 Seung Song	.20	.50
152 Roberto Hernandez	.20	.50
153 Marquis Grissom	.20	.50
154 Billy Wagner	.20	.50
155 Josh Beckett	.20	.50
156A Randall Simon New Logo	.20	.50
156B Randall Simon Old Logo SP	2.00	5.00
157 Ben Broussard	.20	.50
158 Russell Branyan	.20	.50
159 Frank Thomas	.50	1.25
160 Alex Escobar	.20	.50
161 Mark Bellhorn	.20	.50
162 Melvin Mora	.20	.50
163 Andruw Jones	.20	.50
164 Danny Bautista	.20	.50
165 Ramon Ortiz	.20	.50
166 Wily Mo Pena	.20	.50
167 Jose Jimenez	.20	.50
168 Mark Redman	.20	.50
169 Angel Berroa	.20	.50
170 Andy Marte SP RC	2.00	5.00
171 Juan Gonzalez	.20	.50
172 Fernando Vina	.20	.50
173 Joel Pineiro	.20	.50
174 Boof Bonser	.20	.50
175 Bernie Castro SP RC	2.00	5.00
176 Bobby Cox MG	.20	.50
177 Jeff Kent	.20	.50
178 Oliver Perez	.20	.50
179 Chase Utley	.30	.75
180 Mark Mulder	.20	.50
181 Bobby Abreu	.20	.50
182 Ramiro Mendoza	.20	.50
183 Aaron Heilman	.20	.50
184 A.J. Pierzynski	.20	.50
185 Eric Gagne	.20	.50
186 Kirk Saarloos	.20	.50
187 Ron Gardenhire MG	.20	.50
188 Dmitri Young	.20	.50
189 Todd Zeile	.20	.50
190A Jim Thome New Logo	.30	.75
190B Jim Thome Old Logo SP	3.00	8.00
191 Cliff Lee	1.25	3.00
192 Matt Morris	.20	.50
193 Robert Fick	.20	.50
194 C.C. Sabathia	.30	.75
195 Alexis Rios	.20	.50
196 D'Angelo Jimenez	.20	.50
197 Edgar Martinez	.30	.75
198 Robb Nen	.20	.50
199 Taggert Bozied	.20	.50
200 Vladimir Guerrero SP	3.00	8.00
201 Walter Young SP	2.00	5.00
202 Brendan Harris RC	.40	1.00
203 Mike Hargrove MG	.20	.50
204 Vernon Wells	.20	.50
205 Hank Blalock	.20	.50
206 Mike Cameron	.20	.50
207 Tony Batista	.20	.50
208 Matt Williams	.20	.50
209 Tony Womack	.20	.50
210 Ramon Nivar-Martinez RC	.40	1.00
211 Aaron Sele	.20	.50
212 Mark Grace	.30	.75
213 Joe Crede	.20	.50
214 Ryan Dempster	.20	.50
215 Omar Vizquel	.30	.75
216 Juan Pierre	.20	.50
217 Denny Bautista	.20	.50
218 Chuck Knoblauch	.20	.50
219 Eric Karros	.20	.50
220 Victor Diaz	.20	.50
221 Jacque Jones	.20	.50
222 Jose Vidro	.20	.50
223 Joe McEwing	.20	.50
224 Nick Johnson	.20	.50
225 Eric Chavez	.20	.50
226 Jose Mesa	.20	.50
227 Aramis Ramirez	.20	.50
228 John Lackey	.30	.75
229 David Bell	.20	.50
230 John Olerud	.20	.50
231 Tino Martinez	.20	.50
232 Randy Winn	.20	.50
233 Todd Hollandsworth	.20	.50
234 Ruddy Lugo RC	.40	1.00
235 Carlos Delgado	.20	.50
236 Chris Narveson	.20	.50
237 Tim Salmon	.20	.50
238 Orlando Palmeiro	.20	.50
239 Jeff Clark SP RC	2.00	5.00
240 Byung-Hyun Kim	.20	.50
241 Mike Remlinger	.20	.50
242 Johnny Damon	.30	.75
243 Corey Patterson	.20	.50
244 Paul Konerko	.30	.75
245 Danny Graves	.20	.50
246 Ellis Burks	.20	.50
247 Gavin Floyd	.20	.50
248 Jaime Bubela RC	.40	1.00
249 Sean Burroughs	.20	.50
250 Alex Rodriguez SP	5.00	12.00
251 Gabe Gross	.20	.50
252 Rafael Palmeiro	.30	.75
253 Dewon Brazelton	.20	.50
254 Jimmy Journell	.20	.50
255 Rafael Soriano	.20	.50
256 Jerome Williams	.20	.50
257 Xavier Nady	.20	.50
258 Mike Williams	.20	.50
259 Randy Wolf	.20	.50
260A Miguel Tejada Orange	.30	.75
260B Miguel Tejada Black SP	3.00	8.00
261 Juan Rivera	.20	.50
262 Rey Ordonez	.20	.50
263 Bartolo Colon	.20	.50
264 Eric Milton	.20	.50
265 Jeffrey Hammonds	.20	.50
266 Odalis Perez	.20	.50
267 Mike Sweeney	.20	.50
268 Richard Hidalgo	.20	.50
269 Alex Gonzalez	.20	.50
270 Aaron Cook	.20	.50
271 Earl Snyder	.20	.50
272 Todd Walker	.20	.50
273 Aaron Rowand	.20	.50
274 Matt Clement	.20	.50
275 Anastacio Martinez	.20	.50
276 Mike Bordick	.20	.50
277 John Smoltz	.50	1.25
278 Scott Hairston	.20	.50
279 David Eckstein	.20	.50
280 Shannon Stewart	.20	.50
281 Carl Everett	.20	.50
282 Aubrey Huff	.20	.50
283 Mike Mussina	.30	.75
284 Ruben Sierra	.20	.50
285 Russ Ortiz	.20	.50
286 Brian Lawrence	.20	.50
287 Kip Wells	.20	.50
288 Placido Polanco	.20	.50
289 Ted Lilly	.20	.50
290 Andy Pettitte	.30	.75
291 John Buck	.20	.50
292 Orlando Cabrera	.20	.50
293 Cristian Guzman	.20	.50
294 Ruben Quevedo	.20	.50
295 Cesar Izturis	.20	.50
296 Ryan Ludwick	.20	.50
297 Roy Oswalt	.30	.75
298 Jason Stokes	.20	.50
299 Mike Hampton	.20	.50
300 Pedro Martinez	.30	.75
301 Nic Jackson	.20	.50
302A Magglio Ordonez New Logo	.30	.75
302B Magglio Ordonez Old Logo SP	3.00	8.00
303 Manny Ramirez	.50	1.25
304 Jorge Julio	.20	.50
305 Javy Lopez	.20	.50
306 Roy Halladay	.30	.75
307 Kevin Mench	.20	.50
308 Jason Isringhausen	.20	.50
309 Carlos Guillen	.20	.50
310 Tsuyoshi Shinjo	.20	.50
311 Phil Nevin	.20	.50
312 Pokey Reese	.20	.50
313 Jorge Padilla	.20	.50
314 Jermaine Dye	.20	.50
315 David Wells	.20	.50
316 Mo Vaughn	.20	.50
317 Bernie Williams	.30	.75
318 Michael Restovich	.20	.50
319 Jose Hernandez	.20	.50
320 Richie Sexson	.20	.50
321 Daryle Ward	.20	.50
322 Luis Castillo	.20	.50
323 Rene Reyes	.20	.50
324 Victor Martinez	.30	.75
325A Adam Dunn New Logo	.30	.75
325B Adam Dunn Old Logo SP	3.00	8.00
326 Corwin Malone	.20	.50
327 Kerry Wood	.20	.50
328 Rickey Henderson	.50	1.25
329 Marty Cordova	.20	.50
330 Greg Maddux	.60	1.50
331 Miguel Batista	.20	.50
332 Chris Bootcheck	.20	.50
333 Carlos Baerga	.20	.50
334 Antonio Alfonseca	.20	.50
335 Shane Halter	.20	.50
336 Juan Encarnacion	.20	.50
337 Tom Gordon	.20	.50
338 Hideo Nomo	.50	1.25
339 Torii Hunter	.20	.50
340A Alfonso Soriano Yellow	.30	.75
340B Alfonso Soriano Black SP	3.00	8.00
341 Roberto Alomar	.30	.75
342 David Justice	.20	.50
343 Mike Lieberthal	.20	.50
344 Jeff Weaver	.20	.50
345 Timo Perez	.20	.50
346 Travis Lee	.20	.50
347 Sean Casey	.20	.50
348 Willie Harris	.20	.50
349 Derek Lowe	.20	.50
350 Tom Glavine	.30	.75
351 Eric Hinske	.20	.50
352 Rocco Baldelli	.20	.50
353 J.D. Drew	.20	.50
354 Jamie Moyer	.20	.50
355 Todd Linden	.20	.50
356 Benito Santiago	.20	.50
357 Brad Baker	.20	.50
358 Alex Gonzalez	.20	.50
359 Brandon Duckworth	.20	.50
360 John Rheinecker	.20	.50
361 Orlando Hernandez	.20	.50
362 Pedro Astacio	.20	.50
363 Brad Wilkerson	.20	.50
364 David Ortiz SP	5.00	12.00
365 Geoff Jenkins SP	2.00	5.00
366 Brian Jordan SP	2.00	5.00
367 Paul Byrd SP	2.00	5.00
368 Jason Lane SP	2.00	5.00
369 Jeff Bagwell SP	3.00	8.00
370 Bobby Higginson SP	2.00	5.00
371 Juan Uribe SP	2.00	5.00
372 Lee Stevens SP	2.00	5.00
373 Jimmy Haynes SP	2.00	5.00
374 Jose Valentin SP	2.00	5.00
375 Ken Griffey Jr. SP	6.00	15.00
376 Barry Bonds SP	6.00	15.00
377 Gary Matthews Jr. SP	2.00	5.00
378 Gary Sheffield SP	2.00	5.00
379 Rick Helling SP	2.00	5.00
380 Junior Spivey SP	2.00	5.00
381 Francisco Rodriguez SP	3.00	8.00
382 Chipper Jones SP	5.00	12.00
383 Orlando Hudson SP	2.00	5.00
384 Ivan Rodriguez SP	3.00	8.00
385 Chris Snelling SP	2.00	5.00
386 Kenny Lofton SP	2.00	5.00
387 Eric Cyr SP	2.00	5.00
388 Jason Kendall SP	2.00	5.00
389 Marlon Anderson SP	2.00	5.00
390 Billy Koch SP	2.00	5.00
391 Shelley Duncan SP	2.00	5.00
392 Jose Reyes SP	5.00	12.00
393 Fernando Tatis SP	2.00	5.00
394 Michael Cuddyer SP	2.00	5.00
395 Mark Prior SP	3.00	8.00
396 Dontrelle Willis SP	2.00	5.00
397 Jay Payton SP	2.00	5.00
398 Brandon Phillips SP	2.00	5.00
399 Dustin Moseley SP RC	2.00	5.00
400 Jason Giambi SP	2.00	5.00
401 John Mabry SP	2.00	5.00
402 Ron Gant SP	2.00	5.00
403 J.T. Snow SP	2.00	5.00
404 Jeff Cirillo SP	2.00	5.00
405 Darin Erstad SP	2.00	5.00
406 Luis Gonzalez SP	2.00	5.00
407 Marcus Giles SP	2.00	5.00
408 Brian Daubach SP	2.00	5.00
409 Moises Alou SP	2.00	5.00
410 Raul Mondesi SP	2.00	5.00
411 Adrian Beltre SP	5.00	12.00
412 A.J. Burnett SP	2.00	5.00
413 Jason Jennings SP	2.00	5.00
414 Edwin Almonte SP	2.00	5.00
415 Fred McGriff SP	3.00	8.00
416 Tim Raines Jr. SP	2.00	5.00
417 Rafael Furcal SP	2.00	5.00
418 Erubiel Durazo SP	2.00	5.00
419 Drew Henson SP	2.00	5.00
420 Kevin Appier SP	2.00	5.00
421 Chad Tracy SP	2.00	5.00
422 Adam Wainwright SP	3.00	8.00
423 Choo Freeman SP	2.00	5.00
424 Sandy Alomar Jr. SP	2.00	5.00
425 Corey Koskie SP	2.00	5.00
426 Jeromy Burnitz SP	2.00	5.00
427 Jorge Posada SP	3.00	8.00
428 Jason Arnold SP	2.00	5.00
429 Brett Myers SP	2.00	5.00
430 Shawn Green SP	2.00	5.00
CL1 Checklist 1	.20	.50
CL2 Checklist 2	.20	.50
CL3 Checklist 3	.20	.50

2003 Topps Heritage Chrome

STATED ODDS 1:8
STATED PRINT RUN 1954 SERIAL #'d SETS

Card	Low	High
THC1 Alex Rodriguez	4.00	10.00
THC2 Ichiro Suzuki	4.00	10.00
THC3 Brian Giles	1.25	3.00
THC4 Albert Pujols	4.00	10.00
THC5 Derek Jeter	8.00	20.00
THC6 Pat Burrell	1.25	3.00
THC7 Lance Berkman	2.00	5.00
THC8 Todd Helton	2.00	5.00
THC9 Chris Duncan	4.00	10.00
THC10 Rodrigo Lopez	1.25	3.00
THC11 Sammy Sosa	3.00	8.00
THC12 Barry Zito	2.00	5.00
THC13 Marlon Byrd	1.25	3.00
THC14 Al Leiter	1.25	3.00
THC15 Kazuhisa Ishii	1.25	3.00
THC16 Franklin Gutierrez	3.00	8.00
THC17 Roger Clemens	4.00	10.00
THC18 Mark Buehrle	2.00	5.00
THC19 Larry Walker	2.00	5.00
THC20 Curt Schilling	2.00	5.00
THC21 Garret Anderson	1.25	3.00
THC22 Randy Johnson	3.00	8.00
THC23 Cliff Floyd	1.25	3.00
THC24 Austin Kearns	1.25	3.00
THC25 Manuel Ramirez	1.25	3.00
THC26 Raul Ibanez	2.00	5.00
THC27 Jason Perry	1.25	3.00
THC28 Mark Teixeira	2.00	5.00
THC29 Nomar Garciaparra	2.00	5.00
THC30 Wayne Lydon	1.25	3.00
THC31 Preston Wilson	1.25	3.00
THC32 Paul Lo Duca	1.25	3.00
THC33 Edgardo Alfonzo	1.25	3.00
THC34 Jeremy Giambi	1.25	3.00
THC35 Mariano Rivera	4.00	10.00

THC36 Jimmy Rollins 2.00 5.00
THC37 Bret Boone 1.25 3.00
THC38 Scott Rolen 2.00 5.00
THC39 Adam LaRoche 1.25 3.00
THC40 Tim Hudson 2.00 5.00
THC41 Craig Brazell 1.25 3.00
THC42 Daryl Clark 1.25 3.00
THC43 Mauer Brothers 3.00 8.00
THC44 Troy Glaus 1.25 3.00
THC45 Trey Hodges 1.25 3.00
THC46 Carl Crawford 2.00 5.00
THC47 Mike Piazza 3.00 8.00
THC48 Josh Beckett 1.25 3.00
THC49 Randall Simon 1.25 3.00
THC50 Frank Thomas 3.00 8.00
THC51 Andruw Jones 1.25 3.00
THC52 Andy Marte 1.25 3.00
THC53 Bernie Castro 1.25 3.00
THC54 Jim Thome 2.00 5.00
THC55 Alexis Rios 1.25 3.00
THC56 Vladimir Guerrero 2.00 5.00
THC57 Walter Young 1.25 3.00
THC58 Hank Blalock 1.25 3.00
THC59 Ramon Nivar-Martinez 1.25 3.00
THC60 Jacque Jones 1.25 3.00
THC61 Nick Johnson 1.25 3.00
THC62 Ruddy Lugo 1.25 3.00
THC63 Carlos Delgado 1.25 3.00
THC64 Jeff Clark 1.25 3.00
THC65 Johnny Damon 2.00 5.00
THC66 Jaime Bubela 1.25 3.00
THC67 Alex Rodriguez 4.00 10.00
THC68 Rafael Palmeiro 2.00 5.00
THC69 Miguel Tejada 2.00 5.00
THC70 Bartolo Colon 1.25 3.00
THC71 Mike Sweeney 1.25 3.00
THC72 John Smoltz 3.00 8.00
THC73 Shannon Stewart 1.25 3.00
THC74 Mike Mussina 2.00 5.00
THC75 Roy Oswalt 2.00 5.00
THC76 Pedro Martinez 2.00 5.00
THC77 Magglio Ordonez 2.00 5.00
THC78 Manny Ramirez 3.00 8.00
THC79 David Wells 1.25 3.00
THC80 Richie Sexson 1.25 3.00
THC81 Adam Dunn 2.00 5.00
THC82 Greg Maddux 4.00 10.00
THC83 Alfonso Soriano 2.00 5.00
THC84 Roberto Alomar 2.00 5.00
THC85 Derek Lowe 1.25 3.00
THC86 Tom Glavine 2.00 5.00
THC87 Jeff Bagwell 2.00 5.00
THC88 Ken Griffey Jr. 6.00 15.00
THC89 Barry Bonds 5.00 12.00
THC90 Gary Sheffield 1.25 3.00
THC91 Chipper Jones 3.00 8.00
THC92 Orlando Hudson 1.25 3.00
THC93 Jose Cruz Jr. 1.25 3.00
THC94 Mark Prior 2.00 5.00
THC95 Jason Giambi 1.25 3.00
THC96 Luis Gonzalez 1.25 3.00
THC97 Drew Henson 1.25 3.00
THC98 Cristian Guzman 1.25 3.00
THC99 Shawn Green 1.25 3.00
THC100 Jose Vidro 1.25 3.00

2003 Topps Heritage Chrome Refractors

RANDOM INSERTS IN PACKS
STATED PRINT RUN 554 SERIAL #'d SETS

2003 Topps Heritage Clubhouse Collection Relics

BAT A STATED ODDS 1:2569
BAT B STATED ODDS 1:2506
BAT C STATED ODDS 1:2464
BAT D STATED ODDS 1:1989
UNI A STATED ODDS 1:4223
UNI B STATED ODDS 1:1207
UNI C STATED ODDS 1:921
UNI D STATED ODDS 1:171
AD Adam Dunn Uni D 6.00 15.00
AK Al Kaline Bat D 6.00 15.00
AP Albert Pujols Uni D 8.00 20.00
AR Alex Rodriguez Uni D 8.00 20.00
CJ Chipper Jones Uni D 6.00 15.00
DS Duke Snider Uni A 15.00 40.00
EB Ernie Banks Bat C 8.00 20.00
EM Eddie Mathews Bat B 6.00 15.00
JG Jim Gilliam Uni B 6.00 15.00
KW Kerry Wood Uni D 6.00 15.00
SG Shawn Green Uni C 6.00 15.00
WM Willie Mays Bat A 15.00 40.00

2003 Topps Heritage Flashbacks

COMPLETE SET 10) 6.00 15.00
STATED ODDS 1:12
F1 Willie Mays 2.00 5.00
F2 Yogi Berra 1.00 2.50
F3 Ted Kluszewski .60 1.50
F4 Stan Musial 1.50 4.00
F5 Hank Aaron 2.00 5.00
F6 Duke Snider .60 1.50
F7 Richie Ashburn .60 1.50
F8 Robin Roberts .60 1.50
F9 Mickey Vernon .40 1.00
F10 Don Larsen .40 1.00

2003 Topps Heritage Grandstand Glory Stadium Relics

GROUP A ODDS 1:2804
GROUP B ODDS 1:514
GROUP C ODDS 1:1446
GROUP D ODDS 1:1356
GROUP E ODDS 1:654
GROUP F ODDS 1:214
AK Al Kaline F 8.00 20.00
AP Andy Pafko F 4.00 10.00
DG Dick Groat D 6.00 15.00
DS Duke Snider A 10.00 25.00
EB Ernie Banks C 10.00 25.00
EM Eddie Mathews F 6.00 15.00
PR Phil Rizzuto E 8.00 20.00
RA Richie Ashburn B 8.00 20.00
TK Ted Kluszewski B 8.00 20.00
WM Willie Mays B 15.00 40.00
WS Warren Spahn F 8.00 20.00
YB Yogi Berra E 10.00 25.00

2003 Topps Heritage New Age Performers

COMPLETE SET (15) 10.00 25.00
STATED ODDS 1:15
NA1 Mike Piazza 1.00 2.50
NA2 Ichiro Suzuki 1.25 3.00
NA3 Derek Jeter 2.50 6.00
NA4 Alex Rodriguez 1.25 3.00
NA5 Sammy Sosa 1.00 2.50
NA6 Jason Giambi .40 1.00
NA7 Vladimir Guerrero .60 1.50
NA8 Albert Pujols 1.25 3.00
NA9 Todd Helton .60 1.50
NA10 Nomar Garciaparra .60 1.50
NA11 Randy Johnson 1.00 2.50
NA12 Jim Thome .60 1.50
NA13 Barry Bonds 1.50 4.00
NA14 Miguel Tejada .60 1.50
NA15 Alfonso Soriano .60 1.50

2003 Topps Heritage Real One Autographs

RETIRED ODDS 1:188
ACTIVE A ODDS 1:6168
ACTIVE B ODDS 1:1540
ACTIVE C ODDS 1:2802
*RED INK: 1X TO 2X BASIC RETIRED
*RED INK: .75X TO 1.5X BASIC ACTIVE A
*RED INK: .75X TO 1.5X BASIC ACTIVE B
*RED INK: .75X TO 1.5X BASIC ACTIVE C
RED INK STATED ODDS 1:696
RED INK PRINT RUN 54 SERIAL #'d SETS
AK Al Kaline 30.00 80.00
AP Andy Pafko 15.00 40.00
BR Bob Ross 10.00 25.00
BS Bill Skowron 10.00 25.00
BSH Bobby Shantz 10.00 25.00
BT Bob Talbot 10.00 25.00
BWE Bill Werle 10.00 25.00
CH Cal Hogue 10.00 25.00
CK Charlie Kress 15.00 40.00
CS Carl Scheib 12.50 30.00
DG Dick Groat 10.00 25.00
DK Dick Kryhoski 12.00 30.00
DL Don Lenhardt 10.00 25.00
DLU Don Lund 10.00 25.00
DS Duke Snider 25.00 60.00
EB Ernie Banks 75.00 200.00
EM Eddie Mayo 10.00 25.00
GH Gene Hermanski 10.00 25.00
HA Hank Aaron 250.00 500.00
HB Hank Bauer 15.00 40.00
JC Jose Cruz Jr. B 10.00 25.00
JP Joe Presko 12.00 30.00
JPO Johnny Podres 20.00 50.00
JR Jimmy Rollins C 10.00 25.00
JV Jose Vidro B 6.00 15.00
JW Jim Willis 10.00 25.00
LB Lance Berkman A 12.50 30.00
LJ Larry Jansen 15.00 40.00
LW Leroy Wheat 10.00 25.00
MB Matt Batts 12.50 30.00
MBL Mike Blyzka 12.00 30.00
MI Monte Irvin 15.00 40.00
MM Mickey Micelotta 6.00 15.00
MS Mike Sandlock 10.00 25.00
PP Paul Penson 10.00 25.00
PR Phil Rizzuto 30.00 60.00
PRO Preacher Roe 15.00 40.00
RF Roy Face 15.00 40.00
RM Ray Murray 10.00 25.00
TL Tom Lasorda 60.00 150.00
VL Vern Law 10.00 25.00
WF Whitey Ford 50.00 100.00
WM Willie Mays 250.00 500.00
YB Yogi Berra 60.00 150.00

2003 Topps Heritage Then and Now

COMPLETE SET (10) 8.00 20.00
STATED ODDS 1:15
TN1 T.Kluszewski A.Rod HR 1.25 3.00
TN2 T.Kluszewski A.Rod RBI 1.25 3.00
TN3 W.Mays B.Bonds BTG 2.00 5.00
TN4 D.Mueller A.Soriano .60 1.50
TN5 S.Musial G.Anderson 1.50 4.00
TN6 M.Minoso J.Damon .60 1.50
TN7 W.Mays B.Bonds SLG 2.00 5.00
TN8 D.Snider A.Rodriguez 1.25 3.00
TN9 R.Roberts R.Johnson 1.00 2.50
TN10 J.Antonelli P.Martinez .60 1.50

2004 Topps Heritage

COMPLETE SET (499) 100.00 250.00
COMP.SET w/o SP's (389) 30.00 60.00
COMMON CARD .20 .50
COMMON RC .30 .75
COMMON SP 1.50 4.00
COMMON SP RC 1.50 4.00
SP STATED ODDS 1:2
BASIC SP: 2/4/28/47/50/92/123/124/164
BASIC SP: 194/198/210/398-475
VARIATION SP: 1/8/10/30/40/49/60/70
VARIATION SP: 85/100/117/120/180/182
VARIATION SP: 200/213/250/311/342/361
SEE BECKETT.COM FOR VAR.DESCRIPTIONS
1A Jim Thome Fielding .30 .75
1B Jim Thome Hitting SP 3.00 8.00
2 Nomar Garciaparra SP 4.00 10.00
3 Aramis Ramirez .20 .50
4 Rafael Palmeiro SP 3.00 8.00
5 Danny Graves .20 .50
6 Casey Blake .20 .50
7 Juan Uribe .20 .50
8A Dmitri Young New Logo .20 .50
8B Dmitri Young Old Logo SP 2.00 5.00
9 Billy Wagner .20 .50
10A Jason Giambi Swinging .20 .50
10B Jason Giambi Btg Stance SP 2.00 5.00
11 Carlos Beltran .30 .75
12 Chad Hermansen .20 .50
13 B.J. Upton .30 .75
14 Dustan Mohr .20 .50
15 Endy Chavez .20 .50
16 Cliff Floyd .20 .50
17 Bernie Williams .30 .75
18 Eric Chavez .20 .50
19 Chase Utley .30 .75
20 Randy Johnson .60 1.50
21 Vernon Wells .20 .50
22 Juan Gonzalez .20 .50
23 Joe Kennedy .20 .50
24 Bengie Molina .20 .50
25 Carlos Lee .20 .50
26 Horacio Ramirez .20 .50
27 Anthony Acevedo RC .30 .75
28 Sammy Sosa SP 3.00 8.00
29 Jon Garland .20 .50
30A Adam Dunn Fielding .30 .75
30B Adam Dunn Hitting SP 2.00 5.00
31 Aaron Rowand .20 .50
32 Jody Gerut .20 .50
33 Chin-Hui Tsao .20 .50
34 Alex Sanchez .20 .50
35 A.J. Burnett .20 .50
36 Brad Ausmus .20 .50
37 Blake Hawksworth RC .30 .75
38 Francisco Rodriguez .30 .75
39 Alex Cintron .20 .50
40A Chipper Jones Pointing .60 1.50
40B Chipper Jones Fielding SP 3.00 8.00
41 Deivi Cruz .20 .50
42 Bill Mueller .20 .50
43 Joe Borowski .20 .50
44 Jimmy Haynes .20 .50
45 Mark Loretta .20 .50
46 Jerome Williams .20 .50
47 Gary Sheffield Yanks SP 3.00 8.00
48 Richard Hidalgo .20 .50
49A Jason Kendall New Logo .20 .50
49B Jason Kendall Old Logo SP 2.00 5.00
50 Ichiro Suzuki SP 5.00 12.00
51 Jim Edmonds .30 .75
52 Frank Catalanotto .20 .50
53 Jose Contreras .20 .50
54 Mo Vaughn .20 .50
55 Brendan Donnelly .20 .50
56 Luis Gonzalez .20 .50
57 Robert Fick .20 .50
58 Laynce Nix .20 .50
59 Johnny Damon .30 .75
60A Magglio Ordonez Running .30 .75
60B Magglio Ordonez Hitting SP 2.00 5.00
61 Matt Clement .20 .50
62 Ryan Ludwick .20 .50
63 Luis Castillo .20 .50
64 Dave Crouthers RC .30 .75
65 Dave Berg .20 .50
66 Kyle Davies RC .30 .75
67 Tim Salmon .20 .50
68 Marcus Giles .20 .50
69 Marty Cordova .20 .50
70A Todd Helton White Jsy .30 .75
70B Todd Helton Purple Jsy SP 3.00 8.00
71 Jeff Kent .20 .50
72 Michael Tucker .20 .50
73 Cesar Izturis .20 .50
74 Paul Quantrill .20 .50
75 Conor Jackson RC 1.00 2.50
76 Placido Polanco .20 .50
77 Adam Eaton .20 .50
78 Ramon Hernandez .20 .50
79 Edgardo Alfonzo .20 .50
80 Dioner Navarro RC .50 1.25
81 Woody Williams .20 .50
82 Rey Ordonez .20 .50
83 Randy Winn .20 .50
84 Casey Myers RC .30 .75
85A R.Choy Foo New Logo RC .30 .75
85B R.Choy Foo Old Logo SP 2.00 5.00
86 Ray Durham .20 .50
87 Sean Burroughs .20 .50
88 Tim Frend RC .30 .75
89 Shigetoshi Hasegawa .20 .50
90 Jeffrey Allison RC .30 .75
91 Orlando Hudson .20 .50
92 Matt Creighton SP RC .30 .75
93 Tim Worrell .20 .50
94 Kris Benson .20 .50
95 Mike Lieberthal .20 .50
96 David Wells .20 .50
97 Jason Phillips .20 .50
98 Bobby Cox MGR .20 .50
99 Johan Santana .60 1.50
100A Alex Rodriguez Hitting 1.00 2.50
100B Alex Rodriguez Throwing SP 4.00 10.00
101 John Vander Wal .20 .50
102 Orlando Cabrera .20 .50
103 Hideo Nomo .60 1.50
104 Todd Walker .20 .50
105 Jason Johnson .20 .50
106 Matt Mantei .20 .50
107 Jarrod Washburn .20 .50
108 Preston Wilson .20 .50
109 Carl Pavano .20 .50
110 Geoff Blum .20 .50
111 Eric Gagne .20 .50
112 Geoff Jenkins .20 .50
113 Joe Torre MG .30 .75
114 Jon Knott RC .30 .75
115 Hank Blalock .20 .50
116 John Olerud .20 .50
117A Pat Burrell New Logo .20 .50
117B Pat Burrell Old Logo SP 2.00 5.00
118 Aaron Boone .20 .50
119 Zach Day .20 .50
120A Frank Thomas New Logo .60 1.50
120B Frank Thomas Old Logo SP 3.00 8.00
121 Kyle Farnsworth .20 .50
122 Derek Lowe .20 .50
123 Zach Miner SP RC 3.00 8.00
124 Matthew Moses SP RC 3.00 8.00
125 Jesse Roman RC .30 .75
126 Josh Phelps .20 .50
127 Nic Ungs RC .30 .75
128 Dan Haren .20 .50
129 Kirk Rueter .20 .50
130 Jack McKeon MGR .20 .50
131 Keith Foulke .20 .50
132 Garrett Stephenson .20 .50
133 Wes Helms .20 .50
134 Raul Ibanez .30 .75
135 Morgan Ensberg .20 .50
136 Jay Payton .20 .50
137 Billy Koch .20 .50
138 Mark Grudzielanek .20 .50
139 Rodrigo Lopez .20 .50
140 Corey Patterson .20 .50
141 Troy Percival .20 .50
142 Shea Hillenbrand .20 .50
143 Brad Fullmer .20 .50
144 Ricky Nolasco RC .50 1.25
145 Mark Teixeira .30 .75
146 Tydus Meadows RC .30 .75
147 Toby Hall .20 .50
148 Orlando Palmeiro .20 .50
149 Khalid Ballouli RC .30 .75
150 Grady Little MGR .20 .50
151 David Eckstein .20 .50
152 Kenny Perez RC .30 .75
153 Ben Grieve .20 .50
154 Ismael Valdes .20 .50
155 Bret Boone .20 .50
156 Jesse Foppert .20 .50
157 Vicente Padilla .20 .50
158 Bobby Abreu .20 .50
159 Scott Hatteberg .20 .50
160 Carlos Quentin RC 1.25 3.00
161 Anthony Lerew RC .30 .75
162 Lance Carter .20 .50
163 Robb Nen .20 .50
164 Zach Duke SP RC 4.00 10.00
165 Xavier Nady .20 .50
166 Kip Wells .20 .50
167 Kevin Millwood .20 .50
168 Jon Lieber .20 .50
169 Jose Reyes .30 .75
170 Eric Byrnes .20 .50
171 Paul Konerko .30 .75
172 Chris Lubanski .20 .50
173 Jae Weong Seo .20 .50
174 Corey Koskie .20 .50
175 Tim Stauffer RC .50 1.25
176 John Lackey .30 .75
177 Danny Bautista .20 .50
178 Shane Reynolds .20 .50
179 Jorge Julio .20 .50
180A Manny Ramirez New Logo .50 1.25
180B Manny Ramirez Old Logo SP 3.00 8.00
181 Alex Gonzalez .20 .50
182A Moises Alou New Logo .20 .50
182B Moises Alou Old Logo SP 2.00 5.00
183 Mark Buehrle .30 .75
184 Carlos Guillen .20 .50
185 Nate Cornejo .20 .50
186 Billy Traber .20 .50
187 Jason Jennings .20 .50
188 Eric Munson .20 .50
189 Braden Looper .20 .50
190 Juan Encarnacion .20 .50
191 Dusty Baker MGR .20 .50
192 Travis Lee .20 .50
193 Miguel Cairo .20 .50
194 Rich Aurilia SP 2.00 5.00
195 Tom Gordon .20 .50
196 Freddy Garcia .20 .50
197 Brian Lawrence .20 .50
198 Jorge Posada SP 3.00 8.00
199 Javier Vazquez .20 .50
200A Albert Pujols New Logo 1.25 3.00
200B Albert Pujols Old Logo SP 5.00 12.00
201 Victor Zambrano .20 .50
202 Eli Marrero .20 .50
203 Joel Pineiro .20 .50
204 Rondell White .20 .50
205 Craig Ansman RC .30 .75
206 Michael Young .20 .50
207 Carlos Baerga .20 .50
208 Andruw Jones .20 .50
209 Jerry Hairston Jr. .20 .50
210 Shawn Green SP 2.00 5.00
211 Ron Gardenhire MGR .20 .50
212 Darin Erstad .20 .50
213A Brandon Webb Glove Chest .20 .50
213B Brandon Webb Glove Out SP 2.00 5.00
214 Greg Maddux 1.00 2.50
215 Reed Johnson .20 .50
216 John Thomson .20 .50
217 Tino Martinez .30 .75
218 Mike Cameron .20 .50
219 Edgar Martinez .30 .75
220 Eric Young .20 .50
221 Reggie Sanders .20 .50
222 Randy Wolf .20 .50
223 Erubiel Durazo .20 .50
224 Mike Mussina .30 .75
225 Tom Glavine .30 .75
226 Troy Glaus .20 .50
227 Oscar Villarreal .20 .50
228 David Segui .20 .50
229 Jeff Suppan .20 .50
230 Kenny Lofton .20 .50
231 Esteban Loaiza .20 .50
232 Felipe Lopez .20 .50
233 Matt Lawton .20 .50
234 Mark Bellhorn .20 .50
235 Wil Ledezma .20 .50
236 Todd Hollandsworth .20 .50
237 Octavio Dotel .20 .50
238 Darren Dreifort .20 .50
239 Paul Lo Duca .20 .50
240 Richie Sexson .20 .50
241 Doug Mientkiewicz .20 .50
242 Luis Rivas .20 .50
243 Claudio Vargas .20 .50
244 Mark Ellis .20 .50
245 Brett Myers .20 .50
246 Jake Peavy .20 .50
247 Marquis Grissom .20 .50
248 Armando Benitez .20 .50
249 Ryan Franklin .20 .50
250A Alfonso Soriano Throwing .30 .75
250B Alfonso Soriano Fielding SP 2.00 5.00
251 Tim Hudson .30 .75
252 Shannon Stewart .20 .50
253 A.J. Pierzynski .20 .50
254 Runelvys Hernandez .20 .50
255 Roy Oswalt .30 .75
256 Shawn Chacon .20 .50
257 Tony Graffanino .20 .50
258 Tim Wakefield .30 .75
259 Damian Miller .20 .50
260 Joe Crede .20 .50
261 Jason LaRue .20 .50
262 Jose Jimenez .20 .50
263 Juan Pierre .20 .50
264 Wade Miller .20 .50
265 Odalis Perez .20 .50
266 Eddie Guardado .20 .50
267 Rocky Biddle .20 .50
268 Jeff Nelson .20 .50
269 Terrence Long .20 .50
270 Ramon Ortiz .20 .50
271 Raul Mondesi .20 .50
272 Ugueth Urbina .20 .50
273 Jeromy Burnitz .20 .50
274 Brad Radke .20 .50
275 Jose Vidro .20 .50
276 Bobby Jenks .20 .50
277 Ty Wigginton .20 .50
278 Jose Guillen .20 .50
279 Delmon Young .30 .75
280 Brian Giles .20 .50
281 Jason Schmidt .20 .50
282 Nick Markakis .40 1.00
283 Felipe Alou MGR .20 .50
284 Carl Crawford .30 .75
285 Neifi Perez .20 .50
286 Miguel Tejada .30 .75
287 Victor Martinez .30 .75
288 Adam Kennedy .20 .50
289 Kerry Ligtenberg .20 .50
290 Scott Williamson .20 .50
291 Tony Womack .20 .50
292 Travis Hafner .20 .50
293 Bobby Crosby .20 .50
294 Chad Billingsley .30 .75
295 Russ Ortiz .20 .50
296 John Burkett .20 .50
297 Carlos Zambrano .30 .75
298 Randall Simon .20 .50
299 Juan Castro .20 .50
300 Mike Lowell .20 .50
301 Fred McGriff .20 .50
302 Glendon Rusch .20 .50
303 Sung Jung RC .30 .75
304 Rocco Baldelli .20 .50
305 Fernando Vina .20 .50
306 Gil Meche .20 .50
307 Jose Cruz Jr. .20 .50
308 Bernie Castro .20 .50
309 Scott Spiezio .20 .50
310 Paul Byrd .20 .50
311A Jay Gibbons New Logo .20 .50
311B Jay Gibbons Old Logo SP 2.00 5.00
312 Trot Nixon .20 .50
313 Chris O'Riordan RC .30 .75
314 Julio Lugo .20 .50
315 Ben Davis .20 .50
316 Mike Williams .20 .50
317 Trevor Hoffman .30 .75
318 Andy Pettitte .30 .75
319 Orlando Hernandez .20 .50
320 Juan Rivera .20 .50
321 Elizardo Ramirez .20 .50
322 Junior Spivey .20 .50
323 Tony Batista .20 .50
324 Mike Remlinger .20 .50
325 Alex Gonzalez .20 .50
326 Aaron Hill .20 .50
327 Steve Finley .20 .50
328 Vinny Castilla .20 .50
329 Eric Duncan .20 .50
330 Mike Gosling RC .30 .75
331 Eric Hinske .20 .50
332 Scott Rolen .30 .75
333 Benito Santiago .20 .50
334 Jimmy Gobble .20 .50
335 Bobby Higginson .20 .50
336 Kelvim Escobar .20 .50
337 Mike DeJean .20 .50
338 Sidney Ponson .20 .50
339 Todd Self RC .30 .75
340 Jeff Cirillo .20 .50
341 Jimmy Rollins .30 .75
342A Barry Zito White Jsy .30 .75
342B Barry Zito Green Jsy SP 2.00 5.00
343 Felix Pie .20 .50
344 Matt Morris .20 .50
345 Kazuhiro Sasaki .20 .50
346 Jack Wilson .20 .50
347 Nick Johnson .20 .50
348 Wil Cordero .20 .50
349 Ryan Madson .20 .50
350 Torii Hunter .20 .50
351 Andy Ashby .20 .50
352 Aubrey Huff .20 .50
353 Brad Lidge .20 .50
354 Derrek Lee .20 .50
355 Yadier Molina RC 30.00 80.00
356 Paul Wilson .20 .50
357 Omar Vizquel .30 .75
358 Rene Reyes .20 .50
359 Marlon Anderson .20 .50
360 Bobby Kielty .20 .50
361A Ryan Wagner New Logo .20 .50
361B Ryan Wagner Old Logo SP 2.00 5.00
362 Justin Morneau .30 .75
363 Shane Spencer .20 .50
364 David Bell .20 .50
365 Matt Stairs .20 .50
366 Joe Borchard .20 .50
367 Mark Redman .20 .50
368 Dave Roberts .30 .75
369 Desi Relaford .20 .50
370 Rich Harden .20 .50
371 Fernando Tatis .20 .50
372 Eric Karros .20 .50
373 Eric Milton .20 .50
374 Mike Sweeney .20 .50
375 Brian Daubach .20 .50
376 Brian Snyder .20 .50
377 Chris Reitsma .20 .50
378 Kyle Lohse .20 .50
379 Livan Hernandez .20 .50
380 Robin Ventura .20 .50
381 Jacque Jones .20 .50
382 Danny Kolb .20 .50
383 Casey Kotchman .20 .50
384 Cristian Guzman .20 .50
385 Josh Beckett .20 .50
386 Khalil Greene .30 .75
387 Greg Myers .20 .50
388 Francisco Cordero .20 .50
389 Donald Levinski RC .30 .75
390 Roy Halladay .30 .75
391 J.D. Drew .20 .50
392 Jamie Moyer .20 .50
393 Ken Macha MGR .20 .50
394 Jeff Davanon .20 .50
395 Matt Kata .20 .50
396 Jack Cust .20 .50
397 Mike Timlin .20 .50
398 Zack Greinke SP 6.00 15.00
399 Byung-Hyun Kim SP 1.50 4.00
400 Kazuhisa Ishii SP 1.50 4.00
401 Brayan Pena SP RC 1.50 4.00
402 Garret Anderson SP 1.50 4.00
403 Kyle Sleeth SP RC 1.50 4.00
404 Javy Lopez SP 1.50 4.00
405 Damian Moss SP 1.50 4.00
406 David Ortiz SP 4.00 10.00
407 Pedro Martinez SP 2.50 6.00
408 Hee Seop Choi SP 1.50 4.00
409 Carl Everett SP 1.50 4.00
410 Dontrelle Willis SP 1.50 4.00
411 Ryan Harvey SP 1.50 4.00
412 Russell Branyan SP 1.50 4.00
413 Milton Bradley SP 1.50 4.00
414 Marcus McBeth SP RC 1.50 4.00
415 Carlos Pena SP 2.50 6.00
416 Ivan Rodriguez SP 2.50 6.00
417 Craig Biggio SP 2.50 6.00
418 Angel Berroa SP 1.50 4.00
419 Brian Jordan SP 1.50 4.00
420 Scott Podsednik SP 1.50 4.00
421 Omar Falcon SP RC 1.50 4.00
422 Joe Mays SP 1.50 4.00
423 Brad Wilkerson SP 1.50 4.00
424 Al Leiter SP 1.50 4.00
425 Derek Jeter SP 40.00 100.00
426 Mark Mulder SP 1.50 4.00
427 Marlon Byrd SP 1.50 4.00
428 David Murphy SP RC 2.50 6.00
429 Phil Nevin SP 1.50 4.00
430 J.T. Snow SP 1.50 4.00
431 Brad Sullivan SP RC 1.50 4.00
432 Bo Hart SP 1.50 4.00
433 Josh Labandeira SP RC 1.50 4.00
434 Chan Ho Park SP 2.50 6.00
435 Carlos Delgado SP 1.50 4.00
436 Curt Schilling Sox SP 2.50 6.00
437 John Smoltz SP 4.00 10.00
438 Luis Matos SP 1.50 4.00
439 Mark Prior SP 2.50 6.00
440 Roberto Alomar SP 2.50 6.00
441 Coco Crisp SP 1.50 4.00
442 Austin Kearns SP 1.50 4.00
443 Larry Walker SP 2.50 6.00
444 Neal Cotts SP 1.50 4.00
445 Jeff Bagwell SP 2.50 6.00
446 Adrian Beltre SP 4.00 10.00
447 Grady Sizemore SP 2.50 6.00
448 Keith Ginter SP 1.50 4.00
449 Vladimir Guerrero SP 2.50 6.00
450 Lyle Overbay SP 1.50 4.00
451 Rafael Furcal SP 1.50 4.00
452 Melvin Mora SP 1.50 4.00
453 Kerry Wood SP 1.50 4.00
454 Jose Valentin SP 1.50 4.00
455 Ken Griffey Jr. SP 8.00 20.00
456 Brandon Phillips SP 1.50 4.00
457 Miguel Cabrera SP 4.00 10.00
458 Edwin Jackson SP 1.50 4.00
459 Eric Owens SP 1.50 4.00
460 Miguel Batista SP 1.50 4.00
461 Mike Hampton SP 1.50 4.00
462 Kevin Millar SP 1.50 4.00
463 Bartolo Colon SP 1.50 4.00
464 Sean Casey SP 1.50 4.00
465 C.C. Sabathia SP 2.50 6.00
466 Rickie Weeks SP 1.50 4.00
467 Brad Penny SP 1.50 4.00
468 Mike MacDougal SP 1.50 4.00
469 Kevin Brown SP 1.50 4.00
470 Lance Berkman SP 2.50 6.00
471 Ben Sheets SP 1.50 4.00
472 Mariano Rivera SP 20.00 50.00
473 Mike Piazza SP 4.00 10.00
474 Ryan Klesko SP 1.50 4.00
475 Edgar Renteria SP 1.50 4.00
CL1 Checklist 1 .20 .50
CL2 Checklist 2 .20 .50
CL3 Checklist 3 .20 .50
CL4 Checklist 4 .20 .50

2004 Topps Heritage Chrome

COMPLETE SET (110) 150.00 250.00
STATED ODDS 1:7
STATED PRINT RUN 1955 SERIAL #'d SETS
THC1 Sammy Sosa 3.00 8.00
THC2 Nomar Garciaparra 2.00 5.00
THC3 Ichiro Suzuki 4.00 10.00
THC4 Rafael Palmeiro 2.00 5.00
THC5 Carlos Delgado 1.25 3.00
THC6 Troy Glaus 1.25 3.00
THC7 Jay Gibbons 1.25 3.00
THC8 Frank Thomas 3.00 8.00
THC9 Pat Burrell 1.25 3.00
THC10 Albert Pujols 4.00 10.00
THC11 Brandon Webb 1.25 3.00
THC12 Chipper Jones 3.00 8.00
THC13 Magglio Ordonez 2.00 5.00
THC14 Adam Dunn 2.00 5.00
THC15 Todd Helton 2.00 5.00
THC16 Jason Giambi 1.25 3.00
THC17 Alfonso Soriano 2.00 5.00
THC18 Barry Zito 2.00 5.00
THC19 Jim Thome 2.00 5.00
THC20 Alex Rodriguez 4.00 10.00
THC21 Hee Seop Choi 1.25 3.00
THC22 Pedro Martinez 2.00 5.00
THC23 Kerry Wood 1.25 3.00
THC24 Bartolo Colon 1.25 3.00
THC25 Austin Kearns 1.25 3.00
THC26 Ken Griffey Jr. 6.00 15.00
THC27 Coco Crisp 1.25 3.00
THC28 Larry Walker 2.00 5.00
THC29 Ivan Rodriguez 2.00 5.00
THC30 Dontrelle Willis 1.25 3.00
THC31 Miguel Cabrera 3.00 8.00
THC32 Jeff Bagwell 2.00 5.00
THC33 Lance Berkman 2.00 5.00
THC34 Shawn Green 1.25 3.00
THC35 Kevin Brown 1.25 3.00
THC36 Vladimir Guerrero 2.00 5.00
THC37 Mike Piazza 3.00 8.00
THC38 Derek Jeter 15.00 40.00
THC39 John Smoltz 3.00 8.00
40 Mark Prior 2.00 5.00
THC41 Gary Sheffield Yanks 1.25 3.00
THC42 Curt Schilling Sox 2.00 5.00
THC43 Randy Johnson 3.00 8.00
THC44 Luis Gonzalez 1.25 3.00
THC45 Andruw Jones 1.25 3.00
THC46 Greg Maddux 4.00 10.00
THC47 Tony Batista 1.25 3.00
THC48 Esteban Loaiza 1.25 3.00
THC49 Chin-Hui Tsao 1.25 3.00
THC50 Mike Lowell 1.25 3.00
THC51 Jeff Kent 1.25 3.00
THC52 Richie Sexson 1.25 3.00
THC53 Torii Hunter 1.25 3.00
THC54 Jose Vidro 1.25 3.00
THC55 Jose Reyes 2.00 5.00
THC56 Jimmy Rollins 2.00 5.00
THC57 Bret Boone 1.25 3.00
THC58 Rocco Baldelli 1.25 3.00
THC59 Hank Blalock 1.25 3.00
THC60 Rickie Weeks 1.25 3.00
THC61 Rodney Choy Foo 1.25 3.00
THC62 Zach Miner 2.00 5.00
THC63 Brayan Pena 1.25 3.00
THC64 David Murphy 2.00 5.00
THC65 Matt Creighton 1.25 3.00
THC66 Kyle Sleeth 1.25 3.00
THC67 Matthew Moses 2.00 5.00
THC68 Josh Labandeira 1.25 3.00
THC69 Grady Sizemore 2.00 5.00
THC70 Edwin Jackson 1.25 3.00
THC71 Marcus McBeth 1.25 3.00
THC72 Brad Sullivan 1.25 3.00
THC73 Zach Duke 2.00 5.00
THC74 Omar Falcon 1.25 3.00
THC75 Conor Jackson 4.00 10.00
THC76 Carlos Quentin 5.00 12.00
THC77 Craig Ansman 1.25 3.00
THC78 Mike Gosling 1.25 3.00
THC79 Kyle Davies 1.25 3.00
THC80 Anthony Lerew 1.25 3.00
THC81 Sung Jung 1.25 3.00
THC82 Dave Crouthers 1.25 3.00
THC83 Kenny Perez 1.25 3.00
THC84 Jeffrey Allison 1.25 3.00
THC85 Nic Ungs 1.25 3.00
THC86 Donald Levinski 1.25 3.00
THC87 Anthony Acevedo 1.25 3.00
THC88 Todd Self 1.25 3.00
THC89 Tim Frend 1.25 3.00
THC90 Tydus Meadows 1.25 3.00
THC91 Khalid Ballouli 1.25 3.00
THC92 Dioner Navarro 2.00 5.00
THC93 Casey Myers 1.25 3.00
THC94 Jon Knott 1.25 3.00
THC95 Tim Stauffer 2.00 5.00
THC96 Ricky Nolasco 2.00 5.00
THC97 Blake Hawksworth 1.25 3.00
THC98 Jesse Roman 1.25 3.00
THC99 Yadier Molina 125.00 300.00
THC100 Chris O'Riordan 1.25 3.00
THC101 Cliff Floyd 1.25 3.00
THC102 Nick Johnson 1.25 3.00
THC103 Edgar Martinez 2.00 5.00
THC104 Brett Myers 1.25 3.00
THC105 Francisco Rodriguez 2.00 5.00
THC106 Scott Rolen 2.00 5.00
THC107 Mark Teixeira 2.00 5.00
THC108 Miguel Tejada 2.00 5.00
THC109 Vernon Wells 1.25 3.00
THC110 Jerome Williams 1.25 3.00

2004 Topps Heritage Chrome Black Refractors

*BLACK REF: 2.5X TO 6X CHROME
*BLACK REF: 2.5X TO 6X CHROME RC YR
STATED ODDS 1:251
STATED PRINT RUN 55 SERIAL #'d SETS

2004 Topps Heritage Chrome Refractors

*REFRACTOR: .6X TO 1.5X CHROME
*REFRACTOR: .6X TO 1.5X CHROME RC YR
STATED ODDS 1:25
STATED PRINT RUN 555 SERIAL #'d SETS

2004 Topps Heritage Clubhouse Collection Relics

GROUP A ODDS 1:3037
GROUP B ODDS 1:4142
GROUP C ODDS 1:138
GROUP D ODDS 1:92
GROUP A STATED PRINT RUN 100 SETS
GROUP A PRINT RUN PROVIDED BY TOPPS
GROUP A ARE NOT SERIAL-NUMBERED
AD Adam Dunn Jsy D 3.00 8.00
AJ Andruw Jones Jsy C 4.00 10.00
AK Al Kaline Bat A 20.00 50.00
AP Albert Pujols Uni C 6.00 15.00
AR Alex Rodriguez Jsy C 4.00 10.00

AS Alfonso Soriano Uni D 3.00 8.00
BA Bobby Abreu Jsy D 3.00 8.00
BB Bret Boone Jsy D 3.00 8.00
BM Brett Myers Jsy D 3.00 8.00
BZ Barry Zito Uni C 3.00 8.00
CJ Chipper Jones Jsy D 4.00 10.00
CS C.C. Sabathia Jsy D 3.00 8.00
DS Duke Snider Bat A 15.00 40.00
EC Eric Chavez Uni D 3.00 8.00
EG Eric Gagne Uni D 3.00 8.00
FM Fred McGriff Bat C 4.00 10.00
GM Greg Maddux Jsy C 6.00 15.00
GS Gary Sheffield Uni D 3.00 8.00
HB Hank Blalock Jsy D 3.00 8.00
HK Harmon Killebrew Jsy C 10.00 25.00
IR Ivan Rodriguez Bat C 4.00 10.00
JD Johnny Damon Uni D 4.00 10.00
JG Jason Giambi Uni D 3.00 8.00
JL Jay Lopez Jsy D 3.00 8.00
JR Jimmy Rollins Jsy D 3.00 8.00
JRE Jose Reyes Jsy D 3.00 8.00
JS John Smoltz Jsy C 4.00 10.00
JT Jim Thome Bat D 4.00 10.00
KB Kevin Brown Uni D 3.00 8.00
KI Kazuhisa Ishii Uni D 3.00 8.00
KW Kerry Wood Jsy D 3.00 8.00
LB Lance Berkman Jsy C 3.00 8.00
LG Luis Gonzalez Jsy D 3.00 8.00
MG Marcus Giles Jsy C 3.00 8.00
MM Mark Mulder Uni D 3.00 8.00
MR Manny Ramirez Jsy C 4.00 10.00
MS Mike Sweeney Jsy D 3.00 8.00
MT Miguel Tejada Uni D 3.00 8.00
MTB Miguel Tejada Bat C 3.00 8.00
MTE Mark Teixeira Jsy D 4.00 10.00
NG Nomar Garciaparra Uni C 6.00 15.00
PL Paul Lo Duca Uni C 3.00 8.00
PM Pedro Martinez Jsy D 4.00 10.00
RB Rocco Baldelli Jsy D 3.00 8.00
RC Roger Clemens Uni D 6.00 15.00
RF Rafael Furcal Jsy D 3.00 8.00
RJ Randy Johnson Jsy C 4.00 10.00
SG Shawn Green Uni C 3.00 8.00
SM Stan Musial Bat A 30.00 60.00
SR Scott Rolen Uni B 4.00 10.00
SRB Scott Rolen Bat C 4.00 10.00
SS Sammy Sosa Jsy C 4.00 10.00
TG Troy Glaus Uni C 3.00 8.00
TH Tim Hudson Uni D 3.00 8.00
THU Torii Hunter Bat C 3.00 8.00
VW Vernon Wells Jsy C 3.00 8.00
WM Willie Mays Uni A 30.00 60.00
YB Yogi Berra Jsy A 20.00 50.00

2004 Topps Heritage Clubhouse Collection Dual Relics

STATED ODDS 1:9244
STATED PRINT RUN 55 SERIAL #'d SETS
BC Y.Berra Uni/R.Clemens Uni 75.00 150.00
GS S.Green Jsy/D.Snider Uni 75.00 150.00
MP A.Pujols Jsy/S.Musial Uni 75.00 150.00

2004 Topps Heritage Doubleheader

ONE PER SEALED HOBBY BOX
VINTAGE D-HEADERS RANDOMLY SEEDED
12 A.Rodriguez 2.00 5.00
N.Garciaparra
34 I.Suzuki 2.00 5.00
A.Pujols
56 S.Sosa 4.00 10.00
D.Jeter
78 J.Thome 1.00 2.50
A.Dunn
910 J.Giambi 1.00 2.50
I.Rodriguez
1112 T.Helton 1.00 2.50
L.Gonzalez
1314 J.Bagwell 1.00 2.50
L.Berkman
1516 A.Soriano 1.00 2.50
D.Willis
1718 M.Prior 1.00 2.50
V.Guerrero
1920 M.Piazza 2.00 5.00
R.Clemens
2122 R.Johnson 1.50 4.00
C.Schilling
2324 G.Sheffield 1.00 2.50
P.Martinez
2526 C.Delgado 1.00 2.50
J.Rollins
2728 A.Jones 1.50 4.00
C.Jones
2930 R.Baldelli .60 1.50
H.Blalock
NNO Vintage Buyback

2004 Topps Heritage Flashbacks

COMPLETE SET (10) 6.00 15.00
STATED ODDS 1:12
F1 Duke Snider .60 1.50
F2 Johnny Podres .40 1.00
F3 Don Newcombe .40 1.00
F4 Al Kaline 1.00 2.50
F5 Willie Mays 2.00 5.00
F6 Stan Musial 1.50 4.00
F7 Harmon Killebrew 1.00 2.50
F8 Herb Score .40 1.00
F9 Whitey Ford .60 1.50
F10 Robin Roberts .60 1.50

2004 Topps Heritage Grandstand Glory Stadium Seat Relics

GROUP A ODDS 1:27,731
GROUP A ODDS 1:606
GROUP A STATED PRINT RUN 55 CARDS
GROUP A PRINT RUN PROVIDED BY TOPPS
GROUP A IS NOT SERIAL-NUMBERED
AK Al Kaline B 10.00 25.00
HK Harmon Killebrew B 10.00 25.00
SM Stan Musial B 10.00 25.00
WM Willie Mays A 90.00 150.00
WS Warren Spahn B 10.00 25.00
YB Yogi Berra B 10.00 25.00

2004 Topps Heritage New Age Performers

COMPLETE SET (15) 10.00 25.00
STATED ODDS 1:15
NA1 Jason Giambi .40 1.00
NA2 Ichiro Suzuki 1.25 3.00
NA3 Alex Rodriguez 1.25 3.00
NA4 Alfonso Soriano .60 1.50
NA5 Albert Pujols 1.25 3.00
NA6 Nomar Garciaparra .60 1.50
NA7 Mark Prior .60 1.50
NA8 Derek Jeter 2.50 6.00
NA9 Sammy Sosa 1.00 2.50
NA10 Carlos Delgado .40 1.00
NA11 Jim Thome .60 1.50
NA12 Todd Helton .60 1.50
NA13 Gary Sheffield .40 1.00
NA14 Vladimir Guerrero .60 1.50
NA15 Josh Beckett .40 1.00

2004 Topps Heritage Real One Autographs

STATED ODDS 1:230
STATED PRINT RUN 200 SETS
PRINT RUN INFO PROVIDED BY TOPPS
BASIC AUTOS ARE NOT SERIAL-NUMBERED
*RED INK: .75X TO 1.5X RETIRED
*RED INK MAYS: 1.25X TO 2X BASIC MAYS
*RED INK: .75X TO 1.5X ACTIVE
RED INK ODDS 1:835
RED INK PRINT RUN 55 #'d SETS
RED INK ALSO CALLED SPECIAL EDITION
AH Aubrey Huff 10.00 25.00
AK Al Kaline 40.00 100.00
BB Bob Borkowski 10.00 25.00
BC Billy Consolo 10.00 25.00
BG Bill Glynn 10.00 25.00
BK Bob Kline 10.00 25.00
BM Bob Milliken 10.00 25.00
BW Bill Wilson 20.00 50.00
CF Cliff Floyd 10.00 25.00
DN Don Newcombe 12.00 30.00
DP Duane Pillette 10.00 25.00
DS Duke Snider 30.00 60.00
DW Dontrelle Willis 10.00 25.00
EB Ernie Banks 40.00 80.00
FS Frank Smith 10.00 25.00
GA Gair Allie 10.00 25.00
HE Harry Elliott 10.00 25.00
HK Harmon Killebrew 40.00 100.00
HP Harry Perkowski 10.00 25.00
HV Corky Valentine 10.00 25.00
JG Johnny Gray 10.00 25.00
JP Jim Pearce 12.00 30.00
JPO Johnny Podres 10.00 25.00
LL Lou Limmer 10.00 25.00
ML Mike Lowell 10.00 25.00
MO Magglio Ordonez 10.00 25.00
SK Steve Kraly 30.00 60.00
SM Stan Musial 100.00 200.00
SR Scott Rolen 15.00 40.00
TK Thornton Kipper 10.00 25.00
TW Tom Wright 10.00 25.00
VT Jake Thies 10.00 25.00
WM Willie Mays 150.00 300.00
YB Yogi Berra 40.00 100.00

2004 Topps Heritage Then and Now

COMPLETE SET (6) 4.00 10.00
STATED ODDS 1:15
TN1 W.Mays 2.00 5.00
J.Thome
TN2 A.Kaline 1.25 3.00
A.Pujols
TN3 D.Snider .60 1.50
C.Delgado
TN4 R.Roberts .60 1.50
R.Halladay
TN5 D.Newcombe .60 1.50
J.Santana
TN6 H.Score .40 1.00
K.Wood

2005 Topps Heritage

COMPLETE SET (497) 250.00 400.00
COMP.SET w/o SP's (387) 30.00 60.00
COMMON CARD .20 .50
COMMON RC .20 .50
COMMON TEAM CARD .20 .50
COMMON SP 3.00 8.00
COMMON SP RC 3.00 8.00
SP STATED ODDS 1:2 HOBBY/RETAIL
BASIC SP: 5/20/30/31/33/79/101/110/130
BASIC SP: 135/260/292/398-475
VARIATION SP: 3/6/7/31/50/69/78/82/118
VARIATION SP: 125/135/155/261/273/286
VARIATION SP: 296/300/312/353/389
SEE BECKETT.COM FOR VAR.DESCRIPTIONS
1 Will Harridge .20 .50
2 Warren Giles .20 .50
3A Alfonso Soriano Fldg .20 .50
3B Alfonso Soriano Running SP 3.00 8.00
4 Mark Mulder .20 .50
5 Todd Helton SP 3.00 8.00
6A Jason Bay Black Cap .20 .50
6B Jason Bay Yellow Cap SP 3.00 8.00
7A Ichiro Suzuki Running .60 1.50
7B Ichiro Suzuki Crouch SP 4.00 10.00
8 Jim Tracy MG .20 .50
9 Gavin Floyd .20 .50
10 John Smoltz .50 1.25
11 Chicago Cubs TC .30 .75
12 Darin Erstad .20 .50
13 Chad Tracy .20 .50
14 Charles Thomas .20 .50
15 Miguel Tejada .30 .75
16 Andre Ethier RC 1.50 4.00
17 Jeff Francis .20 .50
18 Derrek Lee .20 .50
19 Juan Uribe .20 .50
20 Jim Edmonds SP 3.00 8.00
21 Kenny Lofton .20 .50
22 Brad Ausmus .20 .50
23 Jon Garland .20 .50
24 Edwin Jackson .20 .50
25 Joe Mauer .40 1.00
26 Wes Helms .20 .50
27 Brian Schneider .20 .50
28 Kazuo Matsui .20 .50
29 Flash Gordon .20 .50
30 Hideo Nomo SP 3.00 8.00
31A Albert Pujols Red Hat SP 5.00 12.00
31B Albert Pujols Blue Hat SP 5.00 12.00
32 Carl Crawford .30 .75
33 Vladimir Guerrero SP 3.00 8.00
34 Nick Green .20 .50
35 Jay Gibbons .20 .50
36 Kevin Youkilis .20 .50
37 Billy Wagner .20 .50
38 Terrence Long .20 .50
39 Kevin Mench .20 .50
40 Garret Anderson .20 .50
41 Reed Johnson .20 .50
42 Reggie Sanders .20 .50
43 Kirk Rueter .20 .50
44 Jay Payton .20 .50
45 Tike Redman .20 .50
46 Mike Lieberthal .20 .50
47 Damian Miller .20 .50
48 Zach Day .20 .50
49 Juan Rincon .20 .50
50A Jim Thome At Bat .30 .75
50B Jim Thome Fldg SP 3.00 8.00
51 Jose Guillen .20 .50
52 Richie Sexson .20 .50
53 Juan Cruz .20 .50
54 Byung-Hyun Kim .20 .50
55 Carlos Zambrano .30 .75
56 Carlos Lee .20 .50
57 Adam Dunn .30 .75
58 David Riske .20 .50
59 Carlos Guillen .20 .50
60 Larry Bowa MG .20 .50
61 Barry Bonds .75 2.00
62 Chris Woodward .20 .50
63 Matt DeSalvo RC .20 .50
64 Brian Stavisky RC .20 .50
65 Scot Shields .20 .50
66 J.D. Drew .20 .50
67 Erik Bedard .20 .50
68 Scott Williamson .20 .50
69A M.Prior New C on Cap .30 .75
69B M.Prior Old C on Cap SP 3.00 8.00
70 Ken Griffey Jr. 1.00 2.50
71 Kazuhito Tadano .20 .50
72 Philadelphia Phillies TC .20 .50
73 Jeremy Reed .20 .50
74 Ricardo Rodriguez .20 .50
75 Carlos Delgado .20 .50
76 Eric Milton .20 .50
77 Miguel Olivo .20 .50
78A E.Alfonzo No Socks .20 .50
78B E.Alfonzo Black Socks SP 3.00 8.00
79 Kazuhisa Ishii SP 3.00 8.00
80 Jason Giambi .20 .50
81 Cliff Floyd .20 .50
82A Torii Hunter Twins Cap .20 .50
82B Torii Hunter Wash Cap SP 3.00 8.00
83 Odalis Perez .20 .50
84 Scott Podsednik .20 .50
85 Cleveland Indians TC .20 .50
86 Jeff Suppan .20 .50
87 Ray Durham .20 .50
88 Tyler Clippard RC 1.25 3.00
89 Ryan Howard .40 1.00
90 Cincinnati Reds TC .20 .50
91 Bengie Molina .20 .50
92 Danny Bautista .20 .50
93 Eli Marrero .20 .50
94 Larry Bigbie .20 .50
95 Atlanta Braves TC .30 .75
96 Merkin Valdez .20 .50
97 Rocco Baldelli .20 .50
98 Woody Williams .20 .50
99 Jason Frasor .20 .50
100 Baltimore Orioles TC .20 .50
101 Ivan Rodriguez SP 3.00 8.00
102 Joe Kennedy .20 .50
103 Mike Lowell .20 .50
104 Armando Benitez .20 .50
105 Craig Biggio .30 .75
106 David DeJesus .20 .50
107 Adrian Beltre .50 1.25
108 Phil Nevin .20 .50
109 Cristian Guzman .20 .50
110 Jorge Posada SP 3.00 8.00
111 Boston Red Sox TC .50 1.25
112 Jeff Mathis .30 .75
113 Bartolo Colon .20 .50
114 Alex Cintron .20 .50
115 Russ Ortiz .20 .50
116 Doug Mientkiewicz .20 .50
117 Placido Polanco .20 .50
118A M.Ordonez Black Uni .30 .75
118B M.Ordonez White Uni SP 3.00 8.00
119 Chris Seddon RC .20 .50
120 Bobby Abreu .20 .50
121 Pittsburgh Pirates TC .20 .50
122 Dallas McPherson .20 .50
123 Rodrigo Lopez .20 .50
124 Mark Bellhorn .20 .50
125A N.Garciaparra Red Brim Cap .30 .75
125B N.Garciaparra Blue Brim Cap SP 3.00 8.00
126 Sean Casey .20 .50
127 Ronnie Belliard .20 .50
128 Tom Goodwin .20 .50
129 Preston Wilson .20 .50
130 Andruw Jones SP 3.00 8.00
131 Roberto Alomar .30 .75
132 John Buck .20 .50
133 Jason LaRue .20 .50
134 St. Louis Cardinals TC .30 .75
135A Alex Rodriguez Fldg SP 4.00 10.00
135B Alex Rodriguez At Bat SP 4.00 10.00
136 Nate Robertson .20 .50
137 Juan Pierre .20 .50
138 Morgan Ensberg .20 .50
139 Vinny Castilla .20 .50
140 Jake Dittler .20 .50
141 Chan Ho Park .30 .75
142 Felix Hernandez .60 1.50
143 Jason Isringhausen .20 .50
144 Dustan Mohr .20 .50
145 Khalil Greene .20 .50
146 Minnesota Twins TC .20 .50
147 Vicente Padilla .20 .50
148 Oliver Perez .20 .50
149 Brian Giles .20 .50
150 Shawn Green .20 .50
151 Matt Lawton .20 .50
152 Casey Blake .20 .50
153 Frank Thomas .50 1.25
154 Orlando Hernandez .20 .50
155A Eric Chavez Green Cap .20 .50
155B Eric Chavez Blue Cap SP 3.00 8.00
156 Chase Utley .30 .75
157 John Olerud .20 .50
158 Adam Eaton .20 .50
159 Josh Fogg .20 .50
160 Michael Tucker .20 .50
161 Kevin Brown .20 .50
162 Bobby Crosby .20 .50
163 Jason Schmidt .20 .50
164 Shannon Stewart .20 .50
165 Tony Womack .20 .50
166 Los Angeles Dodgers TC .20 .50
167 Franklin Gutierrez .60 1.50
168 Ted Lilly .20 .50
169 Mark Teixeira .30 .75
170 Matt Morris .20 .50
171 Bucky Jacobsen .20 .50
172 Steve Doetsch RC .20 .50
173 Jeff Weaver .20 .50
174 Tony Graffanino .20 .50
175 Jeff Bagwell .30 .75
176 Carl Pavano .20 .50
177 Junior Spivey .20 .50
178 Carlos Silva .20 .50
179 Tim Redding .20 .50
180 Brett Myers .20 .50
181 Mike Mussina .30 .75
182 Richard Hidalgo .20 .50
183 Nick Johnson .20 .50
184 Lew Ford .20 .50
185 Barry Zito .30 .75
186 Jimmy Rollins .30 .75
187 Jack Wilson .20 .50
188 Chicago White Sox TC .20 .50
189 Guillermo Quiroz .20 .50
190 Mark Hendrickson .20 .50
191 Jeremy Bonderman .20 .50
192 Jason Jennings .20 .50
193 Paul Lo Duca .20 .50
194 A.J. Burnett .20 .50
195 Ken Harvey .20 .50
196 Geoff Jenkins .20 .50
197 Joe Mays .20 .50
198 Jose Vidro .20 .50
199 David Wright .40 1.00
200 Randy Johnson .50 1.25
201 Jeff DaVanon .20 .50
202 Paul Byrd .20 .50
203 David Ortiz .50 1.25
204 Kyle Farnsworth .20 .50
205 Keith Foulke .20 .50
206 Joe Crede .20 .50
207 Austin Kearns .20 .50
208 Jody Gerut .20 .50
209 Shawn Chacon .20 .50
210 Carlos Pena .30 .75
211 Luis Castillo .20 .50
212 Chris Denorfia RC .20 .50
213 Detroit Tigers TC .20 .50
214 Aubrey Huff .20 .50
215 Brad Fullmer .20 .50
216 Frank Catalanotto .20 .50
217 Raul Ibanez .30 .75
218 Ryan Klesko .20 .50
219 Octavio Dotel .20 .50
220 Rob Mackowiak .20 .50
221 Scott Hatteberg .20 .50
222 Pat Burrell .20 .50
223 Bernie Williams .30 .75
224 Kris Benson .20 .50
225 Eric Gagne .20 .50
226 San Francisco Giants TC .20 .50
227 Roy Oswalt .30 .75
228 Josh Beckett .20 .50
229 Lee Mazzilli MG .20 .50
230 Rickie Weeks .20 .50
231 Troy Glaus .20 .50
232 Chone Figgins .20 .50
233 John Thomson .20 .50
234 Trot Nixon .20 .50
235 Brad Penny .20 .50
236 Oakland A's TC .30 .75
237 Miguel Batista .20 .50
238 Ryan Drese .20 .50
239 Aaron Miles .20 .50
240 Randy Wolf .20 .50
241 Brian Lawrence .20 .50
242 A.J. Pierzynski .20 .50
243 Jamie Moyer .20 .50
244 Chris Carpenter .30 .75
245 So Taguchi .20 .50
246 Rob Bell .20 .50
247 Francisco Cordero .20 .50
248 Tom Glavine .30 .75
249 Jermaine Dye .20 .50
250 Cliff Lee .20 .50
251 New York Yankees TC .50 1.25
252 Vernon Wells .20 .50
253 R.A. Dickey .30 .75
254 Larry Walker .30 .75
255 Randy Winn .20 .50
256 Pedro Feliz .20 .50
257 Mark Loretta .20 .50
258 Tim Worrell .20 .50
259 Kip Wells .20 .50
260 Cesar Izturis SP 3.00 8.00
261A Carlos Beltran Fldg .30 .75
261B Carlos Beltran At Bat SP 3.00 8.00
262 Juan Encarnacion .20 .50
263 Luis A. Gonzalez .20 .50
264 Grady Sizemore .30 .75
265 Paul Wilson .20 .50
266 Mark Buehrle .30 .75
267 Todd Hollandsworth .20 .50
268 Orlando Cabrera .20 .50
269 Sidney Ponson .20 .50
270 Mike Hampton .20 .50
271 Luis Gonzalez .20 .50
272 Brendan Donnelly .20 .50
273A Chipper Jones Slide .50 1.25
273B Chipper Jones Fldg SP 3.00 8.00
274 Brandon Webb .30 .75
275 Marty Cordova .20 .50
276 Greg Maddux .60 1.50
277 Jose Contreras .20 .50
278 Aaron Harang .20 .50
279 Coco Crisp .20 .50
280 Bobby Higginson .20 .50
281 Guillermo Mota .20 .50
282 Andy Pettitte .30 .75
283 Jeremy West RC .20 .50
284 Craig Brazell .20 .50
285 Eric Hinske .20 .50
286A Hank Blalock Hitting .20 .50
286B Hank Blalock Fldg SP 3.00 8.00
287 B.J. Upton .30 .75
288 Jason Marquis .20 .50
289 Matt Herges .20 .50
290 Ramon Hernandez .20 .50
291 Marlon Byrd .20 .50
292 Ryan Sweeney SP RC 3.00 8.00
293 Esteban Loaiza .20 .50
294 Al Leiter .20 .50
295 Alex Gonzalez .20 .50
296A J.Santana Twins Cap .30 .75
296B J.Santana Wash Cap SP 3.00 8.00
297 Milton Bradley .20 .50
298 Mike Sweeney .20 .50
299 Wade Miller .20 .50
300A Sammy Sosa Hitting .50 1.25
300B Sammy Sosa Standing SP 3.00 8.00
301 Wily Mo Pena .20 .50
302 Tim Wakefield .30 .75
303 Rafael Palmeiro .30 .75
304 Rafael Furcal .20 .50
305 David Eckstein .20 .50
306 David Segui .20 .50
307 Kevin Millar .20 .50
308 Matt Clement .30 .75
309 Wade Robinson RC .20 .50
310 Brad Radke .20 .50
311 Steve Finley .20 .50
312A Lance Berkman Hitting .30 .75
312B Lance Berkman Fldg SP 3.00 8.00
313 Joe Randa .20 .50
314 Miguel Cabrera .50 1.25
315 Billy Koch .20 .50
316 Alex Sanchez .20 .50
317 Chin-Hui Tsao .20 .50
318 Omar Vizquel .30 .75
319 Ryan Freel .20 .50
320 LaTroy Hawkins .20 .50
321 Aaron Rowand .20 .50
322 Paul Konerko .30 .75
323 Joe Borowski .20 .50
324 Jarrod Washburn .20 .50
325 Jaret Wright .20 .50
326 Johnny Damon .30 .75
327 Corey Patterson .20 .50
328 Travis Hafner .20 .50
329 Shingo Takatsu .20 .50
330 Dmitri Young .20 .50
331 Matt Holliday .50 1.25
332 Jeff Kent .30 .75
333 Desi Relaford .20 .50
334 Jose Hernandez .20 .50
335 Lyle Overbay .20 .50
336 Jacque Jones .20 .50
337 Termel Sledge .20 .50
338 Victor Zambrano .20 .50
339 Gary Sheffield .30 .75
340 Brad Wilkerson .20 .50
341 Ian Kinsler RC 1.00 2.50
342 Jesse Crain .20 .50
343 Orlando Hudson .20 .50
344 Laynce Nix .20 .50
345 Jose Cruz Jr. .30 .75
346 Edgar Renteria .20 .50
347 Eddie Guardado .20 .50
348 Jerome Williams .20 .50
349 Trevor Hoffman .30 .75
350 Mike Piazza .50 1.25
351 Jason Kendall .20 .50
352 Kevin Millwood .20 .50
353A Tim Hudson Atl Cap .30 .75
353B Tim Hudson Milw Cap SP 3.00 8.00
354 Paul Quantrill .20 .50
355 Jon Lieber .20 .50
356 Braden Looper .20 .50
357 Chad Cordero .20 .50
358 Joe Nathan .20 .50
359 Doug Davis .20 .50
360 Ian Bladergroen RC .20 .50
361 Val Majewski .20 .50
362 Francisco Rodriguez .30 .75
363 Kelvim Escobar .20 .50
364 Marcus Giles .20 .50
365 Darren Fenster RC .20 .50
366 David Bell .20 .50
367 Shea Hillenbrand .20 .50
368 Manny Ramirez .50 1.25
369 Ben Broussard .20 .50
370 Luis Ramirez RC .20 .50
371 Dustin Hermanson .20 .50
372 Akinori Otsuka .20 .50
373 Chadd Blasko RC .30 .75
374 Delmon Young .50 1.25
375 Michael Young .30 .75
376 Bret Boone .20 .50
377 Jake Peavy .20 .50
378 Matthew Lindstrom RC .20 .50
379 Sean Burroughs .20 .50
380 Rich Harden .20 .50
381 Chris Robertson RC .20 .50
382 John Lackey .30 .75
383 Johnny Estrada .20 .50
384 Matt Rogelstad RC .20 .50
385 Toby Hall .20 .50
386 Adam LaRoche .20 .50
387 Bill Hall .20 .50
388 Tim Salmon .20 .50
389A Curt Schilling Throw .30 .75
389B Curt Schilling Glove Up SP 3.00 8.00
390 Michael Barrett .20 .50
391 Jose Acevedo .20 .50
392 Nate Schierholtz .20 .50
393 J.T. Snow Jr. .20 .50
394 Mark Redman .20 .50
395 Ryan Madson .20 .50
396 Kevin West RC .20 .50
397 Ramon Ortiz .20 .50
398 Derek Lowe SP 3.00 8.00
399 Kerry Wood SP 3.00 8.00
400 Derek Jeter SP 12.00 30.00
401 Livan Hernandez SP 3.00 8.00
402 Casey Kotchman SP 3.00 8.00
403 Chaz Lytle SP RC 3.00 8.00
404 Alexis Rios SP 3.00 8.00
405 Scott Spiezio SP 3.00 8.00
406 Craig Wilson SP 3.00 8.00
407 Felix Rodriguez SP 3.00 8.00
408 D'Angelo Jimenez SP 3.00 8.00
409 Rondell White SP 3.00 8.00
410 Shawn Estes SP 3.00 8.00
411 Troy Percival SP 3.00 8.00
412 Melvin Mora SP 3.00 8.00
413 Aramis Ramirez SP 3.00 8.00
414 Carl Everett SP 3.00 8.00
415 Elvys Quezada SP RC 3.00 8.00
416 Ben Sheets SP 3.00 8.00
417 Matt Stairs SP 3.00 8.00
418 Adam Everett SP 3.00 8.00
419 Jason Johnson SP 3.00 8.00
420 Billy Butler SP RC 4.00 10.00
421 Justin Morneau SP 3.00 8.00
422 Jose Reyes SP 3.00 8.00
423 Mariano Rivera SP 30.00 80.00
424 Jose Vaquedano SP RC 3.00 8.00
425 Gabe Gross SP 3.00 8.00
426 Scott Rolen SP 3.00 8.00
427 Ty Wigginton SP 3.00 8.00
428 James Jurries SP RC 3.00 8.00
429 Pedro Martinez SP 3.00 8.00
430 Mark Grudzielanek SP 3.00 8.00
431 Josh Phelps SP 3.00 8.00
432 Ryan Goleski SP RC 3.00 8.00
433 Mike Matheny SP 3.00 8.00
434 Bobby Kielty SP 3.00 8.00
435 Tony Batista SP 3.00 8.00
436 Corey Koskie SP 3.00 8.00
437 Brad Lidge SP 3.00 8.00
438 Dontrelle Willis SP 3.00 8.00
439 Angel Berroa SP 3.00 8.00
440 Jason Kubel SP 3.00 8.00
441 Roy Halladay SP 3.00 8.00
442 Brian Roberts SP 3.00 8.00
443 Bill Mueller SP 3.00 8.00
444 Adam Kennedy SP 3.00 8.00
445 Brandon Moss SP RC 3.00 8.00
446 Sean Burnett SP 3.00 8.00
447 Eric Byrnes SP 3.00 8.00
448 Matt Campbell SP RC 3.00 8.00
449 Ryan Webb SP 3.00 8.00
450 Jose Valentin SP 3.00 8.00
451 Jake Westbrook SP 3.00 8.00
452 Glen Perkins SP RC 3.00 8.00
453 Alex Gonzalez SP 3.00 8.00
454 Jeromy Burnitz SP 3.00 8.00
455 Zack Greinke SP 3.00 8.00
456 Sean Marshall SP RC 2.50 6.00
457 Erubiel Durazo SP 3.00 8.00
458 Michael Cuddyer SP 3.00 8.00
459 Hee Seop Choi SP 3.00 8.00
460 Melky Cabrera SP RC 4.00 10.00
461 Jerry Hairston Jr. SP 3.00 8.00
462 Moises Alou SP 3.00 8.00
463 Michael Rogers SP RC 3.00 8.00
464 Javy Lopez SP 3.00 8.00
465 Freddy Garcia SP 3.00 8.00
466 Brett Harper SP RC 3.00 8.00
467 Juan Gonzalez SP 3.00 8.00
468 Kevin Melillo SP RC 3.00 8.00
469 Todd Walker SP 3.00 8.00
470 C.C. Sabathia SP 3.00 8.00
471 Kole Strayhorn SP RC 3.00 8.00
472 Mark Kotsay SP 3.00 8.00
473 Javier Vazquez SP 3.00 8.00
474 Mike Cameron SP 3.00 8.00
475 Wes Swackhamer SP RC 3.00 8.00
CL1 Checklist 1 .20 .50
CL2 Checklist 2 .20 .50

2005 Topps Heritage White Backs

COMPLETE SET (220) 75.00 150.00
*WHITE BACKS: .75X TO 2X BASIC
RANDOM INSERTS IN PACKS
SEE BECKETT.COM FOR FULL CHECKLIST

2005 Topps Heritage Chrome

STATED ODDS 1:7 HOBBY/RETAIL
STATED PRINT RUN 1956 SERIAL #'d SETS
TCH1 Will Harridge 1.50 4.00
THC2 Warren Giles 1.50 4.00
THC3 Alex Rodriguez 5.00 12.00
THC4 Alfonso Soriano 2.50 6.00
THC5 Barry Bonds 6.00 15.00
THC6 Todd Helton 2.50 6.00
THC7 Kazuo Matsui 1.50 4.00
THC8 Garret Anderson 1.50 4.00
THC9 Mark Prior 2.50 6.00
THC10 Jim Thome 2.50 6.00
THC11 Jason Giambi 1.50 4.00
THC12 Ivan Rodriguez 2.50 6.00
THC13 Mike Lowell 1.50 4.00
THC14 Vladimir Guerrero 2.50 6.00
THC15 Adrian Beltre 4.00 10.00
THC16 Andruw Jones 1.50 4.00
THC17 Jose Vidro 1.50 4.00
THC18 Josh Beckett 1.50 4.00
THC19 Mike Sweeney 1.50 4.00
THC20 Sammy Sosa 4.00 10.00
THC21 Scott Rolen 2.50 6.00
THC22 Javy Lopez 1.50 4.00
THC23 Albert Pujols 5.00 12.00
THC24 Adam Dunn 2.50 6.00
THC25 Ken Griffey Jr. 8.00 20.00
THC26 Torii Hunter 1.50 4.00
THC27 Jorge Posada 2.50 6.00
THC28 Magglio Ordonez 2.50 6.00
THC29 Shawn Green 1.50 4.00
THC30 Frank Thomas 4.00 10.00
THC31 Barry Zito 2.50 6.00
THC32 David Ortiz 4.00 10.00
THC33 Pat Burrell 1.50 4.00
THC34 Luis Gonzalez 1.50 4.00
THC35 Chipper Jones 4.00 10.00
THC36 Hank Blalock 1.50 4.00
THC37 Rafael Palmeiro 2.50 6.00
THC38 Lance Berkman 2.50 6.00
THC39 Miguel Cabrera 4.00 10.00
THC40 Paul Konerko 2.50 6.00
THC41 Jeff Kent 1.50 4.00
THC42 Gary Sheffield 1.50 4.00
THC43 Mike Piazza 4.00 10.00
THC44 Bret Boone 1.50 4.00
THC45 Kerry Wood 1.50 4.00
THC46 Derek Jeter 10.00 25.00
THC47 Pedro Martinez 2.50 6.00
THC48 Jason Bay 1.50 4.00
THC49 Ichiro Suzuki 5.00 12.00
THC50 Miguel Tejada 2.50 6.00
THC51 Richie Sexson 1.50 4.00
THC52 Jeff Bagwell 2.50 6.00
THC53 Lew Ford 1.50 4.00
THC54 Randy Johnson 4.00 10.00
THC55 Carlos Beltran 2.50 6.00
THC56 Greg Maddux 5.00 12.00
THC57 Lyle Overbay 1.50 4.00
THC58 Michael Young 1.50 4.00
THC59 Curt Schilling 2.50 6.00
THC60 Jose Reyes 2.50 6.00
THC61 Dontrelle Willis 1.50 4.00
THC62 Nomar Garciaparra 2.50 6.00
THC63 Paul Lo Duca 1.50 4.00
THC64 Larry Walker 2.50 6.00
THC65 Andre Ethier 12.00 30.00
THC66 Matt DeSalvo 1.50 4.00
THC67 Brian Stavisky 1.50 4.00
THC68 Tyler Clippard 10.00 25.00
THC69 Chris Seddon 1.50 4.00
THC70 Steve Doetsch 1.50 4.00
THC71 Chris Denorfia 1.50 4.00
THC72 Jeremy West 1.50 4.00
THC73 Ryan Sweeney 2.50 6.00
THC74 Ian Kinsler 8.00 20.00
THC75 Ian Bladergroen 1.50 4.00
THC76 Darren Fenster 1.50 4.00
THC77 Luis Ramirez 1.50 4.00
THC78 Chadd Blasko 2.50 6.00
THC79 Matthew Lindstrom 1.50 4.00
THC80 Chris Robertson 1.50 4.00
THC81 Matt Rogelstad 1.50 4.00
THC82 Nate Schierholtz 1.50 4.00
THC83 Kevin West 1.50 4.00
THC84 Chaz Lytle 2.50 6.00
THC85 Elvys Quezada 1.50 4.00
THC86 Billy Butler 8.00 20.00
THC87 Jose Vaquedano 1.50 4.00
THC88 James Jurries 1.50 4.00
THC89 Ryan Goleski 1.50 4.00
THC90 Brandon Moss 6.00 15.00
THC91 Matt Campbell 1.50 4.00
THC92 Ryan Webb 1.50 4.00
THC93 Glen Perkins 1.50 4.00
THC94 Sean Marshall 4.00 10.00
THC95 Melky Cabrera 5.00 12.00
THC96 Michael Rogers 1.50 4.00
THC97 Brett Harper 1.50 4.00
THC98 Kevin Melillo 1.50 4.00
THC99 Kole Strayhorn 1.50 4.00
THC100 Wes Swackhamer 1.50 4.00
THC101 Rickie Weeks 1.50 4.00
THC102 Delmon Young 4.00 10.00
THC103 Kazuhito Tadano 1.50 4.00
THC104 Kazuhisa Ishii 1.50 4.00
THC105 David Wright 3.00 8.00
THC106 Eric Gagne 1.50 4.00
THC107 So Taguchi 1.50 4.00
THC108 B.J. Upton 2.50 6.00
THC109 Shingo Takatsu 1.50 4.00
THC110 Akinori Otsuka 1.50 4.00

2005 Topps Heritage Chrome Black Refractors

*BLACK REF: 4X TO 8X CHROME
*BLACK REF: 4X TO 8X CHROME RC YR
STATED ODDS 1:250 HOBBY/RETAIL
STATED PRINT RUN 56 SERIAL #'d SETS

2005 Topps Heritage Chrome Refractors

*REFRACTOR: .6X TO 1.5X CHROME
*REFRACTOR: .6X TO 1.5X CHROME RC YR
STATED ODDS 1:25 HOBBY/RETAIL
STATED PRINT RUN 556 SERIAL #'d SETS

2005 Topps Heritage Clubhouse Collection Relics

GROUP A ODDS 1:291 H, 1:292 R
GROUP B ODDS 1:384 H, 1:387 R
GROUP C ODDS 1:1303 H, 1:1307 R
GROUP D ODDS 1:497 H, 1:499 R
GROUP E ODDS 1:384 H, 1:387 R
AK Al Kaline Bat A 8.00 20.00
AP Albert Pujols Bat B 8.00 20.00
AR Alex Rodriguez Bat D 6.00 15.00
AS Alfonso Soriano Bat C 3.00 8.00
BW Bernie Williams Bat A 4.00 10.00
DW Dontrelle Willis Jsy E 3.00 8.00
EB Ernie Banks Bat A 8.00 20.00
GS Gary Sheffield Bat B 3.00 8.00
HK Harmon Killebrew Bat A 8.00 20.00
LA Luis Aparicio Bat A 4.00 10.00
LB Lance Berkman Bat D 3.00 8.00
MC Miguel Cabrera Bat A 4.00 10.00
MR Manny Ramirez Jsy E 4.00 10.00
MT Miguel Tejada Bat B 3.00 8.00
RS Red Schoendienst Bat B 4.00 10.00

2005 Topps Heritage Clubhouse Collection Dual Relics

STATED ODDS 1:9249 H, 1:9490 R
STATED PRINT RUN 56 SERIAL #'d SETS
BG Banks Bat/Garciaparra Bat 30.00 60.00
KR Kaline Bat/I.Rodriguez Bat 30.00 60.00
MP Musial Jsy/Pujols Jsy 125.00 200.00

2005 Topps Heritage Flashbacks

COMPLETE SET (10) 5.00 12.00
STATED ODDS 1:12 HOBBY/RETAIL
AK Al Kaline 1.00 2.50
BF Bob Feller .60 1.50
DL Don Larsen .40 1.00
DS Duke Snider .60 1.50
EB Ernie Banks 1.00 2.50
FR Frank Robinson .60 1.50
HA Hank Aaron 2.00 5.00
HS Herb Score .40 1.00
LA Luis Aparicio .60 1.50
SM Stan Musial 1.50 4.00

2005 Topps Heritage Flashbacks Seat Relics

STATED ODDS 1:96 HOBBY/RETAIL
AK Al Kaline 6.00 15.00
BF Bob Feller 6.00 15.00
DL Don Larsen 6.00 15.00
DS Duke Snider 6.00 15.00
EB Ernie Banks 6.00 15.00
FR Frank Robinson 4.00 10.00
HA Hank Aaron 8.00 20.00
HS Herb Score 4.00 10.00
LA Luis Aparicio 4.00 10.00
SM Stan Musial 8.00 20.00

2005 Topps Heritage New Age Performers

COMPLETE SET (15) 10.00 25.00
STATED ODDS 1:15 HOBBY/RETAIL
1 Alfonso Soriano .60 1.50
2 Alex Rodriguez 1.25 3.00
3 Ichiro Suzuki 1.25 3.00
4 Albert Pujols 1.25 3.00
5 Vladimir Guerrero .60 1.50
6 Jim Thome .60 1.50
7 Derek Jeter 2.50 6.00
8 Sammy Sosa 1.00 2.50
9 Ivan Rodriguez .60 1.50
10 Manny Ramirez 1.00 2.50
11 Todd Helton .60 1.50
12 David Ortiz 1.00 2.50
13 Gary Sheffield .40 1.00
14 Nomar Garciaparra .60 1.50
15 Randy Johnson 1.00 2.50

2005 Topps Heritage Real One Autographs

STATED ODDS 1:333 H, 1:332 R
STATED PRINT RUN 200 SETS
PRINT RUN INFO PROVIDED BY TOPPS
BASIC AUTOS ARE NOT SERIAL-NUMBERED
*RED INK: .75X TO 1.5X BASIC
RED INK ODDS 1:1195 H, 1:1196 R
RED INK PRINT RUN 56 SERIAL #'d SETS
RED INK ALSO CALLED SPECIAL EDITION
AS Art Swanson 20.00 50.00
BF Bob Feller 40.00 80.00
BN Bob Nelson 15.00 40.00
BT Bill Tremel 10.00 25.00
CD Chuck Diering 10.00 25.00
DS Duke Snider 50.00 100.00
EB Ernie Banks 60.00 150.00
FM Fred Marsh 10.00 25.00
HA Hank Aaron 150.00 250.00
JA Joe Astroth 10.00 25.00
JB Jim Brady 20.00 50.00
JG Jim Greengrass 15.00 40.00
JM Jake Martin 15.00 40.00
JS Johnny Schmitz 20.00 50.00
JSA Jose Santiago 20.00 50.00
LP Laurin Pepper 10.00 25.00
LPO Leroy Powell 10.00 25.00
MI Monte Irvin 20.00 50.00
PM Paul Minner 10.00 25.00
RM Rudy Minarcin 10.00 25.00
SJ Spook Jacobs 10.00 25.00
WW Wally Westlake 10.00 25.00
YB Yogi Berra 50.00 120.00

2005 Topps Heritage Then and Now

COMPLETE SET (10) 5.00 12.00
STATED ODDS 1:15 HOBBY/RETAIL
TN1 H.Aaron 2.00 5.00
I.Suzuki
TN2 D.Newcombe .60 1.50
C.Schilling
TN3 R.Roberts .60 1.50
L.Hernandez
TN4 B.Friend .40 1.00
L.Hernandez
TN5 H.Score 1.00 2.50
R.Johnson
TN6 W.Ford .60 1.50
J.Peavy
TN7 J.Piersall .40 1.00
L.Overbay
TN8 C.Labine 1.25 3.00
M.Rivera
TN9 B.Bruton .60 1.50
C.Crawford
TN10 E.Yost .40 1.00
B.Abreu

2006 Topps Heritage

COMPLETE SET (494) 250.00 400.00
COMP.SET w/o SP's (384) 15.00 40.00
SP STATED ODDS 1:2 HOBBY/RETAIL
SP CL: 1/2/10/18/20B/23B/25/35/55
SP CL: 70/76/80B/91/95A/95B/99/106
SP CL: 123/127/165B/200B/212B/265-269
SP CL: 271-274/276-316/318-323/325A
SP CL: 325B/326-328/330-349/350A/350B
SP CL: 351-352/400/407/475B
VARIATION CL: 20/23/80/95/165/200
VARIATION CL: 212/325/350/475
TWO VERSIONS OF EACH VARIATION EXIST
SEE BECKETT.COM FOR VAR.DESCRIPTIONS
CARD 255 NOT INTENDED FOR RELEASE
COMP.SET EXCLUDES CARD 255 CUT OUT
1 David Ortiz SP 3.00 8.00
2 Mike Piazza SP 4.00 10.00
3 Daryle Ward .20 .50
4 Rafael Furcal .20 .50
5 Derek Lowe .20 .50
6 Eric Chavez .20 .50
7 Juan Uribe .20 .50
8 C.C. Sabathia .30 .75
9 Sean Casey .20 .50
10 Barry Bonds SP 5.00 12.00
11 Gary Sheffield .20 .50
12 Ted Lilly .20 .50
13 Lew Ford .20 .50
14 Tom Gordon .20 .50
15 Curt Schilling .30 .75
16 Jason Kendall .20 .50
17 Frank Catalanotto .20 .50
18 Pedro Martinez SP 3.00 8.00
19 David Dellucci .20 .50
20A A.Jones w .20 .50
o Seats
20B A.Jones w 3.00 8.00
Seats SP
21 Brad Halsey .20 .50
22 Vernon Wells .20 .50
23A D.Jeter Yellow 1.25 3.00
White Ltr
23B D.Jeter Blue Ltr SP 5.00 12.00
24 Todd Helton .30 .75
25 Randy Johnson SP 4.00 10.00
26 Jay Gibbons .20 .50
27 Joe Mays .20 .50
28 Paul Konerko .30 .75
29 Lyle Overbay .20 .50
30 Jorge Posada .30 .75
31 Brandon Webb .30 .75
32 Marcus Giles .20 .50
33 J.T. Snow .20 .50
34 Todd Walker .20 .50
35 Wily Mo Pena SP 3.00 8.00
36 Carlos Delgado .20 .50
37 David Wright .40 1.00
38 Shea Hillenbrand .20 .50
39 Daniel Cabrera .20 .50
40 Trevor Hoffman .30 .75
41 Matt Morris .20 .50
42 Mariano Rivera .60 1.50
43 Jeff Bagwell .30 .75
44 J.D. Drew .20 .50
45 Carl Pavano .20 .50
46 Placido Polanco .20 .50
47 Adrian Beltre .50 1.25
48 J.D. Closser .20 .50
49 Paul Lo Duca .20 .50
50 Scott Rolen .30 .75
51 Bernie Williams .30 .75
52 Jose Guillen .20 .50
53 Aubrey Huff .20 .50
54 Greg Maddux .60 1.50
55 Derrek Lee SP 3.00 8.00
56 Hideki Matsui .50 1.25
57 Jose Bautista .50 1.25
58 Kyle Farnsworth .20 .50
59 Nate Robertson .20 .50
60 Sammy Sosa .50 1.25
61 Javier Vazquez .20 .50
62 Jeff Mathis .20 .50
63 Mark Buehrle .30 .75
64 Orlando Hernandez .20 .50
65 Brandon Claussen .20 .50
66 Miguel Batista .20 .50
67 Eddie Guardado .20 .50
68 Alex Gonzalez .20 .50
69 Kris Benson .20 .50
70 Bobby Abreu SP 3.00 8.00
71 Vinny Castilla .20 .50
72 Ben Broussard .20 .50
73 Travis Hafner .20 .50
74 Dmitri Young .20 .50
75 Alex S. Gonzalez .20 .50
76 Jason Bay SP 3.00 8.00
77 Charlton Jimerson .20 .50
78 Ryan Garko .20 .50
79 Lance Berkman .30 .75
80A T.Hudson Red .30 .75
Blue Ltr
80B T.Hudson Blue Ltr SP 3.00 8.00
81 Guillermo Mota .20 .50
82 Chris B. Young .50 1.25
83 Brad Lidge .20 .50
84 A.J. Pierzynski .20 .50
85 Maicer Izturis .20 .50
86 Vladimir Guerrero .30 .75
87 J.J. Hardy .20 .50
88 Cesar Izturis .20 .50
89 Mark Ellis .20 .50
90 Chipper Jones .50 1.25
91 Chris Snelling SP 3.00 8.00
92 Jose Reyes .30 .75
93 Mike Lieberthal .20 .50
94 Octavio Dotel .20 .50
95A A.Rodriguez Fielding SP 4.00 10.00
95B A.Rodriguez w 4.00 10.00
Bat SP
96 Brett Myers .20 .50
97 New York Yankees TC .30 .75
98 Ryan Klesko .20 .50
99 Brian Jordan SP 3.00 8.00
100 W.Harridge .20 .50
W.Giles
101 Adam Eaton .20 .50
102 Aaron Boone .20 .50
103 Alex Rios .20 .50
104 Andy Pettitte .30 .75
105 Barry Zito .30 .75
106 Bengie Molina SP 3.00 8.00
107 Austin Kearns .20 .50
108 Adam Everett .20 .50
109 A.J. Burnett .20 .50
110 Mark Prior .30 .75
111 Russ Ortiz .20 .50
112 Adam Dunn .30 .75
113 Byung-Hyun Kim
114 Atlanta Braves TC .20 .50
115 Carlos Silva .20 .50
116 Chad Cordero .20 .50
117 Chone Figgins .20 .50
118 Chris Reitsma .20 .50
119 Coco Crisp .20 .50
120 David DeJesus .20 .50
121 Chris Snyder .20 .50
122 Brad Eldred .20 .50
123 Humberto Cota SP 3.00 8.00
124 Erubiel Durazo .20 .50
125 Josh Beckett .20 .50
126 Kenny Lofton .20 .50
127 Joe Nathan SP 3.00 8.00
128 Bryan Bullington .20 .50
129 Jim Thome .30 .75
130 Shawn Green .20 .50
131 LaTroy Hawkins .20 .50
132 Mark Kotsay .20 .50
133 Matt Lawton .20 .50
134 Luis Castillo .20 .50
135 Michael Barrett .20 .50
136 Preston Wilson .20 .50
137 Orlando Cabrera .20 .50
138 Chuck James .20 .50
139 Raul Ibanez .30 .75
140 Frank Thomas .50 1.25
141 Orlando Hudson .20 .50
142 Scott Kazmir .30 .75
143 Steve Finley .20 .50
144 Danny Sandoval RC .20 .50
145 Javy Lopez .20 .50
146 Tony Giarratano .20 .50
147 Terrence Long .20 .50
148 Victor Martinez .30 .75
149 Toby Hall .20 .50
150 Fausto Carmona .20 .50
151 Tim Wakefield .30 .75
152 Troy Percival .20 .50
153 Chris Denorfia .20 .50
154 Junior Spivey .20 .50
155 Desi Relaford .20 .50
156 Francisco Liriano .50 1.25
157 Corey Koskie .20 .50
158 Chris Carpenter .30 .75
159 Robert Andino RC .20 .50
160 Cliff Floyd .20 .50
161 Pittsburgh Pirates TC .20 .50
162 Anderson Hernandez .20 .50
163 Mike Maroth .20 .50
164 Aaron Rowand .20 .50
165A A.Pujols Grey Shirt .60 1.50
165B A.Pujols Red Shirt SP 5.00 12.00
166 David Bell .20 .50
167 Angel Berroa .20 .50
168 B.J. Ryan .20 .50
169 Bartolo Colon .20 .50
170 Hong-Chih Kuo .50 1.25
171 Cincinnati Reds TC .20 .50
172 Bill Mueller .20 .50
173 John Koronka .20 .50
174 Billy Wagner .20 .50
175 Zack Greinke .50 1.25
176 Rick Short .20 .50
177 Yadier Molina .60 1.50
178 Willy Taveras .20 .50
179 Wes Helms .20 .50
180 Wade Miller .20 .50
181 Luis Gonzalez .20 .50
182 Victor Zambrano .20 .50
183 Chicago Cubs TC .20 .50
184 Victor Santos .20 .50
185 Tyler Walker .20 .50
186 Bobby Crosby .20 .50
187 Trot Nixon .20 .50
188 Nick Johnson .20 .50
189 Nick Swisher .30 .75
190 Brian Roberts .20 .50
191 Nomar Garciaparra .30 .75
192 Oliver Perez .20 .50
193 Ramon Hernandez .20 .50
194 Randy Winn .20 .50
195 Ryan Church .20 .50
196 Ryan Wagner .20 .50
197 Todd Hollandsworth .20 .50
198 Detroit Tigers TC .20 .50
199 Tino Martinez .20 .50
200A R.Clemens On Mound .60 1.50
200B R.Clemens Red Shirt SP 4.00 10.00
201 Shawn Estes .20 .50
202 Justin Morneau .30 .75
203 Jeff Francis .20 .50
204 Oakland Athletics TC .20 .50
205 Jeff Francoeur .50 1.25
206 C.J. Wilson .30 .75
207 Francisco Rodriguez .30 .75
208 Edgardo Alfonzo .20 .50
209 David Eckstein .20 .50
210 Cory Lidle .20 .50
211 Chase Utley .30 .75
212A R.Baldelli Yellow .20 .50
White Ltr
212B R.Baldelli Blue Ltr SP 3.00 8.00
213 So Taguchi .20 .50
214 Philadelphia Phillies TC .20 .50
215 Brad Hawpe .20 .50
216 Walter Young .20 .50
217 Tom Gorzelanny .20 .50
218 Shaun Marcum .20 .50
219 Ryan Howard .40 1.00
220 Damian Jackson .20 .50
221 Craig Counsell .20 .50
222 Damian Miller .20 .50
223 Derrick Turnbow .20 .50
224 Hank Blalock .20 .50
225 Brayan Pena .20 .50
226 Grady Sizemore .30 .75
227 Ivan Rodriguez .30 .75
228 Jason Isringhausen .20 .50
229 Brian Fuentes .20 .50
230 Jason Phillips .20 .50
231 Jason Schmidt .20 .50
232 Javier Valentin .20 .50
233 Jeff Kent .20 .50
234 John Buck .20 .50
235 Mike Matheny .20 .50
236 Jorge Cantu .20 .50
237 Jose Castillo .20 .50
238 Kenny Rogers .20 .50
239 Kerry Wood .20 .50
240 Kevin Mench .20 .50
241 Tim Stauffer .20 .50
242 Eric Milton .20 .50
243 St. Louis Cardinals TC .30 .75
244 Shawn Chacon .20 .50
245 Mike Jacobs .20 .50
246 Ryan Dempster .20 .50
247 Todd Jones .20 .50
248 Tom Glavine .30 .75
249 Tony Graffanino .20 .50
250 Ichiro Suzuki .60 1.50
251 Baltimore Orioles TC .20 .50
252 Brad Radke .20 .50
253 Brad Wilkerson .20 .50
254 Carlos Lee .20 .50
255 Alex Gordon Cut Out 125.00 250.00
256 Gustavo Chacin .20 .50
257 Jermaine Dye .20 .50
258 Jose Mesa .20 .50
259 Julio Lugo .20 .50
260 Mark Redman .20 .50
261 Brandon Watson .20 .50
262 Pedro Feliz .20 .50
263 Esteban Loaiza .20 .50
264 Anthony Reyes .20 .50
265 Jose Contreras SP 3.00 8.00
266 Tadahito Iguchi SP 3.00 8.00
267 Mark Loretta SP 3.00 8.00
268 Ray Durham SP 3.00 8.00
269 Neifi Perez SP 3.00 8.00
270 Washington Nationals TC .20 .50
271 Troy Glaus SP 3.00 8.00
272 Matt Holliday SP 4.00 10.00
273 Kevin Millwood SP 3.00 8.00
274 Jon Lieber SP 3.00 8.00
275 Cleveland Indians TC .20 .50
276 Jeremy Reed SP 3.00 8.00
277 Garrett Atkins SP 3.00 8.00
278 Geoff Jenkins SP 3.00 8.00
279 Joey Gathright SP 3.00 8.00
280 Ben Sheets SP 3.00 8.00
281 Melvin Mora SP 3.00 8.00
282 Jonathan Papelbon SP 4.00 10.00
283 John Smoltz SP 3.00 8.00
284 Jake Peavy SP 3.00 8.00
285 Felix Hernandez SP 3.00 8.00
286 Alfonso Soriano SP 3.00 8.00
287 Bronson Arroyo SP 3.00 8.00
288 Adam LaRoche SP 3.00 8.00
289 Aramis Ramirez SP 3.00 8.00
290 Brad Hennessey SP 3.00 8.00
291 Conor Jackson SP 3.00 8.00
292 Rod Barajas SP 3.00 8.00
293 Chris R. Young SP 3.00 8.00
294 Jeremy Bonderman SP 3.00 8.00
295 Jack Wilson SP 3.00 8.00
296 Jay Payton SP 3.00 8.00
297 Danys Baez SP 3.00 8.00
298 Jose Lima SP 3.00 8.00
299 Luis A. Gonzalez SP 3.00 8.00
300 Mike Sweeney SP 3.00 8.00
301 Nelson Cruz SP 3.00 8.00
302 Eric Gagne SP 3.00 8.00
303 Juan Castro SP 3.00 8.00
304 Joe Mauer SP 3.00 8.00
305 Richie Sexson SP 3.00 8.00
306 Roy Oswalt SP 3.00 8.00
307 Rickie Weeks SP 3.00 8.00
308 Pat Borders SP 3.00 8.00
309 Mike Morse SP 3.00 8.00
310 Matt Stairs SP 3.00 8.00
311 Chad Tracy SP 3.00 8.00
312 Matt Cain SP 3.00 8.00
313 Mark Mulder SP 3.00 8.00
314 Mark Grudzielanek SP 3.00 8.00
315 Johnny Damon Yanks SP 4.00 10.00
316 Casey Kotchman SP 3.00 8.00
317 San Francisco Giants TC .20 .50
318 Chris Burke SP 3.00 8.00
319 Carl Crawford SP 3.00 8.00
320 Edgar Renteria SP 3.00 8.00
321 Chan Ho Park SP 3.00 8.00
322 Boston Red Sox TC SP 3.00 8.00
323 Robinson Cano SP 3.00 8.00
324 Los Angeles Dodgers TC .30 .75
325A M.Tejada w/Bat SP 3.00 8.00
325B M.Tejada Hand Up SP 3.00 8.00
326 Jimmy Rollins SP 3.00 8.00
327 Juan Pierre SP 3.00 8.00
328 Dan Johnson SP 3.00 8.00
329 Chicago White Sox TC .20 .50
330 Pat Burrell SP 3.00 8.00
331 Ramon Ortiz SP 3.00 8.00
332 Rondell White SP 3.00 8.00
333 David Wells SP 3.00 8.00
334 Michael Young SP 3.00 8.00
335 Mike Mussina SP 3.00 8.00
336 Moises Alou SP 3.00 8.00
337 Scott Podsednik SP 3.00 8.00
338 Rich Harden SP 3.00 8.00
339 Mark Teahen SP 3.00 8.00
340 Jacque Jones SP 3.00 8.00
341 Jason Giambi SP 3.00 8.00
342 Bill Hall SP 3.00 8.00
343 Jon Garland SP 3.00 8.00
344 Dontrelle Willis SP 3.00 8.00
345 Danny Haren SP 3.00 8.00
346 Brian Giles SP 3.00 8.00
347 Brad Penny SP 3.00 8.00
348 Brandon McCarthy SP 3.00 8.00
349 Chien-Ming Wang SP 4.00 10.00
350A T.Hunter Red 3.00 8.00
Blue Ltr SP
350B T.Hunter Blue Ltr SP 3.00 8.00
351 Yhency Brazoban SP 3.00 8.00
352 Rodrigo Lopez SP 3.00 8.00
353 Paul McAnulty .20 .50
354 Francisco Cordero .20 .50
355 Brandon Inge .20 .50
356 Jason Lane .20 .50
357 Brian Schneider .20 .50
358 Dustin Hermanson .20 .50
359 Eric Hinske .20 .50
360 Jarrod Washburn .20 .50
361 Jayson Werth .30 .75
362 Craig Breslow RC .20 .50
363 Jeff Weaver .20 .50
364 Jeromy Burnitz .20 .50
365 Jhonny Peralta .20 .50
366 Joe Crede .20 .50
367 Johan Santana .30 .75
368 Jose Valentin .20 .50
369 Keith Foulke .20 .50
370 Larry Bigbie .20 .50
371 Manny Ramirez .50 1.25
372 Jim Edmonds .30 .75
373 Horacio Ramirez .20 .50
374 Garret Anderson .20 .50
375 Felipe Lopez .20 .50
376 Eric Byrnes .20 .50
377 Darin Erstad .20 .50
378 Carlos Zambrano .30 .75
379 Craig Biggio .30 .75
380 Darrell Rasner .20 .50
381 Dave Roberts .30 .75
382 Hanley Ramirez .30 .75
383 Geoff Blum .20 .50
384 Joel Pineiro .20 .50
385 Kip Wells .20 .50
386 Kelvim Escobar .20 .50
387 John Patterson .20 .50
388 Jody Gerut .20 .50
389 Marshall McDougall .20 .50
390 Mike MacDougal .20 .50
391 Orlando Palmeiro .20 .50
392 Rich Aurilia .20 .50
393 Ronnie Belliard .20 .50
394 Rich Hill .50 1.25
395 Scott Hatteberg .20 .50
396 Ryan Langerhans .20 .50
397 Richard Hidalgo .20 .50
398 Omar Vizquel .30 .75
399 Mike Lowell .20 .50
400 Astros Aces SP 3.00 8.00
401 Mike Cameron .20 .50
402 Matt Clement .20 .50
403 Miguel Cabrera .50 1.25
404 Milton Bradley .20 .50
405 Laynce Nix .20 .50
406 Rob Mackowiak .20 .50
407 White Sox Power Hitters SP 3.00 8.00
408 Mark Teixeira .30 .75
409 Brady Clark .20 .50
410 Johnny Estrada .20 .50
411 Juan Encarnacion .20 .50
412 Morgan Ensberg .20 .50
413 Nook Logan .20 .50
414 Phil Nevin .20 .50
415 Reggie Sanders .20 .50
416 Roy Halladay .30 .75
417 Livan Hernandez .20 .50
418 Jose Vidro .20 .50
419 Shannon Stewart .20 .50
420 Brian Bruney .20 .50
421 Royce Clayton .20 .50
422 Chris Demaria RC .20 .50
423 Eduardo Perez .20 .50
424 Jeff Suppan .20 .50
425 Jaret Wright .20 .50
426 Joe Randa .20 .50
427 Bobby Kielty .20 .50
428 Jason Ellison .20 .50
429 Gregg Zaun .20 .50
430 Runelvys Hernandez .20 .50
431 Joe McEwing .20 .50
432 Jason LaRue .20 .50
433 Aaron Miles .20 .50
434 Adam Kennedy .20 .50
435 Ambiorix Burgos .20 .50
436 Armando Benitez .20 .50
437 Brad Ausmus .20 .50
438 Brandon Backe .20 .50
439 Brian James Anderson
440 Bruce Chen .20 .50
441 Carlos Guillen .20 .50
442 Casey Blake .20 .50
443 Chris Capuano .20 .50
444 Chris Duffy .20 .50
445 Chris Ray .20 .50
446 Clint Barmes .20 .50
447 Andrew Sisco .20 .50
448 Dallas McPherson .20 .50
449 Tanyon Sturtze .20 .50
450 Carlos Beltran .30 .75
451 Jason Vargas .20 .50
452 Ervin Santana .20 .50
453 Jason Marquis .20 .50
454 Juan Rivera .20 .50
455 Jake Westbrook .20 .50
456 Jason Johnson
457 Joe Blanton .20 .50
458 Kevin Millar .20 .50
459 John Thomson .20 .50
460 J.P. Howell .20 .50
461 Justin Verlander 1.50 4.00
462 Kelly Johnson
463 Kyle Davies .20 .50
464 Lance Niekro .20 .50
465 Magglio Ordonez .30 .75
466 Melky Cabrera .30 .75
467 Nick Punto .20 .50
468 Paul Byrd .20 .50
469 Randy Wolf .20 .50
470 Ruben Gotay .20 .50
471 Ryan Madson .20 .50
472 Victor Diaz .20 .50
473 Xavier Nady .20 .50
474 Zach Duke .20 .50
475A H.Street Yellow .20 .50
White Ltr
475B H.Street Blue Ltr SP 3.00 8.00
476 Brad Thompson .20 .50
477 Jonny Gomes .20 .50
478 B.J. Upton .20 .50
479 Jamey Carroll .20 .50
480 Mike Hampton .20 .50
481 Tony Clark .20 .50
482 Antonio Alfonseca .20 .50
483 Justin Duchscherer .20 .50
484 Mike Timlin .20 .50
485 Joe Saunders .20 .50

2006 Topps Heritage Checklists

COMPLETE SET (5) .75 2.00
COMMON CARD (1-5) .20 .50
RANDOM INSERTS IN PACKS

2006 Topps Heritage Chrome

COMPLETE SET (109) 200.00 300.00
COMMON (1-102/104-110) 1.50 4.00
STATED ODDS 1:9 HOBBY, 1:10 RETAIL
STATED PRINT RUN 1957 SERIAL #'d SETS
CARD 103 DOES NOT EXIST
1 Rafael Furcal 1.25 3.00
2 C.C. Sabathia 2.00 5.00
3 Sean Casey 1.25 3.00
4 Gary Sheffield 1.25 3.00
5 W.Harridge 1.25 3.00
W.Giles
6 Curt Schilling 2.00 5.00
7 Jay Gibbons 1.25 3.00
8 Paul Konerko 2.00 5.00
9 Lyle Overbay 1.25 3.00
10 Jorge Posada 2.00 5.00
11 Todd Walker 1.25 3.00
12 Carlos Delgado 1.25 3.00
13 David Wright 2.50 6.00
14 Matt Morris 1.25 3.00
15 Mariano Rivera 4.00 10.00
16 Jeff Bagwell 2.00 5.00
17 Carl Pavano 1.25 3.00
18 Adrian Beltre 3.00 8.00
19 Scott Rolen 2.00 5.00
20 Aubrey Huff 1.25 3.00
21 Hideki Matsui 3.00 8.00
22 Andruw Jones 1.25 3.00
23 Sammy Sosa 3.00 8.00
24 Mark Buehrle 2.00 5.00
25 Orlando Hernandez 1.25 3.00
26 Travis Hafner 1.25 3.00
27 Vladimir Guerrero 2.00 5.00
28 Chipper Jones 3.00 8.00
29 Jose Reyes 2.00 5.00
30 Roger Clemens 4.00 10.00
31 Aaron Boone 1.25 3.00
32 Andy Pettitte 2.00 5.00
33 David DeJesus 1.25 3.00
34 Shawn Green 1.25 3.00
35 Luis Castillo 1.25 3.00
36 Frank Thomas 3.00 8.00
37 Javy Lopez 1.25 3.00
38 Victor Martinez 2.00 5.00
39 Tim Wakefield 2.00 5.00
40 Cliff Floyd 1.25 3.00
41 Bartolo Colon 1.25 3.00
42 Billy Wagner 1.25 3.00
43 Dmitri Young 1.25 3.00
44 Mark Prior 2.00 5.00
45 Nick Johnson 1.25 3.00
46 Brian Roberts 1.25 3.00
47 Nomar Garciaparra 2.00 5.00
48 Jorge Cantu 1.25 3.00
49 Jeff Francoeur 3.00 8.00
50 Barry Bonds 5.00 12.00
51 Francisco Rodriguez 2.00 5.00
52 Rocco Baldelli 1.25 3.00
53 Ryan Howard 2.50 6.00
54 Hank Blalock 1.25 3.00
55 Ivan Rodriguez 2.00 5.00
56 Jason Schmidt 1.25 3.00
57 Jeff Kent 1.25 3.00
58 Jose Castillo 1.25 3.00
59 Kerry Wood 1.25 3.00
60 Chase Utley 2.00 5.00
61 Shawn Chacon 1.25 3.00
62 Tom Glavine 2.00 5.00
63 Ichiro Suzuki 4.00 10.00
64 Carlos Lee 1.25 3.00
65 Jeff Weaver 1.25 3.00
66 Jeromy Burnitz 1.25 3.00
67 Jhonny Peralta 1.25 3.00
68 Johan Santana 2.00 5.00
69 Keith Foulke 1.25 3.00
70 Manny Ramirez 3.00 8.00
71 Jim Edmonds 2.00 5.00
72 Garret Anderson 1.25 3.00
73 Felipe Lopez 1.25 3.00
74 Craig Biggio 2.00 5.00
75 Ryan Langerhans 1.25 3.00
76 Mike Cameron 1.25 3.00
77 Matt Clement 1.25 3.00
78 Miguel Cabrera 3.00 8.00
79 Mark Teixeira 2.00 5.00
80 Johnny Estrada 1.25 3.00
81 Nook Logan 1.25 3.00
82 Livan Hernandez 1.25 3.00
83 Roy Halladay 2.00 5.00
84 Jose Vidro 1.25 3.00
85 Shannon Stewart 1.25 3.00
86 Brian Bruney 1.25 3.00
87 Jaret Wright 1.25 3.00
88 Gregg Zaun 1.25 3.00
89 Jason LaRue 1.25 3.00
90 Adam Kennedy 1.25 3.00
91 Armando Benitez 1.25 3.00
92 Chris Ray 1.25 3.00
93 Clint Barmes 1.25 3.00
94 Ervin Santana 1.25 3.00
95 Justin Verlander 10.00 25.00
96 Magglio Ordonez 2.00 5.00
97 Todd Helton 2.00 5.00
98 Zach Duke 1.25 3.00
99 Huston Street 1.25 3.00
100 Alex Rodriguez 4.00 10.00
101 Mike Hampton 1.25 3.00
102 Tony Clark 1.25 3.00
104 Barry Zito 2.00 5.00
105 Anderson Hernandez 1.25 3.00
106 B.J. Upton 1.25 3.00
107 Albert Pujols 4.00 10.00
108 Tim Hudson 2.00 5.00
109 Derek Jeter 8.00 20.00
110 Greg Maddux 4.00 10.00

2006 Topps Heritage Chrome Refractors

*CHROME REF: .6X TO 1.5X CHROME
STATED ODDS 1:33 HOBBY, 1:34 RETAIL
STATED PRINT RUN 557 SERIAL #'d SETS
CARD 103 DOES NOT EXIST

2006 Topps Heritage Chrome Black Refractors

*BLACK: 2.5X TO 6X CHROME
STATED ODDS 1:328 HOBBY, 1:328 RETAIL
STATED PRINT RUN 57 SERIAL #'d SETS
CARD 103 DOES NOT EXIST

2006 Topps Heritage Clubhouse Collection Relics

GROUP A ODDS 1:3440 H, 1:3457 R
GROUP B ODDS 1:8164 H, 1:8232 R
GROUP C ODDS 1:1639 H, 1:1650 R
GROUP D ODDS 1:2928 H, 1:2935 R
GROUP E ODDS 1:4082 H, 1:4116 R
GROUP F ODDS 1:3404 H, 1:3426 R
GROUP G ODDS 1:487 H, 1:490 R
GROUP H ODDS 1:2583 H, 1:2600 R
GROUP I ODDS 1:206 H, 1:207 R
GROUP J ODDS 1:257 H, 1:255 R
GROUP K ODDS 1:1370 H, 1:1364 R
GROUP L ODDS 1:421 H, 1:419 R
OVERALL AU-RELIC ODDS 1:36 H, 1:36 R
GROUP A PRINT RUN 99 COPIES PER
GROUP B PRINT RUN 125 COPIES PER
GROUP A-B CARDS ARE NOT SERIAL #'d
A-B PRINT RUN INFO PROVIDED BY TOPPS
AD Adam Dunn Bat G 3.00 8.00
AJ Andruw Jones Uni G 4.00 10.00
AK Al Kaline Bat B/125 * 30.00 60.00
AP Albert Pujols Jsy I 8.00 20.00
AR Alex Rodriguez Bat A/99 * 40.00 80.00
AR2 Alex Rodriguez Jsy D 20.00 50.00
AS Alfonso Soriano Bat I 3.00 8.00
BB Barry Bonds Uni A/99 * 50.00 100.00
BM Bill Mazeroski Jsy A/99 * 50.00 100.00
BR Brian Roberts Bat I 3.00 8.00
BRO Brooks Robinson Bat A/99 * 15.00 40.00
BR2 Brian Roberts Jsy J 3.00 8.00
CB Clint Barmes Jsy J 3.00 8.00
CC Carl Crawford Bat I 3.00 8.00
CJ Conor Jackson Bat I 3.00 8.00
CS Curt Schilling Jsy C 4.00 10.00
DL Derrek Lee Bat I 4.00 10.00
DO David Ortiz Jsy C 20.00 50.00
DW David Wright Jsy L 4.00 10.00
DWI Dontrelle Willis Jsy J 3.00 8.00
EC Eric Chavez Uni L 3.00 8.00
EG Eric Gagne Jsy F 3.00 8.00
FJF Jeff Francis Jsy L 3.00 8.00
FR Frank Robinson Bat B/125 * 30.00 60.00
GS Gary Sheffield Bat I 3.00 8.00
JD Johnny Damon Bat E 4.00 10.00
JD2 Johnny Damon Jsy G 4.00 10.00
JE Jim Edmonds Jsy H 3.00 8.00
JP Jake Peavy Jsy J 3.00 8.00
JS Johan Santana Jsy J 4.00 10.00
KG Khalil Greene Jsy D 4.00 10.00
MC Miguel Cabrera Jsy G 4.00 10.00
ME Morgan Ensberg Bat I 3.00 8.00
MH Matt Holliday Bat I 4.00 10.00
MM Mickey Mantle Bat A/99 * 125.00 200.00
MMU Mark Mulder Uni K 3.00 8.00
MP Mike Piazza Bat C 12.50 30.00
MR Manny Ramirez Jsy C 4.00 10.00
MR2 Manny Ramirez Bat J 4.00 10.00
MT Miguel Tejada Uni I 3.00 8.00
MTE Mark Teixeira Jsy G 4.00 10.00
PM Pedro Martinez Jsy C 4.00 10.00
RC Robinson Cano Bat I 4.00 10.00
RW Rickie Weeks Bat G 3.00 8.00
SC Shin-Soo Choo Bat I 3.00 8.00
SM Stan Musial Bat A/99 * 100.00 200.00
TI Tadahito Iguchi Jsy J 3.00 8.00
VG Vladimir Guerrero Bat J 4.00 10.00

2006 Topps Heritage Clubhouse Collection Autograph Relics

STATED ODDS 1:16,400 H, 1:16,400 R
STATED PRINT RUN 25 SERIAL #'d SETS
EXCHANGE DEADLINE 02/28/08
NO PRICING DUE TO SCARCITY

2006 Topps Heritage Clubhouse Collection Cut Signature Relic

STATED ODDS 1:963,072 HOBBY
STATED PRINT RUN 1 SERIAL #'d CARD
NO PRICING DUE TO SCARCITY

2006 Topps Heritage Clubhouse Collection Dual Relics

STATED ODDS 1:12,067 H, 1:12,067 R
STATED PRINT RUN 57 SERIAL #'d SETS
BR B.Robinson B/B.Roberts J 25.00 60.00
MP S.Musial B/A.Pujols J 125.00 200.00
MR M.Mantle B/A.Rod J 150.00 300.00

2006 Topps Heritage Flashbacks

COMPLETE SET (10) 10.00 25.00
STATED ODDS 1:12 HOBBY, 1:12 RETAIL
AK Al Kaline 1.00 2.50
BM Bill Mazeroski .60 1.50
BR Brooks Robinson .60 1.50
BRI Bobby Richardson .40 1.00
EB Ernie Banks 1.00 2.50
FR Frank Robinson .60 1.50
MM Mickey Mantle 3.00 8.00
SM Stan Musial 1.50 4.00
WF Whitey Ford .60 1.50
YB Yogi Berra 1.00 2.50

2006 Topps Heritage Flashbacks Autographs

STATED ODDS 1:16,400 H, 1:16,400 R
STATED PRINT RUN 25 SERIAL #'d SETS
NO PRICING DUE TO SCARCITY

2006 Topps Heritage Flashbacks Seat Relics

GROUP A ODDS 1:14,607 H, 1:14,607 R
GROUP B ODDS 1:6225 H, 1:6175 R
GROUP C ODDS 1:721 H, 1:719 R
GROUP D ODDS 1:1711 H, 1:1703 R
GROUP E ODDS 1:308 H, 1:306 R
OVERALL AU-RELIC ODDS 1:36 H, 1:36 R
GROUP A PRINT RUN 140 COPIES
GROUP A CARD IS NOT SERIAL #'d
GROUP A PRINT RUN PROVIDED BY TOPPS
AK Al Kaline E 12.50 30.00
BM Bill Mazeroski B 10.00 25.00
BR Brooks Robinson E 6.00 15.00
BR Bobby Richardson C 10.00 25.00
EB Ernie Banks D 10.00 25.00
FR Frank Robinson E 4.00 10.00
MM Mickey Mantle E 10.00 25.00
SM Stan Musial A/140 * 40.00 80.00
WF Whitey Ford C 6.00 15.00
YB Yogi Berra C 10.00 25.00

2006 Topps Heritage New Age Performers

COMPLETE SET (15) 15.00 40.00
STATED ODDS 1:15 HOBBY, 1:15 RETAIL
AP Albert Pujols 1.25 3.00
AR Alex Rodriguez 1.25 3.00
BB Barry Bonds 1.50 4.00
CL Carlos Lee .40 1.00
DL Derrek Lee .40 1.00
DO David Ortiz 1.00 2.50
GM Mark Prior .60 1.50
GS Gary Sheffield .40 1.00
IS Ichiro Suzuki 1.25 3.00
MC Miguel Cabrera 1.00 2.50
MR Manny Ramirez 1.00 2.50
MT Mark Teixeira .60 1.50
PM Pedro Martinez .60 1.50
RC Roger Clemens 1.25 3.00
VG Vladimir Guerrero .60 1.50

2006 Topps Heritage Real One Autographs

STATED ODDS 1:366 HOBBY, 1:366 RETAIL
STATED PRINT RUN 200 SETS
CARDS ARE NOT SERIAL-NUMBERED
PRINT RUN INFO PROVIDED BY TOPPS
*RED INK: .75X TO 1.5X BASIC
RED INK ODDS 1:1280 H, 1:1288 R
RED INK PRINT RUN 57 SERIAL #'d SETS
RED INK ALSO CALLED SPECIAL EDITION
EXCHANGE DEADLINE 02/28/08
BC Bob Chakales 10.00 25.00
BW Bob Wiesler 10.00 25.00
CT Charley Thompson 10.00 25.00
DK Don Kaiser 10.00 25.00
DR Dusty Rhodes 30.00 60.00
DS Duke Snider 40.00 100.00
EB Ernie Banks 75.00 150.00
EO Ernie Oravetz 10.00 25.00
EOB Eddie O'Brien 10.00 25.00
FR Frank Robinson 50.00 100.00
JAC Jackie Collum 20.00 50.00
JCR Jack Crimian 10.00 25.00
JD Jack Dittmer 10.00 25.00
JM Joe Margoneri 10.00 25.00
JP Jim Pyburn 20.00 50.00
JRM Red Murff 10.00 25.00
JSM Jim Small 10.00 25.00
JSN Jerry Snyder UER 30.00 60.00
KO Karl Olson 10.00 25.00
LK Lou Kretlow 20.00 50.00
MP Mel Parnell 10.00 25.00
NK Nellie King 20.00 50.00
PL Paul LaPalme 10.00 25.00
RN Ron Negray 10.00 25.00
SM Stan Musial 125.00 250.00
TB Tommy Byrne 12.50 30.00
WF Whitey Ford 50.00 100.00
WM Windy McCall 12.00 30.00
YB Yogi Berra 60.00 150.00

2006 Topps Heritage Then and Now

COMPLETE SET (10) 10.00 25.00
STATED ODDS 1:15 HOBBY, 1:15 RETAIL
TN1 M.Mantle 3.00 8.00
A.Rodriguez
TN2 T.Williams 2.00 5.00
M.Young
TN3 M.Mantle 3.00 8.00
J.Giambi
TN4 L.Aparicio .60 1.50
C.Figgins
TN5 T.Williams 2.00 5.00
A.Rodriguez
TN6 S.Musial 1.50 4.00
D.Lee
TN7 S.Musial 1.50 4.00
D.Lee
TN8 R.Schoendienst .60 1.50
D.Lee
TN9 J.Podres 1.25 3.00
R.Clemens
TN10 C.Labine .40 1.00
C.Cordero

2007 Topps Heritage

COMPLETE SET (527) 250.00 400.00
COMP.SET w/o SP's (384) 30.00 60.00
COMMON CARD .20 .50
COMMON RC .20 .50
COMMON TEAM CARD .20 .50
COMMON SP 2.50 6.00
SP STATED ODDS 1:2 HOBBY/RETAIL
SEE BECKETT.COM FOR SP CHECKLIST
COMMON YELLOW 2.00 5.00
YELLOW STATED ODDS 1:6 HOBBY/RETAIL
SEE BECKETT.COM FOR YELLOW CL
CARD 145 DOES NOT EXIST
1 David Ortiz .50 1.25
2a Roger Clemens .60 1.50
2b Roger Clemens YT 3.00 8.00
3 David Wells .20 .50
4 Ronny Paulino SP 2.50 6.00
5 Derek Jeter SP 12.00 30.00
6 Felix Hernandez .30 .75
7 Todd Helton .30 .75
8a David Eckstein .20 .50
8b David Eckstein YN 2.00 5.00
9 Craig Wilson .20 .50
10 John Smoltz .50 1.25
11a Rob Mackowiak .20 .50
11b Rob Mackowiak YT 2.00 5.00
12 Scott Hatteberg .20 .50
13a Wilfredo Ledezma SP 2.50 6.00
13b Wilfredo Ledezma YT 2.00 5.00
14 Bobby Abreu SP 2.50 6.00
15 Mike Stanton .20 .50
16 Wilson Betemit .20 .50
17 Darren Oliver .20 .50
18 Josh Beckett .20 .50
19 San Francisco Giants TC .20 .50
20a Robinson Cano .30 .75
20b Robinson Cano YT 2.50 6.00
21 Matt Cain .30 .75
22 Jason Kendall SP 2.50 6.00
23a Mark Kotsay SP 2.50 6.00
23b Mark Kotsay YN 2.00 5.00
24a Yadier Molina .60 1.50
24b Yadier Molina YN 2.00 5.00
25 Brad Penny .20 .50
26 Adrian Gonzalez .40 1.00
27 Danny Haren .20 .50
28 Brian Giles .20 .50
29 Jose Lopez .20 .50
30a Ichiro Suzuki .60 1.50
30b Ichiro Suzuki YN 3.00 8.00
31 Beltran Perez SP (RC) 2.50 6.00
32 Brad Hawpe SP 2.50 6.00
33a Jim Thome .30 .75
33b Jim Thome YT 2.50 6.00
34 Mark DeRosa .20 .50
35a Woody Williams .20 .50
35b Woody Williams YT 2.00 5.00
36 Luis Gonzalez .20 .50
37 Billy Sadler (RC) .20 .50
38 Dave Roberts .30 .75
39 Mitch Maier RC .20 .50
40 Francisco Cordero SP 2.50 6.00
41 Anthony Reyes SP 2.50 6.00
42 Russell Martin .20 .50
43 Scott Proctor .20 .50
44 Washington Nationals TC .20 .50
45 Shane Victorino .20 .50
46a Joel Zumaya .20 .50
46b Joel Zumaya YN 2.50 6.00
47 Delmon Young (RC) .30 .75
48 Alex Rios .20 .50
49 Willy Taveras SP 2.50 6.00
50a Mark Buehrle SP 2.50 6.00
50b Mark Buehrle YT 2.00 5.00
51 Livan Hernandez .20 .50
52a Jason Bay .30 .75
52b Jason Bay YT 2.00 5.00
53a Jose Valentin .20 .50
53b Jose Valentin YN 2.00 5.00
54 Kevin Reese .20 .50
55 Felipe Lopez .20 .50
56 Ryan Sweeney (RC) .20 .50
57a Kelvim Escobar .20 .50
57b Kelvim Escobar YN 2.00 5.00
58a N.Swisher Sm.Print SP 2.50 6.00
58b N.Swisher Lg.Print YT 2.00 5.00
59 Kevin Millwood SP 2.50 6.00
60a Preston Wilson .20 .50
60b Preston Wilson YN 2.00 5.00
61a Mariano Rivera .60 1.50
61b Mariano Rivera YN 2.50 6.00
62 Josh Barfield .20 .50
63 Ryan Freel .20 .50
64 Tim Hudson .30 .75
65a Chris Narveson (RC) .20 .50
65b Chris Narveson YN (RC) 2.00 5.00
66 Matt Murton .20 .50
67 Melvin Mora SP 2.50 6.00
68 Jason Jennings SP 2.50 6.00
69 Emil Brown .20 .50
70a Magglio Ordonez .30 .75
70b Magglio Ordonez YN 2.00 5.00
71 Los Angeles Dodgers TC .20 .50
72 Ross Gload .20 .50
73 David Ross .20 .50
74 Juan Uribe .20 .50
75 Scott Podsednik .20 .50
76a Cole Hamels SP 3.00 8.00
76b Cole Hamels YT 2.50 6.00
77a Rafael Furcal SP 2.50 6.00
77b Rafael Furcal YT 2.00 5.00
78a Ryan Theriot .20 .50
78b Ryan Theriot YN 2.00 5.00
79a Corey Patterson .20 .50
79b Corey Patterson YT 2.00 5.00
80 Jered Weaver .30 .75
81a Stephen Drew .20 .50
81b Stephen Drew YT 2.50 6.00
82 Adam Kennedy .20 .50
83 Tony Gwynn Jr. .20 .50
84 Kazuo Matsui .20 .50
85a Omar Vizquel SP 3.00 8.00
85b Omar Vizquel YT 2.50 6.00
86 Fred Lewis SP (RC) 2.50 6.00
87a Shawn Chacon .20 .50
87b Shawn Chacon YN 2.00 5.00
88 Frank Catalanotto .20 .50
89 Orlando Hudson .20 .50
90 Pat Burrell .20 .50
91 David DeJesus .20 .50
92a David Wright .40 1.00
92b David Wright YN 3.00 8.00
93 Conor Jackson .20 .50
94 Xavier Nady SP 2.50 6.00
95 Bill Hall SP 2.50 6.00
96 Kip Wells .20 .50
97a Jeff Suppan .20 .50
97b Jeff Suppan YN 2.00 5.00
98a Ryan Zimmerman .30 .75
98b Ryan Zimmerman YN 2.50 6.00
99 Wes Helms .20 .50
100a Jose Contreras .20 .50
100b Jose Contreras YT 2.00 5.00
101a Miguel Cairo .20 .50
101b Miguel Cairo YN 2.00 5.00
102 Brian Roberts .20 .50
103 Carl Crawford SP 2.50 6.00
104 Mike Lamb SP 2.50 6.00
105 Mark Ellis .20 .50
106 Scott Rolen .30 .75
107 Garrett Atkins .20 .50
108a Hanley Ramirez .30 .75
108b Hanley Ramirez YT 2.50 6.00
109 Trot Nixon .20 .50
110 Edgar Renteria .20 .50
111 Jeff Francis .20 .50
112 Marcus Thames SP 2.50 6.00
113 Brian Burres SP (RC) 2.50 6.00
114 Brian Schneider .20 .50
115 Jeremy Bonderman .20 .50
116 Ryan Madson .20 .50
117 Gerald Laird .20 .50
118 Roy Halladay .30 .75
119 Victor Martinez .30 .75
120 Greg Maddux .60 1.50
121 Jay Payton SP 2.50 6.00
122 Jacque Jones SP 2.50 6.00
123 Juan Lara RC .20 .50
124 Derrick Turnbow .20 .50
125 Adam Everett .20 .50
126 Michael Cuddyer .20 .50
127 Gil Meche .20 .50
128 Willy Aybar .20 .50
129 Jerry Owens (RC) .20 .50
130 Manny Ramirez SP 3.00 8.00
131 Howie Kendrick SP 2.50 6.00
132 Byung-Hyun Kim .20 .50
133 Kevin Kouzmanoff (RC) .20 .50
134 Philadelphia Phillies TC .20 .50
135 Joe Blanton .20 .50
136 Ray Durham .20 .50
137 Luke Hudson .20 .50
138 Eric Byrnes .20 .50
139 Ryan Braun SP RC 2.50 6.00
140 Johnny Damon SP 3.00 8.00
141 Ambiorix Burgos .20 .50
142 Hideki Matsui .50 1.25
143 Josh Johnson .50 1.25
144 Miguel Cabrera .50 1.25
146 Delwyn Young (RC) .20 .50
147 Chuck James .20 .50
148 Morgan Ensberg .20 .50
149 Jose Vidro SP 2.50 6.00
150 Alex Rodriguez SP 5.00 12.00
151 Carlos Maldonado (RC) .20 .50
152 Jason Schmidt .20 .50
153 Alex Escobar .20 .50
154 Chris Gomez .20 .50
155 Endy Chavez .20 .50
156 Kris Benson .20 .50
157 Bronson Arroyo .20 .50
158 Cleveland Indians TC SP 2.50 6.00
159 Chris Ray SP 2.50 6.00
160 Richie Sexson .20 .50
161 Huston Street .20 .50
162 Kevin Youkilis .20 .50
163 Armando Benitez .20 .50
164 Vinny Rottino (RC) .20 .50
165 Garret Anderson .20 .50
166 Todd Greene .20 .50
167 Brian Stokes SP (RC) 2.50 6.00
168 Albert Pujols SP 6.00 15.00
169 Todd Coffey .20 .50
170 Jason Michaels .20 .50
171 David Dellucci .20 .50
172 Eric Milton .20 .50
173 Austin Kearns .20 .50
174 Oakland Athletics TC .20 .50
175 Andy Cannizaro RC .20 .50
176 David Weathers SP 2.50 6.00
177 Jermaine Dye SP 2.50 6.00
178 Wily Mo Pena .20 .50
179 Chris Burke .20 .50
180 Jeff Weaver .20 .50
181 Edwin Encarnacion .50 1.25
182 Jeremy Hermida .20 .50
183 Tim Wakefield .30 .75
184 Rich Hill .20 .50
185 Aaron Hill SP 2.50 6.00
186 Scot Shields SP 2.50 6.00
187 Randy Johnson .50 1.25
188 Dan Johnson .20 .50
189 Sean Marshall .20 .50
190 Marcus Giles .20 .50
191 Jonathan Broxton .20 .50
192 Mike Piazza .50 1.25
193 Carlos Quentin .20 .50
194 Derek Lowe SP 2.50 6.00
195 Russell Branyan SP 2.50 6.00
196 Jason Marquis .20 .50
197 Khalil Greene .20 .50
198 Ryan Dempster .20 .50
199 Ronnie Belliard .20 .50
200 Josh Fogg .20 .50
201 Carlos Lee .20 .50
202 Chris Denorfia .20 .50
203 Kendry Morales SP 3.00 8.00
204 Rafael Soriano SP 2.50 6.00
205 Brandon Phillips .20 .50
206 Andrew Miller RC .75 2.00
207 John Koronka .20 .50
208 Luis Castillo .20 .50
209 Angel Guzman .20 .50
210 Jim Edmonds .30 .75
211 Patrick Misch (RC) .20 .50
212 Ty Wigginton SP 2.50 6.00
213 Brandon Inge SP 2.50 6.00
214 Royce Clayton .20 .50
215 Ben Broussard .20 .50
216 St. Louis Cardinals TC .20 .50
217 Mark Mulder .20 .50
218 Kenji Johjima .50 1.25
219 Joe Crede .20 .50
220 Shea Hillenbrand .20 .50
221 Josh Fields SP (RC) 2.50 6.00
222 Pat Neshek SP 3.00 8.00
223 Reed Johnson .20 .50
224 Mike Mussina .30 .75
225 Randy Winn .20 .50
226 Brian Rogers .20 .50
227 Juan Rivera .20 .50
228 Shawn Green .20 .50
229 Mike Napoli .20 .50
230 Chase Utley SP 3.00 8.00
231 John Nelson SP (RC) 2.50 6.00
232 Casey Blake .20 .50
233 Lyle Overbay .20 .50
234 Adam LaRoche .20 .50
235 Julio Lugo .20 .50
236 Johnny Estrada .20 .50
237 James Shields .20 .50
238 Jose Castillo .20 .50
239 Doug Davis SP 2.50 6.00
240 Jason Giambi SP 2.50 6.00
241 Mike Gonzalez .20 .50
242 Scott Downs .20 .50
243 Joe Inglett .20 .50
244 Matt Kemp .40 1.00
245 Ted Lilly .20 .50
246 New York Yankees TC .50 1.25
247 Jamey Carroll .20 .50
248 Adam Wainwright SP 2.50 6.00
249 Matt Thornton SP 2.50 6.00
250 Alfonso Soriano .30 .75
251 Tom Gordon .20 .50
252 Dennis Sarfate (RC) .20 .50
253 Zach Duke .20 .50
254 Hank Blalock .20 .50
255 Johan Santana .30 .75
256 Chicago White Sox TC .20 .50
257 Aaron Cook SP 2.50 6.00
258 Cliff Lee SP 2.50 6.00
259 Miguel Tejada .30 .75
260 Mike Lowell .20 .50
261 Ian Snell .20 .50
262 Jason Tyner .20 .50
263 Troy Tulowitzki (RC) .60 1.50
264 Ervin Santana .20 .50
265 Jon Lester .30 .75
266 Andy Pettitte SP 3.00 8.00
267 A.J. Pierzynski SP 2.50 6.00
268 Rich Aurilia .20 .50
269 Phil Nevin .20 .50
270 Tom Glavine .30 .75
271 Chris Coste .20 .50
272 Moises Alou .20 .50
273 J.D. Drew .20 .50
274 Abraham Nunez .20 .50
275 Jorge Posada SP 3.00 8.00
276 Jeff Conine SP 2.50 6.00
277 Chad Cordero .20 .50
278 Nick Johnson .20 .50
279 Kevin Millar .20 .50
280 Mark Grudzielanek .20 .50
281 Chris Stewart RC .20 .50
282 Nate Robertson .20 .50
283 Drew Anderson RC .20 .50
284 Doug Mientkiewicz SP 2.50 6.00
285 Ken Griffey Jr. SP 5.00 12.00
286 Cory Sullivan .20 .50
287 Chris Carpenter .30 .75
288 Gary Matthews .20 .50
289 J.Verlander .50 1.25
Jef.Weaver
290 Vicente Padilla .20 .50
291 Chris Roberson .20 .50
292 Chris R. Young .20 .50
293 Ryan Garko SP 2.50 6.00
294 Miguel Batista SP 2.50 6.00
295 B.J. Upton .20 .50
296 Justin Verlander .50 1.25
297 Ben Zobrist .30 .75
298 Ben Sheets .20 .50
299 Eric Chavez .20 .50
300 Scott Schoeneweis .20 .50
301 Placido Polanco .20 .50
302 Angel Sanchez SP RC 2.50 6.00
303 Freddy Sanchez SP 2.50 6.00
304 M.Ordonez .30 .75
C.Monroe
305 A.J. Burnett .20 .50
306 Juan Perez RC .20 .50
307 Chris Britton .20 .50
308 Jon Garland .20 .50
309 Pedro Feliz .20 .50
310 Ryan Howard .40 1.00
311 Aaron Harang SP 2.50 6.00
312 Boston Red Sox TC SP 3.00 8.00
313 Chad Billingsley .30 .75
314 C.Jones .50 1.25
B.Cox MG
315 Bengie Molina .20 .50
316 Juan Pierre .20 .50
317 Luke Scott .20 .50
318 Javier Valentin .20 .50
319 Mark Loretta .20 .50
320 Kenny Lofton SP 2.50 6.00
321 V.Guerrero 3.00 8.00
I.Rodriguez SP
322 Josh Willingham .30 .75
323 Lance Berkman .30 .75
324 Anibal Sanchez .20 .50
325 Maicer Izturis .20 .50
326 Brett Myers .20 .50
327 Chicago Cubs TC .30 .75
328 Francisco Liriano .20 .50
329 Craig Monroe SP 2.50 6.00
330 Paul LoDuca SP 2.50 6.00
331 Steve Trachsel .20 .50
332 Bernie Williams .30 .75
333 Carlos Guillen .20 .50
334 C.Wang .30 .75
M.Mussina
335 Dave Bush .20 .50
336 Carlos Beltran .30 .75
337 Jason Isringhausen .20 .50
338 Todd Walker SP 2.50 6.00
339 Jarrod Washburn SP 2.50 6.00
340 Brandon Webb .30 .75
341 Pittsburgh Pirates TC .20 .50
342 Daryle Ward .20 .50
343 Chad Santos .20 .50
344 Brad Lidge .20 .50
345 Brad Ausmus .20 .50
346 Carlos Delgado .20 .50
347 Boone Logan SP 2.50 6.00
348 Jimmy Rollins SP 2.50 6.00
349 Orlando Hernandez .20 .50
350 Gary Sheffield .20 .50
351 Pujols .60 1.50
Belliard/Eckstein/Rolen
352 Jake Peavy .20 .50
353 Jason Varitek .50 1.25
354 Freddy Garcia .20 .50
355 Matt Diaz .20 .50
356 Bernie Castro SP 2.50 6.00
357 Eric Stults SP RC 2.50 6.00
358 John Lackey .30 .75
359 Bobby Jenks .20 .50
360 Mark Teixeira .30 .75
361 Jonathan Papelbon .50 1.25
362 Paul Konerko .30 .75
363 Erik Bedard .20 .50
364 Eliezer Alfonzo .20 .50
365 Fernando Rodney SP 2.50 6.00
366 Chris Duncan SP 2.50 6.00
367 Jose Diaz (RC) .20 .50
368 Travis Hafner .20 .50
369 Matt Capps .20 .50
370 Ivan Rodriguez .30 .75
371 David Murphy (RC) .20 .50
372 Carlos Zambrano .30 .75
373 Chris Iannetta .20 .50
374 Jose Mesa SP 2.50 6.00
375 Michael Young SP 2.50 6.00
376 Bill Bray .20 .50
377 Atlanta Braves TC .30 .75
378 Jeff Cirillo .20 .50
379 Barry Zito .30 .75
380 Clay Hensley .20 .50
381 J.J. Putz .20 .50
382 C.C. Sabathia .30 .75
383 Eduardo Perez SP 2.50 6.00
384 Scott Moore SP (RC) 2.50 6.00
385 Scott Olsen .20 .50
386 R.Howard .40 1.00
C.Utley
387 Aaron Rowand .20 .50
388 Mike Rouse .20 .50
389 Alexis Gomez .20 .50
390 Brian McCann .20 .50
391 Ryan Shealy .20 .50
392 Shane Youman SP RC 2.50 6.00
393 Melky Cabrera SP 2.50 6.00
394 Jeremy Sowers .20 .50
395 Casey Janssen .20 .50
396 Travis Chick (RC) .20 .50
397 Detroit Tigers TC .20 .50
398 Reggie Abercrombie .20 .50
399 Ricky Nolasco .20 .50
400 Tadahito Iguchi .20 .50
401 Jose Reyes SP 2.50 6.00
402 Juan Encarnacion SP 2.50 6.00
403 Brandon Harper .20 .50
404 Torii Hunter .20 .50
405 Dan Uggla .20 .50
406 Orlando Cabrera .20 .50
407 Jose Capellan .20 .50
408 Baltimore Orioles TC .20 .50
409 Frank Thomas .50 1.25
410 Francisco Rodriguez SP 2.50 6.00
411 Ian Kinsler SP 3.00 8.00
412 Billy Wagner .20 .50
413 Andy Marte .20 .50
414 Mike Jacobs .20 .50
415 Raul Ibanez .30 .75
416 Jhonny Peralta .20 .50
417 Chris B. Young .20 .50
418 A.Pujols .60 1.50
M.Ordonez
419 Scott Kazmir SP 3.00 8.00
420 Norris Hopper SP 2.50 6.00
421 Chris Capuano .20 .50
422 Troy Glaus .20 .50
423 Roy Oswalt .30 .75
424 Grady Sizemore .30 .75
425 Chone Figgins .20 .50
426 Chad Tracy .20 .50
427 Brian Fuentes .20 .50
428 Cincinnati Reds TC SP 2.50 6.00
429 Ramon Hernandez SP 2.50 6.00
430 Mike Cameron .20 .50
431 Dontrelle Willis .20 .50
432 Josh Sharpless .20 .50
433 Adrian Beltre .50 1.25
434 Curtis Granderson .40 1.00
435 B.J. Ryan .20 .50
436 D.Wright .40 1.00
R.Howard
437 Vernon Wells SP 2.50 6.00
438 Vladimir Guerrero SP 3.00 8.00
439 Jake Westbrook .20 .50
440 Chipper Jones .50 1.25
441 James Loney .20 .50
442 Nook Logan .20 .50
443 Oswaldo Navarro RC .20 .50
444 Joe Mauer .40 1.00
445 Miguel Montero (RC) .20 .50
446 Franklin Gutierrez SP 2.50 6.00
447 Mark Redman SP 2.50 6.00
448 Mike Rabelo RC .20 .50
449 Philip Humber (RC) .20 .50
450 Justin Morneau .30 .75
451 Hector Gimenez (RC) .20 .50
452 Matt Holliday .50 1.25
453 Akinori Otsuka .20 .50
454 Prince Fielder .30 .75
455 Chien-Ming Wang SP 4.00 10.00
456 Shawn Riggans SP 2.50 6.00
457 John Maine .20 .50
458 Adam Lind (RC) .20 .50
459 Ubaldo Jimenez (RC) .60 1.50
460 Jaret Wright .20 .50
461 Cla Meredith .20 .50
462 Joaquin Arias (RC) .20 .50
463 Kenny Rogers .20 .50
464 Jose Garcia SP RC 2.50 6.00
465 Pedro Martinez SP 3.00 8.00
466 Jeff Salazar (RC) .20 .50
467 Glen Perkins .20 .50
468 Travis Ishikawa .20 .50
469 Joe Borowski .20 .50
470 Jeremy Brown .20 .50
471 Andre Ethier .30 .75
472 Taylor Tankersley .20 .50
473 Lastings Milledge SP 3.00 8.00
474 Brian Sanches SP 2.50 6.00
475 O.Guillen AS MG .20 .50
P.Garner AS MG
476 Albert Pujols AS .60 1.50
477 David Ortiz AS .50 1.25
478 Chase Utley AS .30 .75
479 Mark Loretta AS .20 .50
480 David Wright AS .40 1.00
481 Alex Rodriguez AS .60 1.50
482 Edgar Renteria AS SP 2.50 6.00
483 Derek Jeter AS SP 10.00 25.00
484 Alfonso Soriano AS .30 .75
485 Vladimir Guerrero AS .30 .75
486 Carlos Beltran AS .30 .75
487 Vernon Wells AS .20 .50
488 Jason Bay AS .30 .75
489 Ichiro Suzuki AS .60 1.50
490 Paul LoDuca AS .20 .50
491 Ivan Rodriguez AS SP 3.00 8.00
492 Brad Penny AS SP 2.50 6.00
493 Roy Halladay AS .30 .75
494 Brian Fuentes AS .20 .50
495 Kenny Rogers AS .20 .50

2007 Topps Heritage Chrome

STATED ODDS 1:11 HOBBY, 1:12 RETAIL
STATED PRINT RUN 1958 SERIAL #'d SETS
THC1 David Ortiz 2.50 6.00
THC2 John Smoltz 2.50 6.00
THC3 San Francisco Giants TC 1.00 2.50
THC4 Brian Giles 1.00 2.50
THC5 Billy Sadler 1.00 2.50
THC6 Joel Zumaya 1.00 2.50
THC7 Felipe Lopez 1.00 2.50
THC8 Tim Hudson 1.50 4.00
THC9 David Ross 1.00 2.50
THC10 Adam Kennedy 1.00 2.50
THC11 David DeJesus 1.00 2.50
THC12 Jose Contreras 1.00 2.50
THC13 Trot Nixon 1.00 2.50
THC14 Roy Halladay 1.50 4.00
THC15 Gil Meche 1.00 2.50
THC16 Ray Durham 1.00 2.50
THC17 Delwyn Young 1.00 2.50
THC18 Endy Chavez 1.00 2.50
THC19 Vinny Rottino 1.00 2.50
THC20 Austin Kearns 1.00 2.50
THC21 Jeremy Hermida 1.00 2.50
THC22 Jonathan Broxton 1.00 2.50
THC23 Josh Fogg 1.00 2.50
THC24 Angel Guzman 1.00 2.50
THC25 Kenji Johjima 2.50 6.00
THC26 Juan Rivera 1.00 2.50
THC27 Johnny Estrada 1.00 2.50
THC28 Ted Lilly 1.00 2.50
THC29 Hank Blalock 1.00 2.50
THC30 Troy Tulowitzki 3.00 8.00
THC31 Moises Alou 1.00 2.50
THC32 Chris Stewart 1.00 2.50
THC33 Vicente Padilla 1.00 2.50
THC34 Eric Chavez 1.00 2.50
THC35 Jon Garland 1.00 2.50
THC36 Luke Scott 1.00 2.50
THC37 Brett Myers 1.00 2.50
THC38 Dave Bush 1.00 2.50
THC39 Brad Lidge 1.00 2.50
THC40 Jason Varitek 2.50 6.00
THC41 Paul Konerko 1.50 4.00
THC42 David Murphy 1.00 2.50
THC43 Clay Hensley 1.00 2.50
THC44 Alexis Gomez 1.00 2.50
THC45 Reggie Abercrombie 1.00 2.50
THC46 Jose Capellan 1.00 2.50
THC47 Jhonny Peralta 1.00 2.50
THC48 Chone Figgins 1.00 2.50
THC49 Curtis Granderson 2.00 5.00
THC50 Oswaldo Navarro 1.00 2.50
THC51 Matt Holliday 2.50 6.00
THC52 Cla Meredith 1.00 2.50
THC53 Jeremy Brown 1.00 2.50
THC54 Mark Loretta AS 1.00 2.50
THC55 Jason Bay AS 1.50 4.00
THC56 Roger Clemens 3.00 8.00
THC57 Rob Mackowiak 1.00 2.50
THC58 Robinson Cano 1.50 4.00
THC59 Jose Lopez 1.00 2.50
THC60 Dave Roberts 1.50 4.00
THC61 Delmon Young 1.50 4.00
THC62 Ryan Sweeney 1.00 2.50
THC63 Chris Narveson 1.00 2.50
THC64 Juan Uribe 1.00 2.50
THC65 Tony Gwynn Jr. 1.00 2.50
THC66 David Wright 2.00 5.00
THC67 Miguel Cairo 1.00 2.50
THC68 Edgar Renteria 1.00 2.50
THC69 Victor Martinez 1.50 4.00
THC70 Willy Aybar 1.00 2.50
THC71 Luke Hudson 1.00 2.50
THC72 Chuck James 1.00 2.50
THC73 Kris Benson 1.00 2.50
THC74 Garret Anderson 1.00 2.50
THC75 Oakland Athletics TC 1.00 2.50
THC76 Tim Wakefield 1.50 4.00
THC77 Mike Piazza 2.50 6.00
THC78 Carlos Lee 1.00 2.50
THC79 Jim Edmonds 1.50 4.00
THC80 Joe Crede 1.00 2.50
THC81 Shawn Green 1.00 2.50
THC82 James Shields 1.00 2.50
THC83 New York Yankees TC 2.50 6.00
THC84 Johan Santana 1.50 4.00
THC85 Ervin Santana 1.00 2.50
THC86 J.D. Drew 1.00 2.50
THC87 Nate Robertson 1.00 2.50
THC88 Chris Roberson 1.00 2.50
THC89 Scott Schoeneweis 1.00 2.50
THC90 Pedro Feliz 1.00 2.50
THC91 Javier Valentin 1.00 2.50
THC92 Chicago Cubs TC 1.00 2.50
THC93 Carlos Beltran 1.50 4.00
THC94 Brad Ausmus 1.00 2.50
THC95 Freddy Garcia 1.00 2.50
THC96 Erik Bedard 1.00 2.50
THC97 Carlos Zambrano 1.50 4.00
THC98 J.J. Putz 1.00 2.50
THC99 Brian McCann 1.00 2.50
THC100 Ricky Nolasco 1.00 2.50
THC101 Baltimore Orioles TC 1.00 2.50
THC102 Chris B. Young 1.00 2.50
THC103 Chad Tracy 1.00 2.50
THC104 B.J. Ryan 1.00 2.50
THC105 Joe Mauer 2.00 5.00
THC106 Akinori Otsuka 1.00 2.50
THC107 Joaquin Arias 1.00 2.50
THC108 Andre Ethier 1.50 4.00
THC109 David Wright AS 2.00 5.00
THC110 Ichiro Suzuki AS 3.00 8.00

2007 Topps Heritage Chrome Refractors

*CHROME REF: 1X TO 2.5X
STATED ODDS 1:39 HOBBY, 1:40 RETAIL
STATED PRINT RUN 558 SERIAL #'d SETS

2007 Topps Heritage Chrome Black Refractors

STATED ODDS 1:383 HOBBY/RETAIL
STATED PRINT RUN 58 SERIAL #'d SETS
THC1 David Ortiz 30.00 80.00
THC2 John Smoltz 30.00 80.00
THC3 San Francisco Giants TC 12.00 30.00
THC4 Brian Giles 12.00 30.00
THC5 Billy Sadler 12.00 30.00
THC6 Joel Zumaya 12.00 30.00
THC7 Felipe Lopez 12.00 30.00
THC8 Tim Hudson 20.00 50.00
THC9 David Ross 12.00 30.00
THC10 Adam Kennedy 12.00 30.00
THC11 David DeJesus 12.00 30.00
THC12 Jose Contreras 12.00 30.00
THC13 Trot Nixon 12.00 30.00
THC14 Roy Halladay 20.00 50.00
THC15 Gil Meche 12.00 30.00
THC16 Ray Durham 12.00 30.00
THC17 Delwyn Young 12.00 30.00
THC18 Endy Chavez 12.00 30.00
THC19 Vinny Rottino 12.00 30.00
THC20 Austin Kearns 12.00 30.00
THC21 Jeremy Hermida 12.00 30.00
THC22 Jonathan Broxton 12.00 30.00
THC23 Josh Fogg 12.00 30.00
THC24 Angel Guzman 12.00 30.00
THC25 Kenji Johjima 30.00 80.00
THC26 Juan Rivera 12.00 30.00
THC27 Johnny Estrada 12.00 30.00
THC28 Ted Lilly 12.00 30.00
THC29 Hank Blalock 12.00 30.00
THC30 Troy Tulowitzki 40.00 100.00
THC31 Moises Alou 12.00 30.00
THC32 Chris Stewart 12.00 30.00
THC33 Vicente Padilla 12.00 30.00
THC34 Eric Chavez 12.00 30.00
THC35 Jon Garland 12.00 30.00
THC36 Luke Scott 12.00 30.00
THC37 Brett Myers 12.00 30.00
THC38 Dave Bush 12.00 30.00
THC39 Brad Lidge 12.00 30.00
THC40 Jason Varitek 30.00 80.00
THC41 Paul Konerko 20.00 50.00
THC42 David Murphy 12.00 30.00
THC43 Clay Hensley 12.00 30.00
THC44 Alexis Gomez 12.00 30.00
THC45 Reggie Abercrombie 12.00 30.00
THC46 Jose Capellan 12.00 30.00
THC47 Jhonny Peralta 12.00 30.00
THC48 Chone Figgins 12.00 30.00
THC49 Curtis Granderson 25.00 60.00
THC50 Oswaldo Navarro 12.00 30.00
THC51 Matt Holliday 30.00 80.00
THC52 Cla Meredith 12.00 30.00
THC53 Jeremy Brown 12.00 30.00
THC54 Mark Loretta AS 12.00 30.00
THC55 Jason Bay AS 20.00 50.00
THC56 Roger Clemens 40.00 100.00
THC57 Rob Mackowiak 12.00 30.00
THC58 Robinson Cano 20.00 50.00
THC59 Jose Lopez 12.00 30.00
THC60 Dave Roberts 20.00 50.00
THC61 Delmon Young 20.00 50.00
THC62 Ryan Sweeney 12.00 30.00
THC63 Chris Narveson 12.00 30.00
THC64 Juan Uribe 12.00 30.00
THC65 Tony Gwynn Jr. 12.00 30.00
THC66 David Wright 25.00 60.00
THC67 Miguel Cairo 12.00 30.00
THC68 Edgar Renteria 12.00 30.00
THC69 Victor Martinez 20.00 50.00
THC70 Willy Aybar 12.00 30.00
THC71 Luke Hudson 12.00 30.00
THC72 Chuck James 12.00 30.00
THC73 Kris Benson 12.00 30.00
THC74 Garret Anderson 12.00 30.00
THC75 Oakland Athletics TC 12.00 30.00
THC76 Tim Wakefield 20.00 50.00
THC77 Mike Piazza 30.00 80.00
THC78 Carlos Lee 12.00 30.00
THC79 Jim Edmonds 20.00 50.00
THC80 Joe Crede 12.00 30.00
THC81 Shawn Green 12.00 30.00
THC82 James Shields 12.00 30.00
THC83 New York Yankees TC 30.00 80.00
THC84 Johan Santana 20.00 50.00
THC85 Ervin Santana 12.00 30.00
THC86 J.D. Drew 12.00 30.00
THC87 Nate Robertson 12.00 30.00
THC88 Chris Roberson 12.00 30.00
THC89 Scott Schoeneweis 12.00 30.00
THC90 Pedro Feliz 12.00 30.00
THC91 Javier Valentin 12.00 30.00
THC92 Chicago Cubs TC 12.00 30.00
THC93 Carlos Beltran 20.00 50.00
THC94 Brad Ausmus 12.00 30.00
THC95 Freddy Garcia 12.00 30.00
THC96 Erik Bedard 12.00 30.00
THC97 Carlos Zambrano 20.00 50.00
THC98 J.J. Putz 12.00 30.00
THC99 Brian McCann 12.00 30.00
THC100 Ricky Nolasco 12.00 30.00
THC101 Baltimore Orioles TC 12.00 30.00
THC102 Chris B. Young 12.00 30.00
THC103 Chad Tracy 12.00 30.00
THC104 B.J. Ryan 12.00 30.00

THC105 Joe Mauer 25.00 60.00
THC106 Akinori Otsuka 12.00 30.00
THC107 Joaquin Arias 12.00 30.00
THC108 Andre Ethier 20.00 50.00
THC109 David Wright AS 25.00 60.00
THC110 Ichiro Suzuki AS 40.00 100.00

2007 Topps Heritage '58 Home Run Champion

COMPLETE SET (42) 30.00 60.00
COMMON MANTLE .60 1.50
STATED ODDS 1:6 HOBBY, 1:6 RETAIL

2007 Topps Heritage Clubhouse Collection Relics

GROUP A ODDS 1:2425 HOBBY/RETAIL
GROUP B ODDS 1:202 HOBBY/RETAIL
GROUP C ODDS 1:67 HOBBY/RETAIL
GROUP D ODDS 1:808 HOBBY/RETAIL
AJP Albert Pujols Pants C 8.00 20.00
AK Al Kaline Bat C 8.00 20.00
ALR Anthony Reyes Jsy C 3.00 8.00
AR Alex Rodriguez Bat C 8.00 20.00
AW Adam Wainwright Jsy C 4.00 10.00
BR Brian Roberts Jsy B 3.00 8.00
BR Brooks Robinson Pants C 6.00 15.00
BS Ben Sheets Bat B 4.00 10.00
BU B.J. Upton Bat C 3.00 8.00
BW Billy Wagner Jsy C 3.00 8.00
BZ Barry Zito Pants D 3.00 8.00
CC Chris Carpenter Jsy C 3.00 8.00
CD Chris Duncan Jsy C 6.00 15.00
CJ Chipper Jones Jsy C 4.00 10.00
CJ Conor Jackson Bat B 3.00 8.00
CU Chase Utley Jsy B 5.00 12.00
DE David Eckstein Bat B 6.00 15.00
DM Doug Mientkiewicz Bat C 3.00 8.00
DO David Ortiz Jsy C 4.00 10.00
DS Duke Snider Pants C 6.00 15.00
DW David Wright Jsy A 12.50 30.00
DWW Dontrelle Willis Jsy C 3.00 8.00
DY Delmon Young Bat C 3.00 8.00
EC Eric Chavez Pants C 3.00 8.00
ER Edgar Renteria Bat C 3.00 8.00
ES Ervin Santana Jsy C 3.00 8.00
FL Francisco Liriano Jsy C 4.00 10.00
FR Frank Robinson Pants C 3.00 8.00
GS Gary Sheffield Bat C 3.00 8.00
HB Hank Blalock Jsy B 3.00 8.00
IR Ivan Rodriguez Jsy B 10.00 25.00
JBR Jose Reyes Jsy A 8.00 20.00
JD Johnny Damon Bat C 4.00 10.00
JM Justin Morneau Bat A 6.00 15.00
JP Juan Pierre Bat B 3.00 8.00
JR Jimmy Rollins Jsy C 3.00 8.00
JRP Jorge Posada Pants C 4.00 10.00
JS Jeff Suppan Jsy C 3.00 8.00
JSA Johan Santana Jsy C 4.00 10.00
JV Jose Vidro Bat B 3.00 8.00
JW Jeff Weaver Jsy C 3.00 8.00
LB Lance Berkman Jsy B 3.00 8.00
LG Luis Gonzalez Bat C 3.00 8.00
MA Moises Alou Bat C 3.00 8.00
MC Miguel Cabrera Bat B 4.00 10.00
MK Mark Kotsay Bat B 3.00 8.00
MM Melvin Mora Jsy C 3.00 8.00
MO Magglio Ordonez Bat C 3.00 8.00
MOT Miguel Tejada Pants C 3.00 8.00
MP Mike Piazza Bat B 6.00 15.00
MR Manny Ramirez Jsy C 4.00 10.00
MT Mark Teixeira Jsy B 4.00 10.00
NS Nick Swisher Jsy C 3.00 8.00
OV Omar Vizquel Bat C 4.00 10.00
PB Pat Burrell Bat B 3.00 8.00
PP Placido Polanco Bat B 10.00 25.00
RB Ronnie Belliard Bat B 3.00 8.00
RF Rafael Furcal Bat D 3.00 8.00
RH Ryan Howard Bat A 12.50 30.00
RS Richie Sexson Bat B 3.00 8.00
SM Stan Musial Pants B 12.50 30.00
TH Todd Helton Jsy B 4.00 10.00
TKH Torii Hunter Jsy B 3.00 8.00
VM Victor Martinez Jsy B 3.00 8.00
YB Yogi Berra Bat B 12.50 30.00
YM Yadier Molina Jsy B 10.00 25.00

2007 Topps Heritage Clubhouse Collection Relics Autographs

STATED ODDS 1:16,100 HOBBY
STATED ODDS 1:16,275 RETAIL
STATED PRINT RUN 25 SER.#'d SETS
NO PRICING DUE TO SCARCITY

2007 Topps Heritage Clubhouse Collection Relics Dual

STATED ODDS 1:13,900 HOBBY
STATED ODDS 1:14,000 RETAIL
STATED PRINT RUN 58 SER.#'d SETS
BR Y.Berra P/A.Rodriguez P 125.00 250.00
KR A.Kaline B/I.Rodriguez B 75.00 150.00
MP S.Musial P/A.Pujols P 125.00 250.00

2007 Topps Heritage Felt Logos

COMPLETE SET (13) 20.00 50.00
1 PER HOBBY BOX TOPPER
BOS Boston Red Sox 5.00 12.00
CHC Chicago Cubs 2.00 5.00
CHW Chicago White Sox 2.00 5.00
CIN Cincinnati Redlegs 2.00 5.00
KCA Kansas City Athletics 2.00 5.00
LAD Los Angeles Dodgers 2.00 5.00
NYY New York Yankees 5.00 12.00
PHI Philadelphia Phillies 2.00 5.00
PIT Pittsburgh Pirates 2.00 5.00
SFG San Francisco Giants 2.00 5.00
STL St. Louis Cardinals 2.00 5.00
WAS Washington Senators 2.00 5.00
BAL Baltimore Orioles 2.00 5.00

2007 Topps Heritage Flashbacks

COMPLETE SET (10) 5.00 12.00
STATED ODDS 1:12 HOBBY, 1:12 RETAIL
FB1 Al Kaline .75 2.00
FB2 Brooks Robinson .50 1.25
FB3 Red Schoendienst .50 1.25
FB4 Warren Spahn .50 1.25
FB5 Stan Musial 1.25 3.00
FB6 Lew Burdette .30 .75
FB7 Eddie Yost .30 .75
FB8 Jim Bunning .50 1.25
FB9 Richie Ashburn .50 1.25
FB10 Hoyt Wilhelm .50 1.25

2007 Topps Heritage Flashbacks Seat Relics

STATED ODDS 1:484 HOBBY, 1:484 RETAIL
AK Al Kaline 10.00 25.00
BR Brooks Robinson 10.00 25.00
EY Eddie Yost 8.00 20.00
HW Hoyt Wilhelm 8.00 20.00
JB Jim Bunning 10.00 25.00
RA Richie Ashburn 8.00 20.00
LB Lew Burdette 8.00 20.00
RS Red Schoendienst 8.00 20.00
SM Stan Musial 8.00 20.00
WS Warren Spahn 10.00 25.00

2007 Topps Heritage New Age Performers

COMPLETE SET (15) 10.00 25.00
STATED ODDS 1:15 HOBBY, 1:15 RETAIL
NP1 Ryan Howard .75 2.00
NP2 Alex Rodriguez 1.25 3.00
NP3 Alfonso Soriano .60 1.50
NP4 David Ortiz 1.00 2.50
NP5 Trevor Hoffman .60 1.50
NP6 Derek Jeter 2.50 6.00
NP7 Anibal Sanchez .40 1.00
NP8 Roger Clemens 1.25 3.00
NP9 Johan Santana .60 1.50
NP10 Albert Pujols 1.25 3.00
NP11 Chipper Jones 1.00 2.50
NP12 Frank Thomas 1.00 2.50
NP13 Ivan Rodriguez .60 1.50
NP14 Ichiro Suzuki 1.25 3.00
NP15 Craig Biggio .60 1.50

2007 Topps Heritage Real One Autographs

STATED ODDS 1:327 HOBBY, 1:328 RETAIL
STATED PRINT RUN 200 SETS
CARDS ARE NOT SERIAL-NUMBERED
PRINT RUN INFO PROVIDED BY TOPPS
RED INK ODDS 1:1129 HOBBY/RETAIL
RED INK PRINT RUN 58 SERIAL #'d SETS
RED INK ALSO CALLED SPECIAL EDITION
EXCHANGE DEADLINE 02/28/09
AK Al Kaline 30.00 80.00
BH Bob Henrich 10.00 25.00
BM Bobby Morgan 10.00 25.00
BP Buddy Pritchard 10.00 25.00
BR Brooks Robinson 40.00 100.00
BT Bill Taylor 10.00 25.00
BW Bill Wight 10.00 25.00
CH Chuck Harmon 10.00 25.00
CJD Jim Derrington 10.00 25.00
CR Charley Rabe 10.00 25.00
DM Dave Melton 10.00 25.00
DS Duke Snider 30.00 80.00
DW David Wright 30.00 80.00
DWW Dontrelle Willis 10.00 25.00
DY Delmon Young 10.00 25.00
DZ Don Zimmer 25.00 60.00
EN Ed Mayer 12.50 30.00
GK George Kell 12.00 30.00
HP Harding Peterson 12.50 30.00
JB Jim Bunning 25.00 60.00
JC Joe Caffie 10.00 25.00
JD Joe Durham 12.50 30.00
JL Joe Lonnett 12.50 30.00
JM Justin Morneau 20.00 50.00
JP Johnny Podres 10.00 25.00
LA Luis Aparicio 30.00 80.00
LM Lloyd Merritt 10.00 25.00
LS Lou Sleater 10.00 25.00
MB Milt Bolling 10.00 25.00
MEB Mack Burk 10.00 25.00
OH Orlando Hudson 12.50 30.00
PS Paul Smith 10.00 25.00
RC Ray Crone 10.00 25.00
RH Ryan Howard 12.00 30.00
RS Red Schoendienst 25.00 60.00
SP Stan Palys 10.00 25.00
TT Tim Thompson 20.00 50.00

2007 Topps Heritage Real One Autographs Red Ink

*RED INK: .75X TO 2X BASIC
STATED ODDS 1:1129 HOBBY/RETAIL
STATED PRINT RUN 58 SERIAL #'d SETS
RED INK ALSO CALLED SPECIAL EDITION
EXCHANGE DEADLINE 02/28/09

2007 Topps Heritage Then and Now

COMPLETE SET (10) 8.00 20.00
STATED ODDS 1:15 HOBBY, 1:15 RETAIL
TN1 F.Robinson/R.Howard .60 1.50
TN2 M.Mantle/D.Ortiz 2.50 6.00
TN3 T.Williams/J.Mauer 1.50 4.00
TN4 L.Aparicio/J.Reyes .50 1.25
TN5 L.Burdette/J.Santana .50 1.25
TN6 J.Podres/A.Harang .30 .75
TN7 R.Ashburn/I.Suzuki 1.00 2.50
TN8 S.Musial/T.Hafner 1.25 3.00
TN9 J.Bunning/A.Sanchez .50 1.25
TN10 W.Spahn/C.Wang .50 1.25

2007 Topps Heritage National Convention '57

408 Roger Maris 1.50 4.00
409 Roberto Clemente 4.00 10.00
410 Mickey Mantle 5.00 12.00
411 Mickey Mantle/Yogi Berra 5.00 12.00
412 Bob Feller 1.00 2.50

2008 Topps Heritage

COMP.SET w/o SP's (425) 40.00 80.00
COMP.HN SET (220) 125.00 200.00
COMP.HN SET w/o SP's (150) 12.50 30.00
COMMON CARD .15 .40
COMMON RC .40 1.00
COMMON TEAM CARD .15 .40
COMMON GB SP .40 1.00
COMMON SP 2.50 6.00
SP STATED ODDS 1:3 HOBBY/RETAIL
HN SP ODDS 1:3 HOBBY/RETAIL
1 Vladimir Guerrero .25 .60
2 Placido Polanco GB SP .40 1.00
3 Eric Byrnes GB SP .40 1.00
4 Mark Teixeira .25 .60
5 Javier Vazquez GB SP .40 1.00
6 Jacoby Ellsbury .30 .75
7 Joey Gathright GB SP .40 1.00
8 Philadelphia Phillies GB SP .40 1.00
9 Andre Ethier GB SP .60 1.50
10 Alex Rodriguez .50 1.25
11 Luke Scott SP 2.50 6.00
12 Curt Schilling GB SP .60 1.50
13 Billy Wagner GB SP .40 1.00
14 Gary Matthews GB SP .40 1.00
15 Sean Marshall .15 .40
16 I.Suzuki GB SP 1.25 3.00
17 Wilson/Bay/Sanchez .25 .60
18 Dontrelle Willis GB SP .40 1.00
19 Josh Willingham .25 .60
20 Jeff Kent .15 .40
21 Troy Tulowitzki GB SP 1.00 2.50
22 Brian Fuentes GB SP .40 1.00
23 Robinson Cano GB SP .60 1.50
24 Felix Hernandez GB SP .60 1.50
25 Edwin Encarnacion .40 1.00
26 Fausto Carmona .15 .40
27 Greg Maddux .50 1.25
28 Ivan Rodriguez GB SP .60 1.50
29 Joe Nathan .15 .40
30 Paul Konerko .25 .60
31 Nook Logan .15 .40
32 Derek Lowe .15 .40
33 Jose Lopez .15 .40
34 Ordonez/Granderson GB SP .60 1.50
35 Adam LaRoche GB SP .40 1.00
36 Kenny Lofton .15 .40
37 Matt Capps .15 .40
38 Mark Reynolds .15 .40
39 Joe Mauer .30 .75
40 Tim Hudson GB SP .60 1.50
41 Kelvim Escobar GB SP .60 1.50
42 Jason Jennings GB SP .40 1.00
43 Victor Martinez .25 .60
44 Jason Kendall .15 .40
45 Chris Ray GB SP .40 1.00
46 Jason Bergmann .15 .40
47 Jason Marquis .15 .40
48 Baltimore Orioles .15 .40
49 Bill Hall GB SP .40 1.00
50 Ken Griffey Jr. .75 2.00
51 Chad Cordero .15 .40
52 Omar Vizquel GB SP .60 1.50
53 Jim Edmonds .25 .60
54 Justin Upton GB SP .60 1.50
55 Josh Beckett .15 .40
56 Jeff Francis .15 .40
57 Brad Lidge GB SP .40 1.00
58 Paul Lo Duca GB SP .40 1.00
59 John Patterson .15 .40
60 Andy Pettitte GB SP .60 1.50
61 Brendan Harris GB SP .40 1.00
62 Chris Young GB SP .40 1.00
63 Eric Chavez .15 .40
64 Francisco Rodriguez .25 .60
65 Jason Giambi GB SP .40 1.00
66 B.J. Ryan .15 .40
67 Rich Hill GB SP .40 1.00
68 Derek Jeter 1.00 2.50
69 San Francisco Giants GB SP .40 1.00
70 Carlos Guillen .15 .40
71 Trevor Hoffman GB SP .60 1.50
72 Zach Duke .15 .40
73 Dustin Pedroia .40 1.00
74 D.Young/R.Zimmerman .25 .60
75 Cole Hamels .30 .75
76 Carlos Delgado .15 .40
77 Jonathan Broxton .15 .40
78 J.Hamilton GB SP .60 1.50
79 Mark Loretta GB SP .60 1.50
80 Grady Sizemore .25 .60
81 Torii Hunter GB SP .40 1.00
82 Carlos Beltran GB SP .60 1.50
83 Jason Isringhausen GB SP .40 1.00
84 Brad Penny GB SP .40 1.00
85 Jayson Werth .25 .60
86 Alex Gordon .25 .60
87 David DeJesus .15 .40
88 Clay Buchholz .25 .60
89 Conor Jackson .15 .40
90 Hideki Matsui GB SP 1.00 2.50
91 Matt Garza GB SP .40 1.00
92 P.Hughes GB SP .40 1.00
93 Mike Piazza .40 1.00
94 Chicago White Sox GB SP .40 1.00
95 Buddy Carlyle .15 .40
96 Mark DeRosa .15 .40
97 Brandon Webb .25 .60
98 Jon Garland GB SP .40 1.00
99 Mariano Rivera .50 1.25
100 Jack Cust .15 .40
101 Carlos Ruiz .15 .40
102 Moises Alou GB SP .40 1.00
103 Bengie Molina .15 .40
104 Adam Jones .25 .60
105 Alfonso Soriano .25 .60
106 Troy Glaus .25 .60
107 John Maine .15 .40
108 Pat Burrell .15 .40
109 David Eckstein .15 .40
110 Homer Bailey .25 .60
111 Cincinnati Reds .15 .40
112 Corey Hart .15 .40
113 Orlando Hernandez .15 .40
114 Orlando Cabrera .25 .60
115 Ryan Garko .15 .40
116 Wladimir Balentien GB SP (RC) .40 1.00
117 Daric Barton GB SP (RC) .40 1.00
118 Emilio Bonifacio RC 1.00 2.50
119 Lance Broadway (RC) .40 1.00
120 Jeff Clement (RC) .60 1.50
121 Dave Davidson RC .60 1.50
122 Ross Detwiler GB SP RC .60 1.50
123 Sam Fuld RC 1.25 3.00
124 Armando Galarraga RC .60 1.50
125 Harvey Garcia (RC) .40 1.00
126 Dan Giese GB SP (RC) .40 1.00
127 Alberto Gonzalez GB SP RC .60 1.50
128 Kevin Hart (RC) .40 1.00
129 Luke Hochevar GB SP RC .60 1.50
130 Chin-Lung Hu GB SP (RC) .40 1.00
131 Brandon Jones RC 1.00 2.50
132 Joe Koshansky (RC) .40 1.00
133 Radhames Liz RC .60 1.50
134 Donny Lucy (RC) .40 1.00
135 Mitch Stetter GB SP RC .60 1.50
136 Nyjer Morgan (RC) .40 1.00
137 Ross Ohlendorf RC .60 1.50
138 Steve Pearce RC 2.00 5.00
139 Jeff Ridgway RC .60 1.50
140 Bronson Sardinha (RC) .40 1.00
141 Seth Smith (RC) .40 1.00
142 Rich Thompson RC .60 1.50
143 Erick Threets (RC) .40 1.00
144 J.R. Towles RC .60 1.50
145 Eugenio Velez RC .40 1.00
146 Joey Votto (RC) 3.00 8.00
147 Soriano/A.Ramirez/D.Lee .25 .60
148 Hunter Pence .25 .60
149 Barry Zito .25 .60
150 Albert Pujols 1.25 3.00
151 Sammy Sosa .40 1.00
152 Brian Bannister .15 .40
153 Reggie Willits .15 .40
154 Bobby Abreu .15 .40
155 Johnny Damon GB SP .60 1.50
156 B.Webb/J.Peavy .25 .60
157 Aramis Ramirez .15 .40
158 Aaron Cook .15 .40
159 David Weathers .15 .40
160 Jack Wilson .15 .40
161 Josh Fogg .15 .40
162 Garrett Atkins .15 .40
163 Brad Ausmus .15 .40
164 Gil Meche .15 .40
165 Jeff Francoeur .25 .60
166 V.Mart/Hafner/Sizemore .25 .60
167 Juan Pierre .15 .40
168 Rafael Furcal .15 .40
169 J.J. Hardy .15 .40
170 Nick Markakis .30 .75
171 Delmon Young .25 .60
172 Oakland Athletics .15 .40
173 Ronny Paulino GB SP .40 1.00
174 Mike Cameron GB SP .40 1.00
175 Jeff Weaver GB SP .40 1.00
176 Preston Wilson GB SP .40 1.00
177 Robinson Tejeda GB SP .40 1.00
178 Adam Lind GB SP .40 1.00
179 Austin Kearns GB SP .40 1.00
180 Jorge Posada GB SP .60 1.50
181 Tadahito Iguchi .15 .40
182 Matt Cain .25 .60
183 Yuniesky Betancourt .15 .40
184 Bronson Arroyo .15 .40
185 Brad Hawpe GB SP .40 1.00
186 Rickie Weeks GB SP .40 1.00
187 Carlos Silva GB SP .40 1.00
188 Adrian Gonzalez .25 .60
189 Kenji Johjima .15 .40
190 Chris Duncan .15 .40
191 James Shields .15 .40
192 Akinori Iwamura .15 .40
193 David Murphy .15 .40
194 Alex Rios .15 .40
195 Carlos Quentin GB SP .40 1.00
196 Jose Valverde GB SP .40 1.00
197 Derrek Lee GB SP .40 1.00
198 Jerry Owens GB SP .40 1.00
199 Russell Martin .15 .40
200 Yovani Gallardo .15 .40
201a Johan Santana Twins .25 .60
201b J.Santana Mets 30.00 60.00
202 Nick Swisher .25 .60
203 So Taguchi .15 .40
204 Justin Morneau .25 .60
205 Milton Bradley .15 .40
206 Jake Westbrook .15 .40
207 Dave Roberts .25 .60
208 Billy Butler .15 .40
209 Lance Berkman .25 .60
210 J.J. Putz GB SP .40 1.00
211 Mike Sweeney GB SP .40 1.00
212 A.Jones/C.Jones .40 1.00
213 Ricky Nolasco .15 .40
214 Andy LaRoche .15 .40
215 Ray Durham .15 .40
216 Francisco Cordero .15 .40
217 Jered Weaver .25 .60
218 Rafael Soriano .15 .40
219 Orlando Hudson .15 .40
220 Mike Lowell .15 .40
221 Chris Snyder .15 .40
222 Cesar Izturis .15 .40
223 St. Louis Cardinals .15 .40
224 D.Wright GB SP .60 1.50
225 Pedro Martinez GB SP .60 1.50
226 Rich Harden GB SP .40 1.00
227 Shane Victorino GB SP .40 1.00
228 Andrew Miller GB SP .60 1.50
229 Chris Young .15 .40
230 Andruw Jones .15 .40
231 Kevin Gregg SP 2.50 6.00
232 C.C. Sabathia .25 .60
233 Hanley Ramirez .25 .60
234 Wandy Rodriguez .15 .40
235 Roy Oswalt .25 .60
236 Mark Grudzielanek .15 .40
237 Jeter/Wang/Cano 1.00 2.50
238 Todd Helton .25 .60
239 Zack Greinke .40 1.00
240 Carlos Gomez .15 .40
241 Lastings Milledge .15 .40
242 Huston Street .15 .40
243 Dan Haren .15 .40
244 Carlos Pena .25 .60
245 Brad Wilkerson .15 .40
246 Roy Halladay .25 .60
247 Dmitri Young .15 .40
248 Boston Red Sox .60 1.50
249 Jonathan Papelbon .25 .60
250 Felix Pie .15 .40
251 Alex Gonzalez .15 .40
252 Bobby Crosby .15 .40
253 Justin Ruggiano RC .60 1.50
254 Freddy Garcia .15 .40
255 Khalil Greene .15 .40
256 Rich Aurilia .15 .40
257 Jarrod Washburn .15 .40
258 B.J. Upton .25 .60
259 Michael Young .15 .40
260 Carlos Zambrano .25 .60
261 Livan Hernandez .15 .40
262 Billingsley/Lowe/Penny GB SP .60 1.50
263 Melky Cabrera GB SP .40 1.00
264 Shannon Stewart GB SP .40 1.00
265 Aaron Rowand GB SP .40 1.00
266 Matt Morris GB SP .40 1.00
267 Xavier Nady GB SP .40 1.00
268 Jim Thome .25 .60
269 Horacio Ramirez .15 .40
270 Prince Fielder .25 .60
271 Andy Phillips .15 .40
272 Aaron Harang .15 .40
273 Josh Barfield .15 .40
274 Ubaldo Jimenez .15 .40
275 Anibal Sanchez .15 .40
276 Carlos Lee .15 .40
277 Mark Teahen .15 .40
278 Delwyn Young .15 .40
279 Kurt Suzuki .15 .40
280 Nate Schierholtz .15 .40
281 Raul Ibanez .25 .60
282 Jose Vidro .15 .40
283 Miguel Cabrera GB SP 1.00 2.50
284 Luis Gonzalez GB SP .40 1.00
285 Chad Billingsley GB SP .60 1.50
286 Tony Gwynn GB SP .40 1.00
287 Matt Kemp .30 .75
288 James Loney .15 .40
289 Brett Myers .15 .40
290 Nate McLouth .15 .40
291 M.Chico/J.Bergmann GB SP .40 1.00
292 Chad Tracy .15 .40
293 Edgar Renteria .15 .40
294 Jay Payton .15 .40
295 Josh Johnson .25 .60
296 Josh Banks (RC) .40 1.00
297 Bill Murphy (RC) .40 1.00
298 Ben Sheets .15 .40
299 Jose Reyes .25 .60
300 Chase Utley .25 .60
301 Ronnie Belliard GB SP .40 1.00
302 Wily Mo Pena .15 .40
303 Tim Lincecum .25 .60
304 Chicago Cubs .25 .60
305 John Lackey .25 .60
306 Stephen Drew .15 .40
307 Kelly Johnson .15 .40
308 Daisuke Matsuzaka .25 .60
309 Craig Monroe .15 .40
310 Jerry Owens .15 .40
311 Jeff Suppan .15 .40
312 Tom Glavine .25 .60
313 Kei Igawa .15 .40
314 Mark Kotsay .15 .40
315 Jacque Jones SP 2.50 6.00
316 Melvin Mora .15 .40
317 M.Holliday/H.Ramirez .40 1.00
318 Jarrod Saltalamacchia .15 .40
319 A.J. Burnett .15 .40
320 Casey Kotchman .15 .40
321 Randy Winn GB SP .40 1.00
322 Richie Sexson GB SP .40 1.00
323 Juan Encarnacion GB SP .40 1.00
324 Rick Ankiel GB SP .40 1.00
325 Dan Wheeler GB SP .40 1.00
326 Brian Roberts .15 .40
327 David Ortiz .40 1.00
328 Garret Anderson .15 .40
329 Detroit Tigers .15 .40
330 Ty Wigginton GB SP .60 1.50
331 Travis Hafner .15 .40
332 Howie Kendrick GB SP .40 1.00
333 Kevin Kouzmanoff GB SP .40 1.00
334 Matt Holliday GB SP 1.00 2.50
335 Brandon Phillips GB SP .40 1.00
336 Ian Kinsler GB SP .60 1.50
337 Lyle Overbay GB SP .40 1.00
338 Justin Verlander GB SP 1.00 2.50
339 Ian Snell .15 .40
340 Hank Blalock .15 .40
341 Vernon Wells .15 .40
342 Matt Chico .15 .40
343 Tim Wakefield .25 .60
344 Michael Bourn .15 .40
345 Chris Carpenter .25 .60
346 Matsuzaka/Beckett .25 .60
347 Chuck James GB SP .40 1.00
348 Joba Chamberlain .15 .40
349 Erik Bedard .15 .40
350 Jimmy Rollins GB SP .60 1.50
351 Anthony Reyes .15 .40
352 Carl Crawford .25 .60
353 Jeremy Hermida .15 .40
354 Ervin Santana .15 .40
355 Edgar Gonzalez .15 .40
356 Yunel Escobar .15 .40
357 Yorvit Torrealba .15 .40
358 Hideki Okajima .15 .40
359 Paul Byrd .15 .40
360 Magglio Ordonez GB SP .60 1.50
361 Joe Borowski .15 .40
362 Clint Sammons (RC) .40 1.00
363 Chris Duffy .15 .40
364 Fred Lewis .15 .40
365 Adrian Beltre .40 1.00
366 Alex Rodriguez BT .50 1.25
367 Troy Tulowitzki BT .40 1.00
368 Prince Fielder BT .25 .60
369 Clay Buchholz BT .25 .60
370 Justin Verlander BT GB SP 1.00 2.50
371 Pedro Martinez BT GB SP .60 1.50
372 R.Howard BT GB SP .60 1.50
373 Ichiro Suzuki BT .50 1.25
374 Kenny Lofton BT .15 .40
375 Manny Ramirez BT .40 1.00
376 Randy Johnson .40 1.00
377 Chris Capuano .15 .40
378 Johnny Estrada .15 .40
379 Franklin Morales .15 .40
380 Ryan Howard .25 .60
381 Casey Blake SP 2.50 6.00
382 Coco Crisp .15 .40
383 J.Maine/W.Randolph MG .15 .40
384 Jeremy Guthrie .15 .40
385 Geoff Jenkins .15 .40
386 Marlon Byrd .15 .40
387 Jeremy Bonderman .15 .40
388 Jason Varitek .40 1.00
389 Joe Girardi MG .25 .60
390 Ryan Braun .25 .60
391 Ryan Zimmerman .25 .60
392 Lowell/Youkilis/Pedroia .40 1.00
393 Pittsburgh Pirates .15 .40
394 Ryan Spilborghs .15 .40
395 Eric Gagne .15 .40
396 Joe Blanton .15 .40
397 Washington Nationals .15 .40
398 Ryan Church .15 .40
399 Ted Lilly .15 .40
400 Manny Ramirez .40 1.00
401 Chad Gaudin .25 .60
402 Dustin McGowan .15 .40
403 Scott Baker .15 .40
404 Franklin Gutierrez .15 .40
405 Dave Bush .15 .40
406 Aubrey Huff .15 .40
407 Jermaine Dye .15 .40
408 C.Utley/J.Rollins .25 .60
409 Jon Lester SP 5.00 12.00
410 Mark Buehrle .25 .60
411 Sergio Mitre .15 .40
412 Jason Bartlett .15 .40
413 Edwin Jackson .15 .40
414 J.D. Drew .15 .40
415 Freddy Sanchez GB SP .40 1.00
416 Asdrubal Cabrera .25 .60
417 Nate Robertson .15 .40
418 Shaun Marcum .15 .40
419 Atlanta Braves .25 .60
420 Noah Lowry .15 .40
421 Jamie Moyer .15 .40
422 Michael Cuddyer .15 .40
423 Randy Wolf .15 .40
424 Juan Uribe .15 .40
425 Brian McCann .25 .60
426 Kyle Lohse SP 2.50 6.00
427 Doug Davis SP 2.50 6.00
428 Snell/Capps/Gorz/Maholm SP 2.50 6.00
429 Miguel Batista SP 2.50 6.00
430 C.Wang SP 4.00 10.00
431 Jeff Salazar SP 2.50 6.00
432 Yadier Molina SP 2.50 6.00
433 Adam Wainwright SP 2.50 6.00
434 Scott Kazmir SP 2.50 6.00
435 Adam Dunn SP 2.50 6.00
436 Ryan Freel SP 2.50 6.00
437 Jhonny Peralta SP 2.50 6.00
438 Kazuo Matsui SP 2.50 6.00
439 Daniel Cabrera .15 .40
440a John Smoltz .40 1.00
440b J.Smoltz Jon Var 50.00 120.00
441 Emil Brown SP 2.50 6.00
442 Gary Sheffield SP 2.50 6.00
443 Jake Peavy SP 3.00 8.00
444 Scott Rolen SP 3.00 8.00
445 Kason Gabbard SP 2.50 6.00
446 Aaron Hill SP 2.50 6.00
447 Felipe Lopez SP 2.50 6.00
448 Dan Uggla SP 2.50 6.00
449 Willy Taveras SP 2.50 6.00
450 Chipper Jones SP 3.00 8.00
451 Josh Anderson SP (RC) 3.00 8.00
452 Young/Upton/Byrnes SP 3.00 8.00
453 Braden Looper SP 2.50 6.00
454 Brandon Inge SP 2.50 6.00
455 Brian Giles SP 2.50 6.00
456 Corey Patterson SP 2.50 6.00
457 Los Angeles Dodgers SP 3.00 8.00
458 Sean Casey SP 2.50 6.00
459 Pedro Feliz SP 2.50 6.00
460 Tom Gorzelanny .15 .40
461 Chone Figgins SP 2.50 6.00
462 Kyle Kendrick SP 2.50 6.00
463 Tony Pena SP 2.50 6.00
464 Marcus Giles SP 2.50 6.00
465 Augie Ojeda SP 2.50 6.00
466 Micah Owings SP 2.50 6.00
467 Ryan Theriot SP 2.50 6.00
468 Shawn Green SP 2.50 6.00
469 Frank Thomas SP 3.00 8.00
470 Lenny DiNardo SP 2.50 6.00
471 Jose Bautista SP 2.50 6.00
472 Manny Corpas SP 2.50 6.00
473 Kevin Millwood SP 2.50 6.00
474 Kevin Youkilis SP 2.50 6.00
475 Jose Contreras SP 2.50 6.00
476 Cleveland Indians .15 .40
477 Julio Lugo SP 2.50 6.00
478 Jason Bay .25 .60
479 Tony LaRussa AS MG SP 2.50 6.00
480 Jim Leyland AS MG SP 2.50 6.00
481 Derrek Lee AS SP 2.50 6.00
482 Justin Morneau AS SP 2.50 6.00
483 Orlando Hudson AS SP 2.50 6.00
484 Brian Roberts AS SP 2.50 6.00
485 Miguel Cabrera AS SP 3.00 8.00
486 Mike Lowell AS SP 2.50 6.00
487 J.J. Hardy AS SP 2.50 6.00
488 Carlos Guillen AS SP 2.50 6.00
489 K.Griffey Jr. AS SP 5.00 12.00
490 Vladimir Guerrero AS SP 3.00 8.00
491 Alfonso Soriano AS SP 3.00 8.00
492 I.Suzuki AS SP 4.00 10.00
493 Matt Holliday AS SP 3.00 8.00
494 Magglio Ordonez AS SP 3.00 8.00
495 Brian McCann AS SP 2.50 6.00
496 Victor Martinez AS SP 2.50 6.00
497 Brad Penny AS SP 2.50 6.00
498 Josh Beckett AS SP 3.00 8.00
499 Cole Hamels AS SP 3.00 8.00
500 Justin Verlander AS SP 4.00 10.00
501 John Danks .15 .40
502 Jamey Wright .15 .40
503 Johnny Cueto RC 1.00 2.50
504 Todd Wellemeyer .15 .40
505 Chase Headley .15 .40
506 Takashi Saito .15 .40
507 Skip Schumaker .15 .40
508 Tampa Bay Rays .15 .40
509 Marcus Thames .15 .40
510 Joe Saunders .15 .40
511 Jair Jurrjens .15 .40
512 Ryan Sweeney .15 .40
513 Darin Erstad .15 .40
514 Brandon Backe GB SP .40 1.00
515 Chris Volstad (RC) .40 1.00
516 Salomon Torres .15 .40
517 Brian Burres .15 .40
518 Brandon Boggs (RC) .60 1.50
519 Max Scherzer RC 4.00 10.00
520 Cliff Lee .25 .60
521 Angel Pagan .15 .40
522 Jason Kubel .15 .40
523 Jose Molina GB SP .40 1.00
524 Hiroki Kuroda RC 1.00 2.50
525 Matt Harrison (RC) .60 1.50
526 C.J. Wilson .15 .40
527 Robb Quinlan .15 .40
528 Darrell Rasner .40 1.00
529 Frank Catalanotto GB SP .40 1.00
530 Mike Mussina .25 .60
531 Ryan Doumit GB SP .40 1.00
532 Willie Bloomquist GB SP .40 1.00
533 Jonny Gomes .15 .40
534 Jesse Litsch .25 .60
535 Curtis Granderson .25 .60
536 A.J. Pierzynski .15 .40
537 Toronto Blue Jays .15 .40
538 Brian Buscher GB SP .40 1.00
539 Kelly Shoppach GB SP .40 1.00
540 Edinson Volquez .15 .40
541 Jon Rauch GB SP .40 1.00
542 Ramon Castro GB SP .40 1.00
543 Greg Smith RC .40 1.00
544 Sean Gallagher .15 .40
545 Justin Masterson GB SP RC 1.00 2.50
546 Milwaukee Brewers .15 .40
547 Jay Bruce (RC) 1.25 3.00
548 Glendon Rusch .15 .40
549 Jeremy Sowers GB SP .40 1.00
550 Ryan Dempster .15 .40
551 Clete Thomas RC .60 1.50
552 Jose Castillo .15 .40
553 Brandon Lyon .15 .40
554 Vicente Padilla .15 .40
555 Jeff Keppinger .15 .40
556 Colorado Rockies .15 .40
557 Dallas Braden GB SP .60 1.50
558 Adam Kennedy .15 .40
559 Luis Mendoza (RC) .40 1.00
560 Justin Duchscherer .15 .40
561 Mike Aviles RC .60 1.50
562 Jed Lowrie (RC) .40 1.00
563 Doug Mientkiewicz GB SP .40 1.00
564 Chris Burke .15 .40
565 Dana Eveland .15 .40
566 Bryan Lahair RC 3.00 8.00
567 Denard Span (RC) .60 1.50
568 Damion Easley .15 .40
569 Josh Fields .15 .40
570 Geovany Soto .40 1.00
571 Gerald Laird UER .15 .40
572 Bobby Jenks .15 .40
573 Andy Marte .15 .40
574 Mike Pelfrey .15 .40
575 Jerry Hairston .15 .40
576 Mike Lamb .15 .40
577 Ben Zobrist .25 .60
578 Carlos Gonzalez (RC) 1.00 2.50
579 Jose Guillen GB SP .40 1.00
580 Kosuke Fukudome RC 1.25 3.00
581 Gabe Kapler GB SP .40 1.00
582 Florida Marlins .15 .40
583 Ramon Vazquez GB SP .40 1.00
584 Wes Helms GB SP .40 1.00
585 Minnesota Twins .15 .40
586 Cody Ross .15 .40
587 Mike Napoli .25 .60
588 Alexi Casilla .15 .40
589 Emmanuel Burriss RC .60 1.50
590 Brian Wilson .40 1.00
591 Rod Barajas .15 .40
592 Mike Hampton GB SP .40 1.00
593 Nick Blackburn RC .60 1.50
594 Joe Mather RC .60 1.50
595 Clayton Kershaw GB SP RC 12.00 30.00
596 Cliff Floyd GB SP .40 1.00
597 Sidney Ponson GB SP .40 1.00
598 Brian Anderson .15 .40
599 Joe Inglett .15 .40
600 Miguel Tejada .25 .60
601 San Diego Padres .15 .40
602 Scott Hairston GB SP .40 1.00
603 Joel Pineiro .15 .40
604 Fernando Tatis .15 .40
605 Greg Reynolds RC .60 1.50
606 Brian Moehler .15 .40
607 Kevin Millar GB SP .40 1.00
608 Ben Francisco .15 .40
609 Troy Percival .15 .40
610 Kerry Wood .15 .40
611 Max Ramirez RC .40 1.00
612 Jeff Baker .15 .40
613 Houston Astros .15 .40
614 Russell Branyan .15 .40
615 Todd Jones .15 .40
616 Brian Schneider .15 .40
617 Gregorio Petit RC .60 1.50
618 Matt Diaz .15 .40
619 Blake DeWitt GB SP (RC) .60 1.50
620 Cristian Guzman .15 .40
621 Jeff Samardzija GB SP RC 1.25 3.00
622 John Baker (RC) .40 1.00
623 Eric Hinske .15 .40
624 Scott Olsen .15 .40
625 Greg Dobbs .15 .40
626 Carlos Marmol GB SP .60 1.50
627 Kansas City Royals .15 .40
628 Esteban German .15 .40
629 Dennis Sarfate .15 .40
630 Ryan Ludwick .15 .40
631 Mike Jacobs .15 .40
632 Tyler Yates .15 .40
633 Joel Hanrahan .25 .60
634 Manny Parra .15 .40
635 Maicer Izturis .15 .40
636 Juan Rivera .15 .40
637 Tim Redding .15 .40
638 Jose Arredondo RC .60 1.50
639 Mike Redmond GB SP .40 1.00
640 Joe Crede .15 .40
641 Omar Infante .15 .40
642 Nick Punto .15 .40
643 Jeff Mathis .15 .40

644 Andy Sonnanstine .15 .40
645 Masahide Kobayashi RC .60 1.50
646 Marco Scutaro .25 .60
647 Matt Macri (RC) .40 1.00
648 Ian Stewart SP 2.50 6.00
649 David Dellucci GB SP .40 1.00
650 Evan Longoria RC 2.00 5.00
651 Martin Prado GB SP .40 1.00
652 Glen Perkins .15 .40
653 Alfredo Amezaga GB SP .40 1.00
654 Brett Gardner (RC) 1.00 2.50
655 Angel Berroa GB SP .40 1.00
656 Pablo Sandoval RC 5.00 12.00
657 Jody Gerut .15 .40
658 Arizona Diamondbacks .15 4.00
659 Ryan Freel GB SP .40 1.00
660 Dioner Navarro .15 .40
661 Endy Chavez GB SP .40 1.00
662 Jorge Campillo .15 .40
663 Mark Ellis .15 .40
664 John Buck .15 .40
665 Texas Rangers .15 .40
666 Jason Michaels .15 .40
667 Chris Dickerson RC .60 1.50
668 Kevin Mench .15 .40
669 Aaron Miles .15 .40
670 Joakim Soria .15 .40
671 Chris Davis RC .75 2.00
672 Taylor Teagarden GB SP RC .60 1.50
673 Willy Aybar .15 .40
674 Paul Maholm .15 .40
675 Mike Gonzalez .15 .40
676 Seattle Mariners .15 .40
677 Ryan Langerhans SP 2.50 6.00
678 Alex Romero (RC) .60 1.50
679 Erick Aybar .15 .40
680 George Sherrill .15 .40
681 John Bowker (RC) .40 1.00
682 Zach Miner GB SP .40 1.00
683 Jorge Cantu .15 .40
684 Jo-Jo Reyes .15 .40
685 Ryan Raburn .15 .40
686 Gavin Floyd SP 2.50 6.00
687 Kevin Slowey SP 2.50 6.00
688 Gio Gonzalez SP (RC) 2.50 6.00
689 Eric Patterson SP 2.50 6.00
690 Jonathan Sanchez SP 2.50 6.00
691 Oliver Perez SP 2.50 6.00
692 John Lannan SP 2.50 6.00
693 Ramon Hernandez SP 2.50 6.00
694 Mike Fontenot SP 2.50 6.00
695 Ross Gload SP 2.50 6.00
696 Mark Sweeney SP 2.50 6.00
697 Nick Hundley SP (RC) 2.50 6.00
698 Kevin Correia SP 2.50 6.00
699 Jeremy Reed SP 2.50 6.00
700 Eddie Kunz SP RC 2.50 6.00
701 Miguel Montero SP 2.50 6.00
702 Gabe Gross SP 2.50 6.00
703 Matt Stairs SP 2.50 6.00
704 Kenny Rogers SP 2.50 6.00
705 Mark Hendrickson SP 2.50 6.00
706 Heath Bell SP 2.50 6.00
707 Wilson Betemit SP 2.50 6.00
708 Brandon Morrow SP 2.50 6.00
709 Brendan Ryan SP 2.50 6.00
710 Eric Hurley SP (RC) 2.50 6.00
711 Los Angeles Angels SP 2.50 6.00
712 Jack Hannahan SP 2.50 6.00
713 Seth McClung SP 2.50 6.00
714 New York Mets SP 2.50 6.00
715 Chris Perez SP RC 2.50 6.00
716 Clayton Richard SP (RC) 2.50 6.00
717 Jaime Garcia SP RC 2.50 6.00
718 Matt Joyce SP RC 2.50 6.00
719 Brad Ziegler SP RC 2.50 6.00
720 Ivan Ochoa (RC) .60 1.50

2008 Topps Heritage Black Back

*BLK BACK VET: .4X TO 1X BASIC
*BLK BACK RC: .4X TO 1X BASIC RC
RANDOM INSERTS IN PACKS

2008 Topps Heritage Chrome

1-100 ODDS 1:8 HOBBY, 1:18 RETAIL
1-100 INSERTED IN 08 HERITAGE
101-200 ODDS 1:6 HOBBY
101-200 INSERTED IN 08 TOPPS CHROME
201-300 ODDS 1:3 HOBBY
201-300 INSERTED IN 08 HERITAGE HN
STATED PRINT RUN 1959 SERIAL #'d SETS

C1 Hunter Pence 1.50 4.00
C2 Andre Ethier 1.50 4.00
C3 Curt Schilling 1.50 4.00
C4 Gary Matthews 1.00 2.50
C5 Dontrelle Willis 1.00 2.50
C6 Troy Tulowitzki 2.50 6.00
C7 Robinson Cano 1.50 4.00
C8 Felix Hernandez 1.50 4.00
C9 Josh Hamilton 1.50 4.00
C10 Justin Upton 1.50 4.00
C11 Brad Penny 1.00 2.50
C12 Hideki Matsui 2.50 6.00
C13 J.J. Putz 1.00 2.50
C14 Jorge Posada 1.50 4.00
C15 Albert Pujols 3.00 8.00
C16 Aaron Rowand 1.00 2.50
C17 Ronnie Belliard 1.00 2.50
C18 Rick Ankiel 1.00 2.50
C19 Ian Kinsler 1.50 4.00
C20 Justin Verlander 2.50 6.00
C21 Lyle Overbay 1.00 2.50
C22 Tim Hudson 1.50 4.00
C23 Ryan Zimmerman 1.50 4.00
C24 Ryan Braun 1.50 4.00
C25 Jimmy Rollins 1.50 4.00
C26 Kelvim Escobar 1.50 4.00
C27 Adam LaRoche 1.00 2.50
C28 Ivan Rodriguez 1.50 4.00
C29 Billy Wagner 1.00 2.50
C30 Ichiro Suzuki 3.00 8.00
C31 Chris Young 1.00 2.50
C32 Trevor Hoffman 1.50 4.00
C33 Torii Hunter 1.00 2.50
C34 Jason Isringhausen 1.00 2.50
C35 Jose Valverde 1.00 2.50
C36 Derrek Lee 1.00 2.50
C37 Rich Harden 1.00 2.50
C38 Andrew Miller 1.50 4.00
C39 Miguel Cabrera 2.50 6.00
C40 David Wright 1.50 4.00
C41 Brandon Phillips 1.00 2.50
C42 Magglio Ordonez 1.50 4.00
C43 Eric Byrnes 1.00 2.50
C44 John Smoltz 2.50 6.00
C45 Brandon Webb 1.50 4.00
C46 Barry Zito 1.50 4.00
C47 Sammy Sosa 2.50 6.00
C48 James Shields 1.00 2.50
C49 Alex Rios 1.00 2.50
C50 Matt Holliday 2.50 6.00
C51 Chris Young 1.00 2.50
C52 Roy Oswalt 1.50 4.00
C53 Matt Kemp 3.00 8.00
C54 Tim Lincecum 1.50 4.00
C55 Hanley Ramirez 1.50 4.00
C56 Vladimir Guerrero 1.50 4.00
C57 Mark Teixeira 1.50 4.00
C58 Fausto Carmona 1.00 2.50
C59 B.J. Ryan 1.00 2.50
C60 Manny Ramirez 2.50 6.00
C61 Carlos Delgado 1.00 2.50
C62 Matt Cain 1.50 4.00
C63 Brian Bannister 1.00 2.50
C64 Russell Martin 1.00 2.50
C65 Todd Helton 1.50 4.00
C66 Roy Halladay 1.50 4.00
C67 Lance Berkman 1.50 4.00
C68 John Lackey 1.50 4.00
C69 Daisuke Matsuzaka 1.50 4.00
C70 Joe Mauer 2.00 5.00
C71 Francisco Rodriguez 1.50 4.00
C72 Derek Jeter 6.00 15.00
C73 Homer Bailey 1.50 4.00
C74 Jonathan Papelbon 1.50 4.00
C75 Billy Butler 1.00 2.50
C76 B.J. Upton 1.50 4.00
C77 Ubaldo Jimenez 1.00 2.50
C78 Erik Bedard 1.00 2.50
C79 Jeff Kent 1.00 2.50
C80 Ken Griffey Jr. 5.00 12.00
C81 Josh Beckett 1.00 2.50
C82 Jeff Francis 1.00 2.50
C83 Grady Sizemore 1.50 4.00
C84 John Maine 1.00 2.50
C85 Cole Hamels 2.00 5.00
C86 Nick Markakis 2.00 5.00
C87 Ben Sheets 1.00 2.50
C88 Jose Reyes 1.50 4.00
C89 Vernon Wells 1.00 2.50
C90 Justin Morneau 1.50 4.00
C91 Brian McCann 1.50 4.00
C92 Jacoby Ellsbury 2.00 5.00
C93 Clay Buchholz 1.50 4.00
C94 Prince Fielder 1.50 4.00
C95 David Ortiz 2.50 6.00
C96 Joba Chamberlain 1.00 2.50
C97 Chien-Ming Wang 1.50 4.00
C98 Chipper Jones 2.50 6.00
C99 Chase Utley 1.50 4.00
C100 Alex Rodriguez 3.00 8.00
C101 Phil Hughes 1.00 2.50
C102 Hideki Okajima 1.00 2.50
C103 Chone Figgins 1.00 2.50
C104 Jose Vidro 1.00 2.50
C105 Johan Santana 1.50 4.00
C106 Paul Konerko 1.50 4.00
C107 Alfonso Soriano 1.50 4.00
C108 Kei Igawa 1.00 2.50
C109 Lastings Milledge 1.00 2.50
C110 Asdrubal Cabrera 1.50 4.00
C111 Brandon Jones 2.50 6.00
C112 Tom Gorzelanny 1.00 2.50
C113 Delmon Young 1.50 4.00
C114 Daric Barton 1.00 2.50
C115 David DeJesus 1.00 2.50
C116 Ryan Howard 1.50 4.00
C117 Tom Glavine 1.50 4.00
C118 Frank Thomas 2.50 6.00
C119 J.R. Towles 1.50 4.00
C120 Jeremy Bonderman 1.00 2.50
C121 Adrian Beltre 2.50 6.00
C122 Dan Haren 1.00 2.50
C123 Kazuo Matsui 1.00 2.50
C124 Joe Blanton 1.00 2.50
C125 Dan Uggla 1.00 2.50
C126 Stephen Drew 1.00 2.50
C127 Daniel Cabrera 1.00 2.50
C128 Jeff Clement 1.50 4.00
C129 Pedro Martinez 1.50 4.00
C130 Josh Anderson 1.00 2.50
C131 Orlando Hudson 1.00 2.50
C132 Jason Bay 1.50 4.00
C133 Eric Chavez 1.00 2.50
C134 Johnny Damon 1.50 4.00
C135 Lance Broadway 1.00 2.50
C136 Jake Peavy 1.00 2.50
C137 Carl Crawford 1.50 4.00
C138 Kenji Johjima 1.00 2.50
C139 Melky Cabrera 1.00 2.50
C140 Aaron Hill 1.00 2.50
C141 Carlos Lee 1.00 2.50
C142 Mark Buehrle 1.50 4.00
C143 Carlos Beltran 1.50 4.00
C144 Chin-Lung Hu 1.00 2.50
C145 C.C. Sabathia 1.50 4.00
C146 Dustin Pedroia 2.50 6.00
C147 Freddy Sanchez 1.00 2.50
C148 Kevin Youkilis 1.00 2.50
C149 Radhames Liz 1.50 4.00
C150 Jim Thome 1.50 4.00
C151 Greg Maddux 3.00 8.00
C152 Rich Hill 1.00 2.50
C153 Andy LaRoche 1.00 2.50
C154 Gil Meche 1.00 2.50
C155 Victor Martinez 1.50 4.00
C156 Mariano Rivera 3.00 8.00
C157 Kyle Kendrick 1.00 2.50
C158 Jarrod Saltalamacchia 1.00 2.50
C159 Tadahito Iguchi 1.00 2.50
C160 Eric Gagne 1.00 2.50
C161 Garrett Atkins 1.00 2.50
C162 Pat Burrell 1.00 2.50
C163 Akinori Iwamura 1.00 2.50
C164 Melvin Mora 1.00 2.50
C165 Joey Votto 8.00 20.00
C166 Brian Roberts 1.00 2.50
C167 Brett Myers 1.00 2.50
C168 Michael Young 1.00 2.50
C169 Adam Jones 1.50 4.00
C170 Carlos Zambrano 1.50 4.00
C171 Jeff Francoeur 1.50 4.00
C172 Brad Hawpe 1.00 2.50
C173 Andy Pettitte 1.50 4.00
C174 Ryan Garko 1.00 2.50
C175 Adrian Gonzalez 1.50 4.00
C176 Ted Lilly 1.00 2.50
C177 J.J. Hardy 1.00 2.50
C178 Jon Lester 1.50 4.00
C179 Carlos Pena 1.50 4.00
C180 Ross Detwiler 1.50 4.00
C181 Andruw Jones 1.00 2.50
C182 Gary Sheffield 1.00 2.50
C183 Dmitri Young 1.00 2.50
C184 Carlos Guillen 1.00 2.50
C185 Yovani Gallardo 1.00 2.50
C186 Alex Gordon 1.50 4.00
C187 Aaron Harang 1.00 2.50
C188 Travis Hafner 1.00 2.50
C189 Orlando Cabrera 1.50 4.00
C190 Bobby Abreu 1.00 2.50
C191 Randy Johnson 2.50 6.00
C192 Scott Kazmir 1.50 4.00
C193 Jason Varitek 2.50 6.00
C194 Mike Lowell 1.00 2.50
C195 A.J. Burnett 1.00 2.50
C196 Garret Anderson 1.00 2.50
C197 Chris Carpenter 1.50 4.00
C198 Jermaine Dye 1.00 2.50
C199 Luke Hochevar 1.50 4.00
C200 Steve Pearce 5.00 12.00
C201 Joe Saunders 1.00 2.50
C202 Cliff Lee 1.50 4.00
C203 Mike Mussina 1.50 4.00
C204 Ryan Dempster 1.00 2.50
C205 Edinson Volquez 1.00 2.50
C206 Justin Duchscherer 1.00 2.50
C207 Geovany Soto 2.50 6.00
C208 Brian Wilson 2.50 6.00
C209 Kerry Wood 1.00 2.50
C210 Kosuke Fukudome 3.00 8.00
C211 Cristian Guzman 1.00 2.50
C212 Ryan Ludwick 1.00 2.50
C213 Joe Crede 1.00 2.50
C214 Dioner Navarro 1.00 2.50
C215 Miguel Tejada 1.50 4.00
C216 Joakim Soria 1.00 2.50
C217 George Sherrill 1.00 2.50
C218 John Danks 1.00 2.50
C219 Jair Jurrjens 1.00 2.50
C220 Evan Longoria 5.00 12.00
C221 Hiroki Kuroda 2.50 6.00
C222 Greg Smith 1.00 2.50
C223 Dana Eveland 1.00 2.50
C224 Ryan Sweeney 1.00 2.50
C225 Mike Pelfrey 1.00 2.50
C226 Nick Blackburn 1.50 4.00
C227 Scott Olsen 1.00 2.50
C228 Manny Parra 1.00 2.50
C229 Tim Redding 1.00 2.50
C230 Paul Maholm 1.00 2.50
C231 Todd Wellemeyer 1.00 2.50
C232 Jesse Litsch 1.50 4.00
C233 Andy Sonnanstine 1.00 2.50
C234 Johnny Cueto 2.50 6.00
C235 Vicente Padilla 1.00 2.50
C236 Glen Perkins 1.00 2.50
C237 Brian Burres 1.00 2.50
C238 Jamey Wright 1.00 2.50
C239 Chase Headley 1.00 2.50
C240 Takashi Saito 1.00 2.50
C241 Skip Schumaker 1.00 2.50
C242 Curtis Granderson 1.50 4.00
C243 A.J. Pierzynski 1.00 2.50
C244 Jorge Cantu 1.00 2.50
C245 Maicer Izturis 1.00 2.50
C246 Kevin Mench 1.00 2.50
C247 Jason Kubel 1.00 2.50
C248 Rod Barajas 1.00 2.50
C249 Jed Lowrie 1.00 2.50
C250 Bobby Jenks 1.00 2.50
C251 Jonny Gomes 1.00 2.50
C252 Clete Thomas 1.50 4.00
C253 Eric Hinske 1.00 2.50
C254 Brett Gardner 2.50 6.00
C255 Denard Span 1.50 4.00
C256 Brian Anderson 1.00 2.50
C257 Troy Percival 1.00 2.50
C258 Darrell Rasner 1.00 2.50
C259 Willy Aybar 1.00 2.50
C260 John Bowker 1.00 2.50
C261 Marco Scutaro 1.50 4.00
C262 Adam Kennedy 1.00 2.50
C263 Nick Punto 1.00 2.50
C264 Mike Napoli 1.50 4.00
C265 Carlos Gonzalez 2.50 6.00
C266 Matt Macri 1.00 2.50
C267 Marcus Thames 1.00 2.50
C268 Ben Zobrist 1.50 4.00
C269 Mark Ellis 1.00 2.50
C270 Mike Aviles 1.50 4.00
C271 Angel Pagan 1.00 2.50
C272 Erick Aybar 1.00 2.50
C273 Todd Jones 1.00 2.50
C274 Brandon Boggs 1.50 4.00
C275 Mike Jacobs 1.00 2.50
C276 Mike Gonzalez 1.00 2.50
C277 Mike Lamb 1.00 2.50
C278 Robb Quinlan 1.00 2.50
C279 Salomon Torres 1.00 2.50
C280 Jose Castillo 1.00 2.50
C281 Damion Easley 1.00 2.50
C282 Jo-Jo Reyes 1.00 2.50
C283 Cody Ross 1.00 2.50
C284 Alexi Casilla 1.00 2.50
C286 Brandon Lyon 1.00 2.50
C287 Greg Dobbs 1.00 2.50
C288 Joel Pineiro 1.00 2.50
C289 Chris Davis 2.00 5.00
C290 Masahide Kobayashi 1.50 4.00
C291 Darin Erstad 1.00 2.50
C292 Matt Diaz 1.00 2.50
C293 Brian Schneider 1.00 2.50
C294 Gerald Laird 1.00 2.50
C295 Ben Francisco 1.00 2.50
C296 Brian Moehler 1.00 2.50
C297 Aaron Miles 1.00 2.50
C298 Max Scherzer 6.00 15.00
C299 C.J. Wilson 1.00 2.50
C300 Jay Bruce 3.00 8.00

2008 Topps Heritage Chrome Refractors

*CHROME REF: .6X TO 1.5X
1-100 ODDS 1:29 HOBBY, 1:59 RETAIL
1-100 INSERTED IN 08 TOPPS HERITAGE
101-200 ODDS 1:21 HOBBY
101-200 INSERTED IN 08 TOPPS CHROME
201-300 ODDS 1:11 HOBBY
201-300 INSERTED IN 08 HERITAGE HN
STATED PRINT RUN 559 SERIAL #'d SETS

C72 Derek Jeter 12.50 30.00
C100 Alex Rodriguez 12.50 30.00
C220 Evan Longoria 8.00 20.00

2008 Topps Heritage Chrome Refractors Black

1-100 ODDS 1:315 HOB,1:450 RET
1-100 INSERTED IN 08 TOPPS HERITAGE
101-200 ODDS 1:196 HOBBY
201-300 INSERTED IN 08 HERITAGE HN
201-300 ODDS 1:99 HOBBY
101-200 INSERTED IN 08 TOPPS CHROME
STATED PRINT RUN 59 SERIAL #'d SETS

C1 Hunter Pence 15.00 40.00
C2 Andre Ethier 15.00 40.00
C3 Curt Schilling 15.00 40.00
C4 Gary Matthews 10.00 25.00
C5 Dontrelle Willis 10.00 25.00
C6 Troy Tulowitzki 25.00 60.00
C7 Robinson Cano 15.00 40.00
C8 Felix Hernandez 15.00 40.00
C9 Josh Hamilton 15.00 40.00
C10 Justin Upton 15.00 40.00
C11 Brad Penny 10.00 25.00
C12 Hideki Matsui 25.00 60.00
C13 J.J. Putz 10.00 25.00
C14 Jorge Posada 15.00 40.00
C15 Albert Pujols 30.00 80.00
C16 Aaron Rowand 10.00 25.00
C17 Ronnie Belliard 10.00 25.00
C18 Rick Ankiel 10.00 25.00
C19 Ian Kinsler 15.00 40.00
C20 Justin Verlander 25.00 60.00
C21 Lyle Overbay 10.00 25.00
C22 Tim Hudson 15.00 40.00
C23 Ryan Zimmerman 15.00 40.00
C24 Ryan Braun 15.00 40.00
C25 Jimmy Rollins 15.00 40.00
C26 Kelvim Escobar 15.00 40.00
C27 Adam LaRoche 10.00 25.00
C28 Ivan Rodriguez 15.00 40.00
C29 Billy Wagner 10.00 25.00
C30 Ichiro Suzuki 30.00 80.00
C31 Chris Young 10.00 25.00
C32 Trevor Hoffman 15.00 40.00
C33 Torii Hunter 10.00 25.00
C34 Jason Isringhausen 10.00 25.00
C35 Jose Valverde 10.00 25.00
C36 Derrek Lee 10.00 25.00
C37 Rich Harden 10.00 25.00
C38 Andrew Miller 15.00 40.00
C39 Miguel Cabrera 25.00 60.00
C40 David Wright 15.00 40.00
C41 Brandon Phillips 10.00 25.00
C42 Magglio Ordonez 15.00 40.00
C43 Eric Byrnes 10.00 25.00
C44 John Smoltz 25.00 60.00
C45 Brandon Webb 15.00 40.00
C46 Barry Zito 15.00 40.00
C47 Sammy Sosa 25.00 60.00
C48 James Shields 10.00 25.00
C49 Alex Rios 10.00 25.00
C50 Matt Holliday 25.00 60.00
C51 Chris Young 10.00 25.00
C52 Roy Oswalt 15.00 40.00
C53 Matt Kemp 20.00 50.00
C54 Tim Lincecum 15.00 40.00
C55 Hanley Ramirez 15.00 40.00
C56 Vladimir Guerrero 15.00 40.00
C57 Mark Teixeira 15.00 40.00
C58 Fausto Carmona 10.00 25.00
C59 B.J. Ryan 10.00 25.00
C60 Manny Ramirez 25.00 60.00
C61 Carlos Delgado 10.00 25.00
C62 Matt Cain 15.00 40.00
C63 Brian Bannister 10.00 25.00
C64 Russell Martin 10.00 25.00
C65 Todd Helton 15.00 40.00
C66 Roy Halladay 15.00 40.00
C67 Lance Berkman 15.00 40.00
C68 John Lackey 15.00 40.00
C69 Daisuke Matsuzaka 15.00 40.00
C70 Joe Mauer 20.00 50.00
C71 Francisco Rodriguez 15.00 40.00
C72 Derek Jeter 60.00 150.00
C73 Homer Bailey 15.00 40.00
C74 Jonathan Papelbon 15.00 40.00
C75 Billy Butler 10.00 25.00
C76 B.J. Upton 15.00 40.00
C77 Ubaldo Jimenez 10.00 25.00
C78 Erik Bedard 10.00 25.00
C79 Jeff Kent 10.00 25.00
C80 Ken Griffey Jr. 50.00 125.00
C81 Josh Beckett 10.00 25.00
C82 Jeff Francis 10.00 25.00
C83 Grady Sizemore 15.00 40.00
C84 John Maine 10.00 25.00
C85 Cole Hamels 20.00 50.00
C86 Nick Markakis 20.00 50.00
C87 Ben Sheets 10.00 25.00
C88 Jose Reyes 15.00 40.00
C89 Vernon Wells 10.00 25.00
C90 Justin Morneau 15.00 40.00
C91 Brian McCann 15.00 40.00
C92 Jacoby Ellsbury 20.00 50.00
C93 Clay Buchholz 15.00 40.00
C94 Prince Fielder 15.00 40.00
C95 David Ortiz 25.00 60.00
C96 Joba Chamberlain 10.00 25.00
C97 Chien-Ming Wang 15.00 40.00
C98 Chipper Jones 25.00 60.00
C99 Chase Utley 15.00 40.00
C100 Alex Rodriguez 30.00 80.00
C101 Phil Hughes 10.00 25.00
C102 Hideki Okajima 10.00 25.00
C103 Chone Figgins 10.00 25.00
C104 Jose Vidro 10.00 25.00
C105 Johan Santana 15.00 40.00
C106 Paul Konerko 15.00 40.00
C107 Alfonso Soriano 15.00 40.00
C108 Kei Igawa 10.00 25.00
C109 Lastings Milledge 10.00 25.00
C110 Asdrubal Cabrera 15.00 40.00
C111 Brandon Jones 25.00 60.00
C112 Tom Gorzelanny 10.00 25.00
C113 Delmon Young 15.00 40.00
C114 Daric Barton 10.00 25.00
C115 David DeJesus 10.00 25.00
C116 Ryan Howard 15.00 40.00
C117 Tom Glavine 15.00 40.00
C118 Frank Thomas 25.00 60.00
C119 J.R. Towles 15.00 40.00
C120 Jeremy Bonderman 10.00 25.00
C121 Adrian Beltre 25.00 60.00
C122 Dan Haren 10.00 25.00
C123 Kazuo Matsui 10.00 25.00
C124 Joe Blanton 10.00 25.00
C125 Dan Uggla 10.00 25.00
C126 Stephen Drew 10.00 25.00
C127 Daniel Cabrera 10.00 25.00
C128 Jeff Clement 15.00 40.00
C129 Pedro Martinez 15.00 40.00
C130 Josh Anderson 10.00 25.00
C131 Orlando Hudson 10.00 25.00
C132 Jason Bay 15.00 40.00
C133 Eric Chavez 10.00 25.00
C134 Johnny Damon 15.00 40.00
C135 Lance Broadway 10.00 25.00
C136 Jake Peavy 10.00 25.00
C137 Carl Crawford 15.00 40.00
C138 Kenji Johjima 10.00 25.00
C139 Melky Cabrera 10.00 25.00
C140 Aaron Hill 10.00 25.00
C141 Carlos Lee 10.00 25.00
C142 Mark Buehrle 15.00 40.00
C143 Carlos Beltran 15.00 40.00
C144 Chin-Lung Hu 10.00 25.00
C145 C.C. Sabathia 15.00 40.00
C146 Dustin Pedroia 25.00 60.00
C147 Freddy Sanchez 10.00 25.00
C148 Kevin Youkilis 10.00 25.00
C149 Radhames Liz 15.00 40.00
C150 Jim Thome 15.00 40.00
C151 Greg Maddux 30.00 80.00
C152 Rich Hill 10.00 25.00
C153 Andy LaRoche 10.00 25.00
C154 Gil Meche 10.00 25.00
C155 Victor Martinez 15.00 40.00
C156 Mariano Rivera 30.00 80.00
C157 Kyle Kendrick 10.00 25.00
C158 Jarrod Saltalamacchia 10.00 25.00
C159 Tadahito Iguchi 10.00 25.00
C160 Eric Gagne 10.00 25.00
C161 Garrett Atkins 10.00 25.00
C162 Pat Burrell 10.00 25.00
C163 Akinori Iwamura 10.00 25.00
C164 Melvin Mora 10.00 25.00
C165 Joey Votto 80.00 200.00
C166 Brian Roberts 10.00 25.00
C167 Brett Myers 10.00 25.00
C168 Michael Young 10.00 25.00
C169 Adam Jones 15.00 40.00
C170 Carlos Zambrano 15.00 40.00
C171 Jeff Francoeur 15.00 40.00
C172 Brad Hawpe 10.00 25.00
C173 Andy Pettitte 15.00 40.00
C174 Ryan Garko 10.00 25.00
C175 Adrian Gonzalez 15.00 40.00
C176 Ted Lilly 10.00 25.00
C177 J.J. Hardy 10.00 25.00
C178 Jon Lester 15.00 40.00
C179 Carlos Pena 15.00 40.00
C180 Ross Detwiler 15.00 40.00
C181 Andruw Jones 10.00 25.00
C182 Gary Sheffield 10.00 25.00
C183 Dmitri Young 10.00 25.00
C184 Carlos Guillen 10.00 25.00
C185 Yovani Gallardo 10.00 25.00
C186 Alex Gordon 15.00 40.00
C187 Aaron Harang 10.00 25.00
C188 Travis Hafner 10.00 25.00
C189 Orlando Cabrera 15.00 40.00
C190 Bobby Abreu 10.00 25.00
C191 Randy Johnson 25.00 60.00
C192 Scott Kazmir 15.00 40.00
C193 Jason Varitek 25.00 60.00
C194 Mike Lowell 10.00 25.00
C195 A.J. Burnett 10.00 25.00
C196 Garret Anderson 10.00 25.00
C197 Chris Carpenter 15.00 40.00
C198 Jermaine Dye 10.00 25.00
C199 Luke Hochevar 15.00 40.00
C200 Steve Pearce 50.00 125.00
C201 Joe Saunders 10.00 25.00
C202 Cliff Lee 15.00 40.00
C203 Mike Mussina 15.00 40.00
C204 Ryan Dempster 10.00 25.00
C205 Edinson Volquez 10.00 25.00
C206 Justin Duchscherer 10.00 25.00
C207 Geovany Soto 25.00 60.00
C208 Brian Wilson 25.00 60.00
C209 Kerry Wood 10.00 25.00
C210 Kosuke Fukudome 30.00 80.00
C211 Cristian Guzman 10.00 25.00
C212 Ryan Ludwick 10.00 25.00
C213 Joe Crede 10.00 25.00
C214 Dioner Navarro 10.00 25.00
C215 Miguel Tejada 15.00 40.00
C216 Joakim Soria 10.00 25.00
C217 George Sherrill 10.00 25.00
C218 John Danks 10.00 25.00
C219 Jair Jurrjens 10.00 25.00
C220 Evan Longoria 50.00 125.00
C221 Hiroki Kuroda 25.00 60.00
C222 Greg Smith 10.00 25.00
C223 Dana Eveland 10.00 25.00
C224 Ryan Sweeney 10.00 25.00
C225 Mike Pelfrey 10.00 25.00
C226 Nick Blackburn 15.00 40.00
C227 Scott Olsen 10.00 25.00
C228 Manny Parra 10.00 25.00
C229 Tim Redding 10.00 25.00
C230 Paul Maholm 10.00 25.00
C231 Todd Wellemeyer 10.00 25.00
C232 Jesse Litsch 15.00 40.00
C233 Andy Sonnanstine 10.00 25.00
C234 Johnny Cueto 25.00 60.00
C235 Vicente Padilla 10.00 25.00
C236 Glen Perkins 10.00 25.00
C237 Brian Burres 10.00 25.00
C238 Jamey Wright 10.00 25.00
C239 Chase Headley 10.00 25.00
C240 Takashi Saito 10.00 25.00
C241 Skip Schumaker 10.00 25.00
C242 Curtis Granderson 15.00 40.00
C243 A.J. Pierzynski 10.00 25.00
C244 Jorge Cantu 10.00 25.00
C245 Maicer Izturis 10.00 25.00
C246 Kevin Mench 10.00 25.00
C247 Jason Kubel 10.00 25.00
C248 Rod Barajas 10.00 25.00
C249 Jed Lowrie 10.00 25.00
C250 Bobby Jenks 10.00 25.00
C251 Jonny Gomes 10.00 25.00
C252 Clete Thomas 15.00 40.00
C253 Eric Hinske 10.00 25.00
C254 Brett Gardner 25.00 60.00
C255 Denard Span 15.00 40.00
C256 Brian Anderson 10.00 25.00
C257 Troy Percival 10.00 25.00
C258 Darrell Rasner 10.00 25.00
C259 Willy Aybar 10.00 25.00
C260 John Bowker 10.00 25.00
C261 Marco Scutaro 15.00 40.00
C262 Adam Kennedy 10.00 25.00
C263 Nick Punto 10.00 25.00
C264 Mike Napoli 15.00 40.00
C265 Carlos Gonzalez 25.00 60.00
C266 Matt Macri 10.00 25.00
C267 Marcus Thames 10.00 25.00
C268 Ben Zobrist 15.00 40.00
C269 Mark Ellis 10.00 25.00
C270 Mike Aviles 15.00 40.00
C271 Angel Pagan 10.00 25.00
C272 Erick Aybar 10.00 25.00
C273 Todd Jones 10.00 25.00
C274 Brandon Boggs 15.00 40.00
C275 Mike Jacobs 10.00 25.00
C276 Mike Gonzalez 10.00 25.00
C277 Mike Lamb 10.00 25.00
C278 Robb Quinlan 10.00 25.00
C279 Salomon Torres 10.00 25.00
C280 Jose Castillo 10.00 25.00
C281 Damion Easley 10.00 25.00
C282 Jo-Jo Reyes 10.00 25.00
C283 Cody Ross 10.00 25.00
C284 Alexi Casilla 10.00 25.00
C285 Jerry Hairston 10.00 25.00
C286 Brandon Lyon 10.00 25.00
C287 Greg Dobbs 10.00 25.00
C288 Joel Pineiro 10.00 25.00
C289 Chris Davis 20.00 50.00
C290 Masahide Kobayashi 15.00 40.00
C291 Darin Erstad 10.00 25.00
C292 Matt Diaz 10.00 25.00
C293 Brian Schneider 10.00 25.00
C294 Gerald Laird 10.00 25.00
C295 Ben Francisco 10.00 25.00
C296 Brian Moehler 10.00 25.00
C297 Aaron Miles 10.00 25.00
C298 Max Scherzer 100.00 250.00
C299 C.J. Wilson 10.00 25.00
C300 Jay Bruce 30.00 80.00

2008 Topps Heritage Flashbacks

COMPLETE SET (10) 6.00 15.00
STATED ODDS 1:12 HOBBY

FB1 Mark Teixeira .75 2.00
FB2 Tim Lincecum .75 2.00
FB3 Jon Lester .75 2.00
FB4 Ken Griffey Jr. 2.50 6.00
FB5 Kosuke Fukudome 1.50 4.00
FB6 Albert Pujols 1.50 4.00
FB7 Ichiro Suzuki 1.50 4.00
FB8 Felix Hernandez .75 2.00
FB9 Carlos Delgado .50 1.25
FB10 Josh Hamilton .75 2.00

2008 Topps Heritage Advertising Panels

ISSUED AS A BOX TOPPER

1 Bronson Arroyo .60 1.50
J.R. Towles/B.J. Ryan
2 Willy Aybar .40 1.00
Darrell Rasner/Troy Percival HN
3 Lance Berkman .60 1.50
Jeff Francoeur/Hanley Ramirez
4 Yuniesky Betancourt .60 1.50
Tim Lincecum/Jason Kendall
5 Brandon Boggs .60 1.50
Todd Jones/Erick Aybar HN
6 Lance Broadway .60 1.50
Russ Ohlendorf/Matt Capps
7 Jay Bruce 4.00 10.00
C.J. Wilson/Max Scherzer HN
8 Emmanuel Burriss .60 1.50
Tyler Yates/Clayton Richard HN
9 Alexi Casilla .40 1.00
Jerry Hairston/Brandon Lyon HN
10 Jose Castillo .40 1.00
Salomon Torres/Robb Quinlan HN
11 Eric Chavez 1.00 2.50
Zack Greinke/Josh Willingham
12 Chad Cordero .60 1.50
Kenji Johjima/Alfonso Soriano
13 Joe Crede .40 1.00
Ryan Ludwick/Cristian Guzman HN
14 Chicago Cubs 1.25 3.00
Tadahito Iguchi/Mariano Rivera
15 Johnny Cueto 1.00 2.50
Andy Sonnanstine/Jesse Litsch HN
16 Jack Cust .60 1.50
Aaron Harang/Vladimir Guerrero
17 Carlos Delgado .60 1.50
Lance Broadway/Russ Ohlendorf
18 Ryan Dempster .40 1.00
Edinson Volquez/Justin Duchscherer HN
19 Greg Dobbs .75 2.00
Joel Pineiro/Chris Davis HN
20 Stephen Drew .40 1.00
Joe Nathan/Bronson Arroyo
21 Damion Easley .40 1.00
JoJo Reyes/Cody Ross HN
22 Jim Edmonds .60 1.50
Horatio Ramriez/Brian Bannister
23 Dana Eveland .40 1.00
Ryan Sweeney/Mike Pelfrey HN
24 Josh Fields .60 1.50
Emmanuel Burriss/Tyler Yates HN
25 Jeff Francoeur .60 1.50
Hanley Ramirez/Josh Barfield
26 Armando Galarraga .60 1.50
Wandy Rodriguez/Wily Mo Pena
27 Brett Gardner 1.00 2.50
Eric Hinske/Clete Thomas HN
28 Carlos Gomez 1.00 2.50
Sammy Sosa/Russ Martin
29 Mike Gonzalez .60 1.50
Mike Jacobs/Brandon Boggs HN
30 Zack Greinke 1.00 2.50
Josh Willingham/Armando Galarraga
31 Mark Grudzielanek .60 1.50
Jim Thome/Joe Koshansky
32 J.J. Hardy .60 1.50
Alex Rios/Johan Santana
33 Kevin Hart .60 1.50
Radhames Liz/Jack Wilson
34 Todd Helton 1.25 3.00
Kelly Johnson/Alex Rodriguez
35 Eric Hinske .60 1.50
Clete Thomas/Jonny Gomes HN
36 Tadahito Iguchi 1.25 3.00
Mariano Rivera/Brandon Webb
37 Akinori Iwamuri .60 1.50
Yuniesky Betancourt/Tim Lincecum
38 Randy Johnson 1.00 2.50
Brett Myers/Kenny Lofton BT
39 Andruw Jones .40 1.00
Stephen Drew/Joe Nathan
40 Todd Jones .40 1.00
Erick Aybar/Angel Pagan HN
41 Jair Jurrjens .40 1.00
John Danks/George Sherrill HN
42 Matt Kemp .75 2.00
Carlos Pena/Fausto Carmona
43 Adam Kennedy .60 1.50
Nick Punto/Mike Napoli HN
44 Gerald Laird UER .40 1.00
Brian Schneider/Matt Diaz HN
45 Cliff Lee .60 1.50
Mike Mussina/Ryan Dempster HN
46 Rhadhames Liz .40 1.00
Jack Wilson/Carlos Gomez
47 Greg Maddux 1.25 3.00
Carlos Ruiz/Nick Swisher
48 Sean Marshall .40 1.00
Craig Monroe/Aramis Ramirez
49 Victor Martinez .60 1.50
C.C. Sabathia/Carlos Delgado
50 Aaron Miles .40 1.00
Brian Moehler/Ben Francisco HN
51 Lastings Milledge .60 1.50
Dmitri Young/Ryan Zimmerman/Barry Zito
52 Bengie Molina .60 1.50
David Murphy/John Lackey
53 David Murphy .60 1.50
John Lackey/Buddy Carlyle
54 Mike Napoli 1.00 2.50
Carlos Gonzalez/Matt Macri HN
55 Dioner Navarro .40 1.00
Joe Crede/Ryan Ludwick HN
56 Russ Ohlendorf .60 1.50
Matt Capps/Chris Young
57 Scott Olsen .40 1.00
Manny Parra/Tim Redding HN
58 Manny Parra .40 1.00
Tim Redding/Paul Maholm HN
59 Hunter Pence .60 1.50
Carlos Guillen/David Weathers
60 Troy Percival .60 1.50
Brian Anderson/Denard Span HN
61 Glen Perkins 1.00 2.50
Vicente Padilla/Johnny Cueto HN
62 A.J. Pierzynski .40 1.00
Jorge Cantu/Matt Diaz HN
63 Joel Pineiro .75 2.00
Chris Davis/Masahide Kobayashi HN
64 Nick Punto 1.00 2.50
Mike Napoli/Carlos Gonzalez HN
65 Robb Quinlan .40 1.00
Mike Lamb/Mike Gonzalez HN
66 Hanley Ramirez .60 1.50
Josh Barfield/Chad Cordero
67 Horatio Ramirez 1.00 2.50
Brian Bannister/Manny Ramirez
68 Manny Ramirez 1.00 2.50
Randy Johnson/Brett Myers
69 Darrell Rasner .40 1.00
Troy Percival/Brian Anderson HN
70 Alex Rios .60 1.50
Johan Santana/Roy Halladay
71 Alex Rodriguez 1.25 3.00
Huston Street/Mark Grudzielanek
72 Carlos Ruiz .60 1.50
Nick Swisher/Kevin Hart
73 C.C. Sabathia .60 1.50
Carlos Delgado/Lance Broadway
74 Pablo Sandoval 1.50 4.00
Alex Romero/Ivan Ochoa HN
75 Johan Santana .60 1.50
Roy Halladay/Brad Wilkinson
76 Joe Saunders .60 1.50
Cliff Lee/Mike Mussina HN
77 Brian Schneider .40 1.00
Matt Diaz/Darin Erstad HN
78 Skip Schumaker .60 1.50
Curtis Granderson/A.J. Pierzynski HN
79 Marco Scutaro .60 1.50
Adam Kennedy/Nick Punto HN
80 George Sherrill .60 1.50
Joakim Soria/Miguel Tejada HN
81 James Shields .60 1.50
Nate McLouth/Rich Thompson
82 John Smoltz 1.00 2.50
Andruw Jones/Chipper Jones/Andruw Jones
83 Andy Sonnanstine .60 1.50

Jesse Litsch/Todd Wellemeyer HN
84 Sammy Sosa 1.00 2.50
Russ Martin/Mark Buehrle
85 Ryan Sweeney .60 1.50
Mike Pelfrey/Nick Blackburn HN
86 Nick Swisher .60 1.50
Kevin Hart/Rhadhames Liz
87 Mark Teixeira 1.00 2.50
John Smoltz/Andruw Jones/Chipper Jones
88 Marcus Thames .60 1.50
Ben Zobrist/Mark Ellis HN
89 Jim Thome .60 1.50
Joe Koshansky/Adrian Gonzalez
90 Salomon Torres .40 1.00
Rob Quinlan/Mike Lamb HN
91 J.R. Towles .60 1.50
B.J. Ryan/Roy Oswalt
92 Eugenio Velez .40 1.00
Akinori Iwamura/Yuniesky Betancourt
93 Edinson Volquez 1.00 2.50
Justin Duchscherer/Geovany Soto HN
94 Brad Wilkerson .40 1.00
Juan Pierre/Bengie Molina
95 Brian Wilson 1.25 3.00
Kerry Wood/Kosuke Fukudome HN
96 Jamey Wright .40 1.00
Brian Burres/Glen Perkins HN
97 Dmitri Young .60 1.50
Ryan Zimmerman/Barry Zito/Dmitri Young
98 Dmitri Young .40 1.00
Yovanni Gallardo/Chris Duncan
99 Barry Zito .60 1.50
Dmitri Young/Yovanni Gallardo
100 Ben Zobrist .60 1.50
Mark Ellis/Mike Aviles HN
101 C.J. Wilson 4.00 10.00
Max Scherzer/Aaron Miles
102 Chris Volstad .60 1.50
Josh Fields/Emmanuel Burriss
103 Joakim Soria .60 1.50
Miguel Tejada/Dioner Navarro
104 Greg Smith .40 1.00
Dana Eveland/Ryan Sweeney
105 Juan Pierre .40 1.00
Bengie Molina/David Murphy
106 Hiroki Kuroda 1.00 2.50
Greg Smith/Dana Eveland
107 Kelly Johnson 1.25 3.00
Alex Rodriguez/Huston Street
108 Carlos Gonzalez 1.00 2.50
Matt Macri/Marcus Thames

2008 Topps Heritage Baseball Flashbacks

COMPLETE SET (10) 5.00 12.00
STATED ODDS 1:12 HOBBY,1:12 RETAIL
BF1 Minnie Minoso .50 1.25
BF2 Luis Aparicio .75 2.00
BF3 Ernie Banks 1.25 3.00
BF4 Bill Mazeroski .75 2.00
BF5 Bob Gibson .75 2.00
BF6 Frank Robinson .75 2.00
BF7 Brooks Robinson .75 2.00
BF8 Mickey Mantle 2.00 5.00
BF9 Orlando Cepeda .75 2.00
BF10 Eddie Mathews 1.25 3.00

2008 Topps Heritage Clubhouse Collection Relics

GROUP A ODDS 1:4100 H,1:7400 R
GROUP B ODDS 1:18,000 H,1:7800 R
GROUP C ODDS 1:90 H,1:182 R
GROUP D ODDS 1:54 H,1:108 R
HN GROUP A ODDS 1:3600 HOBBY
HN GROUP B ODDS 1:74 HOBBY
HN GROUP C ODDS 1:55 HOBBY
NO HN GRP A PRICING AVAILABLE
AD Adam Dunn C 3.00 8.00
AG Alex Gordon HN C 4.00 10.00
AJ Andruw Jones C 3.00 8.00
AJ Andruw Jones HN B 3.00 8.00
AL Al Kaline HN A 50.00 120.00
AP Albert Pujols HN B 6.00 15.00
AR Aramis Ramirez C 3.00 8.00
AR Aramis Ramirez HN B 3.00 8.00
BA Bobby Abreu C 3.00 8.00
BD Blake DeWitt HN B 6.00 15.00
BG Bob Gibson A 50.00 120.00
BG Bob Gibson HN B 10.00 25.00
BM Bill Mazeroski HN B 10.00 25.00
BR Brooks Robinson HN B 10.00 25.00
BS Bill Skowron HN A 50.00 120.00
CAB Craig Biggio C 4.00 10.00
CB Carlos Beltran C 3.00 8.00
CB Carlos Beltran HN B 3.00 8.00
CC Carl Crawford C 3.00 8.00
CD Carlos Delgado C 3.00 8.00
CG Curtis Granderson HN C 3.00 8.00
CL Carlos Lee C 3.00 8.00
CL Carlos Lee HN B 3.00 8.00
DH Dan Haren HN C 3.00 8.00
DL Derrek Lee C 3.00 8.00
DL Derrek Lee HN B 3.00 8.00
DO David Ortiz C 4.00 10.00
DO David Ortiz HN B 4.00 10.00
DS Duke Snider HN A 50.00 120.00
DY Dmitri Young C 3.00 8.00
DY Dmitri Young HN B 3.00 8.00
EB Erik Bedard HN C 3.00 8.00
EC Eric Chavez C 3.00 8.00
FR Frank Robinson HN A 50.00 120.00
FT Frank Thomas C 4.00 10.00
FT Frank Thomas HN B 4.00 10.00
GA Garret Anderson D 3.00 8.00
HB Hank Blalock D 3.00 8.00
IR Ivan Rodriguez C 4.00 10.00
JB Jeremy Bonderman HN C 3.00 8.00
JD Johnny Damon C 3.00 8.00
JD Jermaine Dye HN C 3.00 8.00
JE Jim Edmonds D 3.00 8.00
JE Johnny Estrada HN C 3.00 8.00
JL Julio Lugo HN C 3.00 8.00
JP Jorge Posada C 4.00 10.00
JS John Smoltz D 4.00 10.00
JV Justin Verlander C 4.00 10.00
LA Luis Aparicio A 30.00 60.00
LB Lance Berkman D 3.00 8.00
MC Miguel Cabrera D 4.00 10.00
MM Minnie Minoso B 8.00 20.00
MM Mike Mussina D 3.00 8.00
MT Miguel Tejada D 3.00 8.00
MT Miguel Tejada HN B 3.00 8.00
NF Nellie Fox HN B 12.50 30.00
PM Pedro Martinez D 4.00 10.00
PM Pedro Martinez HN B 3.00 8.00
RH Ryan Howard D 5.00 12.00
RO Roy Oswalt D 3.00 8.00
RO Roy Oswalt HN B 3.00 8.00
RR Robin Roberts HN B 8.00 20.00
RS Richie Sexson D 3.00 8.00
RS Darrell Rasner HN B 3.00 8.00
RZ Ryan Zimmerman D 4.00 10.00
RZ Ryan Zimmerman HN B 3.00 8.00
SG Shawn Green C 3.00 8.00
ST Steve Pearce HN C 3.00 8.00
TH Todd Helton C 4.00 10.00
TKH Torii Hunter D 3.00 8.00
TLH Travis Hafner D 3.00 8.00
WM Bill Mazeroski A 20.00 50.00
YB Yogi Berra A 25.00 60.00

2008 Topps Heritage Clubhouse Collection Relics Autographs

STATED ODDS 1:6875 HOBBY
STATED ODDS 1:14,200 RETAIL
HN ODDS 1:1815 HOBBY
STATED PRINT RUN 25 SER.#'d SETS
NO PRICING DUE TO SCARCITY
EXCHANGE DEADLINE 2/28/2010
HN EXCH DEADLINE 11/30/2010

2008 Topps Heritage Clubhouse Collection Relics Dual

STATED ODDS 1:5582 H,1:11,000 R
HN STATED ODDS 1:1900 HOBBY
HN PRINT RUN 59 SER.#'d SETS
AK L.Aparicio/P.Konerko 30.00 60.00
BL E.Banks/D.Lee 30.00 60.00
CL Cepeda/Lewis HN 30.00 60.00
GE B.Gibson/J.Edmonds 30.00 60.00
KG Kaline/Granderson HN 30.00 60.00
MB B.Mazeroski/J.Bay 30.00 60.00
MH M.Minoso/T.Hafner 30.00 60.00
RB F.Robinson/Bruce HN 30.00 60.00
SK Snider/Kershaw HN 30.00 60.00
SR Skowron/Rasner HN 30.00 60.00

2008 Topps Heritage Dick Perez

COMPLETE SET (10) 30.00 60.00
THREE PER $9.99 WALMART BOX
SIX PER $19.99 WALMART BOX
HDP1 Manny Ramirez 1.25 3.00
HDP2 Cameron Maybin .50 1.25
HDP3 Ryan Howard .75 2.00
HDP4 David Ortiz 1.25 3.00
HDP5 Tim Lincecum .75 2.00
HDP6 David Wright .75 2.00
HDP7 Mickey Mantle 2.50 6.00
HDP8 Joba Chamberlain .50 1.25
HDP9 Ichiro Suzuki 1.50 4.00
HDP10 Prince Fielder .75 2.00

2008 Topps Heritage Flashbacks Autographs

STATED ODDS 1:14,900 HOBBY
STATED ODDS 1:20,000 RETAIL
STATED PRINT RUN 25 SER.#'d SETS
NO PRICING DUE TO SCARCITY
EXCHANGE DEADLINE 2/28/10

2008 Topps Heritage Flashbacks Seat Relics

STATED ODDS 1:162 H,1:327 R
HN ODDS 1:3175 HOBBY
HN PRINT RUN 59 SER.#'d SETS
BG Bob Gibson 10.00 25.00
BR Brooks Robinson 10.00 25.00
DE Dwight D. Eisenhower HN 30.00 60.00
EB Ernie Banks 10.00 25.00
EM Eddie Mathews 10.00 25.00
FR Frank Robinson 8.00 20.00
LA Luis Aparicio 8.00 20.00
MIM Minnie Minoso 8.00 20.00
MM Mickey Mantle 12.00 30.00
MO Motown HN 30.00 60.00
NK Nikita Khrushchev HN 30.00 60.00
OC Orlando Cepeda 8.00 20.00
WM Bill Mazeroski 10.00 25.00

2008 Topps Heritage High Numbers Then and Now

COMPLETE SET (10) 6.00 15.00
STATED ODDS 1:12 HOBBY
TN1 Ernie Banks/Jimmy Rollins 1.25 3.00
TN2 N.Fox/A.Rodriguez 1.50 4.00
TN3 Larry Sherry/Mike Lowell .50 1.25
TN4 W.McCovey/R.Braun .75 2.00
TN5 B.Allison/D.Pedroia 1.25 3.00
TN6 Del Crandall/Russ Martin .50 1.25
TN7 Luis Aparicio/Orlando Cabrera .75 2.00
TN8 E.Wynn/A.Rodriguez 1.50 4.00
TN9 Early Wynn/Jake Peavy .75 2.00
TN10 Sam Jones/CC Sabathia .75 2.00

2008 Topps Heritage National Convention

1 Ted Williams 2.50 6.00
145 Bob Gibson .75 2.00
150 Mickey Mantle 4.00 10.00
310 Ernie Banks 1.25 3.00
496 Mickey Mantle 4.00 10.00

2008 Topps Heritage New Age Performers

COMPLETE SET (15) 10.00 25.00
STATED ODDS 1:15 HOBBY,1:15 RETAIL
NAP1 Magglio Ordonez .60 1.50
NAP2 Ichiro Suzuki 1.25 3.00
NAP3 Matt Holliday 1.00 2.50
NAP4 Prince Fielder .60 1.50
NAP5 David Wright .60 1.50
NAP6 Jake Peavy .40 1.00
NAP7 Alex Rodriguez 1.25 3.00
NAP8 John Lackey .60 1.50
NAP9 Vladimir Guerrero .60 1.50
NAP10 Ryan Howard .60 1.50
NAP11 Brandon Webb .60 1.50
NAP12 Manny Ramirez 1.00 2.50
NAP13 Josh Beckett .40 1.00
NAP14 Jimmy Rollins .60 1.50
NAP15 David Ortiz 1.00 2.50

2008 Topps Heritage News Flashbacks

COMPLETE SET (10) 4.00 10.00
COMMON CARD .60 1.50
STATED ODDS 1:12 HOBBY,1:12 RETAIL

2008 Topps Heritage Real One Autographs

STATED ODDS 1:247 H,1:495 R
HN ODDS 1:110 HOBBY
EXCHANGE DEADLINE 02/28/2010
HN EXCH DEADLINE 11/30/2010
AJ Al Jackson HN 15.00 40.00
AK Al Kaline HN 50.00 120.00
AR Aramis Ramirez 20.00 50.00
BB Bob Blaylock 10.00 25.00
BM Bob Martyn 10.00 25.00
BM Brian McCann HN 10.00 25.00
BMS Bill Skowron HN 10.00 25.00
BR Bill Renna 10.00 25.00
BS Bob Smith 10.00 25.00
BS Barney Schultz HN 15.00 40.00
BSP Bob Speake 10.00 25.00
CE Carl Erskine 10.00 25.00
CE Chuck Essegian HN 10.00 25.00
CG Curtis Granderson HN 15.00 40.00
CK Chick King 10.00 25.00
CK Clayton Kershaw HN 600.00 1000.00
DP Dustin Pedroia HN 40.00 80.00
DR Dusty Rhodes HN 12.50 30.00
DS Duke Snider HN 50.00 100.00
FL Fred Lewis HN 10.00 25.00
FR Frank Robinson HN 20.00 50.00
FS Freddy Sanchez 10.00 25.00
GEZ Gus Zernial 10.00 25.00
GS Geovany Soto HN 10.00 25.00
GZ George Zuverink 10.00 25.00
HL Hector Lopez HN 20.00 50.00
HP Herb Plews 10.00 25.00
JAB Jay Bruce HN 12.50 30.00
JB Jim Bolger 12.50 30.00
JB Jim Brosnan HN 10.00 25.00
JC Joba Chamberlain 10.00 25.00
JF Jack Fisher HN 10.00 25.00
JH Jay Hook HN 10.00 25.00
JK Jim Kaat HN 15.00 40.00
JO Johnny O'Brien 20.00 50.00
JP J.W. Porter 10.00 25.00
KL Ken Lehman 10.00 25.00
LA Luis Aparicio 20.00 50.00
LM Les Moss 15.00 40.00
LT Lee Tate 10.00 25.00
MB Mike Baxes 10.00 25.00
MIM Minnie Minoso 30.00 60.00
MM Morrie Martin 10.00 25.00
MW Maury Wills HN 10.00 25.00
OC Orlando Cepeda HN 25.00 60.00
PC Phil Clark 10.00 25.00
PG Pumpsie Green HN 12.50 30.00
RC Roger Craig HN 10.00 25.00
RH Russ Heman 10.00 25.00
RJ Randy Jackson 10.00 25.00
SP Scott Podsednik 10.00 25.00
TC Tom Carroll 10.00 25.00
TD Tommy Davis HN 15.00 40.00
TK Ted Kazanski 15.00 40.00
TQ Tom Qualters 10.00 25.00
VV Vito Valentinetti 10.00 25.00
WM Bill Mazeroski 30.00 60.00
YB Yogi Berra 60.00 150.00

2008 Topps Heritage Real One Autographs Red Ink

*RED INK: .6X TO 1.5X BASIC
STATED ODDS 1:635 H,1:1650 R
HN ODDS 1:439 HOBBY
STATED PRINT RUN 59 SERIAL #'d SETS
RED INK ALSO CALLED SPECIAL EDITION
EXCHANGE DEADLINE 02/28/2010
HN EXCH DEADLINE 11/30/2010
CK Clayton Kershaw HN 1200.00 1600.00
DS Duke Snider HN 100.00 200.00
GS Geovany Soto HN 15.00 40.00
MIM Minnie Minoso 60.00 120.00
WM Bill Mazeroski 125.00 250.00

2008 Topps Heritage Rookie Performers

COMPLETE SET (15) 12.50 30.00
STATED ODDS 1:12 HOBBY
RP1 Clayton Kershaw 15.00 40.00
RP2 Mike Aviles .75 2.00
RP3 Armando Galarraga .75 2.00
RP4 Joey Votto 4.00 10.00
RP5 Kosuke Fukudome 1.50 4.00
RP6 Chris Davis 1.00 2.50
RP7 Jeff Samardzija 1.50 4.00
RP8 Carlos Gonzalez 1.25 3.00
RP9 Max Scherzer 5.00 12.00
RP10 Evan Longoria 2.50 6.00
RP11 Johnny Cueto 1.25 3.00
RP12 Hiroki Kuroda 1.25 3.00
RP13 John Bowker .50 1.25
RP14 Justin Masterson 1.25 3.00
RP15 Jay Bruce 1.50 4.00

2008 Topps Heritage T205 Mini

THREE PER $9.99 TARGET BOX
SIX PER $19.99 TARGET BOX
HTCP1 Albert Pujols 2.50 6.00
HTCP2 Clay Buchholz 3.00 8.00
HTCP3 Matt Holliday 2.00 5.00
HTCP4 Luke Hochevar 1.25 3.00
HTCP5 Alex Rodriguez 2.50 6.00
HTCP6 Joey Votto 6.00 15.00
HTCP7 Chin-Lung Hu .75 2.00
HTCP8 Ryan Braun 1.25 3.00
HTCP9 Joba Chamberlain .75 2.00
HTCP10 Ryan Howard 1.25 3.00
HTCP11 Ichiro Suzuki 2.50 6.00
HTCP12 Steve Pearce 4.00 10.00
HTCP13 Vladimir Guerrero 1.25 3.00
HTCP14 Wladimir Balentien .75 2.00
HTCP15 David Ortiz 2.00 5.00

2008 Topps Heritage Then and Now

COMPLETE SET (10) 6.00 15.00
STATED ODDS 1:15 HOBBY,1:15 RETAIL
TN1 A.Rodriguez/E.Mathews 1.50 4.00
TN2 A.Rodriguez/E.Banks 1.50 4.00
TN3 M.Ordonez/O.Cepeda .75 2.00
TN4 J.Reyes/L.Aparicio .75 2.00
TN5 D.Ortiz/M.Mantle 2.50 6.00
TN6 E.Bedard/J.Podres .50 1.25
TN7 J.Beckett/E.Wynn .75 2.00
TN8 I.Suzuki/M.Minoso 1.50 4.00
TN9 D.Ortiz/F.Robinson 1.25 3.00
TN10 J.Peavy/D.Drysdale .75 2.00

2009 Topps Heritage

COMPLETE SET (733)
COMP.LO SET w/o VAR (425) 30.00 60.00
COMP.HI SET w/o VAR (220) 90.00 150.00
COMP.HI SET w/o SP's (185) 15.00 40.00
COMMON CARD (1-733) .15 .40
COMMON ROOKIE (1-733) .40 1.00
COMMON SP (426-500/586-720) 2.50 6.00
SP ODDS 1:3 HOBBY
1 Mark Buehrle .25 .60
2 Nyjer Morgan .15 .40
3 Casey Kotchman .15 .40
4 Edinson Volquez .15 .40
5 Andre Ethier .25 .60
6 Brandon Inge .15 .40
7 T.Lincecum/B.Bochy .25 .60
8 Gil Meche .15 .40
9 Brad Hawpe .15 .40
10 Hanley Ramirez .25 .60
11 Ross Gload .15 .40
12 Jeremy Guthrie .15 .40
13 Garret Anderson .15 .40
14 Jeremy Sowers .15 .40
15a Dustin Pedroia .40 1.00
15b D.Pedroia SP VAR 60.00 120.00
16 Chris Perez .15 .40
17 Adam Lind .15 .40
18 Los Angeles Dodgers TC .15 .40
19 Stephen Drew .15 .40
20 Matt Capps .15 .40
21 Mike Napoli .15 .40
22 Khalil Greene .15 .40
23 Andy Sonnanstine .15 .40
24 Marco Scutaro .25 .60
25 Paul Konerko .25 .60
26 Miguel Tejada .25 .60
27 Nick Blackburn .15 .40
28 Nick Markakis .30 .75
29 Johan Santana .25 .60
30 Grady Sizemore .25 .60
31 Raul Ibanez .25 .60
32 Jay Bruce/Johnny Cueto .25 .60
33 Randy Johnson .40 1.00
34 Ian Kinsler .25 .60
35 Andy Pettitte .25 .60
36 Lyle Overbay .15 .40
37 Jeff Francoeur .25 .60
38 Justin Duchscherer .15 .40
39 Mike Cameron .15 .40
40 Ryan Ludwick .25 .60
41 Dave Bush .15 .40
42 Pablo Sandoval (RC) .75 2.00
43 Washington Nationals TC .15 .40
44 Dana Eveland .15 .40
45 Jeff Keppinger .15 .40
46 Brandon Backe .15 .40
47 Ryan Theriot .15 .40
48 Vernon Wells .15 .40
49 Doug Davis .15 .40
50 Curtis Granderson .30 .75
51 Aaron Laffey .15 .40
52 Chris Young .15 .40
53 Adam Jones .25 .60
54 Jonathan Papelbon .25 .60
55 Nate McLouth .15 .40
56 Hunter Pence .25 .60
57 Scot Shields/Francisco Rodriguez .25 .60
58a Conor Jackson ARI .15 .40
58b C.Jackson TB SP 15.00 40.00
59 John Maine .15 .40
60 Ramon Hernandez .15 .40
61 Jorge De La Rosa .15 .40
62 Greg Maddux .50 1.25
63 Carlos Beltran .25 .60
64 Matt Harrison (RC) .40 1.00
65 Ivan Rodriguez .25 .60
66 Jesse Litsch .15 .40
67 Omar Vizquel .25 .60
68 Edwin Jackson .15 .40
69 Ray Durham .15 .40
70a Tom Glavine .25 .60
70b Tom Glavine UER SP 8.00 20.00
71 Darin Erstad .15 .40
72 Detroit Tigers TC .15 .40
73 David Price RC .75 2.00
74 Marlon Byrd .15 .40
75 Ryan Garko .15 .40
76 Jered Weaver .25 .60
77 Kelly Shoppach .15 .40
78 Joe Saunders .15 .40
79 Carlos Pena .25 .60
80 Brian Wilson .40 1.00
81 Carlos Gonzalez .25 .60
82 Scott Baker .15 .40
83a Derek Jeter 1.00 2.50
83b D.Jeter SP VAR 100.00 200.00
84 Yadier Molina .50 1.25
85 Justin Verlander .40 1.00
86 Jose Lopez .15 .40
87 Jarrod Washburn .15 .40
88 Russell Martin .15 .40
89 Garrett Olson .15 .40
90 Erick Aybar .15 .40
91 Kevin Millwood .15 .40
92 Jose Guillen .15 .40
93 Rickie Weeks .15 .40
94 Yovani Gallardo .15 .40
95 Aramis Ramirez .15 .40
96 Phil Hughes .15 .40
97 Kevin Kouzmanoff .15 .40
98 Shaun Marcum .15 .40
99 Lastings Milledge .15 .40
100 Jair Jurrjens .15 .40
101 Gio Gonzalez .25 .60
102a Adrian Gonzalez .30 .75
102b A.Gonzalez Rgr Logo 20.00 50.00
103 Brad Lidge .15 .40
104 Chris Davis .25 .60
105 Brad Penny .15 .40
106 David Eckstein .15 .40
107 Jo-Jo Reyes .15 .40
108 John Buck .15 .40
109 Delmon Young .25 .60
110 Johnny Cueto .25 .60
111 Kevin Youkilis .15 .40
112 Scott Lewis (RC) .40 1.00
113 Brandon Moss .15 .40
114 Alexi Casilla .15 .40
115 Jonathan Papelbon/Tim Wakefield .25 .60
116 Emil Brown .15 .40
117 Michael Bowden (RC) .40 1.00
118 Chris Lambert (RC) .40 1.00
119 Wilkin Castillo RC .40 1.00
120 Fernando Perez (RC) .40 1.00
121 Angel Salome (RC) .40 1.00
122 Dexter Fowler (RC) .60 1.50
123 Will Venable RC .40 1.00
124 Jason Motte (RC) .60 1.50
125 Jesus Delgado RC .60 1.50
126 Alfredo Simon (RC) .40 1.00
127 Gaby Sanchez RC .60 1.50
128 Scott Elbert (RC) .40 1.00
129 James Parr (RC) .40 1.00
130 Greg Golson (RC) .40 1.00
131 Jonathon Niese RC .60 1.50
132 Mat Gamel RC 1.00 2.50
133 Luis Cruz RC .40 1.00
134 Phil Coke RC .60 1.50
135 Devon Lowery (RC) .40 1.00
136 Matt Tuiasosopo (RC) .40 1.00
137 Kila Ka'aihue (RC) .60 1.50
138 Andrew Carpenter RC .60 1.50
139 Jensen Lewis (RC) .40 1.00
140 Lou Marson (RC) .40 1.00
141 Wade LeBlanc RC .60 1.50
142 Juan Miranda RC .60 1.50
143 Alcides Escobar RC .60 1.50
144 Matt Antonelli RC .60 1.50
145 Jesse Chavez RC .40 1.00
146 Ramon Ramirez (RC) .40 1.00
147 Aaron Cunningham RC .40 1.00
148 Travis Snider RC .60 1.50
149 Adam Dunn .25 .60
150 John Danks .15 .40
151 San Francisco Giants TC .15 .40
152 Jorge Cantu .15 .40
153 Jacoby Ellsbury .30 .75
154 Rich Aurilia .15 .40
155 Jeff Kent .15 .40
156 Salomon Torres .15 .40
157 Juan Uribe .15 .40
158 Gregor Blanco .15 .40
159 Shin-Soo Choo .25 .60
160 D.Wright/A.Rodriguez AS .50 1.25
161 Jose Valverde .15 .40
162 B.J. Upton .25 .60
163 Johnny Damon .25 .60
164 Cincinnati Reds TC .15 .40
165 Tim Lincecum .25 .60
166 Carl Crawford .25 .60
167 Jeff Mathis .15 .40
168 Felipe Lopez .15 .40
169 Joe Nathan .15 .40
170 Brian McCann .25 .60
171 Matt Joyce .15 .40
172 Cameron Maybin .15 .40
173 Brandon Phillips .15 .40
174 Cleveland Indians TC .15 .40
175 Tim Redding .15 .40
176 Corey Patterson .15 .40
177 Joakim Soria .15 .40
178 Jhonny Peralta .15 .40
179 Daniel Murphy RC 1.50 4.00
180 Ryan Church .15 .40
181 Josh Johnson .25 .60
182 Carlos Zambrano .25 .60
183 Pittsburgh Pirates TC .15 .40
184 Boston Red Sox TC .25 .60
185 Kyle Kendrick .15 .40
186 Joel Zumaya .15 .40
187 Bronson Arroyo .15 .40
188 Joey Gathright .15 .40
189 Mike Gonzalez .15 .40
190 Luke Scott .15 .40
191 Jonathan Broxton .15 .40
192 Jeff Baker .15 .40
193 Brian Fuentes .15 .40
194 Pat Burrell .15 .40
195 Ryan Franklin .15 .40
196 Alex Gordon .25 .60
197 Orlando Hudson .15 .40
198 Chris Dickerson .15 .40
199 David Purcey .15 .40
200 Ken Griffey Jr. .75 2.00
201 Chad Tracy .15 .40
202 Troy Percival .15 .40
203 Chris Iannetta .15 .40
204 Baltimore Orioles TC .15 .40
205 Yunel Escobar .15 .40
206 Dan Haren .15 .40
207 Aubrey Huff .15 .40
208 Chicago White Sox TC .15 .40
209 Randy Wolf .15 .40
210 Ryan Zimmerman .25 .60
211 Manny Parra .15 .40
212 Manny Acta MG .15 .40
213 Dusty Baker MG .15 .40
214 Bruce Bochy MG .15 .40
215 Bobby Cox MG .15 .40
216 Terry Francona MG .15 .40
217 Joe Girardi MG .25 .60
218 Ozzie Guillen MG .15 .40
219 Bob Geren MG .15 .40
220 Tony La Russa MG .25 .60
221 Jim Leyland MG .15 .40
222 Charlie Manuel MG .15 .40
223 Lou Piniella MG .15 .40
224 John Russell MG .15 .40
225 Joe Torre MG .25 .60
226 Dave Trembley MG .15 .40
227 Eric Wedge MG .15 .40
228 Jeff Suppan .15 .40
229 Kaz Matsui .15 .40
230 Beckett/Lester/Matsuzaka .25 .60
231 Mark Reynolds .15 .40
232 Jay Payton .15 .40
233 Kerry Wood .15 .40
234 Juan Pierre .15 .40
235 Ryan Freel .15 .40
236 Ryan Feierabend .15 .40
237 Xavier Nady .15 .40
238 Ronny Paulino .15 .40
239 A.J. Burnett .15 .40
240 Orlando Cabrera .15 .40
241 Corey Hart .15 .40
242 St. Louis Cardinals TC .15 .40
243 Andy Marte .15 .40
244 Trevor Hoffman .25 .60
245 Carlos Guillen .15 .40
246 Brandon Jones .15 .40
247 Hideki Matsui .40 1.00
248 Henry Blanco .15 .40
249 Jon Lester .25 .60
250a Albert Pujols .50 1.25
250b A.Pujols SP VAR 100.00 200.00
251 Manny Ramirez .40 1.00
252 Brian Bannister .15 .40
253 Alex Cintron .15 .40
254 Brandon Lyon .15 .40
255 Blake DeWitt .15 .40
256 Luis Castillo .15 .40
257 Mark Teixeira .25 .60
258 Jack Wilson .15 .40
259 Kosuke Fukudome .25 .60
260 Manny Ramirez/Andre Ethier .40 1.00
261 Scott Kazmir .15 .40
262 Mark Teahen .15 .40
263 Dioner Navarro .15 .40
264 Cole Hamels .30 .75
265 Justin Upton .25 .60
266 Ricky Nolasco .15 .40
267 Hank Blalock .15 .40
268 John Lackey .25 .60
269 Jeremy Hermida .15 .40
270 Chien-Ming Wang .25 .60
271 Lance Berkman .25 .60
272 Scott Olsen .15 .40
273 Alex Rios .15 .40
274 Matt Garza .15 .40
275 Skip Schumaker .15 .40
276 Greg Smith .15 .40
277 Bobby Crosby .15 .40
278 Hiroki Kuroda .15 .40
279 Gary Matthews .15 .40
280 Tim Wakefield .25 .60
281 Mike Jacobs .15 .40
282 Chris Volstad .15 .40
283 Jeff Clement .15 .40
284 Max Scherzer .40 1.00
285 Chase Headley .15 .40
286 Francisco Rodriguez .25 .60
287 Moises Alou .15 .40
288 Jeff Francis .15 .40
289 Carlos Delgado .15 .40
290 Jose Reyes .25 .60
291 Ubaldo Jimenez .15 .40
292 Kelly Shoppach/Victor Martinez .25 .60
293 Joe Blanton .15 .40
294 Mark DeRosa .25 .60
295 Casey Blake .15 .40
296 Mike Pelfrey .15 .40
297 Aaron Boone .25 .60
298 Aaron Cook .15 .40
299 Daric Barton .15 .40
300 Ryan Howard .30 .75
301 Ty Wigginton .25 .60
302 Philadelphia Phillies TC .15 .40
303 Barry Zito .25 .60
304 Jake Peavy .15 .40
305 Alfonso Soriano .25 .60
306 Scott Linebrink .15 .40
307 Torii Hunter .15 .40
308 Jason Giambi .40 1.00
309 Ryan Sweeney .15 .40
310 Mike Lowell .15 .40
311 Jason Marquis .15 .40
312 Aaron Rowand .15 .40
313 Brandon Morrow .15 .40
314 Edgar Renteria .15 .40
315 Mariano Rivera .50 1.25
316 Wilson Betemit .15 .40
317 Joey Votto .40 1.00
318 Gavin Floyd .25 .60
319 Mike Aviles .15 .40
320 Jay Bruce .25 .60
321 Denard Span .15 .40
322 David Murphy .15 .40
323 Geovany Soto .25 .60
324 John Lannan .15 .40
325 Brad Ziegler .15 .40
326 Ichiro Suzuki .50 1.25
327 Kyle Lohse .15 .40
328 Jesus Flores .15 .40
329 Edwin Encarnacion .15 .40
330 Franklin Gutierrez .15 .40
331 Troy Glaus .15 .40
332 David Ortiz .40 1.00
333 Anibal Sanchez .15 .40
334 Jimmy Rollins .25 .60
335 Kelly Johnson .15 .40
336 Paul Byrd .15 .40
337 Akinori Iwamura .15 .40
338 Milton Bradley .15 .40
339 Miguel Olivo .15 .40
340 Ian Snell .15 .40
341 Vladimir Guerrero .25 .60
342 Asdrubal Cabrera .25 .60
343 Clayton Kershaw .60 1.50
344 Rafael Furcal .15 .40
345 Aaron Harang .15 .40
346a Fred Lewis .15 .40
346b F.Lewis UER Winn SP 15.00 40.00
347 Jack Cust .15 .40
348 Todd Helton .25 .60
349 Steve Pearce .40 1.00
350 Javier Vazquez .15 .40
351 Ben Sheets .15 .40
352 Joey Votto/Edwin Encarnacion
Jay Bruce .40 1.00
353 Luke Hochevar .15 .40
354 Chris Snyder .15 .40
355 Rick Ankiel .15 .40
356 Emmanuel Burriss .15 .40
357 Vicente Padilla .15 .40
358 Yuniesky Betancourt .15 .40
359 Willy Taveras .15 .40
360 Gavin Floyd .15 .40
361 Gerald Laird .15 .40
362 Roy Oswalt .25 .60
363 Coco Crisp .15 .40
364 Felix Hernandez .25 .60
365 Carlos Quentin .15 .40
366 Ervin Santana .15 .40
367 David DeJesus .15 .40
368 Aaron Miles .15 .40
369 B.J. Ryan .15 .40
370 Jason Giambi .15 .40
371 J.J. Putz .15 .40
372 Brian Schneider .15 .40
373 Andy LaRoche .15 .40
374 Tim Hudson .25 .60
375 Garrett Atkins .15 .40
376 James Shields .15 .40
377 Alex Rodriguez .50 1.25
378 J.J. Hardy .15 .40
379 Michael Young .15 .40
380 Prince Fielder .25 .60
381 Atlanta Braves TC .15 .40
382 Chone Figgins .15 .40
383 David Wright .30 .75
384 Brian Giles .15 .40
385 Chase Utley WS .25 .60
386 Eric Bruntlett WS .15 .40
387 Carlos Ruiz WS .15 .40
388 Ryan Howard WS .30 .75
389 Jayson Werth WS .25 .60
390 B.J. Upton WS .25 .60
391 Brad Lidge .15 .40
392 Chad Cordero .15 .40
393 Ryan Doumit .15 .40
394 James Loney .15 .40
395 George Sherrill .15 .40
396 Gary Sheffield .15 .40
397 Chicago Cubs TC .15 .40
398 Rich Harden .15 .40
399 Kazmir/Price/Shields .30 .75
400 Magglio Ordonez .25 .60
401 Dan Uggla .15 .40
402 Adam LaRoche .15 .40
403 Taylor Teagarden .15 .40
404 Chris Young .15 .40
405 Robinson Cano .25 .60
406 Dustin McGowan .15 .40
407a Randy Winn .15 .40
407b Winn UER Lewis SP 15.00 40.00
408 Carlos Lee .15 .40
409 Kurt Suzuki .15 .40
410 Matt Cain .25 .60
411 Paul Bako .15 .40
412 Ted Lilly .15 .40
413 Kansas City Royals TC .15 .40
414 Miguel Cabrera .40 1.00
415 Jayson Werth .25 .60
416 J.C. Romero .15 .40
417 Martin Prado .15 .40
418 Armando Galarraga .15 .40
419 Brian Roberts .15 .40
420 Chipper Jones .40 1.00
421 Bengie Molina .15 .40
422 Matt Kemp .30 .75
423 Brian Buscher .15 .40
424 Erik Bedard .15 .40
425 Chad Billingsley .25 .60
426 Scott Rolen SP 2.00 5.00
427 Ben Francisco SP 2.50 6.00
428 Jermaine Dye SP 2.50 6.00
429 Dustin Pedroia 3.00 8.00
Ichiro Suzuki SP
430 Kevin Slowey SP 3.00 8.00
431 Jason Bartlett SP 2.50 6.00
432 Glen Perkins SP 2.50 6.00
433 Carlos Gomez SP 2.50 6.00
434 Jon Garland SP 2.50 6.00
435 Joe Crede SP 4.00 10.00
436 Billy Butler SP 2.50 6.00
437 Zach Duke SP 2.50 6.00
438 Chris Coste SP 2.50 6.00
439 Daisuke Matsuzaka SP 1.50 4.00
440 Elijah Dukes SP 2.50 6.00
441 Fausto Carmona SP 2.50 6.00
442 Joe Mauer SP 4.00 10.00
443 Marcus Thames SP 2.50 6.00
444 Mike Fontenot SP 2.50 6.00
445a J.Smoltz ATL SP 3.00 8.00
445b J.Smoltz BOS SP 30.00 60.00
446 Pedro Martinez SP 3.00 8.00
447 Adrian Beltre SP 6.00 15.00
448 Kevin Millar SP 2.50 6.00
449 Nick Swisher SP 4.00 10.00
450 Justin Morneau SP 3.00 8.00
451 Shane Victorino SP 2.50 6.00
452 Placido Polanco SP 2.50 6.00
453 Ryan Dempster SP 2.50 6.00
454 Frank Thomas SP 3.00 8.00
455 Dave Jauss/Juan Samuel
John Shelby CO SP 2.50 6.00
456 Brad Mills/John Farrell
Dave Magadan CO SP 2.50 6.00
457 Alan Trammell/Larry Rothschild
Matt Sinatro CO SP 4.00 10.00
458 Joey Cora/Harold Baines
Jeff Cox CO SP 4.00 10.00
459 Chris Speier/Billy Hatcher
Dick Pole CO SP 2.50 6.00
460 Jeff Datz/Luis Rivera/Carl Willis
Joel Skinner CO SP 2.50 6.00
461 Lloyd McClendon/Andy Van Slyke
Rafael Belliard CO SP 2.50 6.00
462 Jim Hickey/Steve Henderson
Tom Foley CO SP 2.50 6.00

463 Larry Bowa/Rick Honeycutt
Mariano Duncan/Bob Schaefer CO SP 2.50 6.00
464 Roger McDowell/Terry Pendleton
Chino Cadahia/Glenn Hubbard CO SP 2.50 6.00
465 Rob Thomson/Tony Pena/Kevin Long
Dave Eiland CO SP 2.50 6.00
466 Milt Thompson/Rich Dubee
Davey Lopes CO SP 2.50 6.00
467 Tony Beasley/Joe Kerrigan
Don Long CO SP 2.50 6.00
468 Dave Duncan/Hal McRae
Jose Oquendo/Dave McKay CO SP 2.50 6.00
469 Sandy Alomar Sr./Howard Johnson
Dan Warthen CO SP 2.50 6.00
470 Randy St. Claire/Marquis Grissom
Jim Riggleman CO SP 2.50 6.00
471 Brad Ausmus SP 2.50 6.00
472 Melvin Mora SP 2.50 6.00
473 Austin Kearns SP 2.50 6.00
474 Josh Willingham SP 4.00 10.00
475 Derek Lowe SP 2.50 6.00
476 Nick Punto SP 2.50 6.00
477 A.J. Pierzynski SP 2.50 6.00
478 Troy Tulowitzki SP 5.00 12.00
479 CC Sabathia SP 3.00 8.00
480 Jorge Posada SP 3.00 8.00
481 Kevin Youkilis AS SP 2.00 5.00
482 Lance Berkman AS SP 3.00 8.00
483 Dustin Pedroia AS SP 3.00 8.00
484 Chase Utley AS SP 2.00 5.00
485 Alex Rodriguez AS SP 3.00 8.00
486 Chipper Jones AS SP 3.00 8.00
487 Derek Jeter AS SP 5.00 12.00
488a H.Ramirez AS FLA SP 2.00 5.00
488b H.Ramirez AS BOS SP 10.00 25.00
489 Josh Hamilton AS SP 2.00 5.00
490 Ryan Braun AS SP 2.00 5.00
491 Manny Ramirez AS SP 3.00 8.00
492 Kosuke Fukudome AS SP 2.00 5.00
493 Ichiro Suzuki AS SP 3.00 8.00
494 Matt Holliday AS SP 5.00 12.00
495 Joe Mauer AS SP 4.00 10.00
496 Geovany Soto AS SP 3.00 8.00
497 Roy Halladay AS SP 4.00 10.00
498 Ben Sheets AS SP 2.50 6.00
499 Cliff Lee AS SP 3.00 8.00
500 Billy Wagner AS SP 2.50 6.00
501 Shane Robinson RC .40 1.00
502 Mat Latos RC 1.25 3.00
503 Aaron Poreda RC .40 1.00
504 Takashi Saito .15 .40
505 Adam Everett .15 .40
506 Adam Kennedy .15 .40
507 John Smoltz .40 1.00
508 Alex Cora .25 .60
509 Alfredo Aceves .25 .60
510 Alfredo Figaro RC .40 1.00
511 Andrew Bailey RC 1.00 2.50
512 Jhoulys Chacin RC .60 1.50
513 Andruw Jones .15 .40
514 Anthony Swarzak (RC) .40 1.00
515 Antonio Bastardo RC .40 1.00
516 Bartolo Colon .15 .40
517 Michael Saunders RC 1.00 2.50
518 Blake Hawksworth (RC) .40 1.00
519 Bud Norris RC .40 1.00
520 Bobby Scales RC .60 1.50
521 Nick Evans .15 .40
522 Brad Bergensen (RC) .40 1.00
524 Brad Penny .15 .40
525 Braden Looper .15 .40
526 Brandon Lyon .15 .40
527 Brandon Wood .15 .40
528 Aaron Bates RC .40 1.00
529 Brett Cecil RC .40 1.00
530 Brett Gardner .25 .60
531 Brett Hayes (RC) .40 1.00
532 C.J. Wilson .15 .40
533 Carl Pavano .15 .40
534 Cesar Izturis .15 .40
535 Chad Qualls .15 .40
536 Marc Rzepczynski RC .60 1.50
537 Chris Gimenez RC .40 1.00
538 Chris Jakubauskas RC .60 1.50
539 Chris Perez .15 .40
540 Clay Zavada RC .60 1.50
541 Clayton Mortensen RC .40 1.00
542 Clayton Richard .15 .40
543 Cliff Floyd .15 .40
544 Coco Crisp .15 .40
545a Neftali Feliz RC .60 1.50
545b N.Feliz SP VAR 125.00 250.00
546 Craig Counsell .15 .40
547 Craig Stammen RC .40 1.00
548 Cristian Guzman .15 .40
549 Dallas Braden .15 .40
550 Daniel Bard RC .40 1.00
551 Jack Wilson .15 .40
552 Daniel Schlereth RC .40 1.00
553 David Aardsma .15 .40
554 David Eckstein .15 .40
555 David Freese RC 1.25 3.00
556 David Hernandez RC .40 1.00
557 David Huff RC .40 1.00
558 David Ross .15 .40
559 Delwyn Young .25 .60
560 Derek Holland RC .60 1.50
561 Derek Lowe .15 .40
562 Diory Hernandez RC .40 1.00
563a Pedro Martinez .25 .60
563b P.Martinez SP VAR 40.00 80.00
564 Emilio Bonifacio .15 .40
565 Endy Chavez .15 .40
566 Eric Byrnes .15 .40
567 Eric Hinske .15 .40
568 Everth Cabrera RC .60 1.50
569a Alex Rios .15 .40
569b A.Rios SP VAR 40.00 80.00
570 Fernando Nieve .15 .40
571 Francisco Cervelli RC 1.00 2.50
572 Frank Catalanotto .15 .40
573 Fu-Te Ni RC .60 1.50
574 Gabe Kapler .15 .40
575 Scott Rolen .25 .60
576 Garrett Olson .15 .40
577 Adam LaRoche .15 .40
578 Gerardo Parra RC .60 1.50
579 George Sherrill .15 .40
580 Graham Taylor RC .60 1.50
581 Gregg Zaun .15 .40
582 Homer Bailey .15 .40
583 Garrett Jones .25 .60
584 Julio Lugo .15 .40
585 J.A. Happ .25 .60
586 J.J. Putz .15 .40
587 J.P. Howell .15 .40
588 Jake Fox .25 .60
589 Jamey Carroll .15 .40
590 Jarrett Hoffpauir (RC) .40 1.00
591 Felipe Lopez .15 .40
592 Cliff Lee .25 .60
593 Jason Giambi .15 .40
594 Jason Jaramillo (RC) .40 1.00
595 Jason Kubel .15 .40
596 Jason Marquis .15 .40
597 Jason Vargas .15 .40
598 Jeff Baker .15 .40
599 Jeff Francoeur .25 .60
600 Jeremy Reed .15 .40
601 Jerry Hairston .15 .40
602 Jesus Guzman RC .40 1.00
603 Jody Gerut .15 .40
604 Joe Crede .25 .60
605 Alex Gonzalez .15 .40
606 Joel Hanrahan .25 .60
607 John Mayberry Jr (RC) .60 1.50
608 Jon Garland .15 .40
609 Jonny Gomes .15 .40
610 Jordan Schafer (RC) .60 1.50
611 Victor Martinez .25 .60
612 Jose Contreras .15 .40
613 Josh Bard .15 .40
614 Josh Outman .25 .60
615 Juan Rivera .15 .40
616 Juan Uribe .15 .40
617 Julio Borbon RC .40 1.00
618 Jarrod Washburn .15 .40
619 Justin Masterson .15 .40
620 Kenshin Kawakami RC .60 1.50
621 Kevin Correia .15 .40
622 Kevin Gregg .15 .40
623 Kevin Millar .15 .40
624 Koji Uehara RC 1.00 2.50
625 Kris Medlen RC 1.00 2.50
626 Tim Redding .15 .40
627 Kyle Farnsworth .15 .40
628 Landon Powell (RC) .40 1.00
629 Lastings Milledge .15 .40
630 LaTroy Hawkins .15 .40
631 Laynce Nix .15 .40
632 Billy Wagner .15 .40
633 Tony Gwynn Jr. .15 .40
634 Mark Loretta .15 .40
635 Matt Diaz .15 .40
636 Ben Francisco .15 .40
637 Travis Ishikawa .15 .40
638 Matt Maloney (RC) .40 1.00
639 Scott Kazmir .15 .40
640 Melky Cabrera .15 .40
641 Micah Hoffpauir .15 .40
642 Micah Owings .15 .40
643 Mike Carp (RC) .60 1.50
644 Mike Hampton .15 .40
645 Mike Sweeney .15 .40
646 Milton Bradley .15 .40
647 Mitch Jones (RC) .40 1.00
648 Trevor Crowe RC .40 1.00
649 Ty Wigginton .25 .60
650 Jim Thome .25 .60
651 Nick Green .15 .40
652 Tyler Greene (RC) .40 1.00
653 Nyjer Morgan .15 .40
654 Omar Vizquel .25 .60
655 Omir Santos RC .40 1.00
656 Orlando Cabrera .15 .40
657 Vin Mazzaro RC .40 1.00
658 Pat Burrell .15 .40
659 Rafael Soriano .15 .40
660 Ramiro Pena RC .60 1.50
661 Freddy Sanchez .15 .40
662 Ramon Ramirez .15 .40
663 Wilkin Ramirez RC .40 1.00
664 Randy Wells .15 .40
665 Randy Wolf .15 .40
666 Rich Hill .15 .40
667 Willy Taveras .15 .40
668 Xavier Paul (RC) .40 1.00
669 Rocco Baldelli .15 .40
670 Ross Detwiler .15 .40
671 Ross Gload .15 .40
672 Aubrey Huff .15 .40
673 Yuniesky Betancourt .15 .40
674 Ryan Church .15 .40
675 Ryan Garko .15 .40
676 Ryan Perry RC 1.00 2.50
677 Ryan Sadowski RC .40 1.00
678 Ryan Spilborghs .15 .40
679 Scott Downs .15 .40
680 Scott Hairston .15 .40
681 Scott Olsen .15 .40
682 Scott Podsednik .15 .40
683 Bill Hall .15 .40
684 Sean O'Sullivan RC .40 1.00
685 Sean West (RC) .60 1.50
686 Aaron Hill SP 2.50 6.00
687 Adam Dunn SP 4.00 10.00
688 McCutchen SP (RC) 6.00 15.00
689 Ben Zobrist SP 4.00 10.00
690 Chris Tillman SP RC 4.00 10.00
691 Bobby Abreu SP 2.50 6.00
692 Brett Anderson SP RC 4.00 10.00
693 Chris Coghlan SP RC 3.00 8.00
694 Colby Rasmus SP (RC) 3.00 8.00
695 Elvis Andrus SP RC 5.00 12.00
696 Fernando Martinez SP RC 6.00 15.00
697 Garret Anderson SP 2.50 6.00
698 Gary Sheffield SP 2.50 6.00
699 G.Beckham SP RC 1.50 4.00
700 Huston Street SP 2.50 6.00
701 Ivan Rodriguez SP 3.00 8.00
702 Jason Bay SP 3.00 8.00
703 Jordan Zimmermann SP RC 6.00 15.00
704 Ken Griffey Jr. SP 5.00 12.00
705 Kendry Morales SP 2.50 6.00
706 Kyle Blanks SP RC 4.00 10.00
707 T.Hanson SP RC 2.50 6.00
708 Mark DeRosa SP 4.00 10.00
709 Matt Holliday SP 5.00 12.00
710 Matt LaPorta SP RC 2.00 5.00
711 Trevor Cahill SP RC 5.00 12.00
712 Nate McLouth SP 2.50 6.00
713 Trevor Hoffman SP 4.00 10.00
714 Nelson Cruz SP 6.00 15.00
715 Nolan Reimold SP (RC) 2.50 6.00
716 Orlando Hudson SP 2.50 6.00
717 Randy Johnson SP 5.00 12.00
718 R.Porcello SP RC 2.50 6.00
719 Ricky Romero SP (RC) 3.00 8.00
720 Russell Branyan SP 2.50 6.00

2009 Topps Heritage Chrome

COMP.HIGH.SET (100) 100.00 200.00
1-100 STATED ODDS 1:6 HOBBY
101-200 STATED ODDS 1:3 HOBBY
STATED PRINT RUN 1960 SER.#'d SETS
C1 Manny Ramirez 2.50 6.00
C2 Andre Ethier 1.50 4.00
C3 Miguel Tejada 1.50 4.00
C4 Nick Markakis 2.00 5.00
C5 Johan Santana 1.50 4.00
C6 Grady Sizemore 1.50 4.00
C7 Ian Kinsler 1.50 4.00
C8 Ryan Ludwick 1.50 4.00
C9 Jonathan Papelbon 1.50 4.00
C10 Albert Pujols 3.00 8.00
C11 Carlos Beltran 1.50 4.00
C12 David Price 2.00 5.00
C13 Carlos Pena 1.50 4.00
C14 Derek Jeter 6.00 15.00
C15 Mark Teixeira 1.50 4.00
C16 Aramis Ramirez 1.00 2.50
C17 Dexter Fowler 1.50 4.00
C18 Brad Lidge 1.00 2.50
C19 Johnny Cueto 1.50 4.00
C20 David Wright 2.00 5.00
C21 Mat Gamel 2.50 6.00
C22 B.J. Upton 1.50 4.00
C23 Carl Crawford 1.50 4.00
C24 Mariano Rivera 3.00 8.00
C25 Scott Kazmir 1.00 2.50
C26 Vladimir Guerrero 1.50 4.00
C27 Clayton Kershaw 4.00 10.00
C28 Ben Sheets 1.00 2.50
C29 Rick Ankiel 1.00 2.50
C30 Nate McLouth 1.00 2.50
C31 Roy Oswalt 1.50 4.00
C32 Felix Hernandez 1.50 4.00
C33 Ervin Santana 1.00 2.50
C34 Prince Fielder 1.50 4.00
C35 Cole Hamels 2.00 5.00
C36 Jon Lester 1.50 4.00
C37 Kosuke Fukudome 1.50 4.00
C38 Justin Upton 1.50 4.00
C39 John Lackey 1.50 4.00
C40 Lance Berkman 1.50 4.00
C41 Chien-Ming Wang 1.50 4.00
C42 Alex Rios 1.00 2.50
C43 Carlos Delgado 1.00 2.50
C44 Jake Peavy 1.00 2.50
C45 Hanley Ramirez 1.50 4.00
C46 Alfonso Soriano 1.50 4.00
C47 Jimmy Rollins 1.50 4.00
C48 J.J. Hardy 1.00 2.50
C49 James Loney 1.00 2.50
C50 Ryan Howard 2.00 5.00
C51 Rich Harden 1.00 2.50
C52 Dan Uggla 1.00 2.50
C53 Miguel Cabrera 2.50 6.00
C54 Matt Kemp 2.00 5.00
C55 Russell Martin 1.00 2.50
C56 Chipper Jones 2.50 6.00
C57 Stephen Drew 1.00 2.50
C58 Randy Johnson 2.50 6.00
C59 Andy Pettitte 1.50 4.00
C60 Francisco Rodriguez 1.50 4.00
C61 Vernon Wells 1.00 2.50
C62 Ivan Rodriguez 1.50 4.00
C63 Joe Saunders 1.00 2.50
C64 Yadier Molina 3.00 8.00
C65 Ken Griffey Jr. 5.00 12.00
C66 Justin Verlander 2.50 6.00
C67 Edinson Volquez 1.00 2.50
C68 Phil Hughes 1.00 2.50
C69 Yovani Gallardo 1.00 2.50
C70 Jose Reyes 1.50 4.00
C71 Gio Gonzalez 1.50 4.00
C72 Adrian Gonzalez 2.00 5.00
C73 Chris Davis 1.50 4.00
C74 Brad Penny 1.00 2.50
C75 Dustin Pedroia 2.50 6.00
C76 Kevin Youkilis 1.00 2.50
C77 Angel Salome 1.00 2.50
C78 Kila Ka'aihue 1.50 4.00
C79 Lou Marson 1.00 2.50
C80 Ichiro Suzuki 3.00 8.00
C81 Alcides Escobar 1.50 4.00
C82 Travis Snider 1.50 4.00
C83 Adam Dunn 1.50 4.00
C84 Jacoby Ellsbury 2.00 5.00
C85 Jay Bruce 1.50 4.00
C86 Ryan Doumit 1.00 2.50
C87 Tim Lincecum 1.50 4.00
C88 Joe Nathan 1.00 2.50
C89 Brian McCann 1.50 4.00
C90 Evan Longoria 1.50 4.00
C91 Carlos Zambrano 1.50 4.00
C92 Pat Burrell 1.00 2.50
C93 Alex Gordon 1.50 4.00
C94 Ryan Zimmerman 1.50 4.00
C95 Carlos Quentin 1.00 2.50
C96 Xavier Nady 1.00 2.50
C97 Max Scherzer 2.50 6.00
C98 Hiroki Kuroda 1.00 2.50
C99 Carlos Lee 1.00 2.50
C100 Alex Rodriguez 3.00 8.00
CHR101 Chad Qualls 1.00 2.50
CHR102 Daniel Schlereth 1.00 2.50
CHR103 Derek Lowe 1.00 2.50
CHR104 Jason Giambi 1.00 2.50
CHR105 Jason Marquis 1.00 2.50
CHR106 Kevin Correia 1.00 2.50
CHR107 Koji Uehara 2.50 6.00
CHR108 Matt Diaz 1.00 2.50
CHR109 Melky Cabrera 1.00 2.50
CHR110 Milton Bradley 1.00 2.50
CHR111 Rafael Soriano 1.00 2.50
CHR112 Scott Downs 1.00 2.50
CHR113 David Aardsma 1.00 2.50
CHR114 Eric Byrnes 1.00 2.50
CHR115 Gerardo Parra 1.50 4.00
CHR116 Homer Bailey 1.00 2.50
CHR117 J.P. Howell 1.00 2.50
CHR118 Joe Crede 1.50 4.00
CHR119 John Mayberry Jr 1.50 4.00
CHR120 Josh Outman 1.50 4.00
CHR121 Lastings Milledge 1.00 2.50
CHR122 Mike Hampton 1.00 2.50
CHR123 Orlando Cabrera 1.00 2.50
CHR124 Randy Wells 1.00 2.50
CHR125 Michael Saunders 2.50 6.00
CHR126 Tony Gwynn Jr. 1.00 2.50
CHR127 Trevor Crowe 1.00 2.50
CHR128 Vin Mazzaro 1.00 2.50
CHR129 Andruw Jones 1.00 2.50
CHR130 Brad Penny 1.00 2.50
CHR131 Brandon Wood 1.00 2.50
CHR132 Cristian Guzman 1.00 2.50
CHR133 David Huff 1.00 2.50
CHR134 J.A. Happ 1.50 4.00
CHR135 Jason Kubel 1.00 2.50
CHR136 Ryan Garko 1.00 2.50
CHR137 Jose Contreras 1.00 2.50
CHR138 Juan Rivera 1.00 2.50
CHR139 Jhoulys Chacin 1.50 4.00
CHR140 Randy Wolf 1.00 2.50
CHR141 Aaron Hill 1.00 2.50
CHR142 Adam Dunn 1.50 4.00
CHR143 Andrew Bailey 2.50 6.00
CHR144 Andrew McCutchen 5.00 12.00
CHR145 Ben Zobrist 1.50 4.00
CHR146 Bobby Abreu 1.00 2.50
CHR147 Brett Anderson 1.50 4.00
CHR148 Chris Coghlan 2.50 6.00
CHR149 Colby Rasmus 1.50 4.00
CHR150 Elvis Andrus 2.50 6.00
CHR151 Fernando Martinez 2.50 6.00
CHR152 Garret Anderson 1.00 2.50
CHR153 Gary Sheffield 1.00 2.50
CHR154 Gordon Beckham 1.50 4.00
CHR155 Huston Street 1.00 2.50
CHR156 Ivan Rodriguez 1.50 4.00
CHR157 Jason Bay 1.50 4.00
CHR158 Jeff Francoeur 1.50 4.00
CHR159 Jordan Zimmermann 2.50 6.00
CHR160 Ken Griffey Jr. 5.00 12.00
CHR161 Kendry Morales 1.00 2.50
CHR162 Kyle Blanks 1.50 4.00
CHR163 Mark DeRosa 1.50 4.00
CHR164 Matt Holliday 2.50 6.00
CHR165 Matt LaPorta 1.50 4.00
CHR166 Nate McLouth 1.00 2.50
CHR167 Nelson Cruz 2.50 6.00
CHR168 Nolan Reimold 1.00 2.50
CHR169 Orlando Hudson 1.00 2.50
CHR170 Randy Johnson 2.50 6.00
CHR171 Rick Porcello 3.00 8.00
CHR172 Ricky Romero 1.50 4.00
CHR173 Russell Branyan 1.00 2.50
CHR174 Tommy Hanson 2.50 6.00
CHR175 Trevor Cahill 2.50 6.00
CHR176 Trevor Hoffman 1.50 4.00
CHR177 Aaron Poreda 1.00 2.50
CHR178 John Smoltz 2.50 6.00
CHR179 Brad Mills 1.00 2.50
CHR180 Brett Gardner 1.50 4.00
CHR181 Carl Pavano 1.00 2.50
CHR182 Daniel Bard 1.00 2.50
CHR183 David Hernandez 1.00 2.50
CHR184 Fu-Te Ni 1.50 4.00
CHR185 Jerry Hairston 1.00 2.50
CHR186 Jordan Schafer 1.50 4.00
CHR187 Julio Borbon 1.00 2.50
CHR188 Kris Medlen 2.50 6.00
CHR189 Micah Hoffpauir 1.00 2.50
CHR190 Nyjer Morgan 1.00 2.50
CHR191 Derek Holland 1.50 4.00
CHR192 Jack Wilson 1.00 2.50
CHR193 Cliff Lee 1.50 4.00
CHR194 Freddy Sanchez 1.00 2.50
CHR195 Pat Burrell 1.00 2.50
CHR196 Ryan Spilborghs 1.00 2.50
CHR197 Takashi Saito 1.00 2.50
CHR198 Bud Norris 1.00 2.50
CHR199 Chris Tillman 1.50 4.00
CHR200 Everth Cabrera 1.50 4.00

2009 Topps Heritage Chrome Refractors

*REF: .6X TO 1.5X BASIC INSERTS
1-100 STATED ODDS 1:23 HOBBY
101-200 STATED ODDS 1:11 HOBBY
STATED PRINT RUN 560 SER.#'d SETS

2009 Topps Heritage Chrome Refractors Black

1-100 STATED ODDS 1:255 HOBBY
101-200 STATED ODDS 1:102 HOBBY
STATED PRINT RUN 60 SER.#'d SETS
C1 Manny Ramirez 12.00 30.00
C2 Andre Ethier 8.00 20.00
C3 Miguel Tejada 8.00 20.00
C4 Nick Markakis 10.00 25.00
C5 Johan Santana 8.00 20.00
C6 Grady Sizemore 8.00 20.00
C7 Ian Kinsler 8.00 20.00
C8 Ryan Ludwick 8.00 20.00
C9 Jonathan Papelbon 8.00 20.00
C10 Albert Pujols 40.00 100.00
C11 Carlos Beltran 8.00 20.00
C12 David Price 10.00 25.00
C13 Carlos Pena 8.00 20.00
C14 Derek Jeter 125.00 300.00
C15 Mark Teixeira 8.00 20.00
C16 Aramis Ramirez 5.00 12.00
C17 Dexter Fowler 8.00 20.00
C18 Brad Lidge 5.00 12.00
C19 Johnny Cueto 8.00 20.00
C20 David Wright 10.00 25.00
C21 Mat Gamel 12.00 30.00
C22 B.J. Upton 8.00 20.00
C23 Carl Crawford 8.00 20.00
C24 Mariano Rivera 40.00 100.00
C25 Scott Kazmir 5.00 12.00
C26 Vladimir Guerrero 8.00 20.00
C27 Clayton Kershaw 20.00 50.00
C28 Ben Sheets 5.00 12.00
C29 Rick Ankiel 5.00 12.00
C30 Nate McLouth 5.00 12.00
C31 Roy Oswalt 8.00 20.00
C32 Felix Hernandez 8.00 20.00
C33 Ervin Santana 5.00 12.00
C34 Prince Fielder 8.00 20.00
C35 Cole Hamels 10.00 25.00
C36 Jon Lester 8.00 20.00
C37 Kosuke Fukudome 8.00 20.00
C38 Justin Upton 8.00 20.00
C39 John Lackey 8.00 20.00
C40 Lance Berkman 8.00 20.00
C41 Chien-Ming Wang 8.00 20.00
C42 Alex Rios 5.00 12.00
C43 Carlos Delgado 5.00 12.00
C44 Jake Peavy 5.00 12.00
C45 Hanley Ramirez 8.00 20.00
C46 Alfonso Soriano 8.00 20.00
C47 Jimmy Rollins 8.00 20.00
C48 J.J. Hardy 5.00 12.00
C49 James Loney 5.00 12.00
C50 Ryan Howard 10.00 25.00
C51 Rich Harden 5.00 12.00
C52 Dan Uggla 5.00 12.00
C53 Miguel Cabrera 12.00 30.00
C54 Matt Kemp 10.00 25.00
C55 Russell Martin 5.00 12.00
C56 Chipper Jones 12.00 30.00
C57 Stephen Drew 5.00 12.00
C58 Randy Johnson 12.00 30.00
C59 Andy Pettitte 8.00 20.00
C60 Francisco Rodriguez 8.00 20.00
C61 Vernon Wells 5.00 12.00
C62 Ivan Rodriguez 8.00 20.00
C63 Joe Saunders 5.00 12.00
C64 Yadier Molina 15.00 40.00
C65 Ken Griffey Jr. 40.00 100.00
C66 Justin Verlander 12.00 30.00
C67 Edinson Volquez 5.00 12.00
C68 Phil Hughes 5.00 12.00
C69 Yovani Gallardo 5.00 12.00
C70 Jose Reyes 8.00 20.00
C71 Gio Gonzalez 8.00 20.00
C72 Adrian Gonzalez 10.00 25.00
C73 Chris Davis 8.00 20.00
C74 Brad Penny 5.00 12.00
C75 Dustin Pedroia 12.00 30.00
C76 Kevin Youkilis 5.00 12.00
C77 Angel Salome 5.00 12.00
C78 Kila Ka'aihue 8.00 20.00
C79 Lou Marson 5.00 12.00
C80 Ichiro Suzuki 40.00 100.00
C81 Alcides Escobar 8.00 20.00
C82 Travis Snider 8.00 20.00
C83 Adam Dunn 8.00 20.00
C84 Jacoby Ellsbury 10.00 25.00
C85 Jay Bruce 8.00 20.00
C86 Ryan Doumit 5.00 12.00
C87 Tim Lincecum 8.00 20.00
C88 Joe Nathan 5.00 12.00
C89 Brian McCann 8.00 20.00
C90 Evan Longoria 8.00 20.00
C91 Carlos Zambrano 8.00 20.00
C92 Pat Burrell 5.00 12.00
C93 Alex Gordon 8.00 20.00
C94 Ryan Zimmerman 8.00 20.00
C95 Carlos Quentin 5.00 12.00
C96 Xavier Nady 5.00 12.00
C97 Max Scherzer 12.00 30.00
C98 Hiroki Kuroda 5.00 12.00
C99 Carlos Lee 5.00 12.00
C100 Alex Rodriguez 15.00 40.00
CHR101 Chad Qualls 5.00 12.00
CHR102 Daniel Schlereth 5.00 12.00
CHR103 Derek Lowe 5.00 12.00
CHR104 Jason Giambi 5.00 12.00
CHR105 Jason Marquis 5.00 12.00
CHR106 Kevin Correia 5.00 12.00
CHR107 Koji Uehara 12.00 30.00
CHR108 Matt Diaz 5.00 12.00
CHR109 Melky Cabrera 5.00 12.00
CHR110 Milton Bradley 5.00 12.00
CHR111 Rafael Soriano 5.00 12.00
CHR112 Scott Downs 5.00 12.00
CHR113 David Aardsma 5.00 12.00
CHR114 Eric Byrnes 5.00 12.00
CHR115 Gerardo Parra 8.00 20.00
CHR116 Homer Bailey 5.00 12.00
CHR117 J.P. Howell 5.00 12.00
CHR118 Joe Crede 8.00 20.00
CHR119 John Mayberry Jr 8.00 20.00
CHR120 Josh Outman 8.00 20.00
CHR121 Lastings Milledge 5.00 12.00
CHR122 Mike Hampton 5.00 12.00
CHR123 Orlando Cabrera 5.00 12.00
CHR124 Randy Wells 5.00 12.00
CHR125 Michael Saunders 12.00 30.00
CHR126 Tony Gwynn Jr. 5.00 12.00
CHR127 Trevor Crowe 5.00 12.00
CHR128 Vin Mazzaro 5.00 12.00
CHR129 Andruw Jones 5.00 12.00
CHR130 Brad Penny 5.00 12.00
CHR131 Brandon Wood 5.00 12.00
CHR132 Cristian Guzman 5.00 12.00
CHR133 David Huff 5.00 12.00
CHR134 J.A. Happ 8.00 20.00
CHR135 Jason Kubel 5.00 12.00
CHR136 Ryan Garko 5.00 12.00
CHR137 Jose Contreras 5.00 12.00
CHR138 Juan Rivera 5.00 12.00
CHR139 Jhoulys Chacin 8.00 20.00
CHR140 Randy Wolf 5.00 12.00
CHR141 Aaron Hill 5.00 12.00
CHR142 Adam Dunn 8.00 20.00
CHR143 Andrew Bailey 12.00 30.00
CHR144 Andrew McCutchen 25.00 60.00
CHR145 Ben Zobrist 8.00 20.00
CHR146 Bobby Abreu 5.00 12.00
CHR147 Brett Anderson 8.00 20.00
CHR148 Chris Coghlan 12.00 30.00
CHR149 Colby Rasmus 8.00 20.00
CHR150 Elvis Andrus 12.00 30.00
CHR151 Fernando Martinez 12.00 30.00
CHR152 Garret Anderson 5.00 12.00
CHR153 Gary Sheffield 5.00 12.00
CHR154 Gordon Beckham 8.00 20.00
CHR155 Huston Street 5.00 12.00
CHR156 Ivan Rodriguez 8.00 20.00
CHR157 Jason Bay 8.00 20.00
CHR158 Jeff Francoeur 8.00 20.00
CHR159 Jordan Zimmermann 12.00 30.00
CHR160 Ken Griffey Jr. 40.00 100.00
CHR161 Kendry Morales 5.00 12.00
CHR162 Kyle Blanks 8.00 20.00
CHR163 Mark DeRosa 8.00 20.00
CHR164 Matt Holliday 12.00 30.00
CHR165 Matt LaPorta 8.00 20.00
CHR166 Nate McLouth 5.00 12.00
CHR167 Nelson Cruz 12.00 30.00
CHR168 Nolan Reimold 5.00 12.00
CHR169 Orlando Hudson 5.00 12.00
CHR170 Randy Johnson 12.00 30.00
CHR171 Rick Porcello 15.00 40.00
CHR172 Ricky Romero 8.00 20.00
CHR173 Russell Branyan 5.00 12.00
CHR174 Tommy Hanson 12.00 30.00
CHR175 Trevor Cahill 12.00 30.00
CHR176 Trevor Hoffman 8.00 20.00
CHR177 Aaron Poreda 5.00 12.00
CHR178 John Smoltz 12.00 30.00
CHR179 Brad Mills 5.00 12.00
CHR180 Brett Gardner 8.00 20.00
CHR181 Carl Pavano 5.00 12.00
CHR182 Daniel Bard 5.00 12.00
CHR183 David Hernandez 5.00 12.00
CHR184 Fu-Te Ni 8.00 20.00
CHR185 Jerry Hairston 5.00 12.00
CHR186 Jordan Schafer 8.00 20.00
CHR187 Julio Borbon 5.00 12.00
CHR188 Kris Medlen 12.00 30.00
CHR189 Micah Hoffpauir 5.00 12.00
CHR190 Nyjer Morgan 5.00 12.00
CHR191 Derek Holland 8.00 20.00
CHR192 Jack Wilson 5.00 12.00
CHR193 Cliff Lee 8.00 20.00
CHR194 Freddy Sanchez 5.00 12.00
CHR195 Pat Burrell 5.00 12.00
CHR196 Ryan Spilborghs 5.00 12.00
CHR197 Takashi Saito 5.00 12.00
CHR198 Bud Norris 5.00 12.00
CHR199 Chris Tillman 8.00 20.00
CHR200 Everth Cabrera 8.00 20.00

2009 Topps Heritage Advertising Panels

ISSUED AS BOX TOPPER
1 Garret Anderson .60 1.50
Brandon Backe/Shin Soo Choo
2 Matt Antonelli 1.25 3.00
David Wright/Alex Rodriguez/Alfredo Simon
3 Bronson Arroyo .60 1.50
Detroit Tigers TC/Matt Cain
4 Brandon Backe .60 1.50
Shin Soo Choo/Ozzie Guillen
5 Carlos Beltran .60 1.50
Andre Ethier/Kelly Shoppach/Victor Martinez
6 Brad Bergesen .40 1.00
Dallas Braden/Garrett Olson HN
7 Nick Blackburn .40 1.00
Scott Lewis/Ramon Ramirez
8 Aaron Boone .40 1.00
James Loney/Gerald Laird
9 Julio Borbon .40 1.00
Jarrett Hoffpauir/David Hernandez HN
10 Emil Brown .60 1.50
Scott Shields/Francisco Rodriguez/David Murphy
11 Pat Burrell .40 1.00
Brian Bannister/Jesus Flores
12 Mike Cameron .60 1.50
Ted Lilly/John Lackey
13 Mike Carp .60 1.50
Jody Gerut/Daniel Schlereth HN
14 Brett Cecil .40 1.00
Aubrey Huff/Mike Hampton HN
15 Shin-Soo Choo .60 1.50
Ozzie Guillen/Mike Aviles
16 Jeff Clement .40 1.00
Bronson Arroyo/Detroit Tigers TC
17 John Danks .60 1.50
Carlos Beltran/Andre Ethier
18 Jesus Delgado 1.00 2.50
Brian Wilson/Gary Mathews
19 Stephen Drew .60 1.50
Ryan Feirebrand/Andy Pettitte
20 Scott Elbert .40 1.00
Fernando Perez/Jeremy Guthrie
21 Yunel Escobar .60 1.50
Gaby Sanchez/Vernon Wells
22 Andre Ethier .60 1.50
Kelly Shoppach/Victor Martinez/Ronny Paulino
23 Cliff Floyd .40 1.00
Alfredo Figaro/Anthony Swarzak HN
24 Ryan Franklin .60 1.50
Emil Brown/Scott Shields/Francisco Rodriguez
25 David Freese 1.25 3.00
J.J. Putz/Juan Uribe HN
26 Jody Gerut .40 1.00
Daniel Schlereth/Brett Cecil HN
27 Ross Gload .60 1.50
Miguel Tejada/Matt Harrison
28 Khalil Greene .75 2.00
Cole Hamels/Juan Pierre
29 Jeremy Guthrie .40 1.00
Nick Blackburn/Scott Lewis
30 Scott Hairston .40 1.00
Orlando Cabrera/Matt Maloney HN
31 Bill Hall .40 1.00
Randy Wells/Kevin Gregg HN
32 Cole Hamels .75 2.00
Juan Pierre/Yunel Escobar
33 Mike Hampton .40 1.00
Jerry Hairston/Scott Downs HN
34 Dan Haren .60 1.50
John Danks/Carlos Beltran
35 Corey Hart .40 1.00
Aubrey Huff/Rich Aurilia
36 Brad Hawpe .60 1.50
Roy Oswalt/Mike Jacobs
37 David Hernandez 1.00 2.50
Brandon Lyon/Koji Uehara HN
38 Aubrey Huff .40 1.00
Mike Hampton/Jerry Hairston HN
39 Aubrey Huff .40 1.00
Rich Aurilia/Scott Baker
40 Mike Jacobs .75 2.00
Terry Francona/Jacoby Ellsbury
41 Scott Kazmir .40 1.00
Jeff Clement/Bronson Arroyo
42 John Lackey .60 1.50
Lyle Overbay/Chris Lambert
43 Aaron Laffey .60 1.50
Hanley Ramirez/Scott Olsen
44 Gerald Laird .60 1.50
Chien-Ming Wang/Corey Hart
45 Chris Lambert .60 1.50
Carlos Zambrano/Dave Tremblay
46 Ted Lilly .60 1.50
John Lackey/Lyle Overbay
47 James Loney .60 1.50
Gerald Laird/Chien-Ming Wang
48 Los Angeles Dodgers TC 1.00 2.50
Jesus Delgado/Brian Wilson
49 Matt Maloney .40 1.00
Julio Borbon/Jarret Hoffpauir HN
50 Hideki Matsui 1.00 2.50
Ty Wigginton/Vicente Padilla
51 John Mayberry Jr .60 1.50
David Aardsma/Scott Podsednik HN
52 Gil Meche .75 2.00
David Price/Luke Scott
53 Brad Mills .40 1.00
David Ross/Chris Perez HN
54 Daniel Murphy 1.50 4.00
Hideki Matsui/Ty Wigginton
55 Mike Napoli .75 2.00
David Wright/Matt Antonelli
56 Scott Olsen .60 1.50
Ryan Franklin/Emil Brown
57 Roy Oswalt .60 1.50
Mike Jacobs/Terry Francona
58 Josh Outman .60 1.50
Homer Bailey/Daniel Bard HN
59 Lyle Overbay .60 1.50
Chris Lambert/Carlos Zambrano
60 Vicente Padilla .60 1.50
Brad Hawpe/Roy Oswalt
61 Jon Papelbon .60 1.50
Tim Wakefield/Corey Patterson/Pat Burrell
62 Corey Patterson .40 1.00
Pat Burrell/Brian Bannister
63 Xavier Paul .60 1.50
John Mayberry Jr/David Aardsma HN
64 Chris Perez .60 1.50
Ramiro Pena/Rocco Baldelli HN
65 Fernando Perez .40 1.00
Jeremy Guthrie/Nick Blackburn
66 Juan Pierre .60 1.50
Yunel Escobar/Gaby Sanchez
67 Lou Piniella .40 1.00
Scott Kazmir/Jeff Clement
68 Aaron Poreda .40 1.00
Bill Hall/Randy Wells HN
69 David Price .75 2.00
Luke Scott/Jeff Suppan
70 Albert Pujols 1.25 3.00
Dan Haren/John Danks
71 Hanley Ramirez .60 1.50
Scott Olsen/Ryan Franklin
72 Tim Redding .40 1.00
Jamey Carroll/Endy Chavez
73 Jeremy Reed .40 1.00
Laynce Nix/Ryan Sadowski HN
74 Edgar Renteria .40 1.00
Brian Giles/Greg Smith
75 Gaby Sanchez .60 1.50
Vernon Wells/Ross Gload
76 Bobby Scales .60 1.50
Clay Zavada/Jason Jaramillo HN
77 Daniel Schlereth .40 1.00
Brett Cecil/Aubrey Huff HN
78 Kelly Shoppach .60 1.50
Victor Martinez/Ronny Paulino/Mike Gonzalez
79 John Smoltz 1.00 2.50
Mike Carp/Jody Gerut HN
80 Rafael Soriano .40 1.00
Ross Gload/Vin Mazzaro HN
81 Craig Stammen 1.00 2.50
John Smoltz/Mike Carp HN
82 Anthony Swarzak .40 1.00
C.J. Wilson/Derek Lowe HN
83 Miguel Tejada .60 1.50
Matt Harrison/James Parr
84 Detroit Tigers TC .60 1.50
Matt Cain/Jeff Francis
85 Dave Tremblay .40 1.00
Edgar Renteria/Brian Giles
86 Koji Uehara 1.00 2.50
Brad Bergesen/Dallas Braden HN
87 Juan Uribe .40 1.00
Rafael Soriano/Ross Gload HN
88 Jason Vargas .40 1.00
Eric Byrnes/Brad Mills HN
89 Chien-Ming Wang .60 1.50
Corey Hart/Aubrey Huff
90 Randy Wells .40 1.00
Kevin Gregg/J.P. Howell HN
91 Vernon Wells .60 1.50
Ross Gload/Miguel Tejada
92 Sean West .60 1.50
Melky Cabrera/Braden Looper HN
93 Ty Wigginton .60 1.50
Vicente Padilla/Brad Hawpe
94 Brian Wilson 1.00 2.50
Gary Mathews/Ubaldo Jimenez
95 Jack Wilson .40 1.00
Cincinnati Reds TC/Dustin McGowan
96 Kerry Wood .40 1.00
Scott Elbert/Fernando Perez
97 David Wright 1.25 3.00
Matt Antonelli/David Wright/Alex Rodriguez
99 David Aardsma .40 1.00
Scott Podsednik/Milton Bradley
98 Carlos Zambrano .60 1.50
Dave Tremblay/Edgar Renteria
100 Ryan Church .60 1.50
Dexter Fowler/Stephen Drew
101 Mike Gonzalez .60 1.50
Wade LeBlanc/Brandon Inge

102 Ozzie Guillen .40 1.00
Mike Aviles/Gil Meche
103 Jair Jurrjens 1.50 4.00
Daniel Murphy/Hideki Matsui
104 Lastings Milledge .40 1.00
Mitch Jones/Xavier Paul
105 Scot Shields .60 1.50
Francisco Rodriguez/David Murphy/Jack Wilson
106 David Wright 1.25 3.00
Alex Rodriguez/Alfredo Simon/Dodgers TC

2009 Topps Heritage Baseball Flashbacks

COMPLETE SET (10) 5.00 12.00
STATED ODDS 1:12 HOBBY
BF1 Mickey Mantle 1.50 4.00
BF2 Bill Mazeroski .75 2.00
BF3 Juan Marichal .75 2.00
BF4 Paul Richards/Hoyt Wilhelm .75 2.00
BF5 Luis Aparicio .75 2.00
BF6 Frank Robinson .75 2.00
BF7 Brooks Robinson .75 2.00
BF8 Ernie Banks 1.25 3.00
BF9 Mickey Mantle 1.50 4.00
BF10 Bobby Richardson .50 1.25

2009 Topps Heritage Clubhouse Collection Relics

GROUP A ODDS 1:219 HOBBY
GROUP B ODDS 1:52 HOBBY
GROUP C ODDS 1:97 HOBBY
HN ODDDS 1:26 HOBBY
AG Adrian Gonzalez HN 2.50 6.00
AJ Adam Jones HN 2.50 6.00
ALR Alexei Ramirez HN 2.50 6.00
AR Aramis Ramirez HN 2.50 6.00
AR Aramis Ramirez Jsy 2.50 6.00
AS Alfonso Soriano HN 2.50 6.00
BJU B.J. Upton HN 2.50 6.00
BM Brian McCann HN 2.50 6.00
BR Brooks Robinson HN 50.00 100.00
BU B.J. Upton Bat 2.50 6.00
CB Chad Billingsley HN 2.50 6.00
CB Clay Buchholz Jsy 2.50 6.00
CC Carl Crawford Uni 2.50 6.00
CH Cole Hamels HN 4.00 10.00
CJ Chipper Jones HN 4.00 10.00
CM Cameron Maybin Bat 2.50 6.00
CQ Carlos Quentin HN 2.50 6.00
CT Curtis Thigpen Jsy 2.50 6.00
CU Chase Utley HN 5.00 12.00
CU Chase Utley Jsy 5.00 12.00
DJ Dan Johnson Jsy 2.50 6.00
DP Dustin Pedroia Jsy 5.00 12.00
DS Duke Snider HN 20.00 50.00
DU Dan Uggla Jsy 2.50 6.00
DW David Wright HN 4.00 10.00
DW Dontrelle Willis Jsy 2.50 6.00
DWR David Wright Jsy 4.00 10.00
EB Ernie Banks HN 30.00 60.00
EL Evan Longoria HN 5.00 12.00
EVL Evan Longoria HN 5.00 12.00
FH Felix Hernandez HN 4.00 10.00
FR Frank Robinson HN 40.00 80.00
GS Geovany Soto HN 4.00 10.00
HR Hanley Ramirez HN 2.50 6.00
IK Ian Kinsler HN 2.50 6.00
JAB Jay Bruce HN 4.00 10.00
JB Jay Bruce HN 4.00 10.00
JD J.D. Drew Jsy 2.50 6.00
JL Jon Lester Jsy 4.00 10.00
JM Joe Mauer HN 4.00 10.00
JR Jimmy Rollins HN 4.00 10.00
JS Joakim Soria HN 2.50 6.00
JU Justin Upton HN 2.50 6.00
KFM Kevin Mench Jsy 2.50 6.00
KK Kenshin Kawakami HN 4.00 10.00
KM Kevin Millwood Jsy 2.50 6.00
KS Kurt Suzuki Bat 2.50 6.00
KU Koji Uehara HN 4.00 10.00
KY Kevin Youkilis Jsy 4.00 10.00
LM Lastings Milledge Bat 2.50 6.00
MH Matt Holliday HN 4.00 10.00
MIC Miguel Cabrera HN 4.00 10.00
MM Mickey Mantle HN 50.00 100.00
MR Manny Ramirez Jsy 5.00 12.00
MT Miguel Tejada Bat 2.50 6.00
RB Ryan Braun HN 4.00 10.00
RB Rocco Baldelli Jsy 2.50 6.00
RH Ryan Howard HN 4.00 10.00
RM Roger Maris HN 40.00 80.00
SM Stan Musial HN 40.00 80.00
SP Scott Podsednik Jsy 2.50 6.00
TL Tim Lincecum HN 5.00 12.00
VW Vernon Wells Jsy 2.50 6.00
WM Willie McCovey HN 50.00 100.00

2009 Topps Heritage Clubhouse Collection Relics Dual

STATED ODDS 1:4800 HOBBY
HN STATED ODDS 1:2020 HOBBY
STATED PRINT RUN 60 SER.#'d SETS
BR Bruce Bat/Robinson Pants 20.00 50.00
HM M.Holliday/S.Musial HN 40.00 80.00
LM Lincecum/J.Marichal HN 30.00 60.00
MR N.Markakis/Brooks HN 30.00 60.00
PM J.Posada/M.Mantle HN 30.00 60.00
PM Pujols Bat/Musial Pants 40.00 80.00
RM Rodriguez Jsy/Mantle Jsy 40.00 80.00
SB Soriano Bat/Banks Bat 30.00 60.00
SK D.Snider/M.Kemp HN 20.00 50.00
TM Teixeira Bat/Mantle Jsy 60.00 120.00

2009 Topps Heritage Flashback Stadium Relics

STATED ODDS 1:383 HOBBY
HN STATED ODDS 1:925 HOBBY
AK Al Kaline 10.00 25.00
BM Bill Mazeroski 6.00 15.00
BR Brooks Robinson 6.00 15.00
BRI Bobby Richardson 4.00 10.00
EB Ernie Banks 10.00 25.00
FR Frank Robinson 6.00 15.00
LA Luis Aparicio 6.00 15.00
MM Mickey Mantle 15.00 40.00
MM2 Mickey Mantle 15.00 40.00
SM Stan Musial 12.00 30.00

2009 Topps Heritage High Number Flashbacks

COMPLETE SET (10) 5.00 12.00
STATED ODDS 1:12 HOBBY
FB01 Jonathan Sanchez .50 1.25
FB02 Jason Giambi .50 1.25
FB03 Randy Johnson 1.25 3.00
FB04 Ian Kinsler .75 2.00
FB05 Carl Crawford .75 2.00
FB06 Albert Pujols 1.50 4.00
FB07 Todd Helton .75 2.00
FB08 Mariano Rivera 1.50 4.00
FB09 Gary Sheffield .50 1.25
FB10 Ichiro Suzuki 1.50 4.00

2009 Topps Heritage High Number Rookie Performers

COMPLETE SET (15) 12.50 30.00
STATED ODDS 1:12 HOBBY
RP01 Colby Rasmus 1.00 2.50
RP02 Tommy Hanson 1.50 4.00
RP03 Andrew McCutchen 3.00 8.00
RP04 Rick Porcello 2.00 5.00
RP05 Nolan Reimold .60 1.50
RP06 Mat Latos 2.00 5.00
RP07 Gordon Beckham 1.00 2.50
RP08 Brett Anderson 1.00 2.50
RP09 Chris Coghlan 1.50 4.00
RP10 Jordan Zimmermann 1.50 4.00
RP11 Brad Bergesen .60 1.50
RP12 Elvis Andrus 1.50 4.00
RP13 Ricky Romero 1.00 2.50
RP14 Dexter Fowler 1.00 2.50
RP15 David Price 1.25 3.00

2009 Topps Heritage High Number Then and Now

COMPLETE SET (10) 5.00 12.00
STATED ODDS 1:12 HOBBY
TN01 D.Pedroia/R.Maris 1.00 2.50
TN02 Jimmy Rollins/Ernie Banks 1.00 2.50
TN03 Adrian Beltre/Brooks Robinson 1.00 2.50
TN04 Michael Young/Ernie Banks 1.00 2.50
TN05 I.Suzuki/R.Maris 1.25 3.00
TN06 Grady Sizemore/Roger Maris 1.00 2.50
TN07 A.Pujols/R.Maris 1.25 3.00
TN08 D.Wright/B.Robinson .75 2.00
TN09 Cole Hamels/Bobby Richardson .75 2.00
TN10 Torii Hunter/Roger Maris 1.00 2.50

2009 Topps Heritage Mayo

COMPLETE SET (10) 15.00 40.00
RANDOM INSERTS IN PACKS
AP Albert Pujols 2.50 6.00
AR Alex Rodriguez 2.50 6.00
ARI Alex Rios .75 2.00
AS Alfonso Soriano 1.25 3.00
CJ Chipper Jones 2.00 5.00
DM Daisuke Matsuzaka 1.25 3.00
DO David Ortiz 2.00 5.00
DP Dustin Pedroia 2.00 5.00
DW David Wright 1.50 4.00
EL Evan Longoria 1.25 3.00
GS Grady Sizemore 1.25 3.00
HR Hanley Ramirez 1.25 3.00
IS Ichiro Suzuki 2.50 6.00
JH Josh Hamilton 1.25 3.00
JS Johan Santana 1.25 3.00
MR Manny Ramirez 2.00 5.00
RB Ryan Braun 1.25 3.00
RH Ryan Howard 1.50 4.00
TL Tim Lincecum 1.25 3.00
VG Vladimir Guerrero 1.25 3.00

2009 Topps Heritage New Age Performers

COMPLETE SET (15) 12.50 30.00
STATED ODDS 1:15 HOBBY
NAP1 David Wright .75 2.00
NAP2 Manny Ramirez 1.00 2.50
NAP3 Mark Teixeira .60 1.50
NAP4 Josh Hamilton .60 1.50
NAP5 Chase Utley .60 1.50
NAP6 Tim Lincecum .60 1.50
NAP7 Stephen Drew .40 1.00
NAP8 Cliff Lee .60 1.50
NAP9 Carlos Quentin .40 1.00
NAP10 Ryan Braun .60 1.50
NAP11 Cole Hamels .75 2.00
NAP12 Dustin Pedroia 1.00 2.50
NAP13 Geovany Soto .60 1.50
NAP14 Scott Kazmir .40 1.00
NAP15 Evan Longoria .60 1.50

2009 Topps Heritage News Flashbacks

COMPLETE SET (10) 6.00 15.00
STATED ODDS 1:12 HOBBY
NF1 Aswan High Dam .50 1.25
NF2 Bathyscaphe Trieste .50 1.25
NF3 Weather Satellite - TIROS-1 .50 1.25
NF4 Civil Rights Act of 1960 .50 1.25
NF5 Fifty-Star Flag .50 1.25
NF6 USS Seadragon .50 1.25
NF7 Marshall Space Flight Center .50 1.25
NF8 Presidential Debate 1.00 2.50
NF9 John F. Kennedy 1.25 3.00
NF10 Polaris Missle .50 1.25

2009 Topps Heritage Real One Autographs

STATED ODDS 1:308 HOBBY
HN STATED ODDS 1:372 HOBBY
EXCHANGE DEADLINE 2/28/2012
AC Art Ceccarelli 6.00 15.00
AD Alvin Dark HN 30.00 60.00
AS Art Schult 6.00 15.00
BB Brian Barton HN 6.00 15.00
BG Buddy Gilbert 10.00 25.00
BJ Bob Johnson HN 6.00 15.00
BJ Ben Johnson 6.00 15.00
BR Bob Rush 6.00 15.00
BTH Bill Harris 6.00 15.00
BWI Bobby Wine HN 15.00 40.00
CK Clayton Kershaw HN 100.00 200.00
CK Clayton Kershaw 100.00 200.00
CM Carl Mathias 6.00 15.00
CN Cal Neeman 6.00 15.00
CP Cliff Pennington HN 6.00 15.00
CR Curt Raydon 6.00 15.00
DB Dick Burwell HN 6.00 15.00
DG Dick Gray 6.00 15.00
DW Don Williams EXCH 6.00 15.00
FC Fausto Carmona 6.00 15.00
GB Gordon Beckham HN 60.00 120.00
GC Gio Gonzalez HN 6.00 15.00
GM Gil McDougald 6.00 15.00
IN Irv Noren HN 6.00 20.00
IN Irv Noren 6.00 15.00
JB Jay Bruce HN 12.50 30.00
JB Jay Bruce 12.50 30.00
JG Johnny Groth 10.00 25.00
JH Jack Harshman 6.00 15.00
JM Justin Masterson 6.00 15.00
JP Jim Proctor 6.00 15.00
JR John Romonosky 6.00 15.00
JS Joe Shipley 6.00 15.00
JSS Jake Striker 6.00 15.00
MB Milton Bradley HN 6.00 15.00
MG Mat Gamel 6.00 15.00
ML Mike Lee 6.00 15.00
NC Nelson Chittum 6.00 15.00
RI Raul Ibanez HN 20.00 50.00
RJW Red Wilson 6.00 15.00
RS Ron Samford 6.00 15.00
RW Ray Webster 6.00 15.00
SK Steve Korcheck 6.00 15.00
SL Stan Lopata 6.00 15.00
TP Taylor Phillips 6.00 15.00
TW Ted Wieand EXCH 6.00 15.00
WL Whitey Lockman 6.00 15.00
WT Wayne Terwilliger 6.00 15.00

2009 Topps Heritage Real One Autographs Red Ink

STATED ODDS 1:514 HOBBY
HN STATED ODDS 1:623 HOBBY
STATED PRINT RUN 60 SER.#'d SETS
EXCHANGE DEADLINE 2/28/2012
AC Art Ceccarelli 8.00 20.00
AD Alvin Dark HN 40.00 80.00
AS Art Schult 8.00 20.00
BB Brian Barton HN 8.00 20.00
BG Buddy Gilbert 12.50 30.00
BJ Bob Johnson HN 8.00 20.00
BJ Ben Johnson 8.00 20.00
BR Bob Rush 8.00 20.00
BTH Bill Harris 8.00 20.00
BWI Bobby Wine HN 20.00 50.00
CK Clayton Kershaw HN 200.00 400.00
CK Clayton Kershaw 200.00 400.00
CM Carl Mathias 8.00 20.00
CN Cal Neeman 8.00 20.00
CP Cliff Pennington HN 8.00 20.00
CR Curt Raydon 8.00 20.00
DB Dick Burwell HN 8.00 20.00
DG Dick Gray 8.00 20.00
DW Don Williams EXCH 8.00 20.00
FC Fausto Carmona 8.00 20.00
GB Gordon Beckham HN 100.00 200.00
GC Gio Gonzalez HN 8.00 20.00
GM Gil McDougald 8.00 20.00
IN Irv Noren HN 8.00 20.00
IN Irv Noren 6.00 15.00
JB Jay Bruce HN 15.00 40.00
JB Jay Bruce 15.00 40.00
JG Johnny Groth 12.00 30.00
JH Jack Harshman 8.00 20.00
JM Justin Masterson 8.00 20.00
JP Jim Proctor 8.00 20.00
JR John Romonosky 8.00 20.00
JS Joe Shipley 8.00 20.00
JSS Jake Striker 8.00 20.00
MB Milton Bradley HN 8.00 20.00
MG Mat Gamel 8.00 20.00
ML Mike Lee 8.00 20.00
NC Nelson Chittum 8.00 20.00
RI Raul Ibanez HN 30.00 60.00
RJW Red Wilson 8.00 20.00
RS Ron Samford 8.00 20.00
RW Ray Webster 8.00 20.00
SK Steve Korcheck 8.00 20.00
SL Stan Lopata 8.00 20.00
TP Taylor Phillips 8.00 20.00
TW Ted Wieand 8.00 20.00
WL Whitey Lockman 8.00 20.00
WT Wayne Terwilliger 8.00 20.00

2009 Topps Heritage Then and Now

COMPLETE SET (10) 8.00 20.00
STATED ODDS 1:15 HOBBY
TN1 E.Banks/R.Howard 1.00 2.50
TN2 E.Banks/R.Howard 1.00 2.50
TN3 Minnie Minoso/Chipper Jones 1.00 2.50
TN4 Luis Aparicio/Willy Taveras .60 1.50
TN5 M.Mantle/A.Dunn 1.50 4.00
TN6 Bob Friend/Johan Santana .60 1.50
TN7 J.Podres/T.incecum .60 1.50
TN8 Bob Friend/Cliff Lee .60 1.50
TN9 Bob Friend/Roy Halladay .60 1.50
TN10 Whitey Ford/CC Sabathia .60 1.50

2009 Topps Heritage '59 National Convention VIP

COMPLETE SET (5) 8.00 20.00
573A Mickey Mantle Facing Left 4.00 10.00
573B Mickey Mantle Facing Right 4.00 10.00
574 Roy Campanella 1.25 3.00
575 Jackie Robinson 1.25 3.00
576 Roger Maris 1.25 3.00

2010 Topps Heritage

COMP.SET w/o SPs (425) 30.00 60.00
COMMON CARD (1-425) .15 .40
COMMON RC (1-425) .40 1.00
DICE ODDS 1:72 HOBBY
COMMON NAME VAR (1-427) 30.00 60.00
61 CHASE MINORS
61 CHASE SEMIS
61 CHASE UNLISTED
61 CHASE ODDS 1:435 HOBBY
COMMON SP (426-500) 2.50 6.00
SP ODDS 1:3 HOBBY
1a Albert Pujols .50 1.25
1b A.Pujols Dice SP 3.00 8.00
1c A.Pujols Blk Name SP 30.00 60.00
2a Joe Mauer .30 .75
2b Joe Mauer Dice Back SP 2.50 6.00
2c Joe Mauer All Black Nameplate SP 30.00 60.00
3 Joe Blanton .15 .40
4 Delmon Young .25 .60
5 Kelly Shoppach .15 .40
6 Ronald Belisario .15 .40
7 Chicago White Sox .15 .40
8 Rajai Davis .15 .40
9 Aaron Harang .15 .40
10 Brian Roberts .15 .40
11 Adam Wainwright .25 .60
12 Geovany Soto .25 .60
13 Ramon Santiago .15 .40
14 Albert Callaspo .15 .40
15a Grady Sizemore .25 .60
15b Grady Sizemore Dice Back SP 3.00 8.00
15c Grady Sizemore Red-Green
Nameplate SP 30.00 60.00
16 Clay Buchholz .15 .40
17 Checklist .15 .40
18 David Huff .15 .40
19a Alex Rodriguez .50 1.25
20 Cole Hamels .30 .75
21 Orlando Cabrera .15 .40
22 Ross Ohlendorf .15 .40
23a Matt Kemp .30 .75
23b Matt Kemp Dice Back SP 4.00 10.00
24 Andrew Bailey .15 .40
25 Juan Francisco/Jay Bruce/Joey Votto .40 1.00
26 Chris Tillman .15 .40
27 Mike Fontenot .15 .40
28 Melky Cabrera .15 .40
29 Reid Gorecki (RC) .60 1.50
30 Jayson Nix .15 .40
31 Bengie Molina .15 .40
32 Chris Carpenter .25 .60
33 Jason Bay .25 .60
34 Fausto Carmona .15 .40
35 Gordon Beckham .15 .40
36 Glen Perkins .15 .40
37 Curtis Granderson .30 .75
38 Rafael Furcal .15 .40
39 Matt Carson (RC) .40 1.00
40 A.J. Burnett .15 .40
41 Ram/San/Puj/Hel .50 1.25
42 Mau/Ich/Jet/Cab 1.00 2.50
43 Puj/Fie/How/Rey .50 1.25
44 C.Pena/Teixeira/J.Bay/A.Hill .25 .60
45 Car/Lin/Jur/Wai .25 .60
46 Greinke/F.Hernandez/Halladay
Sabathia .40 1.00
47 Wainwright/C. Carpenter
De La Rosa/B.Arroyo .25 .60
48 Felix/CC/Verland/Beck .40 1.00
49 Lin/J.Vaz/Har/Wai .25 .60
50 Verlan/Grein/Lest/Felix .40 1.00
51 Detroit Tigers .15 .40
52 Ronny Cedeno .15 .40
53 Jason Varitek .40 1.00
54 Daniel McCutchen RC .60 1.50
55a Pablo Sandoval .25 .60
55b Pablo Sandoval
Yellow-Green Nameplate SP 30.00 60.00
56a Jake Peavy .15 .40
56b Mickey Mantle SP 15.00 40.00
57 Billy Butler .15 .40
58 Ryan Dempster .15 .40
59 Neil Walker (RC) .60 1.50
60a Asdrubal Cabrera .25 .60
60b Babe Ruth SP 12.00 30.00
61a Ryan Church .15 .40
61b Roger Maris SP 12.00 30.00
62 Nick Markakis .30 .75
63 Nick Blackburn .15 .40
64 Mark DeRosa .15 .40
65 Paul Konerko .25 .60
66 Daniel Ray Herrera .15 .40
67 Brandon Inge .25 .60
68 Josh Thole RC .60 1.50
69 Josh Beckett .15 .40
70 Lastings Milledge .15 .40
71 Robert Andino .15 .40
72 Matt Cain .25 .60
73 Nate McLouth .15 .40
74 Russell Martin .15 .40
75 A.Pujols/D.Wright .50 1.25
76 Jay Bruce .25 .60
77a J.A. Happ .25 .60
77b Happ Org-Blu Name SP 15.00 40.00
78 Jayson Werth .25 .60
79 A.J. Pierzynski .15 .40
80 Michael Cuddyer .15 .40
81 Dustin Richardson RC .40 1.00
82a Justin Upton .25 .60
82b Justin Upton Dice Back SP 3.00 8.00
83 Rick Porcello .25 .60
84 Garret Anderson .15 .40
85 Jeremy Guthrie .15 .40
86 Los Angeles Dodgers .25 .60
87 Juan Uribe .15 .40
88 Alfonso Soriano .25 .60
89 Martin Prado .15 .40
90 Gavin Floyd .15 .40
91 Colby Rasmus .25 .60
92a Mark Teixeira .25 .60
92b Mark Teixeira Dice Back SP 3.00 8.00
93 Raul Ibanez .25 .60
94a Zack Greinke .40 1.00
94b Greinke YB Name SP 50.00 100.00
95 Miguel Cabrera .40 1.00
96 Randy Johnson .40 1.00
97 Chris Dickerson .15 .40
98 Checklist .15 .40
99 Jed Lowrie .15 .40
100 Zach Duke .15 .40
101 Jhonny Peralta .15 .40
102 Nolan Reimold .15 .40
103 Jimmy Rollins .25 .60
104 Jorge Posada .25 .60
105 Tim Hudson .25 .60
106 Scott Hairston .15 .40
107 Rich Harden .15 .40
108 Jason Kubel .15 .40
109 Clayton Kershaw .60 1.50
110 Willy Taveras .15 .40
111 Brett Myers .15 .40
112 Adam Everett .15 .40
113 Jonathan Papelbon .25 .60
114 Buster Posey RC 6.00 15.00
115 Kerry Wood .15 .40
116 Jerry Hairston Jr. .15 .40
117 Adam Dunn .25 .60
118 Yadier Molina .50 1.25
119 David DeJesus/Alex Gordon .25 .60
120a Chipper Jones .40 1.00
120b Chipper Jones Dice Back SP 3.00 8.00
121 John Lackey .25 .60
122 Chicago Cubs .25 .60
123 Nick Punto .15 .40
124 Daniel Hudson RC .60 1.50
125 David Hernandez .15 .40
126 Garrett Jones .15 .40
127 Joel Pineiro .15 .40
128 Jacoby Ellsbury .30 .75
129 Ian Desmond (RC) .60 1.50
130 James Loney .15 .40
131 Dave Trembley MG .15 .40
132 Ozzie Guillen MG .15 .40
133 Joe Girardi MG .25 .60
134 Jim Riggleman MG .15 .40
135 Dusty Baker MG .15 .40
136 Joe Torre MG .25 .60
137 Bobby Cox MG .15 .40
138 John Russell MG .15 .40
139 Tony LaRussa MG .25 .60
140 Jarrod Saltalamacchia .15 .40
141 Kosuke Fukudome .25 .60
142 Mariano Rivera .50 1.25
143 David DeJesus .15 .40
144 Jon Niese .15 .40
145 Jair Jurrjens .15 .40
146 Josh Willingham .25 .60
147 Chris Pettit RC .40 1.00
148 Chris Getz .15 .40
149 Ryan Doumit .15 .40
150 Aaron Rowand .15 .40
151 Brad Kilby RC .40 1.00
152 Prince Fielder .25 .60
153 Scott Baker .15 .40
154 Shane Victorino .25 .60
155 Luis Valbuena .15 .40
156 Drew Stubbs RC 1.00 2.50
157 Mark Buehrle .25 .60
158 Josh Bard .15 .40
159 Baltimore Orioles .15 .40
160 Andy Pettitte .25 .60
161 M.Bumgarner RC 4.00 10.00
162 Johnny Cueto .25 .60
163 Jeff Mathis .15 .40
164 Yunel Escobar .15 .40
165 Steve Pearce .40 1.00
166 Ramon Hernandez .15 .40
167 San Francisco Giants .15 .40
168 Chris Coghlan .15 .40
169 Ted Lilly .15 .40
170 Alex Rios .15 .40
171 Justin Verlander .40 1.00
172 Michael Brantley RC .60 1.50
173 D.Pedroia/J.Ellsbury .40 1.00
174 Craig Stammen .15 .40
175 Scott Rolen .25 .60
176 Howie Kendrick .15 .40
177 Trevor Cahill .15 .40
178 Matt Holliday .40 1.00
179a Chase Utley .25 .60
179b Chase Utley Dice Back SP 3.00 8.00
180 Robinson Cano .25 .60
181 Paul Maholm .15 .40
182a Adam Jones .25 .60
182b Adam Jones Dice Back SP 3.00 8.00
183 Felipe Lopez .15 .40
184 Kendry Morales .15 .40
185 John Danks .15 .40
186 Denard Span .15 .40
187 Nyjer Morgan .15 .40
188 Adrian Gonzalez .30 .75
189 Checklist .15 .40
190 Chad Billingsley .25 .60
191 Travis Hafner .15 .40
192 Gerald Laird .15 .40
193a Daisuke Matsuzaka .25 .60
193b Matsuzaka Dice SP 1.50 4.00
194 Joey Votto .40 1.00
195 Jered Weaver .25 .60
196 Ryan Theriot .15 .40
197 Gio Gonzalez .25 .60
198 Chris Iannetta .15 .40
199 Mike Jacobs .15 .40
19b A.Rod Dice SP 3.00 8.00
200 Javier Vasquez .15 .40
201 Josh Beckett/Johan Santana .25 .60
202 Torii Hunter .15 .40
203 Juan Rivera .15 .40
204 Brandon Phillips .15 .40
205 Edwin Jackson .15 .40
206 Lance Berkman .25 .60
207 Gil Meche .15 .40
208 Jorge Cantu .15 .40
209 Eric Young Jr (RC) .40 1.00
210 Andre Ethier .25 .60
211 Rickie Weeks .15 .40
212 Omir Santos .15 .40
213 Mat Latos .25 .60
214 Tyler Colvin RC .60 1.50
215a Derek Jeter 1.00 2.50
215b D.Jeter Dice SP 6.00 15.00
215c Jeter Red-Yel Name SP 50.00 100.00
216 Carlos Pena .25 .60
217 Carlos Ruiz .15 .40
218 Jason Marquis .15 .40
219 Charlie Manuel MG .15 .40
220 Bruce Bochy MG .25 .60
221 Terry Francona MG .25 .60
222 Manny Acta MG .15 .40
223 Jim Leyland MG .15 .40
224 Bob Geren MG .15 .40
225 Mike Scioscia MG .15 .40
226 Ron Gardenhire MG .15 .40
227 Luis Castillo .15 .40
228 New York Mets .25 .60
229 Carlos Carrasco (RC) 1.00 2.50
230 Chone Figgins .15 .40
231 Johan Santana .25 .60
232 Max Scherzer .40 1.00
233a Ian Kinsler .25 .60
233b Ian Kinsler Dice Back SP 3.00 8.00
234 Jeff Samardzija .15 .40
235 Will Venable .15 .40
236 Cristian Guzman .15 .40
237 Alexei Ramirez .25 .60
238 B.J. Upton .25 .60
239 Derek Lowe .15 .40
240 Elvis Andrus .25 .60
241 Joakim Soria .15 .40
242 Chase Headley .15 .40
243 Adam Lind .25 .60
244a Ichiro Suzuki .50 1.25
244b Ichiro Dice SP 3.00 8.00
245 Ryan Howard .30 .75
246 Johnny Damon .25 .60
247 Casey Blake .15 .40
248 Kevin Millwood .15 .40
249 Cincinnati Reds .15 .40
250 A.McCutchen/G.Jones .40 1.00
251 Jarrod Washburn .15 .40
252 Dan Uggla .15 .40
253 Cliff Lee .25 .60
254 Chris Davis .25 .60
255 Jordan Zimmermann .25 .60
256 Pedro Feliz .15 .40
257 Carlos Quentin .15 .40
258 Derek Holland .15 .40
259 Jose Reyes .25 .60
260 Manny Ramirez .40 1.00
261 David Ortiz .40 1.00
262 Andrew McCutchen .40 1.00
263 Brian Fuentes .15 .40
264 Nelson Cruz .40 1.00
265 Dexter Fowler .25 .60
266 Carlos Beltran .25 .60
267 Michael Young .15 .40
268 Chris Young .15 .40
269 Edgar Renteria .15 .40
270 Vin Mazzaro .15 .40
271 Gary Sheffield .15 .40
272 Roy Oswalt .25 .60
273 Checklist .15 .40
274 Stephen Drew .15 .40
275 John Lannan .15 .40
276 Tyler Flowers RC .60 1.50
277 Coco Crisp UER
Athletics spelled incorrectly .15 .40
278 Luis Durango RC .40 1.00
279 Erick Aybar .15 .40
280 Tobi Stoner RC .60 1.50
281 Cody Ross .15 .40
282 Koji Uehara .15 .40
283 Cleveland Indians .15 .40
284 Yovani Gallardo .15 .40
285 Wilkin Ramirez .15 .40
286 Roy Halladay .25 .60
287 Juan Francisco RC .60 1.50
288 Carlos Zambrano .25 .60
289 Carl Crawford .25 .60
290 Joba Chamberlain .15 .40
291 Fernando Martinez .15 .40
292 Jhoulys Chacin .15 .40
293 Felix Hernandez .25 .60
294 Josh Hamilton .25 .60
295 Rick Ankiel .15 .40
296 Hiroki Kuroda .15 .40
297 Oakland Athletics .15 .40
298 Wade Davis (RC) .60 1.50
299 Derrek Lee .15 .40
300a Hanley Ramirez .25 .60
300b Hanley Ramirez Dice Back SP 3.00 8.00
301 Ryan Spilborghs .15 .40
302 Adrian Beltre .40 1.00
303 James Shields .15 .40
304 Alex Gordon .25 .60
305 Brad Bergesen .15 .40
306 Lee Dominates .25 .60
307 Burnett Outduels Pedro .25 .60
308 AROD Homer .50 1.25
309 Damon Steals 2 Bags on 1 Pitch .25 .60
310 Utley Ties Reggie .25 .60
311 Matsui Knocks in 6 .40 1.00
312 Matsui Named MVP .40 1.00
313 The Winners Celebrate .40 1.00
314 H.Ramirez/E.Longoria .25 .60
315 Brandon Webb .25 .60
316 Kevin Youkilis .15 .40
317 Brent Dlugach (RC) .40 1.00
318 Aubrey Huff .15 .40
319 John Maine .15 .40
320 Pittsburgh Pirates .15 .40
321 Aramis Ramirez .15 .40
322 Michael Dunn RC .40 1.00
323 Shin-Soo Choo .25 .60
324 Mike Pelfrey .15 .40
325 Brett Gardner .25 .60
326 Nick Johnson .15 .40
327 Henry Rodriguez RC .40 1.00
328 Joe Nathan .15 .40
329 Mike Napoli .15 .40
330 Jamie Moyer .15 .40
331 Kyle Blanks .15 .40
332 Ryan Langerhans .15 .40
333 Travis Snider .15 .40
334 Wandy Rodriguez .15 .40
335 Carlos Gonzalez .25 .60
336 Francisco Rodriguez .25 .60
337 Mark Buehrle/Jake Peavy .25 .60
338 Ryan Zimmerman .25 .60
339 Michael Bourn .15 .40
340 Magglio Ordonez .25 .60
341 Brandon Morrow .15 .40
342 Daniel Murphy .30 .75
343 Ricky Romero .15 .40
344 Homer Bailey .15 .40
345 Nick Swisher .25 .60
346 Akinori Iwamura .15 .40
347 St. Louis Cardinals .25 .60
348 Julio Borbon .15 .40
349 Jose Guillen .15 .40
350 Scott Podsednik .15 .40
351 Bobby Crosby .15 .40
352 Ryan Ludwick .15 .40
353 Brett Cecil .15 .40
354 Minnesota Twins .15 .40
355 Ben Zobrist .25 .60
356 Dan Haren .15 .40
357 Vernon Wells .15 .40
358 Skip Schumaker .15 .40
359 Jose Lopez .15 .40
360a Vladimir Guerrero .25 .60
360b Vladimir Guerrero Dice Back SP 2.00 5.00
361 Checklist .15 .40
362 Brandon Allen (RC) .40 1.00
363 Joe Mauer .30 .75
Roy Halladay
364 Todd Helton .25 .60
365 J.J. Hardy .15 .40
366a CC Sabathia .25 .60
366b Sabath Grn-Yel Name SP 50.00 100.00
367 Yuniesky Betancourt .15 .40
368 Placido Polanco .15 .40
369 Josh Johnson .25 .60
370 Mark Reynolds .15 .40
371a Victor Martinez .25 .60
371b Victor Martinez Dice Back SP 3.00 8.00
372 Ian Stewart .15 .40
373 Boston Red Sox .25 .60
374 Brad Hawpe .15 .40
375 Ricky Nolasco .15 .40
376 Marco Scutaro .25 .60
377 Troy Tulowitzki .40 1.00
378 Francisco Liriano .15 .40
379 Randy Wells .15 .40
380 Jeff Francoeur .25 .60
381 Mike Lowell .15 .40
382 Hunter Pence .25 .60
383 T.Lincecum/M.Cain .25 .60
384 Scott Kazmir .15 .40
385 Hideki Matsui .40 1.00
386 Tim Wakefield .25 .60
387 Jeff Niemann .15 .40
388 John Smoltz .40 1.00
389 Franklin Gutierrez .15 .40
390 Matt LaPorta .15 .40
391 Melvin Mora .15 .40
392 Jeremy Bonderman .15 .40
393a Ryan Braun .25 .60
393b Ryan Braun
Blue-Orange Nameplate SP 30.00 60.00
394 Emilio Bonifacio .15 .40
395 Tommy Hanson .15 .40
396 Aaron Hill .15 .40
397 Micah Owings .15 .40
398 Jack Cust .15 .40
399 Jason Bartlett .15 .40
400 Brian McCann .25 .60
401 Babe Ruth BT 1.00 2.50
402 George Sisler BT .25 .60
403 Jackie Robinson BT .40 1.00
404 Rogers Hornsby BT .25 .60
405 Lou Gehrig BT .75 2.00
406 Mickey Mantle BT 1.25 3.00
407 Ty Cobb BT .60 1.50
408 Christy Mathewson BT .40 1.00
409 Walter Johnson BT .40 1.00
410 Honus Wagner BT .40 1.00
411 Pet/Pos/Jet/Riv 12.50 30.00
412 Joe Saunders .15 .40
413 Andrew Miller .25 .60
414 Alcides Escobar .25 .60
415 Luke Hochevar .15 .40
416 Gerardo Parra .15 .40
417 Garrett Atkins .15 .40
418 Jim Thome .25 .60
419 Michael Saunders .25 .60
420 Justin Morneau .25 .60
421 Dustin Pedroia .40 1.00
422 Dioner Navarro .15 .40
423 Checklist .15 .40
424 Chien-Ming Wang .25 .60
425 Marcus Thames .15 .40
426 David Price SP 4.00 10.00
427a David Wright SP 2.50 6.00
427b David Wright
Green-Yellow Nameplate SP 60.00 120.00
428 Tommy Manzella SP (RC) 2.50 6.00
429a Tim Lincecum SP 2.00 5.00
429b T.Lincecum Dice SP 2.00 5.00
430 Ken Griffey Jr. SP 5.00 12.00
431 Justin Masterson SP 2.50 6.00
432 Jermaine Dye SP 2.50 6.00
433 Casey McGehee SP 2.50 6.00
434 Brett Anderson SP 2.50 6.00
435 Matt Garza SP 2.50 6.00
436 Miguel Tejada SP 3.00 8.00
437 Checklist SP 2.50 6.00
438 Kurt Suzuki SP 2.50 6.00
439 Evan Longoria SP 3.00 8.00
440 Edinson Volquez SP 2.50 6.00
441 Doug Fister SP RC 2.50 6.00
442 Carlos Delgado SP 2.50 6.00
443 Philadelphia Phillies SP 2.50 6.00
444 Justin Duchscherer SP 2.50 6.00
445 Chris Volstad SP 2.50 6.00
446 Freddy Sanchez SP 2.50 6.00
447 Carlos Lee SP 2.50 6.00
448 Carlos Guillen SP 2.50 6.00
449 Hank Blalock SP 2.50 6.00
450 Ubaldo Jimenez SP 2.50 6.00
451 D.Jeter/J.Bartlett SP 5.00 12.00
452 Cliff Pennington SP 2.50 6.00
453 Miguel Montero SP 2.50 6.00
454 Corey Hart SP 2.50 6.00
455 Bronson Arroyo SP 2.50 6.00
456 Carlos Gomez SP 2.50 6.00
457 J.D. Drew SP 2.50 6.00
458 Kenshin Kawakami SP 3.00 8.00
459 Neftali Feliz SP 2.00 5.00
460 Bobby Abreu SP 2.50 6.00
461 Joe Maddon MG AS SP 2.50 6.00
462 Charlie Manuel MG AS SP 2.50 6.00
463a Mark Teixeira AS SP 3.00 8.00
463b Atlanta Braves SP 12.50 30.00
464 Albert Pujols AS SP 2.50 6.00
465 Aaron Hill AS SP 2.50 6.00
466 Chase Utley AS SP 3.00 8.00

467 Michael Young AS SP 2.00 5.00
468 David Wright AS SP 2.50 6.00
469 Derek Jeter AS SP 10.00 25.00
470 Hanley Ramirez AS SP 3.00 8.00
471 Jason Giambi SP 2.50 6.00
472 Ichiro Suzuki SP 3.00 8.00
473 Miguel Tejada SP 3.00 8.00
474 Alex Rodriguez SP 3.00 8.00
475 Justin Morneau SP 3.00 8.00
476 Dustin Pedroia SP 3.00 8.00
477 Albert Pujols SP 2.50 6.00
478 Jimmy Rollins SP 3.00 8.00
479 Ryan Howard SP 2.50 6.00
480 Cole Hamels SP 2.50 6.00
481 Manny Ramirez SP 3.00 8.00
482 Jermaine Dye SP 2.50 6.00
483 Mariano Rivera SP 6.00 15.00
484 Roy Oswalt SP 3.00 8.00
485 Matt Garza SP 2.50 6.00
486 Derek Jeter SP 8.00 20.00
487 Ichiro Suzuki AS SP 3.00 8.00
488 Raul Ibanez AS SP 3.00 8.00
489 Josh Hamilton AS SP 2.00 5.00
490 Shane Victorino AS SP 3.00 8.00
491 Jason Bay AS SP 3.00 8.00
492 Ryan Braun AS SP 3.00 8.00
493 Joe Mauer AS SP 2.50 6.00
494 Yadier Molina AS SP 6.00 15.00
495 Roy Halladay AS SP 3.00 8.00
496 Tim Lincecum AS SP 2.00 5.00
497 Mark Buehrle AS SP 4.00 10.00
498 Johan Santana AS SP 3.00 8.00
499 Mariano Rivera AS SP 6.00 15.00
500 Francisco Rodriguez AS SP 3.00 8.00

2010 Topps Heritage Advertising Panels

ISSUED AS BOX TOPPER
1 Rick Ankiel .40 1.00
Jarrod Washburn/Travis Hafner
2 Scott Baker 1.00 2.50
Miguel Cabrera/Reid Gorecki
3 Gordon Beckham 1.00 2.50
Zack Greinke/Prince Fielder
4 Lance Berkman 1.00 2.50
Josh Willingham/AL Strikeout LL
5 Josh Hamilton .60 1.50
Kevin Millwood/Chad Billingsley
6 Melky Cabrera .40 1.00
Mark DeRosa/Dave Trembley
7 Miguel Cabrera 1.00 2.50
Reid Gorecki/Melky Cabrera
8 Luis Castillo 1.00 2.50
Adam Dunn/Honus Wagner
9 Chris Coghlan .60 1.50
Lance Berkman/Josh Willingham
10 Nelson Cruz 1.00 2.50
Adam Jones/John Russell
11 Michael Cuddyer 1.00 2.50
Jim Thome/Adrian Beltre
12 Prince Fielder .60 1.50
Charlie Manuel/Juan Francisco
13 Gio Gonzalez .60 1.50
Jeff Samardzija/Brandon Morrow
14 Reid Gorecki .60 1.50
Melky Cabrera/Mark DeRosa
15 Zack Greinke 1.00 2.50
Prince Fielder/Charlie Manuel
16 Ozzie Guillen .40 1.00
Glen Perkins/Gordon Beckham
17 Jerry Hairston Jr. .60 1.50
Scott Rolen/Joakim Soria
18 Aaron Hill .40 1.00
Joe Saunders/Scott Podsednik
19 Huff/Santos/Kershaw 1.50 4.00
20 Chris Iannetta .60 1.50
Dexter Fowler/CC Sabathia
21 Edwin Jackson .60 1.50
Erick Aybar/Rogers Hornsby
22 Howie Kendrick .75 2.00
Willy Taveras/Joe Mauer
23 Kershaw/Butler/Owings 1.50 4.00
24 Mike Lowell .60 1.50
Chris Coghlan/Lance Berkman
25 Brandon Morrow .40 1.00
Aaron Hill/Joe Saunders
26 Daniel Murphy .75 2.00
Carlos Zambrano/Will Venable
27 Ricky Nolasco .40 1.00
Derek Holland/Felipe Lopez
28 Micah Owings .60 1.50
John Maine/Mat Latos
29 Hunter Pence .60 1.50
Luis Castillo/Adam Dunn
30 Glen Perkins 1.00 2.50
Gordon Beckham/Zack Greinke
31 A.J. Pierzynski .40 1.00
Yuniesky Betancourt/Matt LaPorta
32 Carlos Quentin 2.50 6.00
AL Batting Average LL/Nolan Reimold
33 Nolan Reimold .40 1.00
Baltimore Orioles/Edwin Jackson
34 Scott Rolen .60 1.50
Joakim Soria/Vernon Wells
35 Michael Saunders .40 1.00
Ricky Nolasco/Derek Holland
36 Gary Sheffield .40 1.00
Jose Guillen/Brad Hawpe
37 James Shields .40 1.00
Chase Headley/Howie Kendrick
38 Joakim Soria .40 1.00
Vernon Wells/Franklin Gutierrez
39 Will Venable 1.00 2.50
Scott Baker/Miguel Cabrera
40 Jarrod Washburn .40 1.00
Travis Hafner/David Hernandez
41 Josh Willingham 1.00 2.50
AL Strikeout LL/Alex Rodriguez
42 Carlos Zambrano .60 1.50
Will Venable/Scott Baker
43 Omir Santos 1.50 4.00
Clayton Kershaw/Billy Butler
44 Alfonso Soriano .60 1.50
Chris Iannetta/Dexter Fowler
45 Scott Podsednik .40 1.00
Rick Ankiel/Jarrod Washburn
46 Henry Rodriguez .60 1.50
Hunter Pence/Luis Castillo
47 Travis Snider 1.00 2.50
Nelson Cruz/Adam Jones
48 Paul Konerko .60 1.50
Mike Lowell/Chris Coglan

2010 Topps Heritage Chrome

COMPLETE SET (150) 125.00 250.00
1-100 STATED ODDS 1:5 HERITAGE HOBBY
101-150 ODDS 1:26 T.CHROME HOBBY
STATED PRINT RUN 1961 SER.#'d SETS
C1 Albert Pujols 2.50 6.00
C2 Joe Mauer 2.00 5.00
C3 Rajai Davis 1.50 4.00
C4 Adam Wainwright 2.00 5.00
C5 Grady Sizemore 2.00 5.00
C6 Alex Rodriguez 2.50 6.00
C7 Cole Hamels 2.00 5.00
C8 Matt Kemp 2.50 6.00
C9 Chris Tillman 1.50 4.00
C10 Reid Gorecki 1.25 3.00
C11 Chris Carpenter 1.50 4.00
C12 Jason Bay 2.00 5.00
C13 Gordon Beckham 1.25 3.00
C14 Curtis Granderson 2.50 6.00
C15 Daniel McCutchen 2.00 5.00
C16 Pablo Sandoval 2.00 5.00
C17 Jake Peavy 1.25 3.00
C18 Ryan Church 1.50 4.00
C19 Nick Markakis 2.50 6.00
C20 Josh Beckett 1.25 3.00
C21 Matt Cain 2.00 5.00
C22 Nate McLouth 1.50 4.00
C23 J.A. Happ 2.00 5.00
C24 Justin Upton 2.50 6.00
C25 Rick Porcello 2.50 6.00
C26 Mark Teixeira 1.50 4.00
C27 Raul Ibanez 2.50 6.00
C28 Zack Greinke 3.00 8.00
C29 Nolan Reimold 1.25 3.00
C30 Jimmy Rollins 2.00 5.00
C31 Jorge Posada 2.00 5.00
C32 Clayton Kershaw 4.00 10.00
C33 Buster Posey 25.00 60.00
C34 Adam Dunn 2.00 5.00
C35 Chipper Jones 2.50 6.00
C36 John Lackey 2.50 6.00
C37 Daniel Hudson 2.00 5.00
C38 Jacoby Ellsbury 2.00 5.00
C39 Mariano Rivera 3.00 8.00
C40 Jair Jurrjens 1.50 4.00
C41 Prince Fielder 1.50 4.00
C42 Shane Victorino 2.00 5.00
C43 Mark Buehrle 2.00 5.00
C44 Madison Bumgarner 10.00 25.00
C45 Yunel Escobar 1.50 4.00
C46 Chris Coghlan 1.50 4.00
C47 Justin Verlander 3.00 8.00
C48 Michael Brantley 2.50 6.00
C49 Matt Holliday 2.50 6.00
C50 Chase Utley 1.50 4.00
C51 Adam Jones 2.00 5.00
C52 Kendry Morales 1.50 4.00
C53 Denard Span 1.50 4.00
C54 Nyjer Morgan 1.50 4.00
C55 Adrian Gonzalez 2.50 6.00
C56 Daisuke Matsuzaka 1.25 3.00
C57 Joey Votto 2.50 6.00
C58 Jered Weaver 2.50 6.00
C59 Lance Berkman 2.00 5.00
C60 Andre Ethier 2.00 5.00
C61 Mat Latos 2.50 6.00
C62 Derek Jeter 10.00 25.00
C63 Johan Santana 1.50 4.00
C64 Max Scherzer 4.00 10.00
C65 Ian Kinsler 2.00 5.00
C66 Elvis Andrus 2.00 5.00
C67 Adam Lind 2.00 5.00
C68 Ichiro Suzuki 2.50 6.00
C69 Ryan Howard 2.50 6.00
C70 Dan Uggla 1.25 3.00
C71 Cliff Lee 1.25 3.00
C72 Andrew McCutchen 2.50 6.00
C73 Nelson Cruz 3.00 8.00
C74 Stephen Drew 1.25 3.00
C75 Koji Uehara 1.25 3.00
C76 Roy Halladay 1.50 4.00
C77 Felix Hernandez 1.50 4.00
C78 Josh Hamilton 1.50 4.00
C79 Hanley Ramirez 1.50 4.00
C80 Kevin Youkilis 1.25 3.00
C81 Kyle Blanks 1.50 4.00
C82 Ryan Zimmerman 1.50 4.00
C83 Ricky Romero 1.50 4.00
C84 Julio Borbon 1.50 4.00
C85 Ben Zobrist 2.50 6.00
C86 Vladimir Guerrero 1.50 4.00
C87 CC Sabathia 2.00 5.00
C88 Josh Johnson 2.00 5.00
C89 Mark Reynolds 2.00 5.00
C90 Troy Tulowitzki 3.00 8.00
C91 Hunter Pence 2.00 5.00
C92 Ryan Braun 1.25 3.00
C93 Tommy Hanson 1.25 3.00
C94 Aaron Hill 1.50 4.00
C95 Brian McCann 2.00 5.00
C96 David Wright 2.00 5.00
C97 Tim Lincecum 1.25 3.00
C98 Evan Longoria 1.25 3.00
C99 Ubaldo Jimenez 1.25 3.00
C100 Neftali Feliz 1.50 4.00
C101 Brian Roberts 1.50 4.00
C102 A.J. Burnett 1.25 3.00
C103 Ryan Dempster 1.50 4.00
C104 Russell Martin 1.50 4.00
C105 Jay Bruce 2.00 5.00
C106 Jayson Werth 2.00 5.00
C107 Michael Cuddyer 1.50 4.00
C108 Alfonso Soriano 2.00 5.00
C109 Martin Prado 1.50 4.00
C110 Miguel Cabrera 2.50 6.00
C111 Yadier Molina 4.00 10.00
C112 Kosuke Fukudome 1.50 4.00
C113 Andy Pettitte 2.00 5.00
C114 Johnny Cueto 2.50 6.00
C115 Alex Rios 1.25 3.00
C116 Howie Kendrick 1.50 4.00
C117 Robinson Cano 1.50 4.00
C118 Chad Billingsley 2.50 6.00
C119 Torii Hunter 1.50 4.00
C120 Brandon Phillips 1.50 4.00
C121 Carlos Pena 2.00 5.00
C122 Chone Figgins 1.50 4.00
C123 Alexei Ramirez 2.50 6.00
C124 Carlos Quentin 1.25 3.00
C125 Jose Reyes 2.00 5.00
C126 Manny Ramirez 2.50 6.00
C127 David Ortiz 2.00 5.00
C128 Carlos Beltran 2.50 6.00
C129 Michael Young 1.50 4.00
C130 Roy Oswalt 2.00 5.00
C131 Erick Aybar 1.50 4.00
C132 Yovani Gallardo 1.50 4.00
C133 Carlos Zambrano 2.00 5.00
C134 Carl Crawford 2.00 5.00
C135 Aramis Ramirez 1.50 4.00
C136 Shin-Soo Choo 1.50 4.00
C137 Wandy Rodriguez 1.50 4.00
C138 Magglio Ordonez 2.00 5.00
C139 Dan Haren 1.50 4.00
C140 Victor Martinez 2.00 5.00
C141 Ian Stewart 1.50 4.00
C142 Francisco Liriano 1.50 4.00
C143 Scott Kazmir 1.50 4.00
C144 Hideki Matsui 2.50 6.00
C145 Justin Morneau 1.50 4.00
C146 Dustin Pedroia 2.00 5.00
C147 David Price 2.00 5.00
C148 Ken Griffey Jr. 4.00 10.00
C149 Carlos Lee 1.50 4.00
C150 Bobby Abreu 1.50 4.00

2010 Topps Heritage Chrome Black Refractors

1-100 ODDS 1:255 HERITAGE HOBBY
101-150 ODDS 1:616 T.CHROME HOBBY
STATED PRINT RUN 61SER.#'d SETS
C1 Albert Pujols 25.00 60.00
C2 Joe Mauer 15.00 40.00
C3 Rajai Davis 8.00 20.00
C4 Adam Wainwright 12.00 30.00
C5 Grady Sizemore 12.00 30.00
C6 Alex Rodriguez 25.00 60.00
C7 Cole Hamels 15.00 40.00
C8 Matt Kemp 15.00 40.00
C9 Chris Tillman 8.00 20.00
C10 Reid Gorecki 12.00 30.00
C11 Chris Carpenter 12.00 30.00
C12 Jason Bay 12.00 30.00
C13 Gordon Beckham 8.00 20.00
C14 Curtis Granderson 15.00 40.00
C15 Daniel McCutchen 12.00 30.00
C16 Pablo Sandoval 12.00 30.00
C17 Jake Peavy 8.00 20.00
C18 Ryan Church 8.00 20.00
C19 Nick Markakis 15.00 40.00
C20 Josh Beckett 8.00 20.00
C21 Matt Cain 12.00 30.00
C22 Nate McLouth 8.00 20.00
C23 J.A. Happ 8.00 20.00
C24 Justin Upton 12.00 30.00
C25 Rick Porcello 12.00 30.00
C26 Mark Teixeira 12.00 30.00
C27 Raul Ibanez 12.00 30.00
C28 Zack Greinke 20.00 50.00
C29 Nolan Reimold 8.00 20.00
C30 Jimmy Rollins 12.00 30.00
C31 Jorge Posada 12.00 30.00
C32 Clayton Kershaw 20.00 50.00
C33 Buster Posey 60.00 150.00
C34 Adam Dunn 12.00 30.00
C35 Chipper Jones 20.00 50.00
C36 John Lackey 12.00 30.00
C37 Daniel Hudson 12.00 30.00
C38 Jacoby Ellsbury 15.00 40.00
C39 Mariano Rivera 25.00 60.00
C40 Jair Jurrjens 8.00 20.00
C41 Prince Fielder 12.00 30.00
C42 Shane Victorino 12.00 30.00
C43 Mark Buehrle 12.00 30.00
C44 Madison Bumgarner 80.00 200.00
C45 Yunel Escobar 8.00 20.00
C46 Chris Coghlan 8.00 20.00
C47 Justin Verlander 20.00 50.00
C48 Michael Brantley 12.00 30.00
C49 Matt Holliday 20.00 50.00
C50 Chase Utley 12.00 30.00
C51 Adam Jones 12.00 30.00
C52 Kendry Morales 8.00 20.00
C53 Denard Span 8.00 20.00
C54 Nyjer Morgan 8.00 20.00
C55 Adrian Gonzalez 15.00 40.00
C56 Daisuke Matsuzaka 12.00 30.00
C57 Joey Votto 20.00 50.00
C58 Jered Weaver 20.00 50.00
C59 Lance Berkman 8.00 20.00
C60 Andre Ethier 12.00 30.00
C61 Mat Latos 12.00 30.00
C62 Derek Jeter 50.00 125.00
C63 Johan Santana 12.00 30.00
C64 Max Scherzer 20.00 50.00
C65 Ian Kinsler 12.00 30.00
C66 Elvis Andrus 12.00 30.00
C67 Adam Lind 12.00 30.00
C68 Ichiro Suzuki 25.00 60.00
C69 Ryan Howard 15.00 40.00
C70 Dan Uggla 8.00 20.00
C71 Cliff Lee 8.00 20.00
C72 Andrew McCutchen 20.00 50.00
C73 Nelson Cruz 20.00 50.00
C74 Stephen Drew 8.00 20.00
C75 Koji Uehara 8.00 20.00
C76 Roy Halladay 12.00 30.00
C77 Felix Hernandez 12.00 30.00
C78 Josh Hamilton 12.00 30.00
C79 Hanley Ramirez 12.00 30.00
C80 Kevin Youkilis 8.00 20.00
C81 Kyle Blanks 8.00 20.00
C82 Ryan Zimmerman 8.00 20.00
C83 Ricky Romero 8.00 20.00
C84 Julio Borbon 8.00 20.00
C85 Ben Zobrist 12.00 30.00
C86 Vladimir Guerrero 12.00 30.00
C87 CC Sabathia 12.00 30.00
C88 Josh Johnson 12.00 30.00
C89 Mark Reynolds 12.00 30.00
C90 Troy Tulowitzki 20.00 50.00
C91 Hunter Pence 12.00 30.00
C92 Ryan Braun 12.00 30.00
C93 Tommy Hanson 8.00 20.00
C94 Aaron Hill 8.00 20.00
C95 Brian McCann 12.00 30.00
C96 David Wright 15.00 40.00
C97 Tim Lincecum 12.00 30.00
C98 Evan Longoria 12.00 30.00
C99 Ubaldo Jimenez 8.00 20.00
C100 Neftali Feliz 8.00 20.00
C101 Brian Roberts 8.00 20.00
C102 A.J. Burnett 8.00 20.00
C103 Ryan Dempster 8.00 20.00
C104 Russell Martin 8.00 20.00
C105 Jay Bruce 12.00 30.00
C106 Jayson Werth 12.00 30.00
C107 Michael Cuddyer 8.00 20.00
C108 Alfonso Soriano 12.00 30.00
C109 Martin Prado 8.00 20.00
C110 Miguel Cabrera 20.00 50.00
C111 Yadier Molina 25.00 60.00
C112 Kosuke Fukudome 12.00 30.00
C113 Andy Pettitte 12.00 30.00
C114 Johnny Cueto 12.00 30.00
C115 Alex Rios 8.00 20.00
C116 Howie Kendrick 8.00 20.00
C117 Robinson Cano 12.00 30.00
C118 Chad Billingsley 12.00 30.00
C119 Torii Hunter 8.00 20.00
C120 Brandon Phillips 8.00 20.00
C121 Carlos Pena 12.00 30.00
C122 Chone Figgins 8.00 20.00
C123 Alexei Ramirez 12.00 30.00
C124 Carlos Quentin 8.00 20.00
C125 Jose Reyes 12.00 30.00
C126 Manny Ramirez 20.00 50.00
C127 David Ortiz 20.00 50.00
C128 Carlos Beltran 12.00 30.00
C129 Michael Young 8.00 20.00
C130 Roy Oswalt 12.00 30.00
C131 Erick Aybar 8.00 20.00
C132 Yovani Gallardo 8.00 20.00
C133 Carlos Zambrano 12.00 30.00
C134 Carl Crawford 12.00 30.00
C135 Aramis Ramirez 8.00 20.00
C136 Shin-Soo Choo 12.00 30.00
C137 Wandy Rodriguez 8.00 20.00
C138 Magglio Ordonez 12.00 30.00
C139 Dan Haren 8.00 20.00
C140 Victor Martinez 12.00 30.00
C141 Ian Stewart 8.00 20.00
C142 Francisco Liriano 8.00 20.00
C143 Scott Kazmir 8.00 20.00
C144 Hideki Matsui 20.00 50.00
C145 Justin Morneau 12.00 30.00
C146 Dustin Pedroia 20.00 50.00
C147 David Price 15.00 40.00
C148 Ken Griffey Jr. 40.00 100.00
C149 Carlos Lee 8.00 20.00
C150 Bobby Abreu 8.00 20.00

2010 Topps Heritage Chrome Refractors

*REF: .6X TO 1.5X BASIC INSERTS
1-100 ODDS 1:18 HERITAGE HOBBY
101-150 ODDS 1:68 T.CHROME HOBBY
STATED PRINT RUN 561 SER.#'d SETS

2010 Topps Heritage Baseball Flashbacks

COMPLETE SET (10) 6.00 15.00
STATED ODDS 1:12 HOBBY
BF1 Roger Maris 1.25 3.00
BF2 Warren Spahn .75 2.00
BF3 Whitey Ford .75 2.00
BF4 Frank Robinson .75 2.00
BF5 Whitey Ford .75 2.00
BF6 Candlestick Park .50 1.25
BF7 Carl Yastrzemski 2.00 5.00
BF8 Luis Aparicio .75 2.00
BF9 Al Kaline 1.25 3.00
BF10 Angels/Senators .50 1.25

2010 Topps Heritage Clubhouse Collection Relics

STATED ODDS 1:29 HOBBY
AE Andre Ethier 3.00 8.00
AK Adam Kennedy 2.00 5.00
AL Adam Lind 3.00 8.00
AP Albert Pujols 6.00 15.00
AR Aramis Ramirez 2.00 5.00
AW Adam Wainwright 3.00 8.00
BJ Bobby Jenks 2.00 5.00
BW Billy Wagner 2.00 5.00
CB Clay Buchholz 2.00 5.00
CG Cristian Guzman 2.00 5.00
CH Cole Hamels 4.00 10.00
CM Carlos Marmol 3.00 8.00
CS CC Sabathia 3.00 8.00
CZ Carlos Zambrano 3.00 8.00
DH Dan Haren 2.00 5.00
DN Dioner Navarro 2.00 5.00
DO David Ortiz 5.00 12.00
DU Dan Uggla 2.00 5.00
EL Evan Longoria 3.00 8.00
EV Edinson Volquez 2.00 5.00
GB Gordon Beckham 2.00 5.00
GS Grady Sizemore 3.00 8.00
HK Hiroki Kuroda 2.00 5.00
JB Jason Bulger 2.00 5.00
JC Jose Contreras
JD Jermaine Dye 2.00 5.00
JF Jeff Francis 2.00 5.00
JL James Loney 2.00 5.00
JV Joey Votto 5.00 12.00
JW Jered Weaver 3.00 8.00
KJ Kenji Johjima 2.00 5.00
KM Kendry Morales 2.00 5.00
KW Kerry Wood 2.00 5.00
LB Lance Berkman 3.00 8.00
MB Mark Buehrle 3.00 8.00
ME Mark Ellis 2.00 5.00
MK Matt Kemp 4.00 10.00
MT Miguel Tejada 3.00 8.00
MY Michael Young 2.00 5.00
NM Nate McLouth 2.00 5.00
PK Paul Konerko 3.00 8.00
PS Pablo Sandoval 3.00 8.00
RB Rocco Baldelli 2.00 5.00
RD Ryan Dempster 2.00 5.00
RH Ryan Howard 4.00 10.00
RL Ryan Ludwick 2.00 5.00
RM Russell Martin 2.00 5.00
VG Vladimir Guerrero 3.00 8.00
AJP A.J. Pierzynski 2.00 5.00
ARA Alexei Ramirez 3.00 8.00
BWE Brandon Webb 3.00 8.00
CHE Chase Headley 2.00 5.00
HCK Hong-Chih Kuo 2.00 5.00
JCR Joe Crede 2.00 5.00
KMI Kevin Millwood 2.00 5.00

2010 Topps Heritage Clubhouse Collection Dual Relics

STATED ODDS 1:6150 HOBBY
STATED PRINT RUN 61 SER.#'d SETS
AR L.Aparicio/A.Ramirez 10.00 25.00
BM B.Robinson/N.Markakis 12.50 30.00
MR R.Maris/A.Rodriguez 100.00 200.00
MT M.Mantle/M.Teixeira 100.00 200.00
YE C.Yastrzemski/J.Ellsbury 40.00 80.00

2010 Topps Heritage Cut Signatures

STATED ODDS 1:285,000
STATED PRINT RUN 1 SER.#'d SET

2010 Topps Heritage Flashback Stadium Relics

STATED ODDS 1:475 HOBBY
AK Al Kaline 6.00 15.00
BG Bob Gibson 4.00 10.00
EB Ernie Banks 12.00 30.00
FR Frank Robinson 40.00 100.00
JP Jim Piersall 2.50 6.00
LA Luis Aparicio 4.00 10.00
MM Mickey Mantle 25.00 60.00
RM Roger Maris 20.00 50.00
RS Brooks Robinson 4.00 10.00
SM Stan Musial 10.00 25.00

2010 Topps Heritage Framed Dual Stamps

STATED ODDS 1:193 HOBBY
STATED PRINT RUN 50 SER.#'d SETS
AD Brett Anderson 6.00 15.00
Adam Dunn
AH Bronson Arroyo 4.00 10.00
Luke Hochevar
AP Garret Anderson 6.00 15.00
Andy Pettitte
BA Casey Blake 6.00 15.00
Elvis Andrus
BE Mark Buehrle 6.00 15.00
Yunel Escobar
BF R.Braun/G.Floyd 6.00 15.00
BG Jay Bruce 8.00 20.00
Curtis Granderson
BL Carlos Beltran 6.00 15.00
John Lackey
BT Marlon Byrd 6.00 15.00
Josh Thole
BU Kyle Blanks 6.00 15.00
B.J. Upton
CB Jorge Cantu 4.00 10.00
Scott Baker
CE Michael Cuddyer 6.00 15.00
Andre Ether
CG Johnny Cueto 10.00 25.00
Zack Greinke
CH1 M.Cabrera/F.Hernandez 10.00 25.00
CH2 Chris Coghlan 6.00 15.00
Felix Hernandez
CJ M.Cabrera/G.Jones 10.00 25.00
CK Matt Cain 6.00 15.00
Paul Konerko
CL Melky Cabrera 6.00 15.00
Mat Latos
CM Orlando Cabrera 12.00 30.00
Yadier Molina
CR Shin-Soo Choo 6.00 15.00
Francisco Rodriguez
DA Adam Dunn 6.00 15.00
Bobby Abreu
DF Zach Duke 6.00 15.00
Tyler Flowers
DG David DeJesus 6.00 15.00
Reid Gorecki
DI Johnny Damon 6.00 15.00
Raul Ibanez
DR Rajai Davis 4.00 10.00
Mark Reynolds
DY Ryan Dempster 4.00 10.00
Michael Young
EC Andre Either 6.00 15.00
Robinson Cano
FB Pedro Feliz 10.00 25.00
Adrian Beltre
FG Jeff Francouer 6.00 15.00
Carlos Guillen
GB Cristian Guzman 6.00 15.00
Chad Billingsley
GC Adrian Gonzalez 8.00 20.00
Carl Crawford
GF Matt Garza 6.00 15.00
Prince Fielder
GG Curtis Granderson 8.00 20.00
Adrian Gonzalez
GH Carlos Guillen 4.00 10.00
Rich Harden
GR Zack Greinke 10.00 25.00
Hanley Ramirez
GS Reid Gorecki 6.00 15.00
Joe Saunders
GW Vladimir Guerrero 8.00 20.00
David Wright
HA Orlando Hudson 4.00 10.00
Erick Aybar
HB Rich Harden 4.00 10.00
Marlon Byrd
HC J.Happ/M.Cabrera 10.00 25.00
HM Matt Holliday 10.00 25.00
Justin Morneau
HR Aaron Hill 6.00 15.00
Jimmy Rollins
HU Roy Halladay 6.00 15.00
Justin Upton
IL Raul Ibanez 6.00 15.00
Jon Lester
IU Ian Kinsler 8.00 20.00
Chase Utley
JL Jair Jurrjens 6.00 15.00
Adam Lind
JM Josh Johnson 6.00 15.00
Victor Martinez
JN Garrett Jones 4.00 10.00
Jeff Neimann
JO Ubaldo Jimenez 6.00 15.00
Magglio Ordonez
JZ Adam Jones 6.00 15.00
Ryan Zimmerman
KA Howie Kendrick 4.00 10.00
Bronson Arroyo
KD Jason Kubel 4.00 10.00
Stephen Drew
KJ Paul Konerko 6.00 15.00
Ubaldo Jimenez
KK Matt Kemp 8.00 20.00
Scott Kazmir
KM Scott Kazmir 4.00 10.00
Nate McLouth
KP Hiroki Kuroda 4.00 10.00
Chris Pettit
KQ Kenshin Kawakami 6.00 15.00
Carlos Quentin
KR C.Kershaw/A.Ramirez 15.00 40.00
LC Derek Lowe 4.00 10.00
Orlando Cabrera
LG T.Lincecum/M.Garza 6.00 15.00
LL Adam Lind 6.00 15.00
Felipe Lopez
LM Cliff Lee 10.00 25.00
Hideki Matsui
LT Mat Latos 6.00 15.00
Chris Tillman
LW Jon Lester 6.00 15.00
Jayson Werth
LZ Jose Lopez 6.00 15.00
Jordan Zimmermann
MB Kevin Millwood 4.00 10.00
Casey Blake
MD Yadier Molina 12.00 30.00
David DeJesus
ME Nate McLouth 8.00 20.00
Jacoby Ellsbury
MG M.Montero/K.Griffey 20.00 50.00
ML Hideki Matsui 10.00 25.00
James Loney
MM Kendry Morales 10.00 25.00
Andrew McCutchen
MU Justin Morneau 6.00 15.00
Dan Uggla
MV McCutchen/Verlander 10.00 25.00
NF Ricky Nolasco 4.00 10.00
Scott Feldman
NG Jeff Neimann 4.00 10.00
Cristian Guzman
NL Joe Nathan 4.00 10.00
Derek Lowe
OA Roy Oswalt 6.00 15.00
Brett Anderson
OO Magglio Ordonez 6.00 15.00
Roy Oswalt
OW David Ortiz 10.00 25.00
Brandon Webb
PB D.Pedroia/C.Beltran 10.00 25.00
PF Andy Pettitte 6.00 15.00
Pedro Feliz
PG Hunter Pence 6.00 15.00
Franklin Gutierrez
PR Mike Pelfrey 4.00 10.00
Dustin Richardson
PS David Price 10.00 25.00
Max Scherzer
QP Carlos Quentin 4.00 10.00
Gerardo Parra
RB M.Ramirez/G.Beckham 10.00 25.00
RJ Hanley Ramirez 6.00 15.00
Adam Jones
RL A.Rodriguez/T.Lincecum 12.00 30.00
RM Dustin Richardson 6.00 15.00
Brian McCann
RR J.Reyes/A.Rodriguez 12.00 30.00
RT Mark Reynolds 6.00 15.00
Mark Teixeira
SB I.Suzuki/R.Braun 12.00 30.00
SC Grady Sizemore 6.00 15.00
Johnny Cueto
SD Johan Santana 6.00 15.00
Rajai Davis
SG Pablo Sandoval 6.00 15.00
Vladimir Guerrero
SJ Denard Span 4.00 10.00
Jair Jurrjens
SK K.Suzuki/C.Kershaw 15.00 40.00
SY Nick Swisher 6.00 15.00
Eric Young Jr.
TD Ryan Theriot 6.00 15.00
Johnny Damon
TS Troy Tulowitzki 10.00 25.00
Grady Sizemore
TZ Chris Tillman 6.00 15.00
Carlos Zambrano
UC Koji Uehara 4.00 10.00
Jorge Cantu
UH Dan Uggla 4.00 10.00
Torii Hunter
UK Justin Upton 6.00 15.00
Ian Kinsler
UM B.J. Upton 6.00 15.00
Miguel Montero
UY Chase Utley 6.00 15.00
Kevin Youkilis
VH J.Verlander/R.Howard 10.00 25.00
VM Joey Votto 10.00 25.00
Nick Markakis
VR Shane Victorino 6.00 15.00
Brian Roberts
WF Jered Weaver 6.00 15.00
Dexter Fowler
WL Jayson Werth 6.00 15.00
Jose Lopez
WR Brandon Webb 6.00 15.00
Nolan Reimold
YC Eric Young Jr. 4.00 10.00
Melky Cabrera
YH Michael Young 10.00 25.00
Matt Holiday
YT Kevin Youkilis 10.00 25.00
Troy Tulowitzki
ZL Zimmerman/E.Longoria 6.00 15.00
ZO Carlos Zambrano 10.00 25.00
David Ortiz
ZU Jordan Zimmermann 6.00 15.00
Koji Uehara
AR1 Elvis Andrus 6.00 15.00
Colby Rasmus
AR2 Erick Aybar 4.00 10.00
Jorge De La Rosa
AV1 Bobby Abreu 6.00 15.00
Shane Victorino
AV2 Brandon Allen 4.00 10.00
Will Venable
BB1 Jason Bay 6.00 15.00
Lance Berkman
BB2 Adrian Beltre 10.00 25.00
Kyle Blanks
BB3 Chad Billingsley 6.00 15.00
Nick Blackburn
BH1 Scott Baker 4.00 10.00
Dan Haren
BH2 Gordon Beckham 4.00 10.00
Tommy Hanson
BM1 Jason Bartlett 6.00 15.00
Daniel McCutchen
BM2 Lance Berkman 6.00 15.00
Daisuke Matsuzaka
BP1 Josh Beckett 6.00 15.00
Hunter Pence
BP2 A.J. Burnett 4.00 10.00
Joel Pineiro
BV1 Nick Blackburn 10.00 25.00
Joey Votto
BV2 Billy Butler 4.00 10.00
Javier Vazquez
CD1 Robinson Cano 6.00 15.00
Carlos Delgado
CD2 Carl Crawford 6.00 15.00
Ryan Dempster
DB1 Jorge De La Rosa 4.00 10.00
Jason Bartlett
DB2 Carlos Delgado 4.00 10.00
Billy Butler
DS1 Mark Derosa 4.00 10.00
James Shields
DS2 Stephen Drew 6.00 15.00
CC Sabathia
EP1 J.Ellsbury/B.Posey 50.00 125.00
EP2 Yunel Escobar 6.00 15.00
Rick Porcello
FM1 Prince Fielder 6.00 15.00
Kendry Morales
FM2 Tyler Flowers 8.00 20.00
Daniel Murphy
FS1 Gavin Floyd 6.00 15.00
Alfonso Soriano
FS2 Dexter Fowler 6.00 15.00
Denard Span
FT1 Scott Feldman 4.00 10.00
Ryan Theriot
FT2 Chone Figgins 6.00 15.00
Miguel Tejada
GD1 K.Griffey/Z.Duke 20.00 50.00
GD2 Franklin Gutierrez 4.00 10.00
Mark Derosa
HF1 Tommy Hanson 4.00 10.00
Chone Figgins
HF2 Luke Hochevar 6.00 15.00
Jeff Francouer
HH1 Brad Hawpe 6.00 15.00
Daniel Hudson
HH2 Felix Hernandez 6.00 15.00
Orlando Hudson
HJ1 Josh Hamilton 10.00 25.00
Chipper Jones
HJ2 Daniel Hudson 6.00 15.00
Nick Johnson
HK1 Cole Hamels 8.00 20.00
Jason Kubel
HK2 Todd Helton 6.00 15.00
Howie Kendrick
HK3 Torii Hunter 8.00 20.00
Matt Kemp
HP1 Dan Haren 4.00 10.00
Placido Polanco
HP2 R.Howard/D.Pedroia 10.00 25.00
JS1 D.Jeter/P.Sandoval 25.00 60.00
JS2 Nick Johnson 6.00 15.00
Nick Swisher
JS3 C.Jones/I.Suzuki 12.00 30.00
LB1 John Lackey 6.00 15.00
Jay Bruce
LB2 Derrek Lee 6.00 15.00
Mark Buehrle
LB3 Felipe Lopez 4.00 10.00
A.J. Burnett
LR1 E.Longoria/J.Reyes 6.00 15.00
LR2 James Loney 4.00 10.00
Juan Rivera
MP1 Nick Markakis 8.00 20.00
David Price
MP2 J.Mauer/A.Pujols 12.00 30.00
MR1 Victor Martinez 10.00 25.00
Manny Ramirez
MR2 Daisuke Matsuzaka 6.00 15.00
Aramis Ramirez
MR3 Brian McCann 12.00 30.00
Mariano Rivera
MR4 Daniel Murphy 8.00 20.00
Ricky Romero
MW1 John Maine 4.00 10.00
Vernon Wells
MW2 Daniel McCutchen 6.00 15.00
Jered Weaver
PA1 Jake Peavy 4.00 10.00
Garret Anderson
PA2 Rick Porcello 6.00 15.00
Brandon Allen
PC1 Carlos Pena 6.00 15.00
Matt Cain
PC2 Joel Pineiro 6.00 15.00
Shin-Soo Choo
PJ1 Jorge Posada 6.00 15.00
Josh Johnson
PJ2 A.Pujols/D.Jeter 25.00 60.00
PM1 Chris Pettit 4.00 10.00
John Maine

PM2 Placido Polanco 4.00 10.00
Kevin Millwood
PP1 Gerardo Parra 4.00 10.00
Jake Peavy
PP2 B.Posey/J.Posada 30.00 80.00
RH1 Alexi Ramirez 6.00 15.00
Brad Hawpe
RH2 Colby Rasmus 6.00 15.00
J.A. Happ
RK1 Nolan Reimold 6.00 15.00
Kenshin Kawakami
RK2 Ricky Romero 4.00 10.00
Hiroki Kuroda
RN1 Juan Rivera 4.00 10.00
Ricky Nolasco
RN2 Francisco Rodriguez 6.00 15.00
Joe Nathan
RP1 Aramis Ramirez 6.00 15.00
Carlos Pena
RP2 Brian Roberts 4.00 10.00
Mike Pelfrey
RS1 Mariano Rivera 12.00 30.00
Johan Santana
RS2 Jimmy Rollins 6.00 15.00
Kurt Suzuki
SH1 Max Scherzer 10.00 25.00
Aaron Hill
SH2 James Shields 8.00 20.00
Cole Hamels
SH3 Alfonso Soriano 6.00 15.00
Roy Halladay
SL1 CC Sabathia 6.00 15.00
Derrek Lee
SL2 Joe Saunders 6.00 15.00
Cliff Lee
TC1 Mark Teixeira 6.00 15.00
Chris Coghlan
TC2 Miguel Tejada 6.00 15.00
Michael Cuddyer
VB1 Javier Vazquez 4.00 10.00
Josh Beckett
VB2 Will Venable 6.00 15.00
Jason Bay
WH1 Vernon Wells 6.00 15.00
Todd Helton
WH2 David Wright 8.00 20.00
Josh Hamilton

2010 Topps Heritage Mantle Chase 61

COMPLETE SET (15) 30.00 60.00
COMMON MANTLE 3.00 8.00
RANDOM INSERTS IN TARGET PACKS
MM1 Mickey Mantle 3.00 8.00
MM2 Mickey Mantle 3.00 8.00
MM3 Mickey Mantle 3.00 8.00
MM4 Mickey Mantle 3.00 8.00
MM5 Mickey Mantle 3.00 8.00
MM6 Mickey Mantle 3.00 8.00
MM7 Mickey Mantle 3.00 8.00
MM8 Mickey Mantle 3.00 8.00
MM9 Mickey Mantle 3.00 8.00
MM10 Mickey Mantle 3.00 8.00
MM11 Mickey Mantle 3.00 8.00
MM12 Mickey Mantle 3.00 8.00
MM13 Mickey Mantle 3.00 8.00
MM14 Mickey Mantle 3.00 8.00
MM15 Mickey Mantle 3.00 8.00

2010 Topps Heritage Maris Chase 61

COMPLETE SET (15) 60.00 120.00
COMMON MARIS 5.00 12.00
RANDOM INSERTS IN WAL-MART PACKS
RM1 Roger Maris 5.00 12.00
RM2 Roger Maris 5.00 12.00
RM3 Roger Maris 5.00 12.00
RM4 Roger Maris 5.00 12.00
RM5 Roger Maris 5.00 12.00
RM6 Roger Maris 5.00 12.00
RM7 Roger Maris 5.00 12.00
RM8 Roger Maris 5.00 12.00
RM9 Roger Maris 5.00 12.00
RM10 Roger Maris 5.00 12.00
RM11 Roger Maris 5.00 12.00
RM12 Roger Maris 5.00 12.00
RM13 Roger Maris 5.00 12.00
RM14 Roger Maris 5.00 12.00
RM15 Roger Maris 5.00 12.00

2010 Topps Heritage New Age Performers

COMPLETE SET (15) 15.00 40.00
STATED ODDS 1:15 HOBBY
NA1 Justin Upton .60 1.50
NA2 Jacoby Ellsbury .75 2.00
NA3 Gordon Beckham .40 1.00
NA4 Tommy Hanson .40 1.00
NA5 Hanley Ramirez .60 1.50
NA6 Joe Mauer .75 2.00
NA7 Ichiro Suzuki 1.25 3.00
NA8 Derek Jeter 2.50 6.00
NA9 Albert Pujols 1.25 3.00
NA10 Ryan Howard .75 2.00
NA11 Zack Greinke 1.00 2.50
NA12 Matt Kemp .75 2.00
NA13 Miguel Cabrera 1.00 2.50
NA14 Mariano Rivera 1.25 3.00
NA15 Prince Fielder .60 1.50

2010 Topps Heritage News Flashbacks

COMPLETE SET (10) 5.00 12.00
2009 Topps Heritage News Flashbacks
NF1 Peace Corps .50 1.25
NF2 John F. Kennedy 1.25 3.00
NF3 Ham the Chimp .50 1.25
NF4 Venera 1 .50 1.25
NF5 Hassan II .50 1.25
NF6 Twenty Third Amendment .50 1.25
NF7 Apollo Program Announce .50 1.25
NF8 Berlin Wall .50 1.25
NF9 Vostok 1 .50 1.25
NF10 Ty Cobb 1.25 3.00

2010 Topps Heritage Real One Autographs

STATED ODDS 1:357 HOBBY
*RED INK/61: .5X TO 1.2X BASIC
AN Al Neiger 30.00 60.00
AR Al Rosen 20.00 50.00
BG Bob Gibson 30.00 60.00
BH Billy Harrell 10.00 25.00
BHA Bob Hale 10.00 25.00
BM Bobby Malkmus 30.00 60.00
BP Buster Posey 100.00 200.00
CB Collin Balester 10.00 25.00
DK Danny Kravitz 20.00 50.00
DP Dustin Pedroia 20.00 50.00
FR Frank Robinson 40.00 80.00
GB Gordon Beckham 12.00 30.00
GL Gene Leek 20.00 50.00
JB Jay Bruce 12.00 30.00
JB Julio Becquer 15.00 40.00
JC Jerry Casale 10.00 25.00
JD Joe DeMaestri 20.00 50.00
JG Joe Ginsberg 20.00 50.00
JJ Johnny James 15.00 40.00
JR Jim Rivera 12.00 30.00
JU Justin Upton 10.00 25.00
JW Jim Woods 10.00 25.00
LA Luis Aparicio 30.00 60.00
MH Matt Holliday 40.00 100.00
NG Ned Garver 20.00 50.00
RB Reno Bertoia 10.00 25.00
RB Rocky Bridges 30.00 60.00
RI Raul Ibanez 20.00 50.00
RL Ralph Lumenti 10.00 25.00
RS Ray Semproch 10.00 25.00
RS Red Schoendienst 30.00 60.00
RS R.C. Stevens 12.00 30.00
TB Tom Borland 10.00 25.00
TB Tom Brewer 12.00 30.00
TL Ted Lepcio 20.00 50.00
WD Walt Dropo 10.00 25.00

2010 Topps Heritage Ruth Chase 61

COMPLETE SET (15) 6.00 15.00
COMMON RUTH 1.25 3.00
RANDOM INSERTS IN HOBBY PACKS
BR1 Babe Ruth 1.25 3.00
BR2 Babe Ruth 1.25 3.00
BR3 Babe Ruth 1.25 3.00
BR4 Babe Ruth 1.25 3.00
BR5 Babe Ruth 1.25 3.00
BR6 Babe Ruth 1.25 3.00
BR7 Babe Ruth 1.25 3.00
BR8 Babe Ruth 1.25 3.00
BR9 Babe Ruth 1.25 3.00
BR10 Babe Ruth 1.25 3.00
BR11 Babe Ruth 1.25 3.00
BR12 Babe Ruth 1.25 3.00
BR13 Babe Ruth 1.25 3.00
BR14 Babe Ruth 1.25 3.00
BR15 Babe Ruth 1.25 3.00

2010 Topps Heritage Team Stamp Panels

1 Anaheim Angels 2.00 5.00
2 Arizona Diamondbacks 2.00 5.00
3 Atlanta Braves 3.00 8.00
4 Baltimore Orioles 2.50 6.00
5 Boston Red Sox 3.00 8.00
6 Chicago Cubs 2.00 5.00
7 Chicago White Sox 2.00 5.00
8 Cincinnati Reds 3.00 8.00
9 Cleveland Indians 2.00 5.00
10 Colorado Rockies 3.00 8.00
11 Detroit Tigers 3.00 8.00
12 Florida Marlins 2.00 5.00
13 Houston Astros 2.00 5.00
14 Kansas City Royals 3.00 8.00
15 Los Angeles Dodgers 3.00 8.00
16 Milwaukee Brewers 2.00 5.00
17 Minnesota Twins 2.50 6.00
18 New York Mets 2.50 6.00
19 New York Yankees 8.00 20.00
20 Oakland Athletics 1.25 3.00
21 Philadelphia Phillies 2.50 6.00
22 Pittsburgh Pirates 3.00 8.00
23 San Diego Padres 2.50 6.00
24 San Francisco Giants 2.00 5.00
25 Seattle Mariners 6.00 15.00
26 St. Louis Cardinals 4.00 10.00
27 Tampa Bay Rays 2.50 6.00
28 Texas Rangers 2.00 5.00
29 Toronto Blue Jays 2.00 5.00
30 Washington Nationals 2.00 5.00

2010 Topps Heritage Then and Now

STATED ODDS 1:15 HOBBY
TN1 R.Maris/A.Pujols 1.00 2.50
TN2 Roger Maris/Prince Fielder 1.25 3.00
TN3 Al Kaline/Joe Mauer 1.25 3.00
TN4 Luis Aparicio/Jacoby Ellsbury 1.00 2.50
TN5 M.Mantle/A.Gonzalez 2.00 5.00
TN6 Whitey Ford/Zack Greinke 1.25 3.00
TN7 Ford/J.Verlander 1.25 3.00
TN8 Whitey Ford/Felix Hernandez .75 2.00
TN9 Ford/J.Verlander 1.25 3.00
TN10 Whitey Ford/Roy Halladay .75 2.00

2010 Topps Heritage '60 National Convention VIP

COMPLETE SET (5) 10.00 25.00
573 Mickey Mantle 3.00 8.00
574 Mickey Mantle 3.00 8.00
575 Cal Ripken Jr. 3.00 8.00
576 Yogi Berra 1.00 2.50
577 Nolan Ryan 3.00 8.00

2011 Topps Heritage

COMP.SET w/o SP's (425) 25.00 60.00
COMMON CARD (1-425) .15 .40
COMMON ROOKIE (1-425) .40 1.00
COMPLETE J.ROB SET (10) 50.00 100.00
COMMON J.ROB SP (135-144) 5.00 12.00
STATED J.ROB ODDS 1:50 HOBBY
COMMON SP (426-500) 2.50 6.00
SP ODDS 1:3 HOBBY
1 Josh Hamilton .25 .60
2 Francisco Cordero .15 .40
3 David Ortiz .40 1.00
4 Ben Zobrist .25 .60
5 Clayton Kershaw .60 1.50
6 Brian Roberts .15 .40
7 Carlos Beltran .25 .60
8 John Danks .15 .40
9 Juan Uribe .15 .40
10 Andrew McCutchen .40 1.00
11 Joe Nathan .15 .40
12 Brad Mills MG .15 .40
13 Cliff Pennington .15 .40
14 Carlos Pena .25 .60
15 Fausto Carmona .15 .40
16 John Jaso .15 .40
17 Jayson Werth .25 .60
18 A.Pujols/R.Braun .50 1.25
19 Jake McGee (RC) .75 2.00
20 Johnny Damon .25 .60
21 Carl Pavano .15 .40
22 San Diego Padres .15 .40
23 Carlos Lee .15 .40
24 Detroit Tigers .15 .40
25 Starlin Castro .25 .60
26 Josh Thole .15 .40
27 Adam Kennedy .15 .40
28 Vernon Wells .15 .40
29 Terry Collins MG .15 .40
30 Chipper Jones .40 1.00
31 Ozzie Martinez RC .40 1.00
32 Russell Martin .15 .40
33 Barry Zito .25 .60
34 Ian Kinsler .25 .60
35 Stephen Strasburg .40 1.00
36 Mark Reynolds .15 .40
37 D.Jeter/R.Cano 1.00 2.50
38 Coco Crisp .15 .40
39 Erick Aybar .15 .40
40 Pablo Sandoval .25 .60
41 Chris Valaika RC .40 1.00
42 Nelson Cruz .40 1.00
43 Los Angeles Dodgers .25 .60
44 Justin Upton .25 .60
45 Evan Longoria .25 .60
46 Cole Hamels .30 .75
47 Kosuke Fukudome .25 .60
48 CC Sabathia .25 .60
49 Jordan Brown (RC) .40 1.00
50 Albert Pujols .50 1.25
51 Ham/Cabrera/Mauer/Beltre .40 1.00
52 Carlos Gonzalez/Joey Votto
Omar Infante/Troy Tulowitzki .40 1.00
53 Bautista/Kon/Cabr/Teix .40 1.00
54 Pujols/Dunn/Votto .50 1.25
55 Felix Hernandez/Clay Buchholz
David Price/Trevor Cahill .30 .75
56 Josh Johnson/Adam Wainwright
Roy Halladay/Jaime Garcia .25 .60
57 CC Sabathia/David Price/Jon Lester .30 .75
58 Roy Halladay/Adam Wainwright
Ubaldo Jimenez .25 .60
59 Wea/Felix/Lest/Verlan .40 1.00
60 Lin/Hal/Jim/Wain .25 .60
61 Milwaukee Brewers .15 .40
62 Brandon Inge .15 .40
63 Tommy Hanson .15 .40
64 Nick Markakis .30 .75
65 Robinson Cano .25 .60
66 Geovany Soto .25 .60
67 Zach Duke .15 .40
68 Travis Snider .15 .40
69 Cory Luebke RC .40 1.00
70 Justin Morneau .25 .60
71 Jonathan Sanchez .15 .40
72 Jimmy Rollins/Chase Utley .25 .60
73 Gordon Beckham .15 .40
74 Hanley Ramirez .25 .60
75 Chris Tillman .15 .40
76 Freddie Freeman RC 6.00 15.00
77 Chase Utley .25 .60
78 Matt LaPorta .15 .40
79 Jordan Zimmermann .25 .60
80 Jay Bruce .25 .60
81 Jason Varitek .40 1.00
82 Kevin Kouzmanoff .15 .40
83 Chris Carpenter .25 .60
84 Denard Span .15 .40
85 Ike Davis .15 .40
86 Alex Presley RC .60 1.50
87 Manny Ramirez .40 1.00
88 Joe Girardi MG .25 .60
89 Jake Peavy .15 .40
90 Julio Borbon .15 .40
91 Gaby Sanchez .15 .40
92 Armando Galarraga .15 .40
93 Nick Swisher .25 .60
94 R.A. Dickey .25 .60
95 Ryan Zimmerman .25 .60
96 Jered Weaver .25 .60
97 Grady Sizemore .25 .60
98 Minnesota Twins .15 .40
99 Brandon Snyder (RC) .40 1.00
100 David Price .30 .75
101 Jacoby Ellsbury .30 .75
102 Matt Capps .15 .40
103 Brandon Phillips .15 .40
104 Domonic Brown .30 .75
105 Max Scherzer .40 1.00
106 Yadier Molina .50 1.25
107 Madison Bumgarner .30 .75
108 Matt Kemp .30 .75
109 Ted Lilly .15 .40
110 Mark Teixeira .25 .60
111 Brad Lidge .15 .40
112 Luke Scott .15 .40
113 Chicago White Sox .15 .40
114 Kyle Drabek RC .60 1.50
115 Alfonso Soriano .25 .60
116 Gavin Floyd .15 .40
117 Alex Rios .15 .40
118 Skip Schumaker .15 .40
119 Scott Cousins RC .40 1.00
120 Bronson Arroyo .15 .40
121 Buck Showalter MG .15 .40
122 Trevor Cahill .15 .40
123 Aaron Hill .15 .40
124 Brian Duensing .15 .40
125A Vladimir Guerrero .25 .60
125B V.Guerrero SP 50.00 100.00
126 James Shields .15 .40
127 Dallas Braden/Trevor Cahill .15 .40
128 Joel Pineiro .15 .40
129 Carlos Quentin .15 .40
130 Omar Infante .15 .40
131 Brett Sinkbeil RC .40 1.00
132 Los Angeles Angels .15 .40
133 Andres Torres .15 .40
134 Brett Cecil .15 .40
135A Babe Ruth 1.00 2.50
135B Jackie Robinson/Displays Athletic
Talents At An Early Age SP 5.00 12.00
136A Babe Ruth 1.00 2.50
136B Jackie Robinson/Emerges As
College Star SP 5.00 12.00
137A Babe Ruth 1.00 2.50
137B Jackie Robinson/Serves Three Years
In The Army SP 5.00 12.00
138A Babe Ruth 1.00 2.50
138B Jackie Robinson/Breaks
The Game's Color Barrier SP 5.00 12.00
139A Babe Ruth 1.00 2.50
139B Jackie Robinson/Takes ROY Honors,
Then MVP SP 5.00 12.00
139C Joba Chamberlain SP 40.00 80.00
140A Babe Ruth 1.00 2.50
140B Jackie Robinson/Wraps Up Hall
Of Fame Career SP 5.00 12.00
141A Babe Ruth 1.00 2.50
141B Jackie Robinson/Legacy
Lives On SP 5.00 12.00
142A Babe Ruth 1.00 2.50
142B Jackie Robinson/Racks 'Em Up SP 5.00 12.00
143A Babe Ruth 1.00 2.50
143B Jackie Robinson/Robinson
Shines in the Fall SP 5.00 12.00
144A Babe Ruth 1.00 2.50
144B Jackie Robinson/The Resume SP 5.00 12.00
145 Dallas Braden .15 .40
146 Placido Polanco .15 .40
147 Joakim Soria .15 .40
148 Jonny Gomes .15 .40
149 Ryan Franklin .15 .40
150 Miguel Cabrera .40 1.00
151 Arthur Rhodes .15 .40
152 Jim Riggleman MG .15 .40
153 Marco Scutaro .25 .60
154 Brennan Boesch .25 .60
155 Brian Wilson .40 1.00
156 Hank Conger RC .60 1.50
157 Shane Victorino .25 .60
158 Atlanta Braves .15 .40
159 Joba Chamberlain .15 .40
160 Garrett Jones .15 .40
161 Bobby Jenks .15 .40
162 Alex Gordon .25 .60
163 M.Teixeira/A.Rodriguez .50 1.25
164 Jason Kendall .15 .40
165 Adam Jones .25 .60
166 Kevin Slowey .15 .40
167 Wilson Ramos .15 .40
168 Rajai Davis .15 .40
169 Curtis Granderson .30 .75
170 Aramis Ramirez .15 .40
171 Edinson Volquez .15 .40
172 Dusty Baker MG .15 .40
173 Jhonny Peralta .15 .40
174 Jon Garland .15 .40
175 Adam Dunn .25 .60
176 Chase Headley .15 .40
177 J.A. Happ .25 .60
178 A.J. Pierzynski .15 .40
179 Mat Latos .25 .60
180 Jim Thome .25 .60
181 Dillon Gee RC .60 1.50
182 Cody Ross .15 .40
183 Mike Pelfrey .15 .40
184 Kurt Suzuki .15 .40
185 Mariano Rivera .50 1.25
186 Rick Ankiel .15 .40
187 Jon Lester .25 .60
188 Freddy Sanchez .15 .40
189 Heath Bell .15 .40
190 Todd Helton .25 .60
191 Ryan Dempster .15 .40
192 Florida Marlins .15 .40
193 Miguel Tejada .25 .60
194 Jordan Walden RC .40 1.00
195 Paul Konerko .25 .60
196 Jose Valverde .15 .40
197 Casey Blake .15 .40
198 Tony La Russa MG .25 .60
199 Aroldis Chapman RC 1.25 3.00
200 Derek Jeter 1.00 2.50
201 Josh Beckett .15 .40
202 Corey Hart .15 .40
203 Kevin Millwood .15 .40
204 Brian Bogusevic (RC) .40 1.00
205 Scott Rolen .25 .60
206 Washington Nationals .15 .40
207 C.J. Wilson .15 .40
208 Rickie Weeks .15 .40
209 Andrew Romine RC .40 1.00
210 Evan Meek .15 .40
211 Elvis Andrus/Ian Kinsler .25 .60
212 Roy Oswalt .25 .60
213 Angel Pagan .15 .40
214 Chris Sale RC 3.00 8.00
215 Asdrubal Cabrera .25 .60
216 David Aardsma .15 .40
217 Don Mattingly MG .75 2.00
218 Buster Posey .50 1.25
219 Jeremy Hellickson RC 1.00 2.50
220 Ryan Howard .30 .75
221 Jeremy Guthrie .15 .40
222 Franklin Gutierrez .15 .40
223 Ryan Theriot .15 .40
224 Casey Coleman RC .40 1.00
225 Adrian Beltre .40 1.00
226 San Francisco Giants .15 .40
227 Cliff Lee .25 .60
228 Marlon Byrd .15 .40
229 Pedro Ciriaco RC .60 1.50
230 Francisco Liriano .15 .40
231 Chone Figgins .15 .40
232 Giants Win Opener HL .15 .40
233 Cain Dominates HL .25 .60
234 Rangers Retaliate HL .15 .40
235 Bumgarner Baffles HL .30 .75
236 Giants Crush Rangers HL .15 .40
237 Winners Celebrate HL .25 .60
238 Ichiro Suzuki .50 1.25
239 Brandon Beachy RC 1.00 2.50
240 Xavier Nady .15 .40
241 Josh Johnson .25 .60
242 Manny Acta MG .15 .40
243 A.J. Burnett .15 .40
244 Lars Anderson RC .60 1.50
245 Jason Bartlett .15 .40
246 Andrew Bailey .15 .40
247 Jonathan Lucroy .25 .60
248 Chris Johnson .15 .40
249 Vance Worley (RC) 1.50 4.00
250 Joe Mauer .30 .75
251 Texas Rangers .15 .40
252 James McDonald .15 .40
253 Lou Marson .15 .40
254 Chris Carter
255 Edwin Jackson .15 .40
256 Ruben Tejada .15 .40
257 Scott Kazmir .15 .40
258 Ryan Braun .25 .60
259 Kelly Johnson .15 .40
260 Matt Cain .25 .60
261 Reid Brignac .15 .40
262 Ivan Rodriguez .25 .60
263 Josh Hamilton/Nelson Cruz .40 1.00
264 Jeff Niemann .15 .40
265 Derrek Lee .15 .40
266 Jose Ceda RC .40 1.00
267 B.J. Upton .25 .60
268 Ervin Santana .15 .40
269 Lance Berkman .25 .60
270 Ronny Cedeno .15 .40
271 Jeremy Jeffress RC .40 1.00
272 Delmon Young .25 .60
273 Chris Perez .15 .40
274 Will Venable .15 .40
275 Billy Butler .15 .40
276 Darwin Barney RC 1.25 3.00
277 Pedro Alvarez RC .30 .75
278 Derek Lowe .15 .40
279A Bengie Molina .15 .40
280 Hiroki Kuroda .15 .40
281 Eduardo Nunez RC 1.00 2.50
282 Aaron Harang .15 .40
283 Danny Valencia .25 .60
284 Jimmy Rollins .25 .60
285 Adam Wainwright .25 .60
286 Ozzie Guillen MG .15 .40
287 Neftali Feliz .15 .40
288 Mike Stanton .40 1.00
289 Darren Ford RC .40 1.00
290 Ty Wigginton .15 .40
291 Bobby Cramer RC .40 1.00
292 Orlando Hudson .15 .40
293 Jonathon Niese .15 .40
294 Philadelphia Phillies .15 .40
295 Paul Maholm .15 .40
296 Ian Desmond .15 .40
297 Jonathan Broxton .15 .40
298 Jason Kubel .15 .40
299 Daniel Descalso RC .40 1.00
300 Carl Crawford .25 .60
301 Clay Buchholz .15 .40
302 Ramon Hernandez .15 .40
303 Daric Barton .15 .40
304 Brett Myers .15 .40
305 Mike Aviles .15 .40
306 D.Ortiz/D.Pedroia .40 1.00
307 Jair Jurrjens .15 .40
308 Jason Bay .25 .60
309 Yonder Alonso RC .60 1.50
310 Andy Pettitte .25 .60
311 Derek Jeter IA 1.00 2.50
312 Roy Halladay IA .25 .60
313 Jose Bautista IA .25 .60
314 Miguel Cabrera IA .40 1.00
315 CC Sabathia IA .25 .60
316 Joe Mauer IA .30 .75
317 Ichiro Suzuki IA .50 1.25
318 Mark Teixeira IA .25 .60
319 Tim Lincecum IA .25 .60
320 Jason Heyward .30 .75
321 Matt Mangini RC .40 1.00
322 Bruce Bochy MG .25 .60
323 Jon Jay .15 .40
324 Tommy Hunter .15 .40
325 Alexei Ramirez .25 .60
326 Gregory Infante RC .40 1.00
327 Jose Lopez .15 .40
328 Raul Ibanez .25 .60
329 Yovani Gallardo .15 .40
330 Mike Napoli .15 .40
331 Mike Leake .25 .60
332 Alcides Escobar .25 .60
333 Lucas Duda RC 1.00 2.50
334 Tampa Bay Rays .15 .40
335 Austin Jackson .15 .40
336 John Lackey .25 .60
337 Adam LaRoche .15 .40
338 Brett Gardner .25 .60
339 J.J. Hardy .15 .40
340 Chad Billingsley .25 .60
341 Lorenzo Cain .15 .40
342 Zack Greinke .40 1.00
343 Bobby Abreu .15 .40
344 Fernando Salas (RC) .60 1.50
345 Dustin Pedroia .40 1.00
346 Felix Hernandez .25 .60
347 Nyjer Morgan .15 .40
348 Eric Sogard RC .40 1.00
349 Jeremy Bonderman .15 .40
350 Joey Votto .40 1.00
351 Justin Morneau/Joe Mauer .30 .75
352 Ricky Nolasco .15 .40
353 Neil Walker .25 .60
354 Hunter Pence .25 .60
355 Brian Matusz .15 .40
356 Jose Bautista .25 .60
357 Brett Anderson .15 .40
358 Andre Ethier .25 .60
359 Carlos Zambrano .25 .60
360 Jorge Posada .25 .60
361 Randy Wolf .15 .40
362 Greg Halman RC .60 1.50
363 Nick Hundley .15 .40
364 Russell Branyan .15 .40
365 Howie Kendrick .15 .40
366 Rick Porcello .25 .60
367 Dan Uggla .15 .40
368 J.P. Arencibia .15 .40
369 Dan Haren .15 .40
370 Matt Holliday .40 1.00
371 Victor Martinez .25 .60
372 Jaime Garcia .25 .60
373 Carlos Gonzalez .25 .60
374 Charlie Manuel MG .15 .40
375 James Loney .15 .40
376 Phil Hughes .15 .40
377 Carlos Santana .40 1.00
378 Ubaldo Jimenez .15 .40
379 Travis Hafner .15 .40
380 Tim Hudson .25 .60
381 Orlando Cabrera .15 .40
382 Casey McGehee .15 .40
383 Daniel Hudson .15 .40
384 Oakland Athletics .15 .40
385 Mark Buehrle .25 .60
386 Michael Cuddyer .15 .40
387 Desmond Jennings RC .60 1.50
388 Rafael Soriano .15 .40
389 Ryan Doumit .15 .40
390 Albert Pujols AS .50 1.25
391 Martin Prado AS .15 .40
392A Ryan Zimmerman AS .25 .60
392B R.Zimmerman AS SP 100.00 200.00
393 Hanley Ramirez AS .25 .60
394 Ryan Braun AS .25 .60
395 Matt Holliday AS .40 1.00
396 Carlos Gonzalez AS .25 .60
397 Brian McCann AS .25 .60
398 Joey Votto AS .40 1.00
399 Roy Halladay AS .25 .60
400 Mark Teixeira .25 .60
401 Matt Kemp/Andre Ethier .30 .75
402 David DeJesus .15 .40
403 Jonathan Papelbon .25 .60
404 Mark Trumbo (RC) 1.00 2.50
405 Gio Gonzalez .25 .60
406 Tyler Colvin .15 .40
407 Wade Davis .15 .40
408 Chris Coghlan .15 .40
409 Pittsburgh Pirates .15 .40
410 Juan Pierre .15 .40
411 Michael Young .15 .40
412 Colby Rasmus .25 .60
413 Chris Young .15 .40
414 Jarrod Dyson RC .60 1.50
415 Dexter Fowler .25 .60
416 Jim Leyland MG .15 .40
417 Lucas May RC .40 1.00
418 Ian Stewart .15 .40
419 Wandy Rodriguez .15 .40
420 Miguel Montero .15 .40
421 Francisco Rodriguez .25 .60
422 Kendry Morales .15 .40
423 B.Wilson/B.Posey .50 1.25
424 Leo Nunez .15 .40
425 Kevin Youkilis .15 .40
426 Brent Morel SP RC 2.50 6.00
427 Will Rhymes SP 2.50 6.00
428 Josh Willingham SP 4.00 10.00
429 Tim Lincecum SP 2.00 5.00
430 Troy Tulowitzki SP 5.00 12.00
431 Welington Castillo SP (RC) 2.50 6.00
432 Michael Bourn SP 2.50 6.00
433 Kyle Davies SP 2.50 6.00
434 Carlos Ruiz SP 2.50 6.00
435 Huston Street SP 2.50 6.00
436 Jose Reyes SP 3.00 8.00
437 Adrian Gonzalez SP 4.00 10.00
438 Shaun Marcum SP 2.50 6.00
439 Stephen Drew SP 2.50 6.00
440 Ricky Romero SP 2.50 6.00
441 Jorge de la Rosa SP 2.50 6.00
442 Kevin Gregg SP 2.50 6.00
443 Brian McCann SP 3.00 8.00
444 Rafael Furcal SP 2.50 6.00
445 Prince Fielder SP 3.00 8.00
446 Carlos Marmol SP 3.00 8.00
447 Shin-Soo Choo SP 2.00 5.00
448 Clayton Richard SP 2.50 6.00
449 Elvis Andrus SP 3.00 8.00
450 Johnny Cueto SP 4.00 10.00
451 Ben Revere SP RC 3.00 8.00
452 Adam Lind SP 3.00 8.00
453 Roy Halladay SP 2.00 5.00
454 Jose Tabata SP 2.50 6.00
455 Joe Saunders SP 2.50 6.00
456 Jeff Keppinger SP 2.50 6.00
457 J.D. Drew SP 2.50 6.00
458 Ian Kennedy SP 2.50 6.00
459 John Buck SP 2.50 6.00
460 Justin Verlander SP 5.00 12.00
461 Russ Mitchell SP RC 2.50 6.00
462 Magglio Ordonez SP 3.00 8.00
463 Bob Geren MG SP 2.50 6.00
464 Johan Santana SP 2.00 5.00
465 Cincinnati Reds SP 2.50 6.00
466 Miguel Cabrera AS SP 3.00 8.00
467 Robinson Cano AS SP 2.00 5.00
468 Evan Longoria AS SP 2.00 5.00
469 Evan Longoria AS SP 4.00 10.00
470 Carl Crawford AS SP 3.00 8.00
471 Josh Hamilton AS SP 2.00 5.00
472 Jose Bautista AS SP 3.00 8.00
473 Joe Mauer AS SP 2.50 6.00
474 Vladimir Guerrero AS SP 2.00 5.00
475 Felix Hernandez AS SP 2.00 5.00
476 Baltimore Orioles SP 2.50 6.00
477 Yunel Escobar SP 2.50 6.00
478A David Wright SP 2.50 6.00
478B D.Wright Reds SP 75.00 150.00
479 Lucas Harrell SP (RC) 2.50 6.00
480 Aubrey Huff SP 2.50 6.00
481 Kila Ka'aihue SP 2.50 6.00
482 Ron Gardenhire MG SP 2.50 6.00
483 Trevor Hoffman SP 3.00 8.00
484 David Eckstein SP 2.50 6.00
485 Matt Garza SP 2.50 6.00
486 Martin Prado SP 2.50 6.00
487 Drew Stubbs SP 2.50 6.00
488 Koji Uehara SP 2.50 6.00
489 Brandon Morrow SP 2.50 6.00
490A Alex Rodriguez SP 4.00 10.00
490B A.Rodriguez Rev.Neg SP 60.00 120.00
491 Torii Hunter SP 2.50 6.00
492 Jason Castro SP 2.50 6.00
493 Josh Tomlin/Jeanmar Gomez/Felix Doubront
Jake Arrieta/Andy Oliver SP 5.00 12.00
494 Barry Enright RC/Mike Minor/Travis Wood
Alex Sanabia/Drew Storen SP 2.50 6.00
495 Andrew Cashner/Jonny Venters/Kenley
Jansen/Jenrry Mejia/John Axford SP 4.00 10.00
496 Michael McKenry RC/Max St. Pierre/Chris Hatcher
RC/Mike Nickeas/Steve Hill SP RC 4.00 10.00
497 Argenis Diaz/Brett Wallace/Brandon Hicks
Lance Zawadzki SP 2.50 6.00
498 Josh Bell/Danny Worth/Luke Hughes
Trevor Plouffe SP 2.50 6.00
499 Dayan Viciedo/Jason Donald/Steve Tolleson
Mitch Moreland SP 2.50 6.00
500 Peter Bourjos/Ryan Kalish/Daniel Nava
Chris Heisey/Logan Morrison SP 3.00 8.00

2011 Topps Heritage Blue Tint

110 Mark Teixeira 4.00 10.00
111 Brad Lidge 2.50 6.00
112 Luke Scott 2.50 6.00
113 Chicago White Sox 2.50 6.00
114 Kyle Drabek 4.00 10.00
115 Alfonso Soriano 4.00 10.00
116 Gavin Floyd 2.50 6.00
117 Alex Rios 2.50 6.00
118 Skip Schumaker 2.50 6.00
119 Scott Cousins 2.50 6.00
120 Bronson Arroyo 2.50 6.00
121 Buck Showalter MG 2.50 6.00
122 Trevor Cahill 2.50 6.00
123 Aaron Hill 2.50 6.00
124 Brian Duensing 2.50 6.00
125 Vladimir Guerrero 4.00 10.00
126 James Shields 2.50 6.00
127 Dallas Braden/Trevor Cahill 2.50 6.00
128 Joel Pineiro 2.50 6.00
129 Carlos Quentin 2.50 6.00
130 Omar Infante 2.50 6.00
131 Brett Sinkbeil 2.50 6.00
132 Los Angeles Angels 2.50 6.00
133 Andres Torres 2.50 6.00
134 Brett Cecil 2.50 6.00
135 Babe Ruth 10.00 25.00
136 Babe Ruth 10.00 25.00
137 Babe Ruth 10.00 25.00
138 Babe Ruth 10.00 25.00
139A Babe Ruth 10.00 25.00
139C Joba Chamberlain 2.50 6.00
140 Babe Ruth 10.00 25.00
141 Babe Ruth 10.00 25.00
142 Babe Ruth 10.00 25.00
143 Babe Ruth 10.00 25.00
144 Babe Ruth 10.00 25.00
145 Dallas Braden 2.50 6.00
146 Placido Polanco 2.50 6.00
147 Joakim Soria 2.50 6.00
148 Jonny Gomes 2.50 6.00
149 Ryan Franklin 2.50 6.00
150 Miguel Cabrera 6.00 15.00
151 Arthur Rhodes 2.50 6.00
152 Jim Riggleman MG 2.50 6.00
153 Marco Scutaro 4.00 10.00
154 Brennan Boesch 4.00 10.00
155 Brian Wilson 6.00 15.00
156 Hank Conger 4.00 10.00
157 Shane Victorino 4.00 10.00
158 Atlanta Braves 2.50 6.00
160 Garrett Jones 2.50 6.00
161 Bobby Jenks 2.50 6.00
162 Alex Gordon 4.00 10.00
163 M.Teixeira/A.Rodriguez 8.00 20.00
164 Jason Kendall 2.50 6.00
165 Adam Jones 4.00 10.00
166 Kevin Slowey 2.50 6.00
167 Wilson Ramos 2.50 6.00
168 Rajai Davis 2.50 6.00
169 Curtis Granderson 5.00 12.00
170 Aramis Ramirez 2.50 6.00
171 Edinson Volquez 2.50 6.00
172 Dusty Baker MG 2.50 6.00
173 Jhonny Peralta 2.50 6.00
174 Jon Garland 2.50 6.00
175 Adam Dunn 4.00 10.00
176 Chase Headley 2.50 6.00
177 J.A. Happ 4.00 10.00
178 A.J. Pierzynski 2.50 6.00
179 Mat Latos 4.00 10.00
180 Jim Thome 4.00 10.00
181 Dillon Gee 4.00 10.00
182 Cody Ross 2.50 6.00
183 Mike Pelfrey 2.50 6.00
184 Kurt Suzuki 2.50 6.00
185 Mariano Rivera 8.00 20.00
186 Rick Ankiel 2.50 6.00
187 Jon Lester 4.00 10.00
188 Freddy Sanchez 2.50 6.00
189 Heath Bell 2.50 6.00
190 Todd Helton 4.00 10.00
191 Ryan Dempster 2.50 6.00
192 Florida Marlins 2.50 6.00
193 Miguel Tejada 4.00 10.00
194 Jordan Walden 2.50 6.00
195 Paul Konerko 4.00 10.00
196 Jose Valverde 2.50 6.00

2011 Topps Heritage Green Tint

110 Mark Teixeira 2.50 6.00
111 Brad Lidge 1.50 4.00
112 Luke Scott 1.50 4.00
113 Chicago White Sox 2.00 5.00
114 Kyle Drabek 2.50 6.00
115 Alfonso Soriano 2.50 6.00
116 Gavin Floyd 1.50 4.00
117 Alex Rios 1.50 4.00
118 Skip Schumaker 1.50 4.00
119 Scott Cousins 1.50 4.00
120 Bronson Arroyo 1.50 4.00
121 Buck Showalter MG 1.50 4.00

122 Trevor Cahill 1.50 4.00
123 Aaron Hill 1.50 4.00
124 Brian Duensing 1.50 4.00
125 Vladimir Guerrero 2.50 6.00
126 James Shields 1.50 4.00
127 Dallas Braden/Trevor Cahill 1.50 4.00
128 Joel Pineiro 1.50 4.00
129 Carlos Quentin 1.50 4.00
130 Omar Infante 1.50 4.00
131 Brett Sinkbeil 1.50 4.00
132 Los Angeles Angels 2.00 5.00
133 Andres Torres 1.50 4.00
134 Brett Cecil 1.50 4.00
135 Babe Ruth 10.00 25.00
136 Babe Ruth 10.00 25.00
137 Babe Ruth 10.00 25.00
138 Babe Ruth 10.00 25.00
139A Babe Ruth 10.00 25.00
139C Joba Chamberlain 1.50 4.00
140 Babe Ruth 10.00 25.00
141 Babe Ruth 10.00 25.00
142 Babe Ruth 10.00 25.00
143 Babe Ruth 10.00 25.00
144 Babe Ruth 10.00 25.00
145 Dallas Braden 1.50 4.00
146 Placido Polanco 1.50 4.00
147 Joakim Soria 1.50 4.00
148 Jonny Gomes 1.50 4.00
149 Ryan Franklin 1.50 4.00
150 Miguel Cabrera 4.00 10.00
151 Arthur Rhodes 1.50 4.00
152 Jim Riggleman MG 1.50 4.00
153 Marco Scutaro 2.50 6.00
154 Brennan Boesch 2.50 6.00
155 Brian Wilson 4.00 10.00
156 Hank Conger 2.50 6.00
157 Shane Victorino 2.50 6.00
158 Atlanta Braves 2.50 5.00
160 Garrett Jones 1.50 4.00
161 Bobby Jenks 1.50 4.00
162 Alex Gordon 2.50 6.00
163 M.Teixeira/A.Rodriguez 20.00 30.00
164 Jason Kendall 1.50 4.00
165 Adam Jones 2.50 6.00
166 Kevin Slowey 1.50 4.00
167 Wilson Ramos 1.50 4.00
168 Rajai Davis 1.50 4.00
169 Curtis Granderson 3.00 8.00
170 Aramis Ramirez 1.50 4.00
171 Edinson Volquez 1.50 4.00
172 Dusty Baker MG 1.50 4.00
173 Jhonny Peralta 1.50 4.00
174 Jon Garland 1.50 4.00
175 Adam Dunn 2.50 6.00
176 Chase Headley 1.50 4.00
177 J.A. Happ 2.50 6.00
178 A.J. Pierzynski 1.50 4.00
179 Mat Latos 2.50 6.00
180 Jim Thome 2.50 6.00
181 Dillon Gee 2.50 6.00
182 Cody Ross 1.50 4.00
183 Mike Pelfrey 1.50 4.00
184 Kurt Suzuki 1.50 4.00
185 Mariano Rivera 5.00 12.00
186 Rick Ankiel 1.50 4.00
187 Jon Lester 2.50 6.00
188 Freddy Sanchez 1.50 4.00
189 Heath Bell 1.50 4.00
190 Todd Helton 2.50 6.00
191 Ryan Dempster 1.50 4.00
192 Florida Marlins 2.00 5.00
193 Miguel Tejada 2.50 6.00
194 Jordan Walden 1.50 4.00
195 Paul Konerko 2.50 6.00
196 Jose Valverde 1.50 4.00

2011 Topps Heritage Red Tint

110 Mark Teixeira 5.00 12.00
111 Brad Lidge 3.00 8.00
112 Luke Scott 3.00 8.00
113 Chicago White Sox 3.00 8.00
114 Kyle Drabek 5.00 12.00
115 Alfonso Soriano 5.00 12.00
116 Gavin Floyd 3.00 8.00
117 Alex Rios 3.00 8.00
118 Skip Schumaker 3.00 8.00
119 Scott Cousins 3.00 8.00
120 Bronson Arroyo 3.00 8.00
121 Buck Showalter MG 3.00 8.00
122 Trevor Cahill 3.00 8.00
123 Aaron Hill 3.00 8.00
124 Brian Duensing 3.00 8.00
125 Vladimir Guerrero 5.00 12.00
126 James Shields 3.00 8.00
127 Dallas Braden/Trevor Cahill 3.00 8.00
128 Joel Pineiro 3.00 8.00
129 Carlos Quentin 3.00 8.00
130 Omar Infante 3.00 8.00
131 Brett Sinkbeil 3.00 8.00
132 Los Angeles Angels 3.00 8.00
133 Andres Torres 3.00 8.00
134 Brett Cecil 3.00 8.00
135 Babe Ruth 8.00 20.00
136 Babe Ruth 8.00 20.00
137 Babe Ruth 8.00 20.00
138 Babe Ruth 8.00 20.00
139A Babe Ruth 8.00 20.00
139C Joba Chamberlain 3.00 8.00
140 Babe Ruth 8.00 20.00
141 Babe Ruth 8.00 20.00
142 Babe Ruth 8.00 20.00
143 Babe Ruth 8.00 20.00
144 Babe Ruth 8.00 20.00
145 Dallas Braden 3.00 8.00
146 Placido Polanco 3.00 8.00
147 Joakim Soria 3.00 8.00
148 Jonny Gomes 3.00 8.00
149 Ryan Franklin 3.00 8.00
150 Miguel Cabrera 8.00 20.00
151 Arthur Rhodes 3.00 8.00
152 Jim Riggleman MG 3.00 8.00
153 Marco Scutaro 5.00 12.00
154 Brennan Boesch 5.00 12.00
155 Brian Wilson 8.00 20.00
156 Hank Conger 5.00 12.00
157 Shane Victorino 5.00 12.00
158 Atlanta Braves 3.00 8.00
160 Garrett Jones 3.00 8.00
161 Bobby Jenks 3.00 8.00
162 Alex Gordon 5.00 12.00
163 M.Teixeira/A.Rodriguez 10.00 25.00
164 Jason Kendall 3.00 8.00
165 Adam Jones 5.00 12.00
166 Kevin Slowey 3.00 8.00
167 Wilson Ramos 3.00 8.00
168 Rajai Davis 3.00 8.00
169 Curtis Granderson 6.00 15.00
170 Aramis Ramirez 3.00 8.00
171 Edinson Volquez 3.00 8.00
172 Dusty Baker MG 3.00 8.00
173 Jhonny Peralta 3.00 8.00
174 Jon Garland 3.00 8.00
175 Adam Dunn 5.00 12.00
176 Chase Headley 3.00 8.00
177 J.A. Happ 5.00 12.00
178 A.J. Pierzynski 3.00 8.00
179 Mat Latos 5.00 12.00
180 Jim Thome 5.00 12.00
181 Dillon Gee 5.00 12.00
182 Cody Ross 3.00 8.00
183 Mike Pelfrey 3.00 8.00
184 Kurt Suzuki 3.00 8.00
185 Mariano Rivera 10.00 25.00
186 Rick Ankiel 3.00 8.00
187 Jon Lester 5.00 12.00
188 Freddy Sanchez 3.00 8.00
189 Heath Bell 3.00 8.00
190 Todd Helton 5.00 12.00
191 Ryan Dempster 3.00 8.00
192 Florida Marlins 3.00 8.00
193 Miguel Tejada 5.00 12.00
194 Jordan Walden 3.00 8.00
195 Paul Konerko 5.00 12.00
196 Jose Valverde 3.00 8.00

2011 Topps Heritage '62 Mint Coins

STATED ODDS 1:263 HOBBY
AO 1st American Orbits 15.00 40.00
BF Bob Feller 50.00 100.00
BR Brooks Robinson 40.00 80.00
CE U.S.-Cuba Embargo 12.50 30.00
CM Missile Crisis Begins 12.50 30.00
DS Duke Snider 10.00 25.00
DST Darryl Strawberry 10.00 25.00
EB Ernie Banks 20.00 50.00
ED Eric Davis 15.00 40.00
EK Ed Kranepool 10.00 25.00
FT Frank Thomas 30.00 60.00
GP Gaylord Perry 10.00 25.00
HK Harmon Killebrew 30.00 60.00
JM Jamie Moyer 12.50 30.00
JR Jackie Robinson 50.00 100.00
MM Mickey Mantle 20.00 50.00
NS SEALs Activated 15.00 40.00
SF Sid Fernandez 10.00 25.00
WS Warren Spahn 15.00 40.00
WST Willie Stargell 10.00 25.00

2011 Topps Heritage Advertising Panels

ISSUED AS BOX TOPPER
1 Atlanta Braves .40 1.00
Tyler Colvin/Matt Capps
2 Chris Carter .60 1.50
Ben Zobrist/Billy Butler
3 Jose Cerda 1.25 3.00
Carlos Pena/Ichiro Suzuki
4 Joba Chamberlain .60 1.50
Colby Rasmus/Gavin Floyd
5 Johnny Damon .60 1.50
Rafael Soriano/Jered Weaver
6 John Danks .60 1.50
Adam Wainwright/Adam Kennedy
7 Brian Duensing .40 1.00
A.J. Pierzynski/Rick Ankiel
8 Ryan Howard .75 2.00
Jason Kendall/Leo Nunez
9 Gregory Infante 1.00 2.50
Felix Hernandez/Clay Buchholz/David Price/Trevor Cahill/Joey Votto AS
10 Derek Jeter 2.50 6.00
Robinson Cano/Travis Hafner/Gaby Sanchez
11 Clayton Kershaw 1.50 4.00
Ronny Cedeno/John Jaso
12 Victor Martinez 1.00 2.50
Zach Duke/Mark Trumbo
13 Kendry Morales 1.25 3.00
Brian Wilson/Buster Posey/Brett Cecil
14 Mike Napoli .75 2.00
Nick Markakis/Jonathan Lucroy
15 Ricky Nolasco .60 1.50
Geovany Soto/Wade Davis
16 Cliff Pennington .40 1.00
Brett Myers/Vernon Wells
17 Andy Pettitte .60 1.50
Ian Kinsler/B.J. Upton
18 Joel Pineiro .60 1.50
Marco Scutaro/Andrew Romine
19 Albert Pujols 1.25 3.00
Adam Dunn/Joey Votto/Derek Lowe/San Diego Padres
20 Hanley Ramirez 2.50 6.00
Ted Lilly/Babe Ruth Special
21 Scott Rolen .60 1.50
Rangers Retaliate/Mat Latos
22 Jimmy Rollins .60 1.50
Carlos Lee/Carlos Gonzalez
23 Cody Ross 1.00 2.50
Brandon Beachy/Bruce Bochy
24 Babe Ruth Special 2.50 6.00
Mark Buehrle/Armando Galarraga
25 CC Sabathia .75 2.00
David Price/Jon Lester/Joe Mauer/Francisco Cordero
26 Grady Sizemore .60 1.50
Chris Young/Buck Showalter
27 Brandon Snyder 2.50 6.00
Babe Ruth Special/Francisco Liriano
28 Jim Thome .60 1.50
Franklin Gutierrez/Ryan Theriot
29 Ryan Dempster 1.00 2.50
Jeremy Hellickson/Brian Wilson
30 Luke Scott .40 1.00
Arthur Rhodes/Giants TC
31 Jose Ceda 1.25 3.00
Carlos Pena/Ichiro Suzuki

2011 Topps Heritage Baseball Bucks

RANDOMLY INSERTED BOX TOPPER
BB1 Justin Upton 3.00 8.00
BB2 Miguel Montero 2.00 5.00
BB3 Daniel Hudson 2.00 5.00
BB4 Torii Hunter 2.00 5.00
BB5 Jered Weaver 3.00 8.00
BB6 Kendry Morales 2.00 5.00
BB7 Chipper Jones 5.00 12.00
BB8 Jason Heyward 4.00 10.00
BB9 Martin Prado 2.00 5.00
BB10 Adam Jones 3.00 8.00
BB11 Nick Markakis 4.00 10.00
BB12 Brian Roberts 2.00 5.00
BB13 David Ortiz 5.00 12.00
BB14 Victor Martinez 3.00 8.00
BB15 Clay Buchholz 2.00 5.00
BB16 Starlin Castro 3.00 8.00
BB17 Aramis Ramirez 2.00 5.00
BB18 Tyler Colvin 2.00 5.00
BB19 Manny Ramirez 5.00 12.00
BB20 Carlos Quentin 2.00 5.00
BB21 John Danks 2.00 5.00
BB22 Joey Votto 5.00 12.00
BB23 Brandon Phillips 2.00 5.00
BB24 Jay Bruce 3.00 8.00
BB25 Shin-Soo Choo 3.00 8.00
BB26 Grady Sizemore 3.00 8.00
BB27 Carlos Santana 5.00 12.00
BB28 Troy Tulowitzki 5.00 12.00
BB29 Ubaldo Jimenez 2.00 5.00
BB30 Carlos Gonzalez 3.00 8.00
BB31 Miguel Cabrera 5.00 12.00
BB32 Justin Verlander 5.00 12.00
BB33 Austin Jackson 2.00 5.00
BB34 Hanley Ramirez 3.00 8.00
BB35 Mike Stanton 5.00 12.00
BB36 Logan Morrison 2.00 5.00
BB37 Hunter Pence 3.00 8.00
BB38 Wandy Rodriguez 2.00 5.00
BB39 Brett Wallace 2.00 5.00
BB40 Lorenzo Cain 2.00 5.00
BB41 Billy Butler 2.00 5.00
BB42 Joakim Soria 2.00 5.00
BB43 Clayton Kershaw 8.00 20.00
BB44 Andre Ethier 3.00 8.00
BB45 Matt Kemp 4.00 10.00
BB46 Ryan Braun 3.00 8.00
BB47 Yovani Gallardo 2.00 5.00
BB48 Casey McGehee 2.00 5.00
BB49 Joe Mauer 4.00 10.00
BB50 Justin Morneau 3.00 8.00
BB51 Danny Valencia 3.00 8.00
BB52 David Wright 4.00 10.00
BB53 Johan Santana 3.00 8.00
BB54 Ike Davis 2.00 5.00
BB55 Derek Jeter 12.00 30.00
BB56 CC Sabathia 3.00 8.00
BB57 Alex Rodriguez 6.00 15.00
BB58 Trevor Cahill 2.00 5.00
BB59 Kurt Suzuki 2.00 5.00
BB60 Brett Anderson 2.00 5.00
BB61 Roy Halladay 3.00 8.00
BB62 Ryan Howard 4.00 10.00
BB63 Domonic Brown 4.00 10.00
BB64 Andrew McCutchen 5.00 12.00
BB65 Jose Tabata 2.00 5.00
BB66 Neil Walker 3.00 8.00
BB67 Adrian Gonzalez 4.00 10.00
BB68 Heath Bell 2.00 5.00
BB69 Mat Latos 3.00 8.00
BB70 Tim Lincecum 3.00 8.00
BB71 Brian Wilson 5.00 12.00
BB72 Pablo Sandoval 3.00 8.00
BB73 Buster Posey 6.00 15.00
BB74 Matt Cain 3.00 8.00
BB75 Cody Ross 2.00 5.00
BB76 Ichiro Suzuki 6.00 15.00
BB77 Felix Hernandez 3.00 8.00
BB78 Franklin Gutierrez 2.00 5.00
BB79 Albert Pujols 6.00 15.00
BB80 Adam Wainwright 3.00 8.00
BB81 Yadier Molina 6.00 15.00
BB82 Evan Longoria 3.00 8.00
BB83 David Price 4.00 10.00
BB84 Jeremy Hellickson 5.00 12.00
BB85 Josh Hamilton 3.00 8.00
BB86 Neftali Feliz 2.00 5.00
BB87 Elvis Andrus 3.00 8.00
BB88 Michael Young 2.00 5.00
BB89 Ian Kinsler 3.00 8.00
BB90 Nelson Cruz 5.00 12.00
BB91 Vernon Wells 2.00 5.00
BB92 Jose Bautista 3.00 8.00
BB93 Brandon Morrow 2.00 5.00
BB94 Ryan Zimmerman 3.00 8.00
BB95 Jordan Zimmermann 3.00 8.00
BB96 Ian Desmond 2.00 5.00

2011 Topps Heritage Baseball Flashbacks

COMPLETE SET (10) 6.00 15.00
STATED ODDS 1:12 HOBBY
BF1 Mickey Mantle 3.00 8.00
BF2 Brooks Robinson .60 1.50
BF3 Roger Maris 1.00 2.50
BF4 Robin Roberts .60 1.50
BF5 Carl Yastrzemski 1.50 4.00
BF6 Whitey Ford .60 1.50
BF7 Harmon Killebrew 1.00 2.50
BF8 Warren Spahn .60 1.50
BF9 Frank Robinson .60 1.50
BF10 Bob Gibson .60 1.50

2011 Topps Heritage Black

*BLACK: .75X TO 2X BASIC CHROME

2011 Topps Heritage Checklists

COMPLETE SET (6) 1.50 4.00
COMMON CHECKLIST .40 1.00

2011 Topps Heritage Chrome

HERITAGE ODDS 1:11 HOBBY
TOPPS CHROME ODDS 1:7 HOBBY
STATED PRINT RUN 1962 SER.#'d SETS
1-100 ISSUED IN TOPPS HERITAGE
101-200 ISSUED IN TOPPS CHROME
C1 Andrew McCutchen 2.50 6.00
C2 Joe Nathan 1.00 2.50
C3 Jake McGee 2.00 5.00
C4 Miguel Cabrera 2.50 6.00
C5 Starlin Castro 1.50 4.00
C6 Josh Thole 1.00 2.50
C7 Russell Martin 1.00 2.50
C8 Mark Reynolds 1.00 2.50
C9 Nelson Cruz 2.50 6.00
C10 Cole Hamels 2.00 5.00
C11 CC Sabathia 1.50 4.00
C12 Carlos Gonzalez/Joey Votto/Omar Infante
Troy Tulowitzki 2.50 6.00
C13 Bautista/Kon/Cabr/Teix 2.50 6.00
C14 Weav/Felix/Lest/Verland 2.00 5.00
C15 Lin/Hal/Jim/Wain 1.25 3.00
C16 Tommy Hanson 1.00 2.50
C17 Travis Snider 1.00 2.50
C18 Jonathan Sanchez 1.00 2.50
C19 Ike Davis 1.00 2.50
C20 Nick Swisher 1.50 4.00
C21 Jacoby Ellsbury 2.00 5.00
C22 Brad Lidge 1.00 2.50
C23 Ryan Braun 1.25 3.00
C24 Kyle Drabek 1.50 4.00
C25 Bronson Arroyo 1.00 2.50
C26 Aaron Hill 1.00 2.50
C27 Omar Infante 1.00 2.50
C28 Babe Ruth 5.00 12.00
C29 Jonny Gomes 1.00 2.50
C30 Clay Buchholz 1.00 2.50
C31 Jhonny Peralta 1.00 2.50
C32 Mike Pelfrey 1.00 2.50
C33 Kurt Suzuki 1.00 2.50
C34 Paul Konerko 1.50 4.00
C35 Casey Blake 1.00 2.50
C36 Josh Beckett 1.00 2.50
C37 Corey Hart 1.00 2.50
C38 Kevin Millwood 1.00 2.50
C39 Evan Longoria 1.25 3.00
C40 Rickie Weeks 1.00 2.50
C41 Roy Oswalt 1.50 4.00
C42 Asdrubal Cabrera 1.50 4.00
C43 Don Mattingly 4.00 10.00
C44 Casey Coleman 1.00 2.50
C45 Adrian Beltre 2.50 6.00
C46 Cliff Lee 1.50 4.00
C47 Marlon Byrd 1.00 2.50
C48 Chone Figgins 1.00 2.50
C49 Giants Win Opener HL 1.00 2.50
C50 Giants Crush Rangers HL 1.00 2.50
C51 Xavier Nady 1.00 2.50
C52 Josh Johnson 1.50 4.00
C53 Chris Johnson 1.00 2.50
C54 Vance Worley 4.00 10.00
C55 Lou Marson 1.00 2.50
C56 Edwin Jackson 1.00 2.50
C57 Ruben Tejada 1.00 2.50
C58 Josh Hamilton/Nelson Cruz 2.50 6.00
C59 Delmon Young 1.50 4.00
C60 Will Venable 1.00 2.50
C61 Pedro Alvarez 2.00 5.00
C62 Hiroki Kuroda 1.00 2.50
C63 Neftali Feliz 1.00 2.50
C64 Mike Stanton 2.50 6.00
C65 Ty Wigginton 1.00 2.50
C66 Bobby Cramer 1.00 2.50
C67 Jason Kubel 1.00 2.50
C68 Daniel Descalso 1.00 2.50
C69 Ramon Hernandez 1.00 2.50
C70 Mike Aviles 1.00 2.50
C71 D.Ortiz/D.Pedroia 2.00 5.00
C72 Jason Bay 1.50 4.00
C73 CC Sabathia 1.50 4.00
C74 Joe Mauer 2.00 5.00
C75 Tommy Hunter 1.00 2.50
C76 Alexei Ramirez 1.50 4.00
C77 Raul Ibanez 1.50 4.00
C78 Lucas Duda 2.50 6.00
C79 Chad Billingsley 1.50 4.00
C80 Bobby Abreu 1.00 2.50
C81 Fernando Salas 1.50 4.00
C82 Nyjer Morgan 1.00 2.50
C83 Justin Morneau/Joe Mauer 2.00 5.00
C84 Hunter Pence 1.50 4.00
C85 Jose Bautista 1.50 4.00
C86 Brett Anderson 1.00 2.50
C87 Carlos Zambrano 1.50 4.00
C88 Greg Halman 1.50 4.00
C89 Nick Hundley 1.00 2.50
C90 J.P. Arencibia 1.00 2.50
C91 Dan Haren 1.00 2.50
C92 James Loney 1.00 2.50
C93 Phil Hughes 1.00 2.50
C94 Ubaldo Jimenez 1.00 2.50
C95 Michael Cuddyer 1.00 2.50
C96 Desmond Jennings 1.50 4.00
C97 Ryan Doumit 1.00 2.50
C98 Mark Teixeira 1.50 4.00
C99 Lucas May 1.00 2.50
C100 Wandy Rodriguez 1.00 2.50
C101 A.Pujols/R.Braun 2.50 6.00
C102 D.Jeter/R.Cano 5.00 12.00
C103 M.Teixeira/A.Rodriguez 2.50 6.00
C104 Matt Kemp/Andre Ethier 2.00 5.00
C105 Derek Jeter 5.00 12.00
C106 Roy Halladay 1.50 4.00
C107 Jose Bautista 1.50 4.00
C108 Miguel Cabrera 2.50 6.00
C109 Ichiro Suzuki 2.50 6.00
C110 Mark Teixeira 1.50 4.00
C111 Tim Lincecum 1.25 3.00
C112 Cory Luebke 1.00 2.50
C113 Freddie Freeman 6.00 15.00
C114 Scott Cousins 1.00 2.50
C115 Hank Conger 1.50 4.00
C116 Jordan Walden 1.00 2.50
C117 Aroldis Chapman 2.50 6.00
C118 Chris Sale 8.00 20.00
C119 Jeremy Hellickson 2.00 5.00
C120 Brandon Beachy 2.00 5.00
C121 Eric Sogard 1.00 2.50
C122 Mark Trumbo 2.50 6.00
C123 Brent Morel 1.00 2.50
C124 Stephen Strasburg 2.00 5.00
C125 Gaby Sanchez 1.00 2.50
C126 Buster Posey 2.50 6.00
C127 Danny Valencia 1.50 4.00
C128 Jason Heyward 1.50 4.00
C129 Austin Jackson 1.00 2.50
C130 Neil Walker 1.50 4.00
C131 Jaime Garcia 1.50 4.00
C132 Jose Tabata 1.00 2.50
C133 Josh Hamilton 1.50 4.00
C134 David Ortiz 2.50 6.00
C135 Clayton Kershaw 4.00 10.00
C136 Carlos Beltran 1.50 4.00
C137 Carlos Pena 1.50 4.00
C138 Jayson Werth 1.50 4.00
C139 Vernon Wells 1.00 2.50
C140 Chipper Jones 2.50 6.00
C141 Ian Kinsler 1.50 4.00
C142 Pablo Sandoval 1.50 4.00
C143 Justin Upton 1.50 4.00
C144 Kosuke Fukudome 1.50 4.00
C145 Albert Pujols 2.50 6.00
C146 Nick Markakis 2.00 5.00
C147 Robinson Cano 1.50 4.00
C148 Justin Morneau 1.50 4.00
C149 Gordon Beckham 1.00 2.50
C150 Hanley Ramirez 1.50 4.00
C151 Chase Utley 1.50 4.00
C152 Jay Bruce 1.50 4.00
C153 Nelson Cruz 2.50 6.00
C154 Ryan Zimmerman 1.50 4.00
C155 Jered Weaver 1.50 4.00
C156 David Price 2.00 5.00
C157 Domonic Brown 2.00 5.00
C158 Madison Bumgarner 2.00 5.00
C159 Matt Kemp 2.00 5.00
C160 Mark Teixeira 1.50 4.00
C161 Alfonso Soriano 1.50 4.00
C162 Carlos Quentin 1.00 2.50
C163 Miguel Cabrera 2.50 6.00
C164 Adam Jones 1.50 4.00
C165 Curtis Granderson 2.00 5.00
C166 Adam Dunn 1.50 4.00
C167 Jim Thome 1.50 4.00
C168 Mariano Rivera 3.00 8.00
C169 Jon Lester 1.50 4.00
C170 Derek Jeter 5.00 12.00
C171 Ryan Howard 1.50 4.00
C172 Francisco Liriano 1.00 2.50
C173 Ichiro Suzuki 2.50 6.00
C174 Joe Mauer 2.00 5.00
C175 Ryan Braun 1.25 3.00
C176 Matt Cain 1.50 4.00
C177 Carl Crawford 1.50 4.00
C178 Zack Greinke 2.50 6.00
C179 Dustin Pedroia 2.00 5.00
C180 Felix Hernandez 1.50 4.00
C181 Joey Votto 2.50 6.00
C182 Andre Ethier 1.50 4.00
C183 Jorge Posada 1.50 4.00
C184 Dan Uggla 1.00 2.50
C185 Matt Holliday 2.50 6.00
C186 Victor Martinez 1.50 4.00
C187 Carlos Gonzalez 1.50 4.00
C188 Carlos Santana 2.50 6.00
C189 Kevin Youkilis 1.00 2.50
C190 Tim Lincecum 1.25 3.00
C191 Troy Tulowitzki 2.50 6.00
C192 Jose Reyes 1.50 4.00
C193 Adrian Gonzalez 2.00 5.00
C194 Brian McCann 1.50 4.00
C195 Prince Fielder 1.50 4.00
C196 Roy Halladay 1.50 4.00
C197 David Wright 1.50 4.00
C198 Martin Prado 1.00 2.50
C199 Drew Stubbs 1.00 2.50
C200 Alex Rodriguez 2.50 6.00

2011 Topps Heritage Chrome Refractors

*REF: .6X TO 1.5X BASIC CHROME
HERITAGE ODDS 1:137 HOBBY
TOPPS CHROME ODDS 1:22 HOBBY
STATED PRINT RUN 562 SER.#'d SETS
1-100 ISSUED IN TOPPS HERITAGE
101-200 ISSUED IN TOPPS CHROME

2011 Topps Heritage Chrome Black Refractors

HERITAGE ODDS 1:334 HOBBY
TOPPS CHROME ODDS 1:148 HOBBY
STATED PRINT RUN 62 SER.#'d SETS
1-100 ISSUED IN TOPPS HERITAGE
101-200 ISSUED IN TOPPS CHROME
C1 Andrew McCutchen 12.00 30.00
C2 Joe Nathan 5.00 12.00
C3 Jake McGee 10.00 25.00
C4 Miguel Cabrera 12.00 30.00
C5 Starlin Castro 8.00 20.00
C6 Josh Thole 5.00 12.00
C7 Russell Martin 5.00 12.00
C8 Mark Reynolds 5.00 12.00
C9 Nelson Cruz 12.00 30.00
C10 Cole Hamels 10.00 25.00
C11 CC Sabathia 8.00 20.00
C12 Carlos Gonzalez/Joey Votto/Omar Infante
Troy Tulowitzki 12.00 30.00
C13 Bautista/Kon/Cabr/Teix 12.00 30.00
C14 Weav/Felix/Lest/Verland 12.00 30.00
C15 Lin/Hal/Jim/Wain 8.00 20.00
C16 Tommy Hanson 5.00 12.00
C17 Travis Snider 5.00 12.00
C18 Jonathan Sanchez 5.00 12.00
C19 Ike Davis 5.00 12.00
C20 Nick Swisher 8.00 20.00
C21 Jacoby Ellsbury 10.00 25.00
C22 Brad Lidge 5.00 12.00
C23 Ryan Braun 8.00 20.00
C24 Kyle Drabek 8.00 20.00
C25 Bronson Arroyo 5.00 12.00
C26 Aaron Hill 5.00 12.00
C27 Omar Infante 5.00 12.00
C28 Babe Ruth 30.00 80.00
C29 Jonny Gomes 5.00 12.00
C30 Clay Buchholz 5.00 12.00
C31 Jhonny Peralta 5.00 12.00
C32 Mike Pelfrey 5.00 12.00
C33 Kurt Suzuki 5.00 12.00
C34 Paul Konerko 8.00 20.00
C35 Casey Blake 5.00 12.00
C36 Josh Beckett 5.00 12.00
C37 Corey Hart 5.00 12.00
C38 Kevin Millwood 5.00 12.00
C39 Evan Longoria 8.00 20.00
C40 Rickie Weeks 5.00 12.00
C41 Roy Oswalt 8.00 20.00
C42 Asdrubal Cabrera 8.00 20.00
C43 Don Mattingly 25.00 60.00
C44 Casey Coleman 5.00 12.00
C45 Adrian Beltre 12.00 30.00
C46 Cliff Lee 8.00 20.00
C47 Marlon Byrd 5.00 12.00
C48 Chone Figgins 5.00 12.00
C49 Giants Win Opener HL 5.00 12.00
C50 Giants Crush Rangers HL 5.00 12.00
C51 Xavier Nady 5.00 12.00
C52 Josh Johnson 8.00 20.00
C53 Chris Johnson 5.00 12.00
C54 Vance Worley 20.00 50.00
C55 Lou Marson 5.00 12.00
C56 Edwin Jackson 5.00 12.00
C57 Ruben Tejada 5.00 12.00
C58 Josh Hamilton/Nelson Cruz 12.00 30.00
C59 Delmon Young 8.00 20.00
C60 Will Venable 5.00 12.00
C61 Pedro Alvarez 10.00 25.00
C62 Hiroki Kuroda 5.00 12.00
C63 Neftali Feliz 5.00 12.00
C64 Mike Stanton 12.00 30.00
C65 Ty Wigginton 5.00 12.00
C66 Bobby Cramer 5.00 12.00
C67 Jason Kubel 5.00 12.00
C68 Daniel Descalso 5.00 12.00
C69 Ramon Hernandez 5.00 12.00
C70 Mike Aviles 5.00 12.00
C71 D.Ortiz/D.Pedroia 12.00 30.00
C72 Jason Bay 8.00 20.00
C73 CC Sabathia 8.00 20.00
C74 Joe Mauer 10.00 25.00
C75 Tommy Hunter 5.00 12.00
C76 Alexei Ramirez 8.00 20.00
C77 Raul Ibanez 8.00 20.00
C78 Lucas Duda 12.00 30.00
C79 Chad Billingsley 8.00 20.00
C80 Bobby Abreu 5.00 12.00
C81 Fernando Salas 8.00 20.00
C82 Nyjer Morgan 5.00 12.00
C83 Justin Morneau/Joe Mauer 10.00 25.00
C84 Hunter Pence 8.00 20.00
C85 Jose Bautista 8.00 20.00
C86 Brett Anderson 5.00 12.00
C87 Carlos Zambrano 8.00 20.00
C88 Greg Halman 8.00 20.00
C89 Nick Hundley 5.00 12.00
C90 J.P. Arencibia 5.00 12.00
C91 Dan Haren 5.00 12.00
C92 James Loney 5.00 12.00
C93 Phil Hughes 5.00 12.00
C94 Ubaldo Jimenez 5.00 12.00
C95 Michael Cuddyer 5.00 12.00
C96 Desmond Jennings 8.00 20.00
C97 Ryan Doumit 5.00 12.00
C98 Mark Teixeira 8.00 20.00
C99 Lucas May 5.00 12.00
C100 Wandy Rodriguez 5.00 12.00
C101 A.Pujols/R.Braun 15.00 40.00
C102 D.Jeter/R.Cano 30.00 80.00
C103 Teixeira/ARod 15.00 40.00
C104 Matt Kemp/Andre Ethier 10.00 25.00
C105 Derek Jeter 30.00 80.00
C106 Roy Halladay 8.00 20.00
C107 Jose Bautista 8.00 20.00
C108 Miguel Cabrera 12.00 30.00
C109 Ichiro Suzuki 15.00 40.00
C110 Mark Teixeira 8.00 20.00
C111 Tim Lincecum 8.00 20.00
C112 Cory Luebke 5.00 12.00
C113 Freddie Freeman 30.00 80.00
C114 Scott Cousins 5.00 12.00
C115 Hank Conger 8.00 20.00
C116 Jordan Walden 5.00 12.00
C117 Aroldis Chapman 15.00 40.00
C118 Chris Sale 40.00 100.00
C119 Jeremy Hellickson 12.00 30.00
C120 Brandon Beachy 12.00 30.00
C121 Eric Sogard 5.00 12.00
C122 Mark Trumbo 12.00 30.00
C123 Brent Morel 5.00 12.00
C124 Stephen Strasburg 12.00 30.00
C125 Gaby Sanchez 5.00 12.00
C126 Buster Posey 15.00 40.00
C127 Danny Valencia 8.00 20.00
C128 Jason Heyward 10.00 25.00
C129 Austin Jackson 5.00 12.00
C130 Neil Walker 8.00 20.00
C131 Jaime Garcia 8.00 20.00
C132 Jose Tabata 5.00 12.00
C133 Josh Hamilton 8.00 20.00
C134 David Ortiz 12.00 30.00
C135 Clayton Kershaw 20.00 50.00
C136 Carlos Beltran 8.00 20.00
C137 Carlos Pena 8.00 20.00
C138 Jayson Werth 8.00 20.00
C139 Vernon Wells 5.00 12.00
C140 Chipper Jones 12.00 30.00
C141 Ian Kinsler 8.00 20.00
C142 Pablo Sandoval 8.00 20.00
C143 Justin Upton 8.00 20.00
C144 Kosuke Fukudome 8.00 20.00
C145 Albert Pujols 15.00 40.00
C146 Nick Markakis 10.00 25.00
C147 Robinson Cano 8.00 20.00
C148 Justin Morneau 8.00 20.00
C149 Gordon Beckham 5.00 12.00
C150 Hanley Ramirez 8.00 20.00
C151 Chase Utley 8.00 20.00
C152 Jay Bruce 8.00 20.00
C153 Nelson Cruz 12.00 30.00
C154 Ryan Zimmerman 8.00 20.00
C155 Jered Weaver 8.00 20.00
C156 David Price 10.00 25.00
C157 Domonic Brown 10.00 25.00
C158 Madison Bumgarner 10.00 25.00
C159 Matt Kemp 10.00 25.00
C160 Mark Teixeira 8.00 20.00
C161 Alfonso Soriano 8.00 20.00
C162 Carlos Quentin 5.00 12.00
C163 Miguel Cabrera 12.00 30.00
C164 Adam Jones 8.00 20.00
C165 Curtis Granderson 10.00 25.00
C166 Adam Dunn 8.00 20.00
C167 Jim Thome 8.00 20.00
C168 Mariano Rivera 15.00 40.00
C169 Jon Lester 8.00 20.00
C170 Derek Jeter 30.00 80.00
C171 Ryan Howard 10.00 25.00
C172 Francisco Liriano 5.00 12.00
C173 Ichiro Suzuki 15.00 40.00
C174 Joe Mauer 10.00 25.00
C175 Ryan Braun 8.00 20.00
C176 Matt Cain 8.00 20.00
C177 Carl Crawford 8.00 20.00
C178 Zack Greinke 12.00 30.00
C179 Dustin Pedroia 12.00 30.00
C180 Felix Hernandez 8.00 20.00
C181 Joey Votto 12.00 30.00
C182 Andre Ethier 8.00 20.00
C183 Jorge Posada 8.00 20.00
C184 Dan Uggla 5.00 12.00
C185 Matt Holliday 12.00 30.00
C186 Victor Martinez 8.00 20.00
C187 Carlos Gonzalez 8.00 20.00
C188 Carlos Santana 12.00 30.00
C189 Kevin Youkilis 5.00 12.00
C190 Tim Lincecum 8.00 20.00
C191 Troy Tulowitzki 12.00 30.00
C192 Jose Reyes 8.00 20.00
C193 Adrian Gonzalez 10.00 25.00
C194 Brian McCann 8.00 20.00
C195 Prince Fielder 8.00 20.00
C196 Roy Halladay 8.00 20.00
C197 David Wright 10.00 25.00
C198 Martin Prado 5.00 12.00
C199 Drew Stubbs 5.00 12.00
C200 Alex Rodriguez 15.00 40.00

2011 Topps Heritage Chrome Green Refractors

*GREEN REF: .75X TO 2X BASIC CHROME

2011 Topps Heritage Clubhouse Collection Dual Relic Autographs

STATED ODDS 1:14,883 HOBBY
STATED PRINT RUN 10 SER.#'d SETS
NO PRICING DUE TO SCARCITY
EXCHANGE DEADLINE 2/28/2014

2011 Topps Heritage Clubhouse Collection Dual Relics

STATED ODDS 1:7600 HOBBY
STATED PRINT RUN 62 SER.#'d SETS
FS W.Ford/C.Sabathia 15.00 40.00
GH B.Gibson/R.Halladay 50.00 100.00
KC A.Kaline/M.Cabrera 75.00 200.00
RV F.Robinson/J.Votto 15.00 40.00
RW B.Robinson/D.Wright 20.00 50.00

2011 Topps Heritage Clubhouse Collection Relics

STATED ODDS 1:29 HOBBY
AP Albert Pujols 6.00 15.00
AR Alex Rios 2.00 5.00
BG Brett Gardner 3.00 8.00
CB Carlos Beltran 3.00 8.00
CBU Clay Buchholz 2.00 5.00
CC Carl Crawford 3.00 8.00
CK Clayton Kershaw 8.00 20.00
CL Carlos Lee 2.00 5.00
CS Carlos Santana 5.00 12.00
CU Chase Utley 3.00 8.00
DU Dan Uggla 2.00 5.00
DW David Wright 4.00 10.00
EL Evan Longoria 3.00 8.00
FH Felix Hernandez 3.00 8.00
FL Francisco Liriano 2.00 5.00
GS Gaby Sanchez 2.00 5.00
HR Hanley Ramirez 3.00 8.00
ID Ike Davis 2.00 5.00
IK Ian Kinsler 3.00 8.00
IS Ichiro Suzuki 6.00 15.00
JB Jason Bartlett 2.00 5.00
JBA Jason Bay 3.00 8.00
JE Jacoby Ellsbury 4.00 10.00
JH Josh Hamilton 3.00 8.00
JJ Josh Johnson 3.00 8.00
JM Joe Mauer 4.00 10.00
JMO Justin Morneau 3.00 8.00
JP Jorge Posada 3.00 8.00
JR Jose Reyes 3.00 8.00
JS Johan Santana 3.00 8.00
JT Jim Thome 3.00 8.00
JTA Jose Tabata 2.00 5.00
JV Joey Votto 5.00 12.00
JW Jayson Werth 3.00 8.00
JWI Josh Willingham 3.00 8.00
MC Miguel Cabrera 5.00 12.00
MR Manny Ramirez 5.00 12.00
MRE Mark Reynolds 2.00 5.00
MT Mark Teixeira 3.00 8.00
PF Prince Fielder 3.00 8.00
PP Placido Polanco 2.00 5.00
RB Ryan Braun 3.00 8.00
RC Robinson Cano 3.00 8.00
RH Ryan Howard 4.00 10.00
SR Scott Rolen 3.00 8.00
TT Troy Tulowitzki 5.00 12.00
VG Vladimir Guerrero 3.00 8.00
VM Victor Martinez 3.00 8.00
YM Yadier Molina 6.00 15.00
ZG Zack Greinke 5.00 12.00

2011 Topps Heritage Flashback Stadium Relics

STATED ODDS 1:1175 HOBBY
AK Al Kaline 15.00 40.00
BG Roger Maris 10.00 25.00
BM Bill Mazeroski 15.00 40.00
BR Brooks Robinson 10.00 25.00
FR Luis Aparicio 10.00 25.00

FT Frank Thomas 12.50 30.00
HK Harmon Killebrew 10.00 25.00
HW Hoyt Wilhelm 10.00 25.00
MM Mickey Mantle 20.00 50.00
RR Robin Roberts 10.00 25.00

2011 Topps Heritage Framed Dual Stamps

STATED ODDS 1:211 HOBBY
STATED PRINT RUN 62 SER.#'d SETS
1 Bobby Abreu
Cole Hamels 6.00 15.00
2 Brett Anderson/Vernon Wells 6.00 15.00
3 Elvis Andrus/Curtis Granderson 6.00 15.00
4 Bronson Arroyo/Brad Lidge 8.00 20.00
5 Jason Bartlett/Adam Wainwright 8.00 20.00
6 Daric Barton/Carl Pavano 6.00 15.00
7 Jose Bautista/Clay Buchholz 6.00 15.00
8 Gordon Beckham/Howie Kendrick 6.00 15.00
9 Heath Bell/Alex Rios 6.00 15.00
10 Adrian Beltre/Denard Span 6.00 15.00
11 Chad Billingsley/Kendry Morales 10.00 25.00
12 Michael Bourn/Francisco Liriano 8.00 20.00
13 Dallas Braden/Will Venable 6.00 15.00
14 Ryan Braun/Gaby Sanchez 10.00 25.00
15 Domonic Brown/Stephen Drew 6.00 15.00
16 J.Bruce/M.Cabrera 6.00 15.00
17 Clay Buchholz/Yovani Gallardo 8.00 20.00
18 Billy Butler/Brett Gardner 6.00 15.00
19 Marlon Byrd/Mat Latos 6.00 15.00
20 M.Cabrera/R.Zimmerman 10.00 25.00
21 Trevor Cahill/Jose Tabata 8.00 20.00
22 M.Cain/E.Longoria 15.00 40.00
23 Robinson Cano/Ian Desmond 8.00 20.00
24 M.Capps/A.Jones 12.50 30.00
25 Chris Carpenter/Felix Hernandez 10.00 25.00
26 Starlin Castro/Francisco Cordero 10.00 25.00
27 Choo/L.Morrison 12.50 30.00
28 Chris Coghlan/Carlos Marmol 8.00 20.00
29 Tyler Colvin/Edwin Jackson 6.00 15.00
30 Francisco Cordero/Mike Napoli 6.00 15.00
31 Carl Crawford/Aaron Hill 8.00 20.00
32 Nelson Cruz/Brett Myers 6.00 15.00
33 Michael Cuddyer/Omar Infante 10.00 25.00
34 John Danks/Jorge Posada 8.00 20.00
35 I.Davis/D.Uggla 15.00 40.00
36 Ryan Dempster/Chris Young 6.00 15.00
37 Ian Desmond/Ben Zobrist 6.00 15.00
38 Stephen Drew/Roy Halladay 8.00 20.00
39 Adam Dunn/Adrian Beltre 8.00 20.00
40 J.Ellsbury/C.Rasmus 12.50 30.00
41 Andre Ethier/Wandy Rodriguez 6.00 15.00
42 Neftali Feliz/Alfonso Soriano 8.00 20.00
43 Prince Fielder/Corey Hart 10.00 25.00
44 Yovani Gallardo/Carl Crawford 6.00 15.00
45 Jaime Garcia/Jim Thome 10.00 25.00
46 Brett Gardner/Miguel Tejada 10.00 25.00
47 Matt Garza/Jayson Werth 6.00 15.00
48 Adrian Gonzalez/Jonathan Papelbon 10.00 25.00
49 Carlos Gonzalez/Trevor Cahill 8.00 20.00
50 Gio Gonzalez/Andre Ethier 6.00 15.00
51 C.Granderson/B.Posey 12.50 30.00
52 Vladimir Guerrero/Justin Morneau 8.00 20.00
53 Franklin Gutierrez/Juan Pierre 6.00 15.00
54 Roy Halladay/Daric Barton 8.00 20.00
55 Cole Hamels/Danny Valencia 8.00 20.00
56 J.Hamilton/H.Ramirez 12.50 30.00
57 Tommy Hanson/Vladimir Guerrero 8.00 20.00
58 Dan Haren/Franklin Gutierrez 6.00 15.00
59 Corey Hart/Yadier Molina 8.00 20.00
60 Chase Headley/Josh Johnson 6.00 15.00
61 Felix Hernandez/Matt Kemp 8.00 20.00
62 Jason Heyward/Chase Headley 8.00 20.00
63 Aaron Hill/Kelly Johnson 6.00 15.00
64 M.Holliday/D.Price 12.50 30.00
65 R.Howard/I.Suzuki 12.50 30.00
66 Daniel Hudson/James Shields 6.00 15.00
67 Tim Hudson/Adam Lind 10.00 25.00
68 A.Huff/I.Davis 15.00 40.00
69 Phil Hughes/Torii Hunter 6.00 15.00
70 Torii Hunter/Casey McGehee 8.00 20.00
71 O.Infante/D.Pedroia 15.00 40.00
72 Austin Jackson/Mariano Rivera 8.00 20.00
73 Edwin Jackson/Michael Bourn 6.00 15.00
75 D.Jeter/B.Upton 20.00 50.00
76 Ubaldo Jimenez/Angel Pagan 8.00 20.00
77 Josh Johnson/Ian Kinsler 6.00 15.00
78 Kelly Johnson/Ivan Rodriguez 6.00 15.00
79 Adam Jones/Chris Coghlan 10.00 25.00
80 C.Jones/R.Cano 30.00 60.00
81 Jair Jurrjens/Nick Markakis 8.00 20.00
82 Matt Kemp/John Lackey 8.00 20.00
83 Howie Kendrick/David Ortiz 6.00 15.00
84 C.Kershaw/J.Rollins 10.00 25.00
85 Ian Kinsler/Rafael Soriano 10.00 25.00
86 Paul Konerko/Manny Ramirez 8.00 20.00
87 John Lackey/Tommy Hanson 10.00 25.00
88 Mat Latos/Matt Holliday 6.00 15.00
89 Cliff Lee/Kevin Youkilis 10.00 25.00
90 Derrek Lee/C.J. Wilson 6.00 15.00
91 J.Lester/A.Torres 12.50 30.00
92 Brad Lidge/Bobby Abreu 6.00 15.00
93 T.Lincecum/C.Ruiz 12.50 30.00
94 Adam Lind/Carlos Quentin 8.00 20.00
95 Liriano/Verlander 10.00 25.00
96 J.Loney/A.Rodriguez 30.00 60.00
97 E.Longoria/D.Jeter 30.00 60.00
98 Derek Lowe/Joey Votto 10.00 25.00
99 N.Markakis/A.Gonzalez 12.50 30.00
100 Carlos Marmol/Barry Zito 6.00 15.00
101 Victor Martinez/Jay Bruce 6.00 15.00
102 Brian Matusz/Dallas Braden 10.00 25.00
103 J.Mauer/K.Suzuki 12.50 30.00
104 Brian McCann/Aubrey Huff 8.00 20.00
105 Andrew McCutchen/Max Scherzer 10.00 25.00
106 Casey McGehee/Derrek Lee 6.00 15.00
107 Jenrry Mejia/Brian Roberts 6.00 15.00
108 Yadier Molina/Jason Bartlett 8.00 20.00
109 Miguel Montero/Brett Wallace 6.00 15.00
110 Kendry Morales/Brandon Morrow 8.00 20.00
111 J.Morneau/P.Sandoval 12.50 30.00
112 Logan Morrison/Drew Stubbs 8.00 20.00
113 Brandon Morrow/Jonathan Sanchez 8.00 20.00
114 Brett Myers/Daniel Hudson 6.00 15.00
115 Mike Napoli/CC Sabathia 8.00 20.00
116 David Ortiz/Joakim Soria 15.00 40.00
117 Roy Oswalt/Jaime Garcia 10.00 25.00
118 A.Pagan/M.Cuddyer 12.50 30.00
119 J.Papelbon/D.Young 12.50 30.00
120 Carl Pavano/Grady Sizemore 8.00 20.00
121 D.Pedroia/B.Wilson 15.00 40.00
122 Mike Pelfrey/Domonic Brown 8.00 20.00
123 Hunter Pence/Josh Hamilton 10.00 25.00
124 A.Pettitte/M.Teixeira 15.00 40.00
125 Brandon Phillips/Johan Santana 10.00 25.00
126 Juan Pierre/Jon Jay 6.00 15.00
127 Jorge Posada/Tyler Colvin 10.00 25.00
128 B.Posey/C.Kershaw 15.00 40.00
129 Martin Prado/Elvis Andrus 8.00 20.00
130 David Price/Andy Pettitte 10.00 25.00
131 A.Pujols/M.Garza 20.00 50.00
132 Carlos Quentin/Bronson Arroyo 8.00 20.00
133 Alexei Ramirez/Mike Pelfrey 6.00 15.00
134 Aramis Ramirez/Michael Young 6.00 15.00
135 H.Ramirez/N.Swisher 12.50 30.00
136 Manny Ramirez/Cliff Lee 15.00 40.00
137 C.Rasmus/A.Dunn 12.50 30.00
138 Jose Reyes/Jose Bautista 10.00 25.00
139 Mark Reynolds/Andrew McCutchen 8.00 20.00
140 Alex Rios/Victor Martinez 8.00 20.00
141 Mariano Rivera/Dan Haren 10.00 25.00
142 Brian Roberts/Heath Bell 6.00 15.00
143 A.Rodriguez/J.Jurrjens 15.00 40.00
144 Ivan Rodriguez/Jose Reyes 10.00 25.00
145 Wandy Rodriguez/Billy Butler 6.00 15.00
146 J.Rollins/T.Lincecum 20.00 50.00
147 Ricky Romero/Jered Weaver 6.00 15.00
148 Carlos Ruiz/Martin Prado 6.00 15.00
149 C.Sabathia/A.Pujols 20.00 50.00
150 Gaby Sanchez/Ricky Romero 6.00 15.00
151 Jonathan Sanchez/Nelson Cruz 10.00 25.00
152 P.Sandoval/C.Carpenter 15.00 40.00
153 Carlos Santana/Jon Lester 8.00 20.00
154 Ervin Santana/Shin-Soo Choo 8.00 20.00
155 Johan Santana/Miguel Montero 8.00 20.00
156 M.Scherzer/J.Heyward 15.00 40.00
157 Luke Scott/Mike Stanton 8.00 20.00
158 James Shields/Chad Billingsley 6.00 15.00
159 Grady Sizemore/Alexei Ramirez 8.00 20.00
160 Joakim Soria/Ervin Santana 6.00 15.00
161 Alfonso Soriano/Prince Fielder 8.00 20.00
162 Rafael Soriano/Mark Reynolds 6.00 15.00
163 Denard Span/Carlos Santana 10.00 25.00
164 Mike Stanton/Matt Capps 12.50 30.00
165 Drew Stubbs/Gordon Beckham 10.00 25.00
166 Ichiro Suzuki/Justin Upton 10.00 25.00
167 Kurt Suzuki/Gio Gonzalez 8.00 20.00
168 Nick Swisher/Brian Matusz 10.00 25.00
169 Jose Tabata/Phil Hughes 8.00 20.00
170 Mark Teixeira/Ryan Dempster 10.00 25.00
171 M.Tejada/J.Mauer 15.00 40.00
172 Jim Thome/Brett Anderson 10.00 25.00
173 A.Torres/J.Ellsbury 12.50 30.00
174 Troy Tulowitzki/Hunter Pence 8.00 20.00
175 D.Uggla/M.Cain 12.50 30.00
176 B.J. Upton/Brian McCann 6.00 15.00
177 Justin Upton/Roy Oswalt 8.00 20.00
178 Chase Utley/Luke Scott 8.00 20.00
179 Danny Valencia/Tim Hudson 10.00 25.00
180 Will Venable/Troy Tulowitzki 8.00 20.00
181 Verlander/Victorino 8.00 20.00
182 Shane Victorino/John Danks 8.00 20.00
183 Joey Votto/Austin Jackson 10.00 25.00
184 A.Wainwright/R.Weeks 12.50 30.00
185 Neil Walker/James Loney 10.00 25.00
186 Brett Wallace/Ryan Braun 10.00 25.00
187 Jered Weaver/Brandon Phillips 6.00 15.00
188 Rickie Weeks/Neftali Feliz 8.00 20.00
189 Vernon Wells/Ryan Howard 8.00 20.00
190 J.Werth/D.Wright 12.50 30.00
191 B.Wilson/A.Ramirez 12.50 30.00
192 C.J. Wilson/Carlos Gonzalez 10.00 25.00
193 D.Wright/S.Castro 12.50 30.00
194 K.Youkilis/C.Jones 20.00 50.00
195 Chris Young/Marlon Byrd 6.00 15.00
196 Delmon Young/Neil Walker 10.00 25.00
197 Michael Young/Ubaldo Jimenez 6.00 15.00
198 Ryan Zimmerman/Jenrry Mejia 6.00 15.00
199 Barry Zito/Chase Utley 10.00 25.00
200 Ben Zobrist/Paul Konerko 8.00 20.00

2011 Topps Heritage Jackie Robinson Special Memorabilia

COMMON ROBINSON 20.00 50.00
STATED ODDS 1:1777 HOBBY
STATED PRINT RUN 42 SER.#'d SETS
135 Jackie Robinson 20.00 50.00
136 Jackie Robinson 20.00 50.00
137 Jackie Robinson 20.00 50.00
138 Jackie Robinson 20.00 50.00
139 Jackie Robinson 20.00 50.00
140 Jackie Robinson 20.00 50.00
141 Jackie Robinson 20.00 50.00
142 Jackie Robinson 20.00 50.00
143 Jackie Robinson 20.00 50.00
144 Jackie Robinson 20.00 50.00

2011 Topps Heritage New Age Performers

COMPLETE SET (15) 15.00 40.00
STATED ODDS 1:15 HOBBY
NAP1 Cliff Lee .60 1.50
NAP2 Jim Thome .60 1.50
NAP3 Josh Hamilton .60 1.50
NAP4 Roy Halladay .60 1.50
NAP5 Miguel Cabrera 1.00 2.50
NAP6 Ubaldo Jimenez .40 1.00
NAP7 Joey Votto 1.00 2.50
NAP8 CC Sabathia .60 1.50
NAP9 David Price .75 2.00
NAP10 Alex Rodriguez 1.25 3.00
NAP11 Evan Longoria .60 1.50
NAP12 Carlos Gonzalez .60 1.50
NAP13 Robinson Cano .60 1.50
NAP14 Felix Hernandez .60 1.50
NAP15 Albert Pujols 1.25 3.00

2011 Topps Heritage News Flashbacks

COMPLETE SET (10) 4.00 10.00
COMMON CARD .40 1.00
STATED ODDS 1:12 HOBBY
NF8 Mets Join National League .60 1.50
NF10 Jackie Robinson Enshrined 1.00 2.50

2011 Topps Heritage Real One Autographs

STATED ODDS 1:303
EXCHANGE DEADLINE 2/28/2014
AD Art Ditmar 10.00 25.00
AJ David Wright 30.00 60.00
AK Al Kaline 50.00 120.00
BC Bob Cerv 10.00 25.00
BG Bob Gibson 40.00 80.00
BP Bill Pierce 10.00 25.00
BR Brooks Robinson 30.00 60.00
DB Don Buddin 10.00 25.00
DD Dan Dobbek 10.00 25.00
DG Dick Gernert 8.00 20.00
DGI Don Gile 6.00 15.00
DH Dave Hillman 6.00 15.00
EB Ernie Banks 40.00 80.00
EBO Ed Bouchee 8.00 20.00
EL Evan Longoria 20.00 50.00
EY Eddie Yost 6.00 15.00
FT Frank Thomas 6.00 15.00
GWI Gordon Windhorn 10.00 25.00
HA Hank Aaron 200.00 400.00
HB Howie Bedell 10.00 25.00
HN Hal Naragon 6.00 15.00
HR Hanley Ramirez 10.00 25.00
HS Hal Stowe 15.00 40.00
JA Jim Archer 10.00 25.00
JD Jim Donohue 10.00 25.00
JDE John DeMerit 8.00 20.00
JH Joe Hicks 6.00 15.00
LP Leo Posada 6.00 15.00
MK Marty Kutyna 10.00 25.00
MS Mike Stanton 20.00 50.00
NC Neil Chrisley 10.00 25.00
RR Ray Rippelmeyer 6.00 15.00
SC Starlin Castro 10.00 25.00
SK Sandy Koufax 500.00 700.00
SM Stan Musial 125.00 250.00
TP Tom Parsons 10.00 25.00
TW Ted Wills 6.00 15.00

2011 Topps Heritage Real One Autographs Red Ink

*RED: 5.X TO 1.2X BASIC
STATED ODDS 1:700 HOBBY
STATED PRINT RUN 62 SER.#'d SETS
SM Stan Musial 150.00 300.00

2011 Topps Heritage Then and Now

COMPLETE SET (10) 8.00 20.00
STATED ODDS 1:15 HOBBY
TN1 Harmon Killebrew/Jose Bautista 1.00 2.50
TN2 F.Robinson/M.Cabrera 1.00 2.50
TN3 Frank Robinson/Josh Hamilton .60 1.50
TN4 Luis Aparicio/Juan Pierre .60 1.50
TN5 M.Mantle/P.Fielder 3.00 8.00
TN6 Robin Roberts/Felix Hernandez .60 1.50
TN7 Bob Gibson/Jered Weaver .60 1.50
TN8 Juan Marichal/CC Sabathia .60 1.50
TN9 Warren Spahn/Roy Halladay .60 1.50
TN10 Bob Gibson/Roy Halladay .60 1.50

2011 Topps Heritage Triple Stamp Box Topper

RANDOMLY INSERTED BOX TOPPER
TSBL1 Jered Weaver/Torii Hunter
Dan Haren 2.50 6.00
TSBL2 Stephen Drew/Justin Upton
Miguel Montero 2.50 6.00
TSBL3 McCann/Heyward/Prado 3.00 8.00
TSBL4 Brian Matusz/Adam Jones
Nick Markakis 3.00 8.00
TSBL5 Pedroia/Ortiz/Lester 4.00 10.00
TSBL6 Alfonso Soriano/Starlin Castro
Carlos Marmol 2.50 6.00
TSBL7 Alex Rios/Gordon Beckham
Alexei Ramirez 2.50 6.00
TSBL8 Brandon Phillips/Joey Votto
Jay Bruce 4.00 10.00
TSBL9 Shin-Soo Choo/Carlos Santana
Grady Sizemore 4.00 10.00
TSBL10 Troy Tulowitzki/Carlos Gonzalez
Ubaldo Jimenez 4.00 10.00
TSBL11 Verlander/Cabrera/Jackson 4.00 10.00
TSBL12 Stntn/Rmrz/Jhnsn 4.00 10.00
TSBL13 Michael Bourn/Hunter Pence
Wandy Rodriguez 2.50 6.00
TSBL14 Billy Butler/Lorezno Cain
Joakim Soria 1.50 4.00
TSBL15 Ethier/Kershaw/Kemp 6.00 15.00
TSBL16 Fielder/Braun/Gallardo 2.50 6.00
TSBL17 Justin Morneau/Joe Mauer
Francisco Liriano 3.00 8.00
TSBL18 Santana/Wright/Reyes 3.00 8.00
TSBL19 Cano/Jeter/Sabathia 10.00 25.00
TSBL20 Brett Anderson/Trevor Cahill
Gio Gonzalez 2.50 6.00
TSBL21 Howard/Halladay/Utley 3.00 8.00
TSBL22 Tbt/McCtchn/Wlkr 4.00 10.00
TSBL23 Mat Latos/Chase Headley
Heath Bell 2.50 6.00
TSBL24 Lincecum/Posey/Wilson 5.00 12.00
TSBL25 Hernandez/Ichiro/Gutierrez 5.00 12.00
TSBL26 Holl/Pujols/Wain 5.00 12.00
TSBL27 Price/Longoria/Upton 3.00 8.00
TSBL28 Nelson Cruz/Josh Hamilton
Ian Kinsler 4.00 10.00
TSBL29 Jose Bautista/Ricky Romero
Brandon Morrow 2.50 6.00
TSBL30 Jayson Werth/Ryan Zimmerman
Ian Desmond 2.50 6.00

2012 Topps Heritage

COMP.SET w/o SPs (425) 20.00 50.00
COMP.HN.FACT.SET (101) 300.00 500.00
COMP.HN SET (100) 75.00 150.00
COMMON CARD (1-425) .15 .40
COMMON ROOKIE (1-425) .40 1.00
COMMON SP (426-500) 2.50 6.00
SP ODDS 1:3 HOBBY
ERR SP'S ARE ERROR CARDS
COMMON BW SP (1-425) 2.50 6.00
BW SP FEATURE BLACK/WHITE MAIN PHOTO
COMMON CS SP (1-425) 12.50 30.00
CS SP FEATURE COLOR VARIATIONS
COMMON HN (H576-H675) .50 1.25
COMMON HN RC (H576-H675) .60 1.50
HN FACT SETS SOLD ONLY ON TOPPS.COM
1 NL Batting Leaders .40 1.00
2 AL Batting Leaders .40 1.00
3 NL HR Leaders .50 1.25
4 Jose Bautista/Curtis Granderson/Mark Teixeira
Mark Reynolds/Adrian Beltre/I .40 1.00
5 Kersh/Halla/Lee/Vogel/Lince LL .60 1.50
6 AL ERA Leaders .40 1.00
7 Kenn/Kersh/Halla/Gallar/Lee/Gre .60 1.50
8 AL Pitching Leaders .40 1.00
9 Kersh/Lee/Halla/Lince/Gallar LL .60 1.50
10 AL Strikeout Leaders .40 1.00
11 Francisco Rodriguez .30 .75
12 Jim Johnson .15 .40
13 Philadelphia Phillies TC .15 .40
14A Justin Masterson .25 .60
15A Darwin Barney .25 .60
15B Darwin Barney ERR SP 30.00 60.00
16 Juan Pierre .25 .60
17 Mike Moustakas .30 .75
18 David Ortiz/Adrian Gonzalez .40 1.00
19 Zach Britton .30 .75
20A Derek Jeter 1.00 2.50
20B Derek Jeter CS SP 50.00 100.00
21 Drew Stubbs .25 .60
22A Edwin Jackson .25 .60
23 Ned Yost MG .15 .40
24 Mark Melancon .25 .60
25 Delmon Young .30 .75
26 Scott Baker .25 .60
27 Josh Thole .25 .60
28 Josh Beckett .25 .60
29A Pea RC/Mes RC/De Fra RC/Sav RC.75 2.00
29B Pea/Mes/De Fra/Sav ERR SP 60.00 120.00
30 Cody Ross .25 .60
31 Jeff Samardzija .25 .60
32A Domonic Brown .30 .75
33 Tyler Chatwood .25 .60
34A Josh Collmenter .30 .75
35 Chris Sale .40 1.00
36 Jason Kipnis .30 .75
37 Yonder Alonso .25 .60
38 Andrew Brackman .15 .40
39 Bronson Arroyo .25 .60
40 Chris Parmelee .25 .60
41 John Buck .25 .60
42 David Robertson .25 .60
43 M.Rivera/J.Girardi .50 1.25
44A Justin Verlander .40 1.00
44B Justin Verlander BW SP 4.00 10.00
45 Jimmy Paredes .25 .60
46 Michael Bourn .25 .60
47 Jayson Werth .30 .75
48 Manny Acta MG .15 .40
49 Jordan Walden .25 .60
50 Madison Bumgarner .30 .75
51 Alex Gordon .30 .75
52A Dustin Pedroia .40 1.00
52B Dustin Pedroia BW SP 4.00 10.00
53 Freddie Freeman .50 1.25
54A Ga RC/Re RC/Ch RC/Be RC 1.00 2.50
54B Gaub/Reed/Cham/Bet ERR SP 20.00 50.00
55 Alex Presley .25 .60
56A Cliff Lee .30 .75
56B Cliff Lee BW SP 3.00 8.00
57 Howie Kendrick .25 .60
58 Marlon Byrd .25 .60
59 R.A. Dickey .30 .75
60A Jesus Montero .25 .60
61 Aubrey Huff .25 .60
62 Eric O'Flaherty .25 .60
63 Cincinnati Reds TC .15 .40
64 Victor Martinez .30 .75
65 Nick Markakis .30 .75
66 Sergio Santos .25 .60
67 J.P. Arencibia .25 .60
68 Ryan Vogelsong/Andre Ethier .30 .75
69 Michael Morse .25 .60
70 Homer Bailey .25 .60
71 Placido Polanco .25 .60
72A Carlos Santana .30 .75
73 Fredi Gonzalez MG .15 .40
74 Randy Wolf .25 .60
75 Aaron Crow .25 .60
76A Jon Lester .25 .60
77 J.B. Shuck .15 .40
78 Daniel Murphy .30 .75
79 Kendrys Morales .25 .60
80 Jamey Carroll .25 .60
81 Geovany Soto .30 .75
82 Greg Holland .75 2.00
83A Lance Berkman .30 .75
83B Lance Berkman CS SP 20.00 50.00
84A Doug Fister .25 .60
85A Buster Posey .50 1.25
85B Buster Posey CS SP 20.00 50.00
86 Dayan Viciedo .25 .60
87A Andrew McCutchen .40 1.00
87B Andrew McCutchen CS SP 30.00 60.00
88 J.J. Hardy .25 .60
89 Liam Hendriks .25 .60
90A Joey Votto .40 1.00
90B Joey Votto CS SP 30.00 60.00
91A Roy Halladay .30 .75
91B Roy Halladay BW SP 3.00 8.00
92 Austin Romine .25 .60
93 Johan Santana .30 .75
94 Wilson Ramos .25 .60
95 Joe Benson RC/Adron Chambers RC
Corey Brown RC/Michael Taylor RC 1.00 2.50
96A Carl Crawford .30 .75
97 Kyle Lohse .25 .60
98A Torii Hunter .30 .75
99 Wandy Rodriguez .25 .60
100A Paul Konerko .25 .60
101 Jeff Karstens .25 .60
102 Ron Washington MG .15 .40
103 Michael Brantley .25 .60
104 Danny Duffy .25 .60
105 James Loney .25 .60
106A Tim Lincecum .30 .75
106B Tim Lincecum BW SP 3.00 8.00
107 Ruben Tejada .25 .60
108 Vladimir Guerrero .30 .75
109 Wade Davis .30 .75
110 Chase Headley .25 .60
111 Jeremy Hellickson .25 .60
112 New York Mets TC .25 .60
113A Kerry Wood .25 .60
113B Kerry Wood ERR SP 10.00 25.00
114 St. Louis Cardinals TC .25 .60
115A Jacoby Ellsbury .30 .75
115B Jacoby Ellsbury CS SP 15.00 40.00
116 Vance Worley .30 .75
117 Vernon Wells .25 .60
118 A.J. Pierzynski .25 .60
119 Matt Downs .25 .60
120 Nick Swisher .30 .75
121 Drew Storen .25 .60
122A Hanley Ramirez .30 .75
123 Andre Ethier .30 .75
124 Alcides Escobar .30 .75
125 Ron Gardenhire MG .15 .40
126 Jonathan Lucroy .30 .75
127 Willie Bloomquist .25 .60
128 Seth Smith .25 .60
129 Chris Perez .25 .60
130A David Freese .25 .60
131 Kevin Gregg .25 .60
132 Cole Hamels .30 .75
133 Todd Frazier .25 .60
134 Jim Leyland MG .15 .40
135 Chris Parmelee RC/Steve Lombardozzi RC/Pedro
Florimon RC/Jordan Pacheco RC .60 1.50
136 Jonathan Papelbon .30 .75
137A Nyjer Morgan .25 .60
137B Nyjer Morgan CS SP 20.00 50.00
138 Dan Uggla/Chipper Jones .40 1.00
139 Carlos Ruiz .25 .60
140 Max Scherzer .40 1.00
141 Carlos Lee .25 .60
142 Allen Craig WS HL .30 .75
143 Neftali Feliz WS HL .25 .60
144 Albert Pujols WS HL .50 1.25
145 Derek Holland WS HL .25 .60
146 Mike Napoli WS HL .25 .60
147 David Freese WS HL .25 .60
148 St. Louis Cardinals WS HL .15 .40
149 Ian Desmond .25 .60
150 Hiroki Kuroda .25 .60
151 Pittsburgh Pirates TC .15 .40
152 Nick Hagadone .25 .60
153 Miguel Montero .25 .60
154 Don Mattingly MG .75 2.00
155 Rafael Soriano .25 .60
156 Yuniesky Betancourt .25 .60
157 Melky Cabrera .25 .60
158 Lomb RC/Flor RC/Domin RC/Mes RC.75 2.00
159 Ryan Doumit .25 .60
160 Mark Buehrle .30 .75
161 Ryan Howard .30 .75
162 Minnesota Twins TC .15 .40
163 Matt Cain .30 .75
164A Austin Jackson .30 .75
165 C.J. Wilson .25 .60
166 Kirk Gibson MG .15 .40
167 Erick Aybar .25 .60
168 Ryan Lavarnway .25 .60
169 Luis Marte RC/Brett Pill RC/Efren Navarro
RC/Jared Hughes RC 1.00 2.50
170 Lonnie Chisenhall .25 .60
171 Jordan Zimmermann .30 .75
172A Yadier Molina .50 1.25
173 Bronx Bombers Best 1.00 2.50
174A Jose Reyes .25 .60
175 Matt Garza .25 .60
176 Michael Taylor .25 .60
177A Evan Longoria .30 .75
177B Evan Longoria CS SP 20.00 50.00
178 Devin Mesoraco .25 .60
179 Shaun Marcum .25 .60
180 Mitch Moreland .25 .60
181 Brent Morel .25 .60
182 Peter Bourjos .25 .60
183A Mark Teixeira .30 .75
183B Mark Teixeira BW SP 3.00 8.00
184 Jared Hughes .25 .60
185A Freddy Sanchez .40 1.00
186A Joe Mauer .30 .75
186B Joe Mauer BW SP 3.00 8.00
187 Shelley Duncan .25 .60
188 Marco Scutaro .30 .75
189 Wilton Lopez .40 1.00
190A Matt Holliday .40 1.00
191 He RC/Li RC/Mo RC/Sc RC 1.00 2.50
192 Justin De Fratus .25 .60
193A Starlin Castro .30 .75
193B Starlin Castro BW SP 3.00 8.00
194 Francisco Cordero .25 .60
195 Desmond Jennings .30 .75
196 Tim Federowicz .25 .60
197A Ian Kennedy .25 .60
197B Ian Kennedy BW SP 3.00 8.00
198 Joe Benson .25 .60
199 Jeff Keppinger .25 .60
200A Curtis Granderson .30 .75
200B Curtis Granderson BW SP 3.00 8.00
201A Yovani Gallardo .30 .75
201B Yovani Gallardo CS SP 20.00 50.00
202 Boston Red Sox TC .25 .60
203 Scott Rolen .30 .75
204 Chris Schwinden .30 .75
205 Robert Andino .25 .60
206 Lance Lynn .25 .60
207 Mike Trout 75.00 200.00
208 Pi RC/Ch RC/Fi RC/Po RC 1.00 2.50
209 Chris Iannetta .25 .60
210A Clayton Kershaw .60 1.50
211 Mark Trumbo .25 .60
212 Carlos Marmol .25 .60
213 Buck Showalter MG .15 .40
214 Joakim Soria .25 .60
215A B.J. Upton .30 .75
215B B.J. Upton CS SP 30.00 60.00
216 Kyle Weiland .15 .40
217A Dexter Fowler .30 .75
217B Dexter Fowler CS SP 30.00 60.00
218 Tigers Twirlers .40 1.00
219 Shin-Soo Choo .30 .75
220 Ricky Romero .25 .60
221A Chase Utley .30 .75
222 Jed Lowrie .25 .60
223 Addison Reed .25 .60
224A Alex Avila .25 .60
225A Aroldis Chapman .40 1.00
226 Skip Schumaker .25 .60
227A Ubaldo Jimenez .25 .60
228 Nick Hagadone RC/Josh Satin RC
Jared Hughes RC/Joe Benson RC .75 2.00
229 Brandon Beachy .25 .60
230 Brett Wallace .25 .60
231A Dan Haren .25 .60
231B Dan Haren ERR SP 15.00 40.00
232A Kevin Youkilis .40 1.00
233 Terry Collins MG .15 .40
234 Alejandro De Aza .25 .60
235 Ryan Vogelsong .25 .60
236 Salvador Perez .30 .75
237 Ivan Nova .30 .75
238 Jose Constanza RC .60 1.50
239 Cleveland Indians TC .15 .40
240 Andy Dirks .25 .60
241 Johnny Cueto .30 .75
242 Jay Bruce/Justin Upton .30 .75
243 Jordan Pacheco .25 .60
244 Jason Motte .25 .60
245 Lucas Duda .30 .75
246A Felix Hernandez .30 .75
246B Felix Hernandez BW SP 3.00 8.00
247 Jarrod Parker RC .75 2.00
248 Kosuke Fukudome .30 .75
249 Alberto Callaspo .25 .60
250A Jon Jay .40 1.00
251 Clay Buchholz .25 .60
252 Aramis Ramirez .25 .60
253 Po RC/Re RC/Li RC/Ta RC .60 1.50
254 Carlos Quentin .25 .60
255 John Axford .25 .60
256 Johnny Giavotella .25 .60
257 Jacob Turner .30 .75
258 Bruce Bochy MG .25 .60
259 Neil Walker .25 .60
260A Anthony Rizzo .50 1.25
261 Javy Guerra .25 .60
262 J.D. Martinez .40 1.00
263 Tyler Clippard .25 .60
264A Robinson Cano .30 .75
264B Robinson Cano CS SP 12.50 30.00
265 Adron Chambers RC/Steve Lombardozzi RC/Tim
Federowicz RC/Brad Peacock RC 1.00 2.50
266 Travis Hafner .25 .60
267 Nick Hundley .25 .60
268 Hunter Pence .30 .75
269 Justin Morneau .30 .75
270 Nate Schierholtz .25 .60
271 Alexei Ramirez .30 .75
272 David Murphy .25 .60
273 Wilin Rosario .25 .60
274 Justin De Fratus RC/Jared Hughes RC/Alex Liddi
RC/Kyle Waldrop (RC) .60 1.50
275A Dan Uggla .30 .75
276A Ryan Braun .25 .60
276B Ryan Braun BW SP 4.00 10.00
277A David Price .30 .75
277B David Price CS SP 12.50 30.00
278 Jhonny Peralta .25 .60
279A Matt Kemp .30 .75
279B Matt Kemp BW SP 3.00 8.00
280 Brett Lawrie RC .75 2.00
281 Jason Marquis .25 .60
282A Jeff Francoeur .30 .75
282B Jeff Francoeur CS SP 30.00 60.00
283 Brad Lidge .15 .40
284 Matt Harrison .25 .60
285A Adrian Gonzalez .30 .75
285B Adrian Gonzalez CS SP 12.50 30.00
286 Mi RC/Re RC/Mo RC/Be RC 1.00 2.50
287 Yorvit Torrealba .15 .40
288 Chicago White Sox TC .15 .40
289A Mariano Rivera .50 1.25
289B Mariano Rivera BW SP 3.00 8.00
290A Albert Pujols .50 1.25
290B Albert Pujols CS SP 30.00 60.00
291 Stephen Strasburg .40 1.00
292 Justin Turner .40 1.00
293 Tim Stauffer .25 .60
294 Mike Scioscia MG .15 .40
295 Cory Luebke .25 .60
296A Jim Thome .30 .75
297 Derek Holland .25 .60
298 Martin Prado .25 .60
299 Steve Delabar RC/Tom Milone RC/Luis Marte
RC/Jared Hughes RC .60 1.50
300 Carlos Beltran .30 .75
301 Gio Gonzalez .30 .75
302 Brennan Boesch .25 .60
303 Alexi Ogando .25 .60
304 Brandon Phillips .25 .60
305 Ryan Roberts .25 .60
306 Yadier Molina/Brian McCann .50 1.25
307 J.J. Putz .25 .60
308 Brian McCann .30 .75
309 Ryan Dempster .25 .60
310 Jerry Sands .25 .60
311 Brad Peacock .25 .60
312 Tampa Bay Rays TC .15 .40
313 Jaime Garcia .30 .75
314 Alexi Casilla .25 .60
315 Hector Noesi .25 .60
316 Billy Butler .25 .60
317 Jason Donald .25 .60
318 Charlie Manuel MG .15 .40
319A Adam Jones .30 .75
320 Zack Greinke .40 1.00
321 Po RC/Sp (RC)/Br RC/Ch RC 1.00 2.50
322 Ervin Santana .25 .60
323 Chase d'Arnaud .25 .60
324 Jesus Montero RC/Austin Romine RC
Tim Federowicz RC/Wilin Rosario RC.60 1.50
325A Brian Wilson .40 1.00
326 Ramon Hernandez .25 .60
327 Rick Porcello .25 .60
328 Elvis Andrus .30 .75
329 Francisco Cervelli .25 .60
330 Jorge Posada .25 .60
331 World Series Foes .50 1.25
332 Jorge De La Rosa .25 .60
333 Joe Benson RC/Liam Hendriks RC
Chris Parmelee RC/Kyle Waldrop (RC).60 1.50
334 Mat Latos .30 .75
335 Bobby Abreu .25 .60
336 Fernando Salas .25 .60
337 Adam Dunn .30 .75
338 Brandon McCarthy .25 .60
339 Guillermo Moscoso RC .75 2.00
340 Russell Martin .25 .60
341A Ryan Madson .25 .60
341B R.Madson Red ERR SP 50.00 100.00
341C R.Madson White ERR SP 75.00 150.00
342 Chris Coghlan .25 .60
343 Joe Maddon MG .15 .40
344 Anibal Sanchez .25 .60
345 Mark Reynolds .25 .60
346 Santiago Casilla .25 .60
347 Chipper Jones .40 1.00
348A Miguel Cabrera .40 1.00
348B Miguel Cabrera BW SP 3.00 8.00
349 Alex Gonzalez .25 .60
350 Tommy Hanson .25 .60
351 Danny Espinosa .25 .60
352 Mike Adams .25 .60
353 Cameron Maybin .25 .60
354 Jemile Weeks RC .60 1.50
355 Josh Reddick .25 .60
356A Adrian Beltre .40 1.00
356B David Ortiz CS SP 60.00 120.00
357 Allen Craig .30 .75
358 Steve Delabar .25 .60
359 Cliff Pennington .25 .60
360 Chad Billingsley .25 .60
361 Alex Rodriguez .50 1.25
362 Matt Dominguez RC/Chris Schwinden RC/Joe
Savery RC/Brad Peacock RC .75 2.00
363 Aaron Harang .25 .60
364 Jose Tabata .25 .60
365 Jose Valverde .30 .75
366 Dustin Ackley .25 .60
367 Trayvon Robinson .25 .60
368 Andrew Bailey .25 .60
369 Jason Kubel .25 .60
370 Koji Uehara .25 .60
371 Brett Gardner .30 .75
372 Scott Downs .25 .60
373A Michael Young .25 .60
373B Michael Young CS SP 40.00 80.00
374 Tom Milone .25 .60
375 Daniel Descalso .25 .60
376 Trevor Cahill .25 .60
377 Baltimore Orioles TC .15 .40
378 Jeff Niemann .25 .60
379 Joaquin Benoit .25 .60
380A Carlos Pena .30 .75
380B Carlos Pena ERR VAR SP 75.00 150.00
381 Blake Beavan .25 .60
382 Joe Girardi MG .25 .60
383 Jason Vargas .25 .60
384 Blake DeWitt .15 .40
385 Logan Morrison .25 .60
386 Mo RC/Br RC/Ro RC/Be RC 1.00 2.50
387 Ricky Nolasco .25 .60
388 Pablo Sandoval .30 .75
389 Drew Pomeranz .25 .60
390 Jason Heyward .30 .75
391 Matt Moore RC 1.00 2.50
392 Asdrubal Cabrera/Carlos Santana .30 .75
393 Clint Hurdle MG .15 .40
394 Tim Hudson .30 .75
395 Daniel Hudson .25 .60
396 Emilio Bonifacio .25 .60
397 Kansas City Royals TC .15 .40
398 Craig Kimbrel .30 .75
399 Mike Minor .25 .60
400 Jay Bruce .30 .75
401 Freddy Garcia .25 .60
402 Davey Johnson MG .15 .40
403 Colby Lewis .25 .60
404 Adam Lind .30 .75
405 Michael Pineda .25 .60
406 Al Alburquerque .15 .40
407 Domin RC/Moore RC/Meso RC
Taylor RC .75 2.00
408A Ian Kinsler .30 .75
408B Ian Kinsler CS SP 20.00 50.00
409 Jair Jurrjens .25 .60
410 Jesus Guzman .25 .60
411 Nathan Eovaldi .30 .75
412 Kemp/Ethier/Kershaw .60 1.50
413 Huston Street .25 .60
414A Corey Hart .25 .60
414B Corey Hart CS SP 20.00 50.00
415A Chris Carpenter .30 .75
415B Chris Carpenter BW SP 3.00 8.00
415C Chris Carpenter CS SP 30.00 60.00
416 Stephen Drew .25 .60
417 Jeremy Guthrie .25 .60
418 Johnny Damon .30 .75
419 Casey Janssen .15 .40
420 Eduardo Nunez .25 .60
421 Kyle Farnsworth .30 .75
422 Dusty Baker MG .15 .40
423 Neftali Feliz .25 .60
424 Matt Dominguez .30 .75
425 Wilson Betemit .25 .60
426 Frank Francisco SP 2.50 6.00
427 Dee Gordon SP 3.00 8.00
428 Eric Thames SP 2.50 6.00
429 Jonny Venters SP 2.50 6.00
430 Ben Zobrist SP 2.50 6.00
431 Jerry Hairston SP 2.50 6.00
432 Matt Joyce SP 2.50 6.00
433 Rickie Weeks SP 3.00 8.00
434 Shane Victorino SP 3.00 8.00
435 Asdrubal Cabrera SP 3.00 8.00
436 Ike Davis SP 3.00 8.00
437 Chris Denorfia SP 2.50 6.00
438 Juan Nicasio SP 2.50 6.00
439 Aaron Miles SP 2.50 6.00
440 Jonathan Sanchez SP 2.50 6.00
441 Paul Goldschmidt SP 3.00 8.00
442 Jason Bartlett SP 2.50 6.00
443 Endy Chavez SP 2.50 6.00
444 Brandon League SP 2.50 6.00
445A Gaby Sanchez SP 2.50 6.00
446 CC Sabathia SP 3.00 8.00
447 Jose Iglesias SP 2.50 6.00
448 Heath Bell SP 3.00 8.00
449 Gerardo Parra SP 2.50 6.00
450 Leo Nunez SP 2.50 6.00
451 Steve Lombardozzi SP 2.50 6.00
452 Fautino De Los Santos SP 2.50 6.00
453A Troy Tulowitzki SP 3.00 8.00
453B Troy Tulowitzki BW SP 3.00 8.00
454A Julio Teheran SP 2.50 6.00
454B Julio Teheran ERR SP 40.00 80.00
455 Jimmy Rollins SP 3.00 8.00
456 Greg Dobbs SP 2.50 6.00

457 Dellin Betances SP 3.00 8.00
458 Adron Chambers SP 3.00 8.00
459 Alex Liddi SP 3.00 8.00
460 Brett Pill SP 3.00 8.00
461 Jose Altuve SP 2.50 6.00
462 Chris Young SP 2.50 6.00
463 Edwin Encarnacion SP 2.50 6.00
464 Omar Infante SP 2.50 6.00
465 John Mayberry Jr. SP 2.50 6.00
466 Kyle Seager SP 2.50 6.00
467 David Wright SP 4.00 10.00
468A Nelson Cruz SP 3.00 8.00
468B Nelson Cruz BW SP 3.00 8.00
468C Nelson Cruz CS SP 12.50 30.00
469 Jeremy Affeldt SP 2.50 6.00
470 Ben Revere SP 3.00 8.00
471 Yunel Escobar SP 2.50 6.00
472 Alfonso Soriano SP 3.00 8.00
473 Carlos Zambrano SP 3.00 8.00
474 Barry Zito SP 2.50 6.00
475 Jason Bay SP 3.00 8.00
476A Prince Fielder SP 3.00 8.00
476B Prince Fielder BW SP 3.00 8.00
477 Derrek Lee SP 2.50 6.00
478 Roy Oswalt SP 3.00 8.00
479 Eric Hosmer SP 4.00 10.00
480A Carlos Gonzalez SP 3.00 8.00
480B Carlos Gonzalez CS SP 20.00 50.00
481A Justin Upton SP 3.00 8.00
481B Justin Upton BW SP 3.00 8.00
482 David Ortiz SP 3.00 8.00
483A Mike Stanton SP 3.00 8.00
483B Mike Stanton BW SP 3.00 8.00
483D Stntn ERR VAR SP 60.00 120.00
484A Todd Helton SP 3.00 8.00
485A Mike Napoli SP 3.00 8.00
485B Mike Napoli CS SP 20.00 50.00
486A Josh Hamilton SP 3.00 8.00
486B Josh Hamilton BW SP 3.00 8.00
487 Casey Kotchman SP 2.50 6.00
488 Ryan Adams SP 2.50 6.00
489A Jose Bautista SP 3.00 8.00
489B Jose Bautista BW SP 3.00 8.00
490 Brandon Belt SP 3.00 8.00
491 Ichiro Suzuki SP 4.00 10.00
492 Joel Hanrahan SP 2.50 6.00
493 Josh Willingham SP 2.50 6.00
494A Ryan Zimmerman SP 3.00 8.00
494B Ryan Zimmerman BW SP 3.00 8.00
495A James Shields SP 2.50 6.00
495B James Shields CS SP 12.00 30.00
496 Josh Johnson SP 3.00 8.00
497A Jered Weaver SP 2.50 6.00
497B Jered Weaver BW SP 2.50 6.00
498 Jhoulys Chacin SP 2.50 6.00
499 Jason Bourgeois SP 2.50 6.00
500 Michael Cuddyer SP 2.50 6.00
H576 Adam Wainwright 1.00 2.50
H577 Tsuyoshi Wada RC 1.00 2.50
H578 J.A. Happ 1.00 2.50
H579 Brian Matusz .75 2.00
H580 Chris Capuano .75 2.00
H581 Cody Ross .75 2.00
H582 Jarrod Saltalamacchia .75 2.00
H583 Ryan Hanigan .75 2.00
H584 Wade Miley 1.00 2.50
H585 Jonathon Niese .75 2.00
H586 Mike Aviles .75 2.00
H587 Bryan LaHair .75 2.00
H588 Jake Arrieta 1.00 2.50
H589 Hisashi Iwakuma RC 2.00 5.00
H590 Garrett Richards RC 1.50 4.00
H591 John Danks .75 2.00
H592 Brandon Morrow .75 2.00
H593 Ernesto Frieri .75 2.00
H594 Kenley Jansen 1.00 2.50
H595 Felix Doubront .75 2.00
H596 Vinnie Pestano .75 2.00
H597 Jake Peavy .75 2.00
H598 Jonathan Broxton .75 2.00
H599 Brian Dozier RC 3.00 8.00
H600 Yu Darvish RC 2.50 6.00
H601 Philip Humber .75 2.00
H602 Derek Lowe .75 2.00
H603 Drew Smyly RC 1.00 2.50
H604 Matt Capps .75 2.00
H605 Jamie Moyer .75 2.00
H606 Ichiro Suzuki 1.50 4.00
H607 Jerome Williams .75 2.00
H608 Bruce Chen .75 2.00
H609 Wei-Yin Chen RC 2.50 6.00
H610 Joe Saunders .75 2.00
H611 Alfredo Aceves .75 2.00
H612 Tyler Pastornicky RC 1.00 2.50
H613 Angel Pagan .75 2.00
H614 Juan Pierre .75 2.00
H615 Pedro Alvarez .75 2.00
H616 Sean Marshall .75 2.00
H617 Jack Hannahan .75 2.00
H618 Brett Myers .75 2.00
H619 Zack Cozart (RC) 1.00 2.50
H620 Fernando Rodney .75 2.00
H621 Chris Davis .75 2.00
H622 Reed Johnson .75 2.00
H623 Gordon Beckham .75 2.00
H624 Andrew Cashner .75 2.00
H625 Alex Rios 1.00 2.50
H626 Lorenzo Cain .75 2.00
H627 Wily Peralta RC 1.00 2.50
H628 Andres Torres .75 2.00
H629 Andruw Jones .75 2.00
H630 Denard Span .75 2.00
H631 Raul Ibanez 1.00 2.50
H632 Ryan Sweeney .75 2.00
H633 Cesar Izturis .75 2.00
H634 Chris Getz .75 2.00
H635 Francisco Liriano .75 2.00
H636 Daniel Bard .75 2.00
H637 Daisuke Matsuzaka 1.00 2.50
H638 Matt Adams RC 8.00 20.00
H639 Andy Pettitte 1.00 2.50
H640 Norichika Aoki RC 1.25 3.00
H641 Jordany Valdespin RC 1.25 3.00
H642 Andrelton Simmons RC 1.50 4.00
H643 Johnny Damon 1.00 2.50
H644 Colby Rasmus 1.00 2.50
H645 Bartolo Colon .50 1.25
H646 Kirk Nieuwenhuis RC 1.00 2.50
H647 A.J. Burnett .75 2.00
H648 Edinson Volquez .75 2.00
H649 Jake Westbrook .75 2.00
H650 Bryce Harper RC 250.00 500.00
H651 Will Middlebrooks RC 1.25 3.00
H652 Yoenis Cespedes RC 2.50 6.00
H653 Grant Balfour .75 2.00
H654 Edwin Jackson .75 2.00
H655 Henry Rodriguez .75 2.00
H656 Brandon Inge .75 2.00
H657 Trevor Bauer RC 5.00 12.00
H658 Chris Iannetta .75 2.00
H659 Garrett Jones .75 2.00
H660 Matt Hague RC 1.00 2.50
H661 Rafael Furcal .75 2.00
H662 Luke Scott .75 2.00
H663 Kelly Johnson .75 2.00
H664 Jonny Gomes .75 2.00
H665 Sean Rodriguez .75 2.00
H666 Carl Pavano .75 2.00
H667 Joe Nathan .75 2.00
H668 Juan Uribe .75 2.00
H669 Bobby Abreu .75 2.00
H670 Marco Scutaro 1.00 2.50
H671 Gavin Floyd .75 2.00
H672 Ted Lilly .75 2.00
H673 Drew Hutchison RC 1.25 3.00
H674 Leonys Martin RC 1.00 2.50
H675 Adam LaRoche .75 2.00

2012 Topps Heritage '63 Mint

STATED ODDS 1:288 HOBBY
JFK STATED ODDS 1:26,520 HOBBY
EXCHANGE DEADLINE 02/28/2015
63AK Al Kaline EXCH 15.00 40.00
63AZ Alcatraz 10.00 25.00
63BG Bob Gibson EXCH 10.00 25.00
63CY Carl Yastrzemski EXCH 25.00 60.00
63DS Duke Snider EXCH 15.00 40.00
63EM Eddie Mathews 20.00 50.00
63EMZ Edgar Martinez 8.00 20.00
63JFK John F. Kennedy EXCH 100.00 200.00
63JM Juan Marichal 12.50 30.00
63JM Joe Morgan 10.00 25.00
63MM Mickey Mantle EXCH 50.00 100.00
63PO Paul O'Neill 12.50 30.00
63RC Bob Clemente 40.00 80.00
63SK Sandy Koufax 20.00 50.00
63SM Stan Musial 20.00 50.00
63UA University of Alabama 8.00 20.00
63WF Whitey Ford EXCH 20.00 50.00
63WM Willie Mays 40.00 80.00
63WS Willie Stargell EXCH 15.00 40.00
63WS Warren Spahn EXCH 20.00 50.00
63YB Yogi Berra EXCH 20.00 50.00

2012 Topps Heritage Advertising Panels

ISSUED AS A BOX TOPPER
1 Bobby Abreu .75 2.00
Desmond Jennings/Allen Craig
2 AL HR Leader 1.00 2.50
Matt Holliday/Ramon Hernandez
3 AL Pitching Leaders .60 1.50
Tim Federowicz/Ron Washington
4 Bronson Arroyo .75 2.00
Cameron Maybin/Craig Kimbrel
5 Joaquin Benoit .75 2.00
Placido Polanco/Nathan Eovaldi
6 Joe Benson 1.00 2.50
Adron Chambers/Corey Brown/Michael Taylor/Jon Jay/Dodgers Big Three
7 Wilson Betemit .60 1.50
David Freese/Drew Pomeranz
8 Emilio Bonifacio .75 2.00
Johan Santana/Tom Milone
9 Alexi Casilla .75 2.00
Craig Pinches Rangers In Opener/Adrian Gonzalez
10 Josh Collmenter .75 2.00
Joaquin Benoit/Placido Polanco
11 Allen Craig .75 2.00
Edwin Jackson/Blake DeWitt
12 Craig Pinches Rangers In Opener 1.00 2.50
Adrian Gonzalez/Joe Benson/Adron Chambers/Corey Brown/Michael Taylor
13 Justin De Fratus .60 1.50
Wilson Betemit/David Freese
14 Deep Freese Makes Texas Toast .75 2.00
Jim Thome/Matt Dominguez/Jeremy Moore/Devin Mesoraco/Michael Taylor
15 Ian Desmond .75 2.00
Jesus Guzman/Vladimir Guerrero
16 Matt Dominguez 1.00 2.50
Jeremy Moore/Devin Mesoraco/Michael Taylor/Brad Lidge/Brett Pill/Ardon Chambers/Thomas Field/Drew Pomeranz
17 Tim Federowicz .60 1.50
Ron Washington/Lance Lynn
18 Feliz Finishes Off For Texas .60 1.50
Yorvit Torrealba/Ryan Dempster
19 Frmn/Cvlli/Arncba 1.25 3.00
20 David Freese .60 1.50
Drew Pomeranz/Liam Hendricks
21 Adrian Gonzalez 1.00 2.50
Joe Benson/Adron Chambers/Corey Brown/Michael Taylor/Jon Jay
22 Kevin Gregg .75 2.00
Emilio Bonifacio/Johan Santana
23 Vladimir Guerrero .75 2.00
Jason Vargas/J.B. Shuck
24 Jesus Guzman .75 2.00
Vladimir Guerrero/Jason Vargas
25 Jeremy Hellickson .75 2.00
Cliff Pennington/Josh Collmenter
26 Ramon Hernandez .60 1.50
Ryan Roberts/Justin De Fratus/Jared Hughes/Alex Liddi/Kyle Waldrop
27 Matt Holliday 1.00 2.50
Ramon Hernandez/Ryan Roberts
28 Jared Hughes .60 1.50
AL Pitching Leaders/Tim Federowicz
29 Edwin Jackson .60 1.50
Blake DeWitt/Kendrys Morales
30 Desmond Jennings .75 2.00
Allen Craig/Edwin Jackson
31 Davey Johnson .60 1.50
Jordan Pacheco/Jim Leyland
32 Clayton Kershaw 1.50 4.00
NL ERA Leaders/Justin De Fratus
33 Craig Kimbrel .75 2.00
Alexi Casilla/Craig Pinches Rangers In Opener
34 Jason Kubel .75 2.00
Jordan Walden/Mat Latos
35 Mat Latos .75 2.00
Jeremy Hellickson/Cliff Pennington
36 Ldge/Pill/Chmbrs/Fld/Mrntz 1.00 2.50
37 Wilson Lopez .60 1.50
Veteran Masters/Ian Desmond
38 Steve Lombardozzi .75 2.00
Pedro Florimon/Matt Dominguez/Devin Mesoraco/Carlos Quentin/Kirk Gibson
39 Carlos Marmol .60 1.50
NL Home Run Leaders/Wilton Lopez
40 Mrtnz/Hrdle/Cnstnza 1.00 2.50
41 Don Mattingly 2.00 5.00
Carlos Marmol/NL Home Run Leaders
42 Joe Mauer .75 2.00
Red Sox Smashers/Kevin Gregg
43 Cameron Maybin .75 2.00
Craig Kimbrel/Alexei Casilla
44 Milone/Freeman/Cervelli 1.25 3.00
45 Yadier Molina 1.25 3.00
Bobby Abreu/Desmond Jennings
46 Jesus Montero .60 1.50
Austin Romine/Tim Federowicz/Wilin Rosario/David Murphy/Feliz Finishes Off For Texas
47 Kendrys Morales .75 2.00
Michael Pineda/Tim Lincecum
48 Mitch Moreland .75 2.00
Deep Freese Makes Texas Toast/Jim Thome
49 David Murphy .60 1.50
Feliz Finishes Off For Texas/Yorvit Torrealba
50 NL Batting Leaders .75 2.00
Joe Mauer/Red Sox Smashers
51 NL ERA Leaders .60 1.50
Justin De Fratus/Wilson Betemit
52 NL Home Run Leaders .40 1.00
Wilton Lopez/Veteran Masters
53 Jordan Pacheco 1.50 4.00
Jim Leyland/Clayton Kershaw
54 Jarrod Parker 1.00 2.50
Nate Spears/Corey Brown/Drew Pomeranz/Adron Chambers/Nate Schierholtz
55 Brad Peacock 1.00 2.50
Devin Mesoraco/Justin DeFrautis/Joe Savery/Jarrod Parker/Nate Spears/Corey Brown/Drew Pomeranz/Adron Chambers
56 Pill/Chmbrs/Fld/Pmrnz/Mrtnz/Hrdle 1.00 2.50
57 Michael Pineda .75 2.00
Tim Lincecum/Eduardo Nunez
58 Placido Polanco .75 2.00
Nathan Eovaldi/Wade Davis
59 Power Plus .60 1.50
Michael Taylor/AL Home Run Leaders
60 Pride of NL .60 1.50
Rafael Soriano/Power Plus
61 Carlos Quentin .60 1.50
Kirk Gibson/Joakim Soria
62 Hanely Ramirez .60 1.50
Jesus Montero/Austin Romine/Tim Federowicz/Wilin Rosario/David Murphy
63 Red Sox Smashers .60 1.50
Kevin Gregg/Emilio Bonifacio
64 Ryan Roberts .60 1.50
Justin De Fratus/Jared Hughes/Alex Liddi/Kyle Waldrop/Nick Hundley
65 Santana/Milone/Freeman 1.25 3.00
66 Rafael Soriano .60 1.50
Power Plus/Michael Taylor
67 Nate Spears 1.00 2.50
Corey Brown/Drew Pomeranz/Adron Chambers/Nate Schierholtz/Tigers Twirlers
68 Jose Tabata .60 1.50
Bronson Arroyo/Cameron Maybin
69 Michael Taylor 1.00 2.50
AL Home Run Leaders/Matt Holliday
70 Jim Thome .75 2.00
Matt Dominguez/Jeremy Moore/Devin Mesoraco/Michael Taylor/Brad Lidge
71 Yorvit Torrealba .75 2.00
Ryan Dempster/Steve Lombardozzi/Pedro Florimon/Matt Dominguez/Devin Mesoraco
72 Veteran Masters .60 1.50
Ian Desmond/Jesus Guzman
73 Jordan Walden .75 2.00
Mat Latos/Jeremy Hellickson
74 Ron Washington .75 2.00
Lance Lynn/Brad Peacock/Devin Mesoraco/Justin De Fratus/Joe Savery
75 World Series Foes .60 1.50
Mitch Moreland/Deep Freese Makes Texas Toast

2012 Topps Heritage Baseball Flashbacks

COMPLETE SET (10) 6.00 15.00
STATED ODDS 1:12 HOBBY
AK Al Kaline 1.00 2.50
EB Ernie Banks 1.00 2.50
EW Early Wynn .60 1.50
HA Hank Aaron 2.00 5.00
JM Juan Marichal .60 1.50
SK Sandy Koufax 2.00 5.00
SM Stan Musial 1.50 4.00
WM Willie Mays 2.00 5.00
SKO Sandy Koufax 2.00 5.00
WMC Willie McCovey .60 1.50

2012 Topps Heritage Black

INSERTED IN RETAIL PACKS
HP1 Matt Kemp 1.50 4.00
HP2 Ryan Braun 1.25 3.00
HP3 Adrian Gonzalez 1.50 4.00
HP4 Jacoby Ellsbury 1.50 4.00
HP5 Miguel Cabrera 2.00 5.00
HP6 Joey Votto 2.00 5.00
HP7 Curtis Granderson 1.50 4.00
HP8 Albert Pujols 2.50 6.00
HP9 Dustin Pedroia 2.00 5.00
HP10 Robinson Cano 1.50 4.00
HP11 Michael Young 1.25 3.00
HP12 Alex Gordon 1.50 4.00
HP13 Lance Berkman 1.50 4.00
HP14 Paul Konerko 1.25 3.00
HP15 Ian Kinsler 1.50 4.00
HP16 Aramis Ramirez 1.25 3.00
HP17 Hunter Pence 1.50 4.00
HP18 Jose Reyes 1.50 4.00
HP19 Hanley Ramirez 1.50 4.00
HP20 Victor Martinez 1.50 4.00
HP21 Ryan Howard 1.50 4.00
HP22 Melky Cabrera 1.25 3.00
HP23 Nick Swisher 1.50 4.00
HP24 Jay Bruce 1.50 4.00
HP25 Michael Bourn 1.25 3.00
HP26 Billy Butler 1.25 3.00
HP27 Dan Uggla 1.50 4.00
HP28 Evan Longoria 1.50 4.00
HP29 Adrian Beltre 2.00 5.00
HP30 Elvis Andrus 1.50 4.00
HP31 Mark Reynolds 1.25 3.00
HP32 Neil Walker 1.25 3.00
HP33 Derek Jeter 5.00 12.00
HP34 Torii Hunter 1.50 4.00
HP35 Nick Markakis 1.50 4.00
HP36 Howie Kendrick 1.25 3.00
HP37 Nyjer Morgan 1.25 3.00
HP38 Andre Ethier 1.50 4.00
HP39 Chris Iannetta 1.25 3.00
HP40 Austin Jackson 1.50 4.00
HP41 J.J. Hardy 1.25 3.00
HP42 Danny Espinosa 1.25 3.00
HP43 Alex Rodriguez 2.50 6.00
HP44 Marco Scutaro 1.50 4.00
HP45 Adam Jones 1.50 4.00
HP46 Jayson Werth 1.50 4.00
HP47 Ian Kennedy 1.25 3.00
HP48 Cole Hamels 1.50 4.00
HP49 Josh Beckett 1.25 3.00
HP50 Dan Haren 1.25 3.00
HP51 Ricky Romero 1.25 3.00
HP52 Tim Lincecum 1.50 4.00
HP53 Matt Cain 1.50 4.00
HP54 Felix Hernandez 1.50 4.00
HP55 Doug Fister 1.25 3.00
HP56 Johnny Cueto 1.50 4.00
HP57 Jeremy Hellickson 1.25 3.00
HP58 Justin Masterson 1.25 3.00
HP59 Jon Lester 1.25 3.00
HP60 Tim Hudson 1.50 4.00
HP61 David Price 1.50 4.00
HP62 Daniel Hudson 1.25 3.00
HP63 Vance Worley 1.50 4.00
HP64 Jair Jurrjens 1.25 3.00
HP65 Gio Gonzalez 1.50 4.00
HP66 Madison Bumgarner 1.50 4.00
HP67 Shaun Marcum 1.25 3.00
HP68 Ervin Santana 1.25 3.00
HP69 Ryan Vogelsong 1.25 3.00
HP70 Yovani Gallardo 1.50 4.00
HP71 Matt Harrison 1.25 3.00
HP72 Randy Wolf 1.25 3.00
HP73 Zack Greinke 2.00 5.00
HP74 Derek Holland 1.25 3.00
HP75 Jordan Zimmermann 1.50 4.00
HP76 Hiroki Kuroda 1.25 3.00
HP77 Mark Teixeira 1.50 4.00
HP78 Carlos Beltran 1.50 4.00
HP79 Andrew McCutchen 2.00 5.00
HP80 Starlin Castro 1.50 4.00
HP81 Matt Holliday 2.00 5.00
HP82 Pablo Sandoval 1.50 4.00
HP83 Michael Morse 1.25 3.00
HP84 Brandon Phillips 1.25 3.00
HP85 Alex Avila 1.25 3.00
HP86 Carlos Santana 1.50 4.00
HP87 Chris Carpenter 1.50 4.00
HP88 Max Scherzer 2.00 5.00
HP89 Rick Porcello 1.25 3.00
HP90 Jaime Garcia 1.50 4.00
HP91 Michael Pineda 1.25 3.00
HP92 AL Batting Leaders 2.00 5.00
HP93 NL Home Run Leaders 2.50 6.00
HP94 Kenn/Kersh/Halla/Gallar/Lee/Gre 3.00 8.00
HP95 AL Pitching Leaders 2.00 5.00
HP96 Ga/Re/Ch/Be 2.00 5.00
HP97 Steve Lombardozzi/Pedro Florimon/Matt Dominguez/Devin Mesoraco 1.50 4.00
HP98 Pi/Ch/Fi/Pom 2.00 5.00
HP99 Mil/Ree/Moo/Bet 2.00 5.00
HP100 Chris Parmelee/Steve Lombardozzi/Pedro Florimon/Jordan Pacheco 1.25 3.00

2012 Topps Heritage Chrome

COMPLETE SET (100) 150.00 300.00
STATED ODDS 1:11 HOBBY
STATED PRINT RUN 1963 SER.#'d SETS
HP1 Matt Kemp 2.00 5.00
HP2 Ryan Braun 1.50 4.00
HP3 Adrian Gonzalez 2.00 5.00
HP4 Jacoby Ellsbury 2.00 5.00
HP5 Miguel Cabrera 2.50 6.00
HP6 Joey Votto 2.50 6.00
HP7 Curtis Granderson 2.00 5.00
HP8 Albert Pujols 3.00 8.00
HP9 Dustin Pedroia 2.50 6.00
HP10 Robinson Cano 2.00 5.00
HP11 Michael Young 1.50 4.00
HP12 Alex Gordon 2.00 5.00
HP13 Lance Berkman 2.00 5.00
HP14 Paul Konerko 1.50 4.00
HP15 Ian Kinsler 2.00 5.00
HP16 Aramis Ramirez 1.50 4.00
HP17 Hunter Pence 2.00 5.00
HP18 Jose Reyes 2.00 5.00
HP19 Hanley Ramirez 2.00 5.00
HP20 Victor Martinez 2.00 5.00
HP21 Ryan Howard 2.00 5.00
HP22 Melky Cabrera 1.50 4.00
HP23 Nick Swisher 2.00 5.00
HP24 Jay Bruce 2.00 5.00
HP25 Michael Bourn 1.50 4.00
HP26 Billy Butler 1.50 4.00
HP27 Dan Uggla 2.00 5.00
HP28 Evan Longoria 2.00 5.00
HP29 Adrian Beltre 2.50 6.00
HP30 Elvis Andrus 2.00 5.00
HP31 Mark Reynolds 1.50 4.00
HP32 Neil Walker 1.50 4.00
HP33 Derek Jeter 6.00 15.00
HP34 Torii Hunter 2.00 5.00
HP35 Nick Markakis 2.00 5.00
HP36 Howie Kendrick 1.50 4.00
HP37 Nyjer Morgan 1.50 4.00
HP38 Andre Ethier 2.00 5.00
HP39 Chris Iannetta 1.50 4.00
HP40 Austin Jackson 2.00 5.00
HP41 J.J. Hardy 1.50 4.00
HP42 Danny Espinosa 1.50 4.00
HP43 Alex Rodriguez 3.00 8.00
HP44 Marco Scutaro 2.00 5.00
HP45 Adam Jones 2.00 5.00
HP46 Jayson Werth 2.00 5.00
HP47 Ian Kennedy 1.50 4.00
HP48 Cole Hamels 2.00 5.00
HP49 Josh Beckett 1.50 4.00
HP50 Dan Haren 1.50 4.00
HP51 Ricky Romero 1.50 4.00
HP52 Tim Lincecum 2.00 5.00
HP53 Matt Cain 2.00 5.00
HP54 Felix Hernandez 2.00 5.00
HP55 Doug Fister 1.50 4.00
HP56 Johnny Cueto 2.00 5.00
HP57 Jeremy Hellickson 1.50 4.00
HP58 Justin Masterson 1.50 4.00
HP59 Jon Lester 1.50 4.00
HP60 Tim Hudson 2.00 5.00
HP61 David Price 2.00 5.00
HP62 Daniel Hudson 1.50 4.00
HP63 Vance Worley 2.00 5.00
HP64 Jair Jurrjens 1.50 4.00
HP65 Gio Gonzalez 2.00 5.00
HP66 Madison Bumgarner 2.00 5.00
HP67 Shaun Marcum 1.50 4.00
HP68 Ervin Santana 1.50 4.00
HP69 Ryan Vogelsong 1.50 4.00
HP70 Yovani Gallardo 2.00 5.00
HP71 Matt Harrison 1.50 4.00
HP72 Randy Wolf 1.50 4.00
HP73 Zack Greinke 2.50 6.00
HP74 Derek Holland 1.50 4.00
HP75 Jordan Zimmermann 2.00 5.00
HP76 Hiroki Kuroda 1.50 4.00
HP77 Mark Teixeira 2.00 5.00
HP78 Carlos Beltran 2.00 5.00
HP79 Andrew McCutchen 2.50 6.00
HP80 Starlin Castro 2.00 5.00
HP81 Matt Holliday 2.50 6.00
HP82 Pablo Sandoval 2.00 5.00
HP83 Michael Morse 1.50 4.00
HP84 Brandon Phillips 1.50 4.00
HP85 Alex Avila 1.50 4.00
HP86 Carlos Santana 2.00 5.00
HP87 Chris Carpenter 2.00 5.00
HP88 Max Scherzer 2.50 6.00
HP89 Rick Porcello 1.50 4.00
HP90 Jaime Garcia 2.00 5.00
HP91 Michael Pineda 1.50 4.00
HP92 AL Batting Leaders 2.50 6.00
HP93 NL HR Leaders 3.00 8.00
HP94 Kenn/Kersh/Halla/Gallar/Lee/Gre 4.00 10.00
HP95 AL ERA Leaders 2.50 6.00
HP96 Gaub/Reed/Chamb/Betan 2.50 6.00
HP97 Lomb/Florimon/Doming/Mesor 2.00 5.00
HP98 Pill/Chamb/Field/Pomeranz 2.50 6.00
HP99 Milone/Reed/Moore/Betan 2.50 6.00
HP100 Chris Parmelee/Steve Lombardozzi/Pedro Florimon/Jordan Pacheco 1.50 4.00

2012 Topps Heritage Chrome Black Refractors

*BLACK REF: 4X TO 10X BASIC
STATED ODDS 1:329 HOBBY
STATED PRINT RUN 63 SER.#'d SETS
HP1 Matt Kemp 20.00 50.00
HP4 Jacoby Ellsbury 15.00 40.00
HP10 Robinson Cano 40.00 80.00
HP48 Cole Hamels 15.00 40.00
HP55 Doug Fister 12.50 30.00
HP58 Justin Masterson 15.00 40.00
HP64 Jair Jurrjens 20.00 50.00
HP84 Brandon Phillips 15.00 40.00
HP85 Alex Avila 30.00 60.00
HP89 Rick Porcello 15.00 40.00
HP93 NL HR Leaders 30.00 60.00
HP95 AL ERA Leaders 15.00 40.00
HP96 Gaub/Reed/Chamb/Betan 25.00 60.00
HP97 Lomb/Florimon/Doming/Mesor 20.00 50.00
HP98 Pill/Chamb/Field/Pomeranz 20.00 50.00
HP100 Parm/Lomb/Flor/Pacheco 12.50 30.00

2012 Topps Heritage Chrome Refractors

*REF: .6X TO 1.5X BASIC
STATED ODDS 1:37 HOBBY
STATED PRINT RUN 563 SER.#'d SETS

2012 Topps Heritage Clubhouse Collection Dual Relics

STATED ODDS 1:9280 HOBBY
STATED PRINT RUN 63 SER.#'d SETS
BC E.Banks/S.Castro 30.00 80.00
KC A.Kaline/M.Cabrera 30.00 60.00
MG R.Maris/C.Granderson 30.00 60.00
MP W.Mays/B.Posey 60.00 150.00
YE Yastrzemski/Ellsbury 50.00 100.00

2012 Topps Heritage Clubhouse Collection Relics

STATED ODDS 1:29 HOBBY
SP VAR PRINT RUN 63 SER.#'d SETS
AB Adrian Beltre 3.00 8.00
AC Aroldis Chapman 3.00 8.00
AJ Adam Jones 3.00 8.00
AM Andrew McCutchen 3.00 8.00
AR Aramis Ramirez 3.00 8.00
BJU B.J. Upton 3.00 8.00
BPH Brandon Phillips 3.00 8.00
CB Carlos Beltran 3.00 8.00
CC1 Chris Carpenter 3.00 8.00
CC2 Chris Carpenter SP 15.00 40.00
CCR Carl Crawford 3.00 8.00
CGO Carlos Gonzalez 3.00 8.00
CH Cole Hamels 4.00 10.00
CJW C.J. Wilson 3.00 8.00
CL1 Cliff Lee 4.00 10.00
CL2 Cliff Lee SP 8.00 20.00
CS Carlos Santana 3.00 8.00
CU Chase Utley 4.00 10.00
DH Dan Haren 3.00 8.00
DHU Daniel Hudson 3.00 8.00
DO1 David Ortiz 3.00 8.00
DO2 David Ortiz SP 20.00 50.00
DP1 Dustin Pedroia 4.00 10.00
DP2 Dustin Pedroia SP 20.00 50.00
DPR David Price 3.00 8.00
DU Dan Uggla 3.00 8.00
DW David Wright 3.00 8.00
EA Elvis Andrus 3.00 8.00
EL1 Evan Longoria 3.00 8.00
EL2 Evan Longoria SP 30.00 60.00
FH1 Felix Hernandez 3.00 8.00
FH2 Felix Hernandez SP 10.00 25.00
HP Hunter Pence 4.00 10.00
IK1 Ian Kennedy 3.00 8.00
IK2 Ian Kennedy SP 12.50 30.00
JB1 Jose Bautista 3.00 8.00
JB2 Jose Bautista SP 20.00 50.00
JBR Jay Bruce 3.00 8.00
JE1 Jacoby Ellsbury 5.00 12.00
JE2 Jacoby Ellsbury SP 20.00 50.00
JG Jaime Garcia 3.00 8.00
JH1 Josh Hamilton 4.00 10.00
JH2 Josh Hamilton SP 20.00 50.00
JM1 Joe Mauer 4.00 10.00
JM2 Joe Mauer SP 12.50 30.00
JR Jose Reyes 3.00 8.00
JRO Jimmy Rollins 4.00 10.00
JS James Shields 3.00 8.00
JU1 Justin Upton 3.00 8.00
JU2 Justin Upton SP 10.00 25.00
JV Justin Verlander 12.50 30.00
JW1 Jered Weaver 3.00 8.00
JW2 Jered Weaver SP 12.50 30.00
JWE Jayson Werth 3.00 8.00
LM Logan Morrison 3.00 8.00
MB Madison Bumgarner 4.00 10.00
MC1 Miguel Cabrera 4.00 10.00
MC2 Miguel Cabrera SP 15.00 40.00
MCA Matt Cain 3.00 8.00
MCB Melky Cabrera 3.00 8.00
MG Matt Garza 3.00 8.00
MH Matt Holliday 3.00 8.00
MK Matt Kemp 5.00 12.00
MR1 Mariano Rivera 4.00 10.00
MR2 Mariano Rivera SP 20.00 50.00
MS1 Mike Stanton 3.00 8.00
MS2 Mike Stanton SP 20.00 50.00
MT1 Mark Teixeira 4.00 10.00
MT2 Mark Teixeira SP 20.00 50.00
NC1 Nelson Cruz 3.00 8.00
NC2 Nelson Cruz SP 30.00 60.00
NM Nyjer Morgan 3.00 8.00
NS Nick Swisher 3.00 8.00
PF1 Prince Fielder 3.00 8.00
PF2 Prince Fielder SP 10.00 25.00
PK Paul Konerko 3.00 8.00
PS Pablo Sandoval 3.00 8.00
RB1 Ryan Braun 5.00 12.00
RB2 Ryan Braun SP 20.00 50.00
RH Roy Halladay SP 20.00 50.00
RHO Ryan Howard 4.00 10.00
RV Ryan Vogelsong 3.00 8.00
RW Rickie Weeks 3.00 8.00
RZ1 Ryan Zimmerman 3.00 8.00
RZ2 Ryan Zimmerman SP 15.00 40.00
SC1 Starlin Castro 5.00 12.00
SC2 Starlin Castro SP 12.50 30.00
TH Tommy Hanson 3.00 8.00
THU Tim Hudson 3.00 8.00
TL1 Tim Lincecum 5.00 12.00
TL2 Tim Lincecum SP 30.00 60.00
TT1 Troy Tulowitzki 3.00 8.00
TT2 Troy Tulowitzki SP 20.00 50.00
VM Victor Martinez 3.00 8.00
YG Yovani Gallardo 3.00 8.00
ZG Zack Greinke 3.00 8.00

2012 Topps Heritage Flashback Stadium Relics

STATED ODDS 1:1459 HOBBY
BG Bob Gibson 12.50 30.00
CY Carl Yastrzemski 12.00 30.00
EB Ernie Banks 15.00 40.00
EM Eddie Mathews 12.50 30.00
FR Frank Robinson 20.00 50.00
HA Hank Aaron 12.50 30.00
RC Bob Clemente 30.00 60.00
RM Roger Maris 12.50 30.00
SM Stan Musial 12.50 30.00
WM Willie Mays 20.00 50.00
YB Yogi Berra 12.50 30.00
MMA Mickey Mantle 15.00 40.00

2012 Topps Heritage JFK Stamp Collection

STATED ODDS 1:2950 HOBBY
STATED PRINT RUN 63 SER.#'d SETS
1 Problems 15.00 40.00
2 Liberty 15.00 40.00
3 Risks 15.00 40.00
4 The America 15.00 40.00
5 Our Common Common Link 15.00 40.00
6 A Free Society 15.00 40.00
7 Ask Not 15.00 40.00

2012 Topps Heritage New Age Performers

COMPLETE SET (15) 10.00 25.00
STATED ODDS 1:15 HOBBY
AP Albert Pujols 1.25 3.00
CJ Chipper Jones 1.00 2.50
CL Cliff Lee .75 2.00
DJ Derek Jeter 2.50 6.00
JB Jose Bautista .75 2.00
JB Josh Beckett .60 1.50
JV Joey Votto 1.00 2.50
JW Jered Weaver .75 2.00
MC Miguel Cabrera 1.00 2.50
MK Matt Kemp .75 2.00
RB Ryan Braun .60 1.50
RC Robinson Cano .75 2.00
RH Roy Halladay .75 2.00
TL Tim Lincecum .75 2.00
VM Victor Martinez .75 2.00

2012 Topps Heritage News Flashbacks

COMPLETE SET (10) 5.00 12.00
STATED ODDS 1:12 HOBBY
A Alcatraz .40 1.00
JK John F. Kennedy 1.00 2.50
MK Martin Luther King Jr. .60 1.50
PP Pope Paul VI .40 1.00
PS Penn Station .40 1.00
UA University of Alabama .40 1.00
UC U.S. Cuba Cuba .40 1.00
VT Valentina Tereshkova .40 1.00
JKE John F. Kennedy 1.00 2.50
MKI Martin Luther King Jr. .60 1.50

2012 Topps Heritage Real One Autographs

STATED ODDS 1:289 HOBBY
HN CARDS ISSUED IN HN.FACT.SETS
EXCHANGE DEADLINE 02/28/2015
AG Adrian Gonzalez 10.00 25.00
AGR Alex Grammas 8.00 20.00
AJ Adam Jones 15.00 40.00
AM Andrew McCutchen 30.00 80.00
AP Andy Pettitte HN 100.00 175.00
BA Bob Anderson 8.00 20.00
BD Bobby Del Greco 8.00 20.00
BG Bob Gibson 40.00 80.00
BGA Billy Gardner 8.00 20.00
BH Bryce Harper HN 400.00 800.00
BT Bob Turley 10.00 25.00
BV Bill Virdon 12.50 30.00
CA Craig Anderson 10.00 25.00
CBO Carl Boles 10.00 25.00
CE Chuck Essegian 8.00 20.00
CF Chico Fernandez 8.00 20.00
CG Chris Getz HN 10.00 25.00
CH Carroll Hardy 8.00 20.00
CK Clayton Kershaw 40.00 80.00
CM Charley Maxwell 8.00 20.00
CR Cody Ross HN 15.00 40.00
DB Daniel Bard HN 12.50 30.00
DH Drew Hutchison HN 20.00 50.00
DS Daryl Spencer 15.00 40.00
DST Dean Stone 8.00 20.00
DZ Brian Dozier HN 30.00 80.00
EA Earl Averill 12.50 30.00
EB Ed Bauta 10.00 25.00
EG Eli Grba 12.00 30.00
EK Eddie Kasko 10.00 25.00
ER Ed Roebuck 10.00 25.00
EV Edinson Volquez HN 40.00 100.00
FF Freddie Freeman 15.00 40.00
FR Fernando Rodney HN 30.00 60.00
FS Frank Sullivan 10.00 25.00
FTO Frank Torre 8.00 20.00
GB Gordon Beckham HN 15.00 40.00
GJ Garrett Jones HN 8.00 20.00
HL Hobie Landrith 15.00 40.00
ID Ike Delock 10.00 25.00
JB Jim Brosnan 10.00 25.00
JC Joe Cunningham 10.00 25.00
JK Jerry Kindall 10.00 25.00
JL Johnny Logan 10.00 25.00
JM Juan Marichal 40.00 100.00
JMO Jesus Montero 12.50 30.00
JV Jordany Valdespin HN 15.00 40.00
KN Kirk Nieuwenhuis HN 15.00 40.00
LA Luis Aparicio 15.00 40.00
MH Matt Holliday 20.00 50.00
MHA Matt Hague HN 12.50 30.00
MK Matt Kemp 12.00 30.00
MM Minnie Minoso 20.00 50.00
MMC Mike McCormick 8.00 20.00
OC Orlando Cepeda 60.00 150.00
RK Russ Kemmerer 10.00 25.00
RS Red Schoendienst 10.00 25.00
RZ Ryan Zimmerman 12.50 30.00
SC Starlin Castro 10.00 25.00
SM Stan Musial 40.00 100.00
TB Trevor Bauer HN 40.00 100.00
TC Tex Clevenger 8.00 20.00
TP Tyler Pastornicky HN 8.00 20.00
WM Will Middlebrooks HN 50.00 100.00
WM Willie Mays EXCH 250.00 500.00
WMC Willie McCovey 50.00 100.00
WP Wily Peralta HN 8.00 20.00
YC Yoenis Cespedes HN 60.00 120.00
YD Yu Darvish HN 50.00 120.00
ZC Zack Cozart HN 15.00 40.00

2012 Topps Heritage Real One Autographs Red Ink

*RED: .6X TO 1.5X BASIC
STATED ODDS 1:738 HOBBY
PRINT RUNS B/WN 10-63 COPIES PER
NO PRICING ON QTY 25 OR LESS
EXCHANGE DEADLINE 02/28/2015
AM Andrew McCutchen 75.00 200.00
CK Clayton Kershaw 125.00 250.00

2012 Topps Heritage Stick-Ons

COMPLETE SET (46) 40.00 80.00
STATED ODDS 1:8 HOBBY
1 Miguel Cabrera 1.00 2.50
2 Nelson Cruz 1.00 2.50
3 Jose Bautista .75 2.00
4 David Wright .75 2.00
5 Jose Reyes .75 2.00
6 Carlos Gonzalez .75 2.00
7 Josh Hamilton .75 2.00
8 Pablo Sandoval .75 2.00
9 Jacoby Ellsbury .75 2.00
10 Madison Bumgarner .75 2.00
11 David Price .75 2.00
12 Starlin Castro .75 2.00
13 Robinson Cano .75 2.00
14 Chris Carpenter .75 2.00
15 Matt Kemp .75 2.00
16 Andrew McCutchen 1.00 2.50
17 Ryan Zimmerman .75 2.00
18 Tim Lincecum .75 2.00
19 Ian Kinsler .75 2.00
20 Albert Pujols 1.25 3.00
21 Ryan Braun .60 1.50
22 Evan Longoria .75 2.00
23 Mark Teixeira .75 2.00
24 Ian Kennedy .60 1.50
25 David Ortiz 1.00 2.50

26 Justin Upton .75 2.00
27 Ryan Howard .75 2.00
28 Mike Stanton 1.00 2.50
29 Mariano Rivera 1.25 3.00
30 Roy Halladay .75 2.00
31 Curtis Granderson .75 2.00
32 Felix Hernandez .75 2.00
33 Troy Tulowitzki 1.00 2.50
34 Adrian Beltre 1.00 2.50
35 Joe Mauer .75 2.00
36 Chase Utley .75 2.00
37 Jimmy Rollins .75 2.00
38 Cliff Lee .75 2.00
39 Hunter Pence .75 2.00
40 Dustin Pedroia 1.00 2.50
41 Victor Martinez .75 2.00
42 Justin Verlander 1.00 2.50
43 James Shields .60 1.50
44 Buster Posey 1.25 3.00
45 Matt Moore 1.00 2.50
46 Jesus Montero .60 1.50

2012 Topps Heritage The JFK Story

COMPLETE SET (7) 40.00 80.00
COMMON CARD 6.00 15.00
JFK1 Kennedy at Cambridge 6.00 15.00
JFK2 A Profile in Courage 6.00 15.00
JFK3 Senate's Shining Stars 6.00 15.00
JFK4 Jack and Jackie 6.00 15.00
JFK5 The 35th President 6.00 15.00
JFK6 Call to Serve 6.00 15.00
JFK7 Cuban Crisis 6.00 15.00

2012 Topps Heritage Then and Now

COMPLETE SET (10) 6.00 15.00
STATED ODDS 1:15 HOBBY
AB Luis Aparicio/Michael Bourn .60 1.50
AK H.Aaron/M.Kemp 2.00 5.00
KB Harmon Killebrew/Jose Bautista 1.00 2.50
KK S.Koufax/C.Kershaw 2.00 5.00
KV S.Koufax/J.Verlander 2.00 5.00
MB Eddie Mathews/Jose Bautista 1.00 2.50
MS Juan Marichal/James Shields .60 1.50
MV J.Marichal/J.Verlander 1.00 2.50
SL Warren Spahn/Cliff Lee .75 2.00
YC Yastrzemski/Cabrera 1.50 4.00

2010 Topps Heritage Strasburg National Convention

DIST.AT 2010 NATIONAL CONVENTION
STATED PRINT RUN 999 SER.#'d SETS
NCC1 Stephen Strasburg 12.00 30.00

2011 Topps Heritage National Convention

COMPLETE SET (5) 15.00 40.00
DISTRIBUTED AT 2011 NATIONAL CON.
STATED PRINT RUN 299 SER.#'d SETS
NC1 Dustin Ackley 3.00 8.00
NC2 Dee Gordon 3.00 8.00
NC3 Mike Moustakas 5.00 12.00
NC4 Michael Pineda 5.00 12.00
NC5 Zach Britton 5.00 12.00

2013 Topps Heritage

COMP.SET w/o SPs (425) 20.00 50.00
COMP.HN.FACT.SET (101) 100.00 150.00
COMP.HN SET (100) 50.00 100.00
SP ODDS 1:3 HOBBY
ERROR SP ODDS 1:1567 HOBBY
SENATOR SP ODDS 1:13,058 HOBBY
NO SENATOR PRICING DUE TO SCARCITY
ACTION SP ODDS 1:26 HOBBY
COLOR SP ODDS 1:155 HOBBY
HN FACT SETS SOLD ONLY ON TOPPS.COM
1 Kershaw/Dickey/Cueto .60 1.50
2 Price/Verlander/Weaver .40 1.00
3 Gio Gonzalez .30 .75
R.A. Dickey/Johnny Cueto/Lance Lynn
4A David Price/Jered Weaver
Matt Harrison .30 .75
4B Price/Weav/Har Error SP 20.00 50.00
5 Dickey/Kershaw/Hamels .60 1.50
6 Verlan/Scher/Hernandez .40 1.00
7 Pos/McCut/Brn/Cbrr .50 1.25
8 Cabrera/Trout/Beltre 3.00 8.00
9 Ryan Braun .30 .75
Giancarlo Stanton/Jay Bruce/Adam LaRoche
10 Cabrera/Granderson/Hamilton .40 1.00
11 Chase Headley/Ryan Braun
Alfonso Soriano .30 .75
12 Cabrera/Ham/Encarnacion .40 1.00
13 Adam LaRoche .25 .60
14 Josh Wall RC/Pacq Rodriguez RC .40 1.00
15 Drew Storen .25 .60
16 Cliff Lee .30 .75
17 Nick Markakis .30 .75
18 Adam Lind .30 .75
19 Alex Avila .30 .75
20 James McDonald .25 .60
21 Joe Girardi .30 .75
22 Andrelton Simmons .25 .60
23 Josh Johnson .30 .75
24 Anibal Sanchez .25 .60
25 Andrew Cashner .25 .60
26 Angel Pagan .25 .60
27 Joe Maddon .15 .40
28 Anthony Gose .25 .60
29 Norichika Aoki .25 .60
30 Chad Billingsley .30 .75
31 Asdrubal Cabrera .30 .75
32 C.J. Wilson .25 .60
33 Didi Gregorius RC/Todd Redmond RC .60 1.50
34 Ricky Romero .25 .60
35 Michael Bourn .25 .60
36 Ben Zobrist .30 .75
37 Brandon Crawford .30 .75
38 J.D. Martinez .40 1.00
39 Brandon League .25 .60
40 Carlos Beltran .30 .75
41 D.Jeter/M.Trout 3.00 8.00
42 Tommy Milone .25 .60
43 Brandon Morrow .25 .60
44 Ike Davis .25 .60
45 Brandon Phillips .25 .60
46A Ian Desmond .25 .60
47 Francisco Peguero RC/Jean Machi RC .60 1.50
48 Peter Bourjos .25 .60
49 Brett Jackson .25 .60
50 Curtis Granderson .30 .75
51 Kenley Jansen .30 .75
52 Jayson Werth .30 .75
53 Tyler Pastornicky .15 .40
54 Ron Gardenhire .15 .40
55 Brett Lawrie .30 .75
56A Ross Detwiler .25 .60
57 Brett Wallace .25 .60
58 Austin Jackson .25 .60
59 Adam Wainwright .30 .75
60 Will Middlebrooks .25 .60
61 Kirk Nieuwenhuis .25 .60
62 Starling Marte .30 .75
63 Jason Grilli .25 .60
64 Brian Wilson .40 1.00
65 Carlos Quentin .25 .60
66 Bruce Chen .25 .60
67 Davey Johnson .15 .40
68 Cameron Maybin .25 .60
69 Alex Rodriguez .50 1.25
70 Brian McCann .30 .75
71 Carlos Gomez .25 .60
72 Chase Utley .30 .75
73 Steve Lombardozzi .15 .40
74 Brock Holt RC/Kyle McPherson RC .75 2.00
75 Chris Carpenter .30 .75
76 Ron Washington .15 .40
77 Justin Masterson .25 .60
78 Mike Napoli .25 .60
79 Chris Johnson .25 .60
80A Jay Bruce .30 .75
80B J.Bruce Color SP 10.00 25.00
81 M.Kemp/C.Kershaw .60 1.50
82 Pablo Sandoval .30 .75
83 Carlos Ruiz .25 .60
84 Jonathon Niese .25 .60
85 Todd Frazier .25 .60
86 Ivan Nova .30 .75
87 Bruce Bochy .30 .75
88 A.J. Ellis .25 .60
89A Jose Bautista .30 .75
89B Jose Bautista Action SP 5.00 12.00
90A Joe Mauer .30 .75
90B Joe Mauer Action SP 5.00 12.00
90C J.Mauer Color SP 10.00 25.00
91 Chris Nelson .25 .60
92 Chris Young .25 .60
93 Christian Friedrich .25 .60
94 H.Rod RC/Cingrani RC 1.25 3.00
95 B.J. Upton .30 .75
96 Jeff Samardzija .25 .60
97 Erick Aybar .25 .60
98 Quintin Berry .15 .40
99 Tim Lincecum .30 .75
100A Robinson Cano .30 .75
100B Robinson Cano Action SP 5.00 12.00
100C R.Cano Color SP 10.00 25.00
101 Don Mattingly .75 2.00
102 Kirk Gibson .15 .40
103 Gordon Beckham .25 .60
104 Jonathan Papelbon .30 .75
105 Shin-Soo Choo .30 .75
106 Mike Leake .25 .60
107 Brian Omogrosso RC
Deunte Heath RC .60 1.50
108 Jarrod Parker .25 .60
109 Zack Cozart .25 .60
110 Mark Trumbo .25 .60
111 Clayton Richard .25 .60
112 Jarrod Saltalamacchia .25 .60
113 Johan Santana .30 .75
114 Cody Ross .25 .60
115 Dan Uggla .25 .60
116 Chris Herrmann RC
Nick Maronde RC .75 2.00
117 Colby Rasmus .30 .75
118 Robin Ventura .25 .60
119 Corey Hart .25 .60
120 Josh Beckett .25 .60
121 Ned Yost .15 .40
122 Hisashi Iwakuma .30 .75
123 Yunel Escobar .25 .60
124 Ryan Cook .25 .60
125A Yu Darvish .40 1.00
125B Y.Darvish Action SP 6.00 15.00
125C Y.Darvish Color SP 12.00 30.00
125D Yu Darvish Error SP 30.00 60.00
126A Craig Kimbrel .30 .75
126B Craig Kimbrel Action SP 5.00 12.00
127 Edwin Jackson .25 .60
128 Doug Fister .25 .60
129 Ruben Tejada .25 .60
130 Philip Humber .25 .60
131 Dan Haren .25 .60
132 Rickie Weeks .25 .60
133 Chris Perez .25 .60
134 Daniel Descalso .25 .60
135 Domonic Brown .30 .75
136 Pablo Sandoval .25 .60
137 Madison Bumgarner .30 .75
138 Gregor Blanco .25 .60
139 San Francisco Giants .15 .40
140 Carlos Pena .30 .75
141 Daniel Hudson .25 .60
142 Daniel Murphy .30 .75
143 Clint Hurdle .15 .40
144 Darwin Barney .25 .60
145 David DeJesus .25 .60
146 Thomas Neal RC/Jaye Chapman RC .60 1.50
147 Kyle Lohse .25 .60
148 A.J. Pierzynski .25 .60
149 Zack Greinke .40 1.00
150 Melky Cabrera .25 .60
151 Brett Gardner .30 .75
152 Tim Hudson .30 .75
153 David Murphy .25 .60
154 Dee Gordon .25 .60
155 W.Middlebrooks/D.Ortiz .40 1.00
156 Dayan Viciedo .25 .60
157 Charlie Manuel .15 .40
158 Denard Span .25 .60
159 Desmond Jennings .30 .75
160 David Freese .25 .60
161 Jason Hammel .30 .75
162 B.Harper/C.Jones .60 1.50
163 Gaby Sanchez .25 .60
164 Dexter Fowler .30 .75
165 Omar Infante .25 .60
166 Dustin Ackley .25 .60
167 Christian Garcia (RC)/Eury Perez RC .75 2.00
168 Addison Reed .25 .60
169 Elvis Andrus .30 .75
170 Jon Lester .30 .75
171 Derek Holland .25 .60
172 Emilio Bonifacio .25 .60
173 Bud Black .25 .60
174 Derek Norris .25 .60
175 Alfonso Soriano .30 .75
176 Ervin Santana .25 .60
177 Ben Revere .25 .60
178 Everth Cabrera .25 .60
179 Justin Maxwell .25 .60
180 Carl Crawford .30 .75
181 Jose Valverde .25 .60
182 Felix Doubront .25 .60
183A Fernando Rodney .25 .60
183B Fernando Rodney Color SP 8.00 20.00
184 Franklin Gutierrez .25 .60
185 Ian Kennedy .25 .60
186 Casper Wells .25 .60
187 Tyler Clippard .25 .60
188 Matt Harvey .30 .75
189 Freddie Freeman .50 1.25
190A Derek Jeter 1.00 2.50
190B D.Jeter Action SP 40.00 100.00
191 Anthony Rizzo .50 1.25
192 Brandon McCarthy .25 .60
193 Garrett Jones .25 .60
194 Mike Moustakas .30 .75
195 Alex Rios .30 .75
196 Chris Carter .15 .40
197 Mark Buehrle .30 .75
198 Gavin Floyd .25 .60
199 Greg Dobbs .25 .60
200A Clayton Kershaw .60 1.50
200B C.Kershaw Color SP 15.00 40.00
201 Machado RC/Bundy RC 4.00 10.00
202 Luke Hochevar .25 .60
203 Alcides Escobar .30 .75
204 Gregor Blanco .25 .60
205 Howie Kendrick .25 .60
206 Huston Street .25 .60
207 Dusty Baker .25 .60
208 Juan Pierre .25 .60
209 Kyle Seager .25 .60
210 Jacoby Ellsbury .30 .75
211 Lance Lynn .25 .60
212 Edinson Volquez .25 .60
213 Michael Morse .25 .60
214 Jean Segura .30 .75
215 Francisco Liriano .25 .60
216 Jason Kipnis .30 .75
217 Alex Gordon .30 .75
218 Brandon Beachy .25 .60
219 S.Strasburg/G.Gonzalez .40 1.00
220 Matt Garza .25 .60
221 J.J. Hardy .25 .60
222 J.P. Arencibia .25 .60
223 James Loney .30 .75
224 Jamey Carroll .25 .60
225 Jason Kubel .25 .60
226 Steven Lerud (RC) .60 1.50
Luis Antonio Jimenez RC
227 Jason Motte .25 .60
228 Jason Vargas .25 .60
229 Jed Lowrie .25 .60
230 Mark Reynolds .25 .60
231 Jeff Francoeur .30 .75
232 Bob Melvin .15 .40
233 Jeremy Hellickson .25 .60
234 Adeiny Hechavarria (RC)
Tyson Brummett RC .75 2.00
235 Jhonny Peralta .25 .60
236 Jim Johnson .25 .60
237 Jimmy Rollins .30 .75
238 Joe Nathan .25 .60
239 Joel Hanrahan .25 .60
240 Allen Craig .30 .75
241 Geovany Soto .30 .75
242 John Jaso .25 .60
243 Ruf RC/Cloyd RC 1.25 3.00
244 Jon Jay .25 .60
245 Jordan Pacheco .25 .60
246A Josh Hamilton .30 .75
246B Josh Hamilton Action SP 5.00 12.00
246C J.Hamilton Color SP 10.00 25.00
247 Josh Reddick .25 .60
248 Jim Leyland .15 .40
249 Josh Thole .25 .60
250A Prince Fielder .30 .75
250B Prince Fielder Action SP 5.00 12.00
250C P.Fielder Color SP 10.00 25.00
251 Juan Nicasio .25 .60
252 Yonder Alonso .25 .60
253 Sergio Romo .25 .60
254 Nathan Eovaldi .25 .60
255 Salvador Perez .25 .60
256 Torii Hunter .25 .60
257 Rick Porcello .25 .60
258 Michael Young .25 .60
259 Miguel Montero .25 .60
260 Drew Stubbs .25 .60
261 Olt RC/Profar RC .75 2.00
262 Miller RC/Rosenthal (RC) 1.50 4.00
263 Vance Worley .30 .75
264 Vernon Wells .25 .60
265 Lorenzo Cain .25 .60
266 Lucas Duda .25 .60
267 Marco Estrada .25 .60
268 Justin Ruggiano .25 .60
269 Justin Smoak .25 .60
270 Trevor Plouffe .25 .60
271 Matt Dominguez .25 .60
272 Matt Joyce .25 .60
273 Matt Moore .30 .75
274 Justin Morneau .30 .75
275 Kevin Youkilis .25 .60
276 Nick Swisher .25 .60
277 Seth Smith .25 .60
278 Shaun Marcum .25 .60
279 Victor Martinez .30 .75
280 Ryan Vogelsong .25 .60
281 Adam Warren RC/Melky Mesa RC .75 2.00
282 Wandy Rodriguez .25 .60
283 Wily Peralta .25 .60
284 Yasmani Grandal .25 .60
285 Ricky Nolasco .25 .60
286 Tom Wilhelmsen .25 .60
287 A.J. Ramos RC/Rob Brantly RC .75 2.00
288 Logan Morrison .25 .60
289 Lonnie Chisenhall .25 .60
290 Josh Willingham .25 .60
291 Ryan Ludwick .25 .60
292 Trevor Cahill .25 .60
293 Ubaldo Jimenez .25 .60
294 Liam Hendriks .25 .60
295 Mitch Moreland .25 .60
296 Rafael Soriano .25 .60
297 Jordan Lyles .25 .60
298 Buck Showalter .15 .40
299 Garrett Richards .30 .75
300 Jason Heyward .30 .75
301 Ernesto Frieri .25 .60
302 Neil Walker .25 .60
303 Grant Balfour .25 .60
304 Paul Goldschmidt .40 1.00
305 Todd Helton .30 .75
306 Pablo Sandoval/Hunter Pence .30 .75
307 Dan Straily .25 .60
308 J.J. Putz .25 .60
309 Michael Cuddyer .25 .60
310 Mark Ellis .25 .60
311 Tyler Colvin .25 .60
312 Avisail Garcia RC/Hernan Perez RC .75 2.00
313 Stephen Drew .25 .60
314 Shane Victorino .30 .75
315 Rajai Davis .25 .60
316 Aaron Crow .25 .60
317 Lance Berkman .30 .75
318 Kendrys Morales .25 .60
319 Jason Isringhausen .25 .60
320 Coco Crisp .25 .60
321 Trevor Bauer .50 1.25
322 Scott Baker .25 .60
323 Danny Espinosa .25 .60
324 Terry Collins .25 .60
325A Rafael Betancourt .25 .60
325B Rafael Betancourt Error SP 20.00 50.00
326 Gerardo Parra .25 .60
327 Heath Bell .25 .60
328 Patrick Corbin .30 .75
329 Drew Pomeranz .30 .75
330 Johnny Cueto .30 .75
331 A.Rodriguez/R.Cano .50 1.25
332 John McDonald .15 .40
333 Mike Minor .25 .60
334 Kurt Suzuki .25 .60
335A Jonny Venters .25 .60
335B Jonny Venters Error SP 30.00 60.00
336 Nolan Reimold .25 .60
337 Kevin Mattison RC/Tom Koehler RC .60 1.50
338 Tommy Hunter .25 .60
339 David Robertson .30 .75
340 Paul Konerko .30 .75
341 Luis Ayala .25 .60
342 Homer Bailey .25 .60
343 Daniel Nava .30 .75
344 Andrew Bailey .25 .60
345 Pedro Ciriaco .25 .60
346 Rafael Dolis .25 .60
347 Carlos Marmol .25 .60
348 Miguel Gonzalez .25 .60
349 Ian Stewart .25 .60
350 Matt Cain .30 .75
351 Matt Thornton .25 .60
352 Alexei Ramirez .30 .75
353 Chris Heisey .25 .60
354 Sean Marshall .25 .60
355A Chris Tillman .25 .60
355B Chris Tillman Error SP 20.00 50.00
356 Adam Eaton RC/Tyler Skaggs RC 1.00 2.50
357 Ryan Hanigan .25 .60
358 Casey Kotchman .25 .60
359 Wilton Lopez .15 .40
360 Mark Teixeira .30 .75
361 Vinnie Pestano .25 .60
362 Ezequiel Carrera .25 .60
363 Neftali Feliz .25 .60
364 Russell Martin .25 .60
365 Phil Coke .25 .60
366 Jason Castro .25 .60
367 Jeremy Guthrie .25 .60
368 Ryan Dempster .25 .60
369 Greg Holland .25 .60
370 Bud Norris .25 .60
371 Cole De Vries .25 .60
372 Joe Blanton .25 .60
373 Ted Lilly .25 .60
374 Luis Cruz .25 .60
375 Austin Kearns .25 .60
376 Steve Cishek .25 .60
377 John Axford .25 .60
378 Rafael Ortega RC/Rob Scahill RC .60 1.50
379 Nyjer Morgan .25 .60
380 Phil Hughes .25 .60
381 Fernando Martinez .25 .60
382 Mike Fiers .25 .60
383 Mike Scioscia .15 .40
384 Ryan Doumit .25 .60
385 Glen Perkins .25 .60
386 Jared Burton .25 .60
387 Bobby Parnell .25 .60
388 Ali Solis RC/Casey Kelly RC .75 2.00
389 Frank Francisco .15 .40
390 Brandon Belt .30 .75
391 Andy Pettitte .30 .75
392 Mike Baxter .25 .60
393 Pat Neshek .25 .60
394 Brandon Inge .25 .60
395 Jemile Weeks .25 .60
396 Jeff Karstens .25 .60
397 Clint Barmes .25 .60
398 Jeurys Familia RC/Collin McHugh RC 1.00 2.50
399 Dale Sveum .15 .40
400 Kris Medlen .30 .75
401 Alex Presley .25 .60
402 Will Venable .25 .60
403 Luke Gregerson .25 .60
404 Barry Zito .30 .75
405 Brendan Ryan .25 .60
406 Jaime Garcia .30 .75
407 Rafael Furcal .25 .60
408 David Lough RC/Jake Odorizzi RC .75 2.00
409 Pete Kozma .25 .60
410 John Lackey .30 .75
411 Chris Archer .25 .60
412 Casey Janssen .25 .60
413 Mike Matheny .15 .40
414 Chris Iannetta .25 .60
415 Tommy Hanson .25 .60
416 Paul Maholm .25 .60
417 Juan Francisco .25 .60
418 Bryan Morris RC/Justin Wilson RC .60 1.50
419 Joe Saunders .25 .60
420 Bronson Arroyo .25 .60
421 Wellington Castillo .25 .60
422 Eduardo Nunez .25 .60
423 M.Cain/B.Posey .50 1.25
424 Logan Forsythe .25 .60
425A Joey Votto .40 1.00
425B J.Votto Color SP 12.00 30.00
426A Miguel Cabrera SP 3.00 8.00
426B M.Cabrera Action SP 15.00 40.00
427 Andre Ethier SP 4.00 10.00
428A Ryan Howard SP 2.50 6.00
428B Ryan Howard Color SP 10.00 25.00
429 Aramis Ramirez SP 4.00 10.00
430A Mike Trout SP 40.00 100.00
430B M.Trout Action SP 200.00 400.00
430C M.Trout Color SP 200.00 400.00
431 Hunter Pence SP 4.00 10.00
432A Ryan Zimmerman SP 4.00 10.00
433 Adam Jones SP 4.00 10.00
434 Dustin Pedroia SP 3.00 8.00
435 Carlos Santana SP 5.00 12.00
436 Michael Brantley SP 4.00 10.00
437 Billy Butler SP 4.00 10.00
438A Andrew McCutchen SP 3.00 8.00
438B Andrew McCutchen Action SP 6.00 15.00
439 Evan Longoria SP 4.00 10.00
440A Bryce Harper SP 10.00 25.00
440B B.Harper Action SP 50.00 120.00
440C B.Harper Color SP 30.00 80.00
440D Bryce Harper Error SP 125.00 250.00
441 Jordan Zimmermann SP 5.00 12.00
442 Hanley Ramirez SP 4.00 10.00
443 Hiroki Kuroda SP 4.00 10.00
444 Adrian Beltre SP 6.00 15.00
445 Lucas Harrell SP 4.00 10.00
446 Jose Reyes SP 4.00 10.00
447A Felix Hernandez SP 2.50 6.00
447B Hernandez Action SP 10.00 25.00
447C Felix Hernandez Color SP 10.00 25.00
448A Cole Hamels SP 4.00 10.00
448B C.Hamels Color SP 10.00 25.00
449 Jered Weaver SP 4.00 10.00
450A Matt Kemp SP 2.50 6.00
450B Matt Kemp Action SP 5.00 12.00
450C Matt Kemp Color SP 10.00 25.00
451 Jake Peavy SP 4.00 10.00
452 Troy Tulowitzki SP 3.00 8.00
453 Justin Upton SP 4.00 10.00
454 Gio Gonzalez SP 4.00 10.00
455A Chris Sale SP 5.00 12.00
455B Chris Sale Color SP 12.00 30.00
456A CC Sabathia SP 4.00 10.00
456B CC Sabathia Action SP 5.00 12.00
457 Mat Latos SP 4.00 10.00
458A David Price SP 4.00 10.00
458B David Price Color SP 10.00 25.00
459A Yoenis Cespedes SP 3.00 8.00
459B Y.Cespedes Action SP 6.00 15.00
459C Y.Cespedes Color SP 12.00 30.00
460A Ryan Braun SP 2.50 6.00
460B Ryan Braun Action SP 5.00 12.00
461 Marco Scutaro SP 4.00 10.00
462 Roy Halladay SP 4.00 10.00
463A Giancarlo Stanton SP 3.00 8.00
463B G.Stanton Action SP 15.00 40.00
463C Giancarlo Stanton Color SP 12.00 30.00
464A R.A. Dickey SP 4.00 10.00
464B R.A. Dickey Action SP 5.00 12.00
465A David Wright SP 2.50 6.00
465B David Wright Color SP 10.00 25.00
466 Carlos Gonzalez SP 4.00 10.00
467A Chase Headley SP 4.00 10.00
467B Chase Headley Color SP 8.00 20.00
468 Mariano Rivera SP 4.00 10.00
469 Max Scherzer SP 6.00 15.00
470A Albert Pujols SP 4.00 10.00
470B A.Pujols Action SP 8.00 20.00
471 Matt Holliday SP 3.00 8.00
472 Adrian Gonzalez SP 2.50 6.00
473 Matt Harrison SP 4.00 10.00
474A Wade Miley SP 3.00 8.00
474B Wade Miley Action SP 5.00 12.00
474C Wade Miley Color SP 8.00 20.00
475 Edwin Encarnacion SP 6.00 15.00
476 Yovani Gallardo SP 4.00 10.00
477A Yadier Molina SP 4.00 10.00
477B Y.Molina Action SP 8.00 20.00
478 Madison Bumgarner SP 2.50 6.00
479 Ian Kinsler SP 4.00 10.00
480A Stephen Strasburg SP 3.00 8.00
480B S.Strasburg Action SP 6.00 15.00
480C Stephen Strasburg Color SP 12.00 30.00
481 Martin Prado SP 4.00 10.00
482 Nelson Cruz SP 5.00 12.00
483 James Shields SP 4.00 10.00
484A Adam Dunn SP 4.00 10.00
484B Adam Dunn Action SP 5.00 12.00
485A Starlin Castro SP 2.00 5.00
485B Starlin Castro Color SP 8.00 20.00
486 David Ortiz SP 5.00 12.00
487 Jose Altuve SP 4.00 10.00
488 Wilin Rosario SP 4.00 10.00
489 Aaron Hill SP 4.00 10.00
490A Buster Posey SP 4.00 10.00
490B B.Posey Action SP 8.00 20.00
490C B.Posey Color SP 15.00 40.00
491 Wei-Yin Chen SP 2.00 5.00
492 Eric Hosmer SP 4.00 10.00
493 Aroldis Chapman SP 5.00 12.00
494 A.J. Burnett SP 3.00 8.00
495 Scott Diamond SP 4.00 10.00
496 Clay Buchholz SP 3.00 8.00
497 Jonathan Lucroy SP 5.00 12.00
498 Pedro Alvarez SP 3.00 8.00
499 Jesus Montero SP 3.00 8.00
500 Justin Verlander SP 4.00 10.00
H501 Evan Gattis RC 2.00 5.00
H502 Devin Mesoraco .75 2.00
H503 Hyun-Jin Ryu RC 2.50 6.00
H504 Jose Fernandez RC 2.50 6.00
H505 Marcell Ozuna RC 2.50 6.00
H506 Jedd Gyorko RC 1.25 3.00
H507 Carlos Martinez RC 1.50 4.00
H508 Matt Adams .75 2.00
H509 Anthony Rendon RC 10.00 25.00
H510 Allen Webster RC 1.25 3.00
H511 Jackie Bradley Jr. RC 2.50 6.00
H512 Bruce Rondon RC 1.00 2.50
H513 Drew Smyly .75 2.00
H514 Aaron Hicks RC 1.50 4.00
H515 Oswaldo Arcia RC 1.00 2.50
H516 Michael Pineda .75 2.00
H517 Brandon Maurer RC 1.25 3.00
H518 Alex Cobb .75 2.00
H519 Nolan Arenado RC 30.00 80.00
H520 Eric Chavez .75 2.00
H521 Jorge De La Rosa .75 2.00
H522 Nate Karns RC 1.00 2.50
H523 Kyle Gibson RC 1.50 4.00
H524 Travis Wood .75 2.00
H525 Jarred Cosart RC 1.25 3.00
H526 Matt Magill RC 1.00 2.50
H527 Juan Uribe .75 2.00
H528 Alex Sanabia .75 2.00
H529 Chris Coghlan .75 2.00
H530 Jim Henderson RC 1.25 3.00
H531 Julio Teheran .75 2.00
H532 John Buck 1.00 2.50
H533 Mike Zunino RC 1.50 4.00
H534 Jonathan Pettibone RC 1.50 4.00
H535 John Mayberry Jr. .75 2.00
H536 Christian Yelich RC 25.00 60.00
H537 Jeff Locke .75 2.00
H538 Jose Tabata .75 2.00
H539 Kyle Blanks .75 2.00
H540 Edward Mujica .75 2.00
H541 Brett Cecil .75 2.00
H542 Hank Conger .75 2.00
H543 Freddy Garcia .50 1.25
H544 Brian Matusz .75 2.00
H545 Chris Davis 1.00 2.50
H546 Nate McLouth .75 2.00
H547 Koji Uehara .75 2.00
H548 Jose Iglesias 1.00 2.50
H549 Dylan Axelrod .75 2.00
H550 Jose Quintana .75 2.00
H551 Steve Delabar .75 2.00
H552 Tyler Flowers .75 2.00
H553 Alejandro De Aza .75 2.00
H554 Raul Ibanez 1.00 2.50
H555 Scott Kazmir .75 2.00
H556 Zach McAllister .75 2.00
H557 Corey Kluber RC 3.00 8.00
H558 Jason Giambi .75 2.00
H559 Mark Melancon .75 2.00
H560 Andy Dirks .75 2.00
H561 Erik Bedard .75 2.00
H562 Jose Veras .75 2.00
H563 Matt Carpenter 1.25 3.00
H564 Wil Myers RC 1.50 4.00
H565 Wade Davis .75 2.00
H566 Henry Urrutia RC 1.25 3.00
H567 Miguel Tejada .75 2.00
H568 Zack Wheeler RC 2.00 5.00
H569 Josh Donaldson 1.00 2.50
H570 Mike Pelfrey .75 2.00
H571 Pedro Hernandez RC 1.00 2.50
H572 Josh Phegley RC 1.00 2.50
H573 Boone Logan .75 2.00
H574 Preston Claiborne RC 1.00 2.50
H575 Austin Romine .75 2.00
H576 Travis Hafner .75 2.00
H577 Alex Wood RC 1.25 3.00
H578 Bartolo Colon .75 2.00
H579 A.J. Griffin .75 2.00
H580 Brett Anderson .75 2.00
H581 Nick Franklin RC 1.25 3.00
H582 Aaron Harang .75 2.00
H583 Cody Asche RC 1.50 4.00
H584 Yasiel Puig RC 4.00 10.00
H585 Roberto Hernandez .50 1.25
H586 Jake McGee 1.00 2.50
H587 Alex Colome RC 1.00 2.50
H588 Brad Miller RC 1.25 3.00
H589 Luke Scott .75 2.00
H590 Justin Grimm RC 1.00 2.50
H591 Alexi Ogando .75 2.00
H592 Leury Garcia RC 1.00 2.50
H593 Leonys Martin .75 2.00
H594 Michael Wacha RC 1.25 3.00
H595 J.A. Happ .75 2.00
H596 Gerrit Cole RC 10.00 25.00
H597 Maicer Izturis .75 2.00
H598 Brad Ziegler .75 2.00
H599 Mike Kickham RC 1.00 2.50
H600 Kevin Gausman RC 3.00 8.00

2013 Topps Heritage Mini

STATED ODDS 1:235 HOBBY
STATED PRINT RUN 100 SER.#'d SETS
13 Adam LaRoche 6.00 15.00
35 Michael Bourn 6.00 15.00
40 Carlos Beltran 8.00 20.00
43 Brandon Morrow 6.00 15.00
50 Curtis Granderson 8.00 20.00
58 Austin Jackson 6.00 15.00
80 Jay Bruce 8.00 20.00
89 Jose Bautista 8.00 20.00
90 Joe Mauer 8.00 20.00
100 Robinson Cano 12.50 30.00
108 Jarrod Parker 6.00 15.00
110 Mark Trumbo 10.00 25.00
125 Yu Darvish 10.00 25.00
147 Kyle Lohse 6.00 15.00
160 David Freese 12.50 30.00
183 Fernando Rodney 6.00 15.00
190 Derek Jeter 60.00 120.00
200 Clayton Kershaw 15.00 40.00
210 Jacoby Ellsbury 8.00 20.00
217 Alex Gordon 8.00 20.00
236 Jim Johnson 10.00 25.00
240 Allen Craig 8.00 20.00
246 Josh Hamilton 8.00 20.00
247 Josh Reddick 6.00 15.00
250 Prince Fielder 10.00 25.00
259 Miguel Montero 6.00 15.00
280 Ryan Vogelsong 10.00 25.00
290 Josh Willingham 8.00 20.00
330 Johnny Cueto 6.00 15.00
340 Paul Konerko 8.00 20.00
350 Matt Cain 12.50 30.00
360 Mark Teixeira 8.00 20.00
400 Kris Medlen 6.00 15.00
425 Joey Votto 12.50 30.00
426 Miguel Cabrera 10.00 25.00
427 Andre Ethier 10.00 25.00
428 Ryan Howard 8.00 20.00
429 Aramis Ramirez 6.00 15.00
430 Mike Trout 40.00 100.00
431 Hunter Pence 10.00 25.00
432 Ryan Zimmerman 12.50 30.00
433 Adam Jones 8.00 20.00
434 Dustin Pedroia 10.00 25.00
435 Carlos Santana 6.00 15.00
436 Michael Brantley 6.00 15.00
437 Billy Butler 6.00 15.00
438 Andrew McCutchen 10.00 25.00
439 Evan Longoria 10.00 25.00
440 Bryce Harper 15.00 40.00
441 Jordan Zimmermann 6.00 15.00
442 Hanley Ramirez 8.00 20.00
443 Hiroki Kuroda 6.00 15.00
444 Adrian Beltre 10.00 25.00
446 Jose Reyes 8.00 20.00
447 Felix Hernandez 8.00 20.00
448 Cole Hamels 8.00 20.00
449 Jered Weaver 8.00 20.00
450 Matt Kemp 8.00 20.00
451 Jake Peavy 6.00 15.00
452 Troy Tulowitzki 10.00 25.00
453 Justin Upton 8.00 20.00
454 Gio Gonzalez 8.00 20.00
455 Chris Sale 10.00 25.00
456 CC Sabathia 8.00 20.00
457 Mat Latos 8.00 20.00
458 David Price 8.00 20.00
459 Yoenis Cespedes 10.00 25.00
460 Ryan Braun 8.00 20.00
461 Marco Scutaro 10.00 25.00
462 Roy Halladay 8.00 20.00
463 Giancarlo Stanton 10.00 25.00
464 R.A. Dickey 8.00 20.00
465 David Wright 12.50 30.00
466 Carlos Gonzalez 8.00 20.00
467 Chase Headley 6.00 15.00
468 Mariano Rivera 20.00 50.00
469 Max Scherzer 10.00 25.00
470 Albert Pujols 25.00 60.00
471 Matt Holliday 12.50 30.00
472 Adrian Gonzalez 6.00 15.00
473 Matt Harrison 6.00 15.00
474 Wade Miley 6.00 15.00
475 Edwin Encarnacion 10.00 25.00
476 Yovani Gallardo 6.00 15.00
477 Yadier Molina 12.00 30.00
478 Madison Bumgarner 8.00 20.00
479 Ian Kinsler 8.00 20.00
480 Stephen Strasburg 15.00 40.00
481 Martin Prado 6.00 15.00
482 Nelson Cruz 10.00 25.00
483 James Shields 6.00 15.00
484 Adam Dunn 8.00 20.00
485 Starlin Castro 12.50 30.00
486 David Ortiz 10.00 25.00
488 Wilin Rosario 6.00 15.00
490 Buster Posey 25.00 60.00
492 Eric Hosmer 8.00 20.00
493 Aroldis Chapman 10.00 25.00
499 Jesus Montero 6.00 15.00
500 Justin Verlander 15.00 40.00

2013 Topps Heritage Target Red Border Variations

89 Jose Bautista 1.50 4.00
126 Craig Kimbrel 1.50 4.00
190 Derek Jeter 5.00 12.00
210 Jacoby Ellsbury 1.50 4.00
330 Johnny Cueto 1.50 4.00
350 Matt Cain 1.50 4.00
425 Joey Votto 2.00 5.00
426 Miguel Cabrera 2.00 5.00
428 Ryan Howard 1.50 4.00
438 Andrew McCutchen 2.00 5.00
439 Evan Longoria 1.50 4.00
440 Bryce Harper 3.00 8.00
449 Jered Weaver 1.50 4.00
452 Troy Tulowitzki 2.00 5.00
454 Gio Gonzalez 1.50 4.00
455 Chris Sale 2.00 5.00
456 CC Sabathia 2.00 5.00
458 David Price 1.50 4.00
459 Yoenis Cespedes 2.00 5.00
462 Roy Halladay 1.50 4.00
463 Giancarlo Stanton 2.00 5.00
465 David Wright 1.50 4.00
467 Chase Headley 1.25 3.00
470 Albert Pujols 2.50 6.00
477 Yadier Molina 2.50 6.00

2013 Topps Heritage Venezuelan

*BASIC VENEZUELAN: 3X TO 8X BASIC
NO ERROR PRICING DUE TO SCARCITY
NO SENATOR PRICING DUE TO SCARCITY
NO COLOR PRICING DUE TO SCARCITY
8 Cabrera/Trout/Beltre 3.00 8.00
41 D.Jeter/M.Trout 15.00 40.00
89B Jose Bautista Action SP 6.00 15.00
90B Joe Mauer Action SP 6.00 15.00
100B Robinson Cano Action SP 6.00 15.00
125B Y.Darvish Action SP 8.00 20.00
126B Craig Kimbrel Action SP 6.00 15.00
162 B.Harper/C.Jones 6.00 15.00
190A Derek Jeter 20.00 50.00
190B D.Jeter Action SP 20.00 50.00
246B Josh Hamilton Action SP 6.00 15.00
250B Prince Fielder Action SP 6.00 15.00
426A Miguel Cabrera 6.00 15.00
426B Miguel Cabrera Action SP 8.00 20.00
427 Andre Ethier SP 5.00 12.00
428A Ryan Howard SP 5.00 12.00
429 Aramis Ramirez SP 4.00 10.00
430A Mike Trout SP 40.00 100.00
430B M.Trout Action SP 200.00 400.00
431 Hunter Pence SP 5.00 12.00
432A Ryan Zimmerman SP 5.00 12.00

433 Adam Jones SP 5.00 12.00
434 Dustin Pedroia SP 6.00 15.00
435 Carlos Santana SP 5.00 12.00
436 Michael Brantley SP 4.00 10.00
437 Billy Butler SP 4.00 10.00
438A Andrew McCutchen SP 6.00 15.00
438B Andrew McCutchen Action SP 8.00 20.00
439 Evan Longoria SP 5.00 12.00
440A Bryce Harper SP 10.00 25.00
440B B.Harper Action SP 12.00 30.00
441 Jordan Zimmermann SP 5.00 12.00
442 Hanley Ramirez SP 5.00 12.00
443 Hiroki Kuroda SP 4.00 10.00
444 Adrian Beltre SP 6.00 15.00
445 Lucas Harrell SP 4.00 10.00
446 Jose Reyes SP 5.00 12.00
447A Felix Hernandez SP 5.00 12.00
447B Felix Hernandez Action SP 6.00 15.00
448A Cole Hamels SP 5.00 12.00
449 Jered Weaver SP 5.00 12.00
450A Matt Kemp SP 5.00 12.00
450B Matt Kemp Action SP 6.00 15.00
451 Jake Peavy SP 4.00 10.00
452 Troy Tulowitzki SP 6.00 15.00
453 Justin Upton SP 5.00 12.00
454 Gio Gonzalez SP 5.00 12.00
455A Chris Sale SP 6.00 15.00
456A CC Sabathia SP 5.00 12.00
456B CC Sabathia Action SP 6.00 15.00
457 Mat Latos SP 5.00 12.00
458A David Price SP 5.00 12.00
459A Yoenis Cespedes SP 6.00 15.00
459B Y.Cespedes Action SP 8.00 20.00
460A Ryan Braun SP 5.00 12.00
460B Ryan Braun Action SP 6.00 15.00
461 Marco Scutaro SP 5.00 12.00
462 Roy Halladay SP 5.00 12.00
463A Giancarlo Stanton SP 6.00 15.00
463B Giancarlo Stanton Action SP 8.00 20.00
464A R.A. Dickey SP 5.00 12.00
464B R.A. Dickey Action SP 6.00 15.00
465A David Wright SP 5.00 12.00
466 Carlos Gonzalez SP 5.00 12.00
467A Chase Headley SP 4.00 10.00
468 Mariano Rivera SP 8.00 20.00
469 Max Scherzer SP 6.00 15.00
470A Albert Pujols SP 8.00 20.00
470B A.Pujols Action SP 10.00 25.00
471 Matt Holliday SP 6.00 15.00
472 Adrian Gonzalez SP 5.00 12.00
473 Matt Harrison SP 4.00 10.00
474A Wade Miley SP 4.00 10.00
474B Wade Miley Action SP 5.00 12.00
475 Edwin Encarnacion SP 6.00 15.00
476 Yovani Gallardo SP 4.00 10.00
477A Yadier Molina SP 8.00 20.00
477B Yadier Molina Action SP 10.00 25.00
478 Madison Bumgarner SP 5.00 12.00
479 Ian Kinsler SP 5.00 12.00
480A Stephen Strasburg SP 6.00 15.00
480B S.Strasburg Action SP 8.00 20.00
481 Martin Prado SP 4.00 10.00
482 Nelson Cruz SP 6.00 15.00
483 James Shields SP 4.00 10.00
484A Adam Dunn SP 5.00 12.00
484B Adam Dunn Action SP 6.00 15.00
485A Starlin Castro SP 4.00 10.00
486 David Ortiz SP 6.00 15.00
487 Jose Altuve SP 5.00 12.00
488 Wilin Rosario SP 4.00 10.00
489 Aaron Hill SP 4.00 10.00
490A Buster Posey SP 8.00 20.00
490B B.Posey Action SP 10.00 25.00
491 Wei-Yin Chen SP 4.00 10.00
492 Eric Hosmer SP 5.00 12.00
493 Aroldis Chapman SP 6.00 15.00
494 A.J. Burnett SP 4.00 10.00
495 Scott Diamond SP 4.00 10.00
496 Clay Buchholz SP 4.00 10.00
497 Jonathan Lucroy SP 5.00 12.00
498 Pedro Alvarez SP 4.00 10.00
499 Jesus Montero SP 4.00 10.00
500 Justin Verlander SP 6.00 15.00

2013 Topps Heritage Wal-Mart Blue Border Variations

80 Jay Bruce 1.50 4.00
90 Joe Mauer 1.50 4.00
100 Robinson Cano 1.50 4.00
125 Yu Darvish 2.00 5.00
160 David Freese 1.25 3.00
183 Fernando Rodney 1.25 3.00
200 Clayton Kershaw 3.00 8.00
246 Josh Hamilton 1.50 4.00
250 Prince Fielder 1.50 4.00
430 Mike Trout 60.00 150.00
433 Adam Jones 1.50 4.00
434 Dustin Pedroia 2.00 5.00
447 Felix Hernandez 1.50 4.00
448 Cole Hamels 1.50 4.00
450 Matt Kemp 1.50 4.00
460 Ryan Braun 1.50 4.00
464 R.A. Dickey 1.50 4.00
471 Matt Holliday 2.00 5.00
472 Adrian Gonzalez 1.50 4.00
474 Wade Miley 1.25 3.00
480 Stephen Strasburg 2.00 5.00
484 Adam Dunn 1.50 4.00
485 Starlin Castro 1.25 3.00
490 Buster Posey 2.50 6.00
500 Justin Verlander 2.00 5.00

2013 Topps Heritage Black

INSERTED IN RETAIL PACKS
13 Adam LaRoche 1.25 3.00
35 Michael Bourn 1.25 3.00
40 Carlos Beltran 1.50 4.00
43 Brandon Morrow 1.25 3.00
50 Curtis Granderson 1.50 4.00
58 Austin Jackson 1.25 3.00
74 Brock Holt/Kyle McPherson 1.50 4.00
80 Jay Bruce 1.50 4.00
89 Jose Bautista 1.50 4.00
90 Joe Mauer 1.50 4.00
100 Robinson Cano 1.50 4.00
108 Jarrod Parker 1.25 3.00
110 Mark Trumbo 1.25 3.00
125 Yu Darvish 2.00 5.00
137 Madison Bumgarner 1.50 4.00
147 Kyle Lohse 1.25 3.00
160 David Freese 1.25 3.00
183 Fernando Rodney 1.25 3.00
190 Derek Jeter 8.00 20.00
200 Clayton Kershaw 3.00 8.00
201 M.Machado/D.Bundy 8.00 20.00
210 Jacoby Ellsbury 1.50 4.00
217 Alex Gordon 1.50 4.00
236 Jim Johnson 1.25 3.00
240 Allen Craig 1.50 4.00
243 D.Ruf/T.Cloyd 2.50 6.00
246 Josh Hamilton 1.50 4.00
247 Josh Reddick 1.25 3.00
250 Prince Fielder 1.50 4.00
259 Miguel Montero 1.25 3.00
261 M.Olt/J.Profar 1.50 4.00
262 S.Miller/T.Rosenthal 3.00 8.00
280 Ryan Vogelsong 1.25 3.00
290 Josh Willingham 1.50 4.00
330 Johnny Cueto 1.50 4.00
340 Paul Konerko 1.50 4.00
350 Matt Cain 1.50 4.00
356 Adam Eaton/Tyler Skaggs 2.00 5.00
398 Jeurys Familia/Collin McHugh 2.00 5.00
400 Kris Medlen 1.50 4.00
426 Miguel Cabrera 2.00 5.00
427 Andre Ethier 1.50 4.00
428 Ryan Howard 1.50 4.00
429 Aramis Ramirez 1.25 3.00
430 Mike Trout 300.00 600.00
431 Hunter Pence 1.50 4.00
432 Ryan Zimmerman 1.50 4.00
433 Adam Jones 1.50 4.00
434 Dustin Pedroia 2.00 5.00
435 Carlos Santana 1.50 4.00
437 Billy Butler 1.25 3.00
438 Andrew McCutchen 2.00 5.00
439 Evan Longoria 1.50 4.00
440 Bryce Harper 3.00 8.00
441 Jordan Zimmermann 1.50 4.00
442 Hanley Ramirez 1.50 4.00
443 Hiroki Kuroda 1.25 3.00
444 Adrian Beltre 2.00 5.00
446 Jose Reyes 1.50 4.00
447 Felix Hernandez 1.50 4.00
448 Cole Hamels 1.50 4.00
449 Jered Weaver 1.50 4.00
450 Matt Kemp 1.50 4.00
451 Jake Peavy 1.25 3.00
452 Troy Tulowitzki 2.00 5.00
453 Justin Upton 1.50 4.00
454 Gio Gonzalez 1.50 4.00
455 Chris Sale 2.00 5.00
456 CC Sabathia 1.50 4.00
457 Mat Latos 1.50 4.00
458 David Price 1.50 4.00
459 Yoenis Cespedes 2.00 5.00
460 Ryan Braun 1.50 4.00
461 Marco Scutaro 1.50 4.00
462 Roy Halladay 1.50 4.00
463 Giancarlo Stanton 2.00 5.00
464 R.A. Dickey 1.50 4.00
465 David Wright 1.50 4.00
466 Carlos Gonzalez 1.50 4.00
467 Chase Headley 1.25 3.00
468 Mariano Rivera 2.50 6.00
469 Max Scherzer 2.00 5.00
470 Albert Pujols 2.50 6.00
471 Matt Holliday 2.00 5.00
472 Adrian Gonzalez 1.50 4.00
473 Matt Harrison 1.25 3.00
474 Wade Miley 1.25 3.00
475 Edwin Encarnacion 2.00 5.00
476 Yovani Gallardo 1.25 3.00
477 Yadier Molina 2.50 6.00
479 Ian Kinsler 1.50 4.00
480 Stephen Strasburg 2.00 5.00
481 Martin Prado 1.25 3.00
482 Nelson Cruz 2.00 5.00
483 James Shields 1.25 3.00
484 Adam Dunn 1.50 4.00
485 Starlin Castro 1.25 3.00
488 Wilin Rosario 1.25 3.00
490 Buster Posey 2.50 6.00
500 Justin Verlander 2.00 5.00

2013 Topps Heritage Advertising Panels

ISSUED AS A BOX TOPPER
1 Bronson Arroyo .60 1.50
Josh Wall/Paco Rodriguez/Chris Johnson
2 Homer Bailey .75 2.00
Allen Craig/Matt Dominguez
3 Mike Baxter .60 1.50
Ross Detwiler/Garrett Jones
4 Bud Black .75 2.00
Josh Willingham/Alexei Ramirez
5 Stephen Drew .75 2.00
Christian Garcia/Eury Perez/AL Strikeout Leaders
6 Lucas Duda .75 2.00
Joe Saunders/Chris Nelson
7 Rafael Furcal .75 2.00
Joe Mauer/Gerardo Parra
8 Paul Goldschmidt 1.00 2.50
Johan Santana/John Axford
9 Joel Hanrahan .75 2.00
Andrelton Simmons/Shane Victorino
10 Edwin Jackson .60 1.50
Bryan Morris/Justin Wilson/Buck Showalter
11 John Jaso .75 2.00
Brian McCann/Dee Gordon
12 Kenley Jansen .75 2.00
Jon Lester/Anthony Gose
13 Desmond Jennings .75 2.00
Marco Estrada/Andrew Bailey
14 Ubaldo Jiminez .75 2.00
Brandon Crawford/Ruben Tejada
15 Howie Kendrick .60 1.50
Luis Ayala/Carlos Ruiz
16 Kyle Lohse .60 1.50
Torii Hunter/Todd Frazier
17 Jed Lowrie 1.00 2.50
Nyjer Morgan/Brian Wilson
18 Shaun Marcum .60 1.50
Jose Valverde/Ron Washington
19 Mrtnz/Mstks/Crrra 1.00 2.50
20 Mitch Moreland .60 1.50
Tyler Colvin/Sandoval Pokes Three
21 Glen Perkins .75 2.00
Jonathan Papelbon/Patrick Corbin
22 A.J. Pierzynski .60 1.50
Rafael Ortega/Rob Schaill/Mike Matheny
23 Henry Rodriguez 1.25 3.00
Tony Cingrani/Will Venable/Mark Teixeira
24 Seth Smith 1.25 3.00
AL RBI Leaders/Darin Ruf/Tyler Cloyd
25 Drew Storen .60 1.50
Gaby Sanchez/Jason Grilli
26 Robin Ventura .75 2.00
Curtis Granderson/Elvis Andrus

2013 Topps Heritage Baseball Flashbacks

COMPLETE SET (10) 4.00 10.00
STATED ODDS 1:12 HOBBY
AK Al Kaline .60 1.50
BG Bob Gibson .50 1.25
CY Carl Yastrzemski 1.00 2.50
EB Ernie Banks .60 1.50
FR Frank Robinson .50 1.25
HA Hank Aaron 1.25 3.00
JM Juan Marichal .50 1.25
SK Sandy Koufax 1.25 3.00
SS Shea Stadium .25 .60
WM Willie Mays 1.25 3.00

2013 Topps Heritage Bazooka

AM Andrew McCutchen 10.00 25.00
BG Bob Gibson 30.00 60.00
BH Bryce Harper 30.00 60.00
BP Buster Posey 15.00 40.00
BR Brooks Robinson 12.50 30.00
CY Carl Yastrzemski 20.00 50.00
DJ Derek Jeter 20.00 50.00
EB Ernie Banks 15.00 40.00
EM Eddie Mathews 10.00 25.00
FH Felix Hernandez 8.00 20.00
HK Harmon Killebrew 15.00 40.00
JM Juan Marichal 30.00 60.00
JV Justin Verlander 20.00 50.00
MC Miguel Cabrera 15.00 40.00
MT Mike Trout 30.00 60.00
RB Ryan Braun 15.00 40.00
RC Roberto Clemente 20.00 50.00
SK Sandy Koufax 15.00 40.00
WM Willie Mays 15.00 40.00
YC Yoenis Cespedes 15.00 40.00

2013 Topps Heritage Chrome

STATED ODDS 1:24 HOBBY
STATED PRINT RUN 999 SER.#'d SETS
HC1 Miguel Cabrera 2.50 6.00
HC2 Derek Jeter 6.00 15.00
HC3 Evan Longoria 2.00 5.00
HC4 Yadier Molina 3.00 8.00
HC5 Albert Pujols 3.00 8.00
HC6 Ryan Howard 2.00 5.00
HC7 Joe Mauer 2.00 5.00
HC8 Hunter Pence 2.00 5.00
HC9 Ian Kinsler 2.00 5.00
HC10 Mike Trout 75.00 200.00
HC11 Ryan Zimmerman 2.00 5.00
HC12 Adam Jones 2.00 5.00
HC13 Hanley Ramirez 2.00 5.00
HC14 Martin Prado 1.50 4.00
HC15 Dustin Pedroia 2.50 6.00
HC16 Andre Ethier 2.00 5.00
HC17 Nelson Cruz 2.50 6.00
HC18 Matt Cain 2.00 5.00
HC19 Jose Bautista 2.00 5.00
HC20 Buster Posey 3.00 8.00
HC21 Billy Butler 1.50 4.00
HC22 Andrew McCutchen 2.50 6.00
HC23 David Freese 1.50 4.00
HC24 Robinson Cano 2.00 5.00
HC25 Clayton Kershaw 4.00 10.00
HC26 Kyle Lohse 1.50 4.00
HC27 Matt Kemp 2.00 5.00
HC28 Hiroki Kuroda 1.50 4.00
HC29 Adrian Beltre 2.50 6.00
HC30 Justin Verlander 2.50 6.00
HC31 Josh Willingham 2.00 5.00
HC32 Jay Bruce 2.00 5.00
HC33 James Shields 1.50 4.00
HC34 Felix Hernandez 2.00 5.00
HC35 Cole Hamels 2.00 5.00
HC36 Jered Weaver 2.00 5.00
HC37 Stephen Strasburg 2.50 6.00
HC38 Jarrod Parker 1.50 4.00
HC39 Alex Gordon 2.00 5.00
HC40 Yu Darvish 2.50 6.00
HC41 Carlos Santana 2.00 5.00
HC42 Mariano Rivera 3.00 8.00
HC43 Jim Johnson 1.50 4.00
HC44 Jake Peavy 1.50 4.00
HC45 Troy Tulowitzki 2.50 6.00
HC46 Jacoby Ellsbury 2.00 5.00
HC47 Gio Gonzalez 2.00 5.00
HC48 Adam Dunn 2.00 5.00
HC49 Chris Sale 2.50 6.00
HC50 Bryce Harper 4.00 10.00
HC51 Carlos Beltran 2.00 5.00
HC52 CC Sabathia 2.00 5.00
HC53 Adam LaRoche 1.50 4.00
HC54 Matt Harrison 1.50 4.00
HC55 Mat Latos 2.00 5.00
HC56 Fernando Rodney 1.50 4.00
HC57 Johnny Cueto 2.00 5.00
HC58 Wilin Rosario 1.50 4.00
HC59 Marco Scutaro 2.00 5.00
HC60 David Price 2.00 5.00
HC61 Yoenis Cespedes 2.50 6.00
HC62 Max Scherzer 2.50 6.00
HC63 Aramis Ramirez 1.50 4.00
HC64 Starlin Castro 1.50 4.00
HC65 Mark Trumbo 1.50 4.00
HC66 Roy Halladay 2.00 5.00
HC67 Giancarlo Stanton 2.50 6.00
HC68 Justin Upton 2.00 5.00
HC69 Kris Medlen 2.00 5.00
HC70 R.A. Dickey 2.00 5.00
HC71 David Wright 2.00 5.00
HC72 Jose Reyes 2.00 5.00
HC73 Jordan Zimmermann 2.00 5.00
HC74 Carlos Gonzalez 2.00 5.00
HC75 Prince Fielder 2.00 5.00
HC76 Miguel Montero 1.50 4.00
HC77 Chase Headley 1.50 4.00
HC78 Paul Konerko 2.00 5.00
HC79 Brandon Morrow 1.50 4.00
HC80 Ryan Braun 2.00 5.00
HC81 Madison Bumgarner 2.00 5.00
HC82 Matt Holliday 2.50 6.00
HC83 Adrian Gonzalez 2.00 5.00
HC84 Curtis Granderson 2.00 5.00
HC85 Michael Bourn 1.50 4.00
HC86 Wade Miley 1.50 4.00
HC87 Allen Craig 2.00 5.00
HC88 Edwin Encarnacion 2.50 6.00
HC89 Yovani Gallardo 1.50 4.00
HC90 Josh Hamilton 2.00 5.00
HC91 Ryan Vogelsong 1.50 4.00
HC92 Josh Reddick 1.50 4.00
HC93 Austin Jackson 1.50 4.00
HC94 M.Machado/D.Bundy 10.00 25.00
HC95 M.Olt/J.Profar 2.00 5.00
HC96 S.Miller/T.Rosenthal 4.00 10.00
HC97 Adam Eaton/Tyler Skaggs 2.50 6.00
HC98 D.Ruf/T.Cloyd 3.00 8.00
HC99 Collin McHugh/Jeurys Familia 2.50 6.00
HC100 Brock Holt/Kyle McPherson 2.00 5.00

2013 Topps Heritage Chrome Black Refractors

*BLACK REF: 2X TO 5X BASIC
STATED ODDS 1:368 HOBBY
STATED PRINT RUN 64 SER.#'d SETS
HC2 Derek Jeter 125.00 250.00
HC10 Mike Trout 300.00 600.00
HC50 Bryce Harper 75.00 150.00

2013 Topps Heritage Chrome Purple Refractors

*PURPLE REF: .4X TO 1X BASIC

2013 Topps Heritage Chrome Refractors

*REF: .5X TO 1.2X BASIC
STATED ODDS 1:42 HOBBY
STATED PRINT RUN 554 SER.#'d SETS

2013 Topps Heritage Clubhouse Collection Dual Relics

STATED ODDS 1:5003 HOBBY
STATED PRINT RUN 64 SER.#'d SETS
CM R.Clemente/A.McCutchen 75.00 150.00
KC A.Kaline/M.Cabrera 60.00 120.00
KM H.Killebrew/J.Mauer 40.00 80.00
MP W.Mays/B.Posey 75.00 150.00
YE C.Yastrzemski/J.Ellsbury 40.00 80.00

2013 Topps Heritage Clubhouse Collection Relics

STATED ODDS 1:38 HOBBY
AB Adrian Beltre 3.00 8.00
AD Adam Dunn 3.00 8.00
AG Alex Gordon 3.00 8.00
AJ Adam Jones 3.00 8.00
AW Adam Wainwright 3.00 8.00
BB Brandon Beachy 3.00 8.00
BBE Brandon Belt 4.00 10.00
BBU Billy Butler 3.00 8.00
BM Brandon McCarthy 3.00 8.00
BMO Brandon Morrow 3.00 8.00
BP Brandon Phillips 3.00 8.00
BU B.J. Upton 3.00 8.00
CD Chris Davis 6.00 15.00
CG Carlos Gonzalez 3.00 8.00
CR Colby Rasmus 3.00 8.00
CS Carlos Santana 3.00 8.00
CW C.J. Wilson 3.00 8.00
DE Danny Espinosa 3.00 8.00
DG Dee Gordon 3.00 8.00
DH Dan Haren 3.00 8.00
DJ Desmond Jennings 3.00 8.00
DM Devin Mesoraco 3.00 8.00
DS Drew Stubbs 3.00 8.00
EA Elvis Andrus 3.00 8.00
EE Edwin Encarnacion 3.00 8.00
EL Evan Longoria 4.00 10.00
ID Ian Desmond 3.00 8.00
IK Ian Kinsler 3.00 8.00
IKE Ian Kennedy 3.00 8.00
JB Jay Bruce 4.00 10.00
JC Johnny Cueto 3.00 8.00
JCH Jhoulys Chacin 3.00 8.00
JG Jaime Garcia 3.00 8.00
JH Jason Heyward 4.00 10.00
JHA Josh Hamilton 3.00 8.00
JJ Jon Jay 3.00 8.00
JM Jesus Montero 3.00 8.00
JMO Jason Motte 3.00 8.00
JP Jake Peavy 3.00 8.00
JPA Jordan Pacheco 3.00 8.00
JPE Jhonny Peralta 3.00 8.00
JS Johan Santana 3.00 8.00
JV Justin Verlander 8.00 20.00
JZ Jordan Zimmermann 3.00 8.00
MB Madison Bumgarner 5.00 12.00
MC Matt Cain 4.00 10.00
MG Matt Garza 3.00 8.00
ML Mike Leake 3.00 8.00
MM Mike Moustakas
MMI Mike Minor 3.00 8.00
MMO Miguel Montero 3.00 8.00
MN Mike Napoli 3.00 8.00
MS Max Scherzer 3.00 8.00
MT Mike Trout 15.00 40.00
MY Michael Young 3.00 8.00
NC Nelson Cruz 3.00 8.00
NF Neftali Feliz 3.00 8.00
NM Nick Markakis 3.00 8.00
PA Pedro Alvarez 3.00 8.00
PK Paul Konerko 3.00 8.00
RP Rick Porcello 3.00 8.00
RZ Ryan Zimmerman 3.00 8.00
SC Starlin Castro 3.00 8.00
SM Shaun Marcum 3.00 8.00
SSC Shin-Soo Choo 3.00 8.00
TC Trevor Cahill 3.00 8.00
TH Tim Hudson 3.00 8.00
THA Tommy Hanson 3.00 8.00
THU Torii Hunter 3.00 8.00
WR Wilin Rosario 3.00 8.00
YA Yonder Alonso 3.00 8.00
YC Yoenis Cespedes 4.00 10.00
YG Yovani Gallardo 3.00 8.00

2013 Topps Heritage Clubhouse Collection Relics Gold

STATED ODDS 1:225 HOBBY
STATED PRINT RUN 99 SER.#'d SETS

2013 Topps Heritage Framed Stamps

STATED ODDS 1:4701 HOBBY
STATED PRINT RUN 50 SER.#'d SETS
S Shakespeare 12.50 30.00
AR Amateur Radio 12.50 30.00
CM C.M. Russell 15.00 40.00
DM Doctors Mayo 12.50 30.00
FA Fine Arts 12.50 30.00
HK Harmon Killebrew 15.00 40.00
JFK John F. Kennedy 20.00 50.00
JM John Muir 15.00 40.00
LA Luis Aparicio 15.00 40.00
MW Maury Wills 20.00 50.00
NJ N.J. Tricentenary 12.50 30.00
NS Nevada Statehood 15.00 40.00
RC Roberto Clemente 15.00 40.00
RG Robert H. Goddard 12.50 30.00
SH Sam Houston 12.50 30.00
UC U.S. Customs 15.00 40.00
UH U.S. Homemakers 12.50 30.00
UV U.S. Vote 30.00 60.00
VB Verrazano Bridge 15.00 40.00
WF World's Fair 15.00 40.00

2013 Topps Heritage Giants

STATED ODDS 1:36 HOBBY BOXES
AM Andrew McCutchen 12.00 30.00
BG Bob Gibson 20.00 50.00
BH Bryce Harper 20.00 50.00
DJ Derek Jeter 40.00 80.00
EB Ernie Banks 12.00 30.00
EM Eddie Mathews 30.00 60.00
FH Felix Hernandez 10.00 25.00
GS Giancarlo Stanton 12.00 30.00
HK Harmon Killebrew 15.00 40.00
JB Jose Bautista 10.00 25.00
JV Justin Verlander 12.00 30.00
MC Miguel Cabrera 12.00 30.00
MCA Matt Cain 10.00 25.00
MT Mike Trout 100.00 250.00
RA R.A. Dickey 10.00 25.00
RB Ryan Braun 10.00 25.00
RC Robinson Cano 15.00 40.00
WM Willie Mays 25.00 60.00
YC Yoenis Cespedes 12.00 30.00
YD Yu Darvish 12.00 30.00

2013 Topps Heritage Memorable Moments

COMPLETE SET (15) 6.00 15.00
STATED ODDS 1:12 HOBBY
BH Bryce Harper 1.00 2.50
CB Carlos Beltran .50 1.25
DJ Derek Jeter 1.50 4.00
DO David Ortiz .60 1.50
DP David Price .50 1.25
FH Felix Hernandez .50 1.25
JS Johan Santana .50 1.25
MC Miguel Cabrera .60 1.50
MCA Matt Cain .50 1.25
MM Manny Machado 2.50 6.00
MT Mike Trout 5.00 12.00
PF Prince Fielder .50 1.25
RA R.A. Dickey .50 1.25
TR Teddy Roosevelt .25 .60
YU Yu Darvish .60 1.50

2013 Topps Heritage New Age Performers

COMPLETE SET (30) 12.50 30.00
STATED ODDS 1:8 HOBBY
AB Adrian Beltre .60 1.50
AM Andrew McCutchen .60 1.50
AP Albert Pujols .75 2.00
BB Billy Butler .40 1.00
BH Bryce Harper 1.00 2.50
BP Buster Posey .75 2.00
CG Curtis Granderson .50 1.25
CK Clayton Kershaw 1.00 2.50
DP David Price .50 1.25
DW David Wright .50 1.25
FH Felix Hernandez .50 1.25
GG Gio Gonzalez .50 1.25
JM Joe Mauer .50 1.25
JV Justin Verlander .60 1.50
KM Kris Medlen .50 1.25
MC Miguel Cabrera .60 1.50
MK Matt Kemp .50 1.25
MM Manny Machado 2.50 6.00
MT Mike Trout 5.00 12.00
PF Prince Fielder .50 1.25
RB Ryan Braun .50 1.25
RC Robinson Cano .50 1.25
RD R.A. Dickey .50 1.25
SC Starlin Castro .40 1.00
SS Stephen Strasburg .60 1.50
WM Wade Miley .40 1.00
YC Yoenis Cespedes .60 1.50
YD Yu Darvish .60 1.50
YM Yadier Molina .75 2.00
MCA Matt Cain .50 1.25

2013 Topps Heritage News Flashbacks

COMPLETE SET (10) 3.00 8.00
STATED ODDS 1:12 HOBBY
J Jeopardy .25 .60
CRA Civil Rights Act of 1964 .25 .60
FM Ford Mustang .25 .60
LBJ Lyndon B. Johnson .25 .60
MLK Dr. Martin Luther King Jr. .40 1.00
MP Mary Poppins .25 .60
RS The Rolling Stones .60 1.50
SP Sidney Poitier .25 .60
TB The Beatles .60 1.50
WF 1964 World's Fair .25 .60

2013 Topps Heritage Real One Autographs

STATED ODDS 1:124 HOBBY
HN CARDS ISSUED IN HN.FACT.SETS
EXCHANGE DEADLINE 1/31/2016
HN EXCH.DEADLINE 11/30/2016
AE Adam Eaton HN 6.00 15.00
AG Anthony Gose 6.00 15.00
AH Aaron Hicks HN 10.00 25.00
AHE Adeiny Hechavarria HN 6.00 15.00
AM Al Moran 10.00 25.00
AR Anthony Rendon HN 100.00 250.00
AS Anibal Sanchez 12.50 30.00
ASA Amado Samuel 6.00 15.00
BD Bill Dailey 6.00 15.00
BF Bill Fischer 6.00 15.00
BG Bob Gibson 20.00 50.00
BJ Brett Jackson 6.00 15.00
BL Bob Lillis 10.00 25.00
BM Brandon Maurer HN 6.00 15.00
BP Bill Pierce 12.00 30.00
BR Bruce Rondon HN 6.00 15.00
BR Bobby Richardson 10.00 25.00
BS Bobby Shantz 10.00 25.00
CA Chris Archer 12.00 30.00
CB Carl Bouldin 6.00 15.00
CD Charlie Dees 10.00 25.00
CK Casey Kelly HN 6.00 15.00
CM Charlie Maxwell 10.00 25.00
DF David Freese 15.00 40.00
DG Didi Gregorius HN 30.00 80.00
DG Dick Groat 6.00 15.00
DL Don Leppert 10.00 25.00
DP Dan Pfister 6.00 15.00
DR Darin Ruf HN 6.00 15.00
EB Ernie Banks 50.00 100.00
EBU Ellis Burton 6.00 15.00
EG Evan Gattis HN 6.00 15.00
FF Frank Funk 6.00 15.00
FR Frank Robinson 30.00 60.00
GC Gerrit Cole HN 40.00 80.00
GC Gene Conley 6.00 15.00
GH Glen Hobbie 6.00 15.00
HA Hank Aaron 200.00 400.00
HB Hal Brown 6.00 15.00
HF Hank Foiles 6.00 15.00
HR Hyun-Jin Ryu HN 50.00 100.00
JB Jackie Bradley Jr. HN 25.00 60.00
JB Jose Bautista 15.00 40.00
JC Jim Campbell 6.00 15.00
JF Jose Fernandez HN 40.00 100.00
JG Jedd Gyorko HN 8.00 20.00
JG John Goryl 10.00 25.00
JH Jay Hook 6.00 15.00
JL Jeoff Long 6.00 15.00
JM Juan Marichal 20.00 50.00
JP Jurickson Profar HN 40.00 80.00
JSH James Shields 6.00 15.00
JSP Jack Spring 6.00 15.00
JW Jerry Walker 6.00 15.00
KF Kyuji Fujikawa HN 6.00 15.00
KM Ken MacKenzie 6.00 15.00
LL Lance Lynn 10.00 25.00
LT Luis Tiant 6.00 15.00
MA Matt Adams HN
MJ Mike Joyce 6.00 15.00
MM Manny Machado HN 150.00 400.00
MM Mike Morse 10.00 25.00
MMI Minnie Minoso 8.00 20.00
MO Marcell Ozuna HN 25.00 60.00
MOL Mike Olt HN 8.00 20.00
MR Mike Roarke 10.00 25.00
MT Mark Trumbo 6.00 15.00
MW Maury Wills 6.00 15.00
MZ Mike Zunino HN 8.00 20.00
NA Nolan Arenado HN
NF Nick Franklin HN EXCH 6.00 15.00
OA Oswaldo Arcia HN
OC Orlando Cepeda 10.00 25.00
PB Paul Brown 6.00 15.00
PF Paul Foytack 6.00 15.00
PG Paul Goldschmidt 50.00 120.00
PGR Pumpsie Green 12.00 30.00
PR Paco Rodriguez HN 8.00 20.00
RM Roman Mejias 12.00 30.00
SD Scott Diamond 6.00 15.00
SM Shelby Miller HN 6.00 15.00
SM Stan Musial 150.00 300.00
SMA Starling Marte 6.00 15.00
TB Ted Bowsfield 6.00 15.00
TBR Tom Brown 6.00 15.00
TC Tony Cingrani HN 6.00 15.00
TF Todd Frazier 6.00 15.00
TH Tim Harkness 6.00 15.00
WM Wil Myers HN 20.00 50.00
WM Willie Mays 200.00 400.00
WMI Will Middlebrooks 10.00 25.00
YG Yasmani Grandal 6.00 15.00
YP Yasiel Puig HN EXCH 400.00 600.00
ZW Zack Wheeler HN 8.00 20.00

2013 Topps Heritage Real One Autographs Red Ink

*RED: .6X TO 1.5X BASIC
STATED ODDS 1:480 HOBBY
HN CARDS FOUND IN HIGH NUMBER BOXES
PRINT RUNS B/WN 10-64 COPIES PER
HN PRINT RUN 10 SER.#'d SETS
NO HIGH NUMBER PRICING AVAILABLE
EXCHANGE DEADLINE 1/31/2016
HN EXCH.DEADLINE 11/30/2016

2013 Topps Heritage Then and Now

COMPLETE SET (10) 5.00 12.00
STATED ODDS 1:15 HOBBY
AT L.Aparicio/M.Trout 5.00 12.00
BV J.Bunning/J.Verlander .60 1.50
CP R.Clemente/B.Posey 1.50 4.00
FH Whitey Ford/Felix Hernandez .50 1.25
GV B.Gibson/J.Verlander .60 1.50
KC H.Killebrew/M.Cabrera .60 1.50
KK S.Koufax/C.Kershaw 1.25 3.00
MD Eddie Mathews/Adam Dunn .60 1.50
MG Juan Marichal/Gio Gonzalez .50 1.25
RC B.Robinson/M.Cabrera .60 1.50

2014 Topps Heritage

COMP.SET w/o SPs (425) 20.00 50.00
COMP.HN.FACT.SET (101) 60.00 120.00
COMP.HN SET (100) 50.00 100.00
SP ODDS 1:3 HOBBY
ACTION SP ODDS 1:23 HOBBY
LOGO SP ODDS 1:135 HOBBY
THROWBACK SP ODDS 1:3175 HOBBY
ERROR SP ODDS 1:1473 HOBBY
HN FACT SETS SOLD ONLY
1 Trout/Mauer/Cabrera 1.25 3.00
2 Freeman/Johnson/Cuddyer .30 .75
3 Encarnacion/Cabrera/Davis .25 .60
4 Alvarez/Bruce/Brown/Goldschmidt .25 .60
5 Cano/Jones/Cabrera/Davis .25 .60
6 Frmn/Bruce/Gldschmdt .30 .75
7 A.Sanchez/B.Colon .15 .40
8 J.Fernandez/C.Kershaw .40 1.00
9 Tillman/Wilson/Moore/Colon/Scherzer .20 .50
10 Kershaw/Zimmermann/Wain .40 1.00
11 Sale/Darvish/Scherzer .25 .60
12 Samardzija/Kershaw/Lee .40 1.00
13 Ross Ohlendorf .15 .40
14 Brian Roberts .15 .40
15 Asdrubal Cabrera .20 .50
16 Carlos Ruiz .15 .40
17 John Mayberry .15 .40
18 Felix Doubront .15 .40
19 Jeff Locke .15 .40
20 Cliff Lee .20 .50
21 Jon Jay .15 .40
22 A.J. Ellis .15 .40
23 Joaquin Benoit .15 .40
24 E.Adrianza RC/Z.Walters RC .40 1.00
25 Kyle Lohse .15 .40
26 Ryan Wheeler .15 .40
27 Jarrod Saltalamacchia .15 .40
28 Jose Altuve .20 .50
29 Derek Norris .15 .40
30 Hiroki Kuroda .15 .40
31 Salvador Perez .20 .50
32 Bruce Bochy MG .20 .50
33 Michael Cuddyer .15 .40
34 A.J. Burnett .15 .40
35 Ryan Vogelsong .15 .40
36 Coco Crisp .15 .40
37 Logan Morrison .15 .40
38 Brett Lawrie .20 .50
39 Chris Carter .15 .40
40 Carl Crawford .20 .50
41 A.Rienzo RC/E.Johnson RC .40 1.00
42 Matt Joyce .15 .40
43A Carlos Beltran .20 .50
43B C.Beltran SP ERR 12.00 30.00
44 Aaron Hill .15 .40
45 Brett Wallace .15 .40
46 Stephen Drew .15 .40
47 Rex Brothers .15 .40
48 Marlon Byrd .15 .40
49 J.Schoop RC/X.Bogaerts RC 1.25 3.00
50 Matt Cain .20 .50
51 Denard Span .15 .40
52 Daniel Nava .15 .40
53A Giancarlo Stanton .25 .60
53B Giancarlo Stanton Logo SP 8.00 20.00
54 Andrew Cashner .15 .40
55 Matt Garza .15 .40
56 Alexi Ogando .15 .40
57 Ryne Sandberg .50 1.25
58 A.J. Pierzynski .15 .40
59 Adam Lind .20 .50
60 Aroldis Chapman .25 .60
61 Nate Eovaldi .20 .50
62A Kevin Correia .15 .40
62B K.Correia SP ERR 10.00 25.00
63 Jacob Turner .20 .50
64 Alex Rodriguez .30 .75
65 Garrett Richards .20 .50
66 Joe Maddon MG .15 .40
67 Nick Franklin .15 .40
68 Jake Odorizzi .15 .40
69 Gaby Sanchez .15 .40
70 Paul Konerko .20 .50
71 Heath Bell .15 .40
72 Homer Bailey .15 .40
73 Francisco Liriano .15 .40
74 C.Leesman RC/M.Belfiore RC .40 1.00
75 Cody Asche .20 .50
76 Chris Capuano .15 .40
77 Austin Romine .15 .40
78 Adam Jones .20 .50
79 Dan Haren .15 .40
80 Brett Oberholtzer .15 .40
81 Jed Lowrie .15 .40
82 C.Bethancourt RC/D.Hale RC .40 1.00
83 Justin Smoak .15 .40
84A Hyun-Jin Ryu .20 .50
84B Hyun-Jin Ryu Action SP 2.50 6.00
85 Alex Rios .20 .50
86 Wei-Yin Chen .15 .40
87 Daniel Murphy .20 .50
88 Ricky Nolasco .15 .40
89 Kyle Gibson .20 .50
90 Trevor Plouffe .15 .40
91 Clint Hurdle MG .15 .40
92 C.J. Wilson .15 .40
93 Jenrry Mejia .15 .40
94 Hector Santiago .15 .40
95 Brandon McCarthy .15 .40
96 Andres Torres .15 .40
97 Chris Heisey .15 .40
98 Mark Buehrle .20 .50
99 Walt Weiss MG .15 .40
100A Adam Wainwright .20 .50
100C Adam Wainwright Action SP 2.50 6.00
101 Brian Wilson .25 .60
102 Howie Kendrick .15 .40
103 Alex Gordon .20 .50
104 J.Butler RC/J.Adduci RC .40 1.00
105 Daniel Hudson .15 .40
106 Nick Markakis .20 .50
107 E.Martin RC/C.Rupp RC .40 1.00
108 Justin Masterson .15 .40
109 Miguel Montero .15 .40
110 Starlin Castro .15 .40
111 Yunel Escobar .15 .40
112 Marcell Ozuna .25 .60
113 Lance Berkman .20 .50
114 Addison Reed .15 .40
115 Ubaldo Jimenez .15 .40
116 K.Wong RC/A.Perez RC .50 1.25
117 Chase Headley .15 .40
118 Justin Ruggiano .15 .40
119 Chase Utley .20 .50
120 Shin-Soo Choo .20 .50
121 Kendrys Morales .15 .40
122 Tyler Chatwood .15 .40
123 Johnny Cueto .20 .50
124 Aramis Ramirez .15 .40

125 Nate Schierholtz .15 .40
126 Mike Matheny MG .15 .40
127 Matt Adams .15 .40
128 Mike Leake .15 .40
129 Alejandro De Aza .15 .40
130 Austin Jackson .15 .40
131 Joe Girardi .20 .50
132 World Series Game 1 .25 .60
133 World Series Game 2 .25 .60
134 World Series Game 3 .25 .60
135 World Series Game 4 .25 .60
136 World Series Game 5 .25 .60
137 World Series Game 6 .25 .60
137 Anthony Gose .15 .40
139 Melky Cabrera .15 .40
140A Jered Weaver .20 .50
140B Jered Weaver Action SP 2.50 6.00
141 Torii Hunter .15 .40
142 Michael Saunders .20 .50
143 A.Lambo RC/S.Pimentel RC .40 1.00
144 Brad Miller .20 .50
145 Edwin Encarnacion .25 .60
146 Juan Pierre .15 .40
147 Johan Santana .20 .50
148A Freddie Freeman .30 .75
148B F.Freeman TB SP 100.00 250.00
148C Freddie Freeman Action SP 4.00 10.00
149A Buster Posey .30 .75
149B B.Posey Logo SP 15.00 40.00
150A Manny Machado .25 .60
150B Machado Action SP 3.00 8.00
151 Kirk Gibson .15 .40
152 Todd Frazier .15 .40
153 Joe Kelly .15 .40
154 Kris Medlen .20 .50
155 Gio Gonzalez .20 .50
156 Mark Ellis .15 .40
157 Kyle Seager .15 .40
158 John Gibbons MG .15 .40
159 Clint Barmes .15 .40
160A Andrew McCutchen .25 .60
160B McCutchen Logo SP 10.00 25.00
160C McCutchen SP ERR 20.00 50.00
161 Brett Gardner .20 .50
162 Cameron Maybin .15 .40
163 Wily Peralta .15 .40
164 John Danks .15 .40
165 Gerardo Parra .15 .40
166 A.Almonte RC/L.Watkins RC .40 1.00
167 Raul Ibanez .20 .50
168 Ike Davis .15 .40
169 Brian Dozier .20 .50
170A Justin Upton .20 .50
170B J.Upton TB SP 75.00 150.00
170C Justin Upton Action SP 2.50 6.00
171 Gordon Beckham .15 .40
172 Ivan Nova .20 .50
173 Ryan Ludwick .15 .40
174 Carlos Martinez .20 .50
175 Dayan Viciedo .15 .40
176 J.B. Shuck .15 .40
177 Dan Straily .15 .40
178 Jose Quintana .15 .40
179 Rafael Betancourt .15 .40
180 Oswaldo Arcia .15 .40
181 T.Gosewisch RC/N.Christiani RC .40 1.00
182 Jake Peavy .15 .40
183 Robbie Grossman .15 .40
184 Kole Calhoun .15 .40
185 Matt Holliday .25 .60
186 Jon Niese .15 .40
187 Terry Collins .15 .40
188 Eric Sogard .15 .40
189 T.Medica RC/R.Fuentes RC .40 1.00
190 Allen Craig .20 .50
191 Tommy Milone .15 .40
192 Luke Hochevar .15 .40
193 Ian Kennedy .15 .40
194 B.Boshers RC/M.Shoemaker RC .60 1.50
195 John Jaso .15 .40
196 Jose Iglesias .20 .50
197A Josh Reddick .15 .40
197B J.Reddick TB SP 75.00 150.00
198A Eric Hosmer .20 .50
198B E.Hosmer TB SP 150.00 250.00
199 Jeremy Hefner .15 .40
200A Jason Heyward .20 .50
200B J.Heyward TB SP 75.00 150.00
201 Z.Rosscup RC/J.Pinto RC .40 1.00
202 Wade Miley .15 .40
203 Leonys Martin .15 .40
204 Jonathan Papelbon .20 .50
205 Starling Marte .20 .50
206 John Lackey .20 .50
207 David Murphy .15 .40
208 Roy Halladay .20 .50
209 Jason Vargas .15 .40
210 Erick Aybar .15 .40
211 Bronson Arroyo .15 .40
212 Steve Cishek .15 .40
213 Clay Buchholz .15 .40
214 Doug Fister .15 .40
215 Matt Harrison .15 .40
216 Patrick Corbin .20 .50
217 Don Mattingly .50 1.25
218 Juan Nicasio .15 .40
219 Michael Young .15 .40
220 Junior Lake .15 .40
221 Bartolo Colon .15 .40
222 Desmond Jennings .20 .50
223 Miguel Gonzalez .15 .40
224 Brandon Moss .15 .40
225 Juan Francisco .15 .40
226 C.Cabral RC/J.Murphy RC .40 1.00
227 Jonny Venters .15 .40
228 Mitch Moreland .15 .40
229 Colby Rasmus .20 .50
230 Lance Lynn .15 .40
231 Chris Johnson .15 .40
232 J.P. Arencibia .15 .40
233 Daniel Descalso .15 .40
234 Jonny Gomes .15 .40
235 Kevin Gregg .15 .40
236 Jorge De La Rosa .15 .40
237 Phil Hughes .15 .40
238 Josh Beckett .15 .40
239 Chris Perez .15 .40
240 Jarred Cosart .15 .40
241 Drew Stubbs .15 .40
242 Ross Detwiler .15 .40
243 N.Castellanos RC/B.Hamilton RC 1.25 3.00
244 Mike Napoli .15 .40
245 Neftali Feliz .15 .40
246 Jeremy Guthrie .15 .40
247 Mat Latos .20 .50
248 Pete Kozma .15 .40
249 Martin Prado .15 .40
250A Mike Trout 1.25 3.00
250B M.Trout TB SP 100.00 200.00
250C M.Trout Action SP 25.00 60.00
250D M.Trout Logo SP 20.00 50.00
251 John Farrell MG .15 .40
252 Dan Uggla .15 .40
253 Justin Maxwell .15 .40
254 Charlie Morton .25 .60
255 Darin Ruf .20 .50
256 Wilson Ramos .15 .40
257 Koji Uehara .15 .40
258 Rick Porcello .20 .50
259 T.Beckham RC/E.Romero RC .60 1.50
260 Zack Greinke .25 .60
261 Jose Molina .15 .40
262 Casey Janssen .15 .40
263 Jonathan Lucroy .20 .50
264 Fernando Rodney .15 .40
265 James Loney .15 .40
266 Adam Dunn .20 .50
267 Jason Grilli .15 .40
268 Christian Yelich .30 .75
269 Albert Pujols .30 .75
270 Jim Johnson .15 .40
271 Grant Balfour .15 .40
272 Eric Stults .15 .40
273 C.Bettis RC/D.Holmberg RC .40 1.00
274 Ron Washington MG .15 .40
275 Julio Teheran .20 .50
276 Ryan Dempster .15 .40
277 Will Venable .15 .40
278 David Lough .15 .40
279 Evan Gattis .15 .40
280 Ryan Howard .20 .50
281 Gregor Blanco .15 .40
282 K.Siegrist RC/H.Hembree RC .75 2.00
283 Josh Donaldson .20 .50
284A David Wright .20 .50
284B David Wright Action SP 2.50 6.00
285 Scooter Gennett .20 .50
286 A.Caminero RC/K.Johnson RC .40 1.00
287 Juan Uribe .15 .40
288 Jhonny Peralta .15 .40
289 Will Middlebrooks .15 .40
290 Chris Tillman .15 .40
291 Carlos Quentin .15 .40
292 Jim Henderson .15 .40
293 Shane Victorino .20 .50
294 David Robertson .15 .40
295 Kyle Blanks .15 .40
296 Randall Delgado .15 .40
297 Khris Davis .25 .60
298 Corey Hart .15 .40
299 Mike Moustakas .20 .50
300A Clayton Kershaw .40 1.00
300B Kershaw Action SP 5.00 12.00
301 Terry Francona MG .20 .50
302 Adam Eaton .15 .40
303 Prince Fielder .20 .50
304 Marco Estrada .15 .40
305 Garrett Jones .15 .40
306 R.A. Dickey .20 .50
307 Jonathan Villar .15 .40
308 T.d'Arnaud RC/W.Flores RC .50 1.25
309 Brandon Barnes .15 .40
310A Domonic Brown .20 .50
310B Domonic Brown Logo SP 6.00 15.00
311 Brandon Morrow .15 .40
312 Munenori Kawasaki .20 .50
313 Yonder Alonso .15 .40
314 Avisail Garcia .20 .50
315 Mike Pelfrey .15 .40
316 Ben Zobrist .20 .50
317 Neil Walker .15 .40
318 Dillon Gee .15 .40
319 David Price .20 .50
320 Shelby Miller .20 .50
321 Jason Castro .15 .40
322 Brandon Crawford .20 .50
323 Buck Showalter MG .15 .40
324 Devin Mesoraco .15 .40
325 Alexei Ramirez .20 .50
326 Elvis Andrus .20 .50
327 D.J. LeMahieu .25 .60
328 Jeremy Hellickson .15 .40
329 Ervin Santana .15 .40
330 CC Sabathia .20 .50
331 O.Garcia RC/N.Buss RC .40 1.00
332 Ryan Raburn .15 .40
333 Mark Melancon .15 .40
334 Alcides Escobar .20 .50
335 Tyler Pastornicky .15 .40
336 Andy Dirks .15 .40
337 Jimmy Rollins .20 .50
338 Corey Kluber .20 .50
339 Zack Cozart .15 .40
340 Josh Willingham .20 .50
341 Glen Perkins .15 .40
342 Matt Carpenter .25 .60
343 Russell Martin .15 .40
344 Justin Morneau .20 .50
345 Jose Bautista .20 .50
346 Fredi Gonzalez MG .15 .40
347 Jhoulys Chacin .15 .40
348 Kyuji Fujikawa .20 .50
349 Yovani Gallardo .15 .40
350 Alfonso Soriano .20 .50
351 Adam LaRoche .15 .40
352 Edward Mujica .15 .40
353 Rickie Weeks .15 .40
354 J.Paxton RC/T.Walker RC .60 1.50
355 Cody Ross .15 .40
356 Victor Martinez .20 .50
357 Lonnie Chisenhall .15 .40
358 Vernon Wells .15 .40
359 Huston Street .15 .40
360 Brandon Belt .20 .50
361 M.Choice RC/J.Marisnick RC .40 1.00
362 Eduardo Nunez .15 .40
363 Norichika Aoki .15 .40
364 Darwin Barney .15 .40
365 Adeiny Hechavarria .15 .40
366 A.J. Griffin .15 .40
367 Alex Cobb .15 .40
368 M.Davidson RC/C.Owings RC .40 1.00
369 Omar Infante .15 .40
370A Matt Kemp .20 .50
370B Matt Kemp Action SP 2.50 6.00
371 Edwin Jackson .15 .40
372 Chris Rusin .15 .40
373 Ben Revere .15 .40
374 W.Tovar RC/M.Robles RC .40 1.00
375 Yasmani Grandal .15 .40
376 Michael Brantley .20 .50
377 Kevin Gausman .25 .60
378 Trevor Rosenthal .20 .50
379 Trevor Cahill .15 .40
380 Michael Bourn .15 .40
381 Dustin Ackley .15 .40
382 Bobby Parnell .15 .40
383 Ryan Doumit .15 .40
384 Andre Ethier .20 .50
385 Nate McLouth .15 .40
386 Y.Ventura RC/J.Nelson RC .50 1.25
387 Jedd Gyorko .15 .40
388 Matt Dominguez .15 .40
389 Marco Scutaro .20 .50
390 Alex Avila .20 .50
391 Bob Melvin MG .15 .40
392 Travis Wood .15 .40
393 Lorenzo Cain .15 .40
394 Dexter Fowler .20 .50
395 Brian McCann .20 .50
396 Everth Cabrera .15 .40
397 Peter Bourjos .15 .40
398 D.Webb RC/C.Robinson RC .40 1.00
399 Nick Swisher .20 .50
400A Bryce Harper .40 1.00
400B B.Harper TB SP 200.00 400.00
400C B.Harper Action SP 10.00 25.00
400D B.Harper Logo SP 15.00 40.00
401 Jose Lobaton .15 .40
402 Jayson Werth .20 .50
403 Kenley Jansen .20 .50
404 Charlie Blackmon .25 .60
405 Danny Salazar .20 .50
406 Rajai Davis .15 .40
407A Michael Wacha .20 .50
407B M.Wacha Action SP 2.50 6.00
407C M.Wacha Logo SP 6.00 15.00
408 Didi Gregorius .20 .50
409 J.DeLeon RC/M.Stassi RC .40 1.00
410 J.J. Hardy .15 .40
411 Mike Minor .15 .40
412 Jose Tabata .15 .40
413 A.J. Pollock .20 .50
414 Robin Ventura MG .15 .40
415 Mike Zunino .15 .40
416 Emilio Bonifacio .15 .40
417 Bud Norris .15 .40
418 Joe Nathan .15 .40
419 Aaron Hicks .20 .50
420 Jeff Samardzija .15 .40
421 K.Pillar RC/R.Goins RC .50 1.25
422 Brad Ziegler .15 .40
423 Alex Wood .15 .40
424 Zack Wheeler .20 .50
425A Yoenis Cespedes .25 .60
425B Y.Cespedes TB SP 75.00 150.00
426A Yasiel Puig SP 8.00 20.00
426B Y.Puig Action SP 10.00 25.00
426C Y.Puig Logo SP 8.00 20.00
427 Jurickson Profar SP 2.00 5.00
428 Madison Bumgarner SP 2.00 5.00
429 Sonny Gray SP 2.00 5.00
430A Justin Verlander SP 2.50 6.00
430B Verlander Action SP 3.00 8.00
431 Jon Lester SP 2.00 5.00
432 Jay Bruce SP 2.00 5.00
433A Derek Jeter SP 10.00 25.00
433B DJeter TB SP 450.00 700.00
433C D.Jeter Action SP 12.00 30.00
434 Pedro Alvarez SP 1.50 4.00
435 Andrelton Simmons SP 1.50 4.00
436 Nelson Cruz SP 2.50 6.00
437A Hanley Ramirez SP 2.00 5.00
437B Hanley Ramirez Action SP 2.50 6.00
438 Mark Teixeira SP 2.00 5.00
439 Jose Fernandez SP 2.50 6.00
440 Tim Lincecum SP 2.00 5.00
441A David Ortiz SP 2.50 6.00
441B David Ortiz Action SP 3.00 8.00
442A Mark Trumbo SP 1.50 4.00
442B M.Trumbo SP ERR 20.00 50.00
443 Rafael Soriano SP 1.50 4.00
444A Yu Darvish SP 2.50 6.00
444B Yu Darvish Action SP 3.00 8.00
444C Yu Darvish Logo SP 8.00 20.00
445 Pablo Sandoval SP 2.00 5.00
446A Wil Myers SP 1.50 4.00
446B W.Myers Action SP 2.00 5.00
447A Dustin Pedroia SP 2.50 6.00
447B Dustin Pedroia Logo SP 8.00 20.00
448 Jason Kipnis SP 2.00 5.00
449 James Shields SP 1.50 4.00
450 David Freese SP 1.50 4.00
451 Matt Moore SP 2.00 5.00
452 Anibal Sanchez SP 1.50 4.00
453 Ian Desmond SP 1.50 4.00
454 Jacoby Ellsbury SP 2.00 5.00
455A Jose Reyes SP 2.00 5.00
455B Jose Reyes Logo SP 6.00 15.00
456 Brandon Phillips SP 1.50 4.00
457A Carlos Gomez SP 1.50 4.00
457B C.Gomez TB SP 50.00 100.00
457C Carlos Gomez Logo SP 5.00 12.00
458A Anthony Rizzo SP 3.00 8.00
458B Anthony Rizzo Logo SP 12.00 30.00
459 Ian Kinsler SP 2.00 5.00
460 Josh Hamilton SP 2.00 5.00
461A Evan Longoria SP 2.00 5.00
461B E.Longoria TB SP 150.00 250.00
461C Evan Longoria Action SP 2.50 6.00
461D Evan Longoria Logo SP 6.00 15.00
462A Jarrod Parker SP 1.50 4.00
462B J.Parker SP ERR 20.00 50.00
463A Paul Goldschmidt SP 2.50 6.00
463B Goldschmidt TB SP 75.00 150.00
463C Paul Goldschmidt Action SP 3.00 8.00
463D Paul Goldschmidt Logo SP 8.00 20.00
464A Joe Mauer SP 2.00 5.00
464B J.Mauer TB SP 150.00 250.00
464C Joe Mauer Logo SP 6.00 15.00
465 Anthony Rendon SP 2.50 6.00
466 Chris Archer SP 1.50 4.00
467A Ryan Braun SP 2.00 5.00
467B R.Braun TB SP 150.00 250.00
468A Carlos Santana SP 2.00 5.00
468B Carlos Santana Logo SP 6.00 15.00
469A Ryan Zimmerman SP 2.00 5.00
469B Zimmerman TB SP 150.00 250.00
470 Stephen Strasburg SP 2.50 6.00
471A Chris Sale SP 2.50 6.00
471B C.Sale TB SP 150.00 250.00
471C Chris Sale Logo SP 8.00 20.00
472A Joey Votto SP 2.50 6.00
472B J.Votto TB SP 150.00 250.00
472C Joey Votto Action SP 3.00 8.00
472D J.Votto SP ERR 50.00 100.00
473 Adrian Gonzalez SP 2.00 5.00
474 Billy Butler SP 1.50 4.00
475A Chris Davis SP 1.50 4.00
475B Chris Davis Action SP 2.00 5.00
475C Chris Davis Logo SP 5.00 12.00
476 Adrian Beltre SP 2.50 6.00
477A Robinson Cano SP 2.00 5.00
477B Robinson Cano Logo SP 6.00 15.00
478 Nolan Arenado SP 12.00 30.00
479 Hunter Pence SP 2.00 5.00
480 Craig Kimbrel SP 2.00 5.00
481 Wilin Rosario SP 1.50 4.00
482A Felix Hernandez SP 2.00 5.00
482B Felix Hernandez Logo SP 6.00 15.00
483 Cole Hamels SP 2.00 5.00
484 B.J. Upton SP 2.00 5.00
485 Derek Holland SP 1.50 4.00
486 Angel Pagan SP 1.50 4.00
487 Troy Tulowitzki SP 2.50 6.00
488 Sergio Romo SP 1.50 4.00
489 Jean Segura SP 2.00 5.00
490A Matt Harvey SP 2.00 5.00
490B Matt Harvey Logo SP 6.00 15.00
491A Yadier Molina SP 3.00 8.00
491B Y.Molina TB SP 200.00 300.00
491C Yadier Molina Logo SP 10.00 25.00
492 Jordan Zimmermann SP 2.00 5.00
493A Max Scherzer SP 2.50 6.00
493B Max Scherzer Action SP 3.00 8.00
494A Carlos Gonzalez SP 2.00 5.00
494B Carlos Gonzalez Logo SP 6.00 15.00
495 Hisashi Iwakuma SP 2.00 5.00
496 Tony Cingrani SP 2.00 5.00
497 Curtis Granderson SP 2.00 5.00
498 Greg Holland SP 1.50 4.00
499 Gerrit Cole SP 2.50 6.00
500A Miguel Cabrera SP 2.50 6.00
500B M.Cabrera TB SP 150.00 250.00
500C M.Cabrera Action SP 3.00 8.00
500D M.Cabrera Logo SP 8.00 20.00
H501 Masahiro Tanaka RC 1.50 4.00
H502 Dee Gordon .40 1.00
H503 James Paxton RC .75 2.00
H504 Edinson Volquez .40 1.00
H505 Jonathan Schoop RC .50 1.25
H506 Enny Romero RC .50 1.25
H507 James Jones RC .50 1.25
H508 Michael Choice RC .50 1.25
H509 Taijuan Walker RC .50 1.25
H510 Jimmy Nelson RC .50 1.25
H511 Tommy La Stella RC .50 1.25
H512 Jackie Bradley Jr. .60 1.50
H513 Martin Perez .50 1.25
H514 Marcus Semien RC 2.50 6.00
H515 Tommy Medica RC .50 1.25
H516 Collin McHugh .40 1.00
H517 Oscar Taveras RC .60 1.50
H518 Daisuke Matsuzaka .50 1.25
H519 Randal Grichuk RC 4.00 10.00
H520 Garin Cecchini RC .50 1.25
H521 Jon Singleton RC .60 1.50
H522 Tyson Ross .40 1.00
H523 Eddie Butler RC .50 1.25
H524 Sean Doolittle .40 1.00
H525 Billy Hamilton RC .60 1.50
H526 Josmil Pinto RC .50 1.25
H527 Gregory Polanco RC .75 2.00
H528 Luis Sardinas RC .50 1.25
H529 Kyle Parker RC .60 1.50
H530 Onelki Garcia RC .50 1.25
H531 John Ryan Murphy RC .50 1.25
H532 Tanner Roark .40 1.00
H533 Andrew Heaney RC .50 1.25
H534 Rougned Odor RC 1.25 3.00
H535 Joe Panik RC .75 2.00
H536 Pat Neshek .40 1.00
H537 Mike Morse .40 1.00
H538 Andre Rienzo RC .50 1.25
H539 Casey McGehee .40 1.00
H540 Michael Pineda .40 1.00
H541 Kevin Kiermaier RC .75 2.00
H542 Nelson Cruz .60 1.50
H543 Yangervis Solarte RC .50 1.25
H544 Jesse Hahn RC .60 1.50
H545 Rafael Montero RC .50 1.25
H546 Mike Olt .40 1.00
H547 Alex Guerrero RC .60 1.50
H548 Chris Owings RC .50 1.25
H549 Jacob deGrom RC 100.00 250.00
H550 Xander Bogaerts RC 1.50 4.00
H551 Erisbel Arruebarrena RC .50 1.25
H552 Nick Castellanos RC 1.50 4.00
H553 Jesse Chavez .40 1.00
H554 Stephen Vogt RC .50 1.25
H555 Ken Giles RC .60 1.50
H556 Scott Kazmir .40 1.00
H557 George Springer RC 2.00 5.00
H558 Mookie Betts RC 100.00 250.00
H559 Christian Vasquez RC UER 1.25 3.00
Last name misspelled
H560 Eric Young Jr. .40 1.00
H561 Kevin Siegrist (RC) .50 1.25
H562 Tom Koehler .40 1.00
H563 Arismendy Alcantara RC .50 1.25
H564 Dellin Betances .50 1.25
H565 Shane Greene RC 1.50 4.00
H566 Kennys Vargas RC .50 1.25
H567 Christian Bethancourt RC .50 1.25
H568 Steve Pearce .40 1.00
H569 Jake Marisnick RC .50 1.25
H570 David Phelps .40 1.00
H571 Kyle Hendricks RC 1.50 4.00
H572 Marcus Stroman RC .75 2.00
H573 Zach Walters RC .50 1.25
H574 Brock Holt .40 1.00
H575 LaTroy Hawkins .40 1.00
H576 Fernando Rodney .40 1.00
H577 Andrew Lambo RC .50 1.25
H578 Wilmer Flores RC .60 1.50
H579 Aaron Sanchez RC .50 1.25
H580 Erik Johnson RC .50 1.25
H581 Jesus Aguilar RC 1.50 4.00
H582 Matt Davidson RC .60 1.50
H583 Yordano Ventura RC .60 1.50
H584 Josh Harrison .40 1.00
H585 Kolten Wong RC .60 1.50
H586 Danny Santana RC .60 1.50
H587 Chris Colabello .40 1.00
H588 Eric Campbell RC .60 1.50
H589 Zach Britton .50 1.25
H590 Jose Ramirez RC 4.00 10.00
H591 Jeff Samardzija .40 1.00
H592 Travis d'Arnaud RC .60 1.50
H593 C.J. Cron RC .50 1.25
H594 Alfredo Simon .40 1.00
H595 Dylan Bundy .50 1.25
H596 Chase Whitley RC .50 1.25
H597 Stefen Romero RC .50 1.25
H598 Yan Gomes .40 1.00
H599 Cody Allen .40 1.00
H600 Jose Abreu RC 4.00 10.00

2014 Topps Heritage Mini

STATED ODDS 1:220 HOBBY
STATED PRINT RUN 100 SER.#'d SETS
20 Cliff Lee 12.00 30.00
160 Andrew McCutchen 15.00 40.00
250 Mike Trout 250.00 350.00
442 Mark Trumbo 12.00 30.00
444 Yu Darvish 12.00 30.00
479 Hunter Pence 15.00 40.00

2014 Topps Heritage Black Border

THC20 Cliff Lee 2.50 6.00
THC30 Hiroki Kuroda 2.00 5.00
THC33 Michael Cuddyer 2.00 5.00
THC43 Carlos Beltran 2.50 6.00
THC49 J.Schoop/X.Bogaerts 6.00 15.00
THC50 Matt Cain 2.50 6.00
THC53 Giancarlo Stanton 3.00 8.00
THC60 Aroldis Chapman 3.00 8.00
THC73 Francisco Liriano 2.00 5.00
THC78 Adam Jones 2.50 6.00
THC84 Hyun-Jin Ryu 2.50 6.00
THC100 Adam Wainwright 2.50 6.00
THC140 Jered Weaver 2.50 6.00
THC145 Edwin Encarnacion 3.00 8.00
THC148 Freddie Freeman 4.00 10.00
THC149 Buster Posey 4.00 10.00
THC150 Manny Machado 3.00 8.00
THC160 Andrew McCutchen 3.00 8.00
THC170 Justin Upton 2.50 6.00
THC190 Allen Craig 2.50 6.00
THC200 Jason Heyward 2.50 6.00
THC205 Starling Marte 2.50 6.00
THC213 Clay Buchholz 2.00 5.00
THC216 Patrick Corbin 2.50 6.00
THC243 N.Castellanos/B.Hamilton 6.00 15.00
THC250 Mike Trout 15.00 40.00
THC260 Zack Greinke 3.00 8.00
THC269 Albert Pujols 4.00 10.00
THC275 Julio Teheran 2.50 6.00
THC284 David Wright 2.50 6.00
THC300 Clayton Kershaw 5.00 12.00
THC303 Prince Fielder 2.50 6.00
THC310 Domonic Brown 2.50 6.00
THC320 Shelby Miller 2.50 6.00
THC330 CC Sabathia 2.50 6.00
THC342 Matt Carpenter 3.00 8.00
THC345 Jose Bautista 2.50 6.00
THC350 Alfonso Soriano 2.50 6.00
THC354 J.Paxton/T.Walker 3.00 8.00
THC370 Matt Kemp 2.50 6.00
THC400 Bryce Harper 5.00 12.00
THC407 Michael Wacha 2.50 6.00
THC425 Yoenis Cespedes 3.00 8.00
THC426 Yasiel Puig 3.00 8.00
THC427 Jurickson Profar 2.50 6.00
THC428 Madison Bumgarner 2.50 6.00
THC430 Justin Verlander 3.00 8.00
THC431 Jon Lester 2.50 6.00
THC432 Jay Bruce 2.50 6.00
THC433 Derek Jeter 8.00 20.00
THC434 Pedro Alvarez 2.00 5.00
THC435 Andrelton Simmons 2.00 5.00
THC436 Nelson Cruz 3.00 8.00
THC437 Hanley Ramirez 2.50 6.00
THC439 Jose Fernandez 3.00 8.00
THC441 David Ortiz 3.00 8.00
THC442 Mark Trumbo 2.00 5.00
THC444 Yu Darvish 3.00 8.00
THC445 Pablo Sandoval 2.50 6.00
THC446 Wil Myers 2.00 5.00
THC447 Dustin Pedroia 3.00 8.00
THC448 Jason Kipnis 2.50 6.00
THC449 James Shields 2.00 5.00
THC451 Matt Moore 2.50 6.00
THC453 Ian Desmond 2.00 5.00
THC454 Jacoby Ellsbury 2.50 6.00
THC456 Brandon Phillips 2.00 5.00
THC457 Carlos Gomez 2.00 5.00
THC458 Anthony Rizzo 4.00 10.00
THC459 Ian Kinsler 2.50 6.00
THC460 Josh Hamilton 2.50 6.00
THC461 Evan Longoria 2.50 6.00
THC463 Paul Goldschmidt 3.00 8.00
THC464 Joe Mauer 2.50 6.00
THC467 Ryan Braun 2.50 6.00
THC468 Carlos Santana 2.50 6.00
THC469 Ryan Zimmerman 2.50 6.00
THC470 Stephen Strasburg 3.00 8.00
THC471 Chris Sale 3.00 8.00
THC472 Joey Votto 3.00 8.00
THC473 Adrian Gonzalez 2.50 6.00
THC474 Billy Butler 2.00 5.00
THC475 Chris Davis 2.00 5.00
THC476 Adrian Beltre 3.00 8.00
THC477 Robinson Cano 2.50 6.00
THC478 Nolan Arenado 15.00 40.00
THC479 Hunter Pence 2.50 6.00
THC480 Craig Kimbrel 2.50 6.00
THC482 Felix Hernandez 2.50 6.00
THC487 Troy Tulowitzki 3.00 8.00
THC489 Jean Segura 2.50 6.00
THC490 Matt Harvey 2.50 6.00
THC491 Yadier Molina 4.00 10.00
THC492 Jordan Zimmermann 2.50 6.00
THC493 Max Scherzer 3.00 8.00
THC494 Carlos Gonzalez 2.50 6.00
THC495 Hisashi Iwakuma 2.50 6.00
THC497 Curtis Granderson 2.50 6.00
THC499 Gerrit Cole 3.00 8.00
THC500 Miguel Cabrera 3.00 8.00

2014 Topps Heritage Blue Border

FOUND IN WALMART PACKS
149 Buster Posey 3.00 8.00
160 Andrew McCutchen 2.50 6.00
170 Justin Upton 2.00 5.00
275 Julio Teheran 2.00 5.00
284 David Wright 2.00 5.00
300 Clayton Kershaw 4.00 10.00
303 Prince Fielder 2.00 5.00
407 Michael Wacha 2.00 5.00
426 Yasiel Puig 2.50 6.00
430 Justin Verlander 2.50 6.00
432 Jay Bruce 2.00 5.00
434 Pedro Alvarez 1.50 4.00
439 Jose Fernandez 2.50 6.00
444 Yu Darvish 2.50 6.00
447 Dustin Pedroia 2.50 6.00
457 Carlos Gomez 1.50 4.00
461 Evan Longoria 2.00 5.00
463 Paul Goldschmidt 2.50 6.00
468 Carlos Santana 2.00 5.00
471 Chris Sale 2.50 6.00
475 Chris Davis 1.50 4.00
477 Robinson Cano 2.00 5.00
482 Felix Hernandez 2.00 5.00
487 Troy Tulowitzki 2.50 6.00
499 Gerrit Cole 2.50 6.00

2014 Topps Heritage Red Border

FOUND IN TARGET PACKS
53 Giancarlo Stanton 1.50 4.00
78 Adam Jones 1.25 3.00
84 Hyun-Jin Ryu 1.25 3.00
140 Jered Weaver 1.25 3.00
150 Manny Machado 1.50 4.00
205 Starling Marte 1.25 3.00
250 Mike Trout 8.00 20.00
260 Zack Greinke 1.50 4.00
310 Domonic Brown 1.25 3.00
320 Shelby Miller 1.25 3.00
330 CC Sabathia 1.25 3.00
400 Bryce Harper 2.50 6.00
431 Jon Lester 1.25 3.00
433 Derek Jeter 4.00 10.00
437 Hanley Ramirez 1.25 3.00
446 Wil Myers 1.00 2.50
458 Anthony Rizzo 2.00 5.00
464 Joe Mauer 1.25 3.00
470 Stephen Strasburg 1.50 4.00
472 Joey Votto 1.50 4.00
480 Craig Kimbrel 1.25 3.00
491 Yadier Molina 2.00 5.00
493 Max Scherzer 1.50 4.00
494 Carlos Gonzalez 1.25 3.00
500 Miguel Cabrera 1.50 4.00

2014 Topps Heritage Advertising Panels

ISSUED AS A BOX TOPPER
1 AL Batting Leaders .40 1.00
Dayan Viciedo/Luke Hochevar
2 AL RBI Leaders 3.00 8.00
Brian McCann/Mike Trout
3 Altuve/Showalter/Dempster .50 1.25
4 Cody Asche .50 1.25
Rick Porcello/Martin Prado
5 Peter Bourjos .40 1.00
Andrew Lambo/Stolmy Pimentel/Chris Rusin
6 Chris Capuano .40 1.00
Chris Perez/Ron Washington
7 Cardinals Dealt Losing Hand .40 1.00
Ross Ohlendorf/Matt Joyce
8 Michael Cuddyer .50 1.25
A.J. Burnett/R.A. Dickey
9 A.J. Ellis .50 1.25
Nate Eovaldi/Nate McLouth
10 Edwin Encarnacion .60 1.50
Buddy Boshers/Matt Shoemaker/Juan Uribe
11 Prince Fielder .50 1.25
Torii Hunter/Jonathan Papelbon
12 Todd Frazier .50 1.25
James Loney/Kolten Wong/Audry Perez
13 Jedd Gyorko 1.00 2.50
Brad Miller/Bryce Harper
14 J.J. Hardy .50 1.25
Trevor Rosenthal/Miguel Gonzalez
15 Jeremy Hefner .60 1.50
Manny Machado/Garrett Richards
16 Jeremy Hellickson .60 1.50
Eric Stults/Giancarlo Stanton
17 Omar Infante .40 1.00
Glen Perkins/Kirk Gibson
18 Mat Latos .50 1.25
Shane Victorino/Neil Walker
19 Mike Moustakas .50 1.25
Cody Ross/David Holmberg/Chad Bettis
20 NL Pitching Leaders .40 1.00
Ryan Doumit/Michael Young
21 Derek Norris .50 1.25
Scooter Gennett/Brad Ziegler
22 Papi Pops Two Hs .40 1.00
Joe Kelly/Stephen Drew
23 Tyler Pastornicky .60 1.50
Matt Holliday/Jason Castro
24 Jhonny Peralta .40 1.00
Edward Mujica/Mike Minor
25 Jarrod Saltalamacchia .40 1.00
Yasmani Grandal/Logan Morrison
26 Johan Santana .50 1.25
Jose Tabata/Patrick Corbin
27 Drew Stubbs .40 1.00
Gordon Beckham/Terry Collins
28 Andres Torres .50 1.25
Alfonso Soriano/Dan Straily
29 Jered Weaver .60 1.50
Taijuan Walker/James Paxton/Marco Estrada
30 Jayson Werth .50 1.25
Devin Mesoraco/Nick Christiani/Tuffy Gosewisch

2014 Topps Heritage Baseball Flashbacks

COMPLETE SET (10) 4.00 10.00
STATED ODDS 1:12 HOBBY
BFA Astrodome .30 .75
BFAK Al Kaline .50 1.25
BFBG Bob Gibson .40 1.00
BFEB Ernie Banks .50 1.25
BFHK Frank Robinson .40 1.00
BFJM Juan Marichal .40 1.00
BFJP Jim Palmer .40 1.00
BFRC Roberto Clemente 1.25 3.00
BFSK Sandy Koufax 1.00 2.50
BFWM Willie Mays 1.00 2.50

2014 Topps Heritage Bazooka

STATED PRINT RUN 25 SER.#'d SETS
65BAM Andrew McCutchen 10.00 25.00
65BBH Bryce Harper 12.00 30.00
65BCD Chris Davis 10.00 25.00
65BCG Carlos Gomez 12.00 30.00
65BCK Clayton Kershaw 8.00 20.00
65BCS CC Sabathia 10.00 25.00
65BDJ Derek Jeter 25.00 60.00
65BDW David Wright 12.00 30.00
65BFH Felix Hernandez 5.00 12.00
65BGC Gerrit Cole 6.00 15.00
65BHJR Hyun-Jin Ryu 5.00 12.00
65BJF Jose Fernandez 6.00 15.00
65BJH Josh Hamilton 5.00 12.00
65BJU Justin Upton 5.00 12.00
65BJV Justin Verlander 6.00 15.00
65BMC Miguel Cabrera 12.00 30.00
65BMH Matt Harvey 8.00 20.00
65BMM Manny Machado 12.00 30.00
65BMT Mike Trout 30.00 80.00
65BPF Prince Fielder 5.00 12.00
65BSM Starling Marte 12.00 30.00
65BWM Wil Myers 4.00 10.00
65BYD Yu Darvish 6.00 15.00
65BYM Yadier Molina 8.00 20.00
65BYP Yasiel Puig 6.00 15.00

2014 Topps Heritage Chrome

STATED ODDS 1:14 HOBBY
STATED PRINT RUN 999 SER.#'d SETS
20 Cliff Lee 1.50 4.00
30 Hiroki Kuroda 1.25 3.00
33 Michael Cuddyer 1.25 3.00
43 Carlos Beltran 1.50 4.00
49 J.Schoop/X.Bogaerts 3.00 8.00
50 Matt Cain 1.50 4.00
53 Giancarlo Stanton 2.00 5.00
60 Aroldis Chapman 2.00 5.00
73 Francisco Liriano 1.25 3.00
78 Adam Jones 1.50 4.00
84 Hyun-Jin Ryu 1.50 4.00
100 Adam Wainwright 1.50 4.00
140 Jered Weaver 1.50 4.00
145 Edwin Encarnacion 2.00 5.00
148 Freddie Freeman 2.50 6.00
149 Buster Posey 2.50 6.00
150 Manny Machado 2.00 5.00
160 Andrew McCutchen 2.00 5.00
170 Justin Upton 1.50 4.00
190 Allen Craig 1.50 4.00
200 Jason Heyward 1.50 4.00
205 Starling Marte 1.50 4.00
213 Clay Buchholz 1.25 3.00
216 Patrick Corbin 1.50 4.00
243 N.Castellanos/B.Hamilton 4.00 10.00
250 Mike Trout 10.00 25.00
260 Zack Greinke 2.00 5.00
269 Albert Pujols 2.50 6.00
275 Julio Teheran 1.50 4.00
284 David Wright 1.50 4.00
300 Clayton Kershaw 3.00 8.00
303 Prince Fielder 1.50 4.00
310 Domonic Brown 1.50 4.00
320 Shelby Miller 1.50 4.00
330 CC Sabathia 1.50 4.00
342 Matt Carpenter 2.00 5.00
345 Jose Bautista 1.50 4.00
350 Alfonso Soriano 1.50 4.00
354 J.Paxton/T.Walker 2.00 5.00
370 Matt Kemp 1.50 4.00
400 Bryce Harper 3.00 8.00
407 Michael Wacha 1.50 4.00
425 Yoenis Cespedes 2.00 5.00
427 Jurickson Profar 1.50 4.00
428 Madison Bumgarner 1.50 4.00
430 Justin Verlander 2.00 5.00
431 Jon Lester 1.50 4.00
432 Jay Bruce 1.50 4.00
433 Derek Jeter 10.00 25.00
434 Pedro Alvarez 1.25 3.00
435 Andrelton Simmons 1.25 3.00
436 Nelson Cruz 2.00 5.00
437 Hanley Ramirez 1.50 4.00
439 Jose Fernandez 2.00 5.00
441 David Ortiz 2.00 5.00
442 Mark Trumbo 1.25 3.00
444 Yu Darvish 2.00 5.00
445 Pablo Sandoval 1.50 4.00
446 Wil Myers 1.25 3.00
447 Dustin Pedroia 2.00 5.00
448 Jason Kipnis 1.50 4.00
449 James Shields 1.25 3.00
451 Matt Moore 1.50 4.00
453 Ian Desmond 1.25 3.00
454 Jacoby Ellsbury 1.50 4.00
456 Brandon Phillips 1.25 3.00
457 Carlos Gomez 1.25 3.00
458 Anthony Rizzo 2.50 6.00
459 Ian Kinsler 1.50 4.00
460 Josh Hamilton 1.50 4.00
461 Evan Longoria 1.50 4.00
463 Paul Goldschmidt 2.00 5.00
464 Joe Mauer 1.50 4.00
467 Ryan Braun 1.50 4.00

468 Carlos Santana 1.50 4.00
469 Ryan Zimmerman 1.50 4.00
470 Stephen Strasburg 2.00 5.00
471 Chris Sale 2.00 5.00
472 Joey Votto 2.00 5.00
473 Adrian Gonzalez 1.50 4.00
474 Billy Butler 1.25 3.00
475 Chris Davis 1.25 3.00
476 Adrian Beltre 2.00 5.00
477 Robinson Cano 1.50 4.00
478 Nolan Arenado 6.00 15.00
479 Hunter Pence 1.50 4.00
480 Craig Kimbrel 1.50 4.00
482 Felix Hernandez 1.50 4.00
487 Troy Tulowitzki 2.00 5.00
489 Jean Segura 1.50 4.00
490 Matt Harvey 1.50 4.00
491 Yadier Molina 2.50 6.00
492 Jordan Zimmermann 1.50 4.00
493 Max Scherzer 2.00 5.00
494 Carlos Gonzalez 1.50 4.00
495 Hisashi Iwakuma 1.50 4.00
497 Curtis Granderson 1.50 4.00
499 Gerrit Cole 2.00 5.00
500 Miguel Cabrera 2.00 5.00

2014 Topps Heritage Chrome Black Refractors

*BLACK REF: 2.5X TO 6X BASIC
STATED ODDS 1:225 HOBBY
STATED PRINT RUN 65 SER.#'d SETS
400 Bryce Harper 50.00 100.00
433 Derek Jeter 150.00 250.00
435 Andrelton Simmons 20.00 50.00
461 Evan Longoria 15.00 40.00
470 Stephen Strasburg 20.00 50.00
490 Matt Harvey 25.00 60.00
500 Miguel Cabrera 30.00 80.00

2014 Topps Heritage Chrome Purple Refractors

*PURPLE: .4X TO 1X BASIC

2014 Topps Heritage Chrome Refractors

*REFRACTORS: .75X TO 2X BASIC
STATED ODDS 1:27 HOBBY
STATED PRINT RUN 565 SER.#'d SETS
433 Derek Jeter 25.00 60.00

2014 Topps Heritage Clubhouse Collection Dual Relics

STATED ODDS 1:4451 HOBBY
STATED PRINT RUN 65 SER.#'d SETS
CCDRBC J.Bench/T.Cingrani 25.00 60.00
CCDRGM B.McCann/E.Gattis 20.00 50.00
CCDRLB E.Longoria/W.Boggs 20.00 50.00
CCDRMA P.Alvarez/A.McCutchen 25.00 60.00
CCDRYS C.Yelich/G.Sheffield 30.00 80.00

2014 Topps Heritage Clubhouse Collection Relic Autographs

STATED ODDS 1:5965 HOBBY
STATED PRINT RUN 25 SER.#'d SETS
EXCHANGE DEADLINE 1/31/2017
CCARAG Anthony Gose 60.00 120.00
CCARAH Aaron Hicks 40.00 80.00
CCARCS Chris Sale EXCH 60.00 120.00
CCARDF David Freese 20.00 50.00
CCAREE E.Encarnacion EXCH 30.00 60.00
CCARJK Jason Kipnis 40.00 80.00
CCARMA Matt Adams 60.00 120.00
CCARMC Miguel Cabrera 300.00 400.00
CCARPG P.Goldschmidt EXCH 75.00 150.00
CCARWR Wilin Rosario 40.00 80.00

2014 Topps Heritage Clubhouse Collection Relics

STATED ODDS 1:35 HOBBY
CCRAJ Adam Jones 3.00 8.00
CCRAM Andrew McCutchen 4.00 10.00
CCRAP Andy Pettitte 3.00 8.00
CCRAW Adam Wainwright 3.00 8.00
CCRBH Bryce Harper 6.00 15.00
CCRBL Brett Lawrie 3.00 8.00
CCRBP Buster Posey 5.00 12.00
CCRBR Bruce Rondon 2.50 6.00
CCRBU B.J. Upton 3.00 8.00
CCRCS Chris Sale 4.00 10.00
CCRDB Domonic Brown 3.00 8.00
CCRDP Dustin Pedroia 4.00 10.00
CCRDS Drew Stubbs 2.50 6.00
CCRFH Felix Hernandez 3.00 8.00
CCRFM Fred McGriff 3.00 8.00
CCRHK Howie Kendrick 2.50 6.00
CCRIN Ivan Nova 3.00 8.00
CCRJA Jose Altuve 3.00 8.00
CCRJB Jose Bautista 3.00 8.00
CCRJBR Jay Bruce 3.00 8.00
CCRJS Jean Segura 3.00 8.00
CCRJT Julio Teheran 3.00 8.00
CCRJV Justin Verlander 4.00 10.00
CCRJW Jayson Werth 3.00 8.00
CCRMJ Matt Joyce 2.50 6.00
CCRMM Mike Moustakas 3.00 8.00
CCRMSC Mike Schmidt 6.00 15.00
CCRMT Mike Trout 30.00 60.00
CCRNF Neftali Feliz 2.50 6.00
CCRNFR Nick Franklin 2.50 6.00
CCRPS Pablo Sandoval 3.00 8.00
CCRRC Robinson Cano 3.00 8.00
CCRRD R.A. Dickey 3.00 8.00
CCRSP Salvador Perez 3.00 8.00
CCRTL Tim Lincecum 3.00 8.00
CCRTT Troy Tulowitzki 4.00 10.00
CCRWB Wade Boggs 3.00 8.00
CCRWR Wilin Rosario 2.50 6.00
CCRYO Yonder Alonso 2.50 6.00
CCRZC Zack Cozart 2.50 6.00

2014 Topps Heritage Clubhouse Collection Relics Gold

*GOLD: .6X TO 1.5X BASIC
STATED ODDS 1:365 HOBBY
STATED PRINT RUN 99 SER.#'d SETS

2014 Topps Heritage Clubhouse Collection Triple Relics

STATED ODDS 1:11,650 HOBBY
STATED PRINT RUN 25 SER.#'d SETS
CCTRCMS Star/Clem/McCut 200.00 300.00
CCTRGGE GregorEaton/Goldsch 90.00 150.00
CCTRHJC Jack/Hend/Cesped 90.00 150.00
CCTRKCF Cabrer/Fielder/Kaline 90.00 150.00
CCTRSMG Glav/Smoltz/Maddux 90.00 150.00

2014 Topps Heritage First Draft

COMPLETE SET (4) 2.00 5.00
STATED ODDS 1:12 HOBBY
65MLBGN Graig Nettles .30 .75
65MLBJB Johnny Bench .50 1.25
65MLBNR Nolan Ryan 1.50 4.00
65MLBJB2 Johnny Bench .50 1.25

2014 Topps Heritage Flashback Relic Autographs

STATED ODDS 1:5965 HOBBY
STATED PRINT RUN 25 SER.#'d SETS
EXCHANGE DEADLINE 1/31/2017
FARAK Al Kaline EXCH 75.00 200.00
FARBW B.Williams EXCH 90.00 150.00
FAREB Ernie Banks 200.00 300.00
FARFR Frank Robinson 75.00 150.00
FARJM J.Marichal EXCH 60.00 120.00
FARLT Luis Tiant 20.00 50.00
FARMW Maury Wills 60.00 120.00
FAROC Orlando Cepeda 25.00 60.00
FARWM Willie Mays EXCH 250.00 400.00

2014 Topps Heritage Framed Stamps

STATED ODDS 1:1885 HOBBY
STATED PRINT RUN 50 SER.#'d SETS
65USAK Al Kaline 20.00 50.00
65USBG Bob Gibson 20.00 50.00
65USEB Ernie Banks 25.00 60.00
65USFR Frank Robinson 20.00 50.00
65USJB Johnny Bench 20.00 50.00
65USJBU Jim Bunning 12.00 30.00
65USJM Juan Marichal 20.00 50.00
65USJP Jim Palmer 20.00 50.00
65USLB Lou Brock 12.00 30.00
65USMW Maury Wills 20.00 50.00
65USOC Orlando Cepeda 20.00 50.00
65USRC Roberto Clemente 50.00 120.00
65USSK Sandy Koufax 30.00 60.00
65USWM Willie Mays 20.00 50.00
65USWS Willie Stargell 20.00 50.00
65USYB Yogi Berra 25.00 60.00

2014 Topps Heritage New Age Performers

COMPLETE SET (20) 8.00 20.00
STATED ODDS 1:8 HOBBY
NAPBH Bryce Harper .75 2.00
NAPCD Chris Davis .30 .75
NAPCG Carlos Gomez .30 .75
NAPCGO Carlos Gonzalez .40 1.00
NAPCK Clayton Kershaw .75 2.00
NAPGS Giancarlo Stanton .50 1.25
NAPHR Hyun-Jin Ryu .40 1.00
NAPJF Jose Fernandez .50 1.25
NAPMC Miguel Cabrera .50 1.25
NAPMH Matt Harvey .40 1.00
NAPMS Max Scherzer .50 1.25
NAPMT Mike Trout 2.50 6.00
NAPMW Michael Wacha .40 1.00
NAPPA Pedro Alvarez .30 .75
NAPPG Paul Goldschmidt .50 1.25
NAPSS Stephen Strasburg .40 1.00
NAPWM Wil Myers .30 .75
NAPXB Xander Bogaerts 1.00 2.50
NAPYD Yu Darvish .50 1.25
NAPYP Yasiel Puig .50 1.25

2014 Topps Heritage News Flashbacks

COMPLETE SET (10) 3.00 8.00
STATED ODDS 1:12 HOBBY
NFAL Aleksei Leonov .30 .75
NFBC Bill Cosby .50 1.25
NFGA Gateway Arch .30 .75
NFJN Joe Namath .60 1.50
NFMA Muhammad Ali 1.00 2.50
NFMX The Autobiography of Malcolm X .30 .75
NFTB The Beatles .50 1.25
NFTRS The Rolling Stones .50 1.25
NFTSOM The Sound of Music .30 .75
NFVRA Voting Rights Act of 1965 .30 .75

2014 Topps Heritage Embossed Box Loaders

STATED ODDS 1:35 HOBBY BOX
AK Al Kaline 15.00 40.00
BG Bob Gibson 12.00 30.00
BH Bryce Harper 30.00 80.00
BJ Bo Jackson 15.00 40.00
CB Craig Biggio 12.00 30.00
CC CC Sabathia 12.00 30.00
CD Chris Davis 10.00 25.00
CK Clayton Kershaw 25.00 60.00
DW David Wright 20.00 50.00
EG Evan Gattis 10.00 25.00
JB Johnny Bench 15.00 40.00
JP Jim Palmer 12.00 30.00
JPA Jarrod Parker 10.00 25.00
KG Kevin Gausman 15.00 40.00
MM Mike Mussina 12.00 30.00
MMA Manny Machado 20.00 50.00
MZ Mike Zunino 10.00 25.00
RH Rickey Henderson 15.00 40.00
TG Tom Glavine 12.00 30.00
YD Yu Darvish 15.00 40.00

2014 Topps Heritage Embossed Box Loaders Relics

STATED ODDS 1:70 HOBBY BOXES
STATED PRINT RUN 25 SER.#'d SETS
AKR Al Kaline 30.00 80.00
BGR Bob Gibson 25.00 60.00
BHR Bryce Harper 50.00 120.00
BJR Bo Jackson 30.00 80.00
CBR Craig Biggio 25.00 60.00
CCR CC Sabathia 25.00 60.00
CDR Chris Davis 20.00 50.00
CKR Clayton Kershaw 50.00 120.00
DWR David Wright 25.00 60.00
JBR Johnny Bench 30.00 80.00
JPAR Jarrod Parker 20.00 50.00
KGR Kevin Gausman 30.00 80.00
MMAR Manny Machado 60.00 150.00
MMR Mike Mussina 25.00 60.00
RHR Rickey Henderson 30.00 80.00
TGR Tom Glavine 25.00 60.00

2014 Topps Heritage Mystery Redemption Autograph

MRAJA Jose Abreu 60.00 150.00

2014 Topps Heritage Real One Autographs

STATED ODDS 1:141 HOBBY
OLBERMANN STATED ODDS 1:15,000 HOBBY
HN CARDS ISSUED IN HN.FACT.SETS
EXCHANGE DEADLINE 1/31/2017
HN EXCH.DEADLINE 10/31/2017
ROAAA Arismendy Alcantara HN 8.00 20.00
ROAAG Alex Guerrero HN 10.00 25.00
ROAAH Andrew Heaney HN 8.00 20.00
ROAAS Aaron Sanchez HN 8.00 20.00
ROABD Bennie Daniels 8.00 20.00
ROABDA Bud Daley 8.00 20.00
ROABH Billy Hamilton HN 12.00 30.00
ROABM Billy Moran 8.00 20.00
ROABP Bill Pleis 8.00 20.00
ROABS Bill Spanswick 8.00 20.00
ROABSC Barney Schultz 8.00 20.00
ROABV Bill Virdon 8.00 20.00
ROACJ Chipper Jones 60.00 120.00
ROACJA Charlie James 8.00 20.00
ROACO Chris Owings HN 12.00 30.00
ROADC Dave Concepcion 15.00 40.00
ROADE Doc Edwards 8.00 20.00
ROADG Dallas Green 8.00 20.00
ROADL Don Larsen 10.00 25.00
ROADLE Don Lee 8.00 20.00
ROADLO Davey Lopes 8.00 20.00
ROADM Don Mattingly 40.00 80.00
ROADST Dave Stenhouse 8.00 20.00
ROADV Dave Vineyard 10.00 25.00
ROADZ Don Zimmer 15.00 40.00
ROAEA Erisbel Arruebarrena HN 12.00 30.00
ROAEB Ernie Banks 75.00 150.00
ROAED Eric Davis 12.00 30.00
ROAEG Evan Gattis 8.00 20.00
ROAER Ed Roebuck 8.00 20.00
ROAFB Frank Baumann 8.00 20.00
ROAFBO Frank Bolling 8.00 20.00
ROAFL Frank Lary 8.00 20.00
ROAFT Frank Thomas 8.00 20.00
ROAGP Gregory Polanco HN 12.00 30.00
ROAGS George Springer HN 30.00 80.00
ROAHA Hank Aaron/65 200.00 300.00
ROAHS Herm Starrette 8.00 20.00
ROAJA Jose Abreu HN 90.00 150.00
ROAJA2 Jose Abreu HN 90.00 150.00
ROAJB Jay Bruce 10.00 25.00
ROAJD Jim Duffalo 8.00 20.00
ROAJD Jacob deGrom HN 400.00 1000.00
ROAJF Jerry Fosnow 8.00 20.00
ROAJM Jake Marisnick HN 8.00 20.00
ROAJN Jimmy Nelson HN 8.00 20.00
ROAJO Jake Odorizzi 8.00 20.00
ROAJP Josmil Pinto HN 8.00 20.00
ROAJPA Joe Panik HN 15.00 40.00
ROAJR Jose Ramirez HN 12.00 30.00
ROAJR Jay Ritchie 8.00 20.00
ROAJRI Jim Rice 15.00 40.00
ROAJRM John Ryan Murphy HN 12.00 30.00
ROAJS Jonathan Schoop HN 15.00 40.00
ROAKG Kevin Gausman 12.00 30.00
ROAKM Ken McBride 8.00 20.00
ROAKO Keith Olbermann 60.00 120.00
ROAKO2 Keith Olbermann 60.00 120.00
ROAKR Ken Retzer 8.00 20.00
ROAKS Kevin Siegrist HN 8.00 20.00
ROAKW Kolten Wong HN 15.00 40.00
ROALB Leo Burke 8.00 20.00
ROALS Luis Sardinas HN 8.00 20.00
ROALY Larry Yellen 8.00 20.00
ROAMA Matt Adams 8.00 20.00
ROAMB Mookie Betts HN 150.00 400.00
ROAMC Michael Choice HN 10.00 25.00
ROAMD Matt Davidson HN 10.00 25.00
ROAMST Marcus Stroman HN 12.00 30.00
ROAMW Maury Wills 12.00 30.00
ROAMWA Michael Wacha 10.00 25.00
ROAMZ Mike Zunino 8.00 20.00
ROANC Nick Castellanos HN 25.00 60.00
ROANG Nomar Garciaparra 25.00 60.00
ROANM Nelson Mathews 8.00 20.00
ROAOT Oscar Taveras HN 10.00 25.00
ROAPO Paul O'Neill 15.00 40.00
ROARP Rafael Palmeiro 10.00 25.00
ROARS Roy Sievers 8.00 20.00
ROATD Travis d'Arnaud HN 10.00 25.00
ROATM Tommy Medica HN 8.00 20.00
ROATW Taijuan Walker HN 10.00 25.00
ROATW Ted Wills 8.00 20.00
ROAWF Wilmer Flores HN 10.00 25.00
ROAWM Willie Mays/65 200.00 400.00
ROAWMY Wil Myers 12.00 30.00
ROAYS Yangervis Solarte HN 15.00 40.00
ROAYV Yordano Ventura HN 15.00 40.00

2014 Topps Heritage Real One Autographs Dual

STATED ODDS 1:3386 HOBBY
EXCHANGE DEADLINE 1/31/2017
RODABL Longoria/Boggs 100.00 175.00
RODABP Bench/Posey EXCH 150.00 300.00
RODAGH Griffey/Harper EXCH 350.00 500.00
RODAMB Marich/Bumg EXCH 75.00 200.00
RODAMF McGrff/Frmn 60.00 150.00
RODAMG Gtts/McCnn EXCH 40.00 80.00
RODARB Brce/Rbnsn EXCH 75.00 150.00
RODARM Mchdo/Rpkn EXCH 250.00 350.00

2014 Topps Heritage Real One Autographs Red Ink

*RED INK: ..6X TO 1.5X BASIC
STATED ODDS 1:372 HOBBY
HN CARDS FOUND IN HIGH NUMBER BOXES
PRINT RUNS B/WN 10-65 COPIES PER
NO HIGH NUMBER PRICING AVAILABLE
EXCHANGE DEADLINE 1/31/2017
ROACJ Chipper Jones 75.00 200.00
ROADM Don Mattingly 100.00 250.00
ROAPO Paul O'Neill 25.00 60.00
ROAWM Willie Mays EXCH 300.00 600.00

2014 Topps Heritage Then and Now

COMPLETE SET (10) 3.00 8.00
STATED ODDS 1:10 HOBBY
TANCC R.Clemente/M.Cabrera 1.25 3.00
TANGW B.Gibson/A.Wainwright .40 1.00
TANKD S.Koufax/Y.Darvish 1.00 2.50
TANKK S.Koufax/C.Kershaw 1.00 2.50
TANMC J.Marichal/B.Colon .40 1.00
TANMD W.Mays/C.Davis 1.00 2.50
TANMS J.Marichal/M.Scherzer .50 1.25
TANMV W.McCovey/J.Votto .50 1.25
TANRD F.Robinson/C.Davis .40 1.00
TANWE M.Wills/J.Ellsbury .40 1.00

2015 Topps Heritage

COMP.SET w/o SPs (425) 30.00 80.00
SP ODDS 1:3 HOBBY
HN SP ODDS 1:3 HOBBY
ACTION SP ODDS 1:24 HOBBY
HN ACTION SP ODDS 1:22 HOBBY
COLOR SWAP SP ODDS 1:140 HOBBY
CLR SWAP HN SP ODDS 1:76 HOBBY
THROWBACK SP ODDS 1:3310 HOBBY
ERROR SP ODDS 1:840 HOBBY
TRADED SP ODDS 1:2310 HOBBY
1A Buster Posey .30 .75
1B Posey Action SP 4.00 10.00
1C Posey Color SP 8.00 20.00
2 Melky Cabrera .15 .40
3 Ned Yost MG .15 .40
4 Danny Duffy .15 .40
5 Ryan Vogelsong .15 .40
6 Zach Britton .20 .50
7 Ian Kennedy .15 .40
8 Asdrubal Cabrera .20 .50
9 Jenrry Mejia .15 .40
10A Julio Teheran .20 .50
10B Teheran Thrwbck SP 75.00 150.00
11 Taylor RC/Pederson RC 1.50 4.00
12 Jean Segura .20 .50
13 Stephen Vogt .20 .50
14 Kyle Lohse .15 .40
15 Roenis Elias .15 .40
16 Anibal Sanchez .15 .40
17 Jason Hammel .20 .50
18 David Freese .15 .40
19 San Francisco Giants .20 .50
20 J.D. Martinez .25 .60
21 Mark Teixeira .20 .50
22 Kolten Wong .20 .50
23 Brad Ziegler .15 .40
24 Wil Myers .20 .50
25A Jose Abreu .25 .60
25B Abreu Action SP 3.00 8.00
25C Abreu Color SP 6.00 15.00
26 Ryan Zimmerman .20 .50
27 Cordier (RC)/Garces RC .40 1.00
28 Jason Castro .15 .40
29 Avisail Garcia .20 .50
30A Brandon Phillips .15 .40
30B B.Phillips ERR SP 12.00 30.00
31 Andrew Susac .15 .40
32 Andrelton Simmons .15 .40
33 Dan Haren .15 .40
34 Bob Melvin MG .15 .40
35 Mike Leake .15 .40
36A Sean Doolittle .15 .40
36B S.Doolittle ERR SP 12.00 30.00
37 John Farrell MG .15 .40
38 B.J. Upton .20 .50
39 Marcus Stroman .20 .50
40 Phil Hughes .15 .40
41 Wilmer Flores .20 .50
42 Jonathon Niese .15 .40
43 Juan Uribe .15 .40
44 Escobar RC/Barnes RC .40 1.00
45 Mookie Betts .50 1.25
46 Jason Vargas .15 .40
47 Jeff Locke .15 .40
48 Jeremy Guthrie .15 .40
49 Spangenberg RC/Liriano RC .40 1.00
50 Jacoby Ellsbury .20 .50
51 Francisco Rodriguez .20 .50
52 M.Trout/M.Cabrera 1.25 3.00
53 Hiroki Kuroda .15 .40
54 Lorenzo Cain .15 .40
55 Justin Turner .25 .60
56 Kris Medlen .20 .50
57 Carlos Ruiz .15 .40
58 Brandon Moss .15 .40
59 Cincinnati Reds .15 .40
60 Matt Holliday .25 .60
61 Russell Martin .15 .40
62 Lance Lynn .15 .40
63 Brett Lawrie .20 .50
64 Kelvin Herrera .15 .40
65 Logan Morrison .15 .40
66 Patrick Corbin .20 .50
67 Goeddel RC/Herrera RC .50 1.25
68A George Springer .20 .50
68B Springer Thrwbck SP 150.00 300.00
69 Angel Pagan .15 .40
70A Yoenis Cespedes .20 .50
70B Y.Cespedes Trade SP 20.00 50.00
71 Mark Buehrle .20 .50
72 Nolan Arenado .40 1.00
73 Collin McHugh .15 .40
74A Jarrod Parker .15 .40
74B J.Parker ERR SP 12.00 30.00
75 Matt Kemp .20 .50
76 Mike Matheny .15 .40
77 Casey Janssen .20 .50
78 Joe Panik .20 .50
79 Emilio Bonifacio .15 .40
80 Cody Asche .20 .50
81 Jake McGee .20 .50
82 Scott Kazmir .15 .40
83 Matt Shoemaker .20 .50
84 Brentz RC/Moya RC .50 1.25
85 Derek Holland .15 .40
86A Norichika Aoki .15 .40
86B Aoki Thrwbck SP 150.00 300.00
87 Torii Hunter .15 .40
88 Butler RC/Rivero RC .40 1.00
89 Eduardo Escobar .15 .40
90A Jonathan Schoop .15 .40
90B Schoop Thrwbck SP 150.00 300.00
91 Nick Markakis .20 .50
92 New York Yankees .20 .50
93 Wilin Rosario .15 .40
94 Ken Giles .15 .40
95 Scooter Gennett .20 .50
96 Tim Lincecum .20 .50
97 Wade Davis .15 .40
98 Clay Buchholz .15 .40
99 M.Trout/A.Pujols 1.25 3.00
100A Clayton Kershaw .40 1.00
100B Kershaw Action SP 5.00 12.00
100C Kershaw Color SP 10.00 25.00
101 Bruce Bochy .15 .40
102 Tim Hudson .20 .50
103 Drew Storen .15 .40
104 Miguel Montero .15 .40
105 Marcell Ozuna .25 .60
106 Ender Inciarte RC .40 1.00
107 McCann RC/Ryan RC .60 1.50
108 James Loney .15 .40
109 Didi Gregorius .20 .50
110A Anthony Rizzo .30 .75
110B Rizzo Thrwbck SP 150.00 400.00
111 Garin Cecchini .15 .40
112 Jeremy Hellickson .15 .40
113 Jake Peavy .15 .40
114 Josh Reddick .15 .40
115 Steve Pearce .25 .60
116 Don Mattingly .50 1.25
117 Matt Joyce .15 .40
118 Jonathan Papelbon .20 .50
119 Trevor Rosenthal .20 .50
120 Brian Dozier .20 .50
121 Kevin Kiermaier .20 .50
122 John Danks .15 .40
123 Holdzkom RC/Alvarez RC .40 1.00
124 Yovani Gallardo .15 .40
125 Jon Jay .15 .40
126A Chris Tillman .15 .40
126B C.Tillman ERR SP 12.00 30.00
127 Chafin RC/Lamb RC .60 1.50
128 Juan Perez .15 .40
129 Alex Avila .20 .50
130 Evan Gattis .15 .40
131 Los Angeles Angels .15 .40
132 Travis Ishikawa .15 .40
133 Mike Minor .15 .40
134 Yan Gomes .15 .40
135 Conor Gillaspie .20 .50
136 Jose Iglesias .20 .50
137 Domonic Brown .20 .50
138 Tony Gwynn Jr. .15 .40
139 Soler RC/Baez RC 3.00 8.00
140 Aroldis Chapman .25 .60
141 Dillon Gee .15 .40
142 Jake Petricka .15 .40
143 Joe Nathan .15 .40
144 Aaron Hill .15 .40
145 Ben Zobrist .20 .50
146 Rodriguez RC/Bonilla RC .40 1.00
147 Lloyd McClendon MG .15 .40
148 Cody Allen .15 .40
149 John Jaso .15 .40
150 Michael Brantley .20 .50
151 Andre Ethier .20 .50
152 Joe Kelly .15 .40
153 Tyler Clippard .15 .40
154 Chris Johnson .15 .40
155 Michael Cuddyer .15 .40
156 S.Castro/J.Baez 1.25 3.00
157 Francisco Liriano .15 .40
158 Trevor Cahill .15 .40
159 Joaquin Benoit .15 .40
160 Michael Pineda .15 .40
161 Adeiny Hechavarria .15 .40
162 Brad Miller .20 .50
163 Dexter Fowler .20 .50
164 Rogers RC/Szczur RC .50 1.25
165 Kennys Vargas .15 .40
166 Jhonny Peralta .15 .40
167 Bud Norris .15 .40
168 Jarred Cosart .15 .40
169 Brandon McCarthy .15 .40
170 Chase Utley .20 .50
171 A.J. Ellis .15 .40
172 New York Mets .20 .50
173 Trevor Plouffe .15 .40
174 Neftali Feliz .15 .40
175A Josh Donaldson .20 .50
175B J.Donaldson Trade SP 20.00 50.00
176 Adam Eaton .15 .40
177 Drew Hutchison .15 .40
178 Jake Odorizzi .15 .40
179 Tuivailala RC/Scruggs RC .40 1.00
180 Jay Bruce .20 .50
181 Gio Gonzalez .20 .50
182 Chris Owings .15 .40
183 Terry Francona .20 .50
184 Yasmani Grandal .15 .40
185 Bartolo Colon .15 .40
186 Trevor Bauer .30 .75
187 Brad Ausmus .15 .40
188 Brandon Crawford .20 .50
189 Casey McGehee .15 .40
190 Oswaldo Arcia .15 .40
191 Carlos Carrasco .15 .40
192A Kole Calhoun .15 .40
192B K.Calhoun ERR SP 12.00 30.00
193 Chris Iannetta .15 .40
194 Washington Nationals .15 .40
195 Edinson Volquez .15 .40
196 Matt Moore .20 .50
197 Mark Trumbo .15 .40
198 Derek Norris .15 .40
199 Mrte/Hrrsn/McCtchn .25 .60
200A Freddie Freeman .30 .75
200B Freddie Freeman Color SP 8.00 20.00
201A Jason Heyward .20 .50
201B J.Heyward Trade SP 20.00 50.00
202 Martin Perez .20 .50
203 Jed Lowrie .15 .40
204 Chicago Cubs .20 .50
205 Jorge De La Rosa .15 .40
206 Jarrod Dyson .15 .40
207 Chase Headley .15 .40
208 Devin Mesoraco .15 .40
209 Farmer RC/Lobstein RC .40 1.00
210 Neil Walker .15 .40
211 C.J. Cron .15 .40
212A Matt Carpenter .25 .60
212B Carpenter Thrwbck SP 250.00 400.00
213 Joakim Soria .15 .40
214 Allen Craig .15 .40
215 Mrn/McCtchn/Hrrsn .25 .60
216 Brantley/Altuve/Martinez .20 .50
217 Duda/Rizzo/Stanton .30 .75
218 Carter/Abreu/Cruz .25 .60
219 Upton/Stanton/Gonzalez .25 .60
220 Cruz/Cabrera/Trout 1.25 3.00
221 Cto/Wnwrght/Krshw .40 1.00
222 Kluber/Sale/Hernandez .25 .60
223 Wnwight/Krshw/Cto .40 1.00
224 Scherzer/Weaver/Kluber .25 .60
225 Krshw/Cto/Strsbrg .40 1.00
226 Hernandez/Scherzer/Kluber/Price .25 .60
227 Austin Jackson .15 .40
228 Yonder Alonso .15 .40
229 Buck Showalter MG .15 .40
230 Ben Revere .15 .40
231 Brock Holt .15 .40
232 Martin Prado .15 .40
233 Patton RC/Jokisch RC .40 1.00
234 Pirela RC/Mitchell RC .40 1.00
235 Kevin Gausman .25 .60
236 Ervin Santana .15 .40
237 Dustin Ackley .15 .40
238 Los Angeles Dodgers .20 .50
239 LaTroy Hawkins .15 .40
240 Kurt Suzuki .15 .40
241 Ivan Nova .20 .50
242 Kendrys Morales .15 .40
243 Pablo Sandoval .20 .50
244 Tropeano RC/Foltynewicz RC .40 1.00
245 Matt Adams .15 .40
246 Kyle Gibson .20 .50
247 A.J. Pollock .20 .50
248 Wade Miley .15 .40
249 Mike Scioscia .15 .40
250A Johnny Cueto .20 .50
250B Johnny Cueto Color SP 5.00 12.00
251 David Peralta .15 .40
252 Chase Anderson .15 .40
253 Arismendy Alcantara .15 .40
254 Franco RC/Gonzalez RC .50 1.25
255 Drew Stubbs .15 .40
256 Starling Marte .20 .50
257 Danny Salazar .20 .50
258 Chris Archer .15 .40
259 Boston Red Sox .20 .50
260A Madison Bumgarner .20 .50
260B Bumgarner Thrwbck SP 150.00 300.00
260C Bmgrnr Action SP 2.50 6.00
261 Mark Melancon .15 .40
262 Huston Street .15 .40
263 Randal Grichuk .15 .40
264 May RC/Achter RC .40 1.00
265 Marlon Byrd .15 .40
266A Lonnie Chisenhall .15 .40
266B L.Chisenhall ERR SP 12.00 30.00
267 Santiago Casilla .15 .40
268A Nick Castellanos .25 .60
268B Castellanos Thrwbck SP 75.00 150.00
269 Bryan Price .15 .40
270 Hyun-Jin Ryu .20 .50
271 J.J. Hardy .15 .40
272 Wei-Yin Chen .15 .40
273 C.Kershaw/A.Wainwright .40 1.00
274 Hector Rondon .15 .40
275 Yadier Molina .30 .75
276 Addison Reed .15 .40
277 Josh Collmenter .15 .40
278 Mike Morse .15 .40
279 John Gibbons .15 .40
280 Howie Kendrick .15 .40
281 Mike Napoli .15 .40
282 Tanner Roark .15 .40
283 Daniel Hudson .15 .40
284 Nathan Eovaldi .20 .50
285 Omar Infante .15 .40
286 Colby Lewis .15 .40
287 R.A. Dickey .20 .50
288 Mercedes RC/Garcia RC .40 1.00
289 Will Middlebrooks .15 .40
290 Luis Valbuena .15 .40
291 John Lackey .20 .50
292 Taijuan Walker .15 .40
293 Rick Porcello .20 .50
294 J.A. Happ .20 .50
295 Jayson Werth .20 .50
296 Joe Girardi .20 .50
297 Colby Rasmus .20 .50
298 Carlos Martinez .20 .50
299 Justin Morneau .20 .50
300A Andrew McCutchen .25 .60
300B A.McCutchen Action SP 3.00 8.00
300C A.McCutchen Color SP 6.00 15.00
301 Erick Aybar .15 .40
302 Miguel Gonzalez .15 .40
303 Cleveland Indians .15 .40
304 Yusmeiro Petit .15 .40
305 Chris Young .15 .40
306 Williams RC/Ynoa RC .40 1.00
307 Alfredo Simon .15 .40
308 Salvador Perez .20 .50
309 Dioner Navarro .15 .40
310A Adam Jones .20 .50
310B Adam Jones Action SP 2.50 6.00
310C Adam Jones Color SP 5.00 12.00
311 Corcino RC/Rodriguez RC .40 1.00
312 Jon Singleton .20 .50
313 Gregor Blanco .15 .40
314 Alex Rios .20 .50
315 Koji Uehara .15 .40
316 Hector Santiago .15 .40
317 Tommy La Stella .15 .40
318 Clint Hurdle .15 .40
319 Mike Zunino .15 .40
320 Michael Wacha .20 .50
321 Aramis Ramirez .15 .40
322 Tsuyoshi Wada .15 .40
323 Andrew Cashner .15 .40
324 Alexei Ramirez .20 .50
325A Michael Bourn .15 .40
325B Bourn Thrwbck SP 125.00 300.00
326 Atlanta Braves .15 .40
327 Elvis Andrus .20 .50
328 Denard Span .15 .40
329 Michael Saunders .20 .50
330 Carl Crawford .20 .50
331A Henderson Alvarez .15 .40
331B Alvarez Thrwbck SP 125.00 300.00
332 Brian McCann .20 .50
333 Pompey RC/Norris RC .50 1.25
334 Alex Wood .15 .40
335 Charlie Blackmon .25 .60
336 Fernando Rodney .15 .40
337 Billy Butler .15 .40
338 Pat Neshek .15 .40
339 Alcides Escobar .20 .50
340 Garrett Richards .20 .50
341 Terry Collins .15 .40
342 Tyler Matzek .15 .40
343 Cliff Lee .20 .50
344 Jedd Gyorko .15 .40
345 Scott Van Slyke .15 .40
346 Jurickson Profar .20 .50
347 Danny Santana .15 .40
348 Baltimore Orioles .15 .40
349 Dallas Keuchel .20 .50
350A Masahiro Tanaka .20 .50
350B Tanaka Action SP 2.50 6.00
350C Tanaka Color SP 5.00 12.00
351 Aaron Sanchez .20 .50
352 Seth Smith .15 .40
353 CC Sabathia .20 .50
354 James Paxton .20 .50
355 David Robertson .20 .50
356 Rndo RC/Cstllo RC .50 1.25
357 Khris Davis .25 .60
358 Shane Greene .15 .40
359 Steve Cishek .15 .40
360 Daniel Murphy .20 .50
361 Zack Wheeler .20 .50
362 Carlos Beltran .20 .50
363 Bud Black .15 .40
364 Ryan Howard .20 .50
365A Brett Gardner .20 .50
365B B.Gardner ERR SP 15.00 40.00
366 Alex Cobb .15 .40
367 Kyle Hendricks .25 .60
368 Chris Coghlan .15 .40
369 Brandon Belt .20 .50
370 Zack Cozart .15 .40
371 Homer Bailey .15 .40
372 Juan Lagares .15 .40
373 Brown RC/Strickland RC .40 1.00
374 Jimmy Rollins .20 .50
375 Josh Harrison .15 .40
376 Wily Peralta .15 .40
377 Nick Swisher .20 .50
378 Ricky Nolasco .15 .40
379 St. Louis Cardinals .20 .50
380 Daniel Nava .15 .40
381 Eric Hosmer .20 .50
382 Mat Latos .20 .50
383 Mike Moustakas .20 .50
384 Jake Arrieta .20 .50
385 Wilson Ramos .15 .40
386 Matt Williams .15 .40
387A Shelby Miller .20 .50
387B S.Miller Trade SP 20.00 50.00
388 Dellin Betances .20 .50
389A Shin-Soo Choo .20 .50
389B Choo Thrwbck SP 125.00 300.00
390 Chris Davis .15 .40
391 Christian Vazquez .20 .50
392 Frias RC/Graveman RC .60 1.50
393 Tyson Ross .15 .40
394 Pedro Alvarez .15 .40
395 Lucas Duda .20 .50
396 Jose Quintana .15 .40
397 Kyle Kendrick .15 .40
398 Travis Wood .15 .40
399 Tony Watson .15 .40
400A Joe Mauer .20 .50
400B Mauer Thrwbck SP 125.00 300.00
401 Neris RC/Heston RC .40 1.00
402 Dayan Viciedo .15 .40
403 Adam Lind .20 .50
404 Pittsburgh Pirates .20 .50
405 C.J. Wilson .15 .40
406 Tom Koehler .15 .40
407 Scott Feldman .15 .40
408 Coco Crisp .15 .40
409 Jarrod Saltalamacchia .15 .40
410 Rajai Davis .15 .40
411 Ryne Sandberg MG .50 1.25
412 Rougned Odor .20 .50
413 Travis d'Arnaud .20 .50
414 Alex Rodriguez .30 .75
415 David Murphy .15 .40
416 Glen Perkins .15 .40
417 O'Malley RC/Diaz RC .15 .40
418 Matt Garza .15 .40
419 Vance Worley .15 .40
420 Matt Cain .20 .50
421 Gerardo Parra .15 .40
422 Curtis Granderson .20 .50
423 Matt den Dekker .15 .40
424 Finnegan RC/Gore RC .40 1.00
425 Gerrit Cole .25 .60
426A Giancarlo Stanton SP 2.50 6.00
426B Giancarlo Stanton Action SP 3.00 8.00
426C Giancarlo Stanton Color SP 6.00 15.00
427 Xander Bogaerts SP 2.50 6.00
428A Evan Longoria SP 2.00 5.00
428B Evan Longoria Action SP 2.50 6.00
428C Evan Longoria Color SP 5.00 12.00
429 Jacob deGrom SP 5.00 12.00
430 Prince Fielder SP 2.00 5.00
431 Billy Hamilton SP 2.00 5.00
432 Adam LaRoche SP 1.50 4.00
433 Jered Weaver SP 2.00 5.00
434 Todd Frazier SP 1.50 4.00
435 Gregory Polanco SP 2.00 5.00
436A Justin Upton SP 2.00 5.00
436B Justin Upton Color SP 5.00 12.00
437 Josh Hamilton SP 2.00 5.00
438 Hanley Ramirez SP 2.00 5.00
439 Carlos Gonzalez SP 2.00 5.00
440A Bryce Harper SP 4.00 10.00
440B Harper Action SP 5.00 12.00
440C Harper Color SP 10.00 25.00
441 Dee Gordon SP 1.50 4.00
442A Robinson Cano SP 2.00 5.00
442B Cano Thrwbck SP 100.00 200.00
442C Robinson Cano Color SP 5.00 12.00
443 Kenley Jansen SP 2.00 5.00
444A Jose Bautista SP 2.00 5.00

444B Jose Bautista Action SP 2.50 6.00
444C Jose Bautista Color SP 5.00 12.00
445A Jonathan Lucroy SP 2.00 5.00
445B Jonathan Lucroy Color SP 5.00 12.00
446 Adrian Beltre SP 2.50 6.00
447A Chris Sale SP 2.50 6.00
447B Chris Sale Action SP 3.00 8.00
447C Chris Sale Color SP 6.00 15.00
447D C.Sale ERR SP 40.00 100.00
448 Carlos Santana SP 2.00 5.00
449 Matt Harvey SP 2.00 5.00
450A Yasiel Puig SP 2.50 6.00
450B Puig Action SP 3.00 8.00
451 Joey Votto SP 2.50 6.00
452 Jordan Zimmermann SP 2.00 5.00
453A Troy Tulowitzki SP 2.50 6.00
453B Troy Tulowitzki Color SP 6.00 15.00
454 Manny Machado SP 2.50 6.00
455A Jose Altuve SP 2.00 5.00
455B Altuve Thrwbck SP 125.00 300.00
455C Jose Altuve Action SP 2.50 6.00
455D Jose Altuve Color SP 5.00 12.00
456 Doug Fister SP 1.50 4.00
457 Ian Kinsler SP 2.00 5.00
458 Jon Lester SP 2.00 5.00
459A David Wright SP 2.00 5.00
459B David Wright Color SP 5.00 12.00
460 James Shields SP 1.50 4.00
461 Anthony Rendon SP 2.50 6.00
462A Felix Hernandez SP 2.00 5.00
462B Felix Hernandez Action SP 2.50 6.00
462C Felix Hernandez Color SP 5.00 12.00
463 Jose Fernandez SP 2.50 6.00
464 Jose Reyes SP 2.00 5.00
465 David Price SP 2.00 5.00
466 Corey Dickerson SP 1.50 4.00
467A Paul Goldschmidt SP 2.50 6.00
467B Paul Goldschmidt Action SP 3.00 8.00
468 Zack Greinke SP 2.50 6.00
469 Max Scherzer SP 2.50 6.00
470 Nelson Cruz SP 2.50 6.00
471A Alex Gordon SP 2.00 5.00
471B Gordon Thrwbck SP 125.00 300.00
472A Craig Kimbrel SP 2.00 5.00
472B Craig Kimbrel Action SP 2.50 6.00
473A Adrian Gonzalez SP 2.00 5.00
473B Adrian Gonzalez Action SP 2.50 6.00
474 Ryan Braun SP 2.00 5.00
475A Miguel Cabrera SP 2.50 6.00
475B Cabrera Thrwbck SP 150.00 300.00
475C Cabrera Action SP 3.00 8.00
475D Cabrera Color SP 6.00 15.00
476 Greg Holland SP 1.50 4.00
477 Ian Desmond SP 1.50 4.00
478 Sonny Gray SP 2.00 5.00
479 Yordano Ventura SP 2.00 5.00
480A David Ortiz SP 2.50 6.00
480B David Ortiz Action SP 3.00 8.00
480C David Ortiz Color SP 6.00 15.00
481 Hisashi Iwakuma SP 2.00 5.00
482 Carlos Gomez SP 1.50 4.00
483A Adam Wainwright SP 2.00 5.00
483B Adam Wainwright Action SP 2.50 6.00
484A Corey Kluber SP 2.00 5.00
484B Corey Kluber Color SP 5.00 12.00
485 Chris Carter SP 1.50 4.00
486 Christian Yelich SP 3.00 8.00
487 Edwin Encarnacion SP 2.50 6.00
488 Hunter Pence SP 2.00 5.00
489 Jason Kipnis SP 2.00 5.00
490 Cole Hamels SP 2.00 5.00
491A Victor Martinez SP 2.00 5.00
491B Martinez Thrwbck SP 75.00 150.00
491C Victor Martinez Action SP 2.50 6.00
492A Jeff Samardzija SP 1.50 4.00
492B Jeff Samardzija Color SP 4.00 10.00
493 Kyle Seager SP 1.50 4.00
494A Starlin Castro SP 1.50 4.00
494B Castro Thrwbck SP 125.00 300.00
495 Justin Verlander SP 2.50 6.00
496 Albert Pujols SP 3.00 8.00
497A Yu Darvish SP 2.50 6.00
497B Darvish Thrwbck SP 125.00 300.00
497C Yu Darvish Action SP 3.00 8.00
498A Stephen Strasburg SP 2.50 6.00
498B Stephen Strasburg Action SP 3.00 8.00
499 Dustin Pedroia SP 2.50 6.00
500A Mike Trout SP 6.00 15.00
500B Trout Thrwbck SP 500.00 800.00
500C Trout Action SP 30.00 80.00
500D Trout Color SP 30.00 80.00
501 Christian Walker RC .75 2.00
502 Brett Cecil .15 .40
503 Ryan Rua RC .40 1.00
504 Ike Davis .15 .40
505 Jesse Chavez .15 .40
506 David Buchanan .15 .40
507 Chi Chi Gonzalez RC .60 1.50
508 Angel Nesbitt RC .40 1.00
509 Casey McGehee .15 .40
510 Justin Nicolino RC .40 1.00
511 Nick Ahmed .15 .40
512 Ruben Tejada .15 .40
513 Brad Boxberger .15 .40
514 Grant Balfour .15 .40
515 Zach McAllister .15 .40
516 Vincent Velasquez RC .60 1.50
517 Colby Rasmus .20 .50
518 Jason Marquis .15 .40
519 Cameron Maybin .15 .40
520 A.J. Burnett .15 .40
521 Shane Greene .15 .40
522 Anthony Ranaudo RC .40 1.00
523 Seth Smith .15 .40
524A Alex Rios .20 .50
524B Alex Rios Color SP 5.00 12.00
525 Jimmy Paredes .15 .40
526 Jordan Lyles .15 .40
527 Eduardo Rodriguez RC .40 1.00
528 Taylor Featherston RC .40 1.00
529 Rickie Weeks .15 .40
530 Norichika Aoki .15 .40
531 Mike Aviles .15 .40
532 Daniel Descalso .15 .40
533 Logan Forsythe .15 .40
534 T.J. House .15 .40
535 Dan Uggla .15 .40
536 Jose Urena RC .40 1.00
537 Anthony Gose .15 .40
538 Mike Fiers .15 .40
539 Matt Joyce .15 .40
540 Rafael Betancourt .15 .40
541 John Ryan Murphy .15 .40
542 Brayan Pena .15 .40
543 Tyler Clippard .15 .40
544 Yangervis Solarte .15 .40
545 Asher Wojciechowski RC .40 1.00
546 Will Venable .15 .40
547 J.R. Graham RC .40 1.00
548 Jacob Lindgren RC .50 1.25
549 David Ross .15 .40
550 Sergio Romo .15 .40
551 Grady Sizemore .20 .50
552 Aaron Harang .15 .40
553 Carlos Perez RC .40 1.00
554 Desmond Jennings .20 .50
555 James Shields .15 .40
556 A.J. Pierzynski .15 .40
557 Danny Muno RC .40 1.00
558 Carlos Sanchez .15 .40
559 Joba Chamberlain .15 .40
560 Pat Venditte RC .40 1.00
561 David Phelps .15 .40
562 Jack Leathersich RC .40 1.00
563A Carlos Correa RC 2.00 5.00
563B Correa Action SP 10.00 25.00
563C Correa Color SP 20.00 50.00
564 Delmon Young .20 .50
565 Jordy Mercer .15 .40
566 Yunel Escobar .15 .40
567 Tommy Pham RC .50 1.25
568 Mikie Mahtook RC .40 1.00
569 Jeurys Familia .20 .50
570 Dixon Machado RC .50 1.25
571 Odrisamer Despaigne .15 .40
572 Jonny Gomes .15 .40
573 Ryan Madson .15 .40
574 Sean Rodriguez .15 .40
575A Nathan Eovaldi .20 .50
575B Nathan Eovaldi Color SP 5.00 12.00
576 Tim Beckham .20 .50
577 Tommy Milone .15 .40
578 Ryan Flaherty .15 .40
579 Garrett Jones .15 .40
580 Bobby Parnell .15 .40
581 Chris Capuano .15 .40
582 Joe Smith .15 .40
583 Mitch Moreland .15 .40
584 Shawn Tolleson RC .40 1.00
585 Yasmani Grandal .15 .40
586 Billy Burns RC .40 1.00
587 Jason Grilli .15 .40
588 Jerome Williams .15 .40
589 Mason Williams RC .50 1.25
590 Taylor Jungmann RC .40 1.00
591A Roberto Osuna RC .40 1.00
591B Roberto Osuna Color SP 4.00 10.00
592 Kevin Plawecki RC .40 1.00
593 Matt Wisler RC .40 1.00
594 Gordon Beckham .15 .40
595 Trevor Cahill .15 .40
596 Freddy Galvis .15 .40
597 Justin Masterson .15 .40
598 Travis Snider .15 .40
599A Archie Bradley RC .40 1.00
599B Archie Bradley Action SP 2.00 5.00
599C Archie Bradley Color SP 4.00 10.00
600 Sean Gilmartin RC .40 1.00
601 Michael Blazek .15 .40
602 Justin Maxwell .15 .40
603 Martin Prado .15 .40
604 Pedro Strop .15 .40
605 Lance McCullers Jr. RC .40 1.00
606 Alex Meyer RC .40 1.00
607 Jordan Schafer .15 .40
608 Paulo Orlando RC .60 1.50
609 Leonys Martin .15 .40
610 Everth Cabrera .15 .40
611 Jed Lowrie .15 .40
612 Hansel Robles RC .40 1.00
613 Tyler Olson RC .40 1.00
614 Tyler Moore .15 .40
615 Nick Franklin .15 .40
616 Justin Bour RC .60 1.50
617A Micah Johnson RC .40 1.00
617B Micah Johnson Color SP 4.00 10.00
618A Noah Syndergaard RC .75 2.00
618B Sndrgrd Action SP 4.00 10.00
618C Sndrgrd Color SP 8.00 20.00
619 Melvin Upton Jr. .20 .50
620 Caleb Joseph RC .40 1.00
621 Wil Myers .20 .50
622 Will Middlebrooks .15 .40
623 Sam Fuld .15 .40
624 Johnny Giavotella .15 .40
625 Kelly Johnson .15 .40
626 Mike Olt .15 .40
627 Tony Cingrani .20 .50
628 Matt den Dekker .15 .40
629 Shane Victorino .20 .50
630 Steven Matz RC .50 1.25
631 Jimmy Nelson .15 .40
632 Marlon Byrd .15 .40
633 A.J. Cole RC .40 1.00
634 Emilio Bonifacio .15 .40
635 Drew Pomeranz .20 .50
636 Eric Sogard .15 .40
637 Brandon Morrow .15 .40
638 Eddie Butler .15 .40
639 Corey Hart .15 .40
640 Steven Souza Jr. .20 .50
641 DJ LeMahieu .25 .60
642 Mark Canha RC .60 1.50
643 Alex Torres .15 .40
644 Rene Rivera .15 .40
645 Ubaldo Jimenez .15 .40
646 A.J. Ramos .15 .40
647A Joey Gallo RC .75 2.00
647B Gallo Action SP 4.00 10.00
648 Leonel Campos RC .40 1.00
649 Nick Hundley .15 .40
650 Anthony DeSclafani .15 .40
651 Kyle Blanks .15 .40
652 Eric Young Jr. .15 .40
653 Nate Karns .15 .40
654 Christian Bethancourt .15 .40
655 Mark Reynolds .15 .40
656 Mike Pelfrey .15 .40
657 Stephen Drew .15 .40
658 Nick Martinez .15 .40
659 J.T. Realmuto RC 2.50 6.00
660 Michael Lorenzen RC .40 1.00
661 Roberto Hernandez .15 .40
662 Marcus Semien .25 .60
663 Robinson Chirinos .15 .40
664 Tyler Flowers .15 .40
665 Justin Smoak .15 .40
666 Odubel Herrera RC .60 1.50
667 Gregorio Petit .15 .40
668 Evan Scribner .15 .40
669 Luke Gregerson .15 .40
670 Austin Adams .15 .40
671 Adam Warren .15 .40
672 Tuffy Gosewisch .15 .40
673 Collin Cowgill .15 .40
674 Eddie Rosario RC .75 2.00
675 Jace Peterson .15 .40
676 Williams Perez RC .50 1.25
677 Ervin Santana .15 .40
678 Tim Cooney RC .40 1.00
679 Luis Valbuena .15 .40
680 Alexi Amarista .15 .40
681 Kevin Pillar .15 .40
682 Wilmer Difo RC .40 1.00
683 Eric Campbell .20 .50
684 Jose Ramirez .20 .50
685 Brandon Guyer .15 .40
686 David DeJesus .15 .40
687 Asdrubal Cabrera .20 .50
688 Rubby De La Rosa .15 .40
689 Ross Detwiler .15 .40
690 Jake Marisnick .15 .40
691 Slade Heathcott RC .50 1.25
692 Marco Gonzales RC .50 1.25
693 Francisco Cervelli .15 .40
694 Preston Tucker RC .60 1.50
695 Alex Guerrero .20 .50
696 Brett Anderson .15 .40
697 Orlando Calixte RC .40 1.00
698 John Jaso .15 .40
699 Delino DeShields Jr. RC .40 1.00
700 Casey Janssen .20 .50
701A Matt Kemp SP 1.25 3.00
701B Matt Kemp Color SP 5.00 12.00
702A Justin Upton SP 1.25 3.00
702B Justin Upton Action SP 2.50 6.00
702C Justin Upton Color SP 5.00 12.00
703 Edinson Volquez SP 1.00 2.50
704 Ben Zobrist SP 1.25 3.00
705A Yasmany Tomas SP RC 1.25 3.00
705B Tomas Action SP 2.50 6.00
705C Tomas Color SP 5.00 12.00
706A Ichiro Suzuki SP 2.00 5.00
706B Suzuki Action SP 4.00 10.00
706C Suzuki Color SP 8.00 20.00
707A Evan Gattis SP 1.00 2.50
707B Evan Gattis Color SP 4.00 10.00
708A Max Scherzer SP 1.50 4.00
708B Max Scherzer Action SP 3.00 8.00
708C Max Scherzer Color SP 6.00 15.00
709 Jesse Hahn SP 1.00 2.50
710A Carlos Rodon SP RC 2.50 6.00
710B Rodon Action SP 5.00 12.00
710C Rodon Color SP 10.00 25.00
711 Andrew Miller SP 1.25 3.00
712A Blake Swihart SP RC 1.25 3.00
712B Blake Swihart Action SP 2.50 6.00
712C Blake Swihart Color SP 5.00 12.00
713A Raisel Iglesias SP RC 1.25 3.00
713B Raisel Iglesias Color SP 5.00 12.00
714A Jung Ho Kang SP RC 1.00 2.50
714B Kang Color SP 4.00 10.00
715A Dexter Fowler SP 1.25 3.00
715B Dexter Fowler Color SP 5.00 12.00
716A Devon Travis SP RC 1.00 2.50
716B Devon Travis Color SP 4.00 10.00
717A Francisco Lindor SP RC 20.00 50.00
717B Lindor Action SP 15.00 40.00
717C Lindor Color SP 30.00 80.00
718A Addison Russell SP RC 3.00 8.00
718B Russell Action SP 6.00 15.00
718C Russell Color SP 12.00 30.00
719 Mike Foltynewicz SP RC 1.00 2.50
720 Austin Hedges SP RC 1.00 2.50
721A Jimmy Rollins SP 1.25 3.00
721B Jimmy Rollins Color SP 5.00 12.00
722A Craig Kimbrel SP 1.25 3.00
722B Craig Kimbrel Action SP 2.50 6.00
723A Yovani Gallardo SP 1.00 2.50
723B Yovani Gallardo Color SP 4.00 10.00
724A Byron Buxton SP RC 5.00 12.00
724B Buxton Action SP 10.00 25.00
724C Buxton Color SP 20.00 50.00
725A Kris Bryant SP RC 10.00 25.00
725B Bryant Action SP 20.00 50.00
725C Bryant Color SP 40.00 100.00

2015 Topps Heritage Gum Stained Back

*GUM BACK VET: 6X TO 15X BASIC
*GUM BACK RC: 2.5X TO 6X BASIC RC
*GUM BACK SP: .6X TO 1.5X BASIC SP
*GUM BACK 701-725: 1X TO 2.5X BASIC SP
HN STATED ODDS 1:43 HOBBY
25 Jose Abreu 12.00 30.00
52 Mike Trout 8.00 20.00
Miguel Cabrera
78 Joe Panik 12.00 30.00
99 Mike Trout 8.00 20.00
Albert Pujols
220 Nelson Cruz 8.00 20.00
Miguel Cabrera/Mike Trout
411 Ryne Sandberg 6.00 15.00
429 Jacob deGrom 10.00 25.00
440 Bryce Harper 20.00 50.00
449 Matt Harvey 10.00 25.00
451 Joey Votto 12.00 30.00
454 Manny Machado 10.00 25.00
500 Mike Trout 25.00 60.00
563 Carlos Correa 25.00 60.00
725 Kris Bryant 30.00 80.00

2015 Topps Heritage '66 Punchboards

STATED ODDS 1:137 HOBBY BOXES
HN ODDS 1:40 HOBBY BOXES
STATED PRINT RUN 50 SER.#'d SETS
66P1 J.Altuve/J.Morneau 6.00 15.00
66P2 Abreu/Gonzalez 8.00 20.00
66P3 Trout/Harper 30.00 80.00
66P4 J.Reyes/S.Castro 6.00 15.00
66P5 J.Bautista/G.Stanton 8.00 20.00
66P6 Cespedes/Puig 8.00 20.00
66P7 Jeter/Wright 30.00 80.00
66P8 Cabrera/Goldschmidt 8.00 20.00
66P9 Trout/Mays 30.00 80.00
66P10 Kaline/McCutchen 15.00 40.00
66P11 B.Robinson/E.Banks 8.00 20.00
66P12 I.Desmond/L.Aparicio 6.00 15.00
66P13 Killebrew/Goldschmidt 20.00 50.00
66P14 Hamilton/Ellsbury 6.00 15.00
66P15 Mazeroski/Cano 20.00 50.00
66P16 Perez/Posey 10.00 25.00
66P17 J.Altuve/J.Morgan 6.00 15.00
66P18 A.Jones/J.Upton 6.00 15.00
66P19 Soler/Castillo 6.00 15.00
66P20 Cepeda/Encarnacion 8.00 20.00
66P21 Donaldson/Bryant HN 25.00 60.00
66P22 Russell/Travis HN 10.00 25.00
66P23 Plawecki/Swihart HN 20.00 50.00
66P24 Upton/Gattis HN 6.00 15.00
66P25 Abreu/Bryant HN 25.00 60.00
66P26 Griffey Jr./Suzuki HN 30.00 80.00
66P27 Killebrew/Pederson HN 30.00 80.00
66P28 Harper/Cruz HN 20.00 50.00
66P29 Kaline/Clemente HN 30.00 80.00
66P30 Tomas/Castillo HN 12.00 30.00

2015 Topps Heritage '66 Punchboards Relics

STATED ODDS 1:85 HOBBY BOXES
HN ODDS 1:113 HOBBY BOXES
STATED PRINT RUN 25 SER.#'d SETS
66PRAC Aroldis Chapman HN 25.00 60.00
66PRAM Andrew McCutchen HN 30.00 80.00
66PRAR Anthony Rizzo 25.00 60.00
66PRAW Adam Wainwright HN 15.00 40.00
66PRCY Christian Yelich 15.00 40.00
66PRDW David Wright 20.00 50.00
66PRHJR Hyun-Jin Ryu 20.00 50.00
66PRJD Josh Donaldson 25.00 60.00
66PRJE Jacoby Ellsbury HN 30.00 80.00
66PRJT Julio Teheran 8.00 20.00
66PRJU Justin Upton 8.00 20.00
66PRMC Miguel Cabrera HN 25.00 60.00
66PRMM Manny Machado 25.00 60.00
66PRMP Mike Piazza 40.00 100.00
66PRMT Mark Teixeira 8.00 20.00
66PRPS Pablo Sandoval 20.00 50.00
66PRRB Ryan Braun 25.00 60.00
66PRRC Robinson Cano HN 20.00 50.00
66PRRJ Randy Johnson 30.00 80.00
66PRSM Shelby Miller 25.00 60.00
66PRSS Stephen Strasburg 40.00 100.00
66PRYP Yasiel Puig 10.00 25.00
66PRZG Zack Greinke HN 15.00 40.00

2015 Topps Heritage A Legend Begins

RANDOM INSERTS IN RETAIL PACKS
NR1 Nolan Ryan 3.00 8.00
NR2 Nolan Ryan 3.00 8.00
NR3 Nolan Ryan 3.00 8.00
NR4 Nolan Ryan 3.00 8.00
NR5 Nolan Ryan 3.00 8.00
NR6 Nolan Ryan 3.00 8.00
NR7 Nolan Ryan 3.00 8.00
NR8 Nolan Ryan 3.00 8.00
NR9 Nolan Ryan 3.00 8.00
NR10 Nolan Ryan 3.00 8.00
NR11 Nolan Ryan 3.00 8.00
NR12 Nolan Ryan 3.00 8.00
NR13 Nolan Ryan 3.00 8.00
NR14 Nolan Ryan 3.00 8.00
NR15 Nolan Ryan 3.00 8.00

2015 Topps Heritage A Legend Retires

RANDOM INSERTS IN RETAIL PACKS
SK1 Sandy Koufax 3.00 8.00
SK2 Sandy Koufax 3.00 8.00
SK3 Sandy Koufax 3.00 8.00
SK4 Sandy Koufax 3.00 8.00
SK5 Sandy Koufax 3.00 8.00
SK6 Sandy Koufax 3.00 8.00
SK7 Sandy Koufax 3.00 8.00
SK8 Sandy Koufax 3.00 8.00
SK9 Sandy Koufax 3.00 8.00
SK10 Sandy Koufax 3.00 8.00
SK11 Sandy Koufax 3.00 8.00
SK12 Sandy Koufax 3.00 8.00
SK13 Sandy Koufax 3.00 8.00
SK14 Sandy Koufax 3.00 8.00
SK15 Sandy Koufax 3.00 8.00

2015 Topps Heritage Award Winners

COMPLETE SET (10) 5.00 12.00
STATED ODDS 1:8 HOBBY
AW1 Mike Trout 2.50 6.00
AW2 Clayton Kershaw .75 2.00
AW3 Corey Kluber .40 1.00
AW4 Clayton Kershaw .75 2.00
AW5 Jose Abreu .50 1.25
AW6 Jacob deGrom 1.00 2.50
AW7 Buck Showalter .30 .75
AW8 Matt Williams .30 .75
AW9 Mike Trout 2.50 6.00
AW10 Madison Bumgarner .40 1.00

2015 Topps Heritage Baseball Flashbacks

COMPLETE SET (10) 5.00 12.00
STATED ODDS 1:12 HOBBY
BF1 Ernie Banks .50 1.25
BF2 Luis Aparicio .40 1.00
BF3 Lou Brock .40 1.00
BF4 Steve Carlton .40 1.00
BF5 Orlando Cepeda .40 1.00
BF6 Al Kaline .50 1.25
BF7 Juan Marichal .40 1.00
BF8 Brooks Robinson .40 1.00
BF9 Willie Mays 1.00 2.50
BF10 Sandy Koufax 1.00 2.50

2015 Topps Heritage Bazooka

COMPLETE SET (35)
RANDOM INSERTS IN PACKS
66BAC Aroldis Chapman 4.00 10.00
66BAG Adrian Gonzalez 3.00 8.00
66BAJ Adam Jones 3.00 8.00
66BAM Andrew McCutchen 4.00 10.00
66BAR Addison Russell HN 8.00 20.00
66BAW Adam Wainwright 3.00 8.00
66BBB Byron Buxton HN 12.00 30.00
66BBP Buster Posey 5.00 12.00
66BBS Blake Swihart HN 3.00 8.00
66BCC Carlos Correa HN 12.00 30.00
66BCK Clayton Kershaw 6.00 15.00
66BCR Carlos Rodon HN 6.00 15.00
66BCS Chris Sale 4.00 10.00
66BDO David Ortiz 4.00 10.00
66BFH Felix Hernandez 3.00 8.00
66BGS Giancarlo Stanton 4.00 10.00
66BJA Jose Abreu 4.00 10.00
66BJAL Jose Altuve 3.00 8.00
66BJB Javier Baez 20.00 50.00
66BJBA Jose Bautista 3.00 8.00
66BJF Jose Fernandez 4.00 10.00
66BJU Justin Upton HN 3.00 8.00
66BKB Kris Bryant HN 25.00 60.00
66BMB Madison Bumgarner 3.00 8.00
66BMC Miguel Cabrera 4.00 10.00
66BMK Matt Kemp HN 3.00 8.00
66BMS Max Scherzer HN 4.00 10.00
66BMT Mike Trout 30.00 80.00
66BMTA Masahiro Tanaka 3.00 8.00
66BPG Paul Goldschmidt 4.00 10.00
66BSS Stephen Strasburg 4.00 10.00
66BVM Victor Martinez 3.00 8.00
66BYD Yu Darvish 4.00 10.00
66BYP Yasiel Puig 4.00 10.00
66BYT Yasmany Tomas HN 3.00 8.00

2015 Topps Heritage Chrome

1-100 ODDS 1:23 HOBBY
101-150 ODDS 1:17 HOBBY
STATED PRINT RUN 999 SER.#'d SETS
THC1 Buster Posey 2.50 6.00
THC10 Julio Teheran 1.50 4.00
THC25 Jose Abreu 2.00 5.00
THC50 Jacoby Ellsbury 1.50 4.00
THC60 Matt Holliday 2.00 5.00
THC70 Yoenis Cespedes 1.50 4.00
THC75 Matt Kemp 1.50 4.00
THC100 Clayton Kershaw 3.00 8.00
THC110 Anthony Rizzo 2.50 6.00
THC139 J.Baez/J.Soler 10.00 25.00
THC140 Aroldis Chapman 2.00 5.00
THC150 Michael Brantley 1.50 4.00
THC175 Josh Donaldson 1.50 4.00
THC200 Freddie Freeman 2.50 6.00
THC250 Johnny Cueto 1.50 4.00
THC260 Madison Bumgarner 1.50 4.00
THC270 Hyun-Jin Ryu 1.50 4.00
THC275 Yadier Molina 2.50 6.00
THC300 Andrew McCutchen 2.00 5.00
THC310 Adam Jones 1.50 4.00
THC320 Michael Wacha 1.50 4.00
THC340 Garrett Richards 1.50 4.00
THC350 Masahiro Tanaka 1.50 4.00
THC356 Ranaudo/Castillo 1.50 4.00
THC375 Josh Harrison 1.25 3.00
THC400 Joe Mauer 1.50 4.00
THC426 Giancarlo Stanton 2.00 5.00
THC427 Xander Bogaerts 2.00 5.00
THC428 Evan Longoria 1.50 4.00
THC429 Jacob deGrom 4.00 10.00
THC430 Prince Fielder 1.50 4.00
THC431 Billy Hamilton 1.50 4.00
THC432 Adam LaRoche 1.25 3.00
THC433 Jered Weaver 1.50 4.00
THC434 Todd Frazier 1.25 3.00
THC435 Gregory Polanco 1.50 4.00
THC436 Justin Upton 1.50 4.00
THC437 Josh Hamilton 1.50 4.00
THC438 Hanley Ramirez 1.50 4.00
THC439 Carlos Gonzalez 1.50 4.00
THC440 Bryce Harper 3.00 8.00
THC441 Dee Gordon 1.25 3.00
THC442 Robinson Cano 1.50 4.00
THC443 Kenley Jansen 1.50 4.00
THC444 Jose Bautista 1.50 4.00
THC445 Jonathan Lucroy 1.50 4.00
THC446 Adrian Beltre 2.00 5.00
THC447 Chris Sale 2.00 5.00
THC448 Carlos Santana 1.50 4.00
THC449 Matt Harvey 1.50 4.00
THC450 Yasiel Puig 2.00 5.00
THC451 Joey Votto 2.00 5.00
THC452 Jordan Zimmermann 1.50 4.00
THC453 Troy Tulowitzki 2.00 5.00
THC454 Manny Machado 2.00 5.00
THC455 Jose Altuve 1.50 4.00
THC457 Ian Kinsler 1.50 4.00
THC458 Jon Lester 1.50 4.00
THC459 David Wright 1.50 4.00
THC460 James Shields 1.25 3.00
THC461 Anthony Rendon 2.00 5.00
THC462 Felix Hernandez 1.50 4.00
THC463 Jose Fernandez 2.00 5.00
THC464 Jose Reyes 1.50 4.00
THC465 David Price 1.50 4.00
THC466 Corey Dickerson 1.25 3.00
THC467 Paul Goldschmidt 2.00 5.00
THC468 Zack Greinke 2.00 5.00
THC469 Max Scherzer 2.00 5.00
THC470 Nelson Cruz 2.00 5.00
THC471 Alex Gordon 1.50 4.00
THC472 Craig Kimbrel 1.50 4.00
THC473 Adrian Gonzalez 1.50 4.00
THC474 Ryan Braun 1.50 4.00
THC475 Miguel Cabrera 2.00 5.00
THC476 Greg Holland 1.25 3.00
THC477 Ian Desmond 1.25 3.00
THC478 Sonny Gray 1.50 4.00
THC479 Yordano Ventura 1.50 4.00
THC480 David Ortiz 2.00 5.00
THC481 Hisashi Iwakuma 1.50 4.00
THC482 Carlos Gomez 1.25 3.00
THC483 Adam Wainwright 1.50 4.00
THC484 Corey Kluber 1.50 4.00
THC485 Chris Carter 1.25 3.00
THC486 Christian Yelich 2.50 6.00
THC487 Edwin Encarnacion 2.00 5.00
THC488 Hunter Pence 1.50 4.00
THC489 Jason Kipnis 1.50 4.00
THC490 Cole Hamels 1.50 4.00
THC491 Victor Martinez 1.50 4.00
THC492 Jeff Samardzija 1.25 3.00
THC493 Kyle Seager 1.25 3.00
THC494 Starlin Castro 1.25 3.00
THC495 Justin Verlander 2.00 5.00
THC496 Albert Pujols 2.50 6.00
THC497 Yu Darvish 2.00 5.00
THC498 Stephen Strasburg 2.00 5.00
THC499 Dustin Pedroia 2.00 5.00
THC500 Mike Trout 10.00 25.00
THC501 Christian Walker 2.50 6.00
THC522 Anthony Ranaudo 1.25 3.00
THC523 Seth Smith 1.25 3.00
THC524 Alex Rios 1.50 4.00
THC530 Norichika Aoki 1.25 3.00
THC548 Jacob Lindgren 1.50 4.00
THC555 James Shields 1.25 3.00
THC563 Carlos Correa 6.00 15.00
THC575 Nathan Eovaldi 1.50 4.00
THC585 Yasmani Grandal 1.25 3.00
THC587 Jason Grilli 1.25 3.00
THC591 Roberto Osuna 1.25 3.00
THC592 Kevin Plawecki 1.25 3.00
THC599 Archie Bradley 1.25 3.00
THC603 Martin Prado 1.25 3.00
THC611 Jed Lowrie 1.25 3.00
THC617 Micah Johnson 1.25 3.00
THC618 Noah Syndergaard 2.50 6.00
THC621 Wil Myers 1.50 4.00
THC622 Will Middlebrooks 1.25 3.00
THC640 Steven Souza Jr. 1.50 4.00
THC647 Joey Gallo 2.50 6.00
THC654 Christian Bethancourt 1.25 3.00
THC662 Marcus Semien 2.00 5.00
THC674 Eddie Rosario 2.50 6.00
THC687 Asdrubal Cabrera 1.50 4.00
THC701 Matt Kemp 1.50 4.00
THC702 Justin Upton 1.50 4.00
THC703 Edinson Volquez 1.25 3.00
THC704 Ben Zobrist 1.50 4.00
THC705 Yasmany Tomas 1.50 4.00
THC706 Ichiro Suzuki 2.50 6.00
THC707 Evan Gattis 1.25 3.00
THC708 Max Scherzer 2.00 5.00
THC709 Jesse Hahn 1.25 3.00
THC710 Carlos Rodon 3.00 8.00
THC711 Andrew Miller 1.50 4.00
THC712 Blake Swihart 1.50 4.00
THC713 Raisel Iglesias 1.50 4.00
THC714 Jung Ho Kang 1.25 3.00
THC715 Dexter Fowler 1.50 4.00
THC716 Devon Travis 1.25 3.00
THC717 Francisco Lindor 10.00 25.00
THC718 Addison Russell 4.00 10.00
THC719 Mike Foltynewicz 1.25 3.00
THC721 Jimmy Rollins 1.50 4.00
THC722 Craig Kimbrel 1.50 4.00
THC723 Yovani Gallardo 1.25 3.00
THC724 Byron Buxton 6.00 15.00
THC725 Kris Bryant 60.00 150.00

2015 Topps Heritage Chrome Black Refractors

*BLACK REF: 2X TO 5X BASIC
STATED ODDS 1:350 HOBBY
HN ODDS 1:256 HOBBY
STATED PRINT RUN 66 SER.#'d SETS
THC100 Clayton Kershaw 30.00 80.00
THC139 J.Baez/J.Soler 50.00 120.00
THC275 Yadier Molina 20.00 50.00
THC300 Andrew McCutchen 20.00 50.00
THC426 Giancarlo Stanton 20.00 50.00
THC429 Jacob deGrom 25.00 60.00
THC440 Bryce Harper 50.00 120.00
THC449 Matt Harvey 20.00 50.00
THC500 Mike Trout 75.00 150.00
THC563 Carlos Correa 75.00 150.00
THC618 Noah Syndergaard 25.00 60.00
THC706 Ichiro Suzuki 30.00 80.00
THC724 Byron Buxton 30.00 80.00
THC725 Kris Bryant 400.00 600.00

2015 Topps Heritage Chrome Purple Refractors

*PURPLE REF: .4X TO 1X BASIC
RANDOM INSERTS IN RETAIL PACKS

2015 Topps Heritage Chrome Refractors

*REFRACTORS: .6X TO 1.5X BASIC
STATED ODDS 1:41 HOBBY
HN ODDS 1:30 HOBBY
STATED PRINT RUN 566 SER.#'d SETS

2015 Topps Heritage Chrome Retail Foil

*RETAIL FOIL: .4X TO 1X BASIC
RANDOM INSERTS IN RETAIL PACKS

2015 Topps Heritage Clubhouse Collection Dual Relics

STATED ODDS 1:6950 HOBBY
HN ODDS 1:1491 HOBBY
STATED PRINT RUN 66 SER.#'d SETS
CCDRAH H.Aaron/J.Heyward 25.00 60.00
CCDRBB Baez/Banks HN 25.00 60.00
CCDRBC Castro/Banks HN 25.00 60.00
CCDRBH Bnnng/Hamels HN 25.00 60.00
CCDRCM McCtchn/Clmnte HN 50.00 120.00
CCDRCM Y.Molina/O.Cepeda 40.00 100.00
CCDRCW Cepeda/Wong HN 25.00 60.00
CCDRMB J.Marichal/M.Bumgarner 25.00 60.00
CCDRMJ D.Jeter/R.Maris 30.00 80.00
CCDRPG Plmr/Gsmn HN 20.00 50.00
CCDRRM Mchdo/Rbnsn HN 15.00 40.00
CCDRSM W.Stargell/A.McCutchen 50.00 120.00

2015 Topps Heritage Clubhouse Collection Relic Autographs

STATED ODDS 1:9100 HOBBY
HN ODDS 1:3346 HOBBY
STATED PRINT RUN 25 SER.#'d SETS
EXCHANGE DEADLINE 2/28/2018
HN EXCH DEADLINE 8/31/2017
CCARAR Anthony Rizzo 60.00 150.00
CCARBP Buster Posey 150.00 250.00
CCARDW David Wright 90.00 150.00
CCARFF Freddie Freeman 30.00 80.00
CCARHA H.Aaron HN EXCH 350.00 700.00
CCARJB Javier Baez HN 100.00 200.00
CCARJP J.Pederson HN EXCH 75.00 200.00
CCARJS Jorge Soler HN 75.00 150.00
CCARKW K.Wong HN EXCH 50.00 120.00
CCARMF Maikel Franco HN 30.00 80.00
CCARMM Manny Machado 100.00 200.00
CCARMT Mike Trout 250.00 400.00
CCARMT Michael Taylor HN 50.00 120.00
CCARTW T.Walker HN EXCH 30.00 80.00
CCARYP Yasiel Puig 30.00 80.00

2015 Topps Heritage Clubhouse Collection Relics

STATED ODDS 1:31 HOBBY
HN ODDS 1:38 HOBBY
CCRAB Adrian Beltre 3.00 8.00
CCRAC Aroldis Chapman 3.00 8.00
CCRAC Alex Cobb HN 2.00 5.00
CCRAJ Adam Jones 2.50 6.00
CCRAM Andrew McCutchen HN 5.00 12.00
CCRAW Alex Wood HN 2.00 5.00
CCRAW Adam Wainwright 2.50 6.00
CCRBH Bryce Harper 6.00 15.00
CCRBHA Billy Hamilton 2.50 6.00
CCRCA Chris Archer 2.00 5.00
CCRCD Chris Davis HN 2.00 5.00
CCRCG Carlos Gonzalez HN 2.50 6.00
CCRCK Clayton Kershaw 5.00 12.00
CCRCS Chris Sale HN 3.00 8.00
CCRCY Christian Yelich 4.00 10.00
CCRDB Dellin Betances HN 2.50 6.00
CCRDJ Derek Jeter 12.00 30.00
CCRDO David Ortiz 3.00 8.00
CCRDP Dustin Pedroia 3.00 8.00
CCRDW David Wright 2.50 6.00
CCREG Evan Gattis 2.00 5.00
CCRFF Freddie Freeman 4.00 10.00
CCRFH Felix Hernandez 2.50 6.00
CCRGS Giancarlo Stanton 3.00 8.00
CCRGS Giancarlo Stanton HN 3.00 8.00
CCRHI Hisashi Iwakuma HN 2.50 6.00
CCRHJR Hyun-Jin Ryu 2.50 6.00
CCRHR Hanley Ramirez 2.50 6.00
CCRIK Ian Kinsler HN 2.50 6.00
CCRJA Jose Abreu HN 3.00 8.00
CCRJAL Jose Altuve HN 2.50 6.00
CCRJB Javier Baez HN 15.00 40.00
CCRJB Jose Bautista 2.50 6.00
CCRJC Johnny Cueto HN 2.50 6.00
CCRJD Jacob deGrom HN 6.00 15.00
CCRJF Jose Fernandez HN 3.00 8.00
CCRJH Jason Heyward 2.50 6.00
CCRJMA Joe Mauer 2.50 6.00
CCRJV Justin Verlander 3.00 8.00
CCRJV Justin Verlander HN 3.00 8.00
CCRKW Kolten Wong HN 2.50 6.00
CCRMB Mookie Betts HN 6.00 15.00
CCRMC Miguel Cabrera HN 3.00 8.00
CCRMC Miguel Cabrera 3.00 8.00
CCRMH Matt Harvey HN 2.50 6.00
CCRMK Matt Kemp 2.50 6.00
CCRMM Manny Machado 3.00 8.00
CCRMM Manny Machado HN 3.00 8.00
CCRMS Max Scherzer 3.00 8.00
CCRMT Mike Trout 15.00 40.00
CCRMTA Michael Taylor HN 2.00 5.00
CCRMW Michael Wacha HN 2.50 6.00
CCRNR Nolan Ryan HN 10.00 25.00
CCROC Orlando Cepeda HN 2.50 6.00
CCRPG Paul Goldschmidt 3.00 8.00
CCRPS Pablo Sandoval HN 2.50 6.00
CCRRB Ryan Braun 2.50 6.00
CCRRC Robinson Cano HN 2.50 6.00
CCRTL Tim Lincecum HN 2.50 6.00
CCRTT Troy Tulowitzki 3.00 8.00
CCRTW Taijuan Walker HN 2.00 5.00
CCRXB Xander Bogaerts 3.00 8.00
CCRYD Yu Darvish 3.00 8.00
CCRYM Yadier Molina HN 4.00 10.00
CCRYP Yasiel Puig 3.00 8.00
CCRYV Yordano Ventura HN 2.50 6.00
CCRZG Zack Greinke 3.00 8.00
CCRZW Zack Wheeler 2.50 6.00

2015 Topps Heritage Clubhouse Collection Relics Gold

*GOLD: .8X TO 2X BASIC
STATED ODDS 1:550 HOBBY
HN ODDS 1:266 HOBBY
STATED PRINT RUN 99 SER.#'d SETS
CCRDJ Derek Jeter 50.00 120.00
CCREB Ernie Banks 20.00 50.00
CCRHA Hank Aaron 30.00 80.00
CCRJM Juan Marichal 5.00 12.00
CCRRM Roger Maris 40.00 100.00
CCRWM Willie Mays 40.00 100.00

2015 Topps Heritage Clubhouse Collection Triple Relics

STATED ODDS 1:18,688 HOBBY
HN ODDS 1:5018 HOBBY
STATED PRINT RUN 25 SER.#'d SETS
CCTRAHU Aaron/Upton/Hywrd 50.00 120.00
CCTRATF Arn/Frmn/Thrn HN 50.00 120.00
CCTRBBC Baez/Cstro/Bnks HN 20.00 50.00
CCTRBJT Banks/Jeter/Tulo 100.00 200.00
CCTRCMS McCtchn/Clmnte/Strgll HN 125.00 250.00
CCTRCMW Wnwrght/Cpda/Mlna HN 50.00 120.00
CCTRMMA Maris/Mays/Aaron 250.00 350.00
CCTRMMP Mays/Psy/Mrchl HN 100.00 200.00
CCTRMPB Posey/Bmgrnr/Mrchl 60.00 150.00
CCTRRJM Mchdo/Rbnsn/Jones HN 60.00 150.00
CCTRSMM McCtchn/Strgll/Marte 100.00 200.00

2015 Topps Heritage Combo Cards

COMPLETE SET (10) 5.00 12.00
STATED ODDS 1:8 HOBBY
CC1 Sandoval/Ramirez/Ortiz .50 1.25
CC2 J.Bautista/J.Donaldson .40 1.00
CC3 Cincinnati Reds Mascots .30 .75
CC4 A.Miller/B.McCann .40 1.00
CC5 J.Altuve/G.Springer .40 1.00
CC6 M.Machado/C.Davis .50 1.25
CC7 A.Gordon/E.Hosmer .40 1.00
CC8 K.Plawecki/N.Syndergaard .60 1.50
CC9 K.Bryant/A.Russell 3.00 8.00
CC10 Myers/Upton/Kemp .40 1.00

2015 Topps Heritage Flashback Relic Autographs

STATED ODDS 1:18,688 HOBBY
STATED PRINT RUN 25 SER.#'d SETS
EXCHANGE DEADLINE 2/28/2018
FARHA Hank Aaron EXCH 200.00 300.00
FARSC Steve Carlton 150.00 250.00

2015 Topps Heritage Framed Stamps

STATED ODDS 1:2310 HOBBY
STATED PRINT RUN 50 SER.#'d SETS

66USAK Al Kaline 30.00 80.00
66USBM Bill Mazeroski 25.00 60.00
66USBR Brooks Robinson 25.00 60.00
66USEB Ernie Banks 30.00 80.00
66USEM Eddie Mathews 30.00 80.00
66USFJ Fergie Jenkins 25.00 60.00
66USHK Harmon Killebrew 30.00 80.00
66USJB Jim Bunning 25.00 60.00
66USJM Joe Morgan 25.00 60.00
66USJMA Juan Marichal 50.00 120.00
66USLA Luis Aparicio 25.00 60.00
66USLB Lou Brock 25.00 60.00
66USNR Nolan Ryan 100.00 250.00
66USOC Orlando Cepeda 25.00 60.00
66USPN Phil Niekro 25.00 60.00
66USSC Steve Carlton 25.00 60.00
66USTP Tony Perez 25.00 60.00
66USWF Whitey Ford 25.00 60.00
66USWM Willie McCovey 25.00 60.00
66USWMA Willie Mays 50.00 120.00

2015 Topps Heritage Mini

*MINI: 1.2X TO 3X BASIC CHROME
STATED ODDS 1:231 HOBBY
HN ODDS 1:169 HOBBY
STATED PRINT RUN 100 SER.#'d SETS
1 Buster Posey 30.00 80.00
300 Andrew McCutchen 15.00 40.00
440 Bryce Harper 20.00 50.00
500 Mike Trout 75.00 200.00
725 Kris Bryant 150.00 400.00

2015 Topps Heritage New Age Performers

COMPLETE SET (20) 10.00 25.00
STATED ODDS 1:8 HOBBY
NAP1 Clayton Kershaw .75 2.00
NAP2 Jose Abreu .50 1.25
NAP3 Billy Hamilton .40 1.00
NAP4 Giancarlo Stanton .50 1.25
NAP5 Mike Trout 2.50 6.00
NAP6 Bryce Harper .75 2.00
NAP7 Yu Darvish .50 1.25
NAP8 Buster Posey .60 1.50
NAP9 Miguel Cabrera .50 1.25
NAP10 Andrew McCutchen .50 1.25
NAP11 Adam Jones .40 1.00
NAP12 Felix Hernandez .40 1.00
NAP13 Masahiro Tanaka .40 1.00
NAP14 Evan Longoria .40 1.00
NAP15 Javier Baez 2.50 6.00
NAP16 Aroldis Chapman .50 1.25
NAP17 Yasiel Puig .50 1.25
NAP18 Troy Tulowitzki .50 1.25
NAP19 Jacob deGrom 1.00 2.50
NAP20 Chris Sale .50 1.25

2015 Topps Heritage News Flashbacks

COMPLETE SET (10) 3.00 8.00
STATED ODDS 1:12 HOBBY
NF1 Batman .50 1.25
NF2 Lunar Orbiter 1 .40 1.00
NF3 Star Trek .75 2.00
NF4 Metropolitan Opera House .40 1.00
NF5 Jimi Hendrix Experience .40 1.00
NF6 Ronald Reagan .40 1.00
NF7 NFL/AFL Merger .40 1.00
NF8 Indira Gandhi .40 1.00
NF9 Marvin Miller .40 1.00
NF10 Sheila Scott .40 1.00

2015 Topps Heritage Now and Then

COMPLETE SET (15) 5.00 12.00
STATED ODDS 1:8 HOBBY
NT1 Corey Kluber .40 1.00
NT2 Steven Matz .40 1.00
NT3 Giancarlo Stanton .50 1.25
NT4 Mike Trout 2.50 6.00
NT5 Alex Rodriguez .60 1.50
NT6 Adrian Beltre .50 1.25
NT7 Miguel Cabrera .50 1.25
NT8 Felix Hernandez .40 1.00
NT9 Clayton Kershaw .75 2.00
NT10 Ryan Zimmerman .40 1.00
NT11 Eddie Rosario .60 1.50
NT12 Jose Altuve .40 1.00
NT13 Yasmani Grandal .30 .75
NT14 Andrew Miller .40 1.00
NT15 Bryce Harper .75 2.00

2015 Topps Heritage Real One Autographs

STATED ODDS 1:258 HOBBY
HN ODDS 1:167 HOBBY BOXES
EXCHANGE DEADLINE 2/28/2018
HN EXCH DEADLINE 8/31/2017
ROAAG Aubrey Gatewood 6.00 15.00
ROAAK Al Kaline 30.00 80.00
ROAAM Art Mahaffey 6.00 15.00
ROAAP Albie Pearson 6.00 15.00
ROAAS Aaron Sanchez 8.00 20.00
ROAAST Al Stanek 6.00 15.00
ROABF Bob Friend 6.00 15.00
ROABR Bobby Richardson 6.00 15.00
ROABS Bob Sadowski 6.00 15.00
ROABW Bill Wakefield 6.00 15.00
ROACCC Choo Choo Coleman 20.00 50.00
ROACS Chuck Schilling 12.00 30.00
ROACW Carl Warwick 6.00 15.00
ROADB Dellin Betances 10.00 25.00
ROADS Dick Stigman 6.00 15.00
ROAEB Ernie Bowman 6.00 15.00
ROAEBR Ernie Broglio 6.00 15.00
ROAFC Frank Carpin 6.00 15.00
ROAFK Frank Kreutzer 6.00 15.00
ROAFM Frank Malzone 6.00 15.00
ROAGB Greg Bollo 6.00 15.00
ROAGK Gary Kroll 6.00 15.00
ROAGR Gordon Richardson 6.00 15.00
ROAJAC Jack Cullen 12.00 30.00
ROAJB Javier Baez 30.00 80.00
Signed in red ink
ROAJC Joe Christopher 6.00 15.00
ROAJD Jim Dickson 6.00 15.00
ROAJG Joe Gaines 6.00 15.00
ROAJGE Jim Gentile 6.00 15.00
ROAJH John Herrnstein 12.00 30.00
ROAJM Juan Marichal 30.00 80.00
ROAKH Ken Hamlin 6.00 15.00
ROALB Lou Brock 40.00 100.00
ROAMB Mike Brumley 6.00 15.00
ROAMK Marty Keough 8.00 20.00
ROAOC Orlando Cepeda 30.00 80.00
ROAPN Phil Niekro 30.00 80.00
ROARC Roger Craig 10.00 25.00
ROARCA Rusney Castillo 20.00 50.00
ROARH Ray Herbert 6.00 15.00
ROARN Ron Nischwitz 12.00 30.00
ROASM Shelby Miller 15.00 40.00
ROATS Tracy Stallard 6.00 15.00
ROAHAB Archie Bradley HN 10.00 25.00
ROAHAK Al Kaline HN 40.00 100.00
ROAHAR Addison Russell HN 40.00 100.00
ROAHBB Byron Buxton HN 30.00 80.00
ROAHBS Blake Swihart HN 8.00 20.00
ROAHCC Carlos Correa HN 100.00 250.00
ROAHCR Carlos Rodon HN EXCH 15.00 40.00
ROAHDH Dilson Herrera HN 8.00 20.00
ROAHDN Daniel Norris HN 6.00 15.00
ROAHDP Dalton Pompey HN 8.00 20.00
ROAHFL Francisco Lindor HN 200.00 500.00
ROAHFR Frank Robinson HN 50.00 120.00
ROAHHR Hanley Ramirez HN 10.00 25.00
ROAHJA Jose Abreu HN 15.00 40.00
ROAHJL Jake Lamb HN 10.00 25.00
ROAHJP Joe Panik HN 15.00 40.00
ROAHJS Jorge Soler HN 10.00 25.00
ROAHKB Kris Bryant HN 250.00 500.00
ROAHKP Kevin Plawecki HN 6.00 15.00
ROAHMJ Micah Johnson HN 6.00 15.00
ROAHMS Max Scherzer HN 25.00 60.00
ROAHMT Michael Taylor HN 6.00 15.00
ROAHNR Nolan Ryan HN 125.00 300.00
ROAHNS Noah Syndergaard HN 25.00 60.00
ROAHPN Phil Niekro HN 15.00 40.00
ROAHRC Rusney Castillo HN 8.00 20.00
ROAHRI Raisel Iglesias HN 12.00 30.00
ROAHRO Roberto Osuna HN 6.00 15.00
ROAHSC Steve Carlton HN 40.00 100.00
ROAHYT Yasmany Tomas HN 8.00 20.00
ROAHJHE Jason Heyward HN 30.00 80.00
ROAHJHK Jung Ho Kang HN 6.00 15.00
ROAHJLE Jon Lester HN 12.00 30.00
ROAHJPE Joc Pederson HN 15.00 40.00
ROAHMFR Maikel Franco HN 12.00 30.00

2015 Topps Heritage Real One Autographs Red Ink

*RED INK: .6X TO 1.5X BASIC
STATED ODDS 1:390 HOBBY
HN ODDS 1:245 HOBBY
STATED PRINT RUN 66 SER.#'d SETS
EXCHANGE DEADLINE 2/28/2018
HN EXCH DEADLINE 8/31/2017
ROABH Bryce Harper 200.00 400.00
ROABRO Brooks Robinson 125.00 250.00
ROAMR Mariano Rivera 400.00 600.00
ROAOC Orlando Cepeda 50.00 120.00
ROASC Steve Carlton 150.00 250.00
ROASK Sandy Koufax EXCH 500.00 800.00
ROAHCK Clayton Kershaw HN 125.00 250.00

2015 Topps Heritage Real One Autographs Dual

STATED ODDS 1:3515 HOBBY
HN ODDS 1:5132 HOBBY
STATED PRINT RUN 25 SER.#'d SETS
EXCHANGE DEADLINE 2/28/2018
HN EXCH DEADLINE 8/31/2017
RODAAF Aaron/Freeman EXCH 125.00 300.00
RODABA L.Brock/M.Adams 100.00 200.00
RODABC Brck/Crpntr HN EXCH 60.00 150.00
RODACH Cpda/Hywrd HN EXCH 60.00 150.00
RODACM O.Cepeda/S.Miller 60.00 150.00
RODACW S.Carlton/M.Wacha 60.00 150.00
RODACW Wng/Cpda HN EXCH 50.00 120.00
RODAKC Cspds/Klne HN EXCH 100.00 250.00
RODAKC A.Kaline/M.Cabrera 125.00 300.00
RODAKK Kfx/Krshw HN EXCH 900.00 1200.00
RODANM Nkro/Mllr HN EXCH 60.00 150.00
RODANT Niekro/Teheran EXCH 60.00 150.00
RODAPJ Palmer/Jenkins EXCH 100.00 200.00
RODARG dGrm/Ryan HN EXCH 300.00 800.00
RODARJ Rbnsn/Jns HN 100.00 250.00
RODAWB Hywrd/Brk HN EXCH 50.00 120.00

2015 Topps Heritage Rookie Performers

COMPLETE SET (15) 10.00 25.00
STATED ODDS 1:8 HOBBY
RP1 Jorge Soler .50 1.25
RP2 Francisco Lindor 2.50 6.00
RP3 Joc Pederson 1.25 3.00
RP4 Kris Bryant 3.00 8.00
RP5 Addison Russell 1.00 2.50
RP6 Archie Bradley .30 .75
RP7 Carlos Rodon .75 2.00
RP8 Daniel Norris .30 .75
RP9 Javier Baez 2.50 6.00
RP10 Byron Buxton 1.50 4.00
RP11 Blake Swihart .40 1.00
RP12 Noah Syndergaard .60 1.50
RP13 Yasmany Tomas .40 1.00
RP14 Joey Gallo .60 1.50
RP15 Carlos Correa 1.50 4.00

2015 Topps Heritage Then and Now

COMPLETE SET (10) 5.00 12.00
STATED ODDS 1:10 HOBBY
TAN1 N.Cruz/H.Killebrew .50 1.25
TAN2 A.Gonzalez/W.Mays 1.00 2.50
TAN3 J.Altuve/W.Stargell .40 1.00
TAN4 D.Gordon/L.Brock .40 1.00
TAN5 C.Santana/H.Killebrew .50 1.25
TAN6 C.Kershaw/S.Koufax 1.00 2.50
TAN7 D.Price/S.Koufax 1.00 2.50
TAN8 C.Kershaw/S.Koufax 1.00 2.50
TAN9 S.Koufax/D.Price 1.00 2.50
TAN10 A.Wainwright/S.Koufax 1.00 2.50

2016 Topps Heritage

SP ODDS 1:3 HOBBY
HN SP ODDS 1:3 HOBBY
HN ACTION ODDS 1:25 HOBBY
HN CLR SWP ODDS 1:89 HOBBY
HN THRWBCK ODDS 1:1535 HOBBY
HN ERROR ODDS 1:430 HOBBY
1 Moustakas/Escobar/Hosmer .20 .50
2 Logan Forsythe .15 .40
3 Brad Miller .20 .50
4 Jeremy Hellickson .15 .40
5 Nick Hundley .15 .40
6 Aaron Hicks .20 .50
7 Alcides Escobar .20 .50
8A Shin-Soo Choo .20 .50
8B Choo Thrwbck SP 200.00 300.00
9 Wil Myers .20 .50
10 Gregory Polanco .20 .50
11 Francisco Rodriguez .20 .50
12 Andre Ethier .20 .50
13 Wily Peralta .15 .40
14 Jhonny Peralta .15 .40
15 Yan Gomes .15 .40
16 Nathan Karns .15 .40
17 Brayan Pena .15 .40
18 Luke Gregerson .15 .40
19 Ian Desmond .15 .40
20 Matt Adams .15 .40
21A Didi Gregorius .20 .50
21B Didi Gregorius Action SP 2.50 6.00
22 J.T. Realmuto .25 .60
23A Brandon Phillips .15 .40
23B Phillips Thrwbck SP 150.00 250.00
24 Rajai Davis .15 .40
25A Brian McCann .20 .50
25B Brian McCann Color SP 5.00 12.00
26 Drew Smyly .15 .40
27 Desmond Jennings .20 .50
28 David Freese .15 .40
29 Anthony Gose .15 .40
30 J.D. Martinez .25 .60
31A Alfredo Simon .15 .40
31B Simon Thrwbck SP 150.00 250.00
32 Jered Weaver .20 .50
33 Jason Grilli .15 .40
34 Kevin Kiermaier .20 .50
35 Jeurys Familia .20 .50
36 Carlos Martinez .20 .50
37 Santiago Casilla .15 .40
38 Adrian Gonzalez .20 .50
39 Jake Lamb .20 .50
40 Kole Calhoun .15 .40
41 Francisco Cervelli .15 .40
42 Justin Bour .20 .50
43 Adam Lind .20 .50
44 Jung Ho Kang .15 .40
45A Hanley Ramirez .20 .50
45B Hanley Ramirez Color SP 5.00 12.00
45C Ramirez ERR SP 20.00 50.00
46 Marcus Semien .25 .60
47 Darin Ruf .15 .40
48 Miguel Montero .15 .40
49 Yonder Alonso .15 .40
50A Byron Buxton .25 .60
50B Buxton Color SP 6.00 15.00
51 Kyle Seager .15 .40
52 Jason Hammel .20 .50
53 Cameron Maybin .15 .40
54 Asdrubal Cabrera .20 .50
55 Jeff Locke .15 .40
56 Robinson Chirinos .15 .40
57 Trevor Plouffe .15 .40
58A C.J. Cron .15 .40
58B Cron ERR SP 25.00 60.00
59 Kyle Hendricks .25 .60
60 Chris Davis .15 .40
61 Pat Venditte .15 .40
62 Steven Matz .15 .40
63 Piscotty/Carpenter .25 .60
64 Nick Ahmed .15 .40
65 Nick Martinez .15 .40
66 Eddie Rosario .20 .50
67 Gerardo Parra .15 .40
68 Wellington Castillo .15 .40
69 Freddy Galvis .15 .40
70A Kris Bryant .30 .75
70B Bryant Color SP 30.00 80.00
70C Bryant Thrwbck SP 400.00 800.00
71 Caleb Joseph .15 .40
72 Mark Trumbo .15 .40
73 Jonathan Papelbon .20 .50
74 Brock Holt .15 .40
75 Yangervis Solarte .15 .40
76 Daniel Murphy .20 .50
77A Evan Gattis .15 .40
77B Evan Gattis Color SP 4.00 10.00
78A Jake Arrieta .20 .50
78B Jake Arrieta Action SP 2.50 6.00
79 Jose Iglesias .20 .50
80 Aroldis Chapman .25 .60
81 Kendall Graveman .15 .40
82 Ryan Zimmerman .20 .50
83 Colby Rasmus .20 .50
84 Yasmani Grandal .15 .40
85 Bryan Morris .15 .40
86 Alexei Ramirez .20 .50
87 Jon Lester .20 .50
88A Xander Bogaerts .25 .60
88B Xander Bogaerts Action SP 3.00 8.00
89 Trevor Rosenthal .20 .50
90 Sonny Gray .20 .50
91 Jackie Bradley Jr. .25 .60
92 Jesse Hahn .15 .40
93 Mitch Moreland .15 .40
94 Mark Buehrle .20 .50
95 Chris Heston .15 .40
96 Blake Swihart .20 .50
97 Carlos Beltran .20 .50
98 Matt Wisler .15 .40
99 Roberto Osuna .15 .40
100A Adam Jones .20 .50
100B Adam Jones Color SP 5.00 12.00
101 Nick Castellanos .25 .60
102 Scott Kazmir .15 .40
103 Andrew Cashner .15 .40
104 Jean Segura .20 .50
105 Kendrys Morales .15 .40
106 Anibal Sanchez .15 .40
107 Jeanmar Gomez .15 .40
108 Rougned Odor .20 .50
109 Lindor/Kipnis .25 .60
110 Brandon Belt .20 .50
111 Eugenio Suarez .20 .50
112 Kyle Gibson .20 .50
113 Erick Aybar .15 .40
114 Kevin Gausman .25 .60
115 Hisashi Iwakuma .20 .50
116 Wade Miley .15 .40
117 James Loney .15 .40
118 Giovanny Urshela .25 .60
119 Joaquin Benoit .15 .40
120A Billy Hamilton .20 .50
120B Billy Hamilton Action SP 2.50 6.00
121 Carlos Carrasco .15 .40
122 Derek Norris .15 .40
123 Billy Butler .15 .40
124 Derek Dietrich .20 .50
125 Zach Britton .20 .50
126 Starlin Castro .15 .40
127 David Wright .20 .50
128A Mike Moustakas .20 .50
128B Moustakas ERR SP 30.00 80.00
129 Cesar Hernandez .15 .40
130 Zack Greinke .25 .60
131 Russell Martin .15 .40
132A Ichiro Suzuki .30 .75
132B Ichiro Action SP 4.00 10.00
133 Jeremy Jeffress .15 .40
134 Bartolo Colon .15 .40
135 Nick Swisher .20 .50
136 John Danks .15 .40
137 Jonathan Schoop .15 .40
138 Carlos Ruiz .15 .40
139 Jacob Lindgren .20 .50
140 Starling Marte .20 .50
141 Scooter Gennett .20 .50
142 Melky Cabrera .15 .40
143 Josh Reddick .15 .40
144 Michael Cuddyer .15 .40
145 Collin McHugh .15 .40
146 Kelvin Herrera .15 .40
147 Jace Peterson .15 .40
148 Will Smith .15 .40
149 R.A. Dickey .20 .50
150 Jacoby Ellsbury .20 .50
151A Eric Hosmer .20 .50
151B E.Hosmer Colorized SP 5.00 12.00
152A Johnny Cueto .20 .50
152B Cueto Colorized SP 20.00 50.00
153A Salvador Perez .20 .50
153B Perez Colorized SP 20.00 50.00
154A Wade Davis .15 .40
154B Davis Colorized SP 20.00 50.00
155A Kansas City Royals .20 .50
155B Royals Colorized SP 20.00 50.00
156 Mark Melancon .15 .40
157A Manny Machado .25 .60
157B Manny Machado Action SP 3.00 8.00
158 Yovani Gallardo .15 .40
159 Jose Reyes .20 .50
160 Joc Pederson .20 .50
161A Schwarber RC/Edwards RC 1.00 2.50
161B Kyle Schwarber SP 12.00 30.00
162 P.O'Brien RC/B.Drury RC .50 1.25
163 Mnts RC/Thmpsn RC .50 1.25
164 K.Waldrop RC/K.Sampson RC .40 1.00
165 G.Soto RC/S.Armstrong RC .40 1.00
166 T.Murphy RC/J.Gray RC .30 .75
167 S.Alexander RC/M.Almonte RC .30 .75
168A Seager RC/Peraza RC 3.00 8.00
168B Corey Seager SP 20.00 50.00
169 B.Ellington RC/C.Reed RC .30 .75
170 A.Pena RC/N.Ashley RC .30 .75
171 Pazos RC/Bird RC .40 1.00
172 R.Dull RC/C.Blair RC .30 .75
173 C.Murray RC/J.Eickhoff RC .50 1.25
174 C.Decker RC/T.Jankowski RC .30 .75
175 J.Hicks RC/K.Marte RC .60 1.50
176 L.Maile RC/R.Shaffer RC .30 .75
177A G.Sanchez RC/R.Mondesi RC 1.00 2.50
177B Snchz/Mndsi ERR SP 40.00 100.00
178 D.Alvarez RC/H.Owens RC .40 1.00
179 Z.Godley RC/S.Brito RC .30 .75
180 Turner RC/Olivera RC 1.00 2.50
181A Conforto RC/Nola RC .60 1.50
181B Aaron Nola SP 6.00 15.00
182 L.Jackson RC/T.Duffey RC .30 .75
183A Sweeney RC/Piscotty RC .50 1.25
183B Stephen Piscotty SP 8.00 20.00
184 E.Diaz RC/N.Ogando RC .30 .75
185 C.Hall RC/R.Lazo RC .30 .75
186 C.Granderson/J.Lagares .20 .50
187 T.Brown RC/M.Williamson RC .40 1.00
188 P.Severino RC/T.Tartamella RC .30 .75
189 Trrys RC/Brxtn RC .60 1.50
190A Severino RC/Sano RC .50 1.25
190B Luis Severino SP 6.00 15.00
191 Jimmy Rollins .20 .50
192 Rick Porcello .20 .50
193 A.J. Pierzynski .15 .40
194 Tommy Milone .15 .40
195A Nolan Arenado .40 1.00
195B Nolan Arenado Action SP 5.00 12.00
195C Nolan Arenado Color SP 10.00 25.00
196 Jorge De La Rosa .15 .40
197 Erasmo Ramirez .15 .40
198 Jimmy Paredes .15 .40
199 Shawn Tolleson .15 .40
200A Hunter Pence .20 .50
200B Pence ERR SP 50.00 120.00
201 Luis Valbuena .15 .40
202 Chris Colabello .15 .40
203 Lonnie Chisenhall .15 .40
204 Adam LaRoche .15 .40
205 Khris Davis .25 .60
206 Kevin Pillar .15 .40
207 Brett Lawrie .20 .50
208 Jarrod Dyson .15 .40
209 Ubaldo Jimenez .15 .40
210A Michael Wacha .20 .50
210B Michael Wacha Color SP 5.00 12.00
211 Aaron Harang .15 .40
212 J.J. Hardy .15 .40
213 Brad Ziegler .15 .40
214 Gio Gonzalez .20 .50
215 John Jaso .15 .40
216 Kinsler/Cabrera .25 .60
217 J.P. Howell .15 .40
218 Matt Shoemaker .20 .50
219 Carson Smith .15 .40
220 Matt Duffy .15 .40
221 Christian Bethancourt .15 .40
222 Chris Iannetta .15 .40
223A Mike Zunino .15 .40
223B Zunino ERR SP 40.00 100.00
224 Jedd Gyorko .15 .40
225 Ken Giles .15 .40
226A Carlos Rodon .25 .60
226B Rodon Thrwbck SP 75.00 200.00
227 Carlos Gomez .15 .40
228 Ben Revere .15 .40
229 Ian Kennedy .15 .40
230 James Shields .15 .40
231 Tim Lincecum .20 .50
232 Sergio Romo .15 .40
233 Price/Gray/Keuchel .20 .50
234 Krshw/Grnke/Arrta .40 1.00
235 Price/McHugh/Keuchel .20 .50
236 Bmgrnr/Cole/Grnke/Arrta .25 .60
237 Sale/Archer/Kluber .25 .60
238 Arrieta/Scherzer/Kershaw .40 1.00
239 Altuive/Bogaerts/Cabrera .25 .60
240 Harper/Goldschmidt/Gordon .40 1.00
241 Jose Bautista .20 .50
Chris Davis/Josh Donaldson
242 Rizzo/Arenado/Goldschmidt .40 1.00
243 Cruz/Trout/Davis 1.25 3.00
244 Gonzalez/Harper/Arenado .40 1.00
245 Marco Estrada .15 .40
246 Logan Morrison .15 .40
247 Hector Santiago .15 .40
248 A.J. Ramos .15 .40
249 Lucas Duda .20 .50
250 Nick Markakis .20 .50
251 Yadier Molina .30 .75
252 Jeff Francoeur .20 .50
253 Michael Brantley .20 .50
254A Dee Gordon .15 .40
254B Gordon ERR SP 20.00 50.00
255 Jorge Soler .25 .60
256 Josh Harrison .15 .40
257 Skip Schumaker .15 .40
258 Rubby De La Rosa .15 .40
259 A.Houser RC/M.Reed RC .30 .75
260 Justin Turner .25 .60
261 Chip Hale MG .15 .40
262 Buck Showalter MG .15 .40
263 Joe Maddon MG .15 .40
264 Terry Francona MG .20 .50
265 A.J. Hinch MG .15 .40
266 Marte/McCutchen .25 .60
267 Mike Scioscia MG .15 .40
268 Fredi Gonzalez MG .15 .40
269 Paul Molitor .25 .60
270 Terry Collins MG .15 .40
271 Joe Girardi MG .20 .50
272 Walt Weiss MG .15 .40
273 Clint Hurdle MG .15 .40
274 Bruce Bochy MG .15 .40
275 Bryan Price MG .15 .40
276 Mike Matheny MG .15 .40
277 Kevin Cash MG .15 .40
278 John Gibbons MG .15 .40
279 Jeff Banister MG .15 .40
280 Craig Counsell MG .15 .40
281 Anthony DeSclafani .15 .40
282 Trevor Bauer .30 .75
283 Huston Street .15 .40
284 Stephen Strasburg .25 .60
285 Mike Leake .15 .40
286 Wei-Yin Chen .15 .40
287 Mark Canha .15 .40
288 Slade Heathcott .20 .50
289 Nathan Eovaldi .20 .50
290 Ryan Howard .20 .50
291 John Lackey .20 .50
292 Edwin Encarnacion .25 .60
293 Wade Davis .15 .40
294 Justin Morneau .20 .50
295 Avisail Garcia .20 .50
296 Eduardo Rodriguez .15 .40
297 Joe Panik .20 .50
298 Yohan Flande .15 .40
299 Ervin Santana .15 .40
300 Glen Perkins .15 .40
301 Mike Aviles .15 .40
302A Salvador Perez .20 .50
302B Salvador Perez Color SP 5.00 12.00
303 David Murphy .15 .40
304 Carlos Santana .20 .50
305 Chase Utley .20 .50
306 Yunel Escobar .15 .40
307 Martin Prado .15 .40
308 Chris Carter .15 .40
309 M.Franco/R.Howard .20 .50
310A Chris Sale .25 .60
310B Chris Sale Color SP 6.00 15.00
311 Jason Motte .15 .40
312 Vidal Nuno .15 .40
313 Seth Smith .15 .40
314 Delino DeShields Jr. .15 .40
315 Kolten Wong .20 .50
316 Steven Souza Jr. .20 .50
317 Colby Lewis .15 .40
318 Dexter Fowler .20 .50
319 Archie Bradley .15 .40
320 Madison Bumgarner .20 .50
321 Garrett Richards .20 .50
322A Giancarlo Stanton .25 .60
322B Giancarlo Stanton Action SP 3.00 8.00
322C Giancarlo Stanton Color SP 6.00 15.00
323 Nori Aoki .15 .40
324 Anthony Rendon .25 .60
325 Matt Holliday .25 .60
326A Francisco Liriano .15 .40
326B Liriano ERR SP 50.00 120.00
327A Matt Carpenter .25 .60
327B Carpenter Thrwbck SP 150.00 250.00
328 Denard Span .15 .40
329 Zack Cozart .15 .40
330 Kenley Jansen .20 .50
331 Brad Boxberger .15 .40
332 Ben Paulsen .15 .40
333A Craig Kimbrel .20 .50
333B Kimbrel Traded SP 60.00 150.00
334 Sano/Buxton .25 .60
335 Adam Eaton .15 .40
336 Drew Pomeranz .20 .50
337A Yordano Ventura .20 .50
337B Ventura Thrwbck SP 125.00 250.00
338 Jay Bruce .20 .50
339 Darren O'Day .15 .40
340 Mark Teixeira .20 .50
341 Baltimore Orioles .15 .40
342 Boston Red Sox .20 .50
343 New York Yankees .20 .50
344 Tampa Bay Rays .15 .40
345 Toronto Blue Jays .15 .40
346 Chicago White Sox .15 .40
347 Cleveland Indians .15 .40
348 Detroit Tigers .15 .40
349 Kansas City Royals .20 .50
350 Minnesota Twins .15 .40
351 Houston Astros .15 .40
352 Los Angeles Angels .15 .40
353 Oakland Athletics .15 .40
354 Seattle Mariners .15 .40
355 Texas Rangers .15 .40
356 Atlanta Braves .15 .40
357 Miami Marlins .15 .40
358 New York Mets .20 .50
359 Philadelphia Phillies .15 .40
360 Washington Nationals .15 .40
361 Chicago Cubs .20 .50
362 Cincinnati Reds .15 .40
363 Milwaukee Brewers .15 .40
364 Pittsburgh Pirates .15 .40
365 St. Louis Cardinals .20 .50
366 Arizona Diamondbacks .15 .40
367 Colorado Rockies .15 .40
368 Los Angeles Dodgers .20 .50
369 San Diego Padres .15 .40
370 San Francisco Giants .20 .50
371A Yasmany Tomas .15 .40
371B Yasmany Tomas Color SP 4.00 10.00
372 Cody Allen .15 .40
373 Marcell Ozuna .25 .60
374A Joe Mauer .20 .50
374B Mauer ERR SP 40.00 100.00
375 Tom Wilhelmsen .15 .40
376 Neil Walker .15 .40
377 Andres Blanco .15 .40
378 Jason Castro .15 .40
379 Drew Storen .15 .40
380 Phil Hughes .15 .40
381 Arodys Vizcaino .15 .40
382 Brett Gardner .20 .50
383 John Axford .15 .40
384 David Robertson .15 .40
385 Victor Martinez .20 .50
386 Hector Rondon .15 .40
387 Elvis Andrus .20 .50
388 Jordan Zimmermann .20 .50
389 Jeff Samardzija .15 .40
390 George Springer .20 .50
391 Mike Fiers .15 .40
392 Coco Crisp .15 .40
393 James McCann .20 .50
394 Ender Inciarte .15 .40
395 Jordy Mercer .15 .40
396 Freeman/Markakis .30 .75
397 Kevin Siegrist .15 .40
398 Wilmer Flores .20 .50
399 J.J. Hoover .15 .40
400A Andrew McCutchen .25 .60
400B McCtchn Action SP 3.00 8.00
401 Curtis Granderson .20 .50
402 Joe Kelly .15 .40
403 Danny Salazar .20 .50
404A Daniel Norris .15 .40
404B Norris Thrwbck SP
405 Adrian Beltre .25 .60
406 Alexi Amarista .15 .40
407 Ryan Flaherty .15 .40
408 Tom Koehler .15 .40
409 Pablo Sandoval .20 .50
410A Yasiel Puig .25 .60
410B Puig Action SP 3.00 8.00
411 Lance Lynn .15 .40
412 Andrew Miller .20 .50
413 Michael Pineda .15 .40
414 Clay Buchholz .15 .40
415 CC Sabathia .20 .50
416 Aaron Sanchez .20 .50
417A Julio Teheran .20 .50
417B Teheran ERR SP 40.00 100.00
418 Sean Doolittle .15 .40
419 DJ LeMahieu .25 .60
420 Justin Verlander .25 .60
421 Taijuan Walker .15 .40
422 Ned Yost .15 .40
423 Brandon Belt .20 .50
424 Domonic Brown .20 .50
425A Gerrit Cole .25 .60
425B Gerrit Cole Color SP 6.00 15.00
426A Clayton Kershaw SP 4.00 10.00
426B Kershaw Color SP 10.00 25.00
427 Brian Dozier SP 2.00 5.00
428 Corey Kluber SP 2.00 5.00
429 Jake Odorizzi SP 1.50 4.00
430A Dallas Keuchel SP 2.00 5.00
430B Keuchel Thrwbck SP 400.00 600.00
431A Jose Bautista SP 2.00 5.00
431B Jose Bautista Color SP 5.00 12.00
432A Robinson Cano SP 2.00 5.00
432B Robinson Cano Action SP 2.50 6.00
432C Cano Thrwbck SP 300.00 500.00
433 Prince Fielder SP 2.00 5.00
434 Jonathan Lucroy SP 2.00 5.00
435A Chris Archer SP 1.50 4.00
435B Chris Archer Color SP 4.00 10.00
436A Masahiro Tanaka SP 2.00 5.00
436B Masahiro Tanaka Color SP 5.00 12.00
437 Addison Russell SP 2.50 6.00
438A David Ortiz SP 2.50 6.00
438B Ortiz Thrwbck SP 300.00 500.00
439 Andrelton Simmons SP 1.50 4.00
440 Alex Rodriguez SP 3.00 8.00
441 Greg Holland SP 1.50 4.00
442 Jose Fernandez SP 2.50 6.00
443A Yu Darvish SP 2.50 6.00
443B Yu Darvish Color SP 6.00 15.00
444 Anthony Rizzo SP 3.00 8.00
445 Justin Upton SP 2.00 5.00
446A Troy Tulowitzki SP 2.50 6.00
446B Troy Tulowitzki Action SP 3.00 8.00
447 Brandon Crawford SP 2.00 5.00
448 Tyson Ross SP 1.50 4.00
449A Matt Kemp SP 2.00 5.00
449B Kemp Thrwbck SP 300.00 500.00
450A Bryce Harper SP 4.00 10.00
450B Harper Action SP 15.00 40.00
450C Harper Color SP 25.00 60.00
451 Stephen Vogt SP 2.00 5.00
452A Jose Abreu SP 2.50 6.00
452B Abreu Thrwbck SP 125.00 250.00
453 Michael Taylor SP 1.50 4.00
454 Ian Kinsler SP 2.00 5.00
455 Carlos Gonzalez SP 2.00 5.00
456 Dustin Pedroia SP 2.50 6.00
457 Nelson Cruz SP 2.50 6.00
458A Jason Kipnis SP 2.00 5.00
458B Kipnis Thrwbck SP
459 Max Scherzer SP 2.50 6.00
460A Buster Posey SP 3.00 8.00
460B Posey Action SP 4.00 10.00
460C Posey Color SP 8.00 20.00
461 Felix Hernandez SP 2.00 5.00
462 Dellin Betances SP 2.00 5.00
463 Josh Hamilton SP 2.00 5.00
464A Shelby Miller SP 2.00 5.00
464B Miller Traded SP 30.00 80.00
465A Paul Goldschmidt SP 2.50 6.00
465B Goldschmidt Thrwbck SP 400.00 600.00
466 A.J. Pollock SP 1.50 4.00
467 Christian Yelich SP 3.00 8.00
468 Yoenis Cespedes SP 2.50 6.00
469A Mookie Betts SP 5.00 12.00
469B Betts Actions SP 6.00 15.00
469C Betts Thrwbck SP 300.00 600.00
470 Jose Altuve SP 2.00 5.00
471 Randal Grichuk SP 1.50 4.00
472A Todd Frazier SP 1.50 4.00
472B Todd Frazier Color SP 4.00 10.00
473A Maikel Franco SP 2.00 5.00
473B Franco Thrwbck SP 200.00 400.00
474A Joey Votto SP 2.50 6.00
474B Votto ERR SP 50.00 120.00
474C Votto Throwback SP
475A Carlos Correa SP 2.50 6.00
475B Correa Action SP 12.00 30.00
475C Correa Thrwbck SP 300.00 600.00
476 David Peralta SP 1.50 4.00
477 David Price SP 2.00 5.00
478A Miguel Cabrera SP 2.50 6.00
478B Cabrera Color SP 15.00 40.00
479A Lorenzo Cain SP 1.50 4.00
479B Lorenzo Cain Action SP 2.00 5.00
480 Pedro Alvarez SP 1.50 4.00
481A Albert Pujols SP 3.00 8.00
481B Pujols Color SP 8.00 20.00
482A Francisco Lindor SP 2.50 6.00
482B Lindor Action SP 3.00 8.00
483A Josh Donaldson SP 2.00 5.00
483B Josh Donaldson Color SP 5.00 12.00
484 Billy Burns SP 1.50 4.00
485 Cole Hamels SP 2.00 5.00
486 Rusney Castillo SP 1.50 4.00
487 Freddie Freeman SP 3.00 8.00
488 Joey Gallo SP 2.00 5.00
489 Taylor Jungmann SP 1.50 4.00
490 Eric Hosmer SP 2.00 5.00
491 Edinson Volquez SP 1.50 4.00
492A Noah Syndergaard SP 2.00 5.00
492B Syndrgrd Action SP 2.50 6.00
493 Matt Harvey SP 2.00 5.00
494 Evan Longoria SP 2.00 5.00
495A Jacob deGrom SP 5.00 12.00
495B deGrom Color SP 12.00 30.00
496 Ryan Braun SP 2.00 5.00
497 Charlie Blackmon SP 2.50 6.00
498 Odubel Herrera SP 2.00 5.00
499 Jason Heyward SP 2.00 5.00
500A Mike Trout SP 12.00 30.00
500B Trout Action SP 15.00 40.00
501 Hank Conger .15 .40
502 Juan Lagares .15 .40
503 Travis Shaw .15 .40
504 Danny Valencia .20 .50
505 Willson Contreras RC 1.50 4.00
506 Joe Smith .15 .40
507 Jeimer Candelario RC .40 1.00
508 Pedro Alvarez .15 .40
509 Derek Holland .15 .40
510 Corey Dickerson .15 .40
511 Austin Jackson .15 .40
512 Jim Henderson .15 .40
513 Rich Hill .15 .40
514A Lucas Giolito RC .50 1.25
514B Lucas Giolito ERR SP Golto 25.00 60.00
515 Melvin Upton Jr. .20 .50
516 Shawn Morimando RC .30 .75
517 Jon Jay .15 .40
518A Jayson Werth .20 .50
518B Jayson Werth Action SP 2.50 6.00
518C Jayson Werth Color SP 5.00 12.00
519 Joaquin Benoit .15 .40
520A Ben Revere .15 .40
520B Revere Thrwbck SP 100.00 200.00
521 Aaron Hill .15 .40
522 Keon Broxton RC .30 .75
523 Logan Verrett .15 .40
524 David Ross .15 .40
525 Alex Presley .15 .40
526 Travis d'Arnaud .20 .50
527 Jed Lowrie .15 .40
528A Scott Kazmir .15 .40
528B Scott Kazmir Color SP 4.00 10.00
529 Enrique Hernandez .25 .60
530 Ezequiel Carrera .15 .40
531 Ryan Dull .15 .40
532 Justin Upton .20 .50
533 Adam Conley .15 .40
534 Gavin Floyd .15 .40
535 Chris Young .15 .40
536 Ryan Madson .15 .40
537 Phil Gosselin .15 .40
538 Wei-Yin Chen .15 .40
539 Vance Worley .15 .40
540 Matt Buschmann RC .30 .75

541 Joe Ross .15 .40
542 Chris Coghlan .15 .40
543 Daniel Castro .15 .40
544 Chris Carter .15 .40
545 Peter Bourjos .15 .40
546 Matt Wieters .25 .60
547 Michael Saunders .20 .50
548 Charlie Morton .25 .60
549A Ian Kennedy .15 .40
549B Kennedy Thrwbck SP 200.00 400.00
550 Jonathan Broxton .15 .40
551 Tyler Clippard .15 .40
552 Jon Niese .15 .40
553 Joe Blanton .15 .40
554 Matt Joyce .15 .40
555 Tanner Roark .15 .40
556 Joe Biagini RC .30 .75
557 Chris Tillman .15 .40
558 Mike Napoli .15 .40
559A Edwin Diaz RC .60 1.50
559B Diaz Thrwbck SP 150.00 300.00
560 Charlie Culberson .15 .40
561 David Freese .15 .40
562 Ryan Vogelsong .15 .40
563 Ryan Goins .15 .40
564A Ben Zobrist .20 .50
564B Ben Zobrist Action SP 2.50 6.00
564C Ben Zobrist Color SP 5.00 12.00
564D Zobrist Thrwbck SP 200.00 400.00
565 A.J. Griffin .15 .40
566A Joey Rickard RC .30 .75
566B Joey Rickard Action SP 2.00 5.00
566C Joey Rickard Color SP 4.00 10.00
567 Wilson Ramos .15 .40
568 Angel Pagan .15 .40
569 Craig Breslow .15 .40
570 John Jaso .15 .40
571 Jeff Francoeur .20 .50
572 Doug Fister .15 .40
573 Lance McCullers RC .30 .75
574 Bud Norris .15 .40
575 Howie Kendrick .15 .40
576 Drew Storen .15 .40
577 Nick Tropeano .15 .40
578 Alejandro De Aza .15 .40
579 Will Harris .15 .40
580 Mike Leake .15 .40
581 Patrick Corbin .20 .50
582A Jonathan Villar .15 .40
582B Jonathan Villar Color SP 4.00 10.00
582C Villar Thrwbck SP 200.00 400.00
583 Rickie Weeks .15 .40
584 Yusmeiro Petit .15 .40
585A Jeremy Hazelbaker RC .40 1.00
585B Jeremy Hazelbaker Color SP 5.00 12.00
586 J.A. Happ .20 .50
587 Munenori Kawasaki .15 .40
588A Johnny Cueto .20 .50
588B Johnny Cueto Action SP 2.50 6.00
588C Johnny Cueto Color SP 5.00 12.00
589 Josh Phegley .15 .40
590 Pat Neshek .15 .40
591 Matt Moore .20 .50
592 Adeiny Hechavarria .15 .40
593 Leonys Martin .15 .40
594 Stephen Drew .15 .40
595 Jimmy Nelson .15 .40
596 Adam Warren .15 .40
597 Jabari Blash RC .30 .75
598 Matt Szczur .20 .50
599 Ji-Man Choi RC .40 1.00
600A Julio Urias RC 1.00 2.50
600B Urias Color SP 12.00 30.00
600C Urias ERR SP No Sig 30.00 80.00
601 Devin Mesoraco .15 .40
602 Tony Cingrani .20 .50
603 Brandon Finnegan .15 .40
604 Raisel Iglesias .20 .50
605 Jake McGee .15 .40
606A Alexei Ramirez .20 .50
606B Alexei Ramirez Action SP 2.50 6.00
607 Mark Reynolds .15 .40
608 Cody Reed RC .30 .75
609 Luke Hochevar .15 .40
610 Jarrod Saltalamacchia .15 .40
611 Yovani Gallardo .15 .40
612 Eduardo Nunez .15 .40
613 Fernando Abad .15 .40
614A Drew Pomeranz .20 .50
614B Pomeranz Thrwbck SP 200.00 400.00
615 Junichi Tazawa .15 .40
616 Adonis Garcia .15 .40
617 Jose Quintana .15 .40
618 Chris Capuano .15 .40
619 Johnny Barbato RC .30 .75
620 Matthew Bowman RC .30 .75
621 Chris Johnson .15 .40
622 Khris Davis .25 .60
623 Denard Span .15 .40
624 Ian Desmond .15 .40
625 Gerardo Parra .15 .40
626 Mark Lowe .15 .40
627 Kurt Suzuki .15 .40
628 Jean Segura .20 .50
629 Steve Cishek .15 .40
630A Jameson Taillon RC .40 1.00
630B Jameson Taillon Color SP 5.00 12.00
630C Taillon Thrwbck SP 200.00 400.00
631 Tim Lincecum .20 .50
632 Michael Ynoa RC .30 .75
633 Jason Grilli .15 .40
634 Tyrell Jenkins RC .30 .75
635A Albert Almora RC .40 1.00
635B Albert Almora Color SP 5.00 12.00
636 Jake Barrett RC .30 .75
637 A.J. Reed RC .30 .75
638 Matt Purke RC .30 .75
639 Mike Clevinger RC .60 1.50
640 Adam Wainwright .20 .50
641 Colin Moran RC .30 .75
642 Matt Bush (RC) .20 .50
643 Luis Cessa RC .30 .75
644A Daniel Murphy .20 .50
644B Daniel Murphy Color SP 5.00 12.00
644C Murphy ERR NE Mets 20.00 50.00
645 Pat Dean RC .30 .75
646 Ryan O'Rourke RC .30 .75
647 Carlos Estevez RC .30 .75
648A Michael Fulmer RC .50 1.25
648B Fulmer Action SP 3.00 8.00
648C Fulmer Color SP 6.00 15.00
648D Fulmer ERR SP Pitcher 25.00 60.00
649 Matt Barnes .15 .40
650 Ben Gamel RC .40 1.00
651 Alen Hanson RC .40 1.00
652 Tony Kemp RC .30 .75
653A Steven Wright .15 .40
653B Steven Wright Color SP 4.00 10.00
654 Brad Ziegler .15 .40
655 Matt Reynolds RC .30 .75
656A Adam Duvall .40 1.00
656B Duvall Color SP 10.00 25.00
656C Duvall Thrwbck SP 200.00 400.00
657A James Loney .15 .40
657B Loney Thrwbck SP 150.00 300.00
658 Cameron Rupp .15 .40
659 Zach Eflin RC .40 1.00
660A Johnny Giavotella .15 .40
660B Giavotella Thrwbck SP 150.00 300.00
661 Geovany Soto .15 .40
662 Paulo Orlando .15 .40
663 Sean Manaea RC .30 .75
664 Darwin Barney .15 .40
665 Jurickson Profar .20 .50
666 Fernando Rodney .15 .40
667 Tyler Goeddel RC .30 .75
668 Chad Kuhl RC .40 1.00
669 Mychal Givens .15 .40
670 Danny Santana .15 .40
671A Kevin Plawecki .15 .40
671B Kevin Plawecki Action SP 2.00 5.00
672 Rafael Ortega .15 .40
673 Hunter Cervenka RC .30 .75
674A Tim Anderson RC 1.25 3.00
674B Tim Anderson Color SP 15.00 40.00
674C Anderson Thrwbck SP 200.00 400.00
675 Blaine Boyer .15 .40
676 Brandon Moss .15 .40
677 Michael Bourn .15 .40
678 Drew Stubbs .15 .40
679 Josh Tomlin .15 .40
680 Tyler Chatwood .15 .40
681 Josh Rutledge .15 .40
682A Sandy Leon RC .40 1.00
682B Leon Thrwbck SP 200.00 400.00
683 Whit Merrifield RC 20.00 50.00
684 Nolan Reimold .15 .40
685 Taylor Motter RC .30 .75
686 Tommy Joseph RC .60 1.50
687 Tim Adleman RC .30 .75
688 Tony Barnette RC .30 .75
689 Sam Dyson .15 .40
690 Ivan Nova .20 .50
691 Dillon Gee .15 .40
692 Steven Moya .15 .40
693 C.J. Wilson .15 .40
694 Ryan Hanigan .15 .40
695 Chris Herrmann .15 .40
696 Brad Brach .15 .40
697 Derek Law RC .40 1.00
698 Jose Ramirez .20 .50
699 Hector Neris .15 .40
700 David Price .20 .50
701A Kenta Maeda SP RC 2.00 5.00
701B Maeda Action SP 4.00 10.00
701C Maeda Color SP 8.00 20.00
701D Maeda ERR SP Blank back 25.00 60.00
702 Aaron Blair SP RC 1.00 2.50
703A Seung-hwan Oh SP RC 2.50 6.00
703B Oh Color SP 10.00 25.00
703C Oh Thrwbck SP 150.00 300.00
704A Nomar Mazara SP RC 1.50 4.00
704B Mazara Action SP 3.00 8.00
704C Mazara Color SP 6.00 15.00
705A Blake Snell SP RC 1.25 3.00
705B Blake Snell Color SP 5.00 12.00
706 Robert Stephenson SP RC 1.00 2.50
707A Trevor Story SP RC 5.00 12.00
707B Story Action SP 10.00 25.00
707C Story Color SP 20.00 50.00
707D Story ERR SP No Line 25.00 60.00
708A Byung-Ho Park SP RC 1.25 3.00
708B Byung-Ho Park Color SP 5.00 12.00
709 Jose Berrios SP RC 1.50 4.00
710 Tyler White SP RC 1.00 2.50
711A Marcus Stroman SP 1.25 3.00
711B Marcus Stroman Action SP 2.50 6.00
712 Mallex Smith SP RC 1.00 2.50
713A Aledmys Diaz SP RC 4.00 10.00
713B Diaz Action SP 8.00 20.00
713C Diaz Color SP 20.00 50.00
713D Diaz Thrwbck SP 400.00 600.00
714A Tyler Naquin SP RC 1.50 4.00
714B Tyler Naquin Color SP 6.00 15.00
714C Naquin Thrwbck SP 300.00 500.00
715A Vince Velasquez SP 1.00 2.50
715B Vince Velasquez Color SP 4.00 10.00
716A Christian Vazquez SP 1.25 3.00
716B Christian Vazquez Action SP 2.50 6.00
717 Max Kepler SP RC 1.50 4.00
718A Aroldis Chapman SP 1.50 4.00
718B Aroldis Chapman Action SP 3.00 8.00
718C Aroldis Chapman Color SP 6.00 15.00
719 Domingo Santana SP 1.25 3.00
720 Ross Stripling SP RC 1.00 2.50
721A Hyun Soo Kim SP RC 1.50 4.00
721B Hyun Soo Kim Action SP 3.00 8.00
722 Aaron Sanchez SP 1.25 3.00
723 Javier Baez SP 2.00 5.00
724 Jeff Samardzija SP 1.00 2.50
725 Chase Headley SP 1.00 2.50

2016 Topps Heritage Black

INSERTED IN HN RETAIL PACKS
505 Willson Contreras 3.00 8.00
511 Austin Jackson .50 1.25
514 Lucas Giolito .75 2.00
528 Scott Kazmir .50 1.25
532 Justin Upton .60 1.50
541 Joe Ross .50 1.25
559 Edwin Diaz 1.00 2.50
566 Joey Rickard .50 1.25
588 Johnny Cueto .60 1.50
590 Pat Neshek .50 1.25
600 Julio Urias 1.50 4.00
606 Alexei Ramirez .60 1.50
611 Yovani Gallardo .50 1.25
614 Drew Pomeranz .60 1.50
628 Jean Segura .60 1.50
630 Jameson Taillon .60 1.50
635 Albert Almora .60 1.50
640 Adam Wainwright .60 1.50
644 Daniel Murphy .60 1.50
648 Michael Fulmer .75 2.00
649 Tanner Roark .50 1.25
653 Steven Wright .50 1.25
668 Ben Zobrist .60 1.50
674 Tim Anderson 2.00 5.00
693 C.J. Wilson .50 1.25
701 Kenta Maeda 1.00 2.50
702 Aaron Blair .50 1.25
703 Seung-hwan Oh 1.25 3.00
704 Nomar Mazara .75 2.00
705 Blake Snell .60 1.50
706 Robert Stephenson .50 1.25
707 Trevor Story 2.50 6.00
708 Byung-Ho Park .60 1.50
709 Jose Berrios .75 2.00
710 Tyler White .50 1.25
711 Marcus Stroman .60 1.50
712 Mallex Smith .50 1.25
713 Aledmys Diaz .75 2.00
714 Tyler Naquin .75 2.00
715 Vince Velasquez .50 1.25
716 Christian Vazquez .60 1.50
717 Max Kepler .75 2.00
718 Aroldis Chapman .75 2.00
719 Domingo Santana .60 1.50
720 Ross Stripling .50 1.25
721 Hyun Soo Kim .75 2.00
722 Aaron Sanchez .60 1.50
723 Javier Baez 1.00 2.50
724 Jeff Samardzija .50 1.25
725 Chase Headley .50 1.25

2016 Topps Heritage Gum Stained Back

*GUM BACK VET: 4X TO 10X BASIC
*GUM BACK RC: 2X TO 5X BASIC RC
*GUM BACK SP: .4X TO 1X BASIC SP
RANDOM INSERTS IN PACKS
HN STATED ODDS 1:50 HOBBY
70 Kris Bryant 25.00 60.00
168 Seager/Peraza 12.00 30.00
243 Cruz/Trout/Davis 5.00 12.00
450 Bryce Harper 30.00 80.00
460 Buster Posey 10.00 25.00
475 Carlos Correa 20.00 50.00
500 Mike Trout 30.00 80.00

2016 Topps Heritage '67 Poster Boxloader

STATED ODDS 1:34 HOBBY BOXES
ANNCD PRINT RUN 50 COPIES PER
67PBAG Adrian Gonzalez 8.00 20.00
67PBBH Bryce Harper 25.00 60.00
67PBBP Buster Posey 20.00 50.00
67PBCC Carlos Correa 20.00 50.00
67PBCH Cole Hamels 10.00 25.00
67PBCK Corey Kluber 10.00 25.00
67PBCKE Clayton Kershaw 20.00 50.00
67PBDO David Ortiz 20.00 50.00
67PBGS Giancarlo Stanton 30.00 80.00
67PBJD Josh Donaldson 8.00 20.00
67PBJL Jon Lester 8.00 20.00
67PBJS James Shields 10.00 25.00
67PBKB Kris Bryant 40.00 100.00
67PBMH Matt Harvey 15.00 40.00
67PBMT Mark Teixeira 12.00 30.00
67PBMTR Mike Trout 60.00 150.00
67PBMW Michael Wacha 15.00 40.00
67PBPG Paul Goldschmidt 20.00 50.00
67PBPS Pablo Sandoval 12.00 30.00
67PBSG Sonny Gray 8.00 20.00

2016 Topps Heritage '67 Punch Outs Boxloader

STATED ODDS 1:34 HOBBY BOXES
HN STATED ODDS 1:47 HOBBY BOXES
ANNCD PRINT RUN 50 COPIES PER
67BPAG D/G/N/L/M/C/R/R/H 5.00 12.00
67BPCY G/G/S/W/K/M/H/P/Y 10.00 25.00
67BPFL C/H/L/O/R/B/D/W/J 6.00 15.00
67BPFR R/V/Z/N/P/S/S/N/B 12.00 30.00
67BPGS R/P/T/S/D/S/R/S/D 6.00 15.00
67BPJC J/T/C/H/C/R/S/O/R 6.00 15.00
67BPJF G/F/D/D/J/D/F/P/P 10.00 25.00
67BPMS M/S/F/S/W/C/G/S/R 6.00 15.00
67BPRC S/P/V/C/G/B/R/C/M 8.00 20.00
67BPTT F/G/T/R/L/F/M/P/O 6.00 15.00
67POBAM H/C/C/K/M/S/K/W/K/R 8.00 20.00
67POBAN D/Y/G/P/N/P/O/D/R 8.00 20.00
67POBAP S/C/M/H/B/P/P/C/K 8.00 20.00
67POBAR E/G/V/H/R/A/P/E/B 8.00 20.00
67POBBH H/C/C/W/U/H/W/P/F 10.00 25.00
67POBBP P/R/B/L/d/U/P/P/B 12.00 30.00
67POBCC E/C/C/B/C/G/M/D/M 6.00 15.00
67POBCK K/H/M/C/M/G/P/S/D 10.00 25.00
67POBCS S/G/S/C/C/S/D/B/N 40.00 100.00
67POBDO H/O/S/D/S/S/K/C/P/D 6.00 15.00
67POBJD G/D/A/J/C/A/B/M/K 6.00 15.00
67POBKB S/B/R/M/G/U/S/M/H 8.00 20.00
67POBKS A/S/G/C/H/T/P/A/A 12.00 30.00
67POBLS S/S/E/B/H/A/I/S/T 6.00 15.00
67POBMB F/P/F/M/L/B/C/F/M/L 8.00 20.00
67POBMC M/G/L/I/S/C/T/N/R 6.00 15.00
67POBMH M/M/H/G/P/W/A/E/M 5.00 12.00
67POBMT C/B/T/G/D/C/B/G/P 30.00 80.00
67POBSP M/R/S/P/B/B/F/E/G 6.00 15.00
67POBZG A/Z/E/I/B/H/G/G/B 6.00 15.00

2016 Topps Heritage '67 Punch Outs Boxloader Patches

STATED ODDS 1:67 HOBBY BOXES
HN STATED ODDS 1:307 HOBBY BOXES
STATED PRINT RUN 25 SER.#'d SETS
67PJPRNC Nelson Cruz 12.00 30.00
67PJPRVM Victor Martinez 10.00 25.00
67PJPRYC Yoenis Cespedes 40.00 100.00
67POBPRAC Aroldis Chapman 12.00 30.00
67POBPRAJ Adam Jones 50.00 120.00
67POBPRAM Andrew McCutchen 50.00 120.00
67POBPRAW Adam Wainwright 10.00 25.00
67POBPRCA Chris Archer 8.00 20.00
67POBPRCD Chris Davis 8.00 20.00
67POBPRDP Dustin Pedroia 25.00 60.00
67POBPRFF Freddie Freeman 15.00 40.00
67POBPRGC Gerrit Cole 12.00 30.00
67POBPRI Ichiro Suzuki 15.00 40.00
67POBPRJP Joc Pederson 20.00 50.00
67POBPRJVE Justin Verlander 12.00 30.00
67POBPRJVO Joey Votto 25.00 60.00
67POBPRMC Miguel Cabrera 20.00 50.00
67POBPRNA Nolan Arenado 25.00 60.00
67POBPRRZ Ryan Zimmerman 10.00 25.00
67POBPRSP Salvador Perez 20.00 50.00
67POBPRSS Stephen Strasburg 20.00 50.00
67POBPRTF Todd Frazier 20.00 50.00
67POBPRWF Wilmer Flores 25.00 60.00

2016 Topps Heritage Award Winners

COMPLETE SET (10) 5.00 12.00
HN ODDS 1:8 HOBBY
AW1 Josh Donaldson .40 1.00
AW2 Bryce Harper .75 2.00
AW3 Dallas Keuchel .40 1.00
AW4 Jake Arrieta .40 1.00
AW5 Carlos Correa .50 1.25
AW6 Kris Bryant .60 1.50
AW7 Jeff Banister .30 .75
AW8 Joe Maddon .30 .75
AW9 Salvador Perez .40 1.00
AW10 Mike Trout 2.50 6.00

2016 Topps Heritage Baseball Flashbacks

COMPLETE SET (10) 3.00 8.00
STATED ODDS 1:12 HOBBY
BFBG Bob Gibson .40 1.00
BFCH Catfish Hunter .40 1.00
BFEM Eddie Mathews .50 1.25
BFOC Orlando Cepeda .40 1.00
BFRCA Rod Carew .40 1.00
BFRCL Roberto Clemente 1.25 3.00
BFRM Roger Maris .50 1.25
BFTP Tony Perez .40 1.00
BFTS Tom Seaver .40 1.00
BFWF Whitey Ford .40 1.00

2016 Topps Heritage Bazooka

INSERTED IN RETAIL PACKS
STATED PRINT RUN 25 SER.#'d SETS
HN CARDS ARE NOT SERIAL NUMBERED
67BAM Andrew McCutchen 10.00 25.00
67BAP Albert Pujols 12.00 30.00
67BARI Anthony Rizzo 12.00 30.00
67BARO Alex Rodriguez 12.00 30.00
67BBH Bryce Harper 30.00 80.00
67BBP Buster Posey 12.00 30.00
67BCA Chris Archer 6.00 15.00
67BCC Carlos Correa 25.00 60.00
67BCK Clayton Kershaw 25.00 60.00
67BCS Chris Sale HN 10.00 25.00
67BDK Dallas Keuchel 8.00 20.00
67BDO David Ortiz HN 10.00 25.00
67BDPE Dustin Pedroia 15.00 40.00
67BDPR David Price 8.00 20.00
67BJA Jake Arrieta 8.00 20.00
67BJD Josh Donaldson 8.00 20.00
67BJV Joey Votto 10.00 25.00
67BKB Kris Bryant 30.00 80.00
67BKM Kenta Maeda HN 12.00 30.00
67BLC Lorenzo Cain 6.00 15.00
67BMB Madison Bumgarner 8.00 20.00
67BMC Miguel Cabrera 20.00 50.00
67BMF Michael Fulmer HN 10.00 25.00
67BMH Matt Harvey 12.00 30.00
67BMT Mike Trout 40.00 100.00
67BNA Nolan Arenado HN 15.00 40.00
67BNC Nelson Cruz 10.00 25.00
67BNM Nomar Mazara HN 10.00 25.00
67BNS Noah Syndergaard HN 8.00 20.00
67BPG Paul Goldschmidt 10.00 25.00
67BSS Stephen Strasburg HN 10.00 25.00
67BTS Trevor Story HN 30.00 80.00
67BXB Xander Bogaerts HN 10.00 25.00
67BYM Yadier Molina 12.00 30.00
67BZG Zack Greinke 10.00 25.00

2016 Topps Heritage Chrome

STATED ODDS 1:25 HOBBY
HN ODDS 1:22 HOBBY
STATED PRINT RUN 999 SER.#'d SETS
*PRPLE REF: .4X TO 1X BASIC
*REF/567: .6X TO 1.5X BASIC
THC40 Kole Calhoun 1.25 3.00
THC50 Byron Buxton 2.00 5.00
THC60 Chris Davis 1.25 3.00
THC70 Kris Bryant 2.50 6.00
THC80 Aroldis Chapman 2.00 5.00
THC90 Sonny Gray 1.50 4.00
THC100 Adam Jones 1.50 4.00
THC130 Zack Greinke 2.00 5.00
THC140 Starling Marte 1.50 4.00
THC157 Manny Machado 2.00 5.00
THC161 Schwarber/Edwards Jr. 4.00 10.00
THC190 Luis Severino 2.00 5.00
Miguel Sano
THC210 Michael Wacha 1.50 4.00
THC220 Matt Duffy 1.25 3.00
THC253 Michael Brantley 1.50 4.00
THC290 Ryan Howard 1.50 4.00
THC310 Chris Sale 2.00 5.00
THC320 Madison Bumgarner 1.50 4.00
THC322 Giancarlo Stanton 2.00 5.00
THC340 Mark Teixeira 1.50 4.00
THC390 George Springer 1.50 4.00
THC400 Andrew McCutchen 2.00 5.00
THC410 Yasiel Puig 2.00 5.00
THC420 Justin Verlander 2.00 5.00
THC425 Gerrit Cole 2.00 5.00
THC426 Clayton Kershaw 3.00 8.00
THC427 Brian Dozier 1.50 4.00
THC428 Corey Kluber 1.50 4.00
THC429 Jake Odorizzi 1.25 3.00
THC430 Dallas Keuchel 1.50 4.00
THC431 Jose Bautista 1.50 4.00
THC432 Robinson Cano 1.50 4.00
THC433 Prince Fielder 1.50 4.00
THC434 Jonathan Lucroy 1.50 4.00
THC435 Chris Archer 1.25 3.00
THC436 Masahiro Tanaka 1.50 4.00
THC437 Addison Russell 2.00 5.00
THC438 David Ortiz 2.00 5.00
THC439 Andrelton Simmons 1.25 3.00
THC440 Alex Rodriguez 2.50 6.00
THC441 Greg Holland 1.25 3.00
THC442 Jose Fernandez 2.00 5.00
THC443 Yu Darvish 2.00 5.00
THC444 Anthony Rizzo 2.50 6.00
THC445 Justin Upton 1.50 4.00
THC446 Troy Tulowitzki 2.00 5.00
THC447 Brandon Crawford 1.50 4.00
THC448 Tyson Ross 1.25 3.00
THC449 Matt Kemp 1.50 4.00
THC450 Bryce Harper 3.00 8.00
THC451 Stephen Vogt 1.50 4.00
THC452 Jose Abreu 2.00 5.00
THC453 Michael Taylor 1.25 3.00
THC454 Ian Kinsler 1.50 4.00
THC455 Carlos Gonzalez 1.50 4.00
THC456 Dustin Pedroia 2.00 5.00
THC457 Nelson Cruz 2.00 5.00
THC458 Jason Kipnis 1.50 4.00
THC459 Max Scherzer 2.00 5.00
THC460 Buster Posey 2.50 6.00
THC461 Felix Hernandez 1.50 4.00
THC462 Dellin Betances 1.50 4.00
THC463 Josh Hamilton 1.50 4.00
THC464 Shelby Miller 1.50 4.00
THC465 Paul Goldschmidt 2.00 5.00
THC466 A.J. Pollock 1.25 3.00
THC467 Christian Yelich 2.50 6.00
THC468 Yoenis Cespedes 2.00 5.00
THC469 Mookie Betts 4.00 10.00
THC470 Jose Altuve 1.50 4.00
THC471 Randal Grichuk 1.25 3.00
THC472 Todd Frazier 1.25 3.00
THC473 Maikel Franco 1.50 4.00
THC474 Joey Votto 2.00 5.00
THC475 Carlos Correa 2.00 5.00
THC476 David Peralta 1.25 3.00
THC477 David Price 1.50 4.00
THC478 Miguel Cabrera 2.00 5.00
THC479 Lorenzo Cain 1.25 3.00
THC480 Pedro Alvarez 1.25 3.00
THC481 Albert Pujols 2.50 6.00
THC482 Francisco Lindor 2.00 5.00
THC483 Josh Donaldson 1.50 4.00
THC484 Billy Burns 1.25 3.00
THC485 Cole Hamels 1.50 4.00
THC486 Rusney Castillo 1.25 3.00
THC487 Freddie Freeman 2.50 6.00
THC488 Joey Gallo 1.50 4.00
THC489 Taylor Jungmann 1.25 3.00
THC490 Eric Hosmer 1.50 4.00
THC491 Edinson Volquez 1.25 3.00
THC492 Noah Syndergaard 1.50 4.00
THC493 Matt Harvey 1.50 4.00
THC494 Evan Longoria 1.50 4.00
THC495 Jacob deGrom 4.00 10.00
THC496 Ryan Braun 1.50 4.00
THC497 Charlie Blackmon 2.00 5.00
THC498 Odubel Herrera 1.50 4.00
THC499 Jason Heyward 1.50 4.00
THC500 Mike Trout 10.00 25.00
THC505 Willson Contreras 3.00 8.00
THC511 Austin Jackson 1.25 3.00
THC514 Lucas Giolito 2.00 5.00
THC528 Scott Kazmir 1.25 3.00
THC532 Justin Upton 1.50 4.00
THC541 Joe Ross 1.25 3.00
THC559 Edwin Diaz 2.50 6.00
THC566 Joey Rickard 1.25 3.00
THC588 Johnny Cueto 1.50 4.00
THC590 Pat Neshek 1.25 3.00
THC600 Julio Urias 4.00 10.00
THC606 Alexei Ramirez 1.50 4.00
THC611 Yovani Gallardo 1.25 3.00
THC614 Drew Pomeranz 1.50 4.00
THC628 Jean Segura 1.50 4.00
THC630 Jameson Taillon 1.50 4.00
THC635 Albert Almora 1.50 4.00
THC640 Adam Wainwright 1.50 4.00
THC644 Daniel Murphy 1.50 4.00
THC648 Michael Fulmer 2.00 5.00
THC649 Tanner Roark 1.25 3.00
THC653 Steven Wright 1.25 3.00
THC668 Ben Zobrist 1.50 4.00
THC674 Tim Anderson 5.00 12.00
THC693 C.J. Wilson 1.25 3.00
THC701 Kenta Maeda 2.50 6.00
THC702 Aaron Blair 1.25 3.00
THC703 Seung-hwan Oh 3.00 8.00
THC704 Nomar Mazara 2.00 5.00
THC705 Blake Snell 1.50 4.00
THC706 Robert Stephenson 1.25 3.00
THC707 Trevor Story 6.00 15.00
THC708 Byung-Ho Park 1.50 4.00
THC709 Jose Berrios 2.00 5.00
THC710 Tyler White 1.25 3.00
THC711 Marcus Stroman 1.50 4.00
THC712 Mallex Smith 1.25 3.00
THC713 Aledmys Diaz 5.00 12.00
THC714 Tyler Naquin 2.00 5.00
THC715 Vince Velasquez 1.25 3.00
THC716 Christian Vazquez 1.50 4.00
THC717 Max Kepler 2.00 5.00
THC718 Aroldis Chapman 2.00 5.00
THC719 Domingo Santana 1.50 4.00
THC720 Ross Stripling 1.25 3.00
THC721 Hyun-Soo Kim 2.00 5.00
THC722 Aaron Sanchez 1.50 4.00
THC723 Javier Baez 2.50 6.00
THC724 Jeff Samardzija 1.25 3.00
THC725 Chase Headley 1.25 3.00

2016 Topps Heritage Chrome Black Refractors

*BLACK REF: 2.5X TO 6X BASIC
STATED ODDS 1:359 HOBBY
HN ODDS 1:321 HOBBY
STATED PRINT RUN 67 SER.#'d SETS
THC50 Byron Buxton 20.00 50.00
THC70 Kris Bryant 150.00 300.00
THC190 L.Severino/M.Sano 25.00 60.00
THC320 Madison Bumgarner 20.00 50.00
THC440 Alex Rodriguez 25.00 60.00
THC460 Buster Posey 25.00 60.00
THC475 Carlos Correa 75.00 150.00
THC478 Miguel Cabrera 30.00 80.00
THC492 Noah Syndergaard 25.00 60.00
THC493 Matt Harvey 10.00 25.00
THC500 Mike Trout 100.00 200.00

2016 Topps Heritage Clubhouse Collection Dual Relics

STATED ODDS 1:7211 HOBBY
HN STATED ODDS 1:2451 HOBBY
STATED PRINT RUN 67 SER.#'d SETS
CCDRCW S.Carlton/A.Wainwright 30.00 80.00
CCDRFV T.Frazier/J.Votto 25.00 60.00
CCDRHW D.Wright/M.Harvey 20.00 50.00
CCDRMA J.Altuve/J.Morgan 30.00 80.00
CCDRMP B.Posey/W.Mays 25.00 60.00
CCDRPB M.Bumgarner/B.Posey 30.00 80.00
CCDRPP J.Pederson/Y.Puig 25.00 60.00
CCDRPV T.Perez/J.Votto 30.00 80.00
CCDRTP A.Pujols/M.Trout 50.00 120.00
CCDRYO D.Ortiz/C.Yastrzemski 25.00 60.00

2016 Topps Heritage Clubhouse Collection Relic Autographs

STATED ODDS 1:9645 HOBBY
HN STATED ODDS 1:3248 HOBBY
STATED PRINT RUN 25 SER.#'d SETS
EXCHANGE DEADLINE 2/28/2018
HN EXCH DEADLINE 8/31/2018
CCARAG Alex Gordon
CCARBH Bryce Harper EXCH 250.00 400.00
CCARBP Buster Posey 200.00 300.00
CCARCK Clayton Kershaw EXCH 250.00 400.00
CCARCR Carlos Rodon 30.00 80.00
CCARDG Dee Gordon
CCARFL Francisco Lindor 40.00 100.00
CCARHR Hanley Ramirez EXCH 12.00 30.00
CCARJA Jose Altuve 150.00 400.00
CCARJH Jason Heyward 100.00 250.00
CCARKB Kris Bryant 300.00 500.00
CCARKS Kyle Schwarber 60.00 150.00
CCARLS Luis Severino 100.00 200.00
CCARMM Manny Machado 125.00 250.00
CCARMS Miguel Sano 100.00 200.00
CCARMT Mike Trout
CCARNA Nolan Arenado 125.00 300.00
CCARNS Noah Syndergaard 50.00 120.00
CCARPS Pablo Sandoval 40.00 100.00

2016 Topps Heritage Clubhouse Collection Relics

STATED ODDS 1:33 HOBBY
HN STATED ODDS 1:45 HOBBY
CCRI Ichiro Suzuki HN 4.00 10.00
CCRI Ichiro Suzuki 4.00 10.00
CCRAG Adrian Gonzalez HN 2.50 6.00
CCRAG Adrian Gonzalez 2.50 6.00
CCRAJ Adam Jones HN 2.50 6.00
CCRAM Andrew McCutchen HN 3.00 8.00
CCRAM Andrew McCutchen 3.00 8.00
CCRAP Albert Pujols HN 4.00 10.00
CCRAPU Albert Pujols 4.00 10.00
CCRAR Anthony Rizzo HN 4.00 10.00
CCRARI Anthony Rizzo HN 4.00 10.00
CCRARU Addison Russell HN 3.00 8.00
CCRAW Adam Wainwright HN 2.50 6.00
CCRBH Bryce Harper HN 5.00 12.00
CCRBHAM Billy Hamilton 2.50 6.00
CCRBP Buster Posey 4.00 10.00
CCRBPH Brandon Phillips HN 2.00 5.00
CCRBPO Buster Posey HN 4.00 10.00
CCRCB Charlie Blackmon 3.00 8.00
CCRCD Chris Davis HN 2.00 5.00
CCRCD Chris Davis 2.00 5.00
CCRCH Cole Hamels HN 2.50 6.00
CCRCKE Clayton Kershaw HN 5.00 12.00
CCRCKE Clayton Kershaw 5.00 12.00
CCRCKI Craig Kimbrel HN 2.50 6.00
CCRCKL Corey Kluber 2.50 6.00
CCRCS Chris Sale HN 3.00 8.00
CCRCS Chris Sale 3.00 8.00
CCRDK Dallas Keuchel 2.50 6.00
CCRDO David Ortiz HN 3.00 8.00
CCRDO David Ortiz 3.00 8.00
CCRDP David Price HN 2.50 6.00
CCRDP David Price 2.50 6.00
CCRDW David Wright HN 2.50 6.00
CCRFF Freddie Freeman 4.00 10.00
CCRFH Felix Hernandez HN 2.50 6.00
CCRGC Gerrit Cole HN 3.00 8.00
CCRGC Gerrit Cole 3.00 8.00
CCRGS Giancarlo Stanton HN 3.00 8.00
CCRHR Hanley Ramirez 2.50 6.00
CCRJAB Jose Abreu HN 3.00 8.00
CCRJAB Jose Abreu 3.00 8.00
CCRJC Johnny Cueto HN 2.50 6.00
CCRJDE Jacob deGrom 6.00 15.00
CCRJH Jason Heyward HN 2.50 6.00
CCRJKA Jung Ho Kang 2.00 5.00
CCRJKI Jason Kipnis 2.50 6.00
CCRJM Joe Mauer HN 2.50 6.00
CCRJP Joc Pederson 2.50 6.00
CCRJS Jonathan Schoop 2.00 5.00
CCRJU Justin Upton HN 2.50 6.00
CCRJU Justin Upton 2.50 6.00
CCRJVE Justin Verlander HN 3.00 8.00
CCRJVE Justin Verlander 3.00 8.00
CCRJVO Joey Votto HN 3.00 8.00
CCRJVO Joey Votto 3.00 8.00
CCRKB Kris Bryant 4.00 10.00
CCRKS Kyle Schwarber
CCRLS Luis Severino 2.50 6.00
CCRMA Matt Adams 2.00 5.00
CCRMBR Michael Brantley HN 2.50 6.00
CCRMBU Madison Bumgarner 2.50 6.00
CCRMC Matt Carpenter HN 3.00 8.00
CCRMC Miguel Cabrera 3.00 8.00
CCRMCA Miguel Cabrera HN 3.00 8.00
CCRMH Matt Harvey HN 2.50 6.00
CCRMH Matt Harvey 2.50 6.00
CCRMK Matt Kemp HN 2.50 6.00
CCRMM Manny Machado HN 3.00 8.00
CCRMM Manny Machado 3.00 8.00
CCRMS Max Scherzer HN 3.00 8.00
CCRMSA Miguel Sano HN 3.00 8.00
CCRMT Mike Trout HN 8.00 20.00
CCRMTE Mark Teixeira 2.50 6.00
CCRMTR Mike Trout 8.00 20.00
CCRNA Nolan Arenado 5.00 12.00
CCRNS Noah Syndergaard HN 2.50 6.00
CCRNS Noah Syndergaard 2.50 6.00
CCRPF Prince Fielder HN 2.50 6.00
CCRPF Prince Fielder 2.50 6.00
CCRPG Paul Goldschmidt HN 3.00 8.00
CCRPG Paul Goldschmidt 3.00 8.00
CCRRB Ryan Braun 2.50 6.00
CCRRC Robinson Cano HN 2.50 6.00
CCRRC Robinson Cano 2.50 6.00
CCRRP Rick Porcello 2.50 6.00
CCRSMAR Starling Marte 2.50 6.00
CCRSMAT Steven Matz 2.00 5.00
CCRSMI Shelby Miller 2.50 6.00
CCRSPE Salvador Perez 2.50 6.00
CCRSS Stephen Strasburg 3.00 8.00
CCRTF Todd Frazier 2.00 5.00
CCRTT Troy Tulowitzki HN 3.00 8.00
CCRVM Victor Martinez 2.50 6.00
CCRYC Yoenis Cespedes HN 3.00 8.00
CCRYD Yu Darvish 3.00 8.00
CCRYM Yadier Molina HN 4.00 10.00
CCRYP Yasiel Puig HN 3.00 8.00

2016 Topps Heritage Clubhouse Collection Relics Gold

*GOLD: .6X TO 1.5X BASIC
STATED ODDS 1:405 HOBBY
HN STATED ODDS 1:194 HOBBY
STATED PRINT RUN 99 SER.#'d SETS
CCRKB Kris Bryant 20.00 50.00
CCRKS Kyle Schwarber 15.00 40.00

2016 Topps Heritage Clubhouse Collection Triple Relics

STATED ODDS 1:19,289 HOBBY
HN STATED ODDS 1:6617 HOBBY
STATED PRINT RUN 25 SER.#'d SETS
CCTRBRA Arrieta/Bryant/Rizzo 100.00 200.00
CCTRCVM Martinez/Cabrera/Verlander 30.00 80.00
CCTRFCV Frazier/Votto/Chapman 60.00 150.00
CCTRHDS Harvey/deGrom/Syndergaard 60.00 150.00
CCTRHDS Syndergaard/Harvey/deGrom 100.00200.00
CCTRHSZ Harper/Zimmerman/Strasburg 100.00
200.00
CCTRPBP Bumgarner/Posey/Pence 100.00 200.00
CCTRRSB Schwarber/Bryant/Rizzo 100.00 200.00
CCTRTPF Pujols/Freese/Trout 100.00 200.00
CCTRVCU Upton/Verlander/Cabrera 100.00 200.00

2016 Topps Heritage Combo Cards

COMPLETE SET (20) 8.00 20.00
HN ODDS 1:8 HOBBY
CC1 B.Harper/M.Scherzer .75 2.00
CC2 J.Panik/B.Posey .60 1.50
CC3 R.Cano/N.Cruz .50 1.25
CC4 A.Pujols/M.Trout 2.50 6.00
CC5 A.Jones/M.Machado .50 1.25
CC6 A.Gonzalez/J.Pederson .40 1.00
CC7 N.Mazara/A.Beltre .50 1.25
CC8 T.Story/N.Arenado 1.50 4.00
CC9 W.Castillo/P.Goldschmidt .50 1.25
CC10 D.Pedroia/H.Ramirez .50 1.25
CC11 X.Bogaerts/M.Betts 1.00 2.50
CC12 M.Prado/I.Suzuki .60 1.50
CC13 S.Matz/N.Syndergaard .40 1.00
CC14 J.Votto/B.Phillips .50 1.25
CC15 D.Gregorius/S.Castro .40 1.00
CC16 Y.Cespedes/D.Wright .50 1.25
CC17 J.Bautista/J.Donaldson .40 1.00
CC18 T.Frazier/A.Eaton .30 .75
CC19 J.Altuve/C.Correa .50 1.25
CC20 J.Arrieta/D.Ross .40 1.00

2016 Topps Heritage Discs

RANDOM INSERTS IN PACKS
67TDCAM Andrew McCutchen 1.50 4.00
67TDCBH Bryce Harper 2.50 6.00
67TDCBP Buster Posey 2.00 5.00
67TDCCC Carlos Correa 1.50 4.00
67TDCCK Clayton Kershaw 2.50 6.00
67TDCJA Jake Arrieta 1.00 2.50
67TDCJD Josh Donaldson 1.25 3.00
67TDCKB Kris Bryant 2.00 5.00
67TDCKS Kyle Schwarber 3.00 8.00
67TDCMB Madison Bumgarner 1.25 3.00
67TDCMC Miguel Cabrera 1.50 4.00
67TDCMH Matt Harvey 1.25 3.00
67TDCMT Mike Trout 8.00 20.00
67TDCSP Stephen Piscotty 1.50 4.00
67TDCZG Zack Greinke 1.50 4.00

2016 Topps Heritage Flashback Relic Autographs

STATED ODDS 1:9645 HOBBY
STATED PRINT RUN 25 SER.#'d SETS
EXCHANGE DEADLINE 2/28/2018
FARAK Al Kaline 125.00 300.00
FARFR Frank Robinson EXCH 100.00 250.00
FARJB Johnny Bench 75.00 200.00
FARJM Juan Marichal
FARLB Lou Brock 75.00 200.00
FARNR Nolan Ryan 200.00 400.00
FARPN Phil Niekro 60.00 150.00
FARRC Rod Carew 75.00 200.00
FARRJ Reggie Jackson EXCH 100.00 250.00
FARTP Tony Perez EXCH 60.00 150.00

2016 Topps Heritage Mini

RANDOM INSERTS IN PACKS
STATED ODDS 1:215 HOBBY
STATED PRINT RUN 100 SER.#'d SETS
10 Gregory Polanco 5.00 12.00
23 Brandon Phillips 4.00 10.00
34 Kevin Kiermaier 5.00 12.00
38 Adrian Gonzalez 5.00 12.00
43 Adam Lind 5.00 12.00
44 Jung Ho Kang 10.00 25.00
50 Byron Buxton 10.00 25.00
60 Chris Davis 4.00 10.00
66 Eddie Rosario 8.00 20.00
70 Kris Bryant 75.00 150.00
77 Evan Gattis 4.00 10.00
78 Jake Arrieta 10.00 25.00
80 Aroldis Chapman 6.00 15.00
87 Jon Lester 5.00 12.00
88 Xander Bogaerts 8.00 20.00
90 Sonny Gray 5.00 12.00
100 Adam Jones 5.00 12.00
110 Brandon Belt 5.00 12.00
123 Billy Butler 4.00 10.00
130 Zack Greinke 6.00 15.00
132 Ichiro Suzuki 8.00 20.00
157 Manny Machado 12.00 30.00
195 Nolan Arenado 10.00 25.00
226 Carlos Rodon 6.00 15.00
230 James Shields 4.00 10.00

251 Yadier Molina 10.00 25.00
255 Jorge Soler 6.00 15.00
256 Josh Harrison 4.00 10.00
284 Stephen Strasburg 6.00 15.00
290 Ryan Howard 5.00 12.00
292 Edwin Encarnacion 6.00 15.00
302 Salvador Perez 5.00 12.00
304 Carlos Santana 5.00 12.00
310 Chris Sale 6.00 15.00
320 Madison Bumgarner 20.00 50.00
322 Giancarlo Stanton 6.00 15.00
337 Yordano Ventura 5.00 12.00
371 Yasmany Tomas 4.00 10.00
374 Joe Mauer 6.00 15.00
376 Neil Walker 8.00 20.00
390 George Springer 5.00 12.00
400 Andrew McCutchen 6.00 15.00
405 Adrian Beltre 6.00 15.00
410 Yasiel Puig 6.00 15.00
420 Justin Verlander 12.00 30.00
426 Clayton Kershaw 20.00 50.00
427 Brian Dozier 5.00 12.00
428 Corey Kluber 5.00 12.00
430 Dallas Keuchel 5.00 12.00
431 Jose Bautista 5.00 12.00
432 Robinson Cano 5.00 12.00
433 Prince Fielder 5.00 12.00
435 Chris Archer 4.00 10.00
436 Masahiro Tanaka 5.00 12.00
438 David Ortiz 8.00 20.00
439 Andrelton Simmons 4.00 10.00
440 Alex Rodriguez 8.00 20.00
442 Jose Fernandez 6.00 15.00
443 Yu Darvish 6.00 15.00
444 Anthony Rizzo 10.00 25.00
445 Justin Upton 5.00 12.00
447 Brandon Crawford 5.00 12.00
448 Tyson Ross 4.00 10.00
450 Bryce Harper 40.00 100.00
451 Stephen Vogt 5.00 12.00
452 Jose Abreu 6.00 15.00
454 Ian Kinsler 5.00 12.00
456 Dustin Pedroia 10.00 25.00
457 Nelson Cruz 6.00 15.00
459 Max Scherzer 6.00 15.00
460 Buster Posey 12.00 30.00
461 Felix Hernandez 5.00 12.00
462 Dellin Betances 5.00 12.00
464 Shelby Miller 5.00 12.00
465 Paul Goldschmidt 10.00 25.00
466 A.J. Pollock 4.00 10.00
468 Yoenis Cespedes 6.00 15.00
469 Mookie Betts 12.00 30.00
470 Jose Altuve 8.00 20.00
473 Maikel Franco 5.00 12.00
474 Joey Votto 10.00 25.00
475 Carlos Correa 30.00 80.00
477 David Price 10.00 25.00
478 Miguel Cabrera 20.00 50.00
479 Lorenzo Cain 4.00 10.00
481 Albert Pujols 8.00 20.00
482 Francisco Lindor 6.00 15.00
483 Josh Donaldson 5.00 12.00
485 Cole Hamels 5.00 12.00
487 Freddie Freeman 8.00 20.00
490 Eric Hosmer 5.00 12.00
492 Noah Syndergaard 10.00 25.00
493 Matt Harvey 10.00 25.00
494 Evan Longoria 5.00 12.00
495 Jacob deGrom 10.00 25.00
496 Ryan Braun 5.00 12.00
497 Charlie Blackmon 6.00 15.00
498 Odubel Herrera 5.00 12.00
499 Jason Heyward 5.00 12.00
500 Mike Trout 75.00 150.00
515 Melvin Upton Jr. 5.00 12.00
518 Jayson Werth 5.00 12.00
526 Travis d'Arnaud 5.00 12.00
527 Scott Kazmir 4.00 10.00
532 Justin Upton 5.00 12.00
541 Joe Ross 4.00 10.00
546 Matt Wieters 6.00 15.00
555 Tanner Roark 4.00 10.00
566 Joey Rickard 4.00 10.00
581 Patrick Corbin 4.00 10.00
588 Johnny Cueto 5.00 12.00
590 Pat Neshek 4.00 10.00
598 Matt Szczur 5.00 12.00
600 Julio Urias 12.00 30.00
606 Alexei Ramirez 5.00 12.00
622 Khris Davis 6.00 15.00
624 Ian Desmond 4.00 10.00
628 Jean Segura 5.00 12.00
639 Mike Clevinger 8.00 20.00
640 Adam Wainwright 5.00 12.00
644 Daniel Murphy 5.00 12.00
648 Michael Fulmer 6.00 15.00
649 Matt Barnes 4.00 10.00
651 Alen Hanson 5.00 12.00
653 Steven Wright 4.00 10.00
656 Adam Duvall 10.00 25.00
663 Sean Manaea 4.00 10.00
668 Ben Zobrist 5.00 12.00
679 Josh Tomlin 4.00 10.00
693 C.J. Wilson 4.00 10.00
701 Kenta Maeda 8.00 20.00
702 Aaron Blair 4.00 10.00
703 Seung-hwan Oh 10.00 25.00
704 Nomar Mazara 6.00 15.00
705 Blake Snell 6.00 15.00
707 Trevor Story 20.00 50.00
708 Byung-Ho Park 5.00 12.00
709 Jose Berrios 6.00 15.00
710 Tyler White 4.00 10.00
711 Marcus Stroman 5.00 12.00
712 Mallex Smith 4.00 10.00
713 Aledmys Diaz 15.00 40.00
714 Tyler Naquin 6.00 15.00
716 Christian Vazquez 5.00 12.00
717 Max Kepler 6.00 15.00
718 Aroldis Chapman 6.00 15.00
720 Ross Stripling 4.00 10.00
721 Hyun Soo Kim 6.00 15.00
723 Javier Baez 8.00 20.00
724 Jeff Samardzija 4.00 10.00

2016 Topps Heritage New Age Performers

COMPLETE SET (20) 6.00 15.00
STATED ODDS 1:8 HOBBY
NAPAP A.J. Pollock .30 .75
NAPBH Bryce Harper .75 2.00
NAPCA Chris Archer .30 .75
NAPGS Giancarlo Stanton .50 1.25
NAPJA Jose Abreu .50 1.25
NAPJD Josh Donaldson .40 1.00
NAPJE Jacoby Ellsbury .40 1.00
NAPKB Kris Bryant .60 1.50
NAPKS Kyle Schwarber 1.00 2.50
NAPLC Lorenzo Cain .30 .75
NAPMMA Manny Machado .50 1.25
NAPMME Mark Melancon .30 .75
NAPMSA Miguel Sano .50 1.25
NAPMSC Max Scherzer .50 1.25
NAPNS Noah Syndergaard .40 1.00
NAPSG Sonny Gray .40 1.00
NAPSP Stephen Piscotty .50 1.25
NAPTT Troy Tulowitzki .50 1.25
NAPYD Yu Darvish .50 1.25
NAPYP Yasiel Puig .50 1.25

2016 Topps Heritage News Flashbacks

COMPLETE SET (10) 2.50 6.00
STATED ODDS 1:12 HOBBY
NFCG Che Guevara .40 1.00
NFEK Evel Knievel .40 1.00
NFJH Jimmy Hoffa .40 1.00
NFPW Presley Wedding .40 1.00
NFRM RMS Queen Mary .40 1.00
NFRR Ronald Reagan .40 1.00
NFSV Saturn V .40 1.00
NFTM Thurgood Marshall .40 1.00
NFSOL Summer of Love .40 1.00
NFB737 Boeing 737 .40 1.00

2016 Topps Heritage Now and Then

COMPLETE SET (15) 5.00 12.00
HN ODDS 1:8 HOBBY
NT1 Trevor Story 1.50 4.00
NT2 Victor Martinez .40 1.00
NT3 Ichiro Suzuki .60 1.50
NT4 Bartolo Colon .30 .75
NT5 David Ortiz .50 1.25
NT6 Jake Arrieta .40 1.00
NT7 Max Scherzer .50 1.25
NT8 Michael Fulmer .50 1.25
NT9 Carlos Beltran .40 1.00
NT10 Kenley Jansen .40 1.00
NT11 Freddie Freeman .60 1.50
NT12 Willson Contreras 1.25 3.00
NT13 Jackie Bradley Jr .50 1.25
NT14 Clayton Kershaw .75 2.00
NT15 Khris Davis .50 1.25

2016 Topps Heritage Postal Stamps

STATED ODDS 1:2404 HOBBY
STATED PRINT RUN 50 SER.#'d SETS
67USPSRAK Al Kaline 30.00 80.00
67USPSRBM Bill Mazeroski 25.00 60.00
67USPSRBR Brooks Robinson 25.00 60.00
67USPSRBW Billy Williams 15.00 40.00
67USPSRFJ Fergie Jenkins 12.00 30.00
67USPSRFR Frank Robinson 25.00 60.00
67USPSRHK Harmon Killebrew 25.00 60.00
67USPSRJB Jim Bunning 20.00 50.00
67USPSRJM Juan Marichal 20.00 50.00
67USPSRLA Luis Aparicio 15.00 40.00
67USPSRLB Lou Brock 25.00 60.00
67USPSROC Orlando Cepeda 15.00 40.00
67USPSRPN Phil Niekro 20.00 50.00
67USPSRRC Rod Carew 20.00 50.00
67USPSRTP Tony Perez 25.00 60.00
67USPSRTS Tom Seaver 25.00 60.00
67USPSRWF Whitey Ford 25.00 60.00
67USPSRWMA Willie Mays 40.00 100.00
67USPSRWMC Willie McCovey 25.00 60.00
67USPSRWS Willie Stargell 25.00 60.00

2016 Topps Heritage Real One Autographs

STATED ODDS 1:142 HOBBY
HN STATED ODDS 1:119 HOBBY
EXCHANGE DEADLINE 2/28/2018
HN EXCH DEADLINE 8/31/2018
ROAAA Albert Almora HN 15.00 40.00
ROAAB Aaron Blair HN 6.00 15.00
ROAAD Aledmys Diaz HN 15.00 40.00
ROAAK Al Kaline 50.00 120.00
ROAAN Aaron Nola 25.00 60.00
ROAARE A.J. Reed HN 6.00 15.00
ROABB Bob Bruce 6.00 15.00
ROABBR Bruce Brubaker 6.00 15.00
ROABD Brandon Drury HN 10.00 25.00
ROABD Bob Duliba 6.00 15.00
ROABH Bryce Harper HN
ROABH Bill Hepler 6.00 15.00
ROABL Barry Latman 6.00 15.00
ROABO Billy O'Dell 6.00 15.00
ROABPA Byung-Ho Park HN 8.00 20.00
ROABPO Buster Posey HN EXCH 75.00 200.00
ROABS Blake Snell HN 30.00 80.00
ROACC Carlos Correa HN 60.00 150.00
ROACC Carlos Correa 150.00 300.00
ROACHA Cole Hamels 8.00 20.00
ROACRO Carlos Rodon HN 10.00 25.00
ROACS Curt Simmons 6.00 15.00
ROACSE Corey Seager 125.00 250.00
ROACY Carl Yastrzemski HN
ROADCL Doug Clemens 6.00 15.00
ROADGO Dee Gordon 6.00 15.00
ROADGR Derrell Griffith 6.00 15.00
ROADO David Ortiz HN 60.00 150.00
ROADP Dustin Pedroia HN 25.00 60.00
ROADS Don Schwall 6.00 15.00
ROADSI Dwight Siebler 6.00 15.00
ROAEB Ed Bressoud 6.00 15.00
ROAEL Evan Longoria HN 20.00 50.00
ROAFM Frankie Montas HN 8.00 20.00
ROAFR Frank Robinson HN 60.00 150.00
ROAGA George Altman 6.00 15.00
ROAHA Hank Aaron HN 250.00 500.00
ROAHF Hank Fischer 6.00 15.00
ROAHO Henry Owens 8.00 20.00
ROAHOL Hector Olivera 10.00 25.00
ROAI Ichiro Suzuki HN 400.00 800.00
ROAJA Jose Altuve 30.00 80.00
Signed in red ink
ROAJB Jackie Brandt 6.00 15.00
ROAJBEN Johnny Bench HN 60.00 150.00
ROAJBER Jose Berrios HN 10.00 25.00
ROAJC Jim Coates 6.00 15.00
ROAJG Jon Gray 6.00 15.00
ROAJH Jason Heyward HN 15.00 40.00
ROAJH Josh Harrison 6.00 15.00
ROAJHA Jason Hammel HN 8.00 20.00
ROAJL Jim Landis 6.00 15.00
ROAJM John Miller 6.00 15.00
ROAJOR John Orsino 6.00 15.00
ROAJOT Jim O'Toole 6.00 15.00
ROAJOW Jim Owens 6.00 15.00
ROAJP Jose Peraza HN 12.00 30.00
ROAJSU John Sullivan 6.00 15.00
ROAJTR J.T. Realmuto 30.00 80.00
ROAJU Julio Urias HN 30.00 80.00
ROAJW Jake Wood 6.00 15.00
ROAKB Kris Bryant HN 50.00 250.00
ROAKB Kris Bryant 50.00 300.00
ROAKC Kole Calhoun 6.00 15.00
ROAKMAE Kenta Maeda HN 10.00 25.00
ROAKS Kyle Schwarber 20.00 50.00
ROALG Lucas Giolito HN 12.00 30.00
ROALS Luis Severino 30.00 80.00
ROAMDH Mike de la Hoz 6.00 15.00
ROAMK Max Kepler HN 10.00 25.00
ROAMR Matt Reynolds HN 6.00 15.00
ROAMS Miguel Sano 12.00 30.00
ROAMT Mike Trout HN 300.00 500.00
ROANA Nolan Arenado HN 50.00 120.00
ROANM Nomar Mazara HN 20.00 50.00
ROANR Nolan Ryan 150.00 250.00
ROANS Noah Syndergaard HN 25.00 60.00
ROAPN Phil Niekro HN 12.00 30.00
ROAPO Peter O'Brien HN 6.00 15.00
ROAPS Pablo Sandoval 8.00 20.00
ROARC Rod Carew HN 60.00 150.00
ROARJ Reggie Jackson HN 75.00 200.00
ROAROS Robert Stephenson HN 6.00 15.00
ROARR Rob Refsnyder HN 8.00 20.00
ROARST Ross Stripling HN 6.00 15.00
ROASM Shelby Miller 12.00 30.00
ROASMA Steven Matz 25.00 60.00
ROASP Stephen Piscotty 30.00 80.00
ROATA Tim Anderson HN 50.00 120.00
ROATN Tyler Naquin HN 12.00 30.00
ROATS Trevor Story HN 25.00 60.00
ROATTUL Troy Tulowitzki HN 30.00 80.00
ROATTUR Trea Turner HN 75.00 200.00
ROATW Tyler White HN 6.00 15.00
ROAVL Vern Law 6.00 15.00
ROAYC Yoenis Cespedes HN 20.00 50.00
ROAYG Yan Gomes 6.00 15.00

2016 Topps Heritage Real One Autographs Red Ink

*RED INK: .6X TO 1.5X BASIC
STATED ODDS 1:589 HOBBY
HN STATED ODDS 1:219 HOBBY
STATED PRINT RUN 67 SER.#'d SETS
EXCHANGE DEADLINE 2/28/2018
HN EXCH DEADLINE 8/31/2018
ROACC Carlos Correa 300.00 500.00
ROAKB Kris Bryant 300.00 600.00
ROAMT Mike Trout HN 400.00 600.00

2016 Topps Heritage Real One Autographs Dual

STATED ODDS 1:3229 HOBBY
HN STATED ODDS 1:2197 HOBBY
STATED PRINT RUN 25 SER.#'d SETS
EXCHANGE DEADLINE 2/28/2018
HN EXCH DEADLINE 8/31/2018
RODAAC M.Adams/O.Cepeda
RODAAT Tulo/Alomar EXCH 60.00 150.00
RODABB B.Buxton/R.Carew
RODABM Belt/Mrchl EXCH 50.00 125.00
RODABME J.Bench/D.Mesoraco
RODACB Correa/Biggio EXCH 100.00 250.00
RODACK Correa/Keuchel EXCH 100.00 250.00
RODACS Carew/Sano EXCH 100.00 250.00
RODADW deGrom/Wright EXCH 150.00 400.00
RODAHB Brck/Hywrd EXCH 50.00 120.00
RODAHR Ryan/Harvey EXCH 150.00 300.00
RODAJR Robinson/Jones 125.00 250.00
RODAMK V.Martinez/A.Kaline
RODAMP Psy/Mrchl EXCH 75.00 150.00
RODAMR Robinson/Machado 200.00 300.00
RODAPK Park/Kim EXCH 125.00 300.00
RODAPM W.Mays/B.Posey
RODAPP Phlps/Prz EXCH 50.00 125.00
RODAPS Pdrsn/Seager EXCH 400.00 1000.00
RODARS Bryant/Rizzo EXCH 80.00 200.00
RODASB Schwrbr/Bryant EXCH 200.00 500.00
RODASM P.Niekro/S.Miller 50.00 125.00

2016 Topps Heritage Rookie Performers

COMPLETE SET (15) 6.00 15.00
STATED ODDS 1:8 HOBBY
RPAD Aledmys Diaz 1.50 4.00
RPAN Aaron Nola .60 1.50
RPBS Blake Snell .40 1.00
RPCS Corey Seager 3.00 8.00
RPJB Jose Berrios .50 1.25
RPJU Julio Urias 1.00 2.50
RPKS Kyle Schwarber 1.00 2.50
RPMC Michael Conforto .40 1.00
RPMF Michael Fulmer .50 1.25
RPMS Miguel Sano .50 1.25
RPNM Nomar Mazara .50 1.25
RPSP Stephen Piscotty .50 1.25
RPTN Tyler Naquin .50 1.25
RPTS Trevor Story 1.50 4.00
RPTT Trayce Thompson .50 1.25

2016 Topps Heritage Stand Ups

COMMON CARD 1.00 2.50
SEMISTARS 1.25 3.00
UNLISTED STARS 1.50 4.00
RANDOM INSERTS IN PACKS
1 Bryce Harper 2.50 6.00
2 Madison Bumgarner 1.25 3.00
3 Clayton Kershaw 2.50 6.00
4 Josh Donaldson 1.25 3.00
5 Buster Posey 2.00 5.00
6 Andrew McCutchen 1.50 4.00
7 Carlos Correa 1.50 4.00
8 Zack Greinke 1.50 4.00
9 Kris Bryant 2.00 5.00
10 Jake Arrieta 1.25 3.00
11 Stephen Piscotty 1.50 4.00
12 Matt Harvey 1.25 3.00
13 Kyle Schwarber 2.50 6.00
14 Mike Trout 8.00 20.00
15 Miguel Cabrera 1.50 4.00

2016 Topps Heritage Then and Now

COMPLETE SET (10) 3.00 8.00
STATED ODDS 1:10 HOBBY
TANBG L.Brock/D.Gordon .40 1.00
TANBK C.Kershaw/J.Bunning .75 2.00
TANBS J.Bunning/M.Scherzer .50 1.25
TANCC M.Cabrera/R.Clemente 1.25 3.00
TANCK S.Carlton/C.Kershaw .75 2.00
TANJA J.Arrieta/F.Jenkins .40 1.00
TANKV J.Votto/H.Killebrew .50 1.25
TANNG P.Niekro/Z.Greinke .50 1.25
TANYA Yastrzemski/Arenado .75 2.00
TANYD C.Davis/C.Yastrzemski .75 2.00

2017 Topps Heritage

COMP.SET w/o SPs (600)
SP ODDS 1:3 HOBBY
SP HN ODDS 1:3 HOBBY
ACTION ODDS 1:25 HOBBY
ACTION HN ODDS 1:31 HOBBY
CLR SWP ODDS 1:147 HOBBY
CLR SWP HN ODDS 1:110 HOBBY
ERROR ODDS 1:1057 HOBBY
ERROR ODDS 1:273 WM HANGER
ERROR HN ODDS 1:461 HOBBY
TRADED ODDS 1:1057 HOBBY
TRADED ODDS 1:273 WM HANGER
TRADED HN ODDS 1:461 HOBBY
THRWBCK ODDS 1:1505 HOBBY
THRWBCK ODDS 1:1304 WM HANGER
THRWBCK HN ODDS 1:1648 HOBBY
NO THROWBACK PRICING DUE TO SCARCITY
1 LeMahieu/Votto/Murphy .25 .60
2 Pedroia/Betts/Altuve .50 1.25
3 Kemp/Rizzo/Arenado .40 1.00
4 Encarnacion/Pujols/Ortiz .30 .75
5 Carter/Arenado/Bryant .40 1.00
6 Trumbo/Cruz/Davis .25 .60
7 Hendricks/Lester/Syndergaard .25 .60
8 Verlander/Sanchez/Tanaka .25 .60
9 Scherzer/Arrieta/Lester .25 .60
10A Kluber/Happ/Porcello .25 .60
10B Klbr/Hpp/Prcllo ERR SP 15.00 40.00
11 Ray/Bumgarner/Scherzer .25 .60
12 Verlander/Sale/Archer .25 .60
13 Francisco Cervelli .15 .40
14 Logan Forsythe .15 .40
15 Logan Morrison .15 .40
16 M.Margot RC/H.Renfroe RC .40 1.00
17 Rougned Odor .20 .50
18 Nate Jones .15 .40
19 Corey Dickerson .15 .40
20 Adam Jones .20 .50
21 Lonnie Chisenhall .15 .40
22 Keon Broxton .15 .40
23 David Wright .20 .50
24 Ryan Schimpf RC .30 .75
25 Aaron Hicks .20 .50
26 Howie Kendrick .15 .40
27 Tampa Bay Rays TC .15 .40
28 Jorge Soler .25 .60
29 A.Pluťko RC/P.Garner RC .30 .75
30 Tyler Flowers .15 .40
31 Justin Grimm .15 .40
32 Jorge Polanco .20 .50
33 Jhonny Peralta .15 .40
34 Ryan Madson .15 .40
35 Anthony DeSclafani .15 .40
36 J.Bell RC/T.Glasnow RC 1.25 3.00
37 Mike Napoli .15 .40
38 Philadelphia Phillies TC .15 .40
39 Yasmany Tomas .15 .40
40 Jordan Zimmermann .20 .50
41 Melky Cabrera .15 .40
42 A.Brice RC/Y.Perez RC .50 1.25
43 Arodys Vizcaino .15 .40
44 Eduardo Nunez .15 .40
45 Scott Kazmir .15 .40
46 Lucas Duda .20 .50
47 Collin McHugh .15 .40
48 Seth Smith .15 .40
49 Danny Espinosa .15 .40
50 Denard Span .15 .40
51 Derek Norris .15 .40
52 Wellington Castillo .15 .40
53 C.J. Cron .15 .40
54 J.T. Realmuto .25 .60
55 Josh Phegley .15 .40
56 Hernan Perez .15 .40
57A Cameron Maybin .15 .40
57B Cameron Maybin TRD SP*
Trade with Tigers 8.00 20.00
58 Tony Watson .15 .40
59 Jose Peraza .20 .50
60 Carl Edwards Jr. .15 .40
61 Marco Estrada .15 .40
62 Nick Markakis .20 .50
63 Alex Wilson .15 .40
64 Russell Martin .15 .40
65 Cody Allen .15 .40
66 Kyle Hendricks .25 .60
67 Sean Doolittle .15 .40
68 Yunel Escobar .15 .40
69 T.Renda RC/W.Peralta RC .30 .75
70 Gerrit Cole .25 .60
71A Pat Neshek .15 .40
71B Pat Neshek Traded SP 8.00 20.00
Trade with Astros
72 Jonathan Villar .15 .40
73 Nick Hundley .15 .40
74 Matt Wieters .25 .60
75 Brandon Finnegan .15 .40
76A D.Swanson RC/R.Ruiz RC .75 2.00
76B Swanson Actn SP 15.00 40.00
77 Yadier Molina .30 .75
78 Pedro Baez .15 .40
79 Adrian Gonzalez .20 .50
80 Eddie Rosario .20 .50
81 Adam Rosales .15 .40
82 Leonys Martin .15 .40
83 G.Dayton RC/J.De Leon RC .30 .75
84 Evan Longoria .20 .50
85 Brett Gardner .20 .50
86A Danny Valencia .20 .50
86B Danny Valencia TRD SP*Trade with A's 10.00
25.00
87 Starlin Castro .15 * .40
88 Kyle Seager .15 .40
89 Wilson Ramos .15 .40
90A Billy Hamilton .20 .50
90B Billy Hamilton Throwback SP
'70's V-Neck Jersey
91 J.Lester/J.Arrieta .20 .50
92 R.A. Dickey .20 .50
93 Aaron Nola .20 .50
94 Francisco Liriano .15 .40
95 Eduardo Escobar .15 .40
96 Gerardo Parra .15 .40
97 Javier Baez .30 .75
98 Jace Peterson .15 .40
99 Christian Bethancourt .15 .40
100 Adam Wainwright .20 .50
101 Jose Iglesias .20 .50
102 Richie Shaffer .15 .40
103 Miguel Montero .15 .40
104 Carlos Santana .20 .50
105 Adam Lind .20 .50
106 Dexter Fowler .20 .50
107 Roberto Osuna .15 .40
108 Seung-Hwan Oh .30 .75
109 Chris Iannetta .15 .40
110 Mallex Smith .15 .40
111 Tanner Roark .15 .40
112 Matt Wisler .15 .40
113A A.Bregman RC/Y.Gurriel RC 1.50 4.00
113B Bregman Actn SP 15.00 40.00
114 Tom Koehler .15 .40
115 Elvis Andrus .20 .50
116 Asdrubal Cabrera .20 .50
117A C.Fulmer RC/Y.Moncada RC 1.00 2.50
117B Moncada Actn SP 6.00 15.00
118 Travis Shaw .15 .40
119 Carlos Beltran .20 .50
120 CC Sabathia .20 .50
121 Jeff Samardzija .15 .40
122 Brandon Drury .15 .40
123 Cam Bedrosian .15 .40
124 Chad Qualls .15 .40
125 Steven Wright .15 .40
126 Matt Duffy .15 .40
127 J.Quercuto RC/E.Gamboa RC .30 .75
128 Minnesota Twins TC .15 .40
129 Colorado Rockies TC .15 .40
130 Eugenio Suarez .20 .50
131 Andre Ethier .20 .50
132 Cheslor Cuthbert RC .30 .75
133 Arizona Diamondbacks TC .15 .40
134 Angel Pagan .15 .40
135 Phil Gosselin .15 .40
136 Ricky Nolasco .15 .40
137 Adeiny Hechavarria .15 .40
138 Justin Turner .25 .60
139 J.A. Happ .20 .50
140 Brock Holt .15 .40
141 Glen Perkins .15 .40
142 Byung-Ho Park .20 .50
143 Marwin Gonzalez .15 .40
144 Ryan Zimmerman .20 .50
145 New York Mets TC .15 .40
146 Stephen Vogt .20 .50
147 Chicago White Sox TC .15 .40
148 Clay Buchholz .15 .40
149 Oakland Athletics TC .15 .40
150 Jung Ho Kang .15 .40
151 Corey Kluber WSH .20 .50
152 Kyle Schwarber WSH .25 .60
153 Coco Crisp WSH .15 .40
154 Jason Kipnis WSH .20 .50
155 Aroldis Chapman WSH .25 .60
156 Addison Russell WSH .25 .60
157 Ben Zobrist WSH .20 .50
158 Chicago Cubs WSH .15 .40
159 J.J. Hardy .15 .40
160 Anibal Sanchez .15 .40
161 David Freese .15 .40
162A Weaver RC/Reyes RC .40 1.00
162B Alex Reyes Actn SP 2.50 6.00
163 Brett Wallace .15 .40
164 Tyler Chatwood .15 .40
165 D.Molleken RC/J.Jones RC .40 1.00
166 Jason Heyward .20 .50
167 Billy Butler .15 .40
168 Brett Lawrie .20 .50
169 Chad Bettis .15 .40
170 Andrelton Simmons .15 .40
171 Chicago Cubs TC .15 .40
172 Cristhian Adames .15 .40
173 Matt Shoemaker .20 .50
174 Chris Capuano .15 .40
175 Michael Saunders .20 .50
176 Brandon Phillips .15 .40
177 G.Cecchini RC/R.Gsellman RC .30 .75
178 James Shields .15 .40
179 J.Beresford RC/A.Wimmers RC .30 .75
180 Stephen Piscotty .20 .50
181 Corey Kluber .20 .50
182 Jacoby Ellsbury .20 .50
183 Jose Quintana .15 .40
184 Jeanmar Gomez .15 .40
185 Trayce Thompson .20 .50
186 Henry Owens .15 .40
187 Chase Utley .20 .50
188 Jedd Gyorko .15 .40
189 San Francisco Giants TC .15 .40
190 Tommy Joseph .25 .60
191 Alexi Amarista .15 .40
192 Zack Cozart .15 .40
193 Devon Travis .15 .40
194 Edwin Jackson .15 .40
195 Drew Pomeranz .20 .50
196 Brandon Crawford .20 .50
196B Crawford ERR SP*
Pitcher on front; card number 196 25.00 60.00
197 New York Yankees TC 1.25 3.00
198 Zack Greinke .25 .60
199 J.Cotton RC/R.Healy RC .40 1.00
200 Randal Grichuk .15 .40
201 Martin Maldonado .15 .40
202 Seattle Mariners TC .15 .40
203 H.Dozier RC/M.Strahm RC .30 .75
204 Tyler Thornburg .15 .40
205 Cincinnati Reds TC .15 .40
206 Robbie Grossman .15 .40
207 Chris Tillman .15 .40
208 Andrew Miller .20 .50
209 Nick Castellanos .25 .60
210 Carlos Rodon .25 .60
211 Jake Barrett .15 .40
212 Kevin Pillar .15 .40
213 Jeremy Hellickson .15 .40
214A A.Judge RC/T.Austin RC 4.00 10.00
214B Judge Actn SP 8.00 20.00
215 Freddy Galvis .15 .40
216 Baltimore Orioles TC .15 .40
217 Avisail Garcia .20 .50
218 Jim Johnson .15 .40
219 Pedro Alvarez .15 .40
220 Joe Mauer .20 .50
221 Toronto Blue Jays TC .15 .40
222 John Jaso .15 .40
223 Chris Archer .15 .40
224 Matt Szczur .20 .50
225 Francisco Rodriguez .20 .50
226 Jed Lowrie .15 .40
227 Steven Souza Jr. .20 .50
228 Jonathan Lucroy .20 .50
229 Luke Gregerson .15 .40
230 Adam Duvall .20 .50
231 Matt Garza .15 .40
232 Michael Conforto .20 .50
233 Scott Schebler .20 .50
234 St. Louis Cardinals TC .15 .40
235 Melvin Upton Jr. .20 .50
236 Ryan Vogelsong .15 .40
237 Kole Calhoun .15 .40
238A Joe Panik .20 .50
238B Joe Panik Throwback SP
'70 Orange jersey
239 Salvador Perez .25 .60
240 J.D. Martinez .25 .60
241 Travis Jankowski .15 .40
242 James McCann .20 .50
243 Byron Buxton .25 .60
244 Hanley Ramirez .20 .50
245 Tucker Barnhart .15 .40
246 Neil Walker .15 .40
247A Odubel Herrera .20 .50
247B Odubel Herrera Throwback SP
'76 Jersey
248 Peter Bourjos .15 .40
249 Justin Bour .20 .50
250 Chris Young .15 .40
251 Victor Martinez .20 .50
252 Ender Inciarte .15 .40
253A Lorenzo Cain .15 .40
253B Lorenzo Cain Throwback SP
'76 Baby blue jersey
254 Johnny Cueto .20 .50
255 Yasmani Grandal .15 .40
256 Matt Harvey .20 .50
257 Houston Astros TC .15 .40
258 R.Tapia RC/D.Dahl RC .40 1.00
259 Ken Giles .15 .40
260 Colby Rasmus .20 .50
261 Mitch Moreland .15 .40
262 Scooter Gennett .20 .50
263 K.Bryant/B.Harper .40 1.00
264 Joc Pederson .20 .50
265 Michael Taylor .15 .40
266 Los Angeles Angels TC .15 .40
267 O.Arcia RC/B.Suter RC .50 1.25
268 Garrett Richards .20 .50
269 Michael Brantley .20 .50
270 Jordy Mercer .15 .40
271 Jason Castro .15 .40
272 Wei-Yin Chen .15 .40
273 Chris Owings .15 .40
274 Nelson Cruz .25 .60
275 R.Quinn RC/J.Thompson RC .30 .75
276 Paulo Orlando .15 .40
277 Jason Motte .15 .40
278 Jeurys Familia .20 .50
279 Washington Nationals TC .15 .40
280 Chase Headley .15 .40
281 Brian McCann .20 .50
282A Bartolo Colon .15 .40
282B Bartolo Colon TRD SP*
Signed with Braves 8.00 20.00
283 Pittsburgh Pirates TC .15 .40
284 Alcides Escobar .20 .50
285 Tyler Lyons .15 .40
286 Dellin Betances .20 .50
287A Adrian Beltre .25 .60
287B Adrian Beltre Throwback SP
'90's Jersey
288 Jarrod Dyson .15 .40
289 Atlanta Braves TC .15 .40
290 Brandon Belt .20 .50
291 Wily Peralta .15 .40
292 Carlos Ruiz .15 .40
293 Didi Gregorius .15 .40
294 Cesar Hernandez .15 .40
295 Maikel Franco .20 .50
296 Jurickson Profar .20 .50
297 Ezequiel Carrera .15 .40
298 Ichiro Suzuki .30 .75
299 Cliff Pennington .15 .40
300 Nori Aoki .15 .40
301 Martin Prado .15 .40
302 Khris Davis .25 .60
303 Gio Gonzalez .20 .50
304 Kennys Vargas .15 .40
305 Kansas City Royals TC .15 .40
306A Adam Eaton .25 .60
306B Adam Eaton TRD SP*
Trade with White Sox 12.00 30.00
307 Yordano Ventura .20 .50
308 Marcus Stroman .20 .50
309 A.J. Ramos .15 .40
310 Tyler Saladino .15 .40
311 Rajai Davis .15 .40
312 Darwin Barney .15 .40
313 Max Kepler .20 .50
314A R.Scott RC/A.Benintendi RC 1.00 2.50
314B Benintendi Actn SP 20.00 50.00
315 Detroit Tigers TC .15 .40
316 Kendrys Morales .15 .40
317 Andrew Romine .15 .40
318 Rick Porcello .20 .50
319 B.Goodwin RC/S.Kieboom RC .30 .75
320 Jayson Werth .20 .50
321 Evan Gattis .15 .40
322 Jonathan Schoop .15 .40
323 Los Angeles Dodgers TC .15 .40
324 Chris Carter .15 .40
325 Chris Davis .15 .40
326 Ben Zobrist .20 .50
327 Hisashi Iwakuma .20 .50
328 Ketel Marte .20 .50
329 Brad Miller .20 .50
330 Matt Holliday .25 .60
331 Joe Musgrove .50 1.25
332 Jose Reyes .20 .50
333 John Lackey .20 .50
334 Justin Smoak .15 .40
335 Carlos Gomez .15 .40
336 D.LeMahieu/C.Blackmon .25 .60
337 Ervin Santana .15 .40
338 Ryan Rua .15 .40
339 Alex Gordon .20 .50
340 Jose Ramirez .20 .50
341 Patrick Corbin .20 .50
342 Curtis Granderson .20 .50
343 Marcus Semien .25 .60
344 Kolten Wong .20 .50
345 Jarred Cosart .15 .40
346 Craig Kimbrel .20 .50
347 Miami Marlins TC .15 .40
348 Julio Teheran .20 .50
349 Jake McGee .20 .50
350 David Robertson .15 .40
351 Michael Bourn .15 .40
352 Kevin Kiermaier .20 .50
353 Zach Britton .20 .50
354 Sandy Leon .15 .40
355 Anthony Rendon .25 .60
356 Huston Street .15 .40
357 Mark Reynolds .15 .40
358 San Diego Padres TC .15 .40
359 Sonny Gray .20 .50
360 Tyler Collins .15 .40
361 David Ortiz TNAS .25 .60
362 Mookie Betts TNAS .50 1.25
363 Mike Trout TNAS 1.25 3.00
364 Miguel Cabrera TNAS .25 .60
365 Josh Donaldson TNAS .20 .50
366 Carlos Correa TNAS .25 .60
367 Corey Seager TNAS .25 .60
368 Manny Machado TNAS .25 .60
369 Robinson Cano TNAS .20 .50
370 Jose Altuve TNAS .20 .50
371 Kris Bryant TNAS .30 .75
372 Anthony Rizzo TNAS .30 .75
373 Nolan Arenado TNAS .40 1.00
374 Clayton Kershaw TNAS .40 1.00
375 Buster Posey TNAS .30 .75
376 Madison Bumgarner TNAS .20 .50
377 Bryce Harper TNAS .40 1.00
378 Max Scherzer TNAS .25 .60
379 Noah Syndergaard TNAS .20 .50
380 Corey Kluber TNAS .20 .50
381 Matt Carpenter .25 .60
382 Boston Red Sox TC .15 .40
383 Robbie Ray .15 .40
384 B.Shipley RC/M.Koch RC .30 .75
385 Cleveland Indians TC .15 .40
386 A.J. Pollock .15 .40
387 Mike Moustakas .20 .50
388 Yonder Alonso .15 .40
389 DJ LeMahieu .25 .60
390 Josh Harrison .15 .40
391 Matt Moore .20 .50
392 Rickie Weeks Jr. .15 .40
393 D Barnes RC/M.Dermody RC .30 .75
394 Texas Rangers TC .15 .40
395 Travis Wood .15 .40
396 Hart RC/Mancini RC .60 1.50
397 Milwaukee Brewers TC .15 .40
398 Yasiel Puig .25 .60
399 Sean Manaea .15 .40
400A Clayton Kershaw .40 1.00
400B Kershaw Actn SP 5.00 12.00
400C Clayton Kershaw Color SP 10.00 25.00
401A Giancarlo Stanton SP 2.00 5.00
401B Giancarlo Stanton Clr SP 6.00 15.00
402A Andrew McCutchen SP 2.00 5.00
402B McCutchen Clr SP 10.00 25.00
402C Andrew McCutchen Throwback SP
'90's Jersey
403A Nolan Arenado SP 3.00 8.00
403B Nolan Arenado Actn SP 5.00 12.00
403C Nolan Arenado Clr SP 10.00 25.00
404A Max Scherzer SP 2.00 5.00
404B Max Scherzer Clr SP 6.00 15.00
405A Chris Sale SP 2.00 5.00
405B Chris Sale TRD SP*
Trade with White Sox 12.00 30.00
406A Yoenis Cespedes SP 2.00 5.00
406B Cespedes Clr SP 10.00 25.00
407A Stephen Strasburg SP 2.00 5.00
407B Stephen Strasburg Clr SP 6.00 15.00
408A Felix Hernandez SP 1.50 4.00
408B Felix Hernandez Clr SP 5.00 12.00
409A Eric Hosmer SP 1.50 4.00
409B Eric Hosmer Clr SP 5.00 12.00
410A Anthony Rizzo SP 2.50 6.00
410B Anthony Rizzo Actn SP 4.00 10.00
410C Rizzo Clr SP 12.00 30.00
410D Anthony Rizzo Throwback SP
1916 Jersey
411 Matt Kemp SP 1.50 4.00
412A David Ortiz SP 2.00 5.00
412B Ortiz Clr SP 10.00 25.00
412C David Ortiz Throwback SP
'36 Jersey
413A Albert Pujols SP 2.50 6.00
413B Pujols Actn SP 4.00 10.00
413C Pujols Clr SP 8.00 20.00
414 Masahiro Tanaka SP 1.50 4.00
415A Kenta Maeda SP 1.50 4.00
415B Maeda Clr SP 8.00 20.00
415C Kenta Maeda Throwback SP
Brooklyn Hat

416 Yu Darvish SP 2.00 5.00
417 Justin Verlander SP 2.00 5.00
418 Miguel Cabrera SP 2.00 5.00
419A Francisco Lindor SP 2.00 5.00
419B Lindor Actn SP 3.00 8.00
420A Manny Machado SP 2.00 5.00
420B Manny Machado Actn SP 3.00 8.00
420C Machado Clr SP 12.00 30.00
420D Manny Machado Throwback SP
'66 Jersey
421 Jacob deGrom SP 4.00 10.00
422A Robinson Cano SP 1.50 4.00
422B Robinson Cano Actn SP 2.50 6.00
423 Kyle Schwarber SP 2.00 5.00
424 Addison Russell SP 2.00 5.00
425 Jose Altuve SP 1.50 4.00
426 Paul Goldschmidt SP 2.00 5.00
427A Bryce Harper SP 3.00 8.00
427B Harper Actn SP 10.00 25.00
427C Harper Clr SP 20.00 50.00
427D Bryce Harper ERR SP 60.00 150.00
Nationals in white
427E Bryce Harper Throwback SP
Homestead Grays Jersey
428A Mookie Betts SP 4.00 10.00
428B Betts Actn SP 6.00 15.00
429 Jose Abreu SP 2.00 5.00
430A Carlos Correa SP 2.00 5.00
430B Correa Actn SP 3.00 8.00
430C Correa Clr SP 15.00 40.00
431 Joey Votto SP 2.00 5.00
432 George Springer SP 1.50 4.00
433 Charlie Blackmon SP 2.00 5.00
434 Troy Tulowitzki SP 2.00 5.00
435 Todd Frazier SP 1.25 3.00
436 Miguel Sano SP 1.50 4.00
437 Carlos Gonzalez SP 1.50 4.00
438 Justin Upton SP 1.50 4.00
439 Hunter Pence SP 1.50 4.00
440A Corey Seager SP 2.00 5.00
440B Seager Actn SP 8.00 20.00
440C Seager Clr SP 30.00 80.00
440D Corey Seager ERR
SP*no Rookie Cup;wrong birthday 60.00 150.00
441A Xander Bogaerts SP 2.00 5.00
441B Xander Bogaerts Clr SP 6.00 15.00
442A Wil Myers SP 1.50 4.00
442B Wil Myers Throwback SP
'90's Jersey
443 Trevor Story SP 2.00 5.00
444A Gary Sanchez SP 2.00 5.00
444B Sanchez Actn SP 6.00 15.00
445 Edwin Encarnacion SP 2.00 5.00
446 Jose Bautista SP 1.50 4.00
447 Dee Gordon SP 1.50 4.00
448 Jason Kipnis SP 1.50 4.00
449 Freddie Freeman SP 2.50 6.00
450A Mike Trout SP 10.00 25.00
450B Trout Actn SP 15.00 40.00
450C Trout Clr SP 30.00 80.00
450D Mike Trout Throwback SP
'70's Jersey
451 Ryan Braun SP 1.50 4.00
452 Ian Kinsler SP 1.50 4.00
453 Jay Bruce SP 1.50 4.00
454 Dustin Pedroia SP 2.00 5.00
455 Marcell Ozuna SP 2.00 5.00
456 Jean Segura SP 1.50 4.00
457 Daniel Murphy SP 1.50 4.00
458 Ian Desmond SP 1.25 3.00
459 Starling Marte SP 1.50 4.00
460A Madison Bumgarner SP 1.50 4.00
460B Bumgarner Actn SP 2.50 6.00
460C Bumgarner Clr SP 5.00 12.00
460D Madison Bumgarner ERR
SP*Giants in white 15.00 40.00
461 Mark Trumbo SP 1.25 3.00
462 Jackie Bradley Jr. SP 2.00 5.00
463 Jon Gray SP 1.25 3.00
464 Jake Lamb SP 1.50 4.00
465 Brian Dozier SP 2.00 5.00
466 Christian Yelich SP 2.50 6.00
467 Gregory Polanco SP 1.50 4.00
468 Aaron Sanchez SP 1.50 4.00
469 Jon Lester SP 1.50 4.00
470A Noah Syndergaard SP 1.50 4.00
470B Syndergaard Actn SP 2.50 6.00
470C Syndergaard Clr SP 10.00 25.00
471 Danny Salazar SP 1.50 4.00
472 Aroldis Chapman SP 2.00 5.00
473 Cole Hamels SP 1.50 4.00
474A Danny Duffy SP 1.25 3.00
474B Danny Duffy Throwback SP
K.C. Monarchs Jersey
475A Buster Posey SP 2.50 6.00
475B Posey Actn SP 4.00 10.00
475C Posey Clr SP 8.00 20.00
476A Lucas Giolito SP 1.50 4.00
476B Lucas Giolito TRD
SP*Trade with Nationals 10.00 25.00
477A Julio Urias SP 2.00 5.00
477B Julio Urias Actn SP 3.00 8.00
478 Jameson Taillon SP 1.50 4.00
479 A.J. Reed SP 1.25 3.00
480A David Price SP 1.50 4.00
480B Price Clr SP 8.00 20.00
480C David Price Throwback SP
481 Willson Contreras SP 2.00 5.00
482 Albert Almora SP 1.25 3.00
483 Nomar Mazara SP 1.25 3.00
484 Michael Fulmer SP 1.25 3.00
485 Trea Turner SP 1.50 4.00
486 Ji-Man Choi SP 1.25 3.00
487 Mike Fiers SP 1.25 3.00
488 Greg Bird SP 1.50 4.00
489 Daniel Norris SP 1.25 3.00
490A Josh Donaldson SP 1.50 4.00
490B Josh Donaldson Actn SP 2.50 6.00
490C Josh Donaldson Clr SP 5.00 12.00
491 Jason Hammel SP 1.50 4.00
492 Aledmys Diaz SP 1.50 4.00
493 Sam Dyson SP 1.25 3.00
494 Alex Colome SP 1.25 3.00
495 Jerad Eickhoff SP 1.25 3.00
496 Jake Odorizzi SP 1.25 3.00
497 Kevin Gausman SP 2.00 5.00
498 Dan Straily SP 1.25 3.00
499A Jake Arrieta SP 1.50 4.00
499B Arrieta Clr SP 8.00 20.00
500A Kris Bryant SP 2.50 6.00
500B Bryant Actn SP 20.00 50.00
500C Bryant Clr SP 40.00 100.00
501 Yan Gomes .25 .60
502 Mike Zunino .15 .40
503 Joey Gallo .20 .50
504 Pierce Johnson RC .30 .75
505 Hunter Strickland .15 .40
506 Fernando Rodney .15 .40
507 Brandon McCarthy .15 .40
508A Christian Arroyo RC .50 1.25
508B Arroyo Actn SP 3.00 8.00
508C Arroyo Clr SP 6.00 15.00
508D Christian Arroyo ERR
SP*Giants in white 20.00 50.00
509 Mike Montgomery .15 .40
510A Yovani Gallardo .15 .40
510B Yovani Gallardo TRD SP*
Trade w/Orioles 8.00 20.00
511 Jose Martinez RC .50 1.25
512 Wade Miley .15 .40
513A Amir Garrett RC .30 .75
513B Amir Garrett ERR SP*Reds in yellow 12.00 30.00
514 Andrew Cashner .15 .40
515 Matt Adams .15 .40
516 Mallex Smith .15 .40
517A Jesse Winker RC 1.25 3.00
517B Winker Actn SP 8.00 20.00
517C Winker Clr SP 15.00 40.00
517D Jesse Winker ERR
SP*Reds in yellow 50.00 120.00
518 Lance Lynn .15 .40
519 Gift Ngoepe RC .30 .75
520 Carlos Asuaje RC .30 .75
521 Hector Neris .15 .40
522 Eduardo Rodriguez .15 .40
523A Antonio Senzatela RC .30 .75
523B Senzatela Actn SP 2.00 5.00
523C Antonio Senzatela ERR
SP*Rockies in white 12.00 30.00
524 Zach Davies .15 .40
525 Nick Hundley .15 .40
526 Josh Smoker RC .30 .75
527 Mat Latos .20 .50
528A Logan Forsythe .15 .40
528B Logan Forsythe TRD
SP*Trade w/Rays 8.00 20.00
529A Reynaldo Lopez RC .30 .75
529B Lopez Clr SP 4.00 10.00
529C Reynaldo Lopez TRD
SP*Trade w/Nationals 8.00 20.00
530 Junior Guerra .15 .40
531 Andrew Toles RC .30 .75
532 Derek Dietrich .20 .50
533 Cameron Rupp .15 .40
534A Brandon Phillips .15 .40
534B Phillips Actn SP 2.00 5.00
534C Phillips Clr SP 4.00 10.00
534D Brandon Phillips TRD
SP*Trade w/Reds 8.00 20.00
535A Eric Thames .20 .50
535B Thames Actn SP 2.50 6.00
536 Joe Ross .15 .40
537 Rob Zastryzny RC .30 .75
538 Rob Segedin RC .30 .75
539 Andrew Albers RC .30 .75
540 Michael Wacha .20 .50
541A Yangervis Solarte .15 .40
541B Yangervis Solarte Throwback SP
'80's Jersey
542 Mychal Givens .15 .40
543 Austin Hedges .15 .40
544 Jaime Garcia .15 .40
545 Frankie Montas .15 .40
546 James Paxton .20 .50
547A Dan Straily .15 .40
547B Dan Straily TRD
SP*Trade w/Reds 8.00 20.00
548 Danny Santana .15 .40
549 Brad Brach .15 .40
550 Adalberto Mejia RC .30 .75
551 Phil Ervin RC .30 .75
552 Archie Bradley .15 .40
553 Steve Pearce .25 .60
554 Brandon Kintzler .15 .40
555 Martin Perez .20 .50
556 Mauricio Cabrera RC .30 .75
557 Gabriel Ynoa RC .30 .75
558 Jesus Aguilar .40 1.00
559 Jorge Bonifacio RC .30 .75
560 Stephen Cardullo RC .30 .75
561 Daniel Nava .15 .40
562 Phil Hughes .15 .40
563 Andrew Triggs .15 .40
564 Carlos Carrasco .15 .40
565 Chris Taylor .20 .50
566 Jose Berrios .20 .50
567 Joe Jimenez RC .40 1.00
568A Koda Glover RC .30 .75
568B Glover Actn SP 2.00 5.00
568C Glover Clr SP 4.00 10.00
569 Allen Cordoba RC .30 .75
570 Abraham Almonte .15 .40
571 Hector Santiago .15 .40
572A Addison Reed .15 .40
572B Addison Reed Throwback SP
V-neck Jersey
573 Drew Storen .15 .40
574 Colby Rasmus .20 .50
575 J.T. Riddle RC .30 .75
576A Bradley Zimmer RC .40 1.00
576B Zimmer Actn SP 2.50 6.00
576C Zimmer Clr SP 5.00 12.00
576D Bradley Zimmer ERR
SP*Indians in white 15.00 40.00
577 Kurt Suzuki .15 .40
578 Jered Weaver .20 .50
579 Adam Lind .20 .50
580 Hector Rondon .15 .40
581 Darren O'Day .15 .40
582 Brad Ziegler .15 .40
583 Rafael Bautista RC .30 .75
584 Bruce Maxwell RC .30 .75
585 Joe Biagini .15 .40
586 Tyler Naquin .25 .60
587A Domingo Santana .20 .50
587B Domingo Santana Throwback SP
'80's Jersey
588 Daniel Robertson RC .30 .75
589A Drew Smyly .15 .40
589B Drew Smyly TRD
SP*Trade w/Rays 8.00 20.00
590 Travis d'Arnaud .20 .50
591 Alex Meyer .15 .40
592 Sergio Romo .15 .40
593A Hyun-Soo Kim .20 .50
593B Hyun-Soo Kim Throwback SP
wearing elbow pad
594 Michael Saunders .20 .50
595 Koji Uehara .15 .40
596 Matt Joyce .15 .40
597 Jeremy Jeffress .15 .40
598 Bronson Arroyo .15 .40
599 Renato Nunez RC .60 1.50
600 Erick Aybar .15 .40
601 Blake Snell .20 .50
602 Alex Wood .15 .40
603 Dovydas Neverauskas RC .30 .75
604A Matt Cain .20 .50
604B Matt Cain Throwback SP
Orange Jersey
605 Shelby Miller .20 .50
606 Ian Kennedy .15 .40
607 Mark Canha .15 .40
608 Chris Devenski .15 .40
609 Matt Carasiti RC .30 .75
610 Boog Powell RC .30 .75
611 Devin Mesoraco .15 .40
612 Brandon Moss .15 .40
613A Dan Vogelbach RC .50 1.25
613B Vogelbach Clr SP 6.00 15.00
614 Chad Pinder RC .30 .75
615 Brandon Guyer .15 .40
616A Whit Merrifield .25 .60
616B Whit Merrifield Throwback SP
baby blue jersey
617 Seth Lugo RC .30 .75
618 Wade Davis .15 .40
619A Raisel Iglesias .20 .50
619B Raisel Iglesias Throwback SP
'30's Jersey
620 Joe Kelly .15 .40
621 Tyson Ross .15 .40
622 Sal Romano RC .30 .75
623 Edinson Volquez .15 .40
624 Kendall Graveman .15 .40
625 Brock Stassi RC .40 1.00
626 Austin Jackson .15 .40
627 Neftali Feliz .15 .40
628 Tony Wolters .15 .40
629 Mac Williamson .15 .40
630 Mark Melancon .15 .40
631 Derek Norris .15 .40
632 Joaquin Benoit .15 .40
633A David Peralta .15 .40
633B David Peralta Throwback SP
Pinstripe uniform
634 Matt Albers .15 .40
635 Mike Pelfrey .15 .40
636 Stuart Turner RC .30 .75
637 Ben Gamel .20 .50
638 Jason Grilli .15 .40
639A Jorge Alfaro RC .40 1.00
639B Alfaro Clr SP 5.00 12.00
640A Miguel Gonzalez .15 .40
640B Miguel Gonzalez Throwback SP
'80's Jersey
641 Ivan Nova .20 .50
642A Jose De Leon RC .30 .75
642B De Leon Actn SP 2.00 5.00
642C De Leon Clr SP 4.00 10.00
642D Jose De Leon ERR
SP*Rays in white 12.00 30.00
642E Jose De Leon TRD
SP*Trade w/Dodgers 8.00 20.00
643 Jarlin Garcia RC .30 .75
644A Chase Anderson .15 .40
644B Chase Anderson Throwback SP
90's Uniform
645 Chih-Wei Hu RC .30 .75
646A Jordan Montgomery RC .50 1.25
646B Jordan Montgomery ERR
SP*Yankees in white 12.00 30.00
647A Matt Wieters .25 .60
647B Wieters Actn SP 3.00 8.00
647C Wieters Clr SP 6.00 15.00
647D Matt Wieters TRD
SP*Trade w/Nationals 12.00 30.00
648 Delino DeShields .15 .40
649A Mike Clevinger .20 .50
649B Mike Clevinger Throwback SP
Buckeyes Jersey
650 Tyler Clippard .15 .40
651A Jeff Hoffman RC .30 .75
651B Hoffman Clr SP 4.00 10.00
652 Derek Holland .15 .40
653 Jon Jay .15 .40
654 Teoscar Hernandez RC 1.25 3.00
655 Craig Breslow .15 .40
656 Daniel Descalso .15 .40
657 Nathan Eovaldi .20 .50
658 Wilmer Difo .15 .40
659 Ty Blach RC .30 .75
660A Ian Happ RC .60 1.50
660B Happ Actn SP 4.00 10.00
660C Happ Clr SP 8.00 20.00
660D Ian Happ ERR
SP*Cubs in yellow 20.00 50.00
661 Derek Law .15 .40
662 Martin Maldonado .15 .40
663 Mike Minor .15 .40
664A Edwin Encarnacion .25 .60
664B Encrncn Actn SP 3.00 8.00
664C Encrncn Clr SP 6.00 15.00
664D Edwin Encarnacion TRD
SP*Signed w/Indians 12.00 30.00
665 Trevor Plouffe .15 .40
666 Kyle Freeland RC .40 1.00
667 Aaron Altherr .15 .40
668A Steve Cishek .15 .40
668B Steve Cishek Throwback SP
'80's Jersey
669 Adam Frazier RC .30 .75
670 Jeff Mathis .20 .50
671 Rajai Davis .15 .40
672 Hansel Robles .15 .40
673 Nick Ahmed .15 .40
674 Magneuris Sierra RC .30 .75
675 Joakim Soria .15 .40
676A Mitch Haniger RC .50 1.25
676B Haniger Actn SP 3.00 8.00
676C Haniger Clr SP 6.00 15.00
676D Mitch Haniger ERR
SP*Mariners in white 15.00 40.00
677 Brandon Nimmo .20 .50
678A Cody Bellinger RC 6.00 15.00
678B Bellinger Actn SP 40.00 100.00
678C Bellinger Clr SP 60.00 150.00
678D Cody Bellinger ERR
SP*Dodgers in white 100.00 250.00
679 Jett Bandy .15 .40
680 Jarrod Dyson .15 .40
681 Matt Olson RC 1.50 4.00
682 Rene Rivera .15 .40
683 Brad Peacock .15 .40
684 Santiago Casilla .15 .40
685 German Marquez RC .50 1.25
686A Aroldis Chapman .25 .60
686B Chapman Actn SP 3.00 8.00
686C Chapman Clr SP 6.00 15.00
686D Aroldis Chapman TRD
SP*Signed w/Yankees 12.00 30.00
687 Adam Ottavino .15 .40
688 Ben Revere .15 .40
689 Jason Vargas .15 .40
690 Anthony Alford RC .30 .75
691 Jose Osuna RC .30 .75
692 Pat Valaika RC .40 1.00
693 Corey Knebel .15 .40
694 Ronald Torreyes .15 .40
695 Christian Vazquez .20 .50
696 Luke Maile .15 .40
697 T.J. Rivera RC .50 1.25
698 Adam Conley .15 .40
699 Matt Bush .20 .50
700 Brett Anderson .15 .40
701 Tim Anderson SP 2.00 5.00
702 Edwin Diaz SP 1.50 4.00
703 Tom Murphy SP 1.25 3.00
704 Alex Cobb SP 1.25 3.00
705A Vince Velasquez SP 1.25 3.00
705B Vince Velasquez Throwback SP
'80's Jersey
706A Carlos Martinez SP 1.50 4.00
706B Martinez Actn SP 2.50 6.00
706C Martinez Clr SP 5.00 12.00
707A Steven Matz SP 1.25 3.00
707B Matz Clr SP 4.00 10.00
708 Zack Wheeler SP 1.25 3.00
709 Michael Pineda SP 1.25 3.00
710 Luis Severino SP 1.50 4.00
711 Rich Hill SP 1.25 3.00
712A Kenley Jansen SP 1.50 4.00
712B Jansen Clr SP 5.00 12.00
713A Dylan Bundy SP 1.50 4.00
713B Bundy Clr SP 10.00 25.00
714 Kelvin Herrera SP 1.25 3.00
715A Trevor Bauer SP 1.25 3.00
715B Bauer Clr SP 8.00 20.00
716A Pablo Sandoval SP 1.50 4.00
716B Sandoval Clr SP 5.00 12.00
717A Shin-Soo Choo SP 1.50 4.00
717B Choo Clr SP 5.00 12.00
717C Shin-Soo Choo Throwback SP
'90's Jersey
718 Taijuan Walker SP 1.25 3.00
719A Dallas Keuchel SP 1.50 4.00
719B Keuchel Clr SP 5.00 12.00
720A Lance McCullers SP 1.25 3.00
720B McCullers Clr SP 4.00 10.00
721 Josh Reddick SP 1.25 3.00
722 Greg Holland SP 1.25 3.00
723A Mike Leake SP 1.25 3.00
723B Mike Leake Throwback SP
'56 Jersey
724 Trevor Cahill SP 1.25 3.00
725 Jared Hughes SP 1.25 3.00

2017 Topps Heritage Blue

*BLUE: 8X TO 20X BASIC
*BLUE RC: 4X TO 10X BASIC RC
*BLUE SP: 1X TO 2.5X BASIC SP
STATED ODDS 1:37 HOBBY
STATED HN ODDS 1:61 HOBBY
ANNCD PRINT RUN OF 50 COPIES EACH
5 Carter/Arenado/Bryant 8.00 20.00
76 D.Swanson/R.Ruiz 15.00 40.00
117 C.Fulmer/Y.Moncada 12.00 30.00
177 Cecchini/Gsellman 8.00 20.00
197 New York Yankees TC 10.00 25.00
214 A.Judge/T.Austin 12.00 30.00
298 Ichiro Suzuki 8.00 20.00
314 R.Scott/A.Benintendi 40.00 100.00
363 Mike Trout TNAS 12.00 30.00
364 Miguel Cabrera TNAS 10.00 25.00
367 Corey Seager TNAS 15.00 40.00
368 Manny Machado TNAS 6.00 15.00
371 Kris Bryant TNAS 25.00 60.00
377 Bryce Harper TNAS 8.00 20.00
379 Noah Syndergaard TNAS 10.00 25.00
412 David Ortiz 8.00 20.00
418 Miguel Cabrera 10.00 25.00
420 Manny Machado 12.00 30.00
427 Bryce Harper 10.00 25.00
431 Joey Votto 8.00 20.00
440 Corey Seager 25.00 60.00
444 Gary Sanchez 10.00 25.00
450 Mike Trout 30.00 80.00
470 Noah Syndergaard 8.00 20.00
481 Willson Contreras 10.00 25.00
500 Kris Bryant 30.00 80.00
660 Ian Happ 20.00 50.00
678 Cody Bellinger 100.00 250.00

2017 Topps Heritage Bright Yellow Back

*YELLOW: 10X TO 25X BASIC
*YELLOW RC: 5X TO 25X BASIC RC
*YELLOW SP: 1.2X TO 3X BASIC SP
STATED ODDS 1:212 HOBBY
STATED ODDS 1:55 WM HANGER
STATED HN ODDS 1:205 HOBBY
ANNCD PRINT RUN OF 25 COPIES EACH
5 Carter/Arenado/Bryant 10.00 25.00
76 D.Swanson/R.Ruiz 20.00 50.00
117 C.Fulmer/Y.Moncada 15.00 40.00
177 Cecchini/Gsellman 10.00 25.00
197 New York Yankees TC 12.00 30.00
214 A.Judge/T.Austin 15.00 40.00
298 Ichiro Suzuki 10.00 25.00
314 R.Scott/A.Benintendi 50.00 120.00
363 Mike Trout TNAS 15.00 40.00
364 Miguel Cabrera TNAS 12.00 30.00
367 Corey Seager TNAS 20.00 50.00
368 Manny Machado TNAS 8.00 20.00
371 Kris Bryant TNAS 30.00 80.00
377 Bryce Harper TNAS 10.00 25.00
379 Noah Syndergaard TNAS 12.00 30.00
412 David Ortiz 10.00 25.00
418 Miguel Cabrera 12.00 30.00
427 Bryce Harper 12.00 30.00
431 Joey Votto 10.00 25.00
440 Corey Seager 30.00 80.00
444 Gary Sanchez 12.00 30.00
450 Mike Trout 40.00 100.00
470 Noah Syndergaard 10.00 25.00
481 Willson Contreras 12.00 30.00
500 Kris Bryant 40.00 100.00
660 Ian Happ 25.00 60.00
678 Cody Bellinger 125.00 300.00

2017 Topps Heritage Mini

STATED ODDS 1:204 HOBBY
STATED ODDS 1:53 WM HANGER
STATED HN ODDS 1:231 HOBBY
STATED PRINT RUN 100 SER.#'d SETS
17 Rougned Odor 5.00 12.00
20 Adam Jones 6.00 15.00
23 David Wright 5.00 12.00
67 Sean Doolittle 4.00 10.00
70 Gerrit Cole 6.00 15.00
77 Yadier Molina 8.00 20.00
79 Adrian Gonzalez 5.00 12.00
84 Evan Longoria 5.00 12.00
88 Kyle Seager 4.00 10.00
93 Aaron Nola 5.00 12.00
100 Adam Wainwright 5.00 12.00
106 Dexter Fowler 6.00 15.00
115 Elvis Andrus 5.00 12.00
119 Carlos Beltran 5.00 12.00
166 Jason Heyward 5.00 12.00
180 Stephen Piscotty 5.00 12.00
181 Corey Kluber 8.00 20.00
196 Brandon Crawford 5.00 12.00
198 Zack Greinke 6.00 15.00
208 Andrew Miller 5.00 12.00
220 Joe Mauer 5.00 12.00
223 Chris Archer 4.00 10.00
228 Jonathan Lucroy 5.00 12.00
239 Salvador Perez 5.00 12.00
240 J.D. Martinez 6.00 15.00
243 Byron Buxton 6.00 15.00
244 Hanley Ramirez 5.00 12.00
251 Victor Martinez 5.00 12.00
254 Johnny Cueto 5.00 12.00
256 Matt Harvey 5.00 12.00
274 Nelson Cruz 6.00 15.00
287 Adrian Beltre 6.00 15.00
295 Maikel Franco 5.00 12.00
302 Khris Davis 6.00 15.00
308 Marcus Stroman 5.00 12.00
318 Rick Porcello 5.00 12.00
325 Chris Davis 4.00 10.00
326 Ben Zobrist 5.00 12.00
359 Sonny Gray 5.00 12.00
381 Matt Carpenter 6.00 15.00
386 A.J. Pollock 4.00 10.00
400 Clayton Kershaw 10.00 25.00
401 Giancarlo Stanton 6.00 15.00
402 Andrew McCutchen 6.00 15.00
403 Nolan Arenado 10.00 25.00
404 Max Scherzer 6.00 15.00
405 Chris Sale 10.00 25.00
406 Yoenis Cespedes 6.00 15.00
407 Stephen Strasburg 6.00 15.00
408 Felix Hernandez 5.00 12.00
409 Eric Hosmer 5.00 12.00
410 Anthony Rizzo 8.00 20.00
411 Matt Kemp 5.00 12.00
412 David Ortiz 10.00 25.00
413 Albert Pujols 8.00 20.00
414 Masahiro Tanaka 5.00 12.00
415 Kenta Maeda 5.00 12.00
416 Yu Darvish 6.00 15.00
417 Justin Verlander 6.00 15.00
418 Miguel Cabrera 20.00 50.00
419 Francisco Lindor 10.00 25.00
420 Manny Machado 10.00 25.00
421 Jacob deGrom 8.00 20.00
422 Robinson Cano 5.00 12.00
423 Kyle Schwarber 6.00 15.00
424 Addison Russell 6.00 15.00
425 Jose Altuve 12.00 30.00
426 Paul Goldschmidt 8.00 20.00
427 Bryce Harper 25.00 60.00
428 Mookie Betts 12.00 30.00
429 Jose Abreu 6.00 15.00
430 Carlos Correa 6.00 15.00
431 Joey Votto 6.00 15.00
432 George Springer 5.00 12.00
433 Charlie Blackmon 6.00 15.00
434 Troy Tulowitzki 6.00 15.00
435 Todd Frazier 4.00 10.00
436 Miguel Sano 5.00 12.00
437 Carlos Gonzalez 5.00 12.00
438 Justin Upton 5.00 12.00
439 Hunter Pence 5.00 12.00
440 Corey Seager 20.00 50.00
441 Xander Bogaerts 6.00 15.00
442 Wil Myers 5.00 12.00
443 Trevor Story 6.00 15.00
444 Gary Sanchez 25.00 60.00
445 Edwin Encarnacion 6.00 15.00
446 Jose Bautista 10.00 25.00
447 Dee Gordon 4.00 10.00
448 Jason Kipnis 5.00 12.00
449 Freddie Freeman 8.00 20.00
450 Mike Trout 40.00 100.00
451 Ryan Braun 5.00 12.00
452 Ian Kinsler 5.00 12.00
453 Jay Bruce 5.00 12.00
454 Dustin Pedroia 10.00 25.00
455 Marcell Ozuna 6.00 15.00
456 Jean Segura 5.00 12.00
457 Daniel Murphy 5.00 12.00
458 Ian Desmond 4.00 10.00
459 Starling Marte 5.00 12.00
460 Madison Bumgarner 5.00 12.00
461 Mark Trumbo 4.00 10.00
462 Jackie Bradley Jr. 6.00 15.00
463 Jon Gray 4.00 10.00
464 Jake Lamb 5.00 12.00
465 Brian Dozier 8.00 20.00
466 Christian Yelich 8.00 20.00
467 Gregory Polanco 5.00 12.00
468 Aaron Sanchez 5.00 12.00
469 Jon Lester 5.00 12.00
470 Noah Syndergaard 5.00 12.00
471 Danny Salazar 8.00 20.00
472 Aroldis Chapman 6.00 15.00
473 Cole Hamels 5.00 12.00
474 Danny Duffy 4.00 10.00
475 Buster Posey 8.00 20.00
476 Lucas Giolito 5.00 12.00
477 Julio Urias 8.00 20.00
478 Jameson Taillon 5.00 12.00
479 A.J. Reed 4.00 10.00
480 David Price 5.00 12.00
481 Willson Contreras 6.00 15.00
482 Albert Almora 4.00 10.00
483 Nomar Mazara 4.00 10.00
484 Michael Fulmer 4.00 10.00
485 Trea Turner 5.00 12.00
490 Josh Donaldson 5.00 12.00
499 Jake Arrieta 5.00 12.00
500 Kris Bryant 30.00 80.00
508 Christian Arroyo 6.00 15.00
513 Amir Garrett 4.00 10.00
517 Jesse Winker 15.00 40.00
529 Reynaldo Lopez 4.00 10.00
531 Andrew Toles 4.00 10.00
534 Brandon Phillips 4.00 10.00
537 Rob Zastryzny 4.00 10.00
538 Rob Segedin 4.00 10.00
550 Adalberto Mejia 8.00 20.00
556 Mauricio Cabrera 4.00 10.00
567 Joe Jimenez 5.00 12.00
568 Koda Glover 4.00 10.00
576 Bradley Zimmer 10.00 25.00
584 Bruce Maxwell 4.00 10.00
589 Drew Smyly 4.00 10.00
595 Koji Uehara 4.00 10.00
599 Renato Nunez 8.00 20.00
601 Blake Snell 5.00 12.00
613 Dan Vogelbach 6.00 15.00
617 Seth Lugo 4.00 10.00
639 Jorge Alfaro 5.00 12.00
642 Jose De Leon 4.00 10.00
647 Matt Wieters 12.00 30.00
651 Jeff Hoffman 4.00 10.00
654 Teoscar Hernandez 15.00 40.00
659 Ty Blach 4.00 10.00
660 Ian Happ 8.00 20.00
664 Edwin Encarnacion 10.00 25.00
676 Mitch Haniger 6.00 15.00
678 Cody Bellinger 75.00 200.00
681 Matt Olson 20.00 50.00
685 German Marquez 6.00 15.00
686 Aroldis Chapman 6.00 15.00
697 T.J. Rivera 6.00 15.00
701 Tim Anderson 6.00 15.00
702 Edwin Diaz 5.00 12.00
705 Vince Velasquez 4.00 10.00
706 Carlos Martinez 5.00 12.00
707 Steven Matz 4.00 10.00
708 Zack Wheeler 5.00 12.00
709 Michael Pineda 4.00 10.00
710 Luis Severino 5.00 12.00
712 Kenley Jansen 5.00 12.00
713 Dylan Bundy 10.00 25.00
715 Trevor Bauer 8.00 20.00
716 Pablo Sandoval 5.00 12.00
717 Shin-Soo Choo 5.00 12.00
719 Dallas Keuchel 5.00 12.00
720 Lance McCullers 4.00 10.00
721 Josh Reddick 4.00 10.00

2017 Topps Heritage '68 Poster Boxloader

STATED ODDS 1:39 HOBBY BOXES
STATED HN ODDS 1:29 HOBBY BOXES
68PAB Alex Bregman HN 40.00 100.00
68PAK Al Kaline 20.00 50.00
68PAM Andrew McCutchen HN 30.00 80.00
68PBH Bryce Harper 20.00 50.00
68PBP Buster Posey 15.00 40.00
68PBR Brooks Robinson HN 30.00 80.00
68PCC Carlos Correa 12.00 30.00
68PCK Clayton Kershaw 20.00 50.00
68PCY Carl Yastrzemski 30.00 80.00
68PDP David Price 10.00 25.00
68PDS Dansby Swanson HN 20.00 50.00
68PFL Francisco Lindor 15.00 40.00
68PFR Frank Robinson HN 30.00 80.00
68PGS Gary Sanchez HN 40.00 100.00
68PGS Giancarlo Stanton HN 30.00 80.00
68PHA Hank Aaron 20.00 50.00
68PJA Jake Arrieta 10.00 25.00
68PJB Johnny Bench 30.00 80.00
68PJD Josh Donaldson HN 30.00 80.00
68PJP Jim Palmer HN 30.00 80.00
68PJV Joey Votto HN 25.00 60.00
68PKB Kris Bryant 30.00 80.00
68PKS Kyle Schwarber HN 25.00 60.00
68PLB Lou Brock HN 30.00 80.00
68PMB Mookie Betts HN 25.00 60.00
68PMB Madison Bumgarner 20.00 50.00
68PMC Miguel Cabrera HN 25.00 60.00
68PMM Manny Machado 30.00 80.00
68PMS Max Scherzer HN 30.00 80.00
68PMT Mike Trout 30.00 80.00
68PNR Nolan Ryan 40.00 100.00
68PNS Noah Syndergaard 25.00 60.00
68PRC Rod Carew 20.00 50.00
68PRJ Reggie Jackson HN 60.00 150.00
68PSC Steve Carlton HN 30.00 80.00
68PYM Yoan Moncada HN 25.00 60.00
68PYS Yoenis Cespedes HN 20.00 50.00
68PABR Andrew Benintendi HN 25.00 60.00
68PARI Anthony Rizzo 15.00 40.00
68PCSE Corey Seager 20.00 50.00

2017 Topps Heritage 3D

STATED ODDS 1:12 HOBBY BOXES
683DAR Anthony Rizzo 12.00 30.00
683DBH Bryce Harper 20.00 50.00
683DBP Buster Posey 12.00 30.00
683DCC Carlos Correa 12.00 30.00
683DCK Clayton Kershaw 12.00 30.00
683DCS Corey Seager 20.00 50.00
683DDO David Ortiz 10.00 25.00
683DGS Giancarlo Stanton 8.00 20.00
683DJA Jake Arrieta 5.00 12.00
683DJD Josh Donaldson 8.00 20.00
683DKB Kris Bryant 40.00 100.00
683DMBU Madison Bumgarner 12.00 30.00
683DMM Manny Machado 15.00 40.00
683DMT Mike Trout 30.00 80.00
683DNS Noah Syndergaard 12.00 30.00

2017 Topps Heritage Award Winners

COMPLETE SET (10) 4.00 10.00
STATED HN ODDS 1:8 HOBBY
AW1 Rick Porcello .50 1.25
AW2 Max Scherzer .60 1.50
AW3 Corey Seager .60 1.50
AW4 Michael Fulmer .40 1.00
AW5 Kris Bryant .75 2.00
AW6 Mike Trout 3.00 8.00
AW7 Eric Hosmer .50 1.25
AW8 Ben Zobrist .50 1.25
AW9 Kris Bryant .75 2.00
AW10 David Ortiz .60 1.50

2017 Topps Heritage Baseball Flashbacks

COMPLETE SET (15) 8.00 20.00
STATED ODDS 1:20 HOBBY
STATED ODDS 1:7 WM HANGER
BFBR Brooks Robinson .50 1.25
BFBW Billy Williams .50 1.25
BFCH Catfish Hunter .50 1.25
BFCY Carl Yastrzemski 1.00 2.50
BFFJ Fergie Jenkins .50 1.25
BFFR Frank Robinson .50 1.25
BFHA Hank Aaron 1.25 3.00
BFHK Harmon Killebrew .60 1.50
BFJB Johnny Bench .60 1.50
BFJM Joe Morgan .50 1.25
BFLB Lou Brock .50 1.25
BFNR Nolan Ryan 2.00 5.00
BFRJ Reggie Jackson .50 1.25
BFWM Willie McCovey .50 1.25
BFWS Willie Stargell .50 1.25

2017 Topps Heritage Bazooka

STATED ODDS 1:76 WM HANGER
68BAM Andrew McCutchen 5.00 12.00
68BAR Anthony Rizzo 8.00 20.00
68BBH Bryce Harper 15.00 40.00
68BBP Buster Posey 6.00 15.00
68BCC Carlos Correa 5.00 12.00
68BCK Clayton Kershaw 8.00 20.00
68BCS Chris Sale HN 8.00 20.00
68BCS Corey Seager 10.00 25.00
68BDO David Ortiz 5.00 12.00
68BDP David Price 4.00 10.00
68BEH Eric Hosmer 4.00 10.00
68BFF Freddie Freeman HN 8.00 20.00
68BFH Felix Hernandez 4.00 10.00
68BFL Francisco Lindor HN 10.00 25.00
68BGS Giancarlo Stanton 8.00 20.00
68BJA Jose Altuve HN 12.00 30.00
68BJA Jake Arrieta 4.00 10.00
68BJB Jose Bautista HN 8.00 20.00
68BJD Josh Donaldson 8.00 20.00
68BJU Julio Urias HN 8.00 20.00
68BJV Justin Verlander HN 8.00 20.00
68BJVO Joey Votto HN 10.00 25.00
68BKB Kris Bryant 20.00 50.00
68BKS Kyle Schwarber HN 5.00 12.00
68BMB Mookie Betts 10.00 25.00
68BMBU Madison Bumgarner 4.00 10.00
68BMC Miguel Cabrera 10.00 25.00
68BMM Manny Machado 5.00 12.00
68BMS Max Scherzer 5.00 12.00
68BMT Mike Trout 25.00 60.00
68BNA Nolan Arenado 10.00 25.00
68BNS Noah Syndergaard 4.00 10.00
68BRC Robinson Cano 4.00 10.00
68BTT Trea Turner HN 8.00 20.00
68BYC Yoenis Cespedes 5.00 12.00

2017 Topps Heritage Chrome

STATED ODDS 1:27 HOBBY
STATED ODDS 1:7 WM HANGER
STATED HN ODDS 1:24 HOBBY
STATED PRINT RUN 999 SER.#'d SETS
*PRPLE REF: .4X TO 1X BASIC
*REF/568: .6X TO 1.5X BASIC
16 M.Margot/H.Renfroe 1.50 4.00
36 J.Bell/T.Glasnow 5.00 12.00
76 D.Swanson/R.Ruiz 5.00 12.00
113 A.Bregman/Y.Gurriel 5.00 12.00
117 C.Fulmer/Y.Moncada 4.00 10.00
162 L.Weaver/A.Reyes 1.50 4.00
177 G.Cecchini/R.Gsellman 1.25 3.00
199 J.Cotton/R.Healy 1.50 4.00
214 A.Judge/T.Austin 30.00 80.00
258 R.Tapia/D.Dahl 1.50 4.00
THC400 Clayton Kershaw 3.00 8.00
THC401 Giancarlo Stanton 2.00 5.00
THC402 Andrew McCutchen 2.00 5.00
THC403 Nolan Arenado 3.00 8.00
THC404 Max Scherzer 2.00 5.00
THC405 Chris Sale 2.00 5.00
THC406 Yoenis Cespedes 2.00 5.00
THC407 Stephen Strasburg 2.00 5.00
THC408 Felix Hernandez 1.50 4.00
THC409 Eric Hosmer 1.50 4.00
THC410 Anthony Rizzo 2.50 6.00
THC411 Matt Kemp 1.50 4.00
THC412 David Ortiz 2.00 5.00
THC413 Albert Pujols 2.50 6.00
THC414 Masahiro Tanaka 1.50 4.00
THC415 Kenta Maeda 1.50 4.00
THC416 Yu Darvish 2.00 5.00
THC417 Justin Verlander 2.00 5.00
THC418 Miguel Cabrera 2.00 5.00
THC419 Francisco Lindor 2.00 5.00
THC420 Manny Machado 2.00 5.00

THC421 Jacob deGrom 4.00 10.00
THC422 Robinson Cano 1.50 4.00
THC423 Kyle Schwarber 2.00 5.00
THC424 Addison Russell 2.00 5.00
THC425 Jose Altuve 1.50 4.00
THC426 Paul Goldschmidt 2.00 5.00
THC427 Bryce Harper 4.00 10.00
THC428 Mookie Betts 4.00 10.00
THC429 Jose Abreu 2.00 5.00
THC430 Carlos Correa 2.00 5.00
THC431 Joey Votto 2.00 5.00
THC432 George Springer 1.50 4.00
THC433 Charlie Blackmon 2.00 5.00
THC434 Troy Tulowitzki 2.00 5.00
THC435 Todd Frazier 1.25 3.00
THC436 Miguel Sano 1.50 4.00
THC437 Carlos Gonzalez 1.50 4.00
THC438 Justin Upton 1.50 4.00
THC439 Hunter Pence 1.50 4.00
THC440 Corey Seager 5.00 12.00
THC441 Xander Bogaerts 2.00 5.00
THC442 Wil Myers 1.50 4.00
THC443 Trevor Story 2.00 5.00
THC444 Gary Sanchez 2.00 5.00
THC445 Edwin Encarnacion 2.00 5.00
THC446 Jose Bautista 1.50 4.00
THC447 Dee Gordon 1.25 3.00
THC448 Jason Kipnis 1.50 4.00
THC449 Freddie Freeman 2.50 6.00
THC450 Mike Trout 10.00 25.00
THC451 Ryan Braun 1.50 4.00
THC452 Ian Kinsler 1.50 4.00
THC453 Jay Bruce 1.50 4.00
THC454 Dustin Pedroia 2.00 5.00
THC455 Marcell Ozuna 2.00 5.00
THC456 Jean Segura 1.50 4.00
THC457 Daniel Murphy 1.50 4.00
THC458 Ian Desmond 1.25 3.00
THC459 Starling Marte 1.50 4.00
THC460 Madison Bumgarner 1.50 4.00
THC461 Mark Trumbo 1.25 3.00
THC462 Jackie Bradley Jr. 2.00 5.00
THC463 Jon Gray 1.25 3.00
THC464 Jake Lamb 1.50 4.00
THC465 Brian Dozier 2.00 5.00
THC466 Christian Yelich 2.50 6.00
THC467 Gregory Polanco 1.50 4.00
THC468 Aaron Sanchez 1.50 4.00
THC469 Jon Lester 1.50 4.00
THC470 Noah Syndergaard 1.50 4.00
THC471 Danny Salazar 1.50 4.00
THC472 Aroldis Chapman 2.00 5.00
THC473 Cole Hamels 1.50 4.00
THC474 Danny Duffy 1.25 3.00
THC475 Buster Posey 2.50 6.00
THC476 Lucas Giolito 1.50 4.00
THC477 Julio Urias 2.00 5.00
THC478 Jameson Taillon 1.50 4.00
THC479 A.J. Reed 1.25 3.00
THC480 David Price 1.50 4.00
THC481 Willson Contreras 2.00 5.00
THC482 Albert Almora 1.25 3.00
THC483 Nomar Mazara 1.25 3.00
THC484 Michael Fulmer 1.25 3.00
THC485 Trea Turner 1.50 4.00
THC490 Josh Donaldson 1.50 4.00
THC492 Aledmys Diaz 1.50 4.00
THC499 Jake Arrieta 1.50 4.00
THC500 Kris Bryant 12.00 30.00
THC508 Christian Arroyo 2.00 5.00
THC513 Amir Garrett 1.25 3.00
THC517 Jesse Winker 5.00 12.00
THC529 Reynaldo Lopez 1.25 3.00
THC531 Andrew Toles 1.25 3.00
THC534 Brandon Phillips 1.25 3.00
THC537 Rob Zastryzny 1.25 3.00
THC538 Rob Segedin 1.25 3.00
THC550 Adalberto Mejia 1.25 3.00
THC556 Mauricio Cabrera 1.25 3.00
THC567 Joe Jimenez 1.50 4.00
THC568 Koda Glover 1.25 3.00
THC576 Bradley Zimmer 1.50 4.00
THC584 Bruce Maxwell 1.25 3.00
THC589 Drew Smyly 1.25 3.00
THC599 Renato Nunez 2.50 6.00
THC601 Blake Snell 1.50 4.00
THC613 Dan Vogelbach 2.00 5.00
THC617 Seth Lugo 1.25 3.00
THC622 Sal Romano 1.25 3.00
THC639 Jorge Alfaro 1.50 4.00
THC642 Jose De Leon 1.25 3.00
THC647 Matt Wieters 2.00 5.00
THC651 Jeff Hoffman 1.25 3.00
THC654 Teoscar Hernandez 5.00 12.00
THC659 Ty Blach 1.25 3.00
THC660 Ian Happ 2.50 6.00
THC664 Edwin Encarnacion 2.00 5.00
THC666 Kyle Freeland 1.50 4.00
THC676 Mitch Haniger 2.00 5.00
THC677 Brandon Nimmo 1.50 4.00
THC678 Cody Bellinger 25.00 60.00
THC681 Matt Olson 6.00 15.00
THC685 German Marquez 2.00 5.00
THC686 Aroldis Chapman 2.00 5.00
THC691 Jose Osuna 1.25 3.00
THC697 T.J. Rivera 2.00 5.00
THC706 Carlos Martinez 1.50 4.00
THC707 Steven Matz 1.25 3.00
THC708 Zack Wheeler 1.50 4.00
THC709 Michael Pineda 1.25 3.00
THC710 Luis Severino 1.50 4.00
THC712 Kenley Jansen 1.50 4.00
THC713 Dylan Bundy 1.50 4.00
THC715 Trevor Bauer 2.50 6.00
THC716 Pablo Sandoval 1.50 4.00
THC717 Shin-Soo Choo 1.50 4.00
THC719 Dallas Keuchel 1.50 4.00
THC720 Lance McCullers 1.25 3.00
THC721 Josh Reddick 1.25 3.00

2017 Topps Heritage Chrome Blue Refractors

*BLUE REF: 2X TO 5X BASIC
STATED ODDS 1:389 HOBBY
STATED ODDS 1:100 WM HANGER
STATED HN ODDS 1:339 HOBBY
STATED PRINT RUN 68 SER.#'d SETS
THC418 Miguel Cabrera 30.00 80.00
THC423 Kyle Schwarber 25.00 60.00
THC427 Bryce Harper 40.00 100.00
THC440 Corey Seager 50.00 120.00
THC444 Gary Sanchez 30.00 80.00
THC470 Noah Syndergaard 15.00 40.00
THC500 Kris Bryant 100.00 250.00

2017 Topps Heritage Clubhouse Collection Dual Relics

STATED ODDS 1:5045 HOBBY
STATED ODDS 1:3354 WM HANGER
STATED HN ODDS 1:2667 HOBBY
STATED PRINT RUN 68 SER.#'d SETS
CCDRBV J.Votto/J.Bench 30.00 80.00
CCDRCB Buxton/Carew HN 20.00 50.00
CCDRCM A.McCutchen/R.Clemente 60.00 150.00
CCDRMA J.Altuve/J.Morgan 25.00 60.00
CCDRMOC Correa/Morgan HN 25.00 60.00
CCDRMP McCvy/Posey HN 40.00 100.00
CCDRPV Votto/Perez HN 30.00 80.00
CCDRRM Mchdo/Rbnsn HN 30.00 80.00
CCDRRS N.Ryan/N.Syndergaard 60.00 150.00
CCDRYO C.Yastrzemski/D.Ortiz 50.00 125.00

2017 Topps Heritage Clubhouse Collection Relic Autographs

STATED ODDS 1:6764 HOBBY
STATED ODDS 1:4471 WM HANGER
STATED HN ODDS 1:3190 HOBBY
STATED PRINT RUN 25 SER.#'d SETS
EXCHANGE DEADLINE 1/31/2019
HN EXCH DEADLINE 7/31/2019
CCARAB Benintendi HN 125.00 300.00
CCARABR Bregman HN EXCH 120.00 300.00
CCARAJ Adam Jones HN/25 60.00 150.00
CCARAJU Judge HN 150.00 400.00
CCARARI Anthony Rizzo/25 150.00 250.00
CCARBH Bryce Harper/25 250.00 400.00
CCARCC Carlos Correa/25
CCARCK Corey Kluber HN/25 50.00 210.00
CCARCSE Corey Seager/25 75.00 200.00
CCARDJ Derek Jeter HN/5
CCARDP David Price EXCH/25 30.00 80.00
CCARDS Swanson HN EXCH 60.00 150.00
CCARFF Freddie Freeman HN/25 50.00 125.00
CCARFL Francisco Lindor HN/25 75.00 200.00
CCARJD Donaldson HN EXCH 40.00 100.00
CCARKB Kris Bryant/25 250.00 500.00
CCARMM Manny Machado/25 150.00 300.00
CCARMT Mike Trout/25 200.00 400.00
CCARNS Noah Syndergaard/25 75.00 200.00

2017 Topps Heritage Clubhouse Collection Relics

STATED ODDS 1:36 HOBBY
STATED ODDS 1:24 WM HANGER
STATED HN ODDS 1:47 HOBBY
*GOLD/99: .5X TO 1.2X BASIC
CCRABE Andrew Benintendi HN 5.00 12.00
CCRABR Alex Bregman HN 4.00 10.00
CCRAC Aroldis Chapman HN 3.00 8.00
CCRAG Adrian Gonzalez HN 2.50 6.00
CCRAG Adrian Gonzalez 2.50 6.00
CCRAJ Adam Jones HN 2.50 6.00
CCRAJU Aaron Judge HN 25.00 60.00
CCRAM Andrew McCutchen HN 3.00 8.00
CCRAM Andrew McCutchen 3.00 8.00
CCRAP Albert Pujols 4.00 10.00
CCRAR Alex Reyes HN 3.00 8.00
CCRAR Anthony Rizzo 5.00 12.00
CCRARI Anthony Rizzo HN 4.00 10.00
CCRARU Addison Russell 3.00 8.00
CCRAW Adam Wainwright 2.50 6.00
CCRBB Byron Buxton HN 3.00 8.00
CCRBH Billy Hamilton 2.50 6.00
CCRBHA Bryce Harper 5.00 12.00
CCRBP Buster Posey HN 4.00 10.00
CCRBP Brandon Phillips 2.00 5.00
CCRBPO Buster Posey 4.00 10.00
CCRBZ Ben Zobrist HN 2.50 6.00
CCRCC Carlos Correa 3.00 8.00
CCRCG Carlos Gonzalez 2.50 6.00
CCRCH Cole Hamels 2.50 6.00
CCRCK Clayton Kershaw HN 5.00 12.00
CCRCK Clayton Kershaw 5.00 12.00
CCRCKL Corey Kluber 2.50 6.00
CCRCS Chris Sale HN 3.00 8.00
CCRCSE Corey Seager HN 3.00 8.00
CCRCY Christian Yelich HN 4.00 10.00
CCRDB Dellin Betances 2.50 6.00
CCRDG Dee Gordon 2.00 5.00
CCRDJ Derek Jeter HN 30.00 80.00
CCRDM Daniel Murphy HN 2.50 6.00
CCRDO David Ortiz 3.00 8.00
CCRDP Dustin Pedroia HN 3.00 8.00
CCRDP David Price 2.50 6.00
CCRDS Dansby Swanson HN 5.00 12.00
CCRDW David Wright 2.50 6.00
CCREH Eric Hosmer 2.50 6.00
CCREL Evan Longoria 2.50 6.00
CCRFF Freddie Freeman 4.00 10.00
CCRFH Felix Hernandez 2.50 6.00
CCRFL Francisco Lindor HN 3.00 8.00
CCRGC Gerrit Cole 3.00 8.00
CCRGP Gregory Polanco HN 2.50 6.00
CCRGS Gary Sanchez HN 3.00 8.00
CCRGS George Springer 2.50 6.00
CCRGST Giancarlo Stanton 3.00 8.00
CCRHP Hunter Pence HN 2.50 6.00
CCRHR Hanley Ramirez 2.50 6.00
CCRIK Ian Kinsler 2.50 6.00
CCRI Ichiro HN 4.00 10.00
CCRI Ichiro 4.00 10.00
CCRJA Jake Arrieta HN 2.50 6.00
CCRJA Jose Abreu 3.00 8.00
CCRJAL Jose Altuve 2.50 6.00
CCRJB Jose Bautista HN 2.50 6.00
CCRJB Javier Baez 4.00 10.00
CCRJBR Jackie Bradley Jr. HN 3.00 8.00
CCRJD Jacob deGrom HN 6.00 15.00
CCRJDO Josh Donaldson HN 2.50 6.00
CCRJE Jacoby Ellsbury HN 2.50 6.00
CCRJH Jason Heyward HN 2.50 6.00
CCRJL Jon Lester 4.00 10.00
CCRJM J.D. Martinez HN 3.00 8.00
CCRJM Joe Mauer 2.50 6.00
CCRJP Joc Pederson 2.50 6.00
CCRJT Jameson Taillon HN 2.50 6.00
CCRJU Justin Upton 2.50 6.00
CCRJV Justin Verlander HN 3.00 8.00
CCRJV Justin Verlander 3.00 8.00
CCRJVO Joey Votto 3.00 8.00
CCRKB Kris Bryant HN 10.00 25.00
CCRKB Kris Bryant 10.00 25.00
CCRKM Kenta Maeda HN 2.50 6.00
CCRKS Kyle Seager 2.00 5.00
CCRMB Mookie Betts HN 6.00 15.00
CCRMC Miguel Cabrera HN 3.00 8.00
CCRMC Miguel Cabrera 3.00 8.00
CCRMCA Matt Carpenter HN 3.00 8.00
CCRMF Michael Fulmer HN 2.00 5.00
CCRMH Matt Harvey 2.50 6.00
CCRMM Manny Machado HN 4.00 10.00
CCRMM Manny Machado 4.00 10.00
CCRMS Miguel Sano 2.50 6.00
CCRMST Marcus Stroman HN 2.50 6.00
CCRMT Masahiro Tanaka HN 2.50 6.00
CCRMTR Mike Trout HN 15.00 40.00
CCRMTR Mike Trout 15.00 40.00
CCRNA Nolan Arenado 5.00 12.00
CCRNC Nelson Cruz 3.00 8.00
CCRNS Noah Syndergaard HN 4.00 10.00
CCRNS Noah Syndergaard 4.00 10.00
CCRPG Paul Goldschmidt 3.00 8.00
CCRRB Ryan Braun 2.50 6.00
CCRRC Robinson Cano 2.50 6.00
CCRRO Rougned Odor 2.50 6.00
CCRRP Rick Porcello 2.50 6.00
CCRSG Sonny Gray HN 2.50 6.00
CCRSM Starling Marte 2.50 6.00
CCRSP Stephen Piscotty HN 2.50 6.00
CCRSP Salvador Perez 2.50 6.00
CCRTG Tyler Glasnow HN 8.00 20.00
CCRTS Trevor Story HN 3.00 8.00
CCRTT Troy Tulowitzki HN 3.00 8.00
CCRTTU Trea Turner HN 2.50 6.00
CCRVM Victor Martinez 2.50 6.00
CCRWM Wil Myers 2.50 6.00
CCRXB Xander Bogaerts HN 3.00 8.00
CCRYC Yoenis Cespedes 3.00 8.00
CCRYG Yulieski Gurriel HN 3.00 8.00
CCRYM Yadier Molina 4.00 10.00
CCRZG Zack Greinke HN 3.00 8.00

2017 Topps Heritage Clubhouse Collection Triple Relics

STATED ODDS 1:13,852 HOBBY
STATED ODDS 1:9389 WM HANGER
STATED HN ODDS 1:6139 HOBBY
STATED PRINT RUN 25 SER.#'d SETS
CCTRBBR Rzzo/Brks/Brnt HN 100.00 250.00
CCTRBMC Brock/Molina/Carpenter HN 40.00 100.00
CCTRCAM Morgan/Altuve/Correa 75.00 200.00
CCTRJHM Jcksn/Hndrsn/McGwre HN 50.00 120.00
CCTRMBA Bggo/Altve/Mrgn HN 75.00 200.00
CCTRMJF Frmn/Chppr/Mthws HN 100.00 250.00
CCTROYB Yaz/Ortiz/Betts HN 75.00 200.00
CCTROYG Ortiz/Nomar/Yaz 75.00 200.00
CCTRPMB Bmgrnr/Posey/McCvy 75.00 200.00
CCTRSRD deGrom/Ryan/Sndrgrd 75.00 200.00
CCTRVBP Bench/Votto/Perez 50.00 120.00

2017 Topps Heritage Combo Cards

COMPLETE SET (15) 25.00 60.00
STATED HN ODDS 1:20 HOBBY
CC1 A.Rizzo/K.Bryant 1.50 4.00
CC2 A.Judge/G.Sanchez 10.00 25.00
CC3 G.Springer/C.Correa 1.25 3.00
CC4 G.Stanton/M.Ozuna 1.25 3.00
CC5 R.Zimmerman/D.Murphy 1.00 2.50
CC6 D.Santana/E.Thames 1.00 2.50
CC7 J.Kipnis/F.Lindor 1.25 3.00
CC8 A.Benintendi/M.Betts 2.50 6.00
CC9 J.Turner/C.Bellinger 5.00 12.00
CC10 Y.Alonso/K.Davis 1.25 3.00
CC11 B.Hamilton/J.Votto 1.25 3.00
CC12 M.Sano/J.Mauer 1.00 2.50
CC13 P.Goldschmidt/J.Lamb 1.25 3.00
CC14 E.Hosmer/S.Perez 1.00 2.50
CC15 J.Abreu/A.Garcia 1.25 3.00

2017 Topps Heritage Discs

COMPLETE SET (30) 40.00 100.00
STATED ODDS 1:2 WM HANGER
68TDC1 David Price .75 2.00
68TDC2 Anthony Rizzo 1.25 3.00
68TDC3 Manny Machado 1.00 2.50
68TDC4 Corey Seager 1.00 2.50
68TDC5 Noah Syndergaard .75 2.00
68TDC6 Giancarlo Stanton 1.00 2.50
68TDC7 Nolan Arenado 1.50 4.00
68TDC8 Max Scherzer 1.00 2.50
68TDC9 Mookie Betts 2.00 5.00
68TDC10 Yoenis Cespedes 1.00 2.50
68TDC11 Felix Hernandez .75 2.00
68TDC12 Eric Hosmer .75 2.00
68TDC13 Robinson Cano .75 2.00
68TDC14 David Ortiz 1.00 2.50
68TDC15 Gary Sanchez 1.00 2.50
68TDC16 Joey Votto 1.00 2.50
68TDC17 Bryce Harper 1.50 4.00
68TDC18 Clayton Kershaw 1.50 4.00
68TDC19 Josh Donaldson .75 2.00
68TDC20 Buster Posey 1.25 3.00
68TDC21 Andrew McCutchen 1.00 2.50
68TDC22 Kris Bryant 1.25 3.00
68TDC23 Carlos Correa 1.00 2.50
68TDC24 Kyle Schwarber 1.00 2.50
68TDC25 Mike Trout 5.00 12.00
68TDC26 Miguel Cabrera 1.00 2.50
68TDC27 Jose Altuve .75 2.00
68TDC28 Trea Turner .75 2.00
68TDC29 Francisco Lindor 1.00 2.50
68TDC30 Justin Verlander 1.00 2.50

2017 Topps Heritage Flashback Relic Autographs

STATED ODDS 1:6764 HOBBY
STATED ODDS 1:4471 WM HANGER
STATED PRINT RUN 25 SER.#'d SETS
EXCHANGE DEADLINE 1/31/2019
FARAK Al Kaline 100.00 250.00
FARBR Brooks Robinson 100.00 250.00
FARCY Carl Yastrzemski 100.00 250.00
FARHA Hank Aaron EXCH 300.00 500.00
FARJB Johnny Bench 75.00 200.00
FARLB Lou Brock 60.00 150.00
FARNR Nolan Ryan 200.00 400.00
FARPN Phil Niekro 25.00 60.00
FARRC Rod Carew 75.00 200.00
FARRF Rollie Fingers 25.00 60.00
FARRJ Reggie Jackson 200.00 400.00
FARSC Steve Carlton 100.00 250.00

2017 Topps Heritage High Number Topps Game Rookies

1 Manny Margot 1.25 3.00
2 Hunter Dozier 1.25 3.00
3 Jose De Leon 1.25 3.00
4 Mitch Haniger 2.00 5.00
5 Jorge Alfaro 1.50 4.00
6 Trey Mancini 2.50 6.00
7 JaCoby Jones 1.50 4.00
8 Christian Arroyo 2.00 5.00
9 Cody Bellinger 20.00 50.00
10 Raimel Tapia 1.50 4.00
11 Reynaldo Lopez 1.25 3.00
12 Joe Musgrove 4.00 10.00
13 Andrew Toles 1.25 3.00
14 Gavin Cecchini 1.25 3.00
15 Jharel Cotton 1.25 3.00

2017 Topps Heritage New Age Performers

COMPLETE SET (25) 10.00 25.00
STATED ODDS 1:12 HOBBY
STATED ODDS 1:4 WM HANGER
NAP1 DJ LeMahieu .60 1.50
NAP2 Nolan Arenado 1.00 2.50
NAP3 Mookie Betts 1.25 3.00
NAP4 Jean Segura .40 1.00
NAP5 Mike Trout 3.00 8.00
NAP6 Corey Seager .60 1.50
NAP7 Kenta Maeda .50 1.25
NAP8 Manny Machado .60 1.50
NAP9 Jose Altuve .50 1.25
NAP10 Carlos Correa .60 1.50
NAP11 Francisco Lindor .60 1.50
NAP12 Kris Bryant .75 2.00
NAP13 Anthony Rizzo .75 2.00
NAP14 Kyle Hendricks .60 1.50
NAP15 Christian Yelich .75 2.00
NAP16 Noah Syndergaard .50 1.25
NAP17 Danny Duffy .40 1.00
NAP18 Dellin Betances .50 1.25
NAP19 Gary Sanchez .60 1.50
NAP20 Orlando Arcia .60 1.50
NAP21 Michael Fulmer .40 1.00
NAP22 Starling Marte .50 1.25
NAP23 Blake Snell .50 1.25
NAP24 Khris Davis .60 1.50
NAP25 Wil Myers .50 1.25

2017 Topps Heritage News Flashbacks

COMPLETE SET (15) 6.00 15.00
STATED ODDS 1:20 HOBBY
STATED ODDS 1:7 WM HANGER
NF1 Vietnam War .40 1.00
NF2 MLK Assassination .40 1.00
NF3 Kennedy Assassination .40 1.00
NF4 President Johnson .40 1.00
NF5 60 Minutes .40 1.00
NF6 Apollo 8 .40 1.00
NF7 1968 Summer Games .40 1.00
NF8 Special Olympics Founded .40 1.00
NF9 2001: A Space Odyssey .40 1.00
NF10 The Beatles .60 1.50
NF11 First U.S. Heart Transplant .40 1.00
NF12 Civil Rights Act of 1968 .40 1.00
NF13 Ivy League Schools Start going co-ed .40
1.00
NF14 Computer Mouse Invented .40 1.00
NF15 Arthur Ashe .40 1.00

2017 Topps Heritage Postal Stamps

STATED ODDS 1:1715 HOBBY
STATED ODDS 1:1145 WN HANGER
STATED PRINT RUN 50 SER.#'d SETS
68PSRBM Bill Mazeroski 20.00 50.00
68PSRBR Brooks Robinson 20.00 50.00
68PSRBW Billy Williams 15.00 40.00
68PSRCH Catfish Hunter 20.00 50.00
68PSRCY Carl Yastrzemski 30.00 80.00
68PSRFJ Fergie Jenkins 20.00 50.00
68PSRFR Frank Robinson 20.00 50.00
68PSRHA Hank Aaron 25.00 60.00
68PSRHK Harmon Killebrew 25.00 60.00
68PSRJB Johnny Bench 30.00 80.00
68PSRJM Joe Morgan 20.00 50.00
68PSRLA Luis Aparicio 20.00 50.00
68PSRLB Lou Brock 20.00 50.00
68PSRNR Nolan Ryan 80.00 200.00
68PSROC Orlando Cepeda 20.00 50.00
68PSRRC Rod Carew 20.00 50.00
68PSRRJ Reggie Jackson 20.00 50.00
68PSRTP Tony Perez 20.00 50.00
68PSRWM Willie McCovey 20.00 50.00
68PSRWS Willie Stargell 20.00 50.00

2017 Topps Heritage Real One Autographs

STATED ODDS 1:173 HOBBY
STATED ODDS 1:112 WM HANGER
STATED HN ODDS 106 HOBBY
EXCHANGE DEADLINE 1/31/2019
HN EXCH DEADLINE 7/31/2019
ROAAB Adrian Beltre HN 40.00 100.00
ROAABE Andrew Benintendi HN 60.00 150.00
ROAABE Andrew Benintendi 150.00 300.00
ROAABR Alex Bregman HN 40.00 100.00
ROAABR Alex Bregman 50.00 120.00
ROAAD Aledmys Diaz HN 10.00 25.00
ROAAG Amir Garrett HN 5.00 12.00
ROAAJ Aaron Judge 600.00 800.00
ROAAK Al Kaline 75.00 200.00
ROAARE Alex Reyes 12.00 30.00
ROAARI Anthony Rizzo
Signed in red ink
ROAAT Andrew Toles HN 5.00 12.00
ROAAW Al Worthington 10.00 25.00
ROABB Byron Buxton HN 25.00 60.00
ROABB Bill Bryan 8.00 20.00
ROABD Bill Denehy 8.00 20.00
ROABH Bryce Harper 75.00 200.00
ROABLE Bob Lee 10.00 25.00
ROABLO Bobby Locke 8.00 20.00
ROABR Brooks Robinson 50.00 120.00
ROABSA Bob Saverine 8.00 20.00
ROABSH Braden Shipley 10.00 25.00
ROABZ Bradley Zimmer HN 6.00 15.00
ROACA Christian Arroyo HN 15.00 40.00
ROACB Cody Bellinger HN 150.00 400.00
ROACC Carlos Correa 60.00 150.00
ROACFU Carson Fulmer 8.00 20.00
ROACJ Clarence Jones 8.00 20.00
ROACKL Corey Kluber HN 30.00 80.00
ROACS Chris Sale HN 40.00 100.00
ROACSE Corey Seager HN 75.00 200.00
ROACSE Corey Seager 75.00 200.00
ROACY Carl Yastrzemski HN
ROADD David Dahl 10.00 30.00
ROADJ Derek Jeter HN
ROADJ Derek Jeter EXCH 600.00 900.00
ROADN Dick Nen 8.00 20.00
ROADSW Dansby Swanson HN 30.00 80.00
ROADSW Dansby Swanson 60.00 150.00
ROADV Dan Vogelbach HN 8.00 20.00
ROAFB Franklin Barreto HN 5.00 12.00
ROAFF Freddie Freeman HN 25.00 60.00
ROAFL Francisco Lindor 25.00 60.00
ROAFRO Frank Robinson 40.00 100.00
ROAFV Fred Valentine 8.00 20.00
ROAGC Gavin Cecchini HN 5.00 12.00
ROAGM German Marquez HN 8.00 20.00
ROAGR Garry Roggenburk 8.00 20.00
ROAGS George Springer 10.00 25.00
ROAHA Hank Aaron HN
ROAHD Hunter Dozier HN 8.00 20.00
ROAHR Hunter Renfroe 20.00 50.00
ROAIH Ian Happ HN 50.00 120.00
ROAJA Jorge Alfaro HN 10.00 25.00
ROAJAL Jose Altuve HN 60.00 150.00
ROAJB Javier Baez HN 40.00 100.00
ROAJBE Johnny Bench 150.00 300.00
ROAJBO Jim Bouton 10.00 25.00
ROAJBU Jerry Buchek 8.00 20.00
ROAJC Jharel Cotton HN 5.00 12.00
ROAJD Jose De Leon HN 8.00 20.00
ROAJD Jacob deGrom 40.00 100.00
ROAJDE Jose De Leon 10.00 25.00
ROAJDO Josh Donaldson HN 30.00 80.00
ROAJHO Jeff Hoffman HN 5.00 12.00
ROAJJ Joe Jimenez HN 6.00 15.00
ROAJJO JaCoby Jones HN 6.00 15.00
ROAJM Joe Musgrove 8.00 20.00
ROAJS Jimmie Schaffer 8.00 20.00
ROAJT Jake Thompson 8.00 20.00
ROAJV Joey Votto HN 40.00 100.00
ROAJW Jesse Winker HN 40.00 100.00
ROAKB Kris Bryant HN 30.00 400.00
ROAKB Kris Bryant 300.00 600.00
ROAKM Kenta Maeda HN 12.00 30.00
ROALB Lewis Brinson HN 15.00 40.00
ROALBR Lou Brock 25.00 60.00
ROALG Lucas Giolito 10.00 25.00
ROALT Lee Thomas 8.00 20.00
ROALW Luke Weaver HN 6.00 15.00
ROAMF Michael Fulmer HN 15.00 40.00
ROAMM Manny Machado HN 150.00 300.00
ROAMMA Manny Margot HN 8.00 20.00
ROAMO Matt Olson HN 25.00 60.00
ROAMS Miguel Sano 12.00 30.00
ROAMT Mike Trout HN 300.00 500.00
ROAMT Mike Trout 250.00 400.00
ROANR Nolan Ryan 200.00 400.00
ROANS Noah Syndergaard 25.00 60.00
ROAOC Orlando Cepeda 15.00 40.00
ROAPC Pete Cimino 8.00 20.00
ROAPG Paul Goldschmidt HN 15.00 40.00
ROAPN Phil Niekro 15.00 40.00
ROARCA Rod Carew 75.00 200.00
ROARH Ryon Healy HN 6.00 15.00
ROARJ Reggie Jackson 150.00 300.00
ROARL Reynaldo Lopez HN 8.00 20.00
ROARL Rene Lachemann 8.00 20.00
ROART Raimel Tapia HN 6.00 15.00
ROASC Steve Carlton 25.00 60.00
ROASK Sandy Koufax HN
ROASN Sean Newcomb HN 6.00 15.00
ROASP Stephen Piscotty HN 10.00 25.00
ROATA Tyler Austin HN 6.00 15.00
ROATB Ty Blach HN 6.00 15.00
ROATG Tyler Glasnow 12.00 30.00
ROATM Trey Mancini HN 20.00 50.00
ROATST Trevor Story 8.00 20.00
ROAYG Yulieski Gurriel HN 12.00 30.00
ROAYM Yoan Moncada HN 75.00 200.00
ROAYM Yoan Moncada 150.00 300.00

2017 Topps Heritage Real One Autographs Red Ink

*RED INK: .6X TO 1.5X BASIC
*RED INK HN: 1X TO 2.5X BASIC
STATED ODDS 1:488 HOBBY
STATED ODDS 1:326 WM HANGER
STATED HN ODDS 1:269 HOBBY
PRINT RUNS B/WN 25-68 COPIES PER
EXCHANGE DEADLINE 1/31/2019
HN EXCH DEADLINE 7/31/2019
ROAAB Adrian Beltre HN 60.00 150.00
ROAABE Andrew Benintendi HN 250.00 400.00
Signed in gold ink
ROAABE Andrew Benintendi/68 300.00 600.00
ROAABR Alex Bregman HN 60.00 150.00
ROAABR Alex Bregman/68 100.00 250.00
ROAAD Aledmys Diaz HN 15.00 40.00
ROAAJ Aaron Judge/68 3000.00 5000.00
ROABB Byron Buxton HN 40.00 100.00
ROACB Cody Bellinger HN 800.00 1200.00
ROACS Chris Sale HN 60.00 150.00
ROACSE Corey Seager HN 125.00 300.00
ROACY Carl Yastrzemski/25 HN 200.00 400.00
ROADSW Dansby Swanson HN 50.00 120.00
ROADSW Dansby Swanson/68 200.00 400.00
ROAFB Franklin Barreto HN 12.00 30.00
ROAGC Gavin Cecchini HN 12.00 30.00
ROAIH Ian Happ HN 75.00 200.00
ROAJA Jorge Alfaro HN 30.00 80.00
ROAJAL Jose Altuve HN 75.00 200.00
ROAJB Javier Baez HN 60.00 150.00
ROAJBE Johnny Bench/25 300.00 500.00
ROAJDO Josh Donaldson/25 HN 50.00 120.00
ROAKB Kris Bryant/25 HN 800.00 1200.00
ROAKB Kris Bryant/25 1000.00 1500.00
ROAKM Kenta Maeda HN 20.00 50.00
ROAMF Michael Fulmer HN 25.00 60.00
ROAMM Manny Machado/25 HN 200.00 400.00
ROAMT Mike Trout/25 HN 800.00 1200.00
ROAMT Mike Trout/25 500.00 800.00
ROANR Nolan Ryan/25 500.00 800.00
ROANS Noah Syndergaard/68 50.00 120.00
ROASC Steve Carlton/68 75.00 200.00
ROASN Sean Newcomb HN 15.00 40.00
ROASP Stephen Piscotty HN 15.00 40.00

2017 Topps Heritage Real One Autographs Dual

STATED ODDS 1:3592 HOBBY
STATED HN ODDS 1:2624 HOBBY
STATED PRINT RUN 25 SER.#'d SETS
EXCHANGE DEADLINE 1/31/2019
HN EXCH DEADLINE 7/31/2019
RODAAJ Jeter/Aaron HN EX
RODABC Brck/Crltn HN EX 75.00 200.00
RODACB Brgmn/Crra HN EX 125.00 300.00
RODACB Brock/Cepeda 100.00 250.00
RODADR Ryan/deGrom EXCH 250.00 600.00
RODAFS Swnsn/Frmn HN EX 60.00 150.00
RODAGF Gray/Fingers EXCH 75.00 200.00
RODAKS Seager/Kershaw HN 400.00 600.00
RODAMR Robinson/Machado 100.00 250.00
RODAMRO F.Rob/Machado 100.00 250.00
RODAMY Yaz/Moncada 200.00 400.00
RODAPB Pdra/Bnntndi HN EX 100.00 250.00
RODARB Ryan/Bench 800.00 1300.00
RODARC Carlton/Reyes 100.00 250.00
RODARJ Jones/Robinson HN 125.00 300.00
RODARK Kershaw/Ryan HN EX
RODARP Plmr/Rbnsn HN EX 125.00 300.00
RODARR Rbnsn/RpknHN EX 125.00 300.00
RODASC Sano/Carew 100.00 250.00
RODASR Ryan/Sndrgrd 100.00 250.00
RODATM Thms/Mncda HN 150.00 400.00
RODAYF Fisk/Yaz HN 150.00 400.00

2017 Topps Heritage Then and Now

COMPLETE SET (15) 10.00 25.00
STATED ODDS 1:20 HOBBY
STATED ODDS 1:7 WM HANGER
TAN1 M.Trumbo/F.Howard .40 1.00
TAN2 N.Arenado/F.Howard 1.00 2.50
TAN3 D.LeMahieu/C.Yastrzemski 1.00 2.50
TAN4 J.Villar/L.Brock .50 1.25
TAN5 M.Trout/C.Yastrzemski 3.00 8.00
TAN6 K.Hendricks/F.Jenkins .60 1.50
TAN7 F.Jenkins/M.Scherzer .60 1.50
TAN8 R.Porcello/J.Marichal .50 1.25
TAN9 D.Price/J.Marichal .50 1.25
TAN10 C.Kershaw/J.Marichal 1.00 2.50
TAN11 C.Yastrzemski/J.Altuve 1.00 2.50
TAN12 F.Howard/E.Encarnacion .60 1.50
TAN13 L.Brock/R.Davis .50 1.25
TAN14 M.Scherzer/J.Marichal .60 1.50
TAN15 J.Verlander/F.Jenkins .60 1.50

2017 Topps Heritage Topps Game

COMPLETE SET (30) 25.00 60.00
STATED ODDS 1:10 HOBBY
STATED ODDS 1:4 WM HANGER
1 Max Scherzer .60 1.50
2 Jose Altuve .50 1.25
3 Clayton Kershaw 1.00 2.50
4 Mike Trout 3.00 8.00
5 Kris Bryant .75 2.00
6 Bryce Harper 1.00 2.50
7 Buster Posey .75 2.00
8 Anthony Rizzo .75 2.00
9 Manny Machado .60 1.50
10 Carlos Correa .60 1.50
11 Corey Seager .60 1.50
12 Jake Arrieta .50 1.25
13 Madison Bumgarner .50 1.25
14 Noah Syndergaard .50 1.25
15 Josh Donaldson .50 1.25
16 Giancarlo Stanton .60 1.50
17 Andrew McCutchen .60 1.50
18 Nolan Arenado 1.00 2.50
19 Mookie Betts 1.25 3.00
20 Yoenis Cespedes .60 1.50
21 Miguel Cabrera .60 1.50
22 Felix Hernandez .50 1.25
23 Eric Hosmer .50 1.25
24 Robinson Cano .50 1.25
25 David Ortiz .60 1.50
26 Gary Sanchez .60 1.50
27 Trea Turner .50 1.25
28 Aledmys Diaz .50 1.25
29 Addison Russell .60 1.50
30 Brian Dozier .60 1.50

2017 Topps Heritage Topps Game Rookies

1 Josh Bell 5.00 12.00
2 Tyler Glasnow 8.00 20.00
3 Orlando Arcia 3.00 8.00
4 Alex Bregman 5.00 12.00
5 David Dahl 2.50 6.00
6 Luke Weaver 2.50 6.00
7 Yulieski Gurriel 3.00 8.00
8 Andrew Benintendi 6.00 15.00
9 Yoan Moncada 5.00 12.00
10 Aaron Judge 25.00 60.00
11 Alex Reyes 2.50 6.00
12 Dansby Swanson 5.00 12.00
13 Hunter Renfroe 2.50 6.00
14 Jake Thompson 2.00 5.00
15 Ryon Healy 2.50 6.00

2018 Topps Heritage

SP ODDS 1:3 HOBBY
1 Altve/Hsmr/Rmrz/Grca LL .20 .50
2 Charlie Blackmon .25 .60
Justin Turner
Daniel Murphy LL
3 Judge/Cruz/Davis LL .60 1.50
4 Arndo/Stntn/Ozna LL .40 1.00
5 Judge/Gallo/Davis LL .60 1.50
6 Blckmn/Arndo/Bllngr/Stntn LL .50 1.25
7 Kluber/Sale/Severino .25 .60
8 Schrzr/Strsbrg/Krshw LL .40 1.00
9 Jason Vargas .20 .50
Carlos Carrasco
Corey Kluber LL
10 Dvs/Krshw/Grnke LL .40 1.00
11 Archer/Sale/Kluber .25 .60
12 Robbie Ray .50 1.25
Max Scherzer
Jacob deGrom LL
13 Domingo Santana .20 .50
14 Alex Mejia RC .30 .75
Sandy Alcantara RC
15 Chris Davis .15 .40
16 Ryder Jones RC .30 .75
Reyes Moronta RC
Miguel Gomez RC
17 Zach Davies .15 .40
18 Matt Carpenter .25 .60
19 Wilmer Flores .20 .50
20 Anthony Rizzo .30 .75
21 Mitch Haniger .20 .50
22 Bryce Harper .40 1.00
23 Sean Manaea .15 .40
24 Charlie Blackmon .25 .60
25 Aaron Judge .60 1.50
26 Tommy Pham .15 .40
27 Jacoby Ellsbury .20 .50
28 Craig Kimbrel .20 .50
29 Andrelton Simmons .15 .40
30 Miguel Sano .20 .50
31 Dominic Smith RC .40 1.00
Amed Rosario RC
32 Steven Souza Jr. .20 .50
33 Gio Gonzalez .20 .50
34 Tommy Joseph .25 .60
35 Jose Altuve .20 .50
36 Chris Owings .15 .40
37 Adam Jones .20 .50
38 Fernando Rodney .15 .40
39 Ty Blach .15 .40
40 Miguel Cabrera .25 .60
41 Anthony Rendon .25 .60
42 David Wright .20 .50
43 Jon Lester .20 .50
44 Gregory Polanco .20 .50
45 Corey Seager .25 .60
46 Paul Goldschmidt .25 .60
47 Mike Trout 1.25 3.00
48 Joey Gallo .20 .50
49 Stephen Vogt .20 .50
50 Andrew McCutchen .25 .60
51 Brandon Crawford .20 .50
52 Bryce Harper .40 1.00
53 Dansby Swanson .25 .60
54 Blake Snell .20 .50
55 Aaron Sanchez .20 .50
56 Derek Fisher .15 .40
57 Mike Trout CL 1.25 3.00
58 Justin Verlander .25 .60
59 Albert Pujols .30 .75
60 Justin Upton .20 .50
61 Bradley Zimmer .15 .40
62 Eric Thames .20 .50
63 Ian Happ .20 .50
64 Johnny Cueto .20 .50
65 DJ LeMahieu .25 .60
66 Sisco RC/Hays RC .50 1.25
67 Max Scherzer .25 .60
68 Mikie Mahtook .15 .40
69 James Paxton .20 .50
70 Joey Votto .25 .60
71 Eric Hosmer .20 .50
72 Jacob deGrom .50 1.25
73 Max Kepler .20 .50
74 Giancarlo Stanton .25 .60
75 Jonathan Schoop .15 .40
76 Greg Holland .15 .40
77 Brian McCann .20 .50
78 Jose Altuve .20 .50
79 Anthony Banda RC .30 .75
Jimmie Sherfy RC
80 Kris Bryant .30 .75
81 Luiz Gohara RC 1.25 3.00
Max Fried RC
82 Yonder Alonso .15 .40
83 Dexter Fowler .20 .50
84 Mike Clevinger .20 .50
85 Mike Zunino .15 .40
86 Gradewine RC/Calhoun RC .50 1.25
87 Starlin Castro .15 .40
88 Corey Dickerson .15 .40
89 Adam Duvall .20 .50
90 Noah Syndergaard .20 .50
91 Josh Donaldson .20 .50
92 Stephen Strasburg .25 .60
93 Mike Moustakas .20 .50
94 Kenta Maeda .20 .50
95 Kevin Gausman .25 .60
96 Jonathan Lucroy .20 .50
97 Jose Abreu .25 .60
98 Troy Tulowitzki .25 .60
99 Jorge RC/Granite RC .30 .75
100 Felix Hernandez .20 .50
101 Salvador Perez .20 .50
102 Edwin Diaz .20 .50
103 Justin Upton .20 .50
104 Trea Turner .20 .50
105 Josh Harrison .15 .40
106 Rizzo/Bryant .30 .75
107 Kris Bryant CL .30 .75
108 Billy Hamilton .20 .50
109 Chris Sale .25 .60
110 Rougned Odor .20 .50
111 Michael Pineda .15 .40
112 Nolan Arenado .40 1.00
113 Justin Bour .15 .40
114 Frazier RC/Andujar RC 1.25 3.00
115 Kendall Graveman .15 .40
116 Stephen Piscotty .15 .40
117 auchman RC/McMahon RC 1.50 4.00
118 Cody Bellinger .50 1.25
119 Alex Bregman .25 .60
120 Brad Peacock .15 .40
121 Kolten Wong .20 .50
122 Ian Desmond .15 .40
123 Carson Fulmer .15 .40
124 Kendrys Morales .15 .40
125 Nicholas Castellanos .25 .60
126 Jose Quintana .15 .40
127 Carlos Correa .25 .60
128 Ender Inciarte .15 .40
129 Randal Grichuk .15 .40
130 Andrew Benintendi .25 .60
131 Scott Schebler .20 .50
132 Maikel Franco .20 .50
133 Rick Porcello .20 .50

134 Kevin Kiermaier .20 .50
135 Randy Read RC .30 .75
Erick Fedde RC
136 Bader RC/Flaherty RC 1.25 3.00
137 Martin Prado .15 .40
138 Aaron Hicks .20 .50
139 Jose Bautista .20 .50
140 Aroldis Chapman .25 .60
141 Johan Camargo .15 .40
142 Danny Duffy .15 .40
143 A.J. Pollock .15 .40
144 Travis d'Arnaud .20 .50
145 Francisco Lindor .25 .60
146 Hanley Ramirez .20 .50
147 Jharel Cotton .15 .40
148 Carlos Beltran .20 .50
149 Andrew Cashner .15 .40
150 Josh Hader .20 .50
151 Manny Machado .25 .60
152 Tim Anderson .25 .60
153 Elvis Andrus .20 .50
154 Devon Travis .15 .40
155 Orlando Arcia .15 .40
156 Jordy Mercer .15 .40
157 Cody Allen .15 .40
158 Joe Mauer .20 .50
159 Jay Bruce .20 .50
160 O'Koyea Dickson RC .30 .75
Kyle Farmer RC
Tim Locastro RC
161 Yu Darvish .25 .60
162 Kershaw WS HL .40 1.00
163 George Springer WS HL .20 .50
Game 2
164 Lance McCullers .15 .40
Brad Peacock WS HL
Game 3
165 Bellinger WS HL .50 1.25
166 Alex Bregman WS HL .25 .60
Game 5
167 Joc Pederson WS HL .20 .50
Game 6
168 George Springer WS HL .20 .50
Game 7
169 Astros Celebration WS HL .15 .40
170 Marcell Ozuna .25 .60
171 Javier Baez .30 .75
172 Jean Segura .15 .40
173 Nicky Delmonico RC .30 .75
Aaron Bummer RC
174 Welington Castillo .15 .40
175 Gerrit Cole .25 .60
176 Corey Kluber .25 .60
177 Sonny Gray .20 .50
178 Archie Bradley .15 .40
179 Gary Sanchez .25 .60
180 Jordan Montgomery .15 .40
181 Mark Reynolds .15 .40
182 Mookie Betts .50 1.25
183 Sanchez/Judge .60 1.50
184 Hector Neris .15 .40
185 Starling Marte .20 .50
186 Guillermo Heredia .15 .40
187 Joey Votto .25 .60
188 Aaron Nola .20 .50
189 Martin RC/Devers RC 1.00 2.50
190 Dinelson Lamet .15 .40
191 Gary Sanchez .25 .60
192 Tanner Roark .15 .40
193 Taijuan Walker .15 .40
194 Roberto Osuna .15 .40
195 Adam Wainwright .20 .50
196 Evan Gattis .15 .40
197 Jeff Samardzija .15 .40
198 Hunter Renfroe .15 .40
199 Jason Kipnis .20 .50
200 Pat Neshek .15 .40
201 Yoan Moncada .25 .60
202 Dallas Keuchel .20 .50
203 Carlos Asuaje .15 .40
204 Travis Shaw .15 .40
205 Cameron Maybin .15 .40
206 Hoskins RC/Williams RC 1.25 3.00
207 Jorge Polanco .20 .50
208 Yuli Gurriel .20 .50
209 Dee Gordon .15 .40
210 Jesse Winker .25 .60
211 Brandon Nimmo .20 .50
212 Didi Gregorius .20 .50
213 Ervin Santana .15 .40
214 Carlos Correa CL .25 .60
215 Brett Gardner .20 .50
216 Clayton Kershaw .40 1.00
217 A.J. Ramos .15 .40
218 Masahiro Tanaka .20 .50
219 Freddie Freeman .30 .75
220 Carlos Carrasco .15 .40
221 Yoenis Cespedes .25 .60
222 Steve Pearce .25 .60
223 Caleb Joseph .15 .40
224 Parker Bridwell RC .30 .75
Troy Scribner RC
225 Sean Newcomb .20 .50
226 Giancarlo Stanton .25 .60
227 Delino DeShields .15 .40
228 Wilson Ramos .15 .40
229 Matt Holliday .25 .60
230 Ryan Zimmerman .20 .50
231 Kole Calhoun .15 .40
232 Yadier Molina .30 .75
233 Kyle Seager .15 .40
234 Zack Greinke .25 .60
235 Buster Posey .30 .75
236 Joc Pederson .20 .50
237 Chris Rusin .15 .40
238 Corey Kluber .20 .50
239 Mike Foltynewicz .15 .40
240 Justin Smoak .15 .40
241 Addison Russell .20 .50
242 Jimmy Nelson .15 .40
243 Keon Broxton .15 .40
244 Francisco Mejia RC .40 1.00
Greg Allen RC
245 C.J. Cron .15 .40
246 Jose Reyes UER .20 .50
Missing career stats
247 Willson Contreras .25 .60
248 CC Sabathia .20 .50
249 Marcus Stroman .20 .50
250 Trey Mancini .30 .75
251 Matt Kemp .20 .50
252 Matt Davidson .20 .50
253 Luke Weaver .20 .50
254 Joe Panik .20 .50
255 Adam Eaton .20 .50
256 Clayton Kershaw .40 1.00
257 Hunter Pence .20 .50
258 Tyler Glasnow .25 .60
259 Brandon McCarthy .15 .40
260 Khris Davis .25 .60
261 Kyle Barraclough .15 .40
262 Eddie Rosario .25 .60
263 Alex Wood .15 .40
264 Carl Edwards Jr. .15 .40
265 Carlos Martinez .20 .50
266 Buehler RC/Verdugo RC 1.50 4.00
267 Trevor Bauer .30 .75
268 Kyle Schwarber .25 .60
269 Ken Giles .15 .40
270 Matt Adams .15 .40
271 Christian Vazquez .20 .50
272 Matt Moore .20 .50
273 Crwfrd RC/Arano RC/Rios RC .30 .75
274 Jon Gray .15 .40
275 Mike Trout 1.25 3.00
276 Trevor Story .25 .60
277 Russell Martin .15 .40
278 Aaron Judge .60 1.50
279 Jose Peraza .20 .50
280 Raisel Iglesias .20 .50
281 Cory Spangenberg .15 .40
282 Francisco Cervelli .15 .40
283 Brett Phillips .15 .40
284 Robles RC/Stevenson RC .75 2.00
285 Ian Kinsler .20 .50
286 Chris Archer .15 .40
287 Andrew Miller .20 .50
288 Jake Arrieta .20 .50
289 Dellin Betances .20 .50
290 Jose Berrios .20 .50
291 Jose Ramirez .20 .50
292 Manny Machado .25 .60
293 Buster Posey .30 .75
294 J.D. Martinez .25 .60
295 Corey Seager .25 .60
296 Reynaldo Lopez .20 .50
297 Taylor Davis RC .30 .75
Dillon Maples RC
Jen-Ho Tseng RC
298 Cody Bellinger .50 1.25
299 Andrew Heaney .15 .40
300 Ichiro .30 .75
301 Robinson Cano .20 .50
302 Matt Olson .25 .60
303 Luis Severino .20 .50
304 Christian Villanueva RC .30 .75
Kyle McGrath RC
305 Josh Bell .20 .50
306 Odubel Herrera .20 .50
307 David Robertson .15 .40
308 James Shields .15 .40
309 Charlie Morton .25 .60
310 Kyle Freeland .20 .50
311 Jed Lowrie .15 .40
312 Justin Turner .25 .60
313 Corey Knebel .15 .40
314 Cody Bellinger CL .50 1.25
315 Sean Doolittle .15 .40
316 Chad Green .15 .40
317 Taylor Rogers RC .40 1.00
318 Lance McCullers .15 .40
319 Brandon Belt .20 .50
320 Paul DeJong .25 .60
321 Tyler Wade RC .40 1.00
Garrett Cooper RC
322 Nelson Cruz .25 .60
323 Jack Reinheimer RC .40 1.00
Ildemaro Vargas RC
324 David Price .20 .50
325 Edwin Encarnacion .25 .60
326 Daniel Murphy .20 .50
327 Yasiel Puig .25 .60
328 Avisail Garcia .20 .50
329 Aaron Altherr .15 .40
330 Mookie Betts .50 1.25
331 Albies RC/Sims RC 1.00 2.50
332 Franklin Barreto .15 .40
333 Jedd Gyorko .15 .40
334 Zack Godley .15 .40
335 Nomar Mazara .15 .40
336 Howie Kendrick .15 .40
337 Byron Buxton .25 .60
338 Alex Colome .15 .40
339 Tyler Mahle RC .40 1.00
Jackson Stephens RC
340 Carlos Santana .20 .50
341 Christian Yelich .30 .75
342 Jacob Faria .15 .40
343 Martin Maldonado .15 .40
344 Manny Pina .15 .40
345 Robbie Ray .15 .40
346 Marcus Semien .25 .60
347 Dylan Bundy .20 .50
348 German Marquez .15 .40
349 Dustin Pedroia .25 .60
350 Yan Gomes .25 .60
351 Nolan Arenado .40 1.00
352 Jorge Alfaro .15 .40
353 Pat Valaika .15 .40
354 Felipe Rivero .20 .50
355 Brandon Kintzler .15 .40
356 Brian Dozier .20 .50
357 Lucas Giolito .20 .50
358 Dustin Fowler RC .30 .75
Paul Blackburn RC
359 Wilmer Difo .15 .40
360 George Springer .20 .50
361 Aaron Judge CL .60 1.50
362 Kris Bryant .30 .75
363 Ian Kennedy .15 .40
364 Michael Conforto .20 .50
365 Matt Chapman .25 .60
366 Chris Taylor .20 .50
367 Greg Bird .20 .50
368 Jason Heyward .20 .50
369 Paul Goldschmidt .25 .60
370 Melky Cabrera .15 .40
371 Brad Brach .15 .40
372 Michael Taylor .15 .40
373 Enrique Hernandez .25 .60
374 Austin Hedges .15 .40
375 Whit Merrifield .25 .60
376 Manny Margot .15 .40
377 Jose Abreu .25 .60
378 Magneuris Sierra .25 .60
379 Carlos Ramirez RC .50 1.25
Chris Rowley RC
Richard Urena RC
380 Eric Sogard .15 .40
381 Carlos Correa .25 .60
382 Michael Fulmer .15 .40
383 Jose de Leon .15 .40
384 Jake Lamb .20 .50
385 Michael Brantley .20 .50
386 Alex Gordon .20 .50
387 Wil Myers .20 .50
388 J.T. Realmuto .25 .60
389 Shelby Miller .20 .50
390 Amir Garrett .15 .40
391 Jackie Bradley Jr. .25 .60
392 Jerad Eickhoff .15 .40
393 Marco Estrada .15 .40
394 Brandon Woodruff RC 1.00 2.50
Aaron Wilkerson RC
Taylor Williams RC
395 Dillon Peters RC .40 1.00
Brian Anderson RC
396 Kevin Pillar .15 .40
397 Evan Longoria .20 .50
398 J.A. Happ .20 .50
399 Bryce Harper CL .40 1.00
400 Carlos Gomez .15 .40
401 Scooter Gennett SP 1.50 4.00
402 Logan Morrison SP 1.25 3.00
403 Ben Zobrist SP 1.50 4.00
404 Drew Pomeranz SP 1.25 3.00
405 Xander Bogaerts SP 2.00 5.00
406 Ryan Braun SP 1.50 4.00
407 Lewis Brinson SP 1.25 3.00
408 Cole Hamels SP 1.50 4.00
409 Kelvin Herrera SP 1.25 3.00
410 Chad Kuhl SP 1.25 3.00
411 Albert Almora SP 1.50 4.00
412 Carlos Gonzalez SP 1.50 4.00
413 Todd Frazier SP 1.25 3.00
414 James McCann SP 1.50 4.00
415 Matt Wieters SP 2.00 5.00
416 Matt Harvey SP 1.50 4.00
417 Jason Vargas SP 1.25 3.00
418 Steven Matz SP 1.25 3.00
419 Brandon Drury SP 1.25 3.00
420 Martin Perez SP 1.50 4.00
421 Brandon Finnegan SP 1.25 3.00
422 Yolmer Sanchez SP 1.25 3.00
423 Kyle Hendricks SP 2.00 5.00
424 Kenley Jansen SP 1.50 4.00
425 Marwin Gonzalez SP 1.25 3.00
426 Rich Hill SP 1.25 3.00
427 Victor Martinez SP 1.50 4.00
428 Lorenzo Cain SP 1.50 4.00
429 Mike Leake SP 1.25 3.00
430 Wade Davis SP 1.25 3.00
431 Dan Straily SP 1.25 3.00
432 Chase Anderson SP 1.25 3.00
433 Hyun-Jin Ryu SP 1.25 3.00
434 Jeimer Candelario SP 1.25 3.00
435 Brad Ziegler SP 1.25 3.00
436 Carlos Rodon SP 2.00 5.00
437 Nick Pivetta SP 1.25 3.00
438 Matt Boyd SP 1.25 3.00
439 Lance Lynn SP 1.25 3.00
440 Seung-Hwan Oh SP 1.50 4.00
441 Zach Britton SP 1.25 3.00
442 Josh Reddick SP 1.25 3.00
443 Danny Salazar SP 1.50 4.00
444 Eugenio Suarez SP 1.25 3.00
445 Alcides Escobar SP 1.25 3.00
446 Michael Wacha SP 1.50 4.00
447 Zack Cozart SP 1.25 3.00
448 Jayson Werth SP 1.50 4.00
449 Ryon Healy SP 1.25 3.00
450 Christian Arroyo SP 1.25 3.00
451 Brad Hand SP 1.25 3.00
452 Garrett Richards SP 1.50 4.00
453 Ben Gamel SP 1.25 3.00
454 Shin-Soo Choo SP 1.50 4.00
455 Drew Smyly SP 1.25 3.00
456 Aledmys Diaz SP 1.50 4.00
457 Ivan Nova SP 1.25 3.00
458 Jonathan Villar SP 1.25 3.00
459 Jorge Bonifacio SP 1.25 3.00
460 Patrick Corbin SP 1.50 4.00
461 Jameson Taillon SP 1.25 3.00
462 Mike Napoli SP 1.25 3.00
463 Adrian Beltre SP 2.00 5.00
464 Alex Reyes SP 1.50 4.00
465 Kyle Gibson SP 1.25 3.00
466 Mark Trumbo SP 1.25 3.00
467 Julio Teheran SP 1.50 4.00
468 Alex Cobb SP 1.25 3.00
469 Julio Urias SP 2.00 5.00
470 Yasmani Grandal SP 1.25 3.00
471 Ricky Nolasco SP 1.25 3.00
472 Brandon Phillips SP 1.50 4.00
473 Matt Shoemaker SP 1.50 4.00
474 Yasmany Tomas SP 1.25 3.00
475 Kurt Suzuki SP 1.25 3.00
476 Nick Markakis SP 1.50 4.00
477 R.A. Dickey SP 1.50 4.00
478 Eduardo Rodriguez SP 1.25 3.00
479 Michael Lorenzen SP 1.25 3.00
480 Anthony DeSclafani SP 1.25 3.00
481 Lonnie Chisenhall SP 1.25 3.00
482 Josh Tomlin SP 1.25 3.00
483 Raimel Tapia SP 1.25 3.00
484 Antonio Senzatela SP 1.25 3.00
485 Tyler Anderson SP 1.25 3.00
486 Chad Bettis SP 1.25 3.00
487 Jose Iglesias SP 1.50 4.00
488 Jake Marisnick SP 1.25 3.00
489 Joe Musgrove SP 2.00 5.00
490 Adrian Gonzalez SP 1.50 4.00
491 Jose Urena SP 1.25 3.00
492 Edinson Volquez SP 1.25 3.00
493 Hernan Perez SP 1.25 3.00
494 Jeurys Familia SP 1.50 4.00
495 Bruce Maxwell SP 1.25 3.00
496 Vince Velasquez SP 1.25 3.00
497 David Freese SP 1.25 3.00
498 Yangervis Solarte SP 1.25 3.00
499 Luis Perdomo SP 1.25 3.00
500 Jose Pirela SP 1.25 3.00
501 Jordan Zimmermann .20 .50
502 Juan Soto RC 20.00 50.00
503 Franchy Cordero .15 .40
504 Ketel Marte .20 .50
505 Mallex Smith .15 .40
506 Braxton Lee RC .30 .75
507 Jacob Barnes RC .30 .75
508 Pedro Alvarez .15 .40
509 Alex Blandino RC .30 .75
510 Pablo Sandoval .20 .50
511 Scott Kingery RC .50 1.25
512 Yoshihisa Hirano RC .50 1.25
513 Jaime Garcia .15 .40
514 Matt Duffy .15 .40
515 Hunter Strickland .15 .40
516 Hector Velazquez .25 .60
517 Jonathan Lucroy .20 .50
518 John Axford .15 .40
519 Eduardo Nunez .15 .40
520 Tony Cingrani .20 .50
521 Seth Lugo .15 .40
522 Chris Iannetta .15 .40
523 Danny Farquhar .15 .40
524 Tyler Beede RC .30 .75
525 Daniel Mengden .15 .40
526 Steven Souza Jr. .20 .50
527 Corey Dickerson .15 .40
528 Matt Szczur .20 .50
529 Mitch Garver RC .30 .75
530 Trayce Thompson .20 .50
531 Blake Swihart .20 .50
532 J.D. Davis RC .40 1.00
533 Trevor Cahill .15 .40
534 Niko Goodrum RC .50 1.25
535 Pedro Severino .15 .40
536 Asdrubal Cabrera .20 .50
537 Matt Adams .15 .40
538 Eduardo Escobar .15 .40
539 Jakob Junis .15 .40
540 David Bote RC .75 2.00
541 Freddy Peralta RC .30 .75
542 Marco Gonzales .15 .40
543 Ryan Yarbrough RC .50 1.25
544 Fernando Rodney .15 .40
545 Preston Tucker .15 .40
546 Tommy La Stella .15 .40
547 Clayton Richard .15 .40
548 Dixon Machado .15 .40
549 Jose Martinez .15 .40
550 Leonys Martin .15 .40
551 Tyler Clippard .15 .40
552 Adeiny Hechavarria .15 .40
553 Mark Melancon .15 .40
554 Richard Bleier .15 .40
555 Matt Moore .20 .50
556 Mike Fiers .15 .40
557 Trevor Williams .15 .40
558 Jaime Schultz RC .30 .75
559 Miles Mikolas RC .40 1.00
560 P.J. Conlon RC .30 .75
561 Ryan Flaherty .15 .40
562 Joe Kelly .15 .40
563 Garrett Cooper RC .30 .75
564 Teoscar Hernandez .25 .60
565 Dan Otero .15 .40
566 Adam Ottavino .15 .40
567 Craig Gentry .15 .40
568 Austin Meadows RC .75 2.00
569 Greg Holland .15 .40
570 Adam Engel .15 .40
571 Bryan Shaw .15 .40
572 Tyler Skaggs .15 .40
573 Max Stassi .15 .40
574 Miguel Montero .15 .40
575 Alen Hanson .20 .50
576 Brandon Morrow .15 .40
577 Jesse Biddle RC .40 1.00
578 Victor Caratini RC .40 1.00
579 Gift Ngoepe .15 .40
580 Ronald Acuna Jr. RC 20.00 50.00
581 Sal Romano .15 .40
582 Brian Johnson .15 .40
583 Francisco Liriano .15 .40
584 Jurickson Profar .20 .50
585 Brian Goodwin .15 .40
586 Mike Gerber RC .30 .75
587 Brandon McCarthy .15 .40
588 Lucas Duda .15 .40
589 Rene Rivera .15 .40
590 Dereck Rodriguez RC .40 1.00
591 Kevin Plawecki .15 .40
592 Yairo Munoz RC .40 1.00
593 Jaime Barria RC .40 1.00
594 Harrison Musgrave RC .30 .75
595 Freddy Galvis .15 .40
596 Hector Rondon .15 .40
597 Luis Valbuena .15 .40
598 Jarrod Dyson .15 .40
599 Tony Watson .15 .40
600 Shohei Ohtani RC 12.00 30.00
601 Matt Albers .15 .40
602 Cesar Hernandez .15 .40
603 Gleyber Torres RC 3.00 8.00
604 Taylor Motter .15 .40
605 Marcus Walden RC .40 1.00
606 Bartolo Colon .15 .40
607 Addison Reed .15 .40
608 Jarlin Garcia .15 .40
609 Keone Kela .15 .40
610 C.J. Cron .15 .40
611 Ronald Guzman RC .30 .75
612 Tyler O'Neill RC .50 1.25
613 Christian Arroyo .15 .40
614 Will Smith .25 .60
615 Matt Koch .15 .40
616 Tim Beckham .20 .50
617 Shane Greene .15 .40
618 Denard Span .15 .40
619 Austin Gomber RC .40 1.00
620 Jordan Hicks RC .60 1.50
621 Ross Stripling .15 .40
622 Jake Odorizzi .15 .40
623 Mark Canha .15 .40
624 Nick Ahmed .15 .40
625 Mitch Moreland .15 .40
626 Rajai Davis .15 .40
627 Colin Moran .15 .40
628 Cameron Maybin .15 .40
629 Andrew Suarez RC .30 .75
630 Tyler Naquin .20 .50
631 Robert Gsellman .15 .40
632 Sergio Romo .15 .40
633 Pat Neshek .15 .40
634 Dylan Cozens RC .30 .75
635 Austin Romine .15 .40
636 JaCoby Jones .20 .50
637 Joe Jimenez .15 .40
638 Logan Forsythe .15 .40
639 Anibal Sanchez .15 .40
640 Anthony Santander RC .30 .75
641 Andrew Romine .15 .40
642 Ronald Torreyes .15 .40
643 Willy Adames RC .40 1.00
644 Joey Wendle .30 .75
645 Tyson Ross .15 .40
646 Dwight Smith Jr. .15 .40
647 Caleb Smith .15 .40
648 Austin Jackson .15 .40
649 Tyler Chatwood .15 .40
650 Tomas Nido RC .30 .75
651 Nick Kingham RC .30 .75
652 Seung-Hwan Oh .20 .50
653 Steve Cishek .15 .40
654 Brandon Drury .15 .40
655 Joey Lucchesi RC .30 .75
656 Jorge Soler .25 .60
657 Mike Soroka RC 1.00 2.50
658 Jon Jay .15 .40
659 Logan Morrison .15 .40
660 Austin Barnes .20 .50
661 Darren O'Day .15 .40
662 Bud Norris .15 .40
663 Billy McKinney RC .40 1.00
664 Jeremy Jeffress .15 .40
665 Chase Utley .20 .50
666 Alex Avila .20 .50
667 Jeremy Hellickson .15 .40
668 Shane Carle RC .40 1.00
669 A.J. Minter RC .40 1.00
670 Yonny Chirinos RC .30 .75
671 Carlos Gomez .15 .40
672 Joe Musgrove .25 .60
673 Blake Treinen .15 .40
674 Isiah Kiner-Falefa RC .50 1.25
675 Colby Rasmus .20 .50
676 Keynan Middleton .15 .40
677 Jacob Nottingham RC .30 .75
678 Drew Robinson .15 .40
679 Carson Smith .15 .40
680 Cheslor Cuthbert .15 .40
681 Kelby Tomlinson .15 .40
682 Lance Lynn .15 .40
683 Andrew Cashner .15 .40
684 Lourdes Gurriel Jr. RC .60 1.50
685 Eric Lauer RC .40 1.00
686 Mark Leiter .20 .50
687 Roberto Perez .15 .40
688 Fernando Romero RC .30 .75
689 Wade Davis .15 .40
690 Derek Holland .15 .40
691 Brock Holt .15 .40
692 Steven Brault .15 .40
693 Daniel Palka RC .30 .75
694 Tucker Barnhart .15 .40
695 David Peralta .15 .40
696 Tyler Austin .25 .60
697 Brad Boxberger .15 .40
698 Merandy Gonzalez RC .30 .75
699 Miguel Rojas .15 .40
700 Dan Vogelbach .15 .40
701 Stephen Piscotty SP 1.25 3.00
702 Randal Grichuk SP 1.25 3.00
703 Jay Bruce SP 1.50 4.00
704 Yonder Alonso SP 1.25 3.00
705 Andrew McCutchen SP 2.00 5.00
706 Lorenzo Cain SP 1.25 3.00
707 Yu Darvish SP 2.00 5.00
708 Neil Walker SP 1.25 3.00
709 Eric Hosmer SP 1.50 4.00
710 J.D. Martinez SP 2.50 6.00
711 Carlos Santana SP 1.50 4.00
712 Eduardo Nunez SP 1.25 3.00
713 Matt Kemp SP 1.50 4.00
714 Anthony Banda SP 1.25 3.00
715 Gerrit Cole SP 2.00 5.00
716 Ichiro SP 2.50 6.00
717 Arodys Vizcaino SP 1.25 3.00
718 Todd Frazier SP 1.25 3.00
719 Curtis Granderson SP 1.50 4.00
720 Christian Yelich SP 2.50 6.00
721 Jake Arrieta SP 1.50 4.00
722 Lewis Brinson SP 1.25 3.00
723 Alex Cobb SP 1.25 3.00
724 Brandon Morrow SP 1.25 3.00
725 Evan Longoria SP 1.50 4.00

2018 Topps Heritage '69 Bazooka Ad Panel Boxloader

STATED ODDS 1:3 HOBBY BOXES
1 Carlos Correa 1.00 2.50
2 Mike Trout 5.00 12.00
3 Bryce Harper 1.50 4.00
4 Kris Bryant 1.25 3.00
5 Giancarlo Stanton 1.00 2.50
6 Manny Machado 1.00 2.50
7 Anthony Rizzo 1.25 3.00
8 Amed Rosario .75 2.00
9 Aaron Judge 2.50 6.00
10 Clint Frazier 1.25 3.00
11 Cody Bellinger 2.00 5.00
12 Rhys Hoskins 2.50 6.00
13 Andrew Benintendi 1.00 2.50
14 Rafael Devers 2.00 5.00
15 Clayton Kershaw 1.50 4.00

2018 Topps Heritage '69 Bazooka All Time Greats

RANDOM INSERTS IN PACKS
69BG1 Adrian Beltre 6.00 15.00
69BG2 Albert Pujols 15.00 40.00
69BG3 Mike Trout 30.00 80.00
69BG4 Ichiro 10.00 25.00
69BG5 Miguel Cabrera 6.00 15.00
69BG6 Max Scherzer 6.00 15.00
69BG7 Joey Votto 6.00 15.00
69BG8 Clayton Kershaw 10.00 25.00
69BG9 Buster Posey 8.00 20.00
69BG10 Robinson Cano 5.00 12.00
69BG11 Yadier Molina 8.00 20.00
69BG12 Justin Verlander 6.00 15.00
69BG13 Felix Hernandez 5.00 12.00
69BG14 Bryce Harper 25.00 60.00
69BG15 Giancarlo Stanton 6.00 15.00
69BG16 Carl Yastrzemski 10.00 25.00
69BG17 Willie McCovey 10.00 25.00
69BG18 Orlando Cepeda 8.00 20.00
69BG19 Nolan Ryan 12.00 30.00
69BG20 Harmon Killebrew 10.00 25.00
69BG21 Bob Gibson 10.00 25.00
69BG22 Rollie Fingers 10.00 25.00
69BG23 Willie Stargell 10.00 25.00
69BG24 Reggie Jackson 10.00 25.00
69BG25 Roberto Clemente 12.00 30.00
69BG26 Tom Seaver 12.00 30.00
69BG27 Jim Palmer 10.00 25.00
69BG28 Brooks Robinson 12.00 30.00
69BG29 Steve Carlton 10.00 25.00
69BG30 Johnny Bench 15.00 40.00

2018 Topps Heritage '69 Collector Cards

RANDOM INSERTS IN PACKS
69CCAB Adrian Beltre HN .75 2.00
69CCAJ Aaron Judge 2.00 5.00
69CCAM Andrew McCutchen HN .75 2.00
69CCAR Anthony Rizzo 1.00 2.50
69CCARO Amed Rosario .60 1.50
69CCBH Bryce Harper 1.25 3.00
69CCBP Buster Posey HN 1.25 3.00
69CCCB Cody Bellinger 1.50 4.00
69CCCC Carlos Correa HN .75 2.00
69CCCK Clayton Kershaw HN 1.25 3.00
69CCCS Corey Seager HN .75 2.00
69CCGS Giancarlo Stanton .75 2.00
69CCGT Gleyber Torres HN 5.00 12.00
69CCI Ichiro HN 1.00 2.50
69CCJA Jose Altuve .60 1.50
69CCJV Joey Votto .75 2.00
69CCJV Justin Verlander HN .75 2.00
69CCKB Kris Bryant 1.00 2.50
69CCMB Mookie Betts 1.50 4.00
69CCMM Manny Machado .75 2.00
69CCMS Max Scherzer .75 2.00
69CCMS Miguel Sano HN .60 1.50
69CCMT Mike Trout 4.00 10.00
69CCNA Nolan Arenado HN 1.25 3.00
69CCNS Noah Syndergaard HN .60 1.50
69CCOA Ozzie Albies HN 1.50 4.00
69CCPG Paul Goldschmidt HN .75 2.00
69CCRD Rafael Devers 1.50 4.00
69CCRH Rhys Hoskins 2.00 5.00
69CCSO Shohei Ohtani HN 12.00 30.00

2018 Topps Heritage '69 Postal Stamps

STATED ODDS 1:3524 HOBBY
STATED PRINT RUN 50 SER.#'d SETS
69PSRAK Al Kaline 30.00 80.00
69PSRBR Brooks Robinson 30.00 80.00
69PSRBW Billy Williams 25.00 60.00
69PSRCH Catfish Hunter 30.00 80.00
69PSRFJ Fergie Jenkins 30.00 80.00
69PSRHA Hank Aaron 30.00 80.00
69PSRHK Harmon Killebrew 30.00 80.00
69PSRJB Johnny Bench 40.00 100.00
69PSRJM Joe Morgan 25.00 60.00
69PSRJP Jim Palmer 30.00 80.00
69PSRLB Lou Brock 30.00 80.00
69PSRNR Nolan Ryan 50.00 125.00
69PSROC Orlando Cepeda 25.00 60.00
69PSRRC Rod Carew 25.00 60.00
69PSRRJ Reggie Jackson 30.00 80.00
69PSRSC Steve Carlton
69PSRTP Tony Perez 30.00 80.00
69PSRTS Tom Seaver 30.00 80.00
69PSRWM Willie McCovey 50.00 120.00
69PSRWS Willie Stargell 30.00 80.00

2018 Topps Heritage '69 Poster Boxloader

STATED ODDS 1:36 HOBBY BOXES
ANNCD PRINT RUN OF 50 COPIES EACH
69PA Angels 75.00 200.00
69PAB Braves 30.00 80.00
69PAD Diamondbacks 25.00 60.00
69PBO Orioles 30.00 80.00
69PBR Red Sox 50.00 120.00
69PCC Cubs 50.00 120.00
69PCI Indians 50.00 120.00
69PCR Reds 30.00 80.00
69PCW White Sox 30.00 80.00
69PDT Tigers 30.00 80.00
69PHA Astros 30.00 80.00
69PMB Brewers 30.00 80.00
69PMM Marlins 25.00 60.00
69PMT Twins 30.00 80.00
69POA A's 30.00 80.00
69PPP Phillies 40.00 100.00
69PSM Mariners 25.00 60.00
69PTR Rangers 30.00 80.00
69PWN Nationals 40.00 100.00
69PCOR Rockies 25.00 60.00
69PKCR Royals 30.00 80.00
69PLAD Dodgers 30.00 80.00
69PNYM Mets 40.00 100.00
69PNYY Yankees 40.00 100.00
69PPIP Pirates 25.00 60.00
69PSDP Padres 20.00 50.00
69PSFG Giants 30.00 80.00
69PSLC Cardinals 40.00 100.00
69PTBJ Blue Jays 20.00 50.00
69PTBR Rays 25.00 60.00

2018 Topps Heritage '69 Topps Decals

RANDOM INSERTS IN PACKS
1 Carlos Correa 1.25 3.00
2 Mike Trout 6.00 15.00
3 Bryce Harper 2.00 5.00
4 Kris Bryant 1.50 4.00
5 Giancarlo Stanton 1.25 3.00
6 Manny Machado 1.25 3.00
7 Anthony Rizzo 1.50 4.00
8 Amed Rosario 1.00 2.50
9 Aaron Judge 3.00 8.00
10 Clint Frazier 1.50 4.00
11 Cody Bellinger 2.50 6.00
12 Rhys Hoskins 3.00 8.00
13 Andrew Benintendi 1.25 3.00
14 Rafael Devers 2.50 6.00
15 Clayton Kershaw 2.00 5.00

2018 Topps Heritage '69 Topps Deckle Edge

COMPLETE SET (30) 30.00 80.00
STATED ODDS 1:10 HOBBY
1 Mike Trout 5.00 12.00
2 Jose Altuve .75 2.00
3 Carlos Correa 1.00 2.50
4 Aaron Judge 2.50 6.00
5 Francisco Lindor 1.00 2.50
6 Clayton Kershaw 1.50 4.00
7 Bryce Harper 1.50 4.00
8 Buster Posey 1.25 3.00
9 Cody Bellinger 2.00 5.00
10 Joey Votto 1.00 2.50
11 Ozzie Albies 2.00 5.00
12 Yadier Molina 1.25 3.00
13 Salvador Perez .75 2.00
14 Mookie Betts 2.00 5.00
15 Gary Sanchez 1.00 2.50
16 Giancarlo Stanton 1.00 2.50
17 Andrew Benintendi 1.00 2.50
18 Kris Bryant 1.25 3.00
19 Anthony Rizzo 1.25 3.00
20 Manny Machado 1.00 2.50
21 Rafael Devers 2.00 5.00
22 Clint Frazier 1.25 3.00
23 Rhys Hoskins 2.50 6.00
24 Amed Rosario .75 2.00
25 Victor Robles 1.50 4.00
26 Chris Sale 1.00 2.50
27 Nolan Arenado 1.50 4.00
28 Max Scherzer 1.00 2.50
29 Paul Goldschmidt 1.00 2.50
30 Corey Seager 1.00 2.50

2018 Topps Heritage 100th Anniversary

*100TH: 10X TO 25X BASIC
*100TH RC: 5X TO 12X BASIC RC
*100TH SP: 1.2X TO 3X BASIC SP
STATED ODDS 1:277 HOBBY
STATED HN ODDS 1:370 HOBBY
STATED PRINT RUN 25 SER.#'d SETS
22 Bryce Harper 25.00 60.00
25 Aaron Judge 100.00 250.00
502 Juan Soto 500.00 1200.00
511 Scott Kingery 12.00 30.00
540 David Bote 25.00 60.00
600 Shohei Ohtani 150.00 400.00
603 Gleyber Torres 100.00 250.00
716 Ichiro 12.00 30.00

2018 Topps Heritage Action Variations

STATED ODDS 1:35 HOBBY
STATED HN ODDS 1:24 HOBBY
17 Shohei Ohtani 125.00 300.00
20 Anthony Rizzo 5.00 12.00
22 Bryce Harper 6.00 15.00
25 Aaron Judge 15.00 40.00
31 Amed Rosario 3.00 8.00
35 Jose Altuve 3.00 8.00
45 Corey Seager 4.00 10.00
70 Joey Votto 4.00 10.00
80 Kris Bryant 5.00 12.00
114 Clint Frazier 5.00 12.00
118 Cody Bellinger 10.00 25.00
130 Andrew Benintendi 4.00 10.00
145 Francisco Lindor 4.00 10.00
151 Manny Machado 4.00 10.00
189 Rafael Devers 20.00 50.00
191 Gary Sanchez 4.00 10.00
206 Rhys Hoskins 15.00 40.00
216 Clayton Kershaw 6.00 15.00
275 Mike Trout 25.00 60.00
284 Victor Robles 6.00 15.00
293 Buster Posey 5.00 12.00
330 Mookie Betts 8.00 20.00
351 Nolan Arenado 6.00 15.00
369 Paul Goldschmidt 4.00 10.00
381 Carlos Correa 4.00 10.00
511 Scott Kingery 4.00 10.00
517 Jonathan Lucroy 3.00 8.00
549 Jose Martinez 2.50 6.00
580 Ronald Acuna Jr. 125.00 300.00
600 Shohei Ohtani 30.00 80.00
603 Gleyber Torres 50.00 120.00
606 Bartolo Colon 2.50 6.00
612 Tyler O'Neill 4.00 10.00
620 Jordan Hicks 5.00 12.00
636 JaCoby Jones 3.00 8.00
684 Lourdes Gurriel Jr. 5.00 12.00
696 Tyler Austin 4.00 10.00
701 Stephen Piscotty 2.50 6.00
705 Andrew McCutchen 4.00 10.00
706 Lorenzo Cain 2.50 6.00
707 Yu Darvish 4.00 10.00
709 Eric Hosmer 3.00 8.00
710 J.D. Martinez 4.00 10.00
711 Carlos Santana 3.00 8.00
713 Matt Kemp 3.00 8.00
715 Gerrit Cole 4.00 10.00
716 Ichiro 5.00 12.00
718 Todd Frazier 2.50 6.00
720 Christian Yelich 5.00 12.00
721 Jake Arrieta 3.00 8.00

2018 Topps Heritage Black Border

*BLACK: 8X TO 20X BASIC
*BLACK RC: 4X TO 10X BASIC RC
*BLACK SP: 1X TO 2.5X BASIC SP
STATED ODDS 1:52 HOBBY
STATED HN ODDS 1:77 HOBBY
ANNCD PRINT RUN OF 50 COPIES EACH
22 Bryce Harper 20.00 50.00
25 Aaron Judge 75.00 200.00

502 Juan Soto 400.00 1000.00
540 David Bote 20.00 50.00
600 Shohei Ohtani 125.00 300.00
603 Gleyber Torres 75.00 200.00
716 Ichiro 10.00 25.00

2018 Topps Heritage Error Variations

RANDOM INSERTS IN PACKS
STATED HN ODDS 1:1663 HOBBY
22 Harper Birth year 60.00 150.00
25 Judge Name clr 75.00 200.00
74 Stanton Rev Neg 60.00 150.00
80 Bryant Name clr 75.00 200.00
275 Trout Bat Boy 60.00 150.00
580 AcunaBlue lst nme 100.00 250.00
600 Ohtani Red lst nme 100.00 250.00
603 Torres Blue lst nme 50.00 120.00
705 McCtchn Cubs back 30.00 80.00
716 Ichiro Rvrse neg 30.00 80.00

2018 Topps Heritage Mini

STATED ODDS 1:262 HOBBY
STATED HN ODDS 1:416 HOBBY
STATED PRINT RUN 100 SER.#'d SETS
13 Domingo Santana 5.00 12.00
15 Chris Davis 4.00 10.00
17 Zach Davies 4.00 10.00
18 Matt Carpenter 6.00 15.00
20 Anthony Rizzo 8.00 20.00
21 Mitch Haniger 5.00 12.00
22 Bryce Harper 40.00 100.00
23 Sean Manaea 4.00 10.00
24 Charlie Blackmon 6.00 15.00
25 Aaron Judge 60.00 150.00
26 Tommy Pham 4.00 10.00
30 Miguel Sano 5.00 12.00
35 Jose Altuve 5.00 12.00
37 Adam Jones 5.00 12.00
40 Miguel Cabrera 20.00 50.00
43 Jon Lester 5.00 12.00
45 Corey Seager 6.00 15.00
48 Joey Gallo 5.00 12.00
50 Andrew McCutchen 6.00 15.00
51 Brandon Crawford 5.00 12.00
53 Dansby Swanson 6.00 15.00
58 Justin Verlander 6.00 15.00
59 Albert Pujols 12.00 30.00
60 Justin Upton 5.00 12.00
61 Bradley Zimmer 4.00 10.00
62 Eric Thames 5.00 12.00
63 Ian Happ 5.00 12.00
64 Johnny Cueto 5.00 12.00
67 Max Scherzer 6.00 15.00
70 Joey Votto 6.00 15.00
71 Eric Hosmer 5.00 12.00
72 Jacob deGrom 12.00 30.00
74 Giancarlo Stanton 20.00 50.00
75 Jonathan Schoop 4.00 10.00
80 Kris Bryant 40.00 100.00
83 Dexter Fowler 5.00 12.00
87 Starlin Castro 4.00 10.00
90 Noah Syndergaard 5.00 12.00
91 Josh Donaldson 5.00 12.00
92 Stephen Strasburg 6.00 15.00
93 Mike Moustakas 5.00 12.00
94 Kenta Maeda 5.00 12.00
97 Jose Abreu 6.00 15.00
100 Felix Hernandez 5.00 12.00
101 Salvador Perez 5.00 12.00
104 Trea Turner 5.00 12.00
105 Josh Harrison 4.00 10.00
108 Billy Hamilton 5.00 12.00
109 Chris Sale 6.00 15.00
118 Cody Bellinger 12.00 30.00
119 Alex Bregman 6.00 15.00
124 Kendrys Morales 4.00 10.00
128 Ender Inciarte 4.00 10.00
130 Andrew Benintendi 25.00 60.00
134 Kevin Kiermaier 5.00 12.00
139 Jose Bautista 5.00 12.00
140 Aroldis Chapman 6.00 15.00
143 A.J. Pollock 4.00 10.00
145 Francisco Lindor 6.00 15.00
150 Josh Hader 5.00 12.00
151 Manny Machado 12.00 30.00
153 Elvis Andrus 5.00 12.00
155 Orlando Arcia 4.00 10.00
161 Yu Darvish 6.00 15.00
170 Marcell Ozuna 6.00 15.00
171 Javier Baez 8.00 20.00
176 Corey Kluber 10.00 25.00
180 Jordan Montgomery 4.00 10.00
185 Starling Marte 5.00 12.00
188 Aaron Nola 5.00 12.00
191 Gary Sanchez 6.00 15.00
198 Hunter Renfroe 4.00 10.00
201 Yoan Moncada 6.00 15.00
202 Dallas Keuchel 5.00 12.00
208 Yuli Gurriel 5.00 12.00
209 Dee Gordon 4.00 10.00
212 Didi Gregorius 5.00 12.00
216 Clayton Kershaw 20.00 50.00
218 Masahiro Tanaka 5.00 12.00
219 Freddie Freeman 8.00 20.00
220 Carlos Carrasco 4.00 10.00
221 Yoenis Cespedes 6.00 15.00
230 Ryan Zimmerman 5.00 12.00
232 Yadier Molina 8.00 20.00
233 Kyle Seager 4.00 10.00
234 Zack Greinke 6.00 15.00
240 Justin Smoak 4.00 10.00
241 Addison Russell 5.00 12.00
247 Willson Contreras 6.00 15.00
249 Marcus Stroman 5.00 12.00
250 Trey Mancini 5.00 12.00
260 Khris Davis 6.00 15.00
262 Eddie Rosario 6.00 15.00
265 Carlos Martinez 5.00 12.00
267 Trevor Bauer 8.00 20.00
268 Kyle Schwarber 6.00 15.00
275 Mike Trout 60.00 150.00
286 Chris Archer 4.00 10.00
288 Jake Arrieta 5.00 12.00
290 Jose Berrios 5.00 12.00
291 Jose Ramirez 5.00 12.00
293 Buster Posey 8.00 20.00
294 J.D. Martinez 6.00 15.00
300 Ichiro 8.00 20.00
301 Robinson Cano 5.00 12.00
302 Matt Olson 6.00 15.00
303 Luis Severino 5.00 12.00
305 Josh Bell 5.00 12.00
320 Paul DeJong 6.00 15.00
322 Nelson Cruz 6.00 15.00
325 Edwin Encarnacion 6.00 15.00
326 Daniel Murphy 5.00 12.00
327 Yasiel Puig 6.00 15.00
330 Mookie Betts 12.00 30.00
337 Byron Buxton 6.00 15.00
341 Christian Yelich 8.00 20.00
344 Manny Pina 4.00 10.00
345 Robbie Ray 4.00 10.00
348 German Marquez 4.00 10.00
349 Dustin Pedroia 6.00 15.00
351 Nolan Arenado 10.00 25.00
356 Brian Dozier 5.00 12.00
360 George Springer 5.00 12.00
364 Michael Conforto 5.00 12.00
365 Matt Chapman 6.00 15.00
366 Chris Taylor 5.00 12.00
369 Paul Goldschmidt 6.00 15.00
375 Whit Merrifield 6.00 15.00
381 Carlos Correa 6.00 15.00
384 Jake Lamb 5.00 12.00
387 Wil Myers 5.00 12.00
397 Evan Longoria 5.00 12.00
502 Juan Soto 500.00 1200.00
511 Scott Kingery 6.00 15.00
517 Jonathan Lucroy 5.00 12.00
526 Steven Souza Jr. 5.00 12.00
527 Corey Dickerson 4.00 10.00
537 Matt Adams 4.00 10.00
541 Freddy Peralta 4.00 10.00
549 Jose Martinez 4.00 10.00
555 Matt Moore 5.00 12.00
562 Joe Kelly 4.00 10.00
568 Austin Meadows 10.00 25.00
570 Adam Engel 4.00 10.00
580 Ronald Acuna Jr. 250.00 600.00
583 Francisco Liriano 4.00 10.00
588 Lucas Duda 5.00 12.00
600 Shohei Ohtani 150.00 400.00
603 Gleyber Torres 40.00 100.00
613 Christian Arroyo 4.00 10.00
616 Tim Beckham 5.00 12.00
620 Jordan Hicks 8.00 20.00
622 Jake Odorizzi 4.00 10.00
633 Pat Neshek 4.00 10.00
655 Joey Lucchesi 4.00 10.00
659 Logan Morrison 4.00 10.00
672 Joe Musgrove 6.00 15.00
689 Wade Davis 4.00 10.00
694 Tucker Barnhart 4.00 10.00
701 Stephen Piscotty 4.00 10.00
703 Jay Bruce 5.00 12.00
704 Yonder Alonso 4.00 10.00
705 Andrew McCutchen 12.00 30.00
706 Lorenzo Cain 4.00 10.00
707 Yu Darvish 6.00 15.00
708 Neil Walker 4.00 10.00
709 Eric Hosmer 5.00 12.00
710 J.D. Martinez 6.00 15.00
711 Carlos Santana 5.00 12.00
712 Eduardo Nunez 4.00 10.00
713 Matt Kemp 5.00 12.00
714 Anthony Banda 4.00 10.00
715 Gerrit Cole 6.00 15.00
716 Ichiro 8.00 20.00
717 Arodys Vizcaino 4.00 10.00
718 Todd Frazier 4.00 10.00
719 Curtis Granderson 5.00 12.00
720 Christian Yelich 8.00 20.00
721 Jake Arrieta 5.00 12.00
722 Lewis Brinson 4.00 10.00
724 Brandon Morrow 4.00 10.00
725 Evan Longoria 5.00 12.00

2018 Topps Heritage Nickname Variations

RANDOM INSERTS IN PACKS
STATED HN ODDS 1:1663 HOBBY
22 Bryce Harper 60.00 150.00
25 Aaron Judge 150.00 400.00
50 Andrew McCutchen 20.00 50.00
80 Kris Bryant 60.00 150.00
90 Noah Syndergaard 15.00 40.00
114 Clint Frazier 40.00 100.00
118 Cody Bellinger 30.00 80.00
130 Andrew Benintendi 20.00 50.00
145 Francisco Lindor 20.00 50.00
151 Manny Machado 40.00 100.00
189 Rafael Devers 75.00 200.00
216 Clayton Kershaw 30.00 80.00
275 Mike Trout 100.00 250.00
369 Paul Goldschmidt 20.00 50.00
381 Carlos Correa 20.00 50.00
600 Shohei Ohtani 100.00 250.00
707 Yu Darvish 20.00 50.00
716 Ichiro 25.00 60.00
718 Todd Frazier 12.00 30.00
725 Evan Longoria 15.00 40.00

2018 Topps Heritage Rookie Cup Variations

RANDOM INSERTS IN PACKS
25 Aaron Judge 75.00 200.00
63 Ian Happ 12.00 30.00
118 Cody Bellinger 30.00 80.00
130 Andrew Benintendi 30.00 80.00
150 Josh Hader 12.00 30.00
180 Jordan Montgomery 10.00 25.00
189 Rafael Devers 40.00 100.00
250 Trey Mancini 12.00 30.00
320 Paul DeJong 20.00 50.00
348 German Marquez 10.00 25.00

2018 Topps Heritage Team Color Swap Variations

STATED ODDS 1:205 HOBBY
STATED HN ODDS 1:139 HOBBY
20 Anthony Rizzo 15.00 40.00
22 Bryce Harper 25.00 60.00
25 Aaron Judge 60.00 150.00
31 Amed Rosario 15.00 40.00
67 Max Scherzer 8.00 20.00
70 Joey Votto 12.00 30.00
74 Giancarlo Stanton 25.00 60.00
80 Kris Bryant 10.00 25.00
101 Salvador Perez 6.00 15.00
109 Chris Sale 8.00 20.00
114 Clint Frazier 20.00 50.00
118 Cody Bellinger 20.00 50.00
130 Andrew Benintendi 20.00 50.00
145 Francisco Lindor 8.00 20.00
151 Manny Machado 8.00 20.00
189 Rafael Devers 50.00 120.00
191 Gary Sanchez 15.00 40.00
206 Rhys Hoskins 40.00 60.00
216 Clayton Kershaw 20.00 50.00
232 Yadier Molina 10.00 25.00
275 Mike Trout 40.00 100.00
284 Victor Robles 25.00 60.00
293 Buster Posey 15.00 40.00
330 Mookie Betts 15.00 40.00
381 Carlos Correa 8.00 20.00
510 Pablo Sandoval 6.00 15.00
511 Scott Kingery 8.00 20.00
517 Jonathan Lucroy 6.00 15.00
580 Ronald Acuna Jr. 250.00 600.00
600 Shohei Ohtani 40.00 100.00
603 Gleyber Torres 50.00 125.00
620 Jordan Hicks 10.00 25.00
655 Joey Lucchesi 5.00 12.00
684 Lourdes Gurriel Jr. 10.00 25.00
689 Wade Davis 5.00 12.00
696 Tyler Austin 8.00 20.00
701 Stephen Piscotty 5.00 12.00
705 Andrew McCutchen 8.00 20.00
707 Yu Darvish 8.00 20.00
709 Eric Hosmer 6.00 15.00
710 J.D. Martinez 15.00 40.00
713 Matt Kemp 6.00 15.00
715 Gerrit Cole 8.00 20.00
716 Ichiro 10.00 25.00
718 Todd Frazier 5.00 12.00
719 Curtis Granderson 6.00 15.00
720 Christian Yelich 10.00 25.00
721 Jake Arrieta 6.00 15.00
724 Brandon Morrow 5.00 12.00
725 Evan Longoria 6.00 15.00

2018 Topps Heritage Traded Variations

RANDOM INSERTS IN PACKS
STATED HN ODDS 1:831 HOBBY
58 Justin Verlander 12.00 30.00
60 Justin Upton 10.00 25.00
74 Giancarlo Stanton 50.00 120.00
126 Jose Quintana 8.00 20.00
159 Jay Bruce 10.00 25.00
161 Yu Darvish 12.00 30.00
177 Sonny Gray 10.00 25.00
294 J.D. Martinez 12.00 30.00
315 Sean Doolittle 8.00 20.00
472 Brandon Phillips 8.00 20.00
600 Shohei Ohtani 40.00 100.00
701 Stephen Piscotty 8.00 20.00
705 Andrew McCutchen 12.00 30.00
713 Matt Kemp 10.00 25.00
715 Gerrit Cole 12.00 30.00
716 Ichiro 15.00 40.00
718 Todd Frazier 8.00 20.00
721 Jake Arrieta 10.00 25.00
725 Evan Longoria 10.00 25.00

2018 Topps Heritage Amazin' Mets Autographs

STATED HN ODDS 1:1095 HOBBY
STATED PRINT RUN 69 SER.#'d SETS
EXCHANGE DEADLINE 8/31/2020
AMAAW Al Weis 20.00 50.00
AMACJ Cleon Jones 30.00 80.00
AMAEK Ed Kranepool 75.00 200.00
AMANR Nolan Ryan 300.00 600.00
AMARS Ron Swoboda 25.00 60.00
AMAWG Wayne Garrett 75.00 200.00

2018 Topps Heritage Baseball Flashbacks

COMPLETE SET (15) 8.00 20.00
STATED ODDS 1:20 HOBBY
BFBR Brooks Robinson .50 1.25
BFFJ Fergie Jenkins .50 1.25
BFHA Hank Aaron 1.25 3.00
BFHK Harmon Killebrew .60 1.50
BFJB Johnny Bench .60 1.50
BFJM Juan Marichal .50 1.25
BFJP Jim Palmer .50 1.25
BFLB Lou Brock .50 1.25
BFRC Rod Carew .50 1.25
BFRCL Roberto Clemente 1.50 4.00
BFRJ Reggie Jackson .50 1.25
BFSC Steve Carlton .50 1.25
BFTS Tom Seaver .50 1.25
BFWM Willie McCovey .50 1.25
BFWS Willie Stargell .50 1.25

2018 Topps Heritage Chrome

STATED ODDS 1:35 HOBBY
STATED HN ODDS 1:42 HOBBY
STATED PRINT RUN 999 SER.#'d SETS
*PRPLE REF: .4X TO 1X BASIC
*REF/569: .6X TO 1.5X BASIC
THC15 Chris Davis 1.25 3.00
THC17 Zach Davies 1.25 3.00
THC18 Matt Carpenter 2.00 5.00
THC20 Anthony Rizzo 2.50 6.00
THC22 Bryce Harper 3.00 8.00
THC23 Sean Manaea 1.25 3.00
THC24 Charlie Blackmon 2.00 5.00
THC25 Aaron Judge 5.00 12.00
THC30 Miguel Sano 1.50 4.00
THC31 Dominic Smith 1.50 4.00
Amed Rosario
THC35 Jose Altuve 1.50 4.00
THC37 Adam Jones 1.50 4.00
THC40 Miguel Cabrera 2.00 5.00
THC43 Jon Lester 1.50 4.00
THC45 Corey Seager 2.00 5.00
THC48 Joey Gallo 1.50 4.00
THC50 Andrew McCutchen 2.00 5.00
THC53 Dansby Swanson 2.00 5.00
THC58 Justin Verlander 2.00 5.00
THC59 Albert Pujols 2.50 6.00
THC61 Bradley Zimmer 1.25 3.00
THC62 Eric Thames 1.50 4.00
THC63 Ian Happ 1.50 4.00
THC64 Johnny Cueto 1.50 4.00
THC66 Sisco/Hays 2.00 5.00
THC67 Max Scherzer 2.00 5.00
THC70 Joey Votto 2.00 5.00
THC71 Eric Hosmer 1.50 4.00
THC72 Jacob deGrom 4.00 10.00
THC74 Giancarlo Stanton 2.00 5.00
THC80 Kris Bryant 2.50 6.00
THC87 Starlin Castro 1.25 3.00
THC90 Noah Syndergaard 1.50 4.00
THC91 Josh Donaldson 1.50 4.00
THC92 Stephen Strasburg 2.00 5.00
THC93 Mike Moustakas 1.50 4.00
THC94 Kenta Maeda 1.50 4.00
THC97 Jose Abreu 2.00 5.00
THC100 Freddie Freeman 2.50 6.00
THC109 Chris Sale 2.00 5.00
THC114 Frazier/Andujar 5.00 12.00
THC119 Alex Bregman 2.00 5.00
THC124 Kendrys Morales 1.25 3.00
THC125 Carlos Correa 2.00 5.00
THC128 Ender Inciarte 1.25 3.00
THC130 Andrew Benintendi 2.00 5.00
THC145 Francisco Lindor 2.00 5.00
THC150 Cody Bellinger 4.00 10.00
THC151 Manny Machado 2.00 5.00
THC153 Elvis Andrus 1.50 4.00
THC161 Yu Darvish 2.00 5.00
THC170 Marcell Ozuna 2.00 5.00
THC171 Javier Baez 2.50 6.00
THC176 Corey Kluber 1.50 4.00
THC188 Aaron Nola 1.50 4.00
THC189 Martin/Devers 4.00 10.00
THC191 Gary Sanchez 2.00 5.00
THC202 Dallas Keuchel 1.50 4.00
THC206 Williams/Hoskins 5.00 12.00
THC208 Yuli Gurriel 1.50 4.00
THC209 Dee Gordon 1.25 3.00
THC212 Didi Gregorius 1.50 4.00
THC216 Clayton Kershaw 3.00 8.00
THC220 Carlos Carrasco 1.25 3.00
THC221 Yoenis Cespedes 2.00 5.00
THC230 Ryan Zimmerman 1.50 4.00
THC232 Yadier Molina 2.50 6.00
THC233 Kyle Seager 1.25 3.00
THC247 Willson Contreras 2.00 5.00
THC250 Trey Mancini 1.50 4.00
THC254 Zack Greinke 2.00 5.00
THC260 Khris Davis 2.00 5.00
THC266 Buehler/Verdugo 6.00 15.00
THC267 Trevor Bauer 2.50 6.00
THC268 Kyle Schwarber 2.00 5.00
THC275 Mike Trout 10.00 25.00
THC284 Stevenson/Robles 3.00 8.00
THC288 Jake Arrieta 1.50 4.00
THC290 Jose Berrios 1.50 4.00
THC291 Jose Ramirez 1.50 4.00
THC293 Buster Posey 2.50 6.00
THC294 J.D. Martinez 2.00 5.00
THC300 Ichiro 2.50 6.00
THC301 Robinson Cano 1.50 4.00
THC320 Paul DeJong 2.00 5.00
THC322 Nelson Cruz 2.00 5.00
THC325 Edwin Encarnacion 2.00 5.00
THC326 Daniel Murphy 1.50 4.00
THC327 Yasiel Puig 2.00 5.00
THC330 Mookie Betts 4.00 10.00
THC331 Albies/Sims 6.00 15.00
THC349 Dustin Pedroia 2.00 5.00
THC351 Nolan Arenado 3.00 8.00
THC356 Brian Dozier 1.50 4.00
THC360 George Springer 1.50 4.00
THC364 Michael Conforto 1.50 4.00
THC369 Paul Goldschmidt 2.00 5.00
THC384 Jake Lamb 1.50 4.00
THC387 Wil Myers 1.50 4.00
THC397 Evan Longoria 1.50 4.00
THC502 Juan Soto 75.00 200.00
THC511 Scott Kingery 2.00 5.00
THC517 Jonathan Lucroy 1.50 4.00
THC526 Steven Souza Jr. 1.50 4.00
THC527 Corey Dickerson 1.25 3.00
THC537 Matt Adams 1.25 3.00
THC544 Fernando Rodney 1.25 3.00
THC549 Jose Martinez 1.25 3.00
THC555 Matt Moore 1.50 4.00
THC568 Austin Meadows 3.00 8.00
THC580 Ronald Acuna Jr. 40.00 100.00
THC583 Francisco Liriano 1.25 3.00
THC588 Lucas Duda 1.50 4.00
THC600 Shohei Ohtani 30.00 80.00
THC603 Gleyber Torres 12.00 30.00
THC612 Tyler O'Neill 2.00 5.00
THC613 Christian Arroyo 1.25 3.00
THC616 Tim Beckham 1.50 4.00
THC618 Denard Span 1.25 3.00
THC620 Jordan Hicks 2.50 6.00
THC622 Jake Odorizzi 1.25 3.00
THC633 Pat Neshek 1.25 3.00
THC634 Dylan Cozens 1.25 3.00
THC643 Willy Adames 1.50 4.00
THC655 Joey Lucchesi 1.25 3.00
THC659 Logan Morrison 1.25 3.00
THC689 Wade Davis 1.25 3.00
THC701 Stephen Piscotty 1.25 3.00
THC703 Jay Bruce 1.50 4.00
THC704 Yonder Alonso 1.25 3.00
THC705 Andrew McCutchen 2.00 5.00
THC706 Lorenzo Cain 1.25 3.00
THC707 Yu Darvish 2.00 5.00
THC708 Neil Walker 1.25 3.00
THC709 Eric Hosmer 1.50 4.00
THC710 J.D. Martinez 2.00 5.00
THC711 Carlos Santana 1.50 4.00
THC712 Eduardo Nunez 1.25 3.00
THC713 Matt Kemp 1.50 4.00
THC714 Anthony Banda 1.25 3.00
THC715 Gerrit Cole 2.00 5.00
THC716 Ichiro 2.50 6.00
THC717 Arodys Vizcaino 1.25 3.00
THC718 Todd Frazier 1.25 3.00
THC719 Curtis Granderson 1.50 4.00
THC720 Christian Yelich 2.50 6.00
THC721 Jake Arrieta 1.50 4.00
THC722 Lewis Brinson 1.25 3.00
THC724 Brandon Morrow 1.25 3.00
THC725 Evan Longoria 1.50 4.00

2018 Topps Heritage Chrome Black Refractors

*BLACK REF: 2X TO 5X BASIC
STATED ODDS 1:501 HOBBY
STATED HN ODDS 1:602 HOBBY
STATED PRINT RUN 69 SER.#'d SETS
THC22 Bryce Harper 40.00 100.00
THC25 Aaron Judge 200.00 400.00
THC189 Kyle Martin 30.00 80.00
Rafael Devers
THC266 Buehler/Verdugo 40.00 100.00
THC275 Mike Trout 75.00 200.00
THC502 Juan Soto 500.00 1200.00
THC580 Ronald Acuna Jr. 500.00 1000.00
THC600 Shohei Ohtani 200.00 500.00
THC603 Gleyber Torres 125.00 300.00
THC716 Ichiro 15.00 40.00

2018 Topps Heritage Clubhouse Collection Autograph Relics

STATED ODDS 1:8151 HOBBY
STATED HN ODDS 1:3021 HOBBY
STATED PRINT RUN 25 SER.#'d SETS
EXCHANGE DEADLINE 1/31/2020
HN EXCH DEADLINE 8/31/2020
CCARAB Alex Bregman HN EXCH 50.00 120.00
CCARABE Andrew Benintendi HN 60.00 150.00
CCARAJ Aaron Judge
CCARAR Anthony Rizzo
CCARAR Amed Rosario HN EXCH 40.00 100.00
CCARBG Bob Gibson HN 50.00 120.00
CCARBP Buster Posey HN 60.00 150.00
CCARCB Charlie Blackmon HN
CCARCC Carlos Correa
CCARCK Clayton Kershaw EXCH 100.00 250.00
CCARCS Chris Sale 50.00 120.00
CCARDP Dustin Pedroia HN EXCH 40.00 100.00
CCARIH Ian Happ
CCARJA Jose Altuve HN 40.00 100.00
CCARJD Jacob deGrom 50.00 120.00
CCARJV Joey Votto
CCARKB Kris Bryant 150.00 400.00
CCARMM Manny Machado 100.00 250.00
CCARMT Mike Trout 300.00 600.00
CCARNS Noah Syndergaard EXCH 50.00 120.00
CCARPG Paul Goldschmidt HN EXCH 40.00 100.00
CCARRJ Reggie Jackson HN 50.00 120.00
CCARSM Starling Marte HN
CCARVR Victor Robles HN 25.00 60.00
CCARYM Yadier Molina HN EXCH 125.00 300.00

2018 Topps Heritage Clubhouse Collection Dual Relics

STATED ODDS 1:8490 HOBBY
STATED HN ODDS 1:3356 HOBBY
STATED PRINT RUN 69 SER.#'d SETS
CCDRBV Votto/Bench 40.00 100.00
CCDRBV Bench/Votto HN 20.00 50.00
CCDRCS Carew/Sano 40.00 100.00
CCDRGM Gibson/Molina HN 30.00 80.00
CCDRMA Altuve/Morgan 50.00 120.00
CCDRMC Correa/Morgan 20.00 50.00
CCDRRS Syndergaard/Ryan 75.00 200.00
CCDRSB Stargell/Bell HN 25.00 60.00
CCDRSS Seaver/Syndrgrd HN 15.00 40.00
CCDRYB Yaz/Benint. HN 25.00 60.00

2018 Topps Heritage Clubhouse Collection Relics

STATED ODDS 1:33 HOBBY
STATED HN ODDS 1:45 HOBBY
*GOLD/99: .5X TO 1.2X BASIC
CCRAB Adrian Beltre HN 3.00 8.00
CCRABE Andrew Benintendi HN 4.00 10.00
CCRABR Alex Bregman HN 3.00 8.00
CCRAM Andrew McCutchen 3.00 8.00
CCRAP Albert Pujols 4.00 10.00
CCRAR Anthony Rizzo 4.00 10.00
CCRAR Anthony Rendon HN 3.00 8.00
CCRARI Anthony Rizzo HN 4.00 10.00
CCRARO Amed Rosario HN 2.50 6.00
CCRARU Addison Russell 2.50 6.00
CCRAW Adam Wainwright 2.50 6.00
CCRBH Billy Hamilton 2.50 6.00
CCRBH Bryce Harper HN 5.00 12.00
CCRBHA Bryce Harper 10.00 25.00
CCRBP Buster Posey HN 4.00 10.00
CCRBPO Buster Posey 4.00 10.00
CCRBS Blake Snell HN 2.50 6.00
CCRCA Chris Archer 2.00 5.00
CCRCB Charlie Blackmon 3.00 8.00
CCRCBE Cody Bellinger 6.00 15.00
CCRCC Carlos Correa 3.00 8.00
CCRCF Clint Frazier HN 4.00 10.00
CCRCG Carlos Gonzalez 2.50 6.00
CCRCH Cole Hamels 2.50 6.00
CCRCK Clayton Kershaw 5.00 12.00
CCRCK Clayton Kershaw HN 5.00 12.00
CCRCKI Craig Kimbrel HN 2.50 6.00
CCRCS Chris Sale 3.00 8.00
CCRCS CC Sabathia HN 2.50 6.00
CCRCSE Corey Seager 3.00 8.00
CCRDD Danny Duffy HN 2.00 5.00
CCRDG Dee Gordon 2.00 5.00
CCRDK Dallas Keuchel 2.50 6.00
CCRDK Dallas Keuchel HN 2.50 6.00
CCRDL DJ LeMahieu HN 3.00 8.00
CCRDM Daniel Murphy HN 2.50 6.00
CCRDP David Price 2.50 6.00
CCRDW David Wright 2.50 6.00
CCREA Elvis Andrus HN 2.50 6.00
CCREH Eric Hosmer 2.50 6.00
CCREI Ender Inciarte HN 2.00 5.00
CCREL Evan Longoria 2.50 6.00
CCRFB Franklin Barreto HN 2.00 5.00
CCRFF Freddie Freeman 4.00 10.00
CCRFH Felix Hernandez 2.50 6.00
CCRFM Francisco Mejia HN 2.50 6.00
CCRGC Gerrit Cole 3.00 8.00
CCRGP Gregory Polanco 2.50 6.00
CCRGS George Springer 2.50 6.00
CCRGSA Gary Sanchez 3.00 8.00
CCRGST Giancarlo Stanton 3.00 8.00
CCRGT Gleyber Torres HN 6.00 15.00
CCRHR Hanley Ramirez 2.50 6.00
CCRIK Ian Kinsler 2.50 6.00
CCRI Ichiro 4.00 10.00
CCRIS Ichiro HN 4.00 10.00
CCRJA Jose Abreu 3.00 8.00
CCRJAL Jose Altuve 2.50 6.00
CCRJB Javier Baez 4.00 10.00
CCRJB Josh Bell HN 2.50 6.00
CCRJBE Jose Berrios HN 2.50 6.00
CCRJC J.P. Crawford HN 2.00 5.00
CCRJD Jacob deGrom HN 6.00 15.00
CCRJDO Josh Donaldson HN 2.50 6.00
CCRJG Jon Gray 2.00 5.00
CCRJGA Joey Gallo 2.50 6.00
CCRJL Jon Lester 2.50 6.00
CCRJM Joe Mauer 2.50 6.00
CCRJR Jose Ramirez HN 2.50 6.00
CCRJT Justin Turner HN 3.00 8.00
CCRJU Justin Upton 2.50 6.00
CCRJV Justin Verlander 3.00 8.00
CCRJVO Joey Votto 3.00 8.00
CCRKB Kris Bryant 6.00 15.00
CCRKB Kris Bryant HN 5.00 12.00
CCRKD Khris Davis 3.00 8.00
CCRKS Kyle Seager 2.00 5.00
CCRKSC Kyle Schwarber 3.00 8.00
CCRLC Lorenzo Cain 2.00 5.00
CCRLS Luis Severino HN 2.50 6.00
CCRMB Mookie Betts 6.00 15.00
CCRMC Miguel Cabrera 3.00 8.00
CCRMCO Michael Conforto 2.50 6.00
CCRMF Michael Fulmer HN 2.00 5.00
CCRMM Manny Machado 3.00 8.00
CCRMM Manny Machado HN 3.00 8.00
CCRMS Miguel Sano 2.50 6.00
CCRMSC Max Scherzer 3.00 8.00
CCRMT Masahiro Tanaka HN 2.50 6.00
CCRMTR Mike Trout 15.00 40.00
CCRMTR Mike Trout HN 10.00 25.00
CCRNA Nolan Arenado 5.00 12.00
CCRNC Nelson Cruz 3.00 8.00
CCRNS Noah Syndergaard 2.50 6.00
CCROA Ozzie Albies HN 4.00 10.00
CCRPG Paul Goldschmidt 3.00 8.00
CCRPG Paul Goldschmidt HN 3.00 8.00
CCRRA Ronald Acuna Jr. HN 12.00 30.00
CCRRB Ryan Braun 2.50 6.00
CCRRD Rafael Devers HN 6.00 15.00
CCRRH Rhys Hoskins HN 5.00 12.00
CCRRI Raisel Iglesias HN 2.50 6.00
CCRRO Rougned Odor 2.50 6.00
CCRSM Starling Marte 2.50 6.00
CCRSP Salvador Perez 2.50 6.00
CCRSS Stephen Strasburg 3.00 8.00
CCRWM Wil Myers 2.50 6.00
CCRWM Whit Merrifield HN 3.00 8.00
CCRYC Yoenis Cespedes 3.00 8.00
CCRYM Yadier Molina 4.00 10.00
CCRYP Yasiel Puig HN 3.00 8.00
CCRZD Zach Davies HN 2.00 5.00
CCRZG Zack Greinke 3.00 8.00

2018 Topps Heritage Clubhouse Collection Triple Relics

STATED ODDS 1:23,511 HOBBY
STATED HN ODDS 1:9247 HOBBY
STATED PRINT RUN 25 SER.#'d SETS
CCTRCAM Correa/Altuve/Morgan 60.00 150.00
CCTRJMJ Jtr/Mttngly/Jcksn HN 75.00 200.00
CCTRPMM Mrchl/Posey/McCvy 200.00 400.00
CCTRRMC Reyes/Martinez/Carlton 100.00 200.00
CCTRRMR B.Rob/Murray/CRJ HN 125.00 300.00
CCTRSGS Svr/Gdn/Sndrgrd HN 30.00 80.00
CCTRSPK Sttn/Pzza/Krshw HN 40.00 100.00
CCTRSRD Ryan/deGrom/Sndrgrd 60.00 150.00
CCTRVBP Bench/Votto/Perez 60.00 150.00
CCTRWSR Williams/Sndbrg/Rizzo HN 40.00 100.00

2018 Topps Heritage Flashbacks Autograph Relics

STATED ODDS 1:11,986 HOBBY
STATED HN ODDS 1:32,937 HOBBY
PRINT RUNS B/WN 19-25 COPIES PER
EXCHANGE DEADLINE 1/31/2020
FARAK Al Kaline/25 100.00 250.00
FARCY Carl Yastrzemski/25 75.00 200.00
FARHA Hank Aaron/25 250.00 400.00
FARJB Johnny Bench/25 75.00 200.00
FARJP Jim Palmer/25 60.00 150.00
FARLB Lou Brock/19 50.00 120.00
FARNR Nolan Ryan
FARPN Phil Niekro/25 25.00 60.00
FARRC Rod Carew/25 60.00 150.00
FARRJ Reggie Jackson/25 60.00 150.00
FARSC Steve Carlton/25 60.00 150.00

2018 Topps Heritage High Number '69 Bazooka Ad Panel Boxloader

STATED ODDS 1:2 HOBBY BOXES
1 Ian Happ .60 1.50
2 Shohei Ohtani 12.00 30.00
3 Ichiro 1.00 2.50
4 George Springer .60 1.50
5 Giancarlo Stanton .75 2.00
6 Ryan Braun .60 1.50
7 Shohei Ohtani 12.00 30.00
8 Didi Gregorius .60 1.50
9 Adrian Beltre .75 2.00
10 Adam Jones .60 1.50
11 Andrew McCutchen .75 2.00
12 Xander Bogaerts .75 2.00
13 Jameson Taillon .60 1.50
14 Max Scherzer .75 2.00
15 Walker Buehler 2.50 6.00

2018 Topps Heritage High Number '69 Topps Decals

RANDOM INSERTS IN PACKS
69TDBB Byron Buxton 1.25 3.00
69TDBP Buster Posey 1.50 4.00
69TDCS Corey Seager 1.25 3.00
69TDFL Francisco Lindor 1.25 3.00
69TDJA Jose Altuve 1.00 2.50
69TDJV Joey Votto 1.25 3.00
69TDNR Nolan Ryan 4.00 10.00
69TDNS Noah Syndergaard 1.00 2.50
69TDNW Nick Williams 1.00 2.50
69TDOA Ozzie Albies 2.50 6.00
69TDRC Robinson Cano 1.00 2.50
69TDRJ Reggie Jackson 1.00 2.50
69TDSO Shohei Ohtani 4.00 10.00
69TDTS Tom Seaver 1.00 2.50
69TDVR Victor Robles 2.00 5.00

2018 Topps Heritage High Number '69 Topps Deckle Edge

COMPLETE SET (30) 30.00 80.00
STATED HN ODDS 1:10 HOBBY
1 Shohei Ohtani 15.00 40.00
2 Ichiro 1.25 3.00
3 Andrew McCutchen 1.00 2.50
4 Charlie Blackmon 1.00 2.50
5 Albert Pujols 1.25 3.00
6 Justin Verlander 1.00 2.50
7 Josh Donaldson .75 2.00
8 Freddie Freeman 1.25 3.00
9 Corey Kluber .75 2.00
10 Noah Syndergaard .75 2.00
11 Joe Mauer .75 2.00
12 Miguel Cabrera 1.00 2.50
13 Eric Hosmer .75 2.00
14 Mike Moustakas .75 2.00
15 Javier Baez 1.25 3.00
16 Stephen Piscotty .60 1.50
17 Scott Kingery 1.00 2.50
18 Jordan Hicks 1.25 3.00
19 Alex Bregman 1.00 2.50
20 Christian Yelich 1.25 3.00
21 Adrian Beltre 1.00 2.50
22 Matt Chapman 1.00 2.50
23 Didi Gregorius .75 2.00
24 Jose Abreu 1.00 2.50
25 Starling Marte .75 2.00
26 Trey Mancini .75 2.00
27 Gleyber Torres 5.00 12.00
28 Dansby Swanson 1.00 2.50
29 Patrick Corbin .75 2.00
30 Christian Villanueva .60 1.50

2018 Topps Heritage Miracle of '69

COMPLETE SET (5) 4.00 10.00
STATED HN ODDS 1:24 HOBBY
MO69AW Al Weis .40 1.00
MO69CJ Cleon Jones .40 1.00
MO69NR Nolan Ryan 2.00 5.00
MO69RS Ron Swoboda .40 1.00
MO69TS Tom Seaver .50 1.25

2018 Topps Heritage New Age Performers

COMPLETE SET (25) 12.00 30.00
STATED ODDS 1:12 HOBBY
NAP1 Mookie Betts 1.25 3.00
NAP2 Mike Trout 3.00 8.00
NAP3 Jose Altuve .50 1.25
NAP4 Carlos Correa .60 1.50
NAP5 Aaron Judge 1.50 4.00
NAP6 Francisco Lindor .60 1.50
NAP7 Clayton Kershaw 1.00 2.50
NAP8 Bryce Harper 1.00 2.50
NAP9 Buster Posey .75 2.00
NAP10 Cody Bellinger 1.25 3.00
NAP11 Paul Goldschmidt .60 1.50
NAP12 Corey Seager .60 1.50
NAP13 Joey Votto .60 1.50
NAP14 Nolan Arenado 1.00 2.50
NAP15 Gary Sanchez .60 1.50
NAP16 Giancarlo Stanton .60 1.50
NAP17 Andrew Benintendi .60 1.50
NAP18 Kris Bryant .75 2.00
NAP19 Anthony Rizzo .75 2.00
NAP20 Manny Machado .60 1.50
NAP21 Rafael Devers 1.25 3.00
NAP22 Rhys Hoskins 1.50 4.00
NAP23 Amed Rosario .50 1.25
NAP24 Chris Sale .60 1.50
NAP25 Clint Frazier .75 2.00

2018 Topps Heritage News Flashbacks

2017 Topps Heritage News Flashbacks 8.00 20.00
2017 Topps Heritage News Flashbacks
NF1 Apollo 11 Moon Landing .60 1.50
NF2 Woodstock Music & Art Fair .60 1.50
NF3 The Beatles' Abbey Road Album Released .60 1.50
NF4 Dodge Charger Daytona: American Muscle .60 1.50
NF5 Boeing 747 Jumbo Jet Debuts .60 1.50
NF6 Concorde Test Flight .60 1.50
NF7 Automated Teller Machine .60 1.50
NF8 Apollo 12 .60 1.50
NF9 The Brady Bunch .60 1.50
NF10 Richard Nixon .60 1.50
NF11 Vietnam War Draft Lottery .60 1.50
NF12 Project Blue Book Confirms no UFO's .60 1.50
NF13 Vietnam War Protest March on Washington .60 1.50
NF14 Stonewall Riot .60 1.50
NF15 Sesame Street Debut .60 1.50

2018 Topps Heritage Real One Autographs

STATED ODDS 1:154 HOBBY
STATED HN ODDS 1:118 HOBBY
EXCHANGE DEADLINE 1/31/2020
HN EXCH DEADLINE 8/31/2020
ROAAB Anthony Banda HN 5.00 12.00
ROAABE Andrew Benintendi HN 25.00 60.00
ROAAH Austin Hays 12.00 30.00
ROAAK Al Kaline 50.00 120.00
ROAAN Aaron Nola HN 20.00 50.00
ROAAO Amed Rosario HN 20.00 50.00
ROAAR Anthony Rizzo 60.00 150.00
ROAAR Anthony Rizzo HN 25.00 60.00
ROAARO Amed Rosario 20.00 50.00
ROAAV Alex Verdugo 25.00 60.00
ROABA Brian Anderson HN 10.00 25.00
ROABB Byron Buxton HN 10.00 25.00
ROABP Buster Posey HN 100.00 250.00
ROABRO Bob Rodgers 10.00 25.00
ROABRP Bryce Harper HN 100.00 250.00
ROABW Brandon Woodruff HN 8.00 20.00
ROACC Carlos Correa 30.00 80.00
ROACF Clint Frazier 20.00 50.00
ROACK Corey Kluber HN 20.00 50.00
ROACS Chris Sale 25.00 60.00
ROACSI Chance Sisco 10.00 25.00
ROACT Chris Taylor HN 8.00 20.00
ROACY Carl Yastrzemski 100.00 250.00
ROADF Dustin Fowler 8.00 20.00
ROADG Didi Gregorius 15.00 40.00

ROADH Dick Hughes 8.00 20.00
ROADJ Derek Jeter HN
ROADS Dominic Smith 30.00 80.00
ROADT Dick Tracewski 8.00 20.00
ROAFF Freddie Freeman 30.00 80.00
ROAFM Francisco Mejia 12.00 30.00
ROAFP Freddie Patek HN 10.00 25.00
ROAGA Greg Allen HN 10.00 25.00
ROAGC Garrett Cooper HN 5.00 12.00
ROAGT Gleyber Torres HN 250.00 600.00
ROAHA Hank Aaron
ROAHA Hank Aaron HN 200.00 500.00
ROAHB Harrison Bader 8.00 20.00
ROAIH Ian Happ HN 6.00 15.00
ROAJB Johnny Bench 150.00 400.00
ROAJBR Jose Berrios HN 6.00 15.00
ROAJC J.P. Crawford HN 10.00 25.00
ROAJD J.D. Davis HN 6.00 15.00
ROAJE Jackson Stephens HN 5.00 12.00
ROAJF Jack Flaherty 30.00 80.00
ROAJL Jake Lamb HN 6.00 15.00
ROAJP Jim Palmer 50.00 120.00
ROAJS Justin Smoak HN 8.00 20.00
ROAJSO Juan Soto HN 350.00 700.00
ROAJV Joey Votto HN 40.00 100.00
ROAKB Kris Bryant 150.00 400.00
ROAKB Kris Bryant HN 125.00 300.00
ROAKD Khris Davis 20.00 50.00
ROALB Lou Brock 50.00 120.00
ROALS Lucas Sims 8.00 20.00
ROAMA Miguel Andujar HN 60.00 150.00
ROAMF Max Fried HN 10.00 25.00
ROAMM Manny Machado 60.00 150.00
ROAMO Matt Olson HN 12.00 30.00
ROAMT Mike Trout
ROAMT Mike Trout HN 500.00 800.00
ROAND Nicky Delmonico 8.00 20.00
ROANR Nolan Ryan 300.00 500.00
ROANS Noah Syndergaard HN 20.00 50.00
ROAOA Ozzie Albies HN 75.00 200.00
ROAOC Orlando Cepeda 25.00 60.00
ROAPB Paul Blackburn HN 5.00 12.00
ROAPD Paul DeJong HN 15.00 40.00
ROAPG Paul Goldschmidt 25.00 60.00
ROAPN Phil Niekro HN 10.00 25.00
ROARA Ronald Acuna HN 800.00 1200.00
ROARC Rod Carew 40.00 100.00
ROARD Rafael Devers 60.00 150.00
ROARF Rollie Fingers HN 20.00 50.00
ROARFA Roy Face HN 10.00 25.00
ROARH Rhys Hoskins HN 40.00 100.00
ROARJ Reggie Jackson 150.00 400.00
ROARM Ryan McMahon 10.00 25.00
ROARU Richard Urena HN 6.00 15.00
ROASA Sandy Alcantara HN 6.00 15.00
ROASC Steve Carlton 20.00 50.00
ROASG Sonny Gray HN 6.00 15.00
ROASK Scott Kingery HN 15.00 40.00
ROASO Shohei Ohtani 300.00 800.00
ROASO Shohei Ohtani HN 300.00 800.00
ROATM Trey Mancini 10.00 25.00
ROATMA Tyler Mahle 10.00 25.00
ROATW Tyler Wade HN 10.00 25.00
ROAVR Victor Robles 20.00 50.00
ROAVR Victor Robles HN 50.00 120.00
ROAWB Walker Buehler 50.00 120.00
ROAWC Willson Contreras HN 25.00 60.00
ROAZG Zack Granite HN 5.00 12.00

2018 Topps Heritage Real One Autographs Red Ink

*RED INK: .75X TO 2X BASIC
*RED INK NH: .6X TO 1.5X BASIC
STATED ODDS 1:1003 HOBBY
STATED HN ODDS 1:277 HOBBY
PRINT RUNS B/WN 25-69 COPIES PER
EXCHANGE DEADLINE 1/31/2020
HN EXCH DEADLINE 8/31/2020
ROAABE Andrew Benintendi HN 100.00 250.00
ROAARO Amed Rosario/69 50.00 120.00
ROAAV Alex Verdugo/69 60.00 150.00
ROABA Brian Anderson HN 30.00 80.00
ROACF Clint Frazier/69 75.00 200.00
ROAFM Francisco Mejia/69 40.00 100.00
ROAJSO Juan Soto HN/69 1000.00 1500.00
ROAJV Joey Votto HN/25 125.00 300.00
ROARA Ronald Acuna HN 1500.00 2000.00
ROARH Rhys Hoskins HN 100.00 250.00
ROASO Shohei Ohtani/69 5000.00 8000.00
ROASO Shohei Ohtani HN 1200.00 2000.00
ROAVR Victor Robles/69 30.00 80.00
ROAWB Walker Buehler/69 125.00 300.00

2018 Topps Heritage Real One Dual Autographs

STATED ODDS 1:5045 HOBBY
STATED HN ODDS 1:3371 HOBB8Y
STATED PRINT RUN 25 SER.#'d SETS
HN EXCH DEADLINE 8/31/2020
EXCHANGE DEADLINE 1/31/2020
RODABC Carlton/Brock
RODABV Votto/Bench EXCH 200.00 400.00
RODACN Cepeda/Niekro 75.00 200.00
RODAFA Frmn/Acna HN EX 300.00 500.00
RODAFE Eckersley/Fingers 75.00 200.00
RODAJH Henderson/Jackson 300.00 500.00
RODAJJ Judge/Jackson 300.00 500.00
RODAJM Jcksn/McGwre HN 200.00 400.00
RODAJT Judge/Torres HN 300.00 600.00
RODAKB Krshw/Bllngr HN EX 300.00 500.00
RODAOD Ortz/Dvrs HN EX 75.00 200.00
RODARM Rbnsn/Mchdo EXCH 150.00 300.00
RODARP Plmr/Rbnsn EXCH 150.00 300.00
RODARS Ryan/Svr HN EX 600.00 1000.00
RODASR Syndrgrd/Rsro HN EX 60.00 150.00

2018 Topps Heritage Reggie Jackson Highlights

COMPLETE SET (5) 5.00 12.00
STATED HN ODDS 1:24 HOBBY
RJH1 Reggie Jackson 1.00 2.50
RJH2 Reggie Jackson 1.00 2.50
RJH3 Reggie Jackson 1.00 2.50
RJH4 Reggie Jackson 1.00 2.50
RJH5 Reggie Jackson 1.00 2.50

2018 Topps Heritage Rookie Performers

COMPLETE SET (15) 6.00 15.00
STATED HN ODDS 1:8 HOBBY
RPAR Amed Rosario .30 .75
RPCS Chance Sisco .30 .75
RPCV Christian Villanueva .25 .60
RPGT Gleyber Torres 2.50 6.00
RPJH Jordan Hicks .50 1.25
RPJL Joey Lucchesi .25 .60
RPMA Miguel Andujar 1.00 2.50
RPOA Ozzie Albies .75 2.00
RPRA Ronald Acuna Jr. 8.00 20.00
RPRD Rafael Devers .75 2.00
RPRH Rhys Hoskins 1.00 2.50
RPSK Scott Kingery .40 1.00
RPSO Shohei Ohtani 6.00 15.00
RPVR Victor Robles .60 1.50
RPWB Walker Buehler 1.25 3.00

2018 Topps Heritage Seattle Pilots Autographs

STATED ODDS 1:3464 HOBBY
EXCHANGE DEADLINE 1/31/2020
SPABE Bill Edgerton 40.00 100.00
SPABP Bill Parsons 30.00 80.00
SPABR Bob Richmond 30.00 80.00
SPABS Bernie Smith 30.00 80.00
SPABST Buzz Stephen 30.00 80.00
SPADB Dick Baney 30.00 80.00
SPADBA Dick Bates 30.00 80.00
SPAFK Frank Kimball 30.00 80.00
SPAFS Fred Stanley 30.00 80.00
SPAJB Jim Bouton 75.00 200.00
SPAMR Mike Rollyson 30.00 80.00
SPAPK Pete Koegel 30.00 80.00
SPARH Roric Harrison 30.00 80.00
SPARK Ron Kotick 30.00 80.00
SPARP Ray Peters 40.00 100.00

2018 Topps Heritage Then and Now

COMPLETE SET (15) 12.00 30.00
STATED ODDS 1:20 HOBBY
TN1 Seaver/Kershaw 1.00 2.50
TN2 Corey Kluber .50 1.25
Jim Palmer
TN3 Kershaw/Marichal 1.00 2.50
TN4 Corey Kluber .50 1.25
Jim Palmer
TN5 Judge/Killebrew 1.50 4.00
TN6 Stanton/McCovey .60 1.50
TN7 Harmon Killebrew .60 1.50
Nelson Cruz
TN8 Stanton/McCovey .60 1.50
TN9 Altuve/Carew .50 1.25
TN10 Blackmon/Clemente 1.50 4.00
TN11 Dee Gordon .50 1.25
Lou Brock
TN12 Corey Kluber .50 1.25
Jim Palmer
TN13 Juan Marichal .50 1.25
Carlos Martinez
TN14 Max Scherzer .60 1.50
Fergie Jenkins
TN15 Sale/Hunter .60 1.50

2019 Topps Heritage

SP ODDS 1:3 HOBBY
1 Boston Red Sox WS Champs .25 .60
2 Felix Hernandez .20 .50
3 Jared Hughes .15 .40
4 Kole Calhoun .15 .40
5 Alex Wood .15 .40
6 Nick Pivetta .15 .40
7 Kopech RC/Frare RC 1.00 2.50
8 Josh Harrison .15 .40
9 Brandon Lowe RC .50 1.25
Michael Perez RC
10 Jackie Bradley Jr. .25 .60
11 Daniel Mengden .15 .40
12 Jordan Zimmermann .20 .50
13 Chris Stratton .15 .40
14 Adam Eaton .25 .60
15 Roberto Osuna .15 .40
16 Jake Junis .15 .40
17 Sean Newcomb .15 .40
18 Lucas Giolito .20 .50
19 Russell Martin .15 .40
20 Alex Cobb .15 .40
21 Martini RC/Laureano RC .60 1.50
22 Jose Peraza .20 .50
23 CC Sabathia .20 .50
24 Zach Eflin .15 .40
25 Eddie Rosario .20 .50
26 Juan Lagares .15 .40
27 Leonys Martin .15 .40
28 Tommy Hunter .15 .40
29 Andrelton Simmons .15 .40
30 Gregory Polanco .20 .50
31 Jhoulys Chacin .15 .40
32 Brad Peacock .15 .40
33 Jeimer Candelario .15 .40
34 Cody Bellinger .50 1.25
35 Ketel Marte .20 .50
36 Blake Trahan RC .30 .75
Jesus Reyes RC
37 Danny Duffy .15 .40
38 Randal Grichuk .15 .40
39 Brock Holt .15 .40
40 Jose Martinez .15 .40
41 Yusmeiro Petit .15 .40
42 Evan Longoria .20 .50
43 Luke Voit .40 1.00
44 Joey Lucchesi .15 .40
45 Jonathan Villar .15 .40
46 Kyle Hendricks .25 .60
47 Zack Godley .15 .40
48 Jesse Biddle .15 .40
49 Howie Kendrick .15 .40
50 Yoenis Cespedes .25 .60
51 Robbie Ray .15 .40
52 Chris Archer .15 .40
53 Orlando Arcia .15 .40
54 Ross Stripling .15 .40
55 Lou Trivino .15 .40
56 Ranger Suarez RC .30 .75
Enyel de los Santos RC
57 David Peralta .15 .40
58 Gorkys Hernandez .15 .40
59 Mike Clevinger .20 .50
60 Josh Reddick .15 .40
61 Ylch/Fmn/Gennett LL .30 .75
62 Altuve/Betts/Martinez LL .50 1.25
63 Baez/Aglr/Stry/Ylch/Arndo LL .40 1.00
64 Encrncn/Mrtnz/Davis LL .25 .60
65 Ylch/Crpntr/Story/Arndo LL .40 1.00
66 Gallo/Mrtnz/Davis LL .25 .60
67 Max Scherzer .50 1.25
Aaron Nola
Jacob deGrom LL
68 Justin Verlander .30 .75
Trevor Bauer
Blake Snell LL
69 Kyle Freeland .25 .60
Aaron Nola
Miles Mikolas
Jon Lester
Max Scherzer LL
70 Corey Kluber .20 .50
Luis Severino
Blake Snell LL
71 Jacob deGrom .50 1.25
Patrick Corbin
Max Scherzer LL
72 Sale/Vrlndr/Cole LL .25 .60
73 Tyler Mahle .15 .40
74 David Fletcher RC 1.00 2.50
Taylor Ward RC
75 Jake Lamb .20 .50
76 Dexter Fowler .20 .50
77 Tony Watson .15 .40
78 Mookie Betts .50 1.25
79 Clayton Richard .15 .40
80 Ian Happ .20 .50
81 Archie Bradley .15 .40
82 Austin Romine .15 .40
83 Noah Syndergaard .20 .50
84 Wilmer Difo .15 .40
85 Chris Iannetta .15 .40
86 Martin Prado .15 .40
87 Ken Giles .15 .40
88 Nate Orf RC 2.50 6.00
Corbin Burnes RC
89 Adalberto Mondesi .20 .50
90 J.P. Crawford .15 .40
91 Yolmer Sanchez .15 .40
92 Jack Flaherty .25 .60
93 Brian Anderson .15 .40
94 Francisco Cervelli .15 .40
95 Joe Jimenez .15 .40
96 Dakota Hudson RC .50 1.25
Daniel Poncedeleon RC
97 Rich Hill .15 .40
98 Nicholas Castellanos .25 .60
99 Jay Bruce .20 .50
100 Masahiro Tanaka .20 .50
101 Tim Beckham .20 .50
102 Mark Canha .15 .40
103 Miguel Rojas .15 .40
104 Christian Vazquez .20 .50
105 Ender Inciarte .15 .40
106 Stephen Strasburg .25 .60
107 Joe Panik .20 .50
108 Alex Gordon .20 .50
109 Rowdy Tellez RC .50 1.25
Reese McGuire RC
110 Kyle Crick .15 .40
111 Ryan Braun .20 .50
112 Shane Bieber .25 .60
113 Lance McCullers Jr. .15 .40
114 Didi Gregorius .20 .50
115 Billy Hamilton .20 .50
116 Derek Dietrich .20 .50
117 Kyle Schwarber .25 .60
118 Kyle Barraclough .15 .40
119 Michael Wacha .20 .50
120 Matt Chapman .25 .60
121 Duane Underwood Jr. RC .30 .75
James Norwood RC
122 Julio Teheran .20 .50
123 Sandy Alcantara .15 .40
124 Marcus Stroman .20 .50
125 Maikel Franco .20 .50
126 Max Stassi .15 .40
127 Jurickson Profar .20 .50
128 Robinson Chirinos .15 .40
129 James McCann .20 .50
130 Hunter Renfroe .15 .40
131 Dennis Santana RC .40 1.00
Caleb Ferguson RC
132 Blake Parker .15 .40
133 Sal Romano .15 .40
134 Nelson Cruz .25 .60
135 Alen Hanson .20 .50
136 Carlos Carrasco .15 .40
137 Michael Conforto .20 .50
138 James Paxton .20 .50
139 Jedd Gyorko .15 .40
140 Dustin Fowler .15 .40
141 Nick Burdi RC .30 .75
Alex McRae RC
142 Sonny Gray .20 .50
143 Chasen Shreve .15 .40
144 Joey Gallo .20 .50
145 Adam Duvall .25 .60
146 Nate Jones .15 .40
147 Yangervis Solarte .15 .40
148 Ronald Guzman .15 .40
149 Vince Velasquez .15 .40
150 Mallex Smith .15 .40
151 Craig Stammen .15 .40
152 Matt Boyd .15 .40
153 Seth Lugo .15 .40
154 Austin Voth RC .30 .75
Jimmy Cordero RC
155 Collin McHugh .15 .40
156 Matt Shoemaker .20 .50
157 Enrique Hernandez .25 .60
158 Mike Zunino .15 .40
159 Michael Lorenzen .15 .40
160 Shane Carle .15 .40
161 Joey Wendle .20 .50
162 Kolten Wong .20 .50
163 Rafael Devers .30 .75
164 Aledmys Diaz .15 .40
165 Jorge Soler .25 .60
166 Trevor Williams .15 .40
167 Dellin Betances .20 .50
168 Victor Arano .15 .40
169 Matt Duffy .15 .40
170 Albert Almora Jr. .20 .50
171 Darren O'Day .15 .40
172 Chad Sobotka RC .40 1.00
Bryse Wilson RC
173 Jaime Barria .15 .40
174 Justin Turner .25 .60
175 Daniel Robertson .15 .40
176 Will Smith .15 .40
177 Niko Goodrum .20 .50
178 Hector Rondon .15 .40
179 Manny Margot .15 .40
180 Daniel Palka .15 .40
181 Ryan Yarbrough .15 .40
182 Andrew Cashner .15 .40
183 Wilmer Flores .20 .50
184 Yan Gomes .25 .60
185 Ryon Healy .15 .40
186 Scott Kingery .20 .50
187 Whit Merrifield .25 .60
188 Corey Dickerson .15 .40
189 Adams RC/Loaisiga RC .40 1.00
190 Luke Weaver .15 .40
191 David Price .20 .50
192 Jason Heyward .20 .50
193 Devon Travis .15 .40
194 Tommy Pham .15 .40
195 Justin Turner Playoff HL .25 .60
196 Cody Bellinger Playoff HL .50 1.25
197 Clayton Kershaw Playoff HL .40 1.00
198 Yasiel Puig Playoff HL .25 .60
199 Jackie Bradley Playoff HL .25 .60
200 Jackie Bradley Playoff HL .25 .60
201 Andrew Benintendi Playoff HL .25 .60
202 David Price Playoff HL .20 .50
203 Andrew Heaney .15 .40
204 C.J. Cron .15 .40
205 Marcus Semien .25 .60
206 Johan Camargo .15 .40
207 Dawel Lugo RC .50 1.25
Christin Stewart RC
208 Tony Kemp .15 .40
209 Roberto Perez .15 .40
210 Mark Melancon .15 .40
211 Willy Adames .15 .40
212 Hyun-Jin Ryu .20 .50
213 Mark Trumbo .15 .40
214 Todd Frazier .15 .40
215 Steven Wright .15 .40
216 Josh Bell .20 .50
217 Tim Anderson .25 .60
218 Nick Williams .15 .40
219 Jesus Sucre RC .30 .75
220 Marcell Ozuna .25 .60
221 Kendrys Morales .15 .40
222 Hunter Dozier .15 .40
223 Ben Zobrist .20 .50
224 Chase Anderson .15 .40
225 Scott Schebler .20 .50
226 Miguel Sano .20 .50
227 Tucker RC/Perez RC .75 2.00
228 Kaleb Cowart .15 .40
229 Freddy Peralta .25 .60
230 Chris Davis .15 .40
231 Travis Shaw .15 .40
232 A.J. Minter .20 .50
233 Blake Treinen .15 .40
234 Travis Jankowski .15 .40
235 Ryan Zimmerman .20 .50
236 Jameson Taillon .20 .50
237 Eduardo Rodriguez .15 .40
238 Brandon Drury .15 .40
239 Avisail Garcia .20 .50
240 Yu Darvish .25 .60
241 Viloria RC/O'Hearn RC .30 .75
242 Ian Desmond .15 .40
243 Richard Urena .15 .40
244 Ty Buttrey RC .50 1.25
Francisco Arcia RC
Williams Jerez RC
245 Wade Davis .15 .40
246 Steven Matz .15 .40
247 Jason Kipnis .20 .50
248 Gerardo Parra .15 .40
249 Jeremy Jeffress .15 .40
250 Brandon Belt .20 .50
251 Dustin Pedroia .25 .60
252 Pat Neshek .15 .40
253 Kyle Freeland .20 .50
254 Luis Castillo .20 .50
255 Jon Gray .15 .40
256 David Dahl .15 .40
257 Brad Hand .15 .40
258 Cole Hamels .20 .50
259 Chad Pinder .15 .40
260 German Marquez .15 .40
261 Lewis Brinson .15 .40
262 Nix RC/Urias RC .50 1.25
263 Welington Castillo .15 .40
264 Colin Moran .15 .40
265 Steve Pearce .25 .60
266 Rosell Herrera .15 .40
267 Steven Duggar RC .40 1.00
Ray Black RC
268 Brad Boxberger .15 .40
269 Shane Greene .15 .40
270 Jorge Alfaro .15 .40
271 Kyle Seager .15 .40
272 Tyler White .15 .40
273 Willie Calhoun .15 .40
274 Carlos Rodon .25 .60
275 Yoshihisa Hirano .15 .40
276 Pablo Sandoval .20 .50
277 Cam Bedrosian .15 .40
278 Josh Donaldson .20 .50
279 Rick Porcello .20 .50
280 Nick Ahmed .15 .40
281 Rougned Odor .20 .50
282 Harrison Bader .20 .50
283 Adam Conley .15 .40
284 Austin Hedges .15 .40
285 Isiah Kiner-Falefa .20 .50
286 Edmundo Sosa RC 2.00 5.00
Adolis Garcia RC
287 Mike Fiers .15 .40
288 Cesar Hernandez .15 .40
289 Mike Leake .15 .40
290 Jose Leclerc .15 .40
291 Steve Cishek .15 .40
292 Steven Souza Jr. .20 .50
293 Kevin Pillar .15 .40
294 Justin Anderson .15 .40
295 Kevin Gausman .25 .60
296 Tucker Barnhart .15 .40
297 Greg Bird .20 .50
298 Dereck Rodriguez .15 .40
299 Nicky Delmonico .15 .40
300 Zack Wheeler .20 .50
301 Ben Gamel .20 .50
302 Seranthony Dominguez .15 .40
303 Elvis Andrus .20 .50
304 Chris Taylor .20 .50
305 Eduardo Nunez WS HL .15 .40
306 J.D. Martinez WS HL .25 .60
307 Max Muncy WS HL .20 .50
308 Steve Pearce WS HL .25 .60
309 David Price WS HL .20 .50
310 Boston Red Sox WS HL .25 .60
311 Fernando Rodney .15 .40
312 Yairo Munoz .15 .40
313 Michael Fulmer .15 .40
314 Matt Strahm .15 .40
315 Yoan Moncada .25 .60
316 Dansby Swanson .25 .60
317 Jeffrey Springs RC .30 .75
Jose Trevino RC
318 Carl Edwards Jr. .15 .40
319 Dylan Bundy .20 .50
320 Raisel Iglesias .15 .40
321 Arodys Vizcaino .15 .40
322 Ivan Nova .20 .50
323 Robinson Cano .20 .50
324 Justin Bour .15 .40
325 Frankie Montas .15 .40
326 Tyler Skaggs .15 .40
327 Mike Foltynewicz .25 .60
328 Anthony Rendon .25 .60
329 Robbie Erlin .15 .40
330 John Gant .15 .40
331 Matt Olson .25 .60
332 Hernan Perez .15 .40
333 Manny Pina .15 .40
334 Jose Quintana .15 .40
335 Josh Hader .20 .50
336 Ervin Santana .15 .40
337 Reyes Moronta .15 .40
338 Jarrod Dyson .15 .40
339 Denard Span .15 .40
340 Eduardo Nunez .15 .40
341 Corey Seager .25 .60
342 Alex Colome .15 .40
343 Cedric Mullins RC .60 1.50
Paul Fry RC
Austin Wynns RC
344 Joe Musgrove .25 .60
345 Kirby Yates .20 .50
346 Pedro Strop .15 .40
347 David Bote .20 .50
348 McNeil RC/Smith RC .75 2.00
349 Chris Shaw RC .30 .75
Aramis Garcia RC
350 Chris Sale AS .25 .60
351 Salvador Perez AS .20 .50
352 Jose Abreu AS .25 .60
353 Jose Altuve AS .20 .50
354 Manny Machado AS .25 .60
355 Jose Ramirez AS .20 .50
356 Aaron Judge AS .60 1.50
357 Mike Trout AS 1.25 3.00
358 Mookie Betts AS .50 1.25
359 J.D. Martinez AS .25 .60
360 Max Scherzer AS .25 .60
361 Willson Contreras AS .20 .50
362 Freddie Freeman AS .30 .75
363 Javier Baez AS .30 .75
364 Brandon Crawford AS .20 .50
365 Nolan Arenado AS .40 1.00
366 Matt Kemp AS .20 .50
367 Bryce Harper AS .40 1.00
368 Nick Markakis AS .20 .50
369 Paul Goldschmidt AS .25 .60
370 Mike Moustakas .20 .50
371 Heath Fillmyer RC .30 .75
Brad Keller RC
372 Kevin Newman RC .50 1.25
Kevin Kramer RC
373 Aaron Hicks .20 .50
374 Robert Gsellman .15 .40
375 Brandon Morrow .15 .40
376 Ryan Borucki RC .30 .75
Danny Jansen RC
Sean Reid-Foley RC
377 Marco Gonzales .15 .40
378 Max Kepler .20 .50
379 Jorge Polanco .20 .50
380 Jesse Winker .25 .60
381 Andrew Velazquez RC .30 .75
Nick Ciuffo RC
382 Yuli Gurriel .20 .50
383 Mitch Garver .15 .40
384 Keone Kela .15 .40
385 Mitch Moreland .15 .40
386 Kohl Stewart RC .40 1.00
Willians Astudillo RC
Stephen Gonsalves RC
387 Brent Suter .15 .40
388 Carlos Santana .20 .50
389 Mike Minor .15 .40
390 Joc Pederson .20 .50
391 Austin Dean RC .30 .75
Isaac Galloway RC
Pablo Lopez RC
392 Ryne Stanek .15 .40
393 Wade LeBlanc .15 .40
394 Joakim Soria .15 .40
395 Matt Davidson .20 .50
396 Garrett Hampson RC .50 1.25
Sam Howard RC
Yency Almonte RC
397 Zack Cozart .15 .40
398 Teoscar Hernandez .25 .60
399 Wright RC/Tssnt RC/Allard RC .50 1.25
400 Dean Deetz RC .50 1.25
Framber Valdez RC
Josh James RC
401 Francisco Lindor SP 2.00 5.00
402 Salvador Perez SP 1.50 4.00
403 Jake Arrieta SP 1.50 4.00
404 Kris Bryant SP 2.50 6.00
405 Jon Lester SP 1.50 4.00
406 Anthony Rizzo SP 2.50 6.00
407 George Springer SP 1.50 4.00
408 Sean Manaea SP 1.25 3.00
409 Jose Altuve SP 1.50 4.00
410 Christian Yelich SP 2.50 6.00
411 Blake Snell SP 1.50 4.00
412 Trevor Bauer SP 2.50 6.00
413 Gleyber Torres SP 4.00 10.00
414 Paul DeJong SP 2.00 5.00
415 Bryce Harper SP 3.00 8.00
416 Luis Severino SP 1.50 4.00
417 Jordan Hicks SP 1.50 4.00
418 Gary Sanchez SP 2.00 5.00
419 Jacob deGrom SP 4.00 10.00
420 Kenley Jansen SP 1.50 4.00
421 Justin Upton SP 1.50 4.00
422 Albert Pujols SP 2.50 6.00
423 Carlos Correa SP 2.00 5.00
424 Alex Bregman SP 2.00 5.00
425 Franmil Reyes SP 1.25 3.00
426 Justin Verlander SP 2.00 5.00
427 Walker Buehler SP 2.50 6.00
428 Trey Mancini SP 1.50 4.00
429 Gerrit Cole SP 2.00 5.00
430 Shohei Ohtani SP 3.00 8.00
431 Brandon Nimmo SP 1.50 4.00
432 Khris Davis SP 2.00 5.00
433 Justin Smoak SP 1.25 3.00
434 Stephen Piscotty SP 1.25 3.00
435 Miles Mikolas SP 2.00 5.00
436 Ozzie Albies SP 2.00 5.00
437 Lorenzo Cain SP 1.25 3.00
438 Matt Carpenter SP 2.00 5.00
439 Yadier Molina SP 2.50 6.00
440 Javier Baez SP 2.50 6.00
441 Paul Goldschmidt SP 2.00 5.00
442 Zack Greinke SP 2.00 5.00
443 Matt Kemp SP 1.50 4.00
444 Kenta Maeda SP 1.50 4.00
445 Buster Posey SP 2.50 6.00
446 Max Muncy SP 1.50 4.00
447 Edwin Encarnacion SP 2.00 5.00
448 Corey Kluber SP 1.50 4.00
449 Dee Gordon SP 1.25 3.00
450 Jean Segura SP 2.00 5.00
451 Edwin Diaz SP 1.50 4.00
452 Starlin Castro SP 1.25 3.00
453 J.T. Realmuto SP 2.00 5.00
454 Max Scherzer SP 2.00 5.00
455 Trea Turner SP 1.50 4.00
456 Jonathan Schoop SP 1.25 3.00
457 Eric Hosmer SP 1.50 4.00
458 Rhys Hoskins SP 2.50 6.00
459 Aaron Nola SP 1.50 4.00
460 Felipe Vasquez SP 1.25 3.00
461 Shin-Soo Choo SP 1.50 4.00
462 Nomar Mazara SP 1.25 3.00
463 Kevin Kiermaier SP 1.50 4.00
464 Chris Sale SP 2.00 5.00
465 Joey Votto SP 2.00 5.00
466 Scooter Gennett SP 1.50 4.00
467 Eugenio Suarez SP 1.50 4.00
468 Nolan Arenado SP 3.00 8.00
469 Trevor Story SP 2.00 5.00
470 Starling Marte SP 1.50 4.00
471 Charlie Blackmon SP 2.00 5.00
472 Miguel Cabrera SP 2.00 5.00
473 Miguel Andujar SP 2.00 5.00
474 Giancarlo Stanton SP 2.00 5.00
475 J.D. Martinez SP 2.00 5.00
476 Jesus Aguilar SP 1.50 4.00
477 Mitch Haniger SP 1.50 4.00
478 Brandon Crawford SP 1.50 4.00
479 Jose Berrios SP 1.50 4.00
480 Lourdes Gurriel Jr. SP 1.50 4.00
481 Juan Soto SP 6.00 15.00
482 Carlos Martinez SP 1.50 4.00
483 Jose Abreu SP 2.00 5.00
484 Andrew Benintendi SP 2.00 5.00
485 Mike Trout SP 10.00 25.00
486 Adam Jones SP 1.50 4.00
487 Xander Bogaerts SP 2.00 5.00
488 Odubel Herrera SP 1.50 4.00
489 Freddie Freeman SP 2.50 6.00
490 Clayton Kershaw SP 3.00 8.00
491 Jose Ramirez SP 1.50 4.00
492 Willson Contreras SP 1.50 4.00
493 Aroldis Chapman SP 2.00 5.00
494 Wil Myers SP 1.50 4.00
495 Sean Doolittle SP 1.25 3.00
496 Eric Thames SP 1.25 3.00
497 Yonder Alonso SP 1.25 3.00
498 Amed Rosario SP 1.50 4.00
499 Aaron Judge SP 5.00 12.00
500 Ronald Acuna Jr. SP 8.00 20.00
501 Michael Chavis RC .50 1.25
502 Charlie Morton .25 .60
503 Michael Brantley .20 .50
504 Vladimir Guerrero Jr. RC 4.00 10.00
505 Nick Markakis .20 .50
506 Yasmani Grandal .15 .40
507 Nick Senzel RC 1.00 2.50
508 Brendan Rodgers RC .50 1.25
509 Derek Holland .15 .40
510 Lonnie Chisenhall .15 .40
511 Phil Ervin .15 .40
512 Keston Hiura RC 1.00 2.50
513 Kurt Suzuki .15 .40
514 Eric Stamets RC .30 .75
515 Sam Gaviglio .15 .40
516 Eloy Jimenez RC 1.25 3.00
517 Fernando Tatis Jr. RC 12.00 30.00
518 Bradley Zimmer .15 .40
519 Pete Alonso RC 3.00 8.00
520 Manny Machado .25 .60
521 Andrew Miller .20 .50
522 A.J. Pollock .15 .40
523 Carter Kieboom RC .50 1.25
524 Griffin Canning RC .50 1.25
525 Justus Sheffield RC .50 1.25
526 Yusei Kikuchi RC .50 1.25
527 Jorge Alfaro .15 .40
528 Joe Kelly .15 .40
529 Brian Dozier .20 .50
530 Patrick Corbin .20 .50
531 Taylor Clarke RC .30 .75
532 Richie Martin RC .30 .75
533 Jon Duplantier RC .30 .75
534 Bryce Harper .40 1.00
535 J.T. Realmuto .25 .60
536 Trevor Cahill .15 .40
537 Austin Meadows .25 .60
538 Tyler Glasnow .25 .60
539 Byron Buxton .25 .60
540 Alex Verdugo .20 .50
541 Yasiel Puig .25 .60
542 Nicky Lopez RC .50 1.25
543 Sonny Gray .20 .50
544 Daniel Murphy .20 .50
545 Troy Tulowitzki .25 .60
546 DJ LeMahieu .25 .60
547 J.A. Happ .20 .50
548 Adam Ottavino .15 .40
549 Zack Britton .15 .40
550 Brian Goodwin .15 .40
551 Ian Kinsler .20 .50
552 Josh Harrison .15 .40
553 Marwin Gonzalez .15 .40
554 Tim Beckham .20 .50
555 Jurickson Profar .20 .50
556 Jake Bauers RC .50 1.25
557 Jed Lowrie .15 .40
558 Wilson Ramos .15 .40
559 Jeurys Familia .20 .50
560 Robinson Chirinos .15 .40
561 Lance Lynn .15 .40
562 Wade Miley .15 .40
563 Danny Salazar .20 .50
564 Tyler O'Neill .20 .50
565 Matt Davidson .20 .50
566 Jonathan Lucroy .20 .50
567 Alex Wood .15 .40
568 Nathan Eovaldi .20 .50
569 Cody Allen .15 .40
570 Josh Phegley .15 .40
571 Kendrys Morales .15 .40
572 Clay Buchholz .15 .40
573 Matt Shoemaker .20 .50
574 Craig Kimbrel .20 .50
575 Freddy Galvis .15 .40
576 Elvis Luciano RC .50 1.25
577 Max Fried .25 .60
578 Alex Jackson RC .50 1.25
579 Brian McCann .20 .50
580 Brandon Woodruff .25 .60
581 Zach Davies .15 .40
582 Ben Gamel .20 .50
583 John Brebbia .15 .40
584 Adam Wainwright .20 .50
585 Alex Reyes .20 .50
586 Daniel Descalso .15 .40
587 Victor Caratini .15 .40
588 Brad Brach .15 .40
589 Eduardo Escobar .15 .40
590 Wilmer Flores .20 .50
591 Christian Walker .20 .50
592 Carson Kelly .15 .40
593 Greg Holland .15 .40
594 Merrill Kelly RC .30 .75
595 Corbin Martin RC .50 1.25
596 Russell Martin .15 .40
597 Austin Barnes .15 .40
598 Kevin Pillar .15 .40
599 Gerardo Parra .15 .40
600 Jeff Samardzija .15 .40
601 Drew Pomeranz .15 .40
602 Connor Joe RC .30 .75
603 Tyler Naquin .20 .50
604 Nate Lowe RC 1.50 4.00
605 Adam Cimber .15 .40
606 Domingo Santana .20 .50
607 Omar Narvaez .20 .50
608 Braden Bishop RC .40 1.00
609 Curtis Granderson .20 .50
610 Neil Walker .15 .40
611 Sergio Romo .15 .40
612 Trevor Richards RC .30 .75
613 Cal Quantrill RC .30 .75
614 Austin Riley RC 1.50 4.00
615 Skye Bolt RC .40 1.00
616 Jorge Lopez .15 .40
617 J.D. Davis .15 .40
618 Matt Adams .15 .40
619 Jeremy Hellickson .15 .40
620 Dwight Smith Jr. .15 .40
621 Drew Jackson RC .30 .75
622 David Hess .15 .40
623 Rio Ruiz .15 .40
624 Francisco Mejia .20 .50
625 Nick Margevicius RC .30 .75
626 Eric Lauer .15 .40
627 David Robertson .15 .40
628 Jason Martin RC .40 1.00
629 Melky Cabrera .15 .40
630 Jung Ho Kang .15 .40
631 Adam Frazier .15 .40
632 Francisco Liriano .15 .40
633 Delino DeShields .15 .40
634 Asdrubal Cabrera .20 .50
635 Logan Forsythe .15 .40
636 Yandy Diaz .20 .50
637 Ji-Man Choi .15 .40
638 Avisail Garcia .20 .50
639 Jose Alvarado .15 .40
640 Blake Swihart .20 .50
641 Matt Barnes .15 .40
642 Curt Casali .15 .40
643 Jose Iglesias .20 .50
644 Derek Dietrich .20 .50
645 Tanner Roark .15 .40
646 Amir Garrett .15 .40
647 Josh Fuentes RC .50 1.25
648 Mark Reynolds .15 .40
649 Ryan McMahon .25 .60
650 Homer Bailey .15 .40
651 Martin Maldonado .15 .40
652 Richard Lovelady RC .30 .75
653 Kyle Zimmer RC .30 .75
654 Ian Kennedy .15 .40
655 JaCoby Jones .20 .50
656 Jordy Mercer .15 .40
657 Matt Moore .20 .50
658 Tyson Ross .15 .40
659 Grayson Greiner .15 .40

660 Jake Cave RC .40 1.00
661 Kyle Gibson .20 .50
662 Michael Pineda .15 .40
663 Brett Gardner .20 .50
664 Domingo German .20 .50
665 John Means RC 4.00 10.00
666 Jesus Sucre .15 .40
667 Brandon Kintzler .15 .40
668 Leury Garcia .15 .40
669 Kelvin Herrera .15 .40
670 Kevin Plawecki .15 .40
671 Max Moroff .15 .40
672 Brandon Brennan RC .30 .75
673 Hansel Robles .15 .40
674 Matt Harvey .20 .50
675 Tommy La Stella .15 .40
676 Ryan Pressly .15 .40
677 Brett Anderson .15 .40
678 Billy McKinney .15 .40
679 Aaron Sanchez .20 .50
680 Clayton Richard .15 .40
681 Cole Tucker RC .50 1.25
682 Charlie Culberson .15 .40
683 Junior Guerra .15 .40
684 Pedro Avila RC .30 .75
685 Anthony DeSclafani .15 .40
686 Shelby Miller .20 .50
687 Scott Oberg .15 .40
688 Jake Marisnick .15 .40
689 Terrance Gore .15 .40
690 Scott Alexander .15 .40
691 David Freese .15 .40
692 Nick Anderson RC .30 .75
693 Renato Nunez .20 .50
694 Ryan Brasier .15 .40
695 Raimel Tapia .15 .40
696 Josh Sborz RC .30 .75
697 Travis Bergen RC .30 .75
698 Joe Harvey RC .30 .75
699 Caleb Smith .15 .40
700 Nick Kingham .15 .40
701 Victor Robles SP 2.50 6.00
702 Andrew McCutchen SP 2.00 5.00
703 Chris Paddack SP RC 2.50 6.00
704 Hunter Pence SP 1.50 4.00
705 Adam Jones SP 1.50 4.00
706 Daniel Vogelbach SP 1.25 3.00
707 Dominic Smith SP 1.25 3.00
708 Clint Frazier SP 1.50 4.00
709 Gio Gonzalez SP 1.50 4.00
710 Cameron Maybin SP 1.25 3.00
711 Johnny Cueto SP 1.50 4.00
712 Hunter Strickland SP 1.25 3.00
713 Chris Devenski SP 1.25 3.00
714 Franklin Barreto SP 1.25 3.00
715 Thomas Pannone SP RC 2.00 5.00
716 Alen Hanson SP 1.50 4.00
717 Ryan Helsley SP RC 1.50 4.00
718 Erik Swanson SP RC 1.25 3.00
719 Tayron Guerrero SP 1.25 3.00
720 Anibal Sanchez SP 1.25 3.00
721 Mychal Givens SP 1.25 3.00
722 Hector Neris SP 1.25 3.00
723 Dominic Leone SP 1.25 3.00
724 Luis Cessa SP 1.25 3.00
725 Ichiro SP 2.50 6.00

2019 Topps Heritage Action Variations

STATED ODDS 1:41 HOBBY
STATED HN ODDS 1:26 HOBBY
78 Mookie Betts 8.00 20.00
384 Michael Kopech 10.00 25.00
387 Luis Urias 6.00 15.00
392 Danny Jansen 2.50 6.00
393 Corbin Burnes 20.00 50.00
394 Kyle Tucker 10.00 25.00
401 Francisco Lindor 4.00 10.00
404 Kris Bryant 5.00 12.00
406 Anthony Rizzo 6.00 15.00
409 Jose Altuve 3.00 8.00
410 Christian Yelich 5.00 12.00
413 Gleyber Torres 8.00 20.00
415 Bryce Harper 6.00 15.00
419 Jacob deGrom 8.00 20.00
424 Alex Bregman 4.00 10.00
430 Shohei Ohtani 12.00 30.00
436 Ozzie Albies 4.00 10.00
440 Javier Baez 5.00 12.00
458 Rhys Hoskins 5.00 12.00
468 Nolan Arenado 6.00 15.00
475 J.D. Martinez 4.00 10.00
481 Juan Soto 25.00 60.00
485 Mike Trout 25.00 60.00
499 Aaron Judge 10.00 25.00
500 Ronald Acuna Jr. 25.00 60.00
501 Michael Chavis 4.00 10.00
504 Vladimir Guerrero Jr. 40.00 100.00
506 Yasmani Grandal 2.50 6.00
507 Nick Senzel 8.00 20.00
508 Brendan Rodgers 4.00 10.00
512 Keston Hiura 20.00 50.00
516 Eloy Jimenez 15.00 40.00
517 Fernando Tatis Jr. 50.00 120.00
519 Pete Alonso 40.00 100.00
520 Manny Machado 4.00 10.00
523 Carter Kieboom 4.00 10.00
526 Yusei Kikuchi 4.00 10.00
527 Jorge Alfaro 2.50 6.00
534 Bryce Harper 6.00 15.00
535 J.T. Realmuto 4.00 10.00
537 Austin Meadows 4.00 10.00
539 Byron Buxton 4.00 10.00
540 Alex Verdugo 3.00 8.00
545 Troy Tulowitzki 4.00 10.00
591 Christian Walker 3.00 8.00
701 Victor Robles 5.00 12.00
702 Andrew McCutchen 4.00 10.00
703 Chris Paddack 5.00 12.00
708 Clint Frazier 3.00 8.00
725 Ichiro 5.00 12.00

2019 Topps Heritage Black Border

*BLACK: 10X TO 25X BASIC
*BLACK RC: 5X TO 12X BASIC RC
*BLACK SP: 1.2X TO 3X BASIC SP
STATED ODDS 1:62 HOBBY
STATED HN ODDS 1:86 HOBBY
ANNCD PRINT RUN OF 50 COPIES EACH
357 Mike Trout AS 40.00 100.00
413 Gleyber Torres 20.00 50.00
430 Shohei Ohtani 40.00 100.00
481 Juan Soto 40.00 100.00
485 Mike Trout 75.00 200.00
499 Aaron Judge 60.00 150.00
500 Ronald Acuna Jr. 125.00 300.00
504 Vladimir Guerrero Jr. 75.00 200.00
512 Keston Hiura 25.00 60.00
516 Eloy Jimenez 60.00 150.00
517 Fernando Tatis Jr. 300.00 800.00
519 Pete Alonso 125.00 300.00

2019 Topps Heritage French Text

*FRENCH: 10X TO 25X BASIC
*FRENCH RC: 5X TO 12X BASIC RC
*FRENCH SP: 1.2X TO 3X BASIC SP
STATED ODDS 1:164 HOBBY
STATED HN ODDS 1:345 HOBBY
485 Mike Trout 40.00 100.00
516 Eloy Jimenez 25.00 60.00
517 Fernando Tatis Jr. 100.00 250.00
519 Pete Alonso 50.00 120.00

2019 Topps Heritage Silver Metal

STATED ODDS 1:817 HOBBY
STATED HN ODDS 1:689 HOBBY
ANNCD PRINT RUN 70 SER.#'d SETS
52 Chris Archer 5.00 12.00
78 Mookie Betts 15.00 40.00
83 Noah Syndergaard 6.00 15.00
98 Nicholas Castellanos 8.00 20.00
117 Kyle Schwarber 8.00 20.00
163 Rafael Devers 10.00 25.00
347 David Bote 6.00 15.00
401 Francisco Lindor 8.00 20.00
402 Salvador Perez 6.00 15.00
403 Jake Arrieta 6.00 15.00
404 Kris Bryant 10.00 25.00
405 Jon Lester 6.00 15.00
406 Anthony Rizzo 10.00 25.00
407 George Springer 6.00 15.00
408 Sean Manaea 5.00 12.00
409 Jose Altuve 6.00 15.00
410 Christian Yelich 10.00 25.00
411 Blake Snell 6.00 15.00
412 Trevor Bauer 10.00 25.00
413 Gleyber Torres 30.00 80.00
414 Paul DeJong 8.00 20.00
415 Bryce Harper 30.00 80.00
416 Luis Severino 6.00 15.00
417 Jordan Hicks 6.00 15.00
418 Gary Sanchez 8.00 20.00
419 Jacob deGrom 15.00 40.00
421 Justin Upton 6.00 15.00
422 Albert Pujols 10.00 25.00
423 Carlos Correa 8.00 20.00
424 Alex Bregman 8.00 20.00
425 Franmil Reyes 5.00 12.00
426 Justin Verlander 8.00 20.00
427 Walker Buehler 10.00 25.00
428 Trey Mancini 6.00 15.00
429 Gerrit Cole 8.00 20.00
430 Shohei Ohtani 40.00 100.00
431 Brandon Nimmo 6.00 15.00
432 Khris Davis 8.00 20.00
433 Justin Smoak 5.00 12.00
434 Stephen Piscotty 5.00 12.00
435 Miles Mikolas 8.00 20.00
436 Ozzie Albies 8.00 20.00
437 Lorenzo Cain 5.00 12.00
438 Matt Carpenter 8.00 20.00
439 Yadier Molina 10.00 25.00
440 Javier Baez 10.00 25.00
441 Paul Goldschmidt 8.00 20.00
442 Zack Greinke 8.00 20.00
443 Matt Kemp 6.00 15.00
444 Kenta Maeda 6.00 15.00
445 Buster Posey 10.00 25.00
446 Max Muncy 6.00 15.00
447 Edwin Encarnacion 8.00 20.00
448 Corey Kluber 6.00 15.00
449 Dee Gordon 5.00 12.00
450 Jean Segura 8.00 20.00
451 Edwin Diaz 6.00 15.00
452 Starlin Castro 5.00 12.00
453 J.T. Realmuto 8.00 20.00
454 Max Scherzer 8.00 20.00
455 Trea Turner 6.00 15.00
456 Jonathan Schoop 5.00 12.00
457 Eric Hosmer 6.00 15.00
458 Rhys Hoskins 10.00 25.00
459 Aaron Nola 6.00 15.00
460 Felipe Vasquez 5.00 12.00
461 Shin-Soo Choo 6.00 15.00
462 Nomar Mazara 5.00 12.00
463 Kevin Kiermaier 6.00 15.00
464 Chris Sale 8.00 20.00
465 Joey Votto 8.00 20.00
466 Scooter Gennett 6.00 15.00
467 Eugenio Suarez 6.00 15.00
468 Nolan Arenado 12.00 30.00
469 Trevor Story 8.00 20.00
470 Starling Marte 6.00 15.00
471 Charlie Blackmon 8.00 20.00
472 Miguel Cabrera 8.00 20.00
473 Miguel Andujar 8.00 20.00
474 Giancarlo Stanton 8.00 20.00
475 J.D. Martinez 8.00 20.00
476 Jesus Aguilar 6.00 15.00
477 Mitch Haniger 6.00 15.00
478 Brandon Crawford 6.00 15.00
479 Jose Berrios 6.00 15.00
480 Lourdes Gurriel Jr. 6.00 15.00
481 Juan Soto 25.00 60.00
483 Jose Abreu 8.00 20.00
484 Andrew Benintendi 8.00 20.00
485 Mike Trout 125.00 300.00
486 Adam Jones 6.00 15.00
487 Xander Bogaerts 8.00 20.00
488 Odubel Herrera 6.00 15.00
490 Clayton Kershaw 12.00 30.00
491 Jose Ramirez 6.00 15.00
493 Aroldis Chapman 8.00 20.00
494 Wil Myers 6.00 15.00
498 Amed Rosario 6.00 15.00
499 Aaron Judge 100.00 250.00
500 Ronald Acuna Jr. 50.00 120.00
501 Michael Chavis 8.00 20.00
502 Charlie Morton 8.00 20.00
503 Michael Brantley 6.00 15.00
504 Vladimir Guerrero Jr. 125.00 300.00
505 Nick Markakis 6.00 15.00
506 Yasmani Grandal 5.00 12.00
507 Nick Senzel 15.00 40.00
508 Brendan Rodgers 8.00 20.00
512 Keston Hiura 30.00 80.00
516 Eloy Jimenez 30.00 80.00
517 Fernando Tatis Jr. 300.00 800.00
519 Pete Alonso 125.00 300.00
520 Manny Machado 8.00 20.00
521 Andrew Miller 6.00 15.00
522 A.J. Pollock 5.00 12.00
523 Carter Kieboom 8.00 20.00
525 Justus Sheffield 8.00 20.00
526 Yusei Kikuchi 8.00 20.00
527 Jorge Alfaro 5.00 12.00
529 Brian Dozier 6.00 15.00
530 Patrick Corbin 6.00 15.00
533 Jon Duplantier 5.00 12.00
534 Bryce Harper 30.00 80.00
535 J.T. Realmuto 8.00 20.00
537 Austin Meadows 8.00 20.00
538 Tyler Glasnow 8.00 20.00
539 Byron Buxton 8.00 20.00
540 Alex Verdugo 6.00 15.00
541 Yasiel Puig 8.00 20.00
542 Nicky Lopez 8.00 20.00
543 Sonny Gray 6.00 15.00
544 Daniel Murphy 6.00 15.00
545 Troy Tulowitzki 8.00 20.00
546 DJ LeMahieu 8.00 20.00
547 J.A. Happ 6.00 15.00
548 Adam Ottavino 5.00 12.00
549 Zack Britton 5.00 12.00
551 Ian Kinsler 6.00 15.00
566 Jonathan Lucroy 6.00 15.00
575 Freddy Galvis 5.00 12.00
577 Max Fried 8.00 20.00
580 Brandon Woodruff 8.00 20.00
595 Corbin Martin 8.00 20.00
598 Kevin Pillar 5.00 12.00
624 Francisco Mejia 6.00 15.00
664 Domingo German 6.00 15.00
701 Victor Robles 10.00 25.00
702 Andrew McCutchen 8.00 20.00
703 Chris Paddack 10.00 25.00
725 Ichiro 10.00 25.00

2019 Topps Heritage Team Color Swap Variations

STATED ODDS 1:245 HOBBY
STATED HN ODDS 1:154 HOBBY
78 Mookie Betts 8.00 20.00
401 Francisco Lindor 8.00 20.00
404 Kris Bryant 6.00 15.00
406 Anthony Rizzo 6.00 15.00
409 Jose Altuve 4.00 10.00
410 Christian Yelich 6.00 15.00
413 Gleyber Torres 15.00 40.00
415 Bryce Harper 8.00 20.00
419 Jacob deGrom 10.00 25.00
424 Alex Bregman 5.00 12.00
426 Justin Verlander 5.00 12.00
430 Shohei Ohtani 8.00 20.00
432 Khris Davis 5.00 12.00
436 Ozzie Albies 5.00 12.00
440 Javier Baez 6.00 15.00
442 Zack Greinke 5.00 12.00
451 Edwin Diaz 4.00 10.00
454 Max Scherzer 5.00 12.00
458 Rhys Hoskins 6.00 15.00
468 Nolan Arenado 8.00 20.00
475 J.D. Martinez 5.00 12.00
481 Juan Soto 20.00 40.00
485 Mike Trout 40.00 100.00
499 Aaron Judge 20.00 80.00
500 Ronald Acuna Jr. 25.00 60.00
501 Michael Chavis 5.00 12.00
504 Vladimir Guerrero Jr. 25.00 60.00
506 Yasmani Grandal 3.00 8.00
507 Nick Senzel 10.00 25.00
508 Brendan Rodgers 8.00 20.00
512 Keston Hiura 15.00 40.00
516 Eloy Jimenez 20.00 50.00
517 Fernando Tatis Jr. 60.00 150.00
519 Pete Alonso 25.00 60.00
520 Manny Machado 5.00 12.00
523 Carter Kieboom 5.00 12.00
526 Yusei Kikuchi 5.00 12.00
527 Jorge Alfaro 6.00 15.00
534 Bryce Harper 8.00 20.00
535 J.T. Realmuto 5.00 12.00
537 Austin Meadows 5.00 12.00
539 Byron Buxton 6.00 15.00
540 Alex Verdugo 4.00 10.00
545 Troy Tulowitzki 5.00 12.00
591 Christian Walker 4.00 10.00
701 Victor Robles 6.00 15.00
702 Andrew McCutchen 5.00 12.00
703 Chris Paddack 6.00 15.00
708 Clint Frazier 6.00 15.00
725 Ichiro 8.00 20.00

2019 Topps Heritage '70 Postal Stamps

STATED ODDS 1:5718 HOBBY
STATED PRINT RUN 50 SER.#'d SETS
70USAK Al Kaline 30.00 80.00
70USBR Brooks Robinson 20.00 50.00
70USBW Billy Williams 20.00 50.00
70USFJ Fergie Jenkins 20.00 50.00
70USHA Hank Aaron 40.00 100.00
70USHK Harmon Killebrew 30.00 80.00
70USJB Johnny Bench 30.00 80.00
70USJM Joe Morgan 20.00 50.00
70USJP Jim Palmer 30.00 80.00
70USLA Luis Aparicio 20.00 50.00
70USLB Lou Brock 20.00 50.00
70USNR Nolan Ryan 50.00 120.00
70USOC Orlando Cepeda 20.00 50.00
70USRC Rod Carew 20.00 50.00
70USRJ Reggie Jackson 30.00 80.00
70USSC Steve Carlton 20.00 50.00
70USTP Tony Perez 30.00 80.00
70USTS Tom Seaver 30.00 80.00
70USWM Willie McCovey 30.00 80.00
70USWS Willie Stargell 30.00 80.00

2019 Topps Heritage '70 Poster Boxloader

STATED ODDS 1:31 HOBBY BOX
STATED HN ODDS 1:19 HOBBY BOX
1 Shohei Ohtani 20.00 50.00
2 Jose Altuve 12.00 30.00
3 Khris Davis 10.00 25.00
4 Justin Smoak 15.00 40.00
5 Ronald Acuna Jr. 25.00 60.00
6 Christian Yelich 12.00 30.00
7 Matt Carpenter 15.00 40.00
8 Kris Bryant 12.00 30.00
9 Paul Goldschmidt 20.00 50.00
10 Clayton Kershaw 20.00 50.00
11 Buster Posey 25.00 60.00
12 Francisco Lindor 10.00 25.00
13 Edwin Diaz 8.00 20.00
14 Starlin Castro 6.00 15.00
15 Noah Syndergaard 8.00 20.00
16 Juan Soto 20.00 50.00
17 Trey Mancini 12.00 30.00
18 Eric Hosmer 8.00 20.00
19 Rhys Hoskins 15.00 40.00
20 Starling Marte 12.00 30.00
21 Adrian Beltre 15.00 40.00
22 Blake Snell 12.00 30.00
23 Mookie Betts 20.00 50.00
24 Joey Votto 20.00 50.00
25 Nolan Arenado 15.00 40.00
26 Salvador Perez 8.00 20.00
27 Miguel Cabrera 25.00 60.00
28 Joe Mauer 30.00 50.00
29 Jose Abreu 15.00 40.00
30 Aaron Judge 20.00 50.00
31 Mike Trout 60.00 150.00
32 Carlos Correa 15.00 40.00
33 Stephen Piscotty 6.00 15.00
34 Vladimir Guerrero Jr. 25.00 60.00
35 Freddie Freeman 12.00 30.00
36 Lorenzo Cain 6.00 15.00
37 Yadier Molina 15.00 40.00
38 Anthony Rizzo 12.00 30.00
39 Zack Greinke 10.00 25.00
40 Corey Seager 10.00 25.00
41 Evan Longoria 20.00 50.00
42 Jose Ramirez 8.00 20.00
43 Yusei Kikuchi 15.00 40.00
44 Brian Anderson 6.00 15.00
45 Jacob deGrom 20.00 50.00
46 Max Scherzer 15.00 40.00
47 Jonathan Villar 6.00 15.00
48 Manny Machado 10.00 25.00
49 Bryce Harper 15.00 40.00
50 Felipe Vasquez 6.00 15.00
51 Joey Gallo 8.00 20.00
52 Austin Meadows 10.00 25.00
53 J.D. Martinez 15.00 40.00
54 Yasiel Puig 15.00 40.00
55 Trevor Story 10.00 25.00
56 Whit Merrifield 15.00 40.00
57 Nicholas Castellanos 15.00 40.00
58 Jose Berrios 15.00 40.00
59 Eloy Jimenez 25.00 60.00
60 Giancarlo Stanton 10.00 25.00

2019 Topps Heritage '70 Super Boxloader

STATED ODDS 1:3 HOBBY BOX
STATED HN ODDS 1:3 HOBBY BOX
1 Gleyber Torres 4.00 10.00
2 Mookie Betts 4.00 10.00
3 Mike Trout 10.00 25.00
4 Shohei Ohtani 3.00 8.00
5 Juan Soto 6.00 15.00
6 Kris Bryant 2.50 6.00
7 Ronald Acuna Jr. 10.00 25.00
8 Carl Yastrzemski 8.00 20.00
9 Nolan Ryan 6.00 15.00
10 Bob Gibson 1.50 4.00
11 Al Kaline 5.00 12.00
12 Brooks Robinson 1.50 4.00
13 Johnny Bench 5.00 12.00
14 Roberto Clemente 10.00 25.00
15 Thurman Munson 5.00 12.00
16 Aaron Judge 5.00 12.00
17 Cody Bellinger 4.00 10.00
18 Bryce Harper 3.00 8.00
19 Christian Yelich 2.50 6.00
20 Manny Machado 2.00 5.00
21 Ichiro 5.00 12.00
22 Hank Aaron 4.00 10.00
23 Willie Mays 4.00 10.00
24 Jim Palmer 1.50 4.00
25 Carter Kieboom 2.00 5.00
26 Yusei Kikuchi 2.00 5.00
27 Eloy Jimenez 6.00 15.00
28 Fernando Tatis Jr. 20.00 50.00
29 Pete Alonso 10.00 25.00
30 Vladimir Guerrero Jr. 8.00 20.00

2019 Topps Heritage '70 Topps Candy Lids

STATED ODDS 1:8 RETAIL
1 Max Scherzer .50 1.25
2 Mike Trout 2.50 6.00
3 Aaron Nola .40 1.00
4 Giancarlo Stanton .50 1.25
5 Anthony Rizzo .60 1.50
6 Joey Votto .50 1.25
7 Ozzie Albies .50 1.25
8 Francisco Lindor .50 1.25
9 Jose Altuve .40 1.00
10 Matt Carpenter .50 1.25
11 Blake Snell .40 1.00
12 Buster Posey .60 1.50
13 Carlos Correa .50 1.25
14 Miguel Andujar .50 1.25
15 Bryce Harper .75 2.00
16 Kris Bryant .60 1.50
17 Shohei Ohtani .75 2.00
18 Aaron Judge 1.50 4.00
19 Mookie Betts 1.00 2.50
20 Pete Alonso 2.50 6.00
21 Fernando Tatis Jr. 5.00 12.00
22 Christian Yelich .60 1.50
23 Eloy Jimenez 1.25 3.00
24 Cody Bellinger 1.00 2.50
25 Ronald Acuna Jr. 2.50 6.00
26 Juan Soto 1.50 4.00
27 Manny Machado .50 1.25
28 Paul Goldschmidt .50 1.25
29 Rhys Hoskins .60 1.50
30 Vladimir Guerrero Jr. 2.00 5.00

2019 Topps Heritage '70 Topps Player Story Booklets

STATED ODDS 1:972 RETAIL
ANNCD PRINT RUN 250 COPIES PER
1 Aaron Judge 25.00 60.00
2 Miguel Cabrera 8.00 20.00
3 Salvador Perez 6.00 15.00
4 Jose Altuve 6.00 15.00
5 Mike Trout 30.00 80.00
6 Felix Hernandez 6.00 15.00
7 Adrian Beltre 8.00 20.00
8 Freddie Freeman 10.00 25.00
9 Rhys Hoskins 10.00 25.00
10 Kris Bryant 15.00 40.00
11 Joey Votto 8.00 20.00
12 Yadier Molina 12.00 30.00
13 Buster Posey 10.00 25.00
14 Nolan Arenado 12.00 30.00
15 Clayton Kershaw 12.00 30.00
16 Mookie Betts 15.00 40.00
17 Jacob deGrom 15.00 40.00
18 Christian Yelich 10.00 25.00
19 Manny Machado 8.00 20.00
20 Jose Berrios 6.00 15.00
21 Juan Soto 12.00 30.00
22 Blake Snell 6.00 15.00
23 Francisco Lindor 8.00 20.00
24 Khris Davis 8.00 20.00
25 Lewis Brinson 5.00 12.00
26 Trey Mancini 12.00 30.00
27 Eloy Jimenez 10.00 25.00
28 Zack Greinke 8.00 20.00
29 Vladimir Guerrero Jr. 20.00 50.00
30 Starling Marte 6.00 15.00

2019 Topps Heritage '70 Topps Scratch Offs

STATED ODDS 1:24 HOBBY
1 Mike Trout 3.00 8.00
2 Jose Altuve .50 1.25
3 Khris Davis .60 1.50
4 Justin Smoak .40 1.00
5 Freddie Freeman .75 2.00
6 Lorenzo Cain .40 1.00
7 Yadier Molina .75 2.00
8 Anthony Rizzo .75 2.00
9 Paul Goldschmidt .60 1.50
10 Clayton Kershaw 1.00 2.50
11 Buster Posey .75 2.00
12 Francisco Lindor .60 1.50
13 Robinson Cano .50 1.25
14 Starlin Castro .40 1.00
15 Noah Syndergaard .50 1.25
16 Max Scherzer .60 1.50
17 Trey Mancini .50 1.25
18 Eric Hosmer .50 1.25
19 Rhys Hoskins .75 2.00
20 Starling Marte .50 1.25
21 Elvis Andrus .50 1.25
22 Blake Snell .50 1.25
23 Mookie Betts 1.25 3.00
24 Joey Votto .60 1.50
25 Nolan Arenado 1.00 2.50
26 Salvador Perez .50 1.25
27 Miguel Cabrera .60 1.50
28 Jose Berrios .50 1.25
29 Jose Abreu .60 1.50
30 Aaron Judge 1.50 4.00

2019 Topps Heritage '70 Topps Stickers

INSERTED IN WALMART PACKS
1 Aaron Judge 1.50 4.00
2 Kris Bryant .75 2.00
3 Clayton Kershaw 1.00 2.50
4 Juan Soto 2.00 5.00
5 Gleyber Torres 1.25 3.00
6 Mookie Betts 1.25 3.00
7 Ronald Acuna Jr. 3.00 8.00
8 Paul Goldschmidt .60 1.50
9 Jose Ramirez .50 1.25
10 J.D. Martinez .60 1.50
11 Jacob deGrom 1.25 3.00
12 Rhys Hoskins .75 2.00
13 Khris Davis .60 1.50
14 Justin Verlander .60 1.50
15 Nolan Arenado 1.00 2.50
16 Shohei Ohtani 1.00 2.50
17 Eloy Jimenez 1.50 4.00
18 Fernando Tatis Jr. 10.00 25.00
19 Pete Alonso 3.00 8.00
20 Manny Machado .60 1.50
21 Yusei Kikuchi .60 1.50
22 Bryce Harper 1.00 2.50
23 Ichiro .75 2.00
24 Cody Bellinger 1.25 3.00
25 Christian Yelich .75 2.00
26 Mike Trout 5.00 12.00
27 Jose Altuve .50 1.25
28 Victor Robles .75 2.00
29 Vladimir Guerrero Jr. 2.50 6.00
30 Javier Baez .75 2.00

2019 Topps Heritage Award Winners

STATED HN ODDS 1:8 HOBBY
AW1 Mookie Betts .75 2.00
AW2 Christian Yelich .50 1.25
AW3 Blake Snell .30 .75
AW4 Jacob deGrom .75 2.00
AW5 Shohei Ohtani .60 1.50
AW6 Ronald Acuna Jr. 2.00 5.00
AW7 Steve Pearce .40 1.00
AW8 Alex Bregman .40 1.00
AW9 J.D. Martinez .40 1.00
AW10 Christian Yelich .50 1.25

2019 Topps Heritage Baseball Flashbacks

COMPLETE SET (15) 8.00 20.00
STATED ODDS 1:18 HOBBY
BFAK Al Kaline .60 1.50
BFBG Bob Gibson .50 1.25
BFBR Brooks Robinson .50 1.25
BFCY Carl Yastrzemski 1.00 2.50
BFHA Hank Aaron 1.25 3.00
BFJB Johnny Bench .60 1.50
BFJM Juan Marichal .50 1.25
BFJT Joe Torre .50 1.25
BFNR Nolan Ryan 2.00 5.00
BFRC Rod Carew .50 1.25
BFRJ Reggie Jackson .50 1.25
BFSC Steve Carlton .50 1.25
BFTM Thurman Munson .60 1.50
BFTS Tom Seaver .50 1.25
BFWM Willie McCovey .50 1.25

2019 Topps Heritage Brew Crew Autographs

STATED ODDS 1:3738 HOBBY
STATED PRINT RUN 100 SER.#'d SETS
EXCHANGE DEADLINE 1/31/2021
IBCBL Bob Locker 50.00 210.00
IBCBM Bob Meyer 50.00 120.00
IBCBS Bud Selig 75.00 200.00
IBCDB Dave Baldwin 50.00 120.00
IBCFS Fred Stanley 50.00 120.00
IBCKS Ken Sanders 50.00 120.00
IBCLK Lew Krausse 60.00 150.00
IBCMA Max Alvis 50.00 120.00
IBCRP Ray Peters 60.00 150.00
IBCWC Wayne Comer 50.00 120.00

2019 Topps Heritage Chrome

STATED ODDS 1:58 HOBBY
STATED HN ODDS 1:49 HOBBY
STATED PRINT RUN 999 SER.#'d SETS
*PRPLE REF: .4X TO 1X BASIC
*REF/569: .6X TO 1.5X BASIC
THC2 Felix Hernandez MB 1.50 4.00
THC7 Kopech/Frare 4.00 10.00
THC17 Sean Newcomb MB 1.25 3.00
THC19 Russell Martin MB 1.25 3.00
THC25 Eddie Rosario MB 1.50 4.00
THC29 Andrelton Simmons MB 1.25 3.00
THC30 Gregory Polanco MB 1.50 4.00
THC34 Cody Bellinger MB 4.00 10.00
THC39 Brock Holt MB 1.25 3.00
THC42 Evan Longoria MB 1.50 4.00
THC43 Luke Voit MB 3.00 8.00
THC50 Yoenis Cespedes MB 2.00 5.00
THC52 Chris Archer 1.25 3.00
THC53 Orlando Arcia MB 1.25 3.00
THC55 Lou Trivino MB 1.25 3.00
THC78 Mookie Betts 4.00 10.00
THC80 Ian Happ MB 1.50 4.00
THC83 Noah Syndergaard 1.50 4.00
THC89 Adalberto Mondesi MB 1.50 4.00
THC92 Jack Flaherty MB 2.00 5.00
THC93 Jorge Polanco MB 1.50 4.00
THC98 Nicholas Castellanos MB 2.00 5.00
THC100 Masahiro Tanaka MB 1.50 4.00
THC101 Tim Beckham MB 1.50 4.00
THC105 Ender Inciarte MB 1.25 3.00
THC106 Stephen Strasburg MB 2.00 5.00
THC108 Alex Gordon MB 1.50 4.00
THC111 Ryan Braun MB 1.50 4.00
THC115 Billy Hamilton MB 1.50 4.00
THC117 Kyle Schwarber MB 2.00 5.00
THC119 Michael Wacha MB 1.50 4.00
THC120 Matt Chapman MB 2.00 5.00
THC124 Marcus Stroman MB 1.50 4.00
THC125 Maikel Franco MB 1.50 4.00
THC127 Jurickson Profar MB 1.50 4.00
THC130 Hunter Renfroe MB 1.25 3.00
THC136 Carlos Carrasco MB 1.25 3.00
THC138 James Paxton MB 1.50 4.00
THC144 Joey Gallo MB 1.50 4.00
THC148 Ronald Guzman MB 1.25 3.00
THC163 Rafael Devers 2.50 6.00
THC179 Manny Margot MB 1.25 3.00
THC180 Daniel Palka MB 1.25 3.00
THC181 Ryan Yarbrough MB 1.25 3.00
THC186 Scott Kingery MB 1.50 4.00
THC187 Whit Merrifield MB 2.00 5.00
THC188 Corey Dickerson MB 1.25 3.00
THC189 Adams/Loaisiga 1.50 4.00
THC191 David Price MB 1.50 4.00
THC194 Tommy Pham MB 1.25 3.00
THC211 Willy Adames MB 1.25 3.00
THC213 Mark Trumbo MB 1.25 3.00
THC214 Todd Frazier MB 1.25 3.00
THC216 Josh Bell MB 1.50 4.00
THC220 Marcell Ozuna MB 2.00 5.00
THC223 Ben Zobrist MB 1.50 4.00
THC226 Miguel Sano MB 1.50 4.00
THC227 Perez/Tucker 3.00 8.00
THC229 Freddy Peralta MB 2.00 5.00
THC231 Travis Shaw MB 1.25 3.00
THC232 A.J. Minter MB 1.50 4.00
THC233 Blake Treinen MB 1.25 3.00
THC235 Ryan Zimmerman MB 1.50 4.00
THC236 Jameson Taillon MB 1.50 4.00
THC239 Avisail Garcia MB 1.50 4.00
THC240 Yu Darvish MB 2.00 5.00
THC245 Wade Davis MB 1.25 3.00
THC247 Jason Kipnis MB 1.50 4.00
THC249 Jeremy Jeffress MB 1.25 3.00
THC250 Brandon Belt MB 1.50 4.00
THC252 Pat Neshek MB 1.25 3.00
THC253 Kyle Freeland MB 1.50 4.00
THC254 Luis Castillo MB 1.50 4.00
THC256 David Dahl MB 1.25 3.00
THC258 Cole Hamels MB 1.50 4.00
THC260 German Marquez MB 1.25 3.00
THC261 Lewis Brinson MB 1.25 3.00
THC262 Nix/Urias 2.00 5.00
THC269 Shane Greene MB 1.25 3.00
THC270 Jorge Alfaro MB 1.25 3.00
THC271 Kyle Seager MB 1.25 3.00
THC276 Pablo Sandoval MB 1.50 4.00
THC279 Rick Porcello MB 1.50 4.00
THC281 Rougned Odor MB 1.50 4.00
THC282 Harrison Bader MB 1.50 4.00
THC288 Cesar Hernandez MB 1.25 3.00
THC290 Jose Leclerc MB 1.25 3.00
THC293 Kevin Pillar MB 1.25 3.00
THC295 Kevin Gausman MB 2.00 5.00
THC298 Dereck Rodriguez MB 1.25 3.00
THC300 Zack Wheeler MB 1.50 4.00
THC302 Seranthony Dominguez MB 1.25 3.00
THC303 Elvis Andrus MB 1.50 4.00
THC313 Michael Fulmer MB 1.25 3.00
THC315 Yoan Moncada MB 2.00 5.00
THC316 Dansby Swanson MB 2.00 5.00
THC320 Raisel Iglesias MB 1.25 3.00
THC323 Robinson Cano MB 1.50 4.00
THC327 Mike Foltynewicz MB 2.00 5.00
THC331 Matt Olson MB 2.00 5.00
THC335 Josh Hader MB 1.50 4.00
THC340 Eduardo Nunez MB 1.25 3.00
THC341 Corey Seager MB 2.00 5.00
THC373 Aaron Hicks MB 1.50 4.00
THC382 Yuli Gurriel MB 1.50 4.00
THC388 Carlos Santana MB 1.50 4.00
THC390 Joc Pederson MB 1.50 4.00
THC401 Francisco Lindor 2.00 5.00
THC402 Salvador Perez 1.50 4.00
THC403 Jake Arrieta 1.50 4.00
THC404 Kris Bryant 2.50 6.00
THC405 Jon Lester 1.50 4.00
THC406 Anthony Rizzo 2.50 6.00
THC407 George Springer 1.50 4.00
THC408 Sean Manaea 1.25 3.00
THC409 Jose Altuve 1.50 4.00
THC410 Christian Yelich 2.50 6.00
THC411 Blake Snell 1.50 4.00
THC412 Trevor Bauer 2.50 6.00
THC413 Gleyber Torres 4.00 10.00
THC414 Paul DeJong 2.00 5.00
THC415 Bryce Harper 3.00 8.00
THC416 Luis Severino 1.50 4.00
THC417 Jordan Hicks 1.50 4.00
THC418 Gary Sanchez 2.00 5.00
THC419 Jacob deGrom 4.00 10.00
THC420 Kenley Jansen MB 1.50 4.00
THC421 Justin Upton 1.50 4.00
THC422 Albert Pujols 2.50 6.00
THC423 Carlos Correa 2.00 5.00
THC424 Alex Bregman 2.00 5.00
THC426 Justin Verlander 2.00 5.00
THC427 Walker Buehler 2.50 6.00
THC428 Trey Mancini 1.50 4.00
THC429 Gerrit Cole 2.00 5.00
THC430 Shohei Ohtani 3.00 8.00
THC431 Brandon Nimmo 1.50 4.00
THC432 Khris Davis 2.00 5.00
THC433 Justin Smoak 1.25 3.00
THC434 Stephen Piscotty 1.25 3.00
THC435 Miles Mikolas 2.00 5.00
THC436 Ozzie Albies 2.00 5.00
THC437 Lorenzo Cain 1.25 3.00
THC438 Matt Carpenter 2.00 5.00
THC439 Yadier Molina 2.50 6.00
THC440 Javier Baez 2.50 6.00
THC441 Paul Goldschmidt 2.00 5.00
THC442 Zack Greinke 2.00 5.00
THC443 Matt Kemp 1.50 4.00
THC444 Kenta Maeda 1.50 4.00
THC445 Buster Posey 2.50 6.00
THC446 Max Muncy 1.50 4.00
THC447 Edwin Encarnacion 2.00 5.00
THC448 Corey Kluber 1.50 4.00
THC449 Dee Gordon 1.25 3.00
THC450 Jean Segura 2.00 5.00
THC451 Edwin Diaz 1.50 4.00
THC452 Starlin Castro 1.25 3.00
THC453 J.T. Realmuto 2.00 5.00
THC454 Max Scherzer 2.00 5.00
THC455 Trea Turner 1.50 4.00
THC456 Jonathan Schoop 1.25 3.00
THC457 Eric Hosmer 1.50 4.00
THC458 Rhys Hoskins 2.50 6.00
THC459 Aaron Nola 1.50 4.00
THC460 Felipe Vasquez 1.25 3.00
THC461 Shin-Soo Choo 1.50 4.00
THC462 Nomar Mazara 1.25 3.00
THC463 Kevin Kiermaier 1.50 4.00
THC464 Chris Sale 2.00 5.00
THC465 Joey Votto 2.00 5.00
THC466 Scooter Gennett 1.50 4.00
THC467 Eugenio Suarez 1.50 4.00
THC468 Nolan Arenado 3.00 8.00
THC469 Trevor Story 2.00 5.00
THC470 Starling Marte 1.50 4.00
THC471 Charlie Blackmon 2.00 5.00
THC472 Miguel Cabrera 2.00 5.00
THC473 Miguel Andujar 2.00 5.00
THC474 Giancarlo Stanton 2.00 5.00
THC475 J.D. Martinez 2.00 5.00
THC476 Jesus Aguilar 1.50 4.00
THC477 Mitch Haniger 1.50 4.00
THC478 Brandon Crawford 1.50 4.00
THC479 Jose Berrios 1.50 4.00
THC480 Lourdes Gurriel Jr. 1.50 4.00
THC481 Juan Soto 15.00 40.00
THC483 Jose Abreu 2.00 5.00
THC484 Andrew Benintendi 2.00 5.00
THC485 Mike Trout 20.00 50.00
THC486 Adam Jones 1.50 4.00
THC487 Xander Bogaerts 2.00 5.00
THC488 Odubel Herrera 1.50 4.00
THC490 Clayton Kershaw 3.00 8.00
THC491 Jose Ramirez 1.50 4.00
THC493 Aroldis Chapman 2.00 5.00
THC494 Wil Myers 1.50 4.00
THC498 Amed Rosario 1.50 4.00
THC499 Aaron Judge 5.00 12.00
THC500 Ronald Acuna Jr. 15.00 40.00
THC501 Michael Chavis 2.00 5.00
THC502 Charlie Morton 2.00 5.00
THC503 Michael Brantley 1.50 4.00
THC504 Vladimir Guerrero Jr. 20.00 50.00
THC505 Nick Markakis 1.50 4.00
THC506 Yasmani Grandal 1.25 3.00
THC507 Nick Senzel 4.00 10.00
THC508 Brendan Rodgers 2.00 5.00
THC512 Keston Hiura 10.00 25.00
THC516 Eloy Jimenez 12.00 30.00
THC517 Fernando Tatis Jr. 40.00 100.00
THC519 Pete Alonso 20.00 50.00
THC520 Manny Machado 2.00 5.00
THC521 Andrew Miller 1.50 4.00
THC522 A.J. Pollock 1.25 3.00
THC523 Carter Kieboom 4.00 10.00
THC524 Griffin Canning MB 2.00 5.00
THC525 Justus Sheffield 2.00 5.00
THC526 Yusei Kikuchi 2.00 5.00
THC527 Jorge Alfaro 1.25 3.00
THC529 Brian Dozier 1.50 4.00

THC530 Patrick Corbin 1.50 4.00
THC532 Richie Martin 1.25 3.00
THC533 Jon Duplantier 1.25 3.00
THC534 Bryce Harper 3.00 8.00
THC535 J.T. Realmuto 2.00 5.00
THC537 Austin Meadows 2.00 5.00
THC538 Tyler Glasnow 2.00 5.00
THC539 Byron Buxton 2.00 5.00
THC540 Alex Verdugo 1.50 4.00
THC541 Yasiel Puig 2.00 5.00
THC542 Nicky Lopez 2.00 5.00
THC543 Sonny Gray 1.50 4.00
THC544 Daniel Murphy 1.50 4.00
THC545 Troy Tulowitzki 2.00 5.00
THC546 DJ LeMahieu 2.00 5.00
THC547 J.A. Happ 1.50 4.00
THC548 Adam Ottavino 1.25 3.00
THC549 Zack Britton 1.25 3.00
THC551 Ian Kinsler 1.50 4.00
THC556 Jake Bauers 2.00 5.00
THC558 Wilson Ramos 1.25 3.00
THC560 Robinson Chirinos MB 1.25 3.00
THC562 Wade Miley MB 1.25 3.00
THC563 Danny Salazar 1.50 4.00
THC564 Tyler O'Neill 1.50 4.00
THC568 Nathan Eovaldi 1.50 4.00
THC573 Matt Shoemaker MB 1.50 4.00
THC575 Freddy Galvis MB 1.25 3.00
THC577 Max Fried MB 2.00 5.00
THC579 Brian McCann MB 1.50 4.00
THC580 Brandon Woodruff MB 2.00 5.00
THC581 Zach Davies MB 1.25 3.00
THC584 Adam Wainwright MB 1.50 4.00
THC585 Alex Reyes MB 1.50 4.00
THC591 Christian Walker MB 1.50 4.00
THC594 Merrill Kelly MB 1.25 3.00
THC595 Corbin Martin MB 2.00 5.00
THC596 Russell Martin MB 1.25 3.00
THC598 Kevin Pillar MB 1.25 3.00
THC600 Jeff Samardzija MB 1.25 3.00
THC604 Nate Lowe MB 6.00 15.00
THC605 Adam Cimber MB 1.25 3.00
THC606 Domingo Santana MB 1.50 4.00
THC624 Francisco Mejia MB 1.50 4.00
THC625 Nick Margevicius MB 1.25 3.00
THC629 Melky Cabrera MB 1.25 3.00
THC636 Yandy Diaz MB 1.50 4.00
THC637 Ji-Man Choi MB 1.25 3.00
THC639 Jose Alvarado MB 1.25 3.00
THC646 Amir Garrett MB 1.25 3.00
THC649 Ryan McMahon MB 2.00 5.00
THC654 Ian Kennedy MB 1.25 3.00
THC661 Kyle Gibson MB 1.50 4.00
THC663 Brett Gardner MB 1.50 4.00
THC664 Domingo German MB 1.50 4.00
THC672 Brandon Brennan MB 1.25 3.00
THC676 Ryan Pressly MB 1.25 3.00
THC683 Junior Guerra MB 1.25 3.00
THC692 Nick Anderson MB 1.25 3.00
THC694 Ryan Brasier MB 1.25 3.00
THC699 Caleb Smith MB 1.25 3.00
THC701 Victor Robles 2.50 6.00
THC702 Andrew McCutchen 2.00 5.00
THC703 Chris Paddack 2.50 6.00
THC704 Hunter Pence MB 1.50 4.00
THC705 Adam Jones MB 1.50 4.00
THC706 Daniel Vogelbach MB 1.25 3.00
THC707 Dominic Smith MB 1.25 3.00
THC708 Clint Frazier MB 1.50 4.00
THC709 Gio Gonzalez 1.50 4.00
THC710 Cameron Maybin 1.25 3.00
THC711 Johnny Cueto MB 1.50 4.00
THC712 Hunter Strickland MB 1.25 3.00
THC713 Chris Devenski MB 1.25 3.00
THC714 Franklin Barreto MB 1.25 3.00
THC719 Tayron Guerrero MB 1.25 3.00
THC721 Mychal Givens MB 1.25 3.00
THC722 Hector Neris MB 1.25 3.00
THC725 Ichiro 2.50 6.00

2019 Topps Heritage Chrome Black Refractors

*BLACK REF: 2X TO 5X BASIC
STATED ODDS 1:817 HOBBY
STATED HN ODDS 1:699 HOBBY
THC2-THC500 PRINT RUN 70 SER.#'d SETS
THC501-THC725 PRINT RUN 69 SER.#'d SETS
THC504 Vladimir Guerrero Jr. 200.00 500.00
THC512 Keston Hiura 100.00 250.00
THC516 Eloy Jimenez 100.00 250.00
THC517 Fernando Tatis Jr. 600.00 1200.00
THC519 Pete Alonso 300.00 600.00

2019 Topps Heritage Chrome Refractors

*REF: .6X TO 1.5X BASIC
STATED ODDS 1:101 HOBBY
STATED HN ODDS 1:85 HOBBY
THC2-THC500 PRINT RUN 570 SER.#'d SETS
THC501-THC725 PRINT RUN 569 SER.#'d SETS
THC504 Vladimir Guerrero Jr. 60.00 150.00
THC517 Fernando Tatis Jr. 125.00 300.00
THC523 Carter Kieboom 10.00 25.00

2019 Topps Heritage Clubhouse Collection Autograph Relics

STATED ODDS 1:14,867 HOBBY
STATED HN ODDS 1:6555 HOBBY
HN EXCH DEADLINE 7/31/2021
STATED PRINT RUN 25 SER.#'d SETS
EXCHANGE DEADLINE 1/31/2021
CCARAJ Aaron Judge 150.00 400.00
CCARAK Al Kaline HN 75.00 200.00
CCARBS Blake Snell HN 20.00 50.00
CCARBS Blake Snell 20.00 50.00
CCARCY Carl Yastrzemski HN 75.00 200.00
CCARDG Didi Gregorius 50.00 120.00
CCARDS Don Sutton HN EXCH 40.00 100.00
CCARFL Francisco Lindor HN 30.00 80.00
CCARGT Gleyber Torres 100.00 250.00
CCARJA Jose Altuve 30.00 80.00
CCARJD Jacob deGrom HN 40.00 100.00
CCARJR Jose Ramirez 15.00 40.00
CCARJS Juan Soto HN 75.00 200.00
CCARKB Kris Bryant HN 75.00 200.00
CCARKB Kris Bryant 75.00 200.00
CCARLS Luis Severino
CCARMA Miguel Andujar HN
CCARMC Matt Carpenter HN 50.00 120.00
CCARMM Miles Mikolas HN 30.00 80.00
CCARMT Mike Trout 300.00 600.00
CCARNR Nolan Ryan HN
CCARPG Paul Goldschmidt 25.00 60.00
CCARRA Ronald Acuna Jr. 125.00 300.00
CCARRD Rafael Devers EXCH 50.00 120.00
CCARRH Rhys Hoskins HN 50.00 120.00
CCARRH Rhys Hoskins 50.00 120.00
CCARSO Shohei Ohtani HN 100.00 250.00
CCARSO Shohei Ohtani 100.00 250.00
CCARTP Tony Perez HN 40.00 100.00

2019 Topps Heritage Clubhouse Collection Dual Relics

STATED ODDS 1:16,318 HOBBY
STATED HN ODDS 1:6,934 HOBBY
STATED PRINT RUN 70 SER.#'d SETS
CCDRBR Rizzo/Bryant HN 30.00 80.00
CCDRBV Bench/Votto/HN 15.00 40.00
CCDRCS Stargell/Clemente HN 40.00 100.00
CCDRJS Stanton/Judge HN 30.00 80.00
CCDRKC Kaline/Cabrera 30.00 80.00
CCDRLR Lindor/Ramirez 25.00 60.00
CCDRMB Munson/Bench 30.00 80.00
CCDRTP Trout/Pujols 60.00 150.00
CCDRYB Yaz/Betts 40.00 100.00
CCDRYM Martinez/Yaz HN 25.00 60.00

2019 Topps Heritage Clubhouse Collection Relics

STATED ODDS 1:35 HOBBY
STATED HN ODDS 1:40 HOBBY
*GOLD/99: .6X TO 1.5X BASIC
CCRAA Albert Almora Jr. HN 2.50 6.00
CCRAB Andrew Benintendi HN 3.00 8.00
CCRAB Andrew Benintendi 3.00 8.00
CCRABE Adrian Beltre 3.00 8.00
CCRAC Aroldis Chapman HN 3.00 8.00
CCRAJ Aaron Judge 8.00 20.00
CCRAM Adalberto Mondesi HN 2.50 6.00
CCRAP Albert Pujols 4.00 10.00
CCRAR Anthony Rizzo 4.00 10.00
CCRBB Brandon Belt HN 2.50 6.00
CCRBH Bryce Harper 5.00 12.00
CCRBP Buster Posey HN 4.00 10.00
CCRBP Buster Posey 4.00 10.00
CCRBT Blake Treinen HN 2.00 5.00
CCRBZ Ben Zobrist 2.50 6.00
CCRCB Cody Bellinger HN 6.00 15.00
CCRCC Carlos Correa HN 3.00 8.00
CCRCC Carlos Correa 3.00 8.00
CCRCK Clayton Kershaw 5.00 12.00
CCRCM Carlos Martinez 2.50 6.00
CCRCS CC Sabathia HN 2.50 6.00
CCRCS Chris Sale 3.00 8.00
CCRCSE Corey Seager 3.00 8.00
CCRCY Christian Yelich 4.00 10.00
CCRDB Dellin Betances 2.50 6.00
CCRDG Dee Gordon HN 2.00 5.00
CCRDP David Price 2.50 6.00
CCRDS Dansby Swanson 3.00 8.00
CCREA Elvis Andrus HN 2.50 6.00
CCREE Edwin Encarnacion 3.00 8.00
CCREH Eric Hosmer HN 2.50 6.00
CCREL Evan Longoria 2.50 6.00
CCRER Eddie Rosario 2.50 6.00
CCRFF Freddie Freeman 4.00 10.00
CCRFL Francisco Lindor HN 3.00 8.00
CCRFL Francisco Lindor 3.00 8.00
CCRGC Gerrit Cole HN 3.00 8.00
CCRGS Giancarlo Stanton HN 3.00 8.00
CCRGS George Springer 2.50 6.00
CCRGT Gleyber Torres 6.00 15.00
CCRHR Hyun-Jin Ryu HN 2.50 6.00
CCRI Ichiro HN 4.00 10.00
CCRJA Jesus Aguilar HN 2.50 6.00
CCRJA Jose Abreu 3.00 8.00
CCRJAL Jose Altuve 2.50 6.00
CCRJB Javier Baez HN 4.00 10.00
CCRJD Josh Donaldson HN 2.50 6.00
CCRJD Jacob deGrom 6.00 15.00
CCRJG Joey Gallo HN 2.50 6.00
CCRJH Josh Hader HN 2.50 6.00
CCRJHA Josh Harrison 2.00 5.00
CCRJL Jon Lester 2.50 6.00
CCRJM J.D. Martinez 3.00 8.00
CCRJP James Paxton 2.50 6.00
CCRJR Jose Ramirez 2.50 6.00
CCRJS Justin Smoak HN 2.00 5.00
CCRJT Julio Teheran HN 2.50 6.00
CCRJT Jameson Taillon 2.50 6.00
CCRJU Justin Upton HN 2.50 6.00
CCRJV Justin Verlander HN 3.00 8.00
CCRJV Joey Votto 3.00 8.00
CCRKB Kris Bryant HN 4.00 10.00
CCRKB Kris Bryant 4.00 10.00
CCRKF Kyle Freeland HN 2.50 6.00
CCRKM Ketel Marte HN 2.50 6.00
CCRKS Kyle Seager HN 2.00 5.00
CCRKS Kyle Schwarber 3.00 8.00
CCRLB Lewis Brinson HN 2.00 5.00
CCRLC Lorenzo Cain HN 2.00 5.00
CCRLM Lance McCullers Jr. 2.00 5.00
CCRLS Luis Severino 2.50 6.00
CCRLU Luis Urias HN 3.00 8.00
CCRMA Miguel Andujar HN 3.00 8.00
CCRMB Mookie Betts HN 6.00 15.00
CCRMB Mookie Betts 6.00 15.00
CCRMC Miguel Cabrera 3.00 8.00
CCRMCH Matt Chapman 3.00 8.00
CCRMM Manny Machado HN 3.00 8.00
CCRMMI Miles Mikolas 3.00 8.00
CCRMO Marcell Ozuna HN 3.00 8.00
CCRMS Miguel Sano HN 2.50 6.00
CCRMT Masahiro Tanaka 2.50 6.00
CCRMT Mike Trout HN 10.00 25.00
CCRMTR Mike Trout 10.00 25.00
CCRNA Nolan Arenado 5.00 12.00
CCRNC Nicholas Castellanos 3.00 8.00
CCRNE Nathan Eovaldi HN 2.50 6.00
CCRNM Nick Markakis 2.50 6.00
CCRNMA Nomar Mazara 2.00 5.00
CCRNS Noah Syndergaard 2.50 6.00
CCRNS Noah Syndergaard HN 2.50 6.00
CCROA Ozzie Albies HN 3.00 8.00
CCRPA Pete Alonso HN 12.00 30.00
CCRPG Paul Goldschmidt HN 3.00 8.00
CCRRB Ryan Braun 2.50 6.00
CCRRD Rafael Devers 4.00 10.00
CCRRH Rhys Hoskins HN 4.00 10.00
CCRRI Raisel Iglesias HN 2.00 5.00
CCRRP Rick Porcello 2.50 6.00
CCRSC Shin-Soo Choo 2.50 6.00
CCRSG Scooter Gennett 2.50 6.00
CCRSM Starling Marte 2.50 6.00
CCRSO Shohei Ohtani 5.00 12.00
CCRSO Shohei Ohtani HN 5.00 12.00
CCRSP Salvador Perez 2.50 6.00
CCRSS Stephen Strasburg 3.00 8.00
CCRTG Tyler Glasnow HN 3.00 8.00
CCRTM Trey Mancini 2.50 6.00
CCRTT Touki Toussaint HN 2.50 6.00
CCRVG Vladimir Guerrero Jr. HN 8.00 20.00
CCRVR Victor Robles HN 4.00 10.00
CCRWC Willson Contreras HN 2.50 6.00
CCRWM Wil Myers 2.50 6.00
CCRWME Whit Merrifield 3.00 8.00
CCRXB Xander Bogaerts 3.00 8.00
CCRYC Yoenis Cespedes 3.00 8.00
CCRYM Yadier Molina 4.00 10.00
CCRYP Yasiel Puig HN 3.00 8.00
CCRZG Zack Greinke 3.00 8.00
CCRABR Alex Bregman HN 3.00 8.00
CCRAPU Albert Pujols HN 4.00 10.00
CCRBBU Byron Buxton HN 3.00 8.00
CCRJAL Jose Altuve HN 2.50 6.00
CCRJBE Jose Berrios HN 2.50 6.00
CCRJBR Jackie Bradley Jr. HN 3.00 8.00
CCRJHA Josh Harrison HN 2.00 5.00
CCRJSO Juan Soto HN 10.00 25.00
CCRTTU Trea Turner HN 2.50 6.00
ECCRAB Andrew Benintendi 3.00 8.00
ECCRAJ Aaron Judge 8.00 20.00
ECCRAP Albert Pujols 4.00 10.00
ECCRAR Anthony Rizzo 4.00 10.00
ECCRBP Buster Posey 4.00 10.00
ECCRCC Carlos Correa 3.00 8.00
ECCRCK Clayton Kershaw 5.00 12.00
ECCRCS Chris Sale 3.00 8.00
ECCRDP David Price 2.50 6.00
ECCRFL Francisco Lindor 3.00 8.00
ECCRJA Jose Altuve 2.50 6.00
ECCRJM J.D. Martinez 3.00 8.00
ECCRJV Justin Verlander 3.00 8.00
ECCRKB Kris Bryant 4.00 10.00
ECCRKD Khris Davis 3.00 8.00
ECCRMA Miguel Andujar 3.00 8.00
ECCRMB Mookie Betts 6.00 15.00
ECCRMC Miguel Cabrera 3.00 8.00
ECCRMS Max Scherzer 3.00 8.00
ECCRMT Mike Trout 10.00 25.00
ECCRSO Shohei Ohtani 5.00 12.00
ECCRTS Trevor Story 3.00 8.00
ECCRYM Yadier Molina 4.00 10.00
ECCRABR Alex Bregman 3.00 8.00
ECCRARO Amed Rosario 2.50 6.00

2019 Topps Heritage Clubhouse Collection Triple Relics

STATED ODDS 1:46,148 HOBBY
STATED HN ODDS 1:19,511 HOBBY
STATED PRINT RUN 25 SER.#'d SETS
CCTRACB Altuve/Bregman/Correa HN 30.00 80.00
CCTRBPV Perez/Votto/Bench HN 50.00 120.00
CCTRBRB Bryant/Rizzo/Baez 75.00 200.00
CCTRGSM Gibson/Smith/Molina 75.00 200.00
CCTRJMD Jackson/McGwire/Davis 75.00 200.00
CCTRMJJ Munson/Jeter/Judge HN
CCTRMMJ Munson/Mattingly/Jeter 100.00 250.00
CCTRTOP Pujols/Trout/Ohtani HN 60.00 150.00
CCTRYBB Yaz/Betts/Benintendi 40.00 100.00
CCTRYOB Ortiz/Yaz/Betts HN 40.00 100.00

2019 Topps Heritage Combo Cards

STATED ODDS 1:20 HOBBY
CC1 Tatis Jr/Machado 6.00 15.00
CC2 Harper/Hoskins 1.00 2.50
CC3 Torres/Andujar 1.25 3.00
CC4 Yusei Kikuchi .60 1.50
Ichiro
CC5 Goldschmidt/Molina .75 2.00
CC6 Verlander/Altuve .60 1.50
CC7 Robinson Cano .50 1.25
Amed Rosario
CC8 Muncy/Bellinger 1.25 3.00
CC9 Joey Votto .60 1.50
Yasiel Puig
CC10 Yelich/Cain .75 2.00

2019 Topps Heritage Flashback Autograph Relics

2019 Topps Heritage Action Variations
STATED PRINT RUN 25 SER.#'d SETS
EXCHANGE DEADLINE 1/31/2021
FARAK Al Kaline 150.00 400.00
FARBG Bob Gibson 60.00 150.00
FARCY Carl Yastrzemski
FARJB Johnny Bench 125.00 300.00
FARJT Joe Torre 125.00 300.00
FARNR Nolan Ryan 125.00 300.00
FARRJ Reggie Jackson 100.00 250.00
FARSC Steve Carlton 100.00 250.00

2019 Topps Heritage Mini

STATED ODDS 1:434 HOBBY
STATED HN ODDS 1:482 HOBBY
STATED PRINT RUN 100 SER.#'d SETS
17 Sean Newcomb 5.00 12.00
25 Eddie Rosario 6.00 15.00
29 Andrelton Simmons 5.00 12.00
34 Cody Bellinger 15.00 40.00
47 Zack Godley 5.00 12.00
52 Chris Archer 5.00 12.00
54 Ross Stripling 5.00 12.00
55 Lou Trivino 5.00 12.00
78 Mookie Betts 15.00 40.00
83 Noah Syndergaard 6.00 15.00
98 Nicholas Castellanos 8.00 20.00
100 Masahiro Tanaka 6.00 15.00
113 Lance McCullers Jr. 5.00 12.00
114 Didi Gregorius 6.00 15.00
117 Kyle Schwarber 8.00 20.00
120 Matt Chapman 8.00 20.00
125 Maikel Franco 6.00 15.00
136 Carlos Carrasco 5.00 12.00
138 James Paxton 6.00 15.00
163 Rafael Devers 10.00 25.00
174 Justin Turner 8.00 20.00
188 Corey Dickerson 5.00 12.00
191 David Price 6.00 15.00
253 Kyle Freeland 6.00 15.00
278 Josh Donaldson 6.00 15.00
279 Rick Porcello 6.00 15.00
298 Dereck Rodriguez 5.00 12.00
300 Zack Wheeler 6.00 15.00
335 Josh Hader 6.00 15.00
341 Corey Seager 8.00 20.00
347 David Bote 6.00 15.00
370 Mike Moustakas 6.00 15.00
401 Francisco Lindor 8.00 20.00
402 Salvador Perez 6.00 15.00
403 Jake Arrieta 6.00 15.00
404 Kris Bryant 10.00 25.00
405 Jon Lester 6.00 15.00
406 Anthony Rizzo 10.00 25.00
407 George Springer 6.00 15.00
408 Sean Manaea 5.00 12.00
409 Jose Altuve 6.00 15.00
410 Christian Yelich 10.00 25.00
411 Blake Snell 6.00 15.00
412 Trevor Bauer 10.00 25.00
413 Gleyber Torres 15.00 40.00
414 Paul DeJong 8.00 20.00
415 Bryce Harper 12.00 30.00
416 Luis Severino 6.00 15.00
417 Jordan Hicks 6.00 15.00
418 Gary Sanchez 8.00 20.00
419 Jacob deGrom 15.00 40.00
420 Kenley Jansen 6.00 15.00
421 Justin Upton 6.00 15.00
422 Albert Pujols 10.00 25.00
423 Carlos Correa 8.00 20.00
424 Alex Bregman 8.00 20.00
425 Franmil Reyes 5.00 12.00
426 Justin Verlander 8.00 20.00
427 Walker Buehler 10.00 25.00
428 Trey Mancini 6.00 15.00
429 Gerrit Cole 8.00 20.00
430 Shohei Ohtani 12.00 30.00
431 Brandon Nimmo 6.00 15.00
432 Khris Davis 8.00 20.00
433 Justin Smoak 5.00 12.00
434 Stephen Piscotty 5.00 12.00
435 Miles Mikolas 8.00 20.00
436 Ozzie Albies 8.00 20.00
437 Lorenzo Cain 5.00 12.00
438 Matt Carpenter 8.00 20.00
439 Yadier Molina 10.00 25.00
440 Javier Baez 10.00 25.00
441 Paul Goldschmidt 8.00 20.00
442 Zack Greinke 8.00 20.00
443 Matt Kemp 6.00 15.00
444 Kenta Maeda 6.00 15.00
445 Buster Posey 10.00 25.00
446 Max Muncy 6.00 15.00
447 Edwin Encarnacion 8.00 20.00
448 Corey Kluber 6.00 15.00
449 Dee Gordon 5.00 12.00
450 Jean Segura 8.00 20.00
451 Edwin Diaz 6.00 15.00
452 Starlin Castro 5.00 12.00
453 J.T. Realmuto 8.00 20.00
454 Max Scherzer 8.00 20.00
455 Trea Turner 6.00 15.00
456 Jonathan Schoop 5.00 12.00
457 Eric Hosmer 6.00 15.00
458 Rhys Hoskins 10.00 25.00
459 Aaron Nola 6.00 15.00
460 Felipe Vasquez 5.00 12.00
461 Shin-Soo Choo 6.00 15.00
462 Nomar Mazara 5.00 12.00
463 Kevin Kiermaier 6.00 15.00
464 Chris Sale 8.00 20.00
465 Joey Votto 8.00 20.00
466 Scooter Gennett 6.00 15.00
467 Eugenio Suarez 6.00 15.00
468 Nolan Arenado 12.00 30.00
469 Trevor Story 8.00 20.00
470 Starling Marte 6.00 15.00
471 Charlie Blackmon 8.00 20.00
472 Miguel Cabrera 8.00 20.00
473 Miguel Andujar 8.00 20.00
474 Giancarlo Stanton 8.00 20.00
475 J.D. Martinez 8.00 20.00
476 Jesus Aguilar 6.00 15.00
477 Mitch Haniger 6.00 15.00
478 Brandon Crawford 6.00 15.00
479 Jose Berrios 6.00 15.00
480 Lourdes Gurriel, Jr. 6.00 15.00
481 Juan Soto 25.00 60.00
482 Carlos Martinez 6.00 15.00
483 Jose Abreu 8.00 20.00
484 Andrew Benintendi 8.00 20.00
485 Mike Trout 100.00 250.00
486 Adam Jones 6.00 15.00
487 Xander Bogaerts 8.00 20.00
488 Odubel Herrera 6.00 15.00
489 Freddie Freeman 10.00 25.00
490 Clayton Kershaw 12.00 30.00
491 Jose Ramirez 6.00 15.00
492 Willson Contreras 6.00 15.00
493 Aroldis Chapman 8.00 20.00
494 Wil Myers 6.00 15.00
495 Sean Doolittle 5.00 12.00
496 Eric Thames 5.00 12.00
497 Yonder Alonso 5.00 12.00
498 Amed Rosario 6.00 15.00
499 Aaron Judge 20.00 50.00
500 Ronald Acuna Jr. 40.00 100.00
501 Michael Chavis 8.00 20.00
502 Charlie Morton 8.00 20.00
503 Michael Brantley 6.00 15.00
504 Vladimir Guerrero Jr. 30.00 80.00
505 Nick Markakis 6.00 15.00
506 Yasmani Grandal 5.00 12.00
507 Nick Senzel 15.00 40.00
508 Brendan Rodgers 8.00 20.00
512 Keston Hiura 30.00 80.00
516 Eloy Jimenez 30.00 80.00
517 Fernando Tatis Jr. 100.00 250.00
519 Pete Alonso 50.00 120.00
520 Manny Machado 8.00 20.00
521 Andrew Miller 6.00 15.00
522 A.J. Pollock 5.00 12.00
523 Carter Kieboom 8.00 20.00
525 Justus Sheffield 8.00 20.00
526 Yusei Kikuchi 8.00 20.00
527 Jorge Alfaro 5.00 12.00
529 Brian Dozier 6.00 15.00
530 Patrick Corbin 6.00 15.00
533 Jon Duplantier 5.00 12.00
534 Bryce Harper 12.00 30.00
535 J.T. Realmuto 8.00 20.00
537 Austin Meadows 8.00 20.00
538 Tyler Glasnow 8.00 20.00
539 Byron Buxton 8.00 20.00
540 Alex Verdugo 6.00 15.00
541 Yasiel Puig 8.00 20.00
543 Sonny Gray 6.00 15.00
544 Daniel Murphy 6.00 15.00
545 Troy Tulowitzki 8.00 20.00
546 DJ LeMahieu 8.00 20.00
547 J.A. Happ 6.00 15.00
548 Adam Ottavino 5.00 12.00
549 Zack Britton 5.00 12.00
551 Ian Kinsler 6.00 15.00
558 Wilson Ramos 5.00 12.00
563 Danny Salazar 6.00 15.00
574 Craig Kimbrel 6.00 15.00
577 Max Fried 8.00 20.00
580 Brandon Woodruff 8.00 20.00
595 Corbin Martin 8.00 20.00
598 Kevin Pillar 5.00 12.00
624 Francisco Mejia 6.00 15.00
664 Domingo German 6.00 15.00
701 Victor Robles 10.00 25.00
702 Andrew McCutchen 8.00 20.00
703 Chris Paddack 10.00 25.00
725 Ichiro 10.00 25.00

2019 Topps Heritage Mystery Autograph Redemptions

RANDOM INSERTS IN PACKS
EXCHANGE DEADLINE 9/26/2020
TBAA Vladimir Guerrero 300.00 500.00
Mystery EXCH Player A
TBAB Eloy Jimenez 300.00 500.00
Mystery EXCH Player B

2019 Topps Heritage New Age Performers

COMPLETE SET (25) 15.00 40.00
STATED ODDS 1:6 HOBBY
NAP1 Blake Snell .50 1.25
NAP2 Mookie Betts 1.25 3.00
NAP3 J.D. Martinez .60 1.50
NAP4 Miguel Andujar .60 1.50
NAP5 Aaron Judge 1.50 4.00
NAP6 Gleyber Torres 1.25 3.00
NAP7 Francisco Lindor .60 1.50
NAP8 Jose Ramirez .50 1.25
NAP9 Mitch Haniger .50 1.25
NAP10 Khris Davis .60 1.50
NAP11 Alex Bregman .60 1.50
NAP12 Justin Verlander .60 1.50
NAP13 Mike Trout 3.00 8.00
NAP14 Shohei Ohtani 1.00 2.50
NAP15 Juan Soto 2.00 5.00
NAP16 Max Scherzer .60 1.50
NAP17 Ronald Acuna Jr. 3.00 8.00
NAP18 Ozzie Albies .60 1.50
NAP19 Jacob deGrom 1.25 3.00
NAP20 Aaron Nola .50 1.25
NAP21 Javier Baez .75 2.00
NAP22 Nolan Arenado 1.00 2.50
NAP23 Trevor Story .60 1.50
NAP24 Christian Yelich .75 2.00
NAP25 Walker Buehler .75 2.00

2019 Topps Heritage News Flashbacks

COMPLETE SET (15) 8.00 20.00
STATED ODDS 1:18 HOBBY
NF1 Music World Loses Jimi Hendrix .60 2.00
NF2 Janis Joplin Passes Away .60 1.50
NF3 First Earth Day Celebration .60 1.50
NF4 Apollo 13 Mission .60 1.50
NF5 American Top 40 Premieres .60 1.50
NF6 PBS Begins Broadcasting .60 1.50
NF7 Isle of Wight Music Festival .60 1.50
NF8 Establishment of Environmental Protection Agency .60 1.50
NF9 Voting Age Lowered to 18 .60 1.50
NF10 President Nixon Meets with Elvis Presley .60 1.50
NF11 The Beatles Break Up .60 1.50
NF12 Venera 7 Lands on Venus .60 1.50
NF13 First Women Promoted to U.S. Army Generals .60 1.50
NF14 Marshall University Football .60 1.50
NF15 Diana Ross & The Supremes' Final Concert .60 1.50

2019 Topps Heritage Now and Then

STATED ODDS 1:8 HOBBY
NT1 Paul Goldschmidt .60 1.50
NT2 Christian Yelich .75 2.00
NT3 Elvis Luciano .60 1.50
NT4 Zack Greinke .60 1.50
NT5 Jacob deGrom 1.25 3.00
NT6 Trevor Bauer .75 2.00
NT7 Ryan Braun .50 1.25
NT8 Shane Greene .40 1.00
NT9 Khris Davis .60 1.50
NT10 Taylor Clarke .40 1.00
NT11 Nolan Arenado 1.00 2.50
NT12 Vladimir Guerrero Jr. 2.50 6.00
NT13 Cody Bellinger 1.25 3.00
NT14 Carter Kieboom .60 1.50
NT15 Albert Pujols .75 2.00

2019 Topps Heritage Real One Autographs

STATED ODDS 1:106 HOBBY
STATED HN ODDS 1:86 HOBBY
EXCHANGE DEADLINE 1/31/2021
HN EXCH DEADLINE 7/31/2021
ROAAB Alex Bregman 25.00 60.00
ROAAJ Aaron Judge HN 100.00 250.00
ROAAJ Aaron Judge 150.00 400.00
ROAAK Al Kaline HN 30.00 80.00
ROAAK Al Kaline 50.00 120.00
ROAAR Anthony Rizzo HN 20.00 50.00
ROABBL Bert Blyleven 15.00 40.00
ROABD Bill Dillman 8.00 20.00
ROABG Bob Gibson HN 30.00 80.00
ROABG Bob Gibson 30.00 80.00
ROABR Brendan Rodgers HN EXCH 15.00 40.00
ROABS Blake Snell 10.00 25.00
ROACA Chance Adams 8.00 20.00
ROACBU Corbin Burnes 25.00 60.00
ROACC Cisco Carlos 8.00 20.00
ROACK Carter Kieboom HN 20.00 50.00
ROACM Cedric Mullins HN 25.00 60.00
ROACP Chris Paddack HN EXCH 20.00 50.00
ROACS Chris Sale 12.00 30.00
ROACY Carl Yastrzemski HN 40.00 100.00
ROACY Carl Yastrzemski 75.00 200.00
ROACYE Christian Yelich 40.00 100.00
ROADH Dakota Hudson HN 12.00 30.00
ROADJA Danny Jansen 8.00 20.00
ROADM Danny Murphy 8.00 20.00
ROADP David Price HN 10.00 25.00
ROADR Dereck Rodriguez HN 8.00 20.00
ROADS Don Sutton HN EXCH 15.00 40.00
ROAEJ Eloy Jimenez HN 40.00 100.00
ROAEJ Eloy Jimenez 75.00 200.00
Mystery
ROAFF Freddie Freeman 25.00 60.00
ROAFH Frank Howard HN 8.00 20.00
ROAFL Francisco Lindor HN 20.00 50.00
ROAFT Fernando Tatis Jr. HN 500.00 1200.00
ROAGA Gerry Arrigo 8.00 20.00
ROAHA Hank Aaron HN 200.00 500.00
ROAJA Jose Altuve HN 20.00 50.00
ROAJA Jose Altuve 20.00 50.00
ROAJB Jack Baldschun 8.00 20.00
ROAJBA Jake Bauers 12.00 30.00
ROAJBE Johnny Bench 75.00 200.00
ROAJD Jacob deGrom HN 30.00 80.00
ROAJD Jacob deGrom 30.00 80.00
ROAJH Josh Hader HN 8.00 20.00
ROAJHI Jim Hicks 8.00 20.00
ROAJJ Josh James HN 12.00 30.00
ROAJM Jeff McNeil HN 20.00 50.00
ROAJMA Juan Marichal HN 40.00 100.00
ROAJN Gerry Nyman 8.00 20.00
ROAJS Justus Sheffield HN 12.00 30.00
ROAJS Justus Sheffield 12.00 30.00
ROAJSO Juan Soto HN 75.00 200.00
ROAJSO Juan Soto 75.00 200.00
ROAJT Joe Torre 40.00 100.00
ROAKA Kolby Allard 12.00 30.00
ROAKB Kris Bryant 100.00 250.00
ROAKH Keston Hiura HN 40.00 100.00
ROAKK Kevin Kramer HN 10.00 25.00
ROAKT Kyle Tucker 20.00 50.00
ROAKW Kyle Wright HN 12.00 30.00
ROALB Lou Brock 30.00 80.00
ROALGU Lourdes Gurriel Jr. 8.00 20.00
ROALK Lou Klimchock 8.00 20.00
ROALU Luis Urias 8.00 20.00
ROAMA Miguel Andujar HN 20.00 50.00
ROAMA Max Alvis 10.00 25.00
ROAMCA Miguel Cabrera HN 60.00 150.00
ROAMCH Michael Chavis HN 20.00 50.00
ROAMK Matt Kemp HN 10.00 25.00
ROAMKE Mitch Keller HN 8.00 20.00
ROAMKO Michael Kopech 20.00 50.00
ROAMM Miles Mikolas 12.00 30.00
ROAMMU Max Muncy 10.00 25.00
ROAMO Marcell Ozuna HN 15.00 40.00
ROAMT Mike Trout HN 400.00 800.00
ROAMT Mike Trout 400.00 800.00
ROANR Nolan Ryan HN 75.00 200.00
ROANR Nolan Ryan 75.00 200.00
ROANS Noah Syndergaard HN 10.00 25.00
ROANSE Nick Senzel HN 25.00 60.00
ROAOA Ozzie Albies HN EXCH 20.00 50.00
ROAPA Pete Alonso HN 60.00 150.00
ROAPC Patrick Corbin HN 10.00 25.00
ROAPD Paul DeJong 8.00 20.00
ROAPG Paul Goldschmidt HN 25.00 60.00
ROARA Ronald Acuna Jr. HN 250.00 500.00
ROARC Rod Carew HN 20.00 50.00
ROARC Rod Carew 20.00 50.00
ROARD Rafael Devers HN 30.00 80.00
ROARF Rollie Fingers HN 15.00 40.00
ROARH Rhys Hoskins HN 25.00 60.00
ROARH Rhys Hoskins 25.00 60.00
ROARJ Reggie Jackson HN 50.00 120.00
ROARN Rich Nye 8.00 20.00
ROARP Rico Petrocelli 8.00 20.00
ROART Rowdy Tellez HN 12.00 30.00
ROARW Ray Washburn 8.00 20.00
ROASC Steve Carlton HN 25.00 60.00
ROASG Scooter Gennett HN
ROASO Shohei Ohtani HN 100.00 250.00
ROASO Shohei Ohtani 100.00 250.00
ROASW Steve Whitaker 8.00 20.00
ROATB Trevor Bauer HN 15.00 40.00
ROATO Tony Oliva HN 15.00 40.00
ROATP Tony Perez HN 20.00 50.00
ROATST Trevor Story 12.00 30.00
ROAVF Vern Fuller 10.00 25.00
ROAVG Vladimir Guerrero Jr. HN 150.00 400.00
ROAVG Vladimir Guerrero Jr 150.00 400.00
Mystery
ROAWA Willy Adames HN 8.00 20.00
ROAWAS Willians Astudillo HN 8.00 20.00
ROAWC Willson Contreras 10.00 25.00
ROAYK Yusei Kikuchi HN 12.00 30.00

2019 Topps Heritage Real One Autographs Red Ink

*RED INK: .75X TO 2X BASIC
STATED ODDS 1:1404 HOBBY
STATED HN ODDS 1:348 HOBBY
PRINT RUNS B/WN 25-70 COPIES PER
EXCHANGE DEADLINE 1/31/2021
HN EXCH DEADLINE 7/31/2021
ROAAJ Aaron Judge/70 500.00 1000.00
ROACK Carter Kieboom HN 100.00 250.00
ROAEJ Eloy Jimenez/70 HN 150.00 400.00
ROAEJ Eloy Jimenez/70 250.00 600.00
Mystery
ROAKH Keston Hiura/70 HN 150.00 400.00
ROAMKO Michael Kopech/70 60.00 150.00
ROAMT Mike Trout/25 HN 800.00 1500.00
ROAMT Mike Trout/70 600.00 1200.00
ROAPA Pete Alonso/70 HN 800.00 1200.00
ROASO Shohei Ohtani/25 HN 200.00 500.00
ROASO Shohei Ohtani/70 150.00 400.00
ROAVG Vladimir Guerrero Jr/70 400.00 800.00
Mystery

2019 Topps Heritage Real One Dual Autographs

STATED ODDS 1:5947 HOBBY
STATED ODDS HN 1:3763 HOBBY
STATED PRINT RUN 25 SER.#'d SETS
EXCHANGE DEADLINE 1/31/2021
HN EXCH DEADLINE 7/31/2021
RODAAA Aaron/Acuna 700.00 1000.00
RODAAB Brgmn/Altve HN EXCH 100.00 250.00
RODAAS Acuna/Soto HN 400.00 800.00
RODABR Bryant/Rizzo 125.00 300.00
RODACO Carew/Oliva HN EXCH 75.00 200.00
RODACR Carew/Rosario 50.00 120.00
RODAGB Ryan/Gibson 300.00 600.00
RODAGC Carlton/Gibson HN 125.00 300.00
RODAJA Judge/Andjr HN EXCH
RODAJD Jackson/Davis 100.00 250.00
RODAMG Gldschmdt/Mlna HN EXCH 75.00 200.00
RODAMP Marichal/Posey HN 75.00 200.00
RODAPP Piniella/Perez 40.00 100.00
RODAPV Voto/Perez HN 75.00 200.00
RODARD Ryan/deGrom HN 250.00 600.00
RODASP Price/Sale HN EXCH 75.00 200.00
RODATM Torre/Molina EXCH 75.00 200.00
RODATO Ohtani/Trout HN
RODATO Trout/Ohtani 1200.00 1600.00
RODAYD Yaz./Devers 125.00 300.00
RODAYO Yaz./Ortiz 150.00 400.00

2019 Topps Heritage Rookie Performers

STATED ODDS 1:8 HOBBY
RP1 Vladimir Guerrero Jr. 1.50 4.00
RP2 Yusei Kikuchi .40 1.00
RP3 Pete Alonso 2.00 5.00
RP4 Chris Paddack .50 1.25
RP5 Jon Duplantier .25 .60
RP6 Kyle Tucker .60 1.50
RP7 Eloy Jimenez 1.00 2.50
RP8 Brendan Rodgers .40 1.00
RP9 Nick Senzel .75 2.00
RP10 Michael Chavis .40 1.00
RP11 Willians Astudillo .25 .60
RP12 Fernando Tatis Jr. 4.00 10.00
RP13 Touki Toussaint .30 .75
RP14 Keston Hiura .75 2.00
RP15 Carter Kieboom .40 1.00

2019 Topps Heritage Teammates Boxloader

STATED ODDS 1:51 HOBBY BOX
1 Product Development Team 8.00 20.00
2 Licensing Team 8.00 20.00
3 Art/Packaging Team 8.00 20.00
4 Production Team 8.00 20.00
5 Marketing Team 8.00 20.00
6 Customer Service Team 8.00 20.00
7 E-Commerce Team 8.00 20.00
8 Quality Assurance Team 8.00 20.00
9 Finance Team 8.00 20.00
10 BOM/Logistics Team 8.00 20.00
11 Legal/HR Team 8.00 20.00
12 Sales Team 8.00 20.00
13 Executive Team 8.00 20.00
14 Information Technology Team 8.00 20.00
15 Corporate Finance Team 8.00 20.00
16 Fulfillment Team 8.00 20.00
17 Acquistion Team 8.00 20.00
18 Planning/Manufacturing Team 8.00 20.00

2019 Topps Heritage The Hammer's Greatest Hits

STATED HN ODDS 1:24 HOBBY
THGH1 Hank Aaron 1.00 2.50
THGH2 Hank Aaron 1.00 2.50
THGH3 Hank Aaron 1.00 2.50
THGH4 Hank Aaron 1.00 2.50
THGH5 Hank Aaron 1.00 2.50
THGH6 Hank Aaron 1.00 2.50
THGH7 Hank Aaron 1.00 2.50
THGH8 Hank Aaron 1.00 2.50
THGH9 Hank Aaron 1.00 2.50
THGH10 Hank Aaron 1.00 2.50
THGH11 Hank Aaron 1.00 2.50
THGH12 Hank Aaron 1.00 2.50
THGH13 Hank Aaron 1.00 2.50
THGH14 Hank Aaron 1.00 2.50
THGH15 Hank Aaron 1.00 2.50

2019 Topps Heritage The Hammer's Greatest Hits Autographs

STATED HN ODDS 1:12,338 HOBBY
STATED PRINT RUN 5 SER.#'d SETS
HN EXCH DEADLINE 7/31/2021
THGH1 Hank Aaron 300.00 600.00
THGH2 Hank Aaron 300.00 600.00
THGH3 Hank Aaron 300.00 600.00
THGH4 Hank Aaron 300.00 600.00
THGH5 Hank Aaron 300.00 600.00
THGH6 Hank Aaron 300.00 600.00
THGH7 Hank Aaron 300.00 600.00
THGH8 Hank Aaron 300.00 600.00
THGH9 Hank Aaron 300.00 600.00
THGH10 Hank Aaron 300.00 600.00
THGH11 Hank Aaron 300.00 600.00
THGH12 Hank Aaron 300.00 600.00
THGH13 Hank Aaron 300.00 600.00
THGH14 Hank Aaron 300.00 600.00
THGH15 Hank Aaron 300.00 600.00

2019 Topps Heritage Then and Now

COMPLETE SET (15) 6.00 15.00
STATED ODDS 1:18 HOBBY
TN1 Bob Gibson .60 1.50
Max Scherzer
TN2 Jim Perry .50 1.25
Blake Snell
TN3 Tom Seaver 1.25 3.00
Jacob deGrom
TN4 Jim Palmer .50 1.25
Blake Snell
TN5 Harmon Killebrew .60 1.50
Khris Davis
TN6 Johnny Bench 1.00 2.50
Nolan Arenado
TN7 Killebrew/Martinez .60 1.50
TN8 Bench/Baez .75 2.00
TN9 Ystrzmski/Betts 1.25 3.00

TN10 Torre/Yelich .75 2.00
TN11 Lou Brock .60 1.50
Whit Merrifield
TN12 Jim Palmer .60 1.50
Justin Verlander
TN13 Bob Gibson .60 1.50
Max Scherzer
TN14 Tom Seaver .60 1.50
Max Scherzer
TN15 Jim Palmer .60 1.50
Justin Verlander

2020 Topps Heritage

SP ODDS 1:3 HOBBY
1 Washington Nationals WS Champs .15 .40
2 Trevor Bauer .30 .75
3 Jesse Winker .25 .60
4 Adam Frazier .15 .40
5 Gary Sanchez .25 .60
6 Derek Dietrich .20 .50
7 Seth Lugo .15 .40
8 Gio Urshela .25 .60
9 Donovan Solano .25 .60
10 Jedd Gyorko .15 .40
11 Tom Murphy .15 .40
12 Tony Wolters .15 .40
13 Cease RC/Collins RC .50 1.25
14 Matt Beaty .20 .50
15 Anibal Sanchez .20 .50
16 Johnny Cueto .20 .50
17 Yuli Gurriel .20 .50
18 Josh Reddick .15 .40
19 Vince Velasquez .15 .40
20 Shed Long .20 .50
21 Steven Matz .15 .40
22 Julio Teheran .20 .50
23 Scott Kingery .20 .50
24 Mike Moustakas .20 .50
25 Taylor Rogers .15 .40
26 Jose Quintana .15 .40
27 D.Agrazal RC/J.Marvel RC .40 1.00
28 Omar Narvaez .15 .40
29 Adam Ottavino .20 .50
30 Justin Turner .25 .60
31 Victor Caratini .15 .40
32 Evan Longoria .20 .50
33 Ender Inciarte .15 .40
34 Orlando Arcia .15 .40
35 Jorge Soler .25 .60
36 Kenley Jansen .20 .50
37 Luke Jackson .15 .40
38 Rougned Odor .20 .50
39 J.Rogers RC/T.Alexander RC .50 1.25
40 Joey Votto .25 .60
41 Miguel Cabrera .25 .60
42 Albert Almora .20 .50
43 Emilio Pagan .15 .40
44 Brendan Rodgers .25 .60
45 Kyle Tucker .25 .60
46 Adam Engel .15 .40
47 J.A. Happ .20 .50
48 Matt Adams .15 .40
49 Harold Ramirez .15 .40
50 Chris Bassitt .15 .40
51 Mitch Haniger .20 .50
52 Bichette RC/Kay RC 2.50 6.00
53 Aaron Nola .20 .50
54 Alvarez RC/Aquino RC 3.00 8.00
55 Cavan Biggio .30 .75
56 Carlos Santana .20 .50
57 Chris Taylor .20 .50
58 Andrew Miller .20 .50
59 Scott Oberg .15 .40
60 Mark Canha .15 .40
61 Tim Anderson .25 .60
Yoan Moncada
DJ LeMahieu LL
62 Rndn/Ylch/Mrte LL .30 .75
63 Jorge Soler .25 .60
Jose Abreu
Xander Bogaerts LL
64 Alnso/Frmn/Rndn LL .60 1.50
65 Soler/Brgmn/Cruz/Trout LL 1.25 3.00
66 Srz/Blingr/Alnso LL .60 1.50
67 Vrlndr/Mrtn/Cole LL .40 1.00
68 Mike Soroka .50 1.25
Jacob deGrom
Hyun-Jin Ryu LL
69 Rdrgz/Vrlndr/Cole LL .40 1.00
70 Krshw/Hdsn/Fried/Strsbrg LL .40 1.00
71 Vrlndr/Bbr/Cole LL .40 1.00
72 Max Scherzer .50 1.25
Jacob deGrom
Stephen Strasburg LL
73 Antonio Senzatela .15 .40
74 L.Thorpe RC/B.Graterol RC .50 1.25
75 J.T. Realmuto .25 .60
76 Touki Toussaint .20 .50
77 Dylan Bundy .20 .50
78 Albert Pujols .30 .75
79 Jay Bruce .20 .50
80 Harrison Bader .20 .50
81 Khris Davis .25 .60
82 Max Scherzer .25 .60
83 Bradley RC/Civale RC .60 1.50
84 David Bote .20 .50
85 Christin Stewart .15 .40
86 Colin Moran .15 .40
87 Josh Hader .20 .50
88 Dexter Fowler .20 .50
89 Carlos Carrasco .15 .40
90 Robinson Cano .20 .50
91 Mike Foltynewicz .15 .40
92 Carson Kelly .15 .40
93 Gallen RC/Young RC .75 2.00
94 Marco Gonzales .15 .40
95 Pedro Severino .15 .40
96 Mitch Garver .15 .40
97 Wil Myers .20 .50
98 Marcus Semien .25 .60
99 Tommy La Stella .15 .40
100 Nick Markakis .20 .50
101 Brad Hand .15 .40
102 Abreu RC/Armntrs RC/Toro RC .40 1.00
103 Adalberto Mondesi .20 .50
104 Austin Hedges .15 .40
105 Josh VanMeter .25 .60
106 James McCann .20 .50
107 Tucker Barnhart .15 .40
108 Tyler Flowers .15 .40
109 Joey Lucchesi .15 .40
110 Pablo Sandoval .20 .50
111 Rojas RC/Leyba RC .40 1.00
112 Nick Ahmed .15 .40
113 Eduardo Rodriguez .15 .40
114 Caleb Smith .15 .40
115 Cal Quantrill .15 .40
116 Grisham RC/Dubon RC 1.25 3.00
117 Marcus Stroman .20 .50
118 Whit Merrifield .25 .60
119 Maikel Franco .20 .50
120 Willians Astudillo .15 .40
121 Hoerner RC/Alzolay RC 1.25 3.00
122 Brandon Dixon .15 .40
123 Hilliard RC/Nunez RC .50 1.25
124 Kolten Wong .20 .50
125 Ross Stripling .15 .40
126 Edwin Encarnacion .25 .60
127 Yan Gomes .25 .60
128 Josh James .15 .40
129 Oscar Mercado .25 .60
130 Clint Frazier .20 .50
131 Luke Voit .30 .75
132 Jose Martinez .15 .40
133 Buster Posey .30 .75
134 Willie Calhoun .15 .40
135 Raimel Tapia .15 .40
136 Cesar Hernandez .15 .40
137 Rio Ruiz .15 .40
138 Kyle Seager .15 .40
139 Kevin Newman .25 .60
140 Nathan Eovaldi .20 .50
141 Brandon Belt .20 .50
142 Javier Baez .30 .75
143 Ildemaro Vargas .15 .40
144 Miguel Rojas .15 .40
145 Rafael Devers .30 .75
146 Mallex Smith .15 .40
147 Tyler Naquin .20 .50
148 Adam Plutko .15 .40
149 Zack Greinke .25 .60
150 Shane Greene .15 .40
151 Jon Gray .15 .40
152 M.Thaiss RC/P.Sandoval RC .50 1.25
153 Sandy Alcantara .15 .40
154 Trea Turner .20 .50
155 Jarlin Garcia .15 .40
156 Ranger Suarez .15 .40
157 Ben Gamel .20 .50
158 Daniel Murphy .20 .50
159 Garrett Cooper .15 .40
160 Domingo Santana .20 .50
161 Brosseau RC/McKay RC .50 1.25
162 David Price .20 .50
163 Tyler Beede .15 .40
164 Sam Coonrod .15 .40
165 Kurt Suzuki .15 .40
166 Joe Panik .20 .50
167 Max Muncy .20 .50
168 Ken Giles .15 .40
169 Lance Lynn .15 .40
170 Justin Wilson .15 .40
171 Andrew Stevenson .15 .40
172 Pedro Baez .15 .40
173 Trevor Richards .15 .40
174 Christian Yelich .30 .75
175 Danny Santana .15 .40
176 Dinelson Lamet .15 .40
177 Welington Castillo .15 .40
178 Brandon Crawford .20 .50
179 Austin Dean .15 .40
180 Byron Buxton .25 .60
181 Solak RC/Burke RC 1.25 3.00
182 Chris Paddack .25 .60
183 Ketel Marte .20 .50
184 Manny Margot .15 .40
185 Luis Severino .20 .50
186 Nelson Cruz .25 .60
187 John Gant .15 .40
188 Lux RC/May RC 1.50 4.00
189 Leury Garcia .15 .40
190 Ronald Guzman .15 .40
191 Francisco Mejia .20 .50
192 Victor Reyes .15 .40
193 Brandon Nimmo .20 .50
194 Craig Kimbrel .20 .50
195 Gleyber Torres PO HL .50 1.25
196 Carlos Correa PO HL .25 .60
197 Gerrit Cole PO HL .40 1.00
198 George Springer .25 .60
Carlos Correa PO HL
199 James Paxton PO HL .20 .50
200 Jose Altuve PO HL .20 .50
201 Houston Astros PO HL .15 .40
202 Anibal Sanchez PO HL .20 .50
203 Max Scherzer .25 .60
204 Stephen Strasburg PO HL .25 .60
205 Patrick Corbin PO HL .20 .50
206 Washington Nationals PO HL .15 .40
207 Travis d'Arnaud .20 .50
208 Juan Lagares .15 .40
209 Austin Slater .15 .40
210 Ian Kinsler .20 .50
211 Cam Bedrosian .15 .40
212 Teoscar Hernandez .25 .60
213 Ian Kennedy .15 .40
214 Griffin Canning .25 .60
215 Justin Upton .20 .50
216 Arzrna RC/Frnndz RC 2.50 6.00
217 Archie Bradley .15 .40
218 Lourdes Gurriel Jr. .20 .50
219 Danny Jansen .15 .40
220 Nate Lowe .40 1.00
221 Jacob Stallings RC .40 1.00
222 Anthony DeSclafani .15 .40
223 Jordan Hicks .20 .50
224 Joc Pederson .20 .50
225 Zach Davies .15 .40
226 Ji-Man Choi .15 .40
227 Drew VerHagen .15 .40
228 Mike Fiers .15 .40
229 Dakota Hudson .20 .50
230 Patrick Corbin .20 .50
231 L.Allen RC/Y.Chang RC .50 1.25
232 Joe Musgrove .25 .60
233 Joey Gallo .25 .60
234 Jose Osuna .15 .40
235 Mike Freeman RC .30 .75
236 Jorge Polanco .20 .50
237 Mychal Givens .15 .40
238 Jose Berrios .20 .50
239 Jose Peraza .20 .50
240 Brian Anderson .15 .40
241 Willson Contreras .25 .60
242 Michael Lorenzen .15 .40
243 Aaron Sanchez .20 .50
244 George Springer .20 .50
245 Mike Soroka .25 .60
246 Jesus Aguilar .20 .50
247 Starling RC/Staumont RC .60 1.50
248 Sean Manaea .15 .40
249 Jackie Bradley Jr. .25 .60
250 Erick Fedde .15 .40
251 Ryan Zimmerman .20 .50
252 Nick Wittgren RC .50 1.25
253 Joe Jimenez .15 .40
254 Zach Plesac .25 .60
255 Brandon Lowe .20 .50
256 Brad Peacock .15 .40
257 Cody Bellinger .50 1.25
258 Brad Keller .15 .40
259 Lewis Brinson .15 .40
260 Ryan Pressly .15 .40
261 Jack Flaherty .25 .60
262 A.Munoz RC/M.Baez RC .50 1.25
263 Freddie Freeman .30 .75
264 Jose Altuve .20 .50
265 Keone Kela .15 .40
266 Delino DeShields Jr. .15 .40
267 Ryan Yarbrough .15 .40
268 Tommy Pham .15 .40
269 John Means .25 .60
270 Raisel Iglesias .15 .40
271 Andrew Cashner .15 .40
272 Eugenio Suarez .20 .50
273 Gregory Polanco .20 .50
274 Wilmer Flores .20 .50
275 Franmil Reyes .15 .40
276 L.Webb RC/T.Rogers RC .50 1.25
277 Richie Martin .15 .40
278 Wilson Ramos .15 .40
279 Starlin Castro .15 .40
280 Kirby Yates .15 .40
281 Enrique Hernandez .25 .60
282 Randal Grichuk .15 .40
283 Eric Hosmer .20 .50
284 Mike Minor .15 .40
285 Will Smith .25 .60
286 Ozzie Albies .25 .60
287 Jake Arrieta .20 .50
288 Miles Mikolas .15 .40
289 Willy Adames .15 .40
290 Ian Desmond .15 .40
291 Kris Bryant .30 .75
292 Luis Arraez .30 .75
293 Mike Leake .15 .40
294 Trent Thornton .15 .40
295 Zach Eflin .15 .40
296 Eric Lauer .15 .40
297 Brandon Workman .15 .40
298 Ryan McMahon .25 .60
299 Cam Gallagher .15 .40
300 Renato Nunez .20 .50
301 Freddy Galvis .15 .40
302 Phil Ervin .15 .40
303 Masahiro Tanaka .25 .60
304 Tommy Edman .25 .60
305 Nicky Lopez .15 .40
306 Nomar Mazara .15 .40
307 Kolby Allard .15 .40
308 Manny Machado .25 .60
309 Martin Perez .20 .50
310 Michael Conforto .20 .50
311 Chris Archer .15 .40
312 Carlos Correa .25 .60
313 Thairo Estrada .20 .50
314 Kenta Maeda .20 .50
315 Luke Weaver .15 .40
316 Nick Anderson .15 .40
317 Lzrdo RC/Puk RC/Brwn RC .60 1.50
318 Andrew Heaney .15 .40
319 Kevin Kiermaier .20 .50
320 Adam Eaton .25 .60
321 Ryan Braun .20 .50
322 Nolan Arenado .40 1.00
323 Edwin Diaz .20 .50
324 Jose Ramirez .20 .50
325 Jason Kipnis .20 .50
326 Austin Hays .25 .60
327 Juan Soto WS HL .75 2.00
328 Kurt Suzuki WS HL .15 .40
329 Zack Greinke WS HL .25 .60
330 Alex Bregman WS HL .25 .60
331 Gerrit Cole WS HL .40 1.00
332 Stephen Strasburg WS HL .25 .60
333 Howie Kendrick WS HL .15 .40
334 Washington Nationals WS HL .15 .40
335 Sean Murphy .25 .60
336 Shin-Soo Choo .20 .50
337 Jake Marisnick .15 .40
338 Hector Neris .15 .40
339 Sean Doolittle .15 .40
340 CC Sabathia .20 .50
341 Mike Clevinger .20 .50
342 Jake Junis .15 .40
343 Gonsolin RC/Sborz RC 1.25 3.00
344 Reynaldo Lopez .20 .50
345 Xander Bogaerts .25 .60
346 Trey Mancini .25 .60
347 Jurickson Profar .20 .50
348 Chad Pinder .15 .40
349 C.J. Cron .15 .40
350 Trevor Story .25 .60
351 Ty France .25 .60
352 Mike Tauchman .25 .60
353 J.P. Crawford .15 .40
354 Yoan Moncada .25 .60
355 Amed Rosario .20 .50
356 Jordan Luplow .15 .40
357 Chance Sisco .15 .40
358 Mike Ford .25 .60
359 Roberto Perez .15 .40
360 Andrelton Simmons .15 .40
361 Merrill Kelly .15 .40
362 D.Tate RC/H.Harvey RC .50 1.25
363 Josh Naylor .15 .40
364 Alex Dickerson .15 .40
365 Tyler Glasnow .25 .60
366 Jake Lamb .20 .50
367 Gerrit Cole .40 1.00
368 Junior Guerra .15 .40
369 Yamamoto RC/Diaz RC .50 1.25
370 Matt Carpenter .25 .60
371 Adam Haseley .20 .50
372 Yolmer Sanchez .15 .40
373 Anthony Rizzo .30 .75
374 Brandon Woodruff .25 .60
375 Hansel Robles .15 .40
376 T.Zeuch RC/J.Romano RC .50 1.25
377 Alex Colome .15 .40
378 Tyler Chatwood .15 .40
379 Rowdy Tellez .20 .50
380 Mark Melancon .15 .40
381 Darwinzon Hernandez .15 .40
382 Austin Romine .15 .40
383 Bryan Reynolds .20 .50
384 Chase Anderson .15 .40
385 Clayton Kershaw .40 1.00
386 Dominic Smith .15 .40
387 Matt Boyd .15 .40
388 Niko Goodrum .20 .50
389 Ian Happ .20 .50
390 Dansby Swanson .25 .60
391 Dunn RC/Nola RC/Lewis RC 2.50 6.00
392 Freddy Peralta .15 .40
393 Anthony Santander .15 .40
394 Kevin Pillar .15 .40
395 Aaron Judge .60 1.50
396 Hanser Alberto .15 .40
397 Eric Thames .15 .40
398 Luis Urias .20 .50
399 Jeff Samardzija .15 .40
400 Yadier Molina .30 .75
401 Elvis Andrus SP 1.50 4.00
402 Jorge Alfaro SP 1.25 3.00
403 Juan Soto SP 6.00 15.00
404 Marwin Gonzalez SP 1.25 3.00
405 Dee Gordon SP 1.25 3.00
406 Jacob deGrom SP 4.00 10.00
407 Matt Olson SP 2.00 5.00
408 Yusei Kikuchi SP 1.50 4.00
409 Kyle Schwarber SP 2.00 5.00
410 Corey Seager SP 2.00 5.00
411 Alex Gordon SP 1.50 4.00
412 A.J. Pollock SP 1.25 3.00
413 Keston Hiura SP 2.50 6.00
414 Vladimir Guerrero Jr. SP 3.00 8.00
415 DJ LeMahieu SP 2.00 5.00
416 Lucas Giolito SP 1.50 4.00
417 Blake Snell SP 1.50 4.00
418 Justus Sheffield SP 2.00 5.00
419 Andrew Benintendi SP 2.00 5.00
420 Charlie Blackmon SP 2.00 5.00
421 Stephen Piscotty SP 1.25 3.00
422 Josh Bell SP 1.50 4.00
423 J.D. Martinez SP 2.00 5.00
424 Yasmani Grandal SP 1.25 3.00
425 Michael Brantley SP 1.50 4.00
426 Mike Yastrzemski SP 3.00 8.00
427 Jason Heyward SP 1.50 4.00
428 Noah Syndergaard SP 1.50 4.00
429 Giovanny Gallegos SP 1.25 3.00
430 Sean Newcomb SP 1.25 3.00
431 Robbie Ray SP 1.25 3.00
432 Eddie Rosario SP 1.50 4.00
433 Shohei Ohtani SP 3.00 8.00
434 Dwight Smith Jr. SP 1.25 3.00
435 Lorenzo Cain SP 1.25 3.00
436 Tim Anderson SP 2.00 5.00
437 Fernando Tatis Jr. SP 10.00 25.00
438 German Marquez SP 2.00 5.00
439 Luis Castillo SP 1.50 4.00
440 Jonathan Villar SP 1.25 3.00
441 Miguel Sano SP 1.50 4.00
442 Francisco Lindor SP 2.00 5.00
443 Giancarlo Stanton SP 2.00 5.00
444 Kyle Hendricks SP 2.00 5.00
445 J.D. Davis SP 1.25 3.00
446 Jose Leclerc SP 1.25 3.00
447 Bryce Harper SP 3.00 8.00
448 Amir Garrett SP 1.25 3.00
449 Jon Duplantier SP 1.25 3.00
450 Carlos Martinez SP 1.50 4.00
451 Chris Sale SP 2.00 5.00
452 David Peralta SP 1.25 3.00
453 Alex Bregman SP 2.00 5.00
454 Shane Bieber SP 2.00 5.00
455 Sonny Gray SP 1.50 4.00
456 Andrew McCutchen SP 2.00 5.00
457 Pete Alonso SP 5.00 12.00
458 Jean Segura SP 1.50 4.00
459 Alex Verdugo SP 1.50 4.00
460 Zack Britton SP 1.25 3.00
461 Daniel Vogelbach SP 1.25 3.00
462 Starling Marte SP 1.50 4.00
463 Kole Calhoun SP 1.25 3.00
464 Ronald Acuna Jr. SP 8.00 20.00
465 Max Fried SP 2.00 5.00
466 Mike Trout SP 10.00 25.00
467 Paul Goldschmidt SP 2.00 5.00
468 Matt Chapman SP 2.00 5.00
469 Julio Urias SP 2.00 5.00
470 Ryan O'Hearn SP 1.25 3.00
471 Christian Vazquez SP 1.50 4.00
472 Liam Hendriks SP 1.25 3.00
473 Justin Verlander SP 2.00 5.00
474 Eduardo Escobar SP 1.25 3.00
475 Yu Darvish SP 2.00 5.00
476 Paul DeJong SP 2.00 5.00
477 Hunter Renfroe SP 1.25 3.00
478 David Dahl SP 1.25 3.00
479 Max Kepler SP 1.50 4.00
480 James Paxton SP 1.50 4.00
481 Austin Meadows SP 2.00 5.00
482 Nick Senzel SP 2.00 5.00
483 Gleyber Torres SP 4.00 10.00
484 Aroldis Chapman SP 2.00 5.00
485 David Fletcher SP 2.00 5.00
486 Jon Lester SP 1.50 4.00
487 Hunter Dozier SP 1.25 3.00
488 Christian Walker SP 1.50 4.00
489 Aaron Hicks SP 1.50 4.00
490 Rhys Hoskins SP 2.50 6.00
491 Austin Riley SP 2.50 6.00
492 Jeff McNeil SP 1.50 4.00
493 Mookie Betts SP 4.00 10.00
494 Eloy Jimenez SP 4.00 10.00
495 Ramon Laureano SP 1.50 4.00
496 Walker Buehler SP 2.50 6.00
497 Victor Robles SP 2.50 6.00
498 Charlie Morton SP 2.00 5.00
499 Roberto Osuna SP 1.25 3.00
500 Michael Chavis SP 1.50 4.00
501 Gerrit Cole .40 1.00
502 Mookie Betts .50 1.25
503 Josh Donaldson .20 .50
504 James Karinchak RC .50 1.25
505 Ben Zobrist .20 .50
506 Jonathan Hernandez RC .30 .75
507 Chad Wallach RC .30 .75
508 Corey Kluber .20 .50
509 Brock Holt .15 .40
510 Collin McHugh .15 .40
511 Hunter Pence .20 .50
512 Luis Robert RC 6.00 15.00
513 Freddy Galvis .15 .40
514 Rich Hill .15 .40
515 Jose Rodriguez RC .30 .75
516 Julio Teheran .20 .50
517 Kole Calhoun .15 .40
518 Felix Hernandez .20 .50
519 Chris Davis .15 .40
520 Dallas Keuchel .20 .50
521 Jeremy Jeffress .15 .40
522 Jharel Cotton .15 .40
523 Danny Mendick RC .40 1.00
524 Delino DeShields Jr. .15 .40
525 Rangel Ravelo RC .40 1.00
526 Willi Castro RC .50 1.25
527 Shogo Akiyama .25 .60
528 Robert Dugger RC .30 .75
529 Maikel Franco .20 .50
530 Edwin Rios RC .75 2.00
531 Tom Eshelman RC .40 1.00
532 Francisco Cervelli .15 .40
533 Justin Smoak .15 .40
534 Randy Dobnak RC .60 1.50
535 Dellin Betances .20 .50
536 Michael Wacha .20 .50
537 Tommy Kahnle .15 .40
538 Kenta Maeda .20 .50
539 Sheldon Neuse RC .40 1.00
540 Jon Berti RC .30 .75
541 Kean Wong RC .50 1.25
542 Zack Wheeler .20 .50
543 Garrett Stubbs RC .30 .75
544 Kwang-Hyun Kim .30 .75
545 Emilio Pagan .15 .40
546 Jaylin Davis RC .50 1.25
547 Jake Fraley RC .40 1.00
548 Yoshi Tsutsugo .40 1.00
549 Shun Yamaguchi .20 .50
550 Mitch Moreland .15 .40
551 Miguel Andujar .25 .60
552 Chad Green .15 .40
553 Anthony Rendon .25 .60
554 Yandy Diaz .20 .50
555 Nick Castellanos .25 .60
556 Cole Hamels .20 .50
557 Yasiel Puig .25 .60
558 Stephen Strasburg .25 .60
559 Salvador Perez .20 .50
560 Jose Iglesias .20 .50
561 Jonathan Lucroy .20 .50
562 Andrew Cashner .15 .40
563 Didi Gregorius .20 .50
564 Jose Martinez .15 .40
565 David Price .20 .50
566 Hyun-Jin Ryu .20 .50
567 Michael Kopech .30 .75
568 Robel Garcia RC .30 .75
569 Nomar Mazara .15 .40
570 Corey Dickerson .20 .50
571 Wade Miley .15 .40
572 Jonathan Schoop .15 .40
573 Homer Bailey .15 .40
574 Joey Wendle .20 .50
575 LaMonte Wade Jr. RC .50 1.25
576 Manuel Margot .15 .40
577 Eric Thames .15 .40
578 Steven Souza Jr. .15 .40
579 Austin Dean .15 .40
580 Brad Miller .15 .40
581 Yoenis Cespedes .25 .60
582 Kevin Pillar .15 .40
583 Junior Guerra .15 .40
584 Franchy Cordero .15 .40
585 Jack Mayfield RC .30 .75
586 Tony Kemp .15 .40
587 Edwin Encarnacion .25 .60
588 Carlos Rodon .25 .60
589 Josh Harrison .15 .40
590 Cameron Maybin .15 .40
591 C.J. Cron .15 .40
592 Todd Frazier .15 .40
593 Kyle Gibson .15 .40
594 Kyle Higashioka .25 .60
595 Ehire Adrianza .15 .40
596 Ryan McBroom RC .40 1.00
597 Myles Straw .20 .50
598 Patrick Wisdom .15 .40
599 Eric Lauer .15 .40
600 Ronny Rodriguez .15 .40
601 Brusdar Graterol RC .50 1.25
602 Emmanuel Clase RC .50 1.25
603 Tyrone Taylor RC .30 .75
604 Frankie Montas .15 .40
605 Scott Heineman RC .30 .75
606 Tim Lopes RC .40 1.00
607 Seth Mejias-Brean RC .30 .75
608 Reggie McClain RC .50 1.25
609 Jarrod Dyson .15 .40
610 Brian O'Grady RC .30 .75
611 David Bednar RC .30 .75
612 Tyler Beede .15 .40
613 Carlos Gonzalez .20 .50
614 Tyler Duffey .15 .40
615 Danny Duffy .15 .40
616 Yangervis Solarte .15 .40
617 Wilmer Flores .20 .50
618 Brian Goodwin .15 .40
619 Carl Edwards Jr. .15 .40
620 DJ Stewart .15 .40
621 Michael Taylor .15 .40
622 Lane Thomas .20 .50
623 Daniel Descalso .15 .40
624 Cy Sneed RC .30 .75
625 Trey Wingenter RC .30 .75
626 Alex Avila .15 .40
627 Jason Castro .15 .40
628 Jesus Tinoco RC .30 .75
629 Ryne Harper .15 .40
630 Adolis Garcia .50 1.25
631 Zach Davies .15 .40
632 Dustin Garneau .15 .40
633 Robbie Grossman .15 .40
634 Kelvin Herrera .15 .40
635 Brian Dozier .20 .50
636 Matt Joyce .15 .40
637 Franklin Barreto .15 .40
638 Kyle Farmer .15 .40
639 Travis d'Arnaud .20 .50
640 Peter Fairbanks RC .30 .75
641 Jeff Hoffman .15 .40
642 Luis Torrens .15 .40
643 Tyler Mahle .15 .40
644 Jimmy Nelson .15 .40
645 Jake Diekman .15 .40
646 Greg Bird .20 .50
647 Tanner Roark .15 .40
648 Adrian Houser .15 .40
649 Pedro Strop .15 .40
650 Yohander Mendez RC .30 .75
651 Chris Devenski .15 .40
652 Jalen Beeks .15 .40
653 Jason Kipnis .20 .50
654 Cody Stashak RC .30 .75
655 Drew Steckenrider .15 .40
656 Kevin Ginkel RC .30 .75
657 Matt Wisler .15 .40
658 Keynan Middleton .15 .40
659 Aaron Bummer .15 .40
660 Jeimer Candelario .15 .40
661 Steve Cishek .15 .40
662 Carter Kieboom .20 .50
663 Alex Wood .15 .40
664 Blake Treinen .15 .40
665 Martin Maldonado .15 .40
666 Austin Allen .20 .50
667 Garrett Hampson .15 .40
668 Brad Wieck RC .50 1.25
669 Domingo Santana .20 .50
670 Kevin Kramer .15 .40
671 Matt Strahm .15 .40
672 Johan Camargo .15 .40
673 Howie Kendrick .15 .40
674 Seby Zavala RC .50 1.25
675 Luis Rengifo .15 .40
676 Omar Narvaez .15 .40
677 Brandon Drury .15 .40
678 JaCoby Jones .20 .50
679 Brandon Kintzler .15 .40
680 Robinson Chirinos .15 .40
681 Austin Pruitt .15 .40
682 Luis Guillorme .15 .40
683 Eric Sogard .15 .40
684 Ryan Cordell .15 .40
685 Tyler Clippard .15 .40
686 Luis Cessa .15 .40
687 Sergio Romo .15 .40
688 Josh Phegley .15 .40
689 Shawn Armstrong .15 .40
690 Jeff Mathis .20 .50
691 Roman Quinn .15 .40
692 Jake Bauers .20 .50
693 Jake Marisnick .15 .40
694 Daniel Hudson .15 .40
695 Austin Voth .15 .40
696 Tommy Milone .15 .40
697 Jimmy Cordero .15 .40
698 Tim Locastro .15 .40
699 Tommy Hunter .15 .40
700 Hernan Perez .15 .40
701 Joe Kelly SP 1.25 3.00
702 Rick Porcello SP 1.50 4.00
703 Starling Marte SP 1.50 4.00
704 Ivan Nova SP 1.50 4.00
705 Yonathan Daza SP RC 1.50 4.00
706 Lance McCullers Jr. SP 1.25 3.00
707 Jose Abreu SP 2.00 5.00
708 Kyle Garlick SP RC 2.00 5.00
709 Starlin Castro SP 1.25 3.00
710 Jake Cave SP 1.50 4.00
711 Alec Mills SP RC 1.25 3.00
712 Lucas Sims SP 1.25 3.00
713 Luis Urias SP 1.50 4.00
714 Daniel Ponce de Leon SP 1.25 3.00
715 Wade Davis SP 1.25 3.00
716 Kevin Gausman SP 2.00 5.00
717 Nestor Cortes SP 1.25 3.00
718 Jordan Lyles SP 1.25 3.00
719 Francisco Liriano SP 1.25 3.00
720 Wilmer Difo SP 1.25 3.00
721 Alex Blandino SP 1.25 3.00
722 Tyler O'Neill SP 1.50 4.00
723 Marcell Ozuna SP 2.00 5.00
724 Drew Pomeranz SP 1.25 3.00
725 Alex Verdugo SP 1.50 4.00

2020 Topps Heritage Action Variations

STATED ODDS 1:27 HOBBY
STATED HN ODDS 1:XX HOBBY
52 Bo Bichette 40.00 100.00
54 Yordan Alvarez 25.00 60.00
54 Aristides Aquino 8.00 20.00
121 Nico Hoerner 8.00 20.00
142 Javier Baez 4.00 10.00
145 Rafael Devers 4.00 10.00
174 Christian Yelich 4.00 10.00
188 Gavin Lux 20.00 50.00
257 Cody Bellinger 6.00 15.00
291 Kris Bryant 4.00 10.00
308 Manny Machado 3.00 8.00
322 Nolan Arenado 5.00 12.00
385 Clayton Kershaw 5.00 12.00
403 Juan Soto 10.00 25.00
414 Vladimir Guerrero Jr. 5.00 12.00
430 Shohei Ohtani 5.00 12.00
437 Fernando Tatis Jr. 30.00 80.00
442 Francisco Lindor 6.00 15.00
447 Bryce Harper 8.00 20.00
453 Alex Bregman 3.00 8.00
457 Pete Alonso 8.00 20.00
464 Ronald Acuna Jr. 15.00 40.00
466 Mike Trout 30.00 80.00
473 Justin Verlander 3.00 8.00
493 Mookie Betts 10.00 25.00
502 Mookie Betts 10.00 25.00
503 Josh Donaldson 5.00 12.00
505 Anthony Rizzo 12.00 30.00
512 Luis Robert 50.00 120.00
520 Dallas Keuchel 4.00 10.00
523 Danny Mendick 10.00 25.00
526 Willi Castro 25.00 60.00
527 Shogo Akiyama 10.00 25.00
530 Edwin Rios 5.00 12.00
543 Garrett Stubbs 8.00 20.00
544 Kwang-Hyun Kim 4.00 10.00
548 Yoshi Tsutsugo 4.00 10.00
549 Shun Yamaguchi 2.50 6.00
553 Anthony Rendon 8.00 20.00
555 Nick Castellanos 6.00 15.00
557 Yasiel Puig 5.00 12.00
558 Stephen Strasburg 6.00 15.00
559 Salvador Perez 6.00 15.00
565 David Price 6.00 15.00
579 Yadier Molina 8.00 20.00
601 Brusdar Graterol 10.00 25.00
663 Walker Buehler 12.00 30.00
702 Jacob deGrom 15.00 40.00
723 Marcell Ozuna 8.00 20.00

2020 Topps Heritage French Text

*FRENCH: 6X TO 15X BASIC
*FRENCH RC: 3X TO 8X BASIC RC
STATED ODDS 1:243 HOBBY
STATED HN ODDS 1:XXX HOBBY
40 Joey Votto 10.00 25.00
41 Miguel Cabrera 12.00 30.00
52 Bichette/Kay 40.00 100.00
54 Alvarez/Aquino 75.00 200.00
145 Rafael Devers 8.00 20.00
174 Christian Yelich 12.00 30.00
291 Kris Bryant 25.00 60.00
317 Luzardo/Puk/Brown 10.00 25.00
501 Gerrit Cole 20.00 50.00
502 Mookie Betts 25.00 60.00
512 Luis Robert 250.00 600.00
530 Edwin Rios 12.00 30.00
534 Randy Dobnak 10.00 25.00
567 Michael Kopech 10.00 25.00

2020 Topps Heritage Missing Signature Variations

STATED ODDS 1:2009 HOBBY
STATED HN ODDS 1:XXX HOBBY
145 Rafael Devers 10.00 25.00
174 Christian Yelich 10.00 25.00
257 Cody Bellinger 15.00 40.00
395 Aaron Judge 40.00 100.00
403 Juan Soto 25.00 60.00
414 Vladimir Guerrero Jr. 25.00 60.00
437 Fernando Tatis Jr. 40.00 100.00
453 Alex Bregman 15.00 40.00
457 Pete Alonso 20.00 50.00
464 Ronald Acuna Jr. 30.00 80.00
466 Mike Trout 60.00 150.00
483 Gleyber Torres 20.00 50.00
501 Gerrit Cole 40.00 100.00
502 Mookie Betts 40.00 100.00
503 Josh Donaldson 40.00 100.00
512 Luis Robert 100.00 250.00
527 Shogo Akiyama 10.00 25.00
530 Edwin Rios 20.00 50.00
544 Kwang-Hyun Kim 10.00 25.00
548 Yoshi Tsutsugo 12.00 30.00
549 Shun Yamaguchi 20.00 50.00
553 Anthony Rendon 15.00 40.00
558 Stephen Strasburg 20.00 50.00
565 David Price 12.00 30.00

2020 Topps Heritage Nickname Variations

STATED ODDS 1:2414 HOBBY
STATED HN ODDS 1:XXX HOBBY
174 Christian Yelich 15.00 40.00
257 Cody Bellinger 25.00 60.00
395 Aaron Judge 50.00 120.00
414 Vladimir Guerrero Jr. 20.00 50.00
447 Bryce Harper 30.00 80.00
453 Alex Bregman 8.00 20.00
457 Pete Alonso 40.00 100.00
464 Ronald Acuna Jr. 30.00 80.00
466 Mike Trout 100.00 250.00
483 Gleyber Torres 25.00 60.00
501 Gerrit Cole 25.00 60.00
502 Josh Donaldson 25.00 60.00
512 Luis Robert 100.00 250.00
553 Anthony Rendon 25.00 60.00
723 Marcell Ozuna 8.00 20.00

2020 Topps Heritage Silver Team Name Variations

STATED ODDS 1:265 HOBBY
STATED HN ODDS 1:XXX HOBBY
82 Max Scherzer 10.00 25.00
142 Javier Baez 8.00 20.00
145 Rafael Devers 8.00 20.00
257 Cody Bellinger 12.00 30.00
264 Jose Altuve 5.00 12.00
291 Kris Bryant 8.00 20.00
373 Anthony Rizzo 8.00 20.00
385 Clayton Kershaw 10.00 25.00
395 Aaron Judge 15.00 40.00
403 Juan Soto 20.00 50.00
414 Vladimir Guerrero Jr. 10.00 25.00
415 DJ LeMahieu 6.00 15.00
423 J.D. Martinez 6.00 15.00
433 Shohei Ohtani 10.00 25.00
437 Fernando Tatis Jr. 30.00 80.00
442 Francisco Lindor 6.00 15.00
453 Alex Bregman 6.00 15.00
457 Pete Alonso 25.00 60.00
464 Ronald Acuna Jr. 25.00 60.00
466 Mike Trout 30.00 80.00
473 Justin Verlander 6.00 15.00
483 Gleyber Torres 12.00 30.00
490 Rhys Hoskins 8.00 20.00

494 Eloy Jimenez 12.00 30.00
501 Gerrit Cole 60.00 150.00
502 Mookie Betts 30.00 80.00
503 Josh Donaldson 15.00 40.00
512 Luis Robert 75.00 200.00
520 Dallas Keuchel 12.00 30.00
523 Danny Mendick 10.00 25.00
526 Willi Castro 30.00 80.00
527 Shogo Akiyama 20.00 50.00
530 Edwin Rios 15.00 40.00
541 Kean Wong 10.00 25.00
542 Zack Wheeler 15.00 40.00
543 Garrett Stubbs 20.00 50.00
544 Kwang-Hyun Kim 15.00 40.00
548 Yoshi Tsutsugo 12.00 30.00
549 Shun Yamaguchi 12.00 30.00
555 Nick Castellanos 12.00 30.00
556 Cole Hamels 12.00 30.00
557 Yasiel Puig 12.00 30.00
558 Stephen Strasburg 15.00 40.00
559 Salvador Perez 12.00 30.00
565 David Price 12.00 30.00
601 Brusdar Graterol 30.00 80.00
603 Tyrone Taylor 15.00 40.00
702 Rick Porcello 20.00 50.00
723 Marcell Ozuna 20.00 50.00

2020 Topps Heritage White Border

*WHITE: 10X TO 25X BASIC
*WHITE RC: 6X TO 15X BASIC RC
*WHITE SP: 1.2X TO 3X BASIC SP
STATED ODDS 1:67 HOBBY
ANNCD PRINT RUN 50 SER.#'d SETS
5 Gary Sanchez 10.00 25.00
13 Cease/Collins 20.00 50.00
39 Rogers/Alexander 10.00 25.00
40 Joey Votto 15.00 40.00
41 Miguel Cabrera 20.00 50.00
52 Bichette/Kay 60.00 510.00
54 Alvarez/Aquino 125.00 300.00
145 Rafael Devers 12.00 30.00
174 Christian Yelich 20.00 50.00
188 Lux/May 75.00 200.00
257 Cody Bellinger 40.00 100.00
291 Kris Bryant 15.00 40.00
317 Luzardo/Puk/Brown 30.00 80.00
395 Aaron Judge 60.00 150.00
400 Yadier Molina 15.00 40.00
403 Juan Soto 25.00 60.00
414 Vladimir Guerrero Jr. 40.00 100.00
433 Shohei Ohtani 20.00 50.00
437 Fernando Tatis Jr. 50.00 120.00
447 Bryce Harper 25.00 60.00
457 Pete Alonso 30.00 80.00
464 Ronald Acuna Jr. 75.00 200.00
466 Mike Trout 200.00 500.00
483 Gleyber Torres 25.00 60.00
493 Mookie Betts 15.00 40.00
496 Walker Buehler 25.00 60.00
502 Mookie Betts 60.00 150.00
512 Luis Robert 300.00 800.00
530 Edwin Rios 40.00 100.00
534 Randy Dobnak 20.00 50.00

2020 Topps Heritage '20 Sticker Collection Preview

1 Mike Trout 6.00 15.00
2 Yordan Alvarez 8.00 20.00
3 Gleyber Torres 2.50 6.00
4 Vladimir Guerrero Jr. 2.00 5.00
5 Max Scherzer 1.25 3.00
6 Paul Goldschmidt 1.25 3.00
7 Christian Yelich 1.50 4.00
8 Ronald Acuna Jr. 5.00 12.00
9 Clayton Kershaw 2.00 5.00
10 Francisco Lindor 1.25 3.00

2020 Topps Heritage '71 Bazooka Numbered Test

STATED ODDS 1:8 BLASTER PACKS
1 Mike Trout 10.00 25.00
2 Alex Bregman 1.00 2.50
3 Matt Chapman 1.00 2.50
4 Vladimir Guerrero Jr. 1.50 4.00
5 Ronald Acuna Jr. 4.00 10.00
6 Christian Yelich 1.25 3.00
7 Paul Goldschmidt 1.00 2.50
8 Javier Baez 1.25 3.00
9 Ketel Marte .75 2.00
10 Cody Bellinger 2.00 5.00
11 Buster Posey 1.25 3.00
12 Francisco Lindor 1.00 2.50
13 Daniel Vogelbach .60 1.50
14 Brian Anderson .60 1.50
15 Pete Alonso 2.50 6.00
16 Juan Soto 3.00 8.00
17 Trey Mancini 1.00 2.50
18 Fernando Tatis Jr. 5.00 12.00
19 Bryce Harper 1.50 4.00
20 Josh Bell .75 2.00
21 Rougned Odor .75 2.00
22 Austin Meadows 1.00 2.50
23 Rafael Devers 1.25 3.00
24 Aristides Aquino 1.50 4.00
25 Nolan Arenado 1.50 4.00

2020 Topps Heritage '71 Postal Stamps

STATED ODDS 1:6044 HOBBY
STATED PRINT RUN 50 SER.#'d SETS
71USAK Al Kaline 60.00 150.00
71USBG Bob Gibson
71USBR Brooks Robinson 50.00 120.00
71USCY Carl Yastrzemski 30.00 80.00
71USFJ Fergie Jenkins 20.00 50.00
71USHA Hank Aaron 50.00 120.00
71USHK Harmon Killebrew 25.00 60.00
71USJB Johnny Bench 40.00 100.00
71USJP Jim Palmer
71USJT Joe Torre 20.00 50.00
71USLB Lou Brock 20.00 50.00
71USNR Nolan Ryan 50.00 120.00
71USRC Rod Carew 40.00 100.00
71USRCL Roberto Clemente 75.00 200.00
71USRJ Reggie Jackson 25.00 60.00
71USSC Steve Carlton 40.00 100.00
71USTS Tom Seaver 25.00 60.00
71USWM Willie Mays 60.00 150.00
71USWMC Willie McCovey 25.00 60.00
71USWS Willie Stargell 40.00 100.00

2020 Topps Heritage '71 Topps Baseball Tattoos

STATED ODDS 1:728 BLSTR PACKS
NO HN PRICING DUE TO LACK OF MARKET INFO
1 Yordan Alvarez 25.00 60.00
2 Vladimir Guerrero Jr. 6.00 15.00
3 S.Ohtani/M.Trout 100.00 250.00
4 Christian Yelich 15.00 40.00
5 Paul Goldschmidt 4.00 10.00
6 M.Chapman/R.Laureano 4.00 10.00
7 Zack Greinke 4.00 10.00
8 Buster Posey 5.00 12.00
9 A.Riley/R.Acuna Jr. 15.00 40.00
10 Francisco Lindor 4.00 10.00
11 Pete Alonso 10.00 25.00
12 K.Bryant/J.Baez 15.00 40.00
13 Max Scherzer 8.00 20.00
14 Fernando Tatis Jr. 12.00 30.00
15 C.Bellinger/C.Kershaw 15.00 40.00
16 Josh Bell 8.00 20.00
17 Elvis Andrus 3.00 8.00
18 D.Gordon/D.Vogelbach 2.50 6.00
19 Blake Snell 6.00 15.00
20 Nick Senzel 12.00 30.00
21 J.Yamamoto/J.Alfaro 2.50 6.00
22 Nolan Arenado 8.00 20.00
23 Whit Merrifield 6.00 15.00
24 G.Torres/A.Judge 20.00 50.00
25 Miguel Cabrera 10.00 25.00
26 Mookie Betts 10.00 25.00
27 B.Harper/R.Hoskins 12.00 30.00
28 Eloy Jimenez 8.00 20.00
29 Trey Mancini 8.00 20.00
30 J.Berrios/M.Kepler 10.00 25.00

2020 Topps Heritage '71 Topps Greatest Moments Boxloader

STATED ODDS 1:3 HOBBY BOXES
1 Roberto Clemente 30.00 80.00
2 Tony Oliva 12.00 30.00
3 Joe Torre 8.00 20.00
4 Willie Stargell 12.00 30.00
5 Harmon Killebrew 12.00 30.00
6 Fergie Jenkins 12.00 30.00
7 Lou Brock 10.00 25.00
8 Tom Seaver 10.00 25.00
9 Brooks Robinson 12.00 30.00
10 Hank Aaron 12.00 30.00
11 Johnny Bench 15.00 40.00
12 Bob Gibson 10.00 25.00
13 Reggie Jackson 20.00 50.00
14 Jim Palmer 8.00 20.00
15 Willie Mays 6.00 15.00
16 Rod Carew 8.00 20.00
17 Catfish Hunter 4.00 10.00
18 Al Kaline 15.00 40.00
19 Willie McCovey 10.00 25.00
20 Tony Perez 12.00 30.00
21 Mike Trout 15.00 40.00
22 Alex Bregman 8.00 20.00
23 Vladimir Guerrero Jr. 8.00 20.00
24 Justin Verlander 5.00 12.00
25 Ronald Acuna Jr. 10.00 25.00
26 Christian Yelich 6.00 15.00
27 Yadier Molina 10.00 25.00
28 Kris Bryant 10.00 25.00
29 Max Scherzer 8.00 20.00
30 Cody Bellinger 10.00 25.00
31 Buster Posey 6.00 15.00
32 Francisco Lindor 5.00 12.00
33 Clayton Kershaw 8.00 20.00
34 Pete Alonso 12.00 30.00
35 Juan Soto 10.00 25.00
36 Fernando Tatis Jr. 12.00 30.00
37 Bryce Harper 8.00 20.00
38 Nolan Arenado 8.00 20.00
39 Anthony Rizzo 10.00 25.00
40 Aaron Judge 12.00 30.00
41 Jacob deGrom 6.00 15.00
42 Rafael Devers 6.00 15.00
43 Miguel Cabrera 15.00 40.00
44 Mookie Betts 10.00 25.00
45 Shohei Ohtani 10.00 25.00
46 Manny Machado 8.00 20.00
47 Gleyber Torres 10.00 25.00
48 Keston Hiura 6.00 15.00
49 Rhys Hoskins 6.00 15.00
50 Aristides Aquino 8.00 20.00
51 Yordan Alvarez 10.00 25.00
52 Bo Bichette 8.00 20.00
53 Brendan McKay 5.00 12.00
54 Gavin Lux 8.00 20.00
55 Kyle Lewis 10.00 25.00

2020 Topps Heritage '71 Topps Scratch Offs

1 Shohei Ohtani 1.00 2.50
2 Yordan Alvarez 4.00 10.00
3 Matt Chapman .60 1.50
4 Vladimir Guerrero Jr. 1.00 2.50
5 Ronald Acuna Jr. 2.50 6.00
6 Christian Yelich .75 2.00
7 Paul Goldschmidt .60 1.50
8 Kris Bryant .75 2.00
9 Ketel Marte .50 1.25
10 Cody Bellinger 1.25 3.00
11 Evan Longoria .50 1.25
12 Francisco Lindor .60 1.50
13 Dee Gordon .40 1.00
14 Brian Anderson .40 1.00
15 Pete Alonso 1.50 4.00
16 Luis Robert 3.00 8.00
17 Jorge Soler .60 1.50
18 Miguel Cabrera .60 1.50
19 Aaron Judge 1.50 4.00
20 Jose Berrios .50 1.25
21 Rafael Devers .75 2.00
22 Blake Snell .50 1.25
23 Trey Mancini .60 1.50
24 Bryce Harper 1.00 2.50
25 Juan Soto 2.00 5.00
26 Joey Votto .60 1.50
27 Josh Bell .50 1.25
28 Nolan Arenado 1.00 2.50
29 Fernando Tatis Jr. 3.00 8.00
30 Joey Gallo .60 1.50

2020 Topps Heritage '71 Topps Super Baseball Boxloader

STATED ODDS 1:5 HOBBY BOXES
1 Vladimir Guerrero Jr. 2.50 6.00
2 Fernando Tatis Jr. 8.00 20.00
3 Ronald Acuna Jr. 6.00 15.00
4 Yordan Alvarez 10.00 25.00
5 Mike Trout 15.00 40.00
6 Max Scherzer 3.00 8.00
7 Javier Baez 5.00 12.00
8 Eloy Jimenez 3.00 8.00
9 Christian Yelich 4.00 10.00
10 Clayton Kershaw 2.50 6.00
11 Shohei Ohtani 4.00 10.00
12 Cody Bellinger 5.00 12.00
13 Pete Alonso 4.00 10.00
14 Aaron Judge 6.00 15.00
15 Bo Bichette 8.00 20.00
16 Paul Goldschmidt 10.00 25.00
17 Christian Yelich 12.00 30.00
18 Nick Senzel 10.00 25.00
19 Gerrit Cole 8.00 20.00
20 Gleyber Torres 3.00 8.00
21 Luis Robert 15.00 40.00
22 Rafael Devers 6.00 15.00
23 Keston Hiura 12.00 30.00
24 Juan Soto 10.00 25.00
25 Anthony Rendon 8.00 20.00
26 Jacob deGrom 8.00 20.00
27 Gavin Lux 10.00 25.00
28 Kris Bryant 12.00 30.00
29 Justin Verlander 10.00 25.00
30 Bryce Harper 10.00 25.00

2020 Topps Heritage '71 Topps Super Baseball Boxloader Autographs

STATED ODDS 1:383 HOBBY BOXES
EXCHANGE DEADLINE 1/31/2022
HN EXCH DEADLINE 10/31/2022
STATED HN ODDS 1:XXX HOBBY BOXES
1 Vladimir Guerrero Jr. 100.00 250.00
4 Yordan Alvarez 150.00 400.00
5 Mike Trout
13 Pete Alonso 75.00 200.00
14 Aaron Judge 200.00 500.00
20 Gleyber Torres HN 100.00 250.00
22 Rafael Devers HN
23 Keston Hiura HN 30.00 80.00
24 Juan Soto HN 75.00 200.00

2020 Topps Heritage 20 Gigantic Seasons

COMPLETE SET (20) 15.00 40.00
STATED ODDS 1:14 HOBBY
1 Willie Mays 1.25 3.00
2 Willie Mays 1.25 3.00
3 Willie Mays 1.25 3.00
4 Willie Mays 1.25 3.00
5 Willie Mays 1.25 3.00
6 Willie Mays 1.25 3.00
7 Willie Mays 1.25 3.00
8 Willie Mays 1.25 3.00
9 Willie Mays 1.25 3.00
10 Willie Mays 1.25 3.00
11 Willie Mays 1.25 3.00
12 Willie Mays 1.25 3.00
13 Willie Mays 1.25 3.00
14 Willie Mays 1.25 3.00
15 Willie Mays 1.25 3.00
16 Willie Mays 1.25 3.00
17 Willie Mays 1.25 3.00
18 Willie Mays 1.25 3.00
19 Willie Mays 1.25 3.00
20 Willie Mays 1.25 3.00

2020 Topps Heritage Baseball Flashbacks

COMPLETE SET (15) 8.00 20.00
STATED ODDS 1:18 HOBBY
BF1 Hank Aaron 1.25 3.00
BF2 Bert Blyleven .50 1.25
BF3 Bob Gibson .50 1.25
BF4 Johnny Bench .60 1.50
BF5 Rod Carew .50 1.25
BF6 Reggie Jackson .50 1.25
BF7 Nolan Ryan 2.00 5.00
BF8 Don Sutton .50 1.25
BF9 Carlton Fisk .50 1.25
BF10 Carl Yastrzemski 1.00 2.50
BF11 Roberto Clemente 1.50 4.00
BF12 Joe Torre .50 1.25
BF13 Willie Stargell .50 1.25
BF14 Tom Seaver .50 1.25
BF15 Brooks Robinson .50 1.25

2020 Topps Heritage Chrome

STATED ODDS 1:60 HOBBY
STATED PRINT RUN 999 SER.#'d SETS
*PURPLE REF: .4X TO 1X BASIC
THC8 Gio Urshela 2.00 5.00
THC17 Yuli Gurriel 1.50 4.00
THC18 Josh Reddick 1.25 3.00
THC22 Julio Teheran 1.50 4.00
THC23 Scott Kingery 1.50 4.00
THC24 Mike Moustakas 1.50 4.00
THC32 Evan Longoria 1.50 4.00
THC35 Jorge Soler 2.00 5.00
THC41 Miguel Cabrera 2.00 5.00
THC52 Bo Bichette 12.00 30.00
Anthony Kay
THC53 Aaron Nola 1.50 4.00
THC54 Y.Alvarez/A.Aquino 15.00 40.00
THC56 Carlos Santana 1.50 4.00
THC75 J.T. Realmuto 2.00 5.00
THC78 Albert Pujols 2.50 6.00
THC82 Max Scherzer 2.00 5.00
THC118 Whit Merrifield 2.00 5.00
THC121 N.Hoerner/A.Alzolay 5.00 12.00
THC142 Javier Baez 2.50 6.00
THC145 Rafael Devers 2.50 6.00
THC149 Zack Greinke 2.00 5.00
THC154 Trea Turner 1.50 4.00
THC167 Max Muncy 1.50 4.00
THC174 Christian Yelich 2.50 6.00
THC175 Danny Santana 1.25 3.00
THC182 Chris Paddack 2.00 5.00
THC183 Ketel Marte 1.50 4.00
THC188 G.Lux/D.May 6.00 15.00
THC194 Craig Kimbrel 1.50 4.00
THC229 Dakota Hudson 1.50 4.00
THC230 Patrick Corbin 1.50 4.00
THC236 Jorge Polanco 1.50 4.00
THC240 Brian Anderson 1.25 3.00
THC241 Willson Contreras 2.00 5.00
THC244 George Springer 1.50 4.00
THC245 Mike Soroka 2.00 5.00
THC257 Cody Bellinger 4.00 10.00
THC260 Ryan Pressly 1.25 3.00
THC261 Jack Flaherty 2.00 5.00
THC272 Eugenio Suarez 1.50 4.00
THC285 Will Smith 2.00 5.00
THC286 Ozzie Albies 2.00 5.00
THC310 Michael Conforto 1.50 4.00
THC312 Carlos Correa 2.00 5.00
THC317 Luzardo/Puk/Brown 2.50 6.00
THC320 Adam Eaton 2.00 5.00
THC321 Ryan Braun 1.50 4.00
THC322 Nolan Arenado 3.00 8.00
THC341 Mike Clevinger 1.50 4.00
THC345 Xander Bogaerts 2.00 5.00
THC346 Trey Mancini 2.00 5.00
THC350 Trevor Story 2.00 5.00
THC373 Anthony Rizzo 2.50 6.00
THC383 Bryan Reynolds 1.50 4.00
THC394 Kevin Pillar 1.25 3.00
THC395 Aaron Judge 5.00 12.00
THC401 Elvis Andrus 1.50 4.00
THC403 Juan Soto 6.00 15.00
THC406 Jacob deGrom 4.00 10.00
THC407 Matt Olson 2.00 5.00
THC410 Corey Seager 2.00 5.00
THC413 Keston Hiura 2.50 6.00
THC414 Vladimir Guerrero Jr. 3.00 8.00
THC415 DJ LeMahieu 2.00 5.00
THC416 Lucas Giolito 1.50 4.00
THC419 Andrew Benintendi 2.00 5.00
THC422 Josh Bell 1.50 4.00
THC423 J.D. Martinez 2.00 5.00
THC425 Michael Brantley 1.50 4.00
THC426 Mike Yastrzemski 3.00 8.00
THC432 Eddie Rosario 1.50 4.00
THC433 Shohei Ohtani 3.00 8.00
THC436 Tim Anderson 2.00 5.00
THC437 Fernando Tatis Jr. 30.00 80.00
THC439 Luis Castillo 1.50 4.00
THC442 Francisco Lindor 2.00 5.00
THC445 J.D. Davis 1.25 3.00
THC447 Bryce Harper 3.00 8.00
THC451 Chris Sale 2.00 5.00
THC457 Pete Alonso 5.00 12.00
THC461 Daniel Vogelbach 1.25 3.00
THC464 Ronald Acuna Jr. 8.00 20.00
THC465 Max Fried 2.00 5.00
THC466 Mike Trout 25.00 60.00
THC467 Paul Goldschmidt 2.00 5.00
THC468 Matt Chapman 2.00 5.00
THC473 Justin Verlander 2.00 5.00
THC474 Eduardo Escobar 1.25 3.00
THC476 Paul DeJong 2.00 5.00
THC478 David Dahl 1.25 3.00
THC479 Max Kepler 1.50 4.00
THC481 Austin Meadows 2.00 5.00
THC482 Nick Senzel 2.00 5.00
THC483 Gleyber Torres 4.00 10.00
THC488 Christian Walker 1.50 4.00
THC492 Jeff McNeil 1.50 4.00
THC494 Eloy Jimenez 4.00 10.00
THC495 Ramon Laureano 1.50 4.00
THC496 Walker Buehler 2.50 6.00
THC498 Charlie Morton 2.00 5.00
THC501 Gerrit Cole 3.00 8.00
THC502 Mookie Betts 15.00 40.00
THC503 Josh Donaldson 1.50 4.00
THC505 Ben Zobrist 1.50 4.00
THC508 Corey Kluber 1.50 4.00
THC509 Brock Holt 1.25 3.00
THC510 Collin McHugh 1.25 3.00
THC511 Hunter Pence 1.50 4.00
THC512 Luis Robert 60.00 150.00
THC513 Freddy Galvis 1.25 3.00
THC514 Rich Hill 1.25 3.00
THC515 Jose Rodriguez 1.25 3.00
THC516 Julio Teheran 1.50 4.00
THC517 Kole Calhoun 1.25 3.00
THC518 Felix Hernandez 1.50 4.00
THC519 Chris Davis 1.25 3.00
THC521 Jeremy Jeffress 1.25 3.00
THC522 Jharel Cotton 1.25 3.00
THC523 Danny Mendick 1.50 4.00
THC524 Delino DeShields 1.25 3.00
THC526 Willi Castro 2.00 5.00
THC527 Shogo Akiyama 2.00 5.00
THC529 Maikel Franco 1.50 4.00
THC530 Edwin Rios 3.00 8.00
THC532 Francisco Cervelli 1.25 3.00
THC533 Justin Smoak 1.25 3.00
THC534 Randy Dobnak 2.50 6.00
THC535 Dellin Betances 1.50 4.00
THC536 Michael Wacha 1.50 4.00
THC537 Tommy Kahnle 1.25 3.00
THC538 Kenta Maeda 1.50 4.00
THC539 Sheldon Neuse 1.50 4.00
THC540 Jon Berti 1.25 3.00
THC541 Kean Wong 2.00 5.00
THC542 Zack Wheeler 1.50 4.00
THC543 Garrett Stubbs 1.25 3.00
THC544 Kwang-Hyun Kim 2.50 6.00
THC545 Emilio Pagan 1.25 3.00
THC546 Jaylin Davis 2.00 5.00
THC547 Jake Fraley 1.50 4.00
THC548 Yoshi Tsutsugo 3.00 8.00
THC549 Shun Yamaguchi 1.50 4.00
THC702 Rick Porcello 1.50 4.00
THC705 Yonathan Daza 1.50 4.00
THC706 Lance McCullers Jr. 1.25 3.00
THC707 Jose Abreu 2.00 5.00
THC708 Kyle Garlick 2.00 5.00
THC709 Starlin Castro 1.25 3.00
THC723 Marcell Ozuna 2.00 5.00
THC725 Alex Verdugo 1.50 4.00

2020 Topps Heritage Chrome Refractors

*REF: .6X TO 1.5X BASIC
STATED ODDS 1:106 HOBBY
STATED PRINT RUN 571 SER.#'d SETS
THC403 Juan Soto 12.00 30.00

2020 Topps Heritage Chrome White Refractors

*WHITE REF: 2X TO 5X BASIC
STATED ODDS 1:849 HOBBY
STATED PRINT RUN 71 SER.#'d SETS
THC403 Juan Soto 40.00 100.00
THC464 Ronald Acuna Jr. 75.00 200.00

2020 Topps Heritage Chrome Spring Mega Box

INSERTED IN
STATED PRINT RUN 999 SER.#'d SETS
*REF/571: .6X TO 1.5X BASIC
*WHITE REF/71: 1.2X TO 3X BASIC
THC2 Trevor Bauer 2.50 6.00
THC5 Gary Sanchez 2.00 5.00
THC30 Justin Turner 2.00 5.00
THC33 Ender Inciarte 1.25 3.00
THC36 Kenley Jansen 1.50 4.00
THC40 Joey Votto 2.00 5.00
THC44 Brendan Rodgers 2.00 5.00
THC60 Mark Canha 1.25 3.00
THC81 Khris Davis 2.00 5.00
THC86 Colin Moran 1.25 3.00
THC87 Josh Hader 1.50 4.00
THC93 Z.Gallen/A.Young 3.00 8.00
THC94 Marco Gonzales 1.25 3.00
THC96 Mitch Garver 1.25 3.00
THC98 Marcus Semien 2.00 5.00
THC101 Brad Hand 1.25 3.00
THC103 Adalberto Mondesi 1.50 4.00
THC106 James McCann 1.50 4.00
THC112 Nick Ahmed 1.25 3.00
THC113 Eduardo Rodriguez 1.25 3.00
THC116 T.Grisham/M.Dubon 5.00 12.00
THC117 Marcus Stroman 1.50 4.00
THC120 Willians Astudillo 1.25 3.00
THC124 Kolten Wong 1.50 4.00
THC126 Edwin Encarnacion 2.00 5.00
THC130 Clint Frazier 1.50 4.00
THC131 Luke Voit 2.50 6.00
THC133 Buster Posey 2.50 6.00
THC139 Kevin Newman 2.00 5.00
THC160 Domingo Santana 1.50 4.00
THC162 David Price 1.50 4.00
THC168 Ken Giles 1.25 3.00
THC187 John Gant 1.25 3.00
THC218 Lourdes Gurriel Jr. 1.50 4.00
THC224 Joc Pederson 1.50 4.00
THC228 Mike Fiers 1.25 3.00
THC233 Joey Gallo 2.00 5.00
THC238 Jose Berrios 1.50 4.00
THC242 Michael Lorenzen 1.25 3.00
THC263 Freddie Freeman 2.50 6.00
THC264 Jose Altuve 1.50 4.00
THC267 Ryan Yarbrough 1.25 3.00
THC269 John Means 2.00 5.00
THC278 Wilson Ramos 1.25 3.00
THC279 Starlin Castro 1.25 3.00
THC280 Kirby Yates 1.25 3.00
THC282 Randal Grichuk 1.25 3.00
THC283 Eric Hosmer 1.50 4.00
THC284 Mike Minor 1.25 3.00
THC291 Kris Bryant 2.50 6.00
THC292 Luis Arraez 2.50 6.00
THC298 Ryan McMahon 2.00 5.00
THC300 Renato Nunez 1.50 4.00
THC303 Masahiro Tanaka 2.00 5.00
THC306 Nomar Mazara 1.25 3.00
THC308 Manny Machado 2.00 5.00
THC324 Jose Ramirez 1.50 4.00
THC336 Shin-Soo Choo 1.50 4.00
THC354 Yoan Moncada 2.00 5.00
THC355 Amed Rosario 1.50 4.00
THC360 Andrelton Simmons 1.25 3.00
THC374 Brandon Woodruff 2.00 5.00
THC385 Clayton Kershaw 3.00 8.00
THC387 Matt Boyd 1.25 3.00
THC390 Dansby Swanson 2.00 5.00
THC396 Hanser Alberto 1.25 3.00
THC397 Eric Thames 1.25 3.00
THC400 Yadier Molina 2.50 6.00
THC402 Jorge Alfaro 1.25 3.00
THC405 Dee Gordon 1.25 3.00
THC408 Yusei Kikuchi 1.50 4.00
THC409 Kyle Schwarber 2.00 5.00
THC417 Blake Snell 1.50 4.00
THC420 Charlie Blackmon 2.00 5.00
THC424 Yasmani Grandal 1.25 3.00
THC427 Jason Heyward 1.50 4.00
THC428 Noah Syndergaard 1.50 4.00
THC431 Robbie Ray 1.25 3.00
THC435 Lorenzo Cain 1.25 3.00
THC441 Miguel Sano 1.50 4.00
THC443 Giancarlo Stanton 2.00 5.00
THC444 Kyle Hendricks 2.00 5.00
THC453 Alex Bregman 2.00 5.00
THC454 Shane Bieber 2.00 5.00
THC455 Sonny Gray 1.50 4.00
THC458 Jean Segura 1.50 4.00
THC459 Alex Verdugo 1.50 4.00
THC462 Starling Marte 1.50 4.00
THC463 Kole Calhoun 1.25 3.00
THC472 Liam Hendriks 1.25 3.00
THC477 Hunter Renfroe 1.25 3.00
THC484 Aroldis Chapman 2.00 5.00
THC485 David Fletcher 2.00 5.00
THC486 Jon Lester 1.50 4.00
THC487 Hunter Dozier 1.25 3.00
THC490 Rhys Hoskins 2.50 6.00
THC491 Austin Riley 2.50 6.00
THC493 Mookie Betts 4.00 10.00
THC497 Victor Robles 2.50 6.00
THC500 Michael Chavis 1.50 4.00
THC520 Dallas Keuchel 1.50 4.00
THC553 Anthony Rendon 2.00 5.00
THC555 Nick Castellanos 2.00 5.00
THC556 Cole Hamels 1.50 4.00
THC557 Yasiel Puig 2.00 5.00
THC558 Stephen Strasburg 2.00 5.00
THC559 Salvador Perez 1.50 4.00
THC560 Jose Iglesias 1.50 4.00
THC561 Jonathan Lucroy 1.50 4.00
THC562 Andrew Cashner 1.25 3.00
THC563 Didi Gregorius 1.50 4.00
THC565 David Price 1.50 4.00
THC566 Hyun-Jin Ryu 1.50 4.00
THC567 Michael Kopech 2.50 6.00
THC568 Robel Garcia 1.25 3.00
THC569 Nomar Mazara 1.25 3.00
THC570 Corey Dickerson 1.50 4.00
THC571 Wade Miley 1.25 3.00
THC572 Jonathan Schoop 1.25 3.00
THC573 Homer Bailey 1.25 3.00
THC575 LaMonte Wade Jr. 2.00 5.00
THC576 Manuel Margot 1.25 3.00
THC577 Eric Thames 1.25 3.00
THC578 Steven Souza Jr. 1.25 3.00
THC579 Austin Dean 1.25 3.00
THC580 Brad Miller 1.25 3.00
THC581 Yoenis Cespedes 2.00 5.00
THC582 Kevin Pillar 1.25 3.00
THC583 Junior Guerra 1.25 3.00
THC584 Franchy Cordero 1.25 3.00
THC585 Jack Mayfield 1.25 3.00
THC586 Tony Kemp 1.25 3.00
THC587 Edwin Encarnacion 2.00 5.00
THC588 Carlos Rodon 2.00 5.00
THC589 Josh Harrison 1.25 3.00
THC590 Cameron Maybin 1.25 3.00
THC591 C.J. Cron 1.25 3.00
THC592 Todd Frazier 1.25 3.00
THC593 Kyle Gibson 1.25 3.00
THC594 Kyle Higashioka 2.00 5.00
THC595 Ehire Adrianza 1.25 3.00
THC596 Ryan McBroom 1.50 4.00
THC597 Myles Straw 1.50 4.00
THC598 Patrick Wisdom 1.25 3.00
THC599 Eric Lauer 1.25 3.00
THC600 Ronny Rodriguez 1.25 3.00
THC601 Brusdar Graterol 2.00 5.00
THC602 Emmanuel Clase 2.00 5.00
THC703 Starling Marte 1.50 4.00
THC704 Ivan Nova 1.50 4.00

2020 Topps Heritage Clubhouse Collection Autograph Relics

STATED ODDS 1:15,948 HOBBY
STATED HN ODDS 1:XXX HOBBY
PRINT RUNS B/WN 15-25 COPIES PER
NO PRICING ON QTY 15
EXCHANGE DEADLINE 1/31/2022
HN EXCH DEADLINE 10/31/2022
CCARAA Aristides Aquino HN
CCARAB Andrew Benintendi EXCH 75.00 200.00
CCARAR Anthony Rizzo/25 50.00 120.00
CCARBB Bo Bichette HN
CCARCK Clayton Kershaw/25 EXCH 75.00 200.00
CCARCY Christian Yelich/25 75.00 200.00
CCARDL DJ LeMahieu/25 HN 60.00 150.00
CCARFT Fernando Tatis Jr. EXCH
CCARGT Gleyber Torres 125.00 300.00
CCARJL Jesus Luzardo/25 HN 30.00 80.00
CCARKH Keston Hiura HN
CCARLR Luis Robert HN EXCH
CCARMS Max Scherzer/25 HN 50.00 120.00
CCARMT Mike Trout 250.00 600.00
CCARNA Nolan Arenado/25 60.00 150.00
CCAROA Ozzie Albies EXCH 50.00 120.00
CCARPG Paul Goldschmidt HN
CCARRA Ronald Acuna Jr./25 100.00 250.00
CCARRA Ronald Acuna Jr./25 HN 100.00 250.00
CCARRD Rafael Devers/25 25.00 60.00
CCARRH Rhys Hoskins/25 HN 100.00 250.00
CCARSO Shohei Ohtani HN
CCARVG Vladimir Guerrero Jr. 100.00 250.00
CCARVG Vladimir Guerrero Jr. HN
CCARXB Xander Bogaerts/25 HN 60.00 150.00
CCARYA Yordan Alvarez/25 60.00 150.00

2020 Topps Heritage Clubhouse Collection Dual Relics

STATED ODDS 1:17,063 HOBBY
STATED HN ODDS 1:XXXX HOBBY
PRINT RUNS BW/N 70-71 COPIES PER
CCDRAA R.Acuna Jr./H.Aaron 60.00 150.00
CCDRBA A.Bregman/Y.Alvarez 60.00 150.00
CCDRBV Votto/Bench HN 30.00 80.00
CCDRCS R.Clemente/W.Stargell 75.00 200.00
CCDRMA Altuve/Morgan HN 20.00 50.00
CCDRMJ Munson/Judge HN 75.00 200.00
CCDRRD Ryan/deGrom HN 75.00 200.00
CCDRSA P.Alonso/T.Seaver 25.00 60.00
CCDRSH Schmidt/Harper HN 50.00 120.00
CCDRYD R.Devers/C.Yastrzemski 30.00 80.00

2020 Topps Heritage Clubhouse Collection Relics

STATED ODDS 1:34 HOBBY
STATED HN ODDS 1:XXX HOBBY
*GOLD/99: .6X TO 1.5X BASIC
CCRAA Aristides Aquino 5.00 12.00
CCRAA Albert Almora HN 2.50 6.00
CCRAAQ Aristides Aquino HN 5.00 12.00
CCRAB Alex Bregman 3.00 8.00
CCRAB Alex Bregman HN 3.00 8.00
CCRAJ Aaron Judge 8.00 20.00
CCRAJ Aaron Judge HN 8.00 20.00
CCRAM Andrew McCutchen HN 3.00 8.00
CCRAN Aaron Nola 2.50 6.00
CCRAN Aaron Nola HN 2.50 6.00
CCRAP Albert Pujols 4.00 10.00
CCRAR Anthony Rizzo 4.00 10.00
CCRAR Anthony Rizzo HN 4.00 10.00
CCRARO Amed Rosario 2.50 6.00
CCRBB Bo Bichette 6.00 15.00
CCRBB Bo Bichette HN 6.00 15.00
CCRBC Brandon Crawford HN 2.50 6.00
CCRBH Bryce Harper 5.00 12.00
CCRBH Bryce Harper HN 5.00 12.00
CCRBP Buster Posey 4.00 10.00
CCRBP Buster Posey HN 4.00 10.00
CCRCB Cody Bellinger 5.00 12.00
CCRCB Charlie Blackmon HN 3.00 8.00
CCRCB Cody Bellinger HN 5.00 12.00
CCRCBL Charlie Blackmon 3.00 8.00
CCRCC Carlos Correa HN 3.00 8.00
CCRCK Clayton Kershaw 5.00 12.00
CCRCK Clayton Kershaw HN 5.00 12.00
CCRCM Charlie Morton 3.00 8.00
CCRCP Chris Paddack 3.00 8.00
CCRCS Chris Sale HN 3.00 8.00
CCRCY Christian Yelich 4.00 10.00
CCRCY Christian Yelich HN 4.00 10.00
CCRDL DJ LeMahieu 3.00 8.00
CCRDL DJ LeMahieu HN 3.00 8.00
CCRDS Dansby Swanson HN 3.00 8.00
CCRDV Daniel Vogelbach 2.00 5.00
CCREA Elvis Andrus 2.50 6.00
CCREL Evan Longoria 2.50 6.00
CCRFB Franklin Barreto HN 2.00 5.00
CCRFL Francisco Lindor HN 3.00 8.00
CCRFT Fernando Tatis Jr. 8.00 20.00
CCRFT Fernando Tatis Jr. HN 8.00 20.00
CCRGS George Springer 2.50 6.00
CCRGS Gary Sanchez HN 3.00 8.00
CCRGT Gleyber Torres 4.00 10.00
CCRGT Gleyber Torres HN 4.00 10.00
CCRGU Gio Urshela 3.00 8.00
CCRHR Hyun-Jin Ryu 2.50 6.00
CCRHR Hyun-Jin Ryu HN 2.50 6.00
CCRJA Jose Altuve 2.50 6.00
CCRJA Jose Altuve HN 2.50 6.00
CCRJAB Jose Abreu HN 3.00 8.00
CCRJB Javier Baez 4.00 10.00
CCRJB Javier Baez HN 4.00 10.00
CCRJBE Jose Berrios HN 2.50 6.00
CCRJBJ Jackie Bradley Jr. HN 3.00 8.00
CCRJD Jacob deGrom HN 6.00 15.00
CCRJG Joey Gallo 3.00 8.00
CCRJM J.D. Martinez 3.00 8.00
CCRJM Jeff McNeil HN 2.50 6.00
CCRJMC Jeff McNeil 2.50 6.00
CCRJR Jose Ramirez 2.50 6.00
CCRJR Jose Ramirez HN 2.50 6.00
CCRJRE J.T. Realmuto 3.00 8.00
CCRJRE J.T. Realmuto HN 3.00 8.00
CCRJS Juan Soto HN 6.00 15.00
CCRJV Justin Verlander 3.00 8.00
CCRKB Kris Bryant 4.00 10.00
CCRKB Kris Bryant HN 4.00 10.00
CCRKH Keston Hiura 4.00 10.00
CCRKK Kevin Kiermaier HN 2.50 6.00
CCRKM Ketel Marte 2.50 6.00
CCRKMA Ketel Marte HN 2.50 6.00
CCRKS Kyle Schwarber 3.00 8.00
CCRLC Lorenzo Cain HN 2.00 5.00
CCRLG Lucas Giolito 2.50 6.00
CCRMB Mookie Betts 6.00 15.00
CCRMB Mookie Betts HN 6.00 15.00
CCRMBR Michael Brantley 2.50 6.00
CCRMC Matt Chapman 3.00 8.00
CCRMCO Michael Conforto 2.50 6.00
CCRMF Max Fried 3.00 8.00
CCRMH Mitch Haniger 2.50 6.00
CCRMK Max Kepler 2.50 6.00
CCRMS Max Scherzer HN 3.00 8.00
CCRMSA Miguel Sano HN 2.50 6.00
CCRMSM Mallex Smith HN 2.00 5.00
CCRMT Mike Trout 12.00 30.00
CCRMT Mike Trout HN 12.00 30.00
CCRNA Nolan Arenado 5.00 12.00
CCRNA Nolan Arenado HN 5.00 12.00
CCRNH Nico Hoerner HN 5.00 12.00
CCRNS Noah Syndergaard 2.50 6.00
CCRNS Nick Solak HN 8.00 20.00
CCROA Ozzie Albies 3.00 8.00
CCROA Ozzie Albies HN 3.00 8.00
CCRPA Pete Alonso 8.00 20.00
CCRPA Pete Alonso HN 8.00 20.00
CCRPC Patrick Corbin 2.50 6.00
CCRPG Paul Goldschmidt 3.00 8.00
CCRPG Paul Goldschmidt HN 3.00 8.00
CCRRA Ronald Acuna Jr. 10.00 25.00
CCRRA Ronald Acuna Jr. HN 10.00 25.00
CCRRD Rafael Devers 4.00 10.00
CCRRD Rafael Devers HN 4.00 10.00
CCRRH Rhys Hoskins 4.00 10.00
CCRRH Rhys Hoskins HN 4.00 10.00
CCRSO Shohei Ohtani 8.00 20.00
CCRSO Shohei Ohtani HN 8.00 20.00
CCRSS Stephen Strasburg 3.00 8.00
CCRTM Trey Mancini 3.00 8.00
CCRTM Trey Mancini HN 3.00 8.00
CCRTS Trevor Story HN 3.00 8.00
CCRTT Trea Turner 2.50 6.00
CCRVG Vladimir Guerrero Jr. 4.00 10.00
CCRVG Vladimir Guerrero Jr. HN 4.00 10.00
CCRVR Victor Robles HN 4.00 10.00
CCRWB Walker Buehler 4.00 10.00
CCRWB Walker Buehler HN 4.00 10.00
CCRWC Willson Contreras 3.00 8.00
CCRWC Willson Contreras HN 3.00 8.00
CCRXB Xander Bogaerts 3.00 8.00
CCRYA Yordan Alvarez 20.00 50.00
CCRYA Yordan Alvarez HN 6.00 15.00
CCRYM Yadier Molina 4.00 10.00
CCRYM Yadier Molina HN 4.00 10.00
CCRZG Zack Greinke 3.00 8.00

2020 Topps Heritage Clubhouse Collection Triple Relics

STATED ODDS 1:48,345 HOBBY
STATED HN ODDS 1:XXXX HOBBY
STATED PRINT RUN 25 SER.#'d SETS
CCTRABB Bichette/Biggio/Alomar HN
CCTRACA Yordan/Altuve/Correa HN
CCTRAJA Acuna Jr./Aaron/Jones 100.00 250.00
CCTRCKO Carew/Killebrew/Oliva HN 60.00 150.00
CCTRCSB Bell/Stargell/Clemente 150.00 400.00
CCTRMBA Morgan/Biggio/Altuve 50.00 120.00
CCTRSSS Strasburg/Scherzer/Soto HN 75.00 200.00
CCTRTJR Thomas/Robert/Jimenez
CCTRTMG Molina/Goldschmidt/Torre 40.00 100.00
CCTRYOD Devers/Yastrzemski/Ortiz 40.00 100.00

2020 Topps Heritage Flashback Autograph Relics

STATED ODDS 1:24,173 HOBBY
PRINT RUNS B/WN 10-25 COPIES PER
NO PRICING ON QTY 10
EXCHANGE DEADLINE 1/31/2022
FARBB Bert Blyleven/25 100.00 250.00
FARBG Bob Gibson/25 125.00 300.00
FARCF Carlton Fisk/25 75.00 200.00
FARCY Carl Yastrzemski/25 100.00 250.00
FARDS Don Sutton EXCH 50.00 120.00
FARJB Johnny Bench
FARNR Nolan Ryan/25 125.00 300.00
FARRC Rod Carew EXCH 100.00 250.00
FARRJ Reggie Jackson/25 200.00 500.00

2020 Topps Heritage High Number '71 Topps Greatest Moments Boxloader

STATED ODDS 1:XXX HOBBY BOXES
1 Roberto Clemente 30.00 80.00
2 Jim Kaat 15.00 40.00

3 Brooks Robinson 12.00 30.00
4 Harmon Killebrew 40.00 100.00
5 Bob Gibson 10.00 25.00
6 Frank Robinson 15.00 40.00
7 Johnny Bench 15.00 40.00
8 Rick Wise 20.00 50.00
9 Carl Yastrzemski 15.00 40.00
10 Willie Stargell 12.00 30.00
11 Lou Brock 10.00 25.00
12 Fergie Jenkins 12.00 30.00
13 Tom Seaver 10.00 25.00
14 Tony Oliva 12.00 30.00
15 Willie Mays 20.00 50.00
16 Joe Torre 8.00 20.00
17 Juan Marichal 20.00 50.00
18 Vida Blue 12.00 30.00
19 Al Kaline 15.00 40.00
20 Rollie Fingers 10.00 25.00
21 Javier Baez 6.00 15.00
22 Mike Trout 30.00 80.00
23 Ronald Acuna Jr. 10.00 25.00
24 Aaron Judge 12.00 30.00
25 Pete Alonso 12.00 30.00
26 Nolan Arenado 8.00 20.00
27 Max Scherzer 8.00 20.00
28 Bryce Harper 8.00 20.00
29 Kris Bryant 10.00 25.00
30 Jose Altuve 6.00 15.00
31 Walker Buehler 6.00 15.00
32 Juan Soto 10.00 25.00
33 Fernando Tatis Jr. 12.00 30.00
34 Eloy Jimenez 10.00 25.00
35 Cody Bellinger 10.00 25.00
36 Christian Yelich 6.00 15.00
37 Vladimir Guerrero Jr. 8.00 20.00
38 Anthony Rendon 8.00 20.00
39 Mookie Betts 10.00 25.00
40 Jacob deGrom 6.00 15.00
41 Nelson Cruz 10.00 25.00
42 Yadier Molina 10.00 25.00
43 Gleyber Torres 10.00 25.00
44 Francisco Lindor 5.00 12.00
45 Luis Robert 25.00 60.00
46 Yordan Alvarez 10.00 25.00
47 Bo Bichette 8.00 20.00
48 Aristides Aquino 8.00 20.00
49 Nico Hoerner 12.00 30.00
50 Gavin Lux 8.00 20.00
51 Brendan McKay 5.00 12.00
52 Manny Machado 8.00 20.00
53 Albert Pujols 15.00 40.00
54 Justin Verlander 5.00 12.00
55 Ron Santo 12.00 30.00

2020 Topps Heritage High Number '71 World Champions Autographs

STATED ODDS 1:XXX HOBBY BOXES
STATED PRINT RUN 71 SER.#'d SETS
HN EXCH DEADLINE 10/31/2022
71WSCAO Al Oliver 75.00 200.00
71WSCMS Manny Sanguillen 125.00 300.00
71WSCSB Steve Blass 125.00 300.00

2020 Topps Heritage High Number '71 World Series Highlights

COMPLETE SET (10) 8.00 20.00
STATED ODDS 1:XXX HOBBY
WSH1 Roberto Clemente 2.00 5.00
WSH2 Brooks Robinson .60 1.50
WSH3 Frank Robinson .60 1.50
WSH4 Nelson Briles .50 1.25
WSH5 Pittsburgh Pirates .75 2.00
WSH6 Steve Blass .50 1.25
WSH7 Jim Palmer .60 1.50
WSH8 Willie Stargell .60 1.50
WSH9 Gene Clines .50 1.25
WSH10 Bob Robertson .50 1.25

2020 Topps Heritage High Number Award Winners

COMPLETE SET (10) 5.00 12.00
STATED HN ODDS 1:XXX HOBBY
AW1 Mike Trout 2.00 5.00
AW2 Cody Bellinger .75 2.00
AW3 Justin Verlander .40 1.00
AW4 Jacob deGrom .75 2.00
AW5 Yordan Alvarez 2.50 6.00
AW6 Pete Alonso 1.00 2.50
AW7 Mike Shildt .25 .60
AW8 Rocco Baldelli .25 .60
AW9 Shane Bieber .40 1.00
AW10 Stephen Strasburg .40 1.00

2020 Topps Heritage High Number Combo Cards

COMPLETE SET (10) 12.00 30.00
STATED ODDS 1:XX HOBBY
CC1 Bichette/Guerrero Jr. 3.00 8.00
CC2 Rizzo/Bryant .75 2.00
CC3 Sano/Cruz .60 1.50
CC4 Judge/Torres 1.50 4.00
CC5 Alvarez/Correa 4.00 10.00
CC6 Lux/Bellinger 2.00 5.00
CC7 Harper/Hoskins 1.00 2.50
CC8 Robert/Jimenez 3.00 8.00
CC9 Soto/Turner 2.00 5.00
CC10 Albies/Acuna Jr. 2.50 6.00

2020 Topps Heritage High Number Let's Play 2

COMPLETE SET (15) 60.00 150.00
STATED ODDS 1:XXX HOBBY
LP21 Ernie Banks 4.00 10.00
LP22 Ernie Banks 4.00 10.00
LP23 Ernie Banks 4.00 10.00
LP24 Ernie Banks 4.00 10.00
LP25 Ernie Banks 4.00 10.00
LP26 Ernie Banks 4.00 10.00
LP27 Ernie Banks 4.00 10.00
LP28 Ernie Banks 4.00 10.00
LP29 Ernie Banks 4.00 10.00
LP210 Ernie Banks 4.00 10.00
LP211 Ernie Banks 4.00 10.00
LP212 Ernie Banks 4.00 10.00
LP213 Ernie Banks 4.00 10.00
LP214 Ernie Banks 4.00 10.00
LP215 Ernie Banks 4.00 10.00

2020 Topps Heritage High Number Let's Play 2 Relics

STATED ODDS 1:XXX HOBBY
LP2R1 Ernie Banks 75.00 200.00
LP2R2 Ernie Banks 75.00
LP2R3 Ernie Banks 75.00
LP2R4 Ernie Banks 75.00
LP2R5 Ernie Banks 75.00
LP2R6 Ernie Banks 75.00
LP2R7 Ernie Banks 75.00
LP2R8 Ernie Banks 75.00
LP2R9 Ernie Banks 75.00
LP2R10 Ernie Banks 75.00
LP2R11 Ernie Banks 75.00
LP2R12 Ernie Banks 75.00
LP2R13 Ernie Banks 75.00
LP2R14 Ernie Banks 75.00
LP2R15 Ernie Banks 75.00

2020 Topps Heritage High Number Now and Then

COMPLETE SET (15) 8.00 20.00
STATED ODDS 1:XXX HOBBY
NT1 Pete Alonso 1.00 2.50
NT2 Justin Verlander .40 1.00
NT3 Ronald Acuna Jr. 1.50 4.00
NT4 Bryce Harper .60 1.50
NT5 Aaron Hicks .30 .75
NT6 Albert Pujols .50 1.25
NT7 Shohei Ohtani .60 1.50
NT8 Stevie Wilkerson .30 .75
NT9 Max Muncy .30 .75
NT10 Will Smith .40 1.00
NT11 Tim Anderson .40 1.00
NT12 Mallex Smith .25 .60
NT13 Kris Bryant .50 1.25
NT14 Yordan Alvarez 2.50 6.00
NT15 Bo Bichette 2.00 5.00

2020 Topps Heritage High Number Rookie Performers

COMPLETE SET (15) 10.00 25.00
STATED HN ODDS 1:XX HOBBY
RP1 Yordan Alvarez 2.50 6.00
RP2 Bo Bichette 2.00 5.00
RP3 Shogo Akiyama .40 1.00
RP4 Zac Gallen .60 1.50
RP5 Nico Hoerner 1.00 2.50
RP6 Luis Robert 2.00 5.00
RP7 Yoshi Tsutsugo .60 1.50
RP8 Kyle Lewis 2.00 5.00
RP9 Dustin May .75 2.00
RP10 Brendan McKay .40 1.00
RP11 Gavin Lux 1.25 3.00
RP12 Kwang-Hyun Kim .50 1.25
RP13 Aristides Aquino .60 1.50
RP14 Mauricio Dubon .30 .75
RP15 Shun Yamaguchi .30 .75

2020 Topps Heritage Mini

STATED ODDS 1:457 HOBBY
STATED HN ODDS 1:XXX HOBBY
STATED PRINT RUN 100 SER.#'d SETS
5 Gary Sanchez 6.00 15.00
8 Gio Urshela 6.00 15.00
17 Yuli Gurriel 5.00 12.00
32 Evan Longoria 5.00 12.00
35 Jorge Soler 6.00 15.00
40 Joey Votto 6.00 15.00
41 Miguel Cabrera 20.00 50.00
53 Aaron Nola 5.00 12.00
56 Carlos Santana 5.00 12.00
75 J.T. Realmuto 6.00 15.00
78 Albert Pujols 8.00 20.00
82 Max Scherzer 6.00 15.00
87 Josh Hader 5.00 12.00
96 Mitch Garver 4.00 10.00
98 Marcus Semien 6.00 15.00
118 Whit Merrifield 6.00 15.00
131 Luke Voit 8.00 20.00
142 Javier Baez 8.00 20.00
145 Rafael Devers 8.00 20.00
149 Zack Greinke 6.00 15.00
154 Trea Turner 5.00 12.00
167 Max Muncy 5.00 12.00
174 Christian Yelich 8.00 20.00
182 Chris Paddack 6.00 15.00
183 Ketel Marte 5.00 12.00
185 Luis Severino 5.00 12.00
220 Nate Lowe 10.00 25.00
224 Joc Pederson 5.00 12.00
230 Patrick Corbin 5.00 12.00
236 Jorge Polanco 5.00 12.00
238 Jose Berrios 5.00 12.00
240 Brian Anderson 4.00 10.00
241 Willson Contreras 6.00 15.00
244 George Springer 5.00 12.00
245 Mike Soroka 6.00 15.00
257 Cody Bellinger 12.00 30.00
263 Freddie Freeman 8.00 20.00
264 Jose Altuve 5.00 12.00
272 Eugenio Suarez 5.00 12.00
280 Kirby Yates 4.00 10.00
283 Eric Hosmer 5.00 12.00
285 Will Smith 6.00 15.00
286 Ozzie Albies 6.00 15.00
291 Kris Bryant 12.00 30.00
300 Renato Nunez 5.00 12.00
303 Masahiro Tanaka 6.00 15.00
308 Manny Machado 6.00 15.00
310 Michael Conforto 5.00 12.00
312 Carlos Correa 6.00 15.00
321 Ryan Braun 5.00 12.00
322 Nolan Arenado 10.00 25.00
324 Jose Ramirez 5.00 12.00
341 Mike Clevinger 5.00 12.00
345 Xander Bogaerts 6.00 15.00
346 Trey Mancini 6.00 15.00
350 Trevor Story 6.00 15.00
354 Yoan Moncada 6.00 15.00
355 Amed Rosario 5.00 12.00
373 Anthony Rizzo 8.00 20.00
383 Bryan Reynolds 5.00 12.00
385 Clayton Kershaw 10.00 25.00
394 Kevin Pillar 4.00 10.00
395 Aaron Judge 25.00 60.00
400 Yadier Molina 10.00 25.00
401 Elvis Andrus 5.00 12.00
403 Juan Soto 20.00 50.00
406 Jacob deGrom 12.00 30.00
407 Matt Olson 6.00 15.00
408 Yusei Kikuchi 5.00 12.00
409 Kyle Schwarber 6.00 15.00
410 Corey Seager 6.00 15.00
413 Keston Hiura 8.00 20.00
414 Vladimir Guerrero Jr. 20.00 50.00
415 DJ LeMahieu 6.00 15.00
416 Lucas Giolito 5.00 12.00
417 Blake Snell 5.00 12.00
419 Andrew Benintendi 6.00 15.00
420 Charlie Blackmon 6.00 15.00
422 Josh Bell 5.00 12.00
423 J.D. Martinez 6.00 15.00
424 Yasmani Grandal 4.00 10.00
425 Michael Brantley 5.00 12.00
426 Mike Yastrzemski 10.00 25.00
428 Noah Syndergaard 5.00 12.00
432 Eddie Rosario 5.00 12.00
433 Shohei Ohtani 10.00 25.00
435 Lorenzo Cain 4.00 10.00
436 Tim Anderson 6.00 15.00
437 Fernando Tatis Jr. 40.00 100.00
439 Luis Castillo 5.00 12.00
440 Jonathan Villar 4.00 10.00
441 Miguel Sano 6.00 15.00
442 Francisco Lindor 6.00 15.00
443 Giancarlo Stanton 6.00 15.00
447 Bryce Harper 15.00 40.00
451 Chris Sale 6.00 15.00
453 Alex Bregman 10.00 25.00
454 Shane Bieber 10.00 25.00
455 Sonny Gray 5.00 12.00
456 Andrew McCutchen 6.00 15.00
457 Pete Alonso 20.00 50.00
458 Jean Segura 5.00 12.00
459 Alex Verdugo 5.00 12.00
461 Daniel Vogelbach 4.00 10.00
462 Starling Marte 5.00 12.00
464 Ronald Acuna Jr. 25.00 60.00
465 Max Fried 6.00 15.00
466 Mike Trout 200.00 500.00
467 Paul Goldschmidt 6.00 15.00
468 Matt Chapman 6.00 15.00
472 Liam Hendriks 4.00 10.00
473 Justin Verlander 6.00 15.00
474 Eduardo Escobar 4.00 10.00
476 Paul DeJong 6.00 15.00
478 David Dahl 4.00 10.00
479 Max Kepler 5.00 12.00
480 James Paxton 5.00 12.00
481 Austin Meadows 6.00 15.00
482 Nick Senzel 6.00 15.00
483 Gleyber Torres 12.00 30.00
484 Aroldis Chapman 6.00 15.00
487 Hunter Dozier 4.00 10.00
488 Christian Walker 5.00 12.00
490 Rhys Hoskins 8.00 20.00
491 Austin Riley 8.00 20.00
492 Jeff McNeil 6.00 15.00
493 Mookie Betts 15.00 40.00
494 Eloy Jimenez 12.00 30.00
495 Ramon Laureano 5.00 12.00
496 Walker Buehler 8.00 20.00
497 Victor Robles 8.00 20.00
500 Michael Chavis 5.00 12.00
501 Gerrit Cole 10.00 25.00
502 Mookie Betts 15.00 40.00
503 Josh Donaldson 5.00 12.00
505 Ben Zobrist 5.00 12.00
508 Corey Kluber 5.00 12.00
512 Luis Robert 150.00 400.00
520 Dallas Keuchel 5.00 12.00
523 Danny Mendick 5.00 12.00
525 Rangel Ravelo 5.00 12.00
526 Willi Castro 6.00 15.00
527 Shogo Akiyama 6.00 15.00
530 Edwin Rios 10.00 25.00
540 Jon Berti 4.00 10.00
541 Kean Wong 6.00 15.00
543 Garrett Stubbs 4.00 10.00
546 Jaylin Davis 6.00 15.00
547 Jake Fraley 5.00 12.00
548 Yoshi Tsutsugo 10.00 25.00
549 Shun Yamaguchi 5.00 12.00
553 Anthony Rendon 6.00 15.00
555 Nick Castellanos 6.00 15.00
556 Cole Hamels 5.00 12.00
557 Yasiel Puig 6.00 15.00
558 Stephen Strasburg 6.00 15.00
559 Salvador Perez 5.00 12.00
563 Didi Gregorius 15.00 40.00
565 David Price 5.00 12.00
566 Hyun-Jin Ryu 5.00 12.00
567 Michael Kopech 8.00 20.00
568 Robel Garcia 4.00 10.00
569 Nomar Mazara 4.00 10.00
570 Corey Dickerson 5.00 12.00
572 Jonathan Schoop 4.00 10.00
573 Homer Bailey 4.00 10.00
575 Lamonte Wade Jr. 6.00 15.00
587 Edwin Encarnacion 6.00 15.00
588 Carlos Rodon 6.00 15.00
589 Josh Harrison 4.00 10.00
590 Cameron Maybin 4.00 10.00
595 Ehire Adrianza 4.00 10.00
596 Ryan McBroom 5.00 12.00
601 Brusdar Graterol 6.00 15.00
603 Tyrone Taylor 4.00 10.00
606 Tim Lopes 5.00 12.00
607 Seth Mejias-Brean 4.00 10.00
610 Brian O'Grady 4.00 10.00
611 David Bednar 4.00 10.00
644 Dellin Betances 5.00 12.00
662 Carter Kieboom 5.00 12.00
673 Howie Kendrick 4.00 10.00

2020 Topps Heritage New Age Performers

COMPLETE SET (25) 15.00 40.00
STATED ODDS 1:11 HOBBY
NAP1 Eugenio Suarez .50 1.25
NAP2 Yordan Alvarez 4.00 10.00
NAP3 Mike Soroka .60 1.50
NAP4 Jorge Soler .60 1.50
NAP5 Keston Hiura .75 2.00
NAP6 Lucas Giolito .50 1.25
NAP7 Pete Alonso 1.50 4.00
NAP8 Ketel Marte .50 1.25
NAP9 Jose Berrios .50 1.25
NAP10 Vladimir Guerrero Jr. 1.00 2.50
NAP11 Gio Urshela .60 1.50
NAP12 Josh Hader .50 1.25
NAP13 Shane Bieber .60 1.50
NAP14 Matt Chapman .60 1.50
NAP15 Bo Bichette 3.00 8.00
NAP16 Tim Anderson .60 1.50
NAP17 J.T. Realmuto .60 1.50
NAP18 Mike Yastrzemski 1.00 2.50
NAP19 Josh Bell .50 1.25
NAP20 George Springer .50 1.25
NAP21 Jack Flaherty .60 1.50
NAP22 Austin Meadows .60 1.50
NAP23 Max Fried .60 1.50
NAP24 Fernando Tatis Jr. 3.00 8.00
NAP25 Luis Castillo .50 1.25

2020 Topps Heritage News Flashbacks

STATED ODDS 1:18 HOBBY
NF1 Walt Disney World opens .60 1.50
NF2 First Starbucks opens .60 1.50
NF3 The Ed Sullivan show airs last episode .60 1.50
NF4 Evel Knievel jumps 19 cars .60 1.50
NF5 NASDAQ is founded .60 1.50
NF6 Fight of the Century .60 1.50
NF7 Apollo 14 launches .60 1.50
NF8 Willy Wonka and the Chocolate Factory is released .60 1.50
NF9 Jim Morrison dies at 27 .60 1.50
NF10 Mariner 9 enters Mars' orbit .60 1.50
NF11 First microprocessor released .60 1.50
NF12 All in the Family debuts .60 1.50
NF13 Lunar Roving Vehicle used on moon .60 1.50
NF14 The Mystery of D.B. Cooper .60 1.50
NF15 Louie Armstrong passes away .60 1.50

2020 Topps Heritage Real One Autographs

STATED ODDS 1:110 HOBBY
STATED HN ODDS 1:XXX HOBBY
EXCHANGE DEADLINE 1/31/2022
HN EXCH DEADLINE 10/31/2022
ROAAA Adbert Alzolay 8.00 20.00
ROAAQ Aristides Aquino 20.00 50.00
ROAAF Al Ferrara 10.00 25.00
ROAAK Anthony Kay 6.00 15.00
ROAAM Austin Meadows HN 10.00 25.00
ROAAMO Adalberto Mondesi HN 8.00 20.00
ROAAN Aaron Nola HN 20.00 50.00
ROAAP A.J. Puk 10.00 25.00
ROAAR Austin Riley 12.00 30.00
ROAAR Anthony Rendon HN 25.00 60.00
ROAARI Anthony Rizzo 12.00 30.00
ROABB Bo Bichette 125.00 300.00
ROABB Bert Blyleven HN 20.00 50.00
ROABBR Bobby Bradley 6.00 15.00
ROABBU Bill Burbach 6.00 15.00
ROABG Bob Gibson HN 75.00 200.00
ROABH Bryce Harper HN 100.00 250.00
ROABL Brandon Lowe 8.00 20.00
ROABM Brendan McKay 12.00 30.00
ROABPR Bob Priddy HN 12.00 30.00
ROABR Bryan Reynolds 8.00 20.00
ROACB Cavan Biggio HN 12.00 30.00
ROACBE Cody Bellinger HN 60.00 150.00
ROACK Corey Kluber HN 15.00 40.00
ROACR Claude Raymond 8.00 20.00
ROACY Carl Yastrzemski 50.00 120.00
ROACYE Christian Yelich 30.00 80.00
ROADC Dylan Cease 8.00 20.00
ROADCO Danny Coombs HN 10.00 25.00
ROADL DJ LeMahieu HN 50.00 120.00
ROADM Dustin May 30.00 80.00
ROADSW Dansby Swanson HN 20.00 50.00
ROADW Devin Williams HN 15.00 40.00
ROAEJ Eloy Jimenez 30.00 80.00
ROAFJO Frank Johnson HN 8.00 20.00
ROAFLI Francisco Lindor 25.00 60.00
ROAFT Fernando Tatis Jr. 200.00 500.00
ROAGC Gerrit Cole HN 60.00 150.00
ROAGL Gavin Lux 60.00 150.00
ROAGS George Springer 12.00 30.00
ROAGT Gleyber Torres 30.00 80.00
ROAGTH George Thomas 6.00 15.00
ROAHA Hank Aaron 150.00 400.00
ROAJA Jose Altuve 15.00 40.00
ROAJB Johnny Bench 75.00 200.00
ROAJD Justin Dunn 8.00 20.00
ROAJDM J.D. Martinez HN 15.00 40.00
ROAJF Jim French 6.00 15.00
ROAJG John Gelnar 6.00 15.00
ROAJGI Jake Gibbs 6.00 15.00
ROAJL Jesus Luzardo 15.00 40.00
ROAJM Joe Moeller 10.00 25.00
ROAJM Juan Marichal HN 30.00 80.00
ROAJMC Jeff McNeil HN 12.00 30.00
ROAJR Jose Ramirez HN 8.00 20.00
ROAJRE J.T. Realmuto HN 25.00 60.00
ROAJS Juan Soto HN Red Hat 100.00 250.00
ROAJS Juan Soto HN White Hat 100.00 250.00
ROAJSO Jorge Soler HN 10.00 25.00
ROAJT Joe Torre 30.00 80.00
ROAJY Jordan Yamamoto 6.00 15.00
ROAKB Kris Bryant HN 40.00 100.00
ROAKH Ken Harrelson 12.00 30.00
ROAKHI Keston Hiura 10.00 25.00
ROAKL Kyle Lewis 50.00 120.00
ROAKM Ketel Marte HN 8.00 20.00
ROALA Logan Allen 6.00 15.00
ROALA Luis Arraez HN 12.00 30.00
ROALB Lou Brock HN 75.00 200.00
ROALG Lucas Giolito HN 10.00 25.00
ROALR Luis Robert HN EXCH 200.00 500.00
ROALT Luis Tiant HN 10.00 25.00
ROAMC Miguel Cabrera HN 50.00 120.00
ROAMK Max Kepler HN 8.00 20.00
ROAML Marcel Lachemann 8.00 20.00
ROAMS Mike Soroka HN 20.00 50.00
ROAMT Mike Trout 300.00 800.00
ROAMT Masahiro Tanaka HN 40.00 100.00
ROAMW Maury Wills HN 25.00 60.00
ROANA Nolan Arenado 25.00 60.00
ROANH Nico Hoerner 25.00 60.00
ROANR Nolan Ryan 125.00 300.00
ROAOM Oscar Mercado HN 6.00 15.00
ROAPA Pete Alonso 60.00 150.00
ROAPA Pete Alonso HN 50.00 120.00
ROAPC Patrick Corbin HN 8.00 20.00
ROAPD Paul DeJong 8.00 20.00
ROAPG Paul Goldschmidt HN 40.00 100.00
ROARA Ronald Acuna Jr. 100.00 250.00
ROARA Ronald Acuna Jr. HN 75.00 200.00
ROARC Rod Carew HN 75.00 200.00
ROARD Rafael Devers 30.00 80.00
ROARF Rollie Fingers HN 20.00 50.00
ROARH Rhys Hoskins 25.00 60.00
ROARJ Reggie Jackson 100.00 250.00
ROASB Seth Brown 6.00 15.00
ROASC Sal Campisi 6.00 15.00
ROASCA Steve Carlton 30.00 80.00
ROASO Shohei Ohtani 75.00 200.00
ROASY Shun Yamaguchi HN 8.00 20.00
ROATC Ty Cline 6.00 15.00
ROATD Tommy Dean 6.00 15.00
ROATE Tommy Edman HN 10.00 25.00
ROATG Trent Grisham HN 15.00 40.00
ROATO Tony Oliva HN 30.00 80.00
ROATP Tony Perez HN 30.00 80.00
ROATT Tom Tischinski 6.00 15.00
ROAVB Vida Blue HN 20.00 50.00
ROAVG Vladimir Guerrero Jr. 50.00 120.00
ROAVG Vladimir Guerrero Jr. HN 50.00 120.00
ROAWB Walker Buehler 30.00 80.00
ROAWS Will Smith 10.00 25.00
ROAWW Woody Woodward 6.00 15.00
ROAYA Yordan Alvarez 100.00 250.00
ROAYG Yuli Gurriel HN 8.00 20.00
ROAZW Zack Wheeler HN 12.00 30.00

2020 Topps Heritage Real One Autographs Red Ink

*RED INK: .75X TO 2X BASIC
STATED ODDS 1:1274 HOBBY
STATED HN ODDS 1:XXX HOBBY
STATED PRINT RUN 71 SER.#'d SETS
EXCHANGE DEADLINE 1/31/2022
HN EXCH DEADLINE 10/31/2022

2020 Topps Heritage Real One Dual Autographs

STATED ODDS 1:6446 HOBBY
STATED HN ODDS 1:XXX HOBBY
STATED PRINT RUN 25 SER.#'d SETS
EXCHANGE DEADLINE 1/31/2022
HN EXCH DEADLINE 10/31/2022
RODAAA Y.Alvarez/J.Altuve 150.00 400.00
RODAAR A.Riley/R.Acuna Jr. 150.00 400.00
RODAAS Acuna/Soto HN 1000.00 2000.00
RODABS N.Senzel/J.Bench 150.00 400.00
RODACM Mauer/Carew HN 100.00 250.00
RODAGB Gibson/Brock HN 500.00 1000.00
RODAJR Rbrt/Jmnz HN EXCH 500.00 1000.00
RODAJT Judge/Torres HN 400.00 800.00
RODAKC A.Kaline/M.Cabrera 250.00 600.00
RODATM J.Torre/Y.Molina 125.00 300.00
RODATO S.Ohtani/M.Trout
RODAYB Bnntndi/Yaz EXCH 75.00 200.00
RODAYH Yelich/Hiura HN 125.00 300.00

2020 Topps Heritage Senators Final Season Autographs

STATED ODDS 1:6684 HOBBY
STATED PRINT RUN 25 SER.#'d SETS
EXCHANGE DEADLINE 1/31/2022
WSFSBG Bill Gogolewski 60.00 150.00
WSFSDB Dick Billings 60.00 150.00
WSFSDBO Dick Bosman 60.00 150.00
WSFSDK Darold Knowles 40.00 100.00
WSFSDM Denny McLain 60.00 150.00
WSFSEM Elliott Maddox 60.00 150.00
WSFSFH Frank Howard 75.00 200.00
WSFSJB Jeff Burroughs 60.00 150.00
WSFSJF Jim French 60.00 150.00

2020 Topps Heritage Then and Now

COMPLETE SET (15) 6.00 15.00
STATED ODDS 1:18 HOBBY
TN1 Fergie Jenkins Stephen Strasburg .60 1.50
TN2 Verlander/Hunter .60 1.50
TN3 Hyun-Jin Ryu Tom Seaver .50 1.25
TN4 Gerrit Cole Jim Palmer 1.00 2.50
TN5 Alonso/Stargell 1.50 4.00
TN6 Jorge Soler Reggie Jackson .60 1.50
TN7 Joe Torre Anthony Rendon .60 1.50
TN8 Jose Abreu Harmon Killebrew .60 1.50
TN9 Yelich/Torre .75 2.00
TN10 Tim Anderson Tony Oliva .60 1.50
TN11 Mallex Smith Lou Brock .50 1.25
TN12 Stephen Strasburg Fergie Jenkins .60 1.50
TN13 Palmer/Verlander .60 1.50
TN14 Jacob deGrom Tom Seaver 1.25 3.00
TN15 Gerrit Cole Bert Blyleven 1.00 2.50

2021 Topps Heritage

COMP.SET w/o SPs (400)
SP ODDS 1:3 HOBBY
1 World Champions .15 .40
2 Max Muncy .20 .50
3 Raisel Iglesias .15 .40
4 Ty Buttrey .15 .40
5 D.Peterson RC/A.Gimenez RC .75 2.00
6 Adam Wainwright .20 .50
7 Brandon Belt .20 .50
8 Rio Ruiz .15 .40
9 Miguel Rojas .15 .40
10 Miguel Rojas IA .15 .40
11 A.Bohm RC/S.Howard RC 5.00 12.00
12 Alec Bohm IA 1.50 4.00
13 Bryce Harper .40 1.00
14 Bryce Harper IA .40 1.00
15 S.Sanchez RC/J.Sanchez RC 1.50 4.00
16 Sixto Sanchez IA .75 2.00
17 Yadier Molina .30 .75
18 Yadier Molina IA .30 .75
19 Rhys Hoskins .30 .75
20 Jake Cronenworth IA 1.00 2.50
21 Fernando Tatis Jr. PO HL 1.25 3.00
22 Mike Brosseau PO HL .20 .50
23 Carlos Correa PO HL .25 .60
24 Randy Arozarena PO HL .60 1.50
25 Cody Bellinger PO HL .50 1.25
26 Game 1 WS HL .15 .40
27 Game 2 WS HL .15 .40
28 Game 4 WS HL .15 .40
29 Game 5 WS HL .15 .40
30 Game 6 WS HL .15 .40
31 Pete Alonso .60 1.50
32 Pete Alonso IA .60 1.50
33 Luis Robert 2.00 5.00
34 Luis Robert IA .75 2.00
35 Juan Soto .75 2.00
36 Juan Soto IA .75 2.00
37 Clayton Kershaw .40 1.00
38 Clayton Kershaw IA .40 1.00
39 Freddie Freeman .30 .75
40 Freddie Freeman IA .30 .75
41 Willson Contreras .25 .60
42 Willson Contreras IA .25 .60
43 Jose Altuve .20 .50
44 Jose Altuve IA .20 .50
45 Joey Votto .25 .60
46 Joey Votto IA .25 .60
47 Shane Bieber .25 .60
48 Shane Bieber IA .25 .60
49 R.Jeffers RC/J.Bart RC/D.Varsho RC 2.00 5.00
50 Joey Bart IA .50 1.25
51 Javier Baez .30 .75
52 Javier Baez IA .30 .75
53 Austin Hays .25 .60
54 Michael Brantley .20 .50
55 Adalberto Mondesi .20 .50
56 Tyler Naquin .20 .50
57 Jorge Alfaro .15 .40
58 Mitch Moreland .15 .40
59 Jarlin Garcia .15 .40
60 Tommy La Stella .15 .40
61 Danny Mendick .15 .40
62 Martin Perez .15 .40
63 Maikel Franco .20 .50
64 Spencer Turnbull .15 .40
65 Mike Tauchman .25 .60
66 Asdrubal Cabrera .20 .50
67 Julio Urias .25 .60
68 Carson Kelly .15 .40
69 Archie Bradley .15 .40
70 Joe Kelly .15 .40
71 Beau Burrows RC Rony Garcia RC Kyle Funkhouser RC .50 1.25
72 Miguel Andujar .25 .60
73 Ronald Guzman .15 .40
74 Michael Pineda .15 .40
75 Kole Calhoun .15 .40
76 Alec Mills .15 .40
77 Ryan McMahon .25 .60
78 Brian Anderson .15 .40
79 Bryan Reynolds .20 .50
80 Dallas Keuchel .20 .50
81 T.Stephenson RC/W.Contreras RC 1.50 4.00
82 Rafael Montero .15 .40
83 Ketel Marte .20 .50
84 Yandy Diaz .20 .50
85 J.Soto/M.Ozuna/F.Freeman LL .75 2.00
86 David Fletcher DJ LeMahieu Tim Anderson LL .25 .60
87 M.Machado/M.Ozuna/F.Freeman LL .30 .75
88 L.Voit/J.Ramirez/M.Trout/J.Abreu LL 1.25 3.00
89 Duvall/Machado/Pollock/Calhoun Betts/Tatis/Alonso/Ozuna LL 1.25 3.00
90 M.Trout/J.Abreu/J.Ramirez/L.Voit LL 1.25 3.00
91 D.Lamet/Y.Darvish/T.Bauer LL .30 .75
92 Chris Bassitt Dallas Keuchel Shane Bieber LL .25 .60
93 Zach Davies Max Fried Yu Darvish LL .25 .60
94 G.Cole/M.Gonzales/S.Bieber LL .40 1.00
95 A.Nola/J.deGrom/T.Bauer LL .50 1.25
96 S.Bieber/G.Cole/L.Giolito LL .40 1.00
97 K.Hayes RC/J.Garcia RC 4.00 10.00
98 Ke'Bryan Hayes IA 1.50 4.00
99 Jacob deGrom .50 1.25
100 Jacob deGrom IA .50 1.25
101 Kyle Lewis .60 1.50
102 Kyle Lewis IA .60 1.50
103 Paul Goldschmidt .25 .60
104 Paul Goldschmidt IA .25 .60
105 Pete Fairbanks .15 .40
106 Spencer Howard IA .50 1.25
107 Miguel Cabrera .25 .60
108 Miguel Cabrera IA .25 .60
109 L.Garcia RC/C.Pache RC 3.00 8.00
110 Luis Garcia IA .75 2.00
111 Kyle Tucker .25 .60
112 Ryan Yarbrough .15 .40
113 Jose Berrios .20 .50
114 Jose Berrios IA .20 .50
115 Jalen Beeks .15 .40
116 Tommy Milone .15 .40
117 Martin Maldonado .15 .40
118 A.J. Puk .25 .60
119 Max Kepler .20 .50
120 Max Kepler IA .20 .50
121 Aaron Judge .60 1.50
122 Aaron Judge IA .60 1.50
123 Matt Chapman .25 .60
124 Matt Chapman IA .25 .60
125 Nick Castellanos .25 .60
126 Nick Castellanos IA .25 .60
127 Hanser Alberto .15 .40
128 Hanser Alberto IA .15 .40
129 B.Singer RC/N.Heath RC 1.50 4.00
130 Brady Singer IA .75 2.00
131 Starling Marte .20 .50
132 Starling Marte IA .20 .50
133 Danny Jansen .15 .40
134 Evan White IA 1.00 2.50
135 Mike Yastrzemski .40 1.00
136 Mike Yastrzemski IA .40 1.00
137 Fernando Tatis Jr. 1.25 3.00
138 Fernando Tatis Jr. IA 1.25 3.00
139 Kyle Schwarber .25 .60
140 Kyle Schwarber IA .25 .60
141 Nick Ahmed .15 .40
142 Chance Sisco .15 .40
143 Kenley Jansen .20 .50
144 Jose Abreu .25 .60
145 Orlando Arcia .15 .40
146 Pete Alonso KP .60 1.50
147 Nico Hoerner KP .40 1.00
148 Spencer Howard KP .50 1.25
149 Ryan Mountcastle KP 1.50 4.00
150 Austin Riley KP .30 .75
151 Josh Naylor .15 .40
152 Tyler Mahle .15 .40
153 German Marquez .25 .60
154 Framber Valdez .15 .40
155 Ali Sanchez RC Franklyn Kilome RC .30 .75
156 Justin Turner .25 .60
157 Brett Anderson .15 .40
158 Estevan Florial RC Clarke Schmidt RC .50 1.25
159 Seth Lugo .15 .40
160 Jesus Luzardo .25 .60
161 Dexter Fowler .20 .50
162 Donovan Solano .25 .60
163 Alex Bregman .25 .60
164 Alex Bregman IA .25 .60
165 Jorge Soler .25 .60
166 Jorge Soler IA .25 .60
167 Mookie Betts .50 1.25
168 Mookie Betts IA .50 1.25
169 Mike Trout 2.50 6.00
170 Mike Trout IA 1.25 3.00
171 Jackie Bradley Jr. .25 .60
172 Jackie Bradley Jr. IA .25 .60
173 Cody Bellinger .50 1.25
174 Cody Bellinger IA .50 1.25
175 Anthony Rizzo .30 .75
176 Anthony Rizzo IA .30 .75
177 Keston Hiura .30 .75
178 Keston Hiura IA .30 .75
179 Joey Gallo .25 .60
180 Joey Gallo IA .25 .60
181 Max Scherzer .25 .60
182 Max Scherzer IA .25 .60
183 Trea Turner .20 .50
184 Trea Turner IA .20 .50
185 R.Mountcastle/B.Dalbec 4.00 10.00
186 Ryan Mountcastle IA 1.50 4.00
187 J.Adell RC/N.Madrigal RC 2.50 6.00
188 Jo Adell IA 1.00 2.50
189 Albert Pujols .30 .75
190 Albert Pujols IA .30 .75
191 Eloy Jimenez .50 1.25
192 Eloy Jimenez IA .50 1.25
193 Vladimir Guerrero Jr. .40 1.00
194 Vladimir Guerrero Jr. IA .40 1.00
195 Justin Upton .20 .50
196 Jose Quintana .15 .40
197 C.J. Cron .15 .40
198 Josh Donaldson .20 .50
199 Zach Davies .15 .40
200 Michael Taylor .15 .40
201 Ryan McBroom .15 .40
202 Nomar Mazara .15 .40
203 Hunter Dozier .15 .40
204 Kenta Maeda .20 .50
205 Nathan Eovaldi .20 .50
206 Carlos Santana .20 .50
207 Brad Keller .15 .40
208 M.Foster RC/D.Dunning RC Z.Burdi RC 1.00 2.50
209 Lewin Diaz RC Monte Harrison RC Nick Neidert RC .50 1.25
210 Devin Williams .25 .60
211 Enoli Paredes RC Blake Taylor RC Taylor Jones RC 1.00 2.50
212 Dominic Smith .15 .40
213 Mike Soroka .25 .60
214 Chris Bassitt .15 .40
215 J.P. Crawford .15 .40
216 Cavan Biggio
217 Wilmer Flores .20 .50
218 Tyler Chatwood .15 .40
219 Jaime Barria .15 .40
220 Renato Nunez .20 .50
221 Garrett Hampson .15 .40
222 Blake Treinen .15 .40
223 Adam Haseley .20 .50
224 Kyle Gibson .15 .40
225 Julio Teheran .20 .50
226 Austin Riley .30 .75
227 Michael Chavis .20 .50
228 James Karinchak .20 .50
229 Chris Taylor .20 .50
230 Byron Buxton .25 .60
231 Robbie Grossman .15 .40
232 Trent Grisham .30 .75
233 Randal Grichuk .15 .40
234 Daniel Hudson .15 .40
235 Pedro Severino .15 .40
236 Kevin Pillar .15 .40
237 Eduardo Escobar .15 .40
238 Jose Peraza .20 .50
239 Andrew McCutchen .25 .60
240 Andrew McCutchen IA .25 .60
241 Brandon Lowe .20 .50
242 Brandon Lowe IA .20 .50
243 Tim Anderson .25 .60
244 Tim Anderson IA .25 .60
245 Shohei Ohtani .40 1.00
246 Shohei Ohtani IA .40 1.00
247 Justin Verlander .25 .60
248 Justin Verlander IA .25 .60
249 Gerrit Cole .40 1.00
250 Gerrit Cole IA .40 1.00
251 Christian Yelich .30 .75
252 Christian Yelich IA .30 .75
253 C.Mize RC/T.Skubal RC 2.50 6.00
254 Casey Mize IA 1.25 3.00
255 Matt Barnes .15 .40
256 Victor Reyes .15 .40
257 Jakob Junis .15 .40

258 Thairo Estrada .20 .50
259 Lane Thomas .20 .50
260 Mike Brosseau .20 .50
261 Jimmy Lambert RC .50 1.25
Tyson Miller RC
262 Max Fried .25 .60
263 Yu Darvish .25 .60
264 Lucas Giolito .20 .50
265 Jesus Luzardo KP .25 .60
266 Matt Olson KP .25 .60
267 Whit Merrifield KP .25 .60
268 Kris Bubic KP .25 .60
269 Will Smith KP .25 .60
270 Cesar Hernandez .15 .40
271 Antonio Senzatela .15 .40
272 Myles Straw .20 .50
273 Sandy Alcantara .15 .40
274 Luke Voit .30 .75
275 Aaron Nola .20 .50
276 Justin Dunn .15 .40
277 Nick Solak .25 .60
278 Adam Eaton .25 .60
279 Jeff Samardzija .15 .40
280 Gio Gonzalez .20 .50
281 Shane Greene .15 .40
282 Jason Kipnis .20 .50
283 Freddy Galvis .15 .40
284 Josh Staumont .15 .40
285 Alex Verdugo .20 .50
286 Ian Happ .20 .50
287 Ashton Goudeau RC .50 1.25
Ryan Castellani RC
288 Jon Berti .15 .40
289 Josh Lindblom .15 .40
290 Noah Syndergaard .20 .50
291 Gleyber Torres .50 1.25
292 Gleyber Torres IA .50 1.25
293 Bo Bichette .60 1.50
294 Bo Bichette IA .60 1.50
295 D.Carlson RC/E.White RC 3.00 8.00
296 Dylan Carlson IA 1.25 3.00
297 Jose Ramirez .20 .50
298 Jose Ramirez IA .20 .50
299 Ronald Acuna Jr. 1.00 2.50
300 Ronald Acuna Jr. IA 1.00 2.50
301 T.Hatch RC/N.Pearson RC 1.50 4.00
302 Nate Pearson IA .75 2.00
303 Kodi Whitley RC .50 1.25
Roel Ramirez RC
304 Cristian Pache IA 1.50 4.00
305 Charlie Blackmon .25 .60
306 Charlie Blackmon IA .25 .60
307 Nelson Cruz .25 .60
308 Nelson Cruz IA .25 .60
309 Josh Bell .20 .50
310 Josh Bell IA .20 .50
311 Miguel Castro .15 .40
312 Jesus Sanchez IA .50 1.25
313 Nolan Arenado .40 1.00
314 Nolan Arenado IA .40 1.00
315 J.Mateo RC/E.Olivares RC .75 2.00
316 Jeff McNeil .20 .50
317 Mike Minor .15 .40
318 Zach Eflin .15 .40
319 Chad Kuhl .15 .40
320 Dylan Moore .15 .40
321 Joey Wendle .20 .50
322 Luis Arraez .30 .75
323 Steven Souza Jr. .15 .40
324 Mark Melancon .15 .40
325 I.Anderson RC/D.Garcia
RC/C.Javier RC 2.50 6.00
326 Jon Lester .20 .50
327 Lucas Sims .15 .40
328 Jonathan Schoop .15 .40
329 Gregory Soto .15 .40
330 Yuli Gurriel .20 .50
331 Danny Duffy .15 .40
332 Justin Smoak .15 .40
333 Sean Manaea .15 .40
334 Randy Dobnak .25 .60
335 Michael Conforto .20 .50
336 DJ LeMahieu .25 .60
337 Brandon Workman .15 .40
338 Jean Segura .20 .50
339 Wil Myers .20 .50
340 Jurickson Profar .20 .50
341 Tommy Edman .25 .60
342 Hyun-Jin Ryu .20 .50
343 Mauricio Dubon .15 .40
344 Michael Wacha .20 .50
345 Zack Godley .15 .40
346 James McCann .20 .50
347 Dustin May .25 .60
348 Matt Kemp .20 .50
349 Abraham Toro .20 .50
350 Trevor May .15 .40
351 Jake Odorizzi .15 .40
352 Jacob Stallings .15 .40
353 Justus Sheffield .25 .60
354 Rick Porcello .20 .50
355 Zack Wheeler .20 .50
356 Tyler O'Neill .20 .50
357 M.White RC/K.Ruiz RC 1.00 2.50
358 Robbie Ray .15 .40
359 Eric Thames .15 .40
360 T.Houck RC/S.Huff RC .60 1.50
361 Charlie Morton .25 .60
362 Austin Slater .15 .40
363 Nick Nelson RC .75 2.00
Albert Abreu RC
Miguel Yajure RC
364 Austin Meadows .25 .60
365 Cy Young Award .15 .40
366 MVP Award .15 .40
367 Willie Mays World Series MVP Award .15 .40
368 Rookie of the Year Award .15 .40
369 Taylor Williams .15 .40
370 Dylan Bundy .20 .50
371 Gregory Polanco .20 .50
372 Brandon Crawford .20 .50
373 Kyle Seager .15 .40
374 Ender Inciarte .15 .40
375 Kris Bubic RC 1.00 2.50
Triston McKenzie RC
376 Adam Engel .15 .40
377 Anthony Santander .15 .40
378 Alex Cobb .15 .40
379 Howie Kendrick .15 .40
380 Sonny Gray .20 .50
381 Evan Longoria .20 .50
382 Chris Paddack .25 .60
383 Luis Severino .20 .50
384 Marco Gonzales .15 .40
385 Pablo Lopez .15 .40
386 Christian Walker .20 .50
387 Lance Lynn .15 .40
388 Jesse Winker .25 .60
389 Jeimer Candelario .15 .40
390 Jake Cave .20 .50
391 J.D. Davis .15 .40
392 Mark Canha .15 .40
393 Scott Kingery .20 .50
394 John Means .25 .60
395 Josh Hader .20 .50
396 Yasmani Grandal .15 .40
397 Liam Hendricks .15 .40
398 Patrick Corbin .20 .50
399 Kolten Wong .20 .50
400 A.Tejeda RC/L.Taveras RC 1.00 2.50
401 Griffin Canning SP 2.00 5.00
402 Shed Long SP 1.50 4.00
403 Corey Seager SP 2.50 6.00
404 Eugenio Suarez SP 1.50 4.00
405 Drew Pomeranz SP 1.25 3.00
406 Tyler Alexander SP 1.50 4.00
407 Taijuan Walker SP 1.25 3.00
408 Harrison Bader SP 1.50 4.00
409 Didi Gregorius SP 1.50 4.00
410 Aaron Hicks SP 1.50 4.00
411 Tommy Pham SP 1.25 3.00
412 Christian Vazquez SP 1.50 4.00
413 Edwin Encarnacion SP 2.00 5.00
414 Dwight Smith Jr. SP 1.25 3.00
415 Yoshi Tsutsugo SP 1.50 4.00
416 Lourdes Gurriel Jr. SP 1.50 4.00
417 Wilson Ramos SP 1.25 3.00
418 Shogo Akiyama SP 2.00 5.00
419 Jon Gray SP 1.25 3.00
420 Matt Davidson SP 1.50 4.00
421 Matt Joyce SP 1.25 3.00
422 Frankie Montas SP 2.00 5.00
423 Zack Greinke SP 2.00 5.00
424 Brett Gardner SP 1.50 4.00
425 Tommy Hunter SP 1.25 3.00
426 Robinson Cano SP 1.50 4.00
427 David Fletcher SP 2.00 5.00
428 Lance McCullers Jr. SP 1.25 3.00
429 Nicky Lopez SP 1.25 3.00
430 Aaron Civale SP 2.00 5.00
431 Will Smith SP 1.25 3.00
432 Ben Gamel SP 1.25 3.00
433 Dansby Swanson SP 2.00 5.00
434 Jonathan Villar SP 1.25 3.00
435 Kevin Newman SP 2.00 5.00
436 David Peralta SP 1.25 3.00
437 Rich Hill SP 1.25 3.00
438 Jeremy Jeffress SP 1.25 3.00
439 Cam Gallagher SP 1.25 3.00
440 Brandon Nimmo SP 1.50 4.00
441 Franmil Reyes SP 1.25 3.00
442 Jake Arrieta SP 1.50 4.00
443 Kwang-Hyun Kim SP 1.50 4.00
444 Chris Sale SP 2.00 5.00
445 Junior Guerra SP 1.25 3.00
446 Chad Green SP 1.25 3.00
447 Jorge Polanco SP 1.50 4.00
448 Matt Olson SP 2.50 6.00
449 Mitch Garver SP 1.25 3.00
450 Scott Heineman SP 1.25 3.00
451 Kyle Freeland SP 1.50 4.00
452 Johnny Cueto SP 1.50 4.00
453 J.D. Martinez SP 2.00 5.00
454 Jack Flaherty SP 2.00 5.00
455 Jose Osuna SP 1.25 3.00
456 Miguel Sano SP 1.50 4.00
457 Gio Urshela SP 2.00 5.00
458 Anibal Sanchez SP 1.50 4.00
459 Enrique Hernandez SP 1.50 4.00
460 Oscar Mercado SP 1.50 4.00
461 Andrelton Simmons SP 1.25 3.00
462 Dylan Cease SP 1.50 4.00
463 Elvis Andrus SP 1.50 4.00
464 Craig Kimbrel SP 1.50 4.00
465 Kevin Gausman SP 2.00 5.00
466 Teoscar Hernandez SP 2.00 5.00
467 Tim Lopes SP 1.25 3.00
468 Clint Frazier SP 1.50 4.00
469 Raimel Tapia SP 1.25 3.00
470 Victor Robles SP 2.50 6.00
471 Corbin Burnes SP 2.00 5.00
472 Ryan Braun SP 1.50 4.00
473 Colten Brewer RC SP 2.00 5.00
474 Josh Reddick SP 1.25 3.00
475 Trevor Bauer SP 2.50 6.00
476 Whit Merrifield SP 2.00 5.00
477 Adam Duvall SP 1.50 4.00
478 Ramon Laureano SP 1.50 4.00
479 Jonathan Hernandez SP 1.25 3.00
480 Logan Webb SP 2.00 5.00
481 Jason Heyward SP 1.50 4.00
482 Jesus Aguilar SP 1.50 4.00
483 Kyle Hendricks SP 2.00 5.00
484 Zac Gallen SP 1.50 4.00
485 Pat Valaika SP 1.25 3.00
486 Dee Strange-Gordon SP 1.25 3.00
487 Luke Weaver SP 1.25 3.00
488 Ji-Man Choi SP 1.25 3.00
489 Marwin Gonzalez SP 1.25 3.00
490 Todd Frazier SP 1.25 3.00
491 Joe Jimenez SP 1.25 3.00
492 Brad Boxberger SP 1.25 3.00
493 Ty France SP 2.00 5.00
494 Zack Britton SP 1.25 3.00
495 Stephen Piscotty SP 1.25 3.00
496 JaCoby Jones SP 1.25 3.00
497 Blake Snell SP 1.50 4.00
498 A.J. Pollock SP 1.25 3.00
499 Dinelson Lamet SP 1.25 3.00
500 Yordan Alvarez SP 2.50 6.00

2021 Topps Heritage Black Border

*BLACK: 10X TO 25X BASIC
*BLACK RC: 6X TO 15X BASIC RC
*BLACK SP: 1.2X TO 3X BASIC SP
STATED ODDS 1:78 HOBBY
ANNCD PRINT RUN 50 SER.#'d SETS
5 D.Peterson/A.Gimenez 10.00 25.00
31 Pete Alonso 30.00 80.00
35 Juan Soto 30.00 80.00
39 Freddie Freeman 15.00 40.00
121 Aaron Judge 50.00 120.00
137 Fernando Tatis Jr. 125.00 300.00
167 Mookie Betts 25.00 60.00
169 Mike Trout 125.00 300.00
293 Bo Bichette 25.00 60.00

2021 Topps Heritage French Text

*FRENCH: 6X TO 15X BASIC
*FRENCH RC: 3X TO 8X BASIC RC
STATED ODDS 1:320 HOBBY
137 Fernando Tatis Jr. 75.00 200.00

2021 Topps Heritage Red

*RED: 4X TO 10X BASIC
*RED RC: 2X TO 5X BASIC RC
*RED SP: .5X TO 1.2X BASIC SP
INSERTED 3 PER TARGET MEGA BOX

2021 Topps Heritage Action Variations

STATED ODDS 1:52 HOBBY
11 Alec Bohm 30.00 80.00
13 Bryce Harper 12.00 30.00
15 Sixto Sanchez 10.00 25.00
33 Luis Robert 20.00 50.00
35 Juan Soto 15.00 40.00
47 Shane Bieber 6.00 15.00
51 Javier Baez 6.00 15.00
97 Ke'Bryan Hayes 40.00 100.00
99 Jacob deGrom 6.00 15.00
109 Luis Garcia 10.00 25.00
121 Aaron Judge 10.00 25.00
137 Fernando Tatis Jr. 15.00 40.00
167 Mookie Betts 10.00 25.00
169 Mike Trout 40.00 100.00
173 Cody Bellinger 6.00 15.00
181 Max Scherzer 3.00 8.00
185 Bobby Dalbec 15.00 40.00
187 Nick Madrigal 10.00 25.00
188 Jo Adell 15.00 40.00
251 Christian Yelich 6.00 15.00
253 Casey Mize 15.00 40.00
299 Ronald Acuna Jr. 15.00 40.00
301 Nate Pearson 10.00 25.00
313 Nolan Arenado 5.00 12.00

2021 Topps Heritage Missing Stars Variations

STATED ODDS 1:3072 HOBBY
13 Bryce Harper 40.00 100.00
35 Juan Soto 50.00 120.00
47 Shane Bieber 25.00 60.00
51 Javier Baez 25.00 60.00
99 Jacob deGrom 30.00 80.00
121 Aaron Judge 40.00 100.00
137 Fernando Tatis Jr. 60.00 150.00
167 Mookie Betts 50.00 120.00
169 Mike Trout 150.00 400.00
181 Max Scherzer 30.00 80.00
251 Christian Yelich 25.00 60.00
299 Ronald Acuna Jr. 100.00 250.00

2021 Topps Heritage Nickname Variations

STATED ODDS 1:3681 HOBBY
13 Bryce Harper 40.00 100.00
31 Pete Alonso 60.00 150.00
33 Luis Robert 30.00 80.00
37 Clayton Kershaw 60.00 150.00
51 Javier Baez 50.00 120.00
121 Aaron Judge 60.00 150.00
137 Fernando Tatis Jr. 50.00 125.00
169 Mike Trout 125.00 300.00
239 Andrew McCutchen 25.00 60.00
307 Nelson Cruz 30.00 80.00

2021 Topps Heritage Team Color Swap Variations

STATED ODDS 1:312 HOBBY
13 Bryce Harper 8.00 20.00
17 Yadier Molina 10.00 25.00
33 Luis Robert 15.00 40.00
35 Juan Soto 15.00 40.00
37 Clayton Kershaw 8.00 20.00
45 Joey Votto 15.00 40.00
47 Shane Bieber 12.00 30.00
51 Javier Baez 12.00 30.00
99 Jacob deGrom 15.00 40.00
121 Aaron Judge 12.00 30.00
123 Matt Chapman 8.00 20.00
137 Fernando Tatis Jr. 25.00 60.00
163 Alex Bregman 8.00 20.00
167 Mookie Betts 20.00 50.00
169 Mike Trout 30.00 60.00
173 Cody Bellinger 12.00 30.00
175 Anthony Rizzo 6.00 15.00
181 Max Scherzer 8.00 20.00
230 Byron Buxton 10.00 25.00
239 Andrew McCutchen 8.00 20.00
249 Gerrit Cole 12.00 30.00
251 Christian Yelich 6.00 15.00
293 Bo Bichette 12.00 30.00
299 Ronald Acuna Jr. 20.00 50.00
313 Nolan Arenado 8.00 20.00

2021 Topps Heritage '72 Baseball Poster Boxloader

STATED ODDS 1:6 HOBBY BOXES
BPBAJ Aaron Judge 12.00 30.00
BPBBH Bryce Harper 15.00 40.00
BPBBP Buster Posey 8.00 20.00
BPBCB Cody Bellinger 8.00 20.00
BPBCK Clayton Kershaw 10.00 25.00
BPBCY Christian Yelich 10.00 25.00
BPBFJ Fergie Jenkins 6.00 15.00
BPBFL Francisco Lindor 8.00 20.00
BPBFT Fernando Tatis Jr. 8.00 20.00
BPBHA Hank Aaron 10.00 25.00
BPBHK Harmon Killebrew 10.00 25.00
BPBJA Jose Altuve 8.00 20.00
BPBJB Javier Baez 8.00 20.00
BPBLR Luis Robert 5.00 12.00
BPBMS Max Scherzer 4.00 10.00
BPBMT Mike Trout 20.00 50.00
BPBNR Nolan Ryan 15.00 40.00
BPBPA Pete Alonso 8.00 20.00
BPBRA Ronald Acuna Jr. 8.00 20.00
BPBRC Roberto Clemente 15.00 40.00
BPBRJ Reggie Jackson 10.00 25.00
BPBTO Tony Oliva 8.00 20.00
BPBVG Vladimir Guerrero Jr. 8.00 20.00
BPBYM Yadier Molina 10.00 25.00
BPBJBE Johnny Bench 12.00 30.00

2021 Topps Heritage '72 Die Cuts

STATED ODDS 1:8 TRGT HNGR
72DC1 Cody Bellinger 2.50 6.00
72DC2 Mike Trout 10.00 25.00
72DC3 Jacob deGrom 2.50 6.00
72DC4 Fernando Tatis Jr. 6.00 15.00
72DC5 Harmon Killebrew 1.25 3.00
72DC6 Nolan Arenado 2.00 5.00
72DC7 Sixto Sanchez 4.00 10.00
72DC8 Johnny Bench 1.25 3.00
72DC9 Ronald Acuna Jr. 5.00 12.00
72DC10 Jo Adell 5.00 12.00
72DC11 Alex Bregman 1.25 3.00
72DC12 Alec Bohm 8.00 20.00
72DC13 Nolan Ryan 3.00 8.00
72DC14 Luis Robert 4.00 10.00
72DC15 Roberto Clemente 6.00 15.00
72DC16 Anthony Rizzo 1.50 4.00
72DC17 Bryce Harper 2.00 5.00
72DC18 Yadier Molina 1.50 4.00
72DC20 Hank Aaron 2.50 6.00
72DC21 Juan Soto 4.00 10.00
72DC22 Casey Mize 4.00 10.00
72DC23 Aaron Judge 3.00 8.00
72DC24 Ernie Banks 1.25 3.00
72DC25 Ke'Bryan Hayes 5.00 12.00

2021 Topps Heritage '72 Postage Stamps

STATED ODDS 1:8803 HOBBY
PSRAK Al Kaline 50.00 120.00
PSRBG Bob Gibson 60.00 150.00
PSRBR Brooks Robinson 40.00 100.00
PSRCY Carl Yastrzemski 30.00 80.00
PSREB Ernie Banks 60.00 150.00
PSRHA Hank Aaron 75.00 200.00
PSRHK Harmon Killebrew 60.00 150.00
PSRJB Johnny Bench 75.00 200.00
PSRLB Lou Brock 50.00 120.00
PSRNR Nolan Ryan 60.00 150.00
PSRRC Roberto Clemente 100.00 250.00
PSRRF Rollie Fingers 60.00 150.00
PSRRJ Reggie Jackson 60.00 150.00
PSRRS Ron Santo 30.00 80.00
PSRSC Steve Carlton 60.00 150.00
PSRTO Tony Oliva 60.00 150.00
PSRWM Willie Mays 100.00 250.00
PSRWS Willie Stargell
PSRRCA Rod Carew 40.00 100.00
PSRWMC Willie McCovey 75.00 200.00

2021 Topps Heritage '72 Topps Candy Lids

STATED ODDS 1:8 WALMART
1 Javier Baez .75 2.00
2 Mike Trout 3.00 8.00
3 Joey Bart 1.25 3.00
4 Jo Adell 2.50 6.00
5 Jose Altuve .50 1.25
6 Clayton Kershaw 1.00 2.50
7 Fernando Tatis Jr. 3.00 8.00
8 Alec Bohm 4.00 10.00
9 Reggie Jackson .50 1.25
10 Pete Alonso 1.50 4.00
11 Ke'Bryan Hayes 4.00 10.00
12 Christian Yelich .75 2.00
13 Bob Gibson .50 1.25
14 Aaron Judge 1.50 4.00
15 Luis Garcia 2.00 5.00
16 Blake Snell .50 1.25
17 Ryan Mountcastle 4.00 10.00
18 Ron Santo .50 1.25
19 Mookie Betts 1.25 3.00
20 Hank Aaron 1.25 3.00
21 Nate Pearson 2.00 5.00
22 Roberto Clemente 1.50 4.00
23 Juan Soto 2.00 5.00
24 Luis Robert 2.00 5.00
25 Rod Carew .50 1.25

2021 Topps Heritage '72 Topps Oversized Boxloader Autographs

STATED ODDS 1:128 HOBBY BOXES
EXCHANGE DEADLINE 1/31/2023
OBAPBH Bryce Harper 125.00 300.00
OBAPBS Brady Singer 30.00 80.00
OBAPCM Casey Mize
OBAPCY Christian Yelich 100.00 250.00
OBAPDC Dylan Carlson
OBAPNP Nate Pearson
OBAPPA Pete Alonso
OBAPVG Vladimir Guerrero Jr. 200.00 500.00
OBAPYA Yordan Alvarez 40.00 100.00

2021 Topps Heritage '72 Topps Venezuela Stamps

STATED ODDS 1:1486 BLASTER
1 Mike Trout 50.00 120.00
2 Harmon Killebrew 25.00 60.00
3 Jo Adell 25.00 60.00
4 Luis Garcia 15.00 40.00
5 Alex Bregman 25.00 60.00
6 Ke'Bryan Hayes 40.00 100.00
7 Reggie Jackson 25.00 60.00
8 Aaron Judge 25.00 60.00
9 Javier Baez 20.00 50.00
10 Pete Alonso 30.00 80.00
11 Casey Mize 12.00 30.00
12 Fernando Tatis Jr. 30.00 80.00
13 Hank Aaron 100.00 250.00
14 Alec Bohm 60.00 150.00
15 Yadier Molina 20.00 50.00
16 Johnny Bench
17 Ronald Acuna Jr. 60.00 150.00
18 Juan Soto 60.00 150.00
19 Joey Bart 20.00 50.00
20 Dylan Carlson 40.00 100.00
21 Bryce Harper 25.00 60.00
22 Ernie Banks 12.00 30.00
23 Cody Bellinger 12.00 30.00
24 Mookie Betts 20.00 50.00
25 Ryan Mountcastle 60.00 150.00

2021 Topps Heritage Baseball Flashbacks

STATED ODDS 1:25 HOBBY
BFBAK Al Kaline 2.00 5.00
BFBCF Carlton Fisk .50 1.25
BFBDA Dick Allen .40 1.00
BFBFH Frank Howard .40 1.00
BFBFJ Fergie Jenkins .50 1.25
BFBHA Hank Aaron 1.25 3.00
BFBJB Johnny Bench 1.50 4.00
BFBJM Joe Morgan .50 1.25
BFBLB Lou Brock 1.50 4.00
BFBMP Milt Pappas .40 1.00
BFBRC Rod Carew .50 1.25
BFBRCL Roberto Clemente 2.00 5.00
BFBSC Steve Carlton .50 1.25
BFBWM Willie Mays 2.00 5.00
BFBWMC Willie McCovey .50 1.25

2021 Topps Heritage Chrome

STATED ODDS 1:92 HOBBY
STATED PRINT RUN 999 SER.#'d SETS
*PURPLE REF: .4X TO 1X BASIC
*BLUE SPRKL: .5X TO 1.2X BASIC
2 Max Muncy 1.50 4.00
5 D.Peterson/A.Gimenez 3.00 8.00
9 Miguel Rojas 1.25 3.00
11 A.Bohm/S.Howard 10.00 25.00
13 Bryce Harper 3.00 8.00
15 S.Sanchez/J.Sanchez 6.00 15.00
17 Yadier Molina 2.50 6.00
19 Rhys Hoskins 2.50 6.00
31 Pete Alonso 5.00 12.00
33 Luis Robert 12.00 30.00
35 Juan Soto 25.00 60.00
37 Clayton Kershaw 3.00 8.00
39 Freddie Freeman 2.50 6.00
41 Willson Contreras 2.00 5.00
43 Jose Altuve 1.50 4.00
45 Joey Votto 2.00 5.00
47 Shane Bieber 2.00 5.00
49 R.Jeffers/J.Bart/D.Varsho 12.00 30.00
51 Javier Baez 2.50 6.00
54 Michael Brantley 1.50 4.00
80 Dallas Keuchel 1.50 4.00
81 T.Stephenson/W.Contreras 6.00 15.00
83 Ketel Marte 1.50 4.00
97 K.Hayes/J.Garcia 25.00 60.00
99 Jacob deGrom 4.00 10.00
101 Kyle Lewis 5.00 12.00
103 Paul Goldschmidt 2.00 5.00
107 Miguel Cabrera 2.00 5.00
109 L.Garcia/C.Pache 20.00 50.00
113 Jose Berrios 1.50 4.00
119 Max Kepler 1.50 4.00
121 Aaron Judge 5.00 12.00
123 Matt Chapman 2.00 5.00
125 Nick Castellanos 2.00 5.00
127 Hanser Alberto 1.25 3.00
129 B.Singer/N.Heath 6.00 15.00
131 Starling Marte 1.50 4.00
135 Mike Yastrzemski 3.00 8.00
137 Fernando Tatis Jr. 25.00 60.00
139 Kyle Schwarber 2.00 5.00
142 Beau Burrows 2.00 5.00
Rony Garcia
Kyle Funkhouser
163 Alex Bregman 2.00 5.00
165 Jorge Soler 2.00 5.00
167 Mookie Betts 6.00 15.00
169 Mike Trout 25.00 60.00
171 Jackie Bradley Jr. 2.00 5.00
173 Cody Bellinger 4.00 10.00
175 Anthony Rizzo 2.50 6.00
177 Keston Hiura 2.50 6.00
179 Joey Gallo 2.00 5.00
181 Max Scherzer 2.00 5.00
185 R.Mountcastle RC/B.Dalbec RC 15.00 40.00
187 J.Adell/N.Madrigal 10.00 25.00
189 Albert Pujols 4.00 10.00
191 Eloy Jimenez 4.00 10.00
193 Vladimir Guerrero Jr. 5.00 12.00
213 Mike Soroka 2.00 5.00
239 Andrew McCutchen 2.00 5.00
241 Brandon Lowe 1.50 4.00
243 Tim Anderson 2.00 5.00
245 Shohei Ohtani 3.00 8.00
247 Justin Verlander 2.00 5.00
249 Gerrit Cole 3.00 8.00
251 Christian Yelich 2.50 6.00
253 C.Mize/T.Skubal 10.00 25.00
285 Alex Verdugo 1.50 4.00
291 Gleyber Torres 4.00 10.00
293 Bo Bichette 5.00 12.00
295 D.Carlson/E.White 8.00 20.00
297 Jose Ramirez 1.50 4.00
299 Ronald Acuna Jr. 12.00 30.00
301 T.Hatch/N.Pearson 6.00 15.00
305 Charlie Blackmon 2.00 5.00
307 Nelson Cruz 2.00 5.00
309 Josh Bell 1.50 4.00
313 Nolan Arenado 3.00 8.00
316 Jeff McNeil 1.50 4.00
320 I.Anderson/D.Garcia/C.Javier 10.00 25.00
355 Zack Wheeler 1.50 4.00
372 Brandon Crawford 1.50 4.00
380 Sonny Gray 1.50 4.00
403 Corey Seager 2.00 5.00
404 Eugenio Suarez 1.50 4.00
409 Didi Gregorius 1.50 4.00
419 Jon Gray 1.25 3.00
423 Zack Greinke 2.00 5.00
433 Dansby Swanson 2.00 5.00
440 Brandon Nimmo 1.50 4.00
441 Franmil Reyes 1.25 3.00
444 Chris Sale 2.00 5.00
447 Jorge Polanco 1.50 4.00
454 Jack Flaherty 2.00 5.00
470 Victor Robles 2.50 6.00
472 Ryan Braun 1.50 4.00
475 Trevor Bauer 2.50 6.00
476 Whit Merrifield 2.00 5.00
478 Ramon Laureano 1.50 4.00
483 Kyle Hendricks 2.00 5.00
497 Blake Snell 1.50 4.00
500 Yordan Alvarez 5.00 12.00

2021 Topps Heritage Chrome Black Refractors

*BLACK REF: 1X TO 2.5X BASIC
STATED ODDS 1:1280 HOBBY
STATED PRINT RUN 72 SER.#'d SETS
13 Bryce Harper 40.00 100.00
33 Luis Robert 125.00 300.00
137 Fernando Tatis Jr. 250.00 600.00
295 D.Carlson/E.White 100.00 250.00
299 Ronald Acuna Jr. 75.00 200.00

2021 Topps Heritage Chrome Red Refractors

*RED REF: 1X TO 2.5X BASIC
STATED ODDS 1:247 HOBBY
STATED PRINT RUN 372 SER.#'d SETS
13 Bryce Harper 20.00 50.00
33 Luis Robert 60.00 150.00
137 Fernando Tatis Jr. 125.00 300.00
295 D.Carlson/E.White 50.00 120.00
299 Ronald Acuna Jr. 40.00 100.00

2021 Topps Heritage Chrome Refractors

*REF: .6X TO 1.5X BASIC
STATED ODDS 1:161 HOBBY
STATED PRINT RUN 572 SER.#'d SETS
13 Bryce Harper 12.00 30.00
33 Luis Robert 40.00 100.00
137 Fernando Tatis Jr. 75.00 200.00
295 D.Carlson/E.White 30.00 80.00
299 Ronald Acuna Jr. 25.00 60.00

2021 Topps Heritage Clubhouse Collection Autograph Relics

STATED ODDS 1:7590 HOBBY
STATED PRINT RUN 25 SER.#'d SETS
EXCHANGE DEADLINE 1/31/2023
CCARAJ Aaron Judge
CCARBH Bryce Harper 125.00 300.00
CCARCY Christian Yelich 100.00 250.00
CCARJA Jo Adell
CCARMK Max Kepler 100.00 250.00
CCARMT Mike Trout
CCARPA Pete Alonso 100.00 250.00
CCARRA Ronald Acuna Jr. 100.00 250.00
CCARVG Vladimir Guerrero Jr. 100.00 250.00
CCARWC Willson Contreras 20.00 50.00
CCARXB Xander Bogaerts 40.00 100.00
CCARYM Yoan Moncada

2021 Topps Heritage Clubhouse Collection Dual Relics

STATED ODDS 1:24,395 HOBBY
STATED PRINT RUN 72 SER.#'d SETS
CDRCC C.Kershaw/C.Bellinger 50.00 120.00
CDRCX X.Bogaerts/C.Yastrzemski 50.00 120.00
CDRMA M.Trout/A.Rendon 25.00 60.00
CDRRK R.Santo/K.Bryant 40.00 100.00
CDRTJ T.Seaver/J.deGrom 100.00 250.00

2021 Topps Heritage Clubhouse Collection Relics

STATED ODDS 1:34 HOBBY
CCRAA Aristides Aquino 3.00 8.00
CCRAH Aaron Hicks 2.50 6.00
CCRAJ Aaron Judge 15.00 40.00
CCRAN Aaron Nola 2.50 6.00
CCRAP Albert Pujols 6.00 15.00
CCRAR Anthony Rizzo 4.00 10.00
CCRBB Brandon Belt 2.50 6.00
CCRBH Bryce Harper 8.00 20.00
CCRBL Brandon Lowe 2.50 6.00
CCRBP Buster Posey 8.00 20.00
CCRBS Blake Snell 2.50 6.00
CCRCB Cody Bellinger 6.00 15.00
CCRCC Carlos Correa 3.00 8.00
CCRCS Chris Sale 3.00 8.00
CCRCY Christian Yelich 8.00 20.00
CCRDP David Peralta 2.00 5.00
CCRDS Dansby Swanson 3.00 8.00
CCRER Eddie Rosario 2.50 6.00
CCRFF Freddie Freeman 6.00 15.00
CCRFL Francisco Lindor 10.00 25.00
CCRFT Fernando Tatis Jr. 15.00 40.00
CCRGS Gary Sanchez 3.00 8.00
CCRGT Gleyber Torres 6.00 15.00
CCRHD Hunter Dozier 2.00 5.00
CCRIH Ian Happ 2.50 6.00
CCRJA Jose Altuve 2.50 6.00
CCRJB Javier Baez 4.00 10.00
CCRJH Josh Hader 2.50 6.00
CCRJL Jesus Luzardo 3.00 8.00
CCRJM John Means 3.00 8.00
CCRJS Jorge Soler 3.00 8.00
CCRJV Justin Verlander 3.00 8.00
CCRJW Jesse Winker 3.00 8.00
CCRKB Kris Bryant 4.00 10.00
CCRKH Keston Hiura 4.00 10.00
CCRKW Kolten Wong 2.50 6.00
CCRLC Luis Castillo 2.50 6.00
CCRMA Miguel Andujar 3.00 8.00
CCRMB Mookie Betts 8.00 20.00
CCRMC Matt Chapman 3.00 8.00
CCRMM Max Muncy 2.50 6.00
CCRMS Max Scherzer 3.00 8.00
CCRMT Mike Trout 20.00 50.00
CCRNC Nelson Cruz 3.00 8.00
CCRNM Nick Markakis 2.50 6.00
CCRNS Nick Senzel 3.00 8.00
CCROA Ozzie Albies 3.00 8.00
CCRPA Pete Alonso 8.00 20.00
CCRRA Ronald Acuna Jr. 10.00 25.00
CCRRD Rafael Devers 4.00 10.00
CCRRH Rhys Hoskins 4.00 10.00
CCRSC Shin-Soo Choo 2.50 6.00
CCRSK Scott Kingery 2.50 6.00
CCRSS Stephen Strasburg 3.00 8.00
CCRTH Teoscar Hernandez 3.00 8.00
CCRTS Trevor Story 3.00 8.00
CCRTT Trea Turner 2.50 6.00
CCRWC Willson Contreras 3.00 8.00
CCRWS Will Smith 3.00 8.00
CCRXB Xander Bogaerts 3.00 8.00
CCRYA Yordan Alvarez 8.00 20.00
CCRYM Yadier Molina 4.00 10.00
CCRZG Zac Gallen 2.50 6.00
CCRAPU A.J. Puk 3.00 8.00
CCRCBI Cavan Biggio 4.00 10.00
CCRCBL Charlie Blackmon 3.00 8.00
CCREWH Evan White 5.00 12.00
CCRGSP George Springer 2.50 6.00
CCRJAB Jose Abreu 3.00 8.00
CCRJAL Jorge Alfaro 2.00 5.00
CCRJBE Josh Bell 2.50 6.00
CCRJDD J.D. Davis 2.00 5.00
CCRJHE Jason Heyward 2.50 6.00
CCRJVO Joey Votto 3.00 8.00
CCRMCA Miguel Cabrera 3.00 8.00
CCRMTA Masahiro Tanaka 3.00 8.00

2021 Topps Heritage Clubhouse Collection Relics Gold

*GOLD: .6X TO 1.5X BASIC
STATED ODDS 1:1168 HOBBY
STATED PRINT RUN 99 SER.#'d SETS
CCRBH Bryce Harper 15.00 40.00
CCRFL Francisco Lindor 20.00 50.00
CCRMB Mookie Betts 40.00 100.00
CCRMT Mike Trout 40.00 100.00
CCRRA Ronald Acuna Jr. 20.00 50.00

2021 Topps Heritage Clubhouse Collection Triple Relics

STATED ODDS 1:71,151 HOBBY
STATED PRINT RUN 25 SER.#'d SETS
CTRAGG Judge/Sanchez/Torres 100.00 250.00
CTRHFR Aaron/Acuna Jr/Freeman 100.00 250.00
CTRLTN Helton/Walker/Arenado 30.00 80.00
CTRRKC Yelich/Hiura/Yount 75.00 200.00
CTRWWB McCovey/Posey/Mays 100.00 250.00

2021 Topps Heritage Flashback Autograph Relics

STATED ODDS 1:34,850 HOBBY
STATED PRINT RUN 25 SER.#'d SETS
EXCHANGE DEADLINE 1/31/2023
FARCY Carl Yastrzemski 150.00 400.00
FARHA Hank Aaron 800.00 1500.00
FARJB Johnny Bench 300.00 800.00
FARNR Nolan Ryan
FARRC Rod Carew 125.00 300.00
FARRJ Reggie Jackson 200.00 500.00
FARSG Steve Garvey 100.00 250.00
FARTO Tony Oliva 100.00 250.00

2021 Topps Heritage Mini

STATED ODDS 1:698 HOBBY
STATED PRINT RUN 100 SER.#'d SETS
2 Max Muncy 5.00 12.00
9 Miguel Rojas 4.00 10.00
13 Bryce Harper 15.00 40.00
17 Yadier Molina 15.00 40.00
19 Rhys Hoskins 8.00 20.00
31 Pete Alonso 30.00 80.00
33 Luis Robert 50.00 120.00
35 Juan Soto 30.00 80.00
37 Clayton Kershaw 10.00 25.00
39 Freddie Freeman 15.00 40.00
41 Willson Contreras 6.00 15.00
43 Jose Altuve 5.00 12.00
45 Joey Votto 6.00 15.00
47 Shane Bieber 6.00 15.00
51 Javier Baez 8.00 20.00
53 Austin Hays 6.00 15.00
54 Michael Brantley 5.00 12.00
55 Adalberto Mondesi 5.00 12.00
70 Joe Kelly 4.00 10.00
80 Dallas Keuchel 5.00 12.00
83 Ketel Marte 5.00 12.00
99 Jacob deGrom 12.00 30.00
101 Kyle Lewis 15.00 40.00
103 Paul Goldschmidt 6.00 15.00
105 Pete Fairbanks 4.00 10.00
107 Miguel Cabrera 6.00 15.00
113 Jose Berrios 5.00 12.00
119 Max Kepler 5.00 12.00
121 Aaron Judge 50.00 120.00
123 Matt Chapman 6.00 15.00
125 Nick Castellanos 6.00 15.00
127 Hanser Alberto 4.00 10.00
131 Starling Marte 5.00 12.00
135 Mike Yastrzemski 10.00 25.00
137 Fernando Tatis Jr. 125.00 300.00
139 Kyle Schwarber 6.00 15.00
144 Jose Abreu 6.00 15.00
163 Alex Bregman 6.00 15.00
165 Jorge Soler 6.00 15.00
167 Mookie Betts 25.00 60.00
169 Mike Trout 60.00 150.00
171 Jackie Bradley Jr. 6.00 15.00
173 Cody Bellinger 12.00 30.00
175 Anthony Rizzo 20.00 50.00
177 Keston Hiura 8.00 20.00
179 Joey Gallo 6.00 15.00
181 Max Scherzer 6.00 15.00
189 Albert Pujols 8.00 20.00
191 Eloy Jimenez 12.00 30.00
193 Vladimir Guerrero Jr. 10.00 25.00
198 Josh Donaldson 5.00 12.00
210 Devin Williams 6.00 15.00
213 Mike Soroka 6.00 15.00
216 Cavan Biggio 8.00 20.00
227 Michael Chavis 5.00 12.00
229 Chris Taylor 5.00 12.00
230 Byron Buxton 6.00 15.00
232 Trent Grisham 8.00 20.00
239 Andrew McCutchen 6.00 15.00
241 Brandon Lowe 5.00 12.00
243 Tim Anderson 6.00 15.00
247 Justin Verlander 6.00 15.00
249 Gerrit Cole 10.00 25.00
251 Christian Yelich 12.00 30.00
257 Jakob Junis 4.00 10.00
260 Mike Brosseau 5.00 12.00
262 Max Fried 6.00 15.00
263 Yu Darvish 6.00 15.00
274 Luke Voit 8.00 20.00
275 Aaron Nola 5.00 12.00
285 Alex Verdugo 5.00 12.00
286 Ian Happ 5.00 12.00
290 Noah Syndergaard 10.00 25.00
291 Gleyber Torres 12.00 30.00
293 Bo Bichette 25.00 60.00
297 Jose Ramirez 5.00 12.00
299 Ronald Acuna Jr. 25.00 60.00
305 Charlie Blackmon 6.00 15.00
307 Nelson Cruz 6.00 15.00
309 Josh Bell 5.00 12.00
313 Nolan Arenado 10.00 25.00

316 Jeff McNeil 5.00 12.00
326 Jon Lester 5.00 12.00
339 Wil Myers 5.00 12.00
342 Hyun-Jin Ryu 5.00 12.00
347 Dustin May 6.00 15.00
351 Jake Odorizzi 4.00 10.00
355 Zack Wheeler 5.00 12.00
361 Charlie Morton 6.00 15.00
364 Austin Meadows 6.00 15.00
372 Brandon Crawford 5.00 12.00
380 Sonny Gray 5.00 12.00
387 Lance Lynn 4.00 10.00
388 Jesse Winker 6.00 15.00
403 Corey Seager 8.00 20.00
404 Eugenio Suarez 5.00 12.00
409 Didi Gregorius 5.00 12.00
410 Aaron Hicks 5.00 12.00
411 Tommy Pham 4.00 10.00
419 Jon Gray 4.00 10.00
423 Zack Greinke 6.00 15.00
427 David Fletcher 6.00 15.00
428 Lance McCullers Jr. 4.00 10.00
433 Dansby Swanson 6.00 15.00
436 David Peralta 4.00 10.00
437 Rich Hill 4.00 10.00
440 Brandon Nimmo 5.00 12.00
441 Franmil Reyes 4.00 10.00
442 Jake Arrieta 5.00 12.00
443 Kwang-Hyun Kim 5.00 12.00
444 Chris Sale 6.00 15.00
447 Jorge Polanco 5.00 12.00
448 Matt Olson 8.00 20.00
449 Mitch Garver 4.00 10.00
453 J.D. Martinez 6.00 15.00
454 Jack Flaherty 6.00 15.00
456 Miguel Sano 5.00 12.00
462 Dylan Cease 5.00 12.00
463 Elvis Andrus 5.00 12.00
464 Craig Kimbrel 5.00 12.00
466 Teoscar Hernandez 6.00 15.00
470 Victor Robles 8.00 20.00
472 Ryan Braun 5.00 12.00
475 Trevor Bauer 8.00 20.00
476 Whit Merrifield 6.00 15.00
478 Ramon Laureano 5.00 12.00
482 Jesus Aguilar 5.00 12.00
483 Kyle Hendricks 6.00 15.00
488 Ji-Man Choi 4.00 10.00
495 Stephen Piscotty 4.00 10.00
497 Blake Snell 5.00 12.00
500 Yordan Alvarez 8.00 20.00

2021 Topps Heritage New Age Performers

STATED ODDS 1:15 HOBBY
NAP1 Luis Robert 2.00 5.00
NAP2 David Fletcher .60 1.50
NAP3 Shane Bieber .60 1.50
NAP4 Ryan Mountcastle 4.00 10.00
NAP5 Fernando Tatis Jr. 3.00 8.00
NAP6 Mike Yastrzemski 2.00 5.00
NAP7 Nate Pearson 2.00 5.00
NAP8 Kyle Lewis 2.50 6.00
NAP9 Luke Voit .75 2.00
NAP10 Teoscar Hernandez .60 1.50
NAP11 Brandon Lowe .50 1.25
NAP12 Max Fried .60 1.50
NAP13 Alex Verdugo .50 1.25
NAP14 Ian Happ .50 1.25
NAP15 Alec Bohm 3.00 8.00
NAP16 Casey Mize 1.50 4.00
NAP17 Ke'Bryan Hayes 2.00 5.00
NAP18 Ian Anderson 3.00 8.00
NAP19 Devin Williams .60 1.50
NAP20 Randy Arozarena 1.50 4.00
NAP21 Sixto Sanchez 2.00 5.00
NAP22 Jo Adell 2.50 6.00
NAP23 Jeff McNeil .50 1.25
NAP24 Keston Hiura .75 2.00
NAP25 Dylan Carlson 2.00 5.00

2021 Topps Heritage News Flashbacks

STATED ODDS 1:25 HOBBY
NFBF Bobby Fischer Wins World Chess Championship .75 2.00
NFDJ Dow Jones Closes Above 1,000 for First Time .75 2.00
NFHT President Harry Truman Passes Away .75 2.00
NFRF Roberta Flack Tops the Billboard Hot 100 .75 2.00
NFRN Watergate Scandal Begins with Break-In .75 2.00
NFARP Atari Releases Pong .75 2.00
NFCAM Bilingual Cameroon Unites .75 2.00
NFDWI Digital Watches Introduced .75 2.00
NFERA Equal Rights Admendment Passed .75 2.00
NFGGB Golden Gate National Recreation Area Opens .75 2.00
NFOLY 72 Winter Games Kick Off in Japan .75 2.00
NFPIO Pioneer 10 Spacecraft Launched .75 2.00
NFPIR The Price Is Right Airs on CBS .75 2.00
NFPOS The Poseidon Adventure Tops '72 Box Office .75 2.00
NFAPOL Apollo 17 Lands on the Moon .75 2.00

2021 Topps Heritage Rangers Inagural Season Autographs

STATED ODDS 1:5825 HOBBY
ANNCD PRINT RUN 100 SER.#'d SETS
EXCHANGE DEADLINE 1/31/2023
RISADB Dick Billings 50.00 120.00
RISAFH Frank Howard 75.00 200.00
RISAMP Mike Paul 50.00 120.00
RISARH Rich Hand 75.00 200.00
RISATF Ted Ford 60.00 150.00
RISATG Tom Grieve 75.00 200.00
RISATH Toby Harrah 60.00 150.00

2021 Topps Heritage Real One Autographs

STATED ODDS 1:106 HOBBY
EXCHANGE DEADLINE 1/31/2023
ROAAB Alec Bohm 100.00 250.00
ROAAG Alex Gordon 8.00 20.00
ROAAR Anthony Rendon 25.00 60.00
ROAAV Alex Verdugo 15.00 40.00
ROABD Bobby Dalbec 60.00 150.00
ROABH Bryce Harper EXCH 75.00 200.00
ROABL Brandon Lowe 8.00 20.00
ROABS Brady Singer 15.00 40.00
ROACB Cody Bellinger 75.00 200.00
ROACM Casey Mize 75.00 200.00
ROACP Cristian Pache 50.00 120.00
ROACY Christian Yelich 50.00 120.00
ROADC Dylan Carlson 75.00 200.00
ROADG Deivi Garcia 20.00 50.00
ROADJ Daniel Johnson 10.00 25.00
ROADP David Peterson 20.00 50.00
ROAEJ Eloy Jimenez 20.00 50.00
ROAEW Evan White 12.00 30.00
ROAFJ Fergie Jenkins 20.00 50.00
ROAFR Franmil Reyes 10.00 25.00
ROAGT Gleyber Torres 50.00 120.00
ROAHA Hank Aaron 600.00 1500.00
ROAIA Ian Anderson 30.00 80.00
ROAJA Jo Adell 75.00 200.00
ROAJB Johnny Bench 100.00 250.00
ROAJC Jake Cronenworth 30.00 80.00
ROAJM Jeff McNeil 8.00 20.00
ROAJR Jose Ramirez 15.00 40.00
ROAKH Keston Hiura 12.00 30.00
ROAKS Kyle Schwarber 10.00 25.00
ROALC Luis Castillo 8.00 20.00
ROALP Luis Patino 10.00 25.00
ROALT Leody Taveras 8.00 20.00
ROAMH Monte Harrison 10.00 25.00
ROAMT Mike Trout 400.00 1000.00
ROAMW Maury Wills 15.00 40.00
ROANM Nick Madrigal 40.00 100.00
ROANP Nate Pearson 30.00 80.00
ROANR Nolan Ryan 150.00 400.00
ROAPA Pete Alonso 40.00 100.00
ROAPC Patrick Corbin 8.00 20.00
ROAPR Phil Regan 10.00 25.00
ROARC Rod Carew 25.00 60.00
ROARH Ron Hansen 6.00 15.00
ROARJ Reggie Jackson 100.00 250.00
ROASG Steve Garvey 20.00 50.00
ROASH Spencer Howard 20.00 50.00
ROASM Starling Marte 8.00 20.00
ROASS Sixto Sanchez 20.00 50.00
ROATH Tanner Houck 15.00 40.00
ROATO Tony Oliva 25.00 60.00
ROATP Tommy Pham 10.00 25.00
ROATS Tyler Stephenson 30.00 80.00
ROAVB Vida Blue 25.00 60.00
ROAVG Vladimir Guerrero Jr. 40.00 100.00
ROAWC Willson Contreras 15.00 40.00
ROAWM Whit Merrifield 20.00 50.00
ROAAGI Andres Gimenez 10.00 25.00
ROACYA Carl Yastrzemski 125.00 300.00
ROADVA Daulton Varsho 15.00 40.00
ROAJAL Jose Altuve 15.00 40.00
ROAJBA Joey Bart 50.00 120.00
ROAJCH Jazz Chisholm 40.00 100.00
ROAJMA J.D. Martinez 15.00 40.00
ROAKBH Ke'Bryan Hayes 100.00 250.00
ROALGA Luis Garcia 30.00 80.00
ROARHO Rhys Hoskins 25.00 60.00
ROARJE Ryan Jeffers 12.00 30.00
ROASHU Sam Huff 30.00 80.00
ROAWCO William Contreras 20.00 50.00

2021 Topps Heritage Real One Autographs Red Ink

*RED/72: .75X TO 2X BASIC
STATED ODDS 1:1960 HOBBY
STATED PRINT RUN 72 SER.#'d SETS
ROAAB Alec Bohm 400.00 1000.00
ROABD Bobby Dalbec 200.00 500.00
ROACP Cristian Pache 200.00 500.00
ROADC Dylan Carlson 200.00 500.00
ROAFJ Fergie Jenkins 75.00 200.00
ROAHA Hank Aaron 800.00 2000.00
ROAJA Jo Adell 200.00 500.00
ROAMT Mike Trout 1000.00 2500.00
ROAPA Pete Alonso 100.00 250.00
ROARJ Reggie Jackson 150.00 400.00
ROACYA Carl Yastrzemski 150.00 400.00
ROAJBA Joey Bart 150.00 400.00

2021 Topps Heritage Real One Dual Autographs

STATED ODDS 1:7590 HOBBY
STATED PRINT RUN 25 SER.#'d SETS
EXCHANGE DEADLINE 1/31/2023
RODAAA R.Acuna Jr/H.Aaron 1500.00 2500.00
RODAHH R.Hoskins/B.Harper 125.00 300.00
RODAJB V.Blue/R.Jackson 150.00 400.00
RODARA C.Pache/R.Acuna Jr 400.00 1000.00
RODATA J.Adell/M.Trout
RODAJBE R.Jackson/J.Bench
RODARMO R.Mountcastle/C.Ripken Jr EXCH 300.00 600.00

2021 Topps Heritage The Great One

STATED ODDS 1:18 HOBBY
GO1 Roberto Clemente 1.50 4.00
GO2 Roberto Clemente 1.50 4.00
GO3 Roberto Clemente 1.50 4.00
GO4 Roberto Clemente 1.50 4.00
GO5 Roberto Clemente 1.50 4.00
GO6 Roberto Clemente 1.50 4.00
GO7 Roberto Clemente 1.50 4.00
GO8 Roberto Clemente 1.50 4.00
GO9 Roberto Clemente 1.50 4.00
GO10 Roberto Clemente 1.50 4.00
GO11 Roberto Clemente 1.50 4.00
GO12 Roberto Clemente 1.50 4.00
GO13 Roberto Clemente 1.50 4.00
GO14 Roberto Clemente 1.50 4.00
GO15 Roberto Clemente 1.50 4.00
GO16 Roberto Clemente 1.50 4.00
GO17 Roberto Clemente 1.50 4.00
GO18 Roberto Clemente 1.50 4.00
GO19 Roberto Clemente 1.50 4.00
GO20 Roberto Clemente 1.50 4.00
GO21 Roberto Clemente 1.50 4.00
GO22 Roberto Clemente 1.50 4.00
GO23 Roberto Clemente 1.50 4.00
GO24 Roberto Clemente 1.50 4.00
GO25 Roberto Clemente 1.50 4.00

2021 Topps Heritage Then and Now

STATED ODDS 1:25 HOBBY
TN1 D.Allen/L.Voit .75 2.00
TN2 T.Seaver/J.deGrom 1.25 3.00
TN3 F.Jenkins/Y.Darvish .60 1.50
TN4 S.Bieber/G.Perry .60 1.50
TN5 R.Carew/D.LeMahieu .60 1.50
TN6 F.Tatis Jr/L.Brock 3.00 8.00
TN7 F.Freeman/J.Bench 2.00 5.00
TN8 H.Aaron/M.Ozuna 2.00 5.00
TN9 C.Santana/D.Allen .50 1.25
TN10 T.Bauer/S.Carlton .75 2.00
TN11 J.Palmer/G.Cole 1.00 2.50
TN12 J.Abreu/D.Allen .60 1.50
TN13 B.Harper/J.Morgan 1.00 2.50
TN14 B.Williams/J.Soto 2.00 5.00
TN15 N.Ryan/S.Bieber 2.00 5.00

2015 Topps Heritage '51 Collection

COMPLETE SET (104) 15.00 40.00
ONE COMPLETE BASE SET PER BOX
1 Mike Trout 1.50 4.00
2 Felix Hernandez .25 .60
3 Miguel Cabrera .30 .75
4 Madison Bumgarner .25 .60
5 Masahiro Tanaka .25 .60
6 Joey Votto .30 .75
7 David Price .25 .60
8 Mookie Betts .60 1.50
9 Jake Lamb RC .60 1.50
10 Yasmany Tomas RC .50 1.25
11 Archie Bradley RC .40 1.00
12 Todd Frazier .20 .50
13 Michael Pineda .20 .50
14 Taijuan Walker .20 .50
15 Starling Marte .25 .60
16 Dalton Pompey RC .50 1.25
17 Eric Hosmer .25 .60
18 Paul Goldschmidt .30 .75
19 Kolten Wong .25 .60
20 Kevin Plawecki RC .40 1.00
21 Jorge Soler RC .60 1.50
22 Devon Travis RC .40 1.00
23 Max Scherzer .30 .75
24 Ian Desmond .20 .50
25 Kris Bryant RC 4.00 10.00
26 Steven Souza Jr. .25 .60
27 Joc Pederson RC 1.50 4.00
28 Jason Heyward .25 .60
29 Justin Upton .25 .60
30 Craig Kimbrel .25 .60
31 Jose Altuve .25 .60
32 Michael Brantley .25 .60
33 Ian Kinsler .25 .60
34 Hanley Ramirez .25 .60
35 Matt Harvey .25 .60
36 Yoenis Cespedes .30 .75
37 Ryan Braun .25 .60
38 George Springer .25 .60
39 Hunter Pence .25 .60
40 Carlos Gonzalez .25 .60
41 Manny Machado .30 .75
42 Corey Kluber .25 .60
43 Daniel Norris RC .40 1.00
44 Joey Gallo RC .75 2.00
45 Jose Bautista .25 .60
46 Albert Pujols .40 1.00
47 Michael Wacha .25 .60
48 Christian Yelich .40 1.00
49 Zack Greinke .30 .75
50 Bryce Harper .50 1.25
51 Yasiel Puig .30 .75
52 Jeff Samardzija .20 .50
53 Robinson Cano .25 .60
54 Carlos Rodon RC 1.00 2.50
55 Anthony Rizzo .40 1.00
56 Josh Donaldson .25 .60
57 Rusney Castillo RC .50 1.25
58 Noah Syndergaard RC .75 2.00
59 James Shields .20 .50
60 Giancarlo Stanton .30 .75
61 David Ortiz .30 .75
62 Troy Tulowitzki .30 .75
63 Pablo Sandoval .25 .60
64 Brandon Finnegan RC .40 1.00
65 Lucas Duda .25 .60
66 Chris Sale .30 .75
67 Carlos Correa RC 2.00 5.00
68 Anthony Rendon .30 .75
69 Andrew McCutchen .30 .75
70 Cole Hamels .25 .60
71 Evan Longoria .25 .60
72 Jacoby Ellsbury .25 .60
73 Adrian Gonzalez .25 .60
74 Byron Buxton RC 2.00 5.00
75 Francisco Lindor RC 3.00 8.00
76 Kyle Seager .20 .50
77 Addison Russell RC 1.25 3.00
78 Jacob deGrom .60 1.50
79 Stephen Strasburg .30 .75
80 Andrew Miller .25 .60
81 Billy Hamilton .25 .60
82 Adam Jones .25 .60
83 David Wright .25 .60
84 Aaron Sanchez .25 .60
85 Chris Archer .20 .50
86 Sonny Gray .25 .60
87 Adrian Beltre .30 .75
88 Freddie Freeman .40 1.00
89 Matt Kemp .25 .60
90 Prince Fielder .25 .60
91 Alex Cobb .20 .50
92 Dustin Pedroia .30 .75
93 Jordan Zimmermann .25 .60
94 Johnny Cueto .25 .60
95 Edwin Encarnacion .30 .75
96 Jon Lester .25 .60
97 Buster Posey .40 1.00
98 Nelson Cruz .30 .75
99 Jose Abreu .30 .75
100 Clayton Kershaw .50 1.25
101 Starlin Castro .20 .50
102 Eduardo Rodriguez RC .40 1.00
103 Blake Swihart RC .50 1.25
104 Aroldis Chapman .30 .75

2015 Topps Heritage '51 Collection Mini Black Back

*BLACK: 3X TO 8X BASIC
*BLACK RC: 1.5X TO 4X BASIC
TWO MINI BLACK PER BOX SET

2015 Topps Heritage '51 Collection Mini Blue Back

*BLUE: 1.5X TO 4X BASIC
*BLUE RC: .75X TO 2X BASIC
FIVE MINI BLUE PER BOX SET

2015 Topps Heritage '51 Collection Mini Gold Back

*GOLD: 6X TO 15X BASIC
*GOLD RC: 3X TO 8X BASIC
ONE MINI GOLD PER BOX SET
1 Mike Trout 25.00 60.00

2015 Topps Heritage '51 Collection Mini Green Back

*GREEN: 2X TO 5X BASIC
*GREEN RC: 1X TO 2.5X BASIC
THREE MINI GREEN PER BOX SET

2015 Topps Heritage '51 Collection Mini Red Back

*RED: 1.2X TO 3X BASIC
*RED RC: .6X TO 1.5X BASIC
TEN MINI RED PER BOX SET

2015 Topps Heritage '51 Collection Autographs

OVERALL ONE AUTO PER BOX SET
PRINT RUNS B/WN 50-250 COPIES PER
EXCHANGE DEADLINE 10/31/2017
*BLUE/25: .6X TO 1.5X BASIC
H51AAB Archie Bradley/250 5.00 12.00
H51AAR Addison Russell/250 15.00 40.00
H51ABB Byron Buxton/250 15.00 40.00
H51ABH Bryce Harper/50 125.00 250.00
H51ABP Buster Posey 40.00 100.00
H51ACC Carlos Correa/50 100.00 250.00
H51ACR Carlos Rodon 12.00 30.00
H51ADP Dalton Pompey/250 6.00 15.00
H51ADW David Wright/100 25.00 60.00
H51AER Eduardo Rodriguez/250 5.00 12.00
H51AFL Francisco Lindor/250 25.00 60.00
H51AJA Jose Abreu/250 8.00 20.00
H51AJD Jacob deGrom/250 20.00 50.00
H51AJL Jake Lamb/250 8.00 20.00
H51AJP Joc Pederson/250 8.00 20.00
H51AJS Jorge Soler/250 10.00 25.00
H51AKB Kris Bryant/210 100.00 250.00
H51AKP Kevin Plawecki/250 5.00 12.00
H51ALD Lucas Duda EXCH 6.00 15.00
H51AMT Mike Trout/50 200.00 300.00
H51ANS Noah Syndergaard/250 20.00 50.00
H51ARC Rusney Castillo/250 6.00 15.00
H51ASG Sonny Gray/250 6.00 15.00
H51ASS Steven Souza Jr./250 6.00 15.00
H51ATW Taijuan Walker/250 5.00 12.00
H51AYT Yasmany Tomas EXCH 6.00 15.00

2014 Topps High Tek Wave

*SPIRAL: .5X TO 1.2X WAVE
*SCRIBBLE: .6X TO 1.5X WAVE
*LG SHATTERED: 1.5X TO 4X WAVE
*SMALL MAZE: 3X TO 8X WAVE
HTAB Albert Belle .60 1.50
HTAJ Adam Jones .75 2.00
HTAP Albert Pujols 1.25 3.00
HTBJ Bo Jackson 1.00 2.50
HTCF Carlton Fisk .75 2.00
HTCR Cal Ripken Jr. 3.00 8.00
HTCS Chris Sale 1.00 2.50
HTDE Dennis Eckersley .75 2.00
HTDP Dustin Pedroia 1.00 2.50
HTEL Evan Longoria .75 2.00
HTEM Edgar Martinez .75 2.00
HTFM Fred McGriff .75 2.00
HTFT Frank Thomas 1.00 2.50
HTGS George Springer RC 2.50 6.00
HTIR Ivan Rodriguez .75 2.00
HTJA Jose Abreu RC 5.00 12.00
HTJC Jose Canseco .75 2.00
HTJG Juan Gonzalez .60 1.50
HTJM Joe Mauer .75 2.00
HTJSI Jon Singleton RC .75 2.00
HTKG Ken Griffey Jr. 2.00 5.00
HTMC Miguel Cabrera 1.00 2.50
HTMM Mike Mussina .75 2.00
HTMN Mike Napoli .60 1.50
HTMR Mariano Rivera 1.25 3.00
HTMS Marcus Stroman RC 1.00 2.50
HTMSC Max Scherzer 1.00 2.50
HTMT Mike Trout 5.00 12.00
HTMTA Masahiro Tanaka RC 2.00 5.00
HTNC Nick Castellanos RC 2.00 5.00
HTNG Nomar Garciaparra .75 2.00
HTNR Nolan Ryan 3.00 8.00
HTOH Orlando Hernandez .60 1.50
HTOV Omar Vizquel .75 2.00
HTPF Prince Fielder .75 2.00
HTPM Pedro Martinez .75 2.00
HTPO Paul O'Neill .75 2.00
HTRA Roberto Alomar .75 2.00
HTRC Robinson Cano .75 2.00
HTRCL Roger Clemens 1.25 3.00
HTRE Roenis Elias RC .60 1.50
HTRH Rickey Henderson 1.00 2.50
HTRJA Reggie Jackson .75 2.00
HTRP Rafael Palmeiro .75 2.00
HTRY Robin Yount 1.00 2.50
HTSG Sonny Gray .75 2.00
HTTW Taijuan Walker RC .60 1.50
HTWB Wade Boggs .75 2.00
HTWM Wil Myers .60 1.50
HTYC Yoenis Cespedes 1.00 2.50
HTYD Yu Darvish 1.00 2.50
HTYS Yangervis Solarte RC .60 1.50
HTYV Yordano Ventura RC .75 2.00

2014 Topps High Tek Wave Clouds Diffractor 25

*CLOUDS: 3X TO 8X BASIC
STATED ODDS 1:10 PACKS
STATED PRINT RUN 25 SER.#'d SETS
HTCR Cal Ripken Jr. 20.00 50.00
HTKG Ken Griffey Jr. 20.00 50.00
HTMT Mike Trout 30.00 80.00
HTRH Rickey Henderson 10.00 25.00
HTRJA Reggie Jackson 8.00 20.00

2014 Topps High Tek Wave Disco Diffractor 50

*DISCO: 1.2X TO 3X BASIC
STATED ODDS 1:5 PACKS
STATED PRINT RUN 50 SER.#'d SETS
HTKG Ken Griffey Jr. 8.00 20.00
HTMT Mike Trout 15.00 40.00
HTRH Rickey Henderson 4.00 10.00
HTRJA Reggie Jackson 3.00 8.00

2014 Topps High Tek Wave Gold Diffractor 99

*GOLD: 1.2X TO 3X BASIC
STATED ODDS 1:3 PACKS
STATED PRINT RUN 99 SER.#'d SETS
HTKG Ken Griffey Jr. 8.00 20.00
HTMT Mike Trout 15.00 40.00
HTRH Rickey Henderson 4.00 10.00
HTRJA Reggie Jackson 3.00 8.00

2014 Topps High Tek Wave Ice Diffractor 75

*ICE: 1.2X TO 3X BASIC
STATED ODDS 1:4 PACKS
STATED PRINT RUN 75 SER.#'d SETS
HTKG Ken Griffey Jr. 8.00 20.00
HTMT Mike Trout 15.00 40.00
HTRH Rickey Henderson 4.00 10.00
HTRJA Reggie Jackson 3.00 8.00

2014 Topps High Tek Spiral Bricks

*SPIRAL: .5X TO 1.2X SPIRAL BRICK
*NET: .5X TO 1.2X SPIRAL BRICK
*SHATTER: .5X TO 1.2X SPIRAL BRICK
*LG MAZE: 2X TO 5X SPIRAL BRICK
2014 Topps High Tek Net
*ZIGZAG: 4X TO 10X SPIRAL BRICK
HTAG Alex Guerrero RC .75 2.00
HTAGO Adrian Gonzalez .75 2.00
HTAH Andrew Heaney RC .60 1.50
HTAS Andrelton Simmons .60 1.50
HTBH Bryce Harper 1.50 4.00
HTBPO Buster Posey 1.25 3.00
HTCB Craig Biggio .75 2.00
HTCG Carlos Gonzalez .75 2.00
HTCJ Chipper Jones 1.00 2.50
HTCK Clayton Kershaw 1.50 4.00
HTCO Chris Owings RC .60 1.50
HTCY Christian Yelich 1.25 3.00
HTDW David Wright .75 2.00
HTEB Ernie Banks 1.00 2.50
HTEBU Eddie Butler RC .60 1.50
HTFF Freddie Freeman 1.25 3.00
HTFV Fernando Valenzuela .60 1.50
HTGM Greg Maddux 1.25 3.00
HTGP Gregory Polanco RC 1.00 2.50
HTGST Giancarlo Stanton 1.00 2.50
HTHA Hank Aaron 2.00 5.00
HTHR Hanley Ramirez .75 2.00
HTJB Jeff Bagwell .75 2.00
HTJCU Johnny Cueto .75 2.00
HTJF Jose Fernandez 1.00 2.50
HTJH Jason Heyward .75 2.00
HTJS Jean Segura .75 2.00
HTJT Julio Teheran .75 2.00
HTJV Joey Votto 1.00 2.50
HTMIS Mike Schmidt 1.50 4.00
HTMMC Mark McGwire 2.00 5.00
HTMP Mike Piazza 1.00 2.50
HTMW Michael Wacha .75 2.00
HTOT Oscar Taveras RC .75 2.00
HTPG Paul Goldschmidt 1.00 2.50
HTRB Ryan Braun .75 2.00
HTRJ Randy Johnson 1.00 2.50
HTSK Sandy Koufax 2.00 5.00
HTSM Shelby Miller .75 2.00
HTTG Tom Glavine .75 2.00
HTTGW Tony Gwynn 1.00 2.50
HTTP Terry Pendleton .60 1.50
HTTT Troy Tulowitzki 1.00 2.50
HTVG Vladimir Guerrero .75 2.00
HTWMA Willie Mays 2.00 5.00
HTYM Yadier Molina 1.25 3.00
HTYP Yasiel Puig 1.00 2.50

2014 Topps High Tek Spiral Bricks Clouds Diffractor 25

*CLOUDS: 2.5X TO 6X BASIC
STATED ODDS 1:10 PACKS
STATED PRINT RUN 25 SER.#'d SETS
HTMMC Mark McGwire 20.00 50.00
HTMP Mike Piazza 15.00 40.00
HTTGW Tony Gwynn 12.00 30.00
HTYM Yadier Molina 10.00 25.00

2014 Topps High Tek Spiral Bricks Disco Diffractor 50

*DISCO: 1X TO 2.5X BASIC
STATED ODDS 1:5 PACKS
STATED PRINT RUN 50 SER.#'d SETS
HTMMC Mark McGwire 8.00 20.00
HTMP Mike Piazza 6.00 15.00
HTTGW Tony Gwynn 5.00 12.00
HTYM Yadier Molina 4.00 10.00

2014 Topps High Tek Spiral Bricks Gold Diffractor 99

*GOLD: 1X TO 2.5X BASIC
STATED ODDS 1:3 PACKS
STATED PRINT RUN 99 SER.#'d SETS
HTMMC Mark McGwire 8.00 20.00
HTMP Mike Piazza 6.00 15.00
HTTGW Tony Gwynn 5.00 12.00
HTYM Yadier Molina 4.00 10.00

2014 Topps High Tek Spiral Bricks Ice Diffractor 75

*ICE: 1X TO 2.5X BASIC
STATED ODDS 1:4 PACKS
STATED PRINT RUN 75 SER.#'d SETS
HTMMC Mark McGwire 8.00 20.00
HTMP Mike Piazza 6.00 15.00
HTTGW Tony Gwynn 5.00 12.00
HTYM Yadier Molina 4.00 10.00

2014 Topps High Tek '00 TEKtonics Diffractors

STATED ODDS 1:24 PACKS
STATED PRINT RUN 50 SER.#'d SETS
TDAB Albert Belle 2.00 5.00
TDAM Andrew McCutchen 3.00 8.00
TDBH Bryce Harper 5.00 12.00
TDCJ Chipper Jones 10.00 25.00
TDCR Cal Ripken Jr. 10.00 25.00
TDDE Dennis Eckersley 2.50 6.00
TDDJ Derek Jeter 25.00 60.00
TDDW David Wright 2.50 6.00
TDJA Jose Abreu 15.00 40.00
TDMP Mike Piazza 3.00 8.00
TDMT Masahiro Tanaka 6.00 15.00
TDNG Nomar Garciaparra 2.50 6.00
TDNR Nolan Ryan 10.00 25.00
TDPF Prince Fielder 2.50 6.00
TDPG Paul Goldschmidt 3.00 8.00
TDPM Pedro Martinez 2.50 6.00
TDRC Robinson Cano 2.50 6.00
TDVG Vladimir Guerrero 2.50 6.00
TDWM Willie Mays 6.00 15.00
TDYD Yu Darvish 3.00 8.00

2014 Topps High Tek '99 TEKnicians Diffractors

STATED ODDS 1:19 PACKS
STATED PRINT RUN 50 SER.#'d SETS
99TAC Aroldis Chapman 6.00 15.00
99TAM Andrew McCutchen 6.00 15.00
99TBM Brian McCann 5.00 12.00
99TCS Chris Sale 6.00 15.00
99TFT Frank Thomas 12.00 30.00
99TGC Gerrit Cole 6.00 15.00
99TGM Greg Maddux 20.00 50.00
99TGS Giancarlo Stanton 6.00 15.00
99THJR Hyun-Jin Ryu 5.00 12.00
99THR Hanley Ramirez 5.00 12.00
99TJH Josh Hamilton 5.00 12.00
99TKG Ken Griffey Jr. 15.00 40.00
99TMC Miguel Cabrera 6.00 15.00
99TMM Mark McGwire 12.00 30.00
99TMS Max Scherzer 6.00 15.00
99TMT Mike Trout 30.00 80.00
99TPG Paul Goldschmidt 6.00 15.00
99TPO Paul O'Neill 5.00 12.00
99TRC Roger Clemens 8.00 20.00
99TRH Rickey Henderson 6.00 15.00
99TRJ Randy Johnson 6.00 15.00
99TRP Rafael Palmeiro 5.00 12.00
99TTG Tom Glavine 5.00 12.00
99TXB Xander Bogaerts 10.00 25.00
99TYP Yasiel Puig 10.00 25.00

2014 Topps High Tek Autographs

OVERALL AUTO ODDS 1:1 PACKS
EXCHANGE DEADLINE 11/30/2017
HTAG Alex Guerrero 5.00 12.00
HTAGA Andres Galarraga 5.00 12.00
HTAGO Adrian Gonzalez 10.00 25.00
HTAH Andrew Heaney 4.00 10.00
HTBP Brandon Phillips 5.00 12.00
HTCB Craig Biggio 15.00 40.00
HTCF Carlton Fisk 15.00 40.00
HTCJ Chipper Jones 40.00 80.00
HTCO Chris Owings 4.00 10.00
HTCS Chris Sale 8.00 20.00
HTCY Christian Yelich 30.00 80.00
HTDE Dennis Eckersley 6.00 15.00
HTDW David Wright 15.00 40.00
HTEBU Eddie Butler 4.00 10.00
HTEM Edgar Martinez 10.00 25.00
HTFF Freddie Freeman 6.00 15.00
HTFM Fred McGriff 6.00 15.00
HTFT Frank Thomas 40.00 80.00
HTFV Fernando Valenzuela 15.00 40.00
HTGP Gregory Polanco 6.00 15.00
HTGS George Springer 20.00 50.00
HTHR Hanley Ramirez 5.00 12.00
HTIR Ivan Rodriguez 10.00 25.00
HTJA Jose Abreu 8.00 20.00
HTJC Jose Canseco 6.00 15.00
HTJF Jose Fernandez 12.00 30.00
HTJG Juan Gonzalez 6.00 15.00
HTJH Jason Heyward 6.00 15.00
HTMB Madison Bumgarner 20.00 50.00
HTMN Mike Napoli 4.00 10.00
HTMS Marcus Stroman 6.00 15.00
HTMSC Max Scherzer 15.00 40.00
HTMW Michael Wacha 8.00 20.00
HTNC Nick Castellanos 12.00 30.00
HTNG Nomar Garciaparra 12.00 30.00
HTOH Orlando Hernandez 4.00 10.00
HTOT Oscar Taveras 5.00 12.00
HTOV Omar Vizquel 5.00 12.00
HTPG Paul Goldschmidt 10.00 25.00
HTPO Paul O'Neill 5.00 12.00
HTRA Roberto Alomar 6.00 15.00
HTRB Ryan Braun 8.00 20.00
HTRC Robinson Cano 15.00 40.00
HTRE Roenis Elias 4.00 10.00
HTRG Ron Gant 4.00 10.00
HTRP Rafael Palmeiro 6.00 15.00
HTRY Robin Yount 25.00 60.00
HTSG Sonny Gray 5.00 12.00
HTSM Shelby Miller 5.00 12.00
HTTG Tom Glavine 10.00 25.00
HTTP Terry Pendleton 6.00 15.00
HTTW Taijuan Walker 4.00 10.00
HTWM Wil Myers 6.00 15.00
HTYC Yoenis Cespedes 8.00 20.00
HTYS Yangervis Solarte 4.00 10.00
HTYV Yordano Ventura 5.00 12.00
HTZW Zack Wheeler 5.00 12.00

2014 Topps High Tek Autographs Clouds Diffractor 25

*CLOUDS 25: .6X TO 1.5X BASIC
STATED ODDS 1:13 PACKS
STATED PRINT RUN 25 SER.#'d SETS
EXCHANGE DEADLINE 11/30/2017
HTBJ Bo Jackson 40.00 100.00
HTCK Clayton Kershaw 60.00 120.00
HTEL Evan Longoria 15.00 40.00
HTGST Giancarlo Stanton 30.00 80.00
HTJT Julio Teheran 8.00 20.00
HTJV Joey Votto 25.00 60.00
HTMC Miguel Cabrera 50.00 100.00
HTMIS Mike Schmidt 30.00 60.00
HTMMC Mark McGwire 75.00 150.00
HTMR Mariano Rivera 75.00 150.00
HTMT Mike Trout 200.00 400.00
HTNR Nolan Ryan 100.00 200.00
HTRJA Reggie Jackson 30.00 60.00
HTTT Troy Tulowitzki 12.00 30.00
HTVG Vladimir Guerrero 20.00 50.00
HTWB Wade Boggs 20.00 50.00
HTYD Yu Darvish 60.00 120.00
HTYP Yasiel Puig 60.00 120.00

2014 Topps High Tek Autographs Disco Diffractor 50

*DISCO 50: .5X TO 1.2X BASIC
STATED ODDS 1:8 PACKS
STATED PRINT RUN 50 SER.#'d SETS
EXCHANGE DEADLINE 11/30/2017
HTBJ Bo Jackson 30.00 80.00
HTCG Carlos Gonzalez 8.00 20.00
HTCK Clayton Kershaw 50.00 100.00
HTGST Giancarlo Stanton 25.00 60.00
HTJT Julio Teheran 8.00 20.00
HTJV Joey Votto 20.00 50.00
HTMT Mike Trout 150.00 300.00
HTTT Troy Tulowitzki 10.00 25.00
HTVG Vladimir Guerrero 15.00 40.00

2014 Topps High Tek Low Tek Diffractors

STATED ODDS 1:14 PACKS
STATED PRINT RUN 50 SER.#'d SETS
LTAJ Adam Jones 5.00 12.00
LTCB Craig Biggio 5.00 12.00
LTCF Carlton Fisk 5.00 12.00
LTCG Carlos Gonzalez 5.00 12.00
LTDJ Derek Jeter 20.00 50.00
LTDO David Ortiz 6.00 15.00
LTDP Dustin Pedroia 8.00 20.00
LTEB Ernie Banks 6.00 15.00
LTFF Freddie Freeman 8.00 20.00
LTFH Felix Hernandez 5.00 12.00
LTGS Giancarlo Stanton 6.00 15.00
LTHA Hank Aaron 12.00 30.00
LTIR Ivan Rodriguez 5.00 12.00
LTJA Jose Abreu 12.00 30.00
LTJB Johnny Bench 6.00 15.00
LTJE Jacoby Ellsbury 5.00 12.00
LTJF Jose Fernandez 6.00 15.00
LTJG Juan Gonzalez 10.00 25.00
LTJS John Smoltz 6.00 15.00
LTJU Justin Upton 5.00 12.00
LTJV Justin Verlander 6.00 15.00
LTKG Ken Griffey Jr. 15.00 40.00
LTMM Mike Mussina 12.00 30.00
LTMT Mike Trout 30.00 80.00
LTRA Roberto Alomar 5.00 12.00
LTRB Ryan Braun 5.00 12.00
LTSG Sonny Gray 5.00 12.00
LTSK Sandy Koufax 10.00 25.00
LTSS Stephen Strasburg 6.00 15.00
LTTG Tony Gwynn 6.00 15.00
LTTT Troy Tulowitzki 6.00 15.00
LTWB Wade Boggs 10.00 25.00
LTYD Yu Darvish 6.00 15.00
LTYP Yasiel Puig 10.00 25.00

2015 Topps High Tek

GROUP A = GRASS PATTERN
GROUP B = WAVES PATTERN
HTABY Archie Bradley B RC .75 2.00
HTAG Alex Gordon A 1.00 2.50
HTAJO Adam Jones A 1.00 2.50
HTAJS Andruw Jones A .75 2.00
HTAL Al Leiter B .75 2.00
HTAM Andrew McCutchen A 1.25 3.00
HTAP Albert Pujols A 1.50 4.00
HTAR Addison Russell A RC 2.50 6.00
HTARI Anthony Rizzo A 1.50 4.00
HTBB Byron Buxton A RC 4.00 10.00
HTBC Brandon Crawford B 1.00 2.50
HTBF Brandon Finnegan B RC .75 2.00
HTBH Bryce Harper A 2.00 5.00
HTBJ Bo Jackson A 1.25 3.00
HTBL Barry Larkin B 1.00 2.50
HTBP Buster Posey B 1.50 4.00
HTBS Blake Swihart B RC 1.00 2.50
HTBW Bernie Williams A 1.00 2.50
HTCB Craig Biggio A 1.00 2.50
HTCC Carlos Correa B RC 4.00 10.00
HTCD Carlos Delgado A .75 2.00
HTCJ Chipper Jones B 1.25 3.00
HTCKR Corey Kluber B 1.00 2.50
HTCKW Clayton Kershaw B 2.00 5.00
HTCRN Cal Ripken Jr. B 4.00 10.00
HTCRO Carlos Rodon B RC 2.00 5.00
HTCSE Chris Sale B 1.25 3.00
HTCY Christian Yelich A 1.50 4.00
HTDB Dellin Betances B 1.00 2.50
HTDF Doug Fister B .75 2.00
HTDH Dilson Herrera A RC 1.00 2.50
HTDJ Derek Jeter B 3.00 8.00
HTDN Daniel Norris B RC .75 2.00
HTDO David Ortiz A 1.25 3.00
HTDPA Dustin Pedroia A 1.25 3.00
HTDPY Dalton Pompey A RC 1.00 2.50
HTDT Devon Travis A RC .75 2.00
HTEE Edwin Encarnacion A 1.25 3.00
HTEM Edgar Martinez A 1.00 2.50
HTFF Freddie Freeman A 1.50 4.00
HTFH Felix Hernandez B 1.00 2.50
HTFL Francisco Lindor B RC 6.00 15.00
HTFR Frank Robinson A 1.00 2.50
HTFT Frank Thomas A 1.25 3.00
HTGM Greg Maddux B 1.50 4.00
HTGR Garrett Richards B 1.00 2.50
HTGS George Springer A 1.00 2.50
HTGST Giancarlo Stanton A 1.25 3.00
HTHA Hank Aaron A 2.50 6.00
HTI Ichiro A 1.50 4.00
HTJAE Jose Altuve A 1.00 2.50
HTJAU Jose Abreu A 1.25 3.00
HTJB Javier Baez A RC 6.00 15.00
HTJB Johnny Bench B 1.25 3.00
HTJC Jose Canseco A 1.00 2.50
HTJDM Jacob deGrom B 2.50 6.00
HTJF Jose Fernandez B 1.25 3.00
HTJGZ Juan Gonzalez A .75 2.00
HTJK Jung-Ho Kang B RC .75 2.00
HTJL Jon Lester B 1.00 2.50
HTJM Joe Mauer A 1.00 2.50
HTJPK Joe Panik A 1.00 2.50
HTJPN Joc Pederson A RC 3.00 8.00
HTJSR Jorge Soler A RC 1.25 3.00
HTJSS James Shields B .75 2.00
HTJSZ John Smoltz B 1.25 3.00

HTKB Kris Bryant B RC 10.00 25.00
HTKG Ken Griffey Jr. A 2.50 6.00
HTKP Kevin Plawecki B RC .75 2.00
HTMBR Madison Bumgarner B 1.00 2.50
HTMBS Matt Barnes B RC .75 2.00
HTMC Miguel Cabrera A 1.25 3.00
HTMFO Maikel Franco B RC 1.00 2.50
HTMGE Mark Grace A 1.00 2.50
HTMGM Marquis Grissom A .75 2.00
HTMHY Matt Harvey B 1.00 2.50
HTMJ Micah Johnson A RC .75 2.00
HTMME Mark McGwire A 2.00 5.00
HTMPA Mike Piazza B 1.25 3.00
HTMPR Mark Prior B 1.00 2.50
HTMR Mariano Rivera B 1.50 4.00
HTMSR Matt Shoemaker B 1.00 2.50
HTMSZ Max Scherzer B 1.25 3.00
HTMTA Masahiro Tanaka B 1.00 2.50
HTMTR Michael Taylor A RC .75 2.00
HTMTT Mike Trout A 6.00 15.00
HTNG Nomar Garciaparra B 1.00 2.50
HTNR Nolan Ryan B 4.00 10.00
HTNS Noah Syndergaard B RC 1.50 4.00
HTOS Ozzie Smith B 1.50 4.00
HTOV Omar Vizquel B 1.00 2.50
HTPG Paul Goldschmidt A 1.25 3.00
HTPS Pablo Sandoval B 1.00 2.50
HTRA Roberto Alomar A 1.00 2.50
HTRCA Rusney Castillo A RC 1.00 2.50
HTRCO Robinson Cano A 1.00 2.50
HTRCS Roger Clemens B 1.50 4.00
HTRH Rickey Henderson A 1.25 3.00
HTRI Raisel Iglesias B RC 1.00 2.50
HTRJA Reggie Jackson A 1.00 2.50
HTRJO Randy Johnson B 1.25 3.00
HTRO Roberto Osuna B RC .75 2.00
HTSGY Sonny Gray B 1.00 2.50
HTSK Sandy Koufax B 2.50 6.00
HTSMA Steven Moya A RC 1.00 2.50
HTSME Starling Marte A 1.00 2.50
HTSP Salvador Perez B 1.00 2.50
HTTG Tom Glavine B 1.00 2.50
HTVC Vinny Castilla B .75 2.00
HTVM Victor Martinez A 1.00 2.50
HTYP Yasiel Puig A 1.25 3.00
HTYT Yasmany Tomas A RC 1.00 2.50

2015 Topps High Tek Blade

*BLADE: 2.5X TO 6X BASIC
STATED ODDS 1:24 HOBBY

2015 Topps High Tek Chain Link

*CHAIN LINK: .75X TO 2X BASIC
STATED ODDS 1:3 HOBBY

2015 Topps High Tek Circuit Board

*CIRCUIT BOARD: .5X TO 1.2X BASIC
RANDOM INSERTS IN PACKS

2015 Topps High Tek Clouds Diffractor

*CLDS DFFRCTR: 2.5X TO 6X BASIC
STATED ODDS 1:10 HOBBY
STATED PRINT RUN 25 SER.#'d SETS

2015 Topps High Tek Confetti Diffractor

*CNFTTI DFFRCTR: 1.2X TO 3X BASIC
STATED ODDS 1:5 HOBBY
STATED PRINT RUN 99 SER.#'d SETS

2015 Topps High Tek Cubes

*CUBES: .75X TO 2X BASIC
STATED ODDS 1:3 HOBBY

2015 Topps High Tek Diamonds

*DIAMONDS: 1.2X TO 3X BASIC
STATED ODDS 1:6 HOBBY

2015 Topps High Tek Dots

*DOTS: .4X TO 1X BASIC
RANDOM INSERTS IN PACKS

2015 Topps High Tek Gold Rainbow

*GOLD RNBW: 2X TO 5X BASIC
STATED ODDS 1:7 HOBBY
STATED PRINT RUN 35 SER.#'d SETS

2015 Topps High Tek Grid

*GRID: 1.5X TO 4X BASIC
STATED ODDS 1:12 HOBBY
HTKB Kris Bryant 60.00 150.00

2015 Topps High Tek Home Uniform Photo Variations

*UNIFORM: 2.5X TO 6X BASIC
STATED ODDS 1:42 HOBBY
HTBP Buster Posey 30.00 80.00
HTCKW Clayton Kershaw 25.00 60.00
HTDJ Derek Jeter 40.00 100.00
HTMTT Mike Trout 60.00 150.00
HTOV Omar Vizquel 75.00 150.00

2015 Topps High Tek Pipes

*PIPES: .5X TO 1.2X BASIC
RANDOM INSERTS IN PACKS

2015 Topps High Tek Purple Rainbow

*PRPLE RNBW: .5X TO 1.2X BASIC
STATED ODDS 1:3 HOBBY

2015 Topps High Tek Pyramids

*PYRAMIDS: 1.2X TO 3X BASIC
STATED ODDS 1:6 HOBBY

2015 Topps High Tek Spiral

*SPIRAL: .4X TO 1X BASIC
RANDOM INSERTS IN PACKS

2015 Topps High Tek Stripes

*STRIPES: 1.5X TO 4X BASIC
STATED ODDS 1:12 HOBBY

2015 Topps High Tek Tidal Diffractor

*TDL DFFRCTR: 1.5X TO 4X BASIC
STATED ODDS 1:7 HOBBY
STATED PRINT RUN 75 SER.#'d SETS

2015 Topps High Tek Autographs

OVERALL AUTO ODDS 1:1 HOBBY
EXCHANGE DEADLINE 9/30/2017
HTABY Archie Bradley 3.00 8.00
HTAG Alex Gordon 4.00 10.00
HTAJS Andruw Jones 3.00 8.00
HTAL Al Leiter 4.00 10.00
HTAR Addison Russell 10.00 25.00
HTBB Byron Buxton 15.00 40.00
HTBC Brandon Crawford 5.00 12.00
HTBJ Bo Jackson 25.00 60.00
HTBL Barry Larkin 15.00 40.00
HTBS Blake Swihart 4.00 10.00
HTBW Bernie Williams 10.00 25.00
HTCB Craig Biggio 8.00 20.00
HTCC Carlos Correa 75.00 200.00
HTCD Carlos Delgado 3.00 8.00
HTCJ Chipper Jones 25.00 60.00
HTCKR Corey Kluber 4.00 10.00
HTCKW Clayton Kershaw 25.00 60.00
HTCSE Chris Sale 10.00 25.00
HTDB Dellin Betances 4.00 10.00
HTDF Doug Fister 3.00 8.00
HTDO David Ortiz 15.00 40.00
HTDPA Dustin Pedroia 12.00 30.00
HTDT Devon Travis 3.00 8.00
HTEE Edwin Encarnacion 5.00 12.00
HTEM Edgar Martinez 10.00 25.00
HTFL Francisco Lindor 20.00 50.00
HTFR Frank Robinson 15.00 40.00
HTGR Garrett Richards 4.00 10.00
HTGS George Springer 10.00 25.00
HTI Ichiro Suzuki 250.00 400.00
HTJAE Jose Altuve 12.00 30.00
HTJAU Jose Abreu 12.00 30.00
HTJB Javier Baez 20.00 50.00
HTJC Jose Canseco 10.00 25.00
HTJDM Jacob deGrom 30.00 80.00
HTJGZ Juan Gonzalez 3.00 8.00
HTJL Jon Lester 8.00 20.00
HTJPK Joe Panik 4.00 10.00
HTJPN Joc Pederson 6.00 15.00
HTJSR Jorge Soler 5.00 12.00
HTJSS James Shields 3.00 8.00
HTJSZ John Smoltz 12.00 30.00
HTKP Kevin Plawecki 3.00 8.00
HTMBS Matt Barnes 3.00 8.00
HTMFO Maikel Franco 4.00 10.00
HTMGE Mark Grace 4.00 10.00
HTMGM Marquis Grissom 3.00 8.00
HTMHY Matt Harvey 20.00 50.00
HTMJ Micah Johnson 3.00 8.00
HTMPR Mark Prior 4.00 10.00
HTMSR Matt Shoemaker 4.00 10.00
HTMTR Michael Taylor 3.00 8.00
HTNG Nomar Garciaparra 10.00 25.00
HTNS Noah Syndergaard 12.00 30.00
HTOS Ozzie Smith 15.00 40.00
HTOV Omar Vizquel 4.00 10.00
HTPG Paul Goldschmidt 12.00 30.00
HTRA Roberto Alomar 10.00 25.00
HTRCA Rusney Castillo 4.00 10.00
HTRI Raisel Iglesias 4.00 10.00
HTRO Roberto Osuna 3.00 8.00
HTSGY Sonny Gray 4.00 10.00
HTSME Starling Marte 5.00 12.00
HTSP Salvador Perez 10.00 25.00
HTTG Tom Glavine 10.00 25.00
HTVC Vinny Castilla 3.00 8.00

2015 Topps High Tek Autographs Clouds Diffractor

*CLDS DFFRCTR: .75X TO 2X BASIC
STATED ODDS 1:20 HOBBY
STATED PRINT RUN 25 SER.#'d SETS
EXCHANGE DEADLINE 9/30/2017
HTBH Bryce Harper EXCH 150.00 250.00
HTBP Buster Posey EXCH 100.00 200.00
HTCRN Cal Ripken Jr. 50.00 120.00
HTCRO Carlos Rodon 15.00 40.00
HTFF Freddie Freeman EXCH 12.00 30.00
HTJB Johnny Bench 30.00 80.00
HTJK Jung-Ho Kang EXCH 30.00 80.00
HTMME Mark McGwire 125.00 250.00
HTRH Rickey Henderson 40.00 100.00
HTRJ Randy Johnson EXCH 60.00 150.00
HTYT Yasmany Tomas 30.00 80.00

2015 Topps High Tek Autographs Gold Rainbow

*GLD RNBW: .6X TO 1.5X BASIC
STATED ODDS 1:10 HOBBY
STATED PRINT RUN 50 SER.#'d SETS
EXCHANGE DEADLINE 9/30/2017
HTCRN Cal Ripken Jr. 40.00 100.00
HTCRO Carlos Rodon 12.00 30.00
HTFF Freddie Freeman EXCH 10.00 25.00
HTJB Johnny Bench 25.00 60.00
HTJK Jung-Ho Kang EXCH 25.00 60.00

2015 Topps High Tek Autographs Tidal Diffractor

*TDL DFFRCTR: .5X TO 1.2X BASIC
STATED ODDS 1:5 HOBBY
STATED PRINT RUN 99 SER.#'d SETS
EXCHANGE DEADLINE 9/30/2017
HTCRO Carlos Rodon 10.00 25.00
HTFF Freddie Freeman EXCH 8.00 20.00

2015 Topps High Tek Bright Horizons

STATED ODDS 1:63 HOBBY
STATED PRINT RUN 50 SER.#'d SETS
BHBH Bryce Harper 8.00 20.00
BHGS George Springer 4.00 10.00
BHJA Jose Abreu 5.00 12.00
BHJD Jacob deGrom 10.00 25.00
BHJP Joc Pederson 12.00 30.00
BHJS Jorge Soler 5.00 12.00
BHKB Kris Bryant 25.00 60.00
BHMT Mike Trout 25.00 60.00
BHRC Rusney Castillo 4.00 10.00
BHTW Taijuan Walker 3.00 8.00

2015 Topps High Tek Bright Horizons Autographs

STATED ODDS 1:122 HOBBY
STATED PRINT RUN 50 SER.#'d SETS
EXCHANGE DEADLINE 9/30/2017
BHJA Jose Abreu 20.00 50.00
BHJD Jacob deGrom 60.00 150.00
BHJP Joc Pederson 12.00 30.00
BHJS Jorge Soler 10.00 25.00
BHRC Rusney Castillo 8.00 20.00

2015 Topps High Tek DramaTEK Performers

STATED ODDS 1:42 HOBBY
STATED PRINT RUN 50 SER.#'d SETS
DTPAG Adrian Gonzalez 4.00 10.00
DTPAJ Adam Jones 4.00 10.00
DTPAR Anthony Rizzo 6.00 15.00
DTPBP Buster Posey 6.00 15.00
DTPCK Clayton Kershaw 8.00 20.00
DTPCS Chris Sale 5.00 12.00
DTPDW David Wright 4.00 10.00
DTPEE Edwin Encarnacion 5.00 12.00
DTPFF Freddie Freeman 6.00 15.00
DTPGS Giancarlo Stanton 5.00 12.00
DTPHR Hanley Ramirez 4.00 10.00
DTPMT Mike Trout 25.00 60.00
DTPPG Paul Goldschmidt 5.00 12.00
DTPRC Robinson Cano 4.00 10.00
DTPTT Troy Tulowitzki 5.00 12.00

2015 Topps High Tek DramaTEK Performers Autographs

STATED ODDS 1:122 HOBBY
STATED PRINT RUN 25 SER.#'d SETS
EXCHANGE DEADLINE 9/30/2017
DTPAJ Adam Jones 12.00 30.00
DTPAR Anthony Rizzo 50.00 120.00
DTPBP Buster Posey 125.00 250.00
DTPDW David Wright EXCH 12.00 30.00
DTPFF Freddie Freeman 50.00 120.00
DTPMT Mike Trout 250.00 350.00
DTPPG Paul Goldschmidt 25.00 60.00

2015 Topps High Tek Low TEK Diffractors

STATED ODDS 1:42 HOBBY
STATED PRINT RUN 50 SER.#'d SETS
LTBL Barry Larkin 2.50 6.00
LTBP Buster Posey 4.00 10.00
LTCR Cal Ripken Jr. 10.00 25.00
LTJL Jon Lester 2.50 6.00
LTMM Mark McGwire 5.00 12.00
LTMP Mike Piazza 3.00 8.00
LTNT Nolan Ryan 10.00 25.00
LTOS Ozzie Smith 4.00 10.00
LTRC Roger Clemens 4.00 10.00
LTRS Ryne Sandberg 6.00 15.00
LTWM Willie Mays 6.00 15.00
LTCKR Corey Kluber 2.50 6.00
LTCKW Clayton Kershaw 5.00 12.00
LTRJA Reggie Jackson 2.50 6.00
LTRJO Randy Johnson 3.00 8.00

2015 Topps High Tek Low TEK Diffractors Autographs

STATED ODDS 1:122 HOBBY
STATED PRINT RUN 25 SER.#'d SETS
EXCHANGE DEADLINE 9/30/2017
LTBL Barry Larkin 30.00 80.00
LTBP Buster Posey 100.00 250.00
LTJL Jon Lester 12.00 30.00
LTMP Mike Piazza 50.00 120.00
LTNR Nolan Ryan 100.00 250.00
LTRS Ryne Sandberg 30.00 80.00
LTCKR Corey Kluber 12.00 30.00
LTCKW Clayton Kershaw 60.00 150.00
LTRJA Reggie Jackson 40.00 100.00
LTRJO Randy Johnson 50.00 120.00

2016 Topps High Tek

GROUP A = SPIRAL PATTERN
GROUP B = MAZE PATTERN
PRINTING PROOF ODDS 1:63 HOBBY
PLATE PRINT RUN 1 SET PER COLOR
BLACK-CYAN-MAGENTA-YELLOW ISSUED
NO PLATE PRICING DUE TO SCARCITY
HTAB Aaron Blair A RC .60 1.50
HTAC Aroldis Chapman B 1.00 2.50
HTAG Andres Galarraga A .75 2.00
HTAJ Adam Jones A .75 2.00
HTAM Andrew McCutchen B 1.00 2.50
HTAN Aaron Nola B RC 1.25 3.00
HTAP A.J. Pollock A .60 1.50
HTAPE Andy Pettitte B .75 2.00
HTAPU Albert Pujols A 1.25 3.00
HTAR Anthony Rizzo A 1.25 3.00
HTBH Bryce Harper B 1.50 4.00
HTBHP Byung-Ho Park B RC .75 2.00
HTBP Buster Posey B 1.25 3.00
HTBR Babe Ruth B 2.50 6.00
HTBS Blake Snell B RC .75 2.00
HTBW Billy Wagner A .60 1.50
HTBWI Bernie Williams B .75 2.00
HTCB Craig Biggio A .75 2.00
HTCC Carlos Correa A 1.00 2.50
HTCE Carl Edwards Jr. A RC .75 2.00
HTCJ Chipper Jones A 1.00 2.50
HTCK Clayton Kershaw B 1.50 4.00
HTCR Cal Ripken Jr. A 3.00 8.00
HTCRO Carlos Rodon A 1.00 2.50
HTCS Curt Schilling A .75 2.00
HTCSA Chris Sale A 1.00 2.50
HTCSE Corey Seager B RC 6.00 15.00
HTDG Dee Gordon B .60 1.50
HTDO David Ortiz A 1.00 2.50
HTDP David Price A .75 2.00
HTDW David Wright B .75 2.00
HTER Eddie Rosario B .75 2.00
HTFH Felix Hernandez B .75 2.00
HTFL Francisco Lindor A 1.00 2.50
HTFM Frankie Montas B RC .75 2.00
HTFT Frank Thomas A 1.00 2.50
HTGM Greg Maddux A 1.25 3.00
HTGR Garrett Richards A .75 2.00
HTGS Giancarlo Stanton B 1.00 2.50
HTHA Hank Aaron A 2.00 5.00
HTHO Henry Owens A RC .75 2.00
HTHOL Hector Olivera A RC .75 2.00
HTI Ichiro Suzuki B 1.25 3.00
HTIR Ivan Rodriguez B .75 2.00
HTJAR Jake Arrieta A .75 2.00
HTJB Johnny Bench A 1.00 2.50
HTJBA Jose Bautista B .75 2.00
HTJBE Jose Berrios B RC 1.00 2.50
HTJC Jose Canseco B .75 2.00
HTJD Johnny Damon A .75 2.00
HTJDE Jacob deGrom B 2.00 5.00
HTJDO Josh Donaldson B .75 2.00
HTJG Jon Gray A RC .60 1.50
HTJG Juan Gonzalez B .60 1.50
HTJH Jason Heyward A .75 2.00
HTJM J.D. Martinez A 1.00 2.50
HTJP Jose Peraza A RC .75 2.00
HTJR Jackie Robinson A 1.00 2.50
HTJS John Smoltz A 1.00 2.50
HTJV Jason Varitek A 1.00 2.50
HTKB Kris Bryant A 1.25 3.00
HTKG Ken Griffey Jr. B 2.00 5.00
HTKM Kenta Maeda B RC 1.25 3.00
HTKMA Ketel Marte B RC 1.25 3.00
HTKS Kyle Schwarber A RC 2.00 5.00
HTLG Luis Gonzalez A .75 2.00
HTLS Luis Severino B RC .75 2.00
HTMB Madison Bumgarner B .75 2.00
HTMC Miguel Cabrera A 1.00 2.50
HTMCO Michael Conforto B RC .75 2.00
HTMF Michael Fulmer A RC 1.00 2.50
HTMH Matt Harvey B .75 2.00
HTMK Max Kepler B RC 1.00 2.50
HTMKE Matt Kemp B .75 2.00
HTMM Manny Machado A 1.00 2.50
HTMMC Mark McGwire B 1.50 4.00
HTMP Mike Piazza B 1.00 2.50
HTMS Mallex Smith A RC .60 1.50
HTMS Miguel Sano B RC 1.00 2.50
HTMSC Max Scherzer B 1.00 2.50
HTMST Marcus Stroman B .75 2.00
HTMT Mike Trout A 5.00 12.00
HTMTA Masahiro Tanaka B .75 2.00
HTNA Nolan Arenado A 1.50 4.00
HTNC Nelson Cruz B 1.00 2.50
HTNG Nomar Garciaparra A .75 2.00
HTNM Nomar Mazara B RC 1.00 2.50
HTNS Noah Syndergaard B .75 2.00
HTOV Omar Vizquel A .75 2.00
HTPG Paul Goldschmidt A 1.00 2.50
HTRA Roberto Alomar A .75 2.00
HTRB Ryan Braun B .75 2.00
HTRC Roger Clemens A 1.25 3.00
HTRJ Randy Johnson A 1.00 2.50
HTRP Rafael Palmeiro A .75 2.00
HTRS Robert Stephenson A RC .60 1.50
HTSG Sonny Gray B .75 2.00
HTSK Sandy Koufax B 2.00 5.00
HTSM Sean Manaea B RC .60 1.50
HTSP Stephen Piscotty B RC 1.00 2.50
HTTG Tom Glavine A .75 2.00
HTTS Trevor Story A RC 3.00 8.00
HTTT Troy Tulowitzki B 1.00 2.50
HTTTU Trea Turner B RC 2.00 5.00
HTTW Ted Williams A 2.00 5.00
HTTYW Tyler White A RC .60 1.50
HTVG Vladimir Guerrero B .75 2.00
HTWB Wade Boggs B .75 2.00
HTYC Yoenis Cespedes B 1.00 2.50
HTYD Yu Darvish B 1.00 2.50
HTZG Zack Greinke A 1.00 2.50

2016 Topps High Tek Arrows

*ARROWS: 1X TO 2.5X BASIC
STATED ODDS 1:6 HOBBY
HTCR Cal Ripken Jr. 12.00 30.00
HTKB Kris Bryant 15.00 40.00

2016 Topps High Tek Buckle

*BUCKLE: .4X TO 1X BASIC
RANDOM INSERTS IN PACKS

2016 Topps High Tek Cubes

*CUBES: .4X TO 1X BASIC
RANDOM INSERTS IN PACKS

2016 Topps High Tek Diamonds

*DIAMONDS: 2.5X TO 6X BASIC
STATED ODDS 1:24 HOBBY
HTCR Cal Ripken Jr. 30.00 80.00
HTKB Kris Bryant 40.00 100.00

2016 Topps High Tek Gold Rainbow

*GOLD RAINBOW: 1X TO 2.5X BASIC
RANDOM INSERTS IN PACKS
STATED PRINT RUN 60 SER.#'d SETS
HTCR Cal Ripken Jr. 20.00 50.00
HTCSE Corey Seager 12.00 30.00
HTKB Kris Bryant 20.00 50.00

2016 Topps High Tek Grass

*GRASS: .6X TO 1.5X BASIC
STATED ODDS 1:3 HOBBY
HTCR Cal Ripken Jr. 8.00 20.00
HTKB Kris Bryant 10.00 25.00

2016 Topps High Tek Green Rainbow

*GREEN RAINBOW: 1X TO 2.5X BASIC
STATED ODDS 1:3 HOBBY
STATED PRINT RUN 99 SER.#'d SETS
HTCSE Corey Seager 12.00 30.00
HTKB Kris Bryant 20.00 50.00
HTMT Mike Trout 20.00 50.00

2016 Topps High Tek Lines

*LINES: 1.5X TO 4X BASIC
STATED ODDS 1:12 HOBBY
HTCR Cal Ripken Jr. 20.00 50.00
HTKB Kris Bryant 25.00 60.00

2016 Topps High Tek Orange Magma Diffractor

*ORANGE MAGMA: 3X TO 8X BASIC
STATED ODDS 1:10 HOBBY
STATED PRINT RUN 25 SER.#'d SETS
HTCSE Corey Seager 25.00 60.00
HTKB Kris Bryant 40.00 100.00

2016 Topps High Tek Peak

*PEAK: 1X TO 2.5X BASIC
STATED ODDS 1:6 HOBBY
HTCSE Corey Seager 15.00 40.00
HTSK Sandy Koufax 10.00 25.00

2016 Topps High Tek Red Orbit Diffractor

*RED ORBIT: 4X TO 10X BASIC
STATED ODDS 1:13 HOBBY
HTCSE Corey Seager 30.00 80.00
HTKB Kris Bryant 50.00 120.00

2016 Topps High Tek Tidal Diffractor

*TIDAL: .5X TO 1.2X BASIC
STATED ODDS 1:2 HOBBY

2016 Topps High Tek Triangles

*TRIANGLES: 1.5X TO 4X BASIC
STATED ODDS 1:12 HOBBY
HTCSE Corey Seager 25.00 60.00
HTSK Sandy Koufax 15.00 40.00

2016 Topps High Tek Waves

*WAVES: .6X TO 1.5X BASIC
STATED ODDS 1:3 HOBBY
HTCSE Corey Seager 10.00 25.00
HTSK Sandy Koufax 5.00 12.00

2016 Topps High Tek '66 Short Prints

STATED ODDS 1:19 HOBBY
66FR Frank Robinson 3.00 8.00
66HA Hank Aaron 8.00 20.00
66LB Lou Brock 3.00 8.00
66RC Roberto Clemente 10.00 25.00
66SK Sandy Koufax 8.00 20.00
66WM Willie Mays 8.00 20.00

2016 Topps High Tek '66 Short Prints Autographs

STATED ODDS 1:421 HOBBY
STATED PRINT RUN 35 SER.#'d SETS
EXCHANGE DEADLINE 10/31/2018
66FR Frank Robinson 40.00 100.00
66HA Hank Aaron 125.00 300.00
66LB Lou Brock 40.00 100.00

2016 Topps High Tek Home Uniform Photo Variations

*UNIFORM: 2.5X TO 6X BASIC
STATED ODDS 1:38 HOBBY
STATED PRINT RUN 50 SER.#'d SETS

2016 Topps High Tek Home Uniform Photo Variations Autographs

STATED ODDS 1:85 HOBBY
PRINT RUNS B/WN 15-50 COPIES PER
NO PRICING ON QTY 15
EXCHANGE DEADLINE 10/31/2018
HTAR Anthony Rizzo/50 60.00 150.00
HTBP Buster Posey/20 60.00 150.00
HTCSA Chris Sale/50 10.00 25.00
HTJDE Jacob deGrom/50 20.00 50.00
HTJH Jason Heyward/35 20.00 50.00
HTNA Nolan Arenado/50 25.00 60.00
HTRB Ryan Braun/35 15.00 40.00
HTTT Troy Tulowitzki

2016 Topps High Tek Autographs

PRINTING PROOF ODDS 1:99 HOBBY
PLATE PRINT RUN 1 SET PER COLOR
NO PLATE PRICING DUE TO SCARCITY
EXCHANGE DEADLINE 10/31/2018
HTAB Aaron Blair 3.00 8.00
HTAG Andres Galarraga 5.00 12.00
HTAN Aaron Nola 6.00 15.00
HTAPE Andy Pettitte 12.00 30.00
HTAR Anthony Rizzo 25.00 60.00
HTBH Bryce Harper 75.00 200.00
HTBP Buster Posey
HTBS Blake Snell 5.00 12.00
HTBW Billy Wagner 3.00 8.00
HTBWI Bernie Williams 20.00 50.00
HTCB Craig Biggio 10.00 25.00
HTCC Carlos Correa 25.00 60.00
HTCE Carl Edwards Jr. 4.00 10.00
HTCJ Chipper Jones 25.00 60.00
HTCK Clayton Kershaw 30.00 80.00
HTCR Cal Ripken Jr.
HTCRO Carlos Rodon 5.00 12.00
HTCS Curt Schilling 8.00 20.00
HTCSA Chris Sale 12.00 30.00
HTCSE Corey Seager
HTDO David Ortiz 30.00 80.00
HTDP David Price 6.00 15.00
HTER Eddie Rosario 4.00 10.00
HTFL Francisco Lindor 20.00 50.00
HTFM Frankie Montas 4.00 10.00
HTGM Greg Maddux 40.00 100.00
HTHA Hank Aaron
HTHO Henry Owens 4.00 10.00
HTI Ichiro Suzuki
HTIR Ivan Rodriguez 10.00 25.00
HTJAR Jake Arrieta EXCH
HTJB Johnny Bench
HTJBE Jose Berrios 5.00 12.00
HTJC Jose Canseco 6.00 15.00
HTJD Johnny Damon 4.00 10.00
HTJDE Jacob deGrom 12.00 30.00
HTJG Jon Gray 3.00 8.00
HTJG Juan Gonzalez 5.00 12.00
HTJH Jason Heyward 6.00 15.00
HTJM J.D. Martinez 10.00 25.00
HTJP Jose Peraza 4.00 10.00
HTJS John Smoltz 10.00 25.00
HTJV Jason Varitek 5.00 12.00
HTKB Kris Bryant
HTKG Ken Griffey Jr. 125.00 250.00
HTKM Kenta Maeda
HTKMA Ketel Marte 6.00 15.00
HTKS Kyle Schwarber 15.00 40.00
HTLG Luis Gonzalez 4.00 10.00
HTLS Luis Severino 8.00 20.00
HTMF Michael Fulmer 8.00 20.00
HTMK Max Kepler 5.00 12.00
HTMMC Mark McGwire
HTMP Mike Piazza
HTMS Mallex Smith 3.00 8.00
HTMS Miguel Sano 5.00 12.00
HTMT Mike Trout 150.00 300.00
HTMTA Masahiro Tanaka
HTNA Nolan Arenado 15.00 40.00
HTNG Nomar Garciaparra 10.00 25.00
HTNM Nomar Mazara 6.00 15.00
HTNS Noah Syndergaard 12.00 30.00
HTOV Omar Vizquel 5.00 12.00
HTRA Roberto Alomar 5.00 12.00
HTRB Ryan Braun 6.00 15.00
HTRC Roger Clemens 20.00 50.00
HTRJ Randy Johnson 25.00 60.00
HTRP Rafael Palmeiro 4.00 10.00
HTRS Robert Stephenson 3.00 8.00
HTSK Sandy Koufax
HTSP Stephen Piscotty 5.00 12.00
HTTG Tom Glavine 12.00 30.00
HTTS Trevor Story 12.00 30.00
HTTT Troy Tulowitzki 8.00 20.00
HTTTU Trea Turner 10.00 25.00
HTTYW Tyler White 3.00 8.00
HTVG Vladimir Guerrero 12.00 30.00
HTWB Wade Boggs 10.00 25.00

2016 Topps High Tek Autographs Gold Rainbow

*GOLD RAINBOW: .6X TO 1.5X BASIC
STATED ODDS 1:9 HOBBY
STATED PRINT RUN 50 SER.#'d SETS
EXCHANGE DEADLINE 10/31/2018
HTBP Buster Posey 50.00 120.00
HTCR Cal Ripken Jr. 60.00 150.00
HTCSE Corey Seager 75.00 200.00
HTGM Greg Maddux
HTHA Hank Aaron
HTI Ichiro Suzuki
HTJAR Jake Arrieta EXCH 25.00 60.00
HTJB Johnny Bench 30.00 80.00
HTKB Kris Bryant 150.00 300.00
HTKG Ken Griffey Jr.
HTKM Kenta Maeda 25.00 60.00
HTMMC Mark McGwire 50.00 120.00
HTMP Mike Piazza
HTMT Mike Trout 200.00 400.00
HTMTA Masahiro Tanaka 200.00 400.00
HTOV Omar Vizquel
HTRC Roger Clemens
HTRJ Randy Johnson
HTSK Sandy Koufax

2016 Topps High Tek Autographs Orange Magma Diffractor

*ORANGE MAGMA: .75X TO 2X BASIC
STATED ODDS 1:16 HOBBY
STATED PRINT RUN 25 SER.#'d SETS
EXCHANGE DEADLINE 10/31/2018
HTBP Buster Posey 60.00 150.00
HTCR Cal Ripken Jr. 75.00 200.00
HTCSE Corey Seager 100.00 250.00
HTHA Hank Aaron 150.00 400.00
HTI Ichiro Suzuki 300.00 500.00
HTJAR Jake Arrieta EXCH 30.00 80.00
HTJB Johnny Bench 40.00 100.00
HTKB Kris Bryant 200.00 400.00
HTKG Ken Griffey Jr. 200.00 400.00
HTKM Kenta Maeda 30.00 80.00
HTMMC Mark McGwire 60.00 150.00
HTMP Mike Piazza 75.00 200.00
HTMT Mike Trout 250.00 500.00
HTMTA Masahiro Tanaka 250.00 500.00

2016 Topps High Tek Autographs Sky Rainbow

*SKY RAINBOW: .75X TO 2X BASIC
RANDOM INSERTS IN ASIA PACKS
STATED PRINT RUN 20 SER.#'d SETS
EXCHANGE DEADLINE 10/31/2018
HTBP Buster Posey 60.00 150.00
HTCR Cal Ripken Jr. 75.00 200.00
HTCSE Corey Seager 100.00 250.00
HTHA Hank Aaron 150.00 400.00
HTI Ichiro Suzuki 300.00 500.00
HTJAR Jake Arrieta EXCH 30.00 80.00
HTJB Johnny Bench 40.00 100.00
HTKB Kris Bryant 200.00 400.00
HTKG Ken Griffey Jr. 200.00 400.00
HTKM Kenta Maeda 30.00 80.00
HTMMC Mark McGwire 60.00 150.00
HTMP Mike Piazza 75.00 200.00
HTMT Mike Trout 250.00 500.00
HTMTA Masahiro Tanaka 250.00 500.00

2016 Topps High Tek Bright Horizons

STATED ODDS 1:56 HOBBY
STATED PRINT RUN 50 SER.#'d SETS
BHBP Byung-Ho Park 2.50 6.00
BHBS Blake Snell 3.00 8.00
BHCC Carlos Correa 4.00 10.00
BHCS Corey Seager 25.00 60.00
BHFL Francisco Lindor 4.00 10.00
BHKM Kenta Maeda 5.00 12.00
BHKS Kyle Schwarber 8.00 20.00
BHLS Luis Severino 3.00 8.00
BHMC Michael Conforto 3.00 8.00
BHMS Miguel Sano 4.00 10.00

2016 Topps High Tek Bright Horizons Autographs

STATED ODDS 1:119 HOBBY
STATED PRINT RUN 50 SER.#'d SETS
EXCHANGE DEADLINE 10/31/2018
BHCC Carlos Correa 40.00 100.00
BHCS Corey Seager
BHFL Francisco Lindor 30.00 80.00
BHKM Kenta Maeda 20.00 50.00
BHKS Kyle Schwarber 50.00 120.00
BHMS Miguel Sano 10.00 25.00

2016 Topps High Tek Highlights

STATED ODDS 1:23 HOBBY
STATED PRINT RUN 50 SER.#'d SETS
HAP Albert Pujols 4.00 10.00
HBH Bryce Harper 5.00 12.00
HCB Craig Biggio 2.50 6.00
HCC Carlos Correa 3.00 8.00
HCJ Chipper Jones 3.00 8.00
HCK Clayton Kershaw 5.00 12.00
HCR Cal Ripken Jr. 20.00 50.00
HFH Felix Hernandez 2.50 6.00
HFT Frank Thomas 3.00 8.00
HGM Greg Maddux 4.00 10.00
HHA Hank Aaron 6.00 15.00
HIR Ivan Rodriguez 2.50 6.00
HIS Ichiro Suzuki 4.00 10.00
HJD Jacob deGrom 6.00 15.00
HJS John Smoltz 3.00 8.00
HKB Kris Bryant 15.00 40.00
HKG Ken Griffey Jr. 15.00 40.00
HMM Manny Machado 3.00 8.00
HMP Mike Piazza 3.00 8.00
HMT Mike Trout 15.00 40.00
HNG Nomar Garciaparra 2.50 6.00
HRJ Randy Johnson 3.00 8.00
HTT Troy Tulowitzki 3.00 8.00
HVG Vladimir Guerrero 2.50 6.00
HAPE Andy Pettitte 2.50 6.00

2016 Topps High Tek Highlights Autographs

STATED ODDS 1:79 HOBBY
STATED PRINT RUN 25 SER.#'d SETS
EXCHANGE DEADLINE 10/31/2018
HBH Bryce Harper 150.00 300.00
HCB Craig Biggio 15.00 40.00
HCC Carlos Correa 30.00 80.00
HCJ Chipper Jones 60.00 150.00
HCR Cal Ripken Jr. 75.00 200.00
HFH Felix Hernandez 20.00 50.00
HGM Greg Maddux 60.00 150.00
HHA Hank Aaron 150.00 300.00
HIR Ivan Rodriguez
HIS Ichiro Suzuki 300.00 500.00
HJD Jacob deGrom 30.00 80.00
HJS John Smoltz 60.00 150.00
HKB Kris Bryant 125.00 300.00
HKG Ken Griffey Jr. EXCH 200.00 400.00
HMT Mike Trout 175.00 350.00
HNG Nomar Garciaparra
HRJ Randy Johnson 50.00 120.00
HVG Vladimir Guerrero 25.00 60.00
HAPE Andy Pettitte 30.00 80.00

2017 Topps High Tek

GROUP A = BASEBALL GRUNGE
GROUP B = PIXEL CIRCLE
HTAB Adrian Beltre A .75 2.00
HTABE Andrew Benintendi B RC 1.50 4.00
HTABO Aaron Boone A .50 1.25
HTABR Alex Bregman A RC 2.50 6.00
HTAD Aledmys Diaz A .60 1.50
HTAG Amir Garrett B RC .50 1.25
HTAJ Aaron Judge B RC 6.00 15.00
HTANP Andy Pettitte B .60 1.50
HTAP Albert Pujols A 1.00 2.50
HTAR Addison Russell A .75 2.00
HTARI Anthony Rizzo A 1.00 2.50
HIBA Bobby Abreu B .50 1.25
HTBH Bryce Harper B 1.25 3.00
HTBP Buster Posey B 1.00 2.50
HTBZ Ben Zobrist B .60 1.50
HTCA Christian Arroyo A .75 2.00
HTCBE Cody Bellinger A RC 2.50 6.00
HTCC Carlos Correa A .75 2.00
HTCC Carlos Carrasco B .50 1.25
HTCK Clayton Kershaw B 1.25 3.00
HTCKL Corey Kluber B .60 1.50
HTCP Chad Pinder A RC .50 1.25
HTCRJ Cal Ripken Jr. A 2.50 6.00
HTCS Corey Seager A .75 2.00
HTCSA Chris Sale B .75 2.00
HTDG Didi Gregorius A .60 1.50
HTDJ Derek Jeter A 2.00 5.00
HTDL Derrek Lee A .50 1.25
HTDM Daniel Murphy A .60 1.50
HTDO David Ortiz A .75 2.00
HTDP Dustin Pedroia A .75 2.00
HTDPR David Price B .60 1.50
HTDS Dansby Swanson A RC 1.25 3.00
HTDV Dan Vogelbach A RC .75 2.00
HTER Edgar Renteria A .50 1.25
HTET Eric Thames A .60 1.50
HTFF Freddie Freeman A 1.00 2.50
HTFL Francisco Lindor A .75 2.00
HTGM Greg Maddux B 1.00 2.50
HTGS Gary Sheffield B .50 1.25
HTGSP George Springer B .60 1.50
HTGST Giancarlo Stanton B .75 2.00
HTHA Hank Aaron B 1.50 4.00
HTHO Henry Owens B .50 1.25
HTHR Hunter Renfroe B RC .60 1.50
HTIH Ian Happ B RC 1.00 2.50
HTIR Ivan Rodriguez B .60 1.50
HTI Ichiro B 1.00 2.50
HTJA Jose Altuve A .60 1.50
HTJAB Jose Abreu A .75 2.00
HTJB Jeff Bagwell A .60 1.50
HTJBA Javier Baez A 1.00 2.50
HTJBE Josh Bell A 1.25 3.00
HTJCO Jharel Cotton B RC .50 1.25
HTJD Josh Donaldson A .60 1.50
HTJD Johnny Damon B .60 1.50
HTJDE Jacob deGrom B 1.50 4.00
HTJDL Jose De Leon B RC .50 1.25
HTJE Jim Edmonds B .50 1.25
HTJJ Joe Jimenez B RC .60 1.50
HTJS John Smoltz B .75 2.00
HTJT Jim Thome A .60 1.50
HTJU Julio Urias B .75 2.00
HTJV Jonathan Villar A .50 1.25
HTJVO Joey Votto A .75 2.00
HTJW Jesse Winker B RC 2.00 5.00
HTKB Kris Bryant A 1.00 2.50
HTKGJ Ken Griffey Jr. B 1.50 4.00
HTKH Kelvin Herrera B .50 1.25
HTKS Kyle Seager A .50 1.25
HTKSC Kyle Schwarber B .75 2.00
HTLG Lucas Giolito B .60 1.50
HTLS Luis Severino B .60 1.50
HTLW Luke Weaver B RC .60 1.50
HTMAT Masahiro Tanaka B .60 1.50
HTMB Mookie Betts B 1.50 4.00
HTMC Matt Carpenter A .75 2.00
HTMCA Miguel Cabrera A .75 2.00
HTMF Maikel Franco A .60 1.50
HTMFU Michael Fulmer B .50 1.25
HTMH Mitch Haniger B RC .75 2.00
HTMM Manny Machado A .75 2.00
HTMMA Manny Margot B RC .50 1.25
HTMMC Mark McGwire A 1.25 3.00
HTMP Mike Piazza B .75 2.00
HTMS Max Scherzer B .75 2.00
HTMT Mike Trout B 4.00 10.00
HTNA Nolan Arenado A 1.25 3.00
HTNG Nomar Garciaparra A .60 1.50
HTNS Noah Syndergaard B .60 1.50
HTOA Orlando Arcia A RC .75 2.00
HTPG Paul Goldschmidt A .75 2.00
HTPK Paul Konerko A .60 1.50
HTPM Pedro Martinez B .60 1.50
HTRA Roberto Alomar A .60 1.50
HTRC Roger Clemens B 1.00 2.50
HTRT Raimel Tapia B .60 1.50
HTSK Sandy Koufax B 1.50 4.00
HTSL Seth Lugo B RC .50 1.25
HTSS Stephen Strasburg B .75 2.00

HTTA Tyler Austin A RC .60 1.50
HTTF Todd Frazier A .50 1.25
HTTG Tyler Glasnow B RC 2.00 5.00
HTTGL Tom Glavine B .60 1.50
HTTM Trey Mancini A RC 1.00 2.50
HTTR Tim Raines B .60 1.50
HTTS Trevor Story A .75 2.00
HTTT Trea Turner A .60 1.50
HTWM Wil Myers A .60 1.50
HTXB Xander Bogaerts A .75 2.00
HTYG Yulieski Gurriel A RC .75 2.00
HTYM Yoan Moncada A RC 1.50 4.00

2017 Topps High Tek Blackout

*BLACKOUT: .6X TO 1.5X BASIC
RANDOM INSERTS IN PACKS

2017 Topps High Tek Blackout Braid

*BLCKOUT BRAID: .6X TO 1.5X BASIC
RANDOM INSERTS IN PACKS

2017 Topps High Tek Blackout Chainlink Hexagon

*BLCK CHNLNK HXGN: .6X TO 1.5X BASIC
RANDOM INSERTS IN PACKS

2017 Topps High Tek Blue Rainbow

*BLUE RAINBOW: 1.2X TO 3X BASIC
STATED ODDS 1:2 HOBBY
STATED PRINT RUN 75 SER.#'d SETS
HTCBE Cody Bellinger A 25.00 60.00

2017 Topps High Tek Braid

*BRAID: .5X TO 1.2X BASIC
RANDOM INSERTS IN PACKS

2017 Topps High Tek Camo Stripes

*CAMO STRIPES: .5X TO 1.2X BASIC
RANDOM INSERTS IN PACKS

2017 Topps High Tek Chainlink Hexagon

*CHNLNK HXGN: .5X TO 1.2X BASIC
RANDOM INSERTS IN PACKS

2017 Topps High Tek Diamond X

*DIAMOND X: 1.2X TO 3X BASIC
RANDOM INSERTS IN PACKS

2017 Topps High Tek Green Rainbow

*GREEN RAINBOW: 1X TO 2.5X BASIC
STATED ODDS 1:2 HOBBY
STATED PRINT RUN 99 SER.#'d SETS
HTCBE Cody Bellinger A 20.00 50.00

2017 Topps High Tek Hexagon Circle

*HXGN CRCLE: .6X TO 1.5X BASIC
RANDOM INSERTS IN PACKS

2017 Topps High Tek Lightning

*LIGHTNING: .5X TO 1.2X BASIC
RANDOM INSERTS IN PACKS

2017 Topps High Tek Orange Magma

*ORANGE MAGMA: 3X TO 8X BASIC
STATED ODDS 1:6 HOBBY
STATED PRINT RUN 25 SER.#'d SETS
HTCBE Cody Bellinger A 60.00 150.00

2017 Topps High Tek Shatter

*SHATTER: 1X TO 2.5X BASIC
RANDOM INSERTS IN PACKS

2017 Topps High Tek Spiral Dots

*SPIRAL DOTS: .6X TO 1.5X BASIC
RANDOM INSERTS IN PACKS

2017 Topps High Tek Spiral Grid

*SPIRAL GRID: 1.2X TO 3X BASIC
RANDOM INSERTS IN PACKS

2017 Topps High Tek Squiggle

*SQUIGGLE: .75X TO 2X BASIC
RANDOM INSERTS IN PACKS

2017 Topps High Tek Stadium

*STADIUM: 1X TO 2.5X BASIC
RANDOM INSERTS IN PACKS

2017 Topps High Tek Tidal Diffractors

*TIDAL DIFFRACTORS: .75X TO 2X BASIC
RANDOM INSERTS IN PACKS
STATED PRINT RUN 250 SER.#'d SETS
HTCBE Cody Bellinger A 15.00 40.00

2017 Topps High Tek Wave

*WAVE: .75X TO 2X BASIC
RANDOM INSERTS IN PACKS

2017 Topps High Tek Clubhouse Images

STATED ODDS 1:31 HOBBY
STATED PRINT RUN 50 SER.#'d SETS
CIAR Anthony Rizzo 8.00 20.00
CIBH Bryce Harper 25.00 60.00
CICC Carlos Correa 4.00 10.00
CICS Corey Seager 4.00 10.00
CIDP David Price 3.00 8.00
CIFL Francisco Lindor 4.00 10.00
CIKB Kris Bryant 15.00 40.00
CIMT Mike Trout 25.00 60.00
CINS Noah Syndergaard 3.00 8.00

2017 Topps High Tek Clubhouse Images Autographs

STATED ODDS 1:61 HOBBY
PRINT RUNS B/WN 10-50 COPIES PER
NO PRICING ON QTY 10
EXCHANGE DEADLINE 10/31/2019
CICC Carlos Correa/25 60.00 150.00
CIDP David Price/40 8.00 20.00
CIFL Francisco Lindor/50 20.00 50.00
CINS Noah Syndergaard EXCH 15.00 40.00

2017 Topps High Tek Jubilation

STATED ODDS 1:20 HOBBY
STATED PRINT RUN 50 SER.#'d SETS
JAB Alex Bregman 12.00 30.00
JABE Andrew Benintendi 20.00 50.00
JAJ Aaron Judge 50.00 120.00
JBH Bryce Harper 6.00 15.00
JCC Carlos Correa 6.00 15.00
JCK Clayton Kershaw 6.00 15.00
JDS Dansby Swanson 5.00 12.00
JFL Francisco Lindor 4.00 10.00
JJA Jose Altuve 6.00 15.00
JJD Josh Donaldson 6.00 15.00
JKB Kris Bryant 12.00 30.00
JMB Mookie Betts 8.00 20.00
JMM Manny Machado 4.00 10.00
JMS Max Scherzer 4.00 10.00
JMT Mike Trout 25.00 60.00
JRC Robinson Cano 3.00 8.00

2017 Topps High Tek Jubilation Autographs

STATED ODDS 1:43 HOBBY
STATED PRINT RUN 35 SER.#'d SETS
EXCHANGE DEADLINE 10/31/2019
JAB Alex Bregman 20.00 50.00
JABE Andrew Benintendi 25.00 120.00
JBH Bryce Harper 125.00 300.00
JCC Carlos Correa 60.00 150.00
JFL Francisco Lindor 20.00 50.00
JJD Josh Donaldson 30.00 80.00
JKB Kris Bryant 100.00 250.00
JMM Manny Machado 20.00 50.00
JMT Mike Trout 250.00 400.00

2017 Topps High Tek Rookie Tek

STATED ODDS 1:20 HOBBY
STATED PRINT RUN 50 SER.#'d SETS
RTAB Alex Bregman 12.00 30.00
RTABE Andrew Benintendi 20.00 50.00
RTAJ Aaron Judge 50.00 120.00
RTAR Alex Reyes 3.00 8.00
RTDD David Dahl 3.00 8.00
RTDS Dansby Swanson 5.00 12.00
RTHR Hunter Renfroe 3.00 8.00
RTJA Jorge Alfaro 3.00 8.00
RTJC Jharel Cotton 2.50 6.00
RTJDL Jose De Leon 2.50 6.00
RTLW Luke Weaver 3.00 8.00
RTOA Orlando Arcia 4.00 10.00
RTTG Tyler Glasnow 10.00 25.00
RTYG Yulieski Gurriel 4.00 10.00
RTYM Yoan Moncada 5.00 12.00

2017 Topps High Tek Rookie Tek Autographs

STATED ODDS 1:30 HOBBY
STATED PRINT RUN 50 SER.#'d SETS
EXCHANGE DEADLINE 10/31/2019
RTAB Alex Bregman 20.00 50.00
RTABE Andrew Benintendi 50.00 120.00
RTAJ Aaron Judge 100.00 250.00
RTAR Alex Reyes 8.00 20.00
RTDD David Dahl 8.00 20.00
RTDS Dansby Swanson 10.00 25.00
RTHR Hunter Renfroe 5.00 12.00
RTLW Luke Weaver 5.00 12.00
RTTG Tyler Glasnow 12.00 30.00
RTYG Yulieski Gurriel 10.00 25.00

2017 Topps High Tek TwiliTEK

STATED ODDS 1:21 HOBBY
STATED PRINT RUN 50 SER.#'d SETS
TWAB Alex Bregman 12.00 30.00
TWABE Andrew Benintendi 20.00 50.00
TWBZ Ben Zobrist 3.00 8.00
TWCC Carlos Correa 6.00 15.00
TWCS Corey Seager 4.00 10.00
TWGS Giancarlo Stanton 4.00 10.00
TWGSA Gary Sanchez 4.00 10.00
TWI Ichiro 5.00 12.00
TWKB Kris Bryant 12.00 30.00
TWMAT Masahiro Tanaka 3.00 8.00
TWMT Mike Trout 25.00 60.00
TWNA Nolan Arenado 6.00 15.00
TWPG Paul Goldschmidt 4.00 10.00
TWTS Trevor Story 4.00 10.00
TWYM Yoan Moncada 5.00 12.00

2017 Topps High Tek TwiliTEK Autographs

STATED ODDS 1:41 HOBBY
PRINT RUNS B/WN 10-50 COPIES PER
NO PRICING ON QTY 10
EXCHANGE DEADLINE 10/31/2019
TWAB Alex Bregman/50 20.00 50.00
TWBZ Ben Zobrist/50 20.00 50.00
TWCC Carlos Correa/25
TWCS Corey Seager EXCH 20.00 50.00
TWPG Paul Goldschmidt/40
TWTS Trevor Story/50 10.00 25.00

2017 Topps High Tek Autographs

RANDOM INSERTS IN PACKS
EXCHANGE DEADLINE 10/31/2019
HTAB Adrian Beltre 15.00 40.00
HTABE Andrew Benintendi 25.00 60.00
HTABO Aaron Boone 4.00 10.00
HTABR Alex Bregman 15.00 40.00
HTAD Aledmys Diaz 3.00 8.00
HTAG Amir Garrett 2.50 6.00
HTAJ Aaron Judge 75.00 200.00
HTANP Andy Pettitte 12.00 30.00
HTAP Albert Pujols 60.00 150.00
HTAR Addison Russell 4.00 10.00
HTARI Anthony Rizzo 15.00 40.00
HTBH Bryce Harper 75.00 200.00
HTBP Buster Posey 30.00 80.00
HTBZ Ben Zobrist 12.00 30.00
HTCA Christian Arroyo 4.00 10.00
HTCBE Cody Bellinger 40.00 100.00
HTCC Carlos Carrasco 2.50 6.00
HTCC Carlos Correa 25.00 60.00
HTCKL Corey Kluber 8.00 20.00
HTCP Chad Pinder 2.50 6.00
HTCS Corey Seager 20.00 50.00
HTCSA Chris Sale 12.00 30.00
HTDG Didi Gregorius 10.00 25.00
HTDJ Derek Jeter 300.00 500.00
HTDO David Ortiz 20.00 50.00
HTDPR David Price 5.00 12.00
HTDV Dan Vogelbach 4.00 10.00
HTER Edgar Renteria 4.00 10.00
HTET Eric Thames 3.00 8.00
HTFF Freddie Freeman 8.00 20.00
HTFL Francisco Lindor 12.00 30.00
HTGM Greg Maddux 30.00 80.00
HTGS Gary Sheffield 4.00 10.00
HTHA Hank Aaron 100.00 250.00
HTHR Hunter Renfroe 3.00 8.00
HTI Ichiro 150.00 300.00
HTIH Ian Happ 5.00 12.00
HTIR Ivan Rodriguez 10.00 25.00
HTJA Jose Altuve 12.00 30.00
HTJBA Javier Baez 15.00 40.00
HTJCO Jharel Cotton 2.50 6.00
HTJD Josh Donaldson 6.00 15.00
HTJDE Jacob deGrom 15.00 40.00
HTJJ Joe Jimenez 3.00 8.00
HTJT Jim Thome 25.00 60.00
HTJU Julio Urias 5.00 12.00
HTJV Jonathan Villar 2.50 6.00
HTJW Jesse Winker 12.00 30.00
HTKB Kris Bryant 30.00 80.00
HTKH Kelvin Herrera 2.50 6.00
HTKS Kyle Seager 2.50 6.00
HTLG Lucas Giolito 3.00 8.00
HTLS Luis Severino 3.00 8.00
HTLW Luke Weaver 3.00 8.00
HTMF Maikel Franco 3.00 8.00
HTMFU Michael Fulmer 2.50 6.00
HTMH Mitch Haniger 4.00 10.00
HTMM Manny Machado 20.00 50.00
HTMMA Manny Margot 2.50 6.00
HTMMC Mark McGwire 40.00 100.00
HTMT Mike Trout 150.00 400.00
HTNG Nomar Garciaparra 10.00 25.00
HTNS Noah Syndergaard 10.00 25.00
HTPK Paul Konerko 8.00 20.00
HTPM Pedro Martinez 20.00 50.00
HTRA Roberto Alomar 10.00 25.00
HTRC Roger Clemens 20.00 50.00
HTRT Raimel Tapia 3.00 8.00
HTSK Sandy Koufax
HTSL Seth Lugo 2.50 6.00
HTTA Tyler Austin 3.00 8.00
HTTG Tyler Glasnow 8.00 20.00
HTTGL Tom Glavine 5.00 12.00
HTTM Trey Mancini 5.00 12.00
HTTR Tim Raines 5.00 12.00
HTTS Trevor Story 4.00 10.00
HTWM Wil Myers 3.00 8.00
HTYG Yulieski Gurriel 5.00 12.00

2017 Topps High Tek Autographs Blackout

*BLACKOUT: .5X TO 1.2X BASIC
STATED ODDS 1:7 HOBBY
STATED PRINT RUN 50 SER.#'d SETS
EXCHANGE DEADLINE 10/31/2019

2017 Topps High Tek Autographs Blue Rainbow

*BLUE RAINBOW: .5X TO 1.2X BASIC
STATED ODDS 1:6 HOBBY
STATED PRINT RUN 50 SER.#'d SETS
EXCHANGE DEADLINE 10/31/2019

2017 Topps High Tek Autographs Green Rainbow

*GREEN RAINBOW: .5X TO 1.2X BASIC
RANDOM INSERTS IN PACKS
STATED PRINT RUN 75 SER.#'d SETS
EXCHANGE DEADLINE 10/31/2019

2017 Topps High Tek Autographs Orange Magma

*ORANGE MAGMA: .6X TO 1.5X BASIC
STATED ODDS 1:10 HOBBY
STATED PRINT RUN 25 SER.#'d SETS
EXCHANGE DEADLINE 10/31/2019
HTFF Freddie Freeman 20.00 50.00
HTJVO Joey Votto 40.00 100.00

2018 Topps High Tek

GROUP A = WAVES
GROUP B = DIAGONALS
HTAA Aaron Altherr B .40 1.00
HTAB Anthony Banda A RC .40 1.00
HTABE Andrew Benintendi A .60 1.50
HTAH Austin Hays A RC .60 1.50
HTAJ Aaron Judge A 1.50 4.00
HTAP Andy Pettitte A .50 1.25
HTAR Anthony Rizzo B .75 2.00
HTARD Alex Rodriguez A .75 2.00
HTARO Amed Rosario B RC .50 1.25
HTAS Andrew Stevenson B RC .40 1.00
HTASA Anthony Santander A RC .40 1.00
HTAV Alex Verdugo B RC .60 1.50
HTBB Byron Buxton A .60 1.50
HTBD Brian Dozier A .50 1.25
HTBH Bryce Harper B 1.00 2.50
HTBW Brandon Woodruff B RC 1.25 3.00
HTBWI Bernie Williams A .50 1.25
HTCB Charlie Blackmon B .60 1.50
HTCBE Cody Bellinger B 1.25 3.00
HTCC Carlos Correa A .60 1.50
HTCF Clint Frazier A RC .75 2.00
HTCJ Chipper Jones B .60 1.50
HTCK Clayton Kershaw B 1.00 2.50
HTCKE Carson Kelly B .40 1.00
HTCR Cal Ripken Jr. A 2.00 5.00
HTCS Carlos Santana B .50 1.25
HTCSE Corey Seager B .60 1.50
HTCSI Chance Sisco A RC .50 1.25
HTDF Dustin Fowler A RC .40 1.00
HTDG Didi Gregorius A .50 1.25
HTDGO Dwight Gooden A .40 1.00
HTDJ Derek Jeter A 1.50 4.00
HTDM Don Mattingly A 1.25 3.00
HTDO David Ortiz A .60 1.50
HTDS Dominic Smith B RC .50 1.25
HTDST Darryl Strawberry B .40 1.00
HTEM Edgar Martinez A .50 1.25
HTFF Freddie Freeman B .75 2.00
HTFL Francisco Lindor A .60 1.50
HTFM Francisco Mejia A RC .50 1.25
HTGA Greg Allen A RC .40 1.00
HTGS Gary Sanchez A .60 1.50
HTGSP George Springer A .50 1.25
HTGST Giancarlo Stanton A .60 1.50
HTGT Gleyber Torres A RC 4.00 10.00
HTHA Hank Aaron B 1.25 3.00
HTJA Jose Altuve A .50 1.25
HTJB Jeff Bagwell B .50 1.25
HTJBE Johnny Bench B .60 1.50
HTJC J.P. Crawford B RC .40 1.00
HTJCA Jose Canseco A .50 1.25
HTJD Jacob deGrom B 1.25 3.00
HTJDA J.D. Davis A RC .50 1.25
HTJE Jim Edmonds B .40 1.00
HTJF Jack Flaherty B RC 1.50 4.00
HTJL Jordan Luplow B RC .40 1.00
HTJM Jordan Montgomery A .40 1.00
HTJR Jose Ramirez A .50 1.25
HTJS Justin Smoak A .40 1.00
HTJT Jim Thome A .50 1.25
HTJU Justin Upton A .50 1.25
HTKB Kris Bryant B .75 2.00
HTKBR Keon Broxton B .40 1.00
HTKS Kyle Schwarber B .60 1.50
HTMA Miguel Andujar A RC 1.50 4.00
HTMB Mookie Betts A 1.25 3.00
HTMM Mark McGwire B 1.00 2.50
HTMMA Manny Machado A .60 1.50
HTMO Marcell Ozuna B .60 1.50
HTMOS Matt Olson A .60 1.50
HTMR Mariano Rivera A .75 2.00
HTMS Max Scherzer B .60 1.50
HTMT Mike Trout A 3.00 8.00
HTNA Nolan Arenado B 1.00 2.50
HTND Nicky Delmonico A RC .40 1.00
HTNG Nomar Garciaparra A .50 1.25
HTNR Nolan Ryan A 2.00 5.00
HTNS Noah Syndergaard B .50 1.25
HTNW Nick Williams B RC .50 1.25
HTOA Ozzie Albies B RC 1.25 3.00
HTPB Paul Blackburn A RC .40 1.00
HTPBR Parker Bridwell A RC .40 1.00
HTPD Paul DeJong B .60 1.50
HTPG Paul Goldschmidt B .60 1.50
HTPM Pedro Martinez B .50 1.25
HTRA Ronald Acuna Jr. B RC 12.00 30.00
HTRC Roger Clemens A .75 2.00
HTRD Rafael Devers A RC 1.25 3.00
HTRH Rhys Hoskins B RC 1.50 4.00
HTRI Raisel Iglesias B .50 1.25
HTRJ Randy Johnson B .60 1.50
HTRJA Reggie Jackson A .50 1.25
HTSA Sandy Alcantara B RC .40 1.00
HTSD Sean Doolittle B .40 1.00
HTSK Sandy Koufax B 1.25 3.00
HTSKI Scott Kingery B RC .60 1.50
HTSO Shohei Ohtani A RC 10.00 25.00
HTTG Tom Glavine B .50 1.25
HTTM Tyler Mahle B RC .50 1.25
HTTN Tomas Nido B RC .40 1.00
HTTP Tommy Pham B .40 1.00
HTTT Trea Turner B .50 1.25
HTTV Thyago Vieira A RC .40 1.00
HTTW Ted Williams A 1.25 3.00
HTVR Victor Robles B RC 1.00 2.50
HTWB Walker Buehler B RC 2.00 5.00
HTWBO Wade Boggs A .50 1.25
HTWC Will Clark A .50 1.25
HTWM Whit Merrifield A .60 1.50
HTYM Yadier Molina B .75 2.00
HTZC Zack Cozart A .40 1.00
HTZG Zack Godley B .40 1.00

2018 Topps High Tek Black

*BLACK: 1.2X TO 3X BASIC
*BLACK RC: 1.2X TO 3X BASIC
STATED ODDS 1:3 HOBBY
STATED PRINT RUN 50 SER.#'d SETS

2018 Topps High Tek Blue

*BLUE: .75X TO 2X BASIC
*BLUE RC: .75X TO 2X BASIC
RANDOM INSERTS IN PACKS
STATED PRINT RUN 150 SER.#'d SETS

2018 Topps High Tek Circuit Board

*CIRCUIT BOARD: .6X TO 1.5X BASIC
APPX.FOUR PER PACK

2018 Topps High Tek Diamond Grid

*DIAMOND GRID: .5X TO 1.2X BASIC
APPX.SIX PER PACK

2018 Topps High Tek Dot Grid

*DOTS GRID: .5X TO 1.2X BASIC
APPX.EIGHT PER PACK

2018 Topps High Tek Galactic Wave

*GALACTIC WAVE: .6X TO 1.5X BASIC
APPX.FOUR PER PACK

2018 Topps High Tek Green

*GREEN: 1X TO 2.5X BASIC
*GREEN RC: 1X TO 2.5X BASIC
STATED ODDS 1:2 HOBBY
STATED PRINT RUN 99 SER.#'d SETS

2018 Topps High Tek Lightning

*LIGHTNING: .5X TO 1.2X BASIC
APPX.EIGHT PER PACK

2018 Topps High Tek Orange

*ORANGE: 2.5X TO 6X BASIC
*ORANGE RC: 2.5X TO 6X BASIC
STATED ODDS 1:6 HOBBY
STATED PRINT RUN 25 SER.#'d SETS
HTDJ Derek Jeter A 15.00 40.00
HTDM Don Mattingly A 20.00 50.00

2018 Topps High Tek Triangles

*TRIANGLES: .5X TO 1.2X BASIC
APPX.SIX PER PACK

2018 Topps High Tek Black and White Variations

STATED ODDS 1:67 HOBBY
STATED PRINT RUN 50 SER.#'d SETS
HTAJ Aaron Judge 10.00 25.00
HTKB Kris Bryant 5.00 12.00
HTMR Mariano Rivera 5.00 12.00
HTMT Mike Trout 20.00 50.00
HTSO Shohei Ohtani 60.00 150.00

2018 Topps High Tek Black and White Variations Autographs

STATED ODDS 1:107 HOBBY
PRINT RUNS B/WN 20-40 COPIES PER
EXCHANGE DEADLINE 9/30/2020
HTAJ Aaron Judge EXCH
HTKB Kris Bryant/30 60.00 150.00
HTMR Mariano Rivera/20 75.00 200.00
HTMT Mike Trout/20 250.00 500.00
HTSO Shohei Ohtani/40 100.00 250.00

2018 Topps High Tek Autographs

RANDOM INSERTS IN PACKS
EXCHANGE DEADLINE 9/30/2020
HTAA Aaron Altherr 2.50 6.00
HTAH Austin Hays 4.00 10.00
HTAJ Aaron Judge 60.00 150.00
HTAR Anthony Rizzo 12.00 30.00
HTARD Alex Rodriguez 30.00 80.00
HTARO Amed Rosario 3.00 8.00
HTAV Alex Verdugo 8.00 20.00
HTBB Byron Buxton 4.00 10.00
HTBD Brian Dozier 3.00 8.00
HTBH Bryce Harper 60.00 150.00
HTBWI Bernie Williams 12.00 30.00
HTCB Charlie Blackmon 6.00 15.00
HTCF Clint Frazier 6.00 15.00
HTCJ Chipper Jones 40.00 100.00
HTCK Clayton Kershaw 25.00 60.00
HTCKE Carson Kelly 2.50 6.00
HTCR Cal Ripken Jr. 40.00 100.00
HTCS Carlos Santana 3.00 8.00
HTDF Dustin Fowler 2.50 6.00
HTDGO Dwight Gooden 5.00 12.00
HTDJ Derek Jeter 150.00 400.00
HTDS Dominic Smith 3.00 8.00
HTDST Darryl Strawberry 5.00 12.00
HTFL Francisco Lindor 12.00 30.00
HTFM Francisco Mejia 3.00 8.00
HTGS Gary Sanchez 10.00 25.00
HTGSP George Springer 6.00 15.00
HTGT Gleyber Torres 30.00 80.00
HTHA Hank Aaron 125.00 300.00
HTJA Jose Altuve 12.00 30.00
HTJB Jeff Bagwell 12.00 30.00
HTJCA Jose Canseco 10.00 25.00
HTJDA J.D. Davis 3.00 8.00
HTJM Jordan Montgomery 2.50 6.00
HTJS Justin Smoak 2.50 6.00
HTJT Jim Thome 20.00 50.00
HTJU Justin Upton 3.00 8.00
HTKB Kris Bryant 40.00 100.00
HTKBR Keon Broxton 2.50 6.00
HTMA Miguel Andujar 10.00 25.00
HTMM Mark McGwire 30.00 80.00
HTMO Marcell Ozuna 4.00 10.00
HTMOS Matt Olson 4.00 10.00
HTMR Mariano Rivera 40.00 100.00
HTMT Mike Trout 125.00 300.00
HTND Nicky Delmonico 2.50 6.00
HTNG Nomar Garciaparra 10.00 25.00
HTNS Noah Syndergaard 5.00 12.00
HTNW Nick Williams 3.00 8.00
HTPB Paul Blackburn 2.50 6.00
HTPD Paul DeJong 4.00 10.00
HTPM Pedro Martinez 20.00 50.00
HTRA Ronald Acuna 60.00 150.00
HTRC Roger Clemens 20.00 50.00
HTRH Rhys Hoskins 15.00 40.00
HTRI Raisel Iglesias 3.00 8.00
HTRJA Reggie Jackson 20.00 50.00
HTSA Sandy Alcantara 2.50 6.00
HTSD Sean Doolittle 2.50 6.00
HTSK Sandy Koufax 100.00 250.00
HTSKI Scott Kingery 4.00 10.00
HTSO Shohei Ohtani 125.00 300.00
HTTM Tyler Mahle 3.00 8.00
HTTN Tomas Nido 2.50 6.00
HTTV Thyago Vieira 2.50 6.00
HTVR Victor Robles 8.00 20.00
HTWBO Wade Boggs 10.00 25.00
HTWC Will Clark 6.00 15.00
HTWM Whit Merrifield 4.00 10.00
HTYM Yadier Molina EXCH 20.00 50.00
HTZC Zack Cozart 2.50 6.00
HTZG Zack Godley 2.50 6.00

2018 Topps High Tek Autographs Black Orbit Diffractors

*BLACK ORBIT: .5X TO 1.2X BASIC
RANDOM INSERTS IN PACKS
STATED PRINT RUN 50 SER.#'d SETS
EXCHANGE DEADLINE 9/30/2020
HTGA Greg Allen 10.00 25.00
HTOA Ozzie Albies 15.00 40.00
HTWB Walker Buehler 20.00 50.00

2018 Topps High Tek Autographs Blue

*BLUE: .5X TO 1.2X BASIC
RANDOM INSERTS IN PACKS
STATED PRINT RUN 75 SER.#'d SETS
EXCHANGE DEADLINE 9/30/2020
HTGA Greg Allen 10.00 25.00
HTOA Ozzie Albies 15.00 40.00
HTWB Walker Buehler 20.00 50.00

2018 Topps High Tek Autographs Green

*GREEN: .5X TO 1.2X BASIC
RANDOM INSERTS IN PACKS
STATED PRINT RUN 99 SER.#'d SETS
EXCHANGE DEADLINE 9/30/2020
HTGA Greg Allen 10.00 25.00
HTOA Ozzie Albies 15.00 40.00
HTWB Walker Buehler 20.00 50.00

2018 Topps High Tek Autographs Orange Orbit Diffractors

*ORANGE ORBIT: .6X TO 1.5X BASIC
STATED ODDS 1:10 HOBBY
STATED PRINT RUN 25 SER.#'d SETS
EXCHANGE DEADLINE 9/30/2020
HTGA Greg Allen 12.00 30.00
HTOA Ozzie Albies 20.00 50.00
HTWB Walker Buehler 25.00 60.00

2018 Topps High Tek Galactic Diffractors

*GLCTC DFFRCTRS: .6X TO 1.5X BASIC
*GLCTC DFFRCTRS RC: .6X TO 1.5X BASIC
APPX.ONE GALACTIC PER PACK

2018 Topps High Tek Galactic Diffractors Orange

*GALA ORANGE: 2.5X TO 6X BASIC
*GALA ORANGE RC: 2.5X TO 6X BASIC
STATED ODDS 1:6 HOBBY
STATED PRINT RUN 25 SER.#'d SETS
HTDJ Derek Jeter A 15.00 40.00
HTDM Don Mattingly A 20.00 50.00

2018 Topps High Tek Magma Diffractors

*MGMA DFFRCTRS: .5X TO 1.2X BASIC
*MGMA DFFRCTRS RC: .5X TO 1.2X BASIC
APPX.EIGHT MAGMA PER PACK

2018 Topps High Tek Magma Diffractors Black

*MAG BLACK: 1.2X TO 3X BASIC
*MAG BLACK RC: 1.2X TO 3X BASIC
STATED ODDS 1:3 HOBBY
STATED PRINT RUN 50 SER.#'d SETS

2018 Topps High Tek Magma Diffractors Green

*MAG GREEN: 1X TO 2.5X BASIC
*MAG GREEN RC: 1X TO 2.5X BASIC
STATED ODDS 1:2 HOBBY
STATED PRINT RUN 99 SER.#'d SETS

2018 Topps High Tek Magma Diffractors Orange

*MAGMA ORANGE: 2.5X TO 6X BASIC
*MAGMA ORANGE RC: 2.5X TO 6X BASIC
STATED ODDS 1:6 HOBBY
STATED PRINT RUN 25 SER.#'d SETS
HTDJ Derek Jeter A 15.00 40.00
HTDM Don Mattingly A 20.00 50.00

2018 Topps High Tek Orbit Diffractors

*ORBT DFFRCTRS: .5X TO 1.2X BASIC
*ORBT DFFRCTRS RC: .5X TO 1.2X BASIC
APPX.TWO ORBIT PER PACK

2018 Topps High Tek Orbit Diffractors Black

*ORBIT BLACK: 1.2X TO 3X BASIC
*ORBIT BLACK RC: 1.2X TO 3X BASIC
STATED ODDS 1:3 HOBBY
STATED PRINT RUN 50 SER.#'d SETS

2018 Topps High Tek Orbit Diffractors Orange

*ORBIT ORANGE: 2.5X TO 6X BASIC
*ORBIT ORANGE RC: 2.5X TO 6X BASIC
STATED ODDS 1:6 HOBBY
STATED PRINT RUN 25 SER.#'d SETS
HTDJ Derek Jeter A 15.00 40.00
HTDM Don Mattingly A 20.00 50.00

2018 Topps High Tek PortraiTEK

STATED ODDS 1:16 HOBBY
STATED PRINT RUN 50 SER.#'d SETS
*ORANGE/25: .5X TO 1.2X BASIC
PTAR Amed Rosario 2.50 6.00
PTARI Anthony Rizzo 4.00 10.00
PTBH Bryce Harper 5.00 12.00
PTCJ Chipper Jones 3.00 8.00
PTCR Cal Ripken Jr. 10.00 25.00
PTDJ Derek Jeter 8.00 20.00
PTGS Gary Sanchez 3.00 8.00
PTHA Hank Aaron 6.00 15.00
PTJA Jose Altuve 2.50 6.00
PTJB Jeff Bagwell 2.50 6.00
PTJT Jim Thome 2.50 6.00
PTKB Kris Bryant 4.00 10.00
PTMM Mark McGwire 5.00 12.00
PTMMA Manny Machado 3.00 8.00
PTMR Mariano Rivera 4.00 10.00
PTMT Mike Trout 15.00 40.00
PTPM Pedro Martinez 2.50 6.00
PTRC Roger Clemens 4.00 10.00
PTRD Rafael Devers 6.00 15.00
PTSO Shohei Ohtani 50.00 120.00
PTYM Yadier Molina 4.00 10.00

2018 Topps High Tek PortraiTEK Autographs

STATED ODDS 1:21 HOBBY
PRINT RUNS B/WN 20-99 COPIES PER
EXCHANGE DEADLINE 9/30/2020
PTAR Amed Rosario/99 5.00 12.00
PTBH Bryce Harper 75.00 200.00
PTCJ Chipper Jones/75 30.00 80.00
PTCR Cal Ripken Jr./75 50.00 120.00
PTDJ Derek Jeter
PTHA Hank Aaron/20 125.00 300.00
PTJA Jose Altuve/99 15.00 40.00
PTJT Jim Thome/99 20.00 50.00
PTKB Kris Bryant/55 50.00 120.00
PTMM Mark McGwire/75 40.00 100.00
PTMR Mariano Rivera/30 60.00 150.00
PTMT Mike Trout/25 250.00 500.00
PTPM Pedro Martinez/60 30.00 80.00
PTRD Rafael Devers 12.00 30.00
PTSO Shohei Ohtani/75 100.00 250.00
PTYM Yadier Molina EXCH 25.00 60.00

2018 Topps High Tek PortraiTEK Autographs Black

*BLACK: .4X TO 1X BASIC
STATED ODDS 1:21 HOBBY
STATED PRINT RUN 50 SER.#'d SETS
EXCHANGE DEADLINE 9/30/2020
PTRC Roger Clemens 25.00 60.00

2018 Topps High Tek PyroTEKnics

STATED ODDS 1:12 HOBBY
STATED PRINT RUN 99 SER.#'d SETS
*ORANGE/25: .6X TO 1.5X BASIC
PYTAR Amed Rosario 2.00 5.00
PYTBH Bryce Harper 4.00 10.00
PYTCF Clint Frazier 3.00 8.00
PYTCK Clayton Kershaw 4.00 10.00
PYTFL Francisco Lindor 2.50 6.00
PYTGS Giancarlo Stanton 2.50 6.00
PYTJA Jose Altuve 2.00 5.00
PYTKB Kris Bryant 3.00 8.00
PYTMB Mookie Betts 5.00 12.00
PYTMM Manny Machado 2.50 6.00
PYTMT Mike Trout 12.00 30.00
PYTRD Rafael Devers 5.00 12.00
PYTSO Shohei Ohtani 40.00 100.00
PYTVR Victor Robles 4.00 10.00
PYTYM Yadier Molina 3.00 8.00

2018 Topps High Tek PyroTEKnics Autographs

STATED ODDS 1:54 HOBBY
PRINT RUNS B/WN 20-50 COPIES PER
EXCHANGE DEADLINE 9/30/2020
PYTAR Amed Rosario/25 10.00 25.00
PYTBH Bryce Harper/20 75.00 200.00
PYTCF Clint Frazier/50 12.00 30.00
PYTFL Francisco Lindor/50 20.00 50.00
PYTJA Jose Altuve/50 15.00 40.00
PYTKB Kris Bryant/40 60.00 150.00
PYTMT Mike Trout/20 250.00 500.00
PYTSO Shohei Ohtani/20 300.00 600.00
PYTVR Victor Robles/50 15.00 40.00
PYTYM Yadier Molina EXCH 30.00 80.00

2018 Topps High Tek Rookie Tek

STATED ODDS 1:12 HOBBY
STATED PRINT RUN 99 SER.#'d SETS
*ORANGE/25: .6X TO 1.5X BASIC
RTAH Austin Hays 2.00 5.00
RTAR Amed Rosario 1.50 4.00
RTAV Alex Verdugo 2.00 5.00
RTCF Clint Frazier 2.50 6.00
RTDS Dominic Smith 1.50 4.00
RTFM Francisco Mejia 1.50 4.00
RTJC J.P. Crawford 1.25 3.00
RTMA Miguel Andujar 5.00 12.00
RTNW Nick Williams 1.50 4.00
RTOA Ozzie Albies 4.00 10.00
RTRD Rafael Devers 4.00 10.00
RTRH Rhys Hoskins 5.00 12.00
RTSK Scott Kingery 2.00 5.00
RTSO Shohei Ohtani 25.00 60.00
RTVR Victor Robles 3.00 8.00

2018 Topps High Tek Rookie Tek Autographs

STATED ODDS 1:33 HOBBY
STATED PRINT RUN 50 SER.#'d SETS
EXCHANGE DEADLINE 9/30/2020
RTAH Austin Hays 6.00 15.00
RTAR Amed Rosario 5.00 12.00
RTAV Alex Verdugo
RTCF Clint Frazier 8.00 20.00
RTFM Francisco Mejia 5.00 12.00
RTNW Nick Williams 5.00 12.00
RTOA Ozzie Albies 12.00 30.00
RTRH Rhys Hoskins 20.00 50.00
RTSK Scott Kingery
RTSO Shohei Ohtani 250.00 500.00
RTVR Victor Robles 12.00 30.00

2019 Topps High Tek

1 Cal Ripken Jr. 2.00 5.00
2 Cedric Mullins RC .75 2.00
3 Trey Mancini .50 1.25
4 Roberto Alomar .50 1.25
5 Mookie Betts 1.25 3.00
6 Andrew Benintendi .60 1.50
7 Rafael Devers .75 2.00
8 Chris Sale .60 1.50
9 David Ortiz .60 1.50
10 Pedro Martinez .50 1.25
11 J.D. Martinez .60 1.50
12 Frank Thomas .60 1.50
13 Michael Kopech RC 1.25 3.00
14 Jose Abreu .60 1.50
15 Francisco Lindor .60 1.50
16 Jose Ramirez .50 1.25
17 Corey Kluber .50 1.25
18 Miguel Cabrera .60 1.50
19 Christin Stewart RC .50 1.25
20 Jeff Bagwell .50 1.25
21 Jose Altuve .50 1.25
22 Carlos Correa .60 1.50
23 Alex Bregman .60 1.50
24 Justin Verlander .60 1.50
25 Gerrit Cole .60 1.50
26 George Springer .50 1.25
27 Whit Merrifield .60 1.50
28 Salvador Perez .50 1.25
29 Ryan O'Hearn RC .40 1.00
30 George Brett 1.25 3.00
31 Mike Trout 3.00 8.00
32 Shohei Ohtani 1.00 2.50
33 Albert Pujols .75 2.00
34 Nolan Ryan 2.00 5.00
35 Jose Berrios .50 1.25
36 Miguel Sano .50 1.25
37 Eddie Rosario .50 1.25
38 Derek Jeter 1.50 4.00
39 Tino Martinez .50 1.25
40 Aaron Judge 1.50 4.00
41 Gleyber Torres 1.25 3.00
42 Miguel Andujar .60 1.50
43 Mariano Rivera .75 2.00
44 Luis Severino .50 1.25
45 Khris Davis .60 1.50
46 Matt Chapman .60 1.50
47 Rickey Henderson .60 1.50
48 Ken Griffey Jr. 1.25 3.00
49 Yusei Kikuchi RC .60 1.50
50 Justus Sheffield RC .60 1.50
51 Ichiro .75 2.00
52 Edgar Martinez .50 1.25
53 Blake Snell .50 1.25
54 Austin Meadows .60 1.50
55 Jose Canseco .50 1.25
56 Joey Gallo .50 1.25
57 Nomar Mazara .40 1.00
58 Ivan Rodriguez .50 1.25
59 Rowdy Tellez RC .60 1.50
60 Danny Jansen RC .40 1.00
61 Roy Halladay .50 1.25
62 Randy Johnson .60 1.50
63 Zack Greinke .60 1.50
64 Robbie Ray .40 1.00
65 Chipper Jones .60 1.50
66 Ronald Acuna Jr. 3.00 8.00
67 Touki Toussaint RC .50 1.25
68 Kolby Allard RC .60 1.50
69 John Smoltz .60 1.50
70 Kris Bryant .75 2.00
71 Anthony Rizzo .75 2.00
72 Javier Baez .75 2.00
73 Kyle Schwarber .60 1.50
74 Joey Votto .60 1.50
75 Yasiel Puig .60 1.50
76 Scooter Gennett .50 1.25
77 Nolan Arenado 1.00 2.50
78 Trevor Story .60 1.50

79 Charlie Blackmon .60 1.50
80 Todd Helton .50 1.25
81 Clayton Kershaw 1.00 2.50
82 Sandy Koufax 1.25 3.00
83 Walker Buehler .75 2.00
84 Corey Seager .60 1.50
85 Cody Bellinger 1.25 3.00
86 Max Muncy .50 1.25
87 Brian Anderson .40 1.00
88 Jorge Alfaro .40 1.00
89 Christian Yelich .75 2.00
90 Lorenzo Cain .40 1.00
91 Josh Hader .50 1.25
92 Noah Syndergaard .50 1.25
93 Jacob deGrom 1.25 3.00
94 Bryce Harper 1.00 2.50
95 Robinson Cano .50 1.25
96 Rhys Hoskins .75 2.00
97 Andrew McCutchen .60 1.50
98 Aaron Nola .50 1.25
99 J.T. Realmuto .60 1.50
100 Starling Marte .50 1.25
101 Chris Archer .40 1.00
102 Gregory Polanco .50 1.25
103 Manny Machado .60 1.50
104 Luis Urias RC .60 1.50
105 Tony Gwynn .60 1.50
106 Buster Posey .75 2.00
107 Brandon Crawford .50 1.25
108 Paul Goldschmidt .60 1.50
109 Yadier Molina .75 2.00
110 Juan Soto 2.00 5.00
111 Victor Robles .75 2.00
112 Max Scherzer .60 1.50

2019 Topps High Tek Black

*BLACK: 1.2X TO 3X BASIC
*BLACK RC: 1.2X TO 3X BASIC
STATED ODDS 1:10 HOBBY
STATED PRINT RUN 50 SER.#'d SETS
38 Derek Jeter 10.00 25.00
48 Ken Griffey Jr. 12.00 30.00

2019 Topps High Tek Green

*GREEN: .8X TO 2X BASIC
*GREEN RC: .8X TO 2X BASIC
STATED ODDS 1:4 HOBBY
STATED PRINT RUN 150 SER.#'d SETS
48 Ken Griffey Jr. 6.00 15.00

2019 Topps High Tek Orange

*ORANGE: 2.5X TO 6X BASIC
*ORANGE RC: 2.5X TO 6X BASIC
STATED ODDS 1:19 HOBBY
STATED PRINT RUN 25 SER.#'d SETS
38 Derek Jeter 20.00 50.00
48 Ken Griffey Jr. 30.00 80.00

2019 Topps High Tek Pink

*PINK: 1X TO 2.5X BASIC
*PINK RC: 1X TO 2.5X BASIC
STATED ODDS 1:7 HOBBY
STATED PRINT RUN 75 SER.#'d SETS
38 Derek Jeter 8.00 20.00
48 Ken Griffey Jr. 8.00 20.00

2019 Topps High Tek Purple

*PURPLE: 1X TO 2.5X BASIC
*PURPLE RC: 1X TO 2.5X BASIC
STATED ODDS 1:5 HOBBY
STATED PRINT RUN 99 SER.#'d SETS
38 Derek Jeter 8.00 20.00
48 Ken Griffey Jr. 8.00 20.00

2019 Topps High Tek CelebraTEK

STATED ODDS 1:34 HOBBY
STATED PRINT RUN 99 SER.#'d SETS
*ORANGE/25: .6X TO 1.5X BASIC
CTAB Alex Bregman 5.00 12.00
CTAJ Aaron Judge 12.00 30.00
CTCY Christian Yelich 6.00 15.00
CTFL Francisco Lindor 2.50 6.00
CTJD Jacob deGrom 4.00 10.00
CTJR Jose Ramirez 2.00 5.00
CTJS Juan Soto 8.00 20.00
CTKB Kris Bryant 5.00 12.00
CTKS Kyle Schwarber 4.00 10.00
CTMT Mike Trout 12.00 30.00
CTNS Noah Syndergaard 4.00 10.00
CTOA Ozzie Albies 4.00 10.00
CTRA Ronald Acuna Jr. 15.00 40.00
CTRH Rhys Hoskins 3.00 8.00
CTSO Shohei Ohtani 4.00 10.00

2019 Topps High Tek CelebraTEK Orange

*ORANGE: .6X TO 1.5X BASIC
STATED ODDS 1:135 HOBBY
STATED PRINT RUN 25 SER.#'d SETS
CTAB Alex Bregman 15.00 40.00
CTOA Ozzie Albies 10.00 25.00

2019 Topps High Tek CelebraTEK Autographs

STATED ODDS 1:198 HOBBY
PRINT RUNS B/WN 15-50 COPIES PER
NO PRICING QTY 15 OR LESS
EXCHANGE DEADLINE 10/31/2021
CTAJ Aaron Judge/20 40.00 100.00
CTCY Christian Yelich EXCH
CTFL Francisco Lindor EXCH
CTJS Juan Soto/30 50.00 120.00
CTKS Kyle Schwarber/45 10.00 25.00
CTOA Ozzie Albies/50 15.00 40.00
CTRA Ronald Acuna Jr./25 100.00 250.00
CTRH Rhys Hoskins/30 25.00 60.00

2019 Topps High Tek Future TEK

STATED ODDS 1:34 HOBBY
STATED PRINT RUN 99 SER.#'d SETS
*ORANGE/25: .6X TO 1.5X BASIC
FTCP Cionel Perez 1.50 4.00
FTDB David Bote 4.00 10.00
FTEJ Eloy Jimenez 6.00 15.00
FTJH Josh Hader 2.00 5.00
FTJS Justus Sheffield 2.50 6.00
FTKT Kyle Tucker 4.00 10.00
FTLU Luis Urias 2.50 6.00
FTMC Mike Clevinger 2.00 5.00
FTMK Michael Kopech 5.00 12.00
FTRL Ramon Laureano 3.00 8.00
FTRT Rowdy Tellez 2.50 6.00
FTTT Touki Toussaint 2.00 5.00
FTVG Vladimir Guerrero Jr. 10.00 25.00
FTWA Willy Adames 1.50 4.00
FTYK Yusei Kikuchi 2.50

2019 Topps High Tek Future TEK Orange

*ORANGE: .6X TO 1.5X BASIC
STATED ODDS 1:135 HOBBY
STATED PRINT RUN 25 SER.#'d SETS
FTKT Kyle Tucker 12.00 30.00
FTRL Ramon Laureano 8.00 20.00

2019 Topps High Tek Future TEK Autographs

STATED ODDS 1:99 HOBBY
STATED PRINT RUN 50 SER.#'d SETS
EXCHANGE DEADLINE 10/31/2021
FTEJ Eloy Jimenez 20.00 50.00
FTJS Justus Sheffield 6.00 15.00
FTRT Rowdy Tellez 6.00 15.00
FTVG Vladimir Guerrero Jr. 60.00 150.00

2019 Topps High Tek PortraiTEK

STATED ODDS 1:49 HOBBY
STATED PRINT RUN 50 SER.#'d SETS
*ORANGE/25: .5X TO 1.2X BASIC
PTBH Bryce Harper 10.00 25.00
PTCR Cal Ripken Jr. 15.00 40.00
PTCS Chris Sale 3.00 8.00
PTCY Christian Yelich 8.00 20.00
PTDJ Derek Jeter 15.00 40.00
PTDO David Ortiz 3.00 8.00
PTFL Francisco Lindor 6.00 15.00
PTFT Frank Thomas 6.00 15.00
PTI Ichiro 6.00 15.00
PTJD Jacob deGrom 6.00 15.00
PTJS Juan Soto 10.00 25.00
PTKG Ken Griffey Jr. 30.00 80.00
PTMA Miguel Andujar 3.00 8.00
PTMM Manny Machado 3.00 8.00
PTMT Mike Trout 15.00 40.00
PTPG Paul Goldschmidt 3.00 8.00
PTRA Ronald Acuna Jr. 15.00 40.00
PTRD Rafael Devers 4.00 10.00
PTRJ Randy Johnson 3.00 8.00
PTSO Shohei Ohtani 5.00 12.00
PTSS Sammy Sosa 3.00 8.00

2019 Topps High Tek PortraiTEK Orange

*ORANGE: .5X TO 1.2X BASIC
STATED ODDS 1:96 HOBBY
STATED PRINT RUN 25 SER.#'d SETS
PTDJ Derek Jeter 30.00 80.00
PTFT Frank Thomas 15.00 40.00
PTI Ichiro 10.00 25.00
PTKG Ken Griffey Jr. 25.00 60.00
PTMT Mike Trout 25.00 60.00
PTSS Sammy Sosa 4.00 10.00

2019 Topps High Tek PortraiTEK Autographs

STATED ODDS 1:56 HOBBY
PRINT RUNS B/WN 25-99 COPIES PER
EXCHANGE DEADLINE 10/31/2021
*BLACK: .4X TO 1X p/r 60-70
PTBH Bryce Harper/25 75.00 200.00
PTCR Cal Ripken Jr./60 30.00 80.00
PTCS Chris Sale/70 6.00 15.00
PTCY Christian Yelich EXCH 30.00 80.00
PTDO David Ortiz/60 20.00 50.00
PTFL Francisco Lindor EXCH 20.00 50.00
PTFT Frank Thomas/65 30.00 80.00
PTI Ichiro/25 100.00 250.00
PTJS Juan Soto/70 50.00 120.00
PTMA Miguel Andujar/70 10.00 25.00
PTMT Mike Trout/25 200.00 500.00
PTPG Paul Goldschmidt/65 15.00 40.00
PTRA Ronald Acuna Jr./70 50.00 120.00
PTRD Rafael Devers/70 15.00 40.00
PTRJ Randy Johnson/60 25.00 60.00
PTSO Shohei Ohtani/25 100.00 250.00

2019 Topps High Tek ReflecTEK

STATED ODDS 1:202 HOBBY
STATED PRINT RUN 50 SER.#'d SETS
RTCR Cal Ripken Jr. 10.00 25.00
RTDJ Derek Jeter 15.00 40.00
RTKG Ken Griffey Jr. 30.00 80.00
RTMR Mariano Rivera 10.00 25.00
RTPM David Ortiz 3.00 8.00

2019 Topps High Tek ReflecTEK Autographs

STATED ODDS 1:393 HOBBY
PRINT RUNS B/WN 25-35 COPIES PER
EXCHANGE DEADLINE 10/31/2021
RTDO David Ortiz/35 25.00 60.00
RTKG Ken Griffey Jr./25 150.00 400.00

2019 Topps High Tek Autographs

STATED ODDS 1 PER HOBBY
EXCHANGE DEADLINE 10/31/2021
HTAAG Aramis Garcia 4.00 10.00
HTAAJ Andruw Jones 10.00 25.00
HTAAJU Aaron Judge 50.00 120.00
HTAAM Austin Meadows 5.00 12.00
HTAAR Anthony Rizzo 15.00 40.00
HTABB Byron Buxton 4.00 10.00
HTABH Bryce Harper 75.00 200.00
HTABK Brad Keller 2.50 6.00
HTABL Brandon Lowe 6.00 15.00
HTABT Blake Treinen 2.50 6.00
HTABW Bryse Wilson 8.00 20.00
HTACC Carlos Carrasco 2.50 6.00
HTACK Carter Kieboom 10.00 25.00
HTACT Cole Tucker 4.00 10.00
HTADH Darwinzon Hernandez 2.50 6.00
HTADS DJ Stewart 3.00 8.00
HTAEJ Eloy Jimenez 15.00 40.00
HTAEL Elvis Luciano 4.00 10.00
HTAEM Edgar Martinez 6.00 15.00
HTAFT Fernando Tatis Jr. EXCH 75.00 200.00
HTAFV Framber Valdez 8.00 20.00
HTAHM Hideki Matsui 30.00 80.00
HTAI Ichiro 100.00 250.00
HTAJC Jose Canseco 8.00 20.00
HTAJDA Johnny Damon 5.00 12.00
HTAJDU Jon Duplantier 2.50 6.00
HTAJG Juan Gonzalez 5.00 12.00
HTAJM Jose Martinez 2.50 6.00
HTAJP Jorge Posada 8.00 20.00
HTAJS Justus Sheffield 4.00 10.00
HTAJSM John Smoltz 10.00 25.00
HTAJSO Juan Soto 50.00 120.00
HTAKB Kris Bryant 30.00 80.00
HTAKH Keston Hiura 15.00 40.00
HTAKN Kevin Newman 4.00 10.00
HTAKS Kyle Schwarber 6.00 15.00
HTAKW Kyle Wright 10.00 25.00
HTALM Lance McCullers Jr. 4.00 10.00
HTALT Lane Thomas 4.00 10.00
HTALV Luke Voit 15.00 40.00
HTAMA Miguel Andujar 10.00 25.00
HTAMC Miguel Cabrera 20.00 50.00
HTAMF Mike Foltynewicz 4.00 10.00
HTAMK Merrill Kelly 2.50 6.00
HTAMMU Max Muncy 6.00 15.00
HTAMT Mike Trout 150.00 400.00
HTANL Nate Lowe EXCH 12.00 30.00
HTANM Nick Margevicius 2.50 6.00
HTANR Nolan Ryan 50.00 120.00
HTAOA Ozzie Albies 10.00 25.00
HTAPC Patrick Corbin 3.00 8.00
HTAPD Paul DeJong 4.00 10.00
HTAPG Paul Goldschmidt 15.00 40.00
HTARA Ronald Acuna Jr. 50.00 120.00
HTARAN Rick Ankiel 4.00 10.00
HTARC Roger Clemens 25.00 60.00
HTARD Rafael Devers 12.00 30.00
HTARH Rickey Henderson 25.00 60.00
HTARJ Randy Johnson 40.00 100.00
HTARM Reese McGuire 4.00 10.00
HTART Rowdy Tellez 4.00 10.00
HTASB Skye Bolt 3.00 8.00
HTASK Sandy Koufax 100.00 250.00
HTASKI Scott Kingery 4.00 10.00
HTASO Shohei Ohtani 60.00 150.00
HTATE Thairo Estrada 6.00 15.00
HTATM Tino Martinez 8.00 20.00
HTATP Thomas Pannone 4.00 10.00
HTATT Touki Toussaint 3.00 8.00
HTATTH Trent Thornton 2.50 6.00
HTATW Taylor Ward 2.50 6.00
HTAVG Vladimir Guerrero Jr. 40.00 100.00

2019 Topps High Tek Autographs Black

*BLACK: .5X TO 1.2X BASIC
STATED ODDS 1:14 HOBBY
STATED PRINT RUN 50 SER.#'d SETS
EXCHANGE DEADLINE 10/31/2021
HTAEM Edgar Martinez 12.00 30.00
HTAFL Francisco Lindor EXCH 15.00 40.00
HTAFT Fernando Tatis Jr. EXCH 150.00 400.00
HTAJC Jose Canseco 12.00 30.00
HTAJP Jorge Posada 15.00 40.00
HTALM Lance McCullers Jr. 6.00 15.00
HTANS Nick Senzel EXCH 20.00 50.00
HTAPA Pete Alonso EXCH 100.00 250.00

2019 Topps High Tek Autographs Orange

*ORANGE: .6X TO 1.5X BASIC
STATED ODDS 1:28 HOBBY
STATED PRINT RUN 25 SER.#'d SETS
EXCHANGE DEADLINE 10/31/2021
HTAEJ Eloy Jimenez 30.00 80.00
HTAEM Edgar Martinez 15.00 40.00
HTAFT Fernando Tatis Jr. EXCH 250.00 600.00
HTAJC Jose Canseco 15.00 40.00
HTAJDA Johnny Damon 10.00 25.00
HTAJG Juan Gonzalez 10.00 25.00
HTAJP Jorge Posada 20.00 50.00
HTAKH Keston Hiura 40.00 100.00
HTALM Lance McCullers Jr. 8.00 20.00
HTANS Nick Senzel EXCH 40.00 100.00
HTAPA Pete Alonso EXCH 125.00 300.00
HTAXB Xander Bogaerts 15.00 40.00

2019 Topps High Tek Autographs Pink

*PINK: .5X TO 1.2X BASIC
STATED ODDS 1:11 HOBBY
STATED PRINT RUN 75 SER.#'d SETS
EXCHANGE DEADLINE 10/31/2021
HTAEM Edgar Martinez 12.00 30.00
HTALM Lance McCullers Jr. 6.00 15.00

2019 Topps High Tek Autographs Purple

*PURPLE: .5X TO 1.2X BASIC
STATED ODDS 1:9 HOBBY
STATED PRINT RUN 99 SER.#'d SETS
EXCHANGE DEADLINE 10/31/2021
HTALM Lance McCullers Jr. 6.00 15.00

2005 Topps Hot Button

COMPLETE SET (140) 50.00 100.00
COMMON CARD .40 1.00
1 Alex Rodriguez 1.25 3.00
2 Ronnie Belliard .40 1.00
3 Miguel Cabrera 1.00 2.50
4 Morgan Ensberg .40 1.00
5 Kazuo Matsui .40 1.00
6 Juan Uribe .40 1.00
7 Eric Munson .40 1.00
8 Matt Holliday 1.00 2.50
9 Vladimir Guerrero .60 1.50
10 Manny Ramirez 1.00 2.50
11 Livan Hernandez .40 1.00
12 Sean Burroughs .40 1.00
13 Danny Bautista .40 1.00
14 Aaron Miles .40 1.00
15 Michael Young .40 1.00
16 Tino Martinez .60 1.50
17 Corey Koskie .40 1.00
18 Juan Pierre .40 1.00
19 Benito Santiago .40 1.00
20 Carlos Beltran .60 1.50
21 Dontrelle Willis .40 1.00
22 Orlando Cabrera .40 1.00
23 Brad Wilkerson .40 1.00
24 Eric Milton .40 1.00
25 Jacque Jones .40 1.00
26 Jorge Julio .40 1.00
27 Roberto Alomar .60 1.50
28 Alfonso Soriano .60 1.50
29 Johnny Estrada .40 1.00
30 Derek Jeter 2.50 6.00
31 Rob Mackowiak .40 1.00
32 Keith Foulke .40 1.00
33 Jermaine Dye .40 1.00
34 Jeromy Burnitz .40 1.00
35 Jeff Bagwell .60 1.50
36 Keith Ginter .40 1.00
37 A.J. Pierzynski .40 1.00
38 Toby Hall .40 1.00
39 Pedro Martinez .60 1.50
40 Eric Gagne .40 1.00
41 Ichiro Suzuki 1.25 3.00
42 Alex S. Gonzalez .40 1.00
43 Javy Lopez .40 1.00
44 Lyle Overbay .40 1.00
45 David Ortiz 1.00 2.50
46 Rocco Baldelli .40 1.00
47 Darin Erstad .40 1.00
48 Mike Lowell .40 1.00
49 Orlando Hernandez .40 1.00
50 Sammy Sosa 1.00 2.50
51 J.D. Drew .40 1.00
52 Michael Barrett .40 1.00
53 Albert Pujols 1.25 3.00
54 David Eckstein .40 1.00
55 Shawn Green .40 1.00
56 Matt Morris .40 1.00
57 Carlos Zambrano .60 1.50
58 Justin Morneau .60 1.50
59 Francisco Rodriguez .60 1.50
60 Joe Nathan .40 1.00
61 Mike Lieberthal .40 1.00
62 Miguel Cairo .40 1.00
63 David Bell .40 1.00
64 Julio Lugo .40 1.00
65 Johnny Damon .60 1.50
66 Eric Hinske .40 1.00
67 Eddie Guardado .40 1.00
68 Kerry Wood .40 1.00
69 Carl Pavano .40 1.00
70 Ivan Rodriguez .60 1.50
71 Larry Walker .60 1.50
72 Delvi Cruz .40 1.00
73 Shea Hillenbrand .40 1.00
74 Gregg Zaun .40 1.00
75 Randy Johnson 1.00 2.50
76 Luis Castillo .40 1.00
77 Jason Phillips .40 1.00
78 Garret Anderson .40 1.00
79 David Dellucci .40 1.00
80 Todd Helton .60 1.50
81 Odalis Perez .40 1.00
82 Vinny Castilla .40 1.00
83 Tony Batista .40 1.00
84 Ray Durham .40 1.00
85 Mike Piazza 1.00 2.50
86 Braden Looper .40 1.00
87 Eric Byrnes .40 1.00
88 Angel Berroa .40 1.00
89 Jack Wilson .40 1.00
90 Jim Thome .60 1.50
91 Rafael Palmeiro .60 1.50
92 Pokey Reese .40 1.00
93 Bobby Abreu .40 1.00
94 Ben Sheets .40 1.00
95 Andruw Jones .40 1.00
96 Royce Clayton .40 1.00
97 Charles Johnson .40 1.00
98 Mark Teixeira .60 1.50
99 J.T. Snow .40 1.00
100 Miguel Tejada .60 1.50
101 Torii Hunter .40 1.00
102 Geoff Jenkins .40 1.00
103 Rich Harden .40 1.00
104 Brad Ausmus .40 1.00
105 Joe Mauer .75 2.00
106 Adrian Beltre 1.00 2.50
107 Moises Alou .40 1.00
108 Aubrey Huff .40 1.00
109 Tim Wakefield .60 1.50
110 Lance Berkman .60 1.50
111 Matt Stairs .40 1.00
112 Jerome Williams .40 1.00
113 Troy Percival .40 1.00
114 Khalil Greene .40 1.00
115 Jeff Kent .40 1.00
116 Paul Konerko .60 1.50
117 Alex Cora .60 1.50
118 Jason Kendall .40 1.00
119 Pat Burrell .40 1.00
120 Chipper Jones 1.00 2.50
121 Lew Ford .40 1.00
122 Josh Beckett .40 1.00
123 David Wells .40 1.00
124 Hee Seop Choi .40 1.00
125 Curt Schilling .60 1.50
126 Edgardo Alfonzo .40 1.00
127 Roger Clemens 1.25 3.00
128 Adam Kennedy .40 1.00
129 Brian Roberts .40 1.00
130 Ken Griffey Jr. 2.00 5.00
131 Mike Matheny .40 1.00
132 Carlos Pena .60 1.50
133 Jake Westbrook .40 1.00
134 Freddy Garcia .40 1.00
135 Jorge Posada .60 1.50
136 Derrek Lee .40 1.00
137 Joe Crede .40 1.00
138 Adam Dunn .60 1.50
139 Coco Crisp .40 1.00
140 Magglio Ordonez .60 1.50
NNO Hot Button Gaming Console

2005 Topps Hot Button Refractors

*REF: .5X TO 1.5X BASIC
STATED ODDS 1:3

2017 Topps Inception

COMP.SET w/o AU's (100) 75.00 200.00
AU RC PRINT RUNS B/WN 149-299 COPIES PER
PRINTING PLATE ODDS 1:106 HOBBY
PLATE PRINT RUN 1 SET PER COLOR
BLACK-CYAN-MAGENTA-YELLOW ISSUED
NO PLATE PRICING DUE TO SCARCITY
EXCHANGE DEADLINE 4/30/2019
1 Mike Trout 4.00 10.00
2 Jose Altuve .60 1.50
3 Mookie Betts 1.50 4.00
4 Nolan Arenado 1.25 3.00
5 Paul Goldschmidt .75 2.00
6 Manny Machado .75 2.00
7 Anthony Rizzo 1.00 2.50
8 Josh Donaldson .60 1.50
9 Bryce Harper 1.25 3.00
10 Clayton Kershaw 1.25 3.00
11 Xander Bogaerts .75 2.00
12 Carlos Correa .75 2.00
13 Chris Sale .75 2.00
14 Starling Marte .60 1.50
15 Francisco Lindor .75 2.00
16 Wil Myers .60 1.50
17 Brian Dozier .75 2.00
18 Jake Arrieta .60 1.50
19 Carlos Gonzalez .60 1.50
20 Noah Syndergaard .60 1.50
21 Daniel Murphy .60 1.50
22 Christian Yelich 1.00 2.50
23 J.D. Martinez .75 2.00
24 Jacob deGrom 1.50 4.00
25 Stephen Strasburg .75 2.00
26 George Springer .60 1.50
27 Jose Abreu .75 2.00
28 A.J. Pollock .50 1.25
29 Dee Gordon .50 1.25
30 Rougned Odor .60 1.50
31 Billy Hamilton .60 1.50
32 Yu Darvish .75 2.00
33 Dellin Betances .60 1.50
34 Buster Posey 1.00 2.50
35 Maikel Franco .60 1.50
36 Giancarlo Stanton .75 2.00
37 Andrew McCutchen .75 2.00
38 Kris Bryant 1.00 2.50
39 Joey Votto .75 2.00
40 Miguel Cabrera .75 2.00
41 Freddie Freeman 1.00 2.50
42 Julio Urias .75 2.00
43 Gregory Polanco .60 1.50
44 Chris Archer .50 1.25
45 Carlos Martinez .60 1.50
46 Jonathan Villar .50 1.25
47 Kyle Hendricks .75 2.00
48 Jean Segura .60 1.50
49 Matt Harvey .60 1.50
50 Gerrit Cole .75 2.00
51 Jackie Bradley Jr. .75 2.00
52 Masahiro Tanaka .60 1.50
53 Marcell Ozuna .75 2.00
54 Rick Porcello .60 1.50
55 Randal Grichuk .50 1.25
56 Joc Pederson .60 1.50
57 Willson Contreras .75 2.00
58 Gary Sanchez .75 2.00
59 Corey Seager .75 2.00
60 Byron Buxton .75 2.00
61 Javier Baez 1.00 2.50
62 Max Scherzer .75 2.00
63 Robinson Cano .60 1.50
64 Kyle Seager .50 1.25
65 Yoenis Cespedes .75 2.00
66 Jason Kipnis .60 1.50
67 Aaron Sanchez .60 1.50
68 Lucas Giolito .60 1.50
69 Michael Conforto .60 1.50
70 Marcus Stroman .60 1.50
71 Felix Hernandez .60 1.50
72 Kenta Maeda .60 1.50
73 Lance McCullers .50 1.25
74 Danny Duffy .50 1.25
75 Sonny Gray .60 1.50
76 Yasmany Tomas .50 1.25
77 Kyle Schwarber .75 2.00
78 Jon Gray .50 1.25
79 Jameson Taillon .60 1.50
80 Carlos Rodon .75 2.00
81 Miguel Sano .60 1.50
82 Luis Severino .60 1.50
83 Trevor Story .75 2.00
84 Trea Turner .60 1.50
85 Stephen Piscotty .60 1.50
86 Aledmys Diaz .60 1.50
87 Tyler Naquin .75 2.00
88 Nomar Mazara .50 1.25
89 Addison Russell .75 2.00
90 Aaron Nola .60 1.50
91 Jake Lamb .60 1.50
92 Michael Fulmer .50 1.25
93 Steven Matz .50 1.25
94 Yasiel Puig .75 2.00
95 Jurickson Profar .60 1.50
96 Vince Velasquez .50 1.25
97 Blake Snell .60 1.50
98 A.J. Reed .50 1.25
99 David Price .60 1.50
100 Eric Hosmer .60 1.50
101 Yoan Moncada AU/149 RC 25.00 60.00
102 Orlando Arcia AU/249 RC 4.00 10.00
103 Dansby Swanson AU/199 RC 12.00 30.00
104 Alex Bregman AU/199 RC 25.00 60.00
105 Yulieski Gurriel AU/199 RC 8.00 20.00
106 Andrew Benintendi AU/199 RC 30.00 80.00
107 Jose De Leon AU/199 RC 3.00 8.00
108 Hunter Dozier AU/199 RC 6.00 15.00
109 Hunter Renfroe AU/199 RC 4.00 10.00
110 Jake Thompson AU/299 RC 3.00 8.00
111 Jorge Alfaro AU/199 RC 4.00 10.00
112 Aaron Judge AU/199 RC 100.00 250.00
114 David Dahl AU/199 RC 4.00 15.00
115 Alex Reyes AU/199 RC 4.00 10.00
116 JaCoby Jones AU/199 RC 4.00 10.00
117 Manny Margot AU/249 RC 5.00 12.00
118 Luke Weaver AU/249 RC 4.00 10.00
120 Raimel Tapia AU/199 RC 4.00 10.00
121 Braden Shipley AU/249 RC 3.00 8.00
122 Reynaldo Lopez AU/249 RC 3.00 8.00
123 Joe Musgrove AU/299 RC 10.00 25.00
124 Teoscar Hernandez AU/299 RC 12.00 30.00
125 Jharel Cotton AU/299 RC 3.00 8.00
127 Dan Vogelbach AU/249 RC 5.00 12.00
128 Ty Blach AU/299 RC 5.00 12.00
129 Matt Olson AU/299 RC 8.00 20.00
130 Rob Zastryzny AU/299 RC 3.00 8.00
131 Ryon Healy AU/299 RC 5.00 12.00
132 Robert Gsellman AU/299 RC 3.00 8.00
134 Trey Mancini AU/299 RC 10.00 25.00
135 Carson Fulmer AU/199 RC 5.00 12.00
136 Bruce Maxwell AU/299 RC 3.00 8.00
137 Tyler Austin AU/299 RC 4.00 10.00
138 Matt Strahm AU/299 RC 4.00 10.00
139 German Marquez AU/299 RC 5.00 12.00
140 Seth Lugo AU/299 RC 3.00 8.00
141 Renato Nunez AU/299 RC 6.00 15.00
142 Donnie Hart AU/299 RC 4.00 10.00
145 Chad Pinder AU/299 RC 4.00 10.00

2017 Topps Inception Blue

*BLUE 1-100: 3X TO 8X BASIC
*BLUE 101-145: .75X TO 2X BASIC
1-100 STATED ODDS 1:17 HOBBY
101-145 STATED ODDS 1:33 HOBBY
STATED PRINT RUN 25 SER.#'d SETS
EXCHANGE DEADLINE 4/30/2019
1 Mike Trout 30.00 80.00
38 Kris Bryant 30.00 80.00

2017 Topps Inception Green

*GREEN: .5X TO 1.2X BASIC
RANDOM INSERTS IN PACKS

2017 Topps Inception Magenta

*MAGENTA 1-100: 1.5X TO 4X BASIC
*MAGENTA 101-145: .5X TO 1.2X BASIC
1-100 STATED ODDS 1:5 HOBBY
101-145 STATED ODDS 1:9 HOBBY
STATED PRINT RUN 99 SER.#'d SETS
EXCHANGE DEADLINE 4/30/2019

2017 Topps Inception Orange

*ORANGE 1-100: 2.5X TO 6X BASIC
*ORANGE 101-145: .6X TO 1.5X BASIC
1-100 STATED ODDS 1:9 HOBBY
101-145 STATED ODDS 1:17 HOBBY
STATED PRINT RUN 50 SER.#'d SETS
EXCHANGE DEADLINE 4/30/2019
1 Mike Trout 25.00 60.00
38 Kris Bryant 25.00 60.00

2017 Topps Inception Purple

*PURPLE: 1.2X TO 3X BASIC
STATED ODDS 1:3 HOBBY
STATED PRINT RUN 150 SER.#'d SETS

2017 Topps Inception Red

*RED 1-100: 2X TO 5X BASIC
*RED 101-145: .5X TO 1.2X BASIC
1-100 STATED ODDS 1:6 HOBBY
101-145 STATED ODDS 1:11 HOBBY
STATED PRINT RUN 75 SER.#'d SETS
EXCHANGE DEADLINE 4/30/2019

2017 Topps Inception Autograph Jumbo Patches

STATED ODDS 1:25 HOBBY
PRINT RUNS B/WN 30-75 COPIES PER
EXCHANGE DEADLINE 4/30/2019
*ORANGE/25: .5X TO 1.2X BASIC
IAJAB Andrew Benintendi
IAJABR Alex Bregman/75 25.00 60.00
IAJAD Aledmys Diaz/75 12.00 30.00
IAJAJ Aaron Judge/45 200.00 400.00
IAJAR Alex Reyes/75 12.00 30.00
IAJCC Carlos Correa/50 30.00 80.00
IAJCF Carson Fulmer/30 10.00 25.00
IAJCS Corey Seager/50 40.00 100.00
IAJDD David Dahl/75 12.00 30.00
IAJDS Dansby Swanson/75 20.00 50.00
IAJFL Francisco Lindor/50 50.00 120.00
IAJHR Hunter Renfroe/75 15.00 40.00
IAJJC Jharel Cotton/75 10.00 25.00
IAJJM Joe Musgrove/75 30.00 80.00
IAJJT Jake Thompson/75 10.00 25.00
IAJJU Julio Urias/75 25.00 60.00
IAJKS Kyle Schwarber/75 30.00 80.00
IAJLW Luke Weaver/75 12.00 30.00
IAJMM Manny Machado/50 50.00 120.00
IAJMT Mike Trout/50 150.00 400.00
IAJNS Noah Syndergaard/75 40.00 100.00
IAJRH Ryon Healy/75 12.00 30.00
IAJTG Tyler Glasnow/75 30.00 80.00
IAJTT Trea Turner/75 12.00 30.00
IAJYG Yulieski Gurriel/75 15.00 40.00
IAJYM Yoan Moncada

2017 Topps Inception Autograph Patches

STATED ODDS 1:7 HOBBY
PRINT RUNS B/WN 50-199 COPIES PER
EXCHANGE DEADLINE 4/30/20109
*MAGENTA/50: .6X TO 1.5X BASIC
*RED/25: .75X TO 2X BASIC
IAPAB Andrew Benintendi/199 30.00 80.00
IAPABR Alex Bregman/199 20.00 50.00
IAPAD Aledmys Diaz/199 4.00 10.00
IAPAJ Aaron Judge/199 75.00 200.00
IAPAN Aaron Nola/199 15.00 40.00
IAPARE Alex Reyes/199 6.00 15.00
IAPBSN Blake Snell/199 5.00 12.00
IAPCC Carlos Correa/50 30.00 80.00
IAPCF Carson Fulmer/199 4.00 10.00
IAPCS Corey Seager/50 40.00 100.00
IAPDD David Dahl/199 5.00 12.00
IAPDS Dansby Swanson/149 25.00 60.00
IAPFL Francisco Lindor/149 15.00 40.00
IAPHR Hunter Renfroe/149 6.00 15.00
IAPJA Jorge Alfaro/199 6.00 15.00
IAPJC Jharel Cotton/199 4.00 10.00
IAPJM Joe Musgrove/199 12.00 30.00
IAPJT Jameson Taillon/199 8.00 20.00
IAPJU Julio Urias/199 8.00 20.00
IAPKS Kyle Schwarber EXCH 30.00 80.00
IAPLS Luis Severino/199 10.00 25.00
IAPLW Luke Weaver/199 5.00 12.00
IAPMM Manny Machado/50 30.00 80.00
IAPMS Miguel Sano EXCH 20.00 50.00
IAPMT Mike Trout/50 200.00 400.00
IAPNS Noah Syndergaard/149 10.00 25.00
IAPRG Robert Gsellman EXCH 6.00 15.00
IAPRH Ryon Healy/199 5.00 12.00
IAPSM Steven Matz/199 4.00 10.00
IAPSP Stephen Piscotty/199 5.00 12.00
IAPTA Tim Anderson/199 6.00 15.00
IAPTAU Tyler Austin/199 8.00 20.00
IAPTG Tyler Glasnow/199 15.00 40.00
IAPTTU Trea Turner/199 12.00 30.00
IAPWC Willson Contreras/199 12.00 30.00
IAPYG Yulieski Gurriel/149 10.00 25.00
IAPYM Yoan Moncada/65 30.00 80.00

2017 Topps Inception Legendary Debut Autographs

STATED ODDS 1:138 HOBBY
PRINT RUNS B/WN 10-35 COPIES PER
NO PRICING ON QTY 15 OR LESS
EXCHANGE DEADLINE 4/30/2019
LDABH Bryce Harper/10 50.00 110.00
LDABP Buster Posey/10 60.00 150.00
LDACC Carlos Correa/15 30.00 80.00
LDACS Chris Sale/35 20.00 50.00
LDADP Dustin Pedroia/20 25.00 60.00
LDAFF Freddie Freeman/20 40.00 100.00
LDAFL Francisco Lindor EXCH 30.00 80.00
LDAJA Jose Altuve/35 25.00 60.00
LDAKB Kris Bryant/15
LDAKS Kyle Schwarber EXCH 20.00 50.00
LDAMM Manny Machado/25 50.00 120.00
LDANS Noah Syndergaard/35 30.00 80.00
LDARB Ryan Braun/20 12.00 30.00

2017 Topps Inception Silver Signings

STATED ODDS 1:23 HOBBY
PRINT RUNS B/WN 10-99 COPIES PER
NO PRICING ON QTY 10
EXCHANGE DEADLINE 4/30/20109
*GOLD/25: .5X TO 1.2X BASIC
SSAB Andrew Benintendi/99 30.00 80.00
SSABR Alex Bregman/75 25.00 60.00
SSAD Aledmys Diaz/99 10.00 25.00
SSAJ Aaron Judge/99 200.00 400.00
SSAR Alex Reyes/99 12.00 30.00
SSARU Addison Russell/50 12.00 30.00
SSBH Bryce Harper EXCH
SSCC Carlos Correa EXCH
SSCS Corey Seager/20 75.00 200.00
SSDD David Dahl/99 8.00 20.00
SSDS Dansby Swanson/75 50.00 120.00
SSFL Francisco Lindor/75 30.00 80.00
SSHR Hunter Renfroe/75 12.00 30.00
SSJC Jharel Cotton/50 6.00 15.00
SSJD Jose De Leon/75 6.00 15.00
SSJG Jon Gray/50 10.00 25.00
SSJT Jameson Taillon/50 12.00 30.00
SSJTH Jake Thompson/75 6.00 15.00
SSJU Julio Urias EXCH 15.00 40.00
SSKB Kris Bryant EXCH
SSKS Kyle Schwarber EXCH 10.00 25.00
SSLW Luke Weaver/99 10.00 25.00
SSMC Manny Machado/20
SSMM Manny Margot/50 6.00 15.00
SSMS Miguel Sano EXCH 8.00 20.00
SSNM Nomar Mazara/50 12.00 30.00
SSNS Noah Syndergaard EXCH 25.00 60.00
SSTG Tyler Glasnow EXCH 20.00 50.00
SSTS Trevor Story/99 10.00 25.00
SSTT Trea Turner/99 15.00 40.00
SSYG Yulieski Gurriel/75 10.00 25.00
SSYM Yoan Moncada/25

2017 Topps Inception Stars Autographs

RANDOM INSERTS IN PACKS
PRINT RUNS B/WN 15-299 COPIES PER
NO PRICING ON QTY 15
EXCHANGE DEADLINE 4/30/20109
BSAAD Aledmys Diaz
BSAAN Aaron Nola/75 5.00 12.00
BSAARU Addison Russell
BSABH Bryce Harper EXCH
BSACC Carlos Correa EXCH
BSACS Corey Seager/50 60.00 150.00
BSAJBA Javier Baez EXCH
BSAJT Jameson Taillon EXCH 10.00 25.00
BSAJU Julio Urias EXCH 10.00 25.00
BSAKB Kris Bryant/25 125.00 250.00
BSAKG Ken Giles/199 4.00 10.00
BSAKS Kyle Schwarber EXCH 12.00 30.00
BSALG Lucas Giolito/299 5.00 12.00
BSALS Luis Severino/299 10.00 25.00
BSAMFU Michael Fulmer/75
BSAMM Manny Machado/50 20.00 50.00
BSAMSA Miguel Sano/75 8.00 20.00
BSANS Noah Syndergaard EXCH 15.00 40.00
BSASM Steven Matz/75 4.00 10.00
BSATN Tyler Naquin/75 6.00 15.00
BSATS Trevor Story/75
BSATTU Trea Turner/75 5.00 12.00
BSAZW Zack Wheeler

2017 Topps Inception Stars Autographs Blue

*BLUE: .5X TO 1.2X BASIC
STATED ODDS 1:33 HOBBY
STATED PRINT RUN 25 SER.#'d SETS
EXCHANGE DEADLINE 4/30/2019
BSAAD Aledmys Diaz 15.00 40.00
BSAARU Addison Russell 20.00 50.00
BSAJBA Javier Baez EXCH 25.00 60.00
BSAMFU Michael Fulmer 15.00 40.00
BSAMM Manny Machado 50.00 120.00
BSATS Trevor Story 10.00 25.00
BSAZW Zack Wheeler 6.00 15.00

2017 Topps Inception Stars Autographs Magenta

*MAGENTA: .4X TO 1X BASIC
STATED ODDS 1:9 HOBBY
STATED PRINT RUN 99 SER.#'d SETS
EXCHANGE DEADLINE 4/30/2019
BSAZW Zack Wheeler 5.00 12.00

2017 Topps Inception Stars Autographs Orange

*ORANGE: .4X TO 1X BASIC
STATED ODDS 1:17 HOBBY
STATED PRINT RUN 50 SER.#'d SETS
EXCHANGE DEADLINE 4/30/2019
BSAAD Aledmys Diaz 12.00 30.00
BSAARU Addison Russell 15.00 40.00
BSAJBA Javier Baez EXCH 20.00 50.00
BSAMFU Michael Fulmer 12.00 30.00
BSAMM Manny Machado 40.00 100.00
BSATS Trevor Story 8.00 20.00
BSAZW Zack Wheeler 5.00 12.00

2017 Topps Inception Stars Autographs Red

*RED: .4X TO 1X BASIC
STATED ODDS 1:11 HOBBY
STATED PRINT RUN 75 SER.#'d SETS
EXCHANGE DEADLINE 4/30/2019
BSAAD Aledmys Diaz 12.00 30.00
BSAARU Addison Russell 15.00 40.00
BSAMFU Michael Fulmer 12.00 30.00

BSATS Trevor Story 8.00 20.00
BSAZW Zack Wheeler 5.00 12.00

2018 Topps Inception

1 Aaron Judge 2.00 5.00
2 Luis Severino .60 1.50
3 Jack Flaherty RC 2.50 6.00
4 Noah Syndergaard .60 1.50
5 Nicky Delmonico RC .60 1.50
6 Jacob Faria .50 1.25
7 Ryan McMahon RC 1.50 4.00
8 Tzu-Wei Lin RC .75 2.00
9 Ryon Healy .50 1.25
10 Max Fried RC 2.50 6.00
11 Zack Greinke .75 2.00
12 Trey Mancini .60 1.50
13 Jose Berrios .60 1.50
14 Harrison Bader RC 1.00 2.50
15 Dustin Fowler RC .60 1.50
16 Andrew Stevenson RC .60 1.50
17 Bryce Harper 1.25 3.00
18 Joe Jimenez .50 1.25
19 Kenley Jansen .60 1.50
20 Sean Newcomb .60 1.50
21 Paul Blackburn RC .60 1.50
22 Garrett Cooper RC .60 1.50
23 Ichiro 1.00 2.50
24 Francisco Lindor .75 2.00
25 Victor Robles RC 1.50 4.00
26 Greg Allen RC .60 1.50
27 Anthony Banda RC .60 1.50
28 Nick Williams RC .75 2.00
29 Keon Broxton .50 1.25
30 Brett Phillips .50 1.25
31 Jonathan Schoop .50 1.25
32 Brandon Woodruff RC 2.00 5.00
33 Jose Altuve .60 1.50
34 Lewis Brinson .50 1.25
35 Tyler Austin .75 2.00
36 Alex Verdugo RC 1.00 2.50
37 Corey Seager .75 2.00
38 Raimel Tapia .50 1.25
39 Clayton Kershaw 1.25 3.00
40 Tyler Wade RC .75 2.00
41 Nolan Arenado 1.25 3.00
42 Dominic Smith RC .75 2.00
43 German Marquez .50 1.25
44 Freddie Freeman 1.00 2.50
45 Carlos Correa .75 2.00
46 Matt Olson .75 2.00
47 Jordan Montgomery .60 1.50
48 Austin Hays RC 1.00 2.50
49 Domingo Santana .60 1.50
50 Rafael Devers RC 2.00 5.00
51 Luiz Gohara RC .60 1.50
52 Miguel Gomez RC .60 1.50
53 Hunter Renfroe .50 1.25
54 Miguel Andujar RC 2.50 6.00
55 Andrew Benintendi .75 2.00
56 Tyler Mahle RC .75 2.00
57 Alex Bregman .75 2.00
58 Rhys Hoskins RC 2.50 6.00
59 J.D. Davis RC .75 2.00
60 Brian Anderson RC .75 2.00
61 George Springer .60 1.50
62 Walker Buehler RC 3.00 8.00
63 Adrian Beltre .75 2.00
64 Bradley Zimmer .50 1.25
65 Lucas Sims RC .60 1.50
66 Anthony Rizzo 1.00 2.50
67 Zack Granite RC .60 1.50
68 Francisco Mejia RC .60 1.50
69 Steven Souza Jr. .60 1.50
70 Chance Sisco RC .60 1.50
71 Sandy Alcantara RC .60 1.50
72 Jose Ramirez .60 1.50
73 Ozzie Albies RC 2.00 5.00
74 Billy Hamilton .60 1.50
75 Giancarlo Stanton .75 2.00
76 Cody Bellinger 1.50 4.00
77 Gary Sanchez .75 2.00
78 J.P. Crawford RC .60 1.50
79 Manny Machado .75 2.00
80 Paul DeJong .75 2.00
81 Jake Lamb .60 1.50
82 Jacob deGrom 1.50 4.00
83 Franklin Barreto .50 1.25
84 Jose Abreu .75 2.00
85 Luke Weaver .60 1.50
86 Kris Bryant 1.00 2.50
87 Willie Calhoun RC 1.00 2.50
88 Clint Frazier RC 1.25 3.00
89 Mike Clevinger .60 1.50
90 Mookie Betts 1.50 4.00
91 Lucas Giolito .60 1.50
92 Christian Arroyo .50 1.25
93 Josh Donaldson .60 1.50
94 Parker Bridwell RC .60 1.50
95 Erick Fedde RC .60 1.50
96 Felix Jorge RC .60 1.50
97 Manny Margot .50 1.25
98 Ian Happ .60 1.50
99 Amed Rosario RC .75 2.00
100 Mike Trout 4.00 10.00

2018 Topps Inception Magenta

*MAGENTA: 1X TO 2.5X BASIC
*MAGENTA RC: .75X TO 2X BASIC
STATED ODDS 1:6 HOBBY
STATED PRINT RUN 99 SER.#'d SETS
1 Aaron Judge 15.00 40.00
100 Mike Trout 12.00 30.00

2018 Topps Inception Orange

*ORANGE: 2X TO 5X BASIC
*ORANGE RC: 1.5X TO 4X BASIC
STATED ODDS 1:11 HOBBY
STATED PRINT RUN 50 SER.#'d SETS
1 Aaron Judge 25.00 60.00
100 Mike Trout 20.00 50.00

2018 Topps Inception Purple

*PURPLE: .75X TO 2X BASIC
*PURPLE RC: .6X TO 1.5X BASIC
STATED ODDS 1:4 HOBBY
STATED PRINT RUN 150 SER.#'d SETS
1 Aaron Judge 12.00 30.00
100 Mike Trout 10.00 25.00

2018 Topps Inception Red

*RED: 1.5X TO 4X BASIC
*RED RC: 1.2X TO 3X BASIC
STATED ODDS 1:7 HOBBY
STATED PRINT RUN 75 SER.#'d SETS
1 Aaron Judge 20.00 50.00
100 Mike Trout 15.00 40.00

2018 Topps Inception Blue

*BLUE: 2.5X TO 6X BASIC
*BLUE RC: 2X TO 5X BASIC
STATED ODDS 1:21 HOBBY
STATED PRINT RUN 25 SER.#'d SETS
1 Aaron Judge 30.00 80.00
100 Mike Trout 25.00 60.00

2018 Topps Inception Green

*GREEN: .6X TO 1.5X BASIC
*GREEN RC: .5X TO 1.2X BASIC
RANDOM INSERTS IN PACKS

2018 Topps Inception Jumbo Patch Autographs

STATED ODDS 1:22 HOBBY
PRINT RUNS B/WN 14-150 COPIES PER
NO PRICING ON QTY 14
EXCHANGE DEADLINE 5/31/2020
IAJAB Anthony Banda/150 8.00 20.00
IAJAH Austin Hays/123 10.00 25.00
IAJAS Andrew Stevenson/150 8.00 20.00
IAJBW Brandon Woodruff/60 25.00 60.00
IAJBZ Bradley Zimmer/99 8.00 20.00
IAJCF Clint Frazier/140 15.00 40.00
IAJCS Chance Sisco/150 10.00 25.00
IAJDF Dustin Fowler/70 12.00 30.00
IAJFM Francisco Mejia/80 12.00 30.00
IAJGB Greg Bird/99 10.00 25.00
IAJGC Garrett Cooper/150 8.00 20.00
IAJHR Hunter Renfroe/25 12.00 30.00
IAJIH Ian Happ/70 15.00 40.00
IAJJC J.P. Crawford/150 15.00 40.00
IAJJFL Jack Flaherty/40 30.00 80.00
IAJMO Matt Olson/150 10.00 25.00
IAJOA Ozzie Albies/80 60.00 150.00
IAJPD Paul DeJong/99 15.00 40.00
IAJRD Rafael Devers/99 40.00 100.00
IAJSO Shohei Ohtani/60 300.00 600.00
IAJTM Tyler Mahle/99 12.00 30.00
IAJVR Victor Robles/70 25.00 60.00
IAJZG Zack Granite/60 8.00 20.00

2018 Topps Inception Jumbo Patch Autographs Orange

*ORANGE: .6X TO 1.5X BASE p/r 40-150
*ORANGE: .4X TO 1X BASE p/r 25
STATED ODDS 1:69 HOBBY
STATED PRINT RUN 25 SER.#'d SETS
EXCHANGE DEADLINE 5/31/2020
IAJAR Amed Rosario 15.00 40.00
IAJAV Alex Verdugo 30.00 80.00
IAJFL Francisco Lindor 40.00 100.00
IAJMF Michael Fulmer 12.00 30.00
IAJMM Manny Machado 40.00 100.00
IAJMT Mike Trout 400.00 600.00
IAJSO Shohei Ohtani 400.00 800.00

2018 Topps Inception Legendary Debut Autographs

STATED ODDS 1:161 HOBBY
STATED PRINT RUN 20 SER.#'d SETS
EXCHANGE DEADLINE 5/31/2020
LDAAB Adrian Beltre 30.00 80.00
LDAAD Adam Duvall
LDAAJ Adam Jones
LDAAR Anthony Rizzo 25.00 60.00
LDAARU Addison Russell 15.00 40.00
LDACK Corey Kluber
LDACS Corey Seager 30.00 80.00
LDADJ Derek Jeter 300.00 800.00
LDADP David Price
LDAEE Edwin Encarnacion
LDAEL Evan Longoria 15.00 40.00
LDAET Eric Thames
LDAGS George Springer
LDAJD Josh Donaldson 15.00 40.00
LDAJV Joey Votto 60.00 150.00
LDAPG Paul Goldschmidt 25.00 60.00

2018 Topps Inception Patch Autographs

STATED ODDS 1:7 HOBBY
PRINT RUNS B/WN 20-299 COPIES PER
EXCHANGE DEADLINE 5/31/2020
IAPAB Anthony Banda/99 5.00 12.00
IAPAH Austin Hays/249 12.00 30.00
IAPAR Amed Rosario/122 10.00 25.00
IAPAS Andrew Stevenson/99 5.00 12.00
IAPAT Andrew Toles/199 5.00 12.00
IAPAV Alex Verdugo/109 8.00 20.00
IAPBA Brian Anderson/299 8.00 20.00
IAPBS Blake Snell/249 8.00 20.00
IAPBW Brandon Woodruff/299 15.00 40.00
IAPBZ Bradley Zimmer/199 8.00 20.00
IAPCC Carlos Correa
IAPCF Clint Frazier/249 15.00 40.00
IAPCS Corey Seager
IAPCSI Chance Sisco/249 6.00 15.00
IAPDD David Dahl/30 12.00 30.00
IAPDF Dustin Fowler/249 5.00 12.00
IAPFM Francisco Mejia/99 6.00 15.00
IAPGC Garrett Cooper/99 5.00 12.00
IAPHB Harrison Bader/249 8.00 20.00
IAPHR Hunter Renfroe
IAPIH Ian Happ/99 6.00 15.00
IAPJA Jorge Alfaro/199 8.00 20.00
IAPJC J.P. Crawford/249 10.00 25.00
IAPJFL Jack Flaherty/214 25.00 60.00
IAPKB Kris Bryant
IAPLS Lucas Sims/299 6.00 15.00
IAPLW Luke Weaver/249 6.00 15.00
IAPMA Miguel Andujar/249 25.00 60.00
IAPMF Michael Fulmer/90 10.00 25.00
IAPMG Miguel Gomez/299 6.00 15.00
IAPMM Manny Machado/65 30.00 80.00
IAPMMA Manny Margot/149 5.00 12.00
IAPMO Matt Olson/249 8.00 20.00
IAPND Nicky Delmonico/299 10.00 25.00
IAPNS Noah Syndergaard/30 20.00 50.00
IAPOA Ozzie Albies/99 30.00 80.00
IAPPD Paul DeJong/205 12.00 30.00
IAPRD Rafael Devers/205 30.00 80.00
IAPRM Ryan McMahon/199 12.00 30.00
IAPSO Shohei Ohtani/99 150.00 400.00
IAPTAN Tim Anderson/25 15.00 40.00
IAPTM Trey Mancini/249 6.00 15.00
IAPTMA Tyler Mahle/299 6.00 15.00
IAPTW Tyler Wade/99 12.00 30.00
IAPVR Victor Robles/99 12.00 30.00
IAPYM Yoan Moncada/20 15.00 40.00
IAPZG Zack Granite/299 5.00 12.00

2018 Topps Inception Patch Autographs Magenta

*MAGENTA: .4X TO 1X BASIC
STATED ODDS 1:17 HOBBY
PRINT RUNS B/WN 50-75 COPIES PER
EXCHANGE DEADLINE 5/31/2020
IAPABR Alex Bregman/75 20.00 50.00
IAPDS Dominic Smith/75 10.00 25.00
IAPFL Francisco Lindor/75 25.00 60.00
IAPKB Kris Bryant/50 75.00 200.00
IAPMT Mike Trout/75 300.00 600.00

2018 Topps Inception Patch Autographs Red

*RED: .75X TO 2X BASE p/r 50-199
*RED: .4X TO 1X BASE p/r 30
STATED ODDS 1:45 HOBBY
STATED PRINT RUN 25 SER.#'d SETS
EXCHANGE DEADLINE 5/31/2020
IAPABR Alex Bregman 40.00 100.00
IAPDS Dominic Smith 20.00 50.00
IAPFL Francisco Lindor 50.00 120.00
IAPKB Kris Bryant 125.00 300.00
IAPMT Mike Trout 400.00 800.00
IAPSO Shohei Ohtani 300.00 600.00

2018 Topps Inception Rookies and Emerging Stars Autographs

PRINT RUNS B/WN 230-299 COPIES PER
EXCHANGE DEADLINE 5/31/2020
RESAB Alex Bregman/299 20.00 50.00
RESABA Anthony Banda/230 2.50 6.00
RESAG Amir Garrett/299 2.50 6.00
RESAR Amed Rosario/230 3.00 8.00
RESAS Andrew Stevenson/230 2.50 6.00
RESAV Alex Verdugo/230 6.00 15.00
RESBM Bruce Maxwell/299 2.50 6.00
RESBP Brett Phillips/230 2.50 6.00
RESBW Brandon Woodruff/230 8.00 20.00
RESBZ Bradley Zimmer/230 3.00 8.00
RESCA Christian Arroyo/230 2.50 6.00
RESCF Clint Frazier/230 10.00 25.00
RESCFU Carson Fulmer/299 2.50 6.00
RESCS Chance Sisco/230 6.00 15.00
RESDF Dustin Fowler/230 2.50 6.00
RESFB Franklin Barreto/230 2.50 6.00
RESGA Greg Allen/230 3.00 8.00
RESGCO Garrett Cooper/230 2.50 6.00
RESGM German Marquez/230 2.50 6.00
RESHR Hunter Renfroe/230 2.50 6.00
RESIH Ian Happ/230 3.00 8.00
RESJCR J.P. Crawford/230 2.50 6.00
RESJD J.D. Davis/230 3.00 8.00
RESJF Jacob Faria/230 2.50 6.00
RESJFL Jack Flaherty/230 10.00 25.00
RESJW Jesse Winker/299 4.00 10.00
RESLB Lewis Brinson/230 2.50 6.00
RESLS Lucas Sims/230 3.00 8.00
RESLW Luke Weaver/230 3.00 8.00
RESMA Miguel Andujar/230 10.00 25.00
RESMC Mike Clevinger/230 3.00 8.00
RESMF Max Fried/230 10.00 25.00
RESMM Manny Margot/230 2.50 6.00
RESMO Matt Olson/230 5.00 12.00
RESND Nicky Delmonico/299 2.50 6.00
RESOA Ozzie Albies/230 12.00 30.00
RESPB Parker Bridwell/230 2.50 6.00
RESPBL Paul Blackburn/230 2.50 6.00
RESPD Paul DeJong/230 5.00 12.00
RESRD Rafael Devers/230 15.00 40.00
RESRG Robert Gsellman/299 2.50 6.00
RESRH Ryon Healy/230 2.50 6.00
RESRHO Rhys Hoskins/230 15.00 40.00
RESRM Ryan McMahon/230 6.00 15.00
RESRQ Roman Quinn/299 2.50 6.00
RESRT Raimel Tapia/230 2.50 6.00
RESSA Sandy Alcantara/230 4.00 10.00
RESSL Seth Lugo/299 2.50 6.00
RESSN Sean Newcomb/230 6.00 15.00
RESTA Tyler Austin/230 4.00 10.00
RESTB Ty Blach/299 2.50 6.00
RESTG Tyler Glasnow/299 4.00 10.00
RESTM Trey Mancini/230 3.00 8.00
RESTMA Tyler Mahle/230 3.00 8.00
RESTR T.J. Rivera/299 2.50 6.00
RESTW Tyler Wade/230 6.00 15.00
RESVR Victor Robles/230 10.00 25.00
RESWB Walker Buehler/230 12.00 30.00
RESYG Yulieski Gurriel/299 5.00 12.00
RESZG Zack Granite/230 2.50 6.00

2018 Topps Inception Rookies and Emerging Stars Autographs Blue

*BLUE: .75X TO 2X BASIC
STATED ODDS 1:33 HOBBY
STATED PRINT RUN 25 SER.#'d SETS
EXCHANGE DEADLINE 5/31/2020
RESAH Austin Hays 12.00 30.00
RESAJ Aaron Judge EXCH
RESDS Dominic Smith 6.00 15.00
RESHB Harrison Bader 8.00 20.00
RESJT Jake Thompson 5.00 12.00
RESYM Yoan Moncada 15.00 40.00

2018 Topps Inception Rookies and Emerging Stars Autographs Magenta

*MAGENTA: .5X TO 1.2X BASIC
STATED ODDS 1:9 HOBBY
STATED PRINT RUN 99 SER.#'d SETS
EXCHANGE DEADLINE 5/31/2020
RESAH Austin Hays 8.00 20.00
RESDS Dominic Smith 4.00 10.00
RESHB Harrison Bader 5.00 12.00
RESYM Yoan Moncada 10.00 25.00

2018 Topps Inception Rookies and Emerging Stars Autographs Orange

*ORANGE: .6X TO 1.5X BASIC
STATED ODDS 1:17 HOBBY
STATED PRINT RUN 50 SER.#'d SETS
EXCHANGE DEADLINE 5/31/2020
RESAH Austin Hays 10.00 25.00
RESAJ Aaron Judge EXCH
RESDS Dominic Smith 5.00 12.00
RESHB Harrison Bader 6.00 15.00
RESJT Jake Thompson 4.00 10.00
RESYM Yoan Moncada 12.00 30.00

2018 Topps Inception Rookies and Emerging Stars Autographs Red

*RED: .5X TO 1.2X BASIC
STATED ODDS 1:11 HOBBY
STATED PRINT RUN 75 SER.#'d SETS
EXCHANGE DEADLINE 5/31/2020
RESAH Austin Hays 8.00 20.00
RESDS Dominic Smith 4.00 10.00
RESHB Harrison Bader 5.00 12.00
RESJT Jake Thompson 3.00 8.00
RESYM Yoan Moncada 10.00 25.00

2018 Topps Inception Silver Signings

STATED ODDS 1:18 HOBBY
PRINT RUNS B/WN 25-99 COPIES PER
EXCHANGE DEADLINE 5/31/2020
*GOLD INK/25: .5X TO 1.2X BASIC
SSAB Alex Bregman/99 15.00 40.00
SSAR Amed Rosario/99 8.00 20.00
SSAV Alex Verdugo/90 20.00 50.00
SSBH Bryce Harper/25 200.00 400.00
SSBZ Bradley Zimmer/90 10.00 25.00
SSCA Christian Arroyo/90 6.00 15.00
SSCC Carlos Correa/90 25.00 60.00
SSCS Corey Seager/90 15.00 40.00
SSDF Dustin Fowler/90 6.00 15.00
SSDS Dominic Smith/90 8.00 20.00
SSFB Franklin Barreto/99 6.00 15.00
SSHB Harrison Bader/99 10.00 25.00
SSHR Hunter Renfroe/90 6.00 15.00
SSIH Ian Happ/90 20.00 50.00
SSJC J.P. Crawford
SSJF Jack Flaherty/90 25.00 60.00
SSKB Kris Bryant/90 75.00 200.00
SSLB Lewis Brinson/99 6.00 15.00
SSLW Luke Weaver/99 8.00 20.00
SSMA Miguel Andujar/99 40.00 100.00
SSMF Michael Fulmer/99 10.00 25.00
SSMM Manny Machado/90 20.00 50.00
SSMMA Manny Margot/99 6.00 15.00
SSMT Mike Trout/25 300.00 600.00
SSNS Noah Syndergaard/90 12.00 30.00
SSOA Ozzie Albies/90 20.00 50.00
SSPD Paul DeJong/90 10.00 25.00
SSRD Rafael Devers/90 15.00 40.00
SSRHO Rhys Hoskins/90 40.00 100.00
SSRM Ryan McMahon/90 15.00 40.00
SSRT Raimel Tapia/99 6.00 15.00
Signed in gold ink
SSSN Sean Newcomb/90 8.00 20.00
SSTM Trey Mancini/99 10.00 25.00
SSTW Tyler Wade/99 12.00 30.00
SSVR Victor Robles/90 15.00 40.00
SSYM Yoan Moncada/99 25.00 60.00

2019 Topps Inception

1 Mike Trout 4.00 10.00
2 Max Scherzer .75 2.00
3 Nicholas Ciuffo RC .60 1.50
4 Freddie Freeman 1.00 2.50
5 Francisco Arcia RC 1.00 2.50
6 Aaron Nola .60 1.50
7 Luis Urias RC 1.00 2.50
8 Carlos Correa .75 2.00
9 Kohl Stewart RC .75 2.00
10 Eddie Rosario .60 1.50
11 Clayton Kershaw 1.25 3.00
12 Nick Burdi RC .60 1.50
13 Khris Davis .75 2.00
14 Enyel De Los Santos RC .60 1.50
15 Michael Kopech RC 2.00 5.00
16 Bryce Harper 1.25 3.00
17 Francisco Lindor .75 2.00
18 Dawel Lugo RC 1.00 2.50
19 Daniel Poncedeleon RC 1.00 2.50
20 Cedric Mullins RC 1.25 3.00
21 Christian Yelich 1.00 2.50
22 Bryse Wilson RC .75 2.00
23 Kyle Wright RC 1.00 2.50
24 George Springer .60 1.50
25 Kyle Tucker RC 1.50 4.00
26 Javier Baez 1.00 2.50
27 Sean Reid-Foley RC .60 1.50
28 Miguel Andujar .75 2.00
29 Justin Verlander .75 2.00
30 Chris Shaw RC .60 1.50
31 Corey Seager .75 2.00
32 Ryan Borucki RC .60 1.50
33 Aramis Garcia RC .60 1.50
34 Mitch Haniger .60 1.50
35 Kolby Allard RC 1.00 2.50
36 Kevin Newman RC 1.00 2.50
37 Dennis Santana RC .60 1.50
38 Paul Goldschmidt .75 2.00
39 Alex Bregman .75 2.00
40 Mookie Betts 1.50 4.00
41 Blake Snell .60 1.50
42 Giancarlo Stanton .75 2.00
43 Noah Syndergaard .60 1.50
44 Rhys Hoskins 1.00 2.50
45 Trevor Richards RC .60 1.50
46 Trea Turner .75 2.00
47 Edwin Encarnacion .75 2.00
48 Kevin Kramer RC .75 2.00
49 Jonathan Loaisiga RC .75 2.00
50 Shohei Ohtani 1.25 3.00
51 Edwin Diaz .60 1.50
52 Whit Merrifield .75 2.00
53 David Fletcher RC 2.00 5.00
54 Heath Fillmyer RC .60 1.50
55 Jake Cave RC .75 2.00
56 Joey Votto .75 2.00
57 Ramon Laureano RC 1.25 3.00
58 Steven Duggar RC .75 2.00
59 Chance Adams RC .60 1.50
60 Ozzie Albies .75 2.00
61 Touki Toussaint RC .75 2.00
62 Jose Ramirez .60 1.50
63 Adolis Garcia RC 4.00 10.00
64 Corbin Burnes RC 5.00 12.00
65 Matt Carpenter .75 2.00
66 Jeff McNeil RC 1.50 4.00
67 Luis Severino .60 1.50
68 Pablo Lopez RC .60 1.50
69 Josh Hader .60 1.50
70 Josh Rogers RC .60 1.50
71 Jacob deGrom 1.50 4.00
72 Eugenio Suarez .60 1.50
73 Ray Black RC .60 1.50
74 Masahiro Tanaka .60 1.50
75 Juan Soto 2.50 6.00
76 Charlie Blackmon .75 2.00
77 Jacob Nix RC .75 2.00
78 Christin Stewart RC .75 2.00
79 Jose Altuve .60 1.50
80 Rowdy Tellez RC 1.00 2.50
81 Aaron Judge 2.00 5.00
82 Taylor Ward RC .60 1.50
83 Nolan Arenado 1.25 3.00
84 Andrew Benintendi .75 2.00
85 Brandon Lowe RC 1.00 2.50
86 Jake Bauers RC 1.00 2.50
87 Jalen Beeks RC .60 1.50
88 Gerrit Cole .75 2.00
89 Adam Cimber RC .60 1.50
90 Anthony Rizzo 1.00 2.50
91 Josh James RC 1.00 2.50
92 Chris Sale .75 2.00
93 J.D. Martinez .75 2.00
94 Justus Sheffield RC 1.00 2.50
95 Ryan O'Hearn RC .60 1.50
96 Brad Keller RC .60 1.50
97 Kris Bryant 1.00 2.50
98 Gleyber Torres 1.50 4.00
99 Danny Jansen RC .60 1.50
100 Ronald Acuna Jr. 4.00 10.00

2019 Topps Inception Blue

*BLUE: 3X TO 8X BASIC
*BLUE RC: 2.5X TO 6X BASIC
STATED ODDS 1:23 HOBBY
STATED PRINT RUN 25 SER.#'d SETS
1 Mike Trout 50.00 120.00
50 Shohei Ohtani 40.00 100.00
75 Juan Soto 25.00 60.00
81 Aaron Judge 50.00 120.00
100 Ronald Acuna Jr. 25.00 60.00

2019 Topps Inception Green

*GREEN: .6X TO 1.5X BASIC
*GREEN RC: .5X TO 1.2X BASIC
RANDOM INSERTS IN PACKS

2019 Topps Inception Magenta

*MAGENTA: 1.5X TO 4X BASIC
*MAGENTA RC: 1.2X TO 3X BASIC
STATED ODDS 1:6 HOBBY
STATED PRINT RUN 99 SER.#'d SETS

2019 Topps Inception Orange

*ORANGE: 2X TO 5X BASIC
*ORANGE RC: 1.5X TO 4X BASIC
STATED ODDS 1:12 HOBBY
STATED PRINT RUN 50 SER.#'d SETS
1 Mike Trout 30.00 80.00
75 Juan Soto 15.00 40.00
81 Aaron Judge 30.00 80.00
100 Ronald Acuna Jr. 15.00 40.00

2019 Topps Inception Purple

*PURPLE: 1.2X TO 3X BASIC
*PURPLE RC: 1X TO 2.5X BASIC
STATED ODDS 1:4 HOBBY
STATED PRINT RUN 150 SER.#'d SETS

2019 Topps Inception Red

*RED: 2X TO 5X BASIC
*RED RC: 1.5X TO 4X BASIC
STATED ODDS 1:8 HOBBY
STATED PRINT RUN 75 SER.#'d SETS

2019 Topps Inception Jumbo Patch Autographs

STATED ODDS 1:22 HOBBY
PRINT RUNS B/WN 15-125 COPIES PER
NO PRICING ON QTY 15
EXCHANGE DEADLINE 2/28/2021
*ORANGE/25: .6X TO1.5X BASIC
IAJAB Alex Bregman EXCH 40.00 100.00
IAJAJ Aaron Judge/20 125.00 300.00
IAJAM Austin Meadows/110 12.00 30.00
IAJBK Brad Keller/125 12.00 30.00
IAJBN Brandon Nimmo/110 10.00 25.00
IAJBW Bryse Wilson/125 10.00 25.00
IAJCA Chance Adams/99 8.00 20.00
IAJCB Corbin Burnes/99 25.00 60.00
IAJCM Cedric Mullins/99 25.00 60.00
IAJCS Chris Shaw/99 8.00 20.00
IAJJA Jesus Aguilar/110 10.00 25.00
IAJJB Jake Bauers/99 12.00 30.00
IAJJSH Justus Sheffield/99 12.00 30.00
IAJKA Kolby Allard/125 12.00 30.00
IAJKT Kyle Tucker/99 20.00 50.00
IAJKW Kyle Wright/125 12.00 30.00
IAJLU Luis Urias/99 12.00 30.00
IAJMH Mitch Haniger/110 12.00 30.00
IAJMK Michael Kopech/99 20.00 50.00
IAJMM Miles Mikolas/110 10.00 25.00
IAJOA Ozzie Albies/40 30.00 80.00
IAJRAJ Ronald Acuna Jr./40 75.00 200.00
IAJRH Rhys Hoskins/40 40.00 100.00
IAJROH Ryan O'Hearn/125 8.00 20.00
IAJRT Rowdy Tellez/99 10.00 25.00
IAJSO Shohei Ohtani/125 125.00 300.00

2019 Topps Inception Legendary Debut Autographs

STATED ODDS 1:226 HOBBY
STATED PRINT RUN 20 SER.#'d SETS
EXCHANGE DEADLINE 2/28/2021
LDAAJ Aaron Judge
LDAAM Andrew McCutchen 60.00 150.00
LDAAP Andy Pettitte 60.00 150.00
LDAAPU Albert Pujols
LDADG Didi Gregorius 12.00 30.00
LDADO David Ortiz
LDAER Eddie Rosario 12.00 30.00
LDAHM Hideki Matsui
LDAJA Jesus Aguilar
LDAJD Jacob deGrom 50.00 120.00
LDAJU Justin Upton 12.00 30.00
LDAKD Khris Davis 15.00 40.00
LDAMH Mitch Haniger 25.00 60.00
LDASO Shohei Ohtani
LDATH Torii Hunter 25.00 60.00
LDATS Trevor Story 25.00 60.00
LDAVG Yadier Molina 50.00 120.00

2019 Topps Inception Mystery Redemption Autographs

RANDOM INSERTS IN PACKS
EXCHANGE DEADLINE 2/28/2021
*ORANGE: .5X TO 1.2X BASIC
*BLUE: .6X TO 1.5X BASIC

2019 Topps Inception Patch Autographs

STATED ODDS 1:7 HOBBY
PRINT RUNS B/WN 15-199 COPIES PER
EXCHANGE DEADLINE 2/28/2021
IAPAG Aramis Garcia/199 5.00 12.00
IAPAJ Aaron Judge/30 100.00 250.00
IAPAM Austin Meadows EXCH 10.00 25.00
IAPBK Brad Keller/199 10.00 25.00
IAPBL Brandon Lowe/199 10.00 25.00
IAPBT Blake Treinen/199 10.00 25.00
IAPBW Bryse Wilson/199 10.00 25.00
IAPCB Corbin Burnes/199 15.00 40.00
IAPCM Cedric Mullins/100 10.00 25.00
IAPCS Chris Shaw/199 5.00 12.00
IAPDC Dylan Cozens/199 5.00 12.00
IAPDF David Fletcher/199 15.00 40.00
IAPDH Dakota Hudson/199 10.00 25.00
IAPDJ Danny Jansen/199 10.00 25.00
IAPDL Dawel Lugo/199 8.00 20.00
IAPDS Dennis Santana/199 5.00 12.00
IAPHD Hunter Dozier/199 5.00 12.00
IAPHF Heath Fillmyer/199 5.00 12.00
IAPIKF Isiah Kiner-Falefa/199 6.00 15.00
IAPJA Jesus Aguilar/199 6.00 15.00
IAPJB Jake Bauers/199 8.00 20.00
IAPJM Jeff McNeil/199 20.00 50.00
IAPJN Jacob Nix/199 6.00 15.00
IAPJSH Justus Sheffield/160 8.00 20.00
IAPKA Kolby Allard/199 8.00 20.00
IAPKT Kyle Tucker/199 12.00 30.00
IAPKWR Kyle Wright/199 8.00 20.00
IAPLGJ Lourdes Gurriel Jr./199 8.00 20.00
IAPLU Luis Urias/199 8.00 20.00
IAPMH Mitch Haniger/50 15.00 40.00
IAPMK Michael Kopech/75 12.00 30.00
IAPMM Miles Mikolas/150 8.00 20.00
IAPNK Nick Kingham/199 5.00 12.00
IAPOA Ozzie Albies/99 20.00 50.00
IAPRAJ Ronald Acuna Jr./199 75.00 200.00
IAPRB Ryan Borucki/199 10.00 25.00
IAPRH Rhys Hoskins/199 30.00 80.00
IAPRL Ramon Laureano/199 15.00 40.00
IAPROH Ryan O'Hearn/199 5.00 12.00
IAPRT Rowdy Tellez/199 8.00 20.00
IAPSD Steven Duggar/199 6.00 15.00
IAPSK Scott Kingery/199 6.00 15.00
IAPSO Shohei Ohtani/50 100.00 250.00
IAPTA Tim Anderson/199 8.00 20.00
IAPTM Tyler Mahle/199 5.00 12.00
IAPTP Tommy Pham/199 5.00 12.00
IAPTW Taylor Ward/199 5.00 12.00

2019 Topps Inception Patch Autographs Magenta

*MAGENTA: .4X TO 1X BASIC
STATED ODDS 1:17 HOBBY
STATED PRINT RUN 75 SER.#'d SETS
EXCHANGE DEADLINE 2/28/2021
IAPBN Brandon Nimmo 10.00 25.00
IAPCA Chance Adams 10.00 25.00

2019 Topps Inception Patch Autographs Red

*RED: .75X TO 2X BASE p/r 50-199
*RED: .4X TO 1X BASE p/r 30
STATED ODDS 1:45 HOBBY
STATED PRINT RUN 25 SER.#'d SETS
EXCHANGE DEADLINE 2/28/2021
IAPAB Alex Bregman EXCH 40.00 100.00
IAPBN Brandon Nimmo 20.00 50.00
IAPCA Chance Adams 20.00 50.00

2019 Topps Inception Rookie and Emerging Stars Autographs

PRINT RUNS B/WN 30-250 COPIES PER
EXCHANGE DEADLINE 2/28/2021
*MAGENTA/99: .5X TO 1.2X BASIC
*RED/75: .5X TO 1.2X BASIC
*ORANGE/50: .6X TO 1.5X BASIC
*BLUE/25: .75X TO 2X p/r 60-250
*BLUE/25: .5X TO 1.2X p/r 30
RESAC Adam Cimber/250 2.50 6.00
RESAG Adolis Garcia/225 50.00 120.00
RESAGA Aramis Garcia/225 2.50 6.00
RESAJ Aaron Judge/30 100.00 250.00
RESAM Austin Meadows/200 4.00 10.00
RESAR Amed Rosario/125 6.00 15.00
RESBA Brian Anderson/225 2.50 6.00
RESBK Brad Keller/200 8.00 20.00
RESBKE Brad Keller/200 8.00 20.00
RESBL Brandon Lowe/200 12.00 30.00
RESBW Bryse Wilson/200 8.00 20.00
RESCA Chance Adams/225 2.50 6.00
RESCB Corbin Burnes/225 8.00 20.00
RESCK Carson Kelly/200 2.50 6.00
RESCM Cedric Mullins/200 6.00 15.00
RESCS Christin Stewart/200 12.00 30.00
RESCSH Chris Shaw/200 5.00 12.00
RESDC Dylan Cozens/200 5.00 12.00
RESDJ Danny Jansen/200 6.00 15.00
RESDL Dawel Lugo/225 4.00 10.00
RESDP Daniel Poncedeleon/225 4.00 10.00
RESDS Dennis Santana/225 2.50 6.00
RESEDL Enyel De Los Santos/225 4.00 10.00
RESEJ Eloy Jimenez/125 30.00 80.00
Mystery
RESFA Francisco Arcia/225 4.00 10.00
RESFL Francisco Lindor/60 15.00 40.00
RESFP Freddy Peralta/200 4.00 10.00
RESFR Franmil Reyes/200 5.00 12.00
RESHB Harrison Bader/200 3.00 8.00
RESHF Heath Fillmyer/225 4.00 10.00
RESIKF Isiah Kiner-Falefa/200 3.00 8.00
RESJB Jake Bauers/200 5.00 12.00
RESJBE Jalen Beeks 2.50 6.00
RESJC Johan Camargo/225 10.00 25.00
RESJCA Jake Cave/225 8.00 20.00
RESJF Jack Flaherty/200 10.00 25.00
RESJM Jeff McNeil/225 10.00 25.00
RESJN Jacob Nix/200 3.00 8.00
RESJR Josh Rogers/225 8.00 20.00
RESJS Juan Soto/125 50.00 120.00
RESJSH Justus Sheffield/200 8.00 20.00
RESKA Kolby Allard/200 4.00 10.00
RESKB Kris Bryant EXCH 50.00 120.00
RESKK Kevin Kramer/225 3.00 8.00
RESKN Kevin Newman/200 4.00 10.00
RESKS Kohl Stewart/200 3.00 8.00
RESKT Kyle Tucker/200 12.00 30.00
RESKW Kyle Wright/200 8.00 20.00
RESLGJ Lourdes Gurriel Jr./200 8.00 20.00
RESLU Luis Urias/200 10.00 25.00
RESMC Matt Chapman/200 10.00 25.00
RESMK Michael Kopech/200 8.00 20.00
RESMM Miles Mikolas/200 8.00 20.00
RESMT Mike Trout/30 200.00 500.00
RESNB Nick Burdi/225 2.50 6.00
RESND Nicky Delmonico/200 2.50 6.00
RESNK Nick Kingham/200 2.50 6.00
RESNW Nick Williams/125 2.50 6.00
RESPL Pablo Lopez/225 5.00 12.00
RESPW Patrick Wisdom/225 3.00 8.00
RESRAJ Ronald Acuna Jr./125 50.00 120.00
RESRB Ryan Borucki/200 3.00 8.00
RESRBL Ray Black/225 3.00 8.00
RESRL Ramon Laureano/225 12.00 30.00
RESRMG Reese McGuire/225 6.00 15.00
RESROH Ryan O'Hearn/225 2.50 6.00
RESRT Rowdy Tellez/200 4.00 10.00
RESSA Sandy Alcantara/200 2.50 6.00
RESSD Steven Duggar/225 3.00 8.00
RESSK Scott Kingery/200 5.00 12.00
RESSM Sean Manaea/200 4.00 10.00
RESSO Shohei Ohtani/30 75.00 200.00
RESRF Sean Reid-Foley/225 2.50 6.00
RESTT Touki Toussaint/200 3.00 8.00
RESTW Tyler Wade/225 5.00 12.00
RESTWA Taylor Ward/225 2.50 6.00
RESWA Willy Adames/200 4.00 10.00
RESVGJ Vladimir Guerrero Jr./125 100.00 250.00
Mystery

2019 Topps Inception Silver Signings

STATED ODDS 1:18 HOBBY
PRINT RUNS B/WN 10-99 COPIES PER
NO PRICING ON QTY 15 OR LESS
EXCHANGE DEADLINE 2/28/2021
*GOLD INK/25: .5X TO 1.2X BASIC
SSAM Austin Meadows EXCH 12.00 30.00
SSAR Amed Rosario EXCH 8.00 20.00
SSBA Brian Anderson/99 6.00 15.00
SSCA Chance Adams/99 10.00 25.00
SSCB Corbin Burnes/99 20.00 50.00
SSCM Cedric Mullins/99 12.00 30.00
SSCS Christin Stewart/99 20.00 50.00
SSCSH Chris Shaw/99 12.00 30.00
SSDC Dylan Cozens/99 6.00 15.00
SSDJ Danny Jansen/99 15.00 40.00
SSFA Francisco Arcia/99 12.00 30.00
SSFL Francisco Lindor/30 30.00 80.00
SSHB Harrison Bader/99 8.00 20.00
SSJB Jake Bauers/99 10.00 25.00
SSJF Jack Flaherty/99 10.00 25.00
SSJL Jonathan Loaisiga/99 20.00 50.00
SSJS Juan Soto/60 40.00 100.00
SSJSH Justus Sheffield/99 10.00 25.00
SSKA Kolby Allard/99 10.00 25.00
SSKB Kris Bryant EXCH 60.00 150.00
SSKT Kyle Tucker/99 15.00 40.00
SSKW Kyle Wright/90 20.00 50.00
SSLGJ Lourdes Gurriel Jr./99 12.00 30.00
SSLU Luis Urias/90 10.00 25.00
SSMK Michael Kopech/90 25.00 60.00
SSMM Miles Mikolas/99 8.00 20.00
SSRAJ Ronald Acuna Jr./60 100.00 250.00
SSRB Ryan Borucki/99 10.00 25.00
SSSD Steven Duggar/99 10.00 25.00
SSSK Scott Kingery/90 12.00 30.00
SSSM Sean Manaea/99 12.00 30.00
SSSO Shohei Ohtani
SSTT Touki Toussaint/99 8.00 20.00
SSWA Willy Adames/99 10.00 25.00

2020 Topps Inception

1 Ronald Acuna Jr. 3.00 8.00
2 Matt Thaiss RC .75 2.00
3 Jose Altuve .60 1.50
4 Juan Soto 2.50 6.00
5 Max Scherzer .75 2.00
6 Carlos Correa .75 2.00
7 Abraham Toro RC .75 2.00
8 Robel Garcia RC .60 1.50
9 Sean Murphy RC 1.00 2.50
10 Austin Nola RC 1.00 2.50
11 Logan Allen RC .60 1.50
12 Bryce Harper 1.25 3.00
13 Francisco Lindor .75 2.00
14 Edwin Rios RC 1.50 4.00
15 Josh Hader .60 1.50
16 A.J. Puk RC 1.00 2.50
17 Sam Hilliard RC 1.00 2.50
18 Michel Baez RC .60 1.50
19 Kris Bryant 1.00 2.50
20 Aaron Civale RC 1.25 3.00
21 Tony Gonsolin RC 2.50 6.00
22 Gleyber Torres 1.50 4.00
23 Gavin Lux RC 3.00 8.00
24 Victor Robles 1.00 2.50
25 Yordan Alvarez RC 6.00 15.00
26 Walker Buehler 1.00 2.50
27 Sheldon Neuse RC .75 2.00
28 Trent Grisham RC 2.50 6.00
29 J.T. Realmuto .75 2.00
30 Rafael Devers 1.00 2.50
31 Aaron Judge 2.00 5.00
32 Randy Arozarena RC 5.00 12.00
33 Alex Bregman .75 2.00
34 Cody Bellinger 1.50 4.00
35 Rogelio Armenteros RC .75 2.00
36 Bobby Bradley RC .60 1.50
37 George Springer .60 1.50
38 Adbert Alzolay RC .75 2.00
39 Eloy Jimenez 1.50 4.00
40 Seth Brown RC .60 1.50
41 Trevor Story .75 2.00
42 Isan Diaz RC 1.00 2.50

43 DJ LeMahieu .75 2.00
44 Noah Syndergaard .60 1.50
45 Aristides Aquino RC 1.50 4.00
46 Luis Castillo .60 1.50
47 Charlie Blackmon .75 2.00
48 Nico Hoerner RC 2.50 6.00
49 Dustin May RC 2.00 5.00
50 Christian Yelich 1.00 2.50
51 Justin Dunn RC .75 2.00
52 Jacob deGrom 1.50 4.00
53 Anthony Kay RC .60 1.50
54 Shane Bieber .75 2.00
55 Jordan Yamamoto RC .60 1.50
56 Shohei Ohtani 1.25 3.00
57 Bo Bichette RC 5.00 12.00
58 Domingo Leyba RC .75 2.00
59 Jack Flaherty .75 2.00
60 Dylan Cease RC 1.00 2.50
61 Brusdar Graterol RC 1.00 2.50
62 Zac Gallen RC 1.50 4.00
63 Josh Staumont RC .60 1.50
64 Pete Alonso 2.00 5.00
65 Manny Machado .75 2.00
66 Brock Burke RC .60 1.50
67 Nick Solak RC 2.50 6.00
68 Joey Gallo .75 2.00
69 Tom Eshelman RC .75 2.00
70 Keston Hiura 1.00 2.50
71 Jake Rogers RC .60 1.50
72 Andres Munoz RC 1.00 2.50
73 Fernando Tatis Jr. 4.00 10.00
74 Willi Castro RC 1.00 2.50
75 Anthony Rizzo 1.00 2.50
76 Hunter Harvey RC 1.00 2.50
77 Javier Baez 1.00 2.50
78 Josh Bell .60 1.50
79 Jose Urquidy RC .75 2.00
80 Travis Demeritte RC 1.00 2.50
81 Junior Fernandez RC .60 1.50
82 Justin Verlander .75 2.00
83 Jesus Luzardo RC 1.25 3.00
84 Blake Snell .60 1.50
85 Zack Collins RC .75 2.00
86 Mauricio Dubon RC .75 2.00
87 Adrian Morejon RC .60 1.50
88 Tyler Alexander RC 1.00 2.50
89 Eddie Rosario .60 1.50
90 Paul Goldschmidt .75 2.00
91 Chris Paddack .75 2.00
92 Kyle Lewis RC 5.00 12.00
93 Nolan Arenado 1.25 3.00
94 Freddie Freeman 1.00 2.50
95 Patrick Corbin .60 1.50
96 Giancarlo Stanton .75 2.00
97 Mookie Betts 1.50 4.00
98 Jose Ramirez .60 1.50
99 Ozzie Albies .75 2.00
100 Mike Trout 4.00 10.00

2020 Topps Inception Blue

*BLUE: 3X TO 8X BASIC
*BLUE RC: 2.5X TO 6X BASIC
STATED ODDS 1:25 HOBBY
STATED PRINT RUN 25 SER.#'d SETS
100 Mike Trout 40.00 100.00

2020 Topps Inception Green

*GREEN: .6X TO 1.5X BASIC
*GREEN RC: .5X TO 1.2X BASIC
RANDOM INSERTS IN PACKS

2020 Topps Inception Magenta

*MAGENTA: 1.5X TO 4X BASIC
*MAGENTA RC: 1.2X TO 3X BASIC
STATED ODDS 1:7 HOBBY
STATED PRINT RUN 99 SER.#'d SETS
100 Mike Trout 20.00 50.00

2020 Topps Inception Orange

*ORANGE: 2X TO 5X BASIC
*ORANGE RC: 1.5X TO 4X BASIC
STATED ODDS 1:13 HOBBY
STATED PRINT RUN 50 SER.#'d SETS
100 Mike Trout 25.00 60.00

2020 Topps Inception Purple

*PURPLE: 1.2X TO 3X BASIC
*PURPLE RC: 1X TO 2.5X BASIC
STATED ODDS 1:5 HOBBY
STATED PRINT RUN 150 SER.#'d SETS
100 Mike Trout 15.00 40.00

2020 Topps Inception Red

*RED: 2X TO 5X BASIC
*RED RC: 1.5X TO 4X BASIC
STATED ODDS 1:9 HOBBY
STATED PRINT RUN 75 SER.#'d SETS
100 Mike Trout 25.00 60.00

2020 Topps Inception Dawn of Greatness Autographs

STATED ODDS 1:200 HOBBY
STATED PRINT RUN 20 SER.#'d SETS
EXCHANGE DEADLINE 2/29/2022
DOGAAJ Aaron Judge 150.00 400.00
DOGAAR Anthony Rizzo 25.00 60.00
DOGABH Bryce Harper
DOGACCS CC Sabathia 30.00 80.00
DOGACY Christian Yelich
DOGAHA Hank Aaron
DOGAJA Jose Altuve 25.00 60.00
DOGAJC Jose Canseco 30.00 80.00
DOGAJDM J.D. Martinez 20.00 50.00
DOGAKGJ Ken Griffey Jr.
DOGAMC Miguel Cabrera 75.00 200.00
DOGAMM Mike Mussina 50.00 120.00
DOGAMT Mike Trout
DOGARH Rhys Hoskins 30.00 80.00
DOGASK Sandy Koufax
DOGASO Shohei Ohtani
DOGATM Tino Martinez 20.00 50.00
DOGAWM Whit Merrifield 20.00 50.00
DOGAXB Xander Bogaerts 30.00 80.00

2020 Topps Inception Jumbo Patch Autographs

STATED ODDS 1:28 HOBBY
PRINT RUNS B/WN 10-125 COPIES PER
NO PRICING ON QTY 10
EXCHANGE DEADLINE 2/29/2022
IAJPAA Aristides Aquino/90 50.00 120.00
IAJPAR Austin Riley/90 15.00 40.00
IAJPAY Alex Young/90 10.00 25.00
IAJPBB Bo Bichette/90 60.00 150.00
IAJPBM Brendan McKay/90 20.00 50.00
IAJPCB Cavan Biggio/90 30.00 80.00
IAJPDC Dylan Cease/90 12.00 30.00
IAJPDM Dustin May/90 25.00 60.00
IAJPFTJ Fernando Tatis Jr./90 100.00 250.00
IAJPGL Gavin Lux/90 40.00 100.00
IAJPJC Jake Cave/90 10.00 25.00
IAJPJM Jeff McNeil/90 20.00 50.00
IAJPKH Keston Hiura/90 30.00 80.00
IAJPKL Kyle Lewis/90 40.00 100.00
IAJPLA Logan Allen/45 12.00 30.00
IAJPMD Mauricio Dubon/90 10.00 25.00
IAJPMT Matt Thaiss/90 15.00 40.00
IAJPNH Nico Hoerner/90 20.00 50.00
IAJPPA Pete Alonso/90 60.00 510.00
IAJPRAJ Ronald Acuna Jr./90 75.00 200.00
IAJPRD Rafael Devers/90 20.00 50.00
IAJPTA Tim Anderson/90 25.00 60.00
IAJPVGJ Vladimir Guerrero Jr./90 60.00 150.00
IAJPWS Will Smith/90 15.00 40.00
IAJPYA Yordan Alvarez/90 40.00 100.00

2020 Topps Inception Jumbo Patch Autographs Orange

*ORANGE: .5X TO 1.2X BASIC
STATED ODDS 1:79 HOBBY
STATED PRINT RUN 25 SER.#'d SETS
EXCHANGE DEADLINE 2/29/2022
IAJPAAL Adbert Alzolay 12.00 30.00
IAJPAC Aaron Civale 20.00 50.00
IAJPAJ Aaron Judge 125.00 300.00
IAJPJY Jordan Yamamoto 30.00 80.00
IAJPKB Kris Bryant 75.00 200.00
IAJPRH Rhys Hoskins 40.00 100.00

2020 Topps Inception Patch Autographs

STATED ODDS 1:7 HOBBY
PRINT RUNS B/WN 50-199 COPIES PER
EXCHANGE DEADLINE 2/29/2022
IAPAA Adbert Alzolay/155 8.00 20.00
IAPAAQ Aristides Aquino/199 20.00 50.00
IAPAC Aaron Civale/155 10.00 25.00
IAPAJ Aaron Judge/50 75.00 200.00
IAPAMU Andres Munoz/155 6.00 15.00
IAPAN Austin Nola/155 10.00 25.00
IAPAP A.J. Puk/155 12.00 30.00
IAPAR Austin Riley/199 8.00 20.00
IAPAT Abraham Toro/199 5.00 12.00
IAPAY Alex Young/155 8.00 20.00
IAPBB Bobby Bradley/199 10.00 25.00
IAPBBI Bo Bichette/155 75.00 200.00
IAPBM Brendan McKay/155 12.00 30.00
IAPBR Brendan Rodgers/199 6.00 15.00
IAPCB Cavan Biggio/155 20.00 50.00
IAPCK Carter Kieboom/155 15.00 40.00
IAPDC Dylan Cease/155 10.00 25.00
IAPDL Domingo Leyba/155 5.00 12.00
IAPDM Dustin May/155 20.00 50.00
IAPFTJ Fernando Tatis Jr./155 75.00 200.00
IAPGL Gavin Lux/155 60.00 150.00
IAPGT Gleyber Torres/186 50.00 120.00
IAPID Isan Diaz/199 10.00 25.00
IAPJC Jake Cave/199 8.00 20.00
IAPJL Jesus Luzardo/199 20.00 50.00
IAPJM Jeff McNeil/199 15.00 40.00
IAPJR Jake Rogers/155 10.00 25.00
IAPJS Justus Sheffield/148 10.00 25.00
IAPJST Josh Staumont/165 4.00 10.00
IAPJY Jordan Yamamoto/155 10.00 25.00
IAPKB Kris Bryant
IAPKH Keston Hiura/199 25.00 60.00
IAPKL Kyle Lewis/199 25.00 60.00
IAPKN Kevin Newman/199 10.00 25.00
IAPLA Logan Allen/75 5.00 12.00
IAPMB Michael Brosseau/155 8.00 20.00
IAPMC Michael Chavis/155 5.00 12.00
IAPMD Mauricio Dubon/199 5.00 12.00
IAPMT Matt Thaiss/199 5.00 12.00
IAPNH Nico Hoerner/155 30.00 80.00
IAPNS Nick Senzel/155 15.00 40.00
IAPNSO Nick Solak/155 15.00 40.00
IAPPA Pete Alonso/155 50.00 120.00
IAPPS Patrick Sandoval/155 6.00 15.00
IAPRAJ Ronald Acuna Jr./155 60.00 150.00
IAPRAR Rogelio Armenteros/155 5.00 12.00
IAPRD Rafael Devers/155 20.00 50.00
IAPRG Robel Garcia/199 10.00 25.00
IAPRH Rhys Hoskins
IAPRL Ramon Laureano/199 15.00 40.00
IAPTA Tim Anderson/199 20.00 50.00
IAPTD Travis Demeritte/155 6.00 15.00
IAPVGJ Vladimir Guerrero Jr./155 50.00 120.00
IAPWC Willson Contreras/145 20.00 50.00
IAPWS Will Smith/155 15.00 40.00
IAPYA Yordan Alvarez/199 40.00 100.00

2020 Topps Inception Patch Autographs Magenta

*MAGENTA/75: .5X TO 1.2X BASIC
*MAGENTA/35: .6X TO 1.5X BASIC
STATED ODDS 1:16 HOBBY
PRINT RUNS B/WN 35-75 COPIES PER
EXCHANGE DEADLINE 2/29/2022
IAPRH Rhys Hoskins/75 25.00 60.00

2020 Topps Inception Patch Autographs Red

*RED/25: .6X TO 1.5X BASIC
STATED ODDS 1:45 HOBBY
PRINT RUNS B/WN 15-25 COPIES PER
NO PRICING ON QTY 15
EXCHANGE DEADLINE 2/29/2022
IAPRH Rhys Hoskins/25 30.00 80.00

2020 Topps Inception Rookie and Emerging Stars Autographs

RANDOM INSERTS IN PACKS
PRINT RUNS B/WN 100-249 COPIES PER
EXCHANGE DEADLINE 2/29/2022
RESAAA Adbert Alzolay/245 10.00 25.00
RESAAAQ Aristides Aquino/245 30.00 80.00
RESAAC Aaron Civale/245 5.00 12.00
RESAAJP A.J. Puk/245 8.00 20.00
RESAAK Anthony Kay/245 5.00 12.00
RESAAMU Andres Munoz/245 5.00 12.00
RESAAN Austin Nola/245 6.00 15.00
RESAAR Austin Riley/245 10.00 25.00
RESAAT Abraham Toro/245 3.00 8.00
RESAAY Alex Young/245 5.00 12.00
RESABB Bobby Bradley/245 2.50 6.00
RESABBI Bo Bichette/245 50.00 120.00
RESABM Brendan McKay/245 10.00 25.00
RESABR Brendan Rodgers/245 5.00 12.00
RESABRE Bryan Reynolds/245 8.00 20.00
RESACA Chance Adams/245 2.50 6.00
RESACK Carter Kieboom/245 10.00 25.00
RESACT Cole Tucker/220 4.00 10.00
RESADC Dylan Cease/245 8.00 20.00
RESADF David Fletcher/220 4.00 10.00
RESADJ Danny Jansen/245 2.50 6.00
RESADL Domingo Leyba/245 3.00 8.00
RESADM Dustin May/245 15.00 40.00
RESADSJ Dwight Smith Jr./245 2.50 6.00
RESAGC Griffin Canning/220 4.00 10.00
RESAGH Garrett Hampson/220 2.50 6.00
RESAGL Gavin Lux/245 50.00 120.00
RESAHH Hunter Harvey/245 4.00 10.00
RESAID Isan Diaz/245 4.00 10.00
RESAJAM James Marvel/245 2.50 6.00
RESAJB Jake Bauers/245 3.00 8.00
RESAJD Jon Duplantier/245 2.50 6.00
RESAJL Jesus Luzardo/245 12.00 30.00
RESAJME John Means/245 30.00 80.00
RESAJN Josh Naylor/220 2.50 6.00
RESAJR Jake Rogers/245 6.00 15.00
RESAJST Josh Staumont/220 2.50 6.00
RESAJU Jose Urquidy/245 10.00 25.00
RESAJY Jordan Yamamoto/245 6.00 15.00
RESAKH Keston Hiura/245 15.00 40.00
RESAKN Kevin Newman/245 4.00 10.00
RESALA Logan Allen/245 2.50 6.00
RESALAR Luis Arraez/245 12.00 30.00
RESALR Luis Robert EXCH 150.00 400.00
RESAMBE Matt Beaty/245 6.00 15.00
RESAMBR Michael Brosseau/220 5.00 12.00
RESAMC Michael Chavis/245 10.00 25.00
RESAMD Mauricio Dubon/245 10.00 25.00
RESAMK Mitch Keller/245 4.00 10.00
RESAMKE Merrill Kelly/220 2.50 6.00
RESAMT Matt Thaiss/245 3.00 8.00
RESAMTA Mike Tauchman/245 15.00 40.00
RESAMY Mike Yastrzemski/245 15.00 40.00
RESANH Nico Hoerner/245 10.00 25.00
RESANS Nick Senzel/100 12.00 30.00
RESANSO Nick Solak/245 8.00 20.00
RESARA Rogelio Armenteros/220 3.00 8.00
RESARG Robel Garcia/245 2.50 6.00
RESASA Shaun Anderson/220 4.00 10.00
RESASB Seth Brown/245 2.50 6.00
RESASL Shed Long/245 5.00 12.00
RESASM Sean Murphy/245 6.00 15.00
RESATA Tyler Alexander/220 4.00 10.00
RESATD Travis Demeritte/220 4.00 10.00
RESATE Thairo Estrada/245 3.00 8.00
RESATES Tom Eshelman/220 3.00 8.00
RESATG Trent Grisham/245 6.00 15.00
RESATGO Tony Gonsolin/245 12.00 30.00
RESATW Taylor Ward/220 4.00 10.00
RESAVGJ Vladimir Guerrero Jr./100 40.00 100.00
RESAVR Victor Robles/245 10.00 25.00
RESAWA Willians Astudillo/245 5.00 12.00
RESAWS Will Smith/245 15.00 40.00
RESAYA Yordan Alvarez/245 50.00 120.00
RESAYC Yu Chang/245 EXCH 10.00 25.00
RESAZC Zack Collins/245 3.00 8.00
RESAZP Zach Plesac/220 5.00 12.00

2020 Topps Inception Rookie and Emerging Stars Autographs Blue

*BLUE: .75X TO 2X BASIC
STATED ODDS 1:31 HOBBY
STATED PRINT RUN 25 SER.#'d SETS
EXCHANGE DEADLINE 2/29/2022
RESACP Chris Paddack 20.00 50.00
RESAGT Gleyber Torres 60.00 150.00
RESAJSO Juan Soto EXCH 60.00 150.00
RESASO Shohei Ohtani EXCH 100.00 250.00

2020 Topps Inception Rookie and Emerging Stars Autographs Magenta

*MAGENTA: .5X TO 1.2X BASIC
STATED ODDS 1:8 HOBBY
STATED PRINT RUN 99 SER.#'d SETS
EXCHANGE DEADLINE 2/29/2022
RESACP Chris Paddack 12.00 30.00
RESAGT Gleyber Torres 40.00 100.00
RESAJSO Juan Soto EXCH 40.00 100.00

2020 Topps Inception Rookie and Emerging Stars Autographs Orange

*ORANGE: .6X TO 1.5X BASIC
STATED ODDS 1:16 HOBBY
STATED PRINT RUN 50 SER.#'d SETS
EXCHANGE DEADLINE 2/29/2022
RESACP Chris Paddack 15.00 40.00
RESAGT Gleyber Torres 50.00 120.00
RESAJSO Juan Soto EXCH 50.00 120.00
RESASO Shohei Ohtani EXCH 75.00 200.00

2020 Topps Inception Rookie and Emerging Stars Autographs Red

*RED: .5X TO 1.2X BASIC
STATED ODDS 1:11 HOBBY
STATED PRINT RUN 75 SER.#'d SETS
EXCHANGE DEADLINE 2/29/2022
RESACP Chris Paddack 12.00 30.00
RESAGT Gleyber Torres 40.00 100.00
RESAJSO Juan Soto EXCH 40.00 100.00

2020 Topps Inception Silver Signings

STATED ODDS 1:21 HOBBY
PRINT RUNS B/WN 50-99 COPIES PER
EXCHANGE DEADLINE 2/29/2022
SSAA Adbert Alzolay/99 8.00 20.00
SSAAQ Aristides Aquino/99 40.00 100.00
SSAMU Andres Munoz/90 10.00 25.00
SSAN Austin Nola/90 10.00 25.00
SSAP A.J. Puk/99 20.00 50.00
SSAR Austin Riley/70 30.00 80.00
SSBB Bo Bichette/70 100.00 250.00
SSBM Brendan McKay/60 10.00 25.00
SSCK Carter Kieboom/99 15.00 40.00
SSDC Dylan Cease/99 15.00 40.00
SSDF David Fletcher/90 12.00 30.00
SSDM Dustin May/99 20.00 50.00
SSFTJ Fernando Tatis Jr./70 150.00 400.00
SSGL Gavin Lux/99 75.00 200.00
SSGT Gleyber Torres/50 75.00 200.00
SSID Isan Diaz/99 10.00 25.00
SSJB Jake Bauers/90 8.00 20.00
SSJL Jesus Luzardo/99 30.00 80.00
SSJM Jordan Yamamoto/99 12.00 30.00
SSJME John Means/90 75.00 200.00
SSJN Josh Naylor/90 6.00 15.00
SSJR Jake Rogers/99 12.00 30.00
SSKH Keston Hiura/99 40.00 100.00
SSLA Logan Allen/99 6.00 15.00
SSLAR Luis Arraez/90 30.00 80.00
SSMB Michael Brosseau/90 8.00 20.00
SSMC Michael Chavis/99 20.00 50.00
SSMT Mike Tauchman/99 10.00 25.00
SSNS Nick Senzel/70 20.00 50.00
SSPA Pete Alonso/50 75.00 200.00
SSRAJ Ronald Acuna Jr./50 60.00 150.00
SSRG Robel Garcia/99 6.00 15.00
SSSM Sean Murphy/99 10.00 25.00
SSTG Trent Grisham/99 12.00 30.00
SSTGO Tony Gonsolin/90 15.00 40.00
SSVGJ Vladimir Guerrero Jr./70 75.00 200.00
SSYA Yordan Alvarez/70 75.00 200.00

2020 Topps Inception Silver Signings Gold Ink

*GOLD INK: .5X TO 1.2X BASIC
STATED ODDS 1:66 HOBBY
STATED PRINT RUN 25 SER.#'d SETS
EXCHANGE DEADLINE 2/29/2022
SSCP Chris Paddack 50.00 120.00
SSSO Shohei Ohtani EXCH 20.00 50.00
SSZC Zack Collins 10.00 25.00

2020 Topps Inception Sock Autographs

STATED ODDS 1:200 HOBBY
STATED PRINT RUN 25 SER.#'d SETS
EXCHANGE DEADLINE 2/29/2022
IAGSAA Adbert Alzolay 12.00 30.00
IAGSAAQ Aristides Aquino 60.00 150.00
IAGSAC Aaron Civale 20.00 50.00
IAGSAJP A.J. Puk 25.00 60.00
IAGSAY Alex Young 10.00 25.00
IAGSBB Bobby Bradley 10.00 25.00
IAGSBBI Bo Bichette 80.00 200.00
IAGSDC Dylan Cease 15.00 40.00
IAGSDL Domingo Leyba 12.00 30.00
IAGSDM Dustin May 30.00 80.00
IAGSGL Gavin Lux 100.00 250.00
IAGSID Isan Diaz 25.00 60.00
IAGSJR Jake Rogers 10.00 25.00
IAGSJY Jordan Yamamoto 25.00 60.00
IAGSLA Logan Allen 10.00 25.00
IAGSMB Michael Brosseau 20.00 50.00
IAGSMD Mauricio Dubon 50.00 120.00
IAGSRG Robel Garcia 10.00 25.00
IAGSSM Sean Murphy 40.00 100.00
IAGSYC Yu Chang 20.00 50.00

2021 Topps Inception

1 Daulton Varsho RC 1.50 4.00
2 Stephen Strasburg .60 1.50
3 Deivi Garcia RC 5.00 12.00
4 Ke'Bryan Hayes RC 6.00 15.00
5 Tarik Skubal RC 3.00 8.00
6 Eloy Jimenez 1.25 3.00
7 Luis Robert 4.00 10.00
8 Eddie Rosario .50 1.25
9 Dylan Carlson RC 8.00 20.00
10 Tim Anderson .60 1.50
11 Carlos Correa .60 1.50
12 Ryan Mountcastle RC 8.00 20.00
13 Gerrit Cole 1.00 2.50
14 Anthony Rendon .60 1.50
15 Hanser Alberto .40 1.00
16 Paul Goldschmidt .60 1.50
17 Jake Cronenworth RC 4.00 10.00
18 Buster Posey .75 2.00
19 Fernando Tatis Jr. 8.00 20.00
20 Jo Adell RC 8.00 20.00
21 Nate Pearson RC 3.00 8.00
22 Jesus Sanchez RC 2.00 5.00
23 Jacob deGrom 1.25 3.00
24 Ronald Acuna Jr. 2.50 6.00
25 Bryce Harper 1.00 2.50
26 Starling Marte .50 1.25
27 Ian Anderson RC 4.00 10.00
28 Josh Hader .50 1.25
29 Shane Bieber .60 1.50
30 Joey Votto .60 1.50
31 Mookie Betts 1.25 3.00
32 Aaron Judge 1.50 4.00
33 Keibert Ruiz RC 2.00 5.00
34 DJ LeMahieu .60 1.50
35 Brailyn Marquez RC 3.00 8.00
36 Joey Bart RC 2.00 5.00
37 Devin Williams .60 1.50
38 Alex Bregman .60 1.50
39 Alec Bohm RC 6.00 15.00
40 Freddie Freeman .75 2.00
41 Ozzie Albies .60 1.50
42 Josh Bell .50 1.25
43 Javier Baez .75 2.00
44 Matt Olson .60 1.50
45 Jose Altuve .50 1.25
46 Francisco Lindor .60 1.50
47 Jack Flaherty .60 1.50
48 Trevor Story .60 1.50
49 Pete Alonso 1.50 4.00
50 Pedro Severino .40 1.00
51 Gleyber Torres 1.25 3.00
52 Xander Bogaerts .60 1.50
53 Spencer Howard RC 2.00 5.00
54 Bo Bichette 1.50 4.00
55 Anthony Rizzo .75 2.00
56 Nick Madrigal RC 4.00 10.00
57 Nolan Arenado 1.00 2.50
58 Vladimir Guerrero Jr. 1.00 2.50
59 Brandon Lowe .50 1.25
60 Mike Trout 6.00 15.00
61 Dane Dunning RC 2.00 5.00
62 Luis Garcia RC 3.00 8.00
63 Cristian Pache RC 10.00 25.00
64 Blake Snell .50 1.25
65 Christian Yelich .75 2.00
66 Manny Machado .60 1.50
67 Joey Gallo .60 1.50
68 Yordan Alvarez 1.50 4.00
69 Andres Gimenez RC 1.50 4.00
70 Kris Bryant .75 2.00
71 Rhys Hoskins .75 2.00
72 Charlie Blackmon .60 1.50
73 Matt Chapman .60 1.50
74 Sixto Sanchez RC 3.00 8.00
75 Evan White RC 4.00 10.00
76 Casey Mize RC 5.00 12.00
77 Brady Singer RC 3.00 8.00
78 Shohei Ohtani 1.00 2.50
79 Walker Buehler .75 2.00
80 Kyle Lewis 1.50 4.00
81 Andrew McCutchen .60 1.50
82 Clayton Kershaw 1.00 2.50
83 Whit Merrifield .60 1.50
84 Cristian Javier RC 1.50 4.00
85 Alex Kirilloff RC 2.50 6.00
86 Jorge Polanco .50 1.25
87 Trevor Bauer .75 2.00
88 Chris Sale .60 1.50
89 Miguel Cabrera .60 1.50
90 Cody Bellinger 1.25 3.00
91 Justin Verlander .60 1.50
92 Jose Berrios .50 1.25
93 Juan Soto 2.00 5.00
94 Paul DeJong .60 1.50
95 Max Scherzer .60 1.50
96 Max Kepler .50 1.25
97 Willson Contreras .60 1.50
98 Jorge Soler .60 1.50
99 Kyle Hendricks .60 1.50
100 Alex Verdugo .50 1.25

2021 Topps Inception Blue

*BLUE: 4X TO 10X BASIC
*BLUE RC: 2.5X TO 6X BASIC
STATED ODDS 1:29 HOBBY
STATED PRINT RUN 25 SER.#'d SETS
7 Luis Robert 60.00 150.00
12 Ryan Mountcastle 75.00 200.00
19 Fernando Tatis Jr. 125.00 300.00
20 Jo Adell 75.00 200.00
39 Alec Bohm 150.00 400.00
56 Nick Madrigal 60.00 150.00
60 Mike Trout 125.00 300.00
63 Cristian Pache 75.00 200.00

2021 Topps Inception Green

*GREEN: .8X TO 2X BASIC
*GREEN RC: .5X TO 1.2X BASIC
RANDOM INSERTS IN PACKS
12 Ryan Mountcastle 10.00 25.00

2021 Topps Inception Magenta

*MAGENTA: 2X TO 5X BASIC
*MAGENTA RC: 1.2X TO 3X BASIC
STATED ODDS 1:8 HOBBY
STATED PRINT RUN 99 SER.#'d SETS
7 Luis Robert 30.00 80.00
19 Fernando Tatis Jr. 60.00 150.00
39 Alec Bohm 50.00 120.00
63 Cristian Pache 40.00 100.00

2021 Topps Inception Orange

*ORANGE: 2.5X TO 6X BASIC
*ORANGE RC: 1.5X TO 4X BASIC
STATED ODDS 1:15 HOBBY
STATED PRINT RUN 50 SER.#'d SETS
7 Luis Robert 40.00 100.00
12 Ryan Mountcastle 50.00 120.00
19 Fernando Tatis Jr. 75.00 200.00
20 Jo Adell 50.00 120.00
39 Alec Bohm 100.00 250.00
56 Nick Madrigal 40.00 100.00
63 Cristian Pache 50.00 120.00

2021 Topps Inception Purple

*PURPLE: 1.5X TO 4X BASIC
*PURPLE RC: 1X TO 2.5X BASIC
STATED ODDS 1:5 HOBBY
STATED PRINT RUN 150 SER.#'d SETS
7 Luis Robert 20.00 50.00
39 Alec Bohm 40.00 100.00
63 Cristian Pache 30.00 80.00

2021 Topps Inception Red

*RED; 2X TO 5X BASIC
*RED RC: 1.2X TO 3X BASIC
STATED ODDS 1:10 HOBBY
STATED PRINT RUN 75 SER.#'d SETS
7 Luis Robert 30.00 80.00
19 Fernando Tatis Jr. 60.00 150.00
20 Jo Adell 40.00 100.00
39 Alec Bohm 50.00 120.00
63 Cristian Pache 40.00 100.00

2021 Topps Inception Dawn of Greatness Autographs

STATED ODDS 1:xx HOBBY
STATED PRINT RUN 20 SER.#'d SETS
EXCHANGE DEADLINE 2/28/2023
DOGAAB Adrian Beltre 50.00 120.00
DOGAAR Anthony Rendon
DOGABH Bryce Harper 100.00 250.00
DOGACY Christian Yelich
DOGADJ Derek Jeter
DOGADO David Ortiz 40.00 100.00
DOGAMC Miguel Cabrera 50.00 120.00
DOGAMM Mark McGwire 60.00 150.00
DOGANG Nomar Garciaparra 30.00 80.00
DOGAOS Ozzie Smith 50.00 120.00
DOGARA Roberto Alomar
DOGARC Greg Maddux
DOGATH Torii Hunter 40.00 100.00
DOGACRJ Cal Ripken Jr. 125.00 300.00
DOGAKGJ Ken Griffey Jr. 600.00 1500.00

2021 Topps Inception Jumbo Patch Autographs

STATED ODDS 1:xx HOBBY
PRINT RUNS B/WN 75-125 COPIES PER
EXCHANGE DEADLINE 2/28/2023
AJPAB Alec Bohm/75 200.00 500.00
AJPAJ Aaron Judge
AJPCJ Cristian Javier/100 15.00 40.00
AJPCM Casey Mize/75 60.00 150.00
AJPCP Cristian Pache/75 60.00 150.00
AJPDC Dylan Carlson/75 150.00 400.00
AJPDD Dane Dunning
AJPDP David Peterson/100 30.00 80.00
AJPEW Evan White/100 40.00 100.00
AJPFT Fernando Tatis Jr./75 300.00 600.00
AJPIA Ian Anderson/75 30.00 80.00
AJPJA Jo Adell/75 150.00 400.00
AJPJB Joey Bart/75 50.00 120.00
AJPJC Jake Cronenworth/75 40.00 100.00
AJPJS Jesus Sanchez/82 40.00 100.00
AJPLR Luis Robert/75 75.00 200.00
AJPNM Nick Madrigal/75 50.00 125.00
AJPNP Nate Pearson/75 50.00 120.00
AJPPA Pete Alonso
AJPRA Ronald Acuna Jr.
AJPRD Randy Dobnak
AJPSH Spencer Howard/75 15.00 40.00
AJPSS Sixto Sanchez/75 75.00 200.00
AJPVG Vladimir Guerrero Jr.
AJPWC William Contreras/99 25.00 60.00
AJPYA Yordan Alvarez/125 30.00 80.00
AJPKBH Ke'Bryan Hayes/75 200.00 500.00

2021 Topps Inception Jumbo Patch Autographs Orange

*ORANGE/25: .6X TO 1.5X BASIC
STATED ODDS 1:xx HOBBY
STATED PRINT RUN 25 SER.#'d SETS
EXCHANGE DEADLINE 2/28/2023
AJPAJ Aaron Judge 200.00 500.00
AJPCP Cristian Pache 200.00 500.00
AJPEW Evan White 100.00 250.00
AJPIA Ian Anderson 125.00 300.00
AJPJS Jesus Sanchez 100.00 250.00
AJPLR Luis Robert 250.00 600.00
AJPNM Nick Madrigal 100.00 250.00
AJPRA Ronald Acuna Jr. 125.00 300.00
AJPRD Randy Dobnak 25.00 60.00
AJPVG Vladimir Guerrero Jr. 60.00 150.00
AJPKBH Ke'Bryan Hayes 400.00 1000.00

2021 Topps Inception Jumbo Patch Autographs Red

*RED/50: .5X TO 1.2X BASIC
STATED ODDS 1:xx HOBBY
STATED PRINT RUN 50 SER.#'d SETS
EXCHANGE DEADLINE 2/28/2023
AJPAJ Aaron Judge 150.00 400.00
AJPCP Cristian Pache 150.00 400.00
AJPIA Ian Anderson 100.00 250.00
AJPJS Jesus Sanchez 75.00 200.00
AJPLR Luis Robert 200.00 500.00
AJPRA Ronald Acuna Jr. 100.00 250.00
AJPRD Randy Dobnak 20.00 50.00
AJPVG Vladimir Guerrero Jr. 50.00 120.00
AJPKBH Ke'Bryan Hayes 300.00 800.00

2021 Topps Inception Patch Autographs

STATED ODDS 1:xx HOBBY
PRINT RUNS B/WN 69-200 COPIES PER
EXCHANGE DEADLINE 2/28/2023
APCAB Alec Bohm/120 125.00 300.00
APCAG Andres Gimenez
APCAJ Aaron Judge
APCAK Alex Kirilloff
APCAT Anderson Tejeda/199 10.00 25.00
APCAV Alex Verdugo/125 20.00 50.00
APCBM Brendan McKay/110 10.00 25.00
APCBR Brent Rooker/199 10.00 25.00
APCBS Brady Singer/120 25.00 60.00
APCCJ Cristian Javier/149 20.00 50.00
APCCM Casey Mize/120 40.00 100.00
APCCP Cristian Pache/120 40.00 100.00
APCDB David Bote
APCDC Dylan Carlson/125 75.00 200.00
APCDD Dane Dunning/199 12.00 30.00
APCDG Deivi Garcia/199 15.00 40.00
APCDP David Peterson/199 8.00 20.00
APCDV Daulton Varsho/199 10.00 25.00
APCEO Edward Olivares
APCEW Evan White/199 25.00 60.00
APCFT Fernando Tatis Jr.
APCGT Gleyber Torres/95 50.00 120.00
APCIA Ian Anderson/150 40.00 100.00
APCJA Jo Adell/120 75.00 200.00
APCJB Joey Bart/120 40.00 100.00
APCJC Jake Cronenworth/120 30.00 80.00
APCJG Jose Garcia/199 15.00 40.00
APCJJ Jahmai Jones/199 4.00 10.00
APCJL Jesus Luzardo/125 10.00 25.00
APCJS Jesus Sanchez/199 20.00 50.00
APCKH Keston Hiura
APCKL Kyle Lewis
APCKR Keibert Ruiz/199 12.00 30.00
APCLG Luis Garcia
APCLR Luis Robert/100 100.00 250.00
APCLT Leody Taveras/199 12.00 30.00
APCMY Miguel Yajure/199 10.00 25.00
APCNM Nick Madrigal/120 30.00 80.00
APCNP Nate Pearson/120 20.00 50.00
APCNS Nick Solak/110 6.00 15.00
APCPA Pete Alonso/69 50.00 120.00
APCRA Ronald Acuna Jr./80 125.00 300.00
APCRD Randy Dobnak/199 6.00 15.00
APCRJ Ryan Jeffers/199 8.00 20.00
APCRM Ryan Mountcastle/120 20.00 50.00
APCSE Santiago Espinal/199 15.00 40.00
APCSH Spencer Howard/120 25.00 60.00
APCSS Sixto Sanchez/120 50.00 120.00
APCTR Trevor Rogers/199 30.00 80.00
APCTS Tyler Stephenson/199 20.00 50.00
APCWB Walker Buehler/200 8.00 20.00
APCWC William Contreras/199 25.00 60.00
APCJCH Jazz Chisholm/199 25.00 60.00
APCKBH Ke'Bryan Hayes/150 125.00 300.00
APCSHU Sam Huff/120 25.00 60.00
APCTHO Tanner Houck/120 25.00 60.00
APCTSK Tarik Skubal

2021 Topps Inception Patch Autographs Green

*GREEN/75-99: .5X TO 1.2X p/r 110-200
*GREEN/75-99: .4X TO 1X p/r 69-100
*GREEN/50: .6X TO 1.5X p/r 110-200
*GREEN/50: .5X TO 1.2X p/r 69-100
STATED ODDS 1:xx HOBBY
PRINT RUNS B/WN 50-99 COPIES PER
EXCHANGE DEADLINE 2/28/2023
APCKH Keston Hiura 20.00 50.00

2021 Topps Inception Patch Autographs Magenta

*MAGENTA/75: .5X TO 1.2X p/r 110-200
*MAGENTA/75: .4X TO 1X p/r 69-100
*MAGENTA/30-50: .6X TO 1.5X p/r 110-200
*MAGENTA/30-50: .5X TO 1.2X p/r 69-100
STATED ODDS 1:xx HOBBY
PRINT RUNS B/WN 30-75 COPIES PER
EXCHANGE DEADLINE 2/28/2023
APCAJ Aaron Judge/30 125.00 300.00
APCAK Alex Kirilloff/75 60.00 150.00
APCDB David Bote/75 40.00 100.00
APCFT Fernando Tatis Jr./75 150.00 400.00
APCKH Keston Hiura/50 25.00 60.00
APCKL Kyle Lewis/50 20.00 50.00

2021 Topps Inception Patch Autographs Red

*RED/25: .8X TO 2X p/r 110-200
*RED/25: .6X TO 1.5X p/r 69-100
STATED ODDS 1:xx HOBBY
STATED PRINT RUN 25 SER.#'d SETS
EXCHANGE DEADLINE 2/28/2023
APCAJ Aaron Judge 150.00 400.00
APCAK Alex Kirilloff 100.00 250.00
APCDB David Bote 60.00 150.00
APCEO Edward Olivares 20.00 50.00
APCFT Fernando Tatis Jr. 250.00 600.00
APCKH Keston Hiura 30.00 80.00
APCKL Kyle Lewis 30.00 80.00
APCTSK Tarik Skubal 100.00 250.00

2021 Topps Inception Rookie and Emerging Stars Autographs

STATED ODDS 1:xx HOBBY
PRINT RUNS B/WN 65-299 COPIES PER
EXCHANGE DEADLINE 2/28/2023
RESAAB Alec Bohm/125 100.00 250.00
RESAAC Aaron Civale/299 4.00 10.00
RESAAG Andres Gimenez/249 8.00 20.00
RESAAK Alex Kirilloff/299 40.00 100.00
RESAAM Nick Heath/299 5.00 12.00
RESAAN David Peterson/200 15.00 40.00
RESAAV Alex Verdugo/125 20.00 50.00
RESABD Bobby Dalbec/130 60.00 150.00
RESABM Brendan McKay/125 10.00 25.00
RESABR Bryan Reynolds/299 6.00 15.00
RESABS Brady Singer/208 12.00 30.00
RESABT Blake Taylor/199 8.00 20.00
RESACB Cavan Biggio/200 20.00 50.00
RESACH Codi Heuer/249 20.00 50.00
RESACJ Cristian Javier/249 8.00 20.00
RESACM Casey Mize/100 50.00 120.00
RESACT Cole Tucker/200 6.00 15.00
RESADC Dylan Cease/200 10.00 25.00
RESADD Dane Dunning/200 5.00 12.00
RESADG Deivi Garcia/199 15.00 40.00
RESADJ Daniel Johnson/249 10.00 25.00
RESAEJ Eloy Jimenez/100 30.00 80.00
RESAEO Edward Olivares/249 6.00 15.00
RESAEP Enoli Paredes/249 4.00 10.00
RESAEW Evan White/200 12.00 30.00
RESAGL Gavin Lux/100 40.00 100.00
RESAJA Jo Adell/100 50.00 120.00
RESAJB Joey Bart/100 40.00 100.00
RESAJC Jazz Chisholm/200 30.00 80.00
RESAJH Jordan Holloway/199 2.50 6.00
RESAJL Jesus Luzardo/125 12.00 30.00
RESAJS Juan Soto/65 125.00 300.00
RESAJY Jordan Yamamoto/299 2.50 6.00
RESAKH Keston Hiura/125 12.00 30.00
RESALA Luis Arraez/150 8.00 20.00
RESALG Luis Garcia/150 25.00 60.00
RESALR Luis Robert/100 75.00 200.00
RESALT Leody Taveras/249 10.00 25.00
RESAMD Mauricio Dubon/299 6.00 15.00
RESAMS Mike Soroka/200 20.00 50.00
RESAMW Mitch White/199 4.00 10.00
RESAMY Miguel Yajure/199 12.00 30.00
RESANH Nico Hoerner/125 20.00 50.00
RESANM Nick Madrigal/130 20.00 50.00
RESANN Nick Neidert/249 5.00 12.00
RESANP Nate Pearson/125 25.00 60.00
RESANS Nick Solak/249 10.00 25.00
RESAPA Pete Alonso/75 40.00 100.00
RESARD Randy Dobnak/249 10.00 25.00
RESARM Ryan Mountcastle/150 25.00 60.00
RESASB Seth Brown/249 5.00 12.00
RESASE Santiago Espinal/249 10.00 25.00
RESASH Spencer Howard/125 20.00 50.00
RESASM Sean Murphy/299 12.00 30.00
RESASS Sterling Sharp/249 6.00 15.00
RESATH Tom Hatch/249 3.00 8.00
RESATR Trevor Rogers/249 8.00 20.00
RESATS Tyler Stephenson/200 20.00 50.00
RESATZ Tyler Zuber/199 8.00 20.00
RESAWC William Contreras/200 15.00 40.00
RESAWS Will Smith/200 20.00 50.00
RESAYA Yordan Alvarez/75 40.00 100.00
RESAYM Kodi Whitley/249 8.00 20.00
RESAAAL Adbert Alzolay/299 5.00 12.00
RESAAGO Ashton Goudeau/249 8.00 20.00
RESAAME Austin Meadows/299 12.00 30.00
RESAAVE Alex Vesia/249 8.00 20.00
RESABBU Beau Burrows/249 10.00 25.00
RESABGA Bryan Garcia/249 5.00 12.00
RESACPA Cristian Pache/250 50.00 120.00
RESADCA Dylan Carlson/100 100.00 250.00
RESADWI Devin Williams/199 10.00 25.00
RESAJAR Jonathan Arauz/249 10.00 25.00
RESAJCR Jake Cronenworth/249 30.00 80.00
RESAJLA Jimmy Lambert/249 8.00 20.00
RESAJSA Jesus Sanchez/251 20.00 50.00
RESAKBH Ke'Bryan Hayes/150 100.00 250.00
RESANSN Nick Senzel/100 8.00 20.00
RESARGA Rony Garcia/199 6.00 15.00
RESARJE Ryan Jeffers/249 10.00 25.00
RESASSA Sixto Sanchez/150 30.00 80.00
RESATKS Tarik Skubal/200 20.00 50.00
RESAVGJ Vladimir Guerrero Jr./75 50.00 120.00

2021 Topps Inception Rookie and Emerging Stars Autographs Blue

*BLUE/25: .8X TO 2X p/r 150-299
*BLUE/25: .6X TO 1.5X p/r 65-130
STATED ODDS 1:xx HOBBY
STATED PRINT RUN 50 SER.#'d SETS
EXCHANGE DEADLINE 2/28/2023
RESAAB Alec Bohm 200.00 500.00
RESAAC Aaron Civale 15.00 40.00
RESAAK Alex Kirilloff 100.00 250.00
RESABD Bobby Dalbec 150.00 400.00
RESABS Brady Singer 30.00 80.00

RESABT Blake Taylor 30.00 80.00
RESACJ Cristian Javier 30.00 80.00
RESACM Casey Mize 125.00 300.00
RESACT Cole Tucker 20.00 50.00
RESAEW Evan White 50.00 120.00
RESAKH Keston Hiura 25.00 60.00
RESALA Luis Arraez 20.00 50.00
RESALR Luis Robert 150.00 400.00
RESALT Leody Taveras 30.00 80.00
RESAMD Mauricio Dubon 15.00 40.00
RESAMS Mike Soroka 75.00 200.00
RESANH Nico Hoerner 40.00 100.00
RESANM Nick Madrigal 75.00 200.00
RESANP Nate Pearson 50.00 120.00
RESASB Seth Brown 15.00 40.00
RESATS Tyler Stephenson 50.00 120.00
RESATZ Tyler Zuber 25.00 60.00
RESAWS Will Smith 50.00 120.00
RESACPA Cristian Pache 150.00 400.00
RESADWI Devin Williams 40.00 100.00
RESARJE Ryan Jeffers 25.00 60.00
RESASSA Sixto Sanchez 75.00 200.00

2021 Topps Inception Rookie and Emerging Stars Autographs Green

*GREEN/125: .5X TO 1.2X p/r 150-299
*GREEN/125: .4X TO 1X p/r 65-130
STATED ODDS 1:xx HOBBY
STATED PRINT RUN 125 SER.#'d SETS
EXCHANGE DEADLINE 2/28/2023
RESAEW Evan White 30.00 80.00
RESALA Luis Arraez 12.00 30.00
RESALT Leody Taveras 20.00 50.00
RESAMD Mauricio Dubon 10.00 25.00
RESASB Seth Brown 10.00 25.00

2021 Topps Inception Rookie and Emerging Stars Autographs Magenta

*MAGENTA/99: .5X TO 1.2X p/r 150-299
*MAGENTA/99: .4X TO 1X p/r 65-130
STATED ODDS 1:xx HOBBY
STATED PRINT RUN 99 SER.#'d SETS
EXCHANGE DEADLINE 2/28/2023
RESABT Blake Taylor 12.00 30.00
RESACJ Cristian Javier 20.00 50.00
RESACT Cole Tucker 12.00 30.00
RESAEW Evan White 30.00 80.00
RESALA Luis Arraez 12.00 30.00
RESALT Leody Taveras 20.00 50.00
RESAMD Mauricio Dubon 10.00 25.00
RESASB Seth Brown 10.00 25.00
RESATS Tyler Stephenson 30.00 80.00
RESATZ Tyler Zuber 12.00 30.00
RESADWI Devin Williams 15.00 40.00

2021 Topps Inception Rookie and Emerging Stars Autographs Orange

*ORANGE/50: .6X TO 1.5X p/r 150-299
*ORANGE/50: .5X TO 1.2X p/r 65-130
STATED ODDS 1:xx HOBBY
STATED PRINT RUN 50 SER.#'d SETS
EXCHANGE DEADLINE 2/28/2023
RESAAC Aaron Civale 12.00 30.00
RESAAK Alex Kirilloff 75.00 200.00
RESABD Bobby Dalbec 125.00 300.00
RESABS Brady Singer 25.00 60.00
RESABT Blake Taylor 25.00 60.00
RESACJ Cristian Javier 25.00 60.00
RESACM Casey Mize 100.00 250.00
RESACT Cole Tucker 15.00 40.00
RESAEW Evan White 40.00 100.00
RESALA Luis Arraez 15.00 40.00
RESALR Luis Robert 125.00 300.00
RESALT Leody Taveras 25.00 60.00
RESAMD Mauricio Dubon 12.00 30.00
RESAMS Mike Soroka 60.00 150.00
RESANM Nick Madrigal 60.00 150.00
RESANP Nate Pearson 40.00 100.00
RESASB Seth Brown 12.00 30.00
RESATS Tyler Stephenson 40.00 100.00
RESATZ Tyler Zuber 20.00 50.00
RESAWS Will Smith 40.00 100.00
RESACPA Cristian Pache 125.00 300.00
RESADWI Devin Williams 20.00 50.00
RESASSA Sixto Sanchez 60.00 150.00

2021 Topps Inception Rookie and Emerging Stars Autographs Red

*RED/75: .5X TO 1.2X p/r 150-299
*RED/75: .4X TO 1X p/r 65-130
STATED ODDS 1:xx HOBBY
STATED PRINT RUN 75 SER.#'d SETS
EXCHANGE DEADLINE 2/28/2023
RESABD Bobby Dalbec 75.00 200.00
RESABT Blake Taylor 12.00 30.00
RESACJ Cristian Javier 20.00 50.00
RESACT Cole Tucker 12.00 30.00
RESAEW Evan White 30.00 80.00
RESALA Luis Arraez 12.00 30.00
RESALR Luis Robert 100.00 250.00
RESALT Leody Taveras 20.00 50.00
RESAMD Mauricio Dubon 10.00 25.00
RESAMS Mike Soroka 50.00 120.00
RESANM Nick Madrigal 50.00 120.00
RESANP Nate Pearson 30.00 80.00
RESASB Seth Brown 10.00 25.00
RESATS Tyler Stephenson 30.00 80.00
RESATZ Tyler Zuber 15.00 40.00
RESAWS Will Smith 30.00 80.00
RESACPA Cristian Pache 100.00 250.00
RESADWI Devin Williams 15.00 40.00

2021 Topps Inception Silver Signings

STATED ODDS 1:xx HOBBY
PRINT RUNS B/WN 30-100 COPIES PER
EXCHANGE DEADLINE 2/28/2023
SSAB Alec Bohm/100 200.00 500.00
SSAG Andres Gimenez/100 50.00 120.00
SSAK Alex Kirilloff/100 30.00 80.00
SSBD Bobby Dalbec/100 100.00 250.00
SSBG Bryan Garcia/100 6.00 15.00
SSBS Brady Singer/100 15.00 40.00
SSCH Codi Heuer/100 20.00 50.00
SSCJ Cristian Javier/100 20.00 50.00
SSCM Casey Mize/100 40.00 100.00
SSDC Dylan Carlson/50 75.00 200.00
SSDG Deivi Garcia/100 50.00 125.00
SSDJ Daniel Johnson/100 10.00 25.00
SSDW Nick Heath/100 25.00 60.00
SSEJ Eloy Jimenez/30 50.00 120.00
SSEO Edward Olivares/100 15.00 40.00
SSEW Evan White/100 20.00 50.00
SSGL Gavin Lux/100 50.00 120.00
SSIA Ian Anderson/100 50.00 120.00
SSJA Jo Adell/50 100.00 250.00
SSJB Joey Bart/50 30.00 80.00
SSJC Jazz Chisholm/100 40.00 100.00
SSJS David Peterson/100 30.00 80.00
SSKH Keston Hiura/50 12.00 30.00
SSKW Kodi Whitley/100 10.00 25.00
SSLC Luis Campusano/100 10.00 25.00
SSLG Luis Garcia/64 30.00 80.00
SSLT Leody Taveras/100 20.00 50.00
SSNH Nico Hoerner/100 25.00 60.00
SSNM Nick Madrigal/100 50.00 125.00
SSNP Nate Pearson/100 25.00 60.00
SSRJ Ryan Jeffers/100 20.00 50.00
SSRM Ryan Mountcastle/100 30.00 80.00
SSSE Santiago Espinal/100 10.00 25.00
SSSH Spencer Howard/50 10.00 25.00
SSTH Tanner Houck/100 10.00 25.00
SSTS Tyler Stephenson/100 40.00 100.00
SSWC William Contreras/100 30.00 80.00
SSYA Yordan Alvarez/30
SSJSA Jesus Sanchez/100 20.00 50.00
SSKBH Ke'Bryan Hayes/50 125.00 300.00
SSSSA Sixto Sanchez/100 100.00 250.00
SSTMC Triston McKenzie/100 50.00 120.00

2021 Topps Inception Silver Signings Gold Ink

*GOLD INK/25: .5X TO 1.2X BASIC
STATED ODDS 1:xx HOBBY
STATED PRINT RUN 25 SER.#'d SETS
EXCHANGE DEADLINE 2/28/2023
SSCM Casey Mize 125.00 300.00
SSJB Joey Bart 75.00 200.00
SSNM Nick Madrigal 75.00 200.00

2007 Topps Jumbo Promos

1 David Ortiz 1.00 2.50
2 David Wright .75 2.00
3 Ryan Howard .75 2.00

1996 Topps Laser

The 1996 Topps Laser contains 128 regular cards that are found on one of four perfected designs. Every card is etch foil-stamped and laser-cut. The four-card packs retailed for $5.00 each.

COMPLETE SET (128) 15.00 40.00
COMPLETE SERIES 1 (64) 8.00 20.00
COMPLETE SERIES 2 (64) 8.00 20.00
1 Moises Alou .40 1.00
2 Derek Bell .40 1.00
3 Joe Carter .40 1.00
4 Jeff Conine .40 1.00
5 Darren Daulton .40 1.00
6 Jim Edmonds .40 1.00
7 Ron Gant .40 1.00
8 Juan Gonzalez .40 1.00
9 Brian Jordan .40 1.00
10 Ryan Klesko .40 1.00
11 Paul Molitor .40 1.00
12 Tony Phillips .40 1.00
13 Manny Ramirez .60 1.50
14 Sammy Sosa 1.00 2.50
15 Devon White .40 1.00
16 Bernie Williams .60 1.50
17 Garrett Anderson .40 1.00
18 Jay Bell .40 1.00
19 Craig Biggio .60 1.50
20 Bobby Bonilla .40 1.00
21 Ken Caminiti .40 1.00
22 Shawon Dunston .40 1.00
23 Mark Grace .60 1.50
24 Gregg Jefferies .40 1.00
25 Jeff King .40 1.00
26 Javy Lopez .40 1.00
27 Edgar Martinez .60 1.50
28 Dean Palmer .40 1.00
29 J.T. Snow .40 1.00
30 Mike Stanley .40 1.00
31 Terry Steinbach .40 1.00
32 Robin Ventura .40 1.00
33 Roberto Alomar .60 1.50
34 Jeff Bagwell .60 1.50
35 Dante Bichette .40 1.00
36 Wade Boggs .60 1.50
37 Barry Bonds 2.50 6.00
38 Jose Canseco .60 1.50
39 Vinny Castilla .40 1.00
40 Will Clark .60 1.50
41 Marty Cordova .40 1.00
42 Ken Griffey Jr. 2.00 5.00
43 Tony Gwynn 1.25 3.00
44 Rickey Henderson 1.00 2.50
45 Chipper Jones 1.00 2.50
46 Mark McGwire 2.50 6.00
47 Brian McRae .40 1.00
48 Ryne Sandberg 1.50 4.00
49 Andy Ashby .40 1.00
50 Alan Benes .40 1.00
51 Andy Benes .40 1.00
52 Roger Clemens 2.00 5.00
53 Doug Drabek .40 1.00
54 Dennis Eckersley .40 1.00
55 Tom Glavine .60 1.50
56 Randy Johnson 1.00 2.50
57 Mark Langston .40 1.00
58 Denny Martinez .40 1.00
59 Jack McDowell .40 1.00
60 Hideo Nomo 1.00 2.50
61 Shane Reynolds .40 1.00
62 John Smoltz .60 1.50
63 Paul Wilson .40 1.00
64 Mark Wohlers .40 1.00
65 Shawn Green .40 1.00
66 Marquis Grissom .40 1.00
67 Dave Hollins .40 1.00
68 Todd Hundley .40 1.00
69 David Justice .40 1.00
70 Eric Karros .40 1.00
71 Ray Lankford .40 1.00
72 Fred McGriff .60 1.50
73 Hal Morris .40 1.00
74 Eddie Murray 1.00 2.50
75 Paul O'Neill .60 1.50
76 Rey Ordonez .40 1.00
77 Reggie Sanders .40 1.00
78 Gary Sheffield .40 1.00
79 Jim Thome .60 1.50
80 Rondell White .40 1.00
81 Travis Fryman .40 1.00
82 Derek Jeter 2.50 6.00
83 Chuck Knoblauch .40 1.00
84 Barry Larkin .60 1.50
85 Tino Martinez .60 1.50
86 Raul Mondesi .40 1.00
87 John Olerud .40 1.00
88 Rafael Palmeiro .60 1.50
89 Mike Piazza 1.50 4.00
90 Cal Ripken 3.00 8.00
91 Ivan Rodriguez .60 1.50
92 Frank Thomas 1.00 2.50
93 John Valentin .40 1.00
94 Mo Vaughn .40 1.00
95 Quilvio Veras .40 1.00
96 Matt Williams .40 1.00
97 Brady Anderson .40 1.00
98 Carlos Baerga .40 1.00
99 Albert Belle .40 1.00
100 Jay Buhner .40 1.00
101 Johnny Damon .60 1.50
102 Chili Davis .40 1.00
103 Ray Durham .40 1.00
104 Len Dykstra .40 1.00
105 Cecil Fielder .40 1.00
106 Andres Galarraga .40 1.00
107 Brian L.Hunter .40 1.00
108 Kenny Lofton .40 1.00
109 Kirby Puckett 1.00 2.50
110 Tim Salmon .60 1.50
111 Greg Vaughn .40 1.00
112 Larry Walker .40 1.00
113 Rick Aguilera .40 1.00
114 Kevin Appier .40 1.00
115 Kevin Brown .40 1.00
116 David Cone .40 1.00
117 Alex Fernandez .40 1.00
118 Chuck Finley .40 1.00
119 Joey Hamilton .40 1.00
120 Jason Isringhausen .40 1.00
121 Greg Maddux 1.50 4.00
122 Pedro Martinez .60 1.50
123 Jose Mesa .40 1.00
124 Jeff Montgomery .40 1.00
125 Mike Mussina .60 1.50
126 Randy Myers .40 1.00
127 Kenny Rogers .40 1.00
128 Ismael Valdes .40 1.00

1996 Topps Laser Bright Spots

COMPLETE SET (16) 25.00 60.00
COMPLETE SERIES 1 (8) 10.00 25.00
COMPLETE SERIES 2 (8) 15.00 40.00
STATED ODDS 1:20
1 Brian L.Hunter .75 2.00
2 Derek Jeter 8.00 20.00
3 Jason Kendall .75 2.00
4 Brooks Kieschnick .75 2.00
5 Rey Ordonez .75 2.00
6 Jason Schmidt .75 2.00
7 Chris Snopek .75 2.00
8 Bob Wolcott .75 2.00
9 Alan Benes .75 2.00
10 Marty Cordova .75 2.00
11 Jimmy Haynes .75 2.00
12 Todd Hollandsworth .75 2.00
13 Derek Jeter 5.00 12.00
14 Chipper Jones 2.00 5.00
15 Hideo Nomo 2.00 5.00
16 Paul Wilson .75 2.00

1996 Topps Laser Power Cuts

COMPLETE SET (16) 25.00 60.00
COMPLETE SERIES 1 (8) 10.00 25.00
COMPLETE SERIES 2 (8) 12.50 30.00
STATED ODDS 1:40
1 Albert Belle .75 2.00
2 Jay Buhner .75 2.00
3 Fred McGriff 1.25 3.00
4 Mike Piazza 3.00 8.00
5 Tim Salmon 1.25 3.00
6 Frank Thomas 2.00 5.00
7 Mo Vaughn .75 2.00
8 Matt Williams .75 2.00
9 Jeff Bagwell 1.25 3.00
10 Barry Bonds 5.00 12.00
11 Jose Canseco 1.25 3.00
12 Cecil Fielder .75 2.00
13 Juan Gonzalez .75 2.00
14 Ken Griffey Jr. 4.00 10.00
15 Sammy Sosa 2.00 5.00
16 Larry Walker .75 2.00

1996 Topps Laser Stadium Stars

COMPLETE SET (16) 75.00 150.00
COMPLETE SERIES 1 (8) 30.00 80.00
COMPLETE SERIES 2 (8) 25.00 60.00
STATED ODDS 1:60
1 Carlos Baerga 1.25 3.00
2 Barry Bonds 8.00 20.00
3 Andres Galarraga 1.25 3.00
4 Ken Griffey Jr. 6.00 15.00
5 Barry Larkin 2.00 5.00
6 Raul Mondesi 1.25 3.00
7 Kirby Puckett 3.00 8.00
8 Cal Ripken 10.00 25.00
9 Will Clark 2.00 5.00
10 Roger Clemens 6.00 15.00
11 Tony Gwynn 4.00 10.00
12 Randy Johnson 3.00 8.00
13 Kenny Lofton 1.25 3.00
14 Edgar Martinez 2.00 5.00
15 Ryne Sandberg 5.00 12.00
16 Frank Thomas 8.00 20.00

2016 Topps Legacies of Baseball Vault Metals

RANDOM INSERTS IN PACKS
STATED PRINT RUN 135 SER.#'d SETS
VM1 Wade Boggs 6.00 15.00
VM2 Alex Rodriguez 6.00 15.00
VM3 Roberto Alomar 4.00 10.00
VM4 Sparky Anderson 4.00 10.00
VM5 Adrian Beltre 5.00 12.00
VM6 Johnny Bench 8.00 20.00
VM7 Craig Biggio 4.00 10.00
VM8 Bert Blyleven 4.00 10.00
VM9 George Brett 12.00 30.00
VM10 Lou Brock 6.00 15.00
VM11 Rod Carew 4.00 10.00
VM12 Gary Carter 6.00 15.00
VM13 Orlando Cepeda 6.00 15.00
VM14 Rollie Fingers 4.00 10.00
VM15 Carlton Fisk 10.00 25.00
VM16 Frank Robinson 8.00 20.00
VM17 Adrian Gonzalez 4.00 10.00
VM18 Dwight Gooden 3.00 8.00
VM19 Goose Gossage 10.00 25.00
VM20 Shawn Green 3.00 8.00
VM21 Catfish Hunter 6.00 15.00
VM22 Reggie Jackson 4.00 10.00
VM23 Fergie Jenkins 4.00 10.00
VM24 Randy Johnson 5.00 12.00
VM25 Al Kaline 12.00 30.00
VM26 Eric Karros 3.00 8.00
VM27 Barry Larkin 4.00 10.00
VM28 Tommy Lasorda 4.00 10.00
VM29 Willie Mays 10.00 25.00
VM30 Bill Mazeroski 6.00 15.00
VM31 Willie McCovey 6.00 15.00
VM32 Joe Morgan 4.00 10.00
VM33 Phil Niekro 6.00 15.00
VM34 Jim Palmer 4.00 10.00
VM35 Tony Perez 12.00 30.00
VM36 Cal Ripken Jr. 10.00 25.00
VM37 Nolan Ryan 15.00 40.00
VM38 Tom Seaver 6.00 15.00
VM39 Gary Sheffield 3.00 8.00
VM40 Ozzie Smith 10.00 25.00
VM41 Willie Stargell 6.00 15.00
VM42 Kent Tekulve 3.00 8.00
VM43 Earl Weaver 8.00 20.00
VM44 Bernie Williams 4.00 10.00
VM45 Billy Williams 4.00 10.00
VM46 Stan Musial 8.00 20.00
VM47 Felix Hernandez 4.00 10.00
VM48 Mike Trout 20.00 50.00
VM49 Kyle Schwarber 10.00 25.00
VM50 Bryce Harper 15.00 40.00

2016 Topps Legacies of Baseball Vault Metals Purple Logo

*PURPLE: .5X TO 1.2X BASIC
STATED ODDS 1:4 MINI BOXES
STATED PRINT RUN 50 SER.#'d SETS

2016 Topps Legacies of Baseball Exhilaration Autographs

RANDOM INSERTS IN PACKS
PRINT RUNS B/WN 54-199 COPIES PER
EXCHANGE DEADLINE 3/31/2018
EAAN Aaron Nola/199 8.00 20.00
EAAP A.J. Pollock/199 6.00 15.00
EABS Blake Swihart/199 5.00 12.00
EACS Corey Seager/199 30.00 80.00
EAFL Francisco Lindor/199 20.00 50.00
EAHO Henry Owens/199 5.00 12.00
EAHOL Hector Olivera/199 5.00 12.00
EAJD Jacob deGrom/199 15.00 40.00
EAKS Kyle Schwarber/199 20.00 50.00
EAKW Kolten Wong/199 5.00 12.00
EALS Luis Severino/199 5.00 12.00
EAMS Miguel Sano/199 6.00 15.00
EAMT Mike Trout/54 200.00 500.00
EASP Stephen Piscotty/199 4.00 10.00

2016 Topps Legacies of Baseball Exhilaration Autographs Green

*GREEN: .5X TO 1.2X BASIC
STATED ODDS 1:7 BOXES
STATED PRINT RUN 99 SER.#'d SETS
EXCHANGE DEADLINE 3/31/2018
EAKB Kris Bryant 100.00 200.00

2016 Topps Legacies of Baseball Exhilaration Autographs Purple

*PURPLE: .6X TO 1.5X BASIC
STATED ODDS 1:12 BOXES
STATED PRINT RUN 50 SER.#'d SETS
EXCHANGE DEADLINE 3/31/2018
EACC Carlos Correa EXCH 100.00 200.00
EAKB Kris Bryant 125.00 250.00
EAMT Mike Trout 200.00 500.00

2016 Topps Legacies of Baseball Imminent Arrivals

STATED ODDS 1:14 MINI BOXES
STATED PRINT RUN 70 SER.#'d SETS
*PURPLE/50: .5X TO 1.2X BASIC
IAAN Aaron Nola 6.00 15.00
IACS Corey Seager 25.00 60.00
IAHO Henry Owens 4.00 10.00
IAHOL Hector Olivera 4.00 10.00
IAJG Jon Gray 3.00 8.00
IAKS Kyle Schwarber 4.00 10.00
IALS Luis Severino 4.00 10.00
IAMC Michael Conforto 4.00 10.00
IAMS Miguel Sano 5.00 12.00
IASP Stephen Piscotty 10.00 25.00

2016 Topps Legacies of Baseball Imminent Arrivals Autographs

STATED ODDS 1:19 BOXES
STATED PRINT RUN 99 SER.#'d SETS
EXCHANGE DEADLINE 3/31/2018
IAAN Aaron Nola 12.00 30.00
IACS Corey Seager 20.00 50.00
IAHO Henry Owens 8.00 20.00
IAHOL Hector Olivera 12.00 30.00
IAKM Kenta Maeda EXCH 12.00 30.00
IAKS Kyle Schwarber 10.00 25.00
IALS Luis Severino 8.00 20.00
IAMS Miguel Sano 8.00 20.00

2016 Topps Legacies of Baseball Lasting Imprints

RANDOM INSERTS IN BOXES
STATED PRINT RUN 99 SER.#'d SETS
*PURPLE/50: .4X TO 1X BASIC
LII Ichiro 10.00 25.00
LIAK Al Kaline 3.00 8.00
LIBL Barry Larkin 6.00 15.00
LIBP Buster Posey 4.00 10.00
LIBR Babe Ruth 6.00 15.00
LIBRO Brooks Robinson 6.00 15.00
LICB Craig Biggio 2.50 6.00
LICF Carlton Fisk 2.50 6.00
LICJ Chipper Jones 10.00 25.00
LICK Clayton Kershaw 5.00 12.00
LICR Cal Ripken Jr. 10.00 25.00
LIDE Dennis Eckersley 2.50 6.00
LIDM Don Mattingly 6.00 15.00
LIDO David Ortiz 3.00 8.00
LIDS Duke Snider 2.50 6.00
LIEM Edgar Martinez 2.50 6.00
LIFJ Fergie Jenkins 2.50 6.00
LIFR Frank Robinson 2.50 6.00
LIFT Frank Thomas 10.00 25.00
LIGB George Brett 6.00 15.00
LIGC Gary Carter 2.50 6.00
LIGM Greg Maddux 4.00 10.00
LIHA Hank Aaron 6.00 15.00
LIHK Harmon Killebrew 10.00 25.00
LIHW Honus Wagner 3.00 8.00
LIJB Johnny Bench 3.00 8.00
LIJM Juan Marichal 2.50 6.00
LIJP Jim Palmer 2.50 6.00
LIJR Jim Rice 2.50 6.00
LIJRO Jackie Robinson 3.00 8.00
LIJS John Smoltz 3.00 8.00
LIKB Kris Bryant 4.00 10.00
LIKG Ken Griffey Jr. 6.00 15.00
LILB Lou Brock 2.50 6.00
LILG Lou Gehrig 6.00 15.00
LIMM Mark McGwire 5.00 12.00
LIMR Mariano Rivera 4.00 10.00
LIMS Max Scherzer 3.00 8.00
LIMT Mike Trout 15.00 40.00
LINR Nolan Ryan 10.00 25.00
LIOS Ozzie Smith 4.00 10.00
LIRA Roberto Alomar 2.50 6.00
LIRC Rod Carew 2.50 6.00
LIRCL Roger Clemens 4.00 10.00
LIRH Rickey Henderson 3.00 8.00
LIRJ Randy Johnson 3.00 8.00
LIRK Ralph Kiner 2.50 6.00
LIRS Ryne Sandberg 6.00 15.00
LIRY Robin Yount 3.00 8.00
LISK Sandy Koufax 8.00 20.00
LITS Tom Seaver 2.50 6.00
LITW Ted Williams 15.00 40.00
LIWB Wade Boggs 6.00 15.00
LIWM Willie Mays 6.00 15.00
LIWMC Willie McCovey 8.00 20.00
LIWS Warren Spahn 2.50 6.00

2016 Topps Legacies of Baseball Lasting Imprints Autographs

STATED ODDS 1:15 BOXES
STATED PRINT RUN 25 SER.#'d SETS
EXCHANGE DEADLINE 3/31/2018
LII Ichiro 200.00 400.00
LIAK Al Kaline 25.00 50.00
LIBL Barry Larkin 20.00 50.00
LICB Craig Biggio
LICF Carlton Fisk EXCH 15.00 40.00
LICJ Chipper Jones
LICK Clayton Kershaw
LICR Cal Ripken Jr. 125.00 250.00
LIDE Dennis Eckersley 15.00 40.00
LIDO David Ortiz 40.00 100.00
LIEM Edgar Martinez 25.00 60.00
LIFR Frank Robinson 25.00 60.00
LIFT Frank Thomas EXCH 50.00 120.00
LIGM Greg Maddux
LIHA Hank Aaron
LIJB Johnny Bench 40.00 100.00
LIJR Jim Rice 15.00 40.00
LIJS John Smoltz 40.00 100.00
LIKB Kris Bryant 150.00 300.00
LIMM Mark McGwire 50.00 120.00
LIMT Mike Trout 200.00 300.00
LINR Nolan Ryan 125.00 250.00
LIOS Ozzie Smith 25.00 60.00
LIRC Rod Carew 20.00 50.00
LIRJ Randy Johnson 50.00 120.00
LISK Sandy Koufax EXCH 150.00 300.00
LIWB Wade Boggs EXCH 30.00 80.00

2016 Topps Legacies of Baseball Loyalty Autographs

RANDOM INSERTS IN PACKS
PRINT RUNS B/WN 40-199 COPIES PER
EXCHANGE DEADLINE 3/31/2018
LAAK Al Kaline/199 12.00 30.00
LABP Brandon Phillips/199 6.00 15.00
LABW Bernie Williams/199 10.00 25.00
LACB Craig Biggio/199 12.00 30.00
LACRJ Cal Ripken Jr./40 125.00 250.00
LAEM Edgar Martinez/199 6.00 15.00
LAJB Johnny Bench/75 30.00 80.00
LAJBA Jeff Bagwell/199 15.00 40.00
LAJG Juan Gonzalez/199 6.00 15.00
LAJR Jim Rice/199 6.00 15.00
LAJS John Smoltz/199 10.00 25.00
LAMC Matt Carpenter/199 8.00 20.00
LAMP Mark Prior/199 5.00 12.00
LAOS Ozzie Smith/199 15.00 40.00
LARB Ryan Braun/199 6.00 15.00
LATG Tom Glavine/199 12.00 30.00

2016 Topps Legacies of Baseball Loyalty Autographs Green

*GREEN: .5X TO 1.2X BASIC
STATED ODDS 1:12 BOXES
STATED PRINT RUN 99 SER.#'d SETS
EXCHANGE DEADLINE 3/31/2018
LABL Barry Larkin 20.00 50.00

2016 Topps Legacies of Baseball Loyalty Autographs Purple

*PURPLE: .6X TO 1.5X BASIC
STATED ODDS 1:16 BOXES
STATED PRINT RUN 50 SER.#'d SETS
EXCHANGE DEADLINE 3/31/2018
LABL Barry Larkin 25.00 60.00
LACJ Chipper Jones 50.00 120.00

2016 Topps Legacies of Baseball Tenacity Autographs

RANDOM INSERTS IN PACKS
PRINT RUNS B/WN 70-199 COPIES PER
EXCHANGE DEADLINE 3/31/2018
TAAJ Andruw Jones/199 4.00 10.00
TABJ Bo Jackson/70 40.00 100.00
TACS Chris Sale/199 10.00 25.00
TADE Dennis Eckersley/199 6.00 15.00
TAJA Jose Altuve/199 25.00 60.00
TAJB Jeff Bagwell/178 20.00 50.00
TAJC Jose Canseco/199 10.00 25.00
TAJD Jacob deGrom/199 15.00 40.00
TAJP Joc Pederson/199 3.00 8.00
TAMM Mark McGwire/70 50.00 120.00
TAOV Omar Vizquel/199 5.00 12.00
TAPO Paul O'Neill/199 5.00 12.00
TAYD Yu Darvish EXCH 40.00 100.00

2016 Topps Legacies of Baseball Tenacity Autographs Green

*GREEN: .5X TO 1.2X BASIC
STATED ODDS 1:10 BOXES
STATED PRINT RUN 99 SER.#'d SETS
EXCHANGE DEADLINE 3/31/2018

2016 Topps Legacies of Baseball Tenacity Autographs Purple

*PURPLE: .6X TO 1.5X BASIC
STATED ODDS 1:18 BOXES
STATED PRINT RUN 50 SER.#'d SETS
EXCHANGE DEADLINE 3/31/2018

2016 Topps Legacies of Baseball Tradition Autographs

RANDOM INSERTS IN PACKS
STATED PRINT RUN 199 SER.#'d SETS
EXCHANGE DEADLINE 3/31/2018
TRAI Ichiro/20 250.00 350.00
TRAAG Andres Galarraga/199 10.00 25.00
TRAAK Al Kaline/199 15.00 40.00
TRACR Cal Ripken Jr./50 50.00 120.00
TRADE Dennis Eckersley/199 6.00 15.00
TRAEM Edgar Martinez/199 8.00 20.00
TRAHA Hank Aaron/50 150.00 300.00
TRAJA Jose Altuve/199 12.00 30.00
TRAJS John Smoltz/199 12.00 30.00
TRAMG Mark Grace/199 10.00 25.00
TRAMP Buster Posey/50 40.00 100.00
TRAOS Ozzie Smith/199 15.00 40.00
TRAOV Omar Vizquel/199 10.00 25.00
TRARC Rod Carew/92 12.00 30.00
TRARF Rollie Fingers/199 6.00 15.00
TRASG Sonny Gray/199 5.00 12.00
TRASK Sandy Koufax/40 150.00 250.00

2016 Topps Legacies of Baseball Tradition Autographs Green

*GREEN: .5X TO 1.2X BASIC
STATED ODDS 1:8 BOXES
STATED PRINT RUN 99 SER.#'d SETS
EXCHANGE DEADLINE 3/31/2018
TRAKB Kris Bryant 75.00 200.00
TRAPM Paul Molitor 10.00 25.00
TRATG Tom Glavine 12.00 30.00

2016 Topps Legacies of Baseball Tradition Autographs Purple

*PURPLE: .6X TO 1.5X BASIC
STATED ODDS 1:15 BOXES
STATED PRINT RUN 50 SER.#'d SETS
EXCHANGE DEADLINE 3/31/2018
TRAKB Kris Bryant 100.00 250.00
TRAPM Paul Molitor 12.00 30.00
TRATG Tom Glavine 15.00 40.00

2017 Topps Limited

*LTD: .1.5X TO 4X BASIC
LTD RC: 1X TO 2.5X BASIC RC
ANNCD PRINT RUN OF 1000

2011 Topps Lineage

COMPLETE SET (200) 15.00 40.00
COMMON CARD (1-200) .12 .30
COMMON ROOKIE (1-200) .25 .60
PRINTING PLATE ODDS 1:925 HOBBY
PLATE PRINT RUN 1 SET PER COLOR
BLACK-CYAN-MAGENTA-YELLOW ISSUED
NO PLATE PRICING DUE TO SCARCITY
1 Sandy Koufax .60 1.50
2 Derek Jeter .75 2.00
3 Jimmie Foxx .30 .75
4 Buster Posey .40 1.00
5 Felix Hernandez .20 .50
6 Carlos Beltran .20 .50
7 Mickey Mantle 1.00 2.50
8 Francisco Liriano .12 .30
9 Matt Holliday .30 .75
10 Jim Palmer .20 .50
11 Ryan Zimmerman .20 .50
12 Elvis Andrus .20 .50
13 Cal Ripken Jr. 1.00 2.50
14 Kendry Morales .12 .30
15 Curtis Granderson .25 .60
16 Walter Johnson .30 .75
17 Billy Butler .12 .30
18 Brett Anderson .12 .30
19 Larry Walker .20 .50
20 Justin Morneau .20 .50
21 Edinson Volquez .12 .30
22 Johan Santana .20 .50
23 Carlos Zambrano .20 .50
24 Tsuyoshi Nishioka RC .75 2.00
25 Whitey Ford .20 .50
26 Grady Sizemore .20 .50
27 George Sisler .20 .50
28 Aramis Ramirez .12 .30
29 Chris Sale RC 2.00 5.00
30 Chase Utley .20 .50
31 Jeremy Hellickson RC .60 1.50
32 Jon Lester .20 .50
33 Tony Perez .20 .50
34 Kyle Drabek RC .40 1.00
35 Hanley Ramirez .20 .50
36 Michael Young .12 .30
37 Justin Upton .20 .50
38 Chris Carpenter .20 .50
39 Ricky Romero .12 .30
40 Stan Musial .50 1.25
41 Vladimir Guerrero .20 .50
42 Jackie Robinson .30 .75
43 Victor Martinez .20 .50
44 Jay Bruce .20 .50
45 Ryan Howard .25 .60
46 Logan Morrison .12 .30
47 Lance Berkman .20 .50
48 Carlton Fisk .20 .50
49 Matt Kemp .25 .60
50 Lou Gehrig .60 1.50
51 Hunter Pence .20 .50
52 Andre Dawson .20 .50
53 Mike Schmidt .50 1.25
54 Alfonso Soriano .20 .50
55 Nolan Ryan 1.00 2.50
56 Shane Victorino .20 .50
57 Willie McCovey .20 .50
58 Gordon Beckham .12 .30
59 Duke Snider .20 .50
60 Reggie Jackson .20 .50
61 Zach Britton RC .60 1.50
62 Adrian Beltre .30 .75
63 Ubaldo Jimenez .12 .30
64 Joe Morgan .20 .50
65 Josh Johnson .20 .50
66 Andrew McCutchen .30 .75
67 Nelson Cruz .30 .75
68 Alexei Ramirez .20 .50
69 Jayson Werth .20 .50
70 Carlos Santana .30 .75
71 Kurt Suzuki .12 .30
72 Rickie Weeks .12 .30
73 Kosuke Fukudome .20 .50
74 Brooks Robinson .20 .50
75 Alex Rodriguez .40 1.00
76 Roberto Alomar .20 .50
77 David Wright .25 .60
78 Dan Uggla .12 .30
79 Carl Crawford .20 .50
80 Troy Tulowitzki .30 .75
81 Andruw Jones .12 .30
82 Ike Davis .12 .30
83 Adam Wainwright .20 .50
84 Clayton Kershaw .50 1.25
85 Al Kaline .30 .75
86 Carlos Gonzalez .20 .50
87 David Ortiz .30 .75
88 David Price .25 .60
89 Eddie Murray .20 .50
90 Tris Speaker .20 .50
91 Brent Morel RC .25 .60
92 Clay Buchholz .12 .30
93 Roy Oswalt .20 .50
94 John Smoltz .30 .75
95 Johnny Mize .20 .50
96 Jason Bay .20 .50
97 Aaron Hill .12 .30
98 Evan Longoria .20 .50
99 Honus Wagner .30 .75
100 Babe Ruth .75 2.00
101 Madison Bumgarner .25 .60
102 Cole Hamels .25 .60
103 Joey Votto .30 .75
104 Miguel Montero .12 .30
105 Ty Cobb .50 1.25
106 Cy Young .30 .75
107 Chad Billingsley .20 .50
108 Hank Aaron .60 1.50
109 Mat Latos .20 .50
110 Thurman Munson .30 .75
111 Neil Walker .20 .50
112 Johnny Cueto .20 .50
113 Trevor Cahill .12 .30
114 Dustin Pedroia .30 .75
115 Chipper Jones .30 .75
116 Pedro Alvarez RC .25 .60
117 Torii Hunter .12 .30
118 Todd Helton .20 .50
119 Matt Cain .20 .50
120 Ichiro Suzuki .40 1.00
121 Roy Halladay .20 .50
122 Paul O'Neill .20 .50
123 Andre Ethier .20 .50
124 Franklin Gutierrez .12 .30
125 Mark Teixeira .20 .50
126 Shin-Soo Choo .20 .50
127 Orlando Hudson .12 .30
128 Vernon Wells .12 .30
129 Jason Heyward .25 .60
130 Joe Mauer .25 .60
131 Carlos Lee .12 .30
132 Nick Markakis .25 .60
133 Zack Greinke .30 .75
134 John Danks .12 .30
135 Tim Lincecum .20 .50
136 Starlin Castro .20 .50
137 Johnny Bench .30 .75
138 Prince Fielder .20 .50
139 Michael Pineda RC .60 1.50
140 Albert Belle .12 .30
141 Ozzie Smith .40 1.00
142 Dan Haren .12 .30
143 Miguel Cabrera .30 .75
144 Roy Campanella .30 .75
145 Adrian Gonzalez .25 .60
146 Freddie Freeman RC 4.00 10.00
147 Ryan Braun .20 .50
148 Aroldis Chapman RC .75 2.00
149 Kevin Youkilis .12 .30
150 Robinson Cano .20 .50
151 Johnny Damon .20 .50
152 David DeJesus .12 .30

153 B.J. Upton .20 .50
154 Fergie Jenkins .20 .50
155 Bob Gibson .20 .50
156 Austin Jackson .12 .30
157 Wandy Rodriguez .12 .30
158 Monte Irvin .20 .50
159 Yonder Alonso RC .40 1.00
160 Stephen Strasburg .30 .75
161 Luis Aparicio .20 .50
162 Brandon Belt RC .60 1.50
163 Jered Weaver .20 .50
164 Brandon Beachy RC .60 1.50
165 Jose Reyes .20 .50
166 Yovani Gallardo .12 .30
167 Corey Hart .12 .30
168 Delmon Young .20 .50
169 Cliff Lee .20 .50
170 Tom Seaver .20 .50
171 Ryne Sandberg .60 1.50
172 Jose Bautista .20 .50
173 Adam Dunn .20 .50
174 Adam Jones .20 .50
175 CC Sabathia .20 .50
176 Miguel Tejada .20 .50
177 Phil Hughes .12 .30
178 Albert Pujols .40 1.00
179 Jake McGee (RC) .50 1.25
180 Marlon Byrd .12 .30
181 Frank Thomas .30 .75
182 Frank Robinson .20 .50
183 Brian McCann .20 .50
184 Josh Hamilton .20 .50
185 Ian Kinsler .20 .50
186 Mel Ott .30 .75
187 Justin Verlander .30 .75
188 Daniel Hudson .12 .30
189 Jaime Garcia .20 .50
190 Bert Blyleven .20 .50
191 Johnny Bench .30 .75
192 Willie McCovey .20 .50
193 Joe Morgan .20 .50
194 Cal Ripken Jr 1.00 2.50
195 Chipper Jones .30 .75
196 Ichiro Suzuki .40 1.00
197 Andre Dawson .20 .50
198 Andruw Jones .12 .30
199 CC Sabathia .20 .50
200 Tom Seaver .20 .50

2011 Topps Lineage Diamond Anniversary Refractors

*VET REF: 1.5X TO 4X BASIC
*RC REF: .75X TO 2X BASIC
STATED ODDS 1:4 HOBBY

2011 Topps Lineage Diamond Anniversary Platinum Refractors

*VET PLAT.REF: 1.5X TO 4X BASIC
*RC PLAT.REF: .75X TO 2X BASIC
STATED ODDS 1:4 HOBBY

2011 Topps Lineage '52 Autographs

GROUP A ODDS 1:38 HOBBY
GROUP B ODDS 1:131 HOBBY
GROUP D ODDS 1:327 HOBBY
GROUP C ODDS 1:397 HOBBY
GOLD CANARY ODDS 1:771 HOBBY
GOLD CANARY PRINT RUN 10 SER.#'d SETS
NO GOLD CANARY PRICING AVAILABLE
EXCHANGE DEADLINE 7/31/2014
52ABL Brandon League 3.00 8.00
52ABP Buster Posey 25.00 60.00
52ACB Clay Buchholz 5.00 12.00
52ACM Charlie Morton 6.00 15.00
52ADD David DeJesus 3.00 8.00
52AFF Freddie Freeman 25.00 60.00
52AFR Fernando Rodney 3.00 8.00
52AGS Gaby Sanchez 5.00 12.00
52AID Ike Davis 8.00 20.00
52AJB John Buck 3.00 8.00
52AJG Jonny Gomes 5.00 12.00
52AJM Jason Motte 3.00 8.00
52ALM Logan Morrison 6.00 15.00
52AMB Madison Bumgarner 30.00 80.00
52AMH Matt Harrison 3.00 8.00
52AMM Michael Morse 5.00 12.00
52AMS Mike Stanton 40.00 100.00
52ARZ Ryan Zimmerman 3.00 8.00
52ASV Shane Victorino 6.00 15.00
52ATW Ty Wigginton 3.00 8.00
52AUJ Ubaldo Jimenez 3.00 8.00
52AMBY Marlon Byrd 4.00 10.00

2011 Topps Lineage '75 Mini

COMPLETE SET (200) 250.00 350.00
*MINI VET: 2X TO 5X BASIC
*MINI RC: 1X TO 2.5X BASIC RC
STATED ODDS 1:4 HOBBY

2011 Topps Lineage '75 Mini Relics

GROUP A ODDS 1:28 HOBBY
GROUP B ODDS 1:331 HOBBY
GROUP C ODDS 1:6500 HOBBY
GOLD CANARY ODDS 1:747 HOBBY
GOLD CANARY PRINT RUN 10 SER.#'d SETS
NO GOLD CANARY PRICING AVAILABLE
AB Adrian Beltre 4.00 10.00
ABE Albert Belle 1.50 4.00
AD Andre Dawson 6.00 15.00
ADU Adam Dunn 2.50 6.00
AE Andre Ethier 2.50 6.00
AJ Austin Jackson 1.50 4.00
AK Al Kaline 10.00 25.00
AM Andrew McCutchen 4.00 10.00
AP Albert Pujols 10.00 25.00
AR Aramis Ramirez 1.50 4.00
ARA Alexei Ramirez 2.50 6.00
ARO Alex Rodriguez 5.00 12.00
AS Alfonso Soriano 2.50 6.00
BG Bob Gibson 10.00 25.00
BMC Brian McCann 2.50 6.00
BP Buster Posey 5.00 12.00
BR Brooks Robinson 6.00 15.00
BRU Babe Ruth 75.00 200.00
BU B.J. Upton 2.50 6.00
CBU Clay Buchholz 1.50 4.00
CBE Carlos Beltran 2.50 6.00
CC Chris Carpenter 2.50 6.00
CCS CC Sabathia 2.50 6.00
CF Carlton Fisk 12.00 30.00
CGO Carlos Gonzalez 2.50 6.00
CJ Chipper Jones 4.00 10.00
CK Clayton Kershaw 6.00 15.00
CL Carlos Lee 1.50 4.00
CR Cal Ripken Jr. 6.00 15.00
DO David Ortiz 4.00 10.00
DP David Price 3.00 8.00
DPE Dustin Pedroia 4.00 10.00
DS Duke Snider 10.00 25.00
DU Dan Uggla 1.50 4.00
DW David Wright 3.00 8.00
EA Elvis Andrus 2.50 6.00
EL Evan Longoria 2.50 6.00
EM Eddie Murray 2.50 6.00
EV Edinson Volquez 1.50 4.00
FH Felix Hernandez 2.50 6.00
FJ Fergie Jenkins 6.00 15.00
FT Frank Thomas 20.00 50.00
GS Grady Sizemore 2.50 6.00
HA Hank Aaron 15.00 40.00
HW Honus Wagner 60.00 150.00
ID Ike Davis 1.50 4.00
IK Ian Kinsler 2.50 6.00
IS Ichiro Suzuki 5.00 12.00
JB Jay Bruce 2.50 6.00
JBA Jose Bautista 2.50 6.00
JBE Johnny Bench 6.00 15.00
JBY Jason Bay 2.50 6.00
JC Johnny Cueto 2.50 6.00
JH Jason Heyward 3.00 8.00
JJ Josh Johnson 2.50 6.00
JMA Joe Mauer 3.00 8.00
JMI Johnny Mize 10.00 25.00
JP Jim Palmer 2.50 6.00
JRE Jose Reyes 2.50 6.00
JSM John Smoltz 15.00 40.00
JU Justin Upton 2.50 6.00
JV Joey Votto 4.00 10.00
JVE Justin Verlander 4.00 10.00
JW Jayson Werth 2.50 6.00
JWE Jered Weaver 2.50 6.00
KF Kosuke Fukudome 2.50 6.00
KY Kevin Youkilis 1.50 4.00
MB Madison Bumgarner 3.00 8.00
MBY Marlon Byrd 1.50 4.00
MC Matt Cain 2.50 6.00
MCA Miguel Cabrera 4.00 10.00
MK Matt Kemp 3.00 8.00
MM Mickey Mantle 50.00 120.00
MO Mel Ott 20.00 50.00
MS Mike Schmidt 12.00 30.00
NC Nelson Cruz 4.00 10.00
NR Nolan Ryan 10.00 25.00
OS Ozzie Smith 5.00 12.00
PF Prince Fielder 2.50 6.00
RB Ryan Braun 2.50 6.00
RC Roy Campanella 6.00 15.00
RJ Reggie Jackson 6.00 15.00
RR Ricky Romero 1.50 4.00
RZ Ryan Zimmerman 2.50 6.00
SC Starlin Castro 2.50 6.00
SK Sandy Koufax 75.00 200.00
SM Stan Musial 10.00 25.00
SS Stephen Strasburg 10.00 25.00
SV Shane Victorino 2.50 6.00
TH Todd Helton 2.50 6.00
TL Tim Lincecum 2.50 6.00
TP Tony Perez 2.50 6.00
VM Victor Martinez 2.50 6.00
VW Vernon Wells 1.50 4.00
WF Whitey Ford 6.00 15.00
WM Willie McCovey 10.00 25.00
WM2 Willie McCovey Bat 10.00 25.00
WR Wandy Rodriguez 1.50 4.00
YG Yovani Gallardo 1.50 4.00

2011 Topps Lineage 3-D

COMPLETE SET (25) 30.00 60.00
STATED ODDS 1:12 HOBBY
*BLACK: 2.5X TO 6X BASIC
STATED BLACK ODDS 1:446 HOBBY
STATED RED ODDS 1:30,873 HOBBY
RED PRINT RUN 1 SER.#'d SET
BLACK PRINT RUN 99 SER.#'d SETS
NO RED PRICING DUE TO SCARCITY
T3D1 Ichiro Suzuki 2.00 5.00
T3D2 Buster Posey 2.00 5.00
T3D3 Ryan Howard 1.25 3.00
T3D4 Mark Teixeira 1.00 2.50
T3D5 Joe Mauer 1.25 3.00
T3D6 Ryan Braun 1.00 2.50
T3D7 Carlos Gonzalez 1.00 2.50
T3D8 Joey Votto 1.50 4.00
T3D9 Adrian Gonzalez 1.25 3.00
T3D10 Alex Rodriguez 2.00 5.00
T3D11 David Wright 1.25 3.00
T3D12 Carl Crawford 1.00 2.50
T3D13 Miguel Cabrera 1.50 4.00
T3D14 Chase Utley 1.00 2.50
T3D15 Evan Longoria 1.00 2.50
T3D16 Jason Heyward 1.25 3.00
T3D17 Kendry Morales .60 1.50
T3D18 Shin-Soo Choo 1.00 2.50
T3D19 Hanley Ramirez 1.00 2.50
T3D20 Josh Hamilton 1.00 2.50
T3D21 Justin Upton 1.00 2.50
T3D22 Troy Tulowitzki 1.50 4.00
T3D23 Hunter Pence 1.00 2.50
T3D24 Derek Jeter 4.00 10.00
T3D25 Albert Pujols 2.00 5.00

2011 Topps Lineage Autographs

GROUP A ODDS 1:38 HOBBY
GROUP B-C ODDS 1:131 HOBBY
GROUP D ODDS 1:1810 HOBBY
GOLD CANARY ODDS 1:771 HOBBY
GOLD CANARY PRINT RUN 10 SER.#'d SETS
NO GOLD CANARY PRICING AVAILABLE
EXCHANGE DEADLINE 7/31/2014
AD Al Dark 5.00 12.00
AK Al Kaline EXCH 15.00 40.00
AM Andrew McCutchen 15.00 40.00
AS Al Schoendienst 15.00 40.00
BA Bob Addis EXCH 8.00 20.00
BB Bob Borkowski 8.00 20.00
BD Bob Del Greco 8.00 20.00
BF Bob Friend 8.00 20.00
BK Bob Kelly 6.00 15.00
BK Bob Kuzava 6.00 15.00
BM Bobby Morgan 5.00 12.00
BMI Bob Miller 8.00 20.00
BP Billy Pierce 6.00 15.00
BS Bobby Shantz 6.00 15.00
CB Cloyd Boyer 6.00 15.00
CC Cliff Chambers 5.00 12.00
CD Chuck Diering 6.00 15.00
CS Charlie Silvera 6.00 15.00
CSI Curt Simmons 5.00 12.00
DC Del Crandall 6.00 15.00
DG Dick Groat 8.00 20.00
DGE Dick Gernert 5.00 12.00
DH Daniel Hudson 5.00 12.00
DL Don Lenhardt 6.00 15.00
DP Duane Pillette EXCH 6.00 15.00
EE Ed Erautt 8.00 20.00
ER Eddie Robinson 8.00 20.00
EY Eddie Yost 10.00 25.00
FC Fausto Carmona 5.00 12.00
FJ Fergie Jenkins 30.00 60.00
GC Gil Coan 5.00 12.00
GH Grady Hatton EXCH 5.00 12.00
GS George Spencer EXCH 6.00 15.00
GZ George Zuverink 6.00 15.00
HA Hank Aaron 200.00 400.00
HJ Howie Judson 6.00 15.00
HP Harry Perkowski EXCH 6.00 15.00
ID Ivan Delock 5.00 12.00
IK Ian Kinsler 5.00 12.00
IN Irv Noren 6.00 15.00
JA Joe Astroth 6.00 15.00
JAN John Antonelli 10.00 25.00
JC Jerry Coleman 4.00 10.00
JD Joe DeMaestri 6.00 15.00
JG Johnny Groth 8.00 20.00
JGA Joe Garagiola 20.00 50.00
JM Joe Morgan EXCH 30.00 60.00
JP Joe Presko 8.00 20.00
JS John Smoltz EXCH 40.00 80.00
LB Lou Brissie 6.00 15.00
LS Lou Sleater 6.00 15.00
MB Matt Batts 8.00 20.00
MG Myron Ginsberg EXCH 8.00 20.00
MI Monte Irvin 8.00 20.00
NG Ned Garver 5.00 12.00
NR Nolan Ryan EXCH 100.00 200.00
PS Pablo Sandoval 5.00 12.00
RA Roberto Alomar EXCH 30.00 60.00
RB Rocky Bridges EXCH 5.00 12.00
RBR Ralph Branca 80.00 60.00
RH1 Roy Halladay EXCH 60.00 120.00
RJ Randy Jackson 8.00 20.00
RS Roy Smalley 6.00 15.00
RSI Roy Sievers 8.00 20.00
SK Sandy Koufax 600.00 800.00
SMU Stan Musial 125.00 250.00
TBA Tony Bartirome 8.00 20.00
TL Ted Lepcio 6.00 15.00
VL Vern Law 5.00 12.00
VT Virgil Trucks 8.00 20.00
WT Wayne Terwilliger 6.00 15.00
WW Wally Westlake EXCH 20.00 50.00

2011 Topps Lineage Cloth Stickers

COMMON CARD .50 1.25
SEMISTARS .75 2.00
UNLISTED STARS 1.25 3.00
STATED ODDS 1:12 HOBBY
TCS1 Sandy Koufax 2.50 6.00
TCS2 Derek Jeter 3.00 8.00
TCS3 Buster Posey 1.50 4.00
TCS4 Felix Hernandez .75 2.00
TCS5 Mickey Mantle 4.00 10.00
TCS6 Cal Ripken Jr. 4.00 10.00
TCS7 Whitey Ford .75 2.00
TCS8 George Sisler .75 2.00
TCS9 Hanley Ramirez .75 2.00
TCS10 Stan Musial 2.00 5.00
TCS11 Jackie Robinson 1.25 3.00
TCS12 Ryan Howard 1.00 2.50
TCS13 Lou Gehrig 2.50 6.00
TCS14 Hunter Pence .75 2.00
TCS15 Mike Schmidt 2.00 5.00
TCS16 Nolan Ryan 4.00 10.00
TCS17 Duke Snider .75 2.00
TCS18 Reggie Jackson .75 2.00
TCS19 Alex Rodriguez 1.50 4.00
TCS20 David Wright 1.00 2.50
TCS21 Carl Crawford .75 2.00
TCS22 Troy Tulowitzki 1.25 3.00
TCS23 Victor Martinez .75 2.00
TCS24 Al Kaline 1.25 3.00
TCS25 Carlos Gonzalez .75 2.00
TCS26 Eddie Murray .75 2.00
TCS27 Tris Speaker .75 2.00
TCS28 Evan Longoria .75 2.00
TCS29 Honus Wagner 1.25 3.00
TCS30 Babe Ruth 3.00 8.00
TCS31 Joey Votto 1.25 3.00
TCS32 Ty Cobb 2.00 5.00
TCS33 Cy Young 1.25 3.00
TCS34 Hank Aaron 2.50 6.00
TCS35 Chipper Jones 1.25 3.00
TCS36 Ichiro Suzuki 1.50 4.00
TCS37 Roy Halladay .75 2.00
TCS38 Jason Heyward 1.00 2.50
TCS39 Joe Mauer 1.00 2.50
TCS40 Tim Lincecum .75 2.00
TCS41 Johnny Bench 1.25 3.00
TCS42 Miguel Cabrera 1.25 3.00
TCS43 Adrian Gonzalez 1.00 2.50
TCS44 Ryan Braun .75 2.00
TCS45 Robinson Cano .75 2.00
TCS46 Bob Gibson .75 2.00
TCS47 Tom Seaver .75 2.00
TCS48 Ryne Sandberg 2.50 6.00
TCS49 Albert Pujols 1.50 4.00
TCS50 Josh Hamilton .75 2.00

2011 Topps Lineage Giants

COMPLETE SET (20) 60.00 120.00
ONE PER HOBBY BOX TOPPER
TG1 Albert Pujols 3.00 8.00
TG2 Buster Posey 3.00 8.00
TG3 Jason Heyward 2.00 5.00
TG4 Joe Mauer 2.00 5.00
TG5 Derek Jeter 6.00 15.00
TG6 Roy Halladay 1.50 4.00
TG7 Joey Votto 2.50 6.00
TG8 Ichiro Suzuki 3.00 8.00
TG9 Miguel Cabrera 2.50 6.00
TG10 Mike Stanton 2.50 6.00
TG11 Adrian Gonzalez 2.00 5.00
TG12 Josh Hamilton 1.50 4.00
TG13 Evan Longoria 1.50 4.00
TG14 Tim Lincecum 1.50 4.00
TG15 David Wright 2.00 5.00
TG16 Ryan Braun 1.50 4.00
TG17 Hanley Ramirez 1.50 4.00
TG18 Troy Tulowitzki 2.50 6.00
TG19 Carlos Santana 2.50 6.00
TG20 Vladimir Guerrero 1.50 4.00

2011 Topps Lineage Giants Relics

STATED ODDS 1:24 HOBBY BOXES
STATED PRINT RUN 64 SER.#'d SETS
TG1 Albert Pujols 15.00 40.00
TG2 Buster Posey 30.00 60.00
TG3 Jason Heyward 12.50 30.00
TG4 Joe Mauer 12.50 30.00
TG5 Derek Jeter 50.00 100.00
TG6 Roy Halladay 15.00 40.00
TG7 Joey Votto 20.00 50.00
TG8 Ichiro Suzuki 15.00 40.00
TG9 Miguel Cabrera 15.00 40.00
TG10 Mike Stanton 8.00 20.00
TG11 Adrian Gonzalez 15.00 40.00
TG12 Josh Hamilton 10.00 25.00
TG13 Evan Longoria 15.00 40.00
TG14 Tim Lincecum 15.00 40.00
TG15 David Wright 10.00 25.00
TG16 Ryan Braun 10.00 25.00
TG17 Hanley Ramirez 6.00 15.00
TG18 Troy Tulowitzki 10.00 25.00
TG19 Carlos Santana 15.00 40.00
TG20 Vladimir Guerrero 12.50 30.00

2011 Topps Lineage Rookies

COMPLETE SET (19) 8.00 20.00
STATED ODDS 1:6 HOBBY
TR1 Freddie Freeman 6.00 15.00
TR2 Chris Sale 3.00 8.00
TR3 Brent Morel .40 1.00
TR4 Aroldis Chapman 1.25 3.00
TR5 Jeremy Hellickson 1.00 2.50
TR6 Jake McGee .75 2.00
TR7 Kyle Drabek .60 1.50
TR8 Craig Kimbrel 3.00 8.00
TR9 Mike Minor .40 1.00
TR10 Zach Britton 1.00 2.50
TR11 Brandon Belt 1.00 2.50
TR12 Brandon Beachy 1.00 2.50
TR13 Michael Pineda 1.00 2.50
TR14 Tsuyoshi Nishioka 1.25 3.00
TR16 Hank Conger .60 1.50
TR17 Domonic Brown .75 2.00
TR18 J.P. Arencibia .40 1.00
TR19 Corey Luebke .40 1.00
TR20 Brett Wallace .40 1.00

2011 Topps Lineage Stand-Ups

COMPLETE SET (25) 20.00 50.00
STATED ODDS 1:12 HOBBY
TS1 Jose Bautista .60 1.50
TS2 Ryan Zimmerman .60 1.50
TS3 Albert Pujols 1.25 3.00
TS4 Felix Hernandez .60 1.50
TS5 Tim Lincecum .60 1.50
TS6 Ryan Howard .75 2.00
TS7 Mariano Rivera 1.25 3.00
TS8 Jason Heyward .75 2.00
TS9 Ryan Braun .60 1.50
TS10 Hunter Pence .60 1.50
TS11 Miguel Cabrera 1.00 2.50
TS12 Adam Dunn .60 1.50
TS13 Kevin Youkilis .40 1.00
TS14 Joey Votto 1.00 2.50
TS15 Carlos Gonzalez .60 1.50
TS16 Mike Stanton 1.00 2.50
TS17 Matt Kemp .75 2.00
TS18 Joe Mauer .75 2.00
TS19 Alex Rodriguez 1.25 3.00
TS20 Roy Halladay .60 1.50
TS21 Brooks Robinson .60 1.50
TS22 Hank Aaron 2.00 5.00
TS23 Mickey Mantle 3.00 8.00
TS24 Juan Marichal .60 1.50
TS25 Sandy Koufax 2.00 5.00

2011 Topps Lineage Venezuelan

COMPLETE SET (25) 10.00 25.00
STATED ODDS 1:12 HOBBY
TV1 Derek Jeter 3.00 8.00
TV2 Buster Posey 1.50 4.00
TV3 Felix Hernandez .75 2.00
TV4 Ryan Zimmerman .75 2.00
TV5 Chris Carpenter .75 2.00
TV6 Josh Johnson .75 2.00
TV7 Andrew McCutchen 1.25 3.00
TV8 Carlos Santana 1.25 3.00
TV9 David Wright 1.00 2.50
TV10 Troy Tulowitzki 1.25 3.00
TV11 Clayton Kershaw 2.00 5.00
TV12 David Price 1.00 2.50
TV13 Chipper Jones 1.25 3.00
TV14 Ichiro Suzuki 1.50 4.00
TV15 Mark Teixeira .75 2.00
TV16 Jason Heyward 1.00 2.50
TV17 Joe Mauer 1.00 2.50
TV18 Starlin Castro .75 2.00
TV19 Adrian Gonzalez 1.00 2.50
TV20 Ryan Braun .75 2.00
TV21 Cliff Lee .75 2.00
TV22 Jose Bautista .75 2.00
TV23 Adam Dunn .75 2.00
TV24 Albert Pujols 1.50 4.00
TV25 Ian Kinsler .75 2.00

2018 Topps Living

ISSUED VIA TOPPS.COM
ANNCD PRINT RUNS B/WN 2678-46,809 COPIES PER
1 Aaron Judge/13,256* 12.00 30.00
2 Joe Panik/3650* 40.00 100.00
3 Nicholas Castellanos/3639* 30.00 80.00
4 Rhys Hoskins/5446* 10.00 25.00
5 Ian Happ/3042* 40.00 100.00
6 Nick Markakis/2678* 60.00 150.00
7 Shohei Ohtani/20,966* 8.00 20.00
8 Russell Martin/3953* 12.00 30.00
9 Jackie Bradley Jr./3959* 15.00 40.00
10 Derek Jeter/10,692* 6.00 15.00
11 Alex Gordon/4143* 8.00 20.00
12 Jean Segura/4052* 6.00 15.00
13 Bryce Harper/9515* 5.00 12.00
14 Mallex Smith/4529* 6.00 15.00
15 A.J. Pollock/4221* 6.00 15.00
16 Jose Altuve/6185* 5.00 12.00
17 Chris Taylor/4837* 2.50 6.00
18 Paul DeJong/4936* 5.00 12.00
19 Ronald Acuna/46,809* 10.00 25.00
20 Jose Ramirez/9671* 2.50 6.00
21 Matt Olson/9631* 3.00 8.00
22 Albert Pujols/9403* 4.00 10.00
23 Amed Rosario/7637* 2.50 6.00
24 Chase Headley/6752* 2.00 5.00
25 Ichiro Suzuki/10,713* 4.00 10.00
26 Yoan Moncada/6382* 3.00 8.00
27 Jose Berrios/6065* 2.50 6.00
28 Rickey Henderson/6851* 5.00 12.00
29 Rafael Devers/8403* 4.00 10.00
30 Brandon Morrow/5585* 2.00 5.00
31 Charlie Blackmon/6585* 3.00 8.00
32 Ozzie Albies/14,036* 4.00 10.00
33 Lewis Brinson/5549* 2.00 5.00
34 Gleyber Torres/28,550* 4.00 10.00
35 Adam Duvall/5766* 2.50 6.00
36 Jordy Mercer/5731* 2.00 5.00
37 Manny Machado/6516* 3.00 8.00
38 Christian Villanueva/5296* 2.00 5.00
39 Eric Sogard/4690* 2.00 5.00
40 Scott Kingery/7277* 3.00 8.00
41 Joey Rickard/5731* 2.00 5.00
42 Jackie Robinson/13,147* 3.00 8.00
43 Juan Soto/28,572* 10.00 25.00
44 Bartolo Colon/5630* 2.00 5.00
45 Brad Peacock/5440* 2.00 5.00
46 Hank Aaron/11,233* 6.00 15.00
47 Jordan Hicks/6099* 4.00 10.00
48 Kevin Pillar/5505* 2.00 5.00
49 Miguel Andujar/12,794* 4.00 10.00
50 Noah Syndergaard/6167* 2.50 6.00
51 Austin Hedges/5354* 2.00 5.00
52 Max Scherzer/6277* 3.00 8.00
53 Walker Buehler/7503* 5.00 12.00
54 Mitch Haniger/5218* 2.50 6.00
55 Ted Williams/10,927* 4.00 10.00
56 Brian Anderson/5218* 2.50 6.00
57 Sean Manaea/4792* 2.00 5.00
58 Giancarlo Stanton/7626* 3.00 8.00
59 Freddy Peralta/4915 2.00 5.00
60 Pat Neshek/12,736* 4.00 10.00
61 Francisco Lindor/6714* 3.00 8.00
62 Andrew Benintendi/6239* 3.00 8.00
63 Austin Meadows/5639* 5.00 12.00
64 Ryne Sandberg/7212* 4.00 10.00
65 Dustin Fowler/4808* 2.00 5.00
66 Yasiel Puig/4886* 3.00 8.00
67 Anthony Rizzo/5568* 4.00 10.00
68 Daniel Murphy/4586* 2.50 6.00
69 Willy Adames/4974* 2.50 6.00
70 Bo Jackson/7321* 3.00 8.00
71 Jake Arrieta/5060* 2.50 6.00
72 Dereck Rodriguez/5798* 2.50 6.00
73 Cody Bellinger/5273* 5.00 12.00
74 Lourdes Gurriel Jr./5094* 4.00 10.00
75 Joe Mauer/4725* 2.50 6.00
76 Roberto Clemente/10,922* 4.00 10.00
77 Tyler O'Neill/4851* 3.00 8.00
78 Avisail Garcia/4520* 2.50 6.00
79 Jacob deGrom/5302* 6.00 15.00
80 Victor Robles/6104* 5.00 12.00
81 Jed Lowrie/4348* 2.00 5.00
82 Joey Votto/4915* 3.00 8.00
83 David Bote/5345* 5.00 12.00
84 Trevor Story/4576* 3.00 8.00
85 Don Mattingly/6785* 5.00 12.00
86 Nick Williams/4733* 2.50 6.00
87 David Wright/5524* 2.50 6.00
88 Manny Machado/4802* 3.00 8.00
89 Jack Flaherty/4754* 8.00 20.00
90 Adrian Beltre/4585* 3.00 8.00
91 J.D. Martinez/4532* 3.00 8.00
92 Francisco Mejia/5096* 2.50 6.00
93 Evan Gattis/3990* 2.00 5.00
94 Christian Yelich/5025* 4.00 10.00
95 Clayton Kershaw/5872* 5.00 12.00
96 Ryan McMahon/4549* 5.00 12.00
97 Chris Sale/4622* 3.00 8.00
98 Dominic Smith/4035* 2.50 6.00
99 Ender Inciarte/4248* 2.00 5.00
100 Babe Ruth/14,976* 5.00 12.00
101 Sandy Alcantara/4771* 2.00 5.00
102 Victor Martinez/4634* 2.50 6.00
103 Javier Baez/4499* 4.00 10.00
104 Alex Verdugo/3911* 3.00 8.00
105 Ketel Marte/3644* 2.50 6.00
106 Cal Ripken Jr./6423* 5.00 12.00
107 Blake Snell/4173* 2.50 6.00
108 JP Crawford/4180* 2.00 5.00
109 Nolan Arenado/4065* 5.00 12.00
110 Clint Frazier/4365* 4.00 10.00
111 Andrew Heaney/3602* 2.00 5.00
112 Ralph Kiner/4114* 4.00 10.00
113 Daniel Palka/3923* 2.00 5.00
114 Billy Hamilton/3837* 2.50 6.00
115 Luis Severino/4061* 2.50 6.00
116 Felix Jorge/3472* 2.00 5.00
117 Trey Mancini/3490* 2.50 6.00
118 Nolan Ryan/6745* 5.00 12.00
119 AJ Minter/3994* 2.50 6.00
120 Harrison Bader/4283* 3.00 8.00
121 Buster Posey/3990* 4.00 10.00
122 Jorge Alfaro/3416* 2.00 5.00
123 David Peralta/3353* 2.00 5.00
124 Jim Thome/3753* 4.00 10.00
125 Ryan Yarbrough/3201* 3.00 8.00
126 Justin Upton/3110* 2.50 6.00

2019 Topps Living

ISSUED VIA TOPPS.COM
ANNCD PRINT RUNS B/WN 2009-27,749 COPIES PER
127 Kris Bryant/5361* 4.00 10.00
128 Eugenio Suarez/3766* 2.50 6.00
129 Matthew Boyd/3720* 2.00 5.00
130 George Springer/3541* 2.50 6.00
131 Wil Myers/3239* 2.50 6.00
132 Daniel Mengden/3250* 2.00 5.00
133 Frank Thomas/4163* 3.00 8.00
134 Trea Turner/3402* 2.50 6.00
135 Devon Travis/3205* 2.00 5.00
136 Mariano Rivera/8945* 4.00 10.00
137 Michael Lorenzen/3252* 2.00 5.00
138 Jake Odorizzi/3164* 2.00 5.00
139 Zack Greinke/3094* 3.00 8.00
140 Brandon Crawford/3246* 2.50 6.00
141 Adam Frazier/3074* 2.00 5.00
142 Freddie Freeman/3430* 4.00 10.00
143 Ryan O'Hearn/3145* 2.00 5.00
144 Jedd Gyorko/2974* 2.00 5.00
145 Justin Verlander/3855* 3.00 8.00
146 Cedric Mullins/3190* 4.00 10.00
147 Jose Urena/3053* 2.00 5.00
148 Ivan Rodriguez/3177* 2.50 6.00
149 Aaron Altherr/2964* 2.00 5.00
150 Khris Davis/2976* 3.00 8.00
151 Stephen Strasburg/3084* 3.00 8.00
152 Kyle Tucker/3853* 5.00 12.00
153 Mike Clevinger/2998* 2.50 6.00
154 Stan Musial/4575* 5.00 12.00
155 Luis Urias/3313* 3.00 8.00
156 Ryon Healy/2765* 2.00 5.00
157 Anthony Rendon/2899* 3.00 8.00
158 Garrett Hampson/2897* 3.00 8.00
159 Jose Abreu/2866* 3.00 8.00
160 Randy Johnson/3318* 3.00 8.00
161 Brandon Lowe/2936* 3.00 8.00
162 Enrique Hernandez/2959* 3.00 8.00
163 Bryce Harper/8233* 5.00 12.00
164 Sean Reid-Foley/3052* 2.00 5.00
165 Ryan Braun/3056* 2.50 6.00
166 Robinson Cano/2870* 2.50 6.00
167 Eloy Jimenez/6356* 5.00 12.00
168 Matt Carpenter/2833* 3.00 8.00
169 Corey Kluber/2871* 4.00 10.00
170 Nick Burdi/2873* 2.00 5.00
171 Shin-Soo Choo/2737* 2.50 6.00
172 Evan Longoria/2930* 2.50 6.00
173 Fernando Tatis Jr./10099* 10.00 25.00
174 Andrelton Simmons/2914* 2.00 5.00
175 Jim Palmer/3252* 4.00 10.00
176 Pete Alonso/8695* 6.00 15.00
177 Tim Beckham/2777* 2.50 6.00
178 Xander Bogaerts/3776* 3.00 8.00
179 Vladimir Guerrero Jr./27749* 5.00 12.00
180 Nelson Cruz/3581* 3.00 8.00
181 Paul Goldschmidt/3098* 3.00 8.00
182 Ramon Laureano/2975* 4.00 10.00
183 Howie Kendrick/2633* 6.00 15.00
184 Al Kaline/4278* 3.00 8.00
185 Yusei Kikuchi/3640* 3.00 8.00
186 Ji-Man Choi/2934* 2.00 5.00
187 Lorenzo Cain/2799* 2.00 5.00
188 Nick Senzel/4700* 4.00 10.00
189 Hunter Dozier/2879* 2.00 5.00
190 Justin Turner/2762* 4.00 10.00
191 Carter Kieboom/3338* 3.00 8.00
192 Wade Davis/2605* 2.00 5.00
193 Ken Griffey Jr./8369* 5.00 12.00
194 Jeff McNeil/3713* 5.00 12.00
195 Brian McCann/3243* 2.50 6.00
196 JT Realmuto/2796* 3.00 8.00
197 Keston Hiura/3234* 6.00 15.00
198 Brett Gardner/2928* 2.50 6.00
199 Christin Stewart/4858* 2.50 6.00
200 Mike Trout/22017* 5.00 12.00
201 Martin Prado/4755* 2.00 5.00
202 Rod Carew/3295* 4.00 10.00
203 Michael Chavis/3393* 3.00 8.00
204 Pablo Sandoval/2574* 2.50 6.00
205 Hyun-Jin Ryu/2628* 2.50 6.00
206 Austin Riley/5143* 4.00 10.00
207 Eduardo Escobar/2583* 2.00 5.00
208 Craig Biggio/2680* 2.50 6.00
209 Cavan Biggio/2972* 4.00 10.00
210 Jason Heyward/2573* 2.50 6.00
211 Charlie Morton/2644* 3.00 8.00
212 Brendan Rodgers/2796* 3.00 8.00
213 Tim Anderson/2619* 3.00 8.00
214 Tony Gwynn/3783* 3.00 8.00
215 Oscar Mercado/2853* 5.00 12.00
216 Starling Marte/2659* 2.50 6.00
217 Ernie Banks/5406* 3.00 8.00
218 Dakota Hudson/2639* 2.50 6.00
219 Harold Baines/2821* 2.50 6.00
220 Dansby Swanson/2652* 3.00 8.00
221 John Means/2477* 25.00 60.00
222 Joey Gallo/2499* 2.50 6.00
223 Vladimir Guerrero/2992* 2.50 6.00
224 Spencer Turnbull/2461* 3.00 8.00
225 Max Kepler/2523* 2.50 6.00
226 Marcus Stroman/2372* 2.50 6.00
227 Chris Paddack/2699* 4.00 10.00
228 Jorge Soler/2318* 3.00 8.00
229 Bernie Williams/2788* 2.50 6.00
230 Griffin Canning/2326* 3.00 8.00
231 Adam Eaton/2332* 3.00 8.00
232 Deion Sanders/2564* 4.00 10.00
233 Justus Sheffield/2295* 3.00 8.00
234 Stephen Piscotty/2278* 2.00 5.00
235 Mike Piazza/2984* 3.00 8.00
236 Pablo Lopez/2311* 2.00 5.00
237 Travis d'Arnaud/2280* 2.50 6.00
238 Yasiel Puig/2315* 4.00 10.00
239 Bryan Reynolds/2658* 4.00 10.00
240 Felix Hernandez/2290* 2.50 6.00
241 CC Sabathia/2825* 4.00 10.00
242 Touki Toussaint/2267* 2.50 6.00
243 Maikel Franco/2210* 4.00 10.00
244 Honus Wagner/3707* 4.00 10.00
245 Zach Plesac/2424* 4.00 10.00
246 Mitch Garver/2306* 2.00 5.00
247 Gerrit Cole/2632* 3.00 8.00
248 Will Smith/2781* 4.00 10.00
249 Adam Ottavino/2433* 2.00 5.00
250 Yadier Molina/2695* 4.00 10.00
251 Max Fried/2328* 3.00 8.00
252 Alex Bregman/2888* 3.00 8.00
253 Aroldis Chapman/2472* 3.00 8.00
254 Ryan Zimmerman/2347* 2.50 6.00
255 Ty Cobb/3691* 6.00 15.00
256 Josh James/2285* 3.00 8.00
257 Sean Doolittle/2083* 2.00 5.00
258 Michael Kopech/2157* 6.00 15.00
259 Thurman Munson/3657* 5.00 12.00
260 Jon Duplantier/2128* 2.00 5.00
261 Mike Soroka/2239* 3.00 8.00
262 Tommy Pham/2009* 2.00 5.00
263 Gary Carter/2606* 4.00 10.00
264 Brad Keller/2125* 2.00 5.00
265 Matt Chapman/2187* 3.00 8.00
266 Kyle Hendricks/2074* 3.00 8.00
267 Roy Halladay/2504* 2.50 6.00
268 Mitch Keller/2226* 2.50 6.00
269 Luis Castillo/2020* 2.50 6.00
270 Jonathan Loaisiga/2214* 2.50 6.00
271 Carl Yastrzemski/3129* 5.00 12.00
272 Mike Yastrzemski/3007* 5.00 12.00
CL01 Checklist #1-100/4393* 2.50 6.00
CL02 Checklist #101-200/4393* 2.50 6.00

2020 Topps Living

ISSUED VIA TOPPS.COM
ANNCD PRINT RUNS B/WN 1639-8539 COPIES PER
273 Lucas Giolito/2310* 2.50 6.00
274 Kenley Jansen/2288* 2.50 6.00
275 Todd Helton/2044* 2.50 6.00
276 David Fletcher/1920* 4.00 10.00
277 Whit Merrifield/2137* 3.00 8.00
278 Sonny Gray/2087* 2.50 6.00
279 Jeff Bagwell/2452* 4.00 10.00
280 Caleb Smith/1988* 4.00 10.00
281 Rollie Fingers/2633* 4.00 10.00
282 Seth Lugo/2103* 2.00 5.00
283 Aristides Aquino/3817* 5.00 12.00
284 Kevin Kiermaier/2059* 2.50 6.00
285 Edgar Martinez/2243* 4.00 10.00
286 Brad Ziegler/2021* 2.00 5.00
287 George Brett/3385* 5.00 12.00
288 Mike Minor/1961* 4.00 10.00
289 Yordan Alvarez/6510* 5.00 12.00
290 Carson Kelly/2022* 2.00 5.00
291 Alan Trammell/2488* 4.00 10.00
292 Kirby Yates/1967* 4.00 10.00
293 Didi Gregorius/2052* 2.50 6.00
294 Adrian Morejon/1978* 4.00 10.00
295 A.J. Puk/2285* 3.00 8.00
296 Josh Bell/2114* 2.50 6.00
297 Luis Robert/8539* 12.00 30.00
298 Mike Fiers/2002* 2.00 5.00
299 Eduardo Rodriguez/2498* 2.00 5.00
300 Willie Mays/4787* 6.00 15.00
301 Mookie Betts/2768* 6.00 15.00
302 David Dahl/1927* 4.00 10.00
303 Dellin Betances/2081* 2.50 6.00
304 Bo Bichette/6712* 6.00 15.00
305 Julio Teheran/2018* 2.50 6.00
306 Gavin Lux/6303* 5.00 12.00
307 Gary Sheffield/2076* 4.00 10.00
308 Dylan Cease/2283* 3.00 8.00
309 Salvador Perez/1954* 4.00 10.00
310 Nico Hoerner/3523* 4.00 10.00
311 Avisail Garcia/1898* 4.00 10.00
312 Jesus Luzardo/2504* 4.00 10.00
313 Shane Bieber/2078* 3.00 8.00
314 Jordan Yamamoto/2007* 2.00 5.00
315 Andruw Jones/2246* 4.00 10.00
316 Jose Urquidy/2073* 2.50 6.00
317 Trevor Bauer/1994* 4.00 10.00
318 Zac Gallen/1943* 5.00 12.00
319 Starlin Castro/1810* 4.00 10.00
320 Brendan McKay/2173* 3.00 8.00
321 Larry Walker/2090* 4.00 10.00
322 J.P. Crawford/1781* 4.00 10.00
323 Willson Contreras/2052* 3.00 8.00
324 Nick Solak/1958* 4.00 10.00
325 Jorge Polanco/1891* 4.00 10.00
326 Dustin May/2376* 4.00 10.00
327 Eddie Murray/2453* 4.00 10.00
328 Sean Murphy/2151* 3.00 8.00
329 Josh Donaldson/2077* 2.50 6.00
330 Isan Diaz/1996* 4.00 10.00
331 Kenny Lofton/2096* 4.00 10.00
332 Mauricio Dubon/1955* 4.00 10.00
333 Yasmani Grandal/1917* 4.00 10.00
334 Kyle Lewis/5617* 5.00 12.00
335 Michael Brantley/1790* 4.00 10.00
336 Andres Munoz/1780* 4.00 10.00
337 Jack Morris/2265* 2.50 6.00
338 Anthony Kay/1845* 4.00 10.00
339 Nick Castellanos/1925* 6.00 15.00
340 Aaron Civale/1990* 4.00 10.00
341 Greg Maddux/2851* 4.00 10.00
342 Matt Thaiss/1870* 4.00 10.00
343 Kenta Maeda/1840* 4.00 10.00
344 Dinelson Lamet/1727* 4.00 10.00
345 Dallas Keuchel/1725* 4.00 10.00
346 Kwang-Hyun Kim/1930* 4.00 10.00
347 Zack Wheeler/1822* 4.00 10.00
348 Donovan Solano/1716* 4.00 10.00
349 Adalberto Mondesi/1794* 4.00 10.00
350 Corbin Burnes/1726* 4.00 10.00
351 DJ LeMahieu/2512* 4.00 10.00
352 Alec Mills/1886* 4.00 10.00
353 Randy Arozarena/5093* 6.00 15.00
354 Bob Gibson/3428* 4.00 10.00
355 Trent Grisham/2259* 4.00 10.00
356 Nomar Garciaparra/2043* 4.00 10.00
357 Marcus Semien/1756* 4.00 10.00
358 Tyler Glasnow/1969* 4.00 10.00
359 Corey Seager/2806* 3.00 8.00
360 Masahiro Tanaka/1991* 4.00 10.00
361 Austin Nola/1784* 4.00 10.00
362 Fred McGriff/1904* 4.00 10.00
363 Merrill Kelly/1699* 6.00 15.00
364 Carlos Carrasco/1712* 4.00 10.00
365 Devin Williams/2012* 4.00 10.00
366 Tony Oliva/2291* 4.00 10.00
367 Jorge Posada/2216* 4.00 10.00
368 Teoscar Hernandez/1784* 4.00 10.00
369 Michael Conforto/1808* 4.00 10.00

370 Willi Castro/1894* 4.00 10.00
371 Aaron Nola/1832* 4.00 10.00
372 Renato Nunez/1639* 6.00 15.00
373 Johnny Bench/3164* 4.00 10.00
374 Brandon Woodruff/1747* 4.00 10.00
375 Jose Canseco/2220* 8.00 20.00
376 Tony Gonsolin/1741* 6.00 15.00
CL03 Checklist #201-300/2298* 2.50 6.00

2017 Topps Luminaries Hit Kings Autographs

STATED PRINT RUN 15 SER.#'d SETS
EXCHANGE DEADLINE 10/31/2019
HKAB Alex Bregman 25.00 60.00
HKABE Andrew Benintendi 30.00 80.00
HKAJ Aaron Judge 125.00 300.00
HKAJU Aaron Judge 125.00 300.00
HKANB Andrew Benintendi 30.00 80.00
HKAP Albert Pujols
HKAR Anthony Rizzo 40.00 100.00
HKBH Bryce Harper EXCH 100.00 250.00
HKBL Barry Larkin 25.00 60.00
HKBLA Barry Larkin 25.00 60.00
HKBP Buster Posey 40.00 100.00
HKCB Craig Biggio 20.00 50.00
HKCBI Craig Biggio 20.00 50.00
HKCC Carlos Correa 40.00 100.00
HKCJ Chipper Jones 50.00 120.00
HKCR Cal Ripken Jr. 60.00 150.00
HKCS Corey Seager 30.00 80.00
HKCSE Corey Seager 30.00 80.00
HKCY Carl Yastrzemski 40.00 100.00
HKDJ Derek Jeter
HKDS Dansby Swanson 20.00 50.00
HKDSW Dansby Swanson 20.00 50.00
HKFL Francisco Lindor 20.00 50.00
HKFLI Francisco Lindor 20.00 50.00
HKFR Frank Robinson 30.00 80.00
HKFRO Frank Robinson 30.00 80.00
HKFT Frank Thomas 40.00 100.00
HKFTH Frank Thomas 40.00 100.00
HKHA Hank Aaron 150.00 400.00
HKIR Ivan Rodriguez 30.00 80.00
HKI Ichiro 250.00 400.00
HKJB Johnny Bench 40.00 100.00
HKKB Kris Bryant 75.00 200.00
HKMM Manny Machado 25.00 60.00
HKMMA Manny Machado 25.00 60.00
HKMT Mike Trout 125.00 300.00
HKNG Nomar Garciaparra 20.00 50.00
HKNGA Nomar Garciaparra 20.00 50.00
HKOS Ozzie Smith 25.00 60.00
HKOV Omar Vizquel 12.00 30.00
HKOVI Omar Vizquel 12.00 30.00
HKRA Roberto Alomar 20.00 50.00
HKRC Rod Carew 20.00 50.00
HKRCA Rod Carew 20.00 50.00
HKRH Rickey Henderson 60.00 150.00
HKRJ Reggie Jackson 40.00 100.00
HKWB Wade Boggs 40.00 100.00
HKYG Yulieski Gurriel 20.00 50.00
HKYGU Yulieski Gurriel 20.00 50.00
HKYMO Yoan Moncada 50.00 120.00

2017 Topps Luminaries Hit Kings Relic Autographs

STATED PRINT RUN 15 SER.#'d SETS
EXCHANGE DEADLINE 10/31/2019
HKRAB Alex Bregman 25.00 60.00
HKRABE Andrew Benintendi 30.00 80.00
HKRABR Alex Bregman 25.00 60.00
HKRANB Andrew Benintendi 30.00 80.00
HKRAP Albert Pujols
HKRAR Anthony Rizzo 40.00 100.00
HKRBH Bryce Harper EXCH 100.00 250.00
HKRBL Barry Larkin 15.00 40.00
HKRBP Buster Posey 40.00 100.00
HKRCB Craig Biggio 20.00 50.00
HKRCC Carlos Correa 40.00 100.00
HKRCJ Chipper Jones 50.00 120.00
HKRCR Cal Ripken Jr. 60.00 150.00
HKRCS Corey Seager 30.00 80.00
HKRCY Carl Yastrzemski 40.00 100.00
HKRDJ Derek Jeter
HKRDO David Ortiz 40.00 100.00
HKRDP Dustin Pedroia 25.00 60.00
HKRDS Dansby Swanson 20.00 50.00
HKRFL Francisco Lindor 20.00 50.00
HKRFT Frank Thomas 40.00 100.00
HKRHA Hank Aaron 150.00 400.00
HKRIR Ivan Rodriguez 30.00 80.00
HKRI Ichiro 250.00 400.00
HKRJB Johnny Bench 40.00 100.00
HKRJBA Jeff Bagwell 30.00 80.00
HKRKB Kris Bryant 75.00 200.00
HKRMM Manny Machado 25.00 60.00
HKRMT Mike Trout 125.00 300.00
HKRNG Nomar Garciaparra 20.00 50.00
HKROS Ozzie Smith 25.00 60.00
HKRRA Roberto Alomar 20.00 50.00
HKRRC Rod Carew 20.00 50.00
HKRRH Rickey Henderson 60.00 150.00
HKRRJ Reggie Jackson 40.00 100.00
HKRRS Ryne Sandberg 40.00 100.00
HKRWB Wade Boggs 40.00 100.00
HKRYG Yulieski Gurriel 20.00 50.00

2017 Topps Luminaries Home Run Kings Autographs

STATED PRINT RUN 15 SER.#'d SETS
EXCHANGE DEADLINE 10/31/2019
HRKAB Alex Bregman 25.00 60.00
HRKABE Andrew Benintendi 30.00 80.00
HRKABR Alex Bregman 25.00 60.00
HRKAJ Aaron Judge 125.00 300.00
HRKAJU Aaron Judge 125.00 300.00
HRKANB Andrew Benintendi 30.00 80.00
HRKAP Albert Pujols
HRKAPU Albert Pujols
HRKAR Alex Rodriguez 75.00 200.00
HRKARI Anthony Rizzo 40.00 100.00
HRKBH Bryce Harper 100.00 250.00
HRKBJ Bo Jackson 60.00 150.00
HRKBJA Bo Jackson 60.00 150.00
HRKBP Buster Posey 40.00 100.00
HRKBW Bernie Williams 20.00 50.00
HRKCC Carlos Correa 40.00 100.00
HRKCCO Carlos Correa 40.00 100.00
HRKCJ Chipper Jones 50.00 120.00
HRKCJO Chipper Jones 50.00 120.00
HRKCRJ Cal Ripken Jr. 60.00 150.00
HRKCS Corey Seager 30.00 80.00
HRKCSE Corey Seager 30.00 80.00
HRKCY Carl Yastrzemski 40.00 100.00
HRKDD David Dahl 12.00 30.00
HRKDO David Ortiz 40.00 100.00
HRKDOR David Ortiz 40.00 100.00
HRKDW Dave Winfield 25.00 60.00
HRKFL Francisco Lindor 20.00 50.00
HRKFR Frank Robinson 40.00 100.00
HRKFT Frank Thomas 40.00 100.00
HRKFTH Frank Thomas 40.00 100.00
HRKHA Hank Aaron 150.00 400.00
HRKIR Ivan Rodriguez 30.00 80.00
HRKIRO Ivan Rodriguez 30.00 80.00
HRKJA Jose Altuve 40.00 100.00
HRKJB Johnny Bench 40.00 100.00
HRKJBA Jeff Bagwell 30.00 80.00
HRKJBG Jeff Bagwell 30.00 80.00
HRKJD Josh Donaldson 15.00 40.00
HRKJDO Josh Donaldson 15.00 40.00
HRKKB Kris Bryant 75.00 200.00
HRKKBR Kris Bryant 75.00 200.00
HRKKS Kyle Schwarber 12.00 30.00
HRKKSC Kyle Schwarber 12.00 30.00
HRKMAM Manny Machado 25.00 60.00
HRKMM Mark McGwire 50.00 120.00
HRKMMA Manny Machado 25.00 60.00
HRKMP Mike Piazza 50.00 120.00
HRKMT Mike Trout 125.00 300.00
HRKRC Robinson Cano 20.00 50.00
HRKRJ Reggie Jackson 40.00 100.00
HRKTS Trevor Story 12.00 30.00
HRKTST Trevor Story 12.00 30.00
HRKDAW Dave Winfield 25.00 60.00

2017 Topps Luminaries Home Run Kings Relic Autographs

STATED PRINT RUN 15 SER.#'d SETS
EXCHANGE DEADLINE 10/31/2019
HRKRAB Alex Bregman 25.00 60.00
HRKRAJ Aaron Judge 125.00 300.00
HRKRAP Albert Pujols
HRKRAR Alex Rodriguez 75.00 200.00
HRKRBH Bryce Harper EXCH 100.00 250.00
HRKRBJ Bo Jackson 60.00 150.00
HRKRBP Buster Posey 40.00 100.00
HRKRCJ Chipper Jones 50.00 120.00
HRKRCR Cal Ripken Jr. 60.00 150.00
HRKRCS Corey Seager 30.00 80.00
HRKRCY Carl Yastrzemski 40.00 100.00
HRKRDO David Ortiz 40.00 100.00
HRKRDW Dave Winfield 25.00 60.00
HRKRFT Frank Thomas 40.00 100.00
HRKRHA Hank Aaron 150.00 400.00
HRKRJD Josh Donaldson 15.00 40.00
HRKRKB Kris Bryant 75.00 200.00
HRKRMM Mark McGwire 50.00 120.00
HRKRMP Mike Piazza 50.00 120.00
HRKRMT Mike Trout 125.00 300.00
HRKRRC Robinson Cano 20.00 50.00
HRKRRJ Reggie Jackson 40.00 100.00
HRKRALB Alex Bregman 25.00 60.00
HRKRARI Anthony Rizzo 40.00 100.00
HRKRCCO Carlos Correa 40.00 100.00
HRKRCJO Chipper Jones 50.00 120.00
HRKRDOR David Ortiz 40.00 100.00
HRKRKBR Kris Bryant 75.00 200.00
HRKRMAM Manny Machado 25.00 60.00
HRKRMMA Manny Machado 25.00 60.00

2017 Topps Luminaries Masters of the Mound Autographs

STATED PRINT RUN 15 SER.#'d SETS
EXCHANGE DEADLINE 10/31/2019
MMCK Clayton Kershaw EXCH 60.00 150.00
MMCS Chris Sale
MMGM Greg Maddux 75.00 200.00
MMJS John Smoltz 25.00 60.00
MMJSM John Smoltz 25.00 60.00
MMKM Kenta Maeda 15.00 40.00
MMLG Lucas Giolito 15.00 40.00
MMMT Masahiro Tanaka 75.00 200.00
MMNR Nolan Ryan 100.00 250.00
MMNS Noah Syndergaard 15.00 40.00
MMPM Pedro Martinez 40.00 100.00
MMPMA Pedro Martinez 40.00 100.00
MMRC Roger Clemens 40.00 100.00
MMRCL Roger Clemens 40.00 100.00
MMRJ Randy Johnson 50.00 120.00
MMSK Sandy Koufax
MMTG Tyler Glasnow 40.00 100.00

2017 Topps Luminaries Masters of the Mound Relic Autographs

STATED PRINT RUN 15 SER.#'d SETS
EXCHANGE DEADLINE 10/31/2019
MMRCK Clayton Kershaw EXCH 100.00 250.00
MMRGM Greg Maddux EXCH 75.00 200.00
MMRJS John Smoltz
MMRMT Masahiro Tanaka 75.00 200.00
MMRNR Nolan Ryan
MMRNS Noah Syndergaard 25.00 60.00
MMRPM Pedro Martinez 40.00 100.00
MMRRC Roger Clemens 40.00 100.00
MMRRJ Randy Johnson 50.00 120.00
MMRTG Tom Glavine 20.00 50.00

2018 Topps Luminaries Hit Kings Autograph Relics

STATED ODDS 1:12 HOBBY
STATED PRINT RUN 15 SER.#'d SETS
EXCHANGE DEADLINE 7/31/2020
HKARAD Andre Dawson 20.00 50.00
HKARADA Andre Dawson 20.00 50.00
HKARAJ Aaron Judge 50.00 120.00
HKARAP Albert Pujols 75.00 200.00
HKARAR Anthony Rizzo 25.00 60.00
HKARARO Amed Rosario 15.00 40.00
HKARBH Bryce Harper 100.00 250.00
HKARBL Barry Larkin EXCH 20.00 50.00
HKARBLA Barry Larkin EXCH 20.00 50.00
HKARBP Buster Posey 30.00 80.00
HKARCB Craig Biggio 20.00 50.00
HKARCF Clint Frazier 40.00 100.00
HKARCJ Chipper Jones
HKARCR Cal Ripken Jr. 60.00 150.00
HKARDJ Derek Jeter
HKARDM Don Mattingly 100.00 250.00
HKARDO David Ortiz 30.00 80.00
HKARFL Francisco Lindor 30.00 80.00
HKARFT Frank Thomas 60.00 150.00
HKARGT Gleyber Torres 100.00 250.00
HKARHA Hank Aaron
HKARHM Hideki Matsui 75.00 200.00
HKARJA Jose Altuve 15.00 40.00
HKARJAL Jose Altuve 15.00 40.00
HKARJB Johnny Bench 40.00 100.00
HKARJR Jose Ramirez
HKARJV Joey Votto 30.00 80.00
HKARKB Kris Bryant EXCH 60.00 150.00
HKARMM Manny Machado 30.00 80.00
HKARMT Mike Trout
HKARNG Nomar Garciaparra 20.00 50.00
HKAROA Ozzie Albies 40.00 100.00
HKAROS Ozzie Smith
HKARRA Roberto Alomar 20.00 50.00
HKARRAC Ronald Acuna 300.00 500.00
HKARRC Rod Carew 20.00 50.00
HKARRD Rafael Devers 40.00 100.00
HKARRDE Rafael Devers 40.00 100.00
HKARRH Rhys Hoskins 40.00 100.00
HKARRJ Reggie Jackson 30.00 80.00
HKARRJA Reggie Jackson 30.00 80.00
HKARVR Victor Robles 20.00 50.00
HKARWB Wade Boggs 30.00 80.00

2018 Topps Luminaries Hit Kings Autographs

STATED ODDS 1:10 HOBBY
STATED PRINT RUN 15 SER.#'d SETS
EXCHANGE DEADLINE 7/31/2020
HKAB Adrian Beltre 30.00 80.00
HKAD Andre Dawson 20.00 50.00
HKAJ Aaron Judge 50.00 120.00
HKAK Al Kaline 40.00 100.00
HKAMR Amed Rosario 15.00 40.00
HKAP Albert Pujols 60.00 150.00
HKAR Anthony Rizzo 25.00 60.00
HKBH Bryce Harper 100.00 250.00
HKBL Barry Larkin EXCH 20.00 50.00
HKBLA Barry Larkin EXCH 20.00 50.00
HKBP Buster Posey 30.00 80.00
HKBR Brooks Robinson EXCH 25.00 60.00
HKCB Craig Biggio 20.00 50.00
HKCBI Craig Biggio 15.00 40.00
HKCJ Chipper Jones 40.00 100.00
HKCJO Chipper Jones 40.00 100.00
HKCR Cal Ripken Jr. 60.00 150.00
HKCRJ Cal Ripken Jr. 60.00 150.00
HKDJ Derek Jeter
HKDM Don Mattingly 60.00 150.00
HKDO David Ortiz 30.00 80.00
HKFR Frank Robinson 20.00 50.00
HKFRB Frank Robinson 20.00 50.00
HKFT Frank Thomas 40.00 100.00
HKGT Gleyber Torres 100.00 250.00
HKHA Hank Aaron 125.00 300.00
HKHM Hideki Matsui 75.00 200.00
HKI Ichiro 150.00 400.00
HKJA Jose Altuve 15.00 40.00
HKJB Johnny Bench 40.00 100.00
HKJBE Johnny Bench 40.00 100.00
HKJR Jose Ramirez EXCH 15.00 40.00
HKJVO Joey Votto 30.00 80.00
HKKB Kris Bryant EXCH 60.00 150.00
HKLB Lou Brock 20.00 50.00
HKLBR Lou Brock 20.00 50.00
HKMM Manny Machado 30.00 80.00
HKMT Mike Trout 150.00 400.00
HKNG Nomar Garciaparra
HKOA Ozzie Albies 40.00 100.00
HKOAL Ozzie Albies 40.00 100.00
HKOS Ozzie Smith 25.00 60.00
HKOSM Ozzie Smith 25.00 60.00
HKRA Roberto Alomar 20.00 50.00
HKRAC Ronald Acuna 300.00 500.00
HKRC Rod Carew 20.00 50.00
HKRCA Rod Carew 20.00 50.00
HKRD Rafael Devers 40.00 100.00
HKRDE Rafael Devers 40.00 100.00
HKRH Rhys Hoskins 40.00 100.00
HKRJ Reggie Jackson 30.00 80.00
HKRY Robin Yount 60.00 150.00
HKSO Shohei Ohtani 300.00 600.00
HKVRO Victor Robles 20.00 50.00
HKWB Wade Boggs 30.00 80.00

2018 Topps Luminaries Home Run Kings Autograph Relics

STATED ODDS 1:14 HOBBY
STATED PRINT RUN 15 SER.#'d SETS
EXCHANGE DEADLINE 7/31/2020
HRKRAD Andre Dawson 20.00 50.00
HRKRAJ Aaron Judge 50.00 120.00
HRKRAP Albert Pujols 75.00 200.00
HRKRAR Alex Rodriguez EXCH 75.00 200.00
HRKRARI Anthony Rizzo 25.00 60.00
HRKRBH Bryce Harper EXCH 100.00 250.00
HRKRBJA Bo Jackson 60.00 150.00
HRKRBP Buster Posey 30.00 80.00
HRKRCF Clint Frazier 40.00 100.00
HRKRCJ Chipper Jones
HRKRCR Cal Ripken Jr. 60.00 150.00
HRKRDM Don Mattingly 100.00 250.00
HRKRDO David Ortiz 30.00 80.00
HRKRDW Dave Winfield 30.00 80.00
HRKRFL Francisco Lindor 30.00 80.00
HRKRFT Frank Thomas 60.00 150.00
HRKRGS Gary Sanchez 30.00 80.00
HRKRGSP George Springer 15.00 40.00
HRKRHA Hank Aaron
HRKRHM Hideki Matsui 75.00 200.00
HRKRJA Jose Altuve 15.00 40.00
HRKRJB Johnny Bench 40.00 100.00
HRKRJBA Jeff Bagwell 40.00 100.00
HRKRJV Joey Votto 30.00 80.00
HRKRKB Kris Bryant 60.00 150.00
HRKRMM Mark McGwire 30.00 80.00
HRKRMMA Manny Machado 30.00 80.00
HRKRMMC Mark McGwire 30.00 80.00
HRKRMP Mike Piazza 40.00 100.00
HRKRMPI Mike Piazza 40.00 100.00
HRKRMT Mike Trout
HRKRPG Paul Goldschmidt 20.00 50.00
HRKRRD Rafael Devers 40.00 100.00
HRKRRH Rhys Hoskins 40.00 100.00
HRKRRJ Reggie Jackson 30.00 80.00

2018 Topps Luminaries Home Run Kings Autographs

STATED ODDS 1:8 HOBBY
STATED PRINT RUN 15 SER.#'d SETS
EXCHANGE DEADLINE 7/31/2020
HRKABE Adrian Beltre 30.00 80.00
HRKAD Andre Dawson 20.00 50.00
HRKADA Andre Dawson 20.00 50.00
HRKAJ Aaron Judge 50.00 120.00
HRKAK Al Kaline 40.00 100.00
HRKAKA Al Kaline 40.00 100.00
HRKANR Anthony Rizzo 25.00 60.00
HRKAP Albert Pujols 60.00 150.00
HRKAR Alex Rodriguez EXCH 75.00 200.00
HRKARI Anthony Rizzo 25.00 60.00
HRKBH Bryce Harper 100.00 250.00
HRKBJ Bo Jackson 60.00 150.00
HRKBJA Bo Jackson 60.00 150.00
HRKBP Buster Posey 30.00 80.00
HRKBPO Buster Posey 30.00 80.00
HRKBW Bernie Williams 20.00 50.00
HRKBWI Bernie Williams 20.00 50.00
HRKCF Clint Frazier 15.00 40.00
HRKCFI Carlton Fisk
HRKCJ Chipper Jones 40.00 100.00
HRKCJO Chipper Jones 40.00 100.00
HRKCR Cal Ripken Jr. 60.00 150.00
HRKCRJ Cal Ripken Jr. 60.00 150.00
HRKDM Don Mattingly 60.00 150.00
HRKDO David Ortiz 30.00 80.00
HRKDOR David Ortiz 30.00 80.00
HRKDW Dave Winfield
HRKFL Francisco Lindor 30.00 80.00
HRKFR Frank Robinson 20.00 50.00
HRKFRO Frank Robinson 20.00 50.00
HRKFT Frank Thomas 40.00 100.00
HRKGS Gary Sanchez 30.00 80.00
HRKGSP George Springer
HRKHA Hank Aaron 125.00 300.00
HRKHM Hideki Matsui 75.00 200.00
HRKHMA Hideki Matsui 75.00 200.00
HRKJA Jose Altuve 15.00 40.00
HRKJAL Jose Altuve 15.00 40.00
HRKJB Johnny Bench 40.00 100.00
HRKJBA Jeff Bagwell 40.00 100.00
HRKJBE Johnny Bench 40.00 100.00
HRKJEF Jeff Bagwell 40.00 100.00
HRKJV Joey Votto 30.00 80.00
HRKKB Kris Bryant 60.00 150.00
HRKKBR Kris Bryant 60.00 150.00
HRKMM Mark McGwire 30.00 80.00
HRKMMA Manny Machado 30.00 80.00
HRKMMC Manny Machado 30.00 80.00
HRKMP Mike Piazza 40.00 100.00
HRKMPI Mike Piazza 40.00 100.00
HRKMT Mike Trout 150.00 400.00
HRKPG Paul Goldschmidt 20.00 50.00
HRKPGO Paul Goldschmidt 20.00 50.00
HRKRA Ronald Acuna 300.00 500.00
HRKRD Rafael Devers 40.00 100.00
HRKRDE Rafael Devers 40.00 100.00
HRKRH Rhys Hoskins 40.00 100.00
HRKRJ Reggie Jackson 30.00 80.00
HRKRJA Reggie Jackson 30.00 80.00
HRKRS Ryne Sandberg 30.00 80.00
HRKSO Shohei Ohtani 300.00 600.00

2018 Topps Luminaries Masters of the Mound Autograph Relics

STATED ODDS 1:32 HOBBY
STATED PRINT RUN 15 SER.#'d SETS
EXCHANGE DEADLINE 7/31/2020
MOTMARAND Andy Pettitte 25.00 60.00
MOTMARAP Andy Pettitte 25.00 60.00
MOTMARCK Clayton Kershaw EXCH 60.00 150.00
MOTMARCS Chris Sale 20.00 50.00
MOTMARGM Greg Maddux EXCH 40.00 100.00
MOTMARJS John Smoltz 20.00 50.00
MOTMARMR Mariano Rivera 125.00 300.00
MOTMARNR Nolan Ryan 75.00 200.00
MOTMARNS Noah Syndergaard 15.00 40.00
MOTMARPM Pedro Martinez 40.00 100.00
MOTMARPMA Pedro Martinez 40.00 100.00
MOTMARRJ Randy Johnson 40.00 100.00
MOTMARSC Steve Carlton 20.00 50.00
MOTMARTG Tom Glavine 20.00 50.00

2018 Topps Luminaries Masters of the Mound Autographs

STATED ODDS 1:18 HOBBY
STATED PRINT RUN 15 SER.#'d SETS
EXCHANGE DEADLINE 7/31/2020
MMANP Andy Pettitte 25.00 60.00
MMAP Andy Pettitte 25.00 60.00
MMCK Clayton Kershaw EXCH 60.00 150.00
MMCS Chris Sale 20.00 50.00
MMCSA Chris Sale 20.00 50.00
MMGM Greg Maddux 40.00 100.00
MMGMA Greg Maddux 40.00 100.00
MMGRE Greg Maddux 40.00 100.00
MMJP Jim Palmer EXCH 15.00 40.00
MMJPA Jim Palmer EXCH 15.00 40.00
MMJS John Smoltz 20.00 50.00
MMJSM John Smoltz 20.00 50.00
MMMR Mariano Rivera 75.00 200.00
MMNOL Nolan Ryan 75.00 200.00
MMNR Nolan Ryan 75.00 200.00
MMNRY Nolan Ryan 75.00 200.00
MMNS Noah Syndergaard 15.00 40.00
MMNSY Noah Syndergaard 15.00 40.00
MMPM Pedro Martinez 40.00 100.00
MMPMA Pedro Martinez 40.00 100.00
MMRJ Randy Johnson
MMRJO Randy Johnson
MMSC Steve Carlton 20.00 50.00
MMSCA Steve Carlton 20.00 50.00
MMSK Sandy Koufax
MMSO Shohei Ohtani EXCH 300.00 600.00
MMTG Tom Glavine 20.00 50.00
MMTGL Tom Glavine 20.00 5.00

2019 Topps Luminaries Hit Kings Autograph Patches

STATED ODDS 1:XX HOBBY
STATED PRINT RUN 15 SER.#'d SETS
EXCHANGE DEADLINE 7/31/2021
HKAPAR Alex Rodriguez 60.00 150.00
HKAPARI Anthony Rizzo 30.00 80.00
HKAPARO Alex Rodriguez 60.00 150.00
HKAPBP Buster Posey 40.00 100.00
HKAPCF Carlton Fisk 40.00 100.00
HKAPCRJ Cal Ripken Jr. 100.00 250.00
HKAPDO David Ortiz 50.00 120.00
HKAPGS George Springer 40.00 100.00
HKAPGSP George Springer 40.00 100.00
HKAPIR Ivan Rodriguez 40.00 100.00
HKAPIRO Ivan Rodriguez 40.00 100.00
HKAPJA Jose Altuve 30.00 80.00
HKAPJAL Jose Altuve 30.00 80.00
HKAPJS Juan Soto 60.00 150.00
HKAPJSO Juan Soto 20.00 50.00
HKAPJV Joey Votto 30.00 80.00
HKAPKB Kris Bryant 75.00 200.00
HKAPKGJ Ken Griffey Jr. 150.00 400.00
HKAPMC Miguel Cabrera 60.00 150.00
HKAPMP Mike Piazza 75.00 200.00
HKAPMT Mike Trout 400.00 800.00
HKAPMTR Mike Trout 400.00 800.00
HKAPRC Rod Carew 25.00 60.00
HKAPRH Rickey Henderson 50.00 120.00
HKAPRHO Rhys Hoskins 30.00 80.00
HKAPRHS Rhys Hoskins 30.00 80.00
HKAPRJ Reggie Jackson 50.00 120.00
HKAPVGJ Vladimir Guerrero Jr. 150.00 400.00
HKAPVGU Vladimir Guerrero 30.00 80.00
HKAPVLG Vladimir Guerrero Jr. 150.00 400.00

2019 Topps Luminaries Hit Kings Autograph Relics

STATED ODDS 1:XX HOBBY
STATED PRINT RUN 15 SER.#'d SETS
EXCHANGE DEADLINE 7/31/2021
*BLUE/10: .4X TO 1X BASIC
HKARAD Andre Dawson 25.00 60.00
HKARAK Al Kaline 40.00 100.00
HKARAR Anthony Rizzo 25.00 60.00
HKARBL Barry Larkin
HKARBP Buster Posey 30.00 80.00
HKARBW Bernie Williams 25.00 60.00
HKARCF Carlton Fisk 30.00 80.00
HKARCRJ Cal Ripken Jr. 75.00 200.00
HKARDJ Derek Jeter 250.00 500.00
HKARDM Don Mattingly 75.00 200.00
HKARDO David Ortiz 40.00 100.00
HKARFF Freddie Freeman 40.00 100.00
HKARFT Frank Thomas 60.00 150.00
HKARFTJ Fernando Tatis Jr. 200.00 500.00
HKARGS George Springer 30.00 80.00
HKARHA Hank Aaron 125.00 300.00
HKARHM Hideki Matsui 50.00 120.00
HKARIR Ivan Rodriguez 30.00 80.00
HKARI Ichiro 125.00 300.00
HKARJA Jose Altuve 25.00 60.00
HKARJB Johnny Bench 50.00 120.00
HKARJBA Jeff Bagwell 30.00 80.00
HKARJP Jorge Posada 50.00 120.00
HKARJS Juan Soto 50.00 120.00
HKARJV Joey Votto 25.00 60.00
HKARKB Kris Bryant 60.00 150.00
HKARKGJ Ken Griffey Jr. 200.00 500.00
HKARMC Miguel Cabrera 50.00 120.00
HKARMP Mike Piazza 60.00 150.00
HKARMT Mike Trout 300.00 600.00
HKAROS Ozzie Smith
HKARRAJ Ronald Acuna Jr.
HKARRC Rod Carew 20.00 50.00
HKARRH Rickey Henderson 40.00 100.00
HKARRHO Rhys Hoskins 25.00 60.00
HKARRJ Reggie Jackson 40.00 100.00
HKARSO Shohei Ohtani 100.00 250.00
HKARVGJ Vladimir Guerrero Jr. 125.00 300.00
HKARVGS Vladimir Guerrero 25.00 60.00

2019 Topps Luminaries Hit Kings Autographs

STATED ODDS 1:XX HOBBY
STATED PRINT RUN 15 SER.#'d SETS
EXCHANGE DEADLINE 7/31/2021
*RED/10: .4X TO 1X BASIC
HKAB Adrian Beltre 25.00 60.00
HKABE Andrew Benintendi 40.00 100.00
HKAD Andre Dawson 20.00 50.00
HKAJ Aaron Judge 75.00 200.00
HKAK Al Kaline 50.00 120.00
HKAR Alex Rodriguez 50.00 120.00
HKARI Anthony Rizzo 20.00 50.00
HKBJ Bo Jackson 50.00 120.00
HKBL Barry Larkin 20.00 50.00
HKBP Buster Posey 30.00 80.00
HKBW Bernie Williams 20.00 50.00
HKCF Carlton Fisk 20.00 50.00
HKCJ Chipper Jones 40.00 100.00
HKCRJ Cal Ripken Jr. 60.00 150.00
HKCY Christian Yelich EXCH 75.00 200.00
HKDJ Derek Jeter 250.00 500.00
HKDM Don Mattingly 60.00 150.00
HKDO David Ortiz 30.00 80.00
HKEJ Eloy Jimenez 60.00 150.00
HKFF Freddie Freeman 25.00 60.00
HKFL Francisco Lindor 25.00 60.00
HKFT Frank Thomas 40.00 100.00
HKFTA Fernando Tatis Jr. 200.00 500.00
HKGS George Springer
HKHA Hank Aaron 100.00 250.00
HKHM Hideki Matsui 40.00 100.00
HKIR Ivan Rodriguez 25.00 60.00
HKI Ichiro 150.00 400.00
HKJA Jose Altuve 30.00 80.00
HKJB Johnny Bench 40.00 100.00
HKJBA Jeff Bagwell 25.00 60.00
HKJP Jorge Posada 20.00 50.00
HKJS Juan Soto 50.00 100.00
HKJT Jim Thome 30.00 80.00
HKJV Joey Votto 20.00 50.00
HKKB Kris Bryant 40.00 100.00
HKKGJ Ken Griffey Jr. 125.00 300.00
HKMC Miguel Cabrera 40.00 100.00
HKMP Mike Piazza 30.00 80.00
HKMT Mike Trout 250.00 500.00
HKOA Ozzie Albies 25.00 60.00
HKOS Ozzie Smith 25.00 60.00
HKPG Paul Goldschmidt 20.00 50.00
HKRAJ Ronald Acuna Jr. 100.00 250.00
HKRC Rod Carew 20.00 50.00
HKRD Rafael Devers 25.00 60.00
HKRH Rickey Henderson 50.00 120.00
HKRHO Rhys Hoskins 40.00 100.00
HKRJ Reggie Jackson 30.00 80.00
HKRS Ryne Sandberg 50.00 120.00
HKSO Shohei Ohtani 125.00 300.00
HKTR Tim Raines 15.00 40.00
HKVGJ Vladimir Guerrero Jr. 100.00 250.00
HKVGS Vladimir Guerrero 25.00 60.00

2019 Topps Luminaries Home Run Kings Autograph Patches

STATED ODDS 1:XX HOBBY
STATED PRINT RUN 15 SER.#'d SETS
EXCHANGE DEADLINE 7/31/2021
HRKAPMC Alex Rodriguez 60.00 150.00
HRKAPARO Alex Rodriguez 60.00 150.00
HRKAPBP Buster Posey 40.00 100.00
HRKAPBPO Buster Posey 40.00 100.00
HRKAPCF Carlton Fisk 40.00 100.00
HRKAPCR Cal Ripken Jr. 100.00 250.00
HRKAPDO David Ortiz 50.00 120.00
HRKAPDOR David Ortiz 50.00 120.00
HRKAPFF Freddie Freeman 50.00 120.00
HRKAPFTA Fernando Tatis Jr. 250.00 600.00
HRKAPJS Juan Soto 60.00 150.00
HRKAPKB Kris Bryant 75.00 200.00
HRKAPKBR Kris Bryant 75.00 200.00
HRKAPKGJ Ken Griffey Jr. 150.00 400.00
HRKAPMC Miguel Cabrera 60.00 150.00
HRKAPMP Mike Piazza 75.00 200.00
HRKAPMPI Mike Piazza 75.00 200.00
HRKAPMT Mike Trout 400.00 800.00
HRKAPMTR Mike Trout 400.00 800.00
HRKAPRH Rhys Hoskins 30.00 80.00
HRKAPRJ Reggie Jackson 50.00 120.00
HRKAPVGJ Vladimir Guerrero Jr. 150.00 400.00
HRKAPVLG Vladimir Guerrero 30.00 80.00

2019 Topps Luminaries Home Run Kings Autograph Relics

STATED ODDS 1:XX HOBBY
STATED PRINT RUN 15 SER.#'d SETS
EXCHANGE DEADLINE 7/31/2021
*BLUE/10: .4X TO 1X BASIC
HRKARAD Andre Dawson 25.00 60.00
HRKARAK Al Kaline 40.00 100.00
HRKARAR Alex Rodriguez 50.00 120.00
HRKARARI Anthony Rizzo 25.00 60.00
HRKARARO Alex Rodriguez 50.00 120.00
HRKARBJ Bo Jackson 50.00 120.00
HRKARCF Carlton Fisk 30.00 80.00
HRKARCRJ Cal Ripken Jr. 75.00 200.00
HRKARDM Don Mattingly 75.00 200.00
HRKARDO David Ortiz 40.00 100.00
HRKARFF Freddie Freeman 40.00 100.00
HRKARFT Frank Thomas 60.00 150.00
HRKARFTJ Fernando Tatis Jr. 200.00 500.00
HRKARGS George Springer 30.00 80.00
HRKARHM Hideki Matsui 50.00 120.00
HRKARI Ichiro 125.00 300.00
HRKARJB Johnny Bench 50.00 120.00
HRKARJP Jorge Posada 50.00 120.00
HRKARJS Juan Soto 50.00 120.00
HRKARKB Kris Bryant 60.00 150.00
HRKARKGJ Ken Griffey Jr. 125.00 300.00
HRKARMC Miguel Cabrera 50.00 120.00
HRKARMT Mike Trout 300.00 600.00
HRKARRD Rafael Devers
HRKARRH Rhys Hoskins 25.00 60.00
HRKARRJ Reggie Jackson 40.00 100.00
HRKARSO Shohei Ohtani 100.00 250.00
HRKARVGJ Vladimir Guerrero Jr. 125.00 300.00
HRKARVGS Vladimir Guerrero 25.00 60.00

2019 Topps Luminaries Home Run Kings Autographs

STATED ODDS 1:XX HOBBY
STATED PRINT RUN 15 SER.#'d SETS
EXCHANGE DEADLINE 7/31/2021
*RED/10: .4X TO 1X BASIC
HRKAB Adrian Beltre 25.00 60.00
HRKAJ Aaron Judge 75.00 200.00
HRKAJU Aaron Judge 75.00 200.00
HRKAK Al Kaline 50.00 120.00
HRKAM Andrew McCutchen 40.00 100.00
HRKAR Alex Rodriguez 50.00 120.00
HRKARI Anthony Rizzo 20.00 50.00
HRKARZ Anthony Rizzo 20.00 50.00
HRKBJ Bo Jackson 50.00 120.00
HRKBP Buster Posey 30.00 80.00
HRKBW Bernie Williams 20.00 50.00
HRKBWI Bernie Williams 20.00 50.00
HRKCF Carlton Fisk 20.00 50.00
HRKCJ Chipper Jones 40.00 100.00
HRKCJO Chipper Jones 40.00 100.00
HRKCR Cal Ripken Jr. 60.00 150.00
HRKCY Christian Yelich EXCH 75.00 200.00
HRKDM Don Mattingly 60.00 150.00
HRKDMA Don Mattingly 60.00 150.00
HRKDMU Dale Murphy 30.00 80.00
HRKDO David Ortiz 30.00 80.00
HRKDOR David Ortiz 30.00 80.00
HRKEJ Eloy Jimenez 60.00 150.00
HRKFF Freddie Freeman 25.00 60.00
HRKFL Francisco Lindor 25.00 60.00
HRKFLI Francisco Lindor 25.00 60.00
HRKFT Frank Thomas 40.00 100.00
HRKFTA Fernando Tatis Jr. 200.00 500.00
HRKFTH Frank Thomas 40.00 100.00
HRKFTJ Fernando Tatis Jr. 200.00 500.00
HRKHA Hank Aaron 100.00 250.00
HRKHM Hideki Matsui 40.00 100.00
HRKHMA Hideki Matsui 40.00 100.00
HRKIR Ivan Rodriguez 20.00 50.00
HRKI Ichiro 150.00 400.00
HRKJB Johnny Bench 40.00 100.00
HRKJBA Jeff Bagwell 25.00 60.00
HRKJBG Jeff Bagwell 25.00 60.00
HRKJP Jorge Posada 20.00 50.00
HRKJPO Jorge Posada 20.00 50.00
HRKJS Juan Soto 50.00 120.00
HRKJSO Juan Soto 50.00 120.00
HRKJT Jim Thome 30.00 80.00
HRKJV Joey Votto 20.00 50.00
HRKKB Kris Bryant 40.00 100.00
HRKKGJ Ken Griffey Jr. 125.00 300.00
HRKMC Miguel Cabrera 40.00 100.00
HRKMP Mike Piazza 30.00 80.00
HRKMPI Mike Piazza 30.00 80.00
HRKMT Mike Trout 250.00 500.00
HRKPG Paul Goldschmidt 20.00 50.00
HRKRAC Ronald Acuna Jr. 100.00 250.00
HRKRAJ Ronald Acuna Jr. 100.00 250.00
HRKRH Rhys Hoskins 40.00 100.00
HRKRJ Reggie Jackson 30.00 80.00
HRKRJA Reggie Jackson 30.00 80.00
HRKSO Shohei Ohtani 125.00 300.00
HRKVGJ Vladimir Guerrero Jr. 100.00 250.00
HRKVGR Vladimir Guerrero Jr. 100.00 250.00
HRKVGS Vladimir Guerrero 25.00 60.00
HRKVLG Vladimir Guerrero 25.00 60.00

2019 Topps Luminaries Masters of the Mound Autograph Patches

STATED ODDS 1:XX HOBBY
STATED PRINT RUN 15 SER.#'d SETS
EXCHANGE DEADLINE 7/31/2021
MOMAPANP Andy Pettitte 25.00 60.00
MOMAPAP Andy Pettitte 25.00 60.00
MOMAPCK Clayton Kershaw 75.00 200.00
MOMAPJD Jacob deGrom 50.00 12.00
MOMAPJDE Jacob deGrom 50.00 120.00
MOMAPMR Mariano Rivera 125.00 300.00
MOMAPMRI Mariano Rivera 125.00 300.00
MOMAPNS Noah Syndergaard 20.00 50.00
MOMAPNSY Noah Syndergaard 20.00 50.00
MOMAPRJ Randy Johnson 50.00 120.00

2019 Topps Luminaries Masters of the Mound Autograph Relics

STATED ODDS 1:XX HOBBY
STATED PRINT RUN 15 SER.#'d SETS
EXCHANGE DEADLINE 7/31/2021
*BLUE/10: .4X TO 1X BASIC
MOMARANP Andy Pettitte 20.00 50.00
MOMARAP Andy Pettitte 20.00 50.00
MOMARCK Clayton Kershaw 60.00 150.00
MOMARJD Jacob deGrom 40.00 100.00
MOMARLS Luis Severino
MOMARMR Mariano Rivera 125.00 300.00
MOMARPM Pedro Martinez 30.00 80.00
MOMARRC Roger Clemens 75.00 200.00
MOMARRJ Randy Johnson 40.00 100.00
MOMARSO Shohei Ohtani 100.00 250.00

2019 Topps Luminaries Masters of the Mound Autographs

STATED ODDS 1:XX HOBBY
STATED PRINT RUN 15 SER.#'d SETS
EXCHANGE DEADLINE 7/31/2021
*RED/10: .4X TO 1X BASIC
MOMAP Andy Pettitte 25.00 60.00
MOMBG Bob Gibson 25.00 60.00
MOMCK Clayton Kershaw 50.00 120.00
MOMCS Chris Sale 20.00 50.00
MOMCSA Chris Sale 20.00 50.00
MOMJD Jacob deGrom 50.00 120.00
MOMJM Juan Marichal
MOMJS John Smoltz 25.00 60.00
MOMLS Luis Severino 25.00 60.00
MOMMR Mariano Rivera 75.00 200.00
MOMNR Nolan Ryan 75.00 200.00
MOMPM Pedro Martinez 40.00 100.00
MOMPMA Pedro Martinez 40.00 100.00
MOMRC Roger Clemens 50.00 120.00
MOMRJ Randy Johnson 50.00 120.00
MOMSK Sandy Koufax 150.00 400.00
MOMSO Shohei Ohtani 125.00 300.00
MOMYK Yusei Kikuchi 20.00 50.00

2020 Topps Luminaries Hit Kings Autographs

STATED ODDS 1:XX HOBBY
STATED PRINT RUN 15 SER.#'d SETS
EXCHANGE DEADLINE 7/31/22
*RED/10: .4X TO 1X BASIC
HKI Ichiro 200.00 500.00
HKAA Aristides Aquino 30.00 80.00
HKAB Andrew Benintendi 20.00 50.00
HKAJ Aaron Judge 100.00 250.00
HKAR Alex Rodriguez 60.00 150.00
HKBH Bryce Harper 100.00 250.00
HKBL Barry Larkin 40.00 100.00
HKBP Buster Posey 40.00 100.00
HKCJ Chipper Jones 4.00 150.00
HKCY Carl Yastrzemski 75.00 200.00
HKDJ Derek Jeter 400.00 800.00
HKDM Don Mattingly 50.00 120.00
HKDO David Ortiz 50.00 120.00
HKEM Edgar Martinez 25.00 60.00
HKFT Frank Thomas 60.00 150.00
HKGS George Springer 20.00 50.00
HKGT Gleyber Torres 60.00 150.00
HKHA Hank Aaron 150.00 4001.00
HKJA Jose Altuve 20.00 50.00
HKJB Johnny Bench 50.00 120.00
HKJS Juan Soto 100.00 250.00
HKJT Jim Thome 30.00 80.00
HKJV Joey Votto 20.00 50.00
HKKB Kris Bryant 40.00 100.00
HKKH Keston Hiura 25.00 60.00
HKLR Luis Robert 200.00 500.00
HKMM Mark McGwire 50.00 120.00
HKMS Mike Schmidt 60.00 150.00
HKMT Mike Trout 600.00 1200.00
HKNH Nico Hoerner 50.00 125.00
HKOS Ozzie Smith 40.00 100.00
HKPA Pete Alonso 50.00 125.00
HKRA Roberto Alomar 25.00 60.00
HKRC Rod Carew 25.00 60.00
HKRD Rafael Devers 30.00 80.00
HKRH Rickey Henderson 60.00 150.00
HKRS Ryne Sandberg 50.00 120.00
HKRY Robin Yount 50.00 120.00
HKSO Shohei Ohtani 100.00 250.00
HKTR Tim Raines 15.00 40.00
HKWB Wade Boggs 40.00 100.00
HKXB Xander Bogaerts 40.00 100.00
HKYA Yordan Alvarez 120.00 300.00
HKAAQ Aristides Aquino 30.00 80.00
HKARI Anthony Rizzo 25.00 60.00
HKBBI Bo Bichette 100.00 250.00
HKCRJ Cal Ripken Jr. 75.00 200.00
HKCYE Christian Yelich 50.00 120.00
HKDMA Don Mattingly 50.00 120.00
HKFTJ Fernando Tatis Jr. 125.00 300.00
HKGSP George Springer 20.00 50.00
HKJBA Jeff Bagwell 30.00 80.00
HKJSO Juan Soto 100.00 250.00
HKKGJ Ken Griffey Jr. 200.00 500.00
HKKHI Keston Hiura 25.00 60.00
HKMMC Mark McGwire 50.00 120.00

HKPAL Pete Alonso 50.00 125.00
HKRAJ Ronald Acuna Jr. 80.00 200.00
HKRHO Rhys Hoskins 25.00 60.00
HKROA Ronald Acuna Jr. 80.00 200.00
HKVGJ Vladimir Guerrero Jr. 30.00 80.00
HKVLG Vladimir Guerrero Jr. 30.00 80.00

2020 Topps Luminaries Hit Kings Autograph Patches

STATED ODDS 1:XX HOBBY
STATED PRINT RUN 15 SER.#'d SETS
EXCHANGE DEADLINE 7/31/22
HKAPAA Aristides Aquino 40.00 100.00
HKAPAR Alex Rodriguez 125.00 300.00
HKAPBH Bryce Harper 150.00 400.00
HKAPBP Buster Posey 50.00 120.00
HKAPCY Christian Yelich 75.00 200.00
HKAPDO David Ortiz 50.00 120.00
HKAPGS George Springer 20.00 50.00
HKAPIS Ichiro 150.00 400.00
HKAPJA Jose Altuve 20.00 50.00
HKAPJT Jim Thome 50.00 120.00
HKAPKH Keston Hiura 40.00 100.00
HKAPMT Mike Trout 400.00 800.00
HKAPRA Roberto Alomar 50.00 120.00
HKAPRC Rod Carew 40.00 100.00
HKAPRH Rhys Hoskins 40.00 100.00
HKAPRY Robin Yount 75.00 200.00
HKAPSO Shohei Ohtani 125.00 300.00
HKAPWB Wade Boggs 50.00 120.00
HKAPXB Xander Bogaerts 40.00 100.00
HKAPYA Yordan Alvarez 150.00 400.00
HKAPAAQ Aristides Aquino 40.00 100.00
HKAPBBI Bo Bichette 125.00 300.00
HKAPDOR David Ortiz 50.00 120.00
HKAPFTJ Fernando Tatis Jr. 150.00 400.00
HKAPKGJ Ken Griffey Jr. 400.00 800.00
HKAPMTE Mark Teixeira 40.00 100.00
HKAPRAJ Ronald Acuna Jr. 100.00 250.00

2020 Topps Luminaries Hit Kings Autograph Relics

STATED ODDS 1:XX HOBBY
STATED PRINT RUN 15 SER.#'d SETS
EXCHANGE DEADLINE 7/31/22
HKARI Ichiro 200.00 500.00
HKARAA Aristides Aquino 30.00 80.00
HKARAB Andrew Benintendi 20.00 50.00
HKARAJ Aaron Judge 100.00 250.00
HKARBH Bryce Harper 125.00 300.00
HKARBL Barry Larkin 30.00 80.00
HKARBP Buster Posey 25.00 60.00
HKARCJ Chipper Jones 75.00 200.00
HKARCY Carl Yastrzemski 60.00 150.00
HKARDM Don Mattingly 60.00 150.00
HKARDO David Ortiz 40.00 100.00
HKAREM Edgar Martinez 50.00 120.00
HKARFT Frank Thomas 75.00 200.00
HKARGS George Springer 20.00 50.00
HKARGT Gleyber Torres 60.00 150.00
HKARHA Hank Aaron 150.00 400.00
HKARJA Jose Altuve 25.00 60.00
HKARJB Johnny Bench 60.00 150.00
HKARJS Juan Soto 75.00 200.00
HKARJT Jim Thome 30.00 80.00
HKARJV Joey Votto 40.00 100.00
HKARKB Kris Bryant 50.00 120.00
HKARMT Mike Trout 400.00 800.00
HKARPA Pete Alonso 75.00 200.00
HKARRC Rod Carew 25.00 60.00
HKARRH Rickey Henderson 50.00 120.00
HKARSO Shohei Ohtani 75.00 200.00
HKARVG Vladimir Guerrero 40.00 100.00
HKARYA Yordan Alvarez 75.00 200.00
HKARARO Alex Rodriguez 100.00 250.00
HKARBBI Bo Bichette 100.00 250.00
HKARCRJ Cal Ripken Jr. 75.00 200.00
HKARKGJ Ken Griffey Jr. 200.00 500.00
HKARMTE Mark Teixeira 40.00 100.00
HKARRAJ Ronald Acuna Jr. 80.00 200.00
HKARRAL Roberto Alomar 40.00 100.00
HKARRHO Rhys Hoskins 25.00 60.00
HKARVGJ Vladimir Guerrero Jr. 60.00 150.00

2020 Topps Luminaries Home Run Kings Autograph Patches

STATED ODDS 1:XX HOBBY
STATED PRINT RUN 15 SER.#'d SETS
EXCHANGE DEADLINE 7/31/22
HRKAPAA Aristides Aquino 40.00 100.00
HRKAPBH Bryce Harper 150.00 400.00
HRKAPBP Buster Posey 50.00 120.00
HRKAPCY Christian Yelich 75.00 200.00
HRKAPDO David Ortiz 50.00 120.00
HRKAPFT Frank Thomas 100.00 250.00
HRKAPGS George Springer 20.00 50.00
HRKAPIR Ivan Rodriguez 50.00 120.00
HRKAPJA Jose Altuve 20.00 50.00
HRKAPMT Mike Trout 400.00 800.00
HRKAPRA Ronald Acuna Jr. 100.00 250.00
HRKAPRH Rhys Hoskins 40.00 100.00
HRKAPSO Shohei Ohtani 125.00 300.00
HRKAPYA Yordan Alvarez 150.00 400.00
HRKAPBBI Bo Bichette 125.00 300.00
HRKAPBHA Bryce Harper 150.00 400.00
HRKAPBOB Bo Bichette 125.00 300.00
HRKAPCYE Christian Yelich 75.00 200.00
HRKAPIRO Ivan Rodriguez 50.00 120.00
HRKAPKGJ Ken Griffey Jr. 400.00 800.00
HRKAPMTE Mark Teixeira 40.00 100.00
HRKAPMTR Mike Trout 400.00 800.00
HRKAPRAJ Ronald Acuna Jr. 100.00 250.00
HRKAPYAL Yordan Alvarez 150.00 400.00

2020 Topps Luminaries Home Run Kings Autograph Relics

STATED ODDS 1:XX HOBBY
STATED PRINT RUN 15 SER.#'d SETS
EXCHANGE DEADLINE 7/31/22
HRKARAA Aristides Aquino 30.00 80.00
HRKARAB Andrew Benintendi 20.00 50.00
HRKARAJ Aaron Judge 100.00 250.00
HRKARAR Alex Rodriguez 100.00 250.00
HRKARBH Bryce Harper 125.00 300.00
HRKARCJ Chipper Jones 75.00 200.00
HRKARCY Carl Yastrzemski 60.00 150.00
HRKARDO David Ortiz 40.00 100.00
HRKAREM Edgar Martinez 50.00 120.00
HRKARFT Frank Thomas 75.00 200.00
HRKARGT Gleyber Torres 60.00 150.00
HRKARHA Hank Aaron 150.00 400.00
HRKARIR Ivan Rodriguez 20.00 50.00
HRKARJA Jose Altuve 25.00 60.00
HRKARJS Juan Soto 75.00 200.00
HRKARKB Kris Bryant 50.00 120.00
HRKARMT Mike Trout 400.00 800.00
HRKARNA Nolan Arenado 100.00 250.00
HRKARPA Pete Alonso 75.00 200.00
HRKARPG Paul Goldschmidt 25.00 60.00
HRKARRH Rhys Hoskins 25.00 60.00
HRKARSO Shohei Ohtani 75.00 200.00
HRKARSS Sammy Sosa 125.00 300.00
HRKARVG Vladimir Guerrero 40.00 100.00
HRKARYA Yordan Alvarez 75.00 200.00
HRKARBBI Bo Bichette 100.00 250.00
HRKARCRJ Cal Ripken Jr. 75.00 200.00
HRKARCYE Christian Yelich 125.00 300.00
HRKARKGJ Ken Griffey Jr. 200.00 500.00
HRKARRAJ Ronald Acuna Jr. 80.00 200.00
HRKARVGJ Vladimir Guerrero Jr. 60.00 150.00

2020 Topps Luminaries Home Run Kings Autographs

STATED ODDS 1:XX HOBBY
STATED PRINT RUN 15 SER.#'d SETS
EXCHANGE DEADLINE 7/31/22
*RED/10: .4X TO 1X BASIC
HRKAA Aristides Aquino 30.00 80.00
HRKAB Andrew Benintendi 20.00 50.00
HRKAD Andre Dawson 30.00 80.00
HRKAJ Aaron Judge 100.00 250.00
HRKAR Alex Rodriguez 60.00 150.00
HRKBH Bryce Harper 100.00 250.00
HRKBP Buster Posey 40.00 100.00
HRKBW Bernie Williams 30.00 80.00
HRKCF Carlton Fisk 20.00 50.00
HRKCJ Chipper Jones 60.00 150.00
HRKCY Carl Yastrzemski 75.00 200.00
HRKDO David Ortiz 50.00 120.00
HRKDW David Wright 40.00 100.00
HRKEJ Eloy Jimenez 40.00 100.00
HRKEM Edgar Martinez 40.00 100.00
HRKFT Frank Thomas 60.00 150.00
HRKGS George Springer 20.00 50.00
HRKGT Gleyber Torres 60.00 150.00
HRKHA Hank Aaron 150.00 400.00
HRKIR Ivan Rodriguez 25.00 60.00
HRKJA Jose Altuve 20.00 50.00
HRKJB Johnny Bench 50.00 120.00
HRKJR Jim Rice 25.00 60.00
HRKJS Juan Soto 100.00 250.00
HRKJT Jim Thome 30.00 80.00
HRKJV Joey Votto 40.00 100.00
HRKKB Kris Bryant 40.00 100.00
HRKLR Luis Robert 200.00 500.00
HRKMM Mark McGwire 50.00 120.00
HRKMS Mike Schmidt 60.00 150.00
HRKMT Mike Trout 400.00 800.00
HRKNA Nolan Arenado 60.00 150.00
HRKPA Pete Alonso 50.00 125.00
HRKPG Paul Goldschmidt 30.00 80.00
HRKRH Rhys Hoskins 25.00 60.00
HRKRJ Reggie Jackson 30.00 80.00
HRKSO Shohei Ohtani 75.00 200.00
HRKVG Vladimir Guerrero 40.00 100.00
HRKYA Yordan Alvarez 120.00 300.00
HRKARI Anthony Rizzo 25.00 60.00
HRKBBI Bo Bichette 100.00 250.00
HRKCRJ Cal Ripken Jr. 75.00 200.00
HRKFTH Frank Thomas 60.00 150.00
HRKJAL Jose Altuve 20.00 50.00
HRKJBA Jeff Bagwell 30.00 80.00
HRKJBE Johnny Bench 50.00 120.00
HRKJDM J.D. Martinez 20.00 50.00
HRKJSO Juan Soto 100.00 250.00
HRKKGJ Ken Griffey Jr. 200.00 500.00
HRKMTE Mark Teixeira 30.00 80.00
HRKPAL Pete Alonso 50.00 125.00
HRKRAJ Ronald Acuna Jr. 80.00 200.00
HRKRHO Rhys Hoskins 25.00 60.00
HRKRJA Reggie Jackson 30.00 80.00
HRKROA Ronald Acuna Jr. 80.00 200.00
HRKVGJ Vladimir Guerrero Jr. 30.00 80.00
HRKVLJ Vladimir Guerrero Jr. 30.00 80.00
HRKYAL Yordan Alvarez 120.00 300.00

2020 Topps Luminaries Masters of the Mound Autograph Patches

STATED ODDS 1:XX HOBBY
STATED PRINT RUN 15 SER.#'d SETS
EXCHANGE DEADLINE 7/31/22
MOMAPCK Clayton Kershaw 100.00 250.00
MOMAPGC Gerrit Cole 60.00 150.00
MOMAPMR Mariano Rivera 125.00 300.00
MOMAPMS Max Scherzer 75.00 200.00
MOMAPMT Masahiro Tanaka 50.00 120.00
MOMAPPM Pedro Martinez 60.00 150.00
MOMAPSO Shohei Ohtani 125.00 300.00
MOMAPCKE Clayton Kershaw 100.00 250.00
MOMAPMRI Mariano Rivera 125.00 300.00
MOMAPPMA Pedro Martinez 60.00 150.00

2020 Topps Luminaries Masters of the Mound Autograph Relics

STATED ODDS 1:XX HOBBY
STATED PRINT RUN 15 SER.#'d SETS
EXCHANGE DEADLINE 7/31/22
MOMARAP Andy Pettitte 50.00 120.00
MOMARBB Bert Blyleven 30.00 80.00
MOMARCK Clayton Kershaw 100.00 250.00
MOMARJS John Smoltz 30.00 80.00
MOMARMR Mariano Rivera 125.00 300.00
MOMARMT Masahiro Tanaka 100.00 250.00
MOMARPM Pedro Martinez 40.00 100.00
MOMARRC Roger Clemens 75.00 200.00
MOMARSC Steve Carlton 30.00 80.00
MOMARSO Shohei Ohtani 75.00 200.00
MOMARCCS CC Sabathia 40.00 100.00

2020 Topps Luminaries Masters of the Mound Autographs

STATED ODDS 1:XX HOBBY
STATED PRINT RUN 15 SER.#'d SETS
EXCHANGE DEADLINE 7/31/22
*RED/10: .4X TO 1X BASIC
MOMAP Andy Pettitte 25.00 60.00
MOMBB Bert Blyleven 25.00 60.00
MOMBG Bob Gibson 40.00 100.00
MOMGC Gerrit Cole 100.00 250.00
MOMJM Juan Marichal 30.00 80.00
MOMJS John Smoltz 20.00 50.00
MOMMM Mike Mussina 50.00 120.00
MOMMR Mariano Rivera
MOMMS Max Scherzer 50.00 120.00
MOMNR Nolan Ryan 100.00 250.00
MOMPM Pedro Martinez 40.00 100.00
MOMRC Roger Clemens 40.00 100.00
MOMRJ Randy Johnson 60.00 150.00
MOMSC Steve Carlton 25.00 60.00
MOMSK Sandy Koufax 150.00 400.00
MOMSO Shohei Ohtani 75.00 200.00
MOMCCS CC Sabathia 30.00 80.00

2020 Topps Luminaries Spark of Light Autograph Patches

STATED ODDS 1:XX HOBBY
STATED PRINT RUN 15 SER.#'d SETS
EXCHANGE DEADLINE 7/31/22
SLPAA Aristides Aquino 40.00 100.00
SLPBB Bo Bichette 125.00 300.00
SLPEJ Eloy Jimenez 50.00 125.00
SLPGT Gleyber Torres 75.00 200.00
SLPKH Keston Hiura 40.00 100.00
SLPRH Rhys Hoskins 40.00 100.00
SLPSO Shohei Ohtani 125.00 300.00
SLPYA Yordan Alvarez 150.00 400.00
SLPRAJ Ronald Acuna Jr. 100.00 250.00
SLPVGJ Vladimir Guerrero Jr. 40.00 100.00

2020 Topps Luminaries Spark of Light Dual Autograph Patches

STATED ODDS 1:XX HOBBY
STATED PRINT RUN 15 SER.#'d SETS
EXCHANGE DEADLINE 7/31/22
SLDPBL G.Lux/B.Bichette EXCH 200.00 500.00

2020 Topps Luminaries Spark of Light Dual Autographs

STATED ODDS 1:XX HOBBY
STATED PRINT RUN 15 SER.#'d SETS
EXCHANGE DEADLINE 7/31/22
SLDAAS R.Acuna/J.Soto 200.00 500.00
SLDAJC D.Cease/E.Jimenez 40.00 100.00
SLDATA G.Torres/P.Alonso 200.00 500.00

2011 Topps Marquee

COMPLETE SET (100) 30.00 60.00
COMMON CARD (1-100) .40 1.00
COMMON RC (1-100) .40 1.00
1 Ryan Braun .60 1.50
2 Juan Marichal .60 1.50
3 Cliff Lee .60 1.50
4 Christy Mathewson 1.00 2.50
5 Ozzie Smith 1.25 3.00
6 Robinson Cano .60 1.50
7 Mark Teixeira .60 1.50
8 Jim Palmer .60 1.50
9 Jered Weaver .60 1.50
10 Rogers Hornsby .60 1.50
11 Albert Pujols 1.25 3.00
12 Bob Gibson .60 1.50
13 Dustin Pedroia 1.00 2.50
14 Ryan Zimmerman .60 1.50
15 Nolan Ryan 3.00 8.00
16 Brandon Phillips .40 1.00
17 Starlin Castro .60 1.50
18 George Sisler .60 1.50
19 Lou Gehrig 2.00 5.00
20 CC Sabathia .60 1.50
21 Brian Wilson 1.00 2.50
22 Justin Verlander 1.00 2.50
23 Jon Lester .60 1.50
24 Pee Wee Reese .60 1.50
25 Joey Votto 1.00 2.50
26 Ichiro Suzuki 1.25 3.00
27 Mariano Rivera 1.25 3.00
28 Carlos Gonzalez .60 1.50
29 Chipper Jones 1.00 2.50
30 Cy Young 1.00 2.50
31 Mickey Mantle 3.00 8.00
32 Tony Gwynn 1.00 2.50
33 Tris Speaker .60 1.50
34 Thurman Munson 1.00 2.50
35 Jason Heyward .75 2.00
36 Babe Ruth 2.50 6.00
37 Prince Fielder .60 1.50
38 Cal Ripken Jr. 3.00 8.00
39 Cole Hamels .75 2.00
40 Joe Morgan .60 1.50
41 Justin Morneau .60 1.50
42 Michael Pineda RC 1.00 2.50
43 Stan Musial 1.50 4.00
44 Hanley Ramirez .60 1.50
45 Jackie Robinson 1.00 2.50
46 Derek Jeter 2.50 6.00
47 Frank Robinson .60 1.50
48 Ty Cobb 1.50 4.00
49 Whitey Ford .60 1.50
50 Ian Kinsler .60 1.50
51 Kevin Youkilis .40 1.00
52 Matt Kemp .75 2.00
53 Miguel Cabrera 1.00 2.50
54 Tom Seaver .60 1.50
55 Ryan Howard .75 2.00
56 Andre Ethier .60 1.50
57 Matt Holliday 1.00 2.50
58 Josh Johnson .60 1.50
59 Ryne Sandberg 2.00 5.00
60 Zach Britton RC 1.00 2.50
61 Jose Bautista .60 1.50
62 Mel Ott 1.00 2.50
63 Zack Greinke 1.00 2.50
64 Sandy Koufax 2.00 5.00
65 Mike Schmidt 1.50 4.00
66 Ubaldo Jimenez .40 1.00
67 Clayton Kershaw 1.50 4.00
68 Adrian Gonzalez .75 2.00
69 Nelson Cruz 1.00 2.50
70 Alex Rodriguez 1.25 3.00
71 Shin-Soo Choo .60 1.50
72 Willie McCovey .60 1.50
73 Eddie Murray .60 1.50
74 Justin Upton .60 1.50
75 Duke Snider .60 1.50
76 David Wright .75 2.00
77 Hank Aaron 2.00 5.00
78 Roy Campanella 1.00 2.50
79 Jose Reyes .60 1.50
80 Evan Longoria .60 1.50
81 David Price .75 2.00
82 Tim Lincecum .60 1.50
83 Reggie Jackson .60 1.50
84 Johnny Mize .60 1.50
85 Roberto Alomar .60 1.50
86 Carlos Santana 1.00 2.50
87 Brandon Belt RC 1.00 2.50
88 Josh Hamilton .60 1.50
89 Buster Posey 1.25 3.00
90 Joe DiMaggio 2.00 5.00
91 Troy Tulowitzki 1.00 2.50
92 Brett Anderson .40 1.00
93 Johnny Bench 1.00 2.50
94 Chase Utley .60 1.50
95 Roy Halladay .60 1.50
96 Carl Crawford .60 1.50
97 Honus Wagner 1.00 2.50
98 Felix Hernandez
99 Joe Mauer .75 2.00
100 Brooks Robinson .60 1.50

2011 Topps Marquee Blue

*BLUE: .6X TO 1.5X BASIC
*BLUE RC: .6X TO 1.5X BASIC
STATED ODDS 1:3 HOBBY
STATED PRINT RUN 299 SER.#'d SETS

2011 Topps Marquee Copper

*COPPER: .6X TO 1.5X BASIC
*COPPER RC: .6X TO 1.5X BASIC
STATED ODDS 1:3 HOBBY
STATED PRINT RUN 199 SER.#'d SETS

2011 Topps Marquee Gold

*GOLD: 1X TO 2.5X BASIC
*GOLD RC: 1X TO 2.5X BASIC
STATED ODDS 1:6 HOBBY
STATED PRINT RUN 99 SER.#'d SETS

2011 Topps Marquee Acclaimed Impressions Dual Relic Autographs

STATED ODDS 1:7 HOBBY
PRINT RUNS B/WN 10-590 COPIES PER
EXCHANGE DEADLINE 9/30/2014
AID2 David Ortiz 20.00 50.00
AID6 Starlin Castro/70 8.00 20.00
AID8 Austin Jackson/70 6.00 15.00
AID10 Steve Garvey/126 12.00 30.00
AID11 Kendrys Morales 5.00 12.00
AID14 Andrew McCutchen/70 40.00 80.00
AID16 Tommy Hanson 10.00 25.00
AID18 Matt Kemp 20.00 50.00
AID19 Josh Johnson/50 10.00 25.00
AID21 Shin-Soo Choo 12.00 30.00
AID23 Nelson Cruz 12.50 30.00
AID24 Marlon Byrd/462 6.00 15.00
AID25 Ike Davis/70 10.00 25.00
AID26 Brett Gardner 10.00 25.00
AID27 Ian Kinsler 6.00 15.00
AID28 Andre Ethier/106 6.00 15.00
AID29 Colby Rasmus/150 6.00 15.00
AID30 Zach Britton/70 10.00 25.00
AID31 Brian McCann/50 20.00 50.00
AID33 Kyle Drabek/182 5.00 12.00
AID34 Jonathan Papelbon 6.00 15.00
AID35 Dustin Pedroia/50 30.00 60.00
AID37 Brett Anderson/150 5.00 12.00
AID38 Pablo Sandoval/174 10.00 25.00
AID39 Clay Buchholz 6.00 15.00
AID40 Andrew Cashner/400 5.00 12.00
AID41 Jeff Niemann/400 6.00 15.00
AID42 Jeremy Jeffress/590 5.00 12.00
AID43 Billy Butler 5.00 12.00
AID44 Daniel Descalso/400 5.00 12.00
AID45 Brandon Belt/400 12.00 30.00
AID46 Daniel Hudson/400 6.00 15.00
AID47 Jose Tabata/200 5.00 12.00
AID48 Max Scherzer/70 40.00 100.00
AID49 Fausto Carmona/150 6.00 15.00
AID50 Neftali Feliz/200 6.00 15.00
AID51 Jason Heyward/50 12.00 30.00
AID53 Tyson Ross 5.00 12.00
AID54 Angel Pagan/150 6.00 20.00
AID55 Heath Bell/70 5.00 12.00
AID56 Madison Bumgarner/174 15.00 40.00
AID57 Fernando Martinez/200 5.00 12.00
AID58 Ervin Santana/150 6.00 15.00
AID59 Fergie Jenkins 12.50 30.00
AID60 Danny Valencia/500 8.00 20.00
AID61 Yunel Escobar/150 6.00 15.00
AID62 Drew Storen/200 5.00 12.00
AID63 Ryan Zimmerman/50 12.50 30.00
AID64 Michael Pineda/150 10.00 25.00

2011 Topps Marquee Acclaimed Impressions Triple Relic Autographs

STATED ODDS 1:15 HOBBY
PRINT RUNS B/WN 10-606 COPIES PER
EXCHANGE DEADLINE 9/30/2014
AIT3 Drew Stubbs/606 8.00 20.00
AIT4 Neftali Feliz/470 6.00 15.00
AIT5 Tommy Hanson/50 15.00 40.00
AIT6 Jose Tabata/470 5.00 12.00
AIT7 Trevor Cahill/70 6.00 15.00
AIT11 Heath Bell/150 6.00 15.00
AIT12 Ian Kinsler EXCH 10.00 25.00
AIT13 Josh Johnson/50 5.00 12.00
AIT14 Ryan Zimmerman/50 15.00 40.00
AIT17 Steve Garvey/156 12.50 30.00
AIT18 Nelson Cruz/70 8.00 20.00
AIT19 Shane Victorino/70 8.00 20.00
AIT20 Brett Anderson/350 6.00 15.00
AIT22 Adam Jones/50 10.00 25.00
AIT26 Martin Prado/250 5.00 12.00
AIT27 Clay Buchholz/50 10.00 25.00
AIT28 Austin Jackson/150 10.00 25.00
AIT29 Justin Upton/50 15.00 40.00
AIT30 Andrew McCutchen/150 8.00 20.00
AIT31 Chris Coghlan/250 6.00 15.00
AIT32 Billy Butler EXCH 10.00 25.00
AIT33 Brandon Phillips/50 12.50 30.00

2011 Topps Marquee Gametime Mementos Quad Relics Red

*RED: .4X TO 1X BASIC
STATED ODDS 1:32 HOBBY
PRINT RUNS B/WN 125-150 COPIES PER

2011 Topps Marquee Monumental Markings Autographs

STATED ODDS 1:5 HOBBY
PRINT RUNS B/WN 10-600 COPIES PER
NO PRICING ON QTY 25 OR LESS
EXCHANGE DEADLINE 9/30/2014
AC Aroldis Chapman/185 10.00 25.00
AOG Alexi Ogando/570 5.00 12.00
AP Albert Pujols EXCH 200.00 300.00
APA Angel Pagan/570 6.00 15.00
BA Brett Anderson/570 4.00 10.00
BB Brandon Belt/570 5.00 12.00
BJU B.J. Upton EXCH 8.00 20.00
BWA Brett Wallace/570 4.00 10.00
CKI Craig Kimbrel/570 6.00 15.00
CR Colby Rasmus/570 5.00 12.00
CYO Chris Young/75 6.00 15.00
DP Dustin Pedroia EXCH 20.00 50.00
DS Drew Stubbs/570 6.00 15.00
DST Drew Storen/600 6.00 15.00
EA Elvis Andrus/75 8.00 20.00
ESA Ervin Santana/300 5.00 12.00
FCA Fausto Carmona/300 4.00 10.00
FF Freddie Freeman/185 12.50 30.00
FMA Fernando Martinez/600 5.00 12.00
GF George Foster EXCH 10.00 25.00
HB Heath Bell/190 4.00 10.00
ID Ike Davis/75 6.00 15.00
JB Jay Bruce/75 10.00 25.00
JCU Johnny Cueto/75 8.00 20.00
JFR Jeff Francis/570 4.00 10.00
JH Jeremy Hellickson/185 6.00 15.00
JJE Jeremy Jeffress/600 4.00 10.00
JT Jose Tabata/570 4.00 10.00
KD Kyle Drabek/75 6.00 15.00
MBU Madison Bumgarner EXCH 20.00 50.00
ML Mat Latos EXCH 6.00 15.00
MP Michael Pineda/570 6.00 15.00
MP Manny Pacquiao 100.00 200.00
MS Mike Schmidt EXCH 50.00 100.00
MSZ Max Scherzer/185 30.00 80.00
NF Neftali Feliz/75 10.00 25.00
NWK Neil Walker/185 8.00 20.00
PON Paul O'Neill/75 15.00 40.00
PS Pablo Sandoval/75 12.00 30.00
RED Red Schoendienst/75 15.00 40.00
SC Starlin Castro/75 6.00 15.00
TC Trevor Cahill/75 10.00 25.00
TRO Tyson Ross/600 4.00 10.00
ZB Zach Britton/75 6.00 15.00

2011 Topps Marquee Monumental Markings Autographs Gold

STATED ODDS 1:135 HOBBY
PRINT RUN B/WN 5-50 COPIES PER
NO PRICING ON QTY 5
EXCHANGE DEADLINE 9/30/2014
MP Manny Pacquiao/50 250.00 400.00

2011 Topps Marquee Museum Collection Autographs

STATED ODDS 1:48 HOBBY
STATED PRINT RUN 10 SER.#'d SETS
NO PRICING DUE TO SCARCITY
EXCHANGE DEADLINE 9/30/2014

2011 Topps Marquee Titanic Threads

STATED ODDS 1:6 HOBBY
STATED PRINT RUN 99 SER.#'d SETS
TTJR1 Mike Schmidt 10.00 25.00
TTJR2 Derek Jeter 20.00 50.00
TTJR3 Nolan Ryan 20.00 50.00
TTJR4 Evan Longoria 6.00 15.00
TTJR5 Joe DiMaggio 125.00 250.00
TTJR6 Rickey Henderson 6.00 15.00
TTJR7 Mickey Mantle 125.00 250.00
TTJR8 Ichiro Suzuki 10.00 25.00
TTJR9 Albert Pujols 12.50 30.00
TTJR10 Hank Aaron 30.00 60.00
TTJR11 Sandy Koufax 40.00 80.00
TTJR12 Roy Halladay 12.50 30.00
TTJR13 Stan Musial 40.00 80.00
TTJR14 Bob Gibson 12.50 30.00
TTJR15 Felix Hernandez 8.00 20.00
TTJR16 Tony Gwynn 8.00 20.00
TTJR17 Johnny Bench 10.00 25.00
TTJR18 Rollie Fingers 10.00 25.00
TTJR19 Carlton Fisk 10.00 25.00
TTJR20 Reggie Jackson 6.00 15.00
TTJR21 Fergie Jenkins 12.50 30.00
TTJR22 Al Kaline 10.00 25.00
TTJR23 Juan Marichal 10.00 25.00
TTJR24 Willie McCovey 10.00 25.00
TTJR25 Eddie Murray 12.50 30.00
TTJR26 Tony Perez 10.00 25.00
TTJR27 Gaylord Perry 10.00 25.00
TTJR28 Red Schoendienst 10.00 25.00
TTJR29 Tom Seaver 10.00 25.00
TTJR30 Ozzie Smith 8.00 20.00
TTJR31 Roy Campanella 10.00 25.00
TTJR32 Johnny Mize 10.00 25.00
TTJR33 Mel Ott 8.00 20.00
TTJR34 Roberto Alomar 10.00 25.00
TTJR35 Albert Belle 8.00 20.00
TTJR36 Andre Dawson 8.00 20.00
TTJR37 Steve Garvey 6.00 15.00
TTJR38 Paul Molitor 8.00 20.00
TTJR39 Paul O'Neill 12.50 30.00
TTJR40 Cal Ripken Jr. 8.00 20.00
TTJR41 Frank Robinson 10.00 25.00
TTJR42 John Smoltz 8.00 20.00
TTJR43 Frank Thomas 10.00 25.00
TTJR44 Jered Weaver 6.00 15.00
TTJR45 Torii Hunter 6.00 15.00
TTJR46 Hunter Pence 6.00 15.00
TTJR47 Trevor Cahill 6.00 15.00
TTJR48 Kyle Drabek 6.00 15.00
TTJR49 Martin Prado 6.00 15.00
TTJR50 Chipper Jones 12.50 30.00
TTJR51 Jason Heyward 8.00 20.00
TTJR52 Ryan Braun 10.00 25.00
TTJR53 Prince Fielder 6.00 15.00
TTJR54 Adam Wainwright 10.00 25.00
TTJR55 Starlin Castro 15.00 40.00
TTJR56 Aramis Ramirez 6.00 15.00
TTJR57 Justin Upton 6.00 15.00
TTJR58 Stephen Drew 6.00 15.00
TTJR59 Andre Ethier 6.00 15.00
TTJR60 Matt Kemp 10.00 25.00
TTJR61 Clayton Kershaw 10.00 25.00
TTJR62 Tim Lincecum 6.00 15.00
TTJR63 Pablo Sandoval 8.00 20.00
TTJR64 Brian Wilson 6.00 15.00
TTJR65 Shin-Soo Choo 10.00 25.00
TTJR66 Carlos Santana 6.00 15.00
TTJR67 Grady Sizemore 6.00 15.00
TTJR68 Michael Pineda 8.00 20.00
TTJR69 Carlos Beltran 6.00 15.00
TTJR70 David Wright 8.00 20.00
TTJR71 Jose Reyes 10.00 25.00
TTJR72 Robinson Cano 6.00 15.00
TTJR73 Hanley Ramirez 6.00 15.00
TTJR74 Josh Johnson 6.00 15.00
TTJR75 Ryan Zimmerman 8.00 20.00
TTJR76 Zach Britton 6.00 15.00
TTJR77 Alex Rodriguez 15.00 40.00
TTJR79 Heath Bell 6.00 15.00
TTJR80 Cliff Lee 8.00 20.00
TTJR81 Ryan Howard 10.00 25.00
TTJR84 Nelson Cruz 6.00 15.00
TTJR85 Ian Kinsler 6.00 15.00
TTJR86 Jeremy Hellickson 12.50 30.00
TTJR88 Adrian Gonzalez 8.00 20.00
TTJR89 Josh Beckett 6.00 15.00
TTJR90 Carl Crawford 6.00 15.00
TTJR91 Joey Votto 10.00 25.00
TTJR92 Brandon Phillips 6.00 15.00
TTJR93 Troy Tulowitzki 10.00 25.00
TTJR94 Carlos Gonzalez 8.00 20.00
TTJR95 Billy Butler 8.00 20.00
TTJR96 Miguel Cabrera 8.00 20.00
TTJR97 Justin Verlander 12.50 30.00
TTJR98 Justin Morneau 8.00 20.00
TTJR99 Carlos Quentin 6.00 15.00
TTJR100 Mark Teixeira 6.00 15.00
TTJR102 Jay Bruce 6.00 15.00
TTJR103 Johnny Cueto 6.00 15.00
TTJR104 Drew Stubbs 6.00 15.00
TTJR105 Edwin Encarnacion 6.00 15.00
TTJR106 Vladimir Guerrero 6.00 15.00
TTJR107 A.J. Pierzynski 6.00 15.00
TTJR108 Asdrubal Cabrera 6.00 15.00
TTJR109 Mark Buehrle 8.00 20.00
TTJR110 Jimmy Rollins 10.00 25.00
TTJR111 Alex Gordon 10.00 25.00
TTJR112 Michael Young 6.00 15.00
TTJR113 Fausto Carmona 6.00 15.00
TTJR114 Carlos Marmol 6.00 15.00
TTJR115 B.J. Upton 6.00 15.00

2011 Topps Marquee Titanic Threads Red

*RED: .4X TO 1X BASIC
STATED ODDS 1:28 HOBBY
STATED PRINT RUN 50 SER.#'d SETS

2012 Topps Mini

COMPLETE SET (661) 60.00 120.00
PRINTING PLATE ODDS 1:66
PLATE PRINT RUN 1 SET PER COLOR
BLACK-CYAN-MAGENTA-YELLOW ISSUED
NO PLATE PRICING DUE TO SCARCITY
1 Ryan Braun .30 .75
2 Trevor Cahill .30 .75
3 Jaime Garcia .40 1.00
4 Jeremy Guthrie .30 .75
5 Desmond Jennings .40 1.00
6 Nick Hagadone RC .40 1.00
7 Mickey Mantle 1.50 4.00
8 Mike Adams .30 .75
9 Jesus Montero RC .40 1.00
10 Jon Lester .30 .75
11 Hong-Chih Kuo .30 .75
12 Wilson Ramos .30 .75
13 Vernon Wells .30 .75
14 Jesus Guzman .30 .75
15 Melky Cabrera .30 .75
16 Desmond Jennings .40 1.00
17 Alex Rios .40 1.00
18 Colby Lewis .30 .75
19 Yonder Alonso .30 .75
20 Craig Kimbrel .40 1.00
21 Chris Iannetta .30 .75
22 Alfredo Simon .30 .75
23 Cory Luebke .30 .75
24 Ike Davis .30 .75
25 Neil Walker .30 .75
26 Kyle Lohse .30 .75
27 John Buck .30 .75
28 Placido Polanco .30 .75
29 Livan Hernandez .40 1.00
Roy Oswalt
Randy Wolf LDR
30 Derek Jeter 1.25 3.00
31 Brent Morel .30 .75
32 Detroit Tigers PS HL .20 .50
33 Curtis Granderson .40 1.00
Robinson Cano
Adrian Gonzalez LL
34 Derek Holland .30 .75
35 Eric Hosmer .40 1.00
36 Michael Taylor RC .40 1.00
37 Mike Napoli .30 .75
38 Felipe Paulino .30 .75
39 James Loney .30 .75
40 Tom Milone RC .40 1.00
41 Devin Mesoraco RC .40 1.00
42 Drew Pomeranz RC .40 1.00
43 Brett Wallace .30 .75
44 Edwin Jackson .30 .75
45 Jhoulys Chacin .30 .75
46 Peter Bourjos .30 .75
47 Luke Hochevar .30 .75
48 Wade Davis .40 1.00
49 Jon Niese .30 .75
50 Adrian Gonzalez .40 1.00
51 Alcides Escobar .40 1.00
52 Verland/Weaver/Shields LL .50 1.25
53 St. Louis Cardinals WS HL .20 .50
54 Jhonny Peralta .30 .75
55 Michael Young .30 .75
56 Geovany Soto .40 1.00
57 Yuniesky Betancourt .30 .75
58 Tim Hudson .40 1.00
59 Texas Rangers PS HL .20 .50
60 Hanley Ramirez .40 1.00
61 Daniel Bard .30 .75
62 Ben Revere .40 1.00
63 Nate Schierholtz .30 .75
64 Michael Martinez .30 .75
65 Delmon Young .40 1.00
66 Nyjer Morgan .30 .75
67 Aaron Crow .30 .75
68 Jason Hammel .40 1.00
69 Dee Gordon .30 .75
70 Brett Pill RC .60 1.50
71 Jeff Karstens .30 .75
72 Rex Brothers .30 .75
73 Brandon McCarthy .30 .75
74 Kevin Correia .30 .75
75 Jordan Zimmermann .40 1.00
76 Ian Kennedy .30 .75
77 Kemp/Fielder/Pujols LL .60 1.50
78 Erick Aybar .30 .75
79 Austin Romine RC .40 1.00
80 David Price .40 1.00
81 Liam Hendriks RC .40 1.00
82 Rick Porcello .30 .75
83 Bobby Parnell .30 .75
84 Brian Matusz .30 .75
85 Jason Heyward .40 1.00
86 Brett Cecil .30 .75
87 Craig Kimbrel .40 1.00
88 Javy Guerra .30 .75
89 Dontrelle Willis .30 .75
90 Adron Chambers RC .60 1.50
91 ARod/Thome/Giambi LDR .60 1.50
92 Tim Lincecum .40 1.00
Chris Carpenter
Roy Oswalt LDR
93 Skip Schumaker .30 .75
94 Logan Forsythe .30 .75
95 Chris Parmelee RC .40 1.00
96 Grady Sizemore .40 1.00
97 Jim Thome RB .40 1.00
98 Domonic Brown .40 1.00
99 Michael McKenry .30 .75
100 Jose Bautista .40 1.00
101 David Hernandez .30 .75
102 Chase d'Arnaud .30 .75
103 Madison Bumgarner .40 1.00
104 Brett Anderson .30 .75
105 Paul Konerko .30 .75
106 Mark Trumbo .30 .75
107 Luke Scott .30 .75
108 Albert Pujols WS HL .60 1.50
109 Mariano Rivera RB .60 1.50
110 Mark Teixeira .40 1.00
111 Kevin Slowey .30 .75
112 Juan Nicasio .30 .75
113 Craig Kimbrel RB .40 1.00
114 Matt Garza .30 .75
115 Tommy Hanson .30 .75
116 A.J. Pierzynski .30 .75
117 Carlos Ruiz .30 .75
118 Miguel Olivo .30 .75
119 Ichiro/Mauer/Vlad LDR .60 1.50
120 Hunter Pence .40 1.00
121 Josh Bell .30 .75
122 Ted Lilly .30 .75
123 Scott Downs .30 .75
124 Pujols/Vlad/Helton LDR .60 1.50
125 Adam Jones .40 1.00
126 Eduardo Nunez .30 .75
127 Eli Whiteside .30 .75
128 Lucas Duda .40 1.00
129 Matt Moore RC .60 1.50
130 Asdrubal Cabrera .40 1.00
131 Ian Desmond .30 .75
132 Will Venable .30 .75
133 Ivan Nova .40 1.00
134 Stephen Lombardozzi RC .40 1.00
135 Johnny Cueto .40 1.00
136 Casey McGehee .30 .75
137 Jarrod Saltalamacchia .30 .75
138 Pedro Alvarez .30 .75
139 Scott Sizemore .30 .75
140 Troy Tulowitzki .50 1.25
141 Brandon Belt .40 1.00
142 Travis Wood .30 .75
143 George Kottaras .30 .75
144 Marlon Byrd .30 .75
145 Billy Butler .30 .75
146 Carlos Gomez .30 .75
147 Orlando Hudson .30 .75
148 Chris Getz .30 .75
149 Chris Sale .50 1.25
150 Roy Halladay .40 1.00
151 Chris Davis .30 .75
152 Chad Billingsley .30 .75
153 Mark Melancon .30 .75
154 Ty Wigginton .30 .75
155 Matt Cain .40 1.00
156 Kennedy/Kershaw/Halladay LL .75 2.00
157 Anibal Sanchez .30 .75
158 Josh Reddick .30 .75
159 Chipper/Pujols/Helton LDR .60 1.50
160 Kevin Youkilis .50 1.25
161 Dee Gordon .30 .75
162 Max Scherzer .50 1.25
163 Justin Turner .50 1.25
164 Carl Pavano .30 .75
165 Michael Morse .30 .75
166 Brennan Boesch .30 .75
167 Starlin Castro RB .40 1.00
168 Blake Beavan .30 .75
169 Brett Myers .30 .75
170 Jacoby Ellsbury .40 1.00
171 Koji Uehara .30 .75
172 Reed Johnson .30 .75
173 Ryan Roberts .30 .75
174 Yadier Molina .60 1.50
175 Jared Hughes RC .40 1.00
176 Nolan Reimold .30 .75

177 Josh Thole .30 .75
178 Edward Mujica .30 .75
179 Denard Span .30 .75
180 Mariano Rivera .60 1.50
181 Reyes/Braun/Kemp LL .40 1.00
182 Michael Brantley .30 .75
183 Addison Reed RC .40 1.00
184 Wilin Rosario RC .40 1.00
185 Pablo Sandoval .40 1.00
186 John Lannan .30 .75
187 Jose Altuve .40 1.00
188 Bobby Abreu .30 .75
189 Alberto Callaspo .30 .75
190 Cole Hamels .40 1.00
191 Angel Pagan .30 .75
192 Chipper/Pujols/Jones LDR .60 1.50
193 Kelly Shoppach .30 .75
194 Danny Duffy .30 .75
195 Ben Zobrist .40 1.00
196 Matt Joyce .30 .75
197 Brendan Ryan .30 .75
198 Matt Dominguez RC .50 1.25
199 Adam Dunn .40 1.00
200 Miguel Cabrera .50 1.25
201 Doug Fister .30 .75
202 Andrew Carignan RC .40 1.00
203 Jeff Niemann .30 .75
204 Tom Gorzelanny .30 .75
205 Justin Masterson .30 .75
206 David Robertson .30 .75
207 J.P. Arencibia .30 .75
208 Mark Reynolds .30 .75
209 A.J. Burnett .30 .75
210 Zack Greinke .50 1.25
211 Kelvin Herrera RC .40 1.00
212 Tim Wakefield .40 1.00
CC Sabathia
Mark Buehrle LDR
213 Alex Avila .30 .75
214 Mike Pelfrey .30 .75
215 Freddie Freeman .60 1.50
216 Jason Kipnis .40 1.00
217 Texas Rangers PS HL .20 .50
218 Kyle Hudson RC .40 1.00
219 Jordan Pacheco RC .40 1.00
220 Jay Bruce .40 1.00
221 Luke Gregerson .30 .75
222 Chris Coghlan .30 .75
223 Joe Saunders .30 .75
224 Kemp/Fielder/Howard LL .40 1.00
225 Michael Pineda .30 .75
226 Ryan Hanigan .30 .75
227 Mike Minor .30 .75
228 Brent Lillibridge .30 .75
229 Yunel Escobar .30 .75
230 Justin Morneau .40 1.00
231 Dexter Fowler .40 1.00
232 Rivera/Johan/Felix LDR .60 1.50
233 St. Louis Cardianls PS HL .20 .50
234 Mark Teixeira RB .40 1.00
235 Joe Benson RC .40 1.00
236 Jose Tabata .30 .75
237 Russell Martin .30 .75
238 Emilio Bonifacio .30 .75
239 Cabrera/Young/Gonzalez LL .50 1.25
240 David Wright .40 1.00
241 James McDonald .30 .75
242 Eric Young .30 .75
243 Justin De Fratus RC .40 1.00
244 Sergio Santos .30 .75
245 Adam Lind .40 1.00
246 Bud Norris .30 .75
247 Clay Buchholz .30 .75
248 Stephen Drew .30 .75
249 Trevor Plouffe .30 .75
250 Jered Weaver .40 1.00
251 Jason Bay .40 1.00
252 Dellin Betances RC .60 1.50
253 Tim Federowicz RC .40 1.00
254 Philip Humber .30 .75
255 Scott Rolen .40 1.00
256 Mat Latos .40 1.00
257 Seth Smith .30 .75
258 Jon Jay .50 1.25
259 Michael Stutes .30 .75
260 Brian Wilson .50 1.25
261 Kyle Blanks .30 .75
262 Shaun Marcum .30 .75
263 Steve Delabar RC .40 1.00
264 Chris Carpenter PS HL .40 1.00
265 Aroldis Chapman .50 1.25
266 Carlos Corporan .30 .75
267 Joel Pineiro .30 .75
268 Miguel Cairo .30 .75
269 Jason Vargas .30 .75
270 Starlin Castro .40 1.00
271 John Jaso .30 .75
272 Nyjer Morgan PS HL .30 .75
273 David Freese .30 .75
274 Alex Liddi RC .40 1.00
275 Brad Peacock RC .40 1.00
276 Scott Baker .30 .75
277 Jeremy Moore RC .40 1.00
278 Randy Wells .30 .75
279 R.A. Dickey .40 1.00
280 Ryan Howard .40 1.00
281 Mark Trumbo .30 .75
282 Ryan Raburn .30 .75
283 Brandon Allen .30 .75
284 Tony Gwynn .30 .75
285 Drew Storen .30 .75
286 Franklin Gutierrez .30 .75
287 Antonio Bastardo .30 .75
288 Miguel Montero .30 .75
289 Casey Kotchman .30 .75
290 Curtis Granderson .40 1.00
291 David Freese WS HL .30 .75
292 Ben Revere .40 1.00
293 Eric Thames .40 1.00
294 John Axford .30 .75
295 Jayson Werth .40 1.00
296 Brayan Pena .30 .75
297 Kershaw/Halladay/Lee LL .75 2.00
298 Jeff Keppinger .30 .75
299 Mitch Moreland .30 .75
300 Josh Hamilton .40 1.00
301 Alexi Ogando .30 .75
302 Jose Bautista .40 1.00
Curtis Granderson
Mark Teixeira LL
303 Danny Valencia .40 1.00
304 Brandon Morrow .30 .75
305 Chipper Jones .50 1.25
306 Ubaldo Jimenez .30 .75
307 Vance Worley .40 1.00
308 Mike Leake .30 .75
309 Kurt Suzuki .30 .75
310 Adrian Beltre .50 1.25
311 John Danks .30 .75
312 Nick Hundley .30 .75
313 Phil Hughes .30 .75
314 Matt LaPorta .30 .75
315 Dustin Ackley .30 .75
316 Nick Blackburn .30 .75
317 Tyler Chatwood .30 .75
318 Erik Bedard .30 .75
319 Verland/CC/Weaver LL .50 1.25
320 Matt Holliday .50 1.25
321 Jason Bourgeois .30 .75
322 Ricky Nolasco .30 .75
323 Jason Isringhausen .30 .75
324 ARod/Thome/Giambi LDR .60 1.50
325 Chris Schwinden RC .50 1.25
326 Kevin Gregg .30 .75
327 Mark Kotsay .30 .75
328 John Lackey .40 1.00
329 Allen Craig WS HL .40 1.00
330 Matt Kemp .40 1.00
331 Albert Pujols .60 1.50
332 Jose Reyes .30 .75
333 Roger Bernadina .30 .75
334 Anthony Rizzo .60 1.50
335 Josh Satin RC .50 1.25
336 Gavin Floyd .30 .75
337 Glen Perkins .30 .75
338 Jose Constanza RC .40 1.00
339 Clayton Richard .30 .75
340 Adam LaRoche .30 .75
341 Edwin Encarnacion .50 1.25
342 Kosuke Fukudome .40 1.00
343 Salvador Perez .40 1.00
344 Nelson Cruz .50 1.25
345 Jonathan Papelbon .40 1.00
346 Dillon Gee .30 .75
347 Craig Gentry .30 .75
348 Alfonso Soriano .40 1.00
349 Tim Lincecum .40 1.00
350 Evan Longoria .40 1.00
351 Corey Hart .30 .75
352 Julio Teheran .40 1.00
353 John Mayberry .30 .75
354 Jeremy Hellickson .30 .75
355 Mark Buehrle .40 1.00
356 Endy Chavez .30 .75
357 Aaron Harang .30 .75
358 Jacob Turner .40 1.00
359 Danny Espinosa .30 .75
360 Nelson Cruz RB .50 1.25
361 Chase Utley .40 1.00
362 Dayan Viciedo .30 .75
363 Fernando Salas .30 .75
364 Brandon Beachy .30 .75
365 Aramis Ramirez .30 .75
366 Jose Molina .30 .75
367 Chris Volstad .30 .75
368 Carl Crawford .40 1.00
369 Huston Street .30 .75
370 Lyle Overbay .30 .75
371 Jim Thome .40 1.00
372 Daniel Descalso .30 .75
373 Carlos Gonzalez .40 1.00
374 Coco Crisp .30 .75
375 Drew Stubbs .30 .75
376 Carlos Quentin .30 .75
377 Brandon Inge .30 .75
378 Brandon League .30 .75
379 Sergio Romo RC .40 1.00
380 Daniel Murphy .40 1.00
381 David DeJesus .30 .75
382 Wandy Rodriguez .30 .75
383 Andre Ethier .40 1.00
384 Sean Marshall .30 .75
385 David Murphy .30 .75
386 Ryan Zimmerman .40 1.00
387 Joakim Soria .30 .75
388 Chase Headley .30 .75
389 Alexi Casilla .30 .75
390 Taylor Green RC .40 1.00
391 Rod Barajas .40 1.00
392 Cliff Lee .40 1.00
393 Manny Ramirez .50 1.25
394 Bryan LaHair .30 .75
395 Jonathan Lucroy .40 1.00
396 Yoenis Cespedes RC 1.00 2.50
397 Hector Noesi .30 .75
398 Buster Posey .60 1.50
399 Brian McCann .40 1.00
400 Robinson Cano .40 1.00
401 Kenley Jansen .40 1.00
402 Allen Craig .40 1.00
403 Bronson Arroyo .30 .75
404 Jonathan Sanchez .30 .75
405 Nathan Eovaldi .40 1.00
406 Juan Rivera .30 .75
407 Torii Hunter .40 1.00
408 Jonny Venters .30 .75
409 Greg Holland .40 1.00
410 Jeff Locke RC .60 1.50
411 Tsuyoshi Nishioka .40 1.00
412 Don Kelly .30 .75
413 Frank Francisco .30 .75
414 Ryan Vogelsong .30 .75
415 Rafael Furcal .30 .75
416 Todd Helton .40 1.00
417 Carlos Pena .40 1.00
418 Jarrod Parker RC .50 1.25
419 Cameron Maybin .30 .75
420 Barry Zito .40 1.00
421 Heath Bell .30 .75
422 Austin Jackson .40 1.00
423 Colby Rasmus .40 1.00
424 Vladimir Guerrero RB .40 1.00
425 Carlos Zambrano .40 1.00
426 Eric Hinske .30 .75
427 Rafael Dolis RC .50 1.25
428 Jordan Schafer .30 .75
429 Michael Bourn .30 .75
430 Felix Hernandez .40 1.00
431 Guillermo Moscoso .40 1.00
432 Wei-Yin Chen RC 1.00 2.50
433 Nate McLouth .30 .75
434 Jason Motte .30 .75
435 Jeff Baker .30 .75
436 Chris Perez .30 .75
437 Yoshinori Tateyama RC .50 1.25
438 Juan Uribe .30 .75
439 Elvis Andrus .40 1.00
440 Chien-Ming Wang .40 1.00
441 Mike Aviles .30 .75
442 Johnny Giavotella .30 .75
443 B.J. Upton .40 1.00
444 Rafael Betancourt .30 .75
445 Ramon Santiago .30 .75
446 Mike Trout 20.00 50.00
447 Jair Jurrjens .30 .75
448 Dustin Moseley .30 .75
449 Shane Victorino .40 1.00
450 Justin Upton .40 1.00
451 Jeff Francoeur .40 1.00
452 Robert Andino .30 .75
453 Garrett Jones .30 .75
454 Michael Cuddyer .30 .75
455 Jed Lowrie .30 .75
456 Omar Infante .30 .75
457 J.D. Martinez .50 1.25
458 Kyle Kendrick .30 .75
459 Eric Surkamp RC .60 1.50
460 Thomas Field RC .40 1.00
461 Victor Martinez .40 1.00
462 Brett Lawrie RC .50 1.25
463 Francisco Cordero .30 .75
464 Joe Savery RC .50 1.25
465 Michael Schwimer RC .50 1.25
466 Lance Berkman .40 1.00
467 Juan Francisco .40 1.00
468 Nick Markakis .40 1.00
469 Vinnie Pestano .30 .75
470 Howie Kendrick .30 .75
471 James Shields .30 .75
472 Mat Gamel .30 .75
473 Evan Meek .30 .75
474 Mitch Maier .30 .75
475 Chris Dickerson .30 .75
476 Ramon Hernandez .30 .75
477 Edinson Volquez .30 .75
478 Rajai Davis .30 .75
479 Johan Santana .40 1.00
480 J.J. Putz .30 .75
481 Matt Harrison .30 .75
482 Chris Capuano .30 .75
483 Alex Gordon .40 1.00
484 Hisashi Iwakuma RC .75 2.00
485 Carlos Marmol .30 .75
486 Jerry Sands .30 .75
487 Eric Sogard .30 .75
488 Nick Swisher .40 1.00
489 Andres Torres .30 .75
490 Chris Carpenter .40 1.00
491 Jose Valverde RB .40 1.00
492 Rickie Weeks .30 .75
493 Ryan Madson .30 .75
494 Darwin Barney .30 .75
495 Adam Wainwright .40 1.00
496 Jorge De La Rosa .30 .75
497 Andrew McCutchen .50 1.25
498 Joey Votto .50 1.25
499 Francisco Rodriguez .40 1.00
500 Alex Rodriguez .60 1.50
501 Matt Capps .30 .75
502 Collin Cowgill RC .40 1.00
503 Tyler Clippard .30 .75
504 Ryan Dempster .30 .75
505 Fautino De Los Santos .30 .75
506 David Ortiz .50 1.25
507 Norichika Aoki RC .50 1.25
508 Brandon Phillips .30 .75
509 Travis Snider .30 .75
510 Randall Delgado .30 .75
511 Ervin Santana .30 .75
512 Josh Willingham .40 1.00
513 Gaby Sanchez .40 1.00
514 Brian Roberts .30 .75
515 Willie Bloomquist .30 .75
516 Charlie Morton .50 1.25
517 Francisco Liriano .30 .75
518 Jake Peavy .30 .75
519 Gio Gonzalez .40 1.00
520 Ryan Adams .30 .75
521 Ruben Tejada .30 .75
522 Matt Downs .30 .75
523 Jim Johnson .30 .75
524 Martin Prado .30 .75
525 Paul Maholm .30 .75
526 Casper Wells .30 .75
527 Aaron Hill .30 .75
528 Bryan Petersen .30 .75
529 Luke Hughes .30 .75
530 Cliff Pennington .30 .75
531 Joel Hanrahan .30 .75
532 Tim Stauffer .30 .75
533 Ian Stewart .30 .75
534 Hector Gomez RC .40 1.00
535 Joe Mauer .40 1.00
536 Kendrys Morales .30 .75
537 Ichiro Suzuki .60 1.50
538 Wilson Betemit .30 .75
539 Andrew Bailey .30 .75
540 Dustin Pedroia .50 1.25
541 Jack Hannahan .30 .75
542 Jeff Samardzija .30 .75
543 Josh Johnson .40 1.00
544 Josh Collmenter .40 1.00
545 Randy Wolf .30 .75
546 Matt Thornton .30 .75
547 Jason Giambi .30 .75
548 Charlie Furbush .30 .75
549 Kelly Johnson .30 .75
550 Ian Kinsler .40 1.00
551 Joe Blanton .30 .75
552 Kyle Drabek .30 .75
553 James Darnell RC .40 1.00
554 Raul Ibanez .40 1.00
555 Alex Presley .30 .75
556 Stephen Strasburg .50 1.25
557 Zack Cozart .30 .75
558 Wade Miley RC .50 1.25
559 Brandon Dickson RC .50 1.25
560 J.A. Happ .40 1.00
561 Freddy Sanchez .50 1.25
562 Henderson Alvarez .30 .75
563 Alex White .30 .75
564 Jose Valverde .40 1.00
565 Dan Uggla .40 1.00
566 Jason Donald .30 .75
567 Mike Stanton .50 1.25
568 Jason Castro .30 .75
569 Travis Hafner .30 .75
570 Zach McAllister RC .50 1.25
571 J.J. Hardy .30 .75
572 Hiroki Kuroda .30 .75
573 Kyle Farnsworth .40 1.00
574 Kerry Wood .30 .75
575 Garrett Richards RC .60 1.50
576 Jonathan Herrera .30 .75
577 Dallas Braden .30 .75
578 Wade Davis .40 1.00
579 Dan Uggla RB .40 1.00
580 Tony Campana .30 .75
581 Jason Kubel .30 .75
582 Shin-Soo Choo .40 1.00
583 Josh Tomlin .30 .75
584 Daric Barton .30 .75
585 Jimmy Paredes .30 .75
586 Daisuke Matsuzaka .40 1.00
587 Chris Johnson .30 .75
588 Mark Ellis .30 .75
589 Alex Gonzalez .30 .75
590 Humberto Quintero .30 .75
591 Aubrey Huff .30 .75
592 Carlos Lee .30 .75
593 Marco Scutaro .40 1.00
594 Ricky Romero .30 .75
595 David Carpenter RC .50 1.25
596 Freddy Garcia .30 .75
597 Hank Conger .30 .75
598 Reid Brignac .30 .75
599 Zach Britton .40 1.00
600 Clayton Kershaw .75 2.00
601 Dan Haren .30 .75
602 Alejandro De Aza .30 .75
603 Lonnie Chisenhall .30 .75
604 Juan Abreu RC .50 1.25
605 Jason Bartlett .30 .75
606 Mike Carp .30 .75
607 CC Sabathia .40 1.00
608 Paul Goldschmidt .50 1.25
609 Lorenzo Cain .30 .75
610 Cody Ross .30 .75
611 Neftali Feliz .30 .75
612 Carlos Beltran .40 1.00
613 C.J. Wilson .30 .75
614 Andruw Jones .30 .75
615 Luis Marte RC .40 1.00
616 Tyler Pastornicky RC .40 1.00
617 Jimmy Rollins .40 1.00
618 Eric Chavez .30 .75
619 Tyler Greene .30 .75
620 Trayvon Robinson .30 .75
621 Scott Hairston .30 .75
622 Daniel Hudson .30 .75
623 Clint Barmes .30 .75
624 Gerardo Parra .30 .75
625 Tommy Hunter .30 .75
626 Alexei Ramirez .40 1.00
627 Justin Smoak .40 1.00
628 Sean Rodriguez .30 .75
629 Gordon Beckham .30 .75
630 Logan Morrison .30 .75
631 Ryan Kalish .30 .75
632 Joe Nathan .30 .75
633 Chris Narveson .30 .75
634 Jose Contreras .30 .75
635 Brett Gardner .40 1.00
636 Chris Heisey .30 .75
637 Brad Brach RC .40 1.00
638 Derek Lowe .30 .75
639 Justin Verlander .50 1.25
640 Jemile Weeks RC .30 .75
641 Derek Jeter RB 1.25 3.00
642 Mike Moustakas .40 1.00
643 Chris Young .30 .75
644 Andy Dirks .30 .75
645 Kyle Seager .30 .75
646 Francisco Cervelli .30 .75
647 Bruce Chen .30 .75
648 Josh Beckett .30 .75
649 Brandon Crawford .30 .75
650 Prince Fielder .40 1.00
651 Ryan Sweeney .30 .75
652 Grant Balfour .30 .75
653 Jordan Walden .30 .75
654 Yovani Gallardo .40 1.00
655 Ryan Doumit .30 .75
656 Carlos Santana .40 1.00
657 Dave Sappelt RC .50 1.25
658 Juan Pierre .30 .75
659 Homer Bailey .30 .75
660 Yu Darvish RC 1.00 2.50
661 Bryce Harper RC 20.00 50.00

2012 Topps Mini Gold

*GOLD: 5X TO 12X BASIC
*GOLD RC: .4X TO 10X BASIC RC
STATED ODDS 1:5
STATED PRINT RUN 61 SER.#'d SETS
279 R.A. Dickey 6.00 15.00
432 Wei-Yin Chen 20.00 50.00

2012 Topps Mini Autographs

STATED ODDS 1:143
MA1 Bryce Harper 250.00 400.00
MA2 Neil Walker 8.00 20.00
MA3 Ricky Romero 10.00 25.00
MA4 Brandon Beachy 15.00 40.00
MA5 Jhonny Peralta 12.50 30.00
MA6 David Ortiz 30.00 60.00
MA7 Don Mattingly 40.00 80.00
MA8 Adrian Gonzalez 30.00 60.00
MA9 Al Kaline 40.00 100.00
MA10 Yu Darvish 100.00 200.00
MA11 Mike Trout 400.00 1000.00
MA12 Freddie Freeman 15.00 40.00
MA13 Edgar Martinez 30.00 60.00
MA14 Jesus Montero 6.00 15.00
MA15 Tommy Hanson 12.50 30.00
MA16 Clayton Kershaw 15.00 40.00
MA17 Mark Trumbo 30.00 60.00
MA18 Josh Reddick 15.00 40.00
MA19 Tony Gwynn 60.00 120.00
MA20 Stan Musial 150.00 250.00
MA21 Gio Gonzalez 15.00 40.00
MA22 Dee Gordon 12.50 30.00
MA23 Chad Billingsley 10.00 25.00
MA24 Drew Stubbs 6.00 15.00
MA25 Edinson Volquez 20.00 50.00
MA26 Alcides Escobar 20.00 50.00
MA27 Kyle Drabek 20.00 50.00
MA28 Angel Pagan 15.00 40.00
MA29 Carlos Santana 15.00 40.00
MA30 Frank Robinson 40.00 100.00
MA31 Rickie Weeks 6.00 15.00

2012 Topps Mini Golden Moments

STATED ODDS 1:4
GM1 Tom Seaver .75 2.00
GM2 Derek Jeter 3.00 8.00
GM3 Clayton Kershaw 2.00 5.00
GM4 Prince Fielder 1.00 2.50
GM5 Edgar Martinez .75 2.00
GM6 Felix Hernandez 1.00 2.50
GM7 Ryan Braun .75 2.00
GM8 Barry Larkin .75 2.00
GM9 Andy Pettitte 1.00 2.50
GM10 Albert Belle .50 1.25
GM11 Willie McCovey .75 2.00
GM12 Dennis Eckersley .75 2.00
GM13 Albert Pujols 1.50 4.00
GM14 Jacoby Ellsbury 1.00 2.50
GM15 CC Sabathia 1.00 2.50
GM16 Mike Schmidt 2.00 5.00
GM17 Brooks Robinson .75 2.00
GM18 Frank Thomas 1.25 3.00
GM19 John Smoltz 1.25 3.00
GM20 Matt Kemp 1.00 2.50
GM21 Al Kaline 1.25 3.00
GM22 Dustin Pedroia 1.25 3.00
GM23 Luis Aparicio .75 2.00
GM24 James Shields .75 2.00
GM25 Roy Halladay 1.00 2.50
GM26 Evan Longoria 1.00 2.50
GM27 Johnny Bench 1.25 3.00
GM28 Stan Musial 2.00 5.00
GM29 Alex Rodriguez 1.50 4.00
GM30 Cole Hamels 1.00 2.50
GM31 David Ortiz 1.25 3.00
GM32 Don Mattingly 2.50 6.00
GM33 George Brett 2.50 6.00
GM34 Jim Palmer .75 2.00
GM35 Joe Mauer 1.00 2.50
GM36 Mariano Rivera 1.50 4.00
GM37 Mark Teixeira 1.00 2.50
GM38 Giancarlo Stanton 1.25 3.00
GM39 Ozzie Smith 1.50 4.00
GM40 Reggie Jackson .75 2.00
GM41 Rickey Henderson 1.25 3.00
GM42 Starlin Castro 1.00 2.50
GM43 Stephen Strasburg 1.25 3.00
GM44 Tony Gwynn 1.25 3.00
GM45 Willie Mays 2.50 6.00
GM46 Adrian Gonzalez 1.00 2.50
GM47 Andre Dawson .75 2.00
GM48 Gary Carter .75 2.00
GM49 Josh Hamilton 1.00 2.50
GM50 Ken Griffey Jr. 2.50 6.00

2012 Topps Mini Relics

STATED ODDS 1:29
MR1 Stan Musial 10.00 25.00
MR2 Mike Trout 50.00 120.00
MR3 Mat Latos 4.00 10.00
MR4 Dave Winfield 4.00 10.00
MR5 Curtis Granderson 4.00 10.00
MR6 Ian Kennedy 4.00 10.00
MR7 Dan Haren 4.00 10.00
MR8 Jordan Zimmermann 4.00 10.00
MR9 Nelson Cruz 4.00 10.00
MR10 Carl Yastrzemski 10.00 25.00
MR11 Johan Santana 8.00 20.00
MR12 J.P. Arencibia 4.00 10.00
MR13 Chris Young 4.00 10.00
MR14 Cole Hamels 8.00 20.00
MR15 Tommy Hanson 4.00 10.00
MR16 Kevin Youkilis 4.00 10.00
MR17 Drew Stubbs 4.00 10.00
MR18 Adam Dunn 4.00 10.00
MR19 Tony Gwynn 6.00 15.00
MR20 Harmon Killebrew 8.00 20.00
MR21 Carlos Santana 4.00 10.00
MR22 Troy Tulowitzki 4.00 10.00
MR23 Mark Trumbo 4.00 10.00
MR24 Neftali Feliz 4.00 10.00
MR25 Billy Butler 5.00 12.00
MR26 Jaime Garcia 4.00 10.00
MR27 Jose Reyes 5.00 12.00
MR28 John Axford 4.00 10.00
MR29 C.J. Wilson 4.00 10.00
MR30 Don Mattingly 10.00 25.00
MR31 Justin Upton 4.00 10.00
MR32 Andy Pettitte 5.00 12.00
MR33 Kerry Wood 5.00 12.00
MR34 Cliff Lee 6.00 15.00
MR35 Yovani Gallardo 4.00 10.00
MR36 Matt Cain 6.00 15.00
MR37 Jered Weaver 4.00 10.00
MR38 Brandon League 4.00 10.00
MR39 Rafael Furcal 4.00 10.00
MR40 Ryan Braun 4.00 10.00
MR41 Evan Longoria 4.00 10.00
MR42 Elvis Andrus 4.00 10.00
MR43 Brandon Beachy 4.00 10.00
MR44 Andrew McCutchen 8.00 20.00
MR45 Josh Hamilton 5.00 12.00
MR46 Miguel Cabrera 6.00 15.00
MR47 Clayton Kershaw 10.00 25.00
MR48 Ricky Romero 4.00 10.00
MR49 Ryan Zimmerman 5.00 12.00
MR50 Justin Verlander 6.00 15.00

2012 Topps Mini National Convention

TMB1 Yu Darvish 2.50 6.00
TMB2 Bryce Harper 12.50 30.00
TMB5 Matt Kemp 1.25 3.00
TMB3 Stephen Strasburg 1.50 4.00
TMB4 Roy Halladay 1.25 3.00

2013 Topps Mini

PRINTING PLATE ODDS 1:97
PLATE PRINT RUN 1 SET PER COLOR
BLACK-CYAN-MAGENTA-YELLOW ISSUED
NO PLATE PRICING DUE TO SCARCITY
1 Bryce Harper .75 2.00
2 Derek Jeter 1.25 3.00
3 Hunter Pence .40 1.00
4 Yadier Molina .60 1.50
5 Carlos Gonzalez .40 1.00
6 Ryan Howard .40 1.00
8 Ryan Braun .40 1.00
9 Dee Gordon .30 .75
10 Adam Jones .40 1.00
11 Yu Darvish .50 1.25
12 A.J. Pierzynski .30 .75
13 Brett Lawrie .40 1.00
14 Paul Konerko .40 1.00
15 Dustin Pedroia .50 1.25
16 Andre Ethier .40 1.00
17 Shin-Soo Choo .40 1.00
18 Mitch Moreland .30 .75
19 Joey Votto .50 1.25
20 Kevin Youkilis .30 .75
21 Lucas Duda .40 1.00
22 Clayton Kershaw .75 2.00
23 Jemile Weeks .30 .75
24 Dan Haren .30 .75
25 Mark Teixeira .40 1.00
26 Chase Utley .40 1.00
27 Mike Trout 4.00 10.00
28 Prince Fielder .40 1.00
29 Adrian Beltre .50 1.25
30 Neftali Feliz .30 .75
31 Jose Tabata .30 .75
32 Craig Breslow .30 .75
33 Cliff Lee .40 1.00
34 Felix Hernandez .40 1.00
35 Justin Verlander .50 1.25
36 Jered Weaver .40 1.00
37 Max Scherzer .50 1.25
38 Brian Wilson .50 1.25
39 Scott Feldman .30 .75
40 Chien-Ming Wang .40 1.00
41 Daniel Hudson .30 .75
42 Detroit Tigers .20 .50
43 R.A. Dickey .40 1.00
44 Anthony Rizzo .60 1.50
45 Travis Ishikawa .30 .75
46 Craig Kimbrel .40 1.00
47 Howie Kendrick .30 .75
48 Ryan Cook .30 .75
49 Chris Sale .50 1.25
50 Adam Wainwright .40 1.00
51 Jonathan Broxton .30 .75
52 CC Sabathia .40 1.00
53 Alex Cobb .30 .75
54 Jaime Garcia .40 1.00
55 Tim Lincecum .40 1.00
56 Joe Blanton .30 .75
57 Mark Lowe .30 .75
58 Jeremy Hellickson .30 .75
59 John Axford .30 .75
60 Jon Rauch .30 .75
61 Trevor Bauer .60 1.50
62 Tommy Hunter .30 .75
63 Justin Masterson .30 .75
64 Will Middlebrooks .30 .75
65 J.P. Howell .30 .75
66 Daniel Nava .30 .75
67 San Francisco Giants .20 .50
68 Colby Rasmus .40 1.00
69 Marco Scutaro .40 1.00
70 Todd Frazier .30 .75
71 Kyle Kendrick .30 .75
72 Gerardo Parra .30 .75
73 Brandon Crawford .40 1.00
74 Kenley Jansen .40 1.00
75 Barry Zito .40 1.00
76 Brandon Inge .30 .75
77 Dustin Moseley .30 .75
78 Dylan Bundy .75 2.00
79 Adam Eaton .50 1.25
80 Ryan Zimmerman .40 1.00
81 Kershaw/Cueto/Dickey .75 2.00
82 Jason Vargas .30 .75
83 Darin Ruf .60 1.50
84 Adeiny Hechavarria .40 1.00
85 Sean Doolittle .30 .75
86 Henry Rodriguez .30 .75
87 Mike Olt .40 1.00
88 Jamey Carroll .30 .75
89 Johan Santana .40 1.00
90 Andy Pettitte .40 1.00
91 Alfredo Aceves .30 .75
92 Clint Barmes .30 .75
93 Austin Kearns .30 .75
94 Verlander/Price/Weaver .50 1.25
95 Matt Harrison .40 1.00
David Price
Jered Weaver
96 Edward Mujica .30 .75
97 Danny Espinosa .30 .75
98 Gaby Sanchez .30 .75
99 Paco Rodriguez .50 1.25
100 Mike Moustakas .40 1.00
101 Bryan Shaw .30 .75
102 Denard Span .30 .75
103 Evan Longoria .40 1.00
104 Jed Lowrie .30 .75
105 Freddie Freeman .60 1.50
106 Drew Stubbs .30 .75
107 Joe Mauer .40 1.00
108 Kendrys Morales .30 .75
109 Kirk Nieuwenhuis .30 .75
110 Justin Upton .40 1.00
111 Casey Kelly .40 1.00
112 Mark Reynolds .30 .75
113 Starlin Castro .30 .75
114 Casey McGehee .30 .75
115 Tim Hudson .40 1.00
116 Brian McCann .40 1.00
117 Aubrey Huff .30 .75
118 Daisuke Matsuzaka .40 1.00
119 Chris Davis .40 1.00
120 Ian Desmond .30 .75
121 Delmon Young .40 1.00
122 Andrew McCutchen .50 1.25
123 Rickie Weeks .30 .75
124 Ricky Romero .30 .75
125 Matt Holliday .50 1.25
126 Dan Uggla .30 .75
127 Giancarlo Stanton .50 1.25
128 Buster Posey .60 1.50
129 Ike Davis .30 .75
130 Jason Motte .30 .75
131 Ian Kennedy .30 .75
132 Ryan Vogelsong .30 .75
133 James Shields .30 .75
134 Jake Arrieta .40 1.00
135 Eric Hosmer .40 1.00
136 Tyler Clippard .30 .75
137 Edinson Volquez .30 .75
138 Michael Morse .30 .75
139 Bobby Parnell .30 .75
140 Wade Davis .30 .75
141 Carlos Santana .40 1.00
142 Tony Cingrani .60 1.50
143 Jim Johnson .30 .75
144 Jason Bay .40 1.00
145 Anthony Bass .30 .75
146 Kyle McClellan .30 .75
147 Ivan Nova .40 1.00
148 L.J. Hoes .40 1.00
149 Yovani Gallardo .30 .75
150 John Danks .30 .75
151 Alex Rios .40 1.00
152 Jose Contreras .30 .75
153 Cabrera/Hamilton/Grand .50 1.25
154 Sergio Romo .30 .75
155 Mat Latos .40 1.00
156 Dillon Gee .30 .75
157 Carter Capps .30 .75
158 Chad Billingsley .40 1.00
159 Felipe Paulino .30 .75
160 Stephen Drew .30 .75
161 Bronson Arroyo .30 .75
162 Kyle Seager .30 .75
163 J.A. Happ .40 1.00
164 Lucas Harrell .30 .75
165 Ramon Hernandez .30 .75
166 Logan Ondrusek .30 .75
167 Luke Hochevar .30 .75
168 Kyle Farnsworth .30 .75
169 Brad Ziegler .30 .75
170 Eury Perez .40 1.00
171 Brock Holt .40 1.00
172 Nyjer Morgan .30 .75
173 Tyler Skaggs .50 1.25
174 Jason Grilli .30 .75
175 A.J. Ramos .40 1.00
176 Robert Andino .30 .75
177 Elliot Johnson .30 .75
178 Justin Maxwell .30 .75
179 Detroit Tigers .20 .50
180 Casey Kotchman .30 .75
181 Jeff Keppinger .30 .75
182 Randy Choate .50 1.25
183 Drew Hutchison .40 1.00
184 Geovany Soto .40 1.00
185 Rob Scahill .30 .75
186 Jordan Pacheco .30 .75
187 Nick Maronde .40 1.00
188 Brian Fuentes .30 .75
189 Posey/McCutch/Braun .60 1.50
190 Daniel Descalso .30 .75
191 Chris Capuano .30 .75
192 Javier Lopez .40 1.00
193 Matt Carpenter .50 1.25
194 Encarn/Cabrera/Hamilton .50 1.25
195 Chris Heisey .30 .75
196 Ryan Vogelsong .30 .75
197 Tyler Cloyd .40 1.00
198 Chris Coghlan .30 .75
199 Avisail Garcia .40 1.00
200 Scott Downs .30 .75
201 Jonny Venters .30 .75
202 Zack Cozart .30 .75
203 Wilson Ramos .30 .75
204 Alex Gordon .40 1.00
205 Ryan Theriot .30 .75
206 Jimmy Rollins .40 1.00
207 Matt Holliday .50 1.25
208 Kurt Suzuki .30 .75
209 David DeJesus .30 .75
210 Vernon Wells .30 .75
211 Jarrod Parker .30 .75
212 Eric Chavez .30 .75
213 Alex Rodriguez .60 1.50
214 Curtis Granderson .40 1.00
215 Gordon Beckham .30 .75
216 Josh Willingham .40 1.00
217 Brian Matusz .30 .75
218 Ben Zobrist .40 1.00
219 Josh Beckett .30 .75
220 Octavio Dotel .30 .75
221 Heath Bell .30 .75
222 Jason Heyward .40 1.00
223 Yonder Alonso .30 .75
224 Jon Jay .30 .75
225 Will Venable .30 .75
226 Derek Lowe .30 .75
227 Jose Altuve .40 1.00
228 Adrian Gonzalez .40 1.00
229 Jeff Samardzija .30 .75
230 David Robertson .30 .75
231 Melky Mesa .40 1.00
232 Jake Odorizzi .40 1.00
233 Edwin Jackson .30 .75
234 A.J. Burnett .30 .75
235 Jake Westbrook .30 .75
236 Joe Nathan .30 .75
237 Brandon Lyon .30 .75
238 Carlos Zambrano .40 1.00
239 Ramon Santiago .30 .75
240 J.J. Putz .30 .75
241 Jacoby Ellsbury .40 1.00
242 Matt Kemp .40 1.00
243 Aaron Crow .30 .75
244 Lucas Luetge .30 .75
245 Jason Isringhausen .30 .75
246 Ryan Braun .50 1.25
Giancarlo Stanton

Jay Bruce
247 Luis Perez .30 .75
248 Colby Lewis .30 .75
249 Vance Worley .40 1.00
250 Jonathon Niese .30 .75
251 Sean Marshall .30 .75
252 Dustin Ackley .30 .75
253 Adam Greenberg .40 1.00
254 Sean Burnett .30 .75
255 Josh Johnson .40 1.00
256 Madison Bumgarner .40 1.00
257 Mike Minor .30 .75
258 Doug Fister .30 .75
259 Bartolo Colon .30 .75
260 San Francisco Giants .20 .50
261 Trevor Rosenthal .60 1.50
262 Kevin Correia .30 .75
263 Ted Lilly .30 .75
264 Roy Halladay .40 1.00
265 Tyler Colvin .30 .75
266 Albert Pujols .60 1.50
267 Jason Kipnis .40 1.00
268 David Lough .30 .75
269 St. Louis Cardinals .20 .50
270 Manny Machado 2.00 5.00
271 Jeurys Familia .50 1.25
272 Ryan Braun .40 1.00
Alfonso Soriano
Chase Headley
273 Dexter Fowler .40 1.00
274 Miguel Montero .30 .75
275 Johnny Cueto .40 1.00
276 Luis Ayala .30 .75
277 Brendan Ryan .30 .75
278 Christian Garcia .30 .75
279 Vicente Padilla .30 .75
280 Rafael Dolis .30 .75
281 David Hernandez .30 .75
282 Russell Martin .30 .75
283 CC Sabathia .40 1.00
284 Angel Pagan .30 .75
285 Addison Reed .30 .75
286 Jurickson Profar .40 1.00
287 Johnny Cueto .40 1.00
Gio Gonzalez
R.A. Dickey
288 Starling Marte .40 1.00
289 Jeremy Guthrie .30 .75
290 Tom Layne .30 .75
291 Ryan Sweeney .30 .75
292 Matt Thornton .30 .75
293 Jeff Karstens .30 .75
294 Trout/Beltre/Cabrera 4.00 10.00
295 Brandon League .30 .75
296 Didi Gregorius 1.25 3.00
297 Michael Saunders .40 1.00
298 Pablo Sandoval .40 1.00
299 Darwin Barney .30 .75
300 Daniel Murphy .40 1.00
301 Jarrod Saltalamacchia .30 .75
302 Aaron Hill .30 .75
303 Alex Rodriguez .60 1.50
304 Kyle Drabek .30 .75
305 Shelby Miller .75 2.00
306 Jerry Hairston .30 .75
307 Norichika Aoki .30 .75
308 Desmond Jennings .40 1.00
309 Endy Chavez .30 .75
310 Edwin Encarnacion .50 1.25
311 Rajai Davis .30 .75
312 Scott Hairston .30 .75
313 Maicer Izturis .30 .75
314 A.J. Ellis .30 .75
315 Rafael Furcal .30 .75
316 Josh Reddick .30 .75
317 Baltimore Orioles .20 .50
318 Hiroki Kuroda .30 .75
319 Brian Bogusevic .30 .75
320 Michael Young .30 .75
321 Allen Craig .40 1.00
322 Alex Gonzalez .30 .75
323 Michael Brantley .30 .75
324 Cameron Maybin .30 .75
325 Kevin Millwood .30 .75
326 Andruw Jones .30 .75
327 Jhonny Peralta .30 .75
328 Jayson Werth .40 1.00
329 Rafael Soriano .30 .75
330 Ryan Raburn .30 .75
331 Jose Reyes .40 1.00
332 Cole Hamels .40 1.00
333 Santiago Casilla .30 .75
334 Derek Norris .30 .75
335 Chris Herrmann RC .40 1.00
336 Hank Conger .30 .75
337 Chris Iannetta .30 .75
338 Mike Trout 4.00 10.00
339 Nick Swisher .40 1.00
340 Franklin Gutierrez .30 .75
341 Lonnie Chisenhall .30 .75
342 Matt Dominguez .30 .75
343 Alex Avila .40 1.00
344 Kris Medlen .40 1.00
345 Jenrry Mejia .30 .75
346 Aaron Hicks RC .60 1.50
347 Brett Anderson .30 .75
348 Jonny Gomes .30 .75
349 Ernesto Frieri .30 .75
350 Albert Pujols .60 1.50
351 Asdrubal Cabrera .40 1.00
352 Tommy Hanson .30 .75
353 Bud Norris .30 .75
354 Casey Janssen .30 .75
355 Carlos Marmol .30 .75
356 Greg Dobbs .30 .75
357 Juan Francisco .30 .75
358 Henderson Alvarez .30 .75
359 CC Sabathia .40 1.00
360 Khristopher Davis RC 1.25 3.00
361 Erik Kratz .30 .75
362 Yoenis Cespedes .50 1.25
363 Sergio Santos .30 .75
364 Carlos Pena .40 1.00
365 Mike Baxter .30 .75
366 Ervin Santana .30 .75
367 Carlos Ruiz .30 .75
368 Chris Young .30 .75
369 Bryce Harper .75 2.00
370 A.J. Griffin .30 .75
371 Jeremy Affeldt .30 .75
372 Jeff Locke .30 .75
373 Derek Jeter 1.25 3.00
374 Miguel Cabrera .50 1.25
375 Wilin Rosario .30 .75
376 Juan Pierre .30 .75
377 J.D. Martinez .50 1.25
378 Joe Kelly .30 .75
379 Madison Bumgarner .40 1.00
380 Juan Nicasio .30 .75
381 Wily Peralta .30 .75
382 Jackie Bradley Jr. RC 1.00 2.50
383 Matt Harrison .30 .75
384 Jake McGee .40 1.00
385 Brandon Belt .40 1.00
386 Brandon Phillips .30 .75
387 Jean Segura .40 1.00
388 Justin Turner .50 1.25
389 Phil Hughes .30 .75
390 James McDonald .30 .75
391 Travis Wood .30 .75
392 Tom Koehler RC .40 1.00
393 Andres Torres .30 .75
394 Ubaldo Jimenez .30 .75
395 Alexei Ramirez .40 1.00
396 Aroldis Chapman .50 1.25
397 Mike Aviles .30 .75
398 Mike Fiers .30 .75
399 Shane Victorino .40 1.00
400 David Wright .40 1.00
401 Ryan Dempster .30 .75
402 Tom Wilhelmsen .30 .75
403 Hisashi Iwakuma .40 1.00
404 Ryan Madson .30 .75
405 Hector Sanchez .30 .75
406 Brandon McCarthy .30 .75
407 Juan Pierre .30 .75
408 Coco Crisp .30 .75
409 Logan Morrison .30 .75
410 Roy Halladay .40 1.00
411 Jesus Guzman .30 .75
412 Everth Cabrera .30 .75
413 Brett Gardner .40 1.00
414 Mark Buehrle .40 1.00
415 Leonys Martin .30 .75
416 Jordan Lyles .30 .75
417 Logan Forsythe .30 .75
418 Evan Gattis RC .75 2.00
419 Matt Moore .40 1.00
420 Rick Porcello .40 1.00
421 Jordy Mercer RC .40 1.00
422 Alfredo Marte RC .40 1.00
423 Miguel Gonzalez .30 .75
424 Steven Lerud RC .40 1.00
425 Josh Donaldson .40 1.00
426 Vinnie Pestano .30 .75
427 Chris Nelson .30 .75
428 Kyle McPherson RC .40 1.00
429 David Price .40 1.00
430 Josh Harrison .30 .75
431 Blake Beavan .30 .75
432 Jose Iglesias .40 1.00
433 Andrew Werner RC .40 1.00
434 Wei-Yin Chen .30 .75
435 Brandon Maurer RC .50 1.25
436 Elvis Andrus .40 1.00
437 Dayan Viciedo .30 .75
438 Yasmani Grandal .30 .75
439 Marco Estrada .30 .75
440 Ian Kinsler .40 1.00
441 Jose Bautista .40 1.00
442 Mike Leake .30 .75
443 Lou Marson .30 .75
444 Jordan Walden .30 .75
445 Joe Thatcher .30 .75
446 Chris Parmelee .30 .75
447 Jacob Turner .40 1.00
448 Tim Hudson .40 1.00
449 Michael Cuddyer .30 .75
450 Jay Bruce .40 1.00
451 Pedro Florimon .30 .75
452 Raul Ibanez .40 1.00
453 Troy Tulowitzki .50 1.25
454 Paul Goldschmidt .50 1.25
455 Buster Posey .60 1.50
456 Pablo Sandoval .40 1.00
457 Nate Schierholtz .30 .75
458 Jake Peavy .30 .75
459 Jesus Montero .30 .75
460 Ryan Doumit .30 .75
461 Drew Pomeranz .40 1.00
462 Eduardo Nunez .30 .75
463 Jason Hammel .40 1.00
464 Luis Jimenez RC .40 1.00
465 Placido Polanco .30 .75
466 Jerome Williams .30 .75
467 Brian Duensing .30 .75
468 Anthony Gose .30 .75
469 Adam Warren RC .40 1.00
470 Jeff Francoeur .40 1.00
471 Trevor Cahill .30 .75
472 John Mayberry .30 .75
473 Josh Johnson .40 1.00
474 Brian Omogrosso RC .40 1.00
475 Garrett Jones .30 .75
476 John Buck .40 1.00
477 Paul Maholm .30 .75
478 Gavin Floyd .30 .75
479 Kelly Johnson .30 .75
480 Lance Berkman .40 1.00
481 Justin Wilson RC .40 1.00
482 Emilio Bonifacio .30 .75
483 Jordany Valdespin .30 .75
484 Johan Santana .40 1.00
485 Ruben Tejada .30 .75
486 Jason Kubel .30 .75
487 Hanley Ramirez .40 1.00
488 Ryan Wheeler RC .40 1.00
489 Erick Aybar .30 .75
490 Cody Ross .30 .75
491 Clayton Richard .30 .75
492 Jose Molina .30 .75
493 Johnny Giavotella .30 .75
494 Alberto Callaspo .30 .75
495 Joaquin Benoit .30 .75
496 Scott Sizemore .30 .75
497 Brett Myers .30 .75
498 Martin Prado .30 .75
499 Billy Butler .30 .75
500 Stephen Strasburg .50 1.25
501 Tommy Milone .30 .75
502 Patrick Corbin .40 1.00
503 Clay Buchholz .30 .75
504 Michael Bourn .30 .75
505 Ross Detwiler .30 .75
506 Andy Pettitte .40 1.00
507 Lance Lynn .30 .75
508 Felix Doubront .30 .75
509 Brennan Boesch .30 .75
510 Nate McLouth .30 .75
511 Rob Brantly RC .40 1.00
512 Justin Smoak .30 .75
513 Zach McAllister .30 .75
514 Jonathan Papelbon .40 1.00
515 Brian Roberts .30 .75
516 Omar Infante .30 .75
517 Pedro Alvarez .30 .75
518 Nolan Reimold .30 .75
519 Zack Greinke .50 1.25
520 Peter Bourjos .30 .75
521 Evan Scribner RC .40 1.00
522 Dallas Keuchel .40 1.00
523 Wandy Rodriguez .30 .75
524 Wade LeBlanc .30 .75
525 J.P. Arencibia .30 .75
526 Tyler Flowers .30 .75
527 Carlos Beltran .40 1.00
528 Darin Mastroianni .30 .75
529 Collin McHugh RC .40 1.00
530 Wade Miley .30 .75
531 Craig Gentry .30 .75
532 Todd Helton .40 1.00
533 J.J. Hardy .30 .75
534 Alberto Cabrera RC .40 1.00
535 Philip Humber .30 .75
536 Mike Trout 4.00 10.00
537 Neil Walker .30 .75
538 Brett Wallace .30 .75
539 Phil Coke .30 .75
540 Michael Bourn .30 .75
541 Jon Lester .40 1.00
542 Jeff Niemann .30 .75
543 Donovan Solano .50 1.25
544 Tyler Chatwood .30 .75
545 Alex Presley .30 .75
546 Carlos Quentin .30 .75
547 Glen Perkins .30 .75
548 John Lackey .40 1.00
549 Huston Street .30 .75
550 Matt Joyce .30 .75
551 Wellington Castillo .30 .75
552 Francisco Cervelli .30 .75
553 Josh Rutledge .30 .75
554 R.A. Dickey .40 1.00
555 Joel Hanrahan .30 .75
556 Nick Hundley .30 .75
557 Adam Lind .40 1.00
558 David Murphy .30 .75
559 Travis Snider .30 .75
560 Yunel Escobar .30 .75
561 Josh Vitters .40 1.00
562 Jason Marquis .30 .75
563 Nate Eovaldi .40 1.00
564 Francisco Peguero RC .40 1.00
565 Torii Hunter .30 .75
566 C.J. Wilson .30 .75
567 Alfonso Soriano .40 1.00
568 Steve Lombardozzi .20 .50
569 Ryan Ludwick .30 .75
570 Devin Mesoraco .30 .75
571 Melky Cabrera .30 .75
572 Lorenzo Cain .30 .75
573 Ian Stewart .30 .75
574 Corey Hart .30 .75
575 Justin Morneau .40 1.00
576 Julio Teheran .40 1.00
577 Matt Harvey .40 1.00
578 Brett Jackson .30 .75
579 Adam LaRoche .30 .75
580 Jordan Danks .30 .75
581 Andrelton Simmons .30 .75
582 Seth Smith .30 .75
583 Alejandro De Aza .30 .75
584 Alfonso Soriano .40 1.00
585 Homer Bailey .30 .75
586 Jose Quintana .30 .75
587 Matt Cain .40 1.00
588 Jordan Zimmermann .40 1.00
589 Jose Fernandez RC 1.00 2.50
590 Liam Hendriks .30 .75
591 Derek Holland .30 .75
592 Nick Markakis .40 1.00
593 James Loney .40 1.00
594 Carl Crawford .40 1.00
595 David Ortiz .50 1.25
596 Brian Dozier .40 1.00
597 Marco Scutaro .40 1.00
598 Fernando Martinez .30 .75
599 Carlos Carrasco .30 .75
600 Mariano Rivera .60 1.50
601 Brandon Moss .30 .75
602 Anibal Sanchez .30 .75
603 Chris Perez .30 .75
604 Rafael Betancourt .30 .75
605 Aramis Ramirez .30 .75
606 Mark Trumbo .30 .75
607 Chris Carter .30 .75
608 Ricky Nolasco .30 .75
609 Scott Baker .30 .75
610 Brandon Beachy .30 .75
611 Drew Storen .30 .75
612 Robinson Cano .40 1.00
613 Jhoulys Chacin .30 .75
614 B.J. Upton .40 1.00
615 Mark Ellis .30 .75
616 Grant Balfour .30 .75
617 Fernando Rodney .30 .75
618 Koji Uehara .30 .75
619 Carlos Gomez .30 .75
620 Hector Santiago .30 .75
621 Steve Cishek .30 .75
622 Alcides Escobar .40 1.00
623 Alexi Ogando .30 .75
624 Justin Ruggiano .30 .75
625 Domonic Brown .40 1.00
626 Gio Gonzalez .40 1.00
627 David Price .40 1.00
628 Martin Maldonado RC .40 1.00
629 Trevor Plouffe .30 .75
630 Andy Dirks .30 .75
631 Chris Carpenter .40 1.00
632 R.A. Dickey .40 1.00
633 Victor Martinez .40 1.00
634 Drew Smyly .30 .75
635 Jedd Gyorko RC .50 1.25
636 Cole De Vries RC .40 1.00
637 Ben Revere .30 .75
638 Andrew Cashner .30 .75
639 Josh Hamilton .40 1.00
640 Jason Castro .30 .75
641 Bruce Chen .30 .75
642 Austin Jackson .30 .75
643 Matt Garza .30 .75
644 Ryan Lavarnway .30 .75
645 Luis Cruz .30 .75
646 Phillippe Aumont RC .40 1.00
647 Adam Dunn .40 1.00
648 Dan Straily .30 .75
649 Ryan Hanigan .30 .75
650 Nelson Cruz .50 1.25
651 Gregor Blanco .30 .75
652 Jonathan Lucroy .40 1.00
653 Chase Headley .30 .75
654 Brandon Barnes RC .40 1.00
655 Salvador Perez .40 1.00
656 Scott Diamond .30 .75
657 Jorge De La Rosa .30 .75
658 David Freese .30 .75
659 Mike Napoli .30 .75
660 Miguel Cabrera .50 1.25
661 Hyun-Jin Ryu RC 1.00 2.50

2013 Topps Mini Gold

*GOLD: 3X TO 8X BASIC
*GOLD RC: 2.5X TO 6X BASIC RC
STATED ODDS 1:7
STATED PRINT RUN 62 SER.#'d SETS
4 Yadier Molina 6.00 15.00
27 Mike Trout 15.00 40.00
270 Manny Machado 20.00 50.00
294 Trout/Beltre/Cabrera 15.00 40.00
338 Mike Trout 15.00 40.00
374 Miguel Cabrera 8.00 20.00

2013 Topps Mini Pink

*PINK: 6X TO 15X BASIC
*PINK RC: 5X TO 12X BASIC RC
STATED ODDS 1:16
STATED PRINT RUN 25 SER.#'d SETS
2 Derek Jeter 75.00 150.00
8 Ryan Braun 10.00 25.00
11 Yu Darvish 12.50 30.00
19 Joey Votto 20.00 50.00
373 Derek Jeter 60.00 120.00

2013 Topps Mini Autographs

STATED ODDS 1:147
AJ Adam Jones 10.00 25.00
BP Buster Posey 40.00 80.00
CG Craig Gentry 6.00 15.00
CR Cal Ripken Jr.
CRA Colby Rasmus 6.00 15.00
CS Carlos Santana 6.00 15.00
DS Duke Snider 10.00 25.00
EL Evan Longoria 15.00 40.00
FJ Fergie Jenkins 20.00 50.00
GS Gary Sheffield 6.00 15.00
HR Hanley Ramirez 20.00 50.00
IN Ivan Nova 8.00 20.00
JB Jose Bautista 8.00 20.00
JH Jeremy Hellickson
JK Jason Kipnis 15.00 40.00
JP Johnny Podres 10.00 25.00
JPR Jurickson Profar 10.00 25.00
JS John Smoltz 12.00 30.00
JV Josh Vitters 5.00 12.00
JW Jered Weaver 10.00 25.00
MN Mike Napoli 8.00 20.00
MT Mike Trout 90.00 150.00
NR Nolan Ryan
RB Ryan Braun 8.00 20.00
RK Ralph Kiner 10.00 25.00
SK Sandy Koufax
SM Shelby Miller 10.00 25.00
TC Tyler Colvin 5.00 12.00
TF Tommy Field
TR Tyson Ross 6.00 15.00
TS Tyler Skaggs
UJ Ubaldo Jimenez 6.00 15.00
WR Wilin Rosario 5.00 12.00
YD Yu Darvish 50.00 100.00
YP Yasiel Puig

2013 Topps Mini Chasing History

STATED ODDS 1:4
MCH1 Warren Spahn .60 1.50
MCH2 Cal Ripken Jr. 2.50 6.00
MCH3 Frank Robinson .60 1.50
MCH4 Ted Williams 1.50 4.00
MCH5 Jackie Robinson .75 2.00
MCH6 Ken Griffey Jr. 1.50 4.00
MCH7 Bob Feller .60 1.50
MCH8 Sandy Koufax 1.50 4.00
MCH9 Rod Carew .60 1.50
MCH10 Harmon Killebrew .75 2.00
MCH11 Tom Seaver .60 1.50
MCH12 Yogi Berra .75 2.00
MCH13 Lou Gehrig 1.50 4.00
MCH14 Babe Ruth 2.00 5.00
MCH15 Rickey Henderson .75 2.00
MCH16 Roberto Clemente 2.00 5.00
MCH17 Willie Mays 1.50 4.00
MCH18 Stan Musial 1.25 3.00
MCH19 Ty Cobb 1.25 3.00
MCH20 Adam Dunn .60 1.50
MCH21 Mark Buehrle .60 1.50
MCH22 Hanley Ramirez .60 1.50
MCH23 Johan Santana .60 1.50
MCH24 Mariano Rivera 1.00 2.50
MCH25 Alex Rodriguez 1.00 2.50
MCH26 CC Sabathia .60 1.50
MCH27 Roy Halladay .60 1.50
MCH28 Mike Schmidt 1.25 3.00
MCH29 Lance Berkman .60 1.50
MCH30 Ian Kinsler .60 1.50
MCH31 Carlos Santana .60 1.50
MCH32 Matt Kemp .60 1.50
MCH33 Dylan Bundy 1.25 3.00
MCH34 Miguel Cabrera .75 2.00
MCH35 Matt Cain .60 1.50
MCH36 Yu Darvish .75 2.00
MCH37 Prince Fielder .60 1.50
MCH38 Cliff Lee .60 1.50
MCH39 Tim Lincecum .60 1.50
MCH40 Manny Machado 3.00 8.00
MCH41 Buster Posey 1.00 2.50
MCH42 David Price .60 1.50
MCH43 Mike Schmidt 1.25 3.00
MCH44 Stephen Strasburg .75 2.00
MCH45 Mark Trumbo .50 1.25
MCH46 Troy Tulowitzki .75 2.00
MCH47 Justin Verlander .75 2.00
MCH48 Joey Votto .75 2.00
MCH49 Jered Weaver .60 1.50
MCH50 Reggie Jackson .60 1.50

2013 Topps Mini Relics

STATED ODDS 1:29
AE A.J. Ellis 4.00 10.00
AG Alex Gordon 4.00 10.00
AL Adam Lind 4.00 10.00
AR Alex Rodriguez 5.00 12.00
AS Andrelton Simmons 5.00 12.00
AW Adam Wainwright 3.00 8.00
BB Brandon Beachy 3.00 8.00
BP Brandon Phillips 6.00 15.00
BPO Buster Posey 5.00 12.00
CH Chris Heisey 4.00 10.00
CHA Corey Hart 3.00 8.00
CL Cory Luebke 3.00 8.00
CM Carlos Marmol 3.00 8.00
DD Daniel Descalso 4.00 10.00
DE Danny Espinosa 3.00 8.00
DS Drew Stubbs 5.00 12.00
EA Elvis Andrus 3.00 8.00
EL Evan Longoria 3.00 8.00
FH Felix Hernandez 3.00 8.00
FM Fred McGriff 4.00 10.00
HA Henderson Alvarez 3.00 8.00
HC Hank Conger 5.00 12.00
ID Ian Desmond 4.00 10.00
IDA Ike Davis 3.00 8.00
IN Ivan Nova 4.00 10.00
JB Jay Bruce 5.00 12.00
JD John Danks 3.00 8.00
JL Jon Lester 4.00 10.00
JLY Jordan Lyles 3.00 8.00
JS Justin Smoak 4.00 10.00
JT Jose Tabata 4.00 10.00
JV Justin Verlander 5.00 12.00
JVO Joey Votto 5.00 12.00
JW Jordan Walden 4.00 10.00
JWE Jayson Werth 3.00 8.00
KG Ken Griffey Jr. 10.00 25.00
KW Kerry Wood 4.00 10.00
LL Lance Lynn 5.00 12.00
MB Marlon Byrd 4.00 10.00
MC Matt Cain 4.00 10.00
MH Matt Holliday 4.00 10.00
MK Matt Kemp 3.00 8.00
ML Mike Leake 4.00 10.00
MM Mike Mussina 4.00 10.00
MMO Mike Moustakas 4.00 10.00
MT Mark Teixeira 4.00 10.00
NF Neftali Feliz 4.00 10.00
RR Ricky Romero 3.00 8.00
SC Starlin Castro 4.00 10.00
TL Tim Lincecum 6.00 15.00

2014 Topps Mini

PLATE PRINT RUN 1 SET PER COLOR
BLACK-CYAN-MAGENTA-YELLOW ISSUED
NO PLATE PRICING DUE TO SCARCITY
1 Mike Trout 2.00 5.00
2 Jhonny Peralta .25 .60
3 Jarrod Dyson .25 .60
4 Cody Asche .30 .75
5 Lance Lynn .25 .60
6 Josh Beckett .25 .60
8 Coco Crisp .25 .60
9 Dustin Ackley .25 .60
10 Junior Lake .25 .60
11 Mike Carp .25 .60
12 Aaron Hicks .30 .75
13 Juan Nicasio .25 .60
14 Yoenis Cespedes .40 1.00
15 Paul Goldschmidt .40 1.00
16 Johnny Cueto .30 .75
17 Todd Helton .30 .75
18 Jurickson Profar FS .30 .75
19 Joey Votto .40 1.00
20 Charlie Blackmon .40 1.00
21 Alfredo Simon .25 .60
22 Mike Napoli WS .25 .60
23 Chris Heisey .25 .60
24 Manny Machado FS .40 1.00
25 Troy Tulowitzki .40 1.00
26 Josh Phegley .25 .60
27 Michael Choice RC .30 .75
28 Brayan Pena .25 .60
29 Dvis/Cbrra/Encrncn LL .40 1.00
30 Mark Buehrle .30 .75
31 Victor Martinez .30 .75
32 Reymond Fuentes RC .30 .75
33 Matt Harvey .30 .75
34 Buddy Boshers RC .30 .75
35 Trevor Cahill .25 .60
36 Billy Hamilton RC .40 1.00
37 Nick Hundley .25 .60
38 Alvrz/Gldsmdt/Brce LL .40 1.00
39 David Murphy .25 .60
40 Hyun-Jin Ryu .30 .75
41 Adeiny Hechavarria .25 .60
42 Mariano Rivera .50 1.25
43 Mark Trumbo .25 .60
44 Matt Carpenter .40 1.00
45 Jake Marisnick RC .30 .75
46 Kolten Wong RC .40 1.00
47 Chris Davis HL .25 .60
48 Jarrod Saltalamacchia .25 .60
49 Enny Romero RC .30 .75
50 Buster Posey .50 1.25
51 Kyle Lohse .25 .60
52 Jim Adduci RC .30 .75
53 Clay Buchholz .25 .60
54 Andrew Lambo RC .30 .75
55 Chia-Jen Lo RC .30 .75
56 Taijuan Walker RC .30 .75
57 Yadier Molina .50 1.25
58 Dan Straily .25 .60
59 Nate Schierholtz .25 .60
60 Jon Niese .25 .60
61 Nick Markakis .30 .75
62 Joe Kelly .25 .60
63 Tyler Skaggs FS .25 .60
64 Will Venable .25 .60
65 Hisashi Iwakuma .30 .75
66 Kris Medlen .30 .75
67 Yasmani Grandal .25 .60
68 Sean Burnett .25 .60
69 Jhoulys Chacin .25 .60
70 Marcell Ozuna .40 1.00
71 Anthony Rizzo .50 1.25
72 Michael Young .25 .60
73 Kyle Seager .25 .60
74 John Mayberry .25 .60
75 Brandon Barnes .25 .60
76 Mike Aviles .25 .60
77 Aroldis Chapman .40 1.00
78 Bronson Arroyo .25 .60
79 Garrett Jones .25 .60
80 Jack Hannahan .25 .60
81 Anibal Sanchez .25 .60
82 Leonys Martin .25 .60
83 Jonathan Schoop RC .30 .75
84 Todd Redmond .25 .60
85 Matt Joyce .25 .60
86 Wilmer Flores RC .40 1.00
87 Tyson Ross .25 .60
88 Oswaldo Arcia .25 .60
89 Jarred Cosart FS .25 .60
90 Ethan Martin RC .30 .75
91 Starling Marte FS .30 .75
92 Martin Perez FS .30 .75
93 Ryan Sweeney .25 .60
94 Mitch Moreland .25 .60
95 Brandon Morrow .25 .60
96 Wily Peralta .25 .60
97 Alex Gordon .30 .75
98 Edwin Encarnacion .40 1.00
99 Melky Cabrera .25 .60
100 Bryce Harper .60 1.50
101 Chris Nelson .25 .60
102 Matt Lindstrom .25 .60
103 Cbrra/Mauer/Trout LL 2.00 5.00
104 Kurt Suzuki .25 .60
105 Ryan Howard .30 .75
106 Shin-Soo Choo .30 .75
107 Jordan Zimmermann .30 .75
108 J.D. Martinez .40 1.00
109 David Freese .25 .60
110 Wil Myers .25 .60
111 Mark Ellis .25 .60
112 Torii Hunter .25 .60
113 Krshw/Frnndz/Hrvey LL .60 1.50
114 Francisco Liriano .25 .60
115 Brett Oberholtzer .25 .60
116 Hiroki Kuroda .25 .60
117 Snchz/Clon/Iwkma LL .30 .75
118 Ian Desmond .25 .60
119 Brandon Crawford .30 .75
120 Kevin Correia .25 .60
121 Franklin Gutierrez .25 .60
122 Jonathan Papelbon .30 .75
123 James Paxton RC .50 1.25
124 Jay Bruce .30 .75
125 Joe Mauer .30 .75
126 David DeJesus .25 .60
127 Yusmeiro Petit .25 .60
128 Erasmo Ramirez .25 .60
129 Yonder Alonso .25 .60
130 Scooter Gennett .30 .75
131 Junichi Tazawa .25 .60
132 Henderson Alvarez HL .25 .60
133 Xander Bogaerts RC 1.00 2.50
134 Josh Donaldson .30 .75
135 Eric Sogard .25 .60
136 Will Middlebrooks FS .25 .60
137 Boone Logan .25 .60
138 Wei-Yin Chen .25 .60
139 Rafael Betancourt .25 .60
140 Jonathan Broxton .25 .60
141 Chris Tillman .25 .60
142 Zack Greinke .40 1.00
143 Gldsmdt/Brce/Frman LL .50 1.25
144 Joakim Soria .25 .60
145 Jason Castro .25 .60
146 Jonny Gomes WS .25 .60
147 Jason Frasor .25 .60
148 Chris Sale .40 1.00
149 Miguel Cabrera HL .40 1.00
150 Andrew McCutchen .40 1.00
151 Bruce Chen .25 .60
152 Jonathan Herrera .25 .60
153 Dvis/Cbrra/Jones LL .40 1.00
154 Chris Iannetta .25 .60
155 Daniel Murphy .30 .75
156 Kendrys Morales .25 .60
157 Matt Adams .25 .60
158 Nate McLouth .25 .60
159 Jason Grilli .25 .60
160 Bruce Rondon .25 .60
161 Adrian Beltre .40 1.00
162 Josmil Pinto RC .30 .75
163 Matt Shoemaker RC .50 1.25
164 Jaime Garcia .30 .75
165 Rajai Davis .25 .60
166 Dustin Pedroia .40 1.00
167 Jeremy Guthrie .25 .60
168 Alex Rodriguez .50 1.25
169 Nick Franklin FS .25 .60
170 Wade Miley .25 .60
171 Trevor Rosenthal .30 .75
172 Rickie Weeks .25 .60
173 Brandon League .25 .60
174 Bobby Parnell .25 .60
175 Casey Janssen .25 .60
176 Alex Cobb .25 .60
177 Esmil Rogers .25 .60
178 Erik Johnson RC .30 .75
179 Gerrit Cole FS .40 1.00
180 Ben Revere .25 .60
181 Jim Henderson .25 .60
182 Carlos Ruiz .25 .60
183 Darwin Barney .25 .60
184 Yunel Escobar .25 .60
185 Howie Kendrick .25 .60
186 Clayton Richard .25 .60
187 Justin Turner .40 1.00
188 Mark Melancon .25 .60
189 Adam LaRoche .25 .60
190 Kevin Gausman FS .40 1.00
191 Chris Perez .25 .60
192 Pedro Alvarez .25 .60
193 Ricky Nolasco .25 .60
194 Joel Hanrahan .25 .60
195 Nick Castellanos RC 1.00 2.50
196 Cole Hamels .30 .75
197 Onelki Garcia RC .30 .75
198 Nick Swisher .30 .75
199 Matt Davidson RC .40 1.00
200 Derek Jeter 1.00 2.50
201 Alex Rios .30 .75
202 Jeremy Hellickson .25 .60
203 Cliff Pennington .25 .60
204 Adrian Gonzalez .30 .75
205 Seth Smith .25 .60
206 Jon Lester WS .30 .75
207 Jonathan Villar .25 .60
208 Dayan Viciedo .25 .60
209 Carlos Quentin .25 .60
210 Jose Altuve .30 .75
211 Dioner Navarro .25 .60
212 Jason Heyward .30 .75
213 Justin Smoak .25 .60
214 James Shields .25 .60
215 Jean Segura FS .30 .75
216 Ubaldo Jimenez .25 .60
217 Giancarlo Stanton .40 1.00
218 Matt Dominguez .25 .60
219 Charlie Morton .40 1.00
220 Ryan Doumit .25 .60
221 Brian Dozier .30 .75
222 Vernon Wells .25 .60
223 Joaquin Benoit .25 .60
224 Michael Saunders .30 .75
225 Brian McCann .30 .75
226 Sean Doolittle .25 .60
227 Andrew Cashner .25 .60
228 Jayson Werth .30 .75
229 Justin Upton .30 .75
230 Andre Rienzo RC .30 .75
231 J.R. Murphy RC .30 .75
232 Chris Owings RC .30 .75
233 Rafael Soriano .25 .60
234 Eric Stults .25 .60
235 Jason Kipnis .30 .75
236 Joel Peralta .25 .60
237 Cddyer/Jhnsn/Frman LL .50 1.25
238 Alberto Callaspo .25 .60
239 Jeff Samardzija .25 .60
240 Ernesto Frieri .25 .60
241 Henderson Alvarez .25 .60
242 David Holmberg RC .30 .75
243 Ryan Cook .25 .60
244 Danny Farquhar .25 .60
245 Ross Detwiler .25 .60
246 Eduardo Nunez .25 .60
247 Anthony Gose .25 .60
248 Travis d'Arnaud RC .40 1.00
249 Heath Hembree RC .60 1.50
250 Miguel Cabrera .40 1.00
251 Sergio Romo .25 .60
252 Kevin Pillar RC .30 .75
253 Todd Helton HL .30 .75
254 Brett Gardner .30 .75
255 Billy Butler .25 .60
256 Abraham Almonte RC .30 .75
257 C.J. Wilson .25 .60
258 Jon Lester .30 .75
259 David Ortiz WS .40 1.00
260 Zoilo Almonte .30 .75
261 Michael Brantley .30 .75
262 Jeff Keppinger .25 .60
263 Doug Fister .25 .60
264 Huston Street .25 .60
265 Yordano Ventura RC .40 1.00
266 Zack Wheeler FS .30 .75
267 Ryan Vogelsong .25 .60
268 Don Kelly .25 .60
269 Joe Blanton .25 .60
270 Gregor Blanco .25 .60
271 Justin Ruggiano .25 .60
272 Carlos Villanueva .25 .60
273 Mark DeRosa .25 .60
274 Jonny Gomes .25 .60
275 Nolan Arenado .60 1.50
276 Alfonso Soriano .30 .75
277 Mike Leake .25 .60
278 Tommy Medica RC .30 .75
279 Corey Kluber .30 .75
280 Everth Cabrera .25 .60
281 Robbie Erlin RC .30 .75
282 Rex Brothers .25 .60
283 Andrelton Simmons FS .25 .60
284 Brandon Belt .30 .75
285 Jonathan Lucroy .30 .75
286 Josh Fields RC .30 .75
287 Miguel Montero .25 .60
288 Julio Teheran FS .30 .75
289 Matt Thornton .25 .60
290 Chad Bettis RC .30 .75
291 Brandon McCarthy .25 .60
292 Aaron Hill .25 .60
293 Mike Zunino FS .25 .60
294 Wnwrght/Zmmrmnn/Krshw LL .60 1.50
295 Matt Tuiasosopo .25 .60
296 Domonic Brown .30 .75
297 Max Scherzer .40 1.00
298 Chris Getz .25 .60
299 Schrzr/Clon/Moore LL .40 1.00
300 Yu Darvish .40 1.00
301 Shane Victorino .30 .75
302 Carlos Gomez .25 .60
303 Andres Torres .25 .60
304 Juan Lagares .25 .60
305 Steve Cishek .25 .60
306 Garrett Richards .30 .75
307 Jake Peavy .25 .60

308 Alexei Ramirez .30 .75
309 Drew Stubbs .25 .60
310 Neftali Feliz .25 .60
311 Chris Young .25 .60
312 Jimmy Rollins .30 .75
313 Brad Peacock .25 .60
314 Hanley Ramirez .30 .75
315 Jose Quintana .25 .60
316 Mike Minor .25 .60
317 Lonnie Chisenhall .25 .60
318 Luis Valbuena .25 .60
319 Ryan Goins RC .40 1.00
320 Hector Santiago .25 .60
321 Mariano Rivera HL .50 1.25
322 Emilio Bonifacio .25 .60
323 Jose Bautista .30 .75
324 Elvis Andrus .30 .75
325 Trevor Plouffe .25 .60
326 Khris Davis .40 1.00
327 Pablo Sandoval .30 .75
328 James Loney .25 .60
329 Matt Holliday .40 1.00
330 Evan Longoria .30 .75
331 Yasiel Puig .40 1.00
332 Stephen Strasburg .40 1.00
333 Wil Myers ERR .25 .60
Name spelled Will on back
334 Andy Dirks .25 .60
335 Miguel Cabrera .40 1.00
336 Ben Zobrist .30 .75
337 Zach Walters RC .30 .75
338 Carlos Santana .30 .75
339 Cody Ross .25 .60
340 Casey McGehee .25 .60
341 Mike Moustakas .30 .75
342 Brad Miller .30 .75
343 Nate Freiman .25 .60
344 Kevin Siegrist (RC) .30 .75
345 Darin Ruf .30 .75
346 Derek Norris .25 .60
347 Matt Cain .30 .75
348 Salvador Perez .30 .75
349 Martin Prado .25 .60
350 Carlos Gonzalez .30 .75
351 Matt Garza .25 .60
352 Ryan Wheeler .25 .60
353 A.J. Ramos .25 .60
354 Donnie Murphy .25 .60
355 Jarrod Parker .25 .60
356 Jose Reyes .30 .75
357 Lorenzo Cain .25 .60
358 Christian Yelich .50 1.25
359 Sean Rodriguez .25 .60
360 Russell Martin .25 .60
361 Edwin Jackson .25 .60
362 Daniel Nava .25 .60
363 David Hale RC .30 .75
364 Mike Trout 2.00 5.00
365 Dan Uggla .25 .60
366 Zack Cozart .25 .60
367 Brian Wilson .40 1.00
368 Kyuji Fujikawa .30 .75
369 Erick Aybar .25 .60
370 Jerry Blevins .25 .60
371 Scott Kazmir .25 .60
372 Austin Jackson .25 .60
373 Kyle Drabek .25 .60
374 Taylor Jordan (RC) .25 .60
375 Adam Wainwright .30 .75
376 Jeurys Familia .30 .75
377 J.J. Hardy .25 .60
378 Ryan Zimmerman .30 .75
379 Gerardo Parra .25 .60
380 Tyler Chatwood .25 .60
381 Drew Smyly .25 .60
382 Michael Bourn .25 .60
383 Chris Archer .25 .60
384 Rick Porcello .30 .75
385 Josh Willingham .30 .75
386 Mike Olt .25 .60
387 Ed Lucas .25 .60
388 Yovani Gallardo .25 .60
389 Geovany Soto .30 .75
390 Bryce Harper .60 1.50
391 Blake Parker .25 .60
392 Jacob Turner .30 .75
393 Devin Mesoraco .25 .60
394 Sean Halton .25 .60
395 John Danks .25 .60
396 Brian Roberts .25 .60
397 Tim Lincecum .30 .75
398 Adam Jones .30 .75
399 Hector Sanchez .25 .60
400 Clayton Kershaw .60 1.50
401 Felix Hernandez .30 .75
402 J.J. Putz .25 .60
403 Gordon Beckham .25 .60
404 C.C. Lee RC .30 .75
405 Jason Kubel .25 .60
406 Ramon Santiago .25 .60
407 John Jaso .25 .60
408 Joey Terdoslavich .25 .60
409 Ian Kennedy .25 .60
410 A.J. Griffin .25 .60
411 Josh Rutledge .25 .60
412 Hunter Pence .30 .75
413 Jose Fernandez .40 1.00
414 Michael Wacha .30 .75
415 Andre Ethier .30 .75
416 Josh Reddick .25 .60
417 Chase Headley .25 .60
418 Jordy Mercer .25 .60
419 Lucas Harrell .25 .60
420 Lucas Duda .30 .75
421 R.A. Dickey .30 .75
422 Alexi Ogando .25 .60
423 Marco Scutaro .30 .75
424 Jose Ramirez RC 5.00 12.00
425 Craig Kimbrel .30 .75
426 Koji Uehara .25 .60
427 Cameron Maybin .25 .60
428 Skip Schumaker .25 .60
429 Marcus Semien RC 1.50 4.00
430 Roger Kieschnick RC .30 .75
431 Brett Anderson .25 .60
432 Dillon Gee .25 .60
433 Omar Infante .25 .60
434 Miguel Gonzalez .25 .60
435 Ryan Braun .30 .75
436 Eric Young Jr. .25 .60
437 Alex Wood .25 .60
438 Jake Arrieta .30 .75
439 Jackie Bradley Jr. .40 1.00
440 Ryan Raburn .25 .60
441 Mike Pelfrey .25 .60
442 Angel Pagan .25 .60
443 Jeff Kobernus RC .30 .75
444 Robbie Grossman .25 .60
445 Sean Marshall .25 .60
446 Tim Hudson .30 .75
447 Christian Bethancourt RC .30 .75
448 Brett Lawrie .30 .75
449 Jedd Gyorko .25 .60
450 Justin Verlander .40 1.00
451 Luis Garcia RC .30 .75
452 Andrew McCutchen .40 1.00
453 Nelson Cruz .40 1.00
454 Brandon Beachy .25 .60
455 Danny Espinosa .25 .60
456 Eury De La Rosa RC .30 .75
457 CC Sabathia .30 .75
458 Vinnie Pestano .25 .60
459 Eric Hosmer .30 .75
460 Matt Kemp .30 .75
461 Steve Delabar .25 .60
462 J.A. Happ .30 .75
463 Samuel Deduno .25 .60
464 Evan Gattis .25 .60
465 Justin Morneau .30 .75
466 Ryan Dempster .25 .60
467 Scott Feldman .25 .60
468 Wilin Rosario .25 .60
469 Jesse Crain .25 .60
470 Kole Calhoun .25 .60
471 Brandon Moss .25 .60
472 Caleb Gindl .25 .60
473 Mike Napoli .25 .60
474 Carlos Martinez .30 .75
475 David Ortiz .40 1.00
476 DJ LeMahieu .40 1.00
477 Craig Gentry .25 .60
478 Billy Hamilton .30 .75
479 Ivan Nova .30 .75
480 Peter Bourjos .25 .60
481 Allen Craig .30 .75
482 Dallas Keuchel .30 .75
27-Apr Shane Robinson .25 .60
28-Apr Marlon Byrd .25 .60
29-Apr Gonzalez Germen RC .40 1.00
30-Apr Drew Hutchison .25 .60
1-May Jim Johnson .25 .60
2-May Brian Duensing .25 .60
3-May David Price .30 .75
4-May Logan Morrison .25 .60
5-May Felix Doubront .25 .60
6-May Glen Perkins .25 .60
7-May Ruben Tejada .25 .60
494 Rob Wooten RC .30 .75
495 John Axford .25 .60
10-May Jose Abreu RC 6.00 15.00
11-May Fernando Rodney .25 .60
12-May Steve Susdorf RC .30 .75
13-May Craig Kimbrel .30 .75
14-May Robinson Cano .30 .75
15-May Carlos Carrasco .25 .60
16-May Chase Utley .30 .75
17-May Kyle Kendrick .25 .60
18-May Kelly Johnson .25 .60
19-May Homer Bailey .25 .60
20-May Rafael Furcal .25 .60
507 Justin Masterson .25 .60
508 Sonny Gray FS .30 .75
23-May Brandon Phillips .25 .60
24-May Matt den Dekker RC .40 1.00
25-May Travis Wood .25 .60
26-May Neil Walker .25 .60
27-May Jordan Pacheco .25 .60
28-May Alcides Escobar .30 .75
29-May Curtis Granderson .30 .75
30-May Mike Belfiore RC .30 .75
31-May Norichika Aoki .25 .60
1-Jun Chris Parmelee .25 .60
2-Jun A.J. Ellis .25 .60
520 Jorge De La Rosa .25 .60
521 Anthony Rendon .40 1.00
5-Jun Wandy Rodriguez .25 .60
6-Jun Gio Gonzalez .30 .75
7-Jun Brian Bogusevic .25 .60
8-Jun Chris Davis .25 .60
9-Jun Avisail Garcia .30 .75
10-Jun Travis Snider .25 .60
11-Jun Shelby Miller .30 .75
12-Jun Jesus Montero .25 .60
13-Jun Danny Salazar .30 .75
14-Jun Dylan Bundy .30 .75
15-Jun Danny Duffy .25 .60
533 Jose Veras .25 .60
534 Ian Kinsler .30 .75
18-Jun Juan Francisco .25 .60
19-Jun Matt Harrison .25 .60
20-Jun Madison Bumgarner .30 .75
21-Jun Jon Jay .25 .60
22-Jun Trevor Bauer .50 1.25
23-Jun Ike Davis .25 .60
24-Jun Phil Hughes .25 .60
25-Jun Josh Zeid RC .30 .75
26-Jun Bud Norris .25 .60
27-Jun Jason Vargas .25 .60
28-Jun Jeremy Affeldt .25 .60
546 Heath Bell .25 .60
547 Brian Matusz .25 .60
1-Jul Jered Weaver .30 .75
2-Jul Hank Conger .25 .60
3-Jul Prince Fielder .30 .75
4-Jul Addison Reed .25 .60
5-Jul Yasiel Puig .40 1.00
6-Jul Michael Pineda .25 .60
7-Jul Maicer Izturis .25 .60
8-Jul Adam Eaton .25 .60
9-Jul Brad Ziegler .25 .60
10-Jul Vic Black RC .50 1.25
558 Nolan Reimold .25 .60
559 Asdrubal Cabrera .30 .75
13-Jul Aramis Ramirez .25 .60
14-Jul Wellington Castillo .25 .60
15-Jul Didi Gregorius .30 .75
16-Jul Colt Hynes RC .30 .75
17-Jul Alejandro De Aza .25 .60
18-Jul Roy Halladay .30 .75
19-Jul Carl Crawford .30 .75
20-Jul Donovan Solano .40 1.00
21-Jul Pedro Florimon .25 .60
22-Jul Michael Morse .25 .60
570 Nathan Eovaldi .30 .75
571 Colby Rasmus .30 .75
25-Jul Tommy Milone .25 .60
26-Jul Adam Lind .30 .75
27-Jul Tyler Clippard .25 .60
28-Jul Josh Hamilton .30 .75
29-Jul David Robertson .25 .60
30-Jul Steve Ames RC .30 .75
31-Jul Tyler Thornburg .25 .60
1-Aug Freddie Freeman .50 1.25
2-Aug Todd Frazier .25 .60
3-Aug Tony Cingrani .30 .75
582 Desmond Jennings .30 .75
5-Aug Ryan Ludwick .25 .60
6-Aug Tyler Flowers .25 .60
7-Aug Stephen Drew .25 .60
8-Aug Luke Hochevar .25 .60
9-Aug Dee Gordon .25 .60
10-Aug Matt Moore .30 .75
11-Aug Chris Carter .25 .60
12-Aug Brett Cecil .25 .60
13-Aug Jenrry Mejia .25 .60
14-Aug Simon Castro RC .30 .75
15-Aug Carlos Beltran .30 .75
16-Aug Justin Maxwell .25 .60
17-Aug A.J. Pierzynski .25 .60
18-Aug Juan Uribe .25 .60
19-Aug Mat Latos .30 .75
598 Marco Estrada .25 .60
599 Jason Motte .25 .60
600 David Wright .30 .75
601 Jason Hammel .30 .75
602 Tanner Roark RC .30 .75
603 Starlin Castro .25 .60
604 Clayton Kershaw .60 1.50
605 Tim Beckham RC .50 1.25
606 Kenley Jansen .30 .75
607 Jed Lowrie .25 .60
608 Jeff Locke .25 .60
609 Jonathan Pettibone .25 .60
610 Paul Konerko .30 .75
611 Patrick Corbin .30 .75
612 Jake Petricka RC .30 .75
613 Mark Teixeira .30 .75
614 Moises Sierra .25 .60
615 Drew Storen .25 .60
616 Zach McAllister .25 .60
617 Greg Holland .25 .60
618 Adam Dunn .30 .75
619 Chris Johnson .25 .60
620 Yan Gomes .25 .60
621 B.J. Upton .30 .75
622 Dexter Fowler .30 .75
623 Chad Billingsley .30 .75
624 Alex Presley .25 .60
625 Albert Pujols .50 1.25
626 Tommy Hanson .15 .40
627 J.P. Arencibia .25 .60
628 Joe Nathan .25 .60
629 Cliff Lee .30 .75
630 Max Scherzer .40 1.00
631 Bartolo Colon .25 .60
632 John Lackey .30 .75
633 Alex Avila .30 .75
634 Gaby Sanchez .25 .60
635 Josh Johnson .30 .75
636 Santiago Casilla .25 .60
637 Freddy Galvis .25 .60
638 Michael Cuddyer .25 .60
639 Conor Gillaspie .30 .75
640 Kyle Blanks .25 .60
641 A.J. Burnett .25 .60
642 Brandon Kintzler .25 .60
643 Alex Guerrero RC .40 1.00
644 Grant Green .25 .60
645 Wilson Ramos .25 .60
646 Dan Haren .25 .60
647 L.J. Hoes .25 .60
648 A.J. Pollock .30 .75
649 Jordan Danks .25 .60
650 Jacoby Ellsbury .30 .75
651 Denard Span .25 .60
652 Edinson Volquez .25 .60
653 Jose Iglesias .30 .75
654 Jose Tabata .25 .60
655 Derek Holland .25 .60
656 Grant Balfour .25 .60
657 Corey Hart .25 .60
658 Wade Davis .25 .60
659 Ervin Santana .25 .60
660 Jose Fernandez .40 1.00
661 Masahiro Tanaka RC 6.00 15.00

2014 Topps Mini Gold

*GOLD: 5X TO 12X BASIC
*GOLD RC: 4X TO 10X BASIC
STATED PRINT RUN 63 SER.#'d SETS

2014 Topps Mini Pink

*PINK: 8X TO 20X BASIC
*PINK RC: 6X TO 15X BASIC
STATED PRINT RUN 25 SER.#'d SETS

2014 Topps Mini Autographs

MAAJ Adam Jones 10.00 25.00
MAAR Andre Rienzo 4.00 10.00
MADM Daisuke Matsuzaka 20.00 50.00
MAED Eric Davis 15.00 40.00
MAFF Freddie Freeman 10.00 25.00
MAJA Jose Abreu 40.00 80.00
MAJB Jay Bruce 12.00 30.00
MAJF Jose Fernandez 15.00 40.00
MAJM Joe Mauer 20.00 50.00
MAJS Jonathan Schoop 8.00 20.00
MAKW Kolten Wong 10.00 25.00
MAMA Matt Adams 8.00 20.00
MAMB Madison Bumgarner 30.00 60.00
MANC Nick Castellanos 20.00 50.00
MAOT Oscar Taveras 40.00 80.00
MAPG Paul Goldschmidt 20.00 50.00
MARC Robinson Cano 20.00 50.00
MARH Ryan Howard 12.00 30.00
MATD Travis d'Arnaud 10.00 25.00
MATT Troy Tulowitzki 12.00 30.00
MATW Taijuan Walker 4.00 10.00
MAWF Wilmer Flores 5.00 12.00
MAYC Yoenis Cespedes 15.00 40.00

2014 Topps Mini Relics

MRAG Adrian Gonzalez 3.00 8.00
MRAJ Adam Jones 3.00 8.00
MRAP Albert Pujols 5.00 12.00
MRBHA Bryce Harper 6.00 15.00
MRBP Buster Posey 5.00 12.00
MRCD Chris Davis 2.50 6.00
MRCG Carlos Gonzalez 3.00 8.00
MRCK Clayton Kershaw 6.00 15.00
MRCL Cliff Lee 3.00 8.00
MRDJ Derek Jeter 15.00 40.00
MRDP Dustin Pedroia 6.00 15.00
MRDW David Wright 6.00 15.00
MREE Edwin Encarnacion 4.00 10.00
MREL Evan Longoria 3.00 8.00
MRGG Gio Gonzalez 3.00 8.00
MRHI Hisashi Iwakuma 3.00 8.00
MRHJR Hyun-Jin Ryu 3.00 8.00
MRHR Hanley Ramirez 3.00 8.00
MRIK Ian Kinsler 3.00 8.00
MRJB Jay Bruce 3.00 8.00
MRJM Joe Mauer 3.00 8.00
MRJR Jose Reyes 3.00 8.00
MRJV Justin Verlander 4.00 10.00
MRJVO Joey Votto 6.00 15.00
MRJW Jayson Werth 3.00 8.00
MRKW Kolten Wong 3.00 8.00
MRMC Matt Carpenter 4.00 10.00
MRMCA Miguel Cabrera 4.00 10.00
MRMK Matt Kemp 3.00 8.00
MRMS Max Scherzer 4.00 10.00
MRMT Masahiro Tanaka 8.00 20.00
MRNC Nick Castellanos 8.00 20.00
MRPF Prince Fielder 3.00 8.00
MRPG Paul Goldschmidt 6.00 15.00
MRRB Ryan Braun 3.00 8.00
MRRC Robinson Cano 3.00 8.00
MRSC Starlin Castro 2.50 6.00
MRSS Stephen Strasburg 4.00 10.00
MRSSC Shin-Soo Choo 3.00 8.00
MRTd Travis D'Arnaud 3.00 8.00
MRTL Tim Lincecum 3.00 8.00
MRTT Troy Tulowitzki 4.00 10.00
MRYC Yoenis Cespedes 4.00 10.00
MRYD Yu Darvish 4.00 10.00
MRYP Yasiel Puig 4.00 10.00

2014 Topps Mini The Future Is Now

FN1 Shelby Miller .30 .75
FN2 Shelby Miller .30 .75
FN3 Shelby Miller .30 .75
FN4 Jurickson Profar .30 .75
FN5 Jurickson Profar .30 .75
FN6 Jean Segura .30 .75
FN7 Jean Segura .30 .75
FN8 Zach Wheeler .30 .75
FN9 Zach Wheeler .30 .75
FN10 Michael Wacha .30 .75
FN11 Michael Wacha .30 .75
FN12 Billy Hamilton .30 .75
FN13 Billy Hamilton .30 .75
FN14 Billy Hamilton .30 .75
FN15 Kolten Wong .30 .75
FN16 Kolten Wong .30 .75
FN17 Xander Bogaerts .75 2.00
FN18 Xander Bogaerts .75 2.00
FN19 Xander Bogaerts .75 2.00
FN20 Taijuan Walker .25 .60
FN21 Taijuan Walker .25 .60
FN22 Taijuan Walker .25 .60
FN23 Sonny Gray .30 .75
FN24 Sonny Gray .30 .75
FN25 Jarrod Parker .25 .60
FN26 Jarrod Parker .25 .60
FN27 Freddie Freeman .50 1.25
FN28 Freddie Freeman .50 1.25
FN29 Dylan Bundy .30 .75
FN30 Dylan Bundy .30 .75
FN31 Kevin Gausman .40 1.00
FN32 Kevin Gausman .40 1.00
FN33 Yoenis Cespedes .40 1.00
FN34 Yoenis Cespedes .40 1.00
FN35 Hyun-Jin Ryu .30 .75
FN36 Hyun-Jin Ryu .30 .75
FN37 Wil Myers .25 .60
FN38 Wil Myers .25 .60
FN39 Mike Trout 2.00 5.00
FN40 Mike Trout 2.00 5.00
FN41 Jose Fernandez .40 1.00
FN42 Jose Fernandez .40 1.00
FN43 Manny Machado .40 1.00
FN44 Manny Machado .40 1.00
FN45 Yasiel Puig .40 1.00
FN46 Yasiel Puig .40 1.00
FN47 Yu Darvish .40 1.00
FN48 Yu Darvish .40 1.00
FN49 Bryce Harper .60 1.50
FN50 Bryce Harper .60 1.50

2015 Topps Mini

COMP.FACT.SET (700) 40.00 100.00
1 Derek Jeter 1.25 3.00
2 Altuve/Martinez/Brantley LL .40 1.00
3 Rene Rivera .30 .75
4 Curtis Granderson .40 1.00
5 Josh Donaldson .40 1.00
6 Jayson Werth .40 1.00
8 Miguel Gonzalez .30 .75
9 Hunter Pence WSH .40 1.00
10 Cole Hamels .40 1.00
11 Jon Jay .30 .75
12 James McCann RC .75 2.00
13 Toronto Blue Jays .30 .75
14 Kendall Graveman RC .50 1.25
15 Joey Votto .50 1.25
16 David DeJesus .30 .75
17 Brian McCann .40 1.00
18 Cody Allen .30 .75
19 Baltimore Orioles .30 .75
20 Madison Bumgarner .40 1.00
21 Brett Gardner .40 1.00
22 Tyler Flowers .30 .75
23 Michael Bourn .30 .75
24 New York Mets .30 .75
25 Jose Bautista .40 1.00
26 Bryce Brentz RC .50 1.25
27 Kendrys Morales .30 .75
28 Alex Cobb .30 .75
29 Brandon Belt BH .40 1.00
30 Tanner Roark FS .30 .75
31 Nick Tropeano RC .50 1.25
32 Carlos Quentin .30 .75
33 Oakland Athletics .30 .75
34 Charlie Blackmon .50 1.25
35 Brandon Moss .30 .75
36 Julio Teheran .40 1.00
37 Arismendy Alcantara FS .30 .75
38 Jordan Zimmermann .40 1.00
39 Salvador Perez .40 1.00
40 Joakim Soria .30 .75
41 Chris Colabello .30 .75
42 Todd Frazier .30 .75
43 Starlin Castro .30 .75
44 Gio Gonzalez .40 1.00
45 Carlos Beltran .40 1.00
46 Wilson Ramos .30 .75
47 Anthony Rizzo .60 1.50
48 John Axford .30 .75
49 Dominic Leone RC .50 1.25
50 Yu Darvish .50 1.25
51 Ryan Howard .40 1.00
52 Fernando Rodney .30 .75
53 Nathan Eovaldi .40 1.00
54 Joe Nathan .30 .75
55 Trevor May RC .50 1.25
56 Matt Garza .30 .75
57 Lyle Overbay .30 .75
58 Evan Gattis FS .30 .75
59 Jake Odorizzi .30 .75
60 Michael Wacha .40 1.00
61 Cueto/Kershaw/Wainwright LL .75 2.00
62 Nolan Arenado .75 2.00
63 Chris Owings FS .30 .75
64 Atlanta Braves .30 .75
65 Alexei Ramirez .40 1.00
66 Vance Worley .30 .75
67 Hunter Pence .40 1.00
68 Lonnie Chisenhall .30 .75
69 Justin Upton .40 1.00
70 Charlie Furbush .30 .75
71 Adrian Beltre BH .50 1.25
72 Jordan Lyles .30 .75
73 Freddie Freeman .60 1.50
74 Tyler Skaggs .30 .75
75 Dustin Pedroia .50 1.25
76 Ian Kennedy .30 .75
77 Edwin Escobar RC .50 1.25
78 Yordano Ventura .40 1.00
79 Starling Marte .40 1.00
80 Adam Wainwright .40 1.00
81 Chris Young .30 .75
82 Nick Tepesch .30 .75
83 David Wright .40 1.00
84 Jonathan Schoop .30 .75
85 Wainwright/Cueto/Kershaw LL .75 2.00
86 Tim Hudson .40 1.00
87 Eric Sogard .30 .75
88 Madison Bumgarner WSH .40 1.00
89 Michael Choice .30 .75
90 Marcus Stroman FS .40 1.00
91 Corey Dickerson .30 .75
92 Ian Kinsler .40 1.00
93 Andre Ethier .40 1.00
94 Tommy Kahnle RC .50 1.25
95 Junior Lake .30 .75
96 Sergio Santos .30 .75
97 Dalton Pompey RC .60 1.50
98 Trout/Cruz/Cabrera LL 2.50 6.00
99 Yonder Alonso .30 .75
100 Clayton Kershaw .75 2.00
101 Scooter Gennett .40 1.00
102 Gordon Beckham .30 .75
103 Guilder Rodriguez RC .50 1.25
104 Bud Norris .30 .75
105 Jeff Baker .30 .75
106 Pedro Alvarez .30 .75
107 James Loney .30 .75
108 Jorge Soler RC .75 2.00
109 Doug Fister .30 .75
110 Tony Sipp .30 .75
111 Trevor Bauer .60 1.50
112 Daniel Nava .30 .75
113 Jason Castro .30 .75
114 Mike Zunino .30 .75
115 Khris Davis .50 1.25
116 Vidal Nuno .30 .75
117 Sean Doolittle .30 .75
118 Domonic Brown .40 1.00
119 Anibal Sanchez .30 .75
120 Yoenis Cespedes .40 1.00
121 Garrett Jones .30 .75
122 Corey Kluber .40 1.00
123 Ben Revere .30 .75
124 Mark Melancon .30 .75
125 Troy Tulowitzki .50 1.25
126 Detroit Tigers .30 .75
127 McCutchen/Morneau/Harrison LL .50 1.25
128 Anthony Swarzak .30 .75
129 Jacob deGrom FS 1.00 2.50
130 Mike Napoli .30 .75
131 Edward Mujica .30 .75
132 Michael Taylor RC .50 1.25
133 Daisuke Matsuzaka .40 1.00
134 Brett Lawrie .40 1.00
135 Matt Dominguez .30 .75
136 Manny Machado .50 1.25
137 Alcides Escobar .40 1.00
138 Tim Lincecum .40 1.00
139 Gary Brown RC .50 1.25
140 Alex Avila .40 1.00
141 Cory Spangenberg RC .50 1.25
142 Masahiro Tanaka FS .40 1.00
143 Jonathan Papelbon .40 1.00
144 Rusney Castillo RC .60 1.50
145 Jesse Hahn .30 .75
146 Tony Watson .30 .75
147 Andrew Heaney FS .30 .75
148 J.D. Martinez .50 1.25
149 Daniel Murphy .40 1.00
150 Giancarlo Stanton .50 1.25
151 C.J. Cron FS .30 .75
152 Michael Pineda .30 .75
153 Josh Reddick .30 .75
154 Brandon Finnegan RC .50 1.25
155 Jesse Chavez .30 .75
156 Santiago Casilla .30 .75
157 Ubaldo Jimenez .30 .75
158 Kevin Kiermaier FS .40 1.00
159 Brandon Crawford .40 1.00
160 Washington Nationals .30 .75
161 Howie Kendrick .30 .75
162 Drew Pomeranz .40 1.00
163 Chase Utley .40 1.00
164 Brian Schlitter RC .50 1.25
165 John Jaso .30 .75
166 Jenrry Mejia .30 .75
167 Matt Cain .40 1.00
168 Colorado Rockies .30 .75
169 Adam Jones .40 1.00
170 Tommy Medica .30 .75
171 Mike Foltynewicz RC .50 1.25
172 Didi Gregorius .40 1.00
173 Carlos Torres .30 .75
174 Jesus Guzman .30 .75
175 Adrian Beltre .50 1.25
176 Jose Abreu FS .50 1.25
177 Paul Konerko .40 1.00
178 Christian Yelich .60 1.50
179 Jason Vargas .30 .75
180 Steve Pearce .50 1.25
181 Jason Heyward .40 1.00
182 Devin Mesoraco .30 .75
183 Craig Gentry .30 .75
184 B.J. Upton .40 1.00
185 Ricky Nolasco .30 .75
186 Rex Brothers .30 .75
187 Marlon Byrd .30 .75
188 Madison Bumgarner WSH .40 1.00
189 Dustin Ackley .30 .75
190 Zach Britton .40 1.00
191 Yimi Garcia RC .50 1.25
192 Joc Pederson 1.25 3.00
193 Buck Farmer RC .50 1.25
194 David Murphy .30 .75
195 Garrett Richards .40 1.00
196 Chicago Cubs .30 .75
197 Glen Perkins .30 .75
198 Alexi Ogando .30 .75
199 Eric Young Jr. .30 .75
200 Miguel Cabrera .50 1.25
201 Tommy La Stella .30 .75
202 Mike Minor .30 .75
203 Paul Goldschmidt .50 1.25
204 Eduardo Escobar .30 .75
205 Josh Harrison .30 .75
206 Rick Porcello .40 1.00
207 Bryce Harper .75 2.00
208 Wilin Rosario .30 .75
209 Daniel Corcino RC .50 1.25
210 Salvador Perez BH .40 1.00
211 Clay Buchholz .30 .75
212 Cliff Lee .40 1.00
213 Jered Weaver .40 1.00
214 Kluber/Scherzer/Weaver LL .50 1.25
215 Alejandro De Aza .30 .75
216 Greg Holland .30 .75
217 Daniel Norris RC .50 1.25
218 David Buchanan .30 .75
219 Kennys Vargas .30 .75
220 Shelby Miller .40 1.00
221 Jason Kipnis .40 1.00
222 Antonio Bastardo .30 .75
223 Los Angeles Angels .30 .75
224 Bryan Mitchell RC .50 1.25
225 Jacoby Ellsbury .40 1.00
226 Dioner Navarro .30 .75
227 Madison Bumgarner WSH .40 1.00
228 Jake Peavy .30 .75
229 Bryan Morris .30 .75
230 Jean Segura .40 1.00
231 Andrew Cashner .30 .75
232 Andrew Susac .30 .75
233 Carlos Ruiz .30 .75
234 Brandon Belt .40 1.00
235 Jeremy Guthrie .30 .75
236 Zack Wheeler .40 1.00
237 Lucas Duda .40 1.00
238 Hyun-Jin Ryu .40 1.00
239 Jose Iglesias .40 1.00
240 Anthony Ranaudo RC .50 1.25
241 Dilson Herrera RC .60 1.50
242 Edwin Encarnacion .50 1.25
243 Al Alburquerque .30 .75
244 Bartolo Colon .30 .75
245 Tyler Colvin .30 .75
246 Chris Carter .30 .75
247 Aaron Hill .30 .75
248 Addison Reed .30 .75
249 Jose Reyes .40 1.00
250 Evan Longoria .40 1.00
251 Anthony Rendon .50 1.25
252 Travis Wood .30 .75
253 Gregory Polanco FS .40 1.00
254 Steve Cishek .30 .75
255 James Russell .30 .75
256 Adam Eaton .30 .75
257 Jarrod Saltalamacchia .30 .75
258 Kansas City Royals .30 .75
259 Brian Dozier .40 1.00
260 David Peralta RC .50 1.25
261 Lance Lynn .30 .75
262 Ryan Braun .40 1.00
263 Dillon Gee .30 .75
264 Tony Cingrani .40 1.00
265 Arizona Diamondbacks .30 .75
266 Brandon Phillips .30 .75
267 Zack Greinke .50 1.25
268 Aroldis Chapman .50 1.25
269 Jordy Mercer .30 .75
270 Steven Moya RC .60 1.50
271 Pittsburgh Pirates .30 .75
272 Matt Kemp .40 1.00
273 Brandon Hicks .30 .75
274 Ryan Zimmerman .40 1.00
275 Buster Posey .60 1.50
276 Conor Gillaspie .40 1.00
277 Cincinnati Reds .30 .75
278 David Phelps .30 .75
279 Coco Crisp .30 .75
280 Miguel Montero .30 .75
281 Elvis Andrus .40 1.00
282 Alex Presley .30 .75
283 Chris Johnson .30 .75
284 Brandon League .30 .75
285 Carter/Trout/Cruz LL 2.50 6.00
286 Trevor Rosenthal .40 1.00
287 Everth Cabrera .30 .75
288 Chris Parmelee .30 .75
289 Matt Joyce .30 .75
290 David Lough .30 .75
291 Mark Reynolds .30 .75
292 Neil Walker .30 .75
293 Zach Duke .30 .75
294 Aaron Sanchez FS .40 1.00
295 Erick Aybar .30 .75
296 Charlie Morton .50 1.25
297 Scott Kazmir .30 .75
298 Rymer Liriano RC .50 1.25
299 Joaquin Arias .30 .75
300 Mike Trout 2.50 6.00
301 Zack Cozart .30 .75
302 Martin Prado .30 .75
303 Ike Davis .30 .75
304 Shawn Kelley .30 .75
305 Sonny Gray .40 1.00
306 Juan Lagares FS .30 .75
307 Mark Teixeira .40 1.00
308 Carl Crawford .40 1.00
309 Maikel Franco RC .60 1.50
310 Jake Lamb RC .75 2.00
311 Jhonny Peralta .30 .75
312 Kyle Lobstein RC .50 1.25
313 Rizzo/Stntn/Duda LL .60 1.50
314 Jackie Bradley Jr. .50 1.25
315 Javier Baez RC 4.00 10.00
316 R.A. Dickey .40 1.00
317 Clayton Kershaw BH .75 2.00
318 George Springer FS .40 1.00
319 Derek Jeter BH 1.25 3.00
320 Shin-Soo Choo .40 1.00
321 Josh Hamilton .40 1.00
322 Phil Hughes .30 .75
323 Eric Hosmer .40 1.00
324 Chris Archer .30 .75
325 Felix Hernandez .40 1.00
326 C.J. Wilson .30 .75
327 Xander Bogaerts FS .50 1.25
328 Adrian Gonzalez .40 1.00
329 Logan Forsythe .30 .75
330 Brian Duensing .30 .75
331 Danny Espinosa .30 .75
332 Kyle Seager .30 .75
333 Billy Hamilton FS .40 1.00
334 Gerardo Parra .30 .75
335 Matt Barnes RC .50 1.25
336 Matt Carpenter .50 1.25
337 Jedd Gyorko .30 .75
338 Yasmani Grandal .30 .75
339 Austin Jackson .30 .75
340 Carlos Gomez .30 .75
341 Kluber/Sale/Hernandez LL .50 1.25
342 San Diego Padres .30 .75
343 Shane Greene .30 .75
344 Manny Parra .30 .75
345 Brandon Cumpton .30 .75
346 Trevor Cahill .30 .75
347 Dexter Fowler .40 1.00
348 Carlos Santana .40 1.00
349 Uptn/Gnzlz/Stntn LL .50 1.25
350 Yasiel Puig .50 1.25
351 Tom Koehler .30 .75
352 Jaime Garcia .30 .75
353 Mike Leake .30 .75
354 Kyle Hendricks .50 1.25
355 Travis Snider .30 .75
356 Marcus Semien .50 1.25
357 Derek Holland .30 .75
358 Jon Singleton .40 1.00
359 Robinson Chirinos .30 .75
360 Adam LaRoche .30 .75
361 Matt Holliday .50 1.25
362 Jason Bourgeois .30 .75
363 Avisail Garcia .40 1.00
364 Travis Ishikawa .30 .75
365 L.J. Hoes .30 .75
366 Jhoulys Chacin .30 .75
367 Sam Fuld .30 .75
368 David Robertson .40 1.00
369 Aaron Loup .30 .75
370 Marcell Ozuna .50 1.25
371 Koji Uehara .30 .75
372 Matt Adams .30 .75
373 Kurt Suzuki .30 .75
374 Nick Martinez .30 .75
375 Johnny Cueto .40 1.00
376 Chris Sale .50 1.25
377 Tommy Hunter .30 .75
378 Danny Duffy .30 .75
379 Phil Gosselin .30 .75
380 Hector Noesi .30 .75
381 Stephen Drew .30 .75
382 Ivan Nova .40 1.00
383 Delmon Young .40 1.00
384 Justin Ruggiano .30 .75
385 James Paxton .40 1.00
386 Ben Zobrist .40 1.00
387 Jacob deGrom 1.00 2.50
388 Francisco Liriano .30 .75
389 Mookie Betts 1.00 2.50
390 Cody Ross .30 .75
391 Hisashi Iwakuma .40 1.00
392 Brandon Guyer .30 .75
393 Danny Salazar .40 1.00
394 Marco Scutaro .30 .75
395 Chris Taylor .40 1.00
396 Alex Colome .30 .75
397 Mike Aviles .30 .75
398 Jordan Zimmermann .40 1.00
399 Josmil Pinto .30 .75
400 Andrew McCutchen .50 1.25
401 Chris Coghlan .30 .75
402 Jeurys Familia .40 1.00
403 Leury Garcia .30 .75
404 Tanner Scheppers .30 .75
405 Ross Detwiler .30 .75
406 Jon Lester .40 1.00
407 Jed Lowrie .30 .75
408 Jake Smolinski .30 .75

409 Juan Uribe .30 .75
410 Kyle Lohse .30 .75
411 Nelson Cruz .50 1.25
412 Hector Rondon .30 .75
413 Anthony Gose .30 .75
414 J.A. Happ .40 1.00
415 Ervin Santana .30 .75
416 Francisco Cervelli .30 .75
417 Leonys Martin .30 .75
418 Jung Ho Kang RC .50 1.25
419 Omar Infante .30 .75
420 Cody Asche .40 1.00
421 Joe Kelly .30 .75
422 Prince Fielder .40 1.00
423 Javy Guerra .30 .75
424 Michael Saunders .40 1.00
425 Bryan Shaw .30 .75
426 Trevor Plouffe .30 .75
427 Raisel Iglesias RC .60 1.50
428 Jon Niese .30 .75
429 A.J. Ellis .30 .75
430 Jarred Cosart .30 .75
431 Brandon McCarthy .30 .75
432 Alex Rios .40 1.00
433 Justin Masterson .30 .75
434 Carlos Frias RC .75 2.00
435 Mike Fiers .30 .75
436 Russell Martin .30 .75
437 Jake Marisnick .30 .75
438 DJ LeMahieu .50 1.25
439 Kenley Jansen .40 1.00
440 Denard Span .30 .75
441 Philadelphia Phillies .30 .75
442 Tyler Matzek .30 .75
443 Maicer Izturis .30 .75
444 Lonnie Chisenhall .30 .75
445 Christian Vazquez .40 1.00
446 Nick Franklin .30 .75
447 Jose Ramirez .40 1.00
448 Ryan Hanigan .30 .75
449 Joe Panik .40 1.00
450 Robinson Cano .40 1.00
451 Clayton Kershaw .75 2.00
452 Drew Smyly .30 .75
453 Elian Herrera .30 .75
454 Wade Davis .30 .75
455 Adam Lind .40 1.00
456 Alex Gordon .40 1.00
457 Aaron Hicks .40 1.00
458 Junichi Tazawa .30 .75
459 Tuffy Gosewisch .30 .75
460 San Francisco Giants .30 .75
461 Mike Moustakas .40 1.00
462 Shae Simmons .30 .75
463 Justin Verlander .50 1.25
464 Brett Cecil .30 .75
465 Seattle Mariners .30 .75
466 A.J. Burnett .30 .75
467 Mat Latos .40 1.00
468 CC Sabathia .40 1.00
469 James Shields .30 .75
470 Mark Trumbo .30 .75
471 Pat Neshek .30 .75
472 T.J. House .30 .75
473 Ryan Raburn .30 .75
474 Alexi Amarista .30 .75
475 Juan Perez .30 .75
476 Jose Lobaton .30 .75
477 Dallas Keuchel .40 1.00
478 Los Angeles Dodgers .30 .75
479 Carlos Gonzalez .40 1.00
480 Matt Harvey .40 1.00
481 Freddy Galvis .30 .75
482 Joaquin Benoit .30 .75
483 Randal Grichuk .30 .75
484 Melvin Mercedes RC .50 1.25
485 Daniel Hudson .30 .75
486 Erik Goeddel RC .60 1.50
487 Corey Kluber .40 1.00
488 John Lackey .40 1.00
489 Jeremy Hellickson .30 .75
490 Gavin Floyd .30 .75
491 Rougned Odor .40 1.00
492 Brandon Barnes .30 .75
493 Alex Rodriguez .60 1.50
494 James Jones .30 .75
495 Christian Colon .30 .75
496 Houston Astros .30 .75
497 Hunter Strickland RC .50 1.25
498 Anthony Desclafani .30 .75
499 Eduardo Nunez .30 .75
500 David Ortiz .50 1.25
501 Will Venable .30 .75
502 Kevin Frandsen .30 .75
503 Joe Panik .40 1.00
504 Minnesota Twins .30 .75
505 Arodys Vizcaino .30 .75
506 Chase Anderson .30 .75
507 A.J. Pierzynski .30 .75
508 Collin McHugh .30 .75
509 Danny Santana .30 .75
510 Mike Trout 2.50 6.00
511 Asdrubal Cabrera .40 1.00
512 Jay Bruce .40 1.00
513 Michael Cuddyer .30 .75
514 Will Smith .30 .75
515 Victor Martinez .40 1.00
516 Lorenzo Cain .30 .75
517 Yusmeiro Petit .30 .75
518 Rajai Davis .30 .75
519 Archie Bradley RC .50 1.25
520 Brayan Pena .30 .75
521 Nick Castellanos .50 1.25
522 Sam Tuivailala RC .50 1.25
523 Christian Bethancourt .30 .75
524 John Danks .30 .75
525 Luke Gregerson .30 .75
526 Will Middlebrooks .30 .75
527 Carlos Martinez .40 1.00
528 Brad Ziegler .30 .75
529 Ryan Flaherty .30 .75
530 Chris Heston RC .50 1.25
531 Drew Hutchison .30 .75
532 Dellin Betances .40 1.00
533 Marwin Gonzalez .30 .75
534 Chris Capuano .30 .75
535 Erik Cordier RC .50 1.25
536 Logan Morrison .30 .75
537 Steven Souza Jr. .40 1.00
538 Brad Boxberger RC .50 1.25
539 Jimmy Nelson .30 .75
540 Drew Stubbs .30 .75
541 Homer Bailey .30 .75
542 Yasmany Tomas RC .60 1.50
543 Alberto Callaspo .30 .75
544 Travis d'Arnaud .40 1.00
545 Clayton Kershaw .75 2.00
546 Tyler Clippard .30 .75
547 Kristopher Negron RC .50 1.25
548 Cleveland Indians .30 .75
549 Christian Walker RC 1.00 2.50
550 David Price .40 1.00
551 Corey Hart .30 .75
552 Yovani Gallardo .30 .75
553 Grady Sizemore .40 1.00
554 A.J. Griffin .30 .75
555 Jake Arrieta .40 1.00
556 Jake McGee .40 1.00
557 Nick Markakis .40 1.00
558 Patrick Corbin .40 1.00
559 Dee Gordon .30 .75
560 Jerome Williams .30 .75
561 Ken Giles .30 .75
562 Wilmer Flores .40 1.00
563 J.J. Hardy .30 .75
564 Jose Quintana .30 .75
565 Michael Morse .30 .75
566 Chris Davis .30 .75
567 Brennan Boesch .30 .75
568 Chris Tillman .30 .75
569 Marco Estrada .30 .75
570 Jarrod Dyson .30 .75
571 Devon Travis RC .50 1.25
572 A.J. Pollock .40 1.00
573 Ryan Rua RC .50 1.25
574 Mitch Moreland .30 .75
575 Kris Medlen .40 1.00
576 Chase Headley .30 .75
577 Henderson Alvarez .30 .75
578 Ender Inciarte RC .50 1.25
579 Jason Hammel .40 1.00
580 Chris Bassitt RC .50 1.25
581 John Holdzkom RC .50 1.25
582 Wei-Yin Chen .30 .75
583 Jose Abreu .50 1.25
584 Danny Farquhar .30 .75
585 Matt Moore .40 1.00
586 Max Scherzer .50 1.25
587 Daniel Descalso .30 .75
588 Kolten Wong .40 1.00
589 Jeff Locke .30 .75
590 Torii Hunter .30 .75
591 Josh Collmenter .30 .75
592 Martin Maldonado .30 .75
593 Ruben Tejada .30 .75
594 Jose Pirela RC .50 1.25
595 Craig Kimbrel .40 1.00
596 Bronson Arroyo .30 .75
597 Matt Shoemaker .40 1.00
598 Nick Swisher .40 1.00
599 Michael Brantley .40 1.00
600 Albert Pujols .60 1.50
601 Wade Miley .30 .75
602 Drew Storen .30 .75
603 Jose Fernandez .50 1.25
604 Jordan Schafer .30 .75
605 Huston Street .30 .75
606 Ian Desmond .30 .75
607 Jarrod Parker .30 .75
608 Justin Smoak .30 .75
609 Luke Hochevar .30 .75
610 David Freese .30 .75
611 Gregor Blanco .30 .75
612 Caleb Joseph .30 .75
613 Josh Beckett .30 .75
614 Jordan Walden .30 .75
615 Carlos Sanchez .30 .75
616 Kris Bryant RC 5.00 12.00
617 Terrance Gore RC .50 1.25
618 Billy Butler .30 .75
619 Kevin Gausman .50 1.25
620 Jose Altuve .40 1.00
621 Luis Valbuena .30 .75
622 Yan Gomes .30 .75
623 Melky Cabrera .30 .75
624 Miguel Alfredo Gonzalez RC .50 1.25
625 Mark Buehrle .40 1.00
626 Hanley Ramirez .40 1.00
627 Jason Grilli .30 .75
628 Peter Bourjos .30 .75
629 Robbie Grossman .30 .75
630 Carlos Carrasco .30 .75
631 Chris Iannetta .30 .75
632 Kyle Gibson .40 1.00
633 Skip Schumaker .30 .75
634 Roenis Elias .30 .75
635 Scott Feldman .30 .75
636 Micah Johnson RC .50 1.25
637 Matt Szczur RC .60 1.50
638 Jimmy Rollins .40 1.00
639 Cameron Maybin .30 .75
640 Matt Clark RC .50 1.25
641 Yorman Rodriguez RC .50 1.25
642 Alex Wood .30 .75
643 Oswaldo Arcia .30 .75
644 Chicago White Sox .30 .75
645 Neftali Feliz .30 .75
646 Aramis Ramirez .30 .75
647 Yadier Molina .60 1.50
648 St. Louis Cardinals BB .30 .75
649 Emilio Bonifacio .30 .75
650 Pablo Sandoval .40 1.00
651 Andrelton Simmons .30 .75
652 Stephen Vogt .40 1.00
653 Rafael Montero .30 .75
654 Alfredo Simon .30 .75
655 Taylor Hill .30 .75
656 Adeiny Hechavarria .30 .75
657 Justin Morneau .40 1.00
658 Tsuyoshi Wada .30 .75
659 Jimmy Rollins .40 1.00
660 Roberto Osuna RC .50 1.25
661 Grant Balfour .30 .75
662 Darin Ruf .30 .75
663 Jake Diekman .30 .75
664 Hector Santiago .30 .75
665 Stephen Strasburg .50 1.25
666 Jonathan Broxton .30 .75
667 Kole Calhoun .30 .75
668 Jairo Diaz RC .50 1.25
669 Tampa Bay Rays .30 .75
670 Darren O'Day .30 .75
671 Gerrit Cole .50 1.25
672 Wily Peralta .30 .75
673 Brett Oberholtzer .30 .75
674 Desmond Jennings .40 1.00
675 Jonathan Lucroy .40 1.00
676 Nate McLouth .30 .75
677 Ryan Goins .30 .75
678 Sam Freeman .30 .75
679 Jorge De La Rosa .30 .75
680 Nick Hundley .30 .75
681 Zoilo Almonte .30 .75
682 Christian Bergman .30 .75
683 LaTroy Hawkins .30 .75
684 Wil Myers .40 1.00
685 Yangervis Solarte .30 .75
686 Tyson Ross .30 .75
687 Odubel Herrera RC .75 2.00
688 Angel Pagan .30 .75
689 R.J. Alvarez RC .50 1.25
690 Brett Bochy RC .50 1.25
691 Lisalverto Bonilla RC .50 1.25
692 Andrew Chafin RC .50 1.25
693 Jason Rogers RC .50 1.25
694 Xavier Scruggs RC .50 1.25
695 Rafael Ynoa RC .50 1.25
696 Boston Red Sox .30 .75
697 New York Yankees .30 .75
698 Texas Rangers .30 .75
699 Miami Marlins .30 .75
700 Joe Mauer .40 1.00
701 Milwaukee Brewers .30 .75

2015 Topps Mini '75 Topps

COMPLETE SET (10) 15.00 40.00
ISSUED VIA TOPPS.COM
COMPLETE SET ISSUED WITH FACT.SET
AR Addison Russell 2.00 5.00
BB Byron Buxton 3.00 8.00
BH Bryce Harper 1.50 4.00
CC Carlos Correa 3.00 8.00
CK Clayton Kershaw 1.50 4.00
FL Francisco Lindor 5.00 12.00
JA Jake Arrieta .75 2.00
KB Kris Bryant 6.00 15.00
MT Mike Trout 5.00 12.00
NS Noah Syndergaard 1.25 3.00

2016 Topps Mini

1 Mike Trout 4.00 10.00
2 Jerad Eickhoff .75 2.00
3 Richie Shaffer .50 1.25
4 Sonny Gray .60 1.50
5 Kyle Seager .50 1.25
6 Jimmy Paredes .50 1.25
8 Michael Brantley .60 1.50
9 Eric Hosmer .60 1.50
10 Nelson Cruz .75 2.00
11 Andre Ethier .60 1.50
12 Nolan Arenado 1.25 3.00
13 Craig Kimbrel .60 1.50
14 Chris Davis .50 1.25
15 Ryan Howard .60 1.50
16 Rougned Odor .60 1.50
17 Billy Butler .50 1.25
18 Francisco Rodriguez .60 1.50
19 Delino DeShields Jr. FS .50 1.25
20 Andrew McCutchen .75 2.00
21 Mike Moustakas WSH .60 1.50
22 John Hicks .50 1.25
23 Jeff Francoeur .60 1.50
24 Clayton Kershaw 1.25 3.00
25 Brad Ziegler .50 1.25
26 Chris Davis 4.00 10.00
Mike Trout
Nelson Cruz LL
27 Alec Asher .50 1.25
28 Brian McCann .60 1.50
29 Altuve/Cabrera/Bogaerts .75 2.00
30 Yan Gomes .50 1.25
31 Travis d'Arnaud .60 1.50
32 Zack Greinke .75 2.00
33 Edinson Volquez .50 1.25
34 Omar Infante .50 1.25
35 Luke Hochevar .50 1.25
36 Miguel Montero .50 1.25
37 C.J. Cron .50 1.25
38 Jed Lowrie .50 1.25
39 Mark Trumbo .50 1.25
40 Jedd Gyorko .50 1.25
41 Josh Harrison .50 1.25
42 A.J. Ramos .50 1.25
43 Noah Syndergaard FS .60 1.50
44 David Freese .50 1.25
45 Ryan Zimmerman .60 1.50
46 Jhonny Peralta .50 1.25
47 Gio Gonzalez .60 1.50
48 J.J. Hoover .50 1.25
49 Ike Davis .50 1.25
50 Salvador Perez .60 1.50
51 Dustin Garneau .50 1.25
52 Julio Teheran .60 1.50
53 George Springer .60 1.50
54 Jung Ho Kang FS .50 1.25
55 Jesus Montero .50 1.25
56 Salvador Perez WSH .60 1.50
57 Adam Lind .60 1.50
58 Zack Greinke 1.25 3.00
Clayton Kershaw
Jake Arrieta LL
59 John Lamb .50 1.25
60 Shelby Miller .60 1.50
61 Johnny Cueto WSH .60 1.50
62 Trayce Thompson .75 2.00
63 Zach Britton .60 1.50
64 Corey Kluber .60 1.50
65 Pittsburgh Pirates .50 1.25
66 Kyle Schwarber 1.50 4.00
67 Matt Harvey .60 1.50
68 Odubel Herrera FS .60 1.50
69 Anibal Sanchez .50 1.25
70 Kendrys Morales .50 1.25
71 John Danks .50 1.25
72 Chris Young .50 1.25
73 Ketel Marte 1.00 2.50
74 Troy Tulowitzki .75 2.00
75 Rusney Castillo .50 1.25
76 Glen Perkins .50 1.25
77 Clay Buchholz .50 1.25
78 Miguel Sano .75 2.00
79 Seattle Mariners .50 1.25
80 Carson Smith .50 1.25
81 Alexei Ramirez .60 1.50
82 Michael Bourn .50 1.25
83 Starling Marte .60 1.50
84 Mookie Betts 1.50 4.00
85 Corey Seager 12.00 30.00
86 Wilmer Flores .60 1.50
87 Jorge De La Rosa .50 1.25
88 Ubaldo Jimenez .50 1.25
89 Edwin Encarnacion .75 2.00
90 Koji Uehara .50 1.25
91 Yasmani Grandal FS .50 1.25
92 Darren O'Day .50 1.25
93 Charlie Blackmon .75 2.00
94 Miguel Cabrera .75 2.00
95 Kole Calhoun FS .50 1.25
96 Jose Bautista .60 1.50
97 Ender Inciarte FS .50 1.25
98 Garrett Richards .60 1.50
99 Taijuan Walker .50 1.25
100 Bryce Harper 1.25 3.00
101 Justin Turner .75 2.00
102 Doug Fister .50 1.25
103 Trea Turner 1.50 4.00
104 Jeremy Hellickson .50 1.25
105 Marcus Semien .75 2.00
106 Jordan Walden .50 1.25
107 Kevin Siegrist .50 1.25
108 Ben Paulsen .50 1.25
109 Henry Owens .60 1.50
110 J.D. Martinez FS .75 2.00
111 Coco Crisp .50 1.25
112 Matt Kemp .60 1.50
113 Aaron Sanchez .60 1.50
114 Brett Lawrie .60 1.50
115 Aaron Harang .50 1.25
116 Brett Gardner .60 1.50
117 Liam Hendriks .50 1.25
118 Jose Fernandez .75 2.00
119 Sean Doolittle .50 1.25
120 Alcides Escobar WSH .60 1.50
121 Roberto Osuna FS .50 1.25
122 Melky Cabrera .50 1.25
123 J.P. Howell .50 1.25
124 Melvin Upton Jr. .60 1.50
125 Zack Greinke 1.25 3.00
Clayton Kershaw
Jake Arrieta LL
126 David Ortiz .75 2.00
Albert Pujols
127 Zach Lee .50 1.25
128 Eddie Rosario .60 1.50
129 Kendall Graveman .50 1.25
130 A.J. Pollock .50 1.25
131 Adam LaRoche .50 1.25
132 Joe Ross FS .50 1.25
133 Aaron Nola 1.00 2.50
134 Yadier Molina 1.00 2.50
135 Colby Rasmus .60 1.50
136 Michael Cuddyer .50 1.25
137 Joe Panik .60 1.50
138 Francisco Liriano .50 1.25
139 Yasiel Puig .75 2.00
140 Carlos Carrasco FS .50 1.25
141 Colin Rea .50 1.25
142 CC Sabathia .60 1.50
143 Oliver Perez .50 1.25
144 Jose Iglesias .60 1.50
145 Jon Niese .50 1.25
146 Stephen Piscotty .75 2.00
147 Dee Gordon .50 1.25
148 Yangervis Solarte .50 1.25
149 Chad Bettis .50 1.25
150 Clayton Kershaw 1.25 3.00
151 Jon Lester .60 1.50
152 Kyle Lohse .50 1.25
153 Jason Hammel .60 1.50
154 Hunter Pence .60 1.50
155 New York Yankees .50 1.25
156 Cameron Maybin .50 1.25
157 Darnell Sweeney .50 1.25
158 Henry Urrutia .50 1.25
159 Erick Aybar .50 1.25
160 Chris Sale .75 2.00
161 Phil Hughes .50 1.25
162 Jose Bautista .60 1.50
Josh Donaldson
Chris Davis LL
163 Joaquin Benoit .50 1.25
164 Andrew Heaney .50 1.25
165 Adam Eaton .50 1.25
166 Gldschmdt/Rizzo/Arndo LL 1.25 3.00
167 Jacoby Ellsbury .60 1.50
168 Nathan Eovaldi .60 1.50
169 Charlie Morton .75 2.00
170 Carlos Gomez .50 1.25
171 Matt Cain .60 1.50
172 Carter Capps .50 1.25
173 Jose Abreu .75 2.00
174 Jered Weaver .60 1.50
175 Manny Machado .75 2.00
176 Brandon Phillips .50 1.25
177 Gregor Blanco .50 1.25
178 Rob Refsnyder .60 1.50
179 Jose Peraza .60 1.50
180 Kevin Gausman .75 2.00
181 Minnesota Twins .50 1.25
182 Kevin Pillar .50 1.25
183 Andrelton Simmons .50 1.25
184 Travis Jankowski .50 1.25
185 Dallas Keuchel .60 1.50
Sonny Gray
David Price LL
186 Yasmany Tomas FS .50 1.25
187 Dallas Keuchel .60 1.50
Collin McHugh
David Price LL
188 Greg Bird .60 1.50
189 Jake McGee .60 1.50
190 Jeurys Familia .60 1.50
191 Brian Johnson .50 1.25
192 John Jaso .50 1.25
193 Trevor Bauer 1.00 2.50
194 Chase Headley .50 1.25
195 Jason Kipnis .60 1.50
196 Hunter Strickland .50 1.25
197 Neil Walker .50 1.25
198 Oakland Athletics .50 1.25
199 Jay Bruce .60 1.50
200 Josh Donaldson .60 1.50
201 Adam Jones .60 1.50
202 Colorado Rockies .50 1.25
203 Aaron Hill .50 1.25
204 Mark Teixeira .60 1.50
205 Taylor Jungmann FS .50 1.25
206 Alex Gordon .60 1.50
207 Maikel Franco FS .60 1.50
208 Kurt Suzuki .50 1.25
209 Max Scherzer .75 2.00
210 Mike Zunino .50 1.25
211 Nick Ahmed .50 1.25
212 Starlin Castro .50 1.25
213 Matt Shoemaker .60 1.50
214 Chris Colabello .50 1.25
215 Adrian Gonzalez .60 1.50
216 Logan Forsythe .50 1.25
217 Lance Lynn .50 1.25
218 Andrew Miller .60 1.50
219 Hector Olivera .60 1.50
220 Zack Greinke .75 2.00
Gerrit Cole
Jake Arrieta LL
221 Ryan LaMarre .50 1.25
222 Homer Bailey .50 1.25
223 Christian Yelich 1.00 2.50
224 Billy Burns FS .50 1.25
225 Scooter Gennett .60 1.50
226 Brian Ellington .50 1.25
227 David Murphy .50 1.25
228 Matt Garza .50 1.25
229 Jesse Hahn .50 1.25
230 Ryan Vogelsong .50 1.25
231 Chris Coghlan .50 1.25
232 Michael Conforto .60 1.50
233 J.J. Hardy .50 1.25
234 David Robertson .50 1.25
235 Blaine Boyer .50 1.25
236 Juan Lagares .50 1.25
237 Carlos Ruiz .50 1.25
238 Baltimore Orioles .50 1.25
239 Huston Street .50 1.25
240 Nick Markakis .60 1.50
241 Freddie Freeman 1.00 2.50
242 Matt Wisler FS .50 1.25
243 Luke Gregerson .50 1.25
244 Matt Carpenter .75 2.00
245 Tommy Kahnle .50 1.25
246 Dustin Pedroia .75 2.00
247 Yunel Escobar .50 1.25
248 Atlanta Braves .50 1.25
249 Carlos Gomez .50 1.25
250 Miguel Cabrera .75 2.00
251 Silvino Bracho .50 1.25
252 Jorge Soler .75 2.00
253 Nick Castellanos .75 2.00
254 Matt Holliday .75 2.00
255 Justin Verlander .75 2.00
256 C.J. Wilson .50 1.25
257 Jake Marisnick .50 1.25
258 Devon Travis FS .50 1.25
259 Paul Goldschmidt .75 2.00
260 Ryan Hanigan .50 1.25
261 Russell Martin .50 1.25
262 Ervin Santana .50 1.25
263 Joc Pederson FS .60 1.50
264 Jake Arrieta .60 1.50
265 Luis Severino .60 1.50
266 Jonathan Papelbon .60 1.50
267 Chris Heston FS .50 1.25
268 Robinson Cano .60 1.50
269 Giancarlo Stanton .75 2.00
270 Pat Neshek .50 1.25
271 Kevin Kiermaier .60 1.50
272 Denard Span .50 1.25
273 New York Mets .50 1.25
274 Ryan Goins .50 1.25
275 Ian Kinsler .60 1.50
276 Francisco Cervelli .50 1.25
277 Elvis Andrus .60 1.50
278 Evan Gattis .50 1.25
279 Alex Guerrero FS .60 1.50
280 Brock Holt .50 1.25
281 Alex Dickerson .50 1.25
282 Scott Feldman .50 1.25
283 Felix Hernandez .60 1.50
284 Jon Gray .50 1.25
285 Pablo Sandoval .60 1.50
286 Joe Mauer .60 1.50
287 Alcides Escobar .60 1.50
288 Jake Lamb FS .60 1.50
289 Nick Hundley .50 1.25
290 Zack Godley .50 1.25
291 Asdrubal Cabrera .60 1.50
292 Todd Frazier .50 1.25
293 Hyun-Jin Ryu .60 1.50
294 Chicago White Sox .50 1.25
295 Jonathan Schoop .50 1.25
296 Yordano Ventura .60 1.50
297 Detroit Tigers .50 1.25
298 Ryan Braun .60 1.50
299 Angel Pagan .50 1.25
300 Buster Posey 1.00 2.50
301 Wade Miley .50 1.25
302 Houston Astros .50 1.25
303 Steve Pearce .75 2.00
304 Charlie Furbush .50 1.25
305 Colby Lewis .50 1.25
306 Jarrod Saltalamacchia .50 1.25
307 Wade Davis .50 1.25
308 Brian Dozier .60 1.50
309 Shin-Soo Choo .60 1.50
310 David Wright .60 1.50
311 Dariel Alvarez .50 1.25
312 Curtis Granderson .60 1.50
313 Martin Maldonado .50 1.25
314 Kyle Hendricks .75 2.00
315 San Diego Padres .50 1.25
316 Jake Odorizzi FS .50 1.25
317 Jose Altuve .60 1.50
318 Washington Nationals .50 1.25
319 Adam Wainwright .60 1.50
320 Jake Peavy .50 1.25
321 Hanley Ramirez .60 1.50
322 Kelby Tomlinson .50 1.25
323 Jacob deGrom 1.50 4.00
324 Steven Souza Jr. .60 1.50
325 Kaleb Cowart .50 1.25
326 Kevin Plawecki FS .50 1.25
327 Anthony Rizzo 1.00 2.50
328 Anthony DeSclafani .50 1.25
329 Alex Rodriguez 1.00 2.50
330 Edward Mujica .50 1.25
331 Will Harris .50 1.25
332 Toronto Blue Jays .50 1.25
333 Keyvius Sampson .50 1.25
334 Brandon McCarthy .50 1.25
335 Mitch Moreland .50 1.25
336 Mark Melancon .50 1.25
337 Nolan Arenado 1.25 3.00
Bryce Harper
Carlos Gonzalez LL
338 Paul Goldschmidt 1.25 3.00
Dee Gordon
Bryce Harper LL
339 Carlos Santana .60 1.50
340 Victor Martinez .60 1.50
341 Josh Hamilton .60 1.50
342 Jayson Werth .60 1.50
343 Drew Hutchison .50 1.25
344 Jonathan Lucroy .60 1.50
345 Yonder Alonso .50 1.25
346 Corey Kluber .60 1.50
Dallas Keuchel
Marco Estrada LL
347 Jason Grilli .50 1.25
348 Seth Smith .50 1.25
349 Ben Revere .50 1.25
350 Kris Bryant FS 1.00 2.50
351 Chase Utley .60 1.50
352 Carson Blair .50 1.25
353 Joey Gallo .60 1.50
354 Tyson Ross .50 1.25
355 Avisail Garcia .60 1.50
356 Odrisamer Despaigne .50 1.25
357 Jace Peterson .50 1.25
358 Chris Young .50 1.25
359 Christian Colon .50 1.25
360 Eduardo Escobar .50 1.25
361 Jeff Locke .50 1.25
362 Cory Spangenberg .50 1.25
363 Brett Cecil .50 1.25
364 Keon Broxton .50 1.25
365 James Pazos .60 1.50
366 Scott Alexander .50 1.25
367 Pedro Alvarez .50 1.25
368 Xander Bogaerts .75 2.00
369 Dellin Betances .60 1.50
370 Bud Norris .50 1.25
371 Jason Heyward .60 1.50
372 Zack Cozart .50 1.25
373 Tucker Barnhart .50 1.25
374 Zach McAllister .50 1.25
375 Jordan Lyles .50 1.25
376 Brandon Barnes .50 1.25
377 Scott Kazmir .50 1.25
378 Jeff Mathis .60 1.50
379 Wei-Yin Chen .50 1.25
380 Michael Blazek .50 1.25
381 Bartolo Colon .50 1.25
382 David Ortiz .75 2.00
David Price
383 Andres Blanco .50 1.25
384 Michael Morse .50 1.25
385 Jon Jay .50 1.25
386 Nori Aoki .50 1.25
387 Eric Hosmer .60 1.50
Mike Moustakas
388 Evan Longoria .60 1.50
389 Sam Dyson .50 1.25
390 Danny Espinosa .50 1.25
391 Matt Boyd FS .50 1.25
392 Jon Singleton .60 1.50
393 Kelvin Herrera .50 1.25
394 Abel De Los Santos .50 1.25
395 Raul Mondesi 1.00 2.50
396 Matt Reynolds .50 1.25
397 Mac Williamson .50 1.25
398 Cleveland Indians .50 1.25
399 Kansas City Royals .50 1.25
400 David Ortiz .75 2.00
401 Peter O'Brien .50 1.25
402 Daniel Norris FS .50 1.25
403 David Peralta .50 1.25
404 Miami Marlins .50 1.25
405 Ruben Tejada .50 1.25
406 Marwin Gonzalez .50 1.25
407 Yoenis Cespedes .75 2.00
408 Jason Castro .50 1.25
409 Jean Segura .60 1.50
410 Mike Moustakas .60 1.50
411 Brian Matusz .50 1.25
412 Mark Lowe .50 1.25
413 David Phelps .50 1.25
414 Wily Peralta .50 1.25
415 Brett Wallace .50 1.25
416 Johnny Cueto .60 1.50
417 Brad Boxberger .50 1.25
418 Yu Darvish .75 2.00
419 Aaron Altherr .50 1.25
420 Pedro Severino .50 1.25
421 Cesar Hernandez .50 1.25
422 Miguel Gonzalez .50 1.25
423 Carl Crawford .60 1.50
424 Brandon Belt .60 1.50
425 Jackie Bradley Jr. .75 2.00
426 Joey Votto .75 2.00
427 Travis Shaw .50 1.25
428 Gregory Polanco .60 1.50
429 Kenta Maeda 1.00 2.50
430 Ariel Pena .50 1.25
431 Philadelphia Phillies .50 1.25
432 Cameron Rupp .50 1.25
433 Trevor Brown .60 1.50
434 Matt Adams .50 1.25
435 Enrique Hernandez .75 2.00
436 Raudel Lazo .50 1.25
437 Michael Lorenzen .50 1.25
438 Paulo Orlando .50 1.25
439 Francisco Lindor FS .75 2.00
440 Tommy Pham FS .50 1.25
441 David Ross .50 1.25
442 Brandon Crawford .60 1.50
443 Prince Fielder .60 1.50
444 Jordan Zimmermann .60 1.50
445 Robbie Ray .50 1.25
446 Tom Murphy .50 1.25
447 Ben Zobrist .60 1.50
448 St. Louis Cardinals .50 1.25
449 J.A. Happ .60 1.50
450 David Price .60 1.50
451 Jose Reyes .60 1.50
452 Gerrit Cole .75 2.00
453 Rizzo/Bryant 1.00 2.50
454 Greg Holland .50 1.25
455 Preston Tucker .50 1.25
456 Gordon Beckham .50 1.25
457 Nick Swisher .60 1.50
458 Kenley Jansen .60 1.50
459 James Loney .50 1.25
460 Danny Salazar .60 1.50
461 Freddy Galvis .50 1.25
462 Jumbo Diaz .50 1.25
463 Boston Red Sox .50 1.25
464 Robinson Chirinos .50 1.25
465 Jesse Chavez .50 1.25
466 Marco Estrada .50 1.25
467 Giovanny Urshela .75 2.00
468 Rajai Davis .50 1.25
469 Logan Morrison .50 1.25
470 John Lackey .60 1.50
471 Kolten Wong .60 1.50
472 Josh Reddick .50 1.25
473 Robbie Erlin .50 1.25
474 Chicago Cubs .50 1.25
475 Max Kepler .75 2.00
476 Hisashi Iwakuma .60 1.50
477 Chris Tillman .50 1.25
478 Cody Asche .50 1.25
479 Marcus Stroman .60 1.50
480 Mike Foltynewicz .50 1.25
481 Hector Rondon .50 1.25
482 Drew Smyly .50 1.25
483 Erasmo Ramirez .50 1.25
484 Trevor Rosenthal .60 1.50
485 James Paxton .60 1.50
486 Chris Rusin .50 1.25
487 Martin Prado .50 1.25
488 Colton Murray .50 1.25
489 Adeiny Hechavarria .50 1.25
490 Guido Knudson .50 1.25
491 Rich Hill .50 1.25
492 Yadier Molina 1.00 2.50
Randal Grichuk
Many Healthy Returns
493 R.A. Dickey .60 1.50
494 Luis Avilan .50 1.25
495 Luke Maile .50 1.25
496 Brett Anderson .50 1.25
497 Devin Mesoraco .50 1.25
498 Steve Cishek .50 1.25
499 Carlos Perez .50 1.25
500 Albert Pujols 1.00 2.50
501 Alex Rios .60 1.50
502 Austin Hedges .50 1.25
503 Luis Valbuena .50 1.25
504 Elias Diaz .50 1.25
505 Frankie Montas .60 1.50
506 Stephen Vogt .60 1.50
507 Travis Wood .50 1.25
508 Jaime Garcia .50 1.25
509 Mark Canha .50 1.25
510 Tony Watson .50 1.25
511 Manny Banuelos .75 2.00
512 Ryan Madson .50 1.25
513 Caleb Joseph .50 1.25
514 Michael Taylor .50 1.25
515 Ryan Flaherty .50 1.25
516 Steve Johnson .50 1.25
517 Corey Knebel .50 1.25
518 Matt Duffy .50 1.25
519 Kyle Barraclough .50 1.25
520 Anthony Rendon .75 2.00
521 Chris Archer .50 1.25
522 Alex Avila .60 1.50
523 Blake Swihart FS .60 1.50
524 Justin Nicolino FS .50 1.25
525 Jurickson Profar .60 1.50
526 T.J. McFarland .50 1.25
527 Jordy Mercer .50 1.25
528 Byron Buxton FS .75 2.00
529 Zack Wheeler .60 1.50
530 Caleb Cotham .60 1.50
531 Cody Allen .50 1.25
532 Matt Marksberry .50 1.25
533 Jonathan Villar .50 1.25
534 Eduardo Nunez .50 1.25
535 Ivan Nova .60 1.50
536 Alex Wood .50 1.25
537 Tampa Bay Rays .50 1.25
538 Michael Reed .50 1.25
539 Nate Karns .50 1.25
540 Curt Casali .50 1.25
541 James Shields .50 1.25
542 Scott Van Slyke .50 1.25
543 Carlos Rodon FS .75 2.00
544 Jeremy Jeffress .50 1.25
545 Hector Santiago .50 1.25
546 Ricky Nolasco .50 1.25
547 Nick Goody .60 1.50
548 Lucas Duda .60 1.50
549 Luke Jackson .50 1.25
550 Dallas Keuchel .60 1.50
551 Steven Matz FS .50 1.25
552 Texas Rangers .50 1.25
553 Adrian Houser .50 1.25
554 Daniel Murphy .60 1.50
555 Franklin Gutierrez .50 1.25
556 Abraham Almonte .50 1.25
557 Alexi Amarista .50 1.25
558 Sean Rodriguez .50 1.25
559 Cliff Pennington .50 1.25
560 Kennys Vargas .50 1.25
561 Kyle Gibson .60 1.50
562 Addison Russell FS .75 2.00
563 Lance McCullers FS .50 1.25

564 Tanner Roark	.50	1.25
565 Matt den Dekker	.50	1.25
566 Alex Rodriguez	1.00	2.50
567 Carlos Beltran	.60	1.50
568 Arizona Diamondbacks	.50	1.25
569 Los Angeles Dodgers	.50	1.25
570 Corey Dickerson	.50	1.25
571 Mark Reynolds	.50	1.25
572 Marcell Ozuna	.75	2.00
573 Tom Koehler	.50	1.25
574 Ryan Dull	.50	1.25
575 Ryan Strausborger	.50	1.25
576 Tyler Duffey	.50	1.25
577 Jason Gurka	.50	1.25
578 Mike Leake	.50	1.25
579 Michael Wacha	.60	1.50
580 Socrates Brito	.50	1.25
581 Zach Davies	.60	1.50
582 Jose Quintana	.50	1.25
583 Didi Gregorius	.60	1.50
584 Adam Duvall	1.25	3.00
585 Raisel Iglesias FS	.60	1.50
586 Chris Stewart	.50	1.25
587 Neftali Feliz	.50	1.25
588 Cole Hamels	.60	1.50
589 Derek Holland	.50	1.25
590 Anthony Gose	.50	1.25
591 Trevor Plouffe	.50	1.25
592 Adrian Beltre	.75	2.00
593 Alex Cobb	.50	1.25
594 Lonnie Chisenhall	.50	1.25
595 Mike Napoli	.50	1.25
596 Sergio Romo	.50	1.25
597 Chi Chi Gonzalez	.50	1.25
598 Khris Davis	.75	2.00
599 Domingo Santana	.60	1.50
600 Madison Bumgarner	.60	1.50
601 Leonys Martin	.50	1.25
602 Keith Hessler	.50	1.25
603 Shawn Armstrong	.50	1.25
604 Jeff Samardzija	.50	1.25
605 Santiago Casilla	.50	1.25
606 Miguel Almonte	.50	1.25
607 Brandon Drury	.75	2.00
608 Rick Porcello	.60	1.50
609 Billy Hamilton	.60	1.50
610 Adam Morgan	.50	1.25
611 Darin Ruf	.50	1.25
612 Cincinnati Reds	.50	1.25
613 Milwaukee Brewers	.50	1.25
614 Dalton Pompey	.60	1.50
615 Miguel Castro	.50	1.25
616 Keone Kela	.50	1.25
617 Justin Smoak	.50	1.25
618 Desmond Jennings	.60	1.50
619 Dustin Ackley	.50	1.25
620 Daniel Hudson	.50	1.25
621 Zach Duke	.50	1.25
622 Ken Giles	.50	1.25
623 Tyler Saladino	.50	1.25
624 Tommy Milone	.50	1.25
625 Wil Myers	.60	1.50
626 Danny Valencia	.60	1.50
627 Mike Fiers	.50	1.25
628 Wellington Castillo	.50	1.25
629 Patrick Corbin	.60	1.50
630 Michael Saunders	.60	1.50
631 Chris Reed	.50	1.25
632 Ramon Cabrera	.50	1.25
633 Martin Perez	.60	1.50
634 Jorge Lopez	.50	1.25
635 A.J. Pierzynski	.50	1.25
636 Arodys Vizcaino	.50	1.25
637 Stephen Strasburg	.75	2.00
638 Michael Pineda	.50	1.25
639 Rubby De La Rosa	.50	1.25
640 Carl Edwards Jr.	.60	1.50
641 Vidal Nuno	.50	1.25
642 Mike Pelfrey	.50	1.25
643 Yoenis Cespedes	.75	2.00
David Wright		
644 Los Angeles Angels	.50	1.25
645 Danny Santana	.50	1.25
646 Brad Miller	.60	1.50
647 Eduardo Rodriguez FS	.50	1.25
648 San Francisco Giants	.50	1.25
649 Aroldis Chapman	.75	2.00
650 Carlos Correa FS	.75	2.00
651 Dioner Navarro	.50	1.25
652 Collin McHugh	.50	1.25
653 Chris Iannetta	.50	1.25
654 Brandon Guyer	.50	1.25
655 Domonic Brown	.60	1.50
656 Randal Grichuk FS	.50	1.25
657 Johnny Giavotella	.50	1.25
658 Wilson Ramos	.50	1.25
659 Adonis Garcia	.50	1.25
660 John Axford	.50	1.25
661 DJ LeMahieu	.75	2.00
662 Masahiro Tanaka	.60	1.50
663 Jake Petricka	.50	1.25
664 Mikie Mahtook	.50	1.25
665 Jared Hughes	.50	1.25
666 J.T. Realmuto FS	.75	2.00
667 James McCann FS	.60	1.50
668 Javier Baez FS	1.00	2.50
669 Tyler Skaggs	.50	1.25
670 Will Smith	.50	1.25
671 Tony Cingrani	.60	1.50
672 Shane Peterson	.50	1.25
673 Justin Upton	.60	1.50
674 Tyler Chatwood	.50	1.25
675 Gary Sanchez	1.50	4.00
676 Jarred Cosart	.50	1.25
677 Derek Norris	.50	1.25
678 Carlos Martinez	.60	1.50
679 Nate Jones	.50	1.25
680 Tuffy Gosewisch	.50	1.25
681 Joe Smith	.50	1.25
682 Danny Duffy	.50	1.25
683 Carlos Gonzalez	.60	1.50
684 Jarrod Dyson	.50	1.25
685 Kyle Waldrop	.60	1.50
686 Brandon Finnegan FS	.50	1.25
687 Chris Owings	.50	1.25
688 Shawn Tolleson	.50	1.25
689 Eugenio Suarez	.60	1.50
690 Jimmy Nelson	.50	1.25
691 Kris Medlen	.60	1.50
692 Giovanni Soto	.60	1.50
693 Josh Tomlin	.50	1.25
694 Scott McGough	.50	1.25
695 Kyle Crockett	.50	1.25
696 Lorenzo Cain	.50	1.25
697 Andrew Cashner	.50	1.25
698 Matt Moore	.60	1.50
699 Justin Bour FS	.60	1.50
700 Ichiro Suzuki	1.00	2.50
701 Tyler Flowers	.50	1.25

2016 Topps Mini '75 Topps

COMPLETE SET (10)	15.00	40.00
BC1 Corey Seager	8.00	20.00
BC2 Michael Conforto	1.00	2.50
BC3 Kyle Schwarber	2.50	6.00
BC4 Mike Trout	6.00	15.00
BC5 Bryce Harper	2.00	5.00
BC6 Carlos Correa	1.25	3.00
BC7 Kris Bryant	1.50	4.00
BC8 Chris Sale	1.25	3.00
BC9 Jake Arrieta	1.00	2.50
BC10 Manny Machado	1.25	3.00

2007 Topps Moments and Milestones Red

ALL SAME CARD # VAR.PRICED EQUALLY

1-Jan Albert Pujols	12.00	30.00
1-Feb Albert Pujols	12.00	30.00
1-Mar Albert Pujols	12.00	30.00
1-Apr Albert Pujols	12.00	30.00
1-May Albert Pujols	12.00	30.00
1-Jun Ichiro Suzuki	12.00	30.00
1-Jul Ichiro Suzuki	12.00	30.00
1-Sep Ichiro Suzuki	12.00	30.00
1-Oct Ichiro Suzuki	12.00	30.00
13-1 Greg Maddux	12.00	30.00
15-1 Greg Maddux	12.00	30.00
18-1 Roger Clemens	12.00	30.00
20-1 Roger Clemens	12.00	30.00
21-1 Chipper Jones	10.00	25.00
22-1 Chipper Jones	10.00	25.00
23-1 Chipper Jones	10.00	25.00
24-1 Chipper Jones	10.00	25.00
25-1 Chipper Jones	10.00	25.00
27-1 Alex Rodriguez	12.00	30.00
28-1 Alex Rodriguez	12.00	30.00
29-1 Alex Rodriguez	12.00	30.00
30-1 Alex Rodriguez	12.00	30.00
31-1 Alex Rodriguez	12.00	30.00
33-1 Alex Rodriguez	12.00	30.00
34-1 Alex Rodriguez	12.00	30.00
35-1 Alex Rodriguez	12.00	30.00
36-1 Alex Rodriguez	12.00	30.00
37-1 Alex Rodriguez	12.00	30.00
39-1 Vladimir Guerrero	6.00	15.00
40-1 Vladimir Guerrero	6.00	15.00
41-1 Vladimir Guerrero	6.00	15.00
42-1 Vladimir Guerrero	6.00	15.00
43-1 Vladimir Guerrero	6.00	15.00
45-1 Ken Griffey Jr.	20.00	50.00
46-1 Ken Griffey Jr.	20.00	50.00
47-1 Ken Griffey Jr.	20.00	50.00
49-1 Barry Zito	6.00	15.00
51-1 Randy Johnson	10.00	25.00
55-1 Randy Johnson	10.00	25.00
58-1 Prince Fielder	6.00	15.00
59-1 Prince Fielder	6.00	15.00
60-1 Dan Uggla	4.00	10.00
61-1 Dan Uggla	4.00	10.00
62-1 Dan Uggla	4.00	10.00
64-1 Justin Verlander	10.00	25.00
66-1 Francisco Liriano	4.00	10.00
67-1 Ryan Zimmerman	6.00	15.00
68-1 Ryan Zimmerman	6.00	15.00
69-1 Ryan Zimmerman	6.00	15.00
70-1 Hanley Ramirez	6.00	15.00
71-1 Hanley Ramirez	6.00	15.00
72-1 Hanley Ramirez	6.00	15.00
73-1 Russ Martin	4.00	10.00
74-1 Russ Martin	4.00	10.00
75-1 Mickey Mantle	30.00	80.00
76-1 Mickey Mantle	30.00	80.00
77-1 Mickey Mantle	30.00	80.00
78-1 Mickey Mantle	30.00	80.00
79-1 Mike Piazza	10.00	25.00
80-1 Mike Piazza	10.00	25.00
82-1 Derek Jeter	25.00	60.00
83-1 Derek Jeter	25.00	60.00
85-1 Dontrelle Willis	4.00	10.00
88-1 Bobby Crosby	4.00	10.00
90-1 Ryan Howard	8.00	20.00
92-1 Curt Schilling	6.00	15.00
93-1 Andruw Jones	4.00	10.00
94-1 Andruw Jones	4.00	10.00
97-1 Hideki Matsui	10.00	25.00
98-1 Hideki Matsui	10.00	25.00
99-1 David Wright	8.00	20.00
100-1 David Wright	8.00	20.00
101-1 David Wright	8.00	20.00
103-1 David Ortiz	10.00	25.00
104-1 David Ortiz	10.00	25.00
106-1 Frank Thomas	10.00	25.00
107-1 Frank Thomas	10.00	25.00
108-1 Craig Biggio	6.00	15.00
109-1 Miguel Cabrera	10.00	25.00
110-1 Miguel Cabrera	10.00	25.00
113-1 Michael Young	4.00	10.00
114-1 Joe Mauer	8.00	20.00
115-1 Gary Sheffield	4.00	10.00
116-1 Jim Edmonds	6.00	15.00
119-1 Pat Burrell	4.00	10.00
120-1 Adam Dunn	6.00	15.00
121-1 Johnny Damon	6.00	15.00
122-1 Scott Rolen	6.00	15.00
126-1 Grady Sizemore	6.00	15.00
128-1 Jeff Kent	4.00	10.00
129-1 Billy Wagner	4.00	10.00
131-1 Eric Chavez	4.00	10.00
132-1 Jimmy Rollins	6.00	15.00
134-1 Manny Ramirez	10.00	25.00
135-1 Manny Ramirez	10.00	25.00
136-1 Derrek Lee	4.00	10.00
137-1 Derrek Lee	4.00	10.00
142-1 Pedro Martinez	6.00	15.00
143-1 Mark Teixeira	6.00	15.00
145-1 Carlos Lee	4.00	10.00
148-1 Todd Helton	6.00	15.00
149-1 Mariano Rivera	12.00	30.00
150-1 Travis Hafner	4.00	10.00
152-1 Bobby Abreu	4.00	10.00
154-1 Miguel Tejada	6.00	15.00
155-1 Miguel Tejada	6.00	15.00
157-1 Robinson Cano	6.00	15.00
162-1 Roger Clemens	12.00	30.00
163-1 Mickey Mantle	30.00	80.00
164-1 Mickey Mantle	30.00	80.00
165-1 Mickey Mantle	30.00	80.00
166-1 Mickey Mantle	30.00	80.00
167-1 Mickey Mantle	30.00	80.00
168-1 Mickey Mantle	30.00	80.00
169-1 Mickey Mantle	30.00	80.00

2007 Topps Moments and Milestones Milestone Autographs

GROUP A ODDS 1:63 HOBBY
GROUP B ODDS 1:64 HOBBY
GROUP C ODDS 1:192 HOBBY
GROUP D ODDS 1:74 HOBBY
GROUP E ODDS 1:479 HOBBY
GROUP F ODDS 1:1112 HOBBY
GROUP A PRINT RUN 50 CARDS
GROUP B PRINT RUN 120 CARDS
E-F ARE NOT SERIAL-NUMBERED
E-F PRINT RUNS PROVIDED BY TOPPS
OVERALL PLATE ODDS 1:2361 HOBBY
PLATE PRINT RUN 1 SET PER COLOR
BLACK-CYAN-MAGENTA-YELLOW ISSUED
NO PLATE PRICING DUE TO SCARCITY

AJ Andruw Jones F/100 *	8.00	20.00
AR Alex Rodriguez F/100 *	20.00	50.00
BP Brandon Phillips C	4.00	12.00
BR Brian Roberts D	4.00	10.00
CJ Conor Jackson D	4.00	10.00
DO David Ortiz D	15.00	40.00
DW David Wright D	4.00	10.00
GA Garrett Atkins B	6.00	15.00
GS Gary Sheffield F/100 *	4.00	10.00
HS Huston Street E/200 *	6.00	15.00
JF Jeff Francoeur D	20.00	50.00
JG Jason Giambi F/100 *	10.00	25.00
JJG Jonny Gomes D	3.00	8.00
JL Julio Lugo D	3.00	8.00
JP Jonathan Papelbon B	3.00	8.00
JR Jose Reyes E/200 *	4.00	10.00
JS Jeremy Sowers A	4.00	10.00
KJ Kenji Johjima D	15.00	40.00
KM Kendry Morales B	3.00	8.00
LM Lastings Milledge D	6.00	15.00
MK Matt Kemp B	3.00	8.00
MN Mike Napoli C	3.00	8.00
MP Martin Prado A	6.00	15.00
NS Nick Swisher D	6.00	15.00
RH Ryan Howard E/200 *	8.00	20.00
RP Ronny Paulino A	3.00	8.00
TH Travis Hafner D	3.00	8.00
VG Vladimir Guerrero F/100 *	20.00	50.00
WP Wily Mo Pena F/100 *	6.00	15.00

2007 Topps Moments and Milestones Milestone Autographs Black

*BLACK: .5X TO 1.2X BASIC
STATED ODDS 1:235 HOBBY
STATED PRINT RUN 40 SER.#'d SETS

AR Alex Rodriguez	25.00	60.00
JF Jeff Francoeur	40.00	80.00

2007 Topps Moments and Milestones Rookie Autographs

STATED ODDS 1:19 HOBBY
OVERALL PLATE ODDS 1:2361 HOBBY
PLATE PRINT RUN 1 SET PER COLOR
BLACK-CYAN-MAGENTA-YELLOW ISSUED
NO PLATE PRICING DUE TO SCARCITY

AL Adam Lind	4.00	10.00
AM Andrew Miller	3.00	8.00
DM David Murphy	4.00	10.00
HG Hector Gimenez	3.00	8.00
JA Joaquin Arias	3.00	8.00
KK Kevin Kouzmanoff	4.00	10.00
MB Michael Bourn	3.00	8.00
MM Miguel Montero	4.00	10.00
SR Shawn Riggans	3.00	8.00
TT Troy Tulowitzki	4.00	10.00

2007 Topps Moments and Milestones Rookie Autographs Black

*BLACK: .75X TO 2X BASIC
STATED ODDS 1:235 HOBBY
STATED PRINT RUN 40 SER.#'d SETS

2008 Topps Moments and Milestones

COMMON p/r 11250-78600	.15	.40
COMMON p/r 1650-8100	.25	.60
COMMON ROOKIE	2.00	5.00

STATED PRINT RUN 150 SER.#'d SETS
MILESTONE X 150 = TOTAL PRINT RUN
PRICING BASED ON TOTAL PRINT RUN
ALL VARIATIONS EQUALLY PRICED
PLATES RANDOMLY INSERTED
PLATE PRINT RUN 1 SET PER COLOR
BLACK-CYAN-MAGENTA-YELLOW ISSUED
NO PLATE PRICING DUE TO SCARCITY

1-Jan Alex Rodriguez	.50	1.25
145 Joey Votto (RC)	6.00	15.00
146 Joey Votto (RC)	6.00	15.00
147 Joey Votto (RC)	6.00	15.00
148 Luke Hochevar RC	6.00	15.00
149 Luke Hochevar RC	6.00	15.00
150 Luke Hochevar RC	6.00	15.00
151 Clay Buchholz (RC)	5.00	12.00
152 Clay Buchholz (RC)	5.00	12.00
153 Clay Buchholz (RC)	5.00	12.00
154 Billy Buckner (RC)	2.00	5.00
155 Billy Buckner (RC)	2.00	5.00
156 Billy Buckner (RC)	2.00	5.00
157 Jeff Clement (RC)	2.50	6.00
158 Jeff Clement (RC)	2.50	6.00
159 Jeff Clement (RC)	2.50	6.00
160 Radhames Liz RC	2.00	5.00
161 Radhames Liz RC	2.00	5.00
162 Radhames Liz RC	2.00	5.00
163 Bronson Sardinha (RC)	2.00	5.00
164 Bronson Sardinha (RC)	2.00	5.00
165 Bronson Sardinha (RC)	2.00	5.00
166 Seth Smith (RC)	2.00	5.00
167 Seth Smith (RC)	2.00	5.00
168 Seth Smith (RC)	2.00	5.00
169 Chris Seddon (RC)	2.00	5.00
170 Chris Seddon (RC)	2.00	5.00
171 Chris Seddon (RC)	2.00	5.00
172 Wladimir Balentien (RC)	2.50	6.00
173 Wladimir Balentien (RC)	2.50	6.00
174 Wladimir Balentien (RC)	2.50	6.00
175 Josh Banks (RC)	2.00	5.00
176 Josh Banks (RC)	2.00	5.00
177 Josh Banks (RC)	2.00	5.00
178 Ross Detwiler RC	2.00	5.00
179 Ross Detwiler RC	2.00	5.00
180 Ross Detwiler RC	2.00	5.00
181 Felipe Paulino RC	2.00	5.00
182 Felipe Paulino RC	2.00	5.00
183 Felipe Paulino RC	2.00	5.00
184 Troy Patton (RC)	2.00	5.00
185 Troy Patton (RC)	2.00	5.00
186 Troy Patton (RC)	2.00	5.00
187 Brandon Jones RC	2.00	5.00
188 Brandon Jones RC	2.00	5.00
189 Brandon Jones RC	2.00	5.00
1-Feb Alex Rodriguez	.75	2.00
1-Mar Frank Thomas	.40	1.00
1-Apr Mickey Mantle	.60	1.50
1-May Mickey Mantle	.60	1.50
1-Jun Mickey Mantle	.50	1.25
1-Jul Mickey Mantle	.60	1.50
1-Aug Greg Maddux	.50	1.25
1-Sep Troy Tulowitzki	.40	1.00
1-Oct Hunter Pence	.25	.60
1-Nov Hunter Pence	.40	1.00
1-Dec Albert Pujols	.50	1.25
13-1 Albert Pujols	.50	1.25
14-1 Albert Pujols	.75	2.00
15-1 Albert Pujols	.50	1.25
16-1 David Ortiz	.60	1.50
17-1 David Ortiz	.60	1.50
18-1 David Wright	.40	1.00
19-1 David Wright	.40	1.00
20-1 Aaron Hill	.25	.60
21-1 Eric Byrnes	.25	.60
22-1 Dmitri Young	.25	.60
23-1 Garret Anderson	.25	.60
24-1 Jimmy Rollins	.40	1.00
25-1 Jimmy Rollins	.40	1.00
26-1 Joba Chamberlain	.25	.60
27-1 Magglio Ordonez	.40	1.00
28-1 Ryan Howard	.25	.60
29-1 Ryan Howard	.40	1.00
30-1 Ryan Howard	.25	.60
31-1 Ryan Howard	.40	1.00
32-1 Trevor Hoffman	.25	.60
33-1 Ken Griffey Jr.	.75	2.00
34-1 Travis Hafner	.15	.40
35-1 Joe Mauer	.50	1.25
36-1 Daisuke Matsuzaka	50.00	100.00
37-1 Daisuke Matsuzaka	.40	1.00
38-1 Curtis Granderson	.40	1.00
39-1 Curtis Granderson	.40	1.00
40-1 Curtis Granderson	.40	1.00
41-1 Curtis Granderson	.40	1.00
42-1 Alex Gordon	.40	1.00
43-1 Aramis Ramirez	.15	.40
44-1 Jonathan Papelbon	.25	.60
45-1 B.J. Upton	.40	1.00
46-1 C.C. Sabathia	.40	1.00
47-1 Carl Crawford	.40	1.00
48-1 Jason Bay	.40	1.00
49-1 Carlos Beltran	.40	1.00
50-1 Carlos Guillen	.25	.60
51-1 C.C. Sabathia	.25	.60
52-1 Gary Sheffield	.15	.40
53-1 Chris Young	.25	.60
54-1 Dontrelle Willis	.25	.60
55-1 Dustin Pedroia	.60	1.50
56-1 Alfonso Soriano	.25	.60
57-1 Derek Jeter	1.00	2.50
58-1 Chase Utley	.40	1.00
59-1 Chase Utley	.40	1.00
60-1 Chase Utley	.25	.60
61-1 Chase Utley	.40	1.00
62-1 Ichiro Suzuki	40.00	80.00
63-1 Ichiro Suzuki	.50	1.25
64-1 Jorge Posada	.40	1.00
65-1 Jorge Posada	.40	1.00
66-1 Jose Reyes	.25	.60
67-1 Miguel Tejada	.40	1.00
68-1 Miguel Tejada	.40	1.00
69-1 Nick Swisher	.40	1.00
70-1 Robinson Cano	.25	.60
71-1 Roy Halladay	.40	1.00
72-1 Ryan Zimmerman	.40	1.00
73-1 Scott Rolen	.40	1.00
74-1 Tim Lincecum	.25	.60
75-1 Vernon Wells	.25	.60
76-1 Roger Clemens	.75	2.00
77-1 Roger Clemens	.75	2.00
78-1 Roger Clemens	.75	2.00
79-1 Roger Clemens	.75	2.00
80-1 Roger Clemens	.75	2.00
81-1 Roger Clemens	.75	2.00
82-1 Roger Clemens	.75	2.00
83-1 Michael Young	.25	.60
84-1 John Smoltz	.40	1.00
85-1 Jim Thome	.25	.60
86-1 Johan Santana	.25	.60
87-1 Johan Santana	.25	.60
88-1 Jack Cust	.25	.60
89-1 Jack Cust	.25	.60
90-1 Jake Peavy	.25	.60
91-1 Hanley Ramirez	.40	1.00
92-1 Hanley Ramirez	.25	.60
93-1 Hideki Okajima	.25	.60
94-1 Grady Sizemore	.40	1.00
95-1 Erik Bedard	.15	.40
96-1 Derrek Lee	.25	.60
97-1 Derrek Lee	.25	.60
98-1 Delmon Young	.40	1.00
99-1 Delmon Young	.40	1.00
100-1 Cole Hamels	.50	1.25
101-1 Brad Hawpe	.15	.40
102-1 Mike Lowell	.15	.40
103-1 Placido Polanco	.15	.40
UER Last name misspelled		
104-1 Nick Swisher	.25	.60
105-1 Adrian Gonzalez	.40	1.00
106-1 Adrian Gonzalez	.25	.60
107-1 Scott Kazmir	.25	.60
108-1 Freddy Sanchez	.15	.40
109-1 Jeremy Guthrie	.15	.40
110-1 Chipper Jones	.60	1.50
111-1 Chris Carpenter	.40	1.00
112-1 Andy Pettitte	.25	.60
113-1 Andruw Jones	.25	.60
114-1 Bobby Abreu	.25	.60
115-1 Eric Chavez	.25	.60
116-1 Eric Chavez	.25	.60
117-1 Josh Hamilton	.40	1.00
118-1 Manny Ramirez	.40	1.00
119-1 Manny Ramirez	.40	1.00
120-1 Mariano Rivera	.75	2.00
121-1 Kelly Johnson	.25	.60
122-1 Jeff Kent	.15	.40
123-1 Mark Teixeira	.25	.60
124-1 Matt Holliday	.60	1.50
125-1 Matt Holliday	.40	1.00
126-1 Huston Street	.40	1.00
127-1 Carlos Lee	.25	.60
128-1 Brian Bannister	.25	.60
129-1 Carlos Pena	.40	1.00
130-1 Brian McCann	.40	1.00
131-1 Prince Fielder	.40	1.00
132-1 Randy Johnson	.60	1.50
133-1 Russell Martin	.25	.60
134-1 Ryan Braun	.40	1.00
135-1 Vladimir Guerrero	.25	.60
136-1 Vladimir Guerrero	.40	1.00
137-1 Tom Glavine	.25	.60
138-1 Miguel Cabrera	.40	1.00
139-1 Miguel Cabrera	.40	1.00
140-1 Miguel Cabrera	.60	1.50
141-1 Pedro Martinez	.25	.60
142-1 Daisuke Matsuzaka	.25	.60
143-1 Garrett Atkins	.25	.60
144-1 Brian Roberts	.25	.60

2008 Topps Moments and Milestones Black

*BLACK p/r 1950-13100 : 1.2X TO 3X BASIC
*BLACK p/r 625-1350 : 1.2X TO 3X BASIC
BLACK RC: .5X TO 1.2X BASIC RC
STATED ODDS 1:2 HOBBY
STATED PRINT RUN 25 SER. #'d SETS
MILESTONE X 25 = TOTAL PRINT RUN
PRICING BASED ON TOTAL PRINT RUN
ALL VARIATIONS EQUALLY PRICED
NO PRICING ON QTY 25 OR LESS

145 Joey Votto	8.00	20.00
146 Joey Votto	8.00	20.00
147 Joey Votto	8.00	20.00
148 Luke Hochevar	8.00	20.00
149 Luke Hochevar	8.00	20.00
150 Luke Hochevar	8.00	20.00
151 Clay Buchholz	6.00	15.00
152 Clay Buchholz	6.00	15.00
153 Clay Buchholz	6.00	15.00
154 Billy Buckner	2.50	6.00
155 Billy Buckner	2.50	6.00
156 Billy Buckner	2.50	6.00
157 Jeff Clement	3.00	8.00
158 Jeff Clement	3.00	8.00
159 Jeff Clement	3.00	8.00
160 Radhames Liz	2.50	6.00
161 Radhames Liz	2.50	6.00
162 Radhames Liz	2.50	6.00
163 Bronson Sardinha	2.50	6.00
164 Bronson Sardinha	2.50	6.00
165 Bronson Sardinha	2.50	6.00
166 Seth Smith	2.50	6.00
167 Seth Smith	2.50	6.00
168 Seth Smith	2.50	6.00
169 Chris Seddon	2.50	6.00
170 Chris Seddon	2.50	6.00
171 Chris Seddon	2.50	6.00
172 Wladimir Balentien	3.00	8.00
173 Wladimir Balentien	3.00	8.00
174 Wladimir Balentien	3.00	8.00
175 Josh Banks	2.50	6.00
176 Josh Banks	2.50	6.00
177 Josh Banks	2.50	6.00
178 Ross Detwiler	2.50	6.00
179 Ross Detwiler	2.50	6.00
180 Ross Detwiler	2.50	6.00
181 Felipe Paulino	2.50	6.00
182 Felipe Paulino	2.50	6.00
183 Felipe Paulino	2.50	6.00
184 Troy Patton	2.50	6.00
185 Troy Patton	2.50	6.00
186 Troy Patton	2.50	6.00
187 Brandon Jones	2.50	6.00
188 Brandon Jones	2.50	6.00
189 Brandon Jones	2.50	6.00
36-1 Daisuke Matsuzaka		
62-1 Ichiro Suzuki		

2008 Topps Moments and Milestones Blue

*BLUE p/r 750-5240 : 2.5X TO 6X BASIC
*BLUE p/r 110-540 : 2.5X TO 6X BASIC
BLUE RC: .6X TO 1.5X BASIC RC
STATED ODDS 1:4 HOBBY
STATED PRINT RUN 10 SER. #'d SETS
MILESTONE X 10 = TOTAL PRINT RUN
PRICING BASED ON TOTAL PRINT RUN
ALL VARIATIONS EQUALLY PRICED
NO PRICING ON QTY 25 OR LESS

157 Jeff Clement	6.00	15.00
158 Jeff Clement	6.00	15.00
159 Jeff Clement	6.00	15.00

2008 Topps Moments and Milestones Alex Rodriguez 500 HR Wall Relic

STATED ODDS 1:109
*BLACK: 1X TO 2.5X BASIC
BLACK ODDS 1:4125 HOBBY
BLACK PRINT RUN 99 SER.#'d SETS
BLUE ODDS 1:19,000 HOBBY
BLUE PRINT RUN 25 SER.#'d SETS
NO BLUE PRICING DUE TO SCARCITY
RED ODDS 1:316,440 HOBBY
RED PRINT RUN 1 SER.#'d SET
NO RED PRICING DUE TO SCARCITY

AR Alex Rodriguez	10.00	25.00

2008 Topps Moments and Milestones Milestone Autographs

NO GROUP D PRICING AVAILABLE
GROUP A ODDS 1:69 HOBBY
GROUP B ODDS 1:67 HOBBY
GROUP C ODDS 1:147 HOBBY
GROUP D ODDS 1:9251 HOBBY
OVERALL PLATE ODDS 1:1832 HOBBY
PLATE PRINT RUN 1 SET PER COLOR
BLACK-CYAN-MAGENTA-YELLOW ISSUED
NO PLATE PRICING DUE TO SCARCITY

AC Asdrubal Cabrera B	5.00	12.00
AL Adam Lind A	3.00	8.00
AS Alfonso Soriano C	5.00	12.00
BC Bobby Crosby B	3.00	8.00
BH Brad Hawpe B	4.00	10.00
BR B.J. Ryan A	3.00	8.00
CC Carl Crawford C	5.00	12.00
CM Cameron Maybin B	4.00	10.00
CP Carlos Pena B	3.00	8.00
CR Carlos Ruiz A	8.00	20.00
DH Dan Haren C	3.00	8.00
DW David Wright C	12.50	30.00
FC Fausto Carmona B	3.00	8.00
FS Freddy Sanchez B	3.00	8.00
HR Hanley Ramirez C	4.00	10.00
JD Jermaine Dye B	3.00	8.00
JH Josh Hamilton C	12.50	30.00
JP Jorge Posada C	30.00	60.00
JR Jose Reyes C	5.00	12.00
LM Lastings Milledge B	3.00	8.00
MC Melky Cabrera A	3.00	8.00
MH Matt Holliday C	6.00	15.00
RB Ryan Braun B	6.00	15.00
RC Robinson Cano B	10.00	25.00
RG Ryan Garko C	3.00	8.00
RH Rich Harden C	3.00	8.00
RM Russell Martin B	5.00	12.00
TG Tom Gorzelanny A	3.00	8.00
TH Tim Hudson C	8.00	20.00
TJ Todd Jones B	3.00	8.00
MCA Matt Cain A	6.00	15.00
MIC Miguel Cabrera C	20.00	50.00

2008 Topps Moments and Milestones Rookie Autographs

STATED ODDS 1:11 HOBBY
OVERALL PLATE ODDS 1:1832 HOBBY
PLATE PRINT RUN 1 SET PER COLOR
BLACK-CYAN-MAGENTA-YELLOW ISSUED
NO PLATE PRICING DUE TO SCARCITY

AG Armando Galarraga	3.00	8.00
BJ Brandon Jones	3.00	8.00
CB Clay Buchholz	6.00	15.00
CH Chin-Lung Hu	5.00	12.00
DB Daric Barton	4.00	10.00
FP Felipe Paulino	3.00	8.00
JA Josh Anderson	3.00	8.00
JK Joe Koshansky	3.00	8.00
JM Jonathan Meloan	3.00	8.00
JR Justin Ruggiano	3.00	8.00
JT J.R. Towles	5.00	12.00
LB Lance Broadway	3.00	8.00
NM Nyjer Morgan	3.00	8.00
RJ Rob Johnson	3.00	8.00
RO Ross Ohlendorf	4.00	10.00
RT Rich Thompson	3.00	8.00
SF Sam Fuld	8.00	20.00
SP Steve Pearce	8.00	20.00
WB Wladimir Balentien	3.00	8.00
JMM Jose Morales	3.00	8.00

2012 Topps Museum Collection

COMMON CARD (1-100)	.40	1.00
COMMON RC (1-120)	.40	1.00
1 Jeremy Hellickson	.60	1.50
2 Albert Pujols	1.25	3.00
3 Carlos Santana	.75	2.00
4 Jay Bruce	.75	2.00
5 Don Mattingly	2.00	5.00
6 Justin Upton	.75	2.00
7 Buster Posey	1.25	3.00
8 Stan Musial	1.50	4.00
9 Cole Hamels	.75	2.00
10 Dan Haren	.60	1.50
11 Carl Crawford	.75	2.00
12 Cal Ripken	3.00	8.00
13 Nolan Ryan	3.00	8.00
14 Adrian Gonzalez	.75	2.00
15 Derek Jeter	2.50	6.00
16 Prince Fielder	.75	2.00
17 Clayton Kershaw	1.50	4.00
18 Joe Mauer	.75	2.00
19 Ryne Sandberg	2.00	5.00
20 Matt Holliday	1.00	2.50
21 Joey Votto	1.00	2.50
22 Lou Gehrig	2.00	5.00
23 Tony Gwynn	1.00	2.50
24 Matt Moore RC	1.00	2.50
25 Matt Kemp	.75	2.00
26 Curtis Granderson	.75	2.00
27 Roberto Clemente	2.50	6.00
28 Carlos Gonzalez	.75	2.00
29 Craig Kimbrel	.75	2.00
30 Jim Palmer	.60	1.50
31 Evan Longoria	.75	2.00
32 Babe Ruth	2.50	6.00
33 David Wright	.75	2.00
34 Robinson Cano	.75	2.00
35 Jesus Montero RC	.60	1.50
36 Jose Reyes	.60	1.50
37 Stephen Strasburg	1.00	2.50
38 Edgar Martinez	.60	1.50
39 Eric Hosmer	.75	2.00
40 Frank Robinson	.60	1.50
41 Mark Teixeira	.75	2.00
42 Mickey Mantle	3.00	8.00
43 Mark Trumbo	.60	1.50
44 Eddie Murray	.60	1.50
45 Dustin Ackley	.60	1.50
46 Mike Stanton	1.00	2.50
47 CC Sabathia	.75	2.00
48 Rollie Fingers	.60	1.50
49 Elvis Andrus	.75	2.00
50 Aramis Ramirez	.60	1.50
51 Dustin Pedroia	1.00	2.50
52 Drew Stubbs	.60	1.50
53 Lou Brock	.60	1.50
54 Justin Verlander	1.00	2.50
55 David Price	.75	2.00
56 Jered Weaver	.75	2.00
57 Neftali Feliz	.60	1.50
58 Cliff Lee	.75	2.00
59 Josh Hamilton	.75	2.00
60 Carlton Fisk	.60	1.50
61 Ian Kinsler	.75	2.00
62 Roberto Alomar	.60	1.50
63 Ryan Braun	.60	1.50
64 Roy Halladay	.75	2.00
65 Adrian Beltre	1.00	2.50
66 Andrew McCutchen	1.00	2.50
67 Victor Martinez	.75	2.00
68 Julio Teheran	.75	2.00
69 Felix Hernandez	.75	2.00
70 Ty Cobb	1.50	4.00
71 Willie Mays	3.00	8.00
72 Hanley Ramirez	.75	2.00
73 Paul Molitor	1.00	2.50
74 Troy Tulowitzki	1.00	2.50
75 Paul Konerko	.60	1.50
76 Michael Pineda	.60	1.50
77 Pablo Sandoval	.75	2.00
78 Sandy Koufax	2.00	5.00
79 Ryan Zimmerman	.75	2.00
80 Phil Niekro	.60	1.50
81 Joe DiMaggio	2.00	5.00
82 Jackie Robinson	1.00	2.50
83 Mike Trout	60.00	150.00
84 Dan Uggla	.75	2.00
85 Reggie Jackson	.60	1.50
86 Starlin Castro	.75	2.00
87 Jaime Garcia	.75	2.00
88 Bob Gibson	.60	1.50
89 Ichiro Suzuki	1.25	3.00
90 Alex Rodriguez	1.25	3.00
91 Paul O'Neill	.60	1.50
92 Johnny Bench	1.00	2.50
93 Carl Yastrzemski	1.50	4.00
94 Brooks Robinson	.60	1.50
95 Hunter Pence	.75	2.00
96 Jacoby Ellsbury	.75	2.00
97 Jose Bautista	.75	2.00
98 Steve Carlton	.60	1.50
99 Tim Lincecum	.75	2.00
100 Miguel Cabrera	1.00	2.50

2012 Topps Museum Collection Blue

*BLUE: 1X TO 2.5X BASIC
STATED ODDS 1:6 PACKS
STATED PRINT RUN 99 SER.#'d SETS

2012 Topps Museum Collection Copper

*COPPER: .5X TO 1.2X BASIC
STATED PRINT RUN 299 SER.#'d SETS

2012 Topps Museum Collection Green

*GREEN: .6X TO 1.5X BASIC
STATED ODDS 1:3 PACKS
STATED PRINT RUN 199 SER.#'d SETS

2012 Topps Museum Collection Archival Autographs

STATED ODDS 1:5 PACKS
PRINT RUN B/WN 25-399 COPIES PER
EXCHANGE DEADLINE 3/31/2015

AC Aroldis Chapman/299	10.00	25.00
AC2 Aroldis Chapman/299	10.00	25.00
AG Adrian Gonzalez/25	12.50	30.00
AK Al Kaline/25	60.00	150.00
AM Andrew McCutchen/299	20.00	50.00
AO Alexi Ogando/399	6.00	15.00
AO2 Alexi Ogando/399	6.00	15.00
AP Andy Pettitte/25	40.00	80.00
APU Albert Pujols/25	75.00	150.00
AR Anthony Rizzo/399	20.00	50.00
ARA Aramis Ramirez/100	6.00	15.00
BB Brandon Belt/399	4.00	10.00
BP Buster Posey/25	100.00	200.00
CC Carl Crawford/25	8.00	20.00
CF Carlton Fisk/25	20.00	50.00
CGO Carlos Gonzalez/25	15.00	40.00
CK Clayton Kershaw/100	40.00	80.00
CK2 Clayton Kershaw/100	40.00	80.00
CS CC Sabathia EXCH	30.00	60.00
CY Carl Yastrzemski/25	50.00	100.00
DM Don Mattingly/25	50.00	100.00
DP Drew Pomeranz/299	6.00	15.00
DP2 Drew Pomeranz/299	6.00	15.00
DPE Dustin Pedroia/25	15.00	40.00
DW David Wright/25	12.00	30.00
EA Elvis Andrus/299	6.00	15.00
EH Eric Hosmer/100	10.00	25.00
EH2 Eric Hosmer/100	10.00	25.00
EH3 Eric Hosmer/100	10.00	25.00
EL Evan Longoria/25	30.00	60.00
EM Edgar Martinez/25	12.00	30.00
FF Freddie Freeman/25	20.00	50.00
FH Felix Hernandez/25	30.00	60.00
IK Ian Kennedy/100	8.00	20.00
JB Jay Bruce/100	8.00	20.00
JBE Johnny Bench EXCH	50.00	100.00
JG Jaime Garcia/399	6.00	15.00
JH Jeremy Hellickson/299	6.00	15.00
JH2 Jeremy Hellickson/299	6.00	15.00
JHA Josh Hamilton/25	20.00	50.00
JM Jesus Montero/25	12.50	30.00
JMA Joe Mauer EXCH	30.00	60.00
JR Jim Rice/100	8.00	20.00
JT Julio Teheran/399	8.00	20.00
JW Jered Weaver EXCH	6.00	15.00
KG Ken Griffey Jr. EXCH	300.00	400.00
MC Miguel Cabrera	60.00	120.00
MK Matt Kemp EXCH	30.00	60.00
MK2 Matt Kemp EXCH	30.00	60.00
MM Matt Moore/399	6.00	15.00
MMO Mike Moustakas/299	8.00	20.00
MP Michael Pineda/299	6.00	15.00
MP2 Michael Pineda/299	6.00	15.00
MS Mike Stanton/25	40.00	80.00
MT Mark Trumbo/399	10.00	25.00
MT2 Mark Trumbo/399	10.00	25.00
MT3 Mark Trumbo/399	10.00	25.00
MTR Mike Trout/25	300.00	800.00
NF Neftali Feliz/299	6.00	15.00
NR Nolan Ryan/25	200.00	300.00

PF Prince Fielder/25 10.00 25.00
PO Paul O'Neill/25 12.50 30.00
RC Robinson Cano EXCH 50.00 100.00
RH Roy Halladay EXCH 60.00 120.00
RJ Reggie Jackson/25 50.00 100.00
RR Ricky Romero/399 6.00 15.00
RR2 Ricky Romero/399 6.00 15.00
RZ Ryan Zimmerman/25 40.00 80.00
SC Starlin Castro/100 8.00 20.00
SK Sandy Koufax/25 350.00 500.00
SP Salvador Perez/399 15.00 40.00
WM Willie Mays EXCH 175.00 350.00
YU Yu Darvish EXCH 500.00 1000.00

2012 Topps Museum Collection Canvas Collection

APPX.ODDS 1:4 PACKS
CC1 Babe Ruth 6.00 15.00
CC2 Lou Gehrig 5.00 12.00
CC3 Ty Cobb 4.00 10.00
CC4 Stan Musial 4.00 10.00
CC5 Adrian Gonzalez 2.00 5.00
CC6 Willie Mays 5.00 12.00
CC7 Mickey Mantle 8.00 20.00
CC8 Warren Spahn 1.50 4.00
CC9 Bob Gibson 1.50 4.00
CC10 Johnny Bench 2.50 6.00
CC11 Miguel Cabrera 2.50 6.00
CC12 Frank Robinson 1.50 4.00
CC13 Tom Seaver 1.50 4.00
CC14 Roberto Clemente 6.00 15.00
CC15 Steve Carlton 1.50 4.00
CC16 Yogi Berra 2.50 6.00
CC17 Jim Thome 2.00 5.00
CC18 Jackie Robinson 2.50 6.00
CC19 Ken Griffey 5.00 12.00
CC20 Rickey Henderson 2.50 6.00
CC21 Nolan Ryan 8.00 20.00
CC22 Eddie Mathews 2.50 6.00
CC23 Cal Ripken Jr. 8.00 20.00
CC24 Tony Gwynn 2.50 6.00
CC25 Ichiro Suzuki 3.00 8.00
CC26 Carl Yastrzemski 4.00 10.00
CC27 Joe Mauer 2.00 5.00
CC28 Josh Hamilton 2.00 5.00
CC29 Ozzie Smith 3.00 8.00
CC30 Ryan Braun 1.50 4.00
CC31 Willie McCovey 1.50 4.00
CC32 Jim Palmer 1.50 4.00
CC33 Rod Carew 1.50 4.00
CC34 Derek Jeter 6.00 15.00
CC35 Duke Snider 1.50 4.00
CC36 Al Kaline 2.50 6.00
CC37 Alex Rodriguez 3.00 8.00
CC38 Harmon Killebrew 2.50 6.00
CC39 Reggie Jackson 1.50 4.00
CC40 Vladimir Guerrero 2.00 5.00
CC41 Robinson Cano 2.00 5.00
CC42 Robin Yount 2.50 6.00
CC43 Roy Halladay 2.00 5.00
CC44 Wade Boggs 1.50 4.00
CC45 Eddie Murray 1.00 2.50
CC46 Johan Santana 2.00 5.00
CC47 Mariano Rivera 3.00 8.00
CC48 Carlton Fisk 1.50 4.00

2012 Topps Museum Collection Jumbo Lumber

STATED ODDS 1:38 PACKS
STATED PRINT RUN 30 SER.#'d SETS
AE Andre Ethier 12.00 30.00
AG Adrian Gonzalez 10.00 25.00
AJ Adam Jones 8.00 20.00
AK Al Kaline 20.00 50.00
AR Alexei Ramirez 10.00 25.00
BU B.J. Upton 8.00 20.00
CF Carlton Fisk 12.00 30.00
CG Carlos Gonzalez 6.00 15.00
CP Carlos Pena 8.00 20.00
DU Dan Uggla 6.00 15.00
DW David Wright 15.00 40.00
EL Evan Longoria 10.00 25.00
EM Eddie Murray 12.00 30.00
FR Frank Robinson 10.00 25.00
GB George Brett 12.00 30.00
GS Gary Sheffield 12.00 30.00
HR Hanley Ramirez 10.00 25.00
IR Ivan Rodriguez 10.00 25.00
JB Jose Bautista 12.00 30.00
JD Joe DiMaggio 40.00 100.00
JE Jacoby Ellsbury 12.00 30.00
JH Jason Heyward 6.00 15.00
JV Joey Votto 15.00 40.00
MD Matt Dominguez 6.00 15.00
MK Matt Kemp 15.00 40.00
MS Mike Stanton 10.00 25.00
MT Mark Teixeira 8.00 20.00
OC Orlando Cepeda 10.00 25.00
OS Ozzie Smith 20.00 50.00
PF Prince Fielder 10.00 25.00
RC Rod Carew 10.00 25.00
RI Raul Ibanez 8.00 20.00
RJ Reggie Jackson 10.00 25.00
SC Starlin Castro 10.00 25.00
TG Tony Gwynn 12.00 30.00
TT Troy Tulowitzki 8.00 20.00
VG Vladimir Guerrero 10.00 25.00
WB Wade Boggs 15.00 40.00
YG Yovani Gallardo 10.00 25.00
ARO Alex Rodriguez 15.00 40.00
JBU Jay Bruce 10.00 25.00
MCA Miguel Cabrera 15.00 40.00
NMO Nyjer Morgan 10.00 25.00

2012 Topps Museum Collection Momentous Material Jumbo Relics

STATED ODDS 1:11 PACKS
STATED PRINT RUN 50 SER.#'d SETS
AB Albert Belle 6.00 15.00
ABE Adrian Beltre 6.00 15.00
ABU A.J. Burnett 4.00 10.00
AC Allen Craig 8.00 20.00
ACH Aroldis Chapman 8.00 20.00
AET Andre Ethier 12.00 30.00
AJ Adam Jones 12.00 30.00
AK Al Kaline 10.00 25.00
AM Andrew McCutchen 10.00 25.00
AP Andy Pettitte 8.00 20.00
APU Albert Pujols 15.00 40.00
AR Aramis Ramirez 4.00 10.00
AS Alfonso Soriano 8.00 20.00
BBU Billy Butler 5.00 12.00
BG Brett Gardner 10.00 25.00
BM Brian McCann 4.00 10.00
BP Buster Posey 10.00 25.00
BS Bruce Sutter 5.00 12.00
BU B.J. Upton 4.00 10.00
BW Brian Wilson 10.00 25.00
CB Clay Buchholz 5.00 12.00
CBE Carlos Beltran 5.00 12.00
CC Carl Crawford 6.00 15.00
CCA Chris Carpenter 8.00 20.00
CF Carlton Fisk 8.00 20.00
CG Curtis Granderson 10.00 25.00
CH Cole Hamels 10.00 25.00
CHA Corey Hart 8.00 20.00
CK Craig Kimbrel 6.00 15.00
CLE Cliff Lee 10.00 25.00
CS CC Sabathia 6.00 15.00
CU Chase Utley 8.00 20.00
CW C.J. Wilson 5.00 12.00
DG Dwight Gooden 10.00 25.00
DHA Dan Haren 4.00 10.00
DJ Derek Jeter 30.00 80.00
DM Don Mattingly 10.00 25.00
DO David Ortiz 10.00 25.00
DP Dustin Pedroia 10.00 25.00
DSN Duke Snider 12.50 30.00
DU Dan Uggla 10.00 25.00
DW David Wright 8.00 20.00
EA Elvis Andrus 5.00 12.00
EL Evan Longoria 8.00 20.00
EL2 Evan Longoria 8.00 20.00
FF Freddie Freeman 5.00 12.00
FH Felix Hernandez 5.00 12.00
GB Gordon Beckham 8.00 20.00
HP Hunter Pence 10.00 25.00
HR Hanley Ramirez 5.00 12.00
I Ichiro Suzuki 12.00 30.00
IK Ian Kennedy 5.00 12.00
IKI Ian Kinsler 5.00 12.00
IR Ivan Rodriguez 8.00 20.00
JB Jose Bautista 10.00 25.00
JBR Jay Bruce 8.00 20.00
JE Jacoby Ellsbury 12.00 30.00
JH Josh Hamilton 10.00 25.00
JH Joel Hanrahan 6.00 15.00
JHE Jeremy Hellickson 5.00 12.00
JJH J.J. Hardy 6.00 15.00
JMO Jesus Montero 10.00 25.00
JP Jorge Posada 10.00 25.00
JR Jose Reyes 12.00 30.00
JRO Jimmy Rollins 6.00 15.00
JU Justin Upton 5.00 12.00
LB Lance Berkman 12.00 30.00
LBR Lou Brock 6.00 15.00
LM Logan Morrison 4.00 10.00
MAC Matt Cain 10.00 25.00
MC Miguel Cabrera 12.00 30.00
MH Matt Holliday 5.00 12.00
MK Matt Kemp 12.00 30.00
MMO Matt Moore 10.00 25.00
MR Mariano Rivera 15.00 40.00
MS Mike Stanton 8.00 20.00
NF Neftali Feliz 5.00 12.00
NS Nick Swisher 10.00 25.00
NW Neil Walker 10.00 25.00
PF Prince Fielder 6.00 15.00
PF2 Prince Fielder 6.00 15.00
PN Phil Niekro 6.00 15.00
PO Paul O'Neill 10.00 25.00
RB Ryan Braun 10.00 25.00
RC Robinson Cano 10.00 25.00
RCA Rod Carew 6.00 15.00
RH Roy Halladay 15.00 40.00
RHO Ryan Howard 10.00 25.00
RM Russell Martin 10.00 25.00
RO Roy Oswalt 6.00 15.00
SC Starlin Castro 10.00 25.00
TG Tony Gwynn 10.00 25.00
THE Todd Helton 8.00 20.00
THU Torii Hunter 4.00 10.00
TL Tim Lincecum 10.00 25.00
UJ Ubaldo Jimenez 6.00 15.00
WS Willie Stargell 12.00 30.00
YG Yovani Gallardo 4.00 10.00
YM Yadier Molina 15.00 40.00
ZG Zack Greinke 4.00 10.00

2012 Topps Museum Collection Momentous Material Jumbo Relics Gold 35

*GOLD 35: .4X TO 1X BASIC
STATED ODDS 1:15 PACKS
STATED PRINT RUN 35 SER.#'d SETS

2012 Topps Museum Collection Primary Pieces Four Player Quad Relics

STATED ODDS 1:34 PACKS
STATED PRINT RUN 99 SER.#'d SETS
BWKR Heath Bell 8.00 20.00
Brian Wilson
Craig Kimbrel
Mariano Rivera
CGOF Miguel Cabrera 10.00 25.00
Adrian Gonzalez
David Ortiz
Prince Fielder
CHKA Allen Craig 6.00 15.00
Matt Holliday
Ian Kinsler
Elvis Andrus
CPUU Robinson Cano 8.00 20.00
Dustin Pedroia
Dan Uggla
Chase Utley
GHPT Gonz/How/Puj/Teix 8.00 20.00
GLGB Curtis Granderson 8.00 20.00
Evan Longoria
Adrian Gonzalez
Jose Bautista
LRUV Lee/Rol/Utley/Vict 12.50 30.00
MPRO Matt/Pett/Rivera/O'Neill 10.00 25.00
PCEO Ped/Craw/Ells/Ortiz 12.50 30.00
RHSS Ryan/Hall/CC/Seaver 10.00 25.00
RMKF Aramis Ramirez 6.00 15.00
Brian McCann
Matt Kemp
Prince Fielder
RRTC Jimmy Rollins 8.00 20.00
Hanley Ramirez
Troy Tulowitzki
Starlin Castro
TRAR Troy Tulowitzki 8.00 20.00
Hanley Ramirez
Elvis Andrus
Jose Reyes
VLHK Justin Verlander 10.00 25.00
Cliff Lee
Jeremy Hellickson
Craig Kimbrel
WRJR Wright/Rey/Jeter/ARod 12.50 30.00

2012 Topps Museum Collection Primary Pieces Four Player Quad Relics Red 75

*RED 75: .4X TO 1X BASIC
STATED ODDS 1:45 PACKS
STATED PRINT RUN 75 SER.#'d SETS

2012 Topps Museum Collection Primary Pieces Quad Relics

STATED ODDS 1:12 PACKS
STATED PRINT RUN 99 SER.#'d SETS
AG Adrian Gonzalez 6.00 15.00
AM Andrew McCutchen 10.00 25.00
AP Albert Pujols 12.50 30.00
BW Brian Wilson 12.50 30.00
CC Carl Crawford 8.00 20.00
CG Carlos Gonzalez 6.00 15.00
CL Cliff Lee 8.00 20.00
CU Chase Utley 10.00 25.00
DO David Ortiz 10.00 25.00
DP Dustin Pedroia 12.50 30.00
DU Dan Uggla 8.00 20.00
DW David Wright 8.00 20.00
EA Elvis Andrus 8.00 20.00
EL Evan Longoria 6.00 15.00
FH Felix Hernandez 8.00 20.00
IK Ian Kennedy 6.00 15.00
IR Ivan Rodriguez 8.00 20.00
JB Jose Bautista 12.50 30.00
JE Jacoby Ellsbury 10.00 25.00
JR Jose Reyes 10.00 25.00
JW Jered Weaver 10.00 25.00
MC Miguel Cabrera 10.00 25.00
MH Matt Holliday 10.00 25.00
MK Matt Kemp 12.50 30.00
MR Mariano Rivera 12.50 30.00
MS Mike Stanton 10.00 25.00
MT Mark Teixeira 8.00 20.00
PF Prince Fielder 8.00 20.00
RB Ryan Braun 20.00 50.00
RC Robinson Cano 10.00 25.00
RH Roy Halladay 10.00 25.00
SC Starlin Castro 12.50 30.00
SV Shane Victorino 10.00 25.00
TH Todd Helton 6.00 15.00
TL Tim Lincecum 10.00 25.00
TT Troy Tulowitzki 12.50 30.00
CKI Craig Kimbrel 10.00 25.00
IKI Ian Kinsler 6.00 15.00
JBE Josh Beckett 6.00 15.00
JBR Jay Bruce 6.00 15.00
JHE Jeremy Hellickson 6.00 15.00
JMO Jesus Montero 8.00 20.00
JRO Jimmy Rollins 8.00 20.00
JVO Joey Votto 10.00 25.00
RHO Ryan Howard 8.00 20.00

2012 Topps Museum Collection Primary Pieces Quad Relics Red 75

*RED 75: .4X TO 1X BASIC
STATED ODDS 1:15 PACKS
STATED PRINT RUN 75 SER.#'d SETS

2012 Topps Museum Collection Signature Swatches Dual Relic Autographs

STATED ODDS 1:9 PACKS
PRINT RUN B/WN 30-250 COPIES PER
EXCHANGE DEADLINE 3/31/2015
AC Allen Craig/179 8.00 20.00
ACH Aroldis Chapman/99 30.00 60.00
AE Andre Ethier/50 15.00 40.00
AM Andrew McCutchen/70 40.00 80.00
AR Aramis Ramirez/70 10.00 25.00
BB Brandon Belt/250 6.00 15.00
BBU Billy Butler/70 6.00 15.00
BG Brett Gardner EXCH 15.00 40.00
BM Brian McCann/50 20.00 50.00
BP Brandon Phillips/70 10.00 25.00
BU B.J. Upton/70 10.00 25.00
CB Clay Buchholz/50 6.00 15.00
CC Carl Crawford/30 8.00 20.00
CF Carlton Fisk/30 30.00 60.00
CH Chris Heisey/250 6.00 15.00
CH2 Chris Heisey/250 6.00 15.00
CHA Cole Hamels EXCH 12.50 30.00
CK Craig Kimbrel/179 12.50 30.00
CK2 Craig Kimbrel/30 20.00 50.00
CKE Clayton Kershaw/70 50.00 100.00
DA Dustin Ackley/70 10.00 25.00
DE Danny Espinosa/179 6.00 15.00
DGE Dillon Gee/250 6.00 15.00
DP Dustin Pedroia/30 40.00 80.00
DS Drew Storen/250 6.00 15.00
DSN Duke Snider/30 10.00 25.00
DU Dan Uggla/50 6.00 15.00
GB Gordon Beckham/50 8.00 20.00
GC Gary Carter/50 30.00 60.00
GS Gary Sheffield/99 6.00 15.00
HP Hunter Pence EXCH 40.00 80.00
JB Jay Bruce/70 12.50 30.00
JBA Jose Bautista/30 20.00 50.00
JC Johnny Cueto/179 8.00 20.00
JC2 Johnny Cueto/250 8.00 20.00
JG Jaime Garcia/179 8.00 20.00
JH Jeremy Hellickson/179 6.00 15.00
JJ Jon Jay/250 6.00 15.00
JW Jemile Weeks/250 6.00 15.00
JWA Jordan Walden/179 6.00 15.00
MB Madison Bumgarner/70 40.00 100.00
MMO Matt Moore/99 10.00 25.00
MS Mike Stanton/50 40.00 80.00
MT Mark Trumbo/250 6.00 15.00
NC Nelson Cruz/50 10.00 25.00
NF Neftali Feliz/179 6.00 15.00
PF Prince Fielder/30 10.00 25.00
PS Pablo Sandoval/70 12.50 30.00
RP Rick Porcello/70 10.00 25.00
RZ Ryan Zimmerman/50 12.50 30.00
SC Starlin Castro/70 6.00 15.00
SV Shane Victorino/70 12.50 30.00
VW Vernon Wells/30 8.00 20.00

2012 Topps Museum Collection Signature Swatches Triple Relic Autographs

STATED ODDS 1:18 PACKS
PRINT RUNS B/WN 30-235 COPIES PER
EXCHANGE DEADLINE 3/31/2012
AC Allen Craig/209 12.50 30.00
AG Adrian Gonzalez/30 12.50 30.00
AR Anthony Rizzo/235 10.00 25.00
BB Brandon Belt/209 10.00 25.00
BBU Billy Butler/59 8.00 20.00
CF Carlton Fisk/30 15.00 40.00
CG Carlos Gonzalez/59 15.00 40.00
CH Chris Heisey/235 6.00 15.00
CK Craig Kimbrel/175 15.00 40.00
DB Daniel Bard/235 8.00 20.00
DH Derek Holland/175 10.00 25.00
DS Duke Snider/30 30.00 60.00
GC Gary Carter/59 20.00 50.00
HN Hector Noesi/235 6.00 15.00
HP Hunter Pence EXCH 40.00 80.00
JB Jose Bautista/30 15.00 40.00
JH Jeremy Hellickson/59 6.00 15.00
JM Jesus Montero/175 12.50 30.00
MS Mike Stanton/59 20.00 50.00
MT Mark Trumbo/209 8.00 20.00
NW Neil Walker/209 10.00 25.00
SC Starlin Castro/59 10.00 25.00
SV Shane Victorino/59 6.00 15.00

2013 Topps Museum Collection

1 Derek Jeter 2.00 5.00
2 George Brett 1.50 4.00
3 Juan Marichal .60 1.50
4 Ted Williams 1.50 4.00
5 Bob Gibson .60 1.50
6 Dylan Bundy RC 1.25 3.00
7 Frank Thomas .75 2.00
8 Buster Posey 1.00 2.50
9 Jackie Robinson .75 2.00
10 Gary Carter .60 1.50
11 Adrian Gonzalez .60 1.50
12 Bryce Harper 1.25 3.00
13 Starlin Castro .50 1.25
14 Troy Tulowitzki .75 2.00
15 Ryu Hyun-Jin RC 1.25 3.00
16 Wade Boggs .60 1.50
17 Giancarlo Stanton .75 2.00
18 Matt Cain .60 1.50
19 Hank Aaron 1.50 4.00
20 Will Middlebrooks .50 1.25
21 David Price .60 1.50
22 Miguel Cabrera .75 2.00
23 Yu Darvish .75 2.00
24 Felix Hernandez .60 1.50
25 Chris Sale .75 2.00
26 Bill Mazeroski .60 1.50
27 Robin Yount .75 2.00
28 Adam Jones .60 1.50
29 Johnny Bench .75 2.00
30 Ken Griffey Jr. 1.50 4.00
31 Matt Kemp .60 1.50
32 Stan Musial 1.25 3.00
33 Johnny Cueto .60 1.50
34 Willie McCovey .60 1.50
35 Carlos Gonzalez .60 1.50
36 Joe Mauer .60 1.50
37 Reggie Jackson .60 1.50
38 Yoenis Cespedes .75 2.00
39 Lou Brock .60 1.50
40 Cole Hamels .60 1.50
41 Chase Headley .50 1.25
42 Jose Bautista .60 1.50
43 Cal Ripken Jr. 2.50 6.00
44 John Smoltz .75 2.00
45 Al Kaline .75 2.00
46 Mike Trout 6.00 15.00
47 Justin Verlander .75 2.00
48 Dustin Pedroia .75 2.00
49 Gio Gonzalez .60 1.50
50 Stephen Strasburg .75 2.00
51 Nolan Ryan 2.50 6.00
52 Paul Molitor .75 2.00
53 Lou Gehrig 1.50 4.00
54 Prince Fielder .60 1.50
55 Willie Stargell .60 1.50
56 Norichika Aoki .50 1.25
57 Anthony Rizzo 1.00 2.50
58 Gary Sheffield .50 1.25
59 Brooks Robinson .60 1.50
60 David Wright .60 1.50
61 Joey Votto .75 2.00
62 Adrian Beltre .75 2.00
63 Ryne Sandberg 1.50 4.00
64 Joe Morgan .60 1.50
65 Ryan Braun .60 1.50
66 Pablo Sandoval .60 1.50
67 Aroldis Chapman .75 2.00
68 Babe Ruth 2.00 5.00
69 Sandy Koufax 1.50 4.00
70 Manny Machado RC 3.00 8.00
71 Clayton Kershaw 1.25 3.00
72 Albert Pujols 1.00 2.50
73 Justin Upton .60 1.50
74 Duke Snider .60 1.50
75 Billy Butler .50 1.25
76 Will Clark .60 1.50
77 Mike Schmidt 1.25 3.00
78 Ty Cobb 1.25 3.00
79 Jurickson Profar RC .60 1.50
80 Jake Peavy .50 1.25
81 Evan Longoria .60 1.50
82 R.A. Dickey .60 1.50
83 Eddie Murray .60 1.50
84 Albert Belle .50 1.25
85 Tom Seaver .60 1.50
86 Yadier Molina 1.00 2.50
87 Josh Hamilton .60 1.50
88 Rickey Henderson .75 2.00
89 Ozzie Smith 1.00 2.50
90 Bob Feller .60 1.50
91 Ernie Banks .75 2.00
92 Alex Rodriguez 1.00 2.50
93 Jered Weaver .60 1.50
94 Carlos Beltran .60 1.50
95 Harmon Killebrew .75 2.00
96 Jose Reyes .60 1.50
97 Andrew McCutchen .75 2.00
98 Roy Halladay .60 1.50
99 Tony Gwynn .75 2.00
100 Willie Mays 1.50 4.00

2013 Topps Museum Collection Blue

*BLUE VET: 1.5X TO 4X BASIC
*BLUE RC: 1.5X TO 4X BASIC RC
STATED ODDS 1:8 PACKS
STATED PRINT RUN 99 SER.#'d SETS

2013 Topps Museum Collection Copper

*COPPER VET: .5X TO 1.2X BASIC
*COPPER RC: .5X TO 1.2X BASIC RC
STATED PRINT RUN 424 SER.#'d SETS

2013 Topps Museum Collection Green

*GREEN VET: .75X TO 2X BASIC
*GREEN RC: .75X TO 2X BASIC RC
STATED ODDS 1:4 PACKS
STATED PRINT RUN 199 SER.#'d SETS

2013 Topps Museum Collection Autographs

PRINT RUNS B/WN 27-399 COPIES PER
EXCHANGE DEADLINE 5/31/2016
AB Albert Belle/50 6.00 15.00
AD Andre Dawson/50 8.00 20.00
AG Adrian Gonzalez/25 10.00 25.00
AH Drew Hutchison/399 5.00 12.00
AJ Adam Jones/50 10.00 25.00
AK Al Kaline/50 20.00 50.00
AR Anthony Rizzo/399 20.00 50.00
BB Bill Buckner/399 6.00 15.00
BBL Bert Blyleven/199 8.00 20.00
BBU Billy Butler/399 6.00 15.00
BG Bob Gibson EXCH 20.00 50.00
BS Bruce Sutter/50 10.00 25.00
BW Billy Williams/199 10.00 25.00
CB Craig Biggio/25 30.00 60.00
CF Cecil Fielder/199 6.00 15.00
CKI Craig Kimbrel/50 20.00 50.00
CW C.J. Wilson/399 5.00 12.00
DBU Dylan Bundy/399 5.00 12.00
DE Dennis Eckersley/50 12.00 30.00
DH Derek Holland/399 5.00 12.00
DM Don Mattingly/20 40.00 80.00
DME Devin Mesoraco/399 5.00 12.00
DMU Dale Murphy/50 20.00 50.00
DP Dustin Pedroia/25 30.00 60.00
DS Dave Stewart/159 6.00 15.00
DST Drew Storen/399 5.00 12.00
DSU Don Sutton/399 6.00 15.00
DW David Wright/20 50.00 100.00
EL Evan Longoria/20 50.00 100.00
GS Giancarlo Stanton/199 25.00 60.00
HA Hank Aaron/20 125.00 250.00
JA Jim Abbott/399 5.00 12.00
JB Johnny Bench/110 30.00 80.00
JBA Jose Bautista/25 12.00 30.00
JC Johnny Cueto/50 5.00 12.00
JH Jason Heyward/50 12.00 30.00
JK John Kruk/199 6.00 15.00
JPA Jarrod Parker/399 5.00 12.00
JPR Jurickson Profar/399 5.00 12.00
JR Jim Rice/399 6.00 15.00
JS John Smoltz/25 30.00 60.00
JSE Jean Segura/399 6.00 15.00
JW Jered Weaver/25 15.00 40.00
KG Ken Griffey Jr. EXCH 100.00 200.00
MA Matt Adams/399 5.00 12.00
MC Miguel Cabrera/20 125.00 250.00
MMA Manny Machado/50 30.00 60.00
MMO Matt Moore/399 5.00 12.00
MT Mike Trout/27 175.00 350.00
MW Maury Wills/399 5.00 12.00
NE Nate Eovaldi/399 5.00 12.00
PF Prince Fielder/20 30.00 60.00
PG Paul Goldschmidt/399 12.00 30.00
RD R.A. Dickey/50 12.00 30.00
RV Robin Ventura/199 8.00 20.00
SM Starling Marte/399 5.00 12.00
TB Trevor Bauer/399 6.00 15.00
TF Todd Frazier/399 5.00 12.00
TR Tim Raines/199 8.00 20.00
TSK Tyler Skaggs/399 5.00 12.00
VB Vida Blue/399 5.00 12.00
WC Will Clark/399 12.00 30.00
WJ Wally Joyner/399 6.00 15.00
WM Will Middlebrooks/399 5.00 12.00
WMA Willie Mays/20 150.00 250.00
WMI Wade Miley/399 5.00 12.00
WP Wily Peralta/399 5.00 12.00
WR Wilin Rosario/399 5.00 12.00
YA Yonder Alonso/399 5.00 12.00
YC Yoenis Cespedes/399 6.00 15.00
YD Yu Darvish/25 75.00 150.00
YG Yovani Gallardo/50 6.00 15.00

2013 Topps Museum Collection Canvas Collection

STATED ODDS 1:4 PACKS
1 Albert Pujols 1.25 3.00
2 Andrew McCutchen 1.00 2.50
3 Stephen Strasburg 1.00 2.50
4 David Price .75 2.00
5 Bryce Harper 1.50 4.00
6 Buster Posey 1.25 3.00
7 Prince Fielder .75 2.00
8 Mike Trout 8.00 20.00
9 Willie Mays 2.00 5.00
10 Cal Ripken Jr. 3.00 8.00
11 Ryan Braun .75 2.00
12 Reggie Jackson .75 2.00
13 Johnny Bench 1.00 2.50
14 Roberto Clemente 2.50 6.00
15 Mike Schmidt 1.50 4.00
16 Carlton Fisk .75 2.00
17 Yu Darvish 1.00 2.50
18 Clayton Kershaw 1.50 4.00
19 R.A. Dickey .75 2.00
20 Nolan Ryan 3.00 8.00
21 Tony Gwynn 1.00 2.50
22 Derek Jeter 2.50 6.00
23 Ernie Banks 1.00 2.50
24 Ozzie Smith 1.25 3.00
25 George Brett 2.00 5.00
26 Will Clark .75 2.00
27 Stan Musial 1.50 4.00
28 Miguel Cabrera 1.00 2.50
29 Ken Griffey Jr. 2.00 5.00
30 Ted Williams 2.00 5.00
31 John Smoltz 1.00 2.50
32 Tom Seaver .75 2.00
33 Felix Hernandez .75 2.00
34 Orlando Cepeda .75 2.00
35 Lou Gehrig 2.00 5.00

2013 Topps Museum Collection Jumbo Lumber

STATED ODDS 1:35 PACKS
STATED PRINT RUN 30 SER.#'d SETS
AB Albert Belle 10.00 25.00
AD Adam Dunn 6.00 15.00
AG Anthony Gose 8.00 20.00
AJ Adam Jones 10.00 25.00
AK Al Kaline 15.00 40.00
AP Albert Pujols 10.00 25.00
AROD Alex Rodriguez 15.00 40.00
BB Bill Buckner 8.00 20.00
BE Brandon Belt 12.50 30.00
BM Bill Mazeroski 12.50 30.00
BR Brooks Robinson 20.00 50.00
BW Brett Wallace 6.00 15.00
CF Carlton Fisk 6.00 15.00
CFI Cecil Fielder 12.50 30.00
CH Chris Heisey 5.00 12.00
CK Clayton Kershaw 8.00 20.00
CP Carlos Pena 5.00 12.00
CR Cal Ripken Jr. 30.00 60.00
CRO Cody Ross 5.00 12.00
DD David DeJesus 5.00 12.00
DGO Dee Gordon 5.00 12.00
DH Daniel Hudson 8.00 20.00
DJU David Justice 12.50 30.00
DMA Don Mattingly 30.00 60.00
DME Devin Mesoraco 6.00 15.00
DS Darryl Strawberry 12.50 30.00
DST Drew Stubbs 5.00 12.00
DU Dan Uggla 5.00 12.00
DWR David Wright 10.00 25.00
EA Elvis Andrus 6.00 15.00
EBA Ernie Banks 15.00 40.00
EE Edwin Encarnacion EXCH 6.00 15.00
EL Evan Longoria 8.00 20.00
EM Eddie Murray 12.50 30.00
FJE Fergie Jenkins 5.00 12.00
GG Goose Gossage 10.00 25.00
GSH Gary Sheffield 5.00 12.00
HP Hunter Pence 12.50 30.00
HR Hanley Ramirez 10.00 25.00
ID Ian Desmond 5.00 12.00
IK Ian Kinsler 8.00 20.00
JB Johnny Bench 15.00 40.00
JBR Jay Bruce 8.00 20.00
JC Johnny Cueto 5.00 12.00
JH Josh Hamilton 10.00 25.00
JHE Jason Heyward 12.50 30.00
JJA Jon Jay 10.00 25.00
JK Jason Kubel 5.00 12.00
JL James Loney 5.00 12.00
JR Jim Rice 10.00 25.00
JV Joey Votto 10.00 25.00
JZ Jordan Zimmermann 8.00 20.00
LB Lou Brock 20.00 50.00
MC Melky Cabrera 5.00 12.00
MD Matt Dominguez 5.00 12.00
MK Matt Kemp 8.00 20.00
MM Mike Morse 5.00 12.00
MP Martin Prado 5.00 12.00
MS Mike Schmidt 12.50 30.00
MTE Mark Teixeira 12.50 30.00
NC Nelson Cruz 5.00 12.00
OS Ozzie Smith 10.00 25.00
PS Pablo Sandoval 8.00 20.00
RC Rod Carew 10.00 25.00
RJ Reggie Jackson 12.50 30.00
RY Robin Yount 10.00 25.00
SC Starlin Castro 10.00 25.00
SG Steve Garvey 50.00 100.00
SV Shane Victorino 8.00 20.00
TG Tony Gwynn 15.00 40.00
TL Tim Lincecum 12.50 30.00
TW Ted Williams 40.00 80.00
UJ Ubaldo Jimenez 5.00 12.00
WB Wade Boggs 12.50 30.00
ZG Zack Greinke 6.00 15.00

2013 Topps Museum Collection Momentous Material Jumbo Relics

STATED ODDS 1:11 PACKS
STATED PRINT RUN 50 SER.#'d SETS
AD Adam Dunn 5.00 12.00
AE Andre Ethier 3.00 8.00
AGO Adrian Gonzalez 4.00 10.00
AJ Austin Jackson 5.00 12.00
AJO Adam Jones 6.00 15.00
AK Al Kaline 15.00 40.00
AM Andrew McCutchen 10.00 25.00
APE Andy Pettitte 6.00 15.00
AR Anthony Rizzo 10.00 25.00
AROD Alex Rodriguez 15.00 40.00
AS Alfonso Soriano 4.00 10.00
AW Adam Wainwright 8.00 20.00
BB Billy Butler 4.00 10.00
BF Bob Feller 15.00 40.00
BG Bob Gibson 10.00 25.00
BGA Brett Gardner 6.00 15.00
BH Bryce Harper 12.50 30.00
BM Brandon Morrow 5.00 12.00
BMC Brian McCann 6.00 15.00
BP Brandon Phillips 8.00 20.00
BR Brooks Robinson 15.00 40.00
BW Brett Wallace 3.00 8.00
CBI Chad Billingsley 5.00 12.00
CCS CC Sabathia 10.00 25.00
CF Carlton Fisk 8.00 20.00
CG Carlos Gonzalez 5.00 12.00
CH Cole Hamels 6.00 15.00
CJ Chipper Jones 10.00 25.00
CK Clayton Kershaw 8.00 20.00
CKI Craig Kimbrel 4.00 10.00
CL Cliff Lee 5.00 12.00
CM Carlos Marmol 3.00 8.00
CP Carlos Pena 3.00 8.00
CR Cal Ripken Jr. 12.50 30.00
CRA Colby Rasmus 3.00 8.00
CSA Carlos Santana 6.00 15.00
DA Dustin Ackley 5.00 12.00
DF David Freese 8.00 20.00
DJ Derek Jeter 20.00 50.00
DJE Desmond Jennings 3.00 8.00
DM Don Mattingly 15.00 40.00
DP David Price 3.00 8.00
DS Darryl Strawberry 6.00 15.00
DW David Wright 12.50 30.00
DYB Dylan Bundy 12.50 30.00
EA Elvis Andrus 4.00 10.00
EL Evan Longoria 6.00 15.00
EM Eddie Murray 8.00 20.00
FF Freddie Freeman 6.00 15.00
FH Felix Hernandez 6.00 15.00
GB George Brett 12.50 30.00
GG Gio Gonzalez 4.00 10.00
HK Harmon Killebrew 15.00 40.00
HR Hanley Ramirez 4.00 10.00
HW Hoyt Wilhelm 10.00 25.00
ID Ike Davis 4.00 10.00
IDE Ian Desmond 3.00 8.00
IK Ian Kinsler 4.00 10.00
IKE Ian Kennedy 3.00 8.00
JA Jose Altuve 5.00 12.00
JAR J.P. Arencibia 5.00 12.00
JAX John Axford 4.00 10.00
JB Johnny Bench 10.00 25.00
JBR Jay Bruce 5.00 12.00
JC Johnny Cueto 4.00 10.00
JG Jaime Garcia 5.00 12.00
JH Josh Hamilton 8.00 20.00
JHE Jason Heyward 8.00 20.00
JJ Josh Johnson 4.00 10.00
JK Jason Kipnis 8.00 20.00
JKU Jason Kubel 3.00 8.00
JL Jon Lester 5.00 12.00
JM Justin Morneau 5.00 12.00
JMA Joe Mauer 4.00 10.00
JMC James McDonald 3.00 8.00
JMO Jesus Montero 3.00 8.00
JOZ Jordan Zimmermann 5.00 12.00
JP Jarrod Parker 4.00 10.00
JPE Jake Peavy 3.00 8.00
JR Jose Reyes 6.00 15.00
JRE Josh Reddick 5.00 12.00
JRO Jimmy Rollins 5.00 12.00
JS Johan Santana 5.00 12.00
JSM John Smoltz 6.00 15.00
JT Jacob Turner 3.00 8.00
JU Justin Upton 5.00 12.00
JV Justin Verlander 12.50 30.00
JVO Joey Votto 10.00 25.00
JW Jered Weaver 5.00 12.00
JWE Jemile Weeks 3.00 8.00
LL Lance Lynn 6.00 15.00
MB Madison Bumgarner 12.50 30.00
MC Miguel Cabrera 12.50 30.00
MCA Matt Cain 6.00 15.00
MCB Melky Cabrera 3.00 8.00
MH Matt Harvey 10.00 25.00
MMI Mike Minor 6.00 15.00
MMO Mike Moustakas 4.00 10.00
MS Mike Schmidt 10.00 25.00
MSC Max Scherzer 6.00 15.00
MT Mike Trout 12.00 30.00
MTR Mark Trumbo 8.00 20.00
NC Nelson Cruz 4.00 10.00
NF Neftali Feliz 3.00 8.00
NM Nick Markakis 8.00 20.00
NS Nick Swisher 5.00 12.00
NW Neil Walker 5.00 12.00
PA Pedro Alvarez 5.00 12.00
PF Prince Fielder 8.00 20.00
PK Paul Konerko 4.00 10.00
PN Phil Niekro 6.00 15.00
RB Ryan Braun 6.00 15.00
RC Rod Carew 6.00 15.00
RD R.A. Dickey 4.00 10.00
RH Rickey Henderson 12.50 30.00
RHA Roy Halladay 5.00 12.00
RHO Ryan Howard 5.00 12.00
RJ Reggie Jackson 12.50 30.00
RP Rick Porcello 5.00 12.00
RS Ryne Sandberg 15.00 40.00
RY Robin Yount 10.00 25.00
SC Starlin Castro 8.00 20.00
SM Stan Musial 30.00 60.00
SMA Shaun Marcum 3.00 8.00
SMR Starling Marte 10.00 25.00
SS Stephen Strasburg 6.00 15.00
TG Tony Gwynn 8.00 20.00
TH Torii Hunter 5.00 12.00
TL Tim Lincecum 10.00 25.00
TM Tommy Milone 3.00 8.00
TT Troy Tulowitzki 6.00 15.00
TW Ted Williams 40.00 80.00
VM Victor Martinez 5.00 12.00
WB Wade Boggs 10.00 25.00
WD Wade Davis 3.00 8.00
WMI Will Middlebrooks 6.00 15.00
WR Wilin Rosario 3.00 8.00
YA Yonder Alonso 3.00 8.00
YC Yoenis Cespedes 8.00 20.00
YD Yu Darvish 15.00 40.00
YG Yovani Gallardo 3.00 8.00

2013 Topps Museum Collection Momentous Material Jumbo Relics Gold

*GOLD: .4X TO 1X BASIC
STATED ODDS 1:15 PACKS
STATED PRINT RUN 35 SER.#'d SETS

2013 Topps Museum Collection Primary Pieces Four Player Quad Relics

STATED ODDS 1:32 PACKS
STATED PRINT RUN 99 SER.#'d SETS
1 Mattingly/Strawberry/CC/ARod 15.00 40.00

2 Weaver/Wilson/Trout/Trumbo 12.50 30.00
3 Phillips/Votto/Bench/Bruce 12.50 30.00
4 Koufax/Garvey/Ethier/Kemp 10.00 25.00
5 Prince/Mur/Ripk/Miggy 10.00 25.00
6 Rob/Cano/Kins/Pedr 20.00 50.00
7 Bog/Wright/Schm/Miggy 10.00 25.00
8 Ben/McC/Sant/Mauer 15.00 40.00
9 Uggla/Smoltz/Ryan/Kinsler 10.00 25.00
10 Mays/Griffey/Harper/Trout 50.00 100.00
11 Tulo/Jeter/ARod/Ripken 20.00 50.00
12 Bruce/Votto/Choo/Phillips 15.00 40.00
13 Dickey/Harvey/Sant/Seaver 20.00 50.00
14 Linc/Koufax/Kershaw/Cain 10.00 25.00
15 Smoltz/Posey/Heyward/Cain 15.00 40.00
16 David Ortiz 10.00 25.00
Ryan Howard
Chase Utley
Wade Boggs
17 Yonder Alonso 8.00 20.00
Tony Gwynn
Adrian Gonzalez
Andre Ethier
18 David Price 10.00 25.00
Matt Cain
Justin Verlander
Madison Bumgarner
19 Buster Posey 12.50 30.00
Tim Lincecum
Ian Kinsler
Yu Darvish
20 Andrew McCutchen 12.50 30.00
Yoenis Cespedes
Reggie Jackson
Willie Stargell
21 Mays/Lincecum/Cain/Posey 15.00 40.00
22 Garcia/Gibs/Holl/Musial 12.50 30.00
23 Gio/Zimm/Harper/Strasburg 12.50 30.00
24 Stras/Hernan/Darvish/Price 10.00 25.00
25 Cesped/Darv/Harp/Trout 12.00 30.00

2013 Topps Museum Collection Primary Pieces Four Player Quad Relics Copper

*COPPER: .4X TO 1X BASIC
STATED ODDS 1:42 HOBBY
STATED PRINT RUN 75 SER.#'d SETS

2013 Topps Museum Collection Primary Pieces Quad Relics

STATED ODDS 1:12 PACKS
STATED PRINT RUN 99 SER.#'d SETS
AB Adrian Beltre 4.00 10.00
AC Aroldis Chapman 5.00 12.00
AG Alex Gordon 6.00 15.00
AJ Austin Jackson 8.00 20.00
AM Andrew McCutchen 10.00 25.00
AP Albert Pujols 10.00 25.00
AROD Alex Rodriguez 6.00 15.00
BB Brandon Beachy 4.00 10.00
BBU Billy Butler 4.00 10.00
BP Brandon Phillips 6.00 15.00
BU B.J. Upton 4.00 10.00
CB Chad Billingsley 4.00 10.00
CH Cole Hamels 6.00 15.00
CK Clayton Kershaw 10.00 25.00
CR Colby Rasmus 4.00 10.00
CS Chris Sale 5.00 12.00
CSA Carlos Santana 4.00 10.00
CW C.J. Wilson 4.00 10.00
DA Dustin Ackley 4.00 10.00
DG Dee Gordon 4.00 10.00
DH Dan Haren 4.00 10.00
DO David Ortiz 8.00 20.00
DP Dustin Pedroia 5.00 12.00
DPR David Price 5.00 12.00
DS Drew Stubbs 4.00 10.00
DU Dan Uggla 4.00 10.00
DW David Wright 12.50 30.00
FH Felix Hernandez 6.00 15.00
GB Gordon Beckham 4.00 10.00
GG Gio Gonzalez 4.00 10.00
GS Giancarlo Stanton 6.00 15.00
HI Hisashi Iwakuma 4.00 10.00
HR Hanley Ramirez 6.00 15.00
IK Ian Kinsler 4.00 10.00
IKE Ian Kennedy 4.00 10.00
JBR Jay Bruce 5.00 12.00
JH Jason Heyward 8.00 20.00
JK Jason Kipnis 4.00 10.00
JM Jesus Montero 4.00 10.00
JR Josh Reddick 4.00 10.00
JU Justin Upton 6.00 15.00
JV Joey Votto 6.00 15.00
JVE Justin Verlander 8.00 20.00
JW Jered Weaver 5.00 12.00
MC Miguel Cabrera 12.50 30.00
MCA Matt Cain 6.00 15.00
MH Matt Holliday 8.00 20.00
MK Matt Kemp 4.00 10.00
MM Matt Moore 5.00 12.00
MTE Mark Teixeira 5.00 12.00
MTR Mark Trumbo 12.50 30.00
NA Norichika Aoki 10.00 25.00
NC Nelson Cruz 5.00 12.00
PA Pedro Alvarez 6.00 15.00
PF Prince Fielder 5.00 12.00
RB Ryan Braun 6.00 15.00
RD R.A. Dickey 4.00 10.00
RH Roy Halladay 6.00 15.00
RHO Ryan Howard 4.00 10.00
RZ Ryan Zimmerman 5.00 12.00
SC Starlin Castro 6.00 15.00
TH Tommy Hanson 4.00 10.00
TM Tommy Milone 4.00 10.00
TS Tyler Skaggs 4.00 10.00
TT Troy Tulowitzki 6.00 15.00
VM Victor Martinez 5.00 12.00
YC Yoenis Cespedes 6.00 15.00
YG Yovani Gallardo 4.00 10.00

2013 Topps Museum Collection Primary Pieces Quad Relics Copper

*COPPER: .4X TO 1X BASIC
STATED ODDS 1:16 PACKS
STATED PRINT RUN 75 SER.#'d SETS

2013 Topps Museum Collection Signature Swatches Dual Relic Autographs

STATED ODDS 1:10 PACKS
PRINT RUNS B/WN 25-299 COPIES PER
EXCHANGE DEADLINE 5/31/2016
AA Alex Avila EXCH 6.00 15.00
AC Alex Cobb/299 5.00 12.00
ACA Andrew Cashner/299 5.00 12.00
AE Andre Ethier/50 10.00 25.00
AG Adrian Gonzalez/25 15.00 40.00
AJ Austin Jackson EXCH 8.00 20.00
AK Al Kaline/50 25.00 50.00
AR Anthony Rizzo/99 40.00 100.00
BB Billy Butler/299 6.00 15.00
BBE Brandon Beachy EXCH 8.00 20.00
BG Brett Gardner EXCH 10.00 25.00
BH Bryce Harper/50 125.00 250.00
BP Brandon Phillips/50 10.00 25.00
BS Bruce Sutter/50 15.00 40.00
CG Carlos Gonzalez/50 5.00 12.00
CK Clayton Kershaw/50 30.00 80.00
CKI Craig Kimbrel/50 12.50 30.00
CRA Colby Rasmus/99 6.00 15.00
CS Carlos Santana/99 5.00 12.00
CW C.J. Wilson/50 8.00 20.00
DB Domonic Brown/99 5.00 12.00
DF David Freese/50 20.00 50.00
DH Derek Holland/50 6.00 15.00
DM Devin Mesoraco/299 5.00 12.00
DO David Ortiz/50 20.00 50.00
DP Dustin Pedroia/50 20.00 50.00
DW David Wright/50 20.00 50.00
EA Elvis Andrus/99 10.00 25.00
EL Evan Longoria/50 10.00 25.00
FH Felix Hernandez/50 20.00 50.00
GS Giancarlo Stanton/50 30.00 60.00
GSH Gary Sheffield/99 8.00 20.00
HR Hanley Ramirez/50 12.50 30.00
IN Ivan Nova/99 5.00 12.00
JB Jay Bruce/50 15.00 40.00
JC Johnny Cueto/50 4.00 10.00
JG Jaime Garcia EXCH 5.00 12.00
JH Josh Hamilton/50 12.50 30.00
JJ Jon Jay EXCH 5.00 12.00
JK Jason Kipnis/299 5.00 12.00
JMO Jesus Montero/99 6.00 15.00
JN Jeff Niemann/299 5.00 12.00
JP Jhonny Peralta/99 4.00 10.00
JPA Jarrod Parker/299 5.00 12.00
JR Josh Reddick EXCH 8.00 20.00
JS John Smoltz/85 30.00 60.00
JSE Jean Segura EXCH 15.00 40.00
JZ Jordan Zimmermann/50 5.00 12.00
MB Madison Bumgarner/50 30.00 80.00
MC Miguel Cabrera/50 30.00 80.00
MCA Matt Cain EXCH 15.00 40.00
MH Matt Holliday EXCH 15.00 40.00
MM Manny Machado/50 30.00 60.00
MMO Mike Moustakas EXCH 10.00 25.00
MO Mike Olt/212 5.00 12.00
MP Michael Pineda/99 10.00 25.00
MT Mike Trout/50 125.00 250.00
MTR Mark Trumbo/99 5.00 12.00
NE Nate Eovaldi/299 5.00 12.00
NF Neftali Feliz/99 4.00 10.00
PF Prince Fielder/50 10.00 25.00
PS Pablo Sandoval EXCH 25.00 60.00
RB Ryan Braun EXCH 10.00 25.00
RD R.A. Dickey/50 10.00 25.00
RZ Ryan Zimmerman/50 12.50 30.00
SC Starlin Castro/50 10.00 25.00
SM Starling Marte/50 8.00 20.00
TM Tommy Milone/299 6.00 15.00
TS Tyler Skaggs/299 5.00 12.00
WC Will Clark/50 30.00 60.00
WR Wilin Rosario/299 5.00 12.00
YA Yonder Alonso/99 6.00 15.00
YC Yoenis Cespedes/50 20.00 50.00
YG Yovani Gallardo/99 6.00 15.00
ZC Zack Cozart/299 5.00 12.00

2013 Topps Museum Collection Signature Swatches Triple Relic Autographs

STATED ODDS 1:15 PACKS
PRINT RUNS B/WN 50-299 COPIES PER
EXCHANGE DEADLINE 5/31/2016
AG Adrian Gonzalez/50 15.00 40.00
AK Al Kaline/50 25.00 50.00
BB Billy Butler/299 8.00 20.00
BG Brett Gardner EXCH 10.00 25.00
BP Brandon Phillips/50 12.50 30.00
BS Bruce Sutter/50 15.00 40.00
CG Carlos Gonzalez/50 15.00 40.00
CK Clayton Kershaw/50 50.00 100.00
CR Colby Rasmus/99 5.00 12.00
CSA Carlos Santana/299 4.00 10.00
CW C.J. Wilson/50 8.00 20.00
DH Derek Holland/99 6.00 15.00
DM Devin Mesoraco/299 5.00 12.00
DP Dustin Pedroia/50 20.00 50.00
FD Felix Doubront EXCH 5.00 12.00
GG Gio Gonzalez/50 5.00 12.00
ID Ian Desmond EXCH 8.00 20.00
JH Josh Hamilton/50 4.00 10.00
JJ Jon Jay EXCH 5.00 12.00
JP Jarrod Parker/299 5.00 12.00
JZ Jordan Zimmermann/50 12.00 30.00
KG Ken Griffey Jr. EXCH 100.00 200.00
KN Kirk Nieuwenhuis/299 5.00 12.00
MA Matt Adams/299 10.00 25.00
MC Miguel Cabrera/50 75.00 150.00
MCA Matt Cain EXCH 15.00 40.00
MH Matt Holliday EXCH 15.00 40.00
MM Manny Machado/99 30.00 60.00
MMO Mike Moustakas EXCH 10.00 25.00
MP Michael Pineda/99 8.00 20.00
PF Prince Fielder/50 20.00 50.00
RB Ryan Braun EXCH 10.00 25.00
RD R.A. Dickey/50 12.00 30.00
RZ Ryan Zimmerman/50 15.00 40.00
SM Starling Marte/99 8.00 20.00
TM Tommy Milone/299 5.00 12.00
TS Tyler Skaggs/299 6.00 15.00
WR Wilin Rosario/299 5.00 12.00
YA Yonder Alonso/224 4.00 10.00
YG Yovani Gallardo/50 6.00 15.00

2014 Topps Museum Collection

COMPLETE SET (100) 30.00 80.00
1 Avisail Garcia .50 1.25
2 Christian Yelich .75 2.00
3 Yasiel Puig .60 1.50
4 Nick Castellanos RC 1.25 3.00
5 Andre Dawson .50 1.25
6 Billy Hamilton RC .50 1.25
7 Wade Miley .40 1.00
8 Didi Gregorius .50 1.25
9 Xander Bogaerts RC 1.25 3.00
10 David Ortiz .60 1.50
11 Wilin Rosario .40 1.00
12 Julio Teheran .50 1.25
13 Travis d'Arnaud RC .50 1.25
14 Matt Adams .40 1.00
15 Jose Fernandez .60 1.50
16 Taijuan Walker RC .40 1.00
17 Todd Frazier .40 1.00
18 Ricky Nolasco .40 1.00
19 Mike Zunino .40 1.00
20 Paul Goldschmidt .60 1.50
21 Steve Carlton .50 1.25
22 Starling Marte .50 1.25
23 Kris Medlen .50 1.25
24 Jurickson Profar .50 1.25
25 Wil Myers .40 1.00
26 Juan Gonzalez .40 1.00
27 Yoenis Cespedes .60 1.50
28 Jason Kipnis .50 1.25
29 Shelby Miller .50 1.25
30 Allen Craig .50 1.25
31 David Freese .40 1.00
32 Jordan Zimmermann .50 1.25
33 Paul O'Neill .50 1.25
34 Chris Davis .40 1.00
35 James Shields .40 1.00
36 Jim Rice .50 1.25
37 Rafael Palmeiro .50 1.25
38 Albert Belle .40 1.00
39 Chris Sale .60 1.50
40 Will Clark .50 1.25
41 Adrian Gonzalez .50 1.25
42 Dustin Pedroia .60 1.50
43 Mike Mussina .50 1.25
44 Clayton Kershaw 1.00 2.50
45 Jeff Bagwell .50 1.25
46 Jered Weaver .50 1.25
47 Ivan Rodriguez .50 1.25
48 Manny Machado .60 1.50
49 Tom Glavine .50 1.25
50 Lou Brock .50 1.25
51 Yadier Molina .75 2.00
52 Ozzie Smith .75 2.00
53 Prince Fielder .50 1.25
54 Bob Gibson .50 1.25
55 John Smoltz .60 1.50
56 Don Mattingly 1.25 3.00
57 Nomar Garciaparra .50 1.25
58 Rod Carew .50 1.25
59 Bo Jackson .60 1.50
60 Babe Ruth 1.50 4.00
61 Miguel Cabrera .60 1.50
62 Mike Schmidt 1.00 2.50
63 Roger Clemens .75 2.00
64 Mike Trout 3.00 8.00
65 Pedro Martinez .50 1.25
66 Nolan Ryan 2.00 5.00
67 Robin Yount .50 1.25
68 Randy Johnson .60 1.50
69 Troy Tulowitzki .60 1.50
70 Rickey Henderson .60 1.50
71 Greg Maddux .75 2.00
72 Bryce Harper 1.00 2.50
73 Willie Mays 1.25 3.00
74 Mark McGwire 1.25 3.00
75 Yu Darvish .60 1.50
76 Sandy Koufax 1.25 3.00
77 Ken Griffey Jr. 1.25 3.00
78 Andrew Lambo RC .40 1.00
79 Cal Ripken Jr. 2.00 5.00
80 Hank Aaron 1.25 3.00
81 Devin Mesoraco .40 1.00
82 Oswaldo Arcia .40 1.00
83 Tony Cingrani .50 1.25
84 Mike Olt .40 1.00
85 Alex Cobb .40 1.00
86 Hisashi Iwakuma .50 1.25
87 Jean Segura .50 1.25
88 Felix Doubront .40 1.00
89 Jedd Gyorko .40 1.00
90 Yonder Alonso .40 1.00
91 Domonic Brown .50 1.25
92 Ryan Braun .50 1.25
93 R.A. Dickey .50 1.25
94 Anthony Rizzo .75 2.00
95 Gio Gonzalez .50 1.25
96 Johnny Bench .60 1.50
97 Josh Hamilton .50 1.25
98 Matt Moore .50 1.25
99 Trevor Bauer .75 2.00
100 Tony Gwynn .60 1.50

2014 Topps Museum Collection Blue

*BLUE: 2X TO 5X BASIC
*BLUE RC: 2X TO 5X BASIC RC
STATED ODDS 1:8 PACKS
STATED PRINT RUN 99 SER.#'d SETS
9 Xander Bogaerts 12.00 30.00
64 Mike Trout 12.00 30.00
66 Nolan Ryan 12.00 30.00

2014 Topps Museum Collection Copper

*COPPER: .6X TO 1.5X BASIC
*COPPER RC: .6X TO 1.5X BASIC RC

2014 Topps Museum Collection Green

*GREEN: 1.2X TO 3X BASIC
*GREEN RC: 1.2X TO 3X BASIC RC
STATED ODDS 1:4 PACKS
STATED PRINT RUN 199 SER.#'d SETS

2014 Topps Museum Collection Autographs

PRINT RUNS B/WN 10-399 COPIES PER
NO PRICING ON QTY 15 OR LESS
EXCHANGE DEADLINE 2/24/2016
AAABE Albert Belle/99 6.00 15.00
AAACO Alex Cobb/399 4.00 10.00
AAACR Allen Craig/399 6.00 15.00
AAAGO Adrian Gonzalez/25 6.00 15.00
AAAGOS Anthony Gose/399 4.00 10.00
AAAR Anthony Rizzo/399 15.00 40.00
AABHAM Billy Hamilton/399 5.00 12.00
AACK Clayton Kershaw/25 50.00 120.00
AACR Cal Ripken Jr. EXCH 90.00 150.00
AACS Chris Sale/99 12.00 30.00
AACY Christian Yelich/399 20.00 50.00
AADF David Freese/99 4.00 10.00
AADG Didi Gregorius/399 6.00 15.00
AADME Devin Mesoraco/399 6.00 15.00
AADO David Ortiz/199 40.00 100.00
AADP Dustin Pedroia/25 40.00 80.00
AADR Darin Ruf/399 5.00 12.00
AAFD Felix Doubront/399 4.00 10.00
AAHA Hank Aaron EXCH 150.00 250.00
AAHI Hisashi Iwakuma/199 8.00 20.00
AAJA Jose Abreu/25 20.00 50.00
AAJC Jose Canseco/99 12.00 30.00
AAJH Josh Hamilton/199 5.00 12.00
AAJK Jason Kipnis/399 5.00 12.00
AAJP Jurickson Profar/399 6.00 15.00
AAJR Jim Rice/99 6.00 15.00
AAJS Jean Segura/199 5.00 12.00
AAJSH James Shields/99 4.00 10.00
AAJTE Julio Teheran/399 5.00 12.00
AAJZ Jordan Zimmermann/99 5.00 12.00
AAKM Kris Medlen/399 5.00 12.00
AAKS Kyle Seager/399 4.00 10.00
AALB Lou Brock/99 20.00 50.00
AAMA Matt Adams/399 4.00 10.00
AAMMO Matt Moore/399 5.00 12.00
AAMMU Mike Mussina EXCH 15.00 40.00
AAMO Mike Olt/399 4.00 10.00
AAMZ Mike Zunino/399 4.00 10.00
AANC Nick Castellanos/399 12.00 30.00
AAPG Paul Goldschmidt/399 25.00 60.00
AAPO Paul O'Neill/99 12.00 30.00
AARB Ryan Braun/49 10.00 25.00
AARN Ricky Nolasco/399 4.00 10.00
AARP Rafael Palmeiro/99 8.00 20.00
AASC Steve Carlton/99 10.00 25.00
AASCI Steve Cishek/399 4.00 10.00
AASMI Shelby Miller/399 5.00 12.00
AATB Trevor Bauer/399 8.00 20.00
AATC Tony Cingrani/399 5.00 12.00
AATD Travis d'Arnaud/399 6.00 15.00
AATF Todd Frazier/399 5.00 12.00
AATGL Tom Glavine EXCH 30.00 60.00
AATGW Tony Gwynn/49 30.00 60.00
AATS Tyler Skaggs/399 4.00 10.00
AATW Taijuan Walker/399 4.00 10.00
AAWC Will Clark/99 15.00 40.00
AAWMI Wade Miley/399 4.00 10.00
AAWMY Wil Myers/260 4.00 10.00
AAWR Wilin Rosario/399 4.00 10.00
AAYC Yoenis Cespedes/399 4.00 10.00
AAZW Zack Wheeler/399 5.00 12.00

2014 Topps Museum Collection Canvas Collection

STATED ODDS 1:4 PACKS
CCR1 Mike Trout 5.00 12.00
CCR2 Deion Sanders .75 2.00
CCR3 Yu Darvish 1.00 2.50
CCR4 Bo Jackson 1.00 2.50
CCR5 Joe Mauer .75 2.00
CCR6 Stephen Strasburg 1.00 2.50
CCR7 Nolan Ryan 3.00 8.00
CCR8 Roberto Clemente 2.50 6.00
CCR9 Robinson Cano .75 2.00
CCR10 Mark McGwire 2.00 5.00
CCR11 Miguel Cabrera 1.00 2.50
CCR12 Yoenis Cespedes 1.00 2.50
CCR13 Don Mattingly 2.00 5.00
CCR14 Bryce Harper 1.50 4.00
CCR15 Tommy Lasorda .75 2.00
CCR16 Andrew McCutchen 1.00 2.50
CCR17 Tony Gwynn 1.00 2.50
CCR18 Matt Harvey .75 2.00
CCR19 Pedro Martinez .75 2.00
CCR20 Ernie Banks 1.00 2.50
CCR21 Tom Seaver .75 2.00
CCR22 Wade Boggs .75 2.00
CCR23 David Ortiz 1.00 2.50
CCR24 Brooks Robinson .75 2.00
CCR25 Ozzie Smith 1.25 3.00
CCR26 CC Sabathia .75 2.00
CCR27 Randy Johnson 1.00 2.50
CCR28 Ted Williams 2.00 5.00
CCR29 Jimmie Foxx 1.00 2.50
CCR30 Lou Brock .75 2.00
CCR31 Rickey Henderson 1.00 2.50
CCR32 Yogi Berra 1.00 2.50
CCR33 Dwight Gooden .60 1.50
CCR34 Paul Molitor 1.00 2.50
CCR35 Jackie Robinson 1.00 2.50
CCR36 Robin Yount 1.00 2.50
CCR37 Johnny Bench 1.00 2.50
CCR38 Ty Cobb 1.50 4.00
CCR39 Cal Ripken Jr. 3.00 8.00
CCR40 Justin Verlander 1.00 2.50
CCR41 Yogi Berra 1.00 2.50
CCR42 Reggie Jackson .75 2.00
CCR43 Lou Gehrig 2.00 5.00
CCR44 Johnny Bench 1.00 2.50
CCR45 Buster Posey 1.25 3.00
CCR46 Jose Fernandez 1.00 2.50
CCR47 Darryl Strawberry .60 1.50
CCR48 Lou Brock .75 2.00
CCR49 Joey Votto 1.00 2.50
CCR50 David Wright .75 2.00

2014 Topps Museum Collection Canvas Collection Jumbo

STATED ODDS 1:39 BOXES
STATED PRINT RUN 25 SER.#'d SETS
EXCAHNGE DEADLINE 2/24/2016
CCFAAM Andrew McCutchen EXCH 30.00 80.00
CCFABH Bryce Harper 25.00 60.00
CCFABJ Bo Jackson 30.00 80.00
CCFABP Buster Posey 30.00 80.00
CCFACR Cal Ripken Jr. 30.00 80.00
CCFADM Don Mattingly 20.00 50.00
CCFADO David Ortiz EXCH 30.00 80.00
CCFADS Deion Sanders EXCH 25.00 60.00
CCFAEB Ernie Banks 25.00 60.00
CCFAMC Miguel Cabrera EXCH 20.00 50.00
CCFAMM Mark McGwire 40.00 100.00
CCFAMT Mike Trout 50.00 120.00
CCFANR Nolan Ryan 30.00 80.00
CCFARC Robinson Cano 8.00 20.00
CCFARH Rickey Henderson 20.00 50.00
CCFARJ Randy Johnson EXCH 25.00 60.00
CCFATG Tony Gwynn 20.00 50.00
CCFATS Tom Seaver 15.00 40.00
CCFAYC Yoenis Cespedes 15.00 40.00
CCFAYD Yu Darvish EXCH 25.00 60.00

2014 Topps Museum Collection Jumbo Lumber

STATED ODDS 1:41 PACKS
STATED PRINT RUN 25 SER.#'d SETS
MMJLAB Adrian Beltre 10.00 25.00
MMJLABE Albert Belle 8.00 20.00
MMJLAD Andre Dawson 10.00 25.00
MMJLAJ Adam Jones 12.00 30.00
MMJLBP Brandon Phillips 10.00 25.00
MMJLBR Brooks Robinson 15.00 40.00
MMJLCB Carlos Beltran 8.00 20.00
MMJLCD Chris Davis 15.00 40.00
MMJLCDA Chris Davis 15.00 40.00
MMJLCG Cole Gillespie 6.00 15.00
MMJLCK Clayton Kershaw 15.00 40.00
MMJLCR Cal Ripken Jr. 20.00 50.00
MMJLDJ Derek Jeter 30.00 80.00
MMJLDJE Derek Jeter 30.00 80.00
MMJLDJT Derek Jeter 30.00 80.00
MMJLDM Don Mattingly 25.00 60.00
MMJLDMA Don Mattingly 25.00 60.00
MMJLDO David Ortiz 12.00 30.00
MMJLDOR David Ortiz 12.00 30.00
MMJLDS Drew Stubbs 6.00 15.00
MMJLDW David Wright 20.00 50.00
MMJLEL Evan Longoria 8.00 20.00
MMJLELO Evan Longoria 8.00 20.00
MMJLEM Eddie Mathews 20.00 50.00
MMJLEMD Eddie Murray 10.00 25.00
MMJLEMU Eddie Murray 10.00 25.00
MMJLFM Fred McGriff 10.00 25.00
MMJLHR Hyun-jin Ryu 8.00 20.00
MMJLIK Ian Kinsler 8.00 20.00
MMJLIR Ivan Rodriguez 8.00 20.00
MMJLJB Jay Bruce 10.00 25.00
MMJLJBE Johnny Bench 12.00 30.00
MMJLJBR Jay Bruce 10.00 25.00
MMJLJF Juan Francisco 6.00 15.00
MMJLJG Juan Gonzalez 30.00 80.00
MMJLJJ Jon Jay 8.00 20.00
MMJLJU Justin Upton 8.00 20.00
MMJLJUP Justin Upton 8.00 20.00
MMJLJV Joey Votto 20.00 50.00
MMJLJZ Jordan Zimmermann 8.00 20.00
MMJLMH Matt Harvey 8.00 20.00
MMJLMK Matt Kemp 8.00 20.00
MMJLMM Manny Machado 10.00 25.00
MMJLMN Mike Napoli 12.00 30.00
MMJLMS Mike Schmidt 15.00 40.00
MMJLMSC Mike Schmidt 15.00 40.00
MMJLMSI Mike Schmidt 15.00 40.00
MMJLMT Mark Teixeira 8.00 20.00
MMJLMTE Mark Teixeira 8.00 20.00
MMJLMTR Mike Trout 50.00 120.00
MMJLMZ Mike Zunino 12.00 30.00
MMJLNR Nolan Ryan 50.00 120.00
MMJLNRY Nolan Ryan 50.00 120.00
MMJLNS Nick Swisher 10.00 25.00
MMJLOC Orlando Cepeda 15.00 40.00
MMJLPF Prince Fielder 12.00 30.00
MMJLPM Paul Molitor 8.00 20.00
MMJLRC Roberto Clemente 100.00 175.00
MMJLRC Rod Carew 8.00 20.00
MMJLRH Ryan Howard 20.00 50.00
MMJLRJ Reggie Jackson 12.00 30.00
MMJLRY Robin Yount 8.00 20.00
MMJLSC Starlin Castro 6.00 15.00
MMJLSG Steve Garvey 30.00 80.00
MMJLTD Travis d'Arnaud 8.00 20.00
MMJLTG Tony Gwynn 15.00 40.00
MMJLTGW Tony Gwynn 15.00 40.00
MMJLTGY Tony Gwynn 15.00 40.00
MMJLTT Troy Tulowitzki 10.00 25.00
MMJLWB Wade Boggs 10.00 25.00
MMJLWM Willie McCovey 15.00 40.00
MMJLWMA Willie Mays 30.00 60.00
MMJLWMC Willie McCovey 15.00 40.00
MMJLWMI Willie McCovey 15.00 40.00
MMJLZW Zack Wheeler 8.00 20.00

2014 Topps Museum Collection Momentous Material Jumbo Relics

STATED ODDS 1:10 PACKS
STATED PRINT RUN 50 SER.#'d SETS
MMJRAB Adrian Beltre 6.00 15.00
MMJRAC Alex Cobb 4.00 10.00
MMJRACH Aroldis Chapman 6.00 15.00
MMJRAD Adam Dunn 5.00 12.00
MMJRAE Adam Eaton 4.00 10.00
MMJRAEL A.J. Ellis 4.00 10.00
MMJRAG Alex Gordon 8.00 20.00
MMJRAH Adeiny Hechavarria 4.00 10.00
MMJRAL Adam Lind 5.00 12.00
MMJRAM Andrew McCutchen 25.00 60.00
MMJRAMC Andrew McCutchen 25.00 60.00
MMJRAP Andy Pettitte 5.00 12.00
MMJRAPU Albert Pujols 8.00 20.00
MMJRAR Alex Rodriguez 8.00 20.00
MMJRAW Adam Wainwright 5.00 12.00
MMJRBB Billy Butler 4.00 10.00
MMJRBBE Brandon Beachy 4.00 10.00
MMJRBG Brett Gardner 8.00 20.00
MMJRBH Billy Hamilton 8.00 20.00
MMJRBHA Bryce Harper 10.00 25.00
MMJRBHI Billy Hamilton 8.00 20.00
MMJRBL Brett Lawrie 5.00 12.00
MMJRBM Brian McCann 5.00 12.00
MMJRBMO Brandon Morrow 4.00 10.00
MMJRBP Buster Posey 8.00 20.00
MMJRBR Bruce Rondon 4.00 10.00
MMJRBU B.J. Upton 5.00 12.00
MMJRCA Chris Archer 4.00 10.00
MMJRCB Chad Billingsley 5.00 12.00
MMJRCBE Carlos Beltran 6.00 15.00
MMJRCBU Clay Buchholz 4.00 10.00
MMJRCC CC Sabathia 5.00 12.00
MMJRCG Curtis Granderson 5.00 12.00
MMJRCGO Carlos Gonzalez 6.00 15.00
MMJRCH Chase Headley 4.00 10.00
MMJRCHA Cole Hamels 5.00 12.00
MMJRCK Craig Kimbrel 5.00 12.00
MMJRCO Chris Owings 4.00 10.00
MMJRCR Carlos Ruiz 4.00 10.00
MMJRCS Chris Sale 6.00 15.00
MMJRCSA Carlos Santana 5.00 12.00
MMJRCW C.J. Wilson 4.00 10.00
MMJRDB Domonic Brown 5.00 12.00
MMJRDF David Freese 4.00 10.00
MMJRDG Didi Gregorius 5.00 12.00
MMJRDGR Didi Gregorius 5.00 12.00
MMJRDJ Derek Jeter 40.00 80.00
MMJRDJE Desmond Jennings 5.00 12.00
MMJRDO David Ortiz 8.00 20.00
MMJRDS Drew Storen 4.00 10.00
MMJRDW David Wright 12.00 30.00
MMJRDWR David Wright 12.00 30.00
MMJREA Elvis Andrus 5.00 12.00
MMJREE Edwin Encarnacion 6.00 15.00
MMJREH Eric Hosmer 6.00 15.00
MMJREL Evan Longoria 6.00 15.00
MMJRELO Evan Longoria 6.00 15.00
MMJREN Eduardo Nunez 4.00 10.00
MMJRFF Freddie Freeman 10.00 25.00
MMJRFFR Freddie Freeman 10.00 25.00
MMJRFH Felix Hernandez 6.00 15.00
MMJRFM Fred McGriff 5.00 12.00
MMJRGB Gordon Beckham 4.00 10.00
MMJRGC Gerrit Cole 8.00 20.00
MMJRGS Gary Sheffield 6.00 15.00
MMJRGST Giancarlo Stanton 6.00 15.00
MMJRHK Hiroki Kuroda 8.00 20.00
MMJRHP Hunter Pence 8.00 20.00
MMJRHR Hanley Ramirez 5.00 12.00
MMJRID Ike Davis 4.00 10.00
MMJRIN Ivan Nova 5.00 12.00
MMJRJA Jose Altuve 5.00 12.00
MMJRJB Jackie Bradley Jr. 8.00 20.00
MMJRJBA Jose Bautista 5.00 12.00
MMJRJBR Jay Bruce 5.00 12.00
MMJRJC Jhoulys Chacin 4.00 10.00
MMJRJCH Joba Chamberlain 4.00 10.00
MMJRJH Jeremy Hellickson 4.00 10.00
MMJRJHA Josh Hamilton 5.00 12.00
MMJRJL Jon Lester 5.00 12.00
MMJRJM Justin Masterson 4.00 10.00
MMJRJN Joe Nathan 4.00 10.00
MMJRJPA Jarrod Parker 4.00 10.00
MMJRJPE Jhonny Peralta 4.00 10.00
MMJRJPH Jordan Pacheco 4.00 10.00
MMJRJS Jean Segura 5.00 12.00
MMJRJSA Jarrod Saltalamacchia 4.00 10.00
MMJRJU Justin Upton 6.00 15.00
MMJRJV Joey Votto 6.00 15.00
MMJRJVE Justin Verlander 6.00 15.00
MMJRJW Jayson Werth 5.00 12.00
MMJRJZ Jordan Zimmermann 5.00 12.00
MMJRJZI Jordan Zimmermann 5.00 12.00
MMJRKH Kelvin Herrera 4.00 10.00
MMJRKHE Kelvin Herrera 4.00 10.00
MMJRKM Kris Medlen 8.00 20.00
MMJRKN Kirk Nieuwenhuis 4.00 10.00
MMJRKS Kyle Seager 4.00 10.00
MMJRLM Logan Morrison 4.00 10.00
MMJRMA Matt Adams 6.00 15.00
MMJRMAD Matt Adams 6.00 15.00
MMJRMB Madison Bumgarner 8.00 20.00
MMJRMC Matt Cain 8.00 20.00
MMJRMH Matt Harvey 10.00 25.00
MMJRMHA Matt Harrison 4.00 10.00
MMJRMHO Matt Holliday 10.00 25.00
MMJRMK Matt Kemp 5.00 12.00
MMJRML Mat Latos 5.00 12.00
MMJRMM Manny Machado 12.00 30.00
MMJRMMI Mike Minor 4.00 10.00
MMJRMMO Mitch Moreland 4.00 10.00
MMJRMMU Mike Mussina 5.00 12.00
MMJRMR Mariano Rivera 8.00 20.00
MMJRMS Max Scherzer 8.00 20.00
MMJRMT Mike Trout 25.00 60.00
MMJRMV Matt Davidson 5.00 12.00
MMJRMW Michael Wacha 10.00 25.00
MMJRNA Nolan Arenado 6.00 15.00
MMJRNAR Nolan Arenado 6.00 15.00
MMJRNC Nick Castellanos 8.00 20.00
MMJRNCA Nick Castellanos 8.00 20.00
MMJRNF Nick Franklin 4.00 10.00
MMJRPA Pedro Alvarez 8.00 20.00
MMJRPC Patrick Corbin 5.00 12.00
MMJRPF Prince Fielder 5.00 12.00
MMJRPG Paul Goldschmidt 10.00 25.00
MMJRPGO Paul Goldschmidt 10.00 25.00
MMJRPH Phil Hughes 4.00 10.00
MMJRPS Pablo Sandoval 8.00 20.00
MMJRRB Ryan Braun 5.00 12.00
MMJRRBR Rob Brantly 4.00 10.00
MMJRRC Roberto Clemente 50.00 100.00
MMJRRD R.A. Dickey 5.00 12.00
MMJRRHO Ryan Howard 8.00 20.00
MMJRRV Ryan Vogelsong 6.00 15.00
MMJRRW Rickie Weeks 4.00 10.00
MMJRRZ Ryan Zimmerman 6.00 15.00
MMJRRZI Ryan Zimmerman 6.00 15.00
MMJRSM Shelby Miller 10.00 25.00
MMJRSMA Starling Marte 10.00 25.00
MMJRSP Salvador Perez 5.00 12.00
MMJRSS Stephen Strasburg 8.00 20.00
MMJRTC Tony Cingrani 5.00 12.00
MMJRTD Travis d'Arnaud 5.00 12.00
MMJRTG Tony Gwynn 10.00 25.00
MMJRTH Torii Hunter 4.00 10.00
MMJRTL Tim Lincecum 5.00 12.00
MMJRTT Troy Tulowitzki 6.00 15.00
MMJRUJ Ubaldo Jimenez 4.00 10.00
MMJRVM Victor Martinez 6.00 15.00
MMJRWB Wade Boggs 10.00 25.00
MMJRWM Wade Miley 4.00 10.00
MMJRWMY Wil Myers 12.00 30.00
MMJRWR Wilin Rosario 4.00 10.00
MMJRYA Yonder Alonso 4.00 10.00
MMJRYM Yadier Molina 12.00 30.00
MMJRZC Zack Cozart 4.00 10.00
MMJRZW Zack Wheeler 5.00 12.00

2014 Topps Museum Collection Momentous Material Jumbo Relics Gold

*GOLD: .4X TO 1X BASIC
STATED ODDS 1:14 PACKS
STATED PRINT RUN 35 SER.#'d SETS

2014 Topps Museum Collection Primary Pieces Four Player Quad Relics

STATED ODDS 1:32 PACKS
STATED PRINT RUN 99 SER.#'d SETS
PPFQR1 Parker/Miller/Ryu/Sale 8.00 20.00
PPFQR3 Rosario/McCann/Santana/Perez 6.00 15.00
PPFQR4 Field/Puj/Freem/Goldsc 10.00 25.00
PPFQR5 Utley/Carpenter/Cano/Pedroia 8.00 20.00
PPFQR6 Lngria/Bltr/Cab/Wright 8.00 20.00
PPFQR8 Hey/Stant/Gonz/Harp 12.00 30.00
PPFQR9 Jones/Ellsb/McCut/Trout 40.00 80.00
PPFQR10 Bourn/Upton/Granderson/Kemp 6.00 15.00
PPFQR11 Myers/Price/Hellic/Cobb 6.00 15.00
PPFQR14 Matt/Riv/Jeter/Pettitte 30.00 80.00
PPFQR15 d'Arn/Davis/Harv/Wheel 12.00 30.00
PPFQR16 Pujols/Trum/Trout/Ham 20.00 50.00
PPFQR17 Jone/Dav/Gaus/Mach 20.00 50.00
PPFQR18 Arcia/Hicks/Mauer/Parmelee 6.00 15.00
PPFQR19 Swish/Kip/Bourn/Sant 8.00 20.00
PPFQR20 Scher/Verlan/Field/Cab 15.00 40.00
PPFQR21 Darvish/Sale/Hernandez
Kershaw 10.00 25.00
PPFQR22 McCut/Alvar/Cole/Marte 25.00 60.00
PPFQR23 Beltre/Kinsler/Darvish/Andrus 8.00 20.00
PPFQR24 Belt/Wain/Frees/Miller 6.00 15.00
PPFQR25 Tulowitzki/Gonzalez
Rosario/Chacin 10.00 25.00
PPFQR26 Rasmus/Morrow
Encarnacion/Bautista 8.00 20.00
PPFQR27 Roll/Utley/Hamel/Halla 12.00 30.00
PPFQR28 Beltre/Darvish
Gonzalez/Rodriguez 8.00 20.00
PPFQR30 Grnk/Krshw/Puig/Kemp 12.00 30.00

2014 Topps Museum Collection Primary Pieces Four Player Quad Relics Copper

*COPPER: .4X TO 1X BASIC
STATED ODDS 1:41 PACKS
STATED PRINT RUN 75 SER.#'d SETS

2014 Topps Museum Collection Primary Pieces Four Player Quad Relics Gold

*GOLD: .5X TO 1.2X BASIC
STATED ODDS 1:123 PACKS
STATED PRINT RUN 25 SER.#'d SETS

2014 Topps Museum Collection Primary Pieces Legends Quad Relics

STATED ODDS 1:154 PACKS
STATED PRINT RUN 25 SER.#'d SETS
PPQRLBR Brooks Robinson 15.00 40.00
PPQRLBRU Babe Ruth 250.00 350.00
PPQRLCR Cal Ripken Jr. 30.00 80.00
PPQRLDM Don Mattingly 25.00 60.00
PPQRLDS Duke Snider 20.00 50.00
PPQRLEM Eddie Murray 10.00 25.00
PPQRLFJ Fergie Jenkins 10.00 25.00
PPQRLFM Fred McGriff 10.00 25.00
PPQRLMR Mariano Rivera 20.00 50.00
PPQRLMS Mike Schmidt 20.00 50.00
PPQRLOC Orlando Cepeda 10.00 25.00
PPQRLRC Rod Carew 10.00 25.00
PPQRLRCL Roberto Clemente 75.00 150.00
PPQRLRJ Randy Johnson 12.00 30.00
PPQRLRK Ralph Kiner 10.00 25.00
PPQRLSC Steve Carlton 10.00 25.00
PPQRLTGY Tony Gwynn 12.00 30.00
PPQRLWB Wade Boggs 20.00 50.00
PPQRLWM Willie McCovey 20.00 50.00

2014 Topps Museum Collection Primary Pieces Quad Relics

STATED ODDS 1:12 PACKS
STATED PRINT RUN 99 SER.#'d SETS
PPQRAC Alex Cobb 4.00 10.00
PPQRAM Andrew McCutchen 30.00 80.00
PPQRAP Andy Pettitte 8.00 20.00
PPQRAPJ Albert Pujols 10.00 25.00
PPQRAR Alex Rodriguez 10.00 25.00
PPQRARI Alexei Ramirez 5.00 12.00
PPQRARZ Aramis Ramirez 4.00 10.00
PPQRBH Bryce Harper 15.00 40.00
PPQRBHM Billy Hamilton 5.00 12.00
PPQRBM Brian McCann 5.00 12.00
PPQRBP Buster Posey 12.00 30.00
PPQRBPH Troy Tulowitzki 10.00 25.00
PPQRCB Carlos Beltran 8.00 20.00
PPQRCC CC Sabathia 5.00 12.00
PPQRCCS CC Sabathia 5.00 12.00
PPQRCD Chris Davis 12.00 30.00
PPQRCG Curtis Granderson 5.00 12.00
PPQRCGO Carlos Gonzalez 5.00 12.00
PPQRCH Cole Hamels 5.00 12.00
PPQRCK Craig Kimbrel 10.00 25.00
PPQRCKE Clayton Kershaw 6.00 15.00
PPQRCS Chris Sale 6.00 15.00
PPQRDB Domonic Brown 5.00 12.00
PPQRDH Dan Haren 4.00 10.00
PPQRDO David Ortiz 10.00 25.00
PPQRDS Darryl Strawberry 6.00 15.00
PPQRDS Drew Stubbs 4.00 10.00
PPQRDW David Wright 8.00 20.00
PPQREC Edwin Encarnacion 6.00 15.00
PPQRFF Freddie Freeman 8.00 20.00
PPQRFH Felix Hernandez 6.00 15.00
PPQRGC Gerrit Cole 8.00 20.00
PPQRGG Gio Gonzalez 5.00 12.00
PPQRHC Hank Conger 4.00 10.00
PPQRHP Hunter Pence 8.00 20.00
PPQRJB Jay Bruce 5.00 12.00
PPQRJBU Jose Bautista 5.00 12.00
PPQRJH Jeremy Hellickson 4.00 10.00
PPQRJS James Shields 4.00 10.00
PPQRJV Joey Votto 6.00 15.00
PPQRJVE Justin Verlander 10.00 25.00
PPQRKM Kris Medlen 5.00 12.00
PPQRMA Matt Adams 6.00 15.00
PPQRMC Matt Cain 5.00 12.00
PPQRMH Matt Harvey 12.00 30.00

PPQRMK Matt Kemp 5.00 12.00
PPQRML Mike Leake 4.00 10.00
PPQRMM Manny Machado 12.00 30.00
PPQRMR Mariano Rivera 15.00 40.00
PPQRMS Max Scherzer 6.00 15.00
PPQRPG Paul Goldschmidt 10.00 25.00
PPQRPS Pablo Sandoval 6.00 15.00
PPQRRW Rickie Weeks 4.00 10.00
PPQRSM Starling Marte 8.00 20.00
PPQRSML Shelby Miller 5.00 12.00
PPQRSP Salvador Perez 12.00 30.00
PPQRSS Stephen Strasburg 8.00 20.00
PPQRTG Tony Gwynn 6.00 15.00
PPQRTL Tim Lincecum 5.00 12.00
PPQRYM Yadier Molina 10.00 25.00
PPQRYP Yasiel Puig 10.00 25.00
PPQRZG Zack Greinke 6.00 15.00
PPQRZW Zack Wheeler 10.00 25.00
PPQRMSC Mike Schmidt 10.00 25.00

2014 Topps Museum Collection Primary Pieces Quad Relics Copper

*COPPER: .4X TO 1X BASIC
STATED ODDS 1:16 PACKS
STATED PRINT RUN 75 SER.#'d SETS

2014 Topps Museum Collection Primary Pieces Quad Relics Gold

*GOLD: .5X TO 1.2X BASIC
STATED ODDS 1:146 PACKS
STATED PRINT RUN 25 SER.#'d SETS

2014 Topps Museum Collection Signature Swatches Dual Relic Autographs

STATED ODDS 1:10 PACKS
PRINT RUNS B/WN 50-299 COPIES PER
EXCHANGE DEADLINE 2/24/2016
SSDAB Albert Belle/99 10.00 25.00
SSDAC Allen Craig/99 6.00 15.00
SSDAGA Avisail Garcia/299 6.00 15.00
SSDAGO Adrian Gonzalez/50 15.00 40.00
SSDBH Billy Hamilton/299 6.00 15.00
SSDCK Clayton Kershaw EXCH 40.00 80.00
SSDCS Chris Sale/99 15.00 40.00
SSDCY Christian Yelich/299 25.00 60.00
SSDDB Domonic Brown/50 12.00 30.00
SSDDF David Freese/99 5.00 12.00
SSDDG Didi Gregorius/99 6.00 15.00
SSDDMS Devin Mesoraco/299 8.00 20.00
SSDDO David Ortiz/99 30.00 60.00
SSDDP Dustin Pedroia/50 20.00 50.00
SSDDW David Wright/50 20.00 50.00
SSDFD Felix Doubront/299 5.00 12.00
SSDIR Ivan Rodriguez/50 12.00 30.00
SSDJB Jeff Bagwell/50 20.00 50.00
SSDJBC Johnny Bench/99 20.00 50.00
SSDJG Juan Gonzalez/99 10.00 25.00
SSDJGK Jedd Gyorko/299 5.00 12.00
SSDJH Josh Hamilton/99 10.00 25.00
SSDJP Jurickson Profar/189 6.00 15.00
SSDJR Jim Rice/99 10.00 25.00
SSDJS James Shields/99 5.00 12.00
SSDJSE Jean Segura/99 4.00 10.00
SSDJSM John Smoltz/50 60.00 120.00
SSDJZ Jordan Zimmermann/99 6.00 15.00
SSDKM Kris Medlen/99 8.00 20.00
SSDKS Kyle Seager/299 5.00 12.00
SSDMA Matt Adams/299 5.00 12.00
SSDMM Manny Machado/50 50.00 100.00
SSDMMU Mike Mussina EXCH 15.00 40.00
SSDMO Mike Olt/99 8.00 20.00
SSDMZ Mike Zunino/199 8.00 20.00
SSDNC Nick Castellanos/299 15.00 40.00
SSDNG Nomar Garciaparra/50 12.00 30.00
SSDOS Ozzie Smith/50 30.00 60.00
SSDPG Paul Goldschmidt/199 12.00 30.00
SSDPO Paul O'Neill EXCH 12.00 30.00
SSDRB Ryan Braun/99 15.00 40.00
SSDRC Rod Carew/50 15.00 40.00
SSDRN Ricky Nolasco/106 5.00 12.00
SSDSC Steve Carlton/99 12.00 30.00
SSDSM Shelby Miller/99 6.00 15.00
SSDSMA Starling Marte/99 15.00 40.00
SSDTC Tony Cingrani/299 6.00 15.00
SSDTD Travis d'Arnaud/299 10.00 25.00
SSDTF Todd Frazier/199 5.00 12.00
SSDTG Tom Glavine/50 15.00 40.00
SSDTT Troy Tulowitzki 8.00 20.00
SSDTTU Troy Tulowitzki/299 8.00 20.00
SSDTW Taijuan Walker/299 6.00 15.00
SSDWC Will Clark/99 12.00 30.00
SSDWME Wil Myers/99 10.00 25.00
SSDWR Wilin Rosario/299 5.00 12.00
SSDYC Yoenis Cespedes/99 10.00 25.00
SSDYD Yu Darvish/25 60.00 150.00
SSDYM Yadier Molina EXCH 30.00 60.00

2014 Topps Museum Collection Signature Swatches Triple Relic Autographs

STATED ODDS 1:14 PACKS
PRINT RUNS B/WN 30-299 COPIES PER
EXCHANGE DEADLINE 2/24/2016
SSTAB Albert Belle EXCH 10.00 25.00
SSTAC Allen Craig/50 10.00 25.00
SSTBHL Billy Hamilton EXCH 12.00 30.00
SSTBHL2 Billy Hamilton EXCH 12.00 30.00
SSTBHL3 Billy Hamilton EXCH 12.00 30.00
SSTBJ Bo Jackson EXCH 40.00 80.00
SSTCS Chris Sale/299 10.00 25.00
SSTCS2 Chris Sale/121 15.00 40.00
SSTCY Christian Yelich/70 20.00 50.00
SSTDF David Freese EXCH 5.00 12.00
SSTDFR David Freese EXCH 5.00 12.00
SSTDG Didi Gregorius/299 6.00 15.00
SSTDM Devin Mesoraco/299 8.00 20.00
SSTDM2 Devin Mesoraco/70 8.00 20.00
SSTDO David Ortiz 30.00 60.00
SSTDP Dustin Pedroia/50 20.00 50.00
SSTEL Evan Longoria/50 30.00 60.00
SSTFD Felix Doubront/299 5.00 12.00
SSTFD2 Felix Doubront/70 5.00 12.00
SSTIR Ivan Rodriguez/110 12.00 30.00
SSTJG Juan Gonzalez/110 10.00 25.00
SSTJH Josh Hamilton/110 15.00 40.00
SSTJS Jean Segura/299 8.00 20.00
SSTMA Matt Adams/70 10.00 25.00
SSTMO Mike Olt/299 5.00 12.00
SSTMO2 Mike Olt/70 5.00 12.00
SSTNC Nick Castellanos/299 10.00 25.00
SSTSC Steve Carlton/150 12.00 30.00
SSTTD Travis d'Arnaud/289 10.00 25.00
SSTTD2 Travis d'Arnaud/70 10.00 25.00
SSTTG Tony Cingrani/299 8.00 20.00
SSTTG2 Tony Cingrani/269 8.00 20.00
SSTTGY Tony Gwynn/30 30.00 60.00
SSTWR Wilin Rosario/299 5.00 12.00
SSTWR2 Wilin Rosario/70 5.00 12.00
SSTYC Yoenis Cespedes/50 15.00 40.00
SSTYUD Yu Darvish EXCH 75.00 150.00

2014 Topps Museum Collection Signature Swatches Triple Relic Autographs Gold

*GOLD: .5X TO 1.2X BASIC
STATED ODDS 1:77 PACKS
STATED PRINT RUN 25 SER.#'d SETS
EXCHANGE DEADLINE 2/24/2016

2015 Topps Museum Collection

1 David Ortiz .75 2.00
2 Eric Hosmer .60 1.50
3 Roger Maris .75 2.00
4 Mariano Rivera 1.00 2.50
5 Yu Darvish .75 2.00
6 Shin-Soo Choo .60 1.50
7 Anthony Rendon .75 2.00
8 Anthony Rizzo 1.00 2.50
9 Adrian Beltre .75 2.00
10 Buster Posey 1.00 2.50
11 Ian Kinsler .60 1.50
12 Daniel Norris .50 1.25
13 Dilson Herrera .60 1.50
14 Brandon Belt .60 1.50
15 Matt Adams .50 1.25
16 Albert Pujols 1.00 2.50
17 Jose Altuve .60 1.50
18 Randy Johnson .75 2.00
19 Sandy Koufax 1.50 4.00
20 Joc Pederson RC 2.50 6.00
21 Rusney Castillo RC .75 2.00
22 Cal Ripken Jr. 2.50 6.00
23 Giancarlo Stanton .75 2.00
24 Maikel Franco RC .75 2.00
25 Derek Jeter 2.00 5.00
26 Roberto Clemente 2.00 5.00
27 Jimmie Foxx .75 2.00
28 Mark Teixeira .60 1.50
29 Madison Bumgarner .60 1.50
30 Stephen Strasburg .75 2.00
31 Brandon Finnegan .50 1.25
32 James Shields .50 1.25
33 Mike Schmidt 1.25 3.00
34 Miguel Cabrera .75 2.00
35 Dalton Pompey RC .75 2.00
36 Paul Goldschmidt .75 2.00
37 Warren Spahn .60 1.50
38 Nolan Ryan 2.50 6.00
39 Ryan Howard .60 1.50
40 Dustin Pedroia .75 2.00
41 Masahiro Tanaka .60 1.50
42 Mike Piazza .75 2.00
43 Matt Holliday .75 2.00
44 Jason Heyward .60 1.50
45 Johnny Cueto .60 1.50
46 Hyun-Jin Ryu .60 1.50
47 Yadier Molina 1.00 2.50
48 Reggie Jackson .60 1.50
49 Greg Maddux 1.00 2.50
50 Gregory Polanco .60 1.50
51 Mike Trout 4.00 10.00
52 Jonathan Lucroy .60 1.50
53 Yasiel Puig .75 2.00
54 Roger Clemens 1.00 2.50
55 Prince Fielder .60 1.50
56 Phil Niekro .60 1.50
57 Michael Taylor .50 1.25
58 Fernando Rodney .50 1.25
59 Ken Griffey Jr. 1.50 4.00
60 Lou Gehrig 1.50 4.00
61 Clayton Kershaw 1.25 3.00
62 Ernie Banks .75 2.00
63 Felix Hernandez .60 1.50
64 Joe DiMaggio 1.50 4.00
65 Pablo Sandoval .60 1.50
66 Mike Moustakas .60 1.50
67 Max Scherzer .75 2.00
68 Joey Votto .75 2.00
69 Nelson Cruz .75 2.00
70 Tony Gwynn .75 2.00
71 David Wright .60 1.50
72 Freddie Freeman 1.00 2.50
73 Adam Wainwright .60 1.50
74 Bryce Harper 1.25 3.00
75 Robinson Cano .60 1.50
76 Jacob deGrom 1.50 4.00
77 Jacoby Ellsbury .60 1.50
78 Andrew McCutchen .75 2.00
79 Troy Tulowitzki .75 2.00
80 Jackie Robinson .75 2.00
81 Adrian Gonzalez .60 1.50
82 Yoenis Cespedes .60 1.50
83 Ted Williams 1.50 4.00
84 Ryan Braun .60 1.50
85 Manny Machado .75 2.00
86 Francisco Liriano .50 1.25
87 Jeff Bagwell .60 1.50
88 Ty Cobb 1.25 3.00
89 Jose Bautista .60 1.50
90 Victor Martinez .60 1.50
91 Babe Ruth 2.00 5.00
92 Willie Mays 1.50 4.00
93 Hank Aaron 1.50 4.00
94 Johnny Bench .75 2.00
95 Jose Abreu .75 2.00
96 Javier Baez RC 5.00 12.00
97 Tom Seaver .60 1.50
98 Hanley Ramirez .60 1.50
99 Jorge Soler RC 1.00 2.50
100 Adam Jones .60 1.50

2015 Topps Museum Collection Blue

*BLUE: 2X TO 5X BASIC
*BLUE RC: 1.5X TO 4X BASIC RC
STATED ODDS 1:7 MINI BOXES
STATED PRINT RUN 99 SER.#'d SETS

2015 Topps Museum Collection Copper

*COPPER: .6X TO 1.5X BASIC
*COPPER RC: .5X TO 1.2X BASIC RC
RANDOM INSERTS IN MINI BOXES

2015 Topps Museum Collection Green

*GREEN: 1.2X TO 3X BASIC
*GREEN RC: 1X TO 2.5X BASIC RC
STATED ODDS 1:4 MINI BOXES
STATED PRINT RUN 199 SER.#'d SETS

2015 Topps Museum Collection Archival Autographs

PRINT RUNS B/WN 15-399 COPIES PER
NO PRICING ON QTY 15 OR LESS
EXCHANGE DEADLINE 3/31/2018
AAAD Andre Dawson/99 12.00 30.00
AAAG Adrian Gonzalez/99 5.00 12.00
AAARA Anthony Ranaudo/399 4.00 10.00
AAARI Anthony Rizzo/399 15.00 40.00
AABF Brandon Finnegan/399 4.00 10.00
AABJ Bo Jackson/25 50.00 120.00
AACA Chris Archer/399 4.00 10.00
AACB Craig Biggio/99 10.00 25.00
AACJC C.J. Cron/399 4.00 10.00
AACK Clayton Kershaw/99 50.00 120.00
AACR Cal Ripken Jr./25 40.00 100.00
AACS Chris Sale/99 8.00 20.00
AACY Christian Yelich/399 15.00 40.00
AADB Dellin Betances/399 5.00 12.00
AADC David Cone/199 4.00 10.00
AADE Dennis Eckersley/99 8.00 20.00
AADH Dilson Herrera/399 5.00 12.00
AADMT Don Mattingly/49 20.00 50.00
AADN Daniel Norris/399 4.00 10.00
AADO David Ortiz/25 25.00 60.00
AADP Dustin Pedroia/99 12.00 30.00
AADPO Dalton Pompey/399 5.00 12.00
AADW David Wright/25 12.00 30.00
AAFF Freddie Freeman/199 8.00 20.00
AAFV Fernando Valenzuela/99 15.00 40.00
AAGM Greg Maddux/25 60.00 150.00
AAJA Jose Abreu/99 20.00 50.00
AAJBZ Javier Baez/199 8.00 20.00
AAJC Jose Canseco/199 5.00 12.00
AAJDG Jacob deGrom/299 15.00 40.00
AAJF Jose Fernandez/99 15.00 40.00
AAJGO Juan Gonzalez/299 5.00 12.00
AAJH Jason Heyward/99 8.00 20.00
AAJP Joe Panik/399 5.00 12.00
AAJPE Joc Pederson/299 6.00 15.00
AAJPO Jorge Posada/99 20.00 50.00
AAJR Jim Rice/399 6.00 15.00
AAJS Jorge Soler/399 4.00 10.00
AAJSM John Smoltz/99 15.00 40.00
AAKG Ken Griffey Jr./25 150.00 250.00
AAKV Kennys Vargas/399 4.00 10.00
AAKW Kolten Wong/399 5.00 12.00
AAMAD Matt Adams/399 4.00 10.00
AAMBA Matt Barnes/399 4.00 10.00
AAMC Matt Carpenter/399 6.00 15.00
AAMMC Mark McGwire/25 60.00 150.00
AAMRI Mariano Rivera/25 75.00 200.00
AAMSC Mike Schmidt/25 50.00 120.00
AAMSH Max Scherzer/99 20.00 50.00
AAMTR Mike Trout/25 150.00 250.00
AAMW Michael Wacha/199 5.00 12.00
AANG Nomar Garciaparra/59 20.00 50.00
AAOH Orlando Hernandez/249 4.00 10.00
AAOS Ozzie Smith/59 25.00 60.00
AAOV Omar Vizquel/399 5.00 12.00
AAPG Paul Goldschmidt/199 8.00 20.00
AAPO Paul O'Neill/299 8.00 20.00
AAPP Yasiel Puig/25 40.00 100.00
AARA Roberto Alomar/99 10.00 25.00
AARB Ryan Braun/49 10.00 25.00
AARCA Robinson Cano/25 12.00 30.00
AARCR Rod Carew/99 12.00 30.00
AARCS Rusney Castillo/99 5.00 12.00
AARJO Randy Johnson/25 50.00 120.00
AARY Robin Yount/25 30.00 80.00
AASG Sonny Gray/399 6.00 15.00
AASMA Starling Marte/399 6.00 15.00
AATG Tom Glavine/99 15.00 40.00
AAVG Vladimir Guerrero/99 15.00 40.00
AAYC Yoenis Cespedes/99 10.00 25.00
AAYV Yordano Ventura/399 12.00 30.00

2015 Topps Museum Collection Canvas Collection

STATED ODDS 1:4 MINI BOXES
CCR01 Mike Piazza 1.00 2.50
CCR02 Ken Griffey Jr. 2.00 5.00
CCR03 John Smoltz 1.00 2.50
CCR04 Ken Griffey Jr. 2.00 5.00
CCR05 Nolan Ryan 3.00 8.00
CCR06 Dave Winfield .75 2.00
CCR07 Ivan Rodriguez .75 2.00
CCR08 Stephen Strasburg 1.00 2.50
CCR09 Mike Piazza 1.00 2.50
CCR10 Duke Snider .75 2.00
CCR11 Ozzie Smith 1.25 3.00
CCR12 Warren Spahn .75 2.00
CCR13 Wade Boggs .75 2.00
CCR14 Nolan Ryan 3.00 8.00
CCR15 Ozzie Smith 1.25 3.00
CCR16 Dave Winfield .75 2.00
CCR17 Nolan Ryan 3.00 8.00
CCR18 Johnny Bench 1.00 2.50
CCR19 Derek Jeter 2.50 6.00
CCR20 Harmon Killebrew 1.00 2.50
CCR21 Tom Seaver .75 2.00
CCR22 Jim Palmer .75 2.00
CCR23 Warren Spahn .75 2.00
CCR24 Phil Niekro .75 2.00
CCR25 Al Kaline 1.00 2.50
CCR26 Whitey Ford .75 2.00
CCR27 Wade Boggs .75 2.00
CCR28 George Brett 2.00 5.00
CCR29 Willie Mays 2.00 5.00
CCR30 Steve Carlton .75 2.00
CCR31 Roberto Clemente 2.50 6.00
CCR32 Mariano Rivera 1.25 3.00
CCR33 Don Mattingly 2.00 5.00
CCR34 Randy Johnson 1.00 2.50
CCR35 Chipper Jones 1.00 2.50
CCR36 Masahiro Tanaka .75 2.00
CCR37 Giancarlo Stanton 1.00 2.50
CCR38 Andrew McCutchen 1.00 2.50
CCR39 Clayton Kershaw 1.50 4.00
CCR40 Yasiel Puig 1.00 2.50
CCR41 Miguel Cabrera 1.00 2.50
CCR42 Albert Pujols 1.25 3.00
CCR43 David Ortiz 1.00 2.50
CCR44 Jose Abreu 1.00 2.50
CCR45 Yu Darvish 1.00 2.50
CCR46 Robinson Cano .75 2.00
CCR47 Jose Bautista .75 2.00
CCR48 Buster Posey 1.25 3.00
CCR49 Bryce Harper 1.50 4.00
CCR50 Manny Machado 1.00 2.50

2015 Topps Museum Collection Momentous Material Jumbo Relics

STATED ODDS 1:9 PACKS
STATED PRINT RUN 50 SER.#'d SETS
*COPPER/35: .4X TO 1X BASIC
MMJRAAA Alex Avila 6.00 15.00
MMJRABE Adrian Beltre 6.00 15.00
MMJRABL Adrian Beltre 6.00 15.00
MMJRACH Aroldis Chapman 6.00 15.00
MMJRAGN Alex Gordon 5.00 12.00
MMJRAGO Adrian Gonzalez 5.00 12.00
MMJRAGR Alex Gordon 5.00 12.00
MMJRAGZ Adrian Gonzalez 5.00 12.00
MMJRAJO Adam Jones 5.00 12.00
MMJRALD Adam Lind 5.00 12.00
MMJRAMN Andrew McCutchen 20.00 50.00
MMJRAMU Andrew McCutchen 20.00 50.00
MMJRARD Alex Rodriguez 10.00 25.00
MMJRARE Anthony Rendon 6.00 15.00
MMJRARN Anthony Rendon 6.00 15.00
MMJRARO Anthony Rizzo 8.00 20.00
MMJRARY Anthony Rizzo 8.00 20.00
MMJRARZ Alex Rodriguez 10.00 25.00
MMJRASI Andrelton Simmons 6.00 15.00
MMJRASZ Aaron Sanchez 5.00 12.00
MMJRAWR Adam Wainwright 8.00 20.00
MMJRBBR Billy Butler 4.00 10.00
MMJRBBU Billy Butler 4.00 10.00
MMJRBHA Bryce Harper 10.00 25.00
MMJRBHM Billy Hamilton 5.00 12.00
MMJRBHN Billy Hamilton 5.00 12.00
MMJRBM Brad Miller 5.00 12.00
MMJRBPS Brandon Phillips 4.00 10.00
MMJRCAN Aroldis Chapman 6.00 15.00
MMJRCBG Craig Biggio 8.00 20.00
MMJRCBO Craig Biggio 8.00 20.00
MMJRCBZ Clay Buchholz 4.00 10.00
MMJRCGN Carlos Gonzalez 5.00 12.00
MMJRCGO Carlos Gomez 4.00 10.00
MMJRCGZ Carlos Gonzalez 5.00 12.00
MMJRCJO Chipper Jones 8.00 20.00
MMJRCJS Chipper Jones 8.00 20.00
MMJRCKI Craig Kimbrel 5.00 12.00
MMJRCKL Craig Kimbrel 5.00 12.00
MMJRCKW Clayton Kershaw 10.00 25.00
MMJRCOS Chris Owings 4.00 10.00
MMJRCSA CC Sabathia 6.00 15.00
MMJRCSB CC Sabathia 6.00 15.00
MMJRCSE Chris Sale 6.00 15.00
MMJRCSL Chris Sale 6.00 15.00
MMJRCYE Christian Yelich 8.00 20.00
MMJRDJS Desmond Jennings 5.00 12.00
MMJRDMU Daniel Murphy 5.00 12.00
MMJRDMY Daniel Murphy 5.00 12.00
MMJRDOR David Ortiz 6.00 15.00
MMJRDOZ David Ortiz 6.00 15.00
MMJRDPD Dustin Pedroia 6.00 15.00
MMJRDPR David Price 6.00 15.00
MMJRDSN Drew Storen 4.00 10.00
MMJRDWR David Wright 12.00 30.00
MMJRDWT David Wright 12.00 30.00
MMJREAN Elvis Andrus 5.00 12.00
MMJREAS Elvis Andrus 5.00 12.00
MMJREHO Eric Hosmer 8.00 20.00
MMJRELA Evan Longoria 5.00 12.00
MMJRELO Evan Longoria 5.00 12.00
MMJRFFN Freddie Freeman 8.00 20.00
MMJRFFR Freddie Freeman 8.00 20.00
MMJRFHE Felix Hernandez 6.00 15.00
MMJRFHZ Felix Hernandez 6.00 15.00
MMJRGCE Gerrit Cole 6.00 15.00
MMJRGCO Gerrit Cole 6.00 15.00
MMJRGGZ Gio Gonzalez 5.00 12.00
MMJRGPL Gregory Polanco 8.00 20.00
MMJRGPO Gregory Polanco 8.00 20.00
MMJRGSN Giancarlo Stanton 8.00 20.00
MMJRGST Giancarlo Stanton 8.00 20.00
MMJRHER Eric Hosmer 8.00 20.00
MMJRHIW Hisashi Iwakuma 5.00 12.00
MMJRHRU Hyun-Jin Ryu 8.00 20.00
MMJRIKR Ian Kinsler 6.00 15.00
MMJRJBA Jose Bautista 5.00 12.00
MMJRJBC Jay Bruce 10.00 25.00
MMJRJBE Jay Bruce 10.00 25.00
MMJRJBG Jeff Bagwell 8.00 20.00
MMJRJBL Jeff Bagwell 8.00 20.00
MMJRJCO Johnny Cueto 5.00 12.00
MMJRJFE Jose Fernandez 6.00 15.00
MMJRJFZ Jose Fernandez 6.00 15.00
MMJRJHD Jason Heyward 6.00 15.00
MMJRJJY Jon Jay 4.00 10.00
MMJRJMA Joe Mauer 6.00 15.00
MMJRJMR Joe Mauer 6.00 15.00
MMJRJMY John Ryan Murphy 6.00 15.00
MMJRJPA Jorge Posada 5.00 12.00
MMJRJPI Joe Panik 20.00 50.00
MMJRJPK Joe Panik 20.00 50.00
MMJRJRK Josh Reddick 4.00 10.00
MMJRJRS Jose Reyes 5.00 12.00
MMJRJSA Jean Segura 5.00 12.00
MMJRJSG Jon Singleton 5.00 12.00
MMJRJSN Jon Singleton 5.00 12.00
MMJRJSP Jonathan Schoop 4.00 10.00
MMJRJUP Justin Upton 5.00 12.00
MMJRJVO Joey Votto 8.00 20.00
MMJRKUA Koji Uehara 4.00 10.00
MMJRMCA Miguel Cabrera 6.00 15.00
MMJRMCB Miguel Cabrera 6.00 15.00
MMJRMCD Michael Cuddyer 8.00 20.00
MMJRMCP Matt Carpenter 10.00 25.00
MMJRMCR Matt Carpenter 10.00 25.00
MMJRMCY Michael Cuddyer 8.00 20.00
MMJRMFO Maikel Franco 5.00 12.00
MMJRMHO Matt Holliday 6.00 15.00
MMJRMHY Matt Holliday 6.00 15.00
MMJRMKE Matt Kemp 5.00 12.00
MMJRMKP Matt Kemp 5.00 12.00
MMJRMLS Mat Latos 5.00 12.00
MMJRMMC Mark McGwire 10.00 25.00
MMJRMME Mark McGwire 10.00 25.00
MMJRMMK Mike Moustakas 5.00 12.00
MMJRMMO Manny Machado 10.00 25.00
MMJRMPA Mike Piazza 12.00 30.00
MMJRMPI Mike Piazza 12.00 30.00
MMJRMSR Max Scherzer 6.00 15.00
MMJRMSZ Max Scherzer 6.00 15.00
MMJRMTT Mike Trout 25.00 60.00
MMJRMWA Michael Wacha 5.00 12.00
MMJRNAO Nolan Arenado 10.00 25.00
MMJRNAR Nolan Arenado 10.00 25.00
MMJRNCR Nelson Cruz 6.00 15.00
MMJRNCS Nick Castellanos 6.00 15.00
MMJRNCZ Nelson Cruz 6.00 15.00
MMJRNGP Nomar Garciaparra 8.00 20.00
MMJRNWR Neil Walker 6.00 15.00
MMJRPGO Paul Goldschmidt 6.00 15.00
MMJRPGT Paul Goldschmidt 6.00 15.00
MMJRPKK Paul Konerko 8.00 20.00
MMJRPKO Paul Konerko 8.00 20.00
MMJRPSA Pablo Sandoval 5.00 12.00
MMJRPSL Pablo Sandoval 5.00 12.00
MMJRRHD Ryan Howard 5.00 12.00
MMJRRHO Ryan Howard 5.00 12.00
MMJRROR Rougned Odor 5.00 12.00
MMJRSCA Starlin Castro 4.00 10.00
MMJRSCH Shin-Soo Choo 5.00 12.00
MMJRSCO Shin-Soo Choo 5.00 12.00
MMJRSCS Starlin Castro 4.00 10.00
MMJRSGY Sonny Gray 5.00 12.00
MMJRSPE Salvador Perez 5.00 12.00
MMJRSPZ Salvador Perez 5.00 12.00
MMJRSSG Stephen Strasburg 6.00 15.00
MMJRSST Stephen Strasburg 6.00 15.00
MMJRTDA Travis d'Arnaud 6.00 15.00
MMJRTFR Todd Frazier 8.00 20.00
MMJRTHR Torii Hunter 4.00 10.00
MMJRTLM Tim Lincecum 5.00 12.00
MMJRVMA Victor Martinez 8.00 20.00
MMJRVMZ Victor Martinez 8.00 20.00
MMJRWBS Wade Boggs 5.00 12.00
MMJRWFL Wilmer Flores 5.00 12.00
MMJRWFS Wilmer Flores 5.00 12.00
MMJRWMS Will Middlebrooks 4.00 10.00
MMJRWMY Wil Myers 5.00 12.00
MMJRXBO Xander Bogaerts 10.00 25.00
MMJRXBS Xander Bogaerts 10.00 25.00
MMJRYCE Yoenis Cespedes 5.00 12.00
MMJRYCS Yoenis Cespedes 5.00 12.00
MMJRYDA Yu Darvish 10.00 25.00
MMJRYDH Yu Darvish 10.00 25.00
MMJRYPG Yasiel Puig 8.00 20.00
MMJRZGE Zack Greinke 6.00 15.00
MMJRZWR Zack Wheeler 5.00 12.00

2015 Topps Museum Collection Premium Prints Autographs

STATED ODDS 1:110 MINI BOXES
STATED PRINT RUN 25 SER.#'d SETS
EXCHANGE DEADLINE 3/31/2018
PPAD Andre Dawson 20.00 50.00
PPBJ Bo Jackson 60.00 150.00
PPBP Buster Posey EXCH 100.00 250.00
PPCB Craig Biggio 20.00 50.00
PPDMA Don Mattingly 40.00 100.00
PPDW David Wright 20.00 50.00
PPHA Hank Aaron 125.00 250.00
PPJA Jose Abreu 30.00 80.00
PPJB Jeff Bagwell EXCH 40.00 100.00
PPJC Jose Canseco 20.00 50.00
PPJG Juan Gonzalez 15.00 40.00
PPJP Jorge Posada 20.00 50.00
PPJR Jim Rice 20.00 50.00
PPJS John Smoltz 40.00 100.00
PPMC Miguel Cabrera EXCH 60.00 150.00
PPMS Mike Schmidt 60.00 150.00
PPNG Nomar Garciaparra 60.00 150.00
PPOS Ozzie Smith 30.00 80.00
PPRC Rod Carew 20.00 50.00
PPTG Tom Glavine 20.00 50.00

2015 Topps Museum Collection Primary Pieces Four Player Quad Relics

STATED ODDS 1:35 PACKS
STATED PRINT RUN 99 SER.#'d SETS
PRICING FOR BASIC JSY SWATCHES
*COPPER/75: .4X TO 1X BASIC
*GOLD/25: .5X TO 1.2X BASIC
PPFQAT Abru/dGrm/Hmltn/Tnka 15.00 40.00
PPFQBC Nva/Crg/Btts/Cstllo 15.00 40.00
PPFQBH Hsmr/Mstks/Btlr/Prz 12.00 30.00
PPFQCM Crpntr/Mlna/Adms/Mllr 12.00 30.00
PPFQDG Gry/Rddck/Dnldsn/Nrrs 10.00 25.00
PPFQDS Dvs/Schp/Crz/Jns 10.00 25.00
PPFQFC Fielder/Darvish/Choo/Choice 8.00 20.00
PPFQFS Smmns/Hywrd/Thrn/Frmn 10.00 25.00
PPFQKC Clayton Kershaw
Felix Hernandez
Johnny Cueto
Chris Sale
PPFQKP Rmrz/Krshw/Pg/Gnzlz 12.00 30.00
PPFQLH Lee/Hamels/Howard/Utley 6.00 15.00
PPFQMM Cle/McCtchn/Mrte/Plnco 20.00 50.00
PPFQMP d'Arnd/Mrinz/dGrm/Pizza 15.00 40.00
PPFQPK Hmltn/Pjls/Kndrck/Trt 15.00 40.00
PPFQRH Rosenthal/Holland
Kimbrel/Rodney 6.00 15.00
PPFQRS Sabathia/Ellsbury
Teixeira/Rodriguez 8.00 20.00
PPFQSM Dnld/Stn/Trt/McCtch 30.00 80.00
PPFQSR Bz/Rzzo/Cstro/Slr 30.00 80.00
PPFQVS Cbrra/Vrlndr/Mrtnz/Schrzr 8.00 20.00
PPFQ1WH Hrvy/Whlr/dGrm/d'Arnd 20.00 50.00

2015 Topps Museum Collection Primary Pieces Quad Relics

STATED ODDS 1:12 PACKS
STATED PRINT RUN 99 SER.#'d SETS
*COPPER/75: .4X TO 1X BASIC
*GOLD/25: .5X TO 1.2X BASIC
PPQRAC Aroldis Chapman 6.00 15.00
PPQRAGN Alex Gordon 6.00 15.00
PPQRAGZ Adrian Gonzalez 4.00 10.00
PPQRAJ Adam Jones 6.00 15.00
PPQRAM Andrew McCutchen 15.00 40.00
PPQRAW Adam Wainwright 4.00 10.00
PPQRBB Billy Butler 3.00 8.00
PPQRBHN Billy Hamilton 4.00 10.00
PPQRCBO Craig Biggio 6.00 15.00
PPQRCBZ Clay Buchholz 3.00 8.00
PPQRCGN Carlos Gonzalez 4.00 10.00
PPQRCJ Chipper Jones 5.00 12.00
PPQRCKL Craig Kimbrel 4.00 10.00
PPQRCKW Clayton Kershaw 12.00 30.00
PPQRCSA CC Sabathia 4.00 10.00
PPQRCSE Chris Sale 5.00 12.00
PPQRDO David Ortiz 6.00 15.00
PPQRDPA Dustin Pedroia 5.00 12.00
PPQREA Elvis Andrus 4.00 10.00
PPQREHO Eric Hosmer 4.00 10.00
PPQREL Evan Longoria 4.00 10.00
PPQRFF Freddie Freeman 6.00 15.00
PPQRFH Felix Hernandez 4.00 10.00
PPQRGC Gerrit Cole 5.00 12.00
PPQRGP Gregory Polanco 4.00 10.00
PPQRGSN Giancarlo Stanton 5.00 12.00
PPQRHER Eric Hosmer 4.00 10.00
PPQRHR Hanley Ramirez 4.00 10.00
PPQRJBA Jose Bautista 4.00 10.00
PPQRJBL Jeff Bagwell 6.00 15.00
PPQRJF Jose Fernandez 10.00 25.00
PPQRJM Joe Mauer 6.00 15.00
PPQRJPK Joe Panik 10.00 25.00
PPQRJPN Joc Pederson 5.00 12.00
PPQRJRS Jose Reyes 4.00 10.00
PPQRJSN Jon Singleton 4.00 10.00
PPQRJV Joey Votto 5.00 12.00
PPQRMBS Mookie Betts 10.00 25.00
PPQRMCA Miguel Cabrera 5.00 12.00
PPQRMK Matt Kemp 4.00 10.00
PPQRMMO Manny Machado 5.00 12.00
PPQRMMS Mike Moustakas 4.00 10.00
PPQRMP Mike Piazza 10.00 25.00
PPQRMS Max Scherzer 5.00 12.00
PPQRMW Michael Wacha 6.00 15.00
PPQRNCS Nick Castellanos 5.00 12.00
PPQRNCZ Nelson Cruz 5.00 12.00
PPQRNG Nomar Garciaparra 4.00 10.00
PPQRPG Paul Goldschmidt 5.00 12.00
PPQRPK Paul Konerko 8.00 20.00
PPQRPS Pablo Sandoval 4.00 10.00
PPQRRH Ryan Howard 4.00 10.00
PPQRSCH Shin-Soo Choo 4.00 10.00
PPQRSS Stephen Strasburg 5.00 12.00
PPQRTG Tony Gwynn 8.00 20.00
PPQRTT Troy Tulowitzki 5.00 12.00
PPQRVM Victor Martinez 10.00 25.00
PPQRWB Wade Boggs 4.00 10.00
PPQRXB Xander Bogaerts 5.00 12.00
PPQRYC Yoenis Cespedes 4.00 10.00
PPQRYD Yu Darvish 5.00 12.00
PPQRYP Yasiel Puig 5.00 12.00

2015 Topps Museum Collection Primary Pieces Quad Relics Legends

STATED ODDS 1:137 PACKS
STATED PRINT RUN 25 SER.#'d SETS
PPQLBD Bobby Doerr 30.00 80.00
PPQLBF Bob Feller 25.00 60.00
PPQLBR Babe Ruth 200.00 300.00
PPQLDS Duke Snider 30.00 80.00
PPQLEB Ernie Banks 30.00 80.00
PPQLEM Eddie Mathews 20.00 50.00
PPQLES Enos Slaughter 25.00 60.00
PPQLHA Hank Aaron 90.00 150.00
PPQLJD Joe DiMaggio 90.00 150.00
PPQLJM Juan Marichal 30.00 80.00
PPQLJR Jackie Robinson 50.00 120.00
PPQLMT Masahiro Tanaka 12.00 30.00
PPQLRC Roberto Clemente 90.00 150.00
PPQLRK Ralph Kiner 30.00 80.00
PPQLTC Ty Cobb 50.00 120.00
PPQLTS Tom Seaver 12.00 30.00
PPQLTW Ted Williams 100.00 200.00
PPQLWS Warren Spahn 30.00 80.00
PPQLWMS Willie Mays 60.00 150.00

2015 Topps Museum Collection Signature Swatches Dual Relic Autographs

STATED ODDS 1:9 PACKS
PRINT RUNS B/WN 25-299 COPIES PER
EXCHANGE DEADLINE 3/31/2018
PRICING FOR BASIC JSY SWATCHES
*GOLD: .4X TO 1X BASIC p/r 25-30
*GOLD: .5X TO 1.2X BASIC p/r 50-99
*GOLD: .6X TO 1.5X BASIC p/r 109-299
SSDAC Allen Craig/125 5.00 12.00
SSDARA Anthony Ranaudo/299 5.00 12.00
SSDAS Andrelton Simmons/299 5.00 12.00
SSDBC Brandon Crawford/299 4.00 10.00
SSDBM Brian McCann/75 6.00 15.00
SSDBPS Brandon Phillips/75 5.00 12.00
SSDCAC Chris Archer/299 5.00 12.00
SSDCAR Chris Archer/299 5.00 12.00
SSDCC C.J. Cron/299 5.00 12.00
SSDCK Clayton Kershaw/30 60.00 150.00
SSDCR Cal Ripken Jr./25 60.00 150.00
SSDCSE Chris Sale/99 10.00 25.00
SSDDMO Devin Mesoraco/299 5.00 12.00
SSDDN Daniel Nava/109 5.00 12.00
SSDDPA Dustin Pedroia/25 30.00 80.00
SSDDPY Dalton Pompey/299 6.00 15.00
SSDDW David Wright/30 25.00 60.00
SSDEG Evan Gattis/299 5.00 12.00
SSDFF Freddie Freeman/75 10.00 25.00
SSDGP Gregory Polanco/125 10.00 25.00
SSDHAZ Henderson Alvarez/299 5.00 12.00
SSDJD Jacob deGrom/299 40.00 100.00
SSDJH Jason Heyward/75 6.00 15.00
SSDJPK Joe Panik/189 5.00 12.00
SSDJPN Joc Pederson/299 15.00 40.00
SSDJR Jim Rice/75 6.00 15.00
SSDJT Junichi Tazawa/299 5.00 12.00
SSDKV Kennys Vargas/299 5.00 12.00
SSDKW Kolten Wong/299 6.00 15.00
SSDLH Livan Hernandez/199 5.00 12.00
SSDMBS Matt Barnes/299 6.00 15.00
SSDMC Matt Carpenter/125 10.00 25.00
SSDMFO Maikel Franco/299 6.00 15.00
SSDMMA Mike Mussina/30 25.00 60.00
SSDMMR Mike Minor/299 5.00 12.00
SSDMN Mike Napoli/299 5.00 12.00
SSDMSN Marcus Stroman/241 6.00 15.00
SSDMSR Max Scherzer/50 15.00 40.00
SSDNG Nomar Garciaparra/30 20.00 50.00
SSDRCO Rusney Castillo/75 6.00 15.00
SSDRCS Roger Clemens/30 25.00 60.00
SSDSME Starling Marte/65 20.00 50.00
SSDSMR Shelby Miller/125 6.00 15.00
SSDYV Yordano Ventura/299 12.00 30.00

2015 Topps Museum Collection Signature Swatches Triple Relic Autographs

STATED ODDS 1:14 PACKS
PRINT RUNS B/WN 25-349 COPIES PER
EXCHANGE DEADLINE 3/31/2018
PRICING FOR BASIC JSY SWATCHES
*GOLD: .4X TO 1X BASIC p/r 25-30
*GOLD: .5X TO 1.2X BASIC p/r 50-99
*GOLD: .6X TO 1.5X BASIC p/r 109-349
SSTARO Anthony Ranaudo/75 5.00 12.00
SSTAS Andrelton Simmons/249 12.00 30.00
SSTBH Bryce Harper/25 150.00 300.00
SSTBM Brian McCann/30 8.00 20.00
SSTCC C.J. Cron/249 5.00 12.00
SSTCK Clayton Kershaw/30 60.00 150.00
SSTCSE Chris Sale/50 8.00 20.00
SSTDPA Dustin Pedroia/30 25.00 60.00
SSTEG Evan Gattis/249 5.00 12.00
SSTFF Freddie Freeman/50 20.00 50.00
SSTGM Greg Maddux/30 40.00 100.00
SSTGP Gregory Polanco/50 12.00 30.00
SSTJD Jacob deGrom/249 40.00 100.00
SSTJH Jason Heyward/50 8.00 20.00
SSTJR Jim Rice/199 8.00 20.00
SSTJT Junichi Tazawa/239 5.00 12.00
SSTKV Kennys Vargas/249 5.00 12.00
SSTKW Kolten Wong/349 6.00 15.00
SSTLH Livan Hernandez/249 5.00 12.00
SSTMC Matt Carpenter/199 10.00 25.00
SSTMFO Maikel Franco/249 15.00 40.00
SSTMME Mark McGwire/30 60.00 150.00
SSTMMR Mike Minor/249 5.00 12.00
SSTMN Mike Napoli/249 5.00 12.00
SSTMPA Mike Piazza/30 50.00 120.00
SSTMSN Marcus Stroman/349 6.00 15.00
SSTMSR Max Scherzer/30 20.00 50.00
SSTNG Nomar Garciaparra/30 12.00 30.00
SSTRCS Roger Clemens/30 25.00 60.00
SSTSMR Shelby Miller/199 6.00 15.00
SSTYP Yasiel Puig/30 60.00 150.00
SSTYV Yordano Ventura/329 6.00 15.00

2016 Topps Museum Collection

1 Buster Posey 1.00 2.50
2 Jean Segura .60 1.50
3 Kyle Seager .50 1.25
4 Noah Syndergaard .60 1.50
5 Bryce Harper 1.25 3.00
6 Miguel Cabrera .75 2.00
7 J.D. Martinez .75 2.00
8 Eric Hosmer .60 1.50
9 Kyle Schwarber RC 2.00 5.00
10 Mike Trout 4.00 10.00
11 Starling Marte .60 1.50
12 Carlos Martinez .60 1.50
13 Max Scherzer .75 2.00
14 Lorenzo Cain .50 1.25
15 Joc Pederson .60 1.50
16 Rob Refsnyder RC .75 2.00
17 A.J. Pollock .50 1.25
18 Kaleb Cowart RC .60 1.50
19 Luis Severino RC .75 2.00
20 Ryan Braun .60 1.50
21 Xander Bogaerts .75 2.00
22 Jorge Soler .75 2.00
23 Hector Olivera RC .75 2.00
24 David Price .60 1.50
25 Chris Davis .50 1.25
26 Dee Gordon .50 1.25
27 Craig Kimbrel .60 1.50
28 Hanley Ramirez .60 1.50
29 Yasiel Puig .75 2.00
30 Todd Frazier .50 1.25
31 Jon Gray RC .60 1.50
32 Carlos Carrasco .50 1.25
33 Trevor Rosenthal .60 1.50
34 Addison Russell .75 2.00
35 Billy Hamilton .60 1.50
36 Giancarlo Stanton .75 2.00
37 Zack Greinke .75 2.00
38 Byron Buxton .75 2.00
39 Jake Arrieta .60 1.50
40 Kris Bryant 1.00 2.50
41 Jose Altuve .60 1.50
42 Josh Reddick .50 1.25
43 Nolan Arenado 1.25 3.00
44 Jordan Zimmermann .60 1.50
45 Madison Bumgarner .60 1.50
46 Roberto Clemente 2.00 5.00
47 Jose Fernandez .75 2.00
48 Stephen Strasburg .75 2.00
49 Joey Votto .75 2.00
50 Clayton Kershaw 1.25 3.00
51 Corey Kluber .60 1.50
52 Carlos Gomez .50 1.25
53 Chris Sale .75 2.00
54 Prince Fielder .60 1.50
55 Corey Seager RC 6.00 15.00
56 Mookie Betts 1.50 4.00
57 Felix Hernandez .60 1.50
58 Trea Turner RC 2.00 5.00
59 Justin Upton .60 1.50
60 Kenley Jansen .60 1.50
61 Andrew McCutchen .75 2.00
62 Stephen Piscotty RC 1.00 2.50
63 Francisco Lindor .75 2.00
64 Miguel Sano RC 1.00 2.50
65 Chris Archer .50 1.25
66 Maikel Franco .60 1.50
67 Rougned Odor .60 1.50
68 Michael Conforto RC .75 2.00
69 Gerrit Cole .75 2.00
70 Jose Abreu .75 2.00
71 Carlos Correa .75 2.00
72 Jose Bautista .60 1.50
73 Paul Goldschmidt .75 2.00
74 George Springer .60 1.50

75 Michael Brantley .60 1.50
76 Matt Harvey .60 1.50
77 Aaron Nola RC 1.25 3.00
78 Manny Machado .75 2.00
79 Corey Dickerson .50 1.25
80 Sonny Gray .60 1.50
81 Anthony Rizzo 1.00 2.50
82 Josh Donaldson .60 1.50
83 Michael Wacha .60 1.50
84 Dellin Betances .60 1.50
85 Jacoby Ellsbury .60 1.50
86 Carlos Rodon .75 2.00
87 Charlie Blackmon .75 2.00
88 Kolten Wong .60 1.50
89 Evan Longoria .60 1.50
90 Yoenis Cespedes .75 2.00
91 Jacob deGrom 1.50 4.00
92 Danny Salazar .60 1.50
93 Jason Kipnis .60 1.50
94 Anthony Rendon .75 2.00
95 Adam Jones .60 1.50
96 Freddie Freeman 1.00 2.50
97 Gregory Polanco .60 1.50
98 Edwin Encarnacion .75 2.00
99 Troy Tulowitzki .75 2.00
100 Christian Yelich 1.00 2.50

2016 Topps Museum Collection Blue

*BLUE: 1X TO 2.5X BASIC
*BLUE RC: .75X TO 2X BASIC RC
STATED ODDS 1:8 MINI BOXES
STATED PRINT RUN 99 SER.#'d SETS

2016 Topps Museum Collection Copper

*COPPER: .6X TO 1.5X BASIC
*COPPER RC: .5X TO 1.2X BASIC RC
RANDOM INSERTS IN MINI BOXES

2016 Topps Museum Collection Green

*GREEN: .75X TO 2X BASIC
*GREEN RC: .6X TO 1.5X BASIC RC
STATED ODDS 1:4 MINI BOXES
STATED PRINT RUN 199 SER.#'d SETS

2016 Topps Museum Collection Archival Autographs

RANDOM INSERTS IN MINI BOXES
PRINT RUNS B/WN 25-399 COPIES PER
EXCHANGE DEADLINE 2/28/2018
AAAC Alex Colome/299 3.00 8.00
AAACB Alex Cobb/299 3.00 8.00
AAAD Andre Dawson/50 10.00 25.00
AAAG Andres Galarraga/199 6.00 15.00
AAAGO Alex Gordon EXCH 20.00 50.00
AAAGZ Adrian Gonzalez/75 4.00 10.00
AAAJ Andruw Jones/299 5.00 12.00
AAAN Aaron Nola/299 6.00 15.00
AAARZ Anthony Rizzo/125 20.00 50.00
AABBE Brandon Belt/299 5.00 12.00
AABH Bryce Harper/25 250.00 400.00
AABJ Bo Jackson/25 50.00 120.00
AABL Barry Larkin/50 4.00 10.00
AABS Blake Swihart/299 4.00 10.00
AABW Bernie Williams/75 20.00 50.00
AACH Cole Hamels/75 6.00 15.00
AACK Clayton Kershaw/50 60.00 150.00
AACKL Corey Kluber/299 10.00 25.00
AACM Carlos Martinez/299 5.00 12.00
AACR Carlos Rodon/125 8.00 20.00
AACRJ Cal Ripken Jr./25 60.00 150.00
AACS Corey Seager/125 30.00 80.00
AADC David Cone/125 3.00 8.00
AADF Doug Fister/199 3.00 8.00
AADG Dee Gordon/125 5.00 12.00
AADGR Didi Gregorius/299 6.00 15.00
AADL DJ LeMahieu/299 15.00 40.00
AADM Don Mattingly/50
AADO David Ortiz/25 40.00 100.00
AAEL Evan Longoria/50 4.00 10.00
AAEMA Edgar Martinez/99 4.00 10.00
AAFF Freddie Freeman/75 6.00 15.00
AAFL Francisco Lindor/299 12.00 30.00
AAFV Fernando Valenzuela/75 10.00 25.00
AAGH Greg Holland/299 3.00 8.00
AAGM Greg Maddux EXCH 50.00 120.00
AAGS George Springer/299 4.00 10.00
AAHA Hank Aaron EXCH 150.00 300.00
AAHO Hector Olivera/299 4.00 10.00
AAHOW Henry Owens/125 4.00 10.00
AAI Ichiro Suzuki/25 200.00 300.00
AAJA Jose Altuve/125 25.00 60.00
AAJC Jose Canseco/99 12.00 30.00
AAJD Jacob deGrom/75 15.00 40.00
AAJG Juan Gonzalez/125 8.00 20.00
AAJGR Jon Gray/150 3.00 8.00
AAJHE Jason Heyward EXCH 12.00 30.00
AAJHM Jason Hammel/299 5.00 12.00
AAJS James Shields/125 3.00 8.00
AAJSO Jorge Soler/199 5.00 12.00
AAJSZ John Smoltz/75 15.00 40.00
AAKB Kris Bryant/75 60.00 150.00
AAKC Kole Calhoun/299 5.00 12.00
AAKSC Kyle Schwarber/199 10.00 25.00
AAKSZ Kurt Suzuki/299 3.00 8.00
AALG Luis Gonzalez/125 4.00 10.00
AALS Luis Severino/150 4.00 10.00
AAMA Matt Adams/199 3.00 8.00
AAMC Matt Carpenter/199 5.00 12.00
AAMCA Matt Cain/75 6.00 15.00
AAMCO Michael Conforto EXCH 20.00 50.00
AAMG Mark Grace/125 8.00 20.00
AAMGR Marquis Grissom/299 3.00 8.00
AAMP Mike Piazza/25 60.00 150.00
AAMS Miguel Sano/299 5.00 12.00
AAMT Mike Trout/25 150.00 300.00
AAMW Matt Williams/299 3.00 8.00
AANS Noah Syndergaard/125 20.00 50.00
AAPM Paul Molitor/125 10.00 25.00
AAPO Paul O'Neill/99 10.00 25.00
AAPS Pablo Sandoval/75 4.00 10.00
AARC Rod Carew/75 12.00 30.00
AARI Raisel Iglesias/299 4.00 10.00
AARK Ryan Klesko/299 5.00 12.00
AARPA Rafael Palmeiro/75 6.00 15.00
AARY Robin Yount EXCH 25.00 60.00
AASG Sonny Gray/199 6.00 15.00
AASGR Shawn Green/199 3.00 8.00
AASK Sandy Koufax EXCH 150.00 300.00
AASM Steven Matz/299 6.00 15.00
AASP Stephen Piscotty/299 5.00 12.00
AASS Steven Souza Jr./299 4.00 10.00
AATT Troy Tulowitzki/50 10.00 25.00
AATTU Trea Turner/299 10.00 25.00
AATW Taijuan Walker/199 3.00 8.00
AAVC Vinny Castilla/299 3.00 8.00
AAWM Wil Myers/125 4.00 10.00

2016 Topps Museum Collection Canvas Collection

STATED ODDS 1:4 MINI BOXES
CC1 Hank Aaron 2.00 5.00
CC2 Bernie Williams .75 2.00
CC3 George Brett 2.00 5.00
CC4 Buster Posey 1.25 3.00
CC5 Ichiro Suzuki 1.25 3.00
CC6 Kris Bryant 1.25 3.00
CC7 Noah Syndergaard .75 2.00
CC8 Frank Thomas 1.00 2.50
CC9 Ichiro Suzuki 1.25 3.00
CC10 Bryce Harper 1.50 4.00
CC11 Cal Ripken Jr. 3.00 8.00
CC12 Clayton Kershaw 1.50 4.00
CC13 Mike Trout 5.00 12.00
CC14 Rollie Fingers .75 2.00
CC15 Jose Bautista .75 2.00
CC16 Greg Maddux 1.25 3.00
CC17 Kris Bryant 1.25 3.00
CC18 Reggie Jackson .75 2.00
CC19 David Ortiz 1.00 2.50
CC20 Carl Yastrzemski 1.50 4.00
CC21 Ken Griffey Jr. 2.00 5.00
CC22 Mike Piazza 1.00 2.50
CC23 Andrew McCutchen 1.00 2.50
CC24 Matt Harvey .75 2.00
CC25 Yu Darvish 1.00 2.50

2016 Topps Museum Collection Meaningful Material Prime Relics

STATED ODDS 1:9 PACKS
STATED PRINT RUN 50 SER.#'d SETS
*GOLD/35: .4X TO 1X BASIC
MMPRABE Adrian Beltre 8.00 20.00
MMPRABR Archie Bradley 5.00 12.00
MMPRACH Aroldis Chapman 8.00 20.00
MMPRACO Alex Cobb 5.00 12.00
MMPRAGO Alex Gordon 6.00 15.00
MMPRAGZ Adrian Gonzalez 6.00 15.00
MMPRAJ Adam Jones 6.00 15.00
MMPRAL Adam Lind 6.00 15.00
MMPRAMC Andrew McCutchen 15.00 40.00
MMPRAMI Andrew Miller 6.00 15.00
MMPRARE Anthony Rendon 8.00 20.00
MMPRARI Anthony Rizzo 10.00 25.00
MMPRARU Addison Russell 8.00 20.00
MMPRAS Andrelton Simmons 5.00 12.00
MMPRAW Adam Wainwright 6.00 15.00
MMPRBB Byron Buxton 8.00 20.00
MMPRBBE Brandon Belt 6.00 15.00
MMPRBBU Billy Butler 5.00 12.00
MMPRBC Brandon Crawford 6.00 15.00
MMPRBG Brett Gardner 6.00 15.00
MMPRBHM Billy Hamilton 6.00 15.00
MMPRBM Brian McCann 6.00 15.00
MMPRBPH Brandon Phillips 5.00 12.00
MMPRBPO Buster Posey 10.00 25.00
MMPRBS Blake Swihart 6.00 15.00
MMPRCA Chris Archer 5.00 12.00
MMPRCBE Carlos Beltran 6.00 15.00
MMPRCBL Charlie Blackmon 8.00 20.00
MMPRCBU Clay Buchholz 5.00 12.00
MMPRCCR Carl Crawford 6.00 15.00
MMPRCCS CC Sabathia 6.00 15.00
MMPRCD Chris Davis 5.00 12.00
MMPRCGR Curtis Granderson 6.00 15.00
MMPRCK Clayton Kershaw 12.00 30.00
MMPRCKL Corey Kluber 6.00 15.00
MMPRCM Carlos Martinez 6.00 15.00
MMPRCSA Chris Sale 8.00 20.00
MMPRCSE Corey Seager 15.00 40.00
MMPRDB Dellin Betances 6.00 15.00
MMPRDD Delino DeShields Jr. 5.00 12.00
MMPRDFI Doug Fister 5.00 12.00
MMPRDFR David Freese 5.00 12.00
MMPRDGO Dee Gordon 5.00 12.00
MMPRDGR Didi Gregorius 6.00 15.00
MMPRDK Dallas Keuchel 6.00 15.00
MMPRDL DJ LeMahieu 8.00 20.00
MMPRDME Devin Mesoraco 5.00 12.00
MMPRDO David Ortiz 8.00 20.00
MMPRDPE Dustin Pedroia 8.00 20.00
MMPRDW David Wright 6.00 15.00
MMPREA Elvis Andrus 6.00 15.00
MMPREG Evan Gattis 5.00 12.00
MMPREH Eric Hosmer 6.00 15.00
MMPREI Ender Inciarte 5.00 12.00
MMPREL Evan Longoria 6.00 15.00
MMPRFF Freddie Freeman 10.00 25.00
MMPRFH Felix Hernandez 6.00 15.00
MMPRFL Francisco Lindor 8.00 20.00
MMPRFM Frankie Montas 6.00 15.00
MMPRFR Fernando Rodney 5.00 12.00
MMPRGC Gerrit Cole 8.00 20.00
MMPRGG Gio Gonzalez 6.00 15.00
MMPRGH Greg Holland 5.00 12.00
MMPRGP Gregory Polanco 6.00 15.00
MMPRGSA Gary Sanchez 15.00 40.00
MMPRGSP George Springer 6.00 15.00
MMPRGST Giancarlo Stanton 8.00 20.00
MMPRHI Hisashi Iwakuma 6.00 15.00
MMPRHJR Hyun-Jin Ryu 6.00 15.00
MMPRHO Henry Owens 6.00 15.00
MMPRHP Hunter Pence 10.00 25.00
MMPRID Ian Desmond 5.00 12.00
MMPRIK Ian Kinsler 6.00 15.00
MMPRJBA Javier Baez 10.00 25.00
MMPRJBR Jay Bruce 6.00 15.00
MMPRJD Josh Donaldson 6.00 15.00
MMPRJDG Jacob deGrom 15.00 40.00
MMPRJE Jacoby Ellsbury 6.00 15.00
MMPRJFA Jeurys Familia 6.00 15.00
MMPRJFE Jose Fernandez 8.00 20.00
MMPRJHA Josh Harrison 5.00 12.00
MMPRJHK Jung Ho Kang 5.00 12.00
MMPRJHM Josh Hamilton 6.00 15.00
MMPRJJ Jon Jay 5.00 12.00
MMPRJK Jason Kipnis 6.00 15.00
MMPRJLE Jon Lester 6.00 15.00
MMPRJLU Jonathan Lucroy 6.00 15.00
MMPRJMA Joe Mauer 6.00 15.00
MMPRJMC James McCann 12.00 30.00
MMPRJMR J.D. Martinez 8.00 20.00
MMPRJPD Joc Pederson 6.00 15.00
MMPRJRE Josh Reddick 5.00 12.00
MMPRJRO Jimmy Rollins 6.00 15.00
MMPRJS Jonathan Schoop 5.00 12.00
MMPRJT Julio Teheran 6.00 15.00
MMPRJU Justin Upton 6.00 15.00
MMPRJV Joey Votto 8.00 20.00
MMPRJW Jayson Werth 6.00 15.00
MMPRKB Kris Bryant 10.00 25.00
MMPRKC Kole Calhoun 5.00 12.00
MMPRKJ Kenley Jansen 6.00 15.00
MMPRKM Ketel Marte 10.00 25.00
MMPRKSE Kyle Seager 5.00 12.00
MMPRKW Kolten Wong 6.00 15.00
MMPRLC Lorenzo Cain 5.00 12.00
MMPRLD Lucas Duda 6.00 15.00
MMPRLL Lance Lynn 5.00 12.00
MMPRLS Luis Severino 6.00 15.00
MMPRMA Matt Adams 5.00 12.00
MMPRMBE Mookie Betts 15.00 40.00
MMPRMBR Michael Brantley 6.00 15.00
MMPRMBU Madison Bumgarner 6.00 15.00
MMPRMCA Matt Cain 6.00 15.00
MMPRMCB Miguel Cabrera 8.00 20.00
MMPRMCH Michael Choice 5.00 12.00
MMPRMCO Michael Conforto 6.00 15.00
MMPRMCR Matt Carpenter 8.00 20.00
MMPRMD Matt Duffy 5.00 12.00
MMPRMF Maikel Franco 6.00 15.00
MMPRMHA Matt Harvey 6.00 15.00
MMPRMHO Matt Holliday 8.00 20.00
MMPRMMA Manny Machado 15.00 40.00
MMPRMME Mark Melancon 5.00 12.00
MMPRMP Michael Pineda 5.00 12.00
MMPRMST Marcus Stroman 6.00 15.00
MMPRMTR Mike Trout 40.00 100.00
MMPRMTX Mark Teixeira 6.00 15.00
MMPRMW Michael Wacha 8.00 20.00
MMPRNA Nolan Arenado 12.00 30.00
MMPRNCA Nick Castellanos 8.00 20.00
MMPRNCR Nelson Cruz 8.00 20.00
MMPRNS Noah Syndergaard 6.00 15.00
MMPRPA Pedro Alvarez 5.00 12.00
MMPRPF Prince Fielder 6.00 15.00
MMPRPG Paul Goldschmidt 8.00 20.00
MMPRPS Pablo Sandoval 6.00 15.00
MMPRRA Roberto Alomar 6.00 15.00
MMPRRB Ryan Braun 6.00 15.00
MMPRRC Robinson Cano 6.00 15.00
MMPRRD R.A. Dickey 6.00 15.00
MMPRRH Ryan Howard 6.00 15.00
MMPRRM Russell Martin 5.00 12.00
MMPRROD Rougned Odor 6.00 15.00
MMPRROS Roberto Osuna 5.00 12.00
MMPRRP Rick Porcello 6.00 15.00
MMPRRZ Ryan Zimmerman 6.00 15.00
MMPRSC Starlin Castro 5.00 12.00
MMPRSG Sonny Gray 6.00 15.00
MMPRSMI Shelby Miller 6.00 15.00
MMPRSMR Starling Marte 6.00 15.00
MMPRSMZ Steven Matz 5.00 12.00
MMPRSPE Salvador Perez 6.00 15.00
MMPRSS Stephen Strasburg 8.00 20.00
MMPRSSC Shin-Soo Choo 6.00 15.00
MMPRSV Stephen Vogt 6.00 15.00
MMPRTD Travis d'Arnaud 6.00 15.00
MMPRTF Todd Frazier 5.00 12.00
MMPRTH Torii Hunter 5.00 12.00
MMPRTR Trevor Rosenthal 6.00 15.00
MMPRVM Victor Martinez 6.00 15.00
MMPRWD Wade Davis 5.00 12.00
MMPRWF Wilmer Flores 6.00 15.00
MMPRXB Xander Bogaerts 8.00 20.00
MMPRYC Yoenis Cespedes 8.00 20.00
MMPRYD Yu Darvish 8.00 20.00
MMPRYG Yasmani Grandal 5.00 12.00
MMPRYM Yadier Molina 10.00 25.00
MMPRYP Yasiel Puig 8.00 20.00
MMPRYT Yasmany Tomas 5.00 12.00
MMPRZG Zack Greinke 8.00 20.00
MMPRZW Zack Wheeler 6.00 15.00

2016 Topps Museum Collection Premium Prints Autographs

STATED ODDS 1:109 MINI BOX
STATED PRINT RUN 25 SER.#'d SETS
EXCHANGE DEADLINE 2/28/2018
PPBBE Brandon Belt
PPBH Bryce Harper 200.00 400.00
PPBL Barry Larkin 20.00 50.00
PPBP Buster Posey 50.00 120.00
PPBW Bernie Williams EXCH 25.00 60.00
PPCC Carlos Correa 200.00 400.00
PPCK Corey Kluber 10.00 25.00
PPCR Cal Ripken Jr. 75.00 200.00
PPDG Dee Gordon EXCH 8.00 20.00
PPDP Dustin Pedroia 25.00 60.00
PPFL Franciso Lindor 30.00 80.00
PPGM Greg Maddux EXCH 40.00 100.00
PPHA Hank Aaron 150.00 300.00
PPHR Hanley Ramirez EXCH 10.00 25.00
PPJAL Jose Altuve 25.00 60.00
PPJS Jorge Soler
PPKB Kris Bryant EXCH 150.00 300.00
PPKS Kyle Schwarber 25.00 60.00
PPMAD Matt Adams 8.00 20.00
PPMMA Manny Machado 60.00 150.00
PPPMO Paul Molitor 12.00 30.00
PPSK Sandy Koufax EXCH 150.00 400.00
PPTG Tom Glavine 20.00 50.00

2016 Topps Museum Collection Primary Pieces Four Player Quad Relics

STATED ODDS 1:36 PACKS
STATED PRINT RUN 99 SER.#'d SETS
PRICING FOR BASIC JSY SWATCHES
*COPPER/75: .4X TO 1X BASIC
*GOLD/25: .5X TO 1.2X BASIC
PPFQASSE Sam/Sal/Eat/Abr 6.00 15.00
PPFQCALW Ada/Lyn/Car/Wac 6.00 15.00
PPFQCCHI Iwk/Cru/Hrn/Can 8.00 20.00
PPFQCKVC Ver/Cas/Cab/Kin 12.00 30.00
PPFQDSBE Bau/Str/Don/Enc 6.00 15.00
PPFQFHDC Fie/Ham/Cho/DeS 5.00 12.00
PPFQFVHC Cha/Ham/Fra/Vot 15.00 40.00
PPFQGHHV Hos/Hol/Ven/Gor 12.00 30.00
PPFQHDSM deG/Har/Mat/Syn 30.00 80.00
PPFQJDMH Mac/Dav/Jon/Har 12.00 30.00
PPFQKGGP Gre/Gon/Ker/Pui 10.00 25.00
PPFQLKBS Lin/Bra/Klu/San 6.00 15.00
PPFQMKCM Col/Mar/Kan/McC 25.00 60.00
PPFQPBPC Cai/Pos/Pen/Bum 8.00 20.00
PPFQPSMB Mil/Ser/Pin/Bet 5.00 12.00
PPFQSBPO San/Bog/Ort/Ped 10.00 25.00
PPFQSRBR Sol/Rus/Bry/Riz 20.00 50.00
PPFQTCPF Puj/Tro/Cal/Fre 12.00 30.00
PPFQTTEB Tei/Tan/Bel/Ell 10.00 25.00
PPFQWCGD Wri/Con/Dud/Gra 5.00 12.00

2016 Topps Museum Collection Primary Pieces Quad Relics

STATED ODDS 1:12 PACKS
STATED PRINT RUN 99 SER.#'d SETS
*COPPER/75: .4X TO 1X BASIC
*GOLD/25: .5X TO 1.2X BASIC
PPQRI Ichiro Suzuki 12.00 30.00
PPQRAB Adrian Beltre 6.00 15.00
PPQRAC Aroldis Chapman 5.00 12.00
PPQRAG Adrian Gonzalez 4.00 10.00
PPQRAMC Andrew McCutchen 10.00 25.00
PPQRAMU Andrew McCutchen 10.00 25.00
PPQRAP Albert Pujols 6.00 15.00
PPQRAR Anthony Rizzo 6.00 15.00
PPQRAW Adam Wainwright 6.00 15.00
PPQRBB Byron Buxton 5.00 12.00
PPQRBP Buster Posey 6.00 15.00
PPQRCA Chris Archer 3.00 8.00
PPQRCBI Craig Biggio 4.00 10.00
PPQRCBU Clay Buchholz 3.00 8.00
PPQRCH Cole Hamels 4.00 10.00
PPQRCJ Chipper Jones 10.00 25.00
PPQRCK Clayton Kershaw 8.00 20.00
PPQRCR Cal Ripken Jr. 15.00 40.00
PPQRDM Don Mattingly 10.00 25.00
PPQRDO David Ortiz 10.00 25.00
PPQREA Elvis Andrus 5.00 12.00
PPQRFF Freddie Freeman 6.00 15.00
PPQRFH Felix Hernandez 4.00 10.00
PPQRGC Gerrit Cole 5.00 12.00
PPQRGS Giancarlo Stanton 5.00 12.00
PPQRJAB Jose Abreu 5.00 12.00
PPQRJBA Jose Bautista 4.00 10.00
PPQRJBE Javier Baez 6.00 15.00
PPQRJD Josh Donaldson 4.00 10.00
PPQRJDG Jacob deGrom 10.00 25.00
PPQRJE Jacoby Ellsbury 4.00 10.00
PPQRJF Jose Fernandez 5.00 12.00
PPQRJH Josh Hamilton 4.00 10.00
PPQRJM Joe Mauer 4.00 10.00
PPQRJP Joc Pederson 4.00 10.00
PPQRJV Justin Verlander 8.00 20.00
PPQRKB Kris Bryant 15.00 40.00
PPQRLC Lorenzo Cain 3.00 8.00
PPQRLL Lance Lynn 3.00 8.00
PPQRMA Matt Adams 3.00 8.00
PPQRMB Madison Bumgarner 4.00 10.00
PPQRMCB Miguel Cabrera 8.00 20.00
PPQRMCR Matt Carpenter 5.00 12.00
PPQRMHA Matt Harvey 6.00 15.00
PPQRMHO Matt Holliday 5.00 12.00
PPQRMM Manny Machado 5.00 12.00
PPQRMP Mike Piazza 10.00 25.00
PPQRMT Mike Trout 20.00 50.00
PPQRNA Nolan Arenado 8.00 20.00
PPQROV Omar Vizquel 75.00 200.00
PPQRPA Pedro Alvarez 3.00 8.00
PPQRPF Prince Fielder 4.00 10.00
PPQRPG Paul Goldschmidt 6.00 15.00
PPQRRA Roberto Alomar 4.00 10.00
PPQRRC Roger Clemens 6.00 15.00
PPQRRH Rickey Henderson 8.00 20.00
PPQRSS Stephen Strasburg 5.00 12.00
PPQRTF Todd Frazier 3.00 8.00
PPQRTG Tony Gwynn 15.00 40.00
PPQRVM Victor Martinez 4.00 10.00
PPQRYD Yu Darvish 5.00 12.00
PPQRYM Yadier Molina 8.00 20.00
PPQRYP Yasiel Puig 5.00 12.00
PPQRYV Yordano Ventura 4.00 10.00

2016 Topps Museum Collection Primary Pieces Quad Relics Legends

STATED ODDS 1:140 MINI BOX
STATED PRINT RUN 25 SER.#'d SETS
PPQLBD Bobby Doerr 10.00 25.00
PPQLBF Bob Feller 20.00 50.00
PPQLBL Bob Lemon 10.00 25.00
PPQLCY Carl Yastrzemski 20.00 50.00
PPQLEM Eddie Murray 10.00 25.00
PPQLHA Hank Aaron 60.00 150.00
PPQLJB Jim Bunning 10.00 25.00
PPQLJM Juan Marichal 10.00 25.00
PPQLJP Jim Palmer 10.00 25.00
PPQLJR Jackie Robinson 40.00 100.00
PPQLOC Orlando Cepeda 10.00 25.00
PPQLOS Ozzie Smith 30.00 80.00
PPQLRC Rod Carew 10.00 25.00
PPQLRF Rollie Fingers 20.00 50.00
PPQLRJ Reggie Jackson 20.00 50.00
PPQLRM Roger Maris 40.00 100.00
PPQLSC Steve Carlton 25.00 60.00
PPQLTP Tony Perez 20.00 50.00
PPQLTW Ted Williams 60.00 150.00
PPQLWM Willie Mays 60.00 150.00

2016 Topps Museum Collection Signature Swatches Dual Relic Autographs

STATED ODDS 1:9 PACKS
PRINT RUNS B/WN 30-399 COPIES PER
EXCHANGE DEADLINE 2/28/2018
PRICING FOR BASIC JSY SWATCHES
*GOLD: .4X TO 1X BASIC p/r 30
*GOLD: .5X TO 1.2X BASIC p/r 50-99
*GOLD: .6X TO 1.5X BASIC p/r 150-399
SSDAE Alcides Escobar/199 8.00 20.00
SSDAGN Adrian Gonzalez/99 8.00 20.00
SSDAJO Adam Jones/99 10.00 25.00
SSDAM Andrew Miller/299 6.00 15.00
SSDBB Byron Buxton/99 8.00 20.00
SSDBH Brock Holt/299 5.00 12.00
SSDBP Buster Posey/30 40.00 100.00
SSDBZ Brad Ziegler/90 15.00 40.00
SSDCK Clayton Kershaw/30 50.00 120.00
SSDCKE Clayton Kershaw/50 40.00 100.00
SSDCS Corey Seager/225 30.00 80.00
SSDDG Dee Gordon/299 5.00 12.00
SSDDK Dallas Keuchel/225 6.00 15.00
SSDDL DJ LeMahieu/299 12.00 30.00
SSDDW David Wright/50 8.00 20.00
SSDEL Evan Longoria/30 10.00 25.00
SSDGH Greg Holland/354 5.00 12.00
SSDHOL Hector Olivera/249 6.00 15.00
SSDHOW Henry Owens/299 6.00 15.00
SSDJD Jacob deGrom/199 20.00 50.00
SSDJFA Jeurys Familia/399 6.00 15.00
SSDJK Jung Ho Kang/299 10.00 25.00
SSDJL Jon Lester/99 10.00 25.00
SSDKB Kris Bryant/50 75.00 200.00
SSDKP Kevin Plawecki/399 5.00 12.00
SSDKS Kyle Schwarber/299 20.00 50.00
SSDLS Luis Severino/299 6.00 15.00
SSDMCA Matt Cain/99 6.00 15.00
SSDMCO Michael Conforto/199 25.00 60.00
SSDMH Matt Harvey EXCH 30.00 80.00
SSDMM Mark McGwire/50 50.00 120.00
SSDMTE Mark Teixeira/99 8.00 20.00
SSDMTR Mike Trout/30 150.00 400.00
SSDNS Noah Syndergaard/99 25.00 60.00
SSDPF Prince Fielder/30 10.00 25.00
SSDRC Robinson Cano/30 12.00 30.00
SSDRR Rob Refsnyder/299 6.00 15.00
SSDSH Slade Heathcott/399 6.00 15.00
SSDSMA Steven Matz/399 5.00 12.00
SSDSMI Shelby Miller/225 6.00 15.00
SSDSPE Salvador Perez/30 15.00 40.00
SSDSPI Stephen Piscotty/299 8.00 20.00
SSDTT Troy Tulowitzki/50 12.00 30.00
SSDWM Wil Myers/99 6.00 15.00
SSDYT Yasmany Tomas/99 5.00 12.00
SSDZW Zack Wheeler/299 6.00 15.00

2016 Topps Museum Collection Signature Swatches Triple Relic Autographs

STATED ODDS 1:15 PACKS
PRINT RUNS B/WN 25-299 COPIES PER
EXCHANGE DEADLINE 2/28/2018
PRICING FOR BASIC JSY SWATCHES
*GOLD: .4X TO 1X BASIC p/r 25
*GOLD: .5X TO 1.2X BASIC p/r 50-99
*GOLD: .6X TO 1.5X BASIC p/r 150-299
SSTAM Andrew Miller/179 6.00 15.00
SSTBB Byron Buxton/50 12.00 30.00
SSTBH Brock Holt/299 5.00 12.00
SSTBP Buster Posey/25 60.00 150.00
SSTCS Corey Seager/99 30.00 80.00
SSTDK Dallas Keuchel/99 10.00 25.00
SSTDL DJ LeMahieu/299 12.00 30.00
SSTDW David Wright/55 12.00 30.00
SSTGH Greg Holland/175 5.00 12.00
SSTHOL Hector Olivera/99 6.00 15.00
SSTHOW Henry Owens/299 6.00 15.00
SSTJD Jacob deGrom/99 30.00 80.00
SSTJF Jeurys Familia/299 6.00 15.00
SSTJK Jung Ho Kang/299 12.00 30.00
SSTKP Kevin Plawecki/299 5.00 12.00
SSTKS Kyle Schwarber/150 20.00 50.00
SSTLS Luis Severino/99 6.00 15.00
SSTMC Michael Conforto/99 25.00 60.00
SSTMF Maikel Franco/299 6.00 15.00
SSTMM Mark McGwire/50
SSTMTR Mike Trout/50 150.00 400.00
SSTMTX Mark Teixeira/50 10.00 25.00
SSTNS Noah Syndergaard/99 25.00 60.00
SSTRR Rob Refsnyder/299 6.00 15.00
SSTSH Slade Heathcott/99 6.00 15.00
SSTSMA Steven Matz/299 15.00 40.00
SSTSMI Shelby Miller/99 6.00 15.00
SSTSPE Salvador Perez/99 15.00 40.00
SSTWM Wil Myers/50 6.00 15.00
SSTYD Yu Darvish/50 25.00 60.00
SSTYT Yasmany Tomas/50 5.00 12.00
SSTZW Zack Wheeler/99 6.00 15.00

2017 Topps Museum Collection

1 Kris Bryant 1.00 2.50
2 Mike Trout 4.00 10.00
3 Paul Goldschmidt .75 2.00
4 Manny Machado .75 2.00
5 Mookie Betts 1.50 4.00
6 Anthony Rizzo 1.00 2.50
7 Kyle Schwarber .75 2.00
8 Joey Votto .75 2.00
9 Nolan Arenado 1.25 3.00
10 Miguel Cabrera .75 2.00
11 Justin Verlander .75 2.00
12 Carlos Correa .75 2.00
13 Eric Hosmer .60 1.50
14 Clayton Kershaw 1.25 3.00
15 Corey Seager .75 2.00
16 Julio Urias .75 2.00
17 Giancarlo Stanton .75 2.00
18 Ichiro 1.00 2.50
19 Noah Syndergaard .60 1.50
20 Masahiro Tanaka .60 1.50
21 Gary Sanchez .75 2.00
22 Carl Yastrzemski 1.25 3.00
23 Buster Posey 1.00 2.50
24 Felix Hernandez .60 1.50
25 Robinson Cano .60 1.50
26 Aledmys Diaz .60 1.50
27 Yu Darvish .75 2.00
28 Josh Donaldson .60 1.50
29 Jose Bautista .60 1.50
30 Bryce Harper 1.25 3.00
31 Max Scherzer .75 2.00
32 Francisco Lindor .75 2.00
33 Chris Sale .75 2.00
34 Addison Russell .75 2.00
35 Javier Baez 1.00 2.50
36 Jacob deGrom 1.50 4.00
37 Andrew McCutchen .75 2.00
38 Wil Myers .60 1.50
39 Albert Pujols 1.00 2.50
40 Yoenis Cespedes .75 2.00
41 Jose Altuve .60 1.50
42 Jake Arrieta .60 1.50
43 Edwin Encarnacion .75 2.00
44 David Price .60 1.50
45 Ryan Braun .60 1.50
46 Freddie Freeman 1.00 2.50
47 Troy Tulowitzki .75 2.00
48 Matt Carpenter .75 2.00
49 Carlos Gonzalez .60 1.50
50 Adrian Beltre .75 2.00
51 Hunter Pence .60 1.50
52 Corey Kluber .60 1.50
53 Trea Turner .60 1.50
54 Kenta Maeda .60 1.50
55 Stephen Strasburg .75 2.00
56 Matt Kemp .60 1.50
57 David Wright .60 1.50
58 Xander Bogaerts .75 2.00
59 Adam Jones .60 1.50
60 Daniel Murphy .60 1.50
61 Ken Griffey Jr. 1.50 4.00
62 Roberto Clemente 2.00 5.00
63 Cal Ripken Jr. 2.50 6.00
64 Hank Aaron 1.50 4.00
65 Ted Williams 1.50 4.00
66 Jackie Robinson .75 2.00
67 Sandy Koufax 1.50 4.00
68 Babe Ruth 2.00 5.00
69 Ernie Banks .75 2.00
70 Derek Jeter 2.00 5.00
71 David Ortiz .75 2.00
72 Mark McGwire 1.25 3.00
73 Randy Johnson .75 2.00
74 Honus Wagner .75 2.00
75 Roger Maris .75 2.00
76 Ty Cobb 1.25 3.00
77 Lou Gehrig 1.50 4.00
78 Reggie Jackson .60 1.50
79 George Brett 1.50 4.00
80 Don Mattingly 1.50 4.00
81 Frank Thomas .75 2.00
82 Bo Jackson .75 2.00
83 Johnny Bench .75 2.00
84 Greg Maddux 1.00 2.50
85 Roger Clemens 1.00 2.50
86 Mike Piazza .75 2.00
87 Nolan Ryan 2.50 6.00
88 Brooks Robinson .60 1.50
89 Chipper Jones .75 2.00
90 Ozzie Smith 1.00 2.50
91 Dansby Swanson RC 1.50 4.00
92 Andrew Benintendi RC 2.00 5.00
93 Yoan Moncada RC 2.00 5.00
94 Alex Bregman RC 3.00 8.00
95 Aaron Judge RC 10.00 25.00
96 Tyler Glasnow RC 2.50 6.00
97 Hunter Renfroe RC .75 2.00
98 Alex Reyes RC .75 2.00
99 Yulieski Gurriel RC 1.00 2.50
100 David Dahl RC .75 2.00

2017 Topps Museum Collection Blue

*BLUE: .75X TO 2X BASIC
*BLUE RC: ..6X TO 1.5X BASIC RC
STATED ODDS 1:6 HOBBY
STATED PRINT RUN 150 SER.#'d SETS
70 Derek Jeter 8.00 20.00
95 Aaron Judge 15.00 40.00

2017 Topps Museum Collection Copper

*COPPER: .6X TO 1.5X BASIC
*COPPER RC: .5X TO 1.2X BASIC RC
RANDOM INSERTS IN PACKS
70 Derek Jeter 6.00 15.00

2017 Topps Museum Collection Purple

*PURPLE: 1X TO 2.5X BASIC
*PURPLE RC: .75X TO 2X BASIC RC
STATED ODDS 1:8 HOBBY
STATED PRINT RUN 99 SER.#'d SETS
70 Derek Jeter 10.00 25.00
95 Aaron Judge 20.00 50.00

2017 Topps Museum Collection Red

*RED: 1.5X TO 4X BASIC
*RED RC: 1.2X TO 3X BASIC RC
STATED ODDS 1:16 HOBBY
STATED PRINT RUN 50 SER.#'d SETS
70 Derek Jeter 15.00 40.00
95 Aaron Judge 30.00 80.00

2017 Topps Museum Collection Archival Autographs

STATED ODDS 1:8 HOBBY
PRINT RUNS B/WN 75-299 COPIES PER
EXCHANGE DEADLINE 5/31/2019
AAAB Alex Bregman/299 20.00 50.00
AAADI Aledmys Diaz/199 4.00 10.00
AAAGA Andres Galarraga/99 4.00 10.00
AAAJU Aaron Judge/299 100.00 250.00
AAAK Al Kaline/99 15.00 40.00
AAAN Aaron Nola/199 4.00 10.00
AAARE Alex Reyes/299 4.00 10.00
AAARI Anthony Rizzo/99 20.00 50.00
AAARU Addison Russell/149 12.00 30.00
AABA Bobby Abreu EXCH 5.00 12.00
AABW Billy Wagner/99 5.00 12.00
AACB Craig Biggio/75 12.00 30.00
AACFL Carson Fulmer/299 3.00 8.00
AACSA Chris Sale/75 5.00 12.00
AACSE Corey Seager/75 25.00 60.00
AADD David Dahl/299 4.00 10.00
AADF Dexter Fowler EXCH 10.00 25.00
AADL Derrek Lee/99 3.00 8.00
AADS Dansby Swanson/299 15.00 40.00
AAFL Francisco Lindor/299 15.00 40.00
AAFV Fernando Valenzuela/99 10.00 25.00
AAHO Henry Owens/150 3.00 8.00
AAIR Ivan Rodriguez/75 12.00 30.00
AAJAL Jose Altuve/199 20.00 50.00
AAJCA Jose Canseco/199 6.00 15.00
AAJDG Jacob deGrom/99 15.00 40.00
AAJDL Jose De Leon/299 3.00 8.00
AAJR Jim Rice/199 4.00 10.00
AAJTA Jameson Taillon/75 4.00 10.00
AAJTH Jake Thompson/299 3.00 8.00
AAJTU Justin Turner/199 12.00 30.00
AAJV Jason Varitek/75 12.00 30.00
AAKH Kelvin Herrera/299 3.00 8.00
AAKMA Kenta Maeda/75 6.00 15.00
AAKMO Kendrys Morales/199 3.00 8.00
AAKS Kyle Schwarber/99 12.00 30.00
AALG Lucas Giolito/75 4.00 10.00
AALS Luis Severino/150 10.00 25.00
AAMC Matt Carpenter/199 8.00 20.00
AAMFR Maikel Franco/75 5.00 12.00
AAMFU Michael Fulmer/199 6.00 15.00
AAMMU Mark Mulder/99 5.00 12.00
AAMSA Miguel Sano/75 4.00 10.00
AAMTR Mike Trout
AANM Nomar Mazara/75 6.00 15.00
AANS Noah Syndergaard/199 12.00 30.00
AAOS Ozzie Smith/75 20.00 50.00
AAOV Omar Vizquel/99 6.00 15.00
AAPK Paul Konerko/99 10.00 25.00
AARA Roberto Alomar/75 10.00 25.00
AARCR Rod Carew/75 10.00 25.00
AARF Rollie Fingers/199 4.00 10.00
AARO Roy Oswalt/99 4.00 10.00
AASMZ Steven Matz/99 3.00 8.00
AASW Steven Wright/199 3.00 8.00
AATA Tyler Austin/299 4.00 10.00
AATGS Tyler Glasnow/299 10.00 25.00
AATGV Tom Glavine/75 12.00 30.00
AATS Trevor Story/199 8.00 20.00
AATTH Trayce Thompson/299 4.00 10.00
AATTU Trea Turner/199 10.00 25.00
AAWC Willson Contreras/199 12.00 30.00
AAYG Yulieski Gurriel/299 8.00 20.00
AAYM Yoan Moncada/99 15.00 40.00

2017 Topps Museum Collection Archival Autographs Copper

*COPPER: .5X TO 1.2X BASIC
STATED ODDS 1:22 HOBBY
STATED PRINT RUN 50 SER.#'d SETS
EXCHANGE DEADLINE 5/31/2019
AAAGO Adrian Gonzalez 5.00 12.00
AAAJO Adam Jones 6.00 15.00
AACC Carlos Correa 40.00 100.00
AADM Don Mattingly 25.00 60.00
AADPE Dustin Pedroia 10.00 25.00
AADPR David Price 10.00 25.00
AAJU Julio Urias 8.00 20.00
AAKB Kris Bryant 75.00 200.00
AAMWI Matt Wieters 8.00 20.00

2017 Topps Museum Collection Archival Autographs Gold

*GOLD: .6X TO 1.5X BASIC
STATED ODDS 1:42 HOBBY
STATED PRINT RUN 25 SER.#'d SETS
EXCHANGE DEADLINE 5/31/2019
AAAGO Adrian Gonzalez 6.00 15.00
AAAJO Adam Jones 8.00 20.00
AABH Bryce Harper 150.00 300.00
AACC Carlos Correa 50.00 120.00
AACK Clayton Kershaw 60.00 150.00
AACR Carlos Rodon EXCH 8.00 20.00
AADM Don Mattingly 30.00 80.00
AADPE Dustin Pedroia 12.00 30.00
AADPR David Price 12.00 30.00
AAJU Julio Urias 10.00 25.00
AAKB Kris Bryant 100.00 250.00
AAMMA Manny Machado 30.00 80.00
AAMWI Matt Wieters 10.00 25.00

2017 Topps Museum Collection Canvas Collection

STATED ODDS 1:4 HOBBY
CCRAB Alex Bregman 3.00 8.00
CCRAJ Aaron Judge 8.00 20.00
CCRAM Andrew McCutchen 1.00 2.50
CCRAR Anthony Rizzo 1.25 3.00
CCRBH Bryce Harper 1.50 4.00
CCRCC Carlos Correa 1.00 2.50
CCRCCO Carlos Correa 1.00 2.50
CCRCK Clayton Kershaw 1.50 4.00
CCRCKE Clayton Kershaw 1.50 4.00
CCRCKR Clayton Kershaw 1.50 4.00
CCRCS Corey Seager 1.00 2.50
CCRCSS Corey Seager 1.00 2.50
CCRDM Don Mattingly 2.00 5.00
CCRDO David Ortiz 1.00 2.50
CCRDW David Wright .75 2.00
CCRFL Francisco Lindor 1.00 2.50
CCRGC Gary Carter .75 2.00
CCRGS Giancarlo Stanton 1.00 2.50
CCRGSA Gary Sanchez 1.00 2.50
CCRGST Giancarlo Stanton 1.00 2.50
CCRHA Hank Aaron 2.00 5.00
CCRJA Jose Altuve .75 2.00
CCRJAR Jake Arrieta .75 2.00
CCRKB Kris Bryant 1.25 3.00
CCRKG Ken Griffey Jr. 2.00 5.00
CCRKM Kenta Maeda .75 2.00
CCRKMA Kenta Maeda .75 2.00
CCRKS Kyle Schwarber 1.00 2.50
CCRKSC Kyle Schwarber 1.00 2.50
CCRMB Mookie Betts 2.00 5.00
CCRMC Miguel Cabrera 1.00 2.50
CCRMCA Miguel Cabrera 1.00 2.50
CCRMCB Miguel Cabrera 1.00 2.50
CCRMM Manny Machado 1.00 2.50
CCRMP Mike Piazza 1.00 2.50
CCRMS Max Scherzer 1.00 2.50
CCRMT Mike Trout 5.00 12.00
CCRNA Nolan Arenado 1.50 4.00
CCRNR Nolan Ryan 3.00 8.00
CCRNS Noah Syndergaard .75 2.00
CCRNSN Noah Syndergaard .75 2.00
CCRRC Rod Carew .75 2.00
CCRRJ Reggie Jackson .75 2.00
CCRRM Roger Maris 1.00 2.50
CCRRMA Roger Maris 1.00 2.50
CCRSK Sandy Koufax 2.00 5.00
CCRWB Wade Boggs .75 2.00
CCRWF Whitey Ford .75 2.00
CCRXB Xander Bogaerts 1.00 2.50
CCRYC Yoenis Cespedes 1.00 2.50

2017 Topps Museum Collection Meaningful Materials Relics

STATED ODDS 1:10 HOBBY
STATED PRINT RUN 50 SER.#'d SETS
*COPPER/35: .4X TO 1X BASIC
MRAC Aroldis Chapman 5.00 12.00
MRAD Adam Duvall 20.00 50.00
MRAG Adrian Gonzalez 4.00 10.00
MRAJ Adam Jones 4.00 10.00
MRAN Aaron Nola 4.00 10.00

MRAS Aaron Sanchez 4.00 10.00
MRBH Bryce Harper 15.00 40.00
MRBM Brandon Moss 3.00 8.00
MRBP Buster Posey 6.00 15.00
MRBS Blake Snell 4.00 10.00
MRBZ Ben Zobrist 8.00 20.00
MRCB Charlie Blackmon 5.00 12.00
MRDG Dee Gordon 3.00 8.00
MRDL DJ LeMahieu 5.00 12.00
MRDO David Ortiz 6.00 15.00
MRDP Dustin Pedroia 8.00 20.00
MRDT Devon Travis 3.00 8.00
MREL Evan Longoria 4.00 10.00
MRFF Freddie Freeman 6.00 15.00
MRGP Gregory Polanco UER Wrong Player 4.00 10.00
MRGS George Springer 4.00 10.00
MRHI Hisashi Iwakuma 4.00 10.00
MRHR Hyun-Jin Ryu 4.00 10.00
MMAE Alcides Escobar 4.00 10.00
MMAJ Adam Jones 4.00 10.00
MMAM Andrew McCutchen 8.00 20.00
MMAR Anthony Rendon 6.00 15.00
MMARU Addison Russell 5.00 12.00
MMAW Adam Wainwright 4.00 10.00
MMBF Brandon Finnegan 3.00 8.00
MMBG Brett Gardner 5.00 12.00
MMBH Billy Hamilton 4.00 10.00
MMBP Brandon Phillips 3.00 8.00
MMCA Chris Archer 3.00 8.00
MMCD Chris Davis 6.00 15.00
MMCDI Corey Dickerson 3.00 8.00
MMCG Curtis Granderson 4.00 10.00
MMCGO Carlos Gonzalez 4.00 10.00
MMCH Cole Hamels 4.00 10.00
MMCK Corey Kluber 4.00 10.00
MMCM Carlos Martinez 4.00 10.00
MMCR Carlos Rodon 5.00 12.00
MMCS Carlos Santana 4.00 10.00
MMCY Christian Yelich 6.00 15.00
MMDB Dylan Bundy 6.00 15.00
MMDBE Dellin Betances 4.00 10.00
MMDD Danny Duffy 6.00 15.00
MMDK Dallas Keuchel 4.00 10.00
MMDW David Wright 4.00 10.00
MMEG Evan Gattis 3.00 8.00
MMEH Eric Hosmer 6.00 15.00
MMEL Evan Longoria 4.00 10.00
MMFF Freddie Freeman 6.00 15.00
MMFH Felix Hernandez 4.00 10.00
MMGC Gerrit Cole 6.00 15.00
MMGG Gio Gonzalez 4.00 10.00
MMGP Gregory Polanco 4.00 10.00
MMGR Garrett Richards 4.00 10.00
MMGS George Springer 4.00 10.00
MMGST Giancarlo Stanton 5.00 12.00
MMHR Hanley Ramirez 4.00 10.00
MMHRY Hyun-Jin Ryu 4.00 10.00
MMIK Ian Kinsler 6.00 15.00
MRI Ichiro 10.00 25.00
MMJD Jacob deGrom 10.00 25.00
MMJF Jeurys Familia 4.00 10.00
MMJG Jon Gray 3.00 8.00
MMJH Jason Hammel 4.00 10.00
MMJHA Josh Harrison 8.00 20.00
MMJK Jason Kipnis 6.00 15.00
MMJKA Jung Ho Kang 3.00 8.00
MMJM J.D. Martinez 5.00 12.00
MMJO Jake Odorizzi 3.00 8.00
MMJP Jurickson Profar 4.00 10.00
MMJS Jonathan Schoop 6.00 15.00
MMJT Julio Teheran 4.00 10.00
MMJV Joey Votto 5.00 12.00
MMJVE Justin Verlander 5.00 12.00
MMJW Jayson Werth 4.00 10.00
MMJZ Jordan Zimmermann 4.00 10.00
MMKG Kevin Gausman 6.00 15.00
MMKK Kevin Kiermaier 4.00 10.00
MMKS Kyle Seager 3.00 8.00
MMKU Koji Uehara 3.00 8.00
MMKW Kolten Wong 4.00 10.00
MMLC Lorenzo Cain 10.00 25.00
MMLCH Lonnie Chisenhall 10.00 25.00
MMMA Matt Adams 3.00 8.00
MMMB Mookie Betts 6.00 15.00
MMMC Michael Conforto 4.00 10.00
MMMCA Miguel Cabrera 5.00 12.00
MMMH Matt Harvey 4.00 10.00
MMMM Manny Machado 8.00 20.00
MMMW Matt Wieters 6.00 15.00
MMMWA Michael Wacha 4.00 10.00
MMNC Nelson Cruz 5.00 12.00
MMNCA Nick Castellanos 5.00 12.00
MMNS Noah Syndergaard 4.00 10.00
MMPF Prince Fielder 4.00 10.00
MMPG Paul Goldschmidt 10.00 25.00
MMRI Raisel Iglesias 4.00 10.00
MMRO Roberto Osuna 3.00 8.00
MMROD Rougned Odor 8.00 20.00
MMRP Rick Porcello 4.00 10.00
MMRZ Ryan Zimmerman 4.00 10.00
MMSC Shin-Soo Choo 4.00 10.00
MMSD Sean Doolittle 3.00 8.00
MMSG Sonny Gray 4.00 10.00
MMSM Steven Matz 3.00 8.00
MMSMA Starling Marte 4.00 10.00
MMSP Salvador Perez 6.00 15.00
MMTL Tim Lincecum 12.00 30.00
MMVM Victor Martinez 4.00 10.00
MMWM Wil Myers 4.00 10.00
MMYC Yoenis Cespedes 5.00 12.00
MMZW Zack Wheeler 4.00 10.00
MRAGO Alex Gordon 6.00 15.00
MRARA A.J. Ramos 3.00 8.00
MRBHA Billy Hamilton 4.00 10.00
MRCCA Chris Carpenter 6.00 15.00
MRCKI Craig Kimbrel 4.00 10.00
MRCKL Corey Kluber 4.00 10.00
MRDPR David Price 4.00 10.00
MRGST Giancarlo Stanton 5.00 12.00
MRJB Jackie Bradley Jr. 5.00 12.00
MRJBA Jose Bautista 4.00 10.00
MRJC Johnny Cueto 6.00 15.00
MRJE Jacoby Ellsbury 4.00 10.00
MRJF Jeurys Familia 4.00 10.00
MRJL Jon Lester 5.00 12.00
MRJS Jeff Samardzija 3.00 8.00
MRJT Julio Teheran 4.00 10.00
MRJU Justin Upton 4.00 10.00
MRJV Justin Verlander 5.00 12.00
MRKJ Kenley Jansen 6.00 15.00
MRKSE Kyle Seager 3.00 8.00
MRMBE Mookie Betts 6.00 15.00
MRMCA Matt Cain 4.00 10.00
MRMCB Miguel Cabrera 5.00 12.00
MRME Marco Estrada 3.00 8.00
MRMH Matt Harvey 4.00 10.00
MRMM Manny Machado 8.00 20.00
MRMO Marcell Ozuna 5.00 12.00
MRMP Michael Pineda 3.00 8.00
MRMSA Michael Saunders 4.00 10.00
MRMTA Masahiro Tanaka 4.00 10.00
MRPF Prince Fielder 4.00 10.00
MRRB Ryan Braun 4.00 10.00
MRRBR Ryan Braun 4.00 10.00
MRRC Robinson Cano 4.00 10.00
MRRH Ryan Howard 4.00 10.00
MRSM Starling Marte 4.00 10.00
MRSPE Salvador Perez 6.00 15.00
MRSR Sergio Romo 8.00 20.00
MRSS Stephen Strasburg 5.00 12.00
MRSV Stephen Vogt 5.00 12.00
MRTB Trevor Bauer 6.00 15.00
MRTF Todd Frazier 3.00 8.00
MRWF Wilmer Flores 4.00 10.00
MRWM Wil Myers 4.00 10.00
MRXB Xander Bogaerts 12.00 30.00
MRYC Yoenis Cespedes 5.00 12.00
MRYM Yadier Molina 12.00 30.00
MRYP Yasiel Puig 5.00 12.00
MRZB Zach Britton 6.00 15.00
MRZC Zack Cozart 3.00 8.00
MRZG Zack Greinke 5.00 12.00
MRZW Zack Wheeler 4.00 10.00

2017 Topps Museum Collection Premium Prints Autographs

STATED ODDS 1:100 HOBBY
STATED PRINT RUN 25 SER.#'d SETS
EXCHANGE DEADLINE 5/31/2019
PPAB Alex Bregman 60.00 150.00
PPAG Andres Galarraga 12.00 30.00
PPAN Aaron Nola 12.00 30.00
PPARI Anthony Rizzo
PPARU Addison Russell 20.00 50.00
PPBH Bryce Harper
PPBP Buster Posey 60.00 150.00
PPCC Carlos Correa 50.00 120.00
PPCSE Corey Seager 40.00 100.00
PPDD David Dahl 12.00 30.00
PPDM Don Mattingly 50.00 120.00
PPDP David Price 12.00 30.00
PPDS Dansby Swanson 50.00 120.00
PPFL Francisco Lindor 40.00 100.00
PPFT Frank Thomas 60.00 150.00
PPJC Jose Canseco 30.00 80.00
PPJDG Jacob deGrom 30.00 80.00
PPJU Julio Urias 15.00 40.00
PPJV Jason Varitek 15.00 40.00
PPKB Kris Bryant 200.00 400.00
PPKG Ken Griffey Jr. 200.00 400.00
PPKM Kenta Maeda 20.00 50.00
PPKS Kyle Schwarber 15.00 40.00
PPMM Manny Machado 30.00 80.00
PPMT Mike Trout 200.00 400.00
PPNS Noah Syndergaard 20.00 50.00
PPOS Ozzie Smith 20.00 50.00
PPOV Omar Vizquel 12.00 30.00
PPRA Roberto Alomar 15.00 40.00
PPRB Ryan Braun 20.00 50.00
PPTGS Tyler Glasnow 15.00 40.00
PPTS Trevor Story 15.00 40.00

2017 Topps Museum Collection Primary Pieces Four Player Quad Relics

STATED ODDS 1:46 PACKS
STATED PRINT RUN 75 SER.#'d SETS
PRICING FOR BASIC JSY SWATCHES
*COPPER/75: .4X TO 1X BASIC
*GOLD/25: .5X TO 1.2X BASIC
FPQBBBR Be/Br/Ha/Xa 20.00 50.00
FPQBBGW Br/Bu/Wi/Ga 12.00 30.00
FPQBBRP Ha/Xa/Du/Be 20.00 50.00
FPQCASB Co/Al/Sp/Br 40.00 100.00
FPQCGCS Sy/Co/Ce/Gr 15.00 40.00
FPQCHSC He/Se/Cr/Ca 15.00 40.00
FPQCKVM Ma/Ca/Ki/Ve 15.00 40.00
FPQGHCP Ho/Go/Ca/Pe 25.00 60.00
FPQKCMU Ma/Ca/Up/Ki 10.00 25.00
FPQKCVU Up/Ve/Ca/Ki 6.00 15.00
FPQMCPM Co/Mc/Po/Ma 40.00 100.00
FPQOPPR Pr/Or/Pe/Ra 20.00 50.00
FPQPPOB Or/Be/Po/Pr 20.00 50.00
FPQSCDW Ce/de/Sy/Wr 15.00 40.00
FPQSGYO Go/St/Oz/Ye 15.00 40.00
FPQVPDH Du/Ph/Vo/Ha 20.00 50.00
FPQWCMM Mo/Ca/Ma/Wa 12.00 30.00

2017 Topps Museum Collection Primary Pieces Quad Relics

STATED ODDS 1:14 PACKS
STATED PRINT RUN 99 SER.#'d SETS
*COPPER/75: .4X TO 1X BASIC
SPRAG Alex Gordon 4.00 10.00
SPRAJ Adam Jones 5.00 12.00
SPRAM Andrew McCutchen 20.00 50.00
SPRAR Anthony Rizzo 6.00 15.00
SPRARU Addison Russell 8.00 20.00
SPRBH Bryce Harper
SPRBPO Buster Posey 6.00 15.00
SPRCC Carlos Correa 6.00 15.00
SPRCD Chris Davis 3.00 8.00
SPRCG Curtis Granderson 4.00 10.00
SPRCGO Carlos Gonzalez 5.00 12.00
SPRCK Clayton Kershaw
SPRCSE Corey Seager
SPRDB Dellin Betances 4.00 10.00
SPRDM Daniel Murphy 4.00 10.00
SPRDO David Ortiz 5.00 12.00
SPRDP David Price 4.00 10.00
SPRDPE Dustin Pedroia 5.00 12.00
SPRDW David Wright 4.00 10.00
SPREH Eric Hosmer 12.00 30.00
SPREL Evan Longoria 4.00 10.00
SPRFF Freddie Freeman 6.00 15.00
SPRFH Felix Hernandez 4.00 10.00
SPRFL Francisco Lindor 5.00 12.00
SPRGC Gerrit Cole 8.00 20.00
SPRGS George Springer 8.00 20.00
SPRGST Giancarlo Stanton 5.00 12.00
SPRHR Hanley Ramirez 4.00 10.00
SPRIK Ian Kinsler 4.00 10.00
SPRI Ichiro 6.00 15.00
SPRJA Jake Arrieta 8.00 20.00
SPRJAL Jose Altuve 10.00 25.00
SPRJC Johnny Cueto 4.00 10.00
SPRJD Jacob deGrom 6.00 15.00
SPRJDO Josh Donaldson 4.00 10.00
SPRJV Joey Votto 8.00 20.00
SPRJVE Justin Verlander 5.00 12.00
SPRKB Kris Bryant
SPRKM Kenta Maeda 4.00 10.00
SPRKS Kyle Seager 3.00 8.00
SPRKSC Kyle Schwarber 5.00 12.00
SPRMB Mookie Betts 10.00 25.00
SPRMC Miguel Cabrera 10.00 25.00
SPRMCA Matt Carpenter 5.00 12.00
SPRMH Matt Harvey 4.00 10.00
SPRMM Manny Machado 5.00 12.00
SPRMT Masahiro Tanaka 4.00 10.00
SPRMTR Mike Trout
SPRNA Nolan Arenado 10.00 25.00
SPRNC Nelson Cruz 5.00 12.00
SPRPG Paul Goldschmidt 5.00 12.00
SPRRB Ryan Braun 4.00 10.00
SPRRC Robinson Cano 4.00 10.00
SPRRP Rick Porcello 4.00 10.00
SPRSM Starling Marte 4.00 10.00
SPRSP Salvador Perez 10.00 25.00
SPRSPI Stephen Piscotty 4.00 10.00
SPRTS Trevor Story 5.00 12.00
SPRTT Troy Tulowitzki 5.00 12.00
SPRVM Victor Martinez 4.00 10.00
SPRWM Wil Myers 4.00 10.00
SPRXB Xander Bogaerts 5.00 12.00
SPRYC Yoenis Cespedes 5.00 12.00

2017 Topps Museum Collection Primary Pieces Quad Relics Gold

STATED ODDS 1:50 MINI BOXES
STATED PRINT RUN 25 SER.#'d SETS
SPRBH Bryce Harper 20.00 50.00
SPRCK Clayton Kershaw 15.00 40.00
SPRGC Gerrit Cole 30.00 80.00
SPRKB Kris Bryant 30.00 80.00
SPRMTR Mike Trout 30.00 80.00

2017 Topps Museum Collection Primary Pieces Quad Relics Legends

STATED ODDS 1:153 MINI BOX
STATED PRINT RUN 25 SER.#'d SETS
SPQCB Craig Biggio 4.00 10.00
SPQCJ Chipper Jones 12.00 30.00
SPQCR Cal Ripken Jr. 40.00 100.00
SPQCY Carl Yastrzemski 40.00 100.00
SPQDM Don Mattingly 30.00 80.00
SPQGM Greg Maddux 25.00 60.00
SPQHA Hank Aaron 40.00 100.00
SPQJB Johnny Bench 15.00 40.00
SPQJS John Smoltz 12.00 30.00
SPQKG Ken Griffey Jr. 30.00 80.00
SPQMM Mark McGwire 25.00 60.00
SPQMP Mike Piazza 12.00 30.00
SPQNR Nolan Ryan 30.00 80.00
SPQOS Ozzie Smith 20.00 50.00
SPQRA Roberto Alomar 15.00 40.00
SPQRC Rod Carew 4.00 10.00
SPQRH Rickey Henderson 25.00 60.00
SPQRJ Reggie Jackson 15.00 40.00
SPQRY Robin Yount 20.00 50.00
SPQTW Ted Williams 40.00 100.00

2017 Topps Museum Collection Primary Pieces World Baseball Classic Patches

STATED ODDS 1:57 HOBBY
STATED PRINT RUN 75 SER.#'d SETS
*COPPER/45: .4X TO 1X BASIC
WBCPRBCR Brandon Crawford 8.00 20.00
WBCPRBN Brandon Nimmo 5.00 12.00
WBCPRBP Buster Posey
WBCPRCA Chris Archer 4.00 10.00
WBCPRCM Carlos Martinez 5.00 12.00
WBCPRCY Christian Yelich 6.00 15.00
WBCPRDB Dellin Betances 5.00 12.00
WBCPRDG Didi Gregorius 10.00 25.00
WBCPRDM Daniel Murphy 8.00 20.00
WBCPRGC Gavin Cecchini 4.00 10.00
WBCPRHS Hayato Sakamoto 25.00 60.00
WBCPRIK Ian Kinsler 8.00 20.00
WBCPRJA Jose Altuve 15.00 40.00
WBCPRJP Jurickson Profar 8.00 20.00
WBCPRJQ Jose Quintana 4.00 10.00
WBCPRJT Julio Teheran 5.00 12.00
WBCPRKT Kohsuke Tanaka 8.00 20.00
WBCPRMM Manny Machado
WBCPRNA Norichika Aoki
WBCPRNC Nelson Cruz 6.00 15.00
WBCPRRC Robinson Cano 8.00 20.00
WBCPRSM Starling Marte 20.00 50.00
WBCPRSS Seiya Suzuki 20.00 50.00
WBCPRST Shota Takeda
WBCPRYM Yuki Matsui 8.00 20.00

2017 Topps Museum Collection Primary Pieces World Baseball Classic Quad Relics

STATED ODDS 1:43 HOBBY
STATED PRINT RUN 99 SER.#'d SETS
*COPPER/50: .4X TO 1X BASIC
WBCQRABR Alex Bregman
WBCQRAG Adrian Gonzalez 4.00 10.00
WBCQRAJ Adam Jones 4.00 10.00
WBCQRAM Andrew McCutchen 15.00 40.00
WBCQRBP Buster Posey
WBCQRCG Carlos Gonzalez 4.00 10.00
WBCQREH Eric Hosmer 12.00 30.00
WBCQRGP Gregory Polanco
WBCQRGS Giancarlo Stanton 6.00 15.00
WBCQRJB Javier Baez 12.00 30.00
WBCQRJBA Jose Bautista 4.00 10.00
WBCQRMC Miguel Cabrera 12.00 30.00
WBCQRMM Manny Machado 5.00 12.00
WBCQRMS Marcus Stroman 4.00 10.00
WBCQRPG Paul Goldschmidt 6.00 15.00
WBCQRRC Robinson Cano 4.00 10.00
WBCQRSF Shintaro Fujinami 4.00 10.00
WBCQRSP Salvador Perez 10.00 25.00
WBCQRTN Takahiro Norimoto 6.00 15.00
WBCQRTS Tomoyuki Sugano 6.00 15.00
WBCQRTY Tetsuto Yamada 6.00 15.00
WBCQRVM Victor Martinez 4.00 10.00
WBCQRXB Xander Bogaerts 10.00 25.00
WBCQRYM Yadier Molina 12.00 30.00
WBCQRYT Yoshitomo Tsutsugo 10.00 25.00

2017 Topps Museum Collection Signature Swatches Dual Relic Autographs

STATED ODDS 1:9 PACKS
PRINT RUNS B/WN 75-299 COPIES PER
EXCHANGE DEADLINE 5/31/2019
PRICING FOR BASIC JSY SWATCHES
*COPPER/50: .4X TO 1X p/r 75-99
*COPPER/50: .5X TO 1.2X p/r 149-299
*GOLD/25: .5X TO 1.2X p/r 75-99
*GOLD/25: .6X TO 1.5X p/r 149-299
DRAABN Andrew Benintendi/299 20.00 50.00
DRAAG Alex Gordon/199 8.00 20.00
DRAANO Aaron Nola/299 5.00 12.00
DRAARD A.J. Reed/299 4.00 10.00
DRAARY Alex Reyes/199 6.00 15.00
DRACCO Carlos Correa/75 30.00 80.00
DRACD Chris Davis/99 8.00 20.00
DRACK Corey Kluber/199 12.00 30.00
DRACKE Clayton Kershaw/75 50.00 120.00
DRACS Corey Seager/99 8.00 20.00
DRAEL Evan Longoria/75 10.00 25.00
DRAFF Freddie Freeman/149 12.00 30.00
DRAFL Francisco Lindor/299 12.00 30.00
DRAHR Hunter Renfroe/299 5.00 12.00
DRAIK Ian Kinsler/99 8.00 20.00
DRAJA Jose Altuve/299 25.00 60.00
DRAJBR Jackie Bradley Jr./149 12.00 30.00
DRAJD Jacob deGrom/199 15.00 40.00
DRAJMA J.D. Martinez/75 10.00 25.00
DRAJPA Joe Panik/299 5.00 12.00
DRAJPE Joc Pederson/299 5.00 12.00
DRAKB Kris Bryant/75 75.00 200.00
DRAKK Kevin Kiermaier/299 5.00 12.00
DRAKMA Kenta Maeda/199 5.00 12.00
DRAKS Kyle Schwarber/199 10.00 25.00
DRALS Luis Severino/299 10.00 25.00
DRALW Luke Weaver/299 5.00 12.00
DRAMC Matt Carpenter/299 6.00 15.00
DRAMCO Michael Conforto/199 12.00 30.00
DRAMM Manny Machado/99 20.00 50.00
DRAMSA Miguel Sano/299 6.00 15.00
DRANA Nolan Arenado
DRANM Nomar Mazara/299 6.00 15.00
DRANS Noah Syndergaard/199 12.00 30.00
DRAPF Prince Fielder 5.00 12.00
DRARB Ryan Braun/75 8.00 20.00
DRARH Ryon Healy/299 6.00 15.00
DRARP Rick Porcello/299 5.00 12.00
DRASMR Starling Marte/199 5.00 12.00
DRASP Stephen Piscotty/299 6.00 15.00
DRATST Trevor Story/199 6.00 15.00
DRAWM Wil Myers/99 6.00 15.00
DRAYC Yoenis Cespedes/99 8.00 20.00

2017 Topps Museum Collection Signature Swatches Triple Relic Autographs

STATED ODDS 1:19 PACKS
PRINT RUNS B/WN 30-199 COPIES PER
EXCHANGE DEADLINE 5/31/2019
PRICING FOR BASIC JSY SWATCHES
*COPPER/25: .5X TO 1.2X p/r 30-99
*COPPER/25: .6X TO 1.5X p/r 149-199
TRAAPU Albert Pujols
TRAAR Anthony Rendon/199 8.00 20.00
TRAARI Anthony Rizzo/99 20.00 50.00
TRABB Brandon Belt/199 5.00 12.00
TRABH Bryce Harper
TRABPO Buster Posey/35 40.00 100.00
TRACC Carlos Correa/99 30.00 80.00
TRACH Cole Hamels/99 8.00 20.00
TRACR Carlos Rodon/99 8.00 20.00
TRADB Dellin Betances/99 6.00 15.00
TRADO David Ortiz/35 40.00 100.00
TRAEE Edwin Encarnacion/35 8.00 20.00
TRAFH Felix Hernandez
TRAFL Francisco Lindor/199 12.00 30.00
TRAFT Frank Thomas/30 25.00 60.00
TRAGB Greg Bird/75 6.00 15.00
TRAGP Gregory Polanco/99 6.00 15.00
TRAHI Hisashi Iwakuma/149 5.00 12.00
TRAJA Jose Abreu/99 8.00 20.00
TRAJBA Javier Baez/99 20.00 50.00
TRAJGR Jon Gray/99 8.00 20.00
TRAJH Jason Heyward/99 10.00 25.00
TRAJM Joe Mauer
TRAJTA Jameson Taillon/199 5.00 12.00
TRAKB Kris Bryant/99 75.00 200.00
TRAKSC Kyle Schwarber/149 10.00 25.00
TRAKSE Kyle Seager/99 8.00 20.00
TRALS Luis Severino/99 15.00 40.00
TRAMC Matt Carpenter/199 6.00 15.00
TRAMFL Michael Fulmer/99 10.00 25.00
TRAMFR Maikel Franco/99 6.00 15.00
TRAMM Manny Machado
TRAMSA Miguel Sano/199 8.00 20.00
TRAMT Mike Trout/35 150.00 300.00
TRANS Noah Syndergaard/199 12.00 30.00
TRASM Steven Matz/99 5.00 12.00
TRATS Trevor Story/199 6.00 15.00
TRATTL Troy Tulowitzki/35 8.00 20.00
TRAVM Victor Martinez/99 8.00 20.00
TRAWC Willson Contreras/99 12.00 30.00
TRAYT Yasmany Tomas/50 5.00 12.00

2018 Topps Museum Collection

1 Bryce Harper 1.25 3.00
2 Kris Bryant 1.00 2.50
3 Mike Trout 4.00 10.00
4 Paul Goldschmidt .75 2.00
5 Manny Machado .75 2.00
6 Mookie Betts 1.50 4.00
7 Anthony Rizzo 1.00 2.50
8 Kyle Schwarber .75 2.00
9 Joey Votto .75 2.00
10 Nolan Arenado 1.25 3.00
11 Miguel Cabrera .75 2.00
12 Justin Verlander .75 2.00
13 Carlos Correa .75 2.00
14 Eric Hosmer .60 1.50
15 Clayton Kershaw 1.25 3.00
16 Corey Seager .75 2.00
17 Cody Bellinger 1.50 4.00
18 Giancarlo Stanton .75 2.00
19 Ichiro 1.00 2.50
20 Noah Syndergaard .60 1.50
21 Masahiro Tanaka .60 1.50
22 Gary Sanchez .75 2.00
23 Aaron Judge 2.00 5.00
24 Buster Posey 1.00 2.50
25 Felix Hernandez .60 1.50
26 Robinson Cano .60 1.50
27 Yu Darvish .75 2.00
28 Josh Donaldson .60 1.50
29 Max Scherzer .75 2.00
30 Francisco Lindor .75 2.00
31 Chris Sale .75 2.00
32 Jacob deGrom 1.50 4.00
33 Andrew McCutchen .75 2.00
34 Wil Myers .60 1.50
35 Albert Pujols 1.00 2.50
36 Yoenis Cespedes .75 2.00
37 Jose Altuve .60 1.50
38 Adrian Beltre .75 2.00
39 Corey Kluber .60 1.50
40 Trea Turner .60 1.50
41 Stephen Strasburg .75 2.00
42 Xander Bogaerts .75 2.00
43 Adam Jones .60 1.50
44 Daniel Murphy .60 1.50
45 Roberto Clemente 2.00 5.00
46 Cal Ripken Jr. 2.50 6.00
47 Hank Aaron 1.50 4.00
48 Ted Williams 1.50 4.00
49 Jackie Robinson .75 2.00
50 Sandy Koufax 1.50 4.00
51 Babe Ruth 2.00 5.00
62 Ernie Banks .75 2.00
53 Derek Jeter 2.00 5.00
54 David Ortiz .75 2.00
55 Mark McGwire 1.25 3.00
56 Randy Johnson .75 2.00
57 Honus Wagner .75 2.00
58 Roger Maris .75 2.00
59 Ty Cobb 1.25 3.00
60 Lou Gehrig 1.50 4.00
61 Reggie Jackson .60 1.50
62 George Brett 1.50 4.00
63 Don Mattingly 1.50 4.00
64 Frank Thomas .75 2.00
65 Bo Jackson .75 2.00
66 Johnny Bench .75 2.00
67 Greg Maddux 1.00 2.50
68 Roger Clemens 1.00 2.50
69 Mike Piazza .75 2.00
70 Nolan Ryan 2.50 6.00
71 Byron Buxton .75 2.00
72 Pedro Martinez .60 1.50
73 Ryne Sandberg 1.50 4.00
74 Barry Larkin .60 1.50
75 Chipper Jones .75 2.00
76 Ozzie Smith 1.00 2.50
77 Luis Severino .60 1.50
78 Andrew Benintendi .75 2.00
79 George Springer .60 1.50
80 J.D. Martinez .75 2.00
81 Rhys Hoskins RC 2.50 6.00
82 Michael Conforto .60 1.50
83 Clint Frazier RC 1.25 3.00
84 Trey Mancini .60 1.50
85 Alex Bregman .75 2.00
86 Freddie Freeman 1.00 2.50
87 Ozzie Albies RC 2.00 5.00
88 Rafael Devers RC 2.00 5.00
89 Justin Upton .60 1.50
90 Marcell Ozuna .75 2.00
91 Edwin Encarnacion .75 2.00
92 Javier Baez 1.00 2.50
93 Ryan Braun .60 1.50
94 Miguel Sano .60 1.50
95 Victor Robles RC 1.50 4.00
96 Francisco Mejia RC .75 2.00
97 Salvador Perez .60 1.50
98 Yoan Moncada .75 2.00
99 Mariano Rivera 1.00 2.50
100 Shohei Ohtani RC 15.00 40.00

2018 Topps Museum Collection Copper

*COPPER: .6X TO 1.5X BASIC
*COPPER RC: .5X TO 1.2X BASIC RC
RANDOM INSERTS IN PACKS

2018 Topps Museum Collection Ruby

*RUBY: 1.5X TO 4X BASIC
*RUBY RC: 1.2X TO 3X BASIC RC
STATED ODDS 1:17 HOBBY
STATED PRINT RUN 50 SER.#'d SETS
100 Shohei Ohtani 40.00 100.00

2018 Topps Museum Collection Sapphire

*SAPPHIRE: .75X TO 2X BASIC
*SAPPHIRE RC: ..6X TO 1.5X BASIC RC
STATED ODDS 1:6 HOBBY
STATED PRINT RUN 150 SER.#'d SETS

2018 Topps Museum Collection Amethyst

*PURPLE: 1X TO 2.5X BASIC
*PURPLE RC: .75X TO 2X BASIC RC
STATED ODDS 1:9 HOBBY
STATED PRINT RUN 99 SER.#'d SETS

2018 Topps Museum Collection Archival Autographs

STATED ODDS 1:8 HOBBY
PRINT RUNS B/WN 75-299 COPIES PER
EXCHANGE DEADLINE 5/31/2020
AAABR Alex Bregman/199 20.00 50.00
AAAD Andre Dawson/299 8.00 20.00
AAAH Austin Hays/299 5.00 12.00
AAAK Al Kaline/75 20.00 50.00
AAAN Aaron Nola/299 4.00 10.00
AAARO Amed Rosario/299 4.00 10.00
AABB Byron Buxton/199 5.00 12.00
AABD Brian Dozier/299 6.00 15.00
AABW Brandon Woodruff/299 10.00 25.00
AACKI Craig Kimbrel/299 6.00 15.00
AACKL Corey Kluber/75 10.00 25.00
AACSA Chris Sale/99 12.00 30.00
AACSI Chance Sisco/299 4.00 10.00
AACT Chris Taylor/299 4.00 10.00
AADG Didi Gregorius/299 6.00 15.00
AADSM Dominic Smith/99 4.00 10.00
AADST Darryl Strawberry/199 8.00 20.00
AAET Eric Thames/299 4.00 10.00
AAFF Freddie Freeman/299 12.00 30.00
AAFL Francisco Lindor EXCH 20.00 50.00
AAFM Francisco Mejia/299 6.00 15.00
AAGSP George Springer/75 8.00 20.00
AAJC J.P. Crawford/299 3.00 8.00
AAJCA Jose Canseco/299 10.00 25.00
AAJD J.D. Davis/299 4.00 10.00
AAJDE Jacob deGrom/299 15.00 40.00
AAJF Jack Flaherty/299 12.00 30.00
AAJL Jake Lamb/299 4.00 10.00
AAJR Jose Ramirez/299 12.00 30.00
AAJS Jean Segura/299 3.00 8.00
AAKD Khris Davis/299 8.00 20.00
AAKS Kyle Schwarber/199 5.00 12.00
AALB Lou Brock/299 15.00 40.00
AALS Luis Severino/299 8.00 20.00
AALSI Lucas Sims/299 3.00 8.00
AAMO Matt Olson/299 5.00 12.00
AANS Noah Syndergaard/99 10.00 25.00
AAOA Ozzie Albies/299 10.00 25.00
AAPD Paul DeJong/299 5.00 12.00
AARD Rafael Devers/299 15.00 40.00
AARH Rhys Hoskins/299 15.00 40.00
AARM Ryan McMahon/299 8.00 20.00
AASG Sonny Gray/299 4.00 10.00
AASM Starling Marte/299 4.00 10.00
AASO Shohei Ohtani/99 250.00 500.00
AATG Tom Glavine/299 8.00 20.00
AATM Tyler Mahle/299 4.00 10.00
AATMA Trey Mancini/299 4.00 10.00
AATP Tommy Pham/299 3.00 8.00
AATS Travis Shaw/299 3.00 8.00
AAVR Victor Robles/299 15.00 40.00
AAWCO Willson Contreras/199 5.00 12.00
AAWM Whit Merrifield/299 5.00 12.00

2018 Topps Museum Collection Archival Autographs Copper

*COPPER: .5X TO 1.2X BASIC
STATED ODDS 1:21 HOBBY
STATED PRINT RUN 50 SER.#'d SETS
EXCHANGE DEADLINE 5/31/2020
AAAB Adrian Beltre 20.00 50.00
AAAP Andy Pettitte 12.00 30.00
AABL Barry Larkin 15.00 40.00
AADM Don Mattingly 25.00 60.00
AAJA Jose Altuve 20.00 50.00
AAJSM John Smoltz 20.00 50.00
AARA Roberto Alomar 10.00 25.00
AARC Rod Carew 12.00 30.00
AASC Steve Carlton 12.00 30.00

2018 Topps Museum Collection Archival Autographs Gold

*GOLD: .6X TO 1.5X BASIC
STATED ODDS 1:42 HOBBY
STATED PRINT RUN 25 SER.#'d SETS
EXCHANGE DEADLINE 5/31/2020
AAAB Adrian Beltre 25.00 60.00
AAAP Andy Pettitte 15.00 40.00
AAAR Anthony Rizzo 25.00 60.00
AABH Bryce Harper 125.00 300.00
AABL Barry Larkin 20.00 50.00
AADM Don Mattingly 30.00 80.00
AAI Ichiro 200.00 400.00
AAJA Jose Altuve 25.00 60.00
AAJSM John Smoltz 25.00 60.00
AAJV Joey Votto 40.00 100.00
AAKB Kris Bryant EXCH 75.00 200.00
AAMM Manny Machado 30.00 80.00
AAMTR Mike Trout 400.00 600.00
AARA Roberto Alomar 12.00 30.00
AARC Rod Carew 15.00 40.00
AASC Steve Carlton 15.00 40.00

2018 Topps Museum Collection Canvas Collection

STATED ODDS 1:4 HOBBY
CC1 Roberto Clemente 2.50 6.00
CC2 Mariano Rivera 1.25 3.00
CC3 Harmon Killebrew 1.00 2.50
CC4 Ted Williams 2.00 5.00
CC5 Nolan Arenado 1.50 4.00
CC6 Jimmie Foxx 1.00 2.50
CC7 Frank Thomas 1.00 2.50
CC8 Bryce Harper 1.50 4.00
CC9 Babe Ruth 2.50 6.00
CC10 Mike Trout 5.00 12.00
CC11 Rickey Henderson 1.00 2.50
CC12 Jose Altuve .75 2.00
CC13 Cody Bellinger 2.00 5.00
CC14 Nelson Cruz 1.00 2.50
CC15 Bo Jackson 1.00 2.50
CC16 Aaron Judge 2.50 6.00
CC17 Derek Jeter 2.50 6.00
CC18 Willie Stargell .75 2.00
CC19 Ozzie Smith 1.25 3.00
CC20 Jim Thome .75 2.00
CC21 Giancarlo Stanton 1.00 2.50
CC22 Bryce Harper 1.50 4.00
CC23 Noah Syndergaard .75 2.00
CC24 Wade Boggs .75 2.00
CC25 Mike Piazza 1.00 2.50
CC26 Shohei Ohtani 15.00 40.00
CC27 David Ortiz 1.00 2.50
CC28 Mariano Rivera 1.25 3.00
CC29 Rod Carew .75 2.00
CC30 Roberto Clemente 2.50 6.00
CC31 Reggie Jackson .75 2.00
CC32 Willie McCovey .75 2.00
CC33 Ryne Sandberg 2.00 5.00
CC34 Sandy Koufax 2.00 5.00
CC35 Alex Rodriguez 1.25 3.00
CC36 Chipper Jones 1.00 2.50
CC37 Dave Winfield .75 2.00
CC38 Barry Larkin .75 2.00
CC39 Al Kaline 1.00 2.50
CC40 Nolan Ryan 3.00 8.00
CC41 George Brett 2.00 5.00
CC42 Mike Trout 5.00 12.00
CC43 Babe Ruth 2.50 6.00
CC44 Shohei Ohtani 15.00 40.00
CC45 Derek Jeter 2.50 6.00
CC46 Bryce Harper 1.50 4.00
CC47 Aaron Judge 2.50 6.00
CC48 Mariano Rivera 1.25 3.00
CC49 Mike Piazza 1.00 2.50
CC50 Kris Bryant 1.25 3.00

2018 Topps Museum Collection Dual Meaningful Material Relics

STATED PRINT 1:65 HOBBY
STATED PRINT RUN 50 SER.#'d SETS
*COPPER/35: .4X TO 1X BASIC
DAAC McCutchen/Harrison 20.00 50.00
DAAJ Russell/Baez 20.00 50.00
DABC Arenado/Blackmon 10.00 25.00
DABH Pence/Crawford 10.00 25.00
DABM Buxton/Sano 8.00 20.00
DACC Sale/Kimbrel 15.00 40.00
DACD deGrom/Conforto 20.00 50.00
DACS Kershaw/Seager 15.00 40.00
DADT Murphy/Turner 8.00 20.00
DAES Hosmer/Perez 8.00 20.00
DAFH Hernandez/Cruz 10.00 25.00
DAGA Bregman/Springer 12.00 30.00
DAJS Bell/Marte 12.00 30.00
DAKE Kluber/Encarnacion 10.00 25.00
DAMB Benintendi/Betts
DAMN Castellanos/Cabrera 10.00 25.00
DAMS Strasburg/Scherzer 12.00 30.00
DAMSC Schoop/Machado 10.00 25.00
DAMT Stroman/Tulowitzki 10.00 25.00
DAMY Cespedes/Conforto 10.00 25.00
DAPJ Lamb/Goldschmidt 15.00 40.00
DARN Cruz/Cano 10.00 25.00
DAWF Wainwright/Fowler 8.00 20.00
DAXM Bogaerts/Betts 20.00 50.00
DAYC Molina/Martinez 12.00 30.00

2018 Topps Museum Collection Meaningful Material Relics

STATED ODDS 1:12 HOBBY
STATED PRINT RUN 50 SER.#'d SETS
*COPPER/35: .4X TO 1X BASIC
*GOLD/25: .5X TO 1.2X BASIC
MMRAB Andrew Benintendi 5.00 12.00
MMRABE Adrian Beltre 5.00 12.00
MMRAC Aroldis Chapman 5.00 12.00
MMRAD Adam Duvall 4.00 10.00
MMRAM Andrew McCutchen 12.00 30.00
MMRAN Aaron Nola 4.00 10.00
MMRAP A.J. Pollock 3.00 8.00
MMRAR Addison Russell 4.00 10.00
MMRARE Anthony Rendon 5.00 12.00
MMRARU Addison Russell 4.00 10.00
MMRAS Aaron Sanchez 4.00 10.00
MMRAW Adam Wainwright 4.00 10.00
MMRAWA Adam Wainwright 4.00 10.00
MMRBC Brandon Crawford 10.00 25.00
MMRBCR Brandon Crawford 10.00 25.00
MMRBD Brian Dozier 4.00 10.00
MMRBG Brett Gardner 4.00 10.00
MMRBGA Brett Gardner 4.00 10.00
MMRBH Billy Hamilton 4.00 10.00
MMRBHA Billy Hamilton 4.00 10.00
MMRBHR Bryce Harper
MMRBP Buster Posey 6.00 15.00
MMRBZ Ben Zobrist 4.00 10.00
MMRCA Chris Archer 3.00 8.00
MMRCB Charlie Blackmon 5.00 12.00
MMRCC Carlos Correa 5.00 12.00
MMRCG Carlos Gonzalez 4.00 10.00
MMRCH Cole Hamels 4.00 10.00
MMRCKI Craig Kimbrel 4.00 10.00
MMRCM Carlos Martinez 4.00 10.00
MMRCMA Carlos Martinez 4.00 10.00
MMRCSL Chris Sale 5.00 12.00
MMRCYE Christian Yelich 6.00 15.00
MMRDB Dylan Bundy 4.00 10.00
MMRDBE Dellin Betances 4.00 10.00
MMRDD Danny Duffy 3.00 8.00
MMRDF Dexter Fowler 4.00 10.00
MMRDFO Dexter Fowler 4.00 10.00
MMRDGR Didi Gregorius 4.00 10.00
MMRDK Dallas Keuchel 4.00 10.00
MMRDKE Dallas Keuchel 4.00 10.00
MMRDM Daniel Murphy 4.00 10.00
MMRDO David Ortiz 5.00 12.00
MMRDP Dustin Pedroia 5.00 12.00
MMRDPE Dustin Pedroia 5.00 12.00
MMRDPR David Price 4.00 10.00
MMREG Evan Gattis 3.00 8.00
MMREH Eric Hosmer 4.00 10.00
MMREI Ender Inciarte 3.00 8.00
MMRFFR Freddie Freeman 6.00 15.00
MMRFH Felix Hernandez 4.00 10.00
MMRFHE Felix Hernandez 4.00 10.00
MMRGG Gio Gonzalez 4.00 10.00
MMRGP Gregory Polanco 4.00 10.00
MMRGPO Gregory Polanco 4.00 10.00
MMRGR Garrett Richards 4.00 10.00
MMRGS Giancarlo Stanton 6.00 15.00
MMRGSP George Springer 4.00 10.00
MMRGST Giancarlo Stanton 6.00 15.00
MMRHP Hunter Pence 4.00 10.00
MMRHR Hyun-Jin Ryu 4.00 10.00
MMRHRA Hanley Ramirez 4.00 10.00
MMRHRY Hyun-Jin Ryu 4.00 10.00
MMRI Ichiro 12.00 30.00
MMRJAR Jake Arrieta 4.00 10.00
MMRJB Josh Bell 6.00 15.00
MMRJBA Jose Bautista 4.00 10.00
MMRJBE Josh Bell 6.00 15.00
MMRJBJ Jackie Bradley Jr. 5.00 12.00
MMRJBO Justin Bour 3.00 8.00
MMRJC Johnny Cueto 4.00 10.00
MMRJCU Johnny Cueto 4.00 10.00
MMRJD Josh Donaldson 4.00 10.00
MMRJDE Jacob deGrom 6.00 15.00
MMRJE Jacoby Ellsbury 4.00 10.00
MMRJEL Jacoby Ellsbury 4.00 10.00
MMRJF Jeurys Familia 4.00 10.00
MMRJG Jon Gray 3.00 8.00
MMRJGR Jon Gray 3.00 8.00
MMRJH Josh Harrison 3.00 8.00
MMRJHA Josh Harrison 3.00 8.00
MMRJHE Jason Heyward 4.00 10.00
MMRJK Jason Kipnis 5.00 12.00

MMRJL Jon Lester 4.00 10.00
MMRJP Joe Panik 4.00 10.00
MMRJPA Joe Panik 4.00 10.00
MMRJS Jonathan Schoop 3.00 8.00
MMRJSA Jeff Samardzija 3.00 8.00
MMRJSC Jonathan Schoop 3.00 8.00
MMRJT Julio Teheran 4.00 10.00
MMRJVO Joey Votto 5.00 12.00
MMRJW Jayson Werth 4.00 10.00
MMRKB Kris Bryant 15.00 40.00
MMRKG Kevin Gausman 5.00 12.00
MMRKK Kevin Kiermaier 4.00 10.00
MMRKKI Kevin Kiermaier 4.00 10.00
MMRKSC Kyle Schwarber 5.00 12.00
MMRKSE Kyle Seager 3.00 8.00
MMRMB Mookie Betts 10.00 25.00
MMRMBE Mookie Betts 10.00 25.00
MMRMC Miguel Cabrera 5.00 12.00
MMRMCA Miguel Cabrera 5.00 12.00
MMRMCB Miguel Cabrera 5.00 12.00
MMRMCO Michael Conforto 4.00 10.00
MMRME Marco Estrada 3.00 8.00
MMRMF Michael Fulmer 3.00 8.00
MMRMH Matt Harvey 4.00 10.00
MMRMHA Matt Harvey 4.00 10.00
MMRMK Max Kepler 4.00 10.00
MMRMM Manny Machado 8.00 20.00
MMRMMA Manny Machado 8.00 20.00
MMRMO Matt Olson 5.00 12.00
MMRMS Max Scherzer 6.00 15.00
MMRMT Mike Trout 30.00 80.00
MMRMTA Masahiro Tanaka 4.00 10.00
MMRMW Michael Wacha 4.00 10.00
MMRNC Nelson Cruz 5.00 12.00
MMRNCA Nick Castellanos 5.00 12.00
MMRNCR Nelson Cruz 5.00 12.00
MMRNS Noah Syndergaard 4.00 10.00
MMRPGO Paul Goldschmidt 5.00 12.00
MMRRBR Ryan Braun 4.00 10.00
MMRRC Robinson Cano 4.00 10.00
MMRRO Rougned Odor 4.00 10.00
MMRRZ Ryan Zimmerman 4.00 10.00
MMRSC Shin-Soo Choo 4.00 10.00
MMRSD Sean Doolittle 3.00 8.00
MMRSG Sonny Gray 4.00 10.00
MMRSMA Starling Marte 4.00 10.00
MMRSMT Steven Matz 3.00 8.00
MMRSP Salvador Perez 8.00 20.00
MMRSPE Salvador Perez 8.00 20.00
MMRSS Steven Souza Jr. 4.00 10.00
MMRSST Stephen Strasburg 5.00 12.00
MMRTP Tommy Pham 3.00 8.00
MMRVM Victor Martinez 4.00 10.00
MMRVMA Victor Martinez 4.00 10.00
MMRWM Wil Myers 4.00 10.00
MMRWMY Wil Myers 4.00 10.00
MMRXB Xander Bogaerts 5.00 12.00
MMRYC Yoenis Cespedes 5.00 12.00
MMRYCE Yoenis Cespedes 5.00 12.00
MMRYG Yuli Gurriel 4.00 10.00
MMRYM Yadier Molina 6.00 15.00
MMRZG Zack Greinke 5.00 12.00

2018 Topps Museum Collection Premium Print Autographs

STATED ODDS 1:105 HOBBY
STATED PRINT RUN 25 SER.#'d SETS
EXCHANGE DEADLINE 5/31/2020
PPAARO Amed Rosario 12.00 30.00
PPABB Byron Buxton 12.00 30.00
PPABH Bryce Harper 150.00 400.00
PPABJ Bo Jackson 50.00 120.00
PPABL Barry Larkin 20.00 50.00
PPACJ Chipper Jones 75.00 200.00
PPACKL Corey Kluber 20.00 50.00
PPACR Cal Ripken Jr. 60.00 150.00
PPACS Chris Sale 20.00 50.00
PPADM Don Mattingly 50.00 120.00
PPADS Dominic Smith 6.00 15.00
PPAFF Freddie Freeman 30.00 80.00
PPAFL Francisco Lindor EXCH
PPAFT Frank Thomas 30.00 80.00
PPAHM Hideki Matsui 100.00 250.00
PPAJA Jose Altuve 60.00 150.00
PPAJS John Smoltz
PPAJV Joey Votto
PPAKB Kris Bryant EXCH 75.00 200.00
PPALS Luis Severino 50.00 120.00
PPAMT Mike Trout 400.00 800.00
PPANS Noah Syndergaard 20.00 50.00
PPAOA Ozzie Albies 75.00 200.00
PPARD Rafael Devers 40.00 100.00
PPARHO Rhys Hoskins 60.00 150.00
PPASG Sonny Gray 6.00 15.00
PPAVR Victor Robles 40.00 100.00

2018 Topps Museum Collection Primary Pieces Four Player Quad Relics

STATED PRINT 1:41 HOBBY
STATED PRINT RUN 99 SER.#'d SETS
*COPPER/75: .4X TO 1X BASIC
*GOLD/25: .75X TO 2X BASIC
FPQRARI Goldschmidt/Pollock
Lamb/Greinke 5.00 12.00
FPQRBSN Betts/Bgrts/Pdra/Rmrz 10.00 25.00
FPQRCHI Rssll/Schwrbr/Brynt/Rzzo 6.00 15.00
FPQRCUB Happ/Schwrbr/Baez/Rssll 10.00 25.00
FPQRHOU Sprngr/Crra/Brgmn/Altve 25.00 60.00
FPQRKEE Grgrs/Grdnr/Snchz/Bird 10.00 25.00
FPQRLAA Pjos/Uptn/Clhn/Trt 25.00 60.00
FPQRMIL Braun/Arcia/Thames/Santana 4.00 10.00
FPQRMIN Buxton/Sano/Rosario/Mauer 5.00 12.00
FPQRNAT Trnr/Stasbrg/Mrphy/Schrzr 10.00 25.00
FPQRNYM Cnfrto/Sndrgrd/Cspds/dGrm 10.00 25.00
FPQRNYY Btncs/Grgrs/Snchz/Tnka 8.00 20.00
FPQRSEA Cruz/Cano/Hernandez/Seager 5.00 12.00
FPQRSFG Pnk/Psy/Pnce/Crwfrd 10.00 25.00
FPQRSOX Bnntndi/Btts/Sale/Kmbrl 10.00 25.00
FPQRSTL Carpenter/Wainwright
Martinez/Molina 12.00 30.00
FPQRTEX Odor/Gallo/Hamels/Beltre 5.00 12.00
FPQRTOR Smoak/Stroman/
ulowitzki/Donaldson 5.00 12.00
FPQRWAS Trnr/Hrpr/Strsbrg/Schrzr 8.00 20.00
FPQRYAN Svrno/Chpmn/Gray/Tnka 8.00 20.00

2018 Topps Museum Collection Primary Pieces Quad Relics

STATED ODDS 1:11 HOBBY
STATED PRINT RUN 99 SER.#'d SETS
*COPPER/75: .4X TO 1X BASIC
*GOLD/25: .6X TO 1.5X BASIC
SPQRABE Adrian Beltre 4.00 10.00
SPQRABN Andrew Benintendi 4.00 10.00
SPQRAC Aroldis Chapman 4.00 10.00
SPQRAJ Adam Jones 3.00 8.00
SPQRAM Andrew McCutchen 4.00 10.00
SPQRAN Aaron Nola 3.00 8.00
SPQRARI Anthony Rizzo 5.00 12.00
SPQRARU Addison Russell 3.00 8.00
SPQRAW Adam Wainwright 3.00 8.00
SPQRBC Brandon Crawford 3.00 8.00
SPQRBG Brett Gardner 3.00 8.00
SPQRBHA Bryce Harper 6.00 15.00
SPQRBP Buster Posey 5.00 12.00
SPQRCC Carlos Correa 4.00 10.00
SPQRCD Chris Davis 2.50 6.00
SPQRCG Carlos Gonzalez 3.00 8.00
SPQRCH Cole Hamels 3.00 8.00
SPQRCK Craig Kimbrel 3.00 8.00
SPQRCKE Clayton Kershaw 6.00 15.00
SPQRCM Carlos Martinez 3.00 8.00
SPQRCS Corey Seager 4.00 10.00
SPQRCSA Chris Sale 4.00 10.00
SPQRCY Christian Yelich 5.00 12.00
SPQRDK Dallas Keuchel 3.00 8.00
SPQRDO David Ortiz 4.00 10.00
SPQRDP Dustin Pedroia 4.00 10.00
SPQRDW David Wright 3.00 8.00
SPQREL Evan Longoria 3.00 8.00
SPQRFF Freddie Freeman 5.00 12.00
SPQRFH Felix Hernandez 3.00 8.00
SPQRGP Gregory Polanco 3.00 8.00
SPQRHJR Hyun-Jin Ryu 3.00 8.00
SPQRHP Hunter Pence 3.00 8.00
SPQRHR Hanley Ramirez 3.00 8.00
SPQRI Ichiro 8.00 20.00
SPQRIK Ian Kinsler 3.00 8.00
SPQRJB Josh Bell 3.00 8.00
SPQRJBA Javier Baez 8.00 20.00
SPQRJD Josh Donaldson 3.00 8.00
SPQRJDE Jacob deGrom 6.00 15.00
SPQRJH Josh Harrison 2.50 6.00
SPQRJM J.D. Martinez 4.00 10.00
SPQRJS Jonathan Schoop 2.50 6.00
SPQRJU Justin Upton 3.00 8.00
SPQRJV Justin Verlander 5.00 12.00
SPQRJVO Joey Votto 4.00 10.00
SPQRKB Kris Bryant 5.00 12.00
SPQRKSC Kyle Schwarber 4.00 10.00
SPQRLS Luis Severino 3.00 8.00
SPQRMB Mookie Betts 8.00 20.00
SPQRMC Miguel Cabrera 4.00 10.00
SPQRMCO Michael Conforto 3.00 8.00
SPQRMF Michael Fulmer 2.50 6.00
SPQRMM Manny Machado 4.00 10.00
SPQRMO Marcell Ozuna 4.00 10.00
SPQRMS Max Scherzer 4.00 10.00
SPQRMT Mike Trout 25.00 60.00
SPQRMTA Masahiro Tanaka 3.00 8.00
SPQRNCR Nelson Cruz 4.00 10.00
SPQRNS Noah Syndergaard 3.00 8.00
SPQRPG Paul Goldschmidt 4.00 10.00
SPQRRB Ryan Braun 3.00 8.00
SPQRRC Robinson Cano 3.00 8.00
SPQRRP Rick Porcello 3.00 8.00
SPQRRZ Ryan Zimmerman 3.00 8.00
SPQRSG Sonny Gray 3.00 8.00
SPQRSMA Starling Marte 3.00 8.00
SPQRSP Salvador Perez 3.00 8.00
SPQRSS Stephen Strasburg 4.00 10.00
SPQRTT Trea Turner 3.00 8.00
SPQRWM Wil Myers 3.00 8.00
SPQRXB Xander Bogaerts 4.00 10.00
SPQRYC Yoenis Cespedes 4.00 10.00
SPQRYG Yuli Gurriel 3.00 8.00
SPQRYM Yadier Molina 5.00 12.00
SPQRYP Yasiel Puig 4.00 10.00
SPQRZG Zack Greinke 4.00 10.00

2018 Topps Museum Collection Primary Pieces Quad Relics Legends

STATED ODDS 1:160 HOBBY
STATED PRINT RUN 25 SER.#'d SETS
SPQLAK Al Kaline
SPQLBL Barry Larkin 5.00 12.00
SPQLCR Cal Ripken Jr. 30.00 80.00
SPQLDJ Derek Jeter 20.00 50.00
SPQLDM Don Mattingly 25.00 60.00
SPQLGB George Brett 25.00 60.00
SPQLGM Greg Maddux 20.00 50.00
SPQLHA Hank Aaron 60.00 150.00
SPQLJB Johnny Bench
SPQLMM Mark McGwire 20.00 50.00
SPQLMP Mike Piazza
SPQLNR Nolan Ryan 30.00 80.00
SPQLOS Ozzie Smith 8.00 20.00
SPQLRCE Roger Clemens
SPQLRCL Roberto Clemente 75.00 200.00
SPQLRH Rickey Henderson 12.00 30.00
SPQLRJA Reggie Jackson
SPQLTS Tom Seaver 12.00 30.00
SPQLTW Ted Williams
SPQLWB Wade Boggs 15.00 40.00

2018 Topps Museum Collection Signature Swatches Dual Relic Autographs

STATED ODDS 1:10 HOBBY
PRINT RUNS B/WN 60-299 COPIES PER
NO PRICING DUE TO SCARCITY
EXCHANGE DEADLINE 5/31/2020
*COPPER/50: .4X TO 1X BASIC
*GOLD/25: .6X TO 1.5X BASIC
DRAAB Alex Bregman/199 12.00 30.00
DRAAD Adam Duvall/299 5.00 12.00
DRAAN Aaron Nola/299 10.00 25.00
DRAAR Addison Russell/99 10.00 25.00
DRAARO Amed Rosario/199 5.00 12.00
DRAAW Alex Wood/299 6.00 15.00
DRABD Brian Dozier/99 6.00 15.00
DRABS Blake Snell/299 5.00 12.00
DRACR Carlos Rodon
DRACS Carlos Santana/99 5.00 12.00
DRADG Dee Gordon/60 4.00 10.00
DRADGR Didi Gregorius/299 12.00 30.00
DRADP David Price
DRADS Domingo Santana/299 5.00 12.00
DRAER Eddie Rosario/299 8.00 20.00
DRAET Eric Thames/99 5.00 12.00
DRAGB Greg Bird/299 5.00 12.00
DRAGSA Gary Sanchez
DRAGSE Gary Sheffield/199 8.00 20.00
DRAGSH Gary Sheffield/99 8.00 20.00
DRAIH Ian Happ/199 5.00 12.00
DRAJB Justin Bour/299 4.00 10.00
DRAJC J.P. Crawford/299 5.00 12.00
DRAJD Jacob deGrom/99 15.00 40.00
DRAJDA Johnny Damon/99 8.00 20.00
DRAJH Josh Harrison/299 4.00 10.00
DRAJL Jake Lamb/199 5.00 12.00
DRAJP Joc Pederson/99 5.00 12.00
DRAJSM Justin Smoak/99 4.00 10.00
DRAJT Jameson Taillon/74 5.00 12.00
DRAKD Khris Davis/199 6.00 15.00
DRAKS Kyle Seager/199 4.00 10.00
DRAMC Matt Carpenter/199 6.00 15.00
DRAMF Michael Fulmer/199 4.00 10.00
DRANM Nomar Mazara/175 4.00 10.00
DRANS Noah Syndergaard
DRAOA Ozzie Albies/299 12.00 30.00
DRAPD Paul DeJong
DRARD Rafael Devers/199 20.00 50.00
DRASM Starling Marte/299 5.00 12.00
DRASMA Steven Matz/299 4.00 10.00
DRATM Trey Mancini
DRATP Tommy Pham/299 4.00 10.00
DRATS Trevor Story EXCH 10.00 25.00
DRATSH Travis Shaw/299 6.00 15.00
DRAWM Whit Merrifield/299 6.00 15.00

2018 Topps Museum Collection Signature Swatches Triple Relic Autographs

STATED ODDS 1:15 HOBBY
PRINT RUNS B/WN 45-149 COPIES PER
NO PRICING DUE TO SCARCITY
EXCHANGE DEADLINE 5/31/2020
*COPPER/25: .5X TO 1.2X BASIC
TRAAB Anthony Banda/149 4.00 10.00
TRAABR Alex Bregman/149 15.00 40.00
TRAAD Adam Duvall/149 5.00 12.00
TRAAJ Adam Jones/149 8.00 20.00
TRAAN Aaron Nola/149 6.00 15.00
TRAAR Amed Rosario/149 8.00 20.00
TRABD Brian Dozier/149 10.00 25.00
TRACC Carlos Correa/99 25.00 60.00
TRACF Clint Frazier/149 12.00 30.00
TRACK Corey Kluber/45 25.00 60.00
TRACKI Craig Kimbrel/149 10.00 25.00
TRADGO Dee Gordon/149 4.00 10.00
TRADGR Didi Gregorius/149 15.00 40.00
TRADSM Dominic Smith/149 5.00 12.00
TRAFF Freddie Freeman/149 15.00 40.00
TRAGB Greg Bird/45 5.00 12.00
TRAGS Gary Sanchez/149 15.00 40.00
TRAIH Ian Happ/149 10.00 25.00
TRAJA Jose Altuve/149 25.00 60.00
TRAJB Jose Berrios/149 5.00 12.00
TRAJBA Javier Baez EXCH 25.00 60.00
TRAJC J.P. Crawford/149 4.00 10.00
TRAJD Josh Donaldson/45 12.00 30.00
TRAJF Jack Flaherty/149 15.00 40.00
TRAJH Josh Harrison/149 4.00 10.00
TRAJL Jake Lamb/149 5.00 12.00
TRAJS Justin Smoak/149 10.00 25.00
TRAKB Kris Bryant/149 60.00 150.00
TRAKD Khris Davis/149 10.00 25.00
TRAKS Kyle Seager/149 4.00 10.00
TRAMM Manny Machado/149 25.00 60.00
TRANS Noah Syndergaard/149 10.00 25.00
TRAPG Paul Goldschmidt/149 12.00 30.00
TRARH Rhys Hoskins/149 15.00 40.00
TRASD Sean Doolittle/149 6.00 15.00
TRASM Steven Matz/99 4.00 10.00
TRATP Tommy Pham/45 4.00 10.00
TRAWC Willson Contreras/149 10.00 25.00
TRAYG Yuli Gurriel/149 5.00 12.00

2019 Topps Museum Collection

1 Mike Trout 4.00 10.00
2 Albert Pujols 1.00 2.50
3 Shohei Ohtani 1.25 3.00
4 Freddie Freeman 1.00 2.50
5 Ozzie Albies .75 2.00
6 Ronald Acuna Jr. 4.00 10.00
7 Josh Donaldson .60 1.50
8 Chipper Jones .75 2.00
9 Deion Sanders .60 1.50
10 Cal Ripken Jr. 2.50 6.00
11 Mookie Betts 1.50 4.00
12 Chris Sale .75 2.00
13 Andrew Benintendi .75 2.00
14 J.D. Martinez .75 2.00
15 Ted Williams 1.50 4.00
16 David Ortiz .75 2.00
17 Roger Clemens 1.00 2.50
18 Jackie Robinson .75 2.00
19 Kris Bryant 1.00 2.50
20 Anthony Rizzo 1.00 2.50
21 Javier Baez 1.00 2.50
22 Ernie Banks .75 2.00
23 Ryne Sandberg 1.50 4.00
24 Michael Kopech RC 2.00 5.00
25 Frank Thomas .75 2.00
26 Joey Votto .75 2.00
27 Johnny Bench .75 2.00
28 Barry Larkin .60 1.50
29 Francisco Lindor .75 2.00
30 Corey Kluber .60 1.50
31 Trevor Bauer 1.00 2.50
32 Jose Ramirez .60 1.50
33 Nolan Arenado 1.25 3.00
34 Charlie Blackmon .75 2.00
35 Trevor Story .75 2.00
36 Miguel Cabrera .75 2.00
37 Justin Verlander .75 2.00
38 Carlos Correa .75 2.00
39 Jose Altuve .60 1.50
40 George Springer .60 1.50
41 Alex Bregman .75 2.00
42 Kyle Tucker RC 1.50 4.00
43 Nolan Ryan 2.50 6.00
44 Salvador Perez .60 1.50
45 Whit Merrifield .75 2.00
46 Bo Jackson .75 2.00
47 Clayton Kershaw 1.25 3.00
48 Corey Seager .75 2.00
49 Cody Bellinger 1.50 4.00
50 Sandy Koufax 1.50 4.00
51 Walker Buehler 1.00 2.50
52 Christian Yelich 1.00 2.50
53 Noah Syndergaard .60 1.50
54 Jacob deGrom 1.50 4.00
55 Robinson Cano .60 1.50
56 Mike Piazza .75 2.00
57 Giancarlo Stanton .75 2.00
58 Masahiro Tanaka .60 1.50
59 Gary Sanchez .75 2.00
60 Aaron Judge 2.00 5.00
61 Luis Severino .60 1.50
62 Gleyber Torres 1.50 4.00
63 Miguel Andujar .75 2.00
64 Hideki Matsui .75 2.00
65 Derek Jeter 2.00 5.00
66 Don Mattingly 1.50 4.00
67 Mariano Rivera 1.00 2.50
68 Khris Davis .75 2.00
69 Matt Chapman .75 2.00
70 Rickey Henderson .75 2.00
71 Mark McGwire 1.25 3.00
72 Rhys Hoskins 1.00 2.50
73 Aaron Nola .60 1.50
74 Andrew McCutchen .75 2.00
75 J.T. Realmuto .75 2.00
76 Roberto Clemente 2.00 5.00
77 Chris Archer .50 1.25
78 Manny Machado .75 2.00
79 Pete Alonso RC 6.00 15.00
80 Luis Urias RC 1.00 2.50
81 Tony Gwynn .75 2.00
82 Buster Posey 1.00 2.50
83 Ichiro 1.00 2.50
84 Ken Griffey Jr. 1.50 4.00
85 Yusei Kikuchi RC 1.00 2.50
86 Paul Goldschmidt .75 2.00
87 Fernando Tatis Jr. RC 10.00 25.00
88 Yadier Molina 1.00 2.50
89 Ozzie Smith 1.00 2.50
90 Blake Snell .60 1.50
91 Adrian Beltre .75 2.00
92 Eloy Jimenez RC 2.50 6.00
93 Roberto Alomar .60 1.50
94 Bryce Harper 1.25 3.00
95 Max Scherzer .75 2.00
96 Trea Turner .60 1.50
97 Stephen Strasburg .75 2.00
98 Juan Soto 2.50 6.00
99 Matt Carpenter .75 2.00
100 Vladimir Guerrero Jr. RC 4.00 10.00

2019 Topps Museum Collection Amethyst

*AMETHYST: 1X TO 2.5X BASIC
*AMETHYST RC: .75X TO 2X BASIC RC
STATED ODDS 1:9 HOBBY
STATED PRINT RUN 99 SER.#'d SETS
79 Pete Alonso 20.00 50.00
87 Fernando Tatis Jr. 12.00 30.00
100 Vladimir Guerrero Jr. 15.00 40.00

2019 Topps Museum Collection Ruby

*RUBY: 1.5X TO 4X BASIC
*RUBY RC: 1.2X TO 3X BASIC RC
STATED ODDS 1:18 HOBBY
STATED PRINT RUN 50 SER.#'d SETS
79 Pete Alonso 30.00 80.00
87 Fernando Tatis Jr. 20.00 50.00
100 Vladimir Guerrero Jr. 30.00 80.00

2019 Topps Museum Collection Sapphire

*SAPPHIRE: .75X TO 2X BASIC
*SAPPHIRE RC: ..6X TO 1.5X BASIC RC
STATED ODDS 1:6 HOBBY
STATED PRINT RUN 150 SER.#'d SETS
79 Pete Alonso 15.00 40.00
87 Fernando Tatis Jr. 6.00 15.00

2019 Topps Museum Collection Archival Autographs

STATED ODDS 1:7 HOBBY
PRINT RUNS B/WN 99-299 COPIES PER
EXCHANGE DEADLINE 5/31/2021
*COPPER/50: .5X TO 1.2X BASIC
*GOLD: .6X TO 1.5X BASIC
AAAD Andre Dawson 8.00 20.00
AAAK Al Kaline/99 15.00 40.00
AABG Bob Gibson/199 40.00 100.00
AABN Brandon Nimmo/299 4.00 10.00
AACM Cedric Mullins/299 10.00 25.00
AACST Christin Stewart/299 4.00 10.00
AADE Dennis Eckersley/199 6.00 15.00
AADMU Dale Murphy/199 12.00 30.00
AADS Don Sutton/299 4.00 10.00
AADST Darryl Strawberry/199 8.00 20.00
AAEJ Eloy Jimenez/299 25.00 60.00
AAFF Freddie Freeman/99 25.00 60.00
AAFL Francisco Lindor/99 12.00 30.00
AAFT Fernando Tatis Jr./299 100.00 250.00
AAJAG Jesus Aguilar/299 4.00 10.00
AAJCA Jose Canseco/299 10.00 25.00
AAJDE Jacob deGrom/199 15.00 40.00
AAJG Juan Gonzalez/199 3.00 8.00
AAJHA Josh Hader/299 6.00 15.00
AAJM Jose Martinez/299 3.00 8.00
AAJMA Juan Marichal/199 10.00 25.00
AAJR Jim Rice/299 4.00 10.00
AAJRO Jose Ramirez/199 10.00 25.00
AAJSH Justus Sheffield/299 5.00 12.00
AAJSO Juan Soto/199 60.00 150.00
AAJVA Jason Varitek/199 10.00 25.00
AAKS Kyle Schwarber/199 6.00 15.00
AAKTU Kyle Tucker/299 15.00 40.00
AAKW Kyle Wright/299 5.00 12.00
AALB Lou Brock/99 12.00 30.00
AALS Luis Severino/199 6.00 15.00
AAMA Miguel Andujar/99 8.00 20.00
AAMH Mitch Haniger/299 4.00 10.00
AAMK Michael Kopech/299 10.00 25.00
AAMKE Matt Kemp/199 4.00 10.00
AAMMU Max Muncy/299 4.00 10.00
AANS Noah Syndergaard/99 4.00 10.00
AAOA Ozzie Albies/299 20.00 50.00
AAPA Peter Alonso/299 60.00 150.00
AAPCO Patrick Corbin/299 4.00 10.00
AAPD Paul DeJong/299 5.00 12.00
AARAJ Ronald Acuna Jr./199 75.00 200.00
AARH Rhys Hoskins/199 8.00 20.00
AASGE Scooter Gennett/299 4.00 10.00
AASM Steven Matz/299 3.00 8.00
AASMA Sean Manaea 3.00 8.00
AATH Torii Hunter/199 6.00 15.00
AATMA Trey Mancini/299 4.00 10.00
AATP Tommy Pham/299 3.00 8.00
AATST Trevor Story/299 12.00 30.00
AATT Touki Toussaint/299 4.00 10.00
AAVG Vladimir Guerrero Jr./299 30.00 80.00
AAWC Willson Contreras/199 4.00 10.00
AAWCL Will Clark/199 15.00 40.00
AAWM Whit Merrifield/299 5.00 12.00

2019 Topps Museum Collection Archival Autographs Copper

*COPPER: .5X TO 1.2X BASIC
STATED ODDS 1:27 HOBBY
STATED PRINT RUN 50 SER.#'d SETS
EXCHANGE DEADLINE 5/31/2021
AAAB Adrian Beltre 20.00 50.00
AAAP Andy Pettitte 10.00 25.00
AACF Carlton Fisk 12.00 30.00
AACSA Chris Sale 6.00 15.00
AADM Don Mattingly 30.00 80.00
AAGSP George Springer 5.00 12.00
AAJA Jose Altuve 12.00 30.00
AAJG Juan Gonzalez 8.00 20.00
AARA Roberto Alomar 10.00 25.00
AARC Rod Carew 12.00 30.00
AASC Steve Carlton 15.00 40.00

2019 Topps Museum Collection Archival Autographs Gold

*GOLD: .6X TO 1.5X BASIC
STATED ODDS 1:48 HOBBY
STATED PRINT RUN 25 SER.#'d SETS
EXCHANGE DEADLINE 5/31/2021
AAAK Al Kaline 30.00 80.00
AAAR Anthony Rizzo 15.00 40.00
AAI Ichiro 125.00 300.00
AAJG Juan Gonzalez 20.00 50.00
AAJV Joey Votto 25.00 60.00
AAKB Kris Bryant 60.00 150.00
AAMTR Mike Trout 300.00 600.00
AASO Shohei Ohtani 75.00 200.00
AATG Tom Glavine 25.00 60.00
AATH Torii Hunter 20.00 50.00

2019 Topps Museum Collection Canvas Collection

STATED ODDS 1:4 HOBBY
CC1 Javier Baez 1.25 3.00
CC2 Tony Gwynn 1.00 2.50
CC3 Joey Votto 1.00 2.50
CC4 Mike Trout 5.00 12.00
CC5 Alex Bregman 1.00 2.50
CC6 Mark McGwire 1.50 4.00
CC7 Derek Jeter 2.50 6.00
CC8 Ronald Acuna Jr. 5.00 12.00
CC9 Jose Altuve .75 2.00
CC10 Juan Soto 3.00 8.00
CC11 Mookie Betts 2.00 5.00
CC12 Luis Severino .75 2.00
CC13 Nolan Arenado 1.50 4.00
CC14 Don Mattingly 2.00 5.00
CC15 Aaron Judge 2.50 6.00
CC16 Yadier Molina 1.25 3.00
CC17 Jacob deGrom 2.00 5.00
CC18 Francisco Lindor 1.00 2.50
CC19 Anthony Rizzo 1.25 3.00
CC20 Kris Bryant 1.25 3.00
CC21 Bryce Harper 1.50 4.00
CC22 David Wright .75 2.00
CC23 Gleyber Torres 2.00 5.00
CC24 Max Scherzer 1.00 2.50
CC25 Paul Goldschmidt 1.00 2.50
CC26 Shohei Ohtani 1.50 4.00
CC27 Roberto Clemente 2.50 6.00
CC28 Mariano Rivera 1.25 3.00
CC29 Chris Sale 1.00 2.50
CC30 J.D. Martinez 1.00 2.50
CC31 Andrew Benintendi 6.00 15.00
CC32 Bo Jackson 1.00 2.50
CC33 Rhys Hoskins 1.25 3.00
CC34 Babe Ruth 2.50 6.00
CC35 Albert Pujols 1.25 3.00
CC36 Christian Yelich 1.25 3.00
CC37 Victor Robles 1.25 3.00
CC38 Honus Wagner 1.00 2.50
CC39 Manny Machado 1.00 2.50
CC40 Cal Ripken Jr. 3.00 8.00
CC41 Nolan Ryan 3.00 8.00
CC42 Buster Posey 1.25 3.00
CC43 Ozzie Smith 1.25 3.00
CC44 Hideki Matsui 1.00 2.50
CC45 Rickey Henderson 1.00 2.50
CC46 Ken Griffey Jr. 2.00 5.00
CC47 Ichiro 1.25 3.00
CC48 Lou Gehrig 2.00 5.00
CC49 Ty Cobb 1.50 4.00
CC50 Clayton Kershaw 1.50 4.00

2019 Topps Museum Collection Dual Meaningful Material Relics

STATED PRINT 1:64 HOBBY
STATED PRINT RUN 50 SER.#'d SETS
*COPPER/35: .5X TO 1.2X BASIC
DMRAB Bregman/Altuve 6.00 15.00
DMRAC Altuve/Correa 6.00 15.00
DMRAJ Chris Archer 5.00 12.00
Josh Bell
DMRAM Cabrera/Benintendi 8.00 20.00
DMRAS Trevor Story 10.00 25.00
Nolan Arenado
DMRBB Betts/Benintendi 12.00 30.00
DMRBR Bryant/Rizzo 15.00 40.00
DMRCA Nicholas Castellanos 6.00 15.00
Miguel Cabrera
DMRCC Michael Conforto 6.00 15.00
Yoenis Cespedes
DMRCR Amed Rosario 6.00 15.00
Yoenis Cespedes
DMRFS Freeman/Swanson 8.00 20.00
DMRGM Nomar Mazara 5.00 12.00
Joey Gallo
DMRHH Felix Hernandez 5.00 12.00
Mitch Haniger
DMRHM Eric Hosmer 5.00 12.00
Wil Myers
DMRLH Jason Heyward 5.00 12.00
Jon Lester
DMRLR Jose Ramirez 6.00 15.00
Francisco Lindor
DMROP Dustin Pedroia 6.00 15.00
David Ortiz
DMRPB Xander Bogaerts 6.00 15.00
Dustin Pedroia
DMRPC Crawford/Posey 8.00 20.00
DMRPM Salvador Perez 6.00 15.00
Whit Merrifield
DMRSC Aroldis Chapman 6.00 15.00
Luis Severino
DMRSL Stephen Strasburg 6.00 15.00
Max Scherzer
DMRSS Justin Smoak 5.00 12.00
Marcus Stroman
DMRST Stephen Strasburg 6.00 15.00
Trea Turner
DMRTA Torres/Andujar 12.00 30.00
DMRTM Jameson Taillon 5.00 12.00
Starling Marte
DMRVG Scooter Gennett 6.00 15.00
Joey Votto

2019 Topps Museum Collection Dual Meaningful Material Relics Copper

*COPPER: .5X TO 1.2X BASIC
STATED ODDS 1:111 HOBBY
STATED PRINT RUN 35 SER.#'d SETS
DMRAM Cabrera/Pujols 12.00 30.00
DMRFS Freeman/Swanson 20.00 50.00

2019 Topps Museum Collection Meaningful Material Relics

STATED ODDS 1:12 HOBBY
STATED PRINT RUN 50 SER.#'d SETS
*COPPER/35: .5X TO 1.2X BASIC
*GOLD/25: .5X TO 1.2X BASIC
MMRAA Albert Almora 4.00 10.00
MMRAB Andrew Benintendi 5.00 12.00
MMRAC Aroldis Chapman 5.00 12.00
MMRAM Andrew McCutchen 5.00 12.00
MMRAR Addison Russell 4.00 10.00
MMRAW Adam Wainwright 4.00 10.00
MMRBB Brandon Belt 4.00 10.00
MMRBC Brandon Crawford 4.00 10.00
MMRBM Brian McCann 4.00 10.00
MMRBN Brandon Nimmo 4.00 10.00
MMRBP Buster Posey 6.00 15.00
MMRCA Chris Archer 3.00 8.00
MMRCB Cody Bellinger 10.00 25.00
MMRCC Carlos Correa 5.00 12.00
MMRCD Corey Dickerson 3.00 8.00
MMRCK Craig Kimbrel 4.00 10.00
MMRCM Carlos Martinez 4.00 10.00
MMRCS CC Sabathia 4.00 10.00
MMRCT Chris Taylor 4.00 10.00
MMRCY Christian Yelich 6.00 15.00
MMRDB Dellin Betances 4.00 10.00
MMRDG Dee Gordon 3.00 8.00
MMRDO David Ortiz 5.00 12.00
MMRDP David Price 4.00 10.00
MMRDS Dansby Swanson 5.00 12.00
MMREH Eric Hosmer 4.00 10.00
MMREI Ender Inciarte 3.00 8.00
MMREL Evan Longoria 4.00 10.00
MMRER Eddie Rosario 4.00 10.00
MMRET Eric Thames 3.00 8.00
MMRFB Franklin Barreto 3.00 8.00
MMRFF Freddie Freeman 6.00 15.00
MMRFH Felix Hernandez 4.00 10.00
MMRGP Gregory Polanco 4.00 10.00
MMRGS Giancarlo Stanton 5.00 12.00
MMRHR Hyun-Jin Ryu 4.00 10.00
MMRIH Ian Happ 4.00 10.00
MMRJA Jose Abreu 5.00 12.00
MMRJB Jackie Bradley Jr. 5.00 12.00
MMRJC Johnny Cueto 4.00 10.00
MMRJd Jacob deGrom 10.00 25.00
MMRJE Jacoby Ellsbury 4.00 10.00
MMRJG Joey Gallo 4.00 10.00
MMRJH Jason Heyward 4.00 10.00
MMRJL Jake Lamb 4.00 10.00
MMRJM Joe Mauer 4.00 10.00
MMRJP Joe Panik 4.00 10.00
MMRJS Jeff Samardzija 3.00 8.00
MMRJT Jameson Taillon 4.00 10.00
MMRJV Joey Votto 5.00 12.00
MMRJW Jesse Winker 5.00 12.00
MMRKF Kyle Freeland 4.00 10.00
MMRKK Kevin Kiermaier 4.00 10.00
MMRKM Kenta Maeda 4.00 10.00
MMRKS Kyle Seager 3.00 8.00
MMRKW Kolten Wong 4.00 10.00
MMRLS Luis Severino 4.00 10.00
MMRMA Miguel Andujar 5.00 12.00
MMRMB Mookie Betts 10.00 25.00
MMRMC Miguel Cabrera 5.00 12.00
MMRMF Max Fried 5.00 12.00
MMRMK Max Kepler 4.00 10.00
MMRMO Matt Olson 5.00 12.00
MMRMS Marcus Stroman 4.00 10.00
MMRMW Michael Wacha 4.00 10.00
MMRNA Nolan Arenado 8.00 20.00
MMRNC Nicholas Castellanos 5.00 12.00
MMRNM Nomar Mazara 3.00 8.00
MMRNS Noah Syndergaard 4.00 10.00
MMRPD Paul DeJong 5.00 12.00
MMRPG Paul Goldschmidt 5.00 12.00
MMRRB Ryan Braun 4.00 10.00
MMRRD Rafael Devers 6.00 15.00
MMRRI Raisel Iglesias 3.00 8.00
MMRRO Rougned Odor 4.00 10.00
MMRRP Rick Porcello 4.00 10.00
MMRRZ Ryan Zimmerman 4.00 10.00
MMRSC Shin-Soo Choo 4.00 10.00
MMRSD Sean Doolittle 3.00 8.00
MMRSG Scooter Gennett 4.00 10.00
MMRSM Starling Marte 4.00 10.00
MMRSP Salvador Perez 4.00 10.00
MMRSS Stephen Strasburg 5.00 12.00
MMRTM Trey Mancini 4.00 10.00
MMRTP Tommy Pham 3.00 8.00
MMRTS Travis Shaw 3.00 8.00
MMRTT Trea Turner 4.00 10.00
MMRVM Victor Martinez 4.00 10.00
MMRWM Wil Myers 4.00 10.00
MMRXB Xander Bogaerts 5.00 12.00
MMRYC Yoenis Cespedes 5.00 12.00
MMRYM Yadier Molina 6.00 15.00
MMRYP Yasiel Puig 5.00 12.00
MMRZG Zack Greinke 5.00 12.00
MMRZW Zack Wheeler 4.00 10.00
MMRAMC Andrew McCutchen 5.00 12.00
MMRARE Anthony Rendon 5.00 12.00
MMRARN Anthony Rendon 5.00 12.00
MMRARO Amed Rosario 4.00 10.00
MMRARU Addison Russell 4.00 10.00
MMRAWA Adam Wainwright 4.00 10.00
MMRBBU Byron Buxton 5.00 12.00
MMRBBX Byron Buxton 5.00 12.00
MMRBCR Brandon Crawford 4.00 10.00
MMRCAR Chris Archer 3.00 8.00
MMRCKI Craig Kimbrel 4.00 10.00
MMRCMA Carlos Martinez 4.00 10.00
MMRCSA Chris Sale 5.00 12.00
MMRDBE Dellin Betances 4.00 10.00
MMRDBU Dylan Bundy 4.00 10.00
MMRDGR Didi Gregorius 4.00 10.00
MMRDPD Dustin Pedroia 5.00 12.00
MMRDPE Dustin Pedroia 5.00 12.00
MMRDPR David Price 4.00 10.00
MMRDSW Dansby Swanson 5.00 12.00
MMRELO Evan Longoria 4.00 10.00
MMRGSP George Springer 4.00 10.00
MMRHRY Hyun-Jin Ryu 4.00 10.00
MMRJAG Jesus Aguilar 4.00 10.00
MMRJAL Jose Altuve 4.00 10.00
MMRJBE Josh Bell 4.00 10.00
MMRJBI Jose Berrios 4.00 10.00
MMRJBL Josh Bell 4.00 10.00
MMRJBR Jackie Bradley Jr. 5.00 12.00
MMRJCU Johnny Cueto 4.00 10.00
MMRJDO Josh Donaldson 4.00 10.00
MMRJFL Jack Flaherty 5.00 12.00
MMRJHE Jason Heyward 4.00 10.00
MMRJLE Jon Lester 4.00 10.00
MMRJMA Joe Mauer 4.00 10.00
MMRJMR J.D. Martinez 5.00 12.00
MMRJPD Joc Pederson 4.00 10.00
MMRJPE Jose Peraza 4.00 10.00
MMRJSM Justin Smoak 3.00 8.00
MMRJTA Jameson Taillon 4.00 10.00
MMRJTH Julio Teheran 4.00 10.00
MMRJVE Justin Verlander 5.00 12.00
MMRJVR Justin Verlander 5.00 12.00
MMRKKI Kevin Kiermaier 4.00 10.00
MMRKSE Kyle Seager 3.00 8.00
MMRMBE Mookie Betts 10.00 25.00
MMRMCA Miguel Cabrera 5.00 12.00
MMRMCN Michael Conforto 4.00 10.00
MMRMCO Michael Conforto 4.00 10.00
MMRMFU Michael Fulmer 3.00 8.00
MMRMMI Miles Mikolas 5.00 12.00
MMRMSA Miguel Sano 4.00 10.00
MMRMSC Max Scherzer 5.00 12.00
MMRMST Marcus Stroman 4.00 10.00
MMRNMA Nick Markakis 4.00 10.00
MMRRPO Rick Porcello 4.00 10.00
MMRSGA Sonny Gray 4.00 10.00
MMRSMA Steven Matz 3.00 8.00
MMRSMR Starling Marte 4.00 10.00
MMRSST Stephen Strasburg 5.00 12.00
MMRTMA Trey Mancini 4.00 10.00
MMRWMR Whit Merrifield 5.00 12.00
MMRWMY Wil Myers 4.00 10.00
MMRXBO Xander Bogaerts 5.00 12.00
MMRYCE Yoenis Cespedes 5.00 12.00
MMRYPU Yasiel Puig 5.00 12.00

2019 Topps Museum Collection Meaningful Material Relics Copper

*COPPER: .5X TO 1.2X BASIC
STATED ODDS 1:17 HOBBY
STATED PRINT RUN 35 SER.#'d SETS
MMRBP Buster Posey 10.00 25.00

2019 Topps Museum Collection Meaningful Material Relics Gold

*GOLD: .5X TO 1.2X BASIC
STATED ODDS 1:22 HOBBY
STATED PRINT RUN 25 SER.#'d SETS
MMRAB Andrew Benintendi 15.00 40.00
MMRAP Albert Pujols 8.00 20.00
MMRBP Buster Posey 12.00 30.00
MMRABR Alex Bregman 10.00 25.00

2019 Topps Museum Collection Primary Pieces Four Player Quad Relics

STATED PRINT 1:35 HOBBY
STATED PRINT RUN 99 SER.#'d SETS
*COPPER/75: .4X TO 1X BASIC
*GOLD/25: .75X TO 2X BASIC
FPRABCS Altve/Brgmn/Crra/Sprngr 5.00 12.00
FPRABMT Starling Marte 4.00 10.00
Jameson Taillon
Josh Bell
Chris Archer
FPRBASD Charlie Blackmon 8.00 20.00
David Dahl
Trevor Story
Nolan Arenado
FPRBBRS Brynt/Schwrbr/Rzzo/Baez 12.00 30.00
FPRBPBB Betts/Bgrts/Pdra/Bnntndi 10.00 25.00
FPRBSBM Sale/Mrtnz/Bnntndi/Btts 10.00 25.00
FPRCARN Alnso/Rsro/Nmmo/Cnfrto 25.00 60.00
FPRCDOM Matt Chapman 5.00 12.00
Sean Manaea
Matt Olson
Khris Davis
FPRCPLB Belt/Lngra/Crwfrd/Psy 6.00 15.00
FPRFDSA Frmn/Dnldsn/Swnsn/Albs 6.00 15.00
FPRHMKU Myrs/Knslr/Uris/Hsmr 5.00 12.00
FPRKPBM Krshw/Pdrsn/Bllngr/Muncy 10.00 25.00
FPRLRKB Trevor Bauer 6.00 15.00
Corey Kluber
Jose Ramirez
Francisco Lindor
FPRMGMC Mlna/Gldschmdt
Crpntr/Mrtnz 6.00 15.00

FPRRASC Ryan Braun 4.00 10.00
Jesus Aguilar
Lorenzo Cain
Travis Shaw
FPRRSLH Hywrd/Lstr/Schwrbr/Rizzo 6.00 15.00
FPRSATG Snchz/Trrs/Andjr/Grgous 10.00 25.00
FPRSPBB Prce/Bnntndi/Btts/Sale 10.00 25.00
FPRSSAT Gary Sanchez 5.00 12.00
Luis Severino
Masahiro Tanaka
Miguel Andujar
FPRSSTS Soto/Schrzr/Trnr/Strsbrg 15.00 40.00
FPRSTSC CC Sabathia 5.00 12.00
Masahiro Tanaka
Aroldis Chapman
Luis Severino
FPRTPOU Ohtni/Pjls/Trt/Uptn 25.00 60.00
FPRTRGC Ryan/Trout/Grrro/Crw 25.00 60.00
FPRZTSR Soto/Rndn/Trnr/Zmmrmn 15.00 40.00

2019 Topps Museum Collection Primary Pieces Four Player Quad Relics Copper

*COPPER: .4X TO 1X BASIC
STATED ODDS 1:46 HOBBY
STATED PRINT RUN 75 SER.#'d SETS
FPRMTO Shohei Ohtani 25.00 60.00
Masahiro Tanaka
Ichiro
Hideki Matsui

2019 Topps Museum Collection Primary Pieces Quad Relics

STATED ODDS 1:12 HOBBY
STATED PRINT RUN 99 SER.#'d SETS
*COPPER/75: .4X TO 1X BASIC
*GOLD/25: .6X TO 1.5X BASIC
SPQRAB Andrew Benintendi 4.00 10.00
SPQRAC Aroldis Chapman 4.00 10.00
SPQRAP Albert Pujols 6.00 15.00
SPQRAR Anthony Rizzo 5.00 12.00
SPQRAW Adam Wainwright 3.00 8.00
SPQRBB Byron Buxton 4.00 10.00
SPQRBC Brandon Crawford 3.00 8.00
SPQRBP Buster Posey 5.00 12.00
SPQRCA Chris Archer 2.50 6.00
SPQRCB Charlie Blackmon 4.00 10.00
SPQRCC Carlos Correa 4.00 10.00
SPQRCK Clayton Kershaw 6.00 15.00
SPQRCM Carlos Martinez 3.00 8.00
SPQRCS Chris Sale 4.00 10.00
SPQRDG Didi Gregorius 3.00 8.00
SPQRDP David Price 3.00 8.00
SPQRDS Dansby Swanson 4.00 10.00
SPQREA Elvis Andrus 3.00 8.00
SPQREH Eric Hosmer 3.00 8.00
SPQREL Evan Longoria 3.00 8.00
SPQRFF Freddie Freeman 5.00 12.00
SPQRFL Francisco Lindor 4.00 10.00
SPQRGS George Springer 3.00 8.00
SPQRJA Jose Abreu 4.00 10.00
SPQRJB Javier Baez 5.00 12.00
SPQRJG Joey Gallo 3.00 8.00
SPQRJH Jason Heyward 3.00 8.00
SPQRJL Jon Lester 3.00 8.00
SPQRJM J.D. Martinez 4.00 10.00
SPQRJR Jose Ramirez 3.00 8.00
SPQRJS Justin Smoak 2.50 6.00
SPQRJU Justin Upton 3.00 8.00
SPQRJV Joey Votto 4.00 10.00
SPQRKB Kris Bryant 5.00 12.00
SPQRKK Kevin Kiermaier 3.00 8.00
SPQRKS Kyle Seager 2.50 6.00
SPQRLS Luis Severino 3.00 8.00
SPQRMA Miguel Andujar 4.00 10.00
SPQRMB Mookie Betts 8.00 20.00
SPQRMC Miguel Cabrera 4.00 10.00
SPQRMO Marcell Ozuna 4.00 10.00
SPQRMS Marcus Stroman 3.00 8.00
SPQRNA Nolan Arenado 6.00 15.00
SPQRNC Nicholas Castellanos 4.00 10.00
SPQRNS Noah Syndergaard 3.00 8.00
SPQROA Ozzie Albies 4.00 10.00
SPQRPD Paul DeJong 4.00 10.00
SPQRRB Ryan Braun 3.00 8.00
SPQRRD Rafael Devers 5.00 12.00
SPQRRH Rhys Hoskins 5.00 12.00
SPQRRZ Ryan Zimmerman 3.00 8.00
SPQRSM Starling Marte 3.00 8.00
SPQRSP Salvador Perez 3.00 8.00
SPQRSS Stephen Strasburg 4.00 10.00
SPQRTB Trevor Bauer 5.00 12.00
SPQRTM Trey Mancini 3.00 8.00
SPQRTS Trevor Story 4.00 10.00
SPQRTT Trea Turner 3.00 8.00
SPQRVR Victor Robles 5.00 12.00
SPQRWM Whit Merrifield 4.00 10.00
SPQRXB Xander Bogaerts 4.00 10.00
SPQRYG Yuli Gurriel 3.00 8.00
SPQRYM Yadier Molina 5.00 12.00
SPQRZG Zack Greinke 4.00 10.00
SPQRABR Alex Bregman 6.00 15.00
SPQRARE Anthony Rendon 4.00 10.00
SPQRCBE Cody Bellinger 8.00 20.00
SPQRCSA Carlos Santana 3.00 8.00
SPQRDGO Dee Gordon 2.50 6.00
SPQRDPE Dustin Pedroia 4.00 10.00
SPQRGSA Gary Sanchez 4.00 10.00
SPQRJAL Jose Altuve 3.00 8.00
SPQRJSO Juan Soto 12.00 30.00
SPQRMCA Matt Carpenter 4.00 10.00
SPQRMCO Michael Conforto 3.00 8.00
SPQRMSC Max Scherzer 4.00 10.00
SPQRMTA Masahiro Tanaka 3.00 8.00
SPQRWMY Wil Myers 3.00 8.00

2019 Topps Museum Collection Primary Pieces Quad Relics Gold

*GOLD: .6X TO 1.5X BASIC
STATED ODDS 1:44 HOBBY
STATED PRINT RUN 25 SER.#'d SETS
SPQRFF Freddie Freeman 12.00 30.00
SPQRMB Mookie Betts 12.00 30.00
SPQRMT Mike Trout 40.00 100.00

2019 Topps Museum Collection Primary Pieces Quad Relics Legends

STATED ODDS 1:122 HOBBY
STATED PRINT RUN 25 SER.#'d SETS
SPQLAK Al Kaline 12.00 30.00
SPQLBL Barry Larkin 8.00 20.00
SPQLCR Cal Ripken Jr. 20.00 50.00
SPQLCY Carl Yastrzemski 20.00 50.00
SPQLDJ Derek Jeter 30.00 80.00
SPQLDM Don Mattingly 20.00 50.00
SPQLEM Eddie Mathews 10.00 25.00
SPQLFT Frank Thomas 15.00 40.00
SPQLGB George Brett 20.00 50.00
SPQLJB Johnny Bench 15.00 40.00
SPQLJM Johnny Mize 40.00 100.00
SPQLKG Ken Griffey Jr. 20.00 50.00
SPQLMM Mark McGwire 15.00 40.00
SPQLMP Mike Piazza 25.00 60.00
SPQLNR Nolan Ryan 20.00 50.00
SPQLOS Ozzie Smith 15.00 40.00
SPQLPM Pedro Martinez 5.00 12.00
SPQLPR Pee Wee Reese 5.00 12.00
SPQLRH Rickey Henderson 15.00 40.00
SPQLRJ Reggie Jackson 10.00 25.00
SPQLRY Robin Yount 10.00 25.00
SPQLTG Tony Gwynn 40.00 100.00
SPQLTW Ted Williams 40.00 100.00
SPQLWB Wade Boggs 15.00 40.00
SPQLRCL Roger Clemens 8.00 20.00
SPQLRHO Rogers Hornsby 25.00 60.00
SPQLTSP Tris Speaker 30.00 80.00

2019 Topps Museum Collection Signature Swatches Dual Relic Autographs

STATED ODDS 1:9 HOBBY
PRINT RUNS B/WN 99-299 COPIES PER
EXCHANGE DEADLINE 5/31/2021
*COPPER/50: .5X TO 1.2X BASIC
*GOLD/25: .6X TO 1.5X BASIC
SSDABN Brandon Nimmo/299 5.00 12.00
SSDABS Blake Snell/299 5.00 12.00
SSDACF Clint Frazier/199 5.00 12.00
SSDACM Cedric Mullins/299 12.00 30.00
SSDACS Carlos Santana/299 5.00 12.00
SSDADG Didi Gregorius/299 6.00 15.00
SSDAER Eddie Rosario/199 5.00 12.00
SSDAFR Franmil Reyes/299 4.00 10.00
SSDAHB Harrison Bader/299 5.00 12.00
SSDAJA Jesus Aguilar/199 5.00 12.00
SSDAJB Jose Berrios/299 5.00 12.00
SSDAJF Jack Flaherty/299 6.00 15.00
SSDAJH Josh Hader/199 5.00 12.00
SSDAJM Jose Martinez/299 4.00 10.00
SSDAJS Justin Smoak/149 4.00 10.00
SSDAKD Khris Davis/199 6.00 15.00
SSDALG Lourdes Gurriel Jr./299 5.00 12.00
SSDALV Luke Voit/299 25.00 60.00
SSDAMC Matt Chapman/191 6.00 15.00
SSDAMH Mitch Haniger/199 5.00 12.00
SSDAMM Max Muncy/199 5.00 12.00
SSDAMO Marcell Ozuna/99 6.00 15.00
SSDAOA Ozzie Albies/199 6.00 15.00
SSDAOH Odubel Herrera/199 5.00 12.00
SSDAPD Paul DeJong/299 6.00 15.00
SSDARL Ramon Laureano/299 10.00 25.00
SSDARO Ryan O'Hearn/299 4.00 10.00
SSDASG Scooter Gennett/299 5.00 12.00
SSDASP Salvador Perez/99 5.00 12.00
SSDATM Trey Mancini/199 5.00 12.00
SSDATP Tommy Pham/199 4.00 10.00
SSDATT Touki Toussaint/299 5.00 12.00
SSDAVR Victor Robles/199 8.00 20.00
SSDAWA Willy Adames/299 4.00 10.00
SSDAWM Whit Merrifield/199 6.00 15.00
SSDAZW Zack Wheeler/249 5.00 12.00
SSDAJSE Jean Segura/299 6.00 15.00
SSDAMKO Michael Kopech/299 12.00 30.00
SSDASMA Steven Matz/299 4.00 10.00
SSDATSH Travis Shaw/199 4.00 10.00

2019 Topps Museum Collection Signature Swatches Dual Relic Autographs Copper

*COPPER: .5X TO 1.2X BASIC
STATED ODDS 1:39 HOBBY
STATED PRINT RUN 50 SER.#'d SETS
EXCHANGE DEADLINE 5/31/2021
SSDAET Eric Thames 5.00 12.00
SSDASM Sean Manaea 5.00 12.00
SSDAWC Willson Contreras 6.00 15.00
SSDAGSP George Springer 12.00 30.00
SSDAMCA Matt Carpenter 8.00 20.00

2019 Topps Museum Collection Signature Swatches Dual Relic Autographs Gold

*GOLD: .6X TO 1.5X BASIC
STATED ODDS 1:73 HOBBY
STATED PRINT RUN 25 SER.#'d SETS
EXCHANGE DEADLINE 5/31/2021
SSDAAR Anthony Rizzo 20.00 50.00
SSDAJAL Jose Altuve 15.00 40.00

2019 Topps Museum Collection Signature Swatches Triple Relic Autographs

STATED ODDS 1:18 HOBBY
PRINT RUNS B/WN 80-299 COPIES PER
EXCHANGE DEADLINE 5/31/2021
*COPPER: .6X TO 1.5X BASIC
SSTAAM Adalberto Mondesi 12.00 30.00
SSTACB Charlie Blackmon/199 6.00 15.00
SSTACK Corey Kluber/99 5.00 12.00
SSTACS Chris Sale/99 12.00 30.00
SSTADB Dellin Betances/199 10.00 25.00
SSTADD David Dahl/99 4.00 10.00
SSTADJ Danny Jansen/299 4.00 10.00
SSTAEL Evan Longoria/99 5.00 12.00
SSTAFB Franklin Barreto/199 4.00 10.00
SSTAFF Freddie Freeman 20.00 50.00
SSTAFL Francisco Lindor/99 20.00 50.00
SSTAJd Jacob deGrom/99 15.00 40.00
SSTAJR Jim Rice/99 5.00 12.00
SSTAJU Justin Upton/199 5.00 12.00
SSTAKS Kyle Schwarber/99 6.00 15.00
SSTALS Luis Severino/149 5.00 12.00
SSTALU Luis Urias/299 6.00 15.00
SSTAMA Miguel Andujar/99 6.00 15.00
SSTAMF Maikel Franco/99 5.00 12.00
SSTAMG Mark Grace/149 10.00 25.00
SSTAMK Matt Kemp/199 5.00 12.00
SSTAMO Matt Olson/99 6.00 15.00
SSTANS Noah Syndergaard/99 8.00 20.00
SSTARD Rafael Devers/199 15.00 40.00
SSTARH Rhys Hoskins/99 15.00 40.00
SSTARM Jeff McNeil/299 10.00 25.00
SSTASG Shawn Green/99 6.00 15.00
SSTASP Stephen Piscotty/99 4.00 10.00
SSTAVG Vladimir Guerrero/99 12.00 30.00
SSTAARE Anthony Rendon/95 12.00 30.00
SSTAJHI Jordan Hicks/299 5.00 12.00
SSTAJSO Juan Soto/99 25.00 60.00

2019 Topps Museum Collection Superstar Showpieces Autographs

STATED ODDS 1:112 HOBBY
STATED PRINT RUN 25 SER.#'d SETS
EXCHANGE DEADLINE 5/31/2021
SSAJ Aaron Judge 100.00 250.00
SSBL Barry Larkin 25.00 60.00
SSCR Cal Ripken Jr. 50.00 120.00
SSCS Chris Sale 10.00 25.00
SSCY Christian Yelich EXCH 50.00 120.00
SSDM Don Mattingly 25.00 60.00
SSDO David Ortiz 30.00 80.00
SSFF Freddie Freeman 40.00 100.00
SSFL Francisco Lindor 10.00 25.00
SSFT Frank Thomas 30.00 80.00
SSHM Hideki Matsui 50.00 120.00
SSJA Jose Altuve 15.00 40.00
SSJd Jacob deGrom 50.00 120.00
SSJR Jose Ramirez 8.00 20.00
SSJS John Smoltz 20.00 50.00
SSJV Joey Votto 30.00 80.00
SSKB Kris Bryant 60.00 150.00
SSLS Luis Severino 8.00 20.00
SSMA Miguel Andujar 10.00 25.00
SSMT Mike Trout 300.00 600.00
SSOA Ozzie Albies 10.00 25.00
SSOS Ozzie Smith 25.00 60.00
SSRA Ronald Acuna Jr. 125.00 300.00
SSRH Rhys Hoskins 30.00 80.00
SSTS Trevor Story 10.00 25.00
SSWC Will Clark 25.00 60.00
SSYM Yadier Molina EXCH 40.00 100.00
SSJSO Juan Soto 25.00 60.00

2020 Topps Museum Collection

1 Willie Mays 1.50 4.00
2 Nolan Arenado 1.25 3.00
3 Ted Williams 1.50 4.00
4 Jose Ramirez .60 1.50
5 Robinson Cano .60 1.50
6 Mariano Rivera 1.00 2.50
7 J.D. Martinez .75 2.00
8 Fernando Tatis Jr. 4.00 10.00
9 Matt Chapman .75 2.00
10 Tony Gwynn .75 2.00
11 Ichiro 1.00 2.50
12 Aaron Judge 4.00 10.00
13 Juan Soto 2.50 6.00
14 Manny Machado .75 2.00
15 Noah Syndergaard .60 1.50
16 Kyle Lewis RC 6.00 15.00
17 Don Mattingly 1.50 4.00
18 Nico Hoerner RC 2.50 6.00
19 Joey Votto .75 2.00
20 Trevor Story .75 2.00
21 Kris Bryant 1.00 2.50
22 Babe Ruth 2.00 5.00
23 Whit Merrifield .75 2.00
24 Mike Trout 4.00 10.00
25 Cal Ripken Jr. 2.50 6.00
26 Bryce Harper 1.25 3.00
27 Alex Bregman .75 2.00
28 Aristides Aquino RC 5.00 12.00
29 Charlie Blackmon .75 2.00
30 Ryne Sandberg 1.50 4.00
31 Anthony Rendon .75 2.00
32 Giancarlo Stanton .75 2.00
33 Rhys Hoskins 1.00 2.50
34 Jacob deGrom 1.50 4.00
35 Roberto Clemente 4.00 10.00
36 Bo Bichette RC 5.00 12.00
37 Jack Flaherty .75 2.00
38 Ernie Banks .75 2.00
39 Justin Verlander .75 2.00
40 Carlos Correa .75 2.00
41 Ken Griffey Jr. 5.00 12.00
42 Christian Yelich 1.00 2.50
43 Ozzie Albies .75 2.00
44 Walker Buehler 1.00 2.50
45 Cody Bellinger 1.50 4.00
46 Sandy Koufax 1.50 4.00
47 Buster Posey 1.00 2.50
48 Paul Goldschmidt .75 2.00
49 Shane Bieber .75 2.00
50 Mark McGwire 1.25 3.00
51 Hideki Matsui .75 2.00
52 Pete Alonso 2.00 5.00
53 Luis Robert RC 10.00 25.00
54 Keston Hiura 1.00 2.50
55 Ronald Acuna Jr. 4.00 10.00
56 Johnny Bench .75 2.00
57 David Ortiz .75 2.00
58 Josh Bell .60 1.50
59 Vladimir Guerrero Jr. 1.25 3.00
60 Sonny Gray .60 1.50
61 Freddie Freeman 1.00 2.50
62 Clayton Kershaw 1.25 3.00
63 Rickey Henderson .75 2.00
64 Trea Turner .60 1.50
65 Roberto Alomar .60 1.50
66 Masahiro Tanaka .75 2.00
67 Mike Schmidt 1.25 3.00
68 Eloy Jimenez 1.50 4.00
69 Chipper Jones .75 2.00
70 Roger Clemens 1.00 2.50
71 Mookie Betts 1.50 4.00
72 Javier Baez 1.00 2.50
73 George Springer .60 1.50
74 Lou Gehrig 1.50 4.00
75 Gleyber Torres 1.50 4.00
76 George Brett 1.50 4.00
77 Randy Johnson .75 2.00
78 Jesus Luzardo RC 1.25 3.00
79 Albert Pujols 1.00 2.50
80 Stephen Strasburg .75 2.00
81 Anthony Rizzo 1.00 2.50
82 Max Scherzer .75 2.00
83 Brendan McKay RC 1.00 2.50
84 Yordan Alvarez RC 5.00 12.00
85 Andrew McCutchen .75 2.00
86 Yadier Molina 1.00 2.50
87 Gavin Lux RC 3.00 8.00
88 Barry Larkin .60 1.50
89 Rafael Devers 1.00 2.50
90 Gerrit Cole 1.25 3.00
91 Shohei Ohtani 1.25 3.00
92 Nolan Ryan 2.50 6.00
93 Jackie Robinson .75 2.00
94 Ozzie Smith 1.00 2.50
95 Chris Sale .75 2.00
96 Frank Thomas .75 2.00
97 Jose Altuve .60 1.50
98 J.T. Realmuto .75 2.00
99 Francisco Lindor .75 2.00
100 Miguel Cabrera .75 2.00

2020 Topps Museum Collection Amethyst

*AMETHYST: 1X TO 2.5X BASIC
*AMETHYST RC: .75X TO 2X BASIC RC
STATED ODDS 1:9 HOBBY
STATED PRINT RUN 99 SER.#'d SETS
16 Kyle Lewis 15.00 40.00
24 Mike Trout 20.00 50.00
36 Bo Bichette 20.00 50.00
87 Gavin Lux 12.00 30.00

2020 Topps Museum Collection Ruby

*RUBY: 1.5X TO 4X BASIC
*RUBY RC: 1.2X TO 3X BASIC RC
STATED ODDS 1:18 HOBBY
STATED PRINT RUN 50 SER.#'d SETS
16 Kyle Lewis 25.00 60.00
24 Mike Trout 30.00 80.00
36 Bo Bichette 30.00 80.00
87 Gavin Lux 30.00 80.00

2020 Topps Museum Collection Sapphire

*SAPPHIRE: .75X TO 2X BASIC
*SAPPHIRE RC: ..6X TO 1.5X BASIC RC
STATED ODDS 1:6 HOBBY
STATED PRINT RUN 150 SER.#'d SETS
16 Kyle Lewis 12.00 30.00
24 Mike Trout 15.00 40.00
87 Gavin Lux 10.00 25.00

2020 Topps Museum Collection Archival Autographs

STATED ODDS 1: HOBBY
PRINT RUNS B/WN 99-299 COPIES PER
EXCHANGE DEADLINE 5/31/22
AAAA Adbert Alzolay 6.00 15.00
AAAC Aaron Civale 8.00 20.00
AAAD Andre Dawson 15.00 40.00
AAAH Aaron Hicks 10.00 25.00
AAAN Aaron Nola 10.00 25.00
AAAQ Aristides Aquino 12.00 30.00
AAAR Austin Riley 12.00 30.00
AAAY Alex Young 3.00 8.00
AABB Bo Bichette 75.00 200.00
AABM Brendan McKay 5.00 12.00
AADC Dylan Cease 5.00 12.00
AADE Dennis Eckersley 10.00 25.00
AADL DJ LeMahieu 40.00 100.00
AADM Dustin May 20.00 50.00
AADS Dansby Swanson 15.00 40.00
AAEJ Eloy Jimenez 20.00 50.00
AAFT Fernando Tatis Jr. 75.00 200.00
AAGL Gavin Lux 40.00 100.00
AAJL Jesus Luzardo 6.00 15.00
AAJR Jake Rogers 3.00 8.00
AAJS Jorge Soler 5.00 12.00
AAKH Kyle Hendricks 15.00 40.00
AAKL Kyle Lewis 40.00 100.00
AALA Logan Allen 3.00 8.00
AALB Lou Brock 15.00 40.00
AALG Lucas Giolito 10.00 25.00
AALR Luis Robert 125.00 300.00
AALW Logan Webb 5.00 12.00
AAMD Mauricio Dubon 4.00 10.00
AAMK Max Kepler 4.00 10.00
AAMS Mike Soroka 15.00 40.00
AAMY Mike Yastrzemski 20.00 50.00
AANH Nico Hoerner 12.00 30.00
AANS Nick Solak 6.00 15.00
AARG Robel Garcia 3.00 8.00
AARH Rhys Hoskins 12.00 30.00
AASB Seth Brown 3.00 8.00
AASM Sean Murphy 5.00 12.00
AATA Tim Anderson 10.00 25.00
AATG Trent Grisham 10.00 25.00
AAWC Willson Contreras 10.00 25.00
AAWM Whit Merrifield 6.00 15.00
AAYA Yordan Alvarez 25.00 60.00
AAYG Yasmani Grandal 8.00 20.00
AABRO Brendan Rodgers 5.00 12.00
AADMU Dale Murphy 12.00 30.00
AADST Darryl Strawberry 15.00 40.00
AAJAY Jaylin Davis 5.00 12.00
AAJCA Jose Canseco 15.00 40.00
AAJFL Jack Flaherty 12.00 30.00
AAJMA Juan Marichal 12.00 30.00
AAJMC Jeff McNeil 10.00 25.00
AAJRI Jim Rice 12.00 30.00
AAJSO Juan Soto 100.00 250.00
AAJTR J.T. Realmuto 12.00 30.00
AAJVA Jason Varitek 25.00 60.00
AAKHI Keston Hiura 10.00 25.00
AAMMU Max Muncy 8.00 20.00
AANSE Nick Senzel 8.00 20.00
AAPCO Patrick Corbin 4.00 10.00
AAWCL Will Clark 20.00 50.00

2020 Topps Museum Collection Archival Autographs Copper

AAAR Austin Riley 20.00 50.00
AACF Carlton Fisk 20.00 50.00
AAGT Gleyber Torres 40.00 100.00
AAJA Jose Altuve 5.00 12.00
AAPA Pete Alonso 40.00 100.00
AARA Roberto Alomar 20.00 50.00
AARC Rod Carew 15.00 40.00
AASC Steve Carlton 15.00 40.00
AAVG Vladimir Guerrero Jr. 30.00 80.00
AADMA Don Mattingly 30.00 80.00
AAJSM John Smoltz 25.00 60.00
AAPET Andy Pettitte 20.00 50.00
AARAJ Ronald Acuna Jr. 50.00 120.00
AATGL Tom Glavine 20.00 50.00

2020 Topps Museum Collection Archival Autographs Gold

*GOLD/25: .6X TO 1.5X BASIC
STATED ODDS 1: HOBBY
STATED PRINT RUN 25 SER.#'d SETS
EXCHANGE DEADLINE 5/31/22
AAI Ichiro 150.00 400.00
AAAR Austin Riley 25.00 60.00
AAKB Kris Bryant 40.00 100.00
AAMTR Mike Trout 400.00 800.00

2020 Topps Museum Collection Canvas Collection Reprints

STATED ODDS 1:4 HOBBY
CCR1 Juan Soto 3.00 8.00
CCR2 Mookie Betts 5.00 12.00
CCR3 Mike Trout 5.00 12.00
CCR4 Vladimir Guerrero Jr. 1.50 4.00
CCR5 Ronald Acuna Jr. 4.00 10.00
CCR6 Don Mattingly 8.00 20.00
CCR7 Ernie Banks 4.00 10.00
CCR8 Jacob deGrom 2.00 5.00
CCR9 Gleyber Torres 8.00 20.00
CCR10 Max Scherzer 1.00 2.50
CCR11 Paul Goldschmidt 1.00 2.50
CCR12 Christian Yelich 1.25 3.00
CCR13 Ken Griffey Jr. 8.00 20.00
CCR14 Ty Cobb 8.00 20.00
CCR15 Gerrit Cole 6.00 15.00
CCR16 Rod Carew .75 2.00
CCR17 Frank Thomas 1.00 2.50
CCR18 Cody Bellinger 2.00 5.00
CCR19 Pete Alonso 2.50 6.00
CCR20 Bryce Harper 10.00 25.00
CCR21 Rafael Devers 8.00 20.00
CCR22 Cal Ripken Jr. 5.00 12.00
CCR23 Yordan Alvarez 6.00 15.00
CCR24 Anthony Rendon 10.00 25.00
CCR25 Eloy Jimenez 4.00 10.00
CCR26 Roberto Clemente 6.00 15.00
CCR27 Mike Piazza 6.00 15.00
CCR28 Gavin Lux 3.00 8.00
CCR29 Albert Pujols 1.25 3.00
CCR30 Bo Bichette 10.00 25.00
CCR31 Willie Mays 5.00 12.00
CCR32 Fernando Tatis Jr. 5.00 12.00
CCR33 Shohei Ohtani 1.50 4.00
CCR34 Andre Dawson .75 2.00
CCR35 Ryne Sandberg 2.00 5.00
CCR36 Anthony Rizzo 1.25 3.00
CCR37 Ichiro 5.00 12.00
CCR38 Hank Aaron 5.00 12.00
CCR39 Reggie Jackson 4.00 10.00
CCR40 Ozzie Smith 4.00 10.00
CCR41 Roberto Alomar .75 2.00
CCR42 Nolan Arenado 4.00 10.00
CCR43 Keston Hiura 5.00 12.00
CCR44 Francisco Lindor 5.00 12.00
CCR45 Mike Schmidt 5.00 12.00
CCR46 Wade Boggs 5.00 12.00
CCR47 Luis Robert 15.00 40.00
CCR48 Lou Gehrig 2.00 5.00
CCR49 Jackie Robinson 5.00 12.00
CCR50 Gary Carter 4.00 10.00

2020 Topps Museum Collection Dual Meaningful Material Relics

STATED ODDS 1: HOBBY
STATED PRINT RUN 50 SER.#'d SETS
DMRAC C.Correa/J.Altuve 6.00 15.00
DMRAM A.Pujols/M.Cabrera 10.00 25.00
DMRAS N.Arenado/T.Story 12.00 30.00
DMRBC W.Contreras/J.Baez 10.00 25.00
DMRBD X.Bogaerts/R.Devers 12.00 30.00
DMRBR K.Bryant/A.Rizzo 8.00 20.00
DMRBS A.Bregman/G.Springer 6.00 15.00
DMRFO F.Freeman/O.Albies 8.00 20.00
DMRGA J.Gallo/E.Andrus 6.00 15.00
DMRGB V.Guerrero Jr./B.Bichette 10.00 25.00
DMRHB B.Harper/K.Bryant 10.00 25.00
DMRMM R.Acuna Jr./M.Trout 30.00 80.00
DMROB M.Betts/D.Ortiz 12.00 30.00
DMROP D.Ortiz/D.Pedroia 6.00 15.00
DMRSC L.Severino/A.Chapman 6.00 15.00
DMRSL S.Strasburg/M.Scherzer 6.00 15.00
DMRST T.Turner/S.Strasburg 6.00 15.00
DMRTA G.Torres/M.Andujar 12.00 30.00
DMRTH B.Harper/M.Trout 30.00 80.00
DMRVG J.Votto/S.Gray 10.00 25.00
DMRBAL A.Bregman/J.Altuve 6.00 15.00
DMRBAR C.Archer/J.Bell 5.00 12.00
DMRBBU C.Bellinger/W.Buehler 20.00 50.00
DMRHVO D.Vogelbach/M.Haniger 12.00 30.00
DMRKSA M.Sano/M.Kepler 5.00 12.00
DMRMBO X.Bogaerts/J.Martinez 6.00 15.00
DMRPLO B.Posey/E.Longoria 8.00 20.00
DMRPSA C.Sabathia/A.Pettitte 5.00 12.00
DMRSCO M.Conforto/N.Syndergaard 5.00 12.00
DMRVTJ V.Guerrero Jr./F.Tatis Jr. 30.00 80.00

2020 Topps Museum Collection Dual Meaningful Material Relics Copper

*COPPER/35: .4X TO 1X BASIC
STATED ODDS 1: HOBBY
STATED PRINT RUN 35 SER.#'d SETS
DMRAS N.Arenado/T.Story 25.00 60.00
DMRSL S.Strasburg/M.Scherzer 15.00 40.00
DMRKSA M.Sano/M.Kepler 12.00 30.00
DMRMBO X.Bogaerts/J.Martinez 12.00 30.00
DMRPSA C.Sabathia/A.Pettitte 12.00 30.00

2020 Topps Museum Collection Meaningful Material Relics

STATED ODDS 1: HOBBY
STATED PRINT RUN 50 SER.#'d SETS
MMRAB Andrew Benintendi 5.00 12.00
MMRAC Aroldis Chapman 5.00 12.00
MMRAM Andrew McCutchen 12.00 30.00
MMRAR Austin Riley 6.00 15.00
MMRBC Brandon Crawford 4.00 10.00
MMRBH Bryce Harper 8.00 20.00
MMRBN Brandon Nimmo 4.00 10.00
MMRBP Buster Posey 6.00 15.00
MMRCA Chris Archer 3.00 8.00
MMRCB Cody Bellinger 10.00 25.00
MMRCC Carlos Correa 5.00 12.00
MMRCP Chris Paddack 5.00 12.00
MMRCS CC Sabathia 4.00 10.00
MMRCT Chris Taylor 4.00 10.00
MMRCY Christian Yelich 6.00 15.00
MMRDO David Ortiz 5.00 12.00
MMRDS Dansby Swanson 5.00 12.00
MMREL Evan Longoria 4.00 10.00
MMRFF Freddie Freeman 6.00 15.00
MMRFH Felix Hernandez 6.00 15.00
MMRJB Jackie Bradley Jr. 5.00 12.00
MMRJG Joey Gallo 5.00 12.00
MMRJH Jason Heyward 4.00 10.00
MMRJM Joe Mauer 4.00 10.00
MMRJS Jeff Samardzija 3.00 8.00
MMRJV Craig Kimbrel 4.00 10.00
MMRKK Kevin Kiermaier 4.00 10.00
MMRKM Kenta Maeda 4.00 10.00
MMRKW Kolten Wong 6.00 15.00
MMRKY Kirby Yates 3.00 8.00
MMRLS Luis Severino 4.00 10.00
MMRLV Luke Voit 6.00 15.00
MMRMA Miguel Andujar 5.00 12.00
MMRMB Mookie Betts 10.00 25.00
MMRMC Miguel Cabrera 5.00 12.00
MMRMF Max Fried 10.00 25.00
MMRMT Mike Trout 25.00 60.00
MMRNA Nolan Arenado 8.00 20.00
MMROA Ozzie Albies 5.00 12.00
MMRRB Ryan Braun 6.00 15.00
MMRRD Rafael Devers 6.00 15.00
MMRRO Rougned Odor 4.00 10.00
MMRRZ Ryan Zimmerman 8.00 20.00
MMRSC Shin-Soo Choo 4.00 10.00
MMRSS Stephen Strasburg 5.00 12.00
MMRTM Trey Mancini 5.00 12.00
MMRTT Trea Turner 4.00 10.00
MMRXB Xander Bogaerts 5.00 12.00
MMRYK Yusei Kikuchi 4.00 10.00
MMRAAQ Aristides Aquino 8.00 20.00
MMRABR Alex Bregman 5.00 12.00
MMRAHI Aaron Hicks 4.00 10.00
MMRAME Austin Meadows 5.00 12.00
MMRAMO Adalberto Mondesi 4.00 10.00
MMRANO Aaron Nola 10.00 25.00
MMRARO Amed Rosario 4.00 10.00
MMRBCR Brandon Crawford 4.00 10.00
MMRBLO Brandon Lowe 4.00 10.00
MMRBRO Brendan Rodgers 5.00 12.00
MMRCBL Charlie Blackmon 5.00 12.00
MMRCCA Carlos Carrasco 3.00 8.00
MMRCCS CC Sabathia 4.00 10.00
MMRCHA Matt Chapman 5.00 12.00
MMRCKE Clayton Kershaw 8.00 20.00
MMRDDA David Dahl 3.00 8.00
MMRDHU Dakota Hudson 4.00 10.00
MMRDJ1 DJ LeMahieu 5.00 12.00
MMRDJL DJ LeMahieu 5.00 12.00
MMRDO1 David Ortiz 5.00 12.00
MMRDPD Dustin Pedroia 5.00 12.00
MMRDPE Dustin Pedroia 5.00 12.00
MMRDPR David Price 4.00 10.00
MMRDSM Dominic Smith 5.00 12.00
MMREAN Elvis Andrus 4.00 10.00
MMRELO Evan Longoria 4.00 10.00
MMRESU Eugenio Suarez 4.00 10.00
MMRFFR Freddie Freeman 6.00 15.00
MMRFTJ Fernando Tatis Jr. 25.00 60.00
MMRGM1 German Marquez 5.00 12.00
MMRGSA Gary Sanchez 5.00 12.00
MMRGSP George Springer 4.00 10.00
MMRGTO Gleyber Torres 10.00 25.00
MMRGUR Gio Urshela 5.00 12.00
MMRHDO Hunter Dozier 3.00 8.00
MMRHRY Justus Sheffield 5.00 12.00
MMRJAL Jose Altuve 4.00 10.00
MMRJAR Jake Arrieta 4.00 10.00
MMRJBA Javier Baez 6.00 15.00
MMRJBE Josh Bell 4.00 10.00
MMRJBI Jose Berrios 4.00 10.00
MMRJBR Jackie Bradley Jr. 5.00 12.00
MMRJFL Jack Flaherty 5.00 12.00
MMRJHA Josh Hader 4.00 10.00
MMRJHI Jordan Hicks 4.00 10.00
MMRJLE Jon Lester 4.00 10.00
MMRJLU Joey Lucchesi 3.00 8.00
MMRJMC Jeff McNeil 4.00 10.00
MMRJMR J.D. Martinez 5.00 12.00
MMRJPD Joc Pederson 4.00 10.00
MMRJPO Jorge Polanco 4.00 10.00
MMRJRA Jose Ramirez 4.00 10.00
MMRJSE Jean Segura 6.00 15.00
MMRJTA Jameson Taillon 4.00 10.00
MMRJTR J.T. Realmuto 6.00 15.00
MMRJVR Justin Verlander 5.00 12.00
MMRKDA Khris Davis 5.00 12.00
MMRKHI Keston Hiura 6.00 15.00
MMRKSE Kyle Seager 3.00 8.00
MMRLC1 Lorenzo Cain 3.00 8.00
MMRLCA Lorenzo Cain 3.00 8.00
MMRLG1 Lourdes Gurriel Jr. 4.00 10.00
MMRLGU Lourdes Gurriel Jr. 4.00 10.00
MMRMBE Mookie Betts 10.00 25.00
MMRMCA Miguel Cabrera 5.00 12.00
MMRMCN Michael Conforto 4.00 10.00
MMRMFO Mike Foltynewicz 3.00 8.00
MMRMGA Mitch Garver 3.00 8.00
MMRMHA Mitch Haniger 4.00 10.00
MMRMMI Miles Mikolas 3.00 8.00
MMRMS1 Miguel Sano 4.00 10.00
MMRMSA Miguel Sano 4.00 10.00
MMRMSC Max Scherzer 5.00 12.00
MMRMSE Marcus Semien 5.00 12.00
MMRMSO Mike Soroka 10.00 25.00
MMRMST Marcus Stroman 4.00 10.00
MMRMT1 Mike Trout 25.00 60.00
MMRMTA Masahiro Tanaka 6.00 15.00
MMRNSE Nick Senzel 5.00 12.00
MMROME Oscar Mercado 5.00 12.00
MMRRAJ Ronald Acuna Jr. 20.00 50.00
MMRRHO Rhys Hoskins 10.00 25.00
MMRRLA Ramon Laureano 8.00 20.00
MMRSGA Sonny Gray 4.00 10.00
MMRSKI Scott Kingery 4.00 10.00
MMRSST Stephen Strasburg 5.00 12.00
MMRTEX Mark Teixeira 4.00 10.00
MMRTGL Tyler Glasnow 5.00 12.00
MMRTMA Trey Mancini 5.00 12.00
MMRTSO Trevor Story 5.00 12.00
MMRTST Trevor Story 5.00 12.00
MMRVGJ Vladimir Guerrero Jr. 8.00 20.00
MMRWAS Willians Astudillo 3.00 8.00
MMRWMR Whit Merrifield 5.00 12.00
MMRWSM Will Smith 5.00 12.00
MMRYGU Yuli Gurriel 10.00 25.00
MMRGSA1 Gary Sanchez 5.00 12.00
MMRJMC1 Jeff McNeil 4.00 10.00
MMRLCAS Luis Castillo 4.00 10.00
MMRMCH1 Michael Chavis 4.00 10.00

2020 Topps Museum Collection Meaningful Material Relics Copper

*COPPER/35: .4X TO 1X BASIC
STATED ODDS 1: HOBBY
STATED PRINT RUN 35 SER.#'d SETS
MMRDS Dansby Swanson 12.00 30.00
MMRJG Joey Gallo 10.00 25.00
MMRJM Joe Mauer 12.00 30.00
MMRKW Kolten Wong 8.00 20.00
MMRMF Max Fried 12.00 30.00
MMROA Ozzie Albies 10.00 25.00
MMRRB Ryan Braun 8.00 20.00
MMRCBL Charlie Blackmon 10.00 25.00
MMRCCA Carlos Carrasco 8.00 20.00
MMRCHA Matt Chapman 15.00 40.00
MMRJLE Jon Lester 10.00 25.00
MMRRHO Rhys Hoskins 12.00 30.00

2020 Topps Museum Collection Meaningful Material Relics Gold

*GOLD/25: .5X TO 1.2X BASIC
STATED ODDS 1: HOBBY
STATED PRINT RUN 25 SER.#'d SETS
MMRAM Andrew McCutchen 25.00 60.00
MMRDS Dansby Swanson 15.00 40.00
MMRJG Joey Gallo 12.00 30.00
MMRJM Joe Mauer 15.00 40.00
MMRKW Kolten Wong 10.00 25.00
MMRMF Max Fried 15.00 40.00
MMROA Ozzie Albies 12.00 30.00
MMRRB Ryan Braun 10.00 25.00
MMRCBL Charlie Blackmon 12.00 30.00
MMRCCA Carlos Carrasco 10.00 25.00
MMRCHA Matt Chapman 20.00 50.00
MMRJLE Jon Lester 15.00 40.00
MMRRHO Rhys Hoskins 15.00 40.00

2020 Topps Museum Collection Primary Pieces Four Player Quad Relics

FPRAAJM Andrsn/Jimnz/Abru/Moncda 10.00 25.00
FPRAFAS Albes/Freman/Acuna/Swnsn 15.00 40.00
FPRASBD Dahl/Story/Arnado/Blkmn 8.00 20.00
FPRBACS Corra/Sprngr/Altve/Brgmn 5.00 12.00
FPRBASV Sprngr/Altve/Brgmn/Vrlndr 5.00 12.00
FPRBBTA Tailln/Rynlds/Bell/Archr 4.00 10.00
FPRCGSB Sano/Cruz/Berios/Grvr 5.00 12.00
FPRCOML Manea/Chpmn/Olsn/Lzrdo 6.00 15.00
FPRDASC dGrm/Syndrgrd/Alnso/Cnfrto 12.00 30.00
FPRGACO Gallo/Choo/Andrus/Odor 5.00 12.00
FPRGBBG GureroJr./Bchtte
Bigio/GurielJr. 15.00 40.00
FPRHHNM Hskns/Hrpr/Nola/Relmto 8.00 20.00
FPRJTSL LeMahu/Tores/Stntn/Judge 12.00 30.00
FPRKBBS Seagr/Belli/Krshw/Buhlr 10.00 25.00
FPRLRSR Santna/Lndor/Rmirz/Reyes 5.00 12.00
FPRMBDB Martnz/Devrs/Bentndi/Bgarts 6.00 15.00
FPRMSMP Perz/Mondsi/Solr/Merifield 5.00 12.00
FPRMTPM TatisJr./Machdo/Myrs/Padak 25.00 60.00
FPRRBBC Rizzo/Baez/Contreras/Bryant 6.00 15.00
FPRRBBS Rizzo/Schwrbr/Bryant/Baez 6.00 15.00
FPRSAGT Soto/AcunaJr./GureroJr.
TatisJr. 100.00 250.00
FPRSBDM Mrtnez/Devers/Bogarts/Sale 6.00 15.00
FPRSSST Schrzr/Soto/Strsbrg/Turnr 15.00 40.00
FPRTPOU Upton/Pujols/Ohtani/Trout 25.00 60.00
FPRVSAS Votto/Senzl/Suarez/Aquino 8.00 20.00
FPRYGFD DeJng/Flhrty/Gldschmdt
Molina 6.00 15.00
FPRYHCB Cain/Hiura/Yelich/Braun 6.00 15.00
FPRZSTR Zimermn/Turnr/Robls/Strsbrg 6.00 15.00

2020 Topps Museum Collection Primary Pieces Four Player Quad Relics Gold

*GOLD/25: .8X TO 2X BASIC
STATED ODDS 1:1221 HOBBY
STATED PRINT RUN 25 SER.#'d SETS
FPRIMTO Ohtani/Ichiro/Matsui/Tanaka 75.00 200.00

2020 Topps Museum Collection Primary Pieces Quad Relics

STATED ODDS 1: HOBBY
STATED PRINT RUN 99 SER.#'d SETS
SPQRAB Andrew Benintendi 8.00 20.00
SPQRAC Aroldis Chapman 8.00 20.00
SPQRAJ Aaron Judge 20.00 50.00
SPQRAM Andrew McCutchen 10.00 25.00
SPQRAP Albert Pujols 8.00 20.00
SPQRAR Anthony Rizzo 12.00 30.00
SPQRBC Brandon Crawford 5.00 12.00
SPQRBH Bryce Harper 20.00 50.00
SPQRBP Buster Posey 8.00 20.00
SPQRCA Chris Archer 2.50 6.00
SPQRCB Charlie Blackmon 8.00 20.00
SPQRCC Carlos Correa 8.00 20.00
SPQRCK Clayton Kershaw 8.00 20.00
SPQRCS Chris Sale 4.00 10.00
SPQRCY Christian Yelich 10.00 25.00
SPQRDP David Price 3.00 8.00
SPQRDS Dansby Swanson 8.00 20.00
SPQREA Elvis Andrus 3.00 8.00
SPQREL Evan Longoria 5.00 12.00
SPQRFF Freddie Freeman 5.00 12.00
SPQRGS George Springer 3.00 8.00
SPQRJA Jose Abreu 4.00 10.00
SPQRJB Javier Baez 5.00 12.00
SPQRJG Joey Gallo 4.00 10.00
SPQRJH Jason Heyward 8.00 20.00
SPQRJL Jon Lester 3.00 8.00
SPQRJM J.D. Martinez 4.00 10.00
SPQRJR Jose Ramirez 8.00 20.00
SPQRJS Lourdes Gurriel Jr. 3.00 8.00
SPQRJU Justin Upton 3.00 8.00
SPQRKK Kevin Kiermaier 3.00 8.00
SPQRKW Kolten Wong 8.00 20.00

SPQRLS Luis Severino 3.00 8.00
SPQRMA Miguel Andujar 4.00 10.00
SPQRMC Miguel Cabrera 8.00 20.00
SPQRMH Mitch Haniger 6.00 15.00
SPQRMS Marcus Stroman 3.00 8.00
SPQRMT Mike Trout 25.00 60.00
SPQRNA Nolan Arenado 6.00 15.00
SPQROA Ozzie Albies 8.00 20.00
SPQRPD Paul DeJong 4.00 10.00
SPQRPG Paul Goldschmidt 8.00 20.00
SPQRRB Ryan Braun 3.00 8.00
SPQRRD Rafael Devers 5.00 12.00
SPQRRH Rhys Hoskins 8.00 20.00
SPQRRZ Ryan Zimmerman 3.00 8.00
SPQRSC Shin-Soo Choo 3.00 8.00
SPQRSG Sonny Gray 10.00 25.00
SPQRSM Starling Marte 3.00 8.00
SPQRSS Stephen Strasburg 6.00 15.00
SPQRTM Trey Mancini 4.00 10.00
SPQRTS Trevor Story 4.00 10.00
SPQRTT Trea Turner 3.00 8.00
SPQRVR Victor Robles 5.00 12.00
SPQRXB Xander Bogaerts 4.00 10.00
SPQRYG Yuli Gurriel 3.00 8.00
SPQRYK Yusei Kikuchi 3.00 8.00
SPQRABR Alex Bregman 4.00 10.00
SPQRAME Austin Meadows 6.00 15.00
SPQRAMO Adalberto Mondesi 3.00 8.00
SPQRBLO Brandon Lowe 3.00 8.00
SPQRCBE Cody Bellinger 15.00 40.00
SPQRCPA Chris Paddack 4.00 10.00
SPQRCSA Carlos Santana 3.00 8.00
SPQRDJL DJ LeMahieu 10.00 25.00
SPQRDPE Dustin Pedroia 10.00 25.00
SPQRGSA Gary Sanchez 6.00 15.00
SPQRJAL Jose Altuve 3.00 8.00
SPQRJHA Josh Hader 3.00 8.00
SPQRJMA Joe Mauer 10.00 25.00
SPQRJMc Jeff McNeil 8.00 20.00
SPQRJTA Jameson Taillon 3.00 8.00
SPQRKHI Keston Hiura 8.00 20.00
SPQRLCA Lorenzo Cain 2.50 6.00
SPQRMCA Matt Carpenter 4.00 10.00
SPQRMCH Michael Chavis 3.00 8.00
SPQRMCO Michael Conforto 3.00 8.00
SPQRMSA Miguel Sano 3.00 8.00
SPQRMSC Max Scherzer 6.00 15.00
SPQRMSO Mike Soroka 10.00 25.00
SPQRMTA Masahiro Tanaka 4.00 10.00

2020 Topps Museum Collection Primary Pieces Quad Relics Copper

*COPPER/75: .4X TO 1X BASIC
STATED ODDS 1:15 HOBBY
STATED PRINT RUN 75 SER.#'d SETS
SPQRRA Ronald Acuna Jr. 15.00 40.00

2020 Topps Museum Collection Primary Pieces Quad Relics Gold

*GOLD/25: .6X TO 1.5X BASIC
STATED ODDS 1:43 HOBBY
STATED PRINT RUN 25 SER.#'d SETS
SPQRMT Mike Trout 75.00 200.00
SPQRRA Ronald Acuna Jr. 75.00 200.00

2020 Topps Museum Collection Primary Pieces Quad Relics Legends

STATED ODDS 1: HOBBY
STATED PRINT RUN 50 SER.#'d SETS
SPQLBL Barry Larkin 12.00 30.00
SPQLCR Cal Ripken Jr. 30.00 80.00
SPQLCY Carl Yastrzemski 25.00 60.00
SPQLDM Don Mattingly 25.00 60.00
SPQLEM Eddie Mathews 20.00 50.00
SPQLFT Frank Thomas 20.00 50.00
SPQLGB George Brett 15.00 40.00
SPQLJB Johnny Bench 25.00 60.00
SPQLKG Ken Griffey Jr. 30.00 80.00
SPQLMP Mark McGwire 20.00 50.00
SPQLNR Nolan Ryan 25.00 60.00
SPQLOS Ozzie Smith 20.00 50.00
SPQLPM Pedro Martinez 6.00 15.00
SPQLRH Rickey Henderson 25.00 60.00
SPQLRJ Reggie Jackson 15.00 40.00
SPQLRY Robin Yount 15.00 40.00
SPQLTG Tony Gwynn 15.00 40.00
SPQLTS Tom Seaver 15.00 40.00
SPQLTW Ted Williams 50.00 120.00
SPQLWB Wade Boggs 25.00 60.00
SPQLBRO Brooks Robinson 40.00 100.00
SPQLJMO Joe Morgan 10.00 25.00
SPQLKGJ Ken Griffey Jr. 50.00 120.00
SPQLRCL Roger Clemens 15.00 40.00
SPQLRHO Willie McCovey 15.00 40.00
SPQLRJA Reggie Jackson 15.00 40.00
SPQLRJO Randy Johnson 12.00 30.00

2020 Topps Museum Collection Signature Swatches Dual Relic Autographs

STATED ODDS 1: HOBBY
PRINT RUNS B/WN 99-299 COPIES PER
EXCHANGE DEADLINE 5/31/22
SSDAAH Aaron Hicks 5.00 12.00
SSDAAM Austin Meadows 6.00 15.00
SSDAAN Aaron Nola 12.00 30.00
SSDABN Nico Hoerner 25.00 60.00
SSDABW Brandon Woodruff 6.00 15.00
SSDACP Chris Paddack 10.00 25.00
SSDADL DJ LeMahieu 30.00 80.00
SSDAEJ Eloy Jimenez 20.00 50.00
SSDAES Eugenio Suarez 12.00 30.00
SSDAGS Gary Sheffield 10.00 25.00
SSDAHD Hunter Dozier 4.00 10.00
SSDAHK Howie Kendrick 4.00 10.00
SSDAJA Keston Hiura 10.00 25.00
SSDAJB Jose Berrios 5.00 12.00
SSDAJH Josh Hader 8.00 20.00
SSDAJP Jorge Polanco 6.00 15.00
SSDAJS Cavan Biggio 15.00 40.00
SSDAKH Kyle Hendricks 10.00 25.00
SSDAKY Kirby Yates 4.00 10.00
SSDALC Luis Castillo 5.00 12.00
SSDALG Lourdes Gurriel Jr. 5.00 12.00
SSDALV Luke Voit 10.00 25.00
SSDAMG Mitch Garver 4.00 10.00
SSDAMH Mitch Haniger 5.00 12.00
SSDAMK Max Kepler 5.00 12.00
SSDAMM Max Muncy 8.00 20.00
SSDAMS Mike Soroka 15.00 40.00
SSDANA Nolan Arenado EXCH 40.00 100.00
SSDANS Nick Solak 8.00 20.00
SSDAPC Patrick Corbin 5.00 12.00
SSDAPD Paul DeJong 6.00 15.00
SSDARH Ryan Howard 10.00 25.00
SSDARL Ramon Laureano 10.00 25.00
SSDASG Sonny Gray 10.00 25.00
SSDASM Sean Murphy 6.00 15.00
SSDATA Tim Anderson 12.00 30.00
SSDATE Tommy Edman 15.00 40.00
SSDATP Tommy Pham 4.00 10.00
SSDAVR Victor Robles 8.00 20.00
SSDAYG Yuli Gurriel 10.00 25.00
SSDALGI Lucas Giolito 8.00 20.00
SSDASGR Shawn Green 8.00 20.00
SSDAWSM Will Smith 10.00 25.00
SSDAYGR Yasmani Grandal 4.00 10.00

2020 Topps Museum Collection Signature Swatches Dual Relic Autographs Copper

*COPPER/50: .5X TO 1.2X BASIC
STATED ODDS 1: HOBBY
STATED PRINT RUN 50 SER.#'d SETS
EXCHANGE DEADLINE 5/31/22
SSDAAJ Andruw Jones 20.00 50.00
SSDAJM J.D. Martinez 15.00 40.00
SSDATL Tim Lincecum 25.00 60.00
SSDATM Trey Mancini 12.00 30.00
SSDAGSP George Springer 10.00 25.00
SSDAJLU Jesus Luzardo 10.00 25.00
SSDAJMA Joe Mauer 20.00 50.00
SSDASMA Sean Manaea 5.00 12.00

2020 Topps Museum Collection Signature Swatches Dual Relic Autographs Gold

*GOLD/25: .6X TO 1.5X BASIC
STATED ODDS 1: HOBBY
STATED PRINT RUN 25 SER.#'d SETS
EXCHANGE DEADLINE 5/31/22
SSDADG Didi Gregorius 10.00 25.00
SSDAWM Whit Merrifield 10.00 25.00

2020 Topps Museum Collection Signature Swatches Triple Relic Autographs

COMMON CARD p/r 99-299 4.00 10.00
SEMISTARS p/r 99-299 5.00 12.00
UNLISTED STARS p/r 99-299 6.00 15.00
COMMON CARD p/r 50 5.00 12.00
SEMISTARS p/r 50 6.00 15.00
UNLISTED STARS p/r 50 8.00 20.00
STATED ODDS 1: HOBBY
PRINT RUNS B/WN 50-299 COPIES PER
EXCHANGE DEADLINE 5/31/22
SSTAAA Aristides Aquino 15.00 40.00
SSTABB Byron Buxton 10.00 25.00
SSTABR Brendan Rodgers 6.00 15.00
SSTACB Charlie Blackmon 15.00 40.00
SSTACF Clint Frazier 10.00 25.00
SSTACS Chris Sale 15.00 40.00
SSTAJd Jacob deGrom 40.00 100.00
SSTAJF Jack Flaherty 12.00 30.00
SSTAJG Juan Gonzalez 10.00 25.00
SSTAJR Jose Ramirez 10.00 25.00
SSTAJS Jorge Soler 8.00 20.00
SSTAJU Justin Upton 5.00 12.00
SSTALS Luis Severino 12.00 30.00
SSTAMA Miguel Andujar 10.00 25.00
SSTAMS Max Scherzer 30.00 80.00
SSTAPG Paul Goldschmidt 20.00 50.00
SSTARA Ronald Acuna Jr. 75.00 200.00
SSTARD Rafael Devers 15.00 40.00
SSTARH Rhys Hoskins 10.00 25.00
SSTATB Trevor Bauer 12.00 301.00
SSTAWC Willson Contreras 12.00 30.00
SSTAXB Xander Bogaerts 15.00 40.00
SSTAYA Yordan Alvarez 30.00 80.00
SSTAAMC Andrew McCutchen 30.00 80.00
SSTAARI Austin Riley 8.00 20.00
SSTACSA Carlos Santana 5.00 12.00
SSTAJSO Juan Soto 50.00 120.00
SSTAJTR J.T. Realmuto 12.00 30.00
SSTAMOZ Marcell Ozuna 25.00 60.00
SSTANSE Nick Senzel 15.00 40.00
SSTASSC Shin-Soo Choo 12.00 30.00

2020 Topps Museum Collection Signature Swatches Triple Relic Autographs Copper

*COPPER/50: .5X TO 1.2X p/r 99-299
*COPPER/25: .5X TO 1.2X p/r 50
STATED ODDS 1: HOBBY
PRINT RUNS B/WN 25-50 COPIES PER
EXCHANGE DEADLINE 5/31/22
SSTAAB Adrian Beltre 30.00 80.00
SSTAAR Anthony Rizzo 40.00 100.00
SSTABM Brendan McKay 10.00 25.00
SSTACY Christian Yelich 30.00 80.00
SSTAGL Gavin Lux 60.00 150.00
SSTAGS Gary Sanchez 25.00 60.00
SSTAJA Jose Altuve 20.00 50.00
SSTAMC Miguel Cabrera 50.00 120.00
SSTAMM Manny Machado 25.00 60.00
SSTAVG Vladimir Guerrero 20.00 50.00

2020 Topps Museum Collection Signature Swatches Triple Relic Autographs Gold

*GOLD/25: .6X TO 1.5X p/r 99-299
STATED ODDS 1: HOBBY
PRINT RUNS B/WN 5-25 COPIES PER
NO PRICING ON QTY 15 OR LESS
EXCHANGE DEADLINE 5/31/22 .

2020 Topps Museum Collection Superstar Showpieces Autographs

STATED ODDS 1:116 HOBBY
STATED PRINT RUN 25 SER.#'d SETS
SSAA Aristides Aquino 15.00 40.00
SSAR Anthony Rizzo 30.00 80.00
SSBB Bo Bichette 125.00 300.00
SSDM Don Mattingly 40.00 100.00
SSDO David Ortiz 40.00 100.00
SSEJ Eloy Jimenez 20.00 50.00
SSFT Frank Thomas 30.00 80.00
SSGL Gavin Lux 30.00 80.00
SSGS George Springer 15.00 40.00
SSGT Gleyber Torres 60.00 150.00
SSHM Hideki Matsui 40.00 100.00
SSJA Jose Altuve 15.00 40.00
SSJF Jack Flaherty 10.00 25.00
SSJV Joey Votto 25.00 60.00
SSKB Kris Bryant 60.00 150.00
SSMT Mike Trout 400.00 100.00
SSNH Nico Hoerner 25.00 60.00
SSOS Ozzie Smith 40.00 100.00
SSPA Pete Alonso 75.00 200.00
SSPG Paul Goldschmidt 20.00 50.00
SSRA Ronald Acuna Jr. 100.00 250.00
SSRD Rafael Devers
SSRH Rhys Hoskins 25.00 60.00
SSSO Shohei Ohtani 100.00 250.00
SSWC Will Clark 40.00 100.00
SSYA Yordan Alvarez 125.00 300.00
SSFTJ Fernando Tatis Jr. 125.00 300.00
SSJSO Juan Soto 75.00 200.00

2006 Topps National Baseball Card Day

COMPLETE SET (5) 1.25 3.00
UNLISTED STARS .30 .75
6 Albert Pujols .30 .75
7 Alex Rodriguez .30 .75
8 Mark Teixeira .15 .40
9 David Wright .20 .50
10 Miguel Cabrera .25 .60

2006 Topps National Baseball Card Day Inserts

COMPLETE SET (3) 1.25 3.00
ONE PER NBCD PACK
T1 Vladimir Guerrero FOIL .12 .30
T2 Mickey Mantle FOIL .60 1.50
T3 Ryan Zimmerman .25 .60

2008 Topps National Baseball Card Day

COMPLETE SET (8) 2.50 6.00
COMMON CARD .20 .50
1 Alex Rodriguez .60 1.50
2 David Wright .30 .75
3 Ryan Howard .30 .75
4 David Ortiz .50 1.25
5 Vladimir Guerrero .30 .75
6 Clay Buchholz .30 .75
7 Joey Votto 1.50 4.00
8 Daric Barton .20 .50

2016 Topps National Baseball Card Day

1 Madison Bumgarner .25 .60
2 Buster Posey .40 1.00
3 Clayton Kershaw .50 1.25
4 Mike Trout 1.50 4.00
5 Bryce Harper .50 1.25
6 Anthony Rizzo .40 1.00
7 Matt Harvey .25 .60
8 Andrew McCutchen .30 .75
9 David Wright .25 .60
10 Josh Donaldson .25 .60
11 David Ortiz .30 .75
12 Yadier Molina .40 1.00
13 Carlos Correa .30 .75
14 Jacob deGrom .60 1.50
15 Felix Hernandez .25 .60
16 Albert Pujols .40 1.00
17 Manny Machado .30 .75
18 Masahiro Tanaka .25 .60
19 Luis Severino .25 .60
20 Evan Longoria .25 .60
21 David Price .25 .60
22 Freddie Freeman .40 1.00
24 Jose Fernandez .30 .75
25 Aaron Nola .40 1.00
26 Jose Abreu .30 .75
27 Corey Kluber .25 .60
28 Miguel Cabrera .30 .75
29 Salvador Perez .25 .60
30 Miguel Sano .30 .75
31 Joe Mauer .25 .60
32 Joey Votto .30 .75
33 Ryan Braun .25 .60
34 Sonny Gray .25 .60
35 Prince Fielder .25 .60
36 Paul Goldschmidt .30 .75
37 Nolan Arenado .50 1.25
38 James Shields .20 .50
39 Kyle Schwarber .60 1.50
40 Jose Bautista .25 .60
41 Corey Seager 2.00 5.00
42 Francisco Lindor .30 .75
43 Ichiro .40 1.00
44 Jose Altuve .25 .60
45 Max Scherzer .30 .75
46 Chris Sale .30 .75
47 Cole Hamels .25 .60
48 Zack Greinke .30 .75
49 Jake Arrieta .25 .60
50 Kris Bryant .40 1.00

2017 Topps National Baseball Card Day

COMPLETE SET (29) 6.00 15.00
1 Bryce Harper .50 1.25
2 Carlos Correa .30 .75
3 Corey Seager .30 .75
4 Maikel Franco .25 .60
5 Freddie Freeman .40 1.00
6 Chris Sale .30 .75
7 Paul Goldschmidt .30 .75
8 Nolan Arenado .50 1.25
9 Joey Votto .30 .75
10 Justin Verlander .30 .75
11 Aledmys Diaz .25 .60
12 Dellin Betances .25 .60
13 Eric Hosmer .25 .60
14 Giancarlo Stanton .30 .75
15 Orlando Arcia .30 .75
16 Miguel Sano .25 .60
17 Jharel Cotton .20 .50
18 Andrew McCutchen .30 .75
19 Wil Myers .25 .60
20 Brandon Crawford .25 .60
21 Francisco Lindor .30 .75
22 Kris Bryant .40 1.00
23 Yoan Moncada .60 1.50
24 Robinson Cano .25 .60
25 Manny Machado .30 .75
26 Josh Donaldson .25 .60
27 Jacob deGrom .60 1.50
28 Chris Archer .20 .50
29 Adrian Beltre .30 .75

2017 Topps National Baseball Card Day Autographs

PRINT RUNS B/WN 5-200 COPIES PER
NO PRICING ON QTY 11 OR LESS
AUAB Andrew Benintendi/125 40.00 100.00
AUAD Aledmys Diaz/53 10.00 25.00
AUBH Bryce Harper/20 75.00 200.00
AUCC Carlos Correa/35
AUJA Jose Altuve/73 20.00 50.00
AUJB Justin Bour/200 5.00 12.00
AUTT Trea Turner/105 15.00 40.00
AUYG Yulieski Gurriel/175 8.00 20.00

2017 Topps National Baseball Card Day Gift with Purchase

GWPMT Mike Trout 3.00 8.00

2019 Topps National Baseball Card Day

1 Mike Trout 2.00 5.00
2 David Peralta .25 .60
3 Ronald Acuna Jr. 2.00 5.00
4 Trey Mancini .30 .75
5 Mookie Betts .75 2.00
6 Javier Baez .50 1.25
7 Eloy Jimenez 1.00 2.50
8 Joey Votto .40 1.00
9 Francisco Lindor .40 1.00
10 Nolan Arenado .60 1.50
11 Miguel Cabrera .40 1.00
12 Justin Verlander .40 1.00
13 Alex Gordon .30 .75
14 Clayton Kershaw .60 1.50
15 Jorge Alfaro .25 .60
16 Christian Yelich .50 1.25
17 Jose Berrios .30 .75
18 Pete Alonso 2.00 5.00
19 Gleyber Torres .75 2.00
20 Matt Chapman .40 1.00
21 Rhys Hoskins .50 1.25
22 Josh Bell .30 .75
23 Manny Machado .40 1.00
24 Evan Longoria .30 .75
25 Yusei Kikuchi .40 1.00
26 Paul Goldschmidt .40 1.00
27 Blake Snell .30 .75
28 Elvis Andrus .30 .75
29 Marcus Stroman .30 .75
30 Juan Soto 1.25 3.00
NTCDG1 Bryce Harper .60 1.50
NTCDG2 Vladimir Guerrero Jr 1.50 4.00

2020 Topps National Baseball Card Day

1 Shohei Ohtani .60 1.50
2 David Peralta .25 .60
3 Ronald Acuna Jr. 1.50 4.00
4 John Means .40 1.00
5 J.D. Martinez .40 1.00
6 Kris Bryant .50 1.25
7 Luis Robert 2.00 5.00
8 Joey Votto .40 1.00
9 Francisco Lindor .40 1.00
10 Nolan Arenado .60 1.50
11 Miguel Cabrera .40 1.00
12 Justin Verlander .40 1.00
13 Whit Merrifield .40 1.00
14 Cody Bellinger .75 2.00
15 Jorge Alfaro .25 .60
16 Christian Yelich .50 1.25
17 Jose Berrios .30 .75
18 Jacob deGrom .75 2.00
19 Aaron Judge 1.00 2.50
20 Matt Chapman .40 1.00
21 Bryce Harper .60 1.50
22 Josh Bell .30 .75
23 Manny Machado .40 1.00
24 Buster Posey .50 1.25
25 Yusei Kikuchi .30 .75
26 Yadier Molina .50 1.25
27 Blake Snell .30 .75
28 Corey Kluber .30 .75
29 Vladimir Guerrero Jr. .60 1.50
30 Juan Soto 1.25 3.00

2020 Topps National Baseball Card Day Autographs

PRINT RUNS B/WN 25-750 COPIES PER
AUAJ Aaron Judge
AUAM Austin Meadows/425 5.00 12.00
AUBB Bobby Bradley/675 5.00 12.00
AUFT Fernando Tatis Jr./55 125.00 300.00
AUGL Gavin Lux
AUJF Jack Flaherty/400 6.00 15.00
AUKH Keston Hiura 5.00 12.00
AULG Lourdes Gurriel Jr. 8.00 20.00
AUMC Michael Chavis 5.00 12.00
AUMD Mauricio Dubon 8.00 20.00
AUMM Max Muncy 6.00 15.00
AUMS Mike Soroka 8.00 20.00
AUMT Mike Trout
AUNH Nico Hoerner 10.00 25.00
AUPA Pete Alonso
AUSM Sean Murphy 5.00 12.00
AUTG Trent Grisham 12.00 30.00
AUWM Whit Merrifield 6.00 15.00
AUYA Yordan Alvarez 25.00 60.00
AUMCL Mike Clevinger 12.00 30.00

2010 Topps National Chicle

COMPLETE SET (329) 125.00 250.00
COMP.SET w/o SP's (275) 15.00 40.00
COMMON CARD (1-275) .15 .40
COMMON RC (256-275) .40 1.00
COMMON SP (276-329) 2.00 5.00
SP ODDS 1:4 HOBBY
PRINTING PLATE ODDS 1:300 HOBBY
1 Albert Pujols .50 1.25
2 Grady Sizemore .25 .60
3 Ichiro Suzuki .50 1.25
4 Daisuke Matsuzaka .25 .60
5 Prince Fielder .25 .60
6 Joba Chamberlain .15 .40
7 Joe Mauer .30 .75
8 Jason Bartlett .15 .40
9 Brandon Webb .25 .60
10 Manny Ramirez .40 1.00
11 CC Sabathia .25 .60
12 Raul Ibanez .25 .60
13 Dan Uggla .15 .40
14 Mariano Rivera .50 1.25
15 Brad Hawpe .15 .40
16 James Loney .15 .40
17 Ken Griffey Jr. .75 2.00
18 Josh Johnson .25 .60
19 Jay Bruce .25 .60
20 David DeJesus .15 .40
21 J.A. Happ .25 .60
22 Tim Wakefield .25 .60
23 Shane Victorino .25 .60
24 Kevin Kouzmanoff .15 .40
25 Aaron Hill .15 .40
26 Rick Porcello .25 .60
27 Jacoby Ellsbury .30 .75
28 Andrew McCutchen .40 1.00
29 Hunter Pence .25 .60
30 Michael Cuddyer .15 .40
31 Jayson Werth .25 .60
32 Andy Pettitte .25 .60
33 Evan Longoria .25 .60
34 David Wright .30 .75
35 Justin Morneau .25 .60
36 Derek Jeter 1.00 2.50
37 Ryan Howard .30 .75
38 Russell Martin .15 .40
39 Michael Young .15 .40
40 Johnny Damon .25 .60
41 Carlos Pena .25 .60
42 Robinson Cano .25 .60
43 Ian Kinsler .25 .60
44 Jason Bay .25 .60
45 Adam Lind .25 .60
46 Kevin Youkilis .15 .40
47 Brandon Inge .25 .60
48 Jason Kubel .15 .40
49 Adrian Gonzalez .30 .75
50 David Ortiz .40 1.00
51 Joey Votto .40 1.00
52 Nick Swisher .25 .60
53 Marco Scutaro .25 .60
54 Yunel Escobar .15 .40
55 Carl Crawford .25 .60
56 B.J. Upton .25 .60
57 Kosuke Fukudome .25 .60
58 Matt Cain .25 .60
59 Wandy Rodriguez .15 .40
60 J.J. Hardy .15 .40
61 Gordon Beckham .15 .40
62 Chad Billingsley .25 .60
63 Aramis Ramirez .15 .40
64 Alex Rodriguez .50 1.25
65 Clayton Kershaw .60 1.50
66 Johan Santana .25 .60
67 Mark Buehrle .25 .60
68 Vladimir Guerrero .25 .60
69 Jose Reyes .25 .60
70 Cliff Lee .25 .60
71 Miguel Cabrera .40 1.00
72 Jorge Posada .25 .60
73 Nick Markakis .30 .75
74 Ryan Zimmerman .25 .60
75 Kendry Morales .15 .40
76 Victor Martinez .25 .60
77 Carlos Lee .15 .40
78 Bobby Abreu .15 .40
79 Russell Branyan .15 .40
80 Jermaine Dye .15 .40
81 Hideki Matsui .40 1.00
82 Josh Beckett .15 .40
83 Brian Roberts .15 .40
84 Hanley Ramirez .25 .60
85 Justin Verlander .40 1.00
86 Adam Jones .25 .60
87 Ted Lilly .15 .40
88 Jorge Cantu .15 .40
89 Chone Figgins .15 .40
90 Miguel Tejada .25 .60
91 Asdrubal Cabrera .25 .60
92 Cole Hamels .30 .75
93 Roy Oswalt .25 .60
94 Nyjer Morgan .15 .40
95 Ryan Braun .25 .60
96 Derrek Lee .15 .40
97 Matt Kemp .30 .75
98 Troy Tulowitzki .40 1.00
99 Alexei Ramirez .25 .60
100 Adam Dunn .25 .60
101 Torii Hunter .15 .40
102 Adam Wainwright .25 .60
103 Pablo Sandoval .25 .60
104 Justin Upton .25 .60
105 Mark Reynolds .15 .40
106 Todd Helton .25 .60
107 Mark Teixeira .25 .60
108 Josh Hamilton .25 .60
109 Nelson Cruz .40 1.00
110 Curtis Granderson .30 .75
111 Paul Konerko .25 .60
112 Dustin Pedroia .40 1.00
113 Billy Butler .15 .40
114 Felix Hernandez .25 .60
115 Lance Berkman .25 .60
116 Carlos Beltran .25 .60
117 Jason Marquis .15 .40
118 Ubaldo Jimenez .15 .40
119 Jose Lopez .15 .40
120 Tommy Hanson .15 .40
121 Yovani Gallardo .15 .40
122 Roy Halladay .25 .60
123 Brian McCann .25 .60
124 Carlos Zambrano .25 .60
125 Luis Castillo .15 .40
126 Melky Cabrera .15 .40
127 Kyle Blanks .15 .40
128 Michael Bowden .15 .40
129 Nolan Reimold .15 .40
130 Elvis Andrus .25 .60
131 David Price .30 .75
132 Bengie Molina .15 .40
133 Andrew Bailey .15 .40
134 Felix Pie .15 .40
135 Chris Carpenter .25 .60
136 Julio Borbon .15 .40
137 Zack Greinke .40 1.00
138 Scott Kazmir .15 .40
139 Yadier Molina .50 1.25
140 Javier Vazquez .15 .40
141 Brett Anderson .15 .40
142 Colby Rasmus .25 .60
143 Chris Coghlan .15 .40
144 Jhoulys Chacin .15 .40
145 Kurt Suzuki .15 .40
146 Scott Feldman .15 .40
147 Jon Lester .25 .60
148 Chris Young .15 .40
149 Trevor Cahill .15 .40
150 Zach Duke .15 .40
151 Michael Bourn .15 .40
152 Rick Ankiel .15 .40
153 Alex Gordon .25 .60
154 Derek Lowe .15 .40
155 Vernon Wells .15 .40
156 Luke Scott .15 .40
157 Jimmy Rollins .25 .60
158 Stephen Drew .15 .40
159 Kenshin Kawakami .25 .60
160 Jonathan Sanchez .15 .40
161 Juan Pierre .15 .40
162 Jonathan Papelbon .25 .60
163 Erick Aybar .15 .40
164 Andre Ethier .25 .60
165 Jed Lowrie .15 .40
166 Duke Snider .25 .60
167 Ryan Ludwick .15 .40
168 Jake Peavy .15 .40
169 Denard Span .15 .40
170 Jair Jurrjens .15 .40
171 Mike Cameron .15 .40
172 Gavin Floyd .15 .40
173 Jonathan Broxton .15 .40
174 Marlon Byrd .15 .40
175 Dexter Fowler .25 .60
176 Aaron Rowand .15 .40
177 Koji Uehara .15 .40
178 Joel Pineiro .15 .40
179 Carlos Quentin .15 .40
180 Freddy Sanchez .15 .40
181 John Maine .15 .40
182 Neftali Feliz .15 .40
183 Nate McLouth .15 .40
184 Phil Hughes .15 .40
185 Travis Snider .15 .40
186 Alfonso Soriano .25 .60
187 Joe Saunders .15 .40
188 Rich Harden .15 .40
189 Mat Gamel .15 .40
190 Orlando Hudson .15 .40
191 Chase Utley .25 .60
192 J.D. Drew .15 .40
193 Marc Rzepczynski .15 .40
194 Tim Lincecum .25 .60
195 Alex Rios .15 .40
196 Will Venable .15 .40
197 Dan Haren .15 .40
198 Michael Saunders .25 .60
199 Trevor Crowe .15 .40
200 Chipper Jones .40 1.00
201 A.J. Burnett .15 .40
202 Ian Stewart .15 .40
203 Edinson Volquez .15 .40
204 Carlos Gonzalez .25 .60
205 John Danks .15 .40
206 Hank Greenberg .40 1.00
207 Johnny Bench .40 1.00
208 Luis Aparicio .25 .60
209 Juan Marichal .25 .60
210 Robin Yount .40 1.00
211 Jim Palmer .25 .60
212 Ozzie Smith .50 1.25
213 Paul Molitor .40 1.00
214 Warren Spahn .25 .60
215 Orlando Cepeda .25 .60
216 Bob Gibson .25 .60
217 Frank Robinson .25 .60
218 Carlton Fisk .25 .60
219 Eddie Murray .25 .60
220 Dale Murphy .40 1.00
221 Dennis Eckersley .25 .60
222 Lou Brock .25 .60
223 Carl Yastrzemski .60 1.50
224 Al Kaline .40 1.00
225 Mike Schmidt .60 1.50
226 Phil Rizzuto .25 .60
227 Rogers Hornsby .25 .60
228 Pee Wee Reese .25 .60
229 Lou Gehrig .75 2.00
230 Jimmie Foxx .40 1.00
231 Honus Wagner .40 1.00
232 Roy Campanella .40 1.00
233 Mel Ott .40 1.00
234 Tris Speaker .25 .60
235 Jackie Robinson .40 1.00
236 George Sisler .25 .60
237 Thurman Munson .40 1.00
238 Johnny Mize .25 .60
239 Walter Johnson .40 1.00
240 Cy Young .40 1.00
241 Christy Mathewson .40 1.00
242 Mickey Mantle 1.25 3.00
243 Stan Musial .60 1.50
244 Eddie Mathews .40 1.00
245 Whitey Ford .25 .60
246 Willie McCovey .25 .60
247 Reggie Jackson .25 .60
248 Tom Seaver .25 .60
249 Nolan Ryan 1.25 3.00
250 Joe Morgan .25 .60
251 Richie Ashburn .25 .60
252 Duke Snider .25 .60
253 Ryne Sandberg .75 2.00
254 Ernie Banks .40 1.00
255 Babe Ruth 1.00 2.50
256 Tyler Flowers RC .60 1.50
257 Madison Bumgarner RC 4.00 10.00
258 Gordon Beckham .15 .40
259 Henry Rodriguez RC .40 1.00
260 Drew Stubbs RC 1.00 2.50
261 Kevin Richardson (RC) .40 1.00
262 Reid Gorecki (RC) .60 1.50
263 Eric Young Jr. (RC) .40 1.00
264 Josh Thole RC .60 1.50
265 Neil Walker (RC) .60 1.50
266 Carlos Carrasco (RC) 1.00 2.50
267 Tobi Stoner RC .60 1.50
268 Luis Durango RC .40 1.00
269 Tommy Manzella (RC) .40 1.00
270 Adam Moore RC .40 1.00
271 Brent Dlugach (RC) .40 1.00
272 Michael Brantley RC .60 1.50
273 Juan Francisco RC .60 1.50
274 Ian Desmond (RC) .60 1.50
275 Buster Posey RC 3.00 8.00
276 Babe Ruth SP 5.00 12.00
277 Rogers Hornsby SP 2.00 5.00
278 Pee Wee Reese SP 2.00 5.00
279 Lou Gehrig SP 4.00 10.00
280 Jimmie Foxx SP 2.50 6.00
281 Honus Wagner SP 2.50 6.00
282 Roy Campanella SP 2.50 6.00
283 Mel Ott SP 2.50 6.00
284 Tris Speaker SP 1.25 3.00
285 Jackie Robinson SP 2.50 6.00
286 George Sisler SP 1.50 4.00
287 Ty Cobb SP 3.00 8.00
288 Thurman Munson SP 2.50 6.00
289 Johnny Mize SP 2.00 5.00
290 Walter Johnson SP 2.50 6.00
291 Cy Young SP 2.50 6.00
292 Christy Mathewson SP 2.50 6.00
293 Mickey Mantle SP 6.00 15.00
294 Stan Musial SP 3.00 8.00
295 Eddie Mathews SP 2.50 6.00
296 Ernie Banks SP 2.50 6.00
297 Ryne Sandberg SP 4.00 10.00
298 Joe Morgan SP 3.00 8.00
299 Reggie Jackson SP 2.00 5.00
300 Ian Desmond SP 3.00 8.00
301 Albert Pujols SP 2.50 6.00
302 Ichiro Suzuki SP 2.50 6.00
303 Alex Rodriguez SP 2.50 6.00
304 Ryan Howard SP 1.50 4.00
305 Lance Berkman SP 2.00 5.00
306 Chipper Jones SP 2.50 6.00
307 Manny Ramirez SP 2.50 6.00
308 Dustin Pedroia SP 2.00 5.00
309 Ryan Zimmerman SP 2.00 5.00
310 Joe Mauer SP 2.00 5.00
311 Buster Posey SP 6.00 15.00
312 Tyler Flowers SP 3.00 8.00
313 Madison Bumgarner SP 8.00 20.00
314 Adam Moore SP 2.00 5.00
315 Henry Rodriguez SP 1.25 3.00
316 Drew Stubbs SP 3.00 8.00
317 Kevin Richardson SP 2.00 5.00
318 Reid Gorecki SP 2.00 5.00
319 Eric Young Jr. SP 2.00 5.00
320 Josh Thole SP 2.00 5.00
321 Neil Walker SP 3.00 8.00
322 Carlos Carrasco SP 2.50 6.00
323 Tobi Stoner SP 2.00 5.00
324 Matt Carson SP 2.00 5.00
325 Tommy Manzella SP 2.00 5.00
326 Michael Dunn SP RC 1.25 3.00
327 Brent Dlugach SP 2.00 5.00
328 Michael Brantley SP 3.00 8.00
329 Juan Francisco SP 2.00 5.00

2010 Topps National Chicle Bazooka Back

*1-275 BAZOOKA: 2X TO 5X BASIC
*1-275 BAZOOKA RC: .75X TO 2X BASIC
1-275 BAZOOKA ODDS 1:8 HOBBY
*276-329 BAZOOKA: .5X TO 1.2X BASIC
276-329 BAZOOKA ODDS 1:100 HOBBY

2010 Topps National Chicle National Chicle Back

*1-275 NATIONAL: 1.2X TO 3X BASIC
*1-275 NATIONAL RC: .5X TO 1.2X BASIC
1-275 NATIONAL ODDS 1:4 HOBBY
*276-329 NATIONAL: .4X TO 1X BASIC
276-329 NATIONAL ODDS 1:50 HOBBY

2010 Topps National Chicle Autographs

GROUP A ODDS 1:15 HOBBY
GROUP B ODDS 1:594 HOBBY
PRINTING PLATE ODDS 1:3671 HOBBY
AB Andrew Bailey A 6.00 15.00
BD Brent Dlugach A 3.00 8.00
CC Carlos Carrasco A 3.00 8.00
CR Colby Rasmus B 20.00 50.00
CY Carl Yastrzemski B 30.00 60.00
DS Denard Span A 4.00 10.00
DST Drew Stubbs A 3.00 8.00
GB Gordon Beckham B 8.00 20.00
HR Henry Rodriguez A 3.00 8.00
ID Ian Desmond A 6.00 15.00
JB Jason Bartlett A 3.00 8.00
JF Juan Francisco A 4.00 10.00
JT Josh Thole A 4.00 10.00
KU Koji Uehara A 4.00 10.00
LD Luis Durango A 3.00 8.00
MB Madison Bumgarner A 15.00 40.00
MBR Michael Brantley A 3.00 8.00
NF Neftali Feliz A 3.00 8.00
NM Nate McLouth A 3.00 8.00
NW Neil Walker A 3.00 8.00
PS Pablo Sandoval A 5.00 12.00
RH Ryan Howard B 12.50 30.00
RP Rick Porcello B 12.50 30.00
SM Stan Musial B 40.00 80.00
TH Tommy Hanson B 8.00 20.00
TM Tommy Manzella A 3.00 8.00
TS Tobi Stoner A 3.00 8.00

2010 Topps National Chicle Autographs Bazooka Back

*BAZOOKA: .5X TO 1.2X BASIC
STATED ODDS 1:188 HOBBY
STATED PRINT RUN 99 SER.#'d SETS

2010 Topps National Chicle Autographs National Chicle Back

*NATIONAL: .5X TO 1.2X BASIC
STATED ODDS 1:126 HOBBY
STATED PRINT RUN 199 SER.#'d SETS
GROUP B/199 AUTOS DO NOT EXIST

2010 Topps National Chicle Cabinet

COMPLETE SET (25) 75.00 150.00
BR Babe Ruth 6.00 15.00
CM Christy Mathewson 2.50 6.00
CY Cy Young 2.50 6.00
EM Eddie Mathews 2.50 6.00
GS George Sisler 1.50 4.00
HW Honus Wagner 2.50 6.00
JF Jimmie Foxx 2.50 6.00
JM Johnny Mize 1.50 4.00
JR Jackie Robinson 2.50 6.00
LG Lou Gehrig 5.00 12.00
MM Mickey Mantle 8.00 20.00
MO Mel Ott 2.50 6.00
NR Nolan Ryan 8.00 20.00
RC Roy Campanella 2.50 6.00
RH Rogers Hornsby 1.50 4.00
RJ Reggie Jackson 1.50 4.00
SM Stan Musial 4.00 10.00
TC Ty Cobb 4.00 10.00
TM Thurman Munson 2.50 6.00
TS Tris Speaker 1.50 4.00
WF Whitey Ford 1.50 4.00
WJ Walter Johnson 2.50 6.00
CYA Carl Yastrzemski 4.00 10.00
PWR Pee Wee Reese 1.50 4.00
TSE Tom Seaver 1.50 4.00

2010 Topps National Chicle Cabinet Artist Signatures

RANDOM BOX TOPPER INSERTS
STATED PRINT RUN 50 SER.#'d SETS
CARDS FEATURE ARTIST SIGNATURES
BR Ruth/Hobrecht AU 20.00 50.00
CY Young/Sheldon AU 8.00 20.00
EM Mathews/Lempa AU 8.00 20.00
JF Foxx/Sheldon AU 12.50 30.00
LG Gehrig/Davies AU 20.00 50.00
MM Mantle/Davies AU 30.00 60.00
NR Ryan/Lempa AU 20.00 50.00
RC Campy/Sheldon AU 10.00 25.00
RH Hornsby/Sheldon AU 12.50 30.00
RJ Reggie/Kong AU 10.00 25.00
SM Musial/Sheldon AU 15.00 40.00
TC Cobb/Hobrecht AU 12.50 30.00
TM Munson/Lempa AU 12.50 30.00
TS Speaker/Kupka AU 10.00 25.00
WF Ford/Davies AU 8.00 20.00
WJ Johnson/Kupka AU 15.00 40.00
CYA Yaz/Lempa AU 8.00 20.00
PWR Reese/Kupka AU 10.00 25.00
TSE Seaver/Lempa AU 10.00 25.00

2010 Topps National Chicle Relics

GROUP A ODDS 1:156 HOBBY
GROUP B ODDS 1:65 HOBBY
GROUP C ODDS 1:2061 HOBBY
AE Andre Ethier A 3.00 8.00
AP Albert Pujols B 6.00 15.00
AR Alex Rodriguez A 6.00 15.00
AS Alfonso Soriano B 3.00 8.00
BR Babe Ruth C 40.00 100.00
CB Carlos Beltran B 3.00 8.00
CJ Chipper Jones A 5.00 12.00
CR Colby Rasmus B 3.00 8.00
DM Dale Murphy B 5.00 12.00
DO David Ortiz B 5.00 12.00
DP Dustin Pedroia B 5.00 12.00
EA Elvis Andrus B 3.00 8.00
EL Evan Longoria B 3.00 8.00
EM Eddie Murray A 3.00 8.00
HG Hank Greenberg A 10.00 25.00
JC Joba Chamberlain B 2.00 5.00
JH Josh Hamilton A 3.00 8.00
JM Justin Morneau B 3.00 8.00
KF Kosuke Fukudome B 3.00 8.00
LG Lou Gehrig C 40.00 100.00
MM Mickey Mantle C 15.00 40.00
MR Manny Ramirez B 5.00 12.00
MT Mark Teixeira B 3.00 8.00
NM Nick Markakis B 4.00 10.00
NR Nolan Ryan A 8.00 20.00
NS Nick Swisher B 3.00 8.00
OS Ozzie Smith A 6.00 15.00
PF Prince Fielder B 3.00 8.00
PH Phil Hughes B 2.00 5.00
PM Paul Molitor A 5.00 12.00
PR Phil Rizzuto A 3.00 8.00
PS Pablo Sandoval B 3.00 8.00
RC Robinson Cano B 3.00 8.00
TM Thurman Munson B 5.00 12.00
VG Vladimir Guerrero B 3.00 8.00
WF Whitey Ford A 3.00 8.00
JPA Jim Palmer A 3.00 8.00
PWR Pee Wee Reese A 3.00 8.00

2010 Topps National Chicle Relics Bazooka Back

*BAZOOKA: .5X TO 1.2X BASIC
STATED ODDS 1:174 HOBBY
STATED PRINT RUN 99 SER.#'d SETS
GROUP C/99 RELICS DO NOT EXIST

2010 Topps National Chicle Relics National Chicle Back

*NATIONAL: .5X TO 1.2X BASIC
STATED ODDS 1:87 HOBBY
STATED PRINT RUN 199 SER.#'d SETS
GROUP C/199 RELICS DO NOT EXIST

2011 Topps National Convention VIP

COMPLETE SET (5) 6.00 15.00
590 Lou Gehrig 2.50 6.00
591 Mickey Mantle 4.00 10.00
592 Jackie Robinson 1.25 3.00
593 John F. Kennedy 1.25 3.00
594 Mickey Mantle/Roger Maris 4.00 10.00

2012 Topps National Convention VIP

COMPLETE SET (5) 12.50 30.00
408 Mickey Mantle 5.00 12.00
New York Yankees
409 Mickey Mantle 5.00 12.00
Joplin Miners
410 Willie Mays 3.00 8.00
411 Jackie Robinson 1.50 4.00
412 Babe Ruth 4.00 10.00

2013 Topps National Convention 1952 Bowman

COMPLETE SET (8) 15.00 40.00
1 Frank Thomas
2 Bryce Harper
3 Mike Trout
4 Ernie Banks

2015 Topps National Convention '53 Bowman VIP

COMPLETE SET (5) 10.00 25.00
ISSUED AT '15 NATIONAL CONVENTION
161 Ernie Banks 2.00 5.00
162 Al Kaline 2.00 5.00
163 Ted Williams 4.00 10.00
164 Jackie Robinson 2.00 5.00
165 Willie Mays 4.00 10.00

2015 Topps National Convention Allen and Ginter Die Cut

AGX1 Sandy Koufax 6.00 15.00
AGX2 Ryne Sandberg 6.00 15.00
AGX3 Frank Thomas 3.00 8.00
AGX4 Jose Abreu 5.00 12.00
AGX5 Dalton Pompey 2.00 5.00
AGX6 Drew Hutchison 2.00 5.00
AGX7 Javier Baez 3.00 8.00
AGX8 Jorge Soler 3.00 8.00
AGX9 Anthony Rizzo 3.00 8.00
AGX10 Ernie Banks 3.00 8.00
AGX11 Kennys Vargas 2.50 6.00
AGX12 Joe Panik 3.00 8.00
AGX13 Dilson Herrera 2.00 5.00
AGX14 Madison Bumgarner 4.00 10.00
AGX15 Miguel Cabrera 5.00 12.00
AGX16 Brett Lawrie 2.50 6.00
AGX17 Andrew McCutchen 4.00 10.00
AGX18 Joc Pederson 8.00 20.00
AGX19 Mike Trout 10.00 25.00
AGX20 Albert Pujols 5.00 12.00
AGX21 Paul Goldschmidt 3.00 8.00
AGX22 Adam Jones 2.50 6.00
AGX23 Rusney Castillo 4.00 10.00
AGX24 David Ortiz 2.50 6.00
AGX25 Joey Votto 3.00 8.00
AGX26 Corey Kluber 2.50 6.00
AGX27 Troy Tulowitzki 3.00 8.00
AGX28 Chris Owings 2.00 5.00
AGX29 Carlos Correa 12.00 30.00
AGX30 Alex Gordon 2.50 6.00
AGX31 Yasiel Puig 5.00 12.00
AGX32 Giancarlo Stanton 3.00 8.00
AGX33 Joe Mauer 2.50 6.00
AGX34 Jacob deGrom 4.00 10.00
AGX35 David Wright 3.00 8.00
AGX36 Jacoby Ellsbury 3.00 8.00
AGX37 Matt Kemp 2.50 6.00
AGX38 Jonathan Lucroy 2.00 5.00
AGX39 Buster Posey 5.00 12.00
AGX40 Robinson Cano 3.00 8.00
AGX41 Jason Heyward 2.50 6.00
AGX42 Adam Wainwright 2.50 6.00
AGX43 Evan Longoria 2.50 6.00
AGX44 Todd Frazier 3.00 8.00
AGX45 Jose Bautista 2.50 6.00
AGX46 Bryce Harper 5.00 12.00
AGX47 Anthony Rendon 2.00 5.00
AGX48 Craig Kimbrel 3.00 8.00
AGX49 Julio Teheran 2.50 6.00
AGX50 Sonny Gray 3.00 8.00
AGX51 Chris Sale 3.00 8.00
AGX52 Justin Morneau 2.50 6.00
AGX53 Max Scherzer 2.50 6.00
AGX54 Kris Bryant 40.00 80.00
AGX55 Jose Altuve 2.50 6.00
AGX56 Jonathan Schoop 2.00 5.00
AGX57 Michael Brantley 2.50 6.00
AGX58 Jose Fernandez 3.00 8.00
AGX59 Carlos Gomez 2.00 5.00
AGX60 Mark Teixeira 2.50 6.00
AGX61 Gregory Polanco 2.50 6.00
AGX62 Salvador Perez 2.50 6.00
AGX63 Shin-Soo Choo 2.50 6.00
AGX64 Maikle Franco 5.00 12.00
AGX65 Cole Hamels 2.50 6.00
AGX66 Will Middlebrooks 3.00 8.00
AGX67 Felix Hernandez 2.50 6.00
AGX68 Yadier Molina 3.00 8.00
AGX69 Adrian Beltre 2.00 5.00
AGX70 Asdrubal Cabrera 2.50 6.00

2015 Topps National Convention Allen and Ginter Die Cut Autographs

ISSUED ON '15 NATIONAL CONVENTION
PRINT RUNS B/WN 8-80 COPIES PER
NO PRICING ON QTY 10 OR LESS
AGXAAR Anthony Rizzo/20 150.00 250.00
AGXAAS Andrew Susac
AGXACC C.J. Cron
AGXACR Carlos Rodon
AGXADHA Dilson Herrera/15 4.00 10.00
AGXADHN Drew Hutchison/80
AGXADP Dalton Pompey/40 15.00 40.00
AGXAEB Ernie Banks/5
AGXAFT Frank Thomas/8
AGXAJA Jose Abreu
AGXAJBZ Javier Baez
AGXAJP Joe Panik/28 60.00 150.00
AGXAJS Jorge Soler/40 6.00 15.00
AGXAKV Kennys Vargas/65 10.00 25.00
AGXARS Ryne Sandberg
AGXASK Sandy Koufax

2015 Topps National Convention Gypsy Queen

COMPLETE SET (3) 8.00 20.00
*SILVER/100: 2.5X TO 6X BASIC
*GOLD/25: 4X TO 10X BASIC
NSCC1 Kris Bryant 6.00 15.00
NSCC2 Carlos Correa 3.00 8.00
NSCC3 Byron Buxton 3.00 8.00

2015 Topps National Convention Jose Abreu '90 Topps Autograph

DPI90 Jose Abreu 50.00 120.00

2016 Topps New Era

1 Bryce Harper 3.00 8.00
2 Jacob deGrom 4.00 10.00
3 Andrew McCutchen 2.00 5.00
4 Joc Pederson 1.50 4.00
5 Buster Posey 2.50 6.00
6 Kyle Schwarber 4.00 10.00
7 Marcus Stroman 1.50 4.00
8 Dellin Betances 1.50 4.00
9 Josh Donaldson 1.50 4.00

2016 Topps New Era Blue

STATED ODDS 1:423 PACKS
*BLUE: X TO X BASIC
STATED PRINT RUN 99 SER.#'d SETS

2016 Topps New Era Green

*GREEN: X TO X BASIC
STATED ODDS 1:1673 PACKS
STATED PRINT RUN 25 SER.#'d SETS

2016 Topps New Era Ambassadors Cap Relics

STATED ODDS 1:423 PACKS
STATED PRINT RUN 99 SER.#'d SETS
AM Andrew McCutchen
BH Bryce Harper
BP Buster Posey
DB Dellin Betances
JD Josh Donaldson
JP Joc Pederson
KS Kyle Schwarber
MS Marcus Stroman
JDE Jacob deGrom

2016 Topps New Era Bryce Harper

NEBH1 Bryce Harper
NEBH2 Bryce Harper
NEBH3 Bryce Harper

2017 Topps New Era

1 Mike Trout 12.00 30.00
2 Jose Altuve 2.00 5.00
3 Khris Davis 2.50 6.00
4 Josh Donaldson 2.00 5.00
5 Dansby Swanson 4.00 10.00
6 Eric Thames 2.00 5.00
7 Dexter Fowler 2.00 5.00
8 Kris Bryant 3.00 8.00
9 Kyle Schwarber 2.50 6.00
10 Paul Goldschmidt 2.50 6.00
11 Corey Seager 2.50 6.00
12 Buster Posey 3.00 8.00
13 Francisco Lindor 2.50 6.00
14 Robinson Cano 2.00 5.00
15 Giancarlo Stanton 2.50 6.00
16 Noah Syndergaard 2.00 5.00
17 Bryce Harper 4.00 10.00
18 Manny Machado 2.50 6.00
19 Wil Myers 2.00 5.00
20 Odubel Herrera 2.00 5.00
21 Andrew McCutchen 2.50 6.00
22 Adrian Beltre 2.50 6.00
23 Evan Longoria 2.00 5.00
24 Rick Porcello 2.00 5.00
25 Mookie Betts 5.00 12.00
26 Joey Votto 2.50 6.00
27 Carlos Gonzalez 2.00 5.00
28 Eric Hosmer 2.00 5.00
29 Miguel Cabrera 2.50 6.00
30 Joe Mauer 2.00 5.00
31 Todd Frazier 1.50 4.00
32 Dellin Betances 2.00 5.00

2017 Topps New Era '87 Topps

87T1 Cal Ripken Jr. 3.00 8.00
87T2 Reggie Jackson .75 2.00
87T3 Bo Jackson 1.00 2.50
87T4 Ryne Sandberg 2.00 5.00
87T5 Barry Larkin .75 2.00
87T6 Don Mattingly 2.00 5.00
87T7 Ozzie Smith 1.25 3.00
87T8 Jose Canseco .75 2.00
87T9 Darryl Strawberry .60 1.50
87T10 Roger Clemens 1.25 3.00
87T11 Greg Maddux 1.25 3.00
87T12 Nolan Ryan 3.00 8.00
87T13 Mark McGwire 1.50 4.00
87T14 Rickey Henderson 1.00 2.50
87T15 Tom Glavine .75 2.00
87T16 Fernando Valenzuela .60 1.50
87T17 Dave Winfield .75 2.00
87T18 George Brett 2.00 5.00

2017 Topps New Era Cap Relics

STATED PRINT RUN 99 SER.#'d SETS
1 Jose Altuve 8.00 20.00
2 Dellin Betances 8.00 20.00
3 Mookie Betts 20.00 50.00
4 Josh Donaldson 8.00 20.00
5 Bryce Harper 15.00 40.00
6 Rick Porcello 8.00 20.00
7 Buster Posey 12.00 30.00
8 Kyle Schwarber 10.00 25.00
9 Corey Seager 10.00 25.00
10 Dansby Swanson 15.00 40.00
11 Noah Syndergaard 8.00 20.00

2016 Topps Now

ISSUED VIA TOPPS NOW WEBSITE
PRINT RUNS B/WN 1-11,550 COPIES PER
NO PRICING ON QTY 10 OR LESS
1 Francisco Liriano/266* 400.00 800.00
2 Kansas City Royals/356* 200.00 500.00
3 Bryce Harper/782* 40.00 100.00
4 Trevor Story/981* 6.00 15.00
5 David Ortiz/474* 4.00 10.00
6 Trevor Story/759* 12.00 30.00
7 Kenta Maeda/952* 6.00 15.00
8 Albert Pujols/244* 8.00 20.00
9 Trevor Story/1298* 6.00 15.00
10 Brandon Crawford/316* 6.00 15.00
11 Tyler White/1350* 4.00 10.00
12 Nomar Mazara/1427* 4.00 10.00
13 Chris Davis/266* 6.00 15.00
14 Addison Russell/331* 60.00 150.00
15 Trevor Brown/590* 4.00 10.00
16 Dae-Ho Lee/363* 10.00 25.00
17 Nolan Arenado/268* 12.00 30.00
18 Vincent Velasquez/557* 5.00 12.00
19 Jaime Garcia/300* 12.00 30.00
20 Bryce Harper/1286* 5.00 12.00
21 Jackie Robinson/759* 4.00 10.00
22 Chris Sale/244* 4.00 10.00
23 Mark Trumbo/285* 2.50 6.00
24 Melvin Upton Jr./226* 10.00 25.00
25 Masahiro Tanaka 6.00 15.00
Hisashi Iwakuma/424*
26 John Lackey/244* 75.00 200.00
27 Cincinnati Reds/278* 5.00 12.00
28 Harper/Strasburg/489* 6.00 15.00
29 Kris Bryant/1644* 4.00 10.00
30 Jake Arrieta/1808* 6.00 15.00
31 Curtis Granderson/294* 10.00 25.00
32 Jacoby Ellsbury/326* 5.00 12.00
33 Chicago White Sox/321* 5.00 12.00
34 Brett Gardner/278* 10.00 25.00
35 Kenta Maeda/784* 5.00 12.00
36 Harper/Heisey/400* 8.00 20.00
37 Neil Walker/289* 15.00 40.00
38 Pujols/Jackson/527 4.00 10.00
39 Andrew McCutchen/524* 4.00 10.00
40 Jake Arrieta/365* 60.00 150.00
41 Yoenis Cespedes/325* 12.00 30.00
42 Trevor Story/800* 12.00 30.00
43 Ryan Howard/280* 5.00 12.00
44 David Ortiz/346* 4.00 10.00
45 Clayton Kershaw/453* 12.00 30.00
46 Bartolo Colon/298* 12.00 30.00
47 Nomar Mazara/468* 4.00 10.00
48 Machado/Harper/540* 6.00 15.00
49 Justin Smoak/252* 6.00 15.00
50 Lorenzo Cain/280* 25.00 60.00
51 Corey Kluber/229* 12.00 30.00
52 Piscotty/Holiday/217* 25.00 60.00
53 Colorado Rockies/231* 6.00 15.00
54 Jung Ho Kang/439* 2.50 6.00
55 Giancarlo Stanton/259* 15.00 40.00
56 Matt Carpenter/298* 25.00 60.00
57 Bartolo Colon/8826* 12.00 30.00
58 Aaron Hill/246* 8.00 20.00
59 Bryce Harper/1366* 4.00 10.00
60 Javier Baez/640* 6.00 15.00
61 Ortiz/Yaz/851* 5.00 12.00
62 Todd Frazier/367* 5.00 12.00
63 Felix Hernandez/429* 3.00 8.00
64 Lorenzo Cain/362* 15.00 40.00
65 Trayce Thompson/566* 4.00 10.00
66 Marwin Gonzalez/253* 5.00 12.00
67 Chris Iannetta/215* 10.00 25.00
68 Max Scherzer/3746* 4.00 10.00
69 Noah Syndergaard/3670* 4.00 10.00
70 Boston Red Sox/363* 6.00 15.00
71 Clayton Kershaw/694* 6.00 15.00
72 David Ortiz/919* 5.00 12.00
73 Matt Andriese/284* 3.00 8.00
74 Philadelphia Phillies/398* 4.00 10.00
75 Drew Stubbs/301* 3.00 8.00
76 Carlos Beltran/415* 5.00 12.00
77 Danny Valencia/299* 5.00 12.00
78 Kendrys Morales/227* 15.00 40.00
79 Evan Gattis/212* 12.00 30.00
80 Clayton Kershaw/421* 6.00 15.00
81 Khris Davis/569* 6.00 15.00
82 Justin Verlander/794* 5.00 12.00
83 Francisco Lindor/473* 5.00 12.00
84 George Springer/450* 4.00 10.00
85 Chris Sale/513* 4.00 10.00
86 Jackie Bradley Jr./492* 4.00 10.00
87 Melvin Upton Jr./268* 4.00 10.00
88 David Wright/1014* 5.00 12.00
89 Ichiro Suzuki/551* 6.00 15.00
90 Madison Bumgarner/632* 4.00 10.00
91 Randal Grichuk/428* 3.00 8.00
92 Clayton Kershaw/511* 6.00 15.00
93 Johnny Cueto/428* 4.00 10.00
94 Jackie Bradley Jr./438* 4.00 10.00
95 Francisco Rodriguez/386* 3.00 8.00
96 Carlos Correa/536* 4.00 10.00
97 Leonys Martin/314* 3.00 8.00
98 Nomar Mazara/996* 4.00 10.00
99 Chicago Cubs/724* 5.00 12.00
100A Brandon Crawford/379* 3.00 8.00
101 Houston Astros/357* 6.00 15.00
102 Julio Urias/2992* 4.00 10.00
103 Curtis Granderson/626* 5.00 12.00
104 Buster Posey/577* 4.00 10.00
105 Brett Eibner/904* 4.00 10.00
106 Mike Trout/1245* 4.00 10.00
107 New York Yankees/360* 5.00 12.00
108 Miguel Sano/721* 4.00 10.00
109 Carlos Correa/452* 4.00 10.00
110 Jeff Locke/344* 5.00 12.00
111 Welcome Back Vets/699* 3.00 8.00
112 Christian Bethancourt/330* 4.00 10.00
113 Mookie Betts/784* 5.00 12.00
114 C.J. Cron/273* 5.00 12.00
115 Matt Albers/743* 4.00 10.00
116 Mookie Betts/1075* 5.00 12.00
117 Freddie Freeman/310* 5.00 12.00
118 George Springer/320* 5.00 12.00
119 Madison Bumgarner/479* 4.00 10.00
120 Seattle Mariners/322* 4.00 10.00
121 Jackie Bradley 4.00 10.00
Daniel Murphy
May Players of the Month/456*
122 Trea Turner/1276* 5.00 12.00
123 Corey Seager/1900* 4.00 10.00
124 Melvin Upton Jr./349* 3.00 8.00
125 Stephen Strasburg/496* 5.00 12.00
126 Carlos Correa/381* 5.00 12.00
127 Jose Fernandez/273* 6.00 15.00
128 Evan Longoria/277* 4.00 10.00
129 Chicago Cubs/1278* 5.00 12.00
130 Michael Fulmer/636* 5.00 12.00
131 Rougned Odor/270* 3.00 8.00
132 Joey Votto/354* 5.00 12.00
133 Brian Dozier/293* 4.00 10.00
134 Zack Greinke/281* 4.00 10.00
135 Trayce Thompson/431* 4.00 10.00
136 Albert Almora Jr./766* 4.00 10.00
137 Jameson Taillon/1084* 3.00 8.00
138 Mac Williamson/441* 4.00 10.00
139 Stephen Strasburg/472* 5.00 12.00
140 Adam Wainwright/316* 3.00 8.00
141 Edwin Encarnacion/207* 12.00 30.00
142 Tim Anderson/702* 5.00 12.00
143 Buster Posey/365* 4.00 10.00
144 Matt Shoemaker/216* 8.00 20.00
145 Chris Davis/328* 4.00 10.00
146 Michael Fulmer/658* 4.00 10.00
147 Max Kepler/471* 5.00 12.00
148 Jayson Werth/326* 5.00 12.00
149 Cole Hamels/319* 3.00 8.00
150 Garcia/Eaton/289* 3.00 8.00
151 Whit Merrifield/757* 15.00 40.00
152 Albert Almora Jr./738* 6.00 15.00
153 Jameson Taillon/852* 3.00 8.00
154A Ichiro Suzuki/2798* 4.00 10.00
155 Jayson Werth/478* 3.00 8.00
156 Noah Syndergaard/810* 5.00 12.00
157 Freddie Freeman/432* 5.00 15.00
158 Victor Martinez/336* 4.00 10.00
159 Michael Saunders/280* 3.00 8.00
160 Carlos Santana/269* 3.00 8.00
161 Willie McCovey 4.00 10.00
David Ortiz
Ted Williams
Frank Thomas/1060*
162 Kenta Maeda 5.00 12.00
Francisco Lindor
Mookie Betts
Stand Up To Cancer/431*
163 Julio Teheran/291* 3.00 8.00
164 Willson Contreras/2404* 6.00 15.00
165 Mickey Moniak/2763* 5.00 12.00
166 Colorado Rockies 4.00 10.00
Miami Marlins/323*
167 Miguel Cabrera/430* 4.00 10.00
168 Justin Upton/301* 3.00 8.00
169 Kenley Jansen/310* 5.00 12.00
170 Erik Kratz/552* 5.00 12.00
171 Corey Kluber/274* 3.00 8.00
172 Carlos Correa/315* 5.00 12.00
173 Starlin Castro/299* 4.00 10.00
174 Cleveland Indians/317* 4.00 10.00
175 Yasiel Puig/376* 4.00 10.00
176 Xander Bogaerts/355* 4.00 10.00
177 George Springer/298* 5.00 12.00
178 Adam Lind/230* 6.00 15.00
179 San Francisco Giants/405* 5.00 12.00
180 Drew Pomeranz/232* 3.00 8.00
181 Lindor/Carrasco/255* 4.00 10.00
182 Pujols/Killebrew/413* 6.00 15.00
183 Mark Reynolds/264* 2.50 6.00
184 Bruce Bochy/340* 3.00 8.00
185 Chad Kuhl/750* 4.00 10.00
186 Kris Bryant/3075* 5.00 12.00
187 Texas Rangers/286* 5.00 12.00
188 Lucas Giolito/1891* 4.00 10.00
189 Miguel Cabrera/427* 4.00 10.00
190 Julio Urias/872* 3.00 8.00
191 Javier Baez/651* 6.00 15.00
192 Baltimore Orioles/526* 3.00 8.00
193 Didi Gregorius/355* 4.00 10.00
194 Danny Espinosa/482* 4.00 10.00
195 Carlos Carrasco/318* 2.50 6.00
196 Madison Bumgarner/506* 4.00 10.00
197 Carlos Santana/410* 5.00 12.00
198 Ben Revere/339* 6.00 15.00
199 David Ortiz/756* 4.00 10.00
200 Jose Fernandez/403* 4.00 10.00
201 Altuve/Myers/334* 3.00 8.00
202 Rajai Davis/316* 5.00 12.00
203 Max Kepler/631* 4.00 10.00
204 C.J. Cron/298* 4.00 10.00
205 Melvin Upton Jr./292* 3.00 8.00
206 Wilmer Flores/740* 2.50 6.00
207 Mark Teixeira/339* 5.00 12.00
208 Miami Marlins 3.00 8.00
Atlanta Braves/703*
209 Seager/Thompson/749* 5.00 12.00
210 Billy Hamilton/296* 4.00 10.00
211 Zach Eflin/511* 4.00 10.00
212 Giancarlo Stanton/254* 4.00 10.00
213 Eric Hosmer 3.00 8.00
All-Star Game/372*
214 Jose Altuve 3.00 8.00
All-Star Game/326*
215 Manny Machado 5.00 12.00
All-Star Game/407*
216 Xander Bogaerts 4.00 10.00
All-Star Game/444*
217 Salvador Perez 4.00 10.00
All-Star Game/376*
218 Giancarlo Stanton/335* 4.00 10.00
219 Anthony Rizzo 5.00 12.00
All-Star Game/540*
220 Ben Zobrist 6.00 15.00
All-Star Game/479*
221 Kris Bryant 10.00 25.00
All-Star Game/726*
222 Addison Russell 4.00 10.00
All-Star Game/507*
223 Buster Posey 5.00 12.00
All-Star Game/402*
224 Tyler Glasnow/995* 4.00 10.00
225 Salvador Perez/341* 4.00 10.00
226 Trevor Story/1041* 5.00 12.00
227 Mike Trout 5.00 12.00
All-Star Game/718*
228 Mookie Betts 8.00 20.00
All-Star Game/397*
229 Jackie Bradley Jr. 4.00 10.00
All-Star Game/349*
230 David Ortiz 4.00 10.00
All-Star Game/474*
231 Yasmani Grandal/286* 6.00 15.00
232 Luis Valbuena/236* 4.00 10.00
233 Bryce Harper 5.00 12.00
All-Star Game/708*
234 Yoenis Cespedes 4.00 10.00
All-Star Game/481*
235 Dexter Fowler 5.00 12.00
All-Star Game/386*
236 Josh Bell/925* 5.00 12.00
237 Tyler Anderson/365* 3.00 8.00
238 Yoan Moncada/1452* 4.00 10.00
239 Kenta Maeda/322* 6.00 15.00
240 Madison Bumgarner/386* 4.00 10.00
241 Giancarlo Stanton 5.00 12.00
All-Star Week/812*
242 Mark Trumbo 3.00 8.00
All-Star Week/263*
243 Johnny Cueto 4.00 10.00
All-Star Game/307*
244 Chris Sale 4.00 10.00
All-Star Game/318*
245 David Ortiz 5.00 12.00
All-Star Game/4506*
246 Kris Bryant 12.00 30.00
All-Star Game/246*
247A Eric Hosmer 3.00 8.00
All-Star Game/993*
247B Eric Hosmer Base 30.00 80.00
All-Star Game/99
248 Carew/Gwynn/693* 4.00 10.00
249 Stephen Strasburg/555* 4.00 10.00
250 Carlos Beltran/337* 3.00 8.00
251 Carlos Correa/246* 8.00 20.00
252 Chris Taylor/260* 15.00 40.00
253 Ryon Healy/323* 6.00 15.00
254 Adam Wainwright/272* 5.00 12.00
255 Matt Shoemaker/196* 25.00 60.00
256 Jarrod Saltalamacchia/242* 5.00 12.00
257 Chase d'Arnaud/180* 25.00 60.00
258 Jacob DeGrom/775* 6.00 15.00
259 Billy Hamilton/207* 12.00 30.00
260 Pujols/Robinson/324* 6.00 15.00
261 Jose Fernandez/244* 6.00 15.00
262 Aroldis Chapman/377* 4.00 10.00
263 Adam Lind/267* 3.00 8.00
264 Josh Harrison/319* 10.00 25.00
265 Jeurys Familia/460* 3.00 8.00
266 Danny Salazar/225* 3.00 8.00
267 Albert Pujols/261* 4.00 10.00
268 Leonys Martin/257* 4.00 10.00
269 Hanley Ramirez/317* 4.00 10.00
270 MLB Turns Back The Clock/401* 5.00 12.00
271 Aledmys Diaz/1087* 3.00 8.00
272 Kansas City Royals World Series/1002* 5.00
12.00
273 Zach Eflin/404* 5.00 12.00
274 Miguel Cabrera/448* 4.00 10.00
275 Matt Adams/319* 5.00 12.00
276 Coco Crisp/251* 5.00 12.00
277 Stephen Drew/292* 2.50 6.00
278 Mark Trumbo/256* 2.50 6.00
279 Trevor Story/620* 6.00 15.00
280 Ryon Healy/295* 5.00 12.00
281 Ken Griffey Jr./1930* 5.00 15.00
282 Mike Piazza/1309* 4.00 10.00
283 Nolan Reimold/295* 4.00 10.00
284 Adam Eaton 2.50 6.00
Melky Cabrera/260*
285 Adrian Beltre/280* 4.00 10.00
286 Tyler Saladino/306* 2.50 6.00
287 Alex Bregman/2310* 4.00 10.00
288 Aroldis Chapman/660* 6.00 15.00
289 Francisco Lindor/293* 4.00 10.00
290 A.J. Ellis/261* 4.00 10.00
291 David Dahl/520* 5.00 12.00
292 Gerrit Cole/418* 4.00 10.00
293 Mike Trout 6.00 15.00
Daniel Nava
Albert Pujols/362*
294 Ryan Zimmerman/702* 3.00 8.00
295 Justin Verlander 4.00 10.00
Jose Iglesias/355*
296 Mitch Moreland/296* 2.50 6.00
297 Adam Rosales/262* 2.50 6.00
298 Derek Dietrich/258* 5.00 12.00
299 Dustin Pedroia 4.00 10.00
Xander Bogaerts/405*
300 Matt Cain 5.00 12.00
Madison Bumgarner/389*
301 Jon Lester 6.00 15.00
Jason Heyward/671*
302 Carlos Beltran 8.00 20.00
Jay Bruce
Jonathan Lucroy
Josh Reddick
Matt Moore
Rich Hill/297*
303 Danny Duffy/479* 8.00 20.00
304 Max Kepler/620* 5.00 12.00
305 Kyle Hendricks/347* 40.00 100.00
306 Carlos Correa/269* 5.00 12.00
307 Joe Musgrove/558* 4.00 10.00
308 Carlos Beltran 3.00 8.00
Jonathan Lucroy/284*
309 Jay Bruce/505* 3.00 8.00
310 Josh Reddick/256* 6.00 15.00
311 Scott Schebler/363* 4.00 10.00
312 Andrew Benintendi/1224* 12.00 30.00
313 J.D. Martinez/319* 4.00 10.00
314 Albert Pujols/269* 5.00 12.00
315 Bartolo Colon/741* 3.00 8.00
316 Jay Bruce/489* 2.00 5.00
317 Mark Teixeira/302* 2.00 5.00
318 Steven Wright/322* 4.00 10.00
319 Dallas Keuchel/234* 8.00 20.00
320 Sean Rodriguez/299* 2.50 6.00
321 Mike Trout/679* 5.00 12.00
322 Jorge Soler/317* 8.00 20.00
323 Devon Travis/215* 8.00 20.00
324 Giancarlo Stanton/378* 4.00 10.00
325 Andrew Miller/282* 3.00 8.00
326 Jayson Werth/327* 5.00 12.00
327A Ichiro/11550* 4.00 10.00
327B Ichiro Base/99 125.00 300.00
327C Ichiro Base/49 200.00 400.00
327D Ichiro Base/25 250.00 500.00
328 Mike Trout/761* 6.00 15.00
329 Manny Machado/712* 5.00 12.00
330 Miguel Sano/588* 4.00 10.00
331 Billy Hamilton/444* 5.00 12.00
332 Rob Segedin/524* 4.00 10.00
333 Daniel Murphy 5.00 12.00
Mookie Betts/540*
334 Corey Seager/886* 6.00 15.00
335 Brandon Crawford/522* 3.00 8.00
336 St Louis Cardinals/313* 5.00 12.00
337 Alex Reyes/838* 3.00 8.00
338 Max Scherzer/365* 4.00 10.00
339 Chicago Cubs/962* 6.00 15.00
340 Roberto Clemente 5.00 12.00
Ichiro/668*
341 Gary Sanchez/673* 30.00 80.00
342 Prince Fielder/369* 3.00 8.00
343 Lorenzo Cain/303* 3.00 8.00
344 David Dahl/484* 3.00 8.00
345 Milwaukee Brewers/236* 4.00 10.00
346 Zach Britton/338* 5.00 12.00
347 Alex Rodriguez/1394* 6.00 15.00
348 Charlie Blackmon/273* 5.00 12.00
349 Jake Thompson/349* 3.00 8.00
350 Cleveland Indians/262* 4.00 10.00
351 Austin/Judge/351* 10.00 25.00
352 Tyler Austin/1633* 4.00 10.00
353 Aaron Judge/2537* 25.00 60.00
354 Wilmer Flores/771* 5.00 12.00
355A Mookie Betts 6.00 15.00
Ted Williams/1646*
355B Mookie Betts Base/99 50.00 120.00
355C Mookie Betts Base/49 60.00 150.00
355D Mookie Betts Base/25 75.00 200.00
356 Aaron Judge/1169* 25.00 60.00
357 Michael Fulmer/609* 8.00 20.00
358 Baltimore Orioles/308* 4.00 10.00
359 Stephen Piscotty/527* 4.00 10.00
360 Bartolo Colon/1120* 6.00 15.00
361 Anthony Rizzo/1126* 8.00 20.00
362 Chase Utley/4221* 8.00 20.00
363 Toronto Blue Jays/239* 8.00 20.00
364 Jose Altuve/546* 3.00 8.00
365 Noah Syndergaard 6.00 15.00
Tom Seaver/771*
366 Dansby Swanson 4.00 10.00
Alex Bregman/923*
367 Dansby Swanson/1450* 3.00 8.00
368 Gary Sanchez/740* 12.00 30.00
369 Adam Eaton/411* 8.00 20.00
370A Kris Bryant/1861* 5.00 12.00
370B Kris Bryant Base/99 30.00 80.00
370C Kris Bryant Base/49 40.00 100.00
370D Kris Bryant Base/25 100.00 250.00
371 Madison Bumgarner/489* 5.00 12.00
372 Tyler Naquin/729* 5.00 12.00
373 Ben Revere/357* 3.00 8.00
374 Kendall Graveman/226* 8.00 20.00
375 Baltimore Orioles/298* 3.00 8.00
376 Ryan Raburn/256* 8.00 20.00
377 Ryan Schimpf/378* 8.00 20.00
378 Ichiro 5.00 12.00
Al Kaline/579*
379 Carl Yastrzemski 6.00 15.00
David Ortiz
Ted Williams/884*
380 Brett Gardner/310* 4.00 10.00
381 Yulieski Gurriel/381* 3.00 8.00
382 Jace Peterson/270* 4.00 10.00
383 Adrian Gonzalez/298* 5.00 12.00
384 Andrew Toles 2.00 5.00
Rob Segedin/384*
385 Andrew Benintendi/846* 5.00 12.00
386 Gary Sanchez/1054* 6.00 15.00
387 Paul Goldschmidt/294* 5.00 12.00
388A Gary Sanchez/1395* 6.00 15.00
388B Gary Sanchez Base/99 50.00 120.00
388C Gary Sanchez Base/49 60.00 150.00
388D Gary Sanchez Base/25 75.00 200.00
389A David Ortiz/2394* 4.00 10.00
389B David Ortiz AU/99 40.00 100.00
389C David Ortiz AU/49 50.00 120.00
389D David Ortiz AU/25 60.00 150.00
390 Albert Pujols/670* 3.00 8.00
391 Yu Darvish/753* 4.00 10.00
392 Carlos Gomez/234* 6.00 15.00
393 Albert Pujols/523* 4.00 10.00
394 Matt Moore/366* 5.00 12.00
395 Todd Frazier/240* 5.00 12.00
396 Bartolo Colon/492* 5.00 12.00
397 Carlos Correa 6.00 15.00
Evan Gattis/397*
398 Kris Bryant/870* 6.00 15.00
399 Corey Seager/1084* 4.00 10.00
400 Gary Sanchez/2334* 5.00 12.00
401 Josh Donaldson/524* 6.00 15.00
402 Mark Trumbo/270* 3.00 8.00
403 The Rally Mantis/1029* 3.00 8.00
404 Ichiro 5.00 12.00
Wade Boggs/532*
405 Yoenis Cespedes/841* 4.00 10.00
406 Jason Kipnis/261* 5.00 12.00
407 Jorge Soler 5.00 12.00
Miguel Montero/591*
408 Pat Venditte/412* 5.00 12.00
409 Mike Trout/755* 6.00 15.00
410 Manny Machado/468* 5.00 12.00
411 JaCoby Jones/714* 4.00 10.00
412 Rougned Odor/308* 4.00 10.00
413 Andrew Toles/458* 5.00 12.00
414 Jeurys Familia/503* 3.00 8.00
415 Ricky Nolasco/278* 2.50 6.00
416 Jon Lester/444* 5.00 12.00
417 Eugenio Suarez/223* 6.00 15.00
418 Yoan Moncada/2333* 3.00 8.00
419 Kole Calhoun 6.00 15.00
Mike Trout
Albert Pujols/476*
420A Albert Pujols/656* 5.00 12.00
421 Kris Bryant 8.00 20.00
Gary Sanchez/825*
422 Gary Sanchez/889* 6.00 15.00
423 Jason Heyward/357* 4.00 10.00
424 Khris Davis/188* 12.00 30.00
425 Lonnie Chisenhall/262* 5.00 12.00
426 Jose De Leon/705* 3.00 8.00
427 Brian Dozier/306* 3.00 8.00
428 Chad Bettis/275* 2.50 6.00
429 Dansby Swanson/646* 4.00 10.00

430 Ichiro Suzuki/515* 5.00 12.00
431 St. Louis Cardinals/334* 6.00 15.00
432 St. Louis Cardinals/345* 4.00 10.00
433 Kansas City Royals/314* 4.00 10.00
434 Wilson Ramos/278* 6.00 15.00
435 Cristhian Adames/213*
436 Tyler Austin/592* 5.00 12.00
437 Trea Turner/754* 5.00 12.00
438 Rick Porcello/381* 6.00 15.00
439 Chicago Cubs/544* 5.00 12.00
440 Rich Hill/307* 6.00 15.00
441 Joe Mauer/281* 5.00 12.00
442 Adonis Garcia/273* 4.00 10.00
443 Gary Sanchez/590* 8.00 20.00
444 MLB Tribute to 15th Anniversary of 9/11/551* 4.00 10.00
445 David Ortiz Jimmie Foxx/584* 5.00 12.00
446 Chris Sale/361* 4.00 10.00
447 Kyle Hendricks/538* 6.00 15.00
448 Ichiro Lou Brock/561* 4.00 10.00
449 Brian Dozier Harmon Killebrew/483* 4.00 10.00
450 T.J. Rivera/613* 10.00 25.00
451 Didi Gregorius Jacoby Ellsbury/303* 4.00 10.00
452 Aledmys Diaz/482* 3.00 8.00
453 Taijuan Walker/241* 4.00 10.00
454 Ryan Schimpf/310* 3.00 8.00
455 Daniel Murphy/410* 6.00 15.00
456 Mark Trumbo/275* 2.50 6.00
457 Carlos Sanchez/259* 8.00 20.00
458 Hanley Ramirez/434* 4.00 10.00
459 Mike Trout/410* 5.00 12.00
460A Chicago Cubs N.L. Central Title/878* 5.00 12.00
460B Chicago Cubs N.L Central Title Base/99 40.00 100.00
460C Chicago Cubs N.L Central Title Base/49 50.00 120.00
460D Chicago Cubs N.L Central Title Base/25 60.00 150.00
461 Miguel Montero/556* 4.00 10.00
462 Jimmy Paredes/281* 4.00 10.00
463 Jonathan Lucroy/280* 4.00 10.00
464 Baltimore Orioles/272* 3.00 8.00
465 Daniel Descalso/260 3.00 8.00
466 Jose Ramirez/221* 6.00 15.00
467 Curtis Granderson/467* 5.00 12.00
468 Jeremy Hellickson/204* 10.00 25.00
469 Albert Pujols/316* 4.00 10.00
470 Jon Gray/322* 6.00 15.00
471 Corey Seager/696* 5.00 12.00
472 Miguel Cabrera/462* 3.00 8.00
473 Gary Sanchez/895* 5.00 12.00
474 Carlos Correa Alex Rodriguez/442* ERR 12.00 30.00
Mookie Betts and Nomar Garciaparra pictured
475 Ben Zobrist/2968* 8.00 20.00
476 Rick Porcello/355* 4.00 10.00
477 Jose Abreu/245* 6.00 15.00
478 Ian Desmond/280* 4.00 10.00
479 Aaron Blair/309* 4.00 10.00
480 Adrian Gonzalez/480* 6.00 15.00
481 Trey Mancini/481* 10.00 25.00
482 David Ortiz/759* 4.00 10.00
483 Mookie Betts Nomar Garciaparra/562* 4.00 10.00
484 Brandon Guyer/300* 4.00 10.00
485 Jose Altuve/358* 5.00 12.00
486 Gary Sanchez/3282* 6.00 15.00
487 Robinson Cano/282* 5.00 12.00
488 Asdrubal Cabrera/491* 4.00 10.00
489 Ender Inciarte/273* 4.00 10.00
490 Jose Reyes Asdrubal Cabrera/815* 4.00 10.00
491 Brian Dozier/324* 4.00 10.00
492 Milwaukee Brewers/243* 8.00 20.00
493 Byron Buxton/323* 5.00 12.00
494 Mark Trumbo/299* 3.00 8.00
495 Angels Mike Trout/256* 5.00 12.00
496 Jacob Stallings/374* 4.00 10.00
497 Chicago Cubs Anthony Rizzo/452* 5.00 12.00
498A Texas Rangers A.L. West Title/345*
498B Texas Rangers A.L. West Title Base/99
498C Texas Rangers A.L. West Title Base/49
498D Texas Rangers A.L. West Title Base/25
499 Trey Mancini/432* 4.00 10.00
500 Boston Red Sox/513* 5.00 12.00
501A Washington Nationals N.L. East Title/544* 4.00 10.00
501B Washington Nationals N.L. East Title Base/99 30.00 80.00
501C Washington Nationals N.L. East Title Base/49
501D Washington Nationals N.L. East Title Base/25
502 Edwin Encarnacion/253* 6.00 15.00
503 Boston Red Sox/398* 4.00 10.00
504 David Ross/775* 6.00 15.00
505 Corey Seager Charlie Culberson/704* 5.00 12.00
506 Los Angeles Dodgers N.L. West Title/433*
507A Cleveland Indians A.L. Central Title/415* 5.00 12.00
507B Cleveland Indians A.L. Central Title Base/99 30.00 80.00
507C Cleveland Indians A.L. Central Title Base Francisco Lindor AU/49
507D Cleveland Indians A.L. Central Title Base Francisco Lindor AU/25
508 Chicago Cubs 100 Win Season/902* 4.00 10.00
509A Gary Sanchez/1893* 4.00 10.00
509B Gary Sanchez Base/99 25.00 60.00
509C Gary Sanchez Base/49 30.00 80.00
509D Gary Sanchez Base/25
510 Miguel Cabrera/394* 4.00 10.00
511 Buster Posey/542* 5.00 12.00
512 Hunter Renfroe/512* 5.00 12.00
513 Freddie Freeman/221* 12.00 30.00
514 John Jaso/348* 4.00 10.00
515 Jeurys Familia/461* 5.00 12.00
516 Mark Teixeira/363* 4.00 10.00
517A Boston Red Sox A.L East Title/721* 6.00 15.00
517B Boston Red Sox A.L East Title Base/99 60.00 150.00
517C Boston Red Sox A.L East Title Base/49
517D Boston Red Sox A.L East Title Base/25
518 Hunter Renfroe/1544* 4.00 10.00
519 Hyun-Soo Kim/428* 5.00 12.00
520 Yadier Molina/332* 4.00 10.00
521 Johnny Cueto Jeff Samardzija Matt Moore/339* 4.00 10.00
522 Carlos Rodon/216* 8.00 20.00
523 Chris Carter/178* 4.00 10.00
524 David Oritz/542* 4.00 10.00
525 Yu Darvish/335* 5.00 12.00
526 Madison Bumgarner/406* 5.00 12.00
527 New York Mets Clinch Top NL Wild Card/771* 6.00 15.00
528 Jedd Gyorko/268* 4.00 10.00
529 Ty Blach/425* 12.00 30.00
530 David Ortiz/2690* 5.00 12.00
531 Mark Teixeira/426* 4.00 10.00
532 Martin Prado/281* 5.00 12.00
533 Toronto Blue Jays/315* 5.00 12.00
534 Baltimore Orioles/369* 4.00 10.00
535 Matt Wieters/350* 2.50 6.00
536 San Francisco Giants/422* 5.00 12.00
537 Jose Bautista/255* 6.00 15.00
538A Edwin Encarnacion/365* 10.00 25.00
538B Edwin Encarnacion AU/99 40.00 100.00
538C Edwin Encarnacion AU/49 50.00 120.00
538D Edwin Encarnacion AU/25
539A Toronto Blue Jays Wild Card Win/252* 6.00 15.00
539B Toronto Blue Jays Wild Card Win Base/99 25.00 60.00
539C Toronto Blue Jays Wild Card Win Base/49
539D Toronto Blue Jays Wild Card Win Base/25
540 M.Cabrera/F.Freeman 5.00 12.00
541 San Francisco Giants Wild Card Win/322* 3.00 8.00
542 Conor Gillaspie/361* 4.00 10.00
543 Texas Rangers Yu Darvish/335*
543A Madison Bumgarner/585*
543B Madison Bumgarner Base/99 40.00 100.00
543C Madison Bumgarner Base/49 50.00 120.00
543D Madison Bumgarner Base/25
544 Noah Syndergaard/497* 5.00 12.00
545 Curtis Granderson/417* 10.00 25.00
546 Marco Estrada/186* 6.00 15.00
547 Josh Donaldson/198*
548 Andrew Benintendi/552* 6.00 15.00
549 Jason Kipnis Francisco Lindor/324* 5.00 12.00
550 Toronto Blue Jays HR Record/222* 6.00 15.00
551 Corey Seager/869* 4.00 10.00
552 Lonnie Chisenhall/243* 6.00 15.00
553 Corey Kluber/267* 5.00 12.00
554 Jon Lester/644* 5.00 12.00
555 Javier Baez/756* 6.00 15.00
556 Travis Wood/851* 5.00 12.00
557 Corey Seager/817* 5.00 12.00
558 Jose Lobaton/333* 5.00 12.00
559 Daniel Murphy/340* 5.00 12.00
560A Josh Donaldson ALDS/1041* 5.00 12.00
560B Josh Donaldson ALDS Base/99 30.00 80.00
560C Josh Donaldson ALDS Base/49 40.00 100.00
560D Josh Donaldson ALDS Base/25 50.00 120.00
561 Toronto Blue Jays/433* 6.00 15.00
562 Anthony Rendon Jayson Werth/346* 5.00 12.00
563 Cleveland Indiains/370* 6.00 15.00
564A David Ortiz Final Game/1564* 5.00 12.00
564B David Ortiz Final Game Inscription AU/199 60.00 150.00
564C David Ortiz Final Game Green Monster Edition AU/99 75.00 200.00
564D David Ortiz Final Game Inscription AU/49 125.00 300.00
564E David Ortiz Final Game Inscription AU/25 200.00 500.00
565 Jake Arrieta NLDS/732* 5.00 12.00
566 Kris Bryant NLDS/837* 6.00 15.00
567 Conor Gillaspie NLDS/350* 4.00 10.00
568 Joe Panik NLDS/353* 5.00 12.00
569 Matt Moore NLDS/317* 8.00 20.00
570 Conor Gillaspie NLDS/330* 5.00 12.00
571 Ben Zobrist Willson Contreras Javier Baez NLDS/1316* 6.00 15.00
572A Chicago Cubs NLDS Champs/3836* 8.00 20.00
572B Chicago Cubs NLDS Champs Base/99
572C Chicago Cubs NLDS Champs Base/49
572D Chicago Cubs NLDS Champs Base/25
573 David Ross NLDS/886* 8.00 20.00
574 Chase Utley NLDS/367* 8.00 20.00
575 Daniel Murphy NLDS/367* 4.00 10.00
576 Julio Urias NLDS/817* 5.00 12.00
577 Joc Pederson NLDS/509* 5.00 12.00
578 Chris Heisey NLDS/432* 4.00 10.00
579A Clayton Kershaw 1st Save NLDS /2018* 5.00 12.00
579B Clayton Kershaw 1st Save NLDS AU/199 50.00 120.00
579C Clayton Kershaw 1st Save NLDS Base AU/99 75.00 200.00
579D Clayton Kershaw 1st Save NLDS Base AU/49
579E Clayton Kershaw 1st Save NLDS Base AU/25
580 Los Angeles Dodgers NLDS/486* 4.00 10.00
581 Francisco Lindor ALCS/356* 4.00 10.00
582 Corey Kluber ALCS/273* 5.00 12.00
583 Marco Estrada ALCS/250* 6.00 15.00
584 Andrew Miller Cody Allen ALCS/277* 5.00 12.00
585 Carlos Santana ALCS/339* 5.00 12.00
586 Andrew Miller ALCS/381* 6.00 15.00
587 Javier Baez NLCS/910* 8.00 20.00
588 Dexter Fowler NLCS/739* 4.00 10.00
589 Miguel Montero/926* 6.00 15.00
590 Adrian Gonzalez NLCS/397* 4.00 10.00
591 Clayton Kershaw NLCS/695* 6.00 15.00
592 Kenley Jansen NLCS/381* 6.00 15.00
593 Trevor Bauer ALCS/296* 6.00 15.00
594 Mike Napoli ALCS/272* 4.00 10.00
595 Jason Kipnis ALCS/269* 4.00 10.00
596 Cleveland Indians ALCS/274* 4.00 10.00
597 Josh Donaldson ALCS/269* 6.00 15.00
598 Edwin Encarnacion ALCS/261* 5.00 12.00
599 Corey Seager NLCS/527* 10.00 25.00
600 Yasmani Grandal NLCS/273* 6.00 15.00
601 Justin Turner NLCS/264* 8.00 20.00
602 Rich Hill NLCS/260* 8.00 20.00
603 Carlos Santana ALCS/385* 4.00 10.00
604 Ryan Merritt ALCS/478* 6.00 15.00
605A Andrew Miller ALCS/428*
605B Andrew Miller ALCS Base/99 30.00 80.00
605C Andrew Miller ALCS Base/49 40.00 100.00
605D Andrew Miller ALCS Base/25 60.00 150.00
606 Cleveland Indians ALCS/574* 6.00 15.00
607 Addison Russell NLCS/954* 4.00 10.00
608 Anthony Rizzo NLCS/945* 6.00 15.00
609 Julio Urias NLCS/475* 6.00 15.00
610A Addison Russell NLCS/743* 5.00 12.00
610B Addison Russell NLCS AU/99
610C Addison Russell NLCS AU/49
610D Addison Russell NLCS AU/25
611 Jon Lester NLCS/717* 5.00 12.00
612 Javier Baez NLCS/745* 5.00 12.00
613A Kris Bryant NLCS/1816* 5.00 12.00
613B Kris Bryant NLCS AU/199 60.00 150.00
613C Kris Bryant NLCS AU/99 75.00 200.00
613D Kris Bryant NLCS AU/49 125.00 300.00
613E Kris Bryant NLCS AU/25
614 Kyle Hendricks NLCS/1667* 5.00 12.00
615A Chicago Cubs NLCS/2447* 4.00 10.00
615B Chicago Cubs NLCS Base/99 50.00 120.00
616 Anthony Rizzo NLCS/1745* 5.00 12.00
617 Jon Lester Javier Baez CO-MVPS NLCS/1784* 6.00 15.00
618 Anthony Rizzo Javier Baez Kris Bryant Addison Russell Mike Napoli Jason Kipnis Jose Ramirez Francisco Lindor/1577* 8.00 20.00
621 Kyle Hendricks Jake Arrieta Jon Lester John Lackey Josh Tomlin Trevor Bauer Corey Kluber Danny Salazar/1330* 6.00 15.00
623 Kyle Schwarber WS/1341* 4.00 10.00
624 Danny Salazar/330* 4.00 10.00
625 Cleveland Indians WS/758* 8.00 20.00
626 Francisco Lindor WS/529* 5.00 12.00
627A Corey Kluber WS/692* 5.00 12.00
627B Corey Kluber WS AU/199
627C Corey Kluber WS Base AU//99
627D Corey Kluber WS Base AU/49
627E Corey Kluber WS Base AU/25
628 Kyle Schwarber WS RB/1646* 6.00 15.00
629 Andrew Miller WS/489* 4.00 10.00
630 Roberto Perez WS/493* 5.00 12.00
631A Kyle Schwarber WS/3036* 5.00 12.00
631B Kyle Schwarber WS AU/199 75.00 200.00
631C Kyle Schwarber WS Base AU/99 100.00 250.00
631D Kyle Schwarber WS Base AU/49 125.00 300.00
631E Kyle Schwarber WS Base AU/25
632 Jake Arrieta WS/1272* 5.00 12.00
633 Anthony Rizzo WS/1461* 5.00 12.00
634 Ben Zobrist WS/1175* 6.00 15.00
635 Chicago Cubs Wrigley Field WS/1519* 10.00 25.00
636 Josh Tomlin WS/462* 5.00 12.00
637 Coco Crisp WS/518* 5.00 12.00
638 Andrew Miller WS/552* 3.00 8.00
639A Cleveland Indians WS/553* 4.00 10.00
639B Cleveland Indians WS Base/99 30.00 80.00
639C Cleveland Indians WS Base/49
639D Cleveland Indians WS Base/25
640 Carlos Santana WS/439* 5.00 12.00
641 Corey Kluber WS/473* 5.00 12.00
642 Jason Kipnis WS/515* 5.00 12.00
643 Andrew Miller WS/508* 4.00 10.00
644A Francisco Lindor Corey Kluber WS/665* 4.00 10.00
644B Francisco Lindor Corey Kluber WS AU/99 60.00 150.00
644C Francisco Lindor Corey Kluber WS AU/49 75.00 200.00
644D Francisco Lindor Corey Kluber WS AU/25
645 Jason Heyward WS/1249* 6.00 15.00
646A Kris Bryant WS/1688* 5.00 12.00
646B Kris Bryant WS AU/199 100.00 250.00
646C Kris Bryant WS AU/99 125.00 300.00
646D Kris Bryant WS AU/49 150.00 400.00
646E Kris Bryant WS AU/25 200.00 500.00
647 David Ross WS/1288* 6.00 15.00
648A Aroldis Chapman WS/1384* 4.00 10.00
648B Aroldis Chapman WS Base/99 100.00 250.00
648C Aroldis Chapman WS Base/49 125.00 300.00
648D Aroldis Chapman WS Base/25
649 Chicago Cubs Wrigley Field WS/1516* 5.00 12.00
650 Kris Bryant WS/2628* 5.00 12.00
651 Addison Russell WS/2886* 6.00 15.00
652A Anthony Rizzo WS/2217* 6.00 15.00
652B Anthony Rizzo WS AU/99
652C Anthony Rizzo WS AU/49
652D Anthony Rizzo WS AU/25
653 Jason Kipnis WS/1522* 4.00 10.00
654 Jake Arrieta WS/1967* 5.00 12.00
655 Kris Bryant Anthony Rizzo WS/3105* 6.00 15.00
656A Dexter Fowler WS/2161* 5.00 12.00
656B Dexter Fowler WS AU/99 60.00 150.00
656C Dexter Fowler WS AU/49 75.00 200.00
656D Dexter Fowler WS AU/25
657A Javier Baez WS/2204* 6.00 15.00
657B Javier Baez WS AU/99 75.00 200.00
657C Javier Baez WS AU/49 100.00 250.00
657D Javier Baez WS AU/25 125.00 300.00
658A David Ross WS/2569* 8.00 20.00
658B David Ross WS AU/199 125.00 300.00
658C David Ross WS AU/99
658D David Ross WS AU/49
658E David Ross WS AU/25
659 Rajai Davis WS/1799* 6.00 15.00
660 Ben Zobrist WS/2396* 6.00 15.00
661 Albert Almora Jr. WS/2209* 6.00 15.00
662 Mike Montgomery WS/2103* 12.00 30.00
663A Kris Bryant Anthony Rizzo WS/4516* 8.00 20.00
663B Kris Bryant Anthony Rizzo WS Base AU/99 500.00 800.00
663C Kris Bryant Anthony Rizzo WS Base AU/49 1200.00 1600.00
663D Kris Bryant Anthony Rizzo WS Base AU/25
664A Ben Zobrist WS/4445* 10.00 25.00
664B Ben Zobrist WS Base/99 75.00 200.00
664C Ben Zobrist WS Base/49 100.00 250.00
664D Ben Zobrist WS Base/25 125.00 300.00
665 Chicago Cubs World Series Title/6009* 6.00 15.00
AS1 Ken Griffey Jr. Tony Gwynn/1730* 4.00 10.00
AS2 Mike Trout/1898* 5.00 12.00
BRA Kris Bryant Addison Russell WS Base AU/199 200.00 400.00
BRB Kris Bryant Addison Russell WS Base AU/99 300.00 600.00
BRC Kris Bryant Addison Russell WS Base AU/49 500.00 1000.00
BRD Kris Bryant Addison Russell WS Base AU/25 800.00 1500.00
MNA Mike Napoli AU/99 50.00 120.00
MNB Mike Napoli AU/49
MNC Mike Napoli AU/25
OS1 David Ortiz Kris Bryant Hank Aaron Award/1509* 6.00 15.00
OS2 Curtis Granderson Clemente Award/488*
OS3 Zach Britton Kenley Jansen Top Reliever/452*
OS4 Chicago Cubs World Series Champions/1276*
OS5A Kyle Schwarber WS/981* 4.00 10.00
OS5B Kyle Schwarber WS AU/199
OS5C Kyle Schwarber WS AU/99
OS5D Kyle Schwarber WS AU/49
OS5E Kyle Schwarber WS AU/25
OS6A Willson Contreras WS/898* 4.00 10.00
OS6B Willson Contreras WS AU/99
OS6C Willson Contreras WS AU/49
OS6D Willson Contreras WS AU/25
OS7 Jose Altuve#[Curtis Granderson/266*
OS8 Mark Trumbo Rick Porcello Michael Fulmer Jose Altuve/283*
OS9 Corey Seager Kyle Hendricks Jose Fernandez Daniel Murphy/459*
TFA Terry Francona FWS AU/99 50.00 120.00
TFB Terry Francona FWS AU/49
TFC Terry Francona FWS AU/25
OS10 Daniel Murphy Nolan Arenado Anthony Rizzo Corey Seager Josh Donaldson Jose Altuve Miguel Cabrera Xanders Bogaerts/552* 3.00 8.00
OS11 Mark Trumbo Mike Trout Mookie Betts Christain Yelich Yoenis Cespedes Charlie Blackmon/347*
OS12 David Ortiz Salvador Perez Jake Arrieta Wilson Ramos/450*
OS13 Nolan Arenado Brandon Crawford Dustin Pedroia Anthony Rizzo/441*
OS14 Brett Gardner Kevin Kiermaier Mookie Betts/289*
OS15 Buster Posey Zack Greinke/286*
OS16A Corey Seager Rookie of the Year/1040*
OS16B Corey Seager Rookie of the Year Swatch/199 30.00 80.00
OS16C Corey Seager Rookie of the Year Swatch/99
OS16D Corey Seager Rookie of the Year Patch/49
OS16E Corey Seager Rookie of the Year Patch/25
OS17A Michael Fulmer Rookie of the Year/587* 5.00 12.00
OS17B Michael Fulmer Rookie of the Year AU/99
OS17C Michael Fulmer Rookie of the Year AU/49
OS17D Michael Fulmer Rookie of the Year AU/25
OS18 Gary Sanchez AS Rookie Team/665* 8.00 20.00
OS19 Tommy Joseph AS Rookie Team/665* 4.00 10.00
OS20 Ryan Schimpf AS Rookie Team/665* 5.00 12.00
OS21 Alex Bregman AS Rookie Team/665*
OS22 Corey Seager AS Rookie Team/665*
OS23 Trea Turner AS Rookie Team/665*
OS24 Nomar Mazara AS Rookie Team/665* 4.00 10.00
OS25 Tyler Naquin AS Rookie Team/665*
OS26 Julio Urias AS Rookie Team/665*
OS27 Kenta Maeda AS Rookie Team/665*
OS28 Seung-Hwan Oh AS Rookie Team/665* 4.00 10.00
OS29 Rick Porcello AL Cy Young/398* 4.00 10.00
OS30 Max Scherzer NL Cy Young/499*
OS31A Mike Trout AL MVP/1488*
OS31B Mike Trout AL MVP AU/99
OS31C Mike Trout AL MVP AU/49
OS31D Mike Trout AL MVP AU/25
OS32 Kris Bryant NL MVP/3193* 5.00 12.00
OS33 Rick Porcello AL Comeback POY/265*
OS34 Anthony Rendon NL Comeback POY/283* 4.00 10.00
OS35 Yoenis Cespedes/375*
OS36 Chris Sale/286*
OS37 Yoan Moncada/411* 8.00 20.00
OS38 Wade Davis/311* 4.00 10.00
OS39 Jorge Soler/264* 5.00 12.00
OS40 Adam Eaton/233*
OS41 Lucas Giolito/341*
OS42 Aroldis Chapman/300*
OS43 Chicago Cubs White House W Flag/1200*
OS44 Chicago Cubs White House Obama Jersey/1238*
OS45 Chicago Cubs White House Barack Obama/1301* 4.00 10.00
OS46A Tim Raines Hall of Fame/408*
OS46B Tim Raines Hall of Fame AU/99
OS46C Tim Raines Hall of Fame AU/49
OS46D Tim Raines Hall of Fame AU/25
OS47A Jeff Bagwell Hall of Fame/489* 4.00 10.00
OS47B Jeff Bagwell Hall of Fame AU/99
OS47C Jeff Bagwell Hall of Fame AU/49
OS47D Jeff Bagwell Hall of Fame AU/25
OS48A Ivan Rodriguez Hall of Fame/457*
OS48B Ivan Rodriguez Hall of Fame AU/99 40.00 100.00
OS48C Ivan Rodriguez Hall of Fame AU/49
OS48D Ivan Rodriguez Hall of Fame AU/25
OSBZA Ben Zobrist White House AU/99 50.00 120.00
OSBZB Ben Zobrist White House AU/49
OSBZC Ben Zobrist White House AU/25
OSTBA Mike Trout Kris Bryant MVPs AU/25
OSRBRA Ivan Rodriguez Jeff Bagwell Tim Raines Hall of Fame AU/25

1998 Topps Opening Day

COMPLETE SET (165) 20.00 50.00
*OPEN.DAY: .75X TO 2X BASIC TOPPS
ISSUED IN OPENING DAY PACKS

1999 Topps Opening Day

COMPLETE SET (165) 15.00 40.00
*OPEN.DAY: .75X TO 2X BASIC TOPPS
ISSUED IN OPENING DAY PACKS
AARON AUTO STATED ODDS 1:29,642
1 Hank Aaron 1.00 2.50
HA Hank Aaron AU 175.00 350.00

1999 Topps Opening Day Oversize

COMPLETE SET (3) 3.00 8.00
1 Sammy Sosa .50 1.25
2 Mark McGwire 1.25 3.00
3 Ken Griffey Jr. 1.00 2.50

2000 Topps Opening Day

COMPLETE SET (165) 15.00 40.00
*OPEN.DAY: .75X TO 2X BASIC TOPPS
ISSUED IN OPENING DAY PACKS
NO MM VARIATIONS IN OPENING DAY

2000 Topps Opening Day Autographs

GROUP B STATED ODDS 1:48074
GROUP C STATED ODDS 1:6280
ODA1 Edgardo Alfonzo A 6.00 15.00
ODA2 Wade Boggs A 50.00 100.00
ODA3 Robin Ventura A 6.00 15.00
ODA4 Josh Hamilton 12.00 30.00
ODA5 Vernon Wells C 15.00 40.00

2001 Topps Opening Day

COMPLETE SET (165) 15.00 40.00
*OPEN.DAY: .75X TO 2X BASIC TOPPS
ISSUED IN OPENING DAY PACKS

2001 Topps Opening Day Autographs

GROUP A ODDS 1:31,680
GROUP B ODDS 1:15,020
GROUP C ODDS 1:10,004
GROUP D ODDS 1:5,940
ODACJ Chipper Jones A 60.00 120.00
ODACP Corey Patterson D 10.00 25.00
ODAMO Magglio Ordonez C 10.00 24.00
ODATH Todd Helton B 12.00 30.00

2001 Topps Opening Day Stickers

COMPLETE SET (30) 2.50 6.00
COMMON TEAM (1-30) .08 .25

2002 Topps Opening Day

COMPLETE SET (165) 15.00 40.00
*OPEN.DAY: .75X TO X2 BASIC TOPPS
ISSUED IN OPENING DAY PACKS

2002 Topps Opening Day Autographs

GROUP A STATED ODDS 1:6069
GROUP B STATED ODDS 1:3036
GROUP C STATED ODDS 1:2014
NO PRICING DUE TO SCARCITY

2003 Topps Opening Day

COMPLETE SET (165) 15.00 40.00
*OPEN.DAY: .75X TO 2X BASIC TOPPS
ISSUED IN OPENING DAY PACKS

2003 Topps Opening Day Stickers

*OD STICKERS: 1.5X TO 4X BASIC TOPPS
ONE PER PACK
CARDS LISTED ALPHABETICALLY

2003 Topps Opening Day Autographs

GROUP A ODDS 1:10,623
GROUP B ODDS 1:3539
GROUP C ODDS 1:2654
JD Johnny Damon B 15.00 40.00
LB Lance Berkman A 20.00 50.00
RF Rafael Furcal C 10.00 25.00

2004 Topps Opening Day

COMPLETE SET (165) 15.00 40.00
*OPEN.DAY 1-165: .75X TO 2X BASIC TOPPS
ISSUED IN OPENING DAY PACKS

2004 Topps Opening Day Autographs

STATED ODDS 1:629
AT Andres Torres 6.00 15.00
DW Dontrelle Willis 15.00 40.00
JD Jeff Duncan 6.00 15.00
JW Jerome Williams 6.00 15.00
RH Rich Harden 10.00 25.00
RW Ryan Wagner 6.00 15.00

2005 Topps Opening Day

COMPLETE SET (165) 15.00 40.00
COMMON CARD (1-165) .15 .40
ISSUED IN OPENING DAY PACKS
1 Alex Rodriguez .50 1.25
2 Placido Polanco .15 .40
3 Torii Hunter .15 .40
4 Lyle Overbay .15 .40
5 Johnny Damon .25 .60
6 Mike Cameron .15 .40
7 Ichiro Suzuki .50 1.25
8 Francisco Rodriguez .25 .60
9 Bobby Crosby .15 .40
10 Sammy Sosa .40 1.00
11 Randy Wolf .15 .40
12 Jason Bay .15 .40
13 Mike Lieberthal .15 .40
14 Paul Konerko .25 .60
15 Brian Giles .15 .40
16 Luis Gonzalez .15 .40
17 Jim Edmonds .25 .60
18 Carlos Lee .15 .40
19 Corey Patterson .15 .40
20 Hank Blalock .15 .40
21 Sean Casey .15 .40
22 Dmitri Young .15 .40
23 Mark Mulder .15 .40
24 Bobby Abreu .15 .40
25 Jim Thome .25 .60
26 Jason Kendall .15 .40
27 Jason Giambi .15 .40
28 Vinny Castilla .15 .40
29 Tony Batista .15 .40
30 Ivan Rodriguez .25 .60
31 Craig Biggio .25 .60
32 Chris Carpenter .25 .60
33 Adrian Beltre .40 1.00
34 Scott Podsednik .15 .40
35 Cliff Floyd .15 .40
36 Chad Tracy .15 .40
37 John Smoltz .40 1.00
38 Shingo Takatsu .15 .40
39 Jack Wilson .15 .40
40 Gary Sheffield .15 .40
41 Lance Berkman .25 .60
42 Carl Crawford .25 .60
43 Carlos Guillen .15 .40
44 David Bell .15 .40
45 Kazuo Matsui .15 .40
46 Jason Schmidt .15 .40
47 Jason Marquis .15 .40
48 Melvin Mora .15 .40
49 David Ortiz .40 1.00
50 Andruw Jones .15 .40
51 Miguel Tejada .25 .60
52 Bartolo Colon .15 .40
53 Derrek Lee .15 .40
54 Eric Gagne .15 .40
55 Miguel Cabrera .40 1.00
56 Travis Hafner .15 .40
57 Jose Valentin .15 .40
58 Mark Prior .25 .60
59 Phil Nevin .15 .40
60 Jose Vidro .15 .40
61 Khalil Greene .15 .40
62 Carlos Zambrano .25 .60
63 Erubiel Durazo .15 .40
64 Michael Young UER .15 .40
65 Woody Williams .15 .40
66 Edgardo Alfonzo .15 .40
67 Troy Glaus .15 .40
68 Garret Anderson .15 .40
69 Richie Sexson .15 .40
70 Curt Schilling .25 .60
71 Randy Johnson .40 1.00
72 Chipper Jones .40 1.00
73 J.D. Drew .15 .40
74 Russ Ortiz .15 .40
75 Frank Thomas .40 1.00
76 Jimmy Rollins .25 .60
77 Barry Zito .25 .60
78 Rafael Palmeiro .25 .60
79 Brad Wilkerson .15 .40
80 Adam Dunn .25 .60
81 Doug Mientkiewicz .15 .40
82 Manny Ramirez .40 1.00
83 Pedro Martinez .25 .60
84 Moises Alou .15 .40
85 Mike Sweeney .15 .40
86 Boston Red Sox WC .40 1.00
87 Matt Clement .15 .40
88 Nomar Garciaparra .25 .60
89 Magglio Ordonez .25 .60
90 Bret Boone .15 .40
91 Mark Loretta .15 .40
92 Jose Contreras .15 .40
93 Randy Winn .15 .40
94 Austin Kearns .15 .40
95 Ken Griffey Jr. .75 2.00
96 Jake Westbrook .15 .40
97 Kazuhito Tadano .15 .40
98 C.C. Sabathia .25 .60
99 Todd Helton .25 .60
100 Albert Pujols .50 1.25
101 Jose Molina Bengie Molina .15 .40
102 Aaron Miles .15 .40
103 Mike Lowell .15 .40
104 Paul Lo Duca .15 .40
105 Juan Pierre .15 .40
106 Dontrelle Willis .15 .40
107 Jeff Bagwell .25 .60
108 Carlos Beltran .25 .60
109 Ronnie Belliard .15 .40
110 Roy Oswalt .25 .60
111 Zack Greinke .50 1.25
112 Steve Finley .15 .40
113 Kazuhisa Ishii .15 .40
114 Justin Morneau .25 .60
115 Ben Sheets .15 .40
116 Johan Santana .25 .60
117 Billy Wagner .15 .40
118 Mariano Rivera .50 1.25
119 Corey Koskie .15 .40
120 Akinori Otsuka .15 .40
121 Joe Mauer .30 .75
122 Jacque Jones .15 .40
123 Joe Nathan .15 .40
124 Nick Johnson .15 .40
125 Vernon Wells .15 .40
126 Mike Piazza .40 1.00
127 Jose Guillen .15 .40
128 Jose Reyes .25 .60
129 Marcus Giles .15 .40
130 Javy Lopez .15 .40
131 Kevin Millar .15 .40
132 Jorge Posada .25 .60
133 Carl Pavano .15 .40
134 Bernie Williams .25 .60
135 Kerry Wood .15 .40
136 Matt Holliday .40 1.00
137 Kevin Brown .15 .40
138 Derek Jeter 1.00 2.50
139 Barry Bonds .60 1.50
140 Jeff Kent .15 .40
141 Mark Kotsay .15 .40
142 Shawn Green .15 .40
143 Tim Hudson .25 .60
144 Shannon Stewart .15 .40
145 Pat Burrell .15 .40
146 Gavin Floyd .15 .40
147 Mike Mussina .25 .60
148 Eric Chavez .15 .40
149 Jon Lieber .15 .40
150 Vladimir Guerrero .25 .60
151 Vicente Padilla .15 .40
152 Ryan Klesko .15 .40
153 Jake Peavy .15 .40
154 Scott Rolen .25 .60
155 Greg Maddux .50 1.25
156 Edgar Renteria .15 .40
157 Larry Walker .25 .60
158 Scott Kazmir .40 1.00
159 B.J. Upton .25 .60
160 Mark Teixeira .25 .60
161 Ken Harvey .15 .40
162 Alfonso Soriano .25 .60
163 Carlos Delgado .15 .40
164 Alexis Rios .15 .40
165 Checklist .15 .40

2005 Topps Opening Day Chrome

*REF: .6X TO 1.5X BASIC
ODC1 Albert Pujols 1.25 3.00
ODC2 Alex Rodriguez 1.25 3.00
ODC3 Ivan Rodriguez .60 1.50
ODC4 Jim Thome .60 1.50
ODC5 Sammy Sosa 1.00 2.50
ODC6 Vladimir Guerrero .60 1.50
ODC7 Alfonso Soriano .60 1.50
ODC8 Ichiro Suzuki 1.25 3.00
ODC9 Derek Jeter 2.50 6.00
ODC10 Chipper Jones 1.00 2.50

2005 Topps Opening Day Autographs

GROUP A ODDS 1:852
GROUP B ODDS 1:1192
EXCHANGE DEADLINE 02/28/07
AH Aaron Hill B 4.00 10.00
AW Anthony Whittington A 4.00 10.00
CC Chad Cordero A 6.00 15.00
OQ Omar Quintanilla B 6.00 15.00
PM Paul Maholm A 4.00 10.00

2005 Topps Opening Day MLB Game Worn Jersey Collection

RANDOM INSERTS IN TARGET RETAIL
37 Vladimir Guerrero 3.00 8.00
38 Albert Pujols 6.00 15.00
39 Torii Hunter 2.00 5.00
40 Alfonso Soriano 2.00 5.00
41 Bobby Abreu 2.00 5.00
42 Moises Alou 2.00 5.00
43 Sean Burroughs 2.00 5.00
44 Shannon Stewart 2.00 5.00
45 Troy Glaus 2.00 5.00
46 Fernando Vina 2.00 5.00
47 Dan Wilson 2.00 5.00
48 Paul Konerko 2.00 5.00
49 Jimmy Rollins 2.00 5.00
50 Livan Hernandez 2.00 5.00
51 Sean Casey 2.00 5.00
52 Paul LoDuca 2.00 5.00
53 Richie Sexson 2.00 5.00
54 Aubrey Huff 2.00 5.00

2006 Topps Opening Day

COMPLETE SET (165) 15.00 40.00
COMMON CARD (1-165) .15 .40
OVERALL PLATE SER.1 ODDS 1:246 HTA
PLATE PRINT RUN 1 SET PER COLOR
BLACK-CYAN-MAGENTA-YELLOW ISSUED
NO PLATE PRICING DUE TO SCARCITY
1 Alex Rodriguez .50 1.25
2 Jhonny Peralta .15 .40
3 Garrett Atkins .15 .40
4 Vernon Wells .15 .40
5 Carl Crawford .25 .60
6 Josh Beckett .15 .40
7 Mickey Mantle 1.25 3.00
8 Willy Taveras .15 .40
9 Ivan Rodriguez .25 .60
10 Clint Barmes .15 .40
11 Jose Reyes .25 .60
12 Travis Hafner .15 .40
13 Tadahito Iguchi .15 .40
14 Barry Zito .25 .60
15 Brian Roberts .15 .40
16 David Wright .30 .75
17 Mark Teixeira .25 .60
18 Roy Halladay .25 .60
19 Scott Rolen .25 .60
20 Bobby Abreu .15 .40
21 Lance Berkman .25 .60
22 Moises Alou .15 .40
23 Chone Figgins .15 .40

24 Aaron Rowand .15 .40
25 Chipper Jones .40 1.00
26 Johnny Damon .25 .60
27 Matt Clement .15 .40
28 Nick Johnson .15 .40
29 Freddy Garcia .15 .40
30 Jon Garland .15 .40
31 Torii Hunter .15 .40
32 Mike Sweeney .15 .40
33 Mike Lieberthal .15 .40
34 Rafael Furcal .15 .40
35 Brad Wilkerson .15 .40
36 Brad Penny .15 .40
37 Jorge Cantu .15 .40
38 Paul Konerko .25 .60
39 Rickie Weeks .15 .40
40 Jorge Posada .25 .60
41 Albert Pujols .50 1.25
42 Zack Greinke .40 1.00
43 Jimmy Rollins .25 .60
44 Mark Prior .25 .60
45 Greg Maddux .50 1.25
46 Jeff Francis .15 .40
47 Felipe Lopez .15 .40
48 Dan Johnson .15 .40
49 B.J. Ryan .15 .40
50 Manny Ramirez .40 1.00
51 Melvin Mora .15 .40
52 Javy Lopez .15 .40
53 Garret Anderson .15 .40
54 Jason Bay .15 .40
55 Joe Mauer .25 .60
56 C.C. Sabathia .25 .60
57 Bartolo Colon .15 .40
58 Ichiro Suzuki .50 1.25
59 Andruw Jones .15 .40
60 Rocco Baldelli .15 .40
61 Jeff Kent .15 .40
62 Cliff Floyd .15 .40
63 John Smoltz .40 1.00
64 Shawn Green .15 .40
65 Nomar Garciaparra .25 .60
66 Miguel Cabrera .40 1.00
67 Vladimir Guerrero .25 .60
68 Gary Sheffield .15 .40
69 Jake Peavy .15 .40
70 Carlos Lee .15 .40
71 Tom Glavine .25 .60
72 Craig Biggio .25 .60
73 Steve Finley .15 .40
74 Adrian Beltre .40 1.00
75 Eric Gagne .15 .40
76 Aubrey Huff .15 .40
77 Livan Hernandez .15 .40
78 Scott Podsednik .15 .40
79 Todd Helton .25 .60
80 Kerry Wood .15 .40
81 Randy Johnson .40 1.00
82 Huston Street .15 .40
83 Pedro Martinez .25 .60
84 Roger Clemens .50 1.25
85 Hank Blalock .15 .40
86 Carlos Beltran .25 .60
87 Chien-Ming Wang .25 .60
88 Rich Harden .15 .40
89 Mike Mussina .25 .60
90 Mark Buehrle .25 .60
91 Michael Young .15 .40
92 Mark Mulder .15 .40
93 Khalil Greene .15 .40
94 Johan Santana .25 .60
95 Andy Pettitte .25 .60
96 Derek Jeter 1.00 2.50
97 Jack Wilson .15 .40
98 Ben Sheets .15 .40
99 Miguel Tejada .25 .60
100 Barry Bonds .60 1.50
101 Dontrelle Willis .15 .40
102 Curt Schilling .25 .60
103 Jose Contreras .15 .40
104 Jeremy Bonderman .15 .40
105 David Ortiz .40 1.00
106 Lyle Overbay .15 .40
107 Robinson Cano .25 .60
108 Tim Hudson .25 .60
109 Paul Lo Duca .15 .40
110 Mariano Rivera .50 1.25
111 Derrek Lee .15 .40
112 Morgan Ensberg .15 .40
113 Wily Mo Pena .15 .40
114 Roy Oswalt .25 .60
115 Adam Dunn .25 .60
116 Hideki Matsui .40 1.00
117 Pat Burrell .15 .40
118 Jason Schmidt .15 .40
119 Alfonso Soriano .25 .60
120 Aramis Ramirez .15 .40
121 Jason Giambi .15 .40
122 Orlando Hernandez .15 .40
123 Magglio Ordonez .25 .60
124 Troy Glaus .15 .40
125 Carlos Delgado .15 .40
126 Kevin Millwood .15 .40
127 Shannon Stewart .15 .40
128 Luis Castillo .15 .40
129 Jim Edmonds .25 .60
130 Richie Sexson .15 .40
131 Dmitri Young .15 .40
132 Russ Adams .15 .40
133 Nick Swisher .25 .60
134 Jermaine Dye .15 .40
135 Anderson Hernandez (RC) .15 .40
136 Justin Huber (RC) .15 .40
137 Jason Botts (RC) .15 .40
138 Jeff Mathis (RC) .15 .40
139 Ryan Garko (RC) .15 .40
140 Charlton Jimerson (RC) .15 .40
141 Chris Denorfia (RC) .15 .40
142 Anthony Reyes (RC) .15 .40
143 Bryan Bullington (RC) .15 .40
144 Chuck James (RC) .15 .40
145 Danny Sandoval RC .15 .40
146 Walter Young (RC) .15 .40
147 Fausto Carmona (RC) .15 .40
148 Francisco Liriano (RC) .40 1.00
149 Hong-Chih Kuo (RC) .40 1.00
150 Joe Saunders (RC) .15 .40
151 John Koronka (RC) .15 .40
152 Robert Andino RC .15 .40
153 Shaun Marcum (RC) .15 .40
154 Tom Gorzelanny (RC) .15 .40
155 Craig Breslow RC .15 .40
156 Chris Demaria RC .15 .40
157 Brayan Pena (RC) .15 .40
158 Rich Hill (RC) .40 1.00
159 Rick Short (RC) .15 .40
160 Darrell Rasner (RC) .15 .40
161 C.J. Wilson (RC) .25 .60
162 Brandon Watson (RC) .15 .40
163 Paul McAnulty (RC) .15 .40
164 Marshall McDougall (RC) .15 .40
165 Checklist .15 .40

2006 Topps Opening Day Red Foil

*RED FOIL: 3X TO 8X BASIC
*RED FOIL: 3X TO 8X BASIC RC
STATED ODDS 1:8 HOBBY, 1:11 RETAIL
STATED PRINT RUN 2006 SERIAL #'d SETS

2006 Topps Opening Day Autographs

GROUP A ODDS 1:10928 H, 1:11668 R
GROUP B ODDS 1:3491 H, 1:3491 R
GROUP C ODDS 1:978 H, 1:1185 R
BE Brad Eldred B 4.00 10.00
EM Eli Marrero C 4.00 10.00
JE Johnny Estrada A 6.00 15.00
MK Mark Kotsay B 6.00 15.00
TH Toby Hall C 4.00 10.00
VZ Victor Zambrano C 4.00 10.00

2006 Topps Opening Day Sports Illustrated For Kids

COMPLETE SET (25) 4.00 10.00
STATED ODDS 1:1
1 Vladimir Guerrero .40 1.00
2 Marcus Giles .25 .60
3 Michael Young .25 .60
4 Derek Jeter 1.50 4.00
5 Barry Bonds 1.00 2.50
6 Ivan Rodriguez .40 1.00
7 Miguel Cabrera .60 1.50
8 Jim Edmonds .40 1.00
9 Jack Wilson .25 .60
10 Khalil Greene .25 .60
11 Miguel Tejada .40 1.00
12 Eric Chavez .25 .60
13 Shannon Stewart .25 .60
14 Julio Lugo .25 .60
15 Andruw Jones .25 .60
16 N.Johnson .60 1.50
R.Johnson
17 T.Iguchi .40 1.00
I.Rodriguez
18 R.Oswalt .40 1.00
J.Reyes
19 M.Ramirez .60 1.50
R.Belliard
20 T.Helton .40 1.00
K.Greene
21 D.Ortiz .60 1.50
D.Willis
22 I.Suzuki .75 2.00
J.Damon
23 C.Biggio .40 1.00
J.Wilson
24 B.Roberts .25 .60
R.Sexson
25 C.Jones .60 1.50
M.Giles

2007 Topps Opening Day

COMPLETE SET (220) 20.00 50.00
COMMON CARD (1-220) .15 .40
COMMON RC .15 .40
OVERALL PLATE ODDS 1:370 HOBBY
PLATE PRINT RUN 1 SET PER COLOR
BLACK-CYAN-MAGENTA-YELLOW ISSUED
NO PLATE PRICING DUE TO SCARCITY
1 Bobby Abreu .15 .40
2 Mike Piazza .40 1.00
3 Jake Westbrook .15 .40
4 Zach Duke .15 .40
5 David Wright .30 .75
6 Adrian Gonzalez .30 .75
7 Mickey Mantle 1.25 3.00
8 Bill Hall .15 .40
9 Robinson Cano .25 .60
10 Dontrelle Willis .15 .40
11 J.D. Drew .15 .40
12 Paul Konerko .25 .60
13 Austin Kearns .15 .40
14 Mike Lowell .15 .40
15 Magglio Ordonez .25 .60
16 Rafael Furcal .15 .40
17 Matt Cain .25 .60
18 Craig Monroe .15 .40
19 Matt Holliday .40 1.00
20 Edgar Renteria .15 .40
21 Mark Buehrle .25 .60
22 Carlos Quentin .15 .40
23 C.C. Sabathia .25 .60
24 Nick Markakis .30 .75
25 Chipper Jones .40 1.00
26 Jason Giambi .15 .40
27 Barry Zito .25 .60
28 Jake Peavy .15 .40
29 Hank Blalock .15 .40
30 Johnny Damon .25 .60
31 Chad Tracy .15 .40
32 Nick Swisher .25 .60
33 Willy Taveras .15 .40
34 Chuck James .15 .40
35 Carlos Delgado .15 .40
36 Livan Hernandez .15 .40
37 Freddy Garcia .15 .40
38 Bronson Arroyo .15 .40
39 Jack Wilson .15 .40
40 Dan Uggla .15 .40
41 Chris Carpenter .25 .60
42 Jorge Posada .25 .60
43 Joe Mauer .30 .75
44 Corey Patterson .15 .40
45 Chien-Ming Wang .25 .60
46 Derek Jeter 1.00 2.50
47 Carlos Beltran .25 .60
48 Jim Edmonds .25 .60
49 Jeremy Sowers .15 .40
50 Randy Johnson .40 1.00
51 Jered Weaver .25 .60
52 Josh Barfield .15 .40
53 Scott Rolen .25 .60
54 Ryan Shealy .15 .40
55 Freddy Sanchez .15 .40
56 Javier Vazquez .15 .40
57 Jeremy Bonderman .15 .40
58 Miguel Cabrera .40 1.00
59 Kazuo Matsui .15 .40
60 Curt Schilling .25 .60
61 Alfonso Soriano .25 .60
62 Orlando Hernandez .15 .40
63 Joe Blanton .15 .40
64 Aramis Ramirez .15 .40
65 Ben Sheets .15 .40
66 Jimmy Rollins .25 .60
67 Mark Loretta .15 .40
68 Cole Hamels .30 .75
69 Albert Pujols .50 1.25
70 Moises Alou .15 .40
71 Mark Teahen .15 .40
72 Roy Halladay .25 .60
73 Cory Sullivan .15 .40
74 Frank Thomas .40 1.00
75 Ryan Howard .30 .75
76 Rocco Baldelli .15 .40
77 Manny Ramirez .40 1.00
78 Ray Durham .15 .40
79 Gary Sheffield .15 .40
80 Jay Gibbons .15 .40
81 Todd Helton .25 .60
82 Gary Matthews .15 .40
83 Brandon Inge .15 .40
84 Jonathan Papelbon .40 1.00
85 John Smoltz .40 1.00
86 Chone Figgins .15 .40
87 Hideki Matsui .40 1.00
88 Carlos Lee .15 .40
89 Jose Reyes .25 .60
90 Lyle Overbay .15 .40
91 Johan Santana .25 .60
92 Ian Kinsler .25 .60
93 Scott Kazmir .25 .60
94 Hanley Ramirez .25 .60
95 Greg Maddux .50 1.25
96 Johnny Estrada .15 .40
97 B.J. Upton .15 .40
98 Francisco Liriano .15 .40
99 Chase Utley .25 .60
100 Preston Wilson .15 .40
101 Marcus Giles .15 .40
102 Jeff Kent .15 .40
103 Grady Sizemore .25 .60
104 Ken Griffey .75 2.00
105 Garrett Anderson .15 .40
106 Brian McCann .15 .40
107 Jon Garland .15 .40
108 Troy Glaus .15 .40
109 Brandon Webb .25 .60
110 Jason Schmidt .15 .40
111 Ramon Hernandez .15 .40
112 Justin Morneau .25 .60
113 Mike Cameron .15 .40
114 Andruw Jones .15 .40
115 Russell Martin .15 .40
116 Vernon Wells .15 .40
117 Orlando Hudson .15 .40
118 Derek Lowe .15 .40
119 Alex Rodriguez .50 1.25
120 Chad Billingsley .25 .60
121 Kenji Johjima .40 1.00
122 Nick Johnson .15 .40
123 Dan Haren .15 .40
124 Mark Teixeira .25 .60
125 Jeff Francoeur .40 1.00
126 Ted Lilly .15 .40
127 Jhonny Peralta .15 .40
128 Aaron Harang .15 .40
129 Ryan Zimmerman .25 .60
130 Jermaine Dye .15 .40
131 Orlando Cabrera .15 .40
132 Juan Pierre .15 .40
133 Brian Giles .15 .40
134 Jason Bay .25 .60
135 David Ortiz .40 1.00
136 Chris Capuano .15 .40
137 Carlos Zambrano .25 .60
138 Luis Gonzalez .15 .40
139 Jeff Weaver .15 .40
140 Lance Berkman .25 .60
141 Raul Ibanez .25 .60
142 Jim Thome .25 .60
143 Jose Contreras .15 .40
144 David Eckstein .15 .40
145 Adam Dunn .25 .60
146 Alex Rios .15 .40
147 Garrett Atkins .15 .40
148 A.J. Burnett .15 .40
149 Jeremy Hermida .15 .40
150 Conor Jackson .15 .40
151 Adrian Beltre .40 1.00
152 Torii Hunter .15 .40
153 Andrew Miller RC .60 1.50
154 Ichiro Suzuki .50 1.25
155 Mark Redman .15 .40
156 Paul LoDuca .15 .40
157 Xavier Nady .15 .40
158 Stephen Drew .15 .40
159 Eric Chavez .15 .40
160 Pedro Martinez .25 .60
161 Derrek Lee .15 .40
162 David DeJesus .15 .40
163 Troy Tulowitzki (RC) .50 1.25
164 Vinny Rottino (RC) .15 .40
165 Philip Humber (RC) .15 .40
166 Jerry Owens (RC) .15 .40
167 Ubaldo Jimenez (RC) .50 1.25
168 Michael Young .15 .40
169 Ryan Braun RC .15 .40
170 Kevin Kouzmanoff (RC) .15 .40
171 Oswaldo Navarro RC .15 .40
172 Miguel Montero (RC) .15 .40
173 Roy Oswalt .25 .60
174 Shane Youman RC .15 .40
175 Josh Fields (RC) .15 .40
176 Adam Lind (RC) .15 .40
177 Miguel Tejada .25 .60
178 Delwyn Young (RC) .15 .40
179 Scott Moore (RC) .15 .40
180 Fred Lewis (RC) .25 .60
181 Glen Perkins (RC) .15 .40
182 Vladimir Guerrero .25 .60
183 Drew Anderson RC .15 .40
184 Jeff Salazar (RC) .15 .40
185 Tom Gordon .15 .40
186 The Bird .15 .40
187 Justin Verlander .40 1.00
188 Delmon Young (RC) .25 .60
189 Homer .15 .40
190 Wally the Green Monster .15 .40
191 Southpaw .15 .40
192 Dinger .15 .40
193 Carl Crawford .25 .60
194 Slider .15 .40
195 Gapper .15 .40
196 Paws .15 .40
197 Billy the Marlin .15 .40
198 Ivan Rodriguez .25 .60
199 Slugger .15 .40
200 Junction Jack .15 .40
201 Bernie Brewer .15 .40
202 Travis Hafner .15 .40
203 Stomper .15 .40
204 Mr. Met .15 .40
205 The Moose .15 .40
206 Phillie Phanatic .15 .40
207 Prince Fielder .25 .60
208 Julio Lugo .15 .40
209 Pirate Parrot .15 .40
210 Joel Zumaya .15 .40
211 Swinging Friar .15 .40
212 Jay Payton .15 .40
213 Lou Seal .15 .40
214 Fredbird .15 .40
215 Screech .15 .40
216 TC Bear .15 .40
217 Andre Ethier .25 .60
218 Ervin Santana .15 .40
219 Melvin Mora .15 .40
220 Checklist .15 .40

2007 Topps Opening Day Gold

COMPLETE SET (219) 75.00 150.00
*GOLD: 1.2X TO 3X BASIC
*GOLD: 1.2X TO 3X BASIC RC
STATED ODDS APPX. 1 PER HOBBY PACK
STATED PRINT RUN 2007 SERIAL #'d SETS

2007 Topps Opening Day Autographs

STATED ODDS 1:965 HOBBY, 1:965 RETAIL
EF Emiliano Fruto 10.00 25.00
HK Howie Kendrick 20.00 50.00
JM Juan Morillo 6.00 15.00
MC Matt Cain 5.00 12.00
MK Matt Kemp 5.00 12.00
OH Orlando Hudson 10.00 25.00
SS Shannon Stewart 6.00 15.00

2007 Topps Opening Day Diamond Stars

COMPLETE SET (25) 6.00 15.00
STATED ODDS 1:4 HOBBY, 1:4 RETAIL
DS1 Ryan Howard .50 1.25
DS2 Alfonso Soriano .40 1.00
DS3 Alex Rodriguez .75 2.00
DS4 David Ortiz .60 1.50
DS5 Raul Ibanez .40 1.00
DS6 Matt Holliday .60 1.50
DS7 Delmon Young .40 1.00
DS8 Derrick Turnbow .25 .60
DS9 Freddy Sanchez .25 .60
DS10 Troy Glaus .25 .60
DS11 A.J. Pierzynski .25 .60
DS12 Dontrelle Willis .25 .60
DS13 Justin Morneau .40 1.00
DS14 Jose Reyes .40 1.00
DS15 Derek Jeter 1.50 4.00
DS16 Ivan Rodriguez .40 1.00
DS17 Jay Payton .25 .60
DS18 Adrian Gonzalez .50 1.25
DS19 David Eckstein .25 .60
DS20 Chipper Jones .60 1.50
DS21 Aramis Ramirez .25 .60
DS22 David Wright .50 1.25
DS23 Mark Teixeira .40 1.00
DS24 Stephen Drew .25 .60
DS25 Ichiro Suzuki .75 2.00

2007 Topps Opening Day Movie Gallery

STATED ODDS 1:6 HOBBY
NNO Alex Rodriguez .12 .30

2007 Topps Opening Day Puzzle

COMPLETE SET (28) 6.00 15.00
STATED ODDS 1:3 HOBBY, 1:3 RETAIL
P1 Adam Dunn .40 1.00
P2 Adam Dunn .40 1.00
P3 Miguel Tejada .40 1.00
P4 Miguel Tejada .40 1.00
P5 Hanley Ramirez .40 1.00
P6 Hanley Ramirez .40 1.00
P7 Johan Santana .40 1.00
P8 Johan Santana .40 1.00
P9 Brandon Webb .40 1.00
P10 Brandon Webb .40 1.00
P11 David Wright .50 1.25
P12 David Wright .50 1.25
P13 Alex Rodriguez .75 2.00
P14 Alex Rodriguez .75 2.00
P15 Ryan Howard .50 1.25
P16 Ryan Howard .50 1.25
P17 Albert Pujols .75 2.00
P18 Albert Pujols .75 2.00
P19 Andruw Jones .25 .60
P20 Andruw Jones .25 .60
P21 Alfonso Soriano .40 1.00
P22 Alfonso Soriano .40 1.00
P23 Vladimir Guerrero .40 1.00
P24 Vladimir Guerrero .40 1.00
P25 David Ortiz .60 1.50
P26 David Ortiz .60 1.50
P27 Ichiro Suzuki .75 2.00
P28 Ichiro Suzuki .75 2.00

2008 Topps Opening Day

COMPLETE SET (220) 15.00 40.00
COMMON CARD (1-194) .12 .30
COMMON RC (195-220) .20 .50
OVERALL PLATE ODDS 1:546 HOBBY
PLATE PRINT RUN 1 SET PER COLOR
BLACK-CYAN-MAGENTA-YELLOW ISSUED
NO PLATE PRICING DUE TO SCARCITY
1 Alex Rodriguez .40 1.00
2 Barry Zito .20 .50
3 Jeff Suppan .12 .30
4 Placido Polanco .12 .30
5 Scott Kazmir .20 .50
6 Ivan Rodriguez .20 .50
7 Mickey Mantle 1.00 2.50
8 Stephen Drew .12 .30
9 Ken Griffey Jr. .60 1.50
10 Miguel Cabrera .30 .75
11 Yorvit Torrealba .12 .30
12 Daisuke Matsuzaka .20 .50
13 Kyle Kendrick .12 .30
14 Jimmy Rollins .20 .50
15 Joe Mauer .25 .60
16 Cole Hamels .25 .60
17 Yovani Gallardo .12 .30
18 Miguel Tejada .20 .50
19 Corey Hart .12 .30
20 Nick Markakis .25 .60
21 Zack Greinke .30 .75
22 Orlando Cabrera .20 .50
23 Jake Peavy .12 .30
24 Erik Bedard .12 .30
25 Trevor Hoffman .20 .50
26 Derrek Lee .12 .30
27 Hank Blalock .12 .30
28 Victor Martinez .20 .50
29 Chris Young .12 .30
30 Jose Reyes .20 .50
31 Mike Lowell .12 .30
32 Curtis Granderson .20 .50
33 Dan Uggla .12 .30
34 Mike Piazza .30 .75
35 Garrett Atkins .12 .30
36 Felix Hernandez .20 .50
37 Alex Rios .12 .30
38 Mark Reynolds .12 .30
39 Jason Bay .20 .50
40 Josh Beckett .12 .30
41 Jack Cust .12 .30
42 Vladimir Guerrero .20 .50
43 Marcus Giles .12 .30
44 Kenny Lofton .12 .30
45 John Lackey .20 .50
46 Ryan Howard .20 .50
47 Kevin Youkilis .12 .30
48 Gary Sheffield .12 .30
49 Justin Morneau .20 .50
50 Albert Pujols .40 1.00
51 Ubaldo Jimenez .12 .30
52 Johan Santana .20 .50
53 Chuck James .12 .30
54 Jeremy Hermida .12 .30
55 Andruw Jones .12 .30
56 Jason Varitek .30 .75
57 Tim Hudson .20 .50
58 Justin Upton .20 .50
59 Brad Penny .12 .30
60 Robinson Cano .20 .50
61 Johnny Estrada .12 .30
62 Brandon Webb .20 .50
63 Chris Duncan .12 .30
64 Aaron Hill .12 .30
65 Alfonso Soriano .20 .50
66 Carlos Zambrano .20 .50
67 Ben Sheets .12 .30
68 Andy LaRoche .12 .30
69 Tim Lincecum .20 .50
70 Phil Hughes .12 .30
71 Magglio Ordonez .20 .50
72 Scott Rolen .20 .50
73 John Maine .12 .30
74 Delmon Young .20 .50
75 Chase Utley .20 .50
76 Jose Valverde .12 .30
77 Tadahito Iguchi .12 .30
78 Checklist .12 .30
79 Russell Martin .12 .30
80 B.J. Upton .20 .50
81 Orlando Hudson .12 .30
82 Jim Edmonds .20 .50
83 J.J. Hardy .12 .30
84 Todd Helton .20 .50
85 Melky Cabrera .12 .30
86 Adrian Beltre .30 .75
87 Manny Ramirez .30 .75
88 Rafael Furcal .12 .30
89 Gil Meche .12 .30
90 Grady Sizemore .20 .50
91 Jeff Kent .12 .30
92 David DeJesus .12 .30
93 Lyle Overbay .12 .30
94 Moises Alou .12 .30
95 Frank Thomas .30 .75
96 Ryan Garko .12 .30
97 Kevin Kouzmanoff .12 .30
98 Roy Oswalt .20 .50
99 Mark Buehrle .20 .50
100 David Ortiz .30 .75
101 Hunter Pence .20 .50
102 David Wright .20 .50
103 Dustin Pedroia .30 .75
104 Roy Halladay .20 .50
105 Derek Jeter .75 2.00
106 Casey Blake .12 .30
107 Rich Harden .12 .30
108 Shane Victorino .12 .30
109 Richie Sexson .12 .30
110 Jim Thome .20 .50
111 Akinori Iwamura .12 .30
112 Dan Haren .12 .30
113 Jose Contreras .12 .30
114 Jonathan Papelbon .20 .50
115 Prince Fielder .20 .50
116 Dan Johnson .12 .30
117 Dmitri Young .12 .30
118 Brandon Phillips .12 .30
119 Brett Myers .12 .30
120 James Loney .12 .30
121 C.C. Sabathia .20 .50
122 Jermaine Dye .12 .30
123 Aubrey Huff .12 .30
124 Carlos Ruiz .12 .30
125 Hanley Ramirez .20 .50
126 Edgar Renteria .12 .30
127 Mark Loretta .20 .50
128 Brian McCann .20 .50
129 Paul Konerko .20 .50
130 Jorge Posada .20 .50
131 Chien-Ming Wang .20 .50
132 Jose Vidro .12 .30
133 Carlos Delgado .12 .30
134 Kelvim Escobar .20 .50
135 Pedro Martinez .20 .50
136 Jeremy Guthrie .12 .30
137 Ramon Hernandez .12 .30
138 Ian Kinsler .20 .50
139 Ichiro Suzuki .40 1.00
140 Garret Anderson .12 .30
141 Tom Gorzelanny .12 .30
142 Bobby Crosby .12 .30
143 Jeff Francoeur .20 .50
144 Josh Hamilton .20 .50
145 Mark Teixeira .20 .50
146 Fausto Carmona .12 .30
147 Alex Gordon .20 .50
148 Nick Swisher .20 .50
149 Justin Verlander .30 .75
150 Pat Burrell .12 .30
151 Chris Carpenter .20 .50
152 Matt Holliday .30 .75
153 Adam Dunn .20 .50
154 Curt Schilling .20 .50
155 Kelly Johnson .12 .30
156 Aaron Rowand .12 .30
157 Brian Roberts .12 .30
158 Bobby Abreu .12 .30
159 Carlos Beltran .20 .50
160 Lance Berkman .20 .50
161 Gary Matthews .12 .30
162 Jeff Francis .12 .30
163 Vernon Wells .12 .30
164 Dontrelle Willis .12 .30
165 Travis Hafner .12 .30
166 Brian Bannister .12 .30
167 Carlos Pena .20 .50
168 Raul Ibanez .20 .50
169 Aramis Ramirez .12 .30
170 Eric Byrnes .12 .30
171 Greg Maddux .40 1.00
172 John Smoltz .30 .75
173 Jarrod Saltalamacchia .12 .30
174 Hideki Okajima .20 .50
175 Javier Vazquez .12 .30
176 Aaron Harang .12 .30
177 Jhonny Peralta .12 .30
178 Carlos Lee .12 .30
179 Ryan Braun .30 .75
180 Torii Hunter .12 .30
181 Hideki Matsui .30 .75
182 Eric Chavez .12 .30
183 Freddy Sanchez .12 .30
184 Adrian Gonzalez .20 .50
185 Bengie Molina .12 .30
186 Kenji Johjima .12 .30
187 Carl Crawford .20 .50
188 Chipper Jones .30 .75
189 Chris Young .12 .30
190 Michael Young .12 .30
191 Troy Glaus .12 .30
192 Ryan Zimmerman .20 .50
193 Brian Giles .12 .30
194 Troy Tulowitzki .30 .75
195 Chin-Lung Hu (RC) .20 .50
196 Seth Smith (RC) .20 .50
197 Wladimir Balentien (RC) .20 .50
198 Rich Thompson RC .30 .75
199 Radhames Liz RC .30 .75
200 Ross Detwiler RC .30 .75
201 Sam Fuld RC .60 1.50
202 Clint Sammons (RC) .20 .50
203 Ross Ohlendorf RC .30 .75
204 Jonathan Albaladejo RC .30 .75
205 Brandon Jones RC .50 1.25
206 Steve Pearce RC 1.00 2.50
207 Kevin Hart (RC) .20 .50
208 Luke Hochevar RC .30 .75
209 Troy Patton (RC) .20 .50
210 Josh Anderson (RC) .20 .50
211 Clay Buchholz (RC) .30 .75
212 Joe Koshansky (RC) .20 .50
213 Bronson Sardinha (RC) .20 .50
214 Emilio Bonifacio RC .50 1.25
215 Daric Barton (RC) .20 .50
216 Lance Broadway (RC) .20 .50
217 Jeff Clement (RC) .30 .75
218 Joey Votto (RC) 1.50 4.00
219 J.R. Towles RC .30 .75
220 Nyjer Morgan (RC) .20 .50

2008 Topps Opening Day Gold

COMPLETE SET (220) 50.00 100.00
*GOLD VET: 1X TO 2.5X BASIC
*GOLD RC: 1X TO 2.5X BASIC RC
STATED ODDS APPX. ONE PER PACK
STATED PRINT RUN 2007 SERIAL #'d SETS
7 Mickey Mantle 3.00 8.00

2008 Topps Opening Day Autographs

GROUP A ODDS 1:359
GROUP B ODDS 1:7800
AAL Adam Lind A 6.00 15.00
AL Anthony Lerew A 6.00 15.00
GP Glen Perkins A 3.00 8.00
JAB Jason Bartlett A 3.00 8.00
JB Jeff Baker A 3.00 8.00
JCB Jason Botts B 6.00 15.00
JRB John Buck A 3.00 8.00
KG Kevin Gregg A 5.00 12.00
NS Nate Schierholtz A 5.00 12.00

2008 Topps Opening Day Flapper Cards

COMPLETE SET (18) 6.00 15.00
STATED ODDS 1:8
AP Albert Pujols .75 2.00
AR Alex Rodriguez .75 2.00
CJ Chipper Jones .60 1.50
DJ Derek Jeter 1.50 4.00
DM Daisuke Matsuzaka .40 1.00
DO David Ortiz .60 1.50
DW David Wright .40 1.00
GM Greg Maddux .75 2.00
IS Ichiro Suzuki .75 2.00
JB Josh Beckett .25 .60
JR Jose Reyes .40 1.00
KG Ken Griffey Jr 1.25 3.00
MM Mickey Mantle 1.50 4.00
MR Manny Ramirez .60 1.50
PF Prince Fielder .40 1.00
RC Roger Clemens .75 2.00
RH Ryan Howard .40 1.00
VG Vladimir Guerrero .40 1.00

2008 Topps Opening Day Puzzle

COMPLETE SET (28) 5.00 12.00
STATED ODDS 1:3
1 Matt Holliday .50 1.25
2 Matt Holliday .50 1.25
3 Vladimir Guerrero .30 .75
4 Vladimir Guerrero .30 .75
5 Jose Reyes .30 .75
6 Jose Reyes .30 .75
7 Josh Beckett .20 .50
8 Josh Beckett .20 .50
9 Albert Pujols .60 1.50
10 Albert Pujols .60 1.50
11 Alex Rodriguez .60 1.50
12 Alex Rodriguez .60 1.50
13 Jake Peavy .20 .50
14 Jake Peavy .20 .50
15 David Ortiz .50 1.25
16 David Ortiz .50 1.25
17 Ryan Howard .30 .75
18 Ryan Howard .30 .75
19 Ichiro Suzuki .60 1.50
20 Ichiro Suzuki .60 1.50
21 Hanley Ramirez .30 .75
22 Hanley Ramirez .30 .75
23 Grady Sizemore .30 .75
24 Grady Sizemore .30 .75
25 David Wright .30 .75
26 David Wright .30 .75
27 Alex Rios .20 .50
28 Alex Rios .20 .50

2008 Topps Opening Day Tattoos

STATED ODDS 1:12
AB Atlanta Braves .60 1.50
AD Arizona Diamondbacks .60 1.50
BB Bernie Brewer .60 1.50
BM Billy the Marlin .60 1.50
BRS Boston Red Sox .60 1.50
CC Chicago Cubs .60 1.50
CI Cleveland Indians .60 1.50
CR Cincinnati Reds .60 1.50
CWS Chicago White Sox .60 1.50
FB Fredbird .60 1.50
FM Florida Marlins .60 1.50
JJ Junction Jack .60 1.50
LAA Los Angeles Angels .60 1.50
LS Lou Seal .60 1.50
MM Mr. Met .60 1.50
NYM New York Mets .60 1.50
NYY New York Yankees .60 1.50
PIP Pirate Parrot .60 1.50
PP Phillie Phanatic .60 1.50
PW Paws .60 1.50
SF Swinging Friar .60 1.50
SFG San Francisco Giants .60 1.50
SL Slider .60 1.50
ST Stomper .60 1.50
TB TC Bear .60 1.50
TBJ Toronto Blue Jays .60 1.50
TDR Tampa Bay Rays .60 1.50
TM The Moose .60 1.50
TR Texas Rangers .60 1.50
WM Wally the Green Monster .60 1.50

2010 Topps Opening Day

COMPLETE SET (220) 15.00 40.00
COMMON CARD (1-205/220) .12 .30
COMMON RC (206-219) .20 .50
OVERALL PLATE ODDS 1:2119 HOBBY
1 Prince Fielder .20 .50
2 Derrek Lee .12 .30
3 Clayton Kershaw .50 1.25
4 Orlando Cabrera .12 .30
5 Ted Lilly .12 .30
6 Bobby Abreu .12 .30
7 Mickey Mantle 1.00 2.50
8 Johnny Cueto .20 .50
9 Dexter Fowler .20 .50
10 Felipe Lopez .12 .30
11 Tommy Hanson .12 .30
12 Cristian Guzman .12 .30
13 Shane Victorino .20 .50
14 John Maine .12 .30
15 Adam Jones .20 .50
16 Aubrey Huff .12 .30
17 Victor Martinez .20 .50
18 Rick Porcello .20 .50
19 Garret Anderson .12 .30
20 Josh Johnson .20 .50
21 Marco Scutaro .20 .50
22 Howie Kendrick .12 .30
23 Joey Votto .30 .75

24 Jorge De La Rosa .12 .30
25 Zack Greinke .30 .75
26 Eric Young Jr .12 .30
27 Billy Butler .12 .30
28 John Lackey .20 .50
29 Manny Ramirez .30 .75
30 CC Sabathia .20 .50
31 Kyle Blanks .12 .30
32 David Wright .25 .60
33 Kevin Millwood .12 .30
34 Nick Swisher .20 .50
35 Matt LaPorta .12 .30
36 Brandon Inge .12 .30
37 Cole Hamels .25 .60
38 Adrian Gonzalez .25 .60
39 Joe Saunders .12 .30
40 Kenshin Kawakami .12 .30
41 Tim Lincecum .20 .50
42 Ken Griffey Jr. .60 1.50
43 Ian Kinsler .20 .50
44 Ivan Rodriguez .20 .50
45 Carl Crawford .20 .50
46 Jon Garland .12 .30
47 Albert Pujols .40 1.00
48 Daniel Murphy .25 .60
49 Scott Hairston .12 .30
50 Justin Masterson .12 .30
51 Andrew McCutchen .30 .75
52 Gordon Beckham .12 .30
53 David DeJesus .12 .30
54 Jorge Posada .20 .50
55 Brett Anderson .12 .30
56 Ichiro Suzuki .40 1.00
57 Hank Blalock .12 .30
58 Vladimir Guerrero .20 .50
59 Cliff Lee .20 .50
60 Freddy Sanchez .12 .30
61 Ryan Dempster .12 .30
62 Adam Wainwright .20 .50
63 Matt Holliday .30 .75
64 Chone Figgins .12 .30
65 Tim Hudson .20 .50
66 Rich Harden .12 .30
67 Justin Upton .20 .50
68 Yunel Escobar .12 .30
69 Joe Mauer .25 .60
70 Jeff Niemann .12 .30
71 Vernon Wells .12 .30
72 Miguel Tejada .20 .50
73 Denard Span .12 .30
74 Brandon Phillips .12 .30
75 Jason Bay .20 .50
76 Kendry Morales .12 .30
77 Josh Hamilton .20 .50
78 Yovani Gallardo .12 .30
79 Adam Lind .20 .50
80 Nick Johnson .12 .30
81 Coco Crisp .12 .30
82 Jeff Francoeur .20 .50
83 Hideki Matsui .30 .75
84 Will Venable .12 .30
85 Adrian Beltre .30 .75
86 Pablo Sandoval .20 .50
87 Mat Latos .20 .50
88 James Shields .12 .30
89 R.Halladay UER 2.50 6.00
90 Chris Coghlan .12 .30
91 Colby Rasmus .20 .50
92 Alexei Ramirez .20 .50
93 Josh Beckett .12 .30
94 Kelly Shoppach .12 .30
95 Magglio Ordonez .12 .30
96 Matt Kemp .25 .60
97 Max Scherzer .30 .75
98 Curtis Granderson .25 .60
99 David Price .25 .60
100 Neftali Feliz .12 .30
101 Ian Stewart .12 .30
102 Ricky Romero .12 .30
103 Barry Zito .20 .50
104 Lance Berkman .20 .50
105 Andre Ethier .20 .50
106 Mark Teixeira .20 .50
107 Bengie Molina .12 .30
108 Edwin Jackson .12 .30
109 Akinori Iwamura .12 .30
110 Jermaine Dye .12 .30
111 Jair Jurrjens .12 .30
112 Stephen Drew .12 .30
113 Carlos Delgado .12 .30
114 Mark DeRosa .12 .30
115 Kurt Suzuki .12 .30
116 Javier Vazquez .12 .30
117 Lyle Overbay .12 .30
118 Orlando Hudson .12 .30
119 Adam Dunn .20 .50
120 Kevin Youkilis .12 .30
121 Ben Zobrist .20 .50
122 Chase Utley .20 .50
123 Jack Cust .12 .30
124 Gerald Laird .12 .30
125 Elvis Andrus .20 .50
126 Jason Kubel .12 .30
127 Scott Kazmir .12 .30
128 Ryan Doumit .12 .30
129 Brian McCann .20 .50
130 Jim Thome .20 .50
131 Alex Rios .12 .30
132 Jered Weaver .20 .50
133 Carlos Lee .12 .30
134 Mark Buehrle .20 .50
135 Chipper Jones .30 .75
136 Robinson Cano .20 .50
137 Mark Reynolds .12 .30
138 David Ortiz .30 .75
139 Carlos Gonzalez .20 .50
140 Torii Hunter .12 .30
141 Nick Markakis .25 .60
142 Jose Reyes .20 .50
143 Johnny Damon .20 .50
144 Roy Oswalt .20 .50
145 Alfonso Soriano .20 .50
146 Jimmy Rollins .20 .50
147 Matt Garza .12 .30
148 Michael Cuddyer .12 .30
149 Rick Ankiel .12 .30
150 Miguel Cabrera .30 .75
151 Mike Napoli .12 .30
152 Josh Willingham .20 .50
153 Chris Carpenter .20 .50
154 Paul Konerko .20 .50
155 Jake Peavy .12 .30
156 Nate McLouth .12 .30
157 Daisuke Matsuzaka .20 .50
158 Brad Hawpe .12 .30
159 Johan Santana .20 .50
160 Grady Sizemore .20 .50
161 Chad Billingsley .20 .50
162 Corey Hart .12 .30
163 A.J. Burnett .12 .30
164 Kosuke Fukudome .20 .50
165 Justin Verlander .30 .75
166 Jayson Werth .20 .50
167 Matt Cain .20 .50
168 Carlos Pena .20 .50
169 Hunter Pence .20 .50
170 Russell Martin .12 .30
171 Carlos Quentin .12 .30
172 Jacoby Ellsbury .25 .60
173 Todd Helton .20 .50
174 Derek Jeter .75 2.00
175 Dan Haren .12 .30
176 Nelson Cruz .30 .75
177 Jose Lopez .12 .30
178 Carlos Zambrano .20 .50
179 Hanley Ramirez .20 .50
180 Aaron Hill .12 .30
181 Ubaldo Jimenez .12 .30
182 Brian Roberts .12 .30
183 Jon Lester .20 .50
184 Ryan Braun .20 .50
185 Jay Bruce .20 .50
186 Aramis Ramirez .12 .30
187 Dustin Pedroia .30 .75
188 Troy Tulowitzki .30 .75
189 Justin Morneau .20 .50
190 Jorge Cantu .12 .30
191 Scott Rolen .20 .50
192 B.J. Upton .20 .50
193 Yadier Molina .40 1.00
194 Alex Rodriguez .40 1.00
195 Felix Hernandez .20 .50
196 Raul Ibanez .20 .50
197 Travis Snider .12 .30
198 Brandon Webb .20 .50
199 Ryan Howard .25 .60
200 Michael Young .12 .30
201 Rajai Davis .12 .30
202 Ryan Zimmerman .20 .50
203 Carlos Beltran .20 .50
204 Evan Longoria .20 .50
205 Dan Uggla .12 .30
206 Brandon Allen (RC) .20 .50
207 Buster Posey RC 3.00 8.00
208 Drew Stubbs RC .50 1.25
209 Madison Bumgarner RC 2.00 5.00
210 Reid Gorecki (RC) .30 .75
211 Wade Davis (RC) .30 .75
212 Neil Walker (RC) .30 .75
213 Ian Desmond (RC) .30 .75
214 Josh Thole RC .30 .75
215 Chris Pettit RC .20 .50
216 Daniel McCutchen RC .30 .75
217 Daniel Hudson RC .30 .75
218 Michael Brantley RC .30 .75
219 Tyler Flowers RC .30 .75
220 Checklist .12 .30

2010 Topps Opening Day Blue

*GOLD VET: 1.5X TO 4X BASIC
*GOLD RC: 1.2X TO 3X BASIC RC
STATED ODDS 1:5 HOBBY
STATED PRINT RUN 2010 SERIAL #'d SETS

2010 Topps Opening Day Attax

COMPLETE SET (25) 10.00 25.00
STATED ODDS 1:6 HOBBY
ODTA1 Tim Lincecum .60 1.50
ODTA2 Ichiro Suzuki 1.25 3.00
ODTA3 Miguel Cabrera 1.00 2.50
ODTA4 Ryan Braun .60 1.50
ODTA5 Zack Greinke 1.00 2.50
ODTA6 Alex Rodriguez 1.25 3.00
ODTA7 Albert Pujols 1.25 3.00
ODTA8 Evan Longoria .60 1.50
ODTA9 Roy Halladay .60 1.50
ODTA10 Ryan Howard .75 2.00
ODTA11 Josh Beckett .40 1.00
ODTA12 Hanley Ramirez .60 1.50
ODTA13 Lance Berkman .60 1.50
ODTA14 Dan Haren .40 1.00
ODTA15 Joe Mauer .75 2.00
ODTA16 Adrian Gonzalez .75 2.00
ODTA17 Vladimir Guerrero .60 1.50
ODTA18 Felix Hernandez .60 1.50
ODTA19 Matt Kemp .75 2.00
ODTA20 Mariano Rivera 1.25 3.00
ODTA21 Grady Sizemore .60 1.50
ODTA22 Nick Markakis .75 2.00
ODTA23 CC Sabathia .60 1.50
ODTA24 Ian Kinsler .60 1.50
ODTA25 David Wright .75 2.00

2010 Topps Opening Day Autographs

STATED ODDS 1:746 HOBBY
ODAAC Aaron Cunningham 4.00 10.00
ODACP Cliff Pennington 4.00 10.00
ODACV Chris Volstad 4.00 10.00
ODADS Denard Span 8.00 20.00
ODADSC Daniel Schlereth 6.00 15.00
ODAGP Gerardo Parra 5.00 12.00
ODAMT Matt Tolbert 8.00 20.00

2010 Topps Opening Day Mascots

COMPLETE SET (25) 6.00 15.00
STATED ODDS 1:4 HOBBY
M1 Baxter the Bobcat .40 1.00
M2 Homer the Brave .40 1.00
M3 The Oriole Bird .40 1.00
M4 Wally the Green Monster .40 1.00
M5 Southpaw .40 1.00
M6 Gapper .40 1.00
M7 Slider .40 1.00
M8 Dinger .40 1.00
M9 Paws .40 1.00
M10 Billy the Marlin .40 1.00
M11 Junction Jack .40 1.00
M12 Sluggerrr .40 1.00
M13 Bernie Brewer .40 1.00
M14 TC the Bear .40 1.00
M15 Mr. Met .40 1.00
M16 Stomper .40 1.00
M17 Phillie Phanatic .40 1.00
M18 The Pirate Parrot .40 1.00
M19 The Swinging Friar .40 1.00
M20 Mariner Moose .40 1.00
M21 Fredbird .40 1.00
M22 Raymond .40 1.00
M23 Rangers Captain .40 1.00
M24 ACE .40 1.00
M25 Screech the Eagle .40 1.00

2010 Topps Opening Day Superstar Celebrations

COMPLETE SET (10) 4.00 10.00
STATED ODDS 1:9 HOBBY
SC1 Ryan Braun .40 1.00
SC2 Mark Buehrle .40 1.00
SC3 Alex Rodriguez .75 2.00
SC4 Ichiro Suzuki .75 2.00
SC5 Ryan Zimmerman .40 1.00
SC6 Colby Rasmus .40 1.00
SC7 Andre Ethier .40 1.00
SC8 Michael Young .25 .60
SC9 Evan Longoria .40 1.00
SC10 Aramis Ramirez .25 .60

2010 Topps Opening Day Topps Town Stars

COMPLETE SET (25) 5.00 12.00
STATED ODDS 1:3 HOBBY
TTS1 Vladimir Guerrero .30 .75
TTS2 Justin Upton .30 .75
TTS3 Chipper Jones .50 1.25
TTS4 Nick Markakis .40 1.00
TTS5 David Ortiz .50 1.25
TTS6 Alfonso Soriano .30 .75
TTS7 Jake Peavy .20 .50
TTS8 Jay Bruce .30 .75
TTS9 Grady Sizemore .30 .75
TTS10 Troy Tulowitzki .50 1.25
TTS11 Miguel Cabrera .50 1.25
TTS12 Hanley Ramirez .50 1.25
TTS13 Hunter Pence .30 .75
TTS14 Zack Greinke .50 1.25
TTS15 Manny Ramirez .50 1.25
TTS16 Prince Fielder .30 .75
TTS17 Joe Mauer .40 1.00
TTS18 David Wright .40 1.00
TTS19 Mark Teixeira .30 .75
TTS20 Evan Longoria .30 .75
TTS21 Ryan Howard .40 1.00
TTS22 Albert Pujols .60 1.50
TTS23 Adrian Gonzalez .40 1.00
TTS24 Tim Lincecum .30 .75
TTS25 Ichiro Suzuki .60 1.50

2010 Topps Opening Day Where'd You Go Bazooka Joe

COMPLETE SET (10) 5.00 12.00
STATED ODDS 1:9 HOBBY
WBJ1 David Wright .50 1.25
WBJ2 Ryan Howard .50 1.25
WBJ3 Miguel Cabrera .60 1.50
WBJ4 Albert Pujols .75 2.00
WBJ5 CC Sabathia .40 1.00
WBJ6 Prince Fielder .40 1.00
WBJ7 Evan Longoria .40 1.00
WBJ8 Chipper Jones .60 1.50
WBJ9 Grady Sizemore .40 1.00
WBJ10 Ian Kinsler .40 1.00

2011 Topps Opening Day

COMPLETE SET (220) 15.00 40.00
COMMON CARD (1-220) .12 .30
COMMON RC (1-220) .20 .50
OVERALL PLATE ODDS 1:2660
PLATE PRINT RUN 1 SET PER COLOR
BLACK-CYAN-MAGENTA-YELLOW ISSUED
NO PLATE PRICING DUE TO SCARCITY
1 Carlos Gonzalez .20 .50
2 Shin-Soo Choo .20 .50
3 Jon Lester .20 .50
4 Jason Kubel .12 .30
5 David Wright .25 .60
6 Aramis Ramirez .12 .30
7 Mickey Mantle 1.00 2.50
8 Hanley Ramirez .20 .50
9 Michael Cuddyer .12 .30
10 Joey Votto .30 .75
11 Jaime Garcia .20 .50
12 Neil Walker .20 .50
13 Carl Crawford .20 .50
14 Ben Zobrist .20 .50
15 David Price .20 .50
16 Max Scherzer .30 .75
17 Ryan Dempster .12 .30
18 Justin Upton .20 .50
19 Carlos Marmol .20 .50
20 Mariano Rivera .40 1.00
21 Martin Prado .12 .30
22 Hunter Pence .20 .50
23 Chris Johnson .12 .30
24 Andrew Cashner .12 .30
25 Johan Santana .20 .50
26 Gaby Sanchez .12 .30
27 Andrew McCutchen .30 .75
28 Edinson Volquez .12 .30
29 Jonathan Papelbon .20 .50
30 Alex Rodriguez .40 1.00
31 Chris Sale RC 1.50 4.00
32 James McDonald .12 .30
33 Kyle Drabek RC .30 .75
34 Jair Jurrjens .12 .30
35 Vladimir Guerrero .20 .50
36 Daniel Descalso RC .20 .50
37 Tim Hudson .20 .50
38 Mike Stanton .30 .75
39 Kurt Suzuki .12 .30
40 CC Sabathia .20 .50
41 Aubrey Huff .12 .30
42 Greg Halman RC .30 .75
43 Jered Weaver .20 .50
44 Omar Infante .12 .30
45 Desmond Jennings RC .30 .75
46 Yadier Molina .40 1.00
47 Phil Hughes .12 .30
48 Paul Konerko .20 .50
49 Yonder Alonso RC .30 .75
50 Albert Pujols .40 1.00
51 Ben Revere RC .30 .75
52 Placido Polanco .12 .30
53 Bronson Arroyo .12 .30
54 Ian Stewart .12 .30
55 Cliff Lee .20 .50
56 Brian Bogusevic (RC) .20 .50
57 Zack Greinke .30 .75
58 Howie Kendrick .12 .30
59 Russell Martin .12 .30
60 Aroldis Chapman RC .60 1.50
61 Jason Bay .20 .50
62 Mat Latos .20 .50
63 Manny Ramirez .30 .75
64 Miguel Tejada .20 .50
65 Mike Stanton .30 .75
66 Brett Anderson .12 .30
67 Johnny Cueto .20 .50
68 Jeremy Jeffress RC .12 .30
69 Lance Berkman .20 .50
70 Freddie Freeman RC 3.00 8.00
71 Jon Niese .12 .30
72 Ricky Romero .12 .30
73 David Aardsma .12 .30
74 Fausto Carmona .12 .30
75 Buster Posey .40 1.00
76 Chris Perez .12 .30
77 Koji Uehara .12 .30
78 Garrett Jones .12 .30
79 Heath Bell .12 .30
80 Jeremy Hellickson RC .50 1.25
81 Jay Bruce .20 .50
82 Brennan Boesch .20 .50
83 Daniel Hudson .12 .30
84 Brian Matusz .12 .30
85 Carlos Santana .30 .75
86 Stephen Strasburg .30 .75
87 Brandon Morrow .12 .30
88 Carl Pavano .12 .30
89 Pablo Sandoval .20 .50
90 Chase Utley .20 .50
91 Andres Torres .12 .30
92 Nick Markakis .25 .60
93 Aaron Hill .12 .30
94 Jimmy Rollins .20 .50
95 Josh Johnson .20 .50
96 James Shields .12 .30
97 Mike Napoli .12 .30
98 Angel Pagan .12 .30
99 Clay Buchholz .12 .30
100 Miguel Cabrera .30 .75
101 Brian Wilson .30 .75
102 Carlos Ruiz .12 .30
103 Jose Bautista .20 .50
104 Victor Martinez .20 .50
105 Roy Oswalt .20 .50
106 Todd Helton .20 .50
107 Scott Rolen .20 .50
108 Jonathan Sanchez .12 .30
109 Mark Buehrle .20 .50
110 Ichiro Suzuki .40 1.00
111 Nelson Cruz .30 .75
112 Andre Ethier .20 .50
113 Wandy Rodriguez .12 .30
114 Ervin Santana .12 .30
115 Starlin Castro .20 .50
116 Torii Hunter .12 .30
117 Tyler Colvin .12 .30
118 Rafael Soriano .12 .30
119 Alexei Ramirez .20 .50
120 Roy Halladay .20 .50
121 John Danks .12 .30
122 Rickie Weeks .12 .30
123 Stephen Drew .12 .30
124 Clayton Kershaw .50 1.25
125 Adam Dunn .20 .50
126 Brian Duensing .12 .30
127 Nick Swisher .20 .50
128 Andrew Bailey .12 .30
129 Ike Davis .12 .30
130 Justin Morneau .20 .50
131 Chris Carpenter .20 .50
132 Miguel Montero .12 .30
133 Alex Rios .12 .30
134 Ian Desmond .12 .30
135 David Ortiz .30 .75
136 Gaby Sanchez .12 .30
137 Joel Pineiro .12 .30
138 Chris Young .12 .30
139 Michael Young .12 .30
140 Derek Jeter .75 2.00
141 Brent Morel RC .20 .50
142 C.J. Wilson .12 .30
143 Jeremy Guthrie .12 .30
144 Brett Gardner .20 .50
145 Ubaldo Jimenez .12 .30
146 Gavin Floyd .12 .30
147 Josh Hamilton .20 .50
148 Kevin Youkilis .12 .30
149 Tommy Hanson .12 .30
150 Matt Cain .20 .50
151 Adam Wainwright .20 .50
152 Mark Reynolds .12 .30
153 Kendry Morales .12 .30
154 Dan Haren .12 .30
155 Cole Hamels .25 .60
156 Ryan Zimmerman .20 .50
157 Adam Lind .20 .50
158 Brian McCann .20 .50
159 Dan Uggla .12 .30
160 Carlos Lee .12 .30
161 Jose Tabata .12 .30
162 Gordon Beckham .12 .30
163 Chad Billingsley .20 .50
164 Grady Sizemore .20 .50
165 Carlos Zambrano .20 .50
166 Ian Kinsler .20 .50
167 Geovany Soto .20 .50
168 Tim Lincecum .20 .50
169 Felix Hernandez .20 .50
170 Logan Morrison .12 .30
171 Yovani Gallardo .12 .30
172 Jorge Posada .20 .50
173 Joakim Soria .12 .30
174 Buster Posey .40 1.00
175 Adam Jones .20 .50
176 Jason Heyward .25 .60
177 Magglio Ordonez .30 .75
178 Joe Mauer .25 .60
179 Prince Fielder .30 .75
180 Colby Rasmus .20 .50
181 Josh Beckett .12 .30
182 Troy Tulowitzki .30 .75
183 Jacoby Ellsbury .25 .60
184 Austin Jackson .12 .30
185 Billy Butler .12 .30
186 Evan Longoria .20 .50
187 Brandon Phillips .12 .30
188 Justin Verlander .30 .75
189 B.J. Upton .20 .50
190 Elvis Andrus .20 .50
191 Corey Hart .12 .30
192 Dustin Pedroia .30 .75
193 Trevor Cahill .12 .30
194 Delmon Young .20 .50
195 Shaun Marcum .12 .30
196 Brian Roberts .12 .30
197 Kelly Johnson .12 .30
198 Adrian Gonzalez .25 .60
199 Francisco Liriano .12 .30
200 Robinson Cano .20 .50
201 Madison Bumgarner .25 .60
202 Mike Leake .20 .50
203 Neftali Feliz .12 .30
204 Carlos Beltran .20 .50
205 Carlos Quentin .12 .30
206 Rafael Furcal .12 .30
207 Kosuke Fukudome .20 .50
208 Matt Kemp .25 .60
209 Shane Victorino .20 .50
210 Drew Stubbs .12 .30
211 Ricky Nolasco .12 .30
212 Vernon Wells .12 .30
213 Matt Holliday .30 .75
214 Bobby Abreu .12 .30
215 Mark Teixeira .20 .50
216 Jose Reyes .20 .50
217 Andy Pettitte .20 .50
218 Ryan Howard .25 .60
219 Matt Garza .12 .30
220 Alfonso Soriano .20 .50

2011 Topps Opening Day Blue

*BLUE VET: 3X TO 8X BASIC
*BLUE RC: 1.5X TO 4X BASIC RC
STATED ODDS 1:5
STATED PRINT RUN 2011 SER.#'d SETS

2011 Topps Opening Day Autographs

STATED ODDS 1:480
CC Chris Carter 10.00 25.00
CM Casey McGehee 6.00 15.00
DM Dustin Moseley 10.00 25.00
HK Howie Kendrick 8.00 20.00
JG Justin Germano 8.00 20.00
JM Jose Mijares 8.00 20.00
PH Philip Humber 6.00 15.00
TB Taylor Buchholz 4.00 10.00
JMO Jose Morales 6.00 15.00
JVE Jonathan Van Every 8.00 20.00

2011 Topps Opening Day Mascots

COMPLETE SET (25) 12.50 30.00
STATED ODDS 1:4
M1 Arizona Diamondbacks .60 1.50
M2 Atlanta Braves .60 1.50
M3 Baltimore Orioles .60 1.50
M4 Wally the Green Monster .60 1.50
M5 Chicago White Sox .60 1.50
M6 Gapper .60 1.50
M7 Slider .60 1.50
M8 Dinger .60 1.50
M9 Paws .60 1.50
M10 Billy the Marlin .60 1.50
M11 Junction Jack .60 1.50
M12 Kansas City Royals .60 1.50
M13 Bernie Brewer .60 1.50
M14 TC .60 1.50
M15 Mr. Met .60 1.50
M16 Oakland Athletics .60 1.50
M17 Phillie Phanatic .60 1.50
M18 Pirate Parrot .60 1.50
M19 Swinging Friar .60 1.50
M20 Mariner Moose .60 1.50
M21 Fredbird .60 1.50
M22 Raymond .60 1.50
M23 Rangers Captain .60 1.50
M24 Toronto Blue Jays .60 1.50
M25 Screech .60 1.50

2011 Topps Opening Day Presidential First Pitch

COMPLETE SET (10) 4.00 10.00
STATED ODDS 1:6
PFP1 Barack Obama 1.00 2.50
PFP2 Harry Truman .40 1.00
PFP3 Calvin Coolidge .40 1.00
PFP4 Ronald Reagan .75 2.00
PFP5 Richard Nixon .40 1.00
PFP6 Woodrow Wilson .40 1.00
PFP7 George W. Bush .75 2.00
PFP8 George W. Bush .75 2.00
PFP9 John F. Kennedy .75 2.00
PFP10 Barack Obama 1.00 2.50

2011 Topps Opening Day Spot the Error

COMPLETE SET (10) 4.00 10.00
STATED ODDS 1:6
1 Mark Teixeira .30 .75
2 Jason Heyward .40 1.00
3 Jose Bautista .30 .75
4 Chase Utley .30 .75
5 David Ortiz .50 1.25
6 Ubaldo Jimenez .20 .50
7 David Wright .40 1.00
8 Hanley Ramirez .30 .75
9 Buster Posey .60 1.50
10 Derek Jeter 1.25 3.00

2011 Topps Opening Day Stadium Lights

COMPLETE SET (10) 4.00 10.00
STATED ODDS 1:9
UL1 Joe Mauer .50 1.25
UL2 Troy Tulowitzki .60 1.50
UL3 Robinson Cano .40 1.00
UL4 Alex Rodriguez .75 2.00
UL5 Miguel Cabrera .60 1.50
UL6 Chase Utley .40 1.00
UL7 Pedro Alvarez .50 1.25
UL8 Adrian Gonzalez .50 1.25
UL9 Jason Heyward .50 1.25
UL10 Ryan Braun .40 1.00

2011 Topps Opening Day Stars

COMPLETE SET (10) 5.00 12.00
STATED ODDS 1:12
ODS1 Roy Halladay .40 1.00
ODS2 Carlos Gonzalez .40 1.00
ODS3 Alex Rodriguez .75 2.00
ODS4 Josh Hamilton .40 1.00
ODS5 Miguel Cabrera .60 1.50
ODS6 CC Sabathia .40 1.00
ODS7 Joe Mauer .50 1.25
ODS8 Joey Votto .60 1.50
ODS9 David Price .50 1.25
ODS10 Albert Pujols .75 2.00

2011 Topps Opening Day Superstar Celebrations

COMPLETE SET (25) 5.00 12.00
STATED ODDS 1:4
SC1 Jason Heyward .30 .75
SC2 Buster Posey .50 1.25
SC3 David Ortiz .40 1.00
SC4 Jay Bruce .25 .60
SC5 Ubaldo Jimenez .15 .40
SC6 Evan Longoria .25 .60
SC7 Jim Thome .25 .60
SC8 Vladimir Guerrero .25 .60
SC9 Nick Markakis .30 .75
SC10 Carlos Pena .25 .60
SC11 Jimmy Rollins .25 .60
SC12 Matt Garza .15 .40
SC13 Albert Pujols .50 1.25
SC14 David Wright .30 .75
SC15 Alex Rodriguez .50 1.25
SC16 Jose Reyes .25 .60
SC17 Prince Fielder .25 .60
SC18 Derek Jeter 1.00 2.50
SC19 Bobby Abreu .15 .40
SC20 Ichiro Suzuki .50 1.25
SC21 Matt Holliday .50 1.25
SC22 Cliff Lee .25 .60
SC23 Ryan Braun .25 .60
SC24 Troy Tulowitzki .40 1.00
SC25 Matt Kemp .30 .75

2011 Topps Opening Day Topps Town Codes

COMPLETE SET (25) 8.00 20.00
TTOD1 Clayton Kershaw 1.00 2.50
TTOD2 Hunter Pence .40 1.00
TTOD3 Trevor Cahill .25 .60
TTOD4 Jose Bautista .40 1.00
TTOD5 Jon Lester .40 1.00
TTOD6 Matt Holliday .60 1.50
TTOD7 Carlos Marmol .40 1.00
TTOD8 Justin Upton .40 1.00
TTOD9 Jered Weaver .40 1.00
TTOD10 Tim Lincecum .40 1.00
TTOD11 Logan Morrison .25 .60
TTOD12 Ike Davis .25 .60
TTOD13 Ian Desmond .25 .60
TTOD14 Brian Matusz .25 .60
TTOD15 Justin Morneau .40 1.00
TTOD16 Jose Tabata .25 .60
TTOD17 Ian Kinsler .40 1.00
TTOD18 Desmond Jennings .40 1.00
TTOD19 Martin Prado .25 .60
TTOD20 Alex Rodriguez .75 2.00
TTOD21 Austin Jackson .25 .60
TTOD22 Carlos Ruiz .25 .60
TTOD23 Gordon Beckham .25 .60
TTOD24 Jay Bruce .40 1.00
TTOD25 Derek Jeter 1.50 4.00

2011 Topps Opening Day Toys R Us Geoffrey the Giraffe

COMPLETE SET (5) 3.00 8.00
INSERT IN TRU PACKS
TRU1 Geoffrey 1.50 4.00
TRU2 Geoffrey 1.50 4.00
TRU3 Geoffrey 1.50 4.00
TRU4 Geoffrey 1.50 4.00
TRU5 Geoffrey 1.50 4.00

2012 Topps Opening Day

COMPLETE SET (220) 15.00 40.00
COMMON CARD (1-220) .12 .30
COMMON RC (1-220) .20 .50
OVERALL PLATE ODDS 1:3226 RETAIL
PLATE PRINT RUN 1 SET PER COLOR
BLACK-CYAN-MAGENTA-YELLOW ISSUED
NO PLATE PRICING DUE TO SCARCITY
1 Ryan Braun .12 .30
2 Stephen Drew .12 .30
3 Nelson Cruz .20 .50
4 Jacoby Ellsbury .12 .30
5 Roy Halladay .15 .40
6 Bud Norris .15 .40
7 Mickey Mantle .60 1.50
8 Jordan Zimmermann .15 .40
9 Chris Young .12 .30
10 Jose Valverde .15 .40
11 Michael Morse .12 .30
12 Jason Heyward .15 .40
13 Bobby Abreu .12 .30
14 Buster Posey .25 .60
15 Jeremy Hellickson .12 .30
16 Torii Hunter .15 .40
17 Pedro Alvarez .12 .30
18 David Ortiz .20 .50
19 Mat Latos .15 .40
20 Howie Kendrick .12 .30
21 Matt Moore RC .30 .75
22 Aroldis Chapman .20 .50
23 Troy Tulowitzki .20 .50
24 Brandon Morrow .12 .30
25 Eric Hosmer .15 .40
26 Drew Stubbs .12 .30
27 Chase Utley .15 .40
28 Michael Young .12 .30
29 Mike Napoli .12 .30
30 Shane Victorino .15 .40
31 Evan Longoria .15 .40
32 Anibal Sanchez .12 .30
33 Nick Markakis .15 .40
34 James McDonald .12 .30
35 Brennan Boesch .12 .30
36 Dexter Fowler .15 .40
37 Josh Beckett .12 .30
38 Brett Myers .12 .30
39 Michael Cuddyer .12 .30
40 Domonic Brown .15 .40
41 J.J. Hardy .12 .30
42 Mark Reynolds .12 .30
43 Angel Pagan .12 .30
44 Jay Bruce .15 .40
45 Mark Melancon .12 .30
46 Chris Sale .20 .50
47 Nick Swisher .15 .40
48 Adrian Beltre .20 .50
49 Melky Cabrera .12 .30
50 Ichiro Suzuki .25 .60
51 Prince Fielder .15 .40
52 Matt Joyce .12 .30
53 Alex Rodriguez .25 .60
54 Asdrubal Cabrera .15 .40
55 Miguel Cabrera .20 .50
56 Vance Worley .15 .40
57 Adam Lind .15 .40
58 Justin Masterson .12 .30
59 Alcides Escobar .12 .30
60 Adam Wainwright .15 .40
61 C.J. Wilson .12 .30
62 Ervin Santana .12 .30
63 Pablo Sandoval .15 .40
64 Dan Haren .12 .30
65 Dustin Ackley .12 .30
66 Adam Jones .15 .40
67 Billy Butler .12 .30
68 Shaun Marcum .12 .30
69 Tim Lincecum .15 .40
70 Madison Bumgarner .15 .40
71 Ian Kennedy .12 .30
72 Derek Holland .12 .30
73 Kevin Youkilis .12 .30
74 Cameron Maybin .12 .30
75 Justin Upton .15 .40
76 Gio Gonzalez .15 .40
77 Jimmy Rollins .15 .40
78 Matt Holliday .20 .50
79 Hanley Ramirez .15 .40
80 Joe Mauer .15 .40
81 Brandon Beachy .12 .30
82 Phil Hughes .12 .30
83 Carlos Gonzalez .15 .40
84 Dan Uggla .12 .30
85 Mike Trout 6.00 15.00
86 Jon Lester .12 .30
87 Ryan Howard .15 .40
88 John Axford .12 .30
89 Drew Pomeranz .12 .30
90 Derek Jeter .50 1.25
91 Jayson Werth .15 .40
92 Mike Stanton .20 .50
93 Tim Hudson .15 .40
94 Doug Fister .12 .30
95 Victor Martinez .15 .40
96 Chris Carpenter .15 .40
97 David Price .15 .40
98 Ben Zobrist .15 .40
99 Robinson Cano .15 .40
100 Matt Kemp .15 .40
101 Todd Helton .15 .40
102 Jesus Montero RC .20 .50
103 Mike Leake .12 .30
104 Alexi Ogando .12 .30
105 Curtis Granderson .15 .40
106 Josh Johnson .15 .40
107 Rickie Weeks .12 .30
108 Roy Oswalt .15 .40
109 Brett Gardner .15 .40
110 Scott Rolen .15 .40
111 Carlos Santana .15 .40
112 Dee Gordon .12 .30
113 Justin Verlander .20 .50
114 Paul Konerko .15 .40
115 Yunel Escobar .12 .30
116 Josh Hamilton .15 .40
117 Brandon Belt .15 .40
118 Miguel Montero .12 .30
119 Ricky Nolasco .12 .30
120 Matt Garza .12 .30
121 Mark Teixeira .15 .40
122 Neftali Feliz .12 .30
123 Ryan Roberts .12 .30
124 Grady Sizemore .15 .40
125 Matt Cain .15 .40
126 Danny Valencia .12 .30
127 J.P. Arencibia .12 .30
128 Lance Berkman .15 .40
129 Alex Rios .15 .40
130 Brett Wallace .12 .30
131 Scott Baker .12 .30
132 Kurt Suzuki .12 .30
133 Sergio Santos .12 .30
134 Chipper Jones .20 .50
135 Josh Reddick .12 .30
136 Justin Morneau .15 .40
137 B.J. Upton .15 .40
138 Russell Martin .12 .30
139 Trevor Cahill .12 .30
140 Erick Aybar .12 .30
141 Drew Storen .12 .30
142 Tommy Hanson .12 .30
143 Craig Kimbrel .15 .40
144 Andrew McCutchen .20 .50

145 CC Sabathia .15 .40
146 Ian Desmond .12 .30
147 Corey Hart .12 .30
148 Shin-Soo Choo .15 .40
149 Adrian Gonzalez .15 .40
150 Jose Bautista .15 .40
151 Johnny Cueto .15 .40
152 Neil Walker .12 .30
153 Aramis Ramirez .12 .30
154 Yadier Molina .25 .60
155 Juan Nicasio .12 .30
156 Joey Votto .20 .50
157 Ubaldo Jimenez .12 .30
158 Mark Trumbo .12 .30
159 Max Scherzer .20 .50
160 Carlos Ruiz .12 .30
161 Hunter Pence .15 .40
162 Ricky Romero .12 .30
163 Heath Bell .12 .30
164 Nyjer Morgan .12 .30
165 Yovani Gallardo .15 .40
166 Peter Bourjos .12 .30
167 Orlando Hudson .12 .30
168 Jose Tabata .12 .30
169 Ian Kinsler .15 .40
170 Brian Wilson .20 .50
171 Jaime Garcia .15 .40
172 Dustin Pedroia .20 .50
173 Michael Pineda .15 .40
174 Brian McCann .15 .40
175 Jason Bay .15 .40
176 Geovany Soto .15 .40
177 Jhonny Peralta .12 .30
178 Desmond Jennings .15 .40
179 Zack Greinke .20 .50
180 Ted Lilly .12 .30
181 Clayton Kershaw .30 .75
182 Seth Smith .12 .30
183 Cliff Lee .15 .40
184 Michael Bourn .12 .30
185 Jeff Niemann .12 .30
186 Martin Prado .12 .30
187 David Wright .15 .40
188 Paul Goldschmidt .20 .50
189 Mariano Rivera .25 .60
190 Stephen Strasburg .25 .60
191 Ivan Nova .15 .40
192 James Shields .12 .30
193 Casey McGehee .12 .30
194 Alex Gordon .15 .40
195 Ike Davis .12 .30
196 Cole Hamels .15 .40
197 Elvis Andrus .15 .40
198 Carl Crawford .15 .40
199 Felix Hernandez .15 .40
200 Albert Pujols .25 .60
201 Jose Reyes .12 .30
202 Starlin Castro .15 .40
203 John Danks .12 .30
204 Cory Luebke .12 .30
205 Chad Billingsley .12 .30
206 David Freese .12 .30
207 Brandon McCarthy .12 .30
208 James Loney .12 .30
209 Jered Weaver .15 .40
210 Freddie Freeman .25 .60
211 Ben Revere .15 .40
212 Daniel Hudson .12 .30
213 Jhoulys Chacin .12 .30
214 Alex Avila .12 .30
215 Colby Lewis .12 .30
216 Jason Kipnis .25 .60
217 Ryan Zimmerman .25 .60
218 Clay Buchholz .12 .30
219 Brandon Phillips .20 .50
220 Carlos Lee UER .20 .50
No card number
CL Christian Lopez SP 50.00 100.00

2012 Topps Opening Day Blue

*BLUE VET: 3X TO 8X BASIC
*BLUE RC: 1.5X TO 4X BASIC RC
STATED ODDS 1:6 RETAIL
STATED PRINT RUN 2012 SER.#'d SETS

2012 Topps Opening Day Autographs

STATED ODDS 1:568 RETAIL
AC Andrew Cashner 10.00 25.00
AE Alcides Escobar 8.00 20.00
BA Brett Anderson 6.00 15.00
CC Chris Coghlan 5.00 12.00
CH Chris Heisey 5.00 12.00
DB Daniel Bard 5.00 12.00
DM Daniel McCutchen 5.00 12.00
JJ Jon Jay 12.50 30.00
JN Jon Niese 5.00 12.00
MM Mitch Moreland 8.00 20.00
NF Neftali Feliz 8.00 20.00
NW Neil Walker 6.00 15.00

2012 Topps Opening Day Box Bottom

NNO Justin Verlander 1.50 4.00

2012 Topps Opening Day Elite Skills

COMPLETE SET (25) 5.00 12.00
STATED ODDS 1:4 RETAIL
ES1 Jose Reyes .40 1.00
ES2 Alex Gordon .50 1.25
ES3 Prince Fielder .50 1.25
ES4 Ian Kinsler .50 1.25
ES5 James Shields .40 1.00
ES6 Andrew McCutchen .60 1.50
ES7 Justin Verlander .60 1.50
ES8 Felix Hernandez .50 1.25
ES9 Barry Zito .50 1.25
ES10 R.A. Dickey .50 1.25
ES11 Roy Halladay .50 1.25
ES12 Ichiro Suzuki .75 2.00
ES13 David Wright .50 1.25
ES14 Troy Tulowitzki .60 1.50
ES15 Jose Bautista .50 1.25
ES16 Joey Votto .60 1.50
ES17 Joe Mauer .50 1.25
ES18 Mark Teixeira .50 1.25
ES19 Mike Stanton .60 1.50
ES20 Yadier Molina .75 2.00
ES21 Ryan Zimmerman .50 1.25
ES22 Jacoby Ellsbury .50 1.25
ES23 Carlos Gonzalez .50 1.25
ES24 Jered Weaver .50 1.25
ES25 Elvis Andrus .50 1.25

2012 Topps Opening Day Fantasy Squad

COMPLETE SET (30) 6.00 15.00
STATED ODDS 1:4 RETAIL
FS1 Albert Pujols .75 2.00
FS2 Miguel Cabrera .60 1.50
FS3 Adrian Gonzalez .50 1.25
FS4 Robinson Cano .50 1.25
FS5 Dustin Pedroia .60 1.50
FS6 Ian Kinsler .50 1.25
FS7 Troy Tulowitzki .60 1.50
FS8 Starlin Castro .50 1.25
FS9 Jose Reyes .40 1.00
FS10 David Wright .50 1.25
FS11 Evan Longoria .50 1.25
FS12 Hanley Ramirez .50 1.25
FS13 Victor Martinez .50 1.25
FS14 Brian McCann .50 1.25
FS15 Joe Mauer .50 1.25
FS16 David Ortiz .60 1.50
FS17 Billy Butler .40 1.00
FS18 Michael Young .40 1.00
FS19 Ryan Braun .40 1.00
FS20 Carlos Gonzalez .50 1.25
FS21 Josh Hamilton .50 1.25
FS22 Curtis Granderson .50 1.25
FS23 Matt Kemp .50 1.25
FS24 Jacoby Ellsbury .50 1.25
FS25 Jose Bautista .50 1.25
FS26 Justin Upton .50 1.25
FS27 Mike Stanton .60 1.50
FS28 Justin Verlander .60 1.50
FS29 Roy Halladay .50 1.25
FS30 Tim Lincecum .50 1.25

2012 Topps Opening Day Mascots

COMPLETE SET (25) 10.00 25.00
STATED ODDS 1:4 RETAIL
M1 Bernie Brewer .60 1.50
M2 Baltimore Orioles .60 1.50
M3 Toronto Blue Jays .60 1.50
M4 Arizona Diamondbacks .60 1.50
M5 Fredbird .60 1.50
M6 Raymond .60 1.50
M7 Mr. Met .60 1.50
M8 Atlanta Braves .60 1.50
M9 Rangers Captain .60 1.50
M10 Pirate Parrot .60 1.50
M11 Billy the Marlin .60 1.50
M12 Paws .60 1.50
M13 Dinger .60 1.50
M14 Phillie Phanatic .60 1.50
M15 Kansas City Royals .60 1.50
M16 Wally the Green Monster .60 1.50
M17 Gapper .60 1.50
M18 Slider .60 1.50
M19 TC .60 1.50
M20 Swinging Friar .60 1.50
M21 Chicago White Sox .60 1.50
M22 Screech .60 1.50
M23 Mariner Moose .60 1.50
M24 Oakland Athletics .60 1.50
M25 Junction Jack .60 1.50

2012 Topps Opening Day Stars

COMPLETE SET (25) 12.50 30.00
STATED ODDS 1:8 RETAIL
ODS1 Ryan Braun .60 1.50
ODS2 Albert Pujols 1.25 3.00
ODS3 Miguel Cabrera 1.00 2.50
ODS4 Adrian Gonzalez .75 2.00
ODS5 Troy Tulowitzki 1.00 2.50
ODS6 Matt Kemp .75 2.00
ODS7 Justin Verlander 1.00 2.50
ODS8 Jose Bautista .75 2.00
ODS9 Robinson Cano .75 2.00
ODS10 Roy Halladay .75 2.00
ODS11 Jacoby Ellsbury .75 2.00
ODS12 Prince Fielder .75 2.00
ODS13 Justin Upton .75 2.00
ODS14 Hanley Ramirez .75 2.00
ODS15 Clayton Kershaw 1.50 4.00
ODS16 Felix Hernandez .75 2.00
ODS17 David Wright .75 2.00
ODS18 Mark Teixeira .75 2.00
ODS19 Josh Hamilton .75 2.00
ODS20 Jered Weaver .75 2.00
ODS21 Joey Votto 1.00 2.50
ODS22 Evan Longoria .75 2.00
ODS23 Carlos Gonzalez .75 2.00
ODS24 Dustin Pedroia 1.00 2.50
ODS25 Tim Lincecum .75 2.00

2012 Topps Opening Day Superstar Celebrations

COMPLETE SET (20) 4.00 10.00
STATED ODDS 1:4 RETAIL
SC1 Matt Kemp .40 1.00
SC2 Justin Upton .40 1.00
SC3 Dan Uggla .40 1.00
SC4 Geovany Soto .40 1.00
SC5 Joey Votto .50 1.25
SC6 Alex Rios .40 1.00
SC7 Eric Hosmer .40 1.00
SC8 Troy Tulowitzki .50 1.25
SC9 Ryan Zimmerman .40 1.00
SC10 J.J. Putz .30 .75
SC11 Jacoby Ellsbury .40 1.00
SC12 Ian Kinsler .40 1.00
SC13 David Wright .40 1.00
SC14 Ryan Braun .30 .75
SC15 Miguel Cabrera .50 1.25
SC16 Nelson Cruz .50 1.25
SC17 Adam Jones .40 1.00
SC18 Brett Lawrie .40 1.00
SC19 Mark Trumbo .30 .75
SC20 Martin Prado .30 .75

2013 Topps Opening Day

COMP.SET w/o SP's (220) 12.50 30.00
1A Buster Posey .40 1.00
1B Posey SP Celebrate
2 Ricky Romero .20 .50
3 CC Sabathia .25 .60
4 Matt Dominguez .20 .50
5 Eric Hosmer .25 .60
6 David Wright .25 .60
7 Adrian Beltre .30 .75
8 Ryan Braun .25 .60
9 Mark Buehrle .25 .60
10 Mat Latos .25 .60
11 Hanley Ramirez .25 .60
12 Aroldis Chapman .30 .75
13 Carlos Beltran .25 .60
14 Josh Willingham .25 .60
15 Jim Johnson .20 .50
16 Jesus Montero .20 .50
17 John Axford .20 .50
18 Jemile Weeks .20 .50
19 Joey Votto .30 .75
20 Jacoby Ellsbury .25 .60
21 Yovani Gallardo .20 .50
22 Felix Hernandez .25 .60
23 Logan Morrison .20 .50
24 Tommy Milone .20 .50
25 Jonathan Papelbon .25 .60
26 Howie Kendrick .20 .50
27 Mike Trout 2.50 6.00
28A Prince Fielder .25 .60
28B Fielder SP Celebrate 12.00 30.00
29 Bronson Arroyo .20 .50
30 Jayson Werth .25 .60
31 Jeremy Hellickson .20 .50
32 Jered Weaver .25 .60
33 Trevor Plouffe .20 .50
34 Gerardo Parra .20 .50
35 Justin Verlander .30 .75
36 Tommy Hanson .20 .50
37 Jurickson Profar RC .40 1.00
38 Albert Pujols .40 1.00
39 Heath Bell .20 .50
40 Carlos Quentin .20 .50
41 Dustin Pedroia .30 .75
42 Jon Lester .25 .60
43 Pedro Alvarez .20 .50
44 Gio Gonzalez .25 .60
45 Clayton Kershaw .50 1.25
46A Zack Greinke .30 .75
46B Greinke SP Press 12.00 30.00
47 Jake Peavy .20 .50
48 Ike Davis .20 .50
49 Grant Balfour .20 .50
50A Bryce Harper .50 1.25
50B Harper SP w/Fans 40.00 80.00
51 Elvis Andrus .25 .60
52 Dylan Bundy RC .75 2.00
53 Addison Reed .20 .50
54 Starlin Castro .20 .50
55 Darwin Barney .20 .50
56A Josh Hamilton .25 .60
56B Hamilton SP Press 12.00 30.00
57 Cliff Lee .25 .60
58 Chris Davis .25 .60
59 Matt Harvey .25 .60
60 Carl Crawford .25 .60
61 Drew Hutchison .20 .50
62 Jason Kubel .20 .50
63 Jonathon Niese .20 .50
64 Justin Masterson .20 .50
65 Will Venable .20 .50
66 Shin-Soo Choo .25 .60
67 Marco Scutaro .25 .60
68 Barry Zito .25 .60
69 Brett Gardner .25 .60
70 Danny Espinosa .20 .50
71 Victor Martinez .25 .60
72 Shelby Miller RC .75 2.00
73 Ryan Vogelsong .20 .50
74 Jason Kipnis .25 .60
75 Trevor Cahill .20 .50
76 Adam Jones .25 .60
77 Mark Trumbo .20 .50
78 Hisashi Iwakuma .25 .60
79 Tyler Colvin .20 .50
80 Anthony Rizzo .40 1.00
81 Miguel Cabrera .30 .75
82 Carlos Santana .25 .60
83 Wilin Rosario .20 .50
84 Yonder Alonso .20 .50
85 Jeff Samardzija .20 .50
86 Brandon League .20 .50
87 Adrian Gonzalez .25 .60
88 Edwin Encarnacion .30 .75
89 Drew Stubbs .20 .50
90A Nick Swisher .25 .60
90B Swisher SP Press 40.00 80.00
91 Adam Wainwright .25 .60
92 Aramis Ramirez .20 .50
93A Justin Upton .25 .60
93B Upton SP Press 12.00 30.00
94A James Shields .20 .50
94B Shields SP Press
95 Daniel Murphy .25 .60
96 Jordan Zimmermann .25 .60
97A Matt Cain .25 .60
97B Cain SP w/Mic 8.00 20.00
98 Paul Goldschmidt .30 .75
99 Vernon Wells .20 .50
100 Matt Kemp .25 .60
101 Adeiny Hechavarria RC .40 1.00
102 Andrew McCutchen .30 .75
103 Desmond Jennings .25 .60
104 Tim Lincecum .25 .60
105 James McDonald .20 .50
106 Trevor Bauer .40 1.00
107 Lance Berkman .25 .60
108 Hunter Pence .25 .60
109 Ian Desmond .25 .60
110 Corey Hart .20 .50
111 Jean Segura .25 .60
112 Chase Utley .25 .60
113 Carlos Gonzalez .25 .60
114 Mike Olt RC .40 1.00
115A B.J. Upton .25 .60
115B Upton SP Press
116 Norichika Aoki .20 .50
117 Michael Young .20 .50
118 Max Scherzer .30 .75
119 Angel Pagan .20 .50
120 Alex Rodriguez .40 1.00
121 Nick Markakis .25 .60
122 Aaron Hill .20 .50
123 John Danks .20 .50
124 Josh Reddick .20 .50
125 Bartolo Colon .20 .50
126 Todd Frazier .20 .50
127 Edinson Volquez .20 .50
128 A.J. Burnett .20 .50
129 Sergio Romo .20 .50
130 Chase Headley .20 .50
131A Jose Reyes .25 .60
131B Reyes SP Press 12.00 30.00
132 David Freese .20 .50
133 Billy Butler .20 .50
134 Cameron Maybin .20 .50
135 Josh Johnson .25 .60
136 Ian Kennedy .20 .50
137A Yoenis Cespedes .30 .75
137B Cespedes SP w/Fans
138 Joe Mauer .25 .60
139 Mark Teixeira .25 .60
140 Tyler Skaggs RC .50 1.25
141 Yadier Molina .40 1.00
142 Jarrod Parker .20 .50
143 David Ortiz .30 .75
144 Matt Holliday .30 .75
145 Giancarlo Stanton .30 .75
146 Alex Cobb .20 .50
147 Ryan Zimmerman .25 .60
148 Alex Rios .25 .60
149 C.J. Wilson .20 .50
150 Derek Jeter .75 2.00
151A Torii Hunter .20 .50
151B Hunter SP Press 12.00 30.00
152 Brian Wilson .30 .75
153 Andre Ethier .25 .60
154 Nelson Cruz .30 .75
155 Brandon Crawford .25 .60
156 Adam Dunn .25 .60
157 Madison Bumgarner .25 .60
158 J.J. Putz .20 .50
159 Mike Moustakas .25 .60
160 Johan Santana .25 .60
161 Dan Uggla .20 .50
162 Roy Halladay .25 .60
163 Justin Morneau .25 .60
164 Jose Altuve .25 .60
165 Yu Darvish .30 .75
166 Tyler Clippard .20 .50
167 Starling Marte .25 .60
168 Miguel Montero .20 .50
169 Robinson Cano .25 .60
170 Stephen Strasburg .30 .75
171 Jarrod Saltalamacchia .20 .50
172 Manny Machado RC 2.00 5.00
173 Zack Cozart .20 .50
174 Kendrys Morales .20 .50
175 Brandon Phillips .20 .50
176 Mariano Rivera .40 1.00
177 Chris Sale .30 .75
178 Ben Zobrist .25 .60
179 Wade Miley .25 .60
180 Jason Heyward .25 .60
181 Neftali Feliz .20 .50
182 Freddie Freeman .40 1.00
183 Fernando Rodney .20 .50
184 Denard Span .20 .50
185 Curtis Granderson .25 .60
186 Paul Konerko .25 .60
187 Huston Street .20 .50
188 Coco Crisp .20 .50
189 Austin Jackson .20 .50
190 Chris Carpenter .25 .60
191 Johnny Cueto .25 .60
192 Josh Beckett .20 .50
193 Alex Gordon .25 .60
194 Rickie Weeks .20 .50
195 Tim Hudson .25 .60
196 Kyle Seager .20 .50
197 Jhonny Peralta .20 .50
198 Ryan Howard .25 .60
199 Craig Kimbrel .25 .60
200 Evan Longoria .25 .60
201 Ervin Santana .20 .50
202 Jason Motte .20 .50
203 Daniel Hudson .20 .50
204 Jay Bruce .25 .60
205 Doug Fister .20 .50
206 Cole Hamels .25 .60
207 Jose Bautista .25 .60
208 Jimmy Rollins .25 .60
209 Drew Storen .20 .50
210 Will Middlebrooks .20 .50
211 Allen Craig .25 .60
212A Pablo Sandoval .25 .60
212B Sandoval SP Celebrate 12.00 30.00
213A R.A. Dickey .25 .60
213B Dickey SP Press 12.00 30.00
214 Ian Kinsler .25 .60
215 Ivan Nova .25 .60
216 Kris Medlen .25 .60
217 Carlos Ruiz .20 .50
218 David Price .25 .60
219 Troy Tulowitzki .30 .75
220 Brett Lawrie .25 .60

2013 Topps Opening Day Blue

*BLUE VET: 2.5X TO 6X BASIC
*BLUE RC: 1.5X TO 4X BASIC RC
STATED PRINT RUN 2013 SER.#'d SETS

2013 Topps Opening Day Toys R Us Purple Border

*BLUE VET: 6X TO 15X BASIC
*BLUE RC: 4X TO 10X BASIC RC

2013 Topps Opening Day Autographs

BL Boone Logan 4.00 10.00
CG Craig Gentry 4.00 10.00
DC David Cooper 4.00 10.00
DW David Wright 12.00 30.00
HR Hanley Ramirez 10.00 25.00
ID Ike Davis 4.00 10.00
JT Justin Turner 25.00 60.00
JV Josh Vitters 5.00 12.00
RP Rick Porcello 5.00 12.00
WM Will Middlebrooks 4.00 10.00

2013 Topps Opening Day Ballpark Fun

COMPLETE SET (25) 4.00 10.00
BF1 Dustin Pedroia .50 1.25
BF2 Josh Reddick .30 .75
BF3 Jay Bruce .40 1.00
BF4 Prince Fielder .40 1.00
BF5 Matt Kemp .40 1.00
BF6 Adam Jones .40 1.00
BF7 Manny Machado 2.00 5.00
BF8 Johan Santana .40 1.00
BF9 Bryce Harper .75 2.00
BF10 Miguel Cabrera .50 1.25
BF11 Evan Longoria .40 1.00
BF12 David Ortiz .50 1.25
BF13 Albert Pujols .60 1.50
BF14 Jayson Werth .40 1.00
BF15 Derek Jeter 1.25 3.00
BF16 Elvis Andrus .40 1.00
BF17 Aaron Hill .30 .75
BF18 Darwin Barney .30 .75
BF19 Brandon Phillips .30 .75
BF20 Alfonso Soriano .40 1.00
BF21 Jurickson Profar .40 1.00
BF22 David Price .40 1.00
BF23 Aroldis Chapman .50 1.25
BF24 Hanley Ramirez .40 1.00
BF25 Coco Crisp .30 .75

2013 Topps Opening Day Highlights

ODH1 Ryan Zimmerman 1.25 3.00
ODH2 Miguel Cabrera 1.50 4.00
ODH3 Felix Hernandez 1.25 3.00
ODH4 Jason Heyward 1.25 3.00
ODH5 Jose Altuve 1.25 3.00
ODH6 CC Sabathia 1.25 3.00
ODH7 Clayton Kershaw 2.50 6.00
ODH8 Roy Halladay 1.25 3.00
ODH9 Jay Bruce 1.25 3.00
ODH10 Jose Bautista 1.25 3.00

2013 Topps Opening Day Mascot Autographs

MA1 Mr. Met 30.00 80.00
MA2 Phillie Phanatic 40.00 80.00
MA3 Mariner Moose 15.00 40.00
MA4 Fredbird 15.00 40.00
MA5 Rangers Captain 10.00 25.00

2013 Topps Opening Day Mascots

COMPLETE SET (24) 12.50 30.00
M1 Mr. Met .75 2.00
M2 Phillie Phanatic .75 2.00
M3 Mariner Moose .75 2.00
M4 Fredbird .75 2.00
M5 Rangers Captain .75 2.00
M6 Oakland Athletics .75 2.00
M7 Screech .75 2.00
M8 Bernie Brewer .75 2.00
M9 Chicago White Sox .75 2.00
M10 Swinging Friar .75 2.00
M11 TC .75 2.00
M12 Baltimore Orioles .75 2.00
M13 Atlanta Braves .75 2.00
M14 Raymond .75 2.00
M15 Pirate Parrot .75 2.00
M16 Orbit .75 2.00
M17 Paws .75 2.00
M18 Dinger .75 2.00
M19 Toronto Blue Jays .75 2.00
M20 Arizona Diamondbacks .75 2.00
M21 Kansas City Royals .75 2.00
M22 Wally the Green Monster .75 2.00
M23 Gapper .75 2.00
M24 Slider .75 2.00

2013 Topps Opening Day Play Hard

COMPLETE SET (25) 8.00 20.00
PH1 Buster Posey .75 2.00
PH2 Bryce Harper 1.00 2.50
PH3 Mike Trout 5.00 12.00
PH4 Ian Kinsler .50 1.25
PH5 Brett Lawrie .50 1.25
PH6 Jason Heyward .50 1.25
PH7 Dustin Pedroia .60 1.50
PH8 Josh Reddick .40 1.00
PH9 Starlin Castro .60 1.50
PH10 Miguel Cabrera .60 1.50
PH11 David Ortiz .60 1.50
PH12 Joe Mauer .50 1.25
PH13 Albert Pujols .75 2.00
PH14 David Wright .50 1.25
PH15 Andrew McCutchen .60 1.50
PH16 Matt Kemp .50 1.25
PH17 Jay Bruce .50 1.25
PH18 Carlos Ruiz .40 1.00
PH19 Prince Fielder .50 1.25
PH20 Yadier Molina .75 2.00
PH21 David Freese .40 1.00
PH22 Paul Goldschmidt .60 1.50
PH23 Hanley Ramirez .50 1.25
PH24 Alex Rodriguez .75 2.00
PH25 Alex Gordon .50 1.25

2013 Topps Opening Day Stars

COMPLETE SET (25) 12.50 30.00
ODS1 Prince Fielder .60 1.50
ODS2 Justin Verlander .75 2.00
ODS3 Miguel Cabrera .75 2.00
ODS4 Buster Posey 1.00 2.50
ODS5 Derek Jeter 2.00 5.00
ODS6 Robinson Cano .60 1.50
ODS7 Evan Longoria .60 1.50
ODS8 David Ortiz .75 2.00
ODS9 Joe Mauer .60 1.50
ODS10 Albert Pujols 1.00 2.50
ODS11 Mike Trout 6.00 15.00
ODS12 Josh Hamilton .60 1.50
ODS13 Yu Darvish .75 2.00
ODS14 Felix Hernandez .60 1.50
ODS15 David Wright .60 1.50
ODS16 R.A. Dickey .60 1.50
ODS17 Adrian Gonzalez .60 1.50
ODS18 Cole Hamels .60 1.50
ODS19 Bryce Harper 1.25 3.00
ODS20 Stephen Strasburg .75 2.00
ODS21 Joey Votto .75 2.00
ODS22 Ryan Braun .60 1.50
ODS23 Andrew McCutchen .75 2.00
ODS24 Matt Kemp .60 1.50
ODS25 Yadier Molina 1.00 2.50

2013 Topps Opening Day Superstar Celebrations

COMPLETE SET (25) 8.00 20.00
SC1 Matt Kemp .50 1.25
SC2 Billy Butler .40 1.00
SC3 Albert Pujols .75 2.00
SC4 Joey Votto .60 1.50
SC5 Giancarlo Stanton .60 1.50
SC6 Adam Jones .50 1.25
SC7 Josh Reddick .40 1.00
SC8 Ryan Zimmerman .50 1.25
SC9 Bryce Harper 1.00 2.50
SC10 Joe Mauer .50 1.25
SC11 Jayson Werth .50 1.25
SC12 Justin Morneau .50 1.25
SC13 Corey Hart .40 1.00
SC14 Chipper Jones .60 1.50
SC15 Felix Hernandez .50 1.25
SC16 Mike Olt .50 1.25
SC17 Chase Headley .40 1.00
SC18 Josh Willingham .50 1.25
SC19 Alfonso Soriano .50 1.25
SC20 Prince Fielder .50 1.25
SC21 Buster Posey .75 2.00
SC22 Miguel Cabrera
SC23 Mike Trout 5.00 12.00
SC24 Justin Verlander .60 1.50
SC25 David Ortiz .60 1.50

2014 Topps Opening Day

COMP.SET w/o SP's (220) 12.00 30.00
SP VARIATION ODDS 1:222
PRINTING PLATE ODDS 1:1575
PLATE PRINT RUN 1 SET PER COLOR
BLACK-CYAN-MAGENTA-YELLOW ISSUED
NO PLATE PRICING DUE TO SCARCITY
1A Mike Trout 1.00 2.50
1B Trout SP w/Glove 25.00 60.00
2A Dustin Pedroia .20 .50
2B Pedroia SP Red jsy 20.00 50.00
3 James Paxton RC .30 .75
4 Yordano Ventura RC .25 .60
5 Freddie Freeman .25 .60
6 Adrian Beltre .20 .50
7A Jacoby Ellsbury .15 .40
7B Ellsbury SP Press 15.00 40.00
8 Mike Napoli .12 .30
9 R.A. Dickey .15 .40
10 Pedro Alvarez .12 .30
11 Josh Donaldson .15 .40
12 Mark Teixeira .15 .40
13 Gerrit Cole .20 .50
14 Trevor Rosenthal .15 .40
15 Martin Perez .15 .40
16 Carlos Gonzalez .15 .40
17 Aaron Hicks .15 .40
18 Jered Weaver .15 .40
19A Koji Uehara .12 .30
19B Uehara SP w/Ortiz 10.00 25.00
20 Mike Minor .12 .30
21 Stephen Strasburg .20 .50
22 Clay Buchholz .12 .30
23 Felix Hernandez .15 .40
24 Michael Wacha .15 .40
25 Torii Hunter .12 .30
26 Jonathan Papelbon .15 .40
27 Doug Fister .12 .30
28 Kyle Seager .12 .30
29 C.J. Wilson .12 .30
30 Jason Heyward .15 .40
31 Hunter Pence .15 .40
32 Sergio Romo .12 .30
33 Ben Revere .12 .30
34 Jeremy Hellickson .12 .30
35 Junior Lake .12 .30
36 Wilin Rosario .12 .30
37 Brandon Belt .15 .40
38 Michael Cuddyer .12 .30
39 Allen Craig .15 .40
40 Wil Myers .12 .30
41 Roy Halladay .15 .40
42A Mariano Rivera .25 .60
42B Rivera SP Tipping cap 25.00 60.00
43 Victor Martinez .15 .40
44 Wade Miley .12 .30
45 Carl Crawford .15 .40
46 Todd Helton .15 .40
47 Matt Harvey .15 .40
48 Paul Goldschmidt .20 .50
49 Ian Desmond .12 .30
50A Clayton Kershaw .30 .75
50B Kershaw SP Horizontal 20.00 50.00
51A David Ortiz .20 .50
51B Ortiz SP w/Trophy 20.00 50.00
52 Carlos Santana .15 .40
53 Paul Konerko .15 .40
54 Christian Yelich .25 .60
55 Nelson Cruz .20 .50
56 Jedd Gyorko .12 .30
57 Andrelton Simmons .12 .30
58 Justin Upton .15 .40
59 Francisco Liriano .12 .30
60 Alex Rios .15 .40
61 Yonder Alonso .12 .30
62 Matt Adams .12 .30
63 Starling Marte .15 .40
64 Tyler Skaggs .12 .30
65 Brett Gardner .15 .40
66 Albert Pujols .25 .60
67 Evan Gattis .12 .30
68 Patrick Corbin .15 .40
69 Jason Grilli .12 .30
70 Craig Kimbrel .15 .40
71 Jordan Zimmermann .15 .40
72A Jose Fernandez .20 .50
72B Fernandez SP w/Dino 20.00 50.00
73 Joe Mauer .15 .40
74 Matt Carpenter .20 .50
75 Will Middlebrooks .12 .30
76 Hisashi Iwakuma .15 .40
77 Jose Reyes .15 .40
78 Chris Davis .12 .30
79A Nick Castellanos RC .60 1.50
79B Castellanos SP Dugout 40.00 80.00
80A Justin Verlander .20 .50
80B Verlander SP Arm up 10.00 25.00
81 Hiroki Kuroda .12 .30
82 Rafael Soriano .12 .30
83 Cole Hamels .15 .40
84 Desmond Jennings .15 .40
85 Mike Leake .12 .30
86 Jeff Samardzija .12 .30
87 Jayson Werth .15 .40
88 Yoenis Cespedes .20 .50
89 Julio Teheran .15 .40
90 Jurickson Profar .15 .40
91 Matt Cain .15 .40
92 Coco Crisp .12 .30
93 Elvis Andrus .15 .40
94 Jim Henderson .12 .30
95 Todd Frazier .12 .30
96 Andre Rienzo RC .20 .50
97 Wilmer Flores RC .25 .60
98 Jose Altuve .15 .40
99 Pablo Sandoval .15 .40
100A Miguel Cabrera .20 .50
100B Cabrera SP Dugout 40.00 80.00
101 Zack Wheeler .15 .40
102 James Shields .12 .30
103A Adam Jones .15 .40
103B Jones SP w/Fans 12.00 30.00
104 Jason Kipnis .15 .40
105 Brian Dozier .15 .40
106 Matt Moore .15 .40
107 Joe Nathan .12 .30
108 Troy Tulowitzki .20 .50
109 Jay Bruce .15 .40
110 Jonny Gomes .12 .30
111 Aroldis Chapman .20 .50
112 Billy Butler .12 .30
113 Jon Lester .15 .40
114 Adam Dunn .15 .40
115 Max Scherzer .20 .50
116 Yunel Escobar .12 .30
117 Michael Choice RC .20 .50
118 J.J. Hardy .12 .30
119 Chase Utley .15 .40
120 Shin-Soo Choo .15 .40
121 Brandon Phillips .12 .30
122 Yadier Molina .25 .60
123 Lance Lynn .12 .30
124 Madison Bumgarner .15 .40
125 Tim Lincecum .15 .40
126 David Price .15 .40
127 Adam LaRoche .12 .30
128 Manny Machado .20 .50
129 Joey Votto .20 .50
130 Nick Swisher .15 .40
131 CC Sabathia .15 .40
132A Prince Fielder .15 .40
132B Fielder SP Press 20.00 50.00
133 Greg Holland .12 .30
134 David Wright .15 .40
135 Zack Greinke .20 .50
136 Anthony Rizzo .25 .60
137 Austin Jackson .12 .30
138 Enny Romero RC .20 .50
139 Jarred Cosart .12 .30
140A Brian McCann .15 .40
140B McCann SP Press 20.00 50.00
141A Kolten Wong RC .25 .60
141B Wong SP Arms up 20.00 50.00
142 Starlin Castro .12 .30
143A Taijuan Walker RC .20 .50
143B Walker SP No ball 12.00 30.00
144 Carlos Gomez .15 .40
145 Carlos Beltran .15 .40
146 Howie Kendrick .12 .30
147 Bobby Parnell .12 .30
148A Yu Darvish .20 .50
148B Darvish SP Blue shirt 15.00 40.00
149 Alex Rodriguez .25 .60
150A Buster Posey .25 .60
150B Posey SP Fielding 20.00 50.00
151 Chris Sale .20 .50
152 Darwin Barney .12 .30
153 Chris Archer .12 .30
154 Anthony Rendon .20 .50
155 Kendrys Morales .12 .30
156 Kris Medlen .15 .40
157 Jimmy Rollins .15 .40
158 Nolan Arenado .30 .75
159 Adam Wainwright .15 .40
160 Nate Schierholtz .12 .30
161 Nick Markakis .15 .40
162 Edwin Encarnacion .20 .50
163 Chris Johnson .12 .30
164 Sonny Gray .15 .40
165 Jose Iglesias .15 .40
166 Jose Bautista .15 .40
167 Sean Doolittle .12 .30
168 Kyle Lohse .12 .30
169 Martin Prado .12 .30
170A Billy Hamilton RC .25 .60
170B Hamilton SP Vertical 30.00 60.00
171 Ryan Zimmerman .15 .40
172 Josh Hamilton .15 .40
173 Josh Reddick .12 .30
174 Matt Davidson RC .25 .60
175 Trevor Plouffe .12 .30
176 Yovani Gallardo .12 .30
177 Nick Franklin .12 .30
178A Xander Bogaerts RC .60 1.50
178B Bogaerts SP Sliding 40.00 80.00
179 Johnny Cueto .15 .40
180 Alex Gordon .15 .40
181 Jean Segura .15 .40
182 Adrian Gonzalez .15 .40
183 Aramis Ramirez .12 .30
184 Ubaldo Jimenez .12 .30
185 Ian Kinsler .15 .40
186 Jonathan Schoop RC .20 .50
187 Giancarlo Stanton .20 .50
188 Andrew Lambo RC .20 .50
189 Matt Holliday .20 .50

190A Andrew McCutchen .20 .50
190B McCutch SP Fielding 15.00 40.00
191 Derek Holland .12 .30
192 Kevin Gausman .20 .50
193 Matt Kemp .15 .40
194 Shane Victorino .15 .40
195A Robinson Cano .15 .40
195B Cano SP Press 15.00 40.00
196 Mike Zunino .12 .30
197 David Freese .12 .30
198 Evan Longoria .15 .40
199 Ryan Braun .15 .40
200A Bryce Harper .30 .75
200B Harper SP Horizontal 20.00 50.00
201 Tony Cingrani .15 .40
202 Jake Marisnick RC .20 .50
203 Ryan Howard .15 .40
204 Shelby Miller .15 .40
205 Domonic Brown .15 .40
206 Carlos Ruiz .12 .30
207 Joe Kelly .12 .30
208 Hanley Ramirez .15 .40
209 Alfonso Soriano .15 .40
210 Eric Hosmer .15 .40
211 Mat Latos .15 .40
212 Mark Trumbo .12 .30
213 Hyun-Jin Ryu .15 .40
214 Travis d'Arnaud RC .25 .60
215 Cliff Lee .15 .40
216 Chase Headley .12 .30
217 Robbie Erlin RC .20 .50
218 Everth Cabrera .12 .30
219A Yasiel Puig .20 .50
219B Puig SP Throwing 50.00 100.00
220A Derek Jeter .50 1.25
220B Jeter SP w/Ball 50.00 120.00

2014 Topps Opening Day Blue

*BLUE: 2.5X TO 6X BASIC
*BLUE RC: 1.5X TO 4X BASIC RC
STATED ODDS 1:3
STATED PRINT RUN 2014 SER.#'d SETS

2014 Topps Opening Day Toys R Us Purple Border

*BLUE VET: 4X TO 10X BASIC
*BLUE RC: 2.5X TO 6X BASIC RC
220 Derek Jeter 12.00 30.00

2014 Topps Opening Day Autographs

STATED ODDS 1:278
ODAAL Andrew Lambo 6.00 15.00
ODAGP Glen Perkins 6.00 15.00
ODAJL Junior Lake 10.00 25.00
ODAKS Kyle Seager 6.00 15.00
ODAMO Marcell Ozuna 10.00 25.00
ODASC Steve Cishek 6.00 15.00
ODASD Steve Delabar 6.00 15.00
ODATF Todd Frazier 6.00 15.00
ODAWM Wil Myers 6.00 15.00
ODAZA Zoilo Almonte 8.00 20.00

2014 Topps Opening Day Between Innings

COMPLETE SET (10) 15.00 40.00
STATED ODDS 1:36
BI1 Racing Presidents 2.00 5.00
BI2 Pierogie Race 2.00 5.00
BI3 Hot Dog Race 2.00 5.00
BI4 Cincinnati Mascot Races 2.00 5.00
BI5 Hot Dog Cannon 2.00 5.00
BI6 Famous Racing Sausages 2.00 5.00
BI7 Prank the Opponent 2.00 5.00
BI8 Hug a Mascot 2.00 5.00
BI9 Thank the Fans 2.00 5.00
BI10 Start a Cheer 2.00 5.00

2014 Topps Opening Day Breaking Out

COMPLETE SET (20) 5.00 12.00
STATED ODDS 1:5
BO1 Jason Heyward .30 .75
BO2 Clayton Kershaw .60 1.50
BO3 Bryce Harper .60 1.50
BO4 Mike Trout 2.00 5.00
BO5 Buster Posey .50 1.25
BO6 Yoenis Cespedes .40 1.00
BO7 David Wright .30 .75
BO8 Evan Longoria .30 .75
BO9 Joe Mauer .30 .75
BO10 Jay Bruce .30 .75
BO11 Joey Votto .40 1.00
BO12 Troy Tulowitzki .40 1.00
BO13 Stephen Strasburg .40 1.00
BO14 Andrew McCutchen .40 1.00
BO15 Ryan Braun .30 .75
BO16 Robinson Cano .30 .75
BO17 Justin Verlander .40 1.00
BO18 Felix Hernandez .30 .75
BO19 Manny Machado .40 1.00
BO20 Paul Goldschmidt .40 1.00

2014 Topps Opening Day Fired Up

COMPLETE SET (30) 6.00 15.00
STATED ODDS 1:5
UP1 Bryce Harper .60 1.50
UP2 Yasiel Puig .40 1.00
UP3 Dustin Pedroia .40 1.00
UP4 Jon Lester .30 .75
UP5 Sergio Romo .25 .60
UP6 Jonathan Papelbon .30 .75
UP7 Justin Verlander .40 1.00
UP8 Felix Hernandez .30 .75
UP9 Yadier Molina .50 1.25
UP10 Yu Darvish .40 1.00
UP11 Jacoby Ellsbury .30 .75
UP12 Jered Weaver .30 .75
UP13 Matt Kemp .30 .75
UP14 Koji Uehara .25 .60
UP15 David Wright .30 .75
UP16 Eric Hosmer .30 .75
UP17 Hanley Ramirez .30 .75
UP18 Brandon Phillips .25 .60
UP19 CC Sabathia .30 .75
UP20 David Price .30 .75
UP21 Mike Trout 2.00 5.00
UP22 Allen Craig .30 .75
UP23 Matt Carpenter .40 1.00
UP24 Jason Grilli .25 .60
UP25 Brett Lawrie .30 .75
UP26 Adam Wainwright .30 .75
UP27 Craig Kimbrel .30 .75
UP28 Hunter Pence .30 .75
UP29 Adrian Gonzalez .30 .75
UP30 Jason Kipnis .30 .75

2014 Topps Opening Day Mascot Autographs

STATED ODDS 1:555
MABO Baltimore Orioles 20.00 50.00
MAPP Pirate Parrot 12.00 30.00
MAPAW Paws 12.00 30.00
MARAY Raymond 12.00 30.00
MAWGM Wally the Green Monster 20.00 50.00

2014 Topps Opening Day Mascots

COMPLETE SET (25) 12.00 30.00
COMMON CARD .75 2.00
STATED ODDS 1:5
M1 Kansas City Royals .75 2.00
M2 Orbit .75 2.00
M3 Baltimore Orioles .75 2.00
M4 Bernie Brewer .75 2.00
M5 Oakland Athletics .75 2.00
M6 Fredbird .75 2.00
M7 Chicago White Sox .75 2.00
M8 TC Bear .75 2.00
M9 Raymond .75 2.00
M10 Dinger .75 2.00
M11 Gapper .75 2.00
M12 Wally the Green Monster 1.00 2.50
M13 Phillie Phanatic 1.00 2.50
M14 Rangers Captain .75 2.00
M15 Screech .75 2.00
M16 Atlanta Braves .75 2.00
M17 Paws .75 2.00
M18 Baxter the Bobcat .75 2.00
M19 Slider .75 2.00
M20 Toronto Blue Jays .75 2.00
M21 Pirate Parrot .75 2.00
M22 Swinging Friar .75 2.00
M23 Mariner Moose .75 2.00
M24 Billy the Marlin .75 2.00
M25 Mr. Met 1.00 2.50

2014 Topps Opening Day Relics

STATED ODDS 1:278
ODRAG Alex Gordon 3.00 8.00
ODRDJ Desmond Jennings 3.00 8.00
ODRDJ Derek Jeter 30.00 60.00
ODRFF Freddie Freeman 4.00 10.00
ODRJB Jose Bautista 3.00 8.00
ODRKU Koji Uehara 6.00 15.00
ODRMK Matt Kemp 3.00 8.00
ODRSM Starling Marte 5.00 12.00
ODRTH Torii Hunter 2.50 6.00
ODRJBR Jay Bruce 4.00 10.00

2014 Topps Opening Day Stars

COMPLETE SET (25) 12.00 30.00
STATED ODDS 1:5
ODS1 Mike Trout 3.00 8.00
ODS2 Miguel Cabrera .60 1.50
ODS3 Andrew McCutchen .60 1.50
ODS4 Paul Goldschmidt .60 1.50
ODS5 Ryan Braun .50 1.25
ODS6 Clayton Kershaw 1.00 2.50
ODS7 Carlos Gonzalez .50 1.25
ODS8 Chris Davis .40 1.00
ODS9 Troy Tulowitzki .60 1.50
ODS10 Joe Mauer .50 1.25
ODS11 Buster Posey .75 2.00
ODS12 Stephen Strasburg .60 1.50
ODS13 Felix Hernandez .50 1.25
ODS14 David Ortiz .60 1.50
ODS15 Yasiel Puig .60 1.50
ODS16 Matt Kemp .50 1.25
ODS17 Dustin Pedroia .60 1.50
ODS18 Bryce Harper 1.00 2.50
ODS19 Yu Darvish .60 1.50
ODS20 David Wright .50 1.25
ODS21 Joey Votto .60 1.50
ODS22 Justin Upton .50 1.25
ODS23 Giancarlo Stanton .60 1.50
ODS24 Evan Longoria .50 1.25
ODS25 Derek Jeter 1.50 4.00

2014 Topps Opening Day Superstar Celebrations

COMPLETE SET (25) 5.00 12.00
COMMON CARD .25 .60
SEMISTARS .30 .75
UNLISTED STARS .40 1.00
STATED ODDS 1:5
SC1 Jay Bruce .30 .75
SC2 Alex Gordon .30 .75
SC3 Torii Hunter .25 .60
SC4 Freddie Freeman .50 1.25
SC5 Jose Bautista .30 .75
SC6 Chris Johnson .25 .60
SC7 Barry Zito .30 .75
SC8 Buster Posey .50 1.25
SC9 Chris Davis .25 .60
SC10 Adam Dunn .30 .75
SC11 Salvador Perez .30 .75
SC12 Carl Crawford .30 .75
SC13 Aramis Ramirez .25 .60
SC14 Yoenis Cespedes .40 1.00
SC15 Mike Napoli .25 .60
SC16 Jason Kipnis .30 .75
SC17 Nick Swisher .30 .75
SC18 Justin Upton .30 .75
SC19 Pablo Sandoval .30 .75
SC20 Andrelton Simmons .25 .60
SC21 Paul Goldschmidt .40 1.00
SC22 Bryce Harper .60 1.50
SC23 Josh Donaldson .30 .75
SC24 Jonny Gomes .25 .60
SC25 Yasiel Puig .40 1.00

2015 Topps Opening Day

COMP.SET w/o SP's (200) 12.00 30.00
SP VARIATION ODDS 1:307 HOBBY
PRINTING PLATE ODDS 1:2391 HOBBY
PLATE PRINT RUN 1 SET PER COLOR
BLACK-CYAN-MAGENTA-YELLOW ISSUED
NO PLATE PRICING DUE TO SCARCITY
1 Homer Bailey .12 .30
2 Curtis Granderson .15 .40
3 Todd Frazier .12 .30
4 Lonnie Chisenhall .12 .30
5A Jose Altuve .12 .30
5B Altuve SP w/Fans 15.00 40.00
6 Matt Carpenter .20 .50
7 Matt Garza .12 .30
8 Starling Marte .15 .40
9 Yu Darvish .20 .50
10 Pat Neshek .20 .50
11 Anthony Rizzo .25 .60
12 Chris Tillman .12 .30
13 Drew Hutchison .12 .30
14 Michael Taylor RC .20 .50
15 Gregory Polanco .15 .40
16 Jake Lamb RC .30 .75
17 David Ortiz .20 .50
18A Pablo Sandoval .15 .40
18B Sndvl SP w/Mascot 20.00 50.00
19 Adam Jones .15 .40
20 Miguel Cabrera .20 .50
21 Evan Gattis .12 .30
22 Gerrit Cole .20 .50
23 Greg Holland .12 .30
24 Tim Lincecum .15 .40
25 Jorge Soler RC .30 .75
26A Buster Posey .25 .60
26B Posey SP Parade 25.00 60.00
27 George Springer .15 .40
28 Jedd Gyorko .12 .30
29 John Lackey .15 .40
30A Danny Santana .12 .30
30B Sntna SP In dugout 12.00 30.00
31 David Wright .15 .40
32 Jordan Zimmermann .15 .40
33A Eric Hosmer .15 .40
33B Hosmer SP w/Fans 25.00 60.00
34 Michael Pineda .12 .30
35 Travis d'Arnaud .15 .40
36 Clay Buchholz .12 .30
37 Chris Archer .12 .30
38A Johnny Cueto .15 .40
38B Johnny Cueto SP Sunglasses 15.00 40.00
39 Albert Pujols .25 .60
40A Clayton Kershaw .30 .75
40B Kershaw SP Celebrate 50.00 120.00
41 Carlos Gonzalez .15 .40
42 Anthony Rendon .20 .50
43 Nick Castellanos .20 .50
44 Jonathan Lucroy .15 .40
45 Bryce Harper .30 .75
46 Chris Owings .12 .30
47 Jacoby Ellsbury .15 .40
48 Alex Rodriguez .25 .60
49 Jonny Gomes .12 .30
50 Rougned Odor .15 .40
51 Aramis Ramirez .12 .30
52 Roenis Elias .12 .30
53 Jean Segura .12 .30
54 Jeff Samardzija .12 .30
55 Francisco Liriano .12 .30
56 Elvis Andrus .15 .40
57 Salvador Perez .15 .40
58 Starlin Castro .12 .30
59 Paul Goldschmidt .20 .50
60 Ryan Braun .15 .40
61 Yovani Gallardo .12 .30
62 Jose Bautista .15 .40
63 Adrian Gonzalez .15 .40
64 Anibal Sanchez .12 .30
65 Michael Wacha .15 .40
66A Andrew McCutchen .20 .50
66B McCtchn SP On deck 30.00 80.00
67 Josh Harrison .12 .30
68A Joe Mauer .15 .40
68B Mauer SP In dugout 15.00 40.00
69 James Shields .12 .30
70 Alfredo Simon .12 .30
71 J.D. Martinez .20 .50
72 Coco Crisp .12 .30
73 Kyle Seager .12 .30
74A Derek Norris .12 .30
74B Ellsbury SP Stretching 30.00 80.00
75 Jimmy Rollins .15 .40
76 Matt Shoemaker .15 .40
77A Mike Trout 1.00 2.50
77B Trout SP On deck 400.00 800.00
78 Garrett Richards .15 .40
79 Jered Weaver .15 .40
80 Alexei Ramirez .15 .40
81 Aroldis Chapman .20 .50
82 Joey Votto .20 .50
83 Corey Kluber .15 .40
84 Troy Tulowitzki .20 .50
85 Zack Greinke .20 .50
86 Giancarlo Stanton .20 .50
87 Josh Hamilton .15 .40
88 Christian Yelich .25 .60
89 Brian Dozier .15 .40
90 Daniel Murphy .15 .40
91 Brett Gardner .15 .40
92 Mark Teixeira .15 .40
93 Carlos Beltran .15 .40
94 Sonny Gray .15 .40
95 Jonathan Papelbon .15 .40
96A Madison Bumgarner .15 .40
96B Bmgrnr SP Parade 30.00 80.00
97 Lance Lynn .12 .30
98 Adam Wainwright .15 .40
99 Evan Longoria .15 .40
100 Shin-Soo Choo .15 .40
101 Edwin Encarnacion .20 .50
102 Gio Gonzalez .15 .40
103 Ryan Zimmerman .15 .40
104 Anthony Ranaudo RC .20 .50
105A Jose Abreu .20 .50
105B Abreu SP Pinstripes 20.00 50.00
106A Jacob deGrom .40 1.00
106B deGrom SP Blue jacket 40.00 100.00
107 Erick Aybar .12 .30
108 R.A. Dickey .15 .40
109A Brandon Finnegan RC .20 .50
109B Fnngn SP Gatorade 30.00 80.00
110 Dalton Pompey RC .25 .60
111 Dilson Herrera RC .25 .60
112 Bryce Brentz RC .20 .50
113 Matt Barnes RC .20 .50
114 Hunter Pence .15 .40
115 Jason Kipnis .15 .40
116 David Freese .12 .30
117 Hector Santiago .12 .30
118 Mookie Betts .40 1.00
119A Craig Kimbrel .15 .40
119B Kmbrl SP w/Award 15.00 40.00
120 Jay Bruce .15 .40
121 Mike Leake .12 .30
122A Justin Verlander .20 .50
122B Vrlndr SP w/Fans 25.00 60.00
123A Victor Martinez .15 .40
123B Mrtnz SP Press conference 15.00 40.00
124 Henderson Alvarez .12 .30
125 Adeiny Hechavarria .12 .30
126 Oswaldo Arcia .12 .30
127 Francisco Cervelli .12 .30
128 Chase Headley .12 .30
129 Angel Pagan .12 .30
130 Matt Holliday .20 .50
131 Yadier Molina .25 .60
132 Peter Bourjos .12 .30
133 Jose Molina .12 .30
134 Stephen Strasburg .20 .50
135 Stephen Drew .12 .30
136 Drew Smyly .12 .30
137 Dellin Betances .15 .40
138 Gregor Blanco .12 .30
139 Marcell Ozuna .20 .50
140A Hanley Ramirez .15 .40
140B Rmrz SP Press conference 15.00 40.00
141 Julio Teheran .15 .40
142 Zack Wheeler .15 .40
143 Freddie Freeman .25 .60
144A Robinson Cano .15 .40
144B Cano SP Signing 30.00 80.00
145 Kolten Wong .15 .40
146 Ben Zobrist .15 .40
147 Carlos Martinez .15 .40
148 Ryan Howard .15 .40
149 Jason Castro .12 .30
150 Hisashi Iwakuma .15 .40
151A Rusney Castillo RC .25 .60
151B Cstllo SP w/Ortiz 25.00 60.00
152 Ian Desmond .12 .30
153 Cole Hamels .15 .40
154 Tanner Roark .12 .30
155 Xander Bogaerts .20 .50
156 Daniel Corcino RC .20 .50
157 Cory Spangenberg RC .20 .50
158 Wilmer Flores .15 .40
159A Justin Morneau .15 .40
159B Morneau SP w/ Puig 20.00 50.00
160 Kevin Kiermaier .15 .40
161 Arismendy Alcantara .12 .30
162 Chris Davis .12 .30
163 Rafael Montero .12 .30
164 Jose Reyes .15 .40
165 Ian Kinsler .15 .40
166 Masahiro Tanaka .15 .40
167 Mike Minor .12 .30
168 Kennys Vargas .12 .30
169 Matt Adams .12 .30
170 Marcus Stroman .15 .40
171 Andrelton Simmons .12 .30
172A David Price .15 .40
172B Price SP Glasses 25.00 60.00
173 Alex Cobb .12 .30
174 Michael Brantley .15 .40
175 Manny Machado .20 .50
176 Lucas Duda .15 .40
177 Billy Hamilton .15 .40
178 Carlos Santana .15 .40
179 David Robertson .15 .40
180 Doug Fister .12 .30
181 Jose Fernandez .20 .50
182 Adrian Beltre .20 .50
183 Dustin Pedroia .20 .50
184 Guilder Rodriguez RC .20 .50
185 Maikel Franco RC .25 .60
186 Felix Hernandez .15 .40
187 Daniel Norris RC .20 .50
188A Javier Baez RC 1.50 4.00
188B Baez SP Sunglasses 30.00 80.00
189 CC Sabathia .15 .40
190 Cliff Lee .15 .40
191 Jayson Werth .15 .40
192 Allen Craig .12 .30
193 Joc Pederson RC .75 2.00
194 Andrew Cashner .12 .30
195 Carlos Gomez .12 .30
196 Brandon Phillips .12 .30
197 Brian McCann .15 .40
198A Yasiel Puig .20 .50
198B Puig SP w/Fans 25.00 60.00
199 Aaron Sanchez .15 .40
200 Desmond Jennings .15 .40

2015 Topps Opening Day Blue Foil

*BLUE: 2.5X TO 6X BASIC
*BLUE RC: 1.5X TO 4X BASIC RC
STATED ODDS 1:5 HOBBY

2015 Topps Opening Day Toys R Us Purple Border

*PURPLE VET: 4X TO 10X BASIC
*PURPLE RC: 2.5X TO 6X BASIC RC

2015 Topps Opening Day Autographs

STATED ODDS 1:383 HOBBY
ODAAA Arismendy Alcantara 4.00 10.00
ODACO Chris Owings 4.00 10.00
ODAJB Javier Baez 20.00 50.00
ODAJP Joe Panik 20.00 50.00
ODAJS Jonathan Schoop 12.00 30.00
ODALD Lucas Duda 5.00 12.00
ODAMB Mookie Betts 30.00 80.00
ODAMF Mike Foltynewicz 6.00 15.00
ODAMZ Mike Zunino 4.00 10.00
ODARC Rusney Castillo 12.00 30.00
ODARD Rubby De La Rosa 4.00 10.00
ODARE Roenis Elias 4.00 10.00
ODATT Troy Tulowitzki 20.00 50.00

2015 Topps Opening Day Franchise Flashbacks

COMPLETE SET (20) 4.00 10.00
STATED ODDS 1:5 HOBBY
FF01 Craig Kimbrel .25 .60
FF02 Ryan Braun .25 .60
FF03 George Springer .25 .60
FF04 Robinson Cano .25 .60
FF05 Anthony Rizzo .40 1.00
FF06 Manny Machado .30 .75
FF07 Gregor Blanco .20 .50
FF08 Julio Teheran .25 .60
FF09 Alex Gordon .25 .60
FF10 Tim Lincecum .25 .60
FF11 Adrian Beltre .30 .75
FF12 Nick Castellanos .30 .75
FF13 Jose Altuve .25 .60
FF14 Jered Weaver .25 .60
FF15 Danny Santana .20 .50
FF16 Jonathan Lucroy .25 .60
FF17 Starlin Castro .20 .50
FF18 Chase Utley .25 .60
FF19 Freddie Freeman .40 1.00
FF20 Mike Trout 1.50 4.00

2015 Topps Opening Day Hit the Dirt

COMPLETE SET (15) 4.00 10.00
STATED ODDS 1:5 HOBBY
HTD01 Bryce Harper .60 1.50
HTD02 Lorenzo Cain .25 .60
HTD03 Billy Hamilton .30 .75
HTD04 Mike Trout 2.00 5.00
HTD05 Jacoby Ellsbury .30 .75
HTD06 Ian Kinsler .30 .75
HTD07 Jose Reyes .30 .75
HTD08 Carlos Gomez .25 .60
HTD09 George Springer .30 .75
HTD10 Ben Revere .25 .60
HTD11 Starling Marte .30 .75
HTD12 Yasiel Puig .40 1.00
HTD13 Elvis Andrus .30 .75
HTD14 Denard Span .25 .60
HTD15 Dustin Pedroia .40 1.00

2015 Topps Opening Day Mascot Autographs

STATED ODDS 1:776 HOBBY
MABT Billy the Marlin 12.00 30.00
MAPP Phillie Phanatic 20.00 50.00
MARC Rangers Captain 12.00 30.00
MATB TC Bear 12.00 30.00
MATR Theodore Roosevelt 12.00 30.00

2015 Topps Opening Day Mascots

COMPLETE SET (25) 10.00 25.00
STATED ODDS 1:5 HOBBY
M01 Baxter the Bobcat .60 1.50
M02 Atlanta Braves .60 1.50
M03 Baltimore Orioles .60 1.50
M04 Wally the Green Monster .75 2.00
M05 Clark .60 1.50
M06 Chicago White Sox .60 1.50
M07 Gapper .60 1.50
M08 Rosie Red .60 1.50
M09 Slider .60 1.50
M10 Dinger .60 1.50
M11 Paws .60 1.50
M12 Billy the Marlin .60 1.50
M13 Orbit .60 1.50
M14 Kansas City Royals .60 1.50
M15 TC Bear .60 1.50
M16 Bernie Brewer .60 1.50
M17 Mr. Met .75 2.00
M18 Phillie Phanatic .75 2.00
M19 Pirate Parrot .60 1.50
M20 Swinging Friar .60 1.50
M21 Mariner Moose .60 1.50
M22 Fredbird .60 1.50
M23 Raymond .60 1.50
M24 Rangers Captain .60 1.50
M25 Theodore Roosevelt .60 1.50

2015 Topps Opening Day Relics

STATED ODDS 1:383 HOBBY
ODRAM Andrew McCutchen 6.00 15.00
ODRBP Buster Posey 6.00 15.00
ODRDO David Ortiz 5.00 12.00
ODRDW David Wright 4.00 10.00
ODRKW Kolten Wong 6.00 15.00
ODRMC Miguel Cabrera 6.00 15.00
ODRNC Nick Castellanos 6.00 15.00
ODRTT Troy Tulowitzki 5.00 12.00
ODRYP Yasiel Puig 5.00 12.00
ODRYV Yordano Ventura 6.00 15.00

2015 Topps Opening Day Stadium Scenes

COMPLETE SET (15) 2.50 6.00
STATED ODDS 1:5 HOBBY
STABS Ben Shaw .25 .60
STACP Cameron Payne .25 .60
STADA Dylan Abruscato .25 .60
STADD David Joseph Dick Jr. .25 .60
STADR Donny Racz .25 .60
STAJB Jim Brady .25 .60
STAJF Jordyn Fernandez .25 .60
STAJFJ Juan Fernandez Jr. .25 .60
STAJW Joey Wright .25 .60
STAKR Kevin Ransom .25 .60
STALD Luca Djelosevic .25 .60
STALM Lance McKinnon .25 .60
STARG Robert Grunbaum .25 .60
STARGM Ryan Goose-Meils .25 .60
STATC Tom Cicotello .25 .60
STATCC Tim Culin-Couwels .25 .60
STATV Tony Voda .25 .60

2015 Topps Opening Day Stars

COMPLETE SET (25) 20.00 50.00
STATED ODDS 1:24 HOBBY
ODS01 Mike Trout 5.00 12.00
ODS02 Miguel Cabrera 1.00 2.50
ODS03 Andrew McCutchen 1.00 2.50
ODS04 Jose Abreu 1.00 2.50
ODS05 Clayton Kershaw 1.50 4.00
ODS06 Yasiel Puig 1.00 2.50
ODS07 Felix Hernandez .75 2.00
ODS08 Robinson Cano .75 2.00
ODS09 David Ortiz 1.00 2.50
ODS10 Freddie Freeman 1.25 3.00
ODS11 Buster Posey 1.25 3.00
ODS12 Masahiro Tanaka .75 2.00
ODS13 Paul Goldschmidt 1.00 2.50
ODS14 Bryce Harper 1.50 4.00
ODS15 Yadier Molina 1.25 3.00
ODS16 Adam Jones .75 2.00
ODS17 Evan Longoria .75 2.00
ODS18 David Wright .75 2.00
ODS19 Matt Harvey .75 2.00
ODS20 Joe Mauer .75 2.00
ODS21 Ryan Braun .75 2.00
ODS22 Yu Darvish 1.00 2.50
ODS23 Prince Fielder .75 2.00
ODS24 Troy Tulowitzki 1.00 2.50
ODS25 Jacob deGrom 2.00 5.00

2015 Topps Opening Day Superstar Celebrations

COMPLETE SET (25) 5.00 12.00
STATED ODDS 1:5 HOBBY
SC01 Mike Trout 2.00 5.00
SC02 Madison Bumgarner .30 .75
SC03 Salvador Perez .30 .75
SC04 Giancarlo Stanton .40 1.00
SC05 Tim Lincecum .30 .75
SC06 Rajai Davis .25 .60
SC07 Jordan Zimmermann .30 .75
SC08 Bryce Harper .60 1.50
SC09 Clayton Kershaw .60 1.50
SC10 Chase Utley .30 .75
SC11 Jose Abreu .40 1.00
SC12 Tommy Hunter .25 .60
SC13 Miguel Cabrera .40 1.00
SC14 Albert Pujols .50 1.25
SC15 Anthony Rizzo .50 1.25
SC16 Kolten Wong .30 .75
SC17 Michael Brantley .30 .75
SC18 Mike Napoli .25 .60
SC19 Mike Moustakas .30 .75
SC20 Edwin Encarnacion .40 1.00
SC21 Coco Crisp .25 .60
SC22 Kyle Seager .25 .60
SC23 Jason Castro .25 .60
SC24 Adrian Beltre .40 1.00
SC25 Evan Gattis .25 .60

2015 Topps Opening Day Team Spirit

COMPLETE SET (10) 8.00 20.00
STATED ODDS 1:36 HOBBY
TS01 Mike Trout 4.00 10.00
TS02 Phillie Phanatic .75 2.00
TS03 Madison Bumgarner .60 1.50
TS04 Greg Holland .50 1.25
TS05 Miguel Cabrera .75 2.00
TS06 Clayton Kershaw 1.25 3.00
TS07 Bryce Harper 1.25 3.00
TS08 TC Bear .75 2.00
TS09 Jorge Soler .75 2.00
TS10 Adam Eaton .50 1.25

2016 Topps Opening Day

COMP.SET w/o SP's (200) 10.00 25.00
SP VARIATION ODDS 1:393 HOBBY
PRINTING PLATE ODDS 1:3070 HOBBY
PLATE PRINT RUN 1 SET PER COLOR
BLACK-CYAN-MAGENTA-YELLOW ISSUED
NO PLATE PRICING DUE TO SCARCITY
OD1 Mike Trout 1.00 2.50
OD2A Noah Syndergaard .15 .40
OD2B Syndrgrd SP w/Team 25.00 60.00
OD3 Carlos Santana .15 .40
OD4 Derek Norris .12 .30
OD5A Kenley Jansen .15 .40
OD5B Jansen SP Peace 12.00 30.00
OD6 Luke Jackson RC .20 .50
OD7 Brian Johnson RC .20 .50
OD8 Russell Martin .12 .30
OD9 Rick Porcello .15 .40
OD10 Felix Hernandez .15 .40
OD11 Danny Salazar .15 .40
OD12A Dellin Betances .15 .40
OD12B Btncs SP T-shirt 20.00 50.00
OD13 Rob Refsnyder RC .25 .60
OD14 James Shields .12 .30
OD15 Brandon Crawford .15 .40
OD16 Tom Murphy RC .20 .50
OD17A Kris Bryant .25 .60
OD17B Bryant SP Celebrate 50.00 120.00
OD18 Richie Shaffer RC .20 .50
OD19 Brandon Belt .15 .40
OD20 Anthony Rizzo .25 .60
OD21A Mike Moustakas .15 .40
OD21B Mstks SP Goggles 12.00 30.00
OD22 Roberto Osuna .12 .30
OD23 Jimmy Nelson .12 .30
OD24 Luis Severino RC .25 .60
OD25 Justin Verlander .20 .50
OD26 Ryan Braun .15 .40
OD27 Chris Tillman .12 .30
OD28A Alex Rodriguez .25 .60
OD28B Rdrgz SP Signing autos 20.00 50.00
OD29A Ichiro Suzuki .25 .60
OD29B Ichiro SP Pitching
OD30 R.A. Dickey .15 .40
OD31 Alex Gordon .15 .40
OD32A Raul Mondesi RC .40 1.00
OD32B Mndsi SP w/Trophy
OD33 Josh Reddick .12 .30
OD34 Wilson Ramos .12 .30
OD35 Julio Teheran .15 .40
OD36 Colin Rea RC .20 .50
OD37 Stephen Vogt .15 .40
OD38 Jon Gray RC .20 .50
OD39 DJ LeMahieu .20 .50
OD40 Michael Taylor .12 .30
OD41 Ketel Marte RC .40 1.00
OD42 Albert Pujols .25 .60
OD43 Max Kepler RC .30 .75
OD44 Lorenzo Cain .12 .30
OD45 Carlos Beltran .15 .40
OD46 Carl Edwards Jr. RC .25 .60
OD47A Kyle Schwarber RC .60 1.50
OD47B Schwrbr SP Celebrate 30.00 80.00
OD48 Corey Seager RC .20 .50
OD49 Erasmo Ramirez .12 .30
OD50A Josh Donaldson .12 .30
OD50B Dnldsn SP Press conf 12.00 30.00
OD51A Andrew McCutchen .20 .50
OD51B McCtchn SP Clmnte Awrd 60.00 150.00
OD52A Miguel Sano RC .30 .75
OD52B Sano SP Glasses 40.00 100.00
OD53 Joc Pederson .15 .40
OD54 Marco Estrada .12 .30
OD55 Carlos Rodon .20 .50
OD56 Didi Gregorius .15 .40
OD57 Chris Sale .20 .50
OD58A Carlos Correa .20 .50
OD58B Correa SP Signing autos 15.00 40.00
OD59 David Peralta .12 .30
OD60 Andrew Miller .15 .40
OD61A Adeiny Hechavarria .12 .30
OD61B Hchvrra SP w/Teammate 10.00 25.00
OD62 Yadier Molina .25 .60
OD63 Freddie Freeman .25 .60
OD64 Dalton Pompey .15 .40
OD65 Hector Rondon .12 .30
OD66 Sonny Gray .15 .40
OD67 Max Scherzer .20 .50
OD68 Jacob deGrom .40 1.00
OD69 Yordano Ventura .15 .40
OD70 Aaron Nola RC .40 1.00
OD71 Robbie Ray .12 .30
OD72 Michael Conforto RC .25 .60
OD73 George Springer .15 .40
OD74 Brett Gardner .15 .40
OD75A Prince Fielder .15 .40
OD75B Fielder SP w/Teammate 12.00 30.00
OD76 Adam Jones .15 .40
OD77A Xander Bogaerts .20 .50
OD77B Bogaerts SP w/Fans 25.00 60.00
OD78 Joey Gallo .15 .40
OD79 A.J. Pollock .12 .30
OD80 Jung Ho Kang .12 .30
OD81 Maikel Franco .15 .40
OD82 Delino DeShields Jr. .12 .30
OD83 Chris Heston .12 .30
OD84 Yasmany Tomas .12 .30
OD85 Carlos Carrasco .12 .30
OD86 Devon Travis .12 .30
OD87 Yasmani Grandal .12 .30
OD88 Odubel Herrera .15 .40
OD89 J.D. Martinez .20 .50
OD90 Jonathan Lucroy .15 .40
OD91A Madison Bumgarner .15 .40
OD91B Bmgrnr SP w/Teammate 12.00 30.00
OD92 Jean Segura .15 .40
OD93 Corey Kluber .15 .40
OD94 Lucas Duda .15 .40
OD95 Jon Lester .15 .40
OD96 Gregory Polanco .15 .40
OD97 Joe Mauer .15 .40
OD98 Jackie Bradley Jr. .20 .50
OD99A Ruben Tejada .12 .30
OD99B Tjda SP Tipping cap 10.00 25.00
OD100 Clayton Kershaw .30 .75
OD101 Jose Iglesias .15 .40
OD102 Josh Hamilton .15 .40
OD103 Brock Holt .12 .30
OD104 Manny Machado .20 .50
OD105 Kolten Wong .15 .40
OD106 Victor Martinez .15 .40
OD107A Matt Reynolds RC .20 .50
OD107B Rynlds SP Hand on hip 20.00 50.00
OD108 Adam Wainwright .15 .40
OD109 Michael Reed RC .20 .50
OD110A Francisco Lindor .20 .50
OD110B Lindor SP Signing autos 25.00 60.00
OD111 Edwin Encarnacion .20 .50
OD112 Mookie Betts .40 1.00
OD113 Alex Cobb .12 .30
OD114 Michael Brantley .15 .40
OD115 Carlos Gomez .12 .30
OD116 Jason Kipnis .15 .40
OD117 Michael Pineda .12 .30
OD118 Mike Foltynewicz .12 .30
OD119 Yasiel Puig .20 .50
OD120A Wil Myers .15 .40
OD120B Myers SP No bat 12.00 30.00
OD121 Addison Russell .20 .50
OD122A Masahiro Tanaka .15 .40
OD122B Tanaka SP Goggles 12.00 30.00
OD123 Johnny Giavotella .12 .30
OD124 Trevor Plouffe .12 .30
OD125 Hector Olivera RC .20 .50
OD126 Ian Kinsler .15 .40
OD127 Matt Harvey .15 .40
OD128A Salvador Perez .15 .40
OD128B Perez SP w/Trophy 20.00 50.00
OD129 Dee Gordon .12 .30
OD130 Brian McCann .15 .40
OD131 Carlos Martinez .15 .40
OD132 Brandon Drury RC .30 .75
OD133 Greg Holland .12 .30
OD134 Joe Panik .15 .40
OD135 Adrian Gonzalez .15 .40
OD136 Starling Marte .15 .40
OD137 Mike Fiers .12 .30
OD138 David Ortiz .20 .50
OD139 Dustin Pedroia .20 .50
OD140 Glen Perkins .12 .30
OD141 Christian Yelich .25 .60
OD142 Miguel Almonte RC .20 .50
OD143 Evan Gattis .12 .30
OD144 Adrian Beltre .20 .50
OD145 Domonic Brown .15 .40
OD146 Gary Sanchez RC .60 1.50
OD147 Jose Altuve .15 .40
OD148 Robinson Cano .15 .40
OD149 Nick Markakis .15 .40
OD150 Miguel Cabrera .20 .50
OD151 Kyle Barraclough RC .20 .50
OD152A Carlos Gonzalez .15 .40
OD152B Grulz SP Celebrate 12.00 30.00
OD153 Danny Valencia .15 .40
OD154 Trea Turner RC .60 1.50
OD155 Jake Odorizzi .12 .30
OD156 Greg Bird RC .25 .60
OD157 Odrisamer Despaigne .12 .30
OD158 Peter O'Brien RC .20 .50
OD159 James McCann .15 .40
OD160 Anthony Gose .12 .30
OD161 Stephen Piscotty RC .30 .75
OD162 Frankie Montas RC .25 .60
OD163 Gerrit Cole .20 .50
OD164 Joey Votto .20 .50
OD165 Matt Kemp .15 .40
OD166 Hanley Ramirez .15 .40
OD167 Henry Owens RC .25 .60
OD168 Nick Castellanos .20 .50
OD169 Taylor Jungmann .12 .30
OD170 Jose Quintana .12 .30

2016 Topps Opening Day

OD171 Lance McCullers .12 .30
OD172 Randal Grichuk .12 .30
OD173 Miguel Castro .12 .30
OD174 J.T. Realmuto .20 .50
OD175 Alex Rios .15 .40
OD176 Steven Matz .12 .30
OD177 Eduardo Rodriguez .12 .30
OD178 Drew Smyly .12 .30
OD179 Daniel Norris .12 .30
OD180 Pedro Alvarez .12 .30
OD181 Justin Bour .15 .40
OD182 Matt Adams .12 .30
OD183A Buster Posey .25 .60
OD183B Posey SP Batting 40.00 100.00
OD184 Giancarlo Stanton .20 .50
OD185 Tyson Ross .12 .30
OD186 Jacoby Ellsbury .15 .40
OD187 Jose Bautista .15 .40
OD188 Troy Tulowitzki .20 .50
OD189 Kyle Seager .12 .30
OD190 Billy Hamilton .15 .40
OD191 Jose Fernandez .20 .50
OD192 Luis Valbuena .12 .30
OD193 Hector Santiago .12 .30
OD194 Stephen Strasburg .20 .50
OD195 Jake Arrieta .15 .40
OD196 Jason Castro .12 .30
OD197 Aroldis Chapman .20 .50
OD198 Avisail Garcia .15 .40
OD199 Paul Goldschmidt .20 .50
OD200 Bryce Harper .30 .75

2016 Topps Opening Day Blue Foil

*BLUE: 3X TO 8X BASIC
*BLUE RC: 2X TO 5X BASIC RC
STATED ODDS 1:7 HOBBY

2016 Topps Opening Day Toys R Us Purple Foil

*PURPLE: 10X TO 25X BASIC
*PURPLE RC: 6X TO 15X BASIC RC
INSERTED IN TOYS R US PACKS

2016 Topps Opening Day Alternate Reality

COMPLETE SET (15) 4.00 10.00
STATED ODDS 1:5 HOBBY
AR1 Manny Machado .30 .75
AR2 Mookie Betts .60 1.50
AR3 Troy Tulowitzki .30 .75
AR4 Matt Harvey .25 .60
AR5 Bryce Harper .50 1.25
AR6 Kris Bryant .40 1.00
AR7 Andrew McCutchen .30 .75
AR8 Mike Trout 1.50 4.00
AR9 Eric Hosmer .25 .60
AR10 Miguel Sano .30 .75
AR11 Carlos Correa .30 .75
AR12 Clayton Kershaw .50 1.25
AR13 Buster Posey .40 1.00
AR14 Jose Abreu .30 .75
AR15 Freddie Freeman .40 1.00

2016 Topps Opening Day Autographs

STATED ODDS 1:491 HOBBY
ODAAB Archie Bradley 4.00 10.00
ODAAN Aaron Nola 8.00 20.00
ODABB Brandon Belt 6.00 15.00
ODACC Carlos Correa 100.00 200.00
ODACR Carlos Rodon
ODACS Corey Seager 50.00 100.00
ODADF Doug Fister 4.00 10.00
ODADL DJ LeMahieu 8.00 20.00
ODAFL Francisco Lindor 15.00 40.00
ODAJHA Jesse Hahn 4.00 10.00
ODAJHM Jason Hammel 5.00 12.00
ODAKB Kris Bryant 100.00 200.00
ODAKS Kyle Schwarber 20.00 50.00
ODAKW Kolten Wong 5.00 12.00
ODALS Luis Severino
ODAMC Michael Conforto 25.00 60.00
ODAMS Miguel Sano 20.00 50.00
ODAMSC Matt Shoemaker 5.00 12.00
ODARR Rob Refsnyder

2016 Topps Opening Day Bubble Trouble

COMPLETE SET (10) 12.00 30.00
STATED ODDS 1:36 HOBBY
BT1 Robinson Cano 1.00 2.50
BT2 Felix Hernandez 1.00 2.50
BT3 Salvador Perez 1.00 2.50
BT4 Chris Archer .75 2.00
BT5 Albert Pujols 1.50 4.00
BT6 Manny Machado 1.25 3.00
BT7 Adam Eaton .75 2.00
BT8 Domonic Brown 1.00 2.50
BT9 Nick Castellanos 1.25 3.00
BT10 Troy Tulowitzki 1.25 3.00

2016 Topps Opening Day Heavy Hitters

COMPLETE SET (20) 4.00 10.00
STATED ODDS 1:5 HOBBY
HH1 Bryce Harper .50 1.25
HH2 Giancarlo Stanton .30 .75
HH3 Miguel Cabrera .30 .75
HH4 Kyle Schwarber .60 1.50
HH5 Miguel Sano .30 .75
HH6 Chris Davis .20 .50
HH7 Nelson Cruz .30 .75
HH8 Nolan Arenado .50 1.25
HH9 Jose Bautista .25 .60
HH10 Mike Trout 1.50 4.00
HH11 David Ortiz .30 .75
HH12 Paul Goldschmidt .30 .75
HH13 Joey Votto .30 .75
HH14 Jose Abreu .30 .75
HH15 Prince Fielder .25 .60

2016 Topps Opening Day Mascot Autographs

STATED ODDS 1:482 HOBBY
MAC Clark 15.00 40.00
MAO Orbit 12.00 30.00
MABM Billy the Marlin 12.00 30.00
MAGW George Washington 20.00 50.00
MAMM Mariner Moose 12.00 30.00
MAMR Mr. Red 15.00 40.00
MAWM Wally the Green Monster 12.00 30.00
MAPPA Pirate Parrot 15.00 40.00

2016 Topps Opening Day Mascots

COMPLETE SET (25) 8.00 20.00
STATED ODDS 1:5 HOBBY
M1 Paws .60 1.50
M2 Billy the Marlin .60 1.50
M3 Rally Monkey .60 1.50
M4 Wally the Green Monster .60 1.50
M5 Mr. Red .60 1.50
M6 Diamondbacks Mascot .60 1.50
M7 Orbit .60 1.50
M8 Clark .60 1.50
M9 Mrs. Met .60 1.50
M10 TC Bear .60 1.50
M11 Braves Mascot .60 1.50
M12 Slider .60 1.50
M13 Dinger .60 1.50
M14 Royals Mascot .60 1.50
M15 Hank the Ballpark Pup .60 1.50
M16 Phillie Phanatic .60 1.50
M17 Pirate Parrot .60 1.50
M18 Swinging Friar .60 1.50
M19 Mariner Moose .60 1.50
M20 Fredbird .60 1.50
M21 White Sox Mascot .60 1.50
M22 A's Mascot .60 1.50
M23 Raymond .60 1.50
M24 Rangers Captain .60 1.50
M25 Blue Jays Mascot .60 1.50

2016 Topps Opening Day Relics

STATED ODDS 1:491 HOBBY
ODRI Ichiro Suzuki 6.00 15.00
ODRAR Anthony Rizzo 6.00 15.00
ODRBP Buster Posey 6.00 15.00
ODRCK Clayton Kershaw 8.00 20.00
ODRDO David Ortiz 5.00 12.00
ODRFF Freddie Freeman 6.00 15.00
ODRJM Joe Mauer 4.00 10.00
ODRMW Michael Wacha 4.00 10.00
ODRPF Prince Fielder 4.00 10.00
ODRPS Pablo Sandoval 6.00 15.00
ODRRC Robinson Cano 4.00 10.00

2016 Topps Opening Day Stars

COMPLETE SET (25) 25.00 60.00
STATED ODDS 1:24 HOBBY
ODS1 Mike Trout 5.00 12.00
ODS2 Bryce Harper 1.50 4.00
ODS3 Paul Goldschmidt 1.00 2.50
ODS4 Josh Donaldson .75 2.00
ODS5 Clayton Kershaw 1.50 4.00
ODS6 Nolan Arenado 1.50 4.00
ODS7 Carlos Correa 1.00 2.50
ODS8 Kris Bryant 1.25 3.00
ODS9 Manny Machado 1.00 2.50
ODS10 Ryan Braun .75 2.00
ODS11 Miguel Cabrera 1.00 2.50
ODS12 Andrew McCutchen 1.00 2.50
ODS13 Buster Posey 1.25 3.00
ODS14 Jacob deGrom 2.00 5.00
ODS15 Jose Abreu 1.00 2.50
ODS16 Salvador Perez .75 2.00
ODS17 David Ortiz 1.00 2.50
ODS18 Luis Severino .75 2.00
ODS19 Evan Longoria .75 2.00
ODS20 Freddie Freeman 1.25 3.00
ODS21 Giancarlo Stanton 1.00 2.50
ODS22 Joey Votto 1.00 2.50
ODS23 Miguel Sano 1.00 2.50
ODS24 Yadier Molina 1.25 3.00
ODS25 Prince Fielder .75 2.00

2016 Topps Opening Day Striking Distance

COMPLETE SET (15) 4.00 10.00
STATED ODDS 1:5 HOBBY
SD1 Ichiro Suzuki .40 1.00
SD2 Robinson Cano .25 .60
SD3 Alex Rodriguez .40 1.00
SD4 Miguel Cabrera .25 .60
SD5 Albert Pujols .40 1.00
SD6 David Ortiz .30 .75
SD7 Felix Hernandez .25 .60
SD8 Justin Verlander .30 .75
SD9 Francisco Rodriguez .25 .60
SD10 John Lackey .25 .60
SD11 Ian Kinsler .25 .60
SD12 Ryan Howard .25 .60
SD13 Ichiro Suzuki .40 1.00
SD14 Mark Teixeira .25 .60
SD15 Cole Hamels .25 .60

2016 Topps Opening Day Superstar Celebrations

COMPLETE SET (20) 4.00 10.00
STATED ODDS 1:5 HOBBY
SC1 Mike Trout 1.50 4.00
SC2 Chris Davis .20 .50
SC3 Wilmer Flores .25 .60
SC4 Salvador Perez .25 .60
SC5 Jake Arrieta .25 .60
SC6 Daniel Murphy .25 .60
SC7 Dallas Keuchel .25 .60
SC8 Kris Bryant .40 1.00
SC9 Michael Brantley .25 .60
SC10 Ryan Zimmerman .25 .60
SC11 Brian Dozier .25 .60
SC12 Ian Kinsler .25 .60
SC13 Josh Reddick .20 .50
SC14 Robinson Chirinos .20 .50
SC15 Josh Donaldson .20 .50
SC16 Pedro Alvarez .20 .50
SC17 Derek Norris .20 .50
SC18 Carlos Gonzalez .25 .60
SC19 Andre Ethier .25 .60
SC20 Justin Bour .25 .60

2017 Topps Opening Day

COMP.SET w/o SP's (200) 10.00 25.00
SP VARIATION ODDS 1:256 HOBBY
PRINTING PLATE ODDS 1:3269 HOBBY
PLATE PRINT RUN 1 SET PER COLOR
BLACK-CYAN-MAGENTA-YELLOW ISSUED
NO PLATE PRICING DUE TO SCARCITY
1A Kris Bryant .30 .75
1B Bryant SP WS shirt 40.00 100.00
2 Reynaldo Lopez RC .20 .50
3 Aaron Sanchez .20 .50
4 Justin Turner .25 .60
5A Trevor Story .25 .60
5B Story SP Gray Jrsy 15.00 40.00
6 Robinson Cano .20 .50
7 Drew Smyly .15 .40
8 Victor Martinez .20 .50
9A Max Scherzer .25 .60
9B Schrzr SP High five 10.00 25.00
10 Luke Weaver RC .25 .60
11 Kyle Hendricks .25 .60
12 Marcell Ozuna .25 .60
13 JaCoby Jones RC .25 .60
14 Alex Gordon .20 .50
15 Ben Zobrist .20 .50
16A Ichiro .30 .75
16B Ichiro SP Dugout 40.00 100.00
17 Maikel Franco .20 .50
18A Adam Jones .20 .50
18B Jones SP Cage 8.00 20.00
19A Alex Bregman RC 1.00 2.50
19B Bregman SP Thrwbc 30.00 80.00
20A Bryce Harper .40 1.00
20B Harper SP Laughing 40.00 100.00
20C Harper SP Stppng out 40.00 100.00
21 Ryan Zimmerman .20 .50
22 Lucas Giolito .20 .50
23A Salvador Perez .20 .50
23B Perez SP Mantis cage 8.00 20.00
24 Randal Grichuk .15 .40
25 Adam Eaton .25 .60
26A Freddie Freeman .30 .75
26B Freeman SP White Jrsy 15.00 40.00
27 Nelson Cruz .25 .60
28 Jon Gray .15 .40
29 Wilson Ramos .15 .40
30 Jason Kipnis .20 .50
31 George Springer .20 .50
32 Aaron Nola .20 .50
33 Joey Votto .25 .60
34 David Ortiz .25 .60
35 Nolan Arenado .40 1.00
36 Rougned Odor .20 .50
37 Justin Upton .20 .50
38 David Wright .20 .50
39 Aledmys Diaz .20 .50
40 Adam Duvall .20 .50
41 Jose Bautista .20 .50
42 Yulieski Gurriel RC .30 .75
43 Joe Musgrove RC .60 1.50
44 Danny Salazar .20 .50
45 Jake Lamb .20 .50
46 Kendrys Morales .15 .40
47 Sean Doolittle .15 .40
48 Yadier Molina .30 .75
49 Hunter Pence .20 .50
50A Clayton Kershaw .40 1.00
50B Kershaw SP w/Bat 20.00 50.00
51 Kevin Gausman .25 .60
52 Andrew Miller .20 .50
53 Chase Utley .20 .50
54 Lance McCullers .15 .40
55 Robbie Ray .15 .40
56 Zack Greinke .25 .60
57 Josh Bell RC .50 1.25
58A Andrew Benintendi RC .60 1.50
58B Benintendi SP In chair 75.00 200.00
59 Marcus Semien .25 .60
60A Hanley Ramirez .20 .50
60B Ramirez SP Crouching 15.00 40.00
61 Kenta Maeda .20 .50
62 Carlos Rodon .25 .60
63A Corey Kluber .20 .50
63B Kluber SP Soccer 8.00 20.00
64 Zach Britton .20 .50
65 Adam Wainwright .20 .50
66 Willson Contreras .25 .60
67 Ryan Braun .20 .50
68 Stephen Piscotty .20 .50
69 Jon Lester .20 .50
70 Jay Bruce .20 .50
71 Jacob deGrom .50 1.25
72 Yoenis Cespedes .25 .60
73 Joe Mauer .20 .50
74 Yoan Moncada RC .60 1.50
75A Mike Trout 1.25 3.00
75B Trout SP Into dugout 40.00 100.00
75C Trout SP Puppy 40.00 100.00
76 Felix Hernandez .20 .50
77 Nomar Mazara .15 .40
78 Ian Kinsler .20 .50
79 Sonny Gray .20 .50
80A Manny Machado .20 .50
80B Machado SP Black shirt 15.00 40.00
81 Jean Segura .20 .50
82 Jose De Leon RC .20 .50
83 Carlos Martinez .20 .50
84 James Shields .15 .40
85 Braden Shipley RC .20 .50
86A Addison Russell .20 .50
86B Russell SP High Five 10.00 25.00
87A Jose Altuve .20 .50
87B Altuve SP w/o Jrsy 8.00 20.00
88 Jose Reyes .20 .50
89 Matt Harvey .20 .50
90 Matt Strahm RC .20 .50
91 Tim Anderson .20 .50
92 Masahiro Tanaka .20 .50
93 Michael Fulmer .15 .40
94 Anthony DeSclafani .15 .40
95 Kyle Seager .15 .40
96A Anthony Rizzo .30 .75
96B Rizzo SP Parade 20.00 50.00
97 Brett Gardner .20 .50
98 Lorenzo Cain .15 .40
99 Christian Yelich .20 .50
100 Jonathan Villar .15 .40
101 Starling Marte .20 .50
102 Adrian Beltre .25 .60
103A Daniel Murphy .20 .50
103B Murphy SP Gray jrsy 15.00 40.00
104 Chris Archer .15 .40
105 Danny Duffy .15 .40
106 Xander Bogaerts .25 .60
107 Tommy Joseph .25 .60
108 Tyler Glasnow RC .75 2.00
109 Tyler Austin RC .25 .60
110A Giancarlo Stanton .25 .60
110B Stanton SP Cage 10.00 25.00
111 Craig Kimbrel .20 .50
112 Dustin Pedroia .25 .60
113A Mookie Betts .50 1.25
113B Betts SP Cage 20.00 50.00
114 Jackie Bradley Jr. .25 .60
115 Carlos Gonzalez .20 .50
116 Chris Sale .25 .60
117A Jake Arrieta .20 .50
117B Arrieta SP Red coat 15.00 40.00
118 Curtis Granderson .20 .50
119 Cameron Maybin .15 .40
120A Andrew McCutchen .25 .60
120B McCtchn SP Thrwbck 20.00 50.00
121 Carson Fulmer RC .20 .50
122A Francisco Lindor .25 .60
122B Lindor SP WS shirt 20.00 50.00
123 Khris Davis .25 .60
124 Cole Hamels .20 .50
125 Jake Thompson RC .20 .50
126 David Dahl RC .25 .60
127 Wil Myers .20 .50
128A Eric Hosmer .20 .50
128B Hosmer SP Blue jrsy 8.00 20.00
129A Trea Turner .20 .50
129B Turner SP Gray jrsy 8.00 20.00
130 Jose Abreu .25 .60
131 Orlando Arcia RC .30 .75
132A David Price .20 .50
132B Price SP Glasses 8.00 20.00
133A Javier Baez .30 .75
133B Baez SP Pullover 12.00 30.00
134A Miguel Sano .20 .50
134B Sano SP Dugout 8.00 20.00
135A Madison Bumgarner .20 .50
135B Bumgarner SP Bttng 20.00 50.00
136 Jeff Hoffman RC .20 .50
137 Jonathan Lucroy .20 .50
138 Marcus Stroman .20 .50
139 Rick Porcello .20 .50
140 Albert Pujols .30 .75
141A Evan Longoria .20 .50
141B Longoria SP Football 8.00 20.00
142 Elvis Andrus .20 .50
143 Brandon Finnegan .15 .40
144 Gerrit Cole .25 .60
145 Robert Gsellman RC .25 .60
146 Corey Kluber .20 .50
147A Aaron Judge RC 2.50 6.00
147B Judge SP w/Bat 125.00 300.00
148A Miguel Cabrera .25 .60
148B Cabrera SP Open mouth 10.00 25.00
149 Troy Tulowitzki .25 .60
150A Kyle Schwarber .25 .60
150B Schwrbr SP WS shirt 15.00 40.00
151A Justin Verlander .25 .60
151B Verlander SP Cage 15.00 40.00
152 Brandon Belt .20 .50
153 Matt Moore .20 .50
154 Sean Manaea .15 .40
155 Brandon Phillips .15 .40
156A Matt Carpenter .25 .60
156B Carpenter SP High five 10.00 25.00
157 Gregory Polanco .20 .50
158 Carlos Carrasco .15 .40
159 Ryon Healy RC .25 .60
160 Adrian Gonzalez .20 .50
161 Brian McCann .20 .50
162 Brian Dozier .25 .60
163 Mike Moustakas .20 .50
164 Travis Jankowski .15 .40
165 Alex Reyes RC .25 .60
166 Tyler Naquin .25 .60
167 Byron Buxton .25 .60
168 Brandon Crawford .20 .50
169 Paul Goldschmidt .25 .60
170A Gary Sanchez .25 .60
170B Snchz SP Wearing gear 40.00 100.00
171 Dallas Keuchel .20 .50
172 J.D. Martinez .25 .60
173 Edwin Encarnacion .25 .60
174 Stephen Strasburg .25 .60
175 Carlos Santana .20 .50
176 Teoscar Hernandez RC .75 2.00
177 Tanner Roark .15 .40
178 Mark Trumbo .15 .40
179 Ryan Schimpf .15 .40
180 Jameson Taillon .20 .50
181 Dee Gordon .15 .40
182 Seung-Hwan Oh RC .40 1.00
183 Chris Davis .15 .40
184 Johnny Cueto .20 .50
185 A.J. Pollock .15 .40
186 Julio Urias .25 .60
187 Jason Heyward .20 .50
188 Yu Darvish .25 .60
189 Todd Frazier .15 .40
190A Noah Syndergaard .20 .50
190B Syndrgrd SP Dugout 25.00 60.00
191 Dellin Betances .20 .50
192 Charlie Blackmon .25 .60
193 Kenley Jansen .20 .50
194A Josh Donaldson .20 .50
194B Donaldson SP w/Fans 25.00 60.00
195 Dansby Swanson RC .50 1.25
196 Jacoby Ellsbury .20 .50
197A Carlos Correa .25 .60
197B Correa SP Ornge Jrsy 10.00 25.00
198 Matt Kemp .20 .50
199 Billy Hamilton .20 .50
200 Buster Posey .30 .75

2017 Topps Opening Day Blue Foil

*BLUE: 3X TO 8X BASIC
*BLUE RC: 2X TO 5X BASIC RC
STATED ODDS 1:7 HOBBY

2017 Topps Opening Day Toys R Us Purple Border

*PURPLE: 3X TO 8X BASIC
*PURPLE RC: 3X TO 8X BASIC RC
ISSUED IN TRU PACKS

2017 Topps Opening Day Autographs

STATED ODDS 1:654 HOBBY
ODAABE Andrew Benintendi 40.00 100.00
ODAABR Alex Bregman 30.00 80.00
ODAAD Aledmys Diaz 30.00 80.00
ODAAJ Aaron Judge 100.00 250.00
ODAAN Aaron Nola 8.00 20.00
ODAARU Addison Russell 25.00 60.00
ODACC Carlos Correa
ODADD David Dahl 6.00 15.00
ODAGB Greg Bird 8.00 20.00
ODAJM Joe Musgrove 20.00 50.00
ODAKB Kris Bryant 100.00 250.00
ODANS Noah Syndergaard 20.00 50.00
ODATA Tim Anderson 6.00 15.00
ODATS Trevor Story 15.00 40.00
ODATT Trea Turner 15.00 40.00
ODAYM Yoan Moncada 100.00 250.00

2017 Topps Opening Day Incredible Eats

COMPLETE SET (18) 4.00 10.00
STATED ODDS 1:8 HOBBY
IE1 Italian sausage .30 .75
IE2 Peanuts .30 .75
IE3 Fresh Popcorn .30 .75
IE4 South Philly Dog .30 .75
IE5 Cheesy Corn Brisket-acho .30 .75
IE6 Chicken and Waffle Cone .30 .75
IE7 Classic Pastrami .30 .75
IE8 Foot-long Hot Dog .30 .75
IE9 Nacho bowl .30 .75
IE10 Soft Pretzels .30 .75
IE11 Cotton Candy .30 .75
IE12 Corn on a Stick .30 .75
IE13 Hot Dogs & Onions .30 .75
IE14 Broomstick Hot Dog .30 .75
IE15 Bacon Mac & Cheese .30 .75
IE16 Kayem Fenway Frank .30 .75
IE17 Cracker Jack & Mac Dog .30 .75
IE18 Buffalo Cauliflower Poutine .30 .75

2017 Topps Opening Day Mascot Autographs

STATED ODDS 1:747 HOBBY
MAB Billy the Marlin 12.00 30.00
MAC Clark 20.00 50.00
MAF Fredbird 20.00 50.00
MAO Orbit 15.00 40.00
MAS Slider 15.00 40.00
MAPIP Pirate Parrot 12.00 30.00
MAWGM Wally the Green Monster 20.00 50.00

2017 Topps Opening Day Mascot Relics

STATED ODDS 1:2097 HOBBY
MRB Billy the Marlin 12.00 30.00
MRC Clark 25.00 60.00
MRF Fredbird 20.00 50.00
MRS Slider 25.00 60.00
MRWGM Wally the Green Monster 20.00 50.00

2017 Topps Opening Day Mascots

COMPLETE SET (25) 5.00 12.00
STATED ODDS 1:3 HOBBY
M1 Paws .30 .75
M2 Billy the Marlin .30 .75
M3 Rally Monkey .30 .75
M4 Mr. Red .30 .75
M5 Mr. Met .30 .75
M6 TC Bear .30 .75
M7 Braves Mascot .30 .75
M8 Slider .30 .75
M9 Dinger .30 .75
M10 Royals Mascot .30 .75
M11 Phillie Phanatic .30 .75
M12 Pirate Parrot .30 .75
M13 Swinging Friar .30 .75
M14 Mariner Moose .30 .75
M15 Fredbird .30 .75
M16 White Sox Mascot .30 .75
M17 Athletics Mascot .30 .75
M18 Raymond .30 .75
M19 Rangers Captain .30 .75
M20 Blue Jays Mascot .30 .75
M21 Hank the Ballpark Pup .30 .75
M22 Orbit .30 .75
M23 Clark .30 .75
M24 Wally the Green Monster .30 .75
M25 Brewers Mascot .30 .75

2017 Topps Opening Day MLB Sticker Collection Stars

COMPLETE SET (4)
STATED ODDS 1:288 HOBBY
2 Mike Trout 6.00 15.00
83 David Ortiz 1.25 3.00
194 Kris Bryant 1.50 4.00
212 Clayton Kershaw 2.00 5.00

2017 Topps Opening Day National Anthem

COMPLETE SET (25)
STATED ODDS 1:210 HOBBY
NA1 Addison Russell 3.00 8.00
NA2 Andrew McCutchen 3.00 8.00
NA3 Anthony Rizzo 10.00 25.00
NA4 Bryce Harper 10.00 25.00
NA5 Josh Donaldson 2.50 6.00
NA6 Miguel Cabrera 3.00 8.00
NA7 Carlos Correa 3.00 8.00
NA8 Clayton Kershaw 8.00 20.00
NA9 Felix Hernandez 2.50 6.00
NA10 Francisco Lindor 8.00 20.00
NA11 Jose Altuve 2.50 6.00
NA12 Manny Machado 12.00 30.00
NA13 Mookie Betts 8.00 20.00
NA14 Noah Syndergaard 8.00 20.00
NA15 Robinson Cano 2.50 6.00
NA16 David Ortiz 8.00 20.00
NA17 Khris Davis 3.00 8.00
NA18 Jayson Werth 2.50 6.00
NA19 Jon Lester 2.50 6.00
NA20 Aaron Judge 20.00 50.00
NA21 Eric Hosmer 8.00 20.00
NA22 Mike Trout 15.00 40.00
NA23 Kyle Schwarber 3.00 8.00
NA24 Madison Bumgarner 2.50 6.00
NA25 Adam Jones 6.00 15.00

2017 Topps Opening Day Opening Day

COMPLETE SET (15) 4.00 10.00
STATED ODDS 1:5 HOBBY
ODB1 Pittsburgh Pirates .40 1.00
ODB2 Tampa Bay Rays .40 1.00
ODB3 Kansas City Royals .40 1.00
ODB4 Milwaukee Brewers .40 1.00
ODB5 Baltimore Orioles .40 1.00
ODB6 Texas Rangers .40 1.00
ODB7 Cincinnati Reds .40 1.00
ODB8 Atlanta Braves .40 1.00
ODB9 San Diego Padres .40 1.00
ODB10 Arizona Diamondbacks .40 1.00
ODB11 Los Angeles Angels .40 1.00
ODB12 Oakland Athletics .40 1.00
ODB13 New York Yankees .40 1.00
ODB14 Cleveland Indians .40 1.00
ODB15 Miami Marlins .40 1.00

2017 Topps Opening Day Opening Day Stars

COMPLETE SET (44) 50.00 120.00
STATED ODDS 1:27 HOBBY
ODS1 Adam Jones 1.00 2.50
ODS2 Addison Russell 1.25 3.00
ODS3 Ichiro 1.50 4.00
ODS4 Javier Baez 1.50 4.00
ODS5 Andrew McCutchen 1.25 3.00
ODS6 Anthony Rizzo 1.50 4.00
ODS7 Brandon Phillips .75 2.00
ODS8 Justin Verlander 1.25 3.00
ODS9 Bryce Harper 2.00 5.00
ODS10 Josh Donaldson 1.00 2.50
ODS11 Miguel Cabrera 1.25 3.00
ODS12 Bryce Harper 2.00 5.00
ODS13 Buster Posey 1.50 4.00
ODS14 Max Scherzer 1.25 3.00
ODS15 Clayton Kershaw 2.00 5.00
ODS16 Corey Seager 1.25 3.00
ODS17 Eric Hosmer 1.00 2.50
ODS18 Evan Longoria 1.00 2.50
ODS19 Felix Hernandez 1.00 2.50
ODS20 Hanley Ramirez 1.00 2.50
ODS21 Freddie Freeman 1.50 4.00
ODS22 Jake Arrieta 1.00 2.50
ODS23 Giancarlo Stanton 1.25 3.00
ODS24 Jose Altuve 1.00 2.50
ODS25 Kris Bryant 8.00 20.00
ODS26 Kyle Schwarber 1.25 3.00
ODS27 Gary Sanchez 1.25 3.00
ODS28 Francisco Lindor 1.25 3.00
ODS29 Madison Bumgarner 1.00 2.50
ODS30 Manny Machado 1.25 3.00
ODS31 Matt Carpenter 1.25 3.00
ODS32 Miguel Sano 1.00 2.50
ODS33 Mike Trout 8.00 20.00
ODS34 Mookie Betts 2.50 6.00
ODS35 Noah Syndergaard 1.00 2.50
ODS36 Nolan Arenado 2.00 5.00
ODS37 Paul Goldschmidt 1.25 3.00
ODS38 Robinson Cano 1.00 2.50
ODS39 Ryan Braun 1.00 2.50
ODS40 Salvador Perez 1.00 2.50
ODS41 Trea Turner 1.00 2.50
ODS42 Trevor Story 1.25 3.00
ODS43 Corey Kluber 1.00 2.50
ODS44 Carlos Correa 1.25 3.00

2017 Topps Opening Day Relics

STATED ODDS 1:525 HOBBY
ODRAM Andrew McCutchen 6.00 15.00
ODRBH Bryce Harper 10.00 25.00
ODRBP Buster Posey 6.00 15.00
ODRCC Carlos Correa 5.00 12.00
ODRCK Clayton Kershaw 6.00 15.00
ODRDW David Wright 4.00 10.00
ODRJA Jose Altuve 4.00 10.00
ODRMT Mike Trout
ODRARI Anthony Rizzo 6.00 15.00
ODRJVE Justin Verlander 5.00 12.00

2017 Topps Opening Day Stadium Signatures

COMPLETE SET (25)
STATED ODDS 1:420 HOBBY
SS1 Jose Altuve 5.00 12.00
SS2 Corey Seager 20.00 50.00
SS3 Dee Gordon 4.00 10.00
SS4 Jon Gray 10.00 25.00
SS5 Paul Goldschmidt 6.00 15.00
SS6 Carlos Correa
SS7 Ichiro 25.00 60.00
SS8 Ben Zobrist 20.00 50.00
SS9 David Price 5.00 12.00
SS10 Tyler Naquin 12.00 30.00
SS11 Trevor Story 12.00 30.00
SS12 Mike Trout 60.00 150.00
SS13 Julio Urias 12.00 30.00
SS14 Francisco Lindor 25.00 60.00
SS15 Addison Russell 12.00 30.00
SS16 Michael Conforto 5.00 12.00
SS17 Maikel Franco 5.00 12.00
SS18 Jason Heyward 8.00 20.00
SS19 Bryce Harper 20.00 50.00
SS20 Kyle Schwarber 12.00 30.00
SS21 Trea Turner 20.00 50.00
SS22 Kris Bryant 60.00 150.00
SS23 Nolan Arenado 8.00 20.00
SS24 Charlie Blackmon 10.00 25.00
SS25 Miguel Sano 20.00 50.00

2017 Topps Opening Day Superstar Celebrations

COMPLETE SET (25) 5.00 12.00
STATED ODDS 1:3 HOBBY
SC1 Brian Dozier .30 .75
SC2 Khris Davis .30 .75
SC3 Javier Baez .40 1.00
SC4 Anthony Rizzo .40 1.00
SC5 Francisco Lindor .30 .75
SC6 Jayson Werth .25 .60
SC7 Josh Harrison .20 .50
SC8 Carlos Santana .25 .60
SC9 Andrew McCutchen .30 .75
SC10 Rougned Odor .25 .60
SC11 Adam Eaton .30 .75
SC12 Addison Russell .30 .75
SC13 Robinson Cano .25 .60
SC14 Troy Tulowitzki .30 .75
SC15 David Ortiz .30 .75
SC16 Jonathan Lucroy .25 .60
SC17 Russell Martin .20 .50
SC18 Edwin Encarnacion .25 .60
SC19 Gregory Polanco .25 .60
SC20 Carlos Correa .30 .75
SC21 Giancarlo Stanton .30 .75
SC22 Jose Ramirez .25 .60
SC23 Bryce Harper .50 1.25
SC24 Jackie Bradley Jr. .30 .75
SC25 Yunel Escobar .20 .50

2017 Topps Opening Day Wacky Packages

COMPLETE SET (9)
STATED ODDS 1:1169 HOBBY
WP1 Clam Chowder 8.00 20.00
WP2 Deep Dish Pizza 15.00 40.00
WP3 Alphabet Chili 8.00 20.00
WP4 Royals Mustard 8.00 20.00
WP5 Sssssssarsaparilla 8.00 20.00
WP6 Kielbasa 12.00 30.00
WP7 Hot Salsa 8.00 20.00
WP8 Tuna Steak Marinade 4.00 10.00
WP9 MLB Draft 8.00 20.00

2018 Topps Opening Day

COMPLETE SET (200) 12.00 30.00
PRINTING PLATE ODDS 1:4680 BLASTER
PLATE PRINT RUN 1 SET PER COLOR
BLACK-CYAN-MAGENTA-YELLOW ISSUED
NO PLATE PRICING DUE TO SCARCITY
1 Clayton Kershaw .40 1.00
2 Rafael Devers RC .60 1.50
3 Kris Bryant .30 .75
4 Mike Trout 1.25 3.00
5 Buster Posey .30 .75
6 Anthony Rizzo .30 .75
7 Carlos Correa .25 .60
8 A.J. Pollock .15 .40
9 Jake Lamb .20 .50
10 J.D. Martinez .25 .60
11 Matt Kemp .20 .50
12 Nick Markakis .20 .50
13 Ozzie Albies RC .60 1.50
14 Dansby Swanson .25 .60
15 Adam Jones .20 .50
16 Manny Machado .25 .60
17 Jonathan Schoop .15 .40
18 Trey Mancini .20 .50
19 Craig Kimbrel .20 .50
20 Chris Sale .25 .60
21 Christian Vazquez .20 .50
22 Mookie Betts .50 1.25
23 Willson Contreras .25 .60
24 Kyle Schwarber .20 .50
25 Jon Lester .20 .50
26 Javier Baez .30 .75
27 Ian Happ .20 .50
28 Avisail Garcia .20 .50
29 Carlos Rodon .25 .60
30 Jose Abreu .25 .60
31 Yoan Moncada .25 .60
32 Raisel Iglesias .20 .50
33 Zack Cozart .15 .40
34 Billy Hamilton .20 .50
35 Andrew Miller .20 .50
36 Jason Kipnis .20 .50
37 Carlos Carrasco .15 .40
38 Danny Salazar .20 .50
39 Francisco Lindor .25 .60
40 Raimel Tapia .15 .40
41 Nolan Arenado .40 1.00
42 Jon Gray .15 .40
43 Antonio Senzatela .15 .40
44 David Dahl .15 .40
45 Trevor Story .25 .60
46 Miguel Cabrera .25 .60
47 Michael Fulmer .15 .40
48 George Springer .20 .50
49 Yulieski Gurriel .20 .50
50 Jose Altuve .20 .50
51 Dallas Keuchel .20 .50
52 Justin Verlander .25 .60
53 Alex Bregman .25 .60
54 Danny Duffy .15 .40
55 Mike Moustakas .20 .50
56 Salvador Perez .20 .50
57 Yasiel Puig .25 .60
58 Cody Bellinger .50 1.25
59 Corey Seager .25 .60
60 Giancarlo Stanton .25 .60
61 Ichiro .30 .75
62 Ryan Braun .20 .50
63 Jonathan Villar .15 .40
64 Byron Buxton .25 .60
65 Joe Mauer .20 .50
66 Miguel Sano .20 .50
67 Michael Conforto .20 .50
68 Noah Syndergaard .20 .50
69 Jacob deGrom .50 1.25
70 Amed Rosario RC .25 .60
71 Aaron Judge .60 1.50
72 Gary Sanchez .25 .60
73 Masahiro Tanaka .20 .50
74 Todd Frazier .15 .40
75 Luis Severino .20 .50
76 Khris Davis .25 .60
77 Jharel Cotton .15 .40
78 Sean Manaea .15 .40
79 Odubel Herrera .20 .50
80 Maikel Franco .20 .50
81 Aaron Nola .20 .50
82 Rhys Hoskins RC .75 2.00
83 Andrew McCutchen .25 .60
84 Starling Marte .20 .50
85 Gregory Polanco .20 .50
86 Wil Myers .20 .50
87 Hunter Renfroe .15 .40
88 Johnny Cueto .20 .50
89 Jeff Samardzija .15 .40
90 Hunter Pence .20 .50
91 Nelson Cruz .25 .60
92 Robinson Cano .20 .50
93 Felix Hernandez .20 .50
94 Adam Wainwright .20 .50
95 Dexter Fowler .20 .50
96 Yadier Molina .30 .75
97 Kevin Kiermaier .20 .50
98 Corey Dickerson .15 .40
99 Chris Archer .15 .40
100 Joey Gallo .20 .50
101 Elvis Andrus .20 .50
102 Adrian Beltre .25 .60
103 Rougned Odor .20 .50
104 Nomar Mazara .15 .40
105 Kendrys Morales .15 .40
106 Troy Tulowitzki .25 .60

107 Josh Donaldson .20 .50
108 Marcus Stroman .20 .50
109 Anthony Rendon .25 .60
110 Trea Turner .20 .50
111 Daniel Murphy .20 .50
112 Max Scherzer .25 .60
113 Stephen Strasburg .25 .60
114 Bryce Harper .40 1.00
115 Ryan McMahon RC .50 1.25
116 Jackie Bradley Jr. .25 .60
117 Clint Frazier RC .40 1.00
118 Willie Calhoun RC .30 .75
119 Dominic Smith RC .25 .60
120 Nick Williams RC .25 .60
121 Greg Allen RC .25 .60
122 Brandon Woodruff RC .60 1.50
123 Chance Sisco RC .25 .60
124 Nicky Delmonico RC .20 .50
125 Austin Hays RC .30 .75
126 J.P. Crawford RC .20 .50
127 Victor Robles RC .50 1.25
128 Alex Verdugo RC .30 .75
129 Francisco Mejia RC .25 .60
130 Jack Flaherty RC .75 2.00
131 Brian Anderson RC .25 .60
132 Walker Buehler RC 1.00 2.50
133 Erick Fedde RC .20 .50
134 Harrison Bader RC .30 .75
135 Andrew Stevenson RC .20 .50
136 Anthony Banda RC .20 .50
137 Miguel Andujar RC .75 2.00
138 Luiz Gohara RC .20 .50
139 Joey Votto .25 .60
140 Albert Pujols .30 .75
141 Zack Greinke .25 .60
142 Paul Goldschmidt .25 .60
143 Freddie Freeman .30 .75
144 Julio Teheran .20 .50
145 Zach Britton .15 .40
146 Chris Davis .15 .40
147 Hanley Ramirez .20 .50
148 David Price .20 .50
149 Xander Bogaerts .25 .60
150 Andrew Benintendi .25 .60
151 Jason Heyward .20 .50
152 Jake Arrieta .20 .50
153 Addison Russell .20 .50
154 Tim Anderson .25 .60
155 Melky Cabrera .15 .40
156 Adam Duvall .20 .50
157 Jesse Winker .25 .60
158 Corey Kluber .20 .50
159 Edwin Encarnacion .25 .60
160 Jose Ramirez .20 .50
161 Charlie Blackmon .25 .60
162 DJ LeMahieu .25 .60
163 Ian Kinsler .20 .50
164 Brian McCann .20 .50
165 Alcides Escobar .20 .50
166 Justin Turner .25 .60
167 Chris Taylor .20 .50
168 Yu Darvish .25 .60
169 Kenley Jansen .20 .50
170 Dee Gordon .15 .40
171 Justin Bour .15 .40
172 Eric Thames .20 .50
173 Jose Berrios .20 .50
174 Eddie Rosario .20 .50
175 Didi Gregorius .20 .50
176 Aroldis Chapman .25 .60
177 Sonny Gray .20 .50
178 Ryon Healy .15 .40
179 Matt Olson .25 .60
180 Jeremy Hellickson .15 .40
181 Aaron Altherr .15 .40
182 Josh Bell .20 .50
183 Gerrit Cole .25 .60
184 Yangervis Solarte .15 .40
185 Brandon Crawford .20 .50
186 Kyle Seager .15 .40
187 Matt Carpenter .25 .60
188 Paul DeJong .20 .50
189 Steven Souza Jr. .20 .50
190 Cole Hamels .20 .50
191 Matt Wieters .20 .50
192 Whit Merrifield .25 .60
193 Robbie Ray .15 .40
194 Alex Colome .15 .40
195 Marcell Ozuna .25 .60
196 Alex Wood .15 .40
197 Parker Bridwell RC .20 .50
198 Mark Reynolds .15 .40
199 Jose Quintana .15 .40
200 Shohei Ohtani RC 5.00 12.00

2018 Topps Opening Day Blue Foil

*BLUE: 2X TO 5X BASIC
*BLUE RC: 1.5X TO 4X BASIC RC
STATED ODDS 1:9 BLASTER
ANNCD PRINT RUN 2018 SETS
200 Shohei Ohtani 12.00 30.00

2018 Topps Opening Day Variations

STATED ODDS 1:477 BLASTER
1 Kershaw Hoodie 30.00 80.00
3 Bryant Hat on 30.00 80.00
4 Trout Red jsy 60.00 150.00
5 Posey Mask on 20.00 50.00
7 Correa Helmet 15.00 40.00
16 Machado White jsy 30.00 80.00
30 Abreu No hat 15.00 40.00
39 Lindor Blue jsy 8.00 20.00
41 Arenado Pnstp jsy 8.00 20.00
46 Cabrera Sunglasses 25.00 60.00
55 Moustakas Wht jsy 15.00 40.00
60 Stanton No hat 20.00 50.00
63 Villar Pullover 10.00 25.00
64 Buxton Hat on 15.00 40.00
70 Rosario No helmet 15.00 40.00
71 Judge Pnstp Jsy 125.00 300.00
82 Hoskins High fives 40.00 100.00
83 McCutchen Blk jsy 25.00 60.00
87 Renfroe Diving 8.00 20.00
93 Hernandez Pullover 8.00 20.00
99 Archer Tshirt 8.00 20.00
100 Gallo Hat on 8.00 20.00
107 Donaldson Blue jsy 10.00 25.00
112 Scherzer Ski mask 10.00 25.00
139 Votto Wht jsy 20.00 50.00
142 Goldschmidt Hat on 12.00 30.00
143 Freeman Wht Jsy 20.00 50.00
150 Benintendi Navy jsy 30.00 80.00
179 Olson In dugout 20.00 50.00
187 Carpenter High fives 10.00 25.00

2018 Topps Opening Day At The Ballpark

STATED ODDS 1:6 BLASTER
ODBA Los Angeles Angels .40 1.00
ODBAB Atlanta Braves .40 1.00
ODBAD Arizona Diamondbacks .40 1.00
ODBBO Baltimore Orioles .40 1.00
ODBCC Chicago Cubs .40 1.00
ODBCI Cleveland Indians .40 1.00
ODBCR Cincinnati Reds .40 1.00
ODBDT Detroit Tigers .40 1.00
ODBHA Houston Astros .40 1.00
ODBMB Milwaukee Brewers .40 1.00
ODBPP Pittsburgh Pirates .40 1.00
ODBTR Texas Rangers .40 1.00
ODBWN Washington Nationals .40 1.00
ODBBRS Boston Red Sox .40 1.00
ODBCOR Colorado Rockies .40 1.00
ODBLAD Los Angeles Dodgers .40 1.00
ODBNYM New York Mets .40 1.00
ODBNYY New York Yankees .40 1.00
ODBSLC St. Louis Cardinals .40 1.00
ODBTBR Tampa Bay Rays .40 1.00

2018 Topps Opening Day Autographs

STATED ODDS 1:701 BLASTER
ODAAR Amed Rosario 12.00 30.00
ODACB Charlie Blackmon 10.00 25.00
ODACC Carlos Correa 25.00 60.00
ODAET Eric Thames 4.00 10.00
ODAHB Harrison Bader 5.00 12.00
ODAJB Javier Baez 20.00 50.00
ODAJL Jake Lamb 4.00 10.00
ODAJU Julio Urias 8.00 20.00
ODAKS Kyle Schwarber 15.00 40.00
ODAMK Max Kepler 4.00 10.00
ODAMT Mike Trout
ODANS Noah Syndergaard 20.00 50.00
ODARD Rafael Devers 20.00 50.00
ODART Raimel Tapia 3.00 8.00

2018 Topps Opening Day Before Opening Day

COMPLETE SET (20) 4.00 10.00
STATED ODDS 1:5 BLASTER
BODAB Andrew Benintendi .50 1.25
BODAJ Aaron Judge 1.25 3.00
BODAR Anthony Rizzo .60 1.50
BODBB Byron Buxton .50 1.25
BODBH Bryce Harper .75 2.00
BODBP Buster Posey .60 1.50
BODCB Cody Bellinger 1.00 2.50
BODCD Chris Davis .30 .75
BODCS Chris Sale .50 1.25
BODCV Christian Vazquez .40 1.00
BODDK Dallas Keuchel .40 1.00
BODI Ichiro .60 1.50
BODKB Kris Bryant .60 1.50
BODMB Mookie Betts 1.00 2.50
BODMG Marwin Gonzalez .30 .75
BODMK Mikie Mahtook .30 .75
BODMS Miguel Sano .40 1.00
BODMT Mike Trout 2.50 6.00
BODSP Salvador Perez .40 1.00
BODYP Yasiel Puig .50 1.25

2018 Topps Opening Day Diamond Relics

STATED ODDS 1:1772 BLASTER
DRAB Andrew Benintendi 10.00 25.00
DRAM Andrew McCutchen 20.00 50.00
DRAN Aaron Nola 10.00 25.00
DRCA Chris Archer 8.00 20.00
DRDD Danny Duffy 10.00 25.00
DREL Evan Longoria 8.00 20.00
DRET Eric Thames
DRFL Francisco Lindor 10.00 25.00
DRJD Josh Donaldson 12.00 30.00
DRKB Kris Bryant 12.00 30.00
DRMC Miguel Cabrera 10.00 25.00
DRNA Nolan Arenado 15.00 40.00
DRNC Nicholas Castellanos 15.00 30.00
DRNS Noah Syndergaard 8.00 20.00
DRRB Ryan Braun 12.00 30.00
DRRH Rhys Hoskins 20.00 60.00
DRSM Starling Marte 12.00 30.00
DRTS Trevor Story 10.00 25.00
DRVM Victor Martinez 8.00 20.00
DRYC Yoenis Cespedes 10.00 25.00
DRYM Yadier Molina 15.00 40.00

2018 Topps Opening Day Dugout Peeks

STATED ODDS 1:1791 BLASTER
DPAJ Aaron Judge 50.00 120.00
DPBC Brandon Crawford 15.00 40.00
DPBH Bryce Harper 50.00 120.00
DPBZ Ben Zobrist 15.00 40.00
DPCC Carlos Carrasco 12.00 30.00
DPEE Edwin Encarnacion 20.00 50.00
DPID Ian Desmond 12.00 30.00
DPJA Jose Altuve 15.00 40.00
DPJB Josh Bell 12.00 30.00
DPJS Jonathan Schoop 25.00 60.00
DPKM Kenta Maeda 15.00 40.00
DPMT Mark Trumbo 12.00 30.00
DPPB Parker Bridwell 12.00 30.00
DPRB Ryan Braun 20.00 50.00
DPRH Rhys Hoskins 50.00 125.00
DPRP Rick Porcello
DPTB Tim Beckham
DPWM Wil Myers 12.00 30.00
DPXB Xander Bogaerts 20.00 50.00
DPYP Yasiel Puig 20.00 50.00

2018 Topps Opening Day Mascot Autographs

STATED ODDS 1:1560 BLASTER
MAS Sluggerrr 12.00 30.00
MABB Bernie Brewer 15.00 40.00
MABTM Billy the Marlin 8.00 20.00
MATCB TC Bear 25.00 60.00
MAWGM Wally the Green Monster 15.00 40.00

2018 Topps Opening Day Mascot Relics

STATED ODDS 1:4951 BLASTER
MRC Clark 8.00 20.00
MRF Fredbird 8.00 20.00
MRS Sluggerrr 8.00 20.00
MRBB Bernie Brewer 20.00 50.00
MRBTM Billy the Marlin 8.00 20.00
MRTCB TC Bear 15.00 40.00
MRWGM Wally the Green Monster 15.00 40.00

2018 Topps Opening Day Mascots

COMPLETE SET (25) 6.00 15.00
STATED ODDS 1:4 BLASTER
M1 Sluggerrr .40 1.00
M2 Wally the Green Monster .40 1.00
M3 Tessie .40 1.00
M4 Clark .40 1.00
M5 Gapper .40 1.00
M6 Mr. Red .40 1.00
M7 Mr. Redlegs .40 1.00
M8 Rosie Red .40 1.00
M9 Slider .40 1.00
M10 Dinger .40 1.00
M11 Paws .40 1.00
M12 Billy the Marlin .40 1.00
M13 Orbit .40 1.00
M14 Rally Monkey .40 1.00
M15 TC Bear .40 1.00
M16 Bernie Brewer .40 1.00
M17 Mr. Met .40 1.00
M18 Phillie Phanatic .40 1.00
M19 Pirate Parrot .40 1.00
M20 Swinging Friar .40 1.00
M21 Mariner Moose .40 1.00
M22 Fredbird .40 1.00
M23 Raymond .40 1.00
M24 Rangers Captain .40 1.00
M25 Screech .40 1.00

2018 Topps Opening Day MLB Sticker Collection Stars

STATED ODDS 1:288 BLASTER
ODV1 Aaron Judge 4.00 10.00
ODV2 Francisco Lindor 1.25 3.00
ODV3 Bryce Harper 2.00 5.00
ODV4 Clayton Kershaw 2.00 5.00

2018 Topps Opening Day National Anthem

STATED ODDS 1:286 BLASTER
NAAB Alex Bregman 4.00 10.00
NAAN Andrew Benintendi 10.00 25.00
NACC Carlos Correa 4.00 10.00
NACF Clint Frazier 8.00 20.00
NACH Cesar Hernandez 2.50 6.00
NACS Chris Sale 6.00 15.00
NADF Dexter Fowler 3.00 8.00
NAEE Edwin Encarnacion 4.00 10.00
NAEH Eric Hosmer 6.00 15.00
NAFL Francisco Lindor 4.00 10.00
NAHR Hanley Ramirez 5.00 12.00
NAJA Jose Altuve 3.00 8.00
NAJB Jackie Bradley Jr. 6.00 15.00
NAJC J.P. Crawford 6.00 15.00
NAJD Jacob deGrom 6.00 15.00
NAJK Jason Kipnis 3.00 8.00
NAJM James McCann 6.00 15.00
NAJT Justin Turner 4.00 10.00
NAKD Khris Davis 4.00 10.00
NAKP Kevin Pillar 2.50 6.00
NAKS Kyle Seager 2.50 6.00
NAMB Mookie Betts 8.00 20.00
NAMM Mikie Mahtook 2.50 6.00
NAMT Mike Trout 15.00 40.00
NAYP Yasiel Puig 4.00 10.00

2018 Topps Opening Day Relics

STATED ODDS 1:707 BLASTER
ODRAP Albert Pujols 5.00 12.00
ODRAR Anthony Rizzo 6.00 15.00
ODRCC Carlos Correa 5.00 12.00
ODRCK Clayton Kershaw 6.00 15.00
ODRCS Corey Seager 5.00 12.00
ODRJV Joey Votto 5.00 12.00
ODRKB Kris Bryant 8.00 20.00
ODRMM Manny Machado 5.00 12.00
ODRMS Max Scherzer 5.00 12.00
ODRMT Mike Trout 25.00 60.00

2018 Topps Opening Day Stadium Signatures

STATED ODDS 1:572 BLASTER
SSAJ Aaron Judge 40.00 100.00
SSAP A.J. Pollock 4.00 10.00
SSBB Byron Buxton 6.00 15.00
SSBH Bryce Harper 15.00 40.00
SSCB Cody Bellinger 8.00 20.00
SSCK Clayton Kershaw 8.00 20.00
SSDD Delino Deshields Jr. 4.00 10.00
SSFL Francisco Lindor 6.00 15.00
SSGP Gregory Polanco 5.00 12.00
SSJL Jake Lamb 5.00 12.00
SSJM Joe Musgrove 6.00 15.00
SSKB Kris Bryant 25.00 60.00
SSKM Kenta Maeda 5.00 12.00
SSMB Mookie Betts 12.00 30.00
SSMF Maikel Franco 5.00 12.00
SSMH Matt Shoemaker 5.00 12.00
SSMK Matt Kemp 5.00 12.00
SSMM Manny Machado 15.00 40.00
SSMS Marcus Stroman 5.00 12.00
SSMT Mike Trout 25.00 60.00
SSNA Nolan Arenado 15.00 40.00
SSNC Nicholas Castellanos 6.00 15.00
SSRC Robinson Cano 5.00 12.00
SSTB Tim Beckham 10.00 25.00
SSTM Trey Mancini 12.00 30.00

2018 Topps Opening Day Stars

STATED ODDS 1:27 BLASTER
ODSAD Adam Duvall 1.00 2.50
ODSAG Alex Gordon 1.00 2.50
ODSAJ Adam Jones 1.00 2.50
ODSAP Albert Pujols 1.50 4.00
ODSAS Antonio Senzatela .75 2.00
ODSAU Aaron Judge 5.00 12.00
ODSAV Alex Verdugo 1.25 3.00
ODSBB Brandon Belt 1.00 2.50
ODSBD Brian Dozier 1.00 2.50
ODSCB Charlie Blackmon 1.25 3.00
ODSCF Clint Frazier 1.50 4.00
ODSCH Cole Hamels 1.00 2.50
ODSCI Chance Sisco 1.00 2.50
ODSCK Corey Kluber 1.00 2.50
ODSCS Corey Seager 1.25 3.00
ODSDP Dustin Pedroia 1.25 3.00
ODSDS Dominic Smith 1.00 2.50
ODSDW Dansby Swanson 1.25 3.00
ODSFM Francisco Mejia 1.00 2.50
ODSGS George Springer 1.00 2.50
ODSJC J.P. Crawford .75 2.00
ODSJd Jacob deGrom 2.50 6.00
ODSJH Josh Harrison .75 2.00
ODSJV Justin Verlander 1.25 3.00
ODSKE Kyle Seager .75 2.00
ODSKJ Kenley Jansen 1.00 2.50
ODSKK Kevin Kiermaier 1.00 2.50
ODSKM Kendrys Morales .75 2.00
ODSKS Kyle Schwarber 1.25 3.00
ODSNC Nicholas Castellanos 1.25 3.00
ODSNW Nick Williams 1.00 2.50
ODSOA Ozzie Albies 2.50 6.00
ODSOR Orlando Arcia .75 2.00
ODSPD Paul DeJong 1.25 3.00
ODSRD Rafael Devers 2.50 6.00
ODSRH Rhys Hoskins 3.00 8.00
ODSSM Sean Manaea .75 2.00
ODSSS Stephen Strasburg 1.25 3.00
ODSVR Victor Robles 2.00 5.00
ODSWB Walker Buehler 4.00 10.00
ODSWC Willie Calhoun 1.25 3.00
ODSWM Wil Myers 1.00 2.50
ODSYM Yoan Moncada 1.25 3.00
ODSZG Zack Greinke 1.25 3.00

2018 Topps Opening Day Team Traditions and Celebrations

COMPLETE SET (15) 4.00 10.00
STATED ODDS 1:4 BLASTER
TTCCH Clydesdale Horses .40 1.00
TTCHA Home Run Apple .40 1.00
TTCHS Home Run Slide .40 1.00
TTCHT Home Run Train .40 1.00
TTCKC King's Court .40 1.00
TTCMC McCovey Cove .40 1.00
TTCMS Minnie and Paul Sign .40 1.00
TTCPR Racing Presidents .40 1.00
TTCRM Rally Monkey .40 1.00
TTCSC Sweet Caroline .40 1.00
TTCTF The Freeze .40 1.00
TTCYD Y.M.C.A. Dance .40 1.00
TTCODP Opening Day Parade .40 1.00
TTCOTD Old Timers Day .40 1.00
TTCTMO Take Me Out to the Ballgame .40 1.00

2019 Topps Opening Day

COMPLETE SET (200) 12.00 30.00
PRINTING PLATE ODDS 1:XXX
PLATE PRINT RUN 1 SET PER COLOR
BLACK-CYAN-MAGENTA-YELLOW ISSUED
NO PLATE PRICING DUE TO SCARCITY
1 Billy Hamilton .20 .50
2 Kyle Freeland .20 .50
3 Justin Verlander .25 .60
4 Ryan O'Hearn RC .20 .50
5 Corey Seager .25 .60
6 Scooter Gennett .20 .50
7 Adalberto Mondesi .20 .50
8 Freddie Freeman .30 .75
9 Niko Goodrum .20 .50
10 Jordan Zimmermann .20 .50
11 Nicholas Castellanos .25 .60
12 Zack Greinke .25 .60
13 Kyle Schwarber .25 .60
14 Rick Porcello .20 .50
15 Aaron Judge .60 1.50
16 Brian Anderson .15 .40
17 Sandy Alcantara .15 .40
18 Kyle Tucker RC .50 1.25
19 Charlie Blackmon .25 .60
20 Jon Lester .20 .50
21 Kenley Jansen .20 .50
22 Bryce Harper .40 1.00
23 Miguel Cabrera .25 .60
24 Mike Trout 1.25 3.00
25 Michael Lorenzen .15 .40
26 Zack Godley .15 .40
27 Raisel Iglesias .15 .40
28 Mark Trumbo .15 .40
29 David Dahl .15 .40
30 Eugenio Suarez .20 .50
31 Nolan Arenado .40 1.00
32 Derek Dietrich .20 .50
33 Mookie Betts .50 1.25
34 Trevor Story .25 .60
35 Andrew Benintendi .25 .60
36 Trevor Bauer .30 .75
37 Jose Abreu .25 .60
38 Dansby Swanson .30 .75
39 Christian Yelich .30 .75
40 George Springer .20 .50
41 Jose Altuve .20 .50
42 Rafael Devers .30 .75
43 David Price .20 .50
44 Trey Mancini .20 .50
45 Kris Bryant .30 .75
46 Clayton Kershaw .40 1.00
47 Xander Bogaerts .25 .60
48 Matt Kemp .20 .50
49 Willson Contreras .25 .60
50 Mike Clevinger .20 .50
51 Ronald Acuna Jr. 1.25 3.00
52 Corey Kluber .20 .50
53 Carlos Correa .25 .60
54 Mike Foltynewicz .25 .60
55 Yusei Kikuchi RC .30 .75
56 Justin Upton .20 .50
57 Carlos Rodon .25 .60
58 Alex Gordon .20 .50
59 Joey Votto .25 .60
60 J.T. Realmuto .25 .60
61 Albert Almora .20 .50
62 Ketel Marte .20 .50
63 Avisail Garcia .20 .50
64 Tim Beckham .20 .50
65 Albert Pujols .30 .75
66 Matt Davidson .20 .50
67 Max Muncy .20 .50
68 Christin Stewart RC .25 .60
69 Alex Bregman .25 .60
70 Edwin Encarnacion .25 .60
71 Whit Merrifield .25 .60
72 Carlos Carrasco .15 .40
73 Gerrit Cole .25 .60
74 Jonathan Schoop .15 .40
75 Salvador Perez .20 .50
76 Cedric Mullins RC .40 1.00
77 Jose Ramirez .20 .50
78 Andrelton Simmons .15 .40
79 Justin Turner .25 .60
80 Dylan Bundy .20 .50
81 Jeimer Candelario .15 .40
82 Jonathan Villar .15 .40
83 Kole Calhoun .15 .40
84 Francisco Lindor .25 .60
85 German Marquez .15 .40
86 Anthony Rizzo .30 .75
87 Starlin Castro .15 .40
88 Justus Sheffield RC .30 .75
89 Yoan Moncada .25 .60
90 Jaime Barria .15 .40
91 Brad Keller RC .20 .50
92 David Peralta .15 .40
93 J.D. Martinez .25 .60
94 Paul Goldschmidt .25 .60
95 Javier Baez .30 .75
96 Kevin Gausman .25 .60
97 Brad Boxberger .15 .40
98 Ozzie Albies .25 .60
99 Daniel Palka .15 .40
100 Shohei Ohtani .40 1.00
101 Jose Berrios .20 .50
102 Yadier Molina .30 .75
103 Mitch Garver .15 .40
104 Shane Bieber .25 .60
105 Buster Posey .30 .75
106 Gleyber Torres .50 1.25
107 Rhys Hoskins .30 .75
108 Jose Martinez .15 .40
109 Carlos Martinez .20 .50
110 Jorge Polanco .20 .50
111 Tommy Pham .15 .40
112 Rowdy Tellez RC .30 .75
113 Edwin Diaz .20 .50
114 Matt Duffy .15 .40
115 Josh Hader .20 .50
116 Dakota Hudson RC .25 .60
117 Cionel Perez RC .20 .50
118 Dereck Rodriguez .15 .40
119 Randal Grichuk .15 .40
120 Dee Gordon .15 .40
121 Orlando Arcia .15 .40
122 Ryan Zimmerman .20 .50
123 Eric Hosmer .20 .50
124 Stephen Strasburg .25 .60
125 Franmil Reyes .15 .40
126 Noah Syndergaard .20 .50
127 Mitch Haniger .20 .50
128 Juan Soto .75 2.00
129 Justin Smoak .15 .40
130 Lourdes Gurriel Jr. .20 .50
131 Michael Kopech RC .60 1.50
132 Kevin Pillar .15 .40
133 Jeff McNeil RC .50 1.25
134 Jameson Taillon .20 .50
135 Matt Chapman .25 .60
136 Jesus Aguilar .20 .50
137 Odubel Herrera .20 .50
138 Luis Urias RC .30 .75
139 Jack Flaherty .25 .60
140 Wil Myers .20 .50
141 Ryan Yarbrough .15 .40
142 Eddie Rosario .25 .60
143 Sean Manaea .15 .40
144 Miguel Andujar .25 .60
145 Luis Severino .20 .50
146 Blake Treinen .15 .40
147 Carlos Santana .20 .50
148 Chris Archer .15 .40
149 Todd Frazier .15 .40
150 Jacob deGrom .50 1.25
151 Rougned Odor .20 .50
152 Matt Olson .25 .60
153 Willians Astudillo RC .20 .50
154 Sean Doolittle .15 .40
155 Jose Leclerc .15 .40
156 Aledmys Diaz .15 .40
157 Lorenzo Cain .15 .40
158 Gregory Polanco .20 .50
159 Nick Martini RC .20 .50
160 Ramon Laureano RC .40 1.00
161 Brandon Nimmo .20 .50
162 Jean Segura .25 .60
163 Will Smith .15 .40
164 Willy Adames .15 .40
165 Joey Lucchesi .15 .40
166 Didi Gregorius .20 .50
167 Tyler Glasnow .25 .60
168 Matt Carpenter .25 .60
169 Brandon Belt .20 .50
170 Kyle Gibson .20 .50
171 Corey Dickerson .20 .50
172 Max Kepler .20 .50
173 Amed Rosario .20 .50
174 Harrison Bader .20 .50
175 Hunter Renfroe .15 .40
176 Joey Gallo .20 .50
177 Jake Bauers RC .30 .75
178 Touki Toussaint RC .20 .50
179 Jake Arrieta .20 .50
180 Elvis Andrus .20 .50
181 Josh James RC .30 .75
182 Anthony Rendon .25 .60
183 Max Scherzer .25 .60
184 Maikel Franco .20 .50
185 Khris Davis .25 .60
186 Starling Marte .20 .50
187 Evan Longoria .20 .50
188 Robinson Cano .20 .50
189 Michael Conforto .20 .50
190 Miles Mikolas .20 .50
191 Joey Wendle .20 .50
192 Nomar Mazara .15 .40
193 Masahiro Tanaka .20 .50
194 Stephen Piscotty .15 .40
195 James Paxton .20 .50
196 Blake Snell .20 .50
197 Felipe Vazquez .15 .40
198 Aaron Nola .20 .50
199 Brandon Crawford .20 .50
200 Shin-Soo Choo .20 .50

2019 Topps Opening Day Blue Foil

*BLUE: 2X TO 5X BASIC
*BLUE RC: 1.5X TO 4X BASIC RC
STATED ODDS 1:XX
ANNCD PRINT RUN 2019 SETS

2019 Topps Opening Day Purple Foil

*PURPLE: 5X TO 12X BASIC
*PURPLE RC: 4X TO 10X BASIC RC
FOUND IN MEIJER BLISTER PACKS

2019 Topps Opening Day Red Foil

*RED: 5X TO 12X BASIC
*RED RC: 4X TO 10X BASIC RC
FOUND IN TARGET MEGA BOX

2019 Topps Opening Day Photo Variations

STATED ODDS 1:XXX
15 Judge Blk Jrsy 60.00 150.00
22 Harper Portrait 20.00 50.00
24 Trout w/Bat 150.00 400.00
39 Yelich Tip cap
41 Altuve Sitting
45 Bryant Sngl sses 20.00 50.00
51 Acuna At wall
53 Correa Dugout
67 Muncy Run
84 Lindor Salute 8.00 20.00
95 Baez Blue Jrsy 25.00 60.00
102 Molina Point 30.00 80.00
106 Torres Smile 30.00 80.00
128 Soto Dugout 40.00 100.00
150 deGrom Yllw Jckt 30.00 80.00

2019 Topps Opening Day 150 Years of Fun

COMPLETE SET (25)
STATED ODDS 1:XX
YOF1 Ty Cobb .60 1.50
YOF2 Jackie Robinson .40 1.00
YOF3 Lou Gehrig .75 2.00
YOF4 Ted Williams .75 2.00
YOF5 Babe Ruth 1.00 2.50
YOF6 Hank Aaron .75 2.00
YOF7 Sandy Koufax .75 2.00
YOF8 Roberto Clemente 1.00 2.50
YOF9 Ernie Banks .40 1.00
YOF10 Ozzie Smith .50 1.25
YOF11 Gary Carter .30 .75
YOF12 Joe Morgan .30 .75
YOF13 Tom Seaver .30 .75
YOF14 Jim Palmer .30 .75
YOF15 Reggie Jackson .30 .75
YOF16 Frank Thomas .40 1.00
YOF17 Nolan Ryan 1.25 3.00
YOF18 Cal Ripken Jr. 1.25 3.00
YOF19 Pedro Martinez .30 .75
YOF20 David Ortiz .40 1.00
YOF21 Ichiro .50 1.25
YOF22 Derek Jeter 1.00 2.50
YOF23 Francisco Lindor .40 1.00
YOF24 Ronald Acuna Jr. 2.00 5.00
YOF25 Mike Trout 2.00 5.00

2019 Topps Opening Day Autographs

STATED ODDS 1:XXX
EXCHANGE DEADLINE 1/31/2021
ODAAJ Aaron Judge 75.00 200.00
ODAAR Anthony Rizzo 25.00 60.00
ODABN Brandon Nimmo 12.00 30.00
ODABW Brandon Woodruff 5.00 12.00
ODADR Dereck Rodriguez 10.00 25.00
ODAFL Francisco Lindor 20.00 50.00
ODAJA Jesus Aguilar 4.00 10.00
ODAJAL Jose Altuve 20.00 50.00
ODAJH Josh Hader 8.00 20.00
ODAJS Jean Segura 12.00 30.00
ODAKF Kyle Freeland 4.00 10.00
ODALG Lourdes Gurriel Jr. 6.00 15.00
ODAMC Matt Chapman 5.00 12.00
ODAMK Michael Kopech 10.00 25.00
ODAMMU Max Muncy 8.00 20.00
ODARA Ronald Acuna Jr. 40.00 100.00
ODASB Shane Bieber 5.00 12.00
ODASO Shohei Ohtani 100.00 250.00
ODAWA Willy Adames 3.00 8.00

2019 Topps Opening Day Diamond Autograph Relics

STATED ODDS 1:XXX
STATED PRINT RUN 50 SER.#'d SETS
EXCHANGE DEADLINE 1/31/2021
DARBS Blake Snell 20.00 50.00
DARKD Khris Davis
DARMH Mitch Haniger 20.00 50.00
DARMK Michael Kopech
DARRA Ronald Acuna Jr.
DARRH Rhys Hoskins 60.00 150.00
DARSO Shohei Ohtani
DARSP Salvador Perez
DARTM Trey Mancini 25.00 60.00
DARTS Trevor Story

2019 Topps Opening Day Diamond Relics

STATED ODDS 1:XXX
DRAB Adrian Beltre 10.00 25.00
DRABR Alex Bregman 20.00 50.00
DRAR Anthony Rizzo 12.00 30.00
DRBP Buster Posey 12.00 30.00
DRBS Blake Snell 8.00 20.00
DRCK Clayton Kershaw 15.00 40.00
DRCY Christian Yelich
DREH Eric Hosmer 8.00 20.00
DRGP Gregory Polanco 8.00 20.00
DRJD Jacob deGrom 20.00 50.00
DRJR Jose Ramirez 8.00 20.00
DRJV Joey Votto 10.00 25.00
DRKD Khris Davis 10.00 25.00
DRMB Mookie Betts 20.00 50.00
DRMC Matt Carpenter 10.00 25.00
DRMH Mitch Haniger 8.00 20.00
DRMK Michael Kopech 20.00 50.00
DRNC Nicholas Castellanos 10.00 25.00
DRRA Ronald Acuna Jr. 25.00 60.00
DRRH Rhys Hoskins 15.00 40.00
DRSC Starlin Castro
DRSO Shohei Ohtani 15.00 40.00
DRSP Salvador Perez 15.00 40.00
DRTM Trey Mancini 8.00 20.00
DRTS Trevor Story 10.00 25.00

2019 Topps Opening Day Dugout Peeks

STATED ODDS 1:XX
DP1 Francisco Lindor 30.00 80.00
DP2 Jose Altuve 30.00 80.00
DP3 David Wright 30.00 80.00
DP4 Manny Machado 20.00 50.00
DP5 Starlin Castro 10.00 25.00
DP6 Ichiro 50.00 120.00
DP7 David Price 20.00 50.00
DP8 Marwin Gonzalez 6.00 15.00
DP9 Aaron Judge
DP10 Didi Gregorius 25.00 60.00
DP11 Khris Davis
DP12 Shohei Ohtani 60.00 150.00
DP13 Ronald Acuna Jr.
DP14 Mike Trout 125.00 300.00
DP15 Jose Altuve 30.00 80.00
DP16 Jake Arrieta
DP17 Odubel Herrera 15.00 40.00
DP18 Corey Dickerson 10.00 25.00
DP19 Ronald Acuna Jr.
DP20 Tim Beckham 20.00 50.00

2019 Topps Opening Day Mascot Autograph Relics

STATED ODDS 1:XXX
EXCHANGE DEADLINE 1/31/2021
MARB Blooper
MARO Orbit 30.00 80.00
MARS Screech
MARCC Clark 30.00 80.00
MARMM Mariner Moose
MARSL Slider 30.00 80.00
MARTCB TC Bear 30.00 80.00

2019 Topps Opening Day Mascot Autographs

STATED ODDS 1:XXX
EXCHANGE DEADLINE 1/31/2021
MAB Blooper 20.00 50.00
MAO Orbit 25.00 60.00
MAS Screech 15.00 40.00
MACC Clark 15.00 40.00
MAMM Mariner Moose 12.00 30.00
MAPP Pirate Parrot 12.00 30.00
MASF Swinging Friar 12.00 30.00
MASL Slider 12.00 30.00
MATCB TC Bear 12.00 30.00

2019 Topps Opening Day Mascot Relics

STATED ODDS 1:XXX
MRB Blooper 6.00 15.00
MRO Orbit 6.00 15.00
MRS Screech 6.00 15.00
MRBB Bernie Brewer 6.00 15.00
MRCC Clark the Cub 6.00 15.00
MRMM Mariner Moose 6.00 15.00
MRSL Slider 6.00 15.00
MRTCB TC Bear 6.00 15.00
MRWGM Wally the Green Monster 10.00 25.00

2019 Topps Opening Day Mascots

COMPLETE SET (25) 6.00 15.00
STATED ODDS 1:XX
M1 Blooper .40 1.00
M2 Slider .40 1.00
M3 Clark .40 1.00
M4 Pirate Parrot .40 1.00
M5 Screech .40 1.00
M6 Orbit .40 1.00
M7 Mariner Moose .40 1.00
M8 TC Bear .40 1.00
M9 Swinging Friar .40 1.00
M10 Mascot .40 1.00
M11 Mascot .40 1.00
M12 Rangers Captain .40 1.00
M13 Paws .40 1.00
M14 Sluggerrr .40 1.00
M15 Wally the Green Monster .40 1.00
M16 Mr. Red .40 1.00
M17 Dinger .40 1.00
M18 Billy the Marlin .40 1.00
M19 Bernie Brewer .40 1.00
M20 Mr. Met .40 1.00
M21 Phillie Phanatic .40 1.00
M22 Fredbird .40 1.00
M23 Raymond .40 1.00
M24 Mascot .40 1.00
M25 Mascot .40 1.00

2019 Topps Opening Day Opening Day

COMPLETE SET (15) 4.00 10.00
STATED ODDS 1:XX
ODBAB Atlanta Braves .40 1.00
ODBAD Arizona Diamondbacks .40 1.00
ODBBO Baltimore Orioles .40 1.00
ODBCR Cincinnati Reds .40 1.00
ODBDT Detroit Tigers .40 1.00
ODBMM Miami Marlins .40 1.00
ODBOA Oakland Athletics .40 1.00
ODBSM Seattle Mariners .40 1.00
ODBTR Texas Rangers .40 1.00
ODBKCR Kansas City Royals .40 1.00
ODBLAD Los Angeles Dodgers .40 1.00
ODBNYM New York Mets .40 1.00
ODBSDP San Diego Padres .40 1.00
ODBTBJ Toronto Blue Jays .40 1.00
ODBTBR Tampa Bay Rays .40 1.00

2019 Topps Opening Day Rally Time

STATED ODDS 1:XX
RTA Ozzie Albies 8.00 20.00
RTB Mookie Betts 15.00 40.00
RTC Matt Davidson 6.00 15.00
RTL Clayton Kershaw 15.00 40.00
RTM Christian Yelich 10.00 25.00

RTS Matt Adams 5.00 12.00
RTAB Alex Bregman 15.00 40.00
RTAJ Aaron Judge 40.00 100.00
RTAR Anthony Rizzo 10.00 25.00
RTCY Christian Yelich 10.00 25.00
RTDB David Bote 12.00 30.00
RTEE Enrique Hernandez 8.00 20.00
RTEH Eric Hosmer 6.00 15.00
RTJJ Jeremy Jeffress 5.00 12.00
RTJK Jason Kipnis 6.00 15.00
RTJP Jurickson Profar 6.00 15.00
RTMT Max Kepler 6.00 15.00
RTRA Ronald Acuna Jr. 40.00 100.00
RTRH Rhys Hoskins 10.00 25.00
RTRO Rougned Odor 6.00 15.00
RTSL Matt Carpenter 8.00 20.00
RTWC Willson Contreras 6.00 15.00
RTXB Xander Bogaerts 8.00 20.00
RTYC Yoenis Cespedes 8.00 20.00
RTYM Yadier Molina 15.00 40.00

2019 Topps Opening Day Relics

STATED ODDS 1:XXX
ODRAJ Aaron Judge 20.00 50.00
ODRAP Albert Pujols 5.00 12.00
ODRAR Anthony Rizzo 6.00 15.00
ODRBP Buster Posey 5.00 12.00
ODRCC Carlos Correa 4.00 10.00
ODRCK Clayton Kershaw 6.00 15.00
ODRDG Didi Gregorius 3.00 8.00
ODRJA Jose Abreu 4.00 10.00
ODRJM J.D. Martinez 6.00 15.00
ODRJS Juan Soto 12.00 30.00
ODRJV Justin Verlander 4.00 10.00
ODRKB Kris Bryant 10.00 25.00
ODRMC Miguel Cabrera 4.00 10.00
ODRMS Max Scherzer 4.00 10.00
ODRMT Mike Trout 20.00 50.00
ODRNA Nolan Arenado 6.00 15.00
ODRRH Rhys Hoskins 5.00 12.00
ODRSO Shohei Ohtani 6.00 15.00
ODRYM Yadier Molina 5.00 12.00
ODRJAL Jose Altuve 3.00 8.00
ODRJVO Joey Votto 4.00 10.00

2019 Topps Opening Day Sock it To Me

STATED ODDS 1:XX
SM1 Bryce Harper 30.00 80.00
SM2 Aaron Judge 25.00 60.00
SM3 Javier Baez 12.00 30.00
SM4 Mookie Betts 30.00 80.00
SM5 Ronald Acuna Jr. 50.00 125.00
SM6 Juan Soto 20.00 50.00
SM7 Rhys Hoskins 12.00 30.00
SM8 Jose Altuve 8.00 20.00
SM9 Mike Trout 75.00 200.00
SM10 Francisco Lindor 10.00 25.00
SM11 Trevor Story 10.00 25.00
SM12 Khris Davis 10.00 25.00
SM13 Anthony Rizzo 12.00 30.00
SM14 Chris Archer 6.00 15.00
SM15 Amed Rosario 12.00 30.00
SM16 Joey Votto 10.00 25.00
SM17 Harrison Bader 8.00 20.00
SM18 Chris Taylor 8.00 20.00
SM19 Ozzie Albies 10.00 25.00
SM20 Corey Kluber 8.00 20.00
SM21 Jose Berrios 8.00 20.00
SM22 Andrew Benintendi 10.00 25.00
SM23 Ben Zobrist 8.00 20.00
SM24 Kyle Schwarber 10.00 25.00
SM25 Dee Gordon 6.00 15.00

2019 Topps Opening Day Team Traditions and Celebrations

COMPLETE SET (10) 3.00 8.00
STATED ODDS 1:XX
TTCBM Bobblehead Museum .40 1.00
TTCCS California Spectacular .40 1.00
TTCES Eutaw Street .40 1.00
TTCLB Liberty Bell .40 1.00
TTCOP Outfield Pool .40 1.00
TTCSB Western Metal Building .40 1.00
TTCSF Stadium Fountains .40 1.00
TTCSP Scoreboard Pinwheels .40 1.00
TTCWF Tiger Merry-Go-Round .40 1.00
TTCTGS Tony Gwynn Statue .60 1.50

2020 Topps Opening Day

COMP.SET w/o SP (200) 12.00 30.00
1 Brendan McKay RC .30 .75
2 Jonathan Villar .15 .40
3 Garrett Cooper .15 .40
4 Brandon Woodruff .25 .60
5 Mike Moustakas .20 .50
6 Sean Doolittle .15 .40
7 James Paxton .20 .50
8 Domingo Santana .20 .50
9 Joc Pederson .20 .50
10 Yasmani Grandal .15 .40
11 Luis Arraez .30 .75
12 Nico Hoerner RC .75 2.00
13 Brian Anderson .15 .40
14 Alex Verdugo .20 .50
15 J.T. Realmuto .25 .60
16 Zac Gallen RC .50 1.25
17 Kyle Lewis RC 1.50 4.00
18 Lance Lynn .15 .40
19 Tim Anderson .25 .60
20 Max Scherzer .25 .60
21 Gerrit Cole .40 1.00
22 Anthony Rizzo .30 .75
23 Eduardo Rodriguez .15 .40
24 Willson Contreras .25 .60
25 Omar Narvaez .15 .40
26 Sean Murphy RC .30 .75
27 Juan Soto .75 2.00
28 Mookie Betts .50 1.25
29 Jordan Yamamoto RC .20 .50
30 Nick Solak RC .75 2.00
31 Aaron Judge .60 1.50
32 J.D. Martinez .25 .60
33 Vladimir Guerrero Jr. .40 1.00
34 Jeff McNeil .20 .50
35 Trea Turner .20 .50
36 Ken Giles .15 .40
37 Justin Turner .25 .60
38 Nolan Arenado .40 1.00
39 Carter Kieboom .20 .50
40 Mitch Garver .15 .40
41 Patrick Corbin .20 .50
42 Max Fried .25 .60
43 Shohei Ohtani .40 1.00
44 Albert Pujols .30 .75
45 Dakota Hudson .20 .50
46 Franmil Reyes .15 .40
47 Jose Ramirez .20 .50
48 Francisco Lindor .25 .60
49 Sandy Alcantara .15 .40
50 Kenta Maeda .20 .50
51 Ramon Laureano .20 .50
52 David Dahl .15 .40
53 Jon Lester .20 .50
54 Adalberto Mondesi .20 .50
55 Abraham Toro RC .25 .60
56 Mike Soroka .25 .60
57 Dustin May RC .60 1.50
58 Mike Fiers .15 .40
59 Gary Sanchez .25 .60
60 Lourdes Gurriel Jr. .20 .50
61 Keston Hiura .30 .75
62 Michel Baez RC .20 .50
63 Yordan Alvarez RC 2.00 5.00
64 Mike Yastrzemski .40 1.00
65 Justin Verlander .25 .60
66 Paul Goldschmidt .25 .60
67 Ronald Acuna Jr. 1.00 2.50
68 Dominic Smith .15 .40
69 Tommy La Stella .15 .40
70 Gavin Lux RC 1.00 2.50
71 Ozzie Albies .25 .60
72 Jorge Soler .25 .60
73 Amed Rosario .20 .50
74 Tommy Pham .15 .40
75 Craig Kimbrel .20 .50
76 Jack Flaherty .25 .60
77 Bryan Reynolds .20 .50
78 Matt Chapman .25 .60
79 DJ LeMahieu .25 .60
80 Michael Conforto .20 .50
81 Evan Longoria .20 .50
82 Orlando Arcia .15 .40
83 Eric Hosmer .20 .50
84 Kyle Seager .15 .40
85 Elvis Andrus .20 .50
86 Anthony Rendon .25 .60
87 Giancarlo Stanton .25 .60
88 Matt Carpenter .25 .60
89 Jose Altuve .20 .50
90 Mike Trout 1.25 3.00
91 Marco Gonzales .15 .40
92 Zach Plesac .25 .60
93 Nelson Cruz .25 .60
94 Liam Hendriks .15 .40
95 Eduardo Escobar .15 .40
96 Aroldis Chapman .25 .60
97 Eugenio Suarez .20 .50
98 Oscar Mercado .25 .60
99 Nick Senzel .25 .60
100 John Means .25 .60
101 Kenley Jansen .20 .50
102 Scott Kingery .20 .50
103 Hanser Alberto .15 .40
104 Matthew Boyd .15 .40
105 Jesus Luzardo RC .40 1.00
106 Tyler Glasnow .25 .60
107 Max Muncy .20 .50
108 Corey Seager .25 .60
109 Trevor Story .25 .60
110 Merrill Kelly .15 .40
111 Miguel Cabrera .25 .60
112 Victor Robles .30 .75
113 Charlie Morton .25 .60
114 Randal Grichuk .15 .40
115 Yusei Kikuchi .20 .50
116 Dansby Swanson .25 .60
117 Kris Bryant .30 .75
118 Yoan Moncada .25 .60
119 Joey Lucchesi .15 .40
120 Hunter Dozier .15 .40
121 Zack Greinke .25 .60
122 Jorge Alfaro .15 .40
123 Trey Mancini .25 .60
124 Carlos Correa .25 .60
125 Luis Castillo .20 .50
126 Andres Munoz RC .30 .75
127 Kirby Yates .15 .40
128 Javier Baez .30 .75
129 Cody Bellinger .50 1.25
130 Yadier Molina .30 .75
131 Eddie Rosario .20 .50
132 Clayton Kershaw .40 1.00
133 Christian Walker .20 .50
134 Michael Brantley .20 .50
135 Tommy Edman .25 .60
136 Shane Bieber .25 .60
137 Gregory Polanco .20 .50
138 Eloy Jimenez .50 1.25
139 Paul DeJong .25 .60
140 Michael Chavis .20 .50
141 Lucas Giolito .20 .50
142 Carlos Santana .20 .50
143 Kyle Schwarber .25 .60
144 Buster Posey .30 .75
145 Freddie Freeman .30 .75
146 George Springer .20 .50
147 Aristides Aquino RC .50 1.25
148 Jorge Polanco .20 .50
149 Charlie Blackmon .25 .60
150 Will Smith .25 .60
151 Ian Kennedy .15 .40
152 Marcus Stroman .20 .50
153 Josh Hader .20 .50
154 Whit Merrifield .25 .60
155 J.D. Davis .15 .40
156 Rhys Hoskins .30 .75
157 Pete Alonso .60 1.50
158 Mike Clevinger .20 .50
159 Luke Voit .30 .75
160 Ryan Braun .20 .50
161 Ketel Marte .20 .50
162 Max Kepler .20 .50
163 Christian Yelich .30 .75
164 Alex Bregman .25 .60
165 Brandon Lowe .20 .50
166 Andrew Benintendi .25 .60
167 Adbert Alzolay RC .25 .60
168 A.J. Puk RC .30 .75
169 Rafael Devers .30 .75
170 Starling Marte .20 .50
171 Joey Votto .25 .60
172 Walker Buehler .30 .75
173 Bo Bichette RC 1.50 4.00
174 Sonny Gray .20 .50
175 Austin Meadows .25 .60
176 Jean Segura .20 .50
177 Masahiro Tanaka .25 .60
178 Marcus Semien .25 .60
179 Niko Goodrum .20 .50
180 Austin Riley .30 .75
181 Starlin Castro .15 .40
182 Jameson Taillon .20 .50
183 Yuli Gurriel .20 .50
184 Matt Olson .25 .60
185 Aaron Nola .20 .50
186 Gleyber Torres .50 1.25
187 Jacob deGrom .50 1.25
188 Bryce Harper .40 1.00
189 Fernando Tatis Jr. 1.25 3.00
190 Trent Grisham RC .75 2.00
191 Hunter Renfroe .15 .40
192 Dee Gordon .15 .40
193 Cavan Biggio .30 .75
194 Emilio Pagan .15 .40
195 Brad Hand .15 .40
196 Chris Paddack .25 .60
197 Josh Bell .20 .50
198 Dan Vogelbach .15 .40
199 Jose Berrios .20 .50
200 Manny Machado .25 .60
201 Luis Robert SP RC 25.00 60.00

2020 Topps Opening Day Blue Foil

*BLUE: 1.5X TO 4X BASIC
*BLUE RC: 1.2X TO 3X BASIC RC

2020 Topps Opening Day Blue Jays Maple Leaf Red

DISTRIBUTED IN CANADA
33 Vladimir Guerrero Jr. 4.00 10.00
36 Ken Giles 1.50 4.00
60 Lourdes Gurriel Jr. 2.00 5.00
114 Randal Grichuk 1.50 4.00
173 Bo Bichette 15.00 40.00
193 Cavan Biggio 3.00 8.00

2020 Topps Opening Day Purple Foil

*PURPLE: 3X TO 8X BASIC
*PURPLE RC: 2.5X TO 6X BASIC RC

2020 Topps Opening Day Red Foil

*RED: 2X TO 5X BASIC
*RED RC: 1.5X TO 4X BASIC RC

2020 Topps Opening Day Photo Variations

1 Brendan McKay 8.00 20.00
24 Willson Contreras 15.00 40.00
27 Juan Soto 50.00 120.00
33 Vladimir Guerrero Jr. 12.00 30.00
38 Nolan Arenado 10.00 25.00
39 Carter Kieboom 10.00 25.00
43 Shohei Ohtani 25.00 60.00
61 Keston Hiura 10.00 25.00
63 Yordan Alvarez 50.00 120.00
67 Ronald Acuna Jr. 30.00 80.00
78 Matt Chapman 8.00 20.00
79 DJ LeMahieu 15.00 40.00
105 Jesus Luzardo 10.00 25.00
107 Max Muncy 12.00 30.00
116 Dansby Swanson 8.00 20.00
117 Kris Bryant 12.00 30.00
138 Eloy Jimenez 15.00 40.00
147 Aristides Aquino 20.00 50.00
156 Rhys Hoskins 10.00 25.00
157 Pete Alonso 60.00 150.00
161 Ketel Marte 10.00 25.00
163 Christian Yelich 10.00 25.00
165 Brandon Lowe 10.00 25.00
169 Rafael Devers 30.00 80.00
172 Walker Buehler 10.00 25.00
173 Bo Bichette 50.00 120.00
186 Gleyber Torres 15.00 40.00
187 Jacob deGrom 12.00 30.00
188 Bryce Harper 12.00 30.00
199 Jose Berrios 10.00 25.00

2020 Topps Opening Day Autographs

ODAAA Aristides Aquino 10.00 25.00
ODAAP A.J. Puk 5.00 12.00
ODABB Bo Bichette 40.00 100.00
ODACB Cavan Biggio 10.00 25.00
ODAGL Gavin Lux 30.00 80.00
ODAGT Gleyber Torres 30.00 80.00
ODAJF Jack Flaherty 10.00 25.00
ODAJS Juan Soto 50.00 120.00
ODAJSO Jorge Soler 10.00 25.00
ODAKH Keston Hiura 15.00 40.00
ODAKL Kyle Lewis 50.00 120.00
ODAMK Max Kepler 6.00 15.00
ODAMS Max Scherzer 15.00 40.00
ODAMSO Mike Soroka 10.00 25.00
ODAMT Mike Trout 150.00 400.00
ODAMY Mike Yastrzemski 20.00 50.00
ODARA Ronald Acuna Jr. 60.00 150.00
ODAWA Willians Astudillo 6.00 15.00
ODAWS Will Smith 12.00 30.00
ODAYA Yordan Alvarez 75.00 200.00

2020 Topps Opening Day Ballpark Profile Autographs

BPACC Chip Caray 20.00 50.00
BPADB Dan Baker 12.00 30.00
BPADBR Dick Bremer 25.00 60.00
BPADG Drew Goodman 12.00 30.00
BPADO Don Orsillo 12.00 30.00
BPAGP Gary Pressy 25.00 60.00
BPAJD Jacques Doucet 15.00 40.00
BPAJJ Jaime Jarrin 30.00 80.00
BPAJK John Keating 20.00 50.00
BPARBM Renel Brooks-Moon 15.00 40.00
BPATC Tom Caron 12.00 30.00

2020 Topps Opening Day Diamond Autograph Relics

DARAA Aristides Aquino/40 12.00 30.00
DARBR Bryan Reynolds/49 30.00 80.00
DARCP Chris Paddack/50 20.00 50.00
DARKH Keston Hiura/50 50.00 120.00
DARKL Kyle Lewis/40 15.00 40.00
DARKM Ketel Marte/50 20.00 50.00
DARMCH Matt Chapman/50 15.00 40.00
DARMM Max Muncy/50 20.00 50.00
DARPA Pete Alonso/30 60.00 150.00
DARYA Yordan Alvarez/40 75.00 200.00

2020 Topps Opening Day Diamond Relics

DRAA Aristides Aquino 15.00 40.00
DRBH Bryce Harper 15.00 40.00
DRBR Bryan Reynolds 5.00 12.00
DRCB Clayton Kershaw 10.00 25.00
DRCK Cody Bellinger 10.00 25.00
DRCP Chris Paddack 6.00 15.00
DRCY Christian Yelich 8.00 20.00
DRFF Freddie Freeman 8.00 20.00
DRFT Fernando Tatis Jr. 12.00 30.00
DRJB Javier Baez 8.00 20.00
DRJF Jack Flaherty 10.00 25.00
DRKH Keston Hiura 10.00 25.00
DRKL Kyle Lewis 8.00 20.00
DRKM Ketel Marte 5.00 12.00
DRMC Miguel Cabrera 12.00 30.00
DRMCH Matt Chapman 12.00 30.00
DRMT Mike Trout 30.00 80.00
DRNA Nolan Arenado 12.00 30.00
DRPA Pete Alonso 20.00 50.00
DRPG Paul Goldschmidt 6.00 15.00
DRRA Ronald Acuna Jr. 15.00 40.00
DRRH Rhys Hoskins 8.00 20.00
DRRO Rougned Odor 5.00 12.00
DRSC Shin-Soo Choo 5.00 12.00
DRSO Shohei Ohtani 10.00 25.00
DRYA Yordan Alvarez 25.00 60.00

2020 Topps Opening Day Dugout Peeks

DP1 Ronald Acuna Jr. 60.00 150.00
DP2 Bryce Harper 30.00 80.00
DP3 Nelson Cruz 20.00 50.00
DP4 Kris Bryant 12.00 30.00
DP5 Alex Bregman 10.00 25.00
DP6 Cody Bellinger 20.00 50.00
DP7 Juan Soto 30.00 80.00
DP8 Pete Alonso 20.00 50.00
DP9 Aaron Judge 25.00 60.00
DP10 Mike Trout 150.00 400.00
DP11 Aristides Aquino 40.00 100.00
DP12 Manny Machado 10.00 25.00
DP13 Francisco Lindor 25.00 60.00
DP14 Eloy Jimenez 20.00 50.00
DP15 Ketel Marte 15.00 40.00
DP16 Nolan Arenado 12.00 30.00
DP17 Vladimir Guerrero Jr. 40.00 100.00
DP18 Joey Votto 20.00 50.00
DP19 Mookie Betts 20.00 50.00
DP20 Matt Chapman 10.00 25.00

2020 Topps Opening Day Major League Mementos Relics

MLMBH Bryce Harper 8.00 20.00
MLMBM Brendan McKay 5.00 12.00
MLMBP Buster Posey 6.00 15.00
MLMCY Christian Yelich 6.00 15.00
MLMKB Kris Bryant 6.00 15.00
MLMMT Mike Trout 25.00 60.00
MLMPA Pete Alonso 12.00 30.00
MLMRD Rafael Devers 10.00 25.00

2020 Topps Opening Day Mascot Autograph Relics

MARBB Bernie Brewer 40.00 100.00
MARC Clark 40.00 100.00
MARFB Fredbird 40.00 100.00
MARS Sluggerrr 40.00 100.00
MARWGM Wally the Green Monster 40.00 100.00

2020 Topps Opening Day Mascot Autographs

MABB Bernie Brewer 15.00 40.00
MACC Clark 12.00 30.00
MAFB Fredbird 12.00 30.00
MAMM Mr. Met 25.00 60.00
MAR Raymond 10.00 25.00
MAS Sluggerrr 10.00 25.00
MAWGM Wally the Green Monster 12.00 30.00

2020 Topps Opening Day Mascot Patches

STATED PRINT RUN 99 SER.#'d SETS
MPRCC Clark 30.00 80.00
MPRD Dinger 20.00 50.00
MPRMM Mr. Met 20.00 50.00
MPRMM Mariner Moose 20.00 50.00
MPRO Orbit 20.00 50.00
MPRR Raymond 20.00 50.00
MPRS Screech 20.00 50.00
MPRTCB TC Bear 20.00 50.00
MPRWGM Wally the Green Monster 20.00 50.00

2020 Topps Opening Day Mascot Relics

MRBB Bernie Brewer 8.00 20.00
MRCC Clark 8.00 20.00
MRF Fredbird 8.00 20.00
MRS Sluggerrr 8.00 20.00
MRWGM Wally the Green Monster 8.00 20.00

2020 Topps Opening Day Mascots

COMPLETE SET (24) 6.00 15.00
STATED ODDS 1:XX
M1 Clark .40 1.00
M2 Wally the Green Monster .40 1.00
M3 Mr. Met .40 1.00
M4 Dinger .40 1.00
M5 Fredbird .40 1.00
M6 Paws .40 1.00
M7 Sluggerrr .40 1.00
M8 Bernie Brewer .40 1.00
M9 Raymond .40 1.00
M10 Rosie Red .40 1.00
M11 Blooper .40 1.00
M12 Slider .40 1.00
M13 Pirate Parrot .40 1.00
M14 Screech .40 1.00
M15 Orbit .40 1.00
M16 Mariner Moose .40 1.00
M17 TC Bear .40 1.00
M18 Swinging Friar .40 1.00
M19 Rangers Captain .40 1.00
M20 Mr. Red .40 1.00
M21 Billy the Marlin .40 1.00
M22 Mascot .40 1.00
M23 Mrs. Met .40 1.00
M24 Mascot .40 1.00

2020 Topps Opening Day Opening Day

COMPLETE SET (15) 4.00 10.00
COMMON CARD .40 1.00
OD1 Cincinnati Reds .40 1.00
OD2 Kansas City Royals .40 1.00
OD3 Los Angeles Dodgers .40 1.00
OD4 Miami Marlins .40 1.00
OD5 Milwaukee Brewers .40 1.00
OD6 Minnesota Twins .40 1.00
OD7 New York Yankees .40 1.00
OD8 Oakland Athletics .40 1.00
OD9 Philadelphia Phillies .40 1.00
OD10 San Diego Padres .40 1.00
OD11 Seattle Mariners .40 1.00
OD12 Tampa Bay Rays .40 1.00
OD13 Texas Rangers .40 1.00
OD14 Toronto Blue Jays .40 1.00
OD15 Washington Nationals .40 1.00

2020 Topps Opening Day Relics

ODRAA Aristides Aquino 10.00 25.00
ODRAB Alex Bregman 4.00 10.00
ODRAJ Aaron Judge 10.00 25.00
ODRAR Anthony Rizzo 8.00 20.00
ODRBH Bryce Harper 10.00 25.00
ODRCB Cody Bellinger 6.00 15.00
ODRCK Clayton Kershaw 8.00 20.00
ODRCY Christian Yelich 8.00 20.00
ODRFT Fernando Tatis Jr. 8.00 20.00
ODRGT Gleyber Torres 8.00 20.00
ODRJB Javier Baez 6.00 15.00
ODRJV Justin Verlander 6.00 15.00
ODRKB Kris Bryant 5.00 12.00
ODRKH Keston Hiura 5.00 12.00
ODRMC Miguel Cabrera 8.00 20.00
ODRMS Max Scherzer 6.00 15.00
ODRMT Mike Trout 25.00 60.00
ODRNS Nick Senzel 4.00 10.00
ODRPA Pete Alonso 10.00 25.00
ODRRA Ronald Acuna Jr. 12.00 30.00
ODRRH Rhys Hoskins 6.00 15.00
ODRSO Shohei Ohtani 8.00 20.00
ODRVG Vladimir Guerrero Jr. 6.00 15.00
ODRYA Yordan Alvarez 15.00 40.00
ODRYM Yadier Molina 6.00 15.00

2020 Topps Opening Day Spring Has Sprung

COMPLETE SET (25) 8.00 20.00
SHS1 Babe Ruth .75 2.00
SHS2 Roberto Clemente .75 2.00
SHS3 Ted Williams .60 1.50
SHS4 Sandy Koufax .60 1.50
SHS5 Willie Mays .60 1.50
SHS6 George Brett .60 1.50
SHS7 Reggie Jackson .25 .60
SHS8 Ken Griffey Jr. .60 1.50
SHS9 Cal Ripken Jr. 1.00 2.50
SHS10 Mark McGwire .50 1.25
SHS11 Frank Thomas .30 .75
SHS12 Aaron Judge .75 2.00
SHS13 Cody Bellinger .60 1.50
SHS14 Bryce Harper .50 1.25
SHS15 Ronald Acuna Jr. 1.25 3.00
SHS16 Mike Trout 1.50 4.00
SHS17 Javier Baez .40 1.00
SHS18 Clayton Kershaw .50 1.25
SHS19 Juan Soto 1.00 2.50
SHS20 Rafael Devers .40 1.00
SHS21 Vladimir Guerrero Jr. .50 1.25
SHS22 Fernando Tatis Jr. 1.50 4.00
SHS23 Yordan Alvarez 2.00 5.00
SHS24 Bo Bichette 1.50 4.00
SHS25 Gavin Lux 1.00 2.50

2020 Topps Opening Day Sticker Collection Preview

COMPLETE SET (10) 4.00 10.00
SP1 Justin Verlander .30 .75
SP2 Javier Baez .40 1.00
SP3 Pete Alonso .75 2.00
SP4 Bo Bichette 1.50 4.00
SP5 Nolan Arenado .50 1.25
SP6 Aaron Judge .75 2.00
SP7 Juan Soto 1.00 2.50
SP8 Cody Bellinger .60 1.50
SP9 Mookie Betts .60 1.50
SP10 Bryce Harper .50 1.25

2020 Topps Opening Day Team Traditions and Celebrations

COMPLETE SET (10) 3.00 8.00
TTC1 Judge's Court .75 2.00
TTC2 Jackie Robinson Statue .30 .75
TTC3 Pesky's Pole .20 .50
TTC4 Hand-turned Scoreboard
TTC5 Stan Musial Statue .50 1.25
TTC6 Crown Vision
TTC7 Outfield Cable Car
TTC8 Willie Mays Statue .60 1.50
TTC9 Monument Garden
TTC10 Baseball Bat Chandelier

2020 Topps Opening Day The Lighter Side of Baseball

LSB1 Ronald Acuna Jr. 15.00 40.00
LSB2 Derek Dietrich 8.00 20.00
LSB3 Gerardo Parra 3.00 8.00
LSB4 Francisco Lindor 6.00 15.00
LSB5 Mookie Betts 10.00 25.00
LSB6 Juan Soto 15.00 40.00
LSB7 Vladimir Guerrero Jr. 8.00 20.00
LSB8 Jose Altuve 10.00 25.00
LSB9 Cody Bellinger 10.00 25.00
LSB10 Fernando Tatis Jr. 8.00 20.00
LSB11 Bryce Harper 8.00 20.00
LSB12 Eugenio Suarez 6.00 15.00
LSB13 Tim Anderson 6.00 15.00
LSB14 Anthony Rizzo 10.00 25.00
LSB15 Anthony Rendon 5.00 12.00
LSB16 Shohei Ohtani 8.00 20.00
LSB17 Nelson Cruz 6.00 15.00
LSB18 Walker Buehler 6.00 15.00
LSB19 Pete Alonso 20.00 50.00
LSB20 Max Scherzer 6.00 15.00
LSB21 Mike Trout 30.00 80.00
LSB22 Alex Bregman 8.00 20.00
LSB23 Christian Yelich 8.00 20.00
LSB24 Rafael Devers 6.00 15.00
LSB25 Javier Baez 10.00 25.00

2020 Topps Opening Day Walk This Way

WW1 Ronald Acuna Jr. 20.00 50.00
WW2 Max Muncy 3.00 8.00
WW3 Matt Olson 4.00 10.00
WW4 Keston Hiura 8.00 20.00
WW5 Bryce Harper 6.00 15.00
WW6 Will Smith 4.00 10.00
WW7 Pete Alonso 15.00 40.00
WW8 DJ LeMahieu 4.00 10.00
WW9 Bo Bichette 20.00 50.00
WW10 Christian Yelich 5.00 12.00
WW11 Miguel Sano 3.00 8.00
WW12 Harold Ramirez 2.50 6.00
WW13 Mallex Smith 2.50 6.00
WW14 Tim Locastro 8.00 20.00
WW15 Rafael Devers 5.00 12.00
WW16 Trevor Story 4.00 10.00
WW17 Dominic Smith 6.00 15.00
WW18 Bryan Reynolds 3.00 8.00
WW19 Kurt Suzuki 2.50 6.00
WW20 Harrison Bader 3.00 8.00
WW21 Kevin Newman 4.00 10.00
WW22 Joc Pederson 3.00 8.00
WW23 Nolan Arenado 6.00 15.00
WW24 Carlos Santana 3.00 8.00
WW25 Mike Yastrzemski 6.00 15.00

2021 Topps Opening Day

PRINTING PLATE ODDS 1:4625
PLATE PRINT RUN 1 SET PER COLOR
BLACK-CYAN-MAGENTA-YELLOW ISSUED
NO PLATE PRICING DUE TO SCARCITY
1 Fernando Tatis Jr. 1.25 3.00
2 Luis Castillo .20 .50
3 Cristian Pache RC 2.50 6.00
4 Cavan Biggio .30 .75
5 Yu Darvish .25 .60
6 Trevor Story .25 .60
7 Nolan Arenado .40 1.00
8 Eddy Alvarez RC .40 1.00
9 Spencer Howard RC .75 2.00
10 Ryan Mountcastle RC 2.50 6.00
11 Dansby Swanson .25 .60
12 Mitch White RC .40 1.00
13 Deivi Garcia RC 2.00 5.00
14 Nate Pearson RC 1.25 3.00
15 Tim Anderson .25 .60
16 Aristides Aquino .25 .60
17 Blake Snell .20 .50
18 Ozzie Albies .25 .60
19 Evan White RC 1.50 4.00
20 Tyler Stephenson RC 1.25 3.00
21 Brandon Nimmo .20 .50
22 Keston Hiura .30 .75
23 Nick Heath RC .50 1.25
24 Sixto Sanchez RC 1.25 3.00
25 Shane Bieber .25 .60
26 Brett Gardner .20 .50
27 Mike Trout 1.25 3.00
28 Nick Neidert RC .40 1.00
29 Yordan Alvarez .60 1.50
30 Buster Posey .30 .75
31 JaCoby Jones .20 .50
32 Josh Bell .20 .50
33 Edwin Rios .25 .60
34 Leody Taveras RC .75 2.00
35 Codi Heuer RC .40 1.00
36 Nick Senzel .25 .60
37 Nico Hoerner .40 1.00
38 Gerrit Cole .40 1.00
39 Clayton Kershaw .40 1.00
40 Pete Alonso .60 1.50
41 Yadier Molina .30 .75
42 Charlie Blackmon .25 .60
43 Josh Hader .20 .50
44 Justin Turner .25 .60
45 Whit Merrifield .25 .60
46 John Means .25 .60
47 Marcell Ozuna .25 .60
48 Max Kepler .20 .50
49 James Karinchak .20 .50
50 Bryce Harper .40 1.00
51 Randy Arozarena .60 1.50
52 Byron Buxton .25 .60
53 Andres Gimenez RC .60 1.50
54 Anderson Tejeda RC .60 1.50
55 Andrelton Simmons .15 .40
56 Mookie Betts .50 1.25
57 Santiago Espinal RC .40 1.00
58 Alex Bregman .25 .60
59 Luis Robert .75 2.00
60 Christian Yelich .30 .75
61 Carter Kieboom .20 .50
62 Alec Bohm RC 2.50 6.00
63 Carlos Correa .25 .60
64 Joc Pederson .20 .50
65 Kyle Seager .15 .40
66 Joey Votto .25 .60
67 David Dahl .15 .40
68 Jakob Junis .15 .40
69 Trevor Bauer .30 .75
70 Corey Kluber .20 .50
71 J.T. Realmuto .25 .60
72 Bo Bichette .60 1.50
73 Stephen Strasburg .25 .60
74 Triston McKenzie RC .75 2.00
75 Mike Soroka .25 .60
76 Jesus Aguilar .20 .50
77 Cristian Javier RC .60 1.50
78 Nick Castellanos .25 .60
79 Dee Strange-Gordon .15 .40
80 Cody Bellinger .50 1.25
81 Lorenzo Cain .15 .40
82 Casey Mize RC 2.00 5.00
83 Justus Sheffield .25 .60
84 Teoscar Hernandez .25 .60
85 Jo Adell RC 1.50 4.00
86 Kolten Wong .20 .50
87 Marcus Semien .25 .60
88 Monte Harrison RC .40 1.00
89 Albert Pujols .30 .75
90 Tyler Glasnow .25 .60
91 Alex Verdugo .20 .50
92 Brandon Bielak RC .40 1.00
93 Giancarlo Stanton .25 .60
94 Alex Gordon .20 .50
95 Jose Urquidy .15 .40
96 Manny Machado .25 .60
97 Rafael Devers .30 .75
98 Mauricio Dubon .15 .40
99 Aaron Judge .60 1.50
100 Kris Bryant .30 .75
101 Andrew Benintendi .25 .60
102 Nick Solak .25 .60
103 Rhys Hoskins .30 .75
104 Jose Berrios .20 .50
105 Miguel Cabrera .25 .60
106 Kenta Maeda .20 .50
107 Daulton Varsho RC .60 1.50
108 Niko Goodrum .20 .50
109 Adrian Morejon .15 .40
110 Trea Turner .20 .50
111 Tony Gonsolin .25 .60
112 Rougned Odor .20 .50
113 Kris Bubic RC .40 1.00
114 Zack Greinke .25 .60
115 Brendan McKay .20 .50
116 Amed Rosario .20 .50
117 Willy Adames .15 .40
118 Albert Abreu RC .25 .60
119 Ryan Braun .25 .60
120 Brandon Woodruff .25 .60
121 Starling Marte .20 .50
122 Freddie Freeman .30 .75
123 Tarik Skubal RC 1.25 3.00
124 Kodi Whitley RC .40 1.00
125 Ian Anderson RC 1.50 4.00
126 Sonny Gray .20 .50
127 J.D. Martinez .25 .60
128 Aaron Nola .20 .50
129 Mike Moustakas .20 .50
130 Austin Meadows .25 .60
131 Jacob deGrom .50 1.25
132 Jorge Soler .25 .60
133 Ketel Marte .20 .50
134 Shohei Ohtani .40 1.00
135 Jack Flaherty .25 .60
136 Paul Goldschmidt .25 .60
137 Kyle Schwarber .25 .60
138 Dustin May .25 .60
139 Ian Happ .20 .50
140 Adalberto Mondesi .20 .50
141 Vladimir Guerrero Jr. .40 1.00
142 Salvador Perez .20 .50
143 Luis Patino RC 1.00 2.50
144 Gary Sanchez .25 .60
145 Victor Robles .30 .75
146 Jose Abreu .25 .60
147 Brusdar Graterol .20 .50
148 Beau Burrows RC .40 1.00
149 Zac Gallen .20 .50
150 Ronald Acuna Jr. 1.00 2.50
151 Raisel Iglesias .15 .40
152 Dylan Carlson RC 2.00 5.00
153 Nick Madrigal RC 2.00 5.00
154 Jose Ramirez .20 .50
155 DJ LeMahieu .25 .60
156 Jose Altuve .20 .50
157 Mike Brosseau .20 .50
158 Xander Bogaerts .25 .60
159 Dane Dunning RC .75 2.00
160 Jon Lester .20 .50
161 Josh Donaldson .20 .50
162 Anthony Rendon .25 .60
163 Francisco Lindor .25 .60
164 Adbert Alzolay .15 .40
165 Edward Olivares RC .60 1.50
166 Colin Moran .15 .40
167 Brady Singer RC 1.25 3.00
168 Ramon Laureano .20 .50
169 Miguel Sano .20 .50
170 Javier Baez .30 .75
171 Brandon Crawford .20 .50
172 Justin Dunn .15 .40
173 James Kaprielian RC .40 1.00
174 Corey Seager .25 .60
175 Ryan Castellani RC .40 1.00
176 Joey Bart RC .75 2.00
177 Gleyber Torres .50 1.25
178 Jesus Luzardo .25 .60
179 Isaac Paredes RC 1.00 2.50
180 Jesus Sanchez RC .75 2.00
181 Chris Paddack .25 .60
182 Max Scherzer .25 .60
183 Dylan Cease .20 .50
184 Justin Upton .20 .50
185 Patrick Corbin .20 .50
186 Mark Canha .15 .40
187 Bobby Dalbec RC 2.00 5.00
188 Danny Santana .15 .40
189 Kyle Lewis .60 1.50
190 Gavin Lux .50 1.25
191 Eduardo Rodriguez .15 .40
192 Chris Sale .25 .60
193 Yasmani Grandal .15 .40
194 Craig Kimbrel .20 .50
195 Caleb Smith .15 .40
196 George Springer .20 .50
197 Max Muncy .20 .50
198 Max Fried .25 .60
199 Nelson Cruz .25 .60
200 Matt Chapman .25 .60
201 Miguel Rojas .15 .40
202 Yoan Moncada .25 .60
203 Ryan Yarbrough .15 .40
204 Keibert Ruiz RC .75 2.00
205 Trent Grisham .30 .75
206 David Peterson RC .50 1.25
207 Luis Garcia RC 1.25 3.00
208 Walker Buehler .30 .75
209 Justin Verlander .25 .60
210 Chadwick Tromp RC .40 1.00
211 Willson Contreras .25 .60

212 Eloy Jimenez .50 1.25
213 Juan Soto .75 2.00
214 Humberto Mejia RC .40 1.00
215 Matt Olson .25 .60
216 Mike Clevinger .20 .50
217 Austin Hays .25 .60
218 Daniel Johnson RC .40 1.00
219 Joey Gallo .25 .60
220 Anthony Rizzo .30 .75

2021 Topps Opening Day Blue Foil

*BLUE: 1.5X TO 4X BASIC
*BLUE: 1X TO 2.5X BASIC
STATED ODDS 1:9 HOBBY
27 Mike Trout 10.00 25.00
59 Luis Robert 8.00 20.00
62 Alec Bohm 12.00 30.00
85 Jo Adell 8.00 20.00
152 Dylan Carlson 10.00 25.00
187 Bobby Dalbec 15.00 40.00

2021 Topps Opening Day Ballpark Profile Autographs

STATED ODDS 1:1618 HOBBY
EXCHANGE DEADLINE XX/XX/XX
BPADB Dallas Braden 20.00 50.00
BPADK Duane Kuiper 12.00 30.00
BPADS Dave Sims
BPAGC Gary Cohen 30.00 80.00
BPAGK Glen Kuiper
BPAJB Jason Benetti 20.00 50.00
BPAJZ Joe Zerhusen 20.00 50.00
BPAMF Mike Ferrin 20.00 50.00
BPAPH Pat Hughes
BPARF Ray Fosse 20.00 50.00

2021 Topps Opening Day Diamond Relics

STATED ODDS 1:655 HOBBY
DRAB Alec Bohm 30.00 80.00
DRBB Bo Bichette 12.00 30.00
DRBH Bryce Harper 12.00 30.00
DRBS Blake Snell 6.00 15.00
DRCB Cody Bellinger 10.00 25.00
DRCC Carlos Correa 8.00 20.00
DRCM Casey Mize 8.00 20.00
DRCY Christian Yelich 6.00 15.00
DRFT Fernando Tatis Jr. 25.00 60.00
DRJB Javier Baez 10.00 25.00
DRJV Joey Votto 8.00 20.00
DRKL Kyle Lewis 12.00 30.00
DRLR Luis Robert 15.00 40.00
DRMB Mookie Betts 10.00 25.00
DRMC Matt Chapman 5.00 12.00
DRMK Max Kepler 4.00 10.00
DRNA Nolan Arenado 8.00 20.00
DRRA Ronald Acuna Jr. 20.00 50.00
DRRM Ryan Mountcastle 30.00 80.00
DRSB Shane Bieber 5.00 12.00
DRSS Sixto Sanchez 15.00 40.00
DRTS Trevor Story 8.00 20.00
DRVG Vladimir Guerrero Jr. 8.00 20.00
DRXB Xander Bogaerts 8.00 20.00
DRJBA Joey Bart 6.00 25.00
DRJBE Jose Berrios 4.00 10.00

2021 Topps Opening Day Dugout Peeks

STATED ODDS 1:1595 HOBBY
DP1 Justin Turner
DP2 Kyle Schwarber
DP3 Bobby Dalbec
DP4 Manny Machado
DP5 Fernando Tatis Jr.
DP6 Francisco Lindor
DP7 Mike Trout
DP8 Randy Arozarena
DP9 Xander Bogaerts
DP10 Aaron Judge 30.00 80.00
DP11 Bryce Harper
DP12 Dylan Carlson 75.00 200.00
DP13 Kenta Maeda
DP14 Eloy Jimenez
DP15 Alex Verdugo 12.00 30.00
DP16 Nelson Cruz
DP17 Vladimir Guerrero Jr.
DP18 Eugenio Suarez 25.00 60.00
DP19 Kevin Kiermaier
DP20 Bo Bichette
DP21 Juan Soto
DP22 Matt Olson
DP23 Ronald Acuna Jr.
DP24 Corey Seager
DP25 Ian Happ

2021 Topps Opening Day Legends of Baseball

STATED ODDS 1:3 HOBBY
LOB1 Babe Ruth 1.50 4.00
LOB2 Roberto Clemente 1.50 4.00
LOB3 Harmon Killebrew .60 1.50
LOB4 Ernie Banks .60 1.50
LOB5 George Brett 1.25 3.00
LOB6 Jackie Robinson .60 1.50
LOB7 Hank Aaron 1.25 3.00
LOB8 Cal Ripken Jr. 2.00 5.00
LOB9 Greg Maddux .75 2.00
LOB10 Derek Jeter 1.50 4.00
LOB11 Ken Griffey Jr. 1.25 3.00
LOB12 Reggie Jackson .50 1.25
LOB13 Willie Mays 1.25 3.00
LOB14 Ted Williams 1.25 3.00
LOB15 Randy Johnson .60 1.50
LOB16 Stan Musial 1.00 2.50
LOB17 Craig Biggio .50 1.25
LOB18 Tony Gwynn .60 1.50
LOB19 Ozzie Smith .75 2.00
LOB20 Ichiro .75 2.00
LOB21 Kirby Puckett .60 1.50
LOB22 Roger Clemens .75 2.00
LOB23 Rickey Henderson .60 1.50
LOB24 Mike Schmidt 1.00 2.50
LOB25 Johnny Bench .60 1.50

2021 Topps Opening Day Major League Mementos Relics

STATED ODDS 1:810 HOBBY
MLMRBB Byron Buxton 6.00 15.00
MLMRBS Blake Snell 3.00 8.00
MLMRJB Javier Baez 5.00 12.00
MLMRJD Jacob deGrom 10.00 25.00
MLMRKH Keston Hiura 5.00 12.00
MLMRMC Matt Chapman 4.00 10.00
MLMRRH Rhys Hoskins 8.00 20.00
MLMRRM Ryan Mountcastle 6.00 15.00
MLMRXB Xander Bogaerts 6.00 15.00
MLMRJBA Joey Bart 8.00 20.00

2021 Topps Opening Day Mascot Autograph Relics

COMMON CARD 25.00 60.00
STATED ODDS 1:79,800 HOBBY
EXCHANGE DEADLINE XX/XX/XX
MARRAY Raymond

2021 Topps Opening Day Mascot Relics

COMMON CARD 5.00 12.00
STATED ODDS 1:1030 HOBBY
MRB Blooper 5.00 12.00
MRS Sluggerrr 5.00 12.00
MRMM Mr. Met 5.00 12.00
MRSC Screech 5.00 12.00
MRTB TC Bear 5.00 12.00
MRWT Wally The Green Monster 5.00 12.00
MRMMO Mariner Moose 5.00 12.00
MRRAY Raymond 5.00 12.00

2021 Topps Opening Day Mascots

COMMON CARD 1.25 3.00
STATED ODDS 1:3 HOBBY
M1 Clark 1.25 3.00
M2 Wally the Green Monster 1.25 3.00
M3 Mr. Met 1.25 3.00
M4 Dinger 1.25 3.00
M5 Fredbird 1.25 3.00
M6 Paws 1.25 3.00
M7 Sluggerrr 1.25 3.00
M8 Bernie Brewer 1.25 3.00
M9 Raymond 1.25 3.00
M10 Rosie Red 1.25 3.00
M11 Blooper 1.25 3.00
M12 Slider 1.25 3.00
M13 Pirate Parrot 1.25 3.00
M14 Screech 1.25 3.00
M15 Orbit 1.25 3.00
M16 Mariner Moose 1.25 3.00
M17 TC Bear 1.25 3.00
M18 Swinging Friar 1.25 3.00
M19 Rangers Captain 1.25 3.00
M20 Mr. Red 1.25 3.00
M21 Billy the Marlin 1.25 3.00
M22 Mascot 1.25 3.00
M23 Mrs. Met 1.25 3.00
M24 Mascot 1.25 3.00

2021 Topps Opening Day Opening Day

COMMON CARD 1.25 3.00
STATED ODDS 1:5 HOBBY
OD1 New York Mets 1.25 3.00
OD2 Cincinnati Reds 1.25 3.00
OD3 Tampa Bay Rays 1.25 3.00
OD4 Philadelphia Phillies 1.25 3.00
OD5 Cleveland Indians 1.25 3.00
OD6 Chicago Cubs 1.25 3.00
OD7 Boston Red Sox 1.25 3.00
OD8 Texas Rangers 1.25 3.00
OD9 Chicago White Sox 1.25 3.00
OD10 St. Louis Cardinals BB 1.25 3.00
OD11 San Diego Padres 1.25 3.00
OD12 Houston Astros 1.25 3.00
OD13 Los Angeles Dodgers 1.25 3.00
OD14 Oakland Athletics 1.25 3.00
OD15 Washington Nationals 1.25 3.00

2021 Topps Opening Day Opening Day Origins

STATED ODDS 1:642 HOBBY
ODO1 Bryce Harper 2.50 6.00
ODO2 Aaron Judge 4.00 10.00
ODO3 Jose Altuve 1.25 3.00
ODO4 Jason Heyward 1.25 3.00
ODO5 Christian Yelich 2.00 5.00
ODO6 Rhys Hoskins 2.00 5.00
ODO7 Willson Contreras 1.50 4.00
ODO8 Fernando Tatis Jr. 8.00 20.00
ODO9 Luis Robert 5.00 12.00
ODO10 Shogo Akiyama 6.00 15.00
ODO11 Cody Bellinger 3.00 8.00
ODO12 Anthony Rizzo 2.00 5.00
ODO13 Justin Verlander 1.50 4.00
ODO14 Andrew Benintendi 1.50 4.00
ODO15 Victor Robles 2.00 5.00
ODO16 Max Kepler 5.00 12.00
ODO17 Trevor Story 1.50 4.00
ODO18 Dustin May 1.50 4.00
ODO19 Alex Bregman 1.50 4.00
ODO20 Paul Goldschmidt 1.50 4.00
ODO21 Anthony Rendon 1.50 4.00
ODO22 Nolan Arenado 2.50 6.00
ODO23 Javier Baez 2.00 5.00
ODO24 Francisco Lindor 1.50 4.00
ODO25 Mookie Betts 8.00 20.00

2021 Topps Opening Day Outstanding Opening Days

STATED ODDS 1:8 HOBBY
OOD1 Ivan Rodriguez .50 1.25
OOD2 Albert Pujols .75 2.00
OOD3 Javier Baez .75 2.00
OOD4 Bryce Harper 1.00 2.50
OOD5 Giancarlo Stanton .60 1.50
OOD6 Bob Feller .50 1.25
OOD7 Billy Williams .50 1.25
OOD8 Mark McGwire 1.00 2.50
OOD9 Clayton Kershaw 1.00 2.50
OOD10 Hank Aaron 1.25 3.00

2021 Topps Opening Day Relics

STATED ODDS 1:228 HOBBY
ODRAB Andrew Benintendi 6.00 15.00
ODRCB Cavan Biggio 4.00 10.00
ODRCY Christian Yelich 8.00 20.00
ODRER Eddie Rosario 2.50 6.00
ODRGS Gary Sanchez 3.00 8.00
ODRGT Gleyber Torres 6.00 15.00
ODRHP Hunter Pence 2.50 6.00
ODRJA Jose Altuve 2.50 6.00
ODRJB Josh Bell 2.50 6.00
ODRJH Jason Heyward 2.50 6.00
ODRKB Kris Bryant 4.00 10.00
ODRKK Kevin Kiermaier 2.50 6.00
ODRMC Miguel Cabrera 6.00 15.00
ODRMM Manny Machado 3.00 8.00
ODRMT Mike Trout 15.00 40.00
ODRNG Niko Goodrum 2.50 6.00
ODRNS Nick Senzel 3.00 8.00
ODRPA Pete Alonso 4.00 10.00
ODRRD Rafael Devers 2.00 5.00
ODRSC Shin-Soo Choo 2.50 6.00
ODRSS Stephen Strasburg 5.00 8.00
ODRVG Vladimir Guerrero Jr. 5.00 12.00
ODRYM Yadier Molina 4.00 10.00
ODRJHA Josh Hader 2.50 6.00
ODRMCH Matt Chapman 3.00 8.00

2021 Topps Opening Day Turf War Dual Diamond Relics

STATED ODDS 1:4044 HOBBY
TWDRAS J.Soto/R.Acuna Jr. 25.00 60.00
TWDRBJ X.Bogaerts/A.Judge 25.00 60.00
TWDRBY J.Baez/C.Yelich
TWDRKJ E.Jimenez/M.Kepler 10.00 25.00
TWDRLV J.Votto/F.Lindor 40.00 100.00
TWDRPB C.Bellinger/B.Posey
TWDRPC M.Chapman/B.Posey 12.00 30.00
TWDRRB K.Bryant/L.Robert 40.00 100.00
TWDRRG P.Goldschmidt/A.Rizzo 15.00 40.00
TWDRTB M.Trout/M.Betts 75.00 200.00

2021 Topps Opening Day Walk This Way

STATED ODDS 1:321 HOBBY
WW1 Nelson Cruz 4.00 10.00
WW2 Jose Ramirez 6.00 15.00
WW3 Pete Alonso 10.00 25.00
WW4 Luis Robert 12.00 30.00
WW5 Amed Rosario 8.00 20.00
WW6 Kevin Kiermaier 3.00 8.00
WW7 Adam Duvall 20.00 50.00
WW8 Javier Baez 15.00 40.00
WW9 Matt Olson 12.00 30.00
WW10 Max Kepler 3.00 8.00
WW11 Teoscar Hernandez 4.00 10.00
WW12 Andrew McCutchen 10.00 25.00
WW13 Yasmani Grandal 2.50 6.00
WW14 Kolten Wong 3.00 8.00
WW15 Cody Bellinger 15.00 40.00
WW16 Manny Machado 4.00 10.00
WW17 David Peralta 10.00 25.00
WW18 Kyle Tucker 4.00 10.00
WW19 Marcus Semien 4.00 10.00
WW20 Kevin Newman 10.00 25.00
WW21 Mike Yastrzemski 6.00 15.00
WW22 Charlie Blackmon 4.00 10.00
WW23 Jorge Alfaro 2.50 6.00
WW24 Byron Buxton 4.00 10.00
WW25 Brandon Lowe 3.00 8.00

2004 Topps Originals Signature

ONE AUTO PER PACK
PRINT RUNS B/WN 1-339 COPIES PER
NO PRICING ON QTY OF 14 OR LESS
AD3 Andre Dawson 80/27 20.00 50.00
AD4 Andre Dawson 81/37 20.00 50.00
AD5 Andre Dawson 82/55 12.00 30.00
AD6 Andre Dawson 83/47 20.00 50.00
AD7 Andre Dawson 84/25 20.00 50.00
AD8 Andre Dawson 85/22 20.00 50.00
AD9 Andre Dawson 86/24 20.00 50.00
AH6 Al Hrabosky 78/20 15.00 40.00
AH7 Al Hrabosky 79/40 10.00 25.00
AH8 Al Hrabosky 80/61 6.00 15.00
AH9 Al Hrabosky 81/38 6.00 15.00
AH10 Al Hrabosky 82/62 6.00 15.00
AH11 Al Hrabosky 89 Sr./20 10.00 25.00
AK10 Al Kaline 67/18 60.00 150.00
AK16 Al Kaline 73/25 50.00 120.00
AO6 Al Oliver 79/42 10.00 25.00
AO8 Al Oliver 81/54 6.00 15.00
AO9 Al Oliver 82/45 6.00 15.00
AO10 Al Oliver 83/50 6.00 15.00
AO11 Al Oliver 84/51 6.00 15.00
AO12 Al Oliver 85/46 6.00 15.00
AO13 Al Oliver 86/44 6.00 15.00
AT2 Alan Trammell 80/17 20.00 50.00
AT3 Alan Trammell 81/26 12.00 30.00
AT4 Alan Trammell 82/40 10.00 25.00
AT5 Alan Trammell 83/21 15.00 40.00
AT6 Alan Trammell 84/57 15.00 40.00
AT7 Alan Trammell 85/39 10.00 25.00
AT8 Alan Trammell 86/23 15.00 40.00
AT9 Alan Trammell 87/15 15.00 40.00
AV2 Andy Van Slyke 85/35 10.00 25.00
AV3 Andy Van Slyke 86/37 10.00 25.00
AV4 Andy Van Slyke 87/178 6.00 15.00
AV5 Andy Van Slyke 87 TR/130 6.00 15.00
BB5 Buddy Bell 79/135 8.00 20.00
BB8 Buddy Bell 82/34 8.00 20.00
BB9 Buddy Bell 83/83 4.00 10.00
BB10 Buddy Bell 84/22 10.00 25.00
BB12 Buddy Bell 86/32 8.00 20.00
BBL4 Bert Blyleven 79/45 12.00 30.00
BBL6 Bert Blyleven 81/29 15.00 40.00
BBL7 Bert Blyleven 82 NNO/51 12.00 30.00
BBL8 Bert Blyleven 83/41 12.00 30.00
BBL10 Bert Blyleven 85/40 12.00 30.00
BBL11 Bert Blyleven 86/62 12.00 30.00
BBL12 Bert Blyleven 87/54 12.00 30.00
BC5 Bert Campaneris 79/107 6.00 15.00
BC7 Bert Campaneris 84/28 8.00 20.00
BD5 Bucky Dent 81/16 15.00 40.00
BD6 Bucky Dent 82/49 6.00 15.00
BD7 Bucky Dent 83/92 4.00 10.00
BD8 Bucky Dent 84/63 6.00 15.00
BG2 Bob Grich 79/29 8.00 20.00
BG3 Bob Grich 80/70 8.00 20.00
BG5 Bob Grich 82/45 8.00 20.00
BG6 Bob Grich 83/85 8.00 20.00
BG7 Bob Grich 84/57 8.00 20.00
BG8 Bob Grich 85/36 8.00 20.00
BH4 Bob Horner 82/21 15.00 40.00
BH5 Bob Horner 83/69 6.00 15.00
BH6 Bob Horner 84/63 10.00 15.00
BH7 Bob Horner 85/15 15.00 40.00
BH8 Bob Horner 86/118 4.00 10.00
BH9 Bob Horner 87/38 8.00 20.00
BJ2 Bo Jackson 87/100 30.00 60.00
BJA2 Brook Jacoby 86/133 4.00 10.00
BJA3 Brook Jacoby 87/191 4.00 10.00
BM7 Bill Madlock 82/26 8.00 20.00
BM8 Bill Madlock 83/55 6.00 15.00
BM9 Bill Madlock 84/69 4.00 10.00
BM10 Bill Madlock 85/60 6.00 15.00
BM11 Bill Madlock 86/63 6.00 15.00
BM12 Bill Madlock 87/42 6.00 15.00
BP9 Boog Powell 73/17 20.00 50.00
BP11 Boog Powell 75/19 20.00 50.00
BP13 Boog Powell 77/15 20.00 50.00
BR11 Brooks Robinson 74/20 30.00 80.00
BR13 Brooks Robinson 76/17 30.00 80.00
BS2 Bret Saberhagen 86/23 15.00 40.00
BS3 Bret Saberhagen 87/230 10.00 25.00
BSU6 Bruce Sutter 82/111 8.00 20.00
BSU7 Bruce Sutter 83/45 12.00 30.00
BSU8 Bruce Sutter 84/24 15.00 40.00
BSU9 Bruce Sutter 85/19 15.00 40.00
BSU10 Bruce Sutter 86/78 10.00 25.00
BSU11 Bruce Sutter 87/36 15.00 40.00
BU8 Bill Buckner 81/39 8.00 20.00
BU9 Bill Buckner 82/38 8.00 20.00
BU10 Bill Buckner 83/47 8.00 20.00
BU11 Bill Buckner 84/31 10.00 25.00
BU12 Bill Buckner 84 TR/24 12.00 30.00
BU13 Bill Buckner 85/80 8.00 20.00
BU14 Bill Buckner 86/63 8.00 20.00
BW3 Bob Watson 79/77 6.00 15.00
BW5 Bob Watson 81/16 10.00 25.00
BW6 Bob Watson 82/23 10.00 25.00
BW7 Bob Watson 83/93 4.00 10.00
BW8 Bob Watson 84/64 6.00 15.00
BW9 Bob Watson 85/68 4.00 10.00
CF2 Cecil Fielder 87/208 6.00 15.00
CF3 Cecil Fielder 88/26 12.00 30.00
CF4 Cecil Fielder 89/16 15.00 40.00
CFI3 Carlton Fisk 79/24 40.00 80.00
CFI4 Carlton Fisk 80/32 30.00 60.00
CFI6 Carlton Fisk 82/30 20.00 50.00
CG3 Cesar Geronimo 79/28 20.00 50.00
CG5 Cesar Geronimo 81/21 20.00 50.00
CG6 Cesar Geronimo 82/52 6.00 15.00
CG7 Cesar Geronimo 83/67 4.00 10.00
CG8 Cesar Geronimo 84/70 4.00 10.00
CH2 Charlie Hough 83/19 10.00 25.00
CH3 Charlie Hough 84/50 6.00 15.00
CH4 Charlie Hough 85/57 6.00 15.00
CH5 Charlie Hough 86/66 4.00 10.00
CH6 Charlie Hough 87/46 6.00 15.00
CH7 Charlie Hough 88/19 10.00 25.00
CH8 Charlie Hough 91 TR/70 6.00 15.00
CH9 Charlie Hough 92/25 10.00 25.00
CL3 Carney Lansford 81/184 6.00 15.00
CL5 Carney Lansford 83/40 8.00 20.00
CL6 Carney Lansford 85/35 10.00 25.00
CL7 Carney Lansford 86/76 6.00 15.00
CLE3 Chet Lemon 79/24 12.00 30.00
CLE4 Chet Lemon 80/16 12.00 30.00
CLE6 Chet Lemon 82/23 12.00 30.00
CLE7 Chet Lemon 83/35 12.00 30.00
CLE8 Chet Lemon 84/42 12.00 30.00
CLE9 Chet Lemon 85/32 12.00 30.00
CLE10 Chet Lemon 86/136 8.00 20.00
CLE11 Chet Lemon 87/27 12.00 30.00
CR4 Cal Ripken 86/74 25.00 60.00
CS2 Cory Snyder 87/291 4.00 10.00
CS3 Cory Snyder 91/39 6.00 15.00
CY4 Carl Yastrzemski 80/60 50.00 100.00
CY5 Carl Yastrzemski 81/35 60.00 120.00
DC6 Dave Concepcion 80/21 6.00 15.00
DC8 Dave Concepcion 82/43 6.00 15.00
DC9 Dave Concepcion 83/34 6.00 15.00
DC10 Dave Concepcion 84/24 6.00 15.00
DC11 Dave Concepcion 85/41 6.00 15.00
DC12 Dave Concepcion 86/69 6.00 15.00
DD2 Darren Daulton 87/269 8.00 20.00
DD4 Darren Daulton 92/32 12.00 30.00
DD5 Darren Daulton 94/17 12.00 30.00
DD6 Darren Daulton 96/22 12.00 30.00
DDE2 Doug DeCinces 79/38 6.00 15.00
DDE3 Doug DeCinces 80/24 12.00 30.00
DDE4 Doug DeCinces 81/24 10.00 25.00
DDE5 Doug DeCinces 82/42 6.00 15.00
DDE6 Doug DeCinces 83/75 6.00 15.00
DDE7 Doug DeCinces 84/19 10.00 25.00
DDE8 Doug DeCinces 85/54 6.00 15.00
DDE9 Doug DeCinces 86/74 6.00 15.00
DE3 Dennis Eckersley 79/44 10.00 25.00
DE4 Dennis Eckersley 80/40 10.00 25.00
DEV5 Darrell Evans 79/19 6.00 15.00
DEV7 Darrell Evans 81/15 6.00 15.00
DEV8 Darrell Evans 82/25 6.00 15.00
DEV9 Darrell Evans 83/63 10.00 25.00
DEV10 Darrell Evans 84/81 6.00 15.00
DEV11 Darrell Evans 85/48 6.00 15.00
DEV12 Darrell Evans 86/82 6.00 15.00
DG2 Dwight Gooden 86/16 10.00 25.00
DG3 Dwight Gooden 87/52 6.00 15.00
DG4 Dwight Gooden 89/19 10.00 25.00
DJ1 David Justice 90 DB/69 12.00 30.00
DJ3 David Justice 93/32 12.00 30.00
DK4 Dave Kingman 81/25 15.00 40.00
DK6 Dave Kingman 83/32 12.00 30.00
DK7 Dave Kingman 86/25 15.00 40.00
DL4 Davey Lopes 79/71 6.00 15.00
DL5 Davey Lopes 80/19 12.00 30.00
DL7 Davey Lopes 82/17 10.00 25.00
DL8 Davey Lopes 83/65 6.00 15.00
DL9 Davey Lopes 84/15 10.00 25.00
DL10 Davey Lopes 85/24 10.00 25.00
DL11 Davey Lopes 86/40 6.00 15.00
DL12 Davey Lopes 01 MG/67 6.00 15.00
DL13 Davey Lopes 02 MG/19 10.00 25.00
DM3 Don Mattingly 87/84 30.00 60.00
DMU2 Dale Murphy 79/38 30.00 60.00
DMU6 Dale Murphy 84/29 20.00 50.00
DMU7 Dale Murphy 85/18 30.00 60.00
DMU8 Dale Murphy 86/25 30.00 60.00
DMU9 Dale Murphy 87/91 10.00 25.00
DP5 Dave Parker 81/19 15.00 40.00
DP6 Dave Parker 82/73 6.00 15.00
DP7 Dave Parker 83/30 12.00 30.00
DP9 Dave Parker 85/45 10.00 25.00
DP10 Dave Parker 86/29 12.50 30.00
DS8 Duke Snider 64/18 60.00 120.00
DSE2 Dave Stieb 81/21 20.00 50.00
DSE3 Dave Stieb 82/34 15.00 40.00
DSE4 Dave Stieb 83/70 8.00 20.00
DSE5 Dave Stieb 84/20 20.00 50.00
DSE6 Dave Stieb 85/55 12.50 30.00
DSE7 Dave Stieb 86/69 8.00 20.00
DSE8 Dave Stieb 87/75 8.00 20.00
DSR2 Darryl Strawberry 85/32 15.00 40.00
DSR3 Darryl Strawberry 86/24 15.00 40.00
DSR4 Darryl Strawberry 87/183 15.00 40.00
DSR5 Darryl Strawberry 87 AS/110 15.00 40.00
DSW2 Dave Stewart 83/41 6.00 15.00
DSW3 Dave Stewart 84/60 6.00 15.00
DSW4 Dave Stewart 85/24 10.00 25.00
DSW5 Dave Stewart 86/53 6.00 15.00
DSW6 Dave Stewart 87/171 4.00 10.00
ED3 Eric Davis 87/336 10.00 25.00
EW4 Earl Weaver 78 MG/52 10.00 25.00
EW5 Earl Weaver 83 MG/38 12.00 30.00
EW7 Earl Weaver 86 MG/107 6.00 15.00
EW8 Earl Weaver 87 MG/175 6.00 15.00
FJ8 Fergie Jenkins 78/17 20.00 50.00
FJ10 Fergie Jenkins 80/37 12.00 30.00
FJ11 Fergie Jenkins 81/32 12.00 30.00
FJ12 Fergie Jenkins 82/65 10.00 25.00
FJ13 Fergie Jenkins 83/22 12.00 30.00
FJ14 Fergie Jenkins 84/42 12.00 30.00
FR6 Frank Robinson 72/16 40.00 80.00
FV3 Frank Viola 85/25 15.00 40.00
FV4 Frank Viola 86/99 12.00 30.00
FV5 Frank Viola 87/209 4.00 10.00
GB2 George Bell 84/67 6.00 15.00
GB3 George Bell 85/32 6.00 15.00
GB4 George Bell 86/46 6.00 15.00
GB5 George Bell 87/204 6.00 15.00
GBR4 George Brett 81/19 75.00 150.00
GC3 Gary Carter 79/21 20.00 50.00
GC4 Gary Carter 80/24 30.00 80.00
GC5 Gary Carter 81/22 15.00 40.00
GF6 George Foster 79/20 12.00 30.00
GF10 George Foster 83/39 6.00 15.00
GF11 George Foster 84/112 6.00 15.00
GF12 George Foster 85/76 6.00 15.00
GF13 George Foster 86/64 10.00 25.00
GL7 Greg Luzinski 80/21 20.00 50.00
GL9 Greg Luzinski 82/34 12.00 30.00
GL10 Greg Luzinski 83/75 6.00 15.00
GL11 Greg Luzinski 84/85 6.00 15.00
GL12 Greg Luzinski 85/92 6.00 15.00
GM3 Gary Matthews Sr. 83/20 10.00 25.00
GM4 Gary Matthews Sr. 84/43 6.00 15.00
GM5 Gary Matthews Sr. 85/39 8.00 20.00
GM6 Gary Matthews Sr. 86/38 8.00 20.00
GM7 Gary Matthews Sr. 87/82 8.00 20.00
GM8 Gary Matthews Sr. 88/30 8.00 20.00
HB2 Harold Baines 82/31 12.00 30.00
HB3 Harold Baines 83/19 15.00 40.00
HB5 Harold Baines 85/97 6.00 15.00
HB6 Harold Baines 86/93 6.00 15.00
HB7 Harold Baines 87/115 6.00 15.00
HR2 Harold Reynolds 87/255 8.00 20.00
JA1 Jim Abbott 88 TR/339 10.00 25.00
JA3 Jim Abbott 90 DB/50 15.00 40.00
JB2 Jesse Barfield 83/45 6.00 15.00
JB4 Jesse Barfield 85/60 6.00 15.00
JB5 Jesse Barfield 86/37 6.00 15.00
JB6 Jesse Barfield 87/180 4.00 10.00
JBE5 Johnny Bench 82/16 40.00 80.00
JC2 John Candelaria 79/77 6.00 15.00
JC4 John Candelaria 81/19 15.00 40.00
JC5 John Candelaria 82/42 10.00 25.00
JC6 John Candelaria 83/77 6.00 15.00
JC7 John Candelaria 84/18 15.00 40.00
JC8 John Candelaria 85/61 4.00 10.00
JC9 John Candelaria 86/36 10.00 25.00
JCA2 Jose Canseco 87/99 20.00 50.00
JCR2 Joe Carter 86/24 30.00 60.00
JCR3 Joe Carter 87/23 30.00 60.00
JCU8 Jose Cruz Sr. 82/28 8.00 20.00
JCU9 Jose Cruz Sr. 83/102 4.00 10.00
JCU10 Jose Cruz Sr. 84/67 4.00 10.00
JCU11 Jose Cruz Sr. 85/68 4.00 10.00
JCU12 Jose Cruz Sr. 86/31 8.00 20.00
JK2 Jimmy Key 86/21 15.00 40.00
JK3 Jimmy Key 87/263 6.00 15.00
JK4 Jimmy Key 88/15 15.00 40.00
JK5 Jimmy Key 92/37 10.00 25.00
JKR2 John Kruk 87/214 10.00 25.00
JKR3 John Kruk 92/22 30.00 60.00
JL2 Jim Leyritz 91/38 6.00 15.00
JL3 Jim Leyritz 93/49 6.00 15.00
JL4 Jim Leyritz 94/16 10.00 25.00
JL6 Jim Leyritz 97/62 6.00 15.00
JL7 Jim Leyritz 98/20 10.00 25.00
JL8 Jim Leyritz 99/124 4.00 10.00
JL9 Jim Leyritz 00/40 6.00 15.00
JM2 Jack McDowell 89/36 10.00 25.00
JM3 Jack McDowell 90 TR/61 8.00 20.00
JM4 Jack McDowell 91/33 10.00 25.00
JM5 Jack McDowell 92/38 10.00 25.00
JM6 Jack McDowell 93/27 10.00 25.00
JM9 Jack McDowell 96/15 8.00 20.00
JM10 Jack McDowell 97/27 8.00 20.00
JMO9 Joe Morgan 81/32 12.00 30.00
JMO10 Joe Morgan 82/18 15.00 40.00
JMO11 Joe Morgan 83/49 10.00 25.00
JMO13 Joe Morgan 84/73 6.00 15.00
JMO14 Joe Morgan 85/40 10.00 25.00
JP3 Jim Palmer 80/33 15.00 40.00
JP4 Jim Palmer 81/23 15.00 40.00
JP5 Jim Palmer 82/24 15.00 40.00
JR7 Jim Rice 81/123 10.00 25.00
JR8 Jim Rice 82/24 15.00 40.00
JR9 Jim Rice 83/71 10.00 25.00
JRU9 Joe Rudi 79/24 6.00 15.00
JRU10 Joe Rudi 80/45 4.00 10.00
JRU11 Joe Rudi 82/26 6.00 15.00
JRU12 Joe Rudi 83/75 4.00 10.00
KB2 Kevin Bass 84/71 4.00 10.00
KB3 Kevin Bass 85/30 8.00 20.00
KB4 Kevin Bass 86/44 6.00 15.00
KB5 Kevin Bass 87/74 4.00 10.00
KB6 Kevin Bass 90 TR/35 6.00 15.00
KG5 Ken Griffey Sr. 80/15 20.00 50.00
KG7 Ken Griffey Sr. 82/18 15.00 40.00
KG8 Ken Griffey Sr. 83/70 6.00 15.00
KG9 Ken Griffey Sr. 84/64 10.00 25.00
KG10 Ken Griffey Sr. 85/32 12.00 30.00
KG11 Ken Griffey Sr. 86 TR/32 12.00 30.00
KGI2 Kirk Gibson 82/35 12.00 30.00
KGI3 Kirk Gibson 83/35 12.00 30.00
KGI5 Kirk Gibson 85/44 12.00 30.00
KGI6 Kirk Gibson 86/44 12.00 30.00
KGI7 Kirk Gibson 87/65 12.00 30.00
KGU2 Kelly Gruber 88/77 4.00 10.00
KGU3 Kelly Gruber 89/44 12.00 30.00
KGU4 Kelly Gruber 90/86 10.00 25.00
KGU5 Kelly Gruber 91/52 12.00 30.00
KGU6 Kelly Gruber 92/55 12.00 30.00
KGU7 Kelly Gruber 93/26 15.00 40.00
KH3 Keith Hernandez 80/38 20.00 50.00
KH4 Keith Hernandez 81/19 20.00 50.00
KH5 Keith Hernandez 82/156 12.00 30.00
KH6 Keith Hernandez 83/17 20.00 50.00
KS2 Kevin Seitzer 88/88 4.00 10.00
KS3 Kevin Seitzer 89/39 6.00 15.00
KS4 Kevin Seitzer 90/18 10.00 25.00
KS5 Kevin Seitzer 91/39 6.00 15.00
KS6 Kevin Seitzer 92/49 6.00 15.00
KS9 Kevin Seitzer 93/38 6.00 15.00
KS10 Kevin Seitzer 94/22 10.00 25.00
KS11 Kevin Seitzer 95/16 10.00 25.00
KS13 Kevin Seitzer 97/24 10.00 25.00
KT5 Kent Tekulve 81/17 15.00 40.00
KT6 Kent Tekulve 82/36 10.00 25.00
KT7 Kent Tekulve 83/52 10.00 25.00
KT8 Kent Tekulve 84/71 6.00 15.00
KT9 Kent Tekulve 85/43 10.00 25.00
KT10 Kent Tekulve 86/57 10.00 25.00
KT11 Kent Tekulve 87/32 20.00 50.00
KT12 Kent Tekulve 88/20 15.00 40.00
LA9 Luis Aparicio 69/49 15.00 40.00
LA12 Luis Aparicio 72/15 20.00 50.00
LB4 Lou Brock 70/20 40.00 80.00
LB13 Lou Brock 79/27 30.00 60.00
LD2 Leon Durham 82/51 10.00 25.00
LD3 Leon Durham 83/52 10.00 25.00
LD4 Leon Durham 84/151 8.00 20.00
LD6 Leon Durham 86/19 10.00 25.00
LD7 Leon Durham 87/87 6.00 15.00
LDY2 Len Dykstra 87/200 6.00 15.00
LDY3 Len Dykstra 88/30 12.00 30.00
LDY4 Len Dykstra 89/17 15.00 40.00
LS2 Lee Smith 83/39 10.00 25.00
LS5 Lee Smith 86/29 10.00 25.00
LS6 Lee Smith 87/237 6.00 15.00
LS7 Lee Smith 88/27 12.00 30.00
LT2 Luis Tiant 68/16 20.00 50.00
LT6 Luis Tiant 74/19 20.00 50.00
LT11 Luis Tiant 79/22 12.00 30.00
LT12 Luis Tiant 80/23 12.00 30.00
LT13 Luis Tiant 81/20 10.00 25.00
LT14 Luis Tiant 82/51 10.00 25.00
LT15 Luis Tiant 83/58 6.00 15.00
MB2 Mike Boddicker 84/56 6.00 15.00
MB3 Mike Boddicker 85/139 4.00 10.00
MB4 Mike Boddicker 86/66 4.00 10.00
MB5 Mike Boddicker 87/88 4.00 10.00
MF3 Mark Fidrych 79/74 20.00 50.00
MF4 Mark Fidrych 80/16 40.00 80.00
MR2 Mickey Rivers 79/35 10.00 25.00
MR5 Mickey Rivers 82/49 6.00 15.00
MR6 Mickey Rivers 83/79 4.00 10.00
MR7 Mickey Rivers 84/91 4.00 10.00
MR8 Mickey Rivers 85/34 8.00 20.00
MS2 Mike Schmidt 80/100 30.00 60.00
MSC3 Mike Scott 82/32 8.00 20.00
MSC4 Mike Scott 83/55 6.00 15.00
MSC5 Mike Scott 84/28 8.00 20.00
MSC6 Mike Scott 86/73 8.00 20.00
MSC7 Mike Scott 87/36 6.00 15.00
MSC8 Mike Scott 88/21 10.00 25.00
MW2 Mookie Wilson 82/20 15.00 40.00
MW3 Mookie Wilson 83/41 15.00 40.00
MW5 Mookie Wilson 85/51 15.00 40.00
MW6 Mookie Wilson 86/47 15.00 40.00
MW7 Mookie Wilson 87/67 15.00 40.00
NR5 Nolan Ryan 83/23 100.00 175.00
NR6 Nolan Ryan 84/20 100.00 175.00
NR8 Nolan Ryan 86/20 100.00 175.00
OH2 Orel Hershiser 86/23 30.00 60.00
OH3 Orel Hershiser 87/218 10.00 25.00
OS2 Ozzie Smith 81/28 25.00 60.00
OS3 Ozzie Smith 82/27 25.00 60.00
OS5 Ozzie Smith 84/19 30.00 80.00
OS6 Ozzie Smith 85/16 30.00 80.00
PI2 Pete Incaviglia 87/311 4.00 10.00
PM1 Paul Molitor 79/15 50.00 100.00
PM2 Paul Molitor 80/26 50.00 100.00
PM4 Paul Molitor 82/32 20.00 50.00
PO2 Paul O'Neill 89/24 30.00 60.00
PO3 Paul O'Neill 90/18 30.00 60.00
PO4 Paul O'Neill 91/24 30.00 60.00
PO5 Paul O'Neill 97/33 20.00 50.00
RC4 Rod Carew 79/29 30.00 60.00
RC6 Rod Carew 81/21 30.00 60.00
RC7 Rod Carew 82/18 30.00 60.00
RCE3 Ron Cey 79/55 6.00 15.00
RCE5 Ron Cey 81/16 10.00 25.00
RCE6 Ron Cey 82/34 10.00 25.00
RCE7 Ron Cey 83/87 8.00 20.00
RCE8 Ron Cey 83 TR/68 10.00 25.00
RCE9 Ron Cey 84/15 10.00 25.00
RCE10 Ron Cey 85/19 10.00 25.00
RCE11 Ron Cey 86/43 10.00 25.00
RD3 Ron Darling 87/224 6.00 15.00
RDI2 Rob Dibble 90/31 12.00 30.00
RDI3 Rob Dibble 91/62 8.00 20.00
RDI4 Rob Dibble 92/56 8.00 20.00
RDI5 Rob Dibble 92 Gold/17 12.00 30.00
RDI6 Rob Dibble 93/47 8.00 20.00
RDI7 Rob Dibble 94/37 8.00 20.00
RF3 Rollie Fingers 79/52 15.00 40.00
RF4 Rollie Fingers 80/15 20.00 50.00
RF5 Rollie Fingers 81/18 15.00 40.00
RG6 Rich Gossage 80/15 10.00 25.00
RG7 Rich Gossage 81/21 10.00 25.00
RG8 Rich Gossage 82/30 10.00 25.00
RG9 Rich Gossage 83/34 10.00 25.00
RG10 Rich Gossage 84/90 8.00 20.00
RG12 Rich Gossage 86/30 12.00 30.00
RGU4 Ron Guidry 80/22 20.00 50.00
RGU5 Ron Guidry 81/104 10.00 25.00
RGU6 Ron Guidry 82/53 10.00 25.00
RGU7 Ron Guidry 83/46 10.00 25.00
RGU8 Ron Guidry 84/40 10.00 25.00
RGU9 Ron Guidry 85/50 20.00 50.00
RGU10 Ron Guidry 86/15 15.00 40.00
RJ8 Reggie Jackson 82/21 50.00 100.00
RJ11 Reggie Jackson 85/17 40.00 80.00
RJ12 Reggie Jackson 86/17 40.00 80.00
RK2 Ron Kittle 85/86 6.00 15.00
RK3 Ron Kittle 86/55 8.00 20.00
RK4 Ron Kittle 87/201 6.00 15.00
RKN5 Ray Knight 82/25 15.00 40.00
RKN6 Ray Knight 83/36 6.00 15.00
RKN7 Ray Knight 84/26 12.00 30.00
RKN8 Ray Knight 85/68 6.00 15.00
RKN9 Ray Knight 86/80 4.00 10.00
RKN10 Ray Knight 87 TR/90 4.00 10.00
RM8 Reggie Smith 79/15 12.00 30.00
RM9 Reggie Smith 80/16 12.00 30.00
RM11 Reggie Smith 82/32 8.00 20.00
RM12 Reggie Smith 83/48 6.00 15.00
RS2 Ryne Sandberg 84/37 40.00 100.00
RS5 Ryne Sandberg 87/32 40.00 100.00
RU3 Rick Sutcliffe 82/53 10.00 25.00
RU4 Rick Sutcliffe 83/43 10.00 25.00
RU5 Rick Sutcliffe 84/33 12.50 30.00
RU6 Rick Sutcliffe 85/82 6.00 15.00
RU8 Rick Sutcliffe 87/19 15.00 40.00
RY5 Robin Yount 80/18 50.00 100.00
RY6 Robin Yount 81/23 50.00 100.00
RY9 Robin Yount 84/15 50.00 100.00
RY11 Robin Yount 86/21 50.00 100.00
SA5 Sparky Anderson 83 MG/67 6.00 15.00
SA6 Sparky Anderson 84 MG/97 6.00 15.00
SA7 Sparky Anderson 85 MG/73 6.00 15.00
SF2 Sid Fernandez 86/18 15.00 40.00
SF3 Sid Fernandez 87/211 6.00 15.00
SF4 Sid Fernandez 93/20 15.00 40.00
SG4 Steve Garvey 79/26 15.00 40.00
SG7 Steve Garvey 82/122 10.00 25.00
SG8 Steve Garvey 83/19 15.00 40.00
SG9 Steve Garvey 84/32 12.50 30.00
SG10 Steve Garvey 85/129 10.00 25.00
SM1 Stan Musial 58 AS/15 150.00 250.00
SM5 Stan Musial 62/16 150.00 250.00
SS2 Steve Sax 83/34 10.00 25.00
SS4 Steve Sax 85/33 10.00 25.00
SS5 Steve Sax 86/45 8.00 20.00
SS6 Steve Sax 87/215 6.00 15.00
SY4 Steve Yeager 78/18 15.00 40.00
SY5 Steve Yeager 79/23 15.00 40.00
SY8 Steve Yeager 82/18 15.00 40.00
SY9 Steve Yeager 83/80 5.00 12.00
SY10 Steve Yeager 84/15 15.00 40.00
SY12 Steve Yeager 86/47 6.00 15.00
SY13 Steve Yeager 86 TR/100 5.00 12.00
TB2 Tom Brunansky 83/27 8.00 20.00
TB3 Tom Brunansky 84/62 6.00 15.00
TB5 Tom Brunansky 86/28 8.00 20.00
TB6 Tom Brunansky 87/193 4.00 10.00
TB7 Tom Brunansky 88/18 10.00 25.00
TF2 Tony Fernandez 86/41 6.00 15.00
TF3 Tony Fernandez 87/228 8.00 20.00
TG2 Tony Gwynn 84/95 30.00 60.00
TH2 Tom Herr 81/22 12.50 30.00
TH3 Tom Herr 82/42 12.50 30.00
TH4 Tom Herr 83/80 10.00 25.00
TH5 Tom Herr 84/30 12.50 30.00
TH6 Tom Herr 85/17 12.50 30.00
TH7 Tom Herr 86/28 12.50 30.00
TH8 Tom Herr 87/134 4.00 10.00
TM5 Tim McCarver 79/22 12.50 30.00
TO8 Tony Oliva 73/18 20.00 50.00
TR2 Tim Raines 82/43 10.00 25.00
TR3 Tim Raines 83/26 12.50 30.00
TR5 Tim Raines 85/43 10.00 25.00
TR6 Tim Raines 86/21 20.00 50.00
TR7 Tim Raines 87/211 6.00 15.00
TS2 Tom Seaver 79/44 25.00 60.00
TS4 Tom Seaver 81/16 25.00 60.00
TS5 Tom Seaver 82/25 25.00 60.00
TW2 Tim Wallach 83/49 8.00 20.00
TW4 Tim Wallach 85/46 8.00 20.00
TW5 Tim Wallach 86/44 8.00 20.00
TW6 Tim Wallach 87/197 6.00 15.00
VB5 Vida Blue 79/21 12.50 30.00
VB7 Vida Blue 81/227 6.00 15.00
VB8 Vida Blue 82/53 6.00 15.00
VB9 Vida Blue 83/45 6.00 15.00
VC2 Vince Coleman 87/299 6.00 15.00
VC3 Vince Coleman 88/34 12.50 30.00
VC4 Vince Coleman 91 TR/23 15.00 40.00
WB2 Wade Boggs 84/20 25.00 60.00
WB3 Wade Boggs 85/25 25.00 60.00
WB5 Wade Boggs 87/45 20.00 50.00
WH4 Whitey Herzog 83 MG/63 6.00 15.00
WH5 Whitey Herzog 84 MG/85 4.00 10.00
WH6 Whitey Herzog 85 MG/75 20.00 50.00
WH7 Whitey Herzog 86 MG/66 8.00 20.00
WH8 Whitey Herzog 87 MG/29 8.00 20.00
WH9 Whitey Herzog 88 MG/35 8.00 20.00
WJ2 Wally Joyner 87/335 8.00 20.00
WM9 Willie Mays 72/25 100.00 200.00
WMC2 Willie McGee 84/66 12.50 30.00
WMC3 Willie McGee 85/44 20.00 50.00
WMC4 Willie McGee 86/24 30.00 80.00
WMC5 Willie McGee 87/117 12.50 30.00
WW2 Walt Weiss 89/34 10.00 25.00
WW3 Walt Weiss 91/30 10.00 25.00
WW4 Walt Weiss 92/71 6.00 15.00
WW6 Walt Weiss 94/21 10.00 25.00
WW7 Walt Weiss 97/49 6.00 15.00
WW8 Walt Weiss 98 Rockies/23 10.00 25.00
WW9 Walt Weiss 98 Braves/21 10.00 25.00
WW10 Walt Weiss 99/40 8.00 20.00
WW11 Walt Weiss 01/51 8.00 20.00
YB10 Yogi Berra 85 MG/27 40.00 100.00

2005 Topps Pack Wars

1 Alex Rodriguez 1.25 3.00
2 Eric Chavez .40 1.00
3 Jimmy Rollins .60 1.50
4 Jason Bay .40 1.00

5 Nomar Garciaparra .60 1.50
6 Melvin Mora .40 1.00
7 Bobby Abreu .40 1.00
8 Bartolo Colon .40 1.00
9 Orlando Cabrera Sox .40 1.00
10 Albert Pujols 1.25 3.00
11 Barry Zito .60 1.50
12 Vernon Wells .40 1.00
13 J.D. Drew .40 1.00
14 Darin Erstad .40 1.00
15 Manny Ramirez 1.00 2.50
16 Derrek Lee .40 1.00
17 Juan Uribe .40 1.00
18 Wily Mo Pena .40 1.00
19 Jeromy Burnitz .40 1.00
20 Dontrelle Willis .40 1.00
21 Craig Biggio .60 1.50
22 Cesar Izturis .40 1.00
23 Geoff Jenkins .40 1.00
24 Joe Mauer .75 2.00
25 Derek Jeter 2.50 6.00
26 David Wright .75 2.00
27 Jose Vidro .40 1.00
28 Bobby Crosby .40 1.00
29 Khalil Greene .40 1.00
30 Ichiro Suzuki 1.25 3.00
31 Reggie Sanders .40 1.00
32 A.J. Pierzynski .40 1.00
33 Corey Patterson .40 1.00
34 Frank Thomas 1.00 2.50
35 Craig Wilson .40 1.00
36 Carl Crawford .60 1.50
37 Michael Young .40 1.00
38 Mark Kotsay .40 1.00
39 Javier Vazquez .40 1.00
40 Kazuo Matsui .40 1.00
41 Lew Ford .40 1.00
42 Corey Koskie .40 1.00
43 Larry Walker .60 1.50
44 Mike Lowell .40 1.00
45 Todd Helton .60 1.50
46 Travis Hafner .40 1.00
47 Sean Casey .40 1.00
48 Ken Griffey Jr. 2.00 5.00
49 Milton Bradley .40 1.00
50 Ivan Rodriguez .60 1.50
51 Carlos Lee .40 1.00
52 Aramis Ramirez .40 1.00
53 Curt Schilling .60 1.50
54 Russ Ortiz .40 1.00
55 Randy Johnson 1.00 2.50
56 Preston Wilson .40 1.00
57 Jay Gibbons .40 1.00
58 Mike Lieberthal .40 1.00
59 Johnny Damon .60 1.50
60 Mark Prior .60 1.50
61 Freddy Garcia .40 1.00
62 Casey Blake .40 1.00
63 Chipper Jones 1.00 2.50
64 Carlos Guillen .40 1.00
65 Juan Pierre .40 1.00
66 Tom Glavine .60 1.50
67 Alex Sanchez .40 1.00
68 Tony Batista .40 1.00
69 Paul Lo Duca .40 1.00
70 Hank Blalock .40 1.00
71 Pedro Feliz .40 1.00
72 Jim Edmonds .60 1.50
73 Phil Nevin .40 1.00
74 Rocco Baldelli .40 1.00
75 Alfonso Soriano .60 1.50
76 David Bell .40 1.00
77 Eric Hinske .40 1.00
78 Jose Guillen .40 1.00
79 Marcus Giles .40 1.00
80 Rafael Palmeiro .60 1.50
81 Jeff Bagwell .60 1.50
82 Kerry Wood .40 1.00
83 Johan Santana .60 1.50
84 Troy Glaus .40 1.00
85 Andruw Jones .40 1.00
86 Barry Bonds 1.50 4.00
87 Jermaine Dye .40 1.00
88 Carlos Zambrano .60 1.50
89 Aaron Rowand .40 1.00
90 Garret Anderson .40 1.00
91 Ryan Klesko .40 1.00
92 Paul Konerko .60 1.50
93 Jeff Kent .40 1.00
94 Richie Sexson .40 1.00
95 Lyle Overbay .40 1.00
96 Torii Hunter .40 1.00
97 Mike Cameron .40 1.00
98 Eric Byrnes .40 1.00
99 Jason Kendall .40 1.00
100 Vladimir Guerrero .60 1.50
101 Johnny Estrada .40 1.00
102 Mark Bellhorn .40 1.00
103 Moises Alou .40 1.00
104 Ronnie Belliard .40 1.00
105 Adam Dunn .60 1.50
106 Dmitri Young .40 1.00
107 Luis Castillo .40 1.00
108 Carlos Beltran .60 1.50
109 Steve Finley .40 1.00
110 Shannon Stewart .40 1.00
111 Al Leiter .40 1.00
112 Bernie Williams .60 1.50
113 Roy Oswalt .60 1.50
114 Sean Burroughs .40 1.00
115 Randy Winn .40 1.00
116 Tony Womack .40 1.00
117 Jim Thome .60 1.50
118 Aubrey Huff .40 1.00
119 Bret Boone .40 1.00
120 Carlos Delgado .40 1.00
121 Jason Schmidt .40 1.00
122 Rafael Furcal .40 1.00
123 Miguel Tejada .60 1.50
124 Bill Mueller .40 1.00
125 Pedro Martinez .60 1.50
126 Michael Barrett .40 1.00
127 Jody Gerut .40 1.00
128 Vinny Castilla .40 1.00
129 Rondell White .40 1.00
130 Magglio Ordonez .60 1.50
131 Lance Berkman .60 1.50
132 Alex Gonzalez .40 1.00
133 Mike Sweeney .40 1.00
134 Ben Sheets .40 1.00
135 Jacque Jones .40 1.00
136 Brad Wilkerson .40 1.00
137 Cliff Floyd .40 1.00
138 Kevin Brown .40 1.00
139 Scott Hatteberg .40 1.00
140 Gary Sheffield .40 1.00
141 Justin Morneau .60 1.50
142 Scott Podsednik .40 1.00
143 Shawn Green .40 1.00
144 David Ortiz 1.00 2.50
145 Josh Beckett .40 1.00
146 Tim Hudson .60 1.50
147 Matt Lawton .40 1.00
148 Mark Buehrle .60 1.50
149 Todd Walker .40 1.00
150 Jason Giambi .40 1.00
151 Brian Giles .40 1.00
152 Erubiel Durazo .40 1.00
153 Jack Wilson .40 1.00
154 Jose Reyes .60 1.50
155 Scott Rolen .60 1.50
156 Raul Ibanez .60 1.50
157 Mark Teixeira .60 1.50
158 Luis Gonzalez .40 1.00
159 Javy Lopez .40 1.00
160 Greg Maddux 1.25 3.00
161 Kevin Millar .40 1.00
162 Jose Valentin .40 1.00
163 C.C. Sabathia .60 1.50
164 Carlos Pena .60 1.50
165 Miguel Cabrera 1.00 2.50
166 Adrian Beltre 1.00 2.50
167 Sammy Sosa 1.00 2.50
168 Nick Johnson .40 1.00
169 Jorge Posada .60 1.50
170 Mike Piazza 1.00 2.50
171 Mark Mulder .40 1.00
172 Mark Loretta .40 1.00
173 Edgardo Alfonzo .40 1.00
174 Edgar Renteria .40 1.00
175 Pat Burrell .40 1.00

2005 Topps Pack Wars Foil

*FOIL: 1.5X TO 4X BASIC
STATED ODDS HITTERS 1:6
STATED ODDS PITCHERS 1:35
STATED PRINT RUN 56 SERIAL #'d SETS

2005 Topps Pack Wars Autographs

GROUP A ODDS 1:1950 PRIZE PACKS
GROUP B ODDS 1:975 PRIZE PACKS
GROUP C ODDS 1:9 PRIZE PACKS
GROUP D ODDS 1:8 PRIZE PACKS
GROUP A PRINT RUN 25 CARDS
GROUP B PRINT RUN 50 CARDS
A-B PRINT RUN INFO PROVIDED BY TOPPS
A-B CARDS ARE NOT SERIAL-NUMBERED
NO GROUP A PRICING DUE TO SCARCITY
EXCHANGE DEADLINE 02/26/07
AB Aaron Boone D 6.00 15.00
AR Alex Rodriguez B 100.00 175.00
CB Carlos Beltran C 6.00 15.00
CS C.C. Sabathia C 10.00 25.00
EC Eric Chavez C 6.00 15.00
HB Hank Blalock C 6.00 15.00
JE Johnny Estrada D 4.00 10.00
MC Miguel Cabrera D 12.50 30.00
MY Michael Young C 8.00 20.00
VM Victor Martinez D 8.00 20.00
VW Vernon Wells C 6.00 15.00
ZG Zack Greinke D 10.00 25.00

2005 Topps Pack Wars Autographed Relics

GROUP A ODDS 1:975 PRIZE PACKS
GROUP B ODDS 1:35 PRIZE PACKS
GROUP A PRINT RUN 50 SERIAL #'d SETS
GROUP B PRINT RUN 200 SERIAL #'d SETS
CB Carlos Beltran Bat B/200 10.00 25.00
EC Eric Chavez Uni B/200 10.00 25.00
HB Hank Blalock Bat B/200 10.00 25.00
JE Johnny Estrada Bat B/200 6.00 15.00
MC M.Cabrera Bat UER B/200 30.00 60.00
MY Michael Young Bat B/200 10.00 25.00
VM Victor Martinez Bat B/200 10.00 25.00

2005 Topps Pack Wars Collector Chips Blue

*BLUE: .5X TO 1.2X GREEN
OVERALL ONE CHIP PER SEALED BOX
STATED PRINT RUN 25 SERIAL #'d SETS

2005 Topps Pack Wars Collector Chips Green

STATED PRINT RUN 125 SERIAL #'d SETS
RED PRINT RUN 10 SERIAL #'d SETS
NO RED PRICING DUE TO SCARCITY
ONE CHIP OVERALL PER SEALED BOX
AP Albert Pujols 8.00 20.00
AR Alex Rodriguez 8.00 20.00
AS Alfonso Soriano 4.00 10.00
BB Barry Bonds 10.00 25.00
CJ Chipper Jones 6.00 15.00
DJ Derek Jeter 15.00 40.00
EB Ernie Banks 6.00 15.00
FR Frank Robinson 4.00 10.00
GB George Brett 12.00 30.00
GS Gary Sheffield 2.50 6.00
IR Ivan Rodriguez 4.00 10.00
IS Ichiro Suzuki 8.00 20.00
JP Jorge Posada 4.00 10.00
JT Jim Thome 4.00 10.00
KG Ken Griffey Jr. 12.00 30.00
MP Mike Piazza 6.00 15.00
MP1 Mark Prior 4.00 10.00
MS Mike Schmidt 10.00 25.00
NG Nomar Garciaparra 4.00 10.00
NR Nolan Ryan 20.00 50.00
RJ Reggie Jackson 4.00 10.00
RJ1 Randy Johnson 6.00 15.00
SS Sammy Sosa 6.00 15.00
TH Todd Helton 4.00 10.00
VG Vladimir Guerrero 4.00 10.00

2005 Topps Pack Wars Relics

GROUP A ODDS 1:5 PRIZE PACKS
GROUP B ODDS 1:3 PRIZE PACKS
AP Albert Pujols Bat A 10.00 25.00
AR Alex Rodriguez Bat A 6.00 15.00
AS Alfonso Soriano Uni A 4.00 10.00
CJ Chipper Jones Jsy A 6.00 15.00
CJB Chipper Jones Bat B 4.00 10.00
FT Frank Thomas Bat B 4.00 10.00
GM Greg Maddux Bat A 6.00 15.00
GS Gary Sheffield Bat B 3.00 8.00
IR Ivan Rodriguez Bat A 6.00 15.00
JT Jim Thome Bat B 4.00 10.00
MP Mike Piazza Uni A 6.00 15.00
MR Manny Ramirez Jsy A 6.00 15.00
MRB Manny Ramirez Bat B 4.00 10.00
NG Nomar Garciaparra Bat A 6.00 15.00
PM Pedro Martinez Jsy A 6.00 15.00
RC Roger Clemens Jsy A 6.00 15.00
RP Rafael Palmeiro Bat B 4.00 10.00
SR Scott Rolen Bat A 6.00 15.00
SS Sammy Sosa Bat B 4.00 10.00
TH Todd Helton Jsy B 4.00 10.00
THB Todd Helton Bat B 4.00 10.00
VG Vladimir Guerrero Bat B 4.00 10.00

2019 Topps PKWY

PKWY1 Mike Trout
PKWY2 Shohei Ohtani
PKWY3 Paul Goldschmidt
PKWY4 Ronald Acuna Jr.
PKWY5 Freddie Freeman
PKWY6 Mookie Betts
PKWY7 Christian Yelich
PKWY8 Kris Bryant
PKWY9 Javier Baez
PKWY10 Joey Votto
PKWY11 Francisco Lindor
PKWY12 Nolan Arenado
PKWY13 Carlos Correa
PKWY14 Jose Altuve
PKWY15 Justin Verlander
PKWY16 Clayton Kershaw
PKWY17 Corey Seager
PKWY18 Jacob deGrom
PKWY19 Aaron Judge
PKWY20 Gleyber Torres
PKWY21 Rhys Hoskins
PKWY22 Buster Posey
PKWY23 Matt Carpenter
PKWY24 Yadier Molina
PKWY25 Max Scherzer

2002 Topps Pristine

COMMON CARD (1-140) .50 1.25
COMMON CARD (141-150) .75 2.00
COMMON C CARD (151-210) .50 1.25
COMMON 151-210 SAME ODDS AS 1-150
COMMON U CARD (151-210) 1.00 2.50
UNCOMMON 151-210 STATED ODDS 1:2
COMMON R CARD (151-210) 1.50 4.00
RARE 151-210 STATED ODDS 1:5
RARE PRINT RUN 799 SERIAL #'d SETS
1 Alex Rodriguez 1.50 4.00
2 Carlos Delgado .50 1.25
3 Jimmy Rollins .50 1.25
4 Jason Kendall .50 1.25
5 John Olerud .50 1.25
6 Albert Pujols 2.50 6.00
7 Curt Schilling .50 1.25
8 Gary Sheffield .50 1.25
9 Johnny Damon Sox .75 2.00
10 Ichiro Suzuki 2.50 6.00
11 Pat Burrell .50 1.25
12 Garret Anderson .50 1.25
13 Andruw Jones .75 2.00
14 Kerry Wood .50 1.25
15 Kenny Lofton .50 1.25
16 Adam Dunn .50 1.25
17 Juan Pierre .50 1.25
18 Josh Beckett .50 1.25
19 Roy Oswalt .50 1.25
20 Derek Jeter 3.00 8.00
21 Jose Vidro .50 1.25
22 Richie Sexson .50 1.25
23 Mike Sweeney .50 1.25
24 Jeff Kent .50 1.25
25 Jason Giambi .50 1.25
26 Bret Boone .50 1.25
27 J.D. Drew .50 1.25
28 Shannon Stewart .50 1.25
29 Miguel Tejada .50 1.25
30 Barry Bonds 3.00 8.00
31 Randy Johnson 1.25 3.00
32 Pedro Martinez .75 2.00
33 Magglio Ordonez .50 1.25
34 Todd Helton .75 2.00
35 Craig Biggio .75 2.00
36 Shawn Green .50 1.25
37 Vladimir Guerrero 1.25 3.00
38 Mo Vaughn .50 1.25
39 Alfonso Soriano .50 1.25
40 Barry Zito .50 1.25
41 Aramis Ramirez .50 1.25
42 Ryan Klesko .50 1.25
43 Ruben Sierra .50 1.25
44 Tino Martinez .75 2.00
45 Toby Hall .50 1.25
46 Ivan Rodriguez .75 2.00
47 Raul Mondesi .50 1.25
48 Carlos Pena .50 1.25
49 Darin Erstad .50 1.25
50 Sammy Sosa 1.25 3.00
51 Bartolo Colon .50 1.25
52 Robert Fick .50 1.25
53 Cliff Floyd .50 1.25
54 Brian Jordan .50 1.25
55 Torii Hunter .50 1.25
56 Roberto Alomar .75 2.00
57 Roger Clemens 2.50 6.00
58 Mark Mulder .50 1.25
59 Brian Giles .50 1.25
60 Mike Piazza 2.00 5.00
61 Rich Aurilia .50 1.25
62 Freddy Garcia .50 1.25
63 Jim Edmonds .50 1.25
64 Eric Hinske .50 1.25
65 Vicente Padilla .50 1.25
66 Javier Vazquez .50 1.25
67 Cristian Guzman .50 1.25
68 Paul Lo Duca .50 1.25
69 Bobby Abreu .50 1.25
70 Nomar Garciaparra 2.00 5.00
71 Troy Glaus .50 1.25
72 Chipper Jones 1.25 3.00
73 Scott Rolen .75 2.00
74 Lance Berkman .50 1.25
75 C.C. Sabathia .50 1.25
76 Bernie Williams .75 2.00
77 Rafael Palmeiro .75 2.00
78 Phil Nevin .50 1.25
79 Kazuhiro Sasaki .50 1.25
80 Eric Chavez .50 1.25
81 Jorge Posada .75 2.00
82 Edgardo Alfonzo .50 1.25
83 Geoff Jenkins .50 1.25
84 Preston Wilson .50 1.25
85 Jim Thome .75 2.00
86 Frank Thomas 1.25 3.00
87 Jeff Bagwell .75 2.00
88 Greg Maddux 2.00 5.00
89 Mark Prior .75 2.00
90 Larry Walker .50 1.25
91 Luis Gonzalez .50 1.25
92 Tim Hudson .50 1.25
93 Tsuyoshi Shinjo .50 1.25
94 Juan Gonzalez .50 1.25
95 Shea Hillenbrand .50 1.25
96 Paul Konerko .50 1.25
97 Tom Glavine .75 2.00
98 Marty Cordova .50 1.25
99 Moises Alou .50 1.25
100 Ken Griffey Jr. 2.50 6.00
101 Hank Blalock .75 2.00
102 Matt Morris .50 1.25
103 Robb Nen .50 1.25
104 Mike Cameron .50 1.25
105 Mark Buehrle .50 1.25
106 Sean Burroughs .50 1.25
107 Orlando Cabrera .50 1.25
108 Jeromy Burnitz .50 1.25
109 Juan Uribe .50 1.25
110 Eric Milton .50 1.25
111 Carlos Lee .50 1.25
112 Jose Mesa .50 1.25
113 Morgan Ensberg .50 1.25
114 Derek Lowe .50 1.25
115 Juan Cruz .50 1.25
116 Mike Lieberthal .50 1.25
117 Armando Benitez .50 1.25
118 Vinny Castilla .50 1.25
119 Russ Ortiz .50 1.25
120 Mike Lowell .50 1.25
121 Corey Patterson .50 1.25
122 Mike Mussina .75 2.00
123 Rafael Furcal .50 1.25
124 Mark Grace .75 2.00
125 Ben Sheets .50 1.25
126 John Smoltz .75 2.00
127 Fred McGriff .75 2.00
128 Nick Johnson .50 1.25
129 J.T. Snow .50 1.25
130 Jeff Cirillo .50 1.25
131 Trevor Hoffman .50 1.25
132 Kevin Brown .50 1.25
133 Mariano Rivera 1.25 3.00
134 Marlon Anderson .50 1.25
135 Al Leiter .50 1.25
136 Doug Mientkiewicz .50 1.25
137 Eric Karros .50 1.25
138 Bobby Higginson .50 1.25
139 Sean Casey .50 1.25
140 Troy Percival .50 1.25
141 Willie Mays 2.50 6.00
142 Carl Yastrzemski 2.00 5.00
143 Stan Musial 2.00 5.00
144 Harmon Killebrew 1.25 3.00
145 Mike Schmidt 2.50 6.00
146 Duke Snider .75 2.00
147 Brooks Robinson .75 2.00
148 Frank Robinson .75 2.00
149 Nolan Ryan 3.00 8.00
150 Reggie Jackson .75 2.00
151 Joe Mauer C RC 6.00 15.00
152 Joe Mauer U 10.00 25.00
153 Joe Mauer R 15.00 40.00
154 Colt Griffin C RC .50 1.25
155 Colt Griffin U 1.00 2.50
156 Colt Griffin R 1.50 4.00
157 Jason Simontacchi C RC .50 1.25
158 Jason Simontacchi U 1.00 2.50
159 Jason Simontacchi R 1.50 4.00
160 Casey Kotchman C RC 1.50 4.00
161 Casey Kotchman U 2.50 6.00
162 Casey Kotchman R 4.00 10.00
163 Greg Sain C RC .50 1.25
164 Greg Sain U 1.00 2.50
165 Greg Sain R 1.50 4.00
166 David Wright C RC 2.50 6.00
167 David Wright U 6.00 15.00
168 David Wright R 8.00 20.00
169 Scott Hairston C RC .75 2.00
170 Scott Hairston U 1.50 4.00
171 Scott Hairston R 2.50 6.00
172 Rolando Viera C RC .50 1.25
173 Rolando Viera U 1.00 2.50
174 Rolando Viera R 1.50 4.00
175 Tyrell Godwin C RC .50 1.25
176 Tyrell Godwin U 1.00 2.50
177 Tyrell Godwin R 1.50 4.00
178 Jesus Cota C RC .50 1.25
179 Jesus Cota U 1.00 2.50
180 Jesus Cota R 1.50 4.00
181 Dan Johnson C RC 1.25 3.00
182 Dan Johnson U 2.50 6.00
183 Dan Johnson R 4.00 10.00
184 Mario Ramos C RC .50 1.25
185 Mario Ramos U 1.00 2.50
186 Mario Ramos R 1.50 4.00
187 Jason Dubois C RC .75 2.00
188 Jason Dubois U 1.50 4.00
189 Jason Dubois R 2.50 6.00
190 Jonny Gomes C RC 1.50 4.00
191 Jonny Gomes U 3.00 8.00
192 Jonny Gomes R 5.00 12.00
193 Chris Snelling C RC .60 1.50
194 Chris Snelling U 1.25 3.00
195 Chris Snelling R 2.00 5.00
196 Hansel Izquierdo C RC .50 1.25
197 Hansel Izquierdo U 1.00 2.50
198 Hansel Izquierdo R 1.50 4.00
199 So Taguchi C RC .75 2.00
200 So Taguchi U 1.50 4.00
201 So Taguchi R 2.50 6.00
202 Kazuhisa Ishii C RC .75 2.00
203 Kazuhisa Ishii U 1.50 4.00
204 Kazuhisa Ishii R 2.50 6.00
205 Jorge Padilla C RC .50 1.25
206 Jorge Padilla U 1.00 2.50
207 Jorge Padilla R 1.50 4.00
208 Earl Snyder C RC .50 1.25
209 Earl Snyder U 1.00 2.50
210 Earl Snyder R 1.50 4.00

2002 Topps Pristine Gold Refractors

*GOLD 1-140: 2.5X TO 6X BASIC
*GOLD 141-150: 2.5X TO 6X BASIC
*GOLD C 151-210: 4X TO 10X BASIC C
*GOLD U 151-210: 2X TO 5X BASIC U
*GOLD R 151-210: 1.25X TO 3X BASIC R
ONE PER HOBBY BOX
STATED PRINT RUN 70 SERIAL #'d SETS

2002 Topps Pristine Refractors

*REFRACTORS 1-140: 1.5X TO 4X
*REFRACTORS 141-150: 1.5X TO 4X
1-150 STATED ODDS 1:4
1-150 PRINT RUN 149 SERIAL #'d SETS
*REFRACTORS C 151-210: 1X TO 2.5X
COMMON 151-210 STATED ODDS 1:2
COMMON 151-210 PRINT 1999 #'d SETS
*REFRACTORS U 151-210: .75X TO 2X
UNCOMMON 151-210 STATED ODDS 1:5
*REFRACTORS R 151-210: .75X TO 2X
RARE 151-210 STATED ODDS 1:27
RARE 151-210 PRINT RUN 149 #'d SETS
166 David Wright C 8.00 20.00
167 David Wright U 10.00 25.00
168 David Wright R 12.00 30.00

2002 Topps Pristine Fall Memories

GROUP A ODDS 1:21
GROUP B ODDS 1:8
GROUP C ODDS 1:49
GROUP A PRINT RUN 425 SERIAL #'d SETS
GROUP B PRINT RUN 1000 SERIAL #'d SETS
GROUP C PRINT RUN 1600 SERIAL #'d SETS
AJ Andruw Jones Uni B 4.00 10.00
AS Alfonso Soriano Bat B 3.00 8.00
BB Barry Bonds Bat A 15.00 40.00
BW Bernie Williams Bat B 4.00 10.00
CJ Chipper Jones Bat A 6.00 15.00
CS Curt Schilling Jsy B 3.00 8.00
EM Eddie Murray Bat A 6.00 15.00
GB George Brett Jsy B 12.50 30.00
GS Gary Sheffield Bat C 3.00 8.00
JB Johnny Bench Jsy B 6.00 15.00
JP Jorge Posada Bat B 4.00 10.00
KP Kirby Puckett Bat A 6.00 15.00
LG Luis Gonzalez Bat B 3.00 8.00
MG Mark Grace Bat A 6.00 15.00
RJ Reggie Jackson Bat A 6.00 15.00
SG Shawn Green Bat A 4.00 10.00
TG Tom Glavine Jsy B 4.00 10.00
TH Todd Helton Jsy B 4.00 10.00
TM Tino Martinez Bat A 6.00 15.00
WM Willie Mays Jsy A 10.00 25.00

2002 Topps Pristine In the Gap

GROUP A ODDS 1:12
GROUP B ODDS 1:5
GROUP A PRINT RUN 425 SERIAL #'d SETS
GROUP B PRINT RUN 1000 SERIAL #'d SETS
AD Adam Dunn Jsy B 3.00 8.00
AJ Andruw Jones Jsy B 4.00 10.00
AP Albert Pujols Uni B 8.00 20.00
AR Alex Rodriguez Bat A 6.00 15.00
ARA Aramis Ramirez Bat A 4.00 10.00
AS Alfonso Soriano Bat B 4.00 10.00
BB Bret Boone Bat B 3.00 8.00
BBO Barry Bonds Uni B 12.50 30.00
BW Bernie Williams Bat B 6.00 15.00
CD Carlos Delgado Bat A 4.00 10.00
DE Darin Erstad Bat A 4.00 10.00
EC Eric Chavez Bat A 4.00 10.00
IR Ivan Rodriguez Bat A 6.00 15.00
JE Jim Edmonds Jsy B 3.00 8.00
JK Jeff Kent Jsy B 3.00 8.00
LB Lance Berkman Bat A 4.00 10.00
LW Larry Walker Jsy B 3.00 8.00
MP Mike Piazza Bat A 6.00 15.00
NG Nomar Garciaparra Bat A 6.00 15.00
PL Paul Lo Duca Bat A 4.00 10.00
PW Preston Wilson Jsy B 3.00 8.00
RA Roberto Alomar Bat B 4.00 10.00
RH Rickey Henderson Bat A 6.00 15.00
RK Ryan Klesko Bat A 4.00 10.00
RP Rafael Palmeiro Bat A 6.00 15.00
TG Tony Gwynn Jsy B 6.00 15.00
TH Todd Helton Bat B 4.00 10.00
TS Tsuyoshi Shinjo Bat B 3.00 8.00
WB Wade Boggs Uni B 4.00 10.00
WBE Wilson Betemit Bat B 3.00 8.00

2002 Topps Pristine Personal Endorsements

GROUP A ODDS 1:396
GROUP B ODDS 1:63
GROUP C ODDS 1:79
GROUP D ODDS 1:33
GROUP E ODDS 1:9
GROUP F ODDS 1:53
AP Albert Pujols A 175.00 250.00
BB Barry Bonds E 40.00 100.00
BS Ben Sheets B 8.00 20.00
CG Cristian Guzman C 4.00 10.00
CK Casey Kotchman E 4.00 10.00
CM Corwin Malone E 4.00 10.00
DB Dewon Brazelton D 4.00 10.00
GF Gavin Floyd D 6.00 15.00
IG Irvin Guzman E 30.00 50.00
JD Johnny Damon Sox B 6.00 15.00
JL Jason Lane E 6.00 15.00
JR Jimmy Rollins C 15.00 40.00
JS Juan Silvestre E 4.00 10.00
KB Kenny Baugh F 4.00 10.00
KI Kazuhisa Ishii A 15.00 40.00
LB Lance Berkman B 6.00 15.00
MT Marcus Thames E 4.00 10.00
NN Nick Neugebauer E 4.00 10.00
OH Orlando Hudson D 4.00 10.00
RA Roberto Alomar B 6.00 15.00
ST So Taguchi B 12.00 30.00

2002 Topps Pristine Popular Demand

STATED ODDS 1:4
STATED PRINT RUN 1000 SERIAL #'d SETS
AD Adam Dunn Jsy 3.00 8.00
AP Albert Pujols Jsy 8.00 20.00
AR Alex Rodriguez Bat 6.00 15.00
BB Bret Boone Jsy 3.00 8.00
BBO Barry Bonds Uni 12.50 30.00
CD Carlos Delgado Uni 3.00 8.00
CJ Chipper Jones Jsy 6.00 15.00
CS Curt Schilling Jsy 3.00 8.00
DM Don Mattingly Jsy 15.00 40.00
FT Frank Thomas Jsy 6.00 15.00
IR Ivan Rodriguez Uni 4.00 10.00
JB Jeff Bagwell Jsy 4.00 10.00
LW Larry Walker Jsy 3.00 8.00
MP Mike Piazza Jsy 6.00 15.00
NG Nomar Garciaparra Jsy 6.00 15.00
RA Roberto Alomar Jsy 4.00 10.00
SG Shawn Green Jsy 3.00 8.00
TG Tony Gwynn Jsy 6.00 15.00
TH Todd Helton Jsy 4.00 10.00
WB Wade Boggs Jsy 4.00 10.00

2002 Topps Pristine Portions

GROUP A ODDS 1:21
GROUP B ODDS 1:4
GROUP C ODDS 1:33
GROUP A PRINT RUN 425 SERIAL #'d SETS
GROUP B PRINT RUN 1000 SERIAL #'d SETS
GROUP C PRINT RUN 2400 SERIAL #'d SETS
AD Adam Dunn Bat B 2.00 5.00
AP Albert Pujols Uni B 6.00 15.00
AR Alex Rodriguez Jsy B 4.00 10.00
BB Bret Boone Jsy B 1.25 3.00
BBO Barry Bonds Uni C 5.00 12.00
CB Craig Biggio Jsy B 2.00 5.00
CD Carlos Delgado Jsy B 1.25 3.00
CF Cliff Floyd Jsy B 1.25 3.00
CG Cristian Guzman Jsy B 1.25 3.00
EM Edgar Martinez Bat A 2.00 5.00
GM Greg Maddux Jsy A 5.00 12.00
IR Ivan Rodriguez Bat A 2.00 5.00
JB Jeff Bagwell Uni A 2.00 5.00
JP Jorge Posada Bat A 2.00 5.00
KS Kazuhiro Sasaki Jsy A 1.25 3.00
LB Lance Berkman Bat A 2.00 5.00
LD Paul Lo Duca Jsy B 1.25 3.00
MM Mike Mussina Uni B 2.00 5.00
MO Magglio Ordonez Jsy B 2.00 5.00
MP Mike Piazza Bat A 3.00 8.00
NG Nomar Garciaparra Jsy B 2.00 5.00
NJ Nick Johnson Bat B 1.25 3.00
NR Nolan Ryan Uni B 10.00 25.00
RA Roberto Alomar Bat A 2.00 5.00
RD Ryan Dempster Jsy B 1.25 3.00
RF Rafael Furcal Jsy B 1.25 3.00
RP Rafael Palmeiro Jsy B 2.00 5.00
TH Todd Helton Jsy B 2.00 5.00

2003 Topps Pristine

COMMON CARD (1-100) .60 1.50
COMMON CARD (96-100) .60 1.50
COMMON C (101-190) .30 .75
C 101-190 APPX. 2X EASIER THAN 1-100
COMMON U (101-190) .40 1.00
UNCOMMON 101-190 STATED ODDS 1:2
UNCOMMON PRINT 1499 SERIAL #'d SETS
COMMON R (101-190) .75 2.00
RARE 101-190 STATED ODDS 1:6
RARE PRINT RUN 499 SERIAL #'d SETS
1 Pedro Martinez 1.00 2.50
2 Derek Jeter 4.00 10.00
3 Alex Rodriguez 2.00 5.00
4 Miguel Tejada 1.00 2.50
5 Nomar Garciaparra 1.00 2.50
6 Austin Kearns .60 1.50
7 Jose Vidro .60 1.50
8 Bret Boone .60 1.50
9 Scott Rolen 1.00 2.50
10 Mike Sweeney .60 1.50
11 Jason Schmidt .60 1.50
12 Alfonso Soriano 1.00 2.50
13 Tim Hudson 1.00 2.50
14 A.J. Pierzynski .60 1.50
15 Lance Berkman 1.00 2.50
16 Frank Thomas 1.50 4.00
17 Gary Sheffield .60 1.50
18 Jarrod Washburn .60 1.50
19 Hideo Nomo 1.50 4.00
20 Barry Zito 1.00 2.50
21 Kevin Millwood .60 1.50
22 Matt Morris .60 1.50
23 Carl Crawford 1.00 2.50
24 Carlos Delgado .60 1.50
25 Mike Piazza 1.50 4.00
26 Brad Radke .60 1.50
27 Richie Sexson .60 1.50
28 Kevin Brown .60 1.50
29 Carlos Beltran 1.00 2.50
30 Curt Schilling 1.00 2.50
31 Chipper Jones 1.50 4.00
32 Paul Konerko 1.00 2.50
33 Larry Walker 1.00 2.50
34 Jeff Bagwell 1.00 2.50
35 Jason Giambi .60 1.50
36 Mark Mulder .60 1.50
37 Vicente Padilla .60 1.50
38 Kris Benson .60 1.50
39 Bernie Williams 1.00 2.50
40 Jim Thome 1.00 2.50
41 Roger Clemens 2.00 5.00
42 Roberto Alomar 1.00 2.50
43 Torii Hunter .60 1.50
44 Bobby Abreu .60 1.50
45 Jeff Kent .60 1.50
46 Roy Oswalt 1.00 2.50
47 Bartolo Colon .60 1.50
48 Greg Maddux 2.00 5.00
49 Tom Glavine 1.00 2.50
50 Sammy Sosa 1.50 4.00
51 Ichiro Suzuki 2.00 5.00
52 Mark Prior 1.00 2.50
53 Manny Ramirez 1.50 4.00
54 Andruw Jones .60 1.50
55 Randy Johnson 1.50 4.00
56 Garret Anderson .60 1.50
57 Roy Halladay 1.00 2.50
58 Rafael Palmeiro 1.00 2.50
59 Rocco Baldelli .60 1.50
60 Albert Pujols 2.00 5.00
61 Edgar Renteria .60 1.50
62 John Olerud .60 1.50
63 Rich Aurilia .60 1.50
64 Ryan Klesko .60 1.50
65 Brian Giles .60 1.50
66 Eric Chavez .60 1.50
67 Jorge Posada 1.00 2.50
68 Cliff Floyd .60 1.50
69 Vladimir Guerrero 1.00 2.50
70 Cristian Guzman .60 1.50
71 Raul Ibanez 1.00 2.50
72 Paul Lo Duca .60 1.50
73 A.J. Burnett .60 1.50
74 Ken Griffey Jr. 3.00 8.00
75 Mark Buehrle 1.00 2.50
76 Moises Alou .60 1.50
77 Adam Dunn 1.00 2.50
78 Tony Batista .60 1.50
79 Troy Glaus .60 1.50
80 Luis Gonzalez .60 1.50
81 Shea Hillenbrand .60 1.50
82 Kerry Wood .60 1.50
83 Magglio Ordonez 1.00 2.50
84 Omar Vizquel 1.00 2.50
85 Bobby Higginson .60 1.50
86 Mike Lowell .60 1.50
87 Runelvys Hernandez .60 1.50
88 Shawn Green .60 1.50
89 Erubiel Durazo .60 1.50
90 Pat Burrell .60 1.50
91 Todd Helton 1.00 2.50
92 Jim Edmonds 1.00 2.50
93 Aubrey Huff .60 1.50
94 Eric Hinske .60 1.50
95 Barry Bonds 2.50 6.00
96 Willie Mays 3.00 8.00
97 Bo Jackson 1.50 4.00
98 Carl Yastrzemski 2.50 6.00
99 Don Mattingly 3.00 8.00
100 Gary Carter 1.00 2.50
101 Jose Contreras C RC .75 2.00
102 Jose Contreras U 1.00 2.50
103 Jose Contreras R 2.00 5.00
104 Dan Haren C RC 1.50 4.00
105 Dan Haren U 2.00 5.00
106 Dan Haren R 4.00 10.00
107 Michel Hernandez C RC .30 .75
108 Michel Hernandez U .40 1.00
109 Michel Hernandez R .75 2.00
110 Bobby Basham C RC .30 .75
111 Bobby Basham U .40 1.00
112 Bobby Basham R .75 2.00
113 Bryan Bullington C RC .30 .75
114 Bryan Bullington U .40 1.00
115 Bryan Bullington R .75 2.00
116 Bernie Castro C RC .30 .75
117 Bernie Castro U .40 1.00
118 Bernie Castro R .75 2.00
119 Chien-Ming Wang C RC 1.25 3.00
120 Chien-Ming Wang U 1.50 4.00
121 Chien-Ming Wang R 3.00 8.00
122 Eric Crozier C RC .30 .75
123 Eric Crozier U .40 1.00
124 Eric Crozier R .75 2.00
125 Michael Garciaparra C RC .30 .75
126 Michael Garciaparra U .40 1.00
127 Michael Garciaparra R .75 2.00
128 Joey Gomes C RC .30 .75
129 Joey Gomes U .40 1.00
130 Joey Gomes R .75 2.00
131 Wil Ledezma C RC .30 .75
132 Wil Ledezma U .40 1.00
133 Wil Ledezma R .75 2.00
134 Branden Florence C RC .30 .75
135 Branden Florence U .40 1.00
136 Branden Florence R .75 2.00
137 Jeremy Bonderman C RC 1.25 3.00
138 Jeremy Bonderman U 1.50 4.00
139 Jeremy Bonderman R 3.00 8.00
140 Travis Ishikawa C RC .75 2.00
141 Travis Ishikawa U 1.00 2.50
142 Travis Ishikawa R 2.00 5.00
143 Ben Francisco C RC .30 .75
144 Ben Francisco U .40 1.00
145 Ben Francisco R .75 2.00
146 Jason Kubel C RC 1.00 2.50
147 Jason Kubel U 1.25 3.00
148 Jason Kubel R 2.50 6.00
149 Tyler Martin C RC .30 .75
150 Tyler Martin U .40 1.00
151 Tyler Martin R .75 2.00
152 Jason Perry C RC .30 .75
153 Jason Perry U .40 1.00
154 Jason Perry R .75 2.00
155 Ryan Shealy C RC .30 .75
156 Ryan Shealy U .40 1.00
157 Ryan Shealy R .75 2.00
158 Hanley Ramirez C RC 2.50 6.00
159 Hanley Ramirez U 3.00 8.00
160 Hanley Ramirez R 6.00 15.00
161 Rajai Davis C RC .30 .75
162 Rajai Davis U .40 1.00
163 Rajai Davis R .75 2.00
164 Gary Schneidmiller C RC .30 .75
165 Gary Schneidmiller U .40 1.00
166 Gary Schneidmiller R .75 2.00
167 Haj Turay C RC .30 .75
168 Haj Turay U .40 1.00
169 Haj Turay R .75 2.00
170 Kevin Youkilis C RC 2.00 5.00
171 Kevin Youkilis U 2.50 6.00
172 Kevin Youkilis R 5.00 12.00
173 Shane Bazzell C RC .30 .75
174 Shane Bazzell U .40 1.00
175 Shane Bazzell R .75 2.00
176 Elizardo Ramirez C RC .30 .75
177 Elizardo Ramirez U .40 1.00
178 Elizardo Ramirez R .75 2.00
179 Robinson Cano C RC 5.00 12.00
180 Robinson Cano U 6.00 15.00
181 Robinson Cano R 12.00 30.00
182 Nook Logan C RC .30 .75

183 Nook Logan U .40 1.00
184 Nook Logan R .75 2.00
185 Dustin McGowan C RC .30 .75
186 Dustin McGowan U .40 1.00
187 Dustin McGowan R .75 2.00
188 Ryan Howard C RC 2.50 6.00
189 Ryan Howard U 3.00 8.00
190 Ryan Howard R 6.00 15.00

2003 Topps Pristine Gold Refractors

*GOLD 1-95: 2.5X TO 6X BASIC
*GOLD 96-100: 2.5X TO 6X BASIC
*GOLD C 101-190: 2.5X TO 6X BASIC C
*GOLD U 101-190: 1.5X TO 4X BASIC U
*GOLD R 101-190: 1X TO 2.5X BASIC R
ONE PER SEALED HOBBY BOX
STATED PRINT RUN 69 SERIAL #'d SETS

2003 Topps Pristine Plates

STATED ODDS 1:83
STATED PRINT RUN 4 SETS
BLACK, CYAN, MAGENTA & YELLOW EXIST
NO PRICING DUE TO SCARCITY

2003 Topps Pristine Refractors

*REFRACTORS 1-95: 2X TO 5X BASIC
*REFRACTORS 96-100: 2X TO 5X BASIC
REFRACTORS 1-100 ODDS 1:8
REFRACTORS 1-100 PRINT RUN 99 #'d SETS
*REFRACTORS C 101-190: .6X TO 1.2X
COMMON 101-190 PRINT RUN 1599 #'d SETS
*REFRACTORS U 101-190: 1X TO 2.5X
UNCOMMON 101-190 ODDS 1:6
UNCOMMON 101-190 PRINT 499 #'d SETS
*REFRACTORS R 101-190: 1.5X TO 4X
RARE 101-190 ODDS 1:27
RARE 101-190 PRINT RUN 99 #'d SETS

2003 Topps Pristine Bonds Jersey Relics

STATED ODDS 1:262
REFRACTOR ODDS 1:787
REFRACTOR PRINT RUN 25 SERIAL #'d SETS
NO REFRACTOR PRICING DUE TO SCARCITY
BB Barry Bonds BB 8.00 20.00
GG Barry Bonds GG 8.00 20.00
HR Barry Bonds HR 8.00 20.00
MVP Barry Bonds MVP 8.00 20.00

2003 Topps Pristine Bonds Dual Relics

STATED ODDS 1:262
REFRACTOR STATED ODDS 1:787
REFRACTOR PRINT RUN 25 SERIAL #'d SETS
NO REFRACTOR PRICING DUE TO SCARCITY
BJ B.Bonds Jsy/R.Johnson Jsy 20.00 50.00
BM W.Mays Jsy/B.Bonds Jsy 60.00 120.00
BR A.Rod Jsy/B.Bonds Jsy 20.00 50.00
BT M.Tejada Bat/B.Bonds Bat 12.00 30.00

2003 Topps Pristine Bomb Squad Relics

GROUP A ODDS 1:3
GROUP B ODDS 1:5
GROUP C ODDS 1:9
REFRACTOR ODDS 1:59
REFRACTOR PRINT RUN 25 SERIAL #'d SETS
NO REFRACTOR PRICING DUE TO SCARCITY
AD Adam Dunn Jsy A 3.00 8.00
AJ Andruw Jones Bat B 6.00 15.00
AP1 Albert Pujols Bat A 8.00 20.00
AP2 Albert Pujols Uni B 10.00 25.00
AR1 Alex Rodriguez Bat C 4.00 10.00
AR2 Alex Rodriguez Jsy A 4.00 10.00
AS Alfonso Soriano Uni A 3.00 8.00
BB Barry Bonds Jsy B 10.00 25.00
CC Carl Crawford Bat C 3.00 8.00
CF Cliff Floyd Bat B 4.00 10.00
CJ Chipper Jones Bat B 6.00 15.00
DE1 Darin Erstad Uni B 4.00 10.00
DE2 Darin Erstad Jsy B 4.00 10.00
EC1 Eric Chavez Gray Uni A 3.00 8.00
EC2 Eric Chavez White Uni A 3.00 8.00
FT Frank Thomas Bat C 4.00 10.00
GA1 Garret Anderson Bat A 3.00 8.00
GA2 Garret Anderson Uni B 4.00 10.00
GB1 George Brett Jsy A 8.00 20.00
GB2 George Brett Bat B 8.00 20.00
GC Gary Carter Bat C 3.00 8.00
GS Gary Sheffield Bat A 3.00 8.00
HB Hank Blalock Bat B 4.00 10.00
JAG Juan Gonzalez Jsy B 4.00 10.00
JB Johnny Bench Bat A 4.00 10.00
JG Jason Giambi Bat A 3.00 8.00
JK Jeff Kent Bat B 4.00 10.00
JRB Jeff Bagwell Bat B 6.00 15.00
JT Jim Thome Bat B 6.00 15.00
LB1 Lance Berkman Jsy C 3.00 8.00
LB2 Lance Berkman Bat C 3.00 8.00
LG Luis Gonzalez Jsy B 4.00 10.00
MO Magglio Ordonez Jsy A 3.00 8.00
MO1 Moises Alou Uni A 3.00 8.00
MO2 Moises Alou Bat B 4.00 10.00
MP Mike Piazza Jsy B 6.00 15.00
MR Manny Ramirez Bat A 4.00 10.00
MS1 Mike Schmidt Bat A 8.00 20.00
MS2 Mike Schmidt Uni A 8.00 20.00
MT Miguel Tejada Bat B 4.00 10.00
NG1 Nomar Garciaparra Bat B 6.00 15.00
NG2 Nomar Garciaparra Jsy B 6.00 15.00
RH Rickey Henderson Bat B 6.00 15.00
RP Rafael Palmeiro Jsy B 6.00 15.00
SG Shawn Green Bat B 4.00 10.00
SS1 Sammy Sosa Bat B 6.00 15.00
SS2 Sammy Sosa Jsy A 4.00 10.00
TG1 Troy Glaus Bat A 3.00 8.00
TG2 Troy Glaus Uni B 4.00 10.00
TH Todd Helton Bat B 6.00 15.00
TS Tim Salmon Uni B 6.00 15.00
VG1 Vladimir Guerrero Jsy A 4.00 10.00
VG2 Vladimir Guerrero Bat A 4.00 10.00

2003 Topps Pristine Borders Relics

STATED ODDS 1:9
REFRACTOR ODDS 1:210
REFRACTOR PRINT RUN 25 SERIAL #'d SETS
NO REFRACTOR PRICING DUE TO SCARCITY
AJ Andruw Jones Uni 4.00 10.00
AP Albert Pujols Jsy 8.00 20.00
AS Alfonso Soriano Bat 3.00 8.00
BW Bernie Williams Bat 4.00 10.00
CC Chin Feng Chen Jsy 15.00 40.00
CG Cristian Guzman Bat 3.00 8.00
IR Ivan Rodriguez Bat 4.00 10.00
KI Kazuhisa Ishii Jsy 3.00 8.00
MO Magglio Ordonez Jsy 3.00 8.00
MR Manny Ramirez Jsy 4.00 10.00
MT Miguel Tejada Bat 3.00 8.00
PM Pedro Martinez Jsy 4.00 10.00
SS Sammy Sosa Jsy 4.00 10.00
TS Tsuyoshi Shinjo Bat 3.00 8.00
VG Vladimir Guerrero Jsy 4.00 10.00

2003 Topps Pristine Corners Relics

STATED ODDS 1:12
REFRACTOR ODDS 1:285
REFRACTOR PRINT RUN 25 SERIAL #'d SETS
NO REFRACTOR PRICING DUE TO SCARCITY
AS Alfonzo Bat/Snow Bat 2.50 6.00
BK Burroughs Jsy/Klesko Bat 2.50 6.00
BM Beltre Bat/McGriff Bat 6.00 15.00
BT Bell Bat/Thome Bat 4.00 10.00
CD Chavez Bat/Durazo Bat 2.50 6.00
GS Glaus Jsy/Speizio Jsy 2.50 6.00
KM Koskie Bat/Mientkiewicz Bat 2.50 6.00
RM Rolen Bat/T.Martinez Bat 4.00 10.00
TP Teixeira Bat/Palmeiro Bat 4.00 10.00
VG Ventura Bat/Giambi Bat 2.50 6.00
WG M.Williams Bat/Grace Bat 4.00 10.00

2003 Topps Pristine Factor Bat Relics

STATED ODDS 1:9
REFRACTOR ODDS 1:210
REFRACTOR PRINT RUN 25 SERIAL #'d SETS
NO REFRACTOR PRICING DUE TO SCARCITY
AD Adam Dunn 3.00 8.00
AR Alex Rodriguez 4.00 10.00
AS Alfonso Soriano 3.00 8.00
DE Darin Erstad 3.00 8.00
JG Jason Giambi 3.00 8.00
LB Lance Berkman 3.00 8.00
MO Magglio Ordonez 3.00 8.00
MP Mike Piazza 6.00 15.00
MR Manny Ramirez 4.00 10.00
NG Nomar Garciaparra 6.00 15.00
SS Sammy Sosa 4.00 10.00
TG Troy Glaus 3.00 8.00
TH Todd Helton 4.00 10.00
TKH Torii Hunter 3.00 8.00
VG Vladimir Guerrero 4.00 10.00

2003 Topps Pristine Mini

VETERAN STATED ODDS 1:8
COMMON ROOKIE .60 1.50
ROOKIE STATED ODDS 1:16
AK Austin Kearns V .60 1.50
AR Alex Rodriguez V 2.00 5.00
AS Alfonso Soriano V 1.00 2.50
BB Barry Bonds V 2.50 6.00
BC Bernie Castro R .60 1.50
BG Brian Giles V .60 1.50
BPB Bryan Bullington R .60 1.50
BWB Bobby Basham R .60 1.50
CW Chien-Ming Wang R 2.50 6.00
DH Dan Haren R 3.00 8.00
DJ Derek Jeter V 4.00 10.00
DM Dustin McGowan R .60 1.50
EC Eric Chavez V .60 1.50
ELC Eric Crozier R .60 1.50
ER Elizardo Ramirez R .60 1.50
IS Ichiro Suzuki V 2.00 5.00
JB Jeremy Bonderman R 2.50 6.00
JC Jose Contreras R 1.50 4.00
JG Jason Giambi V .60 1.50
JJK Jason Kubel R 2.00 5.00
JK Jeff Kent V .60 1.50
JT Jim Thome V 1.00 2.50
KY Kevin Youkilis R 4.00 10.00
MH Michel Hernandez R .60 1.50
MJP Mike Piazza V 1.50 4.00
MO Magglio Ordonez V 1.00 2.50
MP Mark Prior V 1.00 2.50
MT Miguel Tejada V 1.00 2.50
NG Nomar Garciaparra V 1.00 2.50
NL Nook Logan R .60 1.50
RB Rocco Baldelli V .60 1.50
RC Roger Clemens V 2.00 5.00
RD Rajai Davis R .60 1.50
RH Ryan Howard R 5.00 12.00
RJC Robinson Cano R 10.00 25.00
RS Ryan Shealy R .60 1.50
SS Sammy Sosa V 1.50 4.00
TM Tyler Martin R .60 1.50
VG Vladimir Guerrero V 1.00 2.50
WL Wil Ledezma R .60 1.50

2003 Topps Pristine Mini Autograph

STATED ODDS 1:636
STATED PRINT RUN 100 CARDS
PRINT RUN INFO PROVIDED BY TOPPS
CARD IS NOT SERIAL-NUMBERED
RC Roger Clemens/100 * 30.00 60.00

2003 Topps Pristine Personal Endorsements

STATED ODDS 1:5
GOLD STATED ODDS 1:184
GOLD PRINT RUN 25 SERIAL #'d SETS
NO GOLD PRICING DUE TO SCARCITY
AB Andrew Brown 4.00 10.00
BM Brett Myers 4.00 15.00
DE David Eckstein 4.00 15.00
FS Felix Sanchez 4.00 10.00
FV Fernando Vina 4.00 10.00
JG Jay Gibbons 4.00 10.00
JP Josh Phelps 4.00 10.00
KH Ken Harvey 4.00 10.00
KS Kelly Shoppach 4.00 10.00
LF Lew Ford 4.00 10.00
ML Mike Lowell 4.00 15.00
MS Mike Sweeney 4.00 10.00
PK Paul Konerko 6.00 15.00
RJH Rich Harden 4.00 10.00
RYC Ryan Church 4.00 10.00
SR Scott Rolen 6.00 15.00
VM Victor Martinez 4.00 10.00

2003 Topps Pristine Primary Elements Patch Relics

STATED ODDS 1:45
STATED PRINT RUN 50 SETS
CARDS ARE NOT SERIAL-NUMBERED
PRINT RUN INFO PROVIDED BY TOPPS
NO PRICING DUE TO SCARCITY
REFRACTOR ODDS 1:224
REFRACTOR PRINT RUN 10 SERIAL #'d SETS
NO REFRACTOR PRICING DUE TO SCARCITY

2004 Topps Pristine

COMMON CARD (1-100) .50 1.25
COMMON C (101-190) .50 1.25
C 101-190 APPROX.EQUAL TO 1-100
COMMON U (101-190) .75 2.00
UNCOMMON 101-190 STATED ODDS 1:2
UNCOMMON 101-190 PRINT 999 #'d SETS
COMMON R (101-190) 1.25 3.00
RARE 101-190 STATED ODDS 1:4
RARE 101-190 PRINT RUN 499 #'d SETS
OVERALL PLATES ODDS 1:52 HOBBY
PLATE PRINT RUN 1 SET PER COLOR
BLACK-CYAN-MAGENTA-YELLOW ISSUED
NO PLATE PRICING DUE TO SCARCITY
1 Jim Thome .75 2.00
2 Ryan Klesko .50 1.25
3 Ichiro Suzuki 1.50 4.00
4 Rocco Baldelli .50 1.25
5 Vernon Wells .50 1.25
6 Javier Vazquez .50 1.25
7 Billy Wagner .50 1.25
8 Jose Reyes .75 2.00
9 Lance Berkman .75 2.00
10 Alex Rodriguez 1.50 4.00
11 Pat Burrell .50 1.25
12 Mark Mulder .50 1.25
13 Mike Piazza 1.25 3.00
14 Miguel Cabrera 1.25 3.00
15 Larry Walker .75 2.00
16 Carlos Lee .50 1.25
17 Mark Prior .75 2.00
18 Pedro Martinez .75 2.00
19 Melvin Mora .50 1.25
20 Sammy Sosa 1.25 3.00
21 Bartolo Colon .50 1.25
22 Luis Gonzalez .50 1.25
23 Marcus Giles .50 1.25
24 Ken Griffey Jr. 2.50 6.00
25 Ivan Rodriguez .75 2.00
26 Carlos Beltran .75 2.00
27 Geoff Jenkins .50 1.25
28 Nick Johnson .50 1.25
29 Gary Sheffield .50 1.25
30 Alfonso Soriano .75 2.00
31 Scott Rolen .75 2.00
32 Garret Anderson .50 1.25
33 Richie Sexson .50 1.25
34 Curt Schilling .75 2.00
35 Greg Maddux 1.50 4.00
36 Adam Dunn .75 2.00
37 Preston Wilson .50 1.25
38 Josh Beckett .50 1.25
39 Roy Oswalt .75 2.00
40 Derek Jeter 3.00 8.00
41 Jason Kendall .50 1.25
42 Bret Boone .50 1.25
43 Torii Hunter .50 1.25
44 Roy Halladay .75 2.00
45 Edgar Renteria .50 1.25
46 Troy Glaus .50 1.25
47 Chipper Jones 1.25 3.00
48 Manny Ramirez 1.25 3.00
49 C.C. Sabathia .75 2.00
50 Albert Pujols 1.50 4.00
51 Randy Wolf .50 1.25
52 Eric Chavez .50 1.25
53 Kevin Brown .50 1.25
54 Cliff Floyd .50 1.25
55 Jeff Bagwell .75 2.00
56 Frank Thomas 1.25 3.00
57 David Ortiz 1.25 3.00
58 Rafael Palmeiro .75 2.00
59 Randy Johnson 1.25 3.00
60 Vladimir Guerrero .75 2.00
61 Carlos Delgado .50 1.25
62 Hank Blalock .50 1.25
63 Jim Edmonds .75 2.00
64 Jason Schmidt .50 1.25
65 Mike Lieberthal .50 1.25
66 Tim Hudson .75 2.00
67 Jorge Posada .75 2.00
68 Jose Vidro .50 1.25
69 Eric Gagne .50 1.25
70 Roger Clemens 1.50 4.00
71 Mike Lowell .50 1.25
72 Dontrelle Willis .50 1.25
73 Austin Kearns .50 1.25
74 Kerry Wood .50 1.25
75 Miguel Tejada .75 2.00
76 Bobby Abreu .50 1.25
77 Edgar Martinez .75 2.00
78 Joe Mauer 1.00 2.50
79 Mike Sweeney .50 1.25
80 Jason Giambi .50 1.25
81 Mark Teixeira .75 2.00
82 Aubrey Huff .50 1.25
83 Brian Giles .50 1.25
84 Barry Zito .75 2.00
85 Mike Mussina .75 2.00
86 Brandon Webb .50 1.25
87 Andruw Jones .50 1.25
88 Javy Lopez .50 1.25
89 Bill Mueller .50 1.25
90 Scott Podsednik .50 1.25
91 Moises Alou .50 1.25
92 Esteban Loaiza .50 1.25
93 Magglio Ordonez .75 2.00
94 Jeff Kent .50 1.25
95 Todd Helton .75 2.00
96 Juan Pierre .50 1.25
97 Jody Gerut .50 1.25
98 Angel Berroa .50 1.25
99 Shawn Green .50 1.25
100 Nomar Garciaparra .75 2.00
101 David Aardsma C RC .50 1.25
102 David Aardsma U .75 2.00
103 David Aardsma R 1.25 3.00
104 Erick Aybar C RC 1.25 3.00
105 Erick Aybar U 2.00 5.00
106 Erick Aybar R 3.00 8.00
107 Chad Bentz C RC .50 1.25
108 Chad Bentz U .75 2.00
109 Chad Bentz R 1.25 3.00
110 Travis Blackley C RC .50 1.25
111 Travis Blackley U .75 2.00
112 Travis Blackley R 1.25 3.00
113 Bobby Brownlie C RC .50 1.25
114 Bobby Brownlie U .75 2.00
115 Bobby Brownlie R 1.25 3.00
116 Alberto Callaspo C RC 1.25 3.00
117 Alberto Callaspo U 2.00 5.00
118 Alberto Callaspo R 3.00 8.00
119 Kazuo Matsui C RC .75 2.00
120 Kazuo Matsui U 1.25 3.00
121 Kazuo Matsui R 2.00 5.00
122 Jesse Crain C RC .75 2.00
123 Jesse Crain U 1.25 3.00
124 Jesse Crain R 2.00 5.00
125 Howie Kendrick C RC 2.50 6.00
126 Howie Kendrick U 4.00 10.00
127 Howie Kendrick R 6.00 15.00
128 Blake Hawksworth C RC .50 1.25
129 Blake Hawksworth U .75 2.00
130 Blake Hawksworth R 1.25 3.00
131 Conor Jackson C RC 1.50 4.00
132 Conor Jackson U 2.50 6.00
133 Conor Jackson R 4.00 10.00
134 Paul Maholm C RC .75 2.00
135 Paul Maholm U 1.25 3.00
136 Paul Maholm R 2.00 5.00
137 Lastings Milledge C RC .75 2.00
138 Lastings Milledge U 1.25 3.00
139 Lastings Milledge R 2.00 5.00
140 Matt Moses C RC .75 2.00
141 Matt Moses U 1.25 3.00
142 Matt Moses R 2.00 5.00
143 David Murphy C RC .75 2.00
144 David Murphy U 1.25 3.00
145 David Murphy R 2.00 5.00
146 Dioner Navarro C RC .75 2.00
147 Dioner Navarro U 1.25 3.00
148 Dioner Navarro R 2.00 5.00
149 Dustin Nippert C RC .50 1.25
150 Dustin Nippert U .75 2.00
151 Dustin Nippert R 1.25 3.00
152 Vito Chiaravalloti C RC .50 1.25
153 Vito Chiaravalloti U .75 2.00
154 Vito Chiaravalloti R 1.25 3.00
155 Akinori Otsuka C RC .50 1.25
156 Akinori Otsuka U .75 2.00
157 Akinori Otsuka R 1.25 3.00
158 Casey Daigle C RC .50 1.25
159 Casey Daigle U .75 2.00
160 Casey Daigle R 1.25 3.00
161 Carlos Quentin C RC 2.00 5.00
162 Carlos Quentin U 3.00 8.00
163 Carlos Quentin R 5.00 12.00
164 Omar Quintanilla C RC .50 1.25
165 Omar Quintanilla U .75 2.00
166 Omar Quintanilla R 1.25 3.00
167 Chris Saenz C RC .50 1.25
168 Chris Saenz U .75 2.00
169 Chris Saenz R 1.25 3.00
170 Ervin Santana C RC 1.25 3.00
171 Ervin Santana U 2.00 5.00
172 Ervin Santana R 3.00 8.00
173 Chris Shelton C RC .50 1.25
174 Chris Shelton U .75 2.00
175 Chris Shelton R 1.25 3.00
176 Kyle Sleeth C RC .50 1.25
177 Kyle Sleeth U .75 2.00
178 Kyle Sleeth R 1.25 3.00
179 Brad Snyder C RC .50 1.25
180 Brad Snyder U .75 2.00
181 Brad Snyder R 1.25 3.00
182 Tim Stauffer C RC .75 2.00
183 Tim Stauffer U 1.25 3.00
184 Tim Stauffer R 2.00 5.00
185 Shingo Takatsu C RC .50 1.25
186 Shingo Takatsu U .75 2.00
187 Shingo Takatsu R 1.25 3.00
188 Merkin Valdez C RC .50 1.25
189 Merkin Valdez U .75 2.00
190 Merkin Valdez R 1.25 3.00

2004 Topps Pristine Gold Refractors

*GOLD 1-100: 2.5X TO 6X BASIC
*GOLD C 101-190: 2.5X TO 6X BASIC
*GOLD U 101-190: 1.5X TO 4X BASIC
*GOLD R 101-190: 1X TO 2.5X BASIC
ONE PER SEALED HOBBY BOX
STATED PRINT RUN 41 SERIAL #'d SETS

2004 Topps Pristine Refractors

*REFRACTORS 1-100: 2.5X TO 6X BASIC
1-100 STATED ODDS 1:11
1-100 PRINT RUN 49 SERIAL #'d SETS
*REFRACTORS C 101-190: .6X TO 1.5X BASIC
COMMON 101-190 RANDOM IN PACKS
COMMON 101-190 PRINT RUN 999 #'d SETS
*REFRACTORS U 101-190: .6X TO 1.5X BASIC
UNCOMMON 101-190 ODDS 1:5
UNCOMMON 101-190 PRINT 399 #'d SETS
*REFRACTORS R 101-190: 1X TO 2.5X BASIC
RARE 101-190 ODDS 1:35
RARE 101-190 PRINT RUN 49 #'d SETS

2004 Topps Pristine 1-2-3 Triple Relics

STATED ODDS 1:171
*REFRACTOR: X TO X BASIC
REFRACTOR ODDS 1:686
REFRACTOR PRINT RUN 25 #'d SETS
B = S BAT; J = S JSY
BOS Damon B/Mueller J/Nomar J 20.00 50.00
CHC Grudz B/A.Gonz B/Sosa B 15.00 40.00
NYY Lofton B/Jeter B/A.Rod B 30.00 60.00

2004 Topps Pristine Fantasy Favorites Relics

RANDOM INSERTS IN PACKS
*REFRACTOR: 2X TO 5X BASIC
REFRACTOR STATED ODDS 1:59
REFRACTOR PRINT RUN 25 #'d SETS
AB Angel Berroa Bat 2.00 5.00
AJ Andruw Jones Jsy 3.00 8.00
AP Albert Pujols Jsy 6.00 15.00
AR Alex Rodriguez Bat 4.00 10.00
BB Bret Boone Jsy 2.00 5.00
BW Brandon Webb Uni 2.00 5.00
CD Carlos Delgado Jsy 2.00 5.00
CJ Chipper Jones Jsy 4.00 10.00
CK Corey Koskie Bat 2.00 5.00
DJ Derek Jeter Bat 10.00 25.00
EG Eric Gagne Jsy 2.00 5.00
FT Frank Thomas Jsy 4.00 10.00
JB Jeff Bagwell Uni 3.00 8.00
JD Johnny Damon Bat 3.00 8.00
JR Jimmy Rollins Jsy 2.00 5.00
JT Jim Thome Uni 3.00 8.00
JV Jose Vidro Bat 2.00 5.00
KL Kenny Lofton Bat 2.00 5.00
KW Kerry Wood Jsy 2.00 5.00
LW Larry Walker Jsy 2.00 5.00
MA Moises Alou Jsy 2.00 5.00
MG Mark Grudzielanek Bat 2.00 5.00
MP Mark Prior Jsy 3.00 8.00
MPI Mike Piazza Jsy 4.00 10.00
MT Mark Teixeira Bat 3.00 8.00
NG Nomar Garciaparra Jsy 4.00 10.00
PM Pedro Martinez Jsy 3.00 8.00
PW Preston Wilson Jsy 2.00 5.00
RB Rocco Baldelli Bat 2.00 5.00
RF Rafael Furcal Bat 2.00 5.00
RFJ Rafael Furcal Jsy 2.00 5.00
SG Shawn Green Jsy 2.00 5.00
TH Tim Hudson Jsy 2.00 5.00
THE Todd Helton Jsy 3.00 8.00
VG Vladimir Guerrero Bat 4.00 10.00

2004 Topps Pristine Going Going Gone Bat Relics

GROUP A ODDS 1:6
GROUP B ODDS 1:11
*REFRACTOR: 2X TO 5X BASIC
REFRACTOR STATED ODDS 1:93
REFRACTOR PRINT RUN 25 #'d SETS
AD Adam Dunn B 2.00 5.00
AP Albert Pujols A 6.00 15.00
AR Alex Rodriguez A 4.00 10.00
AS Alfonso Soriano A 2.00 5.00
BB Bret Boone A 2.00 5.00
CJ Chipper Jones A 4.00 10.00
DO David Ortiz B 4.00 10.00
FT Frank Thomas B 4.00 10.00
JG Juan Gonzalez A 2.00 5.00
JJ Jacque Jones A 2.00 5.00
JK Jeff Kent A 2.00 5.00
JT Jim Thome A 3.00 8.00
LB Lance Berkman A 2.00 5.00
LG Luis Gonzalez A 2.00 5.00
MO Magglio Ordonez A 2.00 5.00
MP Mike Piazza B 4.00 10.00
MR Manny Ramirez B 3.00 8.00
RK Ryan Klesko B 2.00 5.00
SR Scott Rolen A 3.00 8.00
SS Sammy Sosa A 4.00 10.00
VG Vladimir Guerrero A 4.00 10.00
VW Vernon Wells A 2.00 5.00

2004 Topps Pristine Key Acquisition Bat Relics

STATED ODDS 1:8
*REFRACTOR: 2X TO 5X BASIC
REFRACTOR ODDS 1:256
REFRACTOR PRINT RUN 25 #'d SETS
AR Alex Rodriguez 4.00 10.00
AS Alfonso Soriano 2.00 5.00
GS Gary Sheffield 2.00 5.00
HC Hee Seop Choi 2.00 5.00
IR Ivan Rodriguez 3.00 8.00
JG Juan Gonzalez 2.00 5.00
JL Javy Lopez 2.00 5.00
VG Vladimir Guerrero 4.00 10.00

2004 Topps Pristine Mini

STATED ODDS 1:5
AO Akinori Otsuka R .60 1.50
AP Albert Pujols V 2.00 5.00
AR Alex Rodriguez V 2.00 5.00
BH Blake Hawksworth R .60 1.50
CJ Chipper Jones V 1.50 4.00
CJA Conor Jackson R 2.00 5.00
DA David Aardsma R .60 1.50
DJ Derek Jeter V 4.00 10.00
DM David Murphy R 1.00 2.50
DN Dioner Navarro R 1.00 2.50
DW Dontrelle Willis V .60 1.50
EA Erick Aybar R 1.50 4.00
HK Howie Kendrick R 3.00 8.00
IS Ichiro Suzuki V 2.00 5.00
JG Jason Giambi V .60 1.50
JT Jim Thome V 1.00 2.50
KM Kazuo Matsui R 1.00 2.50
KS Kyle Sleeth R .60 1.50
KW Kerry Wood V .60 1.50
LM Lastings Milledge R 1.00 2.50
MM Matt Moses R 1.00 2.50
MP Mark Prior V 1.00 2.50
MPI Mike Piazza V 1.50 4.00
MV Merkin Valdez R .60 1.50
NG Nomar Garciaparra V 1.00 2.50
SS Sammy Sosa V 1.50 4.00
ST Shingo Takatsu R .60 1.50
TS Tim Stauffer R 1.00 2.50
VC Vito Chiaravalloti R .60 1.50
VG Vladimir Guerrero V 1.00 2.50

2004 Topps Pristine Mini Relics

STATED ODDS 1:51
STATED PRINT RUN 100 SETS
CARDS ARE NOT SERIAL-NUMBERED
PRINT RUN INFO PROVIDED BY TOPPS
AP Albert Pujols Jsy 10.00 25.00
CJ Chipper Jones Jsy 6.00 15.00
EG Eric Gagne Jsy 3.00 8.00
JB Jeff Bagwell Uni 5.00 12.00
KW Kerry Wood Jsy 3.00 8.00
MP Mark Prior Jsy 5.00 12.00
NG Nomar Garciaparra Jsy 6.00 15.00
PM Pedro Martinez Jsy 5.00 12.00
PW Preston Wilson Jsy 3.00 8.00
MPI Mike Piazza Jsy 6.00 15.00

2004 Topps Pristine Patch Place Relics

GROUP A ODDS 1:30
GROUP B ODDS 1:34
REFRACTOR STATED ODDS 1:155
REFRACTOR PRINT RUN 10 #'d SETS
NO REF.PRICING DUE TO SCARCITY
LISTED PRICES ARE SINGLE COLOR PATCH
*MULTI-COLOR: ADD 100% PREMIUM
AD Adam Dunn A 4.00 10.00
AJ Andruw Jones A 6.00 15.00
AK Austin Kearns A 4.00 10.00
AP Albert Pujols B 15.00 40.00
BB Bret Boone B 4.00 10.00
BZ Barry Zito A 4.00 10.00
CC Chin-Feng Chen A 25.00 60.00
CD Carlos Delgado A 4.00 10.00
CJ Chipper Jones B 6.00 15.00
DW Dontrelle Willis A 6.00 15.00
EG Eric Gagne A 4.00 10.00
FT Frank Thomas A 6.00 15.00
JB Jeff Bagwell B 6.00 15.00
JBE Josh Beckett B 4.00 10.00
JR Jose Reyes A 4.00 10.00
JS John Smoltz A 6.00 15.00
KW Kerry Wood A 4.00 10.00
LC Luis Castillo A 4.00 10.00
LG Luis Gonzalez B 4.00 10.00
ML Mike Lowell A 4.00 10.00
MP Mark Prior B 6.00 15.00
MPI Mike Piazza B 6.00 15.00
NG Nomar Garciaparra A 6.00 15.00
PL Paul Lo Duca A 4.00 10.00
PM Pedro Martinez B 6.00 15.00
PW Preston Wilson A 4.00 10.00
RB Rocco Baldelli A 4.00 10.00
RF Rafael Furcal A 4.00 10.00
RJ Randy Johnson B 6.00 15.00
SG Shawn Green A 4.00 10.00
SS Sammy Sosa A 6.00 15.00
TH Tim Hudson A 4.00 10.00
THE Todd Helton B 6.00 15.00

2004 Topps Pristine Personal Endorsements

GROUP A ODDS 1:39
GROUP B ODDS 1:41
GROUP C ODDS 1:7
GOLD STATED ODDS 1:73
GOLD PRINT RUN 25 SERIAL #'d SETS
NO GOLD PRICING DUE TO SCARCITY
AH Aubrey Huff C 4.00 10.00
AR Alex Rodriguez A 40.00 80.00
BC Bobby Crosby C 4.00 10.00
BM Brett Myers A 6.00 15.00
BW Brandon Webb B 4.00 10.00
CJ Conor Jackson C 8.00 20.00
CL Chris Lubanski C 4.00 10.00
DA David Aardsma C 6.00 15.00
DM Dustin McGowan C 4.00 10.00
DY Delmon Young A 10.00 25.00
EH Estee Harris C 6.00 15.00
ES Ervin Santana C 5.00 12.00
GA Garret Anderson A 6.00 15.00
GS Gary Sheffield A 15.00 40.00
GSI Grady Sizemore C 6.00 15.00
HB Hank Blalock B 6.00 15.00
IR Ivan Rodriguez A 20.00 50.00
JF Jennie Finch A 30.00 60.00
JM Joe Mauer B 20.00 50.00
JP Jorge Posada A 15.00 40.00
JV Javier Vazquez A 6.00 15.00
LB Lance Berkman A 10.00 25.00
MC Miguel Cabrera B 30.00 60.00
MG Marcus Giles A 6.00 15.00
SP Scott Podsednik B 10.00 25.00
VC Vito Chiaravalloti C 4.00 10.00
VG Vladimir Guerrero A 20.00 50.00
WM Willie Mays A 125.00 200.00

2005 Topps Pristine

COMMON CARD (1-100) .40 1.00
COMMON RC (101-130) .40 1.00
COMMON GU (131-180) 2.00 5.00
GU 131-180 STATED ODDS 1:3
GU 131-180 PRINT RUN 500 #'d SETS
COMMON AU (181-205) 12.50 30.00
COMMON FY AU (181-205) 10.00 25.00
AU 181-205 STATED ODDS 1:22
AU 181-205 PRINT RUN 100 #'d SETS
AU-GU 206-210 STATED ODDS 1:219
AU-GU 206-210 PRINT RUN 49 #'d SETS
AU-GU 206-210 EXCH.DEADLINE 10/31/07
OVERALL PLATE ODDS 1:53 HOBBY
PLATE PRINT RUN 1 SET PER COLOR
BLACK-CYAN-MAGENTA-YELLOW ISSUED
NO PLATE PRICING DUE TO SCARCITY
1 Alex Rodriguez 1.25 3.00
2 Jake Peavy .40 1.00
3 Bobby Crosby .40 1.00
4 J.D. Drew .40 1.00
5 Scott Rolen .60 1.50
6 Bobby Abreu .40 1.00
7 Ken Griffey Jr. 2.00 5.00
8 Jeremy Bonderman .40 1.00
9 Mike Sweeney .40 1.00
10 Mark Prior .60 1.50
11 Tim Hudson .60 1.50
12 Clint Barnes .40 1.00
13 Jeff Bagwell .60 1.50
14 Andruw Jones .40 1.00
15 Carlos Delgado .40 1.00
16 Rocco Baldelli .40 1.00
17 Adam Dunn .60 1.50
18 Greg Maddux 1.25 3.00
19 Torii Hunter .40 1.00
20 Miguel Tejada .60 1.50
21 Lyle Overbay .40 1.00
22 Craig Wilson .40 1.00
23 Scott Kazmir 1.00 2.50
24 Alex Rios .40 1.00
25 Ichiro Suzuki 1.25 3.00
26 Jorge Posada .60 1.50
27 Jose Reyes .60 1.50
28 Hank Blalock .40 1.00
29 Troy Glaus .40 1.00
30 Todd Helton .60 1.50
31 Javy Lopez .40 1.00
32 Barry Zito .60 1.50
33 Jimmy Rollins .60 1.50
34 Mark Loretta .40 1.00
35 Richie Sexson .40 1.00
36 Nick Johnson .40 1.00
37 Ivan Rodriguez .60 1.50
38 Jeff Kent .40 1.00
39 Jake Westbrook .40 1.00
40 Carlos Beltran .60 1.50
41 Rich Harden .40 1.00
42 Joe Mauer .75 2.00
43 Luis Gonzalez .40 1.00
44 Frank Thomas 1.00 2.50
45 Michael Young .40 1.00
46 Jason Schmidt .40 1.00
47 Eric Chavez .40 1.00
48 Vinny Castilla .40 1.00
49 John Smoltz 1.00 2.50
50 Barry Bonds 1.50 4.00
51 Jim Edmonds .60 1.50
52 Edgar Renteria .40 1.00
53 Jose Vidro .40 1.00
54 Chipper Jones 1.00 2.50
55 Curt Schilling .60 1.50
56 Victor Martinez .60 1.50
57 Josh Beckett .60 1.50
58 Derrek Lee .40 1.00
59 Shawn Green .40 1.00
60 Roger Clemens 1.25 3.00
61 Orlando Cabrera .40 1.00
62 Mike Piazza 1.00 2.50
63 Gary Sheffield .40 1.00
64 Carl Crawford .60 1.50
65 Johan Santana .60 1.50
66 Oliver Perez .40 1.00
67 Manny Ramirez 1.00 2.50
68 Paul Konerko .60 1.50
69 Preston Wilson .40 1.00
70 Sammy Sosa 1.00 2.50
71 Eric Gagne .40 1.00
72 Geoff Jenkins .40 1.00
73 Magglio Ordonez .60 1.50
74 Kerry Wood .40 1.00
75 Albert Pujols 1.25 3.00
76 Roy Halladay .60 1.50
77 Aubrey Huff .40 1.00
78 Nomar Garciaparra .60 1.50
79 Brian Roberts .40 1.00
80 Randy Johnson 1.00 2.50
81 Pat Burrell .40 1.00
82 Brian Giles .40 1.00
83 Mike Mussina .60 1.50
84 Mark Teixeira .60 1.50
85 Pedro Martinez .60 1.50
86 Jason Bay .40 1.00
87 Mark Buehrle .60 1.50
88 Rafael Furcal .40 1.00
89 Juan Pierre .40 1.00
90 Jim Thome .60 1.50
91 Ben Sheets .40 1.00
92 Alfonso Soriano .60 1.50
93 Adrian Beltre 1.00 2.50
94 Miguel Cabrera 1.00 2.50
95 Derek Jeter 2.50 6.00
96 Vernon Wells .40 1.00
97 Lance Berkman .60 1.50
98 Hideki Matsui 1.50 4.00
99 David Ortiz 1.00 2.50
100 Vladimir Guerrero .60 1.50
101 Justin Verlander FY RC 8.00 20.00
102 Billy Butler FY RC 2.00 5.00
103 Wladimir Balentien FY RC .60 1.50
104 Jeremy West FY RC .40 1.00
105 Philip Humber FY RC 1.00 2.50
106 Tyler Pelland FY RC .40 1.00
107 Andy LaRoche FY RC .40 1.00
108 Hernan Iribarren FY RC .40 1.00
109 Luke Scott FY RC 1.00 2.50
110 Landon Powell FY RC .40 1.00
111 Alexander Smit FY RC .40 1.00
112 Ryan Garko FY RC .40 1.00
113 Bear Bay FY RC .40 1.00
114 Ian Bladergroen FY RC .40 1.00
115 Manny Parra FY RC 1.00 2.50
116 Andy Sides FY RC .40 1.00
117 Travis Chick FY RC .40 1.00
118 Stefan Bailie FY RC .40 1.00
119 Chuck Tiffany FY RC 1.00 2.50
120 Buck Coats FY RC .40 1.00
121 Jeff Niemann FY RC 1.00 2.50
122 Jake Postlewait FY RC .40 1.00
123 Matt Campbell FY RC .40 1.00
124 Kevin Melillo FY RC .40 1.00
125 Mike Morse FY RC 1.25 3.00
126 Anthony Reyes FY RC .60 1.50
127 Casey McGehee FY RC .60 1.50
128 Cody Haerther FY RC .40 1.00
129 Brandon McCarthy FY RC .60 1.50
130 Glen Perkins FY RC .40 1.00
131 Moises Alou Bat 2.00 5.00
132 Nomar Garciaparra Bat 4.00 10.00
133 Scott Rolen Jsy 3.00 8.00
134 Miguel Tejada Uni 2.00 5.00
135 Alex Rodriguez Bat 6.00 15.00
136 Michael Young Jsy 2.00 5.00
137 Tim Hudson Uni 2.00 5.00
138 Troy Glaus Bat 2.00 5.00
139 Eric Chavez Uni 2.00 5.00
140 David Ortiz Bat 3.00 8.00

141 Andruw Jones Jsy 3.00 8.00
142 Richie Sexson Bat 2.00 5.00
143 Jim Thome Bat 3.00 8.00
144 Javy Lopez Bat 2.00 5.00
145 Lance Berkman Jsy 2.00 5.00
146 Gary Sheffield Bat 2.00 5.00
147 Dontrelle Willis Jsy 2.00 5.00
148 Curt Schilling Jsy 3.00 8.00
149 Jorge Posada Jsy 3.00 8.00
150 Vladimir Guerrero Bat 4.00 10.00
151 Adam Dunn Jsy 2.00 5.00
152 Ryan Drese Jsy 2.00 5.00
153 Hank Blalock Uni 2.00 5.00
154 Kerry Wood Jsy 2.00 5.00
155 Alfonso Soriano Bat 2.00 5.00
156 Aramis Ramirez Bat 2.00 5.00
157 Mark Mulder Uni 2.00 5.00
158 Paul Konerko Bat 2.00 5.00
159 Jim Edmonds Jsy 2.00 5.00
160 Roger Clemens Jsy 5.00 12.00
161 Mariano Rivera Jsy 4.00 10.00
162 Rafael Palmeiro Bat 3.00 8.00
163 Mark Teixeira Bat 3.00 8.00
164 Eric Gagne Jsy 2.00 5.00
165 Sammy Sosa Bat 4.00 10.00
166 Brett Myers Jsy 2.00 5.00
167 Kazuhisa Ishii Uni 2.00 5.00
168 Ken Harvey Bat 2.00 5.00
169 Johnny Estrada Jsy 2.00 5.00
170 Todd Helton Jsy 3.00 8.00
171 Rich Harden Jsy 2.00 5.00
172 Johnny Damon Bat 3.00 8.00
173 Manny Ramirez Bat 3.00 8.00
174 Benito Santiago Bat 2.00 5.00
175 Albert Pujols Jsy 6.00 15.00
176 Chipper Jones Jsy 4.00 10.00
177 Miguel Cabrera Bat 3.00 8.00
178 Jeff Bagwell Uni 3.00 8.00
179 Ivan Rodriguez Jsy 3.00 8.00
180 Mike Piazza Uni 4.00 10.00
181 Chip Cannon FY AU RC 15.00 40.00
182 Erik Cordier FY AU RC 10.00 25.00
183 Billy Butler FY AU 15.00 40.00
184 C.J. Smith FY AU RC 10.00 25.00
185 Alfonso Soriano AU 6.00 15.00
186 Bobby Livingston FY AU RC 10.00 25.00
187 Wladimir Balentien FY AU 15.00 40.00
188 Mike Morse FY AU 10.00 25.00
189 W.Swackhamer FY AU RC 10.00 25.00
190 Justin Verlander FY AU 30.00 60.00
191 Jake Postlewait FY AU 10.00 25.00
192 Michael Rogers FY AU RC 10.00 25.00
193 Matt Campbell FY AU 10.00 25.00
194 Eric Nielsen FY AU RC 10.00 25.00
195 Gary Sheffield AU 10.00 25.00
196 Glen Perkins FY AU 15.00 40.00
197 Kevin Melillo FY AU 10.00 25.00
198 Chad Orvella FY AU RC 10.00 25.00
199 Jeff Niemann FY AU 10.00 25.00
200 Alex Rodriguez AU 25.00 175.00
201 Brian Stavisky FY AU RC 10.00 25.00
202 Brian Miller FY AU RC 10.00 25.00
203 Landon Powell FY AU 15.00 40.00
204 Philip Humber FY AU 15.00 40.00
205 Mariano Rivera AU 60.00 150.00
207 Nolan Ryan AU Jsy 40.00 100.00
208 Albert Pujols AU Jsy 75.00 150.00
209 Stan Musial AU Bat 30.00 80.00
210 Barry Bonds AU Jsy 150.00 250.00

2005 Topps Pristine Die Cut Red

*DC RED 1-100: 2.5X TO 6X BASIC
*DC RED 101-130: 1.5X TO 4X BASIC
1-130 ODDS 1:2 HOBBY BOXES
1-130 PRINT RUN 66 SERIAL #'d SETS
GU 131-180 ODDS 1:59 HOBBY BOXES
AU 181-205 ODDS 1:117 HOBBY BOXES
AU-GU 206-210 ODDS 1:595 HOBBY BOXES
AU-GU 206-210 EXCH.DEADLINE 10/31/07
131-210 PRINT RUN 3 SERIAL #'d SETS
181-210 NO PRICING DUE TO SCARCITY

2005 Topps Pristine Uncirculated Bronze

*BRZ 1-100: 1.5X TO 4X BASIC
*BRZ 101-130: 1X TO 2.5X BASIC
1-130 STATED ODDS 1:2
1-130 PRINT RUN 375 SERIAL #'d SETS
*BRZ 131-180: .6X TO 1.5X BASIC
GU 131-180 STATED ODDS 1:11
GU 131-180 PRINT RUN 100 SERIAL #'d SETS
AU 181-205 STATED ODDS 1:121
AU 181-205 PRINT RUN 18 SERIAL #'d SETS
AU-GU 206-210 STATED ODDS 1:3482
AU-GU 206-210 PRINT RUN 10 #'d SETS
AU-GU 206-210 EXCH.DEADLINE 10/31/07
181-205 NO PRICING DUE TO SCARCITY

2005 Topps Pristine Personal Endorsements Common

STATED ODDS 1:6
STATED PRINT RUN 497 SERIAL #'d SETS
UNCIRCULATED ODDS 1:916
UNCIRCULATED PRINT RUN 3 #'d SETS
NO UNCIRC PRICING DUE TO SCARCITY
BB Billy Butler 6.00 15.00
BJ Blake Johnson 4.00 10.00
BL Bobby Livingston 4.00 10.00
CJS C.J. Smith 4.00 10.00
CO Chad Orvella 4.00 10.00
GP Glen Perkins 6.00 15.00
JF Josh Fields 6.00 15.00
JPH J.P. Howell 4.00 10.00
JS Jeremy Sowers 6.00 15.00
JV Justin Verlander 15.00 40.00
LC Lance Cormier 4.00 10.00
LH Livan Hernandez 6.00 15.00
LP Landon Powell 6.00 15.00
MB Milton Bradley 6.00 15.00
MR Mike Rodriguez 4.00 10.00
MRO Mark Rogers 4.00 10.00
PH Philip Humber 10.00 25.00
SE Scott Elbert 4.00 10.00
TS Termel Sledge 4.00 10.00
ZJ Zach Jackson 4.00 10.00

2005 Topps Pristine Personal Endorsements Uncommon

STATED ODDS 1:18
STATED PRINT RUN 247 SERIAL #'d SETS
UNCIRCULATED ODDS 1:1451
UNCIRCULATED PRINT RUN 3 #'d SETS
NO UNCIRC PRICING DUE TO SCARCITY
AB Aaron Boone 6.00 15.00
BB Billy Butler 8.00 20.00
BL Bobby Livingston 4.00 10.00
CC Chip Cannon 5.00 12.00
CE Carl Erskine 6.00 15.00
CW Craig Wilson 4.00 10.00
DO David Ortiz 12.50 30.00
DW David Wright 10.00 25.00
DZ Don Zimmer 10.00 25.00
HK Harmon Killebrew 10.00 25.00
JB Jason Bay 6.00 15.00
MB Matt Bush 6.00 15.00
ML Mark Loretta 4.00 10.00

2005 Topps Pristine Personal Endorsements Rare

STATED ODDS 1:95
STATED PRINT RUN 97 SERIAL #'d SETS
UNCIRCULATED ODDS 1:3072
UNCIRCULATED PRINT RUN 3 #'d SETS
NO UNCIRC PRICING DUE TO SCARCITY
AS Alfonso Soriano 10.00 25.00
EB Ernie Banks 30.00 60.00
GA Garret Anderson 10.00 25.00
MR Mariano Rivera 60.00 120.00
SM Stan Musial 40.00 80.00
TS Tom Seaver 20.00 50.00

2005 Topps Pristine Personal Pieces Common Relics

STATED ODDS 1:3
STATED PRINT RUN 425 SERIAL #'d SETS
HAFNER PRINT RUN 400 SERIAL #'d CARDS
UNCIRCULATED ODDS 1:363
UNCIRCULATED PRINT RUN 3 #'d SETS
NO UNCIRC PRICING DUE TO SCARCITY
AB Adrian Beltre Bat 2.00 5.00
AD Adam Dunn Bat 2.00 5.00
AJ Andruw Jones Bat 3.00 8.00
AP Albert Pujols Jsy 6.00 15.00
AS Alfonso Soriano Bat 2.00 5.00
BC Bobby Crosby Bat 2.00 5.00
BJU B.J. Upton Bat 2.00 5.00
BM Brett Myers Jsy 2.00 5.00
BR Brad Radke Jsy 2.00 5.00
BW Bernie Williams Bat 3.00 8.00
BZ Barry Zito Uni 2.00 5.00
CG Cristian Guzman Bat 2.00 5.00
CJ Chipper Jones Bat 4.00 10.00
CS Curt Schilling Jsy 3.00 8.00
EC Eric Chavez Uni 2.00 5.00
ER Edgar Renteria Bat 2.00 5.00
FT Frank Thomas Jsy 4.00 10.00
GS Gary Sheffield Bat 2.00 5.00
HB Hank Blalock Jsy 2.00 5.00
JB Jeff Bagwell Jsy 3.00 8.00
JDD J.D. Drew Jsy 2.00 5.00
JE Jim Edmonds Jsy 2.00 5.00
JES Johnny Estrada Jsy 2.00 5.00
JG Jason Giambi Uni 2.00 5.00
JGI Jay Gibbons Bat 2.00 5.00
JL Javy Lopez Bat 2.00 5.00
JT Jim Thome Jsy 3.00 8.00
KM Kevin Millar Bat 2.00 5.00
KW Kerry Wood Jsy 2.00 5.00
LB Lance Berkman Jsy 2.00 5.00
LN Laynce Nix Jsy 2.00 5.00
ML Mark Loretta Bat 2.00 5.00
MLO Mike Lowell Jsy 2.00 5.00
MM Mark Mulder Uni 2.00 5.00
MP Mike Piazza Uni 4.00 10.00
MPR Mark Prior Jsy 3.00 8.00
MR Manny Ramirez Bat 3.00 8.00
MRI Mariano Rivera Jsy 4.00 10.00
MT Miguel Tejada Uni 2.00 5.00
MTE Mark Teixeira Jsy 3.00 8.00
PM Pedro Martinez Jsy 3.00 8.00
RB Ronnie Belliard Bat 2.00 5.00
RC Roger Clemens Jsy 5.00 12.00
SG Shawn Green Bat 2.00 5.00
SR Scott Rolen Jsy 3.00 8.00
TH Todd Helton Jsy 3.00 8.00
THA Travis Hafner Bat/400 2.00 5.00
THU Tim Hudson Uni 2.00 5.00
VG Vladimir Guerrero Bat 4.00 10.00
VM Victor Martinez Bat 2.00 5.00

2005 Topps Pristine Personal Pieces Uncommon Relics

STATED ODDS 1:11
STATED PRINT RUN 200 SERIAL #'d SETS
UNCIRCULATED ODDS 1:726
UNCIRCULATED PRINT RUN 3 #'d SETS
NO UNCIRC PRICING DUE TO SCARCITY
AB Adrian Beltre Bat 2.00 5.00
AJ Andruw Jones Bat 3.00 8.00
AP Albert Pujols Jsy 6.00 15.00
AR Alex Rodriguez Jsy 6.00 15.00
AS Alfonso Soriano Uni 2.00 5.00
CB Carlos Beltran Jsy 2.00 5.00
CJ Chipper Jones Jsy 4.00 10.00
CS Curt Schilling Jsy 3.00 8.00
DO David Ortiz Jsy 4.00 10.00
EG Eric Gagne Jsy 2.00 5.00
IR Ivan Rodriguez Jsy 3.00 8.00
JE Jim Edmonds Jsy 2.00 5.00
JP Jorge Posada Uni 3.00 8.00
JT Jim Thome Jsy 3.00 8.00
MC Miguel Cabrera Jsy 3.00 8.00
MM Mark Mulder Uni 2.00 5.00
MO Magglio Ordonez Bat 2.00 5.00
MP Mike Piazza Jsy 4.00 10.00
MR Manny Ramirez Jsy 3.00 8.00
MRI Mariano Rivera Jsy 4.00 10.00
RC Roger Clemens Jsy 5.00 12.00
SR Scott Rolen Jsy 3.00 8.00
SS Sammy Sosa Bat 4.00 10.00
TG Troy Glaus Bat 2.00 5.00
TH Torii Hunter Jsy 2.00 5.00

2005 Topps Pristine Personal Pieces Rare Relics

STATED ODDS 1:72
STATED PRINT RUN 75 SERIAL #'d SETS
UNCIRCULATED ODDS 1:1801
UNCIRCULATED PRINT RUN 3 #'d SETS
NO UNCIRC PRICING DUE TO SCARCITY
AP Albert Pujols Jsy 12.50 30.00
AR Alex Rodriguez Jsy 12.50 30.00
BB Barry Bonds AS Jsy * 10.00 25.00
CB Carlos Beltran Jsy 4.00 10.00
EG Eric Gagne Jsy 4.00 10.00
JD Johnny Damon Jsy 6.00 15.00
PM Pedro Martinez Jsy 6.00 15.00
RC Roger Clemens Jsy 10.00 25.00
TH Todd Helton Jsy 6.00 15.00
VG Vladimir Guerrero Jsy 6.00 15.00

2005 Topps Pristine Selective Swatch Logo Patch Relics

OVERALL SELECTIVE SWATCH ODDS 1:768
STATED PRINT RUN 1 SERIAL #'d SET
NO PRICING DUE TO SCARCITY

2005 Topps Pristine Legends

COMP. SET w/o SP's (100) 60.00 120.00
COMMON C (1-100) .40 1.00
COMMON U (101-125) .75 2.00
101-125 ODDS 4:5 HOBBY/RETAIL
101-125 PRINT RUN 1999 #'d SETS
101-125 ARE COLLEGE YEARS CARDS
COMMON R (126-135) 1.00 2.50
126-135 ODDS 1:7 HOBBY/RETAIL
126-135 PRINT RUN 999 #'d SETS
126-135 ARE NEGRO LEAGUE CARDS
COMMON S (136-140) 1.25 3.00
136-140 ODDS 1:26 HOBBY/RETAIL
136-140 PRINT RUN 499 #'d SETS
136-140 ARE LITTLE LEAGUE CARDS
OVERALL PLATE ODDS 1:82 HOBBY
PLATE PRINT RUN 1 SET PER COLOR
BLACK-CYAN-MAGENTA-YELLOW ISSUED
NO PLATE PRICING DUE TO SCARCITY
1 Vida Blue C .40 1.00
2 Bert Blyleven C .60 1.50
3 Joe Carter C .40 1.00
4 Bill Buckner C .40 1.00
5 Luis Aparicio C .60 1.50
6 Ernie Banks C 1.00 2.50
7 Wade Boggs C .60 1.50
8 George Brett C 2.00 5.00
9 Lou Brock C .60 1.50
10 Rod Carew C .60 1.50
11 Gary Carter C .60 1.50
12 Andre Dawson C .60 1.50
13 Dennis Eckersley C .60 1.50
14 Rollie Fingers C .60 1.50
15 Steve Garvey C .40 1.00
16 Dwight Gooden C .40 1.00
17 Goose Gossage C .60 1.50
18 Ron Guidry C .40 1.00
19 Keith Hernandez C .40 1.00
20 Charlie Hough C .40 1.00
21 Bo Jackson C 1.00 2.50
22 Monte Irvin C .60 1.50
23 Reggie Jackson C .60 1.50
24 Ferguson Jenkins C .60 1.50
25 Ralph Kiner C .60 1.50
26 Juan Marichal C .60 1.50
27 Stan Musial C 1.50 4.00
28 Tony Oliva C .40 1.00
29 Jim Palmer C .60 1.50
30 Dave Parker C .40 1.00
31 Gaylord Perry C .60 1.50
32 Jimmy Piersall C .40 1.00
33 Johnny Podres C .40 1.00
34 Brooks Robinson C .60 1.50
35 Frank Robinson C .60 1.50
36 Nolan Ryan C 3.00 8.00
37 Tom Seaver C .60 1.50
38 Ozzie Smith C 1.25 3.00
39 Duke Snider C .60 1.50
40 Bobby Thomson C .60 1.50
41 Carl Yastrzemski C 1.25 3.00
42 Maury Wills C .40 1.00
43 Robin Yount C 1.00 2.50
44 Matt Williams C .60 1.50
45 Orel Hershiser C .40 1.00
46 Tim McCarver C .40 1.00
47 Don Newcombe C .40 1.00
48 Paul O'Neill C .60 1.50
49 Al Kaline C 1.00 2.50
50 Harmon Killebrew C 1.00 2.50
51 Dave Kingman C .40 1.00
52 Ken Griffey Sr. C .40 1.00
53 George Foster C .40 1.00
54 Mark Fidrych C .40 1.00
55 Orlando Cepeda C .60 1.50
56 Don Larsen C .40 1.00
57 Bill Madlock C .40 1.00
58 Dale Murphy C 1.00 2.50
59 Graig Nettles C .40 1.00
60 Phil Niekro C .60 1.50
61 Al Oliver C .40 1.00
62 Harold Reynolds C .40 1.00
63 Bobby Richardson C .40 1.00
64 Mike Scott C .40 1.00
65 Dave Stewart C .40 1.00
66 Rick Sutcliffe C .40 1.00
67 Bruce Sutter C .60 1.50
68 Luis Tiant C .40 1.00
69 Bob Watson C .40 1.00
70 Walt Weiss C .40 1.00
71 Don Zimmer C .40 1.00
72 Tommy John C .40 1.00
73 Ray Knight C .40 1.00
74 Jack Morris C .60 1.50
75 Mickey Rivers C .40 1.00
76 Lee Smith C .40 1.00
77 Darryl Strawberry C .40 1.00
78 Dave Justice C .40 1.00
79 Wally Joyner C .40 1.00
80 Jimmy Key C .40 1.00
81 John Kruk C .40 1.00
82 Greg Luzinski C .40 1.00
83 Mookie Wilson C .40 1.00
84 Wilbur Wood C .40 1.00
85 Tim Raines C .60 1.50
86 Jim Rice C .60 1.50
87 Tony Armas C .40 1.00
88 Harold Baines C .60 1.50
89 Bucky Dent C .40 1.00
90 Darrell Evans C .40 1.00
91 Cecil Fielder C .40 1.00
92 Jose Cruz C .40 1.00
93 Dave Concepcion C .40 1.00
94 Ron Cey C .40 1.00
95 Davey Lopes C .40 1.00
96 Boog Powell C .40 1.00
97 Buddy Bell C .40 1.00
98 George Bell C .40 1.00
99 Bert Campaneris C .40 1.00
100 Chet Lemon C .40 1.00
101 Bo Jackson U 2.00 5.00
102 Will Clark U 1.25 3.00
103 Cecil Fielder U .75 2.00
104 Ron Cey U .75 2.00
105 Tony Gwynn U 2.50 6.00
106 Orel Hershiser U .75 2.00
107 Jimmy Key U .75 2.00
108 Paul Molitor U 2.00 5.00
109 Pete Incaviglia U .75 2.00
110 Wally Joyner U .75 2.00
111 Dave Kingman U .75 2.00
112 Ron Guidry U .75 2.00
113 Ron Darling U .75 2.00
114 Mookie Wilson U .75 2.00
115 Reggie Jackson U 1.25 3.00
116 Walt Weiss U .75 2.00
117 Joe Carter U .75 2.00
118 Cory Snyder U .75 2.00
119 Dave Winfield U 1.25 3.00
120 Terry Steinbach U .75 2.00
121 Matt Williams U 1.25 3.00
122 Ozzie Smith U 2.50 6.00
123 Jack McDowell U .75 2.00
124 Bob Horner U .75 2.00
125 Don Kessinger U .75 2.00
126 Minnie Minoso R 1.00 2.50
127 Josh Gibson R 2.50 6.00
128 Buck O'Neil R 1.00 2.50
129 Monte Irvin R 1.50 4.00
130 Jim Gilliam R 1.00 2.50
131 Josh Gibson R 2.50 6.00
132 Ernie Banks R 2.50 6.00
133 Don Newcombe R 1.00 2.50
134 Josh Gibson R 2.50 6.00
135 Josh Gibson R 2.50 6.00
136 Gary Carter S 2.00 5.00
137 Bo Jackson S 3.00 8.00
138 George Brett S 6.00 15.00
139 Joe Carter S 1.25 3.00
140 Nolan Ryan S 10.00 25.00

2005 Topps Pristine Legends Refractors

*REF 1-100: 1X TO 2.5X BASIC
1-100 ONE PER PACK
1-100 PRINT RUN 549 SERIAL #'d SETS
*REF 101-125: 1X TO 2.5X BASIC
101-125 ODDS 1:13 HOBBY/RETAIL
101-125 PRINT RUN 199 SERIAL #'d SETS
*REF 126-135: 1X TO 2.5X BASIC
126-135 ODDS 1:64 HOBBY/RETAIL
126-135 PRINT RUN 99 SERIAL #'d SETS
136-140 ODDS 1:514 HOBBY, 1:480 RETAIL
136-140 PRINT RUN 25 SERIAL #'d SETS
136-140 NO PRICING DUE TO SCARCITY

2005 Topps Pristine Legends Gold Die Cut Refractors

*GOLD DC 1-100: 2X TO 5X BASIC
*GOLD DC 101-125: 1.25X TO 3X BASIC
*GOLD DC 126-135: 1X TO 2.5X BASIC
*GOLD DC 136-140: .6X TO 1.5X BASIC
ONE PER SEALED HOBBY BOX
STATED PRINT RUN 65 SERIAL #'d SETS

2005 Topps Pristine Legends Celebrity Threads

STATED ODDS 1:18 HOBBY/RETAIL
REFRACTOR ODDS 1:1284 H, 1:1440 R
REF PRINT RUN 25 SERIAL #'d SETS
NO REF PRICING DUE TO SCARCITY
EP Elvis Presley Shirt 20.00 50.00
MM Marilyn Monroe Dress 15.00 40.00

2005 Topps Pristine Legends Leading Indicators Relics

GROUP A ODDS 1:210 HOBBY/RETAIL
GROUP B ODDS 1:71 HOBBY/RETAIL
GROUP C ODDS 1:7 HOBBY/RETAIL
GROUP D ODDS 1:20 HOBBY/RETAIL
GROUP E ODDS 1:8 HOBBY/RETAIL
GROUP A PRINT RUN 99 SERIAL #'d SETS
REF GROUP A ODDS 1:14,550 HOBBY
REF GROUP B ODDS 1:111 HOBBY/RETAIL
REF A PRINT RUN 1 SERIAL #'d SET
REF B PRINT RUN 25 SERIAL #'d SETS
NO REF PRICING DUE TO SCARCITY
AD Andre Dawson Bat C 3.00 8.00
AK Al Kaline Bat C 4.00 10.00
BF Bob Feller Uni D 4.00 10.00
CF Cecil Fielder Bat C 3.00 8.00
CY Carl Yastrzemski Bat C 6.00 15.00
DBM Dale Murphy Bat C 4.00 10.00
DK Dave Kingman Bat C 3.00 8.00
DM Don Mattingly Bat D 6.00 15.00
DP Dave Parker Bat E 3.00 8.00
DS Darryl Strawberry Bat C 3.00 8.00
GF George Foster Bat C 3.00 8.00
GP Gaylord Perry Jsy E 3.00 8.00
JR Jim Rice Bat B 3.00 8.00
LB Lou Brock Bat A/99 6.00 15.00
MS Mike Scott Jsy E 3.00 8.00
MW Maury Wills Bat A/99 4.00 10.00
NR Nolan Ryan Jsy C 6.00 15.00
PO Paul O'Neill Bat E 4.00 10.00
RC Rod Carew Bat C 4.00 10.00
RM Roger Maris Bat B 15.00 40.00
TG Tony Gwynn Jsy E 4.00 10.00
TO Tony Oliva Bat D 3.00 8.00
TR Tim Raines Uni C 3.00 8.00
TR2 Tim Raines Bat C 3.00 8.00
TS Tom Seaver Jsy A/99 6.00 15.00
WB Wade Boggs Bat E 4.00 10.00

2005 Topps Pristine Legends Title Threads Relics

GROUP A ODDS 1:66 HOBBY/RETAIL
GROUP B ODDS 1:9 HOBBY/RETAIL
GROUP C ODDS 1:6 HOBBY/RETAIL
REFRACTOR ODDS 1:111 HOBBY/RETAIL
REF PRINT RUN 25 SERIAL #'d SETS
NO REF PRICING DUE TO SCARCITY
BD Bucky Dent Uni B 3.00 8.00
CS Cesar Geronimo Bat C 3.00 8.00
DJ Dave Justice Uni A 4.00 10.00
DS Darryl Strawberry Bat B 3.00 8.00
EK Ed Kranepool Uni C 3.00 8.00
GC Gary Carter Bat C 3.00 8.00
GF George Foster Bat B 3.00 8.00
GG Goose Gossage Uni C 3.00 8.00
GN Graig Nettles Uni C 3.00 8.00
JC Joe Carter Bat B 3.00 8.00
JK Jimmy Key Uni C 3.00 8.00
JP Jim Palmer Uni B 3.00 8.00
KG Ken Griffey Sr. Bat B 3.00 8.00
LD Len Dykstra Bat B 3.00 8.00
MI Monte Irvin Bat B 3.00 8.00
MW Mookie Wilson Uni B 3.00 8.00
OC Orlando Cepeda Jsy C 3.00 8.00
OH Orel Hershiser Jsy A 3.00 8.00
PO Paul O'Neill Uni C 3.00 8.00
RF Rollie Fingers Uni C 3.00 8.00
TM Tim McCarver Uni C 3.00 8.00
WB Wade Boggs Uni C 4.00 10.00
WH Willie Horton Jsy B 3.00 8.00

2005 Topps Pristine Legends Valuable Performance Relics

GROUP A ODDS 1:7275 HOBBY
GROUP B ODDS 1:6 HOBBY/RETAIL
GROUP C ODDS 1:12 HOBBY/RETAIL
GROUP A PRINT RUN 9 SERIAL #'d CARDS
NO GROUP A PRICING DUE TO SCARCITY
REF GROUP A ODDS 1:43,650 HOBBY
REF GROUP B ODDS 1:128 H, 1:125 R
REF A PRINT RUN 1 SERIAL #'d SET
REF B PRINT RUN 25 SERIAL #'d SETS
NO REF PRICING DUE TO SCARCITY
AD Andre Dawson Uni C 3.00 8.00
CF Cecil Fielder Bat B 3.00 8.00
CR Cal Ripken Bat B 10.00 25.00
CY Carl Yastrzemski Bat B 4.00 10.00
DBM Don Mattingly Uni C 8.00 20.00
DE Dennis Eckersley Jsy C 3.00 8.00
DM Dale Murphy Bat B 4.00 10.00
DP Dave Parker Uni C 3.00 8.00
FR Frank Robinson Bat B 3.00 8.00
HK Harmon Killebrew Bat B 4.00 10.00
JC Jose Canseco Bat B 4.00 10.00
JM Joe Morgan Bat B 3.00 8.00
JR Jim Rice Bat B 3.00 8.00
KH Keith Hernandez Bat B 3.00 8.00
MS Mike Schmidt Bat C 6.00 15.00
RJ Reggie Jackson Bat B 4.00 10.00
RY Robin Yount Bat B 4.00 10.00
SG Steve Garvey Bat B 3.00 8.00
SM Stan Musial Bat B 8.00 20.00
YB Yogi Berra Bat B 4.00 10.00

2020 Topps Project 2020

PRINT RUNS B/WN 1065-99177 COPIES PER
1 Ichiro/1334* 1250.00 2500.00
2 Sandy Koufax/1135* 200.00 500.00
3 Jackie Robinson/1302* 250.00 600.00
4 Mike Trout/2911* 300.00 800.00
5 Cal Ripken Jr./1205* 250.00 600.00
6 Ken Griffey Jr./2504* 200.00 500.00
7 Bob Gibson/1205* 200.00 500.00
8 Mariano Rivera/1617* 150.00 400.00
9 Ted Williams/1385* 125.00 300.00
10 Roberto Clemente/1844* 250.00 600.00
11 George Brett/1227* 300.00 800.00
12 Dwight Gooden/1065* 300.00 800.00
13 Don Mattingly/1686* 150.00 400.00
14 Rickey Henderson/1221* 150.00 400.00
15 Willie Mays/1464* 125.00 300.00
16 Tony Gwynn/1302* 125.00 300.00
17 Mark McGwire/1456* 100.00 250.00
18 Nolan Ryan/2623* 100.00 250.00
19 Roberto Clemente/1819* 100.00 250.00
20 Cal Ripken Jr./1576* 75.00 200.00
21 Rickey Henderson/2104* 100.00 250.00
22 Ichiro/1972* 100.00 250.00
23 Frank Thomas/2836* 125.00 300.00
24 Tony Gwynn/1441* 100.00 250.00
25 Ken Griffey Jr./3707* 25.00 60.00
26 Dwight Gooden/1101* 125.00 300.00
27 Willie Mays/1480* 100.00 250.00
28 Mark McGwire/1199* 150.00 400.00
29 Derek Jeter/9873* 20.00 50.00
30 Nolan Ryan/2215* 100.00 250.00
31 Jackie Robinson/2741* 50.00 120.00
32 Ichiro/1798* 100.00 250.00
33 Don Mattingly/2409* 75.00 200.00
34 Ted Williams/1131* 75.00 200.00
35 Mike Trout/13200* 10.00 25.00
36 Sandy Koufax/2488* 40.00 100.00
37 Cal Ripken Jr./2621* 30.00 80.00
38 Dwight Gooden/1864* 100.00 250.00
39 Derek Jeter/9322* 12.00 30.00
40 Tony Gwynn/2319* 40.00 100.00
41 Mariano Rivera/2452* 10.00 25.00
42 Jackie Robinson/2980* 25.00 60.00
43 George Brett/2360* 20.00 50.00
44 Frank Thomas/1480* 60.00 150.00
45 Roberto Clemente/1910* 50.00 120.00
46 Bob Gibson/1268* 100.00 250.00
47 Don Mattingly/2763* 40.00 100.00
48 Willie Mays/1556* 100.00 250.00
49 Sandy Koufax/2149* 50.00 120.00
50 Cal Ripken Jr./2369* 75.00 200.00
51 Mike Trout/34950* 8.00 20.00
52 Nolan Ryan/4103* 30.00 80.00
53 Ken Griffey Jr./4236* 20.00 50.00
54 Bob Gibson/1451* 125.00 300.00
55 George Brett/1992* 50.00 120.00
56 Mariano Rivera/1127* 25.00 60.00
57 Rickey Henderson/3819* 12.00 30.00
58 Ted Williams/4859* 15.00 40.00
59 Derek Jeter/6511* 10.00 25.00
60 Mark McGwire/2687* 20.00 50.00
61 Willie Mays/5459* 8.00 20.00
62 Ichiro/6207* 10.00 25.00
63 Mike Trout/16430* 6.00 15.00
64 Tony Gwynn/3368* 10.00 25.00
65 Dwight Gooden/5041* 6.00 15.00
66 Ken Griffey Jr./9536* 10.00 25.00
67 Nolan Ryan/7383* 10.00 25.00
68 Roberto Clemente/8518* 8.00 20.00
69 Don Mattingly/7900* 6.00 15.00
70 Bob Gibson/6757* 10.00 25.00
71 Rickey Henderson/15741* 8.00 20.00
72 Mariano Rivera/9545* 6.00 15.00
73 Frank Thomas/11969* 8.00 20.00
74 Ted Williams/8897* 8.00 20.00
75 George Brett/5638* 10.00 25.00
76 Sandy Koufax/6607* 8.00 20.00
77 Ichiro/11425* 6.00 15.00
78 Roberto Clemente/8610* 8.00 20.00
79 Jackie Robinson/11643* 6.00 15.00
80 Willie Mays/10480* 6.00 15.00
81 Mark McGwire/18205* 6.00 15.00
82 Derek Jeter/20974* 6.00 15.00
83 Frank Thomas/8806* 6.00 15.00
84 Bob Gibson/14867* 6.00 15.00
85 Mike Trout/33818* 6.00 15.00
86 Dwight Gooden/25928* 6.00 15.00
87 Nolan Ryan/*64629 6.00 15.00
88 Ken Griffey Jr./99177* 6.00 15.00
89 Sandy Koufax/43147* 6.00 15.00
90 Ted Williams/41407* 6.00 15.00
91 Mariano Rivera/35330* 6.00 15.00
92 Cal Ripken Jr/41392* 6.00 15.00
93 Derek Jeter/48465* 6.00 15.00
94 Tony Gwynn/31030* 6.00 15.00
95 Don Mattingly/27299* 6.00 15.00
96 Frank Thomas/22911* 6.00 15.00
97 Mark McGwire/19894* 6.00 15.00
98 Jackie Robinson/20219* 8.00 20.00
99 Sandy Koufax/21535* 6.00 15.00
100 Mike Trout/74862* 8.00 20.00
101 Willie Mays/10568* 6.00 15.00
102 George Brett/10757* 6.00 15.00
103 Roberto Clemente/11577* 6.00 15.00
104 Rickey Henderson/11578* 6.00 15.00
105 Nolan Ryan/12874* 10.00 25.00
106 Dwight Gooden/8854* 6.00 15.00
107 Derek Jeter/24908* 8.00 20.00
108 Bob Gibson/11395* 6.00 15.00
109 Cal Ripken Jr./36466* 8.00 20.00
110 Roberto Clemente/12077* 8.00 20.00
111 Mark McGwire/9169* 6.00 15.00
112 George Brett/6558* 8.00 20.00
113 Tony Gwynn/8401* 6.00 15.00
114 Jackie Robinson/14067* 6.00 15.00
115 Frank Thomas/6763* 6.00 15.00
116 Ken Griffey Jr./10957* 6.00 15.00
117 Mariano Rivera/7460* 10.00 25.00
118 Don Mattingly/8469* 8.00 20.00
119 Dwight Gooden/5868* 6.00 15.00
120 Ichiro/8333* 6.00 15.00
121 Mike Trout/20961* 10.00 25.00
122 Ted Williams/9507* 6.00 15.00
123 Rickey Henderson/4966* 8.00 20.00
124 Bob Gibson/6090* 8.00 20.00
125 Sandy Koufax/4966* 8.00 20.00
126 Nolan Ryan/4859* 6.00 15.00
127 Ken Griffey Jr./10472* 8.00 20.00
128 Willie Mays/7195* 6.00 15.00
129 Rickey Henderson/6609* 8.00 20.00
130 Ichiro/6238* 6.00 15.00
131 Mariano Rivera/9468* 8.00 20.00
132 Derek Jeter/64088* 8.00 20.00
133 George Brett/7757* 6.00 15.00
134 Mark McGwire/5092* 6.00 15.00
135 Tony Gwynn/4863* 8.00 20.00
136 Cal Ripken Jr./4976* 10.00 25.00
137 Dwight Gooden/7141* 12.00 30.00
138 Roberto Clemente/6507* 12.00 30.00
139 Don Mattingly/4682* 8.00 20.00
140 Jackie Robinson/6068* 10.00 25.00
141 Frank Thomas/6678* 8.00 20.00
142 Mike Trout/14821* 8.00 20.00
143 Willie Mays/5930* 8.00 20.00
144 Bob Gibson/4367* 10.00 25.00
145 Sandy Koufax/6385* 10.00 25.00
146 Ted Williams/4693* 10.00 25.00
147 Nolan Ryan/3781* 10.00 25.00
148 Ken Griffey Jr./6021* 8.00 20.00
149 Ichiro/6042* 8.00 20.00
150 George Brett/4085* 10.00 25.00
151 Mariano Rivera/12611* 10.00 25.00
152 Mark McGwire/6977* 12.00 30.00
153 Rickey Henderson/5155* 12.00 30.00
154 Roberto Clemente/5916* 10.00 25.00
155 Don Mattingly/4292* 10.00 25.00
156 Jackie Robinson/4046* 12.00 30.00
157 Derek Jeter/8413* 6.00 15.00
158 Ted Williams/4404* 10.00 25.00
159 Cal Ripken Jr./4158* 10.00 25.00
160 Frank Thomas/5101* 10.00 25.00
161 Tony Gwynn/5543* 10.00 25.00
162 Sandy Koufax/4009* 10.00 25.00
163 Bob Gibson/3484* 10.00 25.00
164 Dwight Gooden/3175* 10.00 25.00
165 Nolan Ryan/4146* 15.00 40.00
166 Willie Mays/3609* 10.00 25.00
167 Mike Trout/11658* 10.00 25.00
168 Rickey Henderson/6650* 12.00 30.00
169 Ichiro/6640* 12.00 30.00
170 Don Mattingly/10210* 12.00 30.00
171 Derek Jeter/6009* 12.00 30.00
172 Ted Williams/3484* 12.00 30.00
173 Cal Ripken Jr./4509* 8.00 20.00
174 Frank Thomas/4239* 10.00 25.00
175 George Brett/3278* 8.00 20.00
176 Jackie Robinson/3253* 10.00 25.00
177 Ken Griffey Jr./6527* 12.00 30.00
178 Mark McGwire/3224* 10.00 25.00
179 Mariano Rivera/3154* 10.00 25.00
180 Tony Gwynn/4292* 10.00 25.00
181 Sandy Koufax/4369* 12.00 30.00
182 Roberto Clemente/3592* 12.00 30.00
183 Ichiro/3652* 10.00 25.00
184 Dwight Gooden/3554* 10.00 25.00
185 Rickey Henderson/4046* 15.00 40.00
186 Nolan Ryan/2981* 15.00 40.00
187 Mike Trout/11405* 10.00 25.00
188 Willie Mays/3858* 10.00 25.00
189 Ted Williams/4684* 10.00 25.00
190 Don Mattingly/3550* 10.00 25.00
191 Mark McGwire/9758* 10.00 25.00
192 George Brett/3851* 10.00 25.00
193 Frank Thomas/3781* 15.00 40.00
194 Jackie Robinson/3268* 10.00 25.00
195 Cal Ripken Jr./4055* 12.00 30.00
196 Ichiro/3930* 10.00 25.00
197 Roberto Clemente/4280* 12.00 30.00
198 Tony Gwynn/3567* 15.00 40.00
199 Mariano Rivera/4952* 15.00 40.00
200 Derek Jeter/7285* 12.00 30.00
201 Ken Griffey Jr/3555* 10.00 25.00
202 Bob Gibson/2769* 12.00 30.00
203 Dwight Gooden/3652* 15.00 40.00
204 Sandy Koufax/3043* 10.00 25.00
205 Cal Ripken Jr/2777* 15.00 40.00
206 Rickey Henderson/2685* 15.00 40.00
207 Mike Trout/8501* 12.00 30.00
208 Don Mattingly/3265* 10.00 25.00
209 Tony Gwynn/7247* 10.00 25.00
210 Jackie Robinson/3415* 10.00 25.00
211 Ken Griffey Jr/5724* 12.00 30.00
212 George Brett/3002* 8.00 20.00
213 Frank Thomas/3415* 10.00 25.00
214 Nolan Ryan/2891* 10.00 25.00
215 Ichiro/3924* 6.00 15.00
216 Mark McGwire/3419* 12.00 30.00
217 Mariano Rivera/2292* 12.00 30.00
218 Willie Mays/2814* 10.00 25.00
219 Derek Jeter/5572* 15.00 40.00
220 Cal Ripken Jr/4937* 12.00 30.00
221 Ted Williams/2443* 15.00 40.00
222 Rickey Henderson/2986* 12.00 30.00
223 Roberto Clemente/4040* 15.00 40.00
224 Jackie Robinson/4931* 12.00 30.00
225 Tony Gwynn/2666* 12.00 30.00
226 Bob Gibson/2567* 10.00 25.00
227 Mike Trout/9739* 10.00 25.00
228 Dwight Gooden/4719* 6.00 15.00
229 Ted Williams/7169* 8.00 20.00
230 Sandy Koufax/2959* 12.00 30.00
231 Ken Griffey Jr/4533* 12.00 30.00
232 George Brett/2243* 12.00 30.00
233 Mariano Rivera/1902* 12.00 30.00
234 Mark McGwire/2793* 12.00 30.00
235 Derek Jeter/4341* 12.00 30.00
236 Nolan Ryan/3186* 10.00 25.00
237 Tony Gwynn/2196* 8.00 20.00
238 Frank Thomas/2871* 10.00 25.00
239 Roberto Clemente/3001* 12.00 30.00
240 Don Mattingly/3547* 12.00 30.00
241 Cal Ripken Jr/2448* 12.00 30.00
242 Mariano Rivera/3196* 10.00 25.00
243 Ichiro/2379* 12.00 30.00
244 Willie Mays/2440* 12.00 30.00
245 Nolan Ryan/3518* 12.00 30.00
246 Ted Williams/2150* 15.00 40.00
247 Mike Trout/7196* 12.00 30.00
248 Rickey Henderson/3299* 12.00 30.00
249 Bob Gibson/5089* 10.00 25.00
250 Sandy Koufax/2959* 12.00 30.00
251 Derek Jeter/4123* 15.00 40.00
252 Ichiro/2961* 15.00 40.00
253 Jackie Robinson/3159* 12.00 30.00
254 George Brett/2300* 10.00 25.00
255 Don Mattingly/2847* 8.00 20.00
256 Willie Mays/2803* 12.00 30.00
257 Ken Griffey Jr/3330* 12.00 30.00
258 Dwight Gooden/2477* 10.00 25.00
259 Frank Thomas/2776* 10.00 25.00
260 Mike Trout/6824* 20.00 50.00
261 Tony Gwynn/2422* 12.00 30.00
262 Ted Williams/2219* 15.00 40.00
263 Nolan Ryan/2649* 10.00 25.00
264 Mark McGwire/2576* 12.00 30.00
265 Mariano Rivera/1959* 20.00 50.00
266 Roberto Clemente/2692* 15.00 40.00
267 Derek Jeter/3561* 12.00 30.00
268 Frank Thomas/2491* 10.00 25.00
269 Don Mattingly/3536* 12.00 30.00
270 Cal Ripken Jr/3339* 12.00 30.00
271 George Brett/4245* 10.00 25.00
272 Ichiro/3843* 25.00 60.00
273 Rickey Henderson/2812* 15.00 40.00
274 Sandy Koufax/2295* 10.00 25.00
275 Willie Mays/2109* 12.00 30.00
276 Mark McGwire/1902* 20.00 50.00
277 Ken Griffey Jr/3355* 15.00 40.00
278 Don Mattingly/2715* 15.00 40.00
279 Bob Gibson/1898* 12.00 30.00
280 Ichiro/2046* 10.00 25.00
281 Jackie Robinson/2703* 10.00 25.00
282 Mike Trout/7656* 12.00 30.00
283 Mark McGwire/1800* 15.00 40.00
284 Dwight Gooden/1995* 10.00 25.00
285 Frank Thomas/1802* 15.00 40.00
286 George Brett/2272* 15.00 40.00
287 Mariano Rivera/3039* 10.00 25.00
288 Willie Mays/3018* 15.00 40.00
289 Derek Jeter/4155* 12.00 30.00
290 Dwight Gooden/2534* 10.00 25.00
291 Roberto Clemente/4975* 12.00 30.00
292 Cal Ripken Jr/2392* 15.00 40.00
293 Ted Williams/1974* 12.00 30.00
294 Rickey Henderson/2194* 15.00 40.00
295 Bob Gibson/1774* 20.00 50.00
296 Tony Gwynn/2334* 15.00 40.00
297 Frank Thomas/1858* 15.00 40.00
298 Sandy Koufax/2279* 12.00 30.00
299 Jackie Robinson/2613* 15.00 40.00
300 Ken Griffey jr/4762* 15.00 40.00
301 Nolan Ryan/2689* 15.00 40.00
302 Mike Trout/6810* 15.00 40.00
303 Cal Ripken Jr/2734* 15.00 40.00
304 Jackie Robinson/3230* 15.00 40.00
305 Rickey Henderson/2149* 12.00 30.00
306 Don Mattingly/2239* 20.00 50.00
307 Ichiro/2516* 12.00 30.00
308 Derek Jeter/3139* 15.00 40.00
309 Willie Mays/4568* 12.00 30.00
310 Mark McGwire/1942* 15.00 40.00
311 Mariano Rivera/2129* 12.00 30.00
312 Bob Gibson/1821* 12.00 30.00
313 George Brett/2495* 15.00 40.00
314 Nolan Ryan/2439* 15.00 40.00
315 Ted Williams/1734* 20.00 50.00
316 Frank Thomas/2647* 15.00 40.00
317 Ken Griffey Jr/3562* 15.00 40.00
318 Tony Gwynn/2498* 15.00 40.00
319 Ichiro/2549* 12.00 30.00
320 Sandy Koufax/1993* 12.00 30.00
321 Jackie Robinson/2232* 12.00 30.00
322 Cal Ripken Jr./1846* 15.00 40.00
323 Bob Gibson/1546* 30.00 80.00
324 Dwight Gooden/1692* 25.00 60.00
325 Mike Trout/8047* 10.00 25.00
326 Rickey Henderson/2584* 15.00 40.00

327 Ted Williams/2588* 15.00 40.00
328 Ken Griffey Jr./2745* 15.00 40.00
329 Nolan Ryan/3871* 12.00 30.00
330 Tony Gwynn/1947* 15.00 40.00
331 Frank Thomas/2841* 12.00 30.00
332 Willie Mays/2087* 12.00 30.00
333 Don Mattingly/2259* 12.00 30.00
334 Bob Gibson/1882* 15.00 40.00
335 Derek Jeter/2893* 25.00 60.00
336 Roberto Clemente/2744* 12.00 30.00
337 George Brett/2067* 15.00 40.00
338 Mark McGwire/1631* 20.00 50.00
339 Jackie Robinson/3057* 12.00 30.00
340 Mariano Rivera/1928* 12.00 30.00
341 Roberto Clemente/2489* 15.00 40.00
342 Ichiro/3383* 20.00 50.00
343 Dwight Gooden/1980* 15.00 40.00
344 George Brett/1705* 12.00 30.00
345 Ted Williams/1923* 15.00 40.00
346 Willie Mays/1753* 15.00 40.00
347 Ken Griffey Jr./11320* 10.00 25.00
348 Mariano Rivera/2147* 10.00 25.00
349 Cal Ripken Jr./2707* 10.00 25.00
350 Ted Williams/2147* 15.00 40.00
351 Mark McGwire/2062* 12.00 30.00
352 Mike Trout/9091* 12.00 30.00
353 George Brett/1736* 15.00 40.00
354 Don Mattingly/2674* 12.00 30.00
355 Tony Gwynn/2397* 15.00 40.00
356 Derek Jeter/3562* 12.00 30.00
357 Nolan Ryan/2695* 15.00 40.00
358 Mark McGwire/2688* 15.00 40.00
359 Rickey Henderson/2094* 15.00 40.00
360 Dwight Gooden/2703* 30.00 80.00
361 Bob Gibson/1752* 15.00 40.00
362 Roberto Clemente/2344* 15.00 40.00
363 Mariano Rivera/1624* 25.00 60.00
364 Don Mattingly/2000* 12.00 30.00
365 Willie Mays/1600* 30.00 80.00
366 Tony Gwynn/2452* 12.00 30.00
367 Nolan Ryan/1974* 15.00 40.00
368 Frank Thomas/2425* 12.00 30.00
369 Sandy Koufax/1907* 10.00 25.00
370 Ted Williams/1734* 20.00 50.00
371 Roberto Clemente/2205* 12.00 30.00
372 Bob Gibson/1978* 12.00 30.00
373 Ken Griffey Jr./3058* 12.00 30.00
374 Sandy Koufax/2018* 15.00 40.00
375 George Brett/1890* 12.00 30.00
376 Mariano Rivera/2529* 10.00 25.00
377 Jackie Robinson/5796* 15.00 40.00
378 Tony Gwynn/2255* 15.00 40.00
379 Dwight Gooden/1807* 12.00 30.00
380 Cal Ripken Jr./2461* 12.00 30.00
381 Derek Jeter/4163* 8.00 20.00
382 Mark McGwire/1762* 12.00 30.00
383 Derek Jeter/4419* 10.00 25.00
384 Jackie Robinson/1948* 30.00 80.00
385 Frank Thomas/2007* 12.00 30.00
386 Don Mattingly/2259* 12.00 30.00
387 Roberto Clemente/2606* 6.00 15.00
388 Willie Mays/1630* 20.00 50.00
389 Dwight Gooden/1585* 20.00 50.00
390 Rickey Henderson/2222* 15.00 40.00
391 Sandy Koufax/1962* 15.00 40.00
392 Bob Gibson/3204* 8.00 20.00
393 Cal Ripken Jr./3321* 10.00 25.00
394 Ken Griffey Jr./4042* 10.00 25.00
395 Ichiro/2738* 10.00 25.00
396 Sandy Koufax/4418* 10.00 25.00
397 Nolan Ryan/4187* 10.00 25.00
398 Rickey Henderson/4527* 12.00 30.00
399 Mike Trout/12632* 10.00 25.00
400 Mike Trout/12452* 8.00 20.00

2020 Topps Project 2020 Rainbow Foil

*RAINBOW: X TO X BASIC
RANDOM INSERTS IN PACKS
325 Mike Trout 125.00 300.00
Gregory Siff
331 Frank Thomas 150.00 400.00
Andrew Thiele
339 Jackie Robinson 200.00 500.00
Ermsy
342 Ichiro 200.00 500.00
Oldmanalan
347 Ken Griffey Jr. 125.00 300.00
Ben Baller
352 Mike Trout 125.00 300.00
Matt Taylor
354 Don Mattingly 125.00 300.00
Efdot
356 Derek Jeter 75.00 200.00
Keith Shore
357 Nolan Ryan 125.00 300.00
JK5
366 Tony Gwynn 100.00 250.00
Tyson Beck
381 Derek Jeter 75.00 200.00
Jacob Rochester
383 Derek Jeter 60.00 150.00
Don C
387 Roberto Clemente 125.00 300.00
Joshua Vides
392 Bob Gibson 100.00 250.00
Blake Jamieson
393 Cal Ripken Jr. 100.00 250.00
Naturel
394 Ken Griffey Jr. 125.00 300.00
Sophia Chang
399 Mike Trout 75.00 200.00
King Saladeen
400 Mike Trout 75.00 200.00
Mister Cartoon

2013 Topps Qubi Stampers Club Logo

1 Chase Headley 1.50 4.00
2 Ian Kennedy 1.50 4.00
3 Billy Butler 1.50 4.00
4 Paul Konerko 2.00 5.00
5 Miguel Cabrera 2.50 6.00
6 Jose Altuve 2.00 5.00
7 Stephen Strasburg 2.50 6.00
8 Evan Longoria 2.00 5.00
9 Adam Jones 2.00 5.00
10 Anthony Rizzo 3.00 8.00
11 Adam Wainwright 2.00 5.00
12 Justin Upton 2.00 5.00
13 Chase Utley 2.00 5.00
14 Edwin Encarnacion 2.50 6.00
15 Tim Lincecum 2.00 5.00

2013 Topps Qubi Stampers Portraits

1 Ichiro Suzuki 3.00 8.00
2 David Ortiz 2.50 6.00
3 Albert Pujols 3.00 8.00
4 Bryce Harper 6.00 15.00
5 Pablo Sandoval 2.00 5.00
6 Yu Darvish 2.50 6.00
7 Mike Trout 6.00 15.00
8 Jose Reyes 2.00 5.00
9 David Wright 2.00 5.00
10 Ryan Howard 2.00 5.00

2013 Topps Qubi Stampers Signature

1 Jose Bautista 2.00 5.00
2 Ryan Braun 2.00 5.00
3 Robinson Cano 2.00 5.00
4 Starlin Castro 1.50 4.00
5 Yoenis Cespedes 2.50 6.00
6 Yu Darvish 2.50 6.00
7 R.A. Dickey 2.00 5.00
8 Prince Fielder 2.00 5.00
9 David Freese 1.50 4.00
10 Adrian Gonzalez 2.00 5.00
11 Gio Gonzalez 2.00 5.00
12 Zack Greinke 2.50 6.00
13 Roy Halladay 2.00 5.00
14 Josh Hamilton 2.00 5.00
15 Bryce Harper 6.00 15.00
16 Felix Hernandez 2.00 5.00
17 Jason Heyward 2.00 5.00
18 Ryan Howard 2.00 5.00
19 Ryu Hyun-Jin 4.00 10.00
20 Derek Jeter 6.00 15.00
21 Matt Kemp 2.00 5.00
22 Clayton Kershaw 4.00 10.00
23 Craig Kimbrel 2.00 5.00
24 Cliff Lee 2.00 5.00
25 Manny Machado 6.00 15.00
26 Joe Mauer 2.00 5.00
27 Andrew McCutchen 2.50 6.00
28 Will Middlebrooks 1.50 4.00
29 Yadier Molina 3.00 8.00
30 David Ortiz 2.50 6.00
31 Dustin Pedroia 2.50 6.00
32 Brandon Phillips 1.50 4.00
33 Buster Posey 3.00 8.00
34 David Price 2.00 5.00
35 Albert Pujols 3.00 8.00
36 Jose Reyes 2.00 5.00
37 Mariano Rivera 3.00 8.00
38 CC Sabathia 2.00 5.00
39 Pablo Sandoval 2.00 5.00
40 Johan Santana 2.00 5.00
41 Giancarlo Stanton 2.50 6.00
42 Ichiro Suzuki 3.00 8.00
43 Nick Swisher 2.00 5.00
44 Mike Trout 6.00 15.00
45 Troy Tulowitzki 2.50 6.00
46 B.J. Upton 2.00 5.00
47 Justin Verlander 2.50 6.00
48 Joey Votto 2.50 6.00
49 David Wright 2.00 5.00
50 Ryan Zimmerman 2.00 5.00

2013 Topps Replacement Autographs

AR Alex Rodriguez 30.00 60.00
BB Bert Blyleven 10.00 25.00
CB Clay Buchholz 6.00 15.00
CU Chase Utley 20.00 50.00
DG Dwight Gooden 6.00 15.00
DJ David Justice 12.50 30.00
DO David Ortiz 12.00 30.00
DS Duke Snider 10.00 25.00
DS Don Sutton 5.00 12.00
DW David Wright 20.00 50.00
FJ Fergie Jenkins 6.00 15.00
FR Frank Robinson 12.50 30.00
GB George Brett 50.00 100.00
GB Gordon Beckham 4.00 10.00
GC Gary Carter 10.00 25.00
GS Gary Sheffield 6.00 15.00
ID Ike Davis 4.00 10.00
JN Jeff Niemann 4.00 10.00
JP Johnny Podres 4.00 10.00
JV Josh Vitters 4.00 10.00
OC Orlando Cepeda 8.00 20.00
RS Ryne Sandberg 20.00 50.00
TH Tommy Hanson 4.00 10.00
VG Vladimir Guerrero 8.00 20.00
WM Willie McCovey 15.00 40.00

2013 Topps Replacement Autographs Gold Refractors

*GOLD: .5X TO 1.2X BASIC
STATED PRINT RUN 199 SER.#'d SETS

2013 Topps Replacement Autographs Green Refractors

*GREEN: X TO X BASIC
STATED PRINT RUN 50 SER.#'d SETS

2013 Topps Replacement Autographs Red Refractors

*RED: X TO X BASIC
STATED PRINT RUN 99 SER.#'d SETS

2013 Topps Replacement Autographs Dual

PS J.Podres/D.Snider 20.00 50.00
RO A.Rodriguez/D.Ortiz 40.00 80.00

2013 Topps Replacement Autographs Triples

GCW Gooden/Carter/Wright 60.00 120.00
ORG Ortiz/ARod/Vlad 60.00 120.00
SPG Snider/Podres/Sheffield 20.00 50.00

2001 Topps Reserve

COMP.SET w/o SP's (100) 40.00 100.00
COMMON CARD (1-100) .40 1.00
COMMON (101-151) 3.00 8.00
101-145/151 ODDS 1:5 HOBBY, 1:52 RETAIL
146-150 ODDS 1:54 RETAIL
101-151 DISPLAY CUMULATIVE PRINT RUNS
101-145 ACTUAL PRINT 945 SERIAL #'d SETS
146-150 ACTUAL PRINT 1170 SER.#'d SETS
CARD 151 ACTUAL PRINT 1500 SERIAL #'d
CARDS 101-145/151 ARE HOBBY/RETAIL
CARDS 146-150 ARE RETAIL ONLY
1 Darin Erstad .40 1.00
2 Moises Alou .40 1.00
3 Tony Batista .40 1.00
4 Andruw Jones .60 1.50
5 Edgar Renteria .40 1.00
6 Eric Young .40 1.00
7 Steve Finley .40 1.00
8 Adrian Beltre .40 1.00
9 Vladimir Guerrero 1.00 2.50
10 Barry Bonds 2.50 6.00
11 Juan Gonzalez .40 1.00
12 Jay Buhner .40 1.00
13 Luis Castillo .40 1.00
14 Cal Ripken 3.00 8.00
15 Bob Abreu .40 1.00
16 Ivan Rodriguez .60 1.50
17 Nomar Garciaparra 1.50 4.00
18 Todd Helton .60 1.50
19 Bobby Higginson .40 1.00
20 Jorge Posada .60 1.50
21 Tim Salmon .60 1.50
22 Jason Giambi .40 1.00
23 Jose Cruz Jr. .40 1.00
24 Chipper Jones 1.00 2.50
25 Jim Edmonds .40 1.00
26 Gerald Williams .40 1.00
27 Randy Johnson 1.00 2.50
28 Gary Sheffield .40 1.00
29 Jeff Kent .40 1.00
30 Jim Thome .60 1.50
31 John Olerud .40 1.00
32 Cliff Floyd .40 1.00
33 Mike Lowell .40 1.00
34 Phil Nevin .40 1.00
35 Scott Rolen .60 1.50
36 Alex Rodriguez 1.25 3.00
37 Ken Griffey Jr. 2.00 5.00
38 Neifi Perez .40 1.00
39 Cristian Guzman .40 1.00
40 Mariano Rivera 1.00 2.50
41 Troy Glaus .40 1.00
42 Johnny Damon .60 1.50
43 Rafael Furcal .40 1.00
44 Jeromy Burnitz .40 1.00
45 Mark McGwire 2.50 6.00
46 Fred McGriff .60 1.50
47 Matt Williams .40 1.00
48 Kevin Brown .40 1.00
49 J.T. Snow .40 1.00
50 Kenny Lofton .40 1.00
51 Al Martin .40 1.00
52 Antonio Alfonseca .40 1.00
53 Edgardo Alfonzo .40 1.00
54 Ryan Klesko .40 1.00
55 Pat Burrell .40 1.00
56 Rafael Palmeiro .60 1.50
57 Sean Casey .40 1.00
58 Jeff Cirillo .40 1.00
59 Ray Durham .40 1.00
60 Derek Jeter 2.50 6.00
61 Jeff Bagwell .60 1.50
62 Carlos Delgado .40 1.00
63 Tom Glavine .60 1.50
64 Richie Sexson .40 1.00
65 J.D. Drew .40 1.00
66 Ben Grieve .40 1.00
67 Mark Grace .60 1.50
68 Shawn Green .40 1.00
69 Robb Nen .40 1.00
70 Omar Vizquel .60 1.50
71 Edgar Martinez .60 1.50
72 Preston Wilson .40 1.00
73 Mike Piazza 1.50 4.00
74 Tony Gwynn 1.25 3.00
75 Jason Kendall .40 1.00
76 Manny Ramirez Sox .60 1.50
77 Pokey Reese .40 1.00
78 Mike Sweeney .40 1.00
79 Magglio Ordonez .40 1.00
80 Bernie Williams .60 1.50
81 Richard Hidalgo .40 1.00
82 Brad Fullmer .40 1.00
83 Greg Maddux 1.50 4.00
84 Geoff Jenkins .40 1.00
85 Sammy Sosa 1.00 2.50
86 Luis Gonzalez .40 1.00
87 Eric Karros .40 1.00
88 Jose Vidro .40 1.00
89 Rich Aurilia .40 1.00
90 Roberto Alomar .60 1.50
91 Mike Cameron .40 1.00
92 Mike Mussina .60 1.50
93 Barry Zito .60 1.50
94 Mike Lieberthal .40 1.00
95 Brian Giles .40 1.00
96 Pedro Martinez .60 1.50
97 Barry Larkin .60 1.50
98 Jermaine Dye .40 1.00
99 Frank Thomas 1.00 2.50
100 David Justice .40 1.00
101 Gary Johnson RC 3.00 8.00
102 Matt Ford RC 3.00 8.00
103 Albert Pujols RC 40.00 100.00
104 Brad Cresse 3.00 8.00
105 Valentino Pascucci RC 3.00 8.00
106 Bob Keppel RC 3.00 8.00
107 Luis Torres RC 3.00 8.00
108 Tony Blanco RC 3.00 8.00
109 Ronnie Corona RC 3.00 8.00
110 Phil Wilson RC 3.00 8.00
111 John Buck RC 4.00 10.00
112 Jim Journell RC 3.00 8.00
113 Victor Hall RC 3.00 8.00
114 Jeff Andra RC 3.00 8.00
115 Greg Nash RC 3.00 8.00
116 Travis Hafner RC 8.00 20.00
117 Casey Fossum RC 3.00 8.00
118 Miguel Olivo 3.00 8.00
119 Elpidio Guzman RC 3.00 8.00
120 Jason Belcher RC 3.00 8.00
121 Esix Snead RC 3.00 8.00
122 Joe Thurston RC 3.00 8.00
123 Rafael Soriano RC 3.00 8.00
124 Ed Rogers RC 3.00 8.00
125 Omar Beltre RC 3.00 8.00
126 Brett Gray RC 3.00 8.00
127 Deivi Mendez RC 3.00 8.00
128 Freddie Bynum RC 3.00 8.00
129 David Krynzel 3.00 8.00
130 Blake Williams RC 3.00 8.00
131 Reggie Abercrombie RC 4.00 10.00
132 Miguel Villilo RC 3.00 8.00
133 Ryan Madson RC 3.00 8.00
134 Matt Thompson RC 3.00 8.00
135 Mark Burnett RC 3.00 8.00
136 Andy Beal RC 3.00 8.00
137 Ryan Ludwick RC 8.00 20.00
138 Roberto Miniel RC 3.00 8.00
139 Steve Smyth RC 3.00 8.00
140 Ben Washburn RC 3.00 8.00
141 Marvin Seale RC 3.00 8.00
142 Reggie Griggs RC 3.00 8.00
143 Seung Song RC 3.00 8.00
144 Chad Petty RC 3.00 8.00
145 Noel Devarez RC 3.00 8.00
146 Matt Butler RC 3.00 8.00
147 Brett Evert RC 3.00 8.00
148 Cesar Izturis 3.00 8.00
149 Troy Farnsworth RC 3.00 8.00
150 Brian Schmitt RC 3.00 8.00
151 Ichiro Suzuki RC 8.00 20.00

2001 Topps Reserve Rookie Autographs

TRA1-45 GROUP A ODDS 1:155 RETAIL
TRA46-50 GROUP B ODDS 1:252 RETAIL
OVERALL STATED ODDS 1:96 RETAIL
ALL CARDS AVAIL.ONLY IN RETAIL PACKS
TRA1 Gary Johnson A 4.00 10.00
TRA2 Matt Ford A 4.00 10.00
TRA3 Albert Pujols A 400.00 1000.00
TRA4 Brad Cresse A 4.00 10.00
TRA5 Valentino Pascucci A 4.00 10.00
TRA6 Bob Keppel A 4.00 10.00
TRA7 Luis Torres A 4.00 10.00
TRA8 Tony Blanco A 4.00 10.00
TRA9 Ronnie Corona A 4.00 10.00
TRA10 Phil Wilson A 4.00 10.00
TRA11 John Buck A 6.00 15.00
TRA12 Jim Journell A 4.00 10.00
TRA13 Victor Hall A 4.00 10.00
TRA14 Jeff Andra A 4.00 10.00
TRA15 Greg Nash A 4.00 10.00
TRA16 Travis Hafner A 6.00 15.00
TRA17 Casey Fossum A 4.00 10.00
TRA18 Miguel Olivo A 4.00 10.00
TRA19 Elpidio Guzman A 4.00 10.00
TRA20 Jason Belcher A 4.00 10.00
TRA21 Esix Snead A 4.00 10.00
TRA22 Joe Thurston A 4.00 10.00
TRA23 Rafael Soriano A 6.00 15.00
TRA24 Ed Rogers A 4.00 10.00
TRA25 Omar Beltre A 4.00 10.00
TRA26 Brett Gray A 4.00 10.00
TRA27 Deivi Mendez A 4.00 10.00
TRA28 Freddie Bynum A 4.00 10.00
TRA29 David Krynzel A 4.00 10.00
TRA30 Blake Williams A 4.00 10.00
TRA31 Reggie Abercrombie A 6.00 15.00
TRA32 Miguel Villilo A 4.00 10.00
TRA33 Ryan Madson A 8.00 20.00
TRA34 Matt Thompson A 4.00 10.00
TRA35 Mark Burnett A 4.00 10.00
TRA36 Andy Beal A 4.00 10.00
TRA37 Ryan Ludwick A 6.00 15.00
TRA38 Roberto Miniel A 4.00 10.00
TRA39 Steve Smyth A 4.00 10.00
TRA40 Ben Washburn A 4.00 10.00
TRA41 Marvin Seale A 4.00 10.00
TRA42 Reggie Griggs A 4.00 10.00
TRA43 Seung Song A 4.00 10.00
TRA44 Chad Petty A 4.00 10.00
TRA45 Noel Devarez A 4.00 10.00
TRA46 Matt Butler B 4.00 10.00
TRA47 Brett Evert B 4.00 10.00
TRA48 Cesar Izturis B 4.00 10.00
TRA49 Troy Farnsworth B 4.00 10.00
TRA50 Brian Schmitt B 4.00 10.00

2001 Topps Reserve Game Bats

OVERALL BAT/JERSEY ODDS 1:5
TRRBW Bernie Williams 6.00 15.00
TRRDE Darin Erstad 6.00 15.00
TRRJB Jeff Bagwell 6.00 15.00
TRRMP Mike Piazza 10.00 25.00
TRRNG Nomar Garciaparra 15.00 40.00
TRRVG Vladimir Guerrero 6.00 15.00
TRRARI Alex Rodriguez 10.00 25.00
TRRBBI Barry Bonds 15.00 40.00
TRRCDI Carlos Delgado 6.00 15.00
TRRCJI Chipper Jones 6.00 15.00
TRRIRI Ivan Rodriguez 6.00 15.00
TRRJEI Jim Edmonds 4.00 10.00
TRRRFI Rafael Furcal 4.00 10.00
TRRTGI Tony Gwynn 6.00 15.00

2001 Topps Reserve Game Jerseys

OVERALL BAT/JERSEY ODDS 1:5
TRRAR Alex Rodriguez 6.00 15.00
TRRBB Barry Bonds 8.00 20.00
TRRCD Carlos Delgado 2.00 5.00
TRRCJ Chipper Jones 5.00 12.00
TRRDJ David Justice 2.00 5.00
TRRFT Frank Thomas 5.00 12.00
TRRGM Greg Maddux 6.00 15.00
TRRIR Ivan Rodriguez 3.00 8.00
TRRJE Jim Edmonds 3.00 8.00
TRRJG Juan Gonzalez 2.00 5.00
TRRNP Nomar Garciaparra 3.00 8.00
TRRPM Pedro Martinez 3.00 8.00
TRRRA Roberto Alomar 3.00 8.00
TRRRJ Randy Johnson 5.00 12.00
TRRRP Rafael Palmeiro 3.00 8.00
TRRSG Shawn Green 2.00 5.00
TRRSR Scott Rolen 3.00 8.00
TRRTG Tony Gwynn 5.00 12.00
TRRTH Todd Helton 3.00 8.00
TRRVG Vladimir Guerrero 5.00 12.00

2001 Topps Reserve Rookie Baseballs

STATED ODDS ONE PER BOX
CABRERA AND LUGO RETAIL ONLY
1 Reggie Abercrombie 10.00 25.00
2 Jeff Andra 6.00 15.00
3 Andy Beal 6.00 15.00
4 Omar Beltre 6.00 15.00
5 Tony Blanco 6.00 15.00
6 Mark Burnett 6.00 15.00
7 Freddie Bynum 6.00 15.00
8 Fernando Cabrera 6.00 15.00
9 Ronnie Corona 6.00 15.00
10 Brad Cresse 6.00 15.00
11 Noel Devarez 6.00 15.00
12 Matt Ford 6.00 15.00
13 Casey Fossum 6.00 15.00
14 Brett Gray 6.00 15.00
15 Reggie Griggs 6.00 15.00
16 Elpidio Guzman 6.00 15.00
17 Travis Hafner 6.00 15.00
18 Victor Hall 6.00 15.00
19 Gary Johnson 6.00 15.00
20 Jim Journell 6.00 15.00
21 Bob Keppel 6.00 15.00
22 David Krynzel 6.00 15.00
23 Ryan Ludwick 6.00 15.00
24 Felix Lugo 6.00 15.00
25 Ryan Madson 8.00 20.00
26 Deivi Mendez 6.00 15.00
27 Roberto Miniel 6.00 15.00
28 Greg Nash 6.00 15.00
29 Miguel Olivo 6.00 15.00
30 Valentino Pascucci 6.00 15.00
31 Chad Petty 6.00 15.00
32 Albert Pujols 250.00 600.00
33 Ed Rogers 6.00 15.00
34 Marvin Seale 6.00 15.00
35 Steve Smyth 6.00 15.00
36 Esix Snead 6.00 15.00
37 Seung Song 6.00 15.00
38 Rafael Soriano 6.00 15.00
39 Matt Thompson 6.00 15.00
40 Joe Thurston 6.00 15.00
41 Luis Torres 6.00 15.00
42 Miguel Villilo 6.00 15.00
43 Ben Washburn 6.00 15.00
44 Blake Williams 6.00 15.00
45 Phil Wilson 6.00 15.00

2002 Topps Reserve

COMP.SET w/o SP's (135) 15.00 40.00
COMMON CARD (1-135) .40 1.00
COMMON CARD (136-150) 1.50 4.00
136-150 STATED ODDS 1:24
136-150 PRINT RUN 999 SERIAL #'d SETS
1 Alex Rodriguez 1.25 3.00
2 Tsuyoshi Shinjo .60 1.50
3 Craig Biggio .60 1.50
4 Troy Glaus .40 1.00
5 Mike Rivera .40 1.00
6 Curt Schilling .40 1.00
7 Garret Anderson .40 1.00
8 Ben Sheets .40 1.00
9 Todd Helton .60 1.50
10 Paul Konerko .60 1.50
11 Sammy Sosa 1.00 2.50
12 Bud Smith .40 1.00
13 Jeff Bagwell .60 1.50
14 Albert Pujols 2.00 5.00
15 Jose Vidro .40 1.00
16 Carlos Delgado .40 1.00
17 Torii Hunter .40 1.00
18 Jerry Hairston .40 1.00
19 Troy Percival .40 1.00
20 Vladimir Guerrero 1.00 2.50
21 Geoff Jenkins .40 1.00
22 Carlos Pena .40 1.00
23 Juan Gonzalez .40 1.00
24 Raul Mondesi .40 1.00
25 Jimmy Rollins .40 1.00
26 Mariano Rivera 1.00 2.50
27 Jorge Posada .60 1.50
28 Magglio Ordonez .40 1.00
29 Roberto Alomar .60 1.50
30 Randy Johnson 1.00 2.50
31 Xavier Nady .40 1.00
32 Terrence Long .40 1.00
33 Chipper Jones 1.00 2.50
34 Rich Aurilia .40 1.00
35 Aramis Ramirez .40 1.00
36 Jim Thome .60 1.50
37 Bret Boone .40 1.00
38 Angel Berroa .40 1.00
39 Jeff Conine .40 1.00
40 Cliff Floyd .40 1.00
41 Pedro Martinez .60 1.50
42 J.D. Drew .40 1.00
43 Kazuhiro Sasaki .40 1.00
44 Jon Rauch .40 1.00
45 Orlando Hudson .40 1.00
46 Scott Rolen .60 1.50
47 Rafael Furcal .40 1.00
48 Brad Penny .40 1.00
49 Miguel Tejada .40 1.00
50 Orlando Cabrera .40 1.00
51 Bob Abreu .40 1.00
52 Darin Erstad .40 1.00
53 Edgar Martinez .60 1.50
54 Ben Grieve .40 1.00
55 Shawn Green .40 1.00
56 Ivan Rodriguez .60 1.50
57 Josh Beckett .40 1.00
58 Ray Durham .40 1.00
59 Jason Hart .40 1.00
60 Nathan Haynes .40 1.00
61 Jason Giambi .40 1.00
62 Eric Chavez .40 1.00
63 Matt Morris .40 1.00
64 Lance Berkman .40 1.00
65 Jeff Kent .40 1.00
66 Andruw Jones .60 1.50
67 Brian Giles .40 1.00
68 Morgan Ensberg .40 1.00
69 Pat Burrell .40 1.00
70 Ken Griffey Jr. 2.00 5.00
71 Carlos Beltran .40 1.00
72 Ichiro Suzuki 2.00 5.00
73 Larry Walker .40 1.00
74 J.J. Putz RC .40 1.00
75 Mike Piazza 1.50 4.00
76 Rafael Palmeiro .60 1.50
77 Mark Prior .60 1.50
78 Toby Hall .40 1.00
79 Pokey Reese .40 1.00
80 Mike Mussina .60 1.50
81 Omar Vizquel .60 1.50
82 Shannon Stewart .40 1.00
83 Jeromy Burnitz .40 1.00
84 Bernie Williams .60 1.50
85 C.C. Sabathia .40 1.00
86 Mike Hampton .40 1.00
87 Kevin Brown .40 1.00
88 Juan Cruz .40 1.00
89 Jeff Weaver .40 1.00
90 Jason Lane .40 1.00
91 Adam Dunn .40 1.00
92 Jose Cruz Jr. .40 1.00
93 Marlon Anderson .40 1.00
94 Jeff Cirillo .40 1.00
95 Mark Buehrle .40 1.00
96 Austin Kearns .40 1.00
97 Tim Hudson .40 1.00
98 Brian Jordan .40 1.00
99 Phil Nevin .40 1.00
100 Barry Bonds 2.50 6.00
101 Derek Jeter 2.50 6.00
102 Javier Vazquez .40 1.00
103 Jason Kendall .40 1.00
104 Jim Edmonds .40 1.00
105 Kenny Kelly .40 1.00
106 Juan Pena .40 1.00
107 Mark Grace .60 1.50
108 Roger Clemens 2.00 5.00
109 Barry Zito .40 1.00
110 Greg Vaughn .40 1.00
111 Greg Maddux 1.50 4.00
112 Richie Sexson .40 1.00
113 Jermaine Dye .40 1.00
114 Kerry Wood .40 1.00
115 Matt Lawton .40 1.00
116 Sean Casey .40 1.00
117 Gary Sheffield .40 1.00
118 Preston Wilson .40 1.00
119 Cristian Guzman .40 1.00
120 Mike Sweeney .40 1.00
121 Neifi Perez .40 1.00
122 Paul LoDuca .40 1.00
123 Luis Gonzalez .40 1.00
124 Ryan Klesko .40 1.00
125 Alfonso Soriano .40 1.00
126 Bobby Higginson .40 1.00
127 Juan Pierre .40 1.00
128 Moises Alou .40 1.00
129 Roy Oswalt .40 1.00
130 Nomar Garciaparra 1.50 4.00
131 Fred McGriff .60 1.50
132 Edgardo Alfonzo .40 1.00
133 Johnny Damon Sox .60 1.50
134 Dewon Brazelton .40 1.00
135 Mark Mulder .40 1.00
136 So Taguchi FYP RC 2.00 5.00
137 Mario Ramos FYP RC 1.50 4.00
138 Dan Johnson FYP RC 2.00 5.00
139 Hansel Izquierdo FYP RC 1.50 4.00
140 Kazuhisa Ishii FYP RC 2.00 5.00
141 Jon Switzer FYP RC 1.50 4.00
142 Chris Tritle FYP RC 1.50 4.00
143 Chris Snelling FYP RC 1.50 4.00
144 Chone Figgins FYP RC 3.00 8.00
145 Dan Phillips FYP RC 1.50 4.00
146 John Rodriguez FYP RC 2.00 5.00
147 Colt Griffin FYP RC 1.50 4.00
148 Jonny Gomes FYP RC 3.00 8.00
149 Josh Barfield FYP RC 4.00 10.00
150 Joe Mauer FYP RC 20.00 50.00

2002 Topps Reserve Parallel

*PARALLEL 1-135: 1.25X TO 3X BASIC
*PARALLEL 136-150: .6X TO 1.5X BASIC
STATED ODDS 1:12
STATED PRINT RUN 150 SERIAL #'d SETS
150 Joe Mauer FYP 30.00 80.00

2002 Topps Reserve Autograph Mini-Helmets

GROUP A ODDS 1:285
GROUP B ODDS 1:39
GROUP C ODDS 1:14
ODDS ARE PER PACK NOT PER BOX
GROUP A PRINT RUN 225 SERIAL #'d SETS
GROUP B PRINT RUN 475 SERIAL #'d SETS
GROUP C PRINT RUN 975 SERIAL #'d SETS
GOLD ODDS 1:279
GOLD ODDS ARE PER PACK NOT PER BOX
GOLD PRINT RUN 25 SERIAL #'d SETS
GOLD HELMETS FEATURE GOLD INK AUTO
NO GOLD PRICING DUE TO SCARCITY
1 Roberto Alomar C 12.50 30.00
2 Moises Alou C 10.00 25.00
3 Lance Berkman C 30.00 60.00
4 Bret Boone B 12.50 30.00
5 Eric Chavez B 12.50 30.00
6 Adam Dunn C 12.50 30.00
7 Cliff Floyd C 10.00 25.00
8 Troy Glaus B 20.00 40.00
9 Luis Gonzalez A 20.00 40.00
10 Todd Helton A 25.00 50.00
11 Magglio Ordonez C 10.00 25.00
12 Rafael Palmeiro B 30.00 60.00
13 Albert Pujols B 150.00 250.00
14 Alex Rodriguez B 60.00 120.00
15 Scott Rolen C 12.50 30.00
16 Jimmy Rollins C 12.50 30.00
17 Alfonso Soriano B 20.00 40.00
18 Barry Zito C 12.50 30.00

2002 Topps Reserve Bat Relics

GROUP A ODDS 1:1563
GROUP B ODDS 1:1180
GROUP C ODDS 1:61
GROUP D ODDS 1:219
GROUP E ODDS 1:31
GROUP F ODDS 1:179
GROUP G ODDS 1:135
GROUP H ODDS 1:46
OVERALL ODDS 1:12
AJ Andruw Jones E 2.00 5.00
AP Albert Pujols F 6.00 15.00
AR Alex Rodriguez E 6.00 15.00
AS Alfonso Soriano E 3.00 8.00
BB Barry Bonds A 8.00 20.00
BW Bernie Williams E 3.00 8.00
CD Carlos Delgado C 2.00 5.00
CJ Chipper Jones C 5.00 12.00
FT Frank Thomas E 5.00 12.00
IR Ivan Rodriguez E 3.00 8.00
JB Jeff Bagwell E 3.00 8.00
JG Juan Gonzalez D 2.00 5.00
LG Luis Gonzalez C 2.00 5.00
MP Mike Piazza H 5.00 12.00
RA Roberto Alomar B 3.00 8.00
RH Rickey Henderson C 5.00 12.00
RP Rafael Palmeiro C 3.00 8.00
TG Tony Gwynn H 5.00 12.00
TM Tino Martinez C 3.00 8.00
TS Tsuyoshi Shinjo G 2.00 5.00

2002 Topps Reserve Patch Relics

STATED ODDS 1:668

2002 Topps Reserve Uniform Relics

GROUP A ODDS 1:376
GROUP B ODDS 1:179
GROUP C ODDS 1:10
GROUP D ODDS 1:14
GROUP E ODDS 1:16
OVERALL ODDS 1:5
AJ Andruw Jones D 4.00 10.00
AP Albert Pujols E 8.00 20.00
AR Alex Rodriguez C 6.00 15.00
BB Barry Bonds E 10.00 25.00
BBO Bret Boone C 4.00 10.00
CJ Chipper Jones C 4.00 10.00
CS Curt Schilling E 4.00 10.00
DE Darin Erstad D 4.00 10.00
FT Frank Thomas C 4.00 10.00
GM Greg Maddux C 6.00 15.00
IR Ivan Rodriguez D 4.00 10.00
KS Kazuhiro Sasaki C 4.00 10.00
KW Kerry Wood E 4.00 10.00
LG Luis Gonzalez C 4.00 10.00
MM Mark Mulder C 4.00 10.00
MO Magglio Ordonez D 4.00 10.00
MP Mike Piazza C 6.00 15.00
NG Nomar Garciaparra D 6.00 15.00
PM Pedro Martinez A 6.00 15.00
RJ Randy Johnson B 4.00 10.00
RP Rafael Palmeiro C 4.00 10.00
SR Scott Rolen C 4.00 10.00
TG Tony Gwynn E 6.00 15.00
TH Todd Helton C 4.00 10.00

2003 Topps Retired Signature

COMPLETE SET (110) 75.00 150.00
COMMON CARD (1-110) .50 1.25
1 Willie Mays 2.50 6.00
2 Tony Perez .75 2.00
3 Tom Seaver .75 2.00
4 Johnny Bench 1.25 3.00
5 Rod Carew .75 2.00
6 Red Schoendienst .75 2.00
7 Phil Rizzuto .75 2.00
8 Ozzie Smith 1.50 4.00
9 Maury Wills .50 1.25
10 Hank Aaron 2.50 6.00
11 Jim Palmer .75 2.00
12 Jose Cruz Sr. .50 1.25
13 Dave Parker .50 1.25
14 Don Sutton .75 2.00
15 Brooks Robinson .75 2.00
16 Bo Jackson 1.25 3.00
17 Andre Dawson .75 2.00
18 Fergie Jenkins .75 2.00
19 George Foster .50 1.25
20 George Brett 2.50 6.00
21 Jerry Koosman .50 1.25
22 John Kruk .50 1.25
23 Kent Tekulve .50 1.25
24 Lee Smith .50 1.25
25 Nolan Ryan 4.00 10.00
26 Paul O'Neill .75 2.00
27 Rich Gossage .75 2.00
28 Ron Santo .75 2.00
29 Tom Lasorda .75 2.00
30 Tony Gwynn 1.25 3.00
31 Vida Blue .50 1.25
32 Whitey Herzog .50 1.25
33 Willie McGee .50 1.25
34 Bill Mazeroski .75 2.00
35 Al Kaline .75 2.00
36 Bobby Richardson .50 1.25
37 Carlton Fisk .75 2.00
38 Darrell Evans .50 1.25
39 Dave Concepcion .50 1.25
40 Cal Ripken 4.00 10.00
41 Dwight Evans .50 1.25

42 Earl Weaver .75 2.00
43 Fred Lynn .50 1.25
44 Greg Luzinski .50 1.25
45 Duke Snider .75 2.00
46 Hank Bauer .50 1.25
47 Jim Rice .75 2.00
48 Johnny Sain .50 1.25
49 Lenny Dykstra .50 1.25
50 Mike Schmidt 2.00 5.00
51 Orlando Cepeda .75 2.00
52 Ralph Kiner .75 2.00
53 Robin Roberts .75 2.00
54 Ron Guidry .50 1.25
55 Steve Garvey .50 1.25
56 Tony Oliva .50 1.25
57 Whitey Ford .75 2.00
58 Willie McCovey .75 2.00
59 Phil Niekro .75 2.00
60 Stan Musial 2.00 5.00
61 Rollie Fingers .75 2.00
62 Robin Yount 1.25 3.00
63 Alan Trammell .75 2.00
64 Bill Buckner .50 1.25
65 Bob Feller .75 2.00
66 Bruce Sutter .75 2.00
67 Dale Murphy 1.25 3.00
68 Dennis Eckersley .75 2.00
69 Don Newcombe .50 1.25
70 Don Mattingly 2.50 6.00
71 Dwight Gooden .50 1.25
72 Frank Robinson .75 2.00
73 Gary Carter .75 2.00
74 Graig Nettles .50 1.25
75 Harmon Killebrew 1.25 3.00
76 Jim Bunning .75 2.00
77 Joe Morgan .75 2.00
78 Joe Rudi .50 1.25
79 Jose Canseco .75 2.00
80 Ernie Banks 1.25 3.00
81 Luis Aparicio .75 2.00
82 Luis Tiant .50 1.25
83 Mark Fidrych .50 1.25
84 Kirk Gibson .50 1.25
85 Lou Brock .75 2.00
86 Juan Marichal .75 2.00
87 Monte Irvin .75 2.00
88 Paul Molitor 1.25 3.00
89 Tommy John .50 1.25
90 Warren Spahn .75 2.00
91 Wade Boggs .75 2.00
92 Reggie Jackson .75 2.00
93 Kirby Puckett 1.25 3.00
94 Boog Powell .50 1.25
95 Carl Yastrzemski 2.00 5.00
96 Bobby Thomson .75 2.00
97 Bill Skowron .50 1.25
98 Bill Madlock .50 1.25
99 Sparky Anderson .75 2.00
100 Yogi Berra 1.25 3.00
101 Bobby Doerr .75 2.00
102 Gaylord Perry .75 2.00
103 George Kell .75 2.00
104 Harold Reynolds .50 1.25
105 Joe Carter .50 1.25
106 Johnny Podres .50 1.25
107 Ron Cey .50 1.25
108 Tim McCarver .50 1.25
109 Tug McGraw .50 1.25
110 Don Larsen .50 1.25

2003 Topps Retired Signature Black

*BLACK: 2.5X TO 6X BASIC
STATED ODDS 1:8
STATED PRINT RUN 99 SERIAL #'d SETS

2003 Topps Retired Signature Autographs

ONE AUTOGRAPH PER PACK
A-B PRINT RUNS PROVIDED BY TOPPS
GROUPS A-B ARE NOT SERIAL-NUMBERED
NO GROUP A PRICING DUE TO SCARCITY
AD Andre Dawson D 6.00 15.00
AK Al Kaline C 25.00 50.00
AT Alan Trammell E 6.00 15.00
BB Bert Blyleven F 10.00 25.00
BBU Bill Buckner C 8.00 20.00
BD Bobby Doerr C 8.00 20.00
BF Bob Feller C 12.00 30.00
BGR Bobby Grich C 6.00 15.00
BH Bob Horner C 5.00 12.00
BJ Bo Jackson C 20.00 50.00
BM Bill Madlock G 6.00 15.00
BMA Bill Mazeroski C 30.00 80.00
BP Boog Powell G 6.00 15.00
BR Bobby Richardson G 8.00 20.00
BRO Brooks Robinson B/75 60.00 150.00
BS Bill Skowron G 6.00 15.00
BSA Bret Saberhagen C 6.00 15.00
BSU Bruce Sutter E 5.00 12.00
BT Bobby Thomson D 5.00 12.00
BW Bob Watson C 5.00 12.00
CF Carlton Fisk C 25.00 60.00
CY Carl Yastrzemski C 30.00 80.00
DE Darrell Evans F 5.00 12.00
DEC Dennis Eckersley C 25.00 60.00
DEV Dwight Evans B/78 6.00 15.00
DG Dwight Gooden C 12.00 30.00
DL Don Larsen G 6.00 15.00
DM Dale Murphy C 12.00 30.00
DN Don Newcombe C 6.00 15.00
DON Don Mattingly B/81 30.00 80.00
DP Dave Parker C 8.00 20.00
DS Dave Stieb C 10.00 25.00
DSN Duke Snider B/75 60.00 150.00
DSU Don Sutton C 6.00 15.00
EB Ernie Banks A/24 60.00 150.00
EW Earl Weaver G 6.00 15.00
FJ Fergie Jenkins D 12.00 30.00
FL Fred Lynn C 12.00 30.00
FR Frank Robinson C 25.00 60.00
GC Gary Carter B/77 25.00 60.00
GF George Foster G 6.00 15.00
GK George Kell C 12.00 30.00
GL Greg Luzinski D 10.00 25.00
GN Graig Nettles G 8.00 20.00
GP Gaylord Perry C 8.00 20.00
HB Harold Baines F 6.00 15.00
HBA Hank Bauer C 6.00 15.00
HK Harmon Killebrew B/76 50.00 120.00
HR Harold Reynolds C 6.00 15.00
JA Jim Abbott E 10.00 25.00
JB Jim Bunning B/76 100.00 200.00
JBE Johnny Bench C 30.00 80.00
JC Joe Carter C 12.00 30.00
JCA Jose Canseco C 12.00 30.00
JCR Jose Cruz Sr. D 6.00 15.00
JK Jerry Koosman C 12.00 30.00
JKR John Kruk C 20.00 50.00
JM Joe Morgan C 20.00 50.00
JMA Juan Marichal C 15.00 40.00
JP Jim Palmer C 10.00 25.00
JPI Jim Piersall G 6.00 15.00
JPO Johnny Podres G 6.00 15.00
JR Jim Rice C 10.00 25.00
JRU Joe Rudi F 5.00 12.00
KG Kirk Gibson C 20.00 50.00
KGR Ken Griffey Sr. C 20.00 50.00
KT Kent Tekulve C 6.00 15.00
LA Luis Aparicio G 6.00 15.00
LB Lou Brock B/76 50.00 120.00
LD Lenny Dykstra D 6.00 15.00
LP Lance Parrish G 8.00 20.00
LS Lee Smith E 5.00 12.00
LT Luis Tiant G 6.00 15.00
MF Mark Fidrych D 20.00 50.00
MI Monte Irvin C 10.00 25.00
MS Mike Schmidt B/83 100.00 200.00
MW Maury Wills F 6.00 15.00
NR Nolan Ryan B/77 150.00 300.00
OC Orlando Cepeda B/75 100.00 200.00
OS Ozzie Smith C 25.00 60.00
PM Paul Molitor C 10.00 25.00
PN Phil Niekro D 10.00 25.00
PO Paul O'Neill C 12.00 30.00
PR Phil Rizzuto B/77 40.00 100.00
RCA Rod Carew C 25.00 60.00
RCE Ron Cey F 6.00 15.00
RF Rollie Fingers C 6.00 15.00
RG Rich Gossage C 12.00 30.00
RGU Ron Guidry D 6.00 15.00
RJ Reggie Jackson C 25.00 60.00
RK Ralph Kiner B/80 25.00 60.00
RR Robin Roberts C 20.00 50.00
RS Red Schoendienst B/83 15.00 40.00
RSA Ron Santo G 30.00 80.00
SA Sparky Anderson C 15.00 40.00
SG Steve Garvey D 6.00 15.00
TJ Tommy John C 10.00 25.00
TL Tom Lasorda B/76 100.00 250.00
TM Tim McCarver C 12.00 30.00
TMC Tug McGraw D 8.00 20.00
TO Tony Oliva C 12.00 30.00
TP Tony Perez C 15.00 40.00
TPE Terry Pendleton D 6.00 15.00
TS Tom Seaver C 40.00 100.00
VB Vida Blue E 6.00 15.00
WB Wade Boggs B/77 25.00 60.00
WF Whitey Ford C 25.00 60.00
WH Whitey Herzog D 8.00 20.00
WMC Willie McCovey C 30.00 80.00
WMG Willie McGee D 20.00 50.00
WS Warren Spahn F 12.00 30.00

2004 Topps Retired Signature

COMPLETE SET (110) 75.00 150.00
COMMON CARD (1-110) .40 1.00
1 Willie Mays 2.00 5.00
2 Tony Gwynn 1.00 2.50
3 Dale Murphy 1.00 2.50
4 Lenny Dykstra .40 1.00
5 Johnny Bench 1.00 2.50
6 Bill Buckner .40 1.00
7 Ferguson Jenkins .40 1.00
8 George Brett 2.00 5.00
9 Ralph Kiner .60 1.50
10 Ernie Banks 1.00 2.50
11 Hal McRae .40 1.00
12 Lou Brock .60 1.50
13 Keith Hernandez .40 1.00
14 Jose Canseco .60 1.50
15 Whitey Ford .60 1.50
16 Dave Kingman .40 1.00
17 Tim Raines .40 1.00
18 Paul O'Neill .60 1.50
19 Lou Whitaker .40 1.00
20 Mike Schmidt 1.50 4.00
21 Wally Joyner .40 1.00
22 Kirk Gibson .40 1.00
23 Ryne Sandberg 2.00 5.00
24 Luis Tiant .40 1.00
25 Al Kaline 1.00 2.50
26 Brooks Robinson .60 1.50
27 Don Zimmer .40 1.00
28 Nolan Ryan 3.00 8.00
29 Maury Wills .40 1.00
30 Stan Musial 1.50 4.00
31 Garry Maddox .40 1.00
32 Tom Brunansky .40 1.00
33 Don Mattingly 2.00 5.00
34 Earl Weaver .60 1.50
35 Bobby Grich .40 1.00
36 Orlando Cepeda .40 1.00
37 Alan Trammell .60 1.50
38 Al Hrabosky .40 1.00
39 Dave Lopes .40 1.00
40 Rod Carew .60 1.50
41 Robin Yount 1.00 2.50
42 Dwight Gooden .40 1.00
43 Andre Dawson .60 1.50
44 Hank Aaron 2.00 5.00
45 Norm Cash .40 1.00
46 Reggie Jackson .60 1.50
47 Jim Rice .60 1.50
48 Carlton Fisk .60 1.50
49 Dave Parker .40 1.00
50 Cal Ripken 3.00 8.00
51 Roy Face .40 1.00
52 Bob Gibson .60 1.50
53 Jimmy Key .40 1.00
54 Al Oliver .40 1.00
55 Don Larsen .40 1.00
56 Tom Seaver .60 1.50
57 Tony Armas .40 1.00
58 Dave Stieb .40 1.00
59 Will Clark .60 1.50
60 Duke Snider .60 1.50
61 Cesar Geronimo .40 1.00
62 Ron Kittle .40 1.00
63 Ron Santo .60 1.50
64 Mickey Rivers .40 1.00
65 Jim Piersall .40 1.00
66 Ron Swoboda .40 1.00
67 Kent Hrbek .40 1.00
68 Dennis Eckersley .60 1.50
69 Greg Luzinski .40 1.00
70 Harmon Killebrew 1.00 2.50
71 Ron Guidry .40 1.00
72 Steve Garvey .40 1.00
73 Andy Van Slyke .40 1.00
74 Goose Gossage .60 1.50
75 Ozzie Smith 1.25 3.00
76 Richie Allen .40 1.00
77 Vida Blue .40 1.00
78 Tony Oliva .40 1.00
79 Darryl Strawberry .40 1.00
80 Frank Robinson .60 1.50
81 Bruce Sutter .60 1.50
82 Dave Concepcion .40 1.00
83 Darrell Evans .40 1.00
84 Jack Morris .60 1.50
85 Bo Jackson 1.00 2.50
86 Orel Hershiser .40 1.00
87 Rob Dibble .40 1.00
88 Wade Boggs .60 1.50
89 Fernando Valenzuela .40 1.00
90 Jim Palmer .60 1.50
91 George Foster .40 1.00
92 Mike Scott .40 1.00
93 Paul Molitor 1.00 2.50
94 Gary Carter .60 1.50
95 Bobby Richardson .40 1.00
96 Rollie Fingers .60 1.50
97 Tim McCarver .40 1.00
98 John Candelaria .40 1.00
99 Dave Winfield .60 1.50
100 Yogi Berra 1.00 2.50
101 Bill Madlock .40 1.00
102 Jack McDowell .40 1.00
103 Luis Aparicio .60 1.50
104 Graig Nettles .40 1.00
105 Dave Stewart .40 1.00
106 Darren Daulton .40 1.00
107 Gary Gaetti .40 1.00
108 Tony Fernandez .40 1.00
109 Buddy Bell .40 1.00
110 Carl Yastrzemski 1.00 2.50

2004 Topps Retired Signature Black

*BLACK: 2.5X TO 6X BASIC
STATED ODDS 1:7
STATED PRINT RUN 99 SERIAL #'d SETS

2004 Topps Retired Signature Autographs

GROUP A ODDS 1:675
GROUP B ODDS 1:338
GROUP C ODDS 1:82
GROUP D ODDS 1:20
GROUP E ODDS 1:8
GROUP F ODDS 1:46
GROUP G ODDS 1:2
GROUP H ODDS 1:33
GROUP A PRINT RUN 25 SETS
GROUP B PRINT RUN 50 SETS
GROUP C PRINT RUN 75 SETS
GROUP A-C ARE NOT SERIAL-NUMBERED
A-C PRINT RUNS PROVIDED BY TOPPS
OVERALL PRESS PLATE ODDS 1:222
PLATE PRINT RUN 1 SET PER COLOR
BLACK-CYAN-MAGENTA-YELLOW ISSUED
NO PLATE PRICING DUE TO SCARCITY
AH Al Hrabosky E 6.00 15.00
AO Al Oliver G 6.00 15.00
AT Alan Trammell E 6.00 15.00
BB Bill Buckner G 8.00 20.00
BBE Buddy Bell E 6.00 15.00
BD Bucky Dent E 6.00 15.00
BG Bob Gibson C 30.00 80.00
BGR Bobby Grich C 6.00 15.00
BM Bill Madlock G 6.00 15.00
BR Bobby Richardson G 6.00 15.00
BRO Brooks Robinson C 40.00 100.00
BS Bruce Sutter G 10.00 25.00
CF Carlton Fisk D 15.00 40.00
CG Cesar Geronimo E 6.00 15.00
CR Cal Ripken A 300.00 500.00
CY Carl Yastrzemski A 100.00 250.00
DD Darren Daulton G 6.00 15.00
DE Darrell Evans G 6.00 15.00
DEC Dennis Eckersley E 12.00 30.00
DG Dwight Gooden C 20.00 50.00
DL Davey Lopes F 6.00 15.00
DM Don Mattingly C 75.00 200.00
DMU Dale Murphy G 10.00 25.00
DP Dave Parker E 10.00 25.00
DS Darryl Strawberry D 10.00 25.00
DSN Duke Snider B 125.00 200.00
DST Dave Stieb G 8.00 20.00
DZ Don Zimmer D 12.00 30.00
EB Ernie Banks B 75.00 200.00
EW Earl Weaver G 8.00 20.00
FJ Ferguson Jenkins G 10.00 25.00
FR Frank Robinson D 15.00 40.00
GC Gary Carter D 20.00 50.00
GF George Foster E 10.00 25.00
GG Goose Gossage E 10.00 25.00
GL Greg Luzinski E 6.00 15.00
GN Graig Nettles G 6.00 15.00
HA Hank Aaron B 150.00 300.00
JB Johnny Bench C 100.00 250.00
JC John Candelaria D 6.00 15.00
JCA Jose Canseco D 20.00 50.00
JK Jimmy Key G 6.00 15.00
JM Jack McDowell G 8.00 20.00
JP Jim Piersall E 6.00 15.00
KG Kirk Gibson E 8.00 20.00
LT Luis Tiant G 6.00 15.00
MS Mike Schmidt C 30.00 60.00
MW Maury Wills G 10.00 25.00
NR Nolan Ryan A 250.00 400.00
OC Orlando Cepeda G 6.00 15.00
OH Orel Hershiser E 15.00 40.00
OS Ozzie Smith C 60.00 120.00
PM Paul Molitor D 20.00 50.00
PO Paul O'Neill D 20.00 50.00
RC Rod Carew E 15.00 40.00
RD Rob Dibble E 8.00 20.00
RF Rollie Fingers E 6.00 15.00
RFA Roy Face H 6.00 15.00
RK Ralph Kiner D 15.00 40.00
RKI Ron Kittle G 6.00 15.00
RS Ron Swoboda G 6.00 15.00
RSA Ryne Sandberg D 30.00 60.00
RSN Ron Santo G 20.00 50.00
RY Robin Yount A 175.00 300.00
SM Stan Musial B 150.00 250.00
TA Tony Armas G 6.00 15.00
TB Tom Brunansky G 6.00 15.00
TF Tony Fernandez E 6.00 15.00
TG Tony Gwynn C 60.00 120.00
TO Tony Oliva E 10.00 25.00
TS Tom Seaver C 60.00 150.00
VB Vida Blue G 6.00 15.00
WB Wade Boggs D 20.00 50.00
WF Whitey Ford C 40.00 100.00
WJ Wally Joyner G 8.00 20.00
YB Yogi Berra C 125.00 250.00

2004 Topps Retired Signature Autographs Refractors

STATED ODDS 1:36
STATED PRINT RUN 25 SERIAL #'d SETS
AH Al Hrabosky 15.00 40.00
AO Al Oliver 15.00 40.00
AT Alan Trammell 15.00 40.00
BB Bill Buckner 20.00 50.00
BBE Buddy Bell 15.00 40.00
BD Bucky Dent 15.00 40.00
BG Bob Gibson 50.00 120.00
BGR Bobby Grich 15.00 40.00
BM Bill Madlock 15.00 40.00
BR Bobby Richardson 40.00 100.00
BRO Brooks Robinson 60.00 150.00
BS Bruce Sutter 15.00 40.00
CF Carlton Fisk 60.00 120.00
CG Cesar Geronimo 15.00 40.00
CR Cal Ripken 300.00 500.00
CY Carl Yastrzemski 100.00 250.00
DD Darren Daulton 30.00 80.00
DE Darrell Evans 25.00 60.00
DEC Dennis Eckersley 40.00 100.00
DG Dwight Gooden 60.00 150.00
DL Davey Lopes 40.00 100.00
DM Don Mattingly 175.00 300.00
DMU Dale Murphy 60.00 120.00
DP Dave Parker 40.00 80.00
DS Darryl Strawberry 15.00 40.00
DSN Duke Snider 60.00 120.00
DST Dave Stieb 50.00 100.00
DZ Don Zimmer 25.00 60.00
EB Ernie Banks 150.00 250.00
EW Earl Weaver 75.00 200.00
FJ Ferguson Jenkins 25.00 60.00
FR Frank Robinson 30.00 80.00
GC Gary Carter 40.00 80.00
GF George Foster 40.00 100.00
GG Goose Gossage 25.00 60.00
GL Greg Luzinski 50.00 120.00
GN Graig Nettles 25.00 60.00
HA Hank Aaron 300.00 600.00
JB Johnny Bench 150.00 400.00
JC John Candelaria 40.00 100.00
JCA Jose Canseco 60.00 120.00
JK Jimmy Key 40.00 80.00
JM Jack McDowell 25.00 60.00
JP Jim Piersall 25.00 60.00
KG Kirk Gibson 30.00 80.00
LT Luis Tiant 25.00 60.00
MS Mike Schmidt 125.00 250.00
MW Maury Wills 25.00 60.00
NR Nolan Ryan 300.00 500.00
OC Orlando Cepeda 25.00 60.00
OH Orel Hershiser 25.00 60.00
OS Ozzie Smith 75.00 150.00
PM Paul Molitor 30.00 80.00
PO Paul O'Neill 50.00 120.00
RC Rod Carew 50.00 120.00
RD Rob Dibble 30.00 80.00
RF Rollie Fingers 30.00 80.00
RFA Roy Face 20.00 50.00
RK Ralph Kiner 50.00 100.00
RKI Ron Kittle 25.00 60.00
RS Ron Swoboda 25.00 60.00
RSA Ryne Sandberg 125.00 250.00
RSN Ron Santo 40.00 80.00
RY Robin Yount 150.00 250.00
SM Stan Musial 200.00 350.00
TA Tony Armas 25.00 60.00
TB Tom Brunansky 15.00 40.00
TF Tony Fernandez 15.00 40.00
TG Tony Gwynn 125.00 200.00
TO Tony Oliva 25.00 60.00
TS Tom Seaver 125.00 300.00
VB Vida Blue 60.00 120.00
WB Wade Boggs 75.00 150.00
WF Whitey Ford 75.00 200.00
WJ Wally Joyner 30.00 80.00
YB Yogi Berra 75.00 200.00

2004 Topps Retired Signature Co-Signers

STATED ODDS 1:675
STATED PRINT RUN 25 SERIAL #'d SETS
NO PRICING DUE TO SCARCITY

2005 Topps Retired Signature

COMMON CARD (1-110) .40 1.00
PLATE ODDS 1:126 HOBBY, 1:127 RETAIL
PLATE PRINT RUN 1 SET PER COLOR
BLACK-CYAN-MAGENTA-YELLOW ISSUED
NO PLATE PRICING DUE TO SCARCITY
1 Josh Gibson 1.00 2.50
2 Andre Dawson .60 1.50
3 Al Kaline 1.00 2.50
4 Andy Van Slyke .40 1.00
5 Brett Butler .40 1.00
6 Bob Gibson .60 1.50
7 Bo Jackson 1.00 2.50
8 Carlton Fisk .60 1.50
9 Chuck Knoblauch .40 1.00
10 Cal Ripken 3.00 8.00
11 Carl Yastrzemski 1.25 3.00
12 Tom Niedenfuer .40 1.00
13 Dennis Eckersley .60 1.50
14 Darryl Strawberry .40 1.00
15 Dwight Gooden .40 1.00
16 Davey Johnson .40 1.00
17 Don Mattingly 2.00 5.00
18 Dave Winfield .60 1.50
19 Don Zimmer .40 1.00
20 Ernie Banks 1.00 2.50
21 George Brett 2.00 5.00
22 Gary Carter .60 1.50
23 Gregg Jefferies .40 1.00
24 Harold Baines .60 1.50
25 Ryne Sandberg 2.00 5.00
26 Howard Johnson .40 1.00
27 Jim Abbott .60 1.50
28 Johnny Bench 1.00 2.50
29 Jay Buhner .40 1.00
30 Johnny Podres .40 1.00
31 Jose Canseco .60 1.50
32 Keith Hernandez .40 1.00
33 Lou Brock Cubs .60 1.50
34 Lou Whitaker .40 1.00
35 Mark Fidrych .40 1.00
36 Orlando Cepeda .60 1.50
37 Ozzie Smith 1.25 3.00
38 Paul O'Neill .60 1.50
39 Reggie Jackson .60 1.50
40 Sid Fernandez .40 1.00
41 Tony Gwynn 1.25 3.00
42 Tim Raines .40 1.00
43 Tom Seaver .60 1.50
44 Vida Blue .40 1.00
45 Brady Anderson .40 1.00
46 Bob Brenly .40 1.00
47 Bob Feller .60 1.50
48 Bill Mazeroski .60 1.50
49 Brooks Robinson .60 1.50
50 Harmon Killebrew 1.00 2.50
51 Bob Welch .40 1.00
52 Carl Erskine .40 1.00
53 Dale Murphy 1.00 2.50
54 Denny McLain .40 1.00
55 Dave Magadan .40 1.00
56 Duke Snider .60 1.50
57 Ed Kranepool .40 1.00
58 Frank Robinson .60 1.50
59 Jesus Alou .40 1.00
60 Joe Girardi .40 1.00
61 John Kruk .40 1.00
62 Jimmy Leyland MG .40 1.00
63 Juan Marichal .60 1.50
64 Johnny Pesky .40 1.00
65 Jesse Orosco .40 1.00
66 Ken Singleton .40 1.00
67 Matty Alou .40 1.00
68 Monte Irvin .60 1.50
69 Matt Williams .60 1.50
70 Pedro Guerrero .40 1.00
71 Ron Blomberg .40 1.00
72 Rod Carew .60 1.50
73 Rafael Santana .40 1.00
74 Ralph Kiner .60 1.50
75 Wade Boggs .60 1.50
76 Roger Craig .40 1.00
77 Robin Yount 1.00 2.50
78 Steve Carlton .60 1.50
79 Shawon Dunston .40 1.00
80 Steve Garvey .40 1.00
81 Stan Musial 1.50 4.00
82 Travis Fryman .40 1.00
83 Tito Fuentes .40 1.00
84 Mike Cuellar .40 1.00
85 Roberto Clemente 2.50 6.00
86 Whitey Ford .60 1.50
87 Yogi Berra 1.00 2.50
88 Atlee Hammaker .40 1.00
89 Bill Freehan .40 1.00
90 Brian Cashman GM .40 1.00
91 Bobby Richardson .40 1.00
92 Bob Boone .40 1.00
93 Charlie Hough .40 1.00
94 Glenn Hubbard .40 1.00
95 Grady Little MG .40 1.00
96 Jimmy Piersall .40 1.00
97 Jim Frey MG .40 1.00
98 Jerry Grote .40 1.00
99 Jim Leyritz .40 1.00
100 Nolan Ryan 3.00 8.00
101 Jim Kaat .40 1.00
102 Joe Pepitone .40 1.00
103 J.R. Richard .40 1.00
104 John Candelaria .40 1.00
105 Moose Skowron .40 1.00
106 Rick Cerone .40 1.00
107 Ron Santo .60 1.50
108 Rick Dempsey .40 1.00
109 Roy White .40 1.00
110 Tippy Martinez .40 1.00

2005 Topps Retired Signature Black

*BLACK: 4X TO 10X BASIC
STATED ODDS 1:9 HOBBY, 1:11 RETAIL
STATED PRINT RUN 54 SERIAL #'d SETS
85 Roberto Clemente 60.00 120.00

2005 Topps Retired Signature Gold

*GOLD: .75X TO 2X BASIC
STATED ODDS 1:2 HOBBY/RETAIL
STATED PRINT RUN 500 SERIAL #'d SETS

2005 Topps Retired Signature Autographs

GROUP A ODDS 1:205 HOBBY/RETAIL
GROUP B ODDS 1:35 HOBBY, 1:34 RETAIL
GROUP C ODDS 1:65 HOBBY, 1:64 RETAIL
GROUP D ODDS 1:11 HOBBY/RETAIL
GROUP E ODDS 1:149 HOBBY/RETAIL
GROUP F ODDS 1:5 HOBBY/RETAIL
GROUP G ODDS 1:16 HOBBY/RETAIL
GROUP H ODDS 1:64 HOBBY/RETAIL
GROUP I ODDS 1:4 HOBBY/RETAIL
GROUP J ODDS 1:6 HOBBY/RETAIL
GROUP A PRINT RUNS B/WN 24-35 PER
GROUP B PRINT RUNS B/WN 60-70 PER
GROUP C PRINT RUNS B/WN 170-175 PER
GROUP D PRINT RUN 220 SETS
A-D ARE NOT SERIAL-NUMBERED
A-D PRINT RUNS PROVIDED BY TOPPS
AU PLATE ODDS 1:121 HOBBY
AU PLATE PRINT RUN 1 SET PER COLOR
BLACK-CYAN-MAGENTA-YELLOW ISSUED
NO AU PLATE PRICING DUE TO SCARCITY
AD Andre Dawson D/220 * 10.00 25.00
AH Atlee Hammaker I 4.00 10.00
AK Al Kaline D/220 * 25.00 50.00
AY Anthony Young H 4.00 10.00
BA Brady Anderson F 4.00 10.00
BAF Bill Freehan I 10.00 25.00
BB Brett Butler F 6.00 15.00
BC Brian Cashman GM B/70 * 50.00 100.00
BCR Bobby Richardson F 8.00 20.00
BD Bob Dernier F 6.00 15.00
BEB Bob Brenly F 6.00 15.00
BF Bob Feller D/220 * 12.50 30.00
BJ Bo Jackson B/70 * 75.00 150.00
BM Bill Mazeroski B/70 * 15.00 40.00
BR Brooks Robinson D/220 * 12.00 30.00
BRB Bob Boone F 6.00 15.00
BW Bob Welch F 8.00 20.00
CDH Charlie Hayes F 4.00 10.00
CE Carl Erskine D/220 * 6.00 15.00
CF Carlton Fisk C/170 * 15.00 40.00
CH Charlie Hough I 4.00 10.00
CR Cal Ripken B/70 * 60.00 120.00
CY Carl Yastrzemski B/70 * 60.00 120.00
DBM Dale Murphy F 8.00 20.00
DDM Denny McLain F 8.00 20.00
DES Darryl Strawberry B/70 * 20.00 50.00
DG Dwight Gooden F 6.00 15.00
DJ Davey Johnson B/70 * 15.00 40.00
DJM Dave Magadan F 4.00 10.00
DLB Daryl Boston J 4.00 10.00
DM Don Mattingly B/70 * 60.00 120.00
DS Duke Snider C/170 * 15.00 40.00
DW Dave Winfield B/70 * 15.00 40.00
DZ Don Zimmer D/220 * 8.00 20.00
EK Ed Kranepool F 6.00 15.00
FR Frank Robinson B/70 * 30.00 60.00
GB George Brett B/70 * 75.00 150.00
GC Gary Carter D/220 * 10.00 25.00
GH Glenn Hubbard I 6.00 15.00
GJ Gregg Jefferies F 6.00 15.00
GL Grady Little MG I 4.00 10.00
HB Harold Baines F 6.00 15.00
HJ Howard Johnson D/220 * 6.00 15.00
HK Harmon Killebrew B/70 * 75.00 150.00
JA Jesus Alou F 8.00 20.00
JAA Jim Abbott F 6.00 15.00
JAP Jimmy Piersall J 6.00 15.00
JC Jose Canseco D/220 * 12.50 30.00
JCB Jay Buhner D/220 * 6.00 15.00
JF Jim Frey MG I 4.00 10.00
JG Jerry Grote I 6.00 15.00
JJL Jim Leyritz I 4.00 10.00
JJP Johnny Podres B/70 * 10.00 25.00
JK John Kruk D/220 * 6.00 15.00
JL Jimmy Leyland MG J 6.00 15.00
JLK Jim Kaat I 6.00 15.00
JM Juan Marichal D/220 * 10.00 25.00
JMP Johnny Pesky F 10.00 25.00
JO Jesse Orosco F 6.00 15.00
JP Joe Pepitone J 10.00 25.00
JR J.R. Richard I 6.00 15.00
JRC John Candelaria I 4.00 10.00
JRL Jim Lonborg I 4.00 10.00
KH Keith Hernandez D/220 * 10.00 25.00
KS Ken Singleton G 6.00 15.00
LB Lou Brock Cubs F 15.00 40.00
LW Lou Whitaker C/175 * 25.00 60.00
MA Matty Alou F 6.00 15.00
MC Mike Cuellar J 8.00 20.00
MI Monte Irvin B/70 * 10.00 25.00
MS Moose Skowron I 8.00 20.00
MW Matt Williams B/70 * 20.00 50.00
NR Nolan Ryan A/35 * 60.00 120.00
OC Orlando Cepeda D/220 * 10.00 25.00
OS Ozzie Smith B/70 * 30.00 60.00
PG Pedro Guerrero F 6.00 15.00
PO Paul O'Neill B/70 * 40.00 80.00
RB Ron Blomberg D/220 * 6.00 15.00
RC Rick Cerone I 4.00 10.00
RCC Rod Carew B/70 * 15.00 40.00
RD Ron Darling I 6.00 15.00
REG Ron Gant D/220 * 8.00 20.00
RES Ron Santo I 15.00 40.00
RFS Rafael Santana G 4.00 10.00
RG Rusty Greer B/70 * 8.00 20.00
RJ Reggie Jackson B/60 * 75.00 150.00
RK Ralph Kiner D/220 * 12.50 30.00
RKD Rob Dibble D/220 * 6.00 15.00
RLC Roger Craig G 6.00 15.00
RRD Rick Dempsey I 6.00 15.00
RS Ryne Sandberg C/170 * 20.00 50.00
RW Roy White J 6.00 15.00
RY Robin Yount B/70 * 40.00 80.00
SC Steve Carlton D/220 * 20.00 50.00
SD Shawon Dunston D/220 * 6.00 15.00
SF Sid Fernandez D/220 * 6.00 15.00
SG Steve Garvey F 6.00 15.00
TDF Travis Fryman F 6.00 15.00
TF Tito Fuentes D/220 * 6.00 15.00
TG Tony Gwynn B/70 * 60.00 120.00
TH Toby Harrah G 6.00 15.00
TL Tony LaRussa D/220 * 10.00 25.00
TM Tippy Martinez J 6.00 15.00
TN Tom Niedenfuer E 6.00 15.00
TR Tim Raines B/70 * 20.00 50.00
VB Vida Blue D/220 * 6.00 15.00
WB Wade Boggs C/170 * 8.00 20.00
ZS Zane Smith F 4.00 10.00

2005 Topps Retired Signature Autographs Refractors

GROUP A ODDS 1:788 HOBBY/RETAIL
GROUP B ODDS 1:21 HOBBY/RETAIL
GROUP A PRINT RUN 10 SERIAL #'d SETS
GROUP B PRINT RUN 25 SERIAL #'d SETS
NO GROUP A PRICING DUE TO SCARCITY
AD Andre Dawson B/25 30.00 60.00
AH Atlee Hammaker B/25 20.00 50.00
AK Al Kaline B/25 75.00 200.00
AY Anthony Young B/25 20.00 50.00
BA Brady Anderson B/25 30.00 60.00
BAF Bill Freehan B/25 15.00 40.00
BB Brett Butler B/25 30.00 60.00
BC Brian Cashman GM B/25 60.00 120.00
BCR Bobby Richardson B/25 40.00 80.00
BD Bob Dernier B/25 15.00 40.00
BEB Bob Brenly B/25 30.00 60.00
BF Bob Feller B/25 50.00 100.00
BJ Bo Jackson B/25 75.00 150.00
BM Bill Mazeroski B/25 30.00 60.00
BR Brooks Robinson B/25 25.00 60.00
BRB Bob Boone B/25 30.00 60.00
BW Bob Welch B/25 40.00 80.00
CDH Charlie Hayes B/25 20.00 50.00
CE Carl Erskine B/25 30.00 60.00
CF Carlton Fisk B/25 30.00 60.00
CH Charlie Hough B/25 20.00 50.00
CR Cal Ripken B/25 100.00 200.00
CY Carl Yastrzemski B/25 125.00 200.00
DBM Dale Murphy B/25 30.00 60.00
DDM Denny McLain B/25 20.00 50.00
DES Darryl Strawberry B/25 30.00 60.00
DG Dwight Gooden B/25 30.00 60.00
DJ Davey Johnson B/25 20.00 50.00
DJM Dave Magadan B/25 20.00 50.00
DLB Daryl Boston B/25 20.00 50.00
DM Don Mattingly B/25 125.00 200.00
DS Duke Snider B/25 75.00 150.00
DW Dave Winfield B/25 30.00 60.00
DZ Don Zimmer B/25 15.00 40.00
EK Ed Kranepool B/25 30.00 60.00
FR Frank Robinson B/25 50.00 100.00
GC Gary Carter B/25 30.00 60.00
GH Glenn Hubbard B/25 20.00 50.00
GJ Gregg Jefferies B/25 20.00 50.00
GL Grady Little MG B/25 20.00 50.00
HB Harold Baines B/25 25.00 60.00
HJ Howard Johnson B/25 20.00 50.00
HK Harmon Killebrew B/25 100.00 200.00
JA Jesus Alou B/25 40.00 80.00
JAA Jim Abbott B/25 30.00 60.00
JAP Jimmy Piersall B/25 30.00 60.00
JC Jose Canseco B/25 50.00 100.00
JCB Jay Buhner B/25 30.00 60.00
JF Jim Frey MG B/25 20.00 50.00
JG Jerry Grote B/25 30.00 80.00
JJL Jim Leyritz B/25 20.00 50.00
JJP Johnny Podres B/25 12.50 30.00
JK John Kruk B/25 30.00 60.00
JL Jimmy Leyland MG B/25 30.00 60.00
JLK Jim Kaat B/25 30.00 60.00
JM Juan Marichal B/25 30.00 60.00
JMP Johnny Pesky B/25 50.00 100.00
JO Jesse Orosco B/25 15.00 40.00
JP Joe Pepitone B/25 40.00 100.00
JR J.R. Richard B/25 30.00 60.00
JRC John Candelaria B/25 20.00 50.00
JRL Jim Lonborg B/25 20.00 50.00
KH Keith Hernandez B/25 30.00 60.00
KS Ken Singleton B/25 30.00 60.00
LB Lou Brock Cubs B/25 50.00 100.00
LW Lou Whitaker B/25 40.00 100.00
MA Matty Alou B/25 30.00 60.00
MC Mike Cuellar B/25 30.00 60.00
MI Monte Irvin B/25 40.00 100.00
MS Moose Skowron B/25 30.00 60.00
MW Matt Williams B/25 30.00 60.00
OC Orlando Cepeda B/25 30.00 60.00
PG Pedro Guerrero B/25 30.00 60.00
PO Paul O'Neill B/25 75.00 150.00
RB Ron Blomberg B/25 20.00 50.00
RC Rick Cerone B/25 20.00 50.00
RCC Rod Carew B/25 30.00 60.00
RD Ron Darling B/25 20.00 50.00
REG Ron Gant B/25 40.00 80.00
RES Ron Santo B/25 75.00 150.00
RFS Rafael Santana B/25 20.00 50.00
RG Rusty Greer B/25 10.00 25.00
RJ Reggie Jackson B/25 75.00 150.00
RK Ralph Kiner B/25 40.00 80.00
RKD Rob Dibble B/25 20.00 50.00
RLC Roger Craig B/25 20.00 50.00
RRD Rick Dempsey B/25 15.00 40.00
RS Ryne Sandberg B/25 100.00 175.00
RW Roy White B/25 20.00 50.00
RY Robin Yount B/25 100.00 200.00
SC Steve Carlton B/25 50.00 100.00
SD Shawon Dunston B/25 15.00 40.00
SF Sid Fernandez B/25 20.00 50.00
SG Steve Garvey B/25 15.00 40.00
TDF Travis Fryman B/25 50.00 100.00
TF Tito Fuentes B/25 30.00 60.00
TH Toby Harrah B/25 15.00 40.00
TL Tony LaRussa B/25 30.00 60.00
TM Tippy Martinez B/25 20.00 50.00
TN Tom Niedenfuer B/25 30.00 60.00
TR Tim Raines B/25 30.00 60.00
TS Tom Seaver B/25 100.00 250.00
VB Vida Blue B/25 20.00 50.00
WB Wade Boggs B/25 50.00 100.00
ZS Zane Smith B/25 20.00 50.00

2005 Topps Retired Signature Co-Signers

GROUP A ODDS 1:6295 H, 1:6192 R
GROUP B ODDS 1:224 HOBBY/RETAIL
GROUP A PRINT RUN 9 SERIAL #'d SETS
GROUP B PRINT RUN 49 SERIAL #'d SETS
NO GROUP A PRICING DUE TO SCARCITY
REFRACTOR ODDS 1:9443 H, 1:12,384 R
REFRACTOR PRINT RUN 1 SERIAL #'d SET
NO REF PRICING DUE TO SCARCITY
BF J.Bench/C.Fisk B/49 75.00 150.00
BS W.Boggs/R.Sandberg B/49 75.00 150.00
GF B.Gibson/W.Ford B/49 60.00 120.00
MS S.Musial/D.Snider B/49 100.00 175.00
SR T.Seaver/N.Ryan B/49 250.00 500.00

2005 Topps Rookie Cup

COMP.SET w/o AU's (150) 20.00 40.00
COMMON CARD (1-150) .40 1.00
COMMON RC (1-150) .40 1.00
COMMON AUTO (151-160) 4.00 10.00

AU 151-160 ODDS 1:62 H, 1:155 R
1-150 OVERALL PLATE ODDS 1:251 H
151-160 OVERALL AU PLATE ODDS 1:3752 H
BLACK-CYAN-MAGENTA-YELLOW ISSUED
NO PLATE PRICING DUE TO SCARCITY
1 Pat Corrales .40 1.00
2 Ron Santo .60 1.50
3 Joe Torre .60 1.50
4 Boog Powell .40 1.00
5 Tom Tresh .40 1.00
6 Jonny Gomes .40 1.00
7 Rico Carty .40 1.00
8 Bert Campaneris .40 1.00
9 Tony Oliva .40 1.00
10 Ron Swoboda .40 1.00
11 Tony Perez .60 1.50
12 Joe Morgan .60 1.50
13 Davey Johnson .40 1.00
14 Cleon Jones .40 1.00
15 Tom Seaver .60 1.50
16 Rod Carew .60 1.50
17 Rick Monday .40 1.00
18 Johnny Bench 1.00 2.50
19 Bobby Cox .40 1.00
20 Jerry Koosman .40 1.00
21 Al Oliver .40 1.00
22 Lou Piniella .40 1.00
23 Larry Bowa .40 1.00
24 Chris Chambliss .40 1.00
25 Bill Buckner .40 1.00
26 Don Baylor .40 1.00
27 Buddy Bell .40 1.00
28 Carlton Fisk .60 1.50
29 Gary Matthews .40 1.00
30 Dave Lopes .40 1.00
31 Bob Boone .40 1.00
32 Bill Madlock .40 1.00
33 Claudell Washington .40 1.00
34 Jim Rice .60 1.50
35 Gary Carter .60 1.50
36 Willie Randolph .40 1.00
37 Chet Lemon .40 1.00
38 Andre Dawson .60 1.50
39 Eddie Murray .60 1.50
40 Paul Molitor 1.00 2.50
41 Ozzie Smith 1.25 3.00
42 Jeffrey Leonard .40 1.00
43 Lonnie Smith .40 1.00
44 Mookie Wilson .40 1.00
45 Tim Wallach .40 1.00
46 Tim Raines .60 1.50
47 Fernando Valenzuela .40 1.00
48 Cal Ripken 3.00 8.00
49 Ryne Sandberg 2.00 5.00
50 Willie McGee .40 1.00
51 Darryl Strawberry .40 1.00
52 Julio Franco .40 1.00
53 Brook Jacoby .40 1.00
54 Dwight Gooden .40 1.00
55 Roger McDowell .40 1.00
56 Ozzie Guillen .40 1.00
57 Vince Coleman .40 1.00
58 Pete Incaviglia .40 1.00
59 Wally Joyner .40 1.00
60 Jose Canseco .60 1.50
61 Cory Snyder .40 1.00
62 Devon White .40 1.00
63 Walt Weiss .40 1.00
64 Mark Grace .60 1.50
65 Ron Gant .40 1.00
66 Chris Sabo .40 1.00
67 Jay Buhner .40 1.00
68 Gary Sheffield .40 1.00
69 Gregg Jefferies .40 1.00
70 Ken Griffey Jr. 2.00 5.00
71 Tom Gordon .40 1.00
72 Jim Abbott .40 1.00
73 Dave Justice .40 1.00
74 Larry Walker .60 1.50
75 Sandy Alomar Jr. .40 1.00
76 Chuck Knoblauch .40 1.00
77 Jeff Bagwell .60 1.50
78 Luis Gonzalez .40 1.00
79 Ivan Rodriguez .60 1.50
80 Eric Karros .40 1.00
81 Jeff Kent .40 1.00
82 Kenny Lofton .40 1.00
83 Moises Alou .40 1.00
84 Reggie Sanders .40 1.00
85 Jeff Conine .40 1.00
86 J.T. Snow .40 1.00
87 Tim Salmon .40 1.00
88 Mike Piazza 1.00 2.50
89 Manny Ramirez 1.00 2.50
90 Ryan Klesko .40 1.00
91 Javy Lopez .40 1.00
92 Chipper Jones 1.00 2.50
93 Ray Durham .40 1.00
94 Garret Anderson .40 1.00
95 Shawn Green .40 1.00
96 Hideo Nomo 1.00 2.50
97 Jermaine Dye .40 1.00
98 Tony Clark .40 1.00
99 Joe Randa .40 1.00
100 Derek Jeter 2.50 6.00
101 Jason Kendall .40 1.00
102 Billy Wagner .40 1.00
103 Andruw Jones .40 1.00
104 Dmitri Young .40 1.00
105 Scott Rolen .60 1.50
106 Nomar Garciaparra .60 1.50
107 Jose Cruz Jr. .40 1.00
108 Scott Hatteberg .40 1.00
109 Mark Kotsay .40 1.00
110 Todd Helton .60 1.50
111 Miguel Cairo .40 1.00
112 Maggio Ordonez .60 1.50
113 Kerry Wood .40 1.00
114 Preston Wilson .40 1.00
115 Alex Gonzalez .40 1.00
116 Carlos Beltran .60 1.50
117 Rafael Furcal .40 1.00
118 Pat Burrell .40 1.00
119 Adam Kennedy .40 1.00
120 Terrence Long .40 1.00
121 Jay Payton .40 1.00
122 Bengie Molina .40 1.00
123 Albert Pujols 1.25 3.00
124 Craig Wilson .40 1.00
125 Alfonso Soriano .60 1.50
126 Jimmy Rollins .60 1.50
127 Adam Dunn .60 1.50
128 Ichiro Suzuki 1.25 3.00
129 Roy Oswalt .60 1.50
130 C.C. Sabathia .60 1.50
131 Brad Wilkerson .40 1.00
132 Nick Johnson .40 1.00
133 Eric Hinske .40 1.00
134 Austin Kearns .40 1.00
135 Dontrelle Willis .40 1.00
136 Mark Teixeira .60 1.50
137 Rocco Baldelli .40 1.00
138 Scott Podsednik .40 1.00
139 Brandon Webb .60 1.50
140 Jason Bay .40 1.00
141 Adam LaRoche .40 1.00
142 Khalil Greene .40 1.00
143 Joe Mauer .75 2.00
144 Matt Holliday 1.00 2.50
145 Chad Tracy .40 1.00
146 Garrett Atkins .40 1.00
147 Tadahito Iguchi RC .60 1.50
148 Russ Adams .40 1.00
149 Huston Street .40 1.00
150 Dan Johnson .40 1.00
151 J. Brent Cox AU RC 5.00 12.00
152 John Drennen AU RC 4.00 10.00
153 Ryan Tucker AU RC 4.00 10.00
154 Yunel Escobar AU RC 5.00 12.00
155 Jacob Marceaux AU RC 4.00 10.00
156 Mark Pawelek AU RC 4.00 10.00
157 Brandon Snyder AU RC 4.00 10.00
158 Wade Townsend AU RC 4.00 10.00
159 Troy Tulowitzki AU RC 12.00 30.00
160 Kevin Whelan AU RC 4.00 10.00

2005 Topps Rookie Cup Blue

*BLUE 1-150: 3X TO 8X BASIC
*BLUE 1-150: 2X TO 5X BASIC RC
1-150 ODDS 1:29 HOBBY, 1:130 RETAIL
*BLUE 151-160: 1X TO 2.5X BASIC AU
151-160 AU ODDS 1:548 H, 1:1385 R
STATED PRINT RUN 50 SERIAL #'d SETS

2005 Topps Rookie Cup Green

*GREEN 1-150: 2X TO 5X BASIC
*BLUE 1-150: 1.25X TO 3X BASIC RC
1-150 ODDS 1:8 HOBBY, 1:33 RETAIL
1-150 PRINT RUN 199 SERIAL #'d SETS
*GREEN 151-160: .75X TO 2X BASIC AU
151-160 AU ODDS 1:274 H, 1:703 R
151-160 PRINT RUN 99 SERIAL #'d SETS

2005 Topps Rookie Cup Orange

*ORANGE 1-150: 1.25X TO 3X BASIC
*BLUE 1-150: .75X TO 2X BASIC RC
1-150 ODDS 1:4 HOBBY, 1:18 RETAIL
1-150 PRINT RUN 399 SERIAL #'d SETS
*ORANGE 151-160: .4X TO 1X BASIC AU
151-160 AU ODDS 1:91 H, 1:232 R
151-160 PRINT RUN 299 SERIAL #'d SETS

2005 Topps Rookie Cup Red

*RED 1-150: 1X TO 2.5X BASIC
*BLUE 1-150: .6X TO 1.5X BASIC RC
1-150 RANDOM INSERTS IN PACKS
1-150 PRINT RUN 499 SERIAL #'d SETS
*RED 151-160: .4X TO 1X BASIC AU
151-160 AU ODDS 1:68 H, 1:174 R
151-160 PRINT RUN 399 SERIAL #'d SETS

2005 Topps Rookie Cup Silver

1-150 ODDS 1:300 HOBBY, 1:1200 RETAIL
151-160 AU ODDS 1:5483 H, 1:13,454 R
STATED PRINT RUN 5 SERIAL #'d SETS
NO PRICING DUE TO SCARCITY

2005 Topps Rookie Cup Yellow

*YELLOW 1-150: 1.5X TO 4X BASIC
*BLUE 1-150: 1X TO 2.5X BASIC RC
1-150 ODDS 1:5 HOBBY, 1:21 RETAIL
1-150 PRINT RUN 299 SERIAL #'d SETS
*YELLOW 151-160: .5X TO 1.2X BASIC AU
151-160 AU ODDS 1:137 H, 1:349 R
151-160 PRINT RUN 199 SERIAL #'d SETS

2005 Topps Rookie Cup Autographs

GROUP A ODDS 1:677 H, 1:1427 R
GROUP B ODDS 1:45 H, 1:51 R
GOLD ODDS 1:5281 HOBBY
GOLD PRINT RUN 1 SERIAL #'d SET
NO GOLD PRICING DUE TO SCARCITY
SILVER ODDS 1:2458 H, 1:3622 R
SILVER PRINT RUN 5 SERIAL #'d SETS
NO SILVER PRICING DUE TO SCARCITY
EXCHANGE DEADLINE 12/31/07
AD Andre Dawson B 6.00 15.00
AJ Andruw Jones A 10.00 25.00
AP Albert Pujols A 150.00 250.00
BP Boog Powell B 6.00 15.00
BW Brad Wilkerson B 4.00 10.00
CJ Chipper Jones B 20.00 50.00
CK Chuck Knoblauch B 6.00 15.00
CR Cal Ripken A 60.00 120.00
DJ Davey Johnson B 6.00 15.00
DJ Dave Justice B 6.00 15.00
DRJ Dan Johnson B 6.00 15.00
DS Darryl Strawberry B 6.00 15.00
DW Dontrelle Willis B 4.00 10.00
EK Eric Karros B 6.00 15.00
GS Gary Sheffield A 8.00 20.00
JB Johnny Bench A 30.00 60.00
JBA Jason Bay B 6.00 15.00
JR Jim Rice A 10.00 25.00
JT Joe Torre A 30.00 60.00
MG Mark Grace B 6.00 15.00
MK Mark Kotsay B 4.00 10.00
MR Manny Ramirez A 40.00 80.00
PM Paul Molitor A 12.00 30.00
RF Rafael Furcal B 6.00 15.00
RM Roger McDowell B 4.00 10.00
RS Ron Swoboda B 6.00 15.00
RSA Ron Santo B 10.00 25.00
TS Tom Seaver A 12.00 30.00

2005 Topps Rookie Cup Dual Autographs

STATED ODDS 1:118 HOBBY
BW J.Bay/D.Willis 12.50 30.00
CS J.Cox/T.Seaver 25.00 60.00
DR J.Drennen/M.Ramirez 8.00 20.00
EF Y.Escobar/R.Furcal 10.00 25.00
GS M.Grace/R.Santo 40.00 80.00
MM J.Marceaux/R.McDowell 8.00 20.00
PG M.Pawelek/M.Grace 8.00 20.00
RTW R.Tucker/D.Willis 12.50 30.00
SP B.Snyder/B.Powell 10.00 25.00
TS W.Townsend/T.Seaver 12.00 30.00
TW T.Tulowitzki/W.Weiss 15.00 40.00
WD B.Wilkerson/A.Dawson 10.00 25.00
WM K.Whelan/R.McDowell 12.50 30.00

2005 Topps Rookie Cup Reprints

COMPLETE SET (150) 40.00 80.00
*REPRINTS: .75X TO 2X BASIC
*REPRINTS: .4X TO 1X BASIC RC
TWO PER HOBBY PACK
ONE PER RETAIL PACK
CHROME ODDS 1:2 BOX-LOADERS
CHROME PRINT RUN 25 #'d SETS
NO CHROME PRICING DUE TO SCARCITY
CHROME REF ODDS 1:3 BOX-LOADERS
CHROME REF PRINT RUN 15 #'d SETS
NO CHR.REF PRICING DUE TO SCARCITY
CHROME GOLD ODDS 1:42 BOX-LOADERS
CHROME GOLD PRINT RUN 1 #'d SET
NO CHR.GOLD PRICING DUE TO SCARCITY

1997 Topps Screenplays

The 1997 Topps Screenplays set was issued in one series totalling 20 cards and distributed in one-card packs with a suggested retail price of 9.99. Each card displays 24 frames of actual game footage with the help of Kodak's revolutionary Kodamotion technology. The cards have a dura clear back. Each card is individually packaged in a fold metal finish collectible tin that resembles a movie reel canister and features a full-color image of the player inside.The tin contains a display stand for it and the card and includes player info, bio, and stats. The cards are unnumbered and checklisted below in alphabetical order.

COMPLETE SET (21) 30.00 80.00
PRICES BELOW ARE FOR TIN/CARD COMBO
PLAYER IS ON BOTTOM OF EACH TIN PACK
1 Jeff Bagwell 1.25 3.00
2 Albert Belle .75 2.00
3 Barry Bonds 5.00 12.00
4 Andres Galarraga .75 2.00
5 Nomar Garciaparra 3.00 8.00
6 Juan Gonzalez .75 2.00
7 Ken Griffey Jr. 4.00 10.00
8 Tony Gwynn 2.50 6.00
9 Derek Jeter 5.00 12.00
10 Randy Johnson 2.00 5.00
11 Andruw Jones 1.25 3.00
12 Chipper Jones 2.00 5.00
13 Kenny Lofton .75 2.00
14 Mark McGwire 5.00 12.00
15 Paul Molitor .75 2.00
16 Hideo Nomo 2.00 5.00
17A Cal Ripken Batting 6.00 15.00
17B Cal Ripken Fielding 6.00 15.00
18 Sammy Sosa 2.00 5.00
19 Frank Thomas 2.00 5.00
20 Jim Thome 1.25 3.00

1997 Topps Screenplays Tins

COMPLETE SET (21) 10.00 25.00
*TINS: .08X TO .2X OF SCREENPLAYS
TINS DIST.AS COLLECTIBLE PACKAGING

1997 Topps Screenplays Premium Series

COMPLETE SET (6) 40.00 100.00
STATED ODDS 1:21
PRICES BELOW ARE FOR TIN/CARD COMBO
ONE SPECIAL INSERT TIN PER SEALED BOX
1 Ken Griffey Jr. 10.00 25.00
2 Chipper Jones 4.00 10.00
3 Mike Piazza 8.00 20.00
4 Cal Ripken 15.00 40.00
5 Frank Thomas 4.00 10.00
6 Larry Walker 4.00 10.00

1997 Topps Screenplays Private Screenings

1 Frank Thomas 8.00 20.00
2 Jim Thome 5.00 12.00
3 Bernie Williams 5.00 12.00

2003 Topps Shoebox

COMP.FACT SET (96) 20.00 50.00
1 Willie Mays 1.00 2.50
2 Monte Irvin .30 .75
3 Bill Mazeroski .30 .75
4 Phil Rizzuto .30 .75
5 Hank Sauer .20 .50
6 Hank Bauer .20 .50
7 Ted Kluszewski .30 .75
8 Robin Roberts .30 .75
9 Red Schoendienst .30 .75
10 Bob Feller .30 .75
11 Duke Snider .30 .75
12 Bobby Thomson .30 .75
13 Hoyt Wilhelm .30 .75
14 John Podres .20 .50
15 Whitey Ford .30 .75
16 Ralph Kiner .30 .75
17 Harmon Killebrew .50 1.25
18 Luis Aparicio .30 .75
19 Bobby Richardson .20 .50
20 Don Newcombe .20 .50
21 Frank Robinson .30 .75
22 Brooks Robinson .30 .75
23 Stan Musial .75 2.00
24 Orlando Cepeda .30 .75
25 Willie McCovey .30 .75
26 Maury Wills .20 .50
27 Carl Yastrzemski .75 2.00
28 Juan Marichal .30 .75
29 Boog Powell .20 .50
30 Willie Stargell .30 .75
31 Bert Campaneris .20 .50
32 Tug McGraw .20 .50
33 Joe Morgan .30 .75
34 Tony Perez .30 .75
35 Luis Tiant .20 .50
36 Fergie Jenkins .30 .75
37 Jim Palmer .30 .75
38 Rod Carew .30 .75
39 Tom Seaver .30 .75
40 Nolan Ryan 1.50 4.00
41 Rollie Fingers .30 .75
42 Reggie Jackson .30 .75
43 Gaylord Perry .30 .75
44 Al Oliver .20 .50
45 Lou Brock .30 .75
46 Johnny Bench .50 1.25
47 Paul Blair .20 .50
48 Phil Niekro .30 .75
49 Bill Buckner .20 .50
50 Darrell Evans .20 .50
51 Bert Blyleven .30 .75
52 Dave Concepcion .20 .50
53 George Foster .20 .50
54 Bob Grich .20 .50
55 Greg Luzinski .20 .50
56 Ron Cey .20 .50
57 Cecil Cooper .20 .50
58 Carlton Fisk .30 .75
59 Mickey Rivers .20 .50
60 Dwight Evans .20 .50
61 Rich Gossage .30 .75
62 Mike Schmidt .75 2.00
63 Dave Parker .20 .50
64 Gary Carter .30 .75
65 Robin Yount .50 1.25
66 Dennis Eckersley .30 .75
67 Ron Guidry .20 .50
68 Jack Clark .20 .50
69 Andre Dawson .30 .75
70 Mark Fidrych .20 .50
Used the League Leader Card
71 Bruce Sutter .30 .75
72 Willie Hernandez .20 .50
73 Ozzie Smith .60 1.50
74 Kirk Gibson .20 .50
75 Don Mattingly 1.00 2.50
76 Joe Carter .20 .50
77 Kirby Puckett .50 1.25
78 Dale Murphy .50 1.25
79 Keith Hernandez .20 .50
80 Tony Armas .20 .50
81 Walt Weiss .20 .50
82 Bill Madlock .20 .50
83 Bo Jackson .50 1.25
84 Buddy Bell .20 .50
85 Dwight Gooden .20 .50
86 Eric Davis .20 .50
87 George Bell .20 .50
88 Harold Reynolds .20 .50
89 Jim Rice .30 .75
90 Ken Griffey .20 .50
91 Lee Smith .20 .50
92 Jose Canseco .30 .75
93 Lance Parrish .20 .50
94 Paul O'Neill .30 .75
95 Paul Molitor .50 1.25
96 Alan Trammell .30 .75

2015 Topps Strata Autographs

OVERALL AUTOS ODDS 1:1 HOBBY
EXCHANGE DEADLINE 11/30/2017
SAAB Archie Bradley 3.00 8.00
SABB Brandon Belt 5.00 12.00
SABS Blake Swihart 5.00 12.00
SACKR Corey Kluber 4.00 10.00
SACRO Carlos Rodon 8.00 20.00
SAFL Francisco Lindor 20.00 50.00
SAJA Jose Altuve 15.00 40.00
SAJL Jake Lamb 5.00 12.00
SAJP Joc Pederson 6.00 15.00
SAJS Jorge Soler 5.00 12.00
SAKG Kendall Graveman 3.00 8.00
SAMG Mark Grace 8.00 20.00
SAMTR Michael Taylor 3.00 8.00
SANS Noah Syndergaard 12.00 30.00
SARI Raisel Iglesias 4.00 10.00
SASG Sonny Gray 4.00 10.00
SAVCA DJ LeMahieu 10.00 25.00
SAYG Yimi Garcia 3.00 8.00
SAYGS Yan Gomes 3.00 8.00
SAYT Yasmany Tomas 6.00 15.00

2015 Topps Strata Autographs Black

*BLACK: .6X TO 1.5X BASIC
STATED ODDS 1:12 HOBBY
STATED PRINT RUN 50 SER.#'d SETS
EXCHANGE DEADLINE 11/30/2017
SAAGN Alex Gordon 12.00 30.00
SAAGZ Adrian Gonzalez 8.00 20.00
SABBU Byron Buxton EXCH 25.00 60.00
SABW Bernie Williams 15.00 40.00
SACC Carlos Correa 60.00 150.00
SACF Carlton Fisk 20.00 50.00
SACH Cole Hamels 6.00 15.00
SACKW Clayton Kershaw 40.00 100.00
SACRN Cal Ripken Jr. 50.00 120.00
SAEE Edwin Encarnacion 8.00 20.00
SAEM Edgar Martinez 6.00 15.00
SAGM Greg Maddux EXCH 50.00 120.00
SAHA Hank Aaron 150.00 300.00
SAJB Johnny Bench 30.00 80.00
SAJG Joey Gallo 8.00 20.00
SAJK Jung Ho Kang EXCH 8.00 20.00
SAKB Kris Bryant 125.00 300.00
SALG Luis Gonzalez 5.00 12.00
SANR Nolan Ryan 40.00 100.00
SAPG Paul Goldschmidt 20.00 50.00
SARC Rusney Castillo 6.00 15.00
SARH Rickey Henderson 40.00 100.00
SARJ Randy Johnson 40.00 100.00
SASK Sandy Koufax 200.00 300.00
SASP Salvador Perez 15.00 40.00

2015 Topps Strata Autographs Blue

*BLUE: .5X TO 1.2X BASIC
STATED ODDS 1:8 HOBBY
STATED PRINT RUN 99 SER.#'d SETS
EXCHANGE DEADLINE 11/30/2017
SAAGN Alex Gordon 10.00 25.00
SAAGZ Adrian Gonzalez 6.00 15.00
SABBU Byron Buxton EXCH 20.00 50.00
SABW Bernie Williams 12.00 30.00
SACF Carlton Fisk 15.00 40.00
SACH Cole Hamels 5.00 12.00
SAEE Edwin Encarnacion 6.00 15.00
SAEM Edgar Martinez 5.00 12.00
SAKB Kris Bryant 100.00 250.00
SALG Luis Gonzalez 4.00 10.00
SARC Rusney Castillo 5.00 12.00
SASP Salvador Perez 12.00 30.00

2015 Topps Strata Autographs Gold

*GOLD: .6X TO 1.5X BASIC
STATED ODDS 1:24 HOBBY
STATED PRINT RUN 25 SER.#'d SETS
EXCHANGE DEADLINE 11/30/2017
SAAGN Alex Gordon 12.00 30.00
SAAGZ Adrian Gonzalez 8.00 20.00
SABBU Byron Buxton EXCH 25.00 60.00
SABW Bernie Williams 15.00 40.00
SACC Carlos Correa 60.00 150.00
SACF Carlton Fisk 20.00 50.00
SACH Cole Hamels 6.00 15.00
SACKW Clayton Kershaw 40.00 100.00
SACRN Cal Ripken Jr. 50.00 120.00
SAEE Edwin Encarnacion 8.00 20.00
SAEM Edgar Martinez 6.00 15.00
SAGM Greg Maddux EXCH 50.00 120.00
SAHA Hank Aaron 150.00 300.00
SAJB Johnny Bench 30.00 80.00
SAJG Joey Gallo 8.00 20.00
SAJK Jung Ho Kang EXCH 8.00 20.00
SAKB Kris Bryant 125.00 300.00
SALG Luis Gonzalez 5.00 12.00
SAMTT Mike Trout 200.00 400.00
SANR Nolan Ryan 40.00 100.00
SAPG Paul Goldschmidt 20.00 50.00
SARC Rusney Castillo 6.00 15.00
SARH Rickey Henderson 40.00 100.00
SARJ Randy Johnson 40.00 100.00
SASK Sandy Koufax 200.00 300.00
SASP Salvador Perez 15.00 40.00

2015 Topps Strata Autographs Green

*GREEN: .5X TO 1.2X BASIC
STATED ODDS 1:9 HOBBY
STATED PRINT RUN 75 SER.#'d SETS
EXCHANGE DEADLINE 11/30/2017
SAAGN Alex Gordon 10.00 25.00
SAAGZ Adrian Gonzalez 6.00 15.00
SABBU Byron Buxton EXCH 20.00 50.00
SABW Bernie Williams 12.00 30.00
SACC Carlos Correa 50.00 120.00
SACF Carlton Fisk 15.00 40.00
SACH Cole Hamels 5.00 12.00
SACKW Clayton Kershaw 30.00 80.00
SACRN Cal Ripken Jr. 40.00 100.00
SAEE Edwin Encarnacion 6.00 15.00
SAEM Edgar Martinez 5.00 12.00
SAGM Greg Maddux EXCH 40.00 100.00
SAJG Joey Gallo 6.00 15.00
SAJK Jung Ho Kang EXCH 6.00 15.00
SAKB Kris Bryant 100.00 250.00
SALG Luis Gonzalez 4.00 10.00
SANR Nolan Ryan 30.00 80.00
SAPG Paul Goldschmidt 15.00 40.00
SARC Rusney Castillo 5.00 12.00
SARJ Randy Johnson 30.00 80.00
SASP Salvador Perez 12.00 30.00

2015 Topps Strata Autographs Orange

*ORANGE: .5X TO 1.2X BASIC
STATED ODDS 1:8 HOBBY
STATED PRINT RUN 125 SER.#'d SETS
EXCHANGE DEADLIN 11/30/2017
SABBU Byron Buxton EXCH 20.00 50.00
SAEE Edwin Encarnacion 6.00 15.00
SAEM Edgar Martinez 5.00 12.00
SALG Luis Gonzalez 4.00 10.00
SARC Rusney Castillo 5.00 12.00
SASP Salvador Perez 12.00 30.00

2015 Topps Strata Clearly Authentic Autograph Relics

STARTED ODDS 1:6 HOBBY
EXCHANGE DEADLINE 11/30/2017
CAARAG Adrian Gonzalez 8.00 20.00
CAARARI Anthony Rizzo 15.00 40.00
CAARBW Blake Swihart 6.00 15.00
CAARCY Christian Yelich 15.00 40.00
CAARDGO Dee Gordon 5.00 12.00
CAARDPA Dustin Pedroia 20.00 50.00
CAARJF Jose Fernandez 30.00 80.00
CAARJHL Jason Hammel 6.00 15.00
CAARJSR Jorge Soler 8.00 20.00
CAARKB Kris Bryant 100.00 200.00
CAARMTA Mark Teixeira 6.00 15.00
CAARPG Paul Goldschmidt 12.00 30.00
CAARPS Pablo Sandoval 8.00 20.00
CAARRP Rick Porcello 6.00 15.00
CAARSG Sonny Gray 6.00 15.00
CAARSM Steven Matz 6.00 15.00
CAARSS Steven Souza Jr. 6.00 15.00
CAARVM Victor Martinez 8.00 20.00
CAARYT Yasmany Tomas 6.00 15.00

2015 Topps Strata Clearly Authentic Autograph Relics Black

*BLACK: 1X TO 2.5X BASIC
STATED ODDS 1:19 HOBBY
STATED PRINT RUN 50 SER.#'d SETS
EXCHANGE DEADLINE 11/30/2017
CAARCKW Clayton Kershaw 60.00 150.00
CAARHR Hanley Ramirez 15.00 40.00
CAARMH Matt Harvey EXCH 25.00 60.00
CAARMTT Mike Trout 150.00 300.00
CAARRB Ryan Braun 25.00 60.00
CAARRCO Robinson Cano 20.00 50.00

2015 Topps Strata Clearly Authentic Autograph Relics Blue

*BLUE: .5X TO 1.2X BASIC
STATED ODDS 1:13 HOBBY
STATED PRINT RUN 99 SER.#'d SETS
EXCHANGE DEADLINE 11/30/2017

2015 Topps Strata Clearly Authentic Autograph Relics Gold

*GOLD: 1.2X TO 3X BASIC
STATED ODDS 1:38 HOBBY
STATED PRINT RUN 25 SER.#'d SETS
EXCHANGE DEADLINE 11/30/2017
CAARCKW Clayton Kershaw 75.00 200.00
CAARHR Hanley Ramirez 20.00 50.00
CAARMH Matt Harvey EXCH 50.00 120.00
CAARMTT Mike Trout 200.00 400.00
CAARRB Ryan Braun 30.00 80.00
CAARRCO Robinson Cano 25.00 60.00

2015 Topps Strata Clearly Authentic Autograph Relics Green

*GREEN: .5X TO 1.2X BASIC
STATED ODDS 1:13 HOBBY
STATED PRINT RUN 75 SER.#'d SETS
EXCHANGE DEADLINE 11/30/2017
CAARCKW Clayton Kershaw 30.00 80.00
CAARHR Hanley Ramirez 8.00 20.00
CAARMH Matt Harvey EXCH 20.00 50.00
CAARRB Ryan Braun 12.00 30.00
CAARRCO Robinson Cano 15.00 40.00

2015 Topps Strata Clearly Authentic Relics

STARTED ODDS 1:5 HOBBY
*BLUE/99: .5X TO 1.2X BASIC
*GREEN/75: .6X TO 1.5X BASIC
*BLACK/50: .75X TO 2X BASIC
*GOLD/25: 1X TO 2.5X BASIC
CARCAG Alex Guerrero 4.00 10.00
CARCAM Andrew McCutchen 4.00 10.00
CARCBH Billy Hamilton 4.00 10.00
CARCCBZ Clay Buchholz 3.00 8.00
CARCCK Craig Kimbrel 4.00 10.00
CARCCU Chase Utley 4.00 10.00
CARCDJ Derek Jeter 12.00 30.00
CARCDN Derek Norris 3.00 8.00
CARCDO David Ortiz 5.00 12.00
CARCEH Eric Hosmer 4.00 10.00
CARCFH Felix Hernandez 5.00 12.00
CARCGC Gerrit Cole 5.00 12.00
CARCIC Ichiro Suzuki 6.00 15.00
CARCJB Jose Bautista 4.00 10.00
CARCJR Jose Reyes 4.00 10.00
CARCJS Jeff Samardzija 3.00 8.00
CARCJU Justin Upton 4.00 10.00
CARCMB Madison Bumgarner 6.00 15.00
CARCMM Mike Moustakas 4.00 10.00
CARCMTA Masahiro Tanaka 6.00 15.00
CARCPF Prince Fielder 4.00 10.00
CARCSS Stephen Strasburg 5.00 12.00
CARCWM Will Middlebrooks 3.00 8.00
CARCYP Yasiel Puig 6.00 15.00
CARCZG Zack Greinke 4.00 10.00

2015 Topps Strata Signature Patches

STATED ODDS 1:18 HOBBY
STATED PRINT RUN 25 SER.#'d SETS
EXCHANGE DEADLINE 11/30/2017
SSPI Ichiro Suzuki 250.00 500.00
SSPAC Alex Colome 20.00 50.00
SSPACB Alex Cobb 20.00 50.00
SSPAG Adrian Gonzalez 40.00 100.00
SSPBB Brandon Belt 40.00 100.00
SSPBH Bryce Harper 100.00 250.00
SSPBP Buster Posey 200.00 400.00
SSPBW Bernie Williams 100.00 250.00
SSPCK Clayton Kershaw EXCH 150.00 300.00
SSPDL DJ LeMahieu 40.00 100.00
SSPDO David Ortiz 100.00 200.00
SSPDW David Wright EXCH 60.00 150.00
SSPEE Edwin Encarnacion 30.00 80.00
SSPEL Evan Longoria 25.00 60.00
SSPFF Freddie Freeman 40.00 100.00
SSPGH Greg Holland EXCH 30.00 80.00
SSPJA Jose Altuve 25.00 60.00
SSPJD Jacob deGrom 100.00 250.00
SSPJF Jose Fernandez 30.00 80.00
SSPJR Josh Reddick EXCH 20.00 50.00
SSPJS John Smoltz 100.00 200.00
SSPJV Joey Votto 50.00 120.00
SSPKG Ken Griffey Jr. 250.00 400.00
SSPKP Kevin Plawecki 20.00 50.00
SSPMA Matt Adams 40.00 100.00
SSPMC Matt Cain 40.00 100.00
SSPMF Maikel Franco 60.00 150.00
SSPMH Matt Harvey EXCH 50.00 120.00
SSPMM Manny Machado 125.00 250.00
SSPMP Mike Piazza 125.00 250.00
SSPMT Mike Trout 300.00 500.00
SSPMW Michael Wacha 30.00 80.00
SSPMZ Mike Zunino 20.00 50.00
SSPPF Prince Fielder 25.00 60.00
SSPPS Pablo Sandoval 30.00 80.00
SSPRB Ryan Braun 25.00 60.00
SSPRH Rickey Henderson 40.00 100.00
SSPRJ Reggie Jackson 30.00 80.00
SSPRP Rafael Palmeiro 25.00 60.00
SSPSG Sonny Gray 25.00 60.00
SSPTR Tyson Ross 20.00 50.00
SSPVM Victor Martinez 20.00 50.00
SSPYC Yoenis Cespedes 25.00 60.00
SSPYT Yasmany Tomas 25.00 60.00

2015 Topps Strata Signatures

STATED ODDS 1:16 HOBBY
EXCHANGE DEADLINE 11/30/2017
SSBJ Bo Jackson 60.00 150.00
SSCK Corey Kluber 8.00 20.00
SSCR Carlos Rodon 15.00 40.00
SSDL DJ LeMahieu 12.00 30.00
SSFF Freddie Freeman 15.00 40.00
SSFT Frank Thomas 50.00 120.00
SSGS George Springer 12.00 30.00
SSJB Johnny Bench 40.00 100.00
SSJG Joey Gallo 10.00 25.00
SSJP Joc Pederson 12.00 30.00
SSKB Kris Bryant 100.00 200.00
SSKP Kevin Plawecki 6.00 15.00
SSMG Mark Grace 20.00 50.00
SSMP Mike Piazza 50.00 120.00
SSMTA Mark Teixeira 15.00 40.00
SSOS Ozzie Smith 20.00 50.00
SSRC Roger Clemens 50.00 120.00
SSSM Shelby Miller 8.00 20.00
SSSP Salvador Perez 8.00 20.00
SSTG Tom Glavine 60.00 150.00

2015 Topps Strata Signatures Gold

*GOLD: .5X TO 1.2X BASIC
STATED ODDS 1:45 HOBBY
STATED PRINT RUN 25 SER.#'d SETS
EXCHANGE DEADLINE 11/30/2017
SSDM Don Mattingly 75.00 200.00
SSIC Ichiro Suzuki 300.00 500.00
SSJS John Smoltz 40.00 100.00
SSRY Robin Yount 60.00 150.00
SSTG Tom Glavine 60.00 150.00

2016 Topps Strata Autographs

OVERALL AUTOS ODDS 1:1 HOBBY
EXCHANGE DEADLINE 7/31/2018
SAAM Andrew Miller 4.00 10.00
SAAN Aaron Nola 6.00 15.00
SAAR Anthony Rizzo 20.00 50.00
SABJ Brian Johnson 3.00 8.00
SABW Billy Wagner 5.00 12.00
SACE Carl Edwards Jr. 4.00 10.00
SAFL Francisco Lindor 20.00 50.00
SAFM Frankie Montas 4.00 10.00
SAHOL Hector Olivera 4.00 10.00
SAJC Jose Canseco 6.00 15.00
SAJD Johnny Damon 8.00 20.00
SAJP Jose Peraza 4.00 10.00
SAJS Jorge Soler 5.00 12.00
SALG Luis Gonzalez 4.00 10.00
SALS Luis Severino 4.00 10.00
SAMA Miguel Almonte 3.00 8.00
SAMD Matt Duffy 3.00 8.00
SAMK Max Kepler 3.00 8.00
SAMR Matt Reynolds 3.00 8.00
SANA Nolan Arenado 25.00 60.00
SAOV Omar Vizquel 4.00 10.00
SARF Rollie Fingers 8.00 20.00
SARR Rob Refsnyder 4.00 10.00
SATM Tom Murphy 3.00 8.00
SATR Tyson Ross 3.00 8.00
SATT Trea Turner 10.00 25.00
SAZL Zach Lee 3.00 8.00

2016 Topps Strata Autographs Black

*BLACK: .6X TO 1.5X BASIC
STATED ODDS 1:13 HOBBY
STATED PRINT RUN 50 SER.#'d SETS
EXCHANGE DEADLINE 7/31/2018
SAAD Andre Dawson 10.00 25.00
SACC Carlos Correa 40.00 100.00
SACJ Chipper Jones 50.00 120.00
SAHA Hank Aaron 100.00 250.00
SAJG Juan Gonzalez 10.00 25.00
SAMT Mike Trout 125.00 300.00
SARC Rod Carew 15.00 40.00

2016 Topps Strata Autographs Blue

*BLUE: .5X TO 1.2X BASIC
STATED ODDS 1:7 HOBBY
STATED PRINT RUN 99 SER.#'d SETS
EXCHANGE DEADLINE 7/31/2018
SAAD Andre Dawson 8.00 20.00
SACC Carlos Correa 30.00 80.00
SACJ Chipper Jones 40.00 100.00
SAJG Juan Gonzalez 8.00 20.00
SARC Rod Carew 12.00 30.00

2016 Topps Strata Autographs Gold

*GOLD: .75X TO 2X BASIC
STATED ODDS 1:25 HOBBY
STATED PRINT RUN 25 SER.#'d SETS
EXCHANGE DEADLINE 7/31/2018
SAAD Andre Dawson 12.00 30.00
SACC Carlos Correa 50.00 120.00
SACJ Chipper Jones 60.00 150.00
SAHA Hank Aaron 125.00 300.00
SAJG Juan Gonzalez 12.00 30.00
SAMT Mike Trout 150.00 400.00
SARC Rod Carew 20.00 50.00

2016 Topps Strata Autographs Green

*GREEN: .5X TO 1.2X BASIC
STATED ODDS 1:9 HOBBY
STATED PRINT RUN 75 SER.#'d SETS
EXCHANGE DEADLINE 7/31/2018
SAAD Andre Dawson 8.00 20.00
SACC Carlos Correa 30.00 80.00
SACJ Chipper Jones 40.00 100.00
SAJG Juan Gonzalez 8.00 20.00
SAMT Mike Trout 100.00 250.00
SARC Rod Carew 12.00 30.00

2016 Topps Strata Autographs Orange

*ORANGE: .5X TO 1.2X BASIC
RANDOM INSERTS IN PACKS
STATED PRINT RUN 125 SER.#'d SETS
EXCHANGE DEADLIN 7/31/2018
SAAD Andre Dawson 8.00 20.00
SAHOW Henry Owens 5.00 12.00

2016 Topps Strata Clearly Authentic Autograph Relics

RANDOM INSERTS IN PACKS
EXCHANGE DEADLINE 7/31/2018
CAARBB Brandon Belt 5.00 12.00
CAARCK Clayton Kershaw 50.00 120.00
CAARCSA Chris Sale 6.00 15.00
CAARDK Dallas Keuchel 12.00 30.00
CAARGB Greg Bird 5.00 12.00
CAARHOW Henry Owens 5.00 12.00
CAARHR Hanley Ramirez EXCH 6.00 15.00
CAARJD Jacob deGrom 25.00 60.00
CAARJG Jon Gray 4.00 10.00
CAARKB Kris Bryant 60.00 150.00
CAARKP Kevin Plawecki 4.00 10.00

CAARKS Kyle Schwarber 12.00 30.00
CAARLS Luis Severino 5.00 12.00
CAARRCA Rusney Castillo 4.00 10.00
CAARRR Rob Refsnyder 6.00 15.00
CAARSG Sonny Gray 6.00 15.00
CAARSMZ Steven Matz 4.00 10.00
CAARSP Stephen Piscotty 8.00 20.00
CAARTR Tyson Ross 6.00 15.00

2016 Topps Strata Clearly Authentic Autograph Relics Black

*BLACK: 1X TO 2.5X BASIC
STATED ODDS 1:20 HOBBY
STATED PRINT RUN 50 SER.#'d SETS
EXCHANGE DEADLINE 7/31/2018
CAARDP Dustin Pedroia 25.00 60.00
CAARDW David Wright 25.00 60.00
CAARMM Manny Machado 60.00 150.00
CAARMT Mike Trout 200.00 500.00
CAARRCN Robinson Cano 30.00 80.00

2016 Topps Strata Clearly Authentic Autograph Relics Blue

*BLUE: .5X TO 1.2X BASIC
STATED ODDS 1:12 HOBBY
STATED PRINT RUN 99 SER.#'d SETS
EXCHANGE DEADLINE 7/31/2018
CAARDP Dustin Pedroia 12.00 30.00
CAARMM Manny Machado 30.00 80.00

2016 Topps Strata Clearly Authentic Autograph Relics Gold

*GOLD: 1.2X TO 3X BASIC
STATED ODDS 1:40 HOBBY
STATED PRINT RUN 25 SER.#'d SETS
EXCHANGE DEADLINE 7/31/2018
CAARDP Dustin Pedroia 30.00 80.00
CAARDW David Wright 30.00 80.00
CAARMM Manny Machado 75.00 200.00
CAARMT Mike Trout 250.00 600.00
CAARRCN Robinson Cano 40.00 100.00

2016 Topps Strata Clearly Authentic Autograph Relics Green

*GREEN: .5X TO 1.2X BASIC
STATED ODDS 1:13 HOBBY
STATED PRINT RUN 75 SER.#'d SETS
EXCHANGE DEADLINE 7/31/2018
CAARDP Dustin Pedroia 12.00 30.00
CAARDW David Wright 12.00 30.00
CAARMM Manny Machado 30.00 80.00
CAARMT Mike Trout 100.00 250.00
CAARRCN Robinson Cano 15.00 40.00

2016 Topps Strata Clearly Authentic Relics

RANDOM INSERTS IN PACKS
*BLUE/99: .5X TO 1.2X BASIC
*GREEN/75: .5X TO 1.2X BASIC
PRICING FOR SINGLE CLR SWATCHES
CARAM Andrew McCutchen 4.00 10.00
CARAP Albert Pujols 6.00 15.00
CARAR Addison Russell 4.00 10.00
CARCG Curtis Granderson 3.00 8.00
CARDO David Ortiz 4.00 10.00
CARGS Giancarlo Stanton 4.00 10.00
CARJAR Jake Arrieta 3.00 8.00
CARJB Jose Bautista 3.00 8.00
CARJDG Jacob deGrom 8.00 20.00
CARJE Jacoby Ellsbury 3.00 8.00
CARJF Jose Fernandez 4.00 10.00
CARJS Jorge Soler 4.00 10.00
CARJV Joey Votto 4.00 10.00
CARKS Kyle Schwarber 8.00 20.00
CARLS Luis Severino 3.00 8.00
CARMB Madison Bumgarner 3.00 8.00
CARMC Miguel Cabrera 6.00 15.00
CARMD Matt Duffy 2.50 6.00
CARMH Matt Harvey 3.00 8.00
CARMM Manny Machado 4.00 10.00
CARMTA Masahiro Tanaka 3.00 8.00
CARMTR Mike Trout 20.00 50.00
CARNS Noah Syndergaard 3.00 8.00
CARYC Yoenis Cespedes 4.00 10.00
CARYM Yadier Molina 5.00 12.00

2016 Topps Strata Clearly Authentic Relics Black

CARAM Andrew McCutchen 30.00 80.00
CARAP Albert Pujols 20.00 50.00
CARDO David Ortiz 25.00 60.00
CARGS Giancarlo Stanton 15.00 40.00
CARJDG Jacob deGrom 10.00 25.00
CARJV Joey Votto 15.00 40.00
CARMD Matt Duffy 10.00 25.00
CARMM Manny Machado 15.00 40.00
CARMTA Masahiro Tanaka 12.00 30.00
CARMTR Mike Trout 30.00 80.00
CARNS Noah Syndergaard 12.00 30.00
CARYC Yoenis Cespedes 12.00 30.00
CARYM Yadier Molina 20.00 50.00

2016 Topps Strata Clearly Authentic Relics Gold

*GOLD: 1X TO 2.5X BASIC
STATED ODDS 1:38 HOBBY
STATED PRINT RUN 25 SER.#'d SETS
CARAM Andrew McCutchen 30.00 80.00
CARAP Albert Pujols 25.00 60.00
CARDO David Ortiz 30.00 80.00
CARGS Giancarlo Stanton 20.00 50.00
CARJDG Jacob deGrom 12.00 30.00
CARJV Joey Votto 20.00 50.00
CARMB Madison Bumgarner 8.00 20.00
CARMD Matt Duffy 20.00 50.00
CARMM Manny Machado 20.00 50.00
CARMTA Masahiro Tanaka 15.00 40.00
CARMTR Mike Trout 40.00 100.00
CARNS Noah Syndergaard 15.00 40.00
CARYC Yoenis Cespedes 15.00 40.00
CARYM Yadier Molina 25.00 60.00

2016 Topps Strata Signature Patches

STATED ODDS 1:40 HOBBY
STATED PRINT RUN 25 SER.#'d SETS
EXCHANGE DEADLINE 7/31/2018
SSPI Ichiro 600.00 800.00
SSPAGR Alex Gordon EXCH 25.00 60.00
SSPAJ Adam Jones 40.00 100.00
SSPAR Anthony Rizzo EXCH 30.00 80.00
SSPBP Buster Posey 60.00 150.00
SSPCJ Chipper Jones 60.00 150.00
SSPCKE Clayton Kershaw EXCH 50.00 125.00
SSPCR Cal Ripken Jr. EXCH 75.00 200.00
SSPCSE Corey Seager
SSPDO David Ortiz 100.00 250.00
SSPDP Dustin Pedroia 40.00 100.00
SSPFH Felix Hernandez EXCH 40.00 100.00
SSPGM Greg Maddux 60.00 150.00
SSPHR Hanley Ramirez EXCH 10.00 25.00
SSPJD Johnny Damon 25.00 60.00
SSPJDE Jacob deGrom 40.00 100.00
SSPMC Michael Conforto EXCH 40.00 100.00
SSPMMA Manny Machado 250.00 400.00
SSPMMG Mark McGwire 75.00 200.00
SSPMP Mike Piazza
SSPPF Prince Fielder EXCH 25.00 60.00
SSPRB Ryan Braun 30.00 80.00
SSPRH Rickey Henderson EXCH 50.00 120.00
SSPRJ Reggie Jackson 40.00 100.00

2016 Topps Strata Signatures

STATED ODDS 1:17 HOBBY
PRINT RUNS B/WN 35-125 COPIES PER
EXCHANGE DEADLINE 7/31/2018
*GOLD/25: .5X TO 1.2X BASIC
SSBP Buster Posey/35 75.00 200.00
SSCC Carlos Correa/35 50.00 120.00
SSCJ Chipper Jones/55 30.00 80.00
SSCK Clayton Kershaw EXCH 40.00 100.00
SSCR Cal Ripken Jr./35 50.00 120.00
SSGB Greg Bird/99 6.00 15.00
SSHO Henry Owens/125 6.00 15.00
SSKG Ken Griffey Jr. EXCH 75.00 200.00
SSKM Kenta Maeda EXCH 20.00 50.00
SSKS Kyle Schwarber/125 15.00 40.00
SSLG Luis Gonzalez/105 6.00 15.00
SSMP Mike Piazza/35 50.00 120.00
SSMR Matt Reynolds/125 5.00 12.00
SSMS Miguel Sano/75 8.00 20.00
SSNR Nolan Ryan/35 75.00 200.00
SSOV Omar Vizquel/125 10.00 25.00
SSRR Rob Refsnyder/125 6.00 15.00
SSSM Steven Matz/125 5.00 12.00
SSRCL Roger Clemens EXCH 25.00 60.00

1997 Topps Stars Promos

COMPLETE SET (3) 2.50 6.00
PP1 Larry Walker .60 1.50
PP2 Roger Clemens 1.25 3.00
PP3 Frank Thomas .60 1.50

1997 Topps Stars

The 1997 Topps Stars set was issued in one series totalling 125 cards and was distributed in seven-card packs with a suggested retail price of $3. A checklist card was added to every fifth pack as an extra card. The set was available exclusively to Home Team Advantage members and features color player photos printed on super-thick, 20-point stock with matte gold foil stamping and a textured matte laminate and spot UV coating. The backs carry another photo of the same player with biographical information and career statistics. Rookie cards include Kris Benson, Lance Berkman, Vernon Wells and Kerry Wood.

COMPLETE SET (125) 12.50 30.00
1 Larry Walker .10 .30
2 Tino Martinez .20 .50
3 Cal Ripken 1.00 2.50
4 Ken Griffey Jr. .60 1.50
5 Chipper Jones .30 .75
6 David Justice .10 .30
7 Mike Piazza .50 1.25
8 Jeff Bagwell .20 .50
9 Ron Gant .10 .30
10 Sammy Sosa .30 .75
11 Tony Gwynn .40 1.00
12 Carlos Baerga .10 .30
13 Frank Thomas .30 .75
14 Moises Alou .10 .30
15 Barry Larkin .20 .50
16 Ivan Rodriguez .20 .50
17 Greg Maddux .50 1.25
18 Jim Edmonds .10 .30
19 Jose Canseco .20 .50
20 Rafael Palmeiro .20 .50
21 Paul Molitor .10 .30
22 Kevin Appier .10 .30
23 Raul Mondesi .10 .30
24 Lance Johnson .10 .30
25 Edgar Martinez .20 .50
26 Andres Galarraga .10 .30
27 Mo Vaughn .10 .30
28 Ken Caminiti .10 .30
29 Cecil Fielder .10 .30
30 Harold Baines .10 .30
31 Roberto Alomar .20 .50
32 Shawn Estes .10 .30
33 Tom Glavine .20 .50
34 Dennis Eckersley .10 .30
35 Manny Ramirez .20 .50
36 John Olerud .10 .30
37 Juan Gonzalez .10 .30
38 Chuck Knoblauch .10 .30
39 Albert Belle .10 .30
40 Vinny Castilla .10 .30
41 John Smoltz .20 .50
42 Barry Bonds .75 2.00
43 Randy Johnson .30 .75
44 Brady Anderson .10 .30
45 Jeff Blauser .10 .30
46 Craig Biggio .20 .50
47 Jeff Conine .10 .30
48 Marquis Grissom .10 .30
49 Mark Grace .20 .50
50 Roger Clemens .60 1.50
51 Mark McGwire .75 2.00
52 Fred McGriff .20 .50
53 Gary Sheffield .10 .30
54 Bobby Jones .10 .30
55 Eric Young .10 .30
56 Robin Ventura .10 .30
57 Wade Boggs .20 .50
58 Joe Carter .10 .30
59 Ryne Sandberg .50 1.25
60 Matt Williams .10 .30
61 Todd Hundley .10 .30
62 Dante Bichette .10 .30
63 Chili Davis .10 .30
64 Kenny Lofton .10 .30
65 Jay Buhner .10 .30
66 Will Clark .20 .50
67 Travis Fryman .10 .30
68 Pat Hentgen .10 .30
69 Ellis Burks .10 .30
70 Mike Mussina .20 .50
71 Hideo Nomo .30 .75
72 Sandy Alomar Jr. .10 .30
73 Bobby Bonilla .10 .30
74 Rickey Henderson .30 .75
75 David Cone .10 .30
76 Terry Steinbach .10 .30
77 Pedro Martinez .20 .50
78 Jim Thome .20 .50
79 Rod Beck .10 .30
80 Randy Myers .10 .30
81 Charles Nagy .10 .30
82 Mark Wohlers .10 .30
83 Paul O'Neill .20 .50
84 Curt Schilling .10 .30
85 Joey Cora .10 .30
86 John Franco .10 .30
87 Kevin Brown .10 .30
88 Benito Santiago .10 .30
89 Ray Lankford .10 .30
90 Bernie Williams .20 .50
91 Jason Dickson .10 .30
92 Jeff Cirillo .10 .30
93 Nomar Garciaparra .50 1.25
94 Mariano Rivera .30 .75
95 Javy Lopez .10 .30
96 Tony Womack RC .20 .50
97 Jose Rosado .10 .30
98 Denny Neagle .10 .30
99 Darryl Kile .10 .30
100 Justin Thompson .10 .30
101 Juan Encarnacion .10 .30
102 Brad Fullmer .10 .30
103 Kris Benson RC .30 .75
104 Todd Helton .30 .75
105 Paul Konerko .20 .50
106 Travis Lee RC .20 .50
107 Todd Greene .10 .30
108 Mark Kotsay RC .50 1.25
109 Carl Pavano .10 .30
110 Kerry Wood RC 2.00 5.00
111 Jason Romano RC .10 .30
112 Geoff Goetz RC .10 .30
113 Scott Hodges RC .10 .30
114 Aaron Akin RC .10 .30
115 Vernon Wells RC 2.00 5.00
116 Chris Stowe RC .10 .30
117 Brett Caradonna RC .10 .30
118 Adam Kennedy RC .30 .75
119 Jayson Werth RC 2.50 6.00
120 Glenn Davis RC .10 .30
121 Troy Cameron RC .10 .30
122 J.J. Davis RC .10 .30
123 Jason Dellaero RC .10 .30
124 Jason Standridge RC .10 .30
125 Lance Berkman RC 4.00 10.00
NNO Checklist .10 .30

1997 Topps Stars Always Mint

*ALWAYS: 4X TO 10X BASIC
*ALWAYS: 2X TO 5X BASIC RC'S
STATED ODDS 1:12

1997 Topps Stars '97 All-Stars

STATED ODDS 1:72
AS1 Greg Maddux 10.00 25.00
AS2 Randy Johnson 6.00 15.00
AS3 Tino Martinez 4.00 10.00
AS4 Jeff Bagwell 4.00 10.00
AS5 Ivan Rodriguez 4.00 10.00
AS6 Mike Piazza 10.00 25.00
AS7 Cal Ripken 20.00 50.00
AS8 Ken Caminiti 2.50 6.00
AS9 Tony Gwynn 8.00 20.00
AS10 Edgar Martinez 4.00 10.00
AS11 Craig Biggio 4.00 10.00
AS12 Roberto Alomar 4.00 10.00
AS13 Larry Walker 2.50 6.00
AS14 Brady Anderson 2.50 6.00
AS15 Barry Bonds 15.00 40.00
AS16 Ken Griffey Jr. 12.50 30.00
AS17 Ray Lankford 2.50 6.00
AS18 Paul O'Neill 4.00 10.00
AS19 Jeff Blauser 2.50 6.00
AS20 Sandy Alomar 2.50 6.00

1997 Topps Stars All-Star Memories

COMPLETE SET (10) 25.00 60.00
STATED ODDS 1:24
ASM1 Cal Ripken 8.00 20.00
ASM2 Jeff Conine 1.00 2.50
ASM3 Mike Piazza 4.00 10.00
ASM4 Randy Johnson 2.50 6.00
ASM5 Ken Griffey Jr. 5.00 12.00
ASM6 Fred McGriff 1.50 4.00
ASM7 Moises Alou 1.00 2.50
ASM8 Hideo Nomo 2.50 6.00
ASM9 Larry Walker 1.00 2.50
ASM10 Sandy Alomar 1.00 2.50

1997 Topps Stars Future All-Stars

COMPLETE SET (15) 15.00 40.00
STATED ODDS 1:12
FAS1 Derek Jeter 5.00 12.00
FAS2 Andruw Jones 1.00 2.50
FAS3 Vladimir Guerrero 1.50 4.00
FAS4 Scott Rolen 1.00 2.50
FAS5 Jose Guillen .75 2.00
FAS6 Jose Cruz Jr. .75 2.00
FAS7 Darin Erstad .75 2.00
FAS8 Tony Clark .40 1.00
FAS9 Scott Spiezio .40 1.00
FAS10 Kevin Orie .40 1.00
FAS11 Pokey Reese .40 1.00
FAS12 Billy Wagner .75 2.00
FAS13 Matt Morris .75 2.00
FAS14 Jeremi Gonzalez .40 1.00
FAS15 Hideki Irabu .75 2.00

1997 Topps Stars Rookie Reprints

COMPLETE SET (15) 20.00 50.00
STATED ODDS 1:6
1 Luis Aparicio 1.50 4.00
2 Richie Ashburn 1.50 4.00
3 Jim Bunning 1.50 4.00
4 Bob Feller 1.50 4.00
5 Rollie Fingers 1.50 4.00
6 Monte Irvin 1.50 4.00
7 Al Kaline 3.00 8.00
8 Ralph Kiner 1.50 4.00
9 Eddie Mathews 3.00 8.00
10 Hal Newhouser 1.50 4.00
11 Gaylord Perry 1.50 4.00
12 Robin Roberts 1.50 4.00
13 Brooks Robinson 1.50 4.00
14 Enos Slaughter 1.50 4.00
15 Earl Weaver 1.50 4.00

1997 Topps Stars Rookie Reprint Autographs

STATED ODDS 1:30
CARD NO.2 DOES NOT EXIST
1 Luis Aparicio 15.00 40.00
3 Jim Bunning 20.00 50.00
4 Bob Feller 15.00 40.00
5 Rollie Fingers 12.00 30.00
6 Monte Irvin 15.00 40.00
7 Al Kaline 30.00 80.00
8 Ralph Kiner 15.00 40.00
9 Eddie Mathews 40.00 100.00
10 Hal Newhouser 40.00 100.00
11 Gaylord Perry 10.00 25.00
12 Robin Roberts 12.00 30.00
13 Brooks Robinson 25.00 60.00
14 Enos Slaughter 15.00 40.00
15 Earl Weaver 10.00 25.00

1998 Topps Stars Pre-Production

COMPLETE SET (6) 2.50 6.00
PP1 Mike Piazza 1.25 3.00
PP2 Darin Erstad .40 1.00
PP3 Vinny Castilla .20 .50
PP4 Craig Biggio .40 1.00
PP5 Ivan Rodriguez .50 1.25
PP6 Pedro Martinez .50 1.25

1998 Topps Stars

Distributed in six-card packs, this 150-card set features color action player photos printed on 20 pt. stock with red foil highlights, luminous diffraction, matte gold foil stamping, textured matte laminate, and spot UV coating. The pictured players are also grouped into five tool categories of baseball: Arm Strength, Hit for Average, Hit for Power, Defense, and Speed. A checklist card was added to every fifth pack as an extra card. The basic set was issued to a stated print run of 9799 cards.

COMP.RED SET (150) 30.00 80.00
ONE RED FOIL CARD PER PACK
RED FOIL PRINT RUN 9799 SERIAL #'d SETS
RED FOIL CARDS PRICED BELOW!
1 Greg Maddux 1.25 3.00
2 Darryl Kile .30 .75
3 Rod Beck .30 .75
4 Ellis Burks .30 .75
5 Gary Sheffield .30 .75
6 David Ortiz 1.00 2.50
7 Marquis Grissom .30 .75
8 Tony Womack .30 .75
9 Mike Mussina .50 1.25
10 Bernie Williams .50 1.25
11 Andy Benes .30 .75
12 Rusty Greer .30 .75
13 Carlos Delgado .30 .75
14 Jim Edmonds .30 .75
15 Raul Mondesi .30 .75
16 Andres Galarraga .30 .75
17 Wade Boggs .50 1.25
18 Paul O'Neill .50 1.25
19 Edgar Renteria .30 .75
20 Tony Clark .30 .75
21 Vladimir Guerrero .75 2.00
22 Moises Alou .30 .75
23 Bernard Gilkey .30 .75
24 Lance Johnson .30 .75
25 Ben Grieve .30 .75
26 Sandy Alomar Jr. .30 .75
27 Ray Durham .30 .75
28 Shawn Estes .30 .75
29 David Segui .30 .75
30 Javy Lopez .30 .75
31 Steve Finley .30 .75
32 Rey Ordonez .30 .75
33 Derek Jeter 2.00 5.00
34 Henry Rodriguez .30 .75
35 Mo Vaughn .30 .75
36 Richard Hidalgo .30 .75
37 Omar Vizquel .50 1.25
38 Johnny Damon .50 1.25
39 Brian Hunter .30 .75
40 Matt Williams .30 .75
41 Chuck Finley .30 .75
42 Jeromy Burnitz .30 .75
43 Livan Hernandez .30 .75
44 Delino DeShields .30 .75
45 Charles Nagy .30 .75
46 Scott Rolen .50 1.25
47 Neifi Perez .30 .75
48 John Wetteland .30 .75
49 Eric Milton .30 .75
50 Mike Piazza 1.25 3.00
51 Cal Ripken 2.50 6.00
52 Mariano Rivera .75 2.00
53 Butch Huskey .30 .75
54 Quinton McCracken .30 .75
55 Jose Cruz Jr. .30 .75
56 Brian Jordan .30 .75
57 Hideo Nomo .75 2.00
58 Masato Yoshii RC .30 .75
59 Cliff Floyd .30 .75
60 Jose Guillen .30 .75
61 Jeff Shaw .30 .75
62 Edgar Martinez .50 1.25
63 Rondell White .30 .75
64 Hal Morris .30 .75
65 Barry Larkin .50 1.25
66 Eric Young .30 .75
67 Ray Lankford .30 .75
68 Derek Bell .30 .75
69 Charles Johnson .30 .75
70 Robin Ventura .30 .75
71 Chuck Knoblauch .30 .75
72 Kevin Brown .50 1.25
73 Jose Valentin .30 .75
74 Jay Buhner .30 .75
75 Tony Gwynn 1.00 2.50
76 Andy Pettitte .50 1.25
77 Edgardo Alfonzo .30 .75
78 Kerry Wood .40 1.00
79 Darin Erstad .30 .75
80 Paul Konerko .30 .75
81 Jason Kendall .30 .75
82 Tino Martinez .50 1.25
83 Brad Radke .30 .75
84 Jeff King .30 .75
85 Travis Lee .30 .75
86 Jeff Kent .30 .75
87 Trevor Hoffman .30 .75
88 David Cone .30 .75
89 Jose Canseco .50 1.25
90 Juan Gonzalez .30 .75
91 Todd Hundley .30 .75
92 John Valentin .30 .75
93 Sammy Sosa .75 2.00
94 Jason Giambi .30 .75
95 Chipper Jones .75 2.00
96 Jeff Blauser .30 .75
97 Brad Fullmer .30 .75
98 Derrek Lee .50 1.25
99 Denny Neagle .30 .75
100 Ken Griffey Jr. 1.50 4.00
101 David Justice .30 .75
102 Tim Salmon .50 1.25
103 J.T. Snow .30 .75
104 Fred McGriff .50 1.25
105 Brady Anderson .30 .75
106 Larry Walker .30 .75
107 Jeff Cirillo .30 .75
108 Andruw Jones .50 1.25
109 Manny Ramirez .50 1.25
110 Justin Thompson .30 .75
111 Vinny Castilla .30 .75
112 Chan Ho Park .30 .75
113 Mark Grudzielanek .30 .75
114 Mark Grace .50 1.25
115 Ken Caminiti .30 .75
116 Ryan Klesko .30 .75
117 Rafael Palmeiro .50 1.25
118 Pat Hentgen .30 .75
119 Eric Karros .30 .75
120 Randy Johnson .75 2.00
121 Roberto Alomar .50 1.25
122 John Olerud .30 .75
123 Paul Molitor .30 .75
124 Dean Palmer .30 .75
125 Nomar Garciaparra 1.25 3.00
126 Curt Schilling .30 .75
127 Jay Bell .30 .75
128 Craig Biggio .50 1.25
129 Marty Cordova .30 .75
130 Ivan Rodriguez .50 1.25
131 Todd Helton .50 1.25
132 Jim Thome .50 1.25
133 Albert Belle .30 .75
134 Mike Lansing .30 .75
135 Mark McGwire 2.00 5.00
136 Roger Clemens 1.50 4.00
137 Tom Glavine .50 1.25
138 Ron Gant .30 .75
139 Alex Rodriguez 1.25 3.00
140 Jeff Bagwell .50 1.25
141 John Smoltz .50 1.25
142 Kenny Lofton .30 .75
143 Dante Bichette .30 .75
144 Pedro Martinez .50 1.25
145 Barry Bonds 2.00 5.00
146 Travis Fryman .30 .75
147 Bobby Jones .30 .75
148 Bobby Higginson .30 .75
149 Reggie Sanders .30 .75
150 Frank Thomas .75 2.00

1998 Topps Stars Bronze

COMPLETE SET (150) 30.00 80.00
*BRONZE: SAME VALUE AS RED
ONE BRONZE PER PACK
STATED PRINT RUN 9799 SERIAL #'d SETS

1998 Topps Stars Gold

COMPLETE SET (150) 150.00 300.00
*STARS: 1.25X TO 3X BASIC CARDS
STATED ODDS 1:2
STATED PRINT RUN 2299 SERIAL #'d SETS

1998 Topps Stars Gold Rainbow

*STARS: 4X TO 10X BASIC CARDS
STATED ODDS 1:46
STATED PRINT RUN 99 SERIAL #'d SETS

1998 Topps Stars Silver

COMPLETE SET (150) 100.00 200.00
*STARS: .75X TO 2X BASIC CARDS
RANDOM INSERTS IN PACKS
STATED PRINT RUN 4399 SERIAL #'d SETS

1998 Topps Stars Galaxy Bronze

BRONZE STATED ODDS 1:682
BRONZE PRINT RUN 100 SERIAL #'d SETS
*SILVER: .5X TO 1.2X BRONZE GAL
SILVER STATED ODDS 1:910
SILVER PRINT RUN 75 SERIAL #'d SETS
*GOLD: .6X TO 1.5X BRONZE GAL
GOLD STATED ODDS 1:1364
GOLD PRINT RUN 50 SERIAL #'d SETS
GOLD RAINBOW STATED ODDS 1:13643
GOLD RBW.PRINT RUN 5 SERIAL #'d SETS
GOLD RBW.NO PRICING DUE TO SCARCITY
BRONZE CARDS LISTED BELOW!
G1 Barry Bonds 25.00 60.00
G2 Jeff Bagwell 6.00 15.00
G3 Nomar Garciaparra 15.00 40.00
G4 Chipper Jones 10.00 25.00
G5 Ken Griffey Jr. 20.00 50.00
G6 Sammy Sosa 10.00 25.00
G7 Larry Walker 4.00 10.00
G8 Alex Rodriguez 15.00 40.00
G9 Craig Biggio 6.00 15.00
G10 Raul Mondesi 4.00 10.00

1998 Topps Stars Luminaries Bronze

COMPLETE SET (15) 200.00 400.00
BRONZE STATED ODDS 1:455
BRONZE PRINT RUN 100 SERIAL #'d SETS
*SILVER: .5X TO 1.2X BRONZE LUM
SILVER STATED ODDS 1:606
SILVER PRINT RUN 75 SERIAL #'d SETS
*GOLD: .6X TO 1.5X BRONZE LUM
GOLD STATED ODDS 1:910
GOLD PRINT RUN 50 SERIAL #'d SETS
GOLD RAINBOW STATED ODDS 1:9095
GOLD RBW.PRINT RUN 5 SERIAL #'d SETS
GOLD RBW.NO PRICING DUE TO SCARCITY
L1 Ken Griffey Jr. 20.00 50.00
L2 Mark McGwire 25.00 60.00
L3 Juan Gonzalez 4.00 10.00
L4 Tony Gwynn 12.50 30.00
L5 Frank Thomas 10.00 25.00
L6 Mike Piazza 15.00 40.00
L7 Chuck Knoblauch 4.00 10.00
L8 Kenny Lofton 4.00 10.00
L9 Barry Bonds 25.00 60.00
L10 Matt Williams 4.00 10.00
L11 Raul Mondesi 4.00 10.00
L12 Ivan Rodriguez 6.00 15.00
L13 Alex Rodriguez 15.00 40.00
L14 Nomar Garciaparra 15.00 40.00
L15 Ken Caminiti 4.00 10.00

1998 Topps Stars Rookie Reprints

COMPLETE SET (5) 15.00 40.00
STATED ODDS 1:24
1 Johnny Bench 3.00 8.00
2 Whitey Ford 2.00 5.00
3 Joe Morgan 2.00 5.00
4 Mike Schmidt 5.00 12.00
5 Carl Yastrzemski 4.00 10.00

1998 Topps Stars Rookie Reprints Autographs

STATED ODDS 1:273
1 Johnny Bench 60.00 150.00
2 Whitey Ford 30.00 80.00
3 Joe Morgan 20.00 50.00
4 Mike Schmidt 40.00 100.00
5 Carl Yastrzemski 50.00 120.00

1998 Topps Stars Supernovas Bronze

BRONZE STATED ODDS 1:682
BRONZE PRINT RUN 100 SERIAL #'d SETS
*SILVER: .5X TO 1.2X BRONZE NOVA
SILVER STATED ODDS 1:910
SILVER PRINT RUN 75 SERIAL #'d SETS
*GOLD: .6X TO 1.5X BRONZE NOVA
GOLD STATED ODDS 1:1364
GOLD PRINT RUN 50 SERIAL #'d SETS
GOLD RAINBOW STATED ODDS 1:13643
GOLD RBW.PRINT RUN 5 SERIAL #'d SETS
GOLD RBW.NO PRICING DUE TO SCARCITY
S1 Ben Grieve 4.00 10.00
S2 Travis Lee 4.00 10.00
S3 Todd Helton 6.00 15.00
S4 Adrian Beltre 4.00 10.00
S5 Derrek Lee 6.00 15.00
S6 David Ortiz 12.50 30.00
S7 Brad Fullmer 4.00 10.00
S8 Mark Kotsay 4.00 10.00
S9 Paul Konerko 4.00 10.00
S10 Kerry Wood 5.00 12.00

1999 Topps Stars Pre-Production

COMPLETE SET (5) 3.00 8.00
PP1 Paul O'Neill No Star .75 2.00
PP2 Vinny Castilla One Star .40 1.00
PP3 Darin Erstad Two Star .75 2.00
PP4 Kerry Wood Three Star .75 2.00
PP5 Chipper Jones Four Star 1.25 3.00

1999 Topps Stars

The 1999 Topps Stars set was issued in one series for a total of 180 cards and distributed in six-card packs with a suggested retail price of $3. The set features action color player photos printed on 20-point card stock with foil-stamping, flood gloss, and metallic inks. The backs carry five-star player evaluation. The set features the following subsets: Luminaries (151-170) and Supernovas (171-180). Rookie Cards include Pat Burrell, Alex Escobar, Nick Johnson and Alfonso Soriano.

COMPLETE SET (180) 20.00 50.00
THREE BASIC CARDS PER PACK
SUBSET CARDS HALF VALUE OF BASE CARDS
1 Ken Griffey Jr. 1.00 2.50
2 Chipper Jones .50 1.25
3 Mike Piazza .75 2.00
4 Nomar Garciaparra .75 2.00
5 Derek Jeter 1.25 3.00
6 Frank Thomas .50 1.25
7 Ben Grieve .20 .50
8 Mark McGwire 1.25 3.00
9 Sammy Sosa .50 1.25
10 Alex Rodriguez .75 2.00
11 Troy Glaus .30 .75
12 Eric Chavez .20 .50
13 Kerry Wood .20 .50
14 Barry Bonds 1.25 3.00
15 Vladimir Guerrero .50 1.25
16 Albert Belle .20 .50
17 Juan Gonzalez .20 .50
18 Roger Clemens 1.00 2.50
19 Ruben Mateo .20 .50
20 Cal Ripken 1.50 4.00
21 Darin Erstad .20 .50
22 Jeff Bagwell .30 .75
23 Roy Halladay .50 1.25
24 Todd Helton .30 .75
25 Michael Barrett .20 .50
26 Manny Ramirez .30 .75
27 Fernando Seguignol .20 .50
28 Pat Burrell RC .75 2.00
29 Andruw Jones .30 .75
30 Randy Johnson .50 1.25
31 Jose Canseco .30 .75
32 Brad Fullmer .20 .50
33 Alex Escobar RC .20 .50
34 Alfonso Soriano RC 2.00 5.00
35 Larry Walker .20 .50
36 Matt Clement .20 .50
37 Mo Vaughn .20 .50
38 Bruce Chen .20 .50
39 Travis Lee .20 .50
40 Adrian Beltre .20 .50
41 Alex Gonzalez .20 .50
42 Jason Tyner RC .20 .50
43 George Lombard .20 .50
44 Scott Rolen .30 .75
45 Mark Mulder RC .60 1.50
46 Gabe Kapler .20 .50
47 Choo Freeman RC .20 .50
48 Tony Gwynn .60 1.50
49 A.J. Burnett RC .40 1.00
50 Matt Belisle RC .20 .50
51 Greg Maddux .75 2.00
52 John Smoltz .30 .75
53 Mark Grace .30 .75
54 Wade Boggs .30 .75
55 Bernie Williams .30 .75
56 Pedro Martinez .30 .75
57 Barry Larkin .30 .75
58 Orlando Hernandez .20 .50
59 Jason Kendall .20 .50
60 Mark Kotsay .20 .50
61 Jim Thome .30 .75
62 Gary Sheffield .20 .50
63 Preston Wilson .20 .50
64 Rafael Palmeiro .30 .75
65 David Wells .20 .50
66 Shawn Green .20 .50
67 Tom Glavine .30 .75
68 Jeromy Burnitz .20 .50
69 Kevin Brown .30 .75
70 Rondell White .20 .50
71 Roberto Alomar .30 .75
72 Cliff Floyd .20 .50
73 Craig Biggio .30 .75
74 Greg Vaughn .20 .50
75 Ivan Rodriguez .30 .75
76 Vinny Castilla .20 .50
77 Todd Walker .20 .50
78 Paul Konerko .20 .50
79 Andy Brown RC .20 .50
80 Todd Hundley .20 .50
81 Dmitri Young .20 .50
82 Tony Clark .20 .50
83 Nick Johnson RC .50 1.25
84 Mike Caruso .20 .50
85 David Ortiz .50 1.25
86 Matt Williams .20 .50
87 Raul Mondesi .20 .50
88 Kenny Lofton .20 .50
89 Miguel Tejada .20 .50
90 Dante Bichette .20 .50
91 Jorge Posada .30 .75
92 Carlos Beltran .20 .50
93 Carlos Delgado .20 .50
94 Javy Lopez .20 .50
95 Aramis Ramirez .20 .50
96 Neifi Perez .20 .50
97 Marlon Anderson .20 .50
98 David Cone .20 .50
99 Moises Alou .20 .50
100 John Olerud .20 .50
101 Tim Salmon .30 .75
102 Jason Giambi .20 .50
103 Sandy Alomar Jr. .20 .50
104 Curt Schilling .20 .50
105 Andres Galarraga .20 .50
106 Rusty Greer .20 .50
107 Bobby Seay RC .20 .50
108 Eric Young .20 .50
109 Brian Jordan .20 .50
110 Eric Davis .20 .50
111 Will Clark .30 .75
112 Andy Ashby .20 .50
113 Edgardo Alfonzo .20 .50
114 Paul O'Neill .30 .75
115 Denny Neagle .20 .50
116 Eric Karros .20 .50
117 Ken Caminiti .20 .50
118 Garret Anderson .20 .50
119 Todd Stottlemyre .20 .50
120 David Justice .20 .50
121 Francisco Cordova .20 .50
122 Robin Ventura .20 .50
123 Mike Mussina .30 .75
124 Hideki Irabu .20 .50
125 Justin Thompson .20 .50
126 Mariano Rivera .50 1.25
127 Delino DeShields .20 .50
128 Steve Finley .20 .50
129 Jose Cruz Jr. .20 .50
130 Ray Lankford .20 .50
131 Jim Edmonds .20 .50
132 Charles Johnson .20 .50
133 Al Leiter .20 .50
134 Jose Offerman .20 .50
135 Eric Milton .20 .50
136 Dean Palmer .20 .50
137 Johnny Damon .30 .75
138 Andy Pettitte .30 .75
139 Ray Durham .20 .50
140 Ugueth Urbina .20 .50
141 Marquis Grissom .20 .50
142 Ryan Klesko .20 .50
143 Brady Anderson .20 .50
144 Bobby Higginson .20 .50
145 Chuck Knoblauch .20 .50
146 Rickey Henderson .50 1.25
147 Kevin Millwood .20 .50
148 Fred McGriff .30 .75
149 Damion Easley .20 .50
150 Tino Martinez .30 .75

151 Greg Maddux LUM .50 1.25
152 Scott Rolen LUM .20 .50
153 Pat Burrell LUM .30 .75
154 Roger Clemens LUM .50 1.25
155 Albert Belle LUM .20 .50
156 Troy Glaus LUM .20 .50
157 Cal Ripken LUM .75 2.00
158 Alfonso Soriano LUM .75 2.00
159 Manny Ramirez LUM .20 .50
160 Eric Chavez LUM .20 .50
161 Kerry Wood LUM .20 .50
162 Tony Gwynn LUM .30 .75
163 Barry Bonds LUM .60 1.50
164 Ruben Mateo LUM .20 .50
165 Todd Helton LUM .20 .50
166 Darin Erstad LUM .20 .50
167 Jeff Bagwell LUM .20 .50
168 Juan Gonzalez LUM .20 .50
169 Mo Vaughn LUM .20 .50
170 Vladimir Guerrero LUM .30 .75
171 Nomar Garciaparra SUP .50 1.25
172 Derek Jeter SUP .60 1.50
173 Alex Rodriguez SUP .50 1.25
174 Ben Grieve SUP .20 .50
175 Mike Piazza SUP .50 1.25
176 Chipper Jones SUP .30 .75
177 Frank Thomas SUP .30 .75
178 Ken Griffey Jr. SUP .60 1.50
179 Sammy Sosa SUP .30 .75
180 Mark McGwire SUP .60 1.50

1999 Topps Stars Foil

*STARS: 3X TO 8X BASIC CARDS
*ROOKIES: 1.5X TO 4X BASIC CARDS
STATED ODDS 1:15
STATED PRINT RUN 299 SERIAL #'d SETS

1999 Topps Stars One Star

COMPLETE SET (100) 15.00 40.00
TWO PER PACK
1 Ken Griffey Jr. .75 2.00
2 Chipper Jones .40 1.00
3 Mike Piazza .60 1.50
4 Nomar Garciaparra .60 1.50
5 Derek Jeter 1.00 2.50
6 Frank Thomas .40 1.00
7 Ben Grieve .15 .40
8 Mark McGwire 1.00 2.50
9 Sammy Sosa .40 1.00
10 Alex Rodriguez .60 1.50
11 Troy Glaus .25 .60
12 Eric Chavez .15 .40
13 Kerry Wood .15 .40
14 Barry Bonds 1.00 2.50
15 Vladimir Guerrero .40 1.00
16 Albert Belle .15 .40
17 Juan Gonzalez .15 .40
18 Roger Clemens .75 2.00
19 Ruben Mateo .15 .40
20 Cal Ripken 1.25 3.00
21 Darin Erstad .15 .40
22 Jeff Bagwell .25 .60
23 Roy Halladay .40 1.00
24 Todd Helton .25 .60
25 Michael Barrett .15 .40
26 Manny Ramirez .25 .60
27 Fernando Seguignol .15 .40
28 Pat Burrell .50 1.25
29 Andruw Jones .25 .60
30 Randy Johnson .40 1.00
31 Jose Canseco .25 .60
32 Brad Fullmer .15 .40
33 Alex Escobar .10 .30
34 Alfonso Soriano 1.50 4.00
35 Larry Walker .15 .40
36 Matt Clement .15 .40
37 Mo Vaughn .15 .40
38 Bruce Chen .15 .40
39 Travis Lee .15 .40
40 Adrian Beltre .15 .40
41 Alex Gonzalez .15 .40
42 Jason Tyner .15 .40
43 George Lombard .15 .40
44 Scott Rolen .25 .60
45 Mark Mulder .50 1.25
46 Gabe Kapler .15 .40
47 Choo Freeman .15 .40
48 Tony Gwynn .50 1.25
49 A.J. Burnett .30 .75
50 Matt Belisle .15 .40
51 Greg Maddux .60 1.50
52 John Smoltz .25 .60
53 Mark Grace .25 .60
54 Wade Boggs .25 .60
55 Bernie Williams .25 .60
56 Pedro Martinez .25 .60
57 Barry Larkin .25 .60
58 Orlando Hernandez .15 .40
59 Jason Kendall .15 .40
60 Mark Kotsay .15 .40
61 Jim Thome .25 .60
62 Gary Sheffield .15 .40
63 Preston Wilson .15 .40
64 Rafael Palmeiro .25 .60
65 David Wells .15 .40
66 Shawn Green .15 .40
67 Tom Glavine .25 .60
68 Jeromy Burnitz .15 .40
69 Kevin Brown .25 .60
70 Rondell White .15 .40
71 Roberto Alomar .25 .60
72 Cliff Floyd .15 .40
73 Craig Biggio .25 .60
74 Greg Vaughn .15 .40
75 Ivan Rodriguez .25 .60
76 Vinny Castilla .15 .40
77 Todd Walker .15 .40
78 Paul Konerko .15 .40
79 Andy Brown .15 .40
80 Todd Hundley .15 .40
81 Dmitri Young .15 .40
82 Tony Clark .15 .40
83 Nick Johnson .40 1.00
84 Mike Caruso .15 .40
85 David Ortiz .40 1.00
86 Matt Williams .15 .40
87 Raul Mondesi .15 .40
88 Kenny Lofton .15 .40
89 Miguel Tejada .15 .40
90 Dante Bichette .15 .40
91 Jorge Posada .25 .60
92 Carlos Beltran .25 .60
93 Carlos Delgado .15 .40
94 Javy Lopez .15 .40
95 Aramis Ramirez .15 .40
96 Neifi Perez .15 .40
97 Marlon Anderson .15 .40
98 David Cone .15 .40
99 Moises Alou .15 .40
100 John Olerud .15 .40

1999 Topps Stars One Star Foil

*STARS: 3X TO 8X BASE CARD HI
*ROOKIES: 1.5X TO 4X BASE CARD HI
STATED ODDS 1:33
STATED PRINT RUN 249 SERIAL #'d SETS

1999 Topps Stars Two Star

COMPLETE SET (50) 12.50 30.00
ONE PER PACK
1 Ken Griffey Jr. .75 2.00
2 Chipper Jones .40 1.00
3 Mike Piazza .60 1.50
4 Nomar Garciaparra .60 1.50
5 Derek Jeter 1.00 2.50
6 Frank Thomas .40 1.00
7 Ben Grieve .15 .40
8 Mark McGwire 1.00 2.50
9 Sammy Sosa .40 1.00
10 Alex Rodriguez .60 1.50
11 Troy Glaus .25 .60
12 Eric Chavez .15 .40
13 Kerry Wood .15 .40
14 Barry Bonds 1.00 2.50
15 Vladimir Guerrero .40 1.00
16 Albert Belle .15 .40
17 Juan Gonzalez .15 .40
18 Roger Clemens .75 2.00
19 Ruben Mateo .15 .40
20 Cal Ripken 1.25 3.00
21 Darin Erstad .15 .40
22 Jeff Bagwell .25 .60
23 Roy Halladay .40 1.00
24 Todd Helton .25 .60
25 Michael Barrett .15 .40
26 Manny Ramirez .25 .60
27 Fernando Seguignol .15 .40
28 Pat Burrell .50 1.25
29 Andruw Jones .25 .60
30 Randy Johnson .40 1.00
31 Jose Canseco .25 .60
32 Brad Fullmer .15 .40
33 Alex Escobar .10 .30
34 Alfonso Soriano 1.50 4.00
35 Larry Walker .15 .40
36 Matt Clement .15 .40
37 Mo Vaughn .15 .40
38 Bruce Chen .15 .40
39 Travis Lee .15 .40
40 Adrian Beltre .15 .40
41 Alex Gonzalez .15 .40
42 Jason Tyner .15 .40
43 George Lombard .15 .40
44 Scott Rolen .25 .60
45 Mark Mulder .50 1.25
46 Gabe Kapler .15 .40
47 Choo Freeman .15 .40
48 Tony Gwynn .50 1.25
49 A.J. Burnett .30 .75
50 Matt Belisle .15 .40

1999 Topps Stars Two Star Foil

*STARS: 4X TO 10X BASE CARD HI
*ROOKIES: 2X TO 5X BASE CARD HI
STATED ODDS 1:82
STATED PRINT RUN 199 SERIAL #'d SETS

1999 Topps Stars Three Star

COMPLETE SET (20) 20.00 50.00
STATED ODDS 1:5
1 Ken Griffey Jr. 1.25 3.00
2 Chipper Jones .60 1.50
3 Mike Piazza 1.00 2.50
4 Nomar Garciaparra 1.00 2.50
5 Derek Jeter 1.50 4.00
6 Frank Thomas .60 1.50
7 Ben Grieve .25 .60
8 Mark McGwire 1.50 4.00
9 Sammy Sosa .60 1.50
10 Alex Rodriguez 1.00 2.50
11 Troy Glaus .40 1.00
12 Eric Chavez .25 .60
13 Kerry Wood .25 .60
14 Barry Bonds 1.50 4.00
15 Vladimir Guerrero .60 1.50
16 Albert Belle .25 .60
17 Juan Gonzalez .25 .60
18 Roger Clemens 1.25 3.00
19 Ruben Mateo .25 .60
20 Cal Ripken 2.00 5.00

1999 Topps Stars Three Star Foil

*STARS: 8X TO 20X BASE CARD HI
STATED ODDS 1:410
STATED PRINT RUN 99 SERIAL #'d SETS

1999 Topps Stars Four Star

COMPLETE SET (10) 15.00 40.00
STATED ODDS 1:10
1 Ken Griffey Jr. 1.25 3.00
2 Chipper Jones .60 1.50
3 Mike Piazza 1.00 2.50
4 Nomar Garciaparra 1.00 2.50
5 Derek Jeter 1.50 4.00
6 Frank Thomas .60 1.50
7 Ben Grieve .25 .60
8 Mark McGwire 1.50 4.00
9 Sammy Sosa .60 1.50
10 Alex Rodriguez 1.00 2.50

1999 Topps Stars Four Star Foil

*STARS: 10X TO 25X BASE CARD HI
STATED ODDS 1:1650
STATED PRINT RUN 49 SERIAL #'d SETS

1999 Topps Stars Bright Futures

COMPLETE SET (10) 15.00 40.00
STATED ODDS 1:41
STATED PRINT RUN 1999 SERIAL #'d SETS
*FOIL: 3X TO 8X BASIC BR.FUTURES
FOIL ODDS 1:2702
FOIL PRINT RUN 30 SERIAL #'d SETS
BF1 Troy Glaus 2.00 5.00
BF2 Eric Chavez 1.25 3.00
BF3 Adrian Beltre 1.25 3.00
BF4 Michael Barrett 1.25 3.00
BF5 Gabe Kapler 1.25 3.00
BF6 Alex Gonzalez 1.25 3.00
BF7 Matt Clement 1.25 3.00
BF8 Pat Burrell 1.25 3.00
BF9 Ruben Mateo 1.25 3.00
BF10 Alfonso Soriano 2.50 6.00

1999 Topps Stars Galaxy

COMPLETE SET (10) 15.00 40.00
STATED ODDS 1:41
STATED PRINT RUN 1999 SERIAL #'d SETS
*FOIL/30: 10X TO 25X BASIC GALAXY
G1 Mark McGwire 3.00 8.00
G2 Roger Clemens 2.50 6.00
G3 Nomar Garciaparra 1.25 3.00
G4 Alex Rodriguez 2.50 6.00
G5 Kerry Wood .75 2.00
G6 Ben Grieve .75 2.00
G7 Derek Jeter 5.00 12.00
G8 Vladimir Guerrero 1.25 3.00
G9 Ken Griffey Jr. 4.00 10.00
G10 Sammy Sosa 2.00 5.00

1999 Topps Stars Rookie Reprints

COMPLETE SET (5) 30.00 80.00
STATED ODDS 1:65
1 Frank Robinson 6.00 15.00
2 Ernie Banks 8.00 20.00
3 Yogi Berra 8.00 20.00
4 Bob Gibson 6.00 15.00
5 Tom Seaver 6.00 15.00

1999 Topps Stars Rookie Reprints Autographs

STATED ODDS 1:406
BANKS STATED ODDS 1:812
1 Frank Robinson 15.00 40.00
2 Ernie Banks DP 50.00 120.00
3 Yogi Berra 25.00 60.00
4 Bob Gibson 50.00 120.00
5 Tom Seaver 60.00 150.00

2000 Topps Stars Pre-Production

COMPLETE SET (5) 2.50 6.00
PP1 Bob Gibson .60 1.50
PP2 Alex Rodriguez 1.25 3.00
PP3 Sammy Sosa 1.00 2.50
PP4 Pat Burrell .40 1.00
PP5 Rick Asadoorian .40 1.00

2000 Topps Stars

COMPLETE SET (200) 20.00 50.00
COMMON CARD (1-200) .20 .50
COMMON RC .20 .50
1 Vladimir Guerrero .30 .75
2 Eric Karros .20 .50
3 Omar Vizquel .30 .75
4 Ken Griffey Jr. 1.00 2.50
5 Preston Wilson .20 .50
6 Albert Belle .20 .50
7 Ryan Klesko .20 .50
8 Bob Abreu .20 .50
9 Warren Morris .20 .50
10 Rafael Palmeiro .30 .75
11 Nomar Garciaparra .30 .75
12 Dante Bichette .20 .50
13 Jeff Cirillo .20 .50
14 Carlos Beltran .30 .75
15 Tony Clark .20 .50
16 Ray Durham .20 .50
17 Mark McGwire .75 2.00
18 Jim Thome .30 .75
19 Todd Walker .20 .50
20 Richie Sexson .20 .50
21 Adrian Beltre .50 1.25
22 Jay Bell .20 .50
23 Craig Biggio .30 .75
24 Ben Grieve .20 .50
25 Greg Maddux .60 1.50
26 Fernando Tatis .20 .50
27 Jeromy Burnitz .20 .50
28 Vinny Castilla .20 .50
29 Mark Grace .30 .75
30 Derek Jeter 1.25 3.00
31 Larry Walker .30 .75
32 Ivan Rodriguez .30 .75
33 Curt Schilling .30 .75
34 Mike Lamb RC .20 .50
35 Kevin Brown .20 .50
36 Andruw Jones .20 .50
37 Chris Mears RC .20 .50
38 Bartolo Colon .20 .50
39 Edgardo Alfonzo .20 .50
40 Brady Anderson .20 .50
41 Andres Galarraga .30 .75
42 Scott Rolen .30 .75
43 Manny Ramirez .50 1.25
44 Carlos Delgado .20 .50
45 David Cone .20 .50
46 Carl Everett .20 .50
47 Chipper Jones .50 1.25
48 Barry Bonds .75 2.00
49 Dean Palmer .20 .50
50 Frank Thomas .50 1.25
51 Paul O'Neill .30 .75
52 Mo Vaughn .20 .50
53 Todd Helton .30 .75
54 Jason Giambi .20 .50
55 Brian Jordan .20 .50
56 Luis Gonzalez .20 .50
57 Alex Rodriguez .60 1.50
58 J.D. Drew .20 .50
59 Javy Lopez .20 .50
60 Tony Gwynn .50 1.25
61 Jason Kendall .20 .50
62 Pedro Martinez .30 .75
63 Matt Williams .20 .50
64 Gary Sheffield .20 .50
65 Roberto Alomar .30 .75
66 Lyle Overbay RC .30 .75
67 Jeff Bagwell .30 .75
68 Tim Hudson .30 .75
69 Sammy Sosa .50 1.25
70 Keith Reed RC .20 .50
71 Robin Ventura .20 .50
72 Cal Ripken 1.50 4.00
73 Alex Gonzalez .20 .50
74 Aaron McNeal RC .20 .50
75 Mike Lieberthal .20 .50
76 Brian Giles .20 .50
77 Kevin Millwood .20 .50
78 Troy O'Leary .20 .50
79 Raul Mondesi .20 .50
80 John Olerud .20 .50
81 David Justice .20 .50
82 Erubiel Durazo .20 .50
83 Shawn Green .20 .50
84 Tino Martinez .20 .50
85 Greg Vaughn .20 .50
86 Tom Glavine .30 .75
87 Jose Canseco .30 .75
88 Kenny Lofton .20 .50
89 Brian Daubach .20 .50
90 Mike Piazza .50 1.25
91 Randy Johnson .50 1.25
92 Pokey Reese .20 .50
93 Troy Glaus .20 .50
94 Kerry Wood .20 .50
95 Sean Casey .20 .50
96 Magglio Ordonez .30 .75
97 Bernie Williams .30 .75
98 Juan Gonzalez .20 .50
99 Barry Larkin .30 .75
100 Orlando Hernandez .20 .50
101 Roger Clemens .60 1.50
102 Bob Gibson .30 .75
103 Gary Carter .30 .75
104 Willie Stargell .30 .75
105 Joe Morgan .30 .75
106 Brooks Robinson .30 .75
107 Ozzie Smith .60 1.50
108 Carl Yastrzemski .75 2.00
109 Al Kaline .50 1.25
110 Frank Robinson .30 .75
111 Lance Berkman .30 .75
112 Adam Piatt .20 .50
113 Vernon Wells .20 .50
114 Rafael Furcal .30 .75
115 Rick Ankiel .30 .75
116 Corey Patterson .20 .50
117 Josh Hamilton .60 1.50
118 Jack Cust .20 .50
119 Josh Girdley .20 .50
120 Pablo Ozuna .20 .50
121 Sean Burroughs .20 .50
122 Pat Burrell .20 .50
123 Chad Hermansen .20 .50
124 Ruben Mateo .20 .50
125 Ben Petrick .20 .50
126 Dee Brown .20 .50
127 Eric Munson .20 .50
128 Ruben Salazar RC .20 .50
129 Kip Wells .20 .50
130 Alfonso Soriano .50 1.25
131 Mark Mulder .20 .50
132 Roosevelt Brown .20 .50
133 Nick Johnson .20 .50
134 Kyle Snyder .20 .50
135 David Walling .20 .50
136 Geraldo Guzman RC .20 .50
137 John Sneed RC .20 .50
138 Ben Christensen RC .20 .50
139 Corey Myers RC .20 .50
140 Jose Ortiz RC .20 .50
141 Ryan Christianson RC .20 .50
142 Brett Myers RC .60 1.50
143 Bobby Bradley RC .20 .50
144 Rick Asadoorian RC .20 .50
145 Julio Zuleta RC .20 .50
146 Ty Howington RC .20 .50
147 Josh Kalinowski RC .20 .50
148 B.J. Garbe RC .20 .50
149 Scott Downs RC .20 .50
150 Dan Wright RC .20 .50
151 Jeff Bagwell SPOT .30 .75
152 Vladimir Guerrero SPOT .30 .75
153 Mike Piazza SPOT .50 1.25
154 Juan Gonzalez SPOT .20 .50
155 Ivan Rodriguez SPOT .30 .75
156 Manny Ramirez SPOT .50 1.25
157 Sammy Sosa SPOT .50 1.25
158 Chipper Jones SPOT .50 1.25
159 Shawn Green SPOT .20 .50
160 Ken Griffey Jr. SPOT 1.00 2.50
161 Cal Ripken SPOT 1.50 4.00
162 Nomar Garciaparra SPOT .30 .75
163 Derek Jeter SPOT 1.25 3.00
164 Barry Bonds SPOT .75 2.00
165 Greg Maddux SPOT .60 1.50
166 Mark McGwire SPOT .75 2.00
167 Roberto Alomar SPOT .30 .75
168 Alex Rodriguez SPOT .60 1.50
169 Randy Johnson SPOT .50 1.25
170 Tony Gwynn SPOT .50 1.25
171 Pedro Martinez SPOT .30 .75
172 Bob Gibson SPOT .30 .75
173 Gary Carter SPOT .30 .75
174 Willie Stargell SPOT .30 .75
175 Joe Morgan SPOT .30 .75
176 Brooks Robinson SPOT .30 .75
177 Ozzie Smith SPOT .60 1.50
178 Carl Yastrzemski SPOT .75 2.00
179 Al Kaline SPOT .50 1.25
180 Frank Robinson SPOT .30 .75
181 Adam Piatt SPOT .20 .50
182 Alfonso Soriano SPOT .50 1.25
183 Corey Patterson SPOT .20 .50
184 Vernon Wells SPOT .20 .50
185 Pat Burrell SPOT .20 .50
186 Mark Mulder SPOT .20 .50
187 Eric Munson SPOT .20 .50
188 Rafael Furcal SPOT .30 .75
189 Rick Ankiel SPOT .30 .75
190 Ruben Mateo SPOT .20 .50
191 Sean Burroughs SPOT .20 .50
192 Josh Hamilton .60 1.50
193 Brett Myers SPOT .60 1.50
194 Ben Christensen SPOT .20 .50
195 Ty Howington SPOT .20 .50
196 Rick Asadoorian SPOT .20 .50
197 Josh Kalinowski SPOT .20 .50
198 Corey Myers SPOT .20 .50
199 Ryan Christianson SPOT .20 .50
200 John Sneed SPOT .20 .50

2000 Topps Stars Metallic Blue

*BLUE 1-150: 2.5X TO 6X BASIC
*BLUE RC 1-150: 2.5X TO 6X BASIC
1-150 STATED ODDS 1:26
1-150 PRINT RUN 299 SERIAL #'d SETS
*BLUE 151-180: 4X TO 10X BASIC
*BLUE RC 193-200: 4X TO 10X BASIC
151-200 STATED ODDS 1:232
151-200 PRINT RUN 99 SERIAL #'d SETS

2000 Topps Stars All-Star Authority

COMPLETE SET (14) 15.00 40.00
STATED ODDS 1:13
AS1 Mark McGwire 1.50 4.00
AS2 Sammy Sosa 1.00 2.50
AS3 Ken Griffey Jr. 2.00 5.00
AS4 Cal Ripken 3.00 8.00
AS5 Tony Gwynn 1.00 2.50
AS6 Barry Bonds 1.50 4.00
AS7 Mike Piazza 1.00 2.50
AS8 Pedro Martinez .60 1.50
AS9 Chipper Jones 1.00 2.50
AS10 Manny Ramirez 1.00 2.50
AS11 Alex Rodriguez 1.25 3.00
AS12 Derek Jeter 2.50 6.00
AS13 Nomar Garciaparra .60 1.50
AS14 Roberto Alomar .60 1.50

2000 Topps Stars Autographs

GROUP A STATED ODDS 1:382
GROUP B STATED ODDS 1:1636
OVERALL STATED ODDS 1:310
AK Al Kaline B 40.00 100.00
BG Bob Gibson A 15.00 40.00
BR Brooks Robinson B 12.50 30.00
CY Carl Yastrzemski B 40.00 80.00
DJ Derek Jeter A 125.00 250.00
FR Frank Robinson B 20.00 50.00
GC Gary Carter B 40.00 80.00
JM Joe Morgan B 20.00 50.00
KM Kevin Millwood A 6.00 15.00
OS Ozzie Smith A 20.00 50.00
RA Rick Ankiel A 10.00 25.00
RF Rafael Furcal A 6.00 15.00
WS Willie Stargell B 60.00 120.00

2000 Topps Stars Game Gear Bats

GROUP A STATED ODDS 1:2289
GROUP B STATED ODDS 1:1353
GROUP C STATED ODDS 1:409
OVERALL STATED ODDS 1:175
EXCH.DEADLINE 05/30/01
GGB1 Rafael Furcal C 4.00 10.00
GGB2 Sean Burroughs B 3.00 8.00
GGB3 Corey Patterson B 3.00 8.00
GGB4 Chipper Jones B 6.00 15.00
GGB5 Vernon Wells C 4.00 10.00
GGB6 Mark Quinn B 3.00 8.00
GGB7 Eric Munson C 3.00 8.00
GGB8 Ben Petrick B 3.00 8.00
GGB9 Dee Brown A 3.00 8.00
GGB10 Lance Berkman C 4.00 10.00

2000 Topps Stars Game Gear Jerseys

STATED ODDS 1:382
EXCHANGE DEADLINE 05/30/01
GGJ1 Kevin Millwood 4.00 10.00
GGJ2 Brad Penny 4.00 10.00
GGJ3 J.D. Drew 4.00 10.00

2000 Topps Stars Progression

COMPLETE SET (9) 8.00 20.00
STATED ODDS 1:13
P1 Gibson .60 1.50
P.Martinez
Ankiel
P2 Carter 1.00 2.50
Piazza
Petrick
P3 Stargell 1.50 4.00
McGwire
Burrell
P4 Morgan .60 1.50
R.Alomar
R.Salazar
P5 B.Rob 1.00 2.50
C.Jones
Burroughs
P6 O.Smith 2.50 6.00
Jeter
Furcal
P7 Carl Yastrzemski 1.25 3.00
Barry Bonds
Josh Hamilton
P8 Kaline 2.00 5.00
Griffey Jr.
Mateo
P9 F.Rob 1.00 2.50
M.Ram
C.Patterson

2000 Topps Stars Walk of Fame

COMPLETE SET (15) 12.50 30.00
STATED ODDS 1:8
WF1 Cal Ripken 2.50 6.00
WF2 Ken Griffey Jr. 1.50 4.00
WF3 Mark McGwire 1.25 3.00
WF4 Sammy Sosa .75 2.00
WF5 Alex Rodriguez 1.00 2.50
WF6 Derek Jeter 2.00 5.00
WF7 Nomar Garciaparra .50 1.25
WF8 Chipper Jones .75 2.00
WF9 Manny Ramirez .75 2.00
WF10 Mike Piazza .75 2.00
WF11 Vladimir Guerrero .50 1.25
WF12 Barry Bonds 1.25 3.00
WF13 Tony Gwynn .75 2.00
WF14 Roberto Alomar .50 1.25
WF15 Pedro Martinez .50 1.25

2001 Topps Stars

COMPLETE SET (200) 40.00 70.00
1 Darin Erstad .20 .50
2 Luis Gonzalez .20 .50
3 Rafael Furcal .20 .50
4 Dante Bichette .20 .50
5 Sammy Sosa .50 1.25
6 Ken Griffey Jr. 1.00 2.50
7 Jim Thome .30 .75
8 Bobby Higginson .20 .50
9 Cliff Floyd .20 .50
10 Lance Berkman .20 .50
11 Eric Karros .20 .50
12 Jeromy Burnitz .20 .50
13 Jose Vidro .15 .40
14 Benny Agbayani .15 .40
15 Jorge Posada .30 .75
16 Ramon Hernandez .15 .40
17 Jason Kendall .20 .50
18 Jeff Kent .20 .50
19 John Olerud .20 .50
20 Al Martin .15 .40
21 Gerald Williams .15 .40
22 Gabe Kapler .20 .50
23 Carlos Delgado .20 .50
24 Mariano Rivera .50 1.25
25 Javy Lopez .20 .50
26 Paul Konerko .20 .50
27 Daryle Ward .15 .40
28 Mike Lieberthal .20 .50
29 Tom Goodwin .15 .40
30 Garret Anderson .20 .50
31 Steve Finley .20 .50
32 Brian Jordan .20 .50
33 Nomar Garciaparra .75 2.00
34 Ray Durham .20 .50
35 Sean Casey .20 .50
36 Kenny Lofton .20 .50
37 Dean Palmer .20 .50
38 Jeff Bagwell .30 .75
39 Mike Sweeney .20 .50
40 Adrian Beltre .20 .50
41 Richie Sexson .20 .50
42 Vladimir Guerrero .50 1.25
43 Derek Jeter 1.25 3.00
44 Miguel Tejada .20 .50
45 Doug Glanville .15 .40
46 Brian Giles .20 .50
47 Marvin Benard .15 .40
48 Edgar Martinez .30 .75
49 Edgar Renteria .20 .50
50 Fred McGriff .30 .75
51 Ivan Rodriguez .30 .75
52 Brad Fullmer .15 .40
53 Antonio Alfonseca .15 .40
54 Tom Glavine .30 .75
55 Warren Morris .15 .40
56 Johnny Damon .30 .75
57 Dmitri Young .20 .50
58 Mo Vaughn .20 .50
59 Randy Johnson .50 1.25
60 Greg Maddux .75 2.00
61 Carl Everett .20 .50
62 Maggio Ordonez .20 .50
63 Pokey Reese .15 .40
64 Todd Helton .30 .75
65 Preston Wilson .20 .50
66 Richard Hidalgo .15 .40
67 Jermaine Dye .20 .50
68 Gary Sheffield .20 .50
69 Geoff Jenkins .15 .40
70 Edgardo Alfonzo .15 .40
71 Paul O'Neill .30 .75
72 Terrence Long .15 .40
73 Bob Abreu .20 .50
74 Kevin Young .15 .40
75 J.T. Snow .20 .50
76 Alex Rodriguez .60 1.50
77 Jim Edmonds .20 .50
78 Mark McGwire 1.25 3.00
79 Tony Batista .15 .40
80 Darrin Fletcher .15 .40
81 Robb Nen .20 .50
82 Jose Offerman .15 .40
83 Travis Fryman .20 .50
84 Joe Randa .20 .50
85 Omar Vizquel .30 .75
86 Tim Salmon .30 .75
87 Andruw Jones .30 .75
88 Albert Belle .20 .50
89 Manny Ramirez Sox .30 .75
90 Frank Thomas .50 1.25
91 Barry Larkin .30 .75
92 Neifi Perez .15 .40
93 Luis Castillo .15 .40
94 Moises Alou .20 .50
95 Mark Quinn .15 .40
96 Kevin Brown .20 .50
97 Cristian Guzman .15 .40
98 Mike Piazza .75 2.00
99 Bernie Williams .30 .75
100 Jason Giambi .20 .50
101 Scott Rolen .30 .75
102 Phil Nevin .20 .50
103 Rich Aurilia .15 .40
104 Mike Cameron .15 .40
105 Fernando Vina .15 .40
106 Greg Vaughn .15 .40
107 Jose Cruz Jr. .15 .40
108 Raul Mondesi .20 .50
109 Ben Molina .15 .40
110 Pedro Martinez .30 .75
111 Todd Hollandsworth .15 .40
112 Jacque Jones .20 .50
113 Rickey Henderson .50 1.25
114 Troy Glaus .20 .50
115 Chipper Jones .50 1.25
116 Delino DeShields .15 .40
117 Eric Young .15 .40
118 Jose Valentin .15 .40
119 Roberto Alomar .30 .75
120 Jeff Cirillo .15 .40
121 Mike Lowell .20 .50
122 Julio Lugo .15 .40
123 Shawn Green .20 .50
124 Marquis Grissom .20 .50
125 Matt Lawton .15 .40
126 Jay Payton .15 .40
127 David Justice .20 .50
128 Eric Chavez .20 .50
129 Pat Burrell .20 .50
130 Ryan Klesko .20 .50
131 Barry Bonds 1.25 3.00
132 Jay Buhner .20 .50
133 J.D. Drew .20 .50
134 Rafael Palmeiro .30 .75
135 Shannon Stewart .20 .50
136 Juan Gonzalez .20 .50
137 Tony Womack .15 .40
138 Carlos Lee .20 .50
139 Derrek Lee .30 .75
140 Ben Grieve .15 .40
141 Ron Belliard .15 .40
142 Stan Musial .75 2.00
143 Ernie Banks .50 1.25
144 Jim Palmer .20 .50
145 Tony Perez .20 .50
146 Duke Snider .30 .75
147 Rod Carew .30 .75
148 Warren Spahn .30 .75
149 Yogi Berra .60 1.50
150 Juan Marichal .20 .50
151 Eric Munson .15 .40
152 Carlos Pena .15 .40
153 Joe Crede .50 1.25
154 Ryan Anderson .15 .40
155 Milton Bradley .20 .50
156 Sean Burroughs .15 .40
157 Corey Patterson .15 .40
158 C.C. Sabathia .20 .50
159 Ben Petrick .15 .40
160 Aubrey Huff .20 .50
161 Gookie Dawkins .15 .40
162 Ben Sheets .30 .75
163 Pablo Ozuna .15 .40
164 Eric Valent .15 .40
165 Rod Barajas .15 .40
166 Chin-Feng Chen .20 .50
167 Josh Hamilton .30 .75
168 Keith Ginter .15 .40
169 Vernon Wells .20 .50
170 Dernell Stenson .15 .40
171 Alfonso Soriano .30 .75
172 Jason Marquis .15 .40
173 Nick Johnson .20 .50
174 Adam Everett .15 .40
175 Jimmy Rollins .20 .50
176 Ben Diggins .15 .40
177 John Lackey .15 .40
178 Scott Heard .15 .40
179 Brian Hitchcox RC .15 .40
180 Odannis Ayala RC .15 .40
181 Scott Pratt RC .15 .40
182 Greg Runser RC .15 .40
183 Chris Russ RC .15 .40
184 Derek Thompson .15 .40
185 Jason Jones RC .15 .40
186 Dominic Rich RC .15 .40
187 Chad Petty RC .15 .40
188 Steve Smyth RC .15 .40
189 Bryan Hebson RC .15 .40
190 Danny Borrell RC .15 .40
191 Bob Keppel RC .15 .40
192 Justin Wayne RC .15 .40
193 Reggie Abercrombie RC .25 .60
194 Travis Baptist RC .15 .40
195 Shawn Fagan RC .15 .40
196 Jose Reyes RC 4.00 10.00
197 Chris Bass RC .15 .40
198 Albert Pujols RC 30.00 80.00
199 Luis Cotto RC .15 .40
200 Jake Peavy RC .75 2.00

2001 Topps Stars Elimination

*STARS: 6X TO 15X BASIC CARDS
STATED ODDS 1:72
STATED PRINT RUN 100 SETS
EXCHANGE DEADLINE 10/19/01

2001 Topps Stars Gold

*STARS: 2X TO 5X BASIC CARDS
*ROOKIES: 1.5X TO 4X BASIC CARDS
STATED ODDS 1:9
STATED PRINT RUN 499 SERIAL #'d SETS
196 Jose Reyes 20.00 50.00
198 Albert Pujols 75.00 200.00
200 Jake Peavy 5.00 12.00

2001 Topps Stars Onyx

*STARS: 5X TO 12X BASIC CARDS
*ROOKIES: 3X TO 8X BASIC CARDS
STATED ODDS 1:48
STATED PRINT RUN 99 SERIAL #'d SETS
196 Jose Reyes 30.00 80.00
198 Albert Pujols 150.00 400.00

2001 Topps Stars Autographs

STATED ODDS 1:353
TSACD Carlos Delgado 6.00 15.00
TSADS Duke Snider 15.00 40.00
TSAEB Ernie Banks 20.00 50.00
TSAEM Eric Munson 6.00 15.00
TSAIR Ivan Rodriguez 20.00 50.00
TSAJM Juan Marichal 10.00 25.00
TSAJP Jim Palmer 10.00 25.00
TSARC Rod Carew 15.00 40.00
TSASM Stan Musial 60.00 120.00
TSATH Todd Helton 15.00 40.00
TSATP Tony Perez 10.00 25.00
TSAWS Warren Spahn 10.00 25.00
TSAYB Yogi Berra 25.00 60.00

2001 Topps Stars Game Gear Bats

GROUP A STATED ODDS 1:216
GROUP B STATED ODDS 1:1368
OVERALL ODDS 1:187
TSRAB Adrian Beltre A 4.00 10.00
TSRAK Adam Kennedy A 4.00 10.00
TSRAP Adam Piatt A 4.00 10.00
TSRBD Ben Davis A 4.00 10.00
TSRCP Corey Patterson B 4.00 10.00
TSRED Erubiel Durazo A 4.00 10.00

TSREM Eric Munson A 4.00 10.00
TSRFL Felipe Lopez A 4.00 10.00
TSRFS Fernando Seguignol A 4.00 10.00
TSRGL George Lombard A 4.00 10.00
TSRGM Gary Matthews Jr. A 4.00 10.00
TSRJE Juan Encarnacion A 4.00 10.00
TSRJDD J.D. Drew A 4.00 10.00
TSRLB Lance Berkman A 4.00 10.00
TSRMC Michael Cuddyer A 4.00 10.00
TSRNP Neifi Perez A 4.00 10.00
TSRRF Rafael Furcal B 4.00 10.00
TSRRS Richie Sexson A 4.00 10.00
TSRSB Sean Burroughs A 4.00 10.00
TSRSR Scott Rolen A 6.00 15.00
TSRTL Terrence Long B 4.00 10.00

2001 Topps Stars Game Gear Jerseys

GROUP A STATED ODDS 1:71
GROUP B STATED ODDS 1:472
OVERALL ODDS 1:61
TSRAJ Andruw Jones A 6.00 15.00
TSRBB Barry Bonds B 12.50 30.00
TSRCJ Chipper Jones A 6.00 15.00
TSREA Edgardo Alfonzo A 4.00 10.00
TSREM Edgar Martinez A 6.00 15.00
TSRFT Frank Thomas A 6.00 15.00
TSRJV Jose Vidro A 4.00 10.00
TSRLC Luis Castillo A 4.00 10.00
TSRMO Magglio Ordonez A 4.00 10.00
TSRMP Mike Piazza A 8.00 20.00
TSRRA Roberto Alomar A 6.00 15.00
TSRSS Sammy Sosa A 6.00 15.00
TSRTG Tony Gwynn A 6.00 15.00
TSRTH Todd Helton B 6.00 15.00
TSRSHS Shannon Stewart A 4.00 10.00

2001 Topps Stars Player's Choice Awards

COMPLETE SET (10) 12.50 30.00
STATED ODDS 1:12
PCA1 Bonds 3.00 8.00
Helton
Delgado
PCA2 E.Davis .50 1.25
Sheff
Wendell
PCA3 Delgado 1.50 4.00
A-Rod
Thomas
PCA4 Pedro .75 2.00
Wells
Pettitte
PCA5 Sasaki .50 1.25
Quinn
Long
PCA6 Thomas 1.25 3.00
Buhner
Higginson
PCA7 Helton 3.00 8.00
Bonds
Kent
PCA8 R.John 2.00 5.00
Glavine
Maddux
PCA9 Furcal .50 1.25
Ankiel
Payton
PCA10 Galarraga .50 1.25
Alou
D'Amico

2001 Topps Stars Player's Choice Awards Relics

STATED ODDS 1:1530
PCAR1 Carlos Delgado 6.00 15.00
PCAR2 Eric Davis 6.00 15.00
PCAR3 Carlos Delgado 6.00 15.00
PCAR4 Pedro Martinez 10.00 25.00
PCAR5 Terrence Long 6.00 15.00
PCAR6 Frank Thomas 10.00 25.00
PCAR7 Todd Helton 10.00 25.00
PCAR8 Randy Johnson 10.00 25.00
PCAR9 Rafael Furcal 6.00 15.00
PCAR10 Andres Galarraga 6.00 15.00

2001 Topps Stars Progression

COMPLETE SET (9) 6.00 15.00
STATED ODDS 1:8
P1 Banks .75 2.00
A-Rod
Soriano
P2 Berra .60 1.50
I-Rod
R.Hernandez
P3 T.Perez .60 1.50
Delg
E.Munson
P4 Carew .60 1.50
R.Alomar
J.Ortiz
P5 Musial 1.00 2.50
Erstad
A.Escobar
P6 Palmer .60 1.50
K.Brown
Ainsworth
P7 Snider .60 1.50
Edmonds
V.Wells
P8 Spahn .60 1.50
R.John
R.Anderson
P9 Marichal .60 1.50
Colon
B.Bradley

1998 Topps Stars 'N Steel

The 1998 Topps Stars 'N Steel set was issued in one series totalling 44 cards and was distributed in three-card tri-fold packs with a suggested retail price of $9.99. The fronts feature color action player photos printed using Serillusion technology on .25 gauge metal stock. The backs carry player information.

COMPLETE SET (44) 25.00 60.00
1 Roberto Alomar .60 1.50
2 Jeff Bagwell .60 1.50
3 Albert Belle .40 1.00
4 Dante Bichette .40 1.00
5 Barry Bonds 1.50 4.00
6 Jay Buhner .40 1.00
7 Ken Caminiti .40 1.00
8 Vinny Castilla .40 1.00
9 Roger Clemens 1.25 3.00
10 Jose Cruz Jr. .40 1.00
11 Andres Galarraga .60 1.50
12 Nomar Garciaparra .60 1.50
13 Juan Gonzalez .40 1.00
14 Mark Grace .60 1.50
15 Ken Griffey Jr. 2.00 5.00
16 Tony Gwynn 1.00 2.50
17 Todd Hundley .40 1.00
18 Derek Jeter 2.50 6.00
19 Randy Johnson 1.00 2.50
20 Andruw Jones .40 1.00
21 Chipper Jones 1.00 2.50
22 David Justice .40 1.00
23 Ray Lankford .40 1.00
24 Barry Larkin .60 1.50
25 Kenny Lofton .40 1.00
26 Greg Maddux 1.25 3.00
27 Edgar Martinez .60 1.50
28 Tino Martinez .40 1.00
29 Mark McGwire 1.50 4.00
30 Paul Molitor .60 1.50
31 Rafael Palmeiro .60 1.50
32 Mike Piazza 1.00 2.50
33 Manny Ramirez 1.00 2.50
34 Cal Ripken 3.00 8.00
35 Ivan Rodriguez .60 1.50
36 Scott Rolen .60 1.50
37 Tim Salmon .60 1.50
38 Gary Sheffield .40 1.00
39 Sammy Sosa 1.00 2.50
40 Frank Thomas 1.00 2.50
41 Jim Thome .60 1.50
42 Mo Vaughn .40 1.00
43 Larry Walker .60 1.50
44 Bernie Williams .60 1.50

1998 Topps Stars 'N Steel Gold

*GOLD: 1X TO 2.5X BASIC CARDS
STATED ODDS 1:12

1998 Topps Stars 'N Steel Gold Holographic

*GOLD HOLO: 3X TO 8X BASIC CARDS
STATED ODDS 1:40

1999 Topps Stars 'N Steel

The 1999 Topps Stars 'N Steel set was issued in one series totalling 44 cards and was distributed in three-card tri-fold packs with a suggested retail price of $9.99. The fronts feature color action player photos printed using Serillusion technology and bonded to 25-gauge metal with a silver border.

COMPLETE SET (44) 30.00 80.00
1 Kerry Wood .60 1.50
2 Ben Grieve .60 1.50
3 Chipper Jones 1.50 4.00
4 Alex Rodriguez 2.00 5.00
5 Mo Vaughn .60 1.50
6 Bernie Williams 1.00 2.50
7 Juan Gonzalez .60 1.50
8 Vinny Castilla .60 1.50
9 Tony Gwynn 1.50 4.00
10 Manny Ramirez 1.50 4.00
11 Raul Mondesi .60 1.50
12 Roger Clemens 2.00 5.00
13 Darin Erstad .60 1.50
14 Barry Bonds 2.50 6.00
15 Cal Ripken 5.00 12.00
16 Barry Larkin 1.00 2.50
17 Scott Rolen 1.00 2.50
18 Albert Belle .60 1.50
19 Craig Biggio 1.00 2.50
20 Tony Clark .60 1.50
21 Mark McGwire 2.50 6.00
22 Andres Galarraga 1.00 2.50
23 Kenny Lofton .60 1.50
24 Pedro Martinez 1.00 2.50
25 Paul O'Neill 1.00 2.50
26 Ken Griffey Jr. 3.00 8.00
27 Travis Lee .60 1.50
28 Tim Salmon .60 1.50
29 Frank Thomas 1.50 4.00
30 Larry Walker 1.00 2.50
31 Moises Alou .60 1.50
32 Vladimir Guerrero 1.00 2.50
33 Ivan Rodriguez 1.00 2.50
34 Derek Jeter 4.00 10.00
35 Greg Vaughn .60 1.50
36 Gary Sheffield .60 1.50
37 Carlos Delgado .60 1.50
38 Greg Maddux 2.00 5.00
39 Sammy Sosa 1.50 4.00
40 Mike Piazza 1.50 4.00
41 Nomar Garciaparra 1.00 2.50
42 Dante Bichette .60 1.50
43 Jeff Bagwell 1.00 2.50
44 Jim Thome 1.00 2.50

1999 Topps Stars 'N Steel Gold

*STARS: 2X TO 5X BASIC CARDS
STATED ODDS 1:12

1999 Topps Stars 'N Steel Gold Domed Holographic

*STARS: 3X TO 8X BASIC CARDS
STATED ODDS 1:24

2006 Topps Sterling

B.BONDS (1-19) 5.00 12.00
B.BONDS ODDS 1:10
M.MANTLE (20-39) 8.00 20.00
M.MANTLE ODDS 1:10
J.GIBSON (40-43) 12.50 30.00
J.GIBSON ODDS 1:191
R.HENDERSON (44-53) 4.00 10.00
R.HENDERSON ODDS 1:22
T.WILLIAMS (54-62) 5.00 12.00
T.WILLIAMS ODDS 1:27
R.CLEMENTE (63-67) 10.00 25.00
R.CLEMENTE ODDS 1:40
N.RYAN (68-77) 8.00 20.00
N.RYAN ODDS 1:20
C.RIPKEN (78-96) 8.00 20.00
C.RIPKEN ODDS 1:10
S.MUSIAL (97-101) 4.00 10.00
S.MUSIAL ODDS 1:40
R.JACKSON (102-106) 4.00 10.00
R.JACKSON ODDS 1:40
J.BENCH (107-111) 4.00 10.00
J.BENCH ODDS 1:43
G.BRETT (112-121) 4.00 10.00
G.BRETT ODDS 1:20
D.MATTINGLY (122-131) 5.00 12.00
D.MATTINGLY ODDS 1:20
R.MARIS (132-136) 5.00 12.00
R.MARIS ODDS 1:40
R.CAREW (137-146) 4.00 10.00
R.CAREW ODDS 1:20
Y.BERRA (147-151) 4.00 10.00
Y.BERRA ODDS 1:40
M.SCHMIDT (152-156) 4.00 10.00
M.SCHMIDT ODDS 1:40
C.YASTRZEMSKI (157-175) 4.00 10.00
C.YASTRZEMSKI ODDS 1:10
T.GWYNN (176-185) 4.00 10.00
T.GWYNN ODDS 1:20
R.SANDBERG (186-190) 4.00 10.00
R.SANDBERG ODDS 1:40
O.SMITH (191-200) 4.00 10.00
O.SMITH ODDS 1:20
STATED PRINT RUN 250 SER.#'d SETS

2006 Topps Sterling Framed Burgundy

B.BONDS (1-19) 30.00 60.00
M.MANTLE (20-39) 50.00 100.00
J.GIBSON (40-43) 30.00 60.00
R.HENDERSON (44-53) 20.00 50.00
T.WILLIAMS (54-62) 30.00 60.00
R.CLEMENTE (63-67) 40.00 80.00
N.RYAN (68-77) 75.00 150.00
C.RIPKEN (78-96) 75.00 150.00
S.MUSIAL (97-101) 20.00 50.00
R.JACKSON (102-106) 20.00 50.00
J.BENCH (107-111) 20.00 50.00
G.BRETT (112-121) 30.00 60.00
D.MATTINGLY (122-131) 30.00 60.00
R.MARIS (132-136) 30.00 60.00
R.CAREW (137-146) 10.00 25.00
Y.BERRA (147-151) 20.00 50.00
M.SCHMIDT (152-156) 20.00 50.00
C.YASTRZEMSKI (157-175) 20.00 50.00
T.GWYNN (176-185) 20.00 50.00
R.SANDBERG (186-190) 20.00 50.00
O.SMITH (191-200) 20.00 50.00
RANDOM INSERTS IN BONUS PACKS
STATED PRINT RUN 10 SER.#'d SETS

2006 Topps Sterling Framed White

*FRAMED WHITE: .6X TO 1.5X BASIC
RANDOM INSERTS IN BONUS PACKS
STATED PRINT RUN 50 SER.#'d SETS

2006 Topps Sterling Baseball Cut Signatures

OVERALL CUT SIGNATURE ODDS 1:5
AK Al Kaline 40.00 100.00
BF Bob Feller 15.00 40.00
BG Bob Gibson 40.00 80.00
BR Brooks Robinson 40.00 80.00
CF Carlton Fisk 30.00 60.00
DS Duke Snider 15.00 40.00
EW Earl Weaver 15.00 40.00
GC Gary Carter 20.00 50.00
GK George Kell 15.00 40.00
GP Gaylord Perry 15.00 40.00
HK Harmon Killebrew 50.00 100.00
JB Johnny Bench 30.00 80.00
JMO Joe Morgan 15.00 40.00
JP Jim Palmer 15.00 40.00
LA Luis Aparicio 30.00 60.00
LB Lou Brock 30.00 60.00
MI Monte Irvin 15.00 40.00
OC Orlando Cepeda 15.00 40.00
PN Phil Niekro 15.00 40.00
RC Rod Carew 20.00 50.00
RF Rollie Fingers 15.00 40.00
RK Ralph Kiner 20.00 50.00
RR Robin Roberts 30.00 60.00
RS Ryne Sandberg 40.00 80.00
RSH Red Schoendienst 15.00 40.00
RY Robin Yount 30.00 60.00
SA Sparky Anderson 20.00 50.00
SC Steve Carlton 30.00 60.00
TP Tony Perez 30.00 60.00

2006 Topps Sterling Cut Signatures

OVERALL CUT SIGNATURE ODDS 1:5
67 Lloyd Waner 20.00 50.00
68 Sal Maglie 20.00 50.00
69 Waite Hoyt 40.00 80.00
70 Warren Spahn 75.00 150.00
72 A.B. Chandler 40.00 80.00
73 Al Barlick 20.00 50.00
74 Bill Dickey 60.00 120.00
75 Bill Terry 20.00 50.00
76 Billy Herman 30.00 60.00
77 Bob Lemon 30.00 60.00
78 Buck Leonard 20.00 50.00
79 Charles Gehringer 60.00 120.00
82 Hoyt Wilhelm 20.00 50.00
83 Catfish Hunter 50.00 100.00
84 Joe Sewell 30.00 60.00
85 Judy Johnson 20.00 50.00
86 Carl Hubbell 30.00 60.00
87 Lou Boudreau 40.00 80.00
88 Luke Appling 20.00 50.00
89 Ray Dandridge 20.00 50.00
90 Rick Ferrell 30.00 60.00
91 Stan Coveleski 40.00 80.00
92 Willie Stargell 50.00 100.00

2006 Topps Sterling Moments Relics

B.BONDS 30.00 80.00
M.MANTLE 3 or 4 RELIC 75.00 150.00
M.MANTLE 5 or 6 RELIC 125.00 250.00
J.GIBSON 500.00 800.00
R.HENDERSON 40.00 100.00
T.WILLIAMS 25.00 60.00
R.CLEMENTE 125.00 250.00
N.RYAN 60.00 150.00
C.RIPKEN 40.00 80.00
S.MUSIAL 25.00 60.00
R.JACKSON 25.00 60.00
J.BENCH 25.00 60.00
G.BRETT 25.00 60.00
R.MARIS 50.00 120.00
Y.BERRA 30.00 80.00
M.SCHMIDT 25.00 60.00
C.YASTRZEMSKI 20.00 50.00
T.GWYNN 25.00 60.00
R.SANDBERG 25.00 60.00
OVERALL AU/GU ODDS 1:3
STATED PRINT RUN 10 SER.#'d SETS
PRIME PRIME RUN 1 SER.#'d SET
NO PRIME PRICING DUE TO SCARCITY

2006 Topps Sterling Moments Relics Autographs

R.HENDERSON 125.00 250.00
N.RYAN 100.00 200.00
C.RIPKEN 150.00 300.00
S.MUSIAL 90.00 150.00
R.JACKSON 40.00 80.00
J.BENCH 75.00 150.00
G.BRETT 75.00 150.00
D.MATTINGLY 75.00 150.00
R.CAREW 40.00 80.00
Y.BERRA 90.00 150.00
M.SCHMIDT 75.00 150.00
C.YASTRZEMSKI 60.00 120.00
T.GWYNN 50.00 100.00
R.SANDBERG 75.00 150.00
O.SMITH 75.00 150.00
OVERALL AU-GU ODDS 1:3
STATED PRINT RUN 10 SERIAL #'d SETS
NO BONDS PRICING DUE TO SCARCITY
PRIME PRINT RUN 1 SER.#'d SET
NO PRIME PRICING DUE TO SCARCITY

2006 Topps Sterling Triple Relics Autographs

OVERALL AU/GU ODDS 1:3
STATED PRINT RUN 10 SERIAL #'d SETS
NO PRICING DUE TO SCARCITY
PRIME PRINT RUN 10 SERIAL #'d SETS
NO PRIME PRICING DUE TO SCARCITY
STER.SIL. PRINT RUN 1 SER. #'d SET
NO STER.SIL. PRICING DUE TO SCARCITY
SS PRIME PRINT RUN 1 SER.#'d SET
NO SS PRIME PRICING DUE TO SCARCITY

2007 Topps Sterling

COMMON MANTLE (1-24) 5.00 12.00
COMMON BONDS (25-48) 5.00 12.00
COMMON ICHIRO (49-56) 4.00 10.00
COMMON YAZ (57-64) 3.00 8.00
COMMON WRIGHT (65-76) 3.00 8.00
COMMON CLEMENTE (77-81) 6.00 15.00
COMMON SANTANA (82-89) 3.00 8.00
COMMON MORNEAU (90-101) 3.00 8.00
COMMON R.JACKSON (102-109) 3.00 8.00
COMMON CLEMENS (110-117) 4.00 10.00
COMMON T.WILLIAMS (118-122) 5.00 12.00
COMMON BERRA (123-130) 3.00 8.00
COMMON MATSUI (131-135) 3.00 8.00
COMMON HOWARD (136-143) 3.00 8.00
COMMON GWYNN (144-151) 3.00 8.00
COMMON ORTIZ (152-159) 2.50 6.00
COMMON SEAVER (160-167) 2.50 6.00
COMMON PUJOLS (168-175) 4.00 10.00
COMMON MUSIAL (176-183) 3.00 8.00
COMMON WANG (184-191) 5.00 12.00
COMMON SANDBERG (192-199) 4.00 10.00
COMMON N.RYAN (200-207) 8.00 20.00
COMMON B.GIBSON (208-215) 2.50 6.00
COMMON MARIS (216-220) 3.00 8.00
COMMON M.RAMIREZ (221-228) 3.00 8.00
COMMON SCHMIDT (229-236) 4.00 10.00
COMMON A.ROD (237-244) 3.00 8.00
COMMON MATSUZAKA (245-249) 6.00 15.00
COMMON DIMAGGIO (250-254) 4.00 10.00
THREE BASE CARDS PER BOX
STATED PRINT RUN 250 SER.#'d SETS
1 Mickey Mantle 5.00 12.00
2 Mickey Mantle 5.00 12.00
3 Mickey Mantle 5.00 12.00
4 Mickey Mantle 5.00 12.00
5 Mickey Mantle 5.00 12.00
6 Mickey Mantle 5.00 12.00
7 Mickey Mantle 5.00 12.00
8 Mickey Mantle 5.00 12.00
9 Mickey Mantle 5.00 12.00
10 Mickey Mantle 5.00 12.00
11 Mickey Mantle 5.00 12.00
12 Mickey Mantle 5.00 12.00
13 Mickey Mantle 5.00 12.00
14 Mickey Mantle 5.00 12.00
15 Mickey Mantle 5.00 12.00
16 Mickey Mantle 5.00 12.00
17 Mickey Mantle 5.00 12.00
18 Mickey Mantle 5.00 12.00
19 Mickey Mantle 5.00 12.00
20 Mickey Mantle 5.00 12.00
21 Mickey Mantle 5.00 12.00
22 Mickey Mantle 5.00 12.00
23 Mickey Mantle 5.00 12.00
24 Mickey Mantle 5.00 12.00
25 Barry Bonds 5.00 12.00
26 Barry Bonds 5.00 12.00
27 Barry Bonds 5.00 12.00
28 Barry Bonds 5.00 12.00
29 Barry Bonds 5.00 12.00
30 Barry Bonds 5.00 12.00
31 Barry Bonds 5.00 12.00
32 Barry Bonds 5.00 12.00
33 Barry Bonds 5.00 12.00
34 Barry Bonds 5.00 12.00
35 Barry Bonds 5.00 12.00
36 Barry Bonds 5.00 12.00
37 Barry Bonds 5.00 12.00
38 Barry Bonds 5.00 12.00
39 Barry Bonds 5.00 12.00
40 Barry Bonds 5.00 12.00
41 Barry Bonds 5.00 12.00
42 Barry Bonds 5.00 12.00
43 Barry Bonds 5.00 12.00
44 Barry Bonds 5.00 12.00
45 Barry Bonds 5.00 12.00
46 Barry Bonds 5.00 12.00
47 Barry Bonds 5.00 12.00
48 Barry Bonds 5.00 12.00
49 Ichiro Suzuki 4.00 10.00
50 Ichiro Suzuki 4.00 10.00
51 Ichiro Suzuki 4.00 10.00
52 Ichiro Suzuki 4.00 10.00
53 Ichiro Suzuki 4.00 10.00
54 Ichiro Suzuki 4.00 10.00
55 Ichiro Suzuki 4.00 10.00
56 Ichiro Suzuki 4.00 10.00
57 Carl Yastrzemski 3.00 8.00
58 Carl Yastrzemski 3.00 8.00
59 Carl Yastrzemski 3.00 8.00
60 Carl Yastrzemski 3.00 8.00
61 Carl Yastrzemski 3.00 8.00
62 Carl Yastrzemski 3.00 8.00
63 Carl Yastrzemski 3.00 8.00
64 Carl Yastrzemski 3.00 8.00
65 David Wright 3.00 8.00
66 David Wright 3.00 8.00
67 David Wright 3.00 8.00
68 David Wright 3.00 8.00
69 David Wright 3.00 8.00
70 David Wright 3.00 8.00
71 David Wright 3.00 8.00
72 David Wright 3.00 8.00
73 David Wright 3.00 8.00
74 David Wright 3.00 8.00
75 David Wright 3.00 8.00
76 David Wright 3.00 8.00
77 Roberto Clemente 6.00 15.00
78 Roberto Clemente 6.00 15.00
79 Roberto Clemente 6.00 15.00
80 Roberto Clemente 6.00 15.00
81 Roberto Clemente 6.00 15.00
82 Johan Santana 3.00 8.00
83 Johan Santana 3.00 8.00
84 Johan Santana 3.00 8.00
85 Johan Santana 3.00 8.00
86 Johan Santana 3.00 8.00
87 Johan Santana 3.00 8.00
88 Johan Santana 3.00 8.00
89 Johan Santana 3.00 8.00
90 Justin Morneau 3.00 8.00
91 Justin Morneau 3.00 8.00
92 Justin Morneau 3.00 8.00
93 Justin Morneau 3.00 8.00
94 Justin Morneau 3.00 8.00
95 Justin Morneau 3.00 8.00
96 Justin Morneau 3.00 8.00
97 Justin Morneau 3.00 8.00
98 Justin Morneau 3.00 8.00
99 Justin Morneau 3.00 8.00
100 Justin Morneau 3.00 8.00
101 Justin Morneau 3.00 8.00
102 Reggie Jackson 3.00 8.00
103 Reggie Jackson 3.00 8.00
104 Reggie Jackson 3.00 8.00
105 Reggie Jackson 3.00 8.00
106 Reggie Jackson 3.00 8.00
107 Reggie Jackson 3.00 8.00
108 Reggie Jackson 3.00 8.00
109 Reggie Jackson 3.00 8.00
110 Roger Clemens 4.00 10.00
111 Roger Clemens 4.00 10.00
112 Roger Clemens 4.00 10.00
113 Roger Clemens 4.00 10.00
114 Roger Clemens 4.00 10.00
115 Roger Clemens 4.00 10.00
116 Roger Clemens 4.00 10.00
117 Roger Clemens 4.00 10.00
118 Ted Williams 5.00 12.00
119 Ted Williams 5.00 12.00
120 Ted Williams 5.00 12.00
121 Ted Williams 5.00 12.00
122 Ted Williams 5.00 12.00
123 Yogi Berra 3.00 8.00
124 Yogi Berra 3.00 8.00
125 Yogi Berra 3.00 8.00
126 Yogi Berra 3.00 8.00
127 Yogi Berra 3.00 8.00
128 Yogi Berra 3.00 8.00
129 Yogi Berra 3.00 8.00
130 Yogi Berra 3.00 8.00
131 Hideki Matsui 3.00 8.00
132 Hideki Matsui 3.00 8.00
133 Hideki Matsui 3.00 8.00
134 Hideki Matsui 3.00 8.00
135 Hideki Matsui 3.00 8.00
136 Ryan Howard 3.00 8.00
137 Ryan Howard 3.00 8.00
138 Ryan Howard 3.00 8.00
139 Ryan Howard 3.00 8.00
140 Ryan Howard 3.00 8.00
141 Ryan Howard 3.00 8.00
142 Ryan Howard 3.00 8.00
143 Ryan Howard 3.00 8.00
144 Tony Gwynn 3.00 8.00
145 Tony Gwynn 3.00 8.00
146 Tony Gwynn 3.00 8.00
147 Tony Gwynn 3.00 8.00
148 Tony Gwynn 3.00 8.00
149 Tony Gwynn 3.00 8.00
150 Tony Gwynn 3.00 8.00
151 Tony Gwynn 3.00 8.00
152 David Ortiz 2.50 6.00
153 David Ortiz 2.50 6.00
154 David Ortiz 2.50 6.00
155 David Ortiz 2.50 6.00
156 David Ortiz 2.50 6.00
157 David Ortiz 2.50 6.00
158 David Ortiz 2.50 6.00
159 David Ortiz 2.50 6.00
160 Tom Seaver 2.50 6.00
161 Tom Seaver 2.50 6.00
162 Tom Seaver 2.50 6.00
163 Tom Seaver 2.50 6.00
164 Tom Seaver 2.50 6.00
165 Tom Seaver 2.50 6.00
166 Tom Seaver 2.50 6.00
167 Tom Seaver 2.50 6.00
168 Albert Pujols 4.00 10.00
169 Albert Pujols 4.00 10.00
170 Albert Pujols 4.00 10.00
171 Albert Pujols 4.00 10.00
172 Albert Pujols 4.00 10.00
173 Albert Pujols 4.00 10.00
174 Albert Pujols 4.00 10.00
175 Albert Pujols 4.00 10.00
176 Stan Musial 3.00 8.00
177 Stan Musial 3.00 8.00
178 Stan Musial 3.00 8.00
179 Stan Musial 3.00 8.00
180 Stan Musial 3.00 8.00
181 Stan Musial 3.00 8.00
182 Stan Musial 3.00 8.00
183 Stan Musial 3.00 8.00
184 Chien-Ming Wang 5.00 12.00
185 Chien-Ming Wang 5.00 12.00
186 Chien-Ming Wang 5.00 12.00
187 Chien-Ming Wang 5.00 12.00
188 Chien-Ming Wang 5.00 12.00
189 Chien-Ming Wang 5.00 12.00
190 Chien-Ming Wang 5.00 12.00
191 Chien-Ming Wang 5.00 12.00
192 Ryne Sandberg 4.00 10.00
193 Ryne Sandberg 4.00 10.00
194 Ryne Sandberg 4.00 10.00
195 Ryne Sandberg 4.00 10.00
196 Ryne Sandberg 4.00 10.00
197 Ryne Sandberg 4.00 10.00
198 Ryne Sandberg 4.00 10.00
199 Ryne Sandberg 4.00 10.00
200 Nolan Ryan 8.00 20.00
201 Nolan Ryan 8.00 20.00
202 Nolan Ryan 8.00 20.00
203 Nolan Ryan 8.00 20.00
204 Nolan Ryan 8.00 20.00
205 Nolan Ryan 8.00 20.00
206 Nolan Ryan 8.00 20.00
207 Nolan Ryan 8.00 20.00
208 Bob Gibson 2.50 6.00
209 Bob Gibson 2.50 6.00
210 Bob Gibson 2.50 6.00
211 Bob Gibson 2.50 6.00
212 Bob Gibson 2.50 6.00
213 Bob Gibson 2.50 6.00
214 Bob Gibson 2.50 6.00
215 Bob Gibson 2.50 6.00
216 Roger Maris 3.00 8.00
217 Roger Maris 3.00 8.00
218 Roger Maris 3.00 8.00
219 Roger Maris 3.00 8.00
220 Roger Maris 3.00 8.00
221 Manny Ramirez 3.00 8.00
222 Manny Ramirez 3.00 8.00
223 Manny Ramirez 3.00 8.00
224 Manny Ramirez 3.00 8.00
225 Manny Ramirez 3.00 8.00
226 Manny Ramirez 3.00 8.00
227 Manny Ramirez 3.00 8.00
228 Manny Ramirez 3.00 8.00
229 Mike Schmidt 4.00 10.00
230 Mike Schmidt 4.00 10.00
231 Mike Schmidt 4.00 10.00
232 Mike Schmidt 4.00 10.00
233 Mike Schmidt 4.00 10.00
234 Mike Schmidt 4.00 10.00
235 Mike Schmidt 4.00 10.00
236 Mike Schmidt 4.00 10.00
237 Alex Rodriguez 3.00 8.00
238 Alex Rodriguez 3.00 8.00
239 Alex Rodriguez 3.00 8.00
240 Alex Rodriguez 3.00 8.00
241 Alex Rodriguez 3.00 8.00
242 Alex Rodriguez 3.00 8.00
243 Alex Rodriguez 3.00 8.00
244 Alex Rodriguez 3.00 8.00
245 Daisuke Matsuzaka RC 6.00 15.00
246 Daisuke Matsuzaka RC 6.00 15.00
247 Daisuke Matsuzaka RC 6.00 15.00
248 Daisuke Matsuzaka RC 6.00 15.00
249 Daisuke Matsuzaka RC 6.00 15.00
250 Joe DiMaggio 4.00 10.00
251 Joe DiMaggio 4.00 10.00
252 Joe DiMaggio 4.00 10.00
253 Joe DiMaggio 4.00 10.00
254 Joe DiMaggio 4.00 10.00

2007 Topps Sterling Framed Burgundy

COMMON MANTLE (1-24) 20.00 50.00
COMMON BONDS (25-48) 12.50 30.00
COMMON ICHIRO (49-56) 12.50 30.00
COMMON YAZ (57-64) 12.50 30.00
COMMON WRIGHT (65-76) 10.00 25.00
COMMON CLEMENTE (77-81) 20.00 50.00
COMMON SANTANA (82-89) 8.00 20.00
COMMON MORNEAU (90-101) 6.00 15.00
COMMON R.JACKSON (102-109) 10.00 25.00
COMMON CLEMENS (110-117) 10.00 25.00
COMMON T.WILLIAMS (118-122) 12.50 30.00
COMMON BERRA (123-130) 6.00 15.00
COMMON MATSUI (131-135) 8.00 20.00
COMMON HOWARD (136-143) 10.00 25.00
COMMON GWYNN (144-151) 20.00 50.00
COMMON ORTIZ (152-159) 6.00 15.00
COMMON SEAVER (160-167) 8.00 20.00
COMMON PUJOLS (168-175) 12.50 30.00
COMMON MUSIAL (176-183) 10.00 25.00
COMMON WANG (184-191) 15.00 40.00
COMMON SANDBERG (192-199) 12.50 30.00
COMMON N.RYAN (200-207) 30.00 60.00
COMMON B.GIBSON (208-215) 8.00 20.00
COMMON MARIS (216-220) 12.50 30.00
COMMON M.RAMIREZ (221-228) 6.00 15.00
COMMON SCHMIDT (229-236) 15.00 40.00
COMMON A.ROD (237-244) 20.00 50.00
COMMON MATSUZAKA (245-249) 20.00 50.00
COMMON DIMAGGIO (250-254) 15.00 40.00
RANDOMLY INSERTED IN MYSTERY PACKS
STATED PRINT RUN 14 SER.#'d SETS

2007 Topps Sterling Framed Gold

COMMON MANTLE (1-24) 40.00 80.00
COMMON BONDS (25-48) 30.00 60.00
COMMON ICHIRO (49-56) 20.00 50.00
COMMON YAZ (57-64) 15.00 40.00
COMMON WRIGHT (65-76) 15.00 40.00
COMMON CLEMENTE (77-81) 30.00 60.00
COMMON SANTANA (82-89) 10.00 25.00
COMMON MORNEAU (90-101) 6.00 15.00
COMMON R.JACKSON (102-109) 12.50 30.00
COMMON CLEMENS (110-117) 12.50 30.00
COMMON T.WILLIAMS (118-122) 15.00 40.00
COMMON BERRA (123-130) 10.00 25.00
COMMON MATSUI (131-135) 15.00 40.00
COMMON HOWARD (136-143) 12.50 30.00
COMMON GWYNN (144-151) 30.00 60.00
COMMON ORTIZ (152-159) 8.00 20.00
COMMON SEAVER (160-167) 10.00 25.00
COMMON PUJOLS (168-175) 20.00 50.00
COMMON MUSIAL (176-183) 12.50 30.00
COMMON WANG (184-191) 30.00 60.00
COMMON SANDBERG (192-199) 15.00 40.00
COMMON N.RYAN (200-207) 30.00 60.00
COMMON B.GIBSON (208-215) 12.50 30.00
COMMON MARIS (216-220) 12.50 30.00
COMMON M.RAMIREZ (221-228) 8.00 20.00
COMMON SCHMIDT (229-236) 20.00 50.00
COMMON A.ROD (237-244) 20.00 50.00
COMMON MATSUZAKA (245-249) 30.00 60.00
COMMON DIMAGGIO (250-254) 20.00 50.00
RANDOMLY INSERTED IN MYSTERY PACKS
STATED PRINT RUN 9 SER.#'d SETS

2007 Topps Sterling Framed White Suede

*FRAMED WHITE: .6X TO 1.5X BASIC
RANDOM INSERTS IN MYSTERY PACKS
STATED PRINT RUN 50 SER.#'d SETS

2007 Topps Sterling Career Stats Relics Five

COMMON MANTLE 100.00 175.00
COMMON BONDS 30.00 60.00
COMMON ICHIRO 75.00 150.00
COMMON YAZ 30.00 60.00
COMMON WRIGHT 40.00 80.00
COMMON CLEMENTE 90.00 150.00
COMMON MORNEAU 12.50 30.00
COMMON CLEMENS 20.00 50.00
COMMON T.WILLIAMS 75.00 150.00
COMMON MATSUI 50.00 100.00
COMMON HOWARD 30.00 60.00
COMMON ORTIZ 20.00 50.00
COMMON PUJOLS 30.00 60.00
COMMON WANG 40.00 80.00
COMMON RYAN 50.00 100.00
COMMON GIBSON 20.00 50.00
COMMON MARIS 50.00 100.00
COMMON M.RAMIREZ 15.00 40.00
COMMON SCHMIDT 12.50 30.00
COMMON A.ROD 60.00 120.00
COMMON MATSUZAKA 60.00 120.00
COMMON DIMAGGIO 60.00 120.00
RANDOM INSERTS IN BOXES
OVERALL ONE AUTO OR MEM PER BOX
STATED PRINT RUN 10 SER.#'d SETS
NO BERRA,GWYNN PRICING
NO SEAVER,SANDBERG PRICING

2007 Topps Sterling Career Stats Relics Quad

COMMON MANTLE 100.00 175.00
COMMON BONDS 20.00 50.00
COMMON ICHIRO 60.00 120.00
COMMON YAZ 30.00 60.00
COMMON CLEMENTE 90.00 150.00
COMMON SANTANA 15.00 40.00
COMMON CLEMENS 20.00 50.00
COMMON T.WILLIAMS 40.00 80.00
COMMON MATSUI 40.00 80.00
COMMON ORTIZ 15.00 40.00
COMMON SEAVER 30.00 60.00
COMMON PUJOLS 20.00 50.00
COMMON GIBSON 20.00 50.00
COMMON MARIS 50.00 100.00
COMMON SCHMIDT 40.00 80.00
COMMON MATSUZAKA 60.00 120.00
COMMON DIMAGGIO 60.00 120.00
RANDOM INSERTS IN BOXES
OVERALL ONE AUTO OR MEM PER BOX
STATED PRINT RUN 10 SER.#'d SETS
NO WRIGHT,MORNEAU,JACKSON PRICING
NO HOWARD,MUSIAL,WANG PRICING
NO SANDBERG PRICING

2007 Topps Sterling Career Stats Relics Six

COMMON MANTLE 75.00 150.00
COMMON BONDS 30.00 60.00
COMMON ICHIRO 75.00 150.00
COMMON D.WRIGHT 40.00 80.00
COMMON CLEMENTE 100.00 200.00
COMMON SANTANA 20.00 50.00
COMMON MORNEAU 12.50 30.00
COMMON R.JACKSON 30.00 60.00
COMMON CLEMENS 20.00 50.00
COMMON T.WILLIAMS 40.00 80.00
COMMON MATSUI 50.00 100.00
COMMON ORTIZ 20.00 50.00
COMMON PUJOLS 40.00 80.00
COMMON WANG 50.00 100.00
COMMON SANDBERG 20.00 50.00
COMMON RYAN 50.00 100.00
COMMON MARIS 50.00 100.00
COMMON M.RAMIREZ 20.00 50.00
COMMON SCHMIDT 40.00 80.00
COMMON AROD 75.00 150.00
COMMON MATSUZAKA 75.00 150.00
COMMON DIMAGGIO 75.00 150.00
RANDOM INSERTS IN BOXES
OVERALL ONE AUTO OR MEM PER BOX
STATED PRINT RUN 10 SER.#'d SETS
NO YAZ,BERRA,GWYNN PRICING
NO MUSIAL OR GIBSON PRICING

2007 Topps Sterling Career Stats Relics Triple

COMMON MANTLE 90.00 150.00
COMMON BONDS 20.00 50.00
COMMON ICHIRO 60.00 120.00
COMMON D.WRIGHT 30.00 60.00
COMMON CLEMENTE 75.00 150.00
COMMON MORNEAU 10.00 25.00
COMMON CLEMENS 15.00 40.00
COMMON T.WILLIAMS 50.00 100.00
COMMON BERRA 30.00 60.00
COMMON MATSUI 30.00 60.00

COMMON ORTIZ 15.00 40.00
COMMON SEAVER 20.00 50.00
COMMON PUJOLS 20.00 50.00
COMMON MUSIAL 30.00 60.00
COMMON GIBSON 15.00 40.00
COMMON MARIS 40.00 80.00
COMMON SCHMIDT 40.00 80.00
COMMON MATSUZAKA 60.00 120.00
COMMON DIMAGGIO 60.00 120.00
RANDOM INSERTS IN BOXES
OVERALL ONE AUTO OR MEM PER BOX
STATED PRINT RUN 10 SER.#'d SETS
NO YAZ,JACKSON,GWYNN PRICING
NO SANDBERG,RYAN PRICING

2007 Topps Sterling Career Stats Relics Autographs Quad

COMMON YAZ 50.00 100.00
COMMON D.WRIGHT 20.00 50.00
COMMON SANTANA 12.00 30.00
COMMON MORNEAU 20.00 50.00
COMMON R.JACKSON 40.00 80.00
COMMON R.CLEMENS 60.00 120.00
COMMON Y.BERRA 60.00 120.00
COMMON R.HOWARD 50.00 100.00
COMMON T.GWYNN 60.00 120.00
COMMON ORTIZ 50.00 100.00
COMMON T.SEAVER 40.00 80.00
COMMON PUJOLS 175.00 300.00
COMMON MUSIAL 60.00 120.00
COMMON WANG 60.00 120.00
COMMON SANDBERG 60.00 120.00
COMMON RYAN 75.00 150.00
COMMON GIBSON 30.00 60.00
COMMON M.RAMIREZ 40.00 80.00
COMMON SCHMIDT 40.00 80.00
COMMON AROD 175.00 300.00
RANDOM INSERTS IN BOXES
OVERALL ONE AUTO OR MEM PER BOX
STATED PRINT RUN 10 SER.#'d SETS
NO MATSUI PRICING DUE TO SCARCITY

2007 Topps Sterling Career Stats Relics Autographs Triple

COMMON BONDS 175.00 300.00
COMMON YAZ 40.00 80.00
COMMON D.WRIGHT 15.00 40.00
COMMON SANTANA 20.00 50.00
COMMON MORNEAU 20.00 50.00
COMMON R.JACKSON 30.00 60.00
COMMON R.CLEMENS 60.00 120.00
COMMON Y.BERRA 50.00 100.00
COMMON R.HOWARD 30.00 60.00
COMMON T.GWYNN 50.00 100.00
COMMON ORTIZ 40.00 80.00
COMMON T.SEAVER 40.00 80.00
COMMON PUJOLS 175.00 300.00
COMMON MUSIAL 75.00 150.00
COMMON WANG 150.00 250.00
COMMON SANDBERG 50.00 100.00
COMMON RYAN 60.00 120.00
COMMON GIBSON 30.00 60.00
COMMON M.RAMIREZ 30.00 60.00
COMMON SCHMIDT 40.00 80.00
COMMON AROD 175.00 300.00
RANDOM INSERTS IN BOXES
OVERALL ONE AUTO OR MEM PER BOX
STATED PRINT RUN 10 SER.#'d SETS

2007 Topps Sterling Moments Relics Eight

COMMON MANTLE 275.00 375.00
COMMON BONDS 150.00 250.00
COMMON MATSUI 75.00 150.00
COMMON ORTIZ 40.00 80.00
RANDOM INSERTS IN BOXES
OVERALL ONE AUTO OR MEM PER BOX
STATED PRINT RUN 10 SER.#'d SETS
NO PRICING ON MOST DUE TO SCARCITY

2007 Topps Sterling Moments Relics Five

COMMON MANTLE 100.00 175.00
COMMON BONDS 30.00 60.00
COMMON ICHIRO 75.00 150.00
COMMON YAZ 30.00 60.00
COMMON WRIGHT 40.00 80.00
COMMON CLEMENTE 90.00 150.00
COMMON MORNEAU 12.50 30.00
COMMON CLEMENS 20.00 50.00
COMMON T.WILLIAMS 75.00 150.00
COMMON MATSUI 50.00 100.00
COMMON HOWARD 30.00 60.00
COMMON ORTIZ 20.00 50.00
COMMON PUJOLS 30.00 60.00
COMMON WANG 40.00 80.00
COMMON RYAN 50.00 100.00
COMMON GIBSON 20.00 50.00
COMMON MARIS 50.00 100.00
COMMON M.RAMIREZ 15.00 40.00
COMMON SCHMIDT 12.50 30.00
COMMON A.ROD 60.00 120.00
COMMON MATSUZAKA 60.00 120.00
COMMON DIMAGGIO 60.00 120.00
RANDOM INSERTS IN BOXES
OVERALL ONE AUTO OR MEM PER BOX
STATED PRINT RUN 10 SER.#'d SETS
NO JOHAN,SEAVER,MUSIAL PRICING

2007 Topps Sterling Moments Relics Quad

COMMON MANTLE 100.00 175.00
COMMON BONDS 20.00 50.00
COMMON ICHIRO 60.00 120.00
COMMON YAZ 30.00 60.00
COMMON CLEMENTE 90.00 150.00
COMMON SANTANA 15.00 40.00
COMMON CLEMENS 20.00 50.00
COMMON T.WILLIAMS 40.00 80.00
COMMON MATUSI 40.00 80.00
COMMON ORTIZ 15.00 40.00
COMMON SEAVER 30.00 60.00
COMMON PUJOLS 20.00 50.00
COMMON GIBSON 20.00 50.00
COMMON MARIS 50.00 100.00
COMMON SCHMIDT 40.00 80.00
COMMON MATSUZAKA 60.00 120.00
COMMON DIMAGGIO 60.00 120.00
RANDOM INSERTS IN BOXES
OVERALL ONE AUTO OR MEM PER BOX
STATED PRINT RUN 10 SER.#'d SETS
NO WRIGHT,MORNEAU,BERRA PRICING
NO GWYNN OR MUSIAL PRICING

2007 Topps Sterling Moments Relics Six

COMMON MANTLE 75.00 150.00
COMMON BONDS 30.00 60.00
COMMON ICHIRO 75.00 150.00
COMMON D.WRIGHT 40.00 100.00
COMMON CLEMENTE 100.00 200.00
COMMON SANTANA 20.00 50.00
COMMON MORNEAU 12.50 30.00
COMMON R.JACKSON 30.00 60.00
COMMON CLEMENS 20.00 50.00
COMMON T.WILLIAMS 40.00 80.00
COMMON MATSUI 50.00 100.00
COMMON ORTIZ 20.00 50.00
COMMON PUJOLS 40.00 80.00
COMMON WANG 50.00 100.00
COMMON SANDBERG 20.00 50.00
COMMON RYAN 50.00 100.00
COMMON MARIS 50.00 100.00
COMMON M.RAMIREZ 20.00 50.00
COMMON SCHMIDT 40.00 80.00
COMMON AROD 75.00 150.00
COMMON MATSUZAKA 75.00 150.00
COMMON DIMAGGIO 75.00 150.00
RANDOM INSERTS IN BOXES
OVERALL ONE AUTO OR MEM PER BOX
STATED PRINT RUN 10 SER.#'d SETS
NO HOWARD PRICING

2007 Topps Sterling Moments Relics Triple

COMMON MANTLE 90.00 150.00
COMMON BONDS 20.00 50.00
COMMON ICHIRO 60.00 120.00
COMMON D.WRIGHT 30.00 60.00
COMMON CLEMENTE 75.00 150.00
COMMON MORNEAU 10.00 25.00
COMMON CLEMENS 15.00 40.00
COMMON T.WILLIAMS 50.00 100.00
COMMON BERRA 30.00 60.00
COMMON MATSUI 30.00 60.00
COMMON ORTIZ 15.00 40.00
COMMON SEAVER 20.00 50.00
COMMON PUJOLS 20.00 50.00
COMMON MUSIAL 30.00 60.00
COMMON GIBSON 15.00 40.00
COMMON MARIS 40.00 80.00
COMMON SCHMIDT 40.00 80.00
COMMON MATSUZAKA 60.00 120.00
COMMON DIMAGGIO 60.00 120.00
RANDOM INSERTS IN BOXES
OVERALL ONE AUTO OR MEM PER BOX
STATED PRINT RUN 10 SER.#'d SETS
NO JACKSON OR GWYNN PRICING

2007 Topps Sterling Moments Relics Autographs Eight

COMMON M.RAMIREZ 60.00 120.00
RANDOM INSERTS IN BOXES
OVERALL ONE AUTO OR MEM PER BOX
STATED PRINT RUN 10 SER.#'d SETS
NO PRICING ON MOST DUE TO SCARCITY

2007 Topps Sterling Moments Relics Autographs Quad

COMMON YAZ 50.00 100.00
COMMON D.WRIGHT 20.00 50.00
COMMON SANTANA 12.00 30.00
COMMON MORNEAU 20.00 50.00
COMMON R.JACKSON 40.00 80.00
COMMON R.CLEMENS 60.00 120.00
COMMON Y.BERRA 60.00 120.00
COMMON R.HOWARD 50.00 100.00
COMMON T.GWYNN 60.00 120.00
COMMON ORTIZ 50.00 100.00
COMMON T.SEAVER 40.00 80.00
COMMON PUJOLS 175.00 300.00
COMMON MUSIAL 60.00 120.00
COMMON WANG 60.00 120.00
COMMON SANDBERG 60.00 120.00
COMMON RYAN 75.00 150.00
COMMON GIBSON 30.00 60.00
COMMON M.RAMIREZ 40.00 80.00
COMMON SCHMIDT 40.00 80.00
COMMON AROD 175.00 300.00
RANDOM INSERTS IN BOXES
OVERALL ONE AUTO OR MEM PER BOX
STATED PRINT RUN 10 SER.#'d SETS
NO BONDS PRICING DUE TO SCARCITY

2007 Topps Sterling Moments Relics Autographs Triple

COMMON BONDS 175.00 300.00
COMMON YAZ 40.00 80.00
COMMON D.WRIGHT 15.00 40.00
COMMON SANTANA 20.00 50.00
COMMON MORNEAU 20.00 50.00
COMMON R.JACKSON 30.00 60.00
COMMON R.CLEMENS 60.00 120.00
COMMON Y.BERRA 50.00 100.00
COMMON R.HOWARD 30.00 60.00
COMMON T.GWYNN 50.00 100.00
COMMON ORTIZ 40.00 80.00
COMMON T.SEAVER 40.00 80.00
COMMON PUJOLS 175.00 300.00
COMMON MUSIAL 75.00 150.00
COMMON WANG 150.00 250.00
COMMON SANDBERG 50.00 100.00
COMMON RYAN 60.00 120.00
COMMON GIBSON 30.00 60.00
COMMON M.RAMIREZ 30.00 60.00
COMMON SCHMIDT 40.00 80.00
COMMON AROD 175.00 300.00
RANDOM INSERTS IN BOXES
OVERALL ONE AUTO OR MEM PER BOX
STATED PRINT RUN 10 SER.#'d SETS

2007 Topps Sterling Stardom Relics Eight

COMMON MANTLE 275.00 375.00
COMMON BONDS 150.00 250.00
COMMON MATSUI 75.00 150.00
COMMON ORTIZ 40.00 80.00
RANDOM INSERTS IN BOXES
OVERALL ONE AUTO OR MEM PER BOX
STATED PRINT RUN 10 SER.#'d SETS
NO PRICING ON MOST DUE TO SCARCITY

2007 Topps Sterling Stardom Relics Five

COMMON MANTLE 100.00 175.00
COMMON BONDS 30.00 60.00
COMMON ICHIRO 75.00 150.00
COMMON YAZ 30.00 60.00
COMMON WRIGHT 40.00 80.00
COMMON CLEMENTE 90.00 150.00
COMMON MORNEAU 12.50 30.00
COMMON CLEMENS 20.00 50.00
COMMON T.WILLIAMS 75.00 150.00
COMMON MATSUI 50.00 100.00
COMMON HOWARD 30.00 60.00
COMMON ORTIZ 20.00 50.00
COMMON PUJOLS 30.00 60.00
COMMON WANG 40.00 80.00
COMMON RYAN 50.00 100.00
COMMON GIBSON 20.00 50.00
COMMON MARIS 50.00 100.00
COMMON M.RAMIREZ 15.00 40.00
COMMON SCHMIDT 12.50 30.00
COMMON A.ROD 60.00 120.00
COMMON MATSUZAKA 60.00 120.00
COMMON DIMAGGIO 60.00 120.00
RANDOM INSERTS IN BOXES
OVERALL ONE AUTO OR MEM PER BOX
STATED PRINT RUN 10 SER.#'d SETS
NO JOHAN,JACKSON,BERRA PRICING

2007 Topps Sterling Stardom Relics Quad

COMMON MANTLE 100.00 175.00
COMMON BONDS 20.00 50.00
COMMON ICHIRO 60.00 120.00
COMMON YAZ 30.00 60.00
COMMON CLEMENTE 90.00 150.00
COMMON SANTANA 15.00 40.00
COMMON CLEMENS 20.00 50.00
COMMON T.WILLIAMS 40.00 80.00
COMMON MATUSI 40.00 80.00
COMMON ORTIZ 15.00 40.00
COMMON SEAVER 30.00 60.00
COMMON PUJOLS 20.00 50.00
COMMON GIBSON 20.00 50.00
COMMON MARIS 50.00 100.00
COMMON SCHMIDT 40.00 80.00
COMMON MATSUZAKA 60.00 120.00
COMMON DIMAGGIO 60.00 120.00
RANDOM INSERTS IN BOXES
OVERALL ONE AUTO OR MEM PER BOX
STATED PRINT RUN 10 SER.#'d SETS
NO BERRA,HOWARD,GWYNN PRICING
NO WANG,SANDBERG, AROD PRICING

2007 Topps Sterling Stardom Relics Six

COMMON MANTLE 75.00 150.00
COMMON BONDS 30.00 60.00
COMMON ICHIRO 75.00 150.00
COMMON D.WRIGHT 40.00 100.00
COMMON CLEMENTE 100.00 200.00
COMMON SANTANA 20.00 50.00
COMMON MORNEAU 12.50 30.00
COMMON R.JACKSON 30.00 60.00
COMMON CLEMENS 20.00 50.00
COMMON T.WILLIAMS 40.00 80.00
COMMON MATSUI 50.00 100.00
COMMON ORTIZ 20.00 50.00
COMMON PUJOLS 40.00 80.00
COMMON WANG 50.00 100.00
COMMON SANDBERG 20.00 50.00
COMMON RYAN 50.00 100.00
COMMON MARIS 50.00 100.00
COMMON M.RAMIREZ 20.00 50.00
COMMON SCHMIDT 40.00 80.00
COMMON AROD 75.00 150.00
COMMON MATSUZAKA 75.00 150.00
COMMON DIMAGGIO 75.00 150.00
RANDOM INSERTS IN BOXES
OVERALL ONE AUTO OR MEM PER BOX
STATED PRINT RUN 10 SER.#'d SETS
NO HOWARD PRICING

2007 Topps Sterling Stardom Relics Triple

COMMON MANTLE 90.00 150.00
COMMON BONDS 20.00 50.00
COMMON ICHIRO 60.00 120.00
COMMON D.WRIGHT 30.00 60.00
COMMON CLEMENTE 75.00 150.00
COMMON MORNEAU 10.00 25.00
COMMON CLEMENS 15.00 40.00
COMMON T.WILLIAMS 50.00 100.00
COMMON BERRA 30.00 60.00
COMMON MATSUI 30.00 60.00
COMMON ORTIZ 15.00 40.00
COMMON SEAVER 20.00 50.00
COMMON PUJOLS 20.00 50.00
COMMON MUSIAL 30.00 60.00
COMMON GIBSON 15.00 40.00
COMMON MARIS 40.00 80.00
COMMON SCHMIDT 40.00 80.00
COMMON MATSUZAKA 60.00 120.00
COMMON DIMAGGIO 60.00 120.00
RANDOM INSERTS IN BOXES
OVERALL ONE AUTO OR MEM PER BOX
STATED PRINT RUN 10 SER.#'d SETS
NO YAZ OR RYAN PRICING

2007 Topps Sterling Stardom Relics Autographs Eight

COMMON M.RAMIREZ 60.00 120.00
RANDOM INSERTS IN BOXES
OVERALL ONE AUTO OR MEM PER BOX
STATED PRINT RUN 10 SER.#'d SETS
NO PRICING ON MOST DUE TO SCARCITY

2007 Topps Sterling Stardom Relics Autographs Quad

COMMON YAZ 50.00 100.00
COMMON D.WRIGHT 20.00 50.00
COMMON SANTANA 12.00 30.00
COMMON MORNEAU 20.00 50.00
COMMON R.JACKSON 40.00 80.00
COMMON R.CLEMENS 60.00 120.00
COMMON Y.BERRA 60.00 120.00
COMMON R.HOWARD 50.00 100.00
COMMON T.GWYNN 60.00 120.00
COMMON ORTIZ 50.00 100.00
COMMON T.SEAVER 40.00 80.00
COMMON PUJOLS 175.00 300.00
COMMON MUSIAL 60.00 120.00
COMMON WANG 60.00 120.00
COMMON SANDBERG 60.00 120.00
COMMON RYAN 75.00 150.00
COMMON GIBSON 30.00 60.00
COMMON M.RAMIREZ 40.00 80.00
COMMON SCHMIDT 40.00 80.00
COMMON AROD 175.00 300.00
RANDOM INSERTS IN BOXES
OVERALL ONE AUTO OR MEM PER BOX
STATED PRINT RUN 10 SER.#'d SETS
NO BONDS OR MATSUI PRICING

2007 Topps Sterling Stardom Relics Autographs Triple

COMMON BONDS 175.00 300.00
COMMON YAZ 40.00 80.00
COMMON D.WRIGHT 15.00 40.00
COMMON SANTANA 20.00 50.00
COMMON MORNEAU 20.00 50.00
COMMON R.JACKSON 30.00 60.00
COMMON R.CLEMENS 60.00 120.00
COMMON Y.BERRA 50.00 100.00
COMMON R.HOWARD 30.00 60.00
COMMON T.GWYNN 50.00 100.00
COMMON ORTIZ 40.00 80.00
COMMON T.SEAVER 40.00 80.00
COMMON PUJOLS 175.00 300.00
COMMON MUSIAL 75.00 150.00
COMMON WANG 150.00 250.00
COMMON SANDBERG 50.00 100.00
COMMON RYAN 60.00 120.00
COMMON GIBSON 30.00 60.00
COMMON M.RAMIREZ 30.00 60.00
COMMON SCHMIDT 40.00 80.00
COMMON AROD 175.00 300.00
RANDOM INSERTS IN BOXES
OVERALL ONE AUTO OR MEM PER BOX
STATED PRINT RUN 10 SER.#'d SETS

2008 Topps Sterling

COMMON MANTLE (1-4) 5.00 12.00
COMMON RUTH (5-8) 6.00 15.00
COMMON OTT (9-12) 2.00 5.00
COMMON BENCH (13-23) 3.00 8.00
COMMON FOXX (24-27) 2.50 6.00
COMMON MURRAY (28-38) 2.00 5.00
COMMON J.ROBINSON (39-42) 3.00 8.00
COMMON SNIDER (43-53) 2.50 6.00
COMMON GIBSON (54-64) 2.50 6.00
COMMON BERRA (65-75) 3.00 8.00
COMMON MUSIAL (76-86) 4.00 10.00
COMMON HORNSBY (87-90) 2.50 6.00
COMMON SEAVER (91-101) 2.50 6.00
COMMON FORD (102-112) 2.50 6.00
COMMON MARIS (124-127) 2.50 6.00
COMMON MUNSON (128-131) 2.50 6.00
COMMON PALMER (132-142) 2.00 5.00
COMMON R.JACKSON (143-153) 2.50 6.00
COMMON SCHMIDT (154-164) 2.50 6.00
COMMON YAZ (165-175) 2.50 6.00
COMMON MATTINGLY (176-186) 3.00 8.00
COMMON CAMPANELLA (187-190) 2.00 5.00
COMMON RYAN (191-201) 6.00 15.00
COMMON COBB (213-216) 3.00 8.00
COMMON YOUNT (217-227) 2.50 6.00
COMMON RIPKEN (228-231) 5.00 12.00
COMMON GEHRIG (232-235) 4.00 10.00
COMMON CLEMENTE (236-239) 5.00 12.00
COMMON SANDBERG (240-250) 3.00 8.00
COMMON T.WILLIAMS (251-254) 3.00 8.00
COMMON F.ROBINSON (255-265) 2.00 5.00
COMMON T.GWYNN (266-276) 2.50 6.00
COMMON BANKS (277-287) 3.00 8.00
COMMON WAGNER (288-291) 2.50 6.00
COMMON MOLITOR (296-308) 2.50 6.00
THREE BASE CARDS PER PACK
STATED PRINT RUN 250 SER.#'d SETS

2008 Topps Sterling Framed Burgundy

COMMON MANTLE (1-4) 30.00 60.00
COMMON RUTH (5-8) 40.00 80.00
COMMON OTT (9-12) 12.50 30.00
COMMON BENCH (13-23) 15.00 40.00
COMMON FOXX (24-27) 12.50 30.00
COMMON MURRAY (28-38) 15.00 40.00
COMMON J.ROBINSON (39-42) 20.00 50.00
COMMON SNIDER (43-53) 10.00 25.00
COMMON GIBSON (54-64) 12.50 30.00
COMMON BERRA (65-75) 20.00 50.00
COMMON MUSIAL (76-86) 12.50 30.00
COMMON HORNSBY (87-90) 10.00 25.00
COMMON SEAVER (91-101) 12.50 30.00
COMMON FORD (102-112) 10.00 25.00
COMMON MARIS (124-127) 20.00 50.00
COMMON MUNSON (128-131) 12.50 30.00
COMMON PALMER (132-142) 10.00 25.00
COMMON R.JACKSON (143-153) 12.50 30.00
COMMON SCHMIDT (154-164) 12.50 30.00
COMMON YAZ (165-175) 12.50 30.00
COMMON MATTINGLY (176-186) 20.00 50.00
COMMON CAMPANELLA (187-190) 12.50 30.00
COMMON RYAN (191-201) 50.00 100.00
COMMON COBB (213-216) 40.00 80.00
COMMON YOUNT (217-227) 15.00 40.00
COMMON RIPKEN (228-231) 60.00 120.00
COMMON GEHRIG (232-235) 20.00 50.00
COMMON CLEMENTE (236-239) 40.00 80.00
COMMON SANDBERG (240-250) 12.50 30.00
COMMON T.WILLIAMS (251-254) 20.00 50.00
COMMON F.ROBINSON (255-265) 10.00 25.00
COMMON T.GWYNN (266-276) 20.00 50.00
COMMON BANKS (277-287) 20.00 50.00
COMMON WAGNER (288-291) 10.00 25.00
COMMON MOLITOR (296-308) 10.00 25.00
RANDOMLY INSERTED IN MYSTERY PACKS
STATED PRINT RUN 10 SER.#'d SETS

2008 Topps Sterling Framed Gold

COMMON MANTLE (1-4) 60.00 120.00
COMMON RUTH (5-8) 75.00 150.00
COMMON OTT (9-12) 30.00 60.00
COMMON BENCH (13-23) 30.00 60.00
COMMON FOXX (24-27) 40.00 80.00
COMMON MURRAY (28-38) 20.00 50.00
COMMON J.ROBINSON (39-42) 30.00 60.00
COMMON SNIDER (43-53) 20.00 50.00
COMMON GIBSON (54-64) 20.00 50.00
COMMON BERRA (65-75) 30.00 60.00
COMMON MUSIAL (76-86) 20.00 50.00
COMMON HORNSBY (87-90) 15.00 40.00
COMMON SEAVER (91-101) 15.00 40.00
COMMON FORD (102-112) 12.50 30.00
COMMON MARIS (124-127) 30.00 60.00
COMMON MUNSON (128-131) 30.00 60.00
COMMON PALMER (132-142) 20.00 50.00
COMMON R.JACKSON (143-153) 40.00 80.00
COMMON SCHMIDT (154-164) 30.00 60.00
COMMON YAZ (165-175) 20.00 50.00
COMMON MATTINGLY (176-186) 50.00 100.00
COMMON CAMPANELLA (187-190) 15.00 40.00
COMMON RYAN (191-201) 100.00 200.00
COMMON COBB (213-216) 50.00 100.00
COMMON YOUNT (217-227) 20.00 50.00
COMMON RIPKEN (228-231) 100.00 175.00
COMMON GEHRIG (232-235) 40.00 80.00
COMMON CLEMENTE (236-239) 75.00 150.00
COMMON SANDBERG (240-250) 40.00 80.00
COMMON T.WILLIAMS (251-254) 30.00 60.00
COMMON F.ROBINSON (255-265) 20.00 50.00
COMMON T.GWYNN (266-276) 30.00 60.00
COMMON BANKS (277-287) 40.00 80.00
COMMON WAGNER (288-291) 30.00 60.00
COMMON MOLITOR (296-308) 30.00 60.00
RANDOMLY INSERTED IN MYSTERY PACKS
STATED PRINT RUN 5 SER.#'d SETS

2008 Topps Sterling Framed White

COMMON MANTLE (1-4) 12.50 30.00
COMMON RUTH (5-8) 12.50 30.00
COMMON OTT (9-12) 8.00 20.00
COMMON BENCH (13-23) 6.00 15.00
COMMON FOXX (24-27) 5.00 12.00
COMMON MURRAY (28-38) 5.00 12.00
COMMON J.ROBINSON (39-42) 8.00 20.00
COMMON SNIDER (43-53) 5.00 12.00
COMMON GIBSON (54-64) 6.00 15.00
COMMON BERRA (65-75) 6.00 15.00
COMMON MUSIAL (76-86) 8.00 20.00
COMMON HORNSBY (87-90) 5.00 12.00
COMMON SEAVER (91-101) 5.00 12.00
COMMON FORD (102-112) 5.00 12.00
COMMON MARIS (124-127) 6.00 15.00
COMMON MUNSON (128-131) 6.00 15.00
COMMON PALMER (132-142) 5.00 12.00
COMMON R.JACKSON (143-153) 5.00 12.00
COMMON SCHMIDT (154-164) 5.00 12.00
COMMON YAZ (165-175) 5.00 12.00
COMMON MATTINGLY (176-186) 5.00 12.00
COMMON CAMPANELLA (187-190) 5.00 12.00
COMMON RYAN (191-201) 12.50 30.00
COMMON COBB (213-216) 8.00 20.00
COMMON YOUNT (217-227) 6.00 15.00
COMMON RIPKEN (228-231) 25.00 60.00
COMMON GEHRIG (232-235) 10.00 25.00
COMMON CLEMENTE (236-239) 15.00 40.00
COMMON SANDBERG (240-250) 6.00 15.00
COMMON T.WILLIAMS (251-254) 8.00 20.00
COMMON F.ROBINSON (255-265) 5.00 12.00
COMMON T.GWYNN (266-276) 8.00 20.00
COMMON BANKS (277-287) 8.00 20.00
COMMON WAGNER (288-291) 6.00 15.00
COMMON MOLITOR (296-308) 5.00 12.00
RANDOMLY INSERTED IN MYSTERY PACKS
STATED PRINT RUN 50 SER.#'d SETS

2008 Topps Sterling Career Stats Relics Five

COMMON MANTLE 75.00 150.00
COMMON RUTH 150.00 250.00
COMMON OTT 50.00 100.00
COMMON BENCH 20.00 50.00
COMMON FOXX 60.00 120.00
COMMON J.ROBINSON 40.00 80.00
COMMON MUSIAL 20.00 50.00
COMMON HORNSBY 40.00 80.00
COMMON SEAVER 15.00 40.00
COMMON MARIS 50.00 100.00
COMMON MUNSON 30.00 60.00
COMMON R.JACKSON 10.00 25.00
COMMON YAZ 20.00 50.00
COMMON CAMPANELLA 30.00 60.00
COMMON RYAN 50.00 100.00
COMMON COBB 100.00 175.00
COMMON RIPKEN 100.00 175.00
COMMON GEHRIG 150.00 250.00
COMMON CLEMENTE 60.00 120.00
COMMON T.WILLIAMS 60.00 120.00
COMMON F.ROBINSON 15.00 40.00
COMMON T.GWYNN 20.00 50.00
COMMON BANKS 15.00 40.00
COMMON WAGNER 100.00 200.00
OVERALL ONE AUTO OR MEM PER BOX
STATED PRINT RUN 10 SER.#'d SETS
5CS1 Mickey Mantle 75.00 150.00
5CS2 Mickey Mantle 75.00 150.00
5CS3 Babe Ruth 150.00 250.00
5CS4 Babe Ruth 150.00 250.00
5CS5 Mel Ott 50.00 100.00
5CS6 Mel Ott 50.00 100.00
5CS7 Johnny Bench 20.00 50.00
5CS8 Johnny Bench 20.00 50.00
5CS9 Johnny Bench 20.00 50.00
5CS10 Johnny Bench 20.00 50.00
5CS11 Jimmie Foxx 60.00 120.00
5CS12 Jimmie Foxx 60.00 120.00
5CS13 Jackie Robinson 40.00 80.00
5CS14 Jackie Robinson 40.00 80.00
5CS15 Stan Musial 20.00 50.00
5CS16 Stan Musial 20.00 50.00
5CS17 Stan Musial 20.00 50.00
5CS18 Stan Musial 20.00 50.00
5CS19 Rogers Hornsby 40.00 80.00
5CS20 Rogers Hornsby 40.00 80.00
5CS21 Tom Seaver 15.00 40.00
5CS22 Tom Seaver 15.00 40.00
5CS23 Tom Seaver 15.00 40.00
5CS24 Tom Seaver 15.00 40.00
5CS29 Roger Maris 50.00 100.00
5CS30 Roger Maris 50.00 100.00
5CS31 Thurman Munson 30.00 60.00
5CS32 Thurman Munson 30.00 60.00
5CS33 Reggie Jackson 10.00 25.00
5CS34 Reggie Jackson 10.00 25.00
5CS35 Reggie Jackson 10.00 25.00
5CS36 Reggie Jackson 10.00 25.00
5CS37 Carl Yastrzemski 20.00 50.00
5CS38 Carl Yastrzemski 20.00 50.00
5CS39 Carl Yastrzemski 20.00 50.00
5CS40 Carl Yastrzemski 20.00 50.00
5CS41 Roy Campanella 30.00 60.00
5CS42 Roy Campanella 30.00 60.00
5CS43 Nolan Ryan 50.00 100.00
5CS44 Nolan Ryan 50.00 100.00
5CS45 Nolan Ryan 50.00 100.00
5CS46 Nolan Ryan 50.00 100.00
5CS51 Ty Cobb 100.00 175.00
5CS52 Ty Cobb 100.00 175.00
5CS53 Cal Ripken 100.00 175.00
5CS54 Lou Gehrig 150.00 250.00
5CS55 Lou Gehrig 150.00 250.00
5CS56 Roberto Clemente 60.00 120.00
5CS57 Roberto Clemente 60.00 120.00
5CS58 Ted Williams 60.00 120.00
5CS59 Ted Williams 60.00 120.00
5CS60 Frank Robinson 15.00 40.00
5CS61 Frank Robinson 15.00 40.00
5CS62 Frank Robinson 15.00 40.00
5CS63 Frank Robinson 15.00 40.00
5CS64 Tony Gwynn 20.00 50.00
5CS65 Tony Gwynn 20.00 50.00
5CS66 Tony Gwynn 20.00 50.00
5CS67 Tony Gwynn 20.00 50.00
5CS68 Ernie Banks 15.00 40.00
5CS69 Ernie Banks 15.00 40.00
5CS70 Ernie Banks 15.00 40.00
5CS71 Ernie Banks 15.00 40.00
5CS72 Honus Wagner 100.00 200.00
5CS73 Honus Wagner 100.00 200.00

2008 Topps Sterling Career Stats Relics Quad

COMMON MANTLE 75.00 150.00
COMMON RUTH 200.00 350.00
COMMON OTT 50.00 100.00
COMMON BENCH 20.00 50.00
COMMON FOXX 40.00 80.00
COMMON J.ROBINSON 40.00 80.00
COMMON MUSIAL 30.00 60.00
COMMON HORNSBY 30.00 60.00
COMMON SEAVER 15.00 40.00
COMMON MARIS 50.00 100.00
COMMON MUNSON 30.00 60.00
COMMON R.JACKSON 15.00 40.00
COMMON YAZ 15.00 40.00
COMMON CAMPANELLA 30.00 60.00
COMMON COBB 40.00 80.00
COMMON RIPKEN 90.00 150.00
COMMON GEHRIG 100.00 250.00
COMMON CLEMENTE 60.00 120.00
COMMON T.WILLIAMS 40.00 80.00
COMMON F.ROBINSON 15.00 40.00
COMMON T.GWYNN 15.00 40.00
COMMON WAGNER 100.00 200.00
OVERALL ONE AUTO OR MEM PER BOX
STATED PRINT RUN 10 SER.#'d SETS
NO RYAN PRICING AVAILABLE
4CS1 Mickey Mantle 75.00 150.00
4CS2 Mickey Mantle 75.00 150.00
4CS3 Babe Ruth 200.00 350.00
4CS4 Babe Ruth 200.00 350.00
4CS5 Mel Ott 50.00 100.00
4CS6 Mel Ott 50.00 100.00
4CS7 Johnny Bench 20.00 50.00
4CS9 Johnny Bench 20.00 50.00
4CS11 Jimmie Foxx 40.00 80.00
4CS12 Jimmie Foxx 40.00 80.00
4CS13 Jackie Robinson 40.00 80.00
4CS14 Jackie Robinson 40.00 80.00
4CS15 Stan Musial 30.00 60.00
4CS16 Stan Musial 30.00 60.00
4CS17 Stan Musial 30.00 60.00
4CS19 Rogers Hornsby 30.00 60.00
4CS20 Rogers Hornsby 30.00 60.00
4CS21 Tom Seaver 15.00 40.00
4CS22 Tom Seaver 15.00 40.00
4CS23 Tom Seaver 15.00 40.00
4CS24 Tom Seaver 15.00 40.00
4CS29 Roger Maris 50.00 100.00
4CS30 Roger Maris 50.00 100.00
4CS31 Thurman Munson 30.00 60.00
4CS32 Thurman Munson 30.00 60.00
4CS34 Reggie Jackson 15.00 40.00
4CS35 Reggie Jackson 15.00 40.00
4CS36 Reggie Jackson 15.00 40.00
4CS40 Carl Yastrzemski 15.00 40.00
4CS41 Roy Campanella 30.00 60.00
4CS42 Roy Campanella 30.00 60.00
4CS54 Ty Cobb 40.00 80.00
4CS55 Ty Cobb 40.00 80.00
4CS56 Cal Ripken 90.00 150.00
4CS57 Lou Gehrig 100.00 250.00
4CS58 Lou Gehrig 100.00 250.00
4CS59 Roberto Clemente 60.00 120.00
4CS60 Roberto Clemente 60.00 120.00
4CS61 Ted Williams 40.00 80.00
4CS62 Ted Williams 40.00 80.00
4CS63 Frank Robinson 15.00 40.00
4CS64 Frank Robinson 15.00 40.00
4CS66 Frank Robinson 15.00 40.00
4CS67 Tony Gwynn 15.00 40.00
4CS68 Tony Gwynn 15.00 40.00
4CS69 Tony Gwynn 15.00 40.00
4CS70 Tony Gwynn 15.00 40.00
4CS77 Honus Wagner 100.00 200.00
4CS78 Honus Wagner 100.00 200.00

2008 Topps Sterling Career Stats Relics Six

COMMON MANTLE 100.00 200.00
COMMON RUTH 250.00 400.00
COMMON OTT 50.00 100.00
COMMON BENCH 20.00 50.00
COMMON FOXX 50.00 100.00
COMMON MURRAY 20.00 50.00
COMMON J.ROBINSON 50.00 100.00
COMMON SNIDER 30.00 60.00
COMMON GIBSON 20.00 50.00
COMMON BERRA 30.00 60.00
COMMON MUSIAL 30.00 60.00
COMMON HORNSBY 40.00 80.00
COMMON SEAVER 20.00 50.00
COMMON FORD 20.00 50.00
COMMON MARIS 60.00 120.00
COMMON MUNSON 40.00 80.00
COMMON PALMER 12.50 30.00
COMMON R.JACKSON 20.00 50.00
COMMON SCHMIDT 20.00 50.00
COMMON YAZ 20.00 50.00
COMMON MATTINGLY 40.00 80.00
COMMON CAMPANELLA 20.00 50.00
COMMON RYAN 30.00 60.00
COMMON COBB 150.00 250.00
COMMON YOUNT 20.00 50.00
COMMON RIPKEN 75.00 150.00
COMMON GEHRIG 175.00 300.00
COMMON CLEMENTE 75.00 150.00
COMMON SANDBERG 20.00 50.00
COMMON T.WILLIAMS 75.00 150.00
COMMON F.ROBINSON 20.00 50.00
COMMON T.GWYNN 20.00 50.00
COMMON BANKS 15.00 40.00
COMMON WAGNER 150.00 250.00
OVERALL ONE AUTO OR MEM PER BOX
STATED PRINT RUN 10 SER.#'d SETS
6CS1 Mickey Mantle 100.00 200.00
6CS2 Mickey Mantle 100.00 200.00
6CS3 Babe Ruth 250.00 400.00
6CS4 Babe Ruth 250.00 400.00
6CS5 Mel Ott 50.00 100.00
6CS6 Mel Ott 50.00 100.00
6CS7 Johnny Bench 20.00 50.00
6CS8 Johnny Bench 20.00 50.00
6CS9 Jimmie Foxx 50.00 100.00
6CS10 Jimmie Foxx 50.00 100.00
6CS11 Eddie Murray 20.00 50.00
6CS12 Jackie Robinson 50.00 100.00
6CS13 Jackie Robinson 50.00 100.00
6CS14 Duke Snider 30.00 60.00
6CS15 Bob Gibson 20.00 50.00
6CS16 Yogi Berra 30.00 60.00
6CS17 Stan Musial 30.00 60.00
6CS18 Stan Musial 30.00 60.00
6CS19 Rogers Hornsby 40.00 80.00
6CS20 Rogers Hornsby 40.00 80.00
6CS21 Tom Seaver 20.00 50.00
6CS22 Tom Seaver 20.00 50.00
6CS23 Whitey Ford 20.00 50.00
6CS26 Roger Maris 60.00 120.00
6CS27 Roger Maris 60.00 120.00
6CS28 Thurman Munson 40.00 80.00
6CS29 Thurman Munson 40.00 80.00
6CS30 Jim Palmer 12.50 30.00
6CS31 Reggie Jackson 20.00 50.00
6CS32 Reggie Jackson 20.00 50.00
6CS33 Mike Schmidt 20.00 50.00
6CS34 Carl Yastrzemski 20.00 50.00
6CS35 Carl Yastrzemski 20.00 50.00
6CS36 Don Mattingly 40.00 80.00
6CS37 Roy Campanella 20.00 50.00
6CS38 Roy Campanella 20.00 50.00
6CS39 Nolan Ryan 30.00 60.00
6CS40 Nolan Ryan 30.00 60.00
6CS41 Nolan Ryan 30.00 60.00
6CS42 Nolan Ryan 30.00 60.00
6CS43 Nolan Ryan 30.00 60.00
6CS44 Nolan Ryan 30.00 60.00
6CS51 Ty Cobb 150.00 250.00
6CS52 Ty Cobb 150.00 250.00
6CS53 Robin Yount 20.00 50.00
6CS54 Cal Ripken 75.00 150.00
6CS55 Cal Ripken 75.00 150.00
6CS56 Lou Gehrig 175.00 300.00
6CS57 Lou Gehrig 175.00 300.00
6CS58 Roberto Clemente 75.00 150.00
6CS59 Roberto Clemente 75.00 150.00
6CS60 Ryne Sandberg 20.00 50.00
6CS61 Ted Williams 75.00 150.00
6CS62 Ted Williams 75.00 150.00
6CS63 Frank Robinson 20.00 50.00
6CS64 Frank Robinson 20.00 50.00
6CS65 Tony Gwynn 20.00 50.00
6CS66 Tony Gwynn 20.00 50.00
6CS67 Ernie Banks 15.00 40.00
6CS68 Ernie Banks 15.00 40.00
6CS69 Ernie Banks 15.00 40.00
6CS70 Ernie Banks 15.00 40.00
6CS71 Ernie Banks 15.00 40.00
6CS72 Honus Wagner 150.00 250.00
6CS73 Honus Wagner 150.00 250.00

2008 Topps Sterling Career Stats Relics Triple

COMMON MANTLE 60.00 120.00
COMMON RUTH 125.00 250.00
COMMON OTT 40.00 80.00
COMMON FOXX 30.00 60.00
COMMON J.ROBINSON 40.00 80.00
COMMON GIBSON 40.00 80.00
COMMON MARIS 40.00 80.00
COMMON MUNSON 50.00 100.00
COMMON CAMPANELLA 20.00 50.00
COMMON COBB 75.00 150.00
COMMON RIPKEN 90.00 150.00
COMMON GEHRIG 150.00 250.00
COMMON CLEMENTE 50.00 100.00
COMMON T.WILLIAMS 40.00 80.00
COMMON WAGNER 90.00 150.00
OVERALL ONE AUTO OR MEM PER BOX
STATED PRINT RUN 10 SER.#'d SETS
3CS1 Mickey Mantle 60.00 120.00
3CS2 Mickey Mantle 60.00 120.00
3CS3 Mickey Mantle 60.00 120.00
3CS4 Babe Ruth 125.00 250.00
3CS5 Babe Ruth 125.00 250.00
3CS6 Babe Ruth 125.00 250.00
3CS7 Mel Ott 40.00 80.00
3CS8 Mel Ott 40.00 80.00
3CS9 Mel Ott 40.00 80.00
3CS13 Jimmie Foxx 30.00 60.00
3CS14 Jimmie Foxx 30.00 60.00
3CS15 Jimmie Foxx 30.00 60.00
3CS16 Jackie Robinson 40.00 80.00
3CS17 Jackie Robinson 40.00 80.00
3CS18 Jackie Robinson 40.00 80.00
3CS22 Rogers Hornsby 40.00 80.00
3CS23 Rogers Hornsby 40.00 80.00
3CS24 Rogers Hornsby 40.00 80.00
3CS31 Roger Maris 40.00 80.00
3CS32 Roger Maris 40.00 80.00
3CS33 Roger Maris 40.00 80.00
3CS34 Thurman Munson 50.00 100.00
3CS35 Thurman Munson 50.00 100.00

3CS36 Thurman Munson 50.00 100.00
3CS43 Roy Campanella 20.00 50.00
3CS44 Roy Campanella 20.00 50.00
3CS45 Roy Campanella 20.00 50.00
3CS54 Ty Cobb 75.00 150.00
3CS55 Ty Cobb 75.00 150.00
3CS56 Ty Cobb 75.00 150.00
3CS57 Cal Ripken 90.00 150.00
3CS58 Lou Gehrig 150.00 250.00
3CS59 Lou Gehrig 150.00 250.00
3CS60 Lou Gehrig 150.00 250.00
3CS61 Roberto Clemente 50.00 100.00
3CS62 Roberto Clemente 50.00 100.00
3CS63 Roberto Clemente 50.00 100.00
3CS64 Ted Williams 40.00 80.00
3CS65 Ted Williams 40.00 80.00
3CS66 Ted Williams 40.00 80.00
3CS77 Honus Wagner 90.00 150.00
3CS78 Honus Wagner 90.00 150.00
3CS79 Honus Wagner 90.00 150.00

2008 Topps Sterling Career Stats Relics Autographs Quad

COMMON BENCH 40.00 80.00
COMMON MURRAY 30.00 60.00
COMMON SNIDER 30.00 60.00
COMMON GIBSON 40.00 80.00
COMMON BERRA 50.00 100.00
COMMON MUSIAL 75.00 150.00
COMMON SEAVER 30.00 60.00
COMMON FORD 40.00 80.00
COMMON PALMER 20.00 50.00
COMMON R.JACKSON 40.00 80.00
COMMON SCHMIDT 40.00 80.00
COMMON YAZ 50.00 100.00
COMMON MATTINGLY 50.00 100.00
COMMON RYAN 100.00 200.00
COMMON YOUNT 40.00 80.00
COMMON RIPKEN 100.00 200.00
COMMON SANDBERG 40.00 80.00
COMMON F.ROBINSON 20.00 50.00
COMMON T.GWYNN 40.00 80.00
COMMON BANKS 30.00 60.00
COMMON MOLITOR 30.00 60.00
OVERALL ONE AUTO OR MEM PER BOX
STATED PRINT RUN 10 SER.#'d SETS
4CSA1 Johnny Bench 40.00 80.00
4CSA2 Johnny Bench 40.00 80.00
4CSA3 Johnny Bench 40.00 80.00
4CSA4 Eddie Murray 30.00 60.00
4CSA5 Eddie Murray 30.00 60.00
4CSA6 Eddie Murray 30.00 60.00
4CSA7 Eddie Murray 30.00 60.00
4CSA8 Eddie Murray 30.00 60.00
4CSA9 Eddie Murray 30.00 60.00
4CSA10 Eddie Murray 30.00 60.00
4CSA11 Eddie Murray 30.00 60.00
4CSA12 Eddie Murray 30.00 60.00
4CSA13 Eddie Murray 30.00 60.00
4CSA15 Eddie Murray 30.00 60.00
4CSA16 Duke Snider 30.00 60.00
4CSA17 Duke Snider 30.00 60.00
4CSA18 Duke Snider 30.00 60.00
4CSA19 Duke Snider 30.00 60.00
4CSA20 Duke Snider 30.00 60.00
4CSA21 Duke Snider 30.00 60.00
4CSA22 Duke Snider 30.00 60.00
4CSA23 Duke Snider 30.00 60.00
4CSA24 Duke Snider 30.00 60.00
4CSA25 Duke Snider 30.00 60.00
4CSA26 Duke Snider 30.00 60.00
4CSA27 Bob Gibson 40.00 80.00
4CSA28 Bob Gibson 40.00 80.00
4CSA29 Bob Gibson 40.00 80.00
4CSA30 Bob Gibson 40.00 80.00
4CSA31 Bob Gibson 40.00 80.00
4CSA32 Bob Gibson 40.00 80.00
4CSA33 Bob Gibson 40.00 80.00
4CSA34 Bob Gibson 40.00 80.00
4CSA35 Bob Gibson 40.00 80.00
4CSA36 Bob Gibson 40.00 80.00
4CSA37 Bob Gibson 40.00 80.00
4CSA38 Bob Gibson 40.00 80.00
4CSA39 Yogi Berra 50.00 120.00
4CSA40 Yogi Berra 50.00 120.00
4CSA41 Yogi Berra 50.00 120.00
4CSA42 Yogi Berra 50.00 120.00
4CSA43 Yogi Berra 50.00 120.00
4CSA44 Yogi Berra 50.00 120.00
4CSA45 Yogi Berra 50.00 120.00
4CSA46 Yogi Berra 50.00 120.00
4CSA47 Yogi Berra 50.00 120.00
4CSA48 Yogi Berra 50.00 120.00
4CSA49 Yogi Berra 50.00 120.00
4CSA50 Stan Musial 75.00 150.00
4CSA51 Stan Musial 75.00 150.00
4CSA52 Stan Musial 75.00 150.00
4CSA53 Stan Musial 75.00 150.00
4CSA54 Tom Seaver 30.00 80.00
4CSA55 Tom Seaver 30.00 80.00
4CSA56 Tom Seaver 30.00 80.00
4CSA57 Whitey Ford 40.00 80.00
4CSA58 Whitey Ford 40.00 80.00
4CSA59 Whitey Ford 40.00 80.00
4CSA60 Whitey Ford 40.00 80.00
4CSA61 Whitey Ford 40.00 80.00
4CSA62 Whitey Ford 40.00 80.00
4CSA63 Whitey Ford 40.00 80.00
4CSA64 Whitey Ford 40.00 80.00
4CSA65 Whitey Ford 40.00 80.00
4CSA66 Whitey Ford 40.00 80.00
4CSA67 Whitey Ford 40.00 80.00
4CSA68 Whitey Ford 40.00 80.00
4CSA73 Jim Palmer 20.00 50.00
4CSA74 Jim Palmer 20.00 50.00
4CSA75 Jim Palmer 20.00 50.00
4CSA76 Jim Palmer 20.00 50.00
4CSA77 Jim Palmer 20.00 50.00
4CSA78 Jim Palmer 20.00 50.00
4CSA79 Jim Palmer 20.00 50.00
4CSA80 Jim Palmer 20.00 50.00
4CSA81 Jim Palmer 20.00 50.00
4CSA82 Jim Palmer 20.00 50.00
4CSA83 Jim Palmer 20.00 50.00
4CSA84 Reggie Jackson 40.00 80.00
4CSA85 Reggie Jackson 40.00 80.00
4CSA86 Reggie Jackson 40.00 80.00
4CSA87 Mike Schmidt 40.00 80.00
4CSA88 Mike Schmidt 40.00 80.00
4CSA89 Mike Schmidt 40.00 80.00
4CSA90 Mike Schmidt 40.00 80.00
4CSA91 Mike Schmidt 40.00 80.00
4CSA92 Mike Schmidt 40.00 80.00
4CSA93 Mike Schmidt 40.00 80.00
4CSA94 Mike Schmidt 40.00 80.00
4CSA95 Mike Schmidt 40.00 80.00
4CSA96 Mike Schmidt 40.00 80.00
4CSA97 Mike Schmidt 40.00 80.00
4CSA98 Mike Schmidt 40.00 80.00
4CSA99 Carl Yastrzemski 50.00 100.00
4CSA100 Carl Yastrzemski 50.00 100.00
4CSA101 Carl Yastrzemski 50.00 100.00
4CSA102 Don Mattingly 50.00 100.00
4CSA103 Don Mattingly 50.00 100.00
4CSA104 Don Mattingly 50.00 100.00
4CSA105 Don Mattingly 50.00 100.00
4CSA106 Don Mattingly 50.00 100.00
4CSA107 Don Mattingly 50.00 100.00
4CSA108 Don Mattingly 50.00 100.00
4CSA109 Don Mattingly 50.00 100.00
4CSA110 Don Mattingly 50.00 100.00
4CSA111 Don Mattingly 50.00 100.00
4CSA112 Don Mattingly 50.00 100.00
4CSA113 Nolan Ryan 100.00 200.00
4CSA114 Nolan Ryan 100.00 200.00
4CSA117 Robin Yount 40.00 80.00
4CSA118 Robin Yount 40.00 80.00
4CSA119 Robin Yount 40.00 80.00
4CSA120 Robin Yount 40.00 80.00
4CSA121 Robin Yount 40.00 80.00
4CSA122 Robin Yount 40.00 80.00
4CSA123 Robin Yount 40.00 80.00
4CSA124 Robin Yount 40.00 80.00
4CSA125 Robin Yount 40.00 80.00
4CSA126 Robin Yount 40.00 80.00
4CSA127 Robin Yount 40.00 80.00
4CSA128 Cal Ripken 100.00 200.00
4CSA129 Ryne Sandberg 40.00 80.00
4CSA130 Ryne Sandberg 40.00 80.00
4CSA131 Ryne Sandberg 40.00 80.00
4CSA132 Ryne Sandberg 40.00 80.00
4CSA133 Ryne Sandberg 40.00 80.00
4CSA134 Ryne Sandberg 40.00 80.00
4CSA135 Ryne Sandberg 40.00 80.00
4CSA136 Ryne Sandberg 40.00 80.00
4CSA137 Ryne Sandberg 40.00 80.00
4CSA138 Ryne Sandberg 40.00 80.00
4CSA139 Ryne Sandberg 40.00 80.00
4CSA140 Frank Robinson 20.00 50.00
4CSA141 Frank Robinson 20.00 50.00
4CSA142 Frank Robinson 20.00 50.00
4CSA143 Frank Robinson 20.00 50.00
4CSA144 Tony Gwynn 40.00 80.00
4CSA145 Tony Gwynn 40.00 80.00
4CSA146 Tony Gwynn 40.00 80.00
4CSA147 Ernie Banks 30.00 60.00
4CSA148 Ernie Banks 30.00 60.00
4CSA149 Paul Molitor 30.00 60.00
4CSA150 Paul Molitor 30.00 60.00
4CSA153 Paul Molitor 30.00 60.00
4CSA155 Paul Molitor 30.00 60.00
4CSA157 Paul Molitor 30.00 60.00
4CSA160 Paul Molitor 30.00 60.00

2008 Topps Sterling Career Stats Relics Autographs Triple

COMMON BENCH 40.00 80.00
COMMON MURRAY 30.00 60.00
COMMON SNIDER 30.00 60.00
COMMON GIBSON 40.00 80.00
COMMON BERRA 40.00 80.00
COMMON SEAVER 30.00 60.00
COMMON FORD 40.00 80.00
COMMON PALMER 20.00 50.00
COMMON R.JACKSON 30.00 60.00
COMMON SCHMIDT 40.00 80.00
COMMON YAZ 30.00 60.00
COMMON MATTINGLY 60.00 120.00
COMMON RYAN 75.00 150.00
COMMON YOUNT 40.00 80.00
COMMON RIPKEN 125.00 250.00
COMMON SANDBERG 40.00 80.00
COMMON T.GWYNN 50.00 100.00
COMMON BANKS 40.00 80.00
COMMON MOLITOR 30.00 60.00
OVERALL ONE AUTO OR MEM PER BOX
STATED PRINT RUN 10 SER.#'d SETS
3CSA3 Johnny Bench 40.00 80.00
3CSA4 Johnny Bench 40.00 80.00
3CSA5 Eddie Murray 30.00 60.00
3CSA6 Eddie Murray 30.00 60.00
3CSA13 Eddie Murray 30.00 60.00
3CSA14 Eddie Murray 30.00 60.00
3CSA15 Eddie Murray 30.00 60.00
3CSA16 Duke Snider 30.00 60.00
3CSA17 Duke Snider 30.00 60.00
3CSA21 Duke Snider 30.00 60.00
3CSA23 Duke Snider 30.00 60.00
3CSA24 Duke Snider 30.00 60.00
3CSA28 Bob Gibson 40.00 80.00
3CSA29 Bob Gibson 40.00 80.00
3CSA31 Bob Gibson 40.00 80.00
3CSA34 Bob Gibson 40.00 80.00
3CSA37 Bob Gibson 40.00 80.00
3CSA40 Yogi Berra 40.00 100.00
3CSA42 Yogi Berra 40.00 100.00
3CSA43 Yogi Berra 40.00 100.00
3CSA45 Yogi Berra 40.00 100.00
3CSA47 Yogi Berra 40.00 100.00
3CSA48 Yogi Berra 40.00 100.00
3CSA49 Yogi Berra 40.00 100.00
3CSA54 Tom Seaver 30.00 80.00
3CSA56 Tom Seaver 30.00 80.00
3CSA59 Whitey Ford 40.00 80.00
3CSA61 Whitey Ford 40.00 80.00
3CSA64 Whitey Ford 40.00 80.00
3CSA66 Whitey Ford 40.00 80.00
3CSA72 Jim Palmer 20.00 50.00
3CSA74 Jim Palmer 20.00 50.00
3CSA76 Jim Palmer 20.00 50.00
3CSA77 Jim Palmer 20.00 50.00
3CSA78 Jim Palmer 20.00 50.00
3CSA82 Jim Palmer 20.00 50.00
3CSA86 Reggie Jackson 30.00 60.00
3CSA89 Mike Schmidt 40.00 80.00
3CSA92 Mike Schmidt 40.00 80.00
3CSA93 Mike Schmidt 40.00 80.00
3CSA98 Mike Schmidt 40.00 80.00
3CSA102 Carl Yastrzemski 30.00 60.00
3CSA103 Don Mattingly 60.00 120.00
3CSA105 Don Mattingly 60.00 120.00
3CSA106 Don Mattingly 60.00 120.00
3CSA108 Don Mattingly 60.00 120.00
3CSA110 Don Mattingly 60.00 120.00
3CSA114 Don Mattingly 60.00 120.00
3CSA115 Nolan Ryan 75.00 150.00
3CSA118 Robin Yount 40.00 80.00
3CSA120 Robin Yount 40.00 80.00
3CSA121 Robin Yount 40.00 80.00
3CSA124 Robin Yount 40.00 80.00
3CSA125 Robin Yount 40.00 80.00
3CSA128 Cal Ripken 125.00 250.00
3CSA130 Ryne Sandberg 40.00 80.00
3CSA133 Ryne Sandberg 40.00 80.00
3CSA136 Ryne Sandberg 40.00 80.00
3CSA139 Ryne Sandberg 40.00 80.00
3CSA140 Ryne Sandberg 40.00 80.00
3CSA146 Tony Gwynn 50.00 100.00
3CSA148 Ernie Banks 40.00 80.00
3CSA157 Paul Molitor 30.00 60.00
3CSA158 Paul Molitor 30.00 60.00
3CSA159 Paul Molitor 30.00 60.00

2008 Topps Sterling Moments Relics Five

COMMON MANTLE 75.00 150.00
COMMON RUTH 150.00 250.00
COMMON OTT 50.00 100.00
COMMON BENCH 20.00 50.00
COMMON FOXX 60.00 120.00
COMMON J.ROBINSON 40.00 80.00
COMMON MUSIAL 20.00 50.00
COMMON HORNSBY 40.00 80.00
COMMON SEAVER 15.00 40.00
COMMON MARIS 50.00 100.00
COMMON MUNSON 30.00 60.00
COMMON R.JACKSON 10.00 25.00
COMMON YAZ 20.00 50.00
COMMON CAMPANELLA 30.00 60.00
COMMON RYAN 50.00 100.00
COMMON COBB 100.00 175.00
COMMON RIPKEN 100.00 175.00
COMMON GEHRIG 150.00 250.00
COMMON CLEMENTE 60.00 120.00
COMMON T.WILLIAMS 60.00 120.00
COMMON F.ROBINSON 15.00 40.00
COMMON T.GWYNN 20.00 50.00
COMMON BANKS 15.00 40.00
COMMON WAGNER 100.00 200.00
OVERALL ONE AUTO OR MEM PER BOX
STATED PRINT RUN 10 SER.#'d SETS
5SM1 Mickey Mantle 75.00 150.00
5SM2 Mickey Mantle 75.00 150.00
5SM3 Babe Ruth 150.00 250.00
5SM4 Babe Ruth 150.00 250.00
5SM5 Mel Ott 50.00 100.00
5SM6 Mel Ott 50.00 100.00
5SM7 Johnny Bench 20.00 50.00
5SM8 Johnny Bench 20.00 50.00
5SM9 Johnny Bench 20.00 50.00
5SM10 Johnny Bench 20.00 50.00
5SM11 Johnny Bench 20.00 50.00
5SM12 Jimmie Foxx 60.00 120.00
5SM13 Jimmie Foxx 60.00 120.00
5SM14 Jackie Robinson 40.00 80.00
5SM15 Jackie Robinson 40.00 80.00
5SM16 Stan Musial 20.00 50.00
5SM17 Stan Musial 20.00 50.00
5SM18 Stan Musial 20.00 50.00
5SM19 Stan Musial 20.00 50.00
5SM20 Stan Musial 20.00 50.00
5SM21 Rogers Hornsby 40.00 80.00
5SM22 Rogers Hornsby 40.00 80.00
5SM23 Tom Seaver 15.00 40.00
5SM24 Tom Seaver 15.00 40.00
5SM25 Tom Seaver 15.00 40.00
5SM26 Tom Seaver 15.00 40.00
5SM27 Tom Seaver 15.00 40.00
5SM33 Roger Maris 50.00 100.00
5SM34 Roger Maris 50.00 100.00
5SM35 Thurman Munson 30.00 60.00
5SM36 Thurman Munson 30.00 60.00
5SM37 Reggie Jackson 10.00 25.00
5SM38 Reggie Jackson 10.00 25.00
5SM39 Reggie Jackson 10.00 25.00
5SM40 Reggie Jackson 10.00 25.00
5SM41 Reggie Jackson 10.00 25.00
5SM42 Carl Yastrzemski 20.00 50.00
5SM43 Carl Yastrzemski 20.00 50.00
5SM44 Carl Yastrzemski 20.00 50.00
5SM45 Carl Yastrzemski 20.00 50.00
5SM46 Carl Yastrzemski 20.00 50.00
5SM47 Roy Campanella 30.00 60.00
5SM48 Roy Campanella 30.00 60.00
5SM51 Nolan Ryan 50.00 100.00
5SM52 Nolan Ryan 50.00 100.00
5SM58 Ty Cobb 100.00 175.00
5SM59 Ty Cobb 100.00 175.00
5SM60 Cal Ripken 100.00 175.00
5SM61 Lou Gehrig 150.00 250.00
5SM62 Lou Gehrig 150.00 250.00
5SM63 Roberto Clemente 60.00 120.00
5SM64 Roberto Clemente 60.00 120.00
5SM65 Ted Williams 60.00 120.00
5SM66 Ted Williams 60.00 120.00
5SM67 Frank Robinson 15.00 40.00
5SM68 Frank Robinson 15.00 40.00
5SM69 Frank Robinson 15.00 40.00
5SM70 Frank Robinson 15.00 40.00
5SM71 Frank Robinson 15.00 40.00
5SM72 Tony Gwynn 20.00 50.00
5SM73 Tony Gwynn 20.00 50.00
5SM74 Tony Gwynn 20.00 50.00
5SM75 Tony Gwynn 20.00 50.00
5SM76 Tony Gwynn 20.00 50.00
5SM77 Ernie Banks 15.00 40.00
5SM78 Ernie Banks 15.00 40.00
5SM79 Ernie Banks 15.00 40.00
5SM80 Ernie Banks 15.00 40.00
5SM81 Ernie Banks 15.00 40.00
5SM82 Honus Wagner 100.00 200.00
5SM83 Honus Wagner 100.00 200.00

2008 Topps Sterling Moments Relics Quad

COMMON MANTLE 75.00 150.00
COMMON RUTH 200.00 350.00
COMMON OTT 50.00 100.00
COMMON BENCH 20.00 50.00
COMMON FOXX 40.00 80.00
COMMON J.ROBINSON 40.00 80.00
COMMON MUSIAL 30.00 60.00
COMMON HORNSBY 30.00 60.00
COMMON SEAVER 15.00 40.00
COMMON MARIS 50.00 100.00
COMMON MUNSON 30.00 60.00
COMMON R.JACKSON 15.00 40.00
COMMON YAZ 15.00 40.00
COMMON CAMPANELLA 30.00 60.00
COMMON COBB 40.00 80.00
COMMON RIPKEN 90.00 150.00
COMMON GEHRIG 100.00 250.00
COMMON CLEMENTE 60.00 120.00
COMMON T.WILLIAMS 40.00 80.00
COMMON F.ROBINSON 12.50 30.00
COMMON T.GWYNN 12.50 30.00
COMMON WAGNER 100.00 200.00
OVERALL ONE AUTO OR MEM PER BOX
STATED PRINT RUN 10 SER.#'d SETS
NO BANKS PRICING AVAILABLE
4SM1 Mickey Mantle 75.00 150.00
4SM2 Mickey Mantle 75.00 150.00
4SM3 Babe Ruth 200.00 350.00
4SM4 Babe Ruth 200.00 350.00
4SM5 Mel Ott 50.00 100.00
4SM6 Mel Ott 50.00 100.00
4SM8 Johnny Bench 20.00 50.00
4SM10 Johnny Bench 20.00 50.00
4SM13 Jimmie Foxx 40.00 80.00
4SM14 Jimmie Foxx 40.00 80.00
4SM15 Jackie Robinson 40.00 80.00
4SM16 Jackie Robinson 40.00 80.00
4SM17 Stan Musial 30.00 60.00
4SM19 Stan Musial 30.00 60.00
4SM20 Stan Musial 30.00 60.00
4SM23 Rogers Hornsby 30.00 60.00
4SM24 Rogers Hornsby 30.00 60.00
4SM27 Tom Seaver 15.00 40.00
4SM29 Tom Seaver 15.00 40.00
4SM37 Roger Maris 50.00 100.00
4SM38 Roger Maris 50.00 100.00
4SM39 Thurman Munson 30.00 60.00
4SM40 Thurman Munson 30.00 60.00
4SM41 Reggie Jackson 15.00 40.00
4SM42 Reggie Jackson 15.00 40.00
4SM43 Reggie Jackson 15.00 40.00
4SM45 Reggie Jackson 15.00 40.00
4SM46 Reggie Jackson 15.00 40.00
4SM48 Carl Yastrzemski 15.00 40.00
4SM50 Carl Yastrzemski 15.00 40.00
4SM51 Carl Yastrzemski 15.00 40.00
4SM52 Carl Yastrzemski 15.00 40.00
4SM53 Roy Campanella 30.00 60.00
4SM54 Roy Campanella 30.00 60.00
4SM65 Ty Cobb 40.00 80.00
4SM66 Ty Cobb 40.00 80.00
4SM67 Cal Ripken 90.00 150.00
4SM68 Lou Gehrig 100.00 250.00
4SM69 Lou Gehrig 100.00 250.00
4SM70 Roberto Clemente 60.00 120.00
4SM71 Roberto Clemente 60.00 120.00
4SM72 Ted Williams 40.00 80.00
4SM73 Ted Williams 40.00 80.00
4SM74 Frank Robinson 12.50 30.00
4SM76 Frank Robinson 12.50 30.00
4SM78 Frank Robinson 12.50 30.00
4SM79 Frank Robinson 12.50 30.00
4SM82 Tony Gwynn 12.50 30.00
4SM83 Tony Gwynn 12.50 30.00
4SM84 Tony Gwynn 12.50 30.00
4SM92 Honus Wagner 100.00 200.00
4SM93 Honus Wagner 100.00 200.00

2008 Topps Sterling Moments Relics Six

COMMON MANTLE 100.00 200.00
COMMON RUTH 250.00 400.00
COMMON OTT 50.00 100.00
COMMON BENCH 20.00 50.00
COMMON FOXX 50.00 100.00
COMMON MURRAY 20.00 50.00
COMMON J.ROBINSON 50.00 100.00
COMMON SNIDER 30.00 60.00
COMMON GIBSON 20.00 50.00
COMMON BERRA 30.00 60.00
COMMON MUSIAL 30.00 60.00
COMMON HORNSBY 40.00 80.00
COMMON SEAVER 20.00 50.00
COMMON FORD 20.00 50.00
COMMON MARIS 60.00 120.00
COMMON MUNSON 40.00 80.00
COMMON PALMER 12.50 30.00
COMMON R.JACKSON 20.00 50.00
COMMON SCHMIDT 20.00 50.00
COMMON YAZ 20.00 50.00
COMMON MATTINGLY 40.00 80.00
COMMON CAMPANELLA 20.00 50.00
COMMON RYAN 30.00 60.00
COMMON COBB 150.00 250.00
COMMON YOUNT 20.00 50.00
COMMON RIPKEN 75.00 150.00
COMMON GEHRIG 175.00 300.00
COMMON CLEMENTE 75.00 150.00
COMMON SANDBERG 20.00 50.00
COMMON T.WILLIAMS 75.00 150.00
COMMON F.ROBINSON 20.00 50.00
COMMON T.GWYNN 20.00 50.00
COMMON BANKS 15.00 40.00
COMMON WAGNER 150.00 250.00
COMMON MOLITOR 20.00 50.00
OVERALL ONE AUTO OR MEM PER BOX
STATED PRINT RUN 10 SER.#'d SETS
6SM1 Mickey Mantle 100.00 200.00
6SM2 Babe Ruth 250.00 400.00
6SM3 Mel Ott 50.00 100.00
6SM4 Johnny Bench 20.00 50.00
6SM5 Johnny Bench 20.00 50.00
6SM6 Johnny Bench 20.00 50.00
6SM7 Jimmie Foxx 50.00 100.00
6SM8 Eddie Murray 20.00 50.00
6SM9 Jackie Robinson 50.00 100.00
6SM10 Duke Snider 30.00 60.00
6SM11 Bob Gibson 20.00 50.00
6SM12 Yogi Berra 30.00 60.00
6SM13 Stan Musial 30.00 60.00
6SM14 Stan Musial 30.00 60.00
6SM15 Stan Musial 30.00 60.00
6SM16 Rogers Hornsby 40.00 80.00
6SM17 Tom Seaver 20.00 50.00
6SM18 Tom Seaver 20.00 50.00
6SM19 Tom Seaver 20.00 50.00
6SM20 Whitey Ford 20.00 50.00
6SM24 Roger Maris 60.00 120.00
6SM25 Thurman Munson 40.00 80.00
6SM26 Jim Palmer 12.50 30.00
6SM27 Reggie Jackson 20.00 50.00
6SM28 Reggie Jackson 20.00 50.00
6SM29 Reggie Jackson 20.00 50.00
6SM30 Mike Schmidt 20.00 50.00
6SM31 Carl Yastrzemski 20.00 50.00
6SM32 Carl Yastrzemski 20.00 50.00
6SM33 Carl Yastrzemski 20.00 50.00
6SM34 Don Mattingly 40.00 80.00
6SM35 Roy Campanella 20.00 50.00
6SM36 Nolan Ryan 30.00 60.00
6SM37 Nolan Ryan 30.00 60.00
6SM38 Nolan Ryan 30.00 60.00
6SM39 Nolan Ryan 30.00 60.00
6SM40 Nolan Ryan 30.00 60.00
6SM41 Nolan Ryan 30.00 60.00
6SM42 Nolan Ryan 30.00 60.00
6SM43 Nolan Ryan 30.00 60.00
6SM44 Nolan Ryan 30.00 60.00
6SM45 Nolan Ryan 30.00 60.00
6SM46 Nolan Ryan 30.00 60.00
6SM47 Nolan Ryan 30.00 60.00
6SM48 Nolan Ryan 30.00 60.00
6SM60 Ty Cobb 150.00 250.00
6SM61 Robin Yount 20.00 50.00
6SM62 Cal Ripken 75.00 150.00
6SM63 Lou Gehrig 175.00 300.00
6SM64 Roberto Clemente 75.00 150.00
6SM65 Ryne Sandberg 20.00 50.00
6SM66 Ted Williams 75.00 150.00
6SM67 Frank Robinson 20.00 50.00
6SM68 Frank Robinson 20.00 50.00
6SM69 Frank Robinson 20.00 50.00
6SM70 Tony Gwynn 20.00 50.00
6SM71 Tony Gwynn 20.00 50.00
6SM72 Tony Gwynn 20.00 50.00
6SM73 Ernie Banks 15.00 40.00
6SM74 Ernie Banks 15.00 40.00
6SM75 Ernie Banks 15.00 40.00
6SM76 Ernie Banks 15.00 40.00
6SM77 Ernie Banks 15.00 40.00
6SM78 Ernie Banks 15.00 40.00
6SM79 Ernie Banks 15.00 40.00
6SM80 Ernie Banks 15.00 40.00
6SM81 Ernie Banks 15.00 40.00
6SM82 Ernie Banks 15.00 40.00
6SM83 Ernie Banks 15.00 40.00
6SM84 Honus Wagner 150.00 250.00
6SM88 Paul Molitor 20.00 50.00

2008 Topps Sterling Moments Relics Triple

COMMON MANTLE 60.00 120.00
COMMON RUTH 125.00 250.00
COMMON OTT 40.00 80.00
COMMON FOXX 30.00 60.00
COMMON J.ROBINSON 40.00 80.00
COMMON HORNSBY 40.00 80.00
COMMON MARIS 40.00 80.00
COMMON MUNSON 50.00 100.00
COMMON CAMPANELLA 20.00 50.00
COMMON COBB 75.00 150.00
COMMON RIPKEN 90.00 150.00
COMMON GEHRIG 150.00 250.00
COMMON CLEMENTE 50.00 100.00
COMMON T.WILLIAMS 40.00 80.00
COMMON WAGNER 90.00 150.00
OVERALL ONE AUTO OR MEM PER BOX
STATED PRINT RUN 10 SER.#'d SETS
NO SEAVER PRICING AVAILABLE
3SM1 Mickey Mantle 60.00 120.00
3SM2 Mickey Mantle 60.00 120.00
3SM3 Mickey Mantle 60.00 120.00
3SM4 Babe Ruth 125.00 250.00
3SM5 Babe Ruth 125.00 250.00
3SM6 Babe Ruth 125.00 250.00
3SM7 Mel Ott 40.00 80.00
3SM8 Mel Ott 40.00 80.00
3SM9 Mel Ott 40.00 80.00
3SM14 Jimmie Foxx 30.00 60.00
3SM15 Jimmie Foxx 30.00 60.00
3SM16 Jimmie Foxx 30.00 60.00
3SM17 Jackie Robinson 40.00 80.00
3SM18 Jackie Robinson 40.00 80.00
3SM19 Jackie Robinson 40.00 80.00
3SM24 Rogers Hornsby 40.00 80.00
3SM25 Rogers Hornsby 40.00 80.00
3SM26 Rogers Hornsby 40.00 80.00
3SM35 Roger Maris 40.00 80.00
3SM36 Roger Maris 40.00 80.00
3SM37 Roger Maris 40.00 80.00
3SM38 Thurman Munson 50.00 100.00
3SM39 Thurman Munson 50.00 100.00
3SM40 Thurman Munson 50.00 100.00
3SM49 Roy Campanella 20.00 50.00
3SM50 Roy Campanella 20.00 50.00
3SM51 Roy Campanella 20.00 50.00
3SM62 Ty Cobb 75.00 150.00
3SM63 Ty Cobb 75.00 150.00
3SM64 Ty Cobb 75.00 150.00
3SM65 Cal Ripken 90.00 150.00
3SM66 Lou Gehrig 150.00 250.00
3SM67 Lou Gehrig 150.00 250.00
3SM68 Lou Gehrig 150.00 250.00
3SM69 Roberto Clemente 50.00 100.00
3SM70 Roberto Clemente 50.00 100.00
3SM71 Roberto Clemente 50.00 100.00
3SM72 Ted Williams 40.00 80.00
3SM73 Ted Williams 40.00 80.00
3SM74 Ted Williams 40.00 80.00
3SM90 Honus Wagner 90.00 150.00
3SM91 Honus Wagner 90.00 150.00
3SM92 Honus Wagner 90.00 150.00

2008 Topps Sterling Moments Relics Autographs Eight

COMMON BENCH 60.00 120.00
COMMON MURRAY 60.00 120.00
COMMON SNIDER 50.00 100.00
COMMON GIBSON 40.00 80.00
COMMON BERRA 75.00 150.00
COMMON MUSIAL 75.00 150.00
COMMON SEAVER 40.00 80.00
COMMON FORD 50.00 100.00
COMMON PALMER 30.00 60.00
COMMON R.JACKSON 40.00 80.00
COMMON SCHMIDT 60.00 120.00
COMMON YAZ 75.00 150.00
COMMON MATTINGLY 75.00 150.00
COMMON RYAN 100.00 175.00
COMMON YOUNT 60.00 120.00
COMMON RIPKEN 100.00 200.00
COMMON SANDBERG 60.00 120.00
COMMON F.ROBINSON 50.00 100.00
COMMON T.GWYNN 75.00 150.00
COMMON BANKS 75.00 150.00
COMMON MOLITOR 50.00 100.00
OVERALL ONE AUTO OR MEM PER BOX
STATED PRINT RUN 10 SER.#'d SETS
8SMA1 Johnny Bench 60.00 120.00
8SMA2 Johnny Bench 60.00 120.00
8SMA3 Eddie Murray 60.00 120.00
8SMA4 Duke Snider 50.00 100.00
8SMA5 Duke Snider 50.00 100.00
8SMA6 Bob Gibson 40.00 80.00
8SMA7 Yogi Berra 75.00 200.00
8SMA8 Stan Musial 75.00 150.00
8SMA9 Stan Musial 75.00 150.00
8SMA10 Tom Seaver 40.00 100.00
8SMA11 Tom Seaver 40.00 100.00
8SMA12 Whitey Ford 50.00 100.00
8SMA14 Jim Palmer 30.00 60.00
8SMA15 Jim Palmer 30.00 60.00
8SMA16 Reggie Jackson 40.00 80.00
8SMA17 Mike Schmidt 60.00 120.00
8SMA18 Carl Yastrzemski 75.00 150.00
8SMA19 Carl Yastrzemski 75.00 150.00
8SMA20 Don Mattingly 75.00 150.00
8SMA21 Nolan Ryan 100.00 175.00
8SMA23 Robin Yount 60.00 120.00
8SMA24 Robin Yount 60.00 120.00
8SMA25 Cal Ripken 100.00 200.00
8SMA26 Ryne Sandberg 60.00 120.00
8SMA27 Ryne Sandberg 60.00 120.00
8SMA28 Frank Robinson 50.00 100.00
8SMA29 Tony Gwynn 75.00 150.00
8SMA30 Ernie Banks 75.00 150.00
8SMA31 Paul Molitor 50.00 100.00

2008 Topps Sterling Moments Relics Autographs Quad

COMMON BENCH 40.00 80.00
COMMON MURRAY 30.00 60.00
COMMON SNIDER 30.00 60.00
COMMON GIBSON 40.00 80.00
COMMON BERRA 50.00 100.00
COMMON MUSIAL 75.00 150.00
COMMON SEAVER 30.00 60.00
COMMON FORD 40.00 80.00
COMMON PALMER 20.00 50.00
COMMON R.JACKSON 40.00 80.00
COMMON SCHMIDT 40.00 80.00
COMMON YAZ 50.00 100.00
COMMON MATTINGLY 50.00 100.00
COMMON RYAN 100.00 200.00
COMMON YOUNT 30.00 60.00
COMMON RIPKEN 100.00 200.00
COMMON SANDBERG 40.00 80.00
COMMON F.ROBINSON 20.00 50.00
COMMON T.GWYNN 40.00 80.00
COMMON BANKS 30.00 60.00
COMMON MOLITOR 30.00 60.00
OVERALL ONE AUTO OR MEM PER BOX
STATED PRINT RUN 10 SER.#'d SETS
4SMA1 Johnny Bench 40.00 80.00
4SMA2 Johnny Bench 40.00 80.00
4SMA3 Johnny Bench 40.00 80.00
4SMA4 Eddie Murray 30.00 60.00
4SMA5 Eddie Murray 30.00 60.00
4SMA6 Eddie Murray 30.00 60.00
4SMA7 Eddie Murray 30.00 60.00
4SMA8 Eddie Murray 30.00 60.00
4SMA9 Eddie Murray 30.00 60.00
4SMA10 Eddie Murray 30.00 60.00
4SMA11 Eddie Murray 30.00 60.00
4SMA12 Eddie Murray 30.00 60.00
4SMA13 Eddie Murray 30.00 60.00
4SMA14 Eddie Murray 30.00 60.00
4SMA15 Eddie Murray 30.00 60.00
4SMA16 Eddie Murray 30.00 60.00
4SMA17 Eddie Murray 30.00 60.00
4SMA18 Duke Snider 30.00 60.00
4SMA19 Duke Snider 30.00 60.00
4SMA20 Duke Snider 30.00 60.00
4SMA21 Duke Snider 30.00 60.00
4SMA22 Duke Snider 30.00 60.00
4SMA23 Duke Snider 30.00 60.00
4SMA24 Duke Snider 30.00 60.00
4SMA25 Duke Snider 30.00 60.00
4SMA26 Duke Snider 30.00 60.00
4SMA27 Duke Snider 30.00 60.00
4SMA28 Duke Snider 30.00 60.00
4SMA29 Duke Snider 30.00 60.00
4SMA30 Duke Snider 30.00 60.00
4SMA31 Duke Snider 30.00 60.00
4SMA32 Bob Gibson 40.00 80.00
4SMA33 Bob Gibson 40.00 80.00
4SMA34 Bob Gibson 40.00 80.00
4SMA35 Bob Gibson 40.00 80.00
4SMA36 Bob Gibson 40.00 80.00
4SMA37 Bob Gibson 40.00 80.00
4SMA38 Bob Gibson 40.00 80.00
4SMA39 Bob Gibson 40.00 80.00
4SMA40 Bob Gibson 40.00 80.00
4SMA41 Bob Gibson 40.00 80.00
4SMA42 Bob Gibson 40.00 80.00
4SMA43 Bob Gibson 40.00 80.00
4SMA44 Bob Gibson 40.00 80.00
4SMA45 Bob Gibson 40.00 80.00
4SMA46 Yogi Berra 50.00 120.00
4SMA47 Yogi Berra 50.00 120.00
4SMA48 Yogi Berra 50.00 120.00
4SMA49 Yogi Berra 50.00 120.00
4SMA50 Yogi Berra 50.00 120.00
4SMA51 Yogi Berra 50.00 120.00
4SMA52 Yogi Berra 50.00 120.00
4SMA53 Yogi Berra 50.00 120.00
4SMA54 Yogi Berra 50.00 120.00
4SMA55 Yogi Berra 50.00 120.00
4SMA56 Yogi Berra 50.00 120.00
4SMA57 Yogi Berra 50.00 120.00
4SMA58 Yogi Berra 50.00 120.00
4SMA59 Yogi Berra 50.00 120.00
4SMA60 Stan Musial 75.00 150.00
4SMA61 Stan Musial 75.00 150.00
4SMA62 Stan Musial 75.00 150.00
4SMA63 Tom Seaver 30.00 80.00
4SMA64 Tom Seaver 30.00 80.00
4SMA65 Tom Seaver 30.00 80.00
4SMA66 Whitey Ford 40.00 80.00
4SMA67 Whitey Ford 40.00 80.00
4SMA68 Whitey Ford 40.00 80.00
4SMA69 Whitey Ford 40.00 80.00
4SMA70 Whitey Ford 40.00 80.00
4SMA71 Whitey Ford 40.00 80.00
4SMA72 Whitey Ford 40.00 80.00
4SMA73 Whitey Ford 40.00 80.00
4SMA74 Whitey Ford 40.00 80.00
4SMA75 Whitey Ford 40.00 80.00
4SMA76 Whitey Ford 40.00 80.00
4SMA77 Whitey Ford 40.00 80.00
4SMA78 Whitey Ford 40.00 80.00
4SMA79 Whitey Ford 40.00 80.00
4SMA84 Jim Palmer 20.00 50.00
4SMA85 Jim Palmer 20.00 50.00
4SMA86 Jim Palmer 20.00 50.00
4SMA87 Jim Palmer 20.00 50.00
4SMA88 Jim Palmer 20.00 50.00
4SMA89 Jim Palmer 20.00 50.00
4SMA90 Jim Palmer 20.00 50.00
4SMA91 Jim Palmer 20.00 50.00
4SMA92 Jim Palmer 20.00 50.00
4SMA93 Jim Palmer 20.00 50.00
4SMA94 Jim Palmer 20.00 50.00
4SMA95 Jim Palmer 20.00 50.00
4SMA96 Jim Palmer 20.00 50.00
4SMA97 Jim Palmer 20.00 50.00
4SMA98 Reggie Jackson 40.00 80.00
4SMA99 Reggie Jackson 40.00 80.00
4SMA100 Reggie Jackson 40.00 80.00
4SMA101 Mike Schmidt 40.00 80.00
4SMA102 Mike Schmidt 40.00 80.00
4SMA103 Mike Schmidt 40.00 80.00
4SMA104 Mike Schmidt 40.00 80.00
4SMA105 Mike Schmidt 40.00 80.00
4SMA106 Mike Schmidt 40.00 80.00
4SMA107 Mike Schmidt 40.00 80.00
4SMA108 Mike Schmidt 40.00 80.00
4SMA109 Mike Schmidt 40.00 80.00
4SMA110 Mike Schmidt 40.00 80.00
4SMA111 Mike Schmidt 40.00 80.00
4SMA112 Mike Schmidt 40.00 80.00
4SMA113 Mike Schmidt 40.00 80.00
4SMA114 Mike Schmidt 40.00 80.00
4SMA115 Carl Yastrzemski 50.00 100.00
4SMA116 Carl Yastrzemski 50.00 100.00
4SMA117 Carl Yastrzemski 50.00 100.00
4SMA118 Don Mattingly 50.00 100.00
4SMA119 Don Mattingly 50.00 100.00
4SMA120 Don Mattingly 50.00 100.00
4SMA121 Don Mattingly 50.00 100.00
4SMA122 Don Mattingly 50.00 100.00
4SMA123 Don Mattingly 50.00 100.00
4SMA124 Don Mattingly 50.00 100.00
4SMA125 Don Mattingly 50.00 100.00
4SMA126 Don Mattingly 50.00 100.00
4SMA127 Don Mattingly 50.00 100.00
4SMA128 Don Mattingly 50.00 100.00
4SMA129 Don Mattingly 50.00 100.00
4SMA130 Don Mattingly 50.00 100.00
4SMA131 Don Mattingly 50.00 100.00
4SMA132 Nolan Ryan 100.00 200.00
4SMA133 Nolan Ryan 100.00 200.00
4SMA135 Robin Yount 40.00 80.00
4SMA136 Robin Yount 40.00 80.00
4SMA137 Robin Yount 40.00 80.00
4SMA138 Robin Yount 40.00 80.00
4SMA139 Robin Yount 40.00 80.00
4SMA140 Robin Yount 40.00 80.00
4SMA141 Robin Yount 40.00 80.00
4SMA142 Robin Yount 40.00 80.00
4SMA143 Robin Yount 40.00 80.00
4SMA144 Robin Yount 40.00 80.00
4SMA145 Robin Yount 40.00 80.00
4SMA146 Robin Yount 40.00 80.00
4SMA147 Robin Yount 40.00 80.00
4SMA148 Robin Yount 40.00 80.00
4SMA149 Cal Ripken 100.00 200.00
4SMA150 Cal Ripken 100.00 200.00
4SMA151 Ryne Sandberg 40.00 80.00
4SMA152 Ryne Sandberg 40.00 80.00
4SMA153 Ryne Sandberg 40.00 80.00
4SMA154 Ryne Sandberg 40.00 80.00
4SMA155 Ryne Sandberg 40.00 80.00
4SMA156 Ryne Sandberg 40.00 80.00
4SMA157 Ryne Sandberg 40.00 80.00
4SMA158 Ryne Sandberg 40.00 80.00
4SMA159 Ryne Sandberg 40.00 80.00
4SMA160 Ryne Sandberg 40.00 80.00
4SMA161 Ryne Sandberg 40.00 80.00
4SMA162 Ryne Sandberg 40.00 80.00
4SMA163 Ryne Sandberg 40.00 80.00
4SMA164 Ryne Sandberg 40.00 80.00
4SMA165 Frank Robinson 20.00 50.00
4SMA166 Frank Robinson 20.00 50.00
4SMA167 Frank Robinson 20.00 50.00
4SMA168 Tony Gwynn 40.00 80.00
4SMA169 Tony Gwynn 40.00 80.00
4SMA170 Tony Gwynn 40.00 80.00
4SMA171 Ernie Banks 30.00 60.00
4SMA172 Ernie Banks 30.00 60.00
4SMA174 Paul Molitor 30.00 60.00
4SMA176 Paul Molitor 30.00 60.00
4SMA177 Paul Molitor 30.00 60.00
4SMA178 Paul Molitor 30.00 60.00
4SMA180 Paul Molitor 30.00 60.00

2008 Topps Sterling Moments Relics Autographs Triple

COMMON BENCH 40.00 80.00
COMMON MURRAY 30.00 60.00
COMMON SNIDER 30.00 60.00
COMMON GIBSON 40.00 80.00
COMMON BERRA 40.00 80.00
COMMON MUSIAL 75.00 150.00
COMMON SEAVER 30.00 60.00
COMMON FORD 40.00 80.00
COMMON PALMER 20.00 50.00
COMMON R.JACKSON 30.00 60.00

COMMON SCHMIDT 40.00 80.00
COMMON YAZ 30.00 60.00
COMMON MATTINGLY 60.00 120.00
COMMON RYAN 75.00 150.00
COMMON YOUNT 40.00 80.00
COMMON RIPKEN 125.00 250.00
COMMON SANDBERG 40.00 80.00
COMMON F.ROBINSON 20.00 50.00
COMMON T.GWYNN 50.00 100.00
COMMON BANKS 40.00 80.00
COMMON MOLITOR 30.00 60.00
OVERALL ONE AUTO OR MEM PER BOX
STATED PRINT RUN 10 SER.#'d SETS
3SMA2 Johnny Bench 40.00 80.00
3SMA6 Eddie Murray 30.00 60.00
3SMA7 Eddie Murray 30.00 60.00
3SMA10 Eddie Murray 30.00 60.00
3SMA11 Eddie Murray 30.00 60.00
3SMA16 Eddie Murray 30.00 60.00
3SMA17 Eddie Murray 30.00 60.00
3SMA20 Duke Snider 30.00 60.00
3SMA21 Duke Snider 30.00 60.00
3SMA26 Duke Snider 30.00 60.00
3SMA27 Duke Snider 30.00 60.00
3SMA28 Duke Snider 30.00 60.00
3SMA34 Bob Gibson 40.00 80.00
3SMA37 Bob Gibson 40.00 80.00
3SMA39 Bob Gibson 40.00 80.00
3SMA40 Bob Gibson 40.00 80.00
3SMA42 Bob Gibson 40.00 80.00
3SMA43 Bob Gibson 40.00 80.00
3SMA47 Yogi Berra 40.00 100.00
3SMA48 Yogi Berra 40.00 100.00
3SMA49 Yogi Berra 40.00 100.00
3SMA52 Yogi Berra 40.00 100.00
3SMA58 Stan Musial 75.00 150.00
3SMA60 Stan Musial 75.00 150.00
3SMA62 Tom Seaver 30.00 80.00
3SMA64 Tom Seaver 30.00 80.00
3SMA67 Whitey Ford 40.00 80.00
3SMA68 Whitey Ford 40.00 80.00
3SMA71 Whitey Ford 40.00 80.00
3SMA75 Whitey Ford 40.00 80.00
3SMA76 Whitey Ford 40.00 80.00
3SMA77 Whitey Ford 40.00 80.00
3SMA85 Jim Palmer 20.00 50.00
3SMA89 Jim Palmer 20.00 50.00
3SMA90 Jim Palmer 20.00 50.00
3SMA93 Jim Palmer 20.00 50.00
3SMA94 Jim Palmer 20.00 50.00
3SMA97 Reggie Jackson 30.00 60.00
3SMA101 Reggie Jackson 30.00 60.00
3SMA102 Mike Schmidt 40.00 80.00
3SMA105 Mike Schmidt 40.00 80.00
3SMA106 Mike Schmidt 40.00 80.00
3SMA109 Mike Schmidt 40.00 80.00
3SMA111 Mike Schmidt 40.00 80.00
3SMA112 Mike Schmidt 40.00 80.00
3SMA115 Carl Yastrzemski 30.00 60.00
3SMA116 Carl Yastrzemski 30.00 60.00
3SMA123 Don Mattingly 60.00 120.00
3SMA126 Don Mattingly 60.00 120.00
3SMA127 Don Mattingly 60.00 120.00
3SMA130 Don Mattingly 60.00 120.00
3SMA132 Don Mattingly 60.00 120.00
3SMA133 Nolan Ryan 75.00 150.00
3SMA136 Robin Yount 40.00 80.00
3SMA138 Robin Yount 40.00 80.00
3SMA139 Robin Yount 40.00 80.00
3SMA141 Robin Yount 40.00 80.00
3SMA143 Robin Yount 40.00 80.00
3SMA145 Robin Yount 40.00 80.00
3SMA146 Robin Yount 40.00 80.00
3SMA148 Cal Ripken 125.00 250.00
3SMA149 Ryne Sandberg 40.00 80.00
3SMA154 Ryne Sandberg 40.00 80.00
3SMA156 Ryne Sandberg 40.00 80.00
3SMA161 Ryne Sandberg 40.00 80.00
3SMA163 Frank Robinson 20.00 50.00
3SMA165 Frank Robinson 20.00 50.00
3SMA170 Tony Gwynn 50.00 100.00
3SMA172 Ernie Banks 40.00 80.00
3SMA174 Paul Molitor 30.00 60.00
3SMA176 Paul Molitor 30.00 60.00

2008 Topps Sterling Stardom Relics Eight

RANDOM INSERTS IN BOXES
OVERALL ONE AUTO OR MEM PER BOX
STATED PRINT RUN 10 SER.#'d SETS
NO PRICING DUE TO SCARCITY

2008 Topps Sterling Stardom Relics Five

COMMON MANTLE 75.00 150.00
COMMON RUTH 150.00 250.00
COMMON OTT 50.00 100.00
COMMON BENCH 20.00 50.00
COMMON FOXX 60.00 120.00
COMMON J.ROBINSON 40.00 80.00
COMMON MUSIAL 20.00 50.00
COMMON HORNSBY 40.00 80.00
COMMON SEAVER 15.00 40.00
COMMON MARIS 50.00 100.00
COMMON MUNSON 30.00 60.00
COMMON R.JACKSON 10.00 25.00
COMMON YAZ 20.00 50.00
COMMON CAMPANELLA 30.00 60.00
COMMON RYAN 50.00 100.00
COMMON COBB 100.00 175.00
COMMON RIPKEN 100.00 175.00
COMMON GEHRIG 150.00 250.00
COMMON CLEMENTE 60.00 120.00
COMMON T.WILLIAMS 60.00 120.00
COMMON F.ROBINSON 15.00 40.00
COMMON T.GWYNN 20.00 50.00
COMMON BANKS 15.00 40.00
COMMON WAGNER 100.00 200.00
OVERALL ONE AUTO OR MEM PER BOX
STATED PRINT RUN 10 SER.#'d SETS
5SS1 Mickey Mantle 75.00 150.00
5SS2 Mickey Mantle 75.00 150.00
5SS3 Babe Ruth 150.00 250.00
5SS4 Babe Ruth 150.00 250.00
5SS5 Mel Ott 50.00 100.00
5SS6 Mel Ott 50.00 100.00
5SS7 Johnny Bench 20.00 50.00
5SS8 Johnny Bench 20.00 50.00
5SS9 Johnny Bench 20.00 50.00
5SS10 Johnny Bench 20.00 50.00
5SS11 Johnny Bench 20.00 50.00
5SS12 Jimmie Foxx 60.00 120.00
5SS13 Jimmie Foxx 60.00 120.00
5SS14 Jackie Robinson 40.00 80.00
5SS15 Jackie Robinson 40.00 80.00
5SS16 Stan Musial 20.00 50.00
5SS17 Stan Musial 20.00 50.00
5SS18 Stan Musial 20.00 50.00
5SS19 Stan Musial 20.00 50.00
5SS20 Stan Musial 20.00 50.00
5SS21 Rogers Hornsby 40.00 80.00
5SS22 Rogers Hornsby 40.00 80.00
5SS23 Tom Seaver 15.00 40.00
5SS24 Tom Seaver 15.00 40.00
5SS25 Tom Seaver 15.00 40.00
5SS26 Tom Seaver 15.00 40.00
5SS27 Tom Seaver 15.00 40.00
5SS33 Roger Maris 50.00 100.00
5SS34 Roger Maris 50.00 100.00
5SS35 Thurman Munson 30.00 60.00
5SS36 Thurman Munson 30.00 60.00
5SS37 Reggie Jackson 10.00 25.00
5SS38 Reggie Jackson 10.00 25.00
5SS39 Reggie Jackson 10.00 25.00
5SS40 Reggie Jackson 10.00 25.00
5SS41 Reggie Jackson 10.00 25.00
5SS42 Carl Yastrzemski 20.00 50.00
5SS43 Carl Yastrzemski 20.00 50.00
5SS44 Carl Yastrzemski 20.00 50.00
5SS45 Carl Yastrzemski 20.00 50.00
5SS46 Carl Yastrzemski 20.00 50.00
5SS47 Roy Campanella 30.00 60.00
5SS48 Roy Campanella 30.00 60.00
5SS49 Nolan Ryan 50.00 100.00
5SS50 Nolan Ryan 50.00 100.00
5SS51 Nolan Ryan 50.00 100.00
5SS52 Nolan Ryan 50.00 100.00
5SS53 Nolan Ryan 50.00 100.00
5SS59 Ty Cobb 100.00 175.00
5SS60 Ty Cobb 100.00 175.00
5SS61 Cal Ripken 100.00 175.00
5SS62 Lou Gehrig 150.00 250.00
5SS63 Lou Gehrig 150.00 250.00
5SS64 Roberto Clemente 60.00 120.00
5SS65 Roberto Clemente 60.00 120.00
5SS66 Ted Williams 60.00 120.00
5SS67 Ted Williams 60.00 120.00
5SS68 Frank Robinson 15.00 40.00
5SS69 Frank Robinson 15.00 40.00
5SS70 Frank Robinson 15.00 40.00
5SS71 Frank Robinson 15.00 40.00
5SS72 Frank Robinson 15.00 40.00
5SS73 Tony Gwynn 20.00 50.00
5SS74 Tony Gwynn 20.00 50.00
5SS75 Tony Gwynn 20.00 50.00
5SS76 Tony Gwynn 20.00 50.00
5SS77 Ernie Banks 15.00 40.00
5SS78 Ernie Banks 15.00 40.00
5SS79 Ernie Banks 15.00 40.00
5SS80 Ernie Banks 15.00 40.00
5SS81 Ernie Banks 15.00 40.00
5SS82 Honus Wagner 100.00 200.00
5SS83 Honus Wagner 100.00 200.00

2008 Topps Sterling Stardom Relics Quad

COMMON MANTLE 75.00 150.00
COMMON RUTH 200.00 350.00
COMMON OTT 50.00 100.00
COMMON BENCH 20.00 50.00
COMMON FOXX 40.00 80.00
COMMON J.ROBINSON 40.00 80.00
COMMON MUSIAL 30.00 60.00
COMMON HORNSBY 30.00 60.00
COMMON SEAVER 15.00 40.00
COMMON MARIS 50.00 100.00
COMMON MUNSON 30.00 60.00
COMMON R.JACKSON 15.00 40.00
COMMON YAZ 15.00 40.00
COMMON CAMPANELLA 30.00 60.00
COMMON COBB 40.00 80.00
COMMON RIPKEN 90.00 150.00
COMMON GEHRIG 100.00 250.00
COMMON CLEMENTE 60.00 120.00
COMMON T.WILLIAMS 40.00 80.00
COMMON F.ROBINSON 15.00 40.00
COMMON T.GWYNN 15.00 40.00
COMMON WAGNER 100.00 200.00
OVERALL ONE AUTO OR MEM PER BOX
STATED PRINT RUN 10 SER.#'d SETS
NO RYAN PRICING AVAILABLE
4SS1 Mickey Mantle 75.00 150.00
4SS2 Mickey Mantle 75.00 150.00
4SS3 Babe Ruth 200.00 350.00
4SS4 Babe Ruth 200.00 350.00
4SS5 Mel Ott 50.00 100.00
4SS6 Mel Ott 50.00 100.00
4SS7 Johnny Bench 20.00 50.00
4SS8 Johnny Bench 20.00 50.00
4SS10 Johnny Bench 20.00 50.00
4SS11 Johnny Bench 20.00 50.00
4SS12 Jimmie Foxx 40.00 80.00
4SS13 Jimmie Foxx 40.00 80.00
4SS14 Jackie Robinson 40.00 80.00
4SS15 Jackie Robinson 40.00 80.00
4SS16 Stan Musial 30.00 60.00
4SS17 Stan Musial 30.00 60.00
4SS19 Stan Musial 30.00 60.00
4SS21 Stan Musial 30.00 60.00
4SS22 Rogers Hornsby 30.00 60.00
4SS23 Rogers Hornsby 30.00 60.00
4SS24 Tom Seaver 15.00 40.00
4SS27 Tom Seaver 15.00 40.00
4SS35 Roger Maris 50.00 100.00
4SS36 Roger Maris 50.00 100.00
4SS37 Thurman Munson 30.00 60.00
4SS38 Thurman Munson 30.00 60.00
4SS41 Reggie Jackson 15.00 40.00
4SS42 Reggie Jackson 15.00 40.00
4SS44 Carl Yastrzemski 15.00 40.00
4SS46 Carl Yastrzemski 15.00 40.00
4SS47 Carl Yastrzemski 15.00 40.00
4SS48 Carl Yastrzemski 15.00 40.00
4SS49 Carl Yastrzemski 15.00 40.00
4SS50 Roy Campanella 30.00 60.00
4SS51 Roy Campanella 30.00 60.00
4SS63 Ty Cobb 40.00 80.00
4SS64 Ty Cobb 40.00 80.00
4SS65 Cal Ripken 90.00 150.00
4SS66 Lou Gehrig 100.00 250.00
4SS67 Lou Gehrig 100.00 250.00
4SS68 Roberto Clemente 60.00 120.00
4SS69 Roberto Clemente 60.00 120.00
4SS70 Ted Williams 40.00 80.00
4SS71 Ted Williams 40.00 80.00
4SS72 Frank Robinson 15.00 40.00
4SS74 Frank Robinson 15.00 40.00
4SS76 Frank Robinson 15.00 40.00
4SS78 Tony Gwynn 15.00 40.00
4SS81 Tony Gwynn 15.00 40.00
4SS82 Tony Gwynn 15.00 40.00
4SS87 Honus Wagner 100.00 200.00
4SS88 Honus Wagner 100.00 200.00

2008 Topps Sterling Stardom Relics Six

COMMON MANTLE 100.00 200.00
COMMON RUTH 250.00 400.00
COMMON OTT 50.00 100.00
COMMON BENCH 20.00 50.00
COMMON FOXX 50.00 100.00
COMMON MURRAY 20.00 50.00
COMMON J.ROBINSON 50.00 100.00
COMMON SNIDER 30.00 60.00
COMMON GIBSON 20.00 50.00
COMMON BERRA 30.00 60.00
COMMON MUSIAL 30.00 60.00
COMMON HORNSBY 40.00 80.00
COMMON SEAVER 20.00 50.00
COMMON FORD 20.00 50.00
COMMON MARIS 60.00 120.00
COMMON MUNSON 40.00 80.00
COMMON PALMER 12.50 30.00
COMMON R.JACKSON 20.00 50.00
COMMON SCHMIDT 20.00 50.00
COMMON YAZ 20.00 50.00
COMMON MATTINGLY 40.00 80.00
COMMON CAMPANELLA 20.00 50.00
COMMON RYAN 30.00 60.00
COMMON COBB 150.00 250.00
COMMON YOUNT 20.00 50.00
COMMON RIPKEN 75.00 150.00
COMMON GEHRIG 175.00 300.00
COMMON CLEMENTE 75.00 150.00
COMMON SANDBERG 20.00 50.00
COMMON T.WILLIAMS 75.00 150.00
COMMON F.ROBINSON 20.00 50.00
COMMON T.GWYNN 20.00 50.00
COMMON BANKS 15.00 40.00
COMMON WAGNER 150.00 250.00
COMMON MOLITOR 20.00 50.00
OVERALL ONE AUTO OR MEM PER BOX
STATED PRINT RUN 10 SER.#'d SETS
6SS1 Mickey Mantle 100.00 200.00
6SS2 Babe Ruth 250.00 400.00
6SS3 Mel Ott 50.00 100.00
6SS4 Johnny Bench 20.00 50.00
6SS5 Johnny Bench 20.00 50.00
6SS6 Johnny Bench 20.00 50.00
6SS7 Johnny Bench 20.00 50.00
6SS8 Jimmie Foxx 50.00 100.00
6SS9 Eddie Murray 20.00 50.00
6SS10 Jackie Robinson 50.00 100.00
6SS11 Duke Snider 30.00 60.00
6SS12 Bob Gibson 20.00 50.00
6SS13 Yogi Berra 30.00 60.00
6SS14 Stan Musial 30.00 60.00
6SS15 Stan Musial 30.00 60.00
6SS16 Stan Musial 30.00 60.00
6SS17 Stan Musial 30.00 60.00
6SS18 Rogers Hornsby 40.00 80.00
6SS19 Tom Seaver 20.00 50.00
6SS20 Tom Seaver 20.00 50.00
6SS21 Tom Seaver 20.00 50.00
6SS22 Tom Seaver 20.00 50.00
6SS23 Whitey Ford 20.00 50.00
6SS28 Roger Maris 60.00 120.00
6SS29 Thurman Munson 40.00 80.00
6SS30 Jim Palmer 12.50 30.00
6SS31 Reggie Jackson 20.00 50.00
6SS32 Reggie Jackson 20.00 50.00
6SS33 Reggie Jackson 20.00 50.00
6SS34 Reggie Jackson 20.00 50.00
6SS35 Mike Schmidt 20.00 50.00
6SS36 Carl Yastrzemski 20.00 50.00
6SS37 Carl Yastrzemski 20.00 50.00
6SS38 Carl Yastrzemski 20.00 50.00
6SS39 Carl Yastrzemski 20.00 50.00
6SS40 Don Mattingly 40.00 80.00
6SS41 Roy Campanella 20.00 50.00
6SS42 Nolan Ryan 30.00 60.00
6SS43 Nolan Ryan 30.00 60.00
6SS44 Nolan Ryan 30.00 60.00
6SS45 Nolan Ryan 30.00 60.00
6SS46 Nolan Ryan 30.00 60.00
6SS47 Nolan Ryan 30.00 60.00
6SS48 Nolan Ryan 30.00 60.00
6SS49 Nolan Ryan 30.00 60.00
6SS50 Nolan Ryan 30.00 60.00
6SS60 Ty Cobb 150.00 250.00
6SS61 Robin Yount 20.00 50.00
6SS62 Cal Ripken 75.00 150.00
6SS63 Lou Gehrig 175.00 300.00
6SS64 Roberto Clemente 75.00 150.00
6SS65 Ryne Sandberg 20.00 50.00
6SS66 Ted Williams 75.00 150.00
6SS67 Frank Robinson 20.00 50.00
6SS68 Frank Robinson 20.00 50.00
6SS69 Frank Robinson 20.00 50.00
6SS70 Frank Robinson 20.00 50.00
6SS71 Tony Gwynn 20.00 50.00
6SS72 Tony Gwynn 20.00 50.00
6SS73 Tony Gwynn 20.00 50.00
6SS74 Tony Gwynn 20.00 50.00
6SS75 Ernie Banks 15.00 40.00
6SS76 Ernie Banks 15.00 40.00
6SS77 Ernie Banks 15.00 40.00
6SS78 Ernie Banks 15.00 40.00
6SS79 Ernie Banks 15.00 40.00
6SS80 Ernie Banks 15.00 40.00
6SS81 Ernie Banks 15.00 40.00
6SS82 Ernie Banks 15.00 40.00
6SS83 Ernie Banks 15.00 40.00
6SS84 Honus Wagner 150.00 250.00
6SS87 Paul Molitor 20.00 50.00
6SS94 Paul Molitor 20.00 50.00

2008 Topps Sterling Stardom Relics Triple

COMMON MANTLE 60.00 120.00
COMMON RUTH 125.00 250.00
COMMON OTT 40.00 80.00
COMMON FOXX 30.00 60.00
COMMON J.ROBINSON 40.00 80.00
COMMON HORNSBY 40.00 80.00
COMMON MARIS 40.00 80.00
COMMON MUNSON 50.00 100.00
COMMON CAMPANELLA 20.00 50.00
COMMON COBB 75.00 150.00
COMMON RIPKEN 90.00 150.00
COMMON GEHRIG 150.00 250.00
COMMON CLEMENTE 50.00 100.00
COMMON T.WILLIAMS 40.00 80.00
COMMON WAGNER 90.00 150.00
OVERALL ONE AUTO OR MEM PER BOX
STATED PRINT RUN 10 SER.#'d SETS
NO RYAN PRICING AVAILABLE
3SS1 Mickey Mantle 60.00 120.00
3SS2 Mickey Mantle 60.00 120.00
3SS3 Mickey Mantle 60.00 120.00
3SS4 Babe Ruth 125.00 250.00
3SS5 Babe Ruth 125.00 250.00
3SS6 Babe Ruth 125.00 250.00
3SS7 Mel Ott 40.00 80.00
3SS8 Mel Ott 40.00 80.00
3SS9 Mel Ott 40.00 80.00
3SS14 Jimmie Foxx 30.00 60.00
3SS15 Jimmie Foxx 30.00 60.00
3SS16 Jimmie Foxx 30.00 60.00
3SS17 Jackie Robinson 40.00 80.00
3SS18 Jackie Robinson 40.00 80.00
3SS19 Jackie Robinson 40.00 80.00
3SS24 Rogers Hornsby 40.00 80.00
3SS25 Rogers Hornsby 40.00 80.00
3SS26 Rogers Hornsby 40.00 80.00
3SS35 Roger Maris 40.00 80.00
3SS36 Roger Maris 40.00 80.00
3SS37 Roger Maris 40.00 80.00
3SS38 Thurman Munson 50.00 100.00
3SS39 Thurman Munson 50.00 100.00
3SS40 Thurman Munson 50.00 100.00
3SS49 Roy Campanella 20.00 50.00
3SS50 Roy Campanella 20.00 50.00
3SS51 Roy Campanella 20.00 50.00
3SS60 Ty Cobb 75.00 150.00
3SS61 Ty Cobb 75.00 150.00
3SS62 Ty Cobb 75.00 150.00
3SS63 Cal Ripken 90.00 150.00
3SS64 Lou Gehrig 150.00 250.00
3SS65 Lou Gehrig 150.00 250.00
3SS66 Lou Gehrig 150.00 250.00
3SS67 Roberto Clemente 50.00 100.00
3SS68 Roberto Clemente 50.00 100.00
3SS69 Roberto Clemente 50.00 100.00
3SS70 Ted Williams 40.00 80.00
3SS71 Ted Williams 40.00 80.00
3SS72 Ted Williams 40.00 80.00
3SS85 Honus Wagner 90.00 150.00
3SS86 Honus Wagner 90.00 150.00
3SS87 Honus Wagner 90.00 150.00

2008 Topps Sterling Stardom Relics Autographs Eight

COMMON BENCH 60.00 120.00
COMMON MURRAY 60.00 120.00
COMMON SNIDER 50.00 100.00
COMMON GIBSON 40.00 80.00
COMMON BERRA 75.00 150.00
COMMON MUSIAL 75.00 150.00
COMMON SEAVER 40.00 80.00
COMMON FORD 50.00 100.00
COMMON PALMER 30.00 60.00
COMMON R.JACKSON 40.00 80.00
COMMON SCHMIDT 60.00 120.00
COMMON YAZ 75.00 150.00
COMMON MATTINGLY 75.00 150.00
COMMON RYAN 100.00 175.00
COMMON YOUNT 60.00 120.00
COMMON RIPKEN 100.00 200.00
COMMON SANDBERG 60.00 120.00
COMMON F.ROBINSON 50.00 100.00
COMMON T.GWYNN 75.00 150.00
COMMON BANKS 75.00 150.00
COMMON MOLITOR 50.00 100.00
OVERALL ONE AUTO OR MEM PER BOX
STATED PRINT RUN 10 SER.#'d SETS
8SSA1 Johnny Bench 60.00 120.00
8SSA2 Johnny Bench 60.00 120.00
8SSA3 Eddie Murray 60.00 120.00
8SSA4 Duke Snider 50.00 100.00
8SSA5 Bob Gibson 40.00 80.00
8SSA6 Bob Gibson 40.00 80.00
8SSA7 Yogi Berra 75.00 200.00
8SSA8 Stan Musial 75.00 150.00
8SSA9 Stan Musial 75.00 150.00
8SSA10 Tom Seaver 40.00 100.00
8SSA11 Whitey Ford 50.00 100.00
8SSA14 Jim Palmer 30.00 60.00
8SSA15 Reggie Jackson 40.00 80.00
8SSA16 Mike Schmidt 60.00 120.00
8SSA17 Carl Yastrzemski 75.00 150.00
8SSA18 Carl Yastrzemski 75.00 150.00
8SSA19 Don Mattingly 75.00 150.00
8SSA20 Don Mattingly 75.00 150.00
8SSA21 Nolan Ryan 100.00 175.00
8SSA23 Robin Yount 60.00 120.00
8SSA24 Cal Ripken 100.00 200.00
8SSA25 Ryne Sandberg 60.00 120.00
8SSA26 Frank Robinson 50.00 100.00
8SSA27 Frank Robinson 50.00 100.00
8SSA28 Tony Gwynn 75.00 150.00
8SSA29 Tony Gwynn 75.00 150.00
8SSA30 Ernie Banks 75.00 150.00
8SSA31 Paul Molitor 50.00 100.00

2008 Topps Sterling Stardom Relics Autographs Quad

COMMON BENCH 40.00 80.00
COMMON MURRAY 30.00 60.00
COMMON SNIDER 30.00 60.00
COMMON GIBSON 40.00 80.00
COMMON BERRA 50.00 100.00
COMMON MUSIAL 75.00 150.00
COMMON SEAVER 30.00 60.00
COMMON FORD 40.00 80.00
COMMON PALMER 20.00 50.00
COMMON R.JACKSON 40.00 80.00
COMMON SCHMIDT 40.00 80.00
COMMON YAZ 50.00 100.00
COMMON MATTINGLY 50.00 100.00
COMMON RYAN 100.00 200.00
COMMON YOUNT 30.00 60.00
COMMON RIPKEN 100.00 200.00
COMMON SANDBERG 40.00 80.00
COMMON F.ROBINSON 20.00 50.00
COMMON T.GWYNN 40.00 80.00
COMMON BANKS 30.00 60.00
COMMON MOLITOR 30.00 60.00
OVERALL ONE AUTO OR MEM PER BOX
STATED PRINT RUN 10 SER.#'d SETS
4SSA1 Johnny Bench 40.00 80.00
4SSA2 Johnny Bench 40.00 80.00
4SSA3 Johnny Bench 40.00 80.00
4SSA4 Johnny Bench 40.00 80.00
4SSA5 Johnny Bench 40.00 80.00
4SSA6 Johnny Bench 40.00 80.00
4SSA7 Eddie Murray 30.00 60.00
4SSA8 Eddie Murray 30.00 60.00
4SSA9 Eddie Murray 30.00 60.00
4SSA10 Eddie Murray 30.00 60.00
4SSA11 Eddie Murray 30.00 60.00
4SSA12 Eddie Murray 30.00 60.00
4SSA13 Eddie Murray 30.00 60.00
4SSA14 Eddie Murray 30.00 60.00
4SSA15 Eddie Murray 30.00 60.00
4SSA16 Eddie Murray 30.00 60.00
4SSA17 Eddie Murray 30.00 60.00
4SSA18 Eddie Murray 30.00 60.00
4SSA19 Duke Snider 30.00 60.00
4SSA20 Duke Snider 30.00 60.00
4SSA21 Duke Snider 30.00 60.00
4SSA22 Duke Snider 30.00 60.00
4SSA23 Duke Snider 30.00 60.00
4SSA24 Duke Snider 30.00 60.00
4SSA25 Duke Snider 30.00 60.00
4SSA26 Duke Snider 30.00 60.00
4SSA27 Duke Snider 30.00 60.00
4SSA28 Duke Snider 30.00 60.00
4SSA29 Duke Snider 30.00 60.00
4SSA30 Duke Snider 30.00 60.00
4SSA31 Bob Gibson 40.00 80.00
4SSA32 Bob Gibson 40.00 80.00
4SSA33 Bob Gibson 40.00 80.00
4SSA34 Bob Gibson 40.00 80.00
4SSA35 Bob Gibson 40.00 80.00
4SSA36 Bob Gibson 40.00 80.00
4SSA37 Bob Gibson 40.00 80.00
4SSA38 Bob Gibson 40.00 80.00
4SSA39 Bob Gibson 40.00 80.00
4SSA40 Bob Gibson 40.00 80.00
4SSA41 Bob Gibson 40.00 80.00
4SSA42 Bob Gibson 40.00 80.00
4SSA43 Yogi Berra 50.00 120.00
4SSA44 Yogi Berra 50.00 120.00
4SSA45 Yogi Berra 50.00 120.00
4SSA46 Yogi Berra 50.00 120.00
4SSA47 Yogi Berra 50.00 120.00
4SSA48 Yogi Berra 50.00 120.00
4SSA49 Yogi Berra 50.00 120.00
4SSA50 Yogi Berra 50.00 120.00
4SSA51 Yogi Berra 50.00 120.00
4SSA52 Yogi Berra 50.00 120.00
4SSA53 Yogi Berra 50.00 120.00
4SSA54 Yogi Berra 50.00 120.00
4SSA55 Stan Musial 75.00 150.00
4SSA56 Stan Musial 75.00 150.00
4SSA57 Stan Musial 75.00 150.00
4SSA58 Stan Musial 75.00 150.00
4SSA59 Stan Musial 75.00 150.00
4SSA60 Tom Seaver 30.00 80.00
4SSA61 Tom Seaver 30.00 80.00
4SSA62 Tom Seaver 30.00 80.00
4SSA63 Tom Seaver 30.00 80.00
4SSA64 Tom Seaver 30.00 80.00
4SSA65 Whitey Ford 40.00 80.00
4SSA66 Whitey Ford 40.00 80.00
4SSA67 Whitey Ford 40.00 80.00
4SSA68 Whitey Ford 40.00 80.00
4SSA69 Whitey Ford 40.00 80.00
4SSA70 Whitey Ford 40.00 80.00
4SSA71 Whitey Ford 40.00 80.00
4SSA72 Whitey Ford 40.00 80.00
4SSA73 Whitey Ford 40.00 80.00
4SSA74 Whitey Ford 40.00 80.00
4SSA75 Whitey Ford 40.00 80.00
4SSA76 Whitey Ford 40.00 80.00
4SSA82 Jim Palmer 20.00 50.00
4SSA83 Jim Palmer 20.00 50.00
4SSA84 Jim Palmer 20.00 50.00
4SSA85 Jim Palmer 20.00 50.00
4SSA86 Jim Palmer 20.00 50.00
4SSA87 Jim Palmer 20.00 50.00
4SSA88 Jim Palmer 20.00 50.00
4SSA89 Jim Palmer 20.00 50.00
4SSA90 Jim Palmer 20.00 50.00
4SSA91 Jim Palmer 20.00 50.00
4SSA92 Jim Palmer 20.00 50.00
4SSA93 Jim Palmer 20.00 50.00
4SSA94 Reggie Jackson 40.00 80.00
4SSA95 Reggie Jackson 40.00 80.00
4SSA96 Reggie Jackson 40.00 80.00
4SSA97 Reggie Jackson 40.00 80.00
4SSA98 Reggie Jackson 40.00 80.00
4SSA99 Reggie Jackson 40.00 80.00
4SSA100 Mike Schmidt 40.00 80.00
4SSA101 Mike Schmidt 40.00 80.00
4SSA102 Mike Schmidt 40.00 80.00
4SSA103 Mike Schmidt 40.00 80.00
4SSA104 Mike Schmidt 40.00 80.00
4SSA105 Mike Schmidt 40.00 80.00
4SSA106 Mike Schmidt 40.00 80.00
4SSA107 Mike Schmidt 40.00 80.00
4SSA108 Mike Schmidt 40.00 80.00
4SSA109 Mike Schmidt 40.00 80.00
4SSA110 Mike Schmidt 40.00 80.00
4SSA111 Mike Schmidt 40.00 80.00
4SSA112 Carl Yastrzemski 50.00 100.00
4SSA113 Carl Yastrzemski 50.00 100.00
4SSA114 Carl Yastrzemski 50.00 100.00
4SSA115 Carl Yastrzemski 50.00 100.00
4SSA116 Carl Yastrzemski 50.00 100.00
4SSA117 Don Mattingly 50.00 100.00
4SSA118 Don Mattingly 50.00 100.00
4SSA119 Don Mattingly 50.00 100.00
4SSA120 Don Mattingly 50.00 100.00
4SSA121 Don Mattingly 50.00 100.00
4SSA122 Don Mattingly 50.00 100.00
4SSA123 Don Mattingly 50.00 100.00
4SSA124 Don Mattingly 50.00 100.00
4SSA125 Don Mattingly 50.00 100.00
4SSA126 Don Mattingly 50.00 100.00
4SSA127 Don Mattingly 50.00 100.00
4SSA128 Don Mattingly 50.00 100.00
4SSA129 Nolan Ryan 100.00 200.00
4SSA132 Robin Yount 40.00 80.00
4SSA133 Robin Yount 40.00 80.00
4SSA134 Robin Yount 40.00 80.00
4SSA135 Robin Yount 40.00 80.00
4SSA136 Robin Yount 40.00 80.00
4SSA137 Robin Yount 40.00 80.00
4SSA138 Robin Yount 40.00 80.00
4SSA139 Robin Yount 40.00 80.00
4SSA140 Robin Yount 40.00 80.00
4SSA141 Robin Yount 40.00 80.00
4SSA142 Robin Yount 40.00 80.00
4SSA143 Cal Ripken 100.00 200.00
4SSA144 Cal Ripken 100.00 200.00
4SSA145 Ryne Sandberg 40.00 80.00
4SSA146 Ryne Sandberg 40.00 80.00
4SSA147 Ryne Sandberg 40.00 80.00
4SSA148 Ryne Sandberg 40.00 80.00
4SSA149 Ryne Sandberg 40.00 80.00
4SSA150 Ryne Sandberg 40.00 80.00
4SSA151 Ryne Sandberg 40.00 80.00
4SSA152 Ryne Sandberg 40.00 80.00
4SSA153 Ryne Sandberg 40.00 80.00
4SSA154 Ryne Sandberg 40.00 80.00
4SSA155 Ryne Sandberg 40.00 80.00
4SSA156 Ryne Sandberg 40.00 80.00
4SSA157 Frank Robinson 20.00 50.00
4SSA158 Frank Robinson 20.00 50.00
4SSA159 Frank Robinson 20.00 50.00
4SSA160 Frank Robinson 20.00 50.00
4SSA161 Frank Robinson 20.00 50.00
4SSA162 Frank Robinson 20.00 50.00
4SSA163 Tony Gwynn 40.00 80.00
4SSA164 Tony Gwynn 40.00 80.00
4SSA165 Tony Gwynn 40.00 80.00
4SSA166 Tony Gwynn 40.00 80.00
4SSA167 Tony Gwynn 40.00 80.00
4SSA168 Tony Gwynn 40.00 80.00
4SSA169 Ernie Banks 30.00 60.00
4SSA170 Ernie Banks 30.00 60.00
4SSA173 Paul Molitor 30.00 60.00
4SSA176 Paul Molitor 30.00 60.00

2008 Topps Sterling Stardom Relics Autographs Triple

COMMON BENCH 40.00 80.00
COMMON MURRAY 30.00 60.00
COMMON SNIDER 30.00 60.00
COMMON GIBSON 40.00 80.00
COMMON BERRA 40.00 80.00
COMMON MUSIAL 75.00 150.00
COMMON SEAVER 30.00 60.00
COMMON FORD 40.00 80.00
COMMON PALMER 20.00 50.00
COMMON R.JACKSON 30.00 60.00
COMMON SCHMIDT 40.00 80.00
COMMON YAZ 30.00 60.00
COMMON MATTINGLY 60.00 120.00
COMMON RYAN 75.00 150.00
COMMON YOUNT 40.00 80.00
COMMON RIPKEN 125.00 250.00
COMMON SANDBERG 40.00 80.00
COMMON F.ROBINSON 20.00 50.00
COMMON T.GWYNN 50.00 100.00
COMMON BANKS 40.00 80.00
OVERALL ONE AUTO OR MEM PER BOX
STATED PRINT RUN 10 SER.#'d SETS
3SSA1 Johnny Bench 40.00 80.00
3SSA9 Eddie Murray 30.00 60.00
3SSA11 Eddie Murray 30.00 60.00
3SSA12 Eddie Murray 30.00 60.00
3SSA14 Eddie Murray 30.00 60.00
3SSA16 Eddie Murray 30.00 60.00
3SSA21 Duke Snider 30.00 60.00
3SSA24 Duke Snider 30.00 60.00
3SSA26 Duke Snider 30.00 60.00
3SSA28 Duke Snider 30.00 60.00
3SSA30 Duke Snider 30.00 60.00
3SSA34 Bob Gibson 40.00 80.00
3SSA40 Bob Gibson 40.00 80.00
3SSA41 Bob Gibson 40.00 80.00
3SSA45 Yogi Berra 40.00 100.00
3SSA49 Yogi Berra 40.00 100.00
3SSA51 Yogi Berra 40.00 100.00
3SSA53 Yogi Berra 40.00 100.00
3SSA54 Yogi Berra 40.00 100.00
3SSA59 Stan Musial 75.00 150.00
3SSA62 Stan Musial 75.00 150.00
3SSA63 Tom Seaver 30.00 80.00
3SSA65 Tom Seaver 30.00 80.00
3SSA71 Whitey Ford 40.00 80.00
3SSA73 Whitey Ford 40.00 80.00
3SSA76 Whitey Ford 40.00 80.00
3SSA77 Whitey Ford 40.00 80.00
3SSA79 Whitey Ford 40.00 80.00
3SSA89 Jim Palmer 20.00 50.00
3SSA91 Jim Palmer 20.00 50.00
3SSA94 Jim Palmer 20.00 50.00
3SSA97 Jim Palmer 20.00 50.00
3SSA101 Reggie Jackson 30.00 60.00
3SSA103 Reggie Jackson 30.00 60.00
3SSA107 Reggie Jackson 30.00 60.00
3SSA111 Mike Schmidt 40.00 80.00
3SSA113 Mike Schmidt 40.00 80.00
3SSA114 Mike Schmidt 40.00 80.00
3SSA115 Mike Schmidt 40.00 80.00
3SSA119 Mike Schmidt 40.00 80.00
3SSA120 Carl Yastrzemski 30.00 60.00
3SSA125 Carl Yastrzemski 30.00 60.00
3SSA128 Don Mattingly 60.00 120.00
3SSA129 Don Mattingly 60.00 120.00
3SSA134 Don Mattingly 60.00 120.00
3SSA135 Don Mattingly 60.00 120.00
3SSA139 Nolan Ryan 75.00 150.00
3SSA142 Robin Yount 40.00 80.00
3SSA148 Robin Yount 40.00 80.00
3SSA149 Robin Yount 40.00 80.00
3SSA153 Cal Ripken 125.00 250.00
3SSA155 Ryne Sandberg 40.00 80.00
3SSA156 Ryne Sandberg 40.00 80.00
3SSA158 Ryne Sandberg 40.00 80.00
3SSA159 Ryne Sandberg 40.00 80.00
3SSA162 Ryne Sandberg 40.00 80.00
3SSA163 Ryne Sandberg 40.00 80.00
3SSA165 Ryne Sandberg 40.00 80.00
3SSA168 Frank Robinson 20.00 50.00
3SSA171 Frank Robinson 20.00 50.00
3SSA176 Tony Gwynn 50.00 100.00
3SSA178 Tony Gwynn 50.00 100.00
3SSA179 Tony Gwynn 50.00 100.00
3SSA180 Ernie Banks 40.00 80.00

2009 Topps Sterling

COMMON CARD .75 2.00
THREE BASE CARDS PER BOX
STATED PRINT RUN 250 SER.#'d SETS
1 Babe Ruth 5.00 12.00
2 Bob Feller 1.25 3.00
3 Orlando Cepeda 1.25 3.00
4 Curt Schilling 1.25 3.00
5 Mickey Mantle 6.00 15.00
6 Joey Votto 2.00 5.00
7 Koji Uehara RC 2.00 5.00
8 Mel Ott 2.00 5.00
9 Miguel Cabrera 2.00 5.00
10 Prince Fielder 1.25 3.00
11 Jose Reyes 1.25 3.00
12 Carlos Beltran 1.25 3.00
13 David Price RC 1.50 4.00
14 Tommy Hanson RC 2.00 5.00
15 Roger Maris 2.00 5.00
16 Roger Maris 2.00 5.00
17 Mike Schmidt 3.00 8.00
18 Lou Gehrig 4.00 10.00
19 Ozzie Smith 2.50 6.00
20 Reggie Jackson 1.25 3.00
21 Reggie Jackson 1.25 3.00
22 Reggie Jackson 1.25 3.00
23 Tim Lincecum 1.25 3.00
24 Warren Spahn 1.25 3.00
25 Duke Snider 1.25 3.00
26 Yogi Berra 2.00 5.00
27 Ty Cobb 3.00 8.00
28 Stan Musial 3.00 8.00
29 Jimmie Foxx 2.00 5.00
30 Jimmie Foxx 2.00 5.00
31 Rick Porcello RC 2.50 6.00
32 Dwight Gooden .75 2.00
33 Ichiro Suzuki 2.50 6.00
34 CC Sabathia 1.25 3.00
35 Willie McCovey 1.25 3.00
36 Albert Pujols 2.50 6.00
37 Gary Sheffield .75 2.00
38 Cal Ripken Jr. 6.00 15.00
39 Daisuke Matsuzaka 1.25 3.00
40 Gary Carter 1.25 3.00
41 Josh Hamilton 1.25 3.00
42 Joe Mauer 1.50 4.00
43 Pedro Martinez 1.25 3.00
44 Whitey Ford 1.25 3.00
45 Johnny Damon 1.25 3.00
46 Frank Thomas 2.00 5.00
47 Dale Murphy 2.00 5.00
48 George Sisler 1.25 3.00
50 Lou Brock 1.25 3.00
51 Paul Molitor 2.00 5.00
52 David Ortiz 2.00 5.00
53 Tris Speaker 1.25 3.00
54 Tris Speaker 1.25 3.00
55 Carl Yastrzemski 3.00 8.00
56 Nolan Ryan 6.00 15.00
57 Nolan Ryan 6.00 15.00
58 Nolan Ryan 6.00 15.00
59 Eddie Mathews 2.00 5.00
60 Joe Morgan 1.25 3.00
61 Honus Wagner 2.00 5.00
62 Andre Dawson 1.25 3.00
63 Justin Morneau 1.25 3.00
64 Manny Ramirez 2.00 5.00
65 Manny Ramirez 2.00 5.00
66 Manny Ramirez 2.00 5.00
67 Vladimir Guerrero 1.25 3.00
68 Hanley Ramirez 1.25 3.00
69 Ryan Braun 1.25 3.00
70 Dan Haren .75 2.00
71 Dave Winfield 1.25 3.00
72 Robin Yount 2.00 5.00
73 Ryne Sandberg 4.00 10.00
74 Johnny Mize 1.25 3.00
75 Johnny Mize 1.25 3.00
76 Johnny Mize 1.25 3.00
77 Don Mattingly 4.00 10.00
78 Ivan Rodriguez 1.25 3.00
79 Ralph Kiner 1.25 3.00
80 Steve Garvey .75 2.00
81 Carlos Delgado .75 2.00
82 Dustin Pedroia 2.00 5.00
83 Hank Greenberg 2.00 5.00
84 Al Kaline 2.00 5.00
85 Fergie Jenkins 1.25 3.00
86 David Wright 1.50 4.00
87 Frank Robinson 1.25 3.00
88 Brandon Webb 1.25 3.00
89 Colby Rasmus (RC) 1.25 3.00
90 Alfonso Soriano 1.25 3.00
91 Jackie Robinson 2.00 5.00
92 Lance Berkman 1.25 3.00
93 Chase Utley 1.25 3.00
94 Mark Teixeira 1.25 3.00
95 Mike Piazza 2.00 5.00
96 Johan Santana 1.25 3.00
97 Rogers Hornsby 1.25 3.00
98 Rogers Hornsby 1.25 3.00
99 Dennis Eckersley 1.25 3.00
100 Evan Longoria 1.25 3.00
101 Bob Gibson 1.25 3.00
102 Tom Seaver 1.25 3.00
103 Tony Gwynn 2.00 5.00
104 Johnny Bench 2.00 5.00
105 Carlton Fisk 1.25 3.00
106 Ernie Banks 2.00 5.00
107 Mariano Rivera 2.50 6.00
108 Tony Perez 1.25 3.00
109 Roy Campanella 2.00 5.00
110 Francisco Rodriguez 1.25 3.00
111 Luis Aparicio 1.25 3.00
112 Monte Irvin 1.25 3.00
113 Zack Greinke 2.00 5.00
114 Jim Thome 1.25 3.00

115 Jimmy Piersall .75 2.00
116 Eddie Murray 1.25 3.00
117 Jim Palmer 1.25 3.00
118 Carl Erskine .75 2.00
119 Juan Marichal 1.25 3.00
120 Joba Chamberlain .75 2.00
121 Chipper Jones 2.00 5.00
122 Johnny Podres .75 2.00
123 Wade Boggs 1.25 3.00
124 Michael Young .75 2.00
125 Steve Carlton 1.25 3.00
126 Ryan Howard 1.50 4.00
127 Jay Bruce 1.25 3.00
128 Alex Rodriguez 2.50 6.00
129 Alex Rodriguez 2.50 6.00
130 Alex Rodriguez 2.50 6.00

2009 Topps Sterling Framed White

*WHITE VET: 1X TO 2.5X BASIC
*WHITE RC: 1X TO 2.5X BASIC RC
OVERALL PARALLEL ODDS 1:1
STATED PRINT RUN 50 SER.#'d SETS

2009 Topps Sterling Career Chronicles Relics Quad

OVERALL MEM ODDS 1:1
STATED PRINT RUN 25 SER.#'d SETS
ALL VARIATIONS PRICED EQUALLY
10 PRINT RUN 10 SER.#'d SETS
NO 10 PRICING DUE TO SCARCITY
SS PRINT RUN 1 SER.#'d SET
NO SS PRICING DUE TO SCARCITY
1 Babe Ruth 200.00 400.00
2 Ichiro Suzuki 30.00 60.00
3 Ichiro Suzuki 30.00 60.00
4 Jackie Robinson 30.00 60.00
5 Jackie Robinson 30.00 60.00
6 Cal Ripken Jr. 30.00 60.00
7 Cal Ripken Jr. 30.00 60.00
8 David Ortiz 8.00 20.00
9 David Ortiz 8.00 20.00
10 Vladimir Guerrero 8.00 20.00
11 Vladimir Guerrero 8.00 20.00
12 Reggie Jackson 15.00 40.00
13 Reggie Jackson 15.00 40.00
14 Prince Fielder 10.00 25.00
15 Prince Fielder 10.00 25.00
16 Chase Utley 15.00 40.00
17 Chase Utley 15.00 40.00
18 Francisco Rodriguez 8.00 20.00
19 Francisco Rodriguez 8.00 20.00
20 Lou Brock 15.00 40.00
21 Lou Brock 15.00 40.00
22 Carl Yastrzemski 12.50 30.00
23 Carl Yastrzemski 12.50 30.00
24 Jimmie Foxx 20.00 50.00
25 Jimmie Foxx 20.00 50.00
26 Eddie Mathews 15.00 40.00
27 Eddie Mathews 15.00 40.00
28 Yogi Berra 20.00 50.00
29 Yogi Berra 20.00 50.00
30 Mike Schmidt 12.50 30.00
31 Mike Schmidt 12.50 30.00
32 Tim Lincecum 20.00 50.00
33 Tim Lincecum 20.00 50.00
34 Mark Teixeira 10.00 25.00
35 Mark Teixeira 10.00 25.00
36 Ernie Banks 12.50 30.00
37 Ernie Banks 12.50 30.00
38 Joe Morgan 8.00 20.00
39 Joe Morgan 8.00 20.00
40 Al Kaline 15.00 40.00
41 Al Kaline 15.00 40.00
42 Carlos Beltran 8.00 20.00
43 Carlos Beltran 8.00 20.00
44 Mel Ott 20.00 50.00
45 Mickey Mantle 60.00 120.00
46 Mickey Mantle 60.00 120.00
47 Albert Pujols 20.00 50.00
48 Albert Pujols 20.00 50.00
49 Chipper Jones 12.50 30.00
50 Chipper Jones 12.50 30.00
51 Daisuke Matsuzaka 10.00 25.00
52 Daisuke Matsuzaka 10.00 25.00
53 Carlos Delgado 8.00 20.00
54 Carlos Delgado 8.00 20.00
55 Joba Chamberlain 10.00 25.00
56 Joba Chamberlain 10.00 25.00
57 Dennis Eckersley 8.00 20.00
58 Dennis Eckersley 8.00 20.00
59 Luis Aparicio 10.00 25.00
60 Luis Aparicio 10.00 25.00
61 CC Sabathia 10.00 25.00
62 CC Sabathia 10.00 25.00
63 Evan Longoria 12.50 30.00
64 Evan Longoria 12.50 30.00
65 Honus Wagner 60.00 120.00
66 Ryan Howard 15.00 40.00
67 Ryan Howard 15.00 40.00
68 Mariano Rivera 15.00 40.00
69 Mariano Rivera 15.00 40.00
70 Ty Cobb 50.00 100.00
71 Nolan Ryan 30.00 60.00
72 Nolan Ryan 30.00 60.00
73 Lou Gehrig 100.00 175.00
74 Dale Murphy 20.00 50.00
75 Dale Murphy 20.00 50.00
76 Eddie Murray 12.50 30.00
77 Eddie Murray 12.50 30.00
78 Don Mattingly 15.00 40.00
79 Don Mattingly 15.00 40.00
80 Johnny Bench 10.00 25.00
81 Johnny Bench 10.00 25.00
82 Joe Mauer 15.00 40.00
83 Joe Mauer 15.00 40.00
84 Dave Winfield 10.00 25.00
85 Dave Winfield 10.00 25.00
86 David Wright 10.00 25.00
87 David Wright 10.00 25.00
88 Carlton Fisk 10.00 25.00
89 Carlton Fisk 10.00 25.00
90 Frank Robinson 8.00 20.00
91 Frank Robinson 8.00 20.00
92 Johan Santana 8.00 20.00
93 Johan Santana 8.00 20.00
94 Duke Snider 12.50 30.00
95 Duke Snider 12.50 30.00
96 Bob Gibson 10.00 25.00
97 Bob Gibson 10.00 25.00
98 Tom Seaver 10.00 25.00
99 Tom Seaver 10.00 25.00
100 Warren Spahn 15.00 40.00
101 Warren Spahn 15.00 40.00
102 Paul Molitor 10.00 25.00
103 Paul Molitor 10.00 25.00
104 Orlando Cepeda 8.00 20.00
105 Orlando Cepeda 8.00 20.00
106 Roger Maris 30.00 60.00
107 Roger Maris 30.00 60.00
108 Tris Speaker 30.00 60.00
109 Manny Ramirez 12.50 30.00
110 Manny Ramirez 12.50 30.00
111 Hank Greenberg 20.00 50.00
112 Hank Greenberg 20.00 50.00
113 Rogers Hornsby 20.00 50.00
114 Tony Gwynn 15.00 40.00
115.Tony Gwynn 15.00 40.00
116 Ozzie Smith 20.00 50.00
117 Ozzie Smith 20.00 50.00
118 Stan Musial 15.00 40.00
119 Stan Musial 15.00 40.00
120 George Sisler 30.00 60.00
121 Roy Campanella 15.00 40.00
122 Roy Campanella 15.00 40.00
123 Jim Palmer 10.00 25.00
124 Jim Palmer 10.00 25.00
125 Ryan Braun 10.00 25.00
126 Ryan Braun 10.00 25.00
127 Johnny Mize 10.00 25.00
128 Johnny Mize 10.00 25.00
129 Ryne Sandberg 12.50 30.00
130 Ryne Sandberg 12.50 30.00
131 Robin Yount 12.50 30.00
132 Robin Yount 12.50 30.00
133 Juan Marichal 15.00 40.00
134 Juan Marichal 15.00 40.00
135 Alex Rodriguez 30.00 60.00
136 Alex Rodriguez 30.00 60.00

2009 Topps Sterling Career Chronicles Relics Triple

OVERALL MEM ODDS 1:1
STATED PRINT RUN 25 SER.#'d SETS
ALL VARIATIONS PRICED EQUALLY
10 PRINT RUN 10 SER.#'d SETS
NO 10 PRICING DUE TO SCARCITY
SS PRINT RUN 1 SER.#'d SET
NO SS PRICING DUE TO SCARCITY
1 Babe Ruth 150.00 300.00
2 Babe Ruth 150.00 300.00
3 Babe Ruth 150.00 300.00
4 Ichiro Suzuki 20.00 50.00
5 Ichiro Suzuki 20.00 50.00
6 Ichiro Suzuki 20.00 50.00
7 Jackie Robinson 30.00 60.00
8 Jackie Robinson 30.00 60.00
9 Jackie Robinson 30.00 60.00
10 Cal Ripken Jr. 20.00 50.00
11 Cal Ripken Jr. 20.00 50.00
12 Cal Ripken Jr. 20.00 50.00
13 David Ortiz 6.00 15.00
14 David Ortiz 6.00 15.00
15 David Ortiz 6.00 15.00
16 Vladimir Guerrero 6.00 15.00
17 Vladimir Guerrero 6.00 15.00
18 Vladimir Guerrero 6.00 15.00
19 Reggie Jackson 12.50 30.00
20 Reggie Jackson 12.50 30.00
21 Reggie Jackson 12.50 30.00
22 Prince Fielder 10.00 25.00
23 Prince Fielder 10.00 25.00
24 Chase Utley 15.00 40.00
25 Chase Utley 15.00 40.00
26 Francisco Rodriguez 8.00 20.00
27 Francisco Rodriguez 8.00 20.00
28 Lou Brock 15.00 40.00
29 Lou Brock 15.00 40.00
30 Carl Yastrzemski 10.00 25.00
31 Carl Yastrzemski 10.00 25.00
32 Carl Yastrzemski 10.00 25.00
33 Jimmie Foxx 20.00 50.00
34 Jimmie Foxx 20.00 50.00
35 Eddie Mathews 15.00 40.00
36 Eddie Mathews 15.00 40.00
37 Yogi Berra 15.00 40.00
38 Yogi Berra 15.00 40.00
39 Yogi Berra 15.00 40.00
40 Mike Schmidt 10.00 25.00
41 Mike Schmidt 10.00 25.00
42 Mike Schmidt 10.00 25.00
43 Tim Lincecum 15.00 40.00
44 Tim Lincecum 15.00 40.00
45 Tim Lincecum 15.00 40.00
46 Mark Teixeira 10.00 25.00
47 Mark Teixeira 10.00 25.00
48 Ernie Banks 10.00 25.00
49 Ernie Banks 10.00 25.00
50 Ernie Banks 10.00 25.00
51 Joe Morgan 8.00 20.00
52 Joe Morgan 8.00 20.00
53 Al Kaline 15.00 40.00
54 Al Kaline 15.00 40.00
55 Carlos Beltran 8.00 20.00
56 Carlos Beltran 8.00 20.00
57 Mel Ott 15.00 40.00
58 Mel Ott 15.00 40.00
59 Mel Ott 15.00 40.00
60 Mickey Mantle 50.00 100.00
61 Mickey Mantle 50.00 100.00
62 Mickey Mantle 50.00 100.00
63 Albert Pujols 15.00 40.00
64 Albert Pujols 15.00 40.00
65 Albert Pujols 15.00 40.00
66 Chipper Jones 12.50 30.00
67 Chipper Jones 12.50 30.00
68 Daisuke Matsuzaka 8.00 20.00
69 Daisuke Matsuzaka 8.00 20.00
70 Daisuke Matsuzaka 8.00 20.00
71 Carlos Delgado 8.00 20.00
72 Carlos Delgado 8.00 20.00
73 Joba Chamberlain 8.00 20.00
74 Joba Chamberlain 8.00 20.00
75 Joba Chamberlain 8.00 20.00
76 Dennis Eckersley 8.00 20.00
77 Dennis Eckersley 8.00 20.00
78 Luis Aparicio 10.00 25.00
79 Luis Aparicio 10.00 25.00
80 CC Sabathia 10.00 25.00
81 CC Sabathia 10.00 25.00
82 Evan Longoria 12.50 30.00
83 Evan Longoria 12.50 30.00
84 Honus Wagner 60.00 120.00
85 Honus Wagner 60.00 120.00
86 Honus Wagner 60.00 120.00
87 Ryan Howard 12.50 30.00
88 Ryan Howard 12.50 30.00
89 Ryan Howard 12.50 30.00
90 Mariano Rivera 12.50 30.00
91 Mariano Rivera 12.50 30.00
92 Mariano Rivera 12.50 30.00
93 Ty Cobb 40.00 80.00
94 Ty Cobb 40.00 80.00
95 Ty Cobb 40.00 80.00
96 Nolan Ryan 20.00 50.00
97 Nolan Ryan 20.00 50.00
98 Nolan Ryan 20.00 50.00
99 Lou Gehrig 75.00 150.00
100 Lou Gehrig 75.00 150.00
101 Lou Gehrig 75.00 150.00
102 Dale Murphy 8.00 20.00
103 Dale Murphy 8.00 20.00
104 Dale Murphy 8.00 20.00
105 Eddie Murray 12.50 30.00
106 Eddie Murray 12.50 30.00
107 Don Mattingly 12.50 30.00
108 Don Mattingly 12.50 30.00
109 Don Mattingly 12.50 30.00
110 Johnny Bench 10.00 25.00
111 Johnny Bench 10.00 25.00
112 Johnny Bench 10.00 25.00
113 Joe Mauer 15.00 40.00
114 Joe Mauer 15.00 40.00
115 Dave Winfield 10.00 25.00
116 Dave Winfield 10.00 25.00
117 David Wright 10.00 25.00
118 David Wright 10.00 25.00
119 Carlton Fisk 10.00 25.00
120 Carlton Fisk 10.00 25.00
121 Frank Robinson 6.00 15.00
122 Frank Robinson 6.00 15.00
123 Frank Robinson 6.00 15.00
124 Johan Santana 8.00 20.00
125 Johan Santana 8.00 20.00
126 Duke Snider 12.50 30.00
127 Duke Snider 12.50 30.00
128 Bob Gibson 8.00 20.00
129 Bob Gibson 8.00 20.00
130 Bob Gibson 8.00 20.00
131 Tom Seaver 8.00 20.00
132 Tom Seaver 8.00 20.00
133 Tom Seaver 8.00 20.00
134 Warren Spahn 15.00 40.00
135 Warren Spahn 15.00 40.00
136 Paul Molitor 10.00 25.00
137 Paul Molitor 10.00 25.00
138 Orlando Cepeda 8.00 20.00
139 Orlando Cepeda 8.00 20.00
140 Roger Maris 30.00 60.00
141 Roger Maris 30.00 60.00
142 Roger Maris 30.00 60.00
143 Tris Speaker 20.00 50.00
144 Tris Speaker 20.00 50.00
145 Tris Speaker 20.00 50.00
146 Manny Ramirez 10.00 25.00
147 Manny Ramirez 10.00 25.00
148 Manny Ramirez 10.00 25.00
149 Hank Greenberg 20.00 50.00
150 Hank Greenberg 20.00 50.00
151 Rogers Hornsby 15.00 40.00
152 Rogers Hornsby 15.00 40.00
153 Rogers Hornsby 15.00 40.00
154 Tony Gwynn 15.00 40.00
155 Tony Gwynn 15.00 40.00
156 Ozzie Smith 15.00 40.00
157 Ozzie Smith 15.00 40.00
158 Ozzie Smith 15.00 40.00
159 Stan Musial 15.00 40.00
160 Stan Musial 15.00 40.00
161 Stan Musial 15.00 40.00
162 George Sisler 20.00 40.00
163 George Sisler 20.00 50.00
164 George Sisler 20.00 50.00
165 Roy Campanella 12.50 30.00
166 Roy Campanella 12.50 30.00
167 Roy Campanella 12.50 30.00
168 Jim Palmer 10.00 25.00
169 Jim Palmer 10.00 25.00
170 Ryan Braun 10.00 25.00
171 Ryan Braun 10.00 25.00
172 Johnny Mize 10.00 25.00
173 Johnny Mize 10.00 25.00
174 Ryne Sandberg 10.00 25.00
175 Ryne Sandberg 10.00 25.00
176 Ryne Sandberg 10.00 25.00
177 Robin Yount 12.50 30.00
178 Robin Yount 12.50 30.00
179 Juan Marichal 15.00 40.00
180 Juan Marichal 15.00 40.00
181 Alex Rodriguez 20.00 50.00
182 Alex Rodriguez 20.00 50.00
183 Alex Rodriguez 20.00 50.00

2009 Topps Sterling Jumbo Swatch Relic Autographs

OVERALL AUTO ODDS 1:1
STATED PRINT RUN 10 SER.#'d SETS
NO PRICING DUE TO SCARCITY

2010 Topps Sterling

COMMON CARD .75 2.00
COMMON RC 1.50 4.00
THREE BASE CARDS PER BOX
STATED PRINT RUN 250 SER.#'d SETS
1 Honus Wagner 2.00 5.00
2 Babe Ruth 5.00 12.00
3 Babe Ruth 5.00 12.00
4 Lou Gehrig 4.00 10.00
5 Christy Mathewson 2.00 5.00
6 Starlin Castro RC 4.00 10.00
7 Mickey Mantle 6.00 15.00
8 Carl Yastrzemski 3.00 8.00
9 Clayton Kershaw 3.00 8.00
10 Cal Ripken Jr. 6.00 15.00
11 Willie McCovey 1.25 3.00
12 Johnny Podres .75 2.00
13 Curt Schilling 1.25 3.00
14 Ernie Banks 2.00 5.00
15 Thurman Munson 2.00 5.00
16 Reggie Jackson 1.25 3.00
17 Reggie Jackson 1.25 3.00
18 Reggie Jackson 1.25 3.00
19 Tony Gwynn 2.00 5.00
20 Mike Schmidt 3.00 8.00
21 Ian Kinsler 1.25 3.00
22 Jason Heyward 3.00 8.00
23 Wade Boggs 1.25 3.00
24 Ryan Braun 1.25 3.00
25 Eddie Mathews 2.00 5.00
26 Chase Utley 1.25 3.00
27 Manny Ramirez 2.00 5.00
28 Manny Ramirez 2.00 5.00
29 Manny Ramirez 2.00 5.00
30 Ty Cobb 3.00 8.00
31 Ty Cobb 3.00 8.00
32 Steve Carlton 1.25 3.00
33 Steve Carlton 1.25 3.00
34 Frank Thomas 2.00 5.00
35 Hank Greenberg 2.00 5.00
36 Red Schoendienst 1.25 3.00
37 Stephen Strasburg RC 12.00 30.00
38 Fergie Jenkins 1.25 3.00
39 Roy Campanella 2.00 5.00
40 Mel Ott 2.00 5.00
41 Brooks Robinson 1.25 3.00
42 Jackie Robinson 2.00 5.00
43 Larry Walker 1.25 3.00
44 Juan Marichal 1.25 3.00
45 Bob Gibson 1.25 3.00
46 Duke Snider 1.25 3.00
47 Kevin Youkilis .75 2.00
48 Mike Piazza 2.00 5.00
49 Mike Piazza 2.00 5.00
50 Albert Pujols 2.50 6.00
51 Ichiro Suzuki 2.50 6.00
52 Robin Yount 2.00 5.00
53 Ozzie Smith 2.50 6.00
54 Ozzie Smith 2.50 6.00
55 Tim Lincecum 1.25 3.00
56 Paul Molitor 2.00 5.00
57 Paul Molitor 2.00 5.00
58 Rickey Henderson 2.00 5.00
59 Rickey Henderson 2.00 5.00
60 Joe Mauer 1.50 4.00
61 Willie Stargell 1.25 3.00
62 Joe Morgan 1.25 3.00
63 Johnny Mize 1.25 3.00
64 Johnny Mize 1.25 3.00
65 Johnny Mize 1.25 3.00
66 Whitey Ford 1.25 3.00
67 Carlton Fisk 1.25 3.00
68 Carlton Fisk 1.25 3.00
69 Harmon Killebrew 2.00 5.00
70 Jimmie Foxx 2.00 5.00
71 Jimmie Foxx 2.00 5.00
72 Bernie Williams 1.25 3.00
73 Justin Upton 1.25 3.00
74 Dale Murphy 2.00 5.00
75 Alex Rodriguez 2.50 6.00
76 Alex Rodriguez 2.50 6.00
77 Alex Rodriguez 2.50 6.00
78 Al Kaline 2.00 5.00
79 Justin Morneau 1.25 3.00
80 Yogi Berra 2.00 5.00
81 Dennis Eckersley 1.25 3.00
82 David Ortiz 2.00 5.00
83 Barry Larkin 1.25 3.00
84 Chipper Jones 2.00 5.00
85 Cy Young 2.00 5.00
86 Roberto Alomar 1.25 3.00
87 Tris Speaker 1.25 3.00
88 Eddie Murray 1.25 3.00
89 Adrian Gonzalez 1.50 4.00
90 Roger Maris 2.00 5.00
91 Roger Maris 2.00 5.00
92 Vladimir Guerrero 1.25 3.00
93 Vladimir Guerrero 1.25 3.00
94 Vladimir Guerrero 1.25 3.00
95 Pee Wee Reese 1.25 3.00
96 Robin Roberts 1.25 3.00
97 Johnny Bench 2.00 5.00
98 Josh Hamilton 1.25 3.00
99 Robinson Cano 1.25 3.00
100 Stan Musial 3.00 8.00
101 Dave Winfield 1.25 3.00
102 Dave Winfield 1.25 3.00
103 Mike Stanton RC 12.00 30.00
104 Orlando Cepeda 1.25 3.00
105 Evan Longoria 1.25 3.00
106 Dustin Pedroia 2.00 5.00
107 Luis Aparicio 1.25 3.00
108 Catfish Hunter 1.25 3.00
109 Bill Mazeroski 1.25 3.00
110 Frank Robinson 1.25 3.00
111 Frank Robinson 1.25 3.00
112 Phil Rizzuto 1.25 3.00
113 Prince Fielder 1.25 3.00
114 Gary Carter 1.25 3.00
115 Ryne Sandberg 4.00 10.00
116 Andre Ethier 1.25 3.00
117 Mark Teixeira 1.25 3.00
118 Mark Teixeira 1.25 3.00
119 Victor Martinez 1.25 3.00
120 George Sisler 1.25 3.00
121 Rod Carew 1.25 3.00
122 CC Sabathia 1.25 3.00
123 Craig Biggio 1.25 3.00
124 David Wright 1.50 4.00
125 Ryan Howard 1.50 4.00
126 Miguel Cabrera 2.00 5.00
127 Don Mattingly 4.00 10.00
128 Bob Feller 1.25 3.00
129 Rogers Hornsby 1.25 3.00
130 Rogers Hornsby 1.25 3.00
131 Greg Maddux 2.50 6.00
132 Greg Maddux 2.50 6.00
133 Ralph Kiner 1.25 3.00
134 Roy Halladay 1.25 3.00
135 Walter Johnson 2.00 5.00
136 Warren Spahn 1.25 3.00
137 Andre Dawson 1.25 3.00
138 Andre Dawson 1.25 3.00
139 Tom Seaver 1.25 3.00
140 Tom Seaver 1.25 3.00
141 Tom Seaver 1.25 3.00
142 Mariano Rivera 2.50 6.00
143 Hanley Ramirez 1.25 3.00
144 Ubaldo Jimenez .75 2.00
145 Jim Palmer 1.25 3.00
146 Monte Irvin 1.25 3.00
147 Nolan Ryan 6.00 15.00
148 Nolan Ryan 6.00 15.00
149 Nolan Ryan 6.00 15.00
150 Nolan Ryan 6.00 15.00

2010 Topps Sterling Framed White

*WHITE VET: .75X TO 2X BASIC
*WHITE RC: .5X TO 1.2X BASIC RC
OVERALL PARALLEL ODDS 1:1
STATED PRINT RUN 50 SER.#'d SETS

2010 Topps Sterling Career Chronicles Relics Five

OVERALL MEM ODDS 1:1
STATED PRINT RUN 25 SER.#'d SETS
ALL VARIATIONS PRICED EQUALLY
10 PRINT RUN 10 SER.#'d SETS
SS PRINT RUN 1 SER.#'d SET
CCR1 Ryan Braun 10.00 25.00
CCR2 Ryan Braun 10.00 25.00
CCR3 Harmon Killebrew 20.00 50.00
CCR4 Harmon Killebrew 20.00 50.00
CCR5 Wade Boggs 12.50 30.00
CCR6 Evan Longoria 12.50 30.00
CCR7 Mickey Mantle 60.00 120.00
CCR8 Mickey Mantle 60.00 120.00
CCR9 Cal Ripken Jr. 30.00 60.00
CCR10 Cal Ripken Jr. 30.00 60.00
CCR11 Yogi Berra 15.00 40.00
CCR12 Yogi Berra 15.00 40.00
CCR13 Roy Halladay 15.00 40.00
CCR14 Roy Halladay 15.00 40.00
CCR15 Joe Mauer 12.50 30.00
CCR16 Joe Mauer 12.50 30.00
CCR17 Rogers Hornsby 20.00 50.00
CCR18 Hank Greenberg 20.00 50.00
CCR19 Albert Pujols 30.00 60.00
CCR20 Albert Pujols 30.00 60.00
CCR21 George Sisler 20.00 50.00
CCR22 George Sisler 20.00 50.00
CCR23 Jackie Robinson 30.00 60.00
CCR24 Jackie Robinson 30.00 60.00
CCR25 Manny Ramirez 15.00 40.00
CCR26 Jimmie Foxx 50:00 100.00
CCR27 Carl Yastrzemski 15.00 40.00
CCR28 Carl Yastrzemski 15.00 40.00
CCR29 Hanley Ramirez 12.50 30.00
CCR30 Hanley Ramirez 12.50 30.00
CCR31 Stan Musial 30.00 60.00
CCR32 Stan Musial 30.00 60.00
CCR33 Nolan Ryan 30.00 60.00
CCR34 Nolan Ryan 30.00 60.00
CCR35 Ty Cobb 60.00 120.00
CCR36 Pee Wee Reese 20.00 50.00
CCR37 Reggie Jackson 12.50 30.00
CCR38 Reggie Jackson 12.50 30.00
CCR39 Mike Schmidt 20.00 50.00
CCR40 Jim Palmer 10.00 25.00
CCR41 Miguel Cabrera 10.00 25.00
CCR42 Whitey Ford 15.00 40.00
CCR43 Honus Wagner 50.00 100.00
CCR44 Honus Wagner 50.00 100.00
CCR45 Frank Robinson 10.00 25.00
CCR46 Roy Campanella 20.00 50.00
CCR47 Alex Rodriguez 10.00 25.00
CCR48 Kevin Youkilis 12.50 30.00
CCR49 Mel Ott 20.00 50.00
CCR50 Tom Seaver 15.00 40.00
CCR51 Warren Spahn 12.50 30.00
CCR52 Roger Maris 30.00 60.00
CCR53 Tim Lincecum 15.00 40.00
CCR54 Tim Lincecum 15.00 40.00
CCR55 Johnny Mize 12.50 30.00
CCR56 Johnny Mize 12.50 30.00
CCR57 Lou Gehrig 75.00 150.00
CCR58 Lou Gehrig 75.00 150.00
CCR59 Ichiro Suzuki 40.00 80.00
CCR60 Ichiro Suzuki 40.00 80.00

2010 Topps Sterling Career Chronicles Relics Quad

OVERALL MEM ODDS 1:1
STATED PRINT RUN 25 SER.#'d SETS
ALL VARIATIONS PRICED EQUALLY
10 PRINT RUN 10 SER.#'d SETS
SS PRINT RUN 1 SER.#'d SET
CCR1 Babe Ruth
CCR2 Babe Ruth
CCR3 Harmon Killebrew 15.00 40.00
CCR4 Harmon Killebrew 15.00 40.00
CCR5 Wade Boggs 10.00 25.00
CCR6 Evan Longoria 10.00 25.00
CCR7 Mickey Mantle 50.00 100.00
CCR8 Mickey Mantle 50.00 100.00
CCR9 Cal Ripken Jr. 20.00 50.00
CCR10 Cal Ripken Jr. 20.00 50.00
CCR11 Yogi Berra 12.50 30.00
CCR12 Yogi Berra 12.50 30.00
CCR13 Roy Halladay 12.50 30.00
CCR14 Roy Halladay 12.50 30.00
CCR15 Joe Mauer 10.00 25.00
CCR16 Joe Mauer 10.00 25.00
CCR17 Rogers Hornsby 15.00 40.00
CCR18 Hank Greenberg 15.00 40.00
CCR19 Albert Pujols 20.00 50.00
CCR20 Albert Pujols 20.00 50.00
CCR21 George Sisler 12.50 30.00
CCR22 George Sisler 12.50 30.00
CCR23 Jackie Robinson 20.00 50.00
CCR24 Jackie Robinson 20.00 50.00
CCR25 Manny Ramirez 12.50 30.00
CCR26 Jimmie Foxx 15.00 40.00
CCR27 Carl Yastrzemski 12.50 30.00
CCR28 Carl Yastrzemski 12.50 30.00
CCR29 Hanley Ramirez 10.00 25.00
CCR30 Hanley Ramirez 10.00 25.00
CCR31 Stan Musial 20.00 50.00
CCR32 Stan Musial 20.00 50.00
CCR33 Nolan Ryan 20.00 50.00
CCR34 Nolan Ryan 20.00 50.00
CCR35 Ty Cobb 40.00 80.00
CCR36 Pee Wee Reese 15.00 40.00
CCR37 Reggie Jackson 10.00 25.00
CCR38 Reggie Jackson 10.00 25.00
CCR39 Mike Schmidt 15.00 40.00
CCR40 Jim Palmer 8.00 20.00
CCR41 Miguel Cabrera 8.00 20.00
CCR42 Whitey Ford 12.50 30.00
CCR43 Honus Wagner 40.00 80.00
CCR44 Honus Wagner 40.00 80.00
CCR45 Frank Robinson 8.00 20.00
CCR46 Roy Campanella 15.00 40.00
CCR47 Alex Rodriguez 12.50 30.00
CCR48 Kevin Youkilis 10.00 25.00
CCR49 Mel Ott 15.00 40.00
CCR50 Tom Seaver 12.50 30.00
CCR51 Warren Spahn 10.00 25.00
CCR52 Roger Maris 20.00 50.00
CCR53 Tim Lincecum 12.50 30.00
CCR54 Tim Lincecum 12.50 30.00
CCR55 Johnny Mize 10.00 25.00
CCR56 Johnny Mize 10.00 25.00
CCR57 Lou Gehrig 60.00 120.00
CCR58 Lou Gehrig 60.00 120.00
CCR59 Ichiro Suzuki 30.00 60.00
CCR60 Ichiro Suzuki 30.00 60.00

2010 Topps Sterling Career Chronicles Relics Triple

OVERALL MEM ODDS 1:1
STATED PRINT RUN 25 SER.#'d SETS
ALL VARIATIONS PRICED EQUALLY
10 PRINT RUN 10 SER.#'d SETS
SS PRINT RUN 1 SER.#'d SET
CCR1 Ryan Braun 8.00 20.00
CCR2 Ryan Braun 8.00 20.00
CCR3 Harmon Killebrew 15.00 40.00
CCR4 Harmon Killebrew 15.00 40.00
CCR5 Wade Boggs 10.00 25.00
CCR6 Evan Longoria 10.00 25.00
CCR7 Mickey Mantle 50.00 100.00
CCR8 Mickey Mantle 50.00 100.00
CCR9 Cal Ripken Jr. 20.00 50.00
CCR10 Cal Ripken Jr. 20.00 50.00
CCR11 Yogi Berra 12.50 30.00
CCR12 Yogi Berra 12.50 30.00
CCR13 Roy Halladay 12.50 30.00
CCR14 Roy Halladay 12.50 30.00
CCR15 Joe Mauer 10.00 25.00
CCR16 Joe Mauer 10.00 25.00
CCR17 Rogers Hornsby 15.00 40.00
CCR18 Hank Greenberg 15.00 40.00
CCR19 Albert Pujols 10.00 25.00
CCR20 Albert Pujols 10.00 25.00
CCR21 George Sisler 12.50 30.00
CCR22 George Sisler 12.50 30.00
CCR23 Jackie Robinson 20.00 50.00
CCR24 Jackie Robinson 20.00 50.00
CCR25 Manny Ramirez 12.50 30.00
CCR26 Jimmie Foxx 15.00 40.00
CCR27 Carl Yastrzemski 12.50 30.00
CCR28 Carl Yastrzemski 12.50 30.00
CCR29 Hanley Ramirez 10.00 25.00
CCR30 Hanley Ramirez 10.00 25.00
CCR31 Stan Musial 20.00 50.00
CCR32 Stan Musial 20.00 50.00
CCR33 Nolan Ryan 20.00 50.00
CCR34 Nolan Ryan 20.00 50.00
CCR35 Ty Cobb 40.00 80.00
CCR36 Pee Wee Reese 15.00 40.00
CCR37 Reggie Jackson 10.00 25.00
CCR38 Reggie Jackson 10.00 25.00
CCR39 Mike Schmidt 15.00 40.00
CCR40 Jim Palmer 8.00 20.00
CCR41 Miguel Cabrera 8.00 20.00
CCR42 Whitey Ford 12.50 30.00
CCR43 Honus Wagner 40.00 80.00
CCR44 Honus Wagner 40.00 80.00
CCR45 Frank Robinson 8.00 20.00
CCR46 Roy Campanella 15.00 40.00
CCR47 Alex Rodriguez 12.50 30.00
CCR48 Kevin Youkilis 10.00 25.00
CCR49 Mel Ott 15.00 40.00
CCR50 Tom Seaver 12.50 30.00
CCR51 Warren Spahn 10.00 25.00
CCR52 Roger Maris 10.00 25.00
CCR53 Tim Lincecum 12.50 30.00
CCR54 Tim Lincecum 12.50 30.00
CCR55 Johnny Mize 10.00 25.00
CCR56 Johnny Mize 10.00 25.00
CCR57 Lou Gehrig 60.00 120.00
CCR58 Lou Gehrig 60.00 120.00
CCR59 Ichiro Suzuki 30.00 60.00
CCR60 Ichiro Suzuki 30.00 60.00

2010 Topps Sterling Legendary Leather Relics Five

OVERALL MEM ODDS 1:1
STATED PRINT RUN 25 SER.#'d SETS
ALL VARIATIONS PRICED EQUALLY
10 PRINT RUN 10 SER.#'d SETS
SS PRINT RUN 1 SER.#'d SET
LLR1 Babe Ruth 125.00 250.00
LLR2 Babe Ruth 125.00 250.00
LLR3 Mike Schmidt 20.00 50.00
LLR4 Mike Schmidt 20.00 50.00
LLR5 Joe Mauer 12.50 30.00
LLR6 Rickey Henderson 40.00 80.00
LLR7 Mickey Mantle 60.00 120.00
LLR8 Mickey Mantle 60.00 120.00
LLR9 Mark Teixeira 12.50 30.00
LLR10 Mark Teixeira 12.50 30.00
LLR11 Carl Yastrzemski 15.00 40.00
LLR12 Carl Yastrzemski 15.00 40.00
LLR13 David Wright 15.00 40.00
LLR14 David Wright 15.00 40.00
LLR15 Bob Gibson 15.00 40.00
LLR16 Bob Gibson 15.00 40.00
LLR17 Pee Wee Reese 20.00 50.00
LLR18 Pee Wee Reese 20.00 50.00
LLR19 Luis Aparicio 10.00 25.00
LLR20 Luis Aparicio 10.00 25.00
LLR21 Roberto Alomar 30.00 60.00
LLR22 Roberto Alomar 30.00 60.00
LLR23 Ernie Banks 12.50 30.00
LLR24 Rogers Hornsby 20.00 50.00
LLR25 Greg Maddux 15.00 40.00
LLR26 Greg Maddux 15.00 40.00
LLR27 Yogi Berra 15.00 40.00
LLR28 Johnny Bench 10.00 25.00
LLR29 Alex Rodriguez 10.00 25.00
LLR30 Dave Winfield 10.00 25.00
LLR31 Tony Gwynn 10.00 25.00
LLR32 Tony Gwynn 10.00 25.00
LLR33 Robinson Cano 15.00 40.00
LLR34 Robinson Cano 15.00 40.00
LLR35 Duke Snider 20.00 50.00
LLR36 Duke Snider 20.00 50.00
LLR37 Barry Larkin 10.00 25.00
LLR38 Barry Larkin 10.00 25.00
LLR39 Evan Longoria 12.50 30.00
LLR40 Evan Longoria 12.50 30.00
LLR41 Joe Morgan 10.00 25.00
LLR42 Roy Campanella 20.00 50.00
LLR43 Craig Biggio 12.50 30.00
LLR44 Craig Biggio 12.50 30.00
LLR45 Brooks Robinson 12.50 30.00
LLR46 Brooks Robinson 12.50 30.00
LLR47 Eddie Murray 12.50 30.00
LLR48 Thurman Munson 10.00 25.00
LLR49 Don Mattingly 20.00 50.00
LLR50 Don Mattingly 20.00 50.00
LLR51 Andre Dawson 12.50 30.00
LLR52 Andre Dawson 12.50 30.00
LLR53 Al Kaline 15.00 40.00
LLR54 Al Kaline 15.00 40.00
LLR55 Albert Pujols 30.00 60.00
LLR56 Albert Pujols 30.00 60.00
LLR57 Ichiro Suzuki 40.00 80.00
LLR58 Ichiro Suzuki 40.00 80.00
LLR59 Ozzie Smith 10.00 25.00
LLR60 Phil Rizzuto 10.00 25.00

2010 Topps Sterling Legendary Leather Relics Quad

OVERALL MEM ODDS 1:1
STATED PRINT RUN 25 SER.#'d SETS
ALL VARIATIONS PRICED EQUALLY
10 PRINT RUN 10 SER.#'d SETS
SS PRINT RUN 1 SER.#'d SET
LLR1 Babe Ruth 100.00 200.00
LLR2 Babe Ruth 100.00 200.00
LLR3 Mike Schmidt 15.00 40.00
LLR4 Mike Schmidt 15.00 40.00
LLR5 Joe Mauer 10.00 25.00
LLR6 Rickey Henderson 30.00 60.00
LLR7 Mickey Mantle 50.00 100.00
LLR8 Mickey Mantle 50.00 100.00
LLR9 Mark Teixeira 10.00 25.00
LLR10 Mark Teixeira 10.00 25.00
LLR11 Carl Yastrzemski 12.50 30.00
LLR12 Carl Yastrzemski 12.50 30.00
LLR13 David Wright 12.50 30.00
LLR14 David Wright 12.50 30.00
LLR15 Bob Gibson 12.50 30.00
LLR16 Bob Gibson 12.50 30.00
LLR18 Pee Wee Reese 15.00 40.00
LLR19 Luis Aparicio 8.00 20.00
LLR20 Luis Aparicio 8.00 20.00
LLR21 Roberto Alomar 20.00 50.00
LLR22 Roberto Alomar 20.00 50.00
LLR23 Ernie Banks 10.00 25.00
LLR24 Rogers Hornsby 15.00 40.00
LLR25 Greg Maddux 12.50 30.00
LLR26 Greg Maddux 12.50 30.00
LLR27 Mike Piazza 10.00 25.00
LLR28 Yogi Berra 12.50 30.00
LLR29 Alex Rodriguez 12.50 30.00
LLR30 Dave Winfield 8.00 20.00
LLR31 Tony Gwynn 12.50 30.00
LLR32 Tony Gwynn 12.50 30.00
LLR33 Robinson Cano 12.50 30.00
LLR34 Robinson Cano 12.50 30.00
LLR35 Duke Snider 15.00 40.00
LLR36 Duke Snider 15.00 40.00
LLR37 Barry Larkin 8.00 20.00
LLR38 Barry Larkin 8.00 20.00
LLR39 Evan Longoria 10.00 25.00
LLR40 Evan Longoria 10.00 25.00
LLR41 Joe Morgan 8.00 20.00
LLR42 Roy Campanella 15.00 40.00
LLR43 Craig Biggio 10.00 25.00
LLR44 Craig Biggio 10.00 25.00
LLR45 Brooks Robinson 10.00 25.00
LLR46 Brooks Robinson 10.00 25.00
LLR47 Eddie Murray 10.00 25.00
LLR48 Thurman Munson 15.00 40.00
LLR49 Don Mattingly 15.00 40.00
LLR50 Don Mattingly 15.00 40.00
LLR51 Andre Dawson 10.00 25.00
LLR52 Andre Dawson 10.00 25.00
LLR53 Al Kaline 12.50 30.00
LLR54 Honus Wagner 40.00 80.00
LLR55 Albert Pujols 20.00 50.00
LLR56 Albert Pujols 20.00 50.00
LLR57 Ichiro Suzuki 30.00 60.00
LLR58 Ichiro Suzuki 30.00 60.00
LLR59 Ozzie Smith 20.00 50.00
LLR60 Phil Rizzuto 15.00 40.00

2010 Topps Sterling Legendary Leather Relics Triple

OVERALL MEM ODDS 1:1
STATED PRINT RUN 25 SER.#'d SETS
ALL VARIATIONS PRICED EQUALLY
10 PRINT RUN 10 SER.#'d SETS
SS PRINT RUN 1 SER.#'d SET
LLR1 Babe Ruth 100.00 200.00
LLR2 Babe Ruth 100.00 200.00
LLR3 Mike Schmidt 15.00 40.00
LLR4 Mike Schmidt 15.00 40.00
LLR5 Joe Mauer 10.00 25.00
LLR6 Rickey Henderson 30.00 60.00
LLR7 Mickey Mantle 50.00 100.00
LLR8 Mickey Mantle 50.00 100.00
LLR9 Mark Teixeira 10.00 25.00
LLR10 Mark Teixeira 10.00 25.00
LLR11 Carl Yastrzemski 12.50 30.00
LLR12 Carl Yastrzemski 12.50 30.00
LLR13 David Wright 12.50 30.00

LLR14 David Wright 12.50 30.00
LLR15 Bob Gibson 12.50 30.00
LLR16 Bob Gibson 12.50 30.00
LLR18 Pee Wee Reese 15.00 40.00
LLR19 Luis Aparicio 8.00 20.00
LLR20 Luis Aparicio 8.00 20.00
LLR21 Roberto Alomar 20.00 50.00
LLR22 Roberto Alomar 20.00 50.00
LLR23 Ernie Banks 10.00 25.00
LLR24 Rogers Hornsby 15.00 40.00
LLR25 Greg Maddux 12.50 30.00
LLR26 Greg Maddux 12.50 30.00
LLR27 Yogi Berra 12.50 30.00
LLR28 Mike Piazza 30.00 60.00
LLR29 Alex Rodriguez 12.50 30.00
LLR30 Dave Winfield 8.00 20.00
LLR31 Tony Gwynn 12.50 30.00
LLR32 Tony Gwynn 12.50 30.00
LLR33 Robinson Cano 12.50 30.00
LLR34 Robinson Cano 12.50 30.00
LLR35 Duke Snider 15.00 40.00
LLR36 Duke Snider 15.00 40.00
LLR37 Barry Larkin 8.00 20.00
LLR38 Barry Larkin 8.00 20.00
LLR39 Evan Longoria 10.00 25.00
LLR40 Evan Longoria 10.00 25.00
LLR41 Joe Morgan 8.00 20.00
LLR42 Roy Campanella 15.00 40.00
LLR43 Craig Biggio 10.00 25.00
LLR44 Craig Biggio 10.00 25.00
LLR45 Brooks Robinson 10.00 25.00
LLR46 Brooks Robinson 10.00 25.00
LLR47 Eddie Murray 10.00 25.00
LLR48 Thurman Munson 15.00 40.00
LLR49 Don Mattingly 15.00 40.00
LLR50 Don Mattingly 15.00 40.00
LLR51 Andre Dawson 10.00 25.00
LLR52 Andre Dawson 10.00 25.00
LLR53 Al Kaline 12.50 30.00
LLR54 Al Kaline 12.50 30.00
LLR55 Albert Pujols 10.00 25.00
LLR56 Albert Pujols 10.00 25.00
LLR57 Ichiro Suzuki 30.00 60.00
LLR58 Ichiro Suzuki 30.00 60.00
LLR59 Ozzie Smith 20.00 50.00
LLR60 Phil Rizzuto 15.00 40.00

2010 Topps Sterling Sterling Stats Relics Six

OVERALL MEM ODDS 1:1
STATED PRINT RUN 25 SER.#'d SETS
ALL VARIATIONS PRICED EQUALLY
10 PRINT RUN 10 SER.#'d SETS
SS PRINT RUN 1 SER.#'d SET
SSR3 Babe Ruth 150.00 300.00
SSR4 Babe Ruth 150.00 300.00
SSR5 Rickey Henderson 40.00 80.00
SSR6 Rickey Henderson 40.00 80.00
SSR7 Cal Ripken Jr. 30.00 60.00
SSR8 Cal Ripken Jr. 30.00 60.00
SSR9 George Sisler 50.00 100.00
SSR10 George Sisler 50.00 100.00
SSR11 Al Kaline 15.00 40.00
SSR12 Al Kaline 15.00 40.00
SSR13 Carl Yastrzemski 15.00 40.00
SSR14 Carl Yastrzemski 15.00 40.00
SSR15 Dale Murphy 12.50 30.00
SSR16 Dale Murphy 12.50 30.00
SSR17 Honus Wagner 50.00 100.00
SSR18 Honus Wagner 50.00 100.00
SSR19 Craig Biggio 12.50 30.00
SSR20 Craig Biggio 12.50 30.00
SSR21 Johnny Mize 12.50 30.00
SSR22 Johnny Mize 12.50 30.00
SSR23 Ryan Braun 10.00 25.00
SSR24 Ryan Braun 10.00 25.00
SSR25 Manny Ramirez 15.00 40.00
SSR26 Manny Ramirez 15.00 40.00
SSR27 Alex Rodriguez 12.50 30.00
SSR28 Alex Rodriguez 12.50 30.00
SSR29 Carlton Fisk 12.50 30.00
SSR30 Carlton Fisk 12.50 30.00
SSR31 Lou Gehrig 75.00 150.00
SSR32 Lou Gehrig 75.00 150.00
SSR33 Ozzie Smith 12.50 30.00
SSR34 Ozzie Smith 12.50 30.00
SSR35 Hank Greenberg 20.00 50.00
SSR36 Hank Greenberg 20.00 50.00
SSR37 Roy Campanella 20.00 50.00
SSR38 Roy Campanella 20.00 50.00
SSR39 Ernie Banks 10.00 25.00
SSR40 Ernie Banks 10.00 25.00
SSR41 Jackie Robinson 30.00 60.00
SSR42 Jackie Robinson 30.00 60.00
SSR43 Phil Rizzuto 20.00 50.00
SSR44 Phil Rizzuto 20.00 50.00
SSR45 Harmon Killebrew 20.00 50.00
SSR46 Harmon Killebrew 20.00 50.00
SSR47 Yogi Berra 15.00 40.00
SSR48 Yogi Berra 15.00 40.00
SSR49 Tom Seaver 10.00 25.00
SSR50 Tom Seaver 10.00 25.00
SSR51 Rogers Hornsby 40.00 80.00
SSR52 Rogers Hornsby 40.00 80.00
SSR53 Dustin Pedroia 20.00 50.00
SSR54 Dustin Pedroia 20.00 50.00
SSR55 Reggie Jackson 12.50 30.00
SSR56 Reggie Jackson 12.50 30.00
SSR57 Miguel Cabrera 10.00 25.00
SSR58 Miguel Cabrera 10.00 25.00
SSR59 Mel Ott 20.00 50.00
SSR60 Mel Ott 20.00 50.00
SSR61 Roger Maris 30.00 60.00
SSR62 Roger Maris 30.00 60.00
SSR63 Prince Fielder 8.00 20.00
SSR64 Prince Fielder 8.00 20.00
SSR65 Eddie Murray 12.50 30.00
SSR66 Eddie Murray 12.50 30.00
SSR67 Johnny Bench 12.50 30.00
SSR68 Johnny Bench 12.50 30.00
SSR69 Frank Robinson 10.00 25.00
SSR70 Frank Robinson 10.00 25.00
SSR71 Greg Maddux 15.00 40.00
SSR72 Greg Maddux 15.00 40.00
SSR73 Ty Cobb 60.00 120.00
SSR74 Ty Cobb 60.00 120.00
SSR75 Mike Schmidt 10.00 25.00
SSR76 Mike Schmidt 10.00 25.00
SSR77 Warren Spahn 40.00 80.00
SSR78 Warren Spahn 40.00 80.00
SSR79 Bob Gibson 15.00 40.00
SSR80 Bob Gibson 15.00 40.00
SSR81 Mark Teixeira 12.50 30.00
SSR82 Mark Teixeira 12.50 30.00
SSR83 Andre Dawson 12.50 30.00
SSR84 Andre Dawson 12.50 30.00
SSR85 Ryan Howard 15.00 40.00
SSR86 Ryan Howard 15.00 40.00
SSR87 Brooks Robinson 12.50 30.00
SSR88 Brooks Robinson 12.50 30.00
SSR89 Joe Morgan 10.00 25.00
SSR90 Joe Morgan 10.00 25.00
SSR91 Roy Halladay 15.00 40.00
SSR92 Roy Halladay 15.00 40.00
SSR93 Stan Musial 30.00 60.00
SSR94 Stan Musial 30.00 60.00
SSR95 Evan Longoria 12.50 30.00
SSR96 Evan Longoria 12.50 30.00
SSR97 Nolan Ryan 30.00 60.00
SSR98 Nolan Ryan 30.00 60.00
SSR99 Chase Utley 10.00 25.00
SSR100 Chase Utley 10.00 25.00
SSR101 Pee Wee Reese 10.00 25.00
SSR102 Pee Wee Reese 10.00 25.00
SSR103 Jim Palmer 10.00 25.00
SSR104 Jim Palmer 10.00 25.00
SSR105 Dave Winfield 10.00 25.00
SSR106 Dave Winfield 10.00 25.00
SSR107 David Ortiz 8.00 20.00
SSR108 David Ortiz 8.00 20.00
SSR109 Hanley Ramirez 12.50 30.00
SSR110 Hanley Ramirez 12.50 30.00
SSR111 Thurman Munson 20.00 50.00
SSR112 Thurman Munson 20.00 50.00
SSR113 David Wright 15.00 40.00
SSR114 David Wright 15.00 40.00
SSR115 Tim Lincecum 10.00 25.00
SSR116 Tim Lincecum 10.00 25.00
SSR117 Chipper Jones 15.00 40.00
SSR118 Chipper Jones 15.00 40.00
SSR119 Wade Boggs 12.50 30.00
SSR120 Wade Boggs 12.50 30.00
SSR121 Don Mattingly 50.00 100.00
SSR122 Don Mattingly 50.00 100.00
SSR123 Vladimir Guerrero 8.00 20.00
SSR124 Vladimir Guerrero 8.00 20.00
SSR125 Jimmie Foxx 20.00 50.00
SSR126 Jimmie Foxx 20.00 50.00
SSR127 CC Sabathia 8.00 20.00
SSR128 CC Sabathia 8.00 20.00
SSR129 Tony Gwynn 15.00 40.00
SSR130 Tony Gwynn 15.00 40.00
SSR133 Mariano Rivera 15.00 40.00
SSR134 Mariano Rivera 15.00 40.00
SSR135 Duke Snider 10.00 25.00
SSR136 Duke Snider 10.00 25.00
SSR137 Whitey Ford 10.00 25.00
SSR138 Whitey Ford 10.00 25.00
SSR139 Jason Heyward 20.00 50.00
SSR140 Jason Heyward 20.00 50.00

2020 Topps Sterling Sterling Seasons Relic Autographs

STATED ODDS 1:xx HOBBY
PRINT RUNS B/WN 15-25 COPIES PER
NO PRICING ON QTY 15 OR LESS
EXCHANGE DEADLINE 6/30/22
SSARI Ichiro
SSARAJ Aaron Judge
SSARAR Alex Rodriguez
SSARBB Bo Bichette RC EXCH 100.00 250.00
SSARBG Bob Gibson 50.00 120.00
SSARBL Barry Larkin 30.00 80.00
SSARBP Buster Posey
SSARCR Cal Ripken Jr. 75.00 200.00
SSARCS CC Sabathia 25.00 60.00
SSARCY Carl Yastrzemski 60.00 150.00
SSARDM Dale Murphy 30.00 80.00
SSARDW David Wright 30.00 80.00
SSARFT Frank Thomas 60.00 150.00
SSARGS George Springer 20.00 50.00
SSARHA Hank Aaron
SSARHM Hideki Matsui 40.00 100.00
SSARIC Ichiro
SSARJA Jose Altuve 25.00 60.00
SSARJB Jeff Bagwell 40.00 100.00
SSARJd Jacob deGrom 75.00 200.00
SSARJS John Smoltz 30.00 80.00
SSARJV Joey Votto 30.00 80.00
SSARKB Kris Bryant 75.00 200.00
SSARKG Ken Griffey Jr.
SSARMC Miguel Cabrera 60.00 150.00
SSARMM Mark McGwire 40.00 100.00
SSARMS Max Scherzer
SSARMT Mike Trout
SSARPA Pete Alonso 75.00 200.00
SSARPM Pedro Martinez
SSARRA Ronald Acuna Jr. 100.00 250.00
SSARRH Rickey Henderson 75.00 200.00
SSARRJ Randy Johnson
SSARRS Ryne Sandberg 60.00 150.00
SSARRY Robin Yount 30.00 80.00
SSARSC Steve Carlton 30.00 80.00
SSARSO Shohei Ohtani
SSARTG Tom Glavine 30.00 80.00
SSARTL Tim Lincecum
SSARVG Vladimir Guerrero 40.00 100.00
SSARWB Wade Boggs 30.00 80.00
SSARWC Will Clark 30.00 80.00
SSARYA Yordan Alvarez RC 60.00 150.00
SSARAAQ Aristides Aquino RC 40.00 100.00
SSARCYE Christian Yelich 50.00 120.00
SSARDMA Don Mattingly 50.00 120.00
SSARDOR David Ortiz 50.00 120.00
SSARJBE Johnny Bench 50.00 120.00
SSARJSO Juan Soto 100.00 250.00
SSARKGR Ken Griffey Jr.
SSARMMC Mark McGwire 40.00 100.00
SSARMSC Mike Schmidt 60.00 150.00
SSARMTR Mike Trout
SSARNRY Nolan Ryan 100.00 250.00
SSARPMA Pedro Martinez
SSARRAL Roberto Alomar 30.00 80.00
SSARRCA Rod Carew 40.00 100.00
SSARRCL Roger Clemens
SSARRHE Rickey Henderson 75.00 200.00
SSARRJA Reggie Jackson
SSARRJO Randy Johnson
SSARVGR Vladimir Guerrero Jr. 40.00 100.00

2020 Topps Sterling Sterling Strikes Relic Autographs

STATED ODDS 1:xx HOBBY
PRINT RUNS B/WN 15-25 COPIES PER
NO PRICING ON QTY 15 OR LESS
EXCHANGE DEADLINE 6/30/22
STARAP Andy Pettitte 30.00 80.00
STARBG Bob Gibson 10.00 25.00
STARBM Brendan McKay 15.00 40.00
STARCC CC Sabathia 25.00 60.00
STARCS Chris Sale 25.00 60.00
STARDM Dustin May 75.00 200.00
STARJd Jacob deGrom 75.00 200.00
STARJL Jesus Luzardo 15.00 40.00
STARJS John Smoltz 30.00 80.00
STARMR Mariano Rivera
STARMT Masahiro Tanaka 50.00 120.00
STARNR Nolan Ryan
STARRJ Randy Johnson
STARSC Steve Carlton 30.00 80.00
STARSO Shohei Ohtani
STARTG Tom Glavine 30.00 80.00
STARTL Tim Lincecum 60.00 150.00
STARWB Walker Buehler 40.00 100.00
STARCKE Clayton Kershaw
STARMSC Max Scherzer
STARPMA Pedro Martinez
STARRCL Roger Clemens
STARRJO Randy Johnson

2020 Topps Sterling Sterling Swings Relic Autographs

STATED ODDS 1:xx HOBBY
PRINT RUNS B/WN 15-25 COPIES PER
NO PRICING ON QTY 15 OR LESS
EXCHANGE DEADLINE 6/30/22
SWARAA Aristides Aquino 40.00 100.00
SWARAK Al Kaline
SWARBL Barry Larkin 30.00 80.00
SWARBP Buster Posey
SWARCJ Chipper Jones 75.00 200.00
SWARCR Cal Ripken Jr. 75.00 200.00
SWARCY Christian Yelich 50.00 120.00
SWARDM Don Mattingly 50.00 120.00
SWARDO David Ortiz 50.00 120.00
SWAREM Edgar Martinez 30.00 80.00
SWARGL Gavin Lux 100.00 250.00
SWARGS George Springer 20.00 50.00
SWARHA Hank Aaron
SWARHM Hideki Matsui 40.00 100.00
SWARJB Jeff Bagwell 40.00 100.00
SWARJS Juan Soto 100.00 250.00
SWARJV Joey Votto 30.00 80.00
SWARMC Miguel Cabrera 60.00 150.00
SWARMM Mark McGwire 40.00 100.00
SWARMT Mike Trout
SWARNA Nolan Arenado 75.00 200.00
SWARPA Pete Alonso 75.00 200.00
SWARPG Paul Goldschmidt 30.00 80.00
SWARRA Roberto Alomar 30.00 80.00
SWARRC Rod Carew 40.00 100.00
SWARRD Rafael Devers 25.00 60.00
SWARRS Ryne Sandberg 60.00 150.00
SWARRY Robin Yount 30.00 80.00
SWARSO Shohei Ohtani
SWARVG Vladimir Guerrero 40.00 100.00
SWARWB Wade Boggs 30.00 80.00
SWARWC Will Clark 30.00 80.00
SWARYA Yordan Alvarez 60.00 150.00
SWARARI Anthony Rizzo 40.00 100.00
SWARBBI Bo Bichette 100.00 250.00
SWARCYA Carl Yastrzemski 60.00 150.00
SWARDMU Dale Murphy 30.00 80.00
SWARDWR David Wright 30.00 80.00
SWARFTH Frank Thomas 60.00 150.00
SWARGTO Gleyber Torres 200.00 500.00
SWARJAL Jose Altuve 25.00 60.00
SWARJBE Johnny Bench 50.00 120.00
SWARKBR Kris Bryant
SWARMSC Mike Schmidt 60.00 150.00
SWARRAJ Ronald Acuna Jr. 100.00 250.00
SWARRHE Rickey Henderson 75.00 200.00
SWARRHO Rhys Hoskins 40.00 100.00
SWARVGJ Vladimir Guerrero Jr. 40.00 100.00

2011 Topps Stickers

COMMON CARD (1-309) .08 .20
COMMON FOIL (286-294) .15 .40
1 Luke Scott .07 .20
2 Adam Jones .12 .30
3 Nick Markakis .15 .40
4 Mark Reynolds .07 .20
5 J.J. Hardy .07 .20
6 Brian Roberts .07 .20
7 Derrek Lee .07 .20
8 Vladimir Guerrero .12 .30
9 Brian Matusz .07 .20
10 Carl Crawford .12 .30
11 Jacoby Ellsbury .15 .40
12 J.D. Drew .07 .20
13 Kevin Youkilis .07 .20
14 Jed Lowrie .07 .20
15 Dustin Pedroia .20 .50
16 Adrian Gonzalez .15 .40
17 David Ortiz .20 .50
18 Jon Lester .12 .30
19 Brett Gardner .12 .30
20 Curtis Granderson .15 .40
21 Nick Swisher .12 .30
22 Alex Rodriguez .25 .60
23 Derek Jeter .50 1.25
24 Robinson Cano .12 .30
25 Mark Teixeira .12 .30
26 Jorge Posada .12 .30
27 CC Sabathia .12 .30
28 Johnny Damon .12 .30
29 B.J. Upton .12 .30
30 Ben Zobrist .12 .30
31 Evan Longoria .12 .30
32 Reid Brignac .07 .20
33 Sean Rodriguez .07 .20
34 Casey Kotchman .07 .20
35 Sam Fuld .07 .20
36 David Price .15 .40
37 Juan Rivera .07 .20
38 Rajai Davis .07 .20
39 Edwin Encarnacion .20 .50
40 Jose Bautista .12 .30
41 Yunel Escobar .07 .20
42 Aaron Hill .07 .20
43 Adam Lind .12 .30
44 J.P. Arencibia .07 .20
45 Brandon Morrow .07 .20
46 Juan Pierre .07 .20
47 Alex Rios .07 .20
48 Carlos Quentin .07 .20
49 Adam Dunn .12 .30
50 Alexei Ramirez .12 .30
51 Gordon Beckham .07 .20
52 Paul Konerko .12 .30
53 A.J. Pierzynski .07 .20
54 Mark Buehrle .12 .30
55 Michael Brantley .07 .20
56 Grady Sizemore .12 .30
57 Shin-Soo Choo .12 .30
58 Travis Hafner .07 .20
59 Asdrubal Cabrera .12 .30
60 Orlando Cabrera .07 .20
61 Matt LaPorta .07 .20
62 Carlos Santana .20 .50
63 Fausto Carmona .07 .20
64 Alex Avila .12 .30
65 Austin Jackson .07 .20
66 Magglio Ordonez .12 .30
67 Brandon Inge .07 .20
68 Jhonny Peralta .07 .20
69 Brennan Boesch .12 .30
70 Miguel Cabrera .20 .50
71 Victor Martinez .12 .30
72 Justin Verlander .20 .50
73 Alex Gordon .12 .30
74 Melky Cabrera .07 .20
75 Jeff Francoeur .12 .30
76 Mike Moustakas .20 .50
77 Alcides Escobar .12 .30
78 Chris Getz .07 .20
79 Eric Hosmer .50 1.25
80 Billy Butler .07 .20
81 Luke Hochevar .07 .20
82 Delmon Young .12 .30
83 Denard Span .07 .20
84 Michael Cuddyer .07 .20
85 Danny Valencia .12 .30
86 Jason Kubel .07 .20
87 Tsuyoshi Nishioka .25 .60
88 Justin Morneau .12 .30
89 Joe Mauer .15 .40
90 Francisco Liriano .07 .20
91 Vernon Wells .07 .20
92 Torii Hunter .07 .20
93 Bobby Abreu .07 .20
94 Maicer Izturis .07 .20
95 Erick Aybar .07 .20
96 Howie Kendrick .07 .20
97 Kendrys Morales .07 .20
98 Jeff Mathis .07 .20
99 Jered Weaver .12 .30
100 Josh Willingham .12 .30
101 Coco Crisp .07 .20
102 David DeJesus .07 .20
103 Kevin Kouzmanoff .07 .20
104 Cliff Pennington .07 .20
105 Mark Ellis .07 .20
106 Daric Barton .07 .20
107 Kurt Suzuki .07 .20
108 Brett Anderson .07 .20
109 Carlos Peguero .12 .30
110 Franklin Gutierrez .07 .20
111 Ichiro Suzuki .25 .60
112 Chone Figgins .07 .20
113 Brendan Ryan .07 .20
114 Jack Wilson .07 .20
115 Jack Cust .07 .20
116 Miguel Olivo .07 .20
117 Felix Hernandez .12 .30
118 Josh Hamilton .12 .30
119 Julio Borbon .07 .20
120 Nelson Cruz .20 .50
121 Adrian Beltre .20 .50
122 Elvis Andrus .12 .30
123 Ian Kinsler .12 .30
124 Mitch Moreland .07 .20
125 Michael Young .07 .20
126 Neftali Feliz .07 .20
127 Baltimore Orioles
309 San Francisco Giants .07 .20
128 New York Yankees
305 Houston Astros .12 .30
129 Toronto Blue Jays/298 Detroit Tigers.07 .20
130 Cleveland Indians
303 Philadelphia Phillies .07 .20
131 Kansas City Royals
306 Pittsburgh Pirates .07 .20
132 Los Angeles Angels
299 Minnesota Twins .07 .20
133 Seattle Mariners
307 Arizona Diamondbacks .07 .20
134 Atlanta Braves/296 Tampa Bay Rays.07 .20
135 New York Mets/295 Boston Red Sox.12 .30
136 Washington Nationals
302 Florida Marlins .07 .20
137 Cincinnati Reds
306 Los Angeles Dodgers .07 .20
138 Milwaukee Brewers
301 Texas Rangers .07 .20
139 St. Louis Cardinals
297 Chicago White Sox .07 .20
140 Colorado Rockies
300 Oakland Athletics .07 .20
141 San Diego Padres/304 Chicago Cubs.07 .20
142 Martin Prado .07 .20
143 Nate McLouth .07 .20
144 Jason Heyward .15 .40
145 Chipper Jones .20 .50
146 Alex Gonzalez .07 .20
147 Dan Uggla .07 .20
148 Freddie Freeman 1.25 3.00
149 Brian McCann .12 .30
150 Tim Hudson .12 .30
151 Logan Morrison .07 .20
152 Chris Coghlan .07 .20
153 Mike Stanton .20 .50
154 Wes Helms .07 .20
155 Hanley Ramirez .12 .30
156 Omar Infante .07 .20
157 Gaby Sanchez .07 .20
158 John Buck .07 .20
159 Josh Johnson .12 .30
160 Jason Bay .12 .30
161 Angel Pagan .07 .20
162 Carlos Beltran .12 .30
163 David Wright .15 .40
164 Jose Reyes .12 .30
165 Daniel Murphy .15 .40
166 Ike Davis .07 .20
167 Josh Thole .07 .20
168 Johan Santana .12 .30
169 Raul Ibanez .12 .30
170 Shane Victorino .12 .30
171 Ben Francisco .07 .20
172 Placido Polanco .07 .20
173 Jimmy Rollins .12 .30
174 Chase Utley .12 .30
175 Ryan Howard .15 .40
176 Carlos Ruiz .07 .20
177 Roy Halladay .12 .30
178 Mike Morse .07 .20
179 Rick Ankiel .07 .20
180 Jayson Werth .12 .30
181 Lance Nix .07 .20
182 Ryan Zimmerman .12 .30
183 Ian Desmond .07 .20
184 Adam LaRoche .07 .20
185 Ivan Rodriguez .12 .30
186 Jordan Zimmermann .12 .30
187 Alfonso Soriano .12 .30
188 Marlon Byrd .07 .20
189 Kosuke Fukudome .12 .30
190 Aramis Ramirez .07 .20
191 Starlin Castro .12 .30
192 Blake DeWitt .07 .20
193 Carlos Pena .12 .30
194 Geovany Soto .12 .30
195 Matt Garza .07 .20
196 Jonny Gomes .07 .20
197 Drew Stubbs .07 .20
198 Jay Bruce .12 .30
199 Scott Rolen .12 .30
200 Paul Janish .07 .20
201 Brandon Phillips .07 .20
202 Joey Votto .20 .50
203 Ramon Hernandez .07 .20
204 Aroldis Chapman .25 .60
205 Carlos Lee .07 .20
206 Michael Bourn .07 .20
207 Hunter Pence .12 .30
208 Chris Johnson .07 .20
209 Clint Barmes .07 .20
210 Bill Hall .07 .20
211 Brett Wallace .07 .20
212 Humberto Quintero .07 .20
213 Wandy Rodriguez .07 .20
214 Ryan Braun .12 .30
215 Carlos Gomez .07 .20
216 Corey Hart .07 .20
217 Casey McGehee .07 .20
218 Yuniesky Betancourt .07 .20
219 Rickie Weeks .07 .20
220 Prince Fielder .12 .30
221 Jonathan Lucroy .12 .30
222 Zack Greinke .20 .50
223 Jose Tabata .07 .20
224 Andrew McCutchen .20 .50
225 Garrett Jones .07 .20
226 Pedro Alvarez .15 .40
227 Ronny Cedeno .07 .20
228 Neil Walker .12 .30
229 Lyle Overbay .07 .20
230 Chris Snyder .07 .20
231 James McDonald .07 .20
232 Matt Holliday .20 .50
233 Colby Rasmus .12 .30
234 Lance Berkman .12 .30
235 David Freese .07 .20
236 Ryan Theriot .07 .20
237 Skip Schumaker .07 .20
238 Albert Pujols .25 .60
239 Yadier Molina .25 .60
240 Adam Wainwright .12 .30
241 Xavier Nady .07 .20
242 Chris Young .07 .20
243 Justin Upton .12 .30
244 Melvin Mora .07 .20
245 Stephen Drew .07 .20
246 Kelly Johnson .07 .20
247 Juan Miranda .07 .20
248 Miguel Montero .07 .20
249 Daniel Hudson .07 .20
250 Carlos Gonzalez .12 .30
251 Dexter Fowler .12 .30
252 Seth Smith .07 .20
253 Ty Wigginton .07 .20
254 Troy Tulowitzki .20 .50
255 Jonathan Herrera .07 .20
256 Todd Helton .12 .30
257 Chris Iannetta .07 .20
258 Ubaldo Jimenez .07 .20
259 Jerry Sands .20 .50
260 Matt Kemp .15 .40
261 Andre Ethier .12 .30
262 Casey Blake .07 .20
263 Rafael Furcal .07 .20
264 Juan Uribe .07 .20
265 James Loney .07 .20
266 Dee Gordon .12 .30
267 Clayton Kershaw .30 .75
268 Ryan Ludwick .07 .20
269 Cameron Maybin .07 .20
270 Will Venable .07 .20
271 Chase Headley .07 .20
272 Jason Bartlett .07 .20
273 Orlando Hudson .07 .20
274 Anthony Rizzo .75 2.00
275 Nick Hundley .07 .20
276 Mat Latos .12 .30
277 Mark DeRosa .07 .20
278 Andres Torres .07 .20
279 Cody Ross .07 .20
280 Pablo Sandoval .12 .30
281 Miguel Tejada .12 .30
282 Freddy Sanchez .07 .20
283 Aubrey Huff .07 .20
284 Buster Posey .25 .60
285 Tim Lincecum .12 .30
286 Hank Aaron FOIL .75 2.00
287 Babe Ruth FOIL 1.00 2.50
288 Stan Musial FOIL .60 1.50
289 Joe DiMaggio FOIL .75 2.00
290 Mike Schmidt FOIL .60 1.50
291 Jackie Robinson FOIL .40 1.00
292 Lou Gehrig FOIL .75 2.00
293 Roy Campanella FOIL .40 1.00
294 Sandy Koufax FOIL .75 2.00

2012 Topps Stickers

COMMON CARD (1-309) .07 .20
1 Jeremy Guthrie .12 .30
2 Adam Jones .15 .40
3 Nick Markakis .15 .40
4 Mark Reynolds .12 .30
5 J.J. Hardy .12 .30
6 Brian Roberts .12 .30
7 Zach Britton .15 .40
8 Vladimir Guerrero .15 .40
9 Mascot .07 .20
10 Carl Crawford .15 .40
11 Jacoby Ellsbury .15 .40
12 Kevin Youkilis .20 .50
13 Jon Lester .12 .30
14 Dustin Pedroia .20 .50
15 Adrian Gonzalez .15 .40
16 David Ortiz .20 .50
17 Josh Beckett .12 .30
18 Wally the Green Monster .12 .30
19 Curtis Granderson .15 .40
20 Alex Rodriguez .25 .60
21 Derek Jeter .50 1.25
22 Robinson Cano .15 .40
23 Mark Teixeira .15 .40
24 CC Sabathia .15 .40
25 Mariano Rivera .25 .60
26 Babe Ruth .50 1.25
27 Mickey Mantle .60 1.50
28 James Shields .12 .30
29 B.J. Upton .15 .40
30 Matt Joyce .12 .30
31 Evan Longoria .15 .40
32 Ben Zobrist .15 .40
33 Desmond Jennings .15 .40
34 David Price .15 .40
35 Jeremy Hellickson .12 .30
36 Raymond .07 .20
37 Colby Rasmus .15 .40
38 Ricky Romero .12 .30
39 Brett Lawrie .15 .40
40 Jose Bautista .15 .40
41 Yunel Escobar .12 .30
42 Adam Lind .15 .40
43 J.P. Arencibia .12 .30
44 Brandon Morrow .12 .30
45 Blue Jays Mascot .07 .20
46 Juan Pierre .12 .30
47 Alex Rios .15 .40
48 Adam Dunn .15 .40
49 Alexei Ramirez .15 .40
50 Gordon Beckham .12 .30
51 Paul Konerko .12 .30
52 A.J. Pierzynski .12 .30
53 John Danks .12 .30
54 Mascot .07 .20
55 Matt LaPorta .12 .30
56 Grady Sizemore .15 .40
57 Shin-Soo Choo .15 .40
58 Travis Hafner .12 .30
59 Asdrubal Cabrera .15 .40
60 Jason Kipnis .15 .40
61 Carlos Santana .15 .40
62 Ubaldo Jimenez .12 .30
63 Slider .07 .20
64 Alex Avila .12 .30
65 Austin Jackson .15 .40
66 Prince Fielder .15 .40
67 Justin Verlander .20 .50
68 Jhonny Peralta .12 .30
69 Miguel Cabrera .20 .50
70 Victor Martinez .15 .40
71 Jose Valverde .15 .40
72 Paws .07 .20
73 Alex Gordon .15 .40
74 Jeff Francoeur .15 .40
75 Mike Moustakas .15 .40
76 Alcides Escobar .15 .40
77 Eric Hosmer .15 .40
78 Billy Butler .12 .30
79 Luke Hochevar .12 .30
80 Joakim Soria .12 .30
81 Kansas City Royals .07 .20
82 Ben Revere .15 .40
83 Danny Valencia .15 .40
84 Tsuyoshi Nishioka .15 .40
85 Justin Morneau .15 .40
86 Joe Mauer .15 .40
87 Francisco Liriano .12 .30
88 Carl Pavano .12 .30
89 Josh Willingham .15 .40
90 TC .07 .20
91 Jered Weaver .15 .40
92 Torii Hunter .15 .40
93 Mike Trout 15.00 40.00
94 Erick Aybar .12 .30
95 Howie Kendrick .12 .30
96 Mark Trumbo .12 .30
97 Dan Haren .12 .30
98 Albert Pujols .25 .60
99 C.J. Wilson .12 .30
100 Coco Crisp .12 .30
101 Brandon McCarthy .12 .30
102 Cliff Pennington .12 .30
103 Jemile Weeks .12 .30
104 Kurt Suzuki .12 .30
105 Brett Anderson .12 .30
106 Josh Reddick .12 .30
107 Dallas Braden .12 .30
108 Oakland Athletics .07 .20
109 Ichiro Suzuki .25 .60
110 Kyle Seager .12 .30
111 Jesus Montero .12 .30
112 Dustin Ackley .12 .30
113 Justin Smoak .15 .40
114 Mike Carp .12 .30
115 Miguel Olivo .12 .30
116 Felix Hernandez .15 .40
117 Mariner Moose .07 .20
118 Neftali Feliz .07 .20
119 Josh Hamilton .15 .40
120 Nelson Cruz .20 .50
121 Adrian Beltre .20 .50
122 Elvis Andrus .15 .40
123 Ian Kinsler .15 .40
124 Michael Young .12 .30
125 Mike Napoli .12 .30
126 Rangers Captain .07 .20
127 Martin Prado .12 .30
128 Chipper Jones .20 .50
129 Jason Heyward .15 .40
130 Dan Uggla .15 .40
131 Freddie Freeman .25 .60
132 Brian McCann .15 .40
133 Tommy Hanson .12 .30
134 Craig Kimbrel .15 .40
135 Atlanta Braves .07 .20
136 Los Angeles Angels
158 Milwaukee Brewers .07 .20
137 Baltimore Orioles
144 New York Yankees .12 .30
138 Boston Red Sox
145 Oakland Athletics .07 .20
139 Chicago White Sox
161 Pittsburgh Pirates .07 .20
140 Cleveland Indians
163 San Francisco Giants .07 .20
141 Detroit Tigers/164 St. Louis Cardinals.12 .30
142 Kansas City Royals
149 Toronto Blue Jays .07 .20
150 Arizona Diamondbacks
143 Minnesota Twins .07 .20
151 Atlanta Braves/159 New York Mets.12 .30
152 Chicago Cubs
160 Philadelphia Phillies .12 .30
153 Cincinnati Reds
162 San Diego Padres .07 .20
154 Colorado Rockies
146 Seattle Mariners .07 .20
155 Miami Marlins/147 Tampa Bay Rays.07 .20
156 Houston Astros/148 Texas Rangers.07 .20
157 Los Angeles Dodgers
165 Washington Nationals .12 .30
166 Gaby Sanchez .15 .40
167 Josh Johnson .15 .40
168 Mark Buehrle .15 .40
169 Logan Morrison .12 .30
170 Mike Stanton .20 .50
171 Jose Reyes .12 .30
172 Hanley Ramirez .15 .40
173 Heath Bell .12 .30
174 Billy the Marlin .07 .20
175 R.A. Dickey .15 .40
176 Jason Bay .15 .40
177 David Wright .15 .40
178 Lucas Duda .15 .40
179 Ike Davis .12 .30
180 Ruben Tejada .12 .30
181 Josh Thole .12 .30
182 Johan Santana .15 .40
183 Mr. Met .12 .30
184 Roy Halladay .15 .40
185 Shane Victorino .15 .40
186 Hunter Pence .15 .40
187 Jimmy Rollins .15 .40
188 Chase Utley .15 .40
189 Ryan Howard .15 .40
190 Carlos Ruiz .12 .30
191 Cliff Lee .15 .40
192 Phillie Phanatic .07 .20
193 Gio Gonzalez .15 .40
194 Mike Morse .12 .30
195 Jayson Werth .15 .40
196 Danny Espinosa .12 .30
197 Ryan Zimmerman .15 .40
198 Ian Desmond .12 .30
199 Drew Storen .12 .30
200 Stephen Strasburg .20 .50
201 Screech .07 .20
202 Ryan Dempster .12 .30
203 Matt Garza .12 .30
204 Alfonso Soriano .15 .40
205 Marlon Byrd .12 .30
206 Carlos Marmol .12 .30
207 Starlin Castro .15 .40
208 Darwin Barney .12 .30
209 Carlos Pena .15 .40
210 Geovany Soto .15 .40
211 Mat Latos .15 .40
212 Joey Votto .20 .50
213 Aroldis Chapman .20 .50
214 Drew Stubbs .12 .30
215 Jay Bruce .15 .40
216 Scott Rolen .15 .40
217 Brandon Phillips .12 .30
218 Johnny Bench .20 .50
219 Gapper .07 .20
220 Wandy Rodriguez .12 .30
221 Brett Myers .12 .30
222 Carlos Lee .12 .30
223 J.D. Martinez .20 .50
224 Brian Bogusevic .12 .30
225 Chris Johnson .12 .30
226 Jose Altuve .15 .40
227 Brett Wallace .12 .30
228 Junction Jack .07 .20
229 John Axford .12 .30
230 Nyjer Morgan .12 .30
231 Aramis Ramirez .12 .30
232 Ryan Braun .12 .30
233 Yovani Gallardo .15 .40
234 Corey Hart .12 .30
235 Zack Greinke .20 .50
236 Rickie Weeks .12 .30
237 Bernie Brewer .07 .20
238 Andrew McCutchen .20 .50
239 Derrek Lee .07 .20
240 James McDonald .12 .30
241 Pedro Alvarez .12 .30
242 Neil Walker .12 .30
243 Jose Tabata .12 .30
244 Joel Hanrahan .12 .30
245 Roberto Clemente .50 1.25
246 Pirate Parrot .07 .20
247 David Freese .12 .30
248 Yadier Molina .25 .60
249 Carlos Beltran .15 .40
250 Matt Holliday .20 .50

251 Adam Wainwright .15 .40
252 Lance Berkman .15 .40
253 Chris Carpenter .15 .40
254 Stan Musial .30 .75
255 Fredbird .07 .20
256 Miguel Montero .12 .30
257 Ian Kennedy .12 .30
258 Chris Young .12 .30
259 Justin Upton .15 .40
260 Ryan Roberts .12 .30
261 Stephen Drew .12 .30
262 Daniel Hudson .12 .30
263 Paul Goldschmidt .20 .50
264 Arizona Diamondbacks .07 .20
265 Michael Cuddyer .12 .30
266 Todd Helton .15 .40
267 Ramon Hernandez .12 .30
268 Carlos Gonzalez .15 .40
269 Dexter Fowler .15 .40
270 Jhoulys Chacin .12 .30
271 Troy Tulowitzki .20 .50
272 Eric Young .12 .30
273 Dinger .07 .20
274 Dee Gordon .12 .30
275 Ted Lilly .12 .30
276 Mark Ellis .12 .30
277 Matt Kemp .15 .40
278 Andre Ethier .15 .40
279 Juan Rivera .12 .30
280 James Loney .12 .30
281 Clayton Kershaw .30 .75
282 Sandy Koufax .40 1.00
283 Cory Luebke .12 .30
284 Jesus Guzman .12 .30
285 Carlos Quentin .12 .30
286 Huston Street .12 .30
287 Cameron Maybin .12 .30
288 Will Venable .12 .30
289 Chase Headley .12 .30
290 Orlando Hudson .12 .30
291 Swinging Friar .07 .20
292 Matt Cain .15 .40
293 Freddy Sanchez .20 .50
294 Buster Posey .25 .60
295 Madison Bumgarner .15 .40
296 Tim Lincecum .15 .40
297 Pablo Sandoval .15 .40
298 Brian Wilson .20 .50
299 Brandon Belt .15 .40
300 Willie Mays .40 1.00
301 Adam Jones .15 .40
302 Ian Kennedy .12 .30
303 Matt Kemp .15 .40
304 Neftali Feliz .12 .30
305 Michael Morse .12 .30
306 Justin Upton .15 .40
307 Eric Hosmer .15 .40
308 Tsuyoshi Nishioka .15 .40
309 Billy Butler .12 .30

2013 Topps Stickers

1 Adam Jones .20 .50
2 Cal Ripken Jr. .75 2.00
3 Nick Markakis .20 .50
4 Chris Davis .20 .50
5 J.J. Hardy .15 .40
6 Jim Johnson .15 .40
7 Manny Machado 1.00 2.50
8 Dylan Bundy .40 1.00
9 Baltimore Orioles .10 .25
10 Jacoby Ellsbury .20 .50
11 Jon Lester .20 .50
12 Ted Williams .50 1.25
13 Will Middlebrooks .15 .40
14 Jarrod Saltalamacchia .15 .40
15 David Ortiz .25 .60
16 Dustin Pedroia .25 .60
17 Joel Hanrahan .15 .40
18 Wally the Green Monster .10 .25
19 Derek Jeter .60 1.50
20 Alex Rodriguez .30 .75
21 Babe Ruth .60 1.50
22 Robinson Cano .20 .50
23 Curtis Granderson .20 .50
24 Mariano Rivera .30 .75
25 CC Sabathia .20 .50
26 Andy Pettitte .20 .50
27 Lou Gehrig .50 1.25
28 Raymond .10 .25
29 James Loney .20 .50
30 Fernando Rodney .15 .40
31 David Price .20 .50
32 Jeff Niemann .15 .40
33 Matt Moore .20 .50
34 Ben Zobrist .20 .50
35 Evan Longoria .20 .50
36 Jeremy Hellickson .15 .40
37 R.A. Dickey .20 .50
38 Colby Rasmus .20 .50
39 Jose Bautista .20 .50
40 Brett Lawrie .20 .50
41 Mark Buehrle .20 .50
42 Josh Johnson .20 .50
43 Jose Reyes .20 .50
44 Edwin Encarnacion .25 .60
45 Toronto Blue Jays .10 .25
46 Jake Peavy .15 .40
47 Paul Konerko .20 .50
48 Adam Dunn .20 .50
49 Addison Reed .15 .40
50 Chris Sale .25 .60
51 Alex Rios .20 .50
52 Dayan Viciedo .15 .40
53 Frank Thomas .25 .60
54 Chicago White Sox .10 .25
55 Mark Reynolds .15 .40
56 Carlos Santana .20 .50
57 Ubaldo Jimenez .15 .40
58 Asdrubal Cabrera .20 .50
59 Jason Kipnis .20 .50
60 Michael Brantley .15 .40
61 Chris Perez .15 .40
62 Trevor Bauer .30 .75
63 Slider .10 .25
64 Austin Jackson .15 .40
65 Prince Fielder .20 .50
66 Miguel Cabrera .25 .60
67 Justin Verlander .25 .60
68 Jose Valverde .15 .40
69 Victor Martinez .20 .50
70 Al Kaline .25 .60
71 Max Scherzer .25 .60
72 Paws .10 .25
73 Alex Gordon .20 .50
74 Alcides Escobar .20 .50
75 George Brett .50 1.25
76 Mike Moustakas .20 .50
77 Ervin Santana .15 .40
78 Billy Butler .15 .40
79 Salvador Perez .20 .50
80 Eric Hosmer .20 .50
81 Kansas City Royals .10 .25
82 Josh Willingham .20 .50
83 Trevor Plouffe .15 .40
84 Jamey Carroll .15 .40
85 Justin Morneau .20 .50
86 Joe Mauer .20 .50
87 Ryan Doumit .15 .40
88 Harmon Killebrew .25 .60
89 Scott Diamond .15 .40
90 TC .10 .25
91 Mike Trout 2.00 5.00
92 Ryan Madson .15 .40
93 Jered Weaver .20 .50
94 C.J. Wilson .15 .40
95 Albert Pujols .30 .75
96 Ernesto Frieri .15 .40
97 Howie Kendrick .15 .40
98 Josh Hamilton .20 .50
99 Mark Trumbo .20 .50
100 Brett Wallace .15 .40
101 Lucas Harrell .15 .40
102 Matt Dominguez .15 .40
103 Jed Lowrie .15 .40
104 Jose Altuve .20 .50
105 Craig Biggio .20 .50
106 Jordan Lyles .15 .40
107 Bud Norris .15 .40
108 Carlos Pena .20 .50
109 Coco Crisp .15 .40
110 Reggie Jackson .25 .60
111 Yoenis Cespedes .25 .60
112 Tom Milone .15 .40
113 Jarrod Parker .15 .40
114 A.J. Griffin .15 .40
115 Josh Reddick .15 .40
116 Rickey Henderson .25 .60
117 Oakland Athletics .10 .25
118 Michael Saunders .20 .50
119 Ken Griffey Jr. .50 1.25
120 Dustin Ackley .15 .40
121 Franklin Gutierrez .15 .40
122 Kyle Seager .15 .40
123 Felix Hernandez .20 .50
124 Justin Smoak .15 .40
125 Jesus Montero .15 .40
126 Mariner Moose .10 .25
127 A.J. Pierzynski .15 .40
128 Yu Darvish .25 .60
129 Nolan Ryan .75 2.00
130 Mike Olt .20 .50
131 Ian Kinsler .20 .50
132 Adrian Beltre .25 .60
133 David Murphy .15 .40
134 Derek Holland .15 .40
135 Rangers Captain .10 .25
136 Kris Medlen .20 .50
137 Tim Hudson .20 .50
138 Freddie Freeman .30 .75
139 Dan Uggla .15 .40
140 Craig Kimbrel .20 .50
141 John Smoltz .25 .60
142 Brian McCann .20 .50
143 Jason Heyward .20 .50
144 Atlanta Braves .10 .25
145 Adeiny Hechavarria .20 .50
146 Jacob Turner .20 .50
147 Steve Cishek .15 .40
148 Donovan Solano .20 .50
149 Giancarlo Stanton .25 .60
150 Ricky Nolasco .15 .40
151 Gary Sheffield .15 .40
152 Justin Ruggiano .15 .40
153 Logan Morrison .15 .40
154 Tom Seaver .20 .50
155 David Wright .20 .50
156 Ruben Tejada .20 .50
157 Jon Niese .15 .40
158 Matt Harvey .20 .50
159 Ike Davis .15 .40
160 Johan Santana .20 .50
161 Kirk Nieuwenhuis .15 .40
162 Mr. Met .10 .25
163 Roy Halladay .20 .50
164 Jimmy Rollins .20 .50
165 Chase Utley .20 .50
166 Mike Schmidt .40 1.00
167 Ryan Howard .20 .50
168 Cole Hamels .20 .50
169 Cliff Lee .20 .50
170 Michael Young .15 .40
171 Phillie Phanatic .10 .25
172 Bryce Harper .40 1.00
173 Gio Gonzalez .20 .50
174 Ryan Zimmerman .20 .50
175 Jordan Zimmermann .20 .50
176 Mike Morse .15 .40
177 Stephen Strasburg .25 .60
178 Ian Desmond .20 .50
179 Jayson Werth .20 .50
180 Screech .10 .25
181 Alfonso Soriano .20 .50
182 Matt Garza .15 .40
183 Brett Jackson .15 .40
184 Jeff Samardzija .15 .40
185 Anthony Rizzo .30 .75
186 Starlin Castro .15 .40
187 Darwin Barney .15 .40
188 Ernie Banks .25 .60
189 Carlos Marmol .15 .40
190 Mat Latos .20 .50
191 Johnny Cueto .20 .50
192 Homer Bailey .15 .40
193 Zack Cozart .15 .40
194 Joey Votto .25 .60
195 Johnny Bench .25 .60
196 Aroldis Chapman .25 .60
197 Brandon Phillips .15 .40
198 Gapper .10 .25
199 Yovani Gallardo .15 .40
200 Ryan Braun .20 .50
201 Rickie Weeks .15 .40
202 Aramis Ramirez .15 .40
203 John Axford .15 .40
204 Norichika Aoki .20 .50
205 Jean Segura .20 .50
206 Robin Yount .25 .60
207 Bernie Brewer .10 .25
208 Andrew McCutchen .25 .60
209 Starling Marte .20 .50
210 Neil Walker .15 .40
211 Pirate Parrot .10 .25
212 Roberto Clemente .60 1.50
213 A.J. Burnett .15 .40
214 Pedro Alvarez .15 .40
215 Garrett Jones .15 .40
216 James McDonald .15 .40
217 Matt Holliday .25 .60
218 Lance Lynn .15 .40
219 Carlos Beltran .20 .50
220 David Freese .15 .40
221 Stan Musial .40 1.00
222 Adam Wainwright .20 .50
223 Chris Carpenter .20 .50
224 Yadier Molina .30 .75
225 Fredbird .10 .25
226 Ian Kennedy .15 .40
227 Jason Kubel .15 .40
228 Adam Eaton .25 .60
229 Paul Goldschmidt .25 .60
230 Miguel Montero .15 .40
231 Trevor Cahill .15 .40
232 Wade Miley .15 .40
233 J.J. Putz .15 .40
234 Arizona Diamondbacks .10 .25
235 Carlos Gonzalez .20 .50
236 Josh Rutledge .15 .40
237 Todd Helton .20 .50
238 Troy Tulowitzki .25 .60
239 Michael Cuddyer .15 .40
240 Rafael Betancourt .15 .40
241 Wilin Rosario .15 .40
242 Dexter Fowler .20 .50
243 Dinger .10 .25
244 Sandy Koufax .50 1.25
245 Brandon League .15 .40
246 Matt Kemp .20 .50
247 Hanley Ramirez .20 .50
248 Clayton Kershaw .40 1.00
249 Adrian Gonzalez .20 .50
250 Carl Crawford .20 .50
251 Josh Beckett .15 .40
252 Andre Ethier .20 .50
253 Yonder Alonso .15 .40
254 Chase Headley .15 .40
255 Carlos Quentin .15 .40
256 Cameron Maybin .15 .40
257 Tony Gwynn .25 .60
258 Yasmani Grandal .15 .40
259 Swinging Friar .10 .25
260 Everth Cabrera .15 .40
261 Clayton Richard .15 .40
262 Angel Pagan .15 .40
263 Willie Mays .50 1.25
264 Matt Cain .20 .50
265 Buster Posey .30 .75
266 Madison Bumgarner .20 .50
267 Tim Lincecum .20 .50
268 Hunter Pence .20 .50
269 Sergio Romo .15 .40
270 Pablo Sandoval .20 .50
271 Giants Puzzle .25 .60
272 Giants Puzzle .25 .60
273 Giants Puzzle .25 .60
274 Giants Puzzle .25 .60
275 Giants Puzzle .25 .60
276 Giants Puzzle .25 .60
277 Giants Puzzle .25 .60
278 Giants Puzzle .25 .60
279 Giants Puzzle .25 .60
280 Giants Puzzle .25 .60
281 Giants Puzzle .25 .60
282 Giants Puzzle .25 .60
283 Giants Puzzle .25 .60
284 Giants Puzzle .25 .60
285 Giants Puzzle .25 .60
286 Baltimore Orioles
Washington Nationals .10 .25
287 Boston Red Sox/Atlanta Braves .10 .25
288 Chicago White Sox/Chicago Cubs .10 .25
289 Los Angeles Angels
Los Angeles Dodgers .10 .25
290 Cleveland Indians/Houston Astros .10 .25
291 Detroit Tigers/Colorado Rockies .10 .25
292 Kansas City Royals
St. Louis Cardinals .10 .25
293 Oakland Athletics
San Francisco Giants .10 .25
294 New York Yankees/New York Mets .10 .25
295 Minnesota Twins/Milwaukee Brewers .10 .25
296 Seattle Mariners/Toronto Blue Jays .10 .25
297 Tampa Bay Rays/Miami Marlins .10 .25
298 Texas Rangers/Cincinnati Reds .10 .25
300 Arizona Diamondbacks
San Diego Padres .10 .25
308 Pittsburgh Pirates
Philadelphia Phillies .10 .25

2014 Topps Stickers

1 Adam Jones .12 .30
2 Cal Ripken Jr .50 1.25
3 Nick Markakis .12 .30
4 Chris Davis .10 .25
5 J.J. Hardy .10 .25
6 Chris Tillman .10 .25
7 Kevin Gausman .15 .40
8 Manny Machado .15 .40
9 Baltimore Orioles Mascot .10 .25
10 Koji Uehara .10 .25
11 Jon Lester .10 .25
12 Xander Bogaerts .30 .75
13 Will Middlebrooks .10 .25
14 Clay Buchholz .10 .25
15 David Ortiz .15 .40
16 Dustin Pedroia .15 .40
17 Shane Victorino .12 .30
18 Wally The Green Monster .10 .25
19 Derek Jeter .40 1.00
20 Alfonso Soriano .12 .30
21 Babe Ruth .40 1.00
22 Jacoby Ellsbury .12 .30
23 Mark Teixeira .12 .30
24 Mariano Rivera .20 .50
25 CC Sabathia .12 .30
26 Carlos Beltran .12 .30
27 Brian McCann .12 .30
28 James Loney .10 .25
29 Desmond Jennings .12 .30
30 Wil Myers .10 .25
31 Alex Cobb .10 .25
32 Matt Moore .12 .30
33 Ben Zobrist .12 .30
34 Evan Longoria .12 .30
35 Chris Archer .10 .25
36 Raymond .10 .25
37 R.A. Dickey .12 .30
38 Colby Rasmus .12 .30
39 Jose Bautista .12 .30
40 Brett Lawrie .12 .30
41 Mark Buehrle .12 .30
42 Brandon Morrow .10 .25
43 Jose Reyes .12 .30
44 Edwin Encarnacion .12 .30
45 Toronto Blue Jays Mascot .10 .25
46 Avisail Garcia .12 .30
47 Alexei Ramirez .12 .30
48 John Danks .10 .25
49 Adam Eaton .10 .25
50 Chris Sale .15 .40
51 Andre Rienzo .10 .25
52 Dayan Viciedo .10 .25
53 Adam Dunn .12 .30
54 Chicago White Sox Mascot .10 .25
55 Nick Swisher .12 .30
56 Carlos Santana .12 .30
57 Justin Masterson .10 .25
58 Asdrubal Cabrera .12 .30
59 Jason Kipnis .12 .30
60 Michael Brantley .12 .30
61 Danny Salazar .12 .30
62 Michael Bourn .10 .25
63 Slider .10 .25
64 Austin Jackson .12 .30
65 Ian Kinsler .12 .30
66 Miguel Cabrera .15 .40
67 Justin Verlander .12 .30
68 Jose Iglesias .12 .30
69 Nick Castellanos .30 .75
70 Torii Hunter .12 .30
71 Max Scherzer .15 .40
72 Paws .10 .25
73 Alex Gordon .12 .30
74 Salvador Perez .12 .30
75 George Brett .30 .75
76 Eric Hosmer .12 .30
77 James Shields .10 .25
78 Billy Butler .10 .25
79 Yordano Ventura .12 .30
80 Mike Moustakas .12 .30
81 Kansas City Royals Mascot .10 .25
82 Josh Willingham .12 .30
83 Trevor Plouffe .10 .25
84 Oswaldo Arcia .10 .25
85 Brian Dozier .12 .30
86 Joe Mauer .12 .30
87 Kevin Correia .10 .25
88 Harmon Killebrew .15 .40
89 Glen Perkins .10 .25
90 TC Bear Mascot .10 .25
91 Mike Trout .75 2.00
92 David Freese .12 .30
93 Jered Weaver .12 .30
94 C.J. Wilson .12 .30
95 Albert Pujols .20 .50
96 Ernesto Frieri .10 .25
97 Howie Kendrick .10 .25
98 Josh Hamilton .12 .30
99 Erick Aybar .10 .25
100 Chris Carter .10 .25
101 Brett Oberholtzer .10 .25
102 Matt Dominguez .12 .30
103 Dexter Fowler .12 .30
104 Jose Altuve .12 .30
105 Jason Castro .10 .25
106 Jarred Cosart .12 .30
107 Jonathan Villar .10 .25
108 Orbit .10 .25
109 Coco Crisp .10 .25
110 Jim Johnson .10 .25
111 Yoenis Cespedes .15 .40
112 Josh Donaldson .12 .30
113 Jarrod Parker .10 .25
114 Sonny Gray .12 .30
115 Josh Reddick .10 .25
116 Jed Lowrie .10 .25
117 Oakland Athletics Mascot .10 .25
118 Michael Saunders .12 .30
119 Robinson Cano .12 .30
120 Hisashi Iwakuma .12 .30
121 Felix Hernandez .12 .30
122 Kyle Seager .10 .25
123 Randy Johnson .15 .40
124 Justin Smoak .10 .25
125 Taijuan Walker .10 .25
126 Mariner Moose .10 .25
127 Martin Perez .12 .30
128 Yu Darvish .15 .40
129 Jurickson Profar .12 .30
130 Prince Fielder .12 .30
131 Adrian Beltre .15 .40
132 Elvis Andrus .12 .30
133 Derek Holland .10 .25
134 Nolan Ryan .50 1.25
135 Rangers Captain .10 .25
136 Los Angeles Angels .15 .40
156 Los Angeles Dodgers
137 Baltimore Orioles .10 .25
165 Washington Nationals
138 Boston Red Sox .15 .40
152 Atlanta Braves
139 Chicago White Sox .15 .40
153 Chicago Cubs
140 Cleveland Indians .10 .25
142 Houston Astros
141 Detroit Tigers .10 .25
155 Colorado Rockies
143 Kansas City Royals .15 .40
164 St. Louis Cardinals
144 Minnesota Twins .10 .25
158 Milwaukee Brewers
145 New York Yankees .15 .40
159 New York Mets
146 Oakland Athletics .10 .25
163 San Francisco Giants
147 Seattle Mariners .10 .25
150 Toronto Blue Jays
148 Tampa Bay Rays .10 .25
157 Miami Marlins
149 Texas Rangers .10 .25
154 Cincinnati Reds
151 Arizona Diamondbacks .10 .25
162 San Diego Padres
161 Pittsburgh Pirates .10 .25
Philadelphia Phillies
166 Greg Maddux .20 .50
167 Kris Medlen .12 .30
168 Freddie Freeman .20 .50
169 Justin Upton .12 .30
170 Craig Kimbrel .10 .25
171 Jason Heyward .12 .30
172 Evan Gattis .10 .25
173 Chris Johnson .10 .25
174 Atlanta Braves Mascot .10 .25
175 Adeiny Hechavarria .10 .25
176 Jose Fernandez .15 .40
177 Steve Cishek .10 .25
178 Christian Yelich .20 .50
179 Giancarlo Stanton .15 .40
180 Henderson Alvarez .10 .25
181 Nate Eovaldi .12 .30
182 Jake Marisnick .10 .25
183 Billy The Marlin .10 .25
184 Tom Seaver .12 .30
185 David Wright .12 .30
186 Daniel Murphy .12 .30
187 Travis d'Arnaud .12 .30
188 Matt Harvey .12 .30
189 Bartolo Colon .10 .25
190 Curtis Granderson .12 .30
191 Zack Wheeler .12 .30
192 Mr Met .10 .25
193 Cole Hamels .12 .30
194 Jimmy Rollins .12 .30
195 Chase Utley .12 .30
196 Mike Schmidt .25 .60
197 Ryan Howard .12 .30
198 Cliff Lee .12 .30
199 Carlos Ruiz .10 .25
200 Domonic Brown .12 .30
201 Phillie Phanatic .10 .25
202 Bryce Harper .25 .60
203 Gio Gonzalez .12 .30
204 Ryan Zimmerman .12 .30
205 Jordan Zimmermann .12 .30
206 Anthony Rendon .15 .40
207 Stephen Strasburg .15 .40
208 Ian Desmond .10 .25
209 Jayson Werth .12 .30
210 Screech .10 .25
211 Junior Lake .10 .25
212 Nate Schierholtz .10 .25
213 Travis Wood .10 .25
214 Jeff Samardzija .10 .25
215 Anthony Rizzo .20 .50
216 Starlin Castro .12 .30
217 Darwin Barney .10 .25
218 Ernie Banks .15 .40
219 Ryne Sandberg .30 .75
220 Mat Latos .12 .30
221 Johnny Cueto .12 .30
222 Billy Hamilton .12 .30
223 Brandon Phillips .12 .30
224 Joey Votto .15 .40
225 Jay Bruce .12 .30
226 Aroldis Chapman .15 .40
227 Todd Frazier .10 .25
228 Gapper .10 .25
229 Yovani Gallardo .10 .25
230 Ryan Braun .12 .30
231 Kyle Lohse .10 .25
232 Aramis Ramirez .10 .25
233 Carlos Gomez .10 .25
234 Jim Henderson .10 .25
235 Jean Segura .12 .30
236 Robin Yount .15 .40
237 Bernie Brewer .10 .25
238 Andrew McCutchen .15 .40
239 Starling Marte .10 .25
240 Neil Walker .10 .25
241 Gerrit Cole .15 .40
242 Roberto Clemente .40 1.00
243 A.J. Burnett .10 .25
244 Pedro Alvarez .10 .25
245 Francisco Liriano .10 .25
246 Pirate Parrot .10 .25
247 Matt Holliday .12 .30
248 Michael Wacha .12 .30
249 Matt Carpenter .15 .40
250 Matt Adams .10 .25
251 Allen Craig .12 .30
252 Adam Wainwright .12 .30
253 Shelby Miller .12 .30
254 Yadier Molina .20 .50
255 Fredbird Mascot .10 .25
256 Patrick Corbin .12 .30
257 Martin Prado .12 .30
258 Mark Trumbo .12 .30
259 Paul Goldschmidt .15 .40
260 Miguel Montero .10 .25
261 Trevor Cahill .10 .25
262 Wade Miley .10 .25
263 Aaron Hill .10 .25
264 Baxter .10 .25
265 Carlos Gonzalez .12 .30
266 Jhoulys Chacin .10 .25
267 Jorge De La Rosa .10 .25
268 Troy Tulowitzki .15 .40
269 Michael Cuddyer .10 .25
270 Nolan Arenado .25 .60
271 Wilin Rosario .10 .25
272 Brett Anderson .10 .25
273 Dinger Mascot .10 .25
274 Yasiel Puig .15 .40
275 Matt Kemp .12 .30
276 Hanley Ramirez .12 .30
277 Clayton Kershaw .25 .60
278 Adrian Gonzalez .12 .30
279 Carl Crawford .12 .30
280 Zack Greinke .15 .40
281 Hyun-Jin Ryu .12 .30
282 Jackie Robinson .15 .40
283 Yonder Alonso .10 .25
284 Chase Headley .10 .25
285 Andrew Cashner .10 .25
286 Jedd Gyorko .10 .25
287 Tony Gwynn .15 .40
288 Will Venable .10 .25
289 Everth Cabrera .10 .25
290 Robbie Erlin .10 .25
291 Swinging Friar .10 .25
292 Angel Pagan .10 .25
293 Willie Mays .30 .75
294 Matt Cain .12 .30
295 Buster Posey .20 .50
296 Madison Bumgarner .12 .30
297 Tim Lincecum .12 .30
298 Hunter Pence .12 .30
299 Sergio Romo .10 .25
300 Pablo Sandoval .12 .30
301 Red Sox Puzzle .15 .40
302 Red Sox Puzzle .15 .40
303 Red Sox Puzzle .15 .40
304 Red Sox Puzzle .15 .40
305 Red Sox Puzzle .15 .40
306 Red Sox Puzzle .15 .40
307 Red Sox Puzzle .15 .40
308 Red Sox Puzzle .15 .40
309 Red Sox Puzzle .15 .40
310 Red Sox Puzzle .15 .40
311 Red Sox Puzzle .15 .40
312 Red Sox Puzzle .15 .40
313 Red Sox Puzzle .15 .40
314 Red Sox Puzzle .15 .40
315 Red Sox Puzzle .15 .40

2015 Topps Stickers

1 Topps Logo .10 .25
2 Chris Davis .10 .25
3 Jonathan Schoop .10 .25
4 Manny Machado .15 .40
5 Adam Jones .12 .30
6 Zach Britton .12 .30
7 Chris Tillman .10 .25
8 Kevin Gausman .15 .40
9 Cal Ripken Jr. .50 1.25
10 Baltimore Orioles .10 .25
Mascot
11 Mookie Betts .30 .75
12 Brock Holt .10 .25
13 Pedro Martinez .12 .30
14 Dustin Pedroia .15 .40
15 Shane Victorino .12 .30
16 Clay Buchholz .10 .25
17 David Ortiz .15 .40
18 Xander Bogaerts .15 .40
19 Wally the Green Monster .10 .25
Mascot
20 Mark Teixeira .12 .30
21 Jacoby Ellsbury .12 .30
22 Brett Gardner .12 .30
23 Michael Pineda .10 .25
24 CC Sabathia .12 .30
25 Dellin Betances .12 .30
26 Brian McCann .12 .30
27 Masahiro Tanaka .12 .30
28 Derek Jeter .40 1.00
29 Kevin Kiermaier .12 .30
30 Chris Archer .10 .25
31 Evan Longoria .12 .30
32 Yunel Escobar .10 .25
33 Matt Joyce .10 .25
34 Jake Odorizzi .10 .25
35 Alex Cobb .10 .25
36 Wade Boggs .12 .30
37 Raymond .10 .25
Mascot
38 Jose Reyes .12 .30
39 Edwin Encarnacion .15 .40
40 Jose Bautista .12 .30
41 Brett Lawrie .12 .30
42 Drew Hutchison .10 .25
43 R.A. Dickey .12 .30
44 Marcus Stroman .12 .30
45 Dioner Navarro .10 .25
46 Toronto Blue Jays .10 .25
Mascot
47 Jose Abreu .15 .40
48 John Danks .10 .25
49 Adam Eaton .10 .25
50 Chris Sale .15 .40
51 Jose Quintana .10 .25
52 Conor Gillaspie .10 .25
53 Alexei Ramirez .10 .25
54 Dayan Viciedo .10 .25
55 Frank Thomas .15 .40
56 Carlos Santana .12 .30
57 Nick Swisher .12 .30
58 Michael Brantley .12 .30
59 Jason Kipnis .12 .30
60 Corey Kluber .12 .30
61 Trevor Bauer .20 .50
62 Cody Allen .10 .25
63 Lonnie Chisenhall .10 .25
64 Roberto Alomar .12 .30
65 Miguel Cabrera .15 .40
66 Justin Verlander .15 .40
67 Ian Kinsler .12 .30
68 Nick Castellanos .15 .40
69 J.D. Martinez .15 .40
70 Max Scherzer .15 .40
71 Anibal Sanchez .10 .25
72 David Price .12 .30
73 Paws .10 .25
Mascot
74 Eric Hosmer .12 .30
75 Alcides Escobar .12 .30
76 George Brett .30 .75
77 Salvador Perez .12 .30
78 Alex Gordon .12 .30
79 Omar Infante .10 .25
80 Yordano Ventura .12 .30
81 Greg Holland .10 .25
82 Kansas City Royals .10 .25
Mascot
83 Glen Perkins .10 .25
84 Phil Hughes .10 .25
85 Joe Mauer .12 .30
86 Kennys Vargas .10 .25
87 Brian Dozier .12 .30
88 Kurt Suzuki .10 .25
89 Trevor Plouffe .10 .25
90 Eduardo Escobar .10 .25
91 Harmon Killebrew .15 .40
92 Josh Hamilton .12 .30
93 Jered Weaver .12 .30
94 Garrett Richards .12 .30
95 Albert Pujols .20 .50
96 Erick Aybar .10 .25
97 Howie Kendrick .10 .25
98 C.J. Cron .10 .25
99 Mike Trout .75 2.00
100 Rod Carew .12 .30
101 George Springer .12 .30
102 Jose Altuve .12 .30
103 Jon Singleton .12 .30
104 Dallas Keuchel .12 .30
105 Matt Dominguez .10 .25
106 Collin McHugh .10 .25
107 Dexter Fowler .12 .30
108 Jason Castro .10 .25
109 Orbit .10 .25
Mascot
110 Scott Kazmir .10 .25
111 Coco Crisp .10 .25
112 Josh Donaldson .12 .30
113 Sonny Gray .12 .30
114 Derek Norris .10 .25
115 Josh Reddick .10 .25
116 Brandon Moss .10 .25
117 Sean Doolittle .10 .25
118 Oakland Athletics .10 .25
Mascot
119 Kyle Seager .12 .30
120 Robinson Cano .12 .30
121 Dustin Ackley .10 .25
122 Felix Hernandez .12 .30
123 Hisashi Iwakuma .12 .30
124 Roenis Elias .10 .25
125 Ken Griffey Jr. .30 .75
126 Fernando Rodney .10 .25
127 Chris Young .10 .25
128 Yu Darvish .15 .40
129 Prince Fielder .12 .30
130 Elvis Andrus .12 .30
131 Adrian Beltre .15 .40
132 Shin-Soo Choo .12 .30
133 Leonys Martin .10 .25
134 Jurickson Profar .12 .30
135 Neftali Feliz .10 .25
136 Nolan Ryan .50 1.25
137 Los Angeles Angels .12 .30
157 Los Angeles Dodgers
138 Baltimore Orioles .10 .25
166 Washington Nationals
139 Boston Red Sox .12 .30
153 Atlanta Braves
140 Chicago White Sox .10 .25
154 Chicago Cubs
141 Cleveland Indians .10 .25
155 Cincinnati Reds
142 Detroit Tigers .12 .30
165 St. Louis Cardinals
143 Houston Astros .10 .25
161 Philadelphia Phillies
144 Kansas City Royals .10 .25
162 Pittsburgh Pirates
145 Minnesota Twins .10 .25
152 Arizona Diamondbacks
146 New York Yankees .12 .30
160 New York Mets
147 Oakland Athletics .10 .25
164 San Francisco Giants
148 Seattle Mariners .10 .25
156 Colorado Rockies
149 Tampa Bay Rays .10 .25
158 Miami Marlins
150 Texas Rangers .10 .25
153 San Diego Padres
151 Toronto Blue Jays .10 .25
159 Milwaukee Brewers
167 Justin Upton .12 .30
168 Evan Gattis .10 .25
169 Jason Heyward .12 .30
170 Tom Glavine .12 .30
171 Andrelton Simmons .10 .25
172 Tommy La Stella .10 .25
173 Freddie Freeman .20 .50
174 Craig Kimbrel .12 .30
175 Julio Teheran .12 .30
176 Christian Yelich .20 .50
177 Giancarlo Stanton .15 .40
178 Marcell Ozuna .15 .40
179 Garrett Jones .10 .25
180 Nathan Eovaldi .12 .30
181 Henderson Alvarez .10 .25
182 Steve Cishek .10 .25
183 Adeiny Hechavarria .10 .25
184 Billy the Marlin .10 .25
Mascot
185 David Wright .12 .30
186 Travis d'Arnaud .12 .30
187 Daniel Murphy .12 .30
188 Jonathon Niese .10 .25
189 Rafael Montero .10 .25
190 Juan Lagares .10 .25
191 Curtis Granderson .12 .30
192 Jacob deGrom .30 .75
193 Mr. Met .10 .25
Mascot
194 Cole Hamels .12 .30
195 Chase Utley .12 .30
196 Ryan Howard .12 .30
197 Jimmy Rollins .12 .30
198 Maikel Franco .12 .30
199 Carlos Ruiz .10 .25
200 Cliff Lee .12 .30
201 Jonathan Papelbon .12 .30
202 Phillie Phanatic .10 .25
Mascot

203 Bryce Harper .25 .60
204 Jayson Werth .12 .30
205 Anthony Rendon .15 .40
206 Ian Desmond .10 .25
207 Stephen Strasburg .15 .40
208 Jordan Zimmermann .12 .30
209 Doug Fister .10 .25
210 Gio Gonzalez .12 .30
211 Screech .10 .25
212 Edwin Jackson .10 .25
213 Starlin Castro .10 .25
214 Anthony Rizzo .20 .50
215 Jorge Soler .15 .40
216 Hector Rondon .10 .25
217 Jake Arrieta .12 .30
218 Javier Baez .75 2.00
219 Luis Valbuena .10 .25
220 Ernie Banks .15 .40
221 Todd Frazier .10 .25
222 Billy Hamilton .12 .30
223 Jay Bruce .12 .30
224 Joey Votto .15 .40
225 Devin Mesoraco .10 .25
226 Johnny Cueto .12 .30
227 Alfredo Simon .10 .25
228 Aroldis Chapman .15 .40
229 Johnny Bench .15 .40
230 Khris Davis .15 .40
231 Carlos Gomez .10 .25
232 Ryan Braun .12 .30
233 Scooter Gennett .12 .30
234 Jean Segura .12 .30
235 Jonathan Lucroy .12 .30
236 Paul Molitor .15 .40
237 Matt Garza .10 .25
238 Bernie Brewer Mascot .10 .25
239 Andrew McCutchen .15 .40
240 Josh Harrison .10 .25
241 Starling Marte .12 .30
242 Pedro Alvarez .10 .25
243 Gregory Polanco .12 .30
244 Mark Melancon .10 .25
245 Francisco Liriano .10 .25
246 Roberto Clemente .40 1.00
247 Pirate Parrot Mascot .10 .25
248 Matt Holliday .15 .40
249 Randal Grichuk .10 .25
250 Matt Carpenter .15 .40
251 Stan Musial .25 .60
252 Adam Wainwright .12 .30
253 Shelby Miller .12 .30
254 Michael Wacha .12 .30
255 Yadier Molina .20 .50
256 Matt Adams .10 .25
257 Paul Goldschmidt .15 .40
258 David Peralta .10 .25
259 Chris Owings .10 .25
260 Miguel Montero .10 .25
261 Chase Anderson .10 .25
262 Addison Reed .10 .25
263 Wade Miley .10 .25
264 Brad Ziegler .10 .25
265 Baxter the Bobcat Mascot .10 .25
266 Charlie Blackmon .15 .40
267 Carlos Gonzalez .12 .30
268 Corey Dickerson .12 .30
269 Nolan Arenado .25 .60
270 Justin Morneau .12 .30
271 Drew Stubbs .10 .25
272 Jorge De La Rosa .10 .25
273 Troy Tulowitzki .15 .40
274 Dinger Mascot .10 .25
275 Zack Greinke .15 .40
276 Joc Pederson .40 1.00
277 Yasiel Puig .15 .40
278 Matt Kemp .12 .30
279 Dee Gordon .10 .25
280 Mike Piazza .15 .40
281 Hyun-Jin Ryu .12 .30
282 Adrian Gonzalez .12 .30
283 Clayton Kershaw .25 .60
284 Yonder Alonso .10 .25
285 Andrew Cashner .10 .25
286 Joaquin Benoit .10 .25
287 Rene Rivera .10 .25
288 Tyson Ross .10 .25
289 Ian Kennedy .10 .25
290 Cameron Maybin .10 .25
291 Dave Winfield .12 .30
292 Swinging Friar Mascot .10 .25
293 Buster Posey .20 .50
294 Hunter Pence .12 .30
295 Tim Lincecum .12 .30
296 Brandon Crawford .12 .30
297 Madison Bumgarner .12 .30
298 Santiago Casilla .10 .25
299 Tim Hudson .12 .30
300 Gregor Blanco .10 .25
301 Willie McCovey .12 .30

2016 Topps Stickers

1 Topps Logo .10 .25
2 Mike Trout .75 2.00
3 Albert Pujols .20 .50
4 Erick Aybar .10 .25
5 David Freese .10 .25
6 Johnny Giavotella .10 .25
7 Jered Weaver .12 .30
8 Garrett Richards .12 .30
9 Hector Santiago .10 .25
10 Huston Street .10 .25
11 George Springer .12 .30
12 Carlos Gomez .10 .25
13 Carlos Correa .15 .40
14 Jose Altuve .12 .30
15 Jason Castro .10 .25
16 Evan Gattis .10 .25
17 Dallas Keuchel .12 .30
18 Lance McCullers .10 .25
19 Orbit Mascot .10 .25
20 Sonny Gray .12 .30
21 Jesse Hahn .10 .25
22 Brett Lawrie .12 .30
23 Ike Davis .10 .25
24 Billy Butler .10 .25
25 Josh Reddick .10 .25
26 Billy Burns .10 .25
27 Coco Crisp .10 .25
28 Marcus Semien .15 .40
29 Josh Donaldson .12 .30
30 Russell Martin .10 .25
31 Jose Bautista .12 .30
32 Edwin Encarnacion .15 .40
33 Troy Tulowitzki .15 .40
34 David Price .12 .30
35 Devon Travis .10 .25
36 R.A. Dickey .12 .30
37 Aaron Sanchez .12 .30
38 Michael Brantley .12 .30
39 Corey Kluber .12 .30
40 Carlos Carrasco .10 .25
41 Carlos Santana .12 .30
42 Francisco Lindor .15 .40
43 Jason Kipnis .12 .30
44 Danny Salazar .12 .30
45 Yan Gomes .10 .25
46 Slider Mascot .10 .25
47 Felix Hernandez .12 .30
48 Robinson Cano .12 .30
49 Kyle Seager .10 .25
50 Seth Smith .10 .25
51 Mark Trumbo .10 .25
52 Nelson Cruz .15 .40
53 Mike Zunino .10 .25
54 Taijuan Walker .10 .25
55 Mariner Moose .10 .25
56 Adam Jones .12 .30
57 Manny Machado .15 .40
58 J.J. Hardy .10 .25
59 Chris Davis .10 .25
60 Jonathan Schoop .10 .25
61 Chris Tillman .10 .25
62 Miguel Gonzalez .10 .25
63 Ubaldo Jimenez .10 .25
64 Zach Britton .12 .30
65 Prince Fielder .12 .30
66 Cole Hamels .12 .30
67 Adrian Beltre .15 .40
68 Elvis Andrus .12 .30
69 Delino DeShields Jr. .10 .25
70 Shin-Soo Choo .12 .30
71 Josh Hamilton .12 .30
72 Yu Darvish .15 .40
73 Rangers Captain Mascot .10 .25
74 Evan Longoria .12 .30
75 Chris Archer .10 .25
76 Steven Souza Jr. .12 .30
77 Desmond Jennings .12 .30
78 Alex Cobb .10 .25
79 Drew Smyly .10 .25
80 Jake Odorizzi .10 .25
81 Matt Moore .12 .30
82 Raymond Mascot .10 .25
83 David Ortiz .15 .40
84 Dustin Pedroia .15 .40
85 Pablo Sandoval .12 .30
86 Hanley Ramirez .12 .30
87 Xander Bogaerts .15 .40
88 Mookie Betts .30 .75
89 Eduardo Rodriguez .10 .25
90 Rick Porcello .12 .30
91 Clay Buchholz .10 .25
92 Eric Hosmer .12 .30
93 Salvador Perez .12 .30
94 Mike Moustakas .12 .30
95 Alex Gordon .12 .30
96 Lorenzo Cain .10 .25
97 Greg Holland .10 .25
98 Yordano Ventura .12 .30
99 Kendrys Morales .10 .25
100 Omar Infante .10 .25
101 Miguel Cabrera .15 .40
102 Victor Martinez .12 .30
103 Justin Verlander .15 .40
104 Ian Kinsler .12 .30
105 J.D. Martinez .15 .40
106 Daniel Norris .10 .25
107 Jose Iglesias .12 .30
108 Nick Castellanos .15 .40
109 Paws Mascot .10 .25
110 Joe Mauer .12 .30
111 Brian Dozier .12 .30
112 Trevor Plouffe .10 .25
113 Eddie Rosario .12 .30
114 Byron Buxton .15 .40
115 Glen Perkins .10 .25
116 Kurt Suzuki .10 .25
117 Phil Hughes .10 .25
118 Miguel Sano .15 .40
119 Jose Abreu .15 .40
120 Chris Sale .15 .40
121 Melky Cabrera .10 .25
122 Adam Eaton .10 .25
123 Avisail Garcia .12 .30
124 Alexei Ramirez .12 .30
125 David Robertson .10 .25
126 Carlos Rodon .15 .40
127 Adam LaRoche .10 .25
128 Jacoby Ellsbury .12 .30
129 Brett Gardner .12 .30
130 Alex Rodriguez .20 .50
131 Luis Severino .12 .30
132 Mark Teixeira .12 .30
133 Masahiro Tanaka .12 .30
134 Carlos Beltran .12 .30
135 Dellin Betances .12 .30
136 Brian McCann .12 .30
137 Tampa Bay Rays .10 .25
157 Miami Marlins
138 Los Angeles Angels .12 .30
166 Los Angeles Dodgers
139 Boston Red Sox .12 .30
153 Atlanta Braves
140 Chicago White Sox .12 .30
154 Chicago Cubs
141 Cleveland Indians .10 .25
155 Cincinnati Reds
142 Texas Rangers .10 .25
165 San Diego Padres
143 Houston Astros .10 .25
161 Philadelphia Phillies
144 Kansas City Royals .12 .30
162 St. Louis Cardinals
145 Minnesota Twins .10 .25
152 Arizona Diamondbacks
146 Baltimore Orioles .10 .25
160 Washington Nationals
147 Toronto Blue Jays .10 .25
164 Milwaukee Brewers
148 Seattle Mariners .10 .25
156 Colorado Rockies
149 New York Yankees .12 .30
158 New York Mets
150 Detroit Tigers .10 .25
163 Pittsburgh Pirates
151 Oakland Athletics .10 .25
159 San Francisco Giants
167 Freddie Freeman .20 .50
168 Andrelton Simmons .10 .25
169 Julio Teheran .12 .30
170 Matt Wisler .10 .25
171 Shelby Miller .12 .30
172 Jason Grilli .10 .25
173 Cameron Maybin .10 .25
174 Nick Markakis .12 .30
175 A.J. Pierzynski .10 .25
176 Jonathan Lucroy .12 .30
177 Wily Peralta .10 .25
178 Ryan Braun .12 .30
179 Jean Segura .12 .30
180 Scooter Gennett .12 .30
181 Adam Lind .12 .30
182 Francisco Rodriguez .12 .30
183 Matt Garza .10 .25
184 Bernie Brewer Mascot .10 .25
185 Yadier Molina .20 .50
186 Michael Wacha .12 .30
187 Jason Heyward .12 .30
188 Matt Carpenter .15 .40
189 Jhonny Peralta .10 .25
190 Kolten Wong .12 .30
191 Matt Adams .10 .25
192 Lance Lynn .10 .25
193 Adam Wainwright .12 .30
194 Kris Bryant .20 .50
195 Anthony Rizzo .20 .50
196 Addison Russell .15 .40
197 Starlin Castro .10 .25
198 Jorge Soler .15 .40
199 Jon Lester .12 .30
200 Kyle Schwarber .30 .75
201 Jake Arrieta .12 .30
202 Jason Hammel .12 .30
203 Paul Goldschmidt .15 .40
204 Yasmany Tomas .10 .25
205 Jake Lamb .10 .25
206 Chris Owings .10 .25
207 Nick Ahmed .10 .25
208 David Peralta .10 .25
209 A.J. Pollock .12 .30
210 Archie Bradley .10 .25
211 Arizona Diamondbacks Mascot .10 .25
212 Clayton Kershaw .25 .60
213 Yasiel Puig .15 .40
214 Joc Pederson .12 .30
215 Zack Greinke .15 .40
216 Adrian Gonzalez .12 .30
217 Andre Ethier .12 .30
218 Yasmani Grandal .10 .25
219 Kenley Jansen .12 .30
220 Justin Turner .15 .40
221 Buster Posey .20 .50
222 Madison Bumgarner .12 .30
223 Brandon Belt .12 .30
224 Matt Duffy .10 .25
225 Brandon Crawford .12 .30
226 Joe Panik .12 .30
227 Norichika Aoki .10 .25
228 Hunter Pence .12 .30
229 Chris Heston .10 .25
230 Giancarlo Stanton .15 .40
231 Christian Yelich .20 .50
232 Ichiro Suzuki .20 .50
233 Marcell Ozuna .15 .40
234 Dee Gordon .10 .25
235 Adeiny Hechavarria .10 .25
236 Jose Fernandez .15 .40
237 Justin Nicolino .10 .25
238 Billy the Marlin Mascot .10 .25
239 Jacob deGrom .30 .75
240 Matt Harvey .12 .30
241 Noah Syndergaard .12 .30
242 Steven Matz .10 .25
243 David Wright .12 .30
244 Michael Cuddyer .10 .25
245 Curtis Granderson .12 .30
246 Travis d'Arnaud .12 .30
247 Mr. Met Mascot .10 .25
248 Bryce Harper .25 .60
249 Max Scherzer .15 .40
250 Stephen Strasburg .15 .40
251 Gio Gonzalez .12 .30
252 Ryan Zimmerman .12 .30
253 Jayson Werth .12 .30
254 Drew Storen .10 .25
255 Anthony Rendon .15 .40
256 Yunel Escobar .10 .25
257 James Shields .10 .25
258 Craig Kimbrel .12 .30
259 Justin Upton .12 .30
260 Matt Kemp .12 .30
261 Yonder Alonso .10 .25
262 Tyson Ross .10 .25
263 Wil Myers .12 .30
264 Melvin Upton Jr. .12 .30
265 Swinging Friar Mascot .10 .25
266 Aaron Nola .20 .50
267 Ryan Howard .12 .30
268 Maikel Franco .12 .30
269 Carlos Ruiz .10 .25
270 Domonic Brown .12 .30
271 Ken Giles .10 .25
272 Freddy Galvis .10 .25
273 Odubel Herrera .12 .30
274 Phillie Phanatic Mascot .10 .25
275 Andrew McCutchen .15 .40
276 Gerrit Cole .15 .40
277 Starling Marte .12 .30
278 Josh Harrison .10 .25
279 Jung Ho Kang .10 .25
280 Francisco Liriano .10 .25
281 Gregory Polanco .12 .30
282 Mark Melancon .10 .25
283 Francisco Cervelli .10 .25
284 Joey Votto .15 .40
285 Eugenio Suarez .12 .30
286 Todd Frazier .10 .25
287 Zack Cozart .10 .25
288 Aroldis Chapman .15 .40
289 Billy Hamilton .12 .30
290 Jay Bruce .12 .30
291 Devin Mesoraco .10 .25
292 Rosie Red Mascot .10 .25
293 Jose Reyes .12 .30
294 Nolan Arenado .25 .60
295 DJ LeMahieu .15 .40
296 Justin Morneau .12 .30
297 Wilin Rosario .10 .25
298 Charlie Blackmon .15 .40
299 Brandon Barnes .10 .25
300 Carlos Gonzalez .12 .30
301 Dinger Mascot .10 .25

2017 Topps Stickers

1 Topps Logo .10 .25
2 Mike Trout .75 2.00
3 Kole Calhoun .10 .25
4 Yunel Escobar .10 .25
5 Andrelton Simmons .10 .25
6 Garrett Richards .12 .30
7 Albert Pujols .20 .50
8 Jered Weaver .12 .30
9 C.J. Cron .12 .30
10 Geovany Soto .10 .25
11 George Springer .12 .30
12 A.J. Reed .10 .25
13 Carlos Correa .15 .40
14 Jose Altuve .12 .30
15 Alex Bregman .50 1.25
16 Dallas Keuchel .12 .30
17 Evan Gattis .10 .25
18 Jason Castro .10 .25
19 Orbit Mascot .10 .25
20 Khris Davis .15 .40
21 Jake Smolinski .10 .25
22 Danny Valencia .12 .30
23 Ryon Healy .12 .30
24 Marcus Semien .15 .40
25 Stephen Vogt .12 .30
26 Sonny Gray .12 .30
27 Sean Doolittle .10 .25
28 Yonder Alonso .10 .25
29 Melvin Upton Jr. .10 .25
30 Edwin Encarnacion .15 .40
31 Justin Smoak .10 .25
32 Devon Travis .10 .25
33 Troy Tulowitzki .15 .40
34 Josh Donaldson .12 .30
35 Russell Martin .10 .25
36 Jose Bautista .12 .30
37 Marcus Stroman .12 .30
38 Tyler Naquin .15 .40
39 Lonnie Chisenhall .10 .25
40 Mike Napoli .12 .30
41 Jason Kipnis .12 .30
42 Francisco Lindor .15 .40
43 Corey Kluber .12 .30
44 Carlos Santana .12 .30
45 Michael Brantley .12 .30
46 Slider Mascot .10 .25
47 Taijuan Walker .10 .25
48 Nelson Cruz .15 .40
49 Robinson Cano .12 .30
50 Ketel Marte .12 .30
51 Kyle Seager .10 .25
52 Felix Hernandez .12 .30
53 Adam Lind .12 .30
54 Hisashi Iwakuma .12 .30
55 Mariner Moose Mascot .10 .25
56 Hyun-Soo Kim .12 .30
57 Adam Jones .12 .30
58 Mark Trumbo .10 .25
59 Chris Davis .10 .25
60 Jonathan Schoop .10 .25
61 J.J. Hardy .10 .25
62 Manny Machado .15 .40
63 Chris Tillman .10 .25
64 Pedro Alvarez .10 .25
65 Nomar Mazara .12 .30
66 Ian Desmond .10 .25
67 Jonathan Lucroy .12 .30
68 Mitch Moreland .10 .25
69 Rougned Odor .12 .30
70 Elvis Andrus .12 .30
71 Adrian Beltre .15 .40
72 Cole Hamels .12 .30
73 Rangers Captain Mascot .10 .25
74 Corey Dickerson .10 .25
75 Kevin Kiermaier .12 .30
76 Steven Souza Jr. .12 .30
77 Logan Forsythe .10 .25
78 Matt Duffy .10 .25
79 Evan Longoria .12 .30
80 Chris Archer .10 .25
81 Blake Snell .12 .30
82 Raymond Mascot .10 .25
83 David Ortiz .15 .40
84 Mookie Betts .30 .75
85 David Price .12 .30
86 Jackie Bradley Jr. .15 .40
87 Andrew Benintendi .30 .75
88 Hanley Ramirez .12 .30
89 Dustin Pedroia .15 .40
90 Xander Bogaerts .15 .40
91 Wally the Green Monster Mascot .10 .25
92 Lorenzo Cain .10 .25
93 Alex Gordon .12 .30
94 Eric Hosmer .12 .30
95 Alcides Escobar .12 .30
96 Salvador Perez .10 .25
97 Kendrys Morales .10 .25
98 Edinson Volquez .10 .25
99 Yordano Ventura .12 .30
100 Mike Moustakas .12 .30
101 J.D. Martinez .15 .40
102 Nick Castellanos .15 .40
103 Justin Upton .12 .30
104 Miguel Cabrera .15 .40
105 Ian Kinsler .12 .30
106 Justin Verlander .15 .40
107 Michael Fulmer .10 .25
108 Victor Martinez .12 .30
109 Paws Mascot .10 .25
110 Max Kepler .12 .30
111 Trevor Plouffe .10 .25
112 Joe Mauer .12 .30
113 Brian Dozier .15 .40
114 Jose Berrios .12 .30
115 Byron Buxton .15 .40
116 Ervin Santana .10 .25
117 Miguel Sano .12 .30
118 TC Bear Mascot .10 .25
119 Adam Eaton .15 .40
120 Jose Abreu .15 .40
121 Todd Frazier .10 .25
122 Chris Sale .15 .40
123 Dioner Navarro .10 .25
124 Jose Quintana .10 .25
125 Melky Cabrera .10 .25
126 Brett Lawrie .12 .30
127 Austin Jackson .10 .25
128 Aaron Judge 1.25 3.00
129 Jacoby Ellsbury .12 .30
130 Brett Gardner .12 .30
131 Starlin Castro .10 .25
132 Didi Gregorius .12 .30
133 Chase Headley .10 .25
134 Masahiro Tanaka .12 .30
135 CC Sabathia .12 .30
136 Brian McCann .12 .30
137 Tampa Bay Rays .10 .25
157 Miami Marlins
138 Los Angeles Angels .10 .25
166 Los Angeles Dodgers
139 Boston Red Sox .10 .25
153 Atlanta Braves
140 Chicago White Sox .10 .25
154 Chicago Cubs
141 Cleveland Indians .10 .25
155 Cincinnati Reds
142 Texas Rangers .10 .25
165 San Diego Padres
143 Houston Astros#161 Philadelphia Phillies .10 .25
144 Kansas City Royals .10 .25
162 St. Louis Cardinals
145 Minnesota Twins .10 .25
152 Arizona Diamondbacks
146 Baltimore Orioles .10 .25
160 Washington Nationals
147 Toronto Blue Jays .10 .25
164 Milwaukee Brewers
148 Seattle Mariners .10 .25
156 Colorado Rockies
149 New York Yankees .10 .25
158 New York Mets
150 Detroit Tigers .10 .25
163 Pittsburgh Pirates
151 Oakland Athletics .10 .25
159 San Francisco Giants
167 Matt Kemp .12 .30
168 Ender Inciarte .10 .25
169 Nick Markakis .12 .30
170 Freddie Freeman .20 .50
171 Dansby Swanson .25 .60
172 A.J. Pierzynski .10 .25
173 Mike Foltynewicz .10 .25
174 Julio Teheran .12 .30
175 Mallex Smith .10 .25
176 Kirk Nieuwenhuis .10 .25
177 Ryan Braun .12 .30
178 Keon Broxton .10 .25
179 Scooter Gennett .12 .30
180 Orlando Arcia .15 .40
181 Taylor Jungmann .10 .25
182 Will Middlebrooks .10 .25
183 Jimmy Nelson .10 .25
184 Chris Carter .10 .25
185 Stephen Piscotty .12 .30
186 Randal Grichuk .10 .25
187 Kolten Wong .12 .30
188 Matt Carpenter .15 .40
189 Matt Holliday .15 .40
190 Yadier Molina .20 .50
191 Adam Wainwright .12 .30
192 Matt Adams .10 .25
193 Fredbird Mascot .10 .25
194 Kris Bryant .20 .50
195 Jason Heyward .12 .30
196 Dexter Fowler .12 .30
197 Addison Russell .15 .40
198 Anthony Rizzo .20 .50
199 Jake Arrieta .12 .30
200 Willson Contreras .15 .40
201 Ben Zobrist .12 .30
202 Clark Mascot .10 .25
203 Socrates Brito .10 .25
204 Michael Bourn .10 .25
205 Brandon Drury .10 .25
206 Paul Goldschmidt .15 .40
207 Jean Segura .12 .30
208 David Peralta .10 .25
209 Jake Lamb .12 .30
210 A.J. Pollock .10 .25
211 Zack Greinke .15 .40
212 Clayton Kershaw .25 .60
213 Josh Reddick .10 .25
214 Joc Pederson .12 .30
215 Howie Kendrick .10 .25
216 Adrian Gonzalez .12 .30
217 Corey Seager .15 .40
218 Justin Turner .15 .40
219 Kenta Maeda .12 .30
220 Yasmani Grandal .10 .25
221 Buster Posey .20 .50
222 Hunter Pence .12 .30
223 Denard Span .10 .25
224 Angel Pagan .10 .25
225 Brandon Belt .12 .30
226 Joe Panik .12 .30
227 Brandon Crawford .12 .30
228 Madison Bumgarner .12 .30
229 Johnny Cueto .12 .30
230 Ichiro .20 .50
231 Marcell Ozuna .15 .40
232 Christian Yelich .20 .50
233 Dee Gordon .10 .25
234 Martin Prado .10 .25
235 Adam Conley .10 .25
236 J.T. Realmuto .15 .40
237 Giancarlo Stanton .15 .40
238 Billy the Marlin Mascot .10 .25
239 Jay Bruce .12 .30
240 Lucas Duda .12 .30
241 Noah Syndergaard .12 .30
242 Curtis Granderson .12 .30
243 Neil Walker .10 .25
244 Jose Reyes .12 .30
245 Wilmer Flores .12 .30
246 Yoenis Cespedes .15 .40
247 Mr. Met Mascot .10 .25
248 Bryce Harper .25 .60
249 Stephen Strasburg .15 .40
250 Ben Revere .10 .25
251 Jayson Werth .12 .30
252 Clint Robinson .10 .25
253 Daniel Murphy .12 .30
254 Danny Espinosa .10 .25
255 Anthony Rendon .15 .40
256 Max Scherzer .15 .40
257 Wil Myers .12 .30
258 Derek Norris .10 .25
259 Tyson Ross .10 .25
260 Hunter Renfroe .12 .30
261 Yangervis Solarte .10 .25
262 Cory Spangenberg .10 .25
263 Jon Jay .10 .25
264 Jarred Cosart .10 .25
265 Swinging Friar Mascot .10 .25
266 Peter Bourjos .10 .25
267 Odubel Herrera .12 .30
268 Ryan Howard .12 .30
269 Freddy Galvis .10 .25
270 Maikel Franco .12 .30
271 Cameron Rupp .10 .25
272 Jeremy Hellickson .10 .25
273 Aaron Nola .12 .30
274 Phillie Phanatic Mascot .10 .25
275 Andrew McCutchen .15 .40
276 Gregory Polanco .12 .30
277 Starling Marte .12 .30
278 John Jaso .10 .25
279 Josh Harrison .10 .25
280 Jung Ho Kang .10 .25
281 Francisco Cervelli .10 .25
282 Gerrit Cole .15 .40
283 Pirate Parrot Mascot .10 .25
284 Adam Duvall .12 .30
285 Billy Hamilton .12 .30
286 Devin Mesoraco .10 .25
287 Joey Votto .15 .40
288 Brandon Phillips .10 .25
289 Zack Cozart .10 .25
290 Jose Peraza .12 .30
291 Raisel Iglesias .12 .30
292 Mr. Red Mascot .10 .25
293 Trevor Story .15 .40
294 Carlos Gonzalez .12 .30
295 Charlie Blackmon .15 .40
296 David Dahl .12 .30
297 DJ LeMahieu .15 .40
298 Nolan Arenado .25 .60
299 Nick Hundley .10 .25
300 Jorge De La Rosa .10 .25
301 Dinger Mascot .10 .25

2018 Topps Stickers

1 Aaron Judge .40 1.00
2 Andrelton Simmons .10 .25
3 Yunel Escobar .10 .25
4 Mike Trout .75 2.00
5 Matt Shoemaker .12 .30
6 Albert Pujols .20 .50
7 Kole Calhoun .10 .25
8 Martin Maldonado .10 .25
9 C.J. Cron .10 .25
10 J.C. Ramirez .10 .25
11 Alex Bregman .15 .40
12 George Springer .12 .30
13 Brian McCann .12 .30
14 Carlos Correa .15 .40
15 Derek Fisher .10 .25
16 Orbit Mascot .10 .25
17 Jose Altuve .12 .30
18 Yulieski Gurriel .12 .30
19 Dallas Keuchel .12 .30
20 Matt Joyce .10 .25
21 Boog Powell .10 .25
22 Jharel Cotton .10 .25
23 Khris Davis .15 .40
24 Marcus Semien .15 .40
25 Sean Manaea .12 .30
26 Bruce Maxwell .10 .25
27 Ryon Healy .12 .30
28 Jed Lowrie .10 .25
29 Kendrys Morales .10 .25
30 Russell Martin .10 .25
31 Marcus Stroman .12 .30
32 Josh Donaldson .12 .30
33 Justin Smoak .10 .25
34 Kevin Pillar .10 .25
35 Jose Bautista .12 .30
36 Troy Tulowitzki .15 .40
37 Francisco Lindor .15 .40
38 Jose Ramirez .12 .30
39 Corey Kluber .12 .30
40 Edwin Encarnacion .15 .40
41 Carlos Santana .12 .30
42 Jason Kipnis .12 .30
43 Bradley Zimmer .10 .25
44 Yan Gomes .15 .40
45 Michael Brantley .12 .30
46 Jean Segura .10 .25
47 Robinson Cano .12 .30
48 Mariner Moose Mascot .10 .25
49 Nelson Cruz .15 .40
50 Kyle Seager .10 .25
51 Mitch Haniger .12 .30
52 Jarrod Dyson .10 .25
53 Felix Hernandez .12 .30
54 Danny Valencia .10 .25
55 Manny Machado .15 .40
56 Welington Castillo .10 .25
57 Chris Davis .10 .25
58 Adam Jones .12 .30
59 Jonathan Schoop .10 .25
60 Mark Trumbo .10 .25
61 Dylan Bundy .12 .30
62 J.J. Hardy .10 .25
63 Trey Mancini .12 .30
64 Adrian Beltre .15 .40
65 Rougned Odor .12 .30
66 Delino DeShields .10 .25
67 Elvis Andrus .12 .30
68 Andrew Cashner .10 .25
69 Mike Napoli .10 .25
70 Joey Gallo .12 .30
71 Carlos Gomez .10 .25
72 Nomar Mazara .12 .30
73 Alex Cobb .10 .25
74 Raymond Mascot .10 .25
75 Logan Morrison .10 .25
76 Kevin Kiermaier .12 .30
77 Evan Longoria .12 .30
78 Brad Miller .12 .30
79 Steven Souza Jr. .12 .30
80 Corey Dickerson .10 .25
81 Chris Archer .10 .25
82 Andrew Benintendi .15 .40
83 David Price .12 .30
84 Dustin Pedroia .15 .40
85 Hanley Ramirez .12 .30
86 Chris Sale .15 .40
87 Xander Bogaerts .15 .40
88 Jackie Bradley Jr. .15 .40
89 Mitch Moreland .10 .25
90 Mookie Betts .30 .75
91 Eric Hosmer .12 .30
92 Alcides Escobar .12 .30
93 Sluggerr Mascot .10 .25
94 Mike Moustakas .12 .30
95 Jason Vargas .10 .25
96 Brandon Moss .10 .25
97 Alex Gordon .12 .30
98 Salvador Perez .12 .30
99 Lorenzo Cain .10 .25
100 Mikie Mahtook .10 .25
101 Jordan Zimmermann .12 .30
102 Jose Iglesias .12 .30
103 Ian Kinsler .12 .30
104 Michael Fulmer .10 .25
105 James McCann .12 .30
106 Victor Martinez .12 .30
107 Miguel Cabrera .15 .40
108 Nick Castellanos .15 .40
109 Joe Mauer .12 .30
110 Robbie Grossman .10 .25
111 Byron Buxton .15 .40
112 Jason Castro .10 .25
113 Max Kepler .12 .30
114 Eddie Rosario .15 .40
115 Ervin Santana .10 .25
116 Brian Dozier .12 .30
117 Miguel Sano .12 .30
118 Yolmer Sanchez .10 .25
119 Jose Abreu .15 .40
120 Avisail Garcia .12 .30
121 Tim Anderson .15 .40
122 Omar Narvaez .12 .30
123 Leury Garcia .10 .25
124 Derek Holland .10 .25
125 James Shields .10 .25
126 Yoan Moncada .15 .40
127 Luis Severino .12 .30
128 Chase Headley .10 .25
129 Jacoby Ellsbury .12 .30
130 Matt Holliday .15 .40
131 Clint Frazier .20 .50
132 Aaron Sanchez .12 .30
133 Didi Gregorius .12 .30
134 Gary Sanchez .15 .40
135 Masahiro Tanaka .12 .30
136 Starlin Castro .10 .25
137 Tampa Bay Rays .10 .25
157 Miami Marlins
138 Los Angeles Angels .10 .25
166 Los Angeles Dodgers
139 Boston Red Sox .10 .25
153 Atlanta Braves
140 Chicago White Sox .10 .25
154 Chicago Cubs
141 Cleveland Indians .10 .25
155 Cincinnati Reds
142 Texas Rangers .10 .25
165 San Diego Padres
143 Houston Astros .10 .25
161 Philadelphia Phillies
144 Kansas City Royals .10 .25
162 St. Louis Cardinals
145 Minnesota Twins .10 .25

152 Arizona Diamondbacks
146 Baltimore Orioles .10 .25
160 Washington Nationals
147 Toronto Blue Jays .10 .25
164 Milwaukee Brewers
148 Seattle Mariners .10 .25
156 Colorado Rockies
149 New York Yankees .10 .25
158 New York Mets
150 Detroit Tigers .10 .25
163 Pittsburgh Pirates
151 Oakland Athletics .10 .25
159 San Francisco Giants
167 Dansby Swanson .15 .40
168 Sean Newcomb .12 .30
169 Ozzie Albies .30 .75
170 Freddie Freeman .20 .50
171 Tyler Flowers .10 .25
172 Julio Teheran .12 .30
173 Matt Kemp .12 .30
174 Ender Inciarte .10 .25
175 Matt Adams .10 .25
176 Ryan Braun .12 .30
177 Lewis Brinson .10 .25
178 Eric Thames .12 .30
179 Keon Broxton .10 .25
180 Bernie Brewer .10 .25
Mascot
181 Orlando Arcia .10 .25
182 Travis Shaw .10 .25
183 Zach Davies .10 .25
184 Jonathan Villar .10 .25
185 Randal Grichuk .10 .25
186 Jedd Gyorko .10 .25
187 Yadier Molina .20 .50
188 Stephen Piscotty .10 .25
189 Aledmys Diaz .12 .30
190 Dexter Fowler .12 .30
191 Matt Carpenter .15 .40
192 Kolten Wong .12 .30
193 Carlos Martinez .12 .30
194 Kris Bryant .20 .50
195 Anthony Rizzo .20 .50
196 Willson Contreras .15 .40
197 Jason Heyward .12 .30
198 Addison Russell .12 .30
199 Ian Happ .12 .30
200 Jon Lester .12 .30
201 Javier Baez .20 .50
202 Kyle Schwarber .15 .40
203 Zack Greinke .15 .40
204 Paul Goldschmidt .15 .40
205 Brandon Drury .10 .25
206 Nick Ahmed .10 .25
207 A.J. Pollock .10 .25
208 Jake Lamb .12 .30
209 Yasmany Tomas .10 .25
210 Jeff Mathis .12 .30
211 Robbie Ray .10 .25
212 Kenta Maeda .12 .30
213 Yasiel Puig .15 .40
214 Corey Seager .15 .40
215 Yasmani Grandal .10 .25
216 Adrian Gonzalez .12 .30
217 Justin Turner .15 .40
218 Clayton Kershaw .25 .60
219 Joc Pederson .12 .30
220 Cody Bellinger .30 .75
221 Brandon Belt .12 .30
222 Joe Panik .12 .30
223 Denard Span .10 .25
224 Hunter Pence .12 .30
225 Brandon Crawford .12 .30
226 Ty Blach .10 .25
227 Buster Posey .20 .50
228 Matt Moore .12 .30
229 Christian Arroyo .10 .25
230 Derek Dietrich .12 .30
231 Edinson Volquez .10 .25
232 Giancarlo Stanton .15 .40
233 Justin Bour .10 .25
234 Christian Yelich .20 .50
235 Marcell Ozuna .15 .40
236 Dee Gordon .10 .25
237 J.T. Realmuto .15 .40
238 Billy the Marlin .10 .25
Mascot
239 Noah Syndergaard .12 .30
240 Mr. Met .10 .25
Mascot
241 Yoenis Cespedes .15 .40
242 Travis d'Arnaud .12 .30
243 Asdrubal Cabrera .12 .30
244 Jacob deGrom .30 .75
245 Amed Rosario .12 .30
246 Michael Conforto .12 .30
247 Wilmer Flores .12 .30
248 Screech .10 .25
Mascot
249 Ryan Zimmerman .12 .30
250 Trea Turner .12 .30
251 Anthony Rendon .15 .40
252 Bryce Harper .25 .60
253 Gio Gonzalez .12 .30
254 Michael Taylor .10 .25
255 Daniel Murphy .12 .30
256 Max Scherzer .15 .40
257 Cory Spangenberg .10 .25
258 Allen Cordoba .10 .25
259 Manny Margot .10 .25
260 Yangervis Solarte .10 .25
261 Austin Hedges .10 .25
262 Erick Aybar .10 .25
263 Clayton Richard .10 .25
264 Wil Myers .12 .30
265 Hunter Renfroe .10 .25
266 Aaron Altherr .10 .25
267 Freddy Galvis .10 .25
268 Jerad Eickhoff .10 .25
269 Odubel Herrera .12 .30
270 Cameron Rupp .10 .25
271 Maikel Franco .12 .30
272 Tommy Joseph .15 .40
273 Phillie Phanatic .10 .25
Mascot
274 Aaron Nola .12 .30
275 Andrew McCutchen .15 .40
276 Adam Frazier .10 .25
277 Josh Harrison .10 .25
278 Francisco Cervelli .10 .25
279 David Freese .10 .25
280 Josh Bell .12 .30
281 Gerrit Cole .15 .40
282 Gregory Polanco .12 .30
283 Jordy Mercer .10 .25
284 Mr. Redlegs .10 .25
Mascot
285 Scooter Gennett .12 .30
286 Zack Cozart .10 .25
287 Adam Duvall .12 .30
288 Tucker Barnhart .10 .25
289 Billy Hamilton .12 .30
290 Amir Garrett .10 .25
291 Jose Peraza .12 .30
292 Joey Votto .15 .40
293 Charlie Blackmon .15 .40
294 Trevor Story .15 .40
295 DJ LeMahieu .15 .40
296 Carlos Gonzalez .12 .30
297 Kyle Freeland .12 .30
298 Nolan Arenado .25 .60
299 Ian Desmond .10 .25
300 Mark Reynolds .10 .25
301 Tony Wolters .10 .25

2019 Topps Stickers

1 Mookie Betts .30 .75
2 AL MVP TRPH .12 .30
178 NL MVP
Adam Jones
3 Steve Pearce WSH .15 .40
Steven Matz
4 Chris Sale WSH .40 1.00
Eloy Jimenez
5 World Series TRPH .12 .30
6 World Series MVP TRPH
Odubel Herrera
7 Red Sox Celebration p1 .12 .30
Jake Arrieta
8 Red Sox Celebration p2 .12 .30
Tim Beckham
9 Mookie Betts SFF .30 .75
Tyler White
10 Aaron Judge SFF .40 1.00
Luis Severino
11 Javier Baez SFF .20 .50
Brandon Crawford
12 Jose Altuve SFF .12 .30
Mike Clevinger
13 Khris Davis SFF .15 .40
J.A. Happ
14 Josh Harrison SFF .12 .30
Nick Markakis
15 Trey Mancini .30 .75
Mookie Betts
16 Dylan Bundy .12 .30
Jose Ramirez
17 Orioles MASCOT .15 .40
20 Wally The Green Monster MASCOT
27 White Sox MASCOT
30 Slider MASCOT
Miguel Cabrera
18 Jonathan Villar .75 2.00
Mike Trout
19 Cedric Mullins .20 .50
Francisco Lindor
21 David Price .15 .40
J.D. Martinez
22 Andrew Benintendi .15 .40
Trea Turner
23 Chris Sale .15 .40
Max Scherzer
24 Dustin Pedroia .15 .40
Manny Machado
25 Yoan Moncada .15 .40
Corey Kluber
26 Jose Abreu .15 .40
Paul Goldschmidt
28 Tim Anderson .15 .40
Alex Bregman
29 Yonder Alonso .15 .40
Andrew Benintendi
31 Francisco Lindor .25 .60
Bryce Harper
32 Jose Ramirez .20 .50
Christian Yelich
33 Corey Kluber .12 .30
Jose Altuve
34 Carlos Santana .20 .50
Freddie Freeman
35 Nicholas Castellanos .15 .40
Giancarlo Stanton
36 Christin Stewart .20 .50
Javier Baez
37 Paws MASCOT .10 .25
40 Orbit MASCOT
57 Sluggerrr MASCOT
67 TC Bear MASCOT
Michael Fulmer
38 Michael Fulmer .25 .60
Clayton Kershaw
39 Miguel Cabrera .75 2.00
Ronald Acuna Jr.
41 Jose Altuve .12 .30
42 Justin Verlander .15 .40
Justin Verlander
43 Carlos Correa .15 .40
Aaron Nola
44 Alex Bregman .15 .40
Eddie Rosario
45 Mike Trout AS .75 2.00
Adam Eaton
46 Mookie Betts AS .30 .75
Kyle Hendricks
47 Aaron Judge AS .40 1.00
Carlos Rodon
48 Chris Sale AS .15 .40
Miles Mikolas
49 Bryce Harper AS .25 .60
Billy Hamilton
50 Javier Baez AS .20 .50
Nathan Eovaldi
51 Jacob deGrom AS .30 .75
Steve Pearce
52 Max Scherzer AS .15 .40
Trey Mancini
53 Bryce Harper HRD .25 .60
Rick Porcello
54 Aaron Judge HRD .40 1.00
Jose Quintana
55 Giancarlo Stanton HRD .15 .40
Gary Sanchez
56 Todd Frazier HRD .12 .30
Joey Wendle
58 Salvador Perez .20 .50
Anthony Rizzo
59 Whit Merrifield .15 .40
Nelson Cruz
60 Alex Gordon .50 1.25
Juan Soto
61 Brett Phillips .15 .40
Charlie Blackmon
62 Mike Trout .75 2.00
Aaron Judge
63 Shohei Ohtani .25 .60
Khris Davis
64 AL Jackie Robinson TRPH .10 .25
141 NL Jackie Robinson TRPH
Andrelton Simmons
65 Justin Upton .15 .40
Anthony Rendon
66 Albert Pujols .20 .50
Whit Merrifield
68 Byron Buxton .15 .40
Chris Sale
69 Eddie Rosario .15 .40
Edwin Encarnacion
70 Jose Berrios .12 .30
George Springer
71 Miguel Sano .15 .40
Jean Segura
72 Aaron Judge .40 1.00
Jacob deGrom
73 Gleyber Torres .30 .75
Kris Bryant
74 Luis Severino .15 .40
Matt Carpenter
75 Giancarlo Stanton .15 .40
Justin Upton
76 Athletics MASCOT .12 .30
83 Mariner Moose MASCOT
91 Raymond MASCOT
94 Rangers Captain MASCOT
Felix Hernandez
77 Khris Davis .15 .40
Carlos Correa
78 Matt Olson .15 .40
Jose Abreu
79 Matt Chapman .15 .40
Blake Snell
80 Stephen Piscotty .10 .25
Tommy Pham
81 Dee Gordon .12 .30
Eugenio Suarez
82 Mitch Haniger .12 .30
Starling Marte
84 Kyle Seager .15 .40
Gerrit Cole
85 Felix Hernandez .12 .30
Mitch Haniger
86 AL Cy Young TRPH .25 .60
196 NL Cy Young
Shohei Ohtani
87 Blake Snell .12 .30
Scooter Gennett
88 Tommy Pham .20 .50
Rhys Hoskins
89 Willy Adames .15 .40
Joey Votto
90 Kevin Kiermaier .15 .40
Zack Greinke
92 Elvis Andrus .15 .40
Ozzie Albies
93 Rougned Odor .12 .30
A.J. Pollock
95 Joey Gallo .12 .30
Noah Syndergaard
96 Nomar Mazara .10 .25
Lorenzo Cain
97 Blue Jays MASCOT .20 .50
138 Diamondbacks MASCOT
146 Blooper MASCOT
149 Clark MASCOT
Ichiro
98 Aaron Sanchez .12 .30
Carlos Carrasco
99 Marcus Stroman .12 .30
Cole Hamels
100 Lourdes Gurriel Jr. .15 .40
Justin Turner
101 Justin Smoak .15 .40
Nicholas Castellanos
102 Gleyber Torres RRS .30 .75
Chris Taylor
103 Miguel Andujar RRS .15 .40
Eric Hosmer
104 Shohei Ohtani RRS .25 .60
Ian Kinsler
105 Vladimir Guerrero Jr. RRS .60 1.50
Corey Dickerson
106 Michael Kopech RRS .30 .75
Kyle Freeland
107 Justus Sheffield RRS .15 .40
Ronald Torreyes
108 Rafael Devers RRS .20 .50
Josh Donaldson
109 Eloy Jimenez RRS .40 1.00
Albert Pujols
110 Jackie Robinson 150 YRS .15 .40
Jake Odorizzi
111 Babe Ruth 150 YRS .40 1.00
Harrison Bader
112 Hank Aaron 150 YRS .30 .75
Justin Bour
113 Mookie Betts p1 .30 .75
Hunter Renfroe
114 Jose Altuve p2 .12 .30
C.J. Cron
115 Cal Ripken Jr. 150 YRS .50 1.25
Lourdes Gurriel Jr.
116 Carl Yastrzemski 150 YRS .25 .60
Lewis Brinson
117 Sandy Koufax 150 YRS .30 .75
Michael Taylor
118 Anthony Rizzo p1 .20 .50
Lance McCullers Jr.
119 Bryce Harper p2 .25 .60
Jon Gray
120 Khris Davis LL .30 .75
122 Mookie Betts LL
Brad Hand
121 Nolan Arenado LL .25 .60
123 Christian Yelich LL
Amed Rosario
124 Whit Merrifield LL .15 .40
126 J.D. Martinez LL
Carlos Santana
125 Trea Turner LL .20 .50
126 Javier Baez LL
Alex Wood
128 Blake Snell LL .12 .30
130 Blake Snell LL
Dallas Keuchel
129 Jacob deGrom LL .30 .75
131 Max Scherzer LL
Jake Bauers
132 Justin Verlander LL .15 .40
134 Edwin Diaz LL
Michael Wacha
133 Max Scherzer LL .15 .40
135 Wade Davis LL
Zack Godley
136 David Peralta .12 .30
Max Muncy
137 Archie Bradley .15 .40
Jack Flaherty
139 Zack Greinke .30 .75
Cody Bellinger
140 Jake Lamb .12 .30
Dee Gordon
142 Ronald Acuna Jr. .75 2.00
Travis Shaw
143 Ozzie Albies ALB .15 .40
144 Dansby Swanson .15 .40
James Paxton
145 Freddie Freeman .20 .50
Daniel Murphy
147 Kris Bryant .20 .50
Joey Gallo
148 Javier Baez .20 .50
Jesus Aguilar
150 Anthony Rizzo .20 .50
Xander Bogaerts
151 Kyle Schwarber .15 .40
Rougned Odor
152 Rosie Red MASCOT .12 .30
157 Mr. Redlegs MASCOT
166 Dinger MASCOT
175 Billy the Marlin MASCOT
Ryan Zimmerman
153 Joey Votto .30 .75
Gleyber Torres
154 Matt Kemp .12 .30
Nomar Mazara
155 Scooter Gennett .15 .40
Andrew McCutchen
156 Eugenio Suarez .15 .40
DJ LeMahieu
158 Justin Turner GIRI .15 .40
Kyle Seager
159 Francisco Lindor GIRI .15 .40
Matt Olson
160 J.D. Martinez GIRI .15 .40
Ross Stripling
161 Ronald Acuna Jr. GIRI .75 2.00
Josh Hader
162 Joey Votto GIRI .15 .40
Masahiro Tanaka
163 Jose Altuve GIRI .12 .30
Mike Fiers
164 Nolan Arenado .25 .60
Edwin Diaz
165 Charlie Blackmon .15 .40
Craig Kimbrel
167 Daniel Murphy .12 .30
Robinson Cano
168 Trevor Story .15 .40
Tim Anderson
169 Cody Bellinger .30 .75
Mike Moustakas
170 Clayton Kershaw .25 .60
Elvis Andrus
171 Justin Turner .15 .40
David Price
172 Corey Seager .15 .40
Michael Brantley
173 Brian Anderson .10 .25
Jonathan Schoop
174 Starlin Castro .15 .40
J.T. Realmuto
176 Jose Urena .15 .40
Marcell Ozuna
177 Lewis Brinson .15 .40
Charlie Morton
179 Christian Yelich ALB .20 .50
180 Ryan Braun .12 .30
Jon Lester
181 Lorenzo Cain .12 .30
Ben Zobrist
182 Mike Moustakas .20 .50
Walker Buehler
183 Bernie Brewer MASCOT .10 .25
197 Mr. Met MASCOT
200 Phillie Phanatic MASCOT
207 Pirate Parrot MASCOT
Stephen Piscotty
184 Bryce Harper p1 .25 .60
Chris Archer
185 Bryce Harper p2 .25 .60
Nolan Arenado
186 Aaron Judge HRH .40 1.00
Jordan Hicks
187 Mike Trout HRH .75 2.00
Jakob Junis
188 Giancarlo Stanton HRH .15 .40
Wade Davis
189 Miguel Cabrera HRH .15 .40
Willson Contreras
190 J.D. Martinez HRH .20 .50
Yadier Molina
191 Nolan Arenado HRH .25 .60
Brett Gardner
192 Kris Bryant p1 .20 .50
Adalberto Mondesi
193 Kris Bryant p2 1.50 4.00
Fernando Tatis Jr.
194 Noah Syndergaard .12 .30
Blake Treinen
195 Jacob deGrom .30 .75
Stephen Strasburg
198 Yoenis Cespedes .15 .40
Kyle Schwarber
199 Michael Conforto .15 .40
Yoan Moncada
201 Rhys Hoskins .20 .50
Matt Kemp
202 Bryce Harper .25 .60
Jose Martinez
203 Jake Arrieta .15 .40
Miguel Andujar
204 Aaron Nola .12 .30
Wil Myers
205 Josh Bell .12 .30
Ian Desmond
206 Starling Marte .12 .30
Kenley Jansen
208 Gregory Polanco .15 .40
Mike Foltynewicz
209 Chris Archer .10 .25
Ender Inciarte
210 Swinging Friar MASCOT .12 .30
227 Fredbird MASCOT
234 Screech MASCOT
Jason Heyward
211 Hunter Renfroe .12 .30
Jose Berrios
212 Eric Hosmer .15 .40
Austin Meadows
213 Manny Machado .15 .40
Matt Chapman
214 Wil Myers .12 .30
Didi Gregorius
215 Juan Soto RRS .50 1.25
Max Kepler
216 Ronald Acuna Jr. RRS .75 2.00
Jose Urena
217 Rhys Hoskins RRS .20 .50
Brandon Woodruff
218 Ozzie Albies RRS .15 .40
Jackie Bradley Jr.
219 Fernando Tatis Jr. RRS 1.50 4.00
Dustin Fowler
220 Victor Robles RRS .20 .50
Evan Longoria
221 Luis Urias RRS .15 .40
Brandon Nimmo
222 Pete Alonso RRS .75 2.00
Victor Robles
223 Buster Posey .20 .50
Jed Lowrie
224 Brandon Crawford .12 .30
Brandon Belt
225 Brandon Belt .12 .30
Jonathan Villar
226 Evan Longoria .12 .30
Zack Wheeler
228 Matt Carpenter .15 .40
Robbie Ray
229 Yadier Molina .20 .50
Paul DeJong
230 Marcell Ozuna .15 .40
David Peralta
231 Paul DeJong .15 .40
Yasiel Puig
232 Juan Soto .50 1.25
Kevin Gausman
233 Trea Turner .12 .30
Justin Smoak
235 Max Scherzer .20 .50
Trevor Bauer
236 Stephen Strasburg .15 .40
Aaron Hicks

2019 Topps Stickers Cards

2 Adam Jones .12 .30
3 Steven Matz .10 .25
4 Eloy Jimenez .40 1.00
5 Odubel Herrera .12 .30
7 Jake Arrieta .12 .30
8 Tim Beckham .12 .30
9 Tyler White .10 .25
10 Luis Severino .12 .30
11 Brandon Crawford .12 .30
12 Mike Clevinger .12 .30
13 J.A. Happ .12 .30
14 Nick Markakis .12 .30
15 Mookie Betts .30 .75
16 Jose Ramirez .12 .30
17 Miguel Cabrera .15 .40
18 Mike Trout .75 2.00
19 Francisco Lindor .15 .40
21 J.D. Martinez .15 .40
22 Trea Turner .12 .30
23 Max Scherzer .15 .40
24 Manny Machado .15 .40
25 Corey Kluber .12 .30
26 Paul Goldschmidt .15 .40
28 Alex Bregman .15 .40
29 Andrew Benintendi .15 .40
31 Bryce Harper .25 .60
32 Christian Yelich .20 .50
33 Jose Altuve .12 .30
34 Freddie Freeman .20 .50
35 Giancarlo Stanton .15 .40
36 Javier Baez .20 .50
37 Michael Fulmer .10 .25
38 Clayton Kershaw .25 .60
39 Ronald Acuna Jr. .75 2.00
42 Justin Verlander .15 .40
43 Aaron Nola .12 .30
44 Eddie Rosario .12 .30
45 Adam Eaton .15 .40
46 Kyle Hendricks .15 .40
47 Carlos Rodon .15 .40
48 Miles Mikolas .15 .40
49 Billy Hamilton .12 .30
50 Nathan Eovaldi .12 .30
51 Steve Pearce .15 .40
52 Trey Mancini .12 .30
53 Rick Porcello .12 .30
54 Jose Quintana .10 .25
55 Gary Sanchez .15 .40
56 Joey Wendle .12 .30
58 Anthony Rizzo .20 .50
59 Nelson Cruz .15 .40
60 Juan Soto .50 1.25
61 Charlie Blackmon .15 .40
62 Aaron Judge .40 1.00
63 Khris Davis .15 .40
64 Andrelton Simmons .10 .25
65 Anthony Rendon .15 .40
66 Whit Merrifield .15 .40
68 Chris Sale .15 .40
69 Edwin Encarnacion .15 .40
70 George Springer .12 .30
71 Jean Segura .15 .40
72 Jacob deGrom .30 .75
73 Kris Bryant .20 .50
74 Matt Carpenter .15 .40
75 Justin Upton .12 .30
76 Felix Hernandez .12 .30
77 Carlos Correa .15 .40
78 Jose Abreu .15 .40
79 Blake Snell .12 .30
80 Tommy Pham .10 .25
81 Eugenio Suarez .12 .30
82 Starling Marte .12 .30
84 Gerrit Cole .15 .40
85 Mitch Haniger .12 .30
86 Shohei Ohtani .25 .60
87 Scooter Gennett .12 .30
88 Rhys Hoskins .20 .50
89 Joey Votto .15 .40
90 Zack Greinke .15 .40
92 Ozzie Albies .15 .40
93 A.J. Pollock .10 .25
95 Noah Syndergaard .12 .30
96 Lorenzo Cain .10 .25
97 Ichiro .20 .50
98 Carlos Carrasco .10 .25
99 Cole Hamels .12 .30
100 Justin Turner .15 .40
101 Nicholas Castellanos .15 .40
102 Chris Taylor .12 .30
103 Eric Hosmer .12 .30
104 Ian Kinsler .12 .30
105 Corey Dickerson .10 .25
106 Kyle Freeland .12 .30
107 Ronald Torreyes .10 .25
108 Josh Donaldson .12 .30
109 Albert Pujols .20 .50
110 Jake Odorizzi .10 .25
111 Harrison Bader .12 .30
112 Justin Bour .10 .25
113 Hunter Renfroe .10 .25
114 C.J. Cron .10 .25
115 Lourdes Gurriel Jr. .12 .30
116 Lewis Brinson .10 .25
117 Michael Taylor .10 .25
118 Lance McCullers Jr. .10 .25
119 Jon Gray .10 .25
120 Brad Hand .10 .25
121 Amed Rosario .12 .30
124 Carlos Santana .12 .30
125 Alex Wood .10 .25
128 Dallas Keuchel .12 .30
129 Jake Bauers .15 .40
132 Michael Wacha .12 .30
133 Zack Godley .10 .25
136 Max Muncy .12 .30
137 Jack Flaherty .15 .40
139 Cody Bellinger .30 .75
140 Dee Gordon .10 .25
142 Travis Shaw .10 .25
144 James Paxton .12 .30
145 Daniel Murphy .12 .30
147 Joey Gallo .12 .30
148 Jesus Aguilar .12 .30
150 Xander Bogaerts .15 .40
151 Rougned Odor .12 .30
152 Ryan Zimmerman .12 .30
153 Gleyber Torres .30 .75
154 Nomar Mazara .10 .25
155 Andrew McCutchen .15 .40
156 DJ LeMahieu .15 .40
158 Kyle Seager .10 .25
159 Matt Olson .15 .40
160 Ross Stripling .10 .25
161 Josh Hader .12 .30
162 Masahiro Tanaka .12 .30
163 Mike Fiers .10 .25
164 Edwin Diaz .12 .30
165 Craig Kimbrel .12 .30
167 Robinson Cano .12 .30
168 Tim Anderson .15 .40
169 Mike Moustakas .12 .30
170 Elvis Andrus .12 .30
171 David Price .12 .30
172 Michael Brantley .12 .30
173 Jonathan Schoop .10 .25
174 J.T. Realmuto .15 .40
176 Marcell Ozuna .15 .40
177 Charlie Morton .15 .40
180 Jon Lester .12 .30
181 Ben Zobrist .12 .30
182 Walker Buehler .20 .50
183 Stephen Piscotty .10 .25
184 Chris Archer .10 .25
185 Nolan Arenado .25 .60
186 Jordan Hicks .12 .30
187 Jakob Junis .10 .25
188 Wade Davis .10 .25
189 Willson Contreras .12 .30
190 Yadier Molina .20 .50
191 Brett Gardner .12 .30
192 Adalberto Mondesi .12 .30
193 Fernando Tatis Jr. 1.50 4.00
194 Blake Treinen .10 .25
195 Stephen Strasburg .15 .40
198 Kyle Schwarber .15 .40
199 Yoan Moncada .15 .40
201 Matt Kemp .12 .30
202 Jose Martinez .10 .25
203 Miguel Andujar .15 .40
204 Wil Myers .12 .30
205 Ian Desmond .10 .25
206 Kenley Jansen .12 .30
208 Mike Foltynewicz .15 .40
209 Ender Inciarte .10 .25
210 Jason Heyward .12 .30
211 Jose Berrios .12 .30
212 Austin Meadows .15 .40
213 Matt Chapman .15 .40
214 Didi Gregorius .12 .30
215 Max Kepler .12 .30
216 Jose Urena .10 .25
217 Brandon Woodruff .15 .40
218 Jackie Bradley Jr. .15 .40
219 Dustin Fowler .10 .25
220 Evan Longoria .12 .30
221 Brandon Nimmo .12 .30
222 Victor Robles .20 .50
223 Jed Lowrie .10 .25
224 Brandon Belt .12 .30
225 Jonathan Villar .10 .25
226 Zack Wheeler .12 .30
228 Robbie Ray .10 .25
229 Paul DeJong .15 .40
230 David Peralta .10 .25
231 Yasiel Puig .15 .40
232 Kevin Gausman .15 .40
233 Justin Smoak .10 .25
235 Trevor Bauer .20 .50
236 Aaron Hicks .12 .30

2020 Topps Stickers

1 Stephen Strasburg .15 .40
2 Willie Mays World Series MVP Award .30 .75
5 Commissioner's Trophy
3 Washington Nationals .10 .25
4 Washington Nationals .10 .25
6 Anthony Rendon .15 .40
7 Max Scherzer .15 .40
8 Pete Alonso .40 1.00
9 Ozzie Albies .15 .40
10 Manny Machado .15 .40
11 Mookie Betts .30 .75
12 Aaron Judge .40 1.00
13 Cody Bellinger .30 .75
14 Home Run Apple .10 .25
15 Outfield Pool
16 Rally Monkey .10 .25
17 Monument Park
18 Bernie Brewer Slide .10 .25
19 Minute Maid Park Train
20 Green Monster Wall .10 .25
21 Wrigley Field Ivy-Covered Walls
22 Trey Mancini .15 .40
23 Chris Davis .10 .25
24 John Means .15 .40
25 Cedric Mullins .12 .30
26 Orioles MASCOT .10 .25
29 Wally The Green Monster MASCOT
36 White Sox MASCOT
39 Slider MASCOT
27 Jackie Bradley Jr. .15 .40
28 Xander Bogaerts .15 .40
30 Chris Sale .15 .40
31 Andrew Benintendi .15 .40
32 Tim Anderson .15 .40
33 Jose Abreu .15 .40
34 Eloy Jimenez .30 .75
35 Lucas Giolito .12 .30
37 Francisco Lindor .15 .40
38 Jose Ramirez .12 .30
40 Carlos Carrasco .10 .25
41 Carlos Santana .12 .30
42 Miguel Cabrera .15 .40
43 Jake Rogers .10 .25
44 Joe Jimenez .10 .25
45 Niko Goodrum .12 .30
46 Paws MASCOT .10 .25
59 Orbit MASCOT
66 Sluggerrr MASCOT
76 TC Bear MASCOT
47 Max Scherzer .15 .40
48 Aroldis Chapman .15 .40
49 Noah Syndergaard .12 .30
50 Josh Hader .12 .30
51 Gerrit Cole .25 .60
52 Jordan Hicks .12 .30
53 Stephen Strasburg .15 .40
54 Justin Verlander .15 .40
55 Alex Bregman .15 .40
57 AL Cy Young Award .10 .25
197 NL Cy Young Award
58 AL Rookie of the Year Award .10 .25
198 NL Rookie of the Year Award
60 Jose Altuve .12 .30
61 Yordan Alvarez 1.00 2.50
62 Whit Merrifield .15 .40
63 Alex Gordon .12 .30
64 Jakob Junis .10 .25
65 Jorge Soler .15 .40
67 Albert Pujols .20 .50
68 Mike Trout .75 2.00
69 AL MVP Award .10 .25
170 NL MVP Award
70 Shohei Ohtani .25 .60
71 Anthony Rendon .15 .40
72 Jose Berrios .12 .30
73 Jorge Polanco .12 .30
74 Byron Buxton .15 .40
75 Nelson Cruz .15 .40
77 Aaron Judge .40 1.00
78 Gleyber Torres .30 .75
79 Luis Severino .12 .30
80 Gary Sanchez .15 .40
81 Matt Chapman .15 .40
82 Matt Olson .15 .40
83 Khris Davis .15 .40
84 Jesus Luzardo .20 .50
85 Athletics MASCOT .10 .25
88 Mariner Moose MASCOT
95 Raymond MASCOT
98 Rangers Captain MASCOT
86 Dan Vogelbach .10 .25
87 Kyle Lewis .75 2.00
89 Mitch Haniger .12 .30
90 Justus Sheffield .15 .40
91 Blake Snell .12 .30
92 Willy Adames .10 .25
93 Kevin Kiermaier .12 .30
94 Charlie Morton .15 .40
96 Elvis Andrus .12 .30
97 Joey Gallo .15 .40
99 Shin-Soo Choo .12 .30
100 Mike Minor .10 .25
101 Vladimir Guerrero Jr. .25 .60

102 Bo Bichette .75 2.00
103 Cavan Biggio .20 .50
104 Trent Thornton .10 .25
105 Blue Jays MASCOT .10 .25
141 Diamondbacks MASCOT
148 Blooper MASCOT
151 Clark MASCOT
106 Bo Bichette .75 2.00
107 Yordan Alvarez 1.00 2.50
108 Vladimir Guerrero Jr. .25 .60
109 Eloy Jimenez .30 .75
110 Brendan McKay .15 .40
111 Michael Chavis .12 .30
112 Luis Arraez .20 .50
113 Austin Nola .15 .40
114 Stan Musial .25 .60
115 Willie Mays .30 .75
116 Johnny Bench .15 .40
117 Mike Schmidt .25 .60
118 Mike Schmidt .25 .60
119 Ken Griffey Jr. .30 .75
120 Albert Pujols .20 .50
121 Mike Trout .75 2.00
122 Mike Trout .75 2.00
123 Tim Anderson .15 .40
125 Jorge Soler
124 Christian Yelich .20 .50
126 Pete Alonso
127 Jose Abreu .15 .40
129 Mallex Smith
128 Anthony Rendon .15 .40
128 Ronald Acuna Jr.
131 Gerrit Cole .25 .60
133 Justin Verlander
132 Hyun-Jin Ryu .12 .30
134 Stephen Strasburg
135 Gerrit Cole .25 .60
137 Roberto Osuna
136 Jacob deGrom .30 .75
138 Kirby Yates
139 Ketel Marte .12 .30
140 Jake Lamb .12 .30
142 Archie Bradley .10 .25
143 Eduardo Escobar .10 .25
144 Ronald Acuna Jr. .60 1.50
145 Ozzie Albies .15 .40
146 Mike Soroka .15 .40
147 Freddie Freeman .20 .50
149 Kris Bryant .20 .50
150 Anthony Rizzo .20 .50
152 Nico Hoerner .40 1.00
154 Nick Senzel .15 .40
155 Aristides Aquino .25 .60
156 Joey Votto .15 .40
157 Trevor Bauer .20 .50
158 Rosie Red MASCOT .10 .25
167 Dinger MASCOT
177 Billy The Marlin MASCOT
159 Ichiro .20 .50
160 Albert Pujols .20 .50
161 Vladimir Guerrero Jr. .25 .60
162 Justin Verlander .15 .40
163 Pete Alonso .40 1.00
164 Washington Nationals .10 .25
165 Trevor Story .15 .40
166 Nolan Arenado .25 .60
168 German Marquez .15 .40
169 Charlie Blackmon .15 .40
171 Cody Bellinger .30 .75
172 Walker Buehler .20 .50
173 Justin Turner .15 .40
174 Clayton Kershaw .25 .60
175 Jesus Aguilar .12 .30
176 Isan Diaz .15 .40
178 Jose Urena .10 .25
179 Pablo Lopez UER .10 .25
Pedro
180 Christian Yelich .20 .50
181 Lorenzo Cain .10 .25
182 Ryan Braun .12 .30
183 Brandon Woodruff .15 .40
184 Bernie Brewer MASCOT .10 .25
199 Mr Met MASCOT
208 Pirate Parrot MASCOT
185 Christian Yelich .20 .50
186 Christian Yelich .20 .50
187 Pete Alonso .40 1.00
188 Cody Bellinger .30 .75
189 Mike Trout .75 2.00
190 Ronald Acuna Jr. .60 1.50
191 Ronald Acuna Jr. .60 1.50
192 Nolan Arenado .25 .60
193 Nelson Cruz .15 .40
194 Alex Bregman .15 .40
195 Noah Syndergaard .12 .30
196 Jacob deGrom .30 .75
200 Amed Rosario .12 .30
201 Pete Alonso .40 1.00
202 Rhys Hoskins .20 .50
203 Jean Segura .12 .30
204 Andrew McCutchen .15 .40
206 Mitch Keller .15 .40
207 Chris Archer .10 .25
209 Josh Bell .12 .30
210 Jameson Taillon .12 .30
211 Manny Machado .15 .40
212 Eric Hosmer .12 .30
213 Kirby Yates .10 .25
215 Swinging Friar MASCOT .10 .25
232 Fredbird MASCOT
235 Screech MASCOT
216 Nico Hoerner .40 1.00
217 Aristides Aquino .25 .60
218 Fernando Tatis Jr. .75 2.00
219 Pete Alonso .40 1.00
220 Gavin Lux .50 1.25
221 Carter Kieboom .12 .30
222 Isan Diaz .15 .40
223 Mitch Keller .15 .40
224 Brandon Crawford .12 .30
225 Buster Posey .20 .50
226 Brandon Belt .12 .30
227 Mike Yastrzemski .25 .60
228 Yadier Molina .20 .50
229 Carlos Martinez .12 .30
230 Paul DeJong .15 .40
231 Kolten Wong .12 .30
233 Juan Soto .50 1.25
234 Max Scherzer .15 .40
236 Trea Turner .12 .30
237 Victor Robles .20 .50

2020 Topps Stickers Cards

1 Ronald Acuna Jr. .60 1.50
2 Mike Trout .75 2.00
3 Mookie Betts .30 .75
4 Nolan Arenado .25 .60
5 Francisco Lindor .15 .40
6 Max Scherzer .15 .40
7 Jose Altuve .12 .30
8 Alex Bregman .15 .40
9 Christian Yelich .20 .50
10 Jose Ramirez .12 .30
11 Jacob deGrom .30 .75
12 J.D. Martinez .15 .40
13 Aaron Judge .40 1.00
14 Chris Sale .15 .40
15 Manny Machado .15 .40
16 Bryce Harper .25 .60
17 Paul Goldschmidt .15 .40
18 Freddie Freeman .20 .50
19 Joey Votto .15 .40
20 Giancarlo Stanton .15 .40
21 Justin Verlander .15 .40
22 Anthony Rendon .15 .40
23 Justin Turner .15 .40
24 Corey Kluber .12 .30
25 Aaron Nola .12 .30
26 Clayton Kershaw .25 .60
27 Blake Snell .12 .30
28 Matt Chapman .15 .40
29 Lorenzo Cain .10 .25
30 Javier Baez .20 .50
31 Trevor Story .15 .40
32 Carlos Correa .15 .40
33 Kris Bryant .20 .50
34 Matt Carpenter .15 .40
35 Anthony Rizzo .20 .50
36 Juan Soto .50 1.25
37 George Springer .12 .30
38 Charlie Blackmon .15 .40
39 Mitch Haniger .12 .30
40 J.T. Realmuto .15 .40
41 Trevor Bauer .20 .50
42 Gerrit Cole .25 .60
43 Luis Severino .12 .30
44 Cody Bellinger .30 .75
45 Tommy Pham .10 .25
46 Xander Bogaerts .15 .40
47 Andrelton Simmons .10 .25
48 Corey Seager .15 .40
49 Whit Merrifield .15 .40
50 Eugenio Suarez .12 .30
51 Edwin Diaz .12 .30
52 Craig Kimbrel .12 .30
53 Robinson Cano .12 .30
54 Brandon Nimmo .12 .30
55 Andrew Benintendi .15 .40
56 Khris Davis .15 .40
57 Matt Olson .15 .40
58 Rhys Hoskins .20 .50
59 Michael Conforto .12 .30
60 Josh Donaldson .12 .30
61 Jesus Aguilar .12 .30
62 Max Muncy .12 .30
63 Kyle Freeland .12 .30
64 Walker Buehler .20 .50
65 Carlos Carrasco .10 .25
66 Justin Upton .12 .30
67 Aaron Hicks .12 .30
68 Gleyber Torres .30 .75
69 Zack Greinke .15 .40
70 Blake Treinen .10 .25
71 Aroldis Chapman .15 .40
72 Nelson Cruz .15 .40
73 Michael Brantley .12 .30
74 Marcell Ozuna .15 .40
75 Jose Abreu .15 .40
76 Patrick Corbin .12 .30
77 Noah Syndergaard .12 .30
78 Stephen Strasburg .15 .40
79 Shohei Ohtani .25 .60
80 Mike Clevinger .12 .30
81 Jean Segura .12 .30
82 Trea Turner .12 .30
83 Ozzie Albies .15 .40
84 David Peralta .10 .25
85 Nicholas Castellanos .15 .40
86 Kenley Jansen .12 .30
87 Sean Doolittle .10 .25
88 Yasiel Puig .15 .40
89 Buster Posey .20 .50
90 Gary Sanchez .15 .40
91 Andrew McCutchen .15 .40
92 Yasmani Grandal .10 .25
93 Stephen Piscotty .10 .25
94 Jon Lester .12 .30
95 David Price .12 .30
96 Shane Bieber .15 .40
97 Tim Anderson .15 .40
98 Gio Urshela .15 .40
99 Victor Robles .20 .50
100 Miguel Cabrera .15 .40
101 Marcus Semien .15 .40
102 Miguel Sano .12 .30
103 Matthew Boyd .10 .25
104 Jorge Polanco .12 .30
105 Masahiro Tanaka .15 .40
106 Kyle Hendricks .15 .40
107 Jake Arrieta .12 .30
108 Shin-Soo Choo .12 .30
109 Nick Senzel .15 .40
110 Cole Hamels .12 .30
111 Eric Hosmer .12 .30
112 Hunter Dozier .10 .25
113 Yoan Moncada .15 .40
114 Dylan Cease .15 .40
115 Jose Martinez .10 .25
116 Ryan Braun .12 .30
117 Willy Adames .10 .25
118 Sean Doolittle .10 .25
119 Ryan Zimmerman .12 .30
120 Kevin Pillar .10 .25
121 Marcus Stroman .12 .30
122 David Price .12 .30
123 Evan Longoria .12 .30
124 Amed Rosario .12 .30
125 Kolten Wong .12 .30
126 Brett Gardner .12 .30
127 Joe Jimenez .10 .25
128 Jason Heyward .12 .30
129 Wil Myers .12 .30
130 Adam Ottavino .12 .30
131 Dallas Keuchel .12 .30
132 Albert Pujols .20 .50
133 Byron Buxton .15 .40
134 Michael Brantley .12 .30
135 Kyle Schwarber .15 .40
136 Yordan Alvarez 1.00 2.50
137 Aristides Aquino .25 .60
138 Wade Davis .10 .25
139 Kevin Kiermaier .12 .30
140 Domingo Santana .12 .30
141 Paul DeJong .15 .40
142 Mallex Smith .10 .25
143 Ryan Yarbrough .10 .25
144 Willson Contreras .15 .40
145 James Paxton .12 .30
146 Cavan Biggio .20 .50
147 Bo Bichette .75 2.00
148 Elvis Andrus .12 .30
149 Chris Archer .10 .25
150 Yadier Molina .20 .50
151 Josh Bell .12 .30
152 Ketel Marte .12 .30
153 Starling Marte .12 .30
154 Dee Gordon .10 .25
155 Jackie Bradley Jr. .15 .40
156 Archie Bradley .10 .25
157 Brendan McKay .15 .40
158 Nick Solak .40 1.00
159 David Bote .12 .30
160 Rick Porcello .12 .30
161 Mike Yastrzemski .25 .60
162 John Means .15 .40
163 Max Kepler .12 .30
164 Howie Kendrick .10 .25
165 Jose Berrios .12 .30
166 Alex Gordon .12 .30
167 Josh Hader .12 .30
168 Jorge Soler .15 .40
169 Nomar Mazara .10 .25
170 Luis Robert .75 2.00
171 Robel Garcia .10 .25
172 Brandon Belt .12 .30
173 Fernando Tatis Jr. .75 2.00
174 Pete Alonso .40 1.00
175 Eloy Jimenez .30 .75
176 Mike Moustakas .12 .30
177 Nico Hoerner .40 1.00
178 Adam Eaton .15 .40
179 Yuli Gurriel .12 .30
180 Kirby Yates .10 .25
181 Hyun-Jin Ryu .12 .30
182 Gavin Lux .50 1.25
183 Eduardo Escobar .10 .25
184 Kyle Seager .10 .25
185 Trey Mancini .15 .40
186 Joey Gallo .15 .40
187 Chris Paddack .15 .40
188 Raisel Iglesias .10 .25
189 Brad Hand .10 .25
190 Kenley Jansen .12 .30
191 Carlos Santana .12 .30
192 Luis Arraez .20 .50
193 Nick Markakis .12 .30
194 Jack Flaherty .15 .40
195 Mike Soroka .15 .40
196 Isan Diaz .15 .40
197 Brandon Woodruff .15 .40
198 Jake Cave .12 .30
199 Tommy La Stella .10 .25

2005-06 Topps Style

COMPLETE SET (165) 30.00 80.00
UNPRICED SUPERFR.PRINT RUN ONE SET
7 Mickey Mantle 3.00 8.00

2005-06 Topps Style Chrome

*1-130 CHROME: .75X TO 2X BASE HI
*131-165 CHROME: .6X TO 1.5X BASE HI
CHROME PRINT RUN 499 SER.#'d SETS

2005-06 Topps Style Chrome Refractors

*1-130 REF: 1.5X TO 4X BASE HI
*131-165 REF: .75X TO 2X BASE HI
PRINT RUN 299 SER.#'d SETS

2005-06 Topps Style Chrome Refractors Blue

*1-130 REF.BLUE: 2.5X TO 6X BASE HI
*131-165 REF.BLUE: 1X TO 2.5X BASE HI
PRINT RUN 149 SER.#'d SETS

2005-06 Topps Style Chrome Refractors Gold

*1-130 GOLD: 12X TO 30X BASE HI
*131-160 GOLD: 4X TO 10X BASE HI
*161-165 GOLD: 3X TO 8X BASE HI
PRINT RUN 25 SER.#'d SETS
7 Mickey Mantle 150.00 400.00

2000 Topps Subway Series

COMP.FACT SET (101) 25.00 60.00
COMPLETE SET (100) 10.00 25.00
COMMON CARD (1-100) .15 .40
ISSUED ONLY IN FACTORY SET FORM
1 Mike Piazza .40 1.00
2 Jay Payton .15 .40
3 Edgardo Alfonzo .15 .40
4 Todd Pratt .15 .40
5 Todd Zeile .15 .40
6 Mike Bordick .15 .40
7 Robin Ventura .15 .40
8 Benny Agbayani .15 .40
9 Timo Perez .25 .60
10 Kurt Abbott .15 .40
11 Matt Franco .15 .40
12 Bubba Trammell .15 .40
13 Darryl Hamilton .15 .40
14 Lenny Harris .15 .40
15 Joe McEwing .15 .40
16 Mike Hampton .15 .40
17 Al Leiter .15 .40
18 Rick Reed .15 .40
19 Bobby Jones .15 .40
20 Glendon Rusch .15 .40
21 Armando Benitez .15 .40
22 John Franco .15 .40
23 Rick White .15 .40
24 Dennis Cook .15 .40
25 Turk Wendell .15 .40
26 Bobby Valentine MG .15 .40
27 Derek Jeter 1.00 2.50
28 Chuck Knoblauch .15 .40
29 Tino Martinez .15 .40
30 Jorge Posada .25 .60
31 Luis Sojo .15 .40
32 Scott Brosius .15 .40
33 Chris Turner .15 .40
34 Bernie Williams .25 .60
35 David Justice .15 .40
36 Paul O'Neill .25 .60
37 Glenallen Hill .15 .40
38 Jose Vizcaino .15 .40
39 Luis Polonia .15 .40
40 Clay Bellinger .15 .40
41 Orlando Hernandez .15 .40
42 Roger Clemens .50 1.25
43 Andy Pettitte .25 .60
44 Denny Neagle .15 .40
45 Dwight Gooden .15 .40
46 David Cone .15 .40
47 Mariano Rivera .50 1.25
48 Jeff Nelson .15 .40
49 Mike Stanton .15 .40
50 Jason Grimsley .15 .40
51 Jose Canseco .25 .60
52 Joe Torre MG .25 .60
53 Edgardo Alfonzo .15 .40
54 Darryl Hamilton .15 .40
55 John Franco .15 .40
56 Benny Agbayani .15 .40
57 Bobby Jones .15 .40
58 New York Mets .25 .60
59 Bobby Valentine MG .15 .40
60 Mike Piazza .40 1.00
61 Armando Benitez .15 .40
62 Mike Piazza .40 1.00
63 Mike Piazza .40 1.00
64 Todd Zeile .15 .40
65 Timo Perez .25 .60
66 Timo Perez .25 .60
67 Mike Hampton .15 .40
68 Andy Pettitte .25 .60
69 Tino Martinez .15 .40
70 Joe Torre MG .25 .60
71 New York Yankees .25 .60
72 Orlando Hernandez .15 .40
73 Bernie Williams .25 .60
74 Andy Pettitte .25 .60
75 Mariano Rivera .50 1.25
76 New York Yankees .25 .60
77 Roger Clemens .50 1.25
78 Derek Jeter 1.00 2.50
79 David Justice .15 .40
80 Mariano Rivera .50 1.25
81 Tino Martinez .15 .40
82 New York Yankees .25 .60
83 Jorge Posada .25 .60
84 Chuck Knoblauch .15 .40
85 Jose Vizcaino .15 .40
86 Roger Clemens .50 1.25
87 Mike Piazza .40 1.00
88 Clay Bellinger .15 .40
89 Robin Ventura .15 .40
90 Benny Agbayani .15 .40
91 Orlando Hernandez .15 .40
92 Derek Jeter 1.00 2.50
93 Mike Piazza .40 1.00
94 Mariano Rivera .50 1.25
95 Derek Jeter 1.00 2.50
96 Luis Sojo .15 .40
97 New York Yankees .25 .60
98 Mike Hampton .15 .40
99 David Justice .15 .40
100 Derek Jeter 1.00 2.50

2000 Topps Subway Series FanFare Tokens

ONE PER FACTORY SET
SSR1 Timo Perez 30.00 60.00
SSR2 Edgardo Alfonzo 20.00 50.00
SSR3 Mike Piazza 40.00 80.00
SSR4 Robin Ventura 30.00 60.00
SSR5 Todd Zeile 20.00 50.00
SSR6 Benny Agbayani 15.00 40.00
SSR7 Jay Payton 20.00 50.00
SSR8 Mike Bordick 15.00 40.00
SSR9 Matt Franco 20.00 50.00
SSR10 Mike Hampton 30.00 60.00
SSR11 Al Leiter 30.00 60.00
SSR12 Rick Reed 8.00 20.00
SSR13 Bobby Jones 20.00 50.00
SSR14 Glendon Rusch 20.00 50.00
SSR15 Darryl Hamilton 20.00 50.00
SSR16 Turk Wendell 8.00 20.00
SSR17 John Franco 8.00 20.00
SSR18 Armando Benitez 20.00 50.00
SSR19 Chuck Knoblauch 20.00 50.00
SSR20 Derek Jeter 200.00 400.00
SSR21 David Justice 30.00 60.00
SSR22 Bernie Williams 30.00 60.00
SSR23 Jorge Posada 50.00 100.00
SSR24 Paul O'Neill 20.00 50.00
SSR25 Tino Martinez 12.00 30.00
SSR26 Luis Sojo 8.00 20.00
SSR27 Scott Brosius 8.00 20.00
SSR28 Jose Canseco 40.00 80.00
SSR29 Orlando Hernandez 8.00 20.00
SSR30 Roger Clemens 25.00 60.00
SSR31 Andy Pettitte 20.00 50.00
SSR32 Denny Neagle 20.00 50.00
SSR33 David Cone 20.00 50.00
SSR34 Jeff Nelson 20.00 50.00
SSR35 Mike Stanton 12.50 30.00
SSR36 Mariano Rivera 40.00 80.00

1998 Topps SuperChrome

The 1998 Topps SuperChrome set was issued in one series totalling 36 cards. The 3-card packs retail for $4.99 each. The fronts feature color player photos surrounded by a white four-sided border. The player's name and team are written along the bottom of the card.

COMPLETE SET (36) 15.00 40.00
1 Tony Gwynn .60 1.50
2 Larry Walker .20 .50
3 Vladimir Guerrero .50 1.25
4 Mo Vaughn .20 .50
5 Frank Thomas .50 1.25
6 Barry Larkin .30 .75
7 Scott Rolen .30 .75
8 Juan Gonzalez .20 .50
9 Jeff Bagwell .30 .75
10 Ryan Klesko .20 .50
11 Mike Piazza .75 2.00
12 Randy Johnson .50 1.25
13 Derek Jeter 1.25 3.00
14 Gary Sheffield .20 .50
15 Hideo Nomo .50 1.25
16 Tino Martinez .30 .75
17 Ivan Rodriguez .30 .75
18 Bernie Williams .30 .75
19 Greg Maddux .75 2.00
20 Roger Clemens 1.00 2.50
21 Roberto Clemente 1.00 2.50
22 Chipper Jones .50 1.25
23 Sammy Sosa .50 1.25
24 Tony Clark .20 .50
25 Barry Bonds 1.25 3.00
26 Craig Biggio .30 .75
27 Cal Ripken 1.50 4.00
28 Ken Griffey Jr. 1.00 2.50
29 Todd Helton .30 .75
30 Mark McGwire 1.25 3.00
31 Jose Cruz Jr. .20 .50
32 Albert Belle .20 .50
33 Andruw Jones .30 .75
34 Nomar Garciaparra .75 2.00
35 Andy Pettitte .30 .75
36 Alex Rodriguez .75 2.00

1998 Topps SuperChrome Refractors

COMPLETE SET (36) 300.00 600.00
*STARS: 5X TO 12X BASIC CARDS
STATED ODDS 1:12

1999 Topps SuperChrome

This 36-card set was distributed in three-card packs with a suggested retail price of $4.99. The fronts feature color action player photos printed on large cards that measure approximately 4 1/8" by 5 3/4". The backs carry player information.

COMPLETE SET (36) 30.00 80.00
1 Roger Clemens 1.50 4.00
2 Andres Galarraga .30 .75
3 Manny Ramirez .50 1.25
4 Greg Maddux 1.25 3.00
5 Kerry Wood .30 .75
6 Travis Lee .30 .75
7 Nolan Ryan 3.00 8.00
8 Juan Gonzalez .30 .75
9 Vladimir Guerrero .75 2.00
10 Sammy Sosa .75 2.00
11 Mark McGwire 2.00 5.00
12 Javy Lopez .30 .75
13 Tony Gwynn 1.00 2.50
14 Derek Jeter 2.00 5.00
15 Albert Belle .30 .75
16 Pedro Martinez .50 1.25
17 Greg Vaughn .30 .75
18 Ken Griffey Jr. 1.50 4.00
19 Ben Grieve .30 .75
20 Vinny Castilla .30 .75
21 Moises Alou .30 .75
22 Barry Bonds 2.00 5.00
23 Nomar Garciaparra 1.25 3.00
24 Chipper Jones .75 2.00
25 Mike Piazza 1.25 3.00
26 Alex Rodriguez 1.25 3.00
27 Ivan Rodriguez .50 1.25
28 Frank Thomas .75 2.00
29 Larry Walker .30 .75
30 Troy Glaus .50 1.25
31 David Wells HL .30 .75
32 Roger Clemens HL .75 2.00
33 Kerry Wood HL .30 .75
34 Mark McGwire HR 70 10.00 25.00
35 Sammy Sosa HR 66 4.00 10.00
36 Scott Brosius WS .30 .75

1999 Topps SuperChrome Refractors

*STARS: 2X TO 5X BASIC CARDS
STATED ODDS 1:12

2002 Topps Super Teams

COMPLETE SET (146) 20.00 50.00
REPURCHASED VINTAGE ODDS 1:41
REPURCH.VINT.EXCH.DEADLINE 01/01/04
1 Leo Durocher MG .40 1.00
2 Whitey Lockman .25 .60
3 Alvin Dark .25 .60
4 Monte Irvin .25 .60
5 Willie Mays 1.25 3.00
6 Wes Westrum .15 .40
7 Johnny Antonelli .15 .40
8 Sal Maglie .25 .60
9 Dusty Rhodes .15 .40
10 Davey Williams .15 .40
11 Hoyt Wilhelm .25 .60
12 Don Mueller .15 .40
13 Dusty Rhodes .15 .40
14 Mays .40 1.00
Irvin
Rhodes
15 Walt Alston MG .25 .60
16 Gil Hodges .60 1.50
17 Jim Gilliam .25 .60
18 Pee Wee Reese .60 1.50
19 Jackie Robinson .60 1.50
20 Duke Snider .40 1.00
21 Carl Furillo .25 .60
22 Roy Campanella .60 1.50
23 Don Newcombe .25 .60
24 Don Hoak .15 .40
25 Johnny Podres .25 .60
26 Clem Labine .25 .60
27 Johnny Podres .25 .60
28 Reese .40 1.00
J.Robinson
Snider
29 Fred Haney MG .15 .40
30 Joe Adcock .25 .60
31 Frank Torre .15 .40
32 Red Schoendienst .25 .60
33 Johnny Logan .25 .60
34 Eddie Mathews .60 1.50
35 Hank Aaron 1.25 3.00
36 Andy Pafko .25 .60
37 Wes Covington .15 .40
38 Lew Burdette .25 .60
39 Warren Spahn .40 1.00
40 Del Crandall .15 .40
41 Lew Burdette .25 .60
42 Spahn .60 1.50
Mathews
Aaron
43 Danny Murtaugh MG .15 .40
44 Dick Stuart .15 .40
45 Bill Mazeroski .40 1.00
46 Dick Groat .25 .60
47 Don Hoak .15 .40
48 Gino Cimoli .15 .40
49 Bill Virdon .15 .40
50 Roberto Clemente 1.50 4.00
51 Smoky Burgess .25 .60
52 Bob Friend .25 .60
53 Vernon Law .25 .60
54 Roy Face .25 .60
55 Harvey Haddix .15 .40
56 Bill Mazeroski .40 1.00
57 Clemente .75 2.00
Mazeroski
Groat
58 Ralph Houk MG .25 .60
59 Moose Skowron .25 .60
60 Bobby Richardson .25 .60
61 Tony Kubek .40 1.00
62 Clete Boyer .15 .40
63 Yogi Berra .60 1.50
64 Bob Cerv .15 .40
65 Roger Maris .60 1.50
66 Elston Howard .40 1.00
67 Whitey Ford .40 1.00
68 Ralph Terry .15 .40
69 Johnny Blanchard .15 .40
70 Whitey Ford .40 1.00
71 Berra .60 1.50
Maris
Howard
Moose
72 Red Schoendienst MG .25 .60
73 Orlando Cepeda .25 .60
74 Julian Javier .15 .40
75 Dal Maxvill .15 .40
76 Mike Shannon .25 .60
77 Lou Brock .40 1.00
78 Roger Maris .60 1.50
79 Curt Flood .25 .60
80 Tim McCarver .25 .60
81 Steve Carlton .25 .60
82 Bob Gibson .40 1.00
83 Nelson Briles .15 .40
84 Bobby Tolan .15 .40
85 Bob Gibson .40 1.00
86 Gibson .25 .60
Carlton
Cepeda
Brock
87 Gil Hodges MG .60 1.50
88 Ed Kranepool .15 .40
89 Buddy Harrelson .15 .40
90 Wayne Garrett .15 .40
91 Cleon Jones .15 .40
92 Tommie Agee .25 .60
93 Ron Swoboda .25 .60
94 Al Weis .15 .40
95 Jerry Grote .15 .40
96 Tom Seaver .40 1.00
97 Jerry Koosman .25 .60
98 Tug McGraw .25 .60
99 Nolan Ryan 1.50 4.00
100 Donn Clendenon .15 .40
101 Seaver .60 1.50
Koos
McGraw
Ryan
102 Earl Weaver MG .25 .60
103 Boog Powell .40 1.00
104 Davey Johnson .25 .60
105 Mark Belanger .15 .40
106 Brooks Robinson .40 1.00
107 Don Buford .15 .40
108 Paul Blair .15 .40
109 Frank Robinson .40 1.00
110 Dick Hall .15 .40
111 Jim Palmer .25 .60
112 Mike Cuellar .25 .60
113 Dave McNally .25 .60
114 Andy Etchebarren .15 .40
115 Brooks Robinson .40 1.00
116 Hall .25 .60
Palmer
Cuellar
McNally
117 Alvin Dark MG .25 .60
118 Gene Tenace .25 .60
119 Dick Green .15 .40
120 Bert Campaneris .25 .60
121 Sal Bando .25 .60
122 Reggie Jackson .40 1.00
123 Joe Rudi .25 .60
124 Claudell Washington .15 .40
125 Ray Fosse .15 .40
126 Vida Blue .25 .60
127 Rollie Fingers .25 .60
128 Catfish Hunter .40 1.00
129 Ken Holtzman .25 .60
130 Rollie Fingers .25 .60
131 Hunter .40 1.00
Bando
Reggie
Fingers
132 Davey Johnson MG .25 .60
133 Keith Hernandez .25 .60
134 Wally Backman .15 .40
135 Rafael Santana .15 .40
136 Ray Knight .25 .60
137 Len Dykstra .25 .60
138 Darryl Strawberry .25 .60
139 Kevin Mitchell .15 .40
140 Dwight Gooden .25 .60
141 Bob Ojeda .15 .40
142 Sid Fernandez .25 .60
143 Ron Darling .25 .60
144 Gary Carter .25 .60
145 Ray Knight .25 .60
146 Straw .25 .60
Gooden
K.Hern

2002 Topps Super Teams Retrofractors

*RETROFRACTORS: 1.5X TO 4X BASIC
ONE PER PACK
1-14 GIANTS SERIAL #'d TO 1954
15-28 DODGERS SERIAL #'d TO 1955
29-42 BRAVES SERIAL #'d TO 1957
43-57 PIRATES SERIAL #'d TO 1960
58-71 YANKEES SERIAL #'d TO 1961
72-86 CARDINALS SERIAL #'d TO 1967
87-101 METS SERIAL #'d TO 1969
102-116 ORIOLES SERIAL #'d TO 1970
117-131 A'S SERIAL #'d TO 1974
131-146 METS SERIAL #'d TO 1986

2002 Topps Super Teams A View To A Thrill Relics

GROUP 1 STATED ODDS 1:124
GROUP 2 STATED ODDS 1:39
OVERALL STATED ODDS 1:30
ALL CARDS FEATURE SEAT RELICS
VTBG Bob Gibson 2 6.00 15.00
VTBM Bill Mazeroski 1 6.00 15.00
VTBP Boog Powell 2 6.00 15.00
VTBR Brooks Robinson 2 6.00 15.00
VTDS Duke Snider 1 8.00 20.00
VTEM Eddie Mathews 2 8.00 20.00
VTFR Frank Robinson 2 6.00 15.00
VTHA Hank Aaron 2 12.50 30.00
VTJP Jim Palmer 2 6.00 15.00
VTLB Lew Burdette 2 6.00 15.00
VTRC Roberto Clemente 1 30.00 60.00
VTRS Red Schoendienst 2 6.00 15.00
VTRMB R.Maris Cardinals 2 10.00 25.00
VTRMY R.Maris Yankees 1 20.00 50.00
VTWF Whitey Ford 1 6.00 15.00
VTWM Willie Mays 1 15.00 40.00
VTWS Warren Spahn 2 8.00 20.00
VTYB Yogi Berra 1 8.00 20.00

2002 Topps Super Teams A View To A Thrill Relics Autographs

STATED ODDS 1:735
PRINT RUNS B/WN 54-67 COPIES PER
ALL CARDS FEATURE SEAT RELICS
VTBGA Bob Gibson/67 30.00 60.00
VTDSA Duke Snider/55 40.00 80.00
VTWFA Whitey Ford/61 40.00 80.00
VTWMA Willie Mays/54 150.00 250.00
VTWSA Warren Spahn/57 40.00 80.00

2002 Topps Super Teams Autographs

GROUP A STATED ODDS 1:28
GROUP B STATED ODDS 1:75
GROUP C STATED ODDS 1:441
GROUP D STATED ODDS 1:1441
GROUP E STATED ODDS 1:432
OVERALL STATED ODDS 1:19
AP Andy Pafko A 6.00 15.00
BR Bobby Richardson B 6.00 15.00
BRO Brooks Robinson B 10.00 25.00
CB Clete Boyer B 6.00 15.00
HW Hoyt Wilhelm A 10.00 25.00
JP Jim Palmer C 10.00 25.00
JPO Johnny Podres A 6.00 15.00
MI Monte Irvin B 8.00 20.00
MS Moose Skowron B 6.00 15.00
NR Nolan Ryan E 75.00 200.00
RJ Reggie Jackson E 25.00 60.00
SC Steve Carlton C 6.00 15.00
TK Tony Kubek D 20.00 50.00
TM Tug McGraw A 10.00 25.00
TS Tom Seaver E 40.00 100.00
VB Vida Blue A 6.00 15.00
WS Warren Spahn B 15.00 40.00
YB Yogi Berra E 20.00 50.00

2002 Topps Super Teams AutoProofs

GROUP 1 STATED ODDS 1:2162
GROUP 2 STATED ODDS 1:5404

2002 Topps Super Teams Classic Combos Relics

STATED ODDS 1:865
CCAJ Agee Bat/Cleon Bat 20.00 50.00
CCJR Reggie Bat/Rudi Bat 20.00 50.00
CCRR F.Rob Bat/Brooks Bat 20.00 50.00
CCSK Seaver Bat/Koosman Jsy 20.00 50.00
CCSRBK Yankees Infield 50.00 100.00

2002 Topps Super Teams Relics

BAT GROUP 1 ODDS 1:393
BAT GROUP 2 ODDS 1:103
BAT GROUP 3 ODDS 1:1081
BAT OVERALL ODDS 1:76
JACKET ODDS 1:721
UNIFORM/JSY GROUP 1 ODDS 1:865
UNIFORM/JSY GROUP 2 ODDS 1:66
UNIFORM/JSY GROUP 3 ODDS 1:180
UNIFORM/JSY OVERALL ODDS 1:46
BAT GROUP 1 PRINT RUN 50 SETS
BAT GROUP 2 PRINT RUN 100 SETS
BAT GROUP 3 PRINT RUN 200 CARDS
BAT CARDS ARE NOT SERIAL-NUMBERED
BAT PRINT RUNS PROVIDED BY TOPPS
STRAP Andy Pafko Bat 2 6.00 15.00
STRBC Bert Campaneris Jsy 2 6.00 15.00
STRBF Bob Friend Jsy 3 6.00 15.00

STRBR Bobby Richardson Bat 1 12.50 30.00
STRCB Clete Boyer Bat 1 10.00 25.00
STRCJ Cleon Jones Bat 1 10.00 25.00
STRCW Cl. Washington Bat 2 4.00 10.00
STRDC Del Crandall Bat 2 6.00 15.00
STRDG Dwight Gooden Jsy 2 6.00 15.00
STRDH Don Hoak Bat 2 4.00 10.00
STRDJ Davey Johnson Bat 2 6.00 15.00
STRDM Dave McNally Jsy 2 6.00 15.00
STRDS Darryl Strawberry Bat 2 6.00 15.00
STREK Ed Kranepool Jsy 3 6.00 15.00
STRFR Frank Robinson Bat 1 12.50 30.00
STRGC Gary Carter Jsy 2 6.00 15.00
STRJA Joe Adcock Bat 6.00 15.00
STRJK Jerry Koosman Jsy 1 6.00 15.00
STRJR Joe Rudi Bat 1 10.00 25.00
STRKM Kevin Mitchell Bat 2 6.00 15.00
STRLB Lew Burdette Jsy 2 6.00 15.00
STRLD Len Dykstra Bat 2 6.00 15.00
STRMB Mark Belanger Bat 2 6.00 15.00
STRMC Mike Cuellar Jsy 2 6.00 15.00
STRMS Moose Skowron Bat 1 12.50 30.00
STRNR Nolan Ryan Bat 2 20.00 50.00
STROC Orlando Cepeda Bat 2 6.00 15.00
STRPB Paul Blair Bat 2 4.00 10.00
STRRD Ron Darling Jsy 2 6.00 15.00
STRRF Ray Fosse Bat 2 6.00 15.00
STRRH Ralph Houk Uni 2 6.00 15.00
STRRJ Reggie Jackson Bat 1 12.50 30.00
STRRK Ray Knight Bat 2 6.00 15.00
STRRS Red Schoendienst Bat 2 6.00 15.00
STRSB Smoky Burgess Bat 2 6.00 15.00
STRTA Tommie Agee Bat 1 10.00 25.00
STRTK Tony Kubek Bat 1 12.50 30.00
STRTM Tug McGraw Jsy 2 6.00 15.00
STRTS Tom Seaver Bat 1 8.00 20.00
STRWG Wayne Garrett Bat 2 4.00 10.00
STRBCE Bob Cerv Bat 2 10.00 25.00
STRBRO Brooks Robinson Bat 1 12.50 30.00
STREKU Ed Kranepool Uni 2 6.00 15.00
STRGCB Gary Carter Bat 2 6.00 15.00
STRGCI Gino Cimoli Bat 2 6.00 15.00
STRGCJ Gary Carter Jacket 10.00 25.00
STRSBB Sal Bando Bat 3 6.00 15.00
STRSBJ Sal Bando Jsy 2 6.00 15.00

2002 Topps Super Teams Teammates

COMPLETE SET (5) 6.00 15.00
STATED ODDS 1:10
STBG L.Brock/B.Gibson 1.50 4.00
STFB W.Ford/Y.Berra 1.50 4.00
STMI W.Mays/M.Irvin 1.50 4.00
STRR B.Robinson/F.Robinson 1.50 4.00
STSRBK Yankees Infield 1.50 4.00

2002 Topps Super Teams Teammates Autographs

STATED ODDS 1:865
STATED PRINT RUN 50 SERIAL #'d SETS
BGA L.Brock/B.Gibson 60.00 120.00
FBA W.Ford/Y.Berra 125.00 250.00
MIA W.Mays/M.Irvin 125.00 200.00
RRA B.Robinson/F.Robinson 60.00 120.00
SRBKA Yankees Infield 150.00 250.00

2013 Topps Supreme Autographs

STATED PRINT RUN 50 SER.#'d SETS
MOST NOT PRICED DUE TO LACK OF INFO
PLATE PRINT RUN 1 SET PER COLOR
BLACK-CYAN-MAGENTA-YELLOW ISSUED
NO PLATE PRICING DUE TO SCARCITY
EXCHANGE DEADLINE 11/30/2016
SAAG Adrian Gonzalez
SAALC Alex Cobb 5.00 12.00
SAAR Anthony Rizzo
SAAW Alex Wood 8.00 20.00
SABG Brett Gardner 8.00 20.00
SABL Bryan LaHair
SABM Bill Madlock 5.00 12.00
SABMI Brad Miller 6.00 15.00
SABML Brad Miller 6.00 15.00
SABP Brandon Phillips 5.00 12.00
SABZ Ben Zobrist 8.00 20.00
SACA Chris Archer 6.00 15.00
SACAR Chris Archer 6.00 15.00
SACB Craig Biggio 10.00 25.00
SACC CC Sabathia 12.00 30.00
SACF Cecil Fielder 12.00 30.00
SACFI Cecil Fielder 12.00 30.00
SACL Colby Lewis
SACS Carlos Santana 5.00 12.00
SADAS Dan Straily
SADC Dave Concepcion 6.00 15.00
SADG Dan Gladden 6.00 15.00
SADGR Didi Gregorius 5.00 12.00
SADIG Didi Gregorius 5.00 12.00
SADR Darin Ruf 8.00 20.00
SADRU Darin Ruf 8.00 20.00
SADSA Danny Salazar 6.00 15.00
SADSL Danny Salazar 6.00 15.00
SADST Dave Stewart
SADW David Wright 12.00 30.00
SAEB Ernie Banks 15.00 40.00
SAED Eric Davis 15.00 40.00
SAEG Evan Gattis 12.00 30.00
SAEGA Evan Gattis 12.00 30.00
SAFD Felix Doubront 5.00 12.00
SAFJE Fergie Jenkins 6.00 15.00
SAGC Gary Carter 15.00 40.00
SAGN Graig Nettles 6.00 15.00
SAGP Glen Perkins
SAGS Gary Sheffield 6.00 15.00
SAGSH Gary Sheffield 6.00 15.00
SAHA Hank Aaron
SAHI Hisashi Iwakuma 10.00 25.00
SAHIW Hisashi Iwakuma 10.00 25.00
SAHJR Hyun-Jin Ryu
SAIN Ivan Nova 5.00 12.00
SAINO Ivan Nova 5.00 12.00
SAJBA Jesse Barfield 5.00 12.00
SAJC Johnny Cueto
SAJF Jose Fernandez
SAJL Jonathan Lucroy
SAJLA Junior Lake 5.00 12.00
SAJLU Jonathan Lucroy 15.00 40.00
SAJP Johnny Podres 5.00 12.00
SAJPE Jonathan Pettibone
SAJPO Johnny Podres
SAJPR Jurickson Profar 8.00 20.00
SAJR Jose Reyes 15.00 40.00
SAJT Junichi Tazawa 15.00 40.00
SAJTE Julio Teheran 8.00 20.00
SAKF Kyuji Fujikawa
SAKG Kyle Gibson 5.00 12.00
SAKGI Kyle Gibson 5.00 12.00
SAKL Kenny Lofton 10.00 25.00
SAKM Kevin Mitchell 6.00 15.00
SAKU Koji Uehara 30.00 60.00
SAMA Matt Adams 10.00 25.00
SAMAD Matt Adams 10.00 25.00
SAMG Mike Greenwell 10.00 20.00
SAMK Munenori Kawasaki 40.00 80.00
SAMMA Matt Magill
SAMMO Matt Moore 5.00 12.00
SAMW Matt Williams
SAMWA Michael Wacha 12.00 30.00
SAPG Paul Goldschmidt 12.00 30.00
SARS Ryne Sandberg 20.00 50.00
SARV Ryan Vogelsong
SASC Starlin Castro 8.00 20.00
SASG Sonny Gray 20.00 50.00
SASP Salvador Perez 15.00 40.00
SATW Tsuyoshi Wada 10.00 25.00
SATWA Tsuyoshi Wada 10.00 25.00
SATWD Tsuyoshi Wada 10.00 25.00
SAWR Wilin Rosario
SAYG Yovani Gallardo

2013 Topps Supreme Autographs Red

*RED: .5X TO 1.2X BASIC
STATED PRINT RUN 25 SER.#'d SETS
MOST NOT PRICED DUE TO LACK OF INFO
EXCHANGE DEADLINE 11/30/2016

2013 Topps Supreme Autographs Sepia

*SEPIA: .5X TO 1.2X BASIC
STATED PRINT RUN 35 SER.#'d SETS
MOST NOT PRICED DUE TO LACK OF INFO
EXCHANGE DEADLINE 11/30/2016

2013 Topps Supreme Autograph Kanji Relics

STATED PRINT RUN 25 SER.#'d SETS
MOST NOT PRICED DUE TO LACK OF INFO
EXCHANGE DEADLINE 11/30/2016
KARAG Adrian Gonzalez
KARAJ Adam Jones
KARAR Anthony Rizzo 20.00 50.00
KARBP Buster Posey
KARCB Craig Biggio 50.00 100.00
KARCD Chris Davis
KARCF Cecil Fielder
KARCK Craig Kimbrel
KARCS Chris Sale
KARDP Dustin Pedroia 20.00 50.00
KARGS Gary Sheffield
KARJB Jay Bruce 15.00 40.00
KARJW Jered Weaver 15.00 40.00
KARJZ Jordan Zimmermann
KARMC Miguel Cabrera
KARMM Matt Moore 8.00 20.00
KARMT Mark Trumbo
KARNG Nomar Garciaparra
KARNM Nyjer Morgan 10.00 25.00
KARRS Ryne Sandberg
KARSMA Starling Marte
KARSP Salvador Perez
KARYC Yoenis Cespedes 25.00 60.00
KARYD Yu Darvish
KARYG Yovani Gallardo 10.00 25.00

2013 Topps Supreme Autograph Patches

STATED PRINT RUN 25 SER.#'d SETS
MOST NOT PRICED DUE TO LACK OF INFO
EXCHANGE DEADLINE 11/30/2016
APRAC Asdrubal Cabrera
APRAG Adrian Gonzalez
APRAJ Adam Jones 12.00 30.00
APRAR Anthony Rizzo 15.00 40.00
APRBB Billy Butler
APRBP Brandon Phillips
APRBPO Buster Posey
APRCB Craig Biggio
APRCD Chris Davis
APRCF Cecil Fielder 12.00 30.00
APRCG Carlos Gonzalez 15.00 40.00
APRCK Craig Kimbrel 30.00 60.00
APRCS Carlos Santana
APRCSA Chris Sale
APRDM Don Mattingly
APRDP Dustin Pedroia
APRDW David Wright
APRGG Gio Gonzalez
APRGS Gary Sheffield 10.00 25.00
APRGST Giancarlo Stanton
APRHR Hyun-Jin Ryu 40.00 80.00
APRJB Jay Bruce
APRJC Johnny Cueto
APRJK Jason Kipnis 15.00 40.00
APRJR Jose Reyes 30.00 60.00
APRJRE Josh Reddick
APRJS Jean Segura
APRJSM John Smoltz 40.00 80.00
APRJW Jered Weaver 12.00 30.00
APRMC Miguel Cabrera
APRMT Mark Trumbo 30.00 60.00
APRMTR Mike Trout
APRPF Prince Fielder
APRPG Paul Goldschmidt 20.00 50.00
APRRD R.A. Dickey
APRSC Starlin Castro 15.00 40.00
APRSM Starling Marte 12.00 30.00
APRSP Salvador Perez
APRWR Wilin Rosario
APRYG Yovani Gallardo

2013 Topps Supreme Dual Autographs

PRINT RUNS B/WN 10-25 COPIES PER
NO PRICING ON QTY 10
EXCHANGE DEADLINE 11/30/2016
DABC Cain/Bumgarner 50.00 100.00
DABR J.Reyes/J.Bautista 50.00 100.00
DACF M.Cabrera/P.Fielder
DACJ C.Kimbrel/J.Smoltz
DACW G.Carter/D.Wright 100.00 200.00
DADI Y.Darvish/H.Iwakuma 50.00 100.00
DADR Y.Darvish/H.J.Ryu 100.00 200.00
DADS A.Dawson/R.Sandberg 60.00 120.00
DAFM S.Miller/J.Fernandez 20.00 50.00
DAGH T.Gwynn/R.Henderson
DAGN I.Nova/B.Gardner 20.00 50.00
DAGP N.Garciaparra/D.Pedroia
DAGR P.Goldschmidt/A.Rizzo
DAHM R.Henderson/D.Mattingly 100.00 200.00
DAHT B.Harper/M.Trout 400.00 600.00
DAIR H.Iwakuma/H.J.Ryu
DAJS B.Jackson/D.Sanders 150.00 250.00
DAKJ J.Tazawa/K.Uehara 60.00 120.00
DAKR C.Kershaw/H.J.Ryu
DALM M.Moore/E.Longoria
DAMJ D.Mattingly/R.Jackson 100.00 200.00
DAMP D.Pedroia/W.Middlebrooks
DANG E.Nunez/B.Gardner 10.00 25.00
DAPB S.Perez/B.Butler 10.00 25.00
DAPBI C.Biggio/D.Pedroia 30.00 60.00
DAPJ J.Bruce/B.Phillips 12.00 30.00
DAPR J.Profar/A.Rendon 12.00 30.00
DAPS D.Straily/J.Parker 10.00 25.00
DAPSE W.Peralta/J.Segura
DARB B.Revere/D.Brown 20.00 50.00
DARC S.Castro/A.Rizzo 50.00 100.00
DARG A.Gonzalez/H.Ramirez
DARM A.Rendon/M.Machado 60.00 150.00
DASG J.Segura/Y.Gallardo 10.00 25.00
DASGL J.Smoltz/T.Glavine 60.00 120.00
DASM J.Smoltz/D.Murphy 60.00 120.00
DATH J.Hamilton/M.Trout
DATW M.Trumbo/J.Weaver
DAUM D.Murphy/J.Upton 20.00 50.00
DAUT K.Uehara/J.Tazawa 75.00 150.00
DAUU B.Upton/J.Upton
DAVL R.Vogelsong/C.Lewis
DAWI T.Wada/H.Iwakuma 75.00 150.00

2013 Topps Supreme Supreme Stylings Autographs

STATED PRINT RUN 50 SER.#'d SETS
MOST NOT PRICED DUE TO LACK OF INFO
PLATE PRINT RUN 1 SET PER COLOR
BLACK-CYAN-MAGENTA-YELLOW ISSUED
NO PLATE PRICING DUE TO SCARCITY
EXCHANGE DEADLINE 11/30/2016
SSACB Alex Cobb
SSACO Alex Cobb
SSAJ Adam Jones
SSAR Anthony Rizzo
SSARE Anthony Rendon 12.00 30.00
SSAW Alex Wood 6.00 15.00
SSAWO Alex Wood 6.00 15.00
SSBG Brett Gardner
SSBH Bryce Harper
SSBL Bryan LaHair 5.00 12.00
SSBM Bill Madlock 8.00 20.00
SSBMI Brad Miller 5.00 12.00
SSBP Brandon Phillips
SSCA Chris Archer
SSCC CC Sabathia 8.00 20.00
SSCF Cecil Fielder
SSCFI Cecil Fielder 10.00 25.00
SSCL Colby Lewis
SSCS Carlos Santana 5.00 12.00
SSDG Dan Gladden
SSDGR Didi Gregorius
SSDIG Didi Gregorius
SSDR Darin Ruf 8.00 20.00
SSDS Don Sutton 6.00 15.00
SSDSA Danny Salazar
SSDSD Duke Snider 10.00 25.00
SSDSN Duke Snider 10.00 25.00
SSEG Evan Gattis 8.00 20.00
SSFD Felix Doubront
SSFDO Felix Doubront
SSFR Fernando Rodney 5.00 12.00
SSGC Gary Carter 15.00 40.00
SSGCA Gary Carter 15.00 40.00
SSGGO Goose Gossage 8.00 20.00
SSGGR Grant Green 5.00 12.00
SSGN Graig Nettles 5.00 12.00
SSGP Glen Perkins 5.00 12.00
SSGPE Glen Perkins 5.00 12.00
SSGS Gary Sheffield 10.00 25.00
SSGSH Gary Sheffield 10.00 25.00
SSHIK Hisashi Iwakuma 20.00 50.00
SSHIW Hisashi Iwakuma 12.00 30.00
SSIN Ivan Nova 6.00 15.00
SSJBA Jesse Barfield
SSJC Johnny Cueto
SSJH Josh Hamilton 12.00 30.00
SSJK Jason Kipnis 8.00 20.00
SSJL Junior Lake 8.00 20.00
SSJLA Junior Lake 8.00 20.00
SSJLU Jonathan Lucroy 15.00 40.00
SSJOP Jonathan Pettibone 5.00 12.00
SSJPD Johnny Podres
SSJPE Jonathan Pettibone 5.00 12.00
SSJPR Jurickson Profar
SSJT Junichi Tazawa
SSJTE Julio Teheran 8.00 20.00
SSJUT Julio Teheran 8.00 20.00
SSJZ Jordan Zimmermann
SSKF Kyuji Fujikawa 8.00 20.00
SSKG Kyle Gibson
SSKM Kevin Mitchell 5.00 12.00
SSKU Koji Uehara
SSMA Matt Adams 10.00 25.00
SSMAM Matt Magill
SSMC Miguel Cabrera 50.00 100.00
SSMG Mike Greenwell
SSMK Munenori Kawasaki 40.00 80.00
SSMM Matt Moore
SSMMI Matt Magill
SSMT Mark Trumbo 5.00 12.00
SSMTT Mike Trout
SSMW Michael Wacha 12.00 30.00
SSMWA Michael Wacha 12.00 30.00
SSPG Paul Goldschmidt
SSRB Ryan Braun 8.00 20.00
SSSG Sonny Gray 10.00 25.00
SSSK Sandy Koufax
SSSM Starling Marte
SSSP Salvador Perez 10.00 25.00
SSTW Tsuyoshi Wada 8.00 20.00
SSTWA Tsuyoshi Wada 8.00 20.00
SSTWD Tsuyoshi Wada 8.00 20.00
SSWC Will Clark 15.00 40.00
SSYD Yu Darvish 75.00 150.00
SSYP Yasiel Puig

2013 Topps Supreme Supreme Stylings Autographs Red

*RED: .5X TO 1.2X BASIC
STATED PRINT RUN 25 SER.#'d SETS
MOST NOT PRICED DUE TO LACK OF INFO
EXCHANGE DEADLINE 11/30/2016

2013 Topps Supreme Supreme Stylings Autographs Sepia

*SEPIA: .6X TO 1.5X BASIC
STATED PRINT RUN 35 SER.#'d SETS
MOST NOT PRICED DUE TO LACK OF INFO
EXCHANGE DEADLINE 11/30/2016

2014 Topps Supreme Autographs

STATED ODDS 1:8 BOXES
STATED PRINT RUN 50 SER.#'d SETS
EXCHANGE DEADLINE 9/30/2017
SAAA Arismendy Alcantara 4.00 10.00
SAAB Albert Belle 8.00 20.00
SAAH Andrew Heaney 4.00 10.00
SAAR Andre Rienzo 4.00 10.00
SACA Chris Archer 4.00 10.00
SACAR Chris Archer 4.00 10.00
SACB Charlie Blackmon 6.00 15.00
SACC C.J. Cron 5.00 12.00
SACCR C.J. Cron 5.00 12.00
SACJ Chris Johnson 5.00 12.00
SACM Carlos Martinez 6.00 15.00
SACO Chris Owings 4.00 10.00
SACW Chase Whitley 4.00 10.00
SACY Christian Yelich 20.00 50.00
SADK Dallas Keuchel 10.00 25.00
SADM Daisuke Matsuzaka 8.00 20.00
SADP Dave Parker 8.00 20.00
SAEA Erisbel Arruebarrena 4.00 10.00
SAEB Eddie Butler 4.00 10.00
SAEBU Eddie Butler 4.00 10.00
SAEG Evan Gattis 6.00 15.00
SAGC Garin Cecchini 6.00 15.00
SAGCE Garin Cecchini 6.00 15.00
SAGP Gregory Polanco 12.00 30.00
SAGS George Springer 10.00 25.00
SAGSP George Springer 15.00 40.00
SAHI Hisashi Iwakuma 5.00 12.00
SAJA Jose Abreu 25.00 60.00
SAJAG Jesus Aguilar 10.00 25.00
SAJD Jacob deGrom 300.00 800.00
SAJDE Jacob deGrom 300.00 800.00
SAJG Juan Gonzalez 10.00 25.00
SAJK Joe Kelly 4.00 10.00
SAJP Jim Palmer 6.00 15.00
SAJPO Johnny Podres 4.00 10.00
SAJS Jonathan Schoop 4.00 10.00
SAJSE Jean Segura 5.00 12.00
SAJT Julio Teheran 6.00 15.00
SAKP Kyle Parker 5.00 12.00
SAKU Koji Uehara 4.00 10.00
SAKW Kolten Wong 5.00 12.00
SAMA Matt Adams 4.00 10.00
SAMB Mookie Betts 50.00 120.00
SAMBR Michael Brantley 10.00 25.00
SAMC Matt Carpenter 12.00 30.00
SAMCA Melky Cabrera 4.00 10.00
SAMM Mike Minor 4.00 10.00
SAMS Marcus Stroman 8.00 20.00
SAMST Marcus Stroman 8.00 20.00
SAMW Matt Williams 8.00 20.00
SAMWA Michael Wacha 8.00 20.00
SANC Nick Castellanos 12.00 30.00
SANCA Nick Castellanos 12.00 30.00
SANM Nick Martinez 4.00 10.00
SAOT Oscar Taveras 5.00 12.00
SAOTA Oscar Taveras 5.00 12.00
SAOV Omar Vizquel 20.00 50.00
SAPG Paul Goldschmidt 8.00 20.00
SARE Roenis Elias 4.00 10.00
SARM Rafael Montero 4.00 10.00
SARMO Rafael Montero 4.00 10.00
SARO Rougned Odor 10.00 25.00
SAROD Rougned Odor 10.00 25.00
SASG Sonny Gray 5.00 12.00
SASGR Sonny Gray 5.00 12.00
SASK Scott Kazmir 4.00 10.00
SASM Starling Marte 20.00 50.00
SASMI Shelby Miller 6.00 15.00
SATL Tommy La Stella 6.00 15.00
SAYS Yangervis Solarte 4.00 10.00
SAYSO Yangervis Solarte 4.00 10.00

2014 Topps Supreme Autographs Blue

*BLUE: .5X TO 1.2X BASIC
STATED ODDS 1:17 BOXES
STATED PRINT RUN 20 SER.#'d SETS
EXCHANGE DEADLINE 9/30/2017
SAAJ Adam Jones 12.00 30.00
SACBI Craig Biggio 20.00 50.00
SAFF Freddie Freeman 12.00 30.00
SAJSI Jon Singleton 6.00 15.00

2014 Topps Supreme Autographs Green

*GREEN: .4X TO 1X BASIC
STATED ODDS 1:8 BOXES
STATED PRINT RUN 45 SER.#'d SETS
EXCHANGE DEADLINE 9/30/2017
SAAJ Adam Jones 10.00 25.00
SAJSI Jon Singleton 5.00 12.00

2014 Topps Supreme Autographs Purple

*PURPLE: .5X TO 1.2X BASIC
STATED ODDS 1:14 BOXES
STATED PRINT RUN 25 SER.#'d SETS
EXCHANGE DEADLINE 9/30/2017
SAAJ Adam Jones 12.00 30.00
SAFF Freddie Freeman 12.00 30.00
SAJSI Jon Singleton 6.00 15.00

2014 Topps Supreme Autographs Sepia

*SEPIA: .4X TO 1X BASIC
STATED ODDS 1:10 BOXES
STATED PRINT RUN 35 SER.#'d SETS
EXCHANGE DEADLINE 9/30/2017
SAAJ Adam Jones 10.00 25.00
SAFF Freddie Freeman 10.00 25.00
SAJSI Jon Singleton 5.00 12.00

2014 Topps Supreme Autograph Patches

STATED ODDS 1:29 BOXES
STATED PRINT RUN 25 SER.#'d SETS
EXCHANGE DEADLINE 9/30/2017
APRAG Adrian Gonzalez 12.00 30.00
APRAJ Adam Jones 20.00 50.00
APRBC Brandon Crawford 60.00 120.00
APRBH Bryce Harper 100.00 250.00
APRBP Brandon Phillips 10.00 25.00
APRCG Carlos Gonzalez 12.00 30.00
APRDO David Ortiz 40.00 80.00
APRDP Dustin Pedroia 40.00 80.00
APREL Evan Longoria 12.00 30.00
APRGS Giancarlo Stanton 50.00 120.00
APRGSP George Springer 40.00 80.00
APRHK Hiroki Kuroda 100.00 200.00
APRJD Josh Donaldson 12.00 30.00
APRJK Jason Kipnis 12.00 30.00
APRJM Joe Mauer EXCH 40.00 80.00
APRJS John Smoltz 60.00 120.00
APRJT Julio Teheran 15.00 40.00
APRJV Joey Votto 15.00 40.00
APRMA Matt Adams 15.00 40.00
APRMB Madison Bumgarner 60.00 120.00
APRMM Manny Machado 30.00 60.00
APRMP Mike Piazza 75.00 150.00
APRMS Max Scherzer 30.00 80.00
APRNC Nick Castellanos 30.00 80.00
APRPG Paul Goldschmidt 15.00 40.00
APRRB Ryan Braun 12.00 30.00
APRRH Ryan Howard 12.00 30.00
APRRO Rougned Odor 25.00 60.00
APRSM Starling Marte 20.00 50.00
APRTG Tom Glavine 60.00 120.00
APRTT Troy Tulowitzki 15.00 40.00
APRWM Wil Myers 10.00 25.00
APRYC Yoenis Cespedes 15.00 40.00

2014 Topps Supreme Dual Autographs

STATED ODDS 1:25 BOXES
STATED PRINT RUN 25 SER.#'d SETS
EXCHANGE DEADLINE 9/30/2017
DAAC M.Carpenter/M.Adams 15.00 40.00
DAAG A.Guerrero/E.Arruebarrena 25.00 60.00
DABB J.Bagwell/C.Biggio 60.00 120.00
DABJ F.Jenkins/E.Banks 40.00 100.00
DACG Y.Cespedes/S.Gray 15.00 40.00
DADM J.deGrom/R.Montero 100.00 250.00
DAGS T.Glavine/J.Smoltz 75.00 150.00
DAHF F.Freeman/J.Heyward 20.00 50.00
DAHM R.Henderson/M.McGwire 75.00 200.00
DAHS A.Heaney/G.Stanton 25.00 60.00
DAHT M.Trout/B.Harper 250.00 350.00
DAJG K.Griffey Jr./R.Johnson 150.00 250.00
DAJGR K.Griffey Jr./B.Jackson 150.00 250.00
DAJH R.Jackson/R.Henderson 60.00 150.00
DAJM M.Machado/A.Jones 50.00 100.00
DAKI H.Iwakuma/H.Kuroda 75.00 150.00
DALF C.Fisk/F.Lynn 30.00 60.00
DAMP B.Posey/J.Mauer 40.00 80.00
DAOC D.Cone/P.O'Neill 12.00 30.00
DAPB K.Parker/E.Butler 12.00 30.00
DAPC R.Cano/D.Pedroia 30.00 60.00
DAPK Y.Puig/C.Kershaw 100.00 250.00
DAPR R.Palmeiro/I.Rodriguez 15.00 40.00
DAPS G.Polanco/G.Springer 20.00 50.00
DAPT M.Trout/Y.Puig 300.00 400.00
DASCA S.Carlton/M.Schmidt 40.00 100.00
DASCR J.Singleton/C.Cron 12.00 30.00
DASG B.Gibson/O.Smith 20.00 50.00
DASK H.Kuroda/C.Sabathia 75.00 150.00
DASO Y.Solarte/R.Odor 25.00 60.00
DASS G.Springer/J.Singleton 25.00 60.00
DATG T.Tulowitzki/C.Gonzalez 30.00 60.00
DATM J.Teheran/M.Minor 15.00 40.00
DATP Taveras/Polanco 15.00 40.00
DATS G.Springer/O.Taveras 40.00 100.00
DAVC J.Votto/J.Cueto 30.00 60.00
DAVS M.Stroman/Y.Ventura 15.00 40.00
DAWM M.Wacha/S.Miller 30.00 60.00
DAYS G.Stanton/C.Yelich 100.00 250.00

2014 Topps Supreme Simply Supreme Autographs

STATED ODDS 1:8 BOXES
STATED PRINT RUN 50 SER.#'d SETS
EXCHANGE DEADLINE 9/30/2017
SSUAH Andrew Heaney 4.00 10.00
SSUAR Andre Rienzo 4.00 10.00
SSUARI Anthony Rizzo/41 15.00 40.00
SSUCA Chris Archer 4.00 10.00
SSUCB Charlie Blackmon 8.00 20.00
SSUCC C.J. Cron 4.00 10.00
SSUCCR C.J. Cron 4.00 10.00
SSUCJ Chris Johnson 6.00 15.00
SSUCO Chris Owings 4.00 10.00
SSUCW Chase Whitley 4.00 10.00
SSUCY Christian Yelich 20.00 50.00
SSUDC David Cone 8.00 20.00
SSUDK Dallas Keuchel 5.00 12.00
SSUDM Daisuke Matsuzaka 8.00 20.00
SSUDME Devin Mesoraco 5.00 12.00
SSUDP Dave Parker 8.00 20.00
SSUDPA Dave Parker 8.00 20.00
SSUEA Erisbel Arruebarrena 4.00 10.00
SSUEB Eddie Butler 4.00 10.00
SSUEBU Eddie Butler 4.00 10.00
SSUEG Evan Gattis 6.00 15.00
SSUEM Edgar Martinez 5.00 12.00
SSUFL Fred Lynn 8.00 20.00
SSUGC Garin Cecchini 6.00 15.00
SSUGCE Garin Cecchini 6.00 15.00
SSUGP Gregory Polanco 6.00 15.00
SSUGPO Gregory Polanco 6.00 15.00
SSUGS George Springer 15.00 40.00
SSUGSP George Springer 15.00 40.00
SSUGST Giancarlo Stanton 20.00 50.00
SSUHI Hisashi Iwakuma 5.00 12.00
SSUJAG Jesus Aguilar 10.00 25.00
SSUJC Jose Canseco 8.00 20.00
SSUJD Jacob deGrom 300.00 800.00
SSUJDO Josh Donaldson 8.00 20.00
SSUJH Jason Heyward 6.00 15.00
SSUJK Joe Kelly 4.00 10.00
SSUJL Jonathan Lucroy 8.00 20.00
SSUJP Josmil Pinto 4.00 10.00
SSUJS Jonathan Schoop 4.00 10.00
SSUJT Julio Teheran 5.00 12.00
SSUKU Koji Uehara 4.00 10.00
SSUKW Kolten Wong 12.00 30.00
SSUMA Matt Adams 4.00 10.00
SSUMB Michael Brantley 10.00 25.00
SSUMC Melky Cabrera 4.00 10.00
SSUMM Mike Minor 4.00 10.00
SSUMN Mike Napoli 4.00 10.00
SSUMO Marcell Ozuna 6.00 15.00
SSUMW Michael Wacha 8.00 20.00
SSUNC Nick Castellanos 12.00 30.00
SSUNE Nate Eovaldi 5.00 12.00
SSUNM Nick Martinez 4.00 10.00
SSUOT Oscar Taveras 5.00 12.00
SSUOTA Oscar Taveras 5.00 12.00
SSUPG Paul Goldschmidt 8.00 20.00
SSUPO Paul O'Neill 5.00 12.00
SSURE Roenis Elias 4.00 10.00
SSURG Ron Gant 4.00 10.00
SSURM Rafael Montero 4.00 10.00
SSURMO Rafael Montero 4.00 10.00
SSURO Rougned Odor 10.00 25.00
SSUROD Rougned Odor 10.00 25.00
SSURP Rafael Palmeiro 6.00 15.00
SSUSG Sonny Gray 5.00 12.00
SSUSGR Sonny Gray 5.00 12.00
SSUSK Scott Kazmir 4.00 10.00
SSUSM Starling Marte 6.00 15.00
SSUTL Tommy La Stella 4.00 10.00
SSUYS Yangervis Solarte 4.00 10.00
SSUYV Yordano Ventura 15.00 40.00

2014 Topps Supreme Simply Supreme Autographs Blue

*BLUE: .5X TO 1.2X BASIC
STATED ODDS 1:17 BOXES
STATED PRINT RUN 20 SER.#'d SETS
EXCHANGE DEADLINE 9/30/2017
SSUTG Tom Glavine 25.00 60.00
SSUYC Yoenis Cespedes 12.00 30.00

2014 Topps Supreme Simply Supreme Autographs Green

*GREEN: .4X TO 1X BASIC
STATED ODDS 1:8 BOXES
STATED PRINT RUN 45 SER.#'d SETS
EXCHANGE DEADLINE 9/30/2017

2014 Topps Supreme Simply Supreme Autographs Purple

*PURPLE: .5X TO 1.2X BASIC
STATED ODDS 1:14 BOXES
STATED PRINT RUN 25 SER.#'d SETS
EXCHANGE DEADLINE 9/30/2017
SSUTG Tom Glavine 25.00 60.00
SSUYC Yoenis Cespedes 12.00 30.00

2014 Topps Supreme Simply Supreme Autographs Sepia

*SEPIA: .4X TO 1X BASIC
STATED ODDS 1:10 BOXES
STATED PRINT RUN 35 SER.#'d SETS
EXCHANGE DEADLINE 9/30/2017
SSUTG Tom Glavine 20.00 50.00
SSUYC Yoenis Cespedes 10.00 25.00

2014 Topps Supreme Supreme Scope Autograph Patches

STATED ODDS 1:25 BOXES
STATED PRINT RUN 40 SER.#'d SETS
EXCHANGE DEADLINE 9/30/2017
SSCAC Allen Craig 12.00 30.00
SSCAJ Adam Jones 12.00 30.00
SSCBH Bryce Harper 150.00 300.00
SSCBP Buster Posey 30.00 80.00
SSCCG Carlos Gonzalez 12.00 30.00
SSCDW David Wright 12.00 30.00
SSCEG Evan Gattis 10.00 25.00
SSCFF Freddie Freeman 15.00 40.00
SSCGS George Springer 10.00 25.00
SSCGST Giancarlo Stanton 50.00 120.00
SSCHK Hiroki Kuroda 60.00 120.00
SSCJD Josh Donaldson 12.00 30.00
SSCJT Julio Teheran 12.00 30.00
SSCMA Matt Adams 10.00 25.00
SSCMB Madison Bumgarner 60.00 120.00
SSCMM Mike Minor 10.00 25.00
SSCMS Max Scherzer 30.00 80.00
SSCOS Ozzie Smith 30.00 60.00
SSCPG Paul Goldschmidt 15.00 40.00
SSCRB Ryan Braun 12.00 30.00
SSCRH Ryan Howard 12.00 30.00
SSCSC Steve Carlton 20.00 50.00
SSCSM Starling Marte 12.00 30.00
SSCTG Tom Glavine 15.00 40.00
SSCTT Troy Tulowitzki 15.00 40.00

2014 Topps Supreme Supreme Styling Autographs

STATED ODDS 1:8 BOXES
STATED PRINT RUN 50 SER.#'d SETS
EXCHANGE DEADLINE 9/30/2017
SSAA Arismendy Alcantara 4.00 10.00
SSAG Avisail Garcia 6.00 15.00
SSAH Andrew Heaney 4.00 10.00
SSAR Andre Rienzo 4.00 10.00
SSAS Andrelton Simmons 8.00 20.00
SSASA Aaron Sanchez 8.00 20.00
SSCA Chris Archer 4.00 10.00
SSCB Charlie Blackmon/31 8.00 20.00
SSCC C.J. Cron 5.00 12.00
SSCCR C.J. Cron 5.00 12.00
SSCJO Chris Johnson 4.00 10.00
SSCM Carlos Martinez 6.00 15.00
SSCO Chris Owings 4.00 10.00
SSCS Chris Sale 8.00 20.00
SSCW Chase Whitley 4.00 10.00
SSDK Dallas Keuchel 10.00 25.00
SSDM Daisuke Matsuzaka 8.00 20.00
SSDP Dave Parker 8.00 20.00
SSEA Erisbel Arruebarrena 6.00 15.00
SSEB Eddie Butler 4.00 10.00
SSEG Evan Gattis 6.00 15.00
SSEM Edgar Martinez 5.00 12.00
SSGC Garin Cecchini 6.00 15.00
SSGCE Garin Cecchini 6.00 15.00
SSGP Gregory Polanco 12.00 30.00
SSGPO Gregory Polanco 12.00 30.00
SSGS George Springer 15.00 40.00
SSGSP George Springer 15.00 40.00
SSHI Hisashi Iwakuma 5.00 12.00
SSJC Jose Canseco 8.00 20.00
SSJD Jacob deGrom 300.00 800.00
SSJDO Josh Donaldson 8.00 20.00
SSJG Juan Gonzalez 10.00 25.00
SSJK Jason Kipnis 8.00 20.00
SSJL Jonathan Lucroy 8.00 20.00
SSJP Josmil Pinto 4.00 10.00
SSJS Jonathan Schoop 4.00 10.00
SSJSE Jean Segura 5.00 12.00
SSKP Kyle Parker 5.00 12.00
SSKU Koji Uehara 4.00 10.00
SSKW Kolten Wong 12.00 30.00
SSMA Matt Adams 6.00 15.00
SSMB Michael Brantley 10.00 25.00
SSMBU Madison Bumgarner 30.00 80.00
SSMC Melky Cabrera 4.00 10.00
SSMCR Matt Carpenter 12.00 30.00
SSMCAR Matt Carpenter 12.00 30.00
SSMM Mike Minor 4.00 10.00
SSMS Marcus Stroman 8.00 20.00
SSMW Matt Williams 8.00 20.00
SSNC Nick Castellanos 10.00 25.00
SSNE Nate Eovaldi 5.00 12.00
SSNEO Nate Eovaldi 5.00 12.00
SSNM Nick Martinez 4.00 10.00
SSOT Oscar Taveras 5.00 12.00
SSOTA Oscar Taveras 5.00 12.00
SSOV Omar Vizquel 25.00 60.00
SSPG Paul Goldschmidt 8.00 20.00
SSRM Rafael Montero 4.00 10.00
SSRMO Rafael Montero 4.00 10.00
SSRO Rougned Odor 10.00 25.00
SSROD Rougned Odor 10.00 25.00
SSSG Sonny Gray 5.00 12.00
SSSGR Sonny Gray 5.00 12.00
SSSK Scott Kazmir 4.00 10.00
SSSM Starling Marte 12.00 30.00
SSSMA Starling Marte 12.00 30.00
SSSMI Shelby Miller 6.00 15.00
SSTL Tommy La Stella 4.00 10.00
SSYS Yangervis Solarte 4.00 10.00

2014 Topps Supreme Supreme Styling Autographs Blue

*BLUE: .5X TO 1.2X BASIC
STATED ODDS 1:17 BOXES
STATED PRINT RUN 20 SER.#'d SETS
EXCHANGE DEADLINE 9/30/2017
SSCY Christian Yelich 20.00 50.00
SSDE Dennis Eckersley 10.00 25.00
SSFJ Fergie Jenkins 12.00 30.00
SSGST Giancarlo Stanton 25.00 60.00
SSJM Juan Marichal 15.00 40.00
SSMSC Max Scherzer 20.00 50.00
SSMWA Michael Wacha 12.00 30.00

2014 Topps Supreme Supreme Styling Autographs Green

*GREEN: .4X TO 1X BASIC
STATED ODDS 1:8 BOXES
STATED PRINT RUN 45 SER.#'d SETS
EXCHANGE DEADLINE 9/30/2017
SSDE Dennis Eckersley 8.00 20.00
SSJM Juan Marichal 12.00 30.00
SSMSC Max Scherzer 15.00 40.00

2014 Topps Supreme Supreme Styling Autographs Purple

*PURPLE: .5X TO 1.2X BASIC
STATED ODDS 1:14 BOXES
STATED PRINT RUN 25 SER.#'d SETS
EXCHANGE DEADLINE 9/30/2017
SSCY Christian Yelich 20.00 50.00
SSDE Dennis Eckersley 10.00 25.00
SSFJ Fergie Jenkins 12.00 30.00
SSJM Juan Marichal 15.00 40.00
SSMSC Max Scherzer 20.00 50.00
SSMWA Michael Wacha 12.00 30.00

2014 Topps Supreme Supreme Styling Autographs Sepia

*SEPIA: .4X TO 1X BASIC
STATED ODDS 1:10 BOXES
STATED PRINT RUN 35 SER.#'d SETS
EXCHANGE DEADLINE 9/30/2017
SSCY Christian Yelich 20.00 50.00
SSDE Dennis Eckersley 8.00 20.00
SSFJ Fergie Jenkins 10.00 25.00
SSJM Juan Marichal 12.00 30.00
SSMSC Max Scherzer 15.00 40.00

2015 Topps Supreme Autographs

OVERALL AUTO ODDS 2:1 HOBBY
*GREEN/50: .5X TO 1.2X BASIC
PRINTING PLATE ODDS 1:90 HOBBY
PLATE PRINT RUN 1 SET PER COLOR
BLACK-CYAN-MAGENTA-YELLOW ISSUED
NO PLATE PRICING DUE TO SCARCITY
EXCHANGE DEADLINE 8/31/2017
SAAGA Andres Galarraga 6.00 15.00
SAAGN Alex Gordon 8.00 20.00
SAAJS Adam Jones 8.00 20.00
SAAJU Andruw Jones 2.50 6.00
SAARO Anthony Ranaudo 2.50 6.00
SABB Byron Buxton 8.00 20.00
SABC Brandon Crawford 5.00 12.00
SABF Buck Farmer 2.50 6.00
SABFI Brandon Finnegan 2.50 6.00
SACB Craig Biggio 10.00 25.00
SACD Carlos Delgado 3.00 8.00
SACH Chase Headley 5.00 12.00
SACKR Corey Kluber 5.00 12.00
SACKW Clayton Kershaw 40.00 100.00
SACRN Carlos Rodon 6.00 15.00
SACS Chris Sale 10.00 25.00
SACY Christian Yelich 30.00 80.00
SADC David Cone 6.00 15.00
SADF Doug Fister 2.50 6.00
SADFR Dexter Fowler 3.00 8.00
SADH Dilson Herrera 3.00 8.00
SADN Daniel Norris 2.50 6.00
SADP Dustin Pedroia 12.00 30.00
SADPY Dalton Pompey 3.00 8.00
SAFL Francisco Lindor 15.00 40.00
SAFV Fernando Valenzuela 10.00 25.00
SAGR Garrett Richards 3.00 8.00
SAGS George Springer 10.00 25.00
SAJA Jose Abreu 12.00 30.00

SAJAE Jose Altuve 30.00 80.00
SAJBZ Javier Baez 30.00 80.00
SAJDM Jacob deGrom 20.00 50.00
SAJF Jose Fernandez 10.00 25.00
SAJG Juan Gonzalez 2.50 6.00
SAJH Josh Harrison 4.00 10.00
SAJK Jung Ho Kang 4.00 10.00
SAJLS Juan Lagares 2.50 6.00
SAJPK Joe Panik 3.00 8.00
SAJPN Joc Pederson 6.00 15.00
SAJS John Smoltz 15.00 40.00
SAJSR Jorge Soler 4.00 10.00
SAJSS James Shields 3.00 8.00
SAKW Kolten Wong 3.00 8.00
SALB Lou Brock 15.00 40.00
SAMA Matt Adams 2.50 6.00
SAMC Miguel Castro 2.50 6.00
SAMFO Maikel Franco 3.00 8.00
SAMJ Micah Johnson 2.50 6.00
SAMTR Michael Taylor 2.50 6.00
SANS Noah Syndergaard 10.00 25.00
SAOV Omar Vizquel 6.00 15.00
SARA Roberto Alomar 10.00 25.00
SARCO Rusney Castillo 3.00 8.00
SARI Raisel Iglesias 3.00 8.00
SARO Roberto Osuna 3.00 8.00
SARP Rick Porcello 10.00 25.00
SARS Ryne Sandberg 20.00 50.00
SASGY Sonny Gray 6.00 15.00
SASMA Steven Moya 3.00 8.00
SASME Starling Marte 5.00 12.00
SASMR Shelby Miller 3.00 8.00
SATG Tom Glavine 10.00 25.00
SAYG Yan Gomes 2.50 6.00
SAYT Yasmany Tomas 3.00 8.00
SAZW Zack Wheeler 6.00 15.00

2015 Topps Supreme Autographs Orange

*ORANGE: .6X TO 1.5X BASIC
STATED ODDS 1:15 HOBBY
STATED PRINT RUN 25 SER.#'d SETS
EXCHANGE DEADLINE 8/31/2017
SAAK Al Kaline 75.00 200.00
SABL Barry Larkin 25.00 60.00
SABP Buster Posey 150.00 250.00
SABW Bernie Williams 20.00 50.00
SACR Cal Ripken Jr. 60.00 150.00
SADO David Ortiz 40.00 100.00
SAJBS Johnny Bench 20.00 50.00
SAMTT Mike Trout 250.00 400.00
SAPN Phil Niekro 20.00 50.00
SARCS Roger Clemens 30.00 80.00
SARJA Reggie Jackson 30.00 80.00
SASC Steve Carlton 10.00 25.00

2015 Topps Supreme Autographs Relics

STATED ODDS 1:45 HOBBY
STATED PRINT RUN 25 SER.#'D SETS
EXCHANGE DEADLINE 8/31/2017
ARAG Adrian Gonzalez 10.00 25.00
ARCJ Chipper Jones 50.00 120.00
ARCY Christian Yelich 20.00 50.00
ARDO David Ortiz 30.00 80.00
ARDP Dustin Pedroia 15.00 40.00
ARFF Freddie Freeman 15.00 40.00
ARFT Frank Thomas 25.00 60.00
ARJD Jacob deGrom 50.00 120.00
ARJP Jorge Posada 30.00 80.00
ARMM Mark McGwire 60.00 150.00
ARMP Mike Piazza 40.00 100.00
ARRCO Robinson Cano 10.00 25.00
ARRJ Randy Johnson 30.00 80.00
ARTG Tom Glavine 10.00 25.00

2015 Topps Supreme Simply Supreme Autographs

OVERALL AUTO ODDS 2:1 HOBBY
*GREEN/50: .5X TO 1.2X BASIC
PRINTING PLATE ODDS 1:90 HOBBY
PLATE PRINT RUN 1 SET PER COLOR
BLACK-CYAN-MAGENTA-YELLOW ISSUED
NO PLATE PRICING DUE TO SCARCITY
EXCHANGE DEADLINE 8/31/2017
SSAAA Arismendy Alcantara 2.50 6.00
SSAAB Archie Bradley 2.50 6.00
SSAAG Alex Gordon 3.00 8.00
SSABFN Brandon Finnegan 2.50 6.00
SSABM Brandon Moss 2.50 6.00
SSACB Craig Biggio 12.00 30.00
SSACD Carlos Delgado 3.00 8.00
SSACK Corey Kluber 8.00 20.00
SSACS Cory Spangenberg 2.50 6.00
SSACY Christian Yelich 20.00 50.00
SSADB Dellin Betances 3.00 8.00
SSADF Doug Fister 2.50 6.00
SSADG Didi Gregorius 4.00 10.00
SSADH Dilson Herrera 3.00 8.00
SSADM Devin Mesoraco 2.50 6.00
SSADP Dalton Pompey 3.00 8.00
SSADT Devon Travis 2.50 6.00
SSAEEN Edwin Encarnacion 6.00 15.00
SSAEM Edgar Martinez 5.00 12.00
SSAFF Freddie Freeman 6.00 15.00
SSAHR Hanley Ramirez 6.00 15.00
SSAJA Jose Altuve 12.00 30.00
SSAJB Javier Baez 15.00 40.00
SSAJCO Jose Canseco 6.00 15.00
SSAJCT Jarred Cosart 2.50 6.00
SSAJD Jacob deGrom 20.00 50.00
SSAJG Joey Gallo 8.00 20.00
SSAJHD Jason Heyward 12.00 30.00
SSAJHN Josh Harrison 4.00 10.00
SSAJK Jung Ho Kang 12.00 30.00
SSAJL Jake Lamb 4.00 10.00
SSAJPA Jorge Posada 15.00 40.00
SSAJPK Joe Panik 3.00 8.00
SSAJPN Joc Pederson 6.00 15.00
SSAJS Jorge Soler 4.00 10.00
SSAJSH James Shields 3.00 8.00
SSAKB Kris Bryant 60.00 150.00
SSAKGN Kevin Gausman 4.00 10.00
SSAKS Kyle Seager 5.00 12.00
SSAKV Kennys Vargas 2.50 6.00
SSAKW Kolten Wong 3.00 8.00
SSALG Luis Gonzalez 2.50 6.00
SSAMB Matt Barnes 2.50 6.00
SSAMC Matt Carpenter 6.00 15.00
SSAMFO Maikel Franco 3.00 8.00
SSAMG Mark Grace 3.00 8.00
SSAMT Mark Teixeira 5.00 12.00
SSAMTA Michael Taylor 2.50 6.00
SSAOV Omar Vizquel 6.00 15.00
SSAPG Paul Goldschmidt 4.00 10.00
SSARB Ryan Braun 3.00 8.00
SSARCO Rusney Castillo 3.00 8.00
SSASGY Sonny Gray 3.00 8.00
SSASK Sandy Koufax 8.00 20.00
SSATM Trevor May 2.50 6.00
SSAVC Vinny Castilla 2.50 6.00
SSAYT Yasmany Tomas 3.00 8.00

2015 Topps Supreme Simply Supreme Autographs Orange

*ORANGE: .6X TO 1.5X BASIC
STATED ODDS 1:15 HOBBY
STATED PRINT RUN 25 SER.#'d SETS
EXCHANGE DEADLINE 8/31/2017
SSABW Bernie Williams 20.00 50.00
SSACR Cal Ripken Jr. 60.00 150.00
SSAFT Frank Thomas 40.00 100.00
SSAMP Mike Piazza 60.00 150.00
SSAOS Ozzie Smith 25.00 60.00
SSARCA Robinson Cano 10.00 25.00
SSASK Sandy Koufax 300.00 400.00
SSAYD Yu Darvish 30.00 80.00

2015 Topps Supreme Supreme Styling Autographs

STATED ODDS 1:21 HOBBY
PRINT RUNS B/WN 18-45 COPIES PER
EXCHANGE DEADLINE 8/31/2017
SSI Ichiro/32 150.00 400.00
SSAR Addison Russell/32 30.00 80.00
SSBP Buster Posey/32 40.00 100.00
SSCC Carlos Correa EXCH 150.00 300.00
SSCF Carlton Fisk/32 15.00 40.00
SSCKR Corey Kluber/45 10.00 25.00
SSCS Chris Sale/32 12.00 30.00
SSDP Dustin Pedroia/32 20.00 50.00
SSDW David Wright/45 15.00 40.00
SSEE Edwin Encarnacion/32 5.00 12.00
SSFF Freddie Freeman/32 15.00 40.00
SSFT Frank Thomas/32 30.00 80.00
SSGM Greg Maddux/26 30.00 80.00
SSHA Hank Aaron/18 150.00 300.00
SSJA Jose Abreu/32 15.00 40.00
SSJBL Jeff Bagwell/28 30.00 80.00
SSJBZ Javier Baez/45 20.00 50.00
SSJD Jacob deGrom/30 50.00 120.00
SSJP Joc Pederson/29 12.00 30.00
SSJSR Jorge Soler/32 8.00 20.00
SSMP Mike Piazza/18 50.00 120.00
SSMR Mariano Rivera/32 125.00 250.00
SSMT Mike Trout/32 150.00 300.00
SSNR Nolan Ryan/30 125.00 250.00
SSRCA Robinson Cano/32 6.00 15.00
SSRCO Rusney Castillo/32 6.00 15.00
SSTG Tom Glavine/32 20.00 50.00
SSYT Yasmany Tomas/32 15.00 40.00

2002 Topps Ten

COMPLETE SET (200) 20.00 50.00
COMMON CARD (1-190) .10 .30
COMMON CARD (191-200) .40 1.00
1 Ichiro Suzuki HITS .60 1.50
2 Rich Aurilia HITS .10 .30
3 Bret Boone HITS .10 .30
4 Juan Pierre HITS .10 .30
5 Shannon Stewart HITS .10 .30
6 Alex Rodriguez HITS .40 1.00
7 Luis Gonzalez HITS .10 .30
8 Todd Helton HITS .20 .50
9 Garret Anderson HITS .10 .30
10 Albert Pujols HITS .60 1.50
11 Lance Berkman 2B .10 .30
12 Todd Helton 2B .20 .50
13 Jeff Kent 2B .10 .30
14 Bob Abreu 2B .10 .30
15 Jason Giambi 2B .10 .30
16 Albert Pujols 2B .60 1.50
17 Mike Sweeney 2B .10 .30
18 Vladimir Guerrero 2B .30 .75
19 Cliff Floyd 2B .10 .30
20 Shannon Stewart 2B .10 .30
21 Cristian Guzman 3B .10 .30
22 Roberto Alomar 3B .20 .50
23 Carlos Beltran 3B .10 .30
24 Jimmy Rollins 3B .10 .30
25 Roger Cedeno 3B .10 .30
26 Juan Pierre 3B .10 .30
27 Juan Uribe 3B .10 .30
28 Luis Castillo 3B .10 .30
29 Ray Durham 3B .10 .30
30 Mark McLemore 3B .10 .30
31 Barry Bonds HR .75 2.00
32 Sammy Sosa HR .30 .75
33 Luis Gonzalez HR .10 .30
34 Alex Rodriguez HR .40 1.00
35 Shawn Green HR .10 .30
36 Todd Helton HR .20 .50
37 Jim Thome HR .20 .50
38 Rafael Palmeiro HR .20 .50
39 Richie Sexson HR .10 .30
40 Phil Nevin HR .10 .30
41 Troy Glaus HR .10 .30
42 Sammy Sosa RBI .30 .75
43 Todd Helton RBI .20 .50
44 Luis Gonzalez RBI .10 .30
45 Bret Boone RBI .10 .30
46 Juan Gonzalez RBI .10 .30
47 Barry Bonds RBI .75 2.00
48 Alex Rodriguez RBI .40 1.00
49 Jeff Bagwell RBI .20 .50
50 Albert Pujols RBI .60 1.50
51 Phil Nevin RBI .10 .30
52 Ichiro Suzuki AVG .60 1.50
53 Larry Walker AVG .10 .30
54 Jason Giambi AVG .10 .30
55 Roberto Alomar AVG .20 .50
56 Todd Helton AVG .20 .50
57 Moises Alou AVG .10 .30
58 Lance Berkman AVG .10 .30
59 Bret Boone AVG .10 .30
60 Frank Catalanotto AVG .10 .30
61 Chipper Jones AVG .30 .75
62 Barry Bonds SLG .75 2.00
63 Sammy Sosa SLG .30 .75
64 Luis Gonzalez SLG .10 .30
65 Todd Helton SLG .20 .50
66 Larry Walker SLG .10 .30
67 Jason Giambi SLG .10 .30
68 Jim Thome SLG .20 .50
69 Alex Rodriguez SLG .40 1.00
70 Lance Berkman SLG .10 .30
71 Albert Pujols SLG .60 1.50
72 Ichiro Suzuki SB .60 1.50
73 Roger Cedeno SB .10 .30
74 Juan Pierre SB .10 .30
75 Jimmy Rollins SB .10 .30
76 Alfonso Soriano SB .10 .30
77 Mark McLemore SB .10 .30
78 Chuck Knoblauch SB .10 .30
79 Vladimir Guerrero SB .30 .75
80 Bob Abreu SB .10 .30
81 Mike Cameron SB .10 .30
82 Sammy Sosa RUNS .30 .75
83 Alex Rodriguez RUNS .40 1.00
84 Todd Helton RUNS .20 .50
85 Barry Bonds RUNS .75 2.00
86 Luis Gonzalez RUNS .10 .30
87 Ichiro Suzuki RUNS .60 1.50
88 Jeff Bagwell RUNS .20 .50
89 Cliff Floyd RUNS .10 .30
90 Shawn Green RUNS .10 .30
91 Craig Biggio RUNS .20 .50
92 Juan Pierre K/AB .10 .30
93 Fernando Vina K/AB .10 .30
94 Paul LoDuca K/AB .10 .30
95 Mark Grace K/AB .20 .50
96 Eric Young K/AB .10 .30
97 Placido Polanco K/AB .10 .30
98 Jason Kendall K/AB .10 .30
99 Ichiro Suzuki K/AB .60 1.50
100 Orlando Cabrera K/AB .10 .30
101 Rey Sanchez K/AB .10 .30
102 Ichiro Suzuki AS VOTE .60 1.50
103 Edgar Martinez AS VOTE .20 .50
104 Bret Boone AS VOTE .10 .30
105 Barry Bonds AS VOTE .75 2.00
106 Ivan Rodriguez AS VOTE .20 .50
107 Mike Piazza AS VOTE .50 1.25
108 Sammy Sosa AS VOTE .30 .75
109 John Olerud AS VOTE .10 .30
110 Roberto Alomar AS VOTE .20 .50
111 Roberto Alomar AS APP .20 .50
112 Mark McGwire AS APP .75 2.00
113 Barry Larkin AS APP .20 .50
114 Ken Griffey Jr. AS APP .60 1.50
115 Rickey Henderson AS APP .30 .75
116 Barry Bonds AS APP .75 2.00
117 Ivan Rodriguez AS APP .20 .50
118 Mike Piazza AS APP .50 1.25
119 Roger Clemens AS APP .60 1.50
120 Randy Johnson AS APP .30 .75
121 Albert Pujols ROY .60 1.50
122 Ichiro Suzuki ROY .60 1.50
123 Roy Oswalt ROY .10 .30
124 C.C. Sabathia ROY .10 .30
125 Jimmy Rollins ROY .10 .30
126 Alfonso Soriano ROY .10 .30
127 David Eckstein ROY .10 .30
128 Adam Dunn ROY .10 .30
129 Bud Smith ROY .10 .30
130 Tsuyoshi Shinjo ROY .10 .30
131 Matt Morris WINS .10 .30
132 Curt Schilling WINS .10 .30
133 Randy Johnson WINS .30 .75
134 Mark Mulder WINS .10 .30
135 Roger Clemens WINS .60 1.50
136 Jon Lieber WINS .10 .30
137 Jamie Moyer WINS .10 .30
138 Freddy Garcia WINS .10 .30
139 Tim Hudson WINS .10 .30
140 C.C. Sabathia WINS .10 .30
141 Randy Johnson ERA .30 .75
142 Curt Schilling ERA .10 .30
143 John Burkett ERA .10 .30
144 Freddy Garcia ERA .10 .30
145 Greg Maddux ERA .50 1.25
146 Darryl Kile ERA .10 .30
147 Mike Mussina ERA .20 .50
148 Joe Mays ERA .10 .30
149 Matt Morris ERA .10 .30
150 Russ Ortiz ERA .10 .30
151 Randy Johnson K .30 .75
152 Curt Schilling K .10 .30
153 Hideo Nomo K .30 .75
154 Chan Ho Park K .10 .30
155 Kerry Wood K .10 .30
156 Mike Mussina K .20 .50
157 Roger Clemens K .60 1.50
158 Javier Vazquez K .10 .30
159 Barry Zito K .10 .30
160 Bartolo Colon K .10 .30
161 Mariano Rivera SV .30 .75
162 Robb Nen SV .10 .30
163 Kazuhiro Sasaki SV .10 .30
164 Armando Benitez SV .10 .30
165 Trevor Hoffman SV .10 .30
166 Jeff Shaw SV .10 .30
167 Keith Foulke SV .10 .30
168 Jose Mesa SV .10 .30
169 Troy Percival SV .10 .30
170 Billy Wagner SV .10 .30
171 Pat Burrell AST .10 .30
172 Raul Mondesi AST .10 .30
173 Gary Sheffield AST .10 .30
174 Carlos Beltran AST .10 .30
175 Vladimir Guerrero AST .30 .75
176 Torii Hunter AST .10 .30
177 Jeromy Burnitz AST .10 .30
178 Tim Salmon AST .20 .50
179 Jim Edmonds AST .10 .30
180 Tsuyoshi Shinjo AST .10 .30
181 Greg Maddux GLV .50 1.25
182 Roberto Alomar GLV .20 .50
183 Ken Griffey Jr. GLV .60 1.50
184 Ivan Rodriguez GLV .20 .50
185 Omar Vizquel GLV .20 .50
186 Barry Bonds GLV .75 2.00
187 Devon White GLV .10 .30
188 J.T. Snow GLV .10 .30
189 Larry Walker GLV .10 .30
190 Robin Ventura GLV .10 .30
191 Mark Phillips PROS RC .40 1.00
192 Clint Nageotte PROS RC .60 1.50
193 Mauricio Lara PROS RC .40 1.00
194 Nic Jackson PROS RC .40 1.00
195 Chris Tritle PROS RC .40 1.00
196 Ryan Gripp PROS RC .40 1.00
197 Greg Montalbano PROS RC .40 1.00
198 Noochie Varner PROS RC .40 1.00
199 Nick Alvarez PROS RC .40 1.00
200 Craig Kuzmic PROS RC .40 1.00

2002 Topps Ten Die Cuts

*DIE CUTS 1-190: 2X TO 5X BASIC
*DIE CUTS 191-200: 2X TO 5X BASIC
STATED ODDS 1:4

2002 Topps Ten Autographs

GROUP A STATED ODDS 1:1928
GROUP B STATED ODDS 1:123
GROUP C STATED ODDS 1:539
GROUP D STATED ODDS 1:617
OVERALL AUTOGRAPH ODDS 1:67
TTABB Barry Bonds B 50.00 100.00
TTABZ Barry Zito B 6.00 15.00
TTACF Cliff Floyd D 6.00 15.00
TTACG Cristian Guzman C 6.00 15.00
TTAJE Jim Edmonds B 10.00 25.00
TTAJR Jimmy Rollins B 15.00 40.00
TTALG Luis Gonzalez B 8.00 20.00
TTARC Roger Clemens A 30.00 80.00
TTARO Roy Oswalt B 6.00 15.00
TTABBO Bret Boone B 6.00 15.00

2002 Topps Ten Relics

BAT GROUP A 1:108
BAT GROUP B 1:108
BAT GROUP C 1:80
BAT GROUP D 1:539
BAT GROUP E 1:216
OVERALL BAT RELIC ODDS 1:27
UNIFORM GROUP A 1:34
UNIFORM GROUP B 1:120
OVERALL UNIFORM RELIC ODDS 1:26
OVERALL RELIC ODDS 1:13
TTRAB Armando Benitez Jsy A 1.50 4.00
TTRAP Albert Pujols Bat A 8.00 20.00
TTRAR Alex Rodriguez Jsy A 5.00 12.00
TTRAS Alfonso Soriano Bat B 2.50 6.00
TTRBA Bob Abreu Bat A 1.50 4.00
TTRBB Bret Boone Bat E 1.50 4.00
TTRBC Bartolo Colon Jsy A 1.50 4.00
TTRBW Billy Wagner Jsy B 1.50 4.00
TTRBZ Barry Zito Jsy B 1.50 4.00
TTRCB Craig Biggio Jsy A 2.50 6.00
TTRCF Cliff Floyd Bat C 1.50 4.00
TTRCG Cristian Guzman Bat A 1.50 4.00
TTRCJ Chipper Jones Bat B 4.00 10.00
TTRCK Chuck Knoblauch Bat B 1.50 4.00
TTRCP Chan Ho Park Jsy A 2.50 6.00
TTRCS Curt Schilling Jsy A 2.50 6.00
TTRDW Devon White Bat A 1.50 4.00
TTREM Edgar Martinez Jsy A 2.50 6.00
TTRFG Freddy Garcia Jsy A 1.50 4.00
TTRFV Fernando Vina Bat A 1.50 4.00
TTRGA Garret Anderson Bat A 1.50 4.00
TTRGM Greg Maddux Jsy A 6.00 15.00
TTRGS Gary Sheffield Jsy A 1.50 4.00
TTRJB John Burkett Jsy A 1.50 4.00
TTRJE Jim Edmonds Bat B 2.50 6.00
TTRJG Juan Gonzalez Bat B 1.50 4.00
TTRJK Jason Kendall Jsy A 1.50 4.00
TTRJO John Olerud Jsy A 1.50 4.00
TTRJP Juan Pierre Jsy A 1.50 4.00
TTRJS J.T. Snow Bat B 1.50 4.00
TTRJT Jim Thome Bat A 2.50 6.00
TTRLB Lance Berkman Bat A 2.50 6.00
TTRLC Luis Castillo Bat A 1.50 4.00
TTRLG Luis Gonzalez Bat C 1.50 4.00
TTRLW Larry Walker Bat C 2.50 6.00
TTRMA Moises Alou Bat C 1.50 4.00
TTRMC Mike Cameron Bat A 1.50 4.00
TTRMG Mark Grace Bat A 2.50 6.00
TTRMM Mark McLemore Bat A 1.50 4.00
TTRMP Mike Piazza Jsy A 4.00 10.00
TTRMS Mike Sweeney Bat A 1.50 4.00
TTROV Omar Vizquel Bat A 2.50 6.00
TTRPL Paul LoDuca Bat C 1.50 4.00
TTRPN Phil Nevin Bat A 1.50 4.00
TTRPP Placido Polanco Bat A 1.50 4.00
TTRRA Roberto Alomar Bat C 2.50 6.00
TTRRC Roger Cedeno Bat B 1.50 4.00
TTRRD Ray Durham Bat B 1.50 4.00
TTRRJ Randy Johnson Jsy A 4.00 10.00
TTRRM Raul Mondesi Bat A 1.50 4.00
TTRRP Rafael Palmeiro Jsy B 2.50 6.00
TTRRS Richie Sexson Bat B 1.50 4.00
TTRRV Robin Ventura Bat A 1.50 4.00
TTRSG Shawn Green Bat D 1.50 4.00
TTRSS Shannon Stewart Bat C 1.50 4.00
TTRTH Todd Helton Bat C 2.50 6.00
TTRTH Trevor Hoffman Jsy A 2.50 6.00
TTRTH Torii Hunter Bat A 1.50 4.00
TTRTS Tim Salmon Bat B 1.50 4.00
TTRTS Tsuyoshi Shinjo Bat A 1.50 4.00
TTRBAB Barry Bonds Jsy A 6.00 15.00
TTRCBE Carlos Beltran Bat C 1.50 4.00
TTRJBA Jeff Bagwell Jsy A 2.50 6.00
TTRJBU Jeromy Burnitz Jsy A 1.50 4.00
TTRJEK Jeff Kent Jsy A 1.50 4.00

1998 Topps Tek Pre-Production

COMPLETE SET (3) 2.50 6.00
13 Mark McGwire 1.25 3.00
21 Roger Clemens 1.25 3.00
76 Raul Mondesi .20 .50

1998 Topps Tek Pattern 1

The 1998 Topps Tek set consisted of 90 standard size cards. The four-card packs retailed for a suggested price of $5 each. The card fronts present a brand-new way to collect, as each card is marked by not only a player number, but also a pattern number. The backs feature a player head shot along with his expected achievements in the coming years. The set was released in October, 1998. Notable Rookie Cards include Troy Glaus.

COMPLETE SET (90) 60.00 120.00
NINETY PATTERN VARIATIONS AVAILABLE
ALL PATTERN VARIATIONS VALUED EQUALLY
1 Ben Grieve .50 1.25
2 Kerry Wood .50 1.25
3 Barry Bonds 2.00 5.00
4 John Olerud .50 1.25
5 Ivan Rodriguez .75 2.00
6 Frank Thomas 1.25 3.00
7 Bernie Williams .75 2.00
8 Dante Bichette .50 1.25
9 Alex Rodriguez 1.50 4.00
10 Tom Glavine .75 2.00
11 Eric Karros .50 1.25
12 Craig Biggio .75 2.00
13 Mark McGwire 2.00 5.00
14 Derek Jeter 3.00 8.00
15 Nomar Garciaparra .75 2.00
16 Brady Anderson .50 1.25
17 Vladimir Guerrero .75 2.00
18 David Justice .50 1.25
19 Chipper Jones 1.25 3.00
20 Jim Edmonds .75 2.00
21 Roger Clemens 1.50 4.00
22 Mark Kotsay .50 1.25
23 Tony Gwynn 1.25 3.00
24 Todd Walker .50 1.25
25 Tino Martinez .50 1.25
26 Andruw Jones .50 1.25
27 Sandy Alomar Jr. .50 1.25
28 Sammy Sosa 1.25 3.00
29 Gary Sheffield .50 1.25
30 Ken Griffey Jr. 2.50 6.00
31 Aramis Ramirez .50 1.25
32 Curt Schilling .75 2.00
33 Robin Ventura .50 1.25
34 Larry Walker .75 2.00
35 Darin Erstad .50 1.25
36 Todd Dunwoody .50 1.25
37 Paul O'Neill .75 2.00
38 Vinny Castilla .50 1.25
39 Randy Johnson 1.25 3.00
40 Rafael Palmeiro .75 2.00
41 Pedro Martinez .75 2.00
42 Derek Bell .50 1.25
43 Carlos Delgado .50 1.25
44 Matt Williams .50 1.25
45 Kenny Lofton .50 1.25
46 Edgar Renteria .50 1.25
47 Albert Belle .50 1.25
48 Jeromy Burnitz .50 1.25
49 Adrian Beltre 1.25 3.00
50 Greg Maddux 1.50 4.00
51 Cal Ripken 4.00 10.00
52 Jason Kendall .50 1.25
53 Ellis Burks .50 1.25
54 Paul Molitor 1.25 3.00
55 Moises Alou .50 1.25
56 Raul Mondesi .50 1.25
57 Barry Larkin .75 2.00
58 Tony Clark .50 1.25
59 Travis Lee .50 1.25
60 Juan Gonzalez .50 1.25
61 Troy Glaus RC 1.50 4.00
62 Jose Cruz Jr. .50 1.25
63 Paul Konerko .50 1.25
64 Edgar Martinez .75 2.00
65 Javy Lopez .50 1.25
66 Manny Ramirez 1.25 3.00
67 Roberto Alomar .75 2.00
68 Ken Caminiti .50 1.25
69 Todd Helton .75 2.00
70 Chuck Knoblauch .50 1.25
71 Kevin Brown .50 1.25
72 Tim Salmon .50 1.25
73 Orlando Hernandez RC 1.50 4.00
74 Jeff Bagwell .75 2.00
75 Brian Jordan .50 1.25
76 Derrek Lee .50 1.25
77 Brad Fullmer .50 1.25
78 Mark Grace .75 2.00
79 Jeff King .50 1.25
80 Mike Mussina .75 2.00
81 Jay Buhner .50 1.25
82 Quinton McCracken .50 1.25
83 A.J. Hinch .50 1.25
84 Richard Hidalgo .50 1.25
85 Andres Galarraga .75 2.00
86 Mike Piazza 1.25 3.00
87 Mo Vaughn .50 1.25
88 Scott Rolen .75 2.00
89 Jim Thome .75 2.00
90 Ray Lankford .50 1.25

1998 Topps Tek Diffractors Pattern 1

COMPLETE SET (90) 500.00 1000.00
*STARS: 2X TO 5X BASIC CARDS
*ROOKIES: 2X TO 5X BASIC CARDS
STATED ODDS 1:6
NINETY PATTERN VARIATIONS AVAILABLE
ALL PATTERN VARIATIONS VALUED EQUALLY

1999 Topps Tek Pre-Production

COMPLETE SET (3) 2.00 5.00
PP1A Derek Jeter 1.25 3.00
PP2A Moises Alou .40 1.00
PP3A Tony Clark .40 1.00

1999 Topps Tek Pattern 1

The 1999 Topps Tek set was issued in one series for a total of 90 cards and distributed in four-card packs with a suggested retail price of $5. The set features color photos of 45 different players each with a Version A and a Version B which are differentiated by design and uniform printed on 30 different background patterns. The card backs carry the player's headshot and technical merit achievements. Notable Rookie Cards include Pat Burrell.

COMPLETE SET (90) 40.00 100.00
COMMON CARD (1A-45B) .40 1.00
CARD A IS HOME JERSEY VARIATION
CARD B IS AWAY JERSEY VARIATION
HOME AND AWAY B CARDS EQUAL VALUE
THIRTY PATTERN VARIATIONS AVAILABLE
ALL PATTERN VARIATIONS VALUED EQUALLY
1A Ben Grieve .40 1.00
2A Andres Galarraga .60 1.50
3A Travis Lee .40 1.00
4A Larry Walker .60 1.50
5A Ken Griffey Jr. 2.00 5.00
6A Sammy Sosa 1.00 2.50
7A Mark McGwire 1.50 4.00
8A Roberto Alomar .60 1.50
9A Wade Boggs .60 1.50
10A Troy Glaus .60 1.50
11A Craig Biggio .60 1.50
12A Kerry Wood .40 1.00
13A Vladimir Guerrero .60 1.50
14A Albert Belle .40 1.00
15A Mike Piazza 1.00 2.50
16A Chipper Jones 1.00 2.50
17A Randy Johnson 1.00 2.50
18A Adrian Beltre .40 1.00
19A Barry Bonds 1.50 4.00
20A Jim Thome .60 1.50
21A Greg Vaughn .40 1.00
22A Scott Rolen .60 1.50
23A Ivan Rodriguez .60 1.50
24A Derek Jeter 2.50 6.00
25A Cal Ripken 3.00 8.00
26A Mark Grace .60 1.50
27A Bernie Williams .60 1.50
28A Darin Erstad .40 1.00
29A Eric Chavez .40 1.00
30A Tom Glavine .60 1.50
31A Jeff Bagwell .60 1.50
32A Manny Ramirez 1.00 2.50
33A Tino Martinez .40 1.00
34A Todd Helton .60 1.50
35A Jason Kendall .40 1.00
36A Pat Burrell RC 1.50 4.00
37A Tony Gwynn 1.00 2.50
38A Nomar Garciaparra .60 1.50
39A Frank Thomas 1.00 2.50
40A Orlando Hernandez .40 1.00
41A Juan Gonzalez .40 1.00
42A Alex Rodriguez 1.25 3.00
43A Greg Maddux 1.25 3.00
44A Mo Vaughn .40 1.00
45A Roger Clemens 1.25 3.00

1999 Topps Tek Gold Pattern 1

*STARS: 8X TO 20X BASIC
*ROOKIES: 8X TO 20X BASIC
STATED ODDS 1:15
10 SERIAL #'d SETS OF ALL 60 VARIATIONS

1999 Topps Tek Fantastek Phenoms

COMPLETE SET (10) 12.50 30.00
STATED ODDS 1:18
F1 Eric Chavez 1.00 2.50
F2 Troy Glaus 1.50 4.00
F3 Pat Burrell 2.50 6.00
F4 Alex Gonzalez 1.00 2.50
F5 Carlos Lee 1.00 2.50
F6 Ruben Mateo 1.00 2.50
F7 Carlos Beltran 1.50 4.00
F8 Adrian Beltre 1.00 2.50
F9 Bruce Chen 1.00 2.50
F10 Ryan Anderson 1.00 2.50

1999 Topps Tek Teknicians

COMPLETE SET (10) 30.00 80.00
STATED ODDS 1:18
T1 Ken Griffey Jr. 4.00 10.00
T2 Mark McGwire 5.00 12.00
T3 Kerry Wood .75 2.00
T4 Ben Grieve .75 2.00
T5 Sammy Sosa 2.00 5.00
T6 Derek Jeter 5.00 12.00
T7 Alex Rodriguez 3.00 8.00
T8 Roger Clemens 4.00 10.00
T9 Nomar Garciaparra 3.00 8.00
T10 Vladimir Guerrero 2.00 5.00

2000 Topps Tek Pattern 1

COMPLETE SET (45) 20.00 50.00
COMMON CARD (1-40) .20 .50
COMMON ROOKIE (41-45) .30 .75
ROOKIE ODDS 1:2 HTA
RC STATED PRINT RUN 2000 SERIAL #'d SETS
* PATTERN 1-15: .4X TO 1X BASIC
* PATTERN 16-20: 2X TO 5X BASIC
* PATTERN 16-20 RC: .4X TO 1X BASIC
PATTERN 16-20 ODDS 1:10
ALL PATTERN 16 CARDS ARE PURPLE
ALL PATTERN 17 CARDS ARE RED
ALL PATTERN 18 CARDS ARE YELLOW
ALL PATTERN 19 CARDS ARE GREEN
ALL PATTERN 20 CARDS ARE BLUE
1 Mike Piazza .50 1.25
2 Chipper Jones .50 1.25
3 Juan Gonzalez .20 .50
4 Ivan Rodriguez .30 .75
5 Cal Ripken 1.50 4.00
6 A.J. Burnett .20 .50
7 Jim Thome .30 .75
8 Mo Vaughn .20 .50
9 Andruw Jones .20 .50
10 Mark McGwire .75 2.00
11 Jose Canseco .30 .75
12 Shawn Green .20 .50
13 Barry Bonds .75 2.00
14 Bernie Williams .30 .75
15 Manny Ramirez .50 1.25
16 Greg Maddux .60 1.50
17 Carlos Beltran .30 .75
18 Pedro Martinez .30 .75
19 Jeff Bagwell .30 .75
20 Sammy Sosa .50 1.25
21 J.D. Drew .20 .50
22 Randy Johnson .50 1.25
23 Larry Walker .30 .75
24 Frank Thomas .50 1.25
25 Orlando Hernandez .20 .50
26 Scott Rolen .30 .75
27 Tony Gwynn .50 1.25
28 Rick Ankiel .30 .75
29 Roberto Alomar .30 .75
30 Ken Griffey Jr. 1.00 2.50
31 Vladimir Guerrero .30 .75
32 Derek Jeter 1.25 3.00
33 Nomar Garciaparra .30 .75
34 Alex Rodriguez .60 1.50
35 Sean Casey .20 .50
36 Adam Platt .20 .50
37 Corey Patterson .20 .50
38 Josh Hamilton .60 1.50
39 Pat Burrell .20 .50
40 Eric Munson .20 .50
41 Ruben Salazar RC .30 .75
42 John Sneed RC .30 .75
43 Josh Girdley .30 .75
44 Brett Myers RC 1.00 2.50
45 Rick Asadoorian RC .30 .75

2000 Topps Tek Gold Pattern 1

*STARS 1-40: 15X TO 40X BASIC
*ROOKIES 41-45: 10X TO 25X BASIC
STATED ODDS 1:42
10 SERIAL #'d SETS OF ALL 20 VARIATIONS

2000 Topps Tek Architeks

COMPLETE SET (18) 20.00 50.00
STATED ODDS 1:5
A1 Nomar Garciaparra .75 2.00
A2 Derek Jeter 3.00 8.00
A3 Chipper Jones 1.25 3.00
A4 Vladimir Guerrero .75 2.00
A5 Mark McGwire 2.00 5.00
A6 Ken Griffey Jr. 2.50 6.00
A7 Mike Piazza 1.25 3.00
A8 Jeff Bagwell .75 2.00
A9 Larry Walker .75 2.00
A10 Manny Ramirez 1.25 3.00
A11 Alex Rodriguez 1.50 4.00
A12 Sammy Sosa 1.25 3.00
A13 Shawn Green .50 1.25
A14 Juan Gonzalez .50 1.25
A15 Barry Bonds 2.00 5.00
A16 Pedro Martinez .75 2.00
A17 Cal Ripken 4.00 10.00
A18 Ivan Rodriguez .75 2.00

2000 Topps Tek Dramatek Performers

COMPLETE SET (9) 8.00 20.00
STATED ODDS 1:10
DP1 Mark McGwire 1.50 4.00
DP2 Sammy Sosa 1.00 2.50
DP3 Ken Griffey Jr. 2.00 5.00
DP4 Nomar Garciaparra .60 1.50
DP5 Chipper Jones 1.00 2.50
DP6 Mike Piazza 1.00 2.50
DP7 Alex Rodriguez 1.25 3.00
DP8 Derek Jeter 2.50 6.00
DP9 Vladimir Guerrero .60 1.50

2000 Topps Tek Tektonics

COMPLETE SET (9) 15.00 40.00
STATED ODDS 1:30
TT1 Derek Jeter 4.00 10.00
TT2 Mark McGwire 2.50 6.00
TT3 Ken Griffey Jr. 3.00 8.00
TT4 Mike Piazza 1.50 4.00
TT5 Alex Rodriguez 2.00 5.00
TT6 Chipper Jones 1.50 4.00
TT7 Nomar Garciaparra 1.00 2.50
TT8 Sammy Sosa 1.50 4.00
TT9 Cal Ripken 5.00 12.00

2016 Topps The Mint Arrivals Autographs

STATED PRINT RUN 99 SER.#'d SETS
VARIATIONS NOT PRICED DUE TO SCARCITY
EXCHANGE DEADLINE 7/31/2018
*PURPLE/50: .5X TO 1.2X BASIC
AAAN Aaron Nola/99 6.00 15.00
AABP Byung-Ho Park/99 8.00 20.00
AACSA C.Sager EXCH
AAHOW Henry Owens/99 4.00 10.00
AAJG Jon Gray/99 6.00 15.00
AAJU Julio Urias EXCH
AAKM Kenta Maeda/99 15.00 40.00
AAKSA Kyle Schwarber/99 10.00 25.00
AALG L.Giolito EXCH
AALS Luis Severino/99 8.00 20.00
AAMS Miguel Sano/99 20.00 50.00
AASP Stephen Piscotty/99 10.00 25.00

2016 Topps The Mint Authenticated Patch Autographs

STATED PRINT RUN 75 SER.#'d SETS
EXCHANGE DEADLINE 7/31/2018
APAI Ichiro Suzuki
APAAM Andrew Miller 25.00 60.00
APADL DJ LeMahieu 15.00 40.00
APADO David Ortiz 60.00 150.00
APAEL Evan Longoria 20.00 50.00
APAJM J.D. Martinez 30.00 80.00
APAJS James Shields 15.00 40.00
APALS Luis Severino 20.00 50.00
APAMS Miguel Sano 25.00 60.00
APAMT Mike Trout 200.00 400.00

2016 Topps The Mint Franchise Autographs

PRINT RUNS B/WN 40-99 COPIES PER
VARIATIONS NOT PRICED DUE TO SCARCITY
EXCHANGE DEADLINE 7/31/2018
FAAJ Adam Jones/99 12.00 30.00
FAAPO A.J. Pollock/99 6.00 15.00
FAAPU Albert Pujols
FAAR Anthony Rizzo/99 25.00 60.00
FABH Bryce Harper/55 150.00 300.00
FABP Buster Posey/55 40.00 100.00
FACCA Carlos Correa/99 50.00 120.00
FACH Cole Hamels/99 8.00 20.00
FACK C.Kershaw EXCH
FACS Chris Sale/99 10.00 25.00
FADK Dallas Keuchel/99 10.00 25.00
FADO David Ortiz/60 40.00 100.00
FADP Dustin Pedroia/99 15.00 40.00
FADW David Wright/99 8.00 20.00
FAEE Edwin Encarnacion/99 10.00 25.00
FAEL Evan Longoria/99 8.00 20.00
FAFF Freddie Freeman/99 15.00 40.00
FAFL Francisco Lindor/99 15.00 40.00
FAIA Ichiro/55 150.00 400.00
FAJA Jose Altuve/99 15.00 40.00
FAJD Jacob deGrom/99 15.00 40.00
FAJH Jason Heyward/99 10.00 25.00
FAKBA Kris Bryant/99 100.00 250.00
FAMM Manny Machado/99 20.00 50.00
FAMTRA Mike Trout/55 200.00 400.00
FANA Nolan Arenado/99 25.00 60.00
FARB Ryan Braun/99 8.00 20.00
FASM Starling Marte/99
FAYC Yoenis Cespedes/99 6.00 15.00

2016 Topps The Mint Franchise Autographs Purple

*PURPLE: .5X TO 1.2X BASIC
STATED PRINT RUN 50 SER.#'d SETS
EXCHANGE DEADLINE 7/31/2018
FAI Ichiro 150.00 400.00
FAKB Kris Bryant 125.00 300.00

2016 Topps The Mint Gem 10 Autographs
STATED PRINT RUN 99 SER.#'d SETS
EXCHANGE DEADLINE 7/31/2018
G10AAG Andres Galarraga 12.00 30.00
G10AAR Alex Rodriguez 50.00 120.00
G10AJA Jake Arrieta 60.00 150.00
G10AJV Jason Varitek 12.00 30.00
G10ANL Nuke LaLoosh 40.00 100.00
Tim Robbins
G10AOV Omar Vizquel 20.00 50.00
G10APK Paul Konerko 15.00 40.00
G10ARB Sylvester Stallone/99 250.00 500.00
G10AVS Vin Scully 200.00 400.00

2016 Topps The Mint Gem 10 Autographs Purple
*PURPLE: .5X TO 1.2X BASIC
STATED PRINT RUN 50 SER.#'d SETS
EXCHANGE DEADLINE 7/31/2018
G10AAR Alex Rodriguez 100.00 200.00

2016 Topps The Mint Golden Engraving Autographs
PRINT RUNS B/WN 40-99 COPIES PER
VARIATIONS NOT PRICED DUE TO SCARCITY
EXCHANGE DEADLINE 7/31/2018
GEAAD Andre Dawson/99 20.00 50.00
GEAAK Al Kaline/99 30.00 80.00
GEABL Barry Larkin/75 20.00 50.00
GEACBA Craig Biggio/99 20.00 50.00
GEACF Carlton Fisk/99 25.00 60.00
GEACRA Cal Ripken Jr. EXCH 125.00 300.00
GEADE Dennis Eckersley/75 20.00 50.00
GEAFT Frank Thomas/75 25.00 60.00
GEAGMA Greg Maddux/40 50.00 120.00
GEAHA Hank Aaron/40 150.00 300.00
GEAJB Johnny Bench/99 40.00 100.00
GEAJR Jim Rice/99 20.00 50.00
GEAJS John Smoltz/99 25.00 60.00
GEAKG K.Griffey Jr. EXCH 200.00 400.00
GEALB Lou Brock/75 40.00 100.00
GEAMP Mike Piazza/40 75.00 200.00
GEANR Nolan Ryan/40 125.00 250.00
GEAOC Orlando Cepeda/99 20.00 50.00
GEAOS Ozzie Smith/75 30.00 80.00
GEAPM Paul Molitor/75 40.00 100.00
GEARA Roberto Alomar/75 20.00 50.00
GEARC Rod Carew/99 30.00 80.00
GEARF Rollie Fingers/99 20.00 50.00
GEARJA Reggie Jackson/75 20.00 50.00
GEARJO Randy Johnson/40 50.00 120.00
GEARY Robin Yount/99 25.00 60.00
GEASC Steve Carlton/99 30.00 80.00
GEASK Sandy Koufax/40 150.00 400.00
GEAWB Wade Boggs/75 20.00 50.00

2016 Topps The Mint Iconic Jersey Relics
STATED PRINT RUN 250 SER.#'d SETS
*PURPLE/60: 1.2X TO 3X BASIC
*GREEN/25: 2.5X TO 6X BASIC
IJRAJ Adam Jones/250 6.00 15.00
IJRAJ Adam Jones/150
IJRDVO David Ortiz/150 10.00 25.00
IJRDVO David Ortiz/250 10.00 25.00

1981 Topps Thirst Break
This is a 56-card set of individual wax paper gum wrappers, similar to a Bazooka Comic. These wrappers were issued in Thirst Break Orange Gum, which was reportedly distributed in Pennsylvania and Ohio. Each of these small gum wrappers has a comic-style image of a particular great moment in sports. As the checklist below shows, many different sports are represented in this set. The wrappers each measure approximately 2 9/16" by 1 5/8". The wrappers are numbered in small print at the top. The backs of the wrappers are blank. The "1981 Topps" copyright is at the bottom of each card. There was an orange and green outer wrapper that did not have player images.

COMPLETE SET (56) 60.00 150.00
1 Shortest Baseball Game .40 1.00
2 Lefty Gomez .60 1.50
3 Bob Gibson .80 2.00
4 Hoyt Wilhelm .60 1.50
5 Babe Ruth 2.40 6.00
6 Toby Harrah .40 1.00
7 Carl Hubbell .80 2.00
8 Harvey Haddix .60 1.50
9 Steve Carlton .80 2.00
10 N.Ryan 4.80 12.00
Seaver
Carlton
11 Lou Brock 1.00 2.50
12 Mickey Mantle 3.20 8.00
13 Tom Seaver 1.60 4.00
14 Don Drysdale .80 2.00
15 Billy Williams .60 1.50
20 Christy Mathewson .60 1.50
21 Hank Aaron 1.60 4.00
22 Ron Blomberg .40 1.00
23 Joe Nuxhall .40 1.00
24 Reggie Jackson 1.60 4.00

2016 Topps Throwback Thursday
1 Bryce Harper 1.25 3.00
'55 Bowman/1665*
2 Mike Trout 4.00 10.00
'55 Bowman/1665*
3 Clayton Kershaw 1.25 3.00
'55 Bowman/1665*
4 Kris Bryant 1.00 2.50
'55 Bowman/1665*
5 Trevor Story 2.50 6.00
'55 Bowman/1665*
6 Corey Seager 5.00 12.00
'55 Bowman/1665*
7 Yoenis Cespedes 1.00 2.50
'58 Topps/730*
8 Giancarlo Stanton 1.00 2.50
'58 Topps/730*
9 Bryce Harper 1.50 4.00
'58 Topps/730*
10 Carlos Beltran .75 2.00
'58 Topps/730*
11 Nomar Mazara 1.00 2.50
'58 Topps/730*
12 Jose Bautista .75 2.00
'58 Topps/730*
13 Nolan Ryan 3.00 8.00
'58 Topps TV Westerns/785*
14 Clayton Kershaw 1.50 4.00
'58 Topps TV Westerns/785*
15 Noah Syndergaard .75 2.00
'58 Topps TV Westerns/785*
16 Jake Arrieta .75 2.00
'58 Topps TV Westerns/785*
17 Stephen Strasburg 1.00 2.50
'58 Topps TV Westerns/785*
18 Madison Bumgarner .75 2.00
'58 Topps TV Westerns/785*
19 Ted Williams 2.00 5.00
'55 Topps All-American/775*
20 Jackie Robinson 1.00 2.50
'55 Topps All-American/775*
21 Stan Musial 1.50 4.00
'55 Topps All-American/775*
22 Duke Snider .75 2.00
'55 Topps All-American/775*
23 Warren Spahn .75 2.00
'55 Topps All-American/775*
24 Ralph Kiner .75 2.00
'55 Topps All-American/775*
25 Jake Arrieta .75 2.00
'59 Topps/946*
26 Francisco Lindor 1.00 2.50
'59 Topps/946*
27 Corey Seager 6.00 15.00
'59 Topps/946*
28 Xander Bogaerts 1.00 2.50
'59 Topps/946*
29 Noah Syndergaard .75 2.00
'59 Topps/946*
30 Aledmys Diaz 1.00 2.50
'59 Topps/946*
31 Willie Mays 2.00 5.00
'75 Topps/570*
32 Mike Trout 5.00 12.00
'75 Topps/570*
33 Cal Ripken Jr. 3.00 8.00
'75 Topps/570*
34 Gary Carter .75 2.00
'75 Topps/570*
35 Steve Garvey .60 1.50
'75 Topps/570*
36 Ken Griffey Jr 2.00 5.00
'62 Topps/753*
37 Mike Piazza 1.00 2.50
'62 Topps/753*
38 Ken Griffey Jr 2.00 5.00
'62 Topps/753*
42 Roberto Clemente 2.50 6.00
Hank Aaron
'79 Highlights/618*
43 Stan Musial 1.50 4.00
Lou Brock
'79 Highlights/618*
44 Carl Yastrzemski 1.50 4.00
Wade Boggs
'79 Highlights/618*
45 Cal Ripken Jr. 3.00 8.00
George Brett
'79 Highlights/618*
46 Tony Gwynn 1.00 2.50
Dave Winfield
'79 Highlights/618*
47 Rod Carew 2.00 5.00
Willie Mays
'79 Highlights/618*
48 Ichiro 1.25 3.00
1st MLB Hit
Journey to 3000/772*
49 Ichiro 1.25 3.00
3000th MLB Hit
Journey to 3000/772*
50 Ichiro 1.25 3.00
262 Hit Record
Journey to 3000/772*
51 Ichiro 1.25 3.00
Inside the Park HR at AS Game
Journey to 3000/772*
52 Ichiro 1.25 3.00
4,257 Hit Overall
Journey to 3000/772*
53 Ichiro 1.25 3.00
MVP and ROY
Journey to 3000/772*
54 Corey Seager 6.00 15.00
'93 Draft Pick/770*
55 Carlos Correa 1.00 2.50
'93 Draft Pick/770*
56 Francisco Lindor 1.00 2.50
'93 Draft Pick/770*
57 Trevor Story 3.00 8.00
'93 Draft Pick/770*
58 Xander Bogaerts 1.00 2.50
'93 Draft Pick/770*
59 Aledmys Diaz 1.00 2.50
'93 Draft Pick/770*
60 Gary Sanchez 2.00 5.00
'91 Beverly Hills 90210/746*
61 Jose Altuve .75 2.00
'91 Beverly Hills 90210/746*
62 Corey Seager 6.00 15.00
'91 Beverly Hills 90210/746*
63 Kris Bryant 1.25 3.00
'91 Beverly Hills 90210/746*
64 Mookie Betts 2.00 5.00
'91 Beverly Hills 90210/746*
65 Joey Votto 1.00 2.50
'91 Beverly Hills 90210/746*
66 Brooks Robinson 1.25 3.00
Kris Bryant
'57 Past and Present Stars/769*
67 Ernie Banks 1.00 2.50
Carlos Correa
'57 Past and Present Stars/769*
68 Sandy Koufax 2.00 5.00
Clayton Kershaw
'57 Past and Present Stars/769*
69 Roberto Clemente 2.50 6.00
Andrew McCutchen
'57 Past and Present Stars/769*
70 Hank Aaron 5.00 12.00
Mike Trout
'57 Past and Present Stars/769*
71 Ted Williams 2.00 5.00
Mookie Betts
'57 Past and Present Stars/769*
72 Cal Ripken Jr. 3.00 8.00
'82 ROY
'82 Highlights/693*
73 Cal Ripken Jr. 3.00 8.00
'83 WS
'82 Highlights/693*
74 Cal Ripken Jr. 3.00 8.00
'91 AS MVP
'82 Highlights/693*
75 Cal Ripken Jr. 3.00 8.00
Ties The Streak
'82 Highlights/693*
76 Cal Ripken Jr. 3.00 8.00
Breaks the Streak
'82 Highlights/693*
77 Cal Ripken Jr. 3.00 8.00
'07 HOF Induction
'82 Highlights/693*
78 Kris Bryant 1.25 3.00
Jake Arrieta
Anthony Rizzo
'69 Mod Squad/586*
79 Bryce Harper 1.50 4.00
Daniel Murphy
Max Scherzer
'69 Mod Squad/586*
80 Clayton Kershaw 6.00 15.00
Adrian Gonzalez
Corey Seager
'69 Mod Squad/586*
81 David Ortiz 2.00 5.00
Mookie Betts
David Price
'69 Mod Squad/586*
82 Mike Trout 5.00 12.00
Albert Pujols
C.J. Cron
'69 Mod Squad/586*
83 Yoenis Cespedes 2.00 5.00
Noah Syndergaard
Jacob deGrom
'69 Mod Squad/586*
84 Kris Bryant 1.25 3.00
'72 US Presidents/540*
85 Daniel Murphy .75 2.00
'72 US Presidents/540*
86 Mookie Betts 2.00 5.00
'72 US Presidents/540*
87 Jose Altuve .75 2.00
'72 US Presidents/540*
88 Mike Trout 5.00 12.00
'72 US Presidents/540*
89 Josh Donaldson .75 2.00
'72 US Presidents/540*
90 Corey Seager 6.00 15.00
Julio Urias
'72 Rookie Stars/644*
91 Trea Turner 2.00 5.00
Max Kepler
'72 Rookie Stars/644*
92 Gary Sanchez 2.00 5.00
Tyler Naquin
'72 Rookie Stars/644*
93 Trevor Story 3.00 8.00
Aledmys Diaz
'72 Rookie Stars/644*
94 Jameson Taillon 1.00 2.50
Michael Fulmer
'72 Rookie Stars/644*
95 Lucas Giolito 1.25 3.00
Kenta Maeda
'72 Rookie Stars/644*
96 David Ortiz 1.00 2.50
'97 Rookie Year
'97 Stadium Club/687*
97 David Ortiz 1.00 2.50
Welcome to Boston
'97 Stadium Club/687*
98 David Ortiz 1.00 2.50
3x WS Champion
'97 Stadium Club/687*
99 David Ortiz 1.00 2.50
500th HR
'97 Stadium Club/687*
100 David Ortiz 1.00 2.50
Ten-Time AS
'97 Stadium Club/687*
101 David Ortiz 1.00 2.50
Last Regular Season Game
'97 Stadium Club/687*
102 Batting Average Leaders 1.25 3.00
D.J. LeMahieu
Daniel Murphy
Jose Altuve
Joey Votto
'61 Insert/374*
103 Home Run Leaders 1.25 3.00
Mark Trumbo
Nelson Cruz
Brian Dozier
Edwin Encarnacion
'61 Insert/374*
104 RBI Leaders 2.00 5.00
Nolan Arenado
Edwin Encarnacion
David Ortiz
Albert Pujols
'61 Insert/374*
105 ERA Leaders 1.00 2.50
Liam Hendricks
Jon Lester
Noah Syndergaard
Madison Bumgarner
'61 Insert/374*
106 Wins Leaders 1.50 4.00
Rick Porcello
Ian Happ
Max Scherzer
Jon Lester
'61 Insert/374*
107 Saves Leaders 1.00 2.50
Jeurys Familia
Zach Britton
Kenley Jansen
Mark Melancon
'61 Insert/374*
108 Kris Bryant 1.25 3.00
'74 HR King/579*
109 Corey Seager 6.00 15.00
'74 HR King/579*
110 Nolan Arenado 1.50 4.00
'74 HR King/579*
111 Mike Trout 5.00 12.00
'74 HR King/579*
112 David Ortiz 1.00 2.50
'74 HR King/579*
113 Jose Altuve .75 2.00
'74 HR King/579*
114 Kris Bryant 1.00 2.50
Ron Santo
'78 Cubs Then and Now/1321*
115 Javier Baez 1.50 4.00
Ryne Sandberg
'78 Cubs Then and Now/1321*
116 Anthony Rizzo 1.00 2.50
Ernie Banks
'78 Cubs Then and Now/1321*
117 Ben Zobrist .60 1.50
Billy Williams
'78 Cubs Then and Now/1321*
118 Jake Arrieta .60 1.50
Fergie Jenkins
'78 Cubs Then and Now/1321*
119 Kyle Schwarber 1.50 4.00
Andre Dawson
'78 Cubs Then and Now/1321*
120 Corey Kluber 1.00 2.50
Bob Feller
'78 Indians Then and Now/413*
121 Francisco Lindor 1.25 3.00
Omar Vizquel
'78 Indians Then and Now/413*
122 Carlos Baerga 1.00 2.50
Jason Kipnis
'78 Indians Then and Now/413*
123 Mike Napoli .75 2.00
Sandy Alomar
'78 Indians Then and Now/413*
124 Tyler Naquin 1.25 3.00
Larry Doby
'78 Indians Then and Now/413*
125 Andrew Miller 1.00 2.50
Bartolo Colon
'78 Indians Then and Now/413*
132 Kyle Schwarber 2.00 5.00
Cubs Game 2 Win At Cleveland
'69 WS/684*
133 Kris Bryant 1.25 3.00
Cubs Game 5 Win At Chicago
'69 WS/684*
134 Addison Russell 1.00 2.50
Cubs Game 6 Win At Cleveland
'69 WS/684*
135 Ben Zobrist .75 2.00
Cubs Game 7 Win At Cleveland
'69 WS/684*
136 David Ross .60 1.50
HR in Game 7 At Cleveland
'69 WS/684*
137 Cubs Win First World Series Since 1908 In Game
7 At Cleveland 1.25 3.00
'69 WS/684*
138 Gary Sanchez 2.00 5.00
'74 Football/626*
139 Mike Trout 5.00 12.00
'74 Football/626*
140 Kris Bryant 1.25 3.00
'74 Football/626*
141 Derek Jeter 2.50 6.00
'74 Football/626*
142 Ichiro Suzuki 1.25 3.00
'74 Football/626*
143 David Ortiz 1.00 2.50
'74 Football/626*
144 David Ortiz 1.25 3.00
'79-80 Basketball/274*
145 Greg Maddux 1.50 4.00
'79-80 Basketball/274*
146 Andre Dawson 1.00 2.50
'79-80 Basketball/274*
147 Randy Johnson 1.25 3.00
'79-80 Basketball/274*
148 Ichiro Suzuki 1.50 4.00
'79-80 Basketball/274*
149 Reggie Jackson 1.00 2.50
'79-80 Basketball/274*
150 Noah Syndergaard 1.00 2.50
'83 Empire Strikes Back/332*
151 Carlos Correa 1.25 3.00
'83 Empire Strikes Back/332*
152 Francisco Lindor 1.25 3.00
'83 Empire Strikes Back/332*
153 Kyle Schwarber 2.50 6.00
'83 Empire Strikes Back/332*
154 Mookie Betts 2.50 6.00
'83 Empire Strikes Back/332*
155 Corey Seager 8.00 20.00
'83 Empire Strikes Back/332*

2017 Topps Throwback Thursday
1 Jeff Bagwell/327* 1.00 2.50
'88 All Star
2 Craig Biggio/327* 1.00 2.50
'88 All Star
3 Tim Raines/327* 1.00 2.50
'88 All Star
4 Gary Carter/327* 1.00 2.50
'88 All Star
5 Ivan Rodriguez/327* 1.00 2.50
'88 All Star
6 Nolan Ryan/327* 4.00 10.00
'88 All Star
7 Ted Williams/1049* 1.50 4.00
'52 Topps
8 Hank Aaron/1049* 1.50 4.00
'52 Topps
9 Nolan Ryan/1049* 2.50 6.00
'52 Topps
10 Alex Rodriguez/1049* 1.00 2.50
'52 Topps
11 Mike Trout/1049* 4.00 10.00
'52 Topps
12 Kris Bryant/1049* 1.00 2.50
'52 Topps
13 Satchel Paige/339* 1.25 3.00
'57-'58 Basketball
14 Lou Brock/339* 1.00 2.50
'57-'58 Basketball
15 Fergie Jenkins/339* 1.00 2.50
'57-'58 Basketball
16 Tony Gwynn/339* 1.25 3.00
'57-'58 Basketball
17 Dave Winfield/339* 1.00 2.50
'57-'58 Basketball
18 Jackie Robinson/339* 1.25 3.00
'57-'58 Basketball
19 Andrew Benintendi/1329* 1.50 4.00
'62 Topps
20 Alex Bregman/1329* 2.50 6.00
'62 Topps
21 Yoan Moncada/1329* 1.50 4.00
'62 Topps
22 Aaron Judge/1329* 6.00 15.00
'62 Topps
23 Josh Bell/1329* 1.25 3.00
'62 Topps
24 Dansby Swanson/1329* 1.25 3.00
'62 Topps
25 Johnny Bench/475* 1.25 3.00
'68 Topps
26 Nolan Ryan/475* 4.00 10.00
'68 Topps
27 Willie Stargell/475* 1.00 2.50
'68 Topps
28 Carlton Fisk/475* 1.00 2.50
'68 Topps
29 Paul Molitor/475* 1.25 3.00
'68 Topps
30 Andre Dawson/475* 1.00 2.50
'68 Topps
31 Alex Bregman/309* 4.00 10.00
'88 Topps
32 Nori Aoki/309* .75 2.00
'88 Topps
33 Manny Machado/309* 1.25 3.00
'88 Topps
34 Miguel Cabrera/309* 1.25 3.00
'88 Topps
35 Carlos Correa/309* 1.25 3.00
'88 Topps
36 Xander Bogaerts/309* 1.25 3.00
'88 Topps
37 Derek Jeter/353* 3.00 8.00
'86 Topps FB
38 Ken Griffey Jr./353* 2.50 6.00
'86 Topps FB
39 Ichiro Suzuki/353* 1.50 4.00
'86 Topps FB
40 Ivan Rodriguez/353* 1.00 2.50
'86 Topps FB
41 Yoenis Cespedes/353* 1.25 3.00
'86 Topps FB
42 Robinson Cano/353* 1.00 2.50
'86 Topps FB
43 Kris Bryant/615* 1.25 3.00
'57 Topps
44 Corey Seager/615* 1.00 2.50
'57 Topps
45 Bryce Harper/615* 1.50 4.00
'57 Topps
46 Adrian Beltre/615* 1.00 2.50
'57 Topps
47 Mookie Betts/615* 2.00 5.00
'57 Topps
48 Francisco Lindor/615* 1.00 2.50
'57 Topps
49 Andrew McCutchen/398* 1.25 3.00
'72 Topps
50 Mike Trout/398* 6.00 15.00
'72 Topps
51 Ken Griffey Jr./398* 2.50 6.00
'72 Topps
52 Buster Posey/398* 1.50 4.00
'72 Topps
53 Clayton Kershaw/398* 2.00 5.00
'72 Topps
54 Rickey Henderson/398* 1.25 3.00
'72 Topps
55 Ken Griffey Jr./382* 2.50 6.00
'90 Topps FB
56 Adrian Gonzalez/382* 1.00 2.50
'90 Topps FB
57 Stephen Strasburg/382* 1.25 3.00
'90 Topps FB
58 Bryce Harper/382* 2.00 5.00
'90 Topps FB
59 Carlos Correa/382* 1.25 3.00
'90 Topps FB
60 Dansby Swanson/382* 2.00 5.00
'90 Topps FB
61 Rickey Henderson/620* 1.00 2.50
'07 Topps
62 Mike Piazza/620* 1.00 2.50
'07 Topps
63 Frank Thomas/620* 1.00 2.50
'07 Topps
64 Derek Jeter/620* 2.50 6.00
'07 Topps
65 Pedro Martinez/620* .75 2.00
'07 Topps
66 Nolan Ryan/620* 3.00 8.00
'07 Topps
67 Wade Boggs/620* .75 2.00
'07 Topps
68 Aaron Judge/1086* 6.00 15.00
'56 Topps
69 Mike Trout/1086* 4.00 10.00
'56 Topps
70 Francisco Lindor/1086* .75 2.00
'56 Topps
71 Anthony Rizzo/1086* 1.00 2.50
'56 Topps
72 Manny Machado/1086* .75 2.00
'56 Topps
73 Javier Baez/1086* 1.00 2.50
'56 Topps
74 Cody Bellinger/1475* 8.00 20.00
'54 Bowman
75 Ian Happ/1475* 1.00 2.50
'54 Bowman
76 Bradley Zimmer/1475* .60 1.50
'54 Bowman
77 Andrew Benintendi/1475* 1.50 4.00
'54 Bowman
78 Aaron Judge/1475* 6.00 15.00
'54 Bowman
79 Trey Mancini/1475* 1.00 2.50
'54 Bowman
80 Edinson Volquez/289* .75 2.00
'90 Topps
81 Nolan Ryan/289* 4.00 10.00
'90 Topps
82 Clayton Kershaw/289* 2.00 5.00
'90 Topps
83 Randy Johnson/289* 1.25 3.00
'90 Topps
84 Jon Lester/289* 1.00 2.50
'90 Topps
85 Sandy Koufax/289* 2.50 6.00
'90 Topps
86 Aaron Judge/2245* 6.00 15.00
'67 Topps
87 Mike Piazza/2245* .75 2.00
'67 Topps
88 Cody Bellinger/2245* 8.00 20.00
'67 Topps
89 Mark McGwire/2245* 1.25 3.00
'67 Topps
90 Mike Trout/2245* 4.00 10.00
'67 Topps
91 Albert Pujols 1.00 2.50
with Mark McGwire/2245*
'67 Topps
92 Aaron Judge/1118* 6.00 15.00
'96 Topps Star Power
93 David Ortiz/1118* .75 2.00
'96 Topps Star Power
94 Giancarlo Stanton/1118* .75 2.00
'96 Topps Star Power
95 Mark McGwire/1118* 1.25 3.00
'96 Topps Star Power
96 Yoenis Cespedes/1118* .75 2.00
'96 Topps Star Power
97 Frank Thomas/1118* .75 2.00
'96 Topps Star Power
98 Aaron Judge/1029* 6.00 15.00
'76 All Time All Stars
99 Carlos Correa/1029* .75 2.00
'76 All Time All Stars
100 Andrew Benintendi/1029* 1.50 4.00
'76 All Time All Stars
101 Gary Sanchez/1029* .75 2.00
'76 All Time All Stars
102 Mike Trout/1029* 4.00 10.00
'76 All Time All Stars
103 Corey Seager/1029* .75 2.00
'76 All Time All Star
104 Andrew Benintendi/333* 2.50 6.00
'91 Beverly Hills 90210
105 Giancarlo Stanton/333* 1.25 3.00
'91 Beverly Hills 90210
106 Jose Altuve/333* 1.00 2.50
'91 Beverly Hills 90210
107 Nolan Arenado/333* 2.00 5.00
'91 Beverly Hills 90210
108 Alex Bregman/333* 4.00 10.00
'91 Beverly Hills 90210
109 Manny Machado/333* 1.25 3.00
'91 Beverly Hills 90210
110 Albert Pujols/892* 1.25 3.00
'84 Topps
111 Aaron Judge/892* 8.00 20.00
'84 Topps
112 Andrew McCutchen/892* 1.00 2.50
'84 Topps
113 Buster Posey/892* 1.25 3.00
'84 Topps
114 Charlie Blackmon/892* 1.00 2.50
'84 Topps
115 Mookie Betts/892* 2.00 5.00
'84 Topps
116 Aaron Judge/901* 8.00 20.00
'84 Topps FB
117 Jose Altuve/901* .75 2.00
'84 Topps FB
118 Kris Bryant/901* 1.25 3.00
'84 Topps FB
119 Mike Trout/901* 5.00 12.00
'84 Topps FB
120 Giancarlo Stanton/901* 1.00 2.50
'84 Topps FB
121 Bryce Harper/901* 1.50 4.00
'84 Topps FB
122 Cody Bellinger/606* 10.00 25.00
'78 Record Breakers
123 Giancarlo Stanton/606* 1.00 2.50
'78 Record Breakers
124 Aaron Judge/606* 8.00 20.00
'78 Record Breakers
125 J.D. Martinez/606* 1.00 2.50
'78 Record Breakers
126 Edwin Encarnacion/606* 1.00 2.50
'78 Record Breakers
127 Joey Gallo/606* .75 2.00
'78 Record Breakers
128 Aaron Judge/1166* 6.00 15.00
'87 Record Breakers
129 Cody Bellinger/1166* 8.00 20.00
'87 Record Breakers
130 Mark McGwire/1166* 1.25 3.00
'87 Record Breakers
131 Mike Trout/1166* 4.00 10.00
'87 Record Breakers
132 Ichiro/1166* 1.00 2.50
'87 Record Breakers
133 Ted Williams/1166* 1.50 4.00
'87 Record Breakers
134 Los Angeles Dodgers/564* 1.25 3.00
'75 Topps Team Card
135 Boston Red Sox/564* 1.25 3.00
'75 Topps Team Card
136 Chicago Cubs/564* 1.25 3.00
'75 Topps Team Card
137 Cleveland Indians/564* 1.25 3.00
'75 Topps Team Card
138 Houston Astros/564* 1.25 3.00
'75 Topps Team Card
139 Washington Nationals/564* 1.25 3.00
'75 Topps Team Card
140 New York Yankees/564* 1.25 3.00
'75 Topps Team Card
141 Arizona Diamondbacks/564* 1.25 3.00
'75 Topps Team Card
142 Aaron Judge Gives
Mock Interview in Dugout 8.00 20.00
Aaron Judge/591*
'59 Topps Thrills
143 High Fives for Lindor and Zimmer 1.00 2.50
Francisco Lindor
Bradley Zimmer/591*
'59 Topps Thrills
144 Houston...We Have Lift Off 1.00 2.50
Jose Altuve
Carlos Correa/591*
'59 Topps Thrills
145 Killer B's: Benintendi,
Betts, Bradley Jr. 2.00 5.00
Andrew Benintendi
Mookie Betts
Jackie Bradley Jr./591*
'59 Topps Thrills
146 Harper and Goodwin
Low Five Celebrates Win 1.50 4.00
Brian Goodwin
Bryce Harper/591*
'59 Topps Thrills
147 Chicago's Star Trio
Embrace After Wild Win 1.25 3.00
Kris Bryant
Anthony Rizzo
Javier Baez/591*
'59 Topps Thrills
148 Aaron Judge A/692* 8.00 20.00
'74 Topps Monster
149 Jose Altuve L/692* .75 2.00
'74 Topps Monster
150 Didi Gregorius C/692* .75 2.00
'74 Topps Monster
151 Carlos Correa S/692* 1.00 2.50
'74 Topps Monster
152 Clayton Kershaw N/692* 1.50 4.00
'74 Topps Monster
153 Anthony Rizzo L/692* 1.25 3.00
'74 Topps Monster
154 Cody Bellinger C/692* 10.00 25.00
'74 Topps Monster
155 Kris Bryant S/692* 1.25 3.00
'74 Topps Monster
156 Nolan Ryan 4.00 10.00
Justin Verlander/478*
'85 Topps Father & Son
157 Craig Biggio 1.00 2.50
Jose Altuve/478*
'85 Topps Father & Son
158 Jeff Bagwell 1.25 3.00
Carlos Correa/478*
'85 Topps Father & Son
159 Sandy Koufax 2.50 6.00
Clayton Kershaw/478*
'85 Topps Father & Son
160 Jackie Robinson 12.00 30.00
Cody Bellinger/487*
'85 Topps Father & Son
161 Mike Piazza 1.25 3.00
Justin Turner/478*
'85 Topps Father & Son
162 Jose Altuve 1.25 3.00
Carlos Correa/420*
Go Back-to-Back
'65 Topps World Series
163 George Springer/420* 1.00 2.50
Goes Yard in 11th
'65 Topps World Series
164 Brad Peacock/420* .75 2.00
Saves Game 3
'65 Topps World Series
165 Alex Bregman/420* 4.00 10.00
Walk-Off
'65 Topps World Series
166 Jose Altuve/420* 1.00 2.50
Clutch RBI Double
'65 Topps World Series
167 Houston Astros/420* 1.50 4.00
'65 Topps World Series
168 Aaron Judge/453* 10.00 25.00
50th HR Breaks Rookie Record
'08 Topps Year in Review
169 Giancarlo Stanton/453* 1.25 3.00
Slugger Hits 59th HR
'08 Topps Year in Review
170 Houston Astros/453* 1.50 4.00
Astros Win 1st World Series
'08 Topps Year in Review
171 Cody Bellinger/453* 12.00 30.00
39th HR Breaks NL Rookie Record
'08 Topps Year in Review
172 Derek Jeter/453* 3.00 8.00
Yankees Retire Jeters Number
'08 Topps Year in Review
173 Anthony Rizzo/453* 1.50 4.00
Cubs Walk Out with World Series Trophy
'08 Topps Year in Review
174 Mike Trout 6.00 15.00
Jose Altuve/453*
'16-17 AL MVPs
'97-98 Bowman's Best Mirror Image
175 Kris Bryant 1.50 4.00
Giancarlo Stanton/453*
'16-17 NL MVPs
'97-98 Bowman's Best Mirror Image
176 Rick Porcello 1.00 2.50
Corey Kluber/453*
'16-17 AL Cy Young Winners
'97-98 Bowman's Best Mirror Image
177 Max Scherzer/453* 1.25 3.00
'16-17 NL Cy Young Winners
'97-98 Bowman's Best Mirror Image
178 Michael Fulmer 10.00 25.00
Aaron Judge/453*
'16-17 AL ROYs
'97-98 Bowman's Best Mirror Image
179 Corey Seager 12.00 30.00
Cody Bellinger/453*
'16-17 NL ROYs
'97-98 Bowman's Best Mirror Image
180 Reyes and Conforto Party in Queens 1.00 2.50
Jose Reyes

Michael Conforto/276*
'92 Home Alone
181 Judge & Sanchez Combine Powers 10.00 25.00
Aaron Judge
Gary Sanchez/276*
'92 Home Alone
182 Harper and Werth Take Flight 2.00 5.00
Bryce Harper
Jayson Werth/276*
'92 Home Alone
183 Benny and the Betts Rock Out 2.50 6.00
Andrew Benintendi
Mookie Betts/276*
'92 Home Alone
184 Baez Rises to the Occasion 1.50 4.00
Javier Baez/276*
'92 Home Alone
185 Jose and Yuli Get the Last Laugh 1.25 3.00
Jose Altuve
Yulieski Gurriel/276*
'92 Home Alone

2018 Topps Throwback Thursday

1 Giancarlo Stanton/680* 1.00 2.50
'68 Topps FB
2 George Springer/680* .75 2.00
'68 Topps FB
3 Mike Trout/680* 5.00 12.00
'68 Topps FB
4 Ian Happ/680* .75 2.00
'68 Topps FB
5 Yoan Moncada/680* 1.00 2.50
'68 Topps FB
6 Paul Goldschmidt/680* 1.00 2.50
'68 Topps FB
7 Aaron Judge/592* 2.50 6.00
'68 Fabulous Rock Records
8 Cal Ripken Jr./592* 3.00 8.00
'68 Fabulous Rock Records
9 Hank Aaron/592* 2.00 5.00
'68 Fabulous Rock Records
10 Rickey Henderson/592* 1.00 2.50
'68 Fabulous Rock Records
11 Ichiro Suzuki/592* 1.25 3.00
'68 Fabulous Rock Records
12 Nolan Ryan/592* 3.00 8.00
'68 Fabulous Rock Records
13 Noah Syndergaard 1.50 4.00
Bryce Harper/670*
'68 Topps HK
14 Chris Sale 2.50 6.00
Aaron Judge/670*
'68 Topps HK
15 Justin Verlander 1.00 2.50
Giancarlo Stanton/670*
'68 Topps HK
16 Corey Kluber 1.00 2.50
Carlos Correa/670*
'68 Topps HK
17 Clayton Kershaw 5.00 12.00
Mike Trout/670*
'68 Topps HK
18 Adam Wainwright 1.25 3.00
Kris Bryant/670*
'68 Topps HK
19 Bryce Harper/336* 2.00 5.00
'77 King Kong
20 Yasiel Puig/336* 1.25 3.00
'77 King Kong
21 Fireworks at Coors Field/336* 1.50 4.00
'77 King Kong
22 Ryon Healy/336* .75 2.00
'77 King Kong
23 Mookie Betts/336* 2.50 6.00
'77 King Kong
24 Jose Altuve 3.00 8.00
Aaron Judge/336*
'77 King Kong
25 Bryce Harper/445* 2.00 5.00
'89 Turn Back the Clock
26 Mike Trout/445* 6.00 15.00
'89 Turn Back the Clock
27 Derek Jeter/445* 3.00 8.00
'89 Turn Back the Clock
28 Alex Rodriguez/445* 1.50 4.00
'89 Turn Back the Clock
29 Mike Piazza/445* 1.25 3.00
'89 Turn Back the Clock
30 Ted Williams/445* 2.50 6.00
'89 Turn Back the Clock
31 Lindsey Vonn/344*
'84 Team USA BB
32 Chloe Kim/344*
'84 Team USA BB
33 Elana Meyers Taylor/344*
'84 Team USA BB
34 Meryl Davis/344*
'84 Team USA BB
35 Adam Rippon/344*
'84 Team USA BB
36 Karen Chen/344*
'84 Team USA BB
37 Clayton Kershaw/418* 2.00 5.00
'76 Topps BB
38 Chris Sale/418* 1.25 3.00
'76 Topps BB
39 Max Scherzer/418* 1.25 3.00
'76 Topps BB
40 Corey Kluber/418* 1.00 2.50
'76 Topps BB
41 Jacob deGrom/418* 2.50 6.00
'76 Topps BB
42 Jon Lester/418* 1.00 2.50
'76 Topps BB
43 Giancarlo Stanton 2.50 6.00
Aaron Judge/581*
'69 Stamp Booklet
44 Mookie Betts 2.00 5.00
Andrew Benintendi/581*
'69 Stamp Booklet
45 Kris Bryant 1.25 3.00
Anthony Rizzo/581*
'69 Stamp Booklet
46 Clayton Kershaw 2.00 5.00
Cody Bellinger/581*
'69 Stamp Booklet
47 Jose Altuve 1.00 2.50
Carlos Correa/581*
'69 Stamp Booklet
48 Bryce Harper 1.50 4.00
Max Scherzer/581*
'69 Stamp Booklet
49 Rafael Devers/466* 2.50 6.00
'89 New Kids on the Block
50 Miguel Andujar/466* 3.00 8.00
'89 New Kids on the Block
51 Amed Rosario/466* 1.00 2.50
'89 New Kids on the Block
52 Clint Frazier/466* 1.50 4.00
'89 New Kids on the Block
53 Rhys Hoskins/466* 3.00 8.00
'89 New Kids on the Block
54 Victor Robles/466* 2.00 5.00
'89 New Kids on the Block
55 Mike Piazza/320* 1.25 3.00
'94 Stadium Club
56 Nolan Ryan/320* 4.00 10.00
'94 Stadium Club
57 Carlton Fisk/320* 1.00 2.50
'94 Stadium Club
58 Ivan Rodriguez/320* 1.00 2.50
'94 Stadium Club
59 Roberto Alomar/320* 1.00 2.50
'94 Stadium Club
60 Roger Clemens/320* 1.50 4.00
'94 Stadium Club
61 Shohei Ohtani/1720* 12.00 30.00
'73 Topps WS
62 Ichiro Suzuki/1720* 1.00 2.50
'73 Topps WS
63 Yu Darvish/1720* .75 2.00
'73 Topps WS
64 Kenta Maeda/1720* .60 1.50
'73 Topps WS
65 Yasiel Puig/1720* .75 2.00
'73 Topps WS
66 Jose Abreu/1720* .75 2.00
'73 Topps WS
67 Nolan Ryan 12.00 30.00
Shohei Ohtani/1894*
'69 Rookies
68 Rafael Devers 1.50 4.00
David Ortiz/1894*
'69 Rookies
69 Amed Rosario .60 1.50
Darryl Strawberry/1894*
'69 Rookies
70 Rhys Hoskins 2.00 5.00
Chase Utley/1894*
'69 Rookies
71 Chance Sisco 2.50 6.00
Cal Ripken Jr./1894*
'69 Rookies
72 Ozzie Albies 1.50 4.00
Chipper Jones/1894*
'69 Rookies
73 Derek Jeter/384* 3.00 8.00
'09 Topps WBC
74 David Ortiz/384* 1.25 3.00
'09 Topps WBC
75 Ichiro Suzuki/384* 1.50 4.00
'09 Topps WBC
76 Clayton Kershaw/384* 2.00 5.00
'09 Topps WBC
77 Mike Piazza/384* 1.25 3.00
'09 Topps WBC
78 Alex Rodriguez/384* 1.50 4.00
'09 Topps WBC
79 Shohei Ohtani/2289* 12.00 30.00
'93 Star Wars
80 Aaron Judge/2289* 2.00 5.00
'93 Star Wars
81 Mike Trout/2289* 4.00 10.00
'93 Star Wars
82 Kris Bryant/2289* 1.00 2.50
'93 Star Wars
83 Bryce Harper/2289* 1.25 3.00
'93 Star Wars
84 Clayton Kershaw/2289* 1.25 3.00
'93 Star Wars
85 Mike Trout/835* 5.00 12.00
'98 Hardball Royalty
86 Hank Aaron/835* 2.00 5.00
'98 Hardball Royalty
87 Nolan Ryan/835* 3.00 8.00
'98 Hardball Royalty
88 Albert Pujols/835* 1.25 3.00
'98 Hardball Royalty
89 Cal Ripken Jr./835* 3.00 8.00
'98 Hardball Royalty
90 Bryce Harper/835* 1.50 4.00
'98 Hardball Royalty
91 Ozzie Albies/1964* 1.50 4.00
'54-55 Topps HK
92 Kris Bryant/1964* 1.00 2.50
'54-55 Topps HK
93 Gleyber Torres/1964* 5.00 12.00
'54-55 Topps HK
94 Mookie Betts/1964* 1.50 4.00
'54-55 Topps HK
95 Jose Altuve/1964* .60 1.50
'54-55 Topps HK
96 Francisco Lindor/1964* .75 2.00
'54-55 Topps HK
97 Mike Trout/1502* 4.00 10.00
'77 Topps BB
98 Bryce Harper/1502* 1.25 3.00
'77 Topps BB
99 Aaron Judge/1502* 2.00 5.00
'77 Topps BB
100 Kris Bryant/1502* 1.00 2.50
'77 Topps BB
101 Mookie Betts/1502* 1.50 4.00
'77 Topps BB
102 Francisco Lindor/1502* .75 2.00
'77 Topps BB
103 Carlos Correa/1502* .75 2.00
'77 Topps BB
104 Manny Machado/1502* .75 2.00
'77 Topps BB
105 Ronald Acuna/1672* 15.00 40.00
'79-80 Topps SOC
106 Albert Pujols/1672* 1.00 2.50
'79-80 Topps SOC
107 Shohei Ohtani/1672* 12.00 30.00
'79-80 Topps SOC
108 Francisco Lindor/1672* .75 2.00
'79-80 Topps SOC
109 Ozzie Albies/1672* 1.50 4.00
'79-80 Topps SOC
110 Didi Gregorius/1672* .60 1.50
'79-80 Topps SOC
111 Bryce Harper/1672* 1.25 3.00
'79-80 Topps SOC
112 Mike Trout/516* 5.00 12.00
'93 Jurassic Park
113 Jose Altuve/516* .75 2.00
'93 Jurassic Park
114 Freddie Freeman/516* 1.25 3.00
'93 Jurassic Park
115 Joey Votto/516* 1.00 2.50
'93 Jurassic Park
116 Yadier Molina/516* 1.25 3.00
'93 Jurassic Park
117 Brett Gardner/516* .75 2.00
'93 Jurassic Park
118 Aaron Judge/691* 2.50 6.00
'91 American Gladiators
119 Kris Bryant/691* 1.25 3.00
'91 American Gladiators
120 Bryce Harper/691* 1.50 4.00
'91 American Gladiators
121 Cody Bellinger/691* 2.00 5.00
'91 American Gladiators
122 Mookie Betts/691* 2.00 5.00
'91 American Gladiators
123 Justin Verlander/691* 1.00 2.50
'91 American Gladiators
124 Ronald Acuna/872* 20.00 50.00
'83 A-Team
125 Miguel Andujar/872* 2.50 6.00
'83 A-Team
126 Ozzie Albies/872* 2.00 5.00
'83 A-Team
127 Jose Altuve/872* .75 2.00
'83 A-Team
128 Nolan Arenado/872* 1.50 4.00
'83 A-Team
129 Jake Arrieta/872* .75 2.00
'83 A-Team
130 Mike Trout/1198* 4.00 10.00
'69 Topps AS
131 Bryce Harper/1198* 1.25 3.00
'69 Topps AS
132 Aaron Judge/1198* 2.00 5.00
'69 Topps AS
133 Gleyber Torres/1198* 5.00 12.00
'69 Topps AS
134 Ozzie Albies/1198* 1.50 4.00
'69 Topps AS
135 J.D. Martinez/1198* .75 2.00
'69 Topps AS
136 Ozzie Albies/793* 2.00 5.00
'89 Topps AS
137 Gleyber Torres/793* 6.00 15.00
'89 Topps AS
138 Alex Bregman/793* 1.00 2.50
'89 Topps AS
139 Javier Baez/793* 1.25 3.00
'89 Topps AS
140 Nick Markakis/793* .75 2.00
'89 Topps AS
141 Aaron Nola/793* .75 2.00
'89 Topps AS
142 Mookie Betts 2.00 5.00
Andrew Benintendi
Jackie Bradley Jr/899*
'78 Three's Company
143 Ben Zobrist 1.25 3.00
Anthony Rizzo
Kris Bryant/899*
'78 Three's Company
144 Aaron Judge 2.50 6.00
Giancarlo Stanton
Brett Gardner/899*
'78 Three's Company
145 Shohei Ohtani 15.00 40.00
Mike Trout
Justin Upton/899*
'78 Three's Company
146 Alex Bregman 1.00 2.50
Carlos Correa
Jose Altuve/899*
'78 Three's Company
147 Johan Camargo 20.00 50.00
Ozzie Albies
Ronald Acuna/899*
'78 Three's Company
148 Chipper Jones/679* 1.00 2.50
'60 Topps BB
149 Jim Thome/679* .75 2.00
'60 Topps BB
150 Jack Morris/679* .75 2.00
'60 Topps BB
151 Alan Trammell/679* .75 2.00
'60 Topps BB
152 Vladimir Guerrero/679* .75 2.00
'60 Topps BB
153 Trevor Hoffman/679* .75 2.00
'60 Topps BB
154 Mike Trout/658* 5.00 12.00
'78 Jaws 2
155 Giancarlo Stanton/658* 1.00 2.50
'78 Jaws 2
156 Jose Ramirez/658* .75 2.00
'78 Jaws 2
157 Bryce Harper/658* 1.50 4.00
'78 Jaws 2
158 Aaron Judge/658* 2.50 6.00
'78 Jaws 2
159 Rhys Hoskins/658* 2.50 6.00
'78 Jaws 2
160 Ronald Acuna Jr./1588* 20.00 50.00
'59 Topps BB
161 Miguel Andujar/1588* 2.00 5.00
'59 Topps BB
162 Juan Soto/1588* 12.00 30.00
'59 Topps BB
163 Matt Carpenter/1588* .75 2.00
'59 Topps BB
164 Jose Ramirez/1588* .60 1.50
'59 Topps BB
165 Javier Baez/1588* 1.00 2.50
'59 Topps BB
166 Babe Ruth 2.50 6.00
The Sultan of Swat/571*
'05 Topps BB
167 Frank Thomas 1.00 2.50
The Big Hurt/571*
'05 Topps BB
168 Reggie Jackson .75 2.00
Mr. October/571*
'05 Topps BB
169 David Ortiz 1.00 2.50
Big Papi/571*
'05 Topps BB
170 Ryne Sandberg 2.00 5.00
Ryno/571*
'05 Topps BB
171 Ozzie Smith 1.25 3.00
The Wizzard/571*
'05 Topps BB
172 Mike Trout 4.00 10.00
Aaron Judge/1029*
'60 Topps BB
173 Juan Soto 15.00 40.00
Ronald Acuna Jr/1029*
'60 Topps BB
174 Gleyber Torres 12.00 30.00
Shohei Ohtani/1029*
'60 Topps BB
175 Bryce Harper 1.25 3.00
Kris Bryant/1029*
'60 Topps BB
176 Max Scherzer .75 2.00
Chris Sale/1029*
'60 Topps BB
177 Matt Carpenter .75 2.00
Jose Ramirez/1029*
'60 Topps BB
178 Bryce Harper/848* 1.50 4.00
'63 Topps FB
179 Shohei Ohtani/848* 15.00 40.00
'63 Topps FB
180 Miguel Andujar/848* 2.50 6.00
'63 Topps FB
181 David Bote/848* 1.50 4.00
'63 Topps FB
182 Francisco Lindor/848* 1.00 2.50
'63 Topps FB
183 Jacob deGrom/848* 2.00 5.00
'63 Topps FB
184 Juan Soto/1172* 12.00 30.00
'61 Topps BB
185 Mike Trout/1172* 4.00 10.00
'61 Topps BB
186 Kris Bryant/1172* 1.00 2.50
'61 Topps BB
187 Ronald Acuna Jr/1172* 15.00 40.00
'61 Topps BB
188 Justin Verlander/1172* .75 2.00
'61 Topps BB
189 J.D. Martinez/1172* .75 2.00
'61 Topps BB
190 Miguel Andujar 12.00 30.00
Shohei Ohtani/1090*
'78 Topps FB Leaders
191 Ronald Acuna Jr. 15.00 40.00
Juan Soto/1090*
'78 Topps FB Leaders
192 J.D. Martinez 4.00 10.00
Mike Trout/1090*
'78 Topps FB Leaders
193 Javier Baez 1.00 2.50
Christian Yelich/1090*
'78 Topps FB Leaders
194 Jacob deGrom 1.50 4.00
Max Scherzer/1090*
'78 Topps FB Leaders
195 Chris Sale .75 2.00
Blake Snell/1090*
'78 Topps FB Leaders
196 Mookie Betts/477* 2.50 6.00
'74 Topps BB
197 Francisco Lindor/477* 1.25 3.00
'74 Topps BB
198 Alex Bregman/477* 1.25 3.00
'74 Topps BB
199 Ronald Acuna Jr/477* 25.00 60.00
'74 Topps BB
200 Christian Yelich/477* 1.50 4.00
'74 Topps BB
201 Walker Buehler/477* 4.00 10.00
'74 Topps BB
202 Ronald Acuna Jr/1371* 15.00 40.00
'86 Topps BB
203 Ozzie Albies/1371* 1.50 4.00
'86 Topps BB
204 Gleyber Torres/1371* 5.00 12.00
'86 Topps BB
205 Miguel Andujar/1371* 2.00 5.00
'86 Topps BB
206 Walker Buehler/1371* 2.50 6.00
'86 Topps BB
207 David Bote/1371* 1.25 3.00
'86 Topps BB
208 Walker Buehler/875* 3.00 8.00
'64 Topps BB
209 Ronald Acuna Jr/875* 20.00 50.00
'64 Topps BB
210 Aaron Judge/875* 2.50 6.00
'64 Topps BB
211 George Springer/875* .75 2.00
'64 Topps BB
212 Brock Holt/875* .60 1.50
'64 Topps BB
213 Christian Yelich/875* 1.25 3.00
'64 Topps BB
214 Alex Bregman/420* 1.25 3.00
'95 Topps BB
215 Christian Yelich/420* 1.50 4.00
'95 Topps BB
216 Walker Buehler/420* 4.00 10.00
'95 Topps BB
217 Mookie Betts/420* 2.50 6.00
'95 Topps BB
218 Derek Jeter/420* 3.00 8.00
'95 Topps BB
219 Kris Bryant/420* 1.50 4.00
'95 Topps BB
220 Clayton Kershaw/680* 1.50 4.00
'63 Topps BB
221 Chris Sale/680* 1.00 2.50
'63 Topps BB
222 Justin Verlander/680* 1.00 2.50
'63 Topps BB
223 Walker Buehler/680* 3.00 8.00
'63 Topps BB
224 Miguel Andujar/680* 2.50 6.00
'63 Topps BB
225 Ozzie Albies/680* 2.00 5.00
'63 Topps BB
226 Boston Red Sox/667* 2.00 5.00
'81 Topps BB
227 Chicago Cubs/667* 2.00 5.00
'81 Topps BB
228 Washington Nationals/667* 2.00 5.00
'81 Topps BB
229 Los Angeles Angels/667* 2.00 5.00
'81 Topps BB
230 New York Yankees/667* 2.00 5.00
'81 Topps BB
231 Atlanta Braves/667* 2.00 5.00
'81 Topps BB
232 Don Mattingly/475* 2.50 6.00
'75-'76 Topps BK
233 Rickey Henderson/475* 1.25 3.00
'75-'76 Topps BK
234 Hank Aaron/475* 2.50 6.00
'75-'76 Topps BK
235 Cal Ripken Jr./475* 4.00 10.00
'75-'76 Topps BK
236 Sandy Koufax/475* 2.50 6.00
'75-'76 Topps BK
237 Reggie Jackson/475* 1.00 2.50
'75-'76 Topps BK
238 Aaron Judge 15.00 40.00
Shohei Ohtani/756*
'82 Topps BB LL
239 Cody Bellinger 20.00 50.00
Ronald Acuna Jr./756*
'82 Topps BB LL
240 Corey Kluber .75 2.00
Blake Snell/756*
'82 Topps BB LL
241 Max Scherzer 2.00 5.00
Jacob deGrom/756*
'82 Topps BB LL
242 Jose Altuve 2.00 5.00
Mookie Betts/756*
'82 Topps BB LL
243 Giancarlo Stanton 1.25 3.00
Christian Yelich/756*
'82 Topps BB LL
244 Mike Trout/605* 5.00 12.00
'85 Rocky IV
245 Mookie Betts/605* 2.00 5.00
'85 Rocky IV
246 Aaron Judge/605* 2.50 6.00
'85 Rocky IV
247 Javier Baez/605* 1.25 3.00
'85 Rocky IV
248 Ronald Acuna Jr./605* 20.00 50.00
'85 Rocky IV
249 Matt Chapman/605* 1.00 2.50
'85 Rocky IV
250 Shohei Ohtani/842* 15.00 40.00
'54 Topps BB
251 Walker Buehler/842* 3.00 8.00
'54 Topps BB
252 Jack Flaherty/842* 2.50 6.00
'54 Topps BB
253 Ryan Yarbrough/842* 1.00 2.50
'54 Topps BB
254 A.J. Minter/842* .75 2.00
'54 Topps BB
255 Dereck Rodriguez/842* .75 2.00
'54 Topps BB
256 Ronald Acuna Jr./1480* 15.00 40.00
'54 Topps BB
257 Gleyber Torres/1480* 5.00 12.00
'54 Topps BB
258 Miguel Andujar/1480* 2.00 5.00
'54 Topps BB
259 David Bote/1480* 1.25 3.00
'54 Topps BB
260 Juan Soto/1480* 12.00 30.00
'54 Topps BB
261 Rafael Devers/1480* 1.50 4.00
'54 Topps BB

2020 Topps Throwback Thursday

1 Ronald Acuna Jr./580* 4.00 10.00
'10 Topps 2020
2 Juan Soto/580* 3.00 8.00
'10 Topps 2020
3 Gleyber Torres/580* 2.00 5.00
'10 Topps 2020
4 Alex Bregman/580* 1.00 2.50
'10 Topps 2020
5 Rafael Devers/580* 1.25 3.00
'10 Topps 2020
6 Shohei Ohtani/580* 1.50 4.00
'10 Topps 2020
91 Pete Alonso/638* 2.50 6.00
'89 Topps BB
92 Vladimir Guerrero Jr./638* 1.50 4.00
'89 Topps BB
93 Shohei Ohtani/638* 1.50 4.00
'89 Topps BB
94 Yordan Alvarez/638* 6.00 15.00
'89 Topps BB
95 Ronald Acuna Jr./638* 4.00 10.00
'89 Topps BB
96 Cody Bellinger/638* 2.00 5.00
'89 Topps BB
97 Gavin Lux/872* 3.00 8.00
'78-79 Topps HK
98 Bryce Harper/872* 1.50 4.00
'78-79 Topps HK
99 Aaron Judge/872* 2.50 6.00
'78-79 Topps HK
100 Willie Mays/872* 2.00 5.00
'78-79 Topps HK
101 George Brett/872* 2.00 5.00
'78-79 Topps HK
102 Aristides Aquino/872* 1.50 4.00
'78-79 Topps HK
103 Roberto Alomar/335* 1.00 2.50
'62 Topps BB
104 Francisco Lindor/335* 1.25 3.00
'62 Topps BB
105 Tim Raines/335* 1.00 2.50
'62 Topps BB
106 Ozzie Albies/335* 1.25 3.00
'62 Topps BB
107 Chipper Jones/335* 1.25 3.00
'62 Topps BB
108 Jose Ramirez/335* 1.00 2.50
'62 Topps BB
109 Nico Hoerner/1155* 2.00 5.00
'97-98 Topps BK
110 Luis Robert/1155* 4.00 10.00
'97-98 Topps BK
111 Kenny Lofton/1155* .50 1.25
'97-98 Topps BK
112 Tony Gwynn/1155* .75 2.00
'97-98 Topps BK
113 Mike Trout/1155* 4.00 10.00
'97-98 Topps BK
114 Fernando Tatis Jr./1155* 4.00 10.00
'97-98 Topps BK
115 Sandy Koufax/657* 2.00 5.00
'59 Topps FB
116 Bob Gibson/657* .75 2.00
'59 Topps FB
117 Jacob deGrom/657* 2.00 5.00
'59 Topps FB
118 Gerrit Cole/657* 1.50 4.00
'59 Topps FB
119 Jesus Luzardo/657* 1.25 3.00
'59 Topps FB
120 Dylan Cease/657* 1.00 2.50
'59 Topps FB
121 Vladimir Guerrero 1.50 4.00
Vladimir Guerrero Jr./661*
'77 Topps BB
122 Craig Biggio 1.25 3.00
Cavan Biggio/661*
'77 Topps BB
123 Mike Yastrzemski 1.50 4.00
Carl Yastrzemski/661*
'77 Topps BB
124 Corey Seager 1.00 2.50
Kyle Seager/661*
'77 Topps BB
125 Sandy Alomar Jr. .75 2.00
Roberto Alomar/661*
'77 Topps BB
126 Dante Bichette 5.00 12.00
Bo Bichette/661*
'77 Topps BB
131 Ichiro 2.00 5.00
Ken Griffey Jr./620*
'71 Topps Brady Bunch
133 Darryl Strawberry/594* .60 1.50
'89 Topps #1 Draft Picks
134 Stephen Strasburg/594* 1.00 2.50
'89 Topps #1 Draft Picks
135 Joe Mauer/594* .75 2.00
'89 Topps #1 Draft Picks
136 Carlos Correa/594* 1.00 2.50
'89 Topps #1 Draft Picks
137 Harold Baines/594* .75 2.00
'89 Topps #1 Draft Picks
138 Chipper Jones/594* 1.00 2.50
'89 Topps #1 Draft Picks
139 Yordan Alvarez/911* 6.00 15.00
'56 Topps Flags of the World
140 Aristides Aquino/911* 1.50 4.00
'56 Topps Flags of the World
141 Christian Yelich/911* 1.25 3.00
'56 Topps Flags of the World
142 Mookie Betts/911* 2.00 5.00
'56 Topps Flags of the World
143 Ronald Acuna Jr./911* 4.00 10.00
'56 Topps Flags of the World
144 Shohei Ohtani/911* 1.50 4.00
'56 Topps Flags of the World
145 Mark McGwire/801* 1.50 4.00
'92-93 Topps BK
146 Aaron Judge/801* 2.50 6.00
'92-93 Topps BK
147 Ken Griffey Jr./801* 2.00 5.00
'92-93 Topps BK
148 Pete Alonso/801* 2.50 6.00
'92-93 Topps BK
149 Jim Thome/801* .75 2.00
'92-93 Topps BK
150 Babe Ruth/801* 2.50 6.00
'92-93 Topps BK
151 Nolan Ryan/611* 3.00 8.00
'85 Woolworth's
152 Cal Ripken Jr./611* 3.00 8.00
'85 Woolworth's
153 Ichiro Suzuki/611* 1.25 3.00
'85 Woolworth's
154 Mariano Rivera/611* 1.25 3.00
'85 Woolworth's
155 Rickey Henderson/611* 1.00 2.50
'85 Woolworth's
156 Bartolo Colon/611* .60 1.50
'85 Woolworth's
157 Yordan Alvarez/2600* 4.00 10.00
'87 Topps BB
158 Pete Alonso/2600* 1.50 4.00
'87 Topps BB
159 Gavin Lux/2600* 2.00 5.00
'87 Topps BB
160 Vladimir Guerrero Jr/2600* 1.00 2.50
'87 Topps BB
161 Luis Robert/2600* 3.00 8.00
'87 Topps BB
162 Mike Soroka/2600* .60 1.50
'87 Topps BB
163 Aristides Aquino/905* 1.50 4.00
'99 Bowman BB
164 Brendan McKay/905* 1.00 2.50
'99 Bowman BB
165 Dustin May/905* 2.00 5.00
'99 Bowman BB
166 Bo Bichette/905* 5.00 12.00
'99 Bowman BB
167 Dylan Cease/905* 1.00 2.50
'99 Bowman BB
168 Nico Hoerner/905* 2.50 6.00
'99 Bowman BB
169 Francisco Lindor/369* 1.25 3.00
'00 Team USA BK
170 Gerrit Cole/369* 2.00 5.00
'00 Team USA BK
171 Anthony Rendon/369* 1.25 3.00
'00 Team USA BK
172 Alex Bregman/369* 1.25 3.00
'00 Team USA BK
173 Joey Gallo/369* 1.25 3.00
'00 Team USA BK
174 Marcus Stroman/369* 1.00 2.50
'00 Team USA BK
175 Fernando Tatis Jr./460* 6.00 15.00
'01 SC FB
176 Eloy Jimenez/460* 2.50 6.00
'01 SC FB
177 Walker Buehler/460* 1.50 4.00
'01 SC FB
178 Jack Flaherty/460* 1.25 3.00
'01 SC FB
179 Bryce Harper/460* 2.00 5.00
'01 SC FB
180 Charlie Morton/460* 1.25 3.00
'01 SC FB
181 Aaron Judge/646* 2.50 6.00
'70-71 Topps BK
182 Albert Pujols/646* 1.25 3.00
'70-71 Topps BK
183 Mike Piazza/646* 1.00 2.50
'70-71 Topps BK
184 Yordan Alvarez/646* 6.00 15.00
'70-71 Topps BK
185 Dave Winfield/646* .75 2.00
'70-71 Topps BK
186 Tony Gwynn/646* 1.00 2.50
'70-71 Topps BK
187 Christian Yelich/515* 1.25 3.00
'61-62 Topps HK
188 Mike Trout/515* 5.00 12.00
'61-62 Topps HK
189 Kevin Kiermaier/515* .75 2.00
'61-62 Topps HK
190 Juan Soto/515* 3.00 8.00
'61-62 Topps HK
191 Cody Bellinger/515* 2.00 5.00
'61-62 Topps HK
192 Cal Ripken Jr/515* 3.00 8.00
'61-62 Topps HK
193 Derek Jeter/855* 2.50 6.00
'80 Wanted Posters
194 Pete Alonso/855* 2.50 6.00
'80 Wanted Posters
195 Mike Trout/855* 5.00 12.00
'80 Wanted Posters
196 Shane Bieber/855* 1.00 2.50
'80 Wanted Posters
197 Shohei Ohtani/855* 1.50 4.00
'80 Wanted Posters
198 Randy Johnson/855* 1.00 2.50
'80 Wanted Posters
199 Luis Robert/2073* 3.00 8.00
'84 Topps Cereal BB
200 Fernando Tatis Jr/2073* 3.00 8.00
'84 Topps Cereal BB
201 Ronald Acuna Jr/2073* 2.50 6.00
'84 Topps Cereal BB
202 Mookie Betts/2073* 1.25 3.00
'84 Topps Cereal BB
203 Jacob deGrom/2073* 1.25 3.00
'84 Topps Cereal BB
204 Charlie Blackmon/2073* .60 1.50
'84 Topps Cereal BB
205 Rickey Henderson/848* 1.00 2.50
'92 SC FB
206 Babe Ruth/848* 2.50 6.00
'92 SC FB
207 Roberto Clemente/848* 2.50 6.00
'92 SC FB
208 Ichiro/848* 1.25 3.00
'92 SC FB
209 Vladimir Guerrero/848* .75 2.00
'92 SC FB
210 Hank Aaron/848* 2.00 5.00
'92 SC FB
211 Kyle Lewis/1789* 4.00 10.00
'98 Topps WCW
212 Luis Robert/1789* 4.00 10.00
'98 Topps WCW
213 Yoshitomo Tsutsugo/1789* 1.25 3.00
'98 Topps WCW
214 Mike Yastrzemski/1789* 1.25 3.00
'98 Topps WCW
215 Eloy Jimenez/1789* 1.50 4.00
'98 Topps WCW
216 Fernando Tatis Jr./1789* 4.00 10.00
'98 Topps WCW
217 Don Mattingly/432* 2.50 6.00
'60 Topps BB MGRs
218 Ted Williams/432* 2.50 6.00
'60 Topps BB MGRs
219 Tony LaRussa/432* 1.00 2.50
'60 Topps BB MGRs
220 Tommy Lasorda/432* 1.00 2.50
'60 Topps BB MGRs
221 Joe Torre/432* 1.00 2.50
'60 Topps BB MGRs
222 Sparky Anderson/432* 1.00 2.50
'60 Topps BB MGRs
223 Kyle Lewis/579* 5.00 12.00
'95-96 SC HK
224 Jose Abreu/579* 1.00 2.50
'95-96 SC HK
225 Yu Darvish/579* 1.00 2.50
'95-96 SC HK
226 Michael Conforto/579* .75 2.00
'95-96 SC HK
227 Manny Machado/579* 1.00 2.50
'95-96 SC HK
228 Corey Seager/579* 1.00 2.50
'95-96 SC HK
229 Mike Trout/1665* 4.00 10.00
'54 Topps World of Wheels
230 Byron Buxton/1665* .75 2.00
'54 Topps World of Wheels
231 Trea Turner/1665* .60 1.50
'54 Topps World of Wheels
232 Luis Robert/1665* 4.00 10.00
'54 Topps World of Wheels
233 Rickey Henderson/1665* .75 2.00

'54 Topps World of Wheels
234 Ichiro Suzuki/1665* 1.00 2.50
'54 Topps World of Wheels
235 Los Angeles Dodgers/385* .75 2.00
'02 Topps BB
236 San Diego Padres/385* .75 2.00
'02 Topps BB
237 Atlanta Braves/385* .75 2.00
'02 Topps BB
238 New York Yankees/385* .75 2.00
'02 Topps BB
239 Tampa Bay Rays/385* .75 2.00
'02 Topps BB
240 Minnesota Twins/385* .75 2.00
'02 Topps BB
241 Aaron Judge/615* 2.50 6.00
'76 Topps BB Bubble Gum Champ
242 Rafael Devers/615* 1.25 3.00
'76 Topps BB Bubble Gum Champ
243 Cody Bellinger/615* 2.00 5.00
'76 Topps BB Bubble Gum Champ
244 Ronald Acuna Jr./615* 4.00 10.00
'76 Topps BB Bubble Gum Champ
245 Manny Machado/615* 1.00 2.50
'76 Topps BB Bubble Gum Champ
246 Eugenio Suarez/615* .75 2.00
'76 Topps BB Bubble Gum Champ
247 Fernando Tatis Jr./793* 5.00 12.00
'92 Topps Kids BB
248 Dustin May/793* 2.00 5.00
'92 Topps Kids BB
249 Randy Arozarena/793* 5.00 12.00
'92 Topps Kids BB
250 Ted Williams/793* 2.00 5.00
'92 Topps Kids BB
251 Gary Carter/793* .75 2.00
'92 Topps Kids BB
252 Ken Griffey Jr./793* 2.00 5.00
'92 Topps Kids BB
253 Clayton Kershaw/1363* 1.25 3.00
'66 Topps BB
254 Tyler Glasnow/1363* .75 2.00
'66 Topps BB
255 Bo Bichette/1363* 4.00 10.00
'66 Topps BB
256 Luis Robert/1363* 4.00 10.00
'66 Topps BB
257 Luke Voit/1363* 1.00 2.50
'66 Topps BB
258 Trent Grisham/1363* 2.00 5.00
'66 Topps BB
259 Corey Seager/415* 1.25 3.00
'72 Topps BB WS
260 Brandon Lowe/415* 1.00 2.50
'72 Topps BB WS
261 Stephen Strasburg/415* 1.25 3.00
'72 Topps BB WS
262 Anthony Rizzo/415* 1.50 4.00
'72 Topps BB WS
263 Derek Jeter/415* 3.00 8.00
'72 Topps BB WS
264 Bill Mazeroski/415* 1.00 2.50
'72 Topps BB WS
265 Randy Arozarena/2602* 3.00 8.00
'92-93 Topps HK
266 Luis Robert/2602* 3.00 8.00
'92-93 Topps HK
267 Dustin May/2602* 1.25 3.00
'92-93 Topps HK
268 Jesus Luzardo/2602* .75 2.00
'92-93 Topps HK
269 Bo Bichette/2602* 3.00 8.00
'92-93 Topps HK
270 Kyle Lewis/2602* 3.00 8.00
'92-93 Topps HK
271 Aaron Judge/430* 3.00 8.00
'71 Topps FB Posters
272 Nico Hoerner/430* 3.00 8.00
'71 Topps FB Posters
273 Bryce Harper/430* 2.00 5.00
'71 Topps FB Posters
274 Clayton Kershaw/430* 2.00 5.00
'71 Topps FB Posters
275 Dave Winfield/430* 1.00 2.50
'71 Topps FB Posters
276 Frank Thomas/430* 1.25 3.00
'71 Topps FB Posters
277 Jose Abreu/645* 1.00 2.50
'72 Topps BB
278 Freddie Freeman/645* 1.25 3.00
'72 Topps BB
279 Shane Bieber/645* 1.00 2.50
'72 Topps BB
280 Trevor Bauer/645* 1.25 3.00
'72 Topps BB
281 Kyle Lewis/645* 5.00 12.00
'72 Topps BB
282 Devin Williams/645* 1.50 4.00
'72 Topps BB
283 Randy Arozarena/939* 5.00 12.00
'83 Topps FB
284 Corey Seager/939* 1.00 2.50
'83 Topps FB
285 Ronald Acuna Jr./939* 4.00 10.00
'83 Topps FB
286 Luis Robert/939* 5.00 12.00
'83 Topps FB
287 Joey Votto/939* 1.00 2.50
'83 Topps FB
288 Josh Hader/939* .75 2.00
'83 Topps FB
289 Roberto Clemente/503* 2.50 6.00
'88 Topps FB
290 Ichiro/503* 1.25 3.00
'88 Topps FB
291 Willie Mays/503* 2.00 5.00
'88 Topps FB
292 Hank Aaron/503* 2.00 5.00
'88 Topps FB
293 Randy Johnson/503* 1.00 2.50
'88 Topps FB
294 Tom Seaver/503* .75 2.00
'88 Topps FB
295 Shohei Ohtani/501* 1.50 4.00
'71 Topps BB
296 Walker Buehler/501* 1.25 3.00
'71 Topps BB
297 Jesus Luzardo/501* 1.25 3.00
'71 Topps BB
298 Tim Anderson/501* 1.00 2.50
'71 Topps BB
299 Bernie Williams/501* .75 2.00
'71 Topps BB
300 Jackie Robinson/501* 1.00 2.50
'71 Topps BB
301 Fernando Tatis Jr./534* 5.00 12.00
'80 Topps Superman II
302 Ronald Acuna Jr./534* 4.00 10.00
'80 Topps Superman II
303 Byron Buxton/534* 1.00 2.50
'80 Topps Superman II
304 Mike Yastrzemski/534* 1.50 4.00
'80 Topps Superman II
305 Kevin Kiermaier/534* .75 2.00
'80 Topps Superman II
306 Jackie Bradley Jr./534* 1.00 2.50
'80 Topps Superman II
307 Bo Bichette/677* 5.00 12.00
'51 Topps Magic FB
308 Yordan Alvarez/677* 6.00 15.00
'51 Topps Magic FB
309 Trea Turner/677* .75 2.00
'51 Topps Magic FB
310 Gerrit Cole/677* 1.50 4.00
'51 Topps Magic FB
311 Bob Feller/677* .75 2.00
'51 Topps Magic FB
312 Eddie Mathews/677* 1.00 2.50
'51 Topps Magic FB
CL1 Checklist Set 1-17/872* .60 1.50
'78-79 Topps HK
CL2 Checklist Set 18-34/2073* .40 1.00
'84 Topps Cereal BB
CL3 Checklist Set 35-50/501* .60 1.50
'71 Topps BB

2009 Topps Ticket to Stardom

COMP.SET w/o RCs (200) 12.50 30.00
COMMON CARD (1-200) .12 .30
COMMON RC (1-200) .25 .60
COMMON RC (201-225) 1.25 3.00
201-225 RC ODDS 1:45 HOBBY
201-225 RC PRINT RUN 199 SER.#'d SETS
PRINTING PLATE ODDS 1:240 HOBBY
PLATE PRINT RUN 1 SET PER COLOR
BLACK-CYAN-MAGENTA-YELLOW ISSUED
NO PLATE PRICING DUE TO SCARCITY
1 Albert Pujols .40 1.00
2 Ichiro Suzuki .40 1.00
3 Aubrey Huff .12 .30
4 Kevin Youkilis .12 .30
5 David Wright .25 .60
6 Ryan Howard .25 .60
7 Jimmy Rollins .20 .50
8 Justin Morneau .20 .50
9 Joe Saunders .12 .30
10 David DeJesus .12 .30
11 Grady Sizemore .20 .50
12 Brian Roberts .12 .30
13 Alex Rodriguez .40 1.00
14 Alex Rios .12 .30
15 Brad Hawpe .12 .30
16 Gary Matthews Jr. .12 .30
17 Glen Perkins .12 .30
18 Erick Aybar .12 .30
19 Manny Ramirez .30 .75
20 Kosuke Fukudome .20 .50
21 David Ortiz .30 .75
22 Hunter Pence .20 .50
23 Edgar Renteria .12 .30
24 Ken Griffey Jr. .60 1.50
25 Joe Mauer .25 .60
26 Adrian Gonzalez .25 .60
27 Brian McCann .20 .50
28 Paul Konerko .20 .50
29 Francisco Liriano .12 .30
30 Pat Burrell .12 .30
31 Stephen Drew .12 .30
32 Chris Young .12 .30
33 Carlos Pena .20 .50
34 Rich Harden .12 .30
35 Felix Hernandez .20 .50
36 Geoff Jenkins .12 .30
37 Kenji Johjima .20 .50
38 Yovani Gallardo .12 .30
39 Max Scherzer .30 .75
40 Joe Crede .20 .50
41 Miguel Tejada .20 .50
42 Nick Swisher .20 .50
43 Tim Lincecum .20 .50
44 Mat Latos RC .75 2.00
45 Alex Gordon .20 .50
46 Jeff Francoeur .20 .50
47 Jay Bruce .20 .50
48 George Sherrill .12 .30
49 Zack Greinke .30 .75
50 Jeremy Guthrie .12 .30
51 Chris Young .12 .30
52 Melvin Mora .12 .30
53 Tim Wakefield .20 .50
54 Victor Martinez .20 .50
55 Nick Markakis .25 .60
56 Carlos Zambrano .20 .50
57 Ryan Garko .12 .30
58 Hideki Okajima .12 .30
59 Ubaldo Jimenez .12 .30
60 Justin Verlander .30 .75
61 Brad Penny .12 .30
62 Cameron Maybin .12 .30
63 Milton Bradley .12 .30
64 Hideki Matsui .30 .75
65 Jorge Cantu .12 .30
66 Jose Contreras .12 .30
67 Jon Lester .20 .50
68 Torii Hunter .12 .30
69 Jermaine Dye .12 .30
70 Roy Halladay .20 .50
71 Carlos Marmol .20 .50
72 Kerry Wood .12 .30
73 Josh Fields .12 .30
74 Evan Longoria .20 .50
75 Andrew McCutchen (RC) 1.25 3.00
76 Freddy Sanchez .12 .30
77 Mike Cameron .12 .30
78 Josh Hamilton .20 .50
79 A.J. Pierzynski .12 .30
80 Scott Rolen .20 .50
81 Joey Votto .30 .75
82 Brandon Inge .12 .30
83 Vernon Wells .12 .30
84 Armando Galarraga .12 .30
85 Mark Teixeira .20 .50
86 Austin Kearns .12 .30
87 Jason Giambi .12 .30
88 Kevin Millwood .12 .30
89 Josh Willingham .20 .50
90 Ryan Braun .20 .50
91 Chris Davis .20 .50
92 Erik Bedard .12 .30
93 Prince Fielder .20 .50
94 Kurt Suzuki .12 .30
95 Ryan Doumit .12 .30
96 Bill Hall .12 .30
97 Jack Wilson .12 .30
98 Tim Hudson .20 .50
99 Paul Maholm .12 .30
100 Adrian Beltre .30 .75
101 Curtis Granderson .25 .60
102 Travis Hafner .12 .30
103 Edinson Volquez .12 .30
104 Mike Lowell .12 .30
105 Justin Upton .20 .50
106 Eric Chavez .12 .30
107 Bobby Abreu .12 .30
108 Joba Chamberlain .12 .30
109 Gary Sheffield .12 .30
110 Chad Billingsley .20 .50
111 Carlos Beltran .20 .50
112 Rickie Weeks .12 .30
113 Jeremy Hermida .12 .30
114 Bronson Arroyo .12 .30
115 Mark Buehrle .20 .50
116 Jorge Posada .20 .50
117 Derrek Lee .12 .30
118 Dustin Pedroia .30 .75
119 Javier Vazquez .12 .30
120 Derek Jeter .75 2.00
121 Johan Santana .20 .50
122 J.J. Hardy .12 .30
123 Miguel Cabrera .30 .75
124 Daisuke Matsuzaka .20 .50
125 Geovany Soto .20 .50
126 Jason Varitek .30 .75
127 Magglio Ordonez .20 .50
128 Carlos Quentin .12 .30
129 Brandon Webb .20 .50
130 Jonathan Papelbon .20 .50
131 Josh Beckett .12 .30
132 Dan Haren .12 .30
133 Alfonso Soriano .20 .50
134 Yadier Molina .40 1.00
135 John Maine .12 .30
136 Todd Helton .20 .50
137 Troy Tulowitzki .30 .75
138 Luis Castillo .12 .30
139 Andy Pettitte .20 .50
140 Hank Blalock .12 .30
141 Jeremy Sowers .12 .30
142 Nate McLouth .12 .30
143 Carlos Lee .12 .30
144 Gavin Floyd .12 .30
145 Joe Nathan .12 .30
146 Matt Holliday .30 .75
147 Hanley Ramirez .20 .50
148 Akinori Iwamura .12 .30
149 Jeremy Bonderman .12 .30
150 Johnny Damon .20 .50
151 Derek Lowe .12 .30
152 Matt Kemp .25 .60
153 Troy Glaus .12 .30
154 Fausto Carmona .12 .30
155 Jered Weaver .20 .50
156 Orlando Hudson .12 .30
157 Garret Anderson .12 .30
158 Jason Bay .20 .50
159 Lance Berkman .20 .50
160 Randy Johnson .30 .75
161 Chipper Jones .30 .75
162 Conor Jackson .12 .30
163 Adam Dunn .20 .50
164 Jake Peavy .12 .30
165 Vladimir Guerrero .20 .50
166 Jacoby Ellsbury .25 .60
167 Cole Hamels .25 .60
168 J.D. Drew .12 .30
169 Cliff Lee .20 .50
170 Russell Martin .12 .30
171 Derek Holland RC .40 1.00
172 Joakim Soria .12 .30
173 Dan Uggla .12 .30
174 Carlos Delgado .12 .30
175 Jose Reyes .20 .50
176 Chase Utley .20 .50
177 Alexei Ramirez .20 .50
178 Roy Oswalt .20 .50
179 Matt Garza .12 .30
180 Matt Cain .20 .50
181 Chien-Ming Wang .20 .50
182 Gordon Beckham RC 1.50 4.00
183 Johnny Cueto .20 .50
184 Ryan Freel .12 .30
185 James Shields .12 .30
186 Rick Ankiel .12 .30
187 A.J. Burnett .12 .30
188 Adam Jones .20 .50
189 Jim Thome .20 .50
190 Andy Sonnanstine .12 .30
191 Ryan Zimmerman .20 .50
192 Jon Garland .12 .30
193 Robinson Cano .20 .50
194 Michael Young .12 .30
195 Xavier Nady .12 .30
196 B.J. Upton .20 .50
197 Ian Kinsler .20 .50
198 Scott Kazmir .12 .30
199 CC Sabathia .20 .50
200 Justin Masterson .12 .30
201 Colby Rasmus (RC) 2.00 5.00
202 Jordan Schafer (RC) 2.00 5.00
203 Ryan Perry RC 3.00 8.00
204 Brett Anderson RC 2.00 5.00
205 David Hernandez RC 1.25 3.00
206 Brian Duensing RC 2.00 5.00
207 Rick Porcello RC 4.00 10.00
208 Koji Uehara RC 3.00 8.00
209 Trevor Crowe RC 1.25 3.00
210 Andrew Bailey RC 3.00 8.00
211 David Price RC 2.50 6.00
212 Travis Snider RC 2.00 5.00
213 David Patton RC 2.00 5.00
214 Dexter Fowler (RC) 2.00 5.00
215 Phil Coke RC 2.00 5.00
216 Bobby Parnell RC 2.00 5.00
217 Ricky Romero (RC) 2.00 5.00
218 Everth Cabrera RC 2.00 5.00
219 Bobby Scales RC 2.00 5.00
220 Michael Bowden (RC) 1.25 3.00
221 Jordan Zimmermann RC 3.00 8.00
222 Fernando Martinez RC 3.00 8.00
223 David Freese RC 4.00 10.00
224 Elvis Andrus RC 3.00 8.00
225 Kenshin Kawakami RC 2.00 5.00

2009 Topps Ticket to Stardom Blue

*BLUE VET 1-200: 2X TO 5X BASIC
*BLUE RC 1-200: 1X TO 2.5X BASIC RC
*BLUE RC 201-225: .5X TO 1.2X BASIC RC
STATED ODDS 1:10
STATED PRINT RUN 99 SER.#'d SETS
182 Gordon Beckham 2.50 6.00

2009 Topps Ticket to Stardom Gold

*GOLD VET 1-200: 2.5X TO 6X BASIC
*GOLD RC 1-200: 1.2X TO 3X BASIC RC
*GOLD RC 201-225: .6X TO 1.5X BASIC RC
STATED ODDS 1:20 HOBBY
STATED PRINT RUN 50 SER.#'d SETS
182 Gordon Beckham 6.00 15.00

2009 Topps Ticket to Stardom Perforated

*GOLD VET 1-200: 1.2X TO 3X BASIC
*GOLD RC 1-200: .6X TO 1.5X BASIC RC
*GOLD RC 201-225: .3X TO .8X BASIC RC
STATED ODDS 1:1 HOBBY
182 Gordon Beckham 2.00 5.00

2009 Topps Ticket to Stardom Red

STATED ODDS 1:960 HOBBY
STATED PRINT RUN 1 SER.#'d SET
NO PRICING DUE TO SCARCITY

2009 Topps Ticket to Stardom Autograph Relics

GROUP A ODDS 1:23 HOBBY
GROUP B ODDS 1:503 HOBBY
GROUP A PRINT RUN 489 SER.#'d SETS
GROUP B PRINT RUN 89 SER.#'d SETS
AE Andre Ethier A 6.00 15.00
BD Blake DeWitt A 5.00 12.00
CJ Chipper Jones B 30.00 80.00
CK Clayton Kershaw A 40.00 80.00
DP Dustin Pedroia A 15.00 40.00
DW David Wright B 10.00 25.00
EL Evan Longoria A 10.00 25.00
ES Ervin Santana A 4.00 10.00
GA Garrett Atkins A 4.00 10.00
JB Jay Bruce A 4.00 10.00
JC Joba Chamberlain A 3.00 8.00
JM Justin Masterson A 5.00 12.00
JW Jayson Werth A 5.00 12.00
MB Michael Bowden A 10.00 25.00
MC Matt Cain A 6.00 15.00
MG Mat Gamel A 6.00 15.00
ML Mike Lowell B 15.00 40.00
NS Nick Swisher A 4.00 10.00
RH Ryan Howard B 6.00 15.00
SK Scott Kazmir A 3.00 8.00
TT Troy Tulowitzki A 8.00 20.00
UJ Ubaldo Jimenez A 3.00 8.00
VG Vladimir Guerrero B 10.00 25.00
CAJ Conor Jackson A 4.00 10.00
JCC Johnny Cueto A 5.00 12.00

2009 Topps Ticket to Stardom Autograph Relics Dual

GROUP A ODDS 1:601 HOBBY
GROUP B ODDS 1:3329 HOBBY
GROUP A PRINT RUN 39 SER.#'d SETS
GROUP B PRINT RUN 14 SER.#'d SETS
NO GROUP B PRICING DUE TO SCARCITY
AGCY A.Gonzalez/C.Young A 30.00 60.00
BUCP B.Upton/C.Pena A 20.00 50.00
CKMK Kershaw/Kemp A 30.00 60.00
CPEL C.Pena/Longoria A 40.00 80.00
ELMH Longoria/Holliday A 50.00 100.00
MGJH Mat Gamel/J.J. Hardy A 10.00 25.00
MGPF M.Gamel/Prince A 40.00 80.00
MLJP Lowell/Papelbon A 20.00 50.00
NMJG Markakis/Guthrie A 10.00 25.00
RCJC Cano/Joba A 15.00 40.00

2009 Topps Ticket to Stardom Big Ticket

STATED ODDS 1:8 HOBBY
*BLUE: .75X TO 2X BASIC
BLUE ODDS 1:57 HOBBY
BLUE PRINT RUN 99 SER.#'d SETS
*GOLD: 1X TO 2.5X BASIC
GOLD ODDS 1:112 HOBBY
GOLD PRINT RUN 50 SER.#'d SETS
RED ODDS 1:5403 HOBBY
RED PRINT RUN 1 SER.#'d SET
NO RED PRICING DUE TO SCARCITY
PRINTING PLATE ODDS 1:1350 HOBBY
PLATE PRINT RUN 1 SET PER COLOR
BLACK-CYAN-MAGENTA-YELLOW ISSUED
NO PLATE PRICING DUE TO SCARCITY
BT1 Ichiro Suzuki 1.00 2.50
BT2 Josh Hamilton .50 1.25
BT3 Ryan Braun .50 1.25
BT4 Albert Pujols 1.00 2.50
BT5 David Wright .60 1.50
BT6 Dustin Pedroia .75 2.00
BT7 Jose Reyes .50 1.25
BT8 Grady Sizemore .50 1.25
BT9 Tim Lincecum .50 1.25
BT10 Alex Rodriguez 1.00 2.50
BT11 Lance Berkman .50 1.25
BT12 Miguel Cabrera .75 2.00
BT13 Brandon Webb .50 1.25
BT14 Hanley Ramirez .50 1.25
BT15 CC Sabathia .50 1.25

2009 Topps Ticket to Stardom Opening Day Ticket Stubs

STATED ODDS 1:120 HOBBY
PRINT RUNS B/WN 22-262 COPIES PER
NO HALLADAY PRICING AVAILABLE
AG Alex Gordon/50 8.00 20.00
AP Albert Pujols/55 12.50 30.00
AS Alfonso Soriano/50 10.00 25.00
BW Brandon Webb/50 12.50 30.00
CQ Carlos Quentin/78 4.00 10.00
DM D.Matsuzaka/30 40.00 80.00
DW David Wright/107 15.00 40.00
EL Evan Longoria/50 15.00 40.00
GS Grady Sizemore/50 10.00 25.00
HR Hanley Ramirez/50 8.00 20.00
JB Jay Bruce/50 20.00 50.00
JH Josh Hamilton/50 12.50 30.00
JM Justin Morneau/50 8.00 20.00
JP Jake Peavy/50 8.00 20.00
KJ Kenji Johjima/262 6.00 15.00
LB Lance Berkman/50 8.00 20.00
MC Miguel Cabrera/55 10.00 25.00
MH Matt Holliday/52 12.00 30.00
MR Manny Ramirez/54 10.00 25.00
MT Mark Teixeira/50 4.00 10.00
NM Nick Markakis/50 12.00 30.00
PF Prince Fielder/99 10.00 25.00
RZ R.Zimmerman/100 12.00 30.00
TH Todd Helton/50 8.00 20.00
TL Tim Lincecum/50 10.00 25.00
VG V.Guerrero/76 6.00 15.00
NMM Nate McLouth/41 4.00 10.00
RHH Ryan Howard/102 12.00 30.00

2009 Topps Ticket to Stardom Seasoned Vets

STATED ODDS 1:12 HOBBY
*BLUE: .75X TO 2X BASIC
BLUE ODDS 1:57 HOBBY
BLUE PRINT RUN 99 SER.#'d SETS
*GOLD: 1X TO 2.5X BASIC
GOLD ODDS 1:112 HOBBY
GOLD PRINT RUN 50 SER.#'d SETS
RED ODDS 1:5403 HOBBY
RED PRINT RUN 1 SER.#'d SET
NO RED PRICING DUE TO SCARCITY
PRINTING PLATE ODDS 1:1350 HOBBY
PLATE PRINT RUN 1 SET PER COLOR
BLACK-CYAN-MAGENTA-YELLOW ISSUED
NO PLATE PRICING DUE TO SCARCITY
SV1 Alex Rodriguez 1.00 2.50
SV2 David Wright .60 1.50
SV3 Manny Ramirez .75 2.00
SV4 Albert Pujols 1.00 2.50
SV5 Ryan Howard .60 1.50
SV6 Vladimir Guerrero .50 1.25
SV7 Alfonso Soriano .50 1.25
SV8 Magglio Ordonez .50 1.25
SV9 Ryan Braun .50 1.25
SV10 David Ortiz .75 2.00

2009 Topps Ticket to Stardom Ticket Stubs

RANDOM INSERTS IN PACKS
PRINT RUNS B/WN 16-110 COPIES PER
NO KURT SUZUKI PRICING AVAILABLE
TS1 Alex Rodriguez/110 10.00 25.00
TS2 Adrian Gonzalez/110 4.00 10.00
TS4 Chad Billingsley/105 4.00 10.00
TS5 David Wright/110 5.00 12.00
TS6 Felix Hernandez/110 8.00 20.00
TS7 Ichiro Suzuki/110 8.00 20.00
TS8 Andre Ethier/110 5.00 12.00
TS9 Albert Pujols/110 20.00 50.00
TS10 Blake DeWitt/107 12.50 30.00
TS11 Brandon Webb/110 4.00 10.00
TS12 Alexei Ramirez/110 10.00 25.00
TS13 Chris Young/110 4.00 10.00
TS16 Grady Sizemore/110 4.00 10.00
TS17 Johan Santana/110 10.00 25.00
TS19 Manny Ramirez/105 4.00 10.00
TS20 Prince Fielder/110 5.00 12.00
TS21 Ryan Howard/110 8.00 20.00
TS23 Jose Reyes/110 10.00 25.00
TS24 Robinson Cano/110 4.00 10.00
TS25 Vladimir Guerrero/110 5.00 12.00
TS26 Evan Longoria/63 12.50 30.00
TS28 Nick Markakis/59 10.00 25.00
TS30 Jon Lester/102 10.00 25.00
TS31 Chipper Jones/110 6.00 15.00
TS32 Josh Hamilton/110 4.00 10.00
TS34 Prince Fielder/110 5.00 12.00
TS36 Joey Votto/110 4.00 10.00
TS38 M.Young/110 3.00 8.00
TS40 Travis Hafner/110 3.00 8.00
TS41 Adrian Beltre/53 8.00 20.00
TS43 Bobby Crosby/110 3.00 8.00
TS44 Miguel Cabrera/110 6.00 15.00
TS45 Fred Lewis/110 4.00 10.00
TS47 Garrett Atkins/110 3.00 8.00
TS49 Russell Martin/110 4.00 10.00
TS50 Adam Wainwright/110 6.00 15.00
TS52 Corey Hart/110 4.00 10.00
TS53 Kurt Suzuki/110 5.00 12.00
TS54 Geovany Soto/79 3.00 8.00
TS56 Travis Buck/110 6.00 15.00
TS57 Justin Duchscherer/110 4.00 10.00
TS58 Daric Barton/110 8.00 20.00
TS59 Tim Lincecum/110 8.00 20.00
TS62 J.Chamberlain/110 6.00 15.00
TS68 Nate McLouth/110 4.00 10.00
TS70 John Lackey/110 3.00 8.00
TS71 Rick Ankiel/110 4.00 10.00
TS72 Ryan Braun/110 5.00 12.00
TS73 Jose Reyes/110 10.00 25.00
TS74 Prince Fielder/110 4.00 10.00
TS75 Nate McLouth/110 3.00 8.00
TS78 Justin Duchscherer/110 3.00 8.00
TS79 J.J. Hardy/110 3.00 8.00
TS80 Chris Young/110 3.00 8.00
TS81 Chad Billingsley/105 4.00 10.00
TS82 David Wright/110 4.00 10.00
TS83 Felix Hernandez/110 8.00 20.00
TS84 Daric Barton/110 6.00 15.00
TS85 Ichiro Suzuki/110 20.00 50.00
TS86 Blake DeWitt/106 12.50 30.00
TS87 Saltalamacchia/110 3.00 8.00
TS88 Erick Aybar/95 4.00 10.00
TS89 Albert Pujols/110 10.00 25.00
TS90 Corey Hart/110 3.00 8.00
TS91 Adam Wainwright/110 8.00 20.00
TS92 Chris Davis/110 3.00 8.00
TS93 Carlos Delgado/110 5.00 12.00
TS94 K.Kouzmanoff/110 3.00 8.00
TS96 Jose Reyes/110 8.00 20.00
TS97 Russell Martin/110 4.00 10.00
TS98 Felix Hernandez/110 6.00 15.00
TS99 Adrian Gonzalez/110 3.00 8.00
TS100 Ichiro Suzuki/110 8.00 20.00

2009 Topps Ticket to Stardom Ticket Stubs Plus Memorabilia

STATED ODDS 1:22 HOBBY
PRINT RUNS B/WN 33-239 COPIES PER
TSP1 David Wright/224 6.00 15.00
TSP2 Bobby Crosby/239 3.00 8.00
TSP3 Albert Pujols/239 10.00 25.00
TSP4 Chad Billingsley/225 3.00 8.00
TSP5 Blake DeWitt/228 8.00 20.00
TSP6 Carlos Beltran/239 6.00 15.00
TSP7 Ichiro Suzuki/225 10.00 25.00
TSP8 Michael Young/224 3.00 8.00
TSP9 Nate McLouth/239 5.00 12.00
TSP10 Kevin Kouzmanoff/224 3.00 8.00
TSP11 Ryan Braun/224 5.00 12.00
TSP12 Josh Hamilton/239 6.00 15.00
TSP13 R.Cano/224 8.00 20.00
TSP14 Trevor Hoffman/224 5.00 12.00
TSP15 Eric Chavez/225 3.00 8.00
TSP16 Adrian Gonzalez/224 3.00 8.00
TSP17 Nick Swisher/224 5.00 12.00
TSP18 Manny Ramirez/239 6.00 15.00
TSP19 Troy Glaus/160 4.00 10.00
TSP20 Jermaine Dye/151 3.00 8.00
TSP21 M.Ordonez/90 8.00 20.00
TSP22 Rich Harden/225 3.00 8.00
TSP23 Alex Rodriguez/33 20.00 50.00
TSP24 Greg Maddux/79 4.00 10.00
TSP25 Hanley Ramirez/90 6.00 15.00
TSP26 Ryan Zimmerman/81 6.00 15.00
TSP27 Conor Jackson/81 8.00 20.00
TSP28 Ubaldo Jimenez/79 3.00 8.00
TSP29 Alfonso Soriano/79 3.00 8.00
TSP30 Aramis Ramirez/79 3.00 8.00
TSP31 Travis Buck/224 3.00 8.00
TSP32 Brian McCann/79 3.00 8.00
TSP33 Hunter Pence/79 3.00 8.00
TSP34 Clayton Kershaw/79 5.00 12.00
TSP35 D.Matsuzaka/45 8.00 20.00
TSP36 Ichiro Suzuki/225 10.00 25.00
TSP37 Cliff Lee/63 8.00 20.00
TSP38 Derrek Lee/77 10.00 25.00
TSP39 Ichiro Suzuki/225 10.00 25.00
TSP40 Adrian Gonzalez/161 3.00 8.00
TSP41 Bobby Crosby/224 3.00 8.00
TSP42 Jack Cust/239 3.00 8.00
TSP43 Ichiro Suzuki/225 20.00 50.00
TSP44 Adrian Gonzalez/224 3.00 8.00
TSP45 Kevin Kouzmanoff/224 3.00 8.00
TSP46 Josh Hamilton/225 6.00 15.00
TSP47 Brian Giles/224 4.00 10.00
TSP48 Travis Buck/224 3.00 8.00
TSP49 Hanley Ramirez/110 6.00 15.00
TSP50 Miguel Tejada/110 3.00 8.00
TSP51 Jose Reyes/110 10.00 25.00
TSP52 Pedro Martinez/110 6.00 15.00
TSP53 Geovany Soto/110 4.00 10.00
TSP54 Bernie Williams/110 5.00 12.00
TSP55 Jonathan Sanchez/110 4.00 10.00
TSP56 J.C. Romero/110 5.00 12.00
TSP57 M.Enriquez/110 10.00 25.00
TSP58 Yulieski Gourriel/110 4.00 10.00
TSP59 Yoennis Cespedes/110 15.00 40.00
TSP60 F.Cepeda/110 10.00 25.00
TSP61 Jimmy Rollins/110 8.00 20.00
TSP62 Roy Oswalt/110 8.00 20.00
TSP63 Adam Dunn/110 4.00 10.00
TSP64 K.Fukudome/90 10.00 25.00
TSP65 Yu Darvish/90 60.00 120.00
TSP66 M.Tanaka/90 50.00 100.00
TSP67 S.Abe/90 10.00 25.00
TSP68 Norichika Aoki/90 15.00 40.00
TSP69 Kwang-Hyun Kim/90 5.00 12.00
TSP70 Tae Kyun Kim/90 10.00 25.00
TSP71 Jin Young Lee/90 3.00 8.00
TSP72 Shin-Soo Choo/90 15.00 40.00

2009 Topps Ticket to Stardom Ticket Stubs Plus Memorabilia Dual

STATED ODDS 1:22 HOBBY
PRINT RUNS B/WN 14-239 COPIES PER
NO PRICING ON QTY 15 OR LESS
TSP1 Ichiro Suzuki/239 6.00 15.00
TSP2 Ichiro Suzuki/228 6.00 15.00
TSP3 Ichiro Suzuki/36 10.00 25.00
TSP4 David Wright/239 8.00 20.00
TSP5 David Wright/239 8.00 20.00
TSP6 David Wright/228 8.00 20.00
TSP8 Howie Kendrick/224 3.00 8.00
TSP9 Corey Hart/224 4.00 10.00
TSP10 Mike Napoli/224 5.00 12.00
TSP11 Jake Peavy/61 5.00 12.00
TSP12 J.J. Hardy/239 3.00 8.00
TSP13 J.J. Hardy/228 3.00 8.00
TSP14 J.J. Hardy/72 4.00 10.00
TSP15 Josh Hamilton/224 8.00 20.00
TSP16 Michael Young/224 3.00 8.00
TSP17 Robinson Cano/224 10.00 25.00
TSP18 Vladimir Guerrero/228 4.00 10.00
TSP19 Vladimir Guerrero/27 6.00 15.00
TSP20 Travis Buck/224 4.00 10.00
TSP21 Prince Fielder/239 5.00 12.00
TSP22 Prince Fielder/228 5.00 12.00
TSP24 Eric Chavez/224 4.00 10.00
TSP25 Jose Reyes/239 12.50 30.00
TSP26 Jose Reyes/210 12.50 30.00
TSP27 Trevor Hoffman/224 6.00 15.00
TSP28 Troy Glaus/161 5.00 12.00
TSP29 Jack Cust/235 4.00 10.00
TSP30 Russell Martin/223 5.00 12.00
TSP31 Jake Peavy/116 4.00 10.00
TSP32 Alex Rios/180 12.50 30.00
TSP33 Matt Kemp/239 5.00 12.00
TSP34 Matt Kemp/40 6.00 15.00
TSP35 Nick Markakis/59 8.00 20.00
TSP36 Johnny Damon/85 8.00 20.00
TSP37 Bobby Crosby/224 4.00 10.00
TSP38 James Loney/79 6.00 15.00
TSP39 Carlos Delgado/81 6.00 15.00
TSP40 Conor Jackson/81 10.00 25.00
TSP41 Aaron Rowand/79 4.00 10.00
TSP42 Ryan Braun/126 6.00 15.00
TSP43 Kosuke Fukudome/90 12.50 30.00
TSP44 Chin-Lung Hu/77 5.00 12.00
TSP45 Wladimir Balentien/239 3.00 8.00
TSP46 Wladimir Balentien/228 3.00 8.00
TSP47 Wladimir Balentien/185 4.00 10.00
TSP48 Adrian Beltre/53 8.00 20.00
TSP49 Kevin Kouzmanoff/239 4.00 10.00
TSP50 Kevin Kouzmanoff/228 4.00 10.00
TSP51 Kevin Kouzmanoff/200 4.00 10.00
TSP52 Kevin Kouzmanoff/154 4.00 10.00
TSP53 Bobby Crosby/224 4.00 10.00
TSP54 Trevor Hoffman/162 6.00 15.00
TSP55 Wladimir Balentien/224 3.00 8.00
TSP56 Jack Cust/239 4.00 10.00
TSP57 Jack Cust/89 5.00 12.00
TSP58 Eric Chavez/239 4.00 10.00
TSP59 Eric Chavez/75 5.00 12.00
TSP60 Wladimir Balentien/228 3.00 8.00
TSP61 Wladimir Balentien/28 5.00 12.00
TSP62 Travis Buck/224 4.00 10.00
TSP63 Daric Barton/224 4.00 10.00

2009 Topps Ticket to Stardom Ticket To Stardom

STATED ODDS 1:4 HOBBY
*BLUE: .75X TO 2X BASIC
BLUE ODDS 1:57 HOBBY
BLUE PRINT RUN 99 SER.#'d SETS
*GOLD: 1X TO 2.5X BASIC
GOLD ODDS 1:112 HOBBY
GOLD PRINT RUN 50 SER.#'d SETS
RED ODDS 1:5403 HOBBY
RED PRINT RUN 1 SER.#'d SET
NO RED PRICING DUE TO SCARCITY
PRINTING PLATE ODDS 1:1350 HOBBY
PLATE PRINT RUN 1 SET PER COLOR
BLACK-CYAN-MAGENTA-YELLOW ISSUED
NO PLATE PRICING DUE TO SCARCITY
TTS1 David Price .75 2.00
TTS2 Travis Snider .60 1.50
TTS3 Colby Rasmus .60 1.50
TTS4 Cameron Maybin .40 1.00
TTS5 Matt Kemp .75 2.00
TTS6 Jay Bruce .60 1.50
TTS7 Prince Fielder .60 1.50
TTS8 Joba Chamberlain .40 1.00
TTS9 Grady Sizemore .60 1.50
TTS10 Evan Longoria .60 1.50
TTS11 Joe Mauer .75 2.00
TTS12 Joey Votto 1.00 2.50
TTS13 Nick Markakis .75 2.00
TTS14 Jacoby Ellsbury .75 2.00
TTS15 Kenshin Kawakami .60 1.50

2011 Topps Tier One

COMMON CARD (1-100) .60 1.50
COMMON RC (1-100) .60 1.50
STATED PRINT RUN 799 SER.#'d SETS
1 Joe DiMaggio 3.00 8.00
2 Derek Jeter 4.00 10.00
3 Babe Ruth 4.00 10.00
4 Lou Gehrig 3.00 8.00
5 Ty Cobb 2.50 6.00
6 Stan Musial 2.50 6.00
7 Mickey Mantle 5.00 12.00
8 Ryan Braun 1.00 2.50
9 Roger Maris 1.50 4.00
10 Albert Pujols 2.00 5.00
11 Luis Aparicio 1.00 2.50
12 Starlin Castro 1.00 2.50
13 Alex Rodriguez 2.00 5.00
14 Justin Verlander 1.50 4.00
15 Thurman Munson 1.50 4.00
16 Cliff Lee 1.00 2.50
17 Matt Holliday 1.50 4.00
18 Clayton Kershaw 2.50 6.00
19 Tony Gwynn 1.50 4.00
20 Frank Robinson 1.00 2.50
21 Paul O'Neill 1.00 2.50
22 Jim Palmer 1.00 2.50
23 Don Mattingly 3.00 8.00
24 Rickey Henderson 1.50 4.00
25 Matt Kemp 1.25 3.00
26 Chipper Jones 1.50 4.00
27 Juan Marichal 1.00 2.50
28 Bert Blyleven 1.00 2.50
29 Mark Teixeira 1.00 2.50
30 Johnny Mize 1.00 2.50
31 Dustin Pedroia 1.50 4.00
32 Sandy Koufax 3.00 8.00
33 Eddie Murray 1.00 2.50
34 Nolan Ryan 5.00 12.00
35 Frank Thomas 1.50 4.00
36 Michael Pineda RC 1.50 4.00
37 Jose Reyes 1.00 2.50
38 Buster Posey 2.00 5.00
39 Roy Campanella 1.50 4.00
40 Mel Ott 1.50 4.00
41 Tom Seaver 1.00 2.50
42 Jackie Robinson 1.50 4.00
43 Prince Fielder 1.00 2.50
44 Hank Aaron 3.00 8.00
45 Bob Gibson 1.00 2.50
46 Ryne Sandberg 3.00 8.00
47 Duke Snider 1.00 2.50
48 Joe Morgan 1.00 2.50
49 Tim Lincecum 1.00 2.50
50 Walter Johnson 1.50 4.00
51 Ichiro Suzuki 2.00 5.00
52 Cole Hamels 1.25 3.00
53 Zach Britton RC 1.50 4.00
54 Carl Crawford 1.00 2.50
55 Johnny Bench 1.50 4.00
56 Adrian Gonzalez 1.25 3.00
57 Paul Konerko 1.00 2.50
58 Anthony Rizzo RC 6.00 15.00
59 Felix Hernandez 1.00 2.50
60 Jimmie Foxx 1.50 4.00
61 Troy Tulowitzki 1.50 4.00
62 Jay Bruce 1.00 2.50
63 Mariano Rivera 2.00 5.00
64 Roberto Alomar 1.00 2.50
65 Willie McCovey 1.00 2.50
66 Ryan Howard 1.25 3.00

67 Mike Moustakas RC 1.50 4.00
68 Andre Dawson 1.00 2.50
69 Jose Bautista 1.00 2.50
70 Rogers Hornsby 1.00 2.50
71 Ozzie Smith 2.00 5.00
72 Carlton Fisk 1.00 2.50
73 Hunter Pence 1.00 2.50
74 Justin Upton 1.00 2.50
75 Robinson Cano 1.00 2.50
76 Brian Wilson 1.50 4.00
77 CC Sabathia 1.00 2.50
78 Hanley Ramirez 1.00 2.50
79 David Ortiz 1.50 4.00
80 Cal Ripken Jr. 5.00 12.00
81 Barry Larkin 1.00 2.50
82 Roy Halladay 1.00 2.50
83 Tris Speaker 1.00 2.50
84 David Wright 1.25 3.00
85 Brooks Robinson 1.00 2.50
86 Paul Molitor 1.50 4.00
87 Andrew McCutchen 1.50 4.00
88 Reggie Jackson 1.00 2.50
89 Evan Longoria 1.00 2.50
90 Christy Mathewson 1.50 4.00
91 Pee Wee Reese 1.00 2.50
92 Dustin Ackley RC 1.00 2.50
93 Carlos Gonzalez 1.00 2.50
94 Ryan Zimmerman 1.00 2.50
95 Mike Schmidt 2.50 6.00
96 Miguel Cabrera 1.50 4.00
97 Joe Mauer 1.25 3.00
98 Josh Hamilton 1.00 2.50
99 Honus Wagner 1.50 4.00
100 Eric Hosmer RC 4.00 10.00

2011 Topps Tier One Black
*BLACK VET: 1X TO 2.5X BASIC VET
*BLACK RC: 1X TO 2.5X BASIC RC
STATED ODDS 1:11 BOXES
STATED PRINT RUN 50 SER.#'d SETS

2011 Topps Tier One Blue
*BLUE VET: .75X TO 2X BASIC VET
*BLUE RC: .75X TO 2X BASIC RC
STATED ODDS 1:6 BOXES
STATED PRINT RUN 199 SER.#'d SETS

2011 Topps Tier One Crowd Pleaser Autographs
OVERALL AUTO ODDS 2:1 BOXES
PRINT RUNS B/WN 50-699 COPIES PER
GOLD STATED ODDS 1:18 BOXES
GOLD STATED PRINT RUN 25 SER.#'d SETS
NO GOLD PRICING DUE TO SCARCITY
EXCHANGE DEADLINE 11/30/2014
AB Albert Belle/75 6.00 15.00
AE Andre Ethier EXCH 3.00 8.00
AJ Adam Jones/75 10.00 25.00
AK Al Kaline/50 25.00 50.00
AL Adam Lind/649 3.00 8.00
AP Angel Pagan/499 4.00 10.00
AR Aramis Ramirez/50 6.00 15.00
BB Bert Blyleven/50 15.00 40.00
BBU Billy Butler EXCH 10.00 25.00
BG Brett Gardner EXCH 15.00 40.00
BJU B.J. Upton/75 8.00 20.00
BM Brian McCann/50 5.00 12.00
BP Brandon Phillips/75 10.00 25.00
CB Clay Buchholz/50 8.00 20.00
CC Carl Crawford 6.00 15.00
CG Carlos Gonzalez EXCH 12.00 30.00
CJ Chipper Jones/50 40.00 100.00
CK Clayton Kershaw/75 30.00 80.00
CL Cliff Lee EXCH 30.00 60.00
CY Chris Young/75 6.00 15.00
DM Don Mattingly/50 25.00 60.00
DP Dustin Pedroia/50 12.00 30.00
EA Elvis Andrus/50 5.00 12.00
EM Edgar Martinez/75 12.00 30.00
ES Ervin Santana/549 6.00 15.00
FJ Fergie Jenkins/50 15.00 40.00
GF George Foster/50 5.00 12.00
GG Gio Gonzalez/699 5.00 12.00
HR Hanley Ramirez/50 10.00 25.00
IK Ian Kinsler EXCH 10.00 25.00
IKN Ian Kennedy EXCH 5.00 12.00
JB Jay Bruce/75 3.00 8.00
JC Johnny Cueto/699 3.00 8.00
JJ Josh Johnson/50 4.00 10.00
JM Joe Morgan EXCH 20.00 50.00
JP Jhonny Peralta/699 3.00 8.00
JW Jered Weaver/50 15.00 40.00
LA Luis Aparicio/50 20.00 50.00
MC Matt Cain EXCH 40.00 80.00
MG Matt Garza/75 10.00 25.00
MK Matt Kemp/75 6.00 15.00
ML Mat Latos EXCH 8.00 20.00
OS Ozzie Smith EXCH 30.00 60.00
PM Paul Molitor/50 8.00 20.00
PO Paul O'Neill/75 8.00 20.00
PS Pablo Sandoval/699 8.00 20.00
RA Roberto Alomar/50 30.00 60.00
RB Ryan Braun EXCH 6.00 15.00
RED Red Schoendienst/75 12.00 30.00
RN Ricky Nolasco/699 3.00 8.00
RS Ryne Sandberg/50 40.00 80.00
RZ Ryan Zimmerman/75 8.00 20.00
TC Trevor Cahill/699 4.00 10.00
UJ Ubaldo Jimenez/50 8.00 20.00

2011 Topps Tier One On The Rise Autographs
OVERALL AUTO ODDS 2:1 BOXES
PRINT RUNS B/WN 99-999 COPIES PER
GOLD STATED ODDS 1:18 BOXES
GOLD STATED PRINT RUN 25 SER.#'d SETS
NO GOLD PRICING DUE TO SCARCITY
EXCHANGE DEADLINE 11/30/2014
AC Alex Cobb/999 3.00 8.00
ACH Aroldis Chapman/99 12.00 30.00
ACR Allen Craig/999 3.00 8.00
AJ Austin Jackson/99 8.00 20.00
AM Andrew McCutchen/99 30.00 60.00
AO Alexi Ogando/999 3.00 8.00
AR Anthony Rizzo/999 20.00 50.00
AW Alex White/999 3.00 8.00
BB Brandon Belt/699 3.00 8.00
BBE Brandon Beachy/999 3.00 8.00
BC Brandon Crawford/999 3.00 8.00
BG Brandon Guyer/999 4.00 10.00
BH Brad Hand/999 3.00 8.00
BM Brent Morel/699 3.00 8.00
BW Brett Wallace/399 4.00 10.00
CC Carlos Carrasco/999 6.00 15.00
CJ Chris Johnson/699 5.00 12.00
CK Craig Kimbrel/699 6.00 15.00
CP Carlos Peguero/999 3.00 8.00
CR Colby Rasmus/349 5.00 12.00
CS Carlos Santana/399 3.00 8.00
CSA Chris Sale/599 12.00 30.00
DA Dustin Ackley/399 5.00 12.00
DC David Cooper/999 3.00 8.00
DD Danny Duffy/999 5.00 12.00
DG Dee Gordon/999 6.00 15.00
DGE Dillon Gee/999 4.00 10.00
DH Daniel Hudson/699 6.00 15.00
DS Drew Storen/699 4.00 10.00
DV Danny Valencia/999 4.00 10.00
EH Eric Hosmer/399 15.00 40.00
EN Eduardo Nunez/999 3.00 8.00
ES Eric Sogard/999 3.00 8.00
ET Eric Thames/999 15.00 40.00
FF Freddie Freeman/99 10.00 25.00
FM Fernando Martinez/499 3.00 8.00
GS Gaby Sanchez/399 5.00 12.00
HN Hector Noesi/999 3.00 8.00
JH Jason Heyward/99 6.00 15.00
JHE Jeremy Hellickson EXCH 10.00 25.00
JI Jose Iglesias/499 10.00 25.00
JS Jordan Schafer/999 3.00 8.00
JT Josh Thole/999 3.00 8.00
JZ Jordan Zimmermann/999 6.00 15.00
LF Logan Forsythe/999 3.00 8.00
MB Madison Bumgarner/99 30.00 60.00
MM Mike Minor/699 3.00 8.00
MP Michael Pineda/99 12.00 30.00
MS Mike Stanton EXCH 20.00 50.00
MSC Max Scherzer EXCH 20.00 50.00
MT Mark Trumbo/399 3.00 8.00
RT Ruben Tejada/699 4.00 10.00
SC Starlin Castro/99 12.50 30.00
TC Tyler Colvin/999 3.00 8.00
TR Tyson Ross/999 3.00 8.00
ZB Zach Britton/99 5.00 12.00

2011 Topps Tier One Top Shelf Relics
OVERALL RELIC ODDS 1:1 BOXES
STATED PRINT RUN 399 SER.#'d SETS
EXCHANGE DEADLINE 9/30/2014
TSR1 Ichiro Suzuki 8.00 20.00
TSR2 Roberto Alomar 4.00 10.00
TSR3 Thurman Munson 8.00 20.00
TSR4 Carlton Fisk 4.00 10.00
TSR5 Joe DiMaggio 20.00 50.00
TSR6 Jimmie Foxx 10.00 25.00
TSR7 Rogers Hornsby 12.00 30.00
TSR8 Ryan Braun 4.00 10.00
TSR9 Roy Campanella 6.00 15.00
TSR10 Roy Halladay 6.00 15.00
TSR11 Johnny Mize 8.00 20.00
TSR12 Aramis Ramirez 3.00 8.00
TSR13 Pee Wee Reese 8.00 20.00
TSR14 George Sisler 6.00 15.00
TSR15 Tris Speaker 10.00 25.00
TSR16 Babe Ruth 60.00 120.00
TSR17 Carl Crawford 3.00 8.00
TSR18 Ian Kinsler 3.00 8.00
TSR19 Johnny Bench 6.00 15.00
TSR20 Reggie Jackson 4.00 10.00
TSR21 Carlos Beltran 4.00 10.00
TSR22 Ty Cobb 30.00 60.00
TSR23 Joey Votto 4.00 10.00
TSR24 Jose Reyes 4.00 10.00
TSR25 Cole Hamels 4.00 10.00
TSR26 Rickey Henderson EXCH 6.00 15.00
TSR27 Lou Gehrig 40.00 80.00
TSR28 Jered Weaver 4.00 10.00
TSR29 Paul Molitor 4.00 10.00
TSR30 Tim Lincecum 6.00 15.00
TSR31 David Wright 4.00 10.00
TSR32 Jacoby Ellsbury 4.00 10.00
TSR33 Sandy Koufax 15.00 40.00
TSR34 Dustin Pedroia 4.00 10.00
TSR35 Eddie Murray 4.00 10.00
TSR36 Mickey Mantle 30.00 80.00
TSR37 Stan Musial 12.00 30.00
TSR38 Ubaldo Jimenez 3.00 8.00
TSR39 Paul O'Neill 4.00 10.00
TSR40 Willie McCovey 6.00 15.00
TSR41 Brian McCann 3.00 8.00
TSR42 Albert Pujols 10.00 25.00
TSR43 Don Mattingly 12.00 30.00
TSR44 Hank Aaron 12.00 30.00
TSR45 Brooks Robinson 5.00 12.00
TSR46 Ryne Sandberg EXCH 10.00 25.00
TSR47 Tom Seaver 5.00 12.00
TSR48 Willie Mays 12.00 30.00
TSR49 Chipper Jones 5.00 12.00
TSR50 Cal Ripken Jr. 6.00 15.00

2011 Topps Tier One Top Shelf Relics Dual
STATED ODDS 1:6 BOXES
STATED PRINT RUN 99 SER.#'d SETS
EXCHANGE DEADLINE 9/30/2014
TSR1 Ichiro Suzuki 10.00 25.00
TSR2 Roberto Alomar 5.00 12.00
TSR3 Thurman Munson 15.00 40.00
TSR4 Carlton Fisk 4.00 10.00
TSR5 Joe DiMaggio 20.00 50.00
TSR6 Jimmie Foxx 12.00 30.00
TSR7 Rogers Hornsby 12.00 30.00
TSR8 Ryan Braun 5.00 12.00
TSR9 Roy Campanella 10.00 25.00
TSR10 Roy Halladay 6.00 15.00
TSR11 Johnny Mize 12.00 30.00
TSR12 Aramis Ramirez 4.00 10.00
TSR13 Pee Wee Reese 10.00 25.00
TSR14 George Sisler 8.00 20.00
TSR15 Tris Speaker 12.00 30.00
TSR16 Babe Ruth 75.00 150.00
TSR17 Carl Crawford 6.00 15.00
TSR18 Ian Kinsler 4.00 10.00
TSR19 Johnny Bench 10.00 25.00
TSR20 Reggie Jackson 8.00 20.00
TSR21 Carlos Beltran 4.00 10.00
TSR22 Ty Cobb 40.00 80.00
TSR23 Joey Votto 6.00 15.00
TSR24 Jose Reyes 6.00 15.00
TSR25 Cole Hamels 4.00 10.00
TSR26 Rickey Henderson EXCH 8.00 20.00
TSR27 Lou Gehrig 30.00 60.00
TSR28 Jered Weaver 4.00 10.00
TSR29 Paul Molitor 6.00 15.00
TSR30 Tim Lincecum 8.00 20.00
TSR31 David Wright 5.00 12.00
TSR32 Jacoby Ellsbury 10.00 25.00
TSR33 Sandy Koufax 40.00 80.00
TSR34 Dustin Pedroia 6.00 15.00
TSR35 Eddie Murray 8.00 20.00
TSR36 Mickey Mantle 30.00 60.00
TSR37 Stan Musial 8.00 20.00
TSR38 Ubaldo Jimenez 4.00 10.00
TSR39 Paul O'Neill 6.00 15.00
TSR40 Willie McCovey 6.00 15.00
TSR41 Brian McCann 5.00 12.00
TSR42 Albert Pujols 12.00 30.00
TSR43 Don Mattingly 10.00 25.00
TSR44 Hank Aaron 20.00 50.00
TSR45 Brooks Robinson 12.00 30.00
TSR46 Ryne Sandberg EXCH 10.00 25.00
TSR47 Tom Seaver 8.00 20.00
TSR48 Willie Mays 10.00 25.00
TSR49 Chipper Jones 10.00 25.00
TSR50 Cal Ripken Jr. 8.00 20.00

2011 Topps Tier One Top Tier Autographs
STATED ODDS 1:13 BOXES
PRINT RUNS B/WN 99-199 COPIES PER
PACQUIAO NOT SERIAL NUMBERED
GOLD STATED ODDS 1:120 BOXES
GOLD PRINT RUN B/WN 10-25 COPIES PER
NO GOLD PRICING DUE TO SCARCITY
EXCHANGE DEADLINE 11/30/2014
AG Adrian Gonzalez/99 10.00 25.00
AP Albert Pujols EXCH 150.00 300.00
BG Bob Gibson/99 20.00 50.00
CF Carlton Fisk/99 15.00 40.00
EL Evan Longoria/99 12.00 30.00
FH Felix Hernandez/99 20.00 50.00
FR Frank Robinson/99 15.00 40.00
HA Hank Aaron EXCH 150.00 400.00
JB Johnny Bench/99 30.00 60.00
JH Josh Hamilton/99 10.00 25.00
MC Miguel Cabrera/99 50.00 100.00
MP Manny Pacquiao 100.00 200.00
MS Mike Schmidt/99 30.00 60.00
NR Nolan Ryan EXCH 75.00 150.00
PF Prince Fielder/99 8.00 20.00
RH Rickey Henderson/99 50.00 150.00
RH Roy Halladay EXCH 100.00 250.00
RJ Reggie Jackson/99 15.00 40.00
SK Sandy Koufax/199 125.00 250.00
SM Stan Musial/99 60.00 120.00
TG Tony Gwynn/99 60.00 120.00

2012 Topps Tier One Autograph Relics
STATED ODDS 1:11 HOBBY
STATED PRINT RUN 99 SER.#'d SETS
EXCHANGE DEADLINE 05/31/2015
CC Carl Crawford 6.00 15.00
CH Chris Heisey 6.00 15.00
DG Dee Gordon 10.00 25.00
DU Dan Uggla 10.00 25.00
EL Evan Longoria 10.00 25.00
GB Gordon Beckham 6.00 15.00
GS Gary Sheffield 6.00 15.00
GST Giancarlo Stanton 25.00 60.00
JHE Jason Heyward 4.00 10.00
JJ Jon Jay 12.50 30.00
JJO Josh Johnson 8.00 20.00
MK Matt Kemp 8.00 20.00
MT Mark Trumbo 12.00 30.00
NF Neftali Feliz 6.00 15.00
PF Prince Fielder 8.00 20.00
PO Paul O'Neill 12.50 30.00
RB Ryan Braun 12.50 30.00
SC Starlin Castro 8.00 20.00
TG Tony Gwynn 30.00 60.00

2012 Topps Tier One Autographs
STATED ODDS 1:21 HOBBY
PRINT RUNS B/WN 50-225 COPIES PER
EXCHANGE DEADLINE 05/31/2015
AP Albert Pujols EXCH 150.00 250.00
CF Carlton Fisk 20.00 50.00
CR Cal Ripken Jr. 75.00 150.00
CY Carl Yastrzemski 30.00 60.00
DM Don Mattingly 50.00 100.00
EB Ernie Banks 30.00 60.00
FR Frank Robinson 30.00 60.00
HA Hank Aaron 150.00 300.00
JB Johnny Bench 30.00 60.00
JH Josh Hamilton 20.00 50.00
KG Ken Griffey Jr. 125.00 250.00
MS Mike Schmidt 50.00 120.00
NR Nolan Ryan 75.00 150.00
RH Roy Halladay 20.00 50.00
RJ Reggie Jackson 30.00 60.00
RS Ryne Sandberg 30.00 60.00
SK Sandy Koufax 200.00 300.00
WMC Willie McCovey 30.00 60.00
YD Yu Darvish 60.00 150.00

2012 Topps Tier One Clear Rookie Reprint Autographs
STATED ODDS 1:82 HOBBY
STATED PRINT RUN 25 SER.#'d SETS
EXCHANGE DEADLINE 05/31/2015
CJ Chipper Jones 300.00 500.00
CR Cal Ripken Jr. 200.00 400.00
CS CC Sabathia 30.00 60.00
DM Don Mattingly 150.00 250.00
EB Ernie Banks 60.00 150.00
JH Josh Hamilton 150.00 250.00
KG Ken Griffey Jr. 300.00 600.00
MC Miguel Cabrera 75.00 200.00
RS Ryne Sandberg 60.00 150.00
WM Willie Mays 200.00 400.00

2012 Topps Tier One Crowd Pleaser Autographs
PRINT RUNS B/WN 50-399 COPIES PER
EXCHANGE DEADLINE 05/31/2015
AB Albert Belle/50 12.00 30.00
AD Andre Dawson/50 10.00 25.00
AE Andre Ethier/50 6.00 15.00
AK Al Kaline/50 20.00 50.00
AL Adam Lind/399 5.00 12.00
ALI Adam Lind/399 5.00 12.00
AM Andrew McCutchen/50 30.00 60.00
AP Andy Pettitte/50 40.00 80.00
AR Aramis Ramirez/75 4.00 10.00
BB Billy Butler/75 4.00 10.00
BG Brett Gardner/245 6.00 15.00
BM Brian McCann/50 10.00 25.00
BP Boog Powell/399 6.00 15.00
BPH Brandon Phillips/75 6.00 15.00
BPO Buster Posey/50 60.00 120.00
BW Billy Williams/50 12.50 30.00
CC Carl Crawford/50 8.00 20.00
CH Cole Hamels/50 12.50 30.00
CJ Chipper Jones/50 50.00 120.00
DP Dustin Pedroia/50 20.00 50.00
DU Dan Uggla/50 8.00 20.00
DW David Wright EXCH 30.00 60.00
EA Elvis Andrus/245 6.00 15.00
EK Ed Kranepool/399 6.00 15.00
EL Evan Longoria/50 20.00 50.00
EM Edgar Martinez/50 12.00 30.00
GF George Foster/75 4.00 10.00
GS Gaby Sanchez/50 4.00 10.00
GSA Gaby Sanchez/399 4.00 10.00
HK Howie Kendrick/245 5.00 12.00
HKE Howie Kendrick/245 5.00 12.00
HR Hanley Ramirez EXCH 10.00 25.00
ID Ike Davis/75 10.00 25.00
JB Jay Bruce/75 4.00 10.00
JC Johnny Cueto/245 6.00 15.00
JCU Johnny Cueto/245 6.00 15.00
JH Joel Hanrahan/399 6.00 15.00
JHA Joel Hanrahan/399 6.00 15.00
JJ Josh Johnson/50 6.00 15.00
JM Joe Mauer/50 20.00 50.00
JMO Jason Motte/399 5.00 12.00
JMT Jason Motte/399 5.00 12.00
JP Jhonny Peralta/245 6.00 15.00
JPE Jhonny Peralta/245 6.00 15.00
JR Jim Rice/75 12.50 30.00
JV Jose Valverde/399 8.00 20.00
JVA Jose Valverde/399 8.00 20.00
LT Luis Tiant/245 6.00 15.00
MB Marlon Byrd/399 4.00 10.00
MBY Marlon Byrd/399 4.00 10.00
MCA Miguel Cabrera/50 75.00 150.00
MGA Matt Garza/75 6.00 15.00
MH Matt Holliday EXCH 20.00 50.00
MK Matt Kemp/50 12.00 30.00
MM Mike Moustakas/75 8.00 20.00
MMO Mike Morse/399 5.00 12.00
MMS Mike Morse/399 5.00 12.00
NC Nelson Cruz/50 10.00 25.00
PF Prince Fielder/50 10.00 25.00
PM Paul Molitor/50 10.00 25.00
PO Paul O'Neill/50 12.50 30.00
RB Ryan Braun/50 20.00 50.00
RC Robinson Cano/50 20.00 50.00
RS Red Schoendienst/75 15.00 40.00
RZ Ryan Zimmerman/50 10.00 25.00
SC Starlin Castro/75 6.00 15.00
THU Tim Hudson/50 10.00 25.00
UJ Ubaldo Jimenez/50 6.00 15.00
WC Will Clark/245 10.00 25.00
WJ Wally Joyner/399 5.00 12.00
YG Yovani Gallardo/50 10.00 25.00

2012 Topps Tier One Crowd Pleaser Autographs White Ink
STATED ODDS 1:10 HOBBY
STATED PRINT RUN 25 SER.#'d SETS
NO PRICING ON MOST DUE TO SCARCITY
EXCHANGE DEADLINE 05/31/2015
AL Adam Lind 8.00 20.00
ALI Adam Lind 8.00 20.00
GS Gaby Sanchez 8.00 20.00
GSA Gaby Sanchez 8.00 20.00
HK Howie Kendrick 10.00 25.00
HKE Howie Kendrick 10.00 25.00
JC Johnny Cueto 15.00 40.00
JCU Johnny Cueto 15.00 40.00
JH Joel Hanrahan 20.00 50.00
JHA Joel Hanrahan 20.00 50.00
JMO Jason Motte 10.00 25.00
JMT Jason Motte 10.00 25.00
JP Jhonny Peralta 10.00 25.00
JPE Jhonny Peralta 10.00 25.00
JV Jose Valverde 15.00 40.00
JVA Jose Valverde 15.00 40.00
MB Marlon Byrd 5.00 12.00
MBY Marlon Byrd 5.00 12.00
MMO Mike Morse 10.00 25.00
MMS Mike Morse 10.00 25.00
PM Paul Molitor 15.00 40.00

2012 Topps Tier One Dual Relics
STATED ODDS 1:7 HOBBY
STATED PRINT RUN 50 SER.#'d SETS
I Ichiro Suzuki 10.00 25.00
AB Adrian Beltre 4.00 10.00
AE Andre Ethier 4.00 10.00
AG Adrian Gonzalez 4.00 10.00
AM Andrew McCutchen 10.00 25.00
AP Albert Pujols 10.00 25.00
APE Andy Pettitte 8.00 20.00
AR Alex Rodriguez 8.00 20.00
AW Adam Wainwright 8.00 20.00
BP Buster Posey 10.00 25.00
BS Bruce Sutter 12.00 30.00
BW Brian Wilson 6.00 15.00
CF Carlton Fisk 5.00 12.00
CJ Chipper Jones 8.00 20.00
CJ2 Chipper Jones 8.00 20.00
CR Cal Ripken Jr. 12.00 30.00
CS CC Sabathia 6.00 15.00
DH Dan Haren 4.00 10.00
DJ Derek Jeter 15.00 40.00
DO David Ortiz 5.00 12.00
DU Dan Uggla 4.00 10.00
DW David Wright 5.00 12.00
EM Eddie Murray 6.00 15.00
FF Freddie Freeman 5.00 12.00
FT Frank Thomas 10.00 25.00
GB George Bell 5.00 12.00
IK Ian Kennedy 4.00 10.00
IKI Ian Kinsler 4.00 10.00
JBR Jay Bruce 8.00 20.00
JE Jacoby Ellsbury 5.00 12.00
JH Jason Heyward 4.00 10.00
JHE Jeremy Hellickson 4.00 10.00
JJ Josh Johnson 4.00 10.00
JL Jon Lester 5.00 12.00
JM Jason Motte 4.00 10.00
JRI Jim Rice 5.00 12.00
JS James Shields 4.00 10.00
JV Justin Verlander 8.00 20.00
JVO Joey Votto 4.00 10.00
KY Kevin Youkilis 5.00 12.00
MC Miguel Cabrera 6.00 15.00
MR Mariano Rivera 8.00 20.00
MT Mark Trumbo 12.00 30.00
MTR Mike Trout 50.00 120.00
MY Michael Young 4.00 10.00
PF Prince Fielder 4.00 10.00
PK Paul Konerko 5.00 12.00
PM Paul Molitor 5.00 12.00
PO Paul O'Neill 10.00 25.00
RCW Rod Carew 5.00 12.00
RH Ryan Howard 5.00 12.00
RO Roy Oswalt 4.00 10.00
RZ Ryan Zimmerman 5.00 12.00
SC Steve Carlton 4.00 10.00
SCA Starlin Castro 4.00 10.00
SS Stephen Strasburg 12.00 30.00
THU Tim Hudson 6.00 15.00
TL Tim Lincecum 6.00 15.00
TT Troy Tulowitzki 6.00 15.00
UJ Ubaldo Jimenez 5.00 12.00
YG Yovanni Gallardo 4.00 10.00

2012 Topps Tier One Elevated Ink
STATED PRINT RUN 250 SER.#'d SETS
DM Devin Mesoraco 6.00 15.00
HI Hisashi Iwakuma 15.00 40.00
JB Jay Bruce 6.00 15.00

2012 Topps Tier One Legends Relics
STATED ODDS 1:28 HOBBY
STATED PRINT RUN 50 SER.#'d SETS
FR Frank Robinson 10.00 25.00
HK Harmon Killebrew 8.00 20.00
JM Joe Morgan 6.00 15.00
LB Lou Brock 6.00 15.00
MM Mickey Mantle 40.00 80.00
MS Mike Schmidt 6.00 15.00
OS Ozzie Smith 12.50 30.00
RC Roberto Clemente 30.00 60.00
RJ Reggie Jackson 6.00 15.00
RS Ryne Sandberg 12.50 30.00
TC Ty Cobb 30.00 60.00
WB Wade Boggs 6.00 15.00
WM Willie McCovey 10.00 25.00
WS Willie Stargell 10.00 25.00
WMA Willie Mays 20.00 50.00

2012 Topps Tier One On The Rise Autographs
PRINT RUNS B/WN 50-395 COPIES PER
EXCHANGE DEADLINE 05/31/2015
AA Alex Avila/235 6.00 15.00
AC Allen Craig/235 8.00 20.00
ACH Aroldis Chapman/75 15.00 40.00
AJO Adam Jones/50 6.00 15.00
AO Alexi Ogando/75 6.00 15.00
AR Anthony Rizzo/235 10.00 25.00
ARI Anthony Rizzo/235 10.00 25.00
BA Brett Anderson/235 5.00 12.00
BAN Brett Anderson/235 5.00 12.00
BBE Brandon Belt/235 6.00 15.00
BH Bryce Harper EXCH 250.00 400.00
BL Brett Lawrie/50 8.00 20.00
BM Brent Morel/235 5.00 12.00
BP Brad Peacock/350 5.00 12.00
BPE Brad Peacock/350 5.00 12.00
BR Ben Revere/235 5.00 12.00
BRE Ben Revere/235 5.00 12.00
CGO Carlos Gonzalez/50 20.00 50.00
CH Chris Heisey/235 5.00 12.00
CHE Chris Heisey/235 5.00 12.00
CK Craig Kimbrel/50 10.00 25.00
CKE Clayton Kershaw/50 20.00 50.00
CR Colby Rasmus/75 3.00 8.00
CS Carlos Santana/50 5.00 12.00
CSA Chris Sale/75 15.00 40.00
DA Dustin Ackley/50 12.50 30.00
DB Darwin Barney/235 6.00 15.00
DBA Daniel Bard/235 5.00 12.00
DBD Daniel Bard/235 5.00 12.00
DE Danny Espinosa/235 3.00 8.00
DGO Dee Gordon/75 5.00 12.00
DH Derek Holland/75 8.00 20.00
DHU Daniel Hudson/235 3.00 8.00
DM Devin Mesoraco/75 6.00 15.00
DME Devin Mesoraco/75 6.00 15.00
DP Drew Pomeranz/75 6.00 15.00
DS Drew Storen/75 6.00 15.00
DST Drew Stubbs/75 8.00 20.00
EH Eric Hosmer/50 15.00 40.00
EN Eduardo Nunez/75 6.00 15.00
ENU Eduardo Nunez/75 6.00 15.00
FF Freddie Freeman/50 12.50 30.00
GB Gordon Beckham EXCH 8.00 20.00
GG Gio Gonzalez/50 15.00 40.00
HN Hector Noesi/315 4.00 10.00
IN Ivan Nova/75 6.00 15.00
INO Ivan Nova/75 6.00 15.00
JA J.P. Arencibia/75 5.00 12.00
JAR J.P. Arencibia/75 5.00 12.00
JDM J.D. Martinez/350 10.00 25.00
JG Johnny Giavotella/395 5.00 12.00
JH Jeremy Hellickson/50 8.00 20.00
JJ Jon Jay/235 5.00 12.00
JK Jason Kipnis/75 6.00 15.00
JMA J.D. Martinez/350 10.00 25.00
JMO Jesus Montero/50 10.00 25.00
JN Jon Niese/235 4.00 10.00
JP Jarrod Parker/235 3.00 8.00
JPA Jimmy Paredes/350 4.00 10.00
JPR Jimmy Paredes/350 4.00 10.00
JR Josh Reddick/350 8.00 20.00
JRE Josh Reddick/350 8.00 20.00
JTE Julio Teheran/235 5.00 12.00
JW Jemile Weeks/235 5.00 12.00
JWA Jordan Walden/75 4.00 10.00
JWE Jemile Weeks/235 5.00 12.00
JZ Jordan Zimmermann/235 6.00 15.00
KS Kyle Seager/235 6.00 15.00
KSE Kyle Seager/235 6.00 15.00
LM Logan Morrison/50 5.00 12.00
MB Madison Bumgarner/50 50.00 100.00
MM Mitch Moreland/350 5.00 12.00
MMO Matt Moore/75 6.00 15.00
MMR Mitch Moreland/350 5.00 12.00
MP Michael Pineda/75 10.00 25.00
MST Giancarlo Stanton/50 20.00 50.00
MT Mark Trumbo/50 6.00 15.00
MTM Mark Trumbo/50 6.00 15.00
MTR Mike Trout/50 200.00 500.00
NE Nathan Eovaldi/395 4.00 10.00
NF Neftali Feliz/75 5.00 12.00
NW Neil Walker/235 3.00 8.00
PG Paul Goldschmidt/75 8.00 20.00
RD Randall Delgado/395 5.00 12.00
RR Ricky Romero/75 6.00 15.00
SP Salvador Perez/350 10.00 25.00
SPE Salvador Perez/350 10.00 25.00
TC Trevor Cahill/75 6.00 15.00
TW Travis Wood/235 5.00 12.00
VW Vance Worley/355 5.00 12.00
VWO Vance Worley/355 5.00 12.00
WR Wilson Ramos/75 8.00 20.00
YC Yoenis Cespedes/50 20.00 50.00
ZB Zach Britton/50 8.00 20.00

2012 Topps Tier One On The Rise Autographs White Ink
STATED ODDS 1:9 HOBBY
STATED PRINT RUN 25 SER.#'d SETS
NO PRICING ON MOST DUE TO SCARCITY
EXCHANGE DEADLINE 05/31/2015
AR Anthony Rizzo 30.00 60.00
ARI Anthony Rizzo 30.00 60.00
BA Brett Anderson 10.00 25.00
BAN Brett Anderson 10.00 25.00
BP Brad Peacock 10.00 25.00
BPE Brad Peacock 10.00 25.00
BR Ben Revere 10.00 25.00
BRE Ben Revere 10.00 25.00
CH Chris Heisey 8.00 20.00
CHE Chris Heisey 8.00 20.00
DBA Daniel Bard 12.50 30.00
DBD Daniel Bard 12.50 30.00
DM Devin Mesoraco 20.00 50.00
DME Devin Mesoraco 20.00 50.00
EN Eduardo Nunez 8.00 20.00
ENU Eduardo Nunez 8.00 20.00
IN Ivan Nova 12.50 30.00
INO Ivan Nova 12.50 30.00
JA J.P. Arencibia 8.00 20.00
JAR J.P. Arencibia 8.00 20.00
JDM J.D. Martinez 15.00 40.00
JMA J.D. Martinez 15.00 40.00
JPA Jimmy Paredes 10.00 25.00
JPR Jimmy Paredes 10.00 25.00
JR Josh Reddick 15.00 40.00
JRE Josh Reddick 15.00 40.00
JW Jemile Weeks 8.00 20.00
JWE Jemile Weeks 8.00 20.00
KS Kyle Seager 30.00 60.00
KSE Kyle Seager 30.00 60.00
MM Mitch Moreland 10.00 25.00
MMR Mitch Moreland 10.00 25.00
MT Mark Trumbo 15.00 40.00
MTM Mark Trumbo 15.00 40.00
SP Salvador Perez 15.00 40.00
SPE Salvador Perez 15.00 40.00
VW Vance Worley 15.00 40.00
VWO Vance Worley 15.00 40.00

2012 Topps Tier One Relics
PRINT RUNS B/WN 150-399 COPIES PER
I Ichiro Suzuki/150 8.00 20.00
AB Adrian Beltre/399 3.00 8.00
AE Andre Ethier/399 4.00 10.00
AG Adrian Gonzalez/399 4.00 10.00
AM Andrew McCutchen/399 6.00 15.00
AP Albert Pujols/150 6.00 15.00
APE Andy Pettitte/150 5.00 12.00
AR Alex Rodriguez/150 8.00 20.00
AW Adam Wainwright/399 4.00 10.00
BP Buster Posey/399 6.00 15.00
BS Bruce Sutter/150 4.00 10.00
BW Brian Wilson/399 4.00 10.00
CF Carlton Fisk/150 4.00 10.00
CJ Chipper Jones/399 5.00 12.00
CJ2 Chipper Jones/399 5.00 12.00
CR Cal Ripken Jr./150 10.00 25.00
CS CC Sabathia/399 4.00 10.00
DH Dan Haren/399 3.00 8.00
DJ Derek Jeter/150 12.50 30.00
DO David Ortiz/399 4.00 10.00
DU Dan Uggla/399 3.00 8.00
DW David Wright/399 4.00 10.00
EM Eddie Murray/150 4.00 10.00
FF Freddie Freeman/399 3.00 8.00
FT Frank Thomas/150 6.00 15.00
GB George Bell/150 5.00 12.00
IK Ian Kennedy/399 3.00 8.00
IKI Ian Kinsler/399 3.00 8.00
JBR Jay Bruce/399 4.00 10.00
JE Jacoby Ellsbury/399 4.00 10.00
JH Jason Heyward/399 3.00 8.00
JHE Jeremy Hellickson/399 3.00 8.00
JJ Josh Johnson/399 3.00 8.00
JL Jon Lester/399 3.00 8.00
JM Jason Motte/399 3.00 8.00
JRI Jim Rice/150 5.00 12.00
JS James Shields/399 3.00 8.00
JV Justin Verlander/150 5.00 12.00
JVO Joey Votto/399 6.00 15.00
KY Kevin Youkilis/399 3.00 8.00
MC Miguel Cabrera/399 5.00 12.00
MR Mariano Rivera/150 8.00 20.00
MT Mark Trumbo/399 4.00 10.00
MTR Mike Trout/399 40.00 100.00
MY Michael Young/399 3.00 8.00
PF Prince Fielder/399 4.00 10.00
PK Paul Konerko/399 3.00 8.00
PM Paul Molitor/150 5.00 12.00
PO Paul O'Neill/150 4.00 10.00
RCW Rod Carew/150 4.00 10.00
RH Ryan Howard/399 4.00 10.00
RO Roy Oswalt/399 3.00 8.00
RZ Ryan Zimmerman/399 3.00 8.00
SC Steve Carlton/150 4.00 10.00
SCA Starlin Castro/399 4.00 10.00
SS Stephen Strasburg/399 4.00 10.00
THU Tim Hudson/399 3.00 8.00
TL Tim Lincecum/399 5.00 12.00
TT Troy Tulowitzki/399 3.00 8.00
UJ Ubaldo Jimenez/399 3.00 8.00
YG Yovani Gallardo/399 3.00 8.00

2013 Topps Tier One Relics
STATED PRINT RUN 399 SER.#'d SETS
AB Albert Belle 3.00 8.00
AC Aroldis Chapman 3.00 8.00
AG Adrian Gonzalez 3.00 8.00
AJ Adam Jones 3.00 8.00
AK Al Kaline 5.00 12.00
AM Andrew McCutchen 4.00 10.00
AW Adam Wainwright 3.00 8.00
BB Billy Butler 3.00 8.00
BP Buster Posey 4.00 10.00
CB Craig Biggio 3.00 8.00
CCS CC Sabathia 3.00 8.00
CG Carlos Gonzalez 3.00 8.00
CK Clayton Kershaw 6.00 15.00
CRJ Cal Ripken Jr. 8.00 20.00
CS Chris Sale 3.00 8.00
DF David Freese 3.00 8.00
DG Dwight Gooden 3.00 8.00
DO David Ortiz 4.00 10.00
DP Dustin Pedroia 3.00 8.00
DW David Wright 4.00 10.00
EH Eric Hosmer 3.00 8.00
EL Evan Longoria 3.00 8.00
FH Felix Hernandez 3.00 8.00
FT Frank Thomas 6.00 15.00
GSH Gary Sheffield 3.00 8.00
IK Ian Kinsler 3.00 8.00
JB Johnny Bench 5.00 12.00
JBR Jay Bruce 3.00 8.00
JBT Jose Bautista 3.00 8.00
JC Johnny Cueto 3.00 8.00
JH Jason Heyward 3.00 8.00
JK Jason Kipnis 3.00 8.00
JL Jon Lester 3.00 8.00
JM Joe Mauer 3.00 8.00
JP Jake Peavy 3.00 8.00
JR Jim Rice 3.00 8.00
JS John Smoltz 3.00 8.00
JU Justin Upton 3.00 8.00
JV Joey Votto 4.00 10.00
JVR Justin Verlander 5.00 12.00
KGJ Ken Griffey Jr. 8.00 20.00
LB Lou Brock 4.00 10.00
MC Miguel Cabrera 5.00 12.00
MCN Matt Cain 3.00 8.00
MH Matt Harvey 5.00 12.00
MK Matt Kemp 3.00 8.00
MTR Mark Trumbo 3.00 8.00
NC Nelson Cruz 3.00 8.00
NG Nomar Garciaparra 3.00 8.00
OC Orlando Cepeda 3.00 8.00
PA Pedro Alvarez 3.00 8.00
PF Prince Fielder 3.00 8.00
PM Pedro Martinez 5.00 12.00
PO Paul O'Neill 3.00 8.00
PS Pablo Sandoval 3.00 8.00
RAD R.A. Dickey 4.00 10.00
RB Ryan Braun 3.00 8.00
RH Rickey Henderson 5.00 12.00
RHD Ryan Howard 3.00 8.00
RHY Roy Halladay 3.00 8.00
RZ Ryan Zimmerman 3.00 8.00
SC Starlin Castro 3.00 8.00
SCR Steve Carlton 3.00 8.00
SS Stephen Strasburg 5.00 12.00
TF Todd Frazier 3.00 8.00
TG Tony Gwynn 3.00 8.00
TL Tim Lincecum 3.00 8.00
TM Tommy Milone 3.00 8.00
TT Troy Tulowitzki 3.00 8.00
YD Yu Darvish 5.00 12.00
YG Yasmani Grandal 3.00 8.00

2013 Topps Tier One Dual Relics
DUAL: .5X TO 1.5X BASIC
STATED ODDS 1:9 HOBBY
STATED PRINT RUN 50 SER.#'d SETS
CRJ Cal Ripken Jr. 12.50 30.00
KGJ Ken Griffey Jr. 12.50 30.00
RH Rickey Henderson 12.50 30.00

2013 Topps Tier One Triple Relics
*TRIPLE: .75X TO 2X BASIC
STATED ODDS 1:17 HOBBY
STATED PRINT RUN 25 SER.#'d SETS
CRJ Cal Ripken Jr. 40.00 80.00
KGJ Ken Griffey Jr. 30.00 60.00
RH Rickey Henderson 20.00 50.00

2013 Topps Tier One Autograph Dual Relics
STATED ODDS 1:46 HOBBY
STATED PRINT RUN 25 SER.#'d SETS
EXCHANGE DEADLINE 07/31/2016
CB Craig Biggio EXCH 30.00 60.00
CG Carlos Gonzalez EXCH 10.00 25.00
CRJ Cal Ripken Jr. 100.00 200.00
CS Chris Sale 30.00 60.00
CST Carlos Santana 8.00 20.00
DF David Freese 25.00 60.00
DP David Price EXCH 15.00 40.00
DW David Wright 50.00 100.00
EA Elvis Andrus EXCH 12.50 30.00
EL Evan Longoria 40.00 80.00
JS Jean Segura EXCH 20.00 50.00
KGJ Ken Griffey Jr. 200.00 500.00
MB Madison Bumgarner EXCH 25.00 60.00
MC Miguel Cabrera 75.00 150.00
MM Matt Moore 40.00 80.00
MO Mike Olt 15.00 40.00
NR Nolan Ryan 125.00 250.00
PF Prince Fielder EXCH 30.00 60.00
PG Paul Goldschmidt 60.00 120.00
RB Ryan Braun 12.50 30.00
RZ Ryan Zimmerman 10.00 25.00
TS Tyler Skaggs EXCH 8.00 20.00
YD Yu Darvish 100.00 200.00

2013 Topps Tier One Autograph Relics

STATED ODDS 1:12 HOBBY
STATED PRINT RUN 99 SER.#'d SETS
EXCHANGE DEADLINE 07/31/2016

CB Craig Biggio 20.00 50.00
CG Carlos Gonzalez EXCH 6.00 15.00
CRJ Cal Ripken Jr. 50.00 100.00
CS Chris Sale 12.50 30.00
CST Carlos Santana 10.00 25.00
DF David Freese 6.00 15.00
DP David Price 10.00 25.00
DW David Wright 40.00 80.00
EA Elvis Andrus EXCH 6.00 15.00
EL Evan Longoria 20.00 50.00
JS Jean Segura EXCH 10.00 25.00
KGJ Ken Griffey Jr. 125.00 300.00
MB Madison Bumgarner EXCH 40.00 80.00
MC Miguel Cabrera 60.00 120.00
MH Matt Holliday EXCH 12.50 30.00
MM Matt Moore 12.50 30.00
MO Mike Olt 10.00 25.00
NR Nolan Ryan 60.00 120.00
PF Prince Fielder EXCH 15.00 40.00
PG Paul Goldschmidt 15.00 40.00
RB Ryan Braun 10.00 25.00
RZ Ryan Zimmerman 12.50 30.00
SC Starlin Castro 12.50 30.00
TS Tyler Skaggs EXCH 6.00 15.00
YD Yu Darvish 30.00 80.00

2013 Topps Tier One Autographs

STATED ODDS 1:19 HOBBY
PRINT RUNS B/WN 50-199 COPIES PER
EXCHANGE DEADLINE 07/31/2016

AD Andre Dawson EXCH 12.50 30.00
BG Bob Gibson/69 20.00 50.00
CK Clayton Kershaw/90 30.00 80.00
CRJ Cal Ripken Jr./50 60.00 120.00
DM Don Mattingly/199 20.00 50.00
EB Ernie Banks/50 30.00 60.00
FT Frank Thomas 50.00 100.00
HA Hank Aaron EXCH 100.00 200.00
JB Johnny Bench EXCH 30.00 60.00
JH Josh Hamilton/99 10.00 25.00
KGJ Ken Griffey Jr./50 100.00 200.00
MC Miguel Cabrera/50 50.00 100.00
MS Mike Schmidt/50 40.00 80.00
NR Nolan Ryan/50 60.00 120.00
OS Ozzie Smith/199 30.00 60.00
P Pele/50 200.00 300.00
PF Prince Fielder EXCH 15.00 40.00
RB Ryan Braun/50 6.00 15.00
RH Rickey Henderson/50 25.00 60.00
RJ Reggie Jackson EXCH 20.00 50.00
SK Sandy Koufax/50 150.00 300.00
TG Tony Gwynn/50 15.00 40.00
TS Tom Seaver EXCH 50.00 120.00
WM Willie Mays/50 100.00 200.00
YD Yu Darvish EXCH 60.00 120.00

2013 Topps Tier One Clear Reprint Autographs

STATED ODDS 1:46 HOBBY
STATED PRINT RUN 25 SER.#'d SETS
EXCHANGE DEADLINE 07/31/2016

AK Al Kaline 75.00 200.00
BG Bob Gibson 100.00 200.00
BP Buster Posey 150.00 300.00
CRJ Cal Ripken Jr. 125.00 300.00
EL Evan Longoria 60.00 120.00
FT Frank Thomas 150.00 300.00
HA Hank Aaron 500.00 800.00
JB Johnny Bench 60.00 200.00
JH Josh Hamilton 50.00 100.00
JW Jered Weaver 60.00 120.00
MC Miguel Cabrera 200.00 300.00
MS Mike Schmidt 75.00 150.00
MT Mike Trout 300.00 500.00
NG N.Garciaparra EXCH 50.00 100.00
NR Nolan Ryan 175.00 350.00
OS Ozzie Smith 150.00 300.00
PF Prince Fielder 60.00 120.00
PO Paul O'Neill 50.00 100.00
RB Ryan Braun 50.00 100.00
RH Rickey Henderson 200.00 300.00
RJ Reggie Jackson 50.00 80.00
SK Sandy Koufax 400.00 800.00
TG Tony Gwynn 100.00 200.00
TS Tom Seaver 100.00 250.00
WM Willie Mays 300.00 400.00

2013 Topps Tier One Crowd Pleaser Autographs

PRINT RUNS B/WN 50-299 COPIES PER
ALL VERSIONS EQUALLY PRICED
EXCHANGE DEADLINE 07/31/2016

AA1 Alex Avila/299 5.00 12.00
AB1 Albert Belle/299 5.00 12.00
AB2 Albert Belle/299 5.00 12.00
AC1 Allen Craig/299 8.00 20.00
AC2 Allen Craig/299 8.00 20.00
AG Adrian Gonzalez/50 20.00 50.00
AJO Adam Jones/99 8.00 20.00
AK Al Kaline/50 25.00 50.00
BB1 Bill Buckner/299 6.00 15.00
BB2 Bill Buckner/299 6.00 15.00
BBU Billy Butler/206 4.00 10.00
BM Brian McCann/99 10.00 25.00
BP Buster Posey/50 40.00 80.00
BP1 Brandon Phillips/299 6.00 15.00
BP2 Brandon Phillips/299 6.00 15.00
BS Bruce Sutter/99 8.00 20.00
CB Craig Biggio EXCH 20.00 50.00
CF Cecil Fielder/199 10.00 25.00
CG Carlos Gonzalez EXCH 8.00 20.00
CH1 Chase Headley/299 4.00 10.00
CH2 Chase Headley/299 4.00 10.00
CJW C.J. Wilson/99 4.00 8.00
CR Carlos Ruiz/299 4.00 10.00
DF1 Dexter Fowler/299 4.00 10.00
DH1 Derek Holland/299 4.00 10.00
DH2 Derek Holland/299 4.00 10.00
DM Dale Murphy/99 10.00 25.00
DO David Ortiz/50 20.00 50.00
DP David Price/50 8.00 20.00
DPD Dustin Pedroia EXCH 15.00 40.00
DS1 Don Sutton/299 6.00 15.00
DS2 Don Sutton/299 6.00 15.00
DST Dave Stewart/299 4.00 10.00
DST2 Dave Stewart/299 4.00 10.00
DW David Wright/50 15.00 40.00
EL Evan Longoria/50 10.00 25.00
FH Felix Hernandez EXCH 12.50 30.00
FL1 Fred Lynn/99 6.00 15.00
FL2 Fred Lynn/180 6.00 15.00
GB1 Grant Balfour/299 5.00 12.00
GB2 Grant Balfour/299 5.00 12.00
GG Gio Gonzalez EXCH 4.00 10.00
GJ1 Garrett Jones/299 5.00 12.00
GJ2 Garrett Jones/299 5.00 12.00
HI1 Hisashi Iwakuma/299 6.00 15.00
JA1 Jim Abbott/299 5.00 12.00
JA2 Jim Abbott/299 5.00 12.00
JB Jose Bautista/50 12.00 30.00
JBR Jay Bruce/99 6.00 15.00
JC Johnny Cueto/99 4.00 10.00
JJ1 Jon Jay/299 5.00 12.00
JJ2 Jon Jay/299 5.00 12.00
JM Juan Marichal/99 10.00 25.00
JP1 Jhonny Peralta/299 4.00 10.00
JP2 Jhonny Peralta/299 4.00 10.00
JR1 Jim Rice/299 6.00 15.00
JR2 Jim Rice/299 6.00 15.00
JS John Smoltz EXCH 15.00 40.00
JS1 James Shields/299 4.00 10.00
JS2 James Shields/299 4.00 10.00
JU Justin Upton 6.00 15.00
KL Kenny Lofton/59 12.00 30.00
LA Luis Aparicio EXCH 10.00 25.00
MC Matt Cain/50 12.50 30.00
MH Matt Holliday EXCH 12.50 30.00
MH1 Matt Harrison/299 4.00 10.00
MH2 Matt Harrison/299 4.00 10.00
MM Mike Mussina EXCH 12.50 30.00
MMO Mike Morse/299 4.00 10.00
MN1 Mike Napoli/299 10.00 25.00
MN2 Mike Napoli/299 10.00 25.00
MW Maury Wills/299 5.00 12.00
NC Nelson Cruz/99 4.00 10.00
NG Nomar Garciaparra/99 12.00 30.00
PM Pedro Martinez/50 75.00 150.00
PO Paul O'Neill/299 6.00 15.00
RAD R.A. Dickey EXCH 6.00 15.00
RV Robin Ventura/299 4.00 10.00
RZ Ryan Zimmerman/99 8.00 20.00
SM1 Shaun Marcum/299 4.00 10.00
SM2 Shaun Marcum/299 4.00 10.00
TG Tom Glavine EXCH 20.00 50.00
TH Tim Hudson/99 6.00 15.00
TR1 Tim Raines/299 6.00 15.00
TR2 Tim Raines/299 6.00 15.00
VB1 Vida Blue/299 5.00 12.00
VB2 Vida Blue/299 5.00 12.00
WC Will Clark/99 12.50 30.00
WJ Wally Joyner/299 5.00 12.00
YG Yovani Gallardo EXCH 4.00 10.00
YP Yasiel Puig EXCH 200.00 400.00

2013 Topps Tier One Dual Autographs

STATED ODDS 1:76 HOBBY
STATED PRINT RUN 25 SER.#'d SETS

BC Banks/Castro EXCH 60.00 120.00
BM Bundy/Machado EXCH 75.00 150.00
BS Banks/Smith 50.00 120.00
FK Fielder/Kaline 40.00 100.00
KA Aaron/Koufax EXCH 600.00 800.00
KM Kimbrel/Medlen 40.00 80.00
MC Musial/Craig 50.00 100.00
RD Darvish/Ryan EXCH 75.00 200.00
RT Rizzo/Thomas EXCH 60.00 120.00
SL Schmidt/Longoria 50.00 100.00
TH Henderson/Trout EXCH 150.00 400.00
THR Trout/Harper EXCH 500.00 700.00
WB Bundy/Hyun-Jin EXCH 40.00 80.00
WK Kershaw/Weaver EXCH 60.00 120.00
WW Weaver/Wilson EXCH 40.00 80.00

2013 Topps Tier One Legends Dual Relics

*DUAL: .5X TO 1.2X BASIC
STATED ODDS 1:76 HOBBY
STATED PRINT RUN 25 SER.#'d SETS

2013 Topps Tier One Legends Relics

STATED ODDS 1:21 HOBBY
PRINT RUNS B/WN 44-99 COPIES PER

BG Bob Gibson 5.00 12.00
BR Babe Ruth/44 60.00 120.00
CRJ Cal Ripken Jr. 15.00 40.00
EB Ernie Banks/45 12.50 30.00
GB George Brett 10.00 25.00
JR Jackie Robinson 15.00 40.00
KGR Ken Griffey Jr. 12.50 30.00
NR1 Nolan Ryan 15.00 40.00
OC Orlando Cepeda 8.00 20.00
OS Ozzie Smith 12.50 30.00
RC Rod Carew 5.00 12.00
RJ Reggie Jackson 5.00 12.00
TW Ted Williams 15.00 40.00
WM Willie Mays 10.00 25.00
YB Yogi Berra 8.00 20.00

2013 Topps Tier One On the Rise Autographs

PRINT RUNS B/WN 50-399 COPIES PER
ALL VERSIONS EQUALLY PRICED
EXCHANGE DEADLINE 07/31/2016

AC Andrew Cashner/399 3.00 8.00
AC1 Alex Cobb/399 3.00 8.00
AC2 Alex Cobb/399 3.00 8.00
ACS1 Andrew Cashner/399 3.00 8.00
AE1 Adam Eaton/399 3.00 8.00
AE2 Adam Eaton/399 3.00 8.00
AG1 Anthony Gose/399 3.00 8.00
AG2 Anthony Gose/399 3.00 8.00
AGR1 Avisail Garcia/399 6.00 15.00
AGR2 Avisail Garcia/399 6.00 15.00
AR Anthony Rizzo 20.00 50.00
BH Bryce Harper 125.00 250.00
BH1 Brock Holt/399 10.00 25.00
BH2 Brock Holt/399 10.00 25.00
BJ1 Brett Jackson/399 3.00 8.00
BJ2 Brett Jackson/399 3.00 8.00
CA1 Chris Archer/399 4.00 10.00
CA2 Chris Archer/399 4.00 10.00
CK Craig Kimbrel/50 30.00 60.00
CK1 Casey Kelly/399 3.00 8.00
CK2 Casey Kelly/399 3.00 8.00
CS Chris Sale/50 10.00 25.00
CST Carlos Santana/299 4.00 10.00
DBY1 Dylan Bundy/99 8.00 20.00
DBY2 Dylan Bundy/99 8.00 20.00
DF David Freese/50 12.50 30.00
DM Devin Mesoraco/399 3.00 8.00
DS Drew Storen/299 3.00 8.00
DS1 Drew Smyly/399 4.00 10.00
DS2 Drew Smyly/399 4.00 10.00
FD1 Felix Doubront/399 5.00 12.00
FD2 Felix Doubront/399 5.00 12.00
JF1 Jeurys Familia/399 3.00 8.00
JF2 Jeurys Familia/399 3.00 8.00
JK Jason Kipnis/99 8.00 20.00
JP1 Jurickson Profar/99 10.00 25.00
JP2 Jurickson Profar/99 10.00 25.00
JPK Jarrod Parker/199 4.00 10.00
JR Josh Reddick/399 4.00 10.00
JRT Josh Rutledge/399 3.00 8.00
JS1 Jean Segura/399 6.00 15.00
JS2 Jean Segura/399 6.00 15.00
JZ1 Jordan Zimmermann/199 4.00 10.00
JZ2 Jordan Zimmermann/199 4.00 10.00
KM Kris Medlen/99 15.00 40.00
KN1 Kirk Nieuwenhuis/399 3.00 8.00
KN2 Kirk Nieuwenhuis/399 3.00 8.00
LL Lance Lynn/99 3.00 8.00
MA Matt Adams/399 4.00 10.00
MB Madison Bumgarner/50 20.00 50.00
MF1 Michael Fiers/399 4.00 10.00
MM Matt Moore/99 3.00 8.00
MM1 Manny Machado/99 30.00 80.00
MM2 Manny Machado/99 30.00 80.00
MO1 Mike Olt/399 4.00 10.00
MO2 Mike Olt/399 4.00 10.00
MP Michael Pineda/199 5.00 12.00
MT Mike Trout/50 100.00 200.00
MTR Mark Trumbo/99 8.00 20.00
NE1 Nate Eovaldi/399 3.00 8.00
NE2 Nate Eovaldi/399 3.00 8.00
NF Neftali Feliz/199 3.00 8.00
PG Paul Goldschmidt/99 12.50 30.00
SD1 Scott Diamond/399 3.00 8.00
SD2 Scott Diamond/399 3.00 8.00
SM Starling Marte/399 4.00 10.00
SM1 Shelby Miller/99 8.00 20.00
SP1 Salvador Perez/399 8.00 20.00
SP2 Salvador Perez/399 8.00 20.00
TF Todd Frazier/299 6.00 15.00
TM1 Tommy Milone/399 3.00 8.00
TM2 Tommy Milone/399 3.00 8.00
TS1 Tyler Skaggs/399 4.00 10.00
TS2 Tyler Skaggs/399 4.00 10.00
WM Will Middlebrooks EXCH 8.00 20.00
WM1 Wil Myers/199 5.00 12.00
WM2 Wil Myers/399 4.00 10.00
WMY Wade Miley/99 4.00 10.00
WP1 Wily Peralta/399 3.00 8.00
WP2 Wily Peralta/399 3.00 8.00
WR Wilin Rosario/399 3.00 8.00
YC1 Yoenis Cespedes/99 12.50 30.00
YC2 Yoenis Cespedes/99 12.50 30.00
YG1 Yasmani Grandal/399 3.00 8.00
ZC1 Zack Cozart/399 4.00 10.00
ZC2 Zack Cozart/399 4.00 10.00

2014 Topps Tier One Relics

PRINT RUNS B/WN 199-399 COPIES PER

TORABE Adrian Beltre/299 4.00 10.00
TORABL Albert Belle/299 2.50 6.00
TORAC Aroldis Chapman/299 4.00 10.00
TORAD Andre Dawson/399 3.00 8.00
TORAG Adrian Gonzalez/254 3.00 8.00
TORAJ Adam Jones/299 3.00 8.00
TORAK Al Kaline/254 4.00 10.00
TORBBU Billy Butler/299 2.50 6.00
TORBP Buster Posey/254 5.00 12.00
TORBW Billy Williams/299 3.00 8.00
TORBZ Ben Zobrist/399 3.00 8.00
TORCA Chris Archer/299 2.50 6.00
TORCDA Chris Davis/249 2.50 6.00
TORCH Cole Hamels/299 3.00 8.00
TORCKE Clayton Kershaw/254 6.00 15.00
TORCKI Craig Kimbrel/254 3.00 8.00
TORCR Colby Rasmus/254 3.00 8.00
TORCW C.J. Wilson/399 2.50 6.00
TORDJ Derek Jeter/254 10.00 25.00
TORDM Dale Murphy/254 4.00 10.00
TORDOR David Ortiz/199 4.00 10.00
TORDPD Dustin Pedroia/254 4.00 10.00
TORDPE Dustin Pedroia/254 4.00 10.00
TORDSA Deion Sanders/254 3.00 8.00
TORDWR David Wright/254 3.00 8.00
TOREEC Edwin Encarnacion/399 4.00 10.00
TOREEN Edwin Encarnacion/399 4.00 10.00
TORELN Evan Longoria/399 3.00 8.00
TORELO Evan Longoria/299 3.00 8.00
TORFF Freddie Freeman/254 5.00 12.00
TORFH Felix Hernandez/254 3.00 8.00
TORFJ Fergie Jenkins/254 3.00 8.00
TORFM Fred McGriff/254 3.00 8.00
TORHP Hunter Pence/254 3.00 8.00
TORHRA Hanley Ramirez/254 3.00 8.00
TORHRY Hyun-Jin Ryu/254 3.00 8.00
TORJBA Jose Bautista/299 3.00 8.00
TORJBR Jackie Bradley Jr./299 4.00 10.00
TORJBU Jay Bruce/299 3.00 8.00
TORJCA Jose Canseco/299 3.00 8.00
TORJCE Johnny Cueto/299 3.00 8.00
TORJCH Jhoulys Chacin/299 2.50 6.00
TORJCU Johnny Cueto/299 3.00 8.00
TORJEV Joey Votto/254 4.00 10.00
TORJHA Josh Hamilton/254 3.00 8.00
TORJHE Jason Heyward/254 3.00 8.00
TORJOV Joey Votto/254 4.00 10.00
TORJPA Jarrod Parker/254 2.50 6.00
TORJPO Jorge Posada/399 3.00 8.00
TORJSH James Shields/399 2.50 6.00
TORJSM John Smoltz/254 4.00 10.00
TORJVO Joey Votto/254 4.00 10.00
TORJVT Joey Votto/254 4.00 10.00
TORJW Jayson Werth/254 3.00 8.00
TORJZ Jordan Zimmermann/254 3.00 8.00
TORKU Koji Uehara/254 2.50 6.00
TORMB Michael Bourn/299 2.50 6.00
TORMCA Miguel Cabrera/299 4.00 10.00
TORMCB Miguel Cabrera/254 4.00 10.00
TORMMA Manny Machado/254 4.00 10.00
TORMT Mark Trumbo/399 2.50 6.00
TORPF Prince Fielder/254 3.00 8.00
TORPG Paul Goldschmidt/254 4.00 10.00
TORRBR Ryan Braun/299 3.00 8.00
TORRD R.A. Dickey/399 3.00 8.00
TORSC Shin-Soo Choo/299 3.00 8.00
TORTC Tony Cingrani/299 3.00 8.00
TORTG Tom Glavine/254 3.00 8.00
TORTL Tim Lincecum/299 3.00 8.00
TORTTL Troy Tulowitzki/254 4.00 10.00
TORTTU Troy Tulowitzki/254 4.00 10.00
TORYC Yoenis Cespedes/399 4.00 10.00
TORYD Yu Darvish/199 4.00 10.00
TORYM Yadier Molina/399 5.00 12.00
TORZW Zack Wheeler/254 3.00 8.00

2014 Topps Tier One Dual Relics

STATED ODDS 1:7 HOBBY
STATED PRINT RUN 50 SER.#'d SETS

TORDJ Derek Jeter 20.00 50.00
TORYM Yadier Molina 10.00 25.00

2014 Topps Tier One Triple Relics

STATED ODDS 1:13 HOBBY
STATED PRINT RUN 25 SER.#'d SETS

TORDJ Derek Jeter 30.00 80.00
TORYM Yadier Molina 15.00 40.00

2014 Topps Tier One Acclaimed Autographs

PRINT RUNS B/WN 50-299 COPIES PER
EXCHANGE DEADLINE 5/31/2017

AAABL Albert Belle/299 5.00 12.00
AAAD Andre Dawson/50 12.00 30.00
AAAG Adrian Gonzalez/50 10.00 25.00
AAAJN Adam Jones/100 8.00 20.00
AAAJO Adam Jones/100 8.00 20.00
AAAKA Al Kaline/299 15.00 40.00
AAAKL Al Kaline/299 15.00 40.00
AABBU Billy Butler/299 4.00 10.00
AABZ Ben Zobrist/299 5.00 12.00
AACBA Carlos Baerga/299 4.00 10.00
AACKE Clayton Kershaw/50 30.00 80.00
AACRA Colby Rasmus/299 5.00 12.00
AACRS Colby Rasmus/299 5.00 12.00
AACWI C.J. Wilson/50 4.00 10.00
AACWL C.J. Wilson/50 4.00 10.00
AADBA Dusty Baker/299 6.00 15.00
AADBK Dusty Baker/299 6.00 15.00
AADFR David Freese/100 4.00 10.00
AADM Dale Murphy/100 8.00 20.00
AADO David Ortiz/50 20.00 50.00
AADP Dustin Pedroia/50 20.00 50.00
AADW David Wright/50 15.00 40.00
AAEDA Eric Davis/299 8.00 20.00
AAEDV Eric Davis/299 8.00 20.00
AAEL Evan Longoria/50 8.00 20.00
AAEM Edgar Martinez/299 5.00 12.00
AAFL Fred Lynn/100 5.00 12.00
AAFMC Fred McGriff/50 6.00 15.00
AAFMG Fred McGriff/50 6.00 15.00
AAGNE Graig Nettles/299 5.00 12.00
AAGNT Graig Nettles/299 5.00 12.00
AAIR Ivan Rodriguez/50 20.00 50.00
AAJB Jeff Bagwell/50 25.00 60.00
AAJCA Jose Canseco/299 10.00 25.00
AAJCN Jose Canseco/299 10.00 25.00
AAJCU Johnny Cueto/299 6.00 15.00
AAJGO Juan Gonzalez/50 12.00 30.00
AAJGZ Juan Gonzalez/50 12.00 30.00
AAJHA Josh Hamilton/50 6.00 15.00
AAJHE Jason Heyward/50 10.00 25.00
AAJM Juan Marichal/50 8.00 20.00
AAJPA Jim Palmer/100 10.00 25.00
AAJPO Jorge Posada/50 15.00 40.00
AAJR Jim Rice/299 6.00 15.00
AAJSH James Shields/299 4.00 10.00
AAJSI James Shields/299 4.00 10.00
AAJSM John Smoltz/50 15.00 40.00
AAJUI Juan Uribe/299 5.00 12.00
AAJUR Juan Uribe/299 5.00 12.00
AAJV Joey Votto/50 12.00 30.00
AAKL Kenny Lofton/50 4.00 10.00
AALB Lou Brock/50 15.00 40.00
AALGN Luis Gonzalez/299 4.00 10.00
AALGO Luis Gonzalez/299 4.00 10.00
AALHE Livan Hernandez/299 4.00 10.00
AALSI Lee Smith/299 5.00 12.00
AAMCA Miguel Cabrera/50 40.00 100.00
AAMCU Michael Cuddyer/299 8.00 20.00
AAMGE Mike Greenwell/299 8.00 20.00
AAMGR Mike Greenwell/299 8.00 20.00
AAMTR Mark Trumbo/299 4.00 10.00
AAMTU Mark Trumbo/299 4.00 10.00
AAMWI Matt Williams/299 5.00 12.00
AAMWL Matt Williams/299 5.00 12.00
AANG Nomar Garciaparra/50 15.00 40.00
AAOC Orlando Cepeda/50 12.00 30.00
AAOHE Orlando Hernandez/299 10.00 25.00
AAOHR Orlando Hernandez/299 10.00 25.00
AAPGO Paul Goldschmidt/299 10.00 25.00
AAPOE Paul O'Neill/299 8.00 20.00
AAPON Paul O'Neill/299 8.00 20.00
AARB Ryan Braun/50 10.00 25.00
AARD R.A. Dickey/50 6.00 15.00
AARNO Ricky Nolasco/299 4.00 10.00
AARPA Rafael Palmeiro/50 8.00 20.00
AARPL Rafael Palmeiro/50 8.00 20.00
AARZI Ryan Zimmerman/50 8.00 20.00
AATG Tom Glavine/50 15.00 40.00
AATRA Tim Raines/50 5.00 12.00
AATT Troy Tulowitzki EXCH 10.00 25.00
AAYC Yoenis Cespedes/299 8.00 20.00
AAYM Yadier Molina EXCH 40.00 100.00

2014 Topps Tier One Acclaimed Autographs Bronze Ink

*BRONZE: .6X TO 1.5X BASIC
STATED ODDS 1:11 HOBBY
STATED PRINT RUN 25 SER.#'d SETS
EXCHANGE DEADLINE 5/31/2017

2014 Topps Tier One Acetate Autographs

STATED ODDS 1:19 HOBBY
PRINT RUNS B/WN 30-99 COPIES PER
EXCHANGE DEADLINE 5/31/2017

TOABJ Bo Jackson/99 40.00 100.00
TOACR Cal Ripken Jr./30 100.00 200.00
TOAEBA Ernie Banks/99 30.00 80.00
TOAGM Greg Maddux/30 100.00 200.00
TOAHA Hank Aaron/30 125.00 250.00
TOAJB Johnny Bench/99 40.00 100.00
TOAKG Ken Griffey Jr./30 75.00 200.00
TOAMM Mark McGwire/45 125.00 250.00
TOAMR Mariano Rivera/69 60.00 150.00
TOAMSH Mike Schmidt/99 30.00 80.00
TOANR Nolan Ryan/45 100.00 200.00
TOAOSI Ozzie Smith/99 20.00 50.00
TOAPM Pedro Martinez/99 40.00 100.00
TOARH Rickey Henderson/99 40.00 100.00
TOARJA Reggie Jackson/45 50.00 100.00
TOARJO Randy Johnson/30 60.00 150.00
TOASCR Steve Carlton/99 25.00 60.00
TOASK Sandy Koufax 150.00 250.00
TOATGW Tony Gwynn/99 30.00 80.00

2014 Topps Tier One Acetate Autographs Bronze Ink

*BRONZE: .4X TO 1X BASIC
STATED ODDS 1:49 HOBBY
STATED PRINT RUN 25 SER.#'d SETS
EXCHANGE DEADLINE 5/31/2017

TOAWM Mays Signed in Black 125.00 250.00

2014 Topps Tier One Autograph Relics

STATED ODDS 1:10 HOBBY
STATED PRINT RUN 99 SER.#'d SETS
EXCHANGE DEADLINE 5/31/2017

TOARAC Alex Cobb 4.00 10.00
TOARAS A.Simmons EXCH 15.00 40.00
TOARBH Billy Hamilton EXCH 12.00 30.00
TOARBJ Bo Jackson 40.00 100.00
TOARBP Buster Posey 40.00 100.00
TOARCA Chris Archer EXCH 4.00 10.00
TOARCS Chris Sale 6.00 15.00
TOARDO David Ortiz 25.00 60.00
TOAREG Evan Gattis 4.00 10.00
TOARFF Freddie Freeman 12.00 30.00
TOARGM Greg Maddux 25.00 60.00
TOARJBA Jose Bautista 12.00 30.00
TOARJG Juan Gonzalez 4.00 10.00
TOARJH Jason Heyward 8.00 20.00
TOARJP Jorge Posada 20.00 50.00
TOARJV Joey Votto 12.00 30.00
TOARJZ Jordan Zimmermann 10.00 25.00
TOARKU Koji Uehara 4.00 10.00
TOARMT Mike Trout 125.00 250.00
TOARRH Rickey Henderson 40.00 100.00
TOARRJA Reggie Jackson 25.00 60.00
TOARSC Steve Carlton 15.00 40.00
TOARTGL Tom Glavine 25.00 60.00
TOARWB Wade Boggs 10.00 25.00
TOARYD Yu Darvish 50.00 120.00

2014 Topps Tier One Autograph Dual Relics

STATED ODDS 1:39 HOBBY
STATED PRINT RUN 25 SER.#'d SETS
EXCHANGE DEADLINE 5/31/2017

2014 Topps Tier One Dual Autographs

STATED ODDS 1:65 HOBBY
STATED PRINT RUN 25 SER.#'d SETS
EXCHANGE DEADLINE 5/31/2017

DABB Biggio/Bagwell EXCH 100.00 200.00
DACT Trout/Cabrera EXCH 300.00 500.00
DAGB Garciapar/Boggs EXCH 40.00 100.00
DAHJ R.Jackson/R.Henderson 10.00 100.00
DAJM Johnson/Martinez EXCH 100.00 200.00
DAMC Cepeda/Marichal EXCH 40.00 100.00
DAMJ Jones/Machado EXCH 75.00 150.00
DAML W.Myers/E.Longoria 40.00 100.00
DAMP Molina/Posey EXCH 100.00 200.00
DAPV B.Phillips/J.Votto 40.00 100.00
DARG IRod/Gonzalez EXCH 40.00 100.00
DARP M.Rivera/J.Posada 300.00 400.00
DASG J.Smoltz/T.Glavine 100.00 200.00
DASJ Jackson/Sanders EXCH 75.00 150.00
DASR Ryan/Seaver EXCH 125.00 300.00

2014 Topps Tier One Legends Relics

STATED ODDS 1:13 HOBBY
STATED PRINT RUN 99 SER.#'d SETS

TORLAB Albert Belle 4.00 10.00
TORLBJ Bo Jackson 8.00 20.00
TORLBR Babe Ruth 50.00 120.00
TORLCR Cal Ripken Jr. 8.00 20.00
TORLDS Deion Sanders 6.00 15.00
TORLGM Greg Maddux 8.00 20.00
TORLGS Gary Sheffield 4.00 10.00
TORLJG Juan Gonzalez 5.00 12.00
TORLJM Joe Morgan 5.00 12.00
TORLJP Jorge Posada 5.00 12.00
TORLMM Mark McGwire 12.00 30.00
TORLMR Manny Ramirez 6.00 15.00
TORLNG Nomar Garciaparra 5.00 12.00
TORLOC Orlando Cepeda 5.00 12.00
TORLRJA Reggie Jackson 5.00 12.00
TORLRJO Randy Johnson 6.00 15.00
TORLSCA Steve Carlton 5.00 12.00
TORLSCR Steve Carlton 5.00 12.00
TORLTGL Tom Glavine 5.00 12.00
TORLTGY Tony Gwynn 6.00 15.00

2014 Topps Tier One Legends Dual Relics

STATED ODDS 1:49 HOBBY
STATED PRINT RUN 25 SER.#'d SETS

2014 Topps Tier One New Guard Autographs

PRINT RUNS B/WN 50-399 COPIES PER
EXCHANGE DEADLINE 5/31/2017

NGAACO Alex Cobb/399 4.00 10.00
NGAACR Allen Craig/50 5.00 12.00
NGAAG Anthony Gose/399 4.00 10.00
NGAALM Andrew Lambo/399 4.00 10.00
NGAAR Anthony Rizzo/50 10.00 25.00
NGAASI Andrelton Simmons/99 12.00 30.00
NGAASM Andrelton Simmons/99 12.00 30.00
NGAAWE Allen Webster/399 4.00 10.00
NGABHA Billy Hamilton 5.00 12.00
NGABHR Bryce Harper/50 75.00 150.00
NGABMI Brad Miller/399 5.00 12.00
NGACAH Cody Asche/399 6.00 15.00
NGACAR Chris Archer/181 4.00 10.00
NGACSA Chris Sale/50 10.00 25.00
NGACSN Carlos Santana/50 6.00 15.00
NGACY Christian Yelich/181 20.00 50.00
NGADB Dylan Bundy/50 12.00 30.00
NGADG Didi Gregorius/399 5.00 12.00
NGADSA Danny Salazar/399 5.00 12.00
NGAEGA Evan Gattis/182 4.00 10.00
NGAEJ Erik Johnson/399 4.00 10.00
NGAER Enny Romero/399 4.00 10.00
NGAFF Freddie Freeman/50 15.00 40.00
NGAHAL Henderson Alvarez/399 4.00 10.00
NGAJA Jose Abreu/399 8.00 20.00
NGAJCO Jarred Cosart/399 4.00 10.00
NGAJKE Joe Kelly/399 4.00 10.00
NGAJKI Jason Kipnis/50 5.00 12.00
NGAJLA Junior Lake/399 6.00 15.00
NGAJLK Junior Lake/399 6.00 15.00
NGAJN Jimmy Nelson/399 4.00 10.00
NGAJOD Jake Odorizzi/399 4.00 10.00
NGAJPR Jurickson Profar/50 5.00 12.00
NGAJSC Jonathan Schoop/399 4.00 10.00
NGAJSE Jean Segura/182 5.00 12.00
NGAJTE Julio Teheran/182 5.00 12.00
NGAKSE Kyle Seager/399 4.00 10.00
NGAKW Kolten Wong/399 5.00 12.00
NGAMAA Matt Adams/399 6.00 15.00
NGAMAD Matt Adams/399 6.00 15.00
NGAMB Madison Bumgarner/50 25.00 60.00
NGAMCA Matt Carpenter/50 20.00 50.00
NGAMCR Matt Carpenter/50 10.00 25.00
NGAMD Matt Davidson/399 6.00 15.00
NGAMMA Manny Machado/50 20.00 50.00
NGAMMI Mike Minor/182 4.00 10.00
NGAMMN Mike Minor/182 4.00 10.00
NGAMOL Mike Olt/399 4.00 10.00
NGAMT Mike Trout/50 100.00 250.00
NGAMWC Michael Wacha/399 10.00 25.00
NGAMWH Michael Wacha/399 10.00 25.00
NGAMZN Mike Zunino/50 6.00 15.00
NGAMZU Mike Zunino/50 6.00 15.00
NGAPBO Peter Bourjos/399 5.00 12.00
NGAPBU Peter Bourjos/399 5.00 12.00
NGAPCO Patrick Corbin/50 5.00 12.00
NGAPCR Patrick Corbin/50 6.00 15.00
NGASGA Sonny Gray/399 8.00 20.00
NGASGR Sonny Gray/399 8.00 20.00
NGASMA Starling Marte/399 6.00 15.00
NGASMI Shelby Miller/50 12.00 30.00
NGASML Shelby Miller/50 12.00 30.00
NGASPE Salvador Perez/399 12.00 30.00
NGATBA Trevor Bauer/50 8.00 20.00
NGATBU Trevor Bauer/50 8.00 20.00
NGATCI Tony Cingrani/399 5.00 12.00
NGATCN Tony Cingrani/399 5.00 12.00
NGATD Travis d'Arnaud/182 5.00 12.00
NGATFR Todd Frazier/99 12.00 30.00
NGATJO Taylor Jordan/399 4.00 10.00
NGATTH Tyler Thornburg/399 4.00 10.00
NGATTO Tyler Thornburg/399 4.00 10.00
NGATW Taijuan Walker/182 4.00 10.00
NGAWFL Wilmer Flores/399 5.00 12.00
NGAWFO Wilmer Flores/399 5.00 12.00
NGAWME Wil Myers/50 10.00 25.00
NGAWMI Wade Miley/399 4.00 10.00
NGAWMY Wil Myers/50 10.00 25.00
NGAWR Wilin Rosario/399 4.00 10.00
NGAXB Xander Bogaerts/399 12.00 30.00
NGAYD Yu Darvish EXCH 50.00 120.00
NGAYV Yordano Ventura/399 8.00 20.00
NGAZWE Zack Wheeler/50 8.00 20.00
NGAZWH Zack Wheeler/50 8.00 20.00

2014 Topps Tier One New Guard Autographs Bronze Ink

*BRONZE: .6X TO 1.5X BASIC
STATED ODDS 1:11 HOBBY
STATED PRINT RUN 25 SER.#'d SETS
EXCHANGE DEADLINE 5/31/2017

2015 Topps Tier One Relics

RANDOM INSERTS IN PACKS
PRINT RUNS B/WN 175-399 COPIES PER
*DUAL/50: .6X TO 1.5 SNGL RELIC
*TRIPLE/25: .75X TO 2X SNGL RELIC

TSRACG Allen Craig/399 2.50 6.00
TSRAD Andre Dawson/199 3.00 8.00
TSRAGZ Adrian Gonzalez/399 3.00 8.00
TSRAJ Adam Jones/399 3.00 8.00
TSRAM Andrew McCutchen/175 10.00 25.00
TSRAP Albert Pujols/249 5.00 12.00
TSRAW Adam Wainwright/399 3.00 8.00
TSRBHN Billy Hamilton/399 3.00 8.00
TSRBHR Bryce Harper/199 10.00 25.00
TSRBJ Bo Jackson/199 6.00 15.00
TSRBP Buster Posey/299 5.00 12.00
TSRCBN Charlie Blackmon/399 4.00 10.00
TSRCBO Craig Biggio/199 3.00 8.00
TSRCD Chris Davis/399 2.50 6.00
TSRCF Carlton Fisk/199 3.00 8.00
TSRCJ Chipper Jones/299 4.00 10.00
TSRCR Cal Ripken Jr./199 8.00 20.00
TSRCS CC Sabathia/399 3.00 8.00
TSRCU Chase Utley/399 3.00 8.00
TSRDJ Derek Jeter/399 10.00 25.00
TSRDM Don Mattingly/199 6.00 15.00
TSRDW David Wright/399 3.00 8.00
TSREA Elvis Andrus/399 3.00 8.00
TSREL Evan Longoria/399 3.00 8.00
TSRFF Freddie Freeman/199 5.00 12.00
TSRFH Felix Hernandez/399 3.00 8.00
TSRFT Frank Thomas/199 4.00 10.00
TSRGC Gerrit Cole/399 4.00 10.00
TSRGS Giancarlo Stanton/399 4.00 10.00
TSRHRU Hyun-Jin Ryu/399 3.00 8.00
TSRHRZ Hanley Ramirez/249 3.00 8.00
TSRJA Jose Abreu/199 5.00 12.00
TSRJBA Jose Bautista/399 3.00 8.00
TSRJBE Jay Bruce/399 3.00 8.00
TSRJD Jacob deGrom/399 6.00 15.00
TSRJE Jacoby Ellsbury/399 3.00 8.00
TSRJF Jose Fernandez/399 4.00 10.00
TSRJG Juan Gonzalez/199 2.50 6.00
TSRJH Jason Heyward/399 3.00 8.00
TSRJR Jim Rice/199 3.00 8.00
TSRJVR Justin Verlander/399 4.00 10.00
TSRKG Ken Griffey Jr./199 8.00 20.00
TSRMBR Madison Bumgarner/199 6.00 15.00
TSRMBS Mookie Betts/399 8.00 20.00
TSRMC Miguel Cabrera/399 4.00 10.00
TSRMK Matt Kemp/399 3.00 8.00
TSRMM Mark McGwire/199 10.00 25.00
TSRMP Mike Piazza/249 5.00 12.00
TSRMTA Masahiro Tanaka/399 3.00 8.00
TSRMTT Mike Trout/199 15.00 40.00
TSRNCS Nick Castellanos/399 4.00 10.00
TSRPF Prince Fielder/399 3.00 8.00
TSRPG Paul Goldschmidt/199 4.00 10.00
TSRPS Pablo Sandoval/399 3.00 8.00
TSRRB Ryan Braun/399 3.00 8.00
TSRRC Roger Clemens/199 5.00 12.00
TSRRHD Ryan Howard/399 3.00 8.00
TSRRHN Rickey Henderson/399 4.00 10.00
TSRRJA Reggie Jackson/199 3.00 8.00
TSRRJO Randy Johnson/199 4.00 10.00
TSRRS Ryne Sandberg/199 5.00 12.00
TSRSCH Shin-Soo Choo/399 3.00 8.00
TSRSM Shelby Miller/399 3.00 8.00
TSRSS Stephen Strasburg/399 4.00 10.00
TSRTGE Tom Glavine/199 3.00 8.00
TSRTGN Tony Gwynn/199 5.00 12.00
TSRTL Tim Lincecum/399 4.00 10.00
TSRTR Tim Raines/299 3.00 8.00
TSRTT Troy Tulowitzki/399 4.00 10.00
TSRVG Vladimir Guerrero/199 3.00 8.00
TSRWB Wade Boggs/199 5.00 12.00
TSRXB Xander Bogaerts/399 4.00 10.00
TSRYC Yoenis Cespedes/199 3.00 8.00
TSRYD Yu Darvish/199 4.00 10.00
TSRYP Yasiel Puig/249 4.00 10.00
TSRZG Zack Greinke/299 4.00 10.00

2015 Topps Tier One Acclaimed Autographs

RANDOM INSERTS IN PACKS
PRINT RUNS B/WN 50-399 COPIES PER
EXCHANGE DEADLINE 4/30/2018

AAAC Allen Craig/299 4.00 10.00
AAAD Andre Dawson/50 10.00 25.00
AAAG Adrian Gonzalez/50 5.00 12.00
AAAGA Andres Galarraga/399 4.00 10.00
AAAJ Adam Jones/50 10.00 25.00
AABC Brandon Crawford/399 6.00 15.00
AABMN Brian McCann/149 6.00 15.00
AABMO Brandon Moss/399 3.00 8.00
AABMS Brandon Moss/399 3.00 8.00
AABPS Brandon Phillips/199 6.00 15.00
AACB Carlos Baerga/399 3.00 8.00
AACD Carlos Delgado/399 3.00 8.00
AACFD Cliff Floyd/399 3.00 8.00
AACFK Carlton Fisk/50 20.00 50.00
AACHS Cole Hamels/299 12.00 30.00
AACHY Chase Headley/299 5.00 12.00
AACJ Chris Johnson/399 3.00 8.00
AADC David Cone/299 3.00 8.00
AADEN David Eckstein/299 3.00 8.00
AADEY Dennis Eckersley/149 5.00 12.00
AADF David Freese/149 3.00 8.00
AADMP Dale Murphy/149 10.00 25.00
AADMY Don Mattingly/50 30.00 80.00
AADN Daniel Nava/399 3.00 8.00
AADO David Ortiz/50 20.00 50.00
AADPA Dustin Pedroia/50 12.00 30.00
AADW David Wright/50 15.00 40.00
AAED Eric Davis/399 6.00 15.00
AAEL Evan Longoria/50 5.00 12.00
AAEM Edgar Martinez/149 6.00 15.00
AAFM Fred McGriff/50 5.00 12.00
AAFV Fernando Valenzuela/50 10.00 25.00
AAGS Giancarlo Stanton EXCH 20.00 50.00
AAGV Greg Vaughn/399 3.00 8.00
AAHR Hanley Ramirez/50 5.00 12.00
AAHS Hector Santiago/399 3.00 8.00
AAJCA Jose Canseco/175 12.00 30.00
AAJG Juan Gonzalez/299 5.00 12.00
AAJML Juan Marichal/149 10.00 25.00
AAJMR Joe Mauer EXCH 12.00 30.00
AAJR Jim Rice/299 6.00 15.00
AAJS John Smoltz/50 15.00 40.00
AAJV Joey Votto/50 15.00 40.00
AAKGS Ken Griffey Sr./299 6.00 15.00
AAKU Koji Uehara/299 6.00 15.00
AALB Lou Brock/149 15.00 40.00
AALG Luis Gonzalez/249 3.00 8.00
AALH Livan Hernandez/399 3.00 8.00
AAMC Michael Cuddyer/249 3.00 8.00
AAMMY Mike Matheny/299 10.00 25.00
AAMN Mike Napoli/149 3.00 8.00
AAMT Mark Teixeira/149 12.00 30.00
AAMWN Mookie Wilson/399 6.00 15.00
AAMWS Matt Williams/399 3.00 8.00
AANG Nomar Garciaparra/50 12.00 30.00
AAOC Orlando Cepeda/149 10.00 25.00
AAOH Orlando Hernandez/299 3.00 8.00
AAOV Omar Vizquel/299 6.00 15.00
AAPG Paul Goldschmidt/149 6.00 15.00
AAPN Phil Niekro/149 8.00 20.00
AARA Roberto Alomar/50 15.00 40.00
AARB Ryan Braun/50 10.00 25.00
AARCO Robinson Cano/50 15.00 40.00
AARCW Rod Carew/50 12.00 30.00
AARD Rob Dibble/399 3.00 8.00
AARG Ron Gant/399 3.00 8.00
AARP Rafael Palmeiro/149 4.00 10.00
AARW Rondell White/399 3.00 8.00
AARY Robin Yount/50 25.00 60.00
AARZ Ryan Zimmerman/149 4.00 10.00
AATG Tom Glavine/50 12.00 30.00
AATP Terry Pendleton/399 3.00 8.00
AATR Tim Raines/50 6.00 15.00
AATT Troy Tulowitzki/50 12.00 30.00
AAUJ Ubaldo Jimenez/149 3.00 8.00
AAVC Vinny Castilla/399 3.00 8.00
AAVG Vladimir Guerrero/50 10.00 25.00

2015 Topps Tier One Acclaimed Autographs Bronze Ink

*BRONZE: X TO X BASIC
STATED ODDS 1:12 HOBBY
STATED PRINT RUN 25 SER.#'d SETS
NO PRICING DUE TO SCARCITY
EXCHANGE DEADLINE 4/30/2018

2015 Topps Tier One Autograph Relics

STATED ODDS 1:12 HOBBY
STATED PRINT RUN 99 SER.#'d SETS
EXCHANGE DEADLINE 4/30/2018
*DUAL/25: .6X TO 1.5X BASIC

TOARAGO Adrian Gonzalez 10.00 25.00
TOARAR Anthony Rizzo 30.00 80.00

TOARCD Carlos Delgado 8.00 20.00
TOARDB Dellin Betances 10.00 25.00
TOARDWR David Wright 15.00 40.00
TOARDWT David Wright 15.00 40.00
TOAREL Evan Longoria 10.00 25.00
TOARFF Freddie Freeman 15.00 40.00
TOARFV Fernando Valenzuela 15.00 40.00
TOARHR Hanley Ramirez 10.00 25.00
TOARJD Jacob deGrom 25.00 60.00
TOARJH Jason Heyward 10.00 25.00
TOARMA Matt Adams 8.00 20.00
TOARMCR Matt Carpenter 12.00 30.00
TOARMG Mark Grace 15.00 40.00
TOARMTA Mark Teixeira 15.00 40.00
TOARPG Paul Goldschmidt 15.00 40.00
TOARRC Rusney Castillo 10.00 25.00
TOARSG Sonny Gray 10.00 25.00
TOARSM Starling Marte 10.00 25.00
TOARYV Yordano Ventura 12.00 30.00

2015 Topps Tier One Autographs

STATED PRINT RUN 1:20 HOBBY
PRINT RUNS B/WN 30-99 COPIES PER
EXCHANGE DEADLINE 4/30/2018
TOABJ Bo Jackson/30 40.00 100.00
TOABP Buster Posey/99 40.00 100.00
TOACJ Chipper Jones/30 50.00 120.00
TOACK Clayton Kershaw/99 40.00 100.00
TOACR Cal Ripken Jr./30 60.00 150.00
TOAFT Frank Thomas/99 25.00 60.00
TOAGM Greg Maddux/30 30.00 80.00
TOAHA Hank Aaron/30 150.00 250.00
TOAJA Jose Abreu/99 6.00 15.00
TOAJB Johnny Bench/30 30.00 80.00
TOAKB Kris Bryant/75 100.00 250.00
TOAMC Miguel Cabrera/30 60.00 150.00
TOAMM Mark McGwire/30 50.00 125.00
TOAMP Mike Piazza/30 60.00 150.00
TOAMR Mariano Rivera/30 75.00 150.00
TOAMS Mike Schmidt/30 50.00 100.00
TOAMTT Mike Trout/30 150.00 250.00
TOANR Nolan Ryan/30 90.00 150.00
TOAOS Ozzie Smith/99 20.00 50.00
TOARC Roger Clemens/30 40.00 100.00
TOARH Rickey Henderson/30 30.00 80.00
TOARJA Reggie Jackson/30 25.00 60.00
TOARJO Randy Johnson/30 30.00 80.00
TOASC Steve Carlton/99 12.00 30.00
TOASK Sandy Koufax/30 200.00 300.00
TOAWB Wade Boggs/99 20.00 50.00
TOAYP Yasiel Puig/30 40.00 100.00

2015 Topps Tier One Autographs Bronze Ink

*BRONZE: .4X TO 1X BASIC p/r 30
*BRONZE: .6X TO 1.5X BASIC p/r 99
STATED ODDS 1:37 HOBBY
STATED PRINT RUN 25 SER.#'d SETS
NO PRICING DUE TO SCARCITY
EXCHANGE DEADLINE 4/30/2018

2015 Topps Tier One Clear One Autographs

STATE ODDS 1:52 HOBBY
STATED PRINT RUN 25 SER.#'d SETS
EXCHANGE DEADLINE 4/30/2018
COABJ Bo Jackson 40.00 100.00
COABP Buster Posey 60.00 150.00
COACJ Chipper Jones EXCH 60.00 150.00
COACK Clayton Kershaw EXCH 100.00 200.00
COADO David Ortiz 12.00 30.00
COAFT Frank Thomas 40.00 100.00
COAJA Jose Abreu 12.00 30.00
COAJF Jose Fernandez EXCH 25.00 60.00
COAJR Jim Rice 10.00 25.00
COAKG Ken Griffey Jr. 100.00 250.00
COAMC Michael Cuddyer EXCH 8.00 20.00
COANG Nomar Garciaparra 10.00 25.00
COAOS Ozzie Smith 15.00 40.00
COARY Robin Yount 30.00 80.00
COASC Steve Carlton 10.00 25.00
COATT Troy Tulowitzki 12.00 30.00
COAWM Wil Myers 10.00 25.00

2015 Topps Tier One Dual Autographs

STATE ODDS 1:69 HOBBY
STATED PRINT RUN 25 SER.#'d SETS
EXCHANGE DEADLINE 4/30/2018
DAAB Baez/Abreu EXCH 150.00 400.00
DAAM Adms/McGwre EXCH 50.00 120.00
DAFO D.Ortiz/C.Fisk 30.00 80.00
DAGJ L.Gonzalez/R.Johnson 40.00 100.00
DAGR A.Gonzalez/H.Ramirez 25.00 60.00
DAJG T.Glavine/C.Jones 150.00 300.00
DAMG Gonzalez/Mattingly 60.00 150.00
DAMT Txra/Mttngly EXCH 60.00 150.00
DAPW D.Wright/M.Piazza 60.00 150.00
DARP J.Posada/M.Rivera 150.00 250.00
DART M.Teixeira/A.Rizzo 40.00 100.00
DATP M.Trout/Y.Puig 175.00 350.00
DAWJ Jones/Wright EXCH 150.00 250.00

2015 Topps Tier One Legends Relics

STATE ODDS 1:14 HOBBY
STATED PRINT RUN 99 SER.#'d SETS
*DUAL/25: .6X TO 1.5X SNGL RELIC
TORLBD Bobby Doerr 6.00 15.00
TORLDS Duke Snider 6.00 15.00
TORLEB Ernie Banks 10.00 25.00
TORLES Enos Slaughter 6.00 15.00
TORLEW Early Wynn 6.00 15.00
TORLFR Frank Robinson 6.00 15.00
TORLHA Hank Aaron 12.00 30.00
TORLHW Hoyt Wilhelm 12.00 30.00
TORLJB Jim Bunning 6.00 15.00
TORLJD Joe DiMaggio 25.00 60.00
TORLJM Juan Marichal 10.00 25.00
TORLJR Jackie Robinson 20.00 50.00
TORLRC Roberto Clemente 30.00 80.00
TORLRF Rick Ferrell 8.00 20.00
TORLRS Red Schoendienst 6.00 15.00
TORLTC Ty Cobb 25.00 60.00
TORLTW Ted Williams 25.00 60.00
TORLWMS Willie Mays 20.00 50.00
TORLWSL Willie Stargell 10.00 25.00

2015 Topps Tier One New Guard Autographs

RANDOM INSERTS IN PACKS
PRINT RUNS B/WN 50-399 COPIES PER
EXCHANGE DEADLINE 4/30/2018
NGAAAA Arismendy Alcantara/399 3.00 8.00
NGAAAY Arismendy Alcantara/399 3.00 8.00
NGAACB Alex Cobb/299 3.00 8.00
NGAACO Alex Cobb/299 3.00 8.00
NGAARA Anthony Ranaudo/399 3.00 8.00
NGAARI Anthony Rizzo/50 20.00 50.00
NGAASA Aaron Sanchez/399 4.00 10.00
NGAASN Andrelton Simmons EXCH 8.00 20.00
NGAASZ Aaron Sanchez/399 4.00 10.00
NGABH Bryce Harper EXCH 125.00 250.00
NGABOB Brett Oberholtzer/299 3.00 8.00
NGABOZ Brett Oberholtzer/299 3.00 8.00
NGACA Chris Archer/199 3.00 8.00
NGACCJ C.J. Cron/399 3.00 8.00
NGACCN C.J. Cron/399 3.00 8.00
NGACK Corey Kluber/199 6.00 15.00
NGACR Carlos Rodon EXCH 20.00 50.00
NGACSE Chris Sale/50 10.00 25.00
NGACSG Cory Spangenberg/399 3.00 8.00
NGACY Christian Yelich/99 10.00 25.00
NGADBE Dellin Betances/349 4.00 10.00
NGADBS Dellin Betances/349 4.00 10.00
NGADH Dilson Herrera/349 4.00 10.00
NGADMO Devin Mesoraco/99 8.00 20.00
NGADN Daniel Norris/349 3.00 8.00
NGAFF Freddie Freeman/99 10.00 25.00
NGAGP Gregory Polanco/50 5.00 12.00
NGAHAL Henderson Alvarez/349 3.00 8.00
NGAHAZ Henderson Alvarez/349 3.00 8.00
NGAJBA Javier Baez/299 8.00 20.00
NGAJBZ Javier Baez/299 8.00 20.00
NGAJCS Jarred Cosart/399 3.00 8.00
NGAJDM Jacob deGrom/299 40.00 100.00
NGAJDN Josh Donaldson/50 5.00 12.00
NGAJF Jose Fernandez/50 25.00 60.00
NGAJHA Josh Harrison/299 10.00 25.00
NGAJHD Jason Heyward/50 5.00 12.00
NGAJHN Josh Harrison/299 10.00 25.00
NGAJKY Joe Kelly/349 3.00 8.00
NGAJLG Juan Lagares/399 6.00 15.00
NGAJPA Joe Panik/399 12.00 30.00
NGAJPE Joc Pederson/349 8.00 20.00
NGAJPK Joe Panik/399 4.00 10.00
NGAJPN Joc Pederson/349 8.00 20.00
NGAJSC Jonathan Schoop/299 3.00 8.00
NGAJSO Jorge Soler/349 5.00 12.00
NGAJSP Jonathan Schoop/299 3.00 8.00
NGAJSR Jorge Soler/349 10.00 25.00
NGAJT Julio Teheran/50 5.00 12.00
NGAKCN Kole Calhoun/349 3.00 8.00
NGAKGA Kevin Gausman/299 5.00 12.00
NGAKGN Kevin Gausman/299 5.00 12.00
NGAKSE Kyle Seager/225 3.00 8.00
NGAKSR Kyle Seager/225 3.00 8.00
NGAKVA Kennys Vargas/399 3.00 8.00
NGAKVG Kennys Vargas/399 3.00 8.00
NGAMA Matt Adams/199 3.00 8.00
NGAMC Matt Carpenter/50 12.00 30.00
NGAMFO Maikel Franco/349 4.00 10.00
NGAMFR Maikel Franco/349 4.00 10.00
NGAMFZ Mike Foltynewicz/399 3.00 8.00
NGAMSN Marcus Stroman/399 4.00 10.00
NGAMST Marcus Stroman/399 4.00 10.00
NGAMTA Michael Taylor/349 3.00 8.00
NGAMTY Michael Taylor/349 3.00 8.00
NGANC Nick Castellanos/50 12.00 30.00
NGAPC Patrick Corbin/50 5.00 12.00
NGARC Rusney Castillo/50 5.00 12.00
NGARDA Rubby De La Rosa/349 3.00 8.00
NGARDE Rubby De La Rosa/349 3.00 8.00
NGARMN Rafael Montero/399 3.00 8.00
NGARMO Rafael Montero/399 3.00 8.00
NGASDE Sean Doolittle/349 3.00 8.00
NGASDO Sean Doolittle/349 3.00 8.00
NGASGE Shane Greene/349 3.00 8.00
NGASGR Shane Greene/349 3.00 8.00
NGASGY Sonny Gray/99 8.00 20.00
NGASMA Starling Marte/225 8.00 20.00
NGASME Starling Marte/225 8.00 20.00
NGATRO Tyson Ross/225 3.00 8.00
NGATRS Tyson Ross/225 3.00 8.00
NGATW Taijuan Walker/99 8.00 20.00
NGAWM Wil Myers/50 5.00 12.00
NGAYV Yordano Ventura/199 6.00 15.00
NGAZW Zack Wheeler/50 5.00 12.00

2015 Topps Tier One New Guard Autographs Bronze Ink

*BRONZE: X TO X BASIC
STATED ODDS 1:11 HOBBY
STATED PRINT RUN 25 SER.#'d SETS
EXCHANGE DEADLINE 4/30/2018

2016 Topps Tier One Relics

RANDOM INSERTS IN PACKS
PRINT RUNS B/WN 99-399 COPIES PER
*DUAL/50: .6X TO 1.5 SNGL RELIC
*TRIPLE/25: .75X TO 2X SNGL RELIC
T1RAGN Adrian Gonzalez/399 3.00 8.00
T1RAGR Alex Gordon/205 3.00 8.00
T1RAM Andrew McCutchen/99 6.00 15.00
T1RAPO A.J. Pollock/299 2.50 6.00
T1RAPU Albert Pujols/299 5.00 12.00
T1RARI Anthony Rizzo/299 5.00 12.00
T1RARU Addison Russell/199 4.00 10.00
T1RAW Adam Wainwright/199 3.00 8.00
T1RBG Brett Gardner/399 3.00 8.00
T1RBH Bryce Harper/299 6.00 15.00
T1RBM Brian McCann/299 3.00 8.00
T1RBPH Brandon Phillips/299 2.50 6.00
T1RBPO Buster Posey/299 5.00 12.00
T1RCBE Carlos Beltran/399 3.00 8.00
T1RCKE Clayton Kershaw/299 6.00 15.00
T1RCM Carlos Martinez/299 3.00 8.00
T1RCSA Carlos Santana/199 3.00 8.00
T1RCY Christian Yelich/199 5.00 12.00
T1RDK Dallas Keuchel/199 3.00 8.00
T1RDO David Ortiz/299 4.00 10.00
T1RDP Dustin Pedroia/299 4.00 10.00
T1RDW David Wright/199 3.00 8.00
T1REE Edwin Encarnacion/399 4.00 10.00
T1REL Evan Longoria/299 3.00 8.00
T1RFH Felix Hernandez/199 3.00 8.00
T1RFL Francisco Lindor/299 4.00 10.00
T1RGSP George Springer/199 3.00 8.00
T1RGST Giancarlo Stanton/199 4.00 10.00
T1RHP Hunter Pence/299 3.00 8.00
T1RHR Hanley Ramirez/299 3.00 8.00
T1RI Ichiro Suzuki/199 5.00 12.00
T1RJAB Jose Abreu/399 4.00 10.00
T1RJBU Jose Bautista/399 3.00 8.00
T1RJBZ Javier Baez/399 5.00 12.00
T1RJC Jose Canseco/99 6.00 15.00
T1RJDA Johnny Damon/399 3.00 8.00
T1RJDE Jacob deGrom/399 8.00 20.00
T1RJE Jacoby Ellsbury/399 3.00 8.00
T1RJF Jose Fernandez/399 4.00 10.00
T1RJH Josh Harrison/299 2.50 6.00
T1RJK Jung Ho Kang/99 2.50 6.00
T1RJLE Jon Lester/299 3.00 8.00
T1RJLU Jonathan Lucroy/299 3.00 8.00
T1RJS Jorge Soler/199 4.00 10.00
T1RJVE Justin Verlander/199 4.00 10.00
T1RJVO Joey Votto/199 4.00 10.00
T1RKB Kris Bryant/399 8.00 20.00
T1RKC Kole Calhoun/399 2.50 6.00
T1RKP Kevin Plawecki/299 2.50 6.00
T1RKSE Kyle Seager/199 2.50 6.00
T1RKSU Kurt Suzuki/199 2.50 6.00
T1RKW Kolten Wong/199 3.00 8.00
T1RLD Lucas Duda/399 3.00 8.00
T1RMCA Miguel Cabrera/399 4.00 10.00
T1RMCR Matt Carpenter/299 4.00 10.00
T1RMH Matt Harvey/299 3.00 8.00
T1RMMA Manny Machado/299 4.00 10.00
T1RMMC Mark McGwire/299 6.00 15.00
T1RMPI Michael Pineda/299 2.50 6.00
T1RMTA Masahiro Tanaka/199 3.00 8.00
T1RMTE Mark Teixeira/199 3.00 8.00
T1RMTR Mike Trout/199 10.00 25.00
T1RNA Nolan Arenado/399 6.00 15.00
T1RPF Prince Fielder/399 3.00 8.00
T1RPG Paul Goldschmidt/399 4.00 10.00
T1RPS Pablo Sandoval/199 3.00 8.00
T1RRCA Robinson Cano/369 3.00 8.00
T1RRCL Roger Clemens/399 5.00 12.00
T1RRCS Rusney Castillo/99 2.50 6.00
T1RRH Ryan Howard/299 3.00 8.00
T1RSC Shin-Soo Choo/399 3.00 8.00
T1RSM Steven Matz/299 2.50 6.00
T1RTD Travis D'Arnaud/399 3.00 8.00
T1RTT Troy Tulowitzki/99 4.00 10.00
T1RVG Vladimir Guerrero/399 3.00 8.00
T1RVM Victor Martinez/299 3.00 8.00
T1RYM Yadier Molina/299 5.00 12.00
T1RYT Yasmany Tomas/199 2.50 6.00
T1RZW Zack Wheeler/199 3.00 8.00

2016 Topps Tier One Autograph Relics

STATED ODDS 1:10 MINI BOX
PRINT RUNS B/WN 50-149 COPIES PER
EXCHANGE DEADLINE 5/31/2018
*DUAL: .6X TO 1.5X BASIC
AT1RAG Alex Gordon/50 10.00 25.00
AT1RAJ Adam Jones/149 10.00 25.00
AT1RBB Byron Buxton/50 6.00 15.00
AT1RBP Buster Posey/50 40.00 100.00
AT1RCK Clayton Kershaw/50 50.00 120.00
AT1RCSA Chris Sale/149 12.00 30.00
AT1RCSE Corey Seager/149 30.00 80.00
AT1RDG Didi Gregorius/149 5.00 12.00
AT1RDK Dallas Keuchel/149 20.00 50.00
AT1RDL DJ LeMahieu/149 8.00 20.00
AT1RDO David Ortiz/99 40.00 100.00
AT1RDP Dustin Pedroia/149 15.00 40.00
AT1RDW David Wright/99 10.00 25.00
AT1RHO Henry Owens/149 5.00 12.00
AT1RKB Kris Bryant/50 75.00 200.00
AT1RKS Kyle Schwarber/149 12.00 30.00
AT1RMCA Matt Cain/50 5.00 12.00
AT1RMH Matt Harvey
AT1RMM Manny Machado/99 40.00 100.00
AT1RMT Mike Trout/50 150.00 400.00
AT1RNS Noah Syndergaard/75 25.00 60.00
AT1RRB Ryan Braun/99 10.00 25.00
AT1RRR Rob Refsnyder/149 5.00 12.00
AT1RSP Stephen Piscotty/149 6.00 15.00
AT1RWM Wil Myers/149 10.00 25.00

2016 Topps Tier One Autographs

STATED ODDS 1:23 MINI BOX
PRINT RUNS B/WN 30-99 COPIES PER
EXCHANGE DEADLINE 5/31/2018
T1ABH Bryce Harper/30 100.00 250.00
T1ABJ Bo Jackson/50 40.00 100.00
T1ABP Buster Posey/30 60.00 150.00
T1ACB Craig Biggio/75 10.00 25.00
T1ACC Carlos Correa/75 40.00 100.00
T1ACJ Chipper Jones/50 40.00 100.00
T1ACK Clayton Kershaw/75 60.00 150.00
T1ACR Cal Ripken Jr./50 50.00 120.00
T1ACY Carl Yastrzemski/75 40.00 100.00
T1AFT Frank Thomas/50 30.00 80.00
T1AGM Greg Maddux/30 40.00 100.00
T1AHA Hank Aaron
T1AI Ichiro Suzuki
T1AJB Johnny Bench/50 25.00 60.00
T1AKB Kris Bryant/75 75.00 200.00
T1AKG Ken Griffey Jr./30 75.00 200.00
T1AMM Mark McGwire/30 60.00 150.00
T1AMP Mike Piazza/30 50.00 120.00
T1AMT Mike Trout/50 150.00 400.00
T1ANR Nolan Ryan
T1AOS Ozzie Smith/50 15.00 40.00
T1ARC Roger Clemens/30 25.00 60.00
T1ARH Rickey Henderson/50 40.00 100.00
T1ARJA Reggie Jackson/30 25.00 60.00
T1ARJO Randy Johnson/30 25.00 60.00
T1ASC Steve Carlton/75 10.00 25.00
T1ASK Sandy Koufax/50 150.00 300.00
T1AYD Yu Darvish/30 40.00 100.00

2016 Topps Tier One Autographs Copper Ink

*COPPER: .6X TO 1.5X BASE p/r 75-99
STATED ODDS 1:32 MINI BOX
STATED PRINT RUN 25 SER.#'d SETS
EXCHANGE DEADLINE 5/31/2018
T1AHA Hank Aaron 125.00 250.00
T1AI Ichiro Suzuki 300.00 500.00
T1ANR Nolan Ryan 60.00 150.00

2016 Topps Tier One Breakout Autographs

RANDOM INSERTS IN PACKS*
PRINT RUNS B/WN 99-299 COPIES PER
EXCHANGE DEADLINE 5/31/2018
*COPPER/25: .6X TO 1.5X BASIC
BOAAC Alex Colome/299 3.00 8.00
BOAANL Aaron Nola/299 8.00 20.00
BOAANO Aaron Nola/299 8.00 20.00
BOABD Brandon Drury/299 5.00 12.00
BOABDR Brandon Drury/249 5.00 12.00
BOABH Brock Holt/299 5.00 12.00
BOABJ Brian Johnson/299 3.00 8.00
BOABSI Blake Swihart/299 4.00 10.00
BOABSW Blake Swihart/299 4.00 10.00
BOABYP Byung-Ho Park/249 4.00 10.00
BOACED Carl Edwards Jr./299 4.00 10.00
BOACEJ Carl Edwards Jr./249 4.00 10.00
BOACEW Carl Edwards Jr./299 4.00 10.00
BOACHE Chris Heston/299 3.00 8.00
BOACHS Chris Heston/299 3.00 8.00
BOACM Carlos Martinez/249 5.00 12.00
BOACRA Colin Rea/249 3.00 8.00
BOACRE Colin Rea/299 3.00 8.00
BOACRO Carlos Rodon/149 5.00 12.00
BOACSA Corey Seager/149 30.00 80.00
BOACSE Corey Seager/149 30.00 80.00
BOADP Dalton Pompey/299 4.00 10.00
BOADT Devon Travis/299 3.00 8.00
BOAER Eduardo Rodriguez/299 3.00 8.00
BOAFL Francisco Lindor/199 10.00 25.00
BOAGBI Greg Bird/249 4.00 10.00
BOAGBR Greg Bird/249 4.00 10.00
BOAHOE Henry Owens/299 4.00 10.00
BOAHOI Hector Olivera/299 4.00 10.00
BOAHOL Hector Olivera/299 4.00 10.00
BOAHOW Henry Owens/249 4.00 10.00
BOAJD Jacob deGrom/99 30.00 80.00
BOAJFA Jeurys Familia/299 4.00 10.00
BOAJGR Jon Gray/159 3.00 8.00
BOAJHA Jesse Hahn/299 3.00 8.00
BOAJPA Joe Panik/249 4.00 10.00
BOAJPD Joc Pederson/199 8.00 20.00
BOAJR J.T. Realmuto/299 20.00 50.00
BOAJS Jorge Soler/199 5.00 12.00
BOAKM Ketel Marte/299 6.00 15.00
BOAKMA Kenta Maeda/99 8.00 20.00
BOAKP Kevin Plawecki/299 3.00 8.00
BOAKSC Kyle Schwarber/199 15.00 40.00
BOAKWA Kyle Waldrop/299 4.00 10.00
BOAKWL Kyle Waldrop/249 4.00 10.00
BOAKWO Kolten Wong/299 4.00 10.00
BOALJ Luke Jackson/299 3.00 8.00
BOALSE Luis Severino/249 12.00 30.00
BOAMAL Miguel Almonte/299 3.00 8.00
BOAMCN Michael Conforto/199 8.00 20.00
BOAMDF Matt Duffy/299 6.00 15.00
BOAMDU Matt Duffy/299 6.00 15.00
BOAMRE Michael Reed/249 3.00 8.00
BOAMRY Matt Reynolds/249 3.00 8.00
BOAMSA Miguel Sano/199 8.00 20.00
BOAMSE Marcus Semien/299 5.00 12.00
BOAMSH Matt Shoemaker/299 4.00 10.00
BOAMSN Miguel Sano/199 8.00 20.00
BOAMT Michael Taylor/299 3.00 8.00
BOAMWI Matt Wisler/299 4.00 10.00
BOAMWM Mac Williamson/299 3.00 8.00
BOANS Noah Syndergaard/199 15.00 40.00
BOAPOB Peter O'Brien/299 3.00 8.00
BOARMO Raul Mondesi/249 6.00 15.00
BOARRF Rob Refsnyder/299 4.00 10.00
BOARRS Rob Refsnyder/299 4.00 10.00
BOARSA Richie Shaffer/249 3.00 8.00
BOARSH Richie Shaffer/299 3.00 8.00
BOASG Sonny Gray/199 4.00 10.00
BOASH Slade Heathcott/299 4.00 10.00
BOASMA Steven Matz/299 10.00 25.00
BOASMT Steven Matz/299 10.00 25.00
BOASPI Stephen Piscotty/299 5.00 12.00
BOASPS Stephen Piscotty/299 5.00 12.00
BOATH T.J. House/299 3.00 8.00
BOATMU Tom Murphy/249 3.00 8.00
BOATTR Trea Turner/249 8.00 20.00
BOATTU Trea Turner/249 8.00 20.00
BOAZL Zach Lee/299 3.00 8.00
BOAZLE Zach Lee/249 3.00 8.00
BOAZW Zack Wheeler/199 5.00 12.00

2016 Topps Tier One Clear One Autographs

STATED ODDS 1:48 MINI BOX
STATED PRINT RUN 25 SER.#'d SETS
EXCHANGE DEADLINE 5/31/2018
C1AAJ Adam Jones 15.00 40.00
C1AAM Andrew Miller 20.00 50.00
C1ABL Barry Larkin 25.00 60.00
C1ABW Bernie Williams 12.00 30.00
C1ACC Carlos Correa 25.00 60.00
C1ACS Corey Seager 25.00 60.00
C1ADK Dallas Keuchel 10.00 25.00
C1ADM Don Mattingly 25.00 60.00
C1ADP Dustin Pedroia 25.00 60.00
C1AHO Hector Olivera 6.00 15.00
C1AJA Jose Abreu 10.00 25.00
C1AJC Jose Canseco 20.00 50.00
C1AJF Jeurys Familia 15.00 40.00
C1AKS Kyle Schwarber 25.00 60.00
C1ALS Luis Severino 12.00 30.00
C1AMS Miguel Sano 8.00 20.00
C1AMT Mike Trout
C1APM Paul Molitor 15.00 40.00
C1APS Pablo Sandoval 6.00 15.00
C1ARC Rod Carew 15.00 40.00
C1ATT Troy Tulowitzki 10.00 25.00

2016 Topps Tier One Dual Autographs

STATED ODDS 1:63 MINI BOX
STATED PRINT RUN 25 SER.#'d SETS
EXCHANGE DEADLINE 5/31/2018
DAAG Alou/Galarraga EXCH 20.00 50.00
DABA Biggio/Altuve EXCH 60.00 150.00
DACA Altuve/Correa EXCH 40.00 100.00
DAET Encrncn/Tulo EXCH 25.00 60.00
DAGJ Gordon/Jackson 60.00 150.00
DAJR Jones/Robinson 50.00 120.00
DAKK Krshw/Kfx EXCH 600.00 1000.00
DALP Larkin/Phillips 50.00 120.00
DAOJ Jones/Olivera 25.00 60.00
DARG Gregorius/Refsnyder 20.00 50.00
DASM Syndrgrd/Matz EXCH 75.00 200.00
DATA Aaron/Trout 500.00 800.00

2016 Topps Tier One Legends Relics

STATED ODDS 1:16 MINI BOX
PRINT RUNS B/WN 75-149 COPIES PER
*DUAL/25: .6X TO 1.5X SNGL RELIC
T1RLBD Bobby Doerr/75 6.00 15.00
T1RLBF Bob Feller/75 8.00 20.00
T1RLCB Craig Biggio/149 5.00 12.00
T1RLCF Carlton Fisk/75 6.00 15.00
T1RLCR Cal Ripken Jr./149 8.00 20.00
T1RLGB George Brett/75 20.00 50.00
T1RLHA Hank Aaron/75 12.00 30.00
T1RLJG Josh Gibson/75 60.00 150.00
T1RLRA Roberto Alomar/149 6.00 15.00
T1RLRC Roberto Clemente
T1RLRFE Rick Ferrell/75 4.00 10.00
T1RLRFI Rollie Fingers/75 5.00 12.00
T1RLRM Roger Maris/75 12.00 30.00
T1RLSC Steve Carlton/75 5.00 12.00
T1RLTGW Tony Gwynn/149 5.00 12.00
T1RLTW Ted Williams/75 15.00 40.00
T1RLWB Wade Boggs/75 5.00 12.00
T1RLWSP Warren Spahn/75 5.00 12.00

2016 Topps Tier One Prime Performers Autographs

RANDOM INSERTS IN PACKS
PRINT RUNS B/WN 50-299 COPIES PER
EXCHANGE DEADLINE 5/31/2018
*CPPR/25: .6X TO 1.5X BASE p/r 99-299
*CPPR/25: .5X TO 1.2X BASE p/r 50
PPAD Andre Dawson/50 10.00 25.00
PPAE Alcides Escobar/249 6.00 15.00
PPAGA Andres Galarraga/249 5.00 12.00
PPAGN Adrian Gonzalez/50 6.00 15.00
PPAGO Alex Gordon/149 4.00 10.00
PPAJ Adam Jones/50 12.00 30.00
PPAK Al Kaline/99 12.00 30.00
PPAMI Andrew Miller/249 5.00 12.00
PPBBO Bret Boone/299 3.00 8.00
PPBL Barry Larkin/50 20.00 50.00
PPBMC Brian McCann/50 5.00 12.00
PPBMO Brandon Moss/249 3.00 8.00
PPBP Brandon Phillips/149 5.00 12.00
PPBW Bernie Williams/50 12.00 30.00
PPCDE Carlos Delgado/249 3.00 8.00
PPCDL Carlos Delgado/299 3.00 8.00
PPCF Carlton Fisk/50 12.00 30.00
PPCHA Cole Hamels/50 15.00 40.00
PPCHE Chase Headley/249 5.00 12.00
PPCK Corey Kluber/149 5.00 12.00
PPCSA Chris Sale/50 10.00 25.00
PPCSL Chris Sale/50 10.00 25.00
PPCY Christian Yelich/249 20.00 50.00
PPDE Dennis Eckersley/149 5.00 12.00
PPDGO Dee Gordon/249 3.00 8.00
PPDGR Didi Gregorius/249 4.00 10.00
PPDKE Dallas Keuchel/249 4.00 10.00
PPDMA Don Mattingly/50 25.00 60.00
PPDME Devin Mesoraco/249 3.00 8.00
PPDP Dustin Pedroia/50 15.00 40.00
PPDWR David Wright/50 10.00 25.00
PPEE Edwin Encarnacion/50 6.00 15.00
PPEL Evan Longoria/50 8.00 20.00
PPEM Edgar Martinez/149 6.00 15.00
PPFF Freddie Freeman/50 10.00 25.00
PPFM Fred McGriff/50 8.00 20.00
PPFR Frank Robinson/50 15.00 40.00
PPFVA Fernando Valenzuela/50 10.00 25.00
PPFVL Fernando Valenzuela/50 10.00 25.00
PPGR Garrett Richards EXCH 4.00 10.00
PPHR Hanley Ramirez/50 5.00 12.00
PPJA Jose Altuve/249 12.00 30.00
PPJG Juan Gonzalez/249 5.00 12.00
PPJHA Josh Harrison/249 3.00 8.00
PPJPA Jimmy Paredes/249 3.00 8.00
PPJR Jim Rice/249 6.00 15.00
PPJSH James Shields/249 3.00 8.00
PPJSM John Smoltz/50 15.00 40.00
PPKSE Kyle Seager/249 3.00 8.00
PPKSU Kurt Suzuki/299 3.00 8.00
PPLD Lucas Duda/249 4.00 10.00
PPLG Luis Gonzalez/249 4.00 10.00
PPMCA Matt Cain/50 5.00 12.00
PPMMA Mike Matheny/249 8.00 20.00
PPMMC Manny Machado/50 30.00 80.00
PPMP Mark Prior/249 4.00 10.00
PPMT Mark Teixeira/99 4.00 10.00
PPMWI Matt Williams/229 4.00 10.00
PPMZ Mike Zunino/249 3.00 8.00
PPNEO Nathan Eovaldi/299 4.00 10.00
PPNEV Nathan Eovaldi/249 4.00 10.00
PPNG Nomar Garciaparra/50 20.00 50.00
PPOC Orlando Cepeda/149 4.00 10.00
PPOVI Omar Vizquel/249 6.00 15.00
PPOVZ Omar Vizquel/249 6.00 15.00
PPPMO Paul Molitor/50 10.00 25.00
PPPN Phil Niekro/99 6.00 15.00
PPPO Paul O'Neill/149 8.00 20.00
PPPS Pablo Sandoval/50 5.00 12.00
PPRA Roberto Alomar/50 15.00 40.00
PPRB Ryan Braun/50 10.00 25.00
PPRCA Rod Carew/50 15.00 40.00
PPRCN Robinson Cano/50 12.00 30.00
PPRPA Rafael Palmeiro/99 6.00 15.00
PPRPO Rick Porcello/249 4.00 10.00
PPRS Ryne Sandberg/50 20.00 50.00
PPRY Robin Yount/50 20.00 50.00
PPSGE Shawn Green/299 3.00 8.00
PPSGR Shawn Green/249 3.00 8.00
PPSMA Starling Marte/249 5.00 12.00
PPSMT Starling Marte/299 5.00 12.00
PPTG Tom Glavine/50 12.00 30.00
PPTT Troy Tulowitzki/50 6.00 15.00
PPVCO Vince Coleman/249 5.00 12.00
PPVV Vince Coleman/249 5.00 12.00
PPWMY Wil Myers/99 4.00 10.00
PPYGO Yan Gomes/249 3.00 8.00
PPYGR Yasmani Grandal/249 5.00 12.00

2017 Topps Tier One Relics

RANDOM INSERTS IN PACKS
PRINT RUNS B/WN 225-331 COPIES PER
*DUAL/25: .6X TO 1.5X SNGL RELIC
T1RAB Alex Bregman/331 5.00 12.00
T1RABE Andrew Benintendi/331 8.00 20.00
T1RAJ Aaron Judge/331 20.00 50.00
T1RAM Andrew McCutchen/331 5.00 12.00
T1RAPU Albert Pujols/331 4.00 10.00
T1RAR Anthony Rizzo/331 5.00 12.00
T1RARE Alex Reyes/331 2.50 6.00
T1RARU Addison Russell/331 3.00 8.00
T1RBB Brandon Belt/331 2.50 6.00
T1RBD Brian Dozier/331 3.00 8.00
T1RBH Bryce Harper/331 5.00 12.00
T1RBHA Billy Hamilton/331 2.50 6.00
T1RBP Buster Posey/331 4.00 10.00
T1RBZ Ben Zobrist/331 3.00 8.00
T1RCA Chris Archer/331 2.00 5.00
T1RCC Carlos Correa/331 3.00 8.00
T1RCD Chris Davis/225 2.00 5.00
T1RCG Carlos Gonzalez/331 2.50 6.00
T1RCK Clayton Kershaw/331 4.00 10.00
T1RCKL Corey Kluber/331 2.50 6.00
T1RCSE Corey Seager/331 3.00 8.00
T1RCY Christian Yelich/331 4.00 10.00
T1RDB Dellin Betances/331 2.50 6.00
T1RDD David Dahl/331 2.50 6.00
T1RDL DJ LeMahieu/331 3.00 8.00
T1RDM Daniel Murphy/331 2.50 6.00
T1RDP Dustin Pedroia/331 3.00 8.00
T1RDS Dansby Swanson/331 5.00 12.00
T1REH Eric Hosmer/331 2.50 6.00
T1RFF Freddie Freeman/331 4.00 10.00
T1RFH Felix Hernandez/331 2.50 6.00
T1RGP Gregory Polanco/331 2.50 6.00
T1RGS Giancarlo Stanton/331 3.00 8.00
T1RGSA Gary Sanchez/331 6.00 15.00
T1RGSP George Springer/331 2.50 6.00
T1RHR Hunter Renfroe/331 2.50 6.00
T1RJA Jake Arrieta/331 2.50 6.00
T1RJB Jackie Bradley Jr./331 3.00 8.00
T1RJC Johnny Cueto/331 2.50 6.00
T1RJD Josh Donaldson/331 2.50 6.00
T1RJDE Jacob deGrom/331 6.00 15.00
T1RJL Jon Lester/331 2.50 6.00
T1RJM J.D. Martinez/331 3.00 8.00
T1RJV Joey Votto/331 3.00 8.00
T1RJVE Justin Verlander/331 3.00 8.00
T1RKB Kris Bryant/331 4.00 10.00
T1RKS Kyle Seager/331 2.00 5.00
T1RKSC Kyle Schwarber/331 3.00 8.00
T1RLW Luke Weaver/331 2.50 6.00
T1RMB Mookie Betts/331 6.00 15.00
T1RMC Miguel Cabrera/331 3.00 8.00
T1RMCA Matt Carpenter/331 3.00 8.00
T1RMM Manny Machado/331 3.00 8.00
T1RMS Max Scherzer
T1RMT Mike Trout/331 15.00 40.00
T1RMTA Masahiro Tanaka/331 2.50 6.00
T1RNA Nolan Arenado/331 5.00 12.00
T1RNC Nelson Cruz/331 3.00 8.00
T1RNS Noah Syndergaard/331 2.50 6.00
T1RPG Paul Goldschmidt/331 3.00 8.00
T1RRB Ryan Braun/331 2.50 6.00
T1RRC Robinson Cano/331 2.50 6.00
T1RRG Robert Gsellman/331 2.00 5.00
T1RRO Rougned Odor/331 2.50 6.00
T1RSM Starling Marte/331 2.50 6.00
T1RSP Stephen Piscotty/331 2.50 6.00
T1RSS Stephen Strasburg/331 3.00 8.00
T1RTF Todd Frazier/331 2.00 5.00
T1RTG Tyler Glasnow/331 8.00 20.00
T1RTS Trevor Story/331 3.00 8.00
T1RWM Wil Myers/331 2.50 6.00
T1RXB Xander Bogaerts/331 3.00 8.00
T1RYG Yulieski Gurriel/331 3.00 8.00
T1RZB Zach Britton/331 2.50 6.00
T1RZG Zack Greinke/331 3.00 8.00

2017 Topps Tier One Autograph Relics

STATED ODDS 1:9 HOBBY
PRINT RUNS B/WN 20-100 COPIES PER
EXCHANGE DEADLINE 5/31/2018
*DUAL/25: .6X TO 1.5X BASIC
T1ARABE Andrew Benintendi/75 30.00 80.00
T1ARABR Alex Bregman/65 20.00 50.00
T1ARAG Alex Gordon/50 10.00 25.00
T1ARAJ Aaron Judge/100 100.00 250.00
T1ARARD A.J. Reed/100 4.00 10.00
T1ARARE Alex Reyes/75 5.00 12.00
T1ARARY Alex Reyes/75 5.00 12.00
T1ARBB Brandon Belt/75 5.00 12.00
T1ARCC Carlos Correa/30 30.00 80.00
T1ARCD Chris Davis/30 10.00 25.00
T1ARCH Cole Hamels/20 12.00 30.00
T1ARCKE Clayton Kershaw/30 50.00 120.00
T1ARCKL Corey Kluber/40 15.00 40.00
T1ARCS Corey Seager/30 30.00 80.00
T1ARDD David Dahl/75 6.00 15.00
T1ARDP David Price/50 8.00 20.00
T1AREL Evan Longoria/30 10.00 25.00
T1ARFF Freddie Freeman/30 20.00 50.00
T1ARJA Jose Altuve/65 30.00 80.00
T1ARJBE Josh Bell
T1ARJC Jose Canseco/100 20.00 50.00
T1ARJD Jacob deGrom/50 25.00 60.00
T1ARJMR J.D. Martinez/75 15.00 40.00
T1ARJPA Joe Panik/75 5.00 12.00
T1ARJPE Joc Pederson/35 10.00 25.00
T1ARJT Julio Teheran/100 6.00 15.00
T1ARKB Kris Bryant/30 60.00 150.00
T1ARKK Kevin Kiermaier/60 6.00 15.00
T1ARKMA Kenta Maeda/60
T1ARKS Kyle Schwarber
T1ARLS Luis Severino/75 10.00 25.00
T1ARLW Luke Weaver/100 5.00 12.00
T1ARMCA Matt Carpenter/65 6.00 15.00
T1ARMCO Michael Conforto/65 12.00 30.00
T1ARMFR Maikel Franco/30 15.00 40.00
T1ARMFU Michael Fulmer/70 8.00 20.00
T1ARMM Manny Machado/30 50.00 120.00
T1ARMST Marcus Stroman/40 8.00 20.00
T1ARNM Nomar Mazara/75 4.00 10.00
T1ARNS Noah Syndergaard/50 10.00 25.00
T1ARPF Prince Fielder/30
T1ARRB Ryan Braun/30 10.00 25.00
T1ARRP Rick Porcello/75 5.00 12.00
T1ARSMA Starling Marte/30 5.00 12.00
T1ARSMZ Steven Matz/100 4.00 10.00
T1ARSP Stephen Piscotty/75 5.00 12.00
T1ARTG Tyler Glasnow/100 12.00 30.00
T1ARWC Willson Contreras/30 12.00 30.00
T1ARWM Wil Myers/26
T1ARYC Yoenis Cespedes/30 10.00 25.00

2017 Topps Tier One Autographs

STATED ODDS 1:20 HOBBY
PRINT RUNS B/WN 11-99 COPIES PER
EXCHANGE DEADLINE 6/30/2019
NO PRICING ON QTY 11
*CPPR/25: .6X TO 1.5X BASE p/r 99
*CPPR/25: .5X TO 1.2X BASE p/r 30
*CPPR/25: .4X TO 1X BASE p/r 25
T1ABH Bryce Harper/20 75.00 200.00
T1ABJ Bo Jackson/30 30.00 80.00
T1ABP Buster Posey/25 60.00 150.00
T1ACC Carlos Correa/99 20.00 50.00
T1ACJ Chipper Jones/30 40.00 100.00
T1ACK Clayton Kershaw/30 40.00 100.00
T1ACR Cal Ripken Jr./30 60.00 150.00
T1ADJ Derek Jeter/11
T1ADM Don Mattingly/99 25.00 60.00
T1ADO David Ortiz/75 20.00 50.00
T1AFT Frank Thomas/99 20.00 50.00
T1AGM Greg Maddux/20 40.00 100.00
T1AI Ichiro/20 200.00 400.00
T1AIR Ivan Rodriguez/99 12.00 30.00
T1AJB Johnny Bench/30 30.00 80.00
T1AKB Kris Bryant/30 75.00 200.00
T1AKG Ken Griffey Jr./20 150.00 300.00
T1AMMA Manny Machado/30 15.00 40.00
T1AMMG Mark McGwire/30 40.00 100.00
T1AMP Mike Piazza/30
T1AMTA Masahiro Tanaka/20 150.00 300.00
T1AMTR Mike Trout/20 200.00 400.00
T1ANR Nolan Ryan/30 60.00 150.00
T1AOV Omar Vizquel/30 5.00 12.00
T1ARB Ryan Braun/30 8.00 20.00
T1ARCA Rod Carew/30 12.00 30.00
T1ARCL Roger Clemens/20 40.00 100.00
T1ARH Rickey Henderson/30 25.00 60.00
T1ARJA Reggie Jackson/30 25.00 60.00
T1ARJO Randy Johnson/20 30.00 80.00
T1ARS Ryne Sandberg/99 20.00 50.00
T1ASC Steve Carlton/30 12.00 30.00
T1ASK Sandy Koufax
T1ATG Tom Glavine/99 12.00 30.00

2017 Topps Tier One Break Out Autographs

RANDOM INSERTS IN PACKS
PRINT RUNS B/WN 50-300 COPIES PER
EXCHANGE DEADLINE 6/30/2019
*CPPR/25: .6X TO 1.5X BASE p/r 60-300
*CPPR/25: .5X TO 1.2X BASE p/r 50
BOAAB Andrew Benintendi/90 40.00 100.00
BOAABR Alex Bregman/60 25.00 60.00
BOAAC Adam Conley/300 3.00 8.00
BOAADA Aledmys Diaz/140 4.00 10.00
BOAADI Aledmys Diaz/140 4.00 10.00
BOAAJD Aaron Judge/140 200.00 400.00
BOAAJR A.J. Reed/300 3.00 8.00
BOAAJU Aaron Judge/140 200.00 400.00
BOAANL Aaron Nola/300 4.00 10.00
BOAANO Aaron Nola/300 4.00 10.00
BOAARD A.J. Reed/300 3.00 8.00
BOAARE Alex Reyes/140 4.00 10.00
BOAARY Alex Reyes/140 4.00 10.00
BOABM Bruce Maxwell/300 3.00 8.00
BOABS Blake Snell/300 4.00 10.00
BOABSN Blake Snell/300 4.00 10.00
BOACF Carson Fulmer/150 3.00 8.00
BOACP Chad Pinder/300 3.00 8.00
BOACRD Cody Reed/300 3.00 8.00
BOACRE Cody Reed/300 3.00 8.00
BOADDA David Dahl/140 4.00 10.00
BOADDH David Dahl/140 4.00 10.00
BOADG Didi Gregorius/140 20.00 50.00
BOADS Dansby Swanson/60 20.00 50.00
BOAEDD Eddie Rosario/300 4.00 10.00
BOAEI Ender Inciarte/171 8.00 20.00
BOAER Eddie Rosario/300 4.00 10.00
BOAGB Greg Bird/180 4.00 10.00
BOAGM German Marquez/297 5.00 12.00
BOAHD Hunter Dozier/140 4.00 10.00
BOAHOE Henry Owens EXCH 3.00 8.00
BOAHOW Henry Owens EXCH 3.00 8.00
BOAHR Hunter Renfroe/180 5.00 12.00
BOAHRE Hunter Renfroe/200 5.00 12.00
BOAJA Jorge Alfaro/300 4.00 10.00
BOAJBA Javier Baez/65 10.00 25.00
BOAJBZ Javier Baez/65 10.00 25.00
BOAJCO Jharel Cotton/300 3.00 8.00
BOAJCT Jharel Cotton/300 3.00 8.00
BOAJD Jose De Leon/90 3.00 8.00
BOAJG Jon Gray/85 3.00 8.00
BOAJH Jeremy Hazelbaker/300 4.00 10.00
BOAJHO Jeff Hoffman/200 6.00 15.00
BOAJJ JaCoby Jones/140 6.00 15.00
BOAJM Joe Musgrove/300 10.00 25.00
BOAJPA Joe Panik/120 4.00 10.00
BOAJPN Joe Panik/120 4.00 10.00
BOAJT Jameson Taillon/85 4.00 10.00
BOAJU Julio Urias/50 5.00 12.00
BOAKG Ken Giles/300 3.00 8.00
BOAKS Kyle Schwarber/65 15.00 40.00
BOALG Lucas Giolito/65 8.00 20.00
BOALSE Luis Severino/90 8.00 20.00
BOALSV Luis Severino/90 8.00 20.00
BOALWA Luke Weaver/200 4.00 10.00
BOALWE Luke Weaver/200 4.00 10.00
BOAMFA Maikel Franco/100 4.00 10.00
BOAMFL Michael Fulmer/150 8.00 20.00
BOAMFR Maikel Franco/100 4.00 10.00
BOAMFU Michael Fulmer/150 8.00 20.00
BOAMK Max Kepler/300 4.00 10.00
BOAMKE Max Kepler/300 4.00 10.00
BOAMM Manny Margot/300 3.00 8.00
BOAMO Matt Olson/300 6.00 15.00
BOAMSA Miguel Sano/90 6.00 15.00
BOANM Nomar Mazara/85 6.00 15.00
BOARG Randal Grichuk/200 8.00 20.00
BOARGE Robert Gsellman/300 3.00 8.00
BOARGR Randal Grichuk/200 8.00 20.00
BOARGS Robert Gsellman/300 3.00 8.00
BOARHA Ryon Healy/300 4.00 10.00
BOARHE Ryon Healy/300 4.00 10.00
BOARLO Reynaldo Lopez/300 3.00 8.00
BOARLP Reynaldo Lopez/300 3.00 8.00
BOARQI Roman Quinn/300 3.00 8.00
BOARQU Roman Quinn/300 3.00 8.00
BOARSC Ryan Schimpf/300 3.00 8.00
BOARST Robert Stephenson/300 3.00 8.00

BOART Raimel Tapia/200 4.00 10.00
BOASLU Seth Lugo/300 3.00 8.00
BOASP Stephen Piscotty/85 4.00 10.00
BOASPI Stephen Piscotty/85 4.00 10.00
BOATAS Tyler Austin/300 4.00 10.00
BOATAU Tyler Austin/300 4.00 10.00
BOATB Ty Blach/295 3.00 8.00
BOATCN Tim Cooney/300 3.00 8.00
BOATCO Tim Cooney/300 3.00 8.00
BOATG Tyler Glasnow/200 10.00 25.00
BOATGL Tyler Glasnow/200 10.00 25.00
BOATMA Trey Mancini/300 15.00 40.00
BOATMN Trey Mancini/300 15.00 40.00
BOATNA Tyler Naquin/300 5.00 12.00
BOATNQ Tyler Naquin/300 5.00 12.00
BOATSO Trevor Story/140 5.00 12.00
BOATST Trevor Story/140 5.00 12.00
BOATTH Trayce Thompson/300 4.00 10.00
BOATTO Trayce Thompson/300 4.00 10.00
BOATTR Trea Turner/200 10.00 25.00
BOATTU Trea Turner/200 10.00 25.00
BOAWC Willson Contreras/50 12.00 30.00
BOAWCO Willson Contreras/50 12.00 30.00
BOAYG Yulieski Gurriel/65 10.00 25.00
BOAYMO Yoan Moncada

2017 Topps Tier One Dual Autographs

STATED ODDS 1:67 MINI BOX
STATED PRINT RUN 25 SER.#'d SETS
EXCHANGE DEADLINE 6/30/2019
DABS Crra/Brgmn EXCH 75.00 200.00
DAFS Swanson/Freeman 100.00 250.00
DAGB Griffey/Bonds EXCH 700.00 900.00
DAGR Gnzlz/Rdrgz EXCH 60.00 150.00
DAGV Glrrga/Vizquel EXCH 30.00 80.00
DAHT Harper/Turner
DAJS Smoltz/Jones EXCH
DAKS Seager/Kershaw 300.00 500.00
DAMB Mncda/Bnntndi EXCH 150.00 400.00
DAOW Oswalt/Wagner 12.00 30.00
DASG Glavine/Smoltz 60.00 150.00
DATB Bryant/Trout
DAVL Lndr/Vzql EXCH
DAVU Valenzuela/Urias 25.00 60.00

2017 Topps Tier One Legend Relics

STATED ODDS 1:7 MINI BOX
PRINT RUNS B/WN 25-200 COPIES PER
T1RLBR Babe Ruth/30 60.00 150.00
T1RLCJ Chipper Jones/200 4.00 10.00
T1RLCR Cal Ripken Jr./200 8.00 20.00
T1RLCY Carl Yastrzemski/200 5.00 12.00
T1RLDJ Derek Jeter/200 15.00 40.00
T1RLDS Duke Snider
T1RLEB Ernie Banks/25 15.00 40.00
T1RLES Enos Slaughter/200 4.00 10.00
T1RLFT Frank Thomas/200 4.00 10.00
T1RLGB George Brett/200 8.00 20.00
T1RLGC Gary Carter/100 3.00 8.00
T1RLGM Greg Maddux/200 5.00 12.00
T1RLHA Hank Aaron/200 10.00 25.00
T1RLJB Johnny Bench/200 5.00 12.00
T1RLJR Jackie Robinson/40 20.00 50.00
T1RLKGJ Ken Griffey Jr./200 10.00 25.00
T1RLMM Mark McGwire/200 6.00 15.00
T1RLMP Mike Piazza/200 4.00 10.00
T1RLNR Nolan Ryan/200 8.00 20.00
T1RLPR Phil Rizzuto/100 5.00 12.00
T1RLRC Roberto Clemente/200 20.00 50.00
T1RLRJ Randy Johnson/200 4.00 10.00
T1RLRM Roger Maris
T1RLTC Ty Cobb/60 30.00 80.00
T1RLTW Ted Williams/200 12.00 30.00
T1RLWS Willie Stargell

2017 Topps Tier One Legend Dual Relics

*DUAL: .6X TO 1.5X BASIC
STATED ODDS 1:41 MINI BOX
STATED PRINT RUN 25 SER.#'d SETS
T1RLBR Babe Ruth 125.00 300.00
T1RLCR Cal Ripken Jr. 30.00 80.00
T1RLCY Carl Yastrzemski 20.00 50.00
T1RLDJ Derek Jeter 60.00 150.00
T1RLGB George Brett 20.00 50.00
T1RLHA Hank Aaron 40.00 100.00
T1RLNR Nolan Ryan 20.00 50.00
T1RLRM Roger Maris 10.00 25.00
T1RLTW Ted Williams 30.00 80.00
T1RLWS Willie Stargell 25.00 60.00

2017 Topps Tier One Prime Performers Autographs

RANDOM INSERTS IN PACKS
PRINT RUNS B/WN 30-300 COPIES PER
EXCHANGE DEADLINE 6/30/2019
*CPPR/25: .6X TO 1.5X BASE p/r 65-300
*CPPR/25: .4X TO 1X BASE p/r 30-40
PPAADU Adam Duvall/300 6.00 15.00
PPAADV Adam Duvall/300 6.00 15.00
PPAAGA Andres Galarraga/200 4.00 10.00
PPAAGR Andres Galarraga/200 4.00 10.00
PPAAJ Adam Jones/65 8.00 20.00
PPAAPE Andy Pettitte/40 20.00 50.00
PPAARI Anthony Rizzo/75 20.00 50.00
PPABA Bobby Abreu/100 6.00 15.00
PPABF Brandon Finnegan/300 4.00 10.00
PPABL Barry Larkin EXCH 15.00 40.00
PPACCO Carlos Correa EXCH 40.00 100.00
PPACCR Carlos Carrasco/300 5.00 12.00
PPACJ Chipper Jones/30 40.00 100.00
PPACSA Chris Sale/65 20.00 50.00
PPACSC Curt Schilling/40 6.00 15.00
PPACSE Corey Seager/40 30.00 80.00
PPADBE Dellin Betances/200 4.00 10.00
PPADBT Dellin Betances/200 4.00 10.00
PPADDF Danny Duffy/300 3.00 8.00
PPADDU Danny Duffy/300 3.00 8.00
PPADFO Dexter Fowler/100 6.00 15.00
PPADFW Dexter Fowler/100 6.00 15.00
PPADGR Dee Gordon/100 3.00 8.00
PPADL Derrek Lee/200 4.00 10.00
PPADMA Don Mattingly/30 30.00 80.00
PPADO David Ortiz/30 40.00 100.00
PPADPE Dustin Pedroia/40 15.00 40.00
PPADPM Drew Pomeranz/200 5.00 12.00
PPADPO Drew Pomeranz/200 5.00 12.00
PPADPR David Price/40 10.00 25.00
PPAEE Edwin Encarnacion EXCH 10.00 25.00
PPAFF Freddie Freeman/65 15.00 40.00
PPAFLI Francisco Lindor EXCH 20.00 50.00
PPAFLN Francisco Lindor EXCH 20.00 50.00
PPAFR Frank Robinson/30 20.00 50.00
PPAFT Frank Thomas/30 20.00 50.00
PPAFV Fernando Valenzuela/65 15.00 40.00
PPAGS George Springer/200 12.00 30.00
PPAIR Ivan Rodriguez/40 15.00 40.00
PPAJAL Jose Altuve/100 20.00 50.00
PPAJAT Jose Altuve/100 20.00 50.00
PPAJCA Jose Canseco/300 8.00 20.00
PPAJCN Jose Canseco/300 8.00 20.00
PPAJDE Jacob deGrom EXCH 20.00 50.00
PPAJDG Jacob deGrom EXCH 20.00 50.00
PPAJFA Jeurys Familia/300 4.00 10.00
PPAJFM Jeurys Familia/300 4.00 10.00
PPAJH Jason Heyward/40 5.00 12.00
PPAJMA J.D. Martinez/100 12.00 30.00
PPAJMR J.D. Martinez/175 12.00 30.00
PPAJOE John Olerud/300 10.00 25.00
PPAJOL John Olerud/300 10.00 25.00
PPAJRC Jim Rice/100 5.00 12.00
PPAJRI Jim Rice/100 5.00 12.00
PPAJS John Smoltz/40 12.00 30.00
PPAJTR Justin Turner/300 10.00 25.00
PPAJTU Justin Turner/300 10.00 25.00
PPAJV Jason Varitek/40 10.00 25.00
PPAKB Kris Bryant EXCH 75.00 200.00
PPAKDA Khris Davis/300 5.00 12.00
PPAKDV Khris Davis/300 5.00 12.00
PPAKH Kelvin Herrera/300 4.00 10.00
PPAKMA Kenta Maeda/65 8.00 20.00
PPAKMO Kendrys Morales/200 3.00 8.00
PPAKSA Kyle Seager/200 3.00 8.00
PPAKSE Kyle Seager/200 3.00 8.00
PPALB Lou Brock/65 12.00 30.00
PPAMCA Matt Carpenter/100 5.00 12.00
PPAMCR Matt Carpenter/100 5.00 12.00
PPAMMA Manny Machado/30 60.00 150.00
PPAMML Mark Mulder/300 3.00 8.00
PPAMMU Mark Mulder/300 3.00 8.00
PPAMW Matt Wieters/40 6.00 15.00
PPANSN Noah Syndergaard/85 15.00 40.00
PPANSY Noah Syndergaard/85 15.00 40.00
PPAOG Ozzie Guillen/200 5.00 12.00
PPAOS Ozzie Smith/40 15.00 40.00
PPAOVI Omar Vizquel/200 4.00 10.00
PPAOVZ Omar Vizquel/200 4.00 10.00
PPAPF Prince Fielder/30 6.00 15.00
PPAPK Paul Konerko/65 8.00 20.00
PPAPN Phil Niekro/65 4.00 10.00
PPARA Roberto Alomar/40 12.00 30.00
PPARB Ryan Braun/40 10.00 25.00
PPARC Rod Carew/40 15.00 40.00
PPARO Roy Oswalt/200 5.00 12.00
PPARS Ryne Sandberg/30 20.00 50.00
PPARY Robin Yount/30 25.00 60.00
PPASA Sandy Alomar Jr./300 5.00 12.00
PPASMA Steven Matz/300 3.00 8.00
PPASME Starling Marte/200 4.00 10.00
PPASMR Starling Marte/200 4.00 10.00
PPASMT Steven Matz/300 3.00 8.00
PPASWI Steven Wright/300 3.00 8.00
PPASWR Steven Wright/300 3.00 8.00
PPAWB Wade Boggs/30 15.00 40.00
PPAWDA Wade Davis/300 3.00 8.00
PPAWDV Wade Davis/300 3.00 8.00

2018 Topps Tier One Relics

RANDOM INSERTS IN PACKS
PRINT RUNS B/WN 335-400 COPIES PER
*DUAL/25: .6X TO 1.5X SNGL RELIC
T1RAB Andrew Benintendi/335 4.00 10.00
T1RABR Alex Bregman/335 3.00 8.00
T1RAD Adam Duvall/335 2.50 6.00
T1RAJO Adam Jones/335 2.50 6.00
T1RAM Andrew McCutchen/335 3.00 8.00
T1RAMI Andrew Miller/335 2.50 6.00
T1RAN Aaron Nola/335 2.50 6.00
T1RAP A.J. Pollock/335 2.00 5.00
T1RAR Amed Rosario/400 2.50 6.00
T1RARE Anthony Rendon/335 3.00 8.00
T1RARU Addison Russell/335 2.50 6.00
T1RBB Byron Buxton/335 3.00 8.00
T1RBH Bryce Harper/400 5.00 12.00
T1RBP Buster Posey/335 4.00 10.00
T1RBZ Ben Zobrist/335 2.50 6.00
T1RCA Chris Archer/335 2.00 5.00
T1RCB Charlie Blackmon/400 3.00 8.00
T1RCBE Cody Bellinger/335 5.00 12.00
T1RCC Carlos Correa/335 3.00 8.00
T1RCF Clint Frazier/400 4.00 10.00
T1RCK Clayton Kershaw/335 5.00 12.00
T1RCKI Craig Kimbrel/335 2.50 6.00
T1RCKL Corey Kluber/335 2.50 6.00
T1RCM Carlos Martinez/335 2.50 6.00
T1RCS Chris Sale/400 3.00 8.00
T1RCSE Corey Seager/335 3.00 8.00
T1RCY Christian Yelich/335 4.00 10.00
T1RDB Dellin Betances/335 2.50 6.00
T1RDG Didi Gregorius/335 2.50 6.00
T1RDK Dallas Keuchel/335 2.50 6.00
T1RDM Daniel Murphy/335 2.50 6.00
T1RDP Drew Pomeranz/335 2.00 5.00
T1RDS Dominic Smith/335 2.50 6.00
T1RGS Giancarlo Stanton/335 4.00 10.00
T1RGSP George Springer/335 2.50 6.00
T1RIH Ian Happ/335 2.50 6.00
T1RIK Ian Kinsler/335 2.50 6.00
T1RJA Jose Altuve/400 2.50 6.00
T1RJD Josh Donaldson/335 2.50 6.00
T1RJF Jack Flahorty/335 4.00 10.00
T1RJG Joey Gallo/335 2.50 6.00
T1RJH Josh Harrison/335 2.00 5.00
T1RJL Jake Lamb/335 2.50 6.00
T1RJLE Jon Lester/335 2.50 6.00
T1RJS Jonathan Schoop/335 2.00 5.00
T1RJT Justin Turner/335 3.00 8.00
T1RJV Joey Votto/335 3.00 8.00
T1RKB Kris Bryant/400 6.00 15.00
T1RKJ Kenley Jansen/335 2.50 6.00
T1RKS Kyle Seager/335 2.00 5.00
T1RLM Lance McCullers/335 2.00 5.00
T1RLS Luis Severino/400 2.50 6.00
T1RMB Mookie Betts/400 6.00 15.00
T1RMBR Michael Brantley/335 2.50 6.00
T1RMC Miguel Cabrera/335 3.00 8.00
T1RMCO Michael Conforto/335 2.50 6.00
T1RMF Michael Fulmer/335 2.00 5.00
T1RMM Manny Machado/400 3.00 8.00
T1RMO Marcell Ozuna/335 3.00 8.00
T1RMOL Matt Olson/335 3.00 8.00
T1RMS Max Scherzer/400 3.00 8.00
T1RMSA Miguel Sano/335 2.50 6.00
T1RMT Mike Trout/400 12.00 30.00
T1RMTA Masahiro Tanaka/335 2.50 6.00
T1RNA Nolan Arenado/400 5.00 12.00
T1RNC Nelson Cruz/335 3.00 8.00
T1RNS Noah Syndergaard/335 2.50 6.00
T1RPG Paul Goldschmidt/400 3.00 8.00
T1RRC Robinson Cano/335 2.50 6.00
T1RRD Rafael Devers/400 4.00 10.00
T1RRH Rhys Hoskins/335 5.00 12.00
T1RRI Raisel Iglesias/335 2.50 6.00
T1RRM Ryan McMahon/335 5.00 12.00
T1RRO Roberto Osuna/335 2.00 5.00
T1RROD Rougned Odor/335 2.50 6.00
T1RSC Starlin Castro/335 2.00 5.00
T1RSN Sean Newcomb/335 2.50 6.00
T1RSP Salvador Perez/335 2.50 6.00
T1RSS Stephen Strasburg/335 3.00 8.00
T1RSSO Steven Souza Jr./335 2.50 6.00
T1RTP Tommy Pham/335 2.00 5.00
T1RTS Trevor Story/335 3.00 8.00
T1RVR Victor Robles/335 4.00 10.00
T1RWC Willson Contreras/335 3.00 8.00
T1RWM Wil Myers/335 2.50 6.00
T1RYG Yuli Gurriel/335 2.50 6.00
T1RYM Yadier Molina/335 4.00 10.00
T1RYP Yasiel Puig/335 3.00 8.00
T1RZG Zack Greinke/335 3.00 8.00

2018 Topps Tier One Autograph Relics

STATED ODDS 1:9 HOBBY
PRINT RUNS B/WN 5-100 COPIES PER
NO PRICING ON QTY 10 OR LESS
EXCHANGE DEADLINE 4/30/2020
ATRAB Adrian Beltre/35 25.00 60.00
ATRABR Alex Bregman/60 12.00 30.00
ATRAP Andy Pettitte/35 15.00 40.00
ATRAPO A.J. Pollock/25 6.00 15.00
ATRAR Amed Rosario/70 5.00 12.00
ATRARE Anthony Rendon/100 12.00 30.00
ATRBG Brett Gardner/60 10.00 25.00
ATRBS Blake Snell/100 8.00 20.00
ATRCB Charlie Blackmon/90 8.00 20.00
ATRCC Carlos Correa
ATRCF Clint Frazier/80 12.00 30.00
ATRCK Craig Kimbrel/55 8.00 20.00
ATRCSA Chris Sale/45 10.00 25.00
ATRCSI Chance Sisco/100 5.00 12.00
ATRDG Didi Gregorius/100 15.00 40.00
ATRDP David Price/35 8.00 20.00
ATRDPO Drew Pomeranz/90 4.00 10.00
ATRDW Dave Winfield/15 20.00 50.00
ATRFF Freddie Freeman/45 12.00 30.00
ATRFM Fred McGriff/35 15.00 40.00
ATRGS Gary Sanchez/55 15.00 40.00
ATRHB Harrison Bader/100 6.00 15.00
ATRJB Jose Berrios/70 5.00 12.00
ATRJC J.P. Crawford/100 8.00 20.00
ATRJG Joey Gallo/70 5.00 12.00
ATRJH Josh Harrison/100 5.00 12.00
ATRJJ JaCoby Jones/100 5.00 12.00
ATRKB Kris Bryant/15 75.00 200.00
ATRKGJ Ken Griffey Jr.
ATRLS Lucas Sims/100 4.00 10.00
ATRMF Michael Fulmer/62 4.00 10.00
ATRMK Max Kepler/100 5.00 12.00
ATRNS Noah Syndergaard/35 12.00 30.00
ATRRA Roberto Alomar/35 20.00 50.00
ATRRD Rafael Devers/80 12.00 30.00
ATRRG Randal Grichuk/24 4.00 10.00
ATRRJ Reggie Jackson/15 30.00 80.00
ATRRM Ryan McMahon/100 10.00 25.00
ATRRT Raimel Tapia/100 4.00 10.00
ATRSN Sean Newcomb/100 5.00 12.00
ATRST Sam Travis/100 4.00 10.00
ATRTM Trey Mancini/100 5.00 12.00
ATRTP Tommy Pham/100 4.00 10.00
ATRWM Whit Merrifield/100 8.00 20.00

2018 Topps Tier One Autograph Dual Relics

ATRCC Carlos Correa 40.00 100.00
ATRJC J.P. Crawford 25.00 60.00

2018 Topps Tier One Autographs

OVERALL AUTO ODDS 1:19 HOBBY
PRINT RUNS B/WN 15-125 COPIES PER
EXCHANGE DEADLINE 4/30/2020
T1AAJ Aaron Judge/40 100.00 250.00
T1AAP Andy Pettitte/125 12.00 30.00
T1AAR Anthony Rizzo/60 20.00 50.00
T1AARO Alex Rodriguez/20 75.00 200.00
T1ABH Bryce Harper/30 125.00 300.00
T1ABJ Bo Jackson/30 40.00 100.00
T1ABL Barry Larkin/55 15.00 40.00
T1ACJ Chipper Jones/50 30.00 80.00
T1ACR Cal Ripken Jr./50 40.00 100.00
T1ACS Chris Sale EXCH 10.00 25.00
T1ADJ Derek Jeter/15 600.00 1000.00
T1ADM Don Mattingly/80 30.00 80.00
T1ADW Dave Winfield/60 12.00 30.00
T1AFL Francisco Lindor/110 12.00 30.00
T1AFT Frank Thomas/80 25.00 60.00
T1AGM Greg Maddux/30 50.00 120.00
T1AGS Gary Sanchez/110 10.00 25.00
T1AHA Hank Aaron/15 300.00 600.00
T1AI Ichiro/30 200.00 400.00
T1AJB Johnny Bench/45 25.00 60.00
T1AJP Jim Palmer/90 12.00 30.00
T1AKB Kris Bryant EXCH 60.00 150.00
T1AMM Mark McGwire/50 50.00 120.00
T1AMMA Manny Machado/80 12.00 30.00
T1AMR Mariano Rivera/30 75.00 200.00
T1AMT Mike Trout/20 300.00 500.00
T1ANG Nomar Garciaparra/90 15.00 40.00
T1ANR Nolan Ryan/50 50.00 120.00
T1AOS Ozzie Smith/125 20.00 50.00
T1ARC Roger Clemens/30 30.00 80.00
T1ARCA Rod Carew/90 12.00 30.00
T1ARH Rickey Henderson/50 40.00 100.00
T1ARJ Randy Johnson/30 50.00 120.00
T1ARJA Reggie Jackson/50 30.00 80.00
T1ASC Steve Carlton/90 12.00 30.00
T1ASK Sandy Koufax/15
T1ATG Tom Glavine/90 10.00 25.00

2018 Topps Tier One Autographs Bronze Ink

*BRONZE: .6X TO 1.5X BASIC
STATED ODDS 1:49 HOBBY
STATED PRINT RUN 25 SER.#'d SETS
EXCHANGE DEADLINE 4/30/2020
T1AFT Frank Thomas 30.00 80.00

2018 Topps Tier One Break Out Autographs

OVERALL AUTO ODDS 1:19 HOBBY
PRINT RUNS B/WN 45-275 COPIES PER
EXCHANGE DEADLINE 4/30/2020
BAAB Anthony Banda/275 3.00 8.00
BAAG Amir Garrett/275 3.00 8.00
BAAH Austin Hays/275 5.00 12.00
BAAR Amed Rosario/100 6.00 15.00
BAARO Amed Rosario/100 6.00 15.00
BAAS Andrew Stevenson/275 3.00 8.00
BAAV Alex Verdugo/275 5.00 12.00
BABG Ben Gamel/275 4.00 10.00
BABP Brett Phillips/275 3.00 8.00
BABPH Brett Phillips/275 3.00 8.00
BABS Blake Snell/275 4.00 10.00
BABSN Blake Snell/275 4.00 10.00
BABW Brandon Woodruff/275 10.00 25.00
BABZ Bradley Zimmer/225 3.00 8.00
BACAR Christian Arroyo/275 3.00 8.00
BACF Clint Frazier/275 10.00 25.00
BACFR Clint Frazier/275 10.00 25.00
BACS Chance Sisco/275 4.00 10.00
BACT Chris Taylor/275 8.00 20.00
BADF Derek Fisher/275 3.00 8.00
BADFI Derek Fisher/275 3.00 8.00
BADFO Dustin Fowler/275 3.00 8.00
BADUF Dustin Fowler/275 3.00 8.00
BADL Dinelson Lamet/275 3.00 8.00
BADOS Domingo Santana/275 4.00 10.00
BADSA Domingo Santana/275 4.00 10.00
BADR Daniel Robertson/275 3.00 8.00
BADRO Daniel Robertson/275 3.00 8.00
BADS Dominic Smith/100 4.00 10.00
BADSM Dominic Smith/275 4.00 10.00
BAFJ Felix Jorge/275 3.00 8.00
BAFM Francisco Mejia/275 4.00 10.00
BAGB Greg Bird/275 4.00 10.00
BAGC Garrett Cooper/275 3.00 8.00
BAGCO Garrett Cooper/275 3.00 8.00
BAHB Harrison Bader/275 5.00 12.00
BAHBA Harrison Bader/275 5.00 12.00
BAJC J.P. Crawford/250 3.00 8.00
BAJF Jack Flaherty/275 12.00 30.00
BAJFL Jack Flaherty/275 12.00 30.00
BAJFA Jacob Faria/275 3.00 8.00
BAJH Josh Hader/275 4.00 10.00
BAJJ JaCoby Jones/275 4.00 10.00
BAJJI Joe Jimenez/275 3.00 8.00
BAJR Jose Ramirez/100 12.00 30.00
BAJW Jesse Winker/275 5.00 12.00
BAKB Keon Broxton/275 3.00 8.00
BALC Luis Castillo/275 4.00 10.00
BALG Lucas Giolito/100 4.00 10.00
BALGI Lucas Giolito/100 4.00 10.00
BALS Lucas Sims/275 3.00 8.00
BALSI Lucas Sims/275 3.00 8.00
BALW Luke Weaver/275 4.00 10.00
BALWE Luke Weaver/275 4.00 10.00
BAMA Miguel Andujar/275 30.00 80.00
BAMAN Miguel Andujar/275 30.00 80.00
BAMAF Max Fried/275 12.00 30.00
BAMFR Max Fried/275 12.00 30.00
BAMF Michael Fulmer/225 3.00 8.00
BAMFU Michael Fulmer/275 3.00 8.00
BAMK Max Kepler/275 4.00 10.00
BAMKE Max Kepler/275 4.00 10.00
BAND Nicky Delmonico/275 3.00 8.00
BANDO Nicky Delmonico/265 3.00 8.00
BAOA Ozzie Albies/225 30.00 80.00
BAOAL Ozzie Albies/225 30.00 80.00
BAPD Paul DeJong/275 5.00 12.00
BARD Rafael Devers/100 20.00 50.00
BARDE Rafael Devers/275 20.00 50.00
BARH Rhys Hoskins/225 15.00 40.00
BARHO Rhys Hoskins/275 15.00 40.00
BARI Raisel Iglesias/265 4.00 10.00
BARM Ryan McMahon/275 8.00 20.00
BARMC Ryan McMahon/275 8.00 20.00
BART Raimel Tapia/275 3.00 8.00
BARTA Raimel Tapia/275 3.00 8.00
BARTO Ronald Torreyes/275 12.00 30.00
BASN Sean Newcomb/275 6.00 15.00
BASNE Sean Newcomb/275 6.00 15.00
BASO Shohei Ohtani 400.00 800.00
BAST Sam Travis/275 3.00 8.00
BASTR Sam Travis/275 3.00 8.00
BATB Tim Beckham/265 4.00 10.00
BATM Trey Mancini/225 4.00 10.00
BATMA Tyler Mahle/275 5.00 12.00
BATP Tommy Pham/275 3.00 8.00
BATS Travis Shaw/275 3.00 8.00
BATW Tyler Wade/275 5.00 12.00
BATWL Tzu-Wei Lin/275 10.00 25.00
BAVR Victor Robles/250 20.00 50.00
BAWB Walker Buehler/275 15.00 40.00

2018 Topps Tier One Break Out Autographs Bronze Ink

*BRONZE: .6X TO 1.5X BASIC
STATED ODDS 1:18 HOBBY
STATED PRINT RUN 25 SER.#'d SETS
EXCHANGE DEADLINE 4/30/2020
BAAH Austin Hays 20.00 50.00
BAJH Josh Hader 6.00 15.00
BAMA Miguel Andujar 60.00 150.00
BAMAN Miguel Andujar 60.00 150.00
BARH Rhys Hoskins 40.00 100.00
BARHO Rhys Hoskins 40.00 100.00
BATWL Tzu-Wei Lin 20.00 50.00
BAWB Walker Buehler 60.00 150.00

2018 Topps Tier One Dual Autographs

STATED ODDS 1:81 HOBBY
STATED PRINT RUN 25 SER.#'d SETS
EXCHANGE DEADLINE 4/30/2020
T1DAAJ Jones/Albies EXCH 125.00 300.00
T1DABT M.Trout/K.Bryant
T1DAFD Devers/Frazier EXCH 30.00 80.00
T1DAJM R.Johnson/P.Martinez 75.00 200.00
T1DAJR M.Rivera/D.Jeter
T1DAKA Koufax/Aaron EXCH 500.00 1000.00
T1DARS Smith/Rosario EXCH 40.00 100.00
T1DASC Clemens/Sale EXCH 60.00 150.00
T1DASD P.DeJong/O.Smith 75.00 200.00

2018 Topps Tier One Legend Relics

STATED ODDS 1:9 MINI BOX
PRINT RUNS B/WN 7-175 COPIES PER
NO PRICING ON QTY 7
T1RLBJ Bo Jackson/175 4.00 10.00
T1RLBRO Brooks Robinson/100 8.00 20.00
T1RLDJ Derek Jeter/175 12.00 30.00
T1RLDM Don Mattingly/175 4.00 10.00
T1RLDS Duke Snider/100 8.00 20.00
T1RLDW Dave Winfield/175 4.00 10.00
T1RLFT Frank Thomas/175 4.00 10.00
T1RLGB George Brett
T1RLGM Greg Maddux/175 5.00 12.00
T1RLHA Hank Aaron/75 12.00 30.00
T1RLHW Honus Wagner/50 30.00 80.00
T1RLJR Jackie Robinson/30 15.00 40.00
T1RLMM Mark McGwire/175 6.00 15.00
T1RLMP Mike Piazza/175 4.00 10.00
T1RLNR Nolan Ryan/175 8.00 20.00
T1RLOS Ozzie Smith/175 6.00 15.00
T1RLPM Pedro Martinez/175 5.00 12.00
T1RLRA Roberto Alomar/175 5.00 12.00
T1RLRC Roberto Clemente/100 25.00 60.00
T1RLRJ Reggie Jackson/175 4.00 10.00
T1RLRJO Randy Johnson/50 4.00 10.00
T1RLTC Ty Cobb
T1RLTW Ted Williams/175 20.00 50.00
T1RLWS Warren Spahn/100 6.00 15.00

2018 Topps Tier One Legend Dual Relics

*DUAL: .75X TO 2X BASIC
STATED ODDS 1:50 MINI BOX
STATED PRINT RUN 25 SER.#'d SETS
T1RLGB George Brett 40.00 100.00

2018 Topps Tier One Prime Performers Autographs

OVERALL AUTO ODDS 1:19 HOBBY
PRINT RUNS B/WN 50-285 COPIES PER
EXCHANGE DEADLINE 4/30/2020
PPAAB Adrian Beltre/80 15.00 40.00
PPAABR Alex Bregman/145 20.00 50.00
PPAAD Adam Duvall/285 4.00 10.00
PPAAG Andres Galarraga/270 4.00 10.00
PPAAK Al Kaline/90 20.00 50.00
PPAAP Andy Pettitte/80 12.00 30.00
PPAAR Alex Rodriguez
PPAARI Anthony Rizzo/60 20.00 50.00
PPAAW Alex Wood/285 3.00 8.00
PPABD Brian Dozier/285 4.00 10.00
PPABW Bernie Williams/50 20.00 50.00
PPABZ Ben Zobrist/110 12.00 30.00
PPACBL Charlie Blackmon/250 10.00 25.00
PPACCA Carlos Carrasco/285 3.00 8.00
PPACJ Chipper Jones/70 30.00 80.00
PPACK Clayton Kershaw/60 40.00 100.00
PPACKI Craig Kimbrel/130 10.00 25.00
PPACRK Craig Kimbrel/130 10.00 25.00
PPACS Corey Seager
PPACSA Chris Sale/90 10.00 25.00
PPADB Dellin Betances/285 4.00 10.00
PPADBE Dellin Betances/275 4.00 10.00
PPADE Dennis Eckersley/90 4.00 10.00
PPADG Didi Gregorius EXCH 8.00 20.00
PPADP David Price/80 5.00 12.00
PPADPR David Price/80 5.00 12.00
PPADPO Drew Pomeranz/250 3.00 8.00
PPADRP Drew Pomeranz/270 3.00 8.00
PPAEE Edwin Encarnacion/90 8.00 20.00
PPAEM Edgar Martinez/130 8.00 20.00
PPAET Eric Thames/270 4.00 10.00
PPAFL Francisco Lindor/110 20.00 50.00
PPAGS Gary Sanchez/110 12.00 30.00
PPAGSH Gary Sheffield/130 5.00 12.00
PPAGSP George Springer/145 12.00 30.00
PPAIH Ian Happ/270 8.00 20.00
PPAIHA Ian Happ/270 8.00 20.00
PPAJA Jose Altuve/110 20.00 50.00
PPAJB Johnny Bench/70 25.00 60.00
PPAJBA Javier Baez/145 20.00 50.00
PPAJBE Jose Berrios/285 4.00 10.00
PPAJOB Jose Berrios/285 4.00 10.00
PPAJC Jose Canseco/285 10.00 25.00
PPAJDA Johnny Damon/90 8.00 20.00
PPAJDE Jacob deGrom/110 20.00 50.00
PPAJDG Jacob deGrom/90 20.00 50.00
PPAJG Juan Gonzalez/250 5.00 12.00
PPAJH Josh Harrison/285 3.00 8.00
PPAJHA Josh Harrison/275 3.00 8.00
PPAJL Jake Lamb/145 4.00 10.00
PPAJP Jim Palmer/50 12.00 30.00
PPAJR Jim Rice/125 6.00 15.00
PPAJS Justin Smoak/120 6.00 15.00
PPAJT Jim Thome/90 25.00 60.00
PPAKB Kris Bryant/70 60.00 150.00
PPAKD Khris Davis/285 8.00 20.00
PPAKS Kyle Schwarber/130 10.00 25.00
PPAKSC Kyle Schwarber/130 10.00 25.00
PPAKSE Kyle Seager/285 3.00 8.00
PPAMG Marwin Gonzalez/275 3.00 8.00
PPAMGO Marwin Gonzalez/275 3.00 8.00
PPAMM Manny Machado/60 25.00 60.00
PPAOG Ozzie Guillen/275 3.00 8.00
PPAOV Omar Vizquel/130 5.00 12.00
PPAPG Paul Goldschmidt/90 12.00 30.00
PPAPK Paul Konerko/110 8.00 20.00
PPARC Rod Carew/80 12.00 30.00
PPARF Rollie Fingers/250 8.00 20.00
PPASG Sonny Gray/145 5.00 12.00
PPASM Starling Marte/275 4.00 10.00
PPATR Tim Raines/70 8.00 20.00
PPATS Trevor Story/285 5.00 12.00
PPATW Tim Wakefield/250 6.00 15.00
PPAWC Willson Contreras/130 10.00 25.00
PPAYA Yonder Alonso/145 3.00 8.00
PPAYAL Yonder Alonso/125 3.00 8.00
PPAYC Yoenis Cespedes/80 8.00 20.00

2018 Topps Tier One Prime Performers Autographs Bronze Ink

*BRONZE: .6X TO 1.5X BASIC
STATED ODDS 1:19 HOBBY
STATED PRINT RUN 25 SER.#'d SETS
EXCHANGE DEADLINE 4/30/2020
PPACS Corey Seager 30.00 80.00

2018 Topps Tier One Talent Autographs

OVERALL AUTO ODDS 1:19 HOBBY
PRINT RUNS B/WN 30-295 COPIES PER
EXCHANGE DEADLINE 4/30/2020
TTAAB Adrian Beltre/80 15.00 40.00
TTAABR Alex Bregman/160 10.00 25.00
TTAAG Andres Galarraga/275 4.00 10.00
TTAAMR Amed Rosario/245 6.00 15.00
TTAAP Andy Pettitte/90 12.00 30.00
TTAAR Anthony Rizzo/60 20.00 50.00
TTAARO Alex Rodriguez
TTAARU Addison Russell
TTAAV Alex Verdugo/295 5.00 12.00
TTABD Brian Dozier/275 4.00 10.00
TTABS Blake Snell/295 8.00 20.00
TTABZ Bradley Zimmer/295 3.00 8.00
TTABZO Ben Zobrist/90 15.00 40.00
TTACA Christian Arroyo/295 3.00 8.00
TTACF Clint Frazier/295 12.00 30.00
TTACJ Chipper Jones/60 30.00 80.00
TTACK Craig Kimbrel/160 8.00 20.00
TTACR Cal Ripken Jr./60 40.00 100.00
TTACS Corey Seager
TTACSA Chris Sale/130 10.00 25.00
TTACT Chris Taylor/275 4.00 10.00
TTADB Dellin Betances/295 4.00 10.00
TTADM Don Mattingly/60 30.00 80.00
TTADP David Price/80 15.00 40.00
TTADPO Drew Pomeranz/275 3.00 8.00
TTADS Dominic Smith/160 4.00 10.00
TTADW Dave Winfield/60 12.00 30.00
TTAEE Edwin Encarnacion/130 8.00 20.00
TTAEM Edgar Martinez/160 8.00 20.00
TTAET Eric Thames/295 4.00 10.00
TTAFL Francisco Lindor/130 20.00 50.00
TTAFLI Francisco Lindor/160 20.00 50.00
TTAFT Frank Thomas/60 25.00 60.00
TTAGS Gary Sanchez/160 15.00 40.00
TTAGSH Gary Sheffield/110 5.00 12.00
TTAGSP George Springer/245 10.00 25.00
TTAHB Harrison Bader/275 5.00 12.00
TTAIH Ian Happ/295 4.00 10.00
TTAJA Jose Altuve/160 20.00 50.00
TTAJB Javier Baez/245 15.00 40.00
TTAJBE Johnny Bench/40 25.00 60.00
TTAJDE Jacob deGrom/160 25.00 60.00
TTAJL Jake Lamb/245 4.00 10.00
TTAJR Jose Ramirez/245 4.00 10.00
TTAJT Jim Thome/130 20.00 50.00
TTAKS Kyle Schwarber/160 10.00 25.00
TTALG Lucas Giolito/245 4.00 10.00
TTAMF Michael Fulmer/295 3.00 8.00
TTAMG Marwin Gonzalez/160 3.00 8.00
TTAMM Manny Machado/60 15.00 40.00
TTAMMC Mark McGwire/30 50.00 120.00
TTAMP Mike Piazza
TTANR Nolan Ryan/60 50.00 120.00
TTAOA Ozzie Albies/295 15.00 40.00
TTAOS Ozzie Smith/50 20.00 50.00
TTAOV Omar Vizquel/110 5.00 12.00
TTAPD Paul DeJong/295 5.00 12.00
TTAPG Paul Goldschmidt/70 12.00 30.00
TTAPK Paul Konerko/90 4.00 10.00
TTARC Rod Carew/80 15.00 40.00
TTARD Rafael Devers/245 15.00 40.00
TTARHE Rickey Henderson/30 40.00 100.00
TTARHO Rhys Hoskins/295 8.00 20.00
TTARJ Randy Johnson/60 40.00 100.00
TTARJA Reggie Jackson/60 20.00 50.00
TTASG Sonny Gray/245 5.00 12.00
TTASK Sandy Koufax
TTASN Sean Newcomb/295 4.00 10.00
TTATM Trey Mancini/295 4.00 10.00
TTATP Tommy Pham/275 3.00 8.00
TTAVR Victor Robles/295 8.00 20.00
TTAWC Willson Contreras/160 5.00 12.00
TTAYA Yonder Alonso/150 3.00 8.00
TTAYC Yoenis Cespedes/80 10.00 25.00

2018 Topps Tier One Talent Autographs Bronze Ink

*BRONZE: .6X TO 1.5X BASIC
STATED ODDS 1:19 HOBBY
STATED PRINT RUN 25 SER.#'d SETS
EXCHANGE DEADLINE 4/30/2020
TTAARU Addison Russell 20.00 50.00
TTABH Bryce Harper 150.00 400.00
TTACS Corey Seager 30.00 80.00
TTAFT Frank Thomas 30.00 80.00
TTAMR Mariano Rivera 75.00 200.00
TTARJ Randy Johnson 50.00 120.00

2019 Topps Tier One Relics

RANDOM INSERTS IN PACKS
PRINT RUNS B/WN 200-399 COPIES PER
T1RAA Albert Almora/375 2.50 6.00
T1RAB Andrew Benintendi/375 3.00 8.00
T1RABR Alex Bregman/399 3.00 8.00
T1RAC Aroldis Chapman/375 3.00 8.00
T1RAM Andrew McCutchen/375 3.00 8.00
T1RAN Aaron Nola/375 2.50 6.00
T1RAP Albert Pujols/399 4.00 10.00
T1RARI Anthony Rizzo/399 4.00 10.00
T1RBP Buster Posey/375 4.00 10.00
T1RCB Charlie Blackmon/375 3.00 8.00
T1RCBE Cody Bellinger/375 6.00 15.00
T1RCC Carlos Correa/399 3.00 8.00
T1RCCS CC Sabathia/375 2.50 6.00
T1RCK Corey Kluber/375 2.50 6.00
T1RCKE Clayton Kershaw/399 5.00 12.00
T1RCKI Craig Kimbrel/375 2.50 6.00
T1RCS Chris Sale/375 3.00 8.00
T1RCY Carl Yastrzemski/399 5.00 12.00
T1RDB Dellin Betances/375 2.50 6.00
T1RDG Didi Gregorius/375 2.50 6.00
T1RDGO Dee Gordon/399 2.00 5.00
T1RDP David Price/399 2.50 6.00
T1REE Edwin Encarnacion/375 3.00 8.00
T1REH Eric Hosmer/375 2.50 6.00
T1REL Evan Longoria/375 2.50 6.00
T1RER Eddie Rosario/399 2.50 6.00
T1RES Eugenio Suarez/375 2.50 6.00
T1RFF Freddie Freeman/375 4.00 10.00
T1RFL Francisco Lindor/200 3.00 8.00
T1RGP Gregory Polanco/375 2.50 6.00
T1RGS George Springer/375 2.50 6.00
T1RGSA Gary Sanchez/399 3.00 8.00
T1RGT Gleyber Torres/399 6.00 15.00
T1RJA Jose Altuve/375 2.50 6.00
T1RJAB Jose Abreu/375 3.00 8.00
T1RJAG Jesus Aguilar/399 2.50 6.00
T1RJAR Jake Arrieta/399 2.50 6.00
T1RJB Javier Baez/375 4.00 10.00
T1RJBJ Jackie Bradley Jr./375 3.00 8.00
T1RJG Joey Gallo/375 2.50 6.00
T1RJM Joe Mauer/375 2.50 6.00
T1RJMA J.D. Martinez/399 3.00 8.00
T1RJR Jose Ramirez/399 2.50 6.00
T1RJS Justin Smoak/375 2.00 5.00
T1RJSO Juan Soto/399 5.00 12.00
T1RJU Justin Upton/375 2.50 6.00
T1RJV Joey Votto/375 3.00 8.00
T1RJVE Justin Verlander/399 3.00 8.00
T1RKB Kris Bryant/375 4.00 10.00
T1RKD Khris Davis/375 3.00 8.00
T1RKS Kyle Schwarber/399 3.00 8.00
T1RKSE Kyle Seager/399 2.00 5.00
T1RLC Lorenzo Cain/375 2.00 5.00
T1RLS Luis Severino/375 2.50 6.00
T1RMB Mookie Betts/399 6.00 15.00
T1RMC Miguel Cabrera/375 3.00 8.00
T1RMCA Matt Carpenter/375 3.00 8.00
T1RMCH Matt Chapman/375 3.00 8.00
T1RMH Mitch Haniger/375 2.50 6.00
T1RMK Max Kepler/375 2.50 6.00
T1RMKO Michael Kopech/375 2.50 6.00
T1RMO Matt Olson/399 3.00 8.00
T1RMS Max Scherzer/375 3.00 8.00
T1RMST Marcus Stroman/375 2.50 6.00
T1RMT Mike Trout/375 15.00 40.00
T1RMTA Masahiro Tanaka/375 2.50 6.00
T1RNA Nolan Arenado/375 5.00 12.00
T1RNC Nicholas Castellanos/375 3.00 8.00
T1ROA Ozzie Albies/375 3.00 8.00
T1ROH Odubel Herrera/399 2.50 6.00
T1RPG Paul Goldschmidt/375 3.00 8.00
T1RRAJ Ronald Acuna Jr./375 15.00 40.00
T1RRO Rougned Odor/375 2.50 6.00
T1RRP Rick Porcello/375 2.50 6.00
T1RSK Scott Kingery/399 2.50 6.00
T1RSM Starling Marte/375 2.50 6.00
T1RSP Salvador Perez/399 2.50 6.00
T1RSS Stephen Strasburg/375 3.00 8.00
T1RTB Trevor Bauer/375 4.00 10.00
T1RTST Trevor Story/375 3.00 8.00
T1RTT Trea Turner/375 2.50 6.00
T1RWC Willson Contreras/375 2.50 6.00
T1RWM Whit Merrifield/375 3.00 8.00
T1RXB Xander Bogaerts/375 3.00 8.00
T1RYA Yonder Alonso/375 2.00 5.00
T1RYM Yadier Molina/399 4.00 10.00

2019 Topps Tier One Dual Relics

*DUAL: 1X TO 2.5X SNGL RELIC
STATE ODDS 1:16 HOBBY
STATED PRINT RUN 25 SER.#'d SETS
T1RBS Blake Snell 6.00 15.00
T1RJD Jacob deGrom 15.00 40.00
T1RNS Noah Syndergaard 6.00 15.00
T1RTS Travis Shaw 5.00 12.00
T1RWMY Wil Myers 6.00 15.00

2019 Topps Tier One Autograph Relics

STATED ODDS 1:12 HOBBY
PRINT RUNS B/WN 5-100 COPIES PER
NO PRICING ON QTY 15 OR LESS
EXCHANGE DEADLINE 4/30/2021
*DUAL/25: .75X TO 2X BASIC
T1ATRAB Adrian Beltre/30 20.00 50.00
T1ATRAK Al Kaline/50 25.00 50.00
T1ATRAM Andrew McCutchen/30 15.00 40.00
T1ATRAN Aaron Nola/45 20.00 50.00
T1ATRBG Bob Gibson/40 20.00 50.00
T1ATRBS Blake Snell/100 8.00 20.00
T1ATRCK Corey Kluber/50
T1ATRCT Chris Taylor/100 6.00 15.00
T1ATRDM Dale Murphy/70 12.00 30.00
T1ATRFL Francisco Lindor/50 20.00 50.00
T1ATRFT Frank Thomas/30 30.00 80.00
T1ATRFV Felipe Vazquez/100 5.00 12.00
T1ATRGS George Springer/40 25.00 60.00
T1ATRIH Ian Happ/70 5.00 12.00
T1ATRJA Jose Altuve/30 30.00 80.00
T1ATRJAG Jesus Aguilar/100 5.00 12.00
T1ATRJB Jeff Bagwell/40 20.00 50.00
T1ATRJC Jose Canseco/100 10.00 25.00
T1ATRJD Jacob deGrom/50 20.00 50.00
T1ATRJS Jean Segura/100 6.00 15.00
T1ATRJU Justin Upton/50 10.00 25.00
T1ATRLS Luis Severino/50 5.00 12.00
T1ATRMC Matt Carpenter/70 8.00 20.00
T1ATRMCH Matt Chapman/100 10.00 25.00
T1ATRMCO Michael Conforto/100 10.00 25.00
T1ATRMG Marwin Gonzalez/100 6.00 15.00
T1ATRMH Mitch Haniger/100 10.00 25.00
T1ATRMK Michael Kopech/100 10.00 25.00
T1ATROA Ozzie Albies/100 20.00 50.00
T1ATRPG Paul Goldschmidt/40 20.00 50.00
T1ATRRA Roberto Alomar/50 20.00 50.00
T1ATRRCA Rod Carew/50 12.00 30.00
T1ATRRYH Rhys Hoskins/70 20.00 50.00
T1ATRSO Shohei Ohtani/5
T1ATRSP Salvador Perez/70 10.00 25.00
T1ATRTL Tommy Lasorda/40 50.00 120.00
T1ATRVG Vladimir Guerrero/30
T1ATRWM Whit Merrifield/100 20.00 50.00
T1ATRYM Yadier Molina/50 40.00 100.00

2019 Topps Tier One Autographs

OVERALL AUTO ODDS 1:14 HOBBY
PRINT RUNS B/WN 15-125 COPIES PER
NO PRICING ON QTY 15
EXCHANGE DEADLINE 4/30/2021
*BRONZE/25: .6X TO 1.5X p/r 30-125
T1AAB Adrian Beltre/60 20.00 50.00
T1AAJ Aaron Judge/30 100.00 250.00
T1AAK Al Kaline/90 20.00 50.00
T1AAP Andy Pettitte/90 12.00 30.00
T1AAR Anthony Rizzo/40 20.00 50.00
T1ABG Bob Gibson/80 20.00 50.00
T1ACF Carlton Fisk/90 12.00 30.00
T1ACJ Chipper Jones/50 40.00 100.00
T1ADM Don Mattingly/70 25.00 60.00

T1ADO David Ortiz/50 30.00 80.00
T1ADS Deion Sanders/50 30.00 80.00
T1AEJ Eloy Jimenez/125 20.00 50.00
T1AFT Frank Thomas/70 20.00 50.00
T1AHM Hideki Matsui/50 50.00 120.00
T1AI Ichiro/25 150.00 400.00
T1AJA Jose Altuve/70 15.00 40.00
T1AJB Johnny Bench/50 25.00 60.00
T1AJD Jacob deGrom/125 15.00 40.00
T1AJS Juan Soto/125 30.00 80.00
T1AKB Kris Bryant EXCH 30.00 80.00
T1ALS Luis Severino/125 4.00 10.00
T1AMA Miguel Andujar/125 6.00 15.00
T1AMR Mariano Rivera/30 100.00 250.00
T1AMT Mike Trout/25 200.00 500.00
T1ANR Nolan Ryan/50 40.00 100.00
T1ANS Noah Syndergaard/90 10.00 25.00
T1AOA Ozzie Albies/125 12.00 30.00
T1AOS Ozzie Smith/90 12.00 30.00
T1APM Pedro Martinez/40 30.00 80.00
T1ARAJ Ronald Acuna Jr./125 50.00 120.00
T1ARH Rickey Henderson/50 40.00 100.00
T1ASO Shohei Ohtani/25 100.00 250.00
T1ATH Trevor Hoffman/125 8.00 20.00
T1AVG Vladimir Guerrero/70 20.00 50.00

2019 Topps Tier One Break Out Autographs

RANDOM INSERTS IN PACKS
PRINT RUNS B/WN 15-250 COPIES PER
NO PRICING ON QTY 15
EXCHANGE DEADLINE 4/30/2021
*BRONZE/25: .6X TO 1.5X p/r 100-250
BAAG Adolis Garcia/250 30.00 80.00
BAAM Austin Meadows/250 8.00 20.00
BAAME Austin Meadows/250 8.00 20.00
BAAR Amed Rosario/100 5.00 12.00
BAARO Amed Rosario/100 5.00 12.00
BABA Brian Anderson/250 3.00 8.00
BABK Brad Keller/250 3.00 8.00
BABKE Brad Keller/250 3.00 8.00
BABL Brandon Lowe/250 8.00 20.00
BABLO Brandon Lowe/250 8.00 20.00
BABN Brandon Nimmo/250 4.00 10.00
BABNI Brandon Nimmo/250 4.00 10.00
BABW Bryse Wilson/250 4.00 10.00
BABWI Bryse Wilson/250 4.00 10.00
BACA Chance Adams/250 3.00 8.00
BACAD Chance Adams/250 3.00 8.00
BACB Corbin Burnes/250 10.00 25.00
BACBU Corbin Burnes/250 10.00 25.00
BACK Carson Kelly/250 3.00 8.00
BACM Cedric Mullins/250 10.00 25.00
BACMU Cedric Mullins/250 10.00 25.00
BADC Dylan Cozens/250 3.00 8.00
BADCO Dylan Cozens/250 3.00 8.00
BADF Dustin Fowler/250 3.00 8.00
BADJ Danny Jansen/250 3.00 8.00
BADJA Danny Jansen/250 3.00 8.00
BADP Daniel Poncedeleon/250 5.00 12.00
BADS Dennis Santana/250 3.00 8.00
BAEDL Enyel De Los Santos/250 3.00 8.00
BAEJ Eloy Jimenez/100 20.00 50.00
BAFA Francisco Arcia/250 5.00 12.00
BAFAR Francisco Arcia/250 5.00 12.00
BAFR Franmil Reyes/250 3.00 8.00
BAFRE Franmil Reyes/250 3.00 8.00
BAFRO Fernando Romero/250 3.00 8.00
BAFTJ Fernando Tatis Jr./100 75.00 200.00
BAHB Harrison Bader/250 4.00 10.00
BAHFI Heath Fillmyer/250 3.00 8.00
BAIG Isaac Galloway/250 3.00 8.00
BAJB Jake Bauers/250 5.00 12.00
BAJBI Jesse Biddle/250 3.00 8.00
BAJF Jack Flaherty/250 5.00 12.00
BAJM Jeff McNeil/250 12.00 30.00
BAJMC Jeff McNeil/250 12.00 30.00
BAJN Jacob Nix/250 4.00 10.00
BAJR Josh Rogers/250 3.00 8.00
BAJS Juan Soto/100 30.00 80.00
BAJSO Juan Soto/100 30.00 80.00
BAKA Kolby Allard/250 5.00 12.00
BAKAL Kolby Allard/250 5.00 12.00
BAKN Kevin Newman/250 5.00 12.00
BAKT Kyle Tucker/200 8.00 20.00
BAKTU Kyle Tucker/200 8.00 20.00
BAKW Kyle Wright/200 5.00 12.00
BALGJ Lourdes Gurriel Jr./250 4.00 10.00
BALS Lucas Sims EXCH 3.00 8.00
BALV Luke Voit/250 25.00 60.00
BAMA Miguel Andujar/100 10.00 25.00
BAMK Michael Kopech/200 8.00 20.00
BAMKO Michael Kopech/200 8.00 20.00
BAMM Miles Mikolas/250 5.00 12.00
BAOA Ozzie Albies/100 12.00 30.00
BAOAL Ozzie Albies/100 12.00 30.00
BAPA Pete Alonso EXCH 60.00 150.00
BARAJ Ronald Acuna Jr./100 50.00 120.00
BARB Ryan Borucki/250 3.00 8.00
BARBO Ryan Borucki/250 3.00 8.00
BARD Rafael Devers/100 10.00 25.00
BARL Ramon Laureano/250 8.00 20.00
BAROH Ryan O'Hearn/250 3.00 8.00
BART Ronald Torreyes/250 3.00 8.00
BARTE Rowdy Tellez/250 5.00 12.00
BARYH Ryan O'Hearn/250 3.00 8.00
BASA Sandy Alcantara/250 3.00 8.00
BASD Steven Duggar/250 4.00 10.00
BASK Scott Kingery/200 4.00 10.00
BASKI Scott Kingery/200 4.00 10.00
BASM Sean Manaea/250 3.00 8.00
BASMA Sean Manaea/250 3.00 8.00
BASRF Sean Reid-Foley/250 3.00 8.00
BATG Tayron Guerrero/250 3.00 8.00
BATM Tyler Mahle/250 3.00 8.00
BATRW Trevor Williams/250 3.00 8.00
BATT Touki Toussaint/250 4.00 10.00
BATW Taylor Ward/250 3.00 8.00
BATWA Taylor Ward/250 3.00 8.00
BATWI Trevor Williams/250 3.00 8.00
BAWA Willy Adames/250 3.00 8.00
BAWAD Willy Adames/250 3.00 8.00
BAYK Yusei Kikuchi/250 5.00 12.00
BAVGJ Guerrero Jr Mstry EX 150.00 400.00

2019 Topps Tier One Dual Autographs

STATED ODDS 1:83 HOBBY
STATED PRINT RUN 25 SER.#'d SETS
EXCHANGE DEADLINE 4/30/2021
T1DAAA Acuna/Albies 100.00 250.00
T1DABBR Bagwell/Bregman 75.00 200.00
T1DABS Blackmon/Story 20.00 50.00
T1DACS Clemens/Sale
T1DAGD Guerrero/Dawson 60.00 150.00
T1DAHB Hunter/Buxton 30.00 80.00
T1DAIO Ichiro/Ohtani
T1DALR Lindor/Ramirez
T1DAMH McGwire/Henderson EXCH 100.00 250.00
T1DARH Rivera/Hoffman
T1DASA Soto/Acuna 150.00 400.00
T1DASD Syndergaard/deGrom 75.00 200.00
T1DASP Severino/Pettitte 25.00 60.00
T1DATB Trout/Bryant EXCH 300.00 600.00
T1DATM Tanaka/Matsui EXCH 150.00 400.00

2019 Topps Tier One Legends Relics

STATED ODDS 1:11 MINI BOX
PRINT RUNS B/WN 25-175 COPIES PER
*DUAL/25: 1X TO 2.5X p/r 50-175
*DUAL/25: .4X TO 1X p/r 25
T1RLAR Alex Rodriguez/175 5.00 12.00
T1RLBG Bob Gibson/175 3.00 8.00
T1RLCJ Chipper Jones/175 4.00 10.00
T1RLCRJ Cal Ripken Jr./175 10.00 25.00
T1RLCY Carl Yastrzemski/175 10.00 25.00
T1RLDJ Derek Jeter/175 12.00 30.00
T1RLDO David Ortiz/175 10.00 25.00
T1RLEB Ernie Banks/50
T1RLEM Eddie Mathews/175 5.00 12.00
T1RLHW Honus Wagner/50 25.00 60.00
T1RLJB Johnny Bench/175 5.00 12.00
T1RLJR Jackie Robinson/25 25.00 60.00
T1RLMP Mike Piazza/175 4.00 10.00
T1RLMR Mariano Rivera/175 5.00 12.00
T1RLRC Roger Clemens/175 5.00 12.00
T1RLRH Rickey Henderson/175 5.00 12.00
T1RLRJ Reggie Jackson/175 5.00 12.00
T1RLTW Ted Williams/175 20.00 50.00
T1RLVG Vladimir Guerrero/175 3.00 8.00
T1RLWM Willie McCovey/175 4.00 10.00

2019 Topps Tier One Prime Performers Autographs

RANDOM INSERTS IN PACKS
PRINT RUNS B/WN 50-299 COPIES PER
EXCHANGE DEADLINE 4/30/2021
PPAAK Al Kaline/100 20.00 50.00
PPAAKI Al Kaline/100 20.00 50.00
PPAAM Andrew McCutchen/70 30.00 80.00
PPAAMC Andrew McCutchen/70 30.00 80.00
PPAANP Andy Pettitte/60 12.00 30.00
PPAAP Andy Pettitte/60 12.00 30.00
PPAAR Alex Rodriguez
PPAAT Alan Trammell/120 15.00 40.00
PPAAW Alex Wood/299 3.00 8.00
PPAAWO Alex Wood/299 3.00 8.00
PPABB Byron Buxton/150 10.00 25.00
PPABBU Byron Buxton/150 10.00 25.00
PPABL Barry Larkin/70 15.00 40.00
PPABR Bobby Richardson/299 6.00 15.00
PPABRI Bobby Richardson/299 6.00 15.00
PPABS Blake Snell/299 5.00 12.00
PPABSN Blake Snell/299 5.00 12.00
PPABT Blake Treinen/299 3.00 8.00
PPABTR Blake Treinen/299 3.00 8.00
PPACF Carlton Fisk/60 12.00 30.00
PPACHY Christian Yelich/240 30.00 80.00
PPACI Carlton Fisk/60 12.00 30.00
PPACY Carl Yastrzemski/50 40.00 100.00
PPACYE Christian Yelich/240 30.00 80.00
PPADJ Derek Jeter
PPADM Dale Murphy/150 10.00 25.00
PPADMU Dale Murphy/150 10.00 25.00
PPADO David Ortiz/50 30.00 80.00
PPADS Deion Sanders/50 30.00 80.00
PPAER Eddie Rosario/299 8.00 20.00
PPAERO Eddie Rosario/299 8.00 20.00
PPAET Eric Thames/299 3.00 8.00
PPAETH Eric Thames/299 3.00 8.00
PPAFF Freddie Freeman/100 15.00 40.00
PPAFFR Freddie Freeman/100 15.00 40.00
PPAFL Francisco Lindor/100 15.00 40.00
PPAFLI Francisco Lindor/100 15.00 40.00
PPAGS George Springer/60 15.00 40.00
PPAGSP George Springer/60 15.00 40.00
PPAHM Hideki Matsui/50 50.00 120.00
PPAIK Ian Kinsler/150 4.00 10.00
PPAIR Ivan Rodriguez EXCH 15.00 40.00
PPAJA Jose Altuve/70 15.00 40.00
PPAJAG Jesus Aguilar/240 4.00 10.00
PPAJB Johnny Bench/65 30.00 80.00
PPAJBE Jose Berrios/299 4.00 10.00
PPAJD Johnny Damon/240 6.00 15.00
PPAJEA Jesus Aguilar/240 4.00 10.00
PPAJG Juan Gonzalez/299 6.00 15.00
PPAJGO Juan Gonzalez/299 6.00 15.00
PPAJOB Jose Berrios/299 4.00 10.00
PPAJP Jorge Posada/100 20.00 50.00
PPAJR Jose Ramirez/150 4.00 10.00
PPAJRA Jose Ramirez/150 4.00 10.00
PPAJS Jean Segura/299 5.00 12.00
PPAJSE Jean Segura/299 5.00 12.00
PPAJV Joey Votto/65 15.00 40.00
PPAKB Kris Bryant/65 50.00 120.00
PPAKBR Kris Bryant/65 50.00 120.00
PPAMC Matt Chapman/299 8.00 20.00
PPAMCA Matt Carpenter/240 8.00 20.00
PPAMCH Matt Chapman/299 8.00 20.00
PPAMM Mark McGwire/50 40.00 100.00
PPAMMU Max Muncy/299 8.00 20.00
PPAMO Marcell Ozuna/150 5.00 12.00
PPAMOZ Marcell Ozuna/150 5.00 12.00
PPANR Nolan Ryan
PPAOH Odubel Herrera/299 6.00 15.00
PPARA Roberto Alomar/70 10.00 25.00
PPARJ Reggie Jackson/50 20.00 50.00
PPASK Sandy Koufax
PPASP Salvador Perez/150 6.00 15.00
PPASPE Salvador Perez/150 6.00 15.00
PPATH Trevor Hoffman/150 8.00 20.00
PPATHO Trevor Hoffman/150 8.00 20.00
PPATS Trevor Story/299 5.00 12.00
PPATST Trevor Story/299 5.00 12.00
PPAYM Yadier Molina EXCH 30.00 80.00
PPAYMO Yadier Molina EXCH 30.00 80.00
PPAZW Zack Wheeler/240 4.00 10.00
PPAZWH Zack Wheeler/240 4.00 10.00

2019 Topps Tier One Prime Performers Autographs Bronze Ink

*BRONZE: .6X TO 1.5X BASIC
STATED ODDS 1:19 HOBBY
STATED PRINT RUN 25 SER.#'d SETS
EXCHANGE DEADLINE 4/30/2021
PPAAJ Aaron Judge 100.00 250.00
PPARC Roger Clemens 30.00 80.00

2019 Topps Tier One Talent Autographs

RANDOM INSERTS IN PACKS
PRINT RUNS B/WN 10-299 COPIES PER
NO PRICING ON QTY 10
EXCHANGE DEADLINE 4/30/2021
*BRONZE/25: .6X TO 1.5X BASIC
TTAAB Adrian Beltre/70 20.00 50.00
TTAABR Alex Bregman EXCH 20.00 50.00
TTAAD Andre Dawson/60 10.00 25.00
TTAADA Andre Dawson/60 10.00 25.00
TTAAJ Andruw Jones/299 8.00 20.00
TTAAJO Andruw Jones/299 8.00 20.00
TTAALB Alex Bregman EXCH 20.00 50.00
TTAAP Albert Pujols
TTAAR Anthony Rizzo/70 20.00 50.00
TTABB Bert Blyleven/200 8.00 20.00
TTABBL Bert Blyleven/200 8.00 20.00
TTABG Bob Gibson/60 15.00 40.00
TTABGI Bob Gibson/60 15.00 40.00
TTABJ Bo Jackson EXCH 60.00 150.00
TTACB Charlie Blackmon/200 6.00 15.00
TTACBL Charlie Blackmon/200 6.00 15.00
TTACG Chad Green/299 5.00 12.00
TTACGR Chad Green/299 5.00 12.00
TTACJ Chipper Jones/50 40.00 100.00
TTACK Corey Kluber/100 6.00 15.00
TTACKL Corey Kluber/100 6.00 15.00
TTACRJ Cal Ripken Jr./50 50.00 120.00
TTACS Carlos Santana/240 4.00 10.00
TTACSA Carlos Santana/240 4.00 10.00
TTADG Didi Gregorius/240 8.00 20.00
TTADGR Didi Gregorius/240 8.00 20.00
TTADJ David Justice/299 6.00 15.00
TTADJU David Justice/299 6.00 15.00
TTADS Deion Sanders/50 30.00 80.00
TTAFB Franklin Barreto/299 3.00 8.00
TTAFBA Franklin Barreto/299 3.00 8.00
TTAFM Fred McGriff/100 10.00 25.00
TTAFMC Fred McGriff/100 10.00 25.00
TTAFT Frank Thomas/70 20.00 50.00
TTAFV Felipe Vazquez/299 3.00 8.00
TTAFVA Felipe Vazquez/299 3.00 8.00
TTAGS Gary Sanchez/70 20.00 50.00
TTAGSA Gary Sanchez/70 20.00 50.00
TTAI Ichiro
TTAJC Jose Canseco/299 8.00 20.00
TTAJCA Jose Canseco/299 8.00 20.00
TTAJD Jacob deGrom/120 15.00 40.00
TTAJDE Jacob deGrom/120 15.00 40.00
TTAJH Josh Hader/299 5.00 12.00
TTAJHA Josh Hader/299 5.00 12.00
TTAJM Juan Marichal/100 15.00 40.00
TTAJR Jim Rice/240 8.00 20.00
TTAJSM Justin Smoak/200 3.00 8.00
TTAJU Justin Upton EXCH 4.00 10.00
TTAKD Khris Davis/299 6.00 15.00
TTAKDA Khris Davis/299 6.00 15.00
TTAKS Kyle Seager/299 3.00 8.00
TTALS Luis Severino/120 8.00 20.00
TTALSE Luis Severino/120 8.00 20.00
TTAMAK Matt Kemp/200 4.00 10.00
TTAMH Mitch Haniger/240 6.00 15.00
TTAMHA Mitch Haniger/240 6.00 15.00
TTAMK Max Kepler/299 4.00 10.00
TTAMKE Max Kepler/299 4.00 10.00
TTAMR Mariano Rivera
TTAMT Mike Trout
TTANS Noah Syndergaard/100 10.00 25.00
TTANSY Noah Syndergaard/100 10.00 25.00
TTAPG Paul Goldschmidt/60 10.00 25.00
TTAPGO Paul Goldschmidt/60 10.00 25.00
TTAPM Pedro Martinez/40 30.00 80.00
TTARH Rickey Henderson/50 40.00 100.00
TTATA Tim Anderson/299 5.00 12.00
TTATG Tom Glavine/70 12.00 30.00
TTATH Torii Hunter/100 8.00 20.00
TTATHU Torii Hunter/100 8.00 20.00
TTATS Travis Shaw/299 3.00 8.00
TTATSH Travis Shaw/299 3.00 8.00
TTAVG Vladimir Guerrero/70 20.00 50.00
TTAWC Will Clark/100 20.00 50.00
TTAWM Whit Merrifield/299 8.00 20.00
TTAWME Whit Merrifield/299 8.00 20.00
TTAZC Zack Cozart/299 3.00 8.00

2020 Topps Tier One Relics

RANDOM INSERTS IN PACKS
STATED PRINT RUN 395 SER.#'d SETS
T1RAA Aristides Aquino 5.00 12.00
T1RAB Andrew Benintendi 6.00 15.00
T1RAH Aaron Hicks 4.00 10.00
T1RAJ Aaron Judge 8.00 20.00
T1RAM Adrian Morejon 2.00 5.00
T1RAN Aaron Nola 2.50 6.00
T1RAP Albert Pujols 5.00 12.00
T1RAR Austin Riley 4.00 10.00
T1RBB Bobby Bradley 2.00 5.00
T1RBH Bryce Harper 6.00 15.00
T1RBM Brendan McKay 3.00 8.00
T1RBP Buster Posey 4.00 10.00
T1RBR Brendan Rodgers 3.00 8.00
T1RBW Brandon Woodruff 3.00 8.00
T1RCB Cavan Biggio 6.00 15.00
T1RCC Carlos Carrasco 2.00 5.00
T1RCK Clayton Kershaw 5.00 12.00
T1RCP Chris Paddack 5.00 12.00
T1RCS Chris Sale 3.00 8.00
T1RCY Christian Yelich 5.00 12.00
T1RDM Dustin May 6.00 15.00
T1REI Ender Inciarte 2.00 5.00
T1REJ Eloy Jimenez 6.00 15.00
T1RGL Gavin Lux 8.00 20.00
T1RGS George Springer 4.00 10.00
T1RGT Gleyber Torres 6.00 15.00
T1RGU Gio Urshela 3.00 8.00
T1RHD Hunter Dozier 2.00 5.00
T1RID Isan Diaz 4.00 10.00
T1RJA Jose Altuve 4.00 10.00
T1RJF Jack Flaherty 6.00 12.00
T1RJH Josh Hader 3.00 8.00
T1RJL Jesus Luzardo 4.00 10.00
T1RJM Jeff McNeil 5.00 12.00
T1RJR Jake Rogers 2.00 5.00
T1RJS Jorge Soler 3.00 8.00
T1RJV Joey Votto 4.00 10.00
T1RJY Jordan Yamamoto 2.00 5.00
T1RKH Keston Hiura 4.00 10.00
T1RKN Kevin Newman 3.00 8.00
T1RLC Lorenzo Cain 4.00 10.00
T1RLS Luis Severino 4.00 10.00
T1RLV Luke Voit 8.00 20.00
T1RMB Mookie Betts 4.00 10.00
T1RMC Michael Chavis 2.50 6.00
T1RMH Mitch Haniger 3.00 8.00
T1RMM Miles Mikolas 2.00 5.00
T1RMS Max Scherzer 3.00 8.00
T1RMT Mike Trout 15.00 40.00
T1RMY Mike Yastrzemski 5.00 12.00
T1RNL Nate Lowe 5.00 12.00
T1RNS Nick Senzel 3.00 8.00
T1ROA Ozzie Albies 3.00 8.00
T1RPG Paul Goldschmidt 6.00 15.00
T1RRD Rafael Devers 4.00 10.00
T1RRH Rhys Hoskins 4.00 10.00
T1RRL Ramon Laureano 2.50 6.00
T1RSB Shane Bieber 3.00 8.00
T1RSO Shohei Ohtani 5.00 12.00
T1RTS Trevor Story 6.00 15.00
T1RWC Willson Contreras 3.00 8.00
T1RXB Xander Bogaerts 4.00 10.00
T1RYA Yordan Alvarez 8.00 20.00
T1RYC Yu Chang 4.00 10.00
T1RYG Yuli Gurriel 2.50 6.00
T1RAAL Adbert Alzolay 2.50 6.00
T1RABR Alex Bregman 5.00 12.00
T1RAJP A.J. Puk 3.00 8.00
T1RAME Austin Meadows 4.00 10.00
T1RAMU Andres Munoz 3.00 8.00
T1RANO Austin Nola 4.00 10.00
T1RARI Anthony Rizzo 6.00 15.00
T1RBBI Bo Bichette 8.00 20.00
T1RCCO Carlos Correa 4.00 10.00
T1RCCS CC Sabathia 6.00 15.00
T1RCKI Carter Kieboom 2.50 6.00
T1RDJL DJ LeMahieu 3.00 8.00
T1RFTJ Fernando Tatis Jr. 8.00 20.00
T1RGSA Gary Sanchez 5.00 12.00
T1RJDM J.D. Martinez 3.00 8.00
T1RJHE Jason Heyward 2.50 6.00
T1RJME John Means 3.00 8.00
T1RLGJ Lourdes Gurriel Jr. 2.50 6.00
T1RMAC Matt Carpenter 3.00 8.00
T1RMBA Michel Baez 2.00 5.00
T1RMBE Matt Beaty 4.00 10.00
T1RMCA Miguel Cabrera 4.00 10.00
T1RMTA Masahiro Tanaka 3.00 8.00
T1RRAJ Ronald Acuna Jr. 8.00 20.00
T1RSSC Shin-Soo Choo 2.50 6.00
T1RVGJ Vladimir Guerrero Jr. 5.00 12.00

2020 Topps Tier One Dual Relics

*DUAL/25: 1X TO 2.5X BASIC
STATED ODDS 1:16 HOBBY
STATED PRINT RUN 25 SER.#'d SETS
T1RBH Bryce Harper 20.00 50.00
T1RSB Shane Bieber 12.00 30.00
T1RSO Shohei Ohtani 25.00 60.00
T1RWC Willson Contreras 15.00 40.00
T1RBBI Bo Bichette 25.00 60.00

2020 Topps Tier One Autograph Dual Relics

*DUAL/25: .6X TO 1.5X p/r 30-99
*DUAL/25: .4X TO 1X p/r 25
STATED ODDS 1:53 HOBBY
STATED PRINT RUN 25 SER.#'d SETS
T1ATRGL Gavin Lux 75.00 200.00
T1ATRHD Hunter Dozier 20.00 50.00
T1ATRJR Jake Rogers 20.00 50.00
T1ATRTM Tino Martinez 40.00 100.00
T1ATRSSC Shin-Soo Choo 50.00 120.00

2020 Topps Tier One Autograph Relics

STATED ODDS 1:13 HOBBY
PRINT RUNS B/WN 5-99 COPIES PER
NO PRICING ON QTY 15 OR LESS
EXCHANGE DEADLINE 5/31/2022
T1ATRAA Adbert Alzolay 6.00 15.00
T1ATRAM Andres Munoz 8.00 20.00
T1ATRAP A.J. Puk 8.00 20.00
T1ATRBB Bert Blyleven 10.00 25.00
T1ATRBM Brendan McKay 8.00 20.00
T1ATRBR Brendan Rodgers 8.00 20.00
T1ATRDM Dustin May 20.00 50.00
T1ATREM Edgar Martinez 15.00 40.00
T1ATRFM Fred McGriff 15.00 40.00
T1ATRFT Frank Thomas 30.00 80.00
T1ATRGL Gavin Lux 40.00 100.00
T1ATRGU Gio Urshela 10.00 25.00
T1ATRHD Hunter Dozier 5.00 12.00
T1ATRID Isan Diaz 8.00 20.00
T1ATRIR Ivan Rodriguez 15.00 40.00
T1ATRJA Jose Altuve 10.00 25.00
T1ATRJL Jesus Luzardo 10.00 25.00
T1ATRJM Jeff McNeil 10.00 25.00
T1ATRJR Jake Rogers 5.00 12.00
T1ATRJS Jorge Soler 8.00 20.00
T1ATRJY Jordan Yamamoto 5.00 12.00
T1ATRMB Michel Baez 5.00 12.00
T1ATRMH Mitch Haniger 6.00 15.00
T1ATRNS Nick Senzel 8.00 20.00
T1ATROS Ozzie Smith 25.00 60.00
T1ATRRA Roberto Alomar 25.00 60.00
T1ATRRL Ramon Laureano 12.00 30.00
T1ATRTM Tino Martinez 15.00 40.00
T1ATRXB Xander Bogaerts 25.00 60.00
T1ATRYA Yordan Alvarez 60.00 150.00
T1ATRAAQ Aristides Aquino 12.00 30.00
T1ATRARI Austin Riley 10.00 25.00
T1ATRCCS CC Sabathia 20.00 50.00
T1ATRCYE Christian Yelich 50.00 120.00
T1ATRJDM J.D. Martinez 20.00 50.00
T1ATRLGJ Lourdes Gurriel Jr. 6.00 15.00
T1ATRSSC Shin-Soo Choo 15.00 40.00

2020 Topps Tier One Autographs

STATED ODDS 1:15 HOBBY
PRINT RUNS B/WN 15-150 COPIES PER
NO PRICING ON QTY 15 OR LESS
EXCHANGE DEADLINE 5/31/2022
T1AI Ichiro 150.00 400.00
T1AAJ Aaron Judge 60.00 150.00
T1ABB Bo Bichette RC 50.00 120.00
T1ABH Bryce Harper 150.00 400.00
T1ACJ Chipper Jones 75.00 200.00
T1ACK Clayton Kershaw 40.00 100.00
T1ADJ Derek Jeter 400.00 800.00
T1ADM Don Mattingly 30.00 80.00
T1AFL Francisco Lindor 20.00 50.00
T1AFT Frank Thomas 25.00 60.00
T1AHA Hank Aaron
T1AJA Jose Altuve 20.00 50.00
T1AJB Johnny Bench 30.00 80.00
T1AJS Juan Soto 40.00 100.00
T1AMM Mark McGwire 50.00 120.00
T1AMR Mariano Rivera 100.00 250.00
T1AMT Mike Trout 300.00 600.00
T1ANR Nolan Ryan 50.00 120.00
T1AOS Ozzie Smith 20.00 50.00
T1APA Pete Alonso 40.00 100.00
T1ARH Rickey Henderson 50.00 120.00
T1ARJ Randy Johnson 60.00 150.00
T1ASC Steve Carlton 12.00 30.00
T1ASK Sandy Koufax
T1ASO Shohei Ohtani 100.00 250.00
T1ASS Sammy Sosa 60.00 150.00
T1AWC Willson Contreras 10.00 25.00
T1AXB Xander Bogaerts EXCH 20.00 50.00
T1AYA Yordan Alvarez RC 40.00 100.00
T1ACRJ Cal Ripken Jr. 50.00 120.00
T1ACYE Christian Yelich 40.00 100.00
T1AFTJ Fernando Tatis Jr. EXCH 60.00 150.00
T1AKGJ Ken Griffey Jr. 150.00 400.00
T1AMMU Mike Mussina 15.00 40.00
T1ARAJ Ronald Acuna Jr. 60.00 150.00
T1ARHO Rhys Hoskins 15.00 40.00
T1ARJA Reggie Jackson 30.00 80.00
T1AVGJ Vladimir Guerrero Jr. EXCH 40.00 100.00

2020 Topps Tier One Autographs Bronze Ink

*BRONZE/25: .6X TO 1.5X p/r 30-150
*BRONZE/25: .4X TO 1X p/r 25
STATED ODDS 1:98 HOBBY
STATED PRINT RUN 25 SER.#'d SETS
T1AYA Yordan Alvarez 125.00 300.00

2020 Topps Tier One Break Out Autographs

RANDOM INSERTS IN PACKS
PRINT RUNS B/WN 100-299 COPIES PER
EXCHANGE DEADLINE 5/31/2022
BOAAA Adbert Alzolay 4.00 10.00
BOAAC Aaron Civale 6.00 15.00
BOAAP A.J. Puk 5.00 12.00
BOAAR Austin Riley 15.00 40.00
BOAAY Alex Young 3.00 8.00
BOABB Bobby Bradley 3.00 8.00
BOABM Brendan McKay 5.00 12.00
BOABR Brendan Rodgers 5.00 12.00
BOACB Cavan Biggio 12.00 30.00
BOACK Carter Kieboom 4.00 10.00
BOACP Chris Paddack 10.00 25.00
BOADC Dylan Cease 5.00 12.00
BOADL Domingo Leyba 4.00 10.00
BOADM Dustin May 10.00 25.00
BOAEJ Eloy Jimenez 20.00 50.00
BOAGL Gavin Lux 30.00 80.00
BOAID Isan Diaz 8.00 20.00
BOAJB Jake Bauers 4.00 10.00
BOAJL Jesus Luzardo 15.00 40.00
BOAJM John Means 40.00 100.00
BOAJY Jordan Yamamoto 3.00 8.00
BOAKH Keston Hiura 10.00 25.00
BOAKL Kyle Lewis 25.00 60.00
BOAKN Kevin Newman 5.00 12.00
BOALA Logan Allen 3.00 8.00
BOALR Luis Robert 125.00 300.00
BOAMC Michael Chavis 4.00 10.00
BOAMD Mauricio Dubon 4.00 10.00
BOAMK Mitch Keller 5.00 12.00
BOAMT Matt Thaiss 6.00 15.00
BOAMY Mike Yastrzemski 20.00 50.00
BOANH Nico Hoerner 20.00 50.00
BOANS Nick Senzel 6.00 15.00
BOAPA Pete Alonso 40.00 100.00
BOARA Rogelio Armenteros 4.00 10.00
BOARG Robel Garcia 3.00 8.00
BOASA Shaun Anderson 3.00 8.00
BOASL Shed Long 4.00 10.00
BOATD Travis Demeritte 5.00 12.00
BOATG Trent Grisham 12.00 30.00
BOATW Taylor Ward 5.00 12.00
BOAWA Willians Astudillo 3.00 8.00
BOAWS Will Smith 5.00 12.00
BOAYA Yordan Alvarez 30.00 80.00
BOAYC Yu Chang 8.00 20.00
BOAZC Zack Collins 4.00 10.00
BOAZP Zach Plesac 8.00 20.00
BOAAAL Adbert Alzolay 4.00 10.00
BOAAAQ Aristides Aquino 15.00 40.00
BOAACI Aaron Civale 6.00 15.00
BOAAMU Andres Munoz 5.00 12.00
BOAAPU A.J. Puk 5.00 12.00
BOAARA Aristides Aquino 15.00 40.00
BOAARI Austin Riley 15.00 40.00
BOAAYO Alex Young 3.00 8.00
BOABBI Bo Bichette 25.00 60.00
BOABBR Bobby Bradley 3.00 8.00
BOABMC Brendan McKay 5.00 12.00
BOABOB Bo Bichette 25.00 60.00
BOABRE Bryan Reynolds 4.00 10.00
BOABRY Bryan Reynolds 4.00 10.00
BOACBI Cavan Biggio 12.00 30.00
BOACKI Carter Kieboom 4.00 10.00
BOADCE Dylan Cease 5.00 12.00
BOADLE Domingo Leyba 4.00 10.00
BOADMA Dustin May 10.00 25.00
BOADSJ Dwight Smith Jr. 3.00 8.00
BOAFTJ Fernando Tatis Jr. 60.00 150.00
BOAGAL Gavin Lux 30.00 80.00
BOAJYA Jordan Yamamoto 3.00 8.00
BOAKHI Keston Hiura 10.00 25.00
BOAKYL Kyle Lewis 25.00 60.00
BOALAL Logan Allen 3.00 8.00
BOALAR Luis Arraez 8.00 20.00
BOAMAB Matt Beaty 4.00 10.00
BOAMBE Matt Beaty 4.00 10.00
BOAMBR Michael Brosseau 6.00 15.00
BOAMEK Merrill Kelly 3.00 8.00
BOAMIT Mike Tauchman 5.00 12.00
BOAMKE Mitch Keller 5.00 12.00
BOAMTA Mike Tauchman 5.00 12.00
BOAPAL Pete Alonso 40.00 100.00
BOARGA Robel Garcia 3.00 8.00
BOATGR Trent Grisham 12.00 30.00
BOAWAS Willians Astudillo 3.00 8.00
BOAWSM Will Smith 5.00 12.00
BOAYAL Yordan Alvarez 30.00 80.00
BOAZCO Zack Collins 4.00 10.00

2020 Topps Tier One Break Out Autographs Bronze Ink

*BRONZE/25: .6X TO 1.5X BASIC
STATED ODDS 1:15 HOBBY
STATED PRINT RUN 25 SER.#'d SETS
EXCHANGE DEADLINE 5/31/2022
BOACP Chris Paddack 20.00 50.00
BOAGL Gavin Lux 75.00 200.00
BOAJM John Means 60.00 150.00
BOAKH Keston Hiura 25.00 60.00
BOAKN Kevin Newman 12.00 30.00
BOAMT Matt Thaiss 20.00 50.00
BOAAAQ Aristides Aquino 30.00 80.00
BOAARA Aristides Aquino 30.00 80.00
BOAGAL Gavin Lux 75.00 200.00
BOAKHI Keston Hiura 25.00 60.00

2020 Topps Tier One Dual Autographs

STATED ODDS 1:69 HOBBY
PRINT RUNS B/WN 5-25 COPIES PER
NO PRICING ON QTY 15 OR LESS
EXCHANGE DEADLINE 5/31/2022
T1DAAB Y.Alvarez/J.Bagwell 75.00 200.00
T1DAAR A.Riley/R.Acuna Jr. 125.00 300.00
T1DABM M.Muncy/M.Beaty 40.00 100.00
T1DAEP A.Puk/D.Eckersley 30.00 80.00
T1DAGS T.Glavine/J.Smoltz
T1DAHH B.Harper/R.Hoskins
T1DAIG K.Griffey Jr./Ichiro
T1DAJC D.Cease/E.Jimenez 100.00 250.00
T1DAKS C.Kieboom/J.Soto 75.00 200.00
T1DAMJ R.Johnson/P.Martinez
T1DAPC W.Clark/B.Posey 75.00 200.00
T1DARG V.Guerrero/T.Raines 50.00 120.00
T1DASM B.McKay/B.Snell 15.00 40.00
T1DATO S.Ohtani/M.Trout
T1DAWM B.Williams/T.Martinez 60.00 150.00

2020 Topps Tier One Legend Dual Relics

*DUAL/25: 1X TO 2.5X BASIC
STATED ODDS 1:68 HOBBY
STATED PRINT RUN 25 SER.#'d SETS
T1LRBR Babe Ruth 125.00 300.00
T1LRCJ Chipper Jones 25.00 60.00
T1LRDS Deion Sanders 20.00 50.00
T1LRFT Frank Thomas 20.00 50.00
T1LRHA Hank Aaron 40.00 100.00
T1LRTG Tony Gwynn 20.00 50.00
T1LRTM Thurman Munson 40.00 100.00
T1LRTW Ted Williams 30.00 80.00

2020 Topps Tier One Next Level Autographs

STATED ODDS 1:46 HOBBY
STATED PRINT RUN 50 SER.#'d SETS
EXCHANGE DEADLINE 5/31/2022
NLABB Bo Bichette EXCH 50.00 120.00
NLACY Carl Yastrzemski EXCH 50.00 120.00
NLADM Don Mattingly 25.00 60.00
NLAJB Johnny Bench 30.00 80.00
NLAJS Juan Soto 40.00 100.00
NLAPA Pete Alonso 40.00 100.00
NLARH Rickey Henderson 40.00 100.00
NLASS Sammy Sosa 75.00 200.00
NLAXB Xander Bogaerts EXCH 25.00 60.00
NLACRJ Cal Ripken Jr. 60.00 150.00
NLAFTJ Fernando Tatis Jr. EXCH 75.00 200.00
NLARHO Rhys Hoskins 25.00 60.00
NLAVGJ Vladimir Guerrero Jr. EXCH 40.00 100.00

2020 Topps Tier One Next Level Autographs Bronze

*BRONZE/25: .6X TO 1.5X BASIC
STATED ODDS 1:78 HOBBY
STATED PRINT RUN 25 SER.#'d SETS
EXCHANGE DEADLINE 5/31/2022
NLAAJ Aaron Judge 75.00 200.00
NLABH Bryce Harper
NLACJ Chipper Jones 60.00 150.00
NLAMR Mariano Rivera
NLAMT Mike Trout
NLASK Sandy Koufax
NLASO Shohei Ohtani
NLAFTJ Fernando Tatis Jr. EXCH 150.00 400.00
NLAKGJ Ken Griffey Jr. 150.00 400.00

2020 Topps Tier One Prime Performers Autographs

RANDOM INSERTS IN PACKS
PRINT RUNS B/WN 10-299 COPIES PER
NO PRICING ON QTY 15 OR LESS
EXCHANGE DEADLINE 5/31/2022
PPAAG Andres Galarraga 8.00 20.00
PPAAH Aaron Hicks 10.00 25.00
PPAAK Al Kaline 25.00 60.00
PPABB Bert Blyleven 4.00 10.00
PPABT Blake Treinen 3.00 8.00
PPABW Bernie Williams 15.00 40.00
PPACC Carlos Carrasco 3.00 8.00
PPACD Corey Dickerson 4.00 10.00
PPACS CC Sabathia 15.00 40.00
PPADC David Cone 6.00 15.00
PPADM Don Mattingly 30.00 80.00
PPAFL Francisco Lindor 20.00 50.00
PPAGS George Springer 8.00 20.00
PPAHM Hideki Matsui 40.00 100.00
PPAJA Jose Altuve 12.00 30.00
PPAJB Jeff Bagwell 20.00 50.00
PPAJL Jed Lowrie 6.00 15.00
PPAJR Jim Rice 10.00 25.00
PPAJS Juan Soto 40.00 100.00
PPAKB Kris Bryant 40.00 100.00
PPAMH Mitch Haniger 6.00 15.00
PPAMM Max Muncy 4.00 10.00
PPAMT Mark Teixeira 8.00 20.00
PPANA Nolan Arenado EXCH 40.00 100.00
PPAPC Patrick Corbin 4.00 10.00
PPAPD Paul DeJong 5.00 12.00
PPARC Rod Carew 15.00 40.00
PPASB Shane Bieber 5.00 12.00
PPASS Sammy Sosa 50.00 120.00
PPATH Todd Helton 12.00 30.00
PPAVG Vladimir Guerrero 20.00 50.00
PPAXB Xander Bogaerts 20.00 50.00
PPAZW Zack Wheeler 6.00 15.00
PPAAKA Al Kaline 25.00 60.00
PPAANR Anthony Rizzo 25.00 60.00
PPAARI Anthony Rizzo 25.00 60.00
PPABBL Bert Blyleven 4.00 10.00
PPABTR Blake Treinen 3.00 8.00
PPABWI Bernie Williams 15.00 40.00
PPACCA Carlos Carrasco 3.00 8.00
PPACCS CC Sabathia 15.00 40.00
PPACDI Corey Dickerson 4.00 10.00
PPACHS Chris Sale 8.00 20.00
PPACRJ Cal Ripken Jr. 50.00 120.00
PPACSA Chris Sale 8.00 20.00
PPADAM Dale Murphy 15.00 40.00
PPADCO David Cone 6.00 15.00
PPADMA Don Mattingly 30.00 80.00
PPADMU Dale Murphy 15.00 40.00
PPAFLI Francisco Lindor 20.00 50.00
PPAGSP George Springer 8.00 20.00
PPAJAL Jose Altuve 12.00 30.00
PPAJBA Jeff Bagwell 20.00 50.00
PPAJOS Jorge Soler 10.00 25.00
PPAJSO Juan Soto 40.00 100.00
PPALGJ Lourdes Gurriel Jr. 4.00 10.00
PPALGU Lourdes Gurriel Jr. 4.00 10.00
PPAMAC Matt Carpenter 5.00 12.00
PPAMCA Matt Carpenter 5.00 12.00
PPAMMG Mark McGwire 50.00 120.00
PPAMMI Miles Mikolas 3.00 8.00
PPAMMU Max Muncy 4.00 10.00
PPAMTE Mark Teixeira 8.00 20.00
PPANAR Nolan Arenado EXCH 40.00 100.00
PPAPCO Patrick Corbin 4.00 10.00
PPAPDE Paul DeJong 5.00 12.00
PPARCA Rod Carew 15.00 40.00
PPASBI Shane Bieber 5.00 12.00
PPATHE Todd Helton 12.00 30.00
PPAVLG Vladimir Guerrero 20.00 50.00
PPAXBO Xander Bogaerts 20.00 50.00

2020 Topps Tier One Prime Performers Autographs Bronze Ink

*BRONZE/25: .6X TO 1.5X BASIC
STATED ODDS 1:19 HOBBY
STATED PRINT RUN 25 SER.#'d SETS
EXCHANGE DEADLINE 5/31/2022
PPAAG Andres Galarraga 15.00 40.00
PPACK Clayton Kershaw 60.00 150.00
PPAMT Mark Teixeira 15.00 40.00
PPAKGJ Ken Griffey Jr. 300.00 600.00
PPAMTE Mark Teixeira 15.00 40.00

2020 Topps Tier One Talent Autographs

RANDOM INSERTS IN PACKS
PRINT RUNS B/WN 10-299 COPIES PER
NO PRICING ON QTY 15 OR LESS
EXCHANGE DEADLINE 5/31/2022
T1TAAD Andre Dawson 12.00 30.00
T1TAAM Austin Meadows 6.00 15.00
T1TAAN Aaron Nola 8.00 20.00
T1TABL Barry Larkin 20.00 50.00
T1TABP Buster Posey 30.00 80.00
T1TABS Blake Snell 4.00 10.00
T1TABW Brandon Woodruff 5.00 12.00
T1TACF Cecil Fielder 8.00 20.00
T1TACK Corey Kluber 4.00 10.00
T1TACY Carl Yastrzemski 40.00 100.00
T1TADE Dennis Eckersley 10.00 25.00
T1TAFM Fred McGriff 15.00 40.00
T1TAFT Frank Thomas 25.00 60.00
T1TAGT Gleyber Torres 40.00 100.00
T1TAHD Hunter Dozier 6.00 15.00
T1TAIR Ivan Rodriguez 15.00 40.00
T1TAJB Johnny Bench 30.00 80.00
T1TAJC Jose Canseco 10.00 25.00
T1TAJH Josh Hader 4.00 10.00
T1TAJM J.D. Martinez 12.00 30.00
T1TAJP Jorge Posada 15.00 40.00
T1TAJT Jim Thome 20.00 50.00
T1TAKW Kerry Wood 12.00 30.00
T1TALM Lance McCullers Jr. 3.00 8.00
T1TALV Luke Voit 15.00 40.00
T1TAMM Mike Mussina 12.00 30.00
T1TAOS Ozzie Smith 15.00 40.00
T1TARD Rafael Devers 15.00 40.00
T1TARF Rollie Fingers 8.00 20.00
T1TARH Rickey Henderson 30.00 80.00
T1TARJ Reggie Jackson 25.00 60.00
T1TARS Ryne Sandberg 20.00 50.00
T1TATA Tim Anderson 5.00 12.00
T1TATM Tino Martinez 12.00 30.00
T1TATR Tim Raines 8.00 20.00
T1TAVR Victor Robles 6.00 15.00
T1TAWC Will Clark 20.00 50.00
T1TAWM Whit Merrifield 5.00 12.00
T1TAYG Yuli Gurriel 8.00 20.00
T1TAADA Andre Dawson 12.00 30.00
T1TAANO Aaron Nola 8.00 20.00
T1TABLA Barry Larkin 20.00 50.00
T1TABSN Blake Snell 4.00 10.00
T1TABWO Brandon Woodruff 5.00 12.00
T1TACFI Cecil Fielder 8.00 20.00
T1TACKL Corey Kluber 4.00 10.00
T1TADEC Dennis Eckersley 10.00 25.00
T1TAFMC Fred McGriff 15.00 40.00
T1TAFTH Frank Thomas 25.00 60.00
T1TAGTO Gleyber Torres 40.00 100.00
T1TAJDM J.D. Martinez 12.00 30.00
T1TAJHA Josh Hader 4.00 10.00
T1TAJPO Jorge Posada 15.00 40.00
T1TAJTH Jim Thome 20.00 50.00
T1TAKWO Kerry Wood 12.00 30.00
T1TALMJ Lance McCullers Jr. 3.00 8.00
T1TALVO Luke Voit 15.00 40.00
T1TAMMU Mike Mussina 12.00 30.00

T1TAOSM Ozzie Smith 15.00 40.00
T1TARAJ Ronald Acuna Jr. 50.00 120.00
T1TARDE Rafael Devers 15.00 40.00
T1TARFI Rollie Fingers 8.00 20.00
T1TARHO Rhys Hoskins 12.00 30.00
T1TARHY Rhys Hoskins 12.00 30.00
T1TAROJ Ronald Acuna Jr. 50.00 120.00
T1TASSC Shin-Soo Choo 15.00 40.00
T1TATAN Tim Anderson 5.00 12.00
T1TATMA Tino Martinez 12.00 30.00
T1TATRA Tim Raines 8.00 20.00
T1TAVRO Victor Robles 6.00 15.00
T1TAWCL Will Clark 20.00 50.00
T1TAWCO Willson Contreras 8.00 20.00
T1TAWIC Willson Contreras 8.00 20.00
T1TAWME Whit Merrifield 5.00 12.00

2020 Topps Tier One Talent Autographs Bronze Ink

*BRONZE/25: .6X TO 1.5X BASIC
STATED ODDS 1:18 HOBBY
STATED PRINT RUN 25 SER.#'d SETS
EXCHANGE DEADLINE 5/31/2022
T1TAAJ Aaron Judge 20.00 50.00
T1TACJ Chipper Jones 60.00 150.00
T1TAMM Mike Mussina 30.00 80.00
T1TAMT Mike Trout 400.00 800.00
T1TAMMU Mike Mussina 30.00 80.00
T1TARHO Rhys Hoskins 30.00 80.00
T1TARHY Rhys Hoskins 30.00 80.00

2021 Topps Tier One Relics

PRINT RUNS B/WN 199-399 COPIES PER
T1RAC Aroldis Chapman/399 3.00 8.00
T1RAG Andres Gimenez/399 5.00 12.00
T1RAJ Aaron Judge/344 10.00 25.00
T1RAK Alejandro Kirk/399 5.00 12.00
T1RAM Austin Meadows/399 5.00 12.00
T1RAN Aaron Nola/399 2.50 6.00
T1RAP Andy Pettitte/299 2.50 6.00
T1RAR Anthony Rizzo/299 4.00 10.00
T1RBB Brandon Belt/399 2.50 6.00
T1RBH Bryce Harper/399 10.00 25.00
T1RBL Barry Larkin/299 2.50 6.00
T1RBN Brandon Nimmo/399 2.50 6.00
T1RBP Buster Posey/344 4.00 10.00
T1RBR Brent Rooker/299 2.50 6.00
T1RBW Brandon Woodruff/399 3.00 8.00
T1RCB Cavan Biggio/299 4.00 10.00
T1RCC Carlos Correa/299 3.00 8.00
T1RCM Colin Moran/399 2.00 5.00
T1RCS CC Sabathia/399 2.50 6.00
T1RCT Chris Taylor/399 2.50 6.00
T1RCY Christian Yelich/299 8.00 20.00
T1RDB David Bote/299 2.50 6.00
T1RDG Dee Strange-Gordon/399 2.00 5.00
T1RDJ Derek Jeter/299 15.00 40.00
T1RDL Derrek Lee/299 2.00 5.00
T1RDM Dustin May/344 3.00 8.00
T1RDO David Ortiz/299 10.00 25.00
T1RDP David Peralta
T1RDS Dansby Swanson/299 3.00 8.00
T1REJ Eloy Jimenez/299 6.00 15.00
T1REL Evan Longoria/344 2.50 6.00
T1RFF Freddie Freeman/299 4.00 10.00
T1RFL Francisco Lindor/299 3.00 8.00
T1RFT Fernando Tatis Jr./199 15.00 40.00
T1RGS Gary Sheffield/299 2.00 5.00
T1RGT Gleyber Torres/344 6.00 15.00
T1RHD Hunter Dozier/399 2.00 5.00
T1RIH Ian Happ
T1RIR Ivan Rodriguez/399 2.50 6.00
T1RJB Jeff Bagwell/299 4.00 10.00
T1RJC Jeimer Candelario/299 2.00 5.00
T1RJD Johnny Damon/399 4.00 10.00
T1RJH Josh Hader/399 2.50 6.00
T1RJJ JaCoby Jones/399 2.50 6.00
T1RJL Jesus Luzardo/399 3.00 8.00
T1RJP Joc Pederson/344 2.50 6.00
T1RJR J.T. Realmuto/399 3.00 8.00
T1RJS John Smoltz/299 3.00 8.00
T1RJT Jim Thome/299 6.00 15.00
T1RJV Joey Votto/299 3.00 8.00
T1RJW Jesse Winker/399 3.00 8.00
T1RKB Kris Bryant/299 4.00 10.00
T1RKG Ken Griffey Jr./299 12.00 30.00
T1RKH Keston Hiura/399 4.00 10.00
T1RKM Ketel Marte/299 2.50 6.00
T1RKS Kyle Seager/399 2.00 5.00
T1RKW Kolten Wong/399 2.50 6.00
T1RLA Luis Arraez/399 4.00 10.00
T1RLG Luis Garcia/299 10.00 25.00
T1RLS Luis Severino/399 2.50 6.00
T1RLV Luke Voit/399 4.00 10.00
T1RLW Larry Walker/399 4.00 10.00
T1RMB Michael Brantley/344 2.50 6.00
T1RMC Miguel Cabrera/299 8.00 20.00
T1RMG Mitch Garver/399 10.00 25.00
T1RMK Max Kepler/399 2.50 6.00
T1RMO Matt Olson/399 3.00 8.00
T1RMS Miguel Sano/399 2.50 6.00
T1RMT Mike Trout/199 30.00 80.00
T1RNC Nelson Cruz/344 3.00 8.00
T1RNP Nate Pearson/299 10.00 25.00
T1RNS Nick Senzel/399 3.00 8.00
T1ROA Ozzie Albies/299 3.00 8.00
T1RPA Pete Alonso/399 8.00 20.00
T1RPC Patrick Corbin/299 2.50 6.00
T1RRA Roberto Alomar/299 2.50 6.00
T1RRD Rafael Devers/399 4.00 10.00
T1RRH Rhys Hoskins/399 6.00 15.00
T1RRL Ramon Laureano/399 2.50 6.00
T1RRM Ryan Mountcastle/299 6.00 15.00
T1RSS Sammy Sosa/299 6.00 15.00
T1RTH Torii Hunter/399 2.00 5.00
T1RTP Tommy Pham/399 2.00 5.00
T1RTS Trevor Story/399 3.00 8.00
T1RTT Trea Turner/299 4.00 10.00
T1RVG Vladimir Guerrero Jr./299 8.00 20.00
T1RWC Willson Contreras/399 3.00 8.00
T1RWM Wil Myers/399 2.50 6.00
T1RWS Will Smith/344 3.00 8.00
T1RXB Xander Bogaerts/299 3.00 8.00
T1RYA Yordan Alvarez/344 8.00 20.00
T1RYG Yasmani Grandal/399 2.00 5.00
T1RYK Yusei Kikuchi/299 2.50 6.00
T1RYM Yadier Molina/399 6.00 15.00
T1RAJP A.J. Puk/399 3.00 8.00
T1RAMC Andrew McCutchen/299 3.00 8.00
T1RARI Austin Riley/199 4.00 10.00
T1RBLO Brandon Lowe/399 2.50 6.00
T1RCBE Cody Bellinger/325 6.00 15.00
T1RCBL Charlie Blackmon/399 3.00 8.00
T1RCMI Casey Mize/299 8.00 20.00
T1RCSE Corey Seager/299 3.00 8.00
T1RDJA Danny Jansen/399 2.00 5.00
T1RGSA Gary Sanchez/399 3.00 8.00
T1RHJR Hyun-Jin Ryu/299 2.50 6.00
T1RJAB Jose Abreu/399 3.00 8.00
T1RJAL Jose Altuve/399 2.50 6.00
T1RJBA Javier Baez/299 4.00 10.00
T1RJBJ Jackie Bradley Jr./199 3.00 8.00
T1RJDA J.D. Davis/399 2.00 5.00
T1RJDO Josh Donaldson/399 2.50 6.00
T1RJOA Jorge Alfaro/349 2.00 5.00
T1RJOB Joey Bart/388 6.00 15.00
T1RJSO Juan Soto/299 10.00 25.00
T1RKHE Kyle Hendricks/299 3.00 8.00
T1RLRO Luis Robert/399 10.00 25.00
T1RMAC Mark Canha/299 2.00 5.00
T1RMCA Matt Carpenter/399 3.00 8.00
T1RMCH Matt Chapman/399 3.00 8.00
T1RMMA Manny Machado/399 3.00 8.00
T1RMOB Mookie Betts/199 15.00 40.00
T1RMST Marcus Stroman/399 2.50 6.00
T1RNSO Nick Solak/399 3.00 8.00
T1RRAJ Ronald Acuna Jr./199 15.00 40.00
T1RSST Stephen Strasburg/299 3.00 8.00
T1RTHE Todd Helton/299 2.50 6.00
T1RYMO Yoan Moncada/299 3.00 8.00

2021 Topps Tier One Relics Dual Patch

*DUAL/25: 1X TO 2.5X BASIC
STATED ODDS 1:xx HOBBY
STATED PRINT RUN 25 SER.#'d SETS
T1RIH Ian Happ 10.00 25.00
T1RYM Yadier Molina 30.00 80.00

2021 Topps Tier One Autograph Relics

STATED ODDS 1:xx HOBBY
PRINT RUNS B/WN 25-100 COPIES PER
EXCHANGE DEADLINE 3/31/23
T1ARAS Alfonso Soriano/100 20.00 50.00
T1ARCC Carlos Correa/50 25.00 60.00
T1ARCM Casey Mize/75 40.00 100.00
T1ARDW Devin Williams/100 8.00 20.00
T1AREH Eric Hosmer/50 20.00 50.00
T1AREJ Eloy Jimenez/50 15.00 40.00
T1AREW Evan White/100 5.00 12.00
T1ARFF Freddie Freeman/25 40.00 100.00
T1ARFT Fernando Tatis Jr./38 200.00 500.00
T1ARGS Gary Sanchez/37 25.00 60.00
T1ARHP Hunter Pence/50 20.00 50.00
T1ARJB Josh Bell/100 10.00 25.00
T1ARJD Jacob deGrom/25 75.00 200.00
T1ARJH Josh Hader/100 6.00 15.00
T1ARJM J.D. Martinez/50 20.00 50.00
T1ARJR Jim Rice/100 12.00 30.00
T1ARKH Keston Hiura/100 10.00 25.00
T1ARKW Kolten Wong/100 8.00 20.00
T1ARLB Lou Brock/50 20.00 50.00
T1ARMC Miguel Cabrera/30 60.00 150.00
T1ARMG Mark Grace/50 20.00 50.00
T1ARMK Max Kepler/100 10.00 25.00
T1ARMM Manny Machado/35 20.00 50.00
T1ARNA Nolan Arenado/25 30.00 80.00
T1ARRA Ronald Acuna Jr./50 125.00 300.00
T1ARRL Ramon Laureano/100 12.00 30.00
T1ARRM Ryan Mountcastle/50 30.00 80.00
T1ARRS Ron Santo/25 150.00 400.00
T1ARTO Tony Oliva/50 15.00 40.00
T1ARVG Vladimir Guerrero Jr./75 40.00 100.00
T1ARWM Whit Merrifield/100 8.00 20.00
T1ARYM Yadier Molina/50 100.00 250.00
T1ARARI Anthony Rizzo/30 30.00 80.00
T1ARJAL Jose Altuve/35 20.00 50.00
T1ARJBA Joey Bart/50 40.00 100.00
T1ARJRE J.T. Realmuto/78 20.00 50.00
T1ARMCH Matt Chapman/50 40.00 100.00
T1ARMMU Mark Mulder/100 20.00 50.00
T1ARWCL Will Clark/50 30.00 80.00
T1ARWSM Will Smith/100 25.00 60.00

2021 Topps Tier One Autograph Relics Dual Patch

*DUAL/25: .6X TO 1.5X p/r 30-100
*DUAL/25: .4X TO 1X p/r 25
STATED ODDS 1:xx HOBBY
STATED PRINT RUN 25 SER.#'d SETS
EXCHANGE DEADLINE 3/31/23
T1ARBS Blake Snell 15.00 40.00
T1ARCB Cody Bellinger 60.00 150.00
T1ARCY Christian Yelich 75.00 200.00
T1ARFF Freddie Freeman 50.00 120.00
T1ARMP Mike Piazza 75.00 200.00
T1ARRA Ronald Acuna Jr. 400.00 1000.00
T1ARRJ Randy Johnson 50.00 120.00
T1ARWB Wade Boggs 40.00 100.00
T1ARSST Stephen Strasburg 40.00 100.00

2021 Topps Tier One Autographs

PRINT RUNS B/WN 10-200 COPIES PER
NO PRICING ON QTY 15 OR LESS
EXCHANGE DEADLINE 3/31/23
*BRONZE/25: .6X TO 1.5X p/r 50-200
T1ABH Bryce Harper
T1ACJ Chipper Jones/50 50.00 120.00
T1ACY Christian Yelich/150 25.00 60.00
T1ADS Darryl Strawberry/175 20.00 50.00
T1AEJ Eloy Jimenez/192 15.00 40.00
T1AEM Edgar Martinez/150 25.00 60.00
T1AGM Greg Maddux/50 60.00 150.00
T1AIR Ivan Rodriguez/75 20.00 50.00
T1AJB Johnny Bench/100 30.00 80.00
T1AJS Juan Soto/200 60.00 150.00
T1ALW Larry Walker/150 30.00 80.00
T1AMC Miguel Cabrera/100 50.00 120.00
T1AMS Mike Schmidt/100 30.00 80.00
T1AMT Mike Trout/25 300.00 800.00
T1APG Paul Goldschmidt/100 12.00 30.00
T1ARJ Randy Johnson/50 50.00 120.00
T1ASB Shane Bieber/175 20.00 50.00
T1ATG Tom Glavine/200 25.00 60.00
T1AWC Will Clark/100 20.00 50.00
T1AABE Adrian Beltre 20.00 50.00
T1AFTA Frank Thomas/157 25.00 60.00
T1AJMA J.D. Martinez/100 20.00 50.00
T1APMO Paul Molitor/100 20.00 50.00
T1ARJA Reggie Jackson/75 30.00 80.00

2021 Topps Tier One Break Out Autographs

STATED ODDS 1:xx HOBBY
PRINT RUNS B/WN 100-300 COPIES PER
EXCHANGE DEADLINE 3/31/23
*BRONZE/25: .6X TO 1.5X BASIC
BOAAB Alec Bohm/150 40.00 100.00
BOAAG Andres Gimenez/300 4.00 10.00
BOAAK Alex Kirilloff/250 20.00 50.00
BOAAN Austin Nola/300 8.00 20.00
BOAAT Anderson Tejeda/300 8.00 20.00
BOAAV Alex Verdugo/300 12.00 30.00
BOABD Bobby Dalbec/150 25.00 60.00
BOABG Bryan Garcia/300 3.00 8.00
BOABS Brady Singer/200 10.00 25.00
BOACH Codi Heuer/300 6.00 15.00
BOACJ Cristian Javier/300 8.00 20.00
BOACM Casey Mize/300 25.00 60.00
BOACP Cristian Pache/263 25.00 60.00
BOACS Clarke Schmidt/300 5.00 12.00
BOADC Dylan Carlson/150 50.00 120.00
BOADG Deivi Garcia/300 15.00 40.00
BOADP David Peterson/300 6.00 15.00
BOADV Daulton Varsho/300 8.00 20.00
BOADW Devin Williams/300 5.00 12.00
BOAEA Eddy Alvarez/300 5.00 12.00
BOAEO Edward Olivares/300 8.00 20.00
BOAEW Evan White/300 6.00 15.00
BOAFK Franklyn Kilome/300 3.00 8.00
BOAGC Garrett Crochet/300 15.00 40.00
BOAGL Gavin Lux EXCH 15.00 40.00
BOAIA Ian Anderson/275 20.00 50.00
BOAJA Jo Adell/150 40.00 100.00
BOAJB Joey Bart/150 20.00 50.00
BOAJC Jake Cronenworth/300 20.00 50.00
BOAJS Jesus Sanchez/300 10.00 25.00
BOAKB Kris Bubic/300 5.00 12.00
BOAKL Kyle Lewis/200 15.00 40.00
BOALG Luis Garcia/300 10.00 25.00
BOALR Luis Robert/150 50.00 120.00
BOALT Leody Taveras/300 3.00 8.00
BOAMB Michael Brosseau/300 4.00 10.00
BOAMH Monte Harrison/300 5.00 12.00
BOANH Nick Heath/300 6.00 15.00
BOANM Nick Madrigal/200 15.00 40.00
BOANN Nick Nelson/300 4.00 10.00
BOANP Nate Pearson/209 10.00 25.00
BOANS Nick Solak/300 5.00 12.00
BOARA Randy Arozarena/275 25.00 60.00
BOARC Ryan Castellani/300 5.00 12.00
BOARJ Ryan Jeffers/300 6.00 15.00
BOARM Ryan Mountcastle/150 25.00 60.00
BOASH Spencer Howard/150 10.00 25.00
BOASS Sixto Sanchez/300 10.00 25.00
BOATM Triston McKenzie/300 12.00 30.00
BOATS Tyler Stephenson/300 12.00 30.00
BOAWC William Contreras/300 15.00 40.00
BOAYA Yordan Alvarez/100 25.00 60.00
BOAZM Zach McKinstry/300 20.00 50.00
BOAABO Alec Bohm/150 40.00 100.00
BOAAGI Andres Gimenez/300 4.00 10.00
BOAAKI Alex Kirilloff/250 20.00 50.00
BOAANO Austin Nola/300 8.00 20.00
BOAATE Anderson Tejeda/300 8.00 20.00
BOAAVE Alex Verdugo/300 12.00 30.00
BOABBU Beau Burrows/300 5.00 12.00
BOABDE Bobby Dalbec/150 25.00 60.00
BOABEB Beau Burrows/300 5.00 12.00
BOABGA Bryan Garcia/300 3.00 8.00
BOABMA Brailyn Marquez/289 10.00 25.00
BOABMQ Brailyn Marquez/275 10.00 25.00
BOABSI Brady Singer/200 10.00 25.00
BOACHE Codi Heuer/300 6.00 15.00
BOACJA Cristian Javier/300 8.00 20.00
BOACMI Casey Mize/300 25.00 60.00
BOACPA Cristian Pache/300 25.00 60.00
BOACSH Clarke Schmidt/300 5.00 12.00
BOADCA Dylan Carlson/150 50.00 120.00
BOADGA Deivi Garcia/300 15.00 40.00
BOADPE David Peterson/300 6.00 15.00
BOADVA Daulton Varsho/300 8.00 20.00
BOADWI Devin Williams/300 5.00 12.00
BOAEOL Edward Olivares/300 8.00 20.00
BOAEWH Evan White/300 6.00 15.00
BOAFKI Franklyn Kilome/300 3.00 8.00
BOAGLU Gavin Lux EXCH 15.00 40.00
BOAHSK Ha-Seong Kim EXCH 6.00 15.00
BOAIAN Ian Anderson/275 20.00 50.00
BOAJAR Jonathan Arauz EXCH 4.00 10.00
BOAJBA Joey Bart/200 20.00 50.00
BOAJCR Jake Cronenworth/300 20.00 50.00
BOAJOA Jonathan Arauz EXCH 4.00 10.00
BOAJSA Jesus Sanchez/300 10.00 25.00
BOAKBH Ke'Bryan Hayes/300 50.00 120.00
BOAKBU Kris Bubic/300 5.00 12.00
BOAKeH Ke'Bryan Hayes/300 50.00 120.00
BOAKLE Kyle Lewis/200 15.00 40.00
BOALGA Luis Garcia/300 10.00 25.00
BOALRO Luis Robert/150 50.00 120.00
BOALTA Leody Taveras/300 3.00 8.00
BOAMBR Michael Brosseau/300 4.00 10.00
BOAMHA Monte Harrison/300 5.00 12.00
BOANHE Nick Heath/300 6.00 15.00
BOANHO Nico Hoerner/200 10.00 25.00
BOANIH Nico Hoerner/200 10.00 25.00
BOANMA Nick Madrigal/201 15.00 40.00
BOANNE Nick Nelson/300 4.00 10.00
BOANPE Nate Pearson/200 10.00 25.00
BOANSO Nick Solak/300 5.00 12.00
BOARCA Ryan Castellani/300 5.00 12.00
BOARJE Ryan Jeffers/300 6.00 15.00
BOARMO Ryan Mountcastle/150 25.00 60.00
BOASHF Sam Huff/300 6.00 15.00
BOASHO Spencer Howard/150 10.00 25.00
BOASHU Sam Huff/300 6.00 15.00
BOASMC Shane McClanahan/300 4.00 10.00
BOASSA Sixto Sanchez/275 10.00 25.00
BOATAH Tanner Houck/300 5.00 12.00
BOATHO Tanner Houck/300 5.00 12.00
BOAWCO William Contreras/300 15.00 40.00
BOAYAL Yordan Alvarez/100 25.00 60.00
BOAZMC Zach McKinstry/300 20.00 50.00
BOASMCL Shane McClanahan/300 4.00 10.00

2021 Topps Tier One Dual Autographs

STATED ODDS 1:xx HOBBY
STATED PRINT RUN 25 SER.#'d SETS
EXCHANGE DEADLINE 3/31/23
DABK B.Buxton/M.Kepler EXCH 50.00 120.00
DACC W.Contreras/W.Contreras EXCH 50.00 120.00
DADG V.Guerrero/A.Dawson
DAMH J.Mauer/K.Hrbek EXCH 60.00 150.00
DAPP A.Pettitte/J.Posada 60.00 150.00
DARH R.Hoskins/S.Rolen EXCH 50.00 120.00
DASA J.Soto/R.Acuna Jr. 600.00 1500.00
DASB K.Bubic/B.Singer 60.00 150.00
DATA M.Trout/J.Adell EXCH 500.00 1200.00

2021 Topps Tier One Legend Relics

STATED ODDS 1:xx HOBBY
PRINT RUNS B/WN 49-199 COPIES PER
T1LRW Pee Wee Reese/199 12.00 30.00
T1LRAK Al Kaline/149 6.00 15.00
T1LRBR Babe Ruth/49 100.00 250.00
T1LRCR Cal Ripken Jr./199 12.00 30.00
T1LRFT Frank Thomas/199 10.00 25.00
T1LRGM Greg Maddux/199 5.00 12.00
T1LRHA Hank Aaron/99 25.00 60.00
T1LRKG Ken Griffey Jr./199 12.00 30.00
T1LRKP Kirby Puckett/149 25.00 60.00
T1LRLB Lou Brock/149 6.00 15.00
T1LRMP Mike Piazza/199 4.00 10.00
T1LRRC Roberto Clemente/49 40.00 100.00
T1LRRH Rickey Henderson/149 10.00 25.00
T1LRRS Ron Santo/99 15.00 40.00
T1LRTG Tony Gwynn/199 8.00 20.00
T1LRTO Tony Oliva/144 10.00 25.00
T1LRTS Tris Speaker/149 15.00 40.00
T1LRWM Willie Mays/49 25.00 60.00
T1LRWS Warren Spahn/99 6.00 15.00
T1LRRCA Rod Carew/99 15.00 40.00
T1LRRCL Roger Clemens/199 5.00 12.00
T1LRWMC Willie McCovey/149 12.00 30.00

2021 Topps Tier One Legend Relics Dual Patch

*DUAL/25: 1X TO 2.5X p/r 144-199
*DUAL/25: .6X TO 1.5X p/r 49-99
STATED ODDS 1:xx HOBBY
STATED PRINT RUN 25 SER.#'d SETS
T1LRKG Ken Griffey Jr. 40.00 100.00
T1LRWS Warren Spahn 20.00 50.00

2021 Topps Tier One Next Level Autographs

STATED ODDS 1:xx HOBBY
STATED PRINT RUN 50 SER.#'d SETS
EXCHANGE DEADLINE 3/31/23
NLAAB Adrian Beltre 30.00 80.00
NLABS Blake Snell 4.00 10.00
NLACY Christian Yelich 40.00 100.00
NLAGM Greg Maddux 75.00 200.00
NLAMC Miguel Cabrera 75.00 200.00
NLARA Ronald Acuna Jr. 100.00 250.00
NLARH Rhys Hoskins 6.00 15.00
NLARS Ryne Sandberg 40.00 100.00
NLARJA Reggie Jackson 30.00 80.00

2021 Topps Tier One Next Level Autographs Bronze Ink

*BRONZE/25: .6X TO 1.5X BASIC
STATED ODDS 1:xx HOBBY
STATED PRINT RUN 25 SER.#'d SETS
EXCHANGE DEADLINE 3/31/23
NLABH Bryce Harper EXCH 75.00 200.00
NLAMT Mike Trout 300.00 800.00

2021 Topps Tier One Prime Performers Autographs

STATED ODDS 1:xx HOBBY
PRINT RUNS B/WN 25-300 COPIES PER
EXCHANGE DEADLINE 3/31/23
*BRONZE/25: .6X TO 1.5X p/r 30-300
*BRONZE/25: .4X TO 1X p/r 25
PPABB Byron Buxton 15.00 40.00
PPABH Bryce Harper EXCH 75.00 200.00
PPADL DJ LeMahieu/300 20.00 50.00
PPAEA Elvis Andrus EXCH 4.00 10.00
PPAGS Gary Sheffield/300 10.00 25.00
PPAHD Hunter Dozier/300 6.00 15.00
PPAJA Jose Altuve/40 10.00 25.00
PPAJB Johnny Bench/30 25.00 60.00
PPAJC Jose Canseco/300 10.00 25.00
PPAJH Josh Hader/300 8.00 20.00
PPAJK John Kruk/300 8.00 20.00
PPAJS Juan Soto/125 75.00 200.00
PPAKH Kyle Hendricks/300 10.00 25.00
PPAKL Kenny Lofton/300 15.00 40.00
PPAKM Ketel Marte/300 8.00 20.00
PPAKW Kolten Wong/300 4.00 10.00
PPALA Luis Arraez/300 6.00 15.00
PPALC Luis Castillo/300 4.00 10.00
PPAMA Moises Alou EXCH/300 6.00 15.00
PPAMB Mark Buehrle/300 10.00 25.00
PPAMM Mark Mulder/300 3.00 8.00
PPAMS Mike Schmidt/100 8.00 20.00
PPAMT Mike Trout/25 300.00 800.00
PPANC Nick Castellanos/300 25.00 60.00
PPAPA Pete Alonso/70 40.00 100.00
PPAPG Paul Goldschmidt/150 12.00 30.00
PPARA Ronald Acuna Jr./70 75.00 200.00
PPARH Rhys Hoskins/300 6.00 15.00
PPARO Roy Oswalt/300 4.00 10.00
PPASM Starling Marte/300 4.00 10.00
PPATB Trevor Bauer/300 20.00 50.00
PPATG Tom Glavine/100 20.00 50.00
PPATH Torii Hunter/300 6.00 15.00
PPATP Tommy Pham/300 3.00 8.00
PPATS Trevor Story/300 5.00 12.00
PPAVG Vladimir Guerrero Jr./150 40.00 100.00
PPAWB Walker Buehler/300 12.00 30.00
PPAWM Whit Merrifield/300 8.00 20.00
PPAYM Yoan Moncada/300 12.00 30.00
PPADLE DJ LeMahieu/300 20.00 50.00
PPAEAN Elvis Andrus EXCH 4.00 10.00
PPAGIO Gio Urshela/300 12.00 30.00
PPAGSH Gary Sheffield/300 10.00 25.00
PPAGUR Gio Urshela/300 12.00 30.00
PPAJCA Jose Canseco/300 10.00 25.00
PPAJDA Johnny Damon/300 8.00 20.00
PPAJHA Josh Hader/300 8.00 20.00
PPAJKR John Kruk/300 8.00 20.00
PPAJOD Johnny Damon/300 8.00 20.00
PPAJSO Juan Soto/130 75.00 200.00
PPAKEM Kenta Maeda/300 8.00 20.00
PPAKET Ketel Marte/300 8.00 20.00
PPAKHE Kyle Hendricks/300 10.00 25.00
PPAKMA Kenta Maeda/300 8.00 20.00
PPAKWO Kolten Wong/300 4.00 10.00
PPALAR Luis Arraez/300 6.00 15.00
PPAMAL Moises Alou EXCH/300 6.00 15.00
PPAMBU Mark Buehrle/300 10.00 25.00
PPAMTE Miguel Tejada/300 6.00 15.00
PPANCA Nick Castellanos/300 25.00 60.00
PPAPGO Paul Goldschmidt/150 12.00 30.00
PPARAJ Ronald Acuna Jr./70 75.00 200.00
PPARHO Rhys Hoskins/300 6.00 15.00
PPAROS Roy Oswalt/300 4.00 10.00
PPASMA Starling Marte/300 4.00 10.00
PPATHU Torii Hunter/300 6.00 15.00
PPATPH Tommy Pham/300 3.00 8.00
PPATST Trevor Story/300 5.00 12.00
PPAWBU Walker Buehler/300 12.00 30.00
PPAWME Whit Merrifield/300 8.00 20.00
PPAYMO Yoan Moncada/300 12.00 30.00

2021 Topps Tier One Tier One Talent Autographs

STATED ODDS 1:xx HOBBY
PRINT RUNS B/WN 10-300 COPIES PER
NO PRICING ON QTY 15 OR LESS
EXCHANGE DEADLINE 3/31/23
*BRONZE/25: .6X TO 1.5X BASIC
T1TAAD Andre Dawson/150 12.00 30.00
T1TAAG Alex Gordon/300 12.00 30.00
T1TAAM Adalberto Mondesi/300 8.00 20.00
T1TAAP Andy Pettitte/101 25.00 60.00
T1TAAR Anthony Rendon/125 10.00 25.00
T1TABS Blake Snell/300 4.00 10.00
T1TACB Cody Bellinger EXCH 60.00 150.00
T1TACJ Chipper Jones/50 50.00 120.00
T1TACY Christian Yelich/150 25.00 60.00
T1TADB Dusty Baker/300 10.00 25.00
T1TADD David Dahl/300 3.00 8.00
T1TADW David Wright/175 20.00 50.00
T1TAEH Eric Hosmer/250 8.00 20.00
T1TAGS Gary Sheffield/300 10.00 25.00
T1TAHM Hideki Matsui/75 40.00 100.00
T1TAJM Juan Marichal/200 20.00 50.00
T1TAJS Juan Soto/150 60.00 150.00
T1TAKH Keston Hiura/300 6.00 15.00
T1TAKW Kolten Wong/300 4.00 10.00
T1TAMK Max Kepler/300 4.00 10.00
T1TAMM Mike Moustakas/250 8.00 20.00
T1TANG Nomar Garciaparra/125 15.00 40.00
T1TAPA Pete Alonso/100 30.00 80.00
T1TARA Ronald Acuna Jr./100 75.00 200.00
T1TARC Rod Carew/125 15.00 40.00
T1TARD Rafael Devers/200 25.00 60.00
T1TARH Rhys Hoskins/200 6.00 15.00
T1TARJ Reggie Jackson/50 30.00 80.00
T1TASB Shane Bieber/300 12.00 30.00
T1TASM Starling Marte/300 4.00 10.00
T1TASR Scott Rolen/300 12.00 30.00
T1TATA Tim Anderson/300 12.00 30.00
T1TATG Tyler Glasnow EXCH 12.00 30.00
T1TAABE Andrew Benintendi 10.00 25.00
T1TAADA Andre Dawson/200 12.00 30.00
T1TAAGA Andres Galarraga/300 6.00 15.00
T1TAAGO Alex Gordon/300 12.00 30.00
T1TAAME Austin Meadows/300 8.00 20.00
T1TAAMO Adalberto Mondesi/300 8.00 20.00
T1TACSA CC Sabathia/125 12.00 30.00
T1TADBA Dusty Baker/300 10.00 25.00
T1TADDA David Dahl/300 3.00 8.00
T1TADWR David Wright/175 20.00 50.00
T1TAEHO Eric Hosmer/250 8.00 20.00
T1TAEJI Eloy Jimenez/250 20.00 50.00
T1TAGSH Gary Sheffield/300 10.00 25.00
T1TAGSP George Springer/200 12.00 30.00
T1TAHOW Ryan Howard/250 12.00 30.00
T1TAHUD Tim Hudson/300 4.00 10.00
T1TAJOS Jorge Soler/300 5.00 12.00
T1TAJSO Jorge Soler/300 5.00 12.00
T1TAKEH Kent Hrbek/300 8.00 20.00
T1TAKHI Keston Hiura/300 6.00 15.00
T1TAKHR Kent Hrbek/300 8.00 20.00
T1TAKWO Kolten Wong/300 4.00 10.00
T1TAMKE Max Kepler/300 4.00 10.00
T1TAMMC Mark McGwire/50 50.00 120.00
T1TAMMO Mike Moustakas/250 8.00 20.00
T1TARAC Ronald Acuna Jr./100 75.00 200.00
T1TARCA Rod Carew/125 15.00 40.00
T1TARHO Rhys Hoskins/200 6.00 15.00
T1TARJA Reggie Jackson/50 30.00 80.00
T1TASBI Shane Bieber/300 12.00 30.00
T1TASMA Starling Marte/300 4.00 10.00
T1TASRO Scott Rolen/300 12.00 30.00
T1TATAN Tim Anderson/300 12.00 30.00
T1TATHU Torii Hunter/250 6.00 15.00
T1TATIH Tim Hudson/300 4.00 10.00
T1TATIM Tim Hudson/300 4.00 10.00
T1TATOH Torii Hunter/250 6.00 15.00

2002 Topps Total Pre-Production

COMPLETE SET (3) 1.25 3.00
PP1 Barry Bonds .50 1.25
PP2 Ichiro Suzuki .60 1.50
PP3 Hank Blalock .30 .75

2002 Topps Total

COMPLETE SET (990) 75.00 150.00
1 Joe Mauer RC 6.00 15.00
2 Derek Jeter .75 2.00
3 Shawn Green .10 .30
4 Vladimir Guerrero .30 .75
5 Mike Piazza .50 1.25
6 Brandon Duckworth .07 .20
7 Aramis Ramirez .10 .30
8 Josh Barfield RC 1.00 2.50
9 Troy Glaus .10 .30
10 Sammy Sosa .30 .75
11 Rod Barajas .07 .20
12 Tsuyoshi Shinjo .10 .30
13 Larry Bigbie .07 .20
14 Tino Martinez .20 .50
15 Craig Biggio .20 .50
16 Anastacio Martinez RC .15 .40
17 John McDonald .07 .20
18 Kyle Kane RC .08 .25
19 Aubrey Huff .10 .30
20 Juan Cruz .07 .20
21 Doug Creek .07 .20
22 Luther Hackman .07 .20
23 Rafael Furcal .10 .30
24 Andres Torres .07 .20
25 Jason Giambi .10 .30
26 Jose Paniagua .07 .20
27 Jose Offerman .07 .20
28 Alex Arias .07 .20
29 J.M. Gold .07 .20
30 Jeff Bagwell .20 .50
31 Brent Cookson .07 .20
32 Kelly Wunsch .07 .20
33 Larry Walker .10 .30
34 Luis Gonzalez .10 .30
35 John Franco .10 .30
36 Roy Oswalt .10 .30
37 Tom Glavine .20 .50
38 C.C. Sabathia .10 .30
39 Jay Gibbons .07 .20
40 Wilson Betemit .07 .20
41 Tony Armas Jr. .07 .20
42 Mo Vaughn .10 .30
43 Gerard Oakes RC .15 .40
44 Dmitri Young .10 .30
45 Tim Salmon .20 .50
46 Barry Zito .10 .30
47 Adrian Gonzalez .07 .20
48 Joe Davenport .07 .20
49 Adrian Hernandez .07 .20
50 Randy Johnson .30 .75
52 Adam Pettyjohn .07 .20
53 Alex Escobar .07 .20
54 Stevenson Agosto RC .08 .25
55 Omar Daal .07 .20
56 Mike Buddie .07 .20
57 Dave Williams .07 .20
58 Marquis Grissom .10 .30
59 Pat Burrell .10 .30
60 Mark Prior .20 .50
61 Mike Bynum .07 .20
62 Mike Hill RC .15 .40
63 Brandon Backe RC .20 .50
64 Dan Wilson .07 .20
65 Nick Johnson .10 .30
66 Jason Grimsley .07 .20
67 Russ Johnson .07 .20
68 Todd Walker .07 .20
69 Kyle Farnsworth .07 .20
70 Ben Broussard .07 .20
71 Garrett Guzman RC .15 .40
72 Terry Mulholland .07 .20
73 Tyler Houston .07 .20
74 Jace Brewer .07 .20
75 Chris Baker RC .15 .40
76 Frank Catalanotto .07 .20
77 Mike Redmond .07 .20
78 Matt Wise .07 .20
79 Fernando Vina .07 .20
80 Kevin Brown .10 .30
81 Grant Balfour .07 .20
82 Clint Nageotte RC .20 .50
83 Jeff Tam .07 .20
84 Steve Trachsel .07 .20
85 Tomo Ohka .07 .20
86 Keith McDonald .07 .20
87 Jose Ortiz .07 .20
88 Rusty Greer .10 .30
89 Jeff Suppan .07 .20
90 Moises Alou .10 .30
91 Juan Encarnacion .07 .20
92 Tyler Yates RC .15 .40
93 Scott Strickland .07 .20
94 Brent Butler .07 .20
95 Jon Rauch .07 .20
96 Brian Mallette RC .08 .25
97 Joe Randa .10 .30
98 Cesar Crespo .07 .20
99 Felix Rodriguez .07 .20
100 Chipper Jones .30 .75
101 Victor Martinez .30 .75
102 Danny Graves .07 .20
103 Brandon Berger .07 .20
104 Carlos Garcia .07 .20
105 Alfonso Soriano .10 .30
106 Allan Simpson RC .08 .25
107 Brad Thomas .07 .20
108 Devon White .10 .30
109 Scott Chiasson .07 .20
110 Cliff Floyd .10 .30
111 Scott Williamson .07 .20
112 Julio Zuleta .07 .20
113 Terry Adams .07 .20
114 Zach Day .07 .20
115 Ben Grieve .07 .20
116 Mark Ellis .07 .20
117 Bobby Jenks RC .60 1.50
118 LaTroy Hawkins .07 .20
119 Tim Raines Jr. .07 .20
120 Juan Uribe .07 .20
121 Bob Scanlan .07 .20
122 Brad Nelson RC .15 .40
123 Adam Johnson .07 .20
124 Raul Casanova .07 .20
125 Jeff D'Amico .07 .20
126 Aaron Cook RC .15 .40
127 Alan Benes .07 .20
128 Mark Little .07 .20
129 Randy Wolf .07 .20
130 Phil Nevin .10 .30
131 Guillermo Mota .07 .20
132 Nick Neugebauer .07 .20
133 Pedro Borbon Jr. .07 .20
134 Doug Mientkiewicz .10 .30
135 Edgardo Alfonzo .07 .20
136 Dustan Mohr .07 .20
137 Dan Reichert .07 .20
138 Dewon Brazelton .07 .20
139 Orlando Cabrera .10 .30
140 Todd Hollandsworth .07 .20
141 Darren Dreifort .07 .20
142 Jose Valentin .07 .20
143 Josh Kalinowski .07 .20
144 Randy Keisler .07 .20
145 Bret Boone .10 .30
146 Roosevelt Brown .07 .20
147 Brent Abernathy .07 .20
148 Jorge Julio .07 .20
149 Alex Gonzalez .07 .20
150 Juan Pierre .10 .30
151 Roger Cedeno .07 .20
152 Javier Vazquez .10 .30
153 Armando Benitez .07 .20
154 Dave Burba .07 .20
155 Brad Penny .07 .20
156 Ryan Jensen .07 .20
157 Jeromy Burnitz .10 .30
158 Matt Childers RC .15 .40
159 Wilmy Caceres .07 .20
160 Roger Clemens .60 1.50
161 Jamie Cerda RC .15 .40
162 Jason Christiansen .07 .20
163 Pokey Reese .07 .20
164 Ivanon Coffie .07 .20
165 Joaquin Benoit .07 .20
166 Mike Matheny .07 .20
167 Eric Cammack .07 .20
168 Alex Graman .07 .20
169 Brook Fordyce .07 .20
170 Mike Lieberthal .10 .30
171 Giovanni Carrara .07 .20
172 Antonio Perez .07 .20
173 Fernando Tatis .07 .20
174 Jason Bay RC 2.00 5.00
175 Jason Botts RC .20 .50
176 Danys Baez .07 .20
177 Shea Hillenbrand .10 .30
178 Jack Cust .07 .20
179 Clay Bellinger .07 .20
180 Roberto Alomar .20 .50
181 Graeme Lloyd .07 .20
182 Clint Weibl RC .08 .25
183 Royce Clayton .07 .20
184 Ben Davis .07 .20
185 Brian Adams RC .08 .25
186 Jack Wilson .07 .20
187 David Coggin .07 .20
188 Derrick Turnbow .07 .20
189 Vladimir Nunez .07 .20
190 Mariano Rivera .30 .75
191 Wilson Guzman .07 .20
192 Michael Barrett .07 .20
193 Corey Patterson .07 .20
194 Luis Sojo .07 .20
195 Scott Elarton .07 .20
196 Charles Thomas RC .15 .40
197 Ricky Bottalico .07 .20
198 Wilfredo Rodriguez .07 .20
199 Ricardo Rincon .07 .20
200 John Smoltz .20 .50
201 Travis Miller .07 .20
202 Ben Weber .07 .20
203 T.J. Tucker .07 .20
204 Terry Shumpert .07 .20
205 Bernie Williams .20 .50
206 Russ Ortiz .07 .20
207 Nate Rolison .07 .20
208 Jose Cruz Jr. .07 .20
209 Bill Ortega .07 .20
210 Carl Everett .10 .30
211 Luis Lopez .07 .20
212 Brian Wolfe RC .15 .40
213 Doug Davis .07 .20
214 Troy Mattes .07 .20
215 Al Leiter .10 .30
216 Joe Mays .07 .20
217 Bobby Smith .07 .20
218 J.J. Trujillo RC .15 .40
219 Hideo Nomo .30 .75
220 Jimmy Rollins .10 .30
221 Bobby Seay .07 .20
222 Mike Thurman .07 .20
223 Bartolo Colon .10 .30
224 Jesus Sanchez .07 .20
225 Ray Durham .10 .30
226 Juan Diaz .07 .20
227 Lee Stevens .07 .20
228 Ben Howard RC .15 .40
229 James Mouton .07 .20
230 Paul Quantrill .07 .20
231 Randy Knorr .07 .20
232 Abraham Nunez .07 .20
233 Mike Fetters .07 .20
234 Mario Encarnacion .07 .20
235 Jeremy Fikac .07 .20
236 Travis Lee .07 .20
237 Bob File .07 .20
238 Pete Harnisch .07 .20
239 Randy Galvez RC .15 .40
240 Geoff Goetz .07 .20
241 Gary Glover .07 .20
242 Troy Percival .10 .30
243 Len Dinardo RC .15 .40
244 Jonny Gomes RC 1.00 2.50
245 Jesus Medrano RC .15 .40
246 Rey Ordonez .07 .20
247 Juan Gonzalez .10 .30
248 Jose Guillen .10 .30
249 Franklyn German RC .15 .40
250 Mike Mussina .20 .50
251 Ugueth Urbina .07 .20
252 Melvin Mora .10 .30
253 Gerald Williams .07 .20
254 Jared Sandberg .07 .20
255 Darrin Fletcher .07 .20
256 A.J. Pierzynski .10 .30
257 Lenny Harris .07 .20
258 Blaine Neal .07 .20
259 Denny Neagle .07 .20
260 Jason Hart .07 .20
261 Henry Mateo .07 .20
262 Rheal Cormier .07 .20
263 Luis Terrero .07 .20
264 Shigetoshi Hasegawa .10 .30
265 Bill Haselman .07 .20
266 Scott Hatteberg .07 .20
267 Adam Hyzdu .07 .20
268 Mike Williams .07 .20

269 Marlon Anderson .07 .20
270 Bruce Chen .07 .20
271 Eli Marrero .07 .20
272 Jimmy Haynes .07 .20
273 Bronson Arroyo .10 .30
274 Kevin Jordan .07 .20
275 Rick Helling .07 .20
276 Mark Loretta .07 .20
277 Dustin Hermanson .07 .20
278 Pablo Ozuna .07 .20
279 Keto Anderson RC .15 .40
280 Jermaine Dye .10 .30
281 Will Smith .07 .20
282 Brian Daubach .07 .20
283 Eric Hinske .07 .20
284 Joe Jiannetti RC .15 .40
285 Chan Ho Park .10 .30
286 Curtis Legendre RC .15 .40
287 Jeff Reboulet .07 .20
288 Scott Rolen .20 .50
289 Chris Richard .07 .20
290 Eric Chavez .10 .30
291 Scot Shields .07 .20
292 Donnie Sadler .07 .20
293 Dave Veres .07 .20
294 Craig Counsell .07 .20
295 Armando Reynoso .07 .20
296 Kyle Lohse .07 .20
297 Arthur Rhodes .07 .20
298 Sidney Ponson .07 .20
299 Trevor Hoffman .10 .30
300 Kerry Wood .10 .30
301 Danny Bautista .07 .20
302 Scott Sauerbeck .07 .20
303 Johnny Estrada .07 .20
304 Mike Timlin .07 .20
305 Orlando Hernandez .10 .30
306 Tony Clark .07 .20
307 Tomas Perez .07 .20
308 Marcus Giles .10 .30
309 Mike Bordick .10 .30
310 Jorge Posada .20 .50
311 Jason Conti .07 .20
312 Kevin Millar .10 .30
313 Paul Shuey .07 .20
314 Jake Mauer RC .15 .40
315 Luke Hudson .07 .20
316 Angel Berroa .07 .20
317 Fred Bastardo RC .15 .40
318 Shawn Estes .07 .20
319 Andy Ashby .07 .20
320 Ryan Klesko .10 .30
321 Kevin Appier .10 .30
322 Juan Pena .07 .20
323 Alex Herrera .07 .20
324 Robb Nen .10 .30
325 Orlando Hudson .07 .20
326 Lyle Overbay .07 .20
327 Ben Sheets .10 .30
328 Mike DiFelice .07 .20
329 Pablo Arias RC .15 .40
330 Mike Sweeney .10 .30
331 Rick Ankiel .07 .20
332 Tomas De La Rosa .07 .20
333 Kazuhisa Ishii RC .20 .50
334 Jose Reyes .20 .50
335 Jeremy Giambi .07 .20
336 Jose Mesa .07 .20
337 Ralph Roberts RC .15 .40
338 Jose Nunez .07 .20
339 Curt Schilling .10 .30
340 Sean Casey .10 .30
341 Bob Wells .07 .20
342 Carlos Beltran .10 .30
343 Alexis Gomez .07 .20
344 Brandon Claussen .07 .20
345 Buddy Groom .07 .20
346 Mark Phillips RC .15 .40
347 Francisco Cordova .07 .20
348 Joe Oliver .07 .20
349 Danny Patterson .07 .20
350 Joel Pineiro .07 .20
351 J.R. House .07 .20
352 Benny Agbayani .07 .20
353 Jose Vidro .07 .20
354 Reed Johnson RC .40 1.00
355 Mike Lowell .10 .30
356 Scott Schoeneweis .07 .20
357 Brian Jordan .10 .30
358 Steve Finley .10 .30
359 Randy Choate .07 .20
360 Jose Lima .07 .20
361 Miguel Olivo .07 .20
362 Kenny Rogers .10 .30
363 David Justice .10 .30
364 Brandon Knight .07 .20
365 Joe Kennedy .07 .20
366 Eric Valent .07 .20
367 Nelson Cruz .07 .20
368 Brian Giles .10 .30
369 Charles Gipson RC .08 .25
370 Juan Pena .07 .20
371 Mark Redman .07 .20
372 Billy Koch .07 .20
373 Ted Lilly .07 .20
374 Craig Paquette .07 .20
375 Kevin Jarvis .07 .20
376 Scott Erickson .07 .20
377 Josh Paul .07 .20
378 Darwin Cubillan .07 .20
379 Nelson Figueroa .07 .20
380 Darin Erstad .10 .30
381 Jeremy Hill RC .15 .40
382 Elvin Nina .07 .20
383 David Wells .10 .30
384 Jay Caligiuri RC .15 .40
385 Freddy Garcia .10 .30
386 Damian Miller .07 .20
387 Bobby Higginson .10 .30
388 Alejandro Giron RC .15 .40
389 Ivan Rodriguez .20 .50
390 Ed Rogers .07 .20
391 Andy Benes .07 .20
392 Matt Blank .07 .20
393 Ryan Vogelsong .07 .20
394 Kelly Ramos RC .08 .25
395 Eric Karros .10 .30
396 Bobby J. Jones .07 .20
397 Omar Vizquel .20 .50
398 Matt Perisho .07 .20
399 Delino DeShields .07 .20
400 Carlos Hernandez .07 .20
401 Derrek Lee .20 .50
402 Kirk Rueter .07 .20
403 David Wright RC 3.00 8.00
404 Paul LoDuca .10 .30
405 Brian Schneider .07 .20
406 Milton Bradley .10 .30
407 Daryle Ward .07 .20
408 Cody Ransom .07 .20
409 Fernando Rodney .07 .20
410 John Suomi RC .15 .40
411 Joe Girardi .07 .20
412 Demetrius Heath RC .15 .40
413 John Foster RC .15 .40
414 Doug Glanville .07 .20
415 Ryan Kohlmeier .07 .20
416 Mike Matthews .07 .20
417 Craig Wilson .07 .20
418 Jay Witasick .07 .20
419 Jay Payton .07 .20
420 Andruw Jones .20 .50
421 Benji Gil .07 .20
422 Jeff Liefer .07 .20
423 Kevin Young .07 .20
424 Richie Sexson .10 .30
425 Cory Lidle .07 .20
426 Shane Halter .07 .20
427 Jesse Foppert RC .20 .50
428 Jose Molina .07 .20
429 Nick Alvarez RC .15 .40
430 Brian L. Hunter .07 .20
431 Cliff Bartosh RC .15 .40
432 Junior Spivey .07 .20
433 Eric Good RC .15 .40
434 Chin-Feng Chen .10 .30
435 T.J. Mathews .07 .20
436 Rich Rodriguez .07 .20
437 Bobby Abreu .10 .30
438 Joe McEwing .07 .20
439 Michael Tucker .07 .20
440 Preston Wilson .10 .30
441 Mike MacDougal .07 .20
442 Shannon Stewart .10 .30
443 Bob Howry .07 .20
444 Mike Benjamin .07 .20
445 Erik Hiljus .07 .20
446 Ryan Gripp RC .15 .40
447 Jose Vizcaino .07 .20
448 Shawn Wooten .07 .20
449 Steve Kent RC .15 .40
450 Ramiro Mendoza .07 .20
451 Jake Westbrook .07 .20
452 Joe Lawrence .07 .20
453 Jae Seo .07 .20
454 Ryan Fry RC .15 .40
455 Darren Lewis .07 .20
456 Brad Wilkerson .07 .20
457 Gustavo Chacin RC .40 1.00
458 Adrian Brown .07 .20
459 Mike Cameron .07 .20
460 Bud Smith .07 .20
461 Derrick Lewis .07 .20
462 Derek Lowe .10 .30
463 Matt Williams .10 .30
464 Jason Jennings .07 .20
465 Albie Lopez .07 .20
466 Felipe Lopez .07 .20
467 Luke Allen .07 .20
468 Brian Anderson .07 .20
469 Matt Riley .07 .20
470 Ryan Dempster .07 .20
471 Matt Ginter .07 .20
472 David Ortiz .30 .75
473 Cole Barthel RC .08 .25
474 Damian Jackson .07 .20
475 Andy Van Hekken .07 .20
476 Doug Brocail .07 .20
477 Denny Hocking .07 .20
478 Sean Douglass .07 .20
479 Eric Owens .07 .20
480 Ryan Ludwick .07 .20
481 Todd Pratt .07 .20
482 Aaron Sele .07 .20
483 Edgar Renteria .10 .30
484 Raymond Cabrera RC .15 .40
485 Brandon Lyon .07 .20
486 Chase Utley 1.00 2.50
487 Robert Fick .07 .20
488 Wilfredo Cordero .07 .20
489 Octavio Dotel .07 .20
490 Paul Abbott .07 .20
491 Jason Kendall .10 .30
492 Jarrod Washburn .07 .20
493 Dane Sardinha .07 .20
494 Jung Bong .07 .20
495 J.D. Drew .10 .30
496 Jason Schmidt .10 .30
497 Mike Magnante .07 .20
498 Jorge Padilla RC .15 .40
499 Eric Gagne .10 .30
500 Todd Helton .20 .50
501 Jeff Weaver .07 .20
502 Alex Sanchez .07 .20
503 Ken Griffey Jr. .60 1.50
504 Abraham Nunez .07 .20
505 Reggie Sanders .10 .30
506 Casey Kotchman RC .40 1.00
507 Jim Mann .07 .20
508 Matt LeCroy .07 .20
509 Frank Castillo .07 .20
510 Geoff Jenkins .07 .20
511 Jayson Durocher RC .08 .25
512 Ellis Burks .10 .30
513 Aaron Fultz .07 .20
514 Hiram Bocachica .07 .20
515 Nate Espy RC .15 .40
516 Placido Polanco .07 .20
517 Kerry Ligtenberg .07 .20
518 Doug Nickle .07 .20
519 Ramon Ortiz .07 .20
520 Greg Swindell .07 .20
521 J.J. Davis .07 .20
522 Sandy Alomar Jr. .07 .20
523 Chris Carpenter .10 .30
524 Vance Wilson .07 .20
525 Nomar Garciaparra .50 1.25
526 Jim Mecir .07 .20
527 Taylor Buchholz RC .20 .50
528 Brent Mayne .07 .20
529 John Rodriguez RC .20 .50
530 David Segui .07 .20
531 Nate Cornejo .07 .20
532 Gil Heredia .07 .20
533 Esteban Loaiza .07 .20
534 Pat Mahomes .07 .20
535 Matt Morris .10 .30
536 Todd Stottlemyre .07 .20
537 Brian Lesher .07 .20
538 Arturo McDowell .07 .20
539 Felix Diaz .07 .20
540 Mark Mulder .10 .30
541 Kevin Frederick RC .15 .40
542 Andy Fox .07 .20
543 Dionys Cesar RC .08 .25
544 Justin Miller .07 .20
545 Keith Osik .07 .20
546 Shane Reynolds .07 .20
547 Mike Myers .07 .20
548 Raul Chavez RC .08 .25
549 Joe Nathan .10 .30
550 Ryan Anderson .07 .20
551 Jason Marquis .07 .20
552 Marty Cordova .07 .20
553 Kevin Tapani .07 .20
554 Jimmy Anderson .07 .20
555 Pedro Martinez .20 .50
556 Rocky Biddle .07 .20
557 Alex Ochoa .07 .20
558 D'Angelo Jimenez .07 .20
559 Wilkin Ruan .07 .20
560 Terrence Long .07 .20
561 Mark Lukasiewicz .07 .20
562 Jose Santiago .07 .20
563 Brad Fullmer .07 .20
564 Corky Miller .07 .20
565 Matt White .07 .20
566 Mark Grace .20 .50
567 Raul Ibanez .07 .20
568 Josh Towers .07 .20
569 Juan M. Gonzalez RC .15 .40
570 Brian Buchanan .07 .20
571 Ken Harvey .07 .20
572 Jeffrey Hammonds .07 .20
573 Wade Miller .07 .20
574 Elpidio Guzman .07 .20
575 Kevin Olsen .07 .20
576 Austin Kearns .07 .20
577 Tim Kalita RC .15 .40
578 David Dellucci .07 .20
579 Alex Gonzalez .07 .20
580 Joe Orloski RC .15 .40
581 Gary Matthews Jr. .07 .20
582 Ryan Mills .07 .20
583 Erick Almonte .07 .20
584 Jeremy Affeldt .07 .20
585 Chris Tritle RC .08 .25
586 Michael Cuddyer .07 .20
587 Kris Foster .07 .20
588 Russell Branyan .07 .20
589 Darren Oliver .07 .20
590 Freddie Money RC .15 .40
591 Carlos Lee .07 .20
592 Tim Wakefield .10 .30
593 Bubba Trammell .07 .20
594 John Koronka RC .40 1.00
595 Geoff Blum .07 .20
596 Darryl Kile .10 .30
597 Neifi Perez .07 .20
598 Torii Hunter .10 .30
599 Luis Castillo .07 .20
600 Mark Buehrle .10 .30
601 Jeff Zimmerman .07 .20
602 Mike DeJean .07 .20
603 Julio Lugo .07 .20
604 Chad Hermansen .07 .20
605 Keith Foulke .10 .30
606 Lance Davis .07 .20
607 Jeff Bagwell .15 .40
608 Brandon Inge .07 .20
609 Orlando Merced .07 .20
610 Johnny Damon Sox .07 .20
611 Doug Henry .07 .20
612 Adam Kennedy .07 .20
613 Wiki Gonzalez .07 .20
614 Brian West RC .15 .40
615 Andy Pettitte .20 .50
616 Chone Figgins RC .60 1.50
617 Matt Lawton .07 .20
618 Paul Rigdon .07 .20
619 Keith Lockhart .07 .20
620 Tim Redding .07 .20
621 John Parrish .07 .20
622 Homer Bush .07 .20
623 Todd Greene .07 .20
624 David Eckstein .10 .30
625 Greg Montalbano RC .15 .40
626 Joe Beimel .07 .20
627 Adrian Beltre .10 .30
628 Charles Nagy .07 .20
629 Cristian Guzman .07 .20
630 Toby Hall .07 .20
631 Jose Hernandez .07 .20
632 Jose Macias .07 .20
633 Jaret Wright .07 .20
634 Steve Parris .07 .20
635 Gene Kingsale .07 .20
636 Tim Worrell .07 .20
637 Billy Martin .07 .20
638 Jovanny Cedeno .07 .20
639 Curtis Leskanic .07 .20
640 Tim Hudson .10 .30
641 Juan Castro .07 .20
642 Rafael Soriano .07 .20
643 Juan Rincon .07 .20
644 Mark DeRosa .07 .20
645 Carlos Pena .07 .20
646 Robin Ventura .10 .30
647 Odalis Perez .07 .20
648 Damion Easley .07 .20
649 Benito Santiago .10 .30
650 Alex Rodriguez .40 1.00
651 Aaron Rowand .07 .20
652 Alex Cora .07 .20
653 Bobby Kielty .07 .20
654 Jose Rodriguez RC .15 .40
655 Herbert Perry .07 .20
656 Jeff Urban .07 .20
657 Paul Bako .07 .20
658 Shane Spencer .07 .20
659 Pat Hentgen .07 .20
660 Jeff Kent .10 .30
661 Mark McLemore .07 .20
662 Chuck Knoblauch .10 .30
663 Blake Stein .07 .20
664 Brett Roneberg RC .15 .40
665 Josh Phelps .07 .20
666 Byung-Hyun Kim .10 .30
667 Dave Martinez .07 .20
668 Mike Maroth .07 .20
669 Shawn Chacon .07 .20
670 Billy Wagner .10 .30
671 Luis Alicea .07 .20
672 Sterling Hitchcock .07 .20
673 Adam Piatt .07 .20
674 Ryan Franklin .07 .20
675 Luke Prokopec .07 .20
676 Alfredo Amezaga .07 .20
677 Gookie Dawkins .07 .20
678 Eric Byrnes .07 .20
679 Barry Larkin .20 .50
680 Albert Pujols .60 1.50
681 Edwards Guzman .07 .20
682 Jason Bere .07 .20
683 Adam Everett .07 .20
684 Greg Colbrunn .07 .20
685 Brandon Puffer RC .15 .40
686 Mark Kotsay .10 .30
687 Willie Bloomquist .10 .30
688 Hank Blalock .20 .50
689 Travis Hafner .10 .30
690 Lance Berkman .10 .30
691 Joe Crede .10 .30
692 Chuck Finley .10 .30
693 John Grabow .07 .20
694 Randy Winn .07 .20
695 Mike James .07 .20
696 Kris Benson .07 .20
697 Bret Prinz .07 .20
698 Jeff Williams .07 .20
699 Eric Munson .07 .20
700 Mike Hampton .10 .30
701 Ramon E. Martinez .07 .20
702 Hansel Izquierdo RC .15 .40
703 Nathan Haynes .07 .20
704 Eddie Taubensee .07 .20
705 Esteban German .07 .20
706 Ross Gload .07 .20
707 Matt Merricks RC .15 .40
708 Chris Piersoll RC .08 .25
709 Seth Greisinger .07 .20
710 Ichiro Suzuki .60 1.50
711 Cesar Izturis .07 .20
712 Brad Cresse .07 .20
713 Carl Pavano .10 .30
714 Steve Sparks .07 .20
715 Dennis Tankersley .07 .20
716 Kelvim Escobar .07 .20
717 Jason LaRue .07 .20
718 Corey Koskie .07 .20
719 Vinny Castilla .10 .30
720 Tim Drew .07 .20
721 Chin-Hui Tsao .10 .30
722 Paul Byrd .07 .20
723 Alex Cintron .07 .20
724 Orlando Palmeiro .07 .20
725 Ramon Hernandez .07 .20
726 Mark Johnson .07 .20
727 B.J. Ryan .07 .20
728 Wendell Magee .07 .20
729 Michael Coleman .07 .20
730 Mario Ramos RC .15 .40
731 Mike Stanton .07 .20
732 Dee Brown .07 .20
733 Brad Ausmus .07 .20
734 Napoleon Calzado RC .15 .40
735 Woody Williams .07 .20
736 Paxton Crawford .07 .20
737 Jason Karnuth .07 .20
738 Michael Restovich .07 .20
739 Ramon Castro .07 .20
740 Magglio Ordonez .10 .30
741 Tom Gordon .07 .20
742 Mark Grudzielanek .07 .20
743 Jaime Moyer .10 .30
744 Marlyn Tisdale RC .15 .40
745 Steve Kline .07 .20
746 Adam Eaton .07 .20
747 Eric Glaser RC .15 .40
748 Sean DePaula .07 .20
749 Greg Norton .07 .20
750 Steve Reed .07 .20
751 Ricardo Aramboles .07 .20
752 Matt Mantei .07 .20
753 Gene Stechschulte .07 .20
754 Chuck McElroy .07 .20
755 Barry Bonds .75 2.00
756 Matt Anderson .07 .20
757 Yorvit Torrealba .07 .20
758 Jason Standridge .07 .20
759 Desi Relaford .07 .20
760 Jolbert Cabrera .07 .20
761 Chris George .07 .20
762 Erubiel Durazo .07 .20
763 Paul Konerko .10 .30
764 Tike Redman .07 .20
765 Chad Ricketts RC .08 .25
766 Roberto Hernandez .07 .20
767 Mark Lewis .07 .20
768 Livan Hernandez .10 .30
769 Carlos Brackley RC .15 .40
770 Kazuhiro Sasaki .10 .30
771 Bill Hall .10 .30
772 Nelson Castro RC .15 .40
773 Eric Milton .07 .20
774 Tom Davey .07 .20
775 Todd Ritchie .07 .20
776 Seth Etherton .07 .20
777 Chris Singleton .07 .20
778 Robert Averette RC .08 .25
779 Robert Person .07 .20
780 Fred McGriff .20 .50
781 Richard Hidalgo .07 .20
782 Kris Wilson .07 .20
783 John Rocker .10 .30
784 Justin Kaye .07 .20
785 Glendon Rusch .07 .20
786 Greg Vaughn .07 .20
787 Mike Lamb .07 .20
788 Greg Myers .07 .20
789 Nate Field RC .15 .40
790 Jim Edmonds .10 .30
791 Olmedo Saenz .07 .20
792 Jason Johnson .07 .20
793 Mike Lincoln .07 .20
794 Todd Coffey RC .15 .40
795 Jesus Sanchez .07 .20
796 Aaron Myette .07 .20
797 Tony Womack .07 .20
798 Chad Kreuter .07 .20
799 Brady Clark .07 .20
800 Adam Dunn .10 .30
801 Jacque Jones .10 .30
802 Kevin Millwood .10 .30
803 Mike Rivera .07 .20
804 Jim Thome .20 .50
805 Jeff Conine .10 .30
806 Elmer Dessens .07 .20
807 Randy Velarde .07 .20
808 Carlos Delgado .10 .30
809 Steve Karsay .07 .20
810 Casey Fossum .07 .20
811 J.C. Romero .07 .20
812 Chris Truby .07 .20
813 Tony Graffanino .07 .20
814 Wascar Serrano .07 .20
815 Delvin James .07 .20
816 Pedro Feliz .07 .20
817 Damian Rolls .07 .20
818 Scott Linebrink .07 .20
819 Rafael Palmeiro .20 .50
820 Javy Lopez .10 .30
821 Larry Barnes .07 .20
822 Brian Lawrence .07 .20
823 Scotty Layfield RC .15 .40
824 Jeff Cirillo .07 .20
825 Willis Roberts .07 .20
826 Rich Harden RC 1.25 3.00
827 Chris Snelling RC .25 .60
828 Gary Sheffield .10 .30
829 Jeff Heaverlo .07 .20
830 Matt Clement .10 .30
831 Rich Garces .07 .20
832 Rondell White .10 .30
833 Henry Pichardo RC .15 .40
834 Aaron Boone .10 .30
835 Ruben Sierra .10 .30
836 Deivis Santos .07 .20
837 Tony Batista .07 .20
838 Rob Bell .07 .20
839 Frank Thomas .30 .75
840 Jose Silva .07 .20
841 Dan Johnson RC .40 1.00
842 Steve Cox .07 .20
843 Jose Acevedo .07 .20
844 Jay Bell .07 .20
845 Mike Sirotka .10 .30
846 Garret Anderson .10 .30
847 James Shanks RC .15 .40
848 Trot Nixon .10 .30
849 Keith Ginter .07 .20
850 Tim Spooneybarger .07 .20
851 Matt Stairs .07 .20
852 Chris Stynes .07 .20
853 Marvin Benard .07 .20
854 Raul Mondesi .10 .30
855 Jeremy Owens .07 .20
856 Jon Garland .10 .30
857 Mitch Meluskey .07 .20
858 Chad Durbin .07 .20
859 John Burkett .07 .20
860 Jon Switzer RC .15 .40
861 Peter Bergeron .07 .20
862 Jesus Colome .07 .20
863 Todd Hundley .07 .20
864 Ben Petrick .07 .20
865 So Taguchi RC .20 .50
866 Ryan Drese .07 .20
867 Mike Trombley .07 .20
868 Rick Reed .07 .20
869 Mark Teixeira .30 .75
870 Corey Thurman RC .15 .40
871 Brian Roberts .10 .30
872 Mike Timlin .07 .20
873 Chris Reitsma .07 .20
874 Jeff Fassero .07 .20
875 Carlos Valderrama .07 .20
876 John Lackey .07 .20
877 Travis Fryman .10 .30
878 Ismael Valdes .07 .20
879 Rick White .07 .20
880 Edgar Martinez .20 .50
881 Dean Palmer .10 .30
882 Matt Allegra RC .15 .40
883 Greg Sain RC .15 .40
884 Carlos Silva .07 .20
885 Jose Valverde RC .15 .40
886 Dernell Stenson .07 .20
887 Todd Van Poppel .07 .20
888 Wes Anderson .07 .20
889 Bill Mueller .10 .30
890 Morgan Ensberg .10 .30
891 Marcus Thames .07 .20
892 Adam Walker RC .15 .40
893 John Halama .07 .20
894 Frank Menechino .07 .20
895 Greg Maddux .50 1.25
896 Gary Bennett .07 .20
897 Mauricio Lara RC .15 .40
898 Mike Young .30 .75
899 Travis Phelps .07 .20
900 Rich Aurilia .07 .20
901 Henry Blanco .07 .20
902 Carlos Febles .07 .20
903 Scott MacRae .07 .20
904 Lou Merloni .07 .20
905 Dicky Gonzalez .07 .20
906 Jeff DaVanon .07 .20
907 A.J. Burnett .10 .30
908 Einar Diaz .07 .20
909 Julio Franco .10 .30
910 John Olerud .10 .30
911 Mark Hamilton RC .15 .40
912 David Riske .07 .20
913 Jason Tyner .07 .20
914 Britt Reames .07 .20
915 Vernon Wells .10 .30
916 Eddie Perez .07 .20
917 Edwin Almonte RC .15 .40
918 Enrique Wilson .07 .20
919 Chris Gomez .07 .20
920 Jayson Werth .07 .20
921 Jeff Nelson .07 .20
922 Freddy Sanchez RC .75 2.00
923 John Vander Wal .07 .20
924 Chad Qualls RC .20 .50
925 Gabe White .07 .20
926 Chad Harville .07 .20
927 Ricky Gutierrez .07 .20
928 Carlos Guillen .10 .30
929 B.J. Surhoff .10 .30
930 Chris Woodward .07 .20
931 Ricardo Rodriguez .07 .20
932 Jimmy Gobble RC .15 .40
933 Jon Lieber .07 .20
934 Craig Kuzmic RC .15 .40
935 Eric Young .07 .20
936 Greg Zaun .07 .20
937 Miguel Batista .07 .20
938 Danny Wright .07 .20
939 Todd Zeile .10 .30
940 Chad Zerbe .07 .20
941 Jason Young RC .08 .25
942 Ronnie Belliard .07 .20
943 John Ennis RC .15 .40
944 John Flaherty .07 .20
945 Jerry Hairston Jr. .07 .20
946 Al Levine .07 .20
947 Antonio Alfonseca .07 .20
948 Brian Moehler .07 .20
949 Calvin Murray .07 .20
950 Nick Bierbrodt .07 .20
951 Sun Woo Kim .07 .20
952 Noochie Varner RC .15 .40
953 Luis Rivas .07 .20
954 Donnie Bridges .07 .20
955 Ramon Vazquez .07 .20
956 Luis Garcia .07 .20
957 Mark Quinn .07 .20
958 Armando Rios .07 .20
959 Chad Fox .07 .20
960 Hee Seop Choi .07 .20
961 Turk Wendell .07 .20
962 Adam Roller RC .15 .40
963 Grant Roberts .07 .20
964 Ben Molina .07 .20
965 Juan Rivera .07 .20
966 Matt Kinney .07 .20
967 Rod Beck .07 .20
968 Xavier Nady .07 .20
969 Masato Yoshii .07 .20
970 Miguel Tejada .10 .30
971 Danny Kolb .07 .20
972 Mike Remlinger .07 .20
973 Ray Lankford .10 .30
974 Ryan Minor .07 .20
975 J.T. Snow .10 .30
976 Brad Radke .10 .30
977 Jason Lane .10 .30
978 Jamey Wright .07 .20
979 Tom Goodwin .07 .20
980 Erik Bedard .10 .30
981 Gabe Kapler .10 .30
982 Brian Reith .07 .20
983 Nic Jackson RC .15 .40
984 Kurt Ainsworth .07 .20
985 Jason Isringhausen .10 .30
986 Willie Harris .07 .20
987 David Cone .10 .30
988 Bob Wickman .07 .20
989 Wes Helms .07 .20
990 Josh Beckett .10 .30

2002 Topps Total Award Winners

COMPLETE SET (30) 15.00 40.00
STATED ODDS 1:6
AW1 Ichiro Suzuki 1.50 4.00
AW2 Albert Pujols 1.50 4.00
AW3 Barry Bonds 2.00 5.00
AW4 Ichiro Suzuki 1.50 4.00
AW5 Randy Johnson .75 2.00
AW6 Roger Clemens 1.50 4.00
AW7 Jason Giambi A's .30 .75
AW8 Bret Boone .30 .75
AW9 Troy Glaus .30 .75
AW10 Alex Rodriguez 1.00 2.50
AW11 Juan Gonzalez .30 .75
AW12 Ichiro Suzuki 1.50 4.00
AW13 Jorge Posada .50 1.25
AW14 Edgar Martinez .50 1.25
AW15 Todd Helton .50 1.25
AW16 Jeff Kent .30 .75
AW17 Albert Pujols 1.50 4.00
AW18 Rich Aurilia .30 .75
AW19 Barry Bonds 2.00 5.00
AW20 Luis Gonzalez .30 .75
AW21 Sammy Sosa .75 2.00
AW22 Mike Piazza 1.25 3.00
AW23 Mike Hampton .30 .75
AW24 Ruben Sierra .30 .75
AW25 Matt Morris .30 .75
AW26 Curt Schilling .30 .75
AW27 Alex Rodriguez 1.00 2.50
AW28 Barry Bonds 2.00 5.00
AW29 Jim Thome .50 1.25
AW30 Barry Bonds 2.00 5.00

2002 Topps Total Production

COMPLETE SET (10) 8.00 20.00
STATED ODDS 1:12
TP1 Alex Rodriguez 1.00 2.50
TP2 Barry Bonds 2.00 5.00
TP3 Ichiro Suzuki 1.50 4.00
TP4 Edgar Martinez .50 1.25
TP5 Jason Giambi .50 1.25
TP6 Todd Helton .50 1.25
TP7 Nomar Garciaparra 1.25 3.00
TP8 Vladimir Guerrero .75 2.00
TP9 Sammy Sosa .75 2.00
TP10 Chipper Jones .75 2.00

2002 Topps Total Team Checklists

COMPLETE SET (30) 4.00 10.00
RANDOM INSERTS IN PACKS
TTC1 Troy Glaus .07 .20
TTC2 Randy Johnson .20 .50
TTC3 Chipper Jones .20 .50
TTC4 Scott Erickson .07 .20
TTC5 Nomar Garciaparra .30 .75
TTC6 Sammy Sosa .20 .50
TTC7 Magglio Ordonez .07 .20
TTC8 Ken Griffey Jr. .40 1.00
TTC9 Jim Thome .10 .30
TTC10 Todd Helton .10 .30
TTC11 Bobby Higginson .07 .20
TTC12 Josh Beckett .07 .20
TTC13 Jeff Bagwell .10 .30
TTC14 Mike Sweeney .07 .20
TTC15 Shawn Green .07 .20
TTC16 Geoff Jenkins .07 .20
TTC17 Cristian Guzman .07 .20
TTC18 Vladimir Guerrero .20 .50
TTC19 Mike Piazza .30 .75
TTC20 Derek Jeter .50 1.25
TTC21 Eric Chavez .07 .20
TTC22 Pat Burrell .07 .20
TTC23 Brian Giles .07 .20
TTC24 Phil Nevin .07 .20
TTC25 Ichiro Suzuki .40 1.00
TTC26 Barry Bonds .50 1.25
TTC27 J.D. Drew .07 .20
TTC28 Carlos Delgado .07 .20
TTC29 Toby Hall .07 .20

2002 Topps Total Topps

COMPLETE SET (50) 20.00 50.00
STATED ODDS 1:3
TT1 Roberto Alomar .50 1.25
TT2 Moises Alou .30 .75
TT3 Jeff Bagwell .50 1.25
TT4 Lance Berkman .30 .75
TT5 Barry Bonds 2.00 5.00
TT6 Bret Boone .30 .75
TT7 Kevin Brown .30 .75
TT8 Eric Chavez .30 .75
TT9 Roger Clemens 1.50 4.00
TT10 Carlos Delgado .30 .75
TT11 Cliff Floyd .30 .75
TT12 Nomar Garciaparra 1.25 3.00
TT13 Jason Giambi .30 .75
TT14 Brian Giles .30 .75
TT15 Troy Glaus .30 .75
TT16 Tom Glavine .50 1.25
TT17 Luis Gonzalez .30 .75
TT18 Juan Gonzalez .30 .75
TT19 Shawn Green .30 .75
TT20 Ken Griffey Jr. 1.50 4.00
TT21 Vladimir Guerrero .75 2.00
TT22 Jorge Posada .50 1.25
TT23 Todd Helton .50 1.25
TT24 Tim Hudson .30 .75
TT25 Derek Jeter 2.00 5.00
TT26 Randy Johnson .75 2.00
TT27 Andruw Jones .50 1.25
TT28 Chipper Jones .75 2.00
TT29 Jeff Kent .30 .75
TT30 Greg Maddux 1.25 3.00
TT31 Edgar Martinez .50 1.25
TT32 Pedro Martinez .50 1.25
TT33 Magglio Ordonez .30 .75
TT34 Rafael Palmeiro .50 1.25
TT35 Mike Piazza 1.25 3.00
TT36 Albert Pujols 1.50 4.00
TT37 Aramis Ramirez .30 .75
TT38 Mariano Rivera .75 2.00
TT39 Alex Rodriguez 1.00 2.50
TT40 Ivan Rodriguez .50 1.25
TT41 Curt Schilling .30 .75
TT42 Gary Sheffield .30 .75
TT43 Sammy Sosa .75 2.00
TT44 Ichiro Suzuki 1.50 4.00
TT45 Miguel Tejada .30 .75
TT46 Frank Thomas .75 2.00
TT47 Jim Thome .50 1.25
TT48 Larry Walker .30 .75
TT49 Bernie Williams .50 1.25
TT50 Kerry Wood .30 .75

2003 Topps Total

COMPLETE SET (990) 25.00 60.00
COMMON CARD (1-990) .07 .20
COMMON RC .15 .40
1 Brent Abernathy .07 .20
2 Bobby Hill .07 .20
3 Victor Martinez .12 .30
4 Chip Ambres .07 .20
5 Matt Anderson .07 .20
6 Ricardo Aramboles .07 .20
7 Carlos Pena .12 .30
8 Aaron Guiel .07 .20
9 Luke Allen .07 .20
10 Francisco Rodriguez .12 .30
11 Jason Marquis .07 .20
12 Edwin Almonte .07 .20
13 Grant Balfour .07 .20
14 Adam Platt .07 .20
15 Andy Phillips .07 .20
16 Adrian Beltre .20 .50
17 Brandon Backe .07 .20
18 Dave Berg .07 .20
19 Brett Myers .07 .20
20 Brian Meadows .07 .20
21 Chin-Feng Chen .07 .20
22 Blake Williams .07 .20

23 Josh Bard .07 .20
24 Josh Beckett .07 .20
25 Tommy Whiteman .07 .20
26 Matt Childers .07 .20
27 Adam Everett .07 .20
28 Mike Bordick .07 .20
29 Antonio Alfonseca .07 .20
30 Doug Creek .07 .20
31 J.D. Drew .07 .20
32 Milton Bradley .07 .20
33 David Wells .07 .20
34 Vance Wilson .07 .20
35 Jeff Fassero .07 .20
36 Sandy Alomar Jr. .07 .20
37 Ryan Vogelsong .07 .20
38 Roger Clemens .25 .60
39 Juan Gonzalez .07 .20
40 Dustin Hermanson .07 .20
41 Andy Ashby .07 .20
42 Adam Hyzdu .07 .20
43 Ben Broussard .07 .20
44 Ryan Klesko .07 .20
45 Chris Buglovsky FY RC .15 .40
46 Bud Smith .07 .20
47 Aaron Boone .07 .20
48 Cliff Floyd .07 .20
49 Alex Cora .12 .30
50 Curt Schilling .12 .30
51 Michael Cuddyer .07 .20
52 Joe Valentine FY RC .15 .40
53 Carlos Guillen .07 .20
54 Angel Berroa .07 .20
55 Eli Marrero .07 .20
56 A.J. Burnett .07 .20
57 Oliver Perez .07 .20
58 Matt Morris .07 .20
59 Valerio De Los Santos .07 .20
60 Austin Kearns .07 .20
61 Darren Dreifort .07 .20
62 Jason Standridge .07 .20
63 Carlos Silva .07 .20
64 Moises Alou .07 .20
65 Jason Anderson .07 .20
66 Russell Branyan .07 .20
67 B.J. Ryan .07 .20
68 Cory Aldridge .07 .20
69 Ellis Burks .07 .20
70 Troy Glaus .07 .20
71 Kelly Wunsch .07 .20
72 Brad Wilkerson .07 .20
73 Jayson Durocher .07 .20
74 Tony Fiore .07 .20
75 Brian Giles .07 .20
76 Billy Wagner .07 .20
77 Neifi Perez .07 .20
78 Jose Valverde .07 .20
79 Brent Butler .07 .20
80 Mario Ramos .07 .20
81 Kerry Robinson .07 .20
82 Brent Mayne .07 .20
83 Sean Casey .07 .20
84 Danys Baez .07 .20
85 Chase Utley .12 .30
86 Jared Sandberg .07 .20
87 Terrence Long .07 .20
88 Kevin Walker .07 .20
89 Royce Clayton .07 .20
90 Shea Hillenbrand .07 .20
91 Brad Lidge .07 .20
92 Shawn Chacon .07 .20
93 Kenny Rogers .07 .20
94 Chris Snelling .07 .20
95 Omar Vizquel .12 .30
96 Joe Borchard .07 .20
97 Matt Belisle .07 .20
98 Steve Smyth .07 .20
99 Raul Mondesi .07 .20
100 Chipper Jones .20 .50
101 Victor Alvarez .07 .20
102 J.M. Gold .07 .20
103 Willis Roberts .07 .20
104 Eddie Guardado .07 .20
105 Brad Voyles .07 .20
106 Bronson Arroyo .07 .20
107 Juan Castro .07 .20
108 Dan Plesac .07 .20
109 Ramon Castro .07 .20
110 Tim Salmon .07 .20
111 Gene Kingsale .07 .20
112 J.D. Closser .07 .20
113 Mark Buehrle .12 .30
114 Steve Karsay .07 .20
115 Cristian Guerrero .07 .20
116 Brad Ausmus .07 .20
117 Cristian Guzman .07 .20
118 Dan Wilson .07 .20
119 Jake Westbrook .07 .20
120 Manny Ramirez .20 .50
121 Jason Giambi .07 .20
122 Bob Wickman .07 .20
123 Aaron Cook .07 .20
124 Alfredo Amezaga .07 .20
125 Corey Thurman .07 .20
126 Brandon Puffer .07 .20
127 Hee Seop Choi .07 .20
128 Javier Vazquez .07 .20
129 Carlos Valderrama .07 .20
130 Jerome Williams .07 .20
131 Wilson Betemit .07 .20
132 Luke Prokopec .07 .20
133 Esteban Yan .07 .20
134 Brandon Berger .07 .20
135 Bill Hall .07 .20
136 LaTroy Hawkins .07 .20
137 Nate Cornejo .07 .20
138 Jim Mecir .07 .20
139 Joe Crede .07 .20
140 Andres Galarraga .12 .30
141 Reggie Sanders .07 .20
142 Joey Eischen .07 .20
143 Mike Timlin .07 .20
144 Jose Cruz Jr. .07 .20
145 Wes Helms .07 .20
146 Brian Roberts .07 .20
147 Bret Prinz .07 .20
148 Brian Hunter .07 .20
149 Chad Hermansen .07 .20
150 Andruw Jones .07 .20
151 Kurt Ainsworth .07 .20
152 Cliff Bartosh .07 .20
153 Kyle Lohse .07 .20
154 Brian Jordan .07 .20
155 Coco Crisp .07 .20
156 Tomas Perez .07 .20
157 Keith Foulke .07 .20
158 Chris Carpenter .12 .30
159 Mike Remlinger .07 .20
160 Dewon Brazelton .07 .20
161 Brook Fordyce .07 .20
162 Rusty Greer .07 .20
163 Scott Downs .07 .20
164 Jason Dubois .07 .20
165 David Coggin .07 .20
166 Mike DeJean .07 .20
167 Carlos Hernandez .07 .20
168 Matt Williams .07 .20
169 Rheal Cormier .07 .20
170 Duaner Sanchez .07 .20
171 Craig Counsell .07 .20
172 Edgar Martinez .12 .30
173 Zack Greinke 1.00 2.50
174 Pedro Feliz .07 .20
175 Randy Choate .07 .20
176 Jon Garland .07 .20
177 Keith Ginter .07 .20
178 Carlos Febles .07 .20
179 Kerry Wood .07 .20
180 Jack Cust .07 .20
181 Koyie Hill .07 .20
182 Ricky Gutierrez .07 .20
183 Ben Grieve .07 .20
184 Scott Eyre .07 .20
185 Jason Isringhausen .07 .20
186 Gookie Dawkins .07 .20
187 Roberto Alomar .12 .30
188 Eric Junge .07 .20
189 Carlos Beltran .12 .30
190 Denny Hocking .07 .20
191 Jason Schmidt .07 .20
192 Cory Lidle .07 .20
193 Rob Mackowiak .07 .20
194 Charlton Jimerson RC .15 .40
195 Darin Erstad .07 .20
196 Jason Davis .07 .20
197 Luis Castillo .07 .20
198 Juan Encarnacion .07 .20
199 Jeffrey Hammonds .07 .20
200 Nomar Garciaparra .12 .30
201 Ryan Christianson .07 .20
202 Robert Person .07 .20
203 Damian Moss .07 .20
204 Chris Richard .07 .20
205 Todd Hundley .07 .20
206 Paul Bako .07 .20
207 Adam Kennedy .07 .20
208 Scott Hatteberg .07 .20
209 Andy Pratt .07 .20
210 Ken Griffey Jr. .40 1.00
211 Chris George .07 .20
212 Lance Niekro .07 .20
213 Greg Colbrunn .07 .20
214 Herbert Perry .07 .20
215 Cody Ransom .07 .20
216 Craig Biggio .12 .30
217 Miguel Batista .07 .20
218 Alex Escobar .07 .20
219 Willie Harris .07 .20
220 Scott Strickland .07 .20
221 Felix Rodriguez .07 .20
222 Torii Hunter .07 .20
223 Tyler Houston .07 .20
224 Darrell May .07 .20
225 Benito Santiago .07 .20
226 Ryan Dempster .07 .20
227 Andy Fox .07 .20
228 Jung Bong .07 .20
229 Jose Macias .07 .20
230 Shannon Stewart .07 .20
231 Buddy Groom .07 .20
232 Eric Valent .07 .20
233 Scott Schoeneweis .07 .20
234 Corey Hart .07 .20
235 Brett Tomko .07 .20
236 Shane Bazzell RC .15 .40
237 Tim Hummel .07 .20
238 Matt Stairs .07 .20
239 Pete Munro .07 .20
240 Ismael Valdes .07 .20
241 Brian Fuentes .07 .20
242 Cesar Izturis .07 .20
243 Mark Bellhorn .07 .20
244 Geoff Jenkins .07 .20
245 Derek Jeter .50 1.25
246 Anderson Machado .07 .20
247 Dave Roberts .12 .30
248 Jaime Cerda .07 .20
249 Woody Williams .07 .20
250 Vernon Wells .07 .20
251 Jon Lieber .07 .20
252 Franklyn German .07 .20
253 David Segui .07 .20
254 Freddy Garcia .07 .20
255 James Baldwin .07 .20
256 Tony Alvarez .07 .20
257 Walter Young .07 .20
258 Alex Herrera .07 .20
259 Robert Fick .07 .20
260 Rob Bell .07 .20
261 Ben Petrick .07 .20
262 Dee Brown .07 .20
263 Mike Bacsik .07 .20
264 Corey Patterson .07 .20
265 Marvin Benard .07 .20
266 Eddie Rogers .07 .20
267 Elio Serrano .07 .20
268 D'Angelo Jimenez .07 .20
269 Adam Johnson .07 .20
270 Gregg Zaun .07 .20
271 Nick Johnson .07 .20
272 Geoff Goetz .07 .20
273 Ryan Drese .07 .20
274 Eric Dubose .07 .20
275 Barry Zito .12 .30
276 Mike Crudale .07 .20
277 Paul Byrd .07 .20
278 Eric Gagne .07 .20
279 Aramis Ramirez .07 .20
280 Ray Durham .07 .20
281 Tony Graffanino .07 .20
282 Jeremy Guthrie .07 .20
283 Erik Bedard .07 .20
284 Vince Faison .07 .20
285 Bobby Kielty .07 .20
286 Francis Beltran .07 .20
287 Alexis Gomez .07 .20
288 Vladimir Guerrero .12 .30
289 Kevin Appier .07 .20
290 Gil Meche .07 .20
291 Marquis Grissom .07 .20
292 John Burkett .07 .20
293 Vinny Castilla .07 .20
294 Tyler Walker .07 .20
295 Shane Halter .07 .20
296 Geronimo Gil .07 .20
297 Eric Hinske .07 .20
298 Adam Dunn .12 .30
299 Mike Kinkade .07 .20
300 Mark Prior .12 .30
301 Corey Koskie .07 .20
302 David Dellucci .07 .20
303 Todd Helton .12 .30
304 Greg Miller .07 .20
305 Delvin James .07 .20
306 Humberto Cota .07 .20
307 Aaron Harang .07 .20
308 Jeremy Hill .07 .20
309 Billy Koch .07 .20
310 Brandon Claussen .07 .20
311 Matt Ginter .07 .20
312 Jason Lane .07 .20
313 Ben Weber .07 .20
314 Alan Benes .07 .20
315 Matt Walbeck .07 .20
316 Danny Graves .07 .20
317 Jason Johnson .07 .20
318 Jason Grimsley .07 .20
319 Steve Kline .07 .20
320 Johnny Damon .12 .30
321 Jay Gibbons .07 .20
322 J.J. Putz .07 .20
323 Stephen Randolph RC .15 .40
324 Bobby Higginson .07 .20
325 Kazuhisa Ishii .07 .20
326 Carlos Lee .07 .20
327 J.R. House .07 .20
328 Mark Loretta .07 .20
329 Mike Matheny .07 .20
330 Ben Diggins .07 .20
331 Seth Etherton .07 .20
332 Eli Whiteside FY RC .15 .40
333 Juan Rivera .07 .20
334 Jeff Conine .07 .20
335 John McDonald .07 .20
336 Erik Hiljus .07 .20
337 David Eckstein .07 .20
338 Jeff Bagwell .12 .30
339 Matt Holliday .20 .50
340 Jeff Liefer .07 .20
341 Greg Myers .07 .20
342 Scott Sauerbeck .07 .20
343 Omar Infante .07 .20
344 Ryan Langerhans .07 .20
345 Abraham Nunez .07 .20
346 Mike MacDougal .07 .20
347 Travis Phelps .07 .20
348 Terry Shumpert .07 .20
349 Alex Rodriguez .25 .60
350 Bobby Seay .07 .20
351 Ichiro Suzuki .25 .60
352 Brandon Inge .07 .20
353 Jack Wilson .07 .20
354 John Ennis .07 .20
355 Jamal Strong .07 .20
356 Jason Jennings .07 .20
357 Jeff Kent .07 .20
358 Scott Chiasson .07 .20
359 Jeremy Griffiths RC .15 .40
360 Paul Konerko .12 .30
361 Jeff Austin .07 .20
362 Todd Van Poppel .07 .20
363 Sun Woo Kim .07 .20
364 Jerry Hairston Jr. .07 .20
365 Tony Torcato .07 .20
366 Arthur Rhodes .07 .20
367 Jose Jimenez .07 .20
368 Matt LeCroy .07 .20
369 Curtis Leskanic .07 .20
370 Ramon Vazquez .07 .20
371 Joe Randa .07 .20
372 John Franco .07 .20
373 Bobby Estalella .07 .20
374 Craig Wilson .07 .20
375 Michael Young .07 .20
376 Mark Ellis .07 .20
377 Joe Mauer .20 .50
378 Checklist 1 .07 .20
379 Jason Kendall .07 .20
380 Checklist 2 .07 .20
381 Alex Gonzalez .07 .20
382 Tom Gordon .07 .20
383 John Buck .07 .20
384 Shigetoshi Hasegawa .07 .20
385 Scott Stewart .07 .20
386 Luke Hudson .07 .20
387 Todd Jones .07 .20
388 Fred McGriff .12 .30
389 Mike Sweeney .07 .20
390 Marlon Anderson .07 .20
391 Terry Adams .07 .20
392 Mark DeRosa .07 .20
393 Doug Mientkiewicz .07 .20
394 Miguel Cairo .07 .20
395 Jamie Moyer .07 .20
396 Jose Leon .07 .20
397 Matt Clement .07 .20
398 Bengie Molina .07 .20
399 Marcus Thames .07 .20
400 Nick Bierbrodt .07 .20
401 Tim Kalita .07 .20
402 Corwin Malone .07 .20
403 Jesse Orosco .07 .20
404 Brandon Phillips .07 .20
405 Eric Cyr .07 .20
406 Jason Michaels .07 .20
407 Julio Lugo .07 .20
408 Gabe Kapler .07 .20
409 Mark Mulder .07 .20
410 Adam Eaton .07 .20
411 Ken Harvey .07 .20
412 Jolbert Cabrera .07 .20
413 Eric Milton .07 .20
414 Josh Hall RC .15 .40
415 Bob File .07 .20
416 Brett Evert .07 .20
417 Ron Chiavacci .07 .20
418 Jorge De La Rosa .07 .20
419 Quinton McCracken .07 .20
420 Luther Hackman .07 .20
421 Gary Knotts .07 .20
422 Kevin Brown .07 .20
423 Jeff Cirillo .07 .20
424 Damaso Marte .07 .20
425 Chan Ho Park .12 .30
426 Nathan Haynes .07 .20
427 Matt Lawton .07 .20
428 Mike Stanton .07 .20
429 Bernie Williams .12 .30
430 Kevin Jarvis .07 .20
431 Joe McEwing .07 .20
432 Mark Kotsay .07 .20
433 Juan Cruz .07 .20
434 Russ Ortiz .07 .20
435 Jeff Nelson .07 .20
436 Alan Embree .07 .20
437 Miguel Tejada .12 .30
438 Kirk Saarloos .07 .20
439 Cliff Lee .50 1.25
440 Ryan Ludwick .07 .20
441 Derrek Lee .07 .20
442 Bobby Abreu .07 .20
443 Dustan Mohr .07 .20
444 Nook Logan RC .15 .40
445 Seth McClung .07 .20
446 Miguel Olivo .07 .20
447 Henry Blanco .07 .20
448 Seung Song .07 .20
449 Kris Wilson .07 .20
450 Xavier Nady .07 .20
451 Corky Miller .07 .20
452 Jim Thome .12 .30
453 George Lombard .07 .20
454 Rey Ordonez .07 .20
455 Deivis Santos .07 .20
456 Mike Myers .07 .20
457 Edgar Renteria .07 .20
458 Braden Looper .07 .20
459 Guillermo Mota .07 .20
460 Scott Rolen .12 .30
461 Lance Berkman .12 .30
462 Jeff Heaverlo .07 .20
463 Ramon Hernandez .07 .20
464 Jason Simontacchi .07 .20
465 So Taguchi .07 .20
466 Dave Veres .07 .20
467 Shane Loux .07 .20
468 Rodrigo Lopez .07 .20
469 Bubba Trammell .07 .20
470 Scott Sullivan .07 .20
471 Mike Mussina .12 .30
472 Ramon Ortiz .07 .20
473 Lyle Overbay .07 .20
474 Mike Lowell .07 .20
475 Al Martin .07 .20
476 Larry Bigbie .07 .20
477 Rey Sanchez .07 .20
478 Magglio Ordonez .12 .30
479 Rondell White .07 .20
480 Jay Witasick .07 .20
481 Jimmy Rollins .12 .30
482 Mike Maroth .07 .20
483 Alejandro Machado .07 .20
484 Nick Neugebauer .07 .20
485 Victor Zambrano .07 .20
486 Travis Lee .07 .20
487 Bobby Bradley .07 .20
488 Marcus Giles .07 .20
489 Steve Trachsel .07 .20
490 Derek Lowe .07 .20
491 Hideo Nomo .20 .50
492 Brad Hawpe .07 .20
493 Jesus Medrano .07 .20
494 Rick Ankiel .07 .20
495 Pasqual Coco .07 .20
496 Michael Barrett .07 .20
497 Joe Beimel .07 .20
498 Marty Cordova .07 .20
499 Aaron Sele .07 .20
500 Sammy Sosa .20 .50
501 Ivan Rodriguez .12 .30
502 Keith Osik .07 .20
503 Hank Blalock .07 .20
504 Hiram Bocachica .07 .20
505 Junior Spivey .07 .20
506 Edgardo Alfonzo .07 .20
507 Alex Graman .07 .20
508 J.J. Davis .07 .20
509 Roger Cedeno .07 .20
510 Joe Roa .07 .20
511 Wily Mo Pena .07 .20
512 Eric Munson .07 .20
513 Arnie Munoz RC .15 .40
514 Albie Lopez .07 .20
515 Andy Pettitte .12 .30
516 Jim Edmonds .12 .30
517 Jeff Davanon .07 .20
518 Aaron Myette .07 .20
519 C.C. Sabathia .12 .30
520 Gerardo Garcia .07 .20
521 Brian Schneider .07 .20
522 Wes Obermueller .07 .20
523 John Mabry .07 .20
524 Casey Fossum .07 .20
525 Toby Hall .07 .20
526 Denny Neagle .07 .20
527 Willie Bloomquist .07 .20
528 A.J. Pierzynski .07 .20
529 Bartolo Colon .07 .20
530 Chad Harville .07 .20
531 Blaine Neal .07 .20
532 Luis Terrero .07 .20
533 Reggie Taylor .07 .20
534 Melvin Mora .07 .20
535 Tino Martinez .07 .20
536 Peter Bergeron .07 .20
537 Jorge Padilla .07 .20
538 Oscar Villarreal RC .15 .40
539 David Weathers .07 .20
540 Mike Lamb .07 .20
541 Greg Norton .07 .20
542 Michael Tucker .07 .20
543 Ben Kozlowski .07 .20
544 Alex Sanchez .07 .20
545 Trey Lunsford .07 .20
546 Abraham Nunez .07 .20
547 Mike Lincoln .07 .20
548 Orlando Hernandez .07 .20
549 Kevin Mench .07 .20
550 Garret Anderson .07 .20
551 Kyle Farnsworth .07 .20
552 Kevin Olsen .07 .20
553 Joel Pineiro .07 .20
554 Jorge Julio .07 .20
555 Jose Mesa .07 .20
556 Jorge Posada .12 .30
557 Jose Ortiz .07 .20
558 Mike Tonis .07 .20
559 Gabe White .07 .20
560 Rafael Furcal .07 .20
561 Matt Franco .07 .20
562 Trey Hodges .07 .20
563 Esteban German .07 .20
564 Josh Fogg .07 .20
565 Fernando Tatis .07 .20
566 Alex Cintron .07 .20
567 Grant Roberts .07 .20
568 Gene Stechschulte .07 .20
569 Rafael Palmeiro .12 .30
570 Mike Hampton .07 .20
571 Ben Davis .07 .20
572 Dean Palmer .07 .20
573 Jerrod Riggan .07 .20
574 Nate Frese .07 .20
575 Josh Phelps .07 .20
576 Freddie Bynum .07 .20
577 Morgan Ensberg .07 .20
578 Juan Rincon .07 .20
579 Kazuhiro Sasaki .07 .20
580 Yorvit Torrealba .07 .20
581 Tim Wakefield .12 .30
582 Sterling Hitchcock .07 .20
583 Craig Paquette .07 .20
584 Kevin Millwood .07 .20
585 Damian Rolls .07 .20
586 Brad Baisley .07 .20
587 Kyle Snyder .07 .20
588 Paul Quantrill .07 .20
589 Trot Nixon .07 .20
590 J.T. Snow .07 .20
591 Kevin Young .07 .20
592 Tomo Ohka .07 .20
593 Brian Boehringer .07 .20
594 Danny Patterson .07 .20
595 Jeff Tam .07 .20
596 Anastacio Martinez .07 .20
597 Rod Barajas .07 .20
598 Octavio Dotel .07 .20
599 Jason Tyner .07 .20
600 Gary Sheffield .07 .20
601 Ruben Quevedo .07 .20
602 Jay Payton .07 .20
603 Mo Vaughn .07 .20
604 Pat Burrell .07 .20
605 Fernando Vina .07 .20
606 Wes Anderson .07 .20
607 Alex Gonzalez .07 .20
608 Ted Lilly .07 .20
609 Nick Punto .07 .20
610 Ryan Madson .07 .20
611 Odalis Perez .07 .20
612 Chris Woodward .07 .20
613 John Olerud .07 .20
614 Brad Cresse .07 .20
615 Chad Zerbe .07 .20
616 Brad Penny .07 .20
617 Barry Larkin .12 .30
618 Brandon Duckworth .07 .20
619 Brad Radke .07 .20
620 Troy Brohawn .07 .20
621 Juan Pierre .07 .20
622 Rick Reed .07 .20
623 Omar Daal .07 .20
624 Jose Hernandez .07 .20
625 Greg Maddux .25 .60
626 Henry Mateo .07 .20
627 Kip Wells .07 .20
628 Kevin Cash .07 .20
629 Wil Ledezma FY RC .15 .40
630 Luis Gonzalez .07 .20
631 Jason Conti .07 .20
632 Ricardo Rincon .07 .20
633 Mike Bynum .07 .20
634 Mike Redmond .07 .20
635 Chance Caple .07 .20
636 Chris Widger .07 .20
637 Michael Restovich .07 .20
638 Mark Grudzielanek .07 .20
639 Brandon Larson .07 .20
640 Rocco Baldelli .07 .20
641 Javy Lopez .07 .20
642 Rene Reyes .07 .20
643 Orlando Merced .07 .20
644 Jason Phillips .07 .20
645 Luis Ugueto .07 .20
646 Ron Calloway .07 .20
647 Josh Paul .07 .20
648 Todd Greene .07 .20
649 Joe Girardi .07 .20
650 Todd Ritchie .07 .20
651 Kevin Millar Sox .07 .20
652 Shawn Wooten .07 .20
653 David Riske .07 .20
654 Luis Rivas .07 .20
655 Roy Halladay .12 .30
656 Travis Driskill .07 .20
657 Ricky Ledee .07 .20
658 Timo Perez .07 .20
659 Fernando Rodney .07 .20
660 Trevor Hoffman .12 .30
661 Pat Hentgen .07 .20
662 Bret Boone .07 .20
663 Ryan Jensen .07 .20
664 Ricardo Rodriguez .07 .20
665 Jeremy Lambert .07 .20
666 Troy Percival .07 .20
667 Jon Rauch .07 .20
668 Mariano Rivera .25 .60
669 Jason LaRue .07 .20
670 J.C. Romero .07 .20
671 Cody Ross .07 .20
672 Eric Byrnes .07 .20
673 Paul Lo Duca .07 .20
674 Brad Fullmer .07 .20
675 Cliff Politte .07 .20
676 Justin Miller .07 .20
677 Nic Jackson .07 .20
678 Kris Benson .07 .20
679 Carl Sadler .07 .20
680 Joe Nathan .07 .20
681 Julio Santana .07 .20
682 Wade Miller .07 .20
683 Josh Pearce .07 .20
684 Tony Armas Jr. .07 .20
685 Al Leiter .07 .20
686 Raul Ibanez .12 .30
687 Danny Bautista .07 .20
688 Travis Hafner .07 .20
689 Carlos Zambrano .12 .30
690 Pedro Martinez .12 .30
691 Ramon Santiago .07 .20
692 Felipe Lopez .07 .20
693 David Ross .07 .20
694 Chone Figgins .07 .20
695 Antonio Osuna .07 .20
696 Jay Powell .07 .20
697 Ryan Church .07 .20
698 Alexis Rios .07 .20
699 Tanyon Sturtze .07 .20
700 Turk Wendell .07 .20
701 Richard Hidalgo .07 .20
702 Joe Mays .07 .20
703 Jorge Sosa .07 .20
704 Eric Karros .07 .20
705 Steve Finley .07 .20
706 Sean Smith FY RC .15 .40
707 Jeremy Giambi .07 .20
708 Scott Hodges .07 .20
709 Vicente Padilla .07 .20
710 Erubiel Durazo .07 .20
711 Aaron Rowand .07 .20
712 Dennis Tankersley .07 .20
713 Rick Bauer .07 .20
714 Tim Olson FY RC .15 .40
715 Jeff Urban .07 .20
716 Steve Sparks .07 .20
717 Glendon Rusch .07 .20
718 Ricky Stone .07 .20
719 Benji Gil .07 .20
720 Pete Walker .07 .20
721 Tim Worrell .07 .20
722 Michael Tejera .07 .20
723 David Kelton .07 .20
724 Britt Reames .07 .20
725 John Stephens .07 .20
726 Mark McLemore .07 .20
727 Jeff Zimmerman .07 .20
728 Checklist 3 .07 .20
729 Andres Torres .07 .20
730 Checklist 4 .07 .20
731 Johan Santana .12 .30
732 Dane Sardinha .07 .20
733 Rodrigo Rosario .07 .20
734 Frank Thomas .20 .50
735 Tom Glavine .12 .30
736 Doug Mirabelli .07 .20
737 Juan Uribe .07 .20
738 Ryan Anderson .07 .20
739 Sean Burroughs .07 .20
740 Eric Chavez .07 .20
741 Enrique Wilson .07 .20
742 Elmer Dessens .07 .20
743 Marlon Byrd .07 .20
744 Brendan Donnelly .07 .20
745 Gary Bennett .07 .20
746 Roy Oswalt .12 .30
747 Andy Van Hekken .07 .20
748 Jesus Colome .07 .20
749 Erick Almonte .07 .20
750 Frank Catalanotto .07 .20
751 Kenny Lofton .07 .20
752 Carlos Delgado .07 .20
753 Ryan Franklin .07 .20
754 Wilkin Ruan .07 .20
755 Kelvim Escobar .07 .20
756 Tim Drew .07 .20
757 Jarrod Washburn .07 .20
758 Runelvys Hernandez .07 .20
759 Cory Vance .07 .20
760 Doug Glanville .07 .20
761 Ryan Rupe .07 .20
762 Jermaine Dye .07 .20
763 Mike Cameron .07 .20
764 Scott Erickson .07 .20
765 Richie Sexson .07 .20
766 Jose Vidro .07 .20
767 Brian West .07 .20
768 Shawn Estes .07 .20
769 Brian Tallet .07 .20
770 Larry Walker .12 .30
771 Josh Hamilton .12 .30
772 Orlando Hudson .07 .20
773 Justin Morneau .12 .30
774 Ryan Bukvich .07 .20
775 Mike Gonzalez .07 .20
776 Tsuyoshi Shinjo .07 .20
777 Matt Mantei .07 .20
778 Jimmy Journell .07 .20
779 Brian Lawrence .07 .20
780 Mike Lieberthal .07 .20
781 Scott Mullen .07 .20
782 Zach Day .07 .20
783 John Thomson .07 .20
784 Ben Sheets .07 .20
785 Damon Minor .07 .20
786 Jose Valentin .07 .20
787 Armando Benitez .07 .20
788 Jamie Walker RC .15 .40
789 Preston Wilson .07 .20
790 Josh Wilson .07 .20
791 Phil Nevin .07 .20
792 Roberto Hernandez .07 .20
793 Mike Williams .07 .20
794 Jake Peavy .07 .20
795 Paul Shuey .07 .20
796 Chad Bradford .07 .20
797 Bobby Jenks .07 .20
798 Sean Douglass .07 .20
799 Damian Miller .07 .20
800 Mark Wohlers .07 .20
801 Ty Wigginton .07 .20
802 Alfonso Soriano .12 .30
803 Randy Johnson .20 .50
804 Placido Polanco .07 .20
805 Drew Henson .07 .20
806 Tony Womack .07 .20
807 Pokey Reese .07 .20
808 Albert Pujols .25 .60
809 Henri Stanley .07 .20
810 Mike Rivera .07 .20
811 John Lackey .12 .30
812 Brian Wright FY RC .15 .40
813 Eric Good .07 .20
814 Dernell Stenson .07 .20
815 Kirk Rueter .07 .20
816 Todd Zeile .07 .20
817 Brad Thomas .07 .20
818 Shawn Sedlacek .07 .20
819 Garrett Stephenson .07 .20
820 Mark Teixeira .12 .30
821 Tim Hudson .12 .30
822 Mike Koplove .07 .20
823 Chris Reitsma .07 .20
824 Rafael Soriano .07 .20
825 Ugueth Urbina .07 .20
826 Lance Carter .07 .20
827 Colin Young .07 .20
828 Pat Strange .07 .20
829 Juan Pena .07 .20
830 Joe Thurston .07 .20
831 Shawn Green .07 .20
832 Pedro Astacio .07 .20
833 Danny Wright .07 .20
834 Wes O'Brien FY RC .15 .40
835 Luis Lopez .07 .20
836 Randall Simon .07 .20
837 Jaret Wright .07 .20
838 Jayson Werth .12 .30
839 Endy Chavez .07 .20
840 Checklist 5 .07 .20
841 Chad Paronto .07 .20
842 Randy Winn .07 .20
843 Sidney Ponson .07 .20
844 Robin Ventura .07 .20
845 Rich Aurilia .07 .20
846 Joaquin Benoit .07 .20
847 Barry Bonds .30 .75
848 Carl Crawford .12 .30
849 Jeromy Burnitz .07 .20
850 Orlando Cabrera .07 .20
851 Luis Vizcaino .07 .20
852 Randy Wolf .07 .20
853 Todd Walker .07 .20
854 Jeremy Affeldt .07 .20
855 Einar Diaz .07 .20
856 Carl Everett .07 .20
857 Wiki Gonzalez .07 .20
858 Mike Paradis .07 .20
859 Travis Harper .07 .20
860 Mike Piazza .20 .50
861 Will Ohman .07 .20
862 Eric Young .07 .20
863 Jason Grabowski .07 .20
864 Rett Johnson RC .15 .40
865 Aubrey Huff .07 .20
866 John Smoltz .20 .50
867 Mickey Callaway .07 .20
868 Joe Kennedy .07 .20
869 Tim Redding .07 .20
870 Colby Lewis .07 .20
871 Salomon Torres .07 .20
872 Marco Scutaro .50 1.25
873 Tony Batista .07 .20
874 Dmitri Young .07 .20
875 Scott Williamson .07 .20
876 Scott Spiezio .07 .20
877 John Webb .07 .20
878 Jose Acevedo .07 .20
879 Kevin Orie .07 .20
880 Jacque Jones .07 .20
881 Ben Francisco FY RC .15 .40
882 Bobby Basham FY RC .15 .40
883 Corey Shafer FY RC .15 .40
884 J.D. Durbin FY RC .15 .40
885 Chien-Ming Wang FY RC .60 1.50
886 Adam Stern FY RC .15 .40
887 Wayne Lydon FY RC .15 .40
888 Derell McCall FY RC .15 .40
889 Jon Nelson FY RC .15 .40
890 Willie Eyre FY RC .15 .40
891 Ramon Nivar-Martinez FY RC .15 .40
892 Adrian Myers FY RC .15 .40
893 Jamie Athas FY RC .15 .40
894 Ismael Castro FY RC .15 .40
895 David Martinez FY RC .15 .40
896 Terry Tiffee FY RC .15 .40
897 Nathan Panther FY RC .15 .40
898 Kyle Roat FY RC .15 .40
899 Kason Gabbard FY RC .15 .40
900 Hanley Ramirez FY RC 1.25 3.00
901 Bryan Grace FY RC .15 .40
902 B.J. Barns FY RC .15 .40
903 Greg Bruso FY RC .15 .40
904 Mike Neu FY RC .15 .40
905 Dustin Yount FY RC .15 .40
906 Shane Victorino FY RC .50 1.25
907 Brian Burgamy FY RC .15 .40
908 Beau Kemp FY RC .15 .40
909 David Corrente FY RC .15 .40
910 Dexter Cooper FY RC .15 .40
911 Chris Colton FY RC .15 .40
912 David Cash FY RC .15 .40
913 Bernie Castro FY RC .15 .40
914 Luis Hodge FY RC .15 .40
915 Jeff Clark FY RC .15 .40
916 Jason Kubel FY RC .50 1.25
917 T.J. Bohn FY RC .15 .40
918 Luke Steidlmayer FY RC .15 .40

919 Matthew Peterson FY RC .15 .40
920 Darrell Rasner FY RC .15 .40
921 Scott Tyler FY RC .15 .40
922 Gary Schneidmiller FY RC .15 .40
923 Gregor Blanco FY RC .15 .40
924 Ryan Cameron FY RC .15 .40
925 Wilfredo Rodriguez FY .15 .40
926 Rajai Davis FY RC .15 .40
927 Evel Bastida-Martinez FY RC .15 .40
928 Chris Duncan FY RC .50 1.25
929 Dave Pember FY RC .15 .40
930 Branden Florence FY RC .15 .40
931 Eric Eckenstahler FY .15 .40
932 Hong-Chih Kuo FY RC .75 2.00
933 Il Kim FY RC .15 .40
934 Michael Garciaparra FY RC .15 .40
935 Kip Bouknight FY RC .15 .40
936 Gary Harris FY RC .15 .40
937 Derry Hammond FY RC .15 .40
938 Joey Gomes FY RC .15 .40
939 Donnie Hood FY RC .15 .40
940 Clay Hensley FY RC .15 .40
941 David Pahucki FY RC .15 .40
942 Wilton Reynolds FY RC .15 .40
943 Michael Hinckley FY RC .15 .40
944 Josh Willingham FY RC .50 1.25
945 Pete LaForest FY RC .15 .40
946 Pete Smart FY RC .15 .40
947 Jay Sitzman FY RC .15 .40
948 Mark Malaska FY RC .15 .40
949 Mike Gallo FY RC .15 .40
950 Matt Diaz FY RC .25 .60
951 Brennan King FY RC .15 .40
952 Ryan Howard FY RC 1.25 3.00
953 Daryl Clark FY RC .15 .40
954 Dayton Buller FY RC .15 .40
955 Rylan Reed FY RC .15 .40
956 Chris Booker FY .15 .40
957 Brandon Watson FY RC .15 .40
958 Matt DeMarco FY RC .15 .40
959 Doug Waechter FY RC .15 .40
960 Callix Crabbe FY RC .15 .40
961 Jairo Garcia FY RC .15 .40
962 Jason Perry FY RC .15 .40
963 Eric Riggs FY RC .15 .40
964 Travis Ishikawa FY RC .40 1.00
965 Simon Pond FY RC .15 .40
966 Manuel Ramirez FY RC .15 .40
967 Tyler Johnson FY RC .15 .40
968 Jaime Bubela FY RC .15 .40
969 Haj Turay FY RC .15 .40
970 Tyson Graham FY RC .15 .40
971 David DeJesus FY RC .40 1.00
972 Franklin Gutierrez FY RC .40 1.00
973 Craig Brazell FY RC .15 .40
974 Keith Stamler FY RC .15 .40
975 Jemel Spearman FY RC .15 .40
976 Ozzie Chavez FY RC .15 .40
977 Nick Trzesniak FY RC .15 .40
978 Bill Simon FY RC .15 .40
979 Matthew Hagen FY RC .15 .40
980 Chris Kroski FY RC .15 .40
981 Prentice Redman FY RC .15 .40
982 Kevin Randel FY RC .15 .40
983 Thomari Story-Harden FY RC .15 .40
984 Brian Shackelford FY RC .15 .40
985 Mike Adams FY RC .25 .60
986 Brian McCann FY RC 1.25 3.00
987 Mike McNutt FY RC .15 .40
988 Aron Weston FY RC .15 .40
989 Dustin Moseley FY RC .15 .40
990 Bryan Bullington FY RC .15 .40

2003 Topps Total Silver

*SILVER: 1X TO 2.5X BASIC
*SILVER RC'S: 1X TO 2.5X BASIC
STATED ODDS 1:1

2003 Topps Total Award Winners

COMPLETE SET (30) 12.50 30.00
STATED ODDS 1:12
AW1 Barry Zito .50 1.25
AW2 Randy Johnson .75 2.00
AW3 Miguel Tejada .50 1.25
AW4 Barry Bonds 1.25 3.00
AW5 Sammy Sosa .75 2.00
AW6 Barry Bonds 1.25 3.00
AW7 Mike Piazza .75 2.00
AW8 Todd Helton .50 1.25
AW9 Jeff Kent .30 .75
AW10 Edgar Renteria .30 .75
AW11 Scott Rolen .50 1.25
AW12 Vladimir Guerrero .50 1.25
AW13 Mike Hampton .30 .75
AW14 Jason Giambi .30 .75
AW15 Alfonso Soriano .50 1.25
AW16 Alex Rodriguez 1.00 2.50
AW17 Eric Chavez .30 .75
AW18 Jorge Posada .50 1.25
AW19 Bernie Williams .50 1.25
AW20 Magglio Ordonez .50 1.25
AW21 Garret Anderson .30 .75
AW22 Manny Ramirez .75 2.00
AW23 Jason Jennings .30 .75
AW24 Eric Hinske .30 .75
AW25 Billy Koch .30 .75
AW26 John Smoltz .75 2.00
AW27 Alex Rodriguez 1.00 2.50
AW28 Barry Bonds 1.25 3.00
AW29 Tony La Russa MG .50 1.25
AW30 Mike Scioscia MG .30 .75

2003 Topps Total Production

COMPLETE SET (10) 5.00 12.00
STATED ODDS 1:18
TP1 Barry Bonds 1.25 3.00
TP2 Manny Ramirez .75 2.00
TP3 Albert Pujols 1.00 2.50
TP4 Jason Giambi .30 .75
TP5 Magglio Ordonez .50 1.25
TP6 Lance Berkman .50 1.25
TP7 Todd Helton .50 1.25
TP8 Miguel Tejada .50 1.25
TP9 Sammy Sosa .75 2.00
TP10 Alex Rodriguez 1.00 2.50

2003 Topps Total Signatures

STATED ODDS 1:176
TSBP Brandon Phillips 4.00 10.00
TSEM Eli Marrero 4.00 10.00
TSMB Marlon Byrd 4.00 10.00
TSMT Marcus Thames 4.00 10.00
TSTT Tony Torcato 4.00 10.00

2003 Topps Total Team Checklists

COMPLETE SET (30) 5.00 12.00
RANDOM INSERTS IN PACKS
1 Troy Glaus .12 .30
2 Randy Johnson .30 .75
3 Greg Maddux .40 1.00
4 Jay Gibbons .12 .30
5 Nomar Garciaparra .20 .50
6 Sammy Sosa .30 .75
7 Paul Konerko .20 .50
8 Ken Griffey Jr. .60 1.50
9 Omar Vizquel .20 .50
10 Todd Helton .20 .50
11 Carlos Pena .20 .50
12 Mike Lowell .12 .30
13 Lance Berkman .20 .50
14 Mike Sweeney .12 .30
15 Shawn Green .12 .30
16 Richie Sexson .12 .30
17 Torii Hunter .12 .30
18 Vladimir Guerrero .20 .50
19 Mike Piazza .30 .75
20 Jason Giambi .12 .30
21 Eric Chavez .12 .30
22 Jim Thome .20 .50
23 Brian Giles .12 .30
24 Ryan Klesko .12 .30
25 Barry Bonds .50 1.25
26 Ichiro Suzuki .40 1.00
27 Albert Pujols .40 1.00
28 Carl Crawford .20 .50
29 Alex Rodriguez .40 1.00
30 Carlos Delgado .12 .30

2003 Topps Total Team Logo Stickers

COMPLETE SET (3) 2.00 5.00
STATED ODDS 1:24
1 Angels-Rockies .75 2.00
2 Tigers-Yankees .75 2.00
3 Athletics-Blue Jays .75 2.00

2003 Topps Total Topps

COMPLETE SET (50) 20.00 50.00
STATED ODDS 1:7
TT1 Ichiro Suzuki 1.00 2.50
TT2 Alex Rodriguez 1.00 2.50
TT3 Barry Bonds 1.25 3.00
TT4 Jason Giambi .30 .75
TT5 Troy Glaus .30 .75
TT6 Greg Maddux 1.00 2.50
TT7 Albert Pujols 1.00 2.50
TT8 Randy Johnson .75 2.00
TT9 Chipper Jones .75 2.00
TT10 Magglio Ordonez .50 1.25
TT11 Jim Thome .50 1.25
TT12 Jeff Kent .30 .75
TT13 Curt Schilling .50 1.25
TT14 Alfonso Soriano .50 1.25
TT15 Rafael Palmeiro .50 1.25
TT16 Carlos Delgado .30 .75
TT17 Torii Hunter .30 .75
TT18 Pat Burrell .30 .75
TT19 Adam Dunn .50 1.25
TT20 Roberto Alomar .50 1.25
TT21 Eric Chavez .30 .75
TT22 Derek Jeter 2.00 5.00
TT23 Nomar Garciaparra .50 1.25
TT24 Lance Berkman .50 1.25
TT25 Jim Edmonds .50 1.25
TT26 Todd Helton .50 1.25
TT27 Sammy Sosa .75 2.00
TT28 Phil Nevin .30 .75
TT29 Andruw Jones .30 .75
TT30 Barry Zito .50 1.25
TT31 Richie Sexson .30 .75
TT32 Ken Griffey Jr. 1.50 4.00
TT33 Gary Sheffield .30 .75
TT34 Shawn Green .30 .75
TT35 Mike Sweeney .30 .75
TT36 Mike Lowell .30 .75
TT37 Larry Walker .50 1.25
TT38 Manny Ramirez .75 2.00
TT39 Miguel Tejada .50 1.25
TT40 Mike Piazza .75 2.00
TT41 Scott Rolen .50 1.25
TT42 Brian Giles .30 .75
TT43 Garret Anderson .30 .75
TT44 Vladimir Guerrero .50 1.25
TT45 Bartolo Colon .30 .75
TT46 Jorge Posada .50 1.25
TT47 Ivan Rodriguez .50 1.25
TT48 Ryan Klesko .30 .75
TT49 Jose Vidro .30 .75
TT50 Pedro Martinez .50 1.25

2004 Topps Total

COMPLETE SET (880) 40.00 100.00
COMMON CARD (1-880) .10 .30
COMMON RC .10 .30
OVERALL PRESS PLATES ODDS 1:159
PLATES PRINT RUN 1 #'d SET PER COLOR
PLATES: BLACK, CYAN, MAGENTA & YELLOW
NO PLATES PRICING DUE TO SCARCITY
1 Kevin Brown .12 .30
2 Mike Mordecai .12 .30
3 Seung Song .12 .30
4 Mike Maroth .12 .30
5 Mike Lieberthal .12 .30
6 Billy Koch .12 .30
7 Mike Stanton .12 .30
8 Brad Penny .12 .30
9 Brooks Kieschnick .12 .30
10 Carlos Delgado .12 .30
11 Brady Clark .12 .30
12 Ramon Martinez .12 .30
13 Dan Wilson .12 .30
14 Guillermo Mota .12 .30
15 Trevor Hoffman .20 .50
16 Tony Batista .12 .30
17 Rusty Greer .12 .30
18 David Weathers .12 .30
19 Horacio Ramirez .12 .30
20 Aubrey Huff .12 .30
21 Casey Blake .12 .30
22 Ryan Bukvich .12 .30
23 Garrett Atkins .12 .30
24 Jose Contreras .12 .30
25 Chipper Jones .30 .75
26 Neifi Perez .12 .30
27 Scott Linebrink .12 .30
28 Matt Kinney .12 .30
29 Michael Restovich .12 .30
30 Scott Rolen .20 .50
31 John Franco .12 .30
32 Toby Hall .12 .30
33 Wily Mo Pena .12 .30
34 Dennis Tankersley .12 .30
35 Robb Nen .12 .30
36 Jose Valverde .12 .30
37 Chin-Feng Chen .12 .30
38 Gary Knotts .12 .30
39 Mark Sweeney .12 .30
40 Bret Boone .12 .30
41 Josh Phelps .12 .30
42 Jason LaRue .12 .30
43 Tim Redding .12 .30
44 Greg Myers .12 .30
45 Darin Erstad .12 .30
46 Kip Wells .12 .30
47 Matt Ford .12 .30
48 Jerome Williams .12 .30
49 Brian Meadows .12 .30
50 Albert Pujols .40 1.00
51 Kirk Saarloos .12 .30
52 Scott Eyre .12 .30
53 John Flaherty .12 .30
54 Rafael Soriano .12 .30
55 Shea Hillenbrand .12 .30
56 Kyle Farnsworth .12 .30
57 Nate Cornejo .12 .30
58 Julian Tavarez .12 .30
59 Ryan Vogelsong .12 .30
60 Ryan Klesko .12 .30
61 Luke Hudson .12 .30
62 Justin Morneau .20 .50
63 Frank Catalanotto .12 .30
64 Derrick Turnbow .12 .30
65 Marcus Giles .12 .30
66 Mark Mulder .12 .30
67 Matt Anderson .12 .30
68 Mike Matheny .12 .30
69 Brian Lawrence .12 .30
70 Bobby Abreu .12 .30
71 Damian Moss .12 .30
72 Richard Hidalgo .12 .30
73 Mark Kotsay .12 .30
74 Mike Cameron .12 .30
75 Troy Glaus .12 .30
76 Matt Holliday .30 .75
77 Byung-Hyun Kim .12 .30
78 Aaron Sele .12 .30
79 Danny Graves .12 .30
80 Barry Zito .20 .50
81 Matt LeCroy .12 .30
82 Jason Isringhausen .12 .30
83 Colby Lewis .12 .30
84 Franklyn German .12 .30
85 Luis Matos .12 .30
86 Mike Timlin .12 .30
87 Miguel Batista .12 .30
88 John McDonald .12 .30
89 Joey Eischen .12 .30
90 Mike Mussina .20 .50
91 Jack Wilson .12 .30
92 Aaron Cook .12 .30
93 John Parrish .12 .30
94 Jose Valentin .12 .30
95 Johnny Damon .20 .50
96 Pat Burrell .12 .30
97 Brendan Donnelly .12 .30
98 Lance Carter .12 .30
99 Omar Daal .12 .30
100 Ichiro Suzuki .40 1.00
101 Robin Ventura .12 .30
102 Brian Shouse .12 .30
103 Kevin Jarvis .12 .30
104 Jason Young .12 .30
105 Moises Alou .12 .30
106 Wes Obermueller .12 .30
107 David Segui .12 .30
108 Mike MacDougal .12 .30
109 John Buck .12 .30
110 Gary Sheffield .12 .30
111 Yorvit Torrealba .12 .30
112 Matt Kata .12 .30
113 David Bell .12 .30
114 Juan Gonzalez .12 .30
115 Kelvim Escobar .12 .30
116 Ruben Sierra .12 .30
117 Todd Wellemeyer .12 .30
118 Jamie Walker .12 .30
119 Will Cunnane .12 .30
120 Cliff Floyd .12 .30
121 Aramis Ramirez .12 .30
122 Damaso Marte .12 .30
123 Juan Castro .12 .30
124 Chris Woodward .12 .30
125 Andruw Jones .12 .30
126 Ben Weber .12 .30
127 Dee Brown .12 .30
128 Steve Reed .12 .30
129 Gabe Kapler .12 .30
130 Miguel Cabrera .30 .75
131 Billy McMillon .12 .30
132 Julio Mateo .12 .30
133 Preston Wilson .12 .30
134 Tony Clark .12 .30
135 Carlos Lee .12 .30
136 Carlos Baerga .12 .30
137 Mike Crudale .12 .30
138 David Ross .12 .30
139 Josh Fogg .12 .30
140 Dmitri Young .12 .30
141 Cliff Lee .20 .50
142 Mike Lowell .12 .30
143 Jason Lane .12 .30
144 Pedro Feliz .12 .30
145 Ken Griffey Jr. .60 1.50
146 Dustin Hermanson .12 .30
147 Scott Hodges .12 .30
148 Aquilino Lopez .12 .30
149 Wes Helms .12 .30
150 Jason Giambi .12 .30
151 Erasmo Ramirez .12 .30
152 Sean Burroughs .12 .30
153 J.T. Snow .12 .30
154 Eddie Guardado .12 .30
155 C.C. Sabathia .20 .50
156 Kyle Lohse .12 .30
157 Roberto Hernandez .12 .30
158 Jason Simontacchi .12 .30
159 Tim Spooneybarger .12 .30
160 Alfonso Soriano .20 .50
161 Mike Gonzalez .12 .30
162 Alex Cora .20 .50
163 Kevin Gryboski .12 .30
164 Mike Lincoln .12 .30
165 Luis Castillo .12 .30
166 Odalis Perez .12 .30
167 Alex Sanchez .12 .30
168 Rob Mackowiak .12 .30
169 Francisco Rodriguez .20 .50
170 Roy Oswalt .20 .50
171 Omar Infante .12 .30
172 Ryan Jensen .12 .30
173 Ben Broussard .12 .30
174 Mark Hendrickson .12 .30
175 Manny Ramirez .30 .75
176 Rob Bell .12 .30
177 Adam Everett .12 .30
178 Chris George .12 .30
179 Ronnie Belliard .12 .30
180 Eric Gagne .12 .30
181 Scott Schoeneweis .12 .30
182 Kris Benson .12 .30
183 Amaury Telemaco .12 .30
184 John Riedling .12 .30
185 Juan Pierre .12 .30
186 Ramon Ortiz .12 .30
187 Luis Rivas .12 .30
188 Larry Bigbie .12 .30
189 Robby Hammock .12 .30
190 Geoff Jenkins .12 .30
191 Chad Cordero .12 .30
192 Mark Ellis .12 .30
193 Mark Loretta .12 .30
194 Ryan Drese .12 .30
195 Lance Berkman .20 .50
196 Kevin Appier .12 .30
197 Kiko Calero .12 .30
198 Mickey Callaway .12 .30
199 Chase Utley .20 .50
200 Nomar Garciaparra .20 .50
201 Kevin Cash .12 .30
202 Ramiro Mendoza .12 .30
203 Shane Reynolds .12 .30
204 Chris Spurling .12 .30
205 Aaron Guiel .12 .30
206 Mark DeRosa .12 .30
207 Adam Kennedy .12 .30
208 Andy Pettitte .20 .50
209 Rafael Palmeiro .20 .50
210 Luis Gonzalez .12 .30
211 Ryan Franklin .12 .30
212 Bob Wickman .12 .30
213 Ron Calloway .12 .30
214 Jae Weong Seo .12 .30
215 Kazuhisa Ishii .12 .30
216 Sterling Hitchcock .12 .30
217 Jimmy Gobble .12 .30
218 Chad Moeller .12 .30
219 Jake Peavy .12 .30
220 John Smoltz .30 .75
221 Donovan Osborne .12 .30
222 David Wells .12 .30
223 Brad Lidge .12 .30
224 Carlos Zambrano .20 .50
225 Kerry Wood .12 .30
226 Alex Cintron .12 .30
227 Javier A. Lopez .12 .30
228 Jeremy Griffiths .12 .30
229 Jon Garland .12 .30
230 Curt Schilling .20 .50
231 Alex Scott Gonzalez .12 .30
232 Jay Gibbons .12 .30
233 Aaron Miles .12 .30
234 Mike Gallo .12 .30
235 Johan Santana .20 .50
236 Jose Guillen .12 .30
237 Jeff Conine .12 .30
238 Matt Roney .12 .30
239 Desi Relaford .12 .30
240 Frank Thomas .30 .75
241 Danny Patterson .12 .30
242 Kevin Mench .12 .30
243 Mike Redmond .12 .30
244 Jeff Suppan .12 .30
245 Carl Everett .12 .30
246 Jack Cressend .12 .30
247 Matt Mantei .12 .30
248 Enrique Wilson .12 .30
249 Craig Counsell .12 .30
250 Mark Prior .20 .50
251 Jared Sandberg .12 .30
252 Scott Strickland .12 .30
253 Lew Ford .12 .30
254 Hee Seop Choi .12 .30
255 Jason Phillips .12 .30
256 Jason Jennings .12 .30
257 Todd Pratt .12 .30
258 Matt Herges .12 .30
259 Kerry Ligtenberg .12 .30
260 Austin Kearns .12 .30
261 Jay Witasick .12 .30
262 Tony Armas Jr. .12 .30
263 Tom Martin .12 .30
264 Oliver Perez .12 .30
265 Jorge Posada .20 .50
266 Jason Boyd .12 .30
267 Ben Hendrickson .12 .30
268 Reggie Sanders .12 .30
269 Julio Lugo .12 .30
270 Pedro Martinez .20 .50
271 Kyle Snyder .12 .30
272 Felipe Lopez .12 .30
273 Kevin Millar .12 .30
274 Travis Hafner .12 .30
275 Magglio Ordonez .20 .50
276 Marlon Byrd .12 .30
277 Scott Spiezio .12 .30
278 Mark Corey .12 .30
279 Tim Salmon .12 .30
280 Alex Gonzalez .12 .30
281 Marquis Grissom .12 .30
282 Miguel Olivo .12 .30
283 Orlando Hudson .12 .30
284 Rondell White .12 .30
285 Jermaine Dye .12 .30
286 Paul Shuey .12 .30
287 Brandon Inge .12 .30
288 B.J. Surhoff .12 .30
289 Edgar Gonzalez .12 .30
290 Angel Berroa .12 .30
291 Claudio Vargas .12 .30
292 Cesar Izturis .12 .30
293 Brandon Phillips .12 .30
294 Jeff Duncan .12 .30
295 Randy Wolf .12 .30
296 Barry Larkin .20 .50
297 Felix Rodriguez .12 .30
298 Robb Quinlan .12 .30
299 Brian Jordan .12 .30
300 Dontrelle Willis .12 .30
301 Doug Davis .12 .30
302 Ricky Stone .12 .30
303 Travis Harper .12 .30
304 Jaret Wright .12 .30
305 Edgardo Alfonzo .12 .30
306 Quinton McCracken .12 .30
307 Jason Bay .20 .50
308 Joe Randa .12 .30
309 Steve Sparks .12 .30
310 Roy Halladay .20 .50
311 Antonio Alfonseca .12 .30
312 Michael Cuddyer .12 .30
313 John Patterson .12 .30
314 Chris Widger .12 .30
315 Shigetoshi Hasegawa .12 .30
316 Tim Wakefield .20 .50
317 Scott Hatteberg .12 .30
318 Mike Remlinger .12 .30
319 Jose Vizcaino .12 .30
320 Rocco Baldelli .12 .30
321 David Riske .12 .30
322 Steve Karsay .12 .30
323 Peter Bergeron .12 .30
324 Jeff Weaver .12 .30
325 Larry Walker .20 .50
326 Jack Cust .12 .30
327 Bo Hart .12 .30
328 Rod Beck .12 .30
329 Jose Acevedo .12 .30
330 Hank Blalock .12 .30
331 Tom Gordon .12 .30
332 Brian Fuentes .12 .30
333 Tomas Perez .12 .30
334 Lenny Harris .12 .30
335 Matt Morris .12 .30
336 Jeremi Gonzalez .12 .30
337 David Eckstein .12 .30
338 Aaron Rowand .12 .30
339 Rick Bauer .12 .30
340 Jim Edmonds .20 .50
341 Joe Borowski .12 .30
342 Eric DuBose .12 .30
343 D'Angelo Jimenez .12 .30
344 Tomo Ohka .12 .30
345 Victor Zambrano .12 .30
346 Joe McEwing .12 .30
347 Jorge Sosa .12 .30
348 Keith Ginter .12 .30
349 A.J. Pierzynski .12 .30
350 Mike Sweeney .12 .30
351 Shawn Chacon .12 .30
352 Matt Clement .12 .30
353 Vance Wilson .12 .30
354 Benito Santiago .12 .30
355 Eric Hinske .12 .30
356 Vladimir Guerrero .20 .50
357 Kenny Rogers .12 .30
358 Travis Lee .12 .30
359 Jay Powell .12 .30
360 Phil Nevin .12 .30
361 Willie Harris .12 .30
362 Ty Wigginton .12 .30
363 Chad Fox .12 .30
364 Junior Spivey .12 .30
365 Brandon Webb .12 .30
366 Brett Myers .12 .30
367 Alexis Gomez .12 .30
368 Dave Roberts .20 .50
369 LaTroy Hawkins .12 .30
370 Kevin Millwood .12 .30
371 Brian Schneider .12 .30
372 Blaine Neal .12 .30
373 Jeromy Burnitz .12 .30
374 Ted Lilly .12 .30
375 Shawn Green .12 .30
376 Carlos Pena .20 .50
377 Gil Meche .12 .30
378 Jeff Bagwell .20 .50
379 Alex Escobar .12 .30
380 Erubiel Durazo .12 .30
381 Cristian Guzman .12 .30
382 Rocky Biddle .12 .30
383 Craig Wilson .12 .30
384 Rey Sanchez .12 .30
385 Russ Ortiz .12 .30
386 Freddy Garcia .12 .30
387 Luis Vizcaino .12 .30
388 David Ortiz .30 .75
389 Jose Molina .12 .30
390 Edgar Martinez .20 .50
391 Nate Bump .12 .30
392 Brent Mayne .12 .30
393 Ray King .12 .30
394 Paul Wilson .12 .30
395 Melvin Mora .12 .30
396 Morgan Ensberg .12 .30
397 Ramon Hernandez .12 .30
398 Juan Rincon .12 .30
399 Ron Mahay .12 .30
400 Jeff Kent .12 .30
401 Cal Eldred .12 .30
402 Mike Difelice .12 .30
403 Valerio De Los Santos .12 .30
404 Steve Finley .12 .30
405 Trot Nixon .12 .30
406 Akinori Otsuka RC .12 .30
407 Ryan Freel .12 .30
408 Ray Durham .12 .30
409 Aaron Heilman .12 .30
410 Edgar Renteria .12 .30
411 Mike Hampton .12 .30
412 Kirk Rueter .12 .30
413 Jim Mecir .12 .30
414 Brian Roberts .12 .30
415 Paul Konerko .20 .50
416 Reed Johnson .12 .30
417 Roger Clemens .40 1.00
418 Coco Crisp .12 .30
419 Carlos Hernandez .12 .30
420 Scott Podsednik .12 .30
421 Miguel Cairo .12 .30
422 Abraham Nunez .12 .30
423 Endy Chavez .12 .30
424 Eric Munson .12 .30
425 Torii Hunter .12 .30
426 Ben Howard .12 .30
427 Chris Gomez .12 .30
428 Francisco Cordero .12 .30
429 Jeffrey Hammonds .12 .30
430 Shannon Stewart .12 .30
431 Einar Diaz .12 .30
432 Eric Byrnes .12 .30
433 Marty Cordova .12 .30
434 Matt Ginter .12 .30
435 Victor Martinez .20 .50
436 Geronimo Gil .12 .30
437 Grant Balfour .12 .30
438 Ramon Vazquez .12 .30
439 Jose Cruz Jr. .12 .30
440 Orlando Cabrera .12 .30
441 Joe Kennedy .12 .30
442 Scott Williamson .12 .30
443 Troy Percival .12 .30
444 Derrek Lee .12 .30
445 Runelvys Hernandez .12 .30
446 Mark Grudzielanek .12 .30
447 Trey Hodges .12 .30
448 Jimmy Haynes .12 .30
449 Eric Milton .12 .30
450 Todd Helton .20 .50
451 Greg Zaun .12 .30
452 Woody Williams .12 .30
453 Todd Walker .12 .30
454 Juan Cruz .12 .30
455 Fernando Vina .12 .30
456 Omar Vizquel .20 .50
457 Roberto Alomar .20 .50
458 Bill Hall .12 .30
459 Juan Rivera .12 .30
460 Tom Glavine .20 .50
461 Ramon Castro .12 .30
462 Cory Vance .12 .30
463 Dan Miceli .12 .30
464 Lyle Overbay .12 .30
465 Craig Biggio .20 .50
466 Ricky Ledee .12 .30
467 Michael Barrett .12 .30
468 Jason Anderson .12 .30
469 Matt Stairs .12 .30
470 Jarrod Washburn .12 .30
471 Todd Hundley .12 .30
472 Grant Roberts .12 .30
473 Randy Winn .12 .30
474 Pat Hentgen .12 .30
475 Jose Vidro .12 .30
476 Tony Torcato .12 .30
477 Jeremy Affeldt .12 .30
478 Carlos Guillen .12 .30
479 Paul Quantrill .12 .30
480 Rafael Furcal .12 .30
481 Adam Melhuse .12 .30
482 Jerry Hairston Jr. .12 .30
483 Adam Bernero .12 .30
484 Terrence Long .12 .30
485 Paul Lo Duca .12 .30
486 Corey Koskie .12 .30
487 John Lackey .20 .50
488 Chad Zerbe .12 .30
489 Vinny Castilla .12 .30
490 Corey Patterson .12 .30
491 John Olerud .12 .30
492 Josh Bard .12 .30
493 Darren Dreifort .12 .30
494 Jason Standridge .12 .30
495 Ben Sheets .12 .30
496 Jose Castillo .12 .30
497 Jay Payton .12 .30
498 Rob Bowen .12 .30
499 Bobby Higginson .12 .30
500 Alex Rodriguez Yanks .40 1.00
501 Octavio Dotel .12 .30
502 Rheal Cormier .12 .30
503 Felix Heredia .12 .30
504 Dan Wright .12 .30
505 Michael Young .12 .30
506 Wilfredo Ledezma .12 .30
507 Sun Woo Kim .12 .30
508 Michael Tejera .12 .30
509 Herbert Perry .12 .30
510 Esteban Loaiza .12 .30
511 Alan Embree .12 .30
512 Ben Davis .12 .30
513 Greg Colbrunn .12 .30
514 Josh Hall .12 .30
515 Raul Ibanez .20 .50
516 Jason Kershner .12 .30
517 Corky Miller .12 .30
518 Jason Marquis .12 .30
519 Roger Cedeno .12 .30
520 Adam Dunn .20 .50
521 Paul Byrd .12 .30
522 Sandy Alomar Jr. .12 .30
523 Salomon Torres .12 .30
524 John Halama .12 .30
525 Mike Piazza .30 .75
526 Buddy Groom .12 .30
527 Adrian Beltre .30 .75
528 Chad Harville .12 .30
529 Javier Vazquez .12 .30
530 Jody Gerut .12 .30
531 Elmer Dessens .12 .30
532 B.J. Ryan .12 .30
533 Chad Durbin .12 .30
534 Doug Mirabelli .12 .30
535 Bernie Williams .20 .50
536 Jeff DaVanon .12 .30
537 Dave Berg .12 .30
538 Geoff Blum .12 .30
539 John Thomson .12 .30
540 Jeremy Bonderman .12 .30
541 Jeff Zimmerman .12 .30
542 Derek Lowe .12 .30
543 Scot Shields .12 .30
544 Michael Tucker .12 .30
545 Tim Hudson .20 .50
546 Ryan Ludwick .12 .30
547 Rick Reed .12 .30
548 Placido Polanco .12 .30
549 Tony Graffanino .12 .30
550 Garret Anderson .12 .30
551 Timo Perez .12 .30
552 Jesus Colome .12 .30
553 R.A. Dickey .20 .50
554 Tim Worrell .12 .30
555 Jason Kendall .12 .30
556 Tom Goodwin .12 .30
557 Joaquin Benoit .12 .30
558 Stephen Randolph .12 .30
559 Miguel Tejada .20 .50
560 A.J. Burnett .12 .30
561 Ben Diggins .12 .30
562 Kent Mercker .12 .30
563 Zach Day .12 .30
564 Antonio Perez .12 .30
565 Jason Schmidt .12 .30
566 Armando Benitez .12 .30
567 Denny Neagle .12 .30
568 Eric Eckenstahler .12 .30
569 Chan Ho Park .20 .50
570 Carlos Beltran .20 .50
571 Brett Tomko .12 .30
572 Henry Mateo .12 .30
573 Ken Harvey .12 .30
574 Matt Lawton .12 .30
575 Mariano Rivera .40 1.00
576 Darrell May .12 .30
577 Jamie Moyer .12 .30
578 Paul Bako .12 .30
579 Cory Lidle .12 .30
580 Jacque Jones .12 .30
581 Jolbert Cabrera .12 .30
582 Jason Grimsley .12 .30
583 Danny Kolb .12 .30
584 Billy Wagner .12 .30
585 Rich Aurilia .12 .30
586 Vicente Padilla .12 .30
587 Oscar Villarreal .12 .30
588 Rene Reyes .12 .30
589 Jon Lieber .12 .30
590 Nick Johnson .12 .30
591 Bobby Crosby .12 .30
592 Steve Trachsel .12 .30
593 Brian Boehringer .12 .30
594 Juan Uribe .12 .30
595 Bartolo Colon .12 .30
596 Bobby Hill .12 .30
597 Chris Shelton RC .12 .30
598 Carl Pavano .12 .30
599 Kurt Ainsworth .12 .30
600 Derek Jeter .75 2.00
601 Doug Mientkiewicz .12 .30
602 Orlando Palmeiro .12 .30
603 J.C. Romero .12 .30
604 Scott Sullivan .12 .30
605 Brad Radke .12 .30
606 Fernando Rodney .12 .30
607 Jim Brower .12 .30
608 Josh Towers .12 .30
609 Brad Fullmer .12 .30
610 Jose Reyes .20 .50
611 Ryan Wagner .12 .30
612 Joe Mays .12 .30
613 Jung Bong .12 .30
614 Curtis Leskanic .12 .30
615 Al Leiter .12 .30
616 Wade Miller .12 .30
617 Keith Foulke Sox .12 .30
618 Casey Fossum .12 .30
619 Craig Monroe .12 .30
620 Hideo Nomo .30 .75
621 Bob File .12 .30
622 Steve Kline .12 .30
623 Bobby Kielty .12 .30
624 Dewon Brazelton .12 .30
625 Eric Chavez .12 .30
626 Chris Carpenter .20 .50
627 Alexis Rios .12 .30
628 Jason Davis .12 .30
629 Jose Jimenez .12 .30
630 Vernon Wells .12 .30
631 Kenny Lofton .12 .30
632 Chad Bradford .12 .30
633 Brad Wilkerson .12 .30
634 Pokey Reese .12 .30
635 Richie Sexson .12 .30
636 Chin-Hui Tsao .12 .30
637 Eli Marrero .12 .30
638 Chris Reitsma .12 .30
639 Daryle Ward .12 .30
640 Mark Teixeira .20 .50
641 Corwin Malone .12 .30
642 Adam Eaton .12 .30
643 Jimmy Rollins .20 .50
644 Brian Anderson .12 .30
645 Bill Mueller .12 .30
646 Jake Westbrook .12 .30
647 Bengie Molina .12 .30
648 Jorge Julio .12 .30

649 Billy Traber .12 .30
650 Randy Johnson .30 .75
651 Javy Lopez .12 .30
652 Doug Glanville .12 .30
653 Jeff Cirillo .12 .30
654 Tino Martinez .20 .50
655 Mark Buehrle .20 .50
656 Jason Michaels .12 .30
657 Damian Rolls .12 .30
658 Rosman Garcia .12 .30
659 Scott Hairston .12 .30
660 Carl Crawford .20 .50
661 Livan Hernandez .12 .30
662 Danny Bautista .12 .30
663 Brad Ausmus .12 .30
664 Juan Acevedo .12 .30
665 Sean Casey .12 .30
666 Josh Beckett .12 .30
667 Milton Bradley .12 .30
668 Braden Looper .12 .30
669 Paul Abbott .12 .30
670 Joel Pineiro .12 .30
671 Luis Terrero .12 .30
672 Rodrigo Lopez .12 .30
673 Joe Crede .12 .30
674 Mike Koplove .12 .30
675 Brian Giles .12 .30
676 Jeff Nelson .12 .30
677 Russell Branyan .12 .30
678 Mike DeJean .12 .30
679 Brian Daubach .12 .30
680 Ellis Burks .12 .30
681 Ryan Dempster .12 .30
682 Cliff Politte .12 .30
683 Brian Reith .12 .30
684 Scott Stewart .12 .30
685 Allan Simpson .12 .30
686 Shawn Estes .12 .30
687 Jason Johnson .12 .30
688 Wil Cordero .12 .30
689 Kelly Stinnett .12 .30
690 Jose Lima .12 .30
691 Gary Bennett .12 .30
692 T.J. Tucker .12 .30
693 Shane Spencer .12 .30
694 Chris Hammond .12 .30
695 Raul Mondesi .12 .30
696 Xavier Nady .12 .30
697 Cody Ransom .12 .30
698 Ron Villone .12 .30
699 Brook Fordyce .12 .30
700 Sammy Sosa .30 .75
701 Terry Adams .12 .30
702 Ricardo Rincon .12 .30
703 Tike Redman .12 .30
704 Chris Stynes .12 .30
705 Mark Redman .12 .30
706 Juan Encarnacion .12 .30
707 Jhonny Peralta .12 .30
708 Denny Hocking .12 .30
709 Ivan Rodriguez .20 .50
710 Jose Hernandez .12 .30
711 Brandon Duckworth .12 .30
712 Dave Burba .12 .30
713 Joe Nathan .12 .30
714 Dan Smith .12 .30
715 Karim Garcia .12 .30
716 Arthur Rhodes .12 .30
717 Shawn Wooten .12 .30
718 Ramon Santiago .12 .30
719 Luis Ugueto .12 .30
720 Danys Baez .12 .30
721 Alfredo Amezaga PROS .12 .30
722 Sidney Ponson .12 .30
723 Joe Mauer PROS .25 .60
724 Jesse Foppert PROS .12 .30
725 Todd Greene .12 .30
726 Dan Haren PROS .12 .30
727 Brandon Larson PROS .12 .30
728 Bobby Jenks PROS .12 .30
729 Grady Sizemore PROS .20 .50
730 Ben Grieve .12 .30
731 Khalil Greene PROS .20 .50
732 Chad Gaudin PROS .12 .30
733 Johnny Estrada PROS .12 .30
734 Joe Valentine PROS .12 .30
735 Tim Raines Jr. PROS .12 .30
736 Brandon Claussen PROS .12 .30
737 Sam Marsonek PROS .12 .30
738 Delmon Young PROS .20 .50
739 David Dellucci .12 .30
740 Sergio Mitre PROS .12 .30
741 Nick Neugebauer PROS .12 .30
742 Laynce Nix PROS .12 .30
743 Joe Thurston PROS .12 .30
744 Ryan Langerhans PROS .12 .30
745 Pete LaForest PROS .12 .30
746 Arnie Munoz PROS .12 .30
747 Rickie Weeks PROS .12 .30
748 Neal Cotts PROS .12 .30
749 Jonny Gomes PROS .12 .30
750 Jim Thome .20 .50
751 Jon Rauch PROS .12 .30
752 Edwin Jackson PROS .12 .30
753 Ryan Madson PROS .12 .30
754 Andrew Good PROS .12 .30
755 Eddie Perez .12 .30
756 Joe Borchard PROS .12 .30
757 Jeremy Guthrie PROS .12 .30
758 Jose Mesa .12 .30
759 Doug Waechter PROS .12 .30
760 J.D. Drew .12 .30
761 Adam LaRoche PROS .12 .30
762 Rich Harden PROS .12 .30
763 Justin Speier .12 .30
764 Todd Zeile .12 .30
765 Turk Wendell .12 .30
766 Mark Bellhorn Sox .12 .30
767 Mike Jackson .12 .30
768 Chone Figgins .12 .30
769 Mike Neu .12 .30
770 Greg Maddux .40 1.00
771 Frank Menechino .12 .30
772 Alec Zumwalt RC .12 .30
773 Eric Young .12 .30
774 Dustan Mohr .12 .30
775 Shane Halter .12 .30
776 Brian Buchanan .12 .30
777 So Taguchi .12 .30
778 Eric Karros .12 .30
779 Ramon Nivar .12 .30
780 Marlon Anderson .12 .30
781 Brayan Pena FY RC .12 .30
782 Chris O'Riordan FY RC .12 .30
783 Dioner Navarro FY RC .20 .50
784 Alberto Callaspo FY RC .30 .75
785 Hector Gimenez FY RC .12 .30
786 Yadier Molina FY RC 10.00 25.00
787 Kevin Richardson FY RC .12 .30
788 Brian Pilkington FY RC .12 .30
789 Adam Greenberg FY RC .60 1.50
790 Ervin Santana FY RC .30 .75
791 Brant Colamarino FY RC .12 .30
792 Ben Himes FY RC .12 .30
793 Todd Self FY RC .12 .30
794 Brad Vericker FY RC .12 .30
795 Donald Kelly FY RC .20 .50
796 Brock Jacobsen FY RC .12 .30
797 Brock Peterson FY RC .12 .30
798 Carlos Sosa FY RC .12 .30
799 Chad Chop FY RC .12 .30
800 Matt Moses FY RC .20 .50
801 Chris Aguila FY RC .12 .30
802 David Murphy FY RC .20 .50
803 Don Sutton FY RC .12 .30
804 Jereme Milons FY RC .12 .30
805 Jon Coutlangus FY RC .12 .30
806 Greg Thissen FY RC .12 .30
807 Jose Capellan FY RC .12 .30
808 Chad Santos FY RC .12 .30
809 Wardell Starling FY RC .12 .30
810 Kevin Kouzmanoff FY RC .75 2.00
811 Kevin Davidson FY RC .12 .30
812 Michael Mooney FY RC .12 .30
813 Rodney Choy Foo FY RC .12 .30
814 Reid Gorecki FY RC .12 .30
815 Rudy Guillen FY RC .12 .30
816 Harvey Garcia FY RC .12 .30
817 Warner Madrigal FY RC .12 .30
818 Kenny Perez FY RC .12 .30
819 Joaquin Arias FY RC .30 .75
820 Benji DeQuin FY RC .12 .30
821 Lastings Milledge FY RC .20 .50
822 Blake Hawksworth FY RC .12 .30
823 Estee Harris FY RC .12 .30
824 Bobby Brownlie FY RC .12 .30
825 Wanell Severino FY RC .12 .30
826 Bobby Madritsch FY .12 .30
827 Travis Hanson FY RC .12 .30
828 Brandon Medders FY RC .12 .30
829 Kevin Howard FY RC .12 .30
830 Brian Steffek FY RC .12 .30
831 Terry Jones FY RC .12 .30
832 Anthony Acevedo FY RC .12 .30
833 Kory Casto FY RC .12 .30
834 Brooks Conrad FY RC .12 .30
835 Juan Gutierrez FY RC .12 .30
836 Charlie Zink FY RC .12 .30
837 David Aardsma FY RC .12 .30
838 Carl Loadenthal FY RC .12 .30
839 Donald Levinski FY RC .12 .30
840 Dustin Nippert FY RC .12 .30
841 Calvin Hayes FY RC .12 .30
842 Felix Hernandez FY RC 2.00 5.00
843 Tyler Davidson FY RC .12 .30
844 George Sherrill FY RC .12 .30
845 Craig Ansman FY RC .12 .30
846 Jeff Allison FY RC .12 .30
847 Tommy Murphy FY RC .12 .30
848 Jerome Gamble FY RC .12 .30
849 Jesse English FY RC .12 .30
850 Alex Romero FY RC .12 .30
851 Joel Zumaya FY RC .50 1.25
852 Carlos Quentin FY RC .50 1.25
853 Jose Valdez FY RC .12 .30
854 J.J. Furmaniak FY RC .12 .30
855 Juan Cedeno FY RC .12 .30
856 Kyle Sleeth FY RC .12 .30
857 Josh Labandeira FY RC .12 .30
858 Lee Gwaltney FY RC .12 .30
859 Lincoln Holdzkom FY RC .12 .30
860 Ivan Ochoa FY RC .12 .30
861 Luke Anderson FY RC .12 .30
862 Conor Jackson FY RC .40 1.00
863 Matt Capps FY RC .12 .30
864 Merkin Valdez FY RC .12 .30
865 Paul Bacot FY RC .12 .30
866 Erick Aybar FY RC .30 .75
867 Scott Proctor FY RC .12 .30
868 Tim Stauffer FY RC .20 .50
869 Matt Creighton FY RC .12 .30
870 Zach Miner FY RC .20 .50
871 Danny Gonzalez FY RC .12 .30
872 Tom Farmer FY RC .12 .30
873 John Santor FY RC .12 .30
874 Logan Kensing FY RC .12 .30
875 Vito Chiaravalloti FY RC .12 .30
876 Checklist .12 .30
877 Checklist .12 .30
878 Checklist .12 .30
879 Checklist .12 .30
880 Checklist .12 .30

2004 Topps Total Silver

*PARALLEL: 1X TO 2.5X BASIC
*PARALLEL RC's: 1X TO 2.5X BASIC RC's
ONE PER PACK

2004 Topps Total Award Winners

COMPLETE SET (30) 12.50 30.00
STATED ODDS 1:12
OVERALL PRESS PLATES ODDS 1:159
PLATES PRINT RUN 1 #'d SET PER COLOR
PLATES: BLACK, CYAN, MAGENTA & YELLOW
NO PLATES PRICING DUE TO SCARCITY
AW1 Roy Halladay CY .50 1.25
AW2 Eric Gagne CY .30 .75
AW3 Alex Rodriguez MVP 1.00 2.50
AW4 Albert Pujols POY 1.00 2.50
AW5 Alex Rodriguez POY 1.00 2.50
AW6 Jorge Posada SS .50 1.25
AW7 Javy Lopez SS .30 .75
AW8 Carlos Delgado SS .30 .75
AW9 Todd Helton SS .50 1.25
AW10 Bret Boone SS .30 .75
AW11 Jose Vidro SS .30 .75
AW12 Bill Mueller SS .30 .75
AW13 Mike Lowell SS .30 .75
AW14 Alex Rodriguez SS 1.00 2.50
AW15 Edgar Renteria SS .30 .75
AW16 Garret Anderson SS .30 .75
AW17 Albert Pujols SS 1.00 2.50
AW18 Manny Ramirez SS .75 2.00
AW19 Vernon Wells SS .30 .75
AW20 Gary Sheffield SS .30 .75
AW21 Edgar Martinez SS .50 1.25
AW22 Mike Hampton SS .30 .75
AW23 Angel Berroa ROY .30 .75
AW24 Dontrelle Willis ROY .30 .75
AW25 Keith Foulke Rolaids .30 .75
AW26 Eric Gagne Rolaids .30 .75
AW27 Alex Rodriguez HA 1.00 2.50
AW28 Albert Pujols HA 1.00 2.50
AW29 Tony Pena MG .30 .75
AW30 Jack McKeon MG .30 .75

2004 Topps Total Production

COMPLETE SET (10) 6.00 15.00
STATED ODDS 1:18
OVERALL PRESS PLATES ODDS 1:159
PLATES PRINT RUN 1 #'d SET PER COLOR
PLATES: BLACK, CYAN, MAGENTA & YELLOW
NO PLATES PRICING DUE TO SCARCITY
TP1 Alex Rodriguez 1.00 2.50
TP2 Albert Pujols 1.00 2.50
TP3 Sammy Sosa .75 2.00
TP4 Carlos Delgado .30 .75
TP5 Gary Sheffield .30 .75
TP6 Manny Ramirez .75 2.00
TP7 Jim Thome .50 1.25
TP8 Todd Helton .50 1.25
TP9 Garret Anderson .30 .75
TP10 Nomar Garciaparra .50 1.25

2004 Topps Total Signatures

STATED ODDS 1:414
BC Brandon Claussen 4.00 10.00
GB Grant Balfour 4.00 10.00
JJ Jimmy Journell 4.00 10.00
LB Larry Bigbie 6.00 15.00
TB Toby Hall 4.00 10.00

2004 Topps Total Team Checklists

COMPLETE SET (30) 6.00 15.00
STATED ODDS 1:4
OVERALL PRESS PLATES ODDS 1:159
PLATES PRINT RUN 1 #'d SET PER COLOR
PLATES: BLACK, CYAN, MAGENTA & YELLOW
NO PLATES PRICING DUE TO SCARCITY
TTC1 Garret Anderson .12 .30
TTC2 Randy Johnson .30 .75
TTC3 Chipper Jones .30 .75
TTC4 Miguel Tejada .20 .50
TTC5 Nomar Garciaparra .20 .50
TTC6 Mark Prior .20 .50
TTC7 Magglio Ordonez .20 .50
TTC8 Ken Griffey Jr. .60 1.50
TTC9 C.C. Sabathia .20 .50
TTC10 Todd Helton .20 .50
TTC11 Ivan Rodriguez .20 .50
TTC12 Dontrelle Willis .12 .30
TTC13 Roger Clemens .40 1.00
TTC14 Mike Sweeney .12 .30
TTC15 Shawn Green .12 .30
TTC16 Geoff Jenkins .12 .30
TTC17 Torii Hunter .12 .30
TTC18 Jose Vidro .12 .30
TTC19 Mike Piazza .30 .75
TTC20 Alex Rodriguez .40 1.00
TTC21 Eric Chavez .12 .30
TTC22 Jim Thome .20 .50
TTC23 Jason Kendall .12 .30
TTC24 Brian Giles .12 .30
TTC25 Jason Schmidt .12 .30
TTC26 Ichiro Suzuki .40 1.00
TTC27 Albert Pujols .40 1.00
TTC28 Aubrey Huff .12 .30
TTC29 Hank Blalock .12 .30
TTC30 Carlos Delgado .12 .30

2004 Topps Total Topps

COMPLETE SET (50) 20.00 50.00
STATED ODDS 1:7
OVERALL PRESS PLATES ODDS 1:159
PLATES PRINT RUN 1 SERIAL #'d SET
NO PLATES PRICING DUE TO SCARCITY
TT1 Derek Jeter 2.00 5.00
TT2 Jose Reyes .50 1.25
TT3 Miguel Tejada .50 1.25
TT4 Larry Walker .50 1.25
TT5 Frank Thomas .75 2.00
TT6 Carlos Delgado .30 .75
TT7 Vernon Wells .30 .75
TT8 Jeff Bagwell .50 1.25
TT9 Jason Giambi .30 .75
TT10 Mike Lowell .30 .75
TT11 Shannon Stewart .30 .75
TT12 Mike Piazza .75 2.00
TT13 Todd Helton .50 1.25
TT14 Austin Kearns .30 .75
TT15 Jim Edmonds .50 1.25
TT16 Jose Vidro .30 .75
TT17 Andruw Jones .30 .75
TT18 Gary Sheffield .30 .75
TT19 Eric Chavez .30 .75
TT20 Magglio Ordonez .50 1.25
TT21 Geoff Jenkins .30 .75
TT22 Ken Griffey Jr. 1.50 4.00
TT23 Jeff Kent .30 .75
TT24 Jorge Posada .50 1.25
TT25 Albert Pujols 1.00 2.50
TT26 Javy Lopez .30 .75
TT27 Alfonso Soriano .50 1.25
TT28 Brian Giles .30 .75
TT29 Mike Sweeney .30 .75
TT30 Miguel Cabrera .75 2.00
TT31 Luis Gonzalez .30 .75
TT32 Scott Rolen .50 1.25
TT33 Jim Thome .50 1.25
TT34 Garret Anderson .30 .75
TT35 Vladimir Guerrero .50 1.25
TT36 Shawn Green .30 .75
TT37 Hank Blalock .30 .75
TT38 Marcus Giles .30 .75
TT39 Torii Hunter .30 .75
TT40 Sammy Sosa .75 2.00
TT41 Nomar Garciaparra .50 1.25
TT42 Bobby Abreu .30 .75
TT43 Richie Sexson .30 .75
TT44 Manny Ramirez .75 2.00
TT45 Troy Glaus .30 .75
TT46 Preston Wilson .30 .75
TT47 Ivan Rodriguez .50 1.25
TT48 Ichiro Suzuki 1.00 2.50
TT49 Chipper Jones .75 2.00
TT50 Alex Rodriguez 1.00 2.50

2005 Topps Total

COMPLETE SET (770) 40.00 100.00
COMMON (1-575/666) .12 .30
COMMON CARD (576-690) .12 .30
COM (269/588/691-765) .12 .30
COMMON CL (766-770) .10 .30
OVERALL PLATE ODDS 1:85 HOBBY
PLATE PRINT RUN 1 SET PER COLOR
BLACK-CYAN-MAGENTA-YELLOW ISSUED
FRONT AND BACK PLATES PRODUCED
NO PLATE PRICING DUE TO SCARCITY
1 Rafael Furcal .15 .40
2 Tony Clark .15 .40
3 Hideki Matsui .60 1.50
4 Zach Day .15 .40
5 Garret Anderson .15 .40
6 B.J. Surhoff .15 .40
7 Trevor Hoffman .25 .60
8 Kenny Lofton .15 .40
9 Ross Gload .15 .40
10 Jorge Cantu .15 .40
11 Joel Pineiro .15 .40
12 Alex Cintron .15 .40
13 Mike Matheny .15 .40
14 Rod Barajas .15 .40
15 Ray Durham .15 .40
16 Danys Baez .15 .40
17 Brian Schneider .15 .40
18 Tike Redman .15 .40
19 Ricardo Rodriguez .15 .40
20 Mike Sweeney .15 .40
21 Greg Myers .15 .40
22 Chone Figgins .15 .40
23 Brian Lawrence .15 .40
24 Joe Nathan .15 .40
25 Placido Polanco .15 .40
26 Yadier Molina 10.00 25.00
27 Gary Bennett .15 .40
28 Yorvit Torrealba .15 .40
29 Javier Valentin .15 .40
30 Jason Giambi .15 .40
31 Brandon Claussen .15 .40
32 Miguel Olivo .15 .40
33 Josh Bard .15 .40
34 Ramon Hernandez .15 .40
35 Geoff Jenkins .15 .40
36 Bobby Kielty .15 .40
37 Luis A. Gonzalez .15 .40
38 Benito Santiago .15 .40
39 Brandon Inge .15 .40
40 Mark Prior .25 .60
41 Mike Lieberthal .15 .40
42 Toby Hall .15 .40
43 Brad Ausmus .15 .40
44 Damian Miller .15 .40
45 Mark Kotsay .15 .40
46 John Buck .15 .40
47 Oliver Perez .15 .40
48 Matt Morris .15 .40
49 Raul Chavez .15 .40
50 Randy Johnson .40 1.00
51 Dave Bush .15 .40
52 Jose Macias .15 .40
53 Paul Wilson .15 .40
54 Wilfredo Ledezma .15 .40
55 J.D. Drew .15 .40
56 Pedro Martinez .25 .60
57 Josh Towers .15 .40
58 Jamie Moyer .15 .40
59 Scott Elarton .15 .40
60 Ken Griffey Jr. .75 2.00
61 Steve Trachsel .15 .40
62 Bubba Crosby .15 .40
63 Michael Barrett .15 .40
64 Odalis Perez .15 .40
65 B.J. Upton .25 .60
66 Eric Bruntlett .15 .40
67 Victor Zambrano .15 .40
68 Brandon League .15 .40
69 Carlos Silva .15 .40
70 Lyle Overbay .15 .40
71 Runelvys Hernandez .15 .40
72 Brad Penny .15 .40
73 Ty Wigginton .15 .40
74 Orlando Hudson .15 .40
75 Roy Oswalt .25 .60
76 Jason LaRue .15 .40
77 Ismael Valdez .15 .40
78 Calvin Pickering .15 .40
79 Bill Hall .15 .40
80 Carl Crawford .25 .60
81 Tomas Perez .15 .40
82 Joe Kennedy .15 .40
83 Chris Woodward .15 .40
84 Jason Lane .15 .40
85 Steve Finley .15 .40
86 Jeff Francis .15 .40
87 Felipe Lopez .15 .40
88 Chan Ho Park .25 .60
89 Joe Crede .15 .40
90 Jose Vidro .15 .40
91 Casey Kotchman .15 .40
92 Brandon Backe .15 .40
93 Mike Hampton .15 .40
94 Ryan Dempster .15 .40
95 Wily Mo Pena .15 .40
96 Matt Holliday .40 1.00
97 A.J. Pierzynski .15 .40
98 Jason Jennings .15 .40
99 Eli Marrero .15 .40
100 Carlos Beltran .25 .60
101 Scott Kazmir .40 1.00
102 Kenny Rogers .15 .40
103 Roy Halladay .25 .60
104 Alex Cora .25 .60
105 Richie Sexson .15 .40
106 Ben Sheets .15 .40
107 Bartolo Colon .15 .40
108 Eddie Perez .15 .40
109 Vicente Padilla .15 .40
110 Sammy Sosa .40 1.00
111 Mark Ellis .15 .40
112 Woody Williams .15 .40
113 Todd Greene .15 .40
114 Nook Logan .15 .40
115 Francisco Rodriguez .25 .60
116 Miguel Batista .15 .40
117 Livan Hernandez .15 .40
118 Chris Aguila .15 .40
119 Coco Crisp .15 .40
120 Jose Reyes .25 .60
121 Ricky Ledee .15 .40
122 Brad Radke .15 .40
123 Carlos Guillen .15 .40
124 Paul Bako .15 .40
125 Tom Glavine .25 .60
126 Chad Moeller .15 .40
127 Mark Buehrle .25 .60
128 Casey Blake .15 .40
129 Juan Rivera .15 .40
130 Preston Wilson .15 .40
131 Nate Robertson .15 .40
132 Julio Franco .15 .40
133 Derek Lowe .15 .40
134 Rob Bell .15 .40
135 Javy Lopez .15 .40
136 Javier Vazquez .15 .40
137 Desi Relaford .15 .40
138 Danny Graves .15 .40
139 Josh Fogg .15 .40
140 Bobby Crosby .15 .40
141 Ramon Castro .15 .40
142 Jerry Hairston Jr. .15 .40
143 Morgan Ensberg .15 .40
144 Brandon Webb .25 .60
145 Jack Wilson .15 .40
146 Bill Mueller .15 .40
147 Troy Glaus .15 .40
148 Armando Benitez .15 .40
149 Adam LaRoche .15 .40
150 Hank Blalock .15 .40
151 Ryan Franklin .15 .40
152 Kevin Millwood .15 .40
153 Jason Marquis .15 .40
154 Dewon Brazelton .15 .40
155 Al Leiter .15 .40
156 Garrett Atkins .15 .40
157 Todd Walker .15 .40
158 Kris Benson .15 .40
159 Eric Milton .15 .40
160 Bret Boone .15 .40
161 Matt LeCroy .15 .40
162 Chris Widger .15 .40
163 Ruben Gotay .15 .40
164 Craig Monroe .15 .40
165 Travis Hafner .15 .40
166 Vance Wilson .15 .40
167 Jason Grabowski .15 .40
168 Tim Salmon .15 .40
169 Henry Blanco .15 .40
170 Josh Beckett .15 .40
171 Jake Westbrook .15 .40
172 Paul Lo Duca .15 .40
173 Julio Lugo .15 .40
174 Juan Cruz .15 .40
175 Mark Mulder .15 .40
176 Juan Castro .15 .40
177 Damion Easley .15 .40
178 LaTroy Hawkins .15 .40
179 Jon Lieber .15 .40
180 Vernon Wells .15 .40
181 Jeff DaVanon .15 .40
182 Dustan Mohr .15 .40
183 Ryan Freel .15 .40
184 Doug Davis .15 .40
185 Sean Casey .15 .40
186 Robb Quinlan .15 .40
187 J.D. Closser .15 .40
188 Tim Wakefield .25 .60
189 Brian Jordan .15 .40
190 Adam Dunn .25 .60
191 Antonio Perez .15 .40
192 Brett Tomko .15 .40
193 John Flaherty .15 .40
194 Michael Cuddyer .15 .40
195 Ronnie Belliard .15 .40
196 Tony Womack .15 .40
197 Jason Johnson
198 Victor Santos .15 .40
199 Danny Haren .15 .40
200 Derek Jeter 1.00 2.50
201 Brian Anderson .15 .40
202 Carlos Pena .25 .60
203 Jaret Wright .15 .40
204 Paul Byrd .15 .40
205 Shannon Stewart .15 .40
206 Chris Carpenter .25 .60
207 Matt Stairs .15 .40
208 Brad Hawpe .15 .40
209 Bobby Higginson .15 .40
210 Torii Hunter .15 .40
211 Shawn Green .15 .40
212 Todd Hollandsworth .15 .40
213 Scott Erickson .15 .40
214 C.C. Sabathia .25 .60
215 Mike Mussina .25 .60
216 Jason Kendall .15 .40
217 Todd Pratt .15 .40
218 Danny Kolb .15 .40
219 Tony Armas .15 .40
220 Edgar Renteria .15 .40
221 Dave Roberts .25 .60
222 Luis Rivas .15 .40
223 Adam Everett .15 .40
224 Jeff Cirillo .15 .40
225 Orlando Hernandez .15 .40
226 Ken Harvey .15 .40
227 Corey Patterson .15 .40
228 Humberto Cota .15 .40
229 A.J. Burnett .15 .40
230 Roger Clemens .50 1.25
231 Joe Randa .15 .40
232 David Dellucci .15 .40
233 Troy Percival .15 .40
234 Dustin Hermanson .15 .40
235 Eric Gagne .15 .40
236 Terry Tiffee .15 .40
237 Tony Graffanino .15 .40
238 Jayson Werth .25 .60
239 Mark Sweeney .15 .40
240 Chipper Jones .40 1.00
241 Aramis Ramirez .15 .40
242 Frank Catalanotto .15 .40
243 Mike Maroth .15 .40
244 Kelvim Escobar .15 .40
245 Bobby Abreu .15 .40
246 Kyle Lohse .15 .40
247 Jason Isringhausen .15 .40
248 Jose Lima .15 .40
249 Adrian Gonzalez .30 .75
250 Alex Rodriguez .50 1.25
251 Ramon Ortiz .15 .40
252 Frank Menechino .15 .40
253 Keith Ginter .15 .40
254 Kip Wells .15 .40
255 Dmitri Young .15 .40
256 Craig Biggio .25 .60
257 Ramon E. Martinez .15 .40
258 Jason Bartlett .15 .40
259 Brad Lidge .15 .40
260 Brian Giles .15 .40
261 Luis Terrero .15 .40
262 Miguel Ojeda .15 .40
263 Rich Harden .15 .40
264 Jacque Jones .15 .40
265 Marcus Giles .15 .40
266 Carlos Zambrano .25 .60
267 Michael Tucker .15 .40
268 Wes Obermueller .15 .40
269 Pete Orr RC .25 .60
270 Jim Thome .25 .60
271 Omar Vizquel .25 .60
272 Jose Valentin .15 .40
273 Juan Uribe .15 .40
274 Doug Mirabelli .15 .40
275 Jeff Kent .15 .40
276 Brad Wilkerson .15 .40
277 Chris Burke .15 .40
278 Endy Chavez .15 .40
279 Richard Hidalgo .15 .40
280 John Smoltz .40 1.00
281 Jarrod Washburn .15 .40
282 Larry Bigbie .15 .40
283 Edgardo Alfonzo .15 .40
284 Cliff Lee .25 .60
285 Carlos Lee .15 .40
286 Olmedo Saenz .15 .40
287 Tomo Ohka .15 .40
288 Ruben Sierra .15 .40
289 Nick Swisher .25 .60
290 Frank Thomas .40 1.00
291 Aaron Cook .15 .40
292 Cody McKay .15 .40
293 Hee-Seop Choi .15 .40
294 Carl Pavano .15 .40
295 Scott Rolen .25 .60
296 Matt Kata .15 .40
297 Terrence Long .15 .40
298 Jimmy Gobble .15 .40
299 Jason Repko .15 .40
300 Manny Ramirez .40 1.00
301 Dan Wilson .15 .40
302 Jhonny Peralta .15 .40
303 John Mabry .15 .40
304 Adam Melhuse .15 .40
305 Kerry Wood .15 .40
306 Ryan Langerhans .15 .40
307 Antonio Alfonseca .15 .40
308 Marco Scutaro .25 .60
309 Jamey Carroll .15 .40
310 Lance Berkman .25 .60
311 Willie Harris .15 .40
312 Phil Nevin .15 .40
313 Gregg Zaun .15 .40
314 Michael Ryan .15 .40
315 Zack Greinke .50 1.25
316 Ted Lilly .15 .40
317 David Eckstein .15 .40
318 Tony Torcato .15 .40
319 Rob Mackowiak .15 .40
320 Mark Teixeira .25 .60
321 Jason Phillips .15 .40
322 Jeremy Reed .15 .40
323 Bengie Molina .15 .40
324 Termel Sledge .15 .40
325 Justin Morneau .25 .60
326 Sandy Alomar Jr. .15 .40
327 Jon Garland .15 .40
328 Jay Payton .15 .40
329 Tino Martinez .25 .60
330 Jason Bay .15 .40
331 Jeff Conine .15 .40
332 Shawn Chacon .15 .40
333 Angel Berroa .15 .40
334 Reggie Sanders .15 .40
335 Kevin Brown .15 .40
336 Brady Clark .15 .40
337 Casey Fossum .15 .40
338 Raul Ibanez .25 .60
339 Derrek Lee .15 .40
340 Victor Martinez .25 .60
341 Kazuhisa Ishii .15 .40
342 Royce Clayton .15 .40
343 Trot Nixon .15 .40
344 Eric Young .15 .40
345 Aubrey Huff .15 .40
346 Brett Myers .15 .40
347 Joey Gathright .15 .40
348 Mark Grudzielanek .15 .40
349 Scott Spiezio .15 .40
350 Eric Chavez .15 .40
351 Einar Diaz .15 .40
352 Dallas McPherson .15 .40
353 John Thomson .15 .40
354 Neifi Perez .15 .40
355 Larry Walker .25 .60
356 Billy Wagner .15 .40
357 Mike Cameron .15 .40
358 Jimmy Rollins .25 .60
359 Kevin Mench .15 .40
360 Joe Mauer .30 .75
361 Jose Molina .15 .40
362 Joe Borchard .15 .40
363 Kevin Cash .15 .40
364 Jay Gibbons .15 .40
365 Khalil Greene .15 .40
366 Justin Leone .15 .40
367 Eddie Guardado .15 .40
368 Mike Lamb .15 .40
369 Matt Riley .15 .40
370 Luis Gonzalez .15 .40
371 Alfredo Amezaga .15 .40
372 J.J. Hardy .15 .40
373 Hector Luna .15 .40
374 Greg Aquino .15 .40
375 Jim Edmonds .25 .60
376 Joe Blanton .15 .40
377 Russell Branyan .15 .40
378 J.T. Snow .15 .40
379 Magglio Ordonez .25 .60
380 Rafael Palmeiro .25 .60
381 Andruw Jones .15 .40
382 David DeJesus .15 .40
383 Marquis Grissom .15 .40
384 Bobby Hill .15 .40
385 Kazuo Matsui .15 .40
386 Mark Loretta .15 .40
387 Chris Shelton .15 .40
388 Johnny Estrada .15 .40
389 Adam Hyzdu .15 .40
390 Nomar Garciaparra .25 .60
391 Mark Teahen .15 .40
392 Chris Capuano .15 .40
393 Ben Broussard .15 .40
394 Daniel Cabrera .15 .40
395 Jeremy Bonderman .15 .40
396 Darin Erstad .15 .40
397 Alex S. Gonzalez .15 .40
398 Kevin Millar .15 .40
399 Freddy Garcia .15 .40
400 Alfonso Soriano .25 .60
401 Koyie Hill .15 .40
402 Omar Infante .15 .40
403 Alex Gonzalez .15 .40
404 Pat Burrell .15 .40
405 Wes Helms .15 .40
406 Junior Spivey .15 .40
407 Joe Mays .15 .40
408 Jason Stanford .15 .40
409 Gil Meche .15 .40
410 Tim Hudson .25 .60
411 Chase Utley .25 .60
412 Matt Clement .15 .40
413 Nick Green .15 .40
414 Jose Vizcaino .15 .40
415 Ryan Klesko .15 .40
416 Vinny Castilla .15 .40
417 Brian Roberts .15 .40
418 Geronimo Gil .15 .40
419 Gary Matthews .15 .40
420 Jeff Weaver .15 .40
421 Jerome Williams .15 .40
422 Andy Pettitte .25 .60
423 Randy Wolf .15 .40
424 D'Angelo Jimenez .15 .40
425 Moises Alou .15 .40
426 Eric Byrnes .15 .40
427 Mark Redman .15 .40
428 Jermaine Dye .15 .40
429 Cory Lidle .15 .40
430 Jason Schmidt .15 .40
431 Jason W. Smith .15 .40
432 Jose Castillo .15 .40
433 Pokey Reese .15 .40
434 Matt Lawton .15 .40
435 Jose Guillen .15 .40
436 Craig Counsell .15 .40
437 Jose Hernandez .15 .40
438 Braden Looper .15 .40
439 Scott Hatteberg .15 .40
440 Gary Sheffield .15 .40
441 Gabe Gross .15 .40
442 Chris Gomez .15 .40
443 Dontrelle Willis .15 .40
444 Jamey Wright .15 .40
445 Rocco Baldelli .15 .40
446 Bernie Williams .25 .60
447 Sean Burroughs .15 .40
448 Willie Bloomquist .15 .40
449 Luis Castillo .15 .40
450 Mike Piazza .40 1.00
451 Ryan Drese .15 .40
452 Pedro Feliz .15 .40
453 Horacio Ramirez .15 .40
454 Luis Matos .15 .40
455 Craig Wilson .15 .40
456 Russ Ortiz .15 .40
457 Xavier Nady .15 .40
458 Hideo Nomo .40 1.00
459 Miguel Cairo .15 .40
460 Mike Lowell .15 .40
461 Corky Miller .15 .40
462 Bobby Madritsch .15 .40
463 Jose Contreras .15 .40
464 Johnny Damon .25 .60
465 Miguel Cabrera .40 1.00
466 Eric Hinske .15 .40
467 Marlon Byrd .15 .40
468 Aaron Miles .15 .40
469 Ramon Vazquez .15 .40
470 Michael Young .15 .40
471 Alex Sanchez .15 .40
472 Shea Hillenbrand .15 .40
473 Jeff Bagwell .25 .60
474 Erik Bedard .15 .40
475 Jake Peavy .15 .40
476 Jody Gerut .15 .40
477 Randy Winn .15 .40
478 Kevin Youkilis .15 .40

479 Eric Dubose .15 .40
480 David Wright .30 .75
481 Wilson Valdez .15 .40
482 Cliff Floyd .15 .40
483 Jose Mesa .15 .40
484 Doug Mientkiewicz .15 .40
485 Jorge Posada .25 .60
486 Sidney Ponson .15 .40
487 Dave Krynzel .15 .40
488 Octavio Dotel .15 .40
489 Matt Treanor .15 .40
490 Johan Santana .25 .60
491 John Patterson .15 .40
492 So Taguchi .15 .40
493 Carl Everett .15 .40
494 Jason Dubois .15 .40
495 Albert Pujols .50 1.25
496 Kirk Rueter .15 .40
497 Geoff Blum .15 .40
498 Juan Encarnacion .15 .40
499 Mark Hendrickson .15 .40
500 Barry Bonds .60 1.50
501 Cesar Izturis .15 .40
502 David Wells .15 .40
503 Jorge Julio .15 .40
504 Cristian Guzman .15 .40
505 Juan Pierre .15 .40
506 Adam Eaton .15 .40
507 Nick Johnson .15 .40
508 Mike Redmond .15 .40
509 Daryle Ward .15 .40
510 Adrian Beltre .40 1.00
511 Laynce Nix .15 .40
512 Reed Johnson .15 .40
513 Jeremy Affeldt .15 .40
514 R.A. Dickey .25 .60
515 Alex Rios .15 .40
516 Orlando Palmeiro .15 .40
517 Mark Bellhorn .15 .40
518 Adam Kennedy .15 .40
519 Curtis Granderson .30 .75
520 Todd Helton .25 .60
521 Aaron Boone .15 .40
522 Milton Bradley .15 .40
523 Timo Perez .15 .40
524 Jeff Suppan .15 .40
525 Austin Kearns .15 .40
526 Charles Thomas .15 .40
527 Bronson Arroyo .15 .40
528 Roger Cedeno .15 .40
529 Russ Adams .15 .40
530 Barry Zito .25 .60
531 Bob Wickman .15 .40
532 Deivi Cruz .15 .40
533 Mariano Rivera .50 1.25
534 J.J. Davis .15 .40
535 Greg Maddux .50 1.25
536 Ryan Vogelsong .15 .40
537 Josh Phelps .15 .40
538 Scott Hairston .15 .40
539 Vladimir Guerrero .25 .60
540 Ivan Rodriguez .25 .60
541 David Newhan .15 .40
542 David Bell .15 .40
543 Lew Ford .15 .40
544 Grady Sizemore .25 .60
545 David Ortiz .40 1.00
546 Jose Cruz Jr. .15 .40
547 Aaron Rowand .15 .40
548 Marcus Thames .15 .40
549 Scott Podsednik .15 .40
550 Ichiro Suzuki .50 1.25
551 Eduardo Perez .15 .40
552 Chris Snyder .15 .40
553 Corey Koskie .15 .40
554 Miguel Tejada .25 .60
555 Orlando Cabrera .15 .40
556 Rondell White .15 .40
557 Wade Miller .15 .40
558 Rodrigo Lopez .15 .40
559 Chad Tracy .15 .40
560 Paul Konerko .25 .60
561 Wil Cordero .15 .40
562 John McDonald .15 .40
563 Jason Ellison .15 .40
564 Jason Michaels .15 .40
565 Melvin Mora .15 .40
566 Ryan Church .15 .40
567 Ryan Ludwick .15 .40
568 Erubiel Durazo .15 .40
569 Noah Lowry .15 .40
570 Curt Schilling .25 .60
571 Esteban Loaiza .15 .40
572 Freddy Sanchez .15 .40
573 Rich Aurilia .15 .40
574 Travis Lee .15 .40
575 Nick Punto .15 .40
576 J.Christiansen .15 .40
K.Correia
577 B.Baker .15 .40
T.Redding
578 T.Adams .15 .40
G.Floyd
579 S.Etherton .15 .40
D.Meyer
580 J.Lehr .15 .40
D.Turnbow
581 M.Gosling .15 .40
B.Halsey
582 J.Mecir .15 .40
L.Kensing
583 B.Hennessey .15 .40
J.Fassero
584 J.Adkins .15 .40
F.Diaz
585 J.Crain .15 .40
J.Rincon
586 J.Cerda .15 .40
N.Field
587 B.Fortunato .15 .40
J.Seo
588 S.Schmoll RC .15 .40
Y.Brazoban
589 U.Urbina .15 .40
J.Walker
590 J.De Paula .15 .40
S.Proctor
591 J.Davis .15 .40
B.Howry
592 T.Worrell .15 .40
P.Liriano
593 J.Acevedo .15 .40
K.Mercker
594 C.Hammond .15 .40
S.Linebrink
595 F.Nieve .15 .40
J.Franco
596 R.Flores .15 .40
M.Lincoln
597 J.Borowski .15 .40
S.Mitre
598 L.Carter .15 .40
J.Colome
599 J.Halama .15 .40
L.DiNardo
600 C.Bradford .15 .40
K.Calero
601 D.Aardsma .15 .40
J.Brower
602 G.Geary .15 .40
R.Madson
603 B.Moehler .15 .40
N.Bump
604 C.Tsao .15 .40
R.Speier
605 R.Wagner .15 .40
A.Harang
606 S.Kline .15 .40
R.Bauer
607 L.Cormier .15 .40
R.Choate
608 J.Leicester .15 .40
T.Wellemeyer
609 V.Chulk .15 .40
J.Frasor
610 S.Dohmann .15 .40
B.Fuentes
611 S.Colyer .15 .40
R.Hernandez
612 I.Snell .15 .40
S.Torres
613 C.Eldred .25 .60
A.Wainwright
614 R.Bukvich .15 .40
D.Brocail
615 J.Putz .15 .40
A.Sele
616 B.Chen .15 .40
T.Williams
617 D.Weathers .15 .40
B.Weber
618 D.Reyes .15 .40
R.Seanez
619 T.Harikkala .15 .40
R.Rincon
620 S.Camp .15 .40
D.Bautista
621 J.Lopez .15 .40
A.Simpson
622 M.Remlinger .15 .40
G.Rusch
623 R.Colon .15 .40
K.Gryboski
624 T.Martin .15 .40
C.Reitsma
625 C.Qualls .15 .40
D.Wheeler
626 T.Phelps .15 .40
M.Wise
627 S.Schoeneweis .15 .40
J.Speier
628 F.Cordero .15 .40
F.Francisco
629 R.Soriano .15 .40
M.Thornton
630 M.Stanton .15 .40
S.Karsay
631 M.MacDougal .15 .40
S.Sullivan
632 B.Bruney .15 .40
O.Villarreal
633 M.Adams .15 .40
R.Bottalico
634 E.Rodriguez .15 .40
D.Borkowski
635 R.Betancourt .15 .40
D.Riske
636 J.De La Rosa .15 .40
G.Glover
637 M.Perisho .15 .40
B.Howard
638 J.Bajenaru .15 .40
L.Vizcaino
639 R.Mahay .15 .40
E.Ramirez
640 J.Grabow .15 .40
M.Gonzalez
641 J.Romero .15 .40
M.Guerrier
642 C.Hernandez .15 .40
B.Duckworth
643 T.Harper .15 .40
S.McClung
644 M.Herges .15 .40
T.Walker
645 K.Wunsch .15 .40
E.Dessens
646 M.Malaska .15 .40
M.Myers
647 K.Farnsworth .15 .40
G.Knotts
648 J.Duchscherer .15 .40
J.Garcia
649 A.Rakers .15 .40
S.Reed
650 T.Gordon .15 .40
P.Quantrill
651 B.Lyon .15 .40
S.Estes
652 P.Walker .15 .40
G.Chacin
653 J.Lackey .25 .60
S.Shields
654 D.Waechter .15 .40
T.Miller
655 L.Ayala .15 .40
C.Cordero
656 R.Villone .15 .40
J.Mateo
657 M.Mantei .15 .40
B.Neal
658 D.Marte .15 .40
C.Politte
659 J.Valentine .15 .40
L.Hudson
660 T.Jones .15 .40
J.Riedling
661 H.Bell .15 .40
A.Heilman
662 D.May .15 .40
A.Otsuka
663 J.Eischen .15 .40
J.Horgan
664 A.Sisco .15 .40
M.Wood
665 A.Embree .15 .40
M.Timlin
666 Keith Foulke .15 .40
667 R.Cormier .15 .40
A.Fultz
668 J.Woods .15 .40
K.Gregg
669 M.Ginter .15 .40
F.German
670 S.Eyre .15 .40
M.Valdez
671 B.Meadows .15 .40
R.White
672 G.Mota .15 .40
T.Spooneybarger
673 J.Grimsley .15 .40
B.Ryan
674 N.Cotts .15 .40
S.Takatsu
675 M.DeJean .15 .40
F.Heredia
676 M.Belisle .15 .40
J.Hancock
677 J.Rauch .15 .40
T.Tucker
678 N.Regilio .15 .40
B.Shouse
679 J.Tavarez .15 .40
R.King
680 C.Fox .15 .40
M.Wuertz
681 J.Sosa .15 .40
A.Bernero
682 J.Valverde .15 .40
M.Koplove
683 A.Rhodes .15 .40
S.Sauerbeck
684 F.Rodriguez .15 .40
T.Sturtze
685 G.Carrara .15 .40
D.Sanchez
686 M.Gallo .15 .40
C.Harville
687 M.Johnston .15 .40
S.Burnett
688 J.Nelson .15 .40
S.Hasegawa
689 C.Vargas .15 .40
A.Osuna
690 B.Donnelly .15 .40
E.Yan
691 J.Mathis .25 .60
E.Santana
692 C.Everts .15 .40
B.Bray
693 J.Kubel .40 1.00
T.Plouffe
694 J.Stevens .15 .40
A.Marte
695 A.Hill .25 .60
C.Gaudin
696 C.Quentin .25 .60
J.Cota
697 T.Diamond .25 .60
C.Young
698 O.Quintanilla .15 .40
D.Johnson
699 J.Maine .15 .40
V.Majewski
700 J.Houser .15 .40
J.Gomes
701 D.Murphy .25 .60
H.Ramirez
702 C.Lambert .15 .40
R.Ankiel
703 F.Pie .15 .40
A.Guzman
704 F.Lewis .25 .60
N.Schierholtz
705 A.Munoz .25 .60
G.Gonzalez
706 F.Hernandez .50 1.25
T.Blackley
707 R.Olmedo .40 1.00
E.Encarnacion
708 T.Stauffer .15 .40
J.Germano
709 J.Guthrie .25 .60
J.Sowers
710 J.Cortes .25 .60
T.Gorzelanny
711 T.Tankersley .15 .40
E.Reed
712 N.Walker .25 .60
P.Maholm
713 W.Taveras .40 1.00
L.Scott RC
714 R.Howard .30 .75
G.Golson
715 B.DeWitt .25 .60
E.Jackson
716 H.Street .15 .40
D.Putnam
717 R.Weeks .15 .40
M.Rogers
718 R.Cano .50 1.25
P.Hughes
719 K.Waldrop .15 .40
J.Rainville
720 C.Brazell .15 .40
Y.Petit
721 B.Lopez RC .15 .40
M.Brown RC
722 D.Thomp RC .15 .40
E.Chavez RC
723 D.Uggla RC 5.00 12.00
E.Sch'wolf RC
724 I.Ramirez RC .15 .40
J.Tingler RC
725 T.G'tano RC .15 .40
E.de la Cruz RC
726 M.Campbell RC .15 .40
S.Costa RC
727 M.Prado RC 1.00 2.50
Bi.McCarthy RC
728 I.Kinsler RC .75 2.00
J.Senreiso RC
729 L.Ramirez RC .15 .40
Lo.Scott RC
730 C.Seddon RC .15 .40
E.Johnson RC
731 C.Tatum RC .15 .40
J.Moran RC
732 S.Pomeranz RC .25 .60
J.Motte RC
733 J.Vaquedano RC .15 .40
S.Bailie RC
734 M.Albers RC .15 .40
W.Robinson RC
735 M.DeSalvo RC .50 1.25
Me.Cabr RC
736 B.Stavisky RC .15 .40
L.Powell RC
737 S.Mathieson RC .15 .40
S.Mitch RC
738 S.Marshall RC .40 1.00
B.Bay RC
739 B.McCarthy RC .25 .60
P.Lopez RC
740 A.Smit RC .15 .40
R.Barrett RC
741 M.R'stad RC .15 .40
R.F'bend RC
742 N.McLouth RC .25 .60
A.Boeve RC
743 K.Melillo RC .15 .40
M.Rogers RC
744 M.Kemp RC .75 2.00
H.Totten RC
745 J.Miller RC .15 .40
T.Arnerich RC
746 T.Pelland RC .15 .40
J.Gutierrez RC
747 J.West RC .15 .40
W.Mota RC
748 R.Goleski RC .15 .40
R.Garko RC
749 B.Triplett RC .15 .40
J.Gothreaux RC
750 K.West RC .15 .40
G.Perkins RC
751 M.Esposito RC .15 .40
Z.Parker RC
752 R.Sweeney RC .25 .60
B.Miller RC
753 C.McGehee RC .25 .60
B.Coats RC
754 M.Bourn RC .40 1.00
K.Pichardo RC
755 M.Morse RC .50 1.25
B.Livingston RC
756 W.Swack RC .15 .40
B.Ryan RC
757 M.Furtado RC .15 .40
N.Masset RC
758 P.Ramos RC .25 .60
G.Kottaras RC
759 E.Quezada RC .15 .40
T.Beam RC
760 D.Eveland RC .15 .40
T.Hinton RC
761 J.Jurries RC .15 .40
C.Vines RC
762 H.Sanch RC 3.00 8.00
J.Verlander RC
763 P.Humber RC .40 1.00
S.Bowman RC
764 P.Misch RC .15 .40
J.Thurmond RC
765 C.Colonel RC .15 .40
N.Wilson RC
766 Checklist 1 .10 .30
767 Checklist 2 .10 .30
768 Checklist 3 .10 .30
769 Checklist 4 .10 .30
770 Checklist 5 .10 .30

2005 Topps Total Domination

*DOMINATION: .75X TO 2X BASIC
STATED ODDS 1:10 H 1:10 R
CL: 40/50/56/60/100/110/147/150/180/190
CL: 200/230/250/260/270/290/300/345/350
CL: 400/465/490/495/500/510/520/540/545
CL: 575/580

2005 Topps Total Silver

*SILVER 1-575/666: 1X TO 2.5X BASIC
*SILVER 576-690: 1X TO 2.5X BASIC
*SILVER 269/691-765: 1X TO 2.5X BASIC
*SILVER 766-770: 1X TO 2.5X BASIC
ONE PER PACK

2005 Topps Total Award Winners

COMPLETE SET (30) 12.50 30.00
STATED ODDS 1:10 H, 1:10 R
OVERALL INSERT PLATE ODDS 1:726 H
PLATE PRINT RUN 1 SET PER COLOR
BLACK-CYAN-MAGENTA-YELLOW ISSUED
FRONT AND BACK PLATES PRODUCED
NO PLATE PRICING DUE TO SCARCITY
AW1 Barry Bonds MVP 1.25 3.00
AW2 Vladimir Guerrero MVP .50 1.25
AW3 Roger Clemens CY 1.00 2.50
AW4 Johan Santana CY .50 1.25
AW5 Jason Bay ROY .30 .75
AW6 Bobby Crosby ROY .30 .75
AW7 Eric Gagne Rolaids .30 .75
AW8 Mariano Rivera Rolaids 1.00 2.50
AW9 Albert Pujols SS 1.00 2.50
AW10 Mark Teixeira SS .50 1.25
AW11 Mark Loretta SS .30 .75
AW12 Alfonso Soriano SS .50 1.25
AW13 Jack Wilson SS .30 .75
AW14 Miguel Tejada SS .50 1.25
AW15 Adrian Beltre SS .75 2.00
AW16 Melvin Mora SS .30 .75
AW17 Barry Bonds SS 1.25 3.00
AW18 Jim Edmonds SS .50 1.25
AW19 Bobby Abreu SS .30 .75
AW20 Manny Ramirez SS .75 2.00
AW21 Gary Sheffield SS .30 .75
AW22 Vladimir Guerrero SS .50 1.25
AW23 Johnny Estrada SS .30 .75
AW24 Victor Martinez SS .50 1.25
AW25 Ivan Rodriguez SS .50 1.25
AW26 Livan Hernandez SS .30 .75
AW27 David Ortiz SS .75 2.00
AW28 Bobby Cox MG .30 .75
AW29 Buck Showalter MG .30 .75
AW30 Barry Bonds Aaron Award 1.25 3.00

2005 Topps Total Production

COMPLETE SET (10) 6.00 15.00
STATED ODDS 1:15 H, 1:15 R
OVERALL INSERT PLATE ODDS 1:726 H
PLATE PRINT RUN 1 SET PER COLOR
BLACK-CYAN-MAGENTA-YELLOW ISSUED
FRONT AND BACK PLATES PRODUCED
NO PLATE PRICING DUE TO SCARCITY
AB Adrian Beltre .75 2.00
AP Albert Pujols 1.00 2.50
AR Alex Rodriguez 1.00 2.50
AS Alfonso Soriano .50 1.25
BB Barry Bonds 1.25 3.00
JT Jim Thome .50 1.25
MR Manny Ramirez .75 2.00
MT Miguel Tejada .50 1.25
TH Todd Helton .50 1.25
VG Vladimir Guerrero .50 1.25

2005 Topps Total Signatures

GROUP A ODDS 1:4849 H, 1:5484 R
GROUP B ODDS 1:608 H, 1:697 R
GROUP C ODDS 1:974 H, 1:1117 R
OVERALL AU PLATE ODDS 1:19,024 HOBBY
AU PLATE PRINT RUN 1 SET PER COLOR
BLACK-CYAN-MAGENTA-YELLOW ISSUED
NO AU PLATE PRICING DUE TO SCARCITY
EXCHANGE DEADLINE 05/31/07
BB Brian Bruney B 4.00 10.00
DW David Wright B 10.00 25.00
JG Joey Gathright B 4.00 10.00
RC Robinson Cano B 10.00 25.00
TT Terry Tiffee C 4.00 10.00
ZG Zack Greinke C 4.00 10.00

2005 Topps Total Team Checklists

COMPLETE SET (30) 6.00 15.00
STATED ODDS 1:4 H, 1:4 R
1 Luis Gonzalez .12 .30
2 John Smoltz .30 .75
3 Miguel Tejada .20 .50
4 David Ortiz .30 .75
5 Kerry Wood .12 .30
6 Frank Thomas .30 .75
7 Adam Dunn .20 .50
8 Victor Martinez .20 .50
9 Todd Helton .20 .50
10 Ivan Rodriguez .20 .50
11 Miguel Cabrera .30 .75
12 Roger Clemens .40 1.00
13 Zack Greinke .40 1.00
14 Vladimir Guerrero .20 .50
15 Eric Gagne .12 .30
16 Ben Sheets .12 .30
17 Johan Santana .20 .50
18 Carlos Beltran .20 .50
19 Alex Rodriguez .40 1.00
20 Eric Chavez .12 .30
21 Jim Thome .20 .50
22 Jason Bay .12 .30
23 Brian Giles .12 .30
24 Barry Bonds .50 1.25
25 Ichiro Suzuki .40 1.00
26 Albert Pujols .40 1.00
27 Carl Crawford .20 .50
28 Alfonso Soriano .20 .50
29 Vernon Wells .12 .30
30 Jose Vidro .12 .30

2005 Topps Total Topps

COMPLETE SET (20) 12.50 30.00
STATED ODDS 1:15 H, 1:15 R
OVERALL INSERT PLATE ODDS 1:726 H
PLATE PRINT RUN 1 SET PER COLOR
BLACK-CYAN-MAGENTA-YELLOW ISSUED
FRONT AND BACK PLATES PRODUCED
NO PLATE PRICING DUE TO SCARCITY
AB Adrian Beltre .75 2.00
AP Albert Pujols 1.00 2.50
AR Alex Rodriguez 1.00 2.50
AS Alfonso Soriano .50 1.25
BB Barry Bonds 1.25 3.00
CB Carlos Beltran .50 1.25
DJ Derek Jeter 2.00 5.00
EC Eric Chavez .30 .75
GM Greg Maddux 1.00 2.50
IR Ivan Rodriguez .50 1.25
JS Johan Santana .50 1.25
JT Jim Thome .50 1.25
MP Mike Piazza .75 2.00
MR Manny Ramirez .75 2.00
MT Miguel Tejada .50 1.25
RC Roger Clemens 1.00 2.50
RJ Randy Johnson .75 2.00
SS Sammy Sosa .75 2.00
TH Todd Helton .50 1.25
VG Vladimir Guerrero .50 1.25

2016 Topps Transcendent

STATED PRINT RUN 65 SER.#'d SETS
1 Babe Ruth 60.00 150.00
2 Kenta Maeda 25.00 60.00
3 Buster Posey 25.00 60.00
4 Julio Urias RC 40.00 100.00
5 Ty Cobb 40.00 100.00
6 Frank Robinson 20.00 50.00
7 Chipper Jones 20.00 50.00
8 Mark McGwire 25.00 60.00
9 Honus Wagner 40.00 100.00
10 Corey Seager RC 100.00 250.00
11 Manny Machado 30.00 80.00
12 Kris Bryant 20.00 50.00
13 Willie Mays 40.00 100.00
14 Clayton Kershaw 20.00 50.00
15 Mike Piazza 20.00 50.00
16 Randy Johnson 20.00 50.00
17 Albert Pujols 25.00 60.00
18 Madison Bumgarner 15.00 40.00
19 Frank Thomas 30.00 80.00
20 Carl Yastrzemski 30.00 80.00
21 Ken Griffey Jr. 30.00 80.00
22 Satchel Paige 40.00 100.00
23 Johnny Bench 25.00 60.00
24 Bryce Harper 40.00 100.00
25 Hank Aaron 40.00 100.00
26 Don Mattingly 40.00 100.00
27 Ichiro 25.00 60.00
28 Lou Gehrig 40.00 100.00
29 Nolan Ryan 50.00 120.00
30 Ozzie Smith 25.00 60.00
31 Eddie Mathews 20.00 50.00
32 Reggie Jackson 20.00 50.00
33 David Price 15.00 40.00
34 Felix Hernandez 15.00 40.00
35 Harmon Killebrew 20.00 50.00
36 Rickey Henderson 30.00 80.00
37 Kyle Schwarber RC 60.00 150.00
38 Roger Clemens 25.00 60.00
39 Mike Trout 100.00 250.00
40 Greg Maddux 25.00 60.00
41 Carlos Correa 20.00 50.00
42 Jackie Robinson 40.00 100.00
43 John Smoltz 20.00 50.00
44 Barry Larkin 20.00 50.00
45 Roberto Clemente 60.00 150.00
46 Roger Maris 25.00 60.00
47 Ted Williams 50.00 120.00
48 Ryne Sandberg 30.00 80.00
49 Cal Ripken Jr. 40.00 100.00
50 Sandy Koufax 40.00 100.00

2016 Topps Transcendent Autographs

STATED PRINT RUN 52 SER.#'d SETS
EXCHANGE DEADLINE 11/30/2018
*BLUE/25: .4X TO 1X BASIC
TCAAP Albert Pujols 100.00 250.00
TCAAR Alex Rodriguez 100.00 250.00
TCABB Barry Bonds 150.00 400.00
TCABH Bryce Harper 175.00 350.00
TCABP Buster Posey 60.00 150.00
TCACC Carlos Correa 100.00 250.00
TCACJ Chipper Jones 100.00 200.00
TCACK Clayton Kershaw 100.00 250.00
TCACR Cal Ripken Jr. 75.00 200.00
TCACS Corey Seager 200.00 400.00
TCACY Carl Yastrzemski 75.00 200.00
TCADJ Derek Jeter 300.00 600.00
TCADM Don Mattingly 75.00 200.00
TCADO David Ortiz 100.00 250.00
TCADR Daisy Ridley 300.00 600.00
TCAFR Frank Robinson 75.00 200.00
TCAFT Frank Thomas 30.00 80.00
TCAGM Greg Maddux 100.00 250.00
TCAHA Hank Aaron 200.00 400.00
TCAI Ichiro 300.00 500.00
TCAJB Johnny Bench 75.00 200.00
TCAJBA John Boyega 250.00 400.00
TCAKB Kris Bryant 400.00 800.00
TCAKGJ Ken Griffey Jr. 350.00 700.00
TCAKM Kenta Maeda 75.00 200.00
TCAKS Kyle Schwarber 60.00 150.00
TCAMM Mark McGwire 75.00 200.00
TCAMP Mike Piazza 60.00 150.00
TCAMT Mike Trout 400.00 800.00
TCAMTA Masahiro Tanaka 175.00 350.00
TCANR Nolan Ryan 100.00 250.00
TCAOS Ozzie Smith 60.00 150.00
TCAOV Omar Vizquel 40.00 100.00
TCAP Pele 200.00 400.00
TCAPM Pedro Martinez 75.00 200.00
TCARC Roger Clemens 75.00 200.00
TCARH Rickey Henderson 100.00 250.00
TCARJ Randy Johnson 75.00 200.00
TCARJA Reggie Jackson 60.00 150.00
TCARS Ryne Sandberg 75.00 200.00
TCASK Sandy Koufax 200.00 400.00
TCAVS Vin Scully 250.00 500.00

2016 Topps Transcendent Sketch Cards

STATED PRINT RUN 65 SER.#'d SETS
TSCR1 Willie Mays 40.00 100.00
TSCR2 Jackie Robinson 30.00 80.00
TSCR3 Eddie Mathews 15.00 40.00
TSCR4 Phil Rizzuto 12.00 30.00
TSCR5 Monte Irvin 15.00 40.00
TSCR6 Satchel Paige 30.00 80.00
TSCR7 Jackie Robinson 30.00 80.00
TSCR8 Hank Aaron 40.00 100.00
TSCR9 Ted Williams 30.00 80.00
TSCR10 Willie Mays 40.00 100.00
TSCR11 Al Kaline 30.00 80.00
TSCR12 Sandy Koufax 30.00 80.00
TSCR13 Roberto Clemente 40.00 100.00
TSCR14 Ted Williams 30.00 80.00
TSCR15 Jackie Robinson 30.00 80.00
TSCR16 Hank Aaron 40.00 100.00
TSCR17 Frank Robinson 15.00 40.00
TSCR18 Sandy Koufax 30.00 80.00
TSCR19 Roger Maris 30.00 80.00
TSCR20 Orlando Cepeda 15.00 40.00
TSCR21 Roberto Clemente 40.00 100.00
TSCR22 Carl Yastrzemski 25.00 60.00
TSCR23 Willie McCovey 20.00 50.00
TSCR24 Roger Maris 30.00 80.00
TSCR25 Jim Palmer 12.00 30.00
TSCR26 Steve Carlton 15.00 40.00
TSCR27 Rod Carew 15.00 40.00
TSCR28 Reggie Jackson 20.00 50.00
TSCR29 Johnny Bench 20.00 50.00
TSCR30 Nolan Ryan 40.00 100.00
TSCR31 Roberto Clemente 40.00 100.00
TSCR32 Joe Morgan 15.00 40.00
TSCR33 Dave Winfield 15.00 40.00
TSCR34 George Brett 30.00 80.00
TSCR35 Dennis Eckersley 12.00 30.00
TSCR36 Reggie Jackson 20.00 50.00
TSCR37 Robin Yount 20.00 50.00
TSCR38 Eddie Murray 15.00 40.00
TSCR39 Ozzie Smith 20.00 50.00
TSCR40 Rickey Henderson 40.00 100.00
TSCR41 Cal Ripken Jr. 40.00 100.00
TSCR42 Wade Boggs 20.00 50.00
TSCR43 Don Mattingly 30.00 80.00
TSCR44 Darryl Strawberry 15.00 40.00
TSCR45 Mark McGwire 25.00 60.00
TSCR46 Roger Clemens 20.00 50.00
TSCR47 Dwight Gooden 12.00 30.00
TSCR48 Greg Maddux 20.00 50.00
TSCR49 Ken Griffey Jr. 50.00 120.00
TSCR50 Randy Johnson 15.00 40.00
TSCR51 Frank Thomas 20.00 50.00
TSCR52 Chipper Jones 20.00 50.00
TSCR53 Mike Piazza 15.00 40.00
TSCR54 Nomar Garciaparra 20.00 50.00
TSCR55 Alex Rodriguez 20.00 50.00
TSCR56 Miguel Cabrera 15.00 40.00
TSCR57 Albert Pujols 20.00 50.00
TSCR58 Ichiro 20.00 50.00
TSCR59 Clayton Kershaw 20.00 50.00
TSCR60 Buster Posey 20.00 50.00
TSCR61 Mike Trout 60.00 150.00
TSCR62 Bryce Harper 25.00 60.00
TSCR63 Kris Bryant 75.00 200.00
TSCR64 Carlos Correa 20.00 50.00
TSCR65 Jose Bautista 20.00 50.00

2017 Topps Transcendent

STATED PRINT RUN 87 SER.#'d SETS
1 Jackie Robinson 20.00 50.00
2 Aaron Judge RC 30.00 80.00
3 Roberto Clemente 30.00 80.00
4 Bryce Harper 12.00 30.00
5 Randy Johnson 15.00 40.00
6 Alex Bregman RC 30.00 80.00
7 Kris Bryant 30.00 80.00
8 Francisco Lindor 15.00 40.00
9 Bo Jackson 25.00 60.00
10 Greg Maddux 20.00 50.00
11 Ted Williams 20.00 50.00
12 Rickey Henderson 20.00 50.00
13 Reggie Jackson 10.00 25.00
14 Roger Maris 20.00 50.00
15 Honus Wagner 10.00 25.00
16 Roger Clemens 10.00 25.00
17 Ernie Banks 20.00 50.00
18 Miguel Cabrera 15.00 40.00
19 Chris Sale 15.00 40.00
20 Yoan Moncada RC 30.00 80.00
21 Andrew Benintendi RC 60.00 150.00
22 Manny Machado 15.00 40.00
23 Carl Yastrzemski 20.00 50.00
24 Clayton Kershaw 20.00 50.00
25 Babe Ruth 40.00 100.00
26 Nolan Ryan 30.00 80.00
27 Carlos Correa 15.00 40.00
28 Dave Winfield 12.00 30.00
29 Anthony Rizzo 12.00 30.00
30 Albert Pujols 20.00 50.00
31 Mike Piazza 15.00 40.00
32 Hank Aaron 20.00 50.00
33 George Brett 25.00 60.00
34 Pedro Martinez 12.00 30.00
35 Jimmie Foxx 15.00 40.00
36 Cal Ripken Jr. 25.00 60.00
37 Chipper Jones 15.00 40.00
38 David Ortiz 15.00 40.00
39 Ichiro 20.00 50.00
40 Lou Gehrig 30.00 80.00
41 Ken Griffey Jr. 25.00 60.00
42 Hideki Matsui 15.00 40.00
43 Sandy Koufax 20.00 50.00
44 Ty Cobb 10.00 25.00
45 Mike Trout 25.00 60.00
46 Cody Bellinger RC 100.00 250.00
47 Corey Seager 20.00 50.00
48 Max Scherzer 10.00 250.00
49 Buster Posey 20.00 50.00
50 Derek Jeter 40.00 100.00

2017 Topps Transcendent Autographs

STATED PRINT RUN 25 SER.#'d SETS
EXCHANGE DEADLINE 11/30/2019
ALL VERSIONS EQUALLY PRICED
TCAAB Adrian Beltre 40.00 100.00
TCAAB Adrian Beltre 40.00 100.00
TCAABE Andrew Benintendi 125.00 300.00
TCAABE Andrew Benintendi 125.00 300.00
TCAABR Alex Bregman 100.00 250.00
TCAABR Alex Bregman 100.00 250.00
TCAAJ Aaron Judge 400.00 800.00
TCAAJ Aaron Judge 400.00 800.00
TCAARI Anthony Rizzo 60.00 150.00
TCAARI Anthony Rizzo 60.00 150.00
TCABH Bryce Harper 150.00 400.00
TCABH Bryce Harper 150.00 400.00
TCABJ Bo Jackson 75.00 200.00
TCABJ Bo Jackson 75.00 200.00
TCABL Barry Larkin 30.00 80.00
TCABL Barry Larkin 30.00 80.00
TCABP Buster Posey 75.00 200.00
TCABP Buster Posey 75.00 200.00
TCACBE Cody Bellinger EXCH 150.00 400.00
TCACBE Cody Bellinger VAR EXCH 150.00 400.00
TCACC Carlos Correa 60.00 150.00
TCACC Carlos Correa 60.00 150.00
TCACJ Chipper Jones 100.00 250.00
TCACJ Chipper Jones 100.00 250.00
TCACK Clayton Kershaw 75.00 200.00
TCACK Clayton Kershaw 75.00 200.00
TCACR Cal Ripken Jr. 75.00 200.00

TCACR Cal Ripken Jr. 75.00 200.00
TCADJ Derek Jeter 300.00 600.00
TCADJ Derek Jeter 300.00 600.00
TCADM Don Mattingly 60.00 150.00
TCADM Don Mattingly 60.00 150.00
TCADO David Ortiz 75.00 200.00
TCADO David Ortiz 75.00 200.00
TCADW Dave Winfield 40.00 100.00
TCADW Dave Winfield 40.00 100.00
TCAFL Francisco Lindor 40.00 100.00
TCAFL Francisco Lindor 40.00 100.00
TCAFMJ Floyd Mayweather Jr. 150.00 400.00
TCAFMJ Floyd Mayweather Jr. 150.00 400.00
TCAGM Greg Maddux 60.00 150.00
TCAGM Greg Maddux 60.00 150.00
TCAHA Hank Aaron 150.00 400.00
TCAHA Hank Aaron 150.00 400.00
TCAHM Hideki Matsui 100.00 250.00
TCAHM Hideki Matsui 100.00 250.00
TCAI Ichiro 300.00 600.00
TCAI Ichiro 300.00 600.00
TCAIH Ian Happ EXCH 40.00 100.00
TCAIH Ian Happ VAR EXCH 40.00 100.00
TCAJB Johnny Bench 60.00 150.00
TCAJB Johnny Bench 60.00 150.00
TCAJD Josh Donaldson 40.00 100.00
TCAJD Josh Donaldson 40.00 100.00
TCAJT Jim Thome 60.00 150.00
TCAJT Jim Thome 60.00 150.00
TCAKB Kris Bryant 125.00 300.00
TCAKB Kris Bryant 125.00 300.00
TCALV Lindsey Vonn EXCH 125.00 300.00
TCALV Lindsey Vonn VAR EXCH 125.00 300.00
TCAMM Manny Machado 60.00 150.00
TCAMM Manny Machado 60.00 150.00
TCAMMC Mark McGwire 75.00 200.00
TCAMMC Mark McGwire 75.00 200.00
TCAMP Mike Piazza 75.00 200.00
TCAMP Mike Piazza 75.00 200.00
TCAMR Mariano Rivera 125.00 300.00
TCAMR Mariano Rivera 125.00 300.00
TCAMT Mike Trout 250.00 500.00
TCAMT Mike Trout 250.00 500.00
TCANR Nolan Ryan 125.00 300.00
TCANR Nolan Ryan 125.00 300.00
TCANS Noah Syndergaard 50.00 120.00
TCANS Noah Syndergaard 50.00 120.00
TCAPM Pedro Martinez 60.00 150.00
TCAPM Pedro Martinez 60.00 150.00
TCARC Roger Clemens 75.00 200.00
TCARC Roger Clemens 75.00 200.00
TCARCA Rod Carew 50.00 120.00
TCARCA Rod Carew 50.00 120.00
TCARH Rickey Henderson 60.00 150.00
TCARH Rickey Henderson 60.00 150.00
TCARJ Randy Johnson 60.00 150.00
TCARJ Randy Johnson 60.00 150.00
TCARJA Reggie Jackson 50.00 120.00
TCARJA Reggie Jackson 50.00 120.00
TCASK Sandy Koufax 200.00 400.00
TCASK Sandy Koufax 200.00 400.00
TCATE Theo Epstein 75.00 200.00
TCATE Theo Epstein 75.00 200.00
TCATS Tom Seaver 60.00 150.00
TCATS Tom Seaver 60.00 150.00
TCAYM Yoan Moncada 60.00 150.00
TCAYM Yoan Moncada 60.00 150.00

2017 Topps Transcendent Autographs Purple

*PURPLE: .5X TO 1.2X BASIC
STATED PRINT RUN 10 SER.#'d SETS
EXCHANGE DEADLINE 11/30/2019

2017 Topps Transcendent Autographs Silver

*SILVER: .4X TO 1X BASIC
STATED PRINT RUN 15 SER.#'d SETS
EXCHANGE DEADLINE 11/30/2019

2017 Topps Transcendent MLB Moments Sketch Cards

STATED PRINT RUN 87 SER.#'d SETS
MLBMRAR Alex Rodriguez 15.00 40.00
MLBMRARO Alex Rodriguez 15.00 40.00
MLBMRBH Bryce Harper 40.00 100.00
MLBMRBJ Bo Jackson 40.00 100.00
MLBMRBM Bill Mazeroski 10.00 25.00
MLBMRBOS Boston Red Sox 15.00 40.00
MLBMRBR Babe Ruth 30.00 80.00
MLBMRBRI K.Bryant/A.Rizzo 75.00 200.00
MLBMRBRU Babe Ruth 30.00 80.00
MLBMRCB Craig Biggio 10.00 25.00
MLBMRCF Carlton Fisk 20.00 50.00
MLBMRCHI Chicago Cubs 50.00 120.00
MLBMRCK Clayton Kershaw 30.00 80.00
MLBMRCR Cal Ripken Jr. 30.00 80.00
MLBMRCRI Cal Ripken Jr. 30.00 80.00
MLBMRCS Curt Schilling 12.00 30.00
MLBMRCY Carl Yastrzemski 20.00 50.00
MLBMRDEJ Derek Jeter 50.00 120.00
MLBMRDJ Derek Jeter 50.00 120.00
MLBMRDJE Derek Jeter 50.00 120.00
MLBMRDJR Derek Jeter 50.00 120.00
MLBMRDJT Derek Jeter 50.00 120.00
MLBMRDO David Ortiz 20.00 50.00
MLBMREL Evan Longoria 10.00 25.00
MLBMRES Enos Slaughter 12.00 30.00
MLBMRGM Greg Maddux 15.00 40.00
MLBMRGWB George W. Bush 30.00 80.00
MLBMRHA Hank Aaron 30.00 80.00
MLBMRHM Hideki Matsui 12.00 30.00
MLBMRIR Ivan Rodriguez 10.00 25.00
MLBMRI Ichiro 20.00 50.00
MLBMRJB Jose Bautista 20.00 50.00
MLBMRJC Jose Canseco 40.00 100.00
MLBMRJG Josh Gibson 20.00 50.00
MLBMRJR Jackie Robinson 30.00 80.00
MLBMRJRO Jackie Robinson 30.00 80.00
MLBMRKG Ken Griffey Jr. 40.00 100.00
MLBMRKGR Ken Griffey Jr. 40.00 100.00
MLBMRLD Larry Doby 10.00 25.00
MLBMRLG Lou Gehrig 25.00 60.00
MLBMRLGH Lou Gehrig 25.00 60.00
MLBMRMM Manny Machado 20.00 50.00
MLBMRMMC Mark McGwire 20.00 50.00
MLBMRMP Mike Piazza 12.00 30.00
MLBMRMR Mariano Rivera 15.00 40.00
MLBMRMS Max Scherzer 12.00 30.00
MLBMRMT Mike Trout 30.00 80.00
MLBMRMTR Mike Trout 30.00 80.00
MLBMRNR Nolan Ryan 25.00 60.00
MLBMROS Ozzie Smith 15.00 40.00
MLBMROSM Ozzie Smith 15.00 40.00
MLBMRPM Pedro Martinez 12.00 30.00
MLBMRRC Roberto Clemente 40.00 100.00
MLBMRRCL Roger Clemens 15.00 40.00
MLBMRRH Rickey Henderson 15.00 40.00
MLBMRRHA Roy Halladay 20.00 50.00
MLBMRRJ Randy Johnson 12.00 30.00
MLBMRRJA Reggie Jackson 12.00 30.00
MLBMRRM Roger Maris 20.00 50.00
MLBMRRS Ryne Sandberg 30.00 80.00
MLBMRSK Sandy Koufax 25.00 60.00
MLBMRSP Satchel Paige 20.00 50.00
MLBMRTW Ted Williams 30.00 80.00
MLBMRTWI Ted Williams 30.00 80.00
MLBMRWB Wade Boggs 15.00 40.00

2018 Topps Transcendent

ONE COMPLETE SET PER BOX
STATED PRINT RUN 83 SER.#'d SETS
1 Sandy Koufax 10.00 25.00
2 Rhys Hoskins RC 12.00 30.00
3 Ryne Sandberg 10.00 25.00
4 Hideki Matsui 5.00 12.00
5 Gleyber Torres RC 150.00 400.00
6 Mariano Rivera 6.00 15.00
7 Mike Piazza 5.00 12.00
8 Jose Altuve 4.00 10.00
9 Frank Thomas 5.00 12.00
10 Shohei Ohtani RC 75.00 200.00
11 Johnny Bench 5.00 12.00
12 Francisco Lindor 5.00 12.00
13 George Brett 10.00 25.00
14 Roger Clemens 6.00 15.00
15 Tom Seaver 4.00 10.00
16 Aaron Judge 12.00 30.00
17 Lou Gehrig 10.00 25.00
18 Ty Cobb 8.00 20.00
19 Chipper Jones 5.00 12.00
20 Kris Bryant 6.00 15.00
21 Pedro Martinez 4.00 10.00
22 Greg Maddux 6.00 15.00
23 Clayton Kershaw 8.00 20.00
24 Randy Johnson 5.00 12.00
25 Derek Jeter 12.00 30.00
26 Bo Jackson 5.00 12.00
27 Rafael Devers RC 75.00 200.00
28 David Ortiz 5.00 12.00
29 Tommy Lasorda 4.00 10.00
30 Bryce Harper 8.00 20.00
31 Jimmie Foxx 5.00 12.00
32 Gary Sanchez 5.00 12.00
33 Alex Rodriguez 6.00 15.00
34 Ted Williams 10.00 25.00
35 Manny Machado 5.00 12.00
36 Rickey Henderson 5.00 12.00
37 Honus Wagner 5.00 12.00
38 Mark McGwire 8.00 20.00
39 Jackie Robinson 5.00 12.00
40 Ichiro 6.00 15.00
41 Roberto Clemente 12.00 30.00
42 Mike Trout 25.00 60.00
43 Reggie Jackson 4.00 10.00
44 Cal Ripken Jr. 15.00 40.00
45 Albert Pujols 6.00 15.00
46 Don Mattingly 10.00 25.00
47 Anthony Rizzo 6.00 15.00
48 Nolan Ryan 15.00 40.00
49 Ronald Acuna Jr. RC 500.00 1000.00
50 Hank Aaron 10.00 25.00

2018 Topps Transcendent Autographs

ONE COMPLETE SET PER BOX
STATED PRINT RUN 25 SER.#'d SETS
ALL VERSIONS EQUALLY PRICED
*EMERALD/15: .4X TO 1X BASIC
*PURPLE/10: .5X TO 1.2X BASIC
TCAI Ichiro V 150.00 400.00
TCAI Ichiro H 150.00 400.00
TCAAJ Aaron Judge V 125.00 300.00
TCAAJ Aaron Judge H 125.00 300.00
TCAAM Andrew McCutchen V 30.00 80.00
TCAAM Andrew McCutchen H 30.00 80.00
TCAAP Albert Pujols V 60.00 150.00
TCAAP Albert Pujols H 60.00 150.00
TCAAR Alex Rodriguez V 75.00 200.00
TCAAR Alex Rodriguez H 75.00 200.00
TCABH Bryce Harper V 125.00 300.00
TCABH Bryce Harper H 125.00 300.00
TCABJ Bo Jackson V 60.00 150.00
TCABJ Bo Jackson H 60.00 150.00
TCACJ Chipper Jones V 125.00 300.00
TCACJ Chipper Jones H 125.00 300.00
TCACK Clayton Kershaw V 60.00 150.00
TCACK Clayton Kershaw H 60.00 150.00
TCACR Cal Ripken Jr. V 60.00 150.00
TCACR Cal Ripken Jr. H 60.00 150.00
TCADJ Derek Jeter H 250.00 500.00
TCADM Don Mattingly V 50.00 120.00
TCADM Don Mattingly H 50.00 120.00
TCADO David Ortiz V 50.00 120.00
TCADO David Ortiz H 50.00 120.00
TCAFL Francisco Lindor V 40.00 100.00
TCAFL Francisco Lindor H 40.00 100.00
TCAFT Frank Thomas V 60.00 150.00
TCAFT Frank Thomas H 60.00 150.00
TCAGM Greg Maddux V 50.00 120.00
TCAGM Greg Maddux H 50.00 120.00
TCAGS Gary Sanchez V 30.00 80.00
TCAGS Gary Sanchez H 30.00 80.00
TCAGT Gleyber Torres V 60.00 150.00
TCAGT Gleyber Torres H 60.00 150.00
TCAHA Hank Aaron V 150.00 400.00
TCAHA Hank Aaron H 150.00 400.00
TCAHM Hideki Matsui V 60.00 150.00
TCAHM Hideki Matsui H 60.00 150.00
TCAJA Jose Altuve V 40.00 100.00
TCAJA Jose Altuve H 40.00 100.00
TCAJB Johnny Bench V 40.00 100.00
TCAJB Johnny Bench H 40.00 100.00
TCAJS Juan Soto V 250.00 500.00
TCAJS Juan Soto H 250.00 500.00
TCAJT Jim Thome V 50.00 120.00
TCAJT Jim Thome H 50.00 120.00
TCAKB Kris Bryant V 75.00 200.00
TCAKB Kris Bryant H 75.00 200.00
TCAMM Mark McGwire V 60.00 150.00
TCAMM Mark McGwire H 60.00 150.00
TCAMP Mike Piazza V 50.00 120.00
TCAMP Mike Piazza H 50.00 120.00
TCAMR Mariano Rivera V 125.00 300.00
TCAMR Mariano Rivera H 125.00 300.00
TCAMT Mike Trout V 300.00 500.00
TCAMT Mike Trout H 300.00 500.00
TCANR Nolan Ryan V 75.00 200.00
TCANR Nolan Ryan H 75.00 200.00
TCAPM Pedro Martinez V 30.00 80.00
TCAPM Pedro Martinez H 30.00 80.00
TCARC Roger Clemens V 60.00 150.00
TCARC Roger Clemens H 60.00 150.00
TCARD Rafael Devers V 40.00 100.00
TCARD Rafael Devers H 40.00 100.00
TCARH Rickey Henderson V 50.00 120.00
TCARH Rickey Henderson H 50.00 120.00
TCARJ Randy Johnson V 40.00 100.00
TCARJ Randy Johnson H 40.00 100.00
TCARS Ryne Sandberg V 50.00 120.00
TCARS Ryne Sandberg H 50.00 120.00
TCASK Sandy Koufax V 150.00 400.00
TCASK Sandy Koufax H 150.00 400.00
TCASO Shohei Ohtani V 300.00 600.00
TCASO Shohei Ohtani H 300.00 600.00
TCAYM Yadier Molina V 75.00 200.00
TCAYM Yadier Molina H 75.00 200.00
TCAANP Andy Pettitte V 20.00 50.00
TCAARI Anthony Rizzo V 30.00 80.00
TCAARI Anthony Rizzo H 30.00 80.00
TCABG Bob Gibson V 30.00 80.00
TCABG Bob Gibson H 30.00 80.00
TCAMMA Manny Machado V 40.00 100.00
TCAMMA Manny Machado H 40.00 100.00
TCARAC Ronald Acuna Jr. V 300.00 600.00
TCARAC Ronald Acuna Jr. H 300.00 600.00
TCARHO Rhys Hoskins V 50.00 120.00
TCARHO Rhys Hoskins H 50.00 120.00
TCARJA Reggie Jackson V 40.00 100.00
TCARJA Reggie Jackson H 40.00 100.00

2018 Topps Transcendent Mike Trout Through the Years Autographs

STATED ODDS ONE PER BOX
STATED PRINT RUN 1 SER.#'d SET
ALL VERSIONS EQUALLY PRICED
MT1952 Mike Trout 1200.00 2500.00
MT1953 Mike Trout 1200.00 2500.00
MT1954 Mike Trout 1200.00 2500.00
MT1955 Mike Trout 1200.00 2500.00
MT1956 Mike Trout 1200.00 2500.00
MT1957 Mike Trout 1200.00 2500.00
MT1958 Mike Trout 1200.00 2500.00
MT1959 Mike Trout 1200.00 2500.00
MT1960 Mike Trout 1200.00 2500.00
MT1961 Mike Trout 1200.00 2500.00
MT1962 Mike Trout 1200.00 2500.00
MT1963 Mike Trout 1200.00 2500.00
MT1964 Mike Trout 1200.00 2500.00
MT1965 Mike Trout 1200.00 2500.00
MT1966 Mike Trout 1200.00 2500.00
MT1967 Mike Trout 1200.00 2500.00
MT1968 Mike Trout 1200.00 2500.00
MT1969 Mike Trout 1200.00 2500.00
MT1970 Mike Trout 1200.00 2500.00
MT1971 Mike Trout 1200.00 2500.00
MT1972 Mike Trout 1200.00 2500.00
MT1973 Mike Trout 1200.00 2500.00
MT1974 Mike Trout 1200.00 2500.00
MT1975 Mike Trout 1200.00 2500.00
MT1976 Mike Trout 1200.00 2500.00
MT1977 Mike Trout 1200.00 2500.00
MT1978 Mike Trout 1200.00 2500.00
MT1979 Mike Trout 1200.00 2500.00
MT1980 Mike Trout 1200.00 2500.00
MT1981 Mike Trout 1200.00 2500.00
MT1982 Mike Trout 1200.00 2500.00
MT1983 Mike Trout 1200.00 2500.00
MT1984 Mike Trout 1200.00 2500.00
MT1985 Mike Trout 1200.00 2500.00
MT1986 Mike Trout 1200.00 2500.00
MT1987 Mike Trout 1200.00 2500.00
MT1988 Mike Trout 1200.00 2500.00
MT1989 Mike Trout 1200.00 2500.00
MT1990 Mike Trout 1200.00 2500.00
MT1991 Mike Trout 1200.00 2500.00
MT1992 Mike Trout 1200.00 2500.00
MT1993 Mike Trout 1200.00 2500.00
MT1994 Mike Trout 1200.00 2500.00
MT1995 Mike Trout 1200.00 2500.00
MT1996 Mike Trout 1200.00 2500.00
MT1997 Mike Trout 1200.00 2500.00
MT1998 Mike Trout 1200.00 2500.00
MT1999 Mike Trout 1200.00 2500.00
MT2000 Mike Trout 1200.00 2500.00
MT2001 Mike Trout 1200.00 2500.00
MT2002 Mike Trout 1200.00 2500.00
MT2003 Mike Trout 1200.00 2500.00
MT2004 Mike Trout 1200.00 2500.00
MT2005 Mike Trout 1200.00 2500.00
MT2006 Mike Trout 1200.00 2500.00
MT2007 Mike Trout 1200.00 2500.00
MT2008 Mike Trout 1200.00 2500.00
MT2009 Mike Trout 1200.00 2500.00
MT2010 Mike Trout 1200.00 2500.00
MT2011 Mike Trout 1200.00 2500.00
MT2012 Mike Trout 1200.00 2500.00
MT2013 Mike Trout 1200.00 2500.00
MT2014 Mike Trout 1200.00 2500.00
MT2015 Mike Trout 1200.00 2500.00
MT2016 Mike Trout 1200.00 2500.00
MT2017 Mike Trout 1200.00 2500.00
MT2018 Mike Trout 1200.00 2500.00
MT51PB Mike Trout 1200.00 2500.00
MT55BB Mike Trout 1200.00 2500.00
MT58AS Mike Trout 1200.00 2500.00
MT68TG Mike Trout 1200.00 2500.00
MT69TS Mike Trout 1200.00 2500.00
MT72IA Mike Trout 1200.00 2500.00
MT75TH Mike Trout 1200.00 2500.00
MT77TB Mike Trout 1200.00 2500.00
MT78RB Mike Trout 1200.00 2500.00
MT82IA Mike Trout 1200.00 2500.00
MT82TH Mike Trout 1200.00 2500.00
MT88AS Mike Trout 1200.00 2500.00
MT88RB Mike Trout 1200.00 2500.00
MT89RB Mike Trout 1200.00 2500.00
MT90RB Mike Trout 1200.00 2500.00
MT91AS Mike Trout 1200.00 2500.00

2018 Topps Transcendent Origins Sketch Reproductions

ONE COMPLETE SET PER BOX
STATED PRINT RUN 83 SER.#'d SETS
OSI Ichiro 12.00 30.00
OSAB Andrew Benintendi 10.00 25.00
OSAD Andre Dawson 8.00 20.00
OSAJ Aaron Judge 25.00 60.00
OSAP Albert Pujols 12.00 30.00
OSAR Alex Rodriguez 12.00 30.00
OSBF Bob Feller 8.00 20.00
OSBH Bryce Harper 15.00 40.00
OSBJ Bo Jackson 10.00 25.00
OSBP Buster Posey 12.00 30.00
OSBW Billy Williams 8.00 20.00
OSCB Cody Bellinger 20.00 50.00
OSCC Carlos Correa 10.00 25.00
OSCF Carlton Fisk 10.00 25.00
OSCS Corey Seager 10.00 25.00
OSDJ Derek Jeter 20.00 50.00
OSDP Dustin Pedroia 10.00 25.00
OSEM Eddie Murray 8.00 20.00
OSFL Francisco Lindor 10.00 25.00
OSFR Frank Robinson 8.00 20.00
OSGM Greg Maddux 12.00 30.00
OSGS Gary Sanchez 10.00 25.00
OSHA Hank Aaron 25.00 60.00
OSHM Hideki Matsui 10.00 25.00
OSIS Ichiro 12.00 30.00
OSJB Jeff Bagwell 12.00 30.00
OSJR Jackie Robinson 10.00 25.00
OSKB Kris Bryant 12.00 30.00
OSLA Luis Aparicio 8.00 20.00
OSLG Lou Gehrig 20.00 50.00
OSMC Miguel Cabrera 10.00 25.00
OSMM Manny Machado 10.00 25.00
OSMP Mike Piazza 10.00 25.00
OSMR Mariano Rivera 15.00 40.00
OSMT Mike Trout 25.00 60.00
OSNR Nolan Ryan 25.00 60.00
OSOC Orlando Cepeda 8.00 20.00
OSRC Roberto Clemente 30.00 80.00
OSRH Rhys Hoskins 20.00 50.00
OSRJ Randy Johnson 10.00 25.00
OSSK Sandy Koufax 20.00 50.00
OSSO Shohei Ohtani 25.00 60.00
OSTS Tom Seaver 8.00 20.00
OSTW Ted Williams 20.00 50.00
OSWM Willie McCovey 12.00 30.00
OSAAJ Aaron Judge 25.00 60.00
OSAJU Aaron Judge 25.00 60.00
OSARI Anthony Rizzo 12.00 30.00
OSBHA Bryce Harper 15.00 40.00
OSCAR Cal Ripken Jr. 25.00 60.00
OSCRJ Cal Ripken Jr. 25.00 60.00
OSDEJ Derek Jeter 20.00 50.00
OSDJE Derek Jeter 20.00 50.00
OSHMI Hideki Matsui 10.00 25.00
OSICS Ichiro 12.00 30.00
OSJBE Johnny Bench 10.00 25.00
OSJRO Jackie Robinson 10.00 25.00
OSKBR Kris Bryant 12.00 30.00
OSMIT Mike Trout 25.00 60.00
OSMMC Mark McGwire 15.00 40.00
OSMTR Mike Trout 25.00 60.00
OSRCA Rod Carew 15.00 40.00
OSRCL Roger Clemens 12.00 30.00
OSRHE Rickey Henderson 20.00 50.00
OSSOH Shohei Ohtani 25.00 60.00

2018 Topps Transcendent Japan

ISSUED IN ASIAN BOXES
STATED PRINT RUN 50 SER.#'d SETS
ALL VERSIONS EQUALLY PRICED
TI1 Ichiro 25.00 60.00
TI2 Ichiro 25.00 60.00
TI3 Ichiro 25.00 60.00
TI4 Ichiro 25.00 60.00
TI5 Ichiro 25.00 60.00
TI6 Ichiro 25.00 60.00
TI7 Ichiro 25.00 60.00
TI8 Ichiro 25.00 60.00
TI9 Ichiro 25.00 60.00
TI10 Ichiro 25.00 60.00
TI11 Ichiro 25.00 60.00
TI12 Ichiro 25.00 60.00
TI13 Ichiro 25.00 60.00
TI14 Ichiro 25.00 60.00
TI15 Ichiro 25.00 60.00
TI16 Ichiro 25.00 60.00
TI17 Ichiro 25.00 60.00
TI18 Ichiro 25.00 60.00
TI19 Ichiro 25.00 60.00
TI20 Ichiro 25.00 60.00
TS01 Shohei Ohtani 120.00 300.00
TS02 Shohei Ohtani 120.00 300.00
TS03 Shohei Ohtani 120.00 300.00
TS04 Shohei Ohtani 120.00 300.00
TS05 Shohei Ohtani 120.00 300.00
TS06 Shohei Ohtani 120.00 300.00
TS07 Shohei Ohtani 120.00 300.00
TS08 Shohei Ohtani 120.00 300.00
TS09 Shohei Ohtani 120.00 300.00
TS010 Shohei Ohtani 120.00 300.00
TS011 Shohei Ohtani 120.00 300.00
TS012 Shohei Ohtani 120.00 300.00
TS013 Shohei Ohtani 120.00 300.00
TS014 Shohei Ohtani 120.00 300.00
TS015 Shohei Ohtani 120.00 300.00
TS016 Shohei Ohtani 120.00 300.00
TS017 Shohei Ohtani 120.00 300.00
TS018 Shohei Ohtani 120.00 300.00
TS019 Shohei Ohtani 120.00 300.00
TS020 Shohei Ohtani 120.00 300.00
TS021 Shohei Ohtani 120.00 300.00
TS022 Shohei Ohtani 120.00 300.00
TS023 Shohei Ohtani 120.00 300.00
TS024 Shohei Ohtani 120.00 300.00
TS025 Shohei Ohtani 120.00 300.00
TS026 Shohei Ohtani 120.00 300.00
TS027 Shohei Ohtani 120.00 300.00
TS028 Shohei Ohtani 120.00 300.00
TS029 Shohei Ohtani 120.00 300.00
TS030 Shohei Ohtani 120.00 300.00

2018 Topps Transcendent Japan '17 Bowman Chrome Mega Box Ohtani Autographs

ISSUED IN ASIAN BOXES
STATED PRINT RUN 17 SER.#'d SETS
BCP31 S.Otani/17 UER 800.00 1200.00

2018 Topps Transcendent Japan Autographs

ISSUED IN ASIAN BOXES
STATED PRINT RUN 5 SER.#'d SETS
ALL VERSIONS EQUALLY PRICED
*EMERALD/3: .4X TO 1X BASIC
TAI1 Ichiro 250.00 500.00
TAI2 Ichiro 250.00 500.00
TAI3 Ichiro 250.00 500.00
TAI4 Ichiro 250.00 500.00
TAI5 Ichiro 250.00 500.00
TAI6 Ichiro 250.00 500.00
TAI7 Ichiro 250.00 500.00
TAI8 Ichiro 250.00 500.00
TAI9 Ichiro 250.00 500.00
TAI10 Ichiro 250.00 500.00
TAI11 Ichiro 250.00 500.00
TAI12 Ichiro 250.00 500.00
TAI13 Ichiro 250.00 500.00
TAI14 Ichiro 250.00 500.00
TAI15 Ichiro 250.00 500.00
TAI16 Ichiro 250.00 500.00
TAI17 Ichiro 250.00 500.00
TAI18 Ichiro 250.00 500.00
TAI19 Ichiro 250.00 500.00
TAI20 Ichiro 250.00 500.00
TAS01 Shohei Ohtani 400.00 800.00
TAS02 Shohei Ohtani 400.00 800.00
TAS03 Shohei Ohtani 400.00 800.00
TAS04 Shohei Ohtani 400.00 800.00
TAS05 Shohei Ohtani 400.00 800.00
TAS06 Shohei Ohtani 400.00 800.00
TAS07 Shohei Ohtani 400.00 800.00
TAS08 Shohei Ohtani 400.00 800.00
TAS09 Shohei Ohtani 400.00 800.00
TAS010 Shohei Ohtani 400.00 800.00
TAS011 Shohei Ohtani 400.00 800.00
TAS012 Shohei Ohtani 400.00 800.00
TAS013 Shohei Ohtani 400.00 800.00
TAS014 Shohei Ohtani 400.00 800.00
TAS015 Shohei Ohtani 400.00 800.00
TAS016 Shohei Ohtani 400.00 800.00
TAS017 Shohei Ohtani 400.00 800.00
TAS018 Shohei Ohtani 400.00 800.00
TAS019 Shohei Ohtani 400.00 800.00
TAS020 Shohei Ohtani 400.00 800.00
TAS021 Shohei Ohtani 400.00 800.00
TAS022 Shohei Ohtani 400.00 800.00
TAS023 Shohei Ohtani 400.00 800.00
TAS024 Shohei Ohtani 400.00 800.00
TAS025 Shohei Ohtani 400.00 800.00
TAS026 Shohei Ohtani 400.00 800.00
TAS027 Shohei Ohtani 400.00 800.00
TAS028 Shohei Ohtani 400.00 800.00
TAS029 Shohei Ohtani 400.00 800.00
TAS030 Shohei Ohtani 400.00 800.00

2018 Topps Transcendent Japan Shohei Ohtani Through the Years Autographs

ISSUED IN ASIAN BOXES
STATED PRINT RUN 1 SER.#'d SET
ALL VERSIONS EQUALLY PRICED
SO1952 Shohei Ohtani 1200.00 2500.00
SO1953 Shohei Ohtani 1200.00 2500.00
SO1954 Shohei Ohtani 1200.00 2500.00
SO1955 Shohei Ohtani 1200.00 2500.00
SO1956 Shohei Ohtani 1200.00 2500.00
SO1957 Shohei Ohtani 1200.00 2500.00
SO1958 Shohei Ohtani 1200.00 2500.00
SO1959 Shohei Ohtani 1200.00 2500.00
SO1960 Shohei Ohtani 1200.00 2500.00
SO1961 Shohei Ohtani 1200.00 2500.00
SO1962 Shohei Ohtani 1200.00 2500.00
SO1963 Shohei Ohtani 1200.00 2500.00
SO1964 Shohei Ohtani 1200.00 2500.00
SO1965 Shohei Ohtani 1200.00 2500.00
SO1966 Shohei Ohtani 1200.00 2500.00
SO1967 Shohei Ohtani 1200.00 2500.00
SO1968 Shohei Ohtani 1200.00 2500.00
SO1969 Shohei Ohtani 1200.00 2500.00
SO1970 Shohei Ohtani 1200.00 2500.00
SO1971 Shohei Ohtani 1200.00 2500.00
SO1972 Shohei Ohtani 1200.00 2500.00
SO1973 Shohei Ohtani 1200.00 2500.00
SO1975 Shohei Ohtani 1200.00 2500.00
SO1976 Shohei Ohtani 1200.00 2500.00
SO1977 Shohei Ohtani 1200.00 2500.00
SO1979 Shohei Ohtani 1200.00 2500.00
SO1981 Shohei Ohtani 1200.00 2500.00
SO1982 Shohei Ohtani 1200.00 2500.00
SO1983 Shohei Ohtani 1200.00 2500.00
SO1984 Shohei Ohtani 1200.00 2500.00
SO1985 Shohei Ohtani 1200.00 2500.00
SO1986 Shohei Ohtani 1200.00 2500.00
SO1987 Shohei Ohtani 1200.00 2500.00
SO1988 Shohei Ohtani 1200.00 2500.00
SO1989 Shohei Ohtani 1200.00 2500.00
SO1990 Shohei Ohtani 1200.00 2500.00
SO1991 Shohei Ohtani 1200.00 2500.00
SO1992 Shohei Ohtani 1200.00 2500.00
SO1995 Shohei Ohtani 1200.00 2500.00
SO1999 Shohei Ohtani 1200.00 2500.00
SO2001 Shohei Ohtani 1200.00 2500.00
SO2002 Shohei Ohtani 1200.00 2500.00
SO2003 Shohei Ohtani 1200.00 2500.00
SO2005 Shohei Ohtani 1200.00 2500.00
SO2007 Shohei Ohtani 1200.00 2500.00
SO2008 Shohei Ohtani 1200.00 2500.00
SO2010 Shohei Ohtani 1200.00 2500.00
SO2014 Shohei Ohtani 1200.00 2500.00
SO2017 Shohei Ohtani 1200.00 2500.00
SO2018 Shohei Ohtani 1200.00 2500.00

2018 Topps Transcendent VIP Party Aaron Judge Bunt

ISSUED AT TRANSCENDENT VIP PARTY
STATED PRINT RUN 87 SER.#'d SETS
NNO Aaron Judge 20.00 50.00

2018 Topps Transcendent VIP Party Aaron Judge History

ISSUED AT TRANSCENDENT VIP PARTY
STATED PRINT RUN 87 SER.#'d SETS
AJ55B Aaron Judge 60.00 150.00
AJ1952 Aaron Judge 200.00 400.00
AJ1953 Aaron Judge 150.00 300.00
AJ1954 Aaron Judge 75.00 200.00
AJ1955 Aaron Judge 60.00 150.00
AJ1956 Aaron Judge 60.00 150.00
AJ1957 Aaron Judge 40.00 100.00
AJ1958 Aaron Judge 40.00 100.00
AJ1959 Aaron Judge 40.00 100.00
AJ1960 Aaron Judge 40.00 100.00
AJ1961 Aaron Judge 40.00 100.00
AJ1962 Aaron Judge 40.00 100.00
AJ1963 Aaron Judge 40.00 100.00
AJ1964 Aaron Judge 40.00 100.00
AJ1965 Aaron Judge 40.00 100.00
AJ1966 Aaron Judge 40.00 100.00
AJ1967 Aaron Judge 40.00 100.00
AJ1968 Aaron Judge 40.00 100.00
AJ1969 Aaron Judge 40.00 100.00
AJ1970 Aaron Judge 40.00 100.00
AJ1971 Aaron Judge 40.00 100.00
AJ1972 Aaron Judge 40.00 100.00
AJ1973 Aaron Judge 40.00 100.00
AJ1974 Aaron Judge 40.00 100.00
AJ1975 Aaron Judge 40.00 100.00
AJ1976 Aaron Judge 40.00 100.00
AJ1977 Aaron Judge 40.00 100.00
AJ1978 Aaron Judge 40.00 100.00
AJ1979 Aaron Judge 40.00 100.00
AJ1980 Aaron Judge 40.00 100.00
AJ1981 Aaron Judge 40.00 100.00
AJ1982 Aaron Judge 40.00 100.00
AJ1983 Aaron Judge 40.00 100.00
AJ1984 Aaron Judge 40.00 100.00
AJ1985 Aaron Judge 40.00 100.00
AJ1986 Aaron Judge 40.00 100.00
AJ1987 Aaron Judge 40.00 100.00
AJ1988 Aaron Judge 40.00 100.00
AJ1989 Aaron Judge 40.00 100.00
AJ1990 Aaron Judge 40.00 100.00
AJ1991 Aaron Judge 40.00 100.00
AJ1992 Aaron Judge 40.00 100.00
AJ1993 Aaron Judge 40.00 100.00
AJ1994 Aaron Judge 40.00 100.00
AJ1995 Aaron Judge 40.00 100.00
AJ1996 Aaron Judge 40.00 100.00
AJ1997 Aaron Judge 40.00 100.00
AJ1998 Aaron Judge 40.00 100.00
AJ1999 Aaron Judge 40.00 100.00
AJ2000 Aaron Judge 40.00 100.00
AJ2001 Aaron Judge 40.00 100.00
AJ2002 Aaron Judge 40.00 100.00
AJ2003 Aaron Judge 40.00 100.00
AJ2004 Aaron Judge 40.00 100.00
AJ2005 Aaron Judge 40.00 100.00
AJ2006 Aaron Judge 40.00 100.00
AJ2007 Aaron Judge 40.00 100.00
AJ2008 Aaron Judge 40.00 100.00
AJ2009 Aaron Judge 40.00 100.00
AJ2010 Aaron Judge 40.00 100.00
AJ2011 Aaron Judge 40.00 100.00
AJ2012 Aaron Judge 40.00 100.00
AJ2013 Aaron Judge 40.00 100.00
AJ2014 Aaron Judge 40.00 100.00
AJ2015 Aaron Judge 40.00 100.00
AJ2016 Aaron Judge 40.00 100.00
AJ2017 Aaron Judge 40.00 100.00
AJ51PB Aaron Judge 40.00 100.00
AJ58AS Aaron Judge 40.00 100.00
AJ60RS Aaron Judge 40.00 100.00
AJ68TG Aaron Judge 40.00 100.00
AJ69TS Aaron Judge 40.00 100.00
AJ71TH Aaron Judge 40.00 100.00
AJ72IA Aaron Judge 40.00 100.00
AJ75TH Aaron Judge 40.00 100.00
AJ78RB Aaron Judge 40.00 100.00
AJ83TH Aaron Judge 40.00 100.00
AJ87FS Aaron Judge 40.00 100.00
AJ88AS Aaron Judge 40.00 100.00
AJ88RB Aaron Judge 40.00 100.00
AJ89RB Aaron Judge 40.00 100.00
AJ90DR Aaron Judge 40.00 100.00
AJ90TR Aaron Judge 40.00 100.00
AJ91AS Aaron Judge 40.00 100.00
AJ91RB Aaron Judge 40.00 100.00
AJ93CA Aaron Judge 40.00 100.00
AJ93DP Aaron Judge 40.00 100.00

2018 Topps Transcendent VIP Party Clint Frazier Autographs

ISSUED AT TRANSCENDENT VIP PARTY
STATED PRINT RUN 25 SER.#'d SETS
2018RC1 Clint Frazier 75.00 200.00
2018RC2 Clint Frazier 75.00 200.00
2018RC3 Clint Frazier 75.00 200.00
2018RC4 Clint Frazier 75.00 200.00

2018 Topps Transcendent VIP Party Hank Aaron Autographs Gold Frame

ISSUED AT TRANSCENDENT VIP PARTY
STATED PRINT RUN 15 SER.#'d SETS
VIP1 Hank Aaron 200.00 400.00
VIP2 Hank Aaron 200.00 400.00
VIP3 Hank Aaron 200.00 400.00
VIP4 Hank Aaron 200.00 400.00
VIP5 Hank Aaron 200.00 400.00
VIP6 Hank Aaron 200.00 400.00

2018 Topps Transcendent VIP Party Hank Aaron Autographs Silver Frame

ISSUED AT TRANSCENDENT VIP PARTY
STATED PRINT RUN 25 SER.#'d SETS
HANK1 Hank Aaron 200.00 400.00
HANK2 Hank Aaron 200.00 400.00
HANK3 Hank Aaron 200.00 400.00
HANK4 Hank Aaron 200.00 400.00

2019 Topps Transcendent

ONE COMPLETE SET PER CASE
STATED PRINT RUN 100 SER.#'d SETS
1 Babe Ruth 12.00 30.00
2 Nick Senzel RC 20.00 50.00
3 Francisco Lindor 10.00 25.00
4 Cody Bellinger 10.00 25.00
5 Roger Clemens 10.00 25.00
6 Giancarlo Stanton 5.00 12.00
7 Ken Griffey Jr. 25.00 60.00
8 Ernie Banks 6.00 15.00
9 Ronald Acuna Jr. 20.00 50.00
10 Bryce Harper 20.00 50.00
11 Christy Mathewson 10.00 25.00
12 Derek Jeter 20.00 50.00
13 Hank Aaron 12.00 30.00
14 Mookie Betts 10.00 25.00
15 Ty Cobb 12.00 30.00
16 Manny Machado 8.00 20.00
17 Jose Altuve 6.00 15.00
18 Rhys Hoskins 12.00 30.00
19 Lou Gehrig 12.00 30.00
20 Sammy Sosa 6.00 15.00
21 Rogers Hornsby 6.00 15.00
22 Pete Alonso RC 100.00 250.00
23 Carter Kieboom RC 30.00 80.00
24 Ted Williams 10.00 25.00
25 Vladimir Guerrero Jr. RC 100.00 250.00
26 Jacob deGrom 8.00 20.00
27 Shohei Ohtani 20.00 50.00
28 Aaron Judge 12.00 30.00
29 Cal Ripken Jr. 15.00 40.00
30 Thurman Munson 10.00 25.00
31 Mariano Rivera 10.00 25.00
32 Carl Yastrzemski 8.00 20.00
33 Honus Wagner 6.00 15.00
34 Juan Soto 15.00 40.00
35 Roberto Clemente 30.00 80.00
36 Deion Sanders 6.00 15.00
37 Vladimir Guerrero 6.00 15.00
38 Rickey Henderson 12.00 30.00
39 Johnny Bench 10.00 25.00
40 Christian Yelich 12.00 30.00
41 Tony Gwynn 12.00 30.00
42 Kris Bryant 12.00 30.00
43 Willie Mays 20.00 50.00
44 Eloy Jimenez RC 40.00 100.00
45 Nolan Ryan 25.00 60.00
46 Sandy Koufax 10.00 25.00
47 Ichiro 15.00 40.00
48 Jackie Robinson 10.00 25.00
49 Fernando Tatis Jr. RC 100.00 250.00
50 Mike Trout 40.00 100.00

2019 Topps Transcendent Autographs

FIFTY AUTOGRAPHS PER CASE
STATED PRINT RUN 25 SER.#'d SETS
*EMERALD/15: .4X TO 1X BASIC
*VAR/25: .4X TO 1X BASIC
*VAR.EMRLD/15: .4X TO 1X BASIC
TCAAB Adrian Beltre 30.00 80.00
TCAAJ Aaron Judge 60.00 150.00
TCAAP Albert Pujols 60.00 150.00
TCAARI Anthony Rizzo 30.00 80.00
TCABH Bryce Harper 100.00 250.00
TCABJ Bo Jackson 40.00 100.00
TCABL Barry Larkin 30.00 80.00
TCABP Buster Posey 40.00 100.00
TCACJ Chipper Jones 40.00 100.00
TCACRJ Cal Ripken Jr. 60.00 150.00
TCACY Carl Yastrzemski 40.00 100.00
TCACYE Christian Yelich 50.00 120.00
TCADJ Derek Jeter 200.00 500.00
TCADM Don Mattingly 40.00 100.00
TCADO David Ortiz 40.00 100.00
TCADS Deion Sanders 40.00 100.00
TCAEJ Eloy Jimenez 60.00 150.00
TCAEM Edgar Martinez 30.00 80.00
TCAFL Francisco Lindor
TCAFTH Frank Thomas 40.00 100.00
TCAFTJ Fernando Tatis Jr. 200.00 500.00
TCAHA Hank Aaron 125.00 300.00
TCAHM Hideki Matsui 40.00 100.00
TCAI Ichiro 125.00 300.00
TCAJA Jose Altuve 20.00 50.00
TCAJB Johnny Bench 30.00 80.00
TCAJM J.D. Martinez 25.00 60.00
TCAJS Juan Soto 75.00 200.00
TCAJV Joey Votto 25.00 60.00
TCAKB Kris Bryant 40.00 100.00
TCAKGJ Ken Griffey Jr. 150.00 400.00
TCAMC Miguel Cabrera 40.00 100.00
TCAMMC Mark McGwire 40.00 100.00
TCAMR Mariano Rivera 75.00 200.00
TCAMT Mike Trout 200.00 500.00
TCAMTA Masahiro Tanaka 40.00 100.00
TCANR Nolan Ryan 60.00 150.00
TCAOS Ozzie Smith 25.00 60.00
TCAPA Pete Alonso 100.00 250.00
TCAPM Pedro Martinez 60.00 150.00
TCARAJ Ronald Acuna Jr. 75.00 200.00
TCARC Roger Clemens 50.00 120.00
TCARH Rickey Henderson 40.00 100.00
TCARJ Randy Johnson 60.00 150.00
TCASK Sandy Koufax 150.00 400.00
TCASO Shohei Ohtani 75.00 200.00
TCASS Sammy Sosa 40.00 100.00
TCAXB Xander Bogaerts 30.00 80.00
TCARJA Reggie Jackson 25.00 60.00
TCAVGJ Vladimir Guerrero Jr. 100.00 250.00
TCAVGS Vladimir Guerrero 40.00 100.00

2019 Topps Transcendent Franchise Favorites Reproductions

ONE COMPLETE SET PER CASE
STATED PRINT RUN 100 SER.#'d SETS
FFRAB Adrian Beltre 5.00 12.00
FFRAD Andre Dawson 6.00 15.00
FFRAJ Aaron Judge 12.00 30.00
FFRAK Al Kaline 12.00 30.00
FFRAP Albert Pujols 10.00 25.00
FFRAT Alan Trammell 12.00 30.00
FFRBF Bob Feller 6.00 15.00
FFRBG Bob Gibson 4.00 10.00
FFRBH Bryce Harper 8.00 20.00
FFRBJ Bo Jackson 12.00 30.00
FFRBL Barry Larkin 8.00 20.00
FFRBP Buster Posey 12.00 30.00
FFRBR Babe Ruth 8.00 20.00
FFRBRU Babe Ruth 8.00 20.00
FFRBW Billy Williams 8.00 20.00
FFRCC Carlos Correa 8.00 20.00
FFRCJ Chipper Jones 12.00 30.00
FFRCK Clayton Kershaw 8.00 20.00
FFRCRJ Cal Ripken Jr. 15.00 40.00
FFRCY Carl Yastrzemski 8.00 20.00
FFRCYE Christian Yelich 8.00 20.00

Card	Low	High
FFRDE Dennis Eckersley	6.00	15.00
FFRDG Dwight Gooden	3.00	8.00
FFRDJ Derek Jeter	15.00	40.00
FFRDO David Ortiz	8.00	20.00
FFRDS Darryl Strawberry	6.00	15.00
FFRDSN Duke Snider	10.00	25.00
FFRDW Dave Winfield	4.00	10.00
FFREB Ernie Banks	12.00	30.00
FFREM Eddie Murray	10.00	25.00
FFREMA Edgar Martinez	6.00	15.00
FFRFL Francisco Lindor	5.00	12.00
FFRFR Frank Robinson	6.00	15.00
FFRFT Frank Thomas	12.00	30.00
FFRGB George Brett	15.00	40.00
FFRGC Gary Carter	8.00	20.00
FFRGCA Gary Carter	8.00	20.00
FFRGM Greg Maddux	10.00	25.00
FFRGS Giancarlo Stanton	5.00	12.00
FFRHA Hank Aaron	15.00	40.00
FFRHB Harold Baines	4.00	10.00
FFRHK Harmon Killebrew	10.00	25.00
FFRHW Honus Wagner	5.00	12.00
FFRIR Ivan Rodriguez	6.00	15.00
FFRIS Ichiro	12.00	30.00
FFRI Ichiro	12.00	30.00
FFRJB Jeff Bagwell	6.00	15.00
FFRJBE Johnny Bench	6.00	15.00
FFRJBU Jim Bunning	4.00	10.00
FFRJM Joe Morgan	6.00	15.00
FFRJMA Juan Marichal	8.00	20.00
FFRJP Jim Palmer	6.00	15.00
FFRJR Jackie Robinson	10.00	25.00
FFRJT Jim Thome	6.00	15.00
FFRJV Justin Verlander	8.00	20.00
FFRKGJ Ken Griffey Jr.	15.00	40.00
FFRLG Lou Gehrig	10.00	25.00
FFRMB Mookie Betts	10.00	25.00
FFRMC Miguel Cabrera	8.00	20.00
FFRMI Monte Irvin	4.00	10.00
FFRMP Mike Piazza	8.00	20.00
FFRMR Mariano Rivera	8.00	20.00
FFRMS Max Scherzer	6.00	15.00
FFRMT Mike Trout	20.00	50.00
FFRNA Nolan Arenado	8.00	20.00
FFRNOR Nolan Ryan	15.00	40.00
FFRNR Nolan Ryan	15.00	40.00
FFRNRY Nolan Ryan	15.00	40.00
FFROS Ozzie Smith	8.00	20.00
FFRPG Paul Goldschmidt	6.00	15.00
FFRPM Pedro Martinez	4.00	10.00
FFRRA Roberto Alomar	6.00	15.00
FFRRAJ Ronald Acuna Jr.	15.00	40.00
FFRRAN Randy Johnson	5.00	12.00
FFRRC Rod Carew	8.00	20.00
FFRRCL Roberto Clemente	20.00	50.00
FFRREJ Reggie Jackson	4.00	10.00
FFRRF Rollie Fingers	4.00	10.00
FFRRH Roy Halladay	6.00	15.00
FFRRIH Rickey Henderson	10.00	25.00
FFRRJ Reggie Jackson	4.00	10.00
FFRRJO Randy Johnson	5.00	12.00
FFRROY Roy Halladay	4.00	10.00
FFRRS Ryne Sandberg	10.00	25.00
FFRRY Robin Yount	8.00	20.00
FFRSC Steve Carlton	8.00	20.00
FFRSK Sandy Koufax	10.00	25.00
FFRSM Stan Musial	10.00	25.00
FFRSS Sammy Sosa	5.00	12.00
FFRTC Ty Cobb	8.00	20.00
FFRTG Tony Gwynn	12.00	30.00
FFRTH Todd Helton	4.00	10.00
FFRTHO Trevor Hoffman	4.00	10.00
FFRTM Thurman Munson	8.00	20.00
FFRTW Ted Williams	12.00	30.00
FFRVGS Vladimir Guerrero	8.00	20.00
FFRVLG Vladimir Guerrero	8.00	20.00
FFRWB Wade Boggs	8.00	20.00
FFRWM Willie McCovey	6.00	15.00
FFRWS Willie Stargell	8.00	20.00

2019 Topps Transcendent Ohtani VIP Party Autographs

ISSUED AT TOPPS VIP PARTY
PRINT RUNS B/WN 10-25 COPIES PER
NO PRICING ON QTY 10

Card	Low	High
SHAP1 Shohei Ohtani	80.00	200.00
SHAP2 Shohei Ohtani	80.00	200.00

2019 Topps Transcendent Ohtani VIP Party Bunt

ISSUED AT TOPPS VIP PARTY
STATED PRINT RUN 50 SER.#'d SETS

Card	Low	High
NNO Shohei Ohtani	12.00	30.00

2019 Topps Transcendent Ohtani VIP Party On Demand

ISSUED AT TOPPS VIP PARTY
STATED PRINT RUN 83 SER.#'d SETS

Card	Low	High
1 Shohei Ohtani	3.00	8.00
2 Shohei Ohtani	3.00	8.00
3 Shohei Ohtani	3.00	8.00
4 Shohei Ohtani	3.00	8.00
5 Shohei Ohtani	3.00	8.00
6 Shohei Ohtani	3.00	8.00
7 Shohei Ohtani	3.00	8.00
8 Shohei Ohtani	3.00	8.00
9 Shohei Ohtani	3.00	8.00
10 Shohei Ohtani	3.00	8.00

2019 Topps Transcendent Ohtani VIP Party Through the Years

ISSUED AT TOPPS VIP PARTY
STATED PRINT RUN 50 SER.#'d SETS

Card	Low	High
SO1952 Shohei Ohtani	10.00	25.00
SO1953 Shohei Ohtani	10.00	25.00
SO1954 Shohei Ohtani	10.00	25.00
SO1955 Shohei Ohtani	10.00	25.00
SO1956 Shohei Ohtani	10.00	25.00
SO1957 Shohei Ohtani	10.00	25.00
SO1958 Shohei Ohtani	10.00	25.00
SO1959 Shohei Ohtani	10.00	25.00
SO1960 Shohei Ohtani	10.00	25.00
SO1961 Shohei Ohtani	10.00	25.00
SO1962 Shohei Ohtani	10.00	25.00
SO1963 Shohei Ohtani	10.00	25.00
SO1964 Shohei Ohtani	10.00	25.00
SO1965 Shohei Ohtani	10.00	25.00
SO1966 Shohei Ohtani	10.00	25.00
SO1967 Shohei Ohtani	10.00	25.00
SO1968 Shohei Ohtani	10.00	25.00
SO1969 Shohei Ohtani	10.00	25.00
SO1970 Shohei Ohtani	10.00	25.00
SO1971 Shohei Ohtani	10.00	25.00
SO1972 Shohei Ohtani	10.00	25.00
SO1973 Shohei Ohtani	10.00	25.00
SO1975 Shohei Ohtani	10.00	25.00
SO1976 Shohei Ohtani	10.00	25.00
SO1977 Shohei Ohtani	10.00	25.00
SO1979 Shohei Ohtani	10.00	25.00
SO1981 Shohei Ohtani	10.00	25.00
SO1982 Shohei Ohtani	10.00	25.00
SO1983 Shohei Ohtani	10.00	25.00
SO1984 Shohei Ohtani	10.00	25.00
SO1985 Shohei Ohtani	10.00	25.00
SO1986 Shohei Ohtani	10.00	25.00
SO1987 Shohei Ohtani	10.00	25.00
SO1988 Shohei Ohtani	10.00	25.00
SO1989 Shohei Ohtani	10.00	25.00
SO1990 Shohei Ohtani	10.00	25.00
SO1991 Shohei Ohtani	10.00	25.00
SO1992 Shohei Ohtani	10.00	25.00
SO1995 Shohei Ohtani	10.00	25.00
SO1999 Shohei Ohtani	10.00	25.00
SO2001 Shohei Ohtani	10.00	25.00
SO2002 Shohei Ohtani	10.00	25.00
SO2003 Shohei Ohtani	10.00	25.00
SO2005 Shohei Ohtani	10.00	25.00
SO2007 Shohei Ohtani	10.00	25.00
SO2008 Shohei Ohtani	10.00	25.00
SO2010 Shohei Ohtani	10.00	25.00
SO2014 Shohei Ohtani	10.00	25.00
SO2017 Shohei Ohtani	10.00	25.00
SO2018 Shohei Ohtani	10.00	25.00

2019 Topps Transcendent VIP Party Mike Trout Autographs

ISSUED AT TOPPS VIP PARTY
PRINT RUNS B/WN 15-25 COPIES PER

Card	Low	High
MTA1 Mike Trout	300.00	500.00
MTA2 Mike Trout	300.00	500.00
MTA3 Mike Trout	300.00	500.00
MTA4 Mike Trout	300.00	500.00
MTA5 Mike Trout	300.00	500.00
MTA6 Mike Trout	300.00	500.00
MTAP1 Mike Trout	300.00	500.00
MTAP2 Mike Trout	300.00	500.00
MTAP3 Mike Trout	300.00	500.00
MTAP4 Mike Trout	300.00	500.00

2019 Topps Transcendent VIP Party Mike Trout Bunt

ISSUED AT TOPPS VIP PARTY
STATED PRINT RUN 83 SER.#'d SETS

Card	Low	High
NNO Mike Trout	20.00	50.00

2019 Topps Transcendent VIP Party Mike Trout On Demand

ISSUED AT TOPPS VIP PARTY
STATED PRINT RUN 83 SER.#'d SETS

Card	Low	High
1 Mike Trout	10.00	25.00
2 Mike Trout	10.00	25.00
3 Mike Trout	10.00	25.00
4 Mike Trout	10.00	25.00
5 Mike Trout	10.00	25.00
6 Mike Trout	10.00	25.00
7 Mike Trout	10.00	25.00
8 Mike Trout	10.00	25.00
9 Mike Trout	10.00	25.00
10 Mike Trout	10.00	25.00

2019 Topps Transcendent VIP Party Mike Trout Through the Years

ISSUED AT TOPPS VIP PARTY
STATED PRINT RUN 83 SER.#'d SETS

Card	Low	High
MT1952 Mike Trout	15.00	40.00
MT1953 Mike Trout	15.00	40.00
MT1954 Mike Trout	15.00	40.00
MT1955 Mike Trout	15.00	40.00
MT1956 Mike Trout	15.00	40.00
MT1957 Mike Trout	15.00	40.00
MT1958 Mike Trout	15.00	40.00
MT1959 Mike Trout	15.00	40.00
MT1960 Mike Trout	15.00	40.00
MT1961 Mike Trout	15.00	40.00
MT1962 Mike Trout	15.00	40.00
MT1963 Mike Trout	15.00	40.00
MT1964 Mike Trout	15.00	40.00
MT1965 Mike Trout	15.00	40.00
MT1966 Mike Trout	15.00	40.00
MT1967 Mike Trout	15.00	40.00
MT1968 Mike Trout	15.00	40.00
MT1969 Mike Trout	15.00	40.00
MT1970 Mike Trout	15.00	40.00
MT1971 Mike Trout	15.00	40.00
MT1972 Mike Trout	15.00	40.00
MT1973 Mike Trout	15.00	40.00
MT1974 Mike Trout	15.00	40.00
MT1975 Mike Trout	15.00	40.00
MT1976 Mike Trout	15.00	40.00
MT1977 Mike Trout	15.00	40.00
MT1978 Mike Trout	15.00	40.00
MT1979 Mike Trout	15.00	40.00
MT1980 Mike Trout	15.00	40.00
MT1981 Mike Trout	15.00	40.00
MT1982 Mike Trout	15.00	40.00
MT1983 Mike Trout	15.00	40.00
MT1984 Mike Trout	15.00	40.00
MT1985 Mike Trout	15.00	40.00
MT1986 Mike Trout	15.00	40.00
MT1987 Mike Trout	15.00	40.00
MT1988 Mike Trout	15.00	40.00
MT1989 Mike Trout	15.00	40.00
MT1990 Mike Trout	15.00	40.00
MT1991 Mike Trout	15.00	40.00
MT1992 Mike Trout	15.00	40.00
MT1993 Mike Trout	15.00	40.00
MT1994 Mike Trout	15.00	40.00
MT1995 Mike Trout	15.00	40.00
MT1996 Mike Trout	15.00	40.00
MT1997 Mike Trout	15.00	40.00
MT1998 Mike Trout	15.00	40.00
MT1999 Mike Trout	15.00	40.00
MT2000 Mike Trout	15.00	40.00
MT2001 Mike Trout	15.00	40.00
MT2002 Mike Trout	15.00	40.00
MT2003 Mike Trout	15.00	40.00
MT2004 Mike Trout	15.00	40.00
MT2005 Mike Trout	15.00	40.00
MT2006 Mike Trout	15.00	40.00
MT2007 Mike Trout	15.00	40.00
MT2008 Mike Trout	15.00	40.00
MT2009 Mike Trout	15.00	40.00
MT2010 Mike Trout	15.00	40.00
MT2011 Mike Trout	15.00	40.00
MT2012 Mike Trout	15.00	40.00
MT2013 Mike Trout	15.00	40.00
MT2014 Mike Trout	15.00	40.00
MT2015 Mike Trout	15.00	40.00
MT2016 Mike Trout	15.00	40.00
MT2017 Mike Trout	15.00	40.00
MT2018 Mike Trout	15.00	40.00
MT51PB Mike Trout	15.00	40.00
MT55BB Mike Trout	15.00	40.00
MT58AS Mike Trout	15.00	40.00
MT68TG Mike Trout	15.00	40.00
MT69TS Mike Trout	15.00	40.00
MT72IA Mike Trout	15.00	40.00
MT75TH Mike Trout	15.00	40.00
MT77TB Mike Trout	15.00	40.00
MT78RB Mike Trout	15.00	40.00
MT82IA Mike Trout	15.00	40.00
MT82TH Mike Trout	15.00	40.00
MT88AS Mike Trout	15.00	40.00
MT88RB Mike Trout	15.00	40.00
MT89RB Mike Trout	15.00	40.00
MT90RB Mike Trout	15.00	40.00
MT91AS Mike Trout	15.00	40.00

2020 Topps Transcendent

ONE COMPLETE SET PER CASE
STATED PRINT RUN 95 SER.#'d SETS

Card	Low	High
1 Ty Cobb	8.00	20.00
2 Derek Jeter	30.00	80.00
3 Babe Ruth	15.00	40.00
4 Lou Gehrig	10.00	25.00
5 Johnny Bench	12.00	30.00
6 Al Kaline	12.00	30.00
7 Gerrit Cole	12.00	30.00
8 Cal Ripken Jr.	15.00	40.00
9 Ted Williams	20.00	50.00
10 Chipper Jones	5.00	12.00
11 Anthony Rendon	10.00	25.00
12 Juan Soto	25.00	60.00
13 Alex Rodriguez	6.00	15.00
14 Ernie Banks	12.00	30.00
15 Zac Gallen RC	12.00	30.00
16 Aaron Judge	12.00	30.00
17 Matt Chapman	5.00	12.00
18 Pete Alonso	12.00	30.00
19 Tony Gwynn	40.00	100.00
20 Mike Schmidt	15.00	40.00
21 Roberto Clemente	20.00	50.00
22 Brendan McKay RC	8.00	20.00
23 Aristides Aquino RC	10.00	25.00
24 Willie Mays	12.00	30.00
25 Dustin May RC	10.00	25.00
26 Luis Robert RC	150.00	400.00
27 Bo Bichette RC	125.00	300.00
28 Yordan Alvarez RC	40.00	100.00
29 Nico Hoerner RC	12.00	30.00
30 Gavin Lux RC	30.00	80.00
31 Dave Winfield	20.00	50.00
32 Sandy Koufax	20.00	50.00
33 Honus Wagner	15.00	40.00
34 Nolan Ryan	20.00	50.00
35 Paul Goldschmidt	8.00	20.00
36 Kris Bryant	12.00	30.00
37 Bryce Harper	8.00	20.00
38 Jacob deGrom	8.00	20.00
39 Max Scherzer	12.00	30.00
40 Nolan Arenado	8.00	20.00
41 Fernando Tatis Jr.	60.00	150.00
42 Jackie Robinson	15.00	40.00
43 Ronald Acuna Jr.	20.00	50.00
44 Justin Verlander	5.00	12.00
45 Mike Trout	50.00	120.00
46 Shohei Ohtani	15.00	40.00
47 Mookie Betts	15.00	40.00
48 Christian Yelich	10.00	25.00
49 Cody Bellinger	10.00	25.00
50 Ichiro	15.00	40.00

2020 Topps Transcendent Sketch Reproductions

ONE COMPLETE SET PER CASE
STATED PRINT RUN 95 SER.#'d SETS

Card	Low	High
TTCRAJ Aaron Judge	12.00	30.00
TTCRAK Al Kaline	5.00	12.00
TTCRAP Albert Pujols	10.00	25.00
TTCRAR Alex Rodriguez	6.00	15.00
TTCRBB Bert Blyleven	4.00	10.00
TTCRBF Bob Feller	8.00	20.00
TTCRBG Bob Gibson	8.00	20.00
TTCRBR Babe Ruth	12.00	30.00
TTCRCB Craig Biggio	8.00	20.00
TTCRCF Cecil Fielder	12.00	30.00
TTCRCK Clayton Kershaw	8.00	20.00
TTCRCR Cal Ripken Jr.	15.00	40.00
TTCRCY Carl Yastrzemski	8.00	20.00
TTCRDE Dennis Eckersley	8.00	20.00
TTCRDG Dwight Gooden	8.00	20.00
TTCRDO David Ortiz	8.00	20.00
TTCRDS Don Sutton	4.00	10.00
TTCRDW Dave Winfield	8.00	20.00
TTCREB Ernie Banks	5.00	12.00
TTCREM Eddie Mathews	10.00	25.00
TTCREW Early Wynn	4.00	10.00
TTCRFJ Fergie Jenkins	4.00	10.00
TTCRFR Frank Robinson	4.00	10.00
TTCRFT Frank Thomas	15.00	40.00
TTCRGB George Brett	40.00	10.00
TTCRHA Hank Aaron	10.00	25.00
TTCRHK Harmon Killebrew	10.00	25.00
TTCRHN Hal Newhouser	8.00	20.00
TTCRHW Honus Wagner	5.00	12.00
TTCRIS Ichiro	10.00	25.00
TTCRJC Jose Canseco	20.00	50.00
TTCRJS John Smoltz	8.00	20.00
TTCRJT Jim Thome	4.00	10.00
TTCRJV Justin Verlander	5.00	12.00
TTCRKG Ken Griffey Jr.	20.00	50.00
TTCRLB Lou Brock	8.00	20.00
TTCRLG Lou Gehrig	10.00	25.00
TTCRMC Miguel Cabrera	8.00	20.00
TTCRMM Mark McGwire	8.00	20.00
TTCRMR Mariano Rivera	10.00	25.00
TTCRMS Mike Schmidt	8.00	20.00
TTCRNR Nolan Ryan	20.00	50.00
TTCRPA Pete Alonso	12.00	30.00
TTCRPM Paul Molitor	8.00	20.00
TTCRPN Phil Niekro	4.00	10.00
TTCRRB Roberto Clemente	12.00	30.00
TTCRRC Roger Clemens	6.00	15.00
TTCRRH Rickey Henderson	15.00	40.00
TTCRRJ Reggie Jackson	8.00	20.00
TTCRRK Ralph Kiner	8.00	20.00
TTCRRM Roger Maris	8.00	20.00
TTCRRY Robin Yount	10.00	25.00
TTCRSC Steve Carlton	4.00	10.00
TTCRSK Sandy Koufax	12.00	30.00
TTCRSM Stan Musial	15.00	40.00
TTCRTC Ty Cobb	8.00	20.00
TTCRTG Tom Glavine	4.00	10.00
TTCRTH Trevor Hoffman	6.00	15.00
TTCRTS Tom Seaver	4.00	10.00
TTCRTW Ted Williams	12.00	30.00
TTCRWB Wade Boggs	20.00	50.00
TTCRWM Willie Mays	15.00	40.00
TTCRWS Warren Spahn	10.00	25.00
TTCRARD Alex Rodriguez	6.00	15.00
TTCRARO Alex Rodriguez	6.00	15.00
TTCRBBR Babe Ruth	12.00	30.00
TTCRCCS CC Sabathia	4.00	10.00
TTCRCRY Carl Yastrzemski	8.00	20.00
TTCRDNS Don Sutton	4.00	10.00
TTCRDOR David Ortiz	8.00	20.00
TTCREDM Eddie Murray	15.00	40.00
TTCRFRB Frank Robinson	4.00	10.00
TTCRHAA Hank Aaron	10.00	25.00
TTCRJMT Jim Thome	4.00	10.00
TTCRJVR Justin Verlander	5.00	12.00
TTCRKFX Sandy Koufax	12.00	30.00
TTCRKGJ Ken Griffey Jr.	20.00	50.00
TTCRLGZ Luis Gonzalez	10.00	25.00
TTCRMMC Mark McGwire	8.00	20.00
TTCRNOR Nolan Ryan	20.00	50.00
TTCRPDM Pedro Martinez	4.00	10.00
TTCRPHN Phil Niekro	4.00	10.00
TTCRPMR Pedro Martinez	4.00	10.00
TTCRRAJ Randy Johnson	6.00	15.00
TTCRRCL Roger Clemens	6.00	15.00
TTCRRDC Rod Carew	8.00	20.00
TTCRRDJ Randy Johnson	6.00	15.00
TTCRRGC Roger Clemens	6.00	15.00
TTCRRJO Randy Johnson	6.00	15.00
TTCRROG Roger Clemens	6.00	15.00
TTCRSCA Steve Carlton	4.00	10.00
TTCRSDK Sandy Koufax	12.00	30.00
TTCRSTC Steve Carlton	4.00	10.00
TTCRTDW Ted Williams	12.00	30.00
TTCRTMS Tom Seaver	4.00	10.00
TTCRTNY Tony Gwynn	20.00	50.00
TTCRTWL Ted Williams	12.00	30.00
TTCRTYC Ty Cobb	8.00	20.00
TTCRWMC Willie McCovey	10.00	25.00
TTCRWMY Willie Mays	15.00	40.00

2020 Topps Transcendent Transcendent Collection Autographs

FIFTY AUTOGRAPHS PER CASE
STATED PRINT RUN 25 SER.#'d SETS
*EMERALD/15: .4X TO 1X BASIC
*VAR/25: .4X TO 1X BASIC
*VAR.EMERALD: .4X TO 1X BASIC

Card	Low	High
TCAI Ichiro	150.00	400.00
TCAAA Aristides Aquino		
TCAAB Adrian Beltre	40.00	100.00
TCAAP Albert Pujols	125.00	300.00
TCAAR Alex Rodriguez	75.00	200.00
TCABH Bryce Harper	125.00	300.00
TCABM Brendan McKay		
TCACF Carlton Fisk	40.00	100.00
TCACR Cal Ripken Jr.	100.00	250.00
TCACY Christian Yelich	50.00	120.00
TCADJ Derek Jeter	300.00	600.00
TCADM Dustin May	50.00	125.00
TCADO David Ortiz	60.00	150.00
TCAEJ Eloy Jimenez	50.00	125.00
TCAEM Edgar Martinez	50.00	120.00
TCAFF Freddie Freeman	60.00	150.00
TCAFT Fernando Tatis Jr.	200.00	500.00
TCAGR Gerrit Cole	60.00	150.00
TCAGT Gleyber Torres	75.00	200.00
TCAHA Hank Aaron	200.00	500.00
TCAHM Hideki Matsui	40.00	100.00
TCAJA Jose Altuve	20.00	50.00
TCAJD Jacob deGrom	125.00	300.00
TCAJM Joe Mauer	60.00	150.00
TCAKG Ken Griffey Jr.	400.00	800.00
TCALR Luis Robert	300.00	600.00
TCALW Larry Walker	50.00	120.00
TCAMC Miguel Cabrera	75.00	200.00
TCAMS Mike Schmidt	75.00	200.00
TCAMT Mike Trout	500.00	1000.00
TCANA Nolan Arenado	40.00	100.00
TCANH Nico Hoerner	60.00	150.00
TCANR Nolan Ryan	100.00	250.00
TCAPA Pete Alonso	60.00	150.00
TCAPM Pedro Martinez	75.00	200.00
TCARA Ronald Acuna Jr.	150.00	400.00
TCARD Rafael Devers	30.00	80.00
TCARH Rickey Henderson	75.00	200.00
TCARJ Reggie Jackson	60.00	150.00
TCASA Shogo Akiyama		
TCAVG Vladimir Guerrero	40.00	100.00
TCAWB Wade Boggs	40.00	100.00
TCAYA Yordan Alvarez	150.00	400.00
TCAYM Yoan Moncada	25.00	60.00
TCABRG Alex Bregman	25.00	60.00
TCAHJR Hyun-Jin Ryu	100.00	250.00
TCAJSO Juan Soto	125.00	300.00
TCAREN Anthony Rendon	50.00	120.00
TCAVGJ Vladimir Guerrero Jr.	60.00	150.00
TCAWLK Walker Buehler	50.00	120.00
TCAYAZ Carl Yastrzemski	50.00	120.00

2020 Topps Transcendent Hall of Fame

ONE COMPLETE SET PER BOX
STATED PRINT RUN 50 SER.#'d SETS

Card	Low	High
1 Babe Ruth	15.00	40.00
2 Mike Mussina	8.00	20.00
3 Frank Thomas	15.00	40.00
4 Roberto Alomar	6.00	15.00
5 Johnny Bench	8.00	20.00
6 Jeff Bagwell	20.00	50.00
7 Harold Baines	8.00	20.00
8 George Brett	12.00	30.00
9 Edgar Martinez	6.00	15.00
10 Carl Yastrzemski	10.00	25.00
11 Cal Ripken Jr.	15.00	40.00
12 Tom Glavine	6.00	15.00
13 Al Kaline	10.00	25.00
14 Wade Boggs	8.00	20.00
15 Bert Blyleven	6.00	15.00
16 Ken Griffey Jr.	25.00	60.00
17 Jim Thome	6.00	15.00
18 Vladimir Guerrero	6.00	15.00
19 Juan Marichal	10.00	25.00
20 Nolan Ryan	20.00	50.00
21 Ivan Rodriguez	10.00	25.00
22 Rickey Henderson	10.00	25.00
23 Andre Dawson	8.00	20.00
24 Ryne Sandberg	15.00	40.00
25 Sandy Koufax	15.00	40.00
26 Ted Williams	20.00	50.00
27 Honus Wagner	10.00	25.00
28 Chipper Jones	12.00	30.00
29 Jackie Robinson	8.00	20.00
30 Craig Biggio	10.00	25.00
31 Steve Carlton	6.00	15.00
32 John Smoltz	8.00	20.00
33 Lou Gehrig	10.00	25.00
34 Ozzie Smith	10.00	25.00
35 Robin Yount	10.00	25.00
36 Tony Gwynn	10.00	25.00
37 Reggie Jackson	8.00	20.00
38 Bob Gibson	6.00	15.00
39 Barry Larkin	6.00	15.00
40 Randy Johnson	8.00	20.00
41 Rod Carew	6.00	15.00
42 Tony Perez	15.00	40.00
43 Stan Musial	12.00	30.00
44 Tim Raines	6.00	15.00
45 Carlton Fisk	10.00	25.00
46 Alan Trammell	20.00	50.00
47 Lou Brock	8.00	20.00
48 Dennis Eckersley	6.00	15.00
49 Mariano Rivera	12.00	30.00
50 Hank Aaron	12.00	30.00

2020 Topps Transcendent Hall of Fame Sketch Reproductions

ONE COMPLETE SET PER BOX
STATED PRINT RUN 50 SER.#'d SETS

Card	Low	High
HOFRAD Andre Dawson	8.00	20.00
HOFRBF Bob Feller	8.00	20.00
HOFRBG Bob Gibson	6.00	15.00
HOFRBL Barry Larkin	6.00	15.00
HOFRBR Babe Ruth	15.00	40.00
HOFRCJ Chipper Jones	12.00	30.00
HOFRCM Christy Mathewson	8.00	20.00
HOFRCRJ Cal Ripken Jr.	15.00	40.00
HOFRCY Carl Yastrzemski	10.00	25.00
HOFREB Ernie Banks	8.00	20.00
HOFREM Edgar Martinez	6.00	15.00
HOFRFT Frank Thomas	15.00	40.00
HOFRGB George Brett	12.00	30.00
HOFRGC Gary Carter	12.00	30.00
HOFRHA Hank Aaron	12.00	30.00
HOFRHK Harmon Killebrew	8.00	20.00
HOFRHW Honus Wagner	10.00	25.00
HOFRIR Ivan Rodriguez	10.00	25.00
HOFRJB Jeff Bagwell	20.00	50.00
HOFRJBE Johnny Bench	8.00	20.00
HOFRJM Joe Morgan	6.00	15.00
HOFRJR Jackie Robinson	8.00	20.00
HOFRJT Jim Thome	6.00	15.00
HOFRKGJ Ken Griffey Jr.	25.00	60.00
HOFRLG Lou Gehrig	10.00	25.00
HOFRMI Monte Irvin	6.00	15.00
HOFRMP Mike Piazza	10.00	25.00
HOFRMR Mariano Rivera	12.00	30.00
HOFRNR Nolan Ryan	20.00	50.00
HOFROS Ozzie Smith	10.00	25.00
HOFRPM Pedro Martinez	6.00	15.00
HOFRRA Roberto Alomar	6.00	15.00
HOFRRC Rod Carew	6.00	15.00
HOFRRCL Roberto Clemente	30.00	80.00
HOFRRH Rickey Henderson	10.00	25.00
HOFRRHO Rogers Hornsby	6.00	15.00
HOFRRJ Randy Johnson	8.00	20.00
HOFRRJA Reggie Jackson	8.00	20.00
HOFRSC Steve Carlton	6.00	15.00
HOFRSK Sandy Koufax	15.00	40.00
HOFRSM Stan Musial	12.00	30.00
HOFRTC Ty Cobb	10.00	25.00
HOFRTG Tom Glavine	6.00	15.00
HOFRTGW Tony Gwynn	10.00	25.00
HOFRTS Tris Speaker	8.00	20.00
HOFRTW Ted Williams	12.00	30.00
HOFRVG Vladimir Guerrero	6.00	15.00
HOFRWB Wade Boggs	8.00	20.00
HOFRWM Willie Mays	12.00	30.00
HOFRWMC Willie McCovey	10.00	25.00

2020 Topps Transcendent Hall of Fame Sandy Koufax Through the Years Autographs

OVERALL ONE KOUFAX AUTO PER BOX
STATED PRINT RUN 1 SER.#'d SET

2020 Topps Transcendent Hall of Fame Autographs

OVERALL FORTY AUTOS PER BOX
STATED PRINT RUN 25 SER.#'d SETS

Card	Low	High
THOFAD Andre Dawson	30.00	80.00
THOFAK Al Kaline	50.00	120.00
THOFBG Bob Gibson	40.00	100.00
THOFBL Barry Larkin	30.00	80.00
THOFCF Carlton Fisk	30.00	80.00
THOFCJ Chipper Jones	75.00	200.00
THOFCRJ Cal Ripken Jr.	75.00	200.00
THOFCY Carl Yastrzemski	50.00	120.00
THOFFT Frank Thomas	50.00	120.00
THOFHA Hank Aaron	200.00	500.00
THOFJB Johnny Bench	40.00	100.00
THOFJBA Jeff Bagwell	75.00	200.00
THOFJM Juan Marichal	30.00	80.00
THOFJS John Smoltz	40.00	100.00
THOFJT Jim Thome	50.00	120.00
THOFKGJ Ken Griffey Jr.	200.00	500.00
THOFMM Mike Mussina	40.00	100.00
THOFMR Mariano Rivera	100.00	250.00
THOFNR Nolan Ryan	100.00	250.00
THOFOS Ozzie Smith	40.00	100.00
THOFPM Paul Molitor	40.00	100.00
THOFRA Roberto Alomar	30.00	80.00
THOFRC Rod Carew	30.00	80.00
THOFRH Rickey Henderson	50.00	120.00
THOFRJ Randy Johnson	50.00	120.00
THOFRJA Reggie Jackson	40.00	100.00
THOFRS Ryne Sandberg	60.00	150.00
THOFRY Robin Yount	40.00	100.00
THOFSK Sandy Koufax	200.00	500.00
THOFTG Tom Glavine	30.00	80.00
THOFVG Vladimir Guerrero	30.00	80.00
THOFWB Wade Boggs	50.00	120.00

2020 Topps Transcendent Hall of Fame Transcendent Collection Image Variation Autographs

OVERALL FORTY AUTOS PER BOX
STATED PRINT RUN 25 SER.#'d SETS

Card	Low	High
THOFVAD Andre Dawson	30.00	80.00
THOFVAK Al Kaline	50.00	210.00
THOFVBG Bob Gibson	40.00	100.00
THOFVBL Barry Larkin	30.00	80.00
THOFVCF Carlton Fisk	30.00	80.00
THOFVCJ Chipper Jones	75.00	200.00
THOFVCRJ Cal Ripken Jr.	75.00	200.00
THOFVCY Carl Yastrzemski	50.00	120.00
THOFVFT Frank Thomas	50.00	120.00
THOFVHA Hank Aaron	200.00	500.00
THOFVJB Johnny Bench	40.00	100.00
THOFVJBA Jeff Bagwell	75.00	200.00
THOFVJM Juan Marichal	30.00	80.00
THOFVJS John Smoltz	40.00	100.00
THOFVJT Jim Thome	50.00	120.00
THOFVKGJ Ken Griffey Jr.	200.00	500.00
THOFVMM Mike Mussina	40.00	100.00
THOFVMR Mariano Rivera	100.00	250.00
THOFVNR Nolan Ryan	100.00	250.00
THOFVOS Ozzie Smith	40.00	100.00
THOFVPM Paul Molitor	40.00	100.00
THOFVRA Roberto Alomar	30.00	80.00
THOFVRC Rod Carew	30.00	80.00
THOFVRH Rickey Henderson	50.00	120.00
THOFVRJ Randy Johnson	50.00	120.00
THOFVRJA Reggie Jackson	40.00	100.00
THOFVRS Ryne Sandberg	60.00	150.00
THOFVRY Robin Yount	40.00	100.00
THOFVSK Sandy Koufax	200.00	500.00
THOFVTG Tom Glavine	30.00	80.00
THOFVVG Vladimir Guerrero	30.00	80.00
THOFVWB Wade Boggs	50.00	120.00

2001 Topps Tribute

Card	Low	High
COMPLETE SET (90)	60.00	120.00

PSA-GRADED MANTLE EXCH ODDS 1:170
M.MANTLE REPURHCASED ODDS 1:426
J.ROBINSON REPURCHASED ODDS 1:426
T.WILLIAMS REPURCHASED ODDS 1:426
EXCHANGE DEADLINE 11/30/03

Card	Low	High
1 Pee Wee Reese	2.50	6.00
2 Babe Ruth	8.00	20.00
3 Ralph Kiner	2.00	5.00
4 Brooks Robinson	2.00	5.00
5 Don Sutton	2.00	5.00
6 Carl Yastrzemski	4.00	10.00
7 Roger Maris	2.50	6.00
8 Andre Dawson	2.00	5.00
9 Luis Aparicio	2.00	5.00
10 Wade Boggs	2.00	5.00
11 Johnny Bench	2.50	6.00
12 Ernie Banks	2.50	6.00
13 Thurman Munson	2.50	6.00
14 Harmon Killebrew	2.50	6.00
15 Ted Kluszewski	2.00	5.00
16 Bob Feller	2.00	5.00
17 Mike Schmidt	5.00	12.00
18 Warren Spahn	2.00	5.00
19 Jim Palmer	2.00	5.00
20 Don Mattingly	5.00	12.00
21 Willie Mays	5.00	12.00
22 Gil Hodges	2.50	6.00
23 Juan Marichal	2.00	5.00
24 Robin Yount	2.50	6.00
25 Nolan Ryan Angels	6.00	15.00
26 Dave Winfield	2.00	5.00
27 Hank Greenberg	2.50	6.00
28 Honus Wagner	3.00	8.00
29 Nolan Ryan Rangers	6.00	15.00
30 Phil Niekro	2.00	5.00
31 Robin Roberts	2.00	5.00
32 Casey Stengel Yankees	2.00	5.00
33 Willie McCovey	2.00	5.00
34 Roy Campanella	2.50	6.00
35 Rollie Fingers A's	2.00	5.00
36 Tom Seaver	2.00	5.00
37 Jackie Robinson	2.50	6.00
38 Hank Aaron Braves	5.00	12.00
39 Bob Gibson	2.00	5.00
40 Carlton Fisk Red Sox	2.00	5.00
41 Hank Aaron Brewers	5.00	12.00
42 George Brett	5.00	12.00
43 Orlando Cepeda	2.00	5.00
44 Red Schoendienst	2.00	5.00
45 Don Drysdale	2.00	5.00
46 Mel Ott	2.50	6.00
47 Casey Stengel Mets	2.50	6.00
48 Al Kaline	2.50	6.00
49 Reggie Jackson	2.00	5.00
50 Tony Perez	2.00	5.00
51 Ozzie Smith	4.00	10.00
52 Billy Martin	2.00	5.00
53 Bill Dickey	2.00	5.00
54 Catfish Hunter	2.00	5.00
55 Duke Snider	2.00	5.00
56 Dale Murphy	2.00	5.00
57 Bobby Doerr	2.00	5.00
58 Earl Averill	2.00	5.00
59 Carlton Fisk White Sox	2.00	5.00
60 Tom Lasorda	2.00	5.00
61 Lou Gehrig	5.00	12.00
62 Enos Slaughter	2.00	5.00
63 Jim Bunning	2.00	5.00
64 Rollie Fingers Brewers	2.00	5.00
65 Frank Robinson Reds	2.00	5.00
66 Earl Weaver	2.00	5.00
67 Eddie Mathews	2.50	6.00
68 Kirby Puckett	2.50	6.00
69 Phil Rizzuto	2.50	6.00
70 Lou Brock	2.00	5.00
71 Walt Alston	2.00	5.00
72 Billy Pierce	2.00	5.00
73 Joe Morgan	2.00	5.00
74 Roberto Clemente	6.00	15.00
75 Whitey Ford	2.00	5.00
76 Richie Ashburn	2.00	5.00
77 Elston Howard	2.00	5.00
78 Gary Carter	2.00	5.00
79 Carl Hubbell	2.00	5.00
80 Yogi Berra	2.50	6.00
81 Ken Boyer	2.00	5.00
82 Nolan Ryan Astros	6.00	15.00
83 Bill Mazeroski	2.00	5.00
84 Dizzy Dean	2.50	6.00
85 Nellie Fox	2.00	5.00
86 Stan Musial	4.00	10.00
87 Steve Carlton	2.00	5.00
88 Willie Stargell	2.00	5.00
89 Hal Newhouser	2.00	5.00
90 Frank Robinson Orioles	2.00	5.00

2001 Topps Tribute Dual Relics

C.STENGEL ODDS 1:860
F.ROBINSON ODDS 1:860

Card	Low	High
CSYM Casey Stengel Jsy-Jsy	75.00	150.00
FRRO Frank Robinson Bat-Jsy	50.00	100.00

2001 Topps Tribute Franchise Figures Relics

GROUP A STATED ODDS 1:50
GROUP B STATED ODDS 1:106
OVERALL STATED ODDS 1:34

Card	Low	High
AL Alston/Lasorda A	15.00	40.00
CD Carter/Dawson B	15.00	40.00
FY Fisk/Yastrzemski A	75.00	150.00
JM R.Jackson/Martin A	40.00	80.00
KG Kaline/Greenberg A	30.00	60.00
MM Munson/Mattingly A	100.00	200.00
PK Puckett/Killebrew A	75.00	150.00
RG B.Ruth/L.Gehrig A	300.00	600.00
RR B.Rob/F.Rob A	60.00	120.00
AFF Aparicio/Fox/Fisk A	75.00	150.00
HDB Dickey/How/Berra A	125.00	200.00
HSS Hodges/Steng/Seav A	60.00	120.00
MCS Maz/Clem/Starg A	150.00	250.00
MMA Murphy/Math/Aaron A	40.00	80.00
MMC Mays/McCov/Cep A	60.00	120.00
RSC Reese/Duke/Campy A	40.00	80.00
SAC Schm/Ash/Carlton A	100.00	200.00
BPKRM Cincy Reds A	100.00	200.00
SBSM Ozzie Smith	75.00	150.00
Lou Brock		
Red Schoendienst		
Stan Musial A		

2001 Topps Tribute Game Bat Relics

GROUP 1 STATED ODDS 1:2
GROUP 2 STATED ODDS 1:35
OVERALL STATED ODDS 1:2
BAT LOGO & STENCIL CUT-OUT SAME QTY
BAT LOGO & STENCIL CUT-OUT SAME VALUE

Card	Low	High
RBAK Al Kaline 1	10.00	25.00
RBBM Billy Martin 1	10.00	25.00
RBBR Babe Ruth 2	40.00	100.00
RBBRO Brooks Robinson 1	12.00	30.00
RBCFR Carlton Fisk Red Sox 1	10.00	25.00
RBCFW Carlton Fisk W.Sox 1	10.00	25.00
RBCS Casey Stengel 1	10.00	25.00
RBCY Carl Yastrzemski 1	10.00	25.00
RBDM Don Mattingly 1	10.00	25.00
RBFRR Frank Robinson Reds 1	10.00	25.00
RBGB George Brett 1	20.00	50.00
RBGH Gil Hodges 1	10.00	25.00
RBHA Hank Aaron Braves 1	12.50	30.00
RBHAB Hank Aaron Brewers 1	12.50	30.00
RBHG Hank Greenberg 1	12.00	30.00
RBHK Harmon Killebrew 1	10.00	25.00
RBHW Honus Wagner 1	20.00	50.00
RBKB Ken Boyer 1	6.00	15.00
RBLA Luis Aparicio 1	6.00	15.00
RBLB Lou Brock 1	20.00	50.00
RBLG Lou Gehrig 1	60.00	150.00
RBOS Ozzie Smith 1	10.00	25.00
RBPWR Pee Wee Reese 1	10.00	25.00
RBRA Richie Ashburn 1	15.00	40.00
RBRC Roy Campanella 1	12.50	30.00
RBRCL Roberto Clemente 1	30.00	80.00
RBRJ Reggie Jackson 1	12.00	30.00
RBRM Roger Maris 1	20.00	50.00
RBTM Thurman Munson 1	10.00	25.00
RBWM Willie McCovey 1	10.00	25.00

2001 Topps Tribute Game Patch-Number Relics

STATED ODDS 1:61
STATED PRINT RUN 30 SETS
CARDS ARE NOT SERIAL NUMBERED
PRINT RUN INFO PROVIDED BY TOPPS

Card	Low	High
RPNBD Bill Dickey	150.00	250.00
RPNBDO Bobby Doerr	90.00	150.00
RPNCY Carl Yastrzemski	125.00	250.00
RPNDM Don Mattingly	150.00	250.00
RPNDW Dave Winfield	90.00	150.00
RPNEM Eddie Mathews	125.00	200.00
RPNGB George Brett	125.00	200.00
RPNHK Harmon Killebrew	125.00	200.00
RPNJB Johnny Bench	125.00	200.00
RPNJM Juan Marichal	90.00	150.00
RPNJP Jim Palmer	90.00	150.00
RPNKB Kirby Puckett	125.00	200.00
RPNLB Lou Brock	90.00	150.00
RPNMS Mike Schmidt	150.00	300.00
RPNNRA Nolan Ryan Angels	100.00	200.00
RPNNRH Nolan Ryan Astros	100.00	200.00
RPNNRR Nolan Ryan Rgr	100.00	200.00
RPNRS Red Schoendienst	90.00	150.00
RPNRY Robin Yount	125.00	200.00
RPNTL Tom Lasorda	90.00	150.00
RPNWA Walt Alston	90.00	150.00
RPNWB Wade Boggs	125.00	200.00
RPNYB Yogi Berra	125.00	200.00

2001 Topps Tribute Game Worn Relics

GROUP 1 STATED ODDS 1:282
GROUP 2 STATED ODDS 1:13
GROUP 3 STATED ODDS 1:42
GROUP 4 STATED ODDS 1:12
GROUP 5 STATED ODDS 1:9

OVERALL STATED ODDS 1:2

Card	Low	High
RJBD Bill Dickey 5	12.50	30.00
RJBDO Bobby Doerr 2	8.00	20.00
RJCS Casey Stengel 5	10.00	25.00
RJCY Carl Yastrzemski White 3	12.00	30.00
RJCYA Carl Yastrzemski Gray 3	15.00	40.00
RJDD Dizzy Dean Uni 4	20.00	50.00
RJDM Don Mattingly 2	10.00	25.00
RJDW Dave Winfield 2	8.00	20.00
RJEB Ernie Banks White 2	12.50	30.00
RJEM Eddie Mathews 2	12.50	30.00
RJEBA Ernie Banks Gray 2	12.50	30.00
RJFR Frank Robinson 2	8.00	20.00
RJGB George Brett 2	10.00	25.00
RJHK Harmon Killebrew 2	12.50	30.00
RJJB Johnny Bench White 2	8.00	20.00
RJJP Jim Palmer White 2	8.00	20.00
RJJR Jackie Robinson 1	50.00	100.00
RJJBE Johnny Bench Gray 2	8.00	20.00
RJJMG Juan Marichal 2	8.00	20.00
RJJPA Jim Palmer Gray 2	8.00	20.00
RJKP Kirby Puckett 2	15.00	40.00
RJLB Lou Brock 2	12.50	30.00
RJMSB Mike Schmidt Blue 2	15.00	40.00
RJMSW Mike Schmidt White 2	12.50	30.00
RJNF Nellie Fox 2	12.50	30.00
RJNRA Nolan Ryan Angels 2	12.50	30.00
RJNRH Nolan Ryan Astros 2	12.50	30.00
RJNRR Nolan Ryan Rangers 2	12.50	30.00
RJRS Red Schoendienst 2	8.00	20.00
RJRY Robin Yount 2	12.50	30.00
RJSC Steve Carlton 2	8.00	20.00
RJSM Stan Musial 2	12.50	30.00
RJTL Tom Lasorda 4	8.00	20.00
RJWA Walt Alston 4	8.00	20.00
RJWB Wade Boggs 2	12.50	30.00
RJWMF Willie Mays Gray 2	15.00	40.00
RJWMW Willie Mays White 2	15.00	40.00
RJWST Willie Stargell 2	12.50	30.00
RJYB Yogi Berra 2	12.50	30.00

2002 Topps Tribute

Card	Low	High
COMPLETE SET (90)	40.00	80.00
1 Hank Aaron	4.00	10.00
2 Rogers Hornsby	1.25	3.00
3 Bobby Thomson	1.25	3.00
4 Eddie Collins	1.25	3.00
5 Joe Carter	.75	2.00
6 Jim Palmer	1.25	3.00
7 Willie Mays	4.00	10.00
8 Willie Stargell	1.25	3.00
9 Vida Blue	.75	2.00
10 Whitey Ford	1.25	3.00
11 Bob Gibson	1.25	3.00
12 Nellie Fox	1.25	3.00
13 Napoleon Lajoie	2.00	5.00
14 Frankie Frisch	1.25	3.00
15 Nolan Ryan	6.00	15.00
16 Brooks Robinson	1.25	3.00
17 Kirby Puckett	2.00	5.00
18 Fergie Jenkins	1.25	3.00
19 Edd Roush	1.25	3.00
20 Honus Wagner	2.00	5.00
21 Richie Ashburn	1.25	3.00
22 Bob Feller	1.25	3.00
23 Joe Morgan	1.25	3.00
24 Orlando Cepeda	1.25	3.00
25 Steve Garvey	.75	2.00
26 Hank Greenberg	2.00	5.00
27 Stan Musial	3.00	8.00
28 Sam Crawford	1.25	3.00
29 Jim Rice	1.25	3.00
30 Hack Wilson	1.25	3.00
31 Lou Brock	1.25	3.00
32 Mickey Vernon	.75	2.00
33 Chuck Klein	.75	2.00
34 Tony Gwynn	2.00	5.00
35 Duke Snider	1.25	3.00
36 Ryne Sandberg	4.00	10.00
37 Johnny Bench	2.00	5.00
38 Sam Rice	1.25	3.00
30 Lou Gohrig	4.00	10.00
40 Robin Yount	2.00	5.00
41 Don Sutton	1.25	3.00
42 Jim Bottomley	.75	2.00
43 Billy Herman	.75	2.00
44 Zach Wheat	1.25	3.00
45 Juan Marichal	1.25	3.00
46 Bert Blyleven	1.25	3.00
47 Jackie Robinson	2.00	5.00
48 Gil Hodges	1.25	3.00
49 Mike Schmidt	3.00	8.00
50 Dale Murphy	2.00	5.00
51 Phil Rizzuto	1.25	3.00
52 Ty Cobb	3.00	8.00
53 Andre Dawson	1.25	3.00
54 Fred Lindstrom	.75	2.00
55 Roy Campanella	2.00	5.00
56 Don Larsen	.75	2.00
57 Harry Heilmann	1.25	3.00
58 Catfish Hunter	1.25	3.00
59 Frank Robinson	1.25	3.00
60 Bill Mazeroski	1.25	3.00
61 Roger Maris	2.00	5.00
62 Dave Winfield	1.25	3.00
63 Warren Spahn	1.25	3.00
64 Babe Ruth	5.00	12.00
65 Ernie Banks	2.00	5.00
66 Wade Boggs	1.25	3.00
67 Carl Yastrzemski	3.00	8.00
68 Ron Santo	1.25	3.00
69 Dennis Martinez	.75	2.00
70 Yogi Berra	2.00	5.00
71 Paul Waner	1.25	3.00
72 George Brett	4.00	10.00
73 Eddie Mathews	2.00	5.00
74 Bill Dickey	.75	2.00
75 Carlton Fisk	1.25	3.00
76 Thurman Munson	2.00	5.00
77 Reggie Jackson	1.25	3.00
78 Phil Niekro	1.25	3.00
79 Luis Aparicio	1.25	3.00
80 Steve Carlton	1.25	3.00
81 Tris Speaker	1.25	3.00
82 Johnny Mize	1.25	3.00
83 Tom Seaver	1.25	3.00
84 Heinie Manush	.75	2.00
85 Tommy John	.75	2.00
86 Joe Cronin	.75	2.00
87 Don Mattingly	4.00	10.00
88 Kirk Gibson	.75	2.00
89 Bo Jackson	2.00	5.00
90 Mel Ott	2.00	5.00

2002 Topps Tribute First Impressions

*1ST IMP p/r 50-100: .75X TO 2X
*1ST IMP p/r 36-48: 1X TO 2.5X
*1ST IMP p/r 26-31: 1.2X TO 3X
STATED ODDS 1:16
PRINT RUNS BASED ON PLAYER'S 1ST YR
NO PRICING ON QTY OF 25 OR LESS
FIRST IMPRESSIONS FEATURE BLUE FOIL

2002 Topps Tribute Lasting Impressions

*LAST IMP p/r 53-99: .75X TO 2X
*LAST IMP p/r 36-47: 1X TO 2.5X
*LAST IMP p/r 27-35: 1.2X TO 3X
STATED ODDS 1:13
PRINT RUNS BASED ON PLAYER'S LAST YR
NO PRICING ON QTY OF 25 OR LESS
LASTING IMPRESSIONS FEATURE RED FOIL

2002 Topps Tribute The Catch Dual Relic

STATED ODDS 1:1023
JSY NUMBER ODDS 1:3161
JSY NUMBER PRINT RUN 24 #'d CARDS
NO JSY NUM.PRICING DUE TO SCARCITY
*SEASON: .6X TO 1.2X BASIC DUAL RELIC
SEASON ODDS 1:1391
SEASON PRINT RUN 54 SERIAL #'d CARDS

Card	Low	High
MW Wertz Bat/Mays Glove	150.00	300.00

2002 Topps Tribute Marks of Excellence Autograph

STATED ODDS 1:61

Card	Low	High
DL Don Larsen	10.00	25.00
LB Lou Brock	15.00	40.00
MS Mike Schmidt	30.00	60.00
SC Steve Carlton	15.00	40.00
SM Stan Musial	40.00	80.00
WS Warren Spahn	15.00	40.00

2002 Topps Tribute Marks of Excellence Autograph Relics

STATED ODDS 1:61

Card	Low	High
BR Brooks Robinson Bat	30.00	80.00
DM Don Mattingly Jsy	30.00	80.00
DS Duke Snider Uni	12.00	30.00
FJ Fergie Jenkins Jsy	10.00	25.00
JP Jim Palmer Uni	20.00	50.00
RY Robin Yount Uni	30.00	80.00

2002 Topps Tribute Matching Marks Dual Relics

GROUP A ODDS 1:134
GROUP B ODDS 1:368
GROUP C ODDS 1:123
GROUP D ODDS 1:43
GROUP E ODDS 1:105
GROUP F ODDS 1:82
GROUP G ODDS 1:31
OVERALL STATED ODDS 1:11

Card	Low	High
AR Aaron Bat Ruth Bat A	250.00	400.00
BB Boggs Jsy/Brett Jsy C	20.00	50.00
BF Bench Bat/Fisk Bat A	30.00	60.00
BM V.Blue Jsy/D.Martinez Jsy G	6.00	15.00
BMA Brett Jsy/Mattingly Jsy A	75.00	150.00
BS Blyleven Jsy/Sutton Jsy C	8.00	20.00
GA G'berg Bat/Ashburn Bat A	60.00	120.00
GH Garvey Bat/Hodges Bat D	10.00	25.00
JS Jenkins Jsy/Seaver Jsy B	20.00	50.00
MA Mays Uni/Aaron Bat A	150.00	250.00
NS Niekro Uni/Seaver Uni G	6.00	15.00
PJ Palmer Jsy/John Jsy D	10.00	25.00
RJ F.Rob Uni/Reggie Bat A	30.00	60.00
RS Ryan Jsy/Seaver Jsy A	40.00	100.00
SB Speaker Bat/Brett Bat A	200.00	300.00
SBA Santo Bat/Banks Bat D	10.00	25.00
SM Snider Bat/Mays Uni A	50.00	100.00
SR Stargell Uni/Rice Uni E	8.00	20.00
WY Winfield Bat/Yaz Bat D	10.00	25.00
WYO Winfield Uni/Yount Uni F	8.00	20.00
YK Yastrzemski Bat/Klein Bat A	10.00	25.00
YP Yount Uni/Puckett Uni A	30.00	80.00

2002 Topps Tribute Memorable Materials

BAT GROUP A ODDS 1:11,592
BAT GROUP B ODDS 1:6
JSY/UNI GROUP A ODDS 1:246
JSY/UNI GROUP B ODDS 1:12

Card	Low	High
BJ Bo Jackson Jsy B	10.00	25.00
BM Bill Mazeroski Uni B	8.00	20.00
BT Bobby Thomson Bat B	8.00	20.00
CF Carlton Fisk Bat B	10.00	25.00
CK Chuck Klein Bat B	15.00	40.00
CY Carl Yastrzemski Uni B	8.00	20.00
DM Don Mattingly Jsy B	8.00	20.00
GB George Brett Jsy B	8.00	20.00
HA Hank Aaron Bat B	10.00	25.00
HW Hack Wilson Bat B	12.00	30.00
JC Joe Carter Bat B	8.00	20.00
JM Joe Morgan Bat B	8.00	20.00
JR Jackie Robinson Bat B	20.00	50.00
KG Kirk Gibson Bat B	8.00	20.00
KP Kirby Puckett Bat B	10.00	25.00
NR Nolan Ryan Jsy A	10.00	25.00
PR Phil Rizzuto Bat B	15.00	40.00
RC Roy Campanella Bat B	15.00	40.00
RJ Reggie Jackson Bat B	10.00	25.00
RM Roger Maris Bat B	15.00	40.00
TM Thurman Munson Bat B	20.00	50.00

2002 Topps Tribute Memorable Materials Jersey Number

BAT STATED ODDS 1:208
JSY/UNI STATED ODDS 1:644
PRINT RUNS BASED ON JERSEY NUMBER
NO PRICING ON QTY OF 40 OR LESS

Card	Low	High
HA Hank Aaron Bat/44	12.00	30.00
JR Jackie Robinson Bat/42	50.00	120.00
RJ Reggie Jackson Bat/44	25.00	60.00

2002 Topps Tribute Memorable Materials Season

BAT STATED ODDS 1:72
JSY/UNI STATED ODDS 1:152
PRINT RUNS BASED ON KEY SEASON
NO PRICING ON QTY OF 40 OR LESS

Card	Low	High
BJ Bo Jackson Jsy/89	10.00	25.00
BM Bill Mazeroski Uni/60	15.00	40.00
BT Bobby Thomson Bat/51	15.00	40.00
CF Carlton Fisk Bat/75	15.00	40.00
CY Carl Yastrzemski Uni/75 UER	12.50	30.00
DM Don Mattingly Jsy/87	10.00	25.00
GB George Brett Jsy/83	12.00	30.00
HA Hank Aaron Bat/74	12.00	30.00
JC Joe Carter Bat/93	12.00	30.00
JM Joe Morgan Bat/76	12.00	30.00
JR Jackie Robinson Bat/47	20.00	50.00
KG Kirk Gibson Bat/88	12.00	30.00
KP Kirby Puckett Bat/91	10.00	25.00
NR Nolan Ryan Jsy/91	30.00	80.00
PR Phil Rizzuto Bat/50	30.00	80.00
RC Roy Campanella Bat/55	30.00	80.00
RJ Reggie Jackson Bat/77	15.00	40.00
RM Roger Maris Bat/61	30.00	80.00
TM Thurman Munson Bat/76	30.00	80.00

2002 Topps Tribute Milestone Materials

BAT STATED ODDS 1:4
JSY/UNI STATED ODDS 1:5

Card	Low	High
AD Andre Dawson Jsy	6.00	15.00
BD Bill Dickey Uni	10.00	25.00
BF Bob Feller Bat	10.00	25.00
BG Bob Gibson Uni	8.00	20.00
BH Billy Herman Uni	6.00	15.00
BR Babe Ruth Bat	50.00	100.00
BRO Brooks Robinson Bat	10.00	25.00
CH Catfish Hunter Jsy	8.00	20.00
DM Dale Murphy Jsy	8.00	20.00
DS Duke Snider Uni	6.00	15.00
EB Ernie Banks Uni	10.00	25.00
EC Eddie Collins Bat	50.00	100.00
EM Eddie Mathews Jsy	10.00	25.00
ER Edd Roush Bat	20.00	50.00
FF Frankie Frisch Bat	10.00	25.00
FL Fred Lindstrom Uni	6.00	15.00
FR Frank Robinson Bat	10.00	25.00
HH Harry Heilmann Bat	12.00	30.00
HM Heinie Manush Bat	12.00	30.00
HW Honus Wagner Bat	40.00	80.00
JB Johnny Bench Jsy	10.00	25.00
JBO Jim Bottomley Bat	12.50	30.00
JC Joe Cronin Bat	10.00	25.00
JM Johnny Mize Uni	8.00	20.00
JMA Juan Marichal Jsy	6.00	15.00
JP Jim Palmer Uni	6.00	15.00
LA Luis Aparicio Bat	8.00	20.00
LG Lou Gehrig Bat	40.00	80.00
MO Mel Ott Bat	12.50	30.00
MV Mickey Vernon Bat	8.00	20.00
NF Nellie Fox Uni	10.00	25.00
NL Napoleon Lajoie Bat	50.00	100.00
NR Nolan Ryan Jsy	10.00	25.00
OC Orlando Cepeda Jsy	6.00	15.00
PW Paul Waner Bat	6.00	15.00
RH Rogers Hornsby Bat	15.00	40.00
RJ Reggie Jackson Jsy	8.00	20.00
RS Ryne Sandberg Bat	10.00	25.00
RY Robin Yount Uni	10.00	25.00
SC Sam Crawford Bat	10.00	25.00
SR Sam Rice Bat	15.00	40.00
TC Ty Cobb Bat	20.00	50.00
TS Tom Seaver Jsy	8.00	20.00
TSP Tris Speaker Bat	20.00	50.00
WB Wade Boggs Uni	8.00	20.00
WF Whitey Ford Uni	8.00	20.00
WM Willie Mays Uni	15.00	40.00
WS Willie Stargell Uni	8.00	20.00
YB Yogi Berra Jsy	10.00	25.00
ZW Zach Wheat Bat	15.00	40.00

2002 Topps Tribute Milestone Materials Jersey Number

BAT STATED ODDS 1:443
JSY/UNI STATED ODDS 1:148
PRINT RUNS BASED ON JERSEY NUMBER
NO PRICING ON QTY OF 40 OR LESS

Card	Low	High
BG Bob Gibson Uni/45	20.00	50.00
EM Eddie Mathews Jsy/41	25.00	60.00
RJ Reggie Jackson Jsy/44	20.00	50.00
TS Tom Seaver Jsy/41	20.00	50.00

2002 Topps Tribute Milestone Materials Season

BAT STATED ODDS 1:73
JSY/UNI STATED ODDS 1:41
PRINT RUNS BASED ON KEY SEASON
NO PRICING ON QTY OF 40 OR LESS

Card	Low	High
AD Andre Dawson Jsy/95	12.50	30.00
BD Bill Dickey Uni/46	25.00	60.00
BF Bob Feller Bat/54	25.00	60.00
BG Bob Gibson Uni/74	15.00	40.00
BH Billy Herman Uni/47	15.00	40.00
BRO Brooks Robinson Bat/74	20.00	50.00
CH Catfish Hunter Jsy/79	15.00	40.00
DM Dale Murphy Jsy/91	20.00	50.00
DS Duke Snider Uni/63	15.00	40.00
EB Ernie Banks Uni/70	20.00	50.00
EM Eddie Mathews Jsy/67	25.00	60.00
FR Frank Robinson Bat/71	20.00	50.00
JB Johnny Bench Jsy/80	20.00	50.00
JC Joe Cronin Bat/45	25.00	60.00
JM Johnny Mize Uni/50	20.00	50.00
JP Jim Palmer Uni/82	12.50	30.00
LA Luis Aparicio Bat/73	15.00	40.00
MO Mel Ott Bat/45	60.00	150.00
MV Mickey Vernon Bat/56	20.00	50.00
NF Nellie Fox Uni/41	40.00	100.00
NR Nolan Ryan Jsy/89	20.00	50.00
OC Orlando Cepeda Jsy/73	12.50	30.00
PW Paul Waner Bat/42	12.00	30.00
RJ Reggie Jackson Jsy/84	15.00	40.00
RS Ryne Sandberg Bat/93	20.00	50.00
RY Robin Yount Uni/92	15.00	40.00
TS Tom Seaver Jsy/81	15.00	40.00
WB Wade Boggs Uni/99	15.00	40.00
WF Whitey Ford Uni/62	20.00	50.00
WM Willie Mays Uni/69	12.50	30.00
WS Willie Stargell Uni/80	15.00	40.00
YB Yogi Berra Jsy/61	25.00	60.00

2002 Topps Tribute Pastime Patches

*LOGO PATCHES: 2.5X VALUE
GROUP A ODDS 1:184
GROUP B ODDS 1:184
OVERALL ODDS 1:92

Card	Low	High
BD Bill Dickey B	30.00	80.00
CY Carl Yastrzemski B	125.00	200.00
DM Don Mattingly A	75.00	150.00
DW Dave Winfield A	30.00	60.00
EM Eddie Mathews A	40.00	80.00
GB George Brett A	30.00	60.00
JB Johnny Bench B	75.00	150.00
JP Jim Palmer B	30.00	60.00
KP Kirby Puckett B	50.00	120.00
RY Robin Yount B	75.00	150.00
WB Wade Boggs B	75.00	150.00
NRR Nolan Ryan B	150.00	250.00

2009 Topps Tribute

Card	Low	High
COMPLETE SET (100)	100.00	200.00
COMMON CARD (1-100)	.60	1.50
COMMON RC (1-100)	1.00	2.50

PRINTING PLATE ODDS 1:91 HOBBY
PLATE PRINT RUN 1 SET PER COLOR
BLACK-CYAN-MAGENTA-YELLOW ISSUED
NO PLATE PRICING DUE TO SCARCITY

Card	Low	High
1 Babe Ruth	4.00	10.00
2 Christy Mathewson	1.50	4.00
3 Don Zimmer	.60	1.50
4 Nolan Ryan	5.00	12.00
5 Dennis Eckersley	1.00	2.50
6 Carl Yastrzemski	2.50	6.00
7 Mickey Mantle	5.00	12.00
8 Tony Perez	1.00	2.50
9 Cal Ripken Jr.	5.00	12.00
10 Derek Jeter	4.00	10.00
11 Wade Boggs	1.00	2.50
12 Tom Seaver	1.00	2.50
13 Willie McCovey	1.00	2.50
14 Walter Johnson	1.50	4.00
15 Steve Garvey	.60	1.50
16 George Sisler	1.00	2.50
17 Joe Morgan	1.00	2.50
18 Don Larson	.60	1.50
19 Reggie Jackson	1.00	2.50
20 Thurman Munson	1.50	4.00
21 Howard Johnson	.60	1.50
22 Johnny Bench	1.50	4.00
23 Bo Jackson	1.50	4.00
24 Ray Knight	.60	1.50
25 Cy Young	1.50	4.00
26 Bruce Sutter	1.00	2.50
27 Mike Schmidt	2.50	6.00
28 Roy Campanella	1.50	4.00
29 John Smoltz	1.50	4.00
30 Bob Gibson	1.00	2.50
31 Roy Halladay	1.00	2.50
32 Tris Speaker	1.00	2.50
33 Tony Gwynn	1.50	4.00
34 Whitey Ford	1.00	2.50
35 Carlos Beltran	1.00	2.50
36 Manny Ramirez	1.50	4.00
37 Frank Thomas	1.50	4.00
38 Honus Wagner	1.50	4.00
39 Josh Beckett	.60	1.50
40 Hanley Ramirez	1.00	2.50
41 Ty Cobb	2.50	6.00
42 Darryl Strawberry	.60	1.50
43 Stan Musial	2.50	6.00
44 Duke Snider	1.00	2.50
45 Rollie Fingers	1.00	2.50
46 Juan Marichal	1.00	2.50
47 Eddie Mathews	1.50	4.00
48 Paul Molitor	1.50	4.00
49 Pee Wee Reese	1.00	2.50
50 Ryan Howard	1.25	3.00
51 Johnny Podres	.60	1.50
52 Randy Johnson	1.50	4.00
53 Rogers Hornsby	1.00	2.50
54 Dwight Gooden	.60	1.50
55 Ryne Sandberg	3.00	8.00
56 Robin Yount	1.50	4.00
57 Greg Maddux	2.00	5.00
58 Jackie Robinson	1.50	4.00
59 Adrian Gonzalez	1.25	3.00
60 Jim Palmer	1.00	2.50
61 David Wright	1.25	3.00
62 Ernie Banks	1.50	4.00
63 Chipper Jones	1.50	4.00
64 Gary Carter	1.00	2.50
65 Aramis Ramirez	.60	1.50
66 Jimmie Foxx	1.50	4.00
67 Joe Mauer	1.25	3.00
68 Ozzie Smith	2.00	5.00
69 George Kell	1.00	2.50
70 Derrek Lee	.60	1.50
71 Hank Greenberg	1.50	4.00
72 Joey Votto	1.50	4.00
73 Mel Ott	1.50	4.00
74 Clayton Kershaw	2.50	6.00
75 Josh Hamilton	1.00	2.50
76 Tommy Hanson RC	2.50	6.00
77 Alex Rodriguez	2.00	5.00
78 Andre Dawson	1.00	2.50
79 Johnny Mize	1.00	2.50
80 Sal Bando	.60	1.50
81 Justin Morneau	1.00	2.50
82 Keith Hernandez	.60	1.50
83 Lou Gehrig	3.00	8.00
84 Dustin Pedroia	1.50	4.00
85 Mark Teixeira	1.00	2.50
86 Jay Bruce	1.00	2.50
87 Chase Utley	1.00	2.50
88 Lance Berkman	1.00	2.50
89 Frank Robinson	1.00	2.50
90 Matt LaPorta RC	1.50	4.00
91 Albert Pujols	2.00	5.00
92 Mike Piazza	1.50	4.00
93 Robin Roberts	1.00	2.50
94 Evan Longoria	1.00	2.50
95 Ryan Braun	1.00	2.50
96 Rick Porcello RC	3.00	8.00
97 CC Sabathia	1.00	2.50
98 Brooks Robinson	1.00	2.50
99 Ichiro Suzuki	2.00	5.00
100 Ken Griffey Jr.	3.00	8.00

2009 Topps Tribute Black

*BLACK: .75X TO 2X BASIC
*BLACK RC: .6X TO 1.5X BASIC RC
STATED ODDS 1:4 HOBBY
STATED PRINT RUN 99 SER.#'d SETS

2009 Topps Tribute Blue

*BLUE: .5X TO 1.2X BASIC
*BLUE RC: .5X TO 1.2X BASIC RC
RANDOM INSERTS IN PACKS
STATED PRINT RUN 219 SER.#'d SETS

2009 Topps Tribute Gold

*GOLD: 1.5X TO 4X BASIC
*GOLD RC: .75X TO 2X BASIC RC
STATED ODDS 1:8 HOBBY
STATED PRINT RUN 50 SER.#'d SETS

2009 Topps Tribute Autograph Relics

STATED ODDS 1:7 HOBBY
STATED PRINT RUN 99 SER.#'d SETS
ALL VARIATIONS PRICED EQUALLY

Card	Low	High
JH Josh Hamilton	20.00	50.00
JM Juan Marichal	10.00	25.00
TS Tom Seaver	20.00	50.00
AD1 Andre Dawson	12.50	30.00
AD2 Andre Dawson	12.50	30.00
CC1 Carl Crawford	6.00	15.00
CC2 Carl Crawford	6.00	15.00
CK1 Clayton Kershaw	30.00	60.00
CK2 Clayton Kershaw	30.00	60.00
CK3 Clayton Kershaw	30.00	60.00
CK4 Clayton Kershaw	50.00	100.00
DP1 Dustin Pedroia	15.00	40.00
DP2 Dustin Pedroia	15.00	40.00
DP3 Dustin Pedroia	15.00	40.00
DP4 Dustin Pedroia	15.00	40.00
DS1 Duke Snider	12.50	30.00
DS2 Duke Snider	12.50	30.00
DS3 Duke Snider	12.50	30.00
DS4 Duke Snider	12.50	30.00
DW1 David Wright	15.00	40.00
DW2 David Wright	15.00	40.00
DW3 David Wright	15.00	40.00
DW4 David Wright	15.00	40.00
EL1 Evan Longoria	20.00	50.00
EL2 Evan Longoria	20.00	50.00
EL3 Evan Longoria	20.00	50.00
EL4 Evan Longoria	20.00	50.00
GC1 Gary Carter	15.00	40.00
GC2 Gary Carter	15.00	40.00
GC3 Gary Carter	15.00	40.00
GC4 Gary Carter	15.00	40.00
JB1 Jay Bruce	8.00	20.00
JB2 Jay Bruce	8.00	20.00
JB3 Jay Bruce	8.00	20.00
JB4 Jay Bruce	8.00	20.00
JP1 Johnny Podres	8.00	20.00
JP2 Johnny Podres	8.00	20.00
KH1 Keith Hernandez	6.00	15.00
KH2 Keith Hernandez	6.00	15.00
KH3 Keith Hernandez	6.00	15.00
KH4 Keith Hernandez	6.00	15.00
ML1 Matt LaPorta	12.50	30.00
RB1 Ryan Braun	10.00	25.00
RB2 Ryan Braun	10.00	25.00
RB3 Ryan Braun	10.00	25.00
RB4 Ryan Braun	10.00	25.00
RP1 Rick Porcello	6.00	15.00
RP2 Rick Porcello	6.00	15.00
RP3 Rick Porcello	6.00	15.00
RP4 Rick Porcello	6.00	15.00
SB1 Sal Bando	8.00	20.00
SB2 Sal Bando	8.00	20.00
SB3 Sal Bando	8.00	20.00
SB4 Sal Bando	8.00	20.00
TH1 Tomnmy Hanson	6.00	15.00
TH2 Tomnmy Hanson	6.00	15.00

2009 Topps Tribute Autograph Relics Black

*BLACK: ..5X TO 1.2X BASIC
OVERALL ODDS 1:10 HOBBY
STATED PRINT RUN 50 SER.#'d SETS

2009 Topps Tribute Autograph Relics Blue

*BLUE: .4X TO 1X BASIC
OVERALL ODDS 1:7 HOBBY
STATED PRINT RUN 75 SER.#'d SETS

2009 Topps Tribute Autograph Dual Relics

STATED ODDS 1:21 HOBBY
STATED PRINT RUN 99 SER.#'d SETS
ALL VARIATIONS PRICED EQUALLY

Card	Low	High
AI Akinori Iwamura	6.00	15.00
AR Aramis Ramirez	6.00	15.00
BJ Bo Jackson	30.00	60.00
DG Dwight Gooden	10.00	25.00
DP Dustin Pedroia	20.00	50.00
DS Duke Snider	15.00	40.00
DS Darryl Strawberry	10.00	25.00
DW David Wright	10.00	25.00
EL Evan Longoria	12.50	30.00
GC Gary Carter	15.00	40.00
JB Jay Bruce	10.00	25.00
MC Melky Cabrera	6.00	15.00
PF Prince Fielder	15.00	40.00
RP Rick Porcello	6.00	15.00
DW2 David Wright	10.00	25.00
EL2 Evan Longoria	12.50	30.00
RC1 Robinson Cano	20.00	50.00
RC2 Robinson Cano	20.00	50.00

2009 Topps Tribute Autograph Dual Relics Black

*BLACK: ..5X TO 1.2X BASIC
OVERALL ODDS 1:10 HOBBY
STATED PRINT RUN 50 SER.#'d SETS

2009 Topps Tribute Autograph Dual Relics Blue

*BLUE: .4X TO 1X BASIC
OVERALL ODDS 1:7 HOBBY
STATED PRINT RUN 75 SER.#'d SETS

2009 Topps Tribute Autograph Triple Relics

STATED ODDS 1:75 HOBBY
STATED PRINT RUN 99 SER.#'d SETS

Card	Low	High
AP Albert Pujols	50.00	120.00
CJ Chipper Jones	30.00	60.00
DM Don Mattingly	30.00	60.00
DW David Wright	20.00	50.00
RH Ryan Howard	6.00	15.00

2009 Topps Tribute Autograph Triple Relics Black

*BLACK: ..5X TO 1.2X BASIC
OVERALL ODDS 1:10 HOBBY
STATED PRINT RUN 50 SER.#'d SETS

2009 Topps Tribute Autograph Triple Relics Blue

*BLUE: .4X TO 1X BASIC
OVERALL ODDS 1:7 HOBBY
STATED PRINT RUN 75 SER.#'d SETS

2009 Topps Tribute Relics

STATED ODDS 1:8 HOBBY
STATED PRINT RUN 99 SER.#'d SETS

Card	Low	High
1 Babe Ruth	60.00	120.00
4 Nolan Ryan	12.50	30.00
6 Carl Yastrzemski	5.00	12.00
7 Mickey Mantle	50.00	100.00
9 Cal Ripken Jr.	10.00	25.00
12 Tom Seaver	8.00	20.00
18 Don Larson	4.00	10.00
19 Reggie Jackson	6.00	15.00
20 Thurman Munson	8.00	20.00
22 Johnny Bench	5.00	12.00
23 Bo Jackson	8.00	20.00
27 Mike Schmidt	6.00	15.00
28 Roy Campanella	8.00	20.00
30 Bob Gibson	5.00	12.00
33 Tony Gwynn	5.00	12.00
34 Whitey Ford	8.00	20.00
36 Manny Ramirez	4.00	10.00
40 Hanley Ramirez	3.00	8.00
41 Ty Cobb	20.00	50.00
44 Duke Snider	5.00	12.00
46 Juan Marichal	3.00	8.00
47 Eddie Mathews	6.00	15.00
49 Pee Wee Reese	6.00	15.00
50 Ryan Howard	5.00	12.00
58 Jackie Robinson	20.00	50.00
61 David Wright	6.00	15.00
63 Chipper Jones	5.00	12.00
67 Joe Mauer	5.00	12.00
68 Ozzie Smith	5.00	12.00
72 Joey Votto	4.00	10.00
74 Clayton Kershaw	3.00	8.00
75 Josh Hamilton	4.00	10.00
76 Tommy Hanson	5.00	12.00
77 Alex Rodriguez	10.00	25.00
81 Justin Morneau	5.00	12.00
83 Lou Gehrig	60.00	120.00
84 Dustin Pedroia	4.00	10.00
85 Mark Teixeira	6.00	15.00
87 Chase Utley	5.00	12.00
88 Lance Berkman	3.00	8.00
91 Albert Pujols	6.00	15.00
92 Mike Piazza	6.00	15.00
94 Evan Longoria	5.00	12.00
95 Ryan Braun	4.00	10.00
96 Rick Porcello	3.00	8.00
97 CC Sabathia	3.00	8.00
99 Ichiro Suzuki	12.50	30.00

2009 Topps Tribute Relics Black

*BLACK: .5X TO 1.2X BASIC
STATED ODDS 1:11 HOBBY
STATED PRINT RUN 50 SER.#'d SETS

2009 Topps Tribute Relics Blue

*BLUE: .4X TO 1X BASIC
STATED ODDS 1:8 HOBBY
STATED PRINT RUN 75 SER.#'d SETS

2009 Topps Tribute Relics Dual

STATED ODDS 1:25 HOBBY
STATED PRINT RUN 99 SER.#'d SETS

Card	Low	High
1 Babe Ruth	75.00	150.00
9 Cal Ripken Jr.	12.50	30.00
19 Reggie Jackson	6.00	15.00
22 Johnny Bench	6.00	15.00
27 Mike Schmidt	10.00	25.00
33 Tony Gwynn	6.00	15.00
36 Manny Ramirez	5.00	12.00
41 Ty Cobb	40.00	80.00
44 Duke Snider	6.00	15.00
50 Ryan Howard	6.00	15.00
61 David Wright	6.00	15.00
76 Tommy Hanson	5.00	12.00
94 Evan Longoria	5.00	12.00
95 Ryan Braun	6.00	15.00
99 Ichiro Suzuki	12.50	30.00

2009 Topps Tribute Relics Dual Black

*BLACK: .5X TO 1.2X BASIC
STATED ODDS 1:11 HOBBY
STATED PRINT RUN 50 SER.#'d SETS

2009 Topps Tribute Relics Dual Blue

*BLUE: .4X TO 1X BASIC
STATED ODDS 1:8 HOBBY
STATED PRINT RUN 75 SER.#'d SETS

2009 Topps Tribute Relics Triple

STATED ODDS 1:75 HOBBY
STATED PRINT RUN 99 SER.#'d SETS

Card	Low	High
1 Babe Ruth	75.00	150.00
7 Mickey Mantle	60.00	120.00
58 Jackie Robinson	20.00	50.00
77 Alex Rodriguez	12.50	30.00
91 Albert Pujols	12.50	30.00

2009 Topps Tribute Relics Triple Black

*BLACK: .5X TO 1.2X BASIC
STATED ODDS 1:11 HOBBY
STATED PRINT RUN 50 SER.#'d SETS

2009 Topps Tribute Relics Triple Blue

*BLUE: .4X TO 1X BASIC
STATED ODDS 1:8 HOBBY
STATED PRINT RUN 75 SER.#'d SETS

2010 Topps Tribute

Card	Low	High
COMPLETE SET (100)	100.00	200.00
COMMON CARD (1-75)	.60	1.50
COMMON CARD (75-90)	.60	1.50
COMMON CARD (91-100)	.60	1.50

PRINTING PLATE ODDS 1:161 HOBBY

Card	Low	High
1 Babe Ruth	4.00	10.00
2 Walter Johnson	1.50	4.00
3 Ty Cobb	2.50	6.00
4 Tris Speaker	1.00	2.50
5 Thurman Munson	1.50	4.00
6 Roy Campanella	1.50	4.00
7 Rogers Hornsby	1.00	2.50
8 Orlando Cepeda	1.00	2.50
9 Jackie Robinson	1.50	4.00
10 Mel Ott	1.50	4.00
11 Johnny Mize	1.00	2.50
12 Jimmie Foxx	1.50	4.00
13 Honus Wagner	1.50	4.00
14 Pee Wee Reese	1.00	2.50
15 Christy Mathewson	1.50	4.00
16 Carlton Fisk	1.00	2.50
17 Yogi Berra	1.50	4.00
18 Lou Gehrig	3.00	8.00
19 Jim Bunning	1.00	2.50
20 Reggie Jackson	1.00	2.50
21 Tony Gwynn	1.50	4.00
22 Al Kaline	1.50	4.00
23 Roger Maris	1.50	4.00
24 Harmon Killebrew	1.50	4.00
25 Eddie Mathews	1.50	4.00
26 Willie McCovey	1.00	2.50
27 Joe Morgan	1.00	2.50
28 Eddie Murray	1.00	2.50
29 Jim Palmer	1.00	2.50
30 Tony Perez	1.00	2.50
31 Gaylord Perry	1.00	2.50
32 Phil Rizzuto	1.00	2.50
33 Robin Roberts	1.00	2.50
34 Brooks Robinson	1.00	2.50
35 Nolan Ryan	5.00	12.00
36 Ryne Sandberg	3.00	8.00
37 Mike Schmidt	2.50	6.00
38 Red Schoendienst	1.00	2.50
39 Tom Seaver	1.00	2.50
40 Ozzie Smith	2.00	5.00
41 Warren Spahn	1.00	2.50
42 Willie Stargell	1.00	2.50
43 Stan Musial	2.50	6.00
44 Cy Young	1.50	4.00
45 Bob Gibson	1.00	2.50
46 Dizzy Dean	1.00	2.50
47 Frank Robinson	1.00	2.50
48 Hank Greenberg	1.50	4.00
49 Johnny Bench	1.50	4.00
50 Mickey Mantle	5.00	12.00
51 Albert Pujols	2.00	5.00
52 Ichiro Suzuki	2.00	5.00
53 Alex Rodriguez	2.00	5.00
54 Prince Fielder	1.00	2.50
55 Joe Mauer	1.25	3.00
56 Tim Lincecum	1.00	2.50
57 Hanley Ramirez	1.00	2.50
58 Chase Utley	1.00	2.50
59 Roy Halladay	1.00	2.50
60 Adrian Gonzalez	1.25	3.00
61 Manny Ramirez	1.50	4.00
62 Chipper Jones	1.50	4.00
63 Grady Sizemore	1.00	2.50
64 Mariano Rivera	2.00	5.00
65 Miguel Cabrera	1.50	4.00
66 Johan Santana	1.00	2.50
67 Ryan Braun	1.00	2.50
68 Zack Greinke	1.50	4.00
69 Ryan Howard	1.25	3.00
70 Dustin Pedroia	1.50	4.00
71 Ian Kinsler	1.00	2.50
72 Evan Longoria	1.00	2.50
73 David Wright	1.25	3.00
74 Vladimir Guerrero	1.00	2.50
75 Derek Jeter	4.00	10.00
76 L.Gehrig T205	3.00	8.00
77 I.Suzuki T205	2.00	5.00
78 Jackie Robinson T205	1.50	4.00
79 Cy Young T205	1.50	4.00
80 D.Jeter T205	4.00	10.00
81 T.Cobb T205	2.50	6.00
82 M.Mantle T205	5.00	12.00
83 N.Ryan T205	5.00	12.00
84 Joe Mauer T205	1.25	3.00
85 Honus Wagner T205	1.50	4.00
86 Frank Robinson T205	1.00	2.50
87 A.Pujols T205	2.00	5.00
88 T.Lincecum T205	1.00	2.50
89 B.Ruth T205	4.00	10.00
90 Tom Seaver T205	1.00	2.50
91 Hatfields vs. McCoys	1.00	2.50
92 David vs. Goliath	1.00	2.50
93 Moby Dick vs. Captain Ahab	1.00	2.50
94 Billy the Kid vs. Pat Garrett	1.00	2.50
95 John F. Kennedy vs Richard Nixon	1.50	4.00
96 Obama vs McCain	2.00	5.00
97 Abraham Lincoln vs Jefferson Davis	1.50	4.00
98 Montagues vs Capulets	1.00	2.50
99 USA vs. Russia	1.00	2.50
100 Tortoise vs The Hare	1.00	2.50

2010 Topps Tribute Black

*BLACK: .75X TO 2X BASIC
STATED ODDS 1:7 HOBBY
STATED PRINT RUN 99 SER.#'d SETS

2010 Topps Tribute Black and White

*BW: .75X TO 2X BASIC
STATED ODDS 1:7 HOBBY
STATED PRINT RUN 99 SER.#'d SETS

2010 Topps Tribute Blue
*BLUE: .5X TO 1.2X BASIC
RANDOM INSERTS IN PACKS
STATED PRINT RUN 399 SER.#'d SETS

2010 Topps Tribute Gold
*GOLD: 1.2X TO 3X BASIC
STATED ODDS 1:13 HOBBY
STATED PRINT RUN 50 SER.#'d SETS

2010 Topps Tribute Red
STATED ODDS 1:656 HOBBY
STATED PRINT RUN 1 SER.#'d SET

2010 Topps Tribute Autograph Relics
STATED ODDS 1:35 HOBBY
STATED PRINT RUN 99 SER.#'d SETS
EXCH DEADLINE 7/31/2013
SAME PLAYER VERSIONS EQUALLY PRICED
AH Aaron Hill 5.00 12.00
AI Akinori Iwamura 5.00 12.00
AJ Adam Jones 5.00 12.00
BM Bengie Molina 6.00 15.00
BMC Brian McCann 6.00 15.00
CF Chone Figgins 5.00 12.00
CP Carlos Pena 8.00 20.00
CS Curt Schilling 12.50 30.00
JHE Jason Heyward 4.00 10.00
JL Jon Lester 8.00 20.00
MCA Miguel Cabrera 50.00 100.00
MK M.Kemp 10.00 25.00
ML Mat Latos 6.00 15.00
NM N.Markakis EXCH 8.00 20.00
OC Orlando Cabrera 5.00 12.00
PF Prince Fielder 12.50 30.00
RK Ralph Kiner 12.50 30.00
SS S.Strasburg 20.00 50.00
TH Tommy Hanson 8.00 20.00
TL Tony LaRussa 15.00 40.00
AD1 Andre Dawson 10.00 25.00
AD2 Andre Dawson 10.00 25.00
AD3 Andre Dawson 10.00 25.00
AD4 Andre Dawson 10.00 25.00
BC B.Cox Red jrsy 30.00 60.00
BC B.Cox White jrsy 30.00 60.00
BM2 Bengie Molina 6.00 15.00
CK1 Clayton Kershaw 30.00 60.00
CK2 Clayton Kershaw 30.00 60.00
CK3 Clayton Kershaw 30.00 60.00
CK4 Clayton Kershaw 30.00 60.00
CL1 Cliff Lee 8.00 20.00
CL2 Cliff Lee 8.00 20.00
CL3 Cliff Lee 8.00 20.00
CL4 Cliff Lee 8.00 20.00
DGO1 Dwight Gooden 8.00 20.00
DGO2 Dwight Gooden 8.00 20.00
DP1 Dustin Pedroia 15.00 40.00
DP2 Dustin Pedroia 15.00 40.00
DP3 Dustin Pedroia 15.00 40.00
DP4 Dustin Pedroia 15.00 40.00
DSN1 Duke Snider 12.50 30.00
DS1 Darryl Strawberry 6.00 15.00
DS2 Darryl Strawberry 6.00 15.00
DSN2 Duke Snider 12.50 30.00
DSN3 Duke Snider 12.50 30.00
GC1 Gary Carter 10.00 25.00
GC2 Gary Carter 10.00 25.00
GS1 Gary Sheffield 6.00 15.00
GS2 Gary Sheffield 6.00 15.00
GS3 Gary Sheffield 6.00 15.00
GS4 Gary Sheffield 6.00 15.00
JG1 Joe Girardi 12.50 30.00
JG2 Joe Girardi 12.50 30.00
JH1 Josh Hamilton 12.50 30.00
JH2 Josh Hamilton 12.50 30.00
JH3 Josh Hamilton 12.50 30.00
JH4 Josh Hamilton 12.50 30.00
MK2 Matt Kemp 10.00 25.00
MK3 Matt Kemp 10.00 25.00
MK4 Matt Kemp 10.00 25.00
MS1 Max Scherzer 20.00 50.00
MS2 Max Scherzer 20.00 50.00
MS3 Max Scherzer 20.00 50.00
MS4 Max Scherzer 20.00 50.00
NM2 Nick Markakis 8.00 20.00
NM3 Nick Markakis 8.00 20.00
NM4 Nick Markakis 8.00 20.00
OC2 Orlando Cabrera 5.00 12.00
PS1 Pablo Sandoval 10.00 25.00
PS2 Pablo Sandoval 10.00 25.00
PS3 Pablo Sandoval 10.00 25.00
PS4 Pablo Sandoval 10.00 25.00
RC1 Robinson Cano 12.50 30.00
RC2 Robinson Cano 12.50 30.00
RC3 Robinson Cano 12.50 30.00
RC4 Robinson Cano 12.50 30.00
RP1 Rick Porcello 6.00 15.00
RP2 Rick Porcello 6.00 15.00
RP3 Rick Porcello 6.00 15.00
RP4 Rick Porcello 6.00 15.00
RZ1 Ryan Zimmerman 10.00 25.00
RZ2 Ryan Zimmerman 10.00 25.00
RZ3 Ryan Zimmerman 10.00 25.00
RZ4 Ryan Zimmerman 10.00 25.00
ST1 Starlin Castro 12.50 30.00
ST2 Starlin Castre 12.50 30.00
ST3 Starlin Castro 12.50 30.00
ST4 Starlin Castro 12.50 30.00
TL2 Tony LaRussa 15.00 40.00
TT1 Troy Tulowitzki 10.00 25.00
TT2 Troy Tulowitzki 10.00 25.00
TT3 Troy Tulowitzki 10.00 25.00
TT4 Troy Tulowitzki 10.00 25.00
ADU1 Adam Dunn 8.00 20.00
ADU2 Adam Dunn 8.00 20.00
ADU3 Adam Dunn 8.00 20.00
ADU4 Adam Dunn 8.00 20.00
DGO3 Dwight Gooden 8.00 20.00
DSN4 Duke Snider 12.50 30.00

2010 Topps Tribute Autograph Relics Black
*BLACK: .5X TO 1.2X BASIC
STATED ODDS 1:11 HOBBY
STATED PRINT RUN 50 SER.#'d SETS
EXCH DEADLINE 7/31/2013

2010 Topps Tribute Autograph Relics Blue
*BLUE: .4X TO 1X BASIC
STATED ODDS 1:7 HOBBY
STATED PRINT RUN 75 SER.#'d SETS
EXCH DEADLINE 7/31/2013

2010 Topps Tribute Autograph Dual Relics
STATED ODDS 1:35 HOBBY
STATED PRINT RUN 99 SER.#'d SETS
EXCH DEADLINE 7/31/2013
AJ Adam Jones 10.00 25.00
DO David Ortiz 15.00 40.00
DW David Wright 10.00 25.00
EL Evan Longoria 8.00 20.00
GB Gordon Beckham 10.00 25.00
GC Gary Carter 20.00 50.00
GK George Kell 10.00 25.00
JH Josh Hamilton 10.00 25.00
JH Jason Heyward 40.00 80.00
JU Justin Upton 6.00 15.00
MH Matt Holliday 10.00 25.00
MK Matt Kemp 12.50 30.00
PF Prince Fielder 12.00 30.00
RB Ryan Braun 8.00 20.00
RP Rick Porcello 6.00 15.00
SS S.Strasburg 60.00 120.00
TH Tommy Hanson 6.00 15.00
TT Troy Tulowitzki 8.00 20.00
WM Willie McCovey 20.00 50.00

2010 Topps Tribute Autograph Dual Relics Black
*BLACK: .5X TO 1.2X BASIC
STATED ODDS 1:11 HOBBY
STATED PRINT RUN 50 SER.#'d SETS
EXCH DEADLINE 7/31/2013

2010 Topps Tribute Autograph Dual Relics Blue
*BLUE: .4X TO 1X BASIC
STATED ODDS 1:7 HOBBY
STATED PRINT RUN 75 SER.#'d SETS
EXCH DEADLINE 7/31/2013

2010 Topps Tribute Autograph Triple Relics
GROUP A ODDS 1:73 HOBBY
GROUP B ODDS 1:262 HOBBY
STATED PRINT RUN 99 SER.#'d SETS
EXCH DEADLINE 7/31/2013
AP Albert Pujols 75.00 150.00
AR Alex Rodriguez 100.00 200.00
CR Cal Ripken 50.00 100.00
DS Duke Snider 12.50 30.00
DW David Wright 12.00 30.00
EL Evan Longoria 15.00 40.00
HR Hanley Ramirez 8.00 20.00
MC Miguel Cabrera 50.00 100.00
MK Matt Kemp 10.00 25.00
MR Manny Ramirez 12.50 30.00
NM Nick Markakis 8.00 20.00
RC Robinson Cano 12.50 30.00
RC Rod Carew 15.00 40.00
RH Ryan Howard 12.00 30.00
VG Vladimir Guerrero 15.00 40.00

2010 Topps Tribute Autograph Triple Relics Black
*BLACK: .5X TO 1.2X BASIC
STATED ODDS 1:11 HOBBY
STATED PRINT RUN 50 SER.#'d SETS
EXCH DEADLINE 7/31/2013

2010 Topps Tribute Autograph Triple Relics Blue
*BLUE: .4X TO 1X BASIC
STATED ODDS 1:7 HOBBY
STATED PRINT RUN 75 SER.#'d SETS
EXCH DEADLINE 7/31/2013

2010 Topps Tribute Buyback Relics
STATED ODDS 1:167 HOBBY
PRINT RUNS B/WN 10-50 COPIES PER
AP Albert Pujols/50 15.00 40.00
BR Babe Ruth/35 50.00 100.00
HA Hank Aaron/45 20.00 50.00

2010 Topps Tribute Relics
STATED ODDS 1:7 HOBBY
STATED PRINT RUN 99 SER.#'d SETS
AD Adrian Gonzalez 4.00 10.00
AK Al Kaline 10.00 25.00
AP Albert Pujols 10.00 25.00
AR Alex Rodriguez 6.00 15.00
BD Bobby Doerr 8.00 20.00
BF Bob Feller 6.00 15.00
BG Bob Gibson 6.00 15.00
BL Bob Lemon 5.00 12.00
BM Bill Mazeroski 10.00 25.00
BR Brooks Robinson 6.00 15.00
BS Bruce Sutter 6.00 15.00
BW Billy Williams 4.00 10.00
CF Carlton Fisk 5.00 12.00
CH Catfish Hunter 4.00 10.00
CJ Chipper Jones 8.00 20.00
CS CC Sabathia 6.00 15.00
CU Chase Utley 5.00 12.00
CY Carl Yastrzemski 8.00 20.00
DE Dennis Eckersley 3.00 8.00
DJ Derek Jeter 10.00 25.00
DJ2 Derek Jeter 10.00 25.00
DJ3 Derek Jeter 10.00 25.00
DJ4 Derek Jeter 10.00 25.00
DS Don Sutton 4.00 10.00
DW David Wright 6.00 15.00
EB Ernie Banks 6.00 15.00
EL Evan Longoria 5.00 12.00
EM Eddie Mathews 12.50 30.00
ES Enos Slaughter 8.00 20.00
EW Early Wynn 6.00 15.00
FJ Fergie Jenkins 4.00 10.00
FR Frank Robinson 4.00 10.00
GC Gary Carter 4.00 10.00
GK George Kell 4.00 10.00
GP Gaylord Perry 3.00 8.00
HG Hank Greenberg 10.00 25.00
HK Harmon Killebrew 8.00 20.00
HN Hal Newhouser 4.00 10.00
HR Hanley Ramirez 3.00 8.00
HW Hoyt Wilhelm 5.00 12.00
IS Ichiro Suzuki 12.50 30.00
JB Johnny Bench 8.00 20.00
JF Jimmie Foxx 12.50 30.00
JM Juan Marichal 4.00 10.00
JR Jackie Robinson 12.50 30.00
LA Luis Aparicio 4.00 10.00
LG Lou Gehrig 40.00 80.00
MC Miguel Cabrera 5.00 12.00
MI Monte Irvin 6.00 15.00
MM Mickey Mantle 30.00 60.00
MO Mel Ott 10.00 25.00
MR Mariano Rivera 8.00 20.00
MS Mike Schmidt 12.50 30.00
MT Mark Teixeira 6.00 15.00
NR Nolan Ryan 10.00 25.00
OC Orlando Cepeda 3.00 8.00
OS Ozzie Smith 6.00 15.00
PF Prince Fielder 4.00 10.00
PM Paul Molitor 5.00 12.00
PN Phil Niekro 3.00 8.00
PR Phil Rizzuto 6.00 15.00
RA Richie Ashburn 8.00 20.00
RB Ryan Braun 4.00 10.00
RC Rod Carew 4.00 10.00
RF Rick Ferrell 8.00 20.00
RH Rogers Hornsby 8.00 20.00
RJ Reggie Jackson 8.00 20.00
RK Ralph Kiner 6.00 15.00
RM Roger Maris 12.50 30.00
RR Robin Roberts 8.00 20.00
RS Ryne Sandberg 6.00 15.00
RY Robin Yount 8.00 20.00
SC Steve Carlton 6.00 15.00
SM Stan Musial 8.00 20.00
TC Ty Cobb 30.00 60.00
TG Tony Gwynn 6.00 15.00
TL Tim Lincecum 8.00 20.00
TM Thurman Munson 12.50 30.00
TP Tony Perez 4.00 10.00
TS Tom Seaver 6.00 15.00
VG Vladimir Guerrero 4.00 10.00
WM Willie McCovey 5.00 12.00
WS Warren Spahn 8.00 20.00
BRU Babe Ruth 60.00 120.00
EMU Eddie Murray 4.00 10.00
HWA Honus Wagner 40.00 80.00
JBU Jim Bunning 4.00 10.00
JMA Joe Mauer 6.00 15.00
JMI Johnny Mize 6.00 15.00
JMO Joe Morgan 4.00 10.00
JPI Jimmy Piersall 8.00 20.00
LBR Lou Brock 6.00 15.00
MRA Manny Ramirez 5.00 12.00
RCA Roy Campanella 8.00 20.00
RFI Rollie Fingers 3.00 8.00
RHO Ryan Howard 6.00 15.00
RSC Red Schoendienst 4.00 10.00
TSP Tris Speaker 15.00 40.00
WST Willie Stargell 8.00 20.00

2010 Topps Tribute Relics Black
*BLACK: .5X TO 1.2X BASIC
STATED ODDS 1:10 HOBBY
STATED PRINT RUN 50 SER.#'d SETS

2010 Topps Tribute Relics Blue
*BLUE: .4X TO 1X BASIC
STATED ODDS 1:7 HOBBY
STATED PRINT RUN 75 SER.#'d SETS

2010 Topps Tribute Relics Dual
STATED ODDS 1:7 HOBBY
STATED PRINT RUN 99 SER.#'d SETS
AR Alex Rodriguez 10.00 25.00
CF Carlton Fisk 6.00 15.00
CS CC Sabathia 5.00 12.00
DJ Derek Jeter 12.50 30.00
DP Dustin Pedroia 6.00 15.00
DW David Wright 8.00 20.00
JB Johnny Bench 6.00 15.00
JE Jacoby Ellsbury 10.00 25.00
JP Jorge Posada 5.00 12.00
KY Kevin Youkilis 5.00 12.00
MR Mariano Rivera 8.00 20.00
MS Mike Schmidt 10.00 25.00
MT Mark Teixeira 6.00 15.00
NR Nolan Ryan 10.00 25.00
OS Ozzie Smith 6.00 15.00
RA Richie Ashburn 10.00 25.00
RB Ryan Braun 4.00 10.00
RH Ryan Howard 6.00 15.00
TG Tony Gwynn 4.00 10.00
VM Victor Martinez 4.00 10.00

2010 Topps Tribute Relics Dual Black
*BLACK: .5X TO 1.2X BASIC
STATED ODDS 1:10 HOBBY
STATED PRINT RUN 50 SER.#'d SETS

2010 Topps Tribute Relics Dual Blue
*BLUE: .4X TO 1X BASIC
STATED ODDS 1:7 HOBBY
STATED PRINT RUN 75 SER.#'d SETS

2010 Topps Tribute Relics Triple
STATED ODDS 1:7 HOBBY
STATED PRINT RUN 99 SER.#'d SETS
CR Cal Ripken 10.00 25.00
DJ Derek Jeter 15.00 40.00
JM Justin Morneau 5.00 12.00
PM Paul Molitor 5.00 12.00
RA Richie Ashburn 12.50 30.00
RG Reggie Jackson 4.00 10.00
RP Rick Porcello 4.00 10.00
RY Robin Yount 8.00 20.00
TG Tony Gwynn 5.00 12.00
TM Thurman Munson 12.50 30.00

2010 Topps Tribute Relics Triple Black
*BLACK: .5X TO 1.2X BASIC
STATED ODDS 1:10 HOBBY
STATED PRINT RUN 50 SER.#'d SETS

2010 Topps Tribute Relics Triple Blue
*BLUE: .4X TO 1X BASIC
STATED ODDS 1:7 HOBBY
STATED PRINT RUN 75 SER.#'d SETS

2011 Topps Tribute

COMPLETE SET (100) 150.00 250.00
COMMON CARD (1-100) .60 1.50
PLATES RANDOMLY INSERTED
PLATE PRINT RUN 1 SET PER COLOR
BLACK-CYAN-MAGENTA-YELLOW ISSUED
NO PLATE PRICING DUE TO SCARCITY
1 Babe Ruth 4.00 10.00
2 Cy Young 1.50 4.00
3 Joe Mauer 1.25 3.00
4 Honus Wagner 1.50 4.00
5 Justin Morneau 1.00 2.50
6 Nolan Ryan 5.00 12.00
7 David Wright 1.25 3.00
8 Evan Longoria 1.00 2.50
9 Troy Tulowitzki 1.50 4.00
10 Mark Teixeira 1.00 2.50
11 Stan Musial 2.50 6.00
12 Sandy Koufax 3.00 8.00
13 Ryan Howard 1.25 3.00
14 Joey Votto 1.50 4.00
15 Carlos Gonzalez 1.00 2.50
16 Roy Halladay 1.00 2.50
17 Brooks Robinson 1.00 2.50
18 Hoyt Wilhelm 1.00 2.50
19 Walter Johnson 1.50 4.00
20 Eddie Murray 1.00 2.50
21 Stephen Strasburg 1.50 4.00
22 Lou Gehrig 3.00 8.00
23 Derek Jeter 4.00 10.00
24 Rod Carew 1.00 2.50
25 Felix Hernandez 1.00 2.50
26 Robin Yount 1.50 4.00
27 Jason Heyward 1.25 3.00
28 Hanley Ramirez 1.00 2.50
29 Fergie Jenkins 1.00 2.50
30 Mickey Mantle 5.00 12.00
31 Josh Hamilton 1.00 2.50
32 Al Kaline 1.50 4.00
33 Hank Greenberg 1.50 4.00
34 Miguel Cabrera 1.50 4.00
35 Jackie Robinson 1.50 4.00
36 Cal Ripken Jr. 5.00 12.00
37 Bob Feller 1.00 2.50
38 Ryne Sandberg 3.00 8.00
39 Dizzy Dean 1.00 2.50
40 Catfish Hunter 1.00 2.50
41 Harmon Killebrew 1.50 4.00
42 Goose Gossage 1.00 2.50
43 Bill Mazeroski 1.00 2.50
44 Bob Gibson 1.00 2.50
45 Johnny Mize 1.00 2.50
46 Tom Seaver 1.00 2.50
47 Jim Bunning 1.00 2.50
48 CC Sabathia 1.00 2.50
49 Rogers Hornsby 1.00 2.50
50 Adam Wainwright 1.00 2.50
51 Thurman Munson 1.50 4.00
52 Albert Pujols 2.00 5.00
53 Willie Stargell 1.00 2.50
54 Tony Gwynn 1.50 4.00
55 Whitey Ford 1.00 2.50
56 Pee Wee Reese 1.00 2.50
57 Frank Robinson 1.00 2.50
58 Roy Campanella 1.50 4.00
59 Robin Roberts 1.00 2.50
60 George Sisler 1.00 2.50
61 Alex Rodriguez 2.00 5.00
62 Ozzie Smith 2.00 5.00
63 Jered Weaver 1.00 2.50
64 Lou Brock 1.00 2.50
65 Bobby Doerr 1.00 2.50
66 Josh Johnson 1.00 2.50
67 David Ortiz 1.50 4.00
68 Johan Santana 1.00 2.50
69 Buster Posey 2.00 5.00
70 Ubaldo Jimenez .60 1.50
71 Duke Snider 1.00 2.50
72 Josh Beckett .60 1.50
73 Vladimir Guerrero 1.00 2.50
74 Justin Verlander 1.50 4.00
75 Mike Schmidt 2.50 6.00
76 Chipper Jones 1.50 4.00
77 Jim Palmer 1.00 2.50
78 Ryan Braun 1.00 2.50
79 Tim Lincecum 1.00 2.50
80 Vernon Wells .60 1.50
81 Joe Morgan 1.00 2.50
82 David Price 1.25 3.00
83 Jon Lester 1.00 2.50
84 Reggie Jackson 1.00 2.50
85 Christy Mathewson 1.50 4.00
86 Prince Fielder 1.00 2.50
87 Johnny Bench 1.50 4.00
88 Tris Speaker 1.00 2.50
89 Juan Marichal 1.00 2.50
90 Ichiro Suzuki 2.00 5.00
91 Warren Spahn 1.00 2.50
92 Yogi Berra 1.50 4.00
93 Willie McCovey 1.00 2.50
94 Cliff Lee 1.00 2.50
95 Mel Ott 1.50 4.00
96 Ty Cobb 2.50 6.00
97 Rollie Fingers 1.00 2.50
98 Chase Utley 1.00 2.50
99 Early Wynn .60 1.50
100 Hank Aaron 3.00 8.00

2011 Topps Tribute Blue
*BLUE: .6X TO 1.5X BASIC
RANDOM INSERTS IN PACKS
STATED PRINT RUN 199 SER.#'d SETS

2011 Topps Tribute Gold
*GOLD: 1.5X TO 4X BASIC
STATED ODDS 1:7 HOBBY
STATED PRINT RUN 50 SER.#'d SETS

2011 Topps Tribute Green
*GREEN: 1X TO 2.5X BASIC
STATED ODDS 1:5 HOBBY
STATED PRINT RUN 75 SER.#'d SETS

2011 Topps Tribute Autograph Dual Relics
STATED ODDS 1:23 HOBBY
STATED PRINT RUN 99 SER.#'d SETS
EXCHANGE DEADLINE 3/31/2014
BP Buster Posey 50.00 100.00
BR Brooks Robinson 15.00 40.00
CB Clay Buchholz 10.00 25.00
DW David Wright 15.00 40.00
EB Ernie Banks 30.00 60.00
EL Evan Longoria 8.00 20.00
FR Frank Robinson 15.00 40.00
JR Jim Rice 10.00 25.00
MM Mike Mussina 8.00 20.00
NG Nomar Garciaparra 30.00 60.00
RH Ryan Howard 12.00 30.00
RS Ryne Sandberg 30.00 60.00
WF Whitey Ford 30.00 60.00
WM Willie McCovey 20.00 50.00
YB Yogi Berra EXCH 25.00 60.00

2011 Topps Tribute Autograph Dual Relics Green
*GREEN: .4X TO 1X BASIC
STATED ODDS 1:6 HOBBY
STATED PRINT RUN 75 SER.#'d SETS
EXCHANGE DEADLINE 3/31/2014

2011 Topps Tribute Autograph Relics
STATED ODDS 1:6 HOBBY
RC AU RELIC ODDS 1:110 HOBBY
STATED PRINT RUN 99 SER.#'d SETS
EXCHANGE DEADLINE 3/31/2014
AB Albert Belle 10.00 25.00
AC Aroldis Chapman 10.00 25.00
AK Al Kaline 25.00 50.00
BL Barry Larkin 20.00 50.00
BP Buster Posey 40.00 80.00
BW Bernie Williams 25.00 60.00
CR Cal Ripken Jr. 40.00 80.00
CS Curt Schilling 15.00 40.00
CU Chase Utley 15.00 40.00
CY Carl Yastrzemski 30.00 80.00
DC David Cone 6.00 15.00
DE Dennis Eckersley 10.00 25.00
DM Don Mattingly 30.00 60.00
DW Dave Winfield 12.50 30.00
EB Ernie Banks 30.00 60.00
FF Freddie Freeman 10.00 25.00
FT Frank Thomas 30.00 60.00
HR Hanley Ramirez 10.00 25.00
JH Josh Hamilton 6.00 15.00
JM Joe Morgan 12.50 30.00
JR Jim Rice 10.00 25.00
JS John Smoltz 15.00 40.00
MI Monte Irvin EXCH 10.00 25.00
MR Manny Ramirez 20.00 50.00
PO Paul O'Neill 15.00 40.00
RA Roberto Alomar 10.00 25.00
RB Ryan Braun 8.00 20.00
RC Robinson Cano 20.00 50.00
RG Ron Guidry 10.00 25.00
SK Sandy Koufax 125.00 250.00
TG Tony Gwynn 15.00 40.00
AB2 Albert Belle 6.00 15.00
AD1 Andre Dawson 10.00 25.00
BP2 Buster Posey 40.00 80.00
CBU Clay Buchholz 10.00 25.00
CBU2 Clay Buchholz 6.00 15.00
DM1 Dale Murphy 12.50 30.00
DS1 Duke Snider 8.00 20.00
DS2 Duke Snider 8.00 20.00
DW1 David Wright 20.00 50.00
DW2 David Wright 10.00 25.00
FJ1 Fergie Jenkins 10.00 25.00
GC1 Gary Carter 15.00 40.00
JHE Jason Heyward 10.00 25.00
JHEL Jeremy Hellickson 10.00 25.00
JMA Juan Marichal 10.00 25.00
JS2 John Smoltz 15.00 40.00
MMC Mike Mussina 12.50 30.00
MS1 Mike Stanton 20.00 50.00
MS2 Mike Stanton 20.00 50.00
OC1 Orlando Cepeda 10.00 25.00
OC2 Orlando Cepeda 10.00 25.00
PO2 Paul O'Neill 10.00 25.00
RA2 Roberto Alomar 10.00 25.00
RA3 Roberto Alomar 10.00 25.00
RG2 Ron Guidry 10.00 25.00
RH1 Ryan Howard 6.00 15.00
RH2 Ryan Howard 10.00 25.00
RK1 Ralph Kiner 12.00 30.00
RK2 Ralph Kiner 10.00 25.00
TP1 Tony Perez 15.00 40.00
YA1 Yonder Alonso 10.00 25.00
YA2 Yonder Alonso 10.00 25.00

2011 Topps Tribute Autograph Relics Green
*GREEN: .4X TO 1X BASIC
STATED ODDS 1:6 HOBBY
RC AU RELIC ODDS 1:145 HOBBY
STATED PRINT RUN 75 SER.#'d SETS
EXCHANGE DEADLINE 3/31/2014

2011 Topps Tribute Autograph Triple Relics
STATED ODDS 1:34 HOBBY
STATED PRINT RUN 99 SER.#'d SETS
EXCHANGE DEADLINE 3/31/2014
AP Albert Pujols 75.00 150.00
AR Alex Rodriguez 40.00 100.00
HA Hank Aaron 100.00 200.00
MR Mariano Rivera 100.00 200.00
NR Nolan Ryan 40.00 80.00
OS Ozzie Smith 30.00 60.00
RH Ryan Howard 10.00 25.00
RJ Reggie Jackson 40.00 80.00
TS Tom Seaver 25.00 60.00
CCS CC Sabathia 6.00 15.00

2011 Topps Tribute Autograph Triple Relics Green
*GREEN: .4X TO 1X BASIC
STATED ODDS 1:6 HOBBY
STATED PRINT RUN 75 SER.#'d SETS
EXCHANGE DEADLINE 3/31/2014

2011 Topps Tribute Dual Relics
STATED ODDS 1:7 HOBBY
STATED PRINT RUN 99 SER.#'d SETS
AB Albert Belle 4.00 10.00
AD Andre Dawson 4.00 10.00
AK Al Kaline 10.00 25.00
BD Bobby Doerr 6.00 15.00
BR Babe Ruth 75.00 150.00
CF Carlton Fisk 8.00 20.00
CR Cal Ripken Jr. 12.50 30.00
CY Carl Yastrzemski 10.00 25.00
DM Don Mattingly 12.50 30.00
DW Dave Winfield 5.00 12.00
EM Eddie Mathews 5.00 12.00
FR Frank Robinson 5.00 12.00
FT Frank Thomas 10.00 25.00
GS George Sisler 10.00 25.00
HA Hank Aaron 12.50 30.00
HG Hank Greenberg 10.00 25.00
HK Harmon Killebrew 10.00 25.00
HW Honus Wagner 50.00 100.00
JB Johnny Bench 8.00 20.00
JF Jimmie Foxx 10.00 25.00
JM Johnny Mize 8.00 20.00
JP Jim Palmer EXCH 8.00 20.00
JR Jackie Robinson 20.00 50.00
JS John Smoltz 5.00 12.00
LG Lou Gehrig 60.00 120.00
MM Mickey Mantle 50.00 100.00
MP Mike Piazza 6.00 15.00
MS Mike Schmidt 8.00 20.00
NR Nolan Ryan 15.00 40.00
OC Orlando Cepeda 8.00 20.00
OS Ozzie Smith 8.00 20.00
PR Phil Rizzuto 6.00 15.00
RA Roberto Alomar 8.00 20.00
RC Roy Campanella 8.00 20.00
RH Rogers Hornsby 12.50 30.00
RJ Reggie Jackson 8.00 20.00
RM Roger Maris 15.00 40.00
RR Robin Roberts EXCH 10.00 25.00
RS Ryne Sandberg 10.00 25.00
RY Robin Yount 6.00 15.00
SK Sandy Koufax 25.00 60.00
SM Stan Musial 20.00 50.00
TC Ty Cobb 30.00 60.00
TG Tony Gwynn 6.00 15.00
TM Thurman Munson 12.50 30.00
TP Tony Perez 4.00 10.00
TS Tris Speaker 12.50 30.00
WF Whitey Ford 5.00 12.00
WS Warren Spahn 5.00 12.00
YB Yogi Berra 10.00 25.00
BRO Brooks Robinson 10.00 25.00
DMU Dale Murphy 6.00 15.00
EMU Eddie Murray 5.00 12.00
RCA Rod Carew 6.00 15.00
TSE Tom Seaver 6.00 15.00
WST Willie Stargell 10.00 25.00

2011 Topps Tribute Dual Relics Green
*GREEN: .4X TO 1X BASIC
STATED ODDS 1:5 HOBBY
STATED PRINT RUN 75 SER.#'d SETS

2011 Topps Tribute Quad Relics
STATED ODDS 1:34 HOBBY
STATED PRINT RUN 99 SER.#'d SETS
AR Alex Rodriguez 10.00 25.00
BG Bob Gibson 8.00 20.00
DJ Derek Jeter 12.50 30.00
IS Ichiro Suzuki 20.00 50.00
JV Joey Votto 10.00 25.00
MO Mel Ott 12.50 30.00
NR Nolan Ryan 20.00 50.00
RH Roy Halladay 15.00 40.00
RH Ryan Howard 10.00 25.00
SS Stephen Strasburg 20.00 50.00

2011 Topps Tribute Quad Relics Green
*GREEN: .4X TO 1X BASIC
STATED ODDS 1:5 HOBBY
STATED PRINT RUN 75 SER.#'d SETS

2011 Topps Tribute Tribute to the Stars Dual Autographs
STATED ODDS 1:38 HOBBY
STATED PRINT RUN 74 SER.#'d SETS
DR A.Dawson/J.Rice 15.00 40.00
DS A.Dawson/R.Sandberg 50.00 100.00
GC D.Gooden/G.Carter 20.00 50.00
HU R.Howard/C.Utley 60.00 120.00
KZ G.Kell/R.Zimmerman 12.00 30.00
LH N.Cruz/J.Hamilton 30.00 60.00
MH D.Murphy/J.Heyward 20.00 50.00
MP B.Matusz/J.Palmer 12.50 30.00
PM A.Pujols/S.Musial 250.00 500.00
PS J.Podres/D.Snider 15.00 40.00
PSA B.Posey/C.Santana 30.00 60.00
SG D.Strawberry/D.Gooden 20.00 50.00

2011 Topps Tribute Tribute to the Stars Triple Autographs
STATED ODDS 1:124 HOBBY
STATED PRINT RUN 24 SER.#'d SETS
SRC Ozzie/Hanley/Starlin 30.00 80.00
FFM Podres/Ford/Marichal 60.00 150.00
HCR Hughes/Cano/Rivera 60.00 150.00
JDS Jenkins/Dawson/Sandberg 30.00 80.00
PKL Price/Kershaw/Lester 40.00 100.00
PSM Posey/Santana/McCann 40.00 100.00
PSN Podres/Snider/Newcombe 20.00 50.00
SBH Stanton/Brown/Heyward 40.00 100.00
SGH Strawberry/Gooden/Carter 40.00 100.00
UHV Utley/Howard/Victorino 60.00 150.00
WAB Wells/Alomar/Bautista 30.00 80.00
YMB Yount/Molitor/Braun 75.00 200.00

2011 Topps Tribute Triple Relics
STATED ODDS 1:23 HOBBY
STATED PRINT RUN 99 SER.#'d SETS
AB Albert Belle 5.00 12.00
AP Albert Pujols 12.50 30.00
CR Cal Ripken Jr. 20.00 50.00
DJ Derek Jeter 10.00 25.00
DM Don Mattingly 10.00 25.00
DW Dave Winfield 6.00 15.00
HA Hank Aaron 20.00 50.00
HK Harmon Killebrew 12.50 30.00
JB Johnny Bench 10.00 25.00
JS John Smoltz 6.00 15.00
LG Lou Gehrig 75.00 150.00
MR Mariano Rivera 10.00 25.00
RS Ryne Sandberg 10.00 25.00
TG Tony Gwynn 10.00 25.00
TS Tom Seaver 8.00 20.00

2011 Topps Tribute Triple Relics Green
*GREEN: .4X TO 1X BASIC
STATED ODDS 1:5 HOBBY
STATED PRINT RUN 75 SER.#'d SETS

2012 Topps Tribute
COMPLETE SET (100) 75.00 150.00
COMMON CARD .40 1.00
PLATES RANDOMLY INSERTED
PLATE PRINT RUN 1 SET PER COLOR
BLACK-CYAN-MAGENTA-YELLOW ISSUED
NO PLATE PRICING DUE TO SCARCITY
1 Hank Aaron 2.00 5.00
2 Luis Aparicio .60 1.50
3 Jose Bautista .75 2.00
4 Albert Belle .40 1.00
5 Johnny Bench 1.00 2.50
6 Lance Berkman .75 2.00
7 Ryan Braun .60 1.50
8 Ralph Kiner .60 1.50
9 Miguel Cabrera 1.00 2.50
10 Robinson Cano .75 2.00
11 Starlin Castro .75 2.00
12 Eddie Mathews 1.00 2.50
13 Ty Cobb 1.50 4.00
14 Yogi Berra 1.00 2.50
15 Andre Dawson .60 1.50
16 Joe DiMaggio 2.00 5.00
17 Duke Snider .60 1.50
18 Prince Fielder .75 2.00
19 Carlton Fisk .60 1.50
20 Orlando Cepeda .60 1.50
21 Yovani Gallardo .75 2.00
22 Lou Gehrig 2.00 5.00
23 Bob Gibson .60 1.50
24 Adrian Gonzalez .75 2.00
25 Carlos Gonzalez .75 2.00
26 Rollie Fingers .60 1.50
27 Roy Halladay .75 2.00
28 Josh Hamilton .75 2.00
29 Juan Marichal .60 1.50
30 Felix Hernandez .75 2.00
31 Mike Napoli .60 1.50
32 Matt Holliday 1.00 2.50
33 Ryan Howard .75 2.00
34 Reggie Jackson .60 1.50
35 Derek Jeter 2.50 6.00
36 Larry Doby .60 1.50
37 Al Kaline 1.00 2.50
38 Matt Kemp .75 2.00
39 Ian Kennedy .60 1.50
40 Clayton Kershaw 1.50 4.00
41 Ian Kinsler .75 2.00
42 Sandy Koufax 2.00 5.00
43 Harmon Killebrew 1.00 2.50
44 Cliff Lee .75 2.00
45 Nelson Cruz 1.00 2.50
46 Tim Lincecum .75 2.00
47 Evan Longoria .75 2.00
48 Mickey Mantle 3.00 8.00
49 Roger Maris 1.00 2.50
50 Edgar Martinez .60 1.50
51 Joe Mauer .75 2.00
52 Willie Mays 2.00 5.00
53 Willie McCovey .60 1.50
54 Michael Young .60 1.50
55 Paul Molitor 1.00 2.50
56 Wade Boggs .60 1.50
57 Stan Musial 1.50 4.00
58 Paul O'Neill .60 1.50
59 Dustin Pedroia 1.00 2.50
60 Andy Pettitte .75 2.00
61 Buster Posey 1.25 3.00
62 Albert Pujols 1.25 3.00
63 Tony Gwynn 1.00 2.50
64 Hanley Ramirez .75 2.00
65 Ken Griffey Jr. 2.00 5.00
66 Cal Ripken Jr. 3.00 8.00
67 Mariano Rivera 1.25 3.00
68 Brooks Robinson .60 1.50
69 Frank Robinson .60 1.50
70 Alex Rodriguez 1.25 3.00
71 Nolan Ryan 5.00 12.00
72 CC Sabathia .75 2.00
73 Ryne Sandberg 2.00 5.00
74 David Freese .60 1.50
75 Mike Schmidt 1.50 4.00
76 Red Schoendienst .60 1.50
77 Tom Seaver .60 1.50
78 John Smoltz 1.00 2.50
79 Mike Stanton 1.00 2.50
80 Mark Teixeira .75 2.00
81 Frank Thomas 1.00 2.50
82 Troy Tulowitzki 1.00 2.50
83 Justin Upton .75 2.00
84 Chase Utley .75 2.00
85 Justin Verlander 1.00 2.50
86 Joey Votto 1.00 2.50
87 Jered Weaver .75 2.00
88 Eddie Murray .60 1.50
89 Jacoby Ellsbury .75 2.00
90 Ryan Zimmerman .75 2.00
91 Roberto Clemente 2.50 6.00
92 Jackie Robinson 1.00 2.50
93 Babe Ruth 2.50 6.00
94 Ernie Banks 1.00 2.50
95 Warren Spahn .60 1.50
96 Carl Yastrzemski 1.50 4.00
97 Bob Feller .60 1.50
98 Rod Carew .60 1.50
99 Willie Stargell .60 1.50
100 Lou Brock .60 1.50

2012 Topps Tribute Black
*BLACK: 2.5X TO 6X BASIC
STATED PRINT RUN 60 SER.#'d SETS

2012 Topps Tribute Blue
*BLUE: .75X TO 2X BASIC
STATED PRINT RUN 199 SER.#'d SETS

2012 Topps Tribute Bronze
*BRONZE: .5X TO 1.2X BASIC
STATED PRINT RUN 299 SER.#'d SETS

2012 Topps Tribute Gold
GOLD: 4X TO 10X BASIC
STATED PRINT RUN 25 SER.#'d SETS

2012 Topps Tribute Green
*GREEN: 1.5X TO 4X BASIC
STATED PRINT RUN 75 SER.#'d SETS

2012 Topps Tribute Orange
*ORANGE: 2.5X TO 6X BASIC
STATED PRINT RUN 50 SER.#'d SETS

2012 Topps Tribute 1994 Topps Achives 1954 Buyback Aaron Autograph
STATED PRINT RUN 100 SER.#'d SETS
128 Hank Aaron 150.00 250.00

2012 Topps Tribute Autographs
PLATES RANDOMLY INSERTED
PLATE PRINT RUN 1 SET PER COLOR
BLACK-CYAN-MAGENTA-YELLOW ISSUED
NO PLATE PRICING DUE TO SCARCITY
EXCHANGE DEADLINE 02/28/2015
AB Albert Belle 10.00 25.00
AB1 Albert Belle 10.00 25.00
AC Alex Cobb 6.00 15.00
ACH Aroldis Chapman 15.00 40.00
ACH1 Aroldis Chapman 15.00 40.00
AD Andre Dawson 12.50 30.00
AE Andre Ethier 8.00 20.00
AG Adrian Gonzalez 6.00 15.00
AJ Adam Jones 10.00 25.00
AJ1 Adam Jones 10.00 25.00
AL1 Adam Lind 6.00 15.00
AL2 Adam Lind 6.00 15.00
AM1 Andrew McCutchen 25.00 60.00
AM2 Andrew McCutchen 25.00 60.00
AO1 Alexi Ogando 6.00 15.00
AO2 Alexi Ogando 6.00 15.00
AO3 Alexi Ogando 6.00 15.00
AP Andy Pettitte 30.00 60.00
AR2 Aramis Ramirez 6.00 15.00
ARI Anthony Rizzo 8.00 20.00
ARI2 Anthony Rizzo 8.00 20.00
BB1 Brandon Beachy 12.50 30.00
BB1 Bert Blyleven 10.00 25.00
BB2 Brandon Beachy 6.00 15.00
BBE1 Brandon Belt 8.00 20.00
BBE2 Brandon Belt 8.00 20.00
BBL Bert Blyleven 10.00 25.00
BG1 Brett Gardner 10.00 25.00
BGI Bob Gibson 20.00 50.00
BMC Brian McCann 6.00 15.00
BP Buster Posey 60.00 120.00
BPH Brandon Phillips 10.00 25.00
CC Carl Crawford 6.00 15.00
CF Carlton Fisk 15.00 40.00
CG Carlos Gonzalez 10.00 25.00
CG1 Carlos Gonzalez 10.00 25.00
CH Chris Heisey 6.00 15.00
CKE1 Clayton Kershaw 50.00 100.00
CKE2 Clayton Kershaw 50.00 100.00
CRI Cal Ripken Jr./49 75.00 150.00
CYA Carl Yastrzemski/49 50.00 100.00
DA Dustin Ackley 12.50 30.00
DA1 Dustin Ackley 12.50 30.00
DE Danny Espinosa 6.00 15.00
DE Dennis Eckersley 8.00 20.00
DE1 Dennis Eckersley 8.00 20.00
DG1 Dee Gordon 6.00 15.00
DG2 Dee Gordon 6.00 15.00
DH1 Daniel Hudson 6.00 15.00
DH2 Daniel Hudson 6.00 15.00
DM Don Mattingly 25.00 60.00
DMU Dale Murphy 20.00 50.00
DP Dustin Pedroia 20.00 50.00
DP1 Dustin Pedroia 10.00 25.00
DU1 Dan Uggla 6.00 15.00
EA Elvis Andrus 10.00 25.00
EB Ernie Banks 30.00 80.00
EH1 Eric Hosmer 8.00 20.00
EH2 Eric Hosmer 10.00 25.00
EL1 Evan Longoria 20.00 50.00
EM1 Edgar Martinez 10.00 25.00
EM2 Edgar Martinez 10.00 25.00
EN Eduardo Nunez 8.00 20.00
EN1 Eduardo Nunez 8.00 20.00
EN2 Eduardo Nunez 8.00 20.00
FF Freddie Freeman 12.50 30.00
FH Felix Hernandez 20.00 50.00
FH1 Felix Hernandez 20.00 50.00
FJ Fergie Jenkins 10.00 25.00
FR Frank Robinson/74 15.00 40.00
FT Frank Thomas 40.00 80.00
GF George Foster 6.00 15.00
GG1 Gio Gonzalez 10.00 25.00
GG2 Gio Gonzalez 10.00 25.00
HA Hank Aaron/74 150.00 250.00
IDA Ike Davis 8.00 20.00
IKE Ian Kennedy 6.00 15.00
IKE1 Ian Kennedy 6.00 15.00
IKE2 Ian Kennedy 6.00 15.00
IKI1 Ian Kinsler 8.00 20.00
IKI2 Ian Kinsler 8.00 20.00
IKI3 Ian Kinsler 8.00 20.00
IN Ivan Nova 10.00 25.00
IN1 Ivan Nova 10.00 25.00
JA J.P. Arencibia 8.00 20.00
JB Johnny Bench/74 20.00 50.00
JBR Jay Bruce 10.00 25.00
JBR1 Jay Bruce 10.00 25.00
JC1 Johnny Cueto 6.00 15.00
JC2 Johnny Cueto 6.00 15.00
JG Jaime Garcia 6.00 15.00
JG1 Jaime Garcia 6.00 15.00
JG2 Jaime Garcia 6.00 15.00
JH Jason Heyward 10.00 25.00
JH1 Jeremy Hellickson 8.00 20.00
JH2 Jeremy Hellickson 8.00 20.00
JJ Josh Johnson 6.00 15.00
JJ1 Jon Jay 6.00 15.00
JJ2 Jon Jay 6.00 15.00
JMA Joe Mauer/74 20.00 50.00
JMO Jesus Montero 6.00 15.00
JMO1 Jesus Montero 6.00 15.00
JMO2 Jesus Montero 6.00 15.00
JR Jim Rice 8.00 20.00
JR1 Jim Rice 8.00 20.00
JS John Smoltz 15.00 40.00
JTE Julio Teheran 8.00 20.00
JTE1 Julio Teheran 8.00 20.00
JU1 Justin Upton/49 10.00 25.00
JW1 Jered Weaver 6.00 15.00
JW2 Jered Weaver 6.00 15.00
JWA Jordan Walden 6.00 15.00
JWK Jemile Weeks 6.00 15.00
JWK1 Jemile Weeks 6.00 15.00
JZ1 Jordan Zimmermann 8.00 20.00
JZ2 Jordan Zimmermann 8.00 20.00
KGJ Ken Griffey Jr./49 200.00 400.00
LA Luis Aparicio 10.00 25.00
LM Logan Morrison 6.00 15.00
MB1 Madison Bumgarner 20.00 50.00
MB2 Madison Bumgarner 20.00 50.00
MCA Miguel Cabrera 50.00 100.00
MG1 Matt Garza 6.00 15.00
MG2 Matt Garza 6.00 15.00
MH Matt Holliday/74 20.00 50.00
MK1 Matt Kemp 10.00 25.00
MK2 Matt Kemp 10.00 25.00
MK3 Matt Kemp 10.00 25.00
MM1 Mike Minor 6.00 15.00
MM2 Mike Minor 6.00 15.00
MMI1 Minnie Minoso 10.00 25.00
MMI1 Minnie Minoso 10.00 25.00
MML Mitch Moreland 8.00 20.00
MMO Matt Moore 6.00 15.00
MMO1 Matt Moore 6.00 15.00
MMO2 Matt Moore 6.00 15.00
MMS1 Mike Morse 8.00 20.00
MMS2 Mike Morse 8.00 20.00
MMU Mike Moustakas 10.00 25.00
MP1 Michael Pineda 10.00 25.00
MP2 Michael Pineda 10.00 25.00
MP3 Michael Pineda 10.00 25.00
MS Mike Schmidt 40.00 100.00
MST Mike Stanton 15.00 40.00
MT1 Mark Trumbo 8.00 20.00
MT2 Mark Trumbo 8.00 20.00
MT3 Mark Trumbo 8.00 20.00
MT4 Mark Trumbo 8.00 20.00
MTR Mike Trout 400.00 1000.00
MTR1 Mike Trout 400.00 1000.00
MTR2 Mike Trout 400.00 1000.00
NC Nelson Cruz 6.00 15.00
NE1 Nathan Eovaldi 6.00 15.00
NE2 Nathan Eovaldi 6.00 15.00
NE3 Nathan Eovaldi 6.00 15.00
NR Nolan Ryan 50.00 120.00
NW Neil Walker 8.00 20.00
PF Prince Fielder 12.00 30.00
PM Paul Molitor 10.00 25.00
PO1 Paul O'Neill 8.00 20.00
PO2 Paul O'Neill 8.00 20.00
PO3 Paul O'Neill 8.00 20.00
PS1 Pablo Sandoval 15.00 40.00
PS2 Pablo Sandoval 15.00 40.00
RB Ryan Braun 12.00 30.00
RC Robinson Cano 10.00 25.00
RC1 Robinson Cano 10.00 25.00
RD Randall Delgado 6.00 15.00
RJ Reggie Jackson 40.00 80.00
RS Red Schoendienst 15.00 40.00
RSA Ryne Sandberg 30.00 60.00
RZ Ryan Zimmerman 8.00 20.00
SC1 Starlin Castro 10.00 25.00
SC2 Starlin Castro 10.00 25.00
SC3 Starlin Castro 10.00 25.00
SK Sandy Koufax/49 200.00 400.00
SM Stan Musial 60.00 120.00
SP Salvador Perez 12.00 30.00
SP1 Salvador Perez 12.00 30.00
TH1 Tommy Hanson 6.00 15.00
TH2 Tommy Hanson 6.00 15.00
THU Tim Hudson 8.00 20.00
UJ Ubaldo Jimenez 6.00 15.00
WM Willie Mays/74 150.00 250.00
WMC Willie McCovey 30.00 60.00

2012 Topps Tribute Autographs Blue
*BLUE: .5X TO 1.2X BASIC
PRINT RUNS B/WN 8-50 COPIES PER
NO PRICING ON QTY 25 OR LESS
EXCHANGE DEADLINE 02/28/2015

2012 Topps Tribute Championship Material Dual Relics
STATED PRINT RUN 99 SER.#'d SETS
AR Alex Rodriguez 12.50 30.00
CC Chris Carpenter 10.00 25.00
CH Cole Hamels 12.50 30.00
CJ Chipper Jones 10.00 25.00
CS CC Sabathia 12.50 30.00
CU Chase Utley 10.00 25.00
DF David Freese 10.00 25.00
DJ Derek Jeter 30.00 60.00
DO David Ortiz 10.00 25.00
DP Dustin Pedroia 12.50 30.00
JE Jacoby Ellsbury 10.00 25.00
JP Jorge Posada 10.00 25.00
JR Jimmy Rollins 10.00 25.00
MC Miguel Cabrera 10.00 25.00
MR Mariano Rivera 15.00 40.00
MT Mark Teixeira 10.00 25.00
NS Nick Swisher 4.00 10.00
PK Paul Konerko 10.00 25.00
RH Ryan Howard 10.00 25.00
TL Tim Lincecum 12.00 30.00

2012 Topps Tribute Championship Material Dual Relics Blue
*BLUE: .4X TO 1X BASIC
STATED PRINT RUN 50 SER.#'d SETS

2012 Topps Tribute Debut Digit Relics
PRINT RUNS B/WN 49-99 COPIES PER
AG Adrian Gonzalez 5.00 12.00
AK Al Kaline 6.00 15.00
BL Bob Lemon 6.00 15.00
CB Carlos Beltran 5.00 12.00
CG Carlos Gonzalez 6.00 15.00
CJ Chipper Jones 6.00 15.00
CL Cliff Lee 5.00 12.00
DF David Freese 10.00 25.00
DM Don Mattingly 10.00 25.00
DO David Ortiz 6.00 15.00
FH Felix Hernandez 6.00 15.00
GB George Brett 20.00 50.00
GC Gary Carter 10.00 25.00
HA Hank Aaron 30.00 60.00
JB Jose Bautista 10.00 25.00
JD Joe DiMaggio 30.00 60.00
JH Josh Hamilton 10.00 25.00
JW Jered Weaver 10.00 25.00
LB Lance Berkman 8.00 20.00
MC Miguel Cabrera 10.00 25.00
MM Mickey Mantle 50.00 100.00
MT Mark Teixeira 8.00 20.00
RC Rod Carew 12.50 30.00
RC Robinson Cano 10.00 25.00
RH Ryan Howard 8.00 20.00
RK Ralph Kiner 10.00 25.00
LBR Lou Brock 10.00 25.00
RCL Roberto Clemente 40.00 80.00

2012 Topps Tribute Debut Digit Relics Blue
*BLUE: .4X TO 1X BASIC
STATED PRINT RUN 50 SER.#'d SETS

2012 Topps Tribute Positions of Power Relics
PRINT RUNS B/WN 49-99 COPIES PER
AB Adrian Beltre 6.00 15.00
AG Adrian Gonzalez 5.00 12.00
AR Alex Rodriguez 15.00 40.00
BM Brian McCann 10.00 25.00
CG Carlos Gonzalez 6.00 15.00
DU Dan Uggla 5.00 12.00
EL Evan Longoria 10.00 25.00
IK Ian Kinsler 5.00 12.00
JB Jose Bautista 8.00 20.00
JH Josh Hamilton 10.00 25.00
JU Justin Upton 8.00 20.00
JV Joey Votto 10.00 25.00
MC Miguel Cabrera 10.00 25.00
MS Mike Stanton 8.00 20.00
MT Mark Teixeira 10.00 25.00
NC Nelson Cruz 5.00 12.00
PF Prince Fielder 8.00 20.00
RB Ryan Braun 6.00 15.00
RH Ryan Howard 8.00 20.00
TT Troy Tulowitzki 5.00 12.00
CGR Curtis Granderson 8.00 20.00

2012 Topps Tribute Positions of Power Relics Blue
*BLUE: .4X TO 1X BASIC
STATED PRINT RUN 50 SER.#'d SETS

2012 Topps Tribute Retired Remnants Relics
PRINT RUNS B/WN 49-99 COPIES PER
AK Al Kaline 10.00 25.00
AP Andy Pettitte 8.00 20.00
BB Bert Blyleven 5.00 12.00
CR Cal Ripken Jr. 30.00 60.00
CY Carl Yastrzemski 10.00 25.00
DE Dennis Eckersley 8.00 20.00
DM Don Mattingly 15.00 40.00
DW Dave Winfield 5.00 12.00
EB Ernie Banks 10.00 25.00
GB George Brett 12.50 30.00
HA Hank Aaron 50.00 100.00
HK Harmon Killebrew 10.00 25.00
JB Johnny Bench 15.00 40.00
JD Joe DiMaggio 40.00 80.00
JR Jim Rice 6.00 15.00
MM Mickey Mantle 60.00 120.00
MS Mike Schmidt 10.00 25.00
PO Paul O'Neill 10.00 25.00
RC Rod Carew 8.00 20.00
RJ Reggie Jackson 10.00 25.00
RK Ralph Kiner 5.00 12.00
RM Roger Maris 10.00 25.00
RY Robin Yount 8.00 20.00
SC Steve Carlton 8.00 20.00
TG Tony Gwynn 8.00 20.00
WB Wade Boggs 8.00 20.00
WM Willie Mays 12.00 30.00
RCL Roberto Clemente 30.00 60.00

2012 Topps Tribute Retired Remnants Relics Blue
*BLUE: .4X TO 1X BASIC
PRINT RUNS B/WN 30-50 COPIES PER
EB Ernie Banks/30 15.00 40.00

2012 Topps Tribute Superstar Swatches
PRINT RUNS B/WN 79-99 COPIES PER
CG Carlos Gonzalez 8.00 20.00
CL Cliff Lee 5.00 12.00
CS CC Sabathia 12.50 30.00
DJ Derek Jeter 40.00 100.00
DO David Ortiz 10.00 25.00
DP Dustin Pedroia 12.50 30.00
EL Evan Longoria 10.00 25.00
FH Felix Hernandez 5.00 12.00
JB Jose Bautista 8.00 20.00
JE Jacoby Ellsbury 6.00 15.00
JH Josh Hamilton 10.00 25.00
JM Joe Mauer 8.00 20.00
JR Jose Reyes 8.00 20.00
JU Justin Upton 8.00 20.00
JW Jered Weaver 8.00 20.00
MC Miguel Cabrera 10.00 25.00
SS Stephen Strasburg 15.00 40.00
TL Tim Lincecum 8.00 20.00
TT Troy Tulowitzki 8.00 20.00
DPR David Price 5.00 12.00

2012 Topps Tribute Superstar Swatches Blue
*BLUE: .4X TO 1X BASIC
STATED PRINT RUN 50 SER.#'d SETS

2012 Topps Tribute Tribute to the Stars Autographs
PRINT RUNS B/WN 9-24 COPIES PER
NO PRICING ON QTY LESS THAN 24
EXCHANGE DEADLINE 02/28/2015
AG Adrian Gonzalez 12.00 30.00
BP Buster Posey 75.00 150.00
CC Carl Crawford 8.00 20.00
CCS CC Sabathia 20.00 50.00
CJ Chipper Jones 100.00 175.00
CK Clayton Kershaw 40.00 80.00
DG Doc Gooden 30.00 60.00
DG1 Doc Gooden 30.00 60.00
DJ David Justice 20.00 50.00
DJ1 David Justice 20.00 50.00
DO David Ortiz 50.00 100.00
DS Darryl Strawberry 60.00 120.00
DS1 Darryl Strawberry 20.00 50.00
DS2 Darryl Strawberry 20.00 50.00
DW David Wright 75.00 150.00
GC Gary Carter 50.00 100.00
GC1 Gary Carter 50.00 100.00
GC2 Gary Carter 50.00 100.00
HR Hanley Ramirez 20.00 50.00
JB Jose Bautista 30.00 60.00
MK Matt Kemp 12.00 30.00
MST Mike Stanton 25.00 60.00
NC Nelson Cruz 15.00 40.00
OC Orlando Cepeda 20.00 50.00
OC1 Orlando Cepeda 20.00 50.00
RK Ralph Kiner 50.00 100.00
RK1 Ralph Kiner 20.00 50.00
SC Steve Carlton 20.00 50.00
SG Steve Garvey 40.00 80.00
SG1 Steve Garvey 40.00 80.00
SG2 Steve Garvey 40.00 80.00

2012 Topps Tribute Tribute to the Stars Relics
STATED PRINT RUN 99 SER.#'d SETS
AM Andrew McCutchen 8.00 20.00
CG Carlos Gonzalez 4.00 10.00
CJ Chipper Jones 10.00 25.00
CL Cliff Lee 8.00 20.00
CU Chase Utley 6.00 15.00
DF David Freese 12.50 30.00
DO David Ortiz 6.00 15.00
DP Dustin Pedroia 8.00 20.00
DW David Wright 6.00 15.00
EL Evan Longoria 8.00 20.00
FH Felix Hernandez 4.00 10.00
IK Ian Kinsler 5.00 12.00
JB Jose Bautista 5.00 12.00
JE Jacoby Ellsbury 10.00 25.00
JH Josh Hamilton 10.00 25.00
JM Joe Mauer 8.00 20.00
JU Justin Upton 5.00 12.00
KY Kevin Youkilis 5.00 12.00
LB Lance Berkman 10.00 25.00
MC Miguel Cabrera 8.00 20.00
MH Matt Holliday 8.00 20.00
MM Matt Moore 10.00 25.00
MS Mike Stanton 8.00 20.00
MT Mark Teixeira 12.50 30.00
NC Nelson Cruz 4.00 10.00
RZ Ryan Zimmerman 5.00 12.00
SC Starlin Castro 8.00 20.00
TL Tim Lincecum 12.50 30.00
TT Troy Tulowitzki 6.00 15.00
DPR David Price 5.00 12.00
IKY Ian Kennedy 5.00 12.00
JMO Jesus Montero 8.00 20.00
JRO Jimmy Rollins 8.00 20.00
RHO Ryan Howard 6.00 15.00

2012 Topps Tribute Tribute to the Stars Relics Blue
*BLUE: .4X TO 1X BASIC
STATED PRINT RUN 50 SER.#'d SETS

2012 Topps Tribute World Series Swatches
PRINT RUNS B/WN 49-99 COPIES PER
AK Al Kaline 12.50 30.00
AP Andy Pettitte 6.00 15.00
BB Bert Blyleven 6.00 15.00
BL Bob Lemon 10.00 25.00
BS Bruce Sutter 15.00 40.00
CR Cal Ripken Jr. 40.00 80.00
DE Dennis Eckersley 6.00 15.00
DS Duke Snider 10.00 25.00
DW Dave Winfield 8.00 20.00
EM Eddie Murray 10.00 25.00
EM Eddie Mathews 10.00 25.00
GB George Brett 10.00 25.00
GC Gary Carter 10.00 25.00
HA Hank Aaron/49 40.00 80.00
HW Hoyt Wilhelm 8.00 20.00
JB Johnny Bench 12.50 30.00
JD Joe DiMaggio/49 20.00 50.00
LA Luis Aparicio 8.00 20.00
LB Lou Brock 12.50 30.00
LG Lou Gehrig/49 50.00 100.00
MS Mike Schmidt 10.00 25.00
OS Ozzie Smith 15.00 40.00
PM Paul Molitor 6.00 15.00
PO Paul O'Neill 10.00 25.00
PR Phil Rizzuto 10.00 25.00
RC Roberto Clemente 30.00 60.00
RJ Reggie Jackson/49 10.00 25.00
RM Roger Maris 12.50 30.00
SA Sparky Anderson 8.00 20.00
SC Steve Carlton 8.00 20.00
WB Wade Boggs 8.00 20.00
WM Willie Mays/49 20.00 50.00
WS Willie Stargell 10.00 25.00

2012 Topps Tribute World Series Swatches Blue
*BLUE: .4X TO 1X BASIC
STATED PRINT RUN 50 SER.#'d SETS

2013 Topps Tribute
COMPLETE SET (100) 75.00 150.00
PRINTING PLATE ODDS 1:227 HOBBY
1 Whitey Ford .75 2.00
2 Albert Pujols 1.25 3.00
3 Alex Rodriguez 1.25 3.00
4 Buster Posey 1.25 3.00
5 Andre Dawson .75 2.00
6 Carlos Gonzalez .75 2.00
7 CC Sabathia .75 2.00
8 Clayton Kershaw 1.50 4.00
9 Cliff Lee .75 2.00
10 Sandy Koufax 2.00 5.00
11 David Freese .60 1.50
12 Dustin Pedroia 1.00 2.50
13 Evan Longoria .75 2.00
14 Felix Hernandez .75 2.00
15 Carlton Fisk .75 2.00
16 Frank Thomas 1.00 2.50
17 Giancarlo Stanton 1.00 2.50
18 Hanley Ramirez .75 2.00
19 Jacoby Ellsbury .75 2.00
20 Roberto Clemente 2.50 6.00
21 Jered Weaver .75 2.00
22 Joe Mauer .75 2.00
23 Joey Votto 1.00 2.50
24 John Smoltz 1.00 2.50
25 Derek Jeter 2.50 6.00
26 Jose Bautista .75 2.00
27 Josh Hamilton .75 2.00
28 Justin Verlander 1.00 2.50
29 Ken Griffey Jr. 2.00 5.00
30 Ted Williams 2.00 5.00
31 Mark Teixeira .75 2.00
32 Matt Holliday 1.00 2.50
33 Matt Kemp .75 2.00
34 Miguel Cabrera 1.00 2.50
35 Ernie Banks 1.00 2.50
36 Nolan Ryan 3.00 8.00
37 Prince Fielder .75 2.00
38 Robinson Cano .75 2.00
39 Roy Halladay .75 2.00
40 Cal Ripken Jr. 3.00 8.00
41 Ryan Braun .75 2.00
42 Ryan Howard .75 2.00
43 Ryan Zimmerman .75 2.00
44 Stan Musial 1.50 4.00
45 Ryne Sandberg 2.00 5.00
46 Troy Tulowitzki 1.00 2.50
47 Willie Mays 2.00 5.00
48 Mike Trout 8.00 20.00
49 Bryce Harper 1.50 4.00
50 Babe Ruth 2.50 6.00
51 Don Mattingly 2.00 5.00
52 Billy Williams .75 2.00
53 Stephen Strasburg 1.00 2.50
54 Rickey Henderson 1.00 2.50
55 Mariano Rivera 1.25 3.00
56 David Price .75 2.00
57 Andrew McCutchen 1.00 2.50
58 David Wright .75 2.00
59 Yoenis Cespedes 1.00 2.50
60 Johnny Bench 1.00 2.50
61 Curtis Granderson .75 2.00
62 Juan Marichal .75 2.00
63 R.A. Dickey .75 2.00
64 Adam Jones .75 2.00
65 Mike Schmidt 1.50 4.00
66 Adrian Beltre 1.00 2.50
67 Frank Robinson .75 2.00
68 Chipper Jones 1.00 2.50
69 Madison Bumgarner .75 2.00
70 Al Kaline 1.00 2.50
71 Cole Hamels .75 2.00
72 Yu Darvish 1.00 2.50
73 Adam Wainwright .75 2.00
74 Fergie Jenkins .75 2.00
75 Reggie Jackson .75 2.00
76 Yadier Molina 1.25 3.00
77 Chris Sale 1.00 2.50
78 Aroldis Chapman 1.00 2.50
79 Bob Feller .75 2.00
80 Gary Carter .75 2.00
81 Bob Gibson .75 2.00
82 Dylan Bundy RC 1.50 4.00
83 Larry Doby .60 1.50
84 Lou Brock .75 2.00
85 Ozzie Smith 1.25 3.00
86 Johnny Cueto .75 2.00
87 Harmon Killebrew 1.00 2.50
88 Lou Gehrig 2.00 5.00
89 Matt Cain .75 2.00
90 Willie Stargell .75 2.00
91 Paul Molitor 1.00 2.50
92 Jurickson Profar RC .75 2.00
93 Manny Machado RC 4.00 10.00
94 George Kell .75 2.00
95 Robin Yount 1.00 2.50
96 Wade Boggs .75 2.00
97 Allen Craig .75 2.00
98 Adrian Gonzalez .75 2.00
99 Monte Irvin .60 1.50
100 Ty Cobb 1.50 4.00

2013 Topps Tribute Blue
*BLUE: 1.2X TO 3X BASIC
STATED ODDS 1:9 HOBBY
STATED PRINT RUN 99 SER.#'d SETS

2013 Topps Tribute Green
*GREEN: 1.2X TO 3X BASIC
STATED ODDS 1:12 HOBBY
STATED PRINT RUN 75 SER.#'d SETS

2013 Topps Tribute Orange
*ORANGE: 2.5X TO 6X BASIC
STATED ODDS 1:18 HOBBY
STATED PRINT RUN 50 SER.#'d SETS

2013 Topps Tribute Autographs
STATED ODDS 1:5 HOBBY
PRINT RUNS B/WN 24-99 COPIES PER
ALL VERSIONS EQUALLY PRICED
EXCHANGE DEADLINE 2/28/2016
AB Albert Belle 8.00 20.00
AB2 Albert Belle 8.00 20.00
AB3 Albert Belle 8.00 20.00
AD Andre Dawson 8.00 20.00
AE Andre Ethier 10.00 25.00
AG Anthony Gose 6.00 15.00
AG2 Anthony Gose 6.00 15.00
AGO Adrian Gonzalez 5.00 12.00
AJ Adam Jones 8.00 20.00
AJ2 Adam Jones 8.00 20.00
AJ3 Adam Jones 8.00 20.00
AP Albert Pujols 125.00 250.00
APE Andy Pettitte/31 30.00 60.00
AR Anthony Rizzo 8.00 20.00
AR2 Anthony Rizzo 8.00 20.00
AR3 Anthony Rizzo 10.00 25.00
BB Bill Buckner 8.00 20.00
BB2 Bill Buckner 8.00 20.00
BBU Billy Butler 6.00 15.00
BBU2 Billy Butler 6.00 15.00
BBU3 Billy Butler 6.00 15.00
BBU4 Billy Butler 6.00 15.00
BG Bob Gibson/31 20.00 50.00
BH Bryce Harper/24 125.00 250.00
BJ Brett Jackson 6.00 15.00
BJ2 Brett Jackson 6.00 15.00
BJ3 Brett Jackson 6.00 15.00
BL Brett Lawrie 6.00 15.00
BL2 Brett Lawrie 6.00 15.00
BL3 Brett Lawrie 6.00 15.00
BM Brian McCann 6.00 15.00
BP Buster Posey/31 75.00 150.00
BPH Brandon Phillips 10.00 25.00
CB Craig Biggio 10.00 25.00
CF Carlton Fisk 15.00 40.00
CFI Cecil Fielder 8.00 20.00
CG Carlos Gonzalez 10.00 25.00
CJ Chipper Jones/31 60.00 120.00
CK Clayton Kershaw 30.00 60.00
CK2 Clayton Kershaw 60.00 120.00
CKE Casey Kelly 6.00 15.00
CR Cal Ripken Jr./24 75.00 150.00
CRU Carlos Ruiz 8.00 20.00
CRU2 Carlos Ruiz 8.00 20.00
CS Chris Sale 8.00 20.00
CS2 Chris Sale 8.00 20.00
CW C.J. Wilson 6.00 15.00
CW2 C.J. Wilson 6.00 15.00
DB Dylan Bundy 10.00 25.00
DB2 Dylan Bundy 10.00 25.00
DE Dennis Eckersley 8.00 20.00
DF David Freese 8.00 20.00
DM Dale Murphy 8.00 20.00
DMA Don Mattingly/31 50.00 100.00
DP Dustin Pedroia 15.00 40.00
DP2 Dustin Pedroia 15.00 40.00
DS Dave Stewart 8.00 20.00
DST Darryl Strawberry 10.00 25.00
DW David Wright/31 15.00 40.00
EA Elvis Andrus 8.00 20.00
EB Ernie Banks/31 40.00 80.00
EE Edwin Encarnacion 6.00 15.00
EE2 Edwin Encarnacion 6.00 15.00
EH Eric Hosmer 10.00 25.00
EL Evan Longoria/31 10.00 25.00
EM Edgar Martinez 5.00 15.00
FF Freddie Freeman 10.00 25.00
FH Felix Hernandez 20.00 50.00
FJ Fergie Jenkins 6.00 15.00
FR Frank Robinson/31 30.00 80.00
FT Frank Thomas/31 40.00 80.00
GF George Foster 6.00 15.00
GG Gio Gonzalez 10.00 25.00
GS Giancarlo Stanton 40.00 100.00
HA Hank Aaron/24 150.00 300.00
IN Ivan Nova 6.00 15.00
JA Jim Abbott 8.00 20.00
JA2 Jim Abbott 8.00 20.00
JB Johnny Bench/31 25.00 60.00
JBA Jose Bautista 10.00 25.00
JBR Jay Bruce 6.00 15.00
JC Johnny Cueto 6.00 15.00
JC2 Johnny Cueto 6.00 15.00
JC3 Johnny Cueto 6.00 15.00
JH Jeremy Hellickson 8.00 20.00
JHA Josh Hamilton/31 10.00 25.00
JHE Jason Heyward 12.00 30.00
JK John Kruk 6.00 15.00
JM Juan Marichal 12.00 30.00
JMO Jesus Montero 8.00 20.00
JP Jim Palmer 10.00 25.00
JP2 Jim Palmer 10.00 25.00
JPR Jurickson Profar 10.00 25.00
JR Jim Rice 10.00 25.00
JS Jean Segura 6.00 15.00
JS2 Jean Segura 6.00 15.00
JSH James Shields 6.00 15.00
JSM John Smoltz 20.00 50.00
JT Jacob Turner 6.00 15.00
JW Jered Weaver 6.00 15.00
JW3 Jered Weaver 6.00 15.00
JZ Jordan Zimmermann 8.00 20.00
JZ2 Jordan Zimmermann 8.00 20.00
JZ3 Jordan Zimmermann 8.00 20.00
KG Ken Griffey Jr. 50.00 100.00
KGS Ken Griffey Sr. 8.00 20.00
KL Kenny Lofton 12.00 30.00
LL Lance Lynn 6.00 15.00
LL2 Lance Lynn 6.00 15.00
MA Matt Adams 10.00 25.00
MA2 Matt Adams 10.00 25.00
MB Madison Bumgarner 20.00 50.00
MC Miguel Cabrera/31 25.00 60.00
MCA Matt Cain 12.00 30.00
MK Matt Kemp 12.00 30.00
MM Matt Moore 8.00 20.00
MM2 Matt Moore 8.00 20.00
MM3 Matt Moore 8.00 20.00
MMA Manny Machado 15.00 40.00
MMI Minnie Minoso 15.00 40.00
MMO Mike Moustakas 8.00 20.00
MMU Mike Mussina 10.00 25.00
MN Mike Napoli 6.00 15.00
MO Mike Olt 6.00 15.00
MO2 Mike Olt 6.00 15.00
MS Mike Schmidt/31 30.00 60.00
MT Mike Trout/31 150.00 250.00
MT4 Mark Trumbo 8.00 20.00
MTR Mark Trumbo 8.00 20.00
MTR2 Mark Trumbo 8.00 20.00
MW Maury Wills 6.00 15.00
MW2 Maury Wills 6.00 15.00
NC Nelson Cruz 8.00 20.00
NG Nomar Garciaparra 15.00 40.00
NR Nolan Ryan/24 150.00 250.00
PF Prince Fielder 6.00 15.00
PG Paul Goldschmidt 15.00 40.00
PG2 Paul Goldschmidt 15.00 40.00
PG3 Paul Goldschmidt 15.00 40.00
PM Paul Molitor 10.00 25.00
PMA Pedro Martinez/24 60.00 150.00
PO Paul O'Neill 10.00 25.00
PS Pablo Sandoval 6.00 15.00
RB Ryan Braun 8.00 20.00
RC Robinson Cano 15.00 40.00
RD R.A. Dickey 8.00 20.00
RH Rickey Henderson/31 60.00 120.00
RJ Reggie Jackson 30.00 60.00
RS Ryne Sandberg/31 40.00 80.00
RV Robin Ventura 10.00 25.00
RZ Ryan Zimmerman 8.00 20.00
SC Starlin Castro 10.00 25.00
SD Scott Diamond 12.00 30.00
SK Sandy Koufax 150.00 300.00
SM Starling Marte 10.00 25.00
SM2 Starling Marte 10.00 25.00
SM3 Starling Marte 10.00 25.00
SMI Shelby Miller 6.00 15.00
SMU Stan Musial/24 75.00 200.00
SP Salvador Perez 6.00 15.00
SP2 Salvador Perez 6.00 15.00
SP3 Salvador Perez 10.00 25.00
TB Trevor Bauer 6.00 15.00
TB2 Trevor Bauer 6.00 15.00
TBA3 Trevor Bauer 6.00 15.00
TC Tony Cingrani 10.00 25.00
TC2 Tony Cingrani 10.00 25.00
TF Todd Frazier 6.00 15.00
TF2 Todd Frazier 6.00 15.00
TFR Todd Frazier 6.00 15.00
TG Tony Gwynn/31 50.00 120.00
TGL Tom Glavine 10.00 25.00
TH Tim Hudson 10.00 25.00
TP Terry Pendleton 8.00 20.00
TP2 Terry Pendleton 8.00 20.00
TR Tim Raines 10.00 25.00
TS Tom Seaver 25.00 60.00
TSK Tyler Skaggs 6.00 15.00
VB Vida Blue 10.00 25.00
VB2 Vida Blue 10.00 25.00
WC Will Clark 10.00 25.00
WC2 Will Clark 12.00 30.00
WM Will Middlebrooks 6.00 15.00
WM2 Will Middlebrooks 6.00 15.00
WM3 Will Middlebrooks 6.00 15.00
WM4 Will Middlebrooks 6.00 15.00
WMA Willie Mays 125.00 250.00
WMI Wade Miley 8.00 20.00
WMI2 Wade Miley 8.00 20.00
WR Wilin Rosario 6.00 15.00
WR2 Wilin Rosario 6.00 15.00
YA Yonder Alonso 6.00 15.00
YA2 Yonder Alonso 6.00 15.00
YC Yoenis Cespedes 15.00 40.00
YC3 Yoenis Cespedes 15.00 40.00
YD Yu Darvish 75.00 150.00
YG Yasmani Grandal 6.00 15.00
YG2 Yasmani Grandal 6.00 15.00
YGO Yovani Gallardo 6.00 15.00
YGO2 Yovani Gallardo 6.00 15.00
YGO3 Yovani Gallardo 6.00 15.00

2013 Topps Tribute Autographs Blue
*BLUE: .4X TO 1X BASIC
STATED ODDS 1:11 HOBBY
STATED PRINT RUN 50 SER.#'d SETS
ALL VERSIONS EQUALLY PRICED
EXCHANGE DEADLINE 2/28/2016

2013 Topps Tribute Autographs Orange
*ORANGE: .5X TO 1.2X BASIC #'d/99
*ORANGE: .4X TO 1X BASIC #'d/31
STATED ODDS 1:19 HOBBY
STATED PRINT RUN 25 SER.#'d SETS
ALL VERSIONS EQUALLY PRICED
EXCHANGE DEADLINE 2/28/2016

2013 Topps Tribute Autographs Sepia
*SEPIA: .5X TO 1.2X BASIC
STATED ODDS 1:15 HOBBY
STATED PRINT RUN 35 SER.#'d SETS
ALL VERSIONS EQUALLY PRICED
EXCHANGE DEADLINE 2/28/2016

2013 Topps Tribute Commemorative Cuts Relics
STATED ODDS 1:33 HOBBY
STATED PRINT RUN 99 SER.#'d SETS
AB Adrian Beltre 4.00 10.00
AG Adrian Gonzalez 8.00 20.00
AP Albert Pujols 10.00 25.00
BH Bryce Harper 10.00 25.00
CB Carlos Beltran 8.00 20.00
CGO Carlos Gonzalez 4.00 10.00
CS Chris Sale 5.00 12.00
DJ Derek Jeter 30.00 60.00
DO David Ortiz 10.00 25.00
FH Felix Hernandez 10.00 25.00
GS Giancarlo Stanton 6.00 15.00
JH Josh Hamilton 8.00 20.00
JS Johan Santana 4.00 10.00
JV Joey Votto 8.00 20.00
JW Jered Weaver 5.00 12.00
MC Matt Cain 8.00 20.00
MCA Miguel Cabrera 12.50 30.00
MK Matt Kemp 5.00 12.00
MM Manny Machado 12.50 30.00
MTE Mark Teixeira 5.00 12.00
PF Prince Fielder 6.00 15.00
PK Paul Konerko 4.00 10.00
RB Ryan Braun 5.00 12.00
RD R.A. Dickey 4.00 10.00
WM Wade Miley 4.00 10.00
WMI Will Middlebrooks 8.00 20.00
YC Yoenis Cespedes 10.00 25.00
YD Yu Darvish 10.00 25.00

2013 Topps Tribute Commemorative Cuts Relics Blue
*BLUE: .4X TO 1X BASIC
STATED ODDS 1:65 HOBBY
STATED PRINT RUN 50 SER.#'d SETS

2013 Topps Tribute Famous Four Baggers Relics
STATED ODDS 1:67 HOBBY
STATED PRINT RUN 99 SER.#'d SETS
AB Albert Belle 4.00 10.00
AD Adam Dunn 4.00 10.00
AG Adrian Gonzalez 4.00 10.00
AK Al Kaline 8.00 20.00
AP Albert Pujols 8.00 20.00
AR Alex Rodriguez 5.00 12.00

CF Cecil Fielder 10.00 25.00
CFI Carlton Fisk 5.00 12.00
CGO Carlos Gonzalez 4.00 10.00
CJ Chipper Jones 10.00 25.00
DK Dave Kingman 6.00 15.00
DO David Ortiz 4.00 10.00
EL Evan Longoria 4.00 10.00
EM Eddie Murray 5.00 12.00
GSH Gary Sheffield 4.00 10.00
JBE Johnny Bench 10.00 25.00
JH Josh Hamilton 6.00 15.00
JR Jim Rice 4.00 10.00
MC Miguel Cabrera 6.00 15.00
MK Matt Kemp 6.00 15.00
MS Mike Schmidt 8.00 20.00
MT Mark Teixeira 4.00 10.00
MTR Mark Trumbo 4.00 10.00
PF Prince Fielder 6.00 15.00
PK Paul Konerko 4.00 10.00
RB Ryan Braun 8.00 20.00
RH Ryan Howard 4.00 10.00

2013 Topps Tribute Famous Four Baggers Relics Blue

*BLUE: .4X TO 1X BASIC
STATED ODDS 1:67 HOBBY
STATED PRINT RUN 50 SER.#'d SETS

2013 Topps Tribute Prime Patches

STATED ODDS 1:79 HOBBY
PRINT RUNS B/WN 13-24 COPIES PER
NO PRICING ON QTY 13
AB Adrian Beltre 10.00 25.00
AC Aroldis Chapman 8.00 20.00
AM Andrew McCutchen 20.00 50.00
AR Alex Rodriguez 25.00 60.00
AW Adam Wainwright 25.00 60.00
BH Bryce Harper 25.00 60.00
BP Buster Posey 25.00 60.00
CG Carlos Gonzalez 10.00 25.00
CJ Chipper Jones 25.00 60.00
CK Clayton Kershaw 20.00 50.00
CL Cliff Lee 15.00 40.00
CS Chris Sale 15.00 40.00
DF David Freese 25.00 60.00
DJ Derek Jeter 100.00 200.00
DS Don Sutton 25.00 60.00
DW David Wright 20.00 50.00
EL Evan Longoria 15.00 40.00
FH Felix Hernandez 20.00 50.00
JH Josh Hamilton 15.00 40.00
JHE Jason Heyward 15.00 40.00
JM Joe Mauer 25.00 60.00
JP Jim Palmer 15.00 40.00
JS Johan Santana 10.00 25.00
JSM John Smoltz 20.00 50.00
JW Jered Weaver 10.00 25.00
LB Lou Brock 15.00 40.00
MH Matt Holliday 12.00 30.00
MK Matt Kemp 15.00 40.00
MT Mike Trout 50.00 120.00
OS Ozzie Smith 50.00 120.00
PF Prince Fielder 20.00 50.00
PK Paul Konerko 12.00 30.00
RB Ryan Braun 12.00 30.00
RC Robinson Cano 30.00 80.00
RCA Rod Carew 12.00 30.00
RD R.A. Dickey 12.00 30.00
RH Roy Halladay 15.00 40.00
RHE Rickey Henderson 40.00 100.00
RZ Ryan Zimmerman 15.00 40.00
SS Stephen Strasburg 15.00 40.00
TL Tim Lincecum 20.00 50.00
TLA Tommy LaSorda 20.00 50.00
TT Troy Tulowitzki 12.00 30.00
WB Wade Boggs 20.00 50.00
WM Willie Mays 50.00 120.00
YC Yoenis Cespedes 25.00 60.00
YD Yu Darvish 10.00 25.00

2013 Topps Tribute Retired Remnants Relics

STATED ODDS 1:26 HOBBY
STATED PRINT RUN 99 SER.#'d SETS
AD Andre Dawson 5.00 12.00
AK Al Kaline 10.00 25.00
BG Bob Gibson 6.00 15.00
BW Billy Williams 4.00 10.00
CF Carlton Fisk 5.00 12.00
CR Cal Ripken Jr. 10.00 25.00
DE Dennis Eckersley 5.00 12.00
DG Dwight Gooden 5.00 12.00
DM Don Mattingly 10.00 25.00
DS Darryl Strawberry 8.00 20.00
EM Eddie Murray 6.00 15.00
EMA Eddie Mathews 6.00 15.00
FJ Fergie Jenkins 5.00 12.00
GB George Brett 10.00 25.00
GC Gary Carter 6.00 15.00
JB Johnny Bench 8.00 20.00
JF Jimmie Foxx 12.50 30.00
JS John Smoltz 5.00 12.00
KG Ken Griffey Jr. 12.50 30.00
LB Lou Brock 6.00 15.00
MS Mike Schmidt 8.00 20.00
NR Nolan Ryan 15.00 40.00
PO Paul O'Neill 6.00 15.00
PR Phil Rizzuto 8.00 20.00
RC Roberto Clemente 20.00 50.00
RJ Reggie Jackson 8.00 20.00
RS Ryne Sandberg 8.00 20.00
RY Robin Yount 6.00 15.00
TC Ty Cobb 20.00 50.00
TG Tony Gwynn 8.00 20.00
TS Tom Seaver 6.00 15.00
TW Ted Williams 20.00 50.00
WM Willie Mays 20.00 50.00
WS Willie Stargell 8.00 20.00
WSP Warren Spahn 5.00 12.00
YB Yogi Berra 8.00 20.00

2013 Topps Tribute Retired Remnants Relics Blue

*BLUE: .4X TO 1X BASIC
STATED ODDS 1:52 HOBBY
STATED PRINT RUN 50 SER.#'d SETS

2013 Topps Tribute Superstar Swatches

STATED ODDS 1:21 HOBBY
STATED PRINT RUN 99 SER.#'d SETS
AB Adrian Beltre 4.00 10.00
AC Aroldis Chapman 5.00 12.00
AG Adrian Gonzalez 4.00 10.00
AM Andrew McCutchen 6.00 15.00
AR Alex Rodriguez 5.00 12.00
AW Adam Wainwright 5.00 12.00
BP Buster Posey 12.50 30.00
CG Carlos Gonzalez 4.00 10.00
CJ Chipper Jones 10.00 25.00
CK Clayton Kershaw 6.00 15.00
CL Cliff Lee 6.00 15.00
CS Chris Sale 4.00 10.00
DF David Freese 5.00 12.00
DJ Derek Jeter 20.00 50.00
DP Dustin Pedroia 8.00 20.00
DW David Wright 5.00 12.00
EL Evan Longoria 4.00 10.00
FH Felix Hernandez 6.00 15.00
HR Hanley Ramirez 4.00 10.00
IK Ian Kinsler 4.00 10.00
JE Jacoby Ellsbury 4.00 10.00
JH Josh Hamilton 6.00 15.00
JM Joe Mauer 8.00 20.00
JR Jose Reyes 4.00 10.00
JS Johan Santana 4.00 10.00
JV Joey Votto 8.00 20.00
JVE Justin Verlander 10.00 25.00
JW Jered Weaver 4.00 10.00
MC Matt Cain 6.00 15.00
MH Matt Holliday 8.00 20.00
MK Matt Kemp 6.00 15.00
MT Mike Trout 20.00 50.00
PF Prince Fielder 6.00 15.00
PK Paul Konerko 4.00 10.00
PS Pablo Sandoval 4.00 10.00
RC Robinson Cano 8.00 20.00
RH Roy Halladay 4.00 10.00
RHO Ryan Howard 4.00 10.00
RZ Ryan Zimmerman 5.00 12.00
SS Stephen Strasburg 10.00 25.00
TL Tim Lincecum 8.00 20.00
TT Troy Tulowitzki 5.00 12.00
YC Yoenis Cespedes 8.00 20.00

2013 Topps Tribute Superstar Swatches Blue

*BLUE: .4X TO 1X BASIC
STATED ODDS 1:42 HOBBY
STATED PRINT RUN 50 SER.#'d SETS

2013 Topps Tribute Transitions Relics

STATED ODDS 1:31 HOBBY
PRINT RUNS B/WN 67-99 COPIES PER
AB Albert Belle 6.00 15.00
AD Andre Dawson 8.00 20.00
AG Adrian Gonzalez 8.00 20.00
AJ Adam Jones 8.00 20.00
AR Alex Rodriguez 8.00 20.00
BS Bruce Sutter 8.00 20.00
CF Carlton Fisk 8.00 20.00
CG Carlos Gonzalez 8.00 20.00
DK Dave Kingman 6.00 15.00
DO David Ortiz 10.00 25.00
EM Eddie Murray 8.00 20.00
FJ Fergie Jenkins 8.00 20.00
FR Frank Robinson 8.00 20.00
HK Harmon Killebrew 12.00 30.00
HR Hanley Ramirez 8.00 20.00
JB Jose Bautista 8.00 20.00
JF Jimmie Foxx 12.00 30.00
JH Josh Hamilton 8.00 20.00
JR Jose Reyes 8.00 20.00
KG Ken Griffey Sr. 4.00 10.00
MC Miguel Cabrera 8.00 20.00
MH Matt Holliday 10.00 25.00
MT Mark Teixeira 8.00 20.00
PF Prince Fielder 8.00 20.00
PM Paul Molitor/67 10.00 25.00
RC Rod Carew 8.00 20.00
TS Tom Seaver 8.00 20.00
WB Wade Boggs 8.00 20.00
CFI Cecil Fielder 6.00 15.00

2013 Topps Tribute Tribute to the Stars Autographs

STATED ODDS 1:38 HOBBY
STATED PRINT RUN 24 SER.#'d SETS
ALL VERSIONS EQUALLY PRICED
EXCHANGE DEADLINE 02/28/2016
AD Andre Dawson 20.00 50.00
AG Adrian Gonzalez 30.00 60.00
AJ Adam Jones 10.00 25.00
BB Brandon Beachy 8.00 20.00
BG Bob Gibson 30.00 60.00
BP Buster Posey 75.00 150.00
BR Brooks Robinson 30.00 60.00
CC CC Sabathia 10.00 25.00
DG Dwight Gooden 10.00 25.00
DJ David Justice 15.00 40.00
DS Duke Snider 10.00 25.00
EE Edwin Encarnacion 10.00 25.00
EL Evan Longoria 20.00 50.00
FH Felix Hernandez 20.00 50.00
FJ Fergie Jenkins 12.00 30.00
FT Frank Thomas 50.00 100.00
GC Gary Carter 12.00 30.00
GF George Foster 12.00 30.00
GS Gary Sheffield 10.00 25.00
ID Ike Davis 12.00 30.00
JM Joe Mauer 20.00 50.00
JP Johnny Podres 12.00 30.00
JR Josh Reddick 12.00 30.00
JU Justin Upton 10.00 25.00
LA Luis Aparicio 10.00 25.00
MC Melky Cabrera 12.00 30.00
MH Matt Harrison 10.00 25.00
MI Monte Irvin 15.00 40.00
MM Manny Machado 60.00 50.00
MO Mike Olt EXCH 12.00 30.00
NM Nick Markakis EXCH 10.00 25.00
OC Orlando Cepeda 10.00 25.00
PM Paul Molitor 20.00 50.00
RB Ryan Braun 10.00 25.00
RC Robinson Cano EXCH 15.00 40.00
RJ Reggie Jackson EXCH 20.00 50.00
RK Ralph Kiner 20.00 50.00
RS Red Schoendienst 10.00 25.00
SG Steve Garvey 20.00 50.00
SV Shane Victorino 20.00 50.00
TB Trevor Bauer 20.00 50.00
WF Whitey Ford 30.00 60.00
AD2 Andre Dawson 20.00 50.00
ADA Adam Dunn 10.00 25.00
AG2 Adrian Gonzalez 30.00 60.00
AJA Austin Jackson 10.00 25.00
BG2 Bob Gibson 30.00 60.00
BP2 Buster Posey 75.00 150.00
DG2 Dwight Gooden 10.00 25.00
DG3 Dwight Gooden 10.00 25.00
DG4 Dwight Gooden 10.00 25.00
DG5 Dwight Gooden 10.00 25.00
DG6 Dwight Gooden 10.00 25.00
DJ2 David Justice 15.00 40.00
DS2 Duke Snider 10.00 25.00
DS3 Duke Snider 10.00 25.00
DS4 Duke Snider 10.00 25.00
DSU Don Sutton 12.00 30.00
DWR David Wright 15.00 40.00
EL2 Evan Longoria 12.00 30.00
FH2 Felix Hernandez 20.00 50.00
FJ2 Fergie Jenkins 12.00 30.00
FJ3 Fergie Jenkins 12.00 30.00
GC2 Gary Carter 12.00 30.00
GC3 Gary Carter 12.00 30.00
GC4 Gary Carter 12.00 30.00
GS2 Gary Sheffield 10.00 25.00
GS3 Gary Sheffield 10.00 25.00
GS4 Gary Sheffield 10.00 25.00
GS5 Gary Sheffield 10.00 25.00
GS6 Gary Sheffield 10.00 25.00
ID2 Ike Davis 12.00 30.00
ID3 Ike Davis 12.00 30.00
JMA Juan Marichal 10.00 25.00
JP2 Johnny Podres 12.00 30.00
JP3 Johnny Podres 12.00 30.00
JP4 Johnny Podres 12.00 30.00
JPA Jim Palmer 12.00 30.00
JU2 Justin Upton 10.00 25.00
JU3 Justin Upton 10.00 25.00
LA2 Luis Aparicio 10.00 25.00
MH2 Matt Harrison 10.00 25.00
MM2 Manny Machado 20.00 50.00
MO2 Mike Olt EXCH 12.00 30.00
NM2 Nick Markakis EXCH 10.00 25.00
OC2 Orlando Cepeda 10.00 25.00
OC3 Orlando Cepeda 10.00 25.00
RB2 Ryan Braun 10.00 25.00
RB3 Ryan Braun 10.00 25.00
RS2 Red Schoendienst 10.00 25.00
SG2 Steve Garvey 20.00 50.00
SG3 Steve Garvey 20.00 50.00
SV2 Shane Victorino 20.00 50.00
TB2 Trevor Bauer 20.00 50.00
WF2 Whitey Ford 30.00 60.00
DSU2 Don Sutton 12.50 30.00
DSU3 Don Sutton 12.50 25.00
JMA2 Juan Marichal 10.00 25.00
JPA2 Jim Palmer 12.00 30.00
JPA3 Jim Palmer 12.00 30.00

2013 Topps Tribute Tribute to the Stars Relics

STATED ODDS 1:15 HOBBY
STATED PRINT RUN 99 SER.#'d SETS
AB Adrian Beltre 4.00 10.00
AC Aroldis Chapman 4.00 10.00
AE Andre Ethier 4.00 10.00
AG Adrian Gonzalez 4.00 10.00
AJ Adam Jones 5.00 12.00
AM Andrew McCutchen 6.00 15.00
AR Alex Rodriguez 10.00 25.00
AW Adam Wainwright 6.00 15.00
BB Billy Butler 4.00 10.00
BG Bob Gibson 6.00 15.00
BH Bryce Harper 12.00 30.00
BP Buster Posey 10.00 25.00
BR Babe Ruth 50.00 120.00
CGO Carlos Gonzalez 4.00 10.00
CH Cole Hamels 4.00 10.00
CJ Chipper Jones 4.00 10.00
CK Clayton Kershaw 4.00 10.00
CL Cliff Lee 4.00 10.00
CR Carlos Ruiz 4.00 10.00
CS Chris Sale 4.00 10.00
CU Chase Utley 4.00 10.00
DF David Freese 4.00 10.00
DJ Derek Jeter 12.50 30.00
DP Dustin Pedroia 4.00 10.00
DPR David Price 4.00 10.00
DW David Wright 6.00 15.00
EL Evan Longoria 6.00 15.00
FH Felix Hernandez 5.00 12.00
HR Hanley Ramirez 4.00 10.00
IK Ian Kinsler 4.00 10.00
JB Jose Bautista 4.00 10.00
JC Johnny Cueto 4.00 10.00
JE Jacoby Ellsbury 4.00 10.00
JH Josh Hamilton 5.00 12.00
JHE Jason Heyward 4.00 10.00
JR Jose Reyes 4.00 10.00
JS Johan Santana 4.00 10.00
JV Joey Votto 4.00 10.00
JVE Justin Verlander 4.00 10.00
JW Jered Weaver 4.00 10.00
MB Madison Bumgarner 8.00 20.00
MC Matt Cain 5.00 12.00
MH Matt Holliday 4.00 10.00
MK Matt Kemp 5.00 12.00
MT Mike Trout 10.00 25.00
MTE Mark Teixeira 10.00 25.00
PF Prince Fielder 6.00 15.00
PK Paul Konerko 4.00 10.00
PO Paul O'Neill 6.00 15.00
PS Pablo Sandoval 6.00 15.00
RB Ryan Braun 5.00 12.00
RC Robinson Cano 8.00 20.00
RH Roy Halladay 4.00 10.00
RHO Ryan Howard 5.00 12.00
RZ Ryan Zimmerman 5.00 12.00
SS Stephen Strasburg 10.00 25.00
TL Tim Lincecum 4.00 10.00
TT Troy Tulowitzki 4.00 10.00
TW Ted Williams 20.00 50.00
YC Yoenis Cespedes 4.00 10.00
YD Yu Darvish 8.00 20.00

2013 Topps Tribute Tribute to the Stars Relics Green

*GREEN: .4X TO 1X BASIC
STATED ODDS 1:37 HOBBY
STATED PRINT RUN 40 SER.#'d SETS

2013 Topps Tribute Tribute to the Stars Relics Orange

*ORANGE: .4X TO 1X BASIC
STATED ODDS 1:30 HOBBY
STATED PRINT RUN 50 SER.#'d SETS

2014 Topps Tribute

PRINTING PLATE ODDS 1:238 HOBBY
PLATE PRINT RUN 1 SET PER COLOR
BLACK-CYAN-MAGENTA-YELLOW ISSUED
NO PLATE PRICING DUE TO SCARCITY
1 Buster Posey 1.25 3.00
2 Yoenis Cespedes 1.00 2.50
3 Whitey Ford .75 2.00
4 Willie Stargell .75 2.00
5 Giancarlo Stanton 1.00 2.50
6 Troy Tulowitzki 1.00 2.50
7 Adam Jones .75 2.00
8 Adrian Beltre 1.00 2.50
9 Shelby Miller .75 2.00
10 Jayson Werth .75 2.00
11 Lou Gehrig 2.00 5.00
12 Babe Ruth 2.50 6.00
13 Wade Boggs .75 2.00
14 Adam Wainwright .75 2.00
15 Ozzie Smith 1.25 3.00
16 Don Mattingly 2.00 5.00
17 Jose Bautista .75 2.00
18 Mike Schmidt 1.50 4.00
19 Roberto Clemente 2.50 6.00
20 Prince Fielder .75 2.00
21 Matt Cain .75 2.00
22 Derek Jeter 2.50 6.00
23 Ted Williams 2.00 5.00
24 Robinson Cano .75 2.00
25 Willie Mays 2.00 5.00
26 Miguel Cabrera 1.00 2.50
27 Josh Hamilton .75 2.00
28 Stan Musial 1.50 4.00
29 Bob Gibson .75 2.00
30 Andrew McCutchen 1.00 2.50
31 Joey Votto 1.00 2.50
32 CC Sabathia .75 2.00
33 Mike Trout 5.00 12.00
34 Monte Irvin .75 2.00
35 Cliff Lee .75 2.00
36 Randy Johnson 1.00 2.50
37 Clayton Kershaw 1.50 4.00
38 Matt Harvey .75 2.00
39 Robin Yount 1.00 2.50
40 John Smoltz 1.00 2.50
41 Ken Griffey Jr. 2.00 5.00
42 Al Kaline 1.00 2.50
43 Aroldis Chapman 1.00 2.50
44 Johnny Bench 1.00 2.50
45 Bryce Harper 1.50 4.00
46 Paul Molitor 1.00 2.50
47 Jose Fernandez 1.00 2.50
48 George Kell .75 2.00
49 Yadier Molina 1.25 3.00
50 Juan Marichal .75 2.00
51 Joe DiMaggio 2.00 5.00
52 R.A. Dickey .75 2.00
53 Jurickson Profar .75 2.00
54 Frank Robinson .75 2.00
55 Lou Brock .75 2.00
56 Evan Longoria .75 2.00
57 Bob Feller .75 2.00
58 Gary Carter .75 2.00
59 Harmon Killebrew 1.00 2.50
60 Carlos Gonzalez .75 2.00
61 Stephen Strasburg 1.00 2.50
62 Carlton Fisk .75 2.00
63 Andre Dawson .75 2.00
64 Mariano Rivera 1.25 3.00
65 Joe Mauer .75 2.00
66 Felix Hernandez .75 2.00
67 Ivan Rodriguez .75 2.00
68 Reggie Jackson .75 2.00
69 Manny Machado 1.00 2.50
70 Nolan Ryan 3.00 8.00
71 Ernie Banks 1.00 2.50
72 Adrian Gonzalez .75 2.00
73 Cal Ripken Jr. 3.00 8.00
74 Larry Doby .75 2.00
75 Dustin Pedroia 1.00 2.50
76 Billy Williams .75 2.00
77 Cole Hamels .75 2.00
78 Frank Thomas 1.00 2.50
79 Albert Pujols 1.25 3.00
80 Chipper Jones 1.00 2.50
81 Rickey Henderson 1.00 2.50
82 Sandy Koufax 2.00 5.00
83 Justin Verlander 1.00 2.50
84 David Price .75 2.00
85 Chris Sale 1.00 2.50
86 Jacoby Ellsbury .75 2.00
87 Ryne Sandberg 2.00 5.00
88 David Wright .75 2.00
89 Matt Kemp .75 2.00
90 Ty Cobb 1.50 4.00
91 Yu Darvish 1.00 2.50
92 Yasiel Puig 1.00 2.50
93 Bo Jackson 1.00 2.50
94 Gerrit Cole 1.00 2.50
95 Wil Myers .60 1.50
96 Mike Zunino .60 1.50
97 Zack Wheeler .75 2.00
98 Greg Maddux 1.25 3.00
99 Paul Goldschmidt 1.00 2.50
100 Chris Davis .60 1.50

2014 Topps Tribute Blue

*BLUE: 1.5X TO 4X BASIC
STATED ODDS 1:10 HOBBY
STATED PRINT RUN 99 SER.#'d SETS
1 Buster Posey 6.00 15.00
22 Derek Jeter 15.00 40.00
23 Ted Williams 6.00 15.00
25 Willie Mays 10.00 25.00
28 Stan Musial 5.00 12.00
49 Yadier Molina 5.00 12.00
51 Joe DiMaggio 8.00 20.00
64 Mariano Rivera 12.00 30.00
98 Greg Maddux 6.00 15.00

2014 Topps Tribute Gold

*GOLD: 3X TO 8X BASIC
STATED ODDS 1:39 HOBBY
STATED PRINT RUN 25 SER.#'d SETS
1 Buster Posey 15.00 40.00
22 Derek Jeter 40.00 100.00
23 Ted Williams 12.50 30.00
25 Willie Mays 20.00 50.00
28 Stan Musial 10.00 25.00
33 Mike Trout 30.00 80.00
49 Yadier Molina 10.00 25.00
51 Joe DiMaggio 15.00 40.00
64 Mariano Rivera 12.50 30.00
98 Greg Maddux 12.50 30.00

2014 Topps Tribute Green

*GREEN: 2X TO 5X BASIC
STATED ODDS 1:20 HOBBY
STATED PRINT RUN 50 SER.#'d SETS
1 Buster Posey 10.00 25.00
22 Derek Jeter 25.00 60.00
23 Ted Williams 8.00 20.00
25 Willie Mays 12.50 30.00
28 Stan Musial 6.00 15.00
49 Yadier Molina 6.00 15.00
51 Joe DiMaggio 10.00 25.00
64 Mariano Rivera 8.00 20.00
98 Greg Maddux 8.00 20.00

2014 Topps Tribute Autographs

PRINTING PLATE ODDS 1:948 HOBBY
PLATE PRINT RUN 1 SET PER COLOR
BLACK-CYAN-MAGENTA-YELLOW ISSUED
NO PLATE PRICING DUE TO SCARCITY
EXCHANGE DEADLINE 2/28/2017
TAAB Albert Belle 5.00 12.00
TAAG Adrian Gonzalez 10.00 25.00
TAAH Aaron Hicks 6.00 15.00
TAAJ Adam Jones 10.00 25.00
TAAR Anthony Rizzo 12.00 30.00
TABB Billy Butler 5.00 12.00
TABG Bob Gibson 20.00 50.00
TABPH Brandon Phillips 5.00 12.00
TABZ Ben Zobrist 6.00 15.00
TACF Carlton Fisk 10.00 25.00
TACH Cole Hamels 6.00 15.00
TACKE Clayton Kershaw 50.00 100.00
TACS Chris Sale 10.00 25.00
TACSA Carlos Santana 6.00 15.00
TACW C.J. Wilson 5.00 12.00
TACWI C.J. Wilson 5.00 12.00
TADB Dylan Bundy 8.00 20.00
TADF David Freese 5.00 12.00
TADG Didi Gregorius 6.00 15.00
TADH Derek Holland 5.00 12.00
TADM Dale Murphy 15.00 40.00
TADP Dustin Pedroia 15.00 40.00
TADST Dave Stewart 5.00 12.00
TADW David Wright 12.00 30.00
TAEB Ernie Banks 20.00 50.00
TAED Eric Davis 5.00 12.00
TAEG Evan Gattis 5.00 12.00
TAEL Evan Longoria 6.00 15.00
TAEM Edgar Martinez 10.00 25.00
TAFF Freddie Freeman 10.00 25.00
TAFL Fred Lynn 8.00 20.00
TAFM Fred McGriff 12.00 30.00
TAIR Ivan Rodriguez 8.00 20.00
TAJC Jose Canseco 12.00 30.00
TAJCU Johnny Cueto 6.00 15.00
TAJGR Jason Grilli 5.00 12.00
TAJH Jason Heyward 6.00 15.00
TAJP Jorge Posada 20.00 50.00
TAJR Jim Rice 6.00 15.00
TAJS Jean Segura 6.00 15.00
TAJSH James Shields 5.00 12.00
TAJT Julio Teheran 6.00 15.00
TAKM Kevin Mitchell 5.00 12.00
TAKME Kris Medlen 6.00 15.00
TALB Lou Brock 15.00 40.00
TALG Luis Gonzalez 5.00 12.00
TALL Lance Lynn 5.00 12.00
TALS Lee Smith 5.00 12.00
TAMB Madison Bumgarner 15.00 40.00
TAMM Matt Moore 6.00 15.00
TAMMI Mike Minor 5.00 12.00
TAMT Mark Trumbo 5.00 12.00
TAMW Matt Williams 10.00 25.00
TAPC Patrick Corbin 6.00 15.00
TAPG Paul Goldschmidt 10.00 25.00
TAPO Paul O'Neill 8.00 20.00
TARZ Ryan Zimmerman 6.00 15.00
TATB Trevor Bauer 10.00 25.00
TATC Tony Cingrani 6.00 15.00
TATD Travis d'Arnaud 6.00 15.00
TATR Tim Raines 6.00 15.00
TATS Tyler Skaggs 5.00 12.00
TAWC Will Clark 12.00 30.00
TAWM Wil Myers 12.00 30.00
TAWMI Will Middlebrooks 5.00 12.00
TAWR Wilin Rosario 5.00 12.00
TAZW Zack Wheeler 6.00 15.00

2014 Topps Tribute Autographs Blue

*BLUE: .4X TO 1X BASIC
STATED ODDS 1:31 HOBBY
STATED PRINT RUN 50 SER.#'d SETS
EXCHANGE DEADLINE 2/28/2017

2014 Topps Tribute Autographs Green

*GREEN: .6X TO 1.5X BASIC
STATED ODDS 1:57 HOBBY
STATED PRINT RUN 25 SER.#'d SETS
EXCHANGE DEADLINE 2/28/2017
TABJ Bo Jackson 50.00 120.00
TABP Buster Posey 60.00 150.00
TACR Cal Ripken Jr. 30.00 80.00
TADMA Don Mattingly 50.00 120.00
TAFJ Fergie Jenkins 12.00 30.00

2014 Topps Tribute Autographs Orange

*ORANGE: .4X TO 1X BASIC
STATED ODDS 1:39 HOBBY
STATED PRINT RUN 40 SER.#'d SETS
EXCHANGE DEADLINE 2/28/2017

2014 Topps Tribute Autographs Pink

*PINK: .4X TO 1X BASIC
STATED ODDS 1:34 HOBBY
STATED PRINT RUN 45 SER.#'d SETS
EXCHANGE DEADLINE 2/28/2017

2014 Topps Tribute Autographs Sepia

*SEPIA: .5X TO 1.2X BASIC
STATED ODDS 1:44 HOBBY
STATED PRINT RUN 35 SER.#'d SETS
EXCHANGE DEADLINE 2/28/2017

2014 Topps Tribute Autographs Yellow

*YELLOW: .5X TO 1.2X BASIC
STATED ODDS 1:51 HOBBY
STATED PRINT RUN 30 SER.#'d SETS
EXCHANGE DEADLINE 2/28/2017

2014 Topps Tribute Forever Young Relics

STATED ODDS 1:28 HOBBY
STATED PRINT RUN 99 SER.#'d SETS
FYRAC Aroldis Chapman 5.00 12.00
FYRBH Bryce Harper 8.00 20.00
FYRBHA Billy Hamilton 8.00 20.00
FYRBP Buster Posey 6.00 15.00
FYRCK Clayton Kershaw 8.00 20.00
FYRCS Chris Sale 5.00 12.00
FYRDB Domonic Brown 4.00 10.00
FYREH Eric Hosmer 4.00 10.00
FYRFF Freddie Freeman 6.00 15.00
FYRFH Felix Hernandez 4.00 10.00
FYRGC Gerrit Cole 6.00 15.00
FYRJF Jose Fernandez 4.00 10.00
FYRJH Jason Heyward 4.00 10.00
FYRJP Jurickson Profar 4.00 10.00
FYRJS Jean Segura 4.00 10.00
FYRJU Justin Upton 4.00 10.00
FYRJZ Jordan Zimmermann 4.00 10.00
FYRMH Matt Harvey 4.00 10.00
FYRMM Manny Machado 5.00 12.00
FYRMMO Matt Moore 4.00 10.00
FYRMT Mike Trout 25.00 60.00
FYRMW Michael Wacha 4.00 10.00
FYRPG Paul Goldschmidt 5.00 12.00
FYRRH Hyun-Jin Ryu 4.00 10.00
FYRSM Shelby Miller 4.00 10.00
FYRSS Stephen Strasburg 5.00 12.00
FYRTC Tony Cingrani 4.00 10.00
FYRTD Travis d'Arnaud 4.00 10.00
FYRTW Taijuan Walker 3.00 8.00
FYRWM Wil Myers 3.00 8.00
FYRXB Xander Bogaerts 12.00 30.00
FYRYC Yoenis Cespedes 5.00 12.00
FYRYP Yasiel Puig 10.00 25.00
FYRZW Zack Wheeler 4.00 10.00

2014 Topps Tribute Forever Young Relics Blue

*BLUE: .4X TO 1X BASIC
STATED ODDS 1:55 HOBBY
STATED PRINT RUN 50 SER.#'d SETS

2014 Topps Tribute Forever Young Relics Green

*GREEN: .5X TO 1.2X BASIC
STATED ODDS 1:108 HOBBY
STATED PRINT RUN 25 SER.#'d SETS

2014 Topps Tribute Forever Young Relics Sepia

*SEPIA: .5X TO 1.2X BASIC
STATED ODDS 1:78 HOBBY
STATED PRINT RUN 35 SER.#'d SETS

2014 Topps Tribute Mystery Redemption Autographs

EXCHANGE DEADLINE 2/28/2017
HAMR Hank Aaron 150.00 300.00

2014 Topps Tribute Prime Patches

STATED ODDS 1:79 HOBBY
STATED PRINT RUN 24 SER.#'d SETS
PPAB Adrian Beltre 12.00 30.00
PPAC Allen Craig 20.00 50.00
PPAG Adrian Gonzalez 12.50 30.00
PPAJ Adam Jones 20.00 50.00
PPAM Andrew McCutchen 12.50 30.00
PPAP Albert Pujols 40.00 80.00
PPBH Bryce Harper 30.00 60.00
PPBHA Billy Hamilton 15.00 40.00
PPBP Buster Posey 20.00 50.00
PPCC CC Sabathia 20.00 50.00
PPCF Carlton Fisk 25.00 60.00
PPCG Carlos Gonzalez 20.00 50.00
PPCKE Clayton Kershaw 20.00 50.00
PPCS Chris Sale 40.00 80.00
PPDG Dwight Gooden 20.00 50.00
PPDP David Price 12.50 30.00
PPDPE Dustin Pedroia 15.00 40.00
PPFF Freddie Freeman 12.00 30.00
PPFH Felix Hernandez 20.00 50.00
PPGC Gerrit Cole 40.00 80.00
PPGS Giancarlo Stanton 20.00 50.00
PPJF Jose Fernandez 20.00 50.00
PPJR Jose Reyes 30.00 60.00
PPJU Justin Upton 12.00 30.00
PPJV Joey Votto 50.00 100.00
PPJVE Justin Verlander 20.00 50.00
PPMC Miguel Cabrera 12.00 30.00
PPMH Matt Harvey 15.00 40.00
PPMK Matt Kemp 12.50 30.00
PPMM Manny Machado 50.00 100.00
PPMMO Matt Moore 12.50 30.00
PPMS Max Scherzer 12.50 30.00
PPMT Mike Trout 75.00 200.00
PPPF Prince Fielder 15.00 40.00
PPPG Paul Goldschmidt 40.00 80.00
PPSM Shelby Miller 15.00 40.00
PPSS Stephen Strasburg 12.00 30.00
PPTG Tony Gwynn 15.00 40.00
PPTGL Tom Glavine 15.00 40.00
PPTL Tim Lincecum 20.00 50.00
PPTW Taijuan Walker 12.50 30.00
PPWB Wade Boggs 20.00 50.00
PPWM Wil Myers 15.00 40.00
PPXB Xander Bogaerts 40.00 80.00
PPYC Yoenis Cespedes 20.00 50.00
PPYM Yadier Molina 30.00 60.00
PPYP Yasiel Puig 12.00 30.00

2014 Topps Tribute Timeless Tribute Dual Autographs

STATED ODDS 1:394 HOBBY
STATED PRINT RUN 24 SER.#'d SETS
EXCHANGE DEADLINE 2/28/2017
TTRASW Schmidt/Wright EXCH 90.00 150.00
TTRABH Brock/Henderson 125.00 250.00
TTRABP Bench/Posey 100.00 200.00
TTRABR Bench/IRod 60.00 150.00
TTRAGH Ham/Griffey Jr. EXCH 75.00 200.00
TTRAHT Henderson/Trout 250.00 350.00
TTRAJT Jackson/Trout 250.00 350.00
TTRAKK Kouf/Kersh 400.00 600.00
TTRART Tulowitzki/Ripken 125.00 250.00

2014 Topps Tribute Tribute Titans Relics

STATED ODDS 1:19 HOBBY
STATED PRINT RUN 99 SER.#'d SETS
TTRAB Adrian Beltre 5.00 12.00
TTRAC Allen Craig 4.00 10.00
TTRACH Aroldis Chapman 5.00 12.00
TTRAG Adrian Gonzalez 4.00 10.00
TTRAJ Adam Jones 4.00 10.00
TTRAM Andrew McCutchen 5.00 12.00
TTRAP Albert Pujols 6.00 15.00
TTRBH Bryce Harper 12.50 30.00
TTRBP Buster Posey 6.00 15.00
TTRCC CC Sabathia 4.00 10.00
TTRCD Chris Davis 3.00 8.00
TTRCG Carlos Gonzalez 4.00 10.00
TTRCK Clayton Kershaw 8.00 20.00
TTRCS Chris Sale 5.00 12.00
TTRDF David Freese 3.00 8.00
TTRDO David Ortiz 5.00 12.00
TTRDP David Price 4.00 10.00
TTRDPE Dustin Pedroia 10.00 25.00
TTRDW David Wright 4.00 10.00
TTREE Edwin Encarnacion 5.00 12.00
TTREL Evan Longoria 4.00 10.00
TTRFF Freddie Freeman 6.00 15.00
TTRGC Gerrit Cole 8.00 20.00
TTRGG Gio Gonzalez 4.00 10.00
TTRJB Jose Bautista 4.00 10.00
TTRJF Jose Fernandez 8.00 20.00
TTRJH Jason Heyward 4.00 10.00
TTRJP Jurickson Profar 4.00 10.00
TTRJR Jose Reyes 4.00 10.00
TTRJS Jean Segura 4.00 10.00
TTRJU Justin Upton 4.00 10.00
TTRJV Joey Votto 5.00 12.00
TTRJVE Justin Verlander 5.00 12.00
TTRMC Miguel Cabrera 12.50 30.00
TTRMH Matt Harvey 4.00 10.00
TTRMK Matt Kemp 4.00 10.00
TTRMM Manny Machado 5.00 12.00
TTRMMO Matt Moore 4.00 10.00
TTRMT Mike Trout 25.00 60.00
TTRMTE Mark Teixeira 4.00 10.00
TTRPF Prince Fielder 4.00 10.00
TTRPG Paul Goldschmidt 5.00 12.00
TTRRD R.A. Dickey 4.00 10.00
TTRRH Hyun-Jin Ryu 4.00 10.00
TTRRHA Roy Halladay 4.00 10.00
TTRRZ Ryan Zimmerman 4.00 10.00
TTRSM Shelby Miller 4.00 10.00
TTRSS Stephen Strasburg 5.00 12.00
TTRTT Troy Tulowitzki 5.00 12.00
TTRWM Wil Myers 3.00 8.00
TTRYP Yasiel Puig 10.00 25.00
TTRZG Zack Greinke 5.00 12.00

2014 Topps Tribute Tribute Titans Relics Blue

*BLUE: .4X TO 1X BASIC
STATED ODDS 1:37 HOBBY
STATED PRINT RUN 50 SER.#'d SETS

2014 Topps Tribute Tribute Titans Relics Green

*GREEN: .5X TO 1.2X BASIC
STATED ODDS 1:73 HOBBY
STATED PRINT RUN 25 SER.#'d SETS

2014 Topps Tribute Tribute Titans Relics Sepia

*SEPIA: .5X TO 1.2X BASIC
STATED ODDS 1:52 HOBBY
STATED PRINT RUN 35 SER.#'d SETS

2014 Topps Tribute Tribute to the Pastime Autographs

PRINTING PLATE ODDS 1:437 HOBBY
PLATE PRINT RUN 1 SET PER COLOR
BLACK-CYAN-MAGENTA-YELLOW ISSUED
NO PLATE PRICING DUE TO SCARCITY
EXCHANGE DEADLINE 2/28/2017
TPTAB Albert Belle 8.00 20.00
TPTAG Adrian Gonzalez 10.00 25.00
TPTAH Aaron Hicks 6.00 15.00
TPTAJ Adam Jones 10.00 25.00
TPTAR Anthony Rizzo 12.00 30.00
TPTBB Billy Butler 5.00 12.00
TPTBP Brandon Phillips 6.00 15.00
TPTBZ Ben Zobrist 6.00 15.00
TPTCS Chris Sale 8.00 20.00
TPTCSA Carlos Santana 6.00 15.00
TPTDC Dave Concepcion 5.00 12.00
TPTDF David Freese 5.00 12.00
TPTDG Didi Gregorius 6.00 15.00
TPTDH Derek Holland 5.00 12.00
TPTDP Dustin Pedroia 15.00 40.00
TPTDS Dave Stewart 5.00 12.00
TPTED Eric Davis 6.00 15.00
TPTEG Evan Gattis 5.00 12.00
TPTEM Edgar Martinez 6.00 15.00
TPTFF Freddie Freeman 10.00 25.00
TPTFL Fred Lynn 5.00 12.00
TPTFM Fred McGriff 10.00 25.00
TPTJC Johnny Cueto 6.00 15.00
TPTJGR Jason Grilli 5.00 12.00
TPTJR Jim Rice 6.00 15.00
TPTJS Jean Segura 6.00 15.00
TPTJSH James Shields 5.00 12.00
TPTJT Julio Teheran 6.00 15.00
TPTKM Kevin Mitchell 6.00 15.00
TPTKME Kris Medlen 6.00 15.00
TPTLL Lance Lynn 5.00 12.00

TPTLS Lee Smith 5.00 12.00
TPTMB Madison Bumgarner 40.00 80.00
TPTMMI Mike Minor 5.00 12.00
TPTMMO Matt Moore 6.00 15.00
TPTMT Mark Trumbo 5.00 12.00
TPTMW Matt Williams 6.00 15.00
TPTNG Nomar Garciaparra 10.00 25.00
TPTPC Patrick Corbin 6.00 15.00
TPTPG Paul Goldschmidt 10.00 25.00
TPTPO Paul O'Neill 10.00 25.00
TPTPS Pablo Sandoval 6.00 15.00
TPTRB Ryan Braun 6.00 15.00
TPTRZ Ryan Zimmerman 6.00 15.00
TPTSC Steve Carlton 12.00 30.00
TPTSM Shelby Miller 6.00 15.00
TPTSMA Starling Marte 6.00 15.00
TPTSP Salvador Perez 10.00 25.00
TPTTB Trevor Bauer 10.00 25.00
TPTTC Tony Cingrani 6.00 15.00
TPTTD Travis d'Arnaud 10.00 25.00
TPTTH Tim Hudson 6.00 15.00
TPTTR Tim Raines 6.00 15.00
TPTTSK Tyler Skaggs 5.00 12.00
TPTTT Troy Tulowitzki 12.00 30.00
TPTVG Vladimir Guerrero 6.00 15.00
TPTWC Will Clark 12.00 30.00
TPTWMY Wil Myers 12.00 30.00
TPTWR Wilin Rosario 5.00 12.00
TPTXB Xander Bogaerts 10.00 25.00
TPTYM Yadier Molina 30.00 80.00
TPTZW Zack Wheeler 10.00 25.00

2014 Topps Tribute Tribute to the Pastime Autographs Blue

*BLUE: .4X TO 1X BASIC
STATED ODDS 1:32 HOBBY
STATED PRINT RUN 50 SER.#'d SETS
EXCHANGE DEADLINE 2/28/2017

2014 Topps Tribute Tribute to the Pastime Autographs Green

*GREEN: .6X TO 1.5X BASIC
STATED ODDS 1:48 HOBBY
STATED PRINT RUN 25 SER.#'d SETS
EXCHANGE DEADLINE 2/28/2017
TPTGM Greg Maddux 75.00 200.00
TPTOC Orlando Cepeda 10.00 25.00
TPTPM Pedro Martinez 75.00 150.00
TPTRH Rickey Henderson 60.00 120.00
TPTRY Robin Yount 50.00 100.00
TPTSK Sandy Koufax 200.00 300.00
TPTTGW Tony Gwynn 20.00 50.00

2014 Topps Tribute Tribute to the Pastime Autographs Orange

*ORANGE: .4X TO 1X BASIC
STATED ODDS 1:39 HOBBY
STATED PRINT RUN 40 SER.#'d SETS
EXCHANGE DEADLINE 2/28/2017

2014 Topps Tribute Tribute to the Pastime Autographs Sepia

*SEPIA: .5X TO 1.2X BASIC
STATED ODDS 1:45 HOBBY
STATED PRINT RUN 35 SER.#'d SETS
EXCHANGE DEADLINE 2/28/2017

2014 Topps Tribute Tribute to the Pastime Autographs Yellow

*YELLOW: .5X TO 1.2X BASIC
STATED ODDS 1:52 HOBBY
STATED PRINT RUN 30 SER.#'d SETS
EXCHANGE DEADLINE 2/28/2017

2014 Topps Tribute Tribute to the Stars Autographs

STATED ODDS 1:51 HOBBY
STATED PRINT RUN 24 SER.#'d SETS
ALL VERSIONS EQUALLY PRICED
EXCHANGE DEADLINE 2/28/2017
TSAAR Anthony Rizzo 20.00 50.00
TSABB Billy Butler 10.00 25.00
TSABH Billy Hamilton 10.00 25.00
TSABH1 Billy Hamilton 10.00 25.00
TSABH2 Billy Hamilton 10.00 25.00
TSABH3 Billy Hamilton 10.00 25.00
TSABP Brandon Phillips 20.00 50.00
TSADM Dale Murphy 20.00 50.00
TSADS Duke Snider 10.00 25.00
TSADS1 Duke Snider 10.00 25.00
TSADS2 Duke Snider 10.00 25.00
TSAEG Evan Gattis 15.00 40.00
TSAEJ Erik Johnson 10.00 25.00
TSAEJ1 Erik Johnson 10.00 25.00
TSAEL Evan Longoria 15.00 40.00
TSAEL1 Evan Longoria 15.00 40.00
TSAFF Freddie Freeman 15.00 40.00
TSAFJ Fergie Jenkins 12.50 30.00
TSAFJ1 Fergie Jenkins 12.50 30.00
TSAFJ2 Fergie Jenkins 12.50 30.00
TSAFJ3 Fergie Jenkins 12.50 30.00
TSAGC Gary Carter 20.00 50.00
TSAGC1 Gary Carter 20.00 50.00
TSAGC2 Gary Carter 20.00 50.00
TSAGC3 Gary Carter 20.00 50.00
TSAGC4 Gary Carter 20.00 50.00
TSAGC5 Gary Carter 20.00 50.00
TSAGC6 Gary Carter 20.00 50.00
TSAGG Goose Gossage 12.50 30.00
TSAGG1 Goose Gossage 12.50 30.00
TSAGK George Kell 15.00 40.00
TSAGK1 George Kell 15.00 40.00
TSAGM Greg Maddux 90.00 150.00
TSAHI Hisashi Iwakuma 20.00 50.00
TSAHI1 Hisashi Iwakuma 20.00 50.00
TSAHI2 Hisashi Iwakuma 20.00 50.00
TSAJB Jose Bautista 15.00 40.00
TSAJB1 Jose Bautista 15.00 40.00
TSAJB2 Jose Bautista 15.00 40.00
TSAJP Johnny Podres 15.00 40.00
TSAJP1 Johnny Podres 15.00 40.00
TSAJW Jered Weaver 10.00 25.00
TSAJW1 Jered Weaver 10.00 25.00
TSAJW2 Jered Weaver 10.00 25.00
TSAMA Mariano Rivera 200.00 300.00
TSAMC Miguel Cabrera 75.00 150.00
TSAMM Mike Minor 10.00 25.00
TSAMMO Matt Moore 10.00 25.00
TSAMT Mike Trout 150.00 250.00
TSANC Nick Castellanos 12.00 30.00
TSANC1 Nick Castellanos 12.00 30.00
TSANC2 Nick Castellanos 12.00 30.00
TSAOS Ozzie Smith 30.00 60.00
TSARC Rod Carew 15.00 40.00
TSARC1 Rod Carew 15.00 40.00
TSASC Starlin Castro 10.00 25.00
TSASC1 Starlin Castro 10.00 25.00
TSASK Sandy Koufax 200.00 300.00
TSATB Trevor Bauer 10.00 25.00
TSATC Tony Cingrani 10.00 25.00
TSATD Travis d'Arnaud 10.00 25.00
TSATD1 Travis d'Arnaud 10.00 25.00
TSATG Tom Glavine 20.00 50.00
TSATG1 Tom Glavine 20.00 50.00
TSATR Tim Raines 10.00 25.00
TSATW Taijuan Walker 15.00 40.00
TSATW1 Taijuan Walker 15.00 40.00
TSATW2 Taijuan Walker 15.00 40.00
TSAWB Wade Boggs 50.00 100.00
TSAWM Wil Myers 15.00 40.00
TSAXB Xander Bogaerts 60.00 120.00
TSAXB1 Xander Bogaerts 60.00 120.00
TSAZW Zack Wheeler 12.50 30.00

2014 Topps Tribute Tribute to the Throne Relics

STATED ODDS 1:24 HOBBY
STATED PRINT RUN 99 SER.#'d SETS
EXCHANGE DEADLINE 2/28/2017
THRONEAD Andre Dawson 8.00 20.00
THRONEAK Al Kaline EXCH 10.00 25.00
THRONEBF Bob Feller 10.00 25.00
THRONEBR Babe Ruth 75.00 150.00
THRONECF Carlton Fisk 8.00 20.00
THRONECR Cal Ripken Jr. 10.00 25.00
THRONEDM Don Mattingly 10.00 25.00
THRONEDMU Dale Murphy 10.00 25.00
THRONEDS Don Sutton 8.00 20.00
THRONEEB Ernie Banks 10.00 25.00
THRONEEM Eddie Mathews 10.00 25.00
THRONEEMU Eddie Murray 8.00 20.00
THRONEFJ Fergie Jenkins 8.00 20.00
THRONEGB George Brett 10.00 25.00
THRONEHA Hank Aaron 12.00 30.00
THRONEHK Harmon Killebrew 10.00 25.00
THRONEIR Ivan Rodriguez 8.00 20.00
THRONEJB Johnny Bench 15.00 40.00
THRONEJD Joe DiMaggio 40.00 100.00
THRONEJR Jackie Robinson 20.00 50.00
THRONEKG Ken Griffey Jr. 10.00 25.00
THRONELB Lou Brock 12.00 30.00
THRONEMS Mike Schmidt 12.00 30.00
THRONEOC Orlando Cepeda 10.00 25.00
THRONEPN Phil Niekro 8.00 20.00
THRONERC Roberto Clemente 30.00 60.00
THRONERCA Rod Carew 8.00 20.00
THRONERH Rickey Henderson 10.00 25.00
THRONERJ Reggie Jackson 8.00 20.00
THRONERJO Randy Johnson 10.00 25.00
THRONERY Robin Yount 10.00 25.00
THRONESM Stan Musial 10.00 25.00
THRONETC Ty Cobb 20.00 50.00
THRONETG Tom Glavine 8.00 20.00
THRONETGW Tony Gwynn 10.00 25.00
THRONETW Ted Williams 20.00 50.00
THRONEWB Wade Boggs 8.00 20.00
THRONEWBO Wade Boggs 8.00 20.00
THRONEWM Willie Mays 15.00 40.00
THRONEWMC Willie McCovey 8.00 20.00
THRONEYB Yogi Berra 10.00 25.00

2014 Topps Tribute Tribute to the Throne Relics Blue

*BLUE: .4X TO 1X BASIC
STATED ODDS 1:47 HOBBY
STATED PRINT RUN 50 SER.#'d SETS
EXCHANGE DEADLINE 2/28/2017

2014 Topps Tribute Tribute to the Throne Relics Green

*GREEN: .5X TO 1.2X BASIC
STATED ODDS 1:93 HOBBY
STATED PRINT RUN 25 SER.#'d SETS
EXCHANGE DEADLINE 2/28/2017

2014 Topps Tribute Tribute to the Throne Relics Sepia

*SEPIA: .5X TO 1.2X BASIC
STATED ODDS 1:66 HOBBY
STATED PRINT RUN 35 SER.#'d SETS
EXCHANGE DEADLINE 2/28/2017

2014 Topps Tribute Tribute Traditions Autographs

PRINTING PLATE ODDS 1:580 HOBBY
PLATE PRINT RUN 1 SET PER COLOR
BLACK-CYAN-MAGENTA-YELLOW ISSUED
NO PLATE PRICING DUE TO SCARCITY
EXCHANGE DEADLINE 2/28/2017
TTAB Albert Belle 5.00 12.00
TTAG Adrian Gonzalez 8.00 20.00
TTAH Aaron Hicks 6.00 15.00
TTAJ Adam Jones 10.00 25.00
TTAR Anthony Rizzo 20.00 50.00
TTBB Billy Butler 5.00 12.00
TTBP Brandon Phillips 6.00 15.00
TTBZ Ben Zobrist 6.00 15.00
TTCS Chris Sale 10.00 25.00
TTCSA Carlos Santana 5.00 12.00
TTDC Dave Concepcion 10.00 25.00
TTDF David Freese 5.00 12.00
TTDG Didi Gregorius 6.00 15.00
TTDH Derek Holland 5.00 12.00
TTDP Dustin Pedroia 15.00 40.00
TTDS Dave Stewart 5.00 12.00
TTED Eric Davis 10.00 25.00
TTEG Evan Gattis 5.00 12.00
TTEM Edgar Martinez 6.00 15.00
TTFL Fred Lynn 5.00 12.00
TTFM Fred McGriff 15.00 40.00
TTGS Giancarlo Stanton 40.00 100.00
TTIR Ivan Rodriguez 12.00 30.00
TTJC Johnny Cueto 6.00 15.00
TTJGR Jason Grilli 6.00 15.00
TTJHE Jason Heyward 6.00 15.00
TTJM Juan Marichal 8.00 20.00
TTJP Jim Palmer 12.00 30.00
TTJR Jim Rice 6.00 15.00
TTJS John Smoltz 15.00 40.00
TTJSE Jean Segura 6.00 15.00
TTJSH James Shields 5.00 12.00
TTJU Justin Upton 6.00 15.00
TTKL Kenny Lofton 12.00 30.00
TTKM Kevin Mitchell 5.00 12.00
TTKME Kris Medlen 6.00 15.00
TTLL Lance Lynn 5.00 12.00
TTLS Lee Smith 5.00 12.00
TTMB Madison Bumgarner 40.00 50.00
TTMMI Mike Minor 5.00 12.00
TTMMO Matt Moore 6.00 15.00
TTMTR Mark Trumbo 5.00 12.00
TTMW Matt Williams 6.00 15.00
TTPC Patrick Corbin 6.00 15.00
TTPG Paul Goldschmidt 10.00 25.00
TTPM Paul Molitor 12.00 30.00
TTPO Paul O'Neill 10.00 25.00
TTRP Rafael Palmeiro 10.00 25.00
TTRZ Ryan Zimmerman 10.00 25.00
TTSM Starling Marte 6.00 15.00
TTSP Salvador Perez 10.00 25.00
TTTB Trevor Bauer 10.00 25.00
TTTC Tony Cingrani 6.00 15.00
TTTD Travis d'Arnaud 10.00 25.00
TTTR Tim Raines 6.00 15.00
TTTS Tyler Skaggs 5.00 12.00
TTWC Will Clark 12.00 30.00
TTWM Wil Myers 5.00 12.00
TTWMI Will Middlebrooks 5.00 12.00
TTWR Wilin Rosario 5.00 12.00
TTZW Zack Wheeler 10.00 25.00

2014 Topps Tribute Tribute Traditions Autographs Blue

*BLUE: .4X TO 1X BASIC
STATED ODDS 1:32 HOBBY
STATED PRINT RUN 50 SER.#'d SETS
EXCHANGE DEADLINE 2/28/2017

2014 Topps Tribute Tribute Traditions Autographs Green

*GREEN: .6X TO 1.5X BASIC
STATED ODDS 1:52 HOBBY
STATED PRINT RUN 25 SER.#'d SETS
EXCHANGE DEADLINE 2/28/2017
TTCJ Chipper Jones 100.00 200.00
TTJB Johnny Bench 50.00 120.00
TTKG Ken Griffey Jr. 125.00 250.00
TTMC Matt Cain 10.00 25.00
TTMCA Miguel Cabrera 75.00 150.00
TTMM Manny Machado 25.00 60.00
TTMMU Mike Mussina 20.00 50.00
TTNR Nolan Ryan 125.00 250.00
TTRJ Randy Johnson 75.00 150.00

2014 Topps Tribute Tribute Traditions Autographs Orange

*ORANGE: .4X TO 1X BASIC
STATED ODDS 1:39 HOBBY
STATED PRINT RUN 40 SER.#'d SETS
EXCHANGE DEADLINE 2/28/2017

2014 Topps Tribute Tribute Traditions Autographs Sepia

*SEPIA: .5X TO 1.2X BASIC
STATED ODDS 1:45 HOBBY
STATED PRINT RUN 35 SER.#'d SETS
EXCHANGE DEADLINE 2/28/2017

2014 Topps Tribute Tribute Traditions Autographs Yellow

*YELLOW: .5X TO 1.2X BASIC
STATED ODDS 1:52 HOBBY
STATED PRINT RUN 30 SER.#'d SETS
EXCHANGE DEADLINE 2/28/2017

2015 Topps Tribute

PRINTING PLATE RANDOMLY INSERTED
PLATE PRINT RUN 1 SET PER COLOR
NO PLATE PRICING DUE TO SCARCITY
1 Mike Trout 10.00 25.00
2 Rod Carew 1.50 4.00
3 Yadier Molina 2.50 6.00
4 Chris Sale 2.00 5.00
5 Nomar Garciaparra 1.50 4.00
6 Manny Machado 2.00 5.00
7 Roberto Alomar 1.50 4.00
8 Javier Baez RC 10.00 25.00
9 George Springer 1.50 4.00
10 Madison Bumgarner 1.50 4.00
11 Bryce Harper 3.00 8.00
12 Steve Carlton 1.50 4.00
13 Joe DiMaggio 4.00 10.00
14 Ted Williams 4.00 10.00
15 Albert Pujols 2.50 6.00
16 Joe Morgan 1.50 4.00
17 Tony Gwynn 2.00 5.00
18 Corey Kluber 1.50 4.00
19 Mike Piazza 2.00 5.00
20 Andre Dawson 1.50 4.00
21 Lou Brock 1.50 4.00
22 Jackie Robinson 2.00 5.00
23 Wade Boggs 1.50 4.00
24 Ernie Banks 2.00 5.00
25 Jose Abreu 2.00 5.00
26 Freddie Freeman 2.50 6.00
27 Nelson Cruz 2.00 5.00
28 Adrian Beltre 2.00 5.00
29 Masahiro Tanaka 1.50 4.00
30 Maikel Franco RC 1.50 4.00
31 Josh Donaldson 1.50 4.00
32 Bo Jackson 2.00 5.00
33 David Ortiz 2.00 5.00
34 Roger Clemens 2.50 6.00
35 Carlton Fisk 1.50 4.00
36 Carlos Gonzalez 1.50 4.00
37 Ian Desmond 1.25 3.00
38 Carlos Gomez 1.25 3.00
39 Stephen Strasburg 2.00 5.00
40 Eddie Murray 1.50 4.00
41 Felix Hernandez 1.50 4.00
42 Mariano Rivera 2.50 6.00
43 Reggie Jackson 1.50 4.00
44 David Price 1.50 4.00
45 Jorge Soler RC 6.00 15.00
46 Anthony Rizzo 2.50 6.00
47 Ozzie Smith 2.50 6.00
48 David Wright 1.50 4.00
49 Jonathan Lucroy 1.50 4.00
50 Clayton Kershaw 3.00 8.00
51 Joc Pederson RC 8.00 20.00
52 Michael Wacha 1.50 4.00
53 Johnny Bench 2.00 5.00
54 Victor Martinez 1.50 4.00
55 Mark McGwire 3.00 8.00
56 Dale Murphy 2.00 5.00
57 Rusney Castillo RC 1.50 4.00
58 Jose Fernandez 2.00 5.00
59 Buster Posey 2.50 6.00
60 Justin Upton 1.50 4.00
61 Dustin Pedroia 2.00 5.00
62 Max Scherzer 2.00 5.00
63 Robin Yount 2.00 5.00
64 Tom Seaver 1.50 4.00
65 Roger Maris 2.00 5.00
66 Justin Verlander 2.00 5.00
67 Ty Cobb 3.00 8.00
68 Adam Wainwright 1.50 4.00
69 Jose Altuve 1.50 4.00
70 Sandy Koufax 4.00 10.00
71 Cal Ripken Jr. 6.00 15.00
72 Craig Kimbrel 1.50 4.00
73 Jose Bautista 1.50 4.00
74 Jacoby Ellsbury 1.50 4.00
75 Miguel Cabrera 2.00 5.00
76 Andrew McCutchen 2.00 5.00
77 Yoenis Cespedes 1.50 4.00
78 Ryan Braun 1.50 4.00
79 Jose Reyes 1.50 4.00
80 Yu Darvish 2.00 5.00
81 Adam Jones 1.50 4.00
82 Nolan Ryan 5.00 12.00
83 Jim Palmer 1.50 4.00
84 Edwin Encarnacion 2.00 5.00
85 Jim Rice 1.50 4.00
86 George Brett 4.00 10.00
87 Hunter Pence 1.50 4.00
88 Lou Gehrig 4.00 10.00
89 Yasiel Puig 2.00 5.00
90 Mike Schmidt 3.00 8.00
91 Jon Lester 1.50 4.00
92 Paul Goldschmidt 2.00 5.00
93 Tom Glavine 1.50 4.00
94 Luis Aparicio 1.50 4.00
95 Gregory Polanco 1.50 4.00
96 Whitey Ford 1.50 4.00
97 Billy Hamilton 1.50 4.00
98 Robinson Cano 1.50 4.00
99 Evan Longoria 1.50 4.00
100 Babe Ruth 5.00 12.00

2015 Topps Tribute Black

*BLACK: 1.5X TO 4X BASIC
RANDOM INSERTS IN PACKS
STATED PRINT RUN 50 SER.#'d SETS

2015 Topps Tribute Green

*GREEN: .75X TO 2X BASIC
RANDOM INSERTS IN PACKS
STATED PRINT RUN 99 SER.#'d SETS

2015 Topps Tribute Diamond Cuts Jerseys

RANDOM INSERTS IN PACKS
STATED PRINT RUN 199 SER.#'d SETS
DCAC Aroldis Chapman 4.00 10.00
DCAG Adrian Gonzalez 3.00 8.00
DCAGO Alex Gordon 3.00 8.00
DCAM Andrew McCutchen 4.00 10.00
DCAP Albert Pujols 6.00 15.00
DCAW Adam Wainwright 3.00 8.00
DCBHA Billy Hamilton 3.00 8.00
DCBP Buster Posey 5.00 12.00
DCCC CC Sabathia 3.00 8.00
DCCG Carlos Gonzalez 3.00 8.00
DCCK Clayton Kershaw 6.00 15.00
DCCS Chris Sale 4.00 10.00
DCDO David Ortiz 4.00 10.00
DCDW David Wright 3.00 8.00
DCFF Freddie Freeman 5.00 12.00
DCGC Gerrit Cole 4.00 10.00
DCGP Gregory Polanco 3.00 8.00
DCGS Giancarlo Stanton 4.00 10.00
DCHR Hanley Ramirez 3.00 8.00
DCIK Ian Kinsler 3.00 8.00
DCJS Jorge Soler 4.00 10.00
DCJV Justin Verlander 4.00 10.00
DCJVO Joey Votto 4.00 10.00
DCKU Koji Uehara 2.50 6.00
DCMC Miguel Cabrera 4.00 10.00
DCMS Max Scherzer 4.00 10.00
DCPS Pablo Sandoval 3.00 8.00
DCRB Ryan Braun 3.00 8.00
DCSG Sonny Gray 3.00 8.00
DCTT Troy Tulowitzki 4.00 10.00
DCYD Yu Darvish 4.00 10.00
DCYM Yadier Molina 5.00 12.00
DCYP Yasiel Puig 4.00 10.00
DCYV Yordano Ventura 3.00 8.00
DCZG Zack Greinke 4.00 10.00

2015 Topps Tribute Diamond Cuts Jerseys Black

*BLACK: .4X TO 1X BASIC
RANDOM INSERTS IN PACKS
STATED PRINT RUN 50 SER.#'d SETS

2015 Topps Tribute Diamond Cuts Jerseys Gold Patch

*GOLD: 1.2X TO 3X BASIC
RANDOM INSERTS IN PACKS
STATED PRINT RUN 25 SER.#'d SETS

2015 Topps Tribute Diamond Cuts Jerseys Orange

*ORANGE: .4X TO 1X BASIC
RANDOM INSERTS IN PACKS
STATED PRINT RUN 75 SER.#'d SETS

2015 Topps Tribute Foundations of Greatness Autographs

RANDOM INSERTS IN PACKS
STATED PRINT RUN 89 SER.#'d SETS
EXCHANGE DEADLINE 2/28/2018
PRICING FOR NON-DAMAGED AUTOS
THENAD Andre Dawson 10.00 25.00
THENDC David Cone 8.00 20.00
THENDE Dennis Eckersley 10.00 25.00
THENDM Dale Murphy 20.00 50.00
THENEM Edgar Martinez 10.00 25.00
THENFM Fred McGriff 10.00 25.00
THENGP Gregory Polanco 10.00 25.00
THENJA Jose Abreu 8.00 20.00
THENJG Juan Gonzalez 10.00 25.00
THENJM Juan Marichal 12.00 30.00
THENJR Jim Rice 10.00 25.00
THENLB Lou Brock 20.00 50.00
THENLG Luis Gonzalez 8.00 20.00
THENOC Orlando Cepeda 10.00 25.00
THENOS Ozzie Smith 20.00 50.00
THENPN Phil Niekro 12.00 30.00
THENPO Paul O'Neill 8.00 20.00
THENSC Steve Carlton 20.00 50.00
THENSG Sonny Gray 10.00 25.00

2015 Topps Tribute Foundations of Greatness Autographs Black

*BLACK: .4X TO 1X BASIC
RANDOM INSERTS IN PACKS
STATED PRINT RUN 50 SER.#'d SETS
EXCHANGE DEADLINE 2/28/2018
PRICING FOR NON-DAMAGED AUTOS
THENCF Carlton Fisk 25.00 60.00
THENCK Clayton Kershaw 100.00 200.00
THENRC Rod Carew 15.00 40.00

2015 Topps Tribute Foundations of Greatness Autographs Gold

*GOLD: .5X TO 1.2X BASIC
RANDOM INSERTS IN PACKS
STATED PRINT RUN 25 SER.#'d SETS
EXCHANGE DEADLINE 2/28/2018
PRICING FOR NON-DAMAGED AUTOS
THENAG Adrian Gonzalez 12.00 30.00
THENCK Clayton Kershaw 125.00 250.00
THENNR Nolan Ryan 50.00 125.00

2015 Topps Tribute Framed Autographs

RANDOM INSERTS IN PACKS
STATED PRINT RUN 189 SER.#'d SETS
EXCHANGE DEADLINE 2/28/2018
PRICING FOR NON-DAMAGED AUTOS
TAAC Allen Craig 6.00 15.00
TAAD Andre Dawson 10.00 25.00
TAAJ Adam Jones 6.00 15.00
TAAR Anthony Rizzo 15.00 40.00
TAARA Anthony Ranaudo 6.00 15.00
TACA Chris Archer 6.00 15.00
TACB Craig Biggio 12.00 30.00
TACC Carlos Correa/150 50.00 120.00
TACH Chase Headley 12.00 30.00
TACS Chris Sale 10.00 25.00
TADC David Cone 10.00 25.00
TADE Dennis Eckersley 8.00 20.00
TADMU Dale Murphy 8.00 20.00
TADN Daniel Norris 15.00 40.00
TADPO Dalton Pompey 20.00 50.00
TAFF Freddie Freeman 10.00 25.00
TAFL Francisco Lindor 50.00 120.00
TAFM Fred McGriff 10.00 25.00
TAFV Fernando Valenzuela 10.00 25.00
TAGP Gregory Polanco 10.00 25.00
TAGSP George Springer 12.00 30.00
TAJA Jose Abreu 10.00 25.00
TAJB Javier Baez 20.00 50.00
TAJBA Javier Baez 20.00 50.00
TAJCA Jose Canseco 12.00 30.00
TAJD Josh Donaldson 10.00 25.00
TAJF Jose Fernandez 20.00 50.00
TAJG Juan Gonzalez 6.00 15.00
TAJM Juan Marichal 12.00 30.00
TAJOS Jorge Soler 25.00 60.00
TAJP Joc Pederson 25.00 60.00
TAJPE Joc Pederson 25.00 60.00
TAJR Jim Rice 10.00 25.00
TAJS Jon Singleton 10.00 25.00
TAJSM John Smoltz 10.00 25.00
TAJSO Jorge Soler 25.00 60.00
TAKU Koji Uehara 12.00 30.00
TAKW Kolten Wong 6.00 12.00
TALB Lou Brock 12.00 30.00
TALG Luis Gonzalez 6.00 15.00
TAMA Matt Adams 10.00 25.00
TAMC Matt Carpenter 10.00 25.00
TAMN Mike Napoli 6.00 15.00
TAMS Max Scherzer 15.00 40.00
TAMTA Michael Taylor 8.00 20.00
TAMW Michael Wacha 10.00 25.00
TAOC Orlando Cepeda 15.00 40.00
TAPG Paul Goldschmidt 12.00 30.00
TAPN Phil Niekro 10.00 25.00
TARUC Rusney Castillo 8.00 20.00
TARUS Rusney Castillo 8.00 20.00
TASG Sonny Gray 10.00 25.00
TATW Taijuan Walker 6.00 15.00
TAVG Vladimir Guerrero 10.00 25.00
TAYC Yoenis Cespedes 10.00 25.00
TAYVE Yordano Ventura 10.00 25.00

2015 Topps Tribute Framed Autographs Black

*BLACK: .4X TO 1X BASIC
RANDOM INSERTS IN PACKS
STATED PRINT RUN 50 SER.#'d SETS
EXCHANGE DEADLINE 2/28/2018
PRICING FOR NON-DAMAGED AUTOS

2015 Topps Tribute Framed Autographs Gold

*GOLD: .6X TO 1.5X BASIC
RANDOM INSERTS IN PACKS
STATED PRINT RUN 25 SER.#'d SETS
EXCHANGE DEADLINE 2/28/2018
PRICING FOR NON-DAMAGED AUTOS

2015 Topps Tribute Framed Autographs Green

*GREEN: .4X TO 1X BASIC
RANDOM INSERTS IN PACKS
STATED PRINT RUN 99 SER.#'d SETS
EXCHANGE DEADLINE 2/28/2018
PRICING FOR NON-DAMAGED AUTOS

2015 Topps Tribute Framed Autographs Orange

*ORANGE: X TO X BASIC
RANDOM INSERTS IN PACKS
STATED PRINT RUN 75 SER.#'d SETS
EXCHANGE DEADLINE 2/28/2018
PRICING FOR NON-DAMAGED AUTOS

2015 Topps Tribute Prime Patches

RANDOM INSERTS IN PACKS
STATED PRINT RUN 45 SER.#'d SETS
PPBP Buster Posey 20.00 50.00
PPCJ Chipper Jones 30.00 80.00
PPCK Clayton Kershaw 25.00 60.00
PPCR Cal Ripken Jr. 30.00 80.00
PPDP Dustin Pedroia 25.00 60.00
PPDW David Wright 12.00 30.00
PPEL Evan Longoria 12.00 30.00
PPFF Freddie Freeman 20.00 50.00
PPFT Frank Thomas 25.00 60.00
PPGM Greg Maddux 25.00 60.00
PPGS Giancarlo Stanton 15.00 40.00
PPJE Jacoby Ellsbury 12.00 30.00
PPJV Joey Votto 20.00 50.00
PPMC Miguel Cabrera 20.00 50.00
PPMM Mark McGwire 25.00 60.00
PPMP Mike Piazza 25.00 60.00
PPMTA Masahiro Tanaka 12.00 30.00
PPRB Ryan Braun 12.00 30.00
PPRCA Rod Carew 12.00 30.00
PPRCL Roger Clemens 20.00 50.00
PPRH Rickey Henderson 15.00 40.00
PPRJ Randy Johnson 15.00 40.00
PPROC Robinson Cano 12.00 30.00
PPRP Rafael Palmeiro 12.00 30.00
PPVG Vladimir Guerrero 12.00 30.00
PPWB Wade Boggs 12.00 30.00
PPYD Yu Darvish 15.00 40.00
PPYP Yasiel Puig 15.00 40.00

2015 Topps Tribute Relics

RANDOM INSERTS IN PACKS
STATED PRINT RUN 199 SER.#'d SETS
TRAD Andre Dawson 6.00 15.00
TRAM Andrew McCutchen 10.00 25.00
TRAP Albert Pujols 6.00 15.00
TRAW Adam Wainwright 4.00 10.00
TRBP Buster Posey 12.00 30.00
TRCB Craig Biggio 4.00 10.00
TRCK Clayton Kershaw 4.00 10.00
TRCR Cal Ripken Jr. 15.00 40.00
TRDO David Ortiz 6.00 15.00
TRDP Dustin Pedroia 8.00 20.00
TRDW David Wright 4.00 10.00
TREL Evan Longoria 4.00 10.00
TRFF Freddie Freeman 6.00 15.00
TRFT Frank Thomas 10.00 25.00
TRGP Gregory Polanco 6.00 15.00
TRGS Giancarlo Stanton 5.00 12.00
TRHR Hanley Ramirez 4.00 10.00
TRJA Jose Abreu 5.00 12.00
TRJB Johnny Bench 5.00 12.00
TRJV Justin Verlander 6.00 15.00
TRKG Ken Griffey Jr. 15.00 40.00
TRMC Miguel Cabrera 5.00 12.00
TRMP Mike Piazza 10.00 25.00
TRMS Mike Schmidt 10.00 25.00
TRMSC Max Scherzer 5.00 12.00
TRMT Masahiro Tanaka 15.00 40.00
TRNR Nolan Ryan 15.00 40.00
TROS Ozzie Smith 10.00 25.00
TRRC Roger Clemens 6.00 15.00
TRRCA Rod Carew 4.00 10.00
TRRH Rickey Henderson 8.00 20.00
TRRJ Randy Johnson 8.00 20.00
TRRJA Reggie Jackson 8.00 20.00
TRRS Ryne Sandberg 10.00 25.00
TRRY Robin Yount 6.00 15.00
TRSS Stephen Strasburg 5.00 12.00
TRTT Troy Tulowitzki 5.00 12.00

2015 Topps Tribute Relics Black

*BLACK: .4X TO 1X BASIC
RANDOM INSERTS IN PACKS
STATED PRINT RUN 50 SER.#'d SETS

2015 Topps Tribute Relics Gold

*GOLD: 1.2X TO 3X BASIC
RANDOM INSERTS IN PACKS
STATED PRINT RUN 25 SER.#'d SETS

2015 Topps Tribute Relics Green

*GREEN: .4X TO 1X BASIC
RANDOM INSERTS IN PACKS
STATED PRINT RUN 150 SER.#'d SETS

2015 Topps Tribute Relics Orange

*ORANGE: .4X TO 1X BASIC
RANDOM INSERTS IN PACKS
STATED PRINT RUN 75 SER.#'d SETS

2015 Topps Tribute Rightful Recognition Autographs

RANDOM INSERTS IN PACKS
STATED PRINT RUN 89 SER.#'d SETS
EXCHANGE DEADLINE 2/28/2018
PRICING FOR NON-DAMAGED AUTOS
NOWAC Allen Craig 8.00 20.00
NOWAD Andre Dawson 10.00 25.00
NOWDC David Cone 10.00 25.00
NOWDE Dennis Eckersley 10.00 25.00
NOWDM Dale Murphy 10.00 25.00
NOWEM Edgar Martinez 10.00 25.00
NOWFM Fred McGriff 10.00 25.00
NOWGP Gregory Polanco 15.00 40.00
NOWJG Juan Gonzalez 10.00 25.00
NOWJM Juan Marichal 12.00 30.00
NOWJR Jim Rice 10.00 25.00
NOWLB Lou Brock 20.00 50.00
NOWLG Luis Gonzalez 8.00 20.00
NOWOC Orlando Cepeda 10.00 25.00
NOWOS Ozzie Smith 25.00 60.00
NOWPN Phil Niekro 12.00 30.00
NOWPO Paul O'Neill 15.00 40.00
NOWSC Steve Carlton 10.00 25.00
NOWSG Sonny Gray 10.00 25.00

2015 Topps Tribute Rightful Recognition Autographs Black

*BLACK: .4X TO 1X BASIC
RANDOM INSERTS IN PACKS
STATED PRINT RUN 50 SER.#'d SETS
EXCHANGE DEADLINE 2/28/2018
PRICING FOR NON-DAMAGED AUTOS

2015 Topps Tribute Rightful Recognition Autographs Gold

*GOLD: .5X TO 1.2X BASIC
RANDOM INSERTS IN PACKS
STATED PRINT RUN 25 SER.#'d SETS
EXCHANGE DEADLINE 2/28/2018
PRICING FOR NON-DAMAGED AUTOS

2015 Topps Tribute To The Victors Die Cut Autographs

RANDOM INSERTS IN PACKS
STATED PRINT RUN 30 SER.#'d SETS
EXCHANGE DEADLINE 2/28/2018
PRICING FOR NON-DAMAGED AUTOS
TTVCJ Chipper Jones 60.00 150.00
TTVDC David Cone 20.00 50.00
TTVDEC Dennis Eckersley 25.00 60.00
TTVFV Fernando Valenzuela 25.00 60.00
TTVHA Hank Aaron 200.00 300.00
TTVJB Johnny Bench 40.00 100.00
TTVJP Jim Palmer 40.00 100.00
TTVJPO Jorge Posada 40.00 100.00
TTVLB Lou Brock 30.00 80.00
TTVLG Luis Gonzalez 20.00 50.00
TTVMM Mark McGwire 200.00 300.00
TTVMR Mariano Rivera 100.00 250.00
TTVMS Mike Schmidt 100.00 200.00
TTVOC Orlando Cepeda 25.00 60.00
TTVOH Orlando Hernandez 25.00 60.00
TTVOS Ozzie Smith 20.00 50.00
TTVPM Pedro Martinez 20.00 50.00
TTVRA Roberto Alomar 30.00 80.00
TTVRJO Randy Johnson 125.00 250.00
TTVTS Tom Seaver 50.00 120.00

2016 Topps Tribute

PRINTING PLATE ODDS 1:185 HOBBY
PLATE PRINT RUN 1 SET PER COLOR
NO PLATE PRICING DUE TO SCARCITY
1 Mike Trout 5.00 12.00
2 Willie Stargell .75 2.00
3 Chris Sale 1.00 2.50
4 Kris Bryant 1.25 3.00
5 David Price .75 2.00
6 Rafael Palmeiro .75 2.00
7 Paul Goldschmidt 1.00 2.50
8 Willie Mays 2.00 5.00
9 Ian Kinsler .75 2.00
10 George Brett 2.00 5.00
11 Buster Posey 1.25 3.00
12 Carlos Correa 1.00 2.50
13 Joey Votto 1.00 2.50
14 Randy Johnson 1.00 2.50
15 Goose Gossage .75 2.00
16 Doc Gooden .60 1.50
17 Nolan Arenado 1.50 4.00
18 Zack Greinke 1.00 2.50
19 David Peralta .60 1.50
20 Michael Brantley .75 2.00
21 Paul Molitor 1.00 2.50
22 Satchel Paige 1.00 2.50
23 Yadier Molina 1.25 3.00
24 Sonny Gray .75 2.00
25 Babe Ruth 2.50 6.00
26 Felix Hernandez .75 2.00
27 Larry Doby .75 2.00
28 Bo Jackson 1.00 2.50
29 Cal Ripken Jr. 3.00 8.00
30 Warren Spahn .75 2.00
31 Ralph Kiner .75 2.00
32 Dee Gordon .60 1.50
33 Wade Davis .60 1.50
34 Trevor Rosenthal .75 2.00
35 Adrian Gonzalez .75 2.00
36 Jake Arrieta .75 2.00
37 Tony Perez .75 2.00
38 Gerrit Cole 1.00 2.50
39 Bryce Harper 1.50 4.00
40 Bert Blyleven .75 2.00
41 Xander Bogaerts 1.00 2.50
42 Bobby Doerr .75 2.00
43 Andrew McCutchen 1.00 2.50
44 Jose Abreu 1.00 2.50
45 Phil Rizzuto .75 2.00
46 Matt Kemp .75 2.00
47 Billy Williams .75 2.00
48 David Ortiz 1.00 2.50
49 Ted Williams 2.00 5.00
50 Sandy Koufax 2.00 5.00
51 Albert Pujols 1.25 3.00
52 Jacob deGrom 2.00 5.00
53 Anthony Rizzo 1.25 3.00
54 Jose Bautista .75 2.00
55 Eddie Murray .75 2.00
56 Catfish Hunter .75 2.00
57 Brooks Robinson .75 2.00
58 Miguel Cabrera 1.00 2.50
59 Carlos Martinez .75 2.00
60 Justin Upton .75 2.00
61 Manny Machado 1.00 2.50
62 Wade Boggs .75 2.00
63 Eddie Mathews 1.00 2.50
64 Adam Jones .75 2.00
65 Hoyt Wilhelm .75 2.00
66 Rollie Fingers .75 2.00
67 Robin Roberts .75 2.00
68 Stan Musial 1.50 4.00
69 Harmon Killebrew 1.00 2.50
70 Whitey Ford .75 2.00
71 Chris Archer .60 1.50
72 Bob Feller .75 2.00
73 Honus Wagner 1.00 2.50
74 Josh Donaldson .75 2.00
75 Bruce Sutter .75 2.00
76 Jim Bunning .75 2.00
77 Paul O'Neill .75 2.00
78 Johnny Bench 1.00 2.50
79 Nelson Cruz 1.00 2.50
80 Dellin Betances .75 2.00
81 Jim Palmer .75 2.00
82 Dallas Keuchel .75 2.00
83 Yoenis Cespedes 1.00 2.50
84 Max Scherzer 1.00 2.50
85 J.D. Martinez 1.00 2.50
86 Salvador Perez .75 2.00
87 Matt Carpenter 1.00 2.50
88 Mark Teixeira .75 2.00
89 Madison Bumgarner .75 2.00
90 Clayton Kershaw 1.50 4.00

2016 Topps Tribute Green

*GREEN: 1X TO 2.5X BASIC
STATED ODDS 1:8 HOBBY
STATED PRINT RUN 99 SER.#'d SETS
1 Mike Trout 6.00 15.00

2016 Topps Tribute Purple

*PURPLE: 2X TO 5X BASIC

STATED ODDS 1:15 HOBBY
STATED PRINT RUN 50 SER.#'d SETS

2016 Topps Tribute '16 Rookies

STATED ODDS 1:24 HOBBY
PRINTING PLATE ODDS 1:1627 HOBBY
PLATE PRINT RUN 1 SET PER COLOR
NO PLATE PRICING DUE TO SCARCITY
*PURPLE: .6X TO 1.5X BASIC
16R1 Blake Snell 2.50 6.00
16R2 Corey Seager 20.00 50.00
16R3 Miguel Sano 3.00 8.00
16R4 Kyle Schwarber 6.00 15.00
16R5 Trevor Story 6.00 15.00
16R6 Luis Severino 2.50 6.00
16R7 Aaron Nola 4.00 10.00
16R8 Stephen Piscotty 3.00 8.00
16R9 Michael Conforto 2.50 6.00
16R10 Kenta Maeda 4.00 10.00

2016 Topps Tribute Ageless Accolades Autographs

STATED ODDS 1:66 HOBBY
STATED PRINT RUN 50 SER.#'d SETS
EXCHANGE DEADLINE 6/30/2018
AAI Ichiro Suzuki 250.00 400.00
AABL Barry Larkin 20.00 50.00
AABP Buster Posey 60.00 150.00
AACJ Chipper Jones 40.00 100.00
AACK Clayton Kershaw 50.00 120.00
AACR Cal Ripken Jr. 30.00 80.00
AADE Dennis Eckersley 10.00 25.00
AADM Don Mattingly 30.00 80.00
AADMU Dale Murphy 25.00 60.00
AADP Dustin Pedroia 15.00 40.00
AAFR Frank Robinson 12.00 30.00
AAFT Frank Thomas 25.00 60.00
AAJB Johnny Bench 25.00 60.00
AAJC Jose Canseco 15.00 40.00
AAJG Juan Gonzalez 15.00 40.00
AAJR Jim Rice 12.00 30.00
AAKG Ken Griffey Jr. 60.00 150.00
AAMT Mike Trout 200.00 400.00
AARB Ryan Braun 10.00 25.00
AARH Rickey Henderson 25.00 60.00
AARJ Reggie Jackson 25.00 60.00
AARY Robin Yount 25.00 60.00
AAVG Vladimir Guerrero 15.00 40.00

2016 Topps Tribute Autographs

PRINT RUNS B/WN 20-199 COPIES PER
*BLUE/150: .4X TO 1X BASIC
*GREEN/99: .5X TO 1.2X BASIC
*PURPLE/50: .5X TO 1.2X BASIC
*ORANGE/25: .6X TO 1.5X BASE p/r 50-199
*ORANGE/25: .4X TO 1X BASE p/r 30
EXCHANGE DEADLINE 6/30/2018
TAAD Andre Dawson/75 8.00 20.00
TAADG Adrian Gonzalez/75 6.00 15.00
TAAG Andres Galarraga/199 4.00 10.00
TAAGO Alex Gordon/199 6.00 15.00
TAAJ Andruw Jones/199 3.00 8.00
TAAN Aaron Nola/199 6.00 15.00
TAAW Alex Wood/199 3.00 8.00
TABC Brandon Crawford/199 5.00 12.00
TABH Bryce Harper/30 200.00 400.00
TABJ Brian Johnson/199 3.00 8.00
TABJA Bo Jackson/30 30.00 80.00
TABL Barry Larkin/50 20.00 50.00
TABP Buster Posey/30 50.00 120.00
TABPA Byung-Ho Park 4.00 10.00
TACC Carlos Correa/50 25.00 60.00
TACD Carlos Delgado/199 3.00 8.00
TACF Carlton Fisk/75 15.00 40.00
TACH Cole Hamels/75 4.00 10.00
TACK Corey Kluber/199 10.00 25.00
TACKE Clayton Kershaw/50 60.00 150.00
TACR Carlos Rodon/199 5.00 12.00
TACS Corey Seager/199 30.00 80.00
TADE Dennis Eckersley/199 4.00 10.00
TADG Dee Gordon/199 3.00 8.00
TADL DJ LeMahieu/199 10.00 25.00
TADM Don Mattingly/50 20.00 50.00
TADP Dustin Pedroia/75 12.00 30.00
TADW David Wright/50 10.00 25.00
TAEM Edgar Martinez/199 10.00 25.00
TAFV Fernando Valenzuela/75 10.00 25.00
TAGR Garrett Richards/199 4.00 10.00
TAHA Hank Aaron/20 200.00 400.00
TAHO Henry Owens/199 4.00 10.00
TAHOL Hector Olivera/199 4.00 10.00
TAI Ichiro Suzuki/20 250.00 400.00
TAJA Jose Altuve/199 15.00 40.00
TAJB Jeff Bagwell/75 20.00 50.00
TAJBE Jose Berrios/199 5.00 12.00
TAJC Jose Canseco/199 10.00 25.00
TAJD Jacob deGrom/199 12.00 30.00
TAJG Juan Gonzalez/199 3.00 8.00
TAJGR Jon Gray/199 3.00 8.00
TAJP Joe Panik/199 4.00 10.00
TAJRI Jim Rice/199 5.00 12.00
TAJSM John Smoltz/75 15.00 40.00
TAKB Kris Bryant
TAKG Ken Griffey Jr. 125.00 250.00
TAKM Kenta Maeda 12.00 30.00
TAKS Kyle Schwarber/199 15.00 40.00
TAKW Kolten Wong/199 4.00 10.00
TALB Lou Brock/199 12.00 30.00
TALS Luis Severino/199 10.00 25.00
TAMCO Michael Conforto/199 12.00 30.00
TAMM Mark McGwire/30 50.00 120.00
TAMP Michael Pineda/199 3.00 8.00
TAMPI Mike Piazza/20 60.00 150.00
TAMSA Miguel Sano/199 5.00 12.00
TAMT Mike Trout/20 200.00 400.00
TANR Nolan Ryan/30 60.00 150.00
TANS Noah Syndergaard/199 10.00 25.00
TAOS Ozzie Smith/75 15.00 40.00
TAPM Paul Molitor/75 10.00 25.00
TAPO Paul O'Neill/199 8.00 20.00
TARB Ryan Braun/75 6.00 15.00
TARJ Reggie Jackson/30 20.00 50.00
TARS Robert Stephenson/199 3.00 8.00
TASC Steve Carlton/75 12.00 30.00
TASG Sonny Gray/199 4.00 10.00
TASPI Stephen Piscotty/199 5.00 12.00
TATT Troy Tulowitzki/50 8.00 20.00
TATTU Trea Turner/199 10.00 25.00

2016 Topps Tribute Cuts From the Cloth Autographs

STATED ODDS 1:94 HOBBY
STATED PRINT RUN 50 SER.#'d SETS
EXCHANGE DEADLINE 6/30/2018
CFCAG Adrian Gonzalez 8.00 20.00
CFCCB Craig Biggio 15.00 40.00
CFCCR Cal Ripken Jr. EXCH 40.00 100.00
CFCFF Freddie Freeman EXCH 10.00 25.00
CFCFT Frank Thomas 25.00 60.00
CFCJA Jose Altuve 15.00 40.00
CFCJS John Smoltz 15.00 40.00
CFCKB Kris Bryant 100.00 250.00
CFCMM Mark McGwire 75.00 200.00
CFCOS Ozzie Smith 25.00 60.00
CFCRC Robinson Cano 12.00 30.00

2016 Topps Tribute Foundations of Greatness Autographs

STATED ODDS 1:47 HOBBY
STATED PRINT RUN 99 SER.#'d SETS
EXCHANGE DEADLINE 6/30/2018
THENAK Al Kaline/99 15.00 40.00
THENAR Anthony Rizzo/99 20.00 50.00
THENCB Craig Biggio/99 12.00 30.00
THENCS Chris Sale/99 10.00 25.00
THENDM Don Mattingly/99 20.00 50.00
THENI Ichiro Suzuki/10
THENJB Jeff Bagwell/99 12.00 30.00
THENJP Joc Pederson/99 10.00 25.00
THENJS James Shields/99 3.00 8.00
THENMT Mark Teixeira/99 12.00 30.00
THENOV Omar Vizquel/99 6.00 15.00
THENPM Paul Molitor/99 12.00 30.00
THENRA Roberto Alomar/99 10.00 25.00
THENRP Rafael Palmeiro/99 6.00 15.00
THENTG Tom Glavine/99 12.00 30.00
THENVG Vladimir Guerrero/99 8.00 20.00

2016 Topps Tribute Foundations of Greatness Autographs Orange

*ORANGE: .6X TO 1.5X BASIC
STATED ODDS 1:105 HOBBY
STATED PRINT RUN 25 SER.#'d SETS
EXCHANGE DEADLINE 6/30/2018
THENBL Barry Larkin 25.00 60.00
THENBP Buster Posey 60.00 150.00
THENCJ Chipper Jones 40.00 100.00
THENCR Cal Ripken Jr. EXCH 60.00 150.00
THENDO David Ortiz 40.00 100.00
THENFT Frank Thomas 30.00 80.00
THENGM Greg Maddux 60.00 150.00
THENJBE Johnny Bench 30.00 80.00
THENNG Nomar Garciaparra 15.00 40.00
THENRH Rickey Henderson 30.00 80.00
THENRJ Randy Johnson 50.00 120.00
THENRY Robin Yount 25.00 60.00
THENWB Wade Boggs 20.00 50.00

2016 Topps Tribute Foundations of Greatness Autographs Purple

*PURPLE: .5X TO 1.2X BASIC
STATED ODDS 1:63 HOBBY
STATED PRINT RUN 50 SER.#'d SETS
EXCHANGE DEADLINE 6/30/2018
THENBL Barry Larkin 20.00 50.00
THENCJ Chipper Jones 30.00 80.00
THENDO David Ortiz 30.00 80.00
THENFT Frank Thomas 25.00 60.00
THENJBE Johnny Bench 25.00 60.00
THENNG Nomar Garciaparra 12.00 30.00
THENRH Rickey Henderson 25.00 60.00
THENRS Ryne Sandberg 30.00 80.00
THENRY Robin Yount 20.00 50.00
THENWB Wade Boggs 15.00 40.00

2016 Topps Tribute Prime Patches

STATED ODDS 1:89 HOBBY
STATED PRINT RUN 25 SER.#'d SETS
PPI Ichiro Suzuki 30.00 80.00
PPAM Andrew McCutchen 25.00 60.00
PPBH Bryce Harper 25.00 60.00
PPBP Buster Posey 20.00 50.00
PPCB Craig Biggio 8.00 20.00
PPCJ Chipper Jones 10.00 25.00
PPCK Clayton Kershaw 12.00 30.00
PPDG Doc Gooden 10.00 25.00
PPEM Eddie Murray 15.00 40.00
PPFH Felix Hernandez 8.00 20.00
PPFT-Frank Thomas 25.00 60.00
PPGM Greg Maddux 12.00 30.00
PPJA Jose Altuve 8.00 20.00
PPJB Jose Bautista 12.00 30.00
PPJM Juan Marichal 15.00 40.00
PPJP Jim Palmer 10.00 25.00
PPJS John Smoltz 12.00 30.00
PPJV Joey Votto 15.00 40.00
PPKB Kris Bryant 30.00 80.00
PPKGJ Ken Griffey Jr. 30.00 80.00
PPMC Miguel Cabrera 10.00 25.00
PPMM Mark McGwire 40.00 100.00
PPMP Mike Piazza 20.00 50.00
PPMT Mike Trout 25.00 60.00
PPNR Nolan Ryan 20.00 50.00
PPRJ Randy Johnson 10.00 25.00
PPRJA Reggie Jackson 10.00 25.00
PPWB Wade Boggs 10.00 25.00
PPWS Warren Spahn 20.00 5.00
PPZG Zack Greinke 12.00 30.00

2016 Topps Tribute Relics

PRINT RUNS B/WN 196-199 COPIES PER
*GREEN/99: .4X TO 1X BASIC
*PURPLE/50: .5X TO 1.2X BASIC
*ORANGE/25: .75X TO 2X BASIC
TRI Ichiro Suzuki/199 8.00 20.00
TRAJ Adam Jones/196 3.00 8.00
TRAM Andrew McCutchen/199 5.00 12.00
TRAMI Andrew Miller/196 3.00 8.00
TRAP Albert Pujols/196 5.00 12.00
TRAW Adam Wainwright/196 3.00 8.00
TRBP Buster Posey/196 5.00 12.00
TRCA Chris Archer/196 2.50 6.00
TRCB Craig Biggio/196 3.00 8.00
TRCK Clayton Kershaw/199 5.00 12.00
TRCKL Corey Kluber/199 3.00 8.00
TRCR Cal Ripken Jr./196 6.00 15.00
TRCS Chris Sale/196 4.00 10.00
TRDG Dee Gordon/196 2.50 6.00
TREM Eddie Murray/196 3.00 8.00
TRFH Felix Hernandez/196 3.00 8.00
TRFM Fred McGriff/196 3.00 8.00
TRGC Gerrit Cole/196 4.00 10.00
TRGM Greg Maddux/196 5.00 12.00
TRJB Jeff Bagwell/196 3.00 8.00
TRJD Jacob deGrom/196 8.00 20.00
TRJE Jacoby Ellsbury/196 3.00 8.00
TRJG Juan Gonzalez/196 2.50 6.00
TRJM Juan Marichal/196 3.00 8.00
TRJP Jim Palmer/196 3.00 8.00
TRJS John Smoltz/196 4.00 10.00
TRKB Kris Bryant/196 8.00 20.00
TRKG Ken Griffey Jr./196 5.00 12.00
TRKS Kyle Schwarber/196 5.00 12.00
TRMB Madison Bumgarner/196 3.00 8.00
TRMC Miguel Cabrera/199 4.00 10.00
TRMH Matt Harvey/196 3.00 8.00
TRMM Manny Machado/199 5.00 12.00
TRMMC Mark McGwire/196 5.00 12.00
TRMP Mike Piazza/196 4.00 10.00
TRMS Max Scherzer/199 4.00 10.00
TRMT Mike Trout/199 20.00 50.00
TRNA Nolan Arenado/196 6.00 15.00
TRNR Nolan Ryan/196 8.00 20.00
TRPF Prince Fielder/196 3.00 8.00
TRPG Paul Goldschmidt/196 4.00 10.00
TRRB Ryan Braun/196 3.00 8.00
TRRC Rod Carew/196 3.00 8.00
TRRCA Robinson Cano/196 3.00 8.00
TRRJ Randy Johnson/196 4.00 10.00
TRRJA Reggie Jackson/196 3.00 8.00
TRSG Sonny Gray/196 3.00 8.00
TRSM Starling Marte/196 3.00 8.00
TRTD Todd Frazier/196 2.50 6.00
TRTW Ted Williams/196 12.00 30.00
TRYD Yu Darvish/196 4.00 10.00
TRYP Yasiel Puig/196 4.00 10.00
TRZG Zack Greinke/196 4.00 10.00

2016 Topps Tribute Rightful Recognition Autographs

STATED ODDS 1:47 HOBBY
PRINT RUNS B/WN 10-99 COPIES PER
NO PRICING ON QTY 10
EXCHANGE DEADLINE 6/30/2018
NOWAK Al Kaline/99 15.00 40.00
NOWAR Anthony Rizzo/99 20.00 50.00
NOWCB Craig Biggio/99 12.00 30.00
NOWCS Chris Sale/99 10.00 25.00
NOWDM Don Mattingly/99 20.00 50.00
NOWJB Jeff Bagwell/99 15.00 40.00
NOWJP Joc Pederson/99 8.00 20.00
NOWJS James Shields/99 3.00 8.00
NOWMT Mark Teixeira/99 12.00 30.00
NOWOV Omar Vizquel/99 6.00 15.00
NOWPM Paul Molitor/99 10.00 25.00
NOWRA Roberto Alomar/99 10.00 25.00
NOWRP Rafael Palmeiro/99 6.00 15.00
NOWTG Tom Glavine/99 12.00 30.00
NOWVG Vladimir Guerrero/99 10.00 25.00

2016 Topps Tribute Rightful Recognition Autographs Orange

*ORANGE: .6X TO 1.5X BASIC
STATED ODDS 1:105 HOBBY
STATED PRINT RUN 25 SER.#'d SETS
EXCHANGE DEADLINE 6/30/2018
NOWBL Barry Larkin 25.00 60.00
NOWBP Buster Posey 60.00 150.00
NOWCJ Chipper Jones 40.00 100.00
NOWCR Cal Ripken Jr. 60.00 150.00
NOWDO David Ortiz 50.00 120.00
NOWFT Frank Thomas 30.00 80.00
NOWGM Greg Maddux 60.00 150.00
NOWJBE Johnny Bench 30.00 80.00
NOWNG Nomar Garciaparra 15.00 40.00
NOWRH Rickey Henderson 30.00 80.00
NOWRJ Randy Johnson 60.00 150.00
NOWRS Ryne Sandberg 25.00 60.00
NOWRY Robin Yount 25.00 60.00
NOWWB Wade Boggs 20.00 50.00

2016 Topps Tribute Rightful Recognition Autographs Purple

*PURPLE: .5X TO 1.2X BASIC
STATED ODDS 1:63 HOBBY
STATED PRINT RUN 50 SER.#'d SETS
EXCHANGE DEADLINE 6/30/2018
NOWBL Barry Larkin 20.00 50.00
NOWCJ Chipper Jones 30.00 80.00
NOWDO David Ortiz 40.00 100.00
NOWFT Frank Thomas 25.00 60.00
NOWJBE Johnny Bench 25.00 60.00
NOWNG Nomar Garciaparra 12.00 30.00
NOWRH Rickey Henderson 25.00 60.00
NOWRS Ryne Sandberg 20.00 50.00
NOWRY Robin Yount 20.00 50.00
NOWWB Wade Boggs 15.00 40.00

2016 Topps Tribute Stamp of Approval Relics

STATED PRINT RUN 199 SER.#'d SETS
*GREEN/99: .4X TO 1X BASIC
*PURPLE/50: .5X TO 1.2X BASIC
*ORANGE/25: .75X TO 2X BASIC
SOAAC Aroldis Chapman 4.00 10.00
SOAAE Alcides Escobar 3.00 8.00
SOAAW Adam Wainwright 3.00 8.00
SOABH Billy Hamilton 3.00 8.00
SOACA Chris Archer 2.50 6.00
SOACK Corey Kluber 3.00 8.00
SOACM Carlos Martinez 3.00 8.00
SOACS Corey Seager 4.00 10.00
SOADP Dustin Pedroia 4.00 10.00
SOAEG Evan Gattis 2.50 6.00
SOAEL Evan Longoria 3.00 8.00
SOAGP Gregory Polanco 4.00 10.00
SOAJA Jose Altuve 6.00 15.00
SOAJB Jose Bautista 3.00 8.00
SOAJE Jacoby Ellsbury 3.00 8.00
SOAJHK Jung Ho Kang 2.50 6.00
SOAJP Joc Pederson 3.00 8.00
SOAJZ Jordan Zimmermann 3.00 8.00
SOAKJ Kenley Jansen 3.00 8.00
SOAKS Kyle Schwarber 5.00 12.00
SOAKSE Kyle Seager 2.50 6.00
SOAMB Mookie Betts 5.00 12.00
SOAMC Miguel Cabrera 4.00 10.00
SOAMCO Michael Conforto 3.00 8.00
SOAMT Michael Taylor 2.50 6.00
SOAMTR Mike Trout 20.00 50.00
SOANA Nolan Arenado 6.00 15.00
SOANS Noah Syndergaard 3.00 8.00
SOASM Starling Marte 3.00 8.00
SOASP Salvador Perez 3.00 8.00
SOAYC Yoenis Cespedes 4.00 10.00
SOAYD Yu Darvish 4.00 10.00

2016 Topps Tribute Tribute Tandems Autographs

STATED ODDS 1:516 HOBBY
STATED PRINT RUN 25 SER.#'d SETS
EXCHANGE DEADLINE 6/30/2018
TTAB J.Altuve/C.Biggio 75.00 200.00
TTBS K.Bryant/R.Sandberg 250.00 400.00
TTJR Rbnsn/Jns EXCH 60.00 150.00
TTPB J.Bench/B.Posey 150.00 300.00
TTSJ R.Johnson/C.Sale 60.00 150.00
TTTA H.Aaron/M.Trout 600.00 800.00
TTTM Txra/Mttngly EXCH 60.00 150.00

2016 Topps Tribute Triple Crown Memories Autographs

STATED ODDS 1:721 HOBBY
STATED PRINT RUN 15 SER.#'d SETS
EXCHANGE DEADLINE 6/30/2018
TCFR1 Frank Robinson 25.00 60.00
TCFR2 Frank Robinson 25.00 60.00
TCFR3 Frank Robinson 25.00 60.00
TCSK1 Sandy Koufax 200.00 300.00
TCSK2 Sandy Koufax 200.00 300.00
TCSK3 Sandy Koufax 200.00 300.00

2017 Topps Tribute

1 Babe Ruth 3.00 8.00
2 Justin Verlander 1.25 3.00
3 Whitey Ford 1.00 2.50
4 Andy Pettitte 1.00 2.50
5 Zach Britton 1.00 2.50
6 Yu Darvish 1.25 3.00
7 Wil Myers 1.00 2.50
8 Duke Snider 1.00 2.50
9 Roger Maris 1.25 3.00
10 Ryne Sandberg 2.50 6.00
11 Jim Palmer 1.00 2.50
12 Tommy Lasorda 1.00 2.50
13 Corey Kluber 1.00 2.50
14 Trevor Story 1.25 3.00
15 Roberto Clemente 3.00 8.00
16 Gary Carter 1.00 2.50
17 Ozzie Smith 1.50 4.00
18 Jose Altuve 1.00 2.50
19 Daniel Murphy 1.00 2.50
20 Ichiro 1.50 4.00
21 Michael Fulmer .75 2.00
22 Jose Bautista 1.00 2.50
23 Willie Stargell 1.00 2.50
24 Mookie Betts 2.50 6.00
25 Mike Trout 6.00 15.00
26 Sparky Anderson 1.00 2.50
27 Anthony Rizzo 1.50 4.00
28 Rod Carew 1.00 2.50
29 Lou Brock 1.00 2.50
30 Edwin Encarnacion 1.25 3.00
31 Randy Johnson 1.25 3.00
32 Jeurys Familia 1.00 2.50
33 Madison Bumgarner 1.00 2.50
34 Stephen Piscotty 1.00 2.50
35 Stephen Strasburg 1.25 3.00
36 Manny Machado 1.25 3.00
37 Mark Trumbo .75 2.00
38 Danny Salazar 1.00 2.50
39 Nolan Arenado 2.00 5.00
40 Kris Bryant 1.50 4.00
41 Yoenis Cespedes 1.25 3.00
42 Noah Syndergaard 1.00 2.50
43 Kenta Maeda 1.00 2.50
44 Cole Hamels 1.00 2.50
45 Luis Aparicio 1.00 2.50
46 Starling Marte 1.00 2.50
47 Earl Weaver 1.00 2.50
48 Johnny Cueto 1.00 2.50
49 Corey Seager 1.25 3.00
50 Sandy Koufax 2.50 6.00
51 Carl Yastrzemski 2.00 5.00
52 Harmon Killebrew 1.25 3.00
53 David Price 1.00 2.50
54 Billy Williams 1.00 2.50
55 Xander Bogaerts 1.25 3.00
56 Ivan Rodriguez 1.00 2.50
57 Jackie Robinson 1.25 3.00
58 Buster Posey 1.50 4.00
59 Tom Glavine 1.00 2.50
60 Catfish Hunter 1.00 2.50
61 Joe Morgan 1.00 2.50
62 Bryce Harper 2.00 5.00
63 Giancarlo Stanton 1.25 3.00
64 Chris Sale 1.25 3.00
65 Ken Griffey Jr. 2.50 6.00
66 Ty Cobb 2.00 5.00
67 Clayton Kershaw 2.00 5.00
68 Jake Arrieta 1.00 2.50
69 Tony La Russa 1.00 2.50
70 Wade Boggs 1.00 2.50
71 Lorenzo Cain .75 2.00
72 Jacob deGrom 2.50 6.00
73 Phil Rizzuto 1.00 2.50
74 Yadier Molina 1.50 4.00
75 David Ortiz 1.25 3.00
76 Eddie Mathews 1.25 3.00
77 Francisco Lindor 1.25 3.00
78 Andrew McCutchen 1.25 3.00
79 Mark McGwire 2.00 5.00
80 Carlos Correa 1.25 3.00
81 Nomar Mazara .75 2.00
82 George Brett 2.50 6.00
83 Aledmys Diaz 1.00 2.50
84 Lou Gehrig 2.50 6.00
85 Albert Pujols 1.50 4.00
86 Mike Piazza 1.25 3.00
87 Brooks Robinson 1.00 2.50
88 Josh Donaldson 1.00 2.50
89 Max Scherzer 1.25 3.00
90 Hank Aaron 2.50 6.00

2017 Topps Tribute Green

*GREEN: 1X TO 2.5X BASIC
STATED ODDS 1:6 HOBBY
STATED PRINT RUN 99 SER.#'d SETS

2017 Topps Tribute Purple

*PURPLE: 1.2X TO 3X BASIC
STATED ODDS 1:15 HOBBY
STATED PRINT RUN 50 SER.#'d SETS

2017 Topps Tribute '17 Rookies

STATED ODDS 1:24 HOBBY
*PURPLE/50: .5X TO 1.2X BASIC
17R1 Alex Bregman 12.00 30.00
17R2 Jose De Leon 2.00 5.00
17R3 David Dahl 2.50 6.00
17R4 Andrew Benintendi 30.00 80.00
17R5 Orlando Arcia 5.00 12.00
17R6 Alex Reyes 2.50 6.00
17R7 Tyler Glasnow 8.00 20.00
17R8 Aaron Judge 12.00 30.00
17R9 Dansby Swanson 10.00 25.00
17R10 Yoan Moncada 8.00 20.00

2017 Topps Tribute Autograph Patches

STATED ODDS 1:89 HOBBY
STATED PRINT RUN 50 SER.#'d SETS
EXCHANGE DEADLINE 2/28/2019
TAPAJ Adam Jones EXCH 30.00 80.00
TAPCC Carlos Correa
TAPDF Dexter Fowler 30.00 80.00
TAPDO David Ortiz
TAPDPE Dustin Pedroia 30.00 80.00
TAPFF Freddie Freeman 20.00 50.00
TAPFL Francisco Lindor 50.00 120.00
TAPHR Hanley Ramirez EXCH 8.00 20.00
TAPI Ichiro
TAPJA Jose Altuve 30.00 80.00
TAPJM J.D. Martinez 25.00 60.00
TAPMF Michael Fulmer 20.00 50.00
TAPMM Manny Machado
TAPNM Nomar Mazara EXCH 30.00 80.00
TAPNS Noah Syndergaard 25.00 60.00
TAPSM Starling Marte EXCH 30.00 80.00

2017 Topps Tribute Autographs

STATE ODDS 1:7 HOBBY
PRINT RUNS B/WN 15-199 COPIES PER
*GREEN/99: .5X TO 1.2X BASIC
*BLUE/75: .5X TO 1.2X BASIC
*PURPLE/50: .4X TO 1X BASE p/r 50
*PURPLE/50: .5X TO 1.2X BASE p/r 90-199
*ORANGE/25: .4X TO 1X BASE p/r 20-30
*ORANGE/25: .6X TO 1.5X BASE p/r 90-199
NO PRICING ON QTY 15
EXCHANGE DEADLINE 2/28/2019
TAAB Alex Bregman/199 20.00 50.00
TAABE Andrew Benintendi/199 75.00 200.00
TAAC Adam Conley/199 3.00 8.00
TAAJU Aaron Judge/199 100.00 250.00
TAAP Andy Pettitte/30 12.00 30.00
TAAR Anthony Rizzo
TAARE Alex Reyes/199 4.00 10.00
TABB Barry Bonds/20
TABH Bryce Harper EXCH
TABP Buster Posey/30
TABS Blake Snell/199 4.00 10.00
TABSH Braden Shipley/199 3.00 8.00
TACC Carlos Correa/90 30.00 80.00
TACFU Carson Fulmer/199 3.00 8.00
TACR Cal Ripken Jr./30 60.00 150.00
TACRO Carlos Rodon EXCH 5.00 12.00
TACSE Corey Seager/199 20.00 50.00
TACY Carl Yastrzemski/30 40.00 100.00
TADD David Dahl/199 4.00 10.00
TADF Dexter Fowler/199 6.00 15.00
TADG Didi Gregorius/199 6.00 15.00
TADJ Derek Jeter EXCH
TADO David Ortiz/30 40.00 100.00
TADP David Price/199 8.00 20.00
TADS Dansby Swanson/199 10.00 25.00
TAFL Francisco Lindor/199 20.00 50.00
TAFLI Francisco Lindor/199 20.00 50.00
TAFV Fernando Valenzuela/50 8.00 20.00
TAGS George Springer/199 10.00 25.00
TAIR Ivan Rodriguez/199 15.00 40.00
TAJAL Jose Altuve/199 12.00 30.00
TAJD Jacob deGrom/199 15.00 40.00
TAJDL Jose De Leon/199 5.00 12.00
TAJM J.D. Martinez/199 20.00 50.00
TAJOA Jose Altuve/199 12.00 30.00
TAJP Joc Pederson/199 8.00 20.00
TAJT Jameson Taillon/199 6.00 15.00
TAJU Julio Urias EXCH 5.00 12.00
TAKB Kris Bryant/100 25.00 60.00
TAKGJ Ken Griffey Jr./30 125.00 300.00
TAKMO Kendrys Morales/199 3.00 8.00
TAKS Kyle Schwarber/199 12.00 30.00
TALW Luke Weaver/199 4.00 10.00
TAMAT Masahiro Tanaka EXCH 125.00 300.00
TAMF Michael Fulmer/199 3.00 8.00
TAMS Marcus Stroman/199 5.00 12.00
TAMW Matt Wieters/199 5.00 12.00
TANM Nomar Mazara/199 12.00 30.00
TANMA Nomar Mazara/199 12.00 30.00
TANR Nolan Ryan/30 100.00 250.00
TANS Noah Syndergaard/199 10.00 25.00
TAOS Ozzie Smith/145 20.00 50.00
TAOV Omar Vizquel/110 6.00 15.00
TAPK Paul Konerko/199 4.00 10.00
TARH Ryon Healy/199 6.00 15.00
TARJ Reggie Jackson/30 30.00 80.00
TARS Ryne Sandberg
TASG Sonny Gray/199 5.00 12.00
TASMA Steven Matz/199 3.00 8.00
TASP Stephen Piscotty/199 4.00 10.00
TASW Steven Wright/199 4.00 10.00
TATA Tim Anderson/199 4.00 10.00
TATG Tom Glavine/199 10.00 25.00
TATRS Trevor Story/199 8.00 20.00
TATS Trevor Story/199 8.00 20.00
TATT Trea Turner/199 12.00 30.00
TATTU Trea Turner/199 12.00 30.00
TAWC Willson Contreras/199 8.00 20.00
TAWD Wade Davis/199 3.00 8.00
TAYG Yulieski Gurriel/199 10.00 25.00
TAYM Yoan Moncada/100 30.00 80.00

2017 Topps Tribute Dual Relics

STATED ODDS 1:85 HOBBY
STATED PRINT RUN 50 SER.#'d SETS
EXCHANGE DEADLINE 2/28/2019
DRACA Abreu/Cabrera 5.00 12.00
DRBE Bautista/Encarnacion 20.00 50.00
DRCA Altuve/Correa
DRCE Cain/Escobar
DRCP Perez/Cain 12.00 30.00
DRCS Springer/Correa 12.00 30.00
DRFN Franco/Nola 10.00 25.00
DRFZI Fulmer/Zimmerman 12.00 30.00
DRHC Hernandez/Cano
DRJM Machado/Jones 20.00 50.00
DRKM Martinez/Kinsler
DRLG Gonzalez/LeMahieu
DRMH Mazara/Hamels 8.00 20.00
DRMM McCutchen/Marte 40.00 100.00
DRSW Wright/Syndergaard 20.00 50.00

2017 Topps Tribute Dual Autographs

STATED ODDS 1:356 HOBBY
STATED PRINT RUN 25 SER.#'d SETS
EXCHANGE DEADLINE 2/28/2019
DACG Tom Glavine 25.00 60.00
David Cone
DAJK John Kruk 60.00 150.00
Randy Johnson
DAJP Andy Pettitte 60.00 150.00
Randy Johnson
DAKA Hank Aaron
Sandy Koufax EXCH
DAKP Clayton Kershaw 75.00 200.00
Buster Posey
DAPS Andy Pettitte 60.00 150.00
John Smoltz
DARJ Nolan Ryan
Reggie Jackson

2017 Topps Tribute Generations of Excellence Autographs

STATE ODDS 1:34 HOBBY
STATED PRINT RUN 99 SER.#'d SETS
*PURPLE/50: .4X TO 1X BASIC
*ORANGE/25: .5X TO 1.2X BASIC
EXCHANGE DEADLINE 2/28/2019
GOEAD Andre Dawson 12.00 30.00
GOEAG Andres Galarraga 5.00 12.00
GOEAP Andy Pettitte 15.00 40.00
GOEBL Barry Larkin 25.00 60.00
GOEBW Billy Wagner 6.00 15.00
GOECB Craig Biggio 12.00 30.00
GOECY Carl Yastrzemski
GOEDC David Cone 10.00 25.00
GOEDE Dennis Eckersley 6.00 15.00
GOEDJ Derek Jeter
GOEDM Don Mattingly 40.00 100.00
GOEDO David Ortiz
GOEFT Frank Thomas 30.00 80.00
GOEHA Hank Aaron
GOEIR Ivan Rodriguez 15.00 40.00
GOEJB Johnny Bench
GOEJR Jim Rice 10.00 25.00
GOEJS John Smoltz 15.00 40.00
GOEMM Mark McGwire
GOEMP Mike Piazza
GOENR Nolan Ryan
GOEOS Ozzie Smith 40.00 100.00
GOEOV Omar Vizquel 5.00 12.00
GOEPK Paul Konerko 12.00 30.00
GOEPM Paul Molitor 10.00 25.00
GOEPO Paul O'Neill 12.00 30.00
GOERA Roberto Alomar 15.00 40.00
GOERJ Reggie Jackson
GOERO Roy Oswalt 6.00 15.00
GOERS Ryne Sandberg 25.00 60.00
GOESG Steve Garvey 12.00 30.00
GOESK Sandy Koufax
GOETG Tom Glavine 12.00 30.00

2017 Topps Tribute Relics

STATED ODDS 1:7 HOBBY
PRINT RUNS B/WN 196-199 COPIES PER
*GREEN/99: .4X TO 1X BASIC
*PURPLE/50: .5X TO 1.2X BASIC
*ORANGE/25: .75X TO 2X BASIC
TRAM Andrew McCutchen/192 6.00 15.00
TRAR Anthony Rizzo/199 5.00 12.00
TRARU Addison Russell/192 5.00 12.00
TRBH Bryce Harper/192 6.00 15.00
TRBL Barry Larkin/192 3.00 8.00
TRBP Buster Posey/192 5.00 12.00
TRCB Craig Biggio/192 3.00 8.00
TRCC Carlos Correa/192 6.00 15.00
TRCH Cole Hamels/192 3.00 8.00
TRCJ Chipper Jones/192 5.00 12.00
TRCR Cal Ripken Jr./192 10.00 25.00
TRCSA Carlos Santana/192 3.00 8.00
TRCSE Corey Seager/192 5.00 12.00
TRDB Dellin Betances/192 3.00 8.00
TRDM Don Mattingly/192 8.00 20.00
TRDO David Ortiz/199 4.00 10.00
TRFH Felix Hernandez/199 3.00 8.00
TRFL Francisco Lindor/192 4.00 10.00
TRGS Giancarlo Stanton/199 4.00 10.00
TRGSP George Springer/192 3.00 8.00
TRI Ichiro/192 5.00 12.00
TRJA Jose Altuve/192 3.00 8.00
TRJAR Jake Arrieta/192 3.00 8.00
TRJB Jose Bautista/192 3.00 8.00
TRJBJ Jackie Bradley Jr./192 4.00 10.00
TRJD Josh Donaldson/192 3.00 8.00
TRJDE Jacob deGrom/192 8.00 20.00
TRJFA Jeurys Familia/192 3.00 8.00
TRJS John Smoltz/192 4.00 10.00
TRJU Julio Urias/192 4.00 10.00
TRJV Joey Votto/192 4.00 10.00
TRKS Kyle Seager/192 2.50 6.00
TRKSC Kyle Schwarber/199 4.00 10.00
TRMB Madison Bumgarner/199 3.00 8.00
TRMC Miguel Cabrera/199 4.00 10.00
TRMCA Matt Carpenter/192 4.00 10.00
TRMM Manny Machado/192 4.00 10.00
TRMMC Mark McGwire/192 6.00 15.00
TRMP Mike Piazza/192 4.00 10.00
TRMT Mike Trout/199 20.00 50.00
TRMTA Masahiro Tanaka/192 6.00 15.00
TRNC Nelson Cruz/192 4.00 10.00
TRNM Nomar Mazara/192 2.50 6.00
TRNS Noah Syndergaard/192 5.00 12.00
TRPG Paul Goldschmidt/192 4.00 10.00
TRRC Robinson Cano/192 3.00 8.00
TRRCL Roger Clemens/192 5.00 12.00
TRRO Rougned Odor/199 3.00 8.00
TRTG Tom Glavine/192 3.00 8.00
TRXB Xander Bogaerts/199 4.00 10.00
TRYC Yoenis Cespedes/199 4.00 10.00

2017 Topps Tribute Stamp of Approval Relics

STATED ODDS 1:11 HOBBY
STATED PRINT RUN 199 SER.#'d SETS
*GREEN/99: .4X TO 1X BASIC
*PURPLE/50: .5X TO 1.2X BASIC
*ORANGE/25: .75X TO 2X BASIC
SOAAJ Adam Jones 3.00 8.00
SOAAM Andrew McCutchen 10.00 25.00
SOAAN Aaron Nola 3.00 8.00
SOABH Billy Hamilton 3.00 8.00
SOABZ Ben Zobrist 3.00 8.00
SOACC Carlos Correa 4.00 10.00
SOACH Cole Hamels 3.00 8.00
SOADF Dexter Fowler 3.00 8.00
SOAEE Edwin Encarnacion 4.00 10.00
SOAFH Felix Hernandez 3.00 8.00
SOAGS George Springer 3.00 8.00
SOAHR Hanley Ramirez 3.00 8.00
SOAI Ichiro 5.00 12.00
SOAJA Jose Altuve 3.00 8.00
SOAJAB Jose Abreu 4.00 10.00
SOAJBA Jose Bautista 3.00 8.00
SOAJOB Javier Baez 4.00 10.00
SOAJV Joey Votto 4.00 10.00
SOAJZ Jordan Zimmermann 3.00 8.00
SOALC Lorenzo Cain 2.50 6.00
SOAMC Melky Cabrera 2.50 6.00
SOAMF Michael Fulmer 2.50 6.00
SOAMFR Maikel Franco 3.00 8.00
SOAMM Manny Machado 4.00 10.00
SOANM Nomar Mazara 2.50 6.00
SOANS Noah Syndergaard 5.00 12.00
SOARC Robinson Cano 3.00 8.00
SOASM Starling Marte 8.00 20.00
SOASP Salvador Perez 3.00 8.00
SOAWM Wil Myers 3.00 8.00

2017 Topps Tribute Tandem Autograph Booklets

STATED ODDS 1:192 HOBBY
STATED PRINT RUN 25 SER.#'d SETS
EXCHANGE DEADLINE 2/28/2019
TTCB Biggio/Correa 100.00 250.00
TTFJ Jones/Freeman 125.00 300.00
TTHG Harper/Griffey
TTKK Kershaw/Koufax
TTLB Boggs/Longoria
TTLV Lindor/Vizquel 250.00 400.00
TTMK Kaline/Martinez 75.00 200.00
TTMR Machado/Ripken 250.00 400.00
TTPG Garciaparra/Pedroia
TTPR Posey/Pudge 50.00 120.00
TTSC Carlton/Sale EXCH 20.00 50.00
TTSR Ryan/Syndergaard EXCH 250.00 400.00
TTUV Valenzuela/Urias EXCH 125.00 300.00
TTVH Heyward/Dawson 40.00 100.00

2017 Topps Tribute to the Moment Autographs

STATE ODDS 1:40 HOBBY
PRINT RUNS B/WN 25-99 COPIES PER
*PURPLE/50: .4X TO 1X BASIC
*ORANGE/25: .5X TO 1.2X BASIC
EXCHANGE DEADLINE 2/28/2019
TTMAD Andre Dawson/99 10.00 25.00
TTMAK Al Kaline/99 20.00 50.00
TTMBB Barry Bonds/25 100.00 250.00
TTMCB Craig Biggio/99 12.00 30.00
TTMCK Clayton Kershaw/50 40.00 100.00
TTMCY Carl Yastrzemski 40.00 100.00
TTMDM Don Mattingly/60 40.00 100.00
TTMDP David Price/99 12.00 30.00
TTMFT Frank Thomas/50 25.00 60.00
TTMHA Hank Aaron
TTMIR Ivan Rodriguez/99 15.00 40.00
TTMI Ichiro/25
TTMJG Juan Gonzalez/99 6.00 15.00
TTMJR Jim Rice/99 10.00 25.00
TTMJS John Smoltz/99 8.00 20.00
TTMMM Manny Machado/99 25.00 60.00
TTMMP Mike Piazza/25 60.00 150.00
TTMMT Mike Trout/40 300.00 600.00
TTMNR Nolan Ryan/50 60.00 150.00
TTMPM Paul Molitor/99 12.00 30.00
TTMYM Yoan Moncada/50 40.00 100.00

2017 Topps Tribute Walk Off Autographs

STATE ODDS 1:104 HOBBY
STATED PRINT RUN 99 SER.#'d SETS
*ORANGE/25: .5X TO 1.2X BASIC
EXCHANGE DEADLINE 2/28/2019
WOAAB Aaron Boone 15.00 40.00
WOABW Bernie Williams 20.00 50.00
WOACF Carlton Fisk 25.00 60.00
WOACJ Chipper Jones 50.00 120.00
WOADO David Ortiz 40.00 100.00
WOAEM Edgar Martinez 15.00 40.00
WOAJB Johnny Bench 25.00 60.00
WOAKGJ Ken Griffey Jr.
WOALG Luis Gonzalez 20.00 50.00
WOAMM Mark McGwire 40.00 100.00
WOAOS Ozzie Smith 20.00
WOAOV Omar Vizquel 12.00 30.00

2013 Topps Tribute WBC

1 Miguel Cabrera 1.00 2.50
2 Andre Rienzo .60 1.50
3 Erisbel Arruebarruena 8.00 20.00
4 Mike Aviles .60 1.50
5 Hideaki Wakui .60 1.50
6 Yao-Hsun Yang 1.00 2.50
7 Jae Weong Seo .60 1.50
8 Andrelton Simmons .60 1.50
9 Anthony Rizzo 1.25 3.00
10 Shinnosuke Abe 1.00 2.50
11 Heath Bell .60 1.50
12 Jhoulys Chacin .60 1.50
13 Adam Jones .75 2.00
14 Marco Estrada .60 1.50
15 Yulieski Gourriel 1.25 3.00
16 John Axford .60 1.50
17 Carlos Gonzalez .75 2.00
18 Edwin Encarnacion 1.00 2.50
19 Toshiya Sugiuchi .60 1.50
20 Joe Mauer .75 2.00
21 Eddie Rosario 1.25 3.00

22 Anibal Sanchez .60 1.50
23 Salvador Perez .75 2.00
24 Kelvin Herrera .60 1.50
25 Xander Bogaerts 2.00 5.00
26 Takeru Imamura .40 1.00
27 Yadier Pedroso .40 1.00
28 Steve Cishek .60 1.50
29 Atsunori Inaba .60 1.50
30 Jose Reyes .75 2.00
31 Miguel Montero .60 1.50
32 Kenji Ohtonari 1.00 2.50
33 Angel Pagan .60 1.50
34 Carlos Zambrano .75 2.00
35 Che-Hsuan Lin 1.00 2.50
36 Eric Hosmer .75 2.00
37 Sergio Romo .60 1.50
38 Martin Prado .60 1.50
39 Atsushi Nohmi 1.00 2.50
40 Joey Votto 1.00 2.50
41 Jonatan Isenia 1.00 2.50
42 Yadier Molina 1.25 3.00
43 Giancarlo Stanton 1.00 2.50
44 Edinson Volquez .60 1.50
45 Masahiro Tanaka 6.00 15.00
46 Ben Zobrist .75 2.00
47 Phillippe Aumont .60 1.50
48 Ryan Vogelsong .60 1.50
49 Dae Ho Lee 1.00 2.50
50 David Wright .75 2.00
51 Carlos Beltran .75 2.00
52 Fernando Rodney .60 1.50
53 Odrisamer Despaigne 8.00 20.00
54 Jose Fernandez 1.50 4.00
55 Dai-Kang Yang 2.50 6.00
56 Marco Scutaro .75 2.00
57 Kenta Maeda 4.00 10.00
58 Jameson Taillon .75 2.00
59 Kazuo Matsui .40 1.00
60 Robinson Cano .75 2.00
61 Adrian Gonzalez .75 2.00
62 J.P. Arencibia .60 1.50
63 Henderson Alvarez .60 1.50
64 Hayato Sakamoto 1.25 3.00
65 Justin Morneau .75 2.00
66 Wandy Rodriguez .60 1.50
67 Gio Gonzalez .75 2.00
68 Alex Rios .75 2.00
69 Freddy Alvarez 1.00 2.50
70 Jimmy Rollins .75 2.00
71 Yuichi Honda 1.00 2.50
72 Derek Holland .60 1.50
73 Erick Aybar .60 1.50
74 Chien-Ming Wang .75 2.00
75 Nelson Cruz 1.00 2.50
76 Suk-Min Yoon 1.00 2.50
77 Jose Berrios 1.00 2.50
78 Jonathan Lucroy .75 2.00
79 Elvis Andrus .75 2.00
80 R.A. Dickey .75 2.00
81 Yovani Gallardo .60 1.50
82 Tadashi Settsu 1.00 2.50
83 Jen-Ho Tseng 1.50 4.00
84 Carlos Santana .75 2.00
85 Craig Kimbrel .75 2.00
86 Asdrubal Cabrera .75 2.00
87 Alfredo Despaigne 1.00 2.50
88 Jonathan Schoop .60 1.50
89 Tetsuya Utsumi .60 1.50
90 Pablo Sandoval .75 2.00
91 Nobuhiro Matsuda 1.00 2.50
92 Shane Victorino .75 2.00
93 Jurickson Profar .75 2.00
94 Andruw Jones .60 1.50
95 Brandon Phillips .60 1.50
96 Ross Detwiler .60 1.50
97 Hanley Ramirez .75 2.00
98 Jose Abreu 10.00 25.00
99 Miguel Tejada .60 1.50
100 Ryan Braun .75 2.00

2013 Topps Tribute WBC Gold

*GOLD: 3X TO 8X BASIC
STATED ODDS 1:20 HOBBY
STATED PRINT RUN 25 SER.#'d SETS
25 Xander Bogaerts 10.00 25.00
30 Jose Reyes 10.00 25.00
42 Yadier Molina 15.00 40.00
53 Odrisamer Despaigne 30.00 60.00
98 Jose Abreu

2013 Topps Tribute WBC Autographs

STATED ODDS 1:4 HOBBY
ALL VERSIONS EQUALLY PRICED
EXCHANGE DEADLINE 06/30/2016
AC Asdrubal Cabrera 5.00 12.00
AC2 Asdrubal Cabrera 5.00 12.00
AG Adrian Gonzalez 8.00 20.00
AG2 Adrian Gonzalez 8.00 20.00
AJ Adam Jones 8.00 20.00
AJ2 Adam Jones 8.00 20.00
AJ3 Adam Jones 8.00 20.00
AR Andre Rienzo 4.00 10.00
AR2 Andre Rienzo 4.00 10.00
ARI Anthony Rizzo 8.00 20.00
ARI2 Anthony Rizzo 8.00 20.00
ARI3 Anthony Rizzo 10.00 25.00
AS Andrelton Simmons 10.00 25.00
AS2 Andrelton Simmons 10.00 25.00
BP Brandon Phillips 5.00 12.00
BP2 Brandon Phillips 5.00 12.00
BP3 Brandon Phillips 5.00 12.00
BZ Ben Zobrist 10.00 25.00
BZ2 Ben Zobrist 10.00 25.00
BZ3 Ben Zobrist 10.00 25.00
CK Craig Kimbrel 10.00 25.00
CK2 Craig Kimbrel 10.00 25.00
CS Carlos Santana 5.00 12.00
CS2 Carlos Santana 5.00 12.00
DHO Derek Holland 4.00 10.00
DHO2 Derek Holland 4.00 10.00
DHO3 Derek Holland 4.00 10.00
DW David Wright 12.50 30.00
EE Edwin Encarnacion 6.00 15.00
EE2 Edwin Encarnacion 6.00 15.00
ER Eddie Rosario 8.00 20.00
ER2 Eddie Rosario 8.00 20.00
FR Fernando Rodney EXCH 4.00 10.00
GG Gio Gonzalez EXCH 4.00 10.00
GP Glen Perkins 4.00 10.00
GP2 Glen Perkins 4.00 10.00
HA Henderson Alvarez 4.00 10.00
HA2 Henderson Alvarez 4.00 10.00
HR Hanley Ramirez 10.00 25.00
JA J.P. Arencibia 6.00 15.00
JA2 J.P. Arencibia 6.00 15.00
JAX John Axford 4.00 10.00
JAX2 John Axford 4.00 10.00
JB Jose Berrios 8.00 20.00
JB2 Jose Berrios 8.00 20.00
JG Jason Grilli 6.00 15.00
JG2 Jason Grilli 6.00 15.00
JL Jonathan Lucroy 8.00 20.00
JL2 Jonathan Lucroy 8.00 20.00
JP Jurickson Profar EXCH 8.00 20.00
JR Jose Reyes 6.00 15.00
JSC Jonathan Schoop 4.00 10.00
JSC2 Jonathan Schoop 4.00 10.00
JSC3 Jonathan Schoop 4.00 10.00
JT Jameson Taillon 6.00 15.00
JT2 Jameson Taillon 6.00 15.00
JT3 Jameson Taillon 6.00 15.00
KH Kelvin Herrera 4.00 10.00
KH2 Kelvin Herrera 4.00 10.00
LM Luis Mendoza 4.00 10.00
LM2 Luis Mendoza 4.00 10.00
MC Miguel Cabrera 20.00 50.00
MC2 Miguel Cabrera 20.00 50.00
MM Miguel Montero 4.00 10.00
MM2 Miguel Montero 4.00 10.00
MP Martin Prado 4.00 10.00
MP2 Martin Prado 4.00 10.00
NC Nelson Cruz 4.00 10.00
NC2 Nelson Cruz 4.00 10.00
NC3 Nelson Cruz 4.00 10.00
RD R.A. Dickey 5.00 12.00
RDE Ross Detwiler 4.00 10.00
RDE2 Ross Detwiler 4.00 10.00
RV Ryan Vogelsong 5.00 12.00
RV2 Ryan Vogelsong 5.00 12.00
SP Salvador Perez 6.00 15.00
SP2 Salvador Perez 6.00 15.00
SP3 Salvador Perez 6.00 15.00
SV Shane Victorino 6.00 15.00
SV2 Shane Victorino 6.00 15.00
WR Wandy Rodriguez 4.00 10.00
WR2 Wandy Rodriguez 4.00 10.00
YG Yovani Gallardo 6.00 15.00
YG2 Yovani Gallardo 6.00 15.00
YG3 Yovani Gallardo 6.00 15.00
YLW Yao-Lin Wang 5.00 12.00

2013 Topps Tribute WBC Autographs Blue

*BLUE: .5X TO 1.2X BASIC
STATED ODDS 1:9 HOBBY
STATED PRINT RUN 50 SER.#'d SETS
EXCHANGE DEADLINE 06/30/2016

2013 Topps Tribute WBC Autographs Orange

*ORANGE: .6X TO 1.5X BASIC
STATED ODDS 1:17 HOBBY
STATED PRINT RUN 25 SER.#'d SETS
EXCHANGE DEADLINE 06/30/2016

2013 Topps Tribute WBC Autographs Sepia

*SEPIA: .5X TO 1.2X BASIC
STATED ODDS 1:12 HOBBY
STATED PRINT RUN 35 SER.#'d SETS
EXCHANGE DEADLINE 06/30/2016

2013 Topps Tribute WBC Heroes Autographs

STATED ODDS 1:82 HOBBY
PRINT RUNS B/WN 20-200 COPIES PER
NO PRICING ON QTY 20 OR LESS
EXCHANGE DEADLINE 06/30/2016
AI Akinori Iwamura/200 5.00 12.00
HI Hisashi Iwakuma/100 20.00 50.00
KJ Kenji Johjima EXCH 10.00 25.00

2013 Topps Tribute WBC Prime Patches

PRINT RUNS B/WN 43-131 COPIES PER
AC Asdrubal Cabrera/131 5.00 12.00
AG Adrian Gonzalez/131 8.00 20.00
AIN Atsunori Inaba/43 20.00 50.00
AJ Andruw Jones/125 6.00 15.00
AJO Adam Jones/107 8.00 20.00
ALR Alex Rios/102 10.00 25.00
AP Angel Pagan/111 8.00 20.00
AR Andre Rienzo/95 6.00 15.00
ARI Anthony Rizzo/127 8.00 20.00
AS Andrelton Simmons/89 8.00 20.00
ASA Anibal Sanchez/131 5.00 12.00
BZ Ben Zobrist/126 8.00 20.00
CB Carlos Beltran/118 8.00 20.00
CGO Carlos Gonzalez/91 6.00 15.00
CHL Che-Hsuan Lin/101 8.00 20.00
CK Craig Kimbrel/131 10.00 25.00
CS Carlos Santana/120 6.00 15.00
DH Derek Holland/131 5.00 12.00
DHL Dae Ho Lee/67 10.00 25.00
DN Darien Nunez/117 5.00 12.00
DW David Wright/75 10.00 25.00
EAN Elvis Andrus/79 6.00 15.00
EAY Erick Aybar/87 5.00 12.00
EE Edwin Encarnacion/131 6.00 15.00
EH Eric Hosmer/131 6.00 15.00
ER Eddie Rosario/95 6.00 15.00
FC Frederich Cepeda/113 10.00 25.00
FR Fernando Rodney/131 5.00 12.00
GS Giancarlo Stanton/131 10.00 25.00
HR Hanley Ramirez/118 5.00 12.00
HWC Hung-Wen Chen/119 12.50 30.00
JB Jose Berrios/127 8.00 20.00
JF Jose Fernandez/85 8.00 20.00
JL Jonathan Lucroy/131 8.00 20.00
JM Justin Morneau/131 8.00 20.00
JMA Joe Mauer/55 12.50 30.00
JP J.P. Arencibia/101 10.00 25.00
JR Jose Reyes/53 10.00 25.00
JRO Jimmy Rollins/101 5.00 12.00
JS Jonathan Schoop/122 6.00 15.00
JT Jameson Taillon/131 8.00 20.00
JTT Jen-Ho Tseng/61 15.00 40.00
JV Joey Votto/118 12.50 30.00
JWS Jae Weong Seo/73 12.50 30.00
KM Kenta Maeda/43 40.00 100.00
KO Kenji Ohtonari/43 30.00 60.00
MC Miguel Cabrera/131 12.50 30.00
MM Miguel Montero/131 5.00 12.00
MS Marco Scutaro/129 6.00 15.00
MT Miguel Tejada/95 5.00 12.00
NC Nelson Cruz/95 5.00 12.00
NM Nobuhiro Matsuda/43 8.00 20.00
PA Phillippe Aumont/131 5.00 12.00
RB Ryan Braun/81 6.00 15.00
RC Robinson Cano/131 15.00 40.00
RD R.A. Dickey/131 10.00 25.00
RDE Ross Detwiler/131 5.00 12.00
SP Salvador Perez/131 5.00 12.00
SR Sergio Romo/102 10.00 25.00
SV Shane Victorino/131 5.00 12.00
TI Takeru Imamura/43 8.00 20.00
TS Toshiya Sugiuchi/43 30.00 60.00
TU Tetsuya Utsumi/43 15.00 40.00
XB Xander Bogaerts/67 12.50 30.00
YG Yulieski Gourriel/76 10.00 25.00
YGA Yovani Gallardo/131 8.00 20.00
YH Yuichi Honda/43 20.00 50.00
YHY Yao-Hsun Yang/95 15.00 40.00
YLW Yao-Lin Wang/102 8.00 20.00
YM Yadier Molina/74 15.00 40.00

2013 Topps Tribute WBC Prime Patches Blue

*BLUE: .4X TO 1X BASIC
STATED PRINT RUN 50 SER.#'d SETS

2013 Topps Tribute WBC Prime Patches Green

*GREEN: .5X TO 1.2X BASIC
STATED PRINT RUN 35 SER.#'d SETS

2013 Topps Tribute WBC Prime Patches Orange

*ORANGE: .5X TO 1.2X BASIC
STATED PRINT RUN 25 SER.#'d SETS
NM Nobuhiro Matsuda 30.00 60.00
TU Tetsuya Utsumi 15.00 40.00

2018 Topps Tribute

1 Mike Trout 5.00 12.00
2 Clayton Kershaw 1.50 4.00
3 Kris Bryant 1.25 3.00
4 Monte Irvin .75 2.00
5 Andrew Benintendi 1.00 2.50
6 Jose Ramirez .75 2.00
7 Goose Gossage .75 2.00
8 Roberto Clemente 2.50 6.00
9 Buster Posey 1.25 3.00
10 Ernie Banks 1.00 2.50
11 Nolan Ryan 3.00 8.00
12 Corey Seager 1.00 2.50
13 Manny Machado 1.00 2.50
14 Bo Jackson 1.00 2.50
15 Paul DeJong 1.00 2.50
16 Jonathan Schoop .60 1.50
17 Lorenzo Cain .60 1.50
18 Jacob deGrom 2.00 5.00
19 Cody Bellinger 2.00 5.00
20 Bert Blyleven .75 2.00
21 Anthony Rizzo 1.25 3.00
22 Red Schoendienst .75 2.00
23 Domingo Santana .75 2.00
24 Luis Severino .75 2.00
25 Bryce Harper 1.50 4.00
26 Adrian Beltre 1.00 2.50
27 Craig Kimbrel .75 2.00
28 Carlos Correa 1.00 2.50
29 Johnny Bench 1.00 2.50
30 Nolan Arenado 1.50 4.00
31 Josh Donaldson .75 2.00
32 Honus Wagner 1.00 2.50
33 Tommy Lasorda .75 2.00
34 Freddie Freeman 1.25 3.00
35 Billy Hamilton .75 2.00
36 Tim Raines .75 2.00
37 Robinson Cano .75 2.00
38 Aaron Judge 2.50 6.00
39 Wade Boggs .75 2.00
40 Giancarlo Stanton 1.00 2.50
41 Jose Altuve .75 2.00
42 Jimmie Foxx 1.00 2.50
43 Alex Bregman 1.00 2.50
44 Ichiro 1.25 3.00
45 Catfish Hunter .75 2.00
46 Billy Williams .75 2.00
47 Jose Abreu 1.00 2.50
48 Chris Sale 1.00 2.50
49 Whitey Ford .75 2.00
50 Hank Aaron 2.00 5.00
51 Jake Lamb .75 2.00
52 George Brett 2.00 5.00
53 Brooks Robinson .75 2.00
54 Mookie Betts 2.00 5.00
55 John Smoltz 1.00 2.50
56 Max Scherzer 1.00 2.50
57 Nelson Cruz 1.00 2.50
58 Cal Ripken Jr. 3.00 8.00
59 Jim Palmer .75 2.00
60 Roger Clemens 1.25 3.00
61 Satchel Paige 1.00 2.50
62 Willie Stargell .75 2.00
63 Steven Souza Jr. .75 2.00
64 Kenley Jansen .75 2.00
65 Francisco Lindor 1.00 2.50
66 Pedro Martinez .75 2.00
67 Ted Williams 2.00 5.00
68 Jeff Bagwell .75 2.00
69 Corey Kluber .75 2.00
70 Noah Syndergaard .75 2.00
71 Matt Olson 1.00 2.50
72 Zack Greinke 1.00 2.50
73 Justin Verlander 1.00 2.50
74 Paul Goldschmidt 1.00 2.50
75 Don Sutton .75 2.00
76 Jim Edmonds .60 1.50
77 Stephen Strasburg 1.00 2.50
78 Jim Thome .75 2.00
79 Carlton Fisk .75 2.00
80 Rickey Henderson 1.00 2.50
81 Alex Rodriguez 1.25 3.00
82 Orlando Cepeda .75 2.00
83 Andrew McCutchen 1.00 2.50
84 Carlos Carrasco .60 1.50
85 Justin Smoak .60 1.50
86 Salvador Perez .75 2.00
87 Mariano Rivera 1.25 3.00
88 Frank Thomas 1.00 2.50
89 Duke Snider .75 2.00
90 Sandy Koufax 2.00 5.00

2018 Topps Tribute Green

*GREEN: 1X TO 2.5X BASIC
STATED ODDS 1:9 HOBBY
STATED PRINT RUN 99 SER.#'d SETS

2018 Topps Tribute Purple

*PURPLE: 1.2X TO 3X BASIC
STATED ODDS 1:17 HOBBY
STATED PRINT RUN 50 SER.#'d SETS

2018 Topps Tribute '18 Rookies

STATED ODDS 1:30 HOBBY
STATED PRINT RUN 254 SER.#'d SETS
*GREEN/99: .5X TO 1.2X BASIC
*PURPLE/50: .6X TO 1.5X BASIC
18R1 Rafael Devers 4.00 10.00
18R2 Amed Rosario 1.50 4.00
18R3 Alex Verdugo 2.00 5.00
18R4 Ozzie Albies 4.00 10.00
18R5 Rhys Hoskins 10.00 25.00
18R6 J.P. Crawford 1.25 3.00
18R7 Dominic Smith 1.50 4.00
18R8 Clint Frazier 2.50 6.00
18R9 Nick Williams 1.50 4.00
18R10 Victor Robles 3.00 8.00

2018 Topps Tribute Autograph Patches

STATED ODDS 1:111 HOBBY
STATED PRINT RUN 50 SER. #'d SETS
EXCHANGE DEADLINE 1/31/2020
TAPAB Andrew Benintendi EXCH 40.00 100.00
TAPAR Anthony Rizzo
TAPBP Buster Posey
TAPCC Carlos Correa
TAPCJ Chipper Jones
TAPCRK Craig Kimbrel 25.00 60.00
TAPCSA Chris Sale 25.00 60.00
TAPDB Dellin Betances 10.00 25.00
TAPDJ Derek Jeter
TAPDM Daniel Murphy EXCH 15.00 40.00
TAPDP David Price 20.00 50.00
TAPEL Evan Longoria
TAPJV Joey Votto EXCH
TAPKD Khris Davis 12.00 30.00
TAPKS Kyle Seager 15.00 40.00
TAPLS Luis Severino 30.00 80.00
TAPMM Manny Machado
TAPMT Mike Trout

2018 Topps Tribute Autographs

STATED ODDS 1:6 HOBBY
PRINT RUNS B/WN 15-199 COPIES PER
NO PRICING ON QTY 15 OR LESS
EXCHANGE DEADLINE 1/31/2020
TAAB Adrian Beltre/110 20.00 50.00
TAABA Anthony Banda/199 3.00 8.00
TAABE Andrew Benintendi/199 20.00 50.00
TAABR Alex Bregman/193 20.00 50.00
TAAD Adam Duvall/196 4.00 10.00
TAAG Andres Galarraga/199 4.00 10.00
TAAJ Aaron Judge/100 100.00 250.00
TAAJU Aaron Judge/100 100.00 250.00
TAAK Al Kaline/199 20.00 50.00
TAAP Andy Pettitte/110 15.00 40.00
TAAR Anthony Rizzo/110 25.00 60.00
TAARO Amed Rosario/199 4.00 10.00
TAAV Alex Verdugo/199 5.00 12.00
TABA Bobby Abreu/190 3.00 8.00
TABJ Bo Jackson/85 50.00 120.00
TABRZ Bradley Zimmer/199 3.00 8.00
TABZI Bradley Zimmer/162 3.00 8.00
TABZ Ben Zobrist/191 10.00 25.00
TACA Christian Arroyo/199 3.00 8.00
TACAR Christian Arroyo/199 3.00 8.00
TACC Carlos Correa/80 15.00 40.00
TACCA Carlos Carrasco/199 3.00 8.00
TACF Clint Frazier/199 6.00 15.00
TACK Craig Kimbrel/199 10.00 25.00
TACRJ Cal Ripken Jr./40 50.00 120.00
TACSA Chris Sale/110 12.00 30.00
TADB Dellin Betances/199 4.00 10.00
TADBE Dellin Betances/199 4.00 10.00
TADDU Danny Duffy/195 3.00 8.00
TADF Derek Fisher/199 3.00 8.00
TADFO Dustin Fowler/199 3.00 8.00
TADG Didi Gregorius/199 4.00 10.00
TADJU David Justice/199 5.00 12.00
TADM Daniel Murphy EXCH 8.00 20.00
TADO David Ortiz/60 30.00 80.00
TADP David Price/110 8.00 20.00
TADS Dominic Smith/199 6.00 15.00
TADW Dave Winfield/85 15.00 40.00
TAET Eric Thames/199 4.00 10.00
TAETH Eric Thames/199 4.00 10.00
TAFB Franklin Barreto/199 3.00 8.00
TAFBA Franklin Barreto/199 3.00 8.00
TAFF Freddie Freeman/199 15.00 40.00
TAFME Francisco Mejia/199 10.00 25.00
TAFT Frank Thomas/100 25.00 60.00
TAHA Hank Aaron/20 100.00 400.00
TAHB Harrison Bader/199 5.00 12.00
TAIH Ian Happ/199 8.00 20.00
TAJC J.P. Crawford/199 8.00 20.00
TAJD Josh Donaldson/80 10.00 25.00
TAJDE Jacob deGrom/199 15.00 40.00
TAJT Jim Thome EXCH 20.00 50.00
TAKB Kris Bryant/85 40.00 100.00
TAKD Khris Davis/199 5.00 12.00
TAKDA Khris Davis/199 5.00 12.00
TAKS Kyle Schwarber/199 5.00 12.00
TALB Lewis Brinson/199 3.00 8.00
TALBR Lewis Brinson/198 3.00 8.00
TALG Lucas Giolito/199 4.00 10.00
TALW Luke Weaver/199 4.00 10.00
TAMCO Michael Conforto/186 4.00 10.00
TAMF Michael Fulmer/199 3.00 8.00
TAMFU Michael Fulmer/199 3.00 8.00
TAMH Mitch Haniger/199 8.00 20.00
TAMM Manny Machado/100 20.00 50.00
TAMP Mike Piazza/30 40.00 100.00
TAMR Mariano Rivera/30 60.00 150.00
TAMT Mike Trout/30 200.00 500.00
TANS Noah Syndergaard/110 12.00 30.00
TAOAL Ozzie Albies/199 20.00 50.00
TAPD Paul DeJong/199 5.00 12.00
TAPM Pedro Martinez/30 40.00 100.00
TARB Ryan Braun/152 5.00 12.00
TARD Rafael Devers/199 10.00 25.00
TARHO Rhys Hoskins/199 15.00 40.00
TARJ Reggie Jackson/40 15.00 40.00
TASK Sandy Koufax
TASN Sean Newcomb/199 4.00 10.00
TASNE Sean Newcomb/199 4.00 10.00
TATR Tim Raines/195 8.00 20.00
TAWC Willson Contreras/178 6.00 15.00

2018 Topps Tribute Autographs Blue

*BLUE: .4X TO 1X BASIC
STATED ODDS 1:20 HOBBY
PRINT RUNS B/WN 113-150 COPIES PER
EXCHANGE DEADLINE 1/31/2020
TALS Luis Severino/142 10.00 25.00

2018 Topps Tribute Autographs Green

*GREEN: .5X TO 1.2X BASIC
STATED ODDS 1:13 HOBBY
PRINT RUNS B/WN 78-99 COPIES PER
NO PRICING ON QTY 15 OR LESS
EXCHANGE DEADLINE 1/31/2020
TALS Luis Severino/81 12.00 30.00

2018 Topps Tribute Autographs Orange

*ORANGE: .6X TO 1.5X BASE p/r 100-199
*ORANGE: .5X TO 1.2X BASE p/r 30-85
STATED ODDS 1:39 HOBBY
PRINT RUNS B/WN 16-25 COPIES PER
NO PRICING ON QTY 19 OR LESS
EXCHANGE DEADLINE 1/31/2020
TALS Luis Severino/25 15.00 40.00
TASO Shohei Ohtani 1000.00 1500.00

2018 Topps Tribute Autographs Purple

*PURPLE: .5X TO 1.2X BASE p/r 100-199
*PURPLE: .4X TO 1X BASE p/r 30-85
STATED ODDS 1:22 HOBBY
PRINT RUNS B/WN 40-50 COPIES PER
NO PRICING ON QTY 15 OR LESS
EXCHANGE DEADLINE 1/31/2020
TALS Luis Severino/46 12.00 30.00
TASO Shohei Ohtani 800.00 1200.00

2018 Topps Tribute Dual Player Relics

RANDOM INSERTS IN PACKS
STATED PRINT RUN 150 SER.#'d SETS
*GREEN/99: .4X TO 1X BASIC
*PURPLE/50: .5X TO 1.2X BASIC
*ORANGE/25: 1X TO 2.5X BASIC
DRAB Nolan Arenado 8.00 20.00
Charlie Blackmon
DRBB Mookie Betts 10.00 25.00
Xander Bogaerts
DRBH Bryce Harper 8.00 20.00
Kris Bryant
DRBL Wade Boggs 5.00 12.00
Evan Longoria
DRCB Dellin Betances 5.00 12.00
Aroldis Chapman
DRCC Robinson Cano 5.00 12.00
Nelson Cruz
DRCS Sale/Clemens 6.00 15.00
DRCSE Carlos Correa 5.00 12.00
Corey Seager
DRCSP Carlos Correa 5.00 12.00
George Springer
DRDB Jose Bautista 4.00 10.00
Josh Donaldson
DRDT Yu Darvish 5.00 12.00
Masahiro Tanaka
DRGG Zack Greinke 5.00 12.00
Paul Goldschmidt
DRGM Ken Griffey Jr. 12.00 30.00
Mark McGwire
DRIS Ichiro 6.00 15.00
Giancarlo Stanton
DRJS Dansby Swanson 8.00 20.00
Chipper Jones
DRKJ Kenley Jansen 6.00 15.00
Clayton Kershaw
DROS Giancarlo Stanton 5.00 12.00
Marcell Ozuna
DRPC Mike Piazza 5.00 12.00
Yoenis Cespedes
DRPCR Brandon Crawford 6.00 15.00
Buster Posey
DRRB Bryant/Rizzo 6.00 15.00
DRRM Cal Ripken Jr. 10.00 25.00
Manny Machado
DRSD Noah Syndergaard 8.00 20.00
Jacob deGrom
DRTM Daniel Murphy 4.00 10.00
Trea Turner
DRTP Mike Trout 25.00 60.00
Albert Pujols

2018 Topps Tribute Dual Relics

STATED ODDS 1:12 HOBBY
STATED PRINT RUN 150 SER.#'d SETS
*GREEN/99: .4X TO 1X BASIC
*PURPLE/50: .5X TO 1.2X BASIC
*ORANGE/25: .75X TO 2X BASIC
DRABE Andrew Benintendi 4.00 10.00
DRABR Alex Bregman 4.00 10.00
DRBLA Barry Larkin 3.00 8.00
DRCF Clint Frazier 5.00 12.00
DRCK Craig Kimbrel 3.00 8.00
DRDO David Ortiz 4.00 10.00
DRFL Francisco Lindor 4.00 10.00
DRGS Gary Sanchez 5.00 12.00
DRJV Joey Votto 4.00 10.00
DRLS Luis Severino 3.00 8.00
DRMS Max Scherzer 4.00 10.00
DRNR Nolan Ryan 8.00 20.00
DRPM Pedro Martinez 3.00 8.00
DRRH Rickey Henderson 5.00 12.00
DRRJ Reggie Jackson 5.00 12.00
DRSS Stephen Strasburg 4.00 10.00

2018 Topps Tribute Generations of Excellence Autographs

STATED ODDS 1:56 HOBBY
PRINT RUNS B/WN X-X COPIES PER
NO PRICING ON QTY 15 OR LESS
EXCHANGE DEADLINE 1/31/2020
*ORANGE/23-25: .4X TO 1X BASE p/r 20-30
*ORANGE/23-25: .5X TO 1.2X BASE p/r 35-65
GOEAD Andre Dawson/40 25.00 60.00
GOEAG Andres Galarraga/65 6.00 15.00
GOEAK Al Kaline/65 25.00 50.00
GOEAP Andy Pettitte/40 12.00 30.00
GOEBJ Bo Jackson/30 40.00 100.00
GOEBW Bernie Williams/40 20.00 50.00
GOECJ Chipper Jones/30 60.00 150.00
GOECRJ Cal Ripken Jr./20 75.00 200.00
GOECY Carl Yastrzemski/20 30.00 120.00
GOEDC David Cone/65 10.00 25.00
GOEDE Dennis Eckersley/50 10.00 25.00
GOEDM Don Mattingly/30 50.00 120.00
GOEDO David Ortiz/30 30.00 80.00
GOEDW Dave Winfield/30 20.00 50.00
GOEEM Edgar Martinez/65 12.00 30.00
GOEFT Frank Thomas/30 30.00 80.00
GOEJB Jeff Bagwell/40 20.00 50.00
GOEJD Johnny Damon/65 5.00 12.00
GOEJG Juan Gonzalez/65 10.00 25.00
GOEJS John Smoltz/35 20.00 50.00
GOEJT Jim Thome EXCH 40.00 100.00
GOEMM Mark McGwire/20 50.00 120.00
GOENG Nomar Garciaparra/40 20.00 50.00
GOEOS Ozzie Smith/35 20.00 50.00
GOEOV Omar Vizquel/50 5.00 12.00
GOEPM Pedro Martinez/20 40.00 100.00
GOEPN Phil Niekro/65 12.00 30.00
GOERA Roberto Alomar/40 12.00 30.00
GOERCA Rod Carew/45 15.00 40.00
GOERF Rollie Fingers/65 10.00 25.00
GOERJA Reggie Jackson/20 40.00 100.00
GOETG Tom Glavine/35 20.00 50.00
GOETR Tim Raines/50 10.00 25.00
GOEWB Wade Boggs/30 25.00 60.00

2018 Topps Tribute Iconic Perspectives Autographs

STATED ODDS 1:40 HOBBY
PRINT RUNS B/WN 10-99 COPIES PER
NO PRICING ON QTY 15 OR LESS
EXCHANGE DEADLINE 1/31/2020
*ORANGE/23-25: .4X TO 1X BASE p/r 25-30
*ORANGE/23-25: .5X TO 1.2X BASE p/r 34-99
IPAB Adrian Beltre/35 20.00 50.00
IPAJ Aaron Judge/99 100.00 250.00
IPAK Al Kaline/99 25.00 50.00
IPAP Andy Pettitte/34 12.00 30.00
IPAR Anthony Rizzo/50 20.00 50.00
IPBJ Bo Jackson/30 40.00 100.00
IPCC Carlos Correa/40 40.00 100.00
IPCSA Chris Sale/50 10.00 25.00
IPDB Dellin Betances/99 5.00 12.00
IPDJU David Justice/97 10.00 25.00
IPDO David Ortiz/30 30.00 80.00
IPDP David Price/35 10.00 25.00
IPER Edgar Renteria/99 5.00 12.00
IPHA Hank Aaron
IPJB Jeff Bagwell/35 20.00 50.00
IPJD Josh Donaldson/50 15.00 40.00
IPJDA Johnny Damon/99 5.00 12.00
IPJDE Jacob deGrom/99 15.00 40.00
IPJT Jim Thome EXCH 25.00 60.00
IPKB Kris Bryant EXCH 75.00 200.00
IPKS Kyle Schwarber/99 12.00 30.00
IPMM Manny Machado/40 20.00 50.00
IPNS Noah Syndergaard/50 20.00 50.00
IPOV Omar Vizquel/99 5.00 12.00
IPPM Pedro Martinez/25 40.00 100.00
IPRC Rod Carew/35 15.00 40.00
IPRJ Randy Johnson/25 40.00 100.00
IPRJA Reggie Jackson/30 40.00 100.00
IPSP Stephen Piscotty/97 4.00 10.00
IPTR Tim Raines/50 10.00 25.00
IPWC Willson Contreras/99 12.00 30.00

2018 Topps Tribute League Inauguration Autographs

STATED ODDS 1:96 HOBBY
PRINT RUNS B/WN 69-75 COPIES PER
EXCHANGE DEADLINE 1/31/2020
*ORANGE/25: .5X TO 1.2X BASIC
LAAR Amed Rosario/75 12.00 30.00
LACF Clint Frazier/75 8.00 20.00
LADS Dominic Smith/75 5.00 12.00
LAHB Harrison Bader/75 6.00 15.00
LAJC J.P. Crawford/69 4.00 10.00
LAOA Ozzie Albies/75 25.00 60.00
LARD Rafael Devers/75 12.00 30.00
LARH Rhys Hoskins/75 60.00 150.00
LARM Ryan McMahon/75 10.00 25.00

2018 Topps Tribute Stamp of Approval Relics

STATED ODDS 1:14 HOBBY
STATED PRINT RUN 150 SER.#'d SETS
*GREEN/99: .4X TO 1X BASIC
*PURPLE/50: .5X TO 1.2X BASIC
*ORANGE/25: .75X TO 2X BASIC
SOAAB Andrew Benintendi/150 4.00 10.00
SOAABR Alex Bregman 4.00 10.00
SOAAR Anthony Rizzo/150 5.00 12.00
SOABH Bryce Harper/150 6.00 15.00
SOABP Buster Posey/150 5.00 12.00
SOACB Cody Bellinger/150 6.00 15.00
SOACBL Charlie Blackmon/150 4.00 10.00
SOACC Carlos Correa/150 4.00 10.00
SOACF Clint Frazier/150 5.00 12.00
SOACJ Chipper Jones/150 5.00 12.00
SOACK Clayton Kershaw/150 6.00 15.00
SOACKI Craig Kimbrel/150 3.00 8.00
SOACM Carlos Martinez/150 3.00 8.00
SOACS Corey Seager/150 4.00 10.00
SOACSA Chris Sale/150 4.00 10.00
SOADB Dellin Betances/150 3.00 8.00
SOADJ Derek Jeter/150 25.00 60.00
SOADM Daniel Murphy/150 3.00 8.00
SOADP David Price/150 3.00 8.00
SOADS Dansby Swanson/150 4.00 10.00
SOAEL Evan Longoria/150 3.00 8.00
SOAFL Francisco Lindor/150 4.00 10.00
SOAGS George Springer/150 3.00 8.00
SOAI Ichiro/140 5.00 12.00
SOAJA Jose Altuve/149 3.00 8.00
SOAJM J.D. Martinez/150 4.00 10.00
SOAJV Joey Votto/150 4.00 10.00
SOAKB Kris Bryant/150 5.00 12.00
SOAKD Khris Davis/150 4.00 10.00
SOAKS Kyle Seager/150 2.50 6.00
SOALS Luis Severino/150 3.00 8.00
SOAMAT Masahiro Tanaka/150 3.00 8.00
SOAMM Manny Machado/150 4.00 10.00
SOAMR Mariano Rivera/150 5.00 12.00
SOAMS Marcus Stroman/150 3.00 8.00
SOAMT Mike Trout/150 20.00 50.00
SOANA Nolan Arenado/150 6.00 15.00

2018 Topps Tribute Tandem Autograph Booklets

STATED ODDS 1:240 HOBBY
STATED PRINT RUN 25 SER.#'d SETS
EXCHANGE DEADLINE 1/31/2020
TTAB Altve/Bggo EXCH 30.00 80.00
TTBB Craig Biggio 40.00 100.00
Alex Bregman EXCH
TTDR dGrm/Ryn EXCH 125.00 300.00
TTET Encrncn/Thme EXCH 75.00 200.00
TTGB Bgwll/Gldschmdt EXCH 50.00 120.00
TTJJ Judge/Jeter
TTJJA Jackson/Judge 100.00 250.00
TTJW Winfield/Judge 150.00 400.00
TTPM Mrtnz/Prce EXCH 60.00 150.00
TTRS Sndbrg/Rssll EXCH 60.00 150.00
TTSC Sale/Clemens
TTSW Miguel Sano 30.00 80.00
Dave Winfield EXCH

2018 Topps Tribute Tribute to the Moment Autographs

STATED ODDS 1:62 HOBBY
PRINT RUNS B/WN 10-99 COPIES PER
NO PRICING ON QTY 10 OR LESS
EXCHANGE DEADLINE 1/31/2020
*PRPLE/47-50: .4X TO 1X BASE p/r 40-99
*ORNGE/23-25: .4X TO 1X BASE p/r 30
*ORNGE/23-25: .5X TO 1.2X BASE p/r 40-99
TTMAB Adrian Beltre/75 20.00 50.00
TTMAR Amed Rosario/99 10.00 25.00
TTMCF Carlton Fisk/67 20.00 50.00
TTMCFR Clint Frazier/99 8.00 20.00
TTMCJ Chipper Jones/40 50.00 120.00
TTMCRJ Cal Ripken Jr. EXCH 75.00 200.00
TTMCS Chris Sale/99 10.00 25.00
TTMJB Jeff Bagwell/75 20.00 50.00
TTMJT Jim Thome EXCH 30.00 80.00
TTMKB Kris Bryant/40 75.00 200.00
TTMOV Omar Vizquel/67 5.00 12.00
TTMRA Roberto Alomar/75 8.00 20.00
TTMRC Roger Clemens/30 25.00 60.00
TTMRCA Rod Carew/75 15.00 40.00
TTMRD Rafael Devers/99 12.00 30.00
TTMRF Rollie Fingers/65 10.00 25.00
TTMRJ Reggie Jackson/40 30.00 80.00
TTMRJO Randy Johnson/30 40.00 100.00
TTMTR Tim Raines/62 10.00 25.00
TTMWB Wade Boggs/40 20.00 50.00

2018 Topps Tribute Triple Relics

STATED ODDS 1:13 HOBBY
STATED PRINT RUN 150 SER.#'d SETS
*GREEN/99: .4X TO 1X BASIC
*PURPLE/50: .5X TO 1.2X BASIC
*ORANGE/25: .75X TO 2X BASIC
TTRAB Andrew Benintendi 4.00 10.00
TTRAC Aroldis Chapman 4.00 10.00
TTRAP Albert Pujols 5.00 12.00
TTRAR Anthony Rizzo 5.00 12.00
TTRBH Bryce Harper 6.00 15.00
TTRBL Barry Larkin 3.00 8.00
TTRBP Buster Posey 5.00 12.00
TTRCB Cody Bellinger 6.00 15.00
TTRCBL Charlie Blackmon 4.00 10.00
TTRCC Carlos Correa 4.00 10.00
TTRCJ Chipper Jones 5.00 12.00
TTRCK Clayton Kershaw 6.00 15.00
TTRCRJ Cal Ripken Jr. 12.00 30.00
TTRCS Chris Sale 4.00 10.00
TTRCSE Corey Seager 4.00 10.00
TTRER Edgar Renteria 2.50 6.00
TTRGS Gary Sanchez 5.00 12.00
TTRGST Giancarlo Stanton 5.00 12.00
TTRI Ichiro 5.00 12.00
TTRJA Jose Altuve 3.00 8.00
TTRJD Josh Donaldson 3.00 8.00
TTRJV Joey Votto 4.00 10.00
TTRKB Kris Bryant 5.00 12.00
TTRKGJ Ken Griffey Jr. 10.00 25.00
TTRMB Mookie Betts 8.00 20.00
TTRMM Manny Machado 4.00 10.00
TTRMP Mike Piazza 4.00 10.00
TTRMS Max Scherzer 4.00 10.00
TTRMT Masahiro Tanaka 3.00 8.00
TTRMTR Mike Trout 20.00 50.00
TTRNR Nolan Ryan 12.00 30.00
TTRNS Noah Syndergaard 3.00 8.00
TTRPM Pedro Martinez 3.00 8.00
TTRRC Robinson Cano 3.00 8.00
TTRRHE Rickey Henderson 5.00 12.00
TTRRJ Reggie Jackson 5.00 12.00
TTRTM Trey Mancini 3.00 8.00
TTRWB Wade Boggs 3.00 8.00
TTRYC Yoenis Cespedes 4.00 10.00

2019 Topps Tribute

1 Mike Trout 3.00 8.00
2 Gary Carter .50 1.25
3 Duke Snider .50 1.25
4 Khris Davis .60 1.50
5 Lou Gehrig 1.25 3.00
6 Giancarlo Stanton .60 1.50
7 Bo Jackson .60 1.50
8 Reggie Jackson .50 1.25
9 Eddie Murray .50 1.25
10 Ivan Rodriguez .50 1.25
11 Carl Yastrzemski 1.00 2.50
12 Max Scherzer .60 1.50
13 Will Clark .50 1.25
14 Phil Rizzuto .50 1.25
15 Vladimir Guerrero .50 1.25
16 Nolan Arenado 1.00 2.50
17 Josh Hader .50 1.25
18 Nolan Ryan 2.00 5.00
19 Warren Spahn .50 1.25
20 Noah Syndergaard .50 1.25
21 David Ortiz .60 1.50
22 Jacob deGrom 1.25 3.00

23 Miguel Andujar .60 1.50
24 Clayton Kershaw 1.00 2.50
25 Jackie Robinson .60 1.50
26 Justin Verlander .60 1.50
27 Gerrit Cole .60 1.50
28 Roberto Alomar .50 1.25
29 Catfish Hunter .50 1.25
30 Luis Severino .50 1.25
31 Roberto Clemente 1.50 4.00
32 Ronald Acuna Jr. 3.00 8.00
33 Mitch Haniger .50 1.25
34 Jose Altuve .50 1.25
35 Edwin Encarnacion .60 1.50
36 Francisco Lindor .60 1.50
37 Juan Soto 2.00 5.00
38 Javier Baez .75 2.00
39 Bryce Harper 1.00 2.50
40 Trea Turner .50 1.25
41 Corey Seager .60 1.50
42 Edwin Diaz .50 1.25
43 Red Schoendienst .50 1.25
44 Torii Hunter .40 1.00
45 Shohei Ohtani 1.00 2.50
46 Alex Bregman .60 1.50
47 Christian Yelich .75 2.00
48 Chris Sale .60 1.50
49 Ty Cobb 1.00 2.50
50 Mookie Betts 1.25 3.00
51 Joey Votto .60 1.50
52 Joe Morgan .50 1.25
53 George Springer .50 1.25
54 Sandy Koufax 1.25 3.00
55 Paul Goldschmidt .60 1.50
56 Ozzie Albies .60 1.50
57 Carlos Correa .60 1.50
58 Eddie Mathews .60 1.50
59 Roger Maris .60 1.50
60 Willie Stargell .50 1.25
61 Tommy Lasorda .50 1.25
62 Matt Carpenter .60 1.50
63 Aaron Nola .50 1.25
64 Goose Gossage .50 1.25
65 Hank Aaron 1.25 3.00
66 Don Mattingly 1.25 3.00
67 Whitey Ford .50 1.25
68 Derek Jeter 1.50 4.00
69 Kris Bryant .75 2.00
70 Jose Ramirez .50 1.25
71 Eugenio Suarez .50 1.25
72 Whit Merrifield .60 1.50
73 J.D. Martinez .60 1.50
74 Bob Feller .50 1.25
75 Aaron Judge 1.50 4.00
76 Freddie Freeman .75 2.00
77 Pedro Martinez .50 1.25
78 Anthony Rizzo .75 2.00
79 Rhys Hoskins .75 2.00
80 Harmon Killebrew .60 1.50
81 Blake Snell .50 1.25
82 Gleyber Torres 1.25 3.00
83 Enos Slaughter .50 1.25
84 Charlie Blackmon .60 1.50
85 Mike Piazza .60 1.50
86 Mark McGwire 1.00 2.50
87 George Brett 1.25 3.00
88 Andrew Benintendi .60 1.50
89 Eddie Rosario .50 1.25
90 Babe Ruth 1.50 4.00

2019 Topps Tribute Green

*GREEN: 1.2X TO 3X BASIC
STATED ODDS 1:9 HOBBY
STATED PRINT RUN 99 SER.#'d SETS

2019 Topps Tribute Purple

*PURPLE: 1.5X TO 4X BASIC
STATED ODDS 1:18 HOBBY
STATED PRINT RUN 50 SER.#'d SETS

2019 Topps Tribute '19 Rookies

STATED ODDS 1:18 HOBBY
STATED PRINT RUN 435 SER.#'d SETS
*GREEN/99: .5X TO 1.2X BASIC
*PURPLE/50: .6X TO 1.5X BASIC
19R1 Kyle Tucker 3.00 8.00
19R2 Rowdy Tellez 2.00 5.00
19R3 Cedric Mullins 2.50 6.00
19R4 Luis Urias 2.00 5.00
19R5 Ryan O'Hearn 1.25 3.00
19R6 Jake Bauers 2.00 5.00
19R7 Michael Kopech 4.00 10.00
19R8 Chance Adams 1.25 3.00
19R9 Kolby Allard 2.00 5.00
19R10 Justus Sheffield 2.00 5.00
19R11 Vladimir Guerrero Jr. 10.00 25.00
19R12 Fernando Tatis Jr. 6.00 15.00
19R13 Eloy Jimenez 5.00 12.00
19R14 Nick Senzel 4.00 10.00
19R15 Pete Alonso 10.00 25.00
19R16 Carter Kieboom 2.00 5.00

2019 Topps Tribute Autograph Patches

STATED ODDS 1:99 HOBBY
STATED PRINT RUN 50 SER. #'d SETS
EXCHANGE DEADLINE 7/31/2021
TAPAM Andrew McCutchen 25.00 60.00
TAPAR Amed Rosario 10.00 25.00
TAPDG Didi Gregorius 20.00 50.00
TAPER Eddie Rosario 8.00 20.00
TAPGS George Springer 15.00 40.00
TAPJD Jacob deGrom EXCH 30.00 80.00
TAPJV Joey Votto 30.00 80.00
TAPKS Kyle Schwarber 10.00 25.00
TAPLS Luis Severino 20.00 50.00
TAPMO Matt Olson 10.00 25.00
TAPNS Noah Syndergaard 15.00 40.00
TAPOA Ozzie Albies 20.00 50.00
TAPRI Raisel Iglesias 6.00 15.00
TAPTM Trey Mancini 15.00 40.00
TAPWM Whit Merrifield 12.00 30.00

2019 Topps Tribute Autographs

STATED ODDS 1:6 HOBBY
PRINT RUNS B/WN 5-199 COPIES PER
NO PRICING ON QTY 15 OR LESS
EXCHANGE DEADLINE 7/31/2021
*BLUE/150: .4X TO 1X p/r 125-199
*GREEN/99: .5X TO 1.2X p/r 125-199
*PURPLE/50: .5X TO 1.2X p/r 125-199
*PURPLE/50: .4X TO 1X p/r 30-90
*ORANGE/25: .6X TO 1.5X p/r 125-199
*ORANGE/25: .5X TO 1.2X p/r 30-90
TAAB Adrian Beltre/55 20.00 50.00
TAAJ Aaron Judge/40 60.00 150.00
TAAK Al Kaline/170 15.00 40.00
TAAM Andrew McCutchen/170 20.00 50.00
TAAME Austin Meadows/199 5.00 12.00
TAAP Andy Pettitte/170 8.00 20.00
TAAR Anthony Rizzo/60 20.00 50.00
TAARO Amed Rosario/199 4.00 10.00
TABB Byron Buxton/199 5.00 12.00
TABBL Bert Blyleven/199 4.00 10.00
TABG Bob Gibson/170 50.00 120.00
TABJ Bo Jackson
TABN Brandon Nimmo/199 8.00 20.00
TABP Buster Posey/45 30.00 80.00
TABW Bernie Williams/150 15.00 40.00
TACA Chance Adams/199 3.00 8.00
TACB Charlie Blackmon/199 5.00 12.00
TACBU Corbin Burnes/199 10.00 25.00
TACJ Chipper Jones/40 40.00 100.00
TACK Corey Kluber/170 4.00 10.00
TACY Carl Yastrzemski/40 40.00 100.00
TADE Dennis Eckersley/199 6.00 15.00
TADG Didi Gregorius/199 6.00 15.00
TADJ Derek Jeter/15
TADM Don Mattingly/170 30.00 80.00
TADO David Ortiz/40 25.00 60.00
TADS Deion Sanders EXCH 30.00 80.00
TAEM Edgar Martinez/199 10.00 25.00
TAER Eddie Rosario/199 4.00 10.00
TAFF Freddie Freeman/170 25.00 60.00
TAFT Frank Thomas/170 25.00 60.00
TAFTJ Fernando Tatis Jr./199 125.00 300.00
TAGM Greg Maddux/45 40.00 100.00
TAHM Hideki Matsui/40 40.00 100.00
TAIH Ian Happ/199 4.00 10.00
TAI Ichiro/25 150.00 400.00
TAJA Jose Altuve/170 15.00 40.00
TAJAB Jake Bauers/199 5.00 12.00
TAJAG Jesus Aguilar/199 4.00 10.00
TAJB Johnny Bench/66 20.00 50.00
TAJL Jonathan Loaisiga/199 4.00 10.00
TAJR Jim Rice/199 4.00 10.00
TAJRA Jose Ramirez/199 4.00 10.00
TAJS Juan Soto/199 25.00 60.00
TAJSH Justus Sheffield/199 5.00 12.00
TAJU Justin Upton/170 5.00 12.00
TAJV Joey Votto/60 15.00 40.00
TAKA Kolby Allard/199 5.00 12.00
TAKB Kris Bryant/60 50.00 120.00
TAKGJ Ken Griffey Jr. EXCH 125.00 300.00
TAKT Kyle Tucker
TALM Lance McCullers Jr./199 6.00 15.00
TALU Luis Urias/199 8.00 20.00
TAMA Miguel Andujar/199 8.00 20.00
TAMCA Miguel Cabrera/60 30.00 80.00
TAMH Mitch Haniger/199 4.00 10.00
TAMK Michael Kopech/199 10.00 25.00
TAMM Miles Mikolas/199 5.00 12.00
TAMO Marcell Ozuna/199 8.00 20.00
TAMOL Matt Olson/199 5.00 12.00
TAMP Mike Piazza/125 30.00 80.00
TAMR Mariano Rivera/30 100.00 250.00
TAMT Mike Trout/25 150.00 400.00
TAMTA Masahiro Tanaka/45 40.00 100.00
TANR Nolan Ryan/40 60.00 150.00
TANS Noah Syndergaard/170 10.00 25.00
TAOS Ozzie Smith/170 20.00 50.00
TAPA Peter Alonso/199 50.00 120.00
TAPD Paul DeJong/199 5.00 12.00
TAPDE Paul DeJong/199 5.00 12.00
TARAJ Ronald Acuna Jr./199 50.00 120.00
TARC Roger Clemens/35 30.00 80.00
TARCA Rod Carew/170 15.00 40.00
TARH Rhys Hoskins/199 6.00 15.00
TARJ Randy Johnson/40 50.00 120.00
TARJA Reggie Jackson/40 20.00 50.00
TASCK Scott Kingery/199 4.00 10.00
TASKI Scott Kingery/199 4.00 10.00
TASM Sean Manaea/199 3.00 8.00
TASO Shohei Ohtani/25 125.00 300.00
TATG Tom Glavine/90 10.00 25.00
TATH Trevor Hoffman/199 8.00 20.00
TATHU Torii Hunter/199 5.00 12.00
TATMA Tino Martinez/199 10.00 25.00
TATO Tyler O'Neill/199 4.00 10.00
TATR Tim Raines/170 6.00 15.00
TAVGJ Vladimir Guerrero Jr./199 40.00 100.00
TAWA Willy Adames/199 3.00 8.00
TAWB Walker Buehler/199 20.00 50.00
TAWC Willson Contreras/199 4.00 10.00
TAXB Xander Bogaerts EXCH 15.00 40.00
TAYK Yusei Kikuchi/199 8.00 20.00

2019 Topps Tribute Dual Player Relics

RANDOM INSERTS IN PACKS
STATED PRINT RUN 150 SER.#'d SETS
*GREEN/99: .4X TO 1X BASIC
*PURPLE/50: .5X TO 1.2X BASIC
*ORANGE/25: .75X TO 2X BASIC
DRAM Jose Abreu 4.00 10.00
Yoan Moncada
DRAS Ozzie Albies 4.00 10.00
Dansby Swanson
DRBA Nolan Arenado 6.00 15.00
Charlie Blackmon
DRBAN Brian Anderson 2.50 6.00
Justin Bour
DRBB Betts/Bogaerts 8.00 20.00
DRBR Eddie Rosario 4.00 10.00
Byron Buxton
DRBRI Bryant/Rizzo 5.00 12.00
DRBT Tucker/Bregman 6.00 15.00
DRCC Miguel Cabrera 4.00 10.00
Nicholas Castellanos
DRCM Matt Carpenter 5.00 12.00
Yadier Molina
DRCO Matt Chapman 4.00 10.00
Matt Olson
DRCS Carlos Correa 4.00 10.00
George Springer
DRDS Jacob deGrom 8.00 20.00
Noah Syndergaard
DREK Corey Kluber 4.00 10.00
Edwin Encarnacion
DRGM Joey Gallo 3.00 8.00
Nomar Mazara
DRGP Goldschmidt/Pollock 4.00 10.00
DRNA Aaron Nola 3.00 8.00
Jake Arrieta
DRPB Gregory Polanco 3.00 8.00
Josh Bell
DRPM Whit Merrifield 4.00 10.00
Salvador Perez
DRPMC Posey/McCutchen 5.00 12.00
DRPS Corey Seager 4.00 10.00
Yasiel Puig
DRSK Chris Sale 4.00 10.00
Craig Kimbrel
DRSS Marcus Stroman 3.00 8.00
Justin Smoak
DRST Masahiro Tanaka 3.00 8.00
Luis Severino
DRTP Trout/Pujols 12.00 30.00
DRVH Billy Hamilton 4.00 10.00
Joey Votto

2019 Topps Tribute Dual Relics

STATED ODDS 1:14 HOBBY
STATED PRINT RUN 150 SER.#'d SETS
*GREEN/99: .4X TO 1X BASIC
*PURPLE/50: .5X TO 1.2X BASIC
*ORANGE/25: .75X TO 2X BASIC
DRAP Andy Pettitte 2.50 6.00
DRAR Alex Rodriguez 4.00 10.00
DRCF Carlton Fisk 2.50 6.00
DRCRJ Cal Ripken Jr. 10.00 25.00
DRCY Carl Yastrzemski 5.00 12.00
DRDJ Derek Jeter 10.00 25.00
DRDW Dave Winfield 2.50 6.00
DRFT Frank Thomas 5.00 12.00
DRIR Ivan Rodriguez 2.50 6.00
DRI Ichiro 4.00 10.00
DRJB Johnny Bench 6.00 15.00
DRMP Mike Piazza 3.00 8.00
DRRC Roger Clemens 4.00 10.00
DRRH Rickey Henderson 10.00 25.00
DRRJ Reggie Jackson 6.00 15.00
DRSC Steve Carlton 2.50 6.00
DRWB Wade Boggs 2.50 6.00

2019 Topps Tribute Iconic Perspectives Autographs

STATED ODDS 1:42 HOBBY
PRINT RUNS B/WN 15-99 COPIES PER
NO PRICING ON TY 15 OR LESS
EXCHANGE DEADLINE 7/31/2021
*ORANGE/25: .5X TO 1.2X p/r 30-99
*ORANGE/25: .4X TO 1X p/r 25
IAPAB Adrian Beltre/30 20.00 50.00
IAPAD Andre Dawson/99 10.00 25.00
IAPBB Bert Blyleven/99 10.00 25.00
IAPCF Carlton Fisk/70 15.00 40.00
IAPCY Carl Yastrzemski/25 30.00 80.00
IAPDG Didi Gregorius/99 10.00 25.00
IAPDM Don Mattingly/30 30.00 80.00
IAPFF Freddie Freeman/99 20.00 50.00
IAPJB Johnny Bench/30 30.00 80.00
IAPJBA Jeff Bagwell/70 15.00 40.00
IAPJU Justin Upton/99 5.00 12.00
IAPMO Marcell Ozuna/99 6.00 15.00
IAPNR Nolan Ryan/25 125.00 300.00
IAPOS Ozzie Smith/70 15.00 40.00
IAPSK Scott Kingery/99 8.00 20.00
IAPWC Willson Contreras/99 12.00 30.00
IPAM Andrew McCutchen/30 15.00 40.00
IPAME Austin Meadows/99 6.00 15.00
IPAP Andy Pettitte/70 12.00 30.00
IPAR Anthony Rizzo
IPARO Amed Rosario/99 5.00 12.00
IPBB Byron Buxton/99 8.00 20.00
IPBG Bob Gibson/70 15.00 40.00
IPCB Charlie Blackmon/99 6.00 15.00
IPDJ Derek Jeter
IPDO David Ortiz/25 30.00 80.00
IPFT Frank Thomas/30 25.00 60.00
IPHA Hank Aaron
IPHM Hideki Matsui/25 50.00 21.00
IPJA Jose Altuve/30 15.00 40.00
IPJS Juan Soto/99 30.00 80.00
IPKB Kris Bryant/30 60.00 150.00
IPMA Miguel Andujar/99 8.00 20.00
IPMP Mike Piazza
IPMT Mike Trout
IPNS Noah Syndergaard/99 8.00 20.00
IPRAJ Ronald Acuna Jr./99 60.00 150.00
IPRC Roger Clemens
IPRH Rhys Hoskins/99 12.00 30.00
IPRJ Reggie Jackson/25 30.00 80.00
IPTH Trevor Hoffman/99 8.00 20.00
IPTHU Torii Hunter/99 10.00 25.00

2019 Topps Tribute League Inauguration Autographs

STATED ODDS 1:149 HOBBY
STATED PRINT RUN 75 SER.#'d SETS
EXCHANGE DEADLINE 7/31/2021
*ORANGE/25: .5X TO 1.2X BASIC
LACA Chance Adams 4.00 10.00
LACB Corbin Burnes 12.00 30.00
LAEJ Eloy Jimenez 25.00 60.00
LAFTJ Fernando Tatis Jr. 75.00 200.00
LAJB Jake Bauers 6.00 15.00
LAJS Justus Sheffield 6.00 15.00
LAKA Kolby Allard 6.00 15.00
LAKT Kyle Tucker 20.00 50.00
LALU Luis Urias 6.00 15.00
LANS Nick Senzel
LAPA Peter Alonso 60.00 150.00
LAVGJ Vladimir Guerrero Jr. 100.00 250.00

2019 Topps Tribute Stamp of Approval Relics

STATED ODDS 1:14 HOBBY
STATED PRINT RUN 150 SER.#'d SETS
*GREEN/99: .4X TO 1X BASIC
*PURPLE/50: .5X TO 1.2X BASIC
*ORANGE/25: .75X TO 2X BASIC
SOAAB Adrian Beltre 3.00 8.00
SOAABR Alex Bregman 3.00 8.00
SOAAM Andrew McCutchen 3.00 8.00
SOAAR Anthony Rizzo 4.00 10.00
SOAARO Amed Rosario 2.50 6.00
SOABP Buster Posey 4.00 10.00
SOACC Carlos Correa 3.00 8.00
SOACS Chris Sale 3.00 8.00
SOADG Didi Gregorius 2.50 6.00
SOADO David Ortiz 3.00 8.00
SOAEE Edwin Encarnacion 3.00 8.00
SOAER Eddie Rosario 2.50 6.00
SOAFF Freddie Freeman 4.00 10.00
SOAGS George Springer 2.50 6.00
SOAJA Jose Altuve 2.50 6.00
SOAJD Jacob deGrom 6.00 15.00
SOAJG Joey Gallo 2.50 6.00
SOAJH Josh Harrison 2.00 5.00
SOAJL Jake Lamb 2.50 6.00
SOAJS Justin Smoak 2.00 5.00
SOAJV Joey Votto 3.00 8.00
SOAKB Kris Bryant 4.00 10.00
SOAKD Khris Davis 3.00 8.00
SOAKS Kyle Schwarber 3.00 8.00
SOAKSE Kyle Seager 2.00 5.00
SOALS Luis Severino 2.50 6.00
SOAMC Michael Conforto 2.50 6.00
SOAMO Matt Olson 3.00 8.00
SOAMT Masahiro Tanaka 2.50 6.00
SOAMTR Mike Trout 12.00 30.00
SOANS Noah Syndergaard 2.50 6.00
SOAOA Ozzie Albies 3.00 8.00
SOARI Raisel Iglesias 2.00 5.00
SOASM Starling Marte 2.50 6.00
SOASP Salvador Perez 2.50 6.00
SOATM Trey Mancini 2.50 6.00
SOAWC Willson Contreras 2.50 6.00
SOAWM Whit Merrifield 3.00 8.00
SOAXB Xander Bogaerts 3.00 8.00

2019 Topps Tribute Tandem Autograph Booklets

STATED ODDS 1:647 HOBBY
STATED PRINT RUN 25 SER.#'d SETS
EXCHANGE DEADLINE 7/31/2021
TTAA Acuna/Aaron
TTBB Blyleven/Berrios 30.00 80.00
TTBH Buxton/Hunter 40.00 100.00
TTGR Gregorius/Richardson 40.00 100.00
TTHT Thome/Hoskins EXCH 75.00 200.00
TTJM Matsui/Judge
TTOB Ozuna/Brock 40.00 100.00
TTOR Ohtani/Ryan
TTPB Bench/Posey
TTRS Rizzo/Sandberg 100.00 250.00
TTSD Soto/Dawson 40.00 100.00
TTSR Syndergaard/Ryan 150.00 400.00
TTTJA Trout/Jackson
TTTP Pettitte/Tanaka

2019 Topps Tribute Tribute to Enshrinement Autographs

STATED ODDS 1:57 HOBBY
PRINT RUNS B/WN 10-99 COPIES PER
NO PRICING ON TY 15 OR LESS
EXCHANGE DEADLINE 7/31/2021
*PURPLE/50: .4X TO 1X BASIC
*ORANGE/25: .5X TO 1.2X BASIC
HOFAD Andre Dawson/99 10.00 25.00
HOFAK Al Kaline/99 20.00 50.00
HOFAT Alan Trammell/99 25.00 60.00
HOFBB Bert Blyleven/99 10.00 25.00
HOFBG Bob Gibson/90 15.00 40.00
HOFCF Carlton Fisk/90 15.00 40.00
HOFCJ Chipper Jones/30 50.00 120.00
HOFCRJ Cal Ripken Jr./30 50.00 120.00
HOFCY Carl Yastrzemski/30 30.00 80.00
HOFEM Edgar Martinez/99 12.00 30.00
HOFFT Frank Thomas/40 25.00 60.00
HOFHA Hank Aaron
HOFJB Johnny Bench/30 30.00 80.00
HOFJBA Jeff Bagwell/90 15.00 40.00
HOFJM Juan Marichal
HOFNR Nolan Ryan/30 100.00 250.00
HOFOS Ozzie Smith/90 15.00 40.00
HOFRC Rod Carew/99 15.00 40.00
HOFRH Rickey Henderson
HOFRJ Randy Johnson
HOFRJA Reggie Jackson/30 25.00 60.00
HOFRY Robin Yount/40 30.00 80.00
HOFSC Steve Carlton/90 12.00 30.00
HOFTH Trevor Hoffman/99 8.00 20.00
HOFWB Wade Boggs/30 10.00 25.00

2019 Topps Tribute Tribute to the Postseason Autographs

STATED ODDS 1:48 HOBBY
PRINT RUNS B/WN 15-99 COPIES PER
NO PRICING ON TY 15 OR LESS
EXCHANGE DEADLINE 7/31/2021
*ORANGE/25: .5X TO 1.2X p/r 30-99
*ORANGE/25: .4X TO 1X p/r 20
TTPAB Adrian Beltre/50 25.00 60.00
TTPAK Al Kaline/99 20.00 50.00
TTPAP Andy Pettitte/99 15.00 40.00
TTPAR Anthony Rizzo/40 20.00 50.00
TTPBG Bob Gibson/99 20.00 50.00
TTPBW Bernie Williams/99
TTPCF Carlton Fisk/99 25.00 60.00
TTPCJ Chipper Jones/30 50.00 210.00
TTPCY Carl Yastrzemski/40 30.00 80.00
TTPDE Dennis Eckersley/99 10.00 25.00
TTPDG Didi Gregorius/99 15.00 40.00
TTPDJ Derek Jeter
TTPDO David Ortiz/40 25.00 60.00
TTPGS George Springer/99 12.00 30.00
TTPHM Hideki Matsui/40 50.00 120.00
TTPIR Ivan Rodriguez/99 10.00 25.00
TTPJA Jose Altuve/99 20.00 50.00
TTPJB Johnny Bench/40 30.00 80.00
TTPJD Johnny Damon/99 10.00 25.00
TTPJM Jack Morris/99 12.00 30.00
TTPJS John Smoltz/99 20.00 50.00
TTPKB Kris Bryant/40 60.00 150.00
TTPMR Mariano Rivera
TTPNR Nolan Ryan/40 100.00 250.00
TTPOS Ozzie Smith
TTPRJ Randy Johnson/20 40.00 100.00
TTPRJA Reggie Jackson/40 25.00 60.00
TTPSC Steve Carlton
TTPSK Sandy Koufax
TTPSP Salvador Perez/99 10.00 25.00
TTPTG Tom Glavine/99 20.00 50.00
TTPTH Torii Hunter/99 12.00 30.00
TTPTHO Trevor Hoffman/99 12.00 30.00
TTPVG Vladimir Guerrero/50 20.00 50.00

2019 Topps Tribute Triple Relics

STATED ODDS 1:15 HOBBY
STATED PRINT RUN 150 SER.#'d SETS
*GREEN/99: .4X TO 1X BASIC
*PURPLE/50: .5X TO 1.2X BASIC
*ORANGE/25: .75X TO 2X BASIC
TTRAB Andrew Benintendi 3.00 8.00
TTRABE Adrian Beltre 3.00 8.00
TTRAC Aroldis Chapman 3.00 8.00
TTRAJ Aaron Judge 8.00 20.00
TTRAP A.J. Pollock 2.00 5.00
TTRAR Anthony Rizzo 4.00 10.00
TTRBH Bryce Harper 5.00 12.00
TTRBP Buster Posey 4.00 10.00
TTRCB Charlie Blackmon 3.00 8.00
TTRCK Corey Kluber 2.50 6.00
TTRCKE Clayton Kershaw 5.00 12.00
TTRCS Chris Sale 3.00 8.00
TTRCSE Corey Seager 3.00 8.00
TTRDG Didi Gregorius 2.50 6.00
TTRDL DJ LeMahieu 3.00 8.00
TTREE Edwin Encarnacion 3.00 8.00
TTRER Eddie Rosario 2.50 6.00
TTRFF Freddie Freeman 4.00 10.00
TTRFL Francisco Lindor 3.00 8.00
TTRGS Gary Sanchez 3.00 8.00
TTRGSP George Springer 2.50 6.00
TTRJA Jose Altuve 2.50 6.00
TTRJAB Jose Abreu 3.00 8.00
TTRJB Josh Bell 2.50 6.00
TTRJBA Javier Baez 4.00 10.00
TTRJM J.D. Martinez 3.00 8.00
TTRJV Joey Votto 3.00 8.00
TTRKB Kris Bryant 4.00 10.00
TTRKS Kyle Schwarber 3.00 8.00
TTRKT Kyle Tucker 5.00 12.00
TTRLS Luis Severino 2.50 6.00
TTRMA Miguel Andujar 3.00 8.00
TTRMB Mookie Betts 6.00 15.00
TTRMC Miguel Cabrera 3.00 8.00
TTRMCA Matt Carpenter 3.00 8.00
TTRMS Max Scherzer 3.00 8.00
TTRMT Mike Trout 15.00 40.00
TTRNA Nolan Arenado 5.00 12.00
TTRNC Nicholas Castellanos 3.00 8.00
TTRNS Noah Syndergaard 2.50 6.00
TTROA Ozzie Albies 3.00 8.00
TTRPG Paul Goldschmidt 3.00 8.00
TTRRAJ Ronald Acuna Jr. 15.00 40.00
TTRRD Rafael Devers 4.00 10.00
TTRTS Trevor Story 3.00 8.00
TTRXB Xander Bogaerts 3.00 8.00
TTRYC Yoenis Cespedes 3.00 8.00
TTRYM Yadier Molina 4.00 10.00
TTRYP Yasiel Puig 3.00 8.00

2020 Topps Tribute

1 Mike Trout 3.00 8.00
2 Mike Mussina .50 1.25
3 Alex Rodriguez 2.00 5.00
4 DJ LeMahieu .60 1.50
5 Tom Seaver .50 1.25
6 Clayton Kershaw 1.00 2.50
7 David Cone .40 1.00
8 Khris Davis .60 1.50
9 Shohei Ohtani 1.00 2.50
10 Gleyber Torres 1.25 3.00
11 Joey Gallo .60 1.50
12 Justin Verlander .60 1.50
13 Chipper Jones .60 1.50
14 Alex Bregman .60 1.50
15 Eugenio Suarez .50 1.25
16 Pete Alonso 1.50 4.00
17 Hank Aaron 1.25 3.00
18 Cal Ripken Jr. 2.00 5.00
19 Willie Mays 1.25 3.00
20 Roger Clemens .75 2.00
21 Lou Gehrig 1.25 3.00
22 Ty Cobb 1.00 2.50
23 Harold Baines 1.50 4.00
24 Aaron Judge 1.50 4.00
25 Christian Yelich .75 2.00
26 Edgar Martinez .50 1.25
27 Bryce Harper 1.00 2.50
28 Eloy Jimenez 1.25 3.00
29 Hyun-Jin Ryu .50 1.25
30 Mookie Betts 1.25 3.00
31 Vladimir Guerrero .50 1.25
32 Don Mattingly 1.25 3.00
33 Austin Riley .75 2.00
34 Deion Sanders .50 1.25
35 Charlie Blackmon .60 1.50
36 Ramon Laureano .50 1.25
37 Mariano Rivera .75 2.00
38 Reggie Jackson .50 1.25
39 Yasiel Puig .60 1.50
40 Rhys Hoskins .75 2.00
41 Jose Altuve .50 1.25
42 Jacob deGrom 1.25 3.00
43 Ozzie Albies .60 1.50
44 Gary Sanchez .60 1.50
45 Walker Buehler .75 2.00
46 Ronald Acuna Jr. 2.50 6.00
47 Anthony Rizzo .75 2.00
48 Jackie Robinson .60 1.50
49 J.D. Martinez .60 1.50
50 Cody Bellinger 1.25 3.00
51 Josh Bell .50 1.25
52 Chris Sale .60 1.50
53 Ted Williams 1.25 3.00
54 Kris Bryant .75 2.00
55 Roberto Clemente 1.50 4.00
56 Sammy Sosa .60 1.50
57 Jeff McNeil .50 1.25
58 Rickey Henderson .60 1.50
59 Tony Gwynn .60 1.50
60 Juan Soto 2.00 5.00
61 Carl Yastrzemski 1.00 2.50
63 Trea Turner .50 1.25
64 Nick Senzel .60 1.50
65 Yoan Moncada .60 1.50
66 Max Scherzer .60 1.50
67 Roger Maris .60 1.50
68 Jose Abreu .60 1.50
69 George Brett 1.25 3.00
70 Manny Machado .60 1.50
71 Nolan Arenado 1.00 2.50
72 Francisco Lindor .60 1.50
73 Whit Merrifield .60 1.50
74 Wade Boggs .50 1.25
75 Javier Baez .75 2.00
76 Paul DeJong .60 1.50
77 Brandon Lowe .50 1.25
78 Freddie Freeman .75 2.00
79 Fernando Tatis Jr. 3.00 8.00
80 Paul Goldschmidt .60 1.50
81 Ichiro .75 2.00
82 Ken Griffey Jr. 1.25 3.00
83 Ernie Banks .60 1.50
84 Jim Thome .50 1.25
85 Vladimir Guerrero Jr. 1.00 2.50
86 Chris Paddack .60 1.50
87 Honus Wagner .60 1.50
88 Xander Bogaerts .60 1.50
89 Sandy Koufax 1.25 3.00
90 Babe Ruth 1.50 4.00
62A Gerrit Cole 1.00 2.50
62B Gerrit Cole 1.00 2.50

2020 Topps Tribute '20 Rookies

STATED ODDS 1:18 HOBBY
STATED PRINT RUN 450 SER.#'d SETS
20RAP A.J. Puk 2.00 5.00
20RBB Bo Bichette 12.00 30.00
20RBM Brendan McKay 2.50 6.00
20RDC Dylan Cease 3.00 8.00
20RGL Gavin Lux 15.00 40.00
20RJL Jesus Luzardo 2.50 6.00
20RKL Kyle Lewis 6.00 15.00
20RNH Nico Hoerner 5.00 12.00
20RYA Yordan Alvarez 15.00 40.00

2020 Topps Tribute '20 Rookies Green

*GREEN: ..5X TO 1.2X BASIC
STATED ODDS 1:84 HOBBY
STATED PRINT RUN 99 SER.#'d SETS

2020 Topps Tribute '20 Rookies Purple

*PURPLE: .6X TO 1.5X BASIC
STATED ODDS 1:165 HOBBY
STATED PRINT RUN 50 SER.#'d SETS
20RYA Yordan Alvarez 30.00 80.00

2020 Topps Tribute Autograph Patches

STATED ODDS 1:86 HOBBY
STATED PRINT RUN 50 SER.#'d SETS
TAPAJ Aaron Judge
TAPAN Aaron Nola 20.00 50.00
TAPAR Anthony Rizzo 50.00 120.00
TAPBL Brandon Lowe 20.00 50.00
TAPBP Buster Posey
TAPBS Blake Snell 15.00 40.00
TAPGC Gerrit Cole 30.00 80.00
TAPGS George Springer 25.00 60.00
TAPJA Jose Altuve 25.00 60.00
TAPMC Miguel Cabrera 60.00 150.00
TAPMT Mike Trout
TAPOA Ozzie Albies EXCH 40.00 100.00
TAPRH Rhys Hoskins 25.00 60.00
TAPRT Rowdy Tellez 8.00 20.00
TAPVR Victor Robles 40.00 100.00
TAPWM Whit Merrifield 12.00 30.00
TAPFTJ Fernando Tatis Jr. 150.00 400.00
TAPLGJ Lourdes Gurriel Jr. 8.00 20.00

2020 Topps Tribute Autographs

STATED ODDS 1:8 HOBBY
PRINT RUNS B/WN 10-199 COPIES PER
NO PRICING ON QTY 15 OR LESS
EXCHANGE DEADLINE 1/31/22
TAAA Aristides Aquino/199 12.00 30.00
TAAG Andres Galarraga/199 4.00 10.00
TAAJ Aaron Judge/35 75.00 200.00
TAAK Al Kaline/150 20.00 50.00
TAAM Austin Meadows/199 8.00 20.00
TAAP Andy Pettitte/110 10.00 25.00
TAAPU A.J. Puk/199 8.00 20.00
TAAR Anthony Rizzo/60 25.00 60.00
TABB Bert Blyleven/199 8.00 20.00
TABBI Bo Bichette/199 40.00 100.00
TABBR Bobby Bradley/199 3.00 8.00
TABH Bryce Harper/30 150.00 400.00
TABM Brendan McKay/199 6.00 15.00
TABR Brendan Rodgers/199 6.00 15.00
TABS Blake Snell/199 8.00 20.00
TABW Bernie Williams/110 20.00 50.00
TACB Cavan Biggio/199 20.00 50.00
TACCS CC Sabathia/110 25.00 60.00
TACRJ Cal Ripken Jr./40 60.00 150.00
TACF Carlton Fisk/110 25.00 60.00
TACJ Chipper Jones/40 50.00 120.00
TACY Christian Yelich/110 25.00 60.00
TADC David Cone/199 10.00 25.00
TADCE Dylan Cease/199 8.00 20.00
TADE Dennis Eckersley/199 10.00 25.00
TADM Don Mattingly/60 40.00 100.00
TADMA Dustin May/199 20.00 50.00
TAEJ Eloy Jimenez/199 20.00 50.00
TAEM Edgar Martinez/150 15.00 40.00
TAFL Francisco Lindor/150 20.00 50.00
TAFT Frank Thomas/60 40.00 100.00
TAGL Gavin Lux/199 25.00 60.00
TAGS George Springer/160 8.00 20.00
TAHM Hideki Matsui/40 40.00 100.00
TAJA Jose Altuve/60 15.00 40.00
TAJB Johnny Bench/60 40.00 100.00
TAJC Jose Canseco/199 15.00 40.00
TAJDM J.D. Martinez/150 12.00 30.00
TAJL Jesus Luzardo/199 6.00 15.00
TAJP Jorge Posada/199 15.00 40.00
TAJR Jim Rice/199 10.00 25.00
TAJSM John Smoltz/110 15.00 40.00
TAJY Jordan Yamamoto/199 6.00 15.00
TAKB Kris Bryant/60 60.00 150.00
TAKH Keston Hiura/199 20.00 50.00
TAKHI Keston Hiura/199 20.00 50.00
TALA Logan Allen/199 3.00 8.00
TALMJ Lance McCullers Jr./199 6.00 15.00
TALR Luis Robert/199 100.00 250.00
TALV Luke Voit/199 15.00 40.00
TAMC Miguel Cabrera/60 60.00 150.00
TAMCH Michael Chavis/199 8.00 20.00
TAMMU Mike Mussina/110 25.00 60.00
TAMR Mariano Rivera/30 75.00 200.00
TAMT Mike Trout/25 800.00 1200.00
TAMUN Max Muncy/199 8.00 20.00
TANA Nolan Arenado/110 40.00 100.00
TANR Nolan Ryan/40 75.00 200.00
TANSZ Nick Senzel/199 15.00 40.00
TAOS Ozzie Smith/110 20.00 50.00
TAPD Paul DeJong/199 5.00 12.00
TARC Roger Clemens/35 50.00 120.00
TARCA Rod Carew/160 25.00 60.00
TARF Rollie Fingers/199 10.00 25.00
TARG Robel Garcia/199 3.00 8.00
TARH Rickey Henderson/40 60.00 150.00
TARHO Rhys Hoskins/199 6.00 15.00
TARJ Reggie Jackson/40 30.00 80.00
TASB Seth Brown/199 6.00 15.00
TASC Steve Carlton/110 15.00 40.00
TASM Sean Murphy/199 5.00 12.00
TASN Sheldon Neuse/199 4.00 10.00
TASO Shohei Ohtani/25 75.00 200.00
TATB Trevor Bauer/199 25.00 60.00
TATM Tino Martinez/199 20.00 50.00
TAVG Vladimir Guerrero/60 30.00 80.00
TAVGJ Vladimir Guerrero Jr./199 40.00 100.00
TAWC Willson Contreras/199 10.00 25.00
TAWM Whit Merrifield/199 5.00 12.00
TAWME Whit Merrifield/199 5.00 12.00
TAXB Xander Bogaerts/199 20.00 50.00
TAYA Yordan Alvarez/199 50.00 120.00

2020 Topps Tribute Autographs Blue

*BLUE/150: .4X TO 1X p/r 110-199
STATED ODDS 1:12 HOBBY
STATED PRINT RUN 150 SER.#'d SETS
TAFET Fernando Tatis Jr. 60.00 150.00
TAFTJ Fernando Tatis Jr. 60.00 150.00
TAJY Jordan Yamamoto 10.00 25.00

2020 Topps Tribute Autographs Green

*GREEN/99: .5X TO 1.2X p/r 110-199
STATED ODDS 1:18 HOBBY
STATED PRINT RUN 99 SER.#'d SETS
TAFET Fernando Tatis Jr. 75.00 200.00
TAFTJ Fernando Tatis Jr. 75.00 200.00
TAJY Jordan Yamamoto 12.00 30.00
TAPA Pete Alonso 50.00 120.00
TAPAL Pete Alonso 50.00 120.00
TARG Robel Garcia 8.00 20.00

2020 Topps Tribute Autographs Orange

*ORANGE/25: .6X TO 1.5X p/r 110-199
*ORANGE/25: .5X TO 1.2X p/r 30-60
*ORANGE/25: .4X TO 1X p/r 25
STATED ODDS 1:47 HOBBY
STATED PRINT RUN 25 SER.#'d SETS
TAAA Aristides Aquino 60.00 150.00
TAFET Fernando Tatis Jr. 100.00 250.00
TAFTJ Fernando Tatis Jr. 100.00 250.00
TAJY Jordan Yamamoto 15.00 40.00
TAMS Max Scherzer EXCH 50.00 120.00
TAMT Mike Trout 800.00 1200.00
TAPA Pete Alonso 60.00 150.00
TAPAL Pete Alonso 60.00 150.00
TARAJ Ronald Acuna Jr. 100.00 250.00
TARG Robel Garcia 12.00 30.00
TAYA Yordan Alvarez 100.00 250.00

2020 Topps Tribute Autographs Purple

*PURPLE/50: .5X TO 1.2X p/r 110-199
*PURPLE/50: .4X TO 1X p/r 30-60
STATED ODDS 1:27 HOBBY
STATED PRINT RUN 50 SER.#'d SETS
TAAA Aristides Aquino 30.00 80.00
TAFET Fernando Tatis Jr. 75.00 200.00
TAFTJ Fernando Tatis Jr. 75.00 200.00
TAJY Jordan Yamamoto 12.00 30.00
TAMS Max Scherzer EXCH 40.00 100.00
TAPA Pete Alonso 50.00 120.00
TAPAL Pete Alonso 50.00 120.00
TARAJ Ronald Acuna Jr. 75.00 200.00
TARG Robel Garcia 8.00 20.00
TAYA Yordan Alvarez 75.00 200.00

2020 Topps Tribute Dual Player Relics

STATED ODDS 1:14 HOBBY
STATED PRINT RUN 150 SER.#'d SETS
*GREEN/99: .4X TO 1X BASIC
*PURPLE/50: .5X TO 1.2X BASIC
*ORANGE/25: .8X TO 2X BASIC
DRAA O.Albies/R.Acuna Jr. 15.00 40.00
DRAC J.Altuve/C.Correa 6.00 15.00
DRAS N.Arenado/T.Story 6.00 15.00
DRAY C.Yelich/H.Aaron 15.00 40.00
DRBB X.Bogaerts/M.Betts 8.00 20.00
DRBP J.Bell/G.Polanco 6.00 15.00
DRBR A.Rizzo/J.Baez 15.00 40.00
DRCM J.McNeil/M.Conforto 3.00 8.00
DRGA V.Guerrero Jr./R.Alomar 6.00 15.00
DRGM K.Griffey Jr./E.Martinez 20.00 50.00
DRHH B.Harper/R.Hoskins 12.00 30.00
DRIK Ichiro/Y.Kikuchi 8.00 20.00
DRJH R.Henderson/R.Jackson 15.00 40.00
DRJS A.Judge/G.Stanton 10.00 25.00
DRLA W.Adames/B.Lowe 3.00 8.00
DRMO J.Martinez/D.Ortiz 4.00 10.00
DRMR C.Ripken Jr./E.Murray 12.00 30.00
DROT M.Trout/S.Ohtani 25.00 60.00
DRPS A.Pettitte/C.Sabathia 8.00 20.00
DRRC N.Ryan/G.Cole 12.00 30.00
DRRK C.Kershaw/H.Ryu 4.00 10.00
DRRS V.Robles/J.Soto 12.00 30.00
DRSB C.Seager/C.Bellinger 8.00 20.00
DRSR C.Santana/J.Ramirez 3.00 8.00
DRTR F.Tatis Jr./F.Reyes 8.00 20.00
DRGMA J.Gallo/N.Mazara 4.00 10.00
DRSBR K.Bryant/S.Sosa 10.00 25.00

2020 Topps Tribute Dual Relics

STATED ODDS 1:14 HOBBY
STATED PRINT RUN 150 SER.#'d SETS
*GREEN/99: .4X TO 1X BASIC
*PURPLE/50: .5X TO 1.2X BASIC
*ORANGE/25: .8X TO 2X BASIC
SDRAB Andrew Benintendi 3.00 8.00
SDRCS Carlos Santana 2.50 6.00
SDREM Eddie Murray 2.50 6.00
SDRFF Freddie Freeman 4.00 10.00
SDRHA Hank Aaron 6.00 15.00

SDRKS Kyle Schwarber 6.00 15.00
SDRMB Michael Brantley 2.50 6.00
SDRMC Michael Conforto 2.50 6.00
SDRNR Nolan Ryan 10.00 25.00
SDRRC Rod Carew 10.00 25.00
SDRRJ Randy Johnson 5.00 12.00
SDRXB Xander Bogaerts 10.00 25.00
SDRABR Alex Bregman 4.00 10.00
SDRCSE Corey Seager 4.00 10.00
SDRFTJ Fernando Tatis Jr. 10.00 25.00
SDRRJA Reggie Jackson 10.00 25.00
SDRVGJ Vladimir Guerrero Jr. 5.00 12.00

2020 Topps Tribute Franchise Best Autographs

STATED ODDS 1:150 HOBBY
PRINT RUNS B/WN 15-99 COPIES PER
NO PRICING ON QTY 15 OR LESS
EXCHANGE DEADLINE 1/31/22
FBAI Ichiro/15 300.00 600.00
FBAAJ Aaron Judge/15 150.00 400.00
FBAAP Andy Pettitte/50 25.00 60.00
FBABS Blake Snell/99 8.00 20.00
FBACF Carlton Fisk/50 20.00 50.00
FBACY Christian Yelich/50 50.00 120.00
FBADO David Ortiz/30 40.00 100.00
FBAFL Francisco Lindor/99 25.00 60.00
FBAHA Hank Aaron/15 150.00 400.00
FBAIR Ivan Rodriguez/50 30.00 80.00
FBAJB Johnny Bench/30 60.00 150.00
FBAKB Kris Bryant/30 75.00 200.00
FBAMC Miguel Cabrera/30 75.00 200.00
FBAMM Mike Mussina/50 30.00 80.00
FBAMR Mariano Rivera/15 200.00 500.00
FBAMS Max Scherzer/50 40.00 100.00
FBAMT Mike Trout/15 500.00 1000.00
FBANR Nolan Ryan/30 150.00 400.00
FBANS Nick Senzel/99 15.00 40.00
FBAOS Ozzie Smith/50 50.00 20.00
FBARC Rod Carew/99 20.00 50.00
FBARH Rhys Hoskins/99 20.00 50.00
FBARJ Reggie Jackson/30 40.00 100.00
FBAVG Vladimir Guerrero/50 30.00 80.00
FBAWB Walker Buehler/99 30.00 80.00
FBACCS CC Sabathia/50 30.00 80.00
FBACRJ Cal Ripken Jr./30 75.00 200.00
FBAJDM J.D. Martinez/99 15.00 40.00
FBAJSM John Smoltz/50 15.00 40.00
FBAKGJ Ken Griffey Jr./15 200.00 500.00
FBARAJ Ronald Acuna Jr./99 100.00 250.00
FBARCL Roger Clemens/15 50.00 120.00
FBAVGJ Vladimir Guerrero Jr./99 60.00 150.00

2020 Topps Tribute Franchise Best Autographs Orange

*ORANGE/25: .5X TO 1.2X p/r 30-99
STATED ODDS 1:191 HOBBY
STATED PRINT RUN 25 SER.#'d SETS
FBAAP Andy Pettitte 40.00 100.00
FBABS Blake Snell 12.00 30.00

2020 Topps Tribute Iconic Perspectives Autographs

STATED ODDS 1:28 HOBBY
PRINT RUNS B/WN 5-99 COPIES PER
NO PRICING ON QTY 15 OR LESS
EXCHANGE DEADLINE 1/31/22
IPAG Andres Galarraga/99 8.00 20.00
IPAJ Aaron Judge/15 125.00 300.00
IPAK Al Kaline/70 25.00 60.00
IPAM Austin Meadows/99 8.00 20.00
IPBS Blake Snell/99 8.00 20.00
IPBW Bernie Williams/50 25.00 60.00
IPCF Carlton Fisk/50 20.00 50.00
IPCY Christian Yelich/50 50.00 120.00
IPDC David Cone/99 20.00 50.00
IPDM Don Mattingly/45 40.00 100.00
IPDO David Ortiz/25 60.00 150.00
IPEJ Eloy Jimenez/99 20.00 50.00
IPFL Francisco Lindor/70 25.00 60.00
IPJA Jose Altuve/45 20.00 50.00
IPJC Jose Canseco/99 20.00 50.00
IPJP Jorge Posada/70 15.00 40.00
IPKH Keston Hiura/99 12.00 30.00
IPMC Michael Chavis/99 15.00 40.00
IPNA Nolan Arenado/50 50.00 120.00
IPNS Nick Senzel/99 15.00 40.00
IPOA Ozzie Albies EXCH/99 20.00 50.00
IPOS Ozzie Smith/50 20.00 50.00
IPPA Pete Alonso/99 50.00 120.00
IPPD Paul DeJong/99 6.00 15.00
IPRC Rod Carew/50 20.00 50.00
IPRF Rollie Fingers/99 10.00 25.00
IPRH Rhys Hoskins/80 10.00 25.00
IPSC Steve Carlton/50 20.00 50.00
IPTB Trevor Bauer/99 8.00 20.00
IPTM Tino Martinez/99 15.00 40.00
IPWB Walker Buehler/99 30.00 80.00
IPWC Willson Contreras/99 6.00 15.00
IPWM Whit Merrifield/99 10.00 25.00
IPXB Xander Bogaerts/80 15.00 40.00
IPCCS CC Sabathia/50 30.00 80.00
IPCRJ Cal Ripken Jr./25 75.00 200.00
IPFTJ Fernando Tatis Jr./99 75.00 200.00
IPJDM J.D. Martinez/70 15.00 40.00
IPJSM John Smoltz/50 15.00 40.00
IPLMJ Lance McCullers Jr./99 8.00 20.00
IPMMU Mike Mussina/50 30.00 80.00
IPMUN Max Muncy/99 12.00 30.00
IPRHE Rickey Henderson/25 50.00 120.00
IPVGJ Vladimir Guerrero Jr./99 60.00 150.00
IPWBO Wade Boggs/45 30.00 80.00

2020 Topps Tribute Iconic Perspectives Autographs Orange

*ORANGE/25: .5X TO 1.2X p/r 45-99
*ORANGE/25: .4X TO 1X p/r 25
STATED ODDS 1:102 HOBBY
STATED PRINT RUN 25 SER.#'d SETS
IPAG Andres Galarraga 15.00 40.00
IPAM Austin Meadows 15.00 40.00
IPBS Blake Snell 12.00 30.00
IPRF Rollie Fingers 15.00 40.00

2020 Topps Tribute League Inauguration Autographs

STATED ODDS 1:59 HOBBY
STATED PRINT RUN 99 SER.#'d SETS
EXCHANGE DEADLINE 1/31/22
*ORANGE/25: .5X TO 1.2X
LAAP A.J. Puk 6.00 15.00
LABB Bo Bichette 75.00 200.00
LABM Brendan McKay 12.00 30.00
LADC Dylan Cease 6.00 15.00
LAJL Jesus Luzardo 8.00 20.00
LAJY Jordan Yamamoto 4.00 10.00
LALA Logan Allen 4.00 10.00
LALR Luis Robert 125.00 300.00
LARG Robel Garcia 4.00 10.00
LASM Sean Murphy 6.00 15.00
LAYA Yordan Alvarez 75.00 200.00
LABBR Bobby Bradley 4.00 10.00

2020 Topps Tribute Stamp of Approval Relics

STATED ODDS 1:14 HOBBY
STATED PRINT RUN 150 SER.#'d SETS
*GREEN/99: .4X TO 1X BASIC
*PURPLE/50: .5X TO 1.2X BASIC
*ORANGE/25: .8X TO 2X BASIC
SOAAH Aaron Hicks 4.00 10.00
SOAAJ Aaron Judge 8.00 20.00
SOAAM Austin Meadows 4.00 10.00
SOAAN Aaron Nola 5.00 12.00
SOAAR Anthony Rizzo 6.00 15.00
SOABL Brandon Lowe 2.50 6.00
SOABP Buster Posey 6.00 15.00
SOABS Blake Snell 4.00 10.00
SOACB Cody Bellinger 6.00 15.00
SOACM Charlie Morton 3.00 8.00
SOACS Chris Sale 3.00 8.00
SOAFF Freddie Freeman 4.00 10.00
SOAGC Gerrit Cole 5.00 12.00
SOAGS George Springer 2.50 6.00
SOAJA Jose Altuve 2.50 6.00
SOAJH Josh Hader 4.00 10.00
SOAJV Joey Votto 5.00 12.00
SOAKH Keston Hiura 6.00 15.00
SOAMA Miguel Andujar 4.00 10.00
SOAMB Michael Brantley 2.50 6.00
SOAMC Miguel Cabrera 5.00 12.00
SOAMT Mike Trout 25.00 60.00
SOANS Noah Syndergaard 4.00 10.00
SOAOA Ozzie Albies 6.00 15.00
SOARH Rhys Hoskins 4.00 10.00
SOART Rowdy Tellez 3.00 8.00
SOATM Trey Mancini 3.00 8.00
SOATP Tommy Pham 5.00 12.00
SOATS Trevor Story 5.00 12.00
SOAVR Victor Robles 4.00 10.00
SOAWB Walker Buehler 4.00 10.00
SOAWM Whit Merrifield 5.00 12.00
SOAYK Yusei Kikuchi 4.00 10.00
SOACCS CC Sabathia 2.50 6.00
SOACSE Corey Seager 3.00 8.00
SOAFTJ Fernando Tatis Jr. 15.00 40.00
SOAJDM J.D. Martinez 3.00 8.00
SOALGJ Lourdes Gurriel Jr. 2.50 6.00
SOALMJ Lance McCullers Jr. 2.00 5.00
SOAMAT Masahiro Tanaka 6.00 15.00
SOANSE Nick Senzel 3.00 8.00

2020 Topps Tribute Tandem Autograph Booklets

STATED ODDS 1:269 HOBBY
STATED PRINT RUN 25 SER.#'d SETS
TTAG A.Galarraga/N.Arenado 100.00 250.00
TTCK M.Cabrera/A.Kaline 250.00 500.00
TTGA V.Guerrero Jr./R.Alomar 250.00 500.00
TTGG V.Guerrero Jr./V.Guerrero 250.00 500.00
TTNC S.Carlton/A.Nola 50.00 120.00
TTOC R.Carew/S.Ohtani
TTSP A.Pettitte/C.Sabathia 75.00 200.00
TTTS O.Smith/F.Tatis Jr. 250.00 600.00

2020 Topps Tribute Tribute to Great Hitters Autographs

STATED ODDS 1:60 HOBBY
PRINT RUNS B/WN 15-99 COPIES PER
NO PRICING ON QTY 20 OR LESS
EXCHANGE DEADLINE 1/31/22
*PURPLE/50: .4X TO 1X p/r 75-99
TGHAK Al Kalino/99 25.00 60.00
TGHCJ Chipper Jones/30 40.00 100.00
TGHCY Carl Yastrzemski/30 50.00 120.00
TGHDM Don Mattingly/95 40.00 100.00
TGHDO David Ortiz/30
TGHEM Edgar Martinez/99 20.00 50.00
TGHFL Francisco Lindor/99 25.00 60.00
TGHFT Frank Thomas/70 40.00 100.00
TGHHM Hideki Matsui/25 40.00 100.00
TGHJB Johnny Bench/40 40.00 100.00
TGHKB Kris Bryant/50 60.00 150.00
TGHMC Miguel Cabrera/50 60.00 150.00
TGHRC Rod Carew/70 20.00 50.00
TGHRH Rickey Henderson/30 40.00 100.00
TGHVG Vladimir Guerrero/75 30.00 80.00
TGHXB Xander Bogaerts/99 15.00 40.00
TGHCRJ Cal Ripken Jr./30 50.00 120.00
TGHCYE Christian Yelich/75 50.00 120.00
TGHRHS Rhys Hoskins/99 10.00 25.00
TGHVGJ Vladimir Guerrero Jr./99 60.00 150.00

2020 Topps Tribute Tribute to Great Hitters Autographs Orange

*ORANGE/25: .5X TO 1.2X p/r 30-99
*ORANGE/25: .4X TO 1X p/r 25
STATED ODDS 1:180 HOBBY
STATED PRINT RUN 25 SER.#'d SETS
TGHDO David Ortiz 40.00 100.00

2020 Topps Tribute Triple Relics

STATED ODDS 1:14 HOBBY
STATED PRINT RUN 150 SER.#'d SETS
*GREEN/99: .4X TO 1X BASIC
*PURPLE/50: .5X TO 1.2X BASIC
*ORANGE/25: .8X TO 2X BASIC
TTRAC Aroldis Chapman 6.00 15.00
TTRAJ Aaron Judge 12.00 30.00
TTRAP Andy Pettitte 6.00 15.00
TTRAR Anthony Rizzo 4.00 10.00
TTRBL Brandon Lowe 4.00 10.00
TTRCB Cody Bellinger 8.00 20.00
TTRCM Charlie Morton 3.00 8.00
TTRCS Chris Sale 3.00 8.00
TTRCY Christian Yelich 10.00 25.00
TTRDC David Cone 5.00 12.00
TTRDS Dansby Swanson 6.00 15.00
TTREH Eric Hosmer 2.50 6.00
TTREM Edgar Martinez 8.00 20.00
TTRER Eddie Rosario 2.50 6.00
TTRFR Franmil Reyes 2.00 5.00
TTRGC Gerrit Cole 5.00 12.00
TTRGS George Springer 4.00 10.00
TTRJB Josh Bell 2.50 6.00
TTRJR Jose Ramirez 2.50 6.00
TTRJS Juan Soto 10.00 25.00
TTRMB Mookie Betts 10.00 25.00
TTRMC Matt Chapman 10.00 25.00
TTRMS Mike Soroka 3.00 8.00
TTRMT Mike Trout 25.00 60.00
TTRNA Nolan Arenado 4.00 10.00
TTROA Ozzie Albies 5.00 12.00
TTRPG Paul Goldschmidt 5.00 12.00
TTRPM Pedro Martinez 6.00 15.00
TTRRH Rickey Henderson 12.00 30.00
TTRSC Steve Carlton 2.50 6.00
TTRSO Shohei Ohtani 10.00 25.00
TTRSS Sammy Sosa 8.00 20.00
TTRTM Thurman Munson 15.00 40.00
TTRTS Trevor Story 3.00 8.00
TTRVG Vladimir Guerrero 2.50 6.00
TTRVR Victor Robles 4.00 10.00
TTRWB Wade Boggs 5.00 12.00
TTRYA Yordan Alvarez 20.00 50.00
TTRYP Yasiel Puig 5.00 12.00
TTRCCS CC Sabathia 2.50 6.00
TTRCRJ Cal Ripken Jr. 12.00 30.00
TTRGST Giancarlo Stanton 8.00 20.00
TTRHJR Hyun-Jin Ryu 2.50 6.00
TTRJBA Javier Baez 12.00 30.00
TTRJDM J.D. Martinez 3.00 8.00
TTRKGJ Ken Griffey Jr. 20.00 50.00
TTRLMJ Lance McCullers Jr. 2.00 5.00
TTRRAJ Ronald Acuna Jr. 20.00 50.00
TTRRAL Roberto Alomar 6.00 15.00
TTRRHO Rhys Hoskins 4.00 10.00

2021 Topps Tribute

1 Ichiro .75 2.00
2 Honus Wagner .60 1.50
3 Lou Gehrig 1.25 3.00
4 Xander Bogaerts .60 1.50
5 Roger Clemens .75 2.00
6 Tom Seaver .50 1.25
7 Bryce Harper 1.00 2.50
8 Charlie Blackmon .60 1.50
9 Nolan Arenado 1.00 2.50
10 Kyle Lewis 1.50 4.00
11 Manny Machado .60 1.50
12 J.D. Martinez .60 1.50
13 Mookie Betts 1.25 3.00
14 Yu Darvish .60 1.50
15 Randy Johnson .60 1.50
16 Walker Buehler .75 2.00
17 Johnny Bench .60 1.50
18 Juan Soto 3.00 8.00
19 Paul Goldschmidt .60 1.50
20 George Brett 1.25 3.00
21 Rickey Henderson .60 1.50
22 Jackie Robinson .60 1.50
23 Aaron Nola .50 1.25
24 Whit Merrifield .60 1.50
25 Mike Schmidt 1.00 2.50
26 Frank Thomas .60 1.50
27 Gleyber Torres 1.25 3.00
28 Shohei Ohtani 1.00 2.50
29 Ted Williams 1.25 3.00
30 Francisco Lindor .60 1.50
31 Jose Abreu .60 1.50
32 Aaron Judge 1.50 4.00
33 Ivan Rodriguez .50 1.25
34 Blake Snell .50 1.25
35 Cody Bellinger 1.25 3.00
36 Ernie Banks .60 1.50
37 Willie Mays 1.25 3.00
38 Alex Bregman .60 1.50
39 Mike Trout 4.00 10.00
40 Reggie Jackson .50 1.25
41 Javier Baez .75 2.00
42 Max Scherzer .60 1.50
43 Freddie Freeman .75 2.00
44 Fernando Tatis Jr. 4.00 10.00
45 Max Kepler .50 1.25
46 Christian Yelich .75 2.00
47 Justin Verlander .60 1.50
48 Joey Votto .60 1.50
49 Ronald Acuna Jr. 3.00 8.00
50 Willie Stargell .50 1.25
51 Albert Pujols .75 2.00
52 Josh Bell .50 1.25
53 Buster Posey .75 2.00
54 Ty Cobb 1.00 2.50
55 Duke Snider .50 1.25
56 Jacob deGrom 1.25 3.00
57 Ken Griffey Jr. 6.00 15.00
58 Tony Gwynn .60 1.50
59 Nolan Ryan 6.00 15.00
60 Babe Ruth 1.50 4.00
61 Brooks Robinson .50 1.25
62 Yordan Alvarez 1.50 4.00
63 Robin Yount .60 1.50
64 Mariano Rivera .75 2.00
65 Kris Bryant .75 2.00
66 Gerrit Cole 1.00 2.50
67 Austin Meadows .60 1.50
68 Yadier Molina .75 2.00
69 Trevor Story .60 1.50
70 Matt Chapman .60 1.50
71 Vladimir Guerrero Jr. 1.00 2.50
72 Stephen Strasburg .60 1.50
73 Cal Ripken Jr. 2.00 5.00
74 Josh Donaldson .50 1.25
75 Ketel Marte .50 1.25
76 Giancarlo Stanton .60 1.50
77 Joey Gallo .60 1.50
78 Carl Yastrzemski 1.00 2.50
79 Pete Alonso 1.50 4.00
80 Jose Altuve .50 1.25
81 Hank Aaron 1.25 3.00
82 Shane Bieber .60 1.50
83 Roger Maris .60 1.50
84 Luis Robert 2.00 5.00
85 Anthony Rendon .60 1.50
86 Clayton Kershaw 1.00 2.50
87 Miguel Cabrera .60 1.50
88 Wade Boggs .50 1.25
89 George Springer .50 1.25
90 Bo Bichette 1.50 4.00

2021 Topps Tribute Green

*GREEN/99: 1.2X TO 3X BASIC
STATED ODDS 1:xx HOBBY
STATED PRINT RUN 99 SER.#'d SETS
39 Mike Trout 25.00 60.00
57 Ken Griffey Jr. 40.00 100.00

2021 Topps Tribute Purple

*PURPLE/50: 2X TO 5X BASIC
STATED ODDS 1:xx HOBBY
STATED PRINT RUN 50 SER.#'d SETS
39 Mike Trout 40.00 100.00
49 Ronald Acuna Jr. 30.00 80.00
57 Ken Griffey Jr. 60.00 150.00

2021 Topps Tribute '21 Rookies

STATED ODDS 1:xx HOBBY
21RAB Alec Bohm 12.00 30.00
21RCM Casey Mize 10.00 25.00
21RDC Dylan Carlson 10.00 25.00
21RJA Jo Adell 8.00 20.00
21RJB Joey Bart 5.00 12.00
21RJC Jake Cronenworth 8.00 20.00
21RKH Ke'Bryan Hayes 12.00 30.00
21RNM Nick Madrigal 10.00 25.00
21RRM Ryan Mountcastle 12.00 30.00
21RSS Sixto Sanchez 2.50 6.00

2021 Topps Tribute '21 Rookies Green

*GREEN/99: .5X TO 1.2X BASIC
STATED ODDS 1:xx HOBBY
STATED PRINT RUN 99 SER.#'d SETS
21RAB Alec Bohm 20.00 50.00
21RCM Casey Mize 20.00 50.00
21RDC Dylan Carlson 20.00 50.00
21RJA Jo Adell 12.00 30.00
21RKH Ke'Bryan Hayes 20.00 50.00

2021 Topps Tribute '21 Rookies Purple

*PURPLE/50: .6X TO 1.5X BASIC
STATED ODDS 1:xx HOBBY
STATED PRINT RUN 50 SER.#'d SETS
21RAB Alec Bohm 25.00 60.00
21RCM Casey Mize 40.00 100.00
21RDC Dylan Carlson 40.00 100.00
21RJA Jo Adell 40.00 100.00
21RJC Jake Cronenworth 25.00 60.00
21RKH Ke'Bryan Hayes 40.00 100.00

2021 Topps Tribute Autograph Patches

STATED ODDS 1:xx HOBBY
STATED PRINT RUN 50 SER.#'d SETS
EXCHANGE DEADLINE 2/28/2023
APAJ Aaron Judge
APAM Austin Meadows 20.00 50.00
APAN Aaron Nola 25.00 60.00
APCY Christian Yelich 50.00 120.00
APFF Freddie Freeman 60.00 150.00
APJA Jose Altuve 20.00 50.00
APJB Josh Bell 12.00 30.00
APJV Joey Votto 25.00 60.00
APLG Lourdes Gurriel Jr. 12.00 30.00
APMC Matt Chapman 25.00 60.00
APMM Max Muncy 25.00 60.00
APMT Mike Trout 500.00 1000.00
APRA Ronald Acuna Jr. 150.00 400.00
APRD Rafael Devers
APRH Rhys Hoskins 30.00 80.00
APRL Ramon Laureano 15.00 40.00
APTS Trevor Story 20.00 50.00
APXB Xander Bogaerts 60.00 150.00
APMCO Michael Conforto 25.00 60.00

2021 Topps Tribute Autographs

*GREEN/99: .5X TO 1.2X BASIC p/r 131-199
*GREEN/99: .4X TO 1X BASIC p/r 30-100
STATED ODDS 1:xx HOBBY
PRINT RUNS B/WN 10-199 COPIES PER
NO PRICING ON QTY 15 OR LESS
EXCHANGE DEADLINE 2/28/2023
*BLUE/150: .4X TO 1X BASIC p/r 131-199
TAAB Alec Bohm EXCH 50.00 120.00
TAAG Andres Gimenez 12.00 30.00
TAAJ Aaron Judge 75.00 200.00
TAAM Austin Meadows 5.00 12.00
TAAP Albert Pujols
TAAT Anderson Tejeda 8.00 20.00
TAAY Andy Young 8.00 20.00
TABD Bobby Dalbec 40.00 100.00
TABH Bryce Harper 100.00 250.00
TABS Brady Singer 20.00 50.00
TACB Cody Bellinger 60.00 150.00
TACJ Cristian Javier 8.00 20.00
TACM Casey Mize 30.00 80.00
TACP Cristian Pache 40.00 100.00
TACR Cal Ripken Jr. 75.00 200.00
TACY Christian Yelich 40.00 100.00
TADB David Bote 10.00 25.00
TADE Dennis Eckersley 10.00 25.00
TADV Daulton Varsho 12.00 30.00
TAEJ Eloy Jimenez 20.00 50.00
TAEW Evan White 10.00 25.00
TAFT Frank Thomas 50.00 120.00
TAHA Hank Aaron
TAJA Jo Adell EXCH 40.00 100.00
TAJB Johnny Bench 40.00 100.00
TAJG Jose Garcia 20.00 50.00
TAJH Josh Hader 8.00 20.00
TAJL Jesus Luzardo 5.00 12.00
TAJR J.T. Realmuto 20.00 50.00
TAJS Juan Soto 100.00 250.00
TAKG Ken Griffey Jr. EXCH
TAKH Keston Hiura 8.00 20.00
TALG Luis Garcia 15.00 40.00
TALP Luis Patino 12.00 30.00
TALR Luis Robert 60.00 150.00
TALT Leody Taveras 10.00 25.00
TAMB Mark Buehrle 15.00 40.00
TAMC Michael Chavis 8.00 20.00
TAMH Monte Harrison 5.00 12.00
TAMK Max Kepler 4.00 10.00
TAMM Max Muncy 6.00 15.00
TAMR Mariano Rivera
TAMS Mike Schmidt 60.00 150.00
TAMT Mike Trout
TAMY Mike Yastrzemski 20.00 50.00
TANA Nolan Arenado 40.00 100.00
TANM Nick Madrigal 25.00 60.00
TANP Nate Pearson 15.00 40.00
TANR Nolan Ryan
TANS Nick Solak 5.00 12.00
TAOS Ozzie Smith 30.00 80.00
TAPC Patrick Corbin 10.00 25.00
TARA Ronald Acuna Jr.
TARC Rod Carew 20.00 50.00
TARF Rollie Fingers 10.00 25.00
TARL Ramon Laureano 8.00 20.00
TARM Ryan Mountcastle 40.00 100.00
TASB Shane Bieber 15.00 40.00
TASE Santiago Espinal 6.00 15.00
TASG Steve Garvey 20.00 50.00
TASH Spencer Howard 5.00 12.00
TASS Sixto Sanchez 15.00 40.00
TATH Torii Hunter 15.00 40.00
TATS Tyler Stephenson 10.00 25.00
TAVG Vladimir Guerrero 30.00 80.00
TAWB Walker Buehler 25.00 60.00
TAWC William Contreras 20.00 50.00
TAWM Whit Merrifield 12.00 30.00
TAXB Xander Bogaerts 12.00 30.00
TAABE Adrian Beltre 40.00 100.00
TAAGA Andres Galarraga 6.00 15.00
TAAJO Andruw Jones 15.00 40.00
TABRO Brooks Robinson 25.00 60.00
TABSN Blake Snell 6.00 15.00
TACBI Cavan Biggio 10.00 25.00
TADCA Dylan Carlson 60.00 150.00
TAJBA Joey Bart 30.00 80.00
TAJCH Jazz Chisholm 50.00 120.00
TAJCR Jake Cronenworth 25.00 60.00
TAJRI Jim Rice 8.00 20.00
TAJSO Jorge Soler 6.00 15.00
TAKHA Ke'Bryan Hayes 60.00 150.00
TAVGU Vladimir Guerrero Jr. EXCH 40.00 100.00

2021 Topps Tribute Autographs Orange

*ORANGE/25: .6X TO 1.5X BASIC p/r 131-199
*ORANGE/25: .5X TO 1.2X BASIC p/r 30-100
STATED ODDS 1:xx HOBBY
STATED PRINT RUN 25 SER.#'d SETS
EXCHANGE DEADLINE 2/28/2023
TABD Bobby Dalbec 75.00 200.00
TAVGU Vladimir Guerrero Jr. EXCH 60.00 150.00

2021 Topps Tribute Autographs Purple

*PURPLE/50: .5X TO 1.2X BASIC p/r 131-199
*PURPLE/50: .4X TO 1X BASIC p/r 30-100
STATED ODDS 1:xx HOBBY
STATED PRINT RUN 50 SER.#'d SETS
EXCHANGE DEADLINE 2/28/2023
TAVGU Vladimir Guerrero Jr. EXCH 50.00 120.00

2021 Topps Tribute Dual Player Relics

COMMON CARD 2.50 6.00
SEMISTARS 3.00 8.00
UNLISTED STARS 4.00 10.00
STATED ODDS 1:xx HOBBY
STATED PRINT RUN 150 SER.#'d SETS
DR2AB C.Biggio/J.Altuve 8.00 20.00
DR2AF F.Freeman/R.Acuna Jr. 20.00 50.00
DR2AS T.Story/N.Arenado 6.00 15.00
DR2BA Y.Alvarez/A.Bregman 10.00 25.00
DR2BB M.Betts/C.Bellinger 20.00 50.00
DR2BD X.Bogaerts/R.Devers 8.00 20.00
DR2BG B.Bichette/V.Guerrero Jr. 20.00 50.00
DR2BR J.Baez/A.Rizzo 15.00 40.00
DR2CP B.Posey/W.Clark 15.00 40.00
DR2HY C.Yelich/K.Hiura 12.00 30.00
DR2IG K.Griffey Jr./Ichiro 25.00 60.00
DR2JJ D.Jeter/A.Judge 30.00 80.00
DR2KH T.Hunter/M.Kepler 6.00 15.00
DR2LR F.Lindor/J.Ramirez 10.00 25.00
DR2MO D.Ortiz/JD Martinez 10.00 25.00
DR2MS J.Smoltz/G.Maddux 15.00 40.00
DR2OT S.Ohtani/M.Trout 30.00 80.00
DR2PA M.Piazza/P.Alonso 15.00 40.00
DR2RB J.Bell/B.Reynolds 3.00 8.00
DR2RC M.Cabrera/I.Rodriguez 15.00 40.00
DR2SC M.Chapman/M.Semien 8.00 20.00
DR2SM O.Smith/Y.Molina
DR2SS S.Strasburg/M.Scherzer 4.00 10.00
DR2TH J.Thome/B.Harper 12.00 30.00
DR2TM M.Machado/F.Tatis Jr. 15.00 40.00
DR2TMO F.Thomas/Y.Moncada 8.00 20.00

2021 Topps Tribute Dual Player Relics Green

*GREEN/99: .4X TO 1X BASIC
STATED ODDS 1:xx HOBBY
STATED PRINT RUN 99 SER.#'d SETS
DR2IG K.Griffey Jr./Ichiro 40.00 100.00
DR2SM O.Smith/Y.Molina 25.00 60.00

2021 Topps Tribute Dual Player Relics Orange

*ORANGE/25: .75X TO 2X BASIC
STATED ODDS 1:xx HOBBY
STATED PRINT RUN 25 SER.#'d SETS
DR2IG K.Griffey Jr./Ichiro 100.00 250.00
DR2OT S.Ohtani/M.Trout 75.00 200.00
DR2SM O.Smith/Y.Molina 50.00 120.00

2021 Topps Tribute Dual Player Relics Purple

*PURPLE/50: .5X TO 1.2X BASIC
STATED ODDS 1:xx HOBBY
STATED PRINT RUN 50 SER.#'d SETS
DR2IG K.Griffey Jr./Ichiro 60.00 150.00
DR2OT S.Ohtani/M.Trout 50.00 120.00
DR2SM O.Smith/Y.Molina 30.00 80.00

2021 Topps Tribute Dual Relics

STATED ODDS 1:xx HOBBY
STATED PRINT RUN 150 SER.#'d SETS
DRI Ichiro
DRAB Alex Bregman 3.00 8.00
DRAP Albert Pujols 15.00 40.00
DRDS Dansby Swanson 3.00 8.00
DRJB Josh Bell 2.50 6.00
DRLB Lou Brock 10.00 25.00
DRMC Michael Conforto 2.50 6.00
DRNR Nolan Ryan 20.00 50.00
DRRC Rod Carew
DRRH Rickey Henderson
DRRJ Reggie Jackson
DRTS Trevor Story 3.00 8.00
DRVG Vladimir Guerrero 2.50 6.00
DRWB Wade Boggs 8.00 20.00
DRWC Willson Contreras 3.00 8.00
DRXB Xander Bogaerts 3.00 8.00
DRYM Yadier Molina 15.00 40.00

2021 Topps Tribute Dual Relics Green

*GREEN/99: .4X TO 1X BASIC
STATED ODDS 1:xx HOBBY
STATED PRINT RUN 99 SER.#'d SETS
DRI Ichiro 12.00 30.00

2021 Topps Tribute Dual Relics Orange

*ORANGE/25: .75X TO 2X BASIC
STATED ODDS 1:xx HOBBY
STATED PRINT RUN 25 SER.#'d SETS
DRI Ichiro 25.00 60.00
DRRH Rickey Henderson 20.00 50.00
DRRJ Reggie Jackson 20.00 50.00

2021 Topps Tribute Dual Relics Purple

*PURPLE/50: .5X TO 1.2X BASIC
STATED ODDS 1:xx HOBBY
STATED PRINT RUN 50 SER.#'d SETS
DRI Ichiro 15.00 40.00
DRRH Rickey Henderson 15.00 40.00
DRRJ Reggie Jackson 12.00 30.00

2021 Topps Tribute Engraved Greats Autographs

STATED ODDS 1:xx HOBBY
PRINT RUNS B/WN 10-50 COPIES PER
NO PRICING ON QTY 15 OR LESS
EXCHANGE DEADLINE 2/28/2023
EGAAD Andre Dawson 25.00 60.00
EGAAJ Aaron Judge
EGABS Blake Snell 5.00 12.00
EGACF Carlton Fisk 30.00 80.00
EGACK Corey Kluber
EGACR Cal Ripken Jr. 75.00 200.00
EGADE Dennis Eckersley 12.00 30.00
EGADO David Ortiz 100.00 250.00
EGAEM Edgar Martinez 25.00 60.00
EGAFT Frank Thomas 50.00 120.00
EGAIR Ivan Rodriguez 30.00 80.00
EGAJB Johnny Bench 50.00 120.00
EGAJS John Smoltz 30.00 80.00
EGAKG Ken Griffey Jr. EXCH
EGAMC Miguel Cabrera 75.00 200.00
EGAMS Mike Schmidt 75.00 200.00
EGAMT Mike Trout
EGANG Nomar Garciaparra 30.00 80.00
EGANR Nolan Ryan 75.00 200.00
EGAOS Ozzie Smith 40.00 100.00
EGAPA Pete Alonso 60.00 150.00
EGARC Roger Clemens
EGARJ Reggie Jackson
EGASC Steve Carlton 40.00 100.00
EGAVG Vladimir Guerrero 40.00 100.00
EGAWB Walker Buehler 30.00 80.00
EGAYA Yordan Alvarez 40.00 100.00
EGARCA Rod Carew 20.00 50.00

2021 Topps Tribute Engraved Greats Autographs Orange

*ORANGE/25: .5X TO 1.2X BASIC
STATED ODDS 1:xx HOBBY
STATED PRINT RUN 25 SER.#'d SETS
EXCHANGE DEADLINE 2/28/2023
EGAOS Ozzie Smith 75.00 200.00

2021 Topps Tribute Green Monster Wall Graphs Autograph Relics

STATED ODDS 1:xx HOBBY
STATED PRINT RUN 25 SER.#'d SETS
EXCHANGE DEADLINE 2/28/2023
GMARAB Andrew Benintendi 125.00 300.00
GMARAJ Aaron Judge 300.00 600.00
GMARCY Carl Yastrzemski 150.00 400.00
GMARDE Dennis Eckersley 125.00 300.00
GMARDO David Ortiz 400.00 800.00
GMAREM Edgar Martinez 75.00 200.00
GMARJA Jose Altuve 75.00 200.00
GMARJR Jim Rice 100.00 250.00
GMARMC Miguel Cabrera 100.00 250.00
GMARMT Mike Trout 800.00 2000.00
GMARMY Mike Yastrzemski 100.00 250.00
GMARPM Pedro Martinez 250.00 600.00
GMARRA Ronald Acuna Jr. 300.00 600.00
GMARRD Rafael Devers 100.00 250.00
GMARRF Rollie Fingers
GMARRH Rhys Hoskins 60.00 150.00
GMARTS Trevor Story 60.00 150.00
GMARVG Vladimir Guerrero Jr. EXCH 125.00 300.00
GMARWM Whit Merrifield 60.00 150.00
GMARXB Xander Bogaerts 150.00 400.00
GMARYA Yordan Alvarez 75.00 200.00
GMARABR Alex Bregman
GMARMCH Michael Chavis 100.00 250.00

2021 Topps Tribute Iconic Perspectives Autographs

STATED ODDS 1:xx HOBBY
PRINT RUNS B/WN 15-50 COPIES PER
NO PRICING ON QTY 15 OR LESS
EXCHANGE DEADLINE 2/28/2023
IPAAJ Aaron Judge
IPACR Cal Ripken Jr.
IPAJA Jose Altuve
IPAJS Juan Soto 100.00 250.00
IPAKG Ken Griffey Jr. EXCH
IPALR Luis Robert 100.00 250.00
IPAMK Max Kepler 15.00 40.00
IPAMT Mike Trout
IPANH Nico Hoerner 20.00 50.00
IPAPA Pete Alonso 50.00 120.00
IPAVG Vladimir Guerrero Jr. EXCH 50.00 120.00

2021 Topps Tribute Iconic Perspectives Autographs Orange

*ORANGE/25: .5X TO 1.2X BASIC p/r 45-50
*ORANGE/25: .4X TO 1X BASIC p/r 25
STATED ODDS 1:xx HOBBY
STATED PRINT RUN 25 SER.#'d SETS
EXCHANGE DEADLINE 2/28/2023
IPAMK Max Kepler 40.00 100.00

2021 Topps Tribute League Inaugurations Autographs

STATED ODDS 1:xx HOBBY
STATED PRINT RUN 99 SER.#'d SETS
EXCHANGE DEADLINE 2/28/2023
LIAAB Alec Bohm 100.00 250.00
LIAAG Andres Gimenez 10.00 25.00
LIABS Brady Singer 20.00 50.00
LIACM Casey Mize 40.00 100.00
LIADC Dylan Carlson 60.00 150.00
LIAEW Evan White 25.00 60.00
LIAIA Ian Anderson 25.00 60.00
LIAJA Jo Adell EXCH 50.00 120.00
LIALG Luis Garcia 20.00 50.00
LIANM Nick Madrigal 40.00 100.00
LIANP Nate Pearson 20.00 50.00
LIATS Tyler Stephenson 30.00 80.00

2021 Topps Tribute League Inaugurations Autographs Orange

*ORANGE/25: .5X TO 1.2X BASIC
STATED ODDS 1:xx HOBBY
STATED PRINT RUN 25 SER.#'d SETS
EXCHANGE DEADLINE 2/28/2023
LIAAG Andres Gimenez 20.00 50.00
LIAJA Jo Adell EXCH 75.00 200.00

2021 Topps Tribute Stamp of Approval Relics

STATED ODDS 1:xx HOBBY
STATED PRINT RUN 150 SER.#'d SETS
SOAAJ Aaron Judge 15.00 40.00
SOAAM Austin Meadows 3.00 8.00
SOAAN Aaron Nola 6.00 15.00
SOAAP Albert Pujols 15.00 40.00
SOABP Buster Posey 6.00 15.00
SOABR Bryan Reynolds 2.50 6.00
SOACB Charlie Blackmon 3.00 8.00
SOACY Christian Yelich 8.00 20.00
SOADS Dansby Swanson 3.00 8.00
SOAEH Eric Hosmer 2.50 6.00
SOAER Eddie Rosario 2.50 6.00
SOAFF Freddie Freeman 8.00 20.00
SOAGS Gary Sanchez 3.00 8.00
SOAJA Jose Altuve 2.50 6.00
SOAJB Josh Bell 2.50 6.00
SOAJH Josh Hader 2.50 6.00
SOAJL Jesus Luzardo 3.00 8.00
SOAJP Joc Pederson 2.50 6.00
SOAJV Joey Votto 3.00 8.00
SOAMC Matt Chapman 3.00 8.00
SOAMM Manny Machado 3.00 8.00
SOAMS Marcus Stroman 2.50 6.00
SOAMT Mike Trout 20.00 50.00
SOAPA Pete Alonso 6.00 15.00
SOARD Rafael Devers 4.00 10.00
SOARH Rhys Hoskins 5.00 12.00
SOARL Ramon Laureano 2.50 6.00
SOATA Tim Anderson 3.00 8.00
SOATP Tommy Pham 2.00 5.00
SOATS Trevor Story 3.00 8.00
SOAWS Will Smith 3.00 8.00
SOAXB Xander Bogaerts 8.00 20.00
SOAYA Yordan Alvarez 5.00 12.00
SOAYM Yoan Moncada 3.00 8.00
SOAFTJ Fernando Tatis Jr. 15.00 40.00
SOAJAB Jose Abreu 3.00 8.00
SOAJBA Javier Baez 6.00 15.00
SOALGJ Lourdes Gurriel Jr. 2.50 6.00
SOAMCA Miguel Cabrera 5.00 12.00
SOAMCO Michael Conforto 2.50 6.00
SOAMMU Max Muncy 2.50 6.00
SOAMSA Miguel Sano 2.50 6.00
SOARAJ Ronald Acuna Jr. 20.00 50.00

2021 Topps Tribute Stamp of Approval Relics Green

*GREEN/99: .4X TO 1X BASIC
STATED ODDS 1:xx HOBBY
STATED PRINT RUN 99 SER.#'d SETS
SOAMCA Miguel Cabrera 8.00 20.00

2021 Topps Tribute Stamp of Approval Relics Orange

*ORANGE/25: .75X TO 2X BASIC
STATED ODDS 1:xx HOBBY
STATED PRINT RUN 25 SER.#'d SETS
SOAMT Mike Trout 50.00 120.00
SOAMCA Miguel Cabrera 15.00 40.00

2021 Topps Tribute Stamp of Approval Relics Purple

*PURPLE/50: .5X TO 1.2X BASIC
STATED ODDS 1:xx HOBBY
STATED PRINT RUN 50 SER.#'d SETS
SOAMT Mike Trout 30.00 80.00
SOAMCA Miguel Cabrera 10.00 25.00

2021 Topps Tribute Tandem Autograph Booklets

STATED ODDS 1:xx HOBBY
STATED PRINT RUN 25 SER.#'d SETS
EXCHANGE DEADLINE 2/28/2023
TTAW P.Alonso/D.Wright 300.00 800.00
TTCP G.Cole/A.Pettitte EXCH
TTDB R.Devers/W.Boggs EXCH 125.00 300.00
TTGG V.Guerrero/V.Guerrero Jr. EXCH 500.00 1000.00
TTHH R.Hoskins/R.Howard 40.00 100.00
TTMO D.Ortiz/J.Martinez EXCH
TTNC S.Carlton/A.Nola EXCH 75.00 200.00
TTTG V.Guerrero/M.Trout EXCH
TTTP J.Posada/G.Torres EXCH

2021 Topps Tribute Tribute to Topps Autographs

STATED ODDS 1:xx HOBBY
STATED PRINT RUN 99 SER.#'d SETS
EXCHANGE DEADLINE 2/28/2023
TTAAB Adrian Beltre 40.00 100.00
TTAAJ Aaron Judge 125.00 300.00
TTACF Carlton Fisk 50.00 120.00
TTADO David Ortiz 60.00 150.00
TTAEJ Eloy Jimenez 30.00 80.00
TTAEM Edgar Martinez 25.00 60.00
TTAFT Frank Thomas 50.00 120.00
TTAIR Ivan Rodriguez 40.00 100.00
TTAJA Jo Adell EXCH 60.00 150.00
TTAJS Juan Soto 125.00 300.00
TTALR Luis Robert 100.00 250.00
TTAMS Marcus Stroman 20.00 50.00

TTAOS Ozzie Smith 40.00 100.00
TTAPA Pete Alonso 50.00 120.00
TTARD Rafael Devers 40.00 100.00
TTAVG Vladimir Guerrero Jr. 60.00 150.00
TTAWB Walker Buehler 25.00 60.00
TTAXB Xander Bogaerts 40.00 100.00
TTADMA Don Mattingly 60.00 150.00

2021 Topps Tribute Tribute to Topps Autographs Orange

*ORANGE/25: .5X TO 1.2X BASIC
STATED ODDS 1:xx HOBBY
STATED PRINT RUN 25 SER.#'d SETS
EXCHANGE DEADLINE 2/28/2023
TTAFT Frank Thomas 75.00 200.00
TTAOS Ozzie Smith 60.00 150.00

2021 Topps Tribute Tribute to Topps Autographs Purple

*PURPLE/50: .4X TO 1X BASIC
STATED ODDS 1:xx HOBBY
STATED PRINT RUN 50 SER.#'d SETS
EXCHANGE DEADLINE 2/28/2023
TTAOS Ozzie Smith 50.00 120.00

2021 Topps Tribute Triple Relics

STATED ODDS 1:xx HOBBY
STATED PRINT RUN 150 SER.#'d SETS
TTRAB Andrew Benintendi 3.00 8.00
TTRAM Austin Meadows 6.00 15.00
TTRAP Andy Pettitte 2.50 6.00
TTRAR Anthony Rizzo 8.00 20.00
TTRBL Barry Larkin 6.00 15.00
TTRCB Cavan Biggio 4.00 10.00
TTRCC Carlos Correa 3.00 8.00
TTRCF Carlton Fisk 10.00 25.00
TTRCJ Chipper Jones 10.00 25.00
TTRCS Chris Sale 3.00 8.00
TTRDO David Ortiz 8.00 20.00
TTREJ Eloy Jimenez 6.00 15.00
TTRFF Freddie Freeman 10.00 25.00
TTRGM Greg Maddux 8.00 20.00
TTRGS Gary Sanchez 3.00 8.00
TTRGT Gleyber Torres 8.00 20.00
TTRJB Jeff Bagwell 5.00 12.00
TTRJL Jesus Luzardo 3.00 8.00
TTRJM Joe Mauer 6.00 15.00
TTRJP Joc Pederson 2.50 6.00
TTRJR J.T. Realmuto 3.00 8.00
TTRKH Keston Hiura 4.00 10.00
TTRKS Kyle Schwarber 3.00 8.00
TTRLW Larry Walker 2.50 6.00
TTRMC Michael Conforto 2.50 6.00
TTRMO Matt Olson 3.00 8.00
TTRMP Mike Piazza 10.00 25.00
TTRMR Mariano Rivera 6.00 15.00
TTRMT Mike Trout 30.00 80.00
TTRNS Noah Syndergaard 2.50 6.00
TTRPM Pedro Martinez 2.50 6.00
TTRRA Roberto Alomar 5.00 12.00
TTRRJ Randy Johnson 5.00 12.00
TTRRL Ramon Laureano 2.50 6.00
TTRRY Robin Yount 8.00 20.00
TTRSO Shohei Ohtani 12.00 30.00
TTRSS Stephen Strasburg 3.00 8.00
TTRTG Tony Gwynn 8.00 20.00
TTRTH Todd Helton 2.50 6.00
TTRWM Whit Merrifield 3.00 8.00
TTRYA Yordan Alvarez 5.00 12.00
TTRYM Yoan Moncada 3.00 8.00
TTRAPU A.J. Puk 3.00 8.00
TTRFTJ Fernando Tatis Jr. 15.00 40.00
TTRKGJ Ken Griffey Jr. 30.00 80.00
TTRKSE Kyle Seager 2.00 5.00
TTRLGJ Lourdes Gurriel Jr. 2.50 6.00

2021 Topps Tribute Triple Relics Green

*GREEN/99: .4X TO 1X BASIC
STATED ODDS 1:xx HOBBY
STATED PRINT RUN 99 SER.#'d SETS
TTRCJ Chipper Jones 12.00 30.00
TTRTG Tony Gwynn 12.00 30.00
TTRFTJ Fernando Tatis Jr. 20.00 50.00

2021 Topps Tribute Triple Relics Orange

*ORANGE/25: .75X TO 2X BASIC
STATED ODDS 1:xx HOBBY
STATED PRINT RUN 25 SER.#'d SETS
TTRCJ Chipper Jones 25.00 60.00
TTRFF Freddie Freeman 40.00 100.00
TTRSO Shohei Ohtani 30.00 80.00
TTRTG Tony Gwynn 25.00 60.00
TTRFTJ Fernando Tatis Jr. 40.00 100.00
TTRKGJ Ken Griffey Jr. 75.00 200.00

2021 Topps Tribute Triple Relics Purple

*PURPLE/50: .5X TO 1.2X BASIC
STATED ODDS 1:xx HOBBY
STATED PRINT RUN 50 SER.#'d SETS
TTRCJ Chipper Jones 15.00 40.00
TTRTG Tony Gwynn 15.00 40.00
TTRFTJ Fernando Tatis Jr. 25.00 60.00
TTRKGJ Ken Griffey Jr. 50.00 120.00

2003 Topps Tribute Contemporary

COMMON CARD (1-90) .60 1.50
COMMON CARD (91-100) .60 1.50
COMMON CARD (101-110) 4.00 10.00
101-110 STATED ODDS 1:7
101-110 PRINT RUN 499 SERIAL #'d SETS
J.CONTRERAS EXCH.DEADLINE 08/31/05
1 Jim Thome 1.00 2.50
2 Edgardo Alfonzo .60 1.50
3 Edgar Martinez 1.00 2.50
4 Scott Rolen 1.00 2.50
5 Eric Hinske .60 1.50
6 Mark Mulder .60 1.50
7 Jason Giambi .60 1.50
8 Bernie Williams 1.00 2.50
9 Cliff Floyd .60 1.50
10 Ichiro Suzuki 2.00 5.00
11 Pat Burrell .60 1.50
12 Garret Anderson .60 1.50
13 Gary Sheffield .60 1.50
14 Johnny Damon 1.00 2.50
15 Kerry Wood .60 1.50
16 Bartolo Colon .60 1.50
17 Adam Dunn 1.00 2.50
18 Omar Vizquel 1.00 2.50
19 Todd Helton 1.00 2.50
20 Nomar Garciaparra 1.00 2.50
21 A.J. Burnett .60 1.50
22 Craig Biggio 1.00 2.50
23 Carlos Beltran 1.00 2.50
24 Kazuhisa Ishii .60 1.50
25 Vladimir Guerrero 1.00 2.50
26 Roberto Alomar 1.00 2.50
27 Roger Clemens 2.00 5.00
28 Tim Hudson 1.00 2.50
29 Brian Giles .60 1.50
30 Barry Bonds 2.50 6.00
31 Jim Edmonds 1.00 2.50
32 Rafael Palmeiro 1.00 2.50
33 Francisco Rodriguez 1.00 2.50
34 Andruw Jones .60 1.50
35 Shea Hillenbrand .60 1.50
36 Moises Alou .60 1.50
37 Luis Gonzalez .60 1.50
38 Darin Erstad .60 1.50
39 John Smoltz 1.50 4.00
40 Derek Jeter 4.00 10.00
41 Aubrey Huff .60 1.50
42 Eric Chavez .60 1.50
43 Doug Mientkiewicz .60 1.50
44 Lance Berkman 1.00 2.50
45 Josh Beckett .60 1.50
46 Austin Kearns .60 1.50
47 Frank Thomas 1.50 4.00
48 Pedro Martinez 1.00 2.50
49 Tim Salmon .60 1.50
50 Alex Rodriguez 2.00 5.00
51 Ryan Klesko .60 1.50
52 Tom Glavine 1.00 2.50
53 Shawn Green .60 1.50
54 Jeff Kent .60 1.50
55 Carlos Pena 1.00 2.50
56 Paul Konerko 1.00 2.50
57 Troy Glaus .60 1.50
58 Manny Ramirez 1.50 4.00
59 Jason Jennings .60 1.50
60 Randy Johnson 1.50 4.00
61 Ivan Rodriguez 1.00 2.50
62 Roy Oswalt 1.00 2.50
63 Kevin Brown .60 1.50
64 Jose Vidro .60 1.50
65 Jorge Posada 1.00 2.50
66 Mike Piazza 1.50 4.00
67 Bret Boone .60 1.50
68 Carlos Delgado .60 1.50
69 Jimmy Rollins 1.00 2.50
70 Alfonso Soriano 1.00 2.50
71 Greg Maddux 2.00 5.00
72 Mark Prior 1.00 2.50
73 Jeff Bagwell 1.00 2.50
74 Richie Sexson .60 1.50
75 Sammy Sosa 1.50 4.00
76 Curt Schilling 1.00 2.50
77 Mike Sweeney .60 1.50
78 Torii Hunter .60 1.50
79 Larry Walker 1.00 2.50
80 Miguel Tejada 1.00 2.50
81 Rich Aurilia .60 1.50
82 Bobby Abreu .60 1.50
83 Phil Nevin .60 1.50
84 Rodrigo Lopez .60 1.50
85 Chipper Jones 1.50 4.00
86 Ken Griffey Jr. 3.00 8.00
87 Mike Lowell .60 1.50
88 Magglio Ordonez 1.00 2.50
89 Barry Zito 1.00 2.50
90 Albert Pujols 2.00 5.00
91 Corey Shafer FY RC .60 1.50
92 Dan Haren FY RC 3.00 8.00
93 Jeremy Bonderman FY RC 2.50 6.00
94 Branden Florence FY RC .60 1.50
95 Evel Bastida-Martinez FY RC .60 1.50
96 Brian Wright FY RC .60 1.50
97 Elizardo Ramirez FY RC .60 1.50
98 Michael Garciaparra FY RC .60 1.50
99 Clay Hensley FY RC .60 1.50
100 Bobby Basham FY RC .60 1.50
101 Jose Contreras FY AU RC 6.00 15.00
102 Bryan Bullington FY AU RC 4.00 10.00
103 Joey Gomes FY AU RC 4.00 10.00
104 Craig Brazell FY AU RC 4.00 10.00
105 Andy Marte FY AU RC 4.00 10.00
106 Hanley Ramirez FY AU RC 8.00 20.00
107 Ryan Shealy FY AU RC 4.00 10.00
108 Daryl Clark FY AU RC 4.00 10.00
109 Tyler Johnson FY AU RC 4.00 10.00
110 Ben Francisco FY AU RC 4.00 10.00

2003 Topps Tribute Contemporary Gold

STATED PRINT RUN 25 SERIAL #'d SETS
NO PRICING DUE TO SCARCITY

2003 Topps Tribute Contemporary Red

*RED 1-90: .6X TO 1.5X BASIC CARDS
*RED 91-100: .6X TO 1.5X BASIC CARDS
1-100 PRINT RUN 225 SERIAL #'d SETS
*RED 101-110: .6X TO 1.5X BASIC
101-110 PRINT RUN 99 SERIAL #'d SETS

2003 Topps Tribute Contemporary Bonds Tribute Relics

*RED BONDS: .6X TO 1.5X BASIC BONDS
RED BONDS PRINT RUN 50 #'d SETS
GOLD BONDS PRINT RUN 1 #'d SET
NO GOLD PRICING DUE TO SCARCITY
DB Barry Bonds Bat-Jsy 10.00 25.00
SB Barry Bonds Jsy 8.00 20.00
TB Barry Bonds Bat-Cap-Jsy 15.00 40.00

2003 Topps Tribute Contemporary Bonds Tribute 40-40 Club Relics

RANDOM INSERTS IN PACKS
NO GOLD PRICING DUE TO SCARCITY
CBR Cans/Bonds/Rod 25.00 60.00
CBRR Cans/Bonds/Rod Red/50 75.00 150.00

2003 Topps Tribute Contemporary Bonds Tribute 600 HR Club Relics

*RED 600: .6X TO 1.5X BASIC
RED 600 PRINT RUN 50 SERIAL #'d SETS
GOLD PRINT RUN 1 SERIAL #'d SET
NO GOLD PRICING DUE TO SCARCITY
BB Barry Bonds Bat 8.00 20.00
BR Babe Ruth Bat 75.00 150.00
HA Hank Aaron Bat 15.00 40.00
WM Willie Mays Uni 20.00 50.00

2003 Topps Tribute Contemporary Bonds Tribute 600 HR Club Double Relics

*RED 600 DOUBLE: .6X TO 1.5X BASIC
RED 600 DOUBLE PRINT RUN 50 #'d SETS
GOLD 600 DOUBLE PRINT 1 SERIAL #'d SET
NO GOLD PRICING DUE TO SCARCITY
BA B.Bonds Bat/H.Aaron Bat 20.00 50.00
BM B.Bonds Bat/W.Mays Uni 20.00 50.00
RB B.Ruth Bat/B.Bonds Bat 125.00 200.00

2003 Topps Tribute Contemporary Bonds Tribute 600 HR Club Quad Relics

RANDOM INSERTS IN PACKS
PRINT RUNS B/WN 1-50 COPIES PER
NO GOLD/RED PRICING DUE TO SCARCITY
HR Ruth/Mays/Aar/Bonds/50 300.00 500.00

2003 Topps Tribute Contemporary Matching Marks Dual Relics

*RED MARKS: .6X TO 1.5X BASIC
RED MARKS PRINT RUN 50 SERIAL #'d SETS
GOLD MARKS PRINT RUN 1 SERIAL #'d SET
NO GOLD PRICING DUE TO SCARCITY
AP Alomar Bat 6.00 15.00
Palmeiro Bat
BG Bagwell Uni/J.Gonzalez Bat 6.00 15.00
BP Bonds Bat/Palmeiro Bat 12.00 30.00
GR Nomar Jsy/A.Rod Jsy 10.00 25.00
HR Henderson Bat/Manny Bat 12.50 30.00
MG McGriff Bat/J.Gonzalez Bat 4.00 10.00
MP McGriff Bat/Palmeiro Bat 6.00 15.00
PA Palmeiro Bat/Alomar Uni 6.00 15.00
PH Palmeiro Bat/Henderson Bat 6.00 15.00
PS Palmeiro Uni/Sosa Bat 6.00 15.00
RP Manny Jsy/Piazza Uni 10.00 25.00
SB Sosa Bat/Bagwell Uni 6.00 15.00
SG Soriano Uni/Guerrero Bat 6.00 15.00

2003 Topps Tribute Contemporary Memorable Materials Relics

*RED MEM: .6X TO 1.5X BASIC
RED MEM PRINT RUN 50 SERIAL #'d SETS
GOLD MEM PRINT RUN 1 SERIAL #'d SET
NO GOLD PRICING DUE TO SCARCITY
AJ Andruw Jones Jsy 6.00 15.00
AP Albert Pujols Jsy 10.00 25.00
AR Alex Rodriguez Jsy 8.00 20.00
AS Alfonso Soriano Uni 4.00 10.00
BB Barry Bonds Jsy 8.00 20.00
CR Cal Ripken Bat 10.00 25.00
GM Greg Maddux Jsy 6.00 15.00
JG Jason Giambi Jsy 4.00 10.00
JG2 Jason Giambi Bat 4.00 10.00
KW Kerry Wood Jsy 4.00 10.00
LG Luis Gonzalez Bat 4.00 10.00
MT Miguel Tejada Bat 4.00 10.00
RH Rickey Henderson Uni 6.00 15.00
SG Shawn Green Jsy 4.00 10.00
SS Sammy Sosa Bat 6.00 15.00
SS2 Sammy Sosa Jsy 6.00 15.00
TG Troy Glaus Uni 4.00 10.00
TH Torii Hunter Jsy 4.00 10.00
VG Vladimir Guerrero Bat 6.00 15.00

2003 Topps Tribute Contemporary Milestone Materials Relics

*RED MILE: .6X TO 1.5X BASIC
RED MILE PRINT RUN 50 SERIAL #'d SETS
GOLD PRINT RUN 1 SERIAL #'d SET
NO GOLD PRICING DUE TO SCARCITY
AR Alex Rodriguez Jsy 8.00 20.00
BB1 Barry Bonds 1500 RBI Uni 10.00 25.00
BB2 Barry Bonds 1500 Runs Uni 10.00 25.00
BB3 Barry Bonds 2000 Hits Uni 10.00 25.00
BB4 Barry Bonds 500 2B Uni 10.00 25.00
BB5 Barry Bonds 600 HR Uni 10.00 25.00
CJ Chipper Jones Jsy 6.00 15.00
FM1 Fred McGriff Cubs Bat 4.00 10.00
FM2 Fred McGriff 2000 Hits Bat 4.00 10.00
FM3 Fred McGriff 400 HR Bat 4.00 10.00
FT Frank Thomas Jsy 6.00 15.00
JB1 Jeff Bagwell Jsy 4.00 10.00
JB2 Jeff Bagwell Uni 4.00 10.00
JG1 Juan Gonzalez Indians Bat 3.00 8.00
JG2 Juan Gonzalez Rgr Bat 3.00 8.00
MP1 Mike Piazza Bat 6.00 15.00
MP2 Mike Piazza Uni 6.00 15.00
MR1 Manny Ramirez Bat 4.00 10.00
MR2 Manny Ramirez Jsy 4.00 10.00
NG Nomar Garciaparra Jsy 10.00 25.00
RA Roberto Alomar Uni 6.00 15.00
RH1 R.Henderson Mets Bat 4.00 10.00
RH2 R.Henderson Sox Bat 4.00 10.00
RH3 R.Henderson A's Bat 4.00 10.00
RH4 R.Henderson 3000 Hits Bat 4.00 10.00
RH5 R.Henderson 500 2B Bat 4.00 10.00
RP1 R.Palmeiro 1500 RBI Jsy 4.00 10.00
RP2 R.Palmeiro 2500 Hits Bat 4.00 10.00
RP3 R.Palmeiro 500 HR Uni 4.00 10.00
RP4 R.Palmeiro 500 2B Bat 4.00 10.00
SS1 Sammy Sosa 1250 RBI Jsy 6.00 15.00
SS2 Sammy Sosa 2000 Hits Jsy 6.00 15.00
SS3 Sammy Sosa Bat 6.00 15.00
TH Todd Helton Jsy 6.00 15.00
VG Vladimir Guerrero Bat 6.00 15.00

2003 Topps Tribute Contemporary Modern Marks Autographs

STATED ODDS 1:19
*RED MARKS: .5X TO 1.2X BASIC
RED MARKS STATED ODDS 1:38
RED MARKS PRINT RUN 99 SERIAL #'d SETS
GOLD MARKS STATED ODDS 1:149
GOLD MARKS PRINT RUN 25 SERIAL #'d SETS
NO GOLD PRICING DUE TO SCARCITY
CF Cliff Floyd 6.00 15.00
EH Eric Hinske 6.00 15.00
LB Lance Berkman 10.00 25.00
MO Magglio Ordonez 6.00 15.00
MS Mike Sweeney 6.00 15.00
PK Paul Konerko 10.00 25.00
PL Paul Lo Duca 6.00 15.00
RC Roger Clemens 30.00 60.00
TH Torii Hunter 10.00 25.00

2003 Topps Tribute Contemporary Perennial All-Star Relics

*RED AS: .6X TO 1.5X BASIC
RED AS PRINT RUN 50 SERIAL #'d SETS
GOLD AS PRINT RUN 1 SERIAL #'d SET
NO GOLD PRICING DUE TO SCARCITY
AR Alex Rodriguez Jsy 8.00 20.00
BB Barry Bonds Uni 10.00 25.00
BS Benito Santiago Bat 4.00 10.00
BW Bernie Williams Bat 6.00 15.00
CB Craig Biggio Uni 6.00 15.00
CJ Chipper Jones Jsy 6.00 15.00
CS Curt Schilling Jsy 4.00 10.00
CM Edgar Martinez Bat 6.00 15.00
FT Frank Thomas Bat 6.00 15.00
GM Greg Maddux Jsy 6.00 15.00
GS Gary Sheffield Bat 4.00 10.00
IR Ivan Rodriguez Bat 6.00 15.00
JS John Smoltz Uni 6.00 15.00
LW Larry Walker Bat 4.00 10.00
MM Mike Mussina Uni 6.00 15.00
MP Mike Piazza Bat 6.00 15.00
MR Manny Ramirez Bat 6.00 15.00
PM Pedro Martinez Jsy 6.00 15.00
RA Roberto Alomar Bat 6.00 15.00
RC Roger Clemens Uni 8.00 20.00
RH Rickey Henderson Bat 6.00 15.00
SS Sammy Sosa Bat 6.00 15.00

2003 Topps Tribute Contemporary Performance Double Relics

*RED DOUBLE: .6X TO 1.5X BASIC
RED DOUBLE PRINT RUN 50 #'d SETS
GOLD DOUBLE PRINT RUN 1 #'d SET
NO GOLD PRICING DUE TO SCARCITY
RAMDOM INSERTS IN PACKS
BJ Bonds Uni/Chipper Bat 10.00 25.00
CM Clemens Uni/Maddux Jsy 8.00 20.00
GG L.Gonz Bat/Glaus Uni 4.00 10.00
JP Chipper Bat/Piazza Bat 8.00 20.00
MM Pedro Jsy/Maddux Uni 8.00 20.00
PR Piazza Uni/I.Rod Bat 8.00 20.00
PS Piazza Bat/Santiago Bat 8.00 20.00
PW Pujols Jsy/Wood Jsy 10.00 25.00
RG A.Rod Jsy/Nomar Jsy 10.00 25.00
RR Ripken Bat/A.Rod Jsy 10.00 25.00
RT A.Rod Jsy/Tejada Bat 8.00 20.00
SA Soriano Uni/Alomar Uni 6.00 15.00
SG Sosa Bat/J.Gonz Bat 6.00 15.00
ZJ Zito Uni/Randy Uni 6.00 15.00

2003 Topps Tribute Contemporary Performance Triple Relics

*RED TRIPLE: .6X TO 1.5X BASIC
RED TRIPLE PRINT RUN 50 #'d SETS
GOLD TRIPLE PRINT RUN 1 #'d SET
NO GOLD PRICING DUE TO SCARCITY
BMP Bonds/McGriff/Palmeiro 15.00 40.00
CMJ Clemens/Maddux/Randy 15.00 40.00
RPH Manny/Piazza/Henderson 10.00 25.00
SPM Sosa/Palmeiro/McGriff 12.50 30.00
STB Sosa/Thomas/Bagwell 12.50 30.00

2003 Topps Tribute Contemporary Team Double Relics

*RED DOUBLE: .6X TO 1.5X BASIC
RED DOUBLE PRINT RUN 50 #'d SETS
GOLD DOUBLE PRINT RUN 1 #'d SET
NO GOLD PRICING DUE TO SCARCITY
BB Biggio Jsy/Bagwell Uni 6.00 15.00
GR Nomar Jsy/Manny Jsy 10.00 25.00
IN Ishii Jsy/Nomo Jsy 10.00 25.00
MS Maddux Jsy/Smoltz Jsy 12.50 30.00
RP A.Rod Jsy/Palmeiro Bat 8.00 20.00
WH Walker Jsy/Helton Jsy 6.00 15.00

2003 Topps Tribute Contemporary Team Triple Relics

*RED TRIPLE: .6X TO 1.5X BASIC
RED TRIPLE PRINT RUN 50 SERIAL #'d SETS
GOLD PRINT RUN 1 SERIAL #'d SET
NO GOLD PRICING DUE TO SCARCITY
ASP Alou/Sosa/Patterson 12.50 30.00
BBB Biggio/Berkman/Bagwell 10.00 25.00
CTM Chavez/Tejada/Mulder 10.00 25.00
GRM Nomar/Manny/Pedro 15.00 40.00
HZM Hudson/Zito/Mulder 10.00 25.00
JSJ Andruw/Sheffield/Chipper 12.50 30.00
MHM Mauer/Torii/Mientkiewicz 12.50 30.00
MOB Edgar/Olerud/Boone 10.00 25.00
PER Pujols/Edmonds/Rolen 15.00 40.00
RBT A.Rod/Blalock/Teixeira 12.50 30.00
RGP A.Rod/J.Gonz/Palmeiro 12.50 30.00
SGV Soriano/Giambi/Ventura 10.00 25.00
TBB Thome/Byrd/Burrell 10.00 25.00
TOK Thomas/Magglio/Konerko 12.50 30.00

2003 Topps Tribute Contemporary Tribute to the Stars Dual Relics

*RED DUAL: .6X TO 1.5X BASIC
RED DUAL PRINT RUN 50 #'d SETS
GOLD DUAL PRINT RUN 1 SERIAL #'d SET
NO GOLD PRICING DUE TO SCARCITY
AD Adam Dunn Bat-Jsy 6.00 15.00
AJ Andruw Jones Bat-Jsy 6.00 15.00
AP Albert Pujols Bat-Uni 10.00 25.00
AR Alex Rodriguez Bat-Jsy 12.50 30.00
AS Alfonso Soriano Bat-Uni 6.00 15.00
BB Barry Bonds Bat-Uni 12.00 30.00
CJ Chipper Jones Bat-Jsy 6.00 15.00
EC Eric Chavez Bat-Uni 6.00 15.00
FT Frank Thomas Bat-Jsy 6.00 15.00
GA Garret Anderson Bat-Uni 6.00 15.00
GM Greg Maddux Bat-Uni 8.00 20.00
JT Jim Thome Bat-Jsy 6.00 15.00
LB Lance Berkman Bat-Jsy 6.00 15.00
LW Larry Walker Bat-Jsy 6.00 15.00
MP Mike Piazza Bat-Uni 8.00 20.00
NG Nomar Garciaparra Bat-Jsy 15.00 40.00
PB Pat Burrell Bat-Jsy 6.00 15.00
RA Roberto Alomar Bat-Uni 6.00 15.00
RH Rickey Henderson Bat-Uni 6.00 15.00
RP Rafael Palmeiro Bat-Jsy 6.00 15.00
SS Sammy Sosa Bat-Jsy 6.00 15.00
TG Troy Glaus Bat-Uni 6.00 15.00
TH Todd Helton Bat-Jsy 6.00 15.00
VG Vladimir Guerrero Bat-Jsy 6.00 15.00
THU Torii Hunter Bat-Jsy 6.00 15.00

2003 Topps Tribute Contemporary Tribute to the Stars Patchworks Dual Relics

STATED ODDS 1:34
STATED PRINT RUN 50 SERIAL #'d SETS
AP Albert Pujols 50.00 100.00
AR Alex Rodriguez 30.00 60.00
AR2 Alex Rodriguez Blue 30.00 60.00
BB Barry Bonds 50.00 100.00
CJ Chipper Jones 15.00 40.00
CS Curt Schilling 10.00 25.00
FT Frank Thomas 15.00 40.00
GM Greg Maddux 20.00 50.00
JB Jeff Bagwell 15.00 40.00
KW Kerry Wood 10.00 25.00
LG Luis Gonzalez 10.00 25.00
MR Manny Ramirez 15.00 40.00
NG Nomar Garciaparra 20.00 50.00
PM Pedro Martinez 15.00 40.00
RJ Randy Johnson 15.00 40.00
RP Rafael Palmeiro 15.00 40.00
SG Shawn Green 10.00 25.00
SS Sammy Sosa 15.00 40.00
TH Todd Helton 15.00 40.00
THU Torii Hunter 10.00 25.00

2003 Topps Tribute Contemporary World Series Relics

*RED WS: .6X TO 1.5X BASIC
RED WS PRINT RUN 50 SERIAL #'d SETS
GOLD WS PRINT RUN 1 SERIAL #'d SET
NO GOLD PRICING DUE TO SCARCITY
MR•Mariano Rivera Jsy 10.00 25.00
TG•Troy Glaus Uni 4.00 10.00

2003 Topps Tribute Contemporary World Series Double Relics

*RED WS DOUBLE: .6X TO 1.5X BASIC
RED WS DOUBLE PRINT RUN 50 #'d SETS
GOLD WS DOUBLE PRINT RUN 1 #'d SET
NO GOLD PRICING DUE TO SCARCITY
BG Bonds Uni/Glaus Uni 15.00 40.00
LP Lackey Uni/Percival Uni 4.00 10.00
PC Piazza Bat/Clemens Uni 15.00 40.00
PP Posada Bat/Pettitte Jsy 10.00 25.00
SJ Schilling Jsy/Randy Jsy 6.00 15.00
WG Bernie Bat/L.Gonz Bat 6.00 15.00
WO Bernie Bat/O'Neill Bat 6.00 15.00

2003 Topps Tribute Contemporary World Series Triple Relics

*RED WS TRIPLE: .6X TO 1.5X BASIC
RED WS TRIPLE PRINT RUN 50 #'d SETS
GOLD WS TRIPLE PRINT RUN 1 #'d SET
NO GOLD PRICING DUE TO SCARCITY
EGS Erstad/Glaus/Salmon 10.00 25.00
LGP Lackey/Glaus/Percival 6.00 15.00

2004 Topps Tribute HOF

COMPLETE SET (80) 50.00 100.00
COMMON CARD (1-80) .75 2.00
1 Willie Mays 4.00 10.00
2 Richie Ashburn 1.25 3.00
3 Babe Ruth 5.00 12.00
4 Lou Gehrig 4.00 10.00
5 Carl Yastrzemski 2.00 5.00
6 Fergie Jenkins 1.25 3.00
7 Cool Papa Bell 1.25 3.00
8 Johnny Bench 2.00 5.00
9 Satchel Paige 2.00 5.00
10 Ty Cobb 3.00 8.00
11 Robin Roberts 1.25 3.00
12 Eddie Mathews 2.00 5.00
13 Tom Seaver 1.25 3.00
14 Kirby Puckett 2.00 5.00
15 Stan Musial 3.00 8.00
16 Ralph Kiner 1.25 3.00
17 Reggie Jackson 1.25 3.00
18 Walter Johnson 1.25 3.00
19 Phil Niekro 1.25 3.00
20 Mike Schmidt 3.00 8.00
21 Brooks Robinson 1.25 3.00
22 Jimmie Foxx 2.00 5.00
23 Nellie Fox 1.25 3.00
24 Joe Morgan 1.25 3.00
25 Cy Young 1.25 3.00
26 Hank Greenberg 2.00 5.00
27 Josh Gibson 2.00 5.00
28 Robin Yount 2.00 5.00
29 Hoyt Wilhelm 1.25 3.00
30 Yogi Berra 2.00 5.00
31 Rollie Fingers 1.25 3.00
32 Gaylord Perry 1.25 3.00
33 Ozzie Smith 2.50 6.00
34 Jim Palmer 1.25 3.00
35 Harmon Killebrew 2.00 5.00
36 Bob Feller 1.25 3.00
37 Chuck Klein .75 2.00
38 Mordecai Brown .75 2.00
39 Napoleon Lajoie 2.00 5.00
40 Al Kaline 2.00 5.00
41 Paul Molitor 2.00 5.00
42 Jackie Robinson 2.00 5.00
43 Mel Ott 2.00 5.00
44 Hank Aaron 4.00 10.00
45 Rod Carew 1.25 3.00
46 Rogers Hornsby 1.25 3.00
47 Bob Gibson 1.25 3.00
48 Juan Marichal 1.25 3.00
49 Bill Mazeroski 1.25 3.00
50 Roberto Clemente 5.00 12.00
51 Willie McCovey 1.25 3.00
52 Red Schoendienst 1.25 3.00
53 Nolan Ryan 6.00 15.00
54 Dennis Eckersley 1.25 3.00
55 Monte Irvin 1.25 3.00
56 George Kell 1.25 3.00
57 Gary Carter 1.25 3.00
58 Tony Perez 1.25 3.00
59 Carlton Fisk 1.25 3.00
60 Duke Snider 1.25 3.00
61 Bobby Doerr 1.25 3.00
62 John McGraw 1.25 3.00
63 George Sisler 1.25 3.00
64 Orlando Cepeda 1.25 3.00
65 Earl Weaver 1.25 3.00
66 Roy Campanella 2.00 5.00
67 Tris Speaker 1.25 3.00
68 Sparky Anderson 1.25 3.00
69 Willie Stargell 1.25 3.00
70 Honus Wagner 2.00 5.00
71 Lou Brock 1.25 3.00
72 Whitey Ford 1.25 3.00
73 George Brett 4.00 10.00
74 Luis Aparicio 1.25 3.00
75 Ernie Banks 2.00 5.00
76 Jim Bunning 1.25 3.00
77 Warren Spahn 1.25 3.00
78 Catfish Hunter 1.25 3.00
79 Pee Wee Reese 1.25 3.00
80 Frank Robinson 1.25 3.00

2004 Topps Tribute HOF Gold

*GOLD p/r 80-99: 1.5X TO 4X BASIC
*GOLD p/r 50-79: 2X TO 5X BASIC
*GOLD p/r 36-49: 2.5X TO 6X BASIC
GROUP A ODDS 1:2714
GROUP B ODDS 1:74
GROUP C ODDS 1:38
GROUP D ODDS 1:14
GROUP A PRINT RUNS B/WN 1-4 PER
GROUP B PRINT RUNS B/WN 36-56 PER
GROUP C PRINT RUNS B/WN 62-79 PER
GROUP D PRINT RUNS B/WN 80-99 PER
NO PRICING ON QTY OF 4 OR LESS

2004 Topps Tribute HOF Cooperstown Classmates Dual Relics

GROUP A ODDS 1:4342
GROUP B ODDS 1:229
GROUP C ODDS 1:122
GROUP A PRINT RUN 5 SERIAL #'d SETS
GROUP B PRINT RUN 50 SERIAL #'d SETS
GROUP C PRINT RUN 75 SERIAL #'d SETS
NO GROUP A PRICING DUE TO SCARCITY
*GOLD: .6X TO 1.5X BASIC C
*GOLD: .5X TO 1.2X BASIC B
GOLD STATED ODDS 1:201
GOLD PRINT RUN 25 SERIAL #'d SETS
GOLD OTT/FOXX PRINT RUN 1 #'d CARD
GOLD RUTH/COBB PRINT RUN 1 #'d CARD
NO GOLD OTT/FOXX, RUTH/COBB PRICING
BY J.Bench Uni/C.Yaz Uni C 15.00 40.00
CR O.Cep Bat/N.Ryan Jsy C 15.00 40.00
KK C.Klein Bat/A.Kaline Bat C 30.00 60.00
ME P.Molitor Bat/D.Eck Uni C 10.00 25.00
MP J.Morg Bat/J.Palm Uni C 10.00 25.00
MR J.Marichal Uni/B.Rob Bat B 20.00 50.00
PC G.Perry Uni/R.Carew Uni B 20.00 50.00
RB N.Ryan Uni/G.Brett Uni B 40.00 80.00
SK D.Snider Bat/A.Kaline Uni B 40.00 80.00

2004 Topps Tribute HOF Relics

GROUP A ODDS 1:118
GROUP B ODDS 1:36
GROUP C ODDS 1:22
GROUP D ODDS 1:6
GROUP E ODDS 1:5
GROUP F ODDS 1:6
GROUP G ODDS 1:4
GROUP A PRINT RUNS B/WN 20-85 PER
GROUP B PRINT RUNS B/WN 100-175 PER
GROUP C PRINT RUNS B/WN 200-455 PER
A-C PRINT RUNS PROVIDED BY TOPPS
GROUP A-C ARE NOT SERIAL-NUMBERED
AK Al Kaline Uni B/125 * 10.00 25.00
AKB Al Kaline Bat D 6.00 15.00
BG Bob Gibson Uni E 6.00 15.00
BR Babe Ruth Bat B/163 * 75.00 150.00
BRO Brooks Robinson Bat E 6.00 15.00
CF Carlton Fisk Wall C/300 * 10.00 25.00
CK Chuck Klein Bat B/107 * 10.00 25.00
CY C.Yastrzemski Wall C/300 * 20.00 50.00
CYU Carl Yastrzemski Uni E 15.00 40.00
DS Duke Snider Bat E 6.00 15.00
EW Earl Weaver Jsy A/25 * 10.00 25.00
FR Frank Robinson O's Uni E 10.00 25.00
FRA F.Robinson Angels Uni D 4.00 10.00
FRB Frank Robinson Bat D 4.00 10.00
GB George Brett Uni F 8.00 20.00
GBB George Brett Bat D 8.00 20.00
GC G.Carter Mets Jsy C/200 * 6.00 15.00
GCU Gary Carter Expos Uni D 4.00 10.00
GS George Sisler Bat C/455 * 10.00 25.00
HA Hank Aaron Bat D 15.00 40.00
HG Hank Greenberg Bat E 10.00 25.00
HK H.Killebrew Bat B/135 * 15.00 40.00
HW Honus Wagner Bat B/118 * 40.00 80.00
JB J.Bench w/Glv Uni C/250 * 10.00 25.00
JB2 J.Bench w/o Glv Uni G 6.00 15.00
JF Jimmie Foxx Bat A/25 * 100.00 175.00
JM Joe Morgan Bat E 4.00 10.00
JMA Juan Marichal Uni B/125 * 6.00 15.00
JP J.Palmer Arm Up Uni F 4.00 10.00
JP2 J.Palmer Arm Down Uni F 4.00 10.00
JR Jackie Robinson Bat G 15.00 40.00
KP Kirby Puckett Jsy B/175 * 10.00 25.00
KPB Kirby Puckett Bat G 10.00 25.00
LBB Lou Brock Bat E 6.00 15.00
LG Lou Gehrig Bat A/52 * 175.00 300.00
MO Mel Ott Bat A/25 * 60.00 120.00
MS Mike Schmidt Jsy A/50 * 15.00 40.00
MSB Mike Schmidt Bat G 8.00 20.00
NR Nolan Ryan Rgr Uni F 12.50 30.00
NRA N.Ryan Angels Uni C/425 * 10.00 25.00
NRJ Nolan Ryan Astros Jsy F 12.50 30.00
OC Orl Cepeda Bat B/100 * 6.00 15.00
OS Ozzie Smith Bat F 6.00 15.00
PM Paul Molitor Jsy G 4.00 10.00
PMB Paul Molitor Bat D 4.00 10.00
RC Roberto Clemente Bat E 12.00 30.00
RH Rogers Hornsby Bat D 8.00 20.00
RJ R.Jackson Jsy B/110 * 10.00 25.00
RJB R.Jackson Bat C/200 * 10.00 25.00
RY Robin Yount Uni A/50 * 15.00 40.00
SM Stan Musial Jsy G 10.00 25.00
TCB Ty Cobb Bat D 15.00 40.00
TS Tom Seaver Uni D 6.00 15.00
TSP Tris Speaker Bat A/85 * 40.00 80.00
WF Whitey Ford Uni A/50 * 15.00 40.00
WM1 Willie Mays Glove B/110 * 100.00 175.00
WM2 Willie Mays Giants Bat D 10.00 25.00
WM3 Willie Mays Mets Bat D 10.00 25.00
WM4 Willie Mays Uni Gray F 10.00 25.00
WM5 Willie Mays Uni White G 10.00 25.00

2004 Topps Tribute HOF Relics Gold

*GOLD: 1.25X TO 3X GROUP E-G
*GOLD: 1.25X TO 3X GROUP D
*GOLD: .75X TO 2X GROUP C
*GOLD: .75X TO 2X GROUP B
*GOLD: .6X TO 1.5X GROUP A p/r 50-85
*GOLD: .5X TO 1.2X GROUP A p/r 20-25
STATED ODDS 1:33
STATED PRINT RUN 25 SERIAL #'d SETS
E.WEAVER PRINT RUN 1 SERIAL #'d CARD
J.FOXX PRINT RUN 1 SERIAL #'d CARD
M.OTT PRINT RUN 1 SERIAL #'d CARD
T.COBB UNI PRINT RUN 1 SERIAL #'d CARD
W.FORD PRINT RUN 15 SERIAL #'d CARDS
NO PRICING ON QTY OF 15 OR LESS
BR Babe Ruth Bat 175.00 300.00
CY Carl Yastrzemski Wall 40.00 100.00
GB George Brett Uni 15.00 40.00
GBB George Brett Bat 15.00 40.00
HW Honus Wagner Bat 40.00 80.00
JR Jackie Robinson Bat 50.00 120.00
KP Kirby Puckett Jsy 50.00 100.00
KPB Kirby Puckett Bat 50.00 100.00
MS Mike Schmidt Jsy 30.00 80.00
MSB Mike Schmidt Bat 30.00 80.00
NRA Nolan Ryan Angels Uni 40.00 100.00
OS Ozzie Smith Bat 25.00 60.00
RC Roberto Clemente Bat 40.00 100.00
SM Stan Musial Jsy 40.00 100.00
TCB Ty Cobb Bat 75.00 150.00
TSP Tris Speaker Bat 60.00 120.00
WF Whitey Ford Uni/15 40.00 100.00
WM1 Willie Mays Glove 200.00 350.00

2004 Topps Tribute HOF Relics Autographs

GROUP A ODDS 1:835
GROUP B ODDS 1:120
GROUP A PRINT RUN 55 SERIAL #'d SETS
GROUP B PRINT RUN 95 SERIAL #'d SETS
GOLD STATED ODDS 1:1888
GOLD PRINT RUN 5 SERIAL #'d SETS
NO GOLD PRICING DUE TO SCARCITY
AKB Al Kaline Bat B 30.00 80.00
BRO Brooks Robinson Bat B 30.00 60.00
CYU Carl Yastrzemski Uni B 40.00 80.00
EW Earl Weaver Jsy A 15.00 40.00
NRJ Nolan Ryan Jsy B 75.00 150.00

2004 Topps Tribute HOF Relics Jersey Patch

*3-COLOR PATCH: ADD 20% PREMIUM
GROUP A ODDS 1:172
GROUP B ODDS 1:114
GROUP A PRINT RUNS B/WN 10-50 PER
GROUP B PRINT RUN 100 SERIAL #'d SETS
NO PRICING ON QTY OF 17 OR LESS
*GOLD p/r 25: .75X TO 2X BASIC p/r 100
*GOLD p/r 25: .6X TO 1.5X BASIC p/r 50
GOLD STATED ODDS 1:251
GOLD PRINT RUNS B/WN 1-25 COPIES PER
NO GOLD PRICING ON QTY OF 10 OR LESS
DE Dennis Eckersley A/50 15.00 40.00
FR Frank Robinson A/39 30.00 60.00
GB George Brett A/50 20.00 50.00
MS Mike Schmidt Swing B 20.00 50.00
MS2 Mike Schmidt Stance B 20.00 50.00
NR Nolan Ryan B 20.00 50.00
RC Rod Carew B 15.00 40.00
RJ Reggie Jackson A/50 20.00 50.00
RY Robin Yount A/50 20.00 50.00

2003 Topps Tribute Perennial All-Star

COMPLETE SET (50) 20.00 50.00
COMMON CARD (1-50) .75 2.00
1 Willie Mays 4.00 10.00
2 Don Mattingly 4.00 10.00
3 Hoyt Wilhelm 1.25 3.00
4 Hank Aaron 4.00 10.00
5 Hank Greenberg 2.00 5.00
6 Johnny Bench 2.00 5.00
7 Duke Snider 1.25 3.00
8 Carl Yastrzemski 3.00 8.00
9 Jim Palmer 1.25 3.00
10 Roberto Clemente 5.00 12.00
11 Mike Schmidt 3.00 8.00
12 Joe Cronin .75 2.00
13 Lou Brock 1.25 3.00
14 Orlando Cepeda 1.25 3.00
15 Bill Mazeroski 1.25 3.00
16 Whitey Ford 1.25 3.00
17 Rod Carew 1.25 3.00
18 Joe Morgan 1.25 3.00
19 Luis Aparicio 1.25 3.00
20 Nolan Ryan 6.00 15.00
21 Bobby Doerr 1.25 3.00
22 Dale Murphy 2.00 5.00
23 Bob Feller 1.25 3.00
24 Paul Molitor 2.00 5.00

25 Tom Seaver 1.25 3.00
26 Ozzie Smith 2.50 6.00
27 Stan Musial 3.00 8.00
28 Willie McCovey 1.25 3.00
29 Gary Carter 1.25 3.00
30 Reggie Jackson 1.25 3.00
31 Gaylord Perry 1.25 3.00
32 George Brett 4.00 10.00
33 Robin Roberts 1.25 3.00
34 Wade Boggs 1.25 3.00
35 Cal Ripken 6.00 15.00
36 Carlton Fisk 1.25 3.00
37 Al Kaline 1.25 3.00
38 Kirby Puckett 2.00 5.00
39 Phil Rizzuto 1.25 3.00
40 Willie Stargell 1.25 3.00
41 Harmon Killebrew 2.00 5.00
42 Red Schoendienst 1.25 3.00
43 Tony Gwynn 2.00 5.00
44 Ralph Kiner 1.25 3.00
45 Yogi Berra 2.00 5.00
46 Catfish Hunter 1.25 3.00
47 Frank Robinson 1.25 3.00
48 Ernie Banks 2.00 5.00
49 Warren Spahn 1.25 3.00
50 Brooks Robinson 1.25 3.00

2003 Topps Tribute Perennial All-Star Gold

*GOLD p/r 81-86: 1.5X TO 4X BASIC
*GOLD p/r 66-80: 2X TO 5X BASIC
*GOLD p/r 51-65: 2.5X TO 6X BASIC
*GOLD p/r 36-50: 3X TO 8X BASIC
*GOLD p/r 26-35: 4X TO 10X BASIC
GROUP A ODDS 1:106
GROUP B ODDS 1:49
GROUP C ODDS 1:38
SEE BECKETT.COM FOR PRINT RUNS

2003 Topps Tribute Perennial All-Star Relics

BAT GROUP A ODDS 1:556
BAT GROUP B ODDS 1:368
BAT GROUP C ODDS 1:276
BAT GROUP D ODDS 1:61
BAT GROUP E ODDS 1:158
BAT GROUP F ODDS 1:23
BAT GROUP G ODDS 1:111
BAT GROUP H ODDS 1:46
BAT GROUP I ODDS 1:85
BAT GROUP J ODDS 1:16
BAT GROUP K ODDS 1:18
BAT GROUP L ODDS 1:31
BAT GROUP M ODDS 1:50
BAT GROUP N ODDS 1:46
BAT GROUP O ODDS 1:21
BAT GROUP P ODDS 1:37
JSY/UNI GROUP A ODDS 1:368
JSY/UNI GROUP B ODDS 1:148
JSY/UNI GROUP C ODDS 1:92
JSY/UNI GROUP D ODDS 1:185
JSY/UNI GROUP E ODDS 1:69
JSY/UNI GROUP F ODDS 1:55
JSY/UNI GROUP G ODDS 1:79
JSY/UNI GROUP H ODDS 1:61
JSY/UNI GROUP I ODDS 1:55
JSY/UNI GROUP J ODDS 1:25
JSY/UNI GROUP K ODDS 1:46
JSY/UNI GROUP L ODDS 1:43
JSY/UNI GROUP M ODDS 1:21
JSY/UNI GROUP N ODDS 1:8
JSY/UNI GROUP O ODDS 1:29
JSY/UNI GROUP P ODDS 1:10
AD Andre Dawson Bat F 4.00 10.00
AK Al Kaline Bat E 4.00 10.00
BD Bobby Doerr Jsy N 4.00 10.00
BF Bob Feller Bat I 4.00 10.00
BM Bill Mazeroski Uni C 4.00 10.00
BR Babe Ruth Bat J 60.00 150.00
BRO Brooks Robinson Bat J 4.00 10.00
CF Carlton Fisk Bat J 4.00 10.00
CH Catfish Hunter Jsy B 4.00 10.00
CRB Cal Ripken Bat P 6.00 15.00
CY Carl Yastrzemski Jsy E 6.00 15.00
DD Dizzy Dean Uni E 20.00 50.00
DM Dale Murphy Jsy A 6.00 15.00
DMA Don Mattingly Jsy L 10.00 25.00
DN Don Newcombe Bat K 2.50 6.00
DSN Duke Snider Bat F 4.00 10.00
EB Ernie Banks Bat M 6.00 15.00
EM Eddie Mathews Jsy K 6.00 15.00
FR Frank Robinson Uni G 4.00 10.00
GB George Brett Jsy M 12.00 30.00
GC Gary Carter Jsy I 4.00 10.00
HA Hank Aaron Bat O 12.00 30.00
HG Hank Greenberg Bat D 6.00 15.00
HK Harmon Killebrew Jsy J 6.00 15.00
HW Honus Wagner Bat B 40.00 100.00
HWI Hoyt Wilhelm Uni N 4.00 10.00
JBE Johnny Bench Uni F 6.00 15.00
JCR Joe Cronin Bat N 2.50 6.00
JF Jimmie Foxx Bat F 15.00 40.00
JMI Johnny Mize Uni D 4.00 10.00
JMO Joe Morgan Bat K 4.00 10.00
JP Jim Palmer Uni N 4.00 10.00
JR Jackie Robinson Bat L 12.00 30.00
KP Kirby Puckett Jsy N 6.00 15.00
LA Luis Aparicio Bat C 4.00 10.00
LB Lou Brock Bat A 4.00 10.00
LBU Lou Brock Uni H 4.00 10.00
LG Lou Gehrig Bat F 40.00 100.00
MO Mel Ott Bat D 6.00 15.00
MS Mike Schmidt Uni P 6.00 15.00
NL Nap Lajoie Bat D 20.00 50.00
NR Nolan Ryan Rangers Uni O 12.00 30.00
NRA Nolan Ryan Astros Jsy F 12.00 30.00
OC Orlando Cepeda Jsy C 4.00 10.00
OS Ozzie Smith Uni J 8.00 20.00
PM Paul Molitor Bat K 6.00 15.00
PR Phil Rizzuto Bat H 4.00 10.00
RC Roberto Clemente Bat L 20.00 50.00
RCA Roy Campanella Bat F 6.00 15.00
RH Rogers Hornsby Bat G 15.00 40.00
RJ Reggie Jackson Bat O 4.00 10.00
ROD Rod Carew Jsy N 4.00 10.00
RS Red Schoendienst Bat H 4.00 10.00
SM Stan Musial Bat J 10.00 25.00
TC Ty Cobb Bat F 15.00 40.00
TG Tony Gwynn Jsy P 6.00 15.00
TM Thurman Munson Jsy M 6.00 15.00
TS Tris Speaker Bat A 100.00 250.00
TSE Tom Seaver Jsy A 12.00 30.00
WB Wade Boggs Uni C 4.00 10.00
WF Whitey Ford Uni B 4.00 10.00
WM Willie Mays Bat K 10.00 25.00
WMC Willie McCovey Bat J 4.00 10.00
WST Willie Stargell Uni B 4.00 10.00
YB Yogi Berra Jsy A 20.00 50.00

2003 Topps Tribute Perennial All-Star Patch Relics

STATED ODDS 1:123
STATED PRINT RUN 30 SERIAL #'d SETS
CR Cal Ripken 175.00 300.00
CY Carl Yastrzemski 125.00 200.00
DMU Dale Murphy 40.00 80.00
GB George Brett 150.00 250.00
GC Gary Carter 20.00 50.00
HK Harmon Killebrew 60.00 120.00
JM Joe Morgan 20.00 50.00
MS Mike Schmidt 75.00 150.00
NR Nolan Ryan Rangers 150.00 250.00
NRA Nolan Ryan Astros 150.00 250.00
OS Ozzie Smith 125.00 200.00
TG Tony Gwynn 75.00 150.00
WB Wade Boggs 40.00 80.00
WM Willie McCovey 20.00 50.00
WS Willie Stargell 40.00 80.00

2003 Topps Tribute Perennial All-Star Signing

STATED ODDS 1:34
GOLD STATED ODDS 1:201
GOLD PRINT RUN 25 SERIAL #'d SETS
NO GOLD PRICING DUE TO SCARCITY
AD Andre Dawson Bat 15.00 40.00
AK Al Kaline Bat 30.00 80.00
DM Dale Murphy Jsy 20.00 50.00
DMA Don Mattingly Jsy 30.00 80.00
DSN Duke Snider Bat 40.00 80.00
GC Gary Carter Jsy 20.00 50.00
JP Jim Palmer Uni 15.00 40.00
LB Lou Brock Bat 30.00 60.00
MS Mike Schmidt Uni 40.00 80.00
OC Orlando Cepeda Jsy 15.00 40.00
TG Tony Gwynn Jsy 30.00 60.00

2003 Topps Tribute Perennial All-Star Memorable Match-Up Relics

STATED ODDS 1:41
STATED PRINT RUN 150 SERIAL #'d SETS
GOLD STATED ODDS 1:245
GOLD PRINT RUN 25 SERIAL #'d SETS
NO GOLD PRICING DUE TO SCARCITY
BF J.Bench Bat/C.Fisk Bat 15.00 40.00
BG W.Boggs Bat/T.Gwynn Bat 10.00 25.00
BS G.Brett Jsy/M.Schmidt Uni 15.00 40.00
CM G.Carter Jsy/D.Mattingly Jsy 20.00 50.00
KA H.Killebrew Jsy/H.Aaron Bat 15.00 40.00
MJ W.Mays Bat/R.Jackson Bat 20.00 50.00
PG K.Puckett Bat/T.Gwynn Bat 20.00 50.00
YB C.Yaz Jsy/J.Bench Bat 20.00 50.00
YBR C.Yaz Jsy/L.Brock Bat 10.00 25.00

2003 Topps Tribute World Series

COMMON CARD (1-130) .75 2.00
COMMON CARD (131-150) .75 2.00
1 Willie Mays 54 4.00 10.00
2 Gary Carter 86 1.25 3.00
3 Yogi Berra 47 2.00 5.00
4 Dennis Eckersley 88 1.25 3.00
5 Willie McCovey 62 1.25 3.00
6 Willie Stargell 71 1.25 3.00
7 Mike Schmidt 80 3.00 8.00
8 Robin Yount 82 2.00 5.00
9 Bucky Harris 24 .75 2.00
10 Carl Yastrzemski 67 3.00 8.00
11 Lenny Dykstra 86 .75 2.00
12 Boog Powell 66 .75 2.00
13 Bill Lee 75 .75 2.00
14 Lou Brock 64 1.25 3.00
15 Bob Friend 60 .75 2.00
16 Hank Greenberg 34 2.00 5.00
17 Maury Wills 59 .75 2.00
18 Tom Lasorda 77 1.25 3.00
19 Moose Skowron 55 .75 2.00
20 Frank Robinson 61 1.25 3.00
21 Rollie Fingers 72 1.25 3.00
22 Doug DeCinces 79 .75 2.00
23 Eric Davis 90 .75 2.00
24 Johnny Podres 53 .75 2.00
25 Darrell Evans 84 .75 2.00
26 Ron Cey 74 .75 2.00
27 Ray Knight 86 .75 2.00
28 Don Larsen 55 .75 2.00
29 Harold Baines 90 1.25 3.00
30 Brooks Robinson 66 1.25 3.00
31 Wade Boggs 86 1.25 3.00
32 Joe Morgan 72 1.25 3.00
33 Kirk Gibson 84 .75 2.00
34 Tommy John 77 .75 2.00
35 Monte Irvin 51 1.25 3.00
36 Goose Gossage 78 1.25 3.00
37 Tug McGraw 73 .75 2.00
38 Walt Weiss 88 .75 2.00
39 Bill Madlock 79 .75 2.00
40 Juan Marichal 62 1.25 3.00
41 Willie McGee 82 .75 2.00
42 Joe Cronin 33 .75 2.00
43 Paul Blair 66 .75 2.00
44 Norm Cash 59 .75 2.00
45 Ken Griffey 75 .75 2.00
46 Bret Saberhagen 85 .75 2.00
47 Don Sutton 74 1.25 3.00
48 Kirby Puckett 87 2.00 5.00
49 Keith Hernandez 82 .75 2.00
50 George Brett 80 4.00 10.00
51 Bobby Richardson 57 .75 2.00
52 Jose Canseco 88 1.25 3.00
53 Greg Luzinski 80 .75 2.00
54 Bill Mazeroski 60 1.25 3.00
55 Red Schoendienst 46 1.25 3.00
56 Graig Nettles 76 .75 2.00
57 Jerry Koosman 69 .75 2.00
58 Tony Perez 70 1.25 3.00
59 Jim Rice 86 1.25 3.00
60 Duke Snider 49 1.25 3.00
61 David Justice 91 .75 2.00
62 Johnny Sain 48 .75 2.00
63 Chuck Klein 35 .75 2.00
64 Sparky Anderson 70 1.25 3.00
65 Alan Trammell 84 1.25 3.00
66 Willie Wilson 80 .75 2.00
67 Hoyt Wilhelm 54 1.25 3.00
68 Joe Pepitone 63 .75 2.00
69 Darren Daulton 93 .75 2.00
70 Tom Seaver 69 1.25 3.00
71 Catfish Hunter 72 1.25 3.00
72 Tim McCarver 64 .75 2.00
73 Dave Parker 79 .75 2.00
74 Earl Weaver 69 1.25 3.00
75 Ted Kluszewski 59 1.25 3.00
76 John Kruk 93 .75 2.00
77 Dwight Evans 75 .75 2.00
78 Ron Darling 86 .75 2.00
79 Tony Oliva 65 .75 2.00
80 Johnny Bench 70 2.00 5.00
81 Sam Crawford 07 1.25 3.00
82 Steve Yeager 74 .75 2.00
83 Paul Molitor 82 2.00 5.00
84 Bert Campaneris 72 .75 2.00
85 Mickey Rivers 76 .75 2.00
86 Vince Coleman 87 .75 2.00
87 Kent Tekulve 79 .75 2.00
88 Dwight Gooden 86 .75 2.00
89 Whitey Herzog 82 .75 2.00
90 Whitey Ford 50 1.25 3.00
91 Warren Spahn 48 1.25 3.00
92 Fred Lynn 75 .75 2.00
93 Joe Tinker 06 1.25 3.00
94 Bill Buckner 74 .75 2.00
95 Bob Feller 48 1.25 3.00
96 Hank Bauer 49 .75 2.00
97 Joe Rudi 72 .75 2.00
98 Steve Sax 81 .75 2.00
99 Bruce Sutter 82 1.25 3.00
100 Nolan Ryan 69 6.00 15.00
101 Bobby Thomson 51 1.25 3.00
102 Bob Watson 81 .75 2.00
103 Vida Blue 72 .75 2.00
104 Robin Roberts 50 1.25 3.00
105 Orlando Cepeda 62 1.25 3.00
106 Jim Bottomley 26 .75 2.00
107 Heinie Manush 33 .75 2.00
108 Jim Gilliam 53 .75 2.00
109 Dave Concepcion 70 .75 2.00
110 Al Kaline 68 1.25 3.00
111 Howard Johnson 84 .75 2.00
112 Phil Rizzuto 41 1.25 3.00
113 Steve Garvey 74 .75 2.00
114 George Foster 72 .75 2.00
115 Carlton Fisk 75 1.25 3.00
116 Don Newcombe 49 .75 2.00
117 Lance Parrish 84 .75 2.00
118 Reggie Jackson 73 1.25 3.00
119 Luis Aparicio 59 1.25 3.00
120 Jim Palmer 66 1.25 3.00
121 Ron Guidry 77 .75 2.00
122 Frankie Frisch 21 1.25 3.00
123 Chet Lemon 84 .75 2.00
124 Cecil Cooper 75 .75 2.00
125 Harmon Killebrew 65 2.00 5.00
126 Luis Tiant 75 .75 2.00
127 John McGraw 05 1.25 3.00
128 Paul O'Neill 90 1.25 3.00
129 Jack Clark 85 .75 2.00
130 Stan Musial 42 3.00 8.00
131 Mike Schmidt FC 3.00 8.00
132 Kirby Puckett FC 2.00 5.00
133 Carlton Fisk FC 1.25 3.00
134 Bill Mazeroski FC 1.25 3.00
135 Johnny Podres FC .75 2.00
136 Robin Yount FC 2.00 5.00
137 David Justice FC .75 2.00
138 Bobby Thomson FC 1.25 3.00
139 Joe Carter FC .75 2.00
140 Reggie Jackson FC 1.25 3.00
141 Kirk Gibson FC .75 2.00
142 Whitey Ford FC 1.25 3.00
143 Don Larsen FC .75 2.00
144 Duke Snider FC 1.25 3.00
145 Carl Yastrzemski FC 3.00 8.00
146 Johnny Bench FC 2.00 5.00
147 Lou Brock FC 1.25 3.00
148 Ted Kluszewski FC 1.25 3.00
149 Jim Palmer FC 1.25 3.00
150 Willie Mays FC 4.00 10.00

2003 Topps Tribute World Series Gold

*GOLD 1-130: 1.5X TO 4X BASIC
*GOLD 131-150: 1.5X TO 4X BASIC
RANDOM INSERTS IN PACKS
STATED PRINT RUN 100 SERIAL #'d SETS

2003 Topps Tribute World Series Memorable Match-Up Relics

STATED ODDS 1:28
PRINT RUNS B/WN 9-88 COPIES PER
NO PRICING ON QTY OF 19 OR LESS
AM Sparky Uni/B.Martin Uni/76 15.00 40.00
AS Aparicio Bat/Snider Bat/59 20.00 50.00
EG D.Eck Uni/K.Gibson Bat/88 15.00 40.00
FS Ford Uni/Snider Bat/52 40.00 80.00
GF G'berg Bat/Frisch Bat/34 75.00 150.00
GK G'berg Bat/Klein Bat/35 75.00 150.00
KB Kaline Uni/Brock Bat/68 40.00 80.00
MF Mazeroski Jsy/Ford Uni/64 40.00 80.00
PR Rizzuto Bat/Mays Uni/51 75.00 150.00
RBE B.Rob Bat/Bench Bat/70 40.00 80.00
RS F.Rob Bat/Seaver Uni/69 20.00 50.00
SB Schmidt Uni/Brett Uni/80 50.00 100.00
SP Stargell Bat/Palmer Jsy/79 20.00 50.00
SRI Schmidt Uni/Ripken Uni/83 75.00 150.00
SY O.Smith Bat/Yount Jsy/82 30.00 60.00
TG Trammell Jsy/Gwynn Bat/84 40.00 80.00
WB Mookie Bat/Buckner Jsy/86 20.00 50.00

2003 Topps Tribute World Series Signature Relics

GROUP A ODDS 1:218
GROUP B ODDS 1:94
GROUP C ODDS 1:9
GROUP D ODDS 1:12
GOLD STATED ODDS 1:88
GOLD PRINT RUN 25 SERIAL #'d SETS
NO GOLD PRICING DUE TO SCARCITY
AK Al Kaline Uni C 20.00 50.00
AT Alan Trammell Jsy C 15.00 40.00
BR Brooks Robinson Bat A 40.00 80.00
DJ David Justice Uni B 20.00 50.00
DN Don Newcombe Bat A 20.00 50.00
EW Earl Weaver Jsy D 12.00 30.00
JC Joe Carter Bat C 20.00 50.00
JP Jim Palmer Jsy D 15.00 40.00
KG Kirk Gibson Bat C 40.00 80.00
MS Moose Skowron Bat C 6.00 15.00
MW Maury Wills Jsy D 6.00 15.00
MWI Mookie Wilson Bat B 20.00 50.00
SA Sparky Anderson Uni C 20.00 50.00
SG Steve Garvey Bat C 15.00 40.00
WF Whitey Ford Uni C 30.00 60.00

2003 Topps Tribute World Series Subway Fan Fare Tokens

ONE PER BOX
BM Billy Martin 8.00 20.00
DJ David Justice 5.00 12.00
DL Don Larsen 5.00 12.00
DN Don Newcombe 5.00 12.00
DS Duke Snider 8.00 20.00
HB Hank Bauer 5.00 12.00
JP Johnny Podres 5.00 12.00
MS Moose Skowron 5.00 12.00
PO Paul O'Neill 8.00 20.00
PR Phil Rizzuto 8.00 20.00
WF Whitey Ford 8.00 20.00
YB Yogi Berra 12.00 30.00

2003 Topps Tribute World Series Team Tribute Relics

GROUP A ODDS 1:436
GROUP B ODDS 1:7
GROUP A PRINT RUN 25 SERIAL #'d SETS
GROUP B PRINT RUN 275 SERIAL #'d SETS
NO GROUP A PRICING DUE TO SCARCITY
CM O.Cepeda/J.Marichal B 12.50 30.00
CPM Conc/Perez/Morgan B 20.00 50.00
CYG Cey/Yeager/Garvey B 12.50 30.00
EC D.Eckersley/J.Canseco B 10.00 25.00
FPG Foster/Perez/Griffey Sr. B 15.00 40.00
GT K.Gibson/A.Trammell B 10.00 25.00
HCD K.Hern/G.Carter/Dykstra B 12.50 30.00
HJ C.Hunter/R.Jackson B 12.50 30.00
KCA A.Kaline/N.Cash B 15.00 40.00
MM W.Mays/W.McCovey B 20.00 50.00
OSD O'Neill/Sabo/E.Davis B 15.00 40.00
SB B.Saberhagen/G.Brett B 10.00 25.00
SMC Ozzie/McGee/Coleman B 10.00 25.00
SPM Stargell/Parker/Madlock B 10.00 25.00
SRK Seaver/Ryan/Koosman B 20.00 50.00
TA A.Trammell/S.Anderson B 12.00 30.00
YLK Yastrzemski/Lynn/Fisk B 20.00 50.00
YM R.Yount/P.Molitor B 15.00 40.00

2003 Topps Tribute World Series Tribute Relics

GROUP A ODDS 1:41
GROUP B ODDS 1:3
GROUP A PRINT RUN 50 SERIAL #'d SETS
GROUP B PRINT RUN 425 SERIAL #'d SETS
GOLD STATED ODDS 1:25
GOLD PRINT RUN 25 SERIAL #'d SETS
NO GOLD PRICING DUE TO SCARCITY
BH Bucky Harris Bat B 12.50 30.00
BM Bill Mazeroski Uni B 8.00 20.00
BMA Billy Martin Uni B 6.00 15.00
BR Babe Ruth Bat B 100.00 175.00
BT Bobby Thomson Bat B 4.00 10.00
CF Carlton Fisk Bat-Wall B 15.00 40.00
CH Catfish Hunter Jsy B 6.00 15.00
CK Chuck Klein Bat B 10.00 25.00
CR Cal Ripken Uni B 10.00 25.00
CY Carl Yastrzemski Jsy B 10.00 25.00
ER Edd Roush Bat A 20.00 50.00
FF Frankie Frisch Bat B 12.50 30.00
FR Frank Robinson Bat B 6.00 15.00
GB George Brett Uni B 10.00 25.00
HA Hank Aaron Bat A 12.50 30.00
HB Hank Bauer Bat A 20.00 50.00
HG Hank Greenberg Bat A 15.00 40.00
HK Harmon Killebrew Uni B 8.00 20.00
HM Heinie Manush Bat A 20.00 50.00
HW Honus Wagner Bat A 150.00 250.00
JB Jim Bottomley Bat A 20.00 50.00
JBE Johnny Bench Uni B 10.00 25.00
JC Jose Canseco Jsy B 6.00 15.00
JF Jimmie Foxx Bat A 100.00 200.00
JM Juan Marichal Uni B 6.00 15.00
JR Jackie Robinson Bat B 20.00 50.00
JT Joe Tinker Bat B 15.00 40.00
KP Kirby Puckett Bat B 10.00 25.00
LB Lou Brock Bat B 10.00 25.00
LG Lou Gehrig Bat A 50.00 100.00
MS Mike Schmidt Uni B 10.00 25.00
NC Norm Cash Jsy A 30.00 60.00
OC Orlando Cepeda Bat A 20.00 50.00
OS Ozzie Smith Uni B 10.00 25.00
RC Roberto Clemente Bat A 75.00 150.00
RH Rogers Hornsby Bat B 12.00 30.00
RJ Reggie Jackson Bat B 6.00 15.00
RM Roger Maris Bat A 50.00 100.00
RS Red Schoendienst Bat B 6.00 15.00
RY Robin Yount Jsy B 10.00 25.00
SC Sam Crawford Bat A 20.00 50.00
SM Stan Musial Bat B 10.00 25.00
TC Ty Cobb Uni B 75.00 150.00
TG Tony Gwynn Uni B 10.00 25.00
TK Ted Kluszewski Uni B 6.00 15.00
TM Thurman Munson Bat B 12.00 30.00
TS Tom Seaver Uni B 6.00 15.00
TSP Tris Speaker Bat A 100.00 175.00
WB Wade Boggs Bat B 6.00 15.00
WM Willie Mays Uni B 15.00 40.00
WMC Willie McCovey Uni B 4.00 10.00
WS Willie Stargell Uni A 20.00 50.00
YB Yogi Berra Uni B 15.00 40.00

2003 Topps Tribute World Series Tribute Autograph Relics

STATED ODDS 1:55
GOLD STATED ODDS 1:163
GOLD PRINT RUN 25 SERIAL #'d SETS
NO GOLD PRICING DUE TO SCARCITY
BM Bill Mazeroski Jsy 60.00 150.00
BT Bobby Thomson Bat 15.00 40.00
CF Carlton Fisk Bat-Wall 125.00 250.00
HK Harmon Killebrew Uni 30.00 60.00
JC Jose Canseco Jsy 30.00 60.00
LB Lou Brock Bat 40.00 80.00
MS Mike Schmidt Uni 40.00 100.00
WM Willie Mays Uni 250.00 400.00

2006 Topps Triple Threads

1-100 THREE PER PACK
101-120 ODDS 1:7 MINI
101-120 PRINT RUN 225 SERIAL #'d SETS
OVERALL 1-100 PLATE ODDS 1:80 MINI
PLATE PRINT RUN 1 SET PER COLOR
BLACK-CYAN-MAGENTA-YELLOW ISSUED
NO PLATE PRICING DUE TO SCARCITY
1 Hideki Matsui 2.00 5.00
2 Josh Gibson HOF 2.00 5.00
3 Roger Clemens 2.50 6.00
4 Paul Konerko 1.25 3.00
5 Brooks Robinson HOF 1.25 3.00
6 Stan Musial HOF 3.00 8.00
7 Dontrelle Willis .75 2.00
8 Yogi Berra HOF 2.00 5.00
9 John Smoltz 2.00 5.00
10 Brian Roberts .75 2.00
11 Gary Sheffield .75 2.00
12 Wade Boggs HOF 1.25 3.00
13 Alex Rodriguez 2.50 6.00
14 Ernie Banks HOF 2.00 5.00
15 Ichiro Suzuki 2.50 6.00
16 Whitey Ford HOF 1.25 3.00
17 Vladimir Guerrero 1.25 3.00
18 Tadahito Iguchi .75 2.00
19 Robin Yount HOF 2.00 5.00
20 Jason Schmidt .75 2.00
21 Roberto Clemente HOF 5.00 12.00
22 Andruw Jones .75 2.00
23 Don Mattingly 4.00 10.00
24 Joe Mauer 1.25 3.00
25 Barry Bonds 3.00 8.00
26 Johnny Damon 1.25 3.00
27 Chris Carpenter 1.25 3.00
28 Garret Anderson .75 2.00
29 Scott Rolen 1.25 3.00
30 Tim Hudson 1.25 3.00
31 Dave Winfield HOF 1.25 3.00
32 Steve Carlton HOF 1.25 3.00
33 Miguel Tejada 1.25 3.00
34 Nolan Ryan HOF 6.00 15.00
35 Mark Buehrle 1.25 3.00
36 Travis Hafner .75 2.00
37 Rickie Weeks .75 2.00
38 Sammy Sosa 2.00 5.00
39 Carlos Beltran 1.25 3.00
40 Todd Helton 1.25 3.00
41 Tom Seaver HOF 1.25 3.00
42 Ted Williams HOF 4.00 10.00
43 Alfonso Soriano 1.25 3.00
44 Reggie Jackson HOF 1.25 3.00
45 Pedro Martinez 1.25 3.00
46 Randy Johnson 2.00 5.00
47 Ted Williams HOF 4.00 10.00
48 Torii Hunter .75 2.00
49 Manny Ramirez 2.00 5.00
50 George Brett HOF 4.00 10.00
51 Chipper Jones 2.00 5.00
52 Nomar Garciaparra 1.25 3.00
53 Richie Sexson .75 2.00
54 David Ortiz 2.00 5.00
55 Derek Jeter 5.00 12.00
56 Mickey Mantle HOF 6.00 15.00
57 Michael Young .75 2.00
58 Aramis Ramirez .75 2.00
59 Bartolo Colon .75 2.00
60 Troy Glaus .75 2.00
61 Carlos Delgado .75 2.00
62 Mike Sweeney .75 2.00
63 Jorge Cantu .75 2.00
64 Mike Mussina 1.25 3.00
65 Hank Blalock .75 2.00
66 Frank Robinson HOF 1.25 3.00
67 Carl Yastrzemski HOF 3.00 8.00
68 Adam Dunn 1.25 3.00
69 Eric Chavez .75 2.00
70 Curt Schilling 1.25 3.00
71 Jeff Francoeur 2.00 5.00
72 C.C. Sabathia 1.25 3.00
73 Roy Oswalt 1.25 3.00
74 Carlos Lee .75 2.00
75 Barry Zito 1.25 3.00
76 Derrek Lee .75 2.00
77 Greg Maddux 2.50 6.00
78 Ivan Rodriguez 1.25 3.00
79 Jeff Kent .75 2.00
80 Gary Carter HOF 1.25 3.00
81 Jose Reyes 1.25 3.00
82 Johan Santana 1.25 3.00
83 Magglio Ordonez 1.25 3.00
84 Mark Prior 1.25 3.00
85 Johnny Bench HOF 2.00 5.00
86 Vernon Wells .75 2.00
87 Mark Mulder .75 2.00
88 Cal Ripken 6.00 15.00
89 Mark Teixeira 1.25 3.00
90 Miguel Cabrera 2.00 5.00
91 Duke Snider HOF 1.25 3.00
92 Jason Giambi .75 2.00
93 Albert Pujols 2.50 6.00
94 Carl Crawford 1.25 3.00
95 Jim Edmonds 1.25 3.00
96 Jose Contreras .75 2.00
97 Victor Martinez 1.25 3.00
98 Jeremy Bonderman .75 2.00
99 Lance Berkman 1.25 3.00
100 Rocco Baldelli .75 2.00
101 Zach Duke AU J-J 10.00 25.00
102 Felix Hernandez AU J-J 15.00 40.00
103 Dan Johnson AU J-J 6.00 15.00
104 Brandon McCarthy AU J-J 10.00 25.00
105 Huston Street AU J-J 6.00 15.00
106 Robinson Cano AU J-J 12.50 30.00
107 Jason Bay AU J-J 6.00 15.00
108 Ryan Howard AU B-B 15.00 40.00
109 Ervin Santana AU J-J 6.00 15.00
110 Rich Harden AU J-J 6.00 15.00
111 Aaron Hill AU J-J 6.00 15.00
112 David Wright AU J-J 12.50 30.00
113 Rich Hill AU J-J (RC) 6.00 15.00
114 Nelson Cruz AU J-J (RC) 15.00 40.00
115 F.Liriano AU J-J (RC) 6.00 15.00
116 Hong-Chih Kuo AU J-J (RC) 30.00 60.00
117 Ryan Garko AU J-J (RC) 10.00 25.00
118 Craig Hansen AU J-J RC 6.00 15.00
119 Shin-Soo Choo AU J-J (RC) 6.00 15.00
120 Darrell Rasner AU J-J (RC) 6.00 15.00

2006 Topps Triple Threads Emerald

*EMERALD 1-100: .75X TO 2X BASIC
1-100 ODDS 1:4 MINI
1-100 PRINT RUN 99 SERIAL #'d SETS
*EMERALD 101-112: .5X TO 1.2X BASIC AU
*EMERALD 113-120: .5X TO 1.2X BASIC AU
101-120 AU ODDS 1:21 MINI
101-120 AU PRINT RUN 75 SERIAL #'d SETS

2006 Topps Triple Threads Gold

*GOLD 1-100: 1.25X TO 3X BASIC
1-100 ODDS 1:7 MINI
1-100 PRINT RUN 50 SERIAL #'d SETS
*GOLD 101-112: .6X TO 1.5X BASIC AU
*GOLD 113-120: .6X TO 1.5X BASIC AU
101-120 AU ODDS 1:32 MINI
101-120 AU PRINT RUN 50 SERIAL #'d SETS
116 Hong-Chih Kuo AU J-J 75.00 150.00

2006 Topps Triple Threads Sapphire

*SAPHIRE 1-100: 2X TO 5X BASIC
1-100 ODDS 1:13 MINI
1-100 PRINT RUN 25 SERIAL #'d SETS
101-120 AU ODDS 1:63 MINI
101-120 AU PRINT RUN 25 SERIAL #'d SETS
101-120 NO PRICING DUE TO SCARCITY

2006 Topps Triple Threads Sepia

*SEPIA 1-100: .6X TO 1.5X BASIC
1-100 ODDS 1:3 MINI
1-100 PRINT RUN 150 SERIAL #'d SETS
*SEPIA 101-112: .4X TO 1X BASIC AU
*SEPIA 113-120: .4X TO 1X BASIC AU
101-120 AU ODDS 1:13 MINI
101-120 AU PRINT RUN 125 SERIAL #'d SETS

2006 Topps Triple Threads Heroes

COMM.T.WILL (1-5/42;1-5/47) 5.00 12.00
COMMON MANTLE (1-10) 6.00 15.00
COMMON F.ROB (1-10) .75 2.00
COMMON YAZ (1-10) 3.00 8.00
ONE BASIC OR DIE CUT HEROES PER PACK
*DIE CUT: 1X TO 2.5X BASIC
DIE CUT ODDS 1:16 MINI
DIE CUT PRINT RUN 50 SERIAL #'d SETS

2006 Topps Triple Threads Relic

STATED ODDS 1:7 MINI
STATED PRINT RUN 18 SERIAL #'d SETS
*GOLD: .5X TO 1.2X BASIC
GOLD ODDS 1:15 MINI
GOLD PRINT RUN 9 SERIAL #'d SETS
PLATINUM ODDS 1:43 MINI
PLATINUM PRINT RUN 3 SERIAL #'d SETS
NO PLATINUM PRICING DUE TO SCARCITY
1 Adam Dunn RBI 10.00 25.00
2 Adam Dunn CIN 10.00 25.00
3 Adrian Beltre LAD 10.00 25.00
4 Adrian Beltre SEA 10.00 25.00
5 Al Kaline GG 15.00 40.00
6 Al Kaline HOF 15.00 40.00
7 Al Kaline DET 15.00 40.00
8 Albert Pujols STL 30.00 60.00
9 Albert Pujols 300 30.00 60.00
10 Albert Pujols MVP 30.00 60.00
11 Albert Pujols ROY 30.00 60.00
12 Alex Rodriguez NYY 15.00 40.00
13 Alex Rodriguez #13 15.00 40.00
14 Alex Rodriguez MVP 15.00 40.00
15 Alex Rodriguez 400 15.00 40.00
16 Alex Rodriguez SEA 15.00 40.00
17 Alex Rodriguez 40/40 15.00 40.00
18 Alex Rodriguez TEX 15.00 40.00
19 Alex Rodriguez GG 15.00 40.00
20 Alex Rodriguez MVP 15.00 40.00
21 Alfonso Soriano NYY 10.00 25.00
22 Alfonso Soriano TEX 10.00 25.00
23 Andruw Jones GG 15.00 40.00
24 Andruw Jones ATL 15.00 40.00
25 Andy Pettitte ACE 15.00 40.00
26 Andy Pettitte HOU 15.00 40.00
27 Aramis Ramirez CHC 10.00 25.00
28 B.J. Upton MLB 10.00 25.00
29 Barry Bonds 40/40 40.00 80.00
30 Barry Bonds MVP 40.00 80.00
31 Barry Bonds PIT 40.00 80.00
32 Barry Bonds 700 40.00 80.00
33 Barry Bonds SFG 40.00 80.00
34 Barry Bonds 700 40.00 80.00
35 Barry Bonds #25 40.00 80.00
36 Barry Bonds 7MVP 40.00 80.00
37 Barry Zito OAK 10.00 25.00
38 Barry Zito CY 10.00 25.00
39 Ben Sheets USA 10.00 25.00
40 Bill Mazeroski PIT 15.00 40.00
41 Bob Feller HOF 15.00 40.00
42 Bobby Abreu PHI 10.00 25.00
43 Bobby Cox ATL 10.00 25.00
44 Bobby Doerr BOS 10.00 25.00
45 Brad Lidge HOU 10.00 25.00
46 Brian Giles SDP 10.00 25.00
47 Brian Roberts BAL 10.00 25.00
48 Cal Ripken CAL 40.00 80.00
49 Cal Ripken MVP 40.00 80.00
50 Cal Ripken BAL 40.00 80.00
51 Carl Yastrzemski YAZ 30.00 60.00
52 Carl Yastrzemski MVP 30.00 60.00
53 Carl Yastrzemski BOS 30.00 60.00
54 Carlos Beltran ROY 10.00 25.00
55 Carlos Beltran NYM 10.00 25.00
56 Carlos Delgado RBI 10.00 25.00
57 Carlton Fisk BOS 15.00 40.00
58 Carlton Fisk HOF 15.00 40.00
59 Carlton Fisk CWS 15.00 40.00
60 Chipper Jones MVP 30.00 60.00
61 Chipper Jones 300 30.00 60.00
62 Chipper Jones ATL 30.00 60.00
63 Chris Carpenter STL 15.00 40.00
64 Craig Biggio HBP 15.00 40.00
65 Craig Biggio HOU 15.00 40.00
66 Curt Schilling WS 10.00 25.00
67 Curt Schilling ACE 10.00 25.00
68 Curt Schilling WS 15.00 40.00
69 Curt Schilling BOS 15.00 40.00
70 Dale Murphy ATL 15.00 40.00
71 Darryl Strawberry NYM 10.00 25.00
72 Darryl Strawberry ROY 10.00 25.00
73 Dave Winfield GG 10.00 25.00
74 Dave Winfield NYY 10.00 25.00
75 Dave Winfield HOF 10.00 25.00
76 David Ortiz RBI 15.00 40.00
77 David Ortiz BOS 15.00 40.00
78 David Ortiz MIN 10.00 25.00
79 Derrek Lee CHC 15.00 40.00
80 Don Mattingly NYY 30.00 60.00
81 Don Mattingly #23 30.00 60.00
82 Don Mattingly MVP 30.00 60.00
83 Dontrelle Willis ROY 10.00 25.00
84 Dontrelle Willis FLA 10.00 25.00
85 Duke Snider HOF 15.00 40.00
86 Dwight Gooden Dr.K 10.00 25.00
87 Dwight Gooden ROY 10.00 25.00
88 Eric Chavez OAK 10.00 25.00
89 Ernie Banks CHC 20.00 50.00
90 Ernie Banks 2MVP 20.00 50.00
91 Ernie Banks 512 20.00 50.00
92 Frank Robinson 586 15.00 40.00
93 Frank Robinson MVP 15.00 40.00
94 Frankie Frisch HOF 20.00 50.00
95 Gary Carter NYM 10.00 25.00
96 Gary Sheffield NYY 10.00 25.00
97 Gary Sheffield RBI 10.00 25.00
98 George Brett KC5 40.00 80.00
99 George Brett MVP 40.00 80.00
100 Greg Maddux CHC 40.00 80.00
101 Hank Blalock TEX 10.00 25.00
102 Hank Greenberg HOF 60.00 120.00
103 Hank Greenberg DET 60.00 120.00
104 Hideki Matsui NYY 40.00 80.00
105 Hideki Matsui MLB 40.00 80.00
106 Hideki Matsui RBI 40.00 80.00
107 Ichiro Suzuki SEA 60.00 120.00
108 Ichiro Suzuki ROY 60.00 120.00
109 Ichiro Suzuki 262 60.00 120.00
110 Ivan Rodriguez GG 10.00 25.00
111 Ivan Rodriguez DET 10.00 25.00
112 Ivan Rodriguez FLA 10.00 25.00
113 Ivan Rodriguez TEX 10.00 25.00
114 Jake Peavy SDP 10.00 25.00
115 Javy Lopez BAL 10.00 25.00
116 Jeff Bagwell HOU 15.00 40.00
117 Jim Edmonds STL 10.00 25.00
118 Jim Thome PHI 15.00 40.00
119 Joe Mauer MIN 10.00 25.00
120 Joe Torre STL 10.00 25.00
121 Johan Santana CY 15.00 40.00
122 Johan Santana MIN 15.00 40.00
123 Johnny Bench ROY 30.00 60.00
124 Johnny Bench CIN 30.00 60.00
125 Johnny Damon BOS 15.00 40.00
126 Jon Garland WS 10.00 25.00
127 Jon Garland CWS 10.00 25.00
128 Jorge Posada NYY 8.00 20.00
129 Jorge Posada RBI 8.00 20.00
130 Jose Canseco ROY 40.00 80.00
131 Jose Reyes NYM 10.00 25.00
132 Juan Marichal SFG 10.00 25.00
133 Kerry Wood ROY 10.00 25.00
134 Kerry Wood CHC 10.00 25.00
135 Lance Berkman MLB 10.00 25.00
136 Lance Berkman HOU 10.00 25.00
137 Lloyd Waner HOF 40.00 80.00
138 Lloyd Waner PIT 40.00 80.00
139 Lou Brock HOF 15.00 40.00
140 Manny Ramirez RBI 15.00 40.00
141 Manny Ramirez BOS 15.00 40.00
142 Mariano Rivera NYY 30.00 60.00
143 Mariano Rivera SAV 30.00 60.00
144 Mark Buehrle CWS 10.00 25.00
145 Mark Mulder OAK 10.00 25.00
146 Mark Mulder STL 10.00 25.00
147 Mark Prior CHC 10.00 25.00
148 Mark Teixeira TEX 15.00 40.00
149 Michael Young TEX 10.00 25.00
150 Michael Young BAT 10.00 25.00
151 Mickey Mantle NYY 200.00 350.00
152 Mickey Mantle 536 200.00 350.00
153 Mickey Mantle HOF 200.00 350.00
154 Mickey Mantle NY7 200.00 350.00
155 Mickey Mantle 3MVP 200.00 350.00
156 Miguel Cabrera FLA 15.00 40.00
157 Miguel Tejada #10 10.00 25.00
158 Miguel Tejada RBI 10.00 25.00
159 Miguel Tejada BAL 10.00 25.00
160 Miguel Tejada MVP 10.00 25.00
161 Mike Mussina NYY 15.00 40.00
162 Mike Mussina ACE 15.00 40.00
163 Mike Piazza LAD 40.00 80.00
164 Mike Piazza NYM 40.00 80.00
165 Mike Piazza #31 30.00 60.00
166 Mike Schmidt 548 12.50 30.00
167 Mike Schmidt HOF 12.50 30.00
168 Mike Schmidt MVP 12.50 30.00
169 Monte Irvin HOF 15.00 40.00
170 Morgan Ensberg HOU 10.00 25.00
171 Nolan Ryan HOF 20.00 50.00
172 Nolan Ryan HOU 20.00 50.00
173 Nolan Ryan TEX 20.00 50.00
174 Nolan Ryan 324 20.00 50.00
175 Wade Boggs WS 15.00 40.00
176 Ozzie Smith GG 20.00 50.00
177 Ozzie Smith HOF 20.00 50.00
178 Pat Burrell PHI 10.00 25.00
179 Paul Konerko WS 10.00 25.00
180 Paul Konerko RBI 10.00 25.00

181 Paul Konerko CWS 10.00 25.00
182 Paul Molitor HOF 10.00 25.00
183 Pedro Martinez 3CY 15.00 40.00
184 Pedro Martinez NYM 15.00 40.00
185 Pedro Martinez ACE 15.00 40.00
186 Randy Johnson TC 15.00 40.00
187 Randy Johnson 5CY 15.00 40.00
188 Reggie Jackson OCT 20.00 50.00
189 Reggie Jackson 563 20.00 50.00
190 Rickey Henderson NYY 30.00 60.00
191 Rickey Henderson OAK 30.00 60.00
192 Rickey Henderson MVP 30.00 60.00
193 Rickey Henderson 130 30.00 60.00
194 Rickie Weeks MLB 10.00 25.00
195 Rickie Weeks MIL 10.00 25.00
196 Roberto Clemente 3000 100.00 175.00
197 Roberto Clemente MVP 100.00 175.00
198 Robin Yount 2MVP 30.00 60.00
199 Rod Carew ROY 15.00 40.00
200 Roger Clemens 7CY 30.00 60.00
201 Roger Clemens CY 30.00 60.00
202 Roger Clemens ERA 30.00 60.00
203 Roger Clemens HOU 30.00 60.00
204 Roger Clemens NYY 30.00 60.00
205 Roger Clemens CY 30.00 60.00
206 Roy Halladay CY 10.00 25.00
207 Roy Oswalt 20W 10.00 25.00
208 Roy Oswalt HOU 10.00 25.00
209 Ryne Sandberg HOF 40.00 80.00
210 Ryne Sandberg MVP 40.00 80.00
211 Sammy Sosa 500 30.00 60.00
212 Sammy Sosa BAL 30.00 60.00
213 Sammy Sosa MVP 30.00 60.00
214 Sammy Sosa CHC 30.00 60.00
215 Sammy Sosa 500 30.00 60.00
216 Scott Rolen ROY 15.00 40.00
217 Scott Rolen STL 15.00 40.00
218 Sean Burroughs SDP 10.00 25.00
219 Stan Musial 3MVP 30.00 60.00
220 Steve Carlton PHI 10.00 25.00
221 Steve Carlton 4CY 10.00 25.00
222 Steve Carlton 329 10.00 25.00
223 Steve Garvey MVP 10.00 25.00
224 Tadahito Iguchi CWS 10.00 25.00
225 Ted Williams .406 100.00 200.00
226 Ted Williams 521 100.00 200.00
227 Tim Hudson ATL 10.00 25.00
228 Tim Hudson OAK 10.00 25.00
229 Todd Helton GG 15.00 40.00
230 Todd Helton 300 15.00 40.00
231 Todd Helton COL 15.00 40.00
232 Tom Seaver 311 15.00 40.00
233 Tony Gwynn SDP 30.00 60.00
234 Tony Gwynn 300 30.00 60.00
235 Tony Gwynn 3000 30.00 60.00
236 Torii Hunter GG 10.00 25.00
237 Torii Hunter MIN 10.00 25.00
238 Travis Hafner CLE 10.00 25.00
239 Vladimir Guerrero MVP 20.00 50.00
240 Vladimir Guerrero RBI 20.00 50.00
241 Wade Boggs 3000 15.00 40.00
242 Willie Stargell HOF 15.00 40.00
243 Willie Stargell PIT 15.00 40.00
244 Willie Stargell POP 15.00 40.00
245 Willy Taveras HOU 10.00 25.00

2006 Topps Triple Threads Relic Autograph

STATED ODDS 1:14 MINI
STATED PRINT RUN 18 SERIAL #'d SETS
*GOLD: .5X TO 1.2X BASIC
GOLD ODDS 1:27 MINI
GOLD PRINT RUN 9 SERIAL #'d SETS
PLATINUM ODDS 1:81 MINI
PLATINUM PRINT RUN 3 SERIAL #'d SETS
NO PLATINUM PRICING DUE TO SCARCITY
1 Albert Pujols MVP 300.00 500.00
2 Albert Pujols ROY 300.00 500.00
3 Albert Pujols STL 100.00 200.00
4 Alex Rodriguez MVP 150.00 300.00
5 Alex Rodriguez 40/40 150.00 300.00
6 Alex Rodriguez MVP 150.00 300.00
7 Derrek Lee CHC 25.00 60.00
8 Barry Bonds 700 250.00 400.00
9 Ben Sheets MIL 15.00 40.00
10 Ben Sheets USA 15.00 40.00
11 Brad Lidge HOU 15.00 40.00
12 B.Lidge Pitcher-Ball 15.00 40.00
13 Cal Ripken BAL 100.00 200.00
14 Cal Ripken HIT 100.00 200.00
15 Cal Ripken MVP 100.00 200.00
16 Carl Yastrzemski BOS 60.00 120.00
17 Carl Yastrzemski MVP 60.00 120.00
18 Carl Yastrzemski YAZ 60.00 120.00
19 Chase Utley PHI 25.00 60.00
20 Chase Utley RBI 25.00 60.00
21 C.Wang Chinese 600.00 1000.00
22 Chien-Ming Wang ERA 300.00 500.00
23 Chien-Ming Wang NYY 300.00 500.00
24 C.Wang Pitcher-Ball 300.00 500.00
25 Chris Carpenter CY 60.00 120.00
26 Chris Carpenter STL 60.00 120.00
27 Clint Barmes COL 10.00 25.00
28 Clint Barmes MLB 10.00 25.00
29 Conor Jackson 1ST 25.00 60.00
30 Conor Jackson ARI 25.00 60.00
31 David Ortiz BOS 50.00 100.00
32 Don Mattingly #23 30.00 60.00
33 Don Mattingly MVP 30.00 60.00
34 Don Mattingly NYY 30.00 60.00
35 Duke Snider LAD 15.00 40.00
36 Duke Snider WS 15.00 40.00
37 Ernie Banks CHC 75.00 150.00
38 Frank Robinson MVP 25.00 60.00
39 Frank Robinson CIN 25.00 60.00
40 Frank Robinson TC 25.00 60.00
41 Garrett Atkins 3RD 10.00 25.00
42 Garrett Atkins COL 10.00 25.00
43 Derrek Lee BAT 25.00 60.00
44 Derrek Lee LEE 25.00 60.00
45 Derrek Lee OPS 25.00 60.00
46 J.J. Hardy MIL 10.00 25.00
47 J.J. Hardy SS6 10.00 25.00
48 Jake Peavy ERA 25.00 60.00
49 Jake Peavy SDP 25.00 60.00
50 Jeff Francis COL 10.00 25.00
51 J.Francis Pitcher-Ball 10.00 25.00
52 Joe Mauer MIN 30.00 60.00
53 Joe Mauer RBI 30.00 60.00
54 Joey Devine ATL 15.00 40.00
55 J.Devine Pitcher-Ball 15.00 40.00
56 Johan Santana CY 8.00 20.00
57 Johan Santana ERA 8.00 20.00
58 Johan Santana MIN 8.00 20.00
59 Johan Santana KK 8.00 20.00
60 Johnny Bench CIN 50.00 100.00
61 Johnny Bench MVP 50.00 100.00
62 Johnny Bench ROY 50.00 100.00
63 Johnny Damon BOS 50.00 100.00
64 Jonny Gomes MLB 15.00 40.00
65 Jonny Gomes RBI 15.00 40.00
66 Jose Reyes MLB 20.00 50.00
67 Jose Reyes NYM 20.00 50.00
68 Justin Morneau 1ST 15.00 40.00
69 Justin Morneau MIN 15.00 40.00
70 Lou Brock 938 25.00 60.00
71 Lou Brock 3 Stars 25.00 60.00
72 Lou Brock HOF 25.00 60.00
73 Lou Brock STL 25.00 60.00
74 Manny Ramirez BOS 50.00 100.00
75 Mariano Rivera 0.81 125.00 200.00
76 Mark Prior CHC 15.00 40.00
77 Miguel Cabrera #24 50.00 100.00
78 Miguel Cabrera FLA 50.00 100.00
79 Miguel Cabrera 300 50.00 100.00
80 Miguel Cabrera RBI 50.00 100.00
81 Mike Schmidt HOF 50.00 100.00
82 Mike Schmidt MVP 50.00 100.00
83 Mike Schmidt PHI 50.00 100.00
84 Morgan Ensberg 3 Stars 15.00 40.00
85 Morgan Ensberg HOU 15.00 40.00
86 Nick Swisher OAK 15.00 40.00
87 Nick Swisher RBI 15.00 40.00
88 Nolan Ryan HOF 30.00 60.00
89 Nolan Ryan TEX 30.00 60.00
90 Nolan Ryan 7 NO NO 30.00 60.00
91 Zach Duke PIT 15.00 40.00
92 Zach Duke WIN 15.00 40.00
93 Ozzie Smith GG 50.00 100.00
94 Ozzie Smith HOF 50.00 100.00
95 Ozzie Smith STL 50.00 100.00
96 Pedro Martinez NYM 75.00 150.00
97 Robin Yount HOF 25.00 60.00
98 Robin Yount MIL 25.00 60.00
99 Robin Yount MVP 25.00 60.00
100 Rod Carew BAT 50.00 100.00
101 Rod Carew MIN 50.00 100.00
102 Rod Carew MVP 50.00 100.00
103 Rod Carew ROY 50.00 100.00
104 Roger Clemens CY 125.00 200.00
105 Roger Clemens CY 125.00 200.00
106 Ryan Langerhans ATL 20.00 50.00
107 Ryan Langerhans RBI 20.00 50.00
108 Ryne Sandberg CHC 50.00 100.00
109 Ryne Sandberg HOF 50.00 100.00
110 Ryne Sandberg MVP 50.00 100.00
111 Scott Kazmir ERA 15.00 40.00
112 S.Kazmir Pitcher-Ball 15.00 40.00
113 Stan Musial 3 Stars 60.00 120.00
114 Stan Musial MVP 60.00 120.00
115 Stan Musial STL 60.00 120.00
116 Steve Carlton 329 15.00 40.00
117 Steve Carlton CY 15.00 40.00
118 Steve Carlton PHI 15.00 40.00
119 Steve Garvey LAD 20.00 50.00
120 Steve Garvey MVP 20.00 50.00
121 Tony Gwynn 300 50.00 100.00
122 Tony Gwynn HIT 50.00 100.00
123 Tony Gwynn SDP 50.00 100.00
124 Travis Hafner CLE 15.00 40.00
125 Travis Hafner RBI 15.00 40.00
126 Victor Martinez CLE 15.00 40.00
127 Victor Martinez RBI 15.00 40.00
128 Wade Boggs BAT 25.00 60.00
129 Wade Boggs BOS 25.00 60.00
130 Wade Boggs RBI 25.00 60.00

2006 Topps Triple Threads Relic Combos

STATED ODDS 1:7 MINI
STATED PRINT RUN 18 SERIAL #'d SETS
*GOLD: .5X TO 1.2X BASIC
GOLD ODDS 1:14 MINI
GOLD PRINT RUN 9 SERIAL #'d SETS
PLATINUM ODDS 1:42 MINI
PLATINUM PRINT RUN 3 SERIAL #'d SETS
NO PLATINUM PRICING DUE TO SCARCITY
1 Pujols J/A-Rod PT/Bonds P 60.00 120.00
2 A-Rod J/Bonds J/Pujols J 60.00 120.00
3 Pujols P/A-Rod B/Manny J 15.00 40.00
4 Pujols J/Bonds H/T.Will B 75.00 150.00
5 A-Rod B/Bonds P/Chip J 20.00 50.00
6 A-Rod J/Clem P/Bonds P 60.00 120.00
7 A-Rod J/Vlad H/Ichiro J 50.00 100.00
8 A-Rod B/Musial P/T.Will B 50.00 100.00
9 Andruw H/A.Sor S/Vlad H 15.00 40.00
10 Bonds B/Ichiro J/Clem B 75.00 150.00
11 Bonds B/L.Waner B/Clem B 75.00 150.00
12 Bonds B/Manny S/And BG 30.00 60.00
13 Bonds P/Manny J/T.Will B 50.00 100.00
14 Bonds P/Clem B/Stargell H 75.00 150.00
15 Yaz S/Moli S/Manny S 30.00 60.00
16 Matt J/Moli S/Boggs B 30.00 60.00
17 Matt J/Carew B/Gwy J 30.00 60.00
18 Sheff P/Vlad PT/I-Rod PT 15.00 40.00
19 G'berg B/Musial B/T.Will B 75.00 150.00
20 Ichiro J/Chip PT/Bonds P 50.00 100.00
21 Ichiro J/T.Will B/Clem P 150.00 250.00
22 Morgan H/Moli S/G.Cart H 15.00 40.00
23 Manny J/Vlad B/Clem P 40.00 80.00
24 Piaz BG/Moli BG/Hend BG 30.00 60.00
25 Lajoie B/Musial B/T.Will B 75.00 150.00
26 Moli H/Andruw H/Yount H 20.00 50.00
27 Moli S/Andruw S/A.Sor S 15.00 40.00
28 Reggie PT/Vlad PT/And PT 20.00 50.00
29 Hend S/Boggs S/Gwy S 30.00 60.00
30 Clem B/T.Will B/Gwy B 75.00 150.00
31 Musial B/T.Will B/Gwy B 50.00 100.00
32 T.Will B/Ichiro J/Boggs B 75.00 150.00
33 Pujols J/T.Will B/Mantle J 60.00 120.00
34 Andruw H/Brett H/Chip H 20.00 50.00
35 Madd PT/Ryan B/Carlton P 30.00 60.00
36 Madd PT/Carlton P/Seav P 20.00 50.00
37 Ryan J/Carlton S/Seav B 20.00 50.00
38 Ryan J/Seav H/Roger J 40.00 80.00
39 Roger H/Ryan J/Seav H 40.00 80.00
40 Bonds B/Hend S/Gwy S 30.00 60.00
41 Rip P/Yaz J/Moli J 40.00 80.00
42 Rip P/Brett B/Clem P 60.00 120.00
43 Rip P/Brett B/Gwy S 40.00 80.00
44 Rip J/Moli PT/Hend J 30.00 60.00
45 Rip J/Moli J/Gwy J 30.00 60.00
46 Brett B/Rip P/Carew B 40.00 80.00
47 Brett B/Rip P/Carew PT 40.00 80.00
48 Brett B/Yount J/Carew B 20.00 50.00
49 Brett B/Carew PT/Musial B 30.00 60.00
50 Brett B/Gwy J/Boggs B 30.00 60.00
51 Moli H/Yount J/Boggs J 20.00 50.00
52 P.Waner B/Hend S/Musial P 40.00 80.00
53 P.Waner B/Hend P/Boggs B 25.00 60.00
54 P.Wnr B/Carew B/Boggs B 15.00 40.00
55 Hend J/Musial B/Boggs B 30.00 60.00
56 Clem P/Yount H/Carew B 50.00 100.00
57 Clem P/Yount H/Gwy S 50.00 100.00
58 Clem B/Musial B/Gwy B 50.00 100.00
59 Carew J/Musial P/Gwy J 20.00 50.00
60 Musial P/Gwy J/Boggs PT 20.00 50.00
61 Boggs B/Boggs B/Boggs B 20.00 50.00
62 Bonds B/Mantle B/F.Rob B 100.00 175.00
63 Bonds SU/T.Will B/Mant SU 200.00 350.00
64 Bonds B/F.Rob P/Reggie B 40.00 80.00
65 Bonds P/F.Rob B/Kill J 30.00 60.00
66 F.Rob B/Bonds P/Schmidt J 40.00 80.00
67 F.Rob B/Kill B/Mantle B 100.00 175.00
68 J.Gib B/Bonds P/Mantle PT 200.00 350.00
69 J.Gib B/Bonds J/T.Will B 125.00 200.00
70 Schmidt B/Kill J/Reggie B 30.00 60.00
71 Winfield J/Vlad B/Reggie J 15.00 40.00
72 Carew B/Reggie J/Vlad B 15.00 40.00
73 Andruw S/Chip PT/Franc J 30.00 60.00
74 Cox PT/Andruw S/Chip J 20.00 50.00
75 Chip PT/Madd PT/And PT 15.00 40.00
76 Roberts J/Sosa J/Tejada P 15.00 40.00
77 Brooks B/Rip P/Palm H 40.00 80.00
78 Brooks B/Palm J/F.Rob B 15.00 40.00
79 Rip P/Brooks B/Tejada P 30.00 60.00
80 Rip P/F.Rob B/Sosa J 30.00 60.00
81 F.Rob B/Reggie J/Brooks B 20.00 50.00
82 Palm J/F.Rob B/Reggie J 15.00 40.00
83 Palm P/Reggie J/Sosa J 30.00 60.00
84 Palm P/Sosa B/Tejada P 15.00 40.00
85 Tejada P/Roberts J/Rip P 10.00 25.00
86 Reggie J/F.Rob B/Sosa J 30.00 60.00
87 Doerr B/Yaz S/T.Will B 75.00 150.00
88 Yaz S/Ortiz J/Manny S 30.00 60.00
89 Yaz P/T.Will B/Ortiz J 75.00 150.00
90 Yaz J/T.Will B/Manny S 75.00 150.00
91 Schil J/Ortiz J/Damon J 15.00 40.00
92 Schil PT/Ortiz B/Manny J 15.00 40.00
93 Schil J/Manny B/Damon J 15.00 40.00
94 Ortiz B/Damon P/Manny B 15.00 40.00
95 Damon B/Manny J/T.Will B 40.00 80.00
96 Manny S/Ortiz J/Pedro PT 30.00 60.00
97 Manny J/T.Will B/Ortiz J 30.00 60.00
98 Pedro S/Roger H/Manny S 30.00 60.00
99 Madd J/Randy J/Roger J 20.00 50.00
100 Johan J/Pedro S/Roger J 20.00 50.00
101 Roger J/Roger J/Roger J 50.00 100.00
102 Roger J/Roger J/Roger J 75.00 150.00
103 Randy H/Schil J/Roger H 30.00 60.00
104 D.Lee J/Aramis B/Prior J 15.00 40.00
105 D.Lee J/Ryno B/Sosa J 40.00 80.00
106 Banks P/Ryno B/D.Lee J 40.00 80.00
107 Banks P/Ryno B/Sosa J 40.00 80.00
108 Madd J/Ryno B/Banks P 50.00 100.00
109 Prior J/Wood PT/Madd J 30.00 60.00
110 Sosa J/Banks P/D.Lee J 40.00 80.00
111 F.Rob P/Morgan H/Bench P 20.00 50.00
112 Bench P/F.Rob B/Seav H 20.00 50.00
113 Bench P/Seav H/Morgan J 20.00 50.00
114 Dye P/Pods B/Iguchi J 15.00 40.00
115 Thome B/Koner P/Iguchi B 30.00 60.00
116 Garland P/Pods B/Buehr P 15.00 40.00
117 Garland P/Iguchi J/Buehr P 15.00 40.00
118 Koner J/Sosa B/Fisk P 30.00 60.00
119 Koner P/Iguchi J/Dye P 15.00 40.00
120 Kaline B/I-Rod J/G'berg B 50.00 100.00
121 Madd BG/Johan J/Roger J 30.00 60.00
122 Marichal J/Ryan P/Roger P 30.00 60.00
123 Ryan P/Randy J/Ford B 30.00 60.00
124 Rip J/Ozzie B/Schmidt J 40.00 80.00
125 Schmidt B/Rip P/Ozzie B 40.00 80.00
126 Kaline B/F.Rob P/P.Wnr B 30.00 60.00
127 Kaline B/Kill P/F.Rob B 30.00 60.00
128 Kaline B/Mantle P/Reggie J 100.00 175.00
129 Kaline B/Reggie B/Musial B 40.00 80.00
130 Kaline B/Yount J/P.Waner B 30.00 60.00
131 Bond P/Chip PT/Manny WB 30.00 60.00
132 Feller P/Marichal J/Ryan J 20.00 50.00
133 Feller P/Ford B/Carlton P 15.00 40.00
134 Doerr B/T.Will B/Boggs B 40.00 80.00
135 Brooks B/Ozzie B/Ryno B 30.00 60.00
136 Yaz S/Brett B/Moli S 30.00 60.00
137 Fisk B/Yaz J/Boggs B 20.00 50.00
138 Morgan H/Brett H/Schmidt H 30.00 60.00
139 Berra FG/Fisk B/G.Cart H 20.00 50.00
140 Pettitte J/Ryan P/Lidge J 20.00 50.00
141 Pettitte J/Ryan B/Randy P 20.00 50.00
142 Pettitte J/Ryan P/Roger J 15.00 40.00
143 Pettitte J/Randy P/Lidge J 15.00 40.00
144 Pettitte J/Oswalt J/Roger J 30.00 60.00
145 Lidge J/Oswalt J/Pettitte J 15.00 40.00
146 Bigg PT/Bag H/Berk PT 20.00 50.00
147 Ryan P/Roger J/Randy P 50.00 100.00
148 Roger J/Lidge J/Pettitte J 20.00 50.00
149 Roger J/Randy P/Pettitte J 20.00 50.00
150 Ichiro J/Hideki J/Ichiro J 100.00 175.00
151 Ichiro B/Hideki J/Kaz B 100.00 175.00
152 Ichiro J/Iguchi J/Hideki J 100.00 175.00
153 Gagne PT/Piaz B/Snider P 20.00 50.00
154 Sheff P/Weeks B/Moli J 15.00 40.00
155 Moli P/Sheff P/Yount PT 20.00 50.00
156 Yount B/Moli J/Weeks B 15.00 40.00
157 Kill P/Carew B/Johan J 20.00 50.00
158 Kill B/Torii J/Carew B 20.00 50.00
159 Johan J/Mauer J/Torii J 15.00 40.00
160 Moli P/Carew B/Kill B 30.00 60.00
161 Pujols J/Ichiro J/Bonds P 75.00 150.00
162 A-Rod J/Bonds P/Brett PT 75.00 150.00
163 A-Rod J/Bonds P/Mantle J 125.00 200.00
164 A-Rod J/Ichiro J/Mantle J 75.00 150.00
165 A-Rod B/Reggie B/Berra B 40.00 80.00
166 A-Rod J/T.Will B/Mantle P 100.00 200.00
167 A-Rod J/Berra B/Matt P 60.00 120.00
168 A-Rod S/Bonds B/Matt P 50.00 100.00
169 A-Rod S/Rip P/Tejada P 40.00 80.00
170 Bonds B/Kill J/Reggie B 40.00 80.00
171 Bonds B/Clem P/Stargell B 75.00 150.00
172 Bonds P/A-Rod J/Pujols H 60.00 120.00
173 Bonds P/Rip J/Mantle P 75.00 150.00
174 Bonds P/J.Gib B/Pujols J 75.00 150.00
175 Bonds P/Vlad B/Ichiro J 50.00 100.00
176 Brooks B/Brett B/Schmidt B 30.00 60.00
177 Rip B/Bonds B/Ichiro B 100.00 175.00
178 Rip J/Matt J/Brett B 50.00 100.00
179 Rip P/Brett B/Matt J 50.00 100.00
180 Rip J/Schmidt B/Matt J 50.00 100.00
181 Rip P/Roger J/Matt P 50.00 100.00
182 Chip PT/Murphy B/Matt P 40.00 80.00
183 Matt J/Mantle P/Reggie B 125.00 200.00
184 Brett B/Bench P/Schmidt B 30.00 60.00
185 Brett B/Bench B/Schmidt B 30.00 60.00
186 Ichiro B/Bonds P/Mantle B 150.00 250.00
187 I-Rod P/Vlad B/Tejada P 15.00 40.00
188 I-Rod P/Berra J/Bench P 20.00 50.00
189 I-Rod P/Berra FG/Bench P 20.00 50.00
190 Bench P/Piaz B/Berra P 40.00 80.00
191 Mantle B/Bonds P/T.Will B 50.00 120.00
192 Mantle P/Ichiro J/Clem P 75.00 150.00
193 Mantle J/Clem P/Musial P 125.00 200.00
194 Mantle J/T.Will B/Clem P 100.00 200.00
195 Mantle P/Vlad B/Clem P 60.00 120.00
196 Tejada P/Reggie B/Hend P 20.00 50.00
197 Reggie B/A-Rod J/Berra B 30.00 60.00
198 Clem B/Mantle B/Bonds B 125.00 200.00
199 O'Neil B/J.Gib B/Irvin B 150.00 250.00
200 Beltran J/Delg B/Wright J 20.00 50.00
201 Beltran J/Delg B/Reyes J 15.00 40.00
202 Beltran J/Wright J/Pedro J 20.00 50.00
203 Straw B/Gooden J/G.Cart B 15.00 40.00
204 Wright J/Beltran PT/Piaz J 40.00 80.00
205 Wright B/Piaz PT/Reyes B 40.00 80.00
206 Reyes J/Kaz B/Wright J 15.00 40.00
207 A-Rod J/Matt J/Mantle J 150.00 250.00
208 A-Rod J/Hideki J/Torre P 50.00 100.00
209 A-Rod J/Hideki J/Mantle P 150.00 250.00
210 Matt J/Mantle J/Roger J 75.00 150.00
211 Hideki J/Sheff B/A-Rod J 50.00 100.00
212 Hideki J/Sheff B/Posada J 40.00 80.00
213 Posada J/Roger J/Muss P 30.00 60.00
214 Mantle J/Ford B/Berra FG 150.00 250.00
215 Muss P/Ford B/Roger J 30.00 60.00
216 Roger J/Mantle P/A-Rod J 150.00 250.00
217 Boggs S/Torre P/A.Sor S 15.00 40.00
218 Zito P/Muld PT/Hudson J 15.00 40.00
219 Cans J/Reggie B/Hend S 20.00 50.00
220 Muld P/Tejada P/Hudson P 15.00 40.00
221 Abreu J/Burr B/Thome PT 15.00 40.00
222 Schil H/Schmidt B/Carlton P 20.00 50.00
223 Schmidt B/Burr B/Rolen B 20.00 50.00
224 Bonds B/Clem B/J.Gib B 100.00 175.00
225 P.Waner B/Clem P/L.Wnr B 100.00 200.00
226 Stargell P/Maz B/Clem P 60.00 120.00
227 Pujols P/Beltran B/Willis PT 30.00 60.00
228 Pujols B/Willis PT/Ichiro B 50.00 100.00
229 Rip J/Pujols P/Willis J 40.00 80.00
230 Rip J/Fisk B/Seav P 30.00 60.00
231 Rip P/Carew B/Fisk P 30.00 60.00
232 Rip P/Carew B/Fisk P 30.00 60.00
233 Bag H/Pujols B/Piaz H 30.00 60.00
234 Piaz B/Bag P/Rolen J 30.00 60.00
235 Hend S/Garvey B/Gwy J 30.00 60.00
236 Beltre B/Ichiro J/A-Rod B 50.00 100.00
237 Ichiro J/A-Rod B/Randy H 50.00 100.00
238 Bonds P/J.Mari J/Moises B 40.00 80.00
239 Marichal J/Irvin B/Moises B 15.00 40.00
240 Moises B/Irvin B/Bonds J 30.00 60.00
241 Pujols J/Frisch B/Musial P 50.00 100.00
242 Pujols J/Muld P/Rolen J 15.00 40.00
243 Rolen J/Edm J/Pujols J 40.00 80.00
244 Musial P/Ozzie B/Pujols P 40.00 80.00
245 A-Rod S/I-Rod PT/A.Sor S 20.00 50.00
246 A-Rod J/Teixeira J/A.Sor P 20.00 50.00
247 A-Rod S/Ryan J/A.Sor S 30.00 60.00
248 A.Sor P/Blal J/Teixeira J 15.00 40.00
249 A.Sor S/Blal J/Young J 15.00 40.00
250 Teixeira J/A.Sor S/Young J 15.00 40.00

2006 Topps Triple Threads Relic Combos Autograph

STATED ODDS 1:59 MINI
STATED PRINT RUN 18 SERIAL #'d SETS
*GOLD: .5X TO 1.2X BASIC
GOLD ODDS 1:116 MINI
GOLD PRINT RUN 9 SERIAL #'d SETS
PLATINUM ODDS 1:353 MINI
PLATINUM PRINT RUN 3 SERIAL #'d SETS
NO PLATINUM PRICING DUE TO SCARCITY
1 Pujols J/Bonds J/A-Rod J 400.00 800.00
2 Felix J/A-Rod J/Choo J 100.00 200.00
3 Ryan J/Roger J/Felix J 175.00 350.00
4 Damon B/A-Rod J/Cano P 150.00 300.00
5 Manny J/Yaz J/Ortiz J 100.00 200.00
6 Young J/Rip J/Ozzie S 125.00 250.00
7 Roberts J/Rip J/F.Rob B 100.00 200.00
8 Musial P/Ozzie B/Brock B 100.00 200.00
9 Ozzie S/Musial P/Brock B 100.00 200.00
10 Gwy J/Musial P/Carew PT 100.00 200.00
11 Brooks P/Rip J/Roberts J 100.00 200.00
12 Carew PT/Yount J/Moli J 60.00 120.00
13 D.Lee J/Ryno B/Prior J 50.00 100.00
14 Wang J/Carlton P/Willis PT 125.00 250.00
15 Lidge J/Rivera J/Street J 100.00 200.00
16 Ensb J/Boggs B/Wright J 60.00 120.00
17 Sheets J/Carlton P/Felix J 40.00 80.00
18 V.Mart J/Bench P/Mauer J 75.00 150.00
19 Wright J/Schmidt B/Hill J 40.00 80.00
20 Utley J/Schmidt S/How B 150.00 300.00
21 Felix J/Carlton P/McCar J 40.00 80.00
22 Wright J/Cabrera J/Bay J 50.00 100.00
23 Cano P/Matt J/Wang J 200.00 400.00
24 Morneau B/Matt J/Hafner J 75.00 150.00
25 Garvey B/Matt J/D.John J 30.00 60.00
26 Hafner PT/Cabrera J/Bay J 60.00 120.00
27 Sheets J/Johan J/Peavy J 50.00 100.00
28 Ervin J/Johan J/Sheets B 30.00 60.00
29 Carp J/Johan J/Harden J 40.00 80.00
30 Duke J/Johan J/McCar J 30.00 60.00

2007 Topps Triple Threads

COMP.SET w/o AU's (125) 125.00 200.00
COMMON CARD (1-125) .40 1.00
1-125 STATED PRINT RUN 1350 SER.#'d SETS
COMMON JSY AU 5.00 12.00
126-189 JSY AU ODDS 1:9 MINI
126-189 JSY AU VARIATION ODDS 1:38 MINI
126-189 JSY AU PRINT RUN 99 SER.#'d SETS
TEAM INITIAL DIECUTS ARE VARIATIONS
OVERALL 1-125 PLATE ODDS 1:113 MINI
PLATE PRINT RUN 1 SET PER COLOR
BLACK-CYAN-MAGENTA-YELLOW ISSUED
NO PLATE PRICING DUE TO SCARCITY
1 Alex Rodriguez 1.25 3.00
2 Barry Zito .60 1.50
3 Corey Patterson .40 1.00
4 Roberto Clemente 2.50 6.00
5 David Wright .75 2.00
6 Dontrelle Willis .40 1.00
7 Mickey Mantle 3.00 8.00
8 Adam Dunn .60 1.50
9 Richie Ashburn .60 1.50
10 Ryan Howard .75 2.00
11 Miguel Tejada .60 1.50
12 Ernie Banks 1.00 2.50
13 Ken Griffey Jr. 2.00 5.00
14 Johnny Bench 1.00 2.50
15 Ichiro Suzuki 1.25 3.00
16 Gil Meche .40 1.00
17 Kazuo Matsui .40 1.00
18 Matt Holliday 1.00 2.50
19 Juan Pierre .40 1.00
20 Yogi Berra 1.00 2.50
21 Bill Hall .40 1.00
22 Wade Boggs .60 1.50
23 Jason Bay .60 1.50
24 Troy Glaus .40 1.00
25 Paul Konerko .60 1.50
26 Rod Carew .60 1.50
27 Jay Gibbons .40 1.00
28 Frank Thomas 1.00 2.50
29 Joe Mauer .75 2.00
30 Carlos Beltran .60 1.50
31 Frank Robinson .60 1.50
32 Bobby Abreu .40 1.00
33 Roy Oswalt .60 1.50
34 Edgar Renteria .40 1.00
35 Magglio Ordonez .60 1.50
36 Mike Piazza 1.00 2.50
37 Trevor Hoffman .60 1.50
38 Eddie Mathews 1.00 2.50
39 Albert Pujols 1.25 3.00
40 Dennis Eckersley .60 1.50
41 Andruw Jones .40 1.00
42 Alfonso Soriano .60 1.50
43 Bob Feller .60 1.50
44 J.D. Drew .40 1.00
45 Jason Schmidt .40 1.00
46 Vladimir Guerrero .60 1.50
47 Reggie Jackson .60 1.50
48 Lance Berkman .60 1.50
49 Michael Young .40 1.00
50 Carlton Fisk .60 1.50
51 Brandon Webb .60 1.50
52 Adrian Beltre 1.00 2.50
53 Hideki Matsui 1.00 2.50
54 Bronson Arroyo .40 1.00
55 Tony Gwynn 1.00 2.50
56 Ray Durham .40 1.00
57 Garrett Atkins .40 1.00
58 Nolan Ryan 3.00 8.00
59 Daisuke Matsuzaka RC 1.50 4.00
60 Todd Helton .60 1.50
61 Carl Crawford .60 1.50
62 Jake Peavy .40 1.00
63 Rafael Furcal .40 1.00
64 Joe Morgan .60 1.50
65 Greg Maddux 1.25 3.00
66 Luis Aparicio .60 1.50
67 Derrek Lee .40 1.00
68 Johnny Damon .60 1.50
69 Mike Lowell .40 1.00
70 Roger Maris 1.00 2.50
71 Vernon Wells .40 1.00
72 Monte Irvin .60 1.50
73 Jermaine Dye .40 1.00
74 Miguel Cabrera 1.00 2.50
75 Barry Bonds 1.50 4.00
76 Stan Musial 1.50 4.00
77 Derek Lowe .40 1.00
78 Don Mattingly 2.00 5.00
79 Lyle Overbay .40 1.00
80 Chien-Ming Wang .60 1.50
81 Carlos Zambrano .60 1.50
82 Kei Igawa RC 1.00 2.50
83 Cole Hamels .75 2.00
84 Gary Sheffield .40 1.00
85 Nick Johnson .40 1.00
86 Brooks Robinson .60 1.50
87 Curt Schilling .60 1.50
88 Ryne Sandberg 2.00 5.00
89 Mike Cameron .40 1.00
90 Mike Schmidt 1.50 4.00
91 Chris Carpenter .60 1.50
92 Scott Rolen .60 1.50
93 Rocco Baldelli .40 1.00
94 C.C. Sabathia .60 1.50
95 Jeff Francis .40 1.00
96 Ozzie Smith 1.25 3.00
97 Aramis Ramirez .40 1.00
98 Aaron Harang .40 1.00
99 Duke Snider .60 1.50
100 David Ortiz 1.00 2.50
101 Raul Ibanez .60 1.50
102 Bruce Sutter .60 1.50
103 Gary Matthews .40 1.00
104 Chipper Jones 1.00 2.50
105 Craig Biggio .60 1.50
106 Roy Halladay .60 1.50
107 Hoyt Wilhelm .60 1.50
108 Manny Ramirez 1.00 2.50
109 Randy Johnson 1.00 2.50
110 Carl Yastrzemski 1.50 4.00
111 Mark Teixeira .60 1.50
112 Derek Jeter 2.50 6.00
113 Stephen Drew .40 1.00
114 Darryl Strawberry .40 1.00
115 Travis Hafner .40 1.00
116 Torii Hunter .40 1.00
117 Jim Edmonds .60 1.50
118 John Smoltz 1.00 2.50
119 Bo Jackson 1.00 2.50
120 Roger Clemens 1.25 3.00
121 Pedro Martinez .60 1.50
122 Rickey Henderson 1.00 2.50
123 Ivan Rodriguez .60 1.50
124 Robin Yount 1.00 2.50
125 Johan Santana .60 1.50
126a Robinson Cano Jsy AU 15.00 40.00
126b Robinson Cano Jsy AU 15.00 40.00
127a Jose Reyes Jsy AU 12.50 30.00
127b Jose Reyes Jsy AU 12.50 30.00
128a Justin Morneau Jsy AU 8.00 20.00
128b Justin Morneau Jsy AU 10.00 25.00
129a Curtis Granderson Jsy AU 6.00 15.00
129b Curtis Granderson Jsy AU 6.00 15.00
130a Justin Verlander Jsy AU 20.00 50.00
130b Justin Verlander Jsy AU 20.00 50.00
131 Prince Fielder Jsy AU 8.00 20.00
132a Ryan Zimmerman Jsy AU 10.00 25.00
132b Ryan Zimmerman Jsy AU 10.00 25.00
133 Mike Napoli Jsy AU 10.00 25.00
134 Melky Cabrera Jsy AU 10.00 25.00
135 Jonathan Papelbon Jsy AU 15.00 40.00
136a Nick Markakis Jsy AU 8.00 20.00
136b Nick Markakis Jsy AU BAL 8.00 20.00
137 B.J. Upton Jsy AU 12.50 30.00
138a Joel Zumaya Jsy AU 10.00 25.00
138b Joel Zumaya Jsy AU 10.00 25.00
140 Nick Swisher Jsy AU 10.00 25.00
141 Andre Ethier Jsy AU 10.00 25.00
142a Jered Weaver Jsy AU 8.00 20.00
142b Jered Weaver Jsy AU LAA 8.00 20.00
143 Matt Cain Jsy AU 8.00 20.00
144 Lastings Milledge Jsy AU 8.00 20.00
145 Brian McCann Jsy AU 8.00 20.00
146 Shin-Soo Choo Jsy AU 6.00 15.00
147a Dan Uggla Jsy AU 8.00 20.00
147b Dan Uggla Jsy AU 8.00 20.00
148 Hanley Ramirez Jsy AU 10.00 25.00
149 Russell Martin Jsy AU 5.00 12.00
150 Francisco Liriano Jsy AU 6.00 15.00
151 Anthony Reyes Jsy AU 5.00 12.00
152 Josh Barfield Jsy AU 6.00 15.00
153 Anibal Sanchez Jsy AU 5.00 12.00
154 Jeremy Hermida Jsy AU 6.00 15.00
155 Kendry Morales Jsy AU 6.00 15.00
156 Matt Kemp Jsy AU 20.00 50.00
157 Freddy Sanchez Jsy AU 6.00 15.00
158 Howie Kendrick Jsy AU 8.00 20.00
159 Scott Thorman Jsy AU 8.00 20.00
160 Franklin Gutierrez Bat AU 6.00 15.00
161 Jason Bartlett Jsy AU 6.00 15.00
162 Chris Duncan Jsy AU 6.00 15.00
163 Maicer Izturis Jsy AU 5.00 12.00
164 Jason Botts Jsy AU 5.00 12.00
165 Tony Gwynn Jr. Jsy AU 15.00 40.00
166 Jorge Cantu Jsy AU 5.00 12.00
167 Adam Jones Jsy AU 10.00 25.00
168 Edinson Volquez Jsy AU 8.00 20.00
169 Joey Gathright Jsy AU 5.00 12.00
170 Carlos Marmol Jsy AU 8.00 20.00
171 Ben Zobrist Jsy AU 10.00 25.00
172 Josh Willingham Jsy AU 5.00 12.00
173 Brad Thompson Jsy AU 10.00 25.00
174a Chris Ray Jsy AU 6.00 15.00
174b Ervin Santana Jsy AU 6.00 15.00
175 Ronny Paulino Jsy AU 5.00 12.00
176 Tyler Johnson Jsy AU 5.00 12.00
177 J.J. Hardy Jsy AU 5.00 12.00
178 Adrian Gonzalez Jsy AU 8.00 20.00
179 Scott Kazmir Jsy AU 6.00 15.00
180 Juan Morillo Jsy AU (RC) 5.00 12.00
181a Shawn Riggans JSY AU (RC) 5.00 12.00
181b Shawn Riggans JSY AU (RC) 5.00 12.00
182 Brian Stokes JSY AU (RC) 5.00 12.00
183 Delmon Young JSY AU (RC) 5.00 12.00
184a Troy Tulowitzki JSY AU (RC) 10.00 25.00
184b Troy Tulowitzki JSY AU (RC) 10.00 25.00
185 Adam Lind JSY AU (RC) 6.00 15.00
186 David Murphy JSY AU (RC) 6.00 15.00
187a Philip Humber JSY AU (RC) 6.00 15.00
187b Philip Humber JSY AU (RC) 6.00 15.00
188a Andrew Miller JSY AU RC 6.00 15.00
188b Andrew Miller JSY AU RC 6.00 15.00
189a Glen Perkins JSY AU (RC) 5.00 12.00
189b Glen Perkins JSY AU (RC) 5.00 12.00

2007 Topps Triple Threads Emerald

*EMERALD 1-125: .75X TO 2X BASIC
1-125 ODDS 1:2 MINI
1-125 PRINT RUN 239 SERIAL #'d SETS
*EMERALD AUTO: .5X TO 1.2X BASIC AU
*EMERLD VAR AUTO: .5X TO 1.2X BAS.AU VAR
126-189 AU ODDS 1:18 MINI
126-189 AU VARIATION ODDS 1:75 MINI
126-189 AU PRINT RUN 50 SERIAL #'d SETS
TEAM INITIAL DIECUTS ARE VARIATIONS

2007 Topps Triple Threads Gold

*GOLD 1-125: 1.25X TO 3X BASIC
1-125 ODDS 1:5 MINI
1-125 PRINT RUN 99 SERIAL #'d SETS
*GOLD AUTO: .75X TO 2X BASIC AU
*GOLD VAR AUTO: .75X TO 2X BASIC AU VAR
126-189 AU ODDS 1:35 MINI
126-189 AU VARIATION ODDS 1:149 MINI
126-189 AU PRINT RUN 25 SERIAL #'d SETS
TEAM INITIAL DIECUTS ARE VARIATIONS

2007 Topps Triple Threads Sapphire

*SAPPHIRE 1-125: 3X TO 8X BASIC
1-125 ODDS 1:19 MINI
1-125 PRINT RUN 25 SERIAL #'d SETS
126-189 JSY AU ODDS 1:88 MINI
126-189 JSY AU VAR.ODDS 1:372 MINI
126-189 AU PRINT RUN 10 SERIAL #'d SETS
TEAM INITIAL DIECUTS ARE VARIATIONS
NO SAPPHIRE JSY AUTO PRICING AVAILABLE

2007 Topps Triple Threads Sepia

*SEPIA 1-125: .5X TO 1.2X BASIC
1-125 ODDS XXX MINI
1-125 PRINT RUN 559 SERIAL #'d SETS
*SEPIA AUTO: .5X TO 1.2X BASIC AU
*SEPIA VAR AUTO: .5X TO 1.2X BASIC AU VAR
126-189 AU ODDS 1:12 MINI
126-189 AU VAR.ODDS 1:50 MINI
126-189 AU PRINT RUN 75 SERIAL #'d SETS
TEAM INITIAL DIECUTS ARE VARIATIONS

2007 Topps Triple Threads Relics

STATED ODDS 1:11 MINI
STATED PRINT RUN 36 SER.#'d SETS
EMERALD ODDS 1:21 MINI
GOLD ODDS 1:42 MINI
GOLD PRINT RUN 9 SER.#'d SETS
PLATINUM ODDS 1:373 MINI
PLATINUM PRINT RUN 1 SER.#'d SET
NO PLATINUM PRICING DUE TO SCARCITY
SAPPHIRE ODDS 1:125 MINI
SAPPHIRE PRINT RUN 3 SER.#'d SETS
NO SAPPHIRE PRICING DUE TO SCARCITY
*SEPIA: .4X TO 1X BASIC
SEPIA ODDS 1:14 MINI
SEPIA PRINT RUN 27 SER.#'d SETS
ALL DC VARIATIONS PRICED EQUALLY
1 Carl Yastrzemski 12.50 30.00
2 Carl Yastrzemski 12.50 30.00
3 Carl Yastrzemski 12.50 30.00
4 Roberto Clemente 75.00 150.00
5 Roberto Clemente 75.00 150.00
6 Roberto Clemente 75.00 150.00
7 Roberto Clemente 75.00 150.00
8 Roberto Clemente 75.00 150.00
9 Roberto Clemente 75.00 150.00
10 Alex Rodriguez 12.50 30.00
11 Alex Rodriguez 12.50 30.00
12 Alex Rodriguez 12.50 30.00
13 Alex Rodriguez 12.50 30.00
14 Alex Rodriguez 12.50 30.00
15 Alex Rodriguez 12.50 30.00
16 Ryan Howard 20.00 50.00
17 Ryan Howard 20.00 50.00
18 Ryan Howard 20.00 50.00
19 David Wright 10.00 25.00
20 David Wright 10.00 25.00
21 David Wright 10.00 25.00
22 Chien-Ming Wang 75.00 150.00
23 Chien-Ming Wang 75.00 150.00
24 Chien-Ming Wang 75.00 150.00
25 Ichiro Suzuki 60.00 120.00
26 Ichiro Suzuki 60.00 120.00
27 Ichiro Suzuki 60.00 120.00
28 Hideki Matsui 10.00 25.00
29 Hideki Matsui 10.00 25.00
30 Hideki Matsui 10.00 25.00
31 Luis Aparicio 8.00 20.00
32 Luis Aparicio 8.00 20.00
33 Luis Aparicio 8.00 20.00
34 Joe DiMaggio 40.00 80.00
35 Joe DiMaggio 40.00 80.00
36 Joe DiMaggio 40.00 80.00
37 Ted Williams 40.00 80.00
38 Ted Williams 40.00 80.00
39 Ted Williams 40.00 80.00
40 Mickey Mantle 75.00 150.00
41 Mickey Mantle 75.00 150.00
42 Mickey Mantle 75.00 150.00
43 Mickey Mantle 75.00 150.00
44 Mickey Mantle 75.00 150.00
45 Mickey Mantle 75.00 150.00
46 Mickey Mantle 75.00 150.00
47 Mickey Mantle 75.00 150.00
48 Mickey Mantle 75.00 150.00
49 David Ortiz 10.00 25.00
50 David Ortiz 10.00 25.00
51 David Ortiz 10.00 25.00
52 Albert Pujols 20.00 50.00
53 Albert Pujols 20.00 50.00
54 Albert Pujols 20.00 50.00
55 Justin Morneau 10.00 25.00
56 Justin Morneau 10.00 25.00
57 Justin Morneau 10.00 25.00
58 Nolan Ryan 25.00 60.00
59 Nolan Ryan 25.00 60.00
60 Nolan Ryan 25.00 60.00
61 Nolan Ryan 25.00 60.00
62 Nolan Ryan 25.00 60.00
63 Nolan Ryan 25.00 60.00
64 Manny Ramirez 10.00 25.00
65 Manny Ramirez 10.00 25.00
66 Manny Ramirez 10.00 25.00
67 Roger Maris 30.00 60.00
68 Roger Maris 30.00 60.00
69 Roger Maris 30.00 60.00
70 Daisuke Matsuzaka 10.00 25.00
71 Daisuke Matsuzaka 10.00 25.00
72 Daisuke Matsuzaka 10.00 25.00
73 Brian Cashman 8.00 20.00
74 Brian Cashman 8.00 20.00
75 Brian Cashman 8.00 20.00
76 Ernie Banks 20.00 50.00
77 Ernie Banks 20.00 50.00
78 Ernie Banks 20.00 50.00
79 Stan Musial 25.00 60.00
80 Stan Musial 25.00 60.00
81 Stan Musial 25.00 60.00
82 Duke Snider 12.50 30.00
83 Duke Snider 12.50 30.00
84 Duke Snider 12.50 30.00
85 Yogi Berra 20.00 50.00
86 Yogi Berra 20.00 50.00
87 Yogi Berra 20.00 50.00
88 Harmon Killebrew 15.00 40.00
89 Harmon Killebrew 15.00 40.00
90 Harmon Killebrew 15.00 40.00
91 Joe Mauer 8.00 20.00
92 Joe Mauer 8.00 20.00
93 Joe Mauer 8.00 20.00

94 Alfonso Soriano 10.00 25.00
95 Alfonso Soriano 10.00 25.00
96 Alfonso Soriano 10.00 25.00
97 Reggie Jackson 15.00 40.00
98 Reggie Jackson 15.00 40.00
99 Reggie Jackson 15.00 40.00
100 Reggie Jackson 15.00 40.00
101 Reggie Jackson 15.00 40.00
102 Reggie Jackson 15.00 40.00
103 Vladimir Guerrero 10.00 25.00
104 Vladimir Guerrero 10.00 25.00
105 Vladimir Guerrero 10.00 25.00
106 Pedro Martinez 10.00 25.00
107 Pedro Martinez 10.00 25.00
108 Pedro Martinez 10.00 25.00
109 Roger Clemens 12.50 30.00
110 Roger Clemens 12.50 30.00
111 Roger Clemens 12.50 30.00
112 Randy Johnson 10.00 25.00
113 Randy Johnson 10.00 25.00
114 Randy Johnson 10.00 25.00
115 Don Mattingly 15.00 40.00
116 Don Mattingly 15.00 40.00
117 Don Mattingly 15.00 40.00
118 Bill Dickey 20.00 50.00
119 Bill Dickey 20.00 50.00
120 Bill Dickey 20.00 50.00
121a Barry Bonds 30.00 60.00
121b Bruce Sutter 10.00 25.00
122a Barry Bonds 30.00 60.00
122b Bruce Sutter 10.00 25.00
123a Barry Bonds 30.00 60.00
123b Bruce Sutter 10.00 25.00
124 John F. Kennedy 150.00 250.00
125 John F. Kennedy 150.00 250.00
126 John F. Kennedy 150.00 250.00
127 Johnny Bench 12.50 30.00
128 Johnny Bench 12.50 30.00
129 Johnny Bench 12.50 30.00
130 Mark Teixeira 12.50 30.00
131 Mark Teixeira 12.50 30.00
132 Mark Teixeira 12.50 30.00
133 Johan Santana 10.00 25.00
134 Johan Santana 10.00 25.00
135 Johan Santana 10.00 25.00
136 Alex Rodriguez 12.50 30.00
137 Alex Rodriguez 12.50 30.00
138 Alex Rodriguez 12.50 30.00
139 Brooks Robinson 12.50 30.00
140 Brooks Robinson 12.50 30.00
141 Brooks Robinson 12.50 30.00
142 Rickey Henderson 12.50 30.00
143 Rickey Henderson 12.50 30.00
144 Rickey Henderson 12.50 30.00
145 Ozzie Smith 12.50 30.00
146 Ozzie Smith 12.50 30.00
147 Ozzie Smith 12.50 30.00
148 Chipper Jones 12.50 30.00
149 Chipper Jones 12.50 30.00
150 Chipper Jones 12.50 30.00

2007 Topps Triple Threads Relics Emerald

*EMERALD: .5X TO 1.2X BASIC
STATED ODDS 1:21 MINI
STATED PRINT RUN 18 SER.#'d SETS
ALL DC VARIATIONS PRICED EQUALLY
4 Roberto Clemente 75.00 150.00
40 Mickey Mantle 75.00 150.00
121a Barry Bonds 30.00 60.00
124 John F. Kennedy 150.00 250.00

2007 Topps Triple Threads Relics Gold

*GOLD: .6X TO 1.5X BASIC
STATED ODDS 1:42 MINI
STATED PRINT RUN 9 SER.#'d SETS
ALL DC VARIATIONS PRICED EQUALLY
25 Ichiro Suzuki 150.00 300.00
79 Stan Musial 40.00 80.00
118 Bill Dickey 30.00 60.00
121a Barry Bonds 30.00 60.00
124 John F. Kennedy 150.00 250.00
145 Ozzie Smith 15.00 40.00

2007 Topps Triple Threads Relics Autographs

STATED ODDS 1:18 MINI
STATED PRINT RUN 18 SER.#'d SETS
*GOLD: .5X TO 1.2X BASIC
GOLD ODDS 1:34 MINI
GOLD PRINT RUN 9 SER.#'d SETS
PLATINUM ODDS 1:472 MINI
PLATINUM PRINT RUN 1 SER.#'d SET
NO PLATINUM PRICING DUE TO SCARCITY
SAPPHIRE ODDS 1:104 MINI
SAPPHIRE PRINT RUN 3 SER.#'d SETS
NO SAPPHIRE PRICING DUE TO SCARCITY
WHITE WHALE ODDS 1:118 MINI
WHITE WHALE PRINT RUN 1 SER.#'d SET
NO WHITE WHALE PRICING DUE TO SCARCITY
ALL DC VARIATIONS PRICED EQUALLY
1 Alex Rodriguez 125.00 250.00
2 Alex Rodriguez 125.00 250.00
3 Alex Rodriguez 125.00 250.00
4 Chien-Ming Wang 30.00 60.00
5 Chien-Ming Wang 30.00 60.00
6 Chien-Ming Wang 30.00 60.00
7 David Ortiz 40.00 50.00
8 David Ortiz 40.00 80.00
9 David Ortiz 40.00 80.00
10 Manny Ramirez 60.00 120.00
11 Manny Ramirez 60.00 120.00
12 Manny Ramirez 60.00 120.00
13 Johnny Damon 30.00 60.00
14 Johnny Damon 30.00 60.00
15 Johnny Damon 30.00 60.00
16 Miguel Tejada 20.00 50.00
17 Miguel Tejada 20.00 50.00
18 Miguel Tejada 20.00 50.00
19 Carl Crawford 20.00 50.00
20 Carl Crawford 20.00 50.00
21 Carl Crawford 20.00 50.00
22 Johan Santana 15.00 40.00
23 Johan Santana 15.00 40.00
24 Johan Santana 15.00 40.00
25 Francisco Liriano 10.00 25.00
26 Francisco Liriano 10.00 25.00
27 Francisco Liriano 10.00 25.00
28 Bob Feller 40.00 80.00
29 Bob Feller 40.00 80.00
30 Bob Feller 40.00 80.00
31 Vladimir Guerrero 20.00 50.00
32 Vladimir Guerrero 20.00 50.00
33 Vladimir Guerrero 20.00 50.00
34 Ernie Banks 50.00 100.00
35 Ernie Banks 50.00 100.00
36 Ernie Banks 50.00 100.00
37 Yogi Berra 60.00 150.00
38 Yogi Berra 60.00 150.00
39 Yogi Berra 60.00 150.00
40 Nolan Ryan 100.00 200.00
41 Nolan Ryan 100.00 200.00
42 Nolan Ryan 100.00 200.00
43 Ozzie Smith 50.00 100.00
44 Ozzie Smith 50.00 100.00
45 Ozzie Smith 50.00 100.00
46 David Wright 20.00 50.00
47 David Wright 20.00 50.00
48 David Wright 20.00 50.00
49 Albert Pujols 200.00 350.00
50 Albert Pujols 200.00 350.00
51 Albert Pujols 200.00 350.00
52 Ryan Howard 20.00 50.00
53 Ryan Howard 20.00 50.00
54 Ryan Howard 20.00 50.00
55 Don Mattingly 50.00 100.00
56 Don Mattingly 50.00 100.00
57 Don Mattingly 50.00 100.00
58 Brooks Robinson 30.00 60.00
59 Brooks Robinson 30.00 60.00
60 Brooks Robinson 30.00 60.00
61 Robin Yount 30.00 60.00
62 Robin Yount 30.00 60.00
63 Robin Yount 30.00 60.00
64 Mike Schmidt 60.00 120.00
65 Mike Schmidt 60.00 120.00
66 Mike Schmidt 60.00 120.00
67 Carl Yastrzemski 50.00 100.00
68 Carl Yastrzemski 50.00 100.00
69 Carl Yastrzemski 50.00 100.00
70 Wade Boggs 40.00 80.00
71 Wade Boggs 40.00 80.00
72 Wade Boggs 40.00 80.00
73 Andre Dawson 30.00 60.00
74 Andre Dawson 30.00 60.00
75 Andre Dawson 30.00 60.00
76 Reggie Jackson 40.00 80.00
77 Reggie Jackson 40.00 80.00
78 Reggie Jackson 40.00 80.00
79 Miguel Cabrera 30.00 60.00
80 Miguel Cabrera 30.00 60.00
81 Miguel Cabrera 30.00 60.00
82 Tom Seaver 40.00 100.00
83 Tom Seaver 40.00 100.00
84 Tom Seaver 40.00 100.00
85 Ralph Kiner 30.00 60.00
86 Ralph Kiner 30.00 60.00
87 Ralph Kiner 30.00 60.00
88 Chipper Jones 50.00 100.00
89 Chipper Jones 50.00 100.00
90 Chipper Jones 50.00 100.00
91 Andruw Jones 10.00 25.00
92 Andruw Jones 10.00 25.00
93 Andruw Jones 10.00 25.00
94 Dontrelle Willis 20.00 50.00
95 Dontrelle Willis 20.00 50.00
96 Dontrelle Willis 20.00 50.00
97 Bob Gibson 30.00 60.00
98 Bob Gibson 30.00 60.00
99 Bob Gibson 30.00 60.00
100 Johnny Bench 40.00 80.00
101 Johnny Bench 40.00 80.00
102 Johnny Bench 40.00 80.00
103 Joe Morgan 20.00 50.00
104 Joe Morgan 20.00 50.00
105 Joe Morgan 20.00 50.00
106 Ryne Sandberg 50.00 100.00
107 Ryne Sandberg 50.00 100.00
108 Ryne Sandberg 50.00 100.00
109 Dwight Gooden 20.00 50.00
110 Dwight Gooden 20.00 50.00
111 Dwight Gooden 20.00 50.00
112 Johnny Podres 20.00 50.00
113 Johnny Podres 20.00 50.00
114 Johnny Podres 20.00 50.00
115 Monte Irvin 10.00 25.00
116 Monte Irvin 10.00 25.00
117 Monte Irvin 10.00 25.00
118 Orlando Cepeda 20.00 50.00
119 Orlando Cepeda 20.00 50.00
120 Orlando Cepeda 20.00 50.00
121 Bo Jackson 60.00 120.00
122 Bo Jackson 60.00 120.00
123 Bo Jackson 60.00 120.00
124 Gary Sheffield 20.00 50.00
125 Gary Sheffield 20.00 50.00
126 Gary Sheffield 20.00 50.00
127 Tom Glavine 20.00 50.00
128 Tom Glavine 20.00 50.00
129 Tom Glavine 20.00 50.00
130 Tony LaRussa 20.00 50.00
131 Tony LaRussa 20.00 50.00
132 Tony LaRussa 20.00 50.00
133 Jim Leyland 40.00 80.00
134 Jim Leyland 40.00 80.00
135 Jim Leyland 40.00 80.00
136 Joe Torre 40.00 80.00
137 Joe Torre 40.00 80.00
138 Joe Torre 40.00 80.00
139 Gary Carter 30.00 60.00
140 Gary Carter 30.00 60.00
141 Gary Carter 30.00 60.00
142 Roy Oswalt 20.00 50.00
143 Roy Oswalt 20.00 50.00
144 Roy Oswalt 20.00 50.00
145 Carlos Delgado 20.00 50.00
146 Carlos Delgado 20.00 50.00
147 Carlos Delgado 20.00 50.00
148 Jason Varitek 40.00 80.00
149 Jason Varitek 40.00 80.00
150 Jason Varitek 40.00 80.00
151 Bobby Abreu 20.00 50.00
152 Bobby Abreu 20.00 50.00
153 Bobby Abreu 20.00 50.00
154 Juan Marichal 20.00 50.00
155 Juan Marichal 20.00 50.00
156 Juan Marichal 20.00 50.00
157 Frank Robinson 30.00 60.00
158 Frank Robinson 30.00 60.00
159 Frank Robinson 30.00 60.00
160 Jorge Posada 50.00 100.00
161 Jorge Posada 50.00 100.00
162 Jorge Posada 50.00 100.00
163 Luis Aparicio 20.00 50.00
164 Luis Aparicio 20.00 50.00
165 Luis Aparicio 20.00 50.00
166 Carlton Fisk 30.00 60.00
167 Carlton Fisk 30.00 60.00
168 Carlton Fisk 30.00 60.00
169 Dale Murphy 75.00 150.00
170 Dale Murphy 75.00 150.00
171 Dale Murphy 75.00 150.00
172 Mark Teixeira 20.00 50.00
173 Mark Teixeira 20.00 50.00
174 Mark Teixeira 20.00 50.00
175 Darryl Strawberry 20.00 50.00
176 Darryl Strawberry 20.00 50.00
177 Darryl Strawberry 20.00 50.00
178 Justin Morneau 12.50 30.00
179 Justin Morneau 12.50 30.00
180 Justin Morneau 12.50 30.00

2007 Topps Triple Threads Relics Autographs Gold

*GOLD: .5X TO 1.2X BASIC
STATED ODDS 1:34 MINI
STATED PRINT RUN 9 SER.#'d SETS
ALL DC VARIATIONS PRICED EQUALLY
34 Ernie Banks 50.00 100.00
37 Yogi Berra 60.00 150.00
49 Albert Pujols 250.00 350.00
88 Chipper Jones 75.00 150.00
121 Bo Jackson 75.00 150.00

2007 Topps Triple Threads Relics Combos

STATED ODDS 1:16 MINI
STATED PRINT RUN 36 SER.#'d SETS
*EMERALD: .5X TO 1.2X BASIC
EMERALD ODDS 1:31 MINI
EMERALD PRINT RUN 18 SER.#'d SETS
GOLD ODDS 1:62 MINI
GOLD PRINT RUN 9 SER.#'d SETS
NO GOLD PRICING DUE TO SCARCITY
PLATINUM ODDS 1:558 MINI
PLATINUM PRINT RUN 1 SER.#'d SET
NO PLATINUM PRICING DUE TO SCARCITY
SAPPHIRE ODDS 1:186 MINI
SAPPHIRE PRINT RUN 3 SER.#'d SETS
NO SAPPHIRE PRICING DUE TO SCARCITY
*SEPIA: .4X TO 1X BASIC
SEPIA ODDS 1:21 MINI
SEPIA PRINT RUN 27 SER.#'d SETS
WHITE WHALE RANDOMLY INSERTED
WHITE WHALE PRINT RUN 1 SER.#'d SET
NO WHITE WHALE PRICING DUE TO SCARCITY
1 Pujols/Manny/Ortiz 20.00 50.00
2 Pujols/Pedro/Vlad 20.00 50.00
3 Pudge/Delgado/Clemente 60.00 120.00
4 Clemente/Bernie/Beltran 30.00 60.00
5 J.Reyes/Soriano/Tejada 8.00 20.00
6 Crawford/J.Reyes/Pierre 8.00 20.00
7 Hideki/Ichiro/Taguchi 40.00 80.00
8 Mig.Cabrera/J.Santana/Abreu 12.50 30.00
9 ARod/Mariano/Hideki 30.00 60.00
10 Reggie/ARod/Mattingly 30.00 60.00
11 Berra/Mattingly/Reggie 30.00 60.00
12 Ortiz/Boggs/Manny 12.50 30.00
13 Ortiz/Manny/Pedro 12.50 30.00
14 Tejada/Murray/Brooks 10.00 25.00
15 Mauer/Morneau/J.Santana 15.00 40.00
16 Killebrew/Mauer/Morneau 20.00 50.00
17 Verlander/Pudge/Zumaya 12.50 30.00
18 Zito/Eckersley/Street 8.00 20.00
19 Reggie/Carew/Vlad 10.00 25.00
20 Vlad/Pedro/Alou 12.50 30.00
21 Young/Teixeira/ARod 12.50 30.00
22 Edgar/Ichiro/ARod 40.00 80.00
23 Wright/Delgado/J.Reyes 12.50 30.00
24 J.Reyes/Pedro/Wright 15.00 40.00
25 J.Reyes/Beltran/Wright 10.00 25.00
26 Howard/Utley/Rollins 30.00 60.00
27 Francoeur/Chipper/McCann 8.00 20.00
28 Smoltz/Glavine/Maddux 20.00 50.00
29 Chipper/Francoeur/Andruw 15.00 40.00
30 Ryan/Pedro/Seaver 20.00 50.00
31 Schmidt/Thome/Howard 15.00 40.00
32 Musial/Pujols/Ozzie 30.00 60.00
33 Pujols/Eckstein/Edmonds 15.00 40.00
34 Berkman/Oswalt/Biggio 12.50 30.00
35 Clemens/Oswalt/Ryan 15.00 40.00
36 F.Robinson/Morgan/Bench 20.00 50.00
37 Molitor/Prince/Yount 15.00 40.00
38 Banks/Soriano/Sandberg 20.00 50.00
39 Ethier/Kemp/Jer.Weaver 8.00 20.00
40 Wang/ARod/Mariano 50.00 100.00
41 Pujols/Ichiro/Vlad 10.00 25.00
42 Pujols/ARod/Ichiro 40.00 80.00
43 Howard/Morneau/Pujols 15.00 40.00
44 Pujols/Clemente/Ichiro 50.00 100.00
45 Pujols/Clemente/Mantle 100.00 200.00
46 DiMaggio/Mantle/ARod 100.00 150.00
47 Williams/DiMaggio/Mantle 150.00 250.00
48 Clemente/Mantle/Reggie 75.00 150.00
49 Musial/Clemente/F.Robinson 50.00 100.00
50 Pujols/Bench/Mantle 40.00 80.00
51 Yaz/Williams/Mantle 100.00 150.00
52 Webb/Seaver/J.Santana 12.50 30.00
53 Clemens/Gooden/Pedro 15.00 40.00
54 J.Santana/Maddux/Clemens 12.50 30.00
55 J.Santana/Pedro/Clemens 12.50 30.00
56 Unit/Clemens/Glavine 12.50 30.00
57 Verlander/Howard/Suzuki 20.00 50.00
58 Willis/Beltran/Bay 8.00 20.00
59 Pujols/Rolen/Howard 12.50 30.00
60 Clemente/DiMaggio/Mantle 125.00 200.00
61 Musial/Banks/Mantle 60.00 120.00
62 Schmidt/Morgan/Bench 15.00 40.00
63 Brett/Yount/Ozzie 20.00 50.00
64 Pujols/Ichiro/Carew 30.00 60.00
65 Soriano/Mantle/ARod 30.00 60.00
66 Mattingly/Boggs/Gwynn 20.00 50.00
67 Carew/Vlad/G.Anderson 10.00 25.00
68 Gwynn/Boggs/Brett 30.00 60.00
69 Vlad/Soriano/Abreu 15.00 40.00
70 Strawberry/Beltran/H.Johnson 15.00 40.00
71 Thome/Manny/F.Thomas 12.50 30.00
72 Mantle/Piazza/Schmidt 60.00 120.00
73 Yaz/ARod/Winfield 20.00 50.00
74 J.Santana/Pedro/Clemens 12.50 30.00
75 Maddux/Ryan/Seaver 30.00 60.00
76 Gibson/Gooden/Maddux 20.00 50.00
77 Clemente/Reggie/Manny 30.00 60.00
78 Podres/Larsen/Burdette 10.00 25.00
79 Ichiro/Johjima/Iguchi 30.00 60.00
80 Molitor/Rollins/Utley 10.00 25.00
81 Carter/LoDuca/Piazza 30.00 60.00
82 Brett/ARod/Wright 30.00 60.00
83 Wilhelm/ Niekro/Wakefield 20.00 50.00
84 FDR/Truman/Eisenhower 30.00 60.00
85 Ichiro/Chavez/Hunter 12.50 30.00
86 Nixon/Reagan/Bush 60.00 120.00
87 Smoltz/Delgado/Edgar 8.00 20.00
88 Manny/Vlad/Ortiz 12.50 30.00
89 Livan/Hershiser/Stargell 10.00 25.00
90 Ortiz/Howard/Pujols 10.00 25.00
91 Wang/J.Santana/Garland 15.00 40.00
92 Deion/Bo/B.Jordan 15.00 40.00
93 FDR/JFK/Clinton 75.00 150.00
94 Vlad/Ichiro/Wells 10.00 25.00
95 Thome/Dye/Konerko 10.00 25.00
96 Pierzynski/Escobar/Paul 8.00 20.00
97 Carter/Rickey/Molitor 15.00 40.00
98 Gibson/Eckersley 20.00 50.00
99 L.Castillo/Alou/Prior 8.00 20.00
100 Mookie/Knight/Buckner 20.00 50.00

2007 Topps Triple Threads Relics Combos Autographs

STATED ODDS 1:94 MINI
STATED PRINT RUN 36 SER.#'d SETS
EMERALD: .5X TO 1.2X BASIC
EMERALD ODDS 1:185 MINI
EMERALD PRINT RUN 18 SER.#'d SETS
GOLD ODDS 1:371 MINI
GOLD PRINT RUN 9 SER.#'d SETS
NO GOLD PRICING DUE TO SCARCITY
PLATINUM ODDS 1:2996 MINI
PLATINUM PRINT RUN 1 SER.#'d SET
NO PLATINUM PRICING DUE TO SCARCITY
SAPPHIRE ODDS 1:1145 MINI
SAPPHIRE PRINT RUN 3 SER.#'d SETS
NO SAPPHIRE PRICING DUE TO SCARCITY
*SEPIA: .4X TO 1X BASIC
SEPIA ODDS 1:129 MINI
SEPIA PRINT RUN 27 SER.#'d SETS
WHITE WHALE ODDS 1:1219 MINI
WHITE WHALE PRINT RUN 1 SER.#'d SET
NO WHITE WHALE PRICING DUE TO SCARCITY
1 Brooks/Yount/Bench 40.00 80.00
2 Reggie/Morgan/Sandberg 75.00 150.00
3 Seaver/Gibson/Ryan 150.00 400.00
4 Pujols/ARod/Vlad 175.00 350.00
5 Seaver/Clemens/Gooden 60.00 150.00
6 J.Santana/Glavine/Clemens 40.00 80.00
7 ARod/Wang/Mattingly 100.00 200.00
8 Howard/Schmidt/Abreu 75.00 150.00
9 Howard/Ortiz/Pujols 100.00 200.00
10 ARod/Wright/J.Reyes 125.00 250.00
11 Mig.Cabrera/Manny/Ortiz 75.00 150.00
12 Verlander/Jer.Weaver/Wang 150.00 300.00
13 Kiner/Snider/Berra 125.00 250.00
14 Howard/ARod/Andruw 100.00 200.00
15 Lind/Stokes/Dav.Murphy 12.50 30.00
16 And.Miller/Stokes/Perkins 12.50 30.00
17 Riggans/Tulo/And.Miller 20.00 50.00
18 Perkins/Milledge/Tulo 20.00 50.00

2007 Topps Triple Threads Relics Combos Double

STATED ODDS 1:31 MINI
STATED PRINT RUN 36 SER.#'d SETS
*EMERALD: .4X TO 1X BASIC
EMERALD ODDS 1:62 MINI
EMERALD PRINT RUN 18 SER.#'d SETS
GOLD ODDS 1:125 MINI
PLATINUM ODDS 1:1140 MINI
PLATINUM PRINT RUN 1 SER.#'d SET
GOLD PRINT RUN 9 SER.#'d SETS
NO GOLD PRICING DUE TO SCARCITY
NO PLATINUM PRICING DUE TO SCARCITY
SAPPHIRE ODDS 1:372 MINI
SAPPHIRE PRINT RUN 3 SER.#'d SETS
NO SAPPHIRE PRICING DUE TO SCARCITY
*SEPIA: .4X TO 1X BASIC
SEPIA ODDS 1:42 MINI
SEPIA PRINT RUN 27 SER.#'d SETS
1 Mantle/DiMaggio 200.00 300.00
2 Yankees/Red Sox 125.00 175.00
3 Mets/Braves 30.00 60.00
4 David Wright 30.00 60.00
5 Albert Pujols 50.00 100.00
6 Chien-Ming Wang 100.00 200.00
7 Wright/Howard 30.00 60.00
8 Alex Rodriguez 50.00 100.00
9 Ryan Howard 12.50 30.00
10 Ichiro Suzuki 75.00 150.00
11 Dominican Republic 30.00 60.00
12 Japan 100.00 200.00
13 Puerto Rico 75.00 150.00
14 Venezuelan 40.00 80.00
15 Hall of Famers 150.00 300.00
16 MVPs 250.00 350.00
17 Yankees 60.00 120.00
18 Red Sox 40.00 80.00
19 Twins 50.00 100.00
20 Tigers 50.00 100.00
21 Athletics 60.00 120.00
22 Angels 20.00 50.00
23 Expos 30.00 60.00
24 Rangers 50.00 100.00
25 Mariners 60.00 120.00
26 Mets 20.00 50.00
27 Cardinals 50.00 100.00
28 Astros 100.00 200.00
29 Phillies 125.00 175.00
30 Braves 40.00 80.00
31 Cubs 40.00 80.00
32 Generation Now 20.00 50.00
33 David Ortiz 15.00 40.00
34 MVPs 60.00 120.00
35 Cardinals/Tigers 50.00 100.00
36 Cubs/White Sox 40.00 80.00
37 Mets/Yankees 15.00 40.00
38 06 AVG Leaders 30.00 60.00
39 06 HR Leaders 40.00 80.00
40 06 RBI Leaders 30.00 60.00
41 06 ERA Leaders 30.00 60.00
42 2006 Wins Leaders 50.00 100.00
43 2006 SO Leaders 12.50 30.00
44 LCS MVPs 30.00 60.00
45 Giants/Dodgers 50.00 100.00
46 03-05 HOF 40.00 80.00
47 White Sox 30.00 60.00
48 Active SO Leaders 40.00 80.00
49 Third Baseman 125.00 175.00
50 Active 30-30 40.00 80.00

2008 Topps Triple Threads

COMMON CARD (1-145) .40 1.00
1-145 PRINT RUN 1350 SER.#'d SETS
COMMON JSY AU RC (146-170) 4.00 10.00
JSY AU RC ODDS 1:11 MINI
JSY AU RC VAR.ODDS 1:20 MINI
JSY AU RC PRINT RUN 99 SER.#'d SETS
TEAM INITIAL DIECUTS ARE VARIATIONS
COMMON JSY AU (171-220) 4.00 10.00
JSY AU ODDS 1:11 MINI
JSY AU VAR.ODDS 1:20 MINI
JSY AU PRINT RUN 99 SER.#'d SETS
TEAM INITIAL DIECUTS ARE VARIATIONS
COMMON CARD (221-251) .40 1.00
221-251 PRINT RUN 1350 SER.#'d SETS
COMMON ROOKIE (221-251) .40 1.00
221-251 RC PRINT RUN 1350 SER.#'d SETS
OVERALL 1-145 PLATE ODDS 1:116 MINI
OVERALL 221-251 PLATE ODDS 1:116 MINI
PLATE PRINT RUN 1 SET PER COLOR
BLACK-CYAN-MAGENTA-YELLOW ISSUED
NO PLATE PRICING DUE TO SCARCITY
1 David Wright .60 1.50
2 Nolan Ryan 3.00 8.00
3 Johnny Damon .60 1.50
4 Joe Mauer .75 2.00
5 Francisco Rodriguez .60 1.50
6 Carlos Beltran .60 1.50
7 Mickey Mantle 3.00 8.00
8 Brian Roberts .40 1.00
9 Lou Gehrig 2.00 5.00
10 Babe Ruth 2.50 6.00
11 Ryne Sandberg 2.00 5.00
12 Bob Gibson .60 1.50
13 Greg Maddux 1.25 3.00
14 Jered Weaver .60 1.50
15 Johnny Bench 1.00 2.50
16 Magglio Ordonez .60 1.50
17 Carl Yastrzemski 1.50 4.00
18 Derek Jeter 2.50 6.00
19 Gil Meche .40 1.00
20 Hanley Ramirez .60 1.50
21 Edgar Martinez .60 1.50
22 Steve Carlton .60 1.50
23 C.C. Sabathia .60 1.50
24 Chase Utley .60 1.50
25 Francisco Cordero .40 1.00
26 Mark Ellis .40 1.00
27 Jeff Kent .40 1.00
28 Brian Fuentes .40 1.00
29 Johan Santana .60 1.50
30 Ichiro 1.25 3.00
31 Ken Griffey Jr. 2.00 5.00
32 Steve Garvey .40 1.00
33 Rafael Furcal .40 1.00
34 Chipper Jones 1.00 2.50
35 Roberto Clemente 2.50 6.00
36 Rich Harden .40 1.00
37 Cy Young 1.00 2.50
38 Albert Pujols 1.25 3.00
39 Dontrelle Willis .40 1.00
40 Mark Teixeira .60 1.50
41 Daisuke Matsuzaka .60 1.50
42 Harmon Killebrew 1.00 2.50
43 Darryl Strawberry .40 1.00
44 Eric Chavez .40 1.00
45 Don Larsen .40 1.00
46 Huston Street .60 1.50
47 Jake Peavy .40 1.00
48 Prince Fielder .60 1.50
49 Garret Anderson .40 1.00
50 Matt Holliday 1.00 2.50
51 Travis Buck .60 1.50
52 Ben Sheets .40 1.00
53 George Brett 2.00 5.00
54 Dmitri Young .40 1.00
55 Phil Rizzuto .60 1.50
56 Jimmy Rollins .60 1.50
57 Manny Ramirez 1.00 2.50
58 Ozzie Smith 1.25 3.00
59 Dale Murphy 1.00 2.50
60 Bobby Crosby .40 1.00
61 Trevor Hoffman .60 1.50
62 Chien-Ming Wang .60 1.50
63 Jose Reyes .60 1.50
64 Vladimir Guerrero .60 1.50
65 Vida Blue .40 1.00
66 Rod Carew .60 1.50
67 Aaron Rowand .40 1.00
68 Hong-Chih Kuo .40 1.00
69 Mike Schmidt 1.50 4.00
70 Rogers Hornsby .60 1.50
71 Alex Rodriguez 1.25 3.00
72 Roger Maris 1.00 2.50
73 Travis Hafner .40 1.00
74 Tom Glavine .60 1.50
75 Pat Burrell .40 1.00
76 Pedro Martinez .60 1.50
77 Joba Chamberlain .40 1.00
78 Jason Varitek 1.00 2.50
79 Hideo Nomo 1.00 2.50
80 Frank Thomas 1.00 2.50
81 Rollie Fingers .60 1.50
82 Carl Crawford .60 1.50
83 Bobby Jenks .40 1.00
84 Victor Martinez .60 1.50
85 Ernie Banks 1.00 2.50
86 Josh Beckett .40 1.00
87 Jose Valverde .40 1.00
88 Reggie Jackson .60 1.50
89 Duke Snider .60 1.50
90 Mike Lowell .40 1.00
91 Dom DiMaggio .40 1.00
92 Torii Hunter .40 1.00
93 Alfonso Soriano .60 1.50
94 Justin Morneau .60 1.50
95 Carlos Delgado .40 1.00
96 Ty Cobb 1.50 4.00
97 Andruw Jones .40 1.00
98 Yogi Berra 1.00 2.50
99 Joe DiMaggio 2.00 5.00
100 Willie Randolph .40 1.00
101 Miguel Cabrera 1.00 2.50
102 Grady Sizemore .60 1.50
103 Michael Young .40 1.00
104 Wade Boggs .60 1.50
105 Goose Gossage .60 1.50
106 Robin Roberts .60 1.50
107 Brooks Robinson .60 1.50
108 Jim Palmer .60 1.50
109 Jorge Posada .60 1.50
110 Keith Hernandez .40 1.00
111 Ivan Rodriguez .60 1.50
112 Carlos Lee .40 1.00
113 John Lackey .60 1.50
114 Alex Rios .40 1.00
115 Carlton Fisk .60 1.50
116 Gary Matthews .40 1.00
117 Billy Martin .60 1.50
118 Paul Molitor 1.00 2.50
119 Hideki Matsui 1.00 2.50
120 Al Kaline 1.00 2.50
121 Takashi Saito .40 1.00
122 Stan Musial 1.50 4.00
123 Ryan Howard .60 1.50
124 Whitey Ford .60 1.50
125 John Smoltz 1.00 2.50
126 Roy Oswalt .60 1.50
127 Jim Thome .60 1.50
128 Tony Gwynn 1.00 2.50
129 Dennis Eckersley .60 1.50
130 Ted Williams 2.00 5.00
131 Justin Verlander 1.00 2.50
132 David Ortiz 1.00 2.50
133 Tom Gordon .40 1.00
134 Tom Seaver .60 1.50
135 Red Schoendienst .60 1.50
136 Johnny Podres .40 1.00
137 Paul Konerko .60 1.50
138 Robin Yount 1.00 2.50
139 Todd Helton .60 1.50
140 Frank Robinson .60 1.50
141 J.J. Putz .40 1.00
142 Jackie Robinson 1.00 2.50
143 Brandon Webb .60 1.50
144 Eddie Murray .60 1.50
145 Freddy Sanchez .40 1.00
146 Josh Anderson Jsy AU (RC) 5.00 12.00
147a Daric Barton Jsy AU (RC) 5.00 12.00
147b Daric Barton Jsy AU (RC) 5.00 12.00
148 S.Pearce Jsy AU RC 40.00 100.00
149 C.Hu Jsy AU (RC) 5.00 12.00
150a Buchholz Jsy AU (RC) 10.00 25.00
150b Buchholz Jsy AU (RC) 8.00 20.00
151a J.Towles Jsy AU RC 6.00 15.00
151b J.Towles Jsy AU RC 6.00 15.00
152 Brandon Jones Jsy AU RC 5.00 12.00
153 Broadway Jsy AU (RC) 6.00 15.00
154a Nyjer Morgan Jsy AU (RC) 6.00 15.00
154b Nyjer Morgan Jsy AU (RC) 6.00 15.00
155a Ross Ohlendorf Jsy AU RC 5.00 12.00
155b Ross Ohlendorf Jsy AU RC 5.00 12.00
156 Chris Seddon Jsy AU (RC) 4.00 10.00
157 Jonathan Albaladejo Jsy AU RC 5.00 12.00
158a Seth Smith Jsy AU (RC) 4.00 10.00
158b Seth Smith Jsy AU (RC) 4.00 10.00
159a Kevin Hart Jsy AU (RC) 5.00 12.00
159b Kevin Hart Jsy AU (RC) 5.00 12.00
160 Bill White Jsy AU RC 5.00 12.00
161 Wladimir Balentien Jsy AU (RC) 5.00 12.00
162a Justin Ruggiano Jsy AU RC 4.00 10.00
162b Justin Ruggiano Jsy AU RC 4.00 10.00
163a Clint Sammons Jsy AU (RC) 5.00 12.00
163b Clint Sammons Jsy AU (RC) 5.00 12.00
164 Rich Thompson Jsy AU RC 5.00 12.00
165 Dave Davidson Jsy AU RC 4.00 10.00
166 Troy Patton Jsy AU (RC) 5.00 12.00
167 Joe Koshansky Jsy AU (RC) 5.00 12.00
168a Colt Morton Jsy AU RC 5.00 12.00
168b Colt Morton Jsy AU RC 5.00 12.00
169 Galarraga Jsy AU RC 12.50 30.00
170a Sam Fuld Jsy AU RC 4.00 10.00
170b Sam Fuld Jsy AU RC 4.00 10.00
171 Dustin Moseley Bat AU 4.00 10.00
172 T.Lincecum Jsy AU 20.00 50.00
173a Ryan Braun Jsy AU 15.00 40.00
173b Ryan Braun Jsy AU 15.00 40.00
174 Phil Hughes Jsy AU 8.00 20.00
175a J.Chamberlain Jsy AU 8.00 20.00
175b J.Chamberlain Jsy AU 8.00 20.00
176 H.Pence Jsy AU 12.00 30.00
177a F.Carmona Jsy AU 5.00 12.00
177b F.Carmona Jsy AU 5.00 12.00
178a U.Jimenez Jsy AU 6.00 15.00
178b Ubaldo Jimenez Jsy AU 6.00 15.00
179a C.Maybin Jsy AU 6.00 15.00
179b C.Maybin Jsy AU 6.00 15.00
180a Adam Jones Jsy AU 6.00 15.00
180b Adam Jones Jsy AU 6.00 15.00
181a Brian Bannister Jsy AU 5.00 12.00
181b Brian Bannister Jsy AU 5.00 12.00
182a Saltalamac Jsy AU 8.00 20.00
182b Saltalamac Jsy AU 5.00 12.00
183 Alex Gordon Jsy AU 8.00 20.00
184a R.Martin Jsy AU 6.00 15.00
184b R.Martin Jsy AU 6.00 15.00
185 John Maine Jsy AU 10.00 25.00
186a H.Okajima Jsy AU 5.00 12.00
186b H.Okajima Jsy AU 5.00 12.00
187a Granderson Jsy AU 10.00 25.00
187b Granderson Jsy AU 10.00 25.00
188 Delmon Young Jsy AU 5.00 12.00
189a Jo-Jo Reyes Jsy AU 5.00 12.00
189b Jo-Jo Reyes Jsy AU 5.00 12.00
190 Y.Gallardo Jsy AU 8.00 20.00
191a Zimmerman Jsy AU 10.00 25.00
191b Zimmerman Jsy AU 6.00 15.00
192 J.Guthrie Jsy AU 8.00 20.00
193a Dan Uggla Jsy AU 6.00 15.00
193b Dan Uggla Jsy AU 6.00 15.00
194a Andre Ethier Jsy AU 8.00 20.00
194b Andre Ethier Jsy AU 8.00 20.00
195a C.Young Jsy AU 6.00 15.00
195b C.Young Jsy AU 6.00 15.00
196a Elijah Dukes Jsy AU 5.00 12.00
196b Elijah Dukes Jsy AU 5.00 12.00
197a N.Markakis Jsy AU 8.00 20.00
197b N.Markakis Jsy AU 8.00 20.00
198a M.Cabrera Jsy AU 5.00 12.00
198b M.Cabrera Jsy AU 5.00 12.00
199 Cole Hamels Jsy AU 12.50 30.00
200 J.Loney Jsy AU 5.00 12.00
201a K.Slowey Jsy AU 8.00 20.00
201b K.Slowey Jsy AU 8.00 20.00
202 Carlos Marmol Jsy AU 6.00 15.00
203a A.Iwamura Jsy AU 10.00 25.00
203b A.Iwamura Jsy AU 10.00 25.00
204 A.Gonzalez Jsy AU 6.00 15.00
205a B.Phillips Jsy AU 5.00 12.00
205b B.Phillips Jsy AU 5.00 12.00
206 J.J. Hardy Jsy AU 10.00 25.00
207a Tom Gorzelanny Jsy AU 4.00 10.00
207b Tom Gorzelanny Jsy AU 4.00 10.00
208a Matt Cain Jsy AU 10.00 25.00
208b Matt Cain Jsy AU 10.00 25.00
209a Matt Capps Jsy AU 5.00 12.00
209b Matt Capps Jsy AU 5.00 12.00
210a Jeff Francis Jsy AU 5.00 12.00
210b Jeff Francis Jsy AU 5.00 12.00
211 B.McCann Jsy AU 10.00 25.00
212 Matt Garza Jsy AU 8.00 20.00
213a R.Cano Jsy AU 20.00 50.00
213b R.Cano Jsy AU 20.00 50.00
214 F.Hernandez Jsy AU 10.00 25.00
215 Y.Escobar Jsy AU 8.00 20.00
216a F.Liriano Jsy AU 8.00 20.00
216b F.Liriano Jsy AU 8.00 20.00
217a Rich Hill Jsy AU 5.00 12.00
217b Rich Hill Jsy AU 5.00 12.00
218a Taylor Buchholz Jsy AU 4.00 10.00
218b Taylor Buchholz Jsy AU 4.00 10.00
219 Asdrubal Cabrera Jsy AU 6.00 15.00
220a Lastings Milledge Jsy AU 5.00 12.00
220b Lastings Milledge Jsy AU 5.00 12.00
221 Honus Wagner 1.00 2.50
222 Walter Johnson 1.00 2.50
223 Thurman Munson 1.00 2.50
224 Roy Campanella 1.00 2.50
225 George Sisler .60 1.50
226 Pee Wee Reese .60 1.50
227 Johnny Mize .60 1.50
228 Jimmie Foxx 1.00 2.50
229 Tris Speaker .60 1.50
230 Christy Mathewson 1.00 2.50
231 Mel Ott 1.00 2.50
232 Ralph Kiner .60 1.50
233 Joey Votto (RC) 3.00 8.00
234 Hiroki Kuroda RC 1.00 2.50
235 John Bowker (RC) .40 1.00
236 Lance Berkman .60 1.50
237 Aaron Harang .40 1.00
238 B.J. Upton .60 1.50
239 Zack Greinke 1.00 2.50
240 Cal Ripken Jr. 3.00 8.00
241 Justin Upton .60 1.50
242 Roy Halladay .60 1.50
243 Orlando Hudson .40 1.00
244 Scott Kazmir .60 1.50
245 Matt Kemp .75 2.00
246 Mark Buehrle .60 1.50
247 Adam Dunn .60 1.50
248 Erik Bedard .40 1.00
249 Carlos Zambrano .60 1.50
250 Jeff Francoeur .60 1.50
251 Brad Penny .40 1.00

2008 Topps Triple Threads Black

*BLACK 1-145: 3X TO 8X BASIC
*BLACK 221-251: 3X TO 8X BASIC
1-145/221-251 ODDS 1:16 MINI
1-145/221-251 PNT RUN 30 SER.#'d SETS

2008 Topps Triple Threads Emerald

*EMERALD 1-145: .6X TO 1.5X BASIC
*EMERALD 221-251: .6X TO 1.5X BASIC
1-145/221-251 ODDS 1:2 MINI
1-145/221-251 PNT RUN 240 SER.#'d SETS
*EMERALD AUTO: .5X TO 1.2X BASIC AU
*EMERALD VAR AU: .5X TO 1.2X BASIC AU
146-220 AU ODDS 1:22 MINI
146-220 AU VAR.ODDS 1:39 MINI
146-220 AU PRINT RUN 50 SERIAL #'d SETS
TEAM INITIAL DIECUTS ARE VARIATIONS

2008 Topps Triple Threads Gold

*GOLD 1-145: 1X TO 2.5X BASIC
*GOLD 221-251: 1X TO 2.5X BASIC
1-145/221-251 ODDS 1:5 MINI
1-145/221-251 PNT RUN 99 SER.#'d SETS
*GOLD AUTO: .6X TO 1.5X BASIC AU
*GOLD VAR AU: .6X TO 1.5X BASIC AU
146-220 AU ODDS 1:43 MINI
146-220 AU VAR.ODDS 1:77 MINI
146-220 AU PRINT RUN 25 SERIAL #'d SETS
TEAM INITIAL DIECUTS ARE VARIATIONS

2008 Topps Triple Threads Sapphire

*SAPPHIRE 1-145: 3X TO 8X BASIC
*SAPPHIRE 221-251: 3X TO 8X BASIC
1-145/221-251 ODDS 1:19 MINI
1-145/221-251 PNT RUN 25 SER.#'d SETS
146-220 JSY AU ODDS 1:107 MINI
146-220 JSY AU VAR.ODDS 1:190 MINI
146-220 AU PRINT RUN 10 SERIAL #'d SETS
TEAM INITIAL DIECUTS ARE VARIATIONS
NO SAPPHIRE JSY AUTO PRICING AVAILABLE

2008 Topps Triple Threads Sepia

*SEPIA 1-145: .5X TO 1.2X BASIC
*SEPIA 221-251: .5X TO 1.2X BASIC
1-145/221-251 RANDOMLY INSERTED
1-145/221-251 PNT RUN 525 SER.#'d SETS
*SEPIA AUTO: .4X TO 1X BASIC AU
*SEPIA VAR AU: .4X TO 1X BASIC AU
146-220 AU ODDS 1:15 MINI
146-220 AU VAR.ODDS 1:26 MINI
146-220 AU PRINT RUN 75 SERIAL #'d SETS
TEAM INITIAL DIECUTS ARE VARIATIONS

2008 Topps Triple Threads Relics

STATED ODDS 1:10 MINI
STATED PRINT RUN 36 SER.#'d SETS
*EMERALD: .5X TO 1.2X BASIC
EMERALD ODDS 1:19 MINI
EMERALD PRINT RUN 18 SER.#'d SETS
NO 226-240 EMERALD PRICING
*GOLD: .6X TO 1.5X BASIC
GOLD ODDS 1:38 MINI
GOLD PRINT RUN 9 SER.#'d SETS
NO 226-240 GOLD PRICING
PLATINUM ODDS 1:334 MINI
PLATINUM PRINT RUN 1 SER.#'d SET
NO PLATINUM PRICING DUE TO SCARCITY
SAPPHIRE ODDS 1:111 MINI
SAPPHIRE PRINT RUN 3 SER.#'d SETS
NO SAPPHIRE PRICING DUE TO SCARCITY
*SEPIA: .4X TO 1X BASIC
SEPIA ODDS 1:13 MINI
SEPIA PRINT RUN 27 SER.#'d SETS
ALL DC VARIATIONS PRICED EQUALLY
1 David Wright 10.00 25.00
2 David Wright 10.00 25.00
3 David Wright 10.00 25.00
4 Alex Rodriguez 20.00 50.00
5 Alex Rodriguez 20.00 50.00
6 Alex Rodriguez 20.00 50.00
7 Mickey Mantle 60.00 120.00
8 Mickey Mantle 60.00 120.00
9 Mickey Mantle 60.00 120.00
10 Duke Snider 12.50 30.00
11 Duke Snider 12.50 30.00
12 Duke Snider 12.50 30.00
13 Carlton Fisk 10.00 25.00
14 Carlton Fisk 10.00 25.00
15 Carlton Fisk 10.00 25.00
16 Ichiro Suzuki 12.00 30.00
17 Ichiro Suzuki 12.00 30.00
18 Ichiro Suzuki 12.00 30.00
19 Wade Boggs 10.00 25.00
20 Wade Boggs 10.00 25.00
21 Wade Boggs 10.00 25.00
22 Chien-Ming Wang 6.00 15.00
23 Chien-Ming Wang 6.00 15.00
24 Chien-Ming Wang 6.00 15.00
25 Alfonso Soriano 8.00 20.00
26 Alfonso Soriano 8.00 20.00
27 Alfonso Soriano 8.00 20.00
28 Ernie Banks 12.50 30.00
29 Ernie Banks 12.50 30.00
30 Ernie Banks 12.50 30.00
31 Jimmy Rollins 8.00 20.00
32 Jimmy Rollins 8.00 20.00
33 Jimmy Rollins 8.00 20.00
34 Bob Gibson 10.00 25.00
35 Bob Gibson 10.00 25.00
36 Bob Gibson 10.00 25.00
37 Brooks Robinson 10.00 25.00
38 Brooks Robinson 10.00 25.00
39 Brooks Robinson 10.00 25.00
40 Joe DiMaggio 50.00 100.00
41 Joe DiMaggio 50.00 100.00
42 Joe DiMaggio 30.00 60.00
43 Hideo Nomo 20.00 50.00
44 Hideo Nomo 20.00 50.00
45 Hideo Nomo 20.00 50.00
46 Ted Williams 30.00 60.00
47 Ted Williams 30.00 60.00
48 Ted Williams 30.00 60.00
49 David Ortiz 8.00 20.00
50 David Ortiz 8.00 20.00
51 David Ortiz 8.00 20.00
52 Frank Robinson 12.50 30.00
53 Frank Robinson 12.50 30.00
54 Frank Robinson 12.50 30.00
55 Tony Gwynn 15.00 40.00
56 Tony Gwynn 15.00 40.00
57 Tony Gwynn 15.00 40.00
58 Jose Reyes 10.00 25.00
59 Jose Reyes 10.00 25.00
60 Jose Reyes 10.00 25.00
61 Roger Maris 30.00 60.00
62 Roger Maris 30.00 60.00
63 Roger Maris 30.00 60.00
64 Mike Schmidt 10.00 25.00
65 Mike Schmidt 10.00 25.00
66 Mike Schmidt 10.00 25.00
67 Eddie Murray 10.00 25.00
68 Eddie Murray 10.00 25.00
69 Eddie Murray 10.00 25.00
70 Johnny Bench 12.50 30.00
71 Johnny Bench 12.50 30.00
72 Johnny Bench 12.50 30.00
73 Roberto Clemente 50.00 100.00
74 Roberto Clemente 50.00 100.00
75 Roberto Clemente 50.00 100.00
76 Steve Carlton 8.00 20.00
77 Steve Carlton 8.00 20.00
78 Steve Carlton 8.00 20.00
79 Grady Sizemore 10.00 25.00
80 Grady Sizemore 10.00 25.00
81 Grady Sizemore 10.00 25.00
82 Robin Yount 15.00 40.00
83 Robin Yount 15.00 40.00
84 Robin Yount 15.00 40.00
85 Hanley Ramirez 8.00 20.00
86 Hanley Ramirez 8.00 20.00
87 Hanley Ramirez 8.00 20.00
88 Al Kaline 12.50 30.00
89 Al Kaline 12.50 30.00
90 Al Kaline 12.50 30.00
91 Vladimir Guerrero 8.00 20.00
92 Vladimir Guerrero 8.00 20.00
93 Vladimir Guerrero 8.00 20.00
94 George Kell 10.00 25.00
95 George Kell 10.00 25.00
96 George Kell 10.00 25.00
97 Reggie Jackson 8.00 20.00
98 Reggie Jackson 8.00 20.00
99 Reggie Jackson 8.00 20.00
100 Tom Seaver 12.50 30.00
101 Tom Seaver 12.50 30.00
102 Tom Seaver 12.50 30.00
103 Johan Santana 8.00 20.00
104 Johan Santana 8.00 20.00
105 Johan Santana 8.00 20.00
106 Jason Varitek 10.00 25.00
107 Jason Varitek 10.00 25.00
108 Jason Varitek 10.00 25.00
109 Ryan Howard 10.00 25.00
110 Ryan Howard 10.00 25.00
111 Ryan Howard 10.00 25.00
112 Manny Ramirez 8.00 20.00
113 Manny Ramirez 8.00 20.00
114 Manny Ramirez 8.00 20.00
115 Miguel Cabrera 8.00 20.00
116 Miguel Cabrera 8.00 20.00
117 Miguel Cabrera 8.00 20.00
118 Jorge Posada 8.00 20.00
119 Jorge Posada 8.00 20.00
120 Jorge Posada 8.00 20.00
121 Nolan Ryan 20.00 50.00
122 Nolan Ryan 20.00 50.00
123 Nolan Ryan 20.00 50.00
124 Paul Molitor 8.00 20.00
125 Paul Molitor 8.00 20.00
126 Paul Molitor 8.00 20.00
127 Chipper Jones 10.00 25.00
128 Chipper Jones 10.00 25.00
129 Chipper Jones 10.00 25.00
130 Carl Yastrzemski 15.00 40.00
131 Carl Yastrzemski 15.00 40.00
132 Carl Yastrzemski 15.00 40.00
133 Whitey Ford 15.00 40.00
134 Whitey Ford 15.00 40.00
135 Whitey Ford 15.00 40.00
136 Yogi Berra 12.50 30.00
137 Yogi Berra 12.50 30.00
138 Yogi Berra 12.50 30.00
139 Albert Pujols 12.50 30.00
140 Albert Pujols 12.50 30.00
141 Albert Pujols 10.00 25.00
142 Jim Palmer 8.00 20.00
143 Jim Palmer 8.00 20.00
144 Jim Palmer 8.00 20.00
145 Harmon Killebrew 20.00 50.00
146 Harmon Killebrew 20.00 50.00
147 Harmon Killebrew 20.00 50.00
148 Ozzie Smith 10.00 25.00
149 Ozzie Smith 10.00 25.00
150 Ozzie Smith 10.00 25.00
151 Stan Musial 20.00 50.00
152 Stan Musial 20.00 50.00
153 Stan Musial 20.00 50.00
154 Ryne Sandberg 12.50 30.00
155 Ryne Sandberg 12.50 30.00
156 Ryne Sandberg 12.50 30.00
157 Matt Holliday 8.00 20.00
158 Matt Holliday 8.00 20.00
159 Matt Holliday 8.00 20.00
160 Carlos Beltran 8.00 20.00
161 Carlos Beltran 8.00 20.00
162 Carlos Beltran 8.00 20.00
163 Prince Fielder 8.00 20.00
164 Prince Fielder 8.00 20.00
165 Prince Fielder 8.00 20.00
166 Ivan Rodriguez 8.00 20.00
167 Ivan Rodriguez 8.00 20.00
168 Ivan Rodriguez 8.00 20.00
169 Victor Martinez 8.00 20.00
170 Victor Martinez 8.00 20.00
171 Victor Martinez 8.00 20.00
172 Justin Verlander 8.00 20.00
173 Justin Verlander 8.00 20.00
174 Justin Verlander 8.00 20.00
175 Reggie Jackson 8.00 20.00
176 Reggie Jackson 8.00 20.00
177 Reggie Jackson 8.00 20.00
178 Alfonso Soriano 8.00 20.00
179 Alfonso Soriano 8.00 20.00
180 Alfonso Soriano 8.00 20.00
181 Prince Fielder 8.00 20.00
182 Prince Fielder 8.00 20.00
183 Prince Fielder 8.00 20.00
184 Ichiro Suzuki 20.00 50.00
185 Ichiro Suzuki 20.00 50.00
186 Ichiro Suzuki 20.00 50.00
187 David Wright 10.00 25.00
188 David Wright 10.00 25.00
189 David Wright 10.00 25.00
190 Eddie Murray 10.00 25.00
191 Eddie Murray 10.00 25.00
192 Eddie Murray 10.00 25.00
193 Manny Ramirez 8.00 20.00
194 Manny Ramirez 8.00 20.00
195 Manny Ramirez 8.00 20.00
196 Mike Schmidt 10.00 25.00
197 Mike Schmidt 10.00 25.00
198 Mike Schmidt 10.00 25.00
199 Johnny Bench 12.50 30.00
200 Johnny Bench 12.50 30.00
201 Johnny Bench 12.50 30.00
202 Matt Holliday 8.00 20.00
203 Matt Holliday 8.00 20.00
204 Matt Holliday 8.00 20.00
205 Alex Rodriguez 20.00 50.00
206 Alex Rodriguez 20.00 50.00
207 Alex Rodriguez 20.00 50.00
208 Jose Reyes 10.00 25.00
209 Jose Reyes 10.00 25.00
210 Jose Reyes 10.00 25.00
211 Jimmy Rollins 8.00 20.00
212 Jimmy Rollins 8.00 20.00
213 Jimmy Rollins 8.00 20.00
214 David Ortiz 12.50 30.00
215 David Ortiz 12.50 30.00
216 David Ortiz 12.50 30.00
217 Robin Yount 10.00 25.00
218 Robin Yount 10.00 25.00
219 Robin Yount 10.00 25.00
220 Nolan Ryan 20.00 50.00
221 Nolan Ryan 20.00 50.00
222 Nolan Ryan 20.00 50.00
223 Ryan Howard 10.00 25.00
224 Ryan Howard 10.00 25.00
225 Ryan Howard 10.00 25.00
226 John F. Kennedy 150.00 200.00
227 Ty Cobb 100.00 200.00
228 Jimmie Foxx 20.00 50.00
229 Rogers Hornsby 10.00 25.00
230 George Sisler 15.00 40.00
231 Mel Ott 15.00 40.00
232 Jackie Robinson 60.00 120.00
233 Tris Speaker 40.00 80.00
234 Honus Wagner 150.00 250.00
235 Lou Gehrig 100.00 150.00
236 Pee Wee Reese 12.50 30.00
237 Roy Campanella 30.00 60.00
238 Johnny Mize 10.00 25.00
239 Thurman Munson 30.00 60.00
240 Babe Ruth 75.00 200.00

2008 Topps Triple Threads Relics Autographs

STATED ODDS 1:25 MINI
STATED PRINT RUN 18 SER.#'d SETS
*GOLD: .5X TO 1.2X BASIC
GOLD ODDS 1:50 MINI
GOLD PRINT RUN 9 SER.#'d SETS
PLATINUM ODDS 1:447 MINI
PLATINUM PRINT RUN 1 SER.#'d SET
NO PLATINUM PRICING DUE TO SCARCITY
SAPPHIRE ODDS 1:149 MINI
SAPPHIRE PRINT RUN 3 SER.#'d SETS
NO SAPPHIRE PRICING DUE TO SCARCITY
WHITE WHALE ODDS 1:111 MINI
WHITE WHALE PRINT RUN 1 SER.#'d SET
NO WHITE WHALE PRICING DUE TO SCARCITY
ALL DC VARIATIONS PRICED EQUALLY
1 Prince Fielder 30.00 60.00
2 Prince Fielder 30.00 60.00
3 Prince Fielder 30.00 60.00
4 Vladimir Guerrero 30.00 60.00
5 Vladimir Guerrero 30.00 60.00
6 Vladimir Guerrero 30.00 60.00
7 Bob Gibson 30.00 60.00
8 Bob Gibson 30.00 60.00
9 Bob Gibson 30.00 60.00
10 Chien-Ming Wang 90.00 150.00
11 Chien-Ming Wang 90.00 150.00
12 Chien-Ming Wang 90.00 150.00
13 Johnny Podres 20.00 50.00
14 Johnny Podres 20.00 50.00
15 Johnny Podres 20.00 50.00
16 Frank Robinson 20.00 50.00
17 Frank Robinson 20.00 50.00
18 Frank Robinson 20.00 50.00
19 Robin Yount 30.00 80.00
20 Robin Yount 30.00 80.00
21 Robin Yount 30.00 80.00
22 David Ortiz 40.00 80.00
23 David Ortiz 40.00 80.00
24 David Ortiz 40.00 80.00
25 Chipper Jones 60.00 120.00
26 Chipper Jones 60.00 120.00
27 Chipper Jones 60.00 120.00
28 Cal Ripken Jr. 150.00 250.00
29 Cal Ripken Jr. 150.00 200.00
30 Cal Ripken Jr. 150.00 200.00
31 Carlton Fisk 20.00 50.00
32 Carlton Fisk 20.00 50.00
33 Carlton Fisk 20.00 50.00
34 Jason Varitek 30.00 60.00
35 Jason Varitek 30.00 60.00
36 Jason Varitek 30.00 60.00
37 Ernie Banks 60.00 120.00
38 Ernie Banks 60.00 120.00
39 Ernie Banks 60.00 120.00
40 Harmon Killebrew 60.00 120.00
41 Harmon Killebrew 60.00 120.00
42 Harmon Killebrew 60.00 120.00
43 Travis Hafner 20.00 50.00
44 Travis Hafner 20.00 50.00
45 Travis Hafner 20.00 50.00
46 Manny Ramirez 50.00 100.00
47 Manny Ramirez 50.00 100.00
48 Manny Ramirez 50.00 100.00
49 Tony Gwynn 30.00 60.00
50 Tony Gwynn 30.00 60.00
51 Tony Gwynn 30.00 60.00
52 Alfonso Soriano 20.00 50.00
53 Alfonso Soriano 20.00 50.00
54 Alfonso Soriano 20.00 50.00
55 Carl Yastrzemski 60.00 120.00
56 Carl Yastrzemski 60.00 120.00
57 Carl Yastrzemski 60.00 120.00
58 Jim Palmer 20.00 50.00
59 Jim Palmer 20.00 50.00
60 Jim Palmer 20.00 50.00
61 Jimmy Rollins 30.00 60.00
62 Jimmy Rollins 30.00 60.00
63 Jimmy Rollins 30.00 60.00
64 Frank Thomas 50.00 100.00
65 Frank Thomas 50.00 100.00
66 Frank Thomas 50.00 100.00
67 Brooks Robinson 30.00 60.00
68 Brooks Robinson 30.00 60.00
69 Brooks Robinson 30.00 60.00
70 Dom DiMaggio 20.00 50.00
71 Dom DiMaggio 20.00 50.00
72 Dom DiMaggio 20.00 50.00
73 George Kell 30.00 60.00
74 George Kell 30.00 60.00
75 George Kell 30.00 60.00
76 Wade Boggs 20.00 50.00
77 Wade Boggs 20.00 50.00
78 Wade Boggs 20.00 50.00
79 Johan Santana 40.00 80.00
80 Johan Santana 40.00 80.00
81 Johan Santana 40.00 80.00
82 Jose Reyes 15.00 40.00
83 Jose Reyes 15.00 40.00
84 Jose Reyes 15.00 40.00
85 Hanley Ramirez 10.00 25.00
86 Hanley Ramirez 10.00 25.00
87 Hanley Ramirez 10.00 25.00
88 Johnny Bench 40.00 80.00
89 Johnny Bench 40.00 80.00
90 Johnny Bench 40.00 80.00
91 Mike Lowell 15.00 40.00
92 Mike Lowell 15.00 40.00
93 Mike Lowell 15.00 40.00
94 Tom Seaver 30.00 80.00
95 Tom Seaver 30.00 80.00
96 Tom Seaver 30.00 80.00
97 John Smoltz 40.00 80.00
98 John Smoltz 40.00 80.00
99 John Smoltz 40.00 80.00
100 Ozzie Smith 30.00 60.00
101 Ozzie Smith 30.00 60.00
102 Ozzie Smith 30.00 60.00
103 Duke Snider 30.00 60.00
104 Duke Snider 30.00 60.00
105 Duke Snider 30.00 60.00
106 Steve Carlton 20.00 50.00
107 Steve Carlton 20.00 50.00
108 Steve Carlton 20.00 50.00
109 Jorge Posada 30.00 60.00
110 Jorge Posada 30.00 60.00
111 Jorge Posada 30.00 60.00
112 Andruw Jones 10.00 25.00
113 Andruw Jones 10.00 25.00
114 Andruw Jones 10.00 25.00
115 Reggie Jackson 50.00 100.00
116 Reggie Jackson 50.00 100.00
117 Reggie Jackson 50.00 100.00
118 C.C. Sabathia 20.00 50.00
119 C.C. Sabathia 20.00 50.00
120 C.C. Sabathia 20.00 50.00
121 Jim Thome 30.00 60.00
122 Jim Thome 30.00 60.00
123 Jim Thome 30.00 60.00
124 Mike Schmidt 40.00 80.00
125 Mike Schmidt 40.00 80.00
126 Mike Schmidt 40.00 80.00
127 Yogi Berra 50.00 120.00
128 Yogi Berra 50.00 120.00
129 Yogi Berra 50.00 120.00
130 Dontrelle Willis 20.00 50.00
131 Dontrelle Willis 20.00 50.00
132 Dontrelle Willis 20.00 50.00
133 Nolan Ryan 75.00 150.00
134 Nolan Ryan 75.00 150.00
135 Nolan Ryan 75.00 150.00
136 Goose Gossage 12.50 30.00
137 Goose Gossage 12.50 30.00
138 Goose Gossage 12.50 30.00
139 Al Kaline 30.00 80.00
140 Al Kaline 30.00 80.00
141 Al Kaline 30.00 80.00
142 David Wright 25.00 60.00
143 David Wright 25.00 60.00
144 David Wright 50.00 100.00
145 Miguel Cabrera 50.00 100.00
146 Miguel Cabrera 50.00 100.00
147 Miguel Cabrera 50.00 100.00
148 Ryne Sandberg 40.00 80.00
149 Ryne Sandberg 40.00 80.00
150 Ryne Sandberg 40.00 80.00
151 Tom Glavine 30.00 60.00
152 Tom Glavine 30.00 60.00
153 Tom Glavine 30.00 60.00
154 Paul Molitor 30.00 60.00
155 Paul Molitor 30.00 60.00
156 Paul Molitor 30.00 60.00
157 Eddie Murray 30.00 60.00
158 Eddie Murray 30.00 60.00
159 Eddie Murray 30.00 60.00
160 Justin Verlander 40.00 80.00
161 Justin Verlander 40.00 80.00
162 Justin Verlander 40.00 80.00
163 Dale Murphy 30.00 60.00
164 Dale Murphy 30.00 60.00
165 Dale Murphy 30.00 60.00
166 Whitey Ford 50.00 100.00
167 Whitey Ford 50.00 100.00
168 Whitey Ford 50.00 100.00
169 Matt Holliday 10.00 25.00
170 Matt Holliday 10.00 25.00
171 Matt Holliday 12.50 30.00
172 Albert Pujols 150.00 300.00
173 Albert Pujols 150.00 300.00
174 Albert Pujols 150.00 300.00
175 Stan Musial 60.00 120.00
176 Stan Musial 60.00 120.00
177 Stan Musial 60.00 120.00
178 Ryan Howard 20.00 50.00
179 Ryan Howard 20.00 50.00
180 Ryan Howard 20.00 50.00
181 Johnny Cueto 10.00 25.00
182 Johnny Cueto 10.00 25.00
183 Johnny Cueto 10.00 25.00
184 Evan Longoria 100.00 175.00
185 Evan Longoria 100.00 175.00
186 Evan Longoria 100.00 175.00

2008 Topps Triple Threads Relics Combos

STATED ODDS 1:20 MINI
STATED PRINT RUN 36 SER.#'d SETS
EMERALD ODDS 1:41 MINI
EMERALD PRINT RUN 18 SER.#'d SETS
NO EMERALD PRICING AVAILABLE
GOLD ODDS 1:81 MINI
GOLD PRINT RUN 9 SER.#'d SETS
NO GOLD PRICING AVAILABLE
PLATINUM ODDS 1:727 MINI
PLATINUM PRINT RUN 1 SER.#'d SET
NO PLATINUM PRICING AVAILABLE
SAPPHIRE ODDS 1:241 MINI
SAPPHIRE PRINT RUN 3 SER.#'d SETS
NO SAPPHIRE PRICING AVAILABLE
*SEPIA: .4X TO 1X BASIC COMBO
SEPIA ODDS 1:27 MINI
SEPIA PRINT RUN 27 SER.#'d SETS
1 ARod/Wright/Howard 20.00 50.00
2 Mantle/Williams/DiMaggio 200.00 300.00
3 Williams/Yaz/Manny 40.00 80.00
4 Ordonez/Ichiro/Polanco 12.50 30.00
5 ARod/Prince/Howard 20.00 50.00
6 ARod/Holliday/Ordonez 20.00 50.00
7 Jose Reyes/Juan Pierre/Hanley Ramirez 8.00 20.00
8 Wang/ARod/Rivera 20.00 50.00
9 Jake Peavy/Scott Kazmir/Johan Santana 10.00 25.00
10 DiMaggio/Clemente/Mantle 75.00 150.00
11 Mark Buehrle/Justin Verlander
Clay Buchholz 10.00 25.00
12 Ordonez/Kaline/Grander 15.00 40.00
13 Martin/Andruw/Furcal 15.00 40.00
14 Jason Varitek/Jorge Posada
Ivan Rodriguez 8.00 20.00
15 Berra/Mantle/Maris 75.00 150.00
16 Gary Matthews/Vladimir Guerrero
Torii Hunter 8.00 20.00
17 Troy Tulowitzki/Matt Holliday
Todd Helton 10.00 25.00
18 Clemente/Yaz/Reggie 50.00 100.00
19 Banks/Soriano/Sandberg 15.00 40.00
20 Mantle/Pujols/Clemente 60.00 120.00
21 Lance Berkman/Carlos Lee
Hunter Pence 8.00 20.00
22 Gordon/Braun/Zimmerman 12.50 30.00
23 Mantle/ARod/Williams 75.00 150.00
24 Morneau/Killebrew/Mauer 15.00 40.00
25 Hoffman/Eckersley/Rivera 20.00 50.00
26 Reyes/Wright/Maine 20.00 50.00
27 Matsuzaka/Suzuki/Matsui 40.00 80.00
28 Musial/Pujols/Hornsby 40.00 80.00
29 Vince D/Joe D/Dom D 60.00 120.00
30 Schmidt/Brett/Carlton 20.00 50.00
31 Markakis/Brooks/Roberts 15.00 40.00
32 Prince/Molitor/Braun 10.00 25.00
33 Linc/Joba/Bannister 30.00 60.00
34 Andruw/Howard/Prince 10.00 25.00
35 Manny/ARod/Papi 30.00 60.00
36 Palmer/Pedro/Seaver 15.00 40.00
37 Ichiro/Helton/Pujols 12.50 30.00
38 Pedro Martinez/Roy Oswalt
Greg Maddux 10.00 25.00
39 Berra/Joe D/Rizzuto 75.00 150.00
40 Banks/Clemente/Yaz 40.00 80.00
41 Justin Morneau/Ryan Howard
Prince Fielder 10.00 25.00
42 Gordon/Brett/Bannister 10.00 25.00
43 Howard/Pujols/Manny 20.00 50.00
44 ARod/Vlad/Prince 20.00 50.00
45 Unit/Ryan/Nomo 20.00 50.00
46 Fingers/Reggie/Blue 15.00 40.00
47 Clemente/Ichiro/Mantle 75.00 150.00
48 Brooks/Palmer/F.Robinson 20.00 50.00
49 Reggie Jackson/Steve Garvey
Willie Randolph 10.00 25.00
50 Ortiz/Williams/Manny 30.00 60.00
51 Mantle/ARod/Joe D 75.00 150.00
52 Snider/Martin/Garvey 15.00 40.00
53 Ichiro/Soriano/Beltran 10.00 25.00
54 Chase Utley/Dan Uggla
Dustin Pedroia 12.50 30.00
55 Jose Reyes/Jimmy Rollins
Hanley Ramirez 8.00 20.00
56 Rollins/Joe D/Utley 40.00 80.00
57 Johnny Bench/Ivan Rodriguez
Carlton Fisk 10.00 25.00
58 Pedro/Ryan/Johan 15.00 40.00
59 Reyes/Ozzie/Rollins 15.00 40.00
60 Jimmy Rollins/Jake Peavy/Ryan Braun 12.50 30.00
61 ARod/Sabathia/Pedroia 12.50 30.00
62 Delmon/ARod/J.Upton 15.00 40.00
63 ARod/Big Hurt/Thome 20.00 50.00
64 Maris/Mantle/Killebrew 100.00 200.00
65 Carlos Beltran/Chipper Jones
Jose Reyes 8.00 20.00
66 Jimmy Rollins/Matt Holliday
Prince Fielder 8.00 20.00
67 ARod/Magglio/Vlad 10.00 25.00
68 Jake Peavy/Brandon Webb/Brad Penny 8.00 20.00
69 C.C. Sabathia/Josh Beckett
John Lackey 10.00 25.00
70 Ryan Braun/Troy Tulowitzki
Hunter Pence 10.00 25.00
71 Dustin Pedroia/Delmon Young
Brian Bannister 10.00 25.00
72 Victor Martinez/Grady Sizemore
Travis Hafner 10.00 25.00
73 Magglio Ordonez/Ichiro Suzuki
Vladimir Guerrero 10.00 25.00
74 Dan Uggla/Hanley Ramirez
Cameron Maybin 8.00 20.00
75 Ichiro/Matsuzaka/Iwamura 30.00 60.00
76 Varitek/ARod/Utley 15.00 40.00
77 Speaker/Manny/Hafner 20.00 50.00
78 Mathews/Chipper/Murphy 40.00 80.00
79 Schmidt/Howard/Ashburn 12.50 30.00
80 Rollins/Howard/Utley 10.00 25.00
81 Matt Holliday
Carlos Beltran/Carlos Lee 8.00 20.00
82 Vladimir Guerrero
Magglio Ordonez/Ichiro Suzuki 10.00 25.00
83 Andruw Jones/Jeff Francoeur
Carlos Beltran 8.00 20.00
84 Sizemore/Ichiro/Hunter 8.00 20.00
85 Musial/Yaz/Williams 30.00 60.00
86 ARod/ARod/ARod 20.00 50.00
87 Chipper Jones/Brian McCann
Jeff Francoeur 12.50 30.00
88 Ryan/Ryan/Ryan 60.00 120.00
89 David Ortiz/Paul Molitor
Edgar Martinez 10.00 25.00
90 ARod/Pujols/Manny 20.00 50.00
91 Unit/L.Gonzalez/Rivera 12.00 30.00
92 Gossage/Brett/Martin 20.00 50.00
93 Fausto Carmona/Joba Chamberlain
Grady Sizemore 8.00 20.00
94 Brian Giles/Matt Holliday
Michael Barrett 8.00 20.00
95 FDR/Truman/JFK 40.00 80.00
96 Bush/Reagan/Bush 50.00 100.00
97 Taft/Wilson/Harding 12.50 30.00
98 Johnny Damon/Chipper Jones
Matt Holliday 10.00 25.00
99 David Ortiz/Jose Reyes
Alfonso Soriano 10.00 25.00
100 Beltre/Pujols/Polanco 10.00 25.00
101 Joe D/Gehrig/Mantle 200.00 300.00
102 Cobb/Ruth/Wagner 250.00 350.00
103 Campy/Munson/Bench 30.00 60.00
104 Reese/J.Robinson/Campy 40.00 80.00
105 Clemente/Wagner/Kiner 75.00 150.00
106 Mize/Ott/Hornsby 50.00 100.00
107 Reggie/Munson/Martin 30.00 60.00
108 Foxx/Gehrig/Ott 100.00 175.00
109 Maris/Ruth/Mantle 250.00 350.00
110 Wagner/Cobb/Speaker 200.00 300.00
111 Foxx/Manny/Williams 30.00 60.00

2008 Topps Triple Threads Relics Combos Autographs

STATED ODDS 1:97 MINI
STATED PRINT RUN 36 SER.#'d SETS
EMERALD ODDS 1:193 MINI
EMERALD PRINT RUN 18 SER.#'d SETS
NO EMERALD PRICING AVAILABLE
GOLD ODDS 1:387 MINI
GOLD PRINT RUN 9 SER.#'d SETS
NO GOLD PRICING AVAILABLE
PLATINUM ODDS 1:3383 MINI
PLAT.PRINT RUN 1 SER.#'d SET
NO PLAT.PRICING AVAILABLE
SAPPHIRE ODDS 1:1179 MINI
SAPP.PRINT RUN 3 SER.#'d SETS
NO SAPP.PRICING AVAILABLE
*SEPIA: .4X TO 1X BASIC
SEPIA ODDS 1:129 MINI
SEPIA PRINT RUN 27 SER.#'d SETS
STATED ODDS 1:874 MINI
STATED PRINT RUN 1 SER.#'d SET
NO PRICING DUE TO SCARCITY
1 Reyes/Ozzie/Hanley 50.00 100.00
2 Pujols/Manny/Vlad 125.00 250.00
3 Hernandez/Schmidt/Murphy 50.00 100.00
4 F.Robinson/Yaz/Killebrew 100.00 200.00
5 Gibson/Seaver/Carlton 60.00 150.00
6 Killebrew/Carew/Brooks 60.00 120.00
7 Wright/Howard/Pujols 100.00 250.00
8 Prince/Murray/Howard 20.00 50.00
9 Ryan/Brett/Yount 200.00 400.00
10 Bench/Pudge/Fisk 60.00 120.00
11 Berra/Ford/Posada 75.00 200.00
12 Gwynn/Murphy/Strawberry 50.00 100.00
13 Lowell/Manny/Papi 60.00 120.00
14 Joba/Posada/Wang 75.00 150.00
15 Jeff Francis/Taylor Buchholz
Ubaldo Jimenez 12.50 30.00
16 Melky/Ohlendorf/Cano 20.00 50.00
17 Uggla/Seddon/Hanley 12.00 30.00
18 Gordon/Longoria/Zimmerman 30.00 60.00
19 Chris Young/Melky Cabrera
Lastings Milledge 12.50 30.00
20 Rich Hill/Johnny Cueto
Tom Gorzelanny 12.50 30.00
21 Moseley/Liriano/King Felix 15.00 40.00
22 Hanley/Loney/Hardy 15.00 40.00
23 Armando Galarraga
/Fausto Carmona/Troy Patton 12.50 30.00

2008 Topps Triple Threads Relics Combos Double

STATED ODDS 1:41 MINI
STATED PRINT RUN 36 SER.#'d SETS
EMERALD ODDS 1:81 MINI
EMERALD PRINT RUN 18 SER.#'d SETS
NO EMERALD PRICING AVAILABLE
GOLD ODDS 1:162 MINI
GOLD PRINT RUN 9 SER.#'d SETS
NO GOLD PRICING AVAILABLE
PLATINUM ODDS 1:1496 MINI
PLAT.PRINT RUN 1 SER.#'d SET
NO PLAT.PRICING AVAILABLE
SAPPHIRE ODDS 1:486 MINI
SAPP.PRINT RUN 3 SER.#'d SETS
NO SAPP.PRICING AVAILABLE
*SEPIA: .4X TO 1X BASIC
SEPIA ODDS 1:54 MINI
SEPIA PRINT RUN 27 SER.#'d SETS
1 Vintage OFs 125.00 250.00
2 Batting Avg LDR 250.00 350.00
3 Triple Play 30.00 60.00
4 Cardinals 60.00 120.00
5 Four Baggers 15.00 40.00
6 Vintage Pitchers 30.00 60.00
7 Base Stealers 15.00 40.00
8 Catchers 30.00 60.00
9 J.DiMaggio/M.Mantle 100.00 200.00
10 Vintage Yankees 100.00 200.00
11 MVP-HOF 100.00 200.00
12 Osw/Mun/Saar/Lid/DOt/Wag 20.00 50.00
13 Yanks/Sox/Mets/Phils 75.00 150.00
14 Yankees 50.00 100.00
15 Japanese Stars 50.00 100.00
16 Russell Martin 20.00 50.00
Jason Bay
Erik Bedard
Rich Harden
Justin Morneau
Shawn Hill
17 Carlos Beltran 30.00 60.00
David Wright
Carlos Delgado
Jose Reyes
Pedro Martinez
John Maine
18 Travis Hafner 10.00 25.00
Victor Martinez
Grady Sizemore
C.C. Sabathia
Fausto Carmona
Bob Feller
19 Brooks Robinson 20.00 50.00
Jim Palmer
Eddie Murray
Brian Roberts
Nick Markakis
Melvin Mora
20 Red Sox 40.00 80.00
21 Mariners 40.00 80.00
22 2007 Award Winners 30.00 60.00
23 Mickey Mantle 75.00 150.00
24 Joe DiMaggio 60.00 120.00
25 Roberto Clemente 60.00 120.00
26 Astros 30.00 60.00
27 Phillies 20.00 50.00
28 WS MVPs 40.00 80.00
29 Ted Williams 50.00 100.00
30 Twins 50.00 100.00
31 First Basemen 10.00 25.00
32 Tigers 50.00 100.00
33 Carlton Fisk 20.00 50.00
Jim Thome
Jermaine Dye
Mark Buehrle
Paul Konerko
Luis Aparicio
34 Keith Hernandez 20.00 50.00
Dwight Gooden
Darryl Strawberry
David Wright
Pedro Martinez
Jose Reyes
35 Braves 30.00 60.00
36 Yankees/Red Sox 40.00 80.00
37 R.Maris/M.Mantle 200.00 300.00
38 Ichiro Suzuki 40.00 80.00
39 Albert Pujols 12.00 30.00
40 Brewers 30.00 60.00
41 Rangers 30.00 60.00
42 Vladimir Guerrero 20.00 50.00
John Lackey
Jered Weaver
Garret Anderson
Torii Hunter
Gary Matthews
43 Tim Lincecum 20.00 50.00
Rich Aurilia
Barry Zito
Eric Chavez
Mark Ellis
Bobby Crosby
44 Russell Martin 20.00 50.00
Rafael Furcal
Andruw Jones
Matt Kemp
Jeff Kent
Hong-Chih Kuo
45 Mets/Phillies 20.00 50.00
46 Chien-Ming Wang 20.00 50.00
47 2007 All-Stars 30.00 60.00
48 2007 ALCS 20.00 50.00
49 Matt Holliday 20.00 50.00
Todd Helton
Troy Tulowitzki
Orlando Hudson
Stephen Drew
Chris Young
50 2007 World Series 30.00 60.00
51 A.Rodriguez/M.Mantle 40.00 80.00
52 Dominican Republic 30.00 60.00
53 All-Time Greats 450.00 650.00
54 STL/PHI/NYG/BRK 60.00 120.00
55 1955 World Series 100.00 200.00

2008 Topps Triple Threads Relics Pairs Rookie-Stars Autographs

STATED ODDS 1:160 MINI
STATED PRINT RUN 50 SER.#'d SETS
GLD ODDS 1:322 MINI
GLD.PRINT RUN 25 SER.#'d SETS
NO GLD.PRICING AVAILABLE
PLAT.ODDS 1:7781 MINI
PLAT.PRINT RUN 1 SER.#'d SET
NO PLAT.PRICING AVAILABLE
SAP.ODDS 1:802 MINI
SAP.PRINT RUN 10 SER.#'d SETS
NO SAP.PRICING AVAILABLE
1 S.Pearce/N.Morgan 15.00 40.00
2 C.Maybin/C.Granderson 12.50 30.00
3 M.Cabrera/R.Cano 30.00 60.00
4 L.Milledge/E.Dukes 10.00 25.00
5 R.Hill/S.Fuld 10.00 25.00
6 J.Towles/J.Saltalamacchia 10.00 25.00
7 C.Buchholz/F.Carmona 10.00 25.00
8 R.Braun/R.Zimmerman 15.00 40.00
9 P.Hughes/J.Chamberlain 15.00 40.00
10 B.Phillips/H.Bailey 12.50 30.00

2009 Topps Triple Threads

COMMON CARD (1-100) .40 1.00
1-100 PRINT RUN 1350 SER.#'d SETS
COMMON JSY AU RC (101-138) 6.00 15.00
JSY AU RC ODDS 1:11 MINI
JSY AU RC PRINT RUN 99 SER.#'d SETS
COMMON JSY AU (101-121) 6.00 15.00
JSY AU ODDS 1:11 MINI
JSY AU PRINT RUN 99 SER.#'d SETS
OVERALL 1-100 PLATE ODDS 1:97 MINI
OVERALL 101-138 PLATE ODDS 1:255 MINI
PLATE PRINT RUN 1 SET PER COLOR
BLACK-CYAN-MAGENTA-YELLOW ISSUED
NO PLATE PRICING DUE TO SCARCITY
1 Justin Upton .60 1.50
2 Brian McCann .60 1.50
3 Babe Ruth 2.50 6.00
4 Alfonso Soriano .60 1.50
5 Albert Pujols 1.25 3.00
6 Edinson Volquez .40 1.00
7 Todd Helton .60 1.50
8 Hanley Ramirez .60 1.50
9 Mickey Mantle 3.00 8.00
10 Manny Ramirez 1.00 2.50
11 Francisco Liriano .40 1.00
12 Lou Gehrig 2.00 5.00
13 Carlos Delgado .40 1.00
14 Walter Johnson 1.00 2.50
15 Alex Rodriguez 1.25 3.00
16 Ryan Howard .75 2.00
17 Nate McLouth .40 1.00
18 Cy Young 1.00 2.50
19 Ichiro Suzuki 1.25 3.00
20 Jorge Posada .60 1.50
21 Scott Kazmir .40 1.00
22 Michael Young .40 1.00
23 Brandon Webb .60 1.50
24 George Sisler .60 1.50
25 Chipper Jones 1.00 2.50
26 Adam Jones .60 1.50
27 David Ortiz 1.00 2.50
28 Geovany Soto .60 1.50
29 Tony Gwynn 1.00 2.50
30 Victor Martinez .60 1.50
31 Jose Lopez .40 1.00
32 Lance Berkman .60 1.50
33 Russell Martin .40 1.00
34 Cal Ripken 3.00 8.00
35 Dan Haren .40 1.00
36 Jose Reyes .60 1.50
37 Rogers Hornsby .60 1.50
38 Mark Teixeira .60 1.50
39 Ernie Banks 1.00 2.50
40 Jimmy Rollins .60 1.50
41 Jake Peavy .40 1.00
42 Jackie Robinson 1.00 2.50
43 B.J. Upton .60 1.50
44 Roy Halladay .60 1.50
45 Jimmie Foxx 1.00 2.50
46 Randy Johnson 1.00 2.50
47 Mel Ott 1.00 2.50
48 Carlos Lee .40 1.00
49 Nick Markakis .75 2.00

50 Dustin Pedroia	1.00	2.50
51 Nolan Ryan	3.00	8.00
52 Matt Cain	.60	1.50
53 Grady Sizemore	.60	1.50
54 Christy Mathewson	1.00	2.50
55 Miguel Cabrera	1.00	2.50
56 Roy Campanella	1.00	2.50
57 Prince Fielder	.60	1.50
58 Ty Cobb	1.50	4.00
59 Carlos Beltran	.60	1.50
60 Pee Wee Reese	.60	1.50
61 A.J. Burnett	.40	1.00
62 Carl Crawford	.60	1.50
63 Chase Utley	.60	1.50
64 Adrian Gonzalez	.75	2.00
65 Thurman Munson	1.00	2.50
66 Felix Hernandez	.60	1.50
67 Chris Carpenter	.60	1.50
68 Carl Yastrzemski	1.50	4.00
69 Ian Kinsler	.60	1.50
70 Vernon Wells	.40	1.00
71 Matt Holliday	1.00	2.50
72 Tris Speaker	.60	1.50
73 Roy Oswalt	.60	1.50
74 Ozzie Smith	1.25	3.00
75 Daisuke Matsuzaka	.60	1.50
76 David Wright	.75	2.00
77 Kosuke Fukudome	.60	1.50
78 Johan Santana	.60	1.50
79 Curtis Granderson	.75	2.00
80 Johnny Mize	.60	1.50
81 Derek Jeter	2.50	6.00
82 Vladimir Guerrero	.60	1.50
83 Dan Uggla	.40	1.00
84 Hank Greenberg	1.00	2.50
85 Justin Morneau	.60	1.50
86 CC Sabathia	.60	1.50
87 Mike Schmidt	1.50	4.00
88 Cole Hamels	.75	2.00
89 Alex Rios	.40	1.00
90 Ryne Sandberg	2.00	5.00
91 Ryan Ludwick	.60	1.50
92 Tim Lincecum	.60	1.50
93 Honus Wagner	1.00	2.50
94 Carlos Quentin	.40	1.00
95 Alexei Ramriez	.60	1.50
96 Joe Mauer	.75	2.00
97 Bob Gibson	.60	1.50
98 Reggie Jackson	.60	1.50
99 Carlos Zambrano	.60	1.50
100 Stan Musial	1.50	4.00
101 R.Braun Jsy AU	15.00	40.00
102 J.Bruce Jsy AU	10.00	25.00
103 Fausto Carmona Jsy AU	6.00	15.00
104 M.Kemp Jsy AU	20.00	50.00
105 C.Maybin Jsy AU	8.00	20.00
106 J.Cueto Jsy AU	10.00	25.00
107 J.Hamilton Jsy AU	15.00	40.00
108 U.Jimenez Jsy AU	6.00	15.00
109 G.Soto Jsy AU	6.00	15.00
110 Jon Lester Jsy AU	15.00	40.00
111 C.Kershaw Jsy AU	50.00	100.00
112 L.Hochevar Jsy AU	6.00	15.00
113 E.Longoria Jsy AU	15.00	40.00
114 J.Masterson Jsy AU	6.00	15.00
115 B.DeWitt Jsy AU	6.00	15.00
116 D.Murphy Jsy AU RC	20.00	50.00
117 C.Billingsley Jsy AU	6.00	15.00
118 D.Pedroia Jsy AU	20.00	50.00
119 H.Pence Jsy AU	10.00	25.00
120 Joakim Soria Jsy AU	6.00	15.00
121 Justin Upton Jsy AU	20.00	50.00
122 F.Martinez Jsy AU RC	10.00	25.00
123 N.Reimold Jsy AU (RC)	6.00	15.00
124 M.Gamel Jsy AU RC	6.00	15.00
125 M.Bowden Jsy AU (RC)	6.00	15.00
126 D.Holland Jsy AU RC	6.00	15.00
127 E.Andrus Jsy AU RC	12.50	30.00
128 T.Cahill Jsy AU RC	8.00	20.00
129 Ryan Perry Jsy AU RC	6.00	15.00
130 J.Zimmermann Jsy AU RC	12.50	30.00
131 T.Hanson Jsy AU RC	6.00	15.00
132 D.Price Jsy AU RC	15.00	40.00
133 C.Rasmus Jsy AU (RC)	6.00	15.00
134 R.Porcello Jsy AU RC	12.00	30.00
135 B.Anderson Jsy AU RC	6.00	15.00
136 K.Uehara Jsy AU RC	15.00	40.00
137 L.Marson Jsy AU (RC)	6.00	15.00
138 Matt Tolbert Jsy AU	6.00	15.00

2009 Topps Triple Threads Emerald

*EMERALD 1-100: .6X TO 1.5X BASIC
1-100 ODDS 1:2 MINI
1-100 PRINT RUN 240 SER.#'d SETS
*EMERALD JSY AU: .4X TO 1X BASIC
EMERALD JSY AU ODDS 1:21 MINI
EM.JSY AU PRINT RUN 50 SER.#'d SETS

2009 Topps Triple Threads Gold

*GOLD 1-100: 1X TO 2.5X BASIC
1-100 ODDS 1:4 MINI
1-100 PRINT RUN 99 SER.#'d SETS
GOLD JSY AU ODDS 1:41 MINI
GOLD JSY AU PRINT RUN 25 SER.#'d SETS
NO GOLD JSY AU PRICING AVAILABLE

2009 Topps Triple Threads Legend Relics

STATED ODDS 1:72 MINI
STATED PRINT RUN 36 SER.#'d SETS

1 Babe Ruth	175.00	350.00
2 Rogers Hornsby	15.00	40.00
3 Pee Wee Reese	10.00	25.00
4 Lou Gehrig	150.00	250.00
5 Jimmie Foxx	10.00	25.00
6 Honus Wagner	100.00	175.00
7 Roy Campanella	20.00	50.00
8 Mickey Mantle	100.00	175.00
9 Mel Ott	40.00	80.00
10 Tris Speaker	15.00	40.00
11 Jackie Robinson	40.00	80.00
12 George Sisler	20.00	50.00
13 Ty Cobb	90.00	150.00
14 Thurman Munson	20.00	50.00
15 Johnny Mize	12.50	30.00

2009 Topps Triple Threads Relic Autographs

STATED ODDS 1:13 MINI
STATED PRINT RUN 18 SER.#'d SETS
ALL DC VARIATIONS PRICED EQUALLY

1 David Wright	30.00	60.00
2 David Wright	30.00	60.00
3 David Wright	30.00	60.00
4 David Ortiz	30.00	60.00
5 David Ortiz	30.00	60.00
6 David Ortiz	30.00	60.00
7 Jose Reyes	15.00	40.00
8 Jose Reyes	15.00	40.00
9 Jose Reyes	15.00	40.00
10 Zack Greinke	12.50	30.00
11 Zack Greinke	12.50	30.00
12 Zack Greinke	12.50	30.00
13 Miguel Cabrera	50.00	100.00
14 Miguel Cabrera	50.00	100.00
15 Miguel Cabrera	50.00	100.00
16 Matt Cain	20.00	50.00
17 Matt Cain	20.00	50.00
18 Matt Cain	20.00	50.00
19 Robinson Cano	20.00	50.00
20 Robinson Cano	20.00	50.00
21 Robinson Cano	20.00	50.00
22 Andre Ethier	15.00	40.00
23 Andre Ethier	15.00	40.00
24 Andre Ethier	15.00	40.00
25 Curtis Granderson	20.00	50.00
26 Curtis Granderson	20.00	50.00
27 Curtis Granderson	20.00	50.00
28 Manny Ramirez	50.00	100.00
29 Manny Ramirez	50.00	100.00
30 Manny Ramirez	50.00	100.00
31 Nick Markakis	12.50	30.00
32 Nick Markakis	12.50	30.00
33 Nick Markakis	12.50	30.00
34 Vladimir Guerrero	40.00	80.00
35 Vladimir Guerrero	40.00	80.00
36 Vladimir Guerrero	40.00	80.00
37 Matt Holliday	15.00	40.00
38 Matt Holliday	15.00	40.00
39 Matt Holliday	15.00	40.00
40 Ryan Howard	15.00	40.00
41 Ryan Howard	15.00	40.00
42 Ryan Howard	15.00	40.00
43 Chipper Jones	50.00	100.00
44 Chipper Jones	50.00	100.00
45 Chipper Jones	50.00	100.00
46 Scott Kazmir	10.00	25.00
47 Scott Kazmir	10.00	25.00
48 Scott Kazmir	10.00	25.00
49 Joba Chamberlain	20.00	50.00
50 Joba Chamberlain	20.00	50.00
51 Joba Chamberlain	20.00	50.00
52 Alfonso Soriano	15.00	40.00
53 Alfonso Soriano	15.00	40.00
54 Alfonso Soriano	15.00	40.00
55 Nick Swisher	20.00	50.00
56 Nick Swisher	20.00	50.00
57 Nick Swisher	20.00	50.00
58 Prince Fielder	40.00	80.00
59 Prince Fielder	40.00	80.00
60 Prince Fielder	40.00	80.00
61 Ryan Zimmerman	20.00	50.00
62 Ryan Zimmerman	20.00	50.00
63 Ryan Zimmerman	20.00	50.00
64 Johnny Podres	20.00	50.00
65 Johnny Podres	20.00	50.00
66 Johnny Podres	20.00	50.00
67 George Kell	20.00	50.00
68 George Kell	20.00	50.00
69 George Kell	20.00	50.00
70 Gary Carter	30.00	60.00
71 Gary Carter	30.00	60.00
72 Gary Carter	30.00	60.00
73 Whitey Ford	40.00	80.00
74 Whitey Ford	40.00	80.00
75 Whitey Ford	40.00	80.00
76 Bob Gibson	30.00	60.00
77 Bob Gibson	30.00	60.00
78 Bob Gibson	30.00	60.00
79 Juan Marichal	20.00	50.00
80 Juan Marichal	20.00	50.00
81 Juan Marichal	20.00	50.00
82 Duke Snider	30.00	60.00
83 Duke Snider	30.00	60.00
84 Duke Snider	30.00	60.00
85 Robin Yount	20.00	50.00
86 Robin Yount	20.00	50.00
87 Robin Yount	20.00	50.00
88 Jim Palmer	15.00	40.00
89 Jim Palmer	15.00	40.00
90 Jim Palmer	15.00	40.00
91 Bo Jackson	40.00	80.00
92 Bo Jackson	40.00	80.00
93 Bo Jackson	40.00	80.00
94 Don Larsen	30.00	60.00
95 Don Larsen	30.00	60.00
96 Don Larsen	30.00	60.00
97 Tony Gwynn	40.00	80.00
98 Tony Gwynn	40.00	80.00
99 Tony Gwynn	40.00	80.00
100 Brian McCann	12.00	30.00
101 Brian McCann	12.00	30.00
102 Brian McCann	12.00	30.00
103 Shane Victorino	40.00	80.00
104 Shane Victorino	40.00	80.00
105 Shane Victorino	40.00	80.00
106 Adrian Gonzalez	12.50	30.00
107 Adrian Gonzalez	12.50	30.00
108 Adrian Gonzalez	12.50	30.00
109 Garrett Atkins	8.00	20.00
110 Garrett Atkins	8.00	20.00
111 Garrett Atkins	8.00	20.00
112 Carl Yastrzemski	40.00	80.00
113 Carl Yastrzemski	40.00	80.00
114 Carl Yastrzemski	40.00	80.00
115 Carlos Delgado	15.00	40.00
116 Carlos Delgado	15.00	40.00
117 Carlos Delgado	15.00	40.00
118 Jason Varitek	20.00	50.00
119 Jason Varitek	20.00	50.00
120 Jason Varitek	20.00	50.00
121 Tom Seaver	40.00	100.00
122 Tom Seaver	40.00	100.00
123 Tom Seaver	40.00	100.00
124 Rich Harden	8.00	20.00
125 Rich Harden	8.00	20.00
126 Rich Harden	8.00	20.00
127 Aramis Ramirez	15.00	40.00
128 Aramis Ramirez	15.00	40.00
129 Aramis Ramirez	15.00	40.00
130 Chien-Ming Wang	90.00	150.00
131 Chien-Ming Wang	90.00	150.00
132 Chien-Ming Wang	90.00	150.00
133 Jayson Werth	20.00	50.00
134 Jayson Werth	20.00	50.00
135 Jayson Werth	20.00	50.00
136 Jonathan Papelbon	12.50	30.00
137 Jonathan Papelbon	12.50	30.00
138 Jonathan Papelbon	12.50	30.00
139 Alex Rodriguez	50.00	100.00
140 Alex Rodriguez	50.00	100.00
141 Alex Rodriguez	50.00	100.00
142 Johnny Bench	50.00	100.00
143 Johnny Bench	50.00	100.00
144 Johnny Bench	50.00	100.00
145 Mark Teixeira	90.00	150.00
146 Mark Teixeira	90.00	150.00
147 Mark Teixeira	90.00	150.00
148 Dan Haren	10.00	25.00
149 Dan Haren	10.00	25.00
150 Dan Haren	10.00	25.00
151 Ernie Banks	15.00	40.00
152 Ernie Banks	15.00	40.00
153 Ernie Banks	15.00	40.00
154 Lance Berkman	15.00	40.00
155 Lance Berkman	15.00	40.00
156 Lance Berkman	15.00	40.00
157 Cal Ripken	100.00	200.00
158 Cal Ripken	100.00	200.00
159 Cal Ripken	100.00	200.00
160 Paul Molitor	15.00	40.00
161 Paul Molitor	15.00	40.00
162 Paul Molitor	15.00	40.00
163 Mike Lowell	15.00	40.00
164 Mike Lowell	15.00	40.00
165 Mike Lowell	15.00	40.00
166 Dan Uggla	8.00	20.00
167 Dan Uggla	8.00	20.00
168 Dan Uggla	8.00	20.00
169 Aaron Hill	12.50	30.00
170 Aaron Hill	12.50	30.00
171 Aaron Hill	12.50	30.00
172 Johnny Damon	20.00	50.00
173 Johnny Damon	20.00	50.00
174 Johnny Damon	20.00	50.00

2009 Topps Triple Threads Relic Autographs Gold

*GOLD: .5X TO 1.2X BASIC
STATED ODDS 1:25 MINI
STATED PRINT RUN 9 SER.#'d SETS
ALL DC VARIATIONS PRICED EQUALLY

2009 Topps Triple Threads Relic Combo Autographs

STATED ODDS 1:51 MINI
STATED PRINT RUN 36 SER.#'d SETS

1 Soto/McCann/Martin	10.00	25.00
2 Hanley/Reyes/Tejada	30.00	60.00
3 Cueto/Silva/Soria	6.00	15.00
4 Halladay/Webb/Wang	50.00	100.00
5 Manny/Kemp/Ethier	50.00	100.00
6 F.Rob/Palmer/Murray	40.00	80.00
7 Kazmir/Joba/Lester	30.00	60.00
8 Howard/Pujols/Cabrera	150.00	300.00
9 Reggie/ARod/Cano	90.00	150.00
10 Molitor/Yount/Braun	60.00	120.00
11 Lester/Mast/Papel	30.00	60.00
12 Bruce/Hamilton/Pence	15.00	40.00
13 Ortiz/Varitek/Papel	40.00	80.00
14 Snider/Manny/Kemp	75.00	150.00
15 Roberts/Pedroia/Cano	30.00	60.00
16 Soriano/Aramis/Sandberg	40.00	80.00
17 Wright/Hanley/Pujols	150.00	250.00
18 Kazmir/Longoria/Price	40.00	80.00
19 Teixeira/Cano/ARod	175.00	350.00
20 Papel/Soria/Nathan	12.50	30.00
21 Torii/Vlad/Reggie	20.00	50.00

2009 Topps Triple Threads Relic Combos

STATED ODDS 1:24 MINI
STATED PRINT RUN 36 SER.#'d SETS

1 Seaver/Ryan/Santana	20.00	50.00
2 Howard/Schmidt/Utley	40.00	80.00
3 Posada/Mantle/Teixeira	30.00	60.00
4 Beckett/Lester/Smoltz	12.50	30.00
5 Reyes/Carter/Wright	20.00	50.00
6 Pujols/Cabrera/Howard	20.00	50.00
7 Sandberg/Schmidt/Ozzie	15.00	40.00
8 Matsuzaka/Ichiro/Matsui	30.00	60.00
9 Kawa/Matsuzaka/Uehara	30.00	60.00
10 Manny/Beltran/Soriano	10.00	25.00
11 Hamil/Kins/Young	8.00	20.00
12 Sizemore/Hamilton/Ichiro	15.00	40.00
13 Ramir/Roll/Reyes	8.00	20.00
14 Pedroi/Sand/Kins	10.00	25.00
15 Longoria/ARod/Chipper	15.00	40.00
16 Manny/Pujols/Howard	12.50	30.00
17 Thome/Manny/Sheff	8.00	20.00
18 Mantle/Ruth/Gehrig	200.00	400.00
20 Mantle/F.Rob/Yaz	50.00	100.00
21 Reese/J.Rob/Campy	40.00	80.00
22 Belt/Delg/Wright	10.00	25.00
23 Zimmerman/Wright/Longoria	12.50	30.00
24 Mauer/Bench/McCann	12.50	30.00
25 Howard/ARod/Wright	12.50	30.00
26 incecum/Peavy/Webb	12.50	30.00
27 Youk/Ortiz/Varitek	10.00	25.00
28 Mart/Manny/Kemp	10.00	25.00
29 Soto/Braun/Ramir	10.00	25.00
30 Pujols/Howard/Hanley	12.50	30.00
31 Gonz/Roll/Wright	10.00	25.00
32 Ripken/ARod/Chipper	30.00	60.00
33 Banks/Ozzie/Hanley	12.50	30.00
34 Gonzalez/Gwynn/Peavy	10.00	25.00
35 Banks/Ozzie/Ripken	20.00	50.00
36 Utley/Rollins/Howard	20.00	50.00
37 Reggie/Reggie/Reggie	15.00	40.00
38 Ryan/Ryan/Ryan	30.00	60.00
39 Prince/Pujols/Berkman	12.50	30.00
40 Cantu/Soria/Gonz	10.00	25.00
41 Felix/Ordonez/Cabrera	12.50	30.00
42 Roll/Oswa/Dunn	8.00	20.00
43 Lee/Lee/Choo	15.00	40.00
44 Aumont/Chapman/Lindsay	8.00	20.00
45 Cepeda/Gourriel/Cespedes	40.00	80.00
46 Ichiro/Darvish/Aoki	60.00	120.00

2009 Topps Triple Threads Relic Combos Sepia

*SEPIA: .4X TO 1X BASIC
STATED ODDS 1:32 MINI
STATED PRINT RUN 27 SER.#'d SETS

1 Tom Seaver	20.00	50.00
Nolan Ryan		
Johan Santana		
2 Ryan Howard	40.00	80.00
Mike Schmidt		
Chase Utley		
3 Jorge Posada	30.00	60.00
Mickey Mantle		
Mark Teixeira		
4 Josh Beckett	12.50	30.00
Jon Lester		
John Smoltz		
5 Jose Reyes	20.00	50.00
Gary Carter		
David Wright		
6 Albert Pujols	20.00	50.00
Miguel Cabrera		
Ryan Howard		
7 Ryne Sandberg	15.00	40.00
Mike Schmidt		
Ozzie Smith		
8 Daisuke Matsuzaka	30.00	60.00
Ichiro Suzuki		
Hideki Matsui		
9 Kenshin Kawakami	30.00	60.00
Daisuke Matsuzaka		
Koji Uehara		
10 Manny Ramirez	10.00	25.00
Carlos Beltran		
Alfonso Soriano		
11 Josh Hamilton	8.00	20.00
Ian Kinsler		
Michael Young		
12 Grady Sizemore	15.00	40.00
Josh Hamilton		
Ichiro Suzuki		
13 Hanley Ramirez	8.00	20.00
Jimmy Rollins		
Jose Reyes		
14 Dustin Pedroia	10.00	25.00
Ryne Sandberg		
Ian Kinsler		
15 Evan Longoria	15.00	40.00
Alex Rodriguez		
Chipper Jones		
16 Manny Ramirez	12.50	30.00
Albert Pujols		
Ryan Howard		
17 Jim Thome	8.00	20.00
Manny Ramirez		
Gary Sheffield		
18 Mickey Mantle	400.00	800.00
Babe Ruth		
Lou Gehrig		
20 Mickey Mantle	50.00	100.00
Frank Robinson		
Carl Yastrzemski		
21 Pee Wee Reese	40.00	80.00
Jackie Robinson		
Roy Campanella		
22 Carlos Beltran	10.00	25.00
Carlos Delgado		
David Wright		
23 Ryan Zimmerman	12.50	30.00
David Wright		
Evan Longoria		
24 Joe Mauer	12.50	30.00
Johnny Bench		
Brian McCann		
25 Ryan Howard	12.50	30.00
Alex Rodriguez		
David Wright		
26 Tim Lincecum	12.50	30.00
Jake Peavy		
Brandon Webb		
27 Kevin Youkilis	10.00	25.00
David Ortiz		
Jason Varitek		
28 Russell Martin	10.00	25.00
Manny Ramirez		
Matt Kemp		
29 Geovany Soto	10.00	25.00
Ryan Braun		
Hanley Ramirez		
30 Albert Pujols	12.50	30.00
Ryan Howard		
Hanley Ramirez		
31 Adrian Gonzalez	10.00	25.00
Jimmy Rollins		
David Wright		
32 Cal Ripken	30.00	60.00
Alex Rodriguez		
Chipper Jones		
33 Ernie Banks	12.50	30.00
Ozzie Smith		
Hanley Ramirez		
34 Adrian Gonzalez	10.00	25.00
Tony Gwynn		
Jake Peavy		
35 Ernie Banks	20.00	50.00
Ozzie Smith		
Cal Ripken		
36 Chase Utley	20.00	50.00
Jimmy Rollins		
Ryan Howard		
37 Reggie Jackson	15.00	40.00
Reggie Jackson		
Reggie Jackson		
38 Nolan Ryan	30.00	60.00
Nolan Ryan		
Nolan Ryan		
39 Prince Fielder	12.50	30.00
Albert Pujols		
Lance Berkman		
40 Jorge Cantu	10.00	25.00
Joakim Soria		
Edgar Gonzalez		
41 Felix Hernandez	12.50	30.00
Magglio Ordonez		
Miguel Cabrera		
42 Jimmy Rollins	8.00	20.00
Roy Oswalt		
Adam Dunn		
43 Dae Ho Lee	15.00	40.00
Jin Young Lee		
Shin-Soo Choo		
44 Phillippe Aumont	8.00	20.00
Aroldis Chapman		
Dylan Lindsay		
45 Frederich Cepeda	40.00	80.00
Yulieski Gourriel		
Yoennis Cespedes		
46 Ichiro Suzuki	60.00	120.00
Yu Darvish		
Norichika Aoki		

2009 Topps Triple Threads Relic Combos Double

STATED ODDS 1:90 MINI
STATED PRINT RUN 36 SER.#'d SETS

1 M.Schmidt/R.Howard	30.00	60.00
2 Y.Gourriel/Y.Darvish	100.00	175.00
3 Ryan Howard	20.00	50.00
4 Dustin Pedroia	15.00	40.00
5 R.Howard/D.Pedroia	15.00	40.00
6 C.Ripken/A.Rodriguez	30.00	60.00
7 J.Peavy/T.Lincecum	12.50	30.00
8 Ichiro/D.Matsuzaka	30.00	60.00
9 Ram/Sor/How/Lon/Quen/Vlad	20.00	50.00
10 Riv/Pap/Hof/Nat/Rod/Eck	40.00	80.00
11 ARod/Lon/You/Rios/Mar/Boggs	20.00	50.00
12 Puj/Wri/Ram/ARod/Ham/Long	40.00	80.00

2009 Topps Triple Threads Relic Combos Double Sepia

*SEPIA: .4X TO 1X BASIC
STATED ODDS 1:120 MINI
STATED PRINT RUN 27 SER.#'d SETS

2009 Topps Triple Threads Relics

STATED ODDS 1:10 MINI
STATED PRINT RUN 36 SER.#'d SETS
ALL DC VARIATIONS PRICED EQUALLY

1 Tim Lincecum	12.50	30.00
2 Tim Lincecum	12.50	30.00
3 Tim Lincecum	12.50	30.00
4 David Wright	10.00	25.00
5 David Wright	10.00	25.00
6 David Wright	10.00	25.00
7 Albert Pujols	20.00	50.00
8 Albert Pujols	20.00	50.00
9 Albert Pujols	20.00	50.00
10 Alex Rodriguez	12.50	30.00
11 Alex Rodriguez	12.50	30.00
12 Alex Rodriguez	12.50	30.00
13 David Ortiz	10.00	25.00
14 David Ortiz	10.00	25.00
15 David Ortiz	10.00	25.00
16 Manny Ramirez	12.50	30.00
17 Manny Ramirez	12.50	30.00
18 Manny Ramirez	12.50	30.00
19 Ichiro Suzuki	20.00	50.00
20 Ichiro Suzuki	20.00	50.00
21 Ichiro Suzuki	20.00	50.00
22 Vladimir Guerrero	6.00	15.00
23 Vladimir Guerrero	6.00	15.00
24 Vladimir Guerrero	6.00	15.00
25 Ryan Braun	10.00	25.00
26 Ryan Braun	10.00	25.00
27 Ryan Braun	10.00	25.00
28 Chipper Jones	10.00	25.00
29 Chipper Jones	10.00	25.00
30 Chipper Jones	10.00	25.00
31 Evan Longoria	12.50	30.00
32 Evan Longoria	12.50	30.00
33 Evan Longoria	12.50	30.00
34 Dustin Pedroia	8.00	20.00
35 Dustin Pedroia	8.00	20.00
36 Dustin Pedroia	8.00	20.00
37 Alfonso Soriano	6.00	15.00
38 Alfonso Soriano	6.00	15.00
39 Alfonso Soriano	6.00	15.00
40 Miguel Cabrera	8.00	20.00
41 Miguel Cabrera	8.00	20.00
42 Miguel Cabrera	8.00	20.00
43 Nick Markakis	8.00	20.00
44 Nick Markakis	8.00	20.00
45 Nick Markakis	8.00	20.00
46 Josh Hamilton	8.00	20.00
47 Josh Hamilton	8.00	20.00
48 Josh Hamilton	8.00	20.00
49 Jose Reyes	8.00	20.00
50 Jose Reyes	8.00	20.00
51 Jose Reyes	8.00	20.00
52 Bob Gibson	10.00	25.00
53 Bob Gibson	10.00	25.00
54 Bob Gibson	10.00	25.00
55 Frank Robinson	10.00	25.00
56 Frank Robinson	10.00	25.00
57 Frank Robinson	10.00	25.00
58 Paul Molitor	10.00	25.00
59 Paul Molitor	10.00	25.00
60 Paul Molitor	10.00	25.00
61 Tom Seaver	10.00	25.00
62 Tom Seaver	10.00	25.00
63 Tom Seaver	10.00	25.00
64 Gary Carter	12.50	30.00
65 Gary Carter	12.50	30.00
66 Gary Carter	12.50	30.00
67 Stan Musial	20.00	50.00
68 Stan Musial	20.00	50.00
69 Stan Musial	20.00	50.00
70 Ryne Sandberg	10.00	25.00
71 Ryne Sandberg	10.00	25.00
72 Ryne Sandberg	10.00	25.00
73 Carl Yastrzemski	10.00	25.00
74 Carl Yastrzemski	10.00	25.00
75 Carl Yastrzemski	10.00	25.00
76 Duke Snider	12.50	30.00
77 Duke Snider	12.50	30.00
78 Duke Snider	12.50	30.00
79 Whitey Ford	15.00	40.00
80 Whitey Ford	15.00	40.00
81 Whitey Ford	15.00	40.00
82 Mike Schmidt	15.00	40.00
83 Mike Schmidt	15.00	40.00
84 Mike Schmidt	15.00	40.00
85 Daisuke Matsuzaka	10.00	25.00
86 Daisuke Matsuzaka	10.00	25.00
87 Daisuke Matsuzaka	10.00	25.00
88 Grady Sizemore	6.00	15.00
89 Grady Sizemore	6.00	15.00
90 Grady Sizemore	6.00	15.00
91 Chase Utley	12.50	30.00
92 Chase Utley	12.50	30.00
93 Chase Utley	12.50	30.00
94 Josh Beckett	8.00	20.00
95 Josh Beckett	8.00	20.00
96 Josh Beckett	8.00	20.00
97 Hanley Ramirez	8.00	20.00
98 Hanley Ramirez	8.00	20.00
99 Hanley Ramirez	8.00	20.00
100 Johan Santana	8.00	20.00
101 Johan Santana	8.00	20.00
102 Johan Santana	8.00	20.00
103 Ryan Howard	12.50	30.00
104 Ryan Howard	12.50	30.00
105 Ryan Howard	12.50	30.00
106 Bo Jackson	10.00	25.00
107 Bo Jackson	10.00	25.00
108 Bo Jackson	10.00	25.00
109 Carlos Quentin	6.00	15.00
110 Carlos Quentin	6.00	15.00
111 Carlos Quentin	6.00	15.00
112 Hideki Matsui	15.00	40.00
113 Hideki Matsui	15.00	40.00
114 Hideki Matsui	15.00	40.00
115 Rickey Henderson	20.00	50.00
116 Rickey Henderson	20.00	50.00
117 Rickey Henderson	20.00	50.00

2009 Topps Triple Threads Relics Emerald

*EMERALD: .5X TO 1.2X BASIC
STATED ODDS 1:19 MINI
STATED PRINT RUN 18 SER.#'d SETS
ALL DC VARIATIONS PRICED EQUALLY

2009 Topps Triple Threads Relics Gold

*GOLD: .6X TO 1.5X BASIC
STATED ODDS 1:37 MINI
STATED PRINT RUN 9 SER.#'d SETS
ALL DC VARIATIONS PRICED EQUALLY

2009 Topps Triple Threads Relics Sepia

*SEPIA: .4X TO 1X BASIC
STATED ODDS 1:13 MINI
STATED PRINT RUN 27 SER.#'d SETS
ALL DC VARIATIONS PRICED EQUALLY

2009 Topps Triple Threads WBC Relic Autographs

STATED ODDS 1:178 MINI
STATED PRINT RUN 36 SER.#'d SETS

BCAR1 Miguel Tejada	8.00	20.00
BCAR2 Jose Reyes	20.00	50.00
BCAR3 Geovany Soto	10.00	25.00
BCAR4 David Wright	60.00	150.00
BCAR5 Roy Oswalt	12.50	30.00
BCAR6 Miguel Cabrera	40.00	80.00

2009 Topps Triple Threads WBC Relic Autographs Sepia

*SEPIA: .4X TO 1X BASIC
STATED ODDS 1:239 MINI
STATED PRINT RUN 27 SER.#'d SETS

2010 Topps Triple Threads

COMMON CARD (1-120)	.40	1.00
1-120 PRINT RUN 1350 SER.#'d SETS		
COMMON JSY AU RC (121-189)	6.00	15.00
JSY AU RC ODDS 1:12 HOBBY		
JSY AU RC PRINT RUN 99 SER.#'d SETS		
COMMON JSY AU (121-189)	6.00	15.00
JSY AU ODDS 1:12 HOBBY		
JSY AU PRINT RUN 99 SER.#'d SETS		
EXCHANGE DEADLINE 9/30/2013		
OVERALL 1-120 PLATE ODDS 1:110 HOBBY		
1 Chipper Jones	1.00	2.50
2 Harmon Killebrew	1.00	2.50
3 Robin Roberts	.60	1.50
4 Mark Teixeira	.60	1.50
5 Todd Helton	.60	1.50
6 Roy Halladay	.60	1.50
7 Albert Pujols	1.25	3.00
8 Ryan Braun	.60	1.50
9 Ryne Sandberg	2.00	5.00
10 Tony Perez	.60	1.50
11 Jose Reyes	.60	1.50
12 Al Kaline	1.00	2.50
13 Dustin Pedroia	1.00	2.50
14 Warren Spahn	.60	1.50
15 Jacoby Ellsbury	.75	2.00
16 Carl Yastrzemski	1.50	4.00
17 Jake Peavy	.40	1.00
18 Carl Crawford	.60	1.50
19 Reggie Jackson	.60	1.50
20 Brian McCann	.60	1.50
21 Ichiro Suzuki	1.25	3.00
22 Miguel Cabrera	1.00	2.50
23 Brooks Robinson	.60	1.50
24 Ty Cobb	1.50	4.00
25 Christy Mathewson	1.00	2.50
26 Johnny Bench	1.00	2.50
27 Ozzie Smith	1.25	3.00
28 Bob Feller	.60	1.50
29 Ken Griffey Jr.	2.00	5.00
30 Josh Hamilton	.60	1.50
31 Adrian Gonzalez	.75	2.00
32 Derek Jeter	2.50	6.00
33 Johnny Mize	.60	1.50
34 Victor Martinez	.60	1.50
35 Steve Carlton	.60	1.50
36 Babe Ruth	2.50	6.00
37 Hunter Pence	.60	1.50
38 Honus Wagner	1.00	2.50
39 Jorge Posada	.60	1.50
40 Adam Dunn	.60	1.50
41 Johan Santana	.60	1.50
42 Andre Ethier	.60	1.50
43 Phil Rizzuto	.60	1.50
44 Justin Upton	.60	1.50
45 Prince Fielder	.60	1.50
46 Dave Winfield	.60	1.50
47 Josh Beckett	.40	1.00
48 Jackie Robinson	1.00	2.50
49 Walter Johnson	1.00	2.50
50 CC Sabathia	.60	1.50
51 Ralph Kiner	.60	1.50
52 Cole Hamels	.75	2.00
53 Mark Buehrle	.60	1.50
54 Ian Kinsler	.60	1.50
55 Yogi Berra	1.00	2.50
56 Bobby Doerr	.60	1.50
57 Roy Campanella	1.00	2.50
58 Alfonso Soriano	.60	1.50
59 Tom Seaver	.60	1.50
60 Hanley Ramirez	.60	1.50
61 Mariano Rivera	1.25	3.00
62 Cy Young	1.00	2.50
63 Jimmie Foxx	1.00	2.50
64 Jim Palmer	.60	1.50
65 Mickey Mantle	3.00	8.00
66 Pee Wee Reese	.60	1.50
67 Justin Verlander	1.00	2.50
68 Zack Greinke	1.00	2.50
69 Jimmy Rollins	.60	1.50
70 Felix Hernandez	.60	1.50
71 Nolan Ryan	3.00	8.00
72 Ryan Howard	.75	2.00
73 Manny Ramirez	1.00	2.50
74 Lou Brock	.60	1.50
75 Mike Schmidt	1.50	4.00
76 Grady Sizemore	.60	1.50
77 Alex Rodriguez	1.25	3.00
78 Joe Morgan	.60	1.50
79 Eddie Mathews	1.00	2.50
80 Hideki Matsui	1.00	2.50
81 Mel Ott	1.00	2.50
82 Rogers Hornsby	.60	1.50
83 Tris Speaker	.60	1.50
84 Vladimir Guerrero	.60	1.50
85 Evan Longoria	.60	1.50
86 Dan Haren	.40	1.00
87 Willie McCovey	.60	1.50
88 Lou Gehrig	2.00	5.00
89 Tim Lincecum	.60	1.50
90 Justin Morneau	.60	1.50
91 Kevin Youkilis	.40	1.00
92 B.J. Upton	.60	1.50
93 Rickey Henderson	1.00	2.50
94 Roy Oswalt	.60	1.50
95 Chase Utley	.60	1.50
96 Lance Berkman	.60	1.50
97 Matt Kemp	.75	2.00
98 Dale Murphy	1.00	2.50
99 George Sisler	.60	1.50
100 Nick Markakis	.75	2.00
101 Thurman Munson	1.00	2.50
102 Dan Uggla	.40	1.00
103 Matt Holliday	1.00	2.50
104 Bill Mazeroski	.60	1.50
105 Joe Mauer	.75	2.00
106 Chris Carpenter	.60	1.50
107 David Wright	.75	2.00
108 Ron Guidry	.40	1.00
109 Roger Maris	1.00	2.50
110 Aaron Hill	.40	1.00
111 Torii Hunter	.40	1.00
112 Ubaldo Jimenez	.40	1.00
113 Aramis Ramirez	.40	1.00
114 Whitey Ford	.60	1.50
115 Andrew McCutchen	1.00	2.50
116 Hank Greenberg	1.00	2.50
117 Dizzy Dean	.60	1.50
118 Mark Fidrych	.40	1.00
119 Bob Gibson	.60	1.50
120 Johnny Damon	.60	1.50
121 P.Sandoval Jsy AU	6.00	15.00
122 Denard Span Jsy AU	6.00	15.00
123 Colby Rasmus Jsy AU	6.00	15.00
124 C.Gomez Jsy AU EXCH	8.00	20.00
125 T.Hanson Jsy AU	6.00	15.00
126 Rick Porcello Jsy AU	6.00	15.00
128 Adam Jones Jsy AU	8.00	20.00
129 G.Beckham Jsy AU	10.00	25.00
130 Elvis Andrus Jsy AU	6.00	15.00
131 Adam Lind Jsy AU	6.00	15.00
132 Chris Young Jsy AU	6.00	15.00
134 Chris Coghlan Jsy AU	8.00	20.00
135 A.Escobar Jsy AU	8.00	20.00
136 Nelson Cruz Jsy AU	6.00	15.00
137 Neftali Feliz Jsy AU	6.00	15.00
139 J.Heyward Jsy AU RC	30.00	60.00
140 A.Jackson Jsy AU RC	8.00	20.00
141 S.Sizemore Jsy AU RC	6.00	15.00
142 C.Kershaw Jsy AU	40.00	100.00
143 Ike Davis Jsy AU RC	10.00	25.00
144 Josh Johnson Jsy AU	6.00	15.00
146 Andre Ethier Jsy AU	10.00	25.00
147 S.Castro Jsy AU RC	10.00	25.00
148 J.Happ Jsy AU	6.00	15.00
149 I.Kinsler Jsy AU EXCH	8.00	20.00
150 Will Venable Jsy AU	8.00	20.00
151 Chris Volstad Jsy AU	6.00	15.00
152 D.Stubbs Jsy AU RC	6.00	15.00
153 Chris Getz Jsy AU	6.00	15.00
155 D.McCutchen Jsy AU RC	6.00	15.00
157 A.McCutchen Jsy AU	40.00	80.00
158 Daniel Murphy Jsy AU	15.00	40.00
159 H.Kendrick Jsy AU	6.00	15.00
160 Billy Butler Jsy AU	8.00	20.00
162 J.Mejia Jsy AU RC	6.00	15.00
163 Trevor Cahill Jsy AU	10.00	25.00
164 W.Davis Jsy AU (RC)	6.00	15.00
165 Manny Parra Jsy AU EXCH	6.00	15.00
166 D.Storen Jsy AU RC	6.00	15.00
167 B.Matusz Jsy AU RC	6.00	15.00
169 E.Young Jr. Jsy AU (RC)	6.00	15.00
171 S.Strasburg Jsy AU RC	30.00	80.00
174 Alexei Ramirez Jsy AU	6.00	15.00
178 C.McGehee Jsy AU	6.00	15.00
182 Mark Reynolds Jsy AU	6.00	15.00
186 M.Stanton Jsy AU RC	40.00	80.00
188 C.Santana Jsy AU RC	6.00	15.00
189 M.Brantley Jsy AU RC	6.00	15.00

2010 Topps Triple Threads Emerald

*EMERALD 1-120: .6X TO 1.5X BASIC
1-120 ODDS 1:2 MINI
1-120 PRINT RUN 240 SER.#'d SETS
*EMERALD JSY AU: .4X TO 1X BASIC
EMERALD JSY AU ODDS 1:22 MINI
EM.JSY AU PRINT RUN 50 SER.#'d SETS

2010 Topps Triple Threads Gold

*GOLD 1-120: 1X TO 2.5X BASIC
1-120 ODDS 1:5 MINI
1-120 PRINT RUN 99 SER.#'d SETS

121-189 ODDS 1:44 HOBBY
121-189 PRINT RUN 25 SER.#'d SETS

2010 Topps Triple Threads Sepia

*SEPIA 1-120: .5X TO 1.2X BASIC
1-120 RANDOMLY INSERTED
1-120 PRINT RUN 525 SER.#'d SETS
*SEPIA JSY AU: .4X TO 1X BASIC
SEPIA JSY AU ODDS 1:15 MINI
SEP.JSY AU PRINT RUN 75 SER.#'d SETS

2010 Topps Triple Threads Autograph Relic Combos

STATED ODDS 1:98 MINI
STATED PRINT RUN 36 SER.#'d SETS
ARC1 Wright/Schm/Zimm 40.00 100.00
ARC2 Pujols/Fielder/Howard 150.00 300.00
ARC3 Hill/Cano/Pedroia 20.00 50.00
ARC4 Heyward/Jones/Upton 50.00 100.00
ARC5 Ford/Rivera/Berra 150.00 300.00
ARC6 Longoria/Beckham/Cabrera 60.00 120.00
ARC7 Price/Lester/Sabathia 30.00 60.00
ARC8 Porcello/Cabrera/Damon 40.00 80.00
ARC9 Varitek/Schilling/Ortiz 50.00 100.00
ARC10 Holliday/Braun/Wright 50.00 100.00
ARC11 John Lackey/Jon Lester
Jonathan Papelbon 20.00 50.00
ARC12 Dawson/Carter/Vlad 40.00 80.00
ARC13 Heyward/McCann/Murphy 75.00 150.00
ARC14 Howard/ARod/Pujols 200.00 400.00
ARC15 ARod/Ortiz/Manny 75.00 150.00

2010 Topps Triple Threads Autograph Relic Combos Sepia

*SEPIA: .4X TO 1X BASIC
STATED ODDS 1:130 MINI
STATED PRINT RUN 27 SER.#'d SETS

2010 Topps Triple Threads Autograph MLB Die Cut Relics

STATED ODDS 1:10 MINI
STATED PRINT RUN 18 SER.#'d SETS
ALL DC VARIATIONS PRICED EQUALLY
AD Adam Dunn 12.50 30.00
AD Andre Dawson 40.00 80.00
AG Adrian Gonzalez 8.00 20.00
AP Albert Pujols 200.00 300.00
AR Alex Rodriguez 100.00 175.00
BM Brian McCann 15.00 40.00
BS Bruce Sutter 15.00 40.00
BZ Ben Zobrist 15.00 40.00
CB Chad Billingsley 12.50 30.00
CC Carl Crawford 12.50 30.00
CF Chone Figgins 8.00 20.00
CL Cliff Lee 30.00 60.00
CP Carlos Pena 8.00 20.00
CS CC Sabathia 50.00 100.00
CY Carl Yastrzemski 30.00 60.00
DG Dwight Gooden 20.00 50.00
DM Dale Murphy 40.00 80.00
DO David Ortiz 15.00 40.00
DS Duke Snider 30.00 60.00
DW David Wright 40.00 80.00
EL Evan Longoria 30.00 60.00
FT Frank Thomas 75.00 150.00
GC Gary Carter 20.00 50.00
GK George Kell 15.00 40.00
HR Hanley Ramirez 12.50 30.00
JD Johnny Damon 30.00 60.00
JH Josh Hamilton 30.00 60.00
JH Jason Heyward 30.00 60.00
JL Jon Lester 8.00 20.00
JM Joe Morgan 20.00 50.00
MC Miguel Cabrera 50.00 100.00
MH Matt Holliday 20.00 50.00
MK Matt Kemp 12.50 30.00
MR Manny Ramirez 50.00 100.00
MT Miguel Tejada 8.00 20.00
NS Nick Swisher 30.00 60.00
PF Prince Fielder 12.50 30.00
RB Ryan Braun 20.00 50.00
RC Robinson Cano 30.00 60.00
RH Ryan Howard 12.00 30.00
RK Ralph Kiner 30.00 60.00
RZ Ryan Zimmerman 20.00 50.00
SM Stan Musial 60.00 120.00
SS Stephen Strasburg 150.00 250.00
SV Shane Victorino 30.00 60.00
VW Vernon Wells 10.00 25.00
WF Whitey Ford 30.00 60.00
CSC Curt Schilling 15.00 40.00
DWI Dave Winfield 30.00 60.00
MRI Mariano Rivera 100.00 175.00

2010 Topps Triple Threads Autograph MLB Die Cut Relics Gold

*GOLD: .5X TO 1.2X BASIC
STATED ODDS 1:19 MINI
STATED PRINT RUN 9 SER.#'d SETS
ALL DC VARIATIONS PRICED EQUALLY

2010 Topps Triple Threads Autograph Relics

STATED ODDS 1:10 MINI
STATED PRINT RUN 18 SER.#'d SETS
ALL DC VARIATIONS PRICED EQUALLY
AR1 Cliff Lee 30.00 60.00
AR2 Cliff Lee 30.00 60.00
AR3 Cliff Lee 30.00 60.00
AR4 Duke Snider 30.00 60.00
AR5 Duke Snider 30.00 60.00
AR6 Duke Snider 30.00 60.00
AR7 Gary Carter 20.00 50.00
AR8 Gary Carter 20.00 50.00
AR9 Gary Carter 20.00 50.00
AR10 Robinson Cano 30.00 60.00
AR11 Robinson Cano 30.00 60.00
AR12 Robinson Cano 30.00 60.00
AR13 Prince Fielder 15.00 40.00
AR14 Prince Fielder 15.00 40.00
AR15 Prince Fielder 15.00 40.00
AR16 Ryan Howard 30.00 60.00
AR17 Ryan Howard 30.00 60.00
AR18 Ryan Howard 30.00 60.00
AR19 Alex Rodriguez 100.00 175.00
AR20 Alex Rodriguez 100.00 175.00
AR21 Alex Rodriguez 100.00 175.00
AR22 Josh Hamilton 20.00 50.00
AR23 Josh Hamilton 20.00 50.00
AR24 Josh Hamilton 20.00 50.00
AR25 Chad Billingsley 12.50 30.00
AR26 Chad Billingsley 12.50 30.00
AR27 Chad Billingsley 12.50 30.00
AR28 Dustin Pedroia 15.00 40.00
AR29 Dustin Pedroia 15.00 40.00
AR30 Dustin Pedroia 15.00 40.00
AR31 Manny Ramirez 20.00 50.00
AR32 Manny Ramirez 20.00 50.00
AR33 Manny Ramirez 20.00 50.00
AR34 CC Sabathia 30.00 60.00
AR35 CC Sabathia 30.00 60.00
AR36 CC Sabathia 30.00 60.00
AR37 Jon Lester 12.50 30.00
AR38 Jon Lester 12.50 30.00
AR39 Jon Lester 12.50 30.00
AR40 Curt Schilling 15.00 40.00
AR41 Curt Schilling 15.00 40.00
AR42 Curt Schilling 15.00 40.00
AR43 Ryan Braun 12.50 30.00
AR44 Ryan Braun 12.50 30.00
AR45 Ryan Braun 12.50 30.00
AR46 David Wright 40.00 80.00
AR47 David Wright 40.00 80.00
AR48 David Wright 40.00 80.00
AR49 B.J. Upton 12.50 30.00
AR50 B.J. Upton 12.50 30.00
AR51 B.J. Upton 12.50 30.00
AR52 David Ortiz 15.00 40.00
AR53 David Ortiz 15.00 40.00
AR54 David Ortiz 15.00 40.00
AR55 Frank Thomas 60.00 120.00
AR56 Frank Thomas 60.00 120.00
AR57 Frank Thomas 60.00 120.00
AR58 Dave Winfield 30.00 60.00
AR59 Dave Winfield 30.00 60.00
AR60 Dave Winfield 30.00 60.00
AR61 John Lackey 20.00 50.00
AR62 John Lackey 20.00 50.00
AR63 John Lackey 20.00 50.00
AR64 Evan Longoria 40.00 80.00
AR65 Evan Longoria 40.00 80.00
AR66 Evan Longoria 40.00 80.00
AR67 Adam Dunn 8.00 20.00
AR68 Adam Dunn 8.00 20.00
AR69 Adam Dunn 8.00 20.00
AR70 Joe Morgan 20.00 50.00
AR71 Joe Morgan 20.00 50.00
AR72 Joe Morgan 20.00 50.00
AR73 Matt Cain 20.00 50.00
AR74 Matt Cain 20.00 50.00
AR75 Matt Cain 20.00 50.00
AR76 Dale Murphy 40.00 80.00
AR77 Dale Murphy 40.00 80.00
AR78 Dale Murphy 40.00 80.00
AR79 Whitey Ford 30.00 60.00
AR80 Whitey Ford 30.00 60.00
AR81 Whitey Ford 30.00 60.00
AR82 Michael Young 10.00 25.00
AR83 Michael Young 10.00 25.00
AR84 Michael Young 10.00 25.00
AR85 Matt Holliday 20.00 50.00
AR86 Matt Holliday 20.00 50.00
AR87 Matt Holliday 20.00 50.00
AR88 Ozzie Smith 30.00 60.00
AR89 Ozzie Smith 30.00 60.00
AR90 Ozzie Smith 30.00 60.00
AR91 Barry Larkin 50.00 100.00
AR92 Barry Larkin 50.00 100.00
AR93 Barry Larkin 50.00 100.00
AR94 Aramis Ramirez 8.00 20.00
AR95 Aramis Ramirez 8.00 20.00
AR96 Aramis Ramirez 8.00 20.00
AR97 Hanley Ramirez 12.50 30.00
AR98 Hanley Ramirez 12.50 30.00
AR99 Hanley Ramirez 12.50 30.00
AR100 Mariano Rivera 100.00 200.00
AR101 Mariano Rivera 100.00 200.00
AR102 Mariano Rivera 100.00 200.00
AR103 Reggie Jackson 50.00 100.00
AR104 Reggie Jackson 50.00 100.00
AR105 Reggie Jackson 50.00 100.00
AR106 Nolan Ryan 60.00 120.00
AR107 Nolan Ryan 60.00 120.00
AR108 Nolan Ryan 60.00 120.00
AR109 Torii Hunter 15.00 40.00
AR110 Torii Hunter 15.00 40.00
AR111 Torii Hunter 15.00 40.00
AR112 Albert Pujols 200.00 300.00
AR113 Albert Pujols 200.00 300.00
AR114 Albert Pujols 200.00 300.00
AR115 Shane Victorino 12.50 30.00
AR116 Shane Victorino 12.50 30.00
AR117 Shane Victorino 12.50 30.00
AR118 Justin Verlander 40.00 80.00
AR119 Justin Verlander 40.00 80.00
AR120 Justin Verlander 40.00 80.00
AR121 Miguel Cabrera 75.00 150.00
AR122 Miguel Cabrera 75.00 150.00
AR123 Miguel Cabrera 75.00 150.00
AR124 Adrian Gonzalez 12.50 30.00
AR125 Adrian Gonzalez 12.50 30.00
AR126 Adrian Gonzalez 12.50 30.00
AR127 Chone Figgins 8.00 20.00
AR128 Chone Figgins 8.00 20.00
AR129 Chone Figgins 8.00 20.00
AR130 Nick Swisher 8.00 20.00
AR131 Nick Swisher 8.00 20.00
AR132 Nick Swisher 8.00 20.00
AR133 Phil Hughes 20.00 50.00
AR134 Phil Hughes 20.00 50.00
AR135 Phil Hughes 20.00 50.00
AR136 Aaron Hill 10.00 25.00
AR137 Aaron Hill 10.00 25.00
AR138 Aaron Hill 10.00 25.00
AR139 Johnny Damon 30.00 60.00
AR140 Johnny Damon 30.00 60.00
AR141 Johnny Damon 30.00 60.00
AR142 Miguel Tejada 8.00 20.00
AR143 Miguel Tejada 8.00 20.00
AR144 Miguel Tejada 8.00 20.00
AR145 Vernon Wells 10.00 25.00
AR146 Vernon Wells 10.00 25.00
AR147 Vernon Wells 10.00 25.00
AR148 George Kell 15.00 40.00
AR149 George Kell 15.00 40.00
AR150 George Kell 15.00 40.00
AR151 Carlos Pena 8.00 20.00
AR152 Carlos Pena 8.00 20.00
AR153 Carlos Pena 8.00 20.00
AR154 Andre Dawson 40.00 80.00
AR155 Andre Dawson 40.00 80.00
AR156 Andre Dawson 40.00 80.00
AR157 Dwight Gooden 12.50 30.00
AR158 Dwight Gooden 12.50 30.00
AR159 Dwight Gooden 12.50 30.00
AR160 Ralph Kiner 30.00 60.00
AR161 Ralph Kiner 30.00 60.00
AR162 Ralph Kiner 30.00 60.00
AR163 Bobby Murcer 15.00 40.00
AR164 Bobby Murcer 15.00 40.00
AR165 Bobby Murcer 15.00 40.00
AR166 Tony Perez 30.00 60.00
AR167 Tony Perez 30.00 60.00
AR168 Tony Perez 30.00 60.00
AR169 Rich Harden 8.00 20.00
AR170 Rich Harden 8.00 20.00
AR171 Rich Harden 8.00 20.00
AR172 Joba Chamberlain 12.50 30.00
AR173 Joba Chamberlain 12.50 30.00
AR174 Joba Chamberlain 12.50 30.00
AR175 Cal Ripken Jr. 150.00 250.00
AR176 Cal Ripken Jr. 150.00 250.00
AR177 Cal Ripken Jr. 150.00 250.00
AR178 Carl Yastrzemski 40.00 80.00
AR179 Carl Yastrzemski 40.00 80.00
AR180 Carl Yastrzemski 40.00 80.00
AR181 Bruce Sutter 15.00 40.00
AR182 Bruce Sutter 15.00 40.00
AR183 Bruce Sutter 15.00 40.00
AR184 Stan Musial 100.00 200.00
AR185 Stan Musial 100.00 200.00
AR186 Stan Musial 100.00 200.00
AR187 Frank Robinson 30.00 60.00
AR188 Frank Robinson 30.00 60.00
AR189 Frank Robinson 30.00 60.00
AR190 Ryan Zimmerman 20.00 50.00
AR191 Ryan Zimmerman 20.00 50.00
AR192 Ryan Zimmerman 20.00 50.00
AR193 Felix Hernandez 40.00 80.00
AR194 Felix Hernandez 40.00 80.00
AR195 Felix Hernandez 40.00 80.00
AR196 Carl Crawford 12.50 30.00
AR197 Carl Crawford 12.50 30.00
AR198 Carl Crawford 12.50 30.00
AR199 Raul Ibanez 10.00 25.00
AR200 Raul Ibanez 10.00 25.00
AR201 Raul Ibanez 10.00 25.00
AR202 Brian McCann 12.50 30.00
AR203 Brian McCann 12.50 30.00
AR204 Brian McCann 12.50 30.00
AR205 Matt Garza 10.00 25.00
AR206 Matt Garza 10.00 25.00
AR207 Matt Garza 10.00 25.00
AR208 Chipper Jones 60.00 120.00
AR209 Chipper Jones 60.00 120.00
AR210 Chipper Jones 60.00 120.00
AR211 Jason Heyward 40.00 80.00
AR212 Jason Heyward 40.00 80.00
AR213 Jason Heyward 40.00 80.00
AR214 Stephen Strasburg 100.00 200.00
AR215 Stephen Strasburg 100.00 200.00
AR216 Stephen Strasburg 100.00 200.00
AR217 Al Kaline 30.00 80.00
AR218 Al Kaline 30.00 80.00
AR219 Al Kaline 30.00 80.00
AR220 Ryne Sandberg 50.00 100.00
AR221 Ryne Sandberg 50.00 100.00
AR222 Ryne Sandberg 50.00 100.00
AR226 Ivan Rodriguez 40.00 80.00
AR227 Ivan Rodriguez 40.00 80.00
AR228 Ivan Rodriguez 40.00 80.00
AR229 Alfonso Soriano 12.50 30.00
AR230 Alfonso Soriano 12.50 30.00
AR231 Alfonso Soriano 12.50 30.00
AR232 Ben Zobrist 12.00 30.00
AR233 Ben Zobrist 12.00 30.00
AR234 Ben Zobrist 12.00 30.00
AR235 Roberto Alomar 20.00 50.00
AR236 Roberto Alomar 20.00 50.00
AR237 Roberto Alomar 20.00 50.00
AR238 Tony Gwynn 30.00 60.00
AR239 Tony Gwynn 30.00 60.00
AR240 Tony Gwynn 30.00 60.00
AR241 Mike Schmidt 30.00 60.00
AR242 Mike Schmidt 30.00 60.00
AR243 Mike Schmidt 30.00 60.00
AR244 Matt Kemp 20.00 50.00
AR245 Matt Kemp 20.00 50.00
AR246 Matt Kemp 20.00 50.00
AR247 Johnny Bench 40.00 80.00
AR248 Johnny Bench 40.00 80.00
AR249 Johnny Bench 40.00 80.00
AR250 Ernie Banks 30.00 60.00
AR251 Ernie Banks 30.00 60.00
AR252 Ernie Banks 30.00 60.00
AR262 Ron Santo 60.00 120.00
AR263 Ron Santo 60.00 120.00
AR264 Ron Santo 60.00 120.00
AR265 Hunter Pence 12.50 30.00
AR266 Hunter Pence 12.50 30.00
AR267 Hunter Pence 12.50 30.00
AR274 Carlton Fisk 20.00 50.00
AR275 Carlton Fisk 20.00 50.00
AR276 Carlton Fisk 20.00 50.00
AR280 Shin-Soo Choo 20.00 50.00
AR281 Shin-Soo Choo 20.00 50.00
AR282 Shin-Soo Choo 20.00 50.00
AR283 Bernie Williams 60.00 120.00
AR284 Bernie Williams 60.00 120.00
AR285 Bernie Williams 60.00 120.00

2010 Topps Triple Threads Autograph Relics Gold

*GOLD: .5X TO 1.2X BASIC
STATED ODDS 1:19 MINI
STATED PRINT RUN 9 SER.#'d SETS
ALL DC VARIATIONS PRICED EQUALLY

2010 Topps Triple Threads Legend Relics

STATED ODDS 1:49 MINI
STATED PRINT RUN 36 SER.#'d SETS
RL1 Yogi Berra 20.00 50.00
RL2 Roy Campanella 20.00 50.00
RL3 Ty Cobb 60.00 120.00
RL4 Nolan Ryan 15.00 40.00
RL5 Johnny Bench 12.50 30.00
RL6 Jim Palmer 12.50 30.00
RL7 Whitey Ford 12.50 30.00
RL8 Jimmie Foxx 40.00 80.00
RL9 Lou Gehrig 100.00 175.00
RL10 Bob Gibson 15.00 40.00
RL11 Hank Greenberg 30.00 60.00
RL12 Rogers Hornsby 40.00 80.00
RL13 Ralph Kiner 15.00 40.00
RL14 Mickey Mantle 100.00 175.00
RL15 Roger Maris 50.00 100.00
RL16 Eddie Mathews 20.00 50.00
RL17 Johnny Mize 12.50 30.00
RL18 Thurman Munson 15.00 40.00
RL19 Stan Musial 30.00 60.00
RL20 Frank Robinson 12.50 30.00
RL21 Mel Ott 30.00 60.00
RL22 Pee Wee Reese 20.00 50.00
RL23 Phil Rizzuto 15.00 40.00
RL24 Jackie Robinson 40.00 80.00
RL25 Babe Ruth 350.00 500.00
RL26 Tom Seaver 12.50 30.00
RL27 George Sisler 30.00 60.00
RL28 Warren Spahn 20.00 50.00
RL29 Tris Speaker 20.00 50.00
RL30 Honus Wagner 50.00 100.00

2010 Topps Triple Threads Legend Relics Sepia

*SEPIA: .4X TO 1X BASIC
STATED ODDS 1:66 MINI
STATED PRINT RUN 27 SER.#'d SETS

2010 Topps Triple Threads MLB Die Cut Relics

STATED ODDS 1:10 MINI
STATED PRINT RUN 36 SER.#'d SETS
ALL DC VARIATIONS PRICED EQUALLY
AG Adrian Gonzalez 6.00 15.00
AK Al Kaline 15.00 40.00
CF Carlton Fisk 6.00 15.00
CJ Chipper Jones 12.50 30.00
CR Cal Ripken Jr. 12.50 30.00
CS Curt Schilling 6.00 15.00
CU Chase Utley 12.50 30.00
DJ Derek Jeter 30.00 60.00
DW David Wright 12.50 30.00
EL Evan Longoria 12.50 30.00
HR Hanley Ramirez 6.00 15.00
KY Kevin Youkilis 6.00 15.00
MC Miguel Cabrera 8.00 20.00
MR Manny Ramirez 12.50 30.00
MT Mark Teixeira 12.50 30.00
OC Orlando Cepeda 6.00 15.00
PF Prince Fielder 6.00 15.00
PM Paul Molitor 8.00 20.00
RH Rickey Henderson 30.00 60.00
RH Roy Halladay 15.00 40.00
SC Steve Carlton 8.00 20.00
TG Tony Gwynn 12.50 30.00
WS Willie Stargell 8.00 20.00
DWI Dave Winfield 8.00 20.00
SSC Shin-Soo Choo 10.00 25.00

2010 Topps Triple Threads MLB Die Cut Relics Emerald

*EMERALD: .5X TO 1.2X BASIC
STATED ODDS 1:19 MINI
STATED PRINT RUN 18 SER.#'d SETS
ALL DC VARIATIONS PRICED EQUALLY

2010 Topps Triple Threads MLB Die Cut Relics Sepia

*SEPIA: .4X TO 1X BASIC
STATED ODDS 1:13 MINI
STATED PRINT RUN 27 SER.#'d SETS
ALL DC VARIATIONS PRICED EQUALLY

2010 Topps Triple Threads Relic Combos

STATED ODDS 1:25 MINI
STATED PRINT RUN 36 SER.#'d SETS
RC1 Mauer/Killebrew/Morneau 20.00 50.00
RC2 Rivera/Posada/Pettitte 20.00 50.00
RC3 Tim Lincecum/Roy Halladay
Johan Santana 12.50 30.00
RC4 Pujols/Gibson/Musial 20.00 50.00
RC5 Ripken/Robinson/Palmer 15.00 40.00
RC6 Willie McCovey
Pablo Sandoval/Monte Irvin 15.00 40.00
RC7 Miggy/Teix/Morneau 15.00 40.00
RC8 Evan Longoria/David Wright
Ryan Zimmerman 12.50 30.00
RC9 Utley/Sandberg/Kinsler 12.50 30.00
RC10 Ramirez/Ripken/Tulowitzki 15.00 40.00
RC11 Matsui/Ichiro/Matsuzaka 30.00 60.00
RC12 David Wright/Aramis Ramirez
Pablo Sandoval 8.00 20.00
RC13 Heyward/Jones/McCann 15.00 40.00
RC14 Hunter Pence/Ryan Braun
Matt Holliday 10.00 25.00
RC15 Sandberg/Banks/Dawson 20.00 50.00
RC16 McCann/Mauer/Posada 12.50 30.00
RC17 Crawford/Henderson/Ellsbury 10.00 25.00
RC19 Zack Greinke/Cliff Lee/CC Sabathia 10.00 25.00
RC21 Ichiro/Ripken/Robinson 15.00 40.00
RC22 Rickey/Rickey/Rickey 12.00 30.00
RC23 Adrian Gonzalez
Ryan Zimmerman/Jimmy Rollins 8.00 20.00
RC24 Morneau/Pedroia/ARod 10.00 25.00
RC25 Dawson/Carter/Vlad 15.00 40.00
RC26 Bench/Mauer/Fisk 12.50 30.00
RC27 Guidry/Ford/Pettitte 15.00 40.00
RC28 Chipper Jones/Jorge Posada
Lance Berkman 12.50 30.00
RC29 Stntn/Strsbrg/Hywrd 20.00 50.00
RC30 Adam Jones/Brian Roberts
Nick Markakis 10.00 25.00
RC31 Mantle/Ruth/Maris 250.00 400.00
RC32 Mark Reynolds/Justin Upton
Stephen Drew 8.00 20.00
RC33 Wright/Carter/Bay 10.00 25.00
RC34 Vladimir Guerrero/David Ortiz
Manny Ramirez 8.00 20.00
RC35 Utley/Howard/Werth 30.00 60.00
RC36 Lincecum/Sandoval/Cain 15.00 40.00
RC37 Cruz/Hamilton/Kinsler 30.00 60.00
RC38 Ivan Rodriguez 15.00 40.00
RC39 Pujols/Hanley/ARod 15.00 40.00
RC40 Josh Hamilton/Adrian Gonzalez
Joe Mauer 10.00 25.00
RC41 ARod/Mauer/Upton 12.50 30.00
RC42 Reyes/Pedroia/Ichiro 12.50 30.00
RC43 Kaline/Cobb/Kell 40.00 80.00
RC44 Pujols/Howard/Prince 12.50 30.00
RC45 Teixeira/Cabrera/ARod 10.00 25.00
RC46 Schmidt/Stargell/Bench 20.00 50.00
RC47 Killebrew/Yaz/Robinson 10.00 25.00
RC48 Hernandez/CC/Verlander 12.50 30.00
RC50 Mariano Rivera/Curt Schilling
Cole Hamels 10.00 25.00
RC51 Ryan/Ryan/Ryan 30.00 60.00
RC52 Shane Victorino/Jose Reyes
Jimmy Rollins 8.00 20.00
RC53 Prince Fielder/Justin Morneau
Vladimir Guerrero 8.00 20.00
RC54 Justin Verlander/Rick Porcello
Jim Bunning 12.50 30.00
RC55 Josh Beckett/Jon Lester
John Lackey 10.00 25.00
RC56 Troy Tulowitzki/Jimmy Rollins
Hanley Ramirez 10.00 25.00
RC57 Upton/Ichiro/Sizemore 12.50 30.00
RC58 Sabathia/Greinke/Hernandez 12.00 30.00
RC59 Rivera/Eckersley/Gossage 15.00 40.00
RC60 ARod/ARod/ARod 10.00 25.00

2010 Topps Triple Threads Relic Combos Sepia

*SEPIA: .4X TO 1X BASIC
STATED ODDS 1:33 MINI
STATED PRINT RUN 27 SER.#'d SETS

2010 Topps Triple Threads Relic Combos Double

STATE ODDS 1:82 MINI
STATED PRINT RUN 36 SER.#'d SETS
RDC1 A.Pujols/J.Mauer 15.00 40.00
RDC2 A.Pujols/A.Rodriguez 30.00 60.00
RDC3 Kin/Gre/Mat/Kil/McC/Rob 50.00 100.00
RDC4 Puj/How/Hol/Car/Sch/Mur 15.00 40.00
RDC5 Ryan Howard 15.00 40.00
Matt Holliday
Albert Pujols
CC Sabathia
Josh Beckett
David Ortiz
RDC6 Miguel Cabrera 15.00 40.00
Justin Morneau
Kendry Morales
Ryan Howard
Albert Pujols
Prince Fielder
RDC7 Alex Rodriguez 15.00 40.00
Joe Mauer
Torii Hunter
Ryan Howard
Albert Pujols
Manny Ramirez
RDC8 Tim Lincecum 15.00 40.00
Roy Halladay
Johan Santana
Zack Greinke
Felix Hernandez
CC Sabathia
RDC9 Upt/Bra/Pen/Kem/McC/Hey 40.00 80.00
RDC10 Mau/Pos/Rod/Fis/Ben/Ber 15.00 40.00
RDC11 Adrian Gonzlez 15.00 40.00
Ryan Zimmerman
Jimmy Rollins
Matt Kemp
Shane Victorino
Yadier Molina
RDC12 Mau/Tei/Lon/Suz/Jon/Hunr 15.00 40.00
RDC13 Daw/Hen/Gos/Rip/Gwy/Sut 75.00 150.00
RDC14 Frank Robinson 15.00 40.00
Frank Robinson
RDC15 Lou Brock 15.00 40.00
Rickey Henderson
Jacoby Ellsbury
Carl Crawford
Jose Reyes
Jimmy Rollins
RDC16 Lin/Gre/Car/San/Sea/For 20.00 50.00
RDC17 Catfish Hunter 15.00 40.00
Thurman Munson
RDC18 How/Fie/Puj/Kil/Kin/Rob 40.00 80.00

2010 Topps Triple Threads Relic Combos Double Sepia

*SEPIA: .4X TO 1X BASIC
STATED ODDS 1:109 MINI
STATED PRINT RUN 27 SER.#'d SETS

2010 Topps Triple Threads Relics

STATED ODDS 1:10 MINI
STATED PRINT RUN 36 SER.#'d SETS
ALL DC VARIATIONS PRICED EQUALLY
R1 Albert Pujols 15.00 40.00
R2 Albert Pujols 15.00 40.00
R3 Albert Pujols 15.00 40.00
R4 Chase Utley 12.50 30.00
R5 Chase Utley 12.50 30.00
R6 Chase Utley 12.50 30.00
R7 Ichiro Suzuki 10.00 25.00
R8 Ichiro Suzuki 10.00 25.00
R9 Ichiro Suzuki 10.00 25.00
R10 Grady Sizemore 6.00 15.00
R11 Grady Sizemore 6.00 15.00
R12 Grady Sizemore 6.00 15.00
R13 Mark Teixeira 8.00 20.00
R14 Mark Teixeira 8.00 20.00
R15 Mark Teixeira 8.00 20.00
R16 Shin-Soo Choo 10.00 25.00
R17 Shin-Soo Choo 10.00 25.00
R18 Shin-Soo Choo 10.00 25.00
R22 Hanley Ramirez 6.00 15.00
R23 Hanley Ramirez 6.00 15.00
R24 Hanley Ramirez 6.00 15.00
R25 Evan Longoria 10.00 25.00
R26 Evan Longoria 10.00 25.00
R27 Evan Longoria 10.00 25.00
R28 David Wright 12.50 30.00
R29 David Wright 12.50 30.00
R30 David Wright 12.50 30.00
R31 Hunter Pence 6.00 15.00
R32 Hunter Pence 6.00 15.00
R33 Hunter Pence 6.00 15.00
R34 Joe Mauer 8.00 20.00
R35 Joe Mauer 8.00 20.00
R36 Joe Mauer 8.00 20.00
R37 Rickey Henderson 15.00 40.00
R38 Rickey Henderson 40.00 80.00
R39 Rickey Henderson 40.00 80.00
R40 Al Kaline 15.00 40.00
R41 Al Kaline 15.00 40.00
R42 Al Kaline 15.00 40.00
R43 Catfish Hunter 12.50 30.00
R44 Catfish Hunter 12.50 30.00
R45 Catfish Hunter 12.50 30.00
R46 Dave Winfield 8.00 20.00
R47 Dave Winfield 8.00 20.00
R48 Dave Winfield 8.00 20.00
R49 Carlton Fisk 12.50 30.00
R50 Carlton Fisk 12.50 30.00
R51 Carlton Fisk 12.50 30.00
R52 Curt Schilling 6.00 15.00
R53 Curt Schilling 6.00 15.00
R54 Curt Schilling 6.00 15.00
R58 Mike Schmidt 15.00 40.00
R58 Mike Schmidt 15.00 40.00
R59 Mike Schmidt 15.00 40.00
R61 Steve Carlton 8.00 20.00
R62 Steve Carlton 8.00 20.00
R63 Steve Carlton 8.00 20.00
R64 Orlando Cepeda 6.00 15.00
R65 Orlando Cepeda 6.00 15.00
R65 Orlando Cepeda 6.00 15.00
R67 Prince Fielder 8.00 20.00
R68 Prince Fielder 8.00 20.00
R69 Prince Fielder 8.00 20.00
R70 Ryne Sandberg 12.50 30.00
R71 Ryne Sandberg 12.50 30.00
R72 Ryne Sandberg 12.50 30.00
R73 Tony Gwynn 8.00 20.00
R74 Tony Gwynn 8.00 20.00
R75 Tony Gwynn 8.00 20.00
R75 Willie Stargell 10.00 25.00
R77 Willie Stargell 10.00 25.00
R78 Willie Stargell 10.00 25.00
R79 Miguel Cabrera 12.50 30.00
R80 Miguel Cabrera 12.50 30.00
R81 Miguel Cabrera 12.50 30.00
R82 George Kell 8.00 20.00
R83 George Kell 8.00 20.00
R84 George Kell 8.00 20.00
R85 Cal Ripken Jr. 15.00 40.00
R86 Cal Ripken Jr. 15.00 40.00
R87 Cal Ripken Jr. 15.00 40.00
R88 Joe Morgan 10.00 25.00
R89 Joe Morgan 10.00 25.00
R90 Joe Morgan 10.00 25.00
R91 Chipper Jones 12.50 30.00
R92 Chipper Jones 12.50 30.00
R93 Chipper Jones 12.50 30.00
R94 Paul Molitor 8.00 20.00
R95 Paul Molitor 8.00 20.00
R96 Paul Molitor 8.00 20.00
R97 Phil Niekro 10.00 25.00
R98 Phil Niekro 10.00 25.00
R99 Phil Niekro 10.00 25.00
R100 Manny Ramirez 12.50 30.00
R101 Manny Ramirez 12.50 30.00
R102 Manny Ramirez 12.50 30.00
R103 Kevin Youkilis 6.00 15.00
R104 Kevin Youkilis 6.00 15.00
R105 Kevin Youkilis 6.00 15.00
R106 Josh Beckett 8.00 20.00
R107 Josh Beckett 8.00 20.00
R108 Josh Beckett 8.00 20.00
R109 Victor Martinez 6.00 15.00
R110 Victor Martinez 6.00 15.00
R111 Victor Martinez 6.00 15.00
R112 Adam Dunn 8.00 20.00
R113 Adam Dunn 8.00 20.00
R114 Adam Dunn 8.00 20.00
R115 Justin Morneau 10.00 25.00
R116 Justin Morneau 10.00 25.00
R117 Justin Morneau 10.00 25.00
R118 Roy Halladay 8.00 20.00
R119 Roy Halladay 8.00 20.00
R120 Roy Halladay 8.00 20.00
R121 Andrew McCutchen 20.00 50.00
R122 Andrew McCutchen 20.00 50.00
R123 Andrew McCutchen 20.00 50.00
R124 Ryan Zimmerman 8.00 20.00
R125 Ryan Zimmerman 8.00 20.00
R126 Ryan Zimmerman 8.00 20.00
R127 Adrian Gonzalez 6.00 15.00
R128 Adrian Gonzalez 6.00 15.00
R129 Adrian Gonzalez 6.00 15.00
R130 Derek Jeter 30.00 60.00
R131 Derek Jeter 30.00 60.00
R132 Derek Jeter 30.00 60.00
R136 Reggie Jackson 15.00 40.00
R137 Reggie Jackson 15.00 40.00
R138 Reggie Jackson 15.00 40.00
R139 Monte Irvin 15.00 40.00
R140 Monte Irvin 15.00 40.00
R141 Monte Irvin 15.00 40.00

2010 Topps Triple Threads Relics Emerald

*EMERALD: .5X TO 1.2X BASIC
STATED ODDS 1:19 MINI
STATED PRINT RUN 18 SER.#'d SETS
ALL DC VARIATIONS PRICED EQUALLY

2010 Topps Triple Threads Relics Gold

*GOLD: .6X TO 1.5X BASIC
STATED ODDS 1:38 MINI
STATED PRINT RUN 9 SER.#'d SETS
ALL DC VARIATIONS PRICED EQUALLY

2010 Topps Triple Threads Relics Sepia

*SEPIA: .4X TO 1X BASIC
STATED ODDS 1:13 MINI
STATED PRINT RUN 27 SER.#'d SETS
ALL DC VARIATIONS PRICED EQUALLY

2010 Topps Triple Threads Rookie Rising Stars Autograph Relic Pairs

STATED ODDS 1:176 MINI
STATED PRINT RUN 50 SER.#'d SETS
RRARP1 S.Strasburg/J.Johnson 75.00 150.00
RRARP2 J.Heyward/T.Hanson 100.00 200.00
RRARP3 Gordon Beckham/Chris Coghlan 12.50 30.00
RRARP4 J.Upton/A.Jones 20.00 50.00
RRARP5 R.Porcello/M.Scherzer 30.00 80.00
RRARP6 S.Strasburg/J.Heyward 75.00 150.00

2011 Topps Triple Threads

COMP.SET w/o AU's (100) 40.00 80.00
COMMON CARD (1-100) .30 .75
1-100 PRINT RUN 1500 SER.#'d SETS
COMMON JSY AU RC (101-150) 5.00 12.00
JSY AU RC ODDS 1:11 HOBBY
JSY AU RC PRINT RUN 99 SER.#'d SETS
COMMON JSY AU (101-150) 5.00 12.00
JSY AU ODDS 1:11 HOBBY
JSY AU PRINT RUN 99 SER.#'d SETS
EXCHANGE DEADLINE 9/30/2014
OVERALL 1-100 PLATE ODDS 1:126 HOBBY
PLATE PRINT RUN 1 SET PER COLOR
BLACK-CYAN-MAGENTA-YELLOW ISSUED
NO PLATE PRICING DUE TO SCARCITY
1 Ryan Braun .50 1.25
2 Johnny Mize .50 1.25
3 Bert Blyleven .50 1.25
4 Lou Gehrig 1.50 4.00
5 Albert Pujols 1.00 2.50
6 Cliff Lee .50 1.25
7 Mickey Mantle 2.50 6.00
8 Cal Ripken Jr. 2.50 6.00
9 Dustin Pedroia .75 2.00
10 Nolan Ryan 2.50 6.00
11 Duke Snider .50 1.25
12 Shin-Soo Choo .50 1.25
13 Hanley Ramirez .50 1.25
14 Eddie Murray .50 1.25
15 Josh Hamilton .50 1.25
16 Chase Utley .50 1.25
17 Willie McCovey .50 1.25
18 Roy Campanella .75 2.00
19 Matt Kemp .60 1.50
20 Victor Martinez .50 1.25
21 Ozzie Smith 1.00 2.50
22 Kevin Youkilis .30 .75
23 Evan Longoria .50 1.25
24 Reggie Jackson .50 1.25
25 Jason Heyward .60 1.50
26 Ty Cobb 1.25 3.00
27 Babe Ruth 2.00 5.00
28 Clayton Kershaw 1.25 3.00
29 Andrew McCutchen .75 2.00
30 Justin Verlander .75 2.00
31 Joe Morgan .50 1.25
32 Carl Crawford .50 1.25
33 Johnny Bench .75 2.00
34 Robinson Cano .50 1.25
35 Mike Stanton .75 2.00
36 Honus Wagner .75 2.00
37 Troy Tulowitzki .75 2.00
38 Jackie Robinson .75 2.00
39 Ryan Zimmerman .50 1.25
40 Carlos Gonzalez .50 1.25
41 Ichiro Suzuki 1.00 2.50
42 Mike Schmidt 1.25 3.00
43 Carlton Fisk .50 1.25
44 Mark Teixeira .50 1.25
45 Tim Lincecum .50 1.25
46 Hank Aaron 1.50 4.00
47 Buster Posey 1.00 2.50
48 Jim Palmer .50 1.25
49 David Wright .60 1.50
50 Mel Ott .75 2.00
51 Brooks Robinson .50 1.25
52 Ryan Howard .60 1.50
53 Joe Mauer .60 1.50
54 Josh Johnson .50 1.25
55 Stan Musial 1.25 3.00
56 Derek Jeter 2.00 5.00
57 Ryne Sandberg 1.50 4.00
58 Pee Wee Reese .50 1.25
59 Bob Gibson .50 1.25
60 Carlos Santana .75 2.00
61 Jose Reyes .50 1.25
62 Paul Molitor .75 2.00
63 Frank Robinson .50 1.25
64 Darryl Strawberry .30 .75
65 Adrian Gonzalez .60 1.50
66 Christy Mathewson .75 2.00
67 Roy Halladay .50 1.25
68 Andre Dawson .50 1.25
69 George Sisler .50 1.25
70 Joey Votto .75 2.00
71 Roger Maris .75 2.00
72 Jimmie Foxx .75 2.00
73 Prince Fielder .50 1.25
74 Roberto Alomar .50 1.25
75 CC Sabathia .50 1.25
76 Rogers Hornsby .50 1.25
77 Ian Kinsler .50 1.25
78 Rickey Henderson .75 2.00
79 Andre Ethier .50 1.25
80 Thurman Munson .75 2.00
81 Matt Holliday .75 2.00
82 Walter Johnson .75 2.00
83 Jon Lester .50 1.25
84 Tom Seaver .50 1.25
85 Starlin Castro .50 1.25
86 Joe DiMaggio 1.50 4.00
87 Felix Hernandez .50 1.25
88 Monte Irvin .50 1.25
89 Cy Young .75 2.00
90 Barry Larkin .50 1.25
91 Tony Gwynn .75 2.00
92 Mariano Rivera 1.00 2.50
93 Clay Buchholz .30 .75
94 John Smoltz .75 2.00
95 Alex Rodriguez 1.00 2.50
96 Tris Speaker .50 1.25
97 Miguel Cabrera .75 2.00

98 Whitey Ford .50 1.25
99 Justin Morneau .50 1.25
100 Sandy Koufax 1.50 4.00
101 Buster Posey Bat AU 50.00 100.00
102 G.Beckham Jsy AU 6.00 15.00
103 Jay Bruce Bat AU 10.00 25.00
104 D.Valencia Bat AU 8.00 20.00
105 Neftali Feliz Jsy AU 5.00 12.00
106 Jose Tabata Jsy AU 5.00 12.00
107 Carlos Santana Jsy AU 5.00 12.00
108 Pablo Sandoval Jsy AU 6.00 15.00
109 Mitch Moreland Bat AU 5.00 12.00
110 Gio Gonzalez Jsy AU 10.00 25.00
111 Brett Wallace Bat AU 6.00 15.00
112 Chris Sale Jsy AU RC 10.00 25.00
113 Kyle Drabek Jsy AU RC 4.00 10.00
114 Starlin Castro Jsy AU 12.00 30.00
115 Austin Jackson Bat AU 8.00 20.00
116 M.Scherzer Jsy AU 30.00 80.00
117 A.Chapman Jsy AU RC 20.00 50.00
118 A.McCutchen Jsy AU 30.00 60.00
119 Zach Britton Jsy AU RC 6.00 15.00
120 Bumgarner JSY AU 20.00 50.00
121 Mike Stanton Jsy AU 25.00 60.00
122 J.Heyward Jsy AU 12.00 30.00
123 F.Freeman Bat AU RC 60.00 150.00
124 Logan Morrison Bat AU 5.00 12.00
125 B.Belt Jsy AU RC 15.00 40.00
126 Brett Anderson Jsy AU 5.00 12.00
127 M.Pineda Jsy AU RC 12.00 30.00
128 Drew Stubbs Jsy AU 8.00 20.00
129 Elvis Andrus Jsy AU 12.50 30.00
130 Colby Rasmus Jsy AU 6.00 15.00
131 Chris Coghlan Jsy AU 5.00 12.00
132 T.Hanson Jsy AU 8.00 20.00
133 C.Kershaw Jsy AU 50.00 100.00
134 Brent Morel Jsy AU RC 5.00 12.00
135 Jaime Garcia Jsy AU 12.50 30.00
136 Hosmer Jsy AU RC EXCH 20.00 50.00
137 J.Hellickson Jsy AU RC 6.00 15.00
138 P.Alvarez Jsy AU RC 8.00 20.00
139 Gaby Sanchez Jsy AU 5.00 12.00
140 J.Arencibia Bat AU 8.00 20.00
141 Neil Walker Jsy AU 8.00 20.00
143 J.Zimmerman Bat AU 6.00 15.00
144 Ian Desmond Jsy AU 4.00 10.00
145 Rick Porcello Jsy AU 5.00 12.00
146 Daniel Bard Jsy AU 6.00 15.00
147A Alcides Escobar Jsy AU 8.00 20.00
147B Hank Conger Jsy AU RC EXCH 5.00 12.00
148 Brett Gardner Bat AU 15.00 40.00
149 Ike Davis Jsy AU 10.00 25.00
150 Carlos Gonzalez Jsy AU 12.50 30.00

2011 Topps Triple Threads Emerald

*EMERALD 1-100: .6X TO 1.5X BASIC
1-100 ODDS 1:3 MINI
1-100 PRINT RUN 249 SER.#'d SETS
*EMERALD JSY AU: .4X TO 1X BASIC
EMERALD JSY AU ODDS 1:21 MINI
EM.JSY AU PRINT RUN 50 SER.#'d SETS
EXCHANGE DEADLINE 9/30/2014

2011 Topps Triple Threads Gold

*GOLD 1-100: .75X TO 2X BASIC
1-100 ODDS 1:6 MINI
1-100 PRINT RUN 99 SER.#'d SETS
101-150 ODDS 1:41 HOBBY
101-150 PRINT RUN 25 SER.#'d SETS
NO 101-150 PRICING DUE TO SCARCITY
EXCHANGE DEADLINE 9/30/2014

2011 Topps Triple Threads Sepia

*SEPIA 1-100: .5X TO 1.2X BASIC
1-100 RANDOMLY INSERTED
1-100 PRINT RUN 625 SER.#'d SETS
*SEPIA JSY AU: .4X TO 1X BASIC
SEPIA JSY AU ODDS 1:14 MINI
SEP.JSY AU PRINT RUN 75 SER.#'d SETS
EXCHANGE DEADLINE 9/30/2014

2011 Topps Triple Threads Autograph Relic Combos

STATED ODDS 1:93 MINI
STATED PRINT RUN 36 SER.#'d SETS
EXCHANGE DEADLINE 9/30/2014
TTARC1 Alomar/Utley/Cano 50.00 100.00
TTARC2 Bench/Mauer/Posey 75.00 150.00
TTARC3 Walk/Gonz/Ubaldo EXCH 20.00 50.00
TTARC4 Schmidt/ARod/Longoria 75.00 150.00
TTARC5 McCovey/Howard/Prince 60.00 120.00
TTARC6 Ryno/Pedroia/Kinsler 40.00 80.00
TTARC7 Wright/Zimmer/Chip 60.00 120.00
TTARC8 Ryan/Halladay/Felix 100.00 200.00
TTARC9 Rick/Craw/Gard EXCH 30.00 60.00
TTARC10 Koufax/Kershaw/Aroldis 250.00 350.00
TTARC11 Braun/Grein/Prin EXCH 50.00 100.00
TTARC12 Musial/Holliday/Rasmus 25.00 60.00
TTARC13 Ryno/Daw/Cast EXCH 40.00 80.00
TTARC14 Strawberry/Heyward/Young 15.00 40.00
TTARC15 Gibson/Felix/Johnson 30.00 60.00

2011 Topps Triple Threads Autograph Relic Combos Sepia

*SEPIA: .4X TO 1X BASIC
STATED ODDS 1:124 MINI
STATED PRINT RUN 27 SER.#'d SETS
EXCHANGE DEADLINE 9/30/2014

2011 Topps Triple Threads Flashback Relics

STATED ODDS 1:56 MINI
STATED PRINT RUN 36 SER.#'d SETS
TTFR1 Mickey Mantle 60.00 150.00
TTFR2 Frank Robinson 12.50 30.00
TTFR3 Babe Ruth 175.00 350.00
TTFR4 Ozzie Smith 20.00 50.00
TTFR5 Nolan Ryan 15.00 40.00
TTFR6 Tony Gwynn 12.50 30.00
TTFR7 Mike Schmidt 15.00 40.00
TTFR8 Paul Molitor 12.50 30.00
TTFR9 Brooks Robinson 15.00 40.00
TTFR10 Hank Aaron 40.00 80.00
TTFR11 Willie McCovey 12.50 30.00
TTFR12 Stan Musial 20.00 50.00
TTFR13 Cal Ripken Jr. 30.00 60.00
TTFR14 Roger Maris 40.00 80.00
TTFR15 Reggie Jackson 12.50 30.00
TTFR16 Ryne Sandberg 12.50 30.00
TTFR17 Carlton Fisk 12.50 30.00
TTFR18 Jackie Robinson 30.00 60.00
TTFR19 Rickey Henderson 30.00 60.00
TTFR20 Johnny Bench 15.00 40.00
TTFR21 Lou Gehrig 75.00 150.00
TTFR22 Al Kaline 15.00 40.00
TTFR23 Ty Cobb 50.00 100.00
TTFR24 Rogers Hornsby 30.00 60.00
TTFR25 Sandy Koufax 75.00 150.00

2011 Topps Triple Threads Flashback Relics Sepia

*SEPIA: .4X TO 1X BASIC
STATED ODDS 1:75 MINI
STATED PRINT RUN 27 SER.#'d SETS

2011 Topps Triple Threads Legend Relics

STATED ODDS 1:94 MINI
STATED PRINT RUN 36 SER.#'d SETS
TTRL1 Ty Cobb 30.00 60.00
TTRL2 Brooks Robinson 12.50 30.00
TTRL3 Babe Ruth 150.00 300.00
TTRL4 Mike Schmidt 10.00 25.00
TTRL5 Joe DiMaggio 60.00 120.00
TTRL6 Johnny Bench 10.00 25.00
TTRL7 Mickey Mantle 75.00 150.00
TTRL8 Jackie Robinson 20.00 50.00
TTRL9 Jim Palmer 10.00 25.00
TTRL10 Lou Gehrig 75.00 150.00
TTRL11 Roy Campanella 12.50 30.00
TTRL12 Bob Gibson 10.00 25.00
TTRL13 Willie McCovey 10.00 25.00
TTRL14 Stan Musial 15.00 40.00
TTRL15 Hank Aaron 30.00 60.00

2011 Topps Triple Threads Legend Relics Sepia

*SEPIA: .4X TO 1X BASIC
STATED ODDS 1:124 MINI
STATED PRINT RUN 27 SER.#'D SETS

2011 Topps Triple Threads Relic Autographs

STATED ODDS 1:11 MINI
STATED PRINT RUN 18 SER.#'d SETS
ALL DC VARIATIONS PRICED EQUALLY
NO PRICING ON PLAYERS W/ONE DC VERSION
EXCHANGE DEADLINE 9/30/2014
TTAR4 Ubaldo Jimenez 10.00 25.00
TTAR5 Ubaldo Jimenez 10.00 25.00
TTAR6 Andre Dawson 15.00 40.00
TTAR7 Andre Dawson 15.00 40.00
TTAR9 Aroldis Chapman 30.00 80.00
TTAR10 Aroldis Chapman 30.00 80.00
TTAR11 Aroldis Chapman 30.00 80.00
TTAR12 Aroldis Chapman 30.00 80.00
TTAR13 Elvis Andrus 10.00 25.00
TTAR14 Johnny Cueto 8.00 20.00
TTAR15 Jay Bruce 20.00 50.00
TTAR16 Jeremy Hellickson 15.00 40.00
TTAR17 Andrew McCutchen 40.00 80.00
TTAR28 Justin Upton 12.50 30.00
TTAR29 Justin Upton 12.50 30.00
TTAR30 Luis Aparicio 12.50 30.00
TTAR31 Luis Aparicio 12.50 30.00
TTAR32 Juan Marichal 20.00 50.00
TTAR33 Juan Marichal 20.00 50.00
TTAR34 Carlos Santana 10.00 25.00
TTAR35 Carlos Santana 10.00 25.00
TTAR36 Carlos Santana 10.00 25.00
TTAR37 Carlos Santana 10.00 25.00
TTAR38 Carlos Santana 10.00 25.00
TTAR40 Tommy Hanson 8.00 20.00
TTAR41 Tommy Hanson 8.00 20.00
TTAR42 Tommy Hanson 8.00 20.00
TTAR43 Tommy Hanson 8.00 20.00
TTAR44 Roberto Alomar 15.00 40.00
TTAR45 Roberto Alomar 15.00 40.00
TTAR46 Elvis Andrus 10.00 25.00
TTAR47 Elvis Andrus 10.00 25.00
TTAR48 Elvis Andrus 10.00 25.00
TTAR49 Elvis Andrus 10.00 25.00
TTAR50 Max Scherzer 40.00 100.00
TTAR51 Max Scherzer 40.00 100.00
TTAR52 Max Scherzer 40.00 100.00
TTAR53 Max Scherzer 40.00 100.00
TTAR54 Jose Bautista 15.00 40.00
TTAR55 Jose Bautista 15.00 40.00
TTAR56 Jose Bautista 15.00 40.00
TTAR57 Jose Bautista 15.00 40.00
TTAR58 Joe Morgan 10.00 25.00
TTAR59 Joe Morgan 10.00 25.00
TTAR60 Matt Garza 8.00 20.00
TTAR61 Matt Garza 8.00 20.00
TTAR62 Matt Garza 8.00 20.00
TTAR63 Matt Garza 8.00 20.00
TTAR66 Josh Johnson 8.00 20.00
TTAR67 Josh Johnson 8.00 20.00
TTAR68 Josh Johnson 8.00 20.00
TTAR69 Josh Johnson 8.00 20.00
TTAR70 Red Schoendienst 20.00 50.00
TTAR71 Red Schoendienst 20.00 50.00
TTAR72 Red Schoendienst 20.00 50.00
TTAR73 Jason Heyward 30.00 60.00
TTAR74 Jason Heyward 30.00 60.00
TTAR76 Dustin Pedroia 30.00 60.00
TTAR77 Dustin Pedroia 30.00 60.00
TTAR78 Duke Snider 30.00 60.00
TTAR79 Duke Snider 30.00 60.00
TTAR80 Pablo Sandoval 12.50 30.00
TTAR81 Pablo Sandoval 12.50 30.00
TTAR82 Pablo Sandoval 12.50 30.00
TTAR83 Pablo Sandoval 12.50 30.00
TTAR84 Pablo Sandoval 12.50 30.00
TTAR85 Angel Pagan 10.00 25.00
TTAR86 Angel Pagan 10.00 25.00
TTAR87 Angel Pagan 10.00 25.00
TTAR88 Angel Pagan 10.00 25.00
TTAR89 Angel Pagan 10.00 25.00
TTAR90 Brian McCann 15.00 40.00
TTAR91 Brian McCann 15.00 40.00
TTAR92 Brian McCann 15.00 40.00
TTAR94 Robinson Cano 20.00 50.00
TTAR95 Robinson Cano 20.00 50.00
TTAR96 Aramis Ramirez 8.00 20.00
TTAR97 Aramis Ramirez 8.00 20.00
TTAR98 Aramis Ramirez 8.00 20.00
TTAR99 Steve Garvey 20.00 50.00
TTAR100 Steve Garvey 20.00 50.00
TTAR101 David Wright 30.00 60.00
TTAR102 David Wright 30.00 60.00
TTAR103 John Smoltz 40.00 80.00
TTAR104 John Smoltz 40.00 80.00
TTAR105 Brooks Robinson 30.00 60.00
TTAR106 Brooks Robinson 30.00 60.00
TTAR107 Prince Fielder 12.00 30.00
TTAR108 Prince Fielder 12.00 30.00
TTAR109 Trevor Cahill 8.00 20.00
TTAR110 Trevor Cahill 8.00 20.00
TTAR111 Trevor Cahill 8.00 20.00
TTAR112 Trevor Cahill 8.00 20.00
TTAR113 Trevor Cahill 8.00 20.00
TTAR117 Tim Hudson 15.00 40.00
TTAR118 Tim Hudson 15.00 40.00
TTAR119 Nick Markakis 10.00 25.00
TTAR120 Nick Markakis 10.00 25.00
TTAR121 Nick Markakis 10.00 25.00
TTAR122 Nick Markakis 10.00 25.00
TTAR124 Josh Hamilton 40.00 80.00
TTAR125 Josh Hamilton 40.00 80.00
TTAR129 Ozzie Smith 15.00 40.00
TTAR130 Ozzie Smith 15.00 40.00
TTAR131 Vernon Wells 8.00 20.00
TTAR132 Vernon Wells 8.00 20.00
TTAR133 Billy Butler 10.00 25.00
TTAR134 Billy Butler 10.00 25.00
TTAR135 Billy Butler 10.00 25.00
TTAR136 Billy Butler 10.00 25.00
TTAR138 Ryan Zimmerman 12.50 30.00
TTAR139 Ryan Zimmerman 12.50 30.00
TTAR140 Ryan Zimmerman 12.50 30.00
TTAR141 Miguel Cabrera 60.00 120.00
TTAR142 Miguel Cabrera 60.00 120.00
TTAR143 Jim Palmer 12.50 30.00
TTAR144 Jim Palmer 12.50 30.00
TTAR145 Adrian Gonzalez 15.00 40.00
TTAR146 Adrian Gonzalez 15.00 40.00
TTAR147 Andrew McCutchen 40.00 80.00
TTAR148 Andrew McCutchen 40.00 80.00
TTAR149 Andrew McCutchen 40.00 80.00
TTAR150 Andrew McCutchen 40.00 80.00
TTAR151 Neftali Feliz 8.00 20.00
TTAR152 Neftali Feliz 8.00 20.00
TTAR153 Neftali Feliz 8.00 20.00
TTAR154 Neftali Feliz 8.00 20.00
TTAR155 Neftali Feliz 8.00 20.00
TTAR158 Nelson Cruz 10.00 25.00
TTAR159 Nelson Cruz 10.00 25.00
TTAR160 Nelson Cruz 10.00 25.00
TTAR161 Nelson Cruz 10.00 25.00
TTAR162 Jonathan Papelbon 10.00 25.00
TTAR163 Jonathan Papelbon 10.00 25.00
TTAR165 Buster Posey 50.00 100.00
TTAR166 Buster Posey 50.00 100.00
TTAR167 Gordon Beckham 10.00 25.00
TTAR168 Gordon Beckham 10.00 25.00
TTAR169 Gordon Beckham 10.00 25.00
TTAR170 Paul Molitor 15.00 40.00
TTAR171 Paul Molitor 15.00 40.00
TTAR172 Mike Stanton 30.00 60.00
TTAR173 Mike Stanton 30.00 60.00
TTAR174 Mike Stanton 30.00 60.00
TTAR175 Jeremy Hellickson 15.00 40.00
TTAR176 Jeremy Hellickson 15.00 40.00
TTAR177 Jeremy Hellickson 15.00 40.00
TTAR178 Jeremy Hellickson 15.00 40.00
TTAR180 Joey Votto 20.00 50.00
TTAR181 Joey Votto 20.00 50.00
TTAR182 Cliff Lee 40.00 80.00
TTAR183 Cliff Lee 40.00 80.00
TTAR184 Ian Kinsler 12.50 30.00
TTAR185 Ian Kinsler 12.50 30.00
TTAR186 Ian Kinsler 12.50 30.00
TTAR187 Ian Kinsler 12.50 30.00
TTAR188 Adam Jones 12.50 30.00
TTAR189 Adam Jones 12.50 30.00
TTAR190 Adam Jones 12.50 30.00
TTAR191 Adam Jones 12.50 30.00
TTAR196 Manny Pacquiao 250.00 350.00
TTAR197 Manny Pacquiao 250.00 350.00
TTAR198 Manny Pacquiao 250.00 350.00
TTAR201 Ryan Howard 30.00 60.00
TTAR202 Ryan Howard 30.00 60.00
TTAR203 Austin Jackson 12.50 30.00
TTAR204 Austin Jackson 12.50 30.00
TTAR205 Austin Jackson 12.50 30.00
TTAR206 Austin Jackson 12.50 30.00
TTAR209 Dan Uggla 15.00 40.00
TTAR210 Dan Uggla 15.00 40.00
TTAR211 Paul O'Neill 30.00 60.00
TTAR212 Paul O'Neill 30.00 60.00
TTAR213 Paul O'Neill 30.00 60.00
TTAR214 Shane Victorino 15.00 40.00
TTAR215 Shane Victorino 15.00 40.00
TTAR216 Shane Victorino 15.00 40.00
TTAR217 Shane Victorino 15.00 40.00
TTAR218 Starlin Castro 20.00 50.00
TTAR219 Starlin Castro 20.00 50.00
TTAR220 Starlin Castro 20.00 50.00
TTAR221 Starlin Castro 20.00 50.00
TTAR222 Starlin Castro 20.00 50.00
TTAR223 Johnny Cueto 8.00 20.00
TTAR224 Johnny Cueto 8.00 20.00
TTAR225 Johnny Cueto 8.00 20.00
TTAR226 Johnny Cueto 8.00 20.00
TTAR228 Fergie Jenkins 15.00 40.00
TTAR229 Fergie Jenkins 15.00 40.00
TTAR230 Andre Ethier 10.00 25.00
TTAR231 Andre Ethier 10.00 25.00
TTAR232 Andre Ethier 10.00 25.00
TTAR233 Andre Ethier 10.00 25.00
TTAR234 Bert Blyleven 15.00 40.00
TTAR235 Bert Blyleven 15.00 40.00
TTAR236 Bert Blyleven 15.00 40.00
TTAR237 Hanley Ramirez 8.00 20.00
TTAR238 Hanley Ramirez 8.00 20.00
TTAR239 Rick Porcello 8.00 20.00
TTAR240 Rick Porcello 8.00 20.00
TTAR241 Rick Porcello 8.00 20.00
TTAR242 Rick Porcello 8.00 20.00
TTAR243 Albert Belle 10.00 25.00
TTAR244 Albert Belle 10.00 25.00
TTAR245 Albert Belle 10.00 25.00
TTAR246 B.J. Upton 10.00 25.00
TTAR247 B.J. Upton 10.00 25.00
TTAR248 B.J. Upton 10.00 25.00
TTAR249 B.J. Upton 10.00 25.00
TTAR250 Matt Holliday 30.00 60.00
TTAR251 Matt Holliday 30.00 60.00
TTAR252 Al Kaline 30.00 80.00
TTAR253 Al Kaline 30.00 80.00
TTAR254 Adam Lind 8.00 20.00
TTAR255 Adam Lind 8.00 20.00
TTAR256 Adam Lind 8.00 20.00
TTAR257 Adam Lind 8.00 20.00
TTAR258 Adam Lind 8.00 20.00
TTAR260 Jay Bruce 10.00 25.00
TTAR261 Jay Bruce 10.00 25.00
TTAR262 Jay Bruce 10.00 25.00
TTAR263 Jay Bruce 10.00 25.00
TTAR264 Heath Bell 8.00 20.00
TTAR265 Heath Bell 8.00 20.00
TTAR266 Heath Bell 8.00 20.00
TTAR267 Heath Bell 8.00 20.00
TTAR268 Darryl Strawberry 30.00 60.00
TTAR269 Darryl Strawberry 30.00 60.00

2011 Topps Triple Threads Relic Autographs Gold

*GOLD: .5X TO 1.2X BASIC
STATED ODDS 1:21 MINI
STATED PRINT RUN 9 SER.#'d SETS
ALL DC VARIATIONS PRICED EQUALLY
NO PRICING ON MANY DUE TO SCARCITY
EXCHANGE DEADLINE 9/30/2014

2011 Topps Triple Threads Relic Combos

STATED ODDS 1:24 MINI
STATED PRINT RUN 36 SER.#'d SETS
TTRC1 Rodriguez/Jeter/Cano 20.00 50.00
TTRC2 Hanley/Tulo/Reyes 10.00 25.00
TTRC3 Pujols/Votto/Cabrera 20.00 50.00
TTRC4 Crawford/Gonzalez/Pedroia 8.00 20.00
TTRC5 Long/Wright/Zimm 10.00 25.00
TTRC6 Heyward/Jones/McCann 12.50 30.00
TTRC7 Lincecum/Posey/Cain 20.00 50.00
TTRC8 Howard/Utley/Rollins 15.00 40.00
TTRC9 McCutchen/Upton/Kemp 8.00 20.00
TTRC10 Hamilton/Kinsler/Cruz 12.50 30.00
TTRC11 Jon Lester/CC Sabathia
David Price 6.00 15.00
TTRC12 Hamilton/Braun/Gonzalez 10.00 25.00
TTRC13 Halladay/Lee/Hamels 20.00 50.00
TTRC14 Stanton/Ramirez/Johnson 12.50 30.00
TTRC15 Ichiro/Hernandez/Figgins 10.00 25.00
TTRC16 Mauer/Posey/McCann 12.50 30.00
TTRC17 Verlan/Cabrera/VMart 15.00 40.00
TTRC18 Choo/Santana/Sizemore 8.00 20.00
TTRC19 Carlos Gonzalez
Troy Tulowitzki/Ubaldo Jimenez 6.00 15.00
TTRC20 Cano/Pedroia/Kinsler 10.00 25.00
TTRC21 Kershaw/Lester/Price 8.00 20.00
TTRC22 Chapman/Votto/Phillips 12.50 30.00
TTRC23 Mauer/Morneau/Liriano 10.00 25.00
TTRC24 Stanton/Heyward/Alvarez 10.00 25.00
TTRC25 Rivera/Sabathia/Hughes 12.50 30.00
TTRC26 Wright/Reyes/Davis 10.00 25.00
TTRC27 Pujols/Holliday/Rasmus 8.00 20.00
TTRC28 Brett Anderson
Trevor Cahill/Gio Gonzalez 6.00 15.00
TTRC29 Bautista/Morrow/Drabek 10.00 25.00
TTRC30 Halladay/Lince/Hernan 12.50 30.00
TTRC31 Walker/Morneau/Votto 12.50 30.00
TTRC32 Fisk/Posada/Posey 10.00 25.00
TTRC33 Jack/Straw/Beltran 12.50 30.00
TTRC34 McCov/How/Field 10.00 25.00
TTRC35 Maric/Lince/Cain 15.00 40.00
TTRC36 Aparicio/Reyes/Andrus 10.00 25.00
TTRC37 Morgan/Alomar/Cano 12.50 30.00
TTRC38 Murray/Teixeira/Jones 10.00 25.00
TTRC39 Campy/Mun/Mauer 15.00 40.00
TTRC40 Ruth/DiMaggio/Mantle 175.00 350.00
TTRC41 Robin/Longo/Zimm 10.00 25.00
TTRC42 Snider/Ethier/Kemp 12.50 30.00
TTRC43 Ryan/Hernandez/Jimenez 15.00 40.00
TTRC44 Sandberg/Castro/Ramirez 15.00 40.00
TTRC45 Schm/Rod/Longo 15.00 40.00
TTRC46 Seaver/Volquez/Cueto 10.00 25.00
TTRC47 Smith/Jeter/Rollins 10.00 25.00
TTRC48 Cobb/Ichiro/Cano 40.00 80.00
TTRC49 Foxx/Pujols/Howard 12.50 30.00
TTRC50 Koufax/Kershaw/Price 30.00 60.00
TTRC51 Dawson/Heyward/Gonzalez 8.00 20.00
TTRC52 Ripken/Jeter/Tulowitzki 20.00 50.00
TTRC53 Gib/Wain/Carp 12.50 30.00
TTRC54 Gwynn/Ichiro/Gonzalez 12.50 30.00
TTRC55 Hend/Craw/McCutch 15.00 40.00
TTRC56 Larkin/Ramirez/Tulowitzki 8.00 20.00
TTRC57 Molitor/Braun/Fielder 12.50 30.00
TTRC58 Musial/Holliday/Rasmus 10.00 25.00
TTRC59 Ford/Sabathia/Rivera 15.00 40.00
TTRC60 DiMaggio/Aaron/Koufax 75.00 150.00

2011 Topps Triple Threads Relic Combos Sepia

*SEPIA: .4X TO 1X BASIC
STATED ODDS 1:31 MINI
STATED PRINT RUN 27 SER.#'d SETS

2011 Topps Triple Threads Relic Combos Double

STATED ODDS 1:78 MINI
STATED PRINT RUN 27 SER.#'d SETS
TTRDC1 Shortstop Superstars 75.00 150.00
TTRDC2 J.Hamilton/J.Votto 30.00 60.00
TTRDC3 Outfield Legends 175.00 350.00
TTRDC4 Jered Weaver/Jon Lester/Felix Hernandez/Roy Halladay/Tim Lincecum/Ubaldo Ji 20.00 50.00
TTRDC5 Dinger Kings 30.00 60.00
TTRDC6 Roy Halladay/Felix Hernandez 20.00 50.00
TTRDC7 Austin Jackson/Carlos Santana/Jason Heyward/Buster Posey/Mike Stanton/Starl 20.00 50.00
TTRDC8 Slugging Second Basemen 40.00 80.00
TTRDC9 World Series Champions 100.00 200.00
TTRDC10 3 Time MVPs 100.00 200.00
TTRDC11 Hollywood Heroes 60.00 120.00
TTRDC12 J.DiMaggio/D.Jeter 100.00 200.00
TTRDC13 Light Tower Power 30.00 60.00
TTRDC14 All Time Aces 50.00 100.00
TTRDC15 Meet The Mets 40.00 80.00
TTRDC16 Cas/Gon/Pos/Price/Bau/Buc 20.00 50.00
TTRDC17 Red Sox Re-Load 30.00 60.00
TTRDC18 Throwing Cheese 40.00 80.00

2011 Topps Triple Threads Relic Combos Double Sepia

*SEPIA: .4X TO 1X BASIC
STATED ODDS 1:103 MINI
STATED PRINT RUN 27 SER.#'d SETS

2011 Topps Triple Threads Relics

STATED ODDS 1:11 MINI
STATED PRINT RUN 36 SER.#'d SETS
ALL DC VARIATIONS PRICED EQUALLY
TTR1 Derek Jeter 30.00 60.00
TTR2 Derek Jeter 30.00 60.00
TTR3 Derek Jeter 30.00 60.00
TTR4 Derek Jeter 30.00 60.00
TTR5 Ichiro Suzuki 12.50 30.00
TTR6 Ichiro Suzuki 12.50 30.00
TTR7 Ichiro Suzuki 12.50 30.00
TTR8 Ichiro Suzuki 12.50 30.00
TTR9 Carlos Gonzalez 5.00 12.00
TTR10 Carlos Gonzalez 5.00 12.00
TTR11 Carlos Gonzalez 5.00 12.00
TTR12 Carlos Gonzalez 5.00 12.00
TTR13 Roy Halladay 10.00 25.00
TTR14 Roy Halladay 10.00 25.00
TTR15 Roy Halladay 10.00 25.00
TTR16 Roy Halladay 10.00 25.00
TTR17 Starlin Castro 10.00 25.00
TTR18 Starlin Castro 10.00 25.00
TTR19 Starlin Castro 10.00 25.00
TTR20 Starlin Castro 10.00 25.00
TTR21 CC Sabathia 8.00 20.00
TTR22 CC Sabathia 8.00 20.00
TTR23 CC Sabathia 8.00 20.00
TTR24 Jose Bautista 5.00 12.00
TTR25 Jose Bautista 5.00 12.00
TTR26 Jose Bautista 5.00 12.00
TTR27 Jose Bautista 5.00 12.00
TTR28 Tim Lincecum 12.50 30.00
TTR29 Tim Lincecum 12.50 30.00
TTR30 Tim Lincecum 12.50 30.00
TTR31 Tim Lincecum 12.50 30.00
TTR32 Mark Teixeira 6.00 15.00
TTR33 Mark Teixeira 6.00 15.00
TTR34 Mark Teixeira 6.00 15.00
TTR35 Mark Teixeira 6.00 15.00
TTR36 Josh Johnson 5.00 12.00
TTR37 Josh Johnson 5.00 12.00
TTR38 Josh Johnson 5.00 12.00
TTR39 Josh Johnson 5.00 12.00
TTR40 Shin-Soo Choo 6.00 15.00
TTR41 Shin-Soo Choo 6.00 15.00
TTR42 Shin-Soo Choo 6.00 15.00
TTR43 Ryan Howard 8.00 20.00
TTR44 Ryan Howard 8.00 20.00
TTR45 Ryan Howard 8.00 20.00
TTR46 Ryan Howard 8.00 20.00
TTR47 Dustin Pedroia 10.00 25.00
TTR48 Dustin Pedroia 10.00 25.00
TTR49 Dustin Pedroia 10.00 25.00
TTR50 Dustin Pedroia 10.00 25.00
TTR51 Evan Longoria 6.00 15.00
TTR52 Evan Longoria 6.00 15.00
TTR53 Evan Longoria 6.00 15.00
TTR54 Evan Longoria 6.00 15.00
TTR55 Justin Morneau 6.00 15.00
TTR56 Justin Morneau 6.00 15.00
TTR57 Justin Morneau 6.00 15.00
TTR58 Hanley Ramirez 5.00 12.00
TTR59 Hanley Ramirez 5.00 12.00
TTR60 Hanley Ramirez 5.00 12.00
TTR61 Hanley Ramirez 5.00 12.00
TTR62 Alex Rodriguez 10.00 25.00
TTR63 Alex Rodriguez 10.00 25.00
TTR64 Alex Rodriguez 10.00 25.00
TTR65 Alex Rodriguez 10.00 25.00
TTR66 Joe Mauer 6.00 15.00
TTR67 Joe Mauer 6.00 15.00
TTR68 Joe Mauer 6.00 15.00
TTR69 Joe Mauer 6.00 15.00
TTR70 Joey Votto 12.50 30.00
TTR71 Joey Votto 12.50 30.00
TTR72 Joey Votto 12.50 30.00
TTR73 Joey Votto 12.50 30.00
TTR74 Chase Utley 8.00 20.00
TTR75 Chase Utley 8.00 20.00
TTR76 Chase Utley 8.00 20.00
TTR77 Prince Fielder 8.00 20.00
TTR78 Prince Fielder 8.00 20.00
TTR79 Prince Fielder 8.00 20.00
TTR80 Prince Fielder 8.00 20.00
TTR81 Robinson Cano 10.00 25.00
TTR82 Robinson Cano 10.00 25.00
TTR83 Robinson Cano 10.00 25.00
TTR84 Robinson Cano 10.00 25.00
TTR85 Carlos Santana 5.00 12.00
TTR86 Carlos Santana 5.00 12.00
TTR87 Carlos Santana 5.00 12.00
TTR88 Hunter Pence 6.00 15.00
TTR89 Hunter Pence 6.00 15.00
TTR90 Hunter Pence 6.00 15.00
TTR91 Kevin Youkilis 6.00 15.00
TTR92 Kevin Youkilis 6.00 15.00
TTR93 Kevin Youkilis 6.00 15.00
TTR94 David Wright 6.00 15.00
TTR95 David Wright 6.00 15.00
TTR96 David Wright 6.00 15.00
TTR97 David Wright 6.00 15.00
TTR98 Jon Lester 8.00 20.00
TTR99 Jon Lester 8.00 20.00
TTR100 Jon Lester 8.00 20.00
TTR101 Justin Upton 5.00 12.00
TTR102 Justin Upton 5.00 12.00
TTR103 Justin Upton 5.00 12.00
TTR104 Justin Upton 5.00 12.00
TTR105 Matt Holliday 6.00 15.00
TTR106 Matt Holliday 6.00 15.00
TTR107 Matt Holliday 6.00 15.00
TTR108 Miguel Cabrera 12.50 30.00
TTR109 Miguel Cabrera 12.50 30.00
TTR110 Miguel Cabrera 12.50 30.00
TTR111 Miguel Cabrera 12.50 30.00
TTR112 Jose Reyes 6.00 15.00
TTR113 Jose Reyes 6.00 15.00
TTR114 Jose Reyes 6.00 15.00
TTR115 Josh Hamilton 10.00 25.00
TTR116 Josh Hamilton 10.00 25.00
TTR117 Josh Hamilton 10.00 25.00
TTR118 Josh Hamilton 10.00 25.00
TTR119 Jason Heyward 8.00 20.00
TTR120 Jason Heyward 8.00 20.00
TTR121 Jason Heyward 8.00 20.00
TTR122 Matt Kemp 10.00 25.00
TTR123 Matt Kemp 10.00 25.00
TTR124 Matt Kemp 10.00 25.00
TTR125 Albert Pujols 10.00 25.00
TTR126 Albert Pujols 10.00 25.00
TTR127 Albert Pujols 10.00 25.00
TTR128 Felix Hernandez 6.00 15.00
TTR129 Felix Hernandez 6.00 15.00
TTR130 Felix Hernandez 6.00 15.00
TTR131 Felix Hernandez 6.00 15.00
TTR132 Ryan Braun 10.00 25.00
TTR133 Ryan Braun 10.00 25.00
TTR134 Ryan Braun 10.00 25.00
TTR135 Ryan Braun 10.00 25.00
TTR136 Troy Tulowitzki 8.00 20.00
TTR137 Troy Tulowitzki 8.00 20.00
TTR138 Troy Tulowitzki 8.00 20.00

2011 Topps Triple Threads Relics Emerald

*EMERALD: .5X TO 1.2X BASIC
STATED ODDS 1:21 MINI
STATED PRINT RUN 18 SER.#'d SETS
ALL DC VARIATIONS PRICED EQUALLY

2011 Topps Triple Threads Relics Gold

*GOLD: .6X TO 1.5X BASIC
STATED ODDS 1:41 MINI
STATED PRINT RUN 9 SER.#'d SETS
ALL DC VARIATIONS EQUALLY PRICED

2011 Topps Triple Threads Relics Sepia

*SEPIA: .4X TO 1X BASIC
STATED ODDS 1:14 MINI
STATED PRINT RUN 27 SER.#'d SETS
ALL DC VARIATIONS EQUALLY PRICED

2011 Topps Triple Threads Rookie Phenom Relic Pairs

STATED ODDS 1:168 MINI
STATED PRINT RUN 50 SER.#'d SETS
EXCHANGE DEADLINE 9/30/2014
RFPP1 Aroldis Chapman/Chris Sale 30.00 80.00
RFPP2 B.Posey/N.Feliz 40.00 80.00
RFPP3 Andrew McCutchen/Pedro Alvarez 25.00 60.00
RFPP4 J.Heyward/F.Freeman 25.00 60.00
RFPP5 Mike Stanton/Logan Morrison 25.00 60.00
RFPP6 Starlin Castro/Elvis Andrus 25.00 60.00

2011 Topps Triple Threads Unity Relic Autographs

STATED ODDS 1:6 MINI
STATED PRINT RUN 99 SER.#'d SETS
EXCHANGE DEADLINE 9/30/2014
TTUAR1 Martin Prado 6.00 15.00
TTUAR2 Chipper Jones 20.00 50.00
TTUAR3 Brian McCann 10.00 25.00
TTUAR4 Tim Hudson 6.00 15.00
TTUAR5 Mike Minor 6.00 15.00
TTUAR6 Jason Heyward 8.00 20.00
TTUAR7 Mike Minor 6.00 15.00
TTUAR8 Tommy Hanson 5.00 12.00
TTUAR9 Martin Prado 6.00 15.00
TTUAR10 Colby Rasmus 4.00 10.00
TTUAR11 Matt Holliday 15.00 40.00
TTUAR12 David Freese 10.00 25.00
TTUAR13 Ozzie Smith 20.00 50.00
TTUAR14 Colby Rasmus 4.00 10.00
TTUAR15 Jon Jay 5.00 12.00
TTUAR16 Jason Motte 8.00 20.00
TTUAR17 Allen Craig 6.00 15.00
TTUAR18 Jon Jay 5.00 12.00
TTUAR19 Marlon Byrd 4.00 10.00
TTUAR20 Andrew Cashner 4.00 10.00
TTUAR21 Randy Wells 4.00 10.00
TTUAR22 Marlon Byrd 4.00 10.00
TTUAR23 Aramis Ramirez 4.00 10.00
TTUAR24 Starlin Castro 6.00 15.00
TTUAR25 Marlon Byrd 4.00 10.00
TTUAR26 Tyler Colvin 4.00 10.00
TTUAR27 Andrew Cashner 4.00 10.00
TTUAR28 Pablo Sandoval 10.00 25.00
TTUAR29 Freddy Sanchez 5.00 12.00
TTUAR30 Cody Ross 6.00 15.00
TTUAR31 Pablo Sandoval 10.00 25.00
TTUAR32 Buster Posey 40.00 80.00
TTUAR33 Matt Cain 8.00 20.00
TTUAR34 Cody Ross 6.00 15.00
TTUAR35 Freddy Sanchez 5.00 12.00
TTUAR36 Brian Wilson 15.00 40.00
TTUAR37 Chris Coghlan 4.00 10.00
TTUAR38 Ricky Nolasco 4.00 10.00
TTUAR39 Logan Morrison 5.00 12.00
TTUAR40 Mike Stanton 15.00 40.00
TTUAR41 Hanley Ramirez 8.00 20.00
TTUAR42 Josh Johnson 6.00 15.00
TTUAR43 Gaby Sanchez 4.00 10.00
TTUAR44 Chris Coghlan 4.00 10.00
TTUAR45 Logan Morrison 4.00 10.00
TTUAR46 Angel Pagan 5.00 12.00
TTUAR47 Josh Thole 4.00 10.00
TTUAR48 Ike Davis 6.00 15.00
TTUAR49 Angel Pagan 5.00 12.00
TTUAR50 David Wright 12.50 30.00
TTUAR51 Darryl Strawberry 10.00 25.00
TTUAR52 Angel Pagan 5.00 12.00
TTUAR53 Josh Thole 4.00 10.00
TTUAR54 Jon Niese 5.00 12.00
TTUAR55 Jose Tabata 4.00 10.00
TTUAR56 Garrett Jones 6.00 15.00
TTUAR57 Neil Walker 5.00 12.00
TTUAR58 Jose Tabata 4.00 10.00
TTUAR59 Andrew McCutchen 20.00 50.00
TTUAR60 Pedro Alvarez 6.00 15.00
TTUAR61 Garrett Jones 6.00 15.00
TTUAR62 Neil Walker 5.00 12.00
TTUAR63 Daniel McCutchen 4.00 10.00
TTUAR64 Craig Gentry 6.00 15.00
TTUAR65 Elvis Andrus 6.00 15.00
TTUAR66 Ian Kinsler 10.00 25.00
TTUAR67 Josh Hamilton 30.00 60.00
TTUAR68 Mitch Moreland 5.00 12.00
TTUAR69 Neftali Feliz 6.00 15.00
TTUAR70 Nelson Cruz 6.00 15.00
TTUAR71 Mitch Moreland 5.00 12.00
TTUAR72 Derek Holland 6.00 15.00
TTUAR73 Chris Heisey 8.00 20.00
TTUAR74 Johnny Cueto 4.00 10.00
TTUAR75 Edinson Volquez 5.00 12.00
TTUAR76 Jay Bruce 10.00 25.00
TTUAR77 Johnny Cueto 6.00 15.00
TTUAR78 Aroldis Chapman 10.00 25.00
TTUAR79 Drew Stubbs 5.00 12.00
TTUAR80 Edinson Volquez 5.00 12.00
TTUAR81 Travis Wood 4.00 10.00
TTUAR82 Scott Sizemore 4.00 10.00
TTUAR83 Jhonny Peralta 5.00 12.00
TTUAR84 Ryan Perry 4.00 10.00
TTUAR85 Austin Jackson 8.00 20.00
TTUAR86 Daniel Schlereth 4.00 10.00
TTUAR87 Max Scherzer 20.00 50.00
TTUAR88 Austin Jackson 8.00 20.00
TTUAR89 Rick Porcello 5.00 12.00
TTUAR90 Jhonny Peralta 5.00 12.00
TTUAR91 Torii Hunter 8.00 20.00
TTUAR92 Kendrys Morales 4.00 10.00
TTUAR93 Jered Weaver 8.00 20.00
TTUAR94 Vernon Wells 4.00 10.00
TTUAR95 Kendrys Morales 4.00 10.00
TTUAR96 Jordan Walden 4.00 10.00
TTUAR97 Torii Hunter 8.00 20.00
TTUAR98 Hank Conger 4.00 10.00
TTUAR99 Dan Haren 5.00 12.00

2011 Topps Triple Threads Unity Relic Autographs Emerald

*EMERALD: .5X TO 1.2X BASIC
STATED ODDS 1:11 MINI
STATED PRINT RUN 50 SER.#'d SETS
EXCHANGE DEADLINE 9/30/2014

2011 Topps Triple Threads Unity Relic Autographs Gold

*GOLD: .5X TO 1.2X BASIC
STATED ODDS 1:21 MINI
STATED PRINT RUN 25 SER.#'d SETS
NO PRICING ON MOST DUE TO SCARCITY
EXCHANGE DEADLINE 9/30/2014

2011 Topps Triple Threads Unity Relic Autographs Sepia

*SEPIA: .4X TO 1X BASIC
STATED ODDS 1:7 MINI
STATED PRINT RUN 75 SER.#'d SETS
EXCHANGE DEADLINE 9/30/2014

2011 Topps Triple Threads Unity Relics

STATED ODDS 1:6 MINI
STATED PRINT RUN 36 SER.#'d SETS
TTUS80 Alfonso Soriano 4.00 10.00
TTUS81 Fergie Jenkins 5.00 12.00
TTUS83 Duke Snider 6.00 15.00
TTUS84 Clayton Kershaw 4.00 10.00
TTUS85 Sandy Koufax 30.00 60.00
TTUS86 Andre Ethier 4.00 10.00
TTUS87 Roy Campanella 8.00 20.00
TTUS88 Matt Kemp 4.00 10.00
TTUS89 Clayton Kershaw 4.00 10.00
TTUS90 Andre Ethier 4.00 10.00
TTUS91 Juan Marichal 4.00 10.00
TTUS92 Brian Wilson 6.00 15.00
TTUS93 Matt Cain 4.00 10.00
TTUS94 Willie McCovey 4.00 10.00
TTUS95 Tim Lincecum 6.00 15.00
TTUS96 Buster Posey 6.00 15.00
TTUS97 Willie McCovey 4.00 10.00
TTUS98 Tim Lincecum 6.00 15.00
TTUS99 Buster Posey 6.00 15.00
TTUSR1 Derek Jeter 10.00 25.00
TTUSR2 Reggie Jackson 6.00 15.00
TTUSR3 Mickey Mantle 30.00 60.00
TTUSR4 Reggie Jackson 6.00 15.00
TTUSR5 Babe Ruth 60.00 120.00
TTUSR6 Joe DiMaggio 30.00 60.00
TTUSR7 Lou Gehrig 50.00 100.00
TTUSR8 Joe DiMaggio 50.00 100.00
TTUSR9 Mariano Rivera 5.00 12.00
TTUS100 Carlos Santana 4.00 10.00
TTUS101 Shin-Soo Choo 5.00 12.00
TTUS102 Roberto Alomar 6.00 15.00
TTUS103 Grady Sizemore 4.00 10.00
TTUS104 Roberto Alomar 6.00 15.00
TTUS105 Albert Belle 5.00 12.00
TTUS106 Carlos Santana 4.00 10.00
TTUS107 Grady Sizemore 4.00 10.00
TTUS108 Albert Belle 5.00 12.00
TTUS109 Alex Rodriguez 6.00 15.00
TTUS110 Ichiro Suzuki 12.50 30.00
TTUS111 Felix Hernandez 4.00 10.00
TTUS112 Alex Rodriguez 6.00 15.00
TTUS113 Ichiro Suzuki 12.50 30.00
TTUS114 Felix Hernandez 4.00 10.00
TTUS115 Alex Rodriguez 6.00 15.00
TTUS116 Ichiro Suzuki 12.50 30.00
TTUS117 Felix Hernandez 4.00 10.00
TTUS118 Hanley Ramirez 4.00 10.00
TTUS119 Josh Johnson 4.00 10.00
TTUS120 Logan Morrison 4.00 10.00
TTUS121 Mike Stanton 5.00 12.00
TTUS122 Hanley Ramirez 4.00 10.00
TTUS123 Josh Johnson 4.00 10.00
TTUS124 Mike Stanton 5.00 12.00
TTUS125 Hanley Ramirez 4.00 10.00
TTUS126 Logan Morrison 4.00 10.00
TTUS127 Darryl Strawberry 4.00 10.00
TTUS128 Tom Seaver 5.00 12.00
TTUS129 Johan Santana 4.00 10.00
TTUS130 David Wright 6.00 15.00
TTUS131 Nolan Ryan 12.50 30.00
TTUS132 Jose Reyes 6.00 15.00
TTUS133 Tom Seaver 5.00 12.00
TTUS134 Jose Reyes 6.00 15.00
TTUS135 Darryl Strawberry 4.00 10.00
TTUS136 Nick Markakis 4.00 10.00
TTUS137 Eddie Murray 5.00 12.00
TTUS138 Adam Jones 4.00 10.00
TTUS139 Jim Palmer 4.00 10.00
TTUS140 Cal Ripken Jr. 10.00 25.00
TTUS141 Brooks Robinson 6.00 15.00
TTUS142 Frank Robinson 4.00 10.00
TTUS143 Brian Roberts 4.00 10.00
TTUS144 Brian Matusz 4.00 10.00
TTUS145 Mat Latos 4.00 10.00
TTUS146 Heath Bell 4.00 10.00
TTUS147 Tony Gwynn 6.00 15.00
TTUS148 Tony Gwynn 6.00 15.00
TTUS149 Tony Gwynn 6.00 15.00
TTUS150 Willie McCovey 4.00 10.00

TTUS151 Mat Latos 4.00 10.00
TTUS152 Tony Gwynn 6.00 15.00
TTUS153 Heath Bell 4.00 10.00
TTUS154 Mike Schmidt 6.00 15.00
TTUS155 Roy Halladay 8.00 20.00
TTUS156 Jimmy Rollins 4.00 10.00
TTUS157 Ryan Howard 5.00 12.00
TTUS158 Mike Schmidt 6.00 15.00
TTUS159 Chase Utley 4.00 10.00
TTUS160 Roy Halladay 8.00 20.00
TTUS161 Ryan Howard 5.00 12.00
TTUS162 Chase Utley 4.00 10.00
TTUS163 Andrew McCutchen 4.00 10.00
TTUS164 Jose Tabata 4.00 10.00
TTUS165 Pedro Alvarez 4.00 10.00
TTUS166 Honus Wagner 40.00 80.00
TTUS167 Andrew McCutchen 4.00 10.00
TTUS168 Jose Tabata 4.00 10.00
TTUS169 Andrew McCutchen 4.00 10.00
TTUS170 Jose Tabata 4.00 10.00
TTUS171 Pedro Alvarez 4.00 10.00
TTUS172 Michael Young 4.00 10.00
TTUS173 Nelson Cruz 4.00 10.00
TTUS174 Ian Kinsler 4.00 10.00
TTUS175 Nolan Ryan 12.50 30.00
TTUS176 Josh Hamilton 5.00 12.00
TTUS177 Alex Rodriguez 6.00 15.00
TTUS178 Vladimir Guerrero 4.00 10.00
TTUS179 Josh Hamilton 5.00 12.00
TTUS180 Ian Kinsler 4.00 10.00
TTUS181 Evan Longoria 4.00 10.00
TTUS182 David Price 4.00 10.00
TTUS183 B.J. Upton 4.00 10.00
TTUS184 Evan Longoria 4.00 10.00
TTUS185 David Price 4.00 10.00
TTUS186 B.J. Upton 4.00 10.00
TTUS187 Evan Longoria 4.00 10.00
TTUS188 David Price 4.00 10.00
TTUS189 Jeremy Hellickson 4.00 10.00
TTUS190 Nomar Garciaparra 6.00 15.00
TTUS191 David Ortiz 4.00 10.00
TTUS192 Kevin Youkilis 4.00 10.00
TTUS193 Jimmie Foxx 12.50 30.00
TTUS194 Jon Lester 4.00 10.00
TTUS195 Dustin Pedroia 4.00 10.00
TTUS196 Manny Ramirez 5.00 12.00
TTUS197 Carlton Fisk 5.00 12.00
TTUS199 Barry Larkin 6.00 15.00
TTUS200 Jay Bruce 4.00 10.00
TTUS201 Johnny Cueto 4.00 10.00
TTUS202 Johnny Bench 6.00 15.00
TTUS203 Joey Votto 5.00 12.00
TTUS204 Tom Seaver 5.00 12.00
TTUS205 Frank Robinson 4.00 10.00
TTUS206 Joe Morgan 4.00 10.00
TTUS207 Aroldis Chapman 5.00 12.00
TTUS208 Matt Holliday 4.00 10.00
TTUS209 Ubaldo Jimenez 4.00 10.00
TTUS210 Troy Tulowitzki 4.00 10.00
TTUS211 Larry Walker 4.00 10.00
TTUS212 Carlos Gonzalez 4.00 10.00
TTUS213 Todd Helton 4.00 10.00
TTUS214 Ubaldo Jimenez 4.00 10.00
TTUS215 Troy Tulowitzki 4.00 10.00
TTUS216 Larry Walker 4.00 10.00
TTUS217 Justin Verlander 6.00 15.00
TTUS218 Miguel Cabrera 6.00 15.00
TTUS219 Al Kaline 10.00 25.00
TTUS220 Ty Cobb 30.00 60.00
TTUS221 Miguel Cabrera 6.00 15.00
TTUS222 Al Kaline 10.00 25.00
TTUS223 Austin Jackson 4.00 10.00
TTUS224 Miguel Cabrera 6.00 15.00
TTUS225 Justin Verlander 6.00 15.00
TTUS226 Francisco Liriano 4.00 10.00
TTUS227 Joe Mauer 4.00 10.00
TTUS228 Justin Morneau 5.00 12.00
TTUS229 Bert Blyleven 5.00 12.00
TTUS230 Joe Mauer 4.00 10.00
TTUS231 Justin Morneau 5.00 12.00
TTUS233 Joe Mauer 4.00 10.00
TTUS234 Justin Morneau 5.00 12.00
TTUS235 Luis Aparicio 5.00 12.00
TTUS236 Gordon Beckham 4.00 10.00
TTUS237 John Danks 4.00 10.00
TTUS238 Carlton Fisk 5.00 12.00
TTUS239 Mark Buehrle 4.00 10.00
TTUS240 Paul Konerko 4.00 10.00
TTUS241 Alex Rios 4.00 10.00
TTUS242 Carlos Quentin 4.00 10.00
TTUS243 Alexei Ramirez 4.00 10.00
TTUS244 Justin Upton 4.00 10.00
TTUS245 Stephen Drew 4.00 10.00
TTUS246 Kelly Johnson 4.00 10.00
TTUS247 Justin Upton 4.00 10.00
TTUS248 Stephen Drew 4.00 10.00
TTUS249 Chris Young 4.00 10.00
TTUS250 Justin Upton 4.00 10.00
TTUS251 Stephen Drew 4.00 10.00
TTUS252 Miguel Montero 4.00 10.00
TTUS253 Stephen Strasburg 8.00 20.00
TTUS254 Ryan Zimmerman 4.00 10.00
TTUS255 Jayson Werth 4.00 10.00
TTUS256 Stephen Strasburg 8.00 20.00
TTUS257 Ryan Zimmerman 4.00 10.00
TTUS258 Jayson Werth 4.00 10.00
TTUS259 Stephen Strasburg 8.00 20.00
TTUS260 Ryan Zimmerman 4.00 10.00
TTUS261 Jayson Werth 4.00 10.00
TTUS262 Zack Greinke 4.00 10.00
TTUS263 Billy Butler 4.00 10.00
TTUS264 Joakim Soria 4.00 10.00
TTUS265 Billy Butler 4.00 10.00
TTUS266 Joakim Soria 4.00 10.00
TTUS267 Alex Gordon 4.00 10.00
TTUS268 Billy Butler 4.00 10.00
TTUS269 Joakim Soria 4.00 10.00
TTUS270 Alex Gordon 4.00 10.00
TTUSR10 Torii Hunter 4.00 10.00
TTUSR11 Kendrys Morales 4.00 10.00
TTUSR12 Jered Weaver 4.00 10.00
TTUSR13 Torii Hunter 4.00 10.00
TTUSR14 Nolan Ryan 12.50 30.00
TTUSR15 Reggie Jackson 6.00 15.00
TTUSR16 Torii Hunter 4.00 10.00
TTUSR17 Nolan Ryan 12.50 30.00
TTUSR18 Reggie Jackson 6.00 15.00
TTUSR19 Nolan Ryan 12.50 30.00
TTUSR20 Joe Morgan 4.00 10.00
TTUSR21 Hunter Pence 4.00 10.00
TTUSR22 Nolan Ryan 12.50 30.00
TTUSR23 Joe Morgan 4.00 10.00
TTUSR24 Lance Berkman 4.00 10.00
TTUSR25 Nolan Ryan 12.50 30.00
TTUSR26 Joe Morgan 4.00 10.00
TTUSR27 Hunter Pence 4.00 10.00
TTUSR28 Rickey Henderson 10.00 25.00
TTUSR29 Reggie Jackson 6.00 15.00
TTUSR30 Brett Anderson 4.00 10.00
TTUSR31 Rickey Henderson 10.00 25.00
TTUSR32 Reggie Jackson 6.00 15.00
TTUSR33 Rollie Fingers 4.00 10.00
TTUSR34 Rickey Henderson 10.00 25.00
TTUSR35 Rollie Fingers 4.00 10.00
TTUSR36 Kurt Suzuki 4.00 10.00
TTUSR37 Vernon Wells 4.00 10.00
TTUSR38 Paul Molitor 5.00 12.00
TTUSR39 Aaron Hill 4.00 10.00
TTUSR40 Roberto Alomar 6.00 15.00
TTUSR41 Roy Halladay 8.00 20.00
TTUSR42 Jose Bautista 4.00 10.00
TTUSR43 Roberto Alomar 6.00 15.00
TTUSR44 Roy Halladay 8.00 20.00
TTUSR45 Jose Bautista 4.00 10.00
TTUSR46 Hank Aaron 12.50 30.00
TTUSR47 Chipper Jones 6.00 15.00
TTUSR48 Brian McCann 4.00 10.00
TTUSR49 Hank Aaron 12.50 30.00
TTUSR50 John Smoltz 4.00 10.00
TTUSR51 Jason Heyward 4.00 10.00
TTUSR52 Hank Aaron 12.50 30.00
TTUSR53 Tommy Hanson 4.00 10.00
TTUSR54 Jason Heyward 4.00 10.00
TTUSR55 Paul Molitor 5.00 12.00
TTUSR56 Ryan Braun 6.00 15.00
TTUSR57 Prince Fielder 4.00 10.00
TTUSR58 Paul Molitor 5.00 12.00
TTUSR59 Ryan Braun 6.00 15.00
TTUSR60 Prince Fielder 4.00 10.00
TTUSR61 Paul Molitor 5.00 12.00
TTUSR62 Ryan Braun 6.00 15.00
TTUSR63 Yovani Gallardo 4.00 10.00
TTUSR64 Ozzie Smith 6.00 15.00
TTUSR65 Matt Holliday 4.00 10.00
TTUSR66 Bob Gibson 6.00 15.00
TTUSR67 Stan Musial 10.00 25.00
TTUSR68 Albert Pujols 10.00 25.00
TTUSR69 Rogers Hornsby 10.00 25.00
TTUSR70 Albert Pujols 10.00 25.00
TTUSR71 Adam Wainwright 4.00 10.00
TTUSR72 Johnny Mize 6.00 15.00
TTUSR73 Starlin Castro 4.00 10.00
TTUSR74 Fergie Jenkins 5.00 12.00
TTUSR75 Ryne Sandberg 8.00 20.00
TTUSR76 Andre Dawson 4.00 10.00
TTUSR77 Starlin Castro 4.00 10.00
TTUSR78 Ryne Sandberg 8.00 20.00
TTUSR79 Aramis Ramirez 4.00 10.00

2011 Topps Triple Threads Unity Relics Emerald

*EMERALD: .5X TO 1.2X BASIC
STATED ODDS 1:11 MINI
STATED PRINT RUN 18 SER.#'d SETS
ALL VERSIONS EQUALLY PRICED
SOME NOT PRICED DUE TO SCARCITY

2011 Topps Triple Threads Unity Relics Gold

*GOLD: .6X TO 1.5X BASIC
STATED ODDS 1:21 MINI
STATED PRINT RUN 9 SER.#'d SETS
ALL VERSIONS EQUALLY PRICED
SOME NOT PRICED DUE TO SCARCITY

2011 Topps Triple Threads Unity Relics Sepia

*SEPIA: .4X TO 1X BASIC
STATED ODDS 1:7 MINI
STATED PRINT RUN 27 SER.#'d SETS

2012 Topps Triple Threads

COMMON CARD (1-100) .30 .75
COMMON JSY AU RC (101-165) 5.00 12.00
JSY AU RC ODDS 1:10 MINI
JSY AU RC PRINT RUN 99 SER.#'d SETS
COMMON JSY AU (101-165) 5.00 12.00
JSY AU ODDS 1:10 MINI
JSY AU PRINT RUN 99 SER.#'d SETS
EXCHANGE DEADLINE 8/31/2015
OVERALL 1-100 PLATE ODDS 1:145 HOBBY
PLATE PRINT RUN 1 SET PER COLOR
BLACK-CYAN-MAGENTA-YELLOW ISSUED
NO PLATE PRICING DUE TO SCARCITY
1 Albert Pujols 1.00 2.50
2 Carlos Gonzalez .60 1.50
3 Adam Jones .60 1.50
4 Wade Boggs .50 1.25
5 Evan Longoria .60 1.50
6 Roberto Clemente 2.00 5.00
7 Mickey Mantle 2.50 6.00
8 Chase Utley .60 1.50
9 Dave Winfield .50 1.25
10 Buster Posey 1.00 2.50
11 Babe Ruth 2.00 5.00
12 Matt Kemp .60 1.50
13 Troy Tulowitzki .75 2.00
14 Matt Holliday .75 2.00
15 David Price .60 1.50
16 Jay Bruce .60 1.50
17 Alex Rodriguez 1.00 2.50
18 Reggie Jackson .50 1.25
19 Craig Kimbrel .60 1.50
20 Gary Carter .50 1.25
21 Don Mattingly 1.50 4.00
22 Ryan Braun .50 1.25
23 Giancarlo Stanton .75 2.00
24 Alex Gordon .60 1.50
25 Frank Robinson .50 1.25
26 Tim Lincecum .60 1.50
27 Justin Upton .60 1.50
28 CC Sabathia .60 1.50
29 Hunter Pence .60 1.50
30 Joe DiMaggio 1.50 4.00
31 Justin Verlander .75 2.00
32 Mike Schmidt 1.25 3.00
33 Ryan Zimmerman .60 1.50
34 Sandy Koufax 1.50 4.00
35 Hanley Ramirez .60 1.50
36 Jose Reyes .50 1.25
37 Lou Gehrig 1.50 4.00
38 Ian Kinsler .60 1.50
39 Felix Hernandez .60 1.50
40 Ichiro Suzuki 1.00 2.50
41 Tony Gwynn .75 2.00
42 David Ortiz .75 2.00
43 Miguel Cabrera .75 2.00
44 Tom Seaver .50 1.25
45 Jose Bautista .60 1.50
46 Josh Hamilton .60 1.50
47 Ty Cobb 1.25 3.00
48 David Freese .50 1.25
49 Dan Uggla .60 1.50
50 Andrew McCutchen .75 2.00
51 Stan Musial 1.25 3.00
52 Juan Marichal .50 1.25
53 Adrian Gonzalez .60 1.50
54 Nolan Ryan 2.50 6.00
55 Jacoby Ellsbury .60 1.50
56 Willie Mays 1.50 4.00
57 Eddie Mathews .75 2.00
58 Ryne Sandberg 1.50 4.00
59 Prince Fielder .60 1.50
60 Yogi Berra .75 2.00
61 Duke Snider .50 1.25
62 Kevin Youkilis .75 2.00
63 Willie McCovey .50 1.25
64 Carl Yastrzemski 1.25 3.00
65 Roger Maris .75 2.00
66 Adrian Beltre .75 2.00
67 Stephen Strasburg .75 2.00
68 Rickey Henderson .75 2.00
69 David Wright .60 1.50
70 Brian McCann .60 1.50
71 Jon Lester .50 1.25
72 Jered Weaver .60 1.50
73 Andre Dawson .50 1.25
74 Dustin Pedroia .75 2.00
75 Cole Hamels .60 1.50
76 Robinson Cano .60 1.50
77 Brooks Robinson .50 1.25
78 Curtis Granderson .60 1.50
79 Ozzie Smith 1.00 2.50
80 Pablo Sandoval .60 1.50
81 Cal Ripken Jr. 2.50 6.00
82 Mark Teixeira .60 1.50
83 Ryan Howard .60 1.50
84 Nelson Cruz .75 2.00
85 Bob Feller .50 1.25
86 Bob Gibson .50 1.25
87 Joe Mauer .60 1.50
88 Roy Halladay .60 1.50
89 Johnny Bench .75 2.00
90 George Brett 1.50 4.00
91 Paul Molitor .75 2.00
92 Derek Jeter 2.00 5.00
93 Carlton Fisk .50 1.25
94 Brandon Phillips .50 1.25
95 Clayton Kershaw 1.25 3.00
96 Joey Votto .75 2.00
97 Cliff Lee .60 1.50
98 Jackie Robinson .75 2.00
99 Mariano Rivera 1.00 2.50
100 Ken Griffey Jr. 1.50 4.00
101 Carlos Santana Jsy AU 6.00 15.00
102 Madison Bumgarner Jsy AU 30.00 80.00
103 Brandon Belt Jsy AU 8.00 20.00
104 Ben Revere Jsy AU 8.00 20.00
105 Dee Gordon Jsy AU EXCH 10.00 25.00
106 Derek Holland Jsy AU 6.00 15.00
107 Anthony Rizzo Jsy AU 12.00 30.00
108 Chris Sale Jsy AU 8.00 20.00
109 Drew Storen Jsy AU 6.00 15.00
110 Eduardo Nunez Jsy AU 5.00 12.00
111 Jason Kipnis Jsy AU 6.00 15.00
112 Jemile Weeks Jsy AU RC 6.00 15.00
113 Wilin Rosario Jsy AU RC 8.00 20.00
114 Jordan Walden Jsy AU 5.00 12.00
115 Mike Minor Jsy AU 4.00 10.00
116 Todd Frazier Jsy AU 8.00 20.00
117 Randall Delgado Jsy AU 5.00 12.00
118 Wilson Ramos Jsy AU 5.00 12.00
119 Yonder Alonso Jsy AU 6.00 15.00
120 Aroldis Chapman Jsy AU 10.00 25.00
121 Jacob Turner Jsy AU 8.00 20.00
122 Neftali Feliz Jsy AU 6.00 15.00
123 Drew Pomeranz Jsy AU RC 6.00 15.00
124 Ike Davis Jsy AU 8.00 20.00
125 Jason Heyward Jsy AU 10.00 25.00
126 Daniel Hudson Jsy AU 6.00 15.00
127 Jordan Zimmermann Jsy AU 6.00 15.00
129 Bryce Harper Jsy AU RC 150.00 300.00
131 Addison Reed Jsy AU RC 6.00 15.00
132 Tyler Pastornicky Jsy AU RC 6.00 15.00
134 Zack Cozart Jsy AU 6.00 15.00
135 B.Jackson Jsy AU RC EXCH 6.00 15.00
136 Devin Mesoraco Jsy AU RC 6.00 15.00
137 Vance Worley Jsy AU 6.00 15.00
138 Yoenis Cespedes Jsy AU RC 12.00 30.00
139 Yu Darvish Jsy AU RC 75.00 200.00
140 Jerry Sands Jsy AU 5.00 12.00
141 Ivan Nova Jsy AU 6.00 15.00
142 Matt Moore Jsy AU RC 10.00 25.00
143 Brett Lawrie Jsy AU RC 10.00 25.00
144 Jesus Montero Jsy AU RC 6.00 15.00
145 Mark Trumbo Jsy AU 6.00 15.00
146 Mike Trout Jsy AU 300.00 600.00
147 Michael Pineda Jsy AU 12.50 30.00
148 Dustin Ackley Jsy AU 6.00 15.00
149 Eric Hosmer Jsy AU 12.50 30.00
150 Freddie Freeman Jsy AU EXCH 12.50 30.00
151 Mike Moustakas Jsy AU 10.00 25.00
152 Starlin Castro Jsy AU 8.00 20.00
153 Paul Goldschmidt Jsy AU 20.00 50.00
154 Jeremy Hellickson Jsy AU 8.00 20.00
155 Matt Adams Jsy AU RC 15.00 40.00
156 Logan Morrison Jsy AU 5.00 12.00
157 Lonnie Chisenhall Jsy AU 6.00 15.00
158 Kyle Seager Jsy AU 6.00 15.00
159 Salvador Perez Jsy AU 15.00 40.00
160 J.D. Martinez Jsy AU 12.00 30.00
161 Cory Luebke Jsy AU 5.00 12.00
162 Danny Duffy Jsy AU 6.00 15.00
163 Kirk Nieuwenhuis Jsy AU RC 6.00 15.00
164 Jose Altuve Jsy AU 40.00 100.00
165 Julio Teheran Jsy AU 6.00 15.00

2012 Topps Triple Threads Amber

*AMBER: .75X TO 2X BASIC
STATED ODDS 1:5 MINI
STATED PRINT RUN 125 SER.#'d SETS

2012 Topps Triple Threads Emerald

*EMERALD 1-100: .6X TO 1.5X BASIC
1-100 ODDS 1:3 MINI
1-100 PRINT RUN 250 SER.#'d SETS
*EMERALD JSY AU: .4X TO 1X BASIC
EMERALD JSY AU ODDS 1:18 MINI
EM.JSY AU PRINT RUN 50 SER.#'d SETS
EXCHANGE DEADLINE 8/31/2015
128 Jarrod Parker Jsy AU 15.00 40.00
130 Trevor Bauer Jsy AU 25.00 60.00
133 Ryan Lavarnway Jsy AU 10.00 25.00
139 Yu Darvish Jsy AU 150.00 250.00

2012 Topps Triple Threads Gold

*GOLD 1-100: 1X TO 2.5X BASIC
1-100 ODDS 1:6 MINI
1-100 PRINT RUN 99 SER.#'d SETS
101-165 ODDS 1:36 HOBBY
101-165 PRINT RUN 25 SER.#'d SETS
NO 101-165 PRICING DUE TO SCARCITY
EXCHANGE DEADLINE 8/31/2015

2012 Topps Triple Threads Onyx

*ONYX: 2X TO 5X BASIC
STATED ODDS 1:12 MINI
STATED PRINT RUN 50 SER.#'d SETS

2012 Topps Triple Threads Sepia

*SEPIA 1-100: .5X TO 1.2X BASIC
1-100 RANDOMLY INSERTED
1-100 PRINT RUN 625 SER.#'d SETS
*SEPIA JSY AU: .4X TO 1X BASIC
SEPIA JSY AU ODDS 1:14 MINI
SEP.JSY AU PRINT RUN 75 SER.#'d SETS
EXCHANGE DEADLINE 08/31/2015
130 Trevor Bauer Jsy AU 25.00 60.00

2012 Topps Triple Threads Autograph Relic Combos

STATED ODDS 1:95 MINI
STATED PRINT RUN 36 SER.#'d SETS
EXCHANGE DEADLINE 8/31/2015
ARC1 Verland/Miggy/Prince 200.00 300.00
ARC2 Hamilton/Cruz/Napoli 15.00 40.00
ARC3 Dave Kingman/Ken Griffey Sr./Greg Luzinski
20.00 50.00
ARC4 Fielder/Mattingly/Clark 100.00 200.00
ARC5 Cooper/Buckner/Clark 30.00 80.00
ARC6 George Bell/Andy Van Slyke/Ken Griffey Sr.
20.00 50.00
ARC7 Price/Hellickson/Moore 40.00 80.00
ARC8 Kershaw/Kemp/Ethier 75.00 150.00
ARC9 Cespedes/Montero/Trout 125.00 250.00
ARC10 Golds/Hosmer/Freeman 30.00 60.00
ARC11 Lawrie/ZimmerM/Freese 10.00 25.00
ARC12 Uggla/Heyward/McCann 20.00 50.00
ARC13 Aramis/Braun/Weeks 20.00 50.00
ARC14 Castro/Gordon/Andrus 20.00 50.00
ARC15 Santana/Weaver/Wilson 30.00 60.00
ARC16 Hanley/Stanton/Johnson 30.00 60.00
ARC17 Kershaw/Kemp/Gordon 50.00 100.00

2012 Topps Triple Threads Autograph Relic Combos Sepia

*SEPIA: .4X TO 1X BASIC
STATED ODDS 1:126 MINI
STATED PRINT RUN 27 SER.#'d SETS
EXCHANGE DEADLINE 8/31/2015

2012 Topps Triple Threads Flashback Relics

STATED ODDS 1:65 MINI
STATED PRINT RUN 36 SER.#'d SETS
FR1 Ty Cobb 50.00 100.00
FR2 Joe Morgan 12.50 30.00
FR3 Harmon Killebrew 20.00 50.00
FR4 Alex Rodriguez 12.50 30.00
FR5 Chipper Jones 50.00 100.00
FR6 David Ortiz 6.00 15.00
FR7 Cliff Lee 10.00 25.00
FR8 Roy Halladay 12.50 30.00
FR9 CC Sabathia 12.50 30.00
FR10 Mariano Rivera 15.00 40.00
FR11 Dave Winfield 8.00 20.00
FR12 Rickey Henderson 10.00 25.00
FR13 Albert Pujols 10.00 25.00
FR14 Paul Molitor 12.50 30.00
FR15 Johan Santana 10.00 25.00
FR16 Ozzie Smith 12.50 30.00
FR17 Jose Bautista 6.00 15.00
FR18 Derek Jeter 50.00 100.00
FR19 Tom Seaver 12.50 30.00
FR20 Tony Gwynn 12.50 30.00
FR21 Robin Yount 12.50 30.00
FR22 Cal Ripken Jr. 30.00 60.00
FR23 Gary Carter 15.00 40.00
FR24 Dwight Gooden 12.50 30.00
FR25 George Brett 20.00 50.00

2012 Topps Triple Threads Flashback Relics Sepia

*SEPIA: .4X TO 1X BASIC
STATED ODDS 1:86 MINI
STATED PRINT RUN 27 SER.#'D SETS

2012 Topps Triple Threads Legend Relics

STATED ODDS 1:81 MINI
STATED PRINT RUN 36 SER.#'d SETS
TTRL1 Joe Morgan 10.00 25.00
TTRL2 Rickey Henderson 15.00 40.00
TTRL3 Eddie Murray 12.50 30.00
TTRL4 Dave Winfield 10.00 25.00
TTRL5 Cal Ripken Jr. 40.00 80.00
TTRL6 Carl Yastrzemski 12.50 30.00
TTRL7 Roberto Clemente 60.00 120.00
TTRL8 Harmon Killebrew 15.00 40.00
TTRL9 Brooks Robinson 15.00 40.00
TTRL10 Willie Mays 40.00 80.00
TTRL11 Tony Gwynn 10.00 25.00
TTRL12 Sandy Koufax 50.00 100.00
TTRL13 Jackie Robinson 30.00 60.00
TTRL14 Ty Cobb 50.00 100.00
TTRL15 Joe DiMaggio 50.00 100.00
TTRL16 Mickey Mantle 60.00 120.00
TTRL17 Willie McCovey 10.00 25.00
TTRL18 Stan Musial 30.00 60.00
TTRL19 Mike Schmidt 12.50 30.00
TTRL20 George Brett 15.00 40.00

2012 Topps Triple Threads Legend Relics Sepia

*SEPIA: .4X TO 1X BASIC
STATED ODDS 1:107 MINI
STATED PRINT RUN 27 SER.#'D SETS

2012 Topps Triple Threads Relic Autographs

STATED ODDS 1:12 MINI
STATED PRINT RUN 18 SER.#'d SETS
ALL DC VARIATIONS PRICED EQUALLY
NO PRICING ON PLAYERS W/ONE DC VERSION
EXCHANGE DEADLINE 8/31/2015
TTAR1 Billy Butler 12.50 30.00
TTAR2 Billy Butler 12.50 30.00
TTAR3 Billy Butler 12.50 30.00
TTAR4 Steve Garvey 30.00 60.00
TTAR5 Steve Garvey 30.00 60.00
TTAR6 Steve Garvey 30.00 60.00
TTAR7 Steve Garvey 30.00 60.00
TTAR8 Steve Garvey 30.00 60.00
TTAR9 Yovani Gallardo 8.00 20.00
TTAR10 Yovani Gallardo 8.00 20.00
TTAR11 Yovani Gallardo 8.00 20.00
TTAR12 Yovani Gallardo 8.00 20.00
TTAR13 Yovani Gallardo 8.00 20.00
TTAR14 Tim Hudson 12.50 30.00
TTAR15 Tim Hudson 12.50 30.00
TTAR16 Tim Hudson 12.50 30.00
TTAR17 Tim Hudson 12.50 30.00
TTAR18 Tim Hudson 12.50 30.00
TTAR19 Tommy Hanson 8.00 20.00
TTAR20 Tommy Hanson 8.00 20.00
TTAR21 Tommy Hanson 8.00 20.00
TTAR22 Tommy Hanson 8.00 20.00
TTAR23 Tommy Hanson 8.00 20.00
TTAR24 Albert Belle 12.00 30.00
TTAR25 Albert Belle 12.00 30.00
TTAR26 Albert Belle 12.00 30.00
TTAR28 Andy Van Slyke 12.50 30.00
TTAR29 Andy Van Slyke 12.50 30.00
TTAR30 Andy Van Slyke 12.50 30.00
TTAR31 Carlos Gonzalez EXCH 12.50 30.00
TTAR32 Carlos Gonzalez EXCH 12.50 30.00
TTAR33 Carlos Gonzalez EXCH 12.50 30.00
TTAR34 Carlos Gonzalez EXCH 12.50 30.00
TTAR35 Carlos Gonzalez EXCH 12.50 30.00
TTAR36 Pablo Sandoval 15.00 40.00
TTAR37 Pablo Sandoval 15.00 40.00
TTAR38 Pablo Sandoval 15.00 40.00
TTAR39 Pablo Sandoval 15.00 40.00
TTAR40 Pablo Sandoval 15.00 40.00
TTAR41 Jose Bautista 20.00 50.00
TTAR42 Jose Bautista 20.00 50.00
TTAR43 Jose Bautista 20.00 50.00
TTAR44 Vida Blue 20.00 50.00
TTAR45 Vida Blue 20.00 50.00
TTAR46 Ryan Braun 40.00 80.00
TTAR47 Ryan Braun 10.00 25.00
TTAR48 Andre Ethier EXCH 10.00 25.00
TTAR49 Andre Ethier EXCH 10.00 25.00
TTAR50 Andre Ethier EXCH 10.00 25.00
TTAR51 Andre Ethier EXCH 10.00 25.00
TTAR52 Andre Ethier EXCH 6.00 15.00
TTAR54 Madison Bumgarner 30.00 80.00
TTAR55 Madison Bumgarner 30.00 80.00
TTAR56 Madison Bumgarner 30.00 80.00
TTAR57 Madison Bumgarner 30.00 80.00
TTAR58 Madison Bumgarner 30.00 80.00
TTAR59 Cecil Cooper 12.50 30.00
TTAR60 Cecil Cooper 12.50 30.00
TTAR61 Cecil Cooper 12.50 30.00
TTAR64 Orlando Cepeda 20.00 50.00
TTAR65 Orlando Cepeda 20.00 50.00
TTAR66 Orlando Cepeda 20.00 50.00
TTAR67 James Shields 8.00 20.00
TTAR68 James Shields 8.00 20.00
TTAR69 James Shields 8.00 20.00
TTAR70 James Shields 8.00 20.00
TTAR71 James Shields 8.00 20.00
TTAR72 Dennis Eckersley 15.00 40.00
TTAR73 Dennis Eckersley 15.00 40.00
TTAR76 George Bell 12.50 30.00
TTAR77 George Bell 12.50 30.00
TTAR81 Dale Murphy 40.00 80.00
TTAR82 Dale Murphy 40.00 80.00
TTAR83 Dale Murphy 40.00 80.00
TTAR84 Dale Murphy 40.00 80.00
TTAR86 Ian Kennedy 8.00 20.00
TTAR87 Ian Kennedy 8.00 20.00
TTAR88 Ian Kennedy 8.00 20.00
TTAR89 Ian Kennedy 8.00 20.00
TTAR90 Ian Kennedy 8.00 20.00
TTAR91 Ricky Romero 10.00 25.00
TTAR92 Ricky Romero 10.00 25.00
TTAR93 Giancarlo Stanton 30.00 60.00
TTAR94 Giancarlo Stanton 30.00 60.00
TTAR95 Giancarlo Stanton 30.00 60.00
TTAR96 Alex Gordon 15.00 40.00
TTAR97 Alex Gordon 15.00 40.00
TTAR98 C.J. Wilson 12.50 30.00
TTAR99 C.J. Wilson 12.50 30.00
TTAR100 C.J. Wilson 12.50 30.00
TTAR102 Cole Hamels 10.00 25.00
TTAR103 Cole Hamels 10.00 25.00
TTAR104 Cole Hamels 10.00 25.00
TTAR105 Cole Hamels 10.00 25.00
TTAR106 Eric Hosmer 15.00 40.00
TTAR107 Jered Weaver 15.00 40.00
TTAR108 Jered Weaver 15.00 40.00
TTAR109 Jered Weaver 15.00 40.00
TTAR110 Jered Weaver 15.00 40.00
TTAR111 Jered Weaver 15.00 40.00
TTAR115 Jon Lester 10.00 25.00
TTAR116 Jon Lester 10.00 25.00
TTAR117 Nelson Cruz 8.00 20.00
TTAR118 Nelson Cruz 8.00 20.00
TTAR119 Nelson Cruz 8.00 20.00
TTAR120 Nelson Cruz 8.00 20.00
TTAR121 Rickie Weeks 10.00 25.00
TTAR122 Rickie Weeks 10.00 25.00
TTAR123 Rickie Weeks 10.00 25.00
TTAR124 Billy Butler 10.00 25.00
TTAR125 Duke Snider 40.00 80.00
TTAR127 Billy Butler 10.00 25.00
TTAR128 Ike Davis 12.50 30.00
TTAR129 Ike Davis 12.50 30.00
TTAR130 Ike Davis 12.50 30.00
TTAR131 Steve Carlton 20.00 50.00
TTAR133 Clayton Kershaw 30.00 60.00
TTAR134 Clayton Kershaw 30.00 60.00
TTAR135 Clayton Kershaw 30.00 60.00
TTAR136 Clayton Kershaw 30.00 60.00
TTAR137 Clayton Kershaw 30.00 60.00
TTAR138 Ike Davis 12.50 30.00
TTAR139 Ike Davis 12.50 30.00
TTAR146 Gio Gonzalez 10.00 25.00
TTAR147 Gio Gonzalez 10.00 25.00
TTAR148 Gio Gonzalez 10.00 25.00
TTAR149 Gio Gonzalez 10.00 25.00
TTAR150 Gio Gonzalez 10.00 25.00
TTAR151 Luis Aparicio 15.00 40.00
TTAR152 Luis Aparicio 15.00 40.00
TTAR153 Luis Aparicio 15.00 40.00
TTAR154 Andrew McCutchen 20.00 50.00
TTAR155 Jim Rice 15.00 40.00
TTAR156 Jason Heyward 10.00 25.00
TTAR157 Jason Heyward 10.00 25.00
TTAR158 Jason Heyward 10.00 25.00
TTAR159 Jason Heyward 10.00 25.00
TTAR160 Jason Heyward 10.00 25.00
TTAR161 Greg Luzinski 12.50 30.00
TTAR162 Greg Luzinski 12.50 30.00
TTAR163 Greg Luzinski 12.50 30.00
TTAR164 Carl Crawford 10.00 25.00
TTAR165 Carl Crawford 10.00 25.00
TTAR166 Carl Crawford 10.00 25.00
TTAR167 David Freese 20.00 50.00
TTAR168 David Freese 20.00 50.00
TTAR169 David Freese 20.00 50.00
TTAR170 Ben Zobrist 12.00 30.00
TTAR171 Ben Zobrist 12.00 30.00
TTAR172 Ben Zobrist 12.00 30.00
TTAR173 Fergie Jenkins 15.00 40.00
TTAR174 Fergie Jenkins 15.00 40.00
TTAR175 Fergie Jenkins 15.00 40.00
TTAR177 Robinson Cano 20.00 50.00
TTAR178 Robinson Cano 20.00 50.00
TTAR179 Dan Uggla 10.00 25.00
TTAR180 Dan Uggla 10.00 25.00
TTAR181 Dan Uggla 10.00 25.00
TTAR182 Dan Uggla 10.00 25.00
TTAR183 Dan Uggla 10.00 25.00
TTAR185 Andre Dawson 20.00 50.00
TTAR186 Andre Dawson 20.00 50.00
TTAR187 Andre Dawson 20.00 50.00
TTAR188 Andy Pettitte 40.00 80.00
TTAR189 Andy Pettitte 40.00 80.00
TTAR190 Andy Pettitte 40.00 80.00
TTAR191 Andy Pettitte 40.00 80.00
TTAR192 Andy Pettitte 40.00 80.00
TTAR193 Al Kaline 40.00 100.00
TTAR194 Mike Morse 8.00 20.00
TTAR195 Mike Morse 8.00 20.00
TTAR196 Mike Morse 8.00 20.00
TTAR197 Mike Morse 8.00 20.00
TTAR198 Josh Johnson 8.00 20.00
TTAR199 Josh Johnson 8.00 20.00
TTAR200 Josh Johnson 8.00 20.00
TTAR201 Josh Johnson 8.00 20.00
TTAR202 Josh Johnson 8.00 20.00
TTAR203 Andrew McCutchen 20.00 50.00
TTAR208 Jim Rice 15.00 40.00
TTAR209 Jim Rice 15.00 40.00
TTAR210 Jim Rice 15.00 40.00
TTAR211 Maury Wills 15.00 40.00
TTAR212 Maury Wills 15.00 40.00
TTAR213 Maury Wills 15.00 40.00
TTAR217 Prince Fielder 50.00 100.00
TTAR218 Prince Fielder 50.00 100.00
TTAR219 Mike Napoli 10.00 25.00
TTAR220 Mike Napoli 10.00 25.00
TTAR221 Mike Napoli 10.00 25.00
TTAR222 Mike Napoli 10.00 25.00
TTAR223 Mike Napoli 10.00 25.00
TTAR225 Willie McCovey 40.00 80.00
TTAR226 Willie McCovey 40.00 80.00
TTAR227 Willie McCovey 40.00 80.00
TTAR228 Al Kaline 40.00 100.00
TTAR230 Brian McCann 15.00 40.00
TTAR231 Brian McCann 15.00 40.00
TTAR232 Brian McCann 15.00 40.00
TTAR233 Brian McCann 15.00 40.00
TTAR234 Brian McCann 15.00 40.00
TTAR235 Adam Jones 8.00 20.00
TTAR236 Adam Jones 8.00 20.00
TTAR237 Adam Jones 8.00 20.00
TTAR238 Adam Jones 8.00 20.00
TTAR242 Paul O'Neill 30.00 60.00
TTAR243 Paul O'Neill 30.00 60.00
TTAR244 Paul O'Neill 30.00 60.00
TTAR246 Felix Hernandez 30.00 60.00
TTAR247 Felix Hernandez 30.00 60.00
TTAR248 Felix Hernandez 30.00 60.00
TTAR249 Felix Hernandez 30.00 60.00
TTAR250 Will Clark 20.00 50.00
TTAR251 Will Clark 20.00 50.00
TTAR252 Will Clark 20.00 50.00
TTAR253 Carlton Fisk 20.00 50.00
TTAR254 Carlton Fisk 20.00 50.00
TTAR255 Carlton Fisk 20.00 50.00
TTAR256 Jose Bautista 12.50 30.00
TTAR257 Paul Molitor 20.00 50.00
TTAR258 Paul Molitor 40.00 80.00
TTAR259 Paul Molitor 20.00 50.00
TTAR261 Starlin Castro 20.00 50.00
TTAR262 Starlin Castro 20.00 50.00
TTAR263 Starlin Castro 20.00 50.00
TTAR264 Eric Hosmer 15.00 40.00
TTAR265 Eric Hosmer 15.00 40.00
TTAR266 David Price 15.00 40.00
TTAR267 David Price 15.00 40.00
TTAR268 David Price 15.00 40.00
TTAR269 David Price 15.00 40.00
TTAR270 Bryce Harper 200.00 300.00
TTAR271 Bryce Harper 200.00 300.00
TTAR272 Bryce Harper 200.00 300.00
TTAR273 Bryce Harper 200.00 300.00
TTAR274 Duke Snider 40.00 80.00
TTAR275 Duke Snider 40.00 80.00

2012 Topps Triple Threads Relic Autographs Gold

*GOLD: .5X TO 1.2X BASIC
STATED ODDS 1:24 MINI
STATED PRINT RUN 9 SER.#'d SETS
ALL DC VARIATIONS PRICED EQUALLY
NO PRICING ON MANY DUE TO SCARCITY
EXCHANGE DEADLINE 8/31/2015

2012 Topps Triple Threads Relic Combos

STATED ODDS 1:26 MINI
STATED PRINT RUN 36 SER.#'d SETS
RC1 Mantle/Musial/Yas 60.00 120.00
RC2 Jim Rice/Eddie Murray/Albert Belle 10.00 25.00
RC3 Brock/Henderson/Ichiro 15.00 40.00
RC4 Gwynn/Boggs/Ripken 30.00 60.00
RC5 Molitor/Sandb/Mattingly 12.50 30.00
RC6 Brooks/Schmidt/Boggs 15.00 40.00
RC7 Joe Morgan/Ryne Sandberg
Robinson Cano 12.50 30.00
RC8 Fisk/Thomas/Konerko 30.00 60.00
RC9 Carlton/Hamels/Lee 15.00 40.00
RC10 Carlton/Schmidt/Halla 10.00 25.00
RC11 Trout/Pujols/Weaver 30.00 60.00
RC12 Trout/Harper/Cespedes 75.00 150.00
RC13 Yas/Rice/Ellsbury 10.00 25.00
RC14 Kemp/Ethier/Kershaw 15.00 40.00
RC15 Dave Winfield/Jim Rice/Albert Belle 8.00 20.00
RC16 Mays/DiMaggio/Musial 50.00 100.00
RC17 Ruth/Gehrig/Mantle 175.00 350.00
RC18 David Price/James Shields
Matt Moore 8.00 20.00
RC19 Jeter/ARod/Cano 40.00 80.00
RC20 Ryan Braun/Ike Davis
Kevin Youkilis 8.00 20.00
RC21 Verland/Cabrera/Prince 30.00 60.00
RC22 Chipper/Uggla/Heyward 10.00 25.00
RC23 Jered Weaver
C.J. Wilson/Dan Haren 10.00 25.00
RC24 Longo/Zimmer/Chipper 12.50 30.00
RC25 Hamilton/Darvish/Kinsler 12.50 30.00
RC26 Ryan Zimmerman
Evan Longoria/David Wright 10.00 25.00
RC27 Hanley Ramirez
Evan Longoria/Ryan Zimmerman 10.00 25.00
RC28 Verland/Halla/Kershaw 15.00 40.00
RC29 Mantle/Yas/Musial 50.00 100.00
RC30 Killebrew/Carew/Mauer 20.00 50.00
RC31 Votto/Phillips/Bruce 30.00 60.00
RC32 Lincec/Cain/Bumg 20.00 50.00
RC33 Buster Posey/Joe Mauer
Mike Napoli 12.50 30.00
RC34 McCov/Mays/Cepeda 40.00 80.00
RC35 Tim Hudson/Tommy Hanson
Brandon Beachy 8.00 20.00
RC36 Hanley Ramirez/Jose Reyes
Giancarlo Stanton 8.00 20.00
RC37 Adrian Gonzalez/Dustin Pedroia
David Ortiz 10.00 25.00
RC38 Lincec/Stras/Verlander 20.00 50.00
RC39 CC Sabathia/Clayton Kershaw
Cliff Lee 10.00 25.00
RC40 Kiner/Stargell/McCutch 30.00 60.00
RC41 Billy Butler/Eric Hosmer
Alex Gordon 10.00 25.00
RC42 Nelson Cruz/Michael Young
Mike Napoli 8.00 20.00
RC43 Gard/Grander/Swish 15.00 40.00
RC44 Jose Bautista/Brett Lawrie
Ricky Romero 10.00 25.00
RC45 Jose Bautista/Matt Kemp
Ryan Braun 10.00 25.00
RC46 Harper/Stras/Zimmerm 15.00 40.00
RC47 Troy Tulowitzki/Carlos Gonzalez
Todd Helton 10.00 25.00
RC48 Ryan Zimmerman
David Freese/Evan Longoria 12.50 30.00
RC49 Tulo/Castro/Jeter 15.00 40.00
RC50 Justin Upton/Matt Kemp
Carlos Gonzalez 8.00 20.00
RC51 Trout/McCut/Upton 20.00 50.00
RC52 Ian Kinsler/Adrian Beltre
Michael Young 10.00 25.00
RC53 Ian Kinsler/Dustin Pedroia
Robinson Cano 8.00 20.00
RC54 Brooks/Murray/Ripken 40.00 80.00
RC55 O'Neill/Jeter/Rivera 30.00 60.00
RC56 Pettitte/Rivera/CC 15.00 40.00
RC57 Yovani Gallardo
Zack Greinke/Ryan Braun 8.00 20.00
RC58 Starg/VanSlyke/McCut 30.00 60.00
RC59 Mark Teixeira
Adrian Gonzalez/Prince Fielder 12.50 30.00
RC60 Hender/Morgan/Brock 12.00 30.00
RC61 Winfield/Murray/Matting 12.00 30.00
RC62 Cecil Cooper
Paul Molitor/Ryan Braun 12.00 30.00
RC63 Molitor/Boggs/Gwynn 10.00 25.00

2012 Topps Triple Threads Relic Combos Sepia

*SEPIA: .4X TO 1X BASIC
STATED ODDS 1:35 MINI
STATED PRINT RUN 27 SER.#'d SETS

2012 Topps Triple Threads Relics

STATED ODDS 1:9 MINI
STATED PRINT RUN 36 SER.#'d SETS
ALL DC VARIATIONS PRICED EQUALLY
TTR1 Roy Halladay 12.50 30.00
TTR2 Roy Halladay 12.50 30.00
TTR3 Roy Halladay 12.50 30.00
TTR4 David Price 8.00 20.00
TTR5 David Price 8.00 20.00
TTR6 David Price 8.00 20.00
TTR7 Ian Kinsler 5.00 12.00
TTR8 Ian Kinsler 5.00 12.00
TTR9 Ian Kinsler 5.00 12.00
TTR10 Carlos Gonzalez 6.00 15.00
TTR11 Carlos Gonzalez 6.00 15.00
TTR12 Carlos Gonzalez 6.00 15.00
TTR13 Freddie Freeman 5.00 12.00
TTR14 Freddie Freeman 5.00 12.00
TTR15 David Freese 12.50 30.00
TTR16 David Freese 12.50 30.00
TTR17 Tommy Hanson 5.00 12.00
TTR18 Tommy Hanson 5.00 12.00

TTR19 Starlin Castro 6.00 15.00
TTR20 Starlin Castro 6.00 15.00
TTR21 Starlin Castro 6.00 15.00
TTR22 Joey Votto 12.50 30.00
TTR23 Joey Votto 12.50 30.00
TTR24 Joey Votto 12.50 30.00
TTR25 C.J. Wilson 5.00 12.00
TTR26 C.J. Wilson 5.00 12.00
TTR27 C.J. Wilson 5.00 12.00
TTR28 Madison Bumgarner 12.50 30.00
TTR29 Madison Bumgarner 12.50 30.00
TTR30 Madison Bumgarner 12.50 30.00
TTR31 Andrew McCutchen 8.00 20.00
TTR32 Andrew McCutchen 8.00 20.00
TTR33 Andrew McCutchen 8.00 20.00
TTR34 Zack Greinke 5.00 12.00
TTR35 Zack Greinke 5.00 12.00
TTR36 Zack Greinke 5.00 12.00
TTR37 Stephen Strasburg 12.50 30.00
TTR38 Stephen Strasburg 12.50 30.00
TTR39 Stephen Strasburg 12.50 30.00
TTR40 Matt Moore 5.00 12.00
TTR41 Matt Moore 5.00 12.00
TTR42 Jose Reyes 5.00 12.00
TTR43 Jose Reyes 5.00 12.00
TTR44 Jose Reyes 5.00 12.00
TTR45 Yu Darvish 10.00 25.00
TTR46 Nelson Cruz 5.00 12.00
TTR47 Nelson Cruz 5.00 12.00
TTR48 Nelson Cruz 5.00 12.00
TTR49 Eric Hosmer 5.00 12.00
TTR50 Eric Hosmer 5.00 12.00
TTR51 Eric Hosmer 5.00 12.00
TTR52 Cliff Lee 5.00 12.00
TTR53 Cliff Lee 5.00 12.00
TTR54 Cliff Lee 5.00 12.00
TTR55 Justin Upton 5.00 12.00
TTR56 Justin Upton 5.00 12.00
TTR57 Justin Upton 5.00 12.00
TTR58 Yovani Gallardo 5.00 12.00
TTR59 Yovani Gallardo 5.00 12.00
TTR60 Yovani Gallardo 5.00 12.00
TTR61 Adrian Gonzalez 5.00 12.00
TTR62 Adrian Gonzalez 5.00 12.00
TTR63 Adrian Gonzalez 5.00 12.00
TTR64 Cole Hamels 8.00 20.00
TTR65 Cole Hamels 8.00 20.00
TTR66 Cole Hamels 8.00 20.00
TTR67 Josh Hamilton 8.00 20.00
TTR68 Josh Hamilton 8.00 20.00
TTR69 Josh Hamilton 8.00 20.00
TTR70 Mike Trout 100.00 250.00
TTR71 Mike Trout 100.00 250.00
TTR72 Mike Trout 100.00 250.00
TTR73 Jacoby Ellsbury 5.00 12.00
TTR74 Jacoby Ellsbury 5.00 12.00
TTR75 Jacoby Ellsbury 5.00 12.00
TTR76 Mike Napoli 6.00 15.00
TTR77 Mike Napoli 6.00 15.00
TTR78 Mike Napoli 6.00 15.00
TTR79 Clayton Kershaw 8.00 20.00
TTR80 Clayton Kershaw 8.00 20.00
TTR81 Clayton Kershaw 8.00 20.00
TTR82 Dan Haren 5.00 12.00
TTR83 Dan Haren 5.00 12.00
TTR84 Dan Haren 5.00 12.00
TTR85 Hanley Ramirez 5.00 12.00
TTR86 Hanley Ramirez 5.00 12.00
TTR87 Hanley Ramirez 5.00 12.00
TTR88 Derek Jeter 20.00 50.00
TTR89 Paul Goldschmidt 5.00 12.00
TTR90 Paul Goldschmidt 5.00 12.00
TTR91 Alex Gordon 6.00 15.00
TTR92 Alex Gordon 6.00 15.00
TTR93 Alex Gordon 6.00 15.00
TTR94 Ryan Braun 8.00 20.00
TTR95 Ryan Braun 8.00 20.00
TTR96 Ryan Braun 8.00 20.00
TTR97 Tim Lincecum 12.50 30.00
TTR98 Tim Lincecum 12.50 30.00
TTR99 Tim Lincecum 12.50 30.00
TTR100 Shane Victorino 5.00 12.00
TTR101 Shane Victorino 5.00 12.00
TTR102 Shane Victorino 5.00 12.00
TTR103 Carlos Santana 6.00 15.00
TTR104 Carlos Santana 6.00 15.00
TTR105 Carlos Santana 6.00 15.00
TTR106 Evan Longoria 8.00 20.00
TTR107 Evan Longoria 8.00 20.00
TTR108 Evan Longoria 8.00 20.00
TTR109 Adrian Beltre 5.00 12.00
TTR110 Adrian Beltre 5.00 12.00
TTR111 Adrian Beltre 5.00 12.00
TTR112 Troy Tulowitzki 5.00 12.00
TTR113 Troy Tulowitzki 5.00 12.00
TTR114 Troy Tulowitzki 5.00 12.00
TTR115 Matt Kemp 10.00 25.00
TTR116 Matt Kemp 10.00 25.00
TTR117 Matt Kemp 10.00 25.00
TTR118 Dee Gordon 5.00 12.00
TTR119 Dee Gordon 5.00 12.00
TTR120 Dee Gordon 5.00 12.00
TTR121 Felix Hernandez 6.00 15.00
TTR122 Felix Hernandez 6.00 15.00
TTR123 Felix Hernandez 6.00 15.00
TTR124 Gio Gonzalez 5.00 12.00
TTR125 Gio Gonzalez 5.00 12.00
TTR126 Gio Gonzalez 5.00 12.00
TTR127 Miguel Cabrera 12.50 30.00
TTR128 Miguel Cabrera 12.50 30.00
TTR129 Miguel Cabrera 12.50 30.00
TTR130 Jason Heyward 6.00 15.00
TTR131 Jason Heyward 6.00 15.00
TTR132 Jason Heyward 6.00 15.00
TTR133 Albert Pujols 12.50 30.00
TTR134 Mike Moustakas 5.00 12.00
TTR135 Mike Moustakas 5.00 12.00
TTR136 Mike Moustakas 5.00 12.00
TTR137 Ryan Howard 6.00 15.00
TTR138 Ryan Howard 6.00 15.00
TTR139 Ryan Howard 6.00 15.00
TTR140 David Ortiz 5.00 12.00
TTR141 David Ortiz 5.00 12.00
TTR142 David Ortiz 5.00 12.00
TTR143 Buster Posey 10.00 25.00
TTR144 Buster Posey 10.00 25.00
TTR145 Buster Posey 10.00 25.00
TTR146 Dustin Pedroia 6.00 15.00
TTR147 Dustin Pedroia 6.00 15.00
TTR148 Dustin Pedroia 6.00 15.00
TTR149 Kevin Youkilis 5.00 12.00
TTR150 Kevin Youkilis 5.00 12.00
TTR151 Kevin Youkilis 5.00 12.00
TTR152 Curtis Granderson 8.00 20.00
TTR153 Curtis Granderson 8.00 20.00
TTR154 Jimmy Rollins 6.00 15.00
TTR155 Jimmy Rollins 6.00 15.00
TTR156 Jimmy Rollins 6.00 15.00
TTR157 Paul Konerko 6.00 15.00
TTR158 Paul Konerko 6.00 15.00
TTR159 Paul Konerko 6.00 15.00
TTR160 Ian Kennedy 5.00 12.00
TTR161 Ian Kennedy 5.00 12.00
TTR162 Ian Kennedy 5.00 12.00
TTR163 Jose Bautista 5.00 12.00
TTR164 Robinson Cano 10.00 25.00
TTR165 Freddie Freeman 5.00 12.00
TTR166 David Freese 12.50 30.00
TTR167 Tommy Hanson 5.00 12.00
TTR168 Chipper Jones 15.00 40.00
TTR169 Joe Mauer 6.00 15.00
TTR170 Alex Rodriguez 10.00 25.00
TTR171 Alex Rodriguez 10.00 25.00
TTR172 Giancarlo Stanton 5.00 12.00
TTR173 Dan Uggla 6.00 15.00
TTR174 David Wright 10.00 25.00
TTR175 Chipper Jones 15.00 40.00
TTR176 David Wright 10.00 25.00
TTR177 David Wright 10.00 25.00
TTR178 Matt Moore 5.00 12.00
TTR179 Bryce Harper 50.00 100.00
TTR180 Brett Lawrie 8.00 20.00
TTR181 Brett Lawrie 8.00 20.00
TTR182 Brett Lawrie 8.00 20.00
TTR183 Desmond Jennings 5.00 12.00
TTR184 Desmond Jennings 5.00 12.00
TTR185 Desmond Jennings 5.00 12.00
TTR186 Chipper Jones 15.00 40.00

2012 Topps Triple Threads Relics Emerald

*EMERALD: .5X TO 1.2X BASIC
STATED ODDS 1:18 MINI
STATED PRINT RUN 18 SER.#'d SETS
ALL DC VARIATIONS EQUALLY PRICED
NO PRICING DUE TO SCARCITY ON SOME

2012 Topps Triple Threads Relics Gold

*GOLD: .6X TO 1.5X BASIC
STATED ODDS 1:35 MINI
STATED PRINT RUN 9 SER.#'d SETS
ALL DC VARIATIONS EQUALLY PRICED
NO PRICING ON SOME DUE TO SCARCITY

2012 Topps Triple Threads Relics Sepia

*SEPIA: .4X TO 1X BASIC
STATED ODDS 1:12 MINI
STATED PRINT RUN 27 SER.#'d SETS
ALL DC VARIATIONS EQUALLY PRICED

2012 Topps Triple Threads Unity Relic Autographs

STATED ODDS 1:6 MINI
PRINT RUNS BW/N 22-99 COPIES PER
NO SNIDER/22 PRICING AVAILABLE
ALL VERSIONS EQUALLY PRICED
EXCHANGE DEADLINE 8/31/2015
UAR1 Melky Cabrera 10.00 25.00
UAR2 Alex Avila 4.00 10.00
UAR3 Alex Avila 4.00 10.00
UAR4 Steve Garvey 8.00 20.00
UAR5 Allen Craig 12.50 30.00
UAR6 Anibal Sanchez 4.00 10.00
UAR7 Anibal Sanchez 4.00 10.00
UAR8 Aramis Ramirez 6.00 15.00
UAR9 Aroldis Chapman 12.50 30.00
UAR10 Mike Trout 250.00 600.00
UAR11 Billy Butler 5.00 12.00
UAR12 Brandon Belt 8.00 20.00
UAR13 Brandon Phillips 8.00 20.00
UAR14 Brennan Boesch EXCH 4.00 10.00
UAR15 Brennan Boesch EXCH 4.00 10.00
UAR16 Carlos Ruiz 5.00 12.00
UAR17 Carlos Ruiz 5.00 12.00
UAR18 Chris Heisey 5.00 12.00
UAR19 Chris Heisey 5.00 12.00
UAR20 Chris Sale 8.00 20.00
UAR21 Chris Sale 8.00 20.00
UAR22 Brett Lawrie 8.00 20.00
UAR23 Jesus Montero 8.00 20.00
UAR24 Jesus Montero 8.00 20.00
UAR25 Daniel Bard 5.00 12.00
UAR26 Daniel Bard 5.00 12.00
UAR27 Daniel Murphy 10.00 25.00
UAR28 Daniel Murphy 10.00 25.00
UAR29 Nick Markakis 4.00 10.00
UAR30 Nick Markakis 4.00 10.00
UAR31 Danny Espinosa EXCH 5.00 12.00
UAR32 Danny Espinosa EXCH 5.00 12.00
UAR33 Darryl Strawberry 10.00 25.00
UAR34 Dayan Viciedo EXCH 6.00 15.00
UAR35 Dayan Viciedo EXCH 6.00 15.00
UAR36 Doc Gooden 10.00 25.00
UAR37 Doc Gooden 10.00 25.00
UAR38 Michael Bourn EXCH 8.00 20.00
UAR39 Michael Bourn EXCH 8.00 20.00
UAR40 Hank Aaron/66 100.00 250.00
UAR41 Dustin Pedroia 12.50 30.00
UAR42 Elvis Andrus 5.00 12.00
UAR43 Emilio Bonifacio 4.00 10.00
UAR44 Emilio Bonifacio 4.00 10.00
UAR45 Ervin Santana 5.00 12.00
UAR46 Gaby Sanchez 4.00 10.00
UAR47 Gaby Sanchez 4.00 10.00
UAR48 Gary Carter 15.00 40.00
UAR49 Salvador Perez 12.00 30.00
UAR50 Henderson Alvarez 6.00 15.00
UAR51 Henderson Alvarez 6.00 15.00
UAR52 Tommy Hanson 6.00 15.00
UAR53 Tommy Hanson 6.00 15.00
UAR54 Ike Davis 5.00 12.00
UAR55 J.D. Martinez 12.00 30.00
UAR56 Josh Johnson 5.00 12.00
UAR57 Jason Motte 6.00 15.00
UAR58 J.D. Martinez 12.00 30.00
UAR59 Johnny Cueto 6.00 15.00
UAR60 Jon Jay 6.00 15.00
UAR61 Jordan Zimmermann 5.00 12.00
UAR62 Jose Valverde 4.00 10.00
UAR63 Jose Valverde 4.00 10.00
UAR64 Josh Thole 5.00 12.00
UAR65 Josh Thole 5.00 12.00
UAR66 Justin Masterson 6.00 15.00
UAR67 Lance Lynn 5.00 12.00
UAR68 Lance Lynn 5.00 12.00
UAR69 Logan Morrison 4.00 10.00
UAR70 David Justice 8.00 20.00
UAR71 David Justice 8.00 20.00
UAR72 Lucas Duda 6.00 15.00
UAR73 Lucas Duda 6.00 15.00
UAR74 David Justice 8.00 20.00
UAR75 Johnny Cueto 6.00 15.00
UAR76 Bryan LaHair 5.00 12.00
UAR77 Mike Minor 5.00 12.00
UAR78 Mike Minor 5.00 12.00
UAR79 Matt Garza 4.00 10.00
UAR80 Mitch Moreland 4.00 10.00
UAR81 Mitch Moreland 4.00 10.00
UAR82 Neftali Feliz 5.00 12.00
UAR83 Nyjer Morgan 4.00 10.00
UAR84 Nyjer Morgan 4.00 10.00
UAR85 Edwin Encarnacion 6.00 15.00
UAR86 Edwin Encarnacion 6.00 15.00
UAR87 R.A. Dickey 10.00 25.00
UAR88 Rickie Weeks 5.00 12.00
UAR89 Rickie Weeks 5.00 12.00
UAR90 Ruben Tejada 5.00 12.00
UAR91 Shaun Marcum 5.00 12.00
UAR92 Shaun Marcum 5.00 12.00
UAR93 Vance Worley 6.00 15.00
UAR94 Vance Worley 6.00 15.00
UAR95 Danny Duffy 5.00 12.00
UAR96 Danny Duffy 5.00 12.00
UAR97 Zack Cozart 5.00 12.00
UAR98 Evan Longoria 10.00 25.00
UAR99 Mike Moustakas 8.00 20.00
UAR100 Ruben Tejada 5.00 12.00
UAR101 Jason Kipnis 10.00 25.00
UAR103 Dexter Fowler 4.00 10.00
UAR104 Dexter Fowler 4.00 10.00
UAR105 R.A. Dickey 10.00 25.00
UAR106 Brandon McCarthy 4.00 10.00
UAR107 Brandon McCarthy 4.00 10.00
UAR108 Justin Masterson 6.00 15.00
UAR109 Jay Bruce 8.00 20.00
UAR110 Jose Altuve 40.00 100.00
UAR111 Jose Altuve 40.00 100.00
UAR112 Justin Masterson 6.00 15.00
UAR113 Bryan LaHair 5.00 12.00

2012 Topps Triple Threads Unity Relic Autographs Emerald

*EMERALD: .5X TO 1.2X BASIC
STATED ODDS 1:11 MINI
STATED PRINT RUN 50 SER.#'d SETS
EXCHANGE DEADLINE 8/31/2015
UAR40 Hank Aaron 100.00 250.00
UAR102 Duke Snider 15.00 40.00

2012 Topps Triple Threads Unity Relic Autographs Gold

*GOLD: .5X TO 1.2X BASIC
STATED ODDS 1:21 MINI
STATED PRINT RUN 25 SER.#'d SETS
NO PRICING ON MOST DUE SCARCITY
EXCHANGE DEADLINE 8/31/2015

2012 Topps Triple Threads Unity Relic Autographs Sepia

*SEPIA: .4X TO 1X BASIC
STATED ODDS 1:7 MINI
STATED PRINT RUN 75 SER.#'d SETS
EXCHANGE DEADLINE 8/31/2015

2012 Topps Triple Threads Unity Relics

STATED ODDS 1:6 MINI
STATED PRINT RUN 36 SER.#'d SETS
UR1 Dave Winfield 4.00 10.00
UR2 Dustin Pedroia 5.00 12.00
UR3 Dustin Pedroia 5.00 12.00
UR4 Paul Konerko 5.00 12.00
UR5 Paul Konerko 5.00 12.00
UR6 Paul Konerko 5.00 12.00
UR7 Jim Rice 4.00 10.00
UR8 Jim Rice 4.00 10.00
UR9 Prince Fielder 8.00 20.00
UR10 Dan Haren 4.00 10.00
UR11 Dan Haren 4.00 10.00
UR12 Dan Haren 4.00 10.00
UR13 Giancarlo Stanton 4.00 10.00
UR14 Giancarlo Stanton 4.00 10.00
UR15 Giancarlo Stanton 4.00 10.00
UR16 Carlos Gonzalez 4.00 10.00
UR17 Carlos Gonzalez 4.00 10.00
UR18 Carlos Gonzalez 4.00 10.00
UR19 Joe DiMaggio 30.00 60.00
UR20 Tony Gwynn 8.00 20.00
UR21 Ryan Howard 4.00 10.00
UR22 Ryan Howard 4.00 10.00
UR23 Ryan Howard 4.00 10.00
UR24 Mike Trout 40.00 100.00
UR25 Mike Trout 40.00 100.00
UR26 Mike Trout 40.00 100.00
UR27 Willie Mays 12.00 30.00
UR28 Jordan Zimmermann 4.00 10.00
UR29 Jordan Zimmermann 4.00 10.00
UR30 Jordan Zimmermann 4.00 10.00
UR31 Rickey Henderson 15.00 40.00
UR32 Rickey Henderson 15.00 40.00
UR33 Rickey Henderson 15.00 40.00
UR34 Zack Greinke 4.00 10.00
UR35 Zack Greinke 4.00 10.00
UR36 Zack Greinke 4.00 10.00
UR37 Paul Molitor 5.00 12.00
UR38 Paul Molitor 5.00 12.00
UR39 Kevin Youkilis 4.00 10.00
UR40 Kevin Youkilis 4.00 10.00
UR41 Kevin Youkilis 4.00 10.00
UR42 Tim Lincecum 6.00 15.00
UR43 Tim Lincecum 6.00 15.00
UR44 Tim Lincecum 6.00 15.00
UR45 Don Mattingly 10.00 25.00
UR46 David Wright 10.00 25.00
UR47 David Wright 10.00 25.00
UR48 David Wright 10.00 25.00
UR49 Derek Jeter 15.00 40.00
UR50 Derek Jeter 15.00 40.00
UR51 Derek Jeter 15.00 40.00
UR52 Tommy Hanson 4.00 10.00
UR53 Tommy Hanson 4.00 10.00
UR54 Tommy Hanson 4.00 10.00
UR55 Josh Johnson 4.00 10.00
UR56 Josh Johnson 4.00 10.00
UR57 Josh Johnson 4.00 10.00
UR58 Matt Kemp 6.00 15.00
UR59 Matt Kemp 6.00 15.00
UR60 Matt Kemp 6.00 15.00
UR61 Bob Lemon 5.00 12.00
UR62 Brett Gardner 4.00 10.00
UR63 Brett Gardner 4.00 10.00
UR64 Matt Moore 4.00 10.00
UR65 Matt Moore 4.00 10.00
UR66 Matt Moore 4.00 10.00
UR67 Andrew McCutchen 15.00 40.00
UR68 Andrew McCutchen 15.00 15.00
UR69 Andrew McCutchen 15.00 40.00
UR70 Paul O'Neill 6.00 15.00
UR71 Paul O'Neill 6.00 15.00
UR72 Todd Helton 4.00 10.00
UR73 Todd Helton 4.00 10.00
UR74 Todd Helton 4.00 10.00
UR75 Alex Gordon 4.00 10.00
UR76 Alex Gordon 4.00 10.00
UR77 Alex Gordon 4.00 10.00
UR78 Stan Musial 12.50 30.00
UR79 Carlos Santana 4.00 10.00
UR80 Carlos Santana 4.00 10.00
UR81 Carlos Santana 4.00 10.00
UR82 Willie Stargell 12.50 30.00
UR83 Curtis Granderson 4.00 10.00
UR84 Curtis Granderson 4.00 10.00
UR85 Curtis Granderson 4.00 10.00
UR86 Ichiro Suzuki 12.50 30.00
UR87 Ichiro Suzuki 12.50 30.00
UR88 Adrian Beltre 4.00 8.00
UR89 Adrian Beltre 4.00 10.00
UR90 Adrian Beltre 4.00 10.00
UR91 Mike Schmidt 8.00 20.00
UR92 Nelson Cruz 4.00 10.00
UR93 Nelson Cruz 4.00 10.00
UR94 Nelson Cruz 4.00 10.00
UR95 Clayton Kershaw 5.00 12.00
UR96 Clayton Kershaw 5.00 12.00
UR97 Clayton Kershaw 5.00 12.00
UR98 Ryan Braun 5.00 12.00
UR99 Ryan Braun 5.00 12.00
UR100 Ryan Braun 5.00 12.00
UR101 Albert Pujols 10.00 25.00
UR102 Albert Pujols 10.00 25.00
UR103 Justin Upton 4.00 10.00
UR104 Justin Upton 4.00 10.00
UR105 Justin Upton 4.00 10.00
UR106 Billy Butler 4.00 10.00
UR107 Billy Butler 4.00 10.00
UR108 Billy Butler 4.00 10.00
UR109 Madison Bumgarner 5.00 12.00
UR110 Madison Bumgarner 5.00 12.00
UR111 Madison Bumgarner 5.00 12.00
UR112 Starlin Castro 6.00 15.00
UR113 Starlin Castro 6.00 15.00
UR114 Steve Garvey 10.00 25.00
UR115 Frank Thomas 10.00 25.00
UR116 Freddie Freeman 4.00 10.00
UR117 Freddie Freeman 4.00 10.00
UR118 Freddie Freeman 4.00 10.00
UR119 Jimmy Rollins 6.00 15.00
UR120 Jimmy Rollins 6.00 15.00
UR121 Jimmy Rollins 6.00 15.00
UR122 Tim Hudson 4.00 10.00
UR123 Tim Hudson 4.00 10.00
UR124 Tim Hudson 4.00 10.00
UR125 Cole Hamels 4.00 10.00
UR126 Cole Hamels 4.00 10.00
UR127 Cole Hamels 4.00 10.00
UR128 Cal Ripken Jr. 15.00 40.00
UR129 Josh Hamilton 5.00 12.00
UR130 Josh Hamilton 5.00 12.00
UR131 Josh Hamilton 5.00 12.00
UR132 Warren Spahn 10.00 25.00
UR133 Gio Gonzalez 4.00 10.00
UR134 Gio Gonzalez 4.00 10.00
UR135 Gio Gonzalez 4.00 10.00
UR136 Brian McCann 4.00 10.00
UR137 Brian McCann 4.00 10.00
UR138 Brian McCann 4.00 10.00
UR139 Dustin Pedroia 5.00 12.00
UR140 Brooks Robinson 6.00 15.00
UR141 Brooks Robinson 6.00 15.00
UR142 George Brett 12.50 30.00
UR143 George Brett 12.50 30.00
UR144 Jemile Weeks 4.00 10.00
UR145 Adrian Gonzalez 4.00 10.00
UR146 Adrian Gonzalez 4.00 10.00
UR147 Adrian Gonzalez 4.00 10.00
UR148 David Freese 8.00 20.00
UR149 David Freese 8.00 20.00
UR150 David Freese 8.00 20.00
UR151 Roy Halladay 5.00 12.00
UR152 Roy Halladay 5.00 12.00
UR153 Troy Tulowitzki 4.00 10.00
UR154 Troy Tulowitzki 4.00 10.00
UR155 Troy Tulowitzki 4.00 10.00
UR156 Mariano Rivera 10.00 25.00
UR157 Mariano Rivera 10.00 25.00
UR158 Mariano Rivera 10.00 25.00
UR159 Ian Kinsler 4.00 10.00
UR160 Ian Kinsler 4.00 10.00
UR161 Ian Kinsler 4.00 10.00
UR162 Mat Latos 4.00 10.00
UR163 Mat Latos 4.00 10.00
UR164 Mat Latos 4.00 10.00
UR165 Johan Santana 4.00 10.00
UR166 Johan Santana 4.00 10.00
UR167 Johan Santana 4.00 10.00
UR168 Lou Gehrig 50.00 100.00
UR169 Chase Utley 4.00 10.00
UR170 Chase Utley 4.00 10.00
UR171 Chase Utley 4.00 10.00
UR172 Lance Berkman 4.00 10.00
UR173 Lance Berkman 4.00 10.00
UR174 Lance Berkman 4.00 10.00
UR175 Joe Morgan 4.00 10.00
UR176 Joe Morgan 4.00 10.00
UR177 Joe Morgan 4.00 10.00
UR178 Johnny Cueto 4.00 10.00
UR179 Johnny Cueto 4.00 10.00
UR180 Johnny Cueto 4.00 10.00
UR181 Yu Darvish 12.50 30.00
UR182 Eric Hosmer 4.00 10.00
UR183 Eric Hosmer 4.00 10.00
UR184 Eric Hosmer 4.00 10.00
UR185 Ben Zobrist 4.00 10.00
UR186 Ben Zobrist 4.00 10.00
UR187 Ben Zobrist 4.00 10.00
UR188 Hanley Ramirez 4.00 10.00
UR189 Hanley Ramirez 4.00 10.00
UR190 Hanley Ramirez 4.00 10.00
UR191 Ian Kennedy 4.00 10.00
UR192 Ian Kennedy 4.00 10.00
UR193 Ian Kennedy 4.00 10.00
UR194 Dan Uggla 4.00 10.00
UR195 Dan Uggla 4.00 10.00
UR196 Dan Uggla 4.00 10.00
UR197 Joey Votto 6.00 15.00
UR198 James Shields 4.00 10.00
UR199 James Shields 4.00 10.00
UR200 James Shields 4.00 10.00
UR201 Albert Belle 4.00 10.00
UR202 Albert Belle 4.00 10.00
UR203 Andy Pettitte 6.00 15.00
UR204 Andy Pettitte 6.00 15.00
UR205 Andy Pettitte 6.00 15.00
UR206 Bryce Harper 20.00 50.00
UR207 Jacoby Ellsbury 8.00 20.00
UR208 Jacoby Ellsbury 8.00 20.00
UR209 Jacoby Ellsbury 8.00 20.00
UR210 Mike Moustakas 4.00 10.00
UR211 Mike Moustakas 4.00 10.00
UR212 Mike Moustakas 4.00 10.00
UR213 Yovani Gallardo 4.00 10.00
UR214 Yovani Gallardo 4.00 10.00
UR215 Yovani Gallardo 4.00 10.00
UR216 Joey Votto 6.00 15.00
UR217 Alex Rodriguez 8.00 20.00
UR218 Alex Rodriguez 8.00 20.00
UR219 Jason Heyward 4.00 10.00
UR220 Jason Heyward 4.00 10.00
UR221 Jason Heyward 4.00 10.00
UR222 Miguel Cabrera 10.00 25.00
UR223 Miguel Cabrera 10.00 25.00
UR224 Miguel Cabrera 10.00 25.00
UR225 Ozzie Smith 10.00 25.00
UR226 Bobby Doerr 4.00 10.00
UR227 Bobby Doerr 4.00 10.00
UR228 Bobby Doerr 4.00 10.00
UR229 Matt Cain 5.00 12.00
UR230 Matt Cain 5.00 12.00
UR231 Matt Cain 5.00 12.00
UR232 Reggie Jackson 8.00 20.00
UR233 Torii Hunter 4.00 10.00
UR234 Torii Hunter 4.00 10.00
UR235 Torii Hunter 4.00 10.00
UR236 Brett Lawrie 6.00 15.00
UR237 Brett Lawrie 6.00 15.00
UR239 Felix Hernandez 4.00 10.00
UR240 Felix Hernandez 4.00 10.00
UR241 Felix Hernandez 4.00 10.00
UR242 Rod Carew 5.00 12.00
UR243 Lou Brock 6.00 15.00
UR244 Jered Weaver 4.00 10.00
UR245 Jered Weaver 4.00 10.00
UR246 Jered Weaver 4.00 10.00
UR247 Stephen Strasburg 6.00 15.00
UR248 Stephen Strasburg 6.00 15.00
UR249 Sandy Koufax 20.00 50.00
UR250 Cecil Cooper 4.00 10.00
UR251 Jose Bautista 4.00 10.00
UR252 Jose Bautista 4.00 10.00
UR253 Jose Bautista 4.00 10.00
UR254 Chipper Jones 8.00 20.00
UR255 Chipper Jones 8.00 20.00
UR256 Chipper Jones 8.00 20.00
UR257 Andre Ethier 4.00 10.00
UR258 Andre Ethier 4.00 10.00
UR259 Andre Ethier 4.00 10.00
UR260 Dustin Ackley 4.00 10.00
UR261 Dustin Ackley 4.00 10.00
UR262 Ryan Zimmerman 4.00 10.00
UR263 Ryan Zimmerman 4.00 10.00
UR264 Ryan Zimmerman 4.00 10.00
UR265 Nick Swisher 5.00 12.00
UR266 Harmon Killebrew 10.00 25.00
UR267 Brandon Beachy 4.00 10.00
UR268 Brandon Beachy 4.00 10.00
UR269 Brandon Beachy 4.00 10.00
UR270 Carlos Beltran 8.00 20.00
UR271 Carlos Beltran 8.00 20.00
UR272 Carlos Beltran 8.00 20.00
UR273 Robinson Cano 8.00 20.00
UR274 Robinson Cano 8.00 20.00
UR275 Robinson Cano 8.00 20.00
UR276 Jay Bruce 4.00 10.00
UR277 Jay Bruce 4.00 10.00
UR278 Jay Bruce 4.00 10.00
UR279 Eddie Murray 6.00 15.00
UR280 Eddie Murray 6.00 15.00
UR281 Anibal Sanchez 4.00 10.00
UR282 Anibal Sanchez 4.00 10.00
UR283 Anibal Sanchez 4.00 10.00
UR284 C.J. Wilson 4.00 10.00
UR285 C.J. Wilson 4.00 10.00
UR286 C.J. Wilson 4.00 10.00
UR287 Evan Longoria 5.00 12.00
UR288 Evan Longoria 5.00 12.00
UR289 Evan Longoria 5.00 12.00
UR290 Buster Posey 10.00 25.00
UR291 Buster Posey 10.00 25.00
UR292 Buster Posey 10.00 25.00
UR293 David Ortiz 4.00 10.00
UR294 David Ortiz 4.00 10.00
UR295 David Ortiz 4.00 10.00
UR296 Daniel Murphy 5.00 12.00
UR297 Justin Verlander 8.00 20.00
UR298 Justin Verlander 8.00 20.00
UR299 Justin Verlander 8.00 20.00
UR300 Ryne Sandberg 8.00 20.00
UR301 Mark Teixeira 4.00 10.00
UR302 Mark Teixeira 4.00 10.00
UR303 Mark Teixeira 4.00 10.00
UR304 Carl Yastrzemski 10.00 25.00
UR305 Carl Yastrzemski 10.00 25.00
UR306 David Price 4.00 10.00
UR307 David Price 4.00 10.00
UR308 David Price 4.00 10.00
UR309 Joey Votto 6.00 15.00
UR332 Joe Mauer 4.00 10.00

2012 Topps Triple Threads Unity Relics Emerald

*EMERALD: .5X TO 1.2X BASIC
STATED ODDS 1:11 MINI
STATED PRINT RUN 18 SER.#'d SETS
ALL VERSIONS EQUALLY PRICED
SOME NOT PRICED DUE TO SCARCITY

2012 Topps Triple Threads Unity Relics Gold

*GOLD: .6X TO 1.5X BASIC
STATED ODDS 1:21 MINI
STATED PRINT RUN 9 SER.#'d SETS
ALL VERSIONS EQUALLY PRICED
SOME NOT PRICED DUE TO SCARCITY

2012 Topps Triple Threads Unity Relics Sepia

*SEPIA: .4X TO 1X BASIC
STATED ODDS 1:7 MINI
STATED PRINT RUN 27 SER.#'d SETS

2013 Topps Triple Threads

JSY AU RC ODDS 1:10 MINI
JSY AU RC PRINT RUN 99 SER.#'d SETS
JSY AU ODDS 1:10 MINI
JSY AU PRINT RUN 99 SER.#'d SETS
EXCHANGE DEADLINE 10/31/2016
OVERALL 1-100 PLATE ODDS 1:145 HOBBY
PLATE PRINT RUN 1 SET PER COLOR
BLACK-CYAN-MAGENTA-YELLOW ISSUED
NO PLATE PRICING DUE TO SCARCITY
1 Ted Williams 1.50 4.00
2 Mike Mussina .60 1.50
3 Dustin Pedroia .75 2.00
4 Lou Gehrig 1.50 4.00
5 Albert Pujols 1.00 2.50
6 Justin Verlander .75 2.00
7 Ozzie Smith 1.00 2.50
8 David Wright .60 1.50
9 CC Sabathia .60 1.50
10 Babe Ruth 2.00 5.00
11 Craig Biggio .60 1.50
12 Ryan Zimmerman .60 1.50
13 Stephen Strasburg .75 2.00
14 Gary Carter .60 1.50
15 R.A. Dickey .60 1.50
16 Clayton Kershaw 1.25 3.00
17 Bob Gibson .60 1.50
18 Brooks Robinson .60 1.50
19 Derek Jeter 2.00 5.00
20 Matt Cain .60 1.50
21 George Brett 1.50 4.00
22 Nolan Ryan 2.50 6.00
23 David Ortiz .75 2.00
24 Ian Kinsler .60 1.50
25 Jose Bautista .60 1.50
26 Ryan Braun .60 1.50
27 Torii Hunter .50 1.25
28 Greg Maddux 1.00 2.50
29 Billy Butler .50 1.25
30 Jose Reyes .60 1.50
31 David Freese .50 1.25
32 Justin Upton .60 1.50
33 Yogi Berra .75 2.00
34 Tony Gwynn .75 2.00
35 Bo Jackson .75 2.00
36 Hanley Ramirez .60 1.50
37 Ryan Howard .60 1.50
38 Joey Votto .75 2.00
39 Harmon Killebrew .75 2.00
40 Tom Glavine .50 1.25
41 Roy Halladay .60 1.50
42 Jackie Robinson .75 2.00
43 John Smoltz .75 2.00
44 Hank Aaron 1.50 4.00
45 Cal Ripken Jr. 2.50 6.00
46 Bill Mazeroski .60 1.50
47 Reggie Jackson .60 1.50
48 Wade Boggs .60 1.50
49 Adrian Gonzalez .60 1.50
50 Johnny Bench .75 2.00
51 David Price .60 1.50
52 Joe Morgan .60 1.50
53 Willie Mays 1.50 4.00
54 Tim Lincecum .60 1.50
55 Whitey Ford .60 1.50
56 Albert Belle .50 1.25
57 Yu Darvish .75 2.00
58 Prince Fielder .60 1.50
59 Tom Seaver .60 1.50
60 Giancarlo Stanton .75 2.00
61 Buster Posey 1.00 2.50
62 Andrew McCutchen .75 2.00
63 Pablo Sandoval .60 1.50
64 Al Kaline .75 2.00
65 Troy Tulowitzki .75 2.00
66 Robinson Cano .60 1.50
67 Roberto Clemente 2.00 5.00
68 Rickey Henderson .75 2.00
69 Yasiel Puig RC 2.00 5.00
70 Evan Longoria .60 1.50
71 Matt Holliday .75 2.00
72 Joe DiMaggio 1.50 4.00
73 C.J. Wilson .50 1.25
74 Josh Hamilton .60 1.50
75 Ty Cobb 1.25 3.00
76 Justin Morneau .60 1.50
77 Mike Schmidt 1.25 3.00
78 Fred McGriff .60 1.50
79 Robin Yount .75 2.00
80 Willie Stargell .60 1.50
81 Bob Feller .60 1.50
82 Jimmie Foxx .75 2.00
83 Jered Weaver .60 1.50
84 Ernie Banks .75 2.00
85 Zack Greinke .75 2.00
86 Sandy Koufax 1.50 4.00
87 Frank Thomas .75 2.00
88 Miguel Cabrera .75 2.00
89 Mariano Rivera 1.00 2.50
90 Matt Kemp .60 1.50
91 Don Mattingly 1.50 4.00
92 Duke Snider .60 1.50
93 Felix Hernandez .60 1.50
94 Joe Mauer .60 1.50
95 Cole Hamels .60 1.50
96 James Shields .50 1.25
97 Carlos Gonzalez .60 1.50
98 Gio Gonzalez .60 1.50
99 Cliff Lee .60 1.50
100 Paul Molitor .75 2.00
101 Mike Trout JSY AU 100.00 250.00
102 K.Gausman JSY AU RC 10.00 25.00
103 N.Arenado JSY AU RC 75.00 200.00
104 Todd Frazier JSY AU 6.00 15.00
106 Salvador Perez JSY AU 12.00 30.00
107 Starlin Castro JSY AU 10.00 25.00
108 Tyler Skaggs JSY AU RC 5.00 12.00
109 M.Machado JSY AU RC 50.00 120.00
110 Josh Reddick JSY AU 8.00 20.00
111 Jurickson Profar JSY AU RC 12.50 30.00
112 Jarrod Parker JSY AU 5.00 12.00
113 Anthony Gose JSY AU 5.00 12.00
114 Alex Cobb JSY AU 5.00 12.00
116 Yonder Alonso JSY AU 5.00 12.00
117 H.Ryu JSY AU RC EXCH 20.00 50.00
118 Will Middlebrooks JSY AU 8.00 20.00
119 Brett Jackson JSY AU 5.00 12.00
120 Yasmani Grandal JSY AU 5.00 12.00
122 T.Rosenthal JSY AU RC 5.00 12.00
123 Wade Miley JSY AU 5.00 12.00
124 Andrew Cashner JSY AU 5.00 12.00
125 Felix Doubront JSY AU 5.00 12.00
126 Julio Teheran JSY AU 8.00 20.00
127 Yu Darvish JSY AU EXCH 40.00 100.00
128 Chris Archer JSY AU 6.00 15.00
129 Nate Eovaldi JSY AU 6.00 15.00
130 Derek Norris JSY AU 5.00 12.00
131 Josh Rutledge JSY AU 5.00 12.00
132 Mike Olt JSY AU RC 6.00 15.00
133 Devin Mesoraco JSY AU 5.00 12.00
134 Aaron Hicks JSY AU RC 5.00 12.00
135 Mark Trumbo JSY AU 6.00 15.00
136 Anthony Rizzo JSY AU 15.00 40.00
138 Brett Lawrie JSY AU 5.00 12.00
139 Jedd Gyorko JSY AU RC 5.00 12.00
140 Dylan Bundy JSY AU RC 15.00 40.00
141 Jeurys Familia JSY AU RC 5.00 12.00
142 Tommy Milone JSY AU 5.00 12.00
143 Matt Moore JSY AU 8.00 20.00
144 Shelby Miller JSY AU RC 12.50 30.00
145 Scott Diamond JSY AU 5.00 12.00
146 Starling Marte JSY AU 5.00 12.00
147 Michael Pineda JSY AU 5.00 12.00
148 Brad Jr. JSY AU RC EXCH 30.00 80.00
149 Matt Adams JSY AU 12.50 30.00
151 A.Garcia JSY AU RC EXCH 5.00 12.00
152 Jake Odorizzi JSY AU RC 5.00 12.00
153 D.Brown JSY AU EXCH 5.00 12.00
154 Freddie Freeman JSY AU 15.00 40.00
155 Jason Kipnis JSY AU 8.00 20.00
156 A.Rendon JSY AU RC 20.00 50.00
157 Kirk Nieuwenhuis JSY AU 5.00 12.00
158 Kris Medlen JSY AU EXCH 5.00 12.00
159 Paul Goldschmidt JSY AU 12.50 30.00
160 Tony Cingrani JSY AU RC 8.00 20.00
161 B.Harper JSY AU 75.00 150.00
162 Jean Segura JSY AU EXCH 10.00 25.00
163 Yoenis Cespedes JSY AU 10.00 25.00
164 Trevor Bauer JSY AU 6.00 15.00
165 Wily Peralta JSY AU 5.00 12.00
166 Wilin Rosario JSY AU 5.00 12.00
167 Didi Gregorius JSY AU RC 5.00 12.00
168 Wil Myers JSY AU RC 10.00 25.00
169 G.Cole JSY AU RC EXCH 50.00 120.00
170 Bruce Rondon JSY AU RC EXCH 5.00 12.00
171 Wheeler JSY AU RC EXCH 10.00 25.00

2013 Topps Triple Threads Amber

*AMBER: 1X TO 2.5X BASIC
STATED ODDS 1:5 MINI
STATED PRINT RUN 125 SER.#'d SETS
69 Yasiel Puig 12.50 30.00

2013 Topps Triple Threads Amethyst

*AMETHYST: .5X TO 1.2X BASIC
STATED PRINT RUN 650 SER.#'d SETS
69 Yasiel Puig 6.00 15.00

2013 Topps Triple Threads Emerald

*EMERALD 1-100: .6X TO 1.5X BASIC
1-100 STATED ODDS 1:3 MINI
1-100 PRINT RUN 250 SER.#'d SETS
*EMERALD JSY AU: .4X TO 1X BASIC
EMERALD JSY AU ODDS 1:18 MINI
EMER.JSY AU PRINT RUN 50 SER.#'d SETS
EXCHANGE DEADLINE 10/31/2016
69 Yasiel Puig 8.00 20.00

2013 Topps Triple Threads Gold

*GOLD: 2X TO 5X BASIC
STATED ODDS 1:6 MINI
STATED PRINT RUN 99 SER.#'d SETS
69 Yasiel Puig 20.00 50.00

2013 Topps Triple Threads Onyx

*ONYX: 2.5X TO 6X BASIC
STATED ODDS 1:12 MINI
STATED PRINT RUN 50 SER.#'d SETS
69 Yasiel Puig 25.00 60.00

2013 Topps Triple Threads Sapphire

*SAPPHIRE: 3X TO 8X BASIC
STATED ODDS 1:24 MINI
STATED PRINT RUN 25 SER.#'d SETS
19 Derek Jeter 30.00 60.00

2013 Topps Triple Threads Sepia

*SEPIA JSY AU: .4X TO 1X BASIC
STATED ODDS 1:12 MINI
STATED PRINT RUN 75 SER.#'d SETS
EXCHANGE DEADLINE 10/31/2016

2013 Topps Triple Threads Autograph Relic Combos

STATED ODDS 1:97 MINI
STATED PRINT RUN 36 SER.#'d SETS
EXCHANGE DEADLINE 10/31/2016
BPP Bggio/Phllps/Pdria
BSG Sgra/Braun/Gllrdo 30.00 60.00

CPC Phllps/Cngrni/Czart 15.00 40.00
GZZ R.Zim/J.Zim/Gnzlz 20.00 50.00
HTD Drvsh/Hrper/Trout 250.00 350.00
JGT Grfley/Thmas/Jcksn 250.00 350.00
JTH Jcksn/Hndrsn/Trout 200.00 400.00
KRM Krshw/Mrtnz/Ryu EXCH 100.00 200.00
MGM Gssge/Mssna/Mttngly 75.00 150.00
MGS Mddx/Smltz/Glvne EXCH 150.00 400.00
MHC Cobb/Hllcksn/Moore 15.00 40.00
MOG Ortz/Mrtnz/Grcparra 75.00 150.00
MRW Whler/Mller/Ryu EXCH 20.00 50.00
RDP Ryan/Drvsh/Prfar EXCH 100.00 200.00
SPR Prce/Ryu/Sale 30.00 60.00
WLM Lngria/Wrght/Mchdo 50.00 100.00
WMW Whler/Mrtnez/Wright 40.00 80.00

2013 Topps Triple Threads Autograph Relic Combos Sepia

*SEPIA: .4X TO 1X BASIC
STATED ODDS 1:130 MINI
STATED PRINT RUN 27 SER.#'d SETS
EXCHANGE DEADLINE 10/31/2016

2013 Topps Triple Threads Legend Relics

STATED ODDS 1:83 MINI
STATED PRINT RUN 36 SER.#'d SETS
BG Bob Gibson 12.50 30.00
BR Babe Ruth 100.00 200.00
CR Cal Ripken Jr. 30.00 60.00
FR Frank Robinson 20.00 50.00
HA Hank Aaron 30.00 60.00
HK Harmon Killebrew 12.50 30.00
JB Johnny Bench 12.50 30.00
JF Jimmie Foxx 20.00 50.00
JM Joe Morgan 8.00 20.00
JR Jackie Robinson 40.00 80.00
KG Ken Griffey Jr. 20.00 50.00
LG Lou Gehrig 60.00 120.00
NR Nolan Ryan 30.00 60.00
RC Roberto Clemente 60.00 120.00
RJ Reggie Jackson 12.50 30.00
SM Stan Musial 30.00 60.00
TC Ty Cobb 40.00 80.00
TW Ted Williams 40.00 80.00
WM Willie Mays 20.00 50.00
YB Yogi Berra 15.00 40.00

2013 Topps Triple Threads Legend Relics Sepia

*SEPIA: .4X TO 1X BASIC
STATED ODDS 1:110 MINI
STATED PRINT RUN 27 SER.#'D SETS

2013 Topps Triple Threads Relic Autographs

STATED ODDS 1:12 MINI
STATED PRINT RUN 18 SER.#'d SETS
ALL DC VARIATIONS PRICED EQUALLY
NO PRICING ON PLAYERS W/ONE DC VERSION
EXCHANGE DEADLINE 10/31/2016
AA1 Alex Avila 8.00 20.00
AA2 Alex Avila 8.00 20.00
AA3 Alex Avila 8.00 20.00
AA4 Alex Avila 8.00 20.00
AET1 Andre Ethier 12.50 30.00
AET2 Andre Ethier 12.50 30.00
AG1 Avisail Garcia 10.00 25.00
AG2 Avisail Garcia 10.00 25.00
AG3 Avisail Garcia 10.00 25.00
AG4 Avisail Garcia 10.00 25.00
AG5 Avisail Garcia 10.00 25.00
AGN1 Anthony Gose 8.00 20.00
AGN2 Anthony Gose 8.00 20.00
AGN3 Anthony Gose 8.00 20.00
AGN4 Anthony Gose 8.00 20.00
AR1 Anthony Rizzo 20.00 50.00
AR2 Anthony Rizzo 20.00 50.00
AR3 Anthony Rizzo 20.00 50.00
ARE1 Anthony Rendon 15.00 40.00
ARE2 Anthony Rendon 15.00 40.00
AS1 Anibal Sanchez 8.00 20.00
AS2 Anibal Sanchez 8.00 20.00
AS3 Anibal Sanchez 8.00 20.00
AS4 Anibal Sanchez 8.00 20.00
BG1 Brett Gardner 15.00 40.00
BG2 Brett Gardner 15.00 40.00
BGI1 Bob Gibson 15.00 40.00
BGI2 Bob Gibson 15.00 40.00
BGI3 Bob Gibson 20.00 50.00
BH1 Bryce Harper EXCH 100.00 200.00
BH2 Bryce Harper EXCH 100.00 200.00
BM1 Brian McCann 10.00 25.00
BM2 Brian McCann 10.00 25.00
BM3 Brian McCann 10.00 25.00
BM4 Brian McCann 10.00 25.00
BM5 Brian McCann 10.00 25.00
BPO1 Buster Posey 75.00 150.00
BPO2 Buster Posey 75.00 150.00
BPO3 Buster Posey 75.00 150.00
CA1 Chris Archer 10.00 25.00
CA2 Chris Archer 10.00 25.00
CA3 Chris Archer 10.00 25.00
CA4 Chris Archer 10.00 25.00
CB1 Craig Biggio 30.00 60.00
CB2 Craig Biggio 30.00 60.00
CKI1 Craig Kimbrel EXCH 40.00 80.00
CKI2 Craig Kimbrel EXCH 40.00 80.00
CKI3 Craig Kimbrel EXCH 40.00 80.00
CR1 Colby Rasmus 8.00 20.00
CR2 Colby Rasmus 8.00 20.00
CR3 Colby Rasmus 8.00 20.00
CR4 Colby Rasmus 8.00 20.00
CS1 Carlos Santana 8.00 20.00
CS2 Carlos Santana 8.00 20.00
CS3 Carlos Santana 8.00 20.00
DF1 Dexter Fowler 5.00 12.00
DF2 Dexter Fowler 5.00 12.00
DF3 Dexter Fowler 5.00 12.00
DF4 Dexter Fowler 5.00 12.00
DFR1 David Freese 15.00 40.00
DFR2 David Freese 15.00 40.00
DFR3 David Freese 15.00 40.00
DM1 Devin Mesoraco 10.00 25.00
DM2 Devin Mesoraco 10.00 25.00
DMA1 Don Mattingly 40.00 80.00
DMA2 Don Mattingly 40.00 80.00
DMA3 Don Mattingly 40.00 80.00
DN1 Derek Norris 5.00 12.00
DN2 Derek Norris 5.00 12.00
DN3 Derek Norris 5.00 12.00
DN4 Derek Norris 5.00 12.00
DO1 David Ortiz 50.00 100.00
DO2 David Ortiz 50.00 100.00
DO3 David Ortiz 50.00 100.00
DS1 Dave Stewart EXCH 8.00 20.00
DS2 Dave Stewart EXCH 8.00 20.00
DS3 Dave Stewart EXCH 8.00 20.00
DS4 Dave Stewart EXCH 8.00 20.00
DSN1 Duke Snider 20.00 50.00
DSN2 Duke Snider 20.00 50.00
DSN3 Duke Snider 20.00 50.00
DU1 Dan Uggla EXCH 6.00 15.00
DU2 Dan Uggla EXCH 6.00 15.00
DU3 Dan Uggla EXCH 6.00 15.00
DU4 Dan Uggla EXCH 6.00 15.00
DU5 Dan Uggla EXCH 6.00 15.00
DW1 David Wright 15.00 40.00
DW2 David Wright 15.00 40.00
DW3 David Wright 15.00 40.00
FF1 Freddie Freeman 15.00 40.00
FF2 Freddie Freeman 15.00 40.00
FH1 Felix Hernandez 20.00 50.00
FH2 Felix Hernandez 20.00 50.00
GG1 Gio Gonzalez 8.00 20.00
GG2 Gio Gonzalez 8.00 20.00
GS1 Gary Sheffield 10.00 25.00
GS2 Gary Sheffield 10.00 25.00
GS3 Gary Sheffield 10.00 25.00
GS4 Gary Sheffield 10.00 25.00
GST1 Giancarlo Stanton 15.00 40.00
GST2 Giancarlo Stanton 15.00 40.00
GST3 Giancarlo Stanton 15.00 40.00
GST4 Giancarlo Stanton 15.00 40.00
HA1 Hank Aaron 250.00 350.00
HA2 Hank Aaron 250.00 350.00
JBA1 Jose Bautista 10.00 25.00
JBA2 Jose Bautista 10.00 25.00
JBA3 Jose Bautista 10.00 25.00
JBE1 Johnny Bench 40.00 80.00
JBE2 Johnny Bench 40.00 80.00
JHE1 Jason Heyward 15.00 40.00
JHE2 Jason Heyward 15.00 40.00
JHE3 Jason Heyward 15.00 40.00
JK1 Jason Kipnis 12.00 30.00
JK2 Jason Kipnis 12.00 30.00
JK3 Jason Kipnis 12.00 30.00
JK4 Jason Kipnis 12.00 30.00
JK5 Jason Kipnis 12.00 30.00
JPA1 Jarrod Parker 6.00 15.00
JPA2 Jarrod Parker 6.00 15.00
JPA3 Jarrod Parker 6.00 15.00
JPA4 Jarrod Parker 6.00 15.00
JPO1 Johnny Podres EXCH 8.00 20.00
JPO2 Johnny Podres EXCH 8.00 20.00
JPO3 Johnny Podres EXCH 8.00 20.00
JPO4 Johnny Podres EXCH 8.00 20.00
JPR1 Jurickson Profar 20.00 50.00
JPR2 Jurickson Profar 20.00 50.00
JPR3 Jurickson Profar 20.00 50.00
JPR4 Jurickson Profar 20.00 50.00
JPR5 Jurickson Profar 20.00 50.00
JS1 Jean Segura 12.50 30.00
JS2 Jean Segura 12.50 30.00
JS3 Jean Segura 12.50 30.00
JU1 Justin Upton 12.50 30.00
JU2 Justin Upton 12.50 30.00
JU3 Justin Upton 12.50 30.00
JW1 Jered Weaver 10.00 25.00
JW2 Jered Weaver 10.00 25.00
JW3 Jered Weaver 10.00 25.00
KM1 Kris Medlen EXCH 10.00 25.00
KM2 Kris Medlen EXCH 10.00 25.00
MA1 Matt Adams 10.00 25.00
MC1 Matt Cain 20.00 50.00
MC2 Matt Cain 10.00 50.00
MC3 Matt Cain 20.00 50.00
MHO1 Matt Holliday EXCH 15.00 40.00
MHO2 Matt Holliday EXCH 15.00 40.00
MHO3 Matt Holliday EXCH 15.00 40.00
MIG1 Miguel Cabrera 75.00 150.00
MIG2 Miguel Cabrera 75.00 150.00
MIG3 Miguel Cabrera 75.00 150.00
MMA1 Manny Machado 50.00 100.00
MMA2 Manny Machado 50.00 100.00
MMA3 Manny Machado 50.00 100.00
MMA4 Manny Machado 20.00 50.00
MMA5 Manny Machado 20.00 50.00
MO1 Mike Olt 6.00 15.00
MO2 Mike Olt 6.00 15.00
MO3 Mike Olt 6.00 15.00
MO4 Mike Olt 6.00 15.00
MO5 Mike Olt 6.00 15.00
MS1 Mike Schmidt 40.00 80.00
MS2 Mike Schmidt 40.00 80.00
NG1 Nomar Garciaparra 30.00 60.00
NG2 Nomar Garciaparra 30.00 60.00
PF1 Prince Fielder EXCH 15.00 40.00
PF2 Prince Fielder EXCH 15.00 40.00
PF3 Prince Fielder EXCH 15.00 40.00
PG1 Paul Goldschmidt 12.50 30.00
PM1 Pedro Martinez EXCH 50.00 100.00
PM2 Pedro Martinez EXCH 50.00 100.00
RB1 Ryan Braun 12.50 30.00
RB2 Ryan Braun 12.50 30.00
RB3 Ryan Braun 12.50 30.00
RD1 R.A. Dickey 15.00 40.00
RD2 R.A. Dickey 15.00 40.00
RD3 R.A. Dickey 15.00 40.00
RH1 Rickey Henderson 60.00 120.00
RH2 Rickey Henderson 60.00 120.00
RJ1 Reggie Jackson EXCH 40.00 80.00
RJ2 Reggie Jackson EXCH 40.00 80.00
SM1 Starling Marte 15.00 40.00
SM2 Starling Marte 15.00 40.00
SM3 Starling Marte 15.00 40.00
SMA1 Shaun Marcum 5.00 12.00
SMA2 Shaun Marcum 5.00 12.00
SMA3 Shaun Marcum 5.00 12.00
SMI1 Shelby Miller 15.00 40.00
SMI2 Shelby Miller 15.00 40.00
SMI3 Shelby Miller 15.00 40.00
SP1 Salvador Perez 15.00 40.00
SP2 Salvador Perez 15.00 40.00
SP3 Salvador Perez 15.00 40.00
SP4 Salvador Perez 15.00 40.00
SP5 Salvador Perez 15.00 40.00
TG1 Tony Gwynn 30.00 60.00
TG2 Tony Gwynn 30.00 60.00
TH1 Tim Hudson 10.00 25.00
TH2 Tim Hudson 10.00 25.00
TH3 Tim Hudson 10.00 25.00
TH4 Tim Hudson 10.00 25.00
TH5 Tim Hudson 10.00 25.00
TM1 Tommy Milone 5.00 12.00
TM2 Tommy Milone 5.00 12.00
TM3 Tommy Milone 5.00 12.00
TM4 Tommy Milone 5.00 12.00
TS1 Tyler Skaggs 6.00 15.00
TS2 Tyler Skaggs 6.00 15.00
TS3 Tyler Skaggs 6.00 15.00
TS4 Tyler Skaggs 6.00 15.00
TS5 Tyler Skaggs 6.00 15.00
WM1 Wil Myers 20.00 50.00
WM2 Wil Myers 20.00 50.00
WM3 Wil Myers 20.00 50.00
WM4 Wil Myers 20.00 50.00
WM5 Wil Myers 20.00 50.00
WMI1 Will Middlebrooks 10.00 25.00
WMI2 Will Middlebrooks 10.00 25.00
WMI3 Will Middlebrooks 10.00 25.00
WMIL1 Wade Miley 5.00 12.00
WMIL2 Wade Miley 5.00 12.00
WMIL3 Wade Miley 5.00 12.00
WP1 Wily Peralta 10.00 25.00
WP2 Wily Peralta 10.00 25.00
WP3 Wily Peralta 10.00 25.00
WP4 Wily Peralta 10.00 25.00
YA1 Yonder Alonso 6.00 15.00
YA2 Yonder Alonso 6.00 15.00
YA3 Yonder Alonso 6.00 15.00
YC1 Yoenis Cespedes 15.00 40.00
YC2 Yoenis Cespedes 15.00 40.00
YC3 Yoenis Cespedes 15.00 40.00
YC4 Yoenis Cespedes 15.00 40.00
YD1 Yu Darvish EXCH 90.00 150.00
YD2 Yu Darvish EXCH 90.00 150.00
YD3 Yu Darvish EXCH 90.00 150.00
YD4 Yu Darvish EXCH 90.00 150.00
ZC1 Zack Cozart 6.00 15.00
ZC2 Zack Cozart 6.00 15.00
ZC3 Zack Cozart 6.00 15.00
ZC4 Zack Cozart 6.00 15.00

2013 Topps Triple Threads Relic Autographs Gold

*GOLD: .5X TO 1.2X BASIC
STATED ODDS 1:23 MINI
STATED PRINT RUN 9 SER.#'d SETS
ALL DC VARIATIONS PRICED EQUALLY
NO PRICING ON MANY DUE TO SCARCITY
EXCHANGE DEADLINE 10/31/2016

2013 Topps Triple Threads Relic Combos

STATED ODDS 1:24 MINI
STATED PRINT RUN 36 SER.#'d SETS
AHM Arcia/Mauer/Hcks 8.00 20.00
ATG Arndo/Tlwtzki/Gnzlz 6.00 15.00
BAP Bltre/Andrs/Prfar 8.00 20.00
BCA Cruz/Andrs/Bltre 8.00 20.00
BCL Bmgrnr/Lnccm/Cain 10.00 25.00
BEC Cbrra/Btsta/Encrncn 5.00 12.00
BHM Hlldy/Bltrn/Mlna 8.00 20.00
BHU Braun/Hrpr/Uptn 10.00 25.00
BJJ Brra/Jcksn/Jter 20.00 50.00
BUC Btsta/Uptn/Cspdes 5.00 12.00
CHD Drvsh/Cspdes/Hrpr 12.00 30.00
CJH Jcksn/Cspdes/Hndrsn 20.00 50.00
CKR Kmbrl/Rvra/Chpmn 15.00 40.00
CLS Cain/Lnccm/Sndvl 12.50 30.00
CMR Cstro/Rzzo/McGrff 8.00 20.00
CRN Rddck/Nrrs/Cspdes EXCH 15.00 40.00
FHS Frnkln/Sger/Hrnndz 6.00 15.00
FPB Psey/Bnch/Fisk 20.00 50.00
FSH Sndvl/Frse/Hdley 6.00 15.00
GBV Grffy/Bnch/Vtto 30.00 60.00
GHJ Jcksn/Gwynn/Hndrsn 20.00 50.00
GMB Bggs/Mddlbrks/Grcprra 20.00 50.00
GRC Rzzo/Cstro/Grza 8.00 20.00
GRF Rzzo/Gldschmdt/Frman 8.00 20.00
HGA Alnso/Hdley/Gyrko 8.00 20.00
HHL Lee/Hlldy/Hmls 12.50 30.00
HMC Cngrni/Hrvy/Mller EXCH 8.00 20.00
HMF Mley/Frzier/Hrper 10.00 25.00
HRS Schmdt/Hwrd/Rllins 12.50 30.00
HSV Strsbrg/Hrvy/Vrlnder 12.50 30.00
HVF Hnter/Vrlndr/Flder 12.50 30.00
HWL Hdley/Wrght/Lngria 15.00 40.00
HWW Wrght/Whler/Hrvey 8.00 20.00
JRS Sbthia/Rdrgz/Jter 40.00 80.00
KGG Krshw/Grnke/Gnzlez 10.00 25.00
KKG Krshw/Kemp/Gnzlez 10.00 25.00
KMH Kmbrl/Hdsn/Mdlen 10.00 25.00
KSH Krshw/Hrvy/Strsbrg 15.00 40.00
LHH Hmels/Hwrd/Lee 10.00 25.00
LMP Price/Lngria/Moore 6.00 15.00
LRM Mchdo/Lngria/Rdrgz 15.00 40.00
MBH Braun/McCtchn/Hrper 12.50 30.00
MCR Mttngly/Cano/Rdrgz 12.50 30.00
MHU Uptn/McCtchn/Hnter 6.00 15.00
MML Mlna/Lynn/Mller 15.00 40.00
MPH Hrvy/Prfar/Mchdo 12.50 30.00
MPM Psey/McCvy/Mays 75.00 150.00
MPP Mlna/Psey/Prez 15.00 40.00
MRL Lynn/Mller/Rsnthl 10.00 25.00
MRR Ruiz/Rsrio/Msraco 5.00 12.00
NPM Npoli/Pdroia/Mddlbrks 12.50 30.00
OGS O'Nll/Shffld/Grndrsn 6.00 15.00
PCL Lnccm/Cain/Psey 15.00 40.00
PKG Kpns/Prfar/Gyrko 12.50 30.00
PRC Chpmn/Rvra/Pplbon 10.00 25.00
RTG Gnzlz/Tlwtzki/Rsrio 6.00 15.00
SBG Sgura/Gllrdo/Braun 5.00 12.00
SKL Sale/Krshw/Lee 8.00 20.00
SMC McCtchn/Clmnte/Strgll 75.00 150.00
SMF Frnkln/Sgura/Mchdo 12.50 30.00
SPK Sale/Peavy/Knrko 8.00 20.00
SPW Sbthia/Wlhlm/Pttitte 8.00 20.00
STJ Sgura/Tlwtzki/Jter 8.00 20.00
SVS Snchz/Schrzer/Vrlnder 15.00 40.00
THT Trmbo/Trout/Hmlton 15.00 40.00
UUH Uptn/Hywrd/Uptn 10.00 25.00
VGG Gldschmdt/Vtto/Gnzlez 10.00 25.00
ZGS Zmmrmnn/Strsbrg/Gnzlez 12.50 30.00
HGA1 Alnso/Hwrd/Gnzlz 5.00 12.00
MRR1 Mchdo/Rbnsn/Rpken 20.00 50.00

2013 Topps Triple Threads Relic Combos Sepia

*SEPIA: .4X TO 1X BASIC
STATED ODDS 1:32 MINI
STATED PRINT RUN 27 SER.#'d SETS

2013 Topps Triple Threads Relics

STATED ODDS 1:8 MINI
STATED PRINT RUN 36 SER.#'d SETS
ALL DC VARIATIONS PRICED EQUALLY
ABE1 Adrian Beltre 4.00 10.00
ABE2 Adrian Beltre 4.00 10.00
ABE3 Adrian Beltre 4.00 10.00
AC1 Aroldis Chapman 6.00 15.00
AC2 Aroldis Chapman 6.00 15.00
AC3 Aroldis Chapman 6.00 15.00
AD1 Adam Dunn 4.00 10.00
AD2 Adam Dunn 4.00 10.00
AD3 Adam Dunn 4.00 10.00
AE1 Andre Ethier 6.00 15.00
AE2 Andre Ethier 6.00 15.00
AE3 Andre Ethier 6.00 15.00
AG1 Adrian Gonzalez 6.00 15.00
AG2 Adrian Gonzalez 6.00 15.00
AG3 Adrian Gonzalez 6.00 15.00
AJ1 Adam Jones 8.00 20.00
AJ2 Adam Jones 8.00 20.00
AJ3 Adam Jones 8.00 20.00
AM1 Andrew McCutchen 10.00 25.00
AM2 Andrew McCutchen 10.00 25.00
AM3 Andrew McCutchen 10.00 25.00
AP1 Albert Pujols 10.00 25.00
AP2 Albert Pujols 10.00 25.00
AP3 Albert Pujols 10.00 25.00
AR1 Anthony Rizzo 5.00 12.00
AR2 Anthony Rizzo 5.00 12.00
AR3 Anthony Rizzo 5.00 12.00
ARO1 Alex Rodriguez 10.00 25.00
ARO2 Alex Rodriguez 10.00 25.00
ARO3 Alex Rodriguez 10.00 25.00
BB1 Billy Butler 4.00 10.00
BB2 Billy Butler 4.00 10.00
BB3 Billy Butler 4.00 10.00
BBE1 Brandon Beachy 4.00 10.00
BBE2 Brandon Beachy 4.00 10.00
BBE3 Brandon Beachy 4.00 10.00
BH1 Bryce Harper 10.00 25.00
CB1 Carlos Beltran 10.00 25.00
CB2 Carlos Beltran 10.00 25.00
CB3 Carlos Beltran 10.00 25.00
CBI1 Craig Biggio 8.00 20.00
CBI2 Craig Biggio 8.00 20.00
CBI3 Craig Biggio 8.00 20.00
CC1 Carl Crawford 4.00 10.00
CC2 Carl Crawford 4.00 10.00
CC3 Carl Crawford 4.00 10.00
CG1 Carlos Gonzalez 4.00 10.00
CG2 Carlos Gonzalez 4.00 10.00
CG3 Carlos Gonzalez 4.00 10.00
CGR1 Curtis Granderson 5.00 12.00
CGR2 Curtis Granderson 5.00 12.00
CGR3 Curtis Granderson 5.00 12.00
CH1 Cole Hamels 5.00 12.00
CH2 Cole Hamels 5.00 12.00
CH3 Cole Hamels 5.00 12.00
CHE1 Chase Headley 4.00 10.00
CHE2 Chase Headley 4.00 10.00
CHE3 Chase Headley 4.00 10.00
CK1 Craig Kimbrel 10.00 25.00
CK2 Craig Kimbrel 10.00 25.00
CK3 Craig Kimbrel 10.00 25.00
CL1 Cliff Lee 5.00 12.00
CL2 Cliff Lee 5.00 12.00
CL3 Cliff Lee 5.00 12.00
DF1 David Freese 5.00 12.00
DF2 David Freese 5.00 12.00
DF3 David Freese 5.00 12.00
DJ1 Derek Jeter 20.00 50.00
DJ2 Derek Jeter 20.00 50.00
DJ3 Derek Jeter 20.00 50.00
DM1 Don Mattingly 10.00 25.00
DM2 Don Mattingly 10.00 25.00
DM3 Don Mattingly 10.00 25.00
DO1 David Ortiz 8.00 20.00
DO2 David Ortiz 8.00 20.00
DO3 David Ortiz 8.00 20.00
DP1 Dustin Pedroia 8.00 20.00
DP2 Dustin Pedroia 8.00 20.00
DP3 Dustin Pedroia 8.00 20.00
DPR1 David Price 5.00 12.00
DPR2 David Price 5.00 12.00
DPR3 David Price 5.00 12.00
DW1 David Wright 8.00 20.00
DW2 David Wright 8.00 20.00
DW3 David Wright 8.00 20.00
EA1 Elvis Andrus 4.00 10.00
EA2 Elvis Andrus 4.00 10.00
EA3 Elvis Andrus 4.00 10.00
EL1 Evan Longoria 6.00 15.00
EL2 Evan Longoria 6.00 15.00
EL3 Evan Longoria 6.00 15.00
FH1 Felix Hernandez 8.00 20.00
FH2 Felix Hernandez 8.00 20.00
FH3 Felix Hernandez 8.00 20.00
FM1 Fred McGriff 6.00 15.00
FM2 Fred McGriff 6.00 15.00
FM3 Fred McGriff 6.00 15.00
GF1 George Foster 6.00 15.00
GF2 George Foster 6.00 15.00
GF3 George Foster 6.00 15.00
GG1 Gio Gonzalez 4.00 10.00
GG2 Gio Gonzalez 4.00 10.00
GG3 Gio Gonzalez 4.00 10.00
IK1 Ian Kinsler 4.00 10.00
IK2 Ian Kinsler 4.00 10.00
IK3 Ian Kinsler 4.00 10.00
JB1 Jose Bautista 4.00 10.00
JB2 Jose Bautista 4.00 10.00
JB3 Jose Bautista 4.00 10.00
JBR1 Jay Bruce 5.00 12.00
JBR2 Jay Bruce 5.00 12.00
JBR3 Jay Bruce 5.00 12.00
JC1 Johnny Cueto 5.00 12.00
JC2 Johnny Cueto 5.00 12.00
JC3 Johnny Cueto 5.00 12.00
JE1 Jacoby Ellsbury 6.00 15.00
JE2 Jacoby Ellsbury 6.00 15.00
JE3 Jacoby Ellsbury 6.00 15.00
JG1 Jedd Gyorko 4.00 10.00
JG2 Jedd Gyorko 4.00 10.00
JG3 Jedd Gyorko 4.00 10.00
JHA1 Josh Hamilton 4.00 10.00
JHA2 Josh Hamilton 4.00 10.00
JHA3 Josh Hamilton 4.00 10.00
JHE1 Jason Heyward 4.00 10.00
JHE2 Jason Heyward 4.00 10.00
JHE3 Jason Heyward 4.00 10.00
JP1 Jurickson Profar 5.00 12.00
JP2 Jurickson Profar 5.00 12.00
JR1 Jim Rice 6.00 15.00
JR2 Jim Rice 6.00 15.00
JR3 Jim Rice 6.00 15.00
JS1 John Smoltz 8.00 20.00
JS2 John Smoltz 8.00 20.00
JS3 John Smoltz 8.00 20.00
JV1 Justin Verlander 6.00 15.00
JV2 Justin Verlander 6.00 15.00
JV3 Justin Verlander 6.00 15.00
MB1 Madison Bumgarner 20.00 50.00
MB2 Madison Bumgarner 20.00 50.00
MB3 Madison Bumgarner 20.00 50.00
MC1 Miguel Cabrera 10.00 25.00
MC2 Miguel Cabrera 10.00 25.00
MC3 Miguel Cabrera 10.00 25.00
MCA1 Matt Cain 5.00 12.00
MCA2 Matt Cain 5.00 12.00
MCA3 Matt Cain 5.00 12.00
MH1 Matt Holliday 8.00 20.00
MH2 Matt Holliday 8.00 20.00
MH3 Matt Holliday 8.00 20.00
MK1 Matt Kemp 6.00 15.00
MK2 Matt Kemp 6.00 15.00
MK3 Matt Kemp 6.00 15.00
MM1 Mike Mussina 5.00 12.00
MM2 Mike Mussina 5.00 12.00
MM3 Mike Mussina 5.00 12.00
MR1 Mariano Rivera 25.00 60.00
MR2 Mariano Rivera 25.00 60.00
MR3 Mariano Rivera 25.00 60.00
MS1 Max Scherzer 6.00 15.00
MS2 Max Scherzer 6.00 15.00
MS3 Max Scherzer 6.00 15.00
NA1 Norichika Aoki 8.00 20.00
NA2 Norichika Aoki 8.00 20.00
NA3 Norichika Aoki 8.00 20.00
NC1 Nelson Cruz 4.00 10.00
NC2 Nelson Cruz 4.00 10.00
NC3 Nelson Cruz 4.00 10.00
NG1 Nomar Garciaparra 10.00 25.00
NG2 Nomar Garciaparra 10.00 25.00
NG3 Nomar Garciaparra 10.00 25.00
PF1 Prince Fielder 4.00 10.00
PF2 Prince Fielder 4.00 10.00
PF3 Prince Fielder 4.00 10.00
RB1 Ryan Braun 4.00 10.00
RB2 Ryan Braun 4.00 10.00
RB3 Ryan Braun 4.00 10.00
RC1 Robinson Cano 6.00 15.00
RC2 Robinson Cano 6.00 15.00
RC3 Robinson Cano 6.00 15.00
RD1 R.A. Dickey 5.00 12.00
RD2 R.A. Dickey 5.00 12.00
RD3 R.A. Dickey 5.00 12.00
RH1 Roy Halladay 5.00 12.00
RH2 Roy Halladay 5.00 12.00
RH3 Roy Halladay 5.00 12.00
RHO1 Ryan Howard 5.00 12.00
RHO2 Ryan Howard 5.00 12.00
RHO3 Ryan Howard 5.00 12.00
SC1 Starlin Castro 4.00 10.00
SC2 Starlin Castro 4.00 10.00
SC3 Starlin Castro 4.00 10.00
SS1 Stephen Strasburg 6.00 15.00
SS2 Stephen Strasburg 6.00 15.00
SS3 Stephen Strasburg 6.00 15.00
TC1 Tony Cingrani 6.00 15.00
TC2 Tony Cingrani 6.00 15.00
TC3 Tony Cingrani 6.00 15.00
TG1 Tom Glavine 6.00 15.00
TG2 Tom Glavine 6.00 15.00
TG3 Tom Glavine 6.00 15.00
TH1 Tim Hudson 4.00 10.00
TH2 Tim Hudson 4.00 10.00
TH3 Tim Hudson 4.00 10.00
TL1 Tim Lincecum 8.00 20.00
TL2 Tim Lincecum 8.00 20.00
TL3 Tim Lincecum 8.00 20.00
TS1 Tyler Skaggs EXCH 4.00 10.00
TS2 Tyler Skaggs EXCH 4.00 10.00
WC1 Will Clark 10.00 25.00
WC2 Will Clark 10.00 25.00
WC3 Will Clark 10.00 25.00
YC1 Yoenis Cespedes 6.00 15.00
YC2 Yoenis Cespedes 6.00 15.00
YC3 Yoenis Cespedes 6.00 15.00
YCE1 Yoenis Cespedes 6.00 15.00
YCE2 Yoenis Cespedes 6.00 15.00
YD1 Yu Darvish 10.00 25.00
YD2 Yu Darvish 10.00 25.00
YD3 Yu Darvish 10.00 25.00
ZG1 Zack Greinke 5.00 12.00
ZG2 Zack Greinke 5.00 12.00
ZG3 Zack Greinke 5.00 12.00

2013 Topps Triple Threads Relics Emerald

*EMERALD: .5X TO 1.2X BASIC
STATED ODDS 1:16 MINI
STATED PRINT RUN 18 SER.#'d SETS
ALL DC VARIATIONS EQUALLY PRICED
NO PRICING DUE TO SCARCITY ON SOME

2013 Topps Triple Threads Relics Gold

*GOLD: .6X TO 1.5X BASIC
STATED ODDS 1:31 MINI
STATED PRINT RUN 9 SER.#'d SETS
ALL DC VARIATIONS EQUALLY PRICED
NO PRICING ON SOME DUE TO SCARCITY

2013 Topps Triple Threads Relics Sepia

*SEPIA: .4X TO 1X BASIC
STATED ODDS 1:11 MINI
STATED PRINT RUN 27 SER.#'d SETS
ALL DC VARIATIONS EQUALLY PRICED

2013 Topps Triple Threads Unity Relic Autographs

STATED ODDS 1:6 MINI
STATED PRINT RUN 99 SER.#'d SETS
ALL VERSIONS EQUALLY PRICED
EXCHANGE DEADLINE 10/31/2016
AG1 Avisail Garcia EXCH 6.00 15.00
AG2 Avisail Garcia EXCH 6.00 15.00
AG3 Avisail Garcia EXCH 6.00 15.00
AR1 Anthony Rizzo 25.00 60.00
AS Anibal Sanchez EXCH 6.00 15.00
BP1 Brandon Phillips 6.00 15.00
BP2 Brandon Phillips 6.00 15.00
BP3 Brandon Phillips 6.00 15.00
CB Craig Biggio 12.50 30.00
CK Clayton Kershaw 25.00 60.00
CW1 C.J. Wilson 4.00 10.00
CW2 C.J. Wilson 4.00 10.00
CW3 C.J. Wilson 4.00 10.00
DG1 Didi Gregorius 4.00 10.00
DG2 Didi Gregorius 4.00 10.00
DG3 Didi Gregorius 4.00 10.00
DM1 Devin Mesoraco 4.00 10.00
DM2 Devin Mesoraco 4.00 10.00
DM3 Devin Mesoraco 4.00 10.00
DW David Wright 10.00 25.00
EG1 Evan Gattis 12.50 30.00
EG2 Evan Gattis 12.50 30.00
EG3 Evan Gattis 12.50 30.00
EL Evan Longoria 12.50 30.00
FD1 Felix Doubront 4.00 10.00
FD2 Felix Doubront 4.00 10.00
FD3 Felix Doubront 4.00 10.00
FD4 Felix Doubront 4.00 10.00
FD5 Felix Doubront 4.00 10.00
GS Giancarlo Stanton 20.00 50.00
HR1 Hyun-Jin Ryu EXCH 15.00 40.00
JBR1 Jay Bruce 8.00 20.00
JBR2 Jay Bruce 8.00 20.00
JC1 Johnny Cueto 4.00 10.00
JC2 Johnny Cueto 4.00 10.00
JC3 Johnny Cueto 4.00 10.00
JG1 Jedd Gyorko 4.00 10.00
JG2 Jedd Gyorko 4.00 10.00
JG3 Jedd Gyorko 4.00 10.00
JG4 Jedd Gyorko 4.00 10.00
JG5 Jedd Gyorko 4.00 10.00
JJ1 Jon Jay 4.00 10.00
JJ2 Jon Jay 4.00 10.00
JJ3 Jon Jay 4.00 10.00
JM1 J.D. Martinez 4.00 10.00
JM2 J.D. Martinez 4.00 10.00
JP1 Jurickson Profar 10.00 25.00
JP2 Jurickson Profar 10.00 25.00
JP3 Jurickson Profar 10.00 25.00
JP4 Jurickson Profar 10.00 25.00
JP5 Jurickson Profar 10.00 25.00
JRU1 Josh Rutledge 4.00 10.00
JRU2 Josh Rutledge 4.00 10.00
JRU3 Josh Rutledge 4.00 10.00
JU1 Justin Upton 8.00 20.00
JU2 Justin Upton 8.00 20.00
JU3 Justin Upton 8.00 20.00
JZ1 Jordan Zimmermann 5.00 12.00
JZ2 Jordan Zimmermann 5.00 12.00
JZ3 Jordan Zimmermann 5.00 12.00
JZ4 Jordan Zimmermann 5.00 12.00
JZ5 Jordan Zimmermann 5.00 12.00
KN1 Kirk Nieuwenhuis 4.00 10.00
KN2 Kirk Nieuwenhuis 4.00 10.00
KN3 Kirk Nieuwenhuis 4.00 10.00
LL1 Lance Lynn 5.00 12.00
LL2 Lance Lynn 5.00 12.00
LL3 Lance Lynn 5.00 12.00
MA1 Matt Adams 10.00 25.00
MA2 Matt Adams 10.00 25.00
MA3 Matt Adams 10.00 25.00
MC1 Matt Cain 6.00 15.00
MC2 Matt Cain 6.00 15.00
MM Mike Mussina EXCH 12.50 30.00
MO1 Mike Olt 4.00 10.00
MO2 Mike Olt 4.00 10.00
MO3 Mike Olt 4.00 10.00
MO4 Mike Olt 4.00 10.00
MO5 Mike Olt 4.00 10.00
MT1 Mark Trumbo 6.00 15.00
MT2 Mark Trumbo 6.00 15.00
MT3 Mark Trumbo 6.00 15.00
NG Nomar Garciaparra 15.00 40.00
PF Prince Fielder 12.00 30.00
PG1 Paul Goldschmidt 10.00 25.00
PG2 Paul Goldschmidt 10.00 25.00
PG3 Paul Goldschmidt 10.00 25.00
PG4 Paul Goldschmidt 10.00 25.00
PG5 Paul Goldschmidt 10.00 25.00
RD R.A. Dickey 8.00 20.00
SM1 Shelby Miller 8.00 20.00
SM2 Shelby Miller 8.00 20.00
SM3 Shelby Miller 8.00 20.00
SM4 Shelby Miller 8.00 20.00
SM5 Shelby Miller 8.00 20.00
TC1 Tony Cingrani 6.00 15.00
TC2 Tony Cingrani 6.00 15.00
TC3 Tony Cingrani 6.00 15.00
TC4 Tony Cingrani 6.00 15.00
TC5 Tony Cingrani 6.00 15.00
TG Tom Glavine EXCH 15.00 40.00
TS1 Tyler Skaggs 4.00 10.00
TS2 Tyler Skaggs 4.00 10.00
TS3 Tyler Skaggs 4.00 10.00
WM1 Will Middlebrooks 5.00 12.00
WM2 Will Middlebrooks 5.00 12.00
WM3 Will Middlebrooks 5.00 12.00
WM4 Will Middlebrooks 5.00 12.00
WM5 Will Middlebrooks 5.00 12.00
WMI1 Wade Miley 4.00 10.00
WMI2 Wade Miley 4.00 10.00
WP1 Wily Peralta 4.00 10.00
WP2 Wily Peralta 4.00 10.00
WP3 Wily Peralta 4.00 10.00
WR2 Wilin Rosario 4.00 10.00
YG1 Yovani Gallardo 4.00 10.00
YG2 Yovani Gallardo 4.00 10.00
ZC1 Zack Cozart 4.00 10.00
ZC2 Zack Cozart 4.00 10.00
ZC3 Zack Cozart 4.00 10.00

2013 Topps Triple Threads Unity Relic Autographs Emerald

*EMERALD: .5X TO 1.2X BASIC
STATED ODDS 1:11 MINI
STATED PRINT RUN 50 SER.#'d SETS
EXCHANGE DEADLINE 10/31/2016

2013 Topps Triple Threads Unity Relic Autographs Gold

*GOLD: .5X TO 1.2X BASIC
STATED ODDS 1:21 MINI
STATED PRINT RUN 25 SER.#'d SETS
NO PRICING ON MOST DUE SCARCITY
EXCHANGE DEADLINE 10/31/2016

2013 Topps Triple Threads Unity Relic Autographs Sapphire

*SAPPHIRE: 1X TO 2.5X BASIC
STATED ODDS 1:52 MINI
STATED PRINT RUN 10 SER.#'d SETS
NO PRICING ON MOST DUE SCARCITY
EXCHANGE DEADLINE 10/31/2016

2013 Topps Triple Threads Unity Relic Autographs Sepia

*SEPIA: .4X TO 1X BASIC
STATED ODDS 1:7 MINI
STATED PRINT RUN 75 SER.#'d SETS
EXCHANGE DEADLINE 10/31/2016

2013 Topps Triple Threads Unity Relics

STATED ODDS 1:6 MINI
STATED PRINT RUN 36 SER.#'d SETS
AB1 Adrian Beltre 4.00 10.00
AB2 Adrian Beltre 4.00 10.00
AB3 Adrian Beltre 4.00 10.00
AC1 Asdrubal Cabrera 4.00 10.00
AC2 Asdrubal Cabrera 4.00 10.00
ACR Allen Craig 10.00 25.00
AD Adam Dunn 4.00 10.00
AG Avisail Garcia 4.00 10.00
AGN1 Anthony Gose 4.00 10.00
AGN2 Anthony Gose 4.00 10.00
AGO1 Adrian Gonzalez 4.00 10.00
AGO2 Adrian Gonzalez 4.00 10.00
AGO3 Adrian Gonzalez 4.00 10.00
AGR Alex Gordon 4.00 10.00
AH Aaron Hicks 4.00 10.00
AJ Austin Jackson 4.00 10.00
AJ2 Austin Jackson 4.00 10.00
AJ3 Austin Jackson 4.00 10.00
AM1 Andrew McCutchen 20.00 50.00
AM2 Andrew McCutchen 20.00 50.00
AM3 Andrew McCutchen 20.00 50.00
AP Albert Pujols 5.00 12.00
AP1 Andy Pettitte 4.00 10.00
AP2 Andy Pettitte 4.00 10.00
AP3 Andy Pettitte 4.00 10.00
ARE1 Anthony Rendon 4.00 10.00
ARO1 Alex Rodriguez 8.00 20.00
ARO2 Alex Rodriguez 8.00 20.00
ARO3 Alex Rodriguez 8.00 20.00
BB Brandon Beachy 4.00 10.00
BBU Billy Butler 4.00 10.00
BF Bob Feller 15.00 40.00
BG Brett Gardner 5.00 12.00
BH1 Bryce Harper 10.00 25.00
BH2 Bryce Harper 10.00 25.00
BJ1 Bo Jackson 10.00 25.00
BJ2 Bo Jackson 10.00 25.00
BJ3 Bo Jackson 10.00 25.00
BL1 Brett Lawrie 4.00 10.00
BL2 Brett Lawrie 4.00 10.00
BP1 Brandon Phillips 4.00 10.00
BP2 Brandon Phillips 4.00 10.00
BP3 Brandon Phillips 4.00 10.00
BPO Buster Posey 15.00 40.00
BR Brooks Robinson 12.50 30.00
BU B.J. Upton 4.00 10.00
BZ1 Ben Zobrist 4.00 10.00
BZ2 Ben Zobrist 4.00 10.00
CB1 Clay Buchholz 4.00 10.00
CB2 Clay Buchholz 4.00 10.00
CB3 Clay Buchholz 4.00 10.00
CBH1 Chad Billingsley 4.00 10.00
CBI1 Craig Biggio 5.00 12.00
CBI2 Craig Biggio 5.00 12.00
CBI3 Craig Biggio 5.00 12.00
CC1 CC Sabathia 4.00 10.00
CC2 CC Sabathia 4.00 10.00
CC3 CC Sabathia 4.00 10.00
CF1 Carlton Fisk 5.00 12.00
CF2 Carlton Fisk 5.00 12.00
CF3 Carlton Fisk 5.00 12.00
CG1 Carlos Gonzalez 4.00 10.00
CG2 Carlos Gonzalez 4.00 10.00
CG3 Carlos Gonzalez 4.00 10.00
CGR1 Curtis Granderson 4.00 10.00
CGR2 Curtis Granderson 4.00 10.00
CGR3 Curtis Granderson 4.00 10.00
CH Corey Hart 4.00 10.00
CH1 Chase Headley 4.00 10.00
CH2 Chase Headley 4.00 10.00
CH3 Chase Headley 4.00 10.00
CJ1 Chipper Jones 10.00 25.00
CJ2 Chipper Jones 10.00 25.00
CJ3 Chipper Jones 10.00 25.00
CK1 Craig Kimbrel 6.00 15.00
CK2 Craig Kimbrel 6.00 15.00
CKE Casey Kelly 4.00 10.00
CR1 Carlos Ruiz 4.00 10.00
CR2 Carlos Ruiz 4.00 10.00
CS1 Chris Sale 4.00 10.00
CS2 Chris Sale 4.00 10.00
CS3 Chris Sale 4.00 10.00
CSA Carlos Santana 4.00 10.00
CW1 C.J. Wilson 4.00 10.00
CW2 C.J. Wilson 4.00 10.00
CW3 C.J. Wilson 4.00 10.00
DE1 Dennis Eckersley 4.00 10.00
DF David Freese 5.00 12.00
DH Derek Holland 4.00 10.00
DJ1 Derek Jeter 12.50 30.00
DJ2 Derek Jeter 12.50 30.00
DJ3 Derek Jeter 12.50 30.00
DJE Desmond Jennings 4.00 10.00
DM1 Don Mattingly 12.50 30.00
DM2 Don Mattingly 12.50 30.00
DM3 Don Mattingly 12.50 30.00

DP1 Dustin Pedroia 5.00 12.00
DP2 Dustin Pedroia 5.00 12.00
DP3 Dustin Pedroia 5.00 12.00
DPR1 David Price 4.00 10.00
DPR2 David Price 4.00 10.00
DPR3 David Price 4.00 10.00
DS1 Don Sutton 4.00 10.00
DS2 Don Sutton 4.00 10.00
DS3 Don Sutton 4.00 10.00
EA1 Elvis Andrus 4.00 10.00
EA2 Elvis Andrus 4.00 10.00
EA3 Elvis Andrus 4.00 10.00
EB Ernie Banks 10.00 25.00
EE1 Edwin Encarnacion 4.00 10.00
EE2 Edwin Encarnacion 4.00 10.00
EH Eric Hosmer 4.00 10.00
EL1 Evan Longoria 4.00 10.00
EL2 Evan Longoria 4.00 10.00
EL3 Evan Longoria 4.00 10.00
EM Eddie Murray 8.00 20.00
FF Freddie Freeman 6.00 15.00
FH1 Felix Hernandez 4.00 10.00
FH2 Felix Hernandez 4.00 10.00
FH3 Felix Hernandez 4.00 10.00
FM1 Fred McGriff 5.00 12.00
FM2 Fred McGriff 5.00 12.00
FM3 Fred McGriff 5.00 12.00
GM1 Greg Maddux 10.00 25.00
GM2 Greg Maddux 10.00 25.00
GM3 Greg Maddux 10.00 25.00
GS Gary Sheffield 4.00 10.00
GS2 Gary Sheffield 4.00 10.00
GS3 Gary Sheffield 4.00 10.00
GST1 Giancarlo Stanton 5.00 12.00
GST2 Giancarlo Stanton 5.00 12.00
HW1 Hoyt Wilhelm 8.00 20.00
HW2 Hoyt Wilhelm 8.00 20.00
ID1 Ian Desmond 4.00 10.00
ID2 Ian Desmond 4.00 10.00
JB Johnny Bench 12.50 30.00
JBA1 Jose Bautista 4.00 10.00
JBA2 Jose Bautista 4.00 10.00
JBA3 Jose Bautista 4.00 10.00
JBR1 Jay Bruce 4.00 10.00
JBR2 Jay Bruce 4.00 10.00
JBR3 Jay Bruce 4.00 10.00
JBU1 Jim Bunning 6.00 15.00
JBU2 Jim Bunning 6.00 15.00
JC1 Johnny Cueto 4.00 10.00
JC2 Johnny Cueto 4.00 10.00
JC3 Johnny Cueto 4.00 10.00
JE1 Jacoby Ellsbury 6.00 15.00
JE2 Jacoby Ellsbury 6.00 15.00
JG Jedd Gyorko 5.00 12.00
JG1 Jaime Garcia 4.00 10.00
JG2 Jaime Garcia 4.00 10.00
JG3 Jaime Garcia 4.00 10.00
JH1 Josh Hamilton 4.00 10.00
JH2 Josh Hamilton 4.00 10.00
JH3 Josh Hamilton 4.00 10.00
JHE1 Jason Heyward 4.00 10.00
JHE2 Jason Heyward 4.00 10.00
JK Jason Kubel 4.00 10.00
JL1 Jon Lester 4.00 10.00
JL2 Jon Lester 4.00 10.00
JL3 Jon Lester 4.00 10.00
JM Justin Masterson 6.00 15.00
JMA Joe Mauer 5.00 12.00
JP1 Jake Peavy 4.00 10.00
JP2 Jake Peavy 4.00 10.00
JR1 Jim Rice 6.00 15.00
JR2 Jim Rice 6.00 15.00
JRO1 Jimmy Rollins 4.00 10.00
JRO2 Jimmy Rollins 4.00 10.00
JS Jean Segura 4.00 10.00
JS2 Jean Segura 4.00 10.00
JS3 Jean Segura 4.00 10.00
JT Jose Tabata 4.00 10.00
JU1 Justin Upton 4.00 10.00
JU2 Justin Upton 4.00 10.00
JU3 Justin Upton 4.00 10.00
JV1 Joey Votto 8.00 20.00
JV2 Joey Votto 8.00 20.00
JV3 Joey Votto 8.00 20.00
JVE1 Justin Verlander 5.00 12.00
JVE2 Justin Verlander 5.00 12.00
JVE3 Justin Verlander 5.00 12.00
JW1 Jayson Werth 4.00 10.00
JW2 Jayson Werth 4.00 10.00
JW3 Jayson Werth 4.00 10.00
JZ1 Jordan Zimmermann 4.00 10.00
KG1 Ken Griffey Jr. 10.00 25.00
KG2 Ken Griffey Jr. 10.00 25.00
KG3 Ken Griffey Jr. 10.00 25.00
KS Kyle Seager 5.00 12.00
LL Lance Lynn 5.00 12.00
MB1 Madison Bumgarner 10.00 25.00
MB2 Madison Bumgarner 10.00 25.00
MB3 Madison Bumgarner 10.00 25.00
MC1 Miguel Cabrera 8.00 20.00
MC2 Miguel Cabrera 8.00 20.00
MC3 Miguel Cabrera 8.00 20.00
MCA1 Matt Cain 4.00 10.00
MCA2 Matt Cain 4.00 10.00
MCA3 Matt Cain 4.00 10.00
MH1 Matt Harvey 5.00 12.00
MH2 Matt Harvey 5.00 12.00
MH3 Matt Harvey 5.00 12.00
MHO1 Matt Holliday 5.00 12.00
MHO2 Matt Holliday 5.00 12.00
MHO3 Matt Holliday 5.00 12.00
MJ Matt Joyce 4.00 10.00
MK1 Matt Kemp 4.00 10.00
MK2 Matt Kemp 4.00 10.00
MK3 Matt Kemp 4.00 10.00
ML1 Mat Latos 4.00 10.00
ML2 Mat Latos 4.00 10.00
ML3 Mat Latos 4.00 10.00
MMA1 Matt Moore 4.00 10.00
MMA2 Matt Moore 4.00 10.00
MMA3 Matt Moore 4.00 10.00
MMO Mike Moustakas 4.00 10.00
MMU1 Mike Mussina 4.00 10.00
MMU2 Mike Mussina 4.00 10.00
MMU3 Mike Mussina 4.00 10.00
MO Mike Olt 4.00 10.00
MO2 Mike Olt 4.00 10.00
MR1 Mariano Rivera 12.50 30.00
MR2 Mariano Rivera 12.50 30.00
MR3 Mariano Rivera 12.50 30.00
MS1 Max Scherzer 6.00 15.00
MS2 Max Scherzer 6.00 15.00
MS3 Max Scherzer 6.00 15.00
MSC Mike Schmidt 8.00 20.00
MT1 Mark Teixeira 4.00 10.00
MT2 Mark Teixeira 4.00 10.00
MT3 Mark Teixeira 4.00 10.00
NA1 Nolan Arenado 6.00 15.00
NA2 Nolan Arenado 6.00 15.00
NAO Norichika Aoki 6.00 15.00
NC Nelson Cruz 4.00 10.00
NG1 Nomar Garciaparra 6.00 15.00
NG2 Nomar Garciaparra 6.00 15.00
NG3 Nomar Garciaparra 6.00 15.00
NW Neil Walker 4.00 10.00
NW2 Neil Walker 4.00 10.00
NW3 Neil Walker 4.00 10.00
OC1 Orlando Cepeda 10.00 25.00
OC2 Orlando Cepeda 10.00 25.00
PA Pedro Alvarez 5.00 12.00
PF1 Prince Fielder 6.00 15.00
PF2 Prince Fielder 6.00 15.00
PF3 Prince Fielder 6.00 15.00
PK Paul Konerko 4.00 10.00
PM1 Paul Molitor 5.00 12.00
PM2 Paul Molitor 5.00 12.00
PM3 Paul Molitor 5.00 12.00
PN1 Phil Niekro 5.00 12.00
PN2 Phil Niekro 5.00 12.00
PN3 Phil Niekro 5.00 12.00
PO Paul O'Neill 4.00 10.00
PS1 Pablo Sandoval 4.00 10.00
PS2 Pablo Sandoval 4.00 10.00
PS3 Pablo Sandoval 4.00 10.00
RB1 Ryan Braun 4.00 10.00
RB2 Ryan Braun 4.00 10.00
RB3 Ryan Braun 4.00 10.00
RC1 Robinson Cano 5.00 12.00
RC2 Robinson Cano 5.00 12.00
RC3 Robinson Cano 5.00 12.00
RCL Roberto Clemente 40.00 80.00
RDI1 R.A. Dickey 4.00 10.00
RDI2 R.A. Dickey 4.00 10.00
RDI3 R.A. Dickey 4.00 10.00
RH1 Rickey Henderson 10.00 25.00
RH2 Rickey Henderson 10.00 25.00
RH3 Rickey Henderson 10.00 25.00
RHO Ryan Howard 4.00 10.00
RJ Reggie Jackson 6.00 15.00
RJ2 Reggie Jackson 6.00 15.00
RV Ryan Vogelsong 6.00 15.00
RW Rickie Weeks 4.00 10.00
RW2 Rickie Weeks 4.00 10.00
RY Robin Yount 6.00 15.00
RZ1 Ryan Zimmerman 4.00 10.00
RZ2 Ryan Zimmerman 4.00 10.00
RZ3 Ryan Zimmerman 4.00 10.00
SC1 Starlin Castro 4.00 10.00
SC2 Starlin Castro 4.00 10.00
SC3 Starlin Castro 4.00 10.00
SCH Shin-Soo Choo 6.00 15.00
SR1 Scott Rolen 4.00 10.00
SR2 Scott Rolen 4.00 10.00
SR3 Scott Rolen 4.00 10.00
SS1 Stephen Strasburg 6.00 15.00
SS2 Stephen Strasburg 6.00 15.00
SS3 Stephen Strasburg 6.00 15.00
TB Trevor Bauer 4.00 10.00
TC1 Tony Cingrani 4.00 10.00
TC2 Tony Cingrani 4.00 10.00
TG1 Tony Gwynn 10.00 25.00
TG2 Tony Gwynn 10.00 25.00
TG3 Tony Gwynn 10.00 25.00
TH Tim Hudson 4.00 10.00
TL1 Tim Lincecum 4.00 10.00
TL2 Tim Lincecum 4.00 10.00
TL3 Tim Lincecum 4.00 10.00
TT1 Troy Tulowitzki 4.00 10.00
TT2 Troy Tulowitzki 4.00 10.00
TT3 Troy Tulowitzki 4.00 10.00
UJ Ubaldo Jimenez 4.00 10.00
VM Victor Martinez 4.00 10.00
VM2 Victor Martinez 4.00 10.00
WM1 Wade Miley 4.00 10.00
WM2 Wade Miley 4.00 10.00
WM3 Wade Miley 4.00 10.00
WMC Willie McCovey 8.00 20.00
WS Willie Stargell 8.00 20.00
YA Yonder Alonso 4.00 10.00
YB Yogi Berra 6.00 15.00
YC1 Yoenis Cespedes 5.00 12.00
YC2 Yoenis Cespedes 5.00 12.00
YD1 Yu Darvish 10.00 25.00
YD2 Yu Darvish 10.00 25.00
YD3 Yu Darvish 10.00 25.00
YG1 Yovani Gallardo 4.00 10.00
YG2 Yovani Gallardo 4.00 10.00
YP3 Yasiel Puig 20.00 50.00

2013 Topps Triple Threads Unity Relics Emerald

*EMERALD: .5X TO 1.2X BASIC
STATED ODDS 1:11 MINI
STATED PRINT RUN 18 SER.#'d SETS
ALL VERSIONS EQUALLY PRICED
SOME NOT PRICED DUE TO SCARCITY

2013 Topps Triple Threads Unity Relics Gold

*GOLD: .6X TO 1.5X BASIC
STATED ODDS 1:21 MINI
STATED PRINT RUN 9 SER.#'d SETS
ALL VERSIONS EQUALLY PRICED
SOME NOT PRICED DUE TO SCARCITY

2013 Topps Triple Threads Unity Relics Sepia

*SEPIA: .4X TO 1X BASIC
STATED ODDS 1:7 MINI
STATED PRINT RUN 27 SER.#'d SETS

2014 Topps Triple Threads

COMP.SET w/o AU's (100) 100.00 200.00
JSY AU RC ODDS 1:12 MINI
JSY AU RC PRINT RUN 99 SER.#'d SETS
JSY AU ODDS 1:12 MINI
JSY AU PRINT RUN 99 SER.#'d SETS
EXCHANGE DEADLINE 9/30/2017
1-100 PLATE ODDS 1:109 MINI
102-160 PLATE ODDS 1:266 MINI
PLATE PRINT RUN 1 SET PER COLOR
BLACK-CYAN-MAGENTA-YELLOW ISSUED
NO PLATE PRICING DUE TO SCARCITY
1 Mike Trout 4.00 10.00
2 George Brett 1.50 4.00
3 Babe Ruth 2.00 5.00
4 Gerrit Cole .75 2.00
5 Joe DiMaggio 1.50 4.00
6 Yangervis Solarte RC .50 1.25
7 Ty Cobb 1.25 3.00
8 Roger Clemens 1.00 2.50
9 Yasiel Puig .75 2.00
10 Allen Craig .60 1.50
11 Justin Verlander .75 2.00
12 Al Kaline .75 2.00
13 Shin-Soo Choo .60 1.50
14 Evan Longoria .60 1.50
15 Josh Hamilton .60 1.50
16 Brooks Robinson .60 1.50
17 Carlos Beltran .60 1.50
18 Rickey Henderson .75 2.00
19 Paul Goldschmidt .75 2.00
20 Adrian Gonzalez .60 1.50
21 Robin Yount .75 2.00
22 Eddie Mathews .75 2.00
23 Tom Seaver .60 1.50
24 Mike Schmidt 1.25 3.00
25 Ted Williams 1.50 4.00
26 Jeff Bagwell .60 1.50
27 Willie Mays 1.50 4.00
28 Stephen Strasburg .75 2.00
29 Johnny Bench .75 2.00
30 Miguel Cabrera .75 2.00
31 Mike Piazza .75 2.00
32 Adrian Beltre .75 2.00
33 Jose Bautista .60 1.50
34 Pedro Martinez .60 1.50
35 Jose Abreu RC 4.00 10.00
36 Derek Jeter 2.00 5.00
37 Jon Singleton RC .60 1.50
38 Adam Jones .60 1.50
39 Ozzie Smith 1.00 2.50
40 John Smoltz .75 2.00
41 Masahiro Tanaka RC 1.50 4.00
42 Madison Bumgarner .60 1.50
43 Jacoby Ellsbury .60 1.50
44 Bryce Harper 1.25 3.00
45 Hyun-Jin Ryu .60 1.50
46 David Wright .60 1.50
47 Mariano Rivera 1.00 2.50
48 Robinson Cano .60 1.50
49 Max Scherzer .75 2.00
50 Roberto Clemente 2.00 5.00
51 Yoenis Cespedes .50 1.25
52 Carlos Gonzalez .60 1.50
53 Craig Kimbrel .60 1.50
54 Justin Upton .60 1.50
55 Ryan Braun .60 1.50
56 Ernie Banks .75 2.00
57 Chris Sale .75 2.00
58 Giancarlo Stanton .60 1.50
59 Matt Holliday .75 2.00
60 Joey Votto .75 2.00
61 Randy Johnson .75 2.00
62 Prince Fielder .60 1.50
63 Reggie Jackson .60 1.50
64 Felix Hernandez .60 1.50
65 Don Mattingly 1.50 4.00
66 Jackie Robinson .75 2.00
67 Jim Palmer .60 1.50
68 Gregory Polanco RC .75 2.00
69 Nolan Ryan 2.50 6.00
70 Bo Jackson .75 2.00
71 Pedro Alvarez .50 1.25
72 Albert Pujols 1.00 2.50
73 Dustin Pedroia .75 2.00
74 Jose Canseco .60 1.50
75 Sandy Koufax 1.50 4.00
76 Chris Davis .50 1.25
77 Jose Reyes .60 1.50
78 Joe Mauer .60 1.50
79 Yu Darvish .75 2.00
80 Mark McGwire 1.50 4.00
81 Greg Maddux 1.00 2.50
82 Hanley Ramirez .60 1.50
83 Ian Kinsler .60 1.50
84 Clayton Kershaw 1.25 3.00
85 Jose Fernandez .75 2.00
86 George Springer RC 2.00 5.00
87 Oscar Taveras RC .60 1.50
88 Jim Rice .60 1.50
89 Cliff Lee .60 1.50
90 Adam Wainwright .60 1.50
91 David Ortiz .75 2.00
92 Stan Musial 1.25 3.00
93 Freddie Freeman 1.00 2.50
94 Andrew McCutchen .75 2.00
95 Yadier Molina 1.00 2.50
96 Cal Ripken Jr. 2.50 6.00
97 Tony Gwynn .75 2.00
98 Troy Tulowitzki .75 2.00
99 Buster Posey 1.00 2.50
100 Ken Griffey Jr. 1.50 4.00
102 Jurickson Profar JSY AU EXCH 6.00 15.00
103 Josh Donaldson JSY AU 15.00 40.00
105 Kolten Wong JSY AU RC 8.00 20.00
107 Patrick Corbin JSY AU 6.00 15.00
108 Wilmer Flores JSY AU RC 8.00 20.00
109 Julio Teheran JSY AU 6.00 15.00
110 Enny Romero JSY AU RC 6.00 15.00
112 Tony Cingrani JSY AU 6.00 15.00
113 L.J. Hoes JSY AU 5.00 12.00
114 Tyler Chatwood JSY AU 5.00 12.00
115 Manny Machado JSY AU 20.00 50.00
116 Matt Adams JSY AU 8.00 20.00
117 Andrelton Simmons JSY AU 4.00 10.00
118 Casey Kelly JSY AU 6.00 15.00
119 Matt Carpenter JSY AU 10.00 25.00
120 Travis d'Arnaud JSY AU RC 12.00 30.00
121 Joe Kelly JSY AU 5.00 12.00
122 Jimmy Nelson JSY AU RC 6.00 15.00
123 Jonathan Schoop JSY AU RC 6.00 15.00
124 Christian Yelich JSY AU 25.00 60.00
126 Allen Webster JSY AU 5.00 12.00
127 Carlos Martinez JSY AU 10.00 25.00
128 Taijuan Walker JSY AU RC 12.00 30.00
129 Evan Gattis JSY AU 10.00 25.00
130 Yordano Ventura JSY AU RC 10.00 25.00
131 Chris Owings JSY AU RC 6.00 15.00
132 Zack Wheeler JSY AU 10.00 25.00
133 Kevin Gausman JSY AU 8.00 20.00
135 Junior Lake JSY AU 5.00 12.00
138 Mike Zunino JSY AU 5.00 12.00
139 Cody Asche JSY AU 10.00 25.00
140 Sonny Gray JSY AU 12.00 30.00
141 Michael Choice JSY AU RC 6.00 15.00
142 Taylor Jordan JSY AU (RC) 6.00 15.00
143 Shelby Miller JSY AU 8.00 15.00
145 Jake Odorizzi JSY AU 5.00 12.00
155 Marcell Ozuna JSY AU 8.00 20.00
157 Andrew Lambo JSY AU RC 6.00 15.00
158 Mike Olt JSY AU EXCH 5.00 12.00
160 John Ryan Murphy JSY AU RC 12.00 30.00

2014 Topps Triple Threads Amber

*AMBER: 1.2X TO 3X BASIC
*AMBER RC: 1.2X TO 3X BASIC RC
STATED ODDS 1:4 MINI
STATED PRINT RUN 125 SER.#'d SETS
35 Jose Abreu 10.00 25.00
36 Derek Jeter 10.00 25.00
96 Cal Ripken Jr. 6.00 15.00

2014 Topps Triple Threads Amethyst

*AMETHYST: .75X TO 2X BASIC
*AMETHYST RC: .75X TO 2X BASIC RC
RANDOM INSETS IN PACKS
STATED PRINT RUN 325 SER.#'d SETS
35 Jose Abreu 6.00 15.00
36 Derek Jeter 6.00 15.00
96 Cal Ripken Jr. 4.00 10.00

2014 Topps Triple Threads Black

*BLCK JSY AU: .5X TO 1.2X BASIC
*BLCK JSY AU RC: .5X TO 1.2X BASIC
STATED ODDS 1:31 MINI
STATED PRINT RUN 35 SER.#'d SETS
EXCHANGE DEADLINE 9/30/2017

2014 Topps Triple Threads Emerald

*EMRLD: .75X TO 2X BASIC
*EMRLD RC: .75X TO 2X BASIC RC
1-100 ODDS 1:2 MINI
1-100 PRINT RUN 250 SER.#'d SETS
*EMRLD JSY AU: .4X TO 1X BASIC
*EMRLD JSY AU RC: .4X TO 1X BASIC
102-160 ODDS 1:22 MINI
102-160 PRINT RUN 50 SER.#'d SETS
EXCHANGE DEADLINE 9/30/2017
35 Jose Abreu 6.00 15.00
36 Derek Jeter 6.00 15.00
96 Cal Ripken Jr. 4.00 10.00

2014 Topps Triple Threads Gold

*GOLD: 1.2X TO 3X BASIC
*GOLD RC: 1.2X TO 3X BASIC RC
STATED ODDS 1:5 MINI
STATED PRINT RUN 99 SER.#'d SETS
35 Jose Abreu 15.00 40.00
96 Cal Ripken Jr. 6.00 15.00

2014 Topps Triple Threads Onyx

*BLACK: 2X TO 5X BASIC
*BLACK RC: 2X TO 5X BASIC RC
STATED ODDS 1:9 MINI
STATED PRINT RUN 50 SER.#'d SETS
36 Derek Jeter 20.00 50.00

2014 Topps Triple Threads Sapphire

*SAPPHIRE: 2.5X TO 6X BASIC
*SAPPHIRE RC: 2.5X TO 6X BASIC RC
STATED ODDS 1:18 MINI
STATED PRINT RUN 25 SER.#'d SETS
1 Mike Trout 30.00 80.00
36 Derek Jeter 30.00 80.00
69 Nolan Ryan 30.00 80.00
75 Sandy Koufax 20.00 50.00
80 Mark McGwire 25.00 60.00
96 Cal Ripken Jr. 30.00 80.00

2014 Topps Triple Threads Sepia

*SEPIA JSY AU: .4X TO 1X BASIC
*SEPIA JSY AU RC: .4X TO 1X BASIC
STATED ODDS 1:15 MINI
STATED PRINT RUN 75 SER.#'d SETS
EXCHANGE DEADLINE 9/30/2017

2014 Topps Triple Threads Autograph Relic Combos

STATED ODDS 1:76 MINI
STATED PRINT RUN 36 SER.#'d SETS
EXCHANGE DEADLINE 9/30/2017
PRINTING PLATE ODDS 1:686 MINI
PLATE PRINT RUN 1 SET PER COLOR
BLACK-CYAN-MAGENTA-YELLOW ISSUED
NO PLATE PRICING DUE TO SCARCITY
TTARCCMS Myrs/Cbrr/Schrzr EXCH 60.00 150.00
TTARCCPD Cspds/Dnldsn/Prkr 15.00 40.00
TTARCCTJ Trt/Cspds/Jns 150.00 300.00
TTARCFSS Schrzr/Sl/Frndz 40.00 100.00
TTARCGFA Gldschmdt/Adms/Frmn 30.00 80.00
TTARCGMA McGwr/Almr/Griff Jr. 150.00 400.00
TTARCGMS Mddx/Smltz/Glvne 250.00 400.00
TTARCGRG Rns/Grrr/Gnzlz 25.00 60.00
TTARCHFG Gtts/Hywrd/Frmn 30.00 80.00
TTARCLFS Santana/Longoria/Frazier 20.00 50.00
TTARCMLC Cobb/Longoria/Moore 20.00 50.00
TTARCMMW Miller/Wong/Martinez 20.00 50.00
TTARCMTM Trt/Myrs/Mchdo 100.00 200.00
TTARCPWH Mrtnz/Wrght/Pzza 60.00 150.00
TTARCSFK Schrzr/Krshw/Frnndz 75.00 150.00
TTARCVPF Phillips/Votto/Frazier 30.00 80.00

2014 Topps Triple Threads Autograph Relic Combos Emerald

*EMERALD: .5X TO 1.2X BASIC
STATED ODDS 1:151 MINI
STATED PRINT RUN 18 SER.#'d SETS
OVERALL 1-100 PLATE ODDS 1:109 MINI

2014 Topps Triple Threads Autograph Relic Combos Sepia

*SEPIA: .4X TO 1X BASIC
STATED ODDS 1:101 MINI
STATED PRINT RUN 27 SER.#'d SETS
OVERALL 1-100 PLATE ODDS 1:109 MINI

2014 Topps Triple Threads Legend Relics

STATED ODDS 1:61 MINI
STATED PRINT RUN 36 SER.#'d SETS
TTRLCR Cal Ripken Jr. 12.00 30.00
TTRLEM Eddie Mathews 15.00 40.00
TTRLHA Hank Aaron 50.00 100.00
TTRLJB Johnny Bench 10.00 25.00
TTRLJM Joe Morgan 12.00 30.00
TTRLKG Ken Griffey Jr. 20.00 50.00
TTRLMR Mariano Rivera 12.00 30.00
TTRLMS Mike Schmidt 10.00 25.00
TTRLNR Nolan Ryan 30.00 80.00
TTRLPM Pedro Martinez 12.00 30.00
TTRLRC Roberto Clemente 40.00 100.00
TTRLRCL Roger Clemens 10.00 25.00
TTRLRH Rickey Henderson 15.00 40.00
TTRLRJ Randy Johnson 15.00 40.00
TTRLSC Steve Carlton 12.00 30.00
TTRLTC Ty Cobb 30.00 80.00
TTRLTS Tom Seaver 12.00 30.00
TTRLTW Ted Williams 30.00 80.00
TTRLWM Willie Mays 40.00 80.00

2014 Topps Triple Threads Legend Relics Emerald

*EMERALD: .4X TO 1X BASIC
STATED ODDS 1:121 MINI
STATED PRINT RUN 18 SER.#'d SETS

2014 Topps Triple Threads Legend Relics Sepia

*SEPIA: .4X TO 1X BASIC
STATED ODDS 1:81 MINI
STATED PRINT RUN 27 SER.#'d SETS

2014 Topps Triple Threads Relic Autographs

STATED ODDS 1:10 MINI
STATED PRINT RUN 18 SER.#'d SETS
EXCHANGE DEADLINE 9/30/2017
PRINTING PLATE ODDS 1:43 MINI
PLATE PRINT RUN 1 SET PER COLOR
BLACK-CYAN-MAGENTA-YELLOW ISSUED
NO PLATE PRICING DUE TO SCARCITY
TTARAC1 Allen Craig 12.00 30.00
TTARAC2 Allen Craig 12.00 30.00
TTARAC3 Allen Craig 12.00 30.00
TTARAC4 Allen Craig 12.00 30.00
TTARAC5 Allen Craig 12.00 30.00
TTARAJ1 Adam Jones 15.00 40.00
TTARAR1 Anthony Rizzo 25.00 60.00
TTARAR2 Anthony Rizzo 25.00 60.00
TTARAR3 Anthony Rizzo 25.00 60.00
TTARBG1 Brett Gardner 10.00 25.00
TTARBG2 Brett Gardner 10.00 25.00
TTARBG3 Brett Gardner 10.00 25.00
TTARBH1 Bryce Harper 75.00 150.00
TTARBH2 Bryce Harper 75.00 150.00
TTARBH3 Bryce Harper 75.00 150.00
TTARBHA1 Billy Hamilton 15.00 40.00
TTARBHA2 Billy Hamilton 15.00 40.00
TTARBHA3 Billy Hamilton 15.00 40.00
TTARBHA4 Billy Hamilton 15.00 40.00
TTARBHA5 Billy Hamilton 15.00 40.00
TTARBM1 Brian McCann 15.00 40.00
TTARBM2 Brian McCann 15.00 40.00
TTARBM3 Brian McCann 15.00 40.00
TTARBP1 Brandon Phillips 8.00 20.00
TTARBP2 Brandon Phillips 8.00 20.00
TTARBP3 Brandon Phillips 8.00 20.00
TTARBZ1 Ben Zobrist 15.00 40.00
TTARBZ2 Ben Zobrist 15.00 40.00
TTARBZ3 Ben Zobrist 15.00 40.00
TTARCA1 Chris Archer 5.00 12.00
TTARCA2 Chris Archer 5.00 12.00
TTARCA3 Chris Archer 5.00 12.00
TTARCA4 Chris Archer 5.00 12.00
TTARCA5 Chris Archer 5.00 12.00
TTARCB1 Christian Bethancourt 5.00 12.00
TTARCB2 Christian Bethancourt 5.00 12.00
TTARCB3 Christian Bethancourt 5.00 12.00
TTARCB4 Christian Bethancourt 5.00 12.00
TTARCB5 Christian Bethancourt 5.00 12.00
TTARCH1 Cole Hamels 12.00 30.00
TTARCO1 Chris Owings 8.00 20.00
TTARCO2 Chris Owings 8.00 20.00
TTARCO3 Chris Owings 8.00 20.00
TTARCO4 Chris Owings 8.00 20.00
TTARCO5 Chris Owings 8.00 20.00
TTARCR1 Cal Ripken Jr. 60.00 150.00
TTARCR2 Cal Ripken Jr. 60.00 150.00
TTARCR3 Cal Ripken Jr. 60.00 150.00
TTARCS1 Chris Sale 15.00 40.00
TTARCS2 Chris Sale 15.00 40.00
TTARCS3 Chris Sale 15.00 40.00
TTARCSA1 Carlos Santana 6.00 15.00
TTARCSA2 Carlos Santana 6.00 15.00
TTARCSA3 Carlos Santana 6.00 15.00
TTARCSA4 Carlos Santana 6.00 15.00
TTARCSA5 Carlos Santana 6.00 15.00
TTARCW1 C.J. Wilson 8.00 20.00
TTARCW2 C.J. Wilson 8.00 20.00
TTARCW3 C.J. Wilson 8.00 20.00
TTARCY1 Christian Yelich 20.00 50.00
TTARCY2 Christian Yelich 20.00 50.00
TTARCY3 Christian Yelich 20.00 50.00
TTARDG1 Didi Gregorius 6.00 15.00
TTARDG2 Didi Gregorius 6.00 15.00
TTARDG3 Didi Gregorius 6.00 15.00
TTARDG4 Didi Gregorius 6.00 15.00
TTARDG5 Didi Gregorius 6.00 15.00
TTARDM1 Dale Murphy 30.00 80.00
TTARDM2 Dale Murphy 30.00 80.00
TTARDM3 Dale Murphy 30.00 80.00
TTARDMA1 Daisuke Matsuzaka 40.00 100.00
TTARDMA2 Daisuke Matsuzaka 40.00 100.00
TTARDMA3 Daisuke Matsuzaka 40.00 100.00
TTARDN1 Daniel Nava 12.00 30.00
TTARDN2 Daniel Nava 12.00 30.00
TTARDN3 Daniel Nava 12.00 30.00
TTARDN4 Daniel Nava 12.00 30.00
TTARDN5 Daniel Nava 12.00 30.00
TTARED1 Eric Davis 12.00 30.00
TTARED2 Eric Davis 12.00 30.00
TTARED3 Eric Davis 12.00 30.00
TTARED4 Eric Davis 12.00 30.00
TTARED5 Eric Davis 12.00 30.00
TTARFF1 Freddie Freeman 20.00 50.00
TTARFF2 Freddie Freeman 20.00 50.00
TTARFF3 Freddie Freeman 20.00 50.00
TTARFM1 Fred McGriff 12.00 30.00
TTARFM2 Fred McGriff 12.00 30.00
TTARFM3 Fred McGriff 12.00 30.00
TTARFV1 Fernando Valenzuela 40.00 100.00
TTARFV2 Fernando Valenzuela 40.00 100.00
TTARFV3 Fernando Valenzuela 40.00 100.00
TTARHA1 Hank Aaron 150.00 300.00
TTARHA2 Hank Aaron 150.00 300.00
TTARHA3 Hank Aaron 150.00 300.00
TTARJD1 Josh Donaldson 10.00 25.00
TTARJD2 Josh Donaldson 10.00 25.00
TTARJD3 Josh Donaldson 10.00 25.00
TTARJD4 Josh Donaldson 10.00 25.00
TTARJD5 Josh Donaldson 10.00 25.00
TTARJG1 Juan Gonzalez 25.00 60.00
TTARJG2 Juan Gonzalez 25.00 60.00
TTARJG3 Juan Gonzalez 25.00 60.00
TTARJH1 Jason Heyward 10.00 25.00
TTARJH2 Jason Heyward 10.00 25.00
TTARJH3 Jason Heyward 10.00 25.00
TTARJP1 Jarrod Parker 5.00 12.00
TTARJP2 Jarrod Parker 5.00 12.00
TTARJP3 Jarrod Parker 5.00 12.00
TTARJPR1 Jurickson Profar EXCH 10.00 25.00
TTARJPR2 Jurickson Profar EXCH 10.00 25.00
TTARJPR3 Jurickson Profar EXCH 10.00 25.00
TTARJR1 Jim Rice 12.00 30.00
TTARJR2 Jim Rice 12.00 30.00
TTARJR3 Jim Rice 12.00 30.00
TTARJS1 John Smoltz 25.00 60.00
TTARKG1 Ken Griffey Jr. 150.00 300.00
TTARKG2 Ken Griffey Jr. 150.00 300.00
TTARKG3 Ken Griffey Jr. 150.00 300.00
TTARKU1 Koji Uehara 30.00 80.00
TTARKU2 Koji Uehara 30.00 80.00
TTARKU3 Koji Uehara 30.00 80.00
TTARKW1 Kolten Wong 6.00 15.00
TTARLG1 Luis Gonzalez 8.00 20.00
TTARLG2 Luis Gonzalez 8.00 20.00
TTARLG3 Luis Gonzalez 8.00 20.00
TTARLH1 Livan Hernandez 5.00 12.00
TTARLH2 Livan Hernandez 5.00 12.00
TTARLH3 Livan Hernandez 5.00 12.00
TTARMA1 Matt Adams 10.00 25.00
TTARMA2 Matt Adams 10.00 25.00
TTARMA3 Matt Adams 10.00 25.00
TTARMA4 Matt Adams 10.00 25.00
TTARMA5 Matt Adams 10.00 25.00
TTARMC1 Miguel Cabrera EXCH 75.00 150.00
TTARMC2 Miguel Cabrera EXCH 75.00 150.00
TTARMC3 Miguel Cabrera EXCH 75.00 150.00
TTARMCA1 Matt Carpenter 15.00 40.00
TTARMCA2 Matt Carpenter 15.00 40.00
TTARMCA3 Matt Carpenter 15.00 40.00
TTARMCN1 Matt Cain 10.00 25.00
TTARMCN2 Matt Cain 10.00 25.00
TTARMCN3 Matt Cain 10.00 25.00
TTARMCU1 Michael Cuddyer 5.00 12.00
TTARMCU2 Michael Cuddyer 5.00 12.00
TTARMCU3 Michael Cuddyer 5.00 12.00
TTARMD1 Matt Davidson 6.00 15.00
TTARMD2 Matt Davidson 6.00 15.00
TTARMD3 Matt Davidson 6.00 15.00
TTARMM1 Mike Minor 6.00 15.00
TTARMM2 Mike Minor 6.00 15.00
TTARMM3 Mike Minor 6.00 15.00
TTARMM4 Mike Minor 6.00 15.00
TTARMM5 Mike Minor 6.00 15.00
TTARMMA1 Manny Machado 30.00 60.00
TTARMMA2 Manny Machado 30.00 60.00
TTARMMA3 Manny Machado 30.00 60.00
TTARMMC1 Mark McGwire 75.00 150.00
TTARMN1 Mike Napoli 10.00 25.00
TTARMN2 Mike Napoli 10.00 25.00
TTARMN3 Mike Napoli 10.00 25.00
TTARMP1 Mike Piazza 50.00 120.00
TTARMP2 Mike Piazza 50.00 120.00
TTARMP3 Mike Piazza 50.00 120.00
TTARMS1 Max Scherzer 30.00 80.00
TTARMW1 Michael Wacha EXCH 12.00 30.00
TTARMW2 Michael Wacha EXCH 12.00 30.00
TTARMW3 Michael Wacha EXCH 12.00 30.00
TTAROC1 Orlando Cepeda 20.00 50.00
TTAROC2 Orlando Cepeda 20.00 50.00
TTAROC3 Orlando Cepeda 20.00 50.00
TTAROH1 Orlando Hernandez EXCH 8.00 20.00
TTAROH2 Orlando Hernandez EXCH 8.00 20.00
TTAROH3 Orlando Hernandez EXCH 8.00 20.00
TTAROV1 Omar Vizquel 60.00 150.00
TTAROV2 Omar Vizquel 60.00 150.00
TTAROV3 Omar Vizquel 60.00 150.00
TTARPG1 Paul Goldschmidt 15.00 40.00
TTARPG2 Paul Goldschmidt 15.00 40.00
TTARPG3 Paul Goldschmidt 15.00 40.00
TTARRA1 Roberto Alomar 25.00 60.00
TTARRA2 Roberto Alomar 25.00 60.00
TTARRA3 Roberto Alomar 25.00 60.00
TTARRB1 Ryan Braun 12.00 30.00
TTARRB2 Ryan Braun 12.00 30.00
TTARRB3 Ryan Braun 12.00 30.00
TTARRC1 Roger Clemens 30.00 80.00
TTARRC2 Roger Clemens 30.00 80.00
TTARRC3 Roger Clemens 30.00 80.00
TTARRH1 Ryan Howard 20.00 50.00
TTARRJ1 Reggie Jackson 25.00 60.00
TTARSC1 Steve Carlton 20.00 50.00
TTARSG1 Sonny Gray 8.00 20.00
TTARSG2 Sonny Gray 8.00 20.00
TTARSG3 Sonny Gray 8.00 20.00
TTARSG4 Sonny Gray 8.00 20.00
TTARSG5 Sonny Gray 8.00 20.00
TTARSM1 Shelby Miller 10.00 25.00
TTARSM2 Shelby Miller 10.00 25.00
TTARSM3 Shelby Miller 10.00 25.00
TTARSMA1 Starling Marte 15.00 40.00
TTARSMA2 Starling Marte 15.00 40.00
TTARSMA3 Starling Marte 15.00 40.00
TTARSMA4 Starling Marte 15.00 40.00
TTARSMA5 Starling Marte 15.00 40.00
TTARSP1 Salvador Perez 12.00 30.00
TTARSP2 Salvador Perez 12.00 30.00
TTARSP3 Salvador Perez 12.00 30.00
TTARSP4 Salvador Perez 12.00 30.00
TTARSP5 Salvador Perez 12.00 30.00
TTARTC1 Tony Cingrani 6.00 15.00
TTARTC2 Tony Cingrani 6.00 15.00
TTARTC3 Tony Cingrani 6.00 15.00
TTARTC4 Tony Cingrani 6.00 15.00
TTARTC5 Tony Cingrani 6.00 15.00
TTARTF1 Todd Frazier 12.00 30.00
TTARTF2 Todd Frazier 12.00 30.00
TTARTF3 Todd Frazier 12.00 30.00
TTARTF4 Todd Frazier 12.00 30.00
TTARTF5 Todd Frazier 12.00 30.00
TTARTR1 Tim Raines 12.00 30.00
TTARTR2 Tim Raines 12.00 30.00
TTARTR3 Tim Raines 12.00 30.00
TTARTT1 Troy Tulowitzki 15.00 40.00
TTARTT2 Troy Tulowitzki 15.00 40.00
TTARTT3 Troy Tulowitzki 15.00 40.00
TTARVG1 Vladimir Guerrero 10.00 25.00
TTARVG2 Vladimir Guerrero 10.00 25.00
TTARVG3 Vladimir Guerrero 10.00 25.00
TTARWM1 Wil Myers 10.00 25.00
TTARWM2 Wil Myers 10.00 25.00
TTARWM3 Wil Myers 10.00 25.00
TTARYA1 Yonder Alonso 5.00 12.00
TTARYA2 Yonder Alonso 5.00 12.00
TTARYA3 Yonder Alonso 5.00 12.00
TTARYC1 Yoenis Cespedes 12.00 30.00
TTARYC2 Yoenis Cespedes 12.00 30.00
TTARYC3 Yoenis Cespedes 12.00 30.00
TTARZW1 Zack Wheeler 10.00 25.00
TTARZW2 Zack Wheeler 10.00 25.00
TTARZW3 Zack Wheeler 10.00 25.00
TTARZW4 Zack Wheeler 10.00 25.00
TTARZW5 Zack Wheeler 10.00 25.00

2014 Topps Triple Threads Relic Autographs Gold

*GOLD: .5X TO 1.2X BASIC
STATED ODDS 1:19 MINI
STATED PRINT RUN 9 SER.#'d SETS
SOME NOT PRICED DUE TO SCARCITY
EXCHANGE DEADLINE 9/30/2017

2014 Topps Triple Threads Relic Combos

STATED ODDS 1:24 MINI
STATED PRINT RUN 36 SER.#'d SETS
TTRCBAP Andrus/Profar/Beltre 8.00 20.00
TTRCBAS Alvarez/Sandoval/Beltre 8.00 20.00
TTRCBEC Btsta/Encrncn/Cbrra 10.00 25.00
TTRCBMC Cspds/McCtchn/Btsta 12.00 30.00
TTRCBSK Kpns/Sntna/Brn 8.00 20.00
TTRCCCC Cngrni/Chpmn/Cto 10.00 25.00
TTRCCHD Hrpr/Cspds/Drvsh 12.00 30.00
TTRCCMS Myrs/Schrzr/Cbrra 8.00 20.00
TTRCCPD Donaldson/Cespedes/Parker 8.00 20.00
TTRCDFE Encarnacion/Davis/Fielder 8.00 20.00
TTRCFHI Iwkma/Hrnndz/Frnkln 8.00 20.00
TTRCFRC Cstro/Rzzo/Fjkwa 10.00 25.00
TTRCFSH Sandoval/Headley/Freese 6.00 15.00
TTRCGCT Cspds/Trt/Gnzlz 20.00 50.00
TTRCGFA Freeman/Adams/Goldschmidt 10.00 25.00
TTRCGMA Almr/McGwre/Griff Jr. 20.00 50.00
TTRCGMG Goldschmidt/Miley/Gregorius 8.00 20.00
TTRCGRG Rns/Gnzlz/Grrro 10.00 25.00
TTRCHFG Heyward/Gattis/Freeman 10.00 25.00
TTRCHMM Mllr/Hlldy/Mlna 15.00 40.00
TTRCHSG Segura/Hart/Gomez 6.00 15.00
TTRCIDK Iwkma/Drvsh/Krda 10.00 25.00
TTRCIHW Iwkma/Wlkr/Hrnndz 12.00 30.00
TTRCJBS Bltrn/CC/Jeter 40.00 100.00
TTRCJPR Rvr/Psd/Jeter 30.00 80.00
TTRCKEP Puig/Ellis/Kemp 10.00 25.00
TTRCLHH Howard/Hamels/Lee 6.00 15.00
TTRCLMP Pice/Lngra/Mre 8.00 20.00
TTRCLUB Lee/Brown/Utley 8.00 20.00
TTRCMAC McCthn/Alvrz/Cole 20.00 50.00
TTRCMDJ Mchdo/Dvs/Jns 15.00 40.00
TTRCMEK Krda/McCnn/Ellsbry 12.00 30.00
TTRCMLC Cbb/Lngra/Mre 8.00 20.00
TTRCMMW Mlna/Mllr/Wnwrght 12.00 30.00
TTRCMMW1 Mllr/Mrtnz/Wong 15.00 40.00
TTRCNPM Pedroia/Middlebrooks/Napoli 8.00 20.00
TTRCPCL Cain/Lncm/Psey 10.00 25.00
TTRCPNC Papelbon/Chapman/Nathan 8.00 20.00
TTRCPWM Piazza/Martinez/Wright 8.00 20.00
TTRCRGA Alomar/Ramirez/Guerrero 8.00 20.00
TTRCRGS Strasburg/Gonzalez/Rodriguez 8.00 20.00
TTRCRPG Puig/Gordon/Ryu 8.00 20.00
TTRCSMF Sgra/Mchdo/Frnkln 6.00 15.00
TTRCSSS Schrzr/Sle/Stasbrg 10.00 25.00
TTRCSVS1 Schrzr/Vrlndr/Snchz 12.00 30.00
TTRCSYF Ylch/Stntn/Frnndz 10.00 25.00
TTRCTCG Tulowitzki/Gonzalez/Cuddyer 8.00 20.00
TTRCUUH Upton/Heyward/Upton 6.00 15.00
TTRCVFG Gonzalez/Freeman/Votto 10.00 25.00
TTRCVPF Phllps/Vtto/Frzr 10.00 25.00
TTRCWHG Gnzlz/Wrth/Hrpr 12.00 30.00

2014 Topps Triple Threads Relic Combos Emerald

*EMERALD: .5X TO 1.2X BASIC
STATED ODDS 1:48 MINI
STATED PRINT RUN 18 SER.#'d SETS

2014 Topps Triple Threads Relic Combos Sepia

*SEPIA: .4X TO 1X BASIC
STATED ODDS 1:32 MINI
STATED PRINT RUN 27 SER.#'d SETS

2014 Topps Triple Threads Relic Combos Double

STATED ODDS 1:406 MINI
STATED PRINT RUN 18 SER.#'d SETS
TTRDC2 McC/Blt/Ell/Krd/Jtr/Sbt 75.00 150.00
TTRDC5 Frm/Vtt/Gnz/Cbr/Gld/Dvs 90.00 150.00
TTRDC8 Parker/Gray/Reddick/Cespedes
Donaldson/Lowrie 25.00 60.00
TTRDC12 Freeman/Gattis/Kimbrel/Heyward
Teheran/Simmons 30.00 80.00
TTRDC13 Cuddyer/Gonzalez/Rosario
Tulowitzki/Arenado/Morneau 40.00 100.00

2014 Topps Triple Threads Relics

STATED ODDS 1:9 MINI
STATED PRINT RUN 36 SER.#'d SETS
TTRAC1 Allen Craig 5.00 12.00
TTRAC2 Allen Craig 5.00 12.00
TTRAC3 Allen Craig 5.00 12.00

TTRAJ1 Adam Jones 8.00 20.00
TTRAJ2 Adam Jones 8.00 20.00
TTRAJ3 Adam Jones 8.00 20.00
TTRAR1 Anthony Rizzo 8.00 20.00
TTRAR2 Anthony Rizzo 8.00 20.00
TTRAR3 Anthony Rizzo 8.00 20.00
TTRBB1 Billy Butler 4.00 10.00
TTRBB2 Billy Butler 4.00 10.00
TTRBB3 Billy Butler 4.00 10.00
TTRBG1 Brett Gardner 10.00 25.00
TTRBG2 Brett Gardner 10.00 25.00
TTRBG3 Brett Gardner 10.00 25.00
TTRBHA1 Billy Hamilton 10.00 25.00
TTRBHA2 Billy Hamilton 10.00 25.00
TTRBHA3 Billy Hamilton 10.00 25.00
TTRBM1 Brian McCann 5.00 12.00
TTRBM2 Brian McCann 5.00 12.00
TTRBM3 Brian McCann 5.00 12.00
TTRBP1 Brandon Phillips 4.00 10.00
TTRBP2 Brandon Phillips 4.00 10.00
TTRBP3 Brandon Phillips 4.00 10.00
TTRBZ1 Ben Zobrist 5.00 12.00
TTRBZ2 Ben Zobrist 5.00 12.00
TTRBZ3 Ben Zobrist 5.00 12.00
TTRCA1 Chris Archer 4.00 10.00
TTRCA2 Chris Archer 4.00 10.00
TTRCA3 Chris Archer 4.00 10.00
TTRCB1 Christian Bethancourt 6.00 15.00
TTRCB2 Christian Bethancourt 6.00 15.00
TTRCB3 Christian Bethancourt 6.00 15.00
TTRCO1 Chris Owings 4.00 10.00
TTRCO2 Chris Owings 4.00 10.00
TTRCO3 Chris Owings 4.00 10.00
TTRCY1 Christian Yelich 8.00 20.00
TTRCY2 Christian Yelich 8.00 20.00
TTRCY3 Christian Yelich 8.00 20.00
TTRDJ1 Derek Jeter 40.00 100.00
TTRDJ2 Derek Jeter 40.00 100.00
TTRDJ3 Derek Jeter 40.00 100.00
TTRDMA1 Daisuke Matsuzaka 5.00 12.00
TTRDMA2 Daisuke Matsuzaka 5.00 12.00
TTRDMA3 Daisuke Matsuzaka 5.00 12.00
TTRDO1 David Ortiz 8.00 20.00
TTRDO2 David Ortiz 8.00 20.00
TTRDO3 David Ortiz 8.00 20.00
TTRFF1 Freddie Freeman 8.00 20.00
TTRFF2 Freddie Freeman 8.00 20.00
TTRFF3 Freddie Freeman 8.00 20.00
TTRFM1 Fred McGriff 5.00 12.00
TTRFM2 Fred McGriff 5.00 12.00
TTRFM3 Fred McGriff 5.00 12.00
TTRJD1 Josh Donaldson 5.00 12.00
TTRJD2 Josh Donaldson 5.00 12.00
TTRJD3 Josh Donaldson 5.00 12.00
TTRJG1 Juan Gonzalez 15.00 40.00
TTRJG2 Juan Gonzalez 15.00 40.00
TTRJG3 Juan Gonzalez 15.00 40.00
TTRJGR1 Jason Grilli 4.00 10.00
TTRJGR2 Jason Grilli 4.00 10.00
TTRJGR3 Jason Grilli 4.00 10.00
TTRJH1 Jason Heyward 5.00 12.00
TTRJH2 Jason Heyward 5.00 12.00
TTRJH3 Jason Heyward 5.00 12.00
TTRJP1 Jarrod Parker 4.00 10.00
TTRJP2 Jarrod Parker 4.00 10.00
TTRJP3 Jarrod Parker 4.00 10.00
TTRJPR1 Jurickson Profar 5.00 12.00
TTRJPR2 Jurickson Profar 5.00 12.00
TTRJPR3 Jurickson Profar 5.00 12.00
TTRJR1 Jim Rice 5.00 12.00
TTRJR2 Jim Rice 5.00 12.00
TTRJR3 Jim Rice 5.00 12.00
TTRKG1 Ken Griffey Jr. 12.00 30.00
TTRKG2 Ken Griffey Jr. 12.00 30.00
TTRKG3 Ken Griffey Jr. 12.00 30.00
TTRKW1 Kolten Wong 8.00 20.00
TTRKW2 Kolten Wong 8.00 20.00
TTRKW3 Kolten Wong 8.00 20.00
TTRMA1 Matt Adams 6.00 15.00
TTRMA2 Matt Adams 6.00 15.00
TTRMA3 Matt Adams 6.00 15.00
TTRMC1 Miguel Cabrera 12.00 30.00
TTRMC2 Miguel Cabrera 12.00 30.00
TTRMC3 Miguel Cabrera 12.00 30.00
TTRMCN1 Matt Cain 6.00 15.00
TTRMCN2 Matt Cain 6.00 15.00
TTRMCN3 Matt Cain 6.00 15.00
TTRMCU1 Michael Cuddyer 4.00 10.00
TTRMCU2 Michael Cuddyer 4.00 10.00
TTRMCU3 Michael Cuddyer 4.00 10.00
TTRMM1 Mike Minor 4.00 10.00
TTRMM2 Mike Minor 4.00 10.00
TTRMM3 Mike Minor 4.00 10.00
TTRMMC1 Mark McGwire 12.00 30.00
TTRMMC2 Mark McGwire 12.00 30.00
TTRMMC3 Mark McGwire 12.00 30.00
TTRMN1 Mike Napoli 4.00 10.00
TTRMN2 Mike Napoli 4.00 10.00
TTRMN3 Mike Napoli 4.00 10.00
TTRMRA1 Manny Ramirez 6.00 15.00
TTRMRA2 Manny Ramirez 6.00 15.00
TTRMRA3 Manny Ramirez 6.00 15.00
TTRMT1 Mike Trout 25.00 60.00
TTRMT2 Mike Trout 25.00 60.00
TTRMT3 Mike Trout 25.00 60.00
TTRMTA1 Masahiro Tanaka 20.00 50.00
TTRMTA2 Masahiro Tanaka 20.00 50.00
TTRMTA3 Masahiro Tanaka 20.00 50.00
TTROC1 Orlando Cepeda 6.00 15.00
TTROC2 Orlando Cepeda 6.00 15.00
TTROC3 Orlando Cepeda 6.00 15.00
TTROV1 Omar Vizquel 8.00 20.00
TTROV2 Omar Vizquel 8.00 20.00
TTROV3 Omar Vizquel 8.00 20.00
TTRPG1 Paul Goldschmidt 6.00 15.00
TTRPG2 Paul Goldschmidt 6.00 15.00
TTRPG3 Paul Goldschmidt 6.00 15.00
TTRRA1 Roberto Alomar 10.00 25.00
TTRRA2 Roberto Alomar 10.00 25.00
TTRRA3 Roberto Alomar 10.00 25.00
TTRRB1 Ryan Braun 5.00 12.00
TTRRB2 Ryan Braun 5.00 12.00
TTRRB3 Ryan Braun 5.00 12.00
TTRRC1 Roger Clemens 12.00 30.00
TTRRC2 Roger Clemens 12.00 30.00
TTRRC3 Roger Clemens 12.00 20.00
TTRSG1 Sonny Gray 5.00 12.00
TTRSG2 Sonny Gray 5.00 12.00
TTRSG3 Sonny Gray 5.00 12.00
TTRSMA1 Starling Marte 5.00 12.00
TTRSMA2 Starling Marte 5.00 12.00
TTRSMA3 Starling Marte 5.00 12.00
TTRTF1 Todd Frazier 4.00 10.00
TTRTF2 Todd Frazier 4.00 10.00
TTRTF3 Todd Frazier 4.00 10.00
TTRVG1 Vladimir Guerrero 5.00 12.00
TTRVG2 Vladimir Guerrero 5.00 12.00
TTRVG3 Vladimir Guerrero 5.00 12.00
TTRWM1 Wil Myers 4.00 10.00
TTRWM2 Wil Myers 4.00 10.00
TTRWM3 Wil Myers 4.00 10.00
TTRYA1 Yonder Alonso 4.00 10.00
TTRYA2 Yonder Alonso 4.00 10.00
TTRYA3 Yonder Alonso 4.00 10.00
TTRYC1 Yoenis Cespedes 8.00 20.00
TTRYC2 Yoenis Cespedes 8.00 20.00
TTRYC3 Yoenis Cespedes 8.00 20.00

2014 Topps Triple Threads Relics Emerald

*EMERALD: .5X TO 1.2X BASIC
STATED ODDS 1:17 MINI
STATED PRINT RUN 18 SER.#'d SETS

2014 Topps Triple Threads Relics Gold

*GOLD: .6X TO 1.5X BASIC
STATED ODDS 1:33 MINI
STATED PRINT RUN 9 SER.#'d SETS

2014 Topps Triple Threads Relics Sepia

*SEPIA: .4X TO 1X BASIC
STATED ODDS 1:11 MINI
STATED PRINT RUN 27 SER.#'d SETS

2014 Topps Triple Threads Rookie Autographs

RANDOM INSERTS IN PACKS
STATED PRINT RUN 100 SER.#'d SETS
EXCHANGE DEADLINE 9/30/2017
TRAAH Andrew Heaney 5.00 12.00
TRAEA Erisbel Arruebarrena 12.00 30.00
TRAEB Eddie Butler 5.00 12.00
TRAGP Gregory Polanco 10.00 25.00
TRAGS George Springer 10.00 25.00
TRAJA Jose Abreu 30.00 80.00
TRAJS Jon Singleton 6.00 15.00
TRANC Nick Castellanos 15.00 40.00
TRAOT Oscar Taveras 6.00 15.00
TRARE Roenis Elias 5.00 12.00
TRARO Rougned Odor 12.00 30.00
TRAYS Yangervis Solarte 5.00 12.00

2014 Topps Triple Threads Transparencies Relic Autographs

STATED ODDS 1:88 MINI
STATED PRINT RUN 25 SER.#'d SETS
EXCHANGE DEADLINE 9/30/2017
TTTAJ Adam Jones 12.00 30.00
TTTAP Albert Pujols 75.00 200.00
TTTBH Bryce Harper 100.00 200.00
TTTBP Buster Posey EXCH 25.00 60.00
TTTDP Dustin Pedroia EXCH 20.00 50.00
TTTDW David Wright 15.00 40.00
TTTFF Freddie Freeman EXCH 30.00 80.00
TTTGS Giancarlo Stanton 30.00 80.00
TTTJF Jose Fernandez EXCH 25.00 60.00
TTTJV Joey Votto 30.00 80.00
TTTMC Miguel Cabrera 30.00 80.00
TTTMS Max Scherzer 30.00 80.00
TTTPG Paul Goldschmidt 25.00 60.00
TTTRB Ryan Braun 15.00 40.00
TTTRC Robinson Cano 25.00 60.00
TTTTT Troy Tulowitzki 25.00 60.00
TTTYM Yadier Molina 60.00 120.00

2014 Topps Triple Threads Unity Relic Autographs

STATED ODDS 1:6 MINI
STATED PRINT RUN 99 SER.#'d SETS
EXCHANGE DEADLINE 9/30/2017
UAJRAB Albert Belle 5.00 12.00
UAJRAC Alex Cobb 4.00 10.00
UAJRACR Allen Craig 5.00 12.00
UAJRAE Adam Eaton 4.00 10.00
UAJRAG Adrian Gonzalez 10.00 25.00
UAJRAJ Adam Jones 6.00 15.00
UAJRBP Buster Posey 30.00 80.00
UAJRCHA Cole Hamels 5.00 12.00
UAJRCO Chris Owings 4.00 10.00
UAJRCO1 Chris Owings 4.00 10.00
UAJRCS Chris Sale 10.00 30.00
UAJRCSA Carlos Santana 5.00 12.00
UAJRDF David Freese 4.00 10.00
UAJRDG Didi Gregorius 5.00 12.00
UAJRDP Dustin Pedroia 15.00 40.00
UAJRDW David Wright 5.00 12.00
UAJRED Eric Davis 10.00 25.00
UAJREG Evan Gattis 4.00 10.00
UAJREL Evan Longoria 5.00 12.00
UAJREM Edgar Martinez 10.00 25.00
UAJRER Enny Romero 4.00 10.00
UAJRFF Freddie Freeman 10.00 25.00
UAJRFL Fred Lynn 10.00 25.00
UAJRFM Fred McGriff 6.00 15.00
UAJRFV Fernando Valenzuela 15.00 40.00
UAJRIR Ivan Rodriguez 6.00 15.00
UAJRJG Juan Gonzalez 6.00 15.00
UAJRJGR Jason Grilli 4.00 10.00
UAJRJH Josh Hamilton 12.00 30.00
UAJRJHE Jason Heyward 5.00 12.00
UAJRJO Jake Odorizzi 4.00 10.00
UAJRJP Jorge Posada 20.00 50.00
UAJRJPA Jarrod Parker 4.00 10.00
UAJRJPR Jurickson Profar 6.00 15.00
UAJRJR Jim Rice 10.00 25.00
UAJRJSA Jarrod Saltalamacchia 4.00 10.00
UAJRJSE Jean Segura 5.00 12.00
UAJRJT Julio Teheran 6.00 15.00
UAJRJV Joey Votto 15.00 40.00
UAJRKG Kevin Gausman 6.00 15.00
UAJRKM Kris Medlen 5.00 12.00
UAJRKS Kevin Siegrist 4.00 10.00
UAJRKU Koji Uehara 10.00 25.00
UAJRKW Kolten Wong 5.00 12.00
UAJRMA Matt Adams 6.00 15.00
UAJRMC Michael Cuddyer 4.00 10.00
UAJRMMA Manny Machado EXCH 20.00 50.00
UAJRMMO Matt Moore 5.00 12.00
UAJRMN Mike Napoli 8.00 20.00
UAJRMS Max Scherzer 12.00 30.00
UAJRMSC Mike Schmidt 20.00 50.00
UAJRNE Nathan Eovaldi 5.00 12.00
UAJRNG Nomar Garciaparra 10.00 25.00
UAJRNR Nolan Ryan 40.00 100.00
UAJRPC Patrick Corbin 5.00 12.00
UAJRPC1 Patrick Corbin 5.00 12.00
UAJRSCA Steve Carlton 12.00 30.00
UAJRPG Paul Goldschmidt 10.00 25.00
UAJRPM Pedro Martinez 25.00 60.00
UAJRRB Ryan Braun 8.00 20.00
UAJRRD R.A. Dickey 6.00 15.00
UAJRRN Ricky Nolasco 4.00 10.00
UAJRRZ Ryan Zimmerman 5.00 12.00
UAJRSC Starlin Castro 8.00 20.00
UAJRSG Sonny Gray 6.00 15.00
UAJRSM Shelby Miller 5.00 12.00
UAJRSMA Starling Marte 10.00 25.00
UAJRTC Tony Cingrani 5.00 12.00
UAJRTD Travis d'Arnaud 5.00 12.00
UAJRTD1 Travis d'Arnaud 5.00 12.00
UAJRTF Todd Frazier 4.00 10.00
UAJRTG Tom Glavine 15.00 40.00
UAJRTRA Tim Raines 4.00 10.00
UAJRVG Vladimir Guerrero 10.00 25.00
UAJRVG1 Vladimir Guerrero 10.00 25.00
UAJRWB Wade Boggs 12.00 30.00
UAJRWB1 Wade Boggs 12.00 30.00
UAJRWC Will Clark 12.00 30.00
UAJRWM Wil Myers 4.00 10.00
UAJRWR Wilin Rosario 4.00 10.00
UAJRYC Yoenis Cespedes 10.00 25.00
UAJRZW Zack Wheeler 6.00 15.00

2014 Topps Triple Threads Unity Relic Autographs Emerald

*EMERALD: .5X TO 1.2X BASIC
STATED ODDS 1:11 MINI
STATED PRINT RUN 50 SER.#'d SETS
EXCHANGE DEADLINE 9/30/2017

2014 Topps Triple Threads Unity Relic Autographs Gold

*GOLD: .6X TO 1.5X BASIC
STATED ODDS 1:22 MINI
STATED PRINT RUN 25 SER.#'d SETS
EXCHANGE DEADLINE 9/30/2017

2014 Topps Triple Threads Unity Relic Autographs Sepia

*SEPIA: .4X TO 1X BASIC
STATED ODDS 1:8 MINI
STATED PRINT RUN 75 SER.#'d SETS
EXCHANGE DEADLINE 9/30/2017

2014 Topps Triple Threads Unity Relics

STATED ODDS 1:6 MINI
UJRAA Albert Almora 6.00 15.00
UJRAB Adrian Beltre 6.00 15.00
UJRAC Aroldis Chapman 6.00 15.00
UJRACA Andrew Cashner 4.00 10.00
UJRACA1 Andrew Cashner 4.00 10.00
UJRACH Aroldis Chapman 6.00 15.00
UJRAD Andre Dawson 8.00 20.00
UJRADU Adam Dunn 5.00 12.00
UJRAE A.J. Ellis 4.00 10.00
UJRAE1 A.J. Ellis 4.00 10.00
UJRAE2 A.J. Ellis 4.00 10.00
UJRAEA Adam Eaton 4.00 10.00
UJRAES Alcides Escobar 5.00 12.00
UJRAG Alex Gordon 5.00 12.00
UJRAGO Adrian Gonzalez 5.00 12.00
UJRAJ Adam Jones 5.00 12.00
UJRAL Adam Lind 5.00 12.00
UJRAL1 Adam Lind 5.00 12.00
UJRAL2 Adam Lind 5.00 12.00
UJRAM Andrew McCutchen 25.00 60.00
UJRAP Albert Pujols 6.00 15.00
UJRAR Anthony Rizzo 12.00 30.00
UJRAR1 Anthony Rizzo 12.00 30.00
UJRARA Alexei Ramirez 5.00 12.00
UJRAW Adam Wainwright 5.00 12.00
UJRBHA Bryce Harper 10.00 25.00
UJRBJ Bo Jackson 10.00 25.00
UJRBL Brett Lawrie 5.00 12.00
UJRBLE Bob Lemon 10.00 25.00
UJRBM Brandon Morrow 4.00 10.00
UJRBMC Brian McCann 5.00 12.00
UJRBP Buster Posey 8.00 20.00
UJRBPH Brandon Phillips 4.00 10.00
UJRBPO Buster Posey 8.00 20.00
UJRBW Brett Wallace 4.00 10.00
UJRCB Chad Billingsley 5.00 12.00
UJRCBE Carlos Beltran 5.00 12.00
UJRCBI Craig Biggio 5.00 12.00
UJRCBU Clay Buchholz 4.00 10.00
UJRCG Carlos Gonzalez 5.00 12.00
UJRCGO Carlos Gonzalez 5.00 12.00
UJRCGO1 Carlos Gonzalez 5.00 12.00
UJRCGR Curtis Granderson 5.00 12.00
UJRCH Chris Heisey 4.00 10.00
UJRCH1 Chris Heisey 4.00 10.00
UJRCH2 Chris Heisey 4.00 10.00
UJRCL Cliff Lee 5.00 12.00
UJRCLU Cory Luebke 4.00 10.00
UJRCS CC Sabathia 10.00 25.00
UJRCSA CC Sabathia 10.00 25.00
UJRCSA1 Carlos Santana 5.00 12.00
UJRCSA2 Chris Sale 6.00 15.00
UJRCSA3 Carlos Santana 5.00 12.00
UJRCSE Chris Sale 6.00 15.00
UJRCW C.J. Wilson 4.00 10.00
UJRDB Domonic Brown 5.00 12.00
UJRDE Danny Espinosa 4.00 10.00
UJRDGD Dee Gordon 4.00 10.00
UJRDGO1 Dee Gordon 4.00 10.00
UJRDJ Desmond Jennings 5.00 12.00
UJRDJ1 Desmond Jennings 5.00 12.00
UJRDJE Derek Jeter 30.00 80.00
UJRDMA Don Mattingly 12.00 30.00
UJRDO David Ortiz 6.00 15.00
UJRDP Dustin Pedroia 6.00 15.00
UJRDS Drew Storen 4.00 10.00
UJRDST Drew Storen 4.00 10.00
UJRDW David Wright 5.00 12.00
UJREE Edwin Encarnacion 6.00 15.00
UJREG Evan Gattis 4.00 10.00
UJREL Evan Longoria 5.00 12.00
UJREM Eddie Murray 6.00 15.00
UJRFH Felix Hernandez 5.00 12.00
UJRFH1 Felix Hernandez 5.00 12.00
UJRFH2 Felix Hernandez 5.00 12.00
UJRFH3 Felix Hernandez 5.00 12.00
UJRFH4 Felix Hernandez 5.00 12.00
UJRFM Franklin Morales 4.00 10.00
UJRFMO Franklin Morales 4.00 10.00
UJRFV Fernando Valenzuela 10.00 25.00
UJRGB Gordon Beckham 4.00 10.00
UJRGB1 Gordon Beckham 4.00 10.00
UJRGC Gerrit Cole 6.00 15.00
UJRGCO Gerrit Cole 6.00 15.00
UJRGG Gio Gonzalez 5.00 12.00
UJRGG1 Gio Gonzalez 5.00 12.00
UJRGM Greg Maddux 12.00 30.00
UJRHC Hank Conger 4.00 10.00
UJRHI Hisashi Iwakuma 5.00 12.00
UJRHIW Hisashi Iwakuma 5.00 12.00
UJRHK Howie Kendrick 4.00 10.00
UJRHKU Hiroki Kuroda 4.00 10.00
UJRHR Hanley Ramirez 5.00 12.00
UJRHRY Hyun-jin Ryu 5.00 12.00
UJRIK Ian Kinsler 5.00 12.00
UJRIK1 Ian Kinsler 5.00 12.00
UJRIR Ivan Rodriguez 5.00 12.00
UJRJB Jackie Bradley Jr. 6.00 15.00
UJRJBE Josh Beckett 4.00 10.00
UJRJBR Jackie Bradley Jr. 6.00 15.00
UJRJCH Jhoulys Chacin 4.00 10.00
UJRJCU Johnny Cueto 5.00 12.00
UJRJD John Danks 4.00 10.00
UJRJD1 John Danks 4.00 10.00
UJRJDA John Danks 4.00 10.00
UJRJE Jacoby Ellsbury 5.00 12.00
UJRJF Jeurys Familia 5.00 12.00
UJRJG Jaime Garcia 5.00 12.00
UJRJH Jeremy Hellickson 4.00 10.00
UJRJHA Josh Hamilton 5.00 12.00
UJRJHY J.J. Hardy 4.00 10.00
UJRJK Jason Kipnis 5.00 12.00
UJRJK1 Jason Kipnis 5.00 12.00
UJRJL Junior Lake 4.00 10.00
UJRJL1 Junior Lake 4.00 10.00
UJRJLE Jon Lester 5.00 12.00
UJRJM Joe Mauer 5.00 12.00
UJRJMA Joe Mauer 5.00 12.00
UJRJMN Joe Morgan 8.00 20.00
UJRJMU Justin Morneau 5.00 12.00
UJRJN Joe Nathan 4.00 10.00
UJRJP Jorge Posada 5.00 12.00
UJRJPA James Paxton 6.00 15.00
UJRJPO Jordan Pacheco 4.00 10.00
UJRJR Josh Reddick 4.00 10.00
UJRJRU Josh Rutledge 4.00 10.00
UJRJS Justin Smoak 4.00 10.00
UJRJSM John Smoltz 6.00 15.00
UJRJT Jose Tabata 4.00 10.00
UJRJTA Jose Tabata 4.00 10.00
UJRJV Joey Votto 6.00 15.00
UJRJV1 Joey Votto 6.00 15.00
UJRJVE Jonny Venters 4.00 10.00
UJRJVL Justin Verlander 6.00 15.00
UJRJVO Joey Votto 6.00 15.00
UJRJWE Jayson Werth 5.00 12.00
UJRJZ Jordan Zimmermann 5.00 12.00
UJRKD Kyle Drabek 4.00 10.00
UJRKF Kyuji Fujikawa 5.00 12.00
UJRKFJ Kyuji Fujikawa 5.00 12.00
UJRKG Ken Griffey Jr. 25.00 60.00
UJRKGA Kevin Gausman 6.00 15.00
UJRKH Kelvin Herrera 4.00 10.00
UJRKM Kris Medlen 5.00 12.00
UJRKN Kirk Nieuwenhuis 4.00 10.00
UJRKW Kolten Wong 5.00 12.00
UJRKWO Kolten Wong 5.00 12.00
UJRLM Leonys Martin 4.00 10.00
UJRMA Matt Adams 4.00 10.00
UJRMB Michael Bourn 4.00 10.00
UJRMBO Michael Bourn 4.00 10.00
UJRMBO1 Michael Bourn 4.00 10.00
UJRMC Michael Cuddyer 4.00 10.00
UJRMCA1 Miguel Cabrera 6.00 15.00
UJRMCU Michael Cuddyer 4.00 10.00
UJRMD Matt Davidson 5.00 12.00
UJRMH Matt Holliday 10.00 25.00
UJRMIG Miguel Cabrera 6.00 15.00
UJRMK Matt Kemp 5.00 12.00
UJRML Mike Leake 4.00 10.00
UJRML1 Mike Leake 4.00 10.00
UJRMLA Mat Latos 5.00 12.00
UJRMM Mitch Moreland 4.00 10.00
UJRMMC Mark McGwire 15.00 40.00
UJRMMC1 Mark McGwire 15.00 40.00
UJRMMI Mike Minor 4.00 10.00
UJRMMO Matt Moore 5.00 12.00
UJRMN Mike Napoli 4.00 10.00
UJRMR Manny Ramirez 6.00 15.00
UJRMR1 Manny Ramirez 6.00 15.00
UJRMRI Mariano Rivera 8.00 20.00
UJRMSC Max Scherzer 6.00 15.00
UJRMT Mike Trout 15.00 40.00
UJRMTE Mark Teixeira 5.00 12.00
UJRMY Michael Young 4.00 10.00
UJRMZ Mike Zunino 4.00 10.00
UJRNA Nolan Arenado 10.00 25.00
UJRNA2 Nolan Arenado 10.00 25.00
UJRNF Nick Franklin 4.00 10.00
UJRNF1 Nick Franklin 4.00 10.00
UJRNF2 Nick Franklin 4.00 10.00
UJRNS Nick Swisher 5.00 12.00
UJRNS1 Nick Swisher 5.00 12.00
UJRNW Neil Walker 4.00 10.00
UJRPA Pedro Alvarez 4.00 10.00
UJRPAL Pedro Alvarez 4.00 10.00
UJRPB Peter Bourjos 4.00 10.00
UJRPC Patrick Corbin 5.00 12.00
UJRPG Paul Goldschmidt 5.00 12.00
UJRPK Paul Konerko 5.00 12.00
UJRPS Pablo Sandoval 5.00 12.00
UJRRB Ryan Braun 5.00 12.00
UJRRB1 Ryan Braun 5.00 12.00
UJRRH Rickey Henderson 6.00 15.00
UJRRHA Roy Halladay 5.00 12.00
UJRRR Ricky Romero 4.00 10.00
UJRRR1 Ricky Romero 4.00 10.00
UJRRZ Ryan Zimmerman 5.00 12.00
UJRSC Starlin Castro 4.00 10.00
UJRSC1 Starlin Castro 4.00 10.00
UJRSC2 Starlin Castro 4.00 10.00
UJRSC3 Starlin Castro 4.00 10.00
UJRSCH Shin-Soo Choo 5.00 12.00
UJRSD Scott Diamond 4.00 10.00
UJRSM Starling Marte 6.00 15.00
UJRSP Salvador Perez 5.00 12.00
UJRSS Stephen Strasburg 6.00 15.00
UJRSST Stephen Strasburg 6.00 15.00
UJRSV Shane Victorino 5.00 12.00
UJRTC1 Tony Cingrani 5.00 12.00
UJRTF Todd Frazier 4.00 10.00
UJRTFR Todd Frazier 4.00 10.00
UJRTHE Todd Helton 5.00 12.00
UJRTHU Torii Hunter 4.00 10.00
UJRTL Tim Lincecum 5.00 12.00
UJRTL1 Tim Lincecum 5.00 12.00
UJRTM Tommy Milone 4.00 10.00
UJRTR Trevor Rosenthal 5.00 12.00
UJRTT Troy Tulowitzki 5.00 12.00
UJRTW Taijuan Walker 5.00 12.00
UJRVG Vladimir Guerrero 5.00 12.00
UJRVG1 Vladimir Guerrero 5.00 12.00
UJRWB Wade Boggs 6.00 15.00
UJRWB1 Wade Boggs 6.00 15.00
UJRWB2 Wade Boggs 6.00 15.00
UJRXB Xander Bogaerts 12.00 30.00
UJRYC Yoenis Cespedes 6.00 15.00
UJRYM Yadier Molina 10.00 25.00
UJRYP Yasiel Puig 6.00 15.00
UJRYP1 Yasiel Puig 6.00 15.00
UJRZC1 Zack Cozart 4.00 10.00
UJRZG Zack Greinke 6.00 15.00
UJRZWH Zack Wheeler 5.00 12.00

2014 Topps Triple Threads Unity Relics Emerald

*EMERALD: .5X TO 1.2X BASIC
STATED ODDS 1:11 MINI
STATED PRINT RUN 18 SER.#'d SETS

2014 Topps Triple Threads Unity Relics Gold

*GOLD: .5X TO 1.5X BASIC
STATED ODDS 1:21 MINI
STATED PRINT RUN 9 SER.#'d SETS
NO PRICING ON MOST DUE TO SCARCITY

2014 Topps Triple Threads Unity Relics Sepia

*SEPIA: .4X TO 1X BASIC
STATED ODDS 1:7 MINI
STATED PRINT RUN 27 SER.#'d SETS

2015 Topps Triple Threads

COMP.SET w/o AU's (100) 100.00 200.00
JSY AU RC ODDS 1:11 MINI BOX
JSY AU RC PRINT RUN 99 SER.#'d SETS
JSY AU ODDS 1:11 MINI BOX
JSY AU PRINT RUN 99 SER.#'d SETS
EXCHANGE DEADLINE 9/30/2017
1-100 PLATE ODDS 1:114 MINI BOX
101-172 PLATE ODDS 1:267 MINI BOX
PLATE PRINT RUN 1 SET PER COLOR
BLACK-CYAN-MAGENTA-YELLOW ISSUED
NO PLATE PRICING DUE TO SCARCITY
1 Babe Ruth 1.50 4.00
2 Matt Kemp .50 1.25
3 Mike Schmidt 1.00 2.50
4 Johnny Bench .60 1.50
5 Paul Goldschmidt .60 1.50
6 Clayton Kershaw 1.00 2.50
7 Chris Sale .60 1.50
8 Reggie Jackson .50 1.25
9 Madison Bumgarner .50 1.25
10 Honus Wagner .60 1.50
11 Carlos Gomez .40 1.00
12 John Smoltz .60 1.50
13 Troy Tulowitzki .60 1.50
14 Cal Ripken Jr. 2.00 5.00
15 Francisco Lindor RC 5.00 12.00
16 Jose Abreu .60 1.50
17 Evan Longoria .50 1.25
18 Greg Maddux .75 2.00
19 Hank Aaron 1.25 3.00
20 Michael Brantley .50 1.25
21 Wade Boggs .50 1.25
22 Johnny Cueto .50 1.25
23 Miguel Cabrera .60 1.50
24 Nolan Ryan 2.00 5.00
25 Warren Spahn .50 1.25
26 David Price .50 1.25
27 Ted Williams 1.25 3.00
28 Devin Mesoraco .40 1.00
29 Edwin Encarnacion .60 1.50
30 Don Mattingly 1.25 3.00
31 Anthony Rizzo .75 2.00
32 Joe DiMaggio 1.25 3.00
33 Jose Altuve .50 1.25
34 Jose Fernandez .60 1.50
35 Joe Mauer .50 1.25
36 Carlos Gonzalez .50 1.25
37 Yordano Ventura .50 1.25
38 Bryce Harper 1.00 2.50
39 Cole Hamels .50 1.25
40 Mike Piazza .60 1.50
41 Adam Wainwright .50 1.25
42 Dave Winfield .50 1.25
43 Jason Heyward .50 1.25
44 Albert Pujols .75 2.00
45 Masahiro Tanaka .50 1.25
46 Steve Carlton .50 1.25
47 David Ortiz .60 1.50
48 Jacob deGrom 1.25 3.00
49 Mariano Rivera .75 2.00
50 Lou Gehrig 1.25 3.00
51 Freddie Freeman .75 2.00
52 Randy Johnson .60 1.50
53 Felix Hernandez .50 1.25
54 Chase Utley .50 1.25
55 Stan Musial 1.00 2.50
56 Jose Bautista .50 1.25
57 David Peralta .40 1.00
58 Adam Jones .50 1.25
59 Bo Jackson .60 1.50
60 Andrew McCutchen .60 1.50
61 Craig Biggio .50 1.25
62 Gregory Polanco .50 1.25
63 Satchel Paige .60 1.50
64 Mike Trout 3.00 8.00
65 Sean Doolittle .40 1.00
66 Giancarlo Stanton .60 1.50
67 Ozzie Smith .75 2.00
68 Whitey Ford .50 1.25
69 Frank Thomas .60 1.50
70 Craig Kimbrel .50 1.25
71 Wil Myers .50 1.25
72 Adrian Beltre .60 1.50
73 Kris Bryant RC 6.00 15.00
74 Rickey Henderson .60 1.50
75 Rod Carew .50 1.25
76 Jacoby Ellsbury .50 1.25
77 Jackie Robinson .60 1.50
78 Adrian Gonzalez .50 1.25
79 Buster Posey .75 2.00
80 Joey Gallo RC 1.25 3.00
81 Corey Kluber .50 1.25
82 Manny Machado .60 1.50
83 Chipper Jones .60 1.50
84 Robinson Cano .50 1.25
85 Alex Gordon .50 1.25
86 Addison Russell RC 2.00 5.00
87 Sonny Gray .50 1.25
88 Jonathan Lucroy .50 1.25
89 Yu Darvish .60 1.50
90 Daniel Murphy .50 1.25
91 Roger Clemens .75 2.00
92 Mark McGwire 1.00 2.50
93 Yasiel Puig .60 1.50
94 Carlos Correa RC 6.00 15.00
95 Byron Buxton RC 3.00 8.00
96 Ken Griffey Jr. 1.25 3.00
97 Barry Larkin .50 1.25
98 Anthony Rendon .60 1.50
99 Chris Archer .40 1.00
100 Derek Jeter 1.50 4.00
103 Bryce Brentz JSY AU RC 3.00 8.00
104 Edwin Escobar JSY AU RC 3.00 8.00
106 Kendall Graveman JSY AU RC 3.00 8.00
107 Dilson Herrera JSY AU RC 15.00 40.00
109 Rymer Liriano JSY AU RC 3.00 8.00
110 Daniel Norris JSY AU RC EXCH 3.00 8.00
111 Aaron Sanchez JSY AU 5.00 12.00
112 Arismendy Alcantara JSY AU 3.00 8.00
113 McCann JSY AU RC EXCH 5.00 12.00
114 Marcus Stroman JSY AU 4.00 10.00
116 Matt Barnes JSY AU RC 3.00 8.00
117 Dellin Betances JSY AU 6.00 15.00
118 Jarred Cosart JSY AU 3.00 8.00
123 Steven Moya JSY AU RC 6.00 15.00
124 Chris Owings JSY AU 3.00 8.00
125 Anthony Ranaudo JSY AU RC EXCH 3.00 8.00
126 Kolten Wong JSY AU 8.00 20.00
127 Gary Brown JSY AU RC 5.00 12.00
128 Sonny Gray JSY AU 8.00 20.00
129 Carlos Martinez JSY AU 6.00 15.00
131 Dalton Pompey JSY AU RC 5.00 12.00
132 Tyson Ross JSY AU 3.00 8.00
133 Taijuan Walker JSY AU 3.00 8.00
134 Javier Baez JSY AU RC 12.00 30.00
135 Nick Castellanos JSY AU 6.00 15.00
136 J.Pederson JSY AU RC 10.00 25.00
137 Jorge Soler JSY AU RC 5.00 12.00
138 Zack Wheeler JSY AU 4.00 10.00
139 Jacob deGrom JSY AU 25.00 60.00
141 R.Castillo JSY AU RC 4.00 10.00
142 Jose Fernandez JSY AU 20.00 50.00
153 Matt Adams JSY AU 6.00 15.00
155 Archie Bradley JSY AU 3.00 8.00
158 Syndergaard JSY AU RC 25.00 60.00
161 Shelby Miller JSY AU 4.00 10.00
163 G.Polanco JSY AU 12.00 30.00
164 Michael Wacha JSY AU 8.00 20.00
165 Wil Myers JSY AU 4.00 10.00
168 Alex Colome JSY AU (RC) 3.00 8.00
172 Addison Russell JSY AU 15.00 40.00

2015 Topps Triple Threads Amber

*AMBER VET: 1.2X TO 3X BASIC
*AMBER RC: .75X TO 2X BASIC RC
STATED ODDS 1:4 MINI BOX
STATED PRINT RUN 125 SER.#'d SETS

2015 Topps Triple Threads Amethyst

*AMETHYST VET: 1X TO 2.5X BASIC
*AMETHYST RC: .6X TO 1.5X BASIC RC
STATED ODDS 1:2 MINI BOX
STATED PRINT RUN 354 SER.#'d SETS

2015 Topps Triple Threads Black

*BLACK: .6X TO 1.5X BASIC
STATED ODDS 1:31 MINI BOX
STATED PRINT RUN 35 SER.#'d SETS
EXCHANGE DEADLINE 8/31/2017

2015 Topps Triple Threads Emerald

*EMERALD VET: 1X TO 2.5X BASIC
*EMERALD RC: .6X TO 1.5X BASIC RC
1-100 ODDS 1:2 MINI BOX
1-100 PRINT RUN 250 SER.#'d SETS
*EMERALD JSY AU: .5X TO 1.2X BASIC
JSY AU ODDS 1:22 MINI BOX
JSY AU PRINT RUN 50 SER.#'d SETS
EXCHANGE DEADLINE 8/31/2017

2015 Topps Triple Threads Gold

*GOLD VET: 1.5X TO 4X BASIC
*GOLD RC: 1X TO 2.5X BASIC RC
STATED ODDS 1:5 MINI BOX
STATED PRINT RUN 99 SER.#'d SETS

2015 Topps Triple Threads Onyx

*ONYX VET: 2.5X TO 6X BASIC
*ONYX RC: 1.5X TO 4X BASIC RC
STATED ODDS 1:10 MINI BOX
STATED PRINT RUN 50 SER.#'d SETS
100 Derek Jeter 20.00 50.00

2015 Topps Triple Threads Sapphire

*SAPPHIRE VET: 3X TO 8X BASIC
*SAPPHIRE RC: 2X TO 5X BASIC RC
STATED ODDS 1:19 MINI BOX
STATED PRINT RUN 25 SER.#'d SETS

2015 Topps Triple Threads Sepia

*SEPIA: .4X TO 1X BASIC
STATED ODDS 1:15 MINI BOX
STATED PRINT RUN 75 SER.#'d SETS
EXCHANGE DEADLINE 8/31/2017

2015 Topps Triple Threads Autograph Relic Combos

STATED ODDS 1:76 MINI BOX
STATED PRINT RUN 36 SER.#'d SETS
EXCHANGE DEADLINE 8/31/2017
*SEPIA/27: .4X TO 1X BASIC
*EMERALD/18: .5X TO 1.2 BASIC
TTARCAHC Hywrd/Adms/Crpntr 60.00 150.00
TTARCALB Lester/Rizzo/Baez 50.00 120.00
TTARCBFP Baez/Frnco/Pdrsn 15.00 40.00
TTARCDWW Whlr/dGrm/Wrght 125.00 300.00
TTARCEDP Encrncn/Pmpy/Dnldsn 30.00 80.00
TTARCFRG Frmn/Rizzo/Gnzlz 30.00 80.00
TTARCMSJ Smltz/Jnes/Mddx 125.00 250.00
TTARCMZF Mesoraco/Zunino/McCann 20.00 50.00
TTARCOPC Pdra/Cstllo/Ortz 60.00 150.00
TTARCRSP Sandoval/Porcello/Ramirez 20.00 50.00
TTARCSCT Tomas/Soler/Castillo 25.00 60.00

2015 Topps Triple Threads Legend Relics

STATED ODDS 1:64 MINI BOX
STATED PRINT RUN 36 SER.#'d SETS
*SEPIA/27: .4X TO 1X BASIC
*EMERALD/18: .4X TO 1X BASIC
TTRLCF Carlton Fisk 4.00 10.00
TTRLCR Cal Ripken Jr. 15.00 40.00
TTRLDM Don Mattingly 10.00 25.00
TTRLEW Early Wynn 10.00 25.00
TTRLFR Frank Robinson 6.00 15.00
TTRLFT Frank Thomas 15.00 40.00
TTRLHN Hal Newhouser 10.00 25.00
TTRLJM Juan Marichal 8.00 20.00
TTRLJPA Jorge Posada 4.00 10.00
TTRLJPR Jim Palmer 4.00 10.00
TTRLJS John Smoltz 5.00 12.00
TTRLMM Mark McGwire 8.00 20.00
TTRLMS Mike Schmidt 15.00 40.00
TTRLNR Nolan Ryan 15.00 40.00
TTRLRCS Roger Clemens 6.00 15.00
TTRLRCW Rod Carew 4.00 10.00
TTRLRJ Reggie Jackson 4.00 10.00
TTRLRS Ryne Sandberg 10.00 25.00
TTRLRY Robin Yount 12.00 30.00
TTRLTG Tony Gwynn 12.00 30.00

2015 Topps Triple Threads Relic Autographs

STATED ODDS 1:10 MINI BOX
STATED PRINT RUN 18 SER.#'d SETS
EXCHANGE DEADLINE 8/31/2017
*GOLD/9: .5X TO 1.2X BASIC
SOME GOLD NOT PRICED DUE TO SCARCITY
ALL VERSIONS EQUALLY PRICED
TTARAC1 Alex Colome 5.00 12.00
TTARAC2 Alex Colome 5.00 12.00
TTARAC3 Alex Colome 5.00 12.00
TTARAC4 Alex Colome 5.00 12.00
TTARAC5 Alex Colome 5.00 12.00
TTARAG1 Adrian Gonzalez 15.00 40.00
TTARAG2 Adrian Gonzalez 15.00 40.00
TTARAG3 Adrian Gonzalez 15.00 40.00
TTARAJ1 Adam Jones 15.00 40.00
TTARAJ2 Adam Jones 15.00 40.00
TTARAJ3 Adam Jones 15.00 40.00
TTARAR1 Anthony Rizzo 30.00 80.00
TTARAR2 Anthony Rizzo 30.00 80.00
TTARAR3 Anthony Rizzo 30.00 80.00
TTARAR4 Anthony Rizzo 30.00 80.00
TTARAR5 Anthony Rizzo 30.00 80.00
TTARBB1 Brandon Belt 12.00 30.00
TTARBB2 Brandon Belt 12.00 30.00
TTARBB3 Brandon Belt 12.00 30.00
TTARBHR1 Bryce Harper 150.00 250.00
TTARBHR2 Bryce Harper 150.00 250.00
TTARBHR3 Bryce Harper 150.00 250.00
TTARBHT1 Brock Holt 10.00 20.00
TTARBHT2 Brock Holt 10.00 20.00
TTARBHT3 Brock Holt 10.00 25.00
TTARBJ1 Bo Jackson 60.00 150.00
TTARBM1 Brian McCann 12.00 30.00
TTARBM2 Brian McCann 12.00 30.00
TTARBM3 Brian McCann 12.00 30.00
TTARBP1 Buster Posey 75.00 200.00
TTARBP2 Buster Posey 75.00 200.00
TTARBS1 Blake Swihart 15.00 40.00
TTARBS2 Blake Swihart 15.00 40.00
TTARBS3 Blake Swihart 15.00 40.00
TTARBS4 Blake Swihart 15.00 40.00
TTARBS5 Blake Swihart 15.00 40.00
TTARBZ1 Ben Zobrist 20.00 50.00
TTARCBN1 Charlie Blackmon 8.00 20.00
TTARCBN2 Charlie Blackmon 8.00 20.00
TTARCBN3 Charlie Blackmon 8.00 20.00
TTARCBN4 Charlie Blackmon 8.00 20.00
TTARCBO1 Craig Biggio 20.00 50.00
TTARCD1 Carlos Delgado 10.00 25.00
TTARCF1 Cliff Floyd 10.00 25.00
TTARCF2 Cliff Floyd 10.00 25.00
TTARCF3 Cliff Floyd 10.00 25.00
TTARCF4 Cliff Floyd 10.00 25.00
TTARCKW1 Clayton Kershaw 75.00 200.00
TTARCR1 Cal Ripken Jr. 75.00 200.00
TTARCR2 Cal Ripken Jr. 75.00 200.00
TTARCR3 Cal Ripken Jr. 75.00 200.00
TTARCSA1 CC Sabathia 12.00 30.00
TTARCSA2 CC Sabathia 12.00 30.00
TTARCSA3 CC Sabathia 12.00 30.00
TTARCSE1 Chris Sale 15.00 40.00
TTARCSE2 Chris Sale 15.00 40.00
TTARCSE3 Chris Sale 15.00 40.00
TTARCY1 Christian Yelich 20.00 50.00
TTARCY2 Christian Yelich 20.00 50.00
TTARCY3 Christian Yelich 20.00 50.00
TTARCY4 Christian Yelich 20.00 50.00
TTARCY5 Christian Yelich 20.00 50.00
TTARDE1 Dennis Eckersley 15.00 40.00
TTARDFE1 David Freese 8.00 20.00
TTARDFE2 David Freese 8.00 20.00
TTARDFE3 David Freese 8.00 20.00
TTARDG1 Didi Gregorius 15.00 40.00
TTARDG2 Didi Gregorius 15.00 40.00

TTARDG3 Didi Gregorius 15.00 40.00
TTARDG4 Didi Gregorius 15.00 40.00
TTARDG5 Didi Gregorius 15.00 40.00
TTARDMO1 Devin Mesoraco 5.00 12.00
TTARDMO2 Devin Mesoraco 5.00 12.00
TTARDMO3 Devin Mesoraco 5.00 12.00
TTARDMO4 Devin Mesoraco 5.00 12.00
TTARDMO5 Devin Mesoraco 5.00 12.00
TTARDMY1 Don Mattingly 50.00 120.00
TTARDO1 David Ortiz 30.00 80.00
TTARDO2 David Ortiz 30.00 80.00
TTARDO3 David Ortiz 30.00 80.00
TTARDP1 Dustin Pedroia 20.00 50.00
TTARDP2 Dustin Pedroia 20.00 50.00
TTARDP3 Dustin Pedroia 20.00 50.00
TTARDW1 David Wright 15.00 40.00
TTARDW2 David Wright 15.00 40.00
TTARDW3 David Wright 15.00 40.00
TTAREL1 Evan Longoria 12.00 30.00
TTAREL2 Evan Longoria 12.00 30.00
TTAREL3 Evan Longoria 12.00 30.00
TTARFF1 Freddie Freeman 10.00 25.00
TTARFF2 Freddie Freeman 10.00 25.00
TTARFF3 Freddie Freeman 10.00 25.00
TTARFR1 Frank Robinson 30.00 80.00
TTARFR2 Frank Robinson 30.00 80.00
TTARFT1 Frank Thomas 40.00 100.00
TTARGR1 Garrett Richards 6.00 15.00
TTARGR2 Garrett Richards 6.00 15.00
TTARGR3 Garrett Richards 6.00 15.00
TTARGR4 Garrett Richards 6.00 15.00
TTARHA1 Hank Aaron 150.00 250.00
TTARHA2 Hank Aaron 150.00 250.00
TTARHR1 Hanley Ramirez 10.00 25.00
TTARHR2 Hanley Ramirez 10.00 25.00
TTARHR3 Hanley Ramirez 10.00 25.00
TTARIR1 Ivan Rodriguez 20.00 50.00
TTARIS1 Ichiro Suzuki
TTARIS2 Ichiro Suzuki
TTARJBL1 Jeff Bagwell 60.00 150.00
TTARJD1 Josh Donaldson 30.00 80.00
TTARJD2 Josh Donaldson 30.00 80.00
TTARJD3 Josh Donaldson 30.00 80.00
TTARJHD1 Jason Heyward 20.00 50.00
TTARJHD2 Jason Heyward 20.00 50.00
TTARJHD3 Jason Heyward 20.00 50.00
TTARJL1 Jon Lester 20.00 50.00
TTARJL2 Jon Lester 20.00 50.00
TTARJL3 Jon Lester 20.00 50.00
TTARJM1 Joe Mauer 20.00 50.00
TTARJM2 Joe Mauer 20.00 50.00
TTARJM3 Joe Mauer 20.00 50.00
TTARJR1 Jim Rice 15.00 40.00
TTARJR2 Jim Rice 15.00 40.00
TTARKC1 Kole Calhoun 10.00 25.00
TTARKC2 Kole Calhoun 10.00 25.00
TTARKC3 Kole Calhoun 10.00 25.00
TTARKC4 Kole Calhoun 10.00 25.00
TTARKC5 Kole Calhoun 10.00 25.00
TTARKGS1 Ken Griffey Sr. 10.00 25.00
TTARKGS2 Ken Griffey Sr. 10.00 25.00
TTARKGS3 Ken Griffey Sr. 10.00 25.00
TTARKGS4 Ken Griffey Sr. 10.00 25.00
TTARLB1 Lou Brock 20.00 50.00
TTARLD1 Lucas Duda 10.00 25.00
TTARLD2 Lucas Duda 10.00 25.00
TTARLD3 Lucas Duda 10.00 25.00
TTARLD4 Lucas Duda 10.00 25.00
TTARLG1 Luis Gonzalez 8.00 20.00
TTARLG2 Luis Gonzalez 8.00 20.00
TTARLG3 Luis Gonzalez 8.00 20.00
TTARLG4 Luis Gonzalez 8.00 20.00
TTARMB1 Matt Barnes 5.00 12.00
TTARMB2 Matt Barnes 5.00 12.00
TTARMB3 Matt Barnes 5.00 12.00
TTARMCN1 Matt Cain 12.00 30.00
TTARMCN2 Matt Cain 12.00 30.00
TTARMCN3 Matt Cain 12.00 30.00
TTARMCR1 Matt Carpenter 12.00 30.00
TTARMCR2 Matt Carpenter 12.00 30.00
TTARMCR3 Matt Carpenter 12.00 30.00
TTARMCR4 Matt Carpenter 12.00 30.00
TTARMCR5 Matt Carpenter 12.00 30.00
TTARMR1 Mariano Rivera 100.00 250.00
TTARMR2 Mariano Rivera 100.00 250.00
TTARMS1 Marcus Semien 8.00 20.00
TTARMS2 Marcus Semien 8.00 20.00
TTARMS3 Marcus Semien 8.00 20.00
TTARMS4 Marcus Semien 8.00 20.00
TTARMS5 Marcus Semien 8.00 20.00
TTARMSH1 Matt Shoemaker 6.00 15.00
TTARMSH2 Matt Shoemaker 6.00 15.00
TTARMSH3 Matt Shoemaker 6.00 15.00
TTARMSH4 Matt Shoemaker 6.00 15.00
TTARMT1 Mike Trout 150.00 300.00
TTARMT2 Mike Trout 150.00 300.00
TTARMT3 Mike Trout 150.00 300.00
TTARMZ1 Mike Zunino 5.00 12.00
TTARMZ2 Mike Zunino 5.00 12.00
TTARMZ3 Mike Zunino 5.00 12.00
TTARMZ4 Mike Zunino 5.00 12.00
TTARNR1 Nolan Ryan 60.00 150.00
TTARNR2 Nolan Ryan 60.00 150.00
TTARNG Nomar Garciaparra 15.00 40.00
TTAROS1 Ozzie Smith 30.00 80.00
TTAROV1 Omar Vizquel 175.00 350.00
TTAROV2 Omar Vizquel 175.00 350.00
TTAROV3 Omar Vizquel 175.00 350.00
TTARPF1 Prince Fielder 15.00 40.00
TTARPF2 Prince Fielder 15.00 40.00
TTARPF3 Prince Fielder 15.00 40.00
TTARPG3 Paul Goldschmidt 20.00 50.00
TTARPS1 Pablo Sandoval 8.00 20.00
TTARPS2 Pablo Sandoval 8.00 20.00
TTARPS3 Pablo Sandoval 8.00 20.00
TTARRB1 Ryan Braun 10.00 25.00
TTARRB2 Ryan Braun 10.00 25.00
TTARRB3 Ryan Braun 10.00 25.00
TTARRCO1 Robinson Cano 15.00 40.00
TTARRCO2 Robinson Cano 15.00 40.00
TTARRCO3 Robinson Cano 15.00 40.00
TTARRCS1 Roger Clemens 40.00 100.00
TTARRCS2 Roger Clemens 40.00 100.00
TTARRHD1 Ryan Howard 10.00 25.00
TTARRHD2 Ryan Howard 10.00 25.00
TTARRHD3 Ryan Howard 10.00 25.00
TTARRJA1 Reggie Jackson 30.00 80.00
TTARRJA2 Reggie Jackson 30.00 80.00
TTARRJO1 Randy Johnson 75.00 150.00
TTARRJO2 Randy Johnson 75.00 150.00
TTARRP1 Rick Porcello 8.00 20.00
TTARRP2 Rick Porcello 8.00 20.00
TTARRP3 Rick Porcello 8.00 20.00
TTARRP4 Rick Porcello 8.00 20.00
TTARRS1 Ryne Sandberg 30.00 80.00
TTARSM1 Starling Marte 15.00 40.00
TTARSM2 Starling Marte 15.00 40.00
TTARSM3 Starling Marte 15.00 40.00
TTARSM4 Starling Marte 15.00 40.00
TTARSM5 Starling Marte 15.00 40.00
TTARTG1 Tom Glavine 12.00 30.00
TTARTT1 Troy Tulowitzki 10.00 25.00
TTARTT2 Troy Tulowitzki 10.00 25.00
TTARTT3 Troy Tulowitzki 10.00 25.00
TTARVG1 Vladimir Guerrero 12.00 30.00
TTARVG2 Vladimir Guerrero 12.00 30.00
TTARVG3 Vladimir Guerrero 12.00 30.00
TTARWP1 Wily Peralta 5.00 12.00
TTARWP2 Wily Peralta 5.00 12.00
TTARWP3 Wily Peralta 5.00 12.00
TTARWP4 Wily Peralta 5.00 12.00
TTARWP5 Wily Peralta 5.00 12.00
TTARYC1 Yoenis Cespedes 20.00 50.00
TTARYC2 Yoenis Cespedes 20.00 50.00
TTARYC3 Yoenis Cespedes 20.00 50.00
TTARZW1 Zack Wheeler 10.00 25.00
TTARZW2 Zack Wheeler 10.00 25.00
TTARZW3 Zack Wheeler 10.00 25.00
TTARZW4 Zack Wheeler 10.00 25.00

2015 Topps Triple Threads Relic Combos

STATED ODDS 1:25 MINI BOX
STATED PRINT RUN 36 SER.#'d SETS
*SEPIA/27: .4X TO 1X BASIC
*EMERALD/18: .5X TO 1.2X BASIC
TTRCACS Ackley/Seager/Cano 6.00 15.00
TTRCAHC Carpenter/Adams/Heyward 8.00 20.00
TTRCASR Abreu/Sale/Ramirez 8.00 20.00
TTRCBCH Cn/Hdsn/Bmgrnr 6.00 15.00
TTRCBFC Beltre/Fielder/Choo 8.00 20.00
TTRCBFT Tomas/Baez/Franco 8.00 20.00
TTRCBPB Bmgrnr/Blt/Psy 40.00 100.00
TTRCBRE Encarnacion/Bautista/Reyes 8.00 20.00
TTRCBTJ Jns/Btsta/Trt 20.00 50.00
TTRCCAM Cole/Alvarez/Melancon 8.00 20.00
TTRCCDC Castellanos
Donaldson/Carpenter 6.00 15.00
TTRCCKC Knslr/Cbrra/Cspds 10.00 25.00
TTRCCSF Fernandez/Cishek/Stanton 6.00 15.00
TTRCCVM Cbrra/Vrlndr/Mrtnz 8.00 20.00
TTRCDHF Holland/Darvish/Feliz 8.00 20.00
TTRCDJM Mchdo/Jns/Dvs 20.00 50.00
TTRCDWW deGrm/Whlr/Wrght 15.00 40.00
TTRCEDP Dnldsn/Encrncn/Pmpy 20.00 50.00
TTRCFRG Frmn/Rzzo/Gnzlz 10.00 25.00
TTRCFSK Kimbrel/Simmons/Freeman 6.00 15.00
TTRCGAC Cbrra/Abru/Gldschmdt 8.00 20.00
TTRCGKP Puig/Krshw/Gnzlz 12.00 30.00
TTRCGOT Tomas/Owings/Goldschmidt 8.00 20.00
TTRCGRB Ramirez/Gomez/Braun 6.00 15.00
TTRCGTB Blackmon/Gonzalez/Tulowitzki 8.00 20.00
TTRCGVP Grdn/Vntra/Prz 12.00 30.00
TTRCHCI Iwakuma/Cano/Hernandez 6.00 15.00
TTRCHDW deGrm/Hrvy/Whlr 15.00 40.00
TTRCHJH Jay/Hlldy/Hywrd 10.00 25.00
TTRCHRZ Zmmrmn/Hrpr/Rndn 12.00 30.00
TTRCHSP Price/Hernandez/Sale 8.00 20.00
TTRCHUL Hamels/Utley/Lee 6.00 15.00
TTRCHVC Vtto/Cto/Hmltn 10.00 25.00
TTRCKGR Grnke/Ryu/Krshw 15.00 40.00
TTRCLJL Loney/Jennings/Longoria 6.00 15.00
TTRCMJS McCnn/Sbtha/Jtr 20.00 50.00
TTRCMMP McCtchn/Plnco/Mrte 15.00 40.00
TTRCMMZ McCann/Zunino/Mesoraco 6.00 15.00
TTRCMSJ Mddx/Jns/Smltz 25.00 60.00
TTRCOPC Ortz/Cstllo/Pdra 15.00 40.00
TTRCPJR Rvra/Psda/Jtr 25.00 60.00
TTRCPTH Trt/Pjls/Hmlton 20.00 50.00
TTRCRGB Reddick/Butler/Gray 6.00 15.00
TTRCRSP Porcello/Ramirez/Sandoval 6.00 15.00
TTRCSAS Springer/Singleton/Altuve 6.00 15.00
TTRCSCP Castillo/Pederson/Soler 20.00 50.00
TTRCSHM Mchdo/Schp/Hrdy 20.00 50.00
TTRCWML Wnwrght/Lynn/Mlna 10.00 25.00

2015 Topps Triple Threads Relics

STATED ODDS 1:9 MINI BOX
STATED PRINT RUN 36 SER.#'d SETS
*SEPIA/27: .4X TO 1X BASIC
*EMERALD/18: .5X TO 1.2X BASIC
*GOLD/9: .6X TO 1.5X BASIC
ALL VERSIONS EQUALLY PRICED
TTRAGN1 Alex Gordon 5.00 12.00
TTRAGN2 Alex Gordon 5.00 12.00
TTRAGZ1 Adrian Gonzalez 5.00 12.00
TTRAGZ2 Adrian Gonzalez 5.00 12.00
TTRAGZ3 Adrian Gonzalez 5.00 12.00
TTRAM1 Andrew McCutchen 12.00 30.00
TTRAM2 Andrew McCutchen 12.00 30.00
TTRAM3 Andrew McCutchen 12.00 30.00
TTRAP1 Albert Pujols 8.00 20.00
TTRAP2 Albert Pujols 8.00 20.00
TTRAP3 Albert Pujols 8.00 20.00
TTRAS1 Andrelton Simmons 8.00 20.00
TTRAWD1 Alex Wood 4.00 10.00
TTRAWD2 Alex Wood 4.00 10.00
TTRAWD3 Alex Wood 4.00 10.00
TTRAWT1 Adam Wainwright 6.00 15.00
TTRAWT2 Adam Wainwright 6.00 15.00
TTRAWT3 Adam Wainwright 6.00 15.00
TTRBM1 Brian McCann 5.00 12.00
TTRBM2 Brian McCann 5.00 12.00
TTRBM3 Brian McCann 5.00 12.00
TTRBP1 Buster Posey 8.00 20.00
TTRBP2 Buster Posey 8.00 20.00
TTRBP3 Buster Posey 8.00 20.00
TTRCBN1 Carlos Beltran 6.00 15.00
TTRCBN2 Carlos Beltran 6.00 15.00
TTRCBN3 Carlos Beltran 6.00 15.00
TTRCBZ1 Clay Buchholz 4.00 10.00
TTRCBZ2 Clay Buchholz 4.00 10.00
TTRCBZ3 Clay Buchholz 4.00 10.00
TTRCKL1 Craig Kimbrel 5.00 12.00
TTRCKL2 Craig Kimbrel 5.00 12.00
TTRCKL3 Craig Kimbrel 5.00 12.00
TTRCSA1 CC Sabathia 5.00 12.00
TTRCSA2 CC Sabathia 5.00 12.00
TTRCSA3 CC Sabathia 5.00 12.00
TTRCSE1 Chris Sale 6.00 15.00
TTRDJ1 Derek Jeter 20.00 50.00
TTRDJ2 Derek Jeter 20.00 50.00
TTRDJ3 Derek Jeter 20.00 50.00
TTRDO1 David Ortiz 8.00 20.00
TTRDO2 David Ortiz 8.00 20.00
TTRDO3 David Ortiz 8.00 20.00
TTRDPA1 Dustin Pedroia 6.00 15.00
TTRDPA2 Dustin Pedroia 6.00 15.00
TTRDPA3 Dustin Pedroia 6.00 15.00
TTRDPE1 David Price 10.00 25.00
TTRDPE2 David Price 10.00 25.00
TTRDPE3 David Price 10.00 25.00
TTRDW1 David Wright 5.00 12.00
TTRDW2 David Wright 5.00 12.00
TTRDW3 David Wright 5.00 12.00
TTRFF1 Freddie Freeman 8.00 20.00
TTRFF2 Freddie Freeman 8.00 20.00
TTRFF3 Freddie Freeman 8.00 20.00
TTRGS1 Giancarlo Stanton 6.00 15.00
TTRGS2 Giancarlo Stanton 6.00 15.00
TTRGS3 Giancarlo Stanton 6.00 15.00
TTRHP1 Hunter Pence 8.00 20.00
TTRHP2 Hunter Pence 8.00 20.00
TTRHP3 Hunter Pence 8.00 20.00
TTRHRR1 Hyun-Jin Ryu 6.00 15.00
TTRHRR2 Hyun-Jin Ryu 6.00 15.00
TTRHRR3 Hyun-Jin Ryu 6.00 15.00
TTRHRZ1 Hanley Ramirez 5.00 12.00
TTRHRZ2 Hanley Ramirez 5.00 12.00
TTRHRZ3 Hanley Ramirez 5.00 12.00
TTRIS1 Ichiro 12.00 30.00
TTRJB1 Javier Baez 30.00 80.00
TTRJB2 Javier Baez 30.00 80.00
TTRJB3 Javier Baez 30.00 80.00
TTRJD1 Jacob deGrom 12.00 30.00
TTRJD2 Jacob deGrom 12.00 30.00
TTRJD3 Jacob deGrom 12.00 30.00
TTRJE1 Jacoby Ellsbury 12.00 30.00
TTRJE2 Jacoby Ellsbury 12.00 30.00
TTRJE3 Jacoby Ellsbury 12.00 30.00
TTRJF1 Jose Fernandez 6.00 15.00
TTRJF2 Jose Fernandez 6.00 15.00
TTRJF3 Jose Fernandez 6.00 15.00
TTRJH1 Jason Heyward 6.00 15.00
TTRJH2 Jason Heyward 6.00 15.00
TTRJH3 Jason Heyward 6.00 15.00
TTRJS1 Jorge Soler 6.00 15.00
TTRJS2 Jorge Soler 6.00 15.00
TTRJS3 Jorge Soler 6.00 15.00
TTRJVO1 Joey Votto 8.00 20.00
TTRJVO2 Joey Votto 8.00 20.00
TTRJVO3 Joey Votto 8.00 20.00
TTRJVR1 Justin Verlander 8.00 20.00
TTRJVR2 Justin Verlander 8.00 20.00
TTRJVR3 Justin Verlander 8.00 20.00
TTRKB1 Kris Bryant 30.00 80.00
TTRKB2 Kris Bryant 30.00 80.00
TTRKB3 Kris Bryant 30.00 80.00
TTRLL1 Lance Lynn 4.00 10.00
TTRMC1 Miguel Cabrera 8.00 20.00
TTRMC2 Miguel Cabrera 8.00 20.00
TTRMC3 Miguel Cabrera 8.00 20.00
TTRMHO1 Matt Holliday 6.00 15.00
TTRMHO2 Matt Holliday 6.00 15.00
TTRMHO3 Matt Holliday 6.00 15.00
TTRMHY1 Matt Harvey 8.00 20.00
TTRMT1 Mike Trout 30.00 80.00
TTRMT2 Mike Trout 30.00 80.00
TTRMT3 Mike Trout 30.00 80.00
TTRMTA1 Masahiro Tanaka 8.00 20.00
TTRMTA2 Masahiro Tanaka 8.00 20.00
TTRMTX1 Mark Teixeira 6.00 15.00
TTRMTX2 Mark Teixeira 6.00 15.00
TTRMTX3 Mark Teixeira 6.00 15.00
TTRPF1 Prince Fielder 5.00 12.00
TTRPF2 Prince Fielder 5.00 12.00
TTRPF3 Prince Fielder 5.00 12.00
TTRPS1 Pablo Sandoval 6.00 15.00
TTRPS2 Pablo Sandoval 6.00 15.00
TTRPS3 Pablo Sandoval 6.00 15.00
TTRRB1 Ryan Braun 5.00 12.00
TTRRB2 Ryan Braun 5.00 12.00
TTRRB3 Ryan Braun 5.00 12.00
TTRRCA1 Rusney Castillo 5.00 12.00
TTRRCA2 Rusney Castillo 5.00 12.00
TTRRCO1 Robinson Cano 5.00 12.00
TTRRCO2 Robinson Cano 5.00 12.00
TTRRCO3 Robinson Cano 5.00 12.00
TTRSC1 Shin-Soo Choo 5.00 12.00
TTRSC2 Shin-Soo Choo 5.00 12.00
TTRSM1 Starling Marte 8.00 20.00
TTRSM2 Starling Marte 8.00 20.00
TTRSM3 Starling Marte 8.00 20.00
TTRSS1 Stephen Strasburg 6.00 15.00
TTRSS2 Stephen Strasburg 6.00 15.00
TTRSS3 Stephen Strasburg 6.00 15.00
TTRTT1 Troy Tulowitzki 6.00 15.00
TTRTT2 Troy Tulowitzki 6.00 15.00
TTRTT3 Troy Tulowitzki 6.00 15.00
TTRVM1 Victor Martinez 8.00 20.00
TTRXB1 Xander Bogaerts 8.00 20.00
TTRXB2 Xander Bogaerts 8.00 20.00
TTRXB3 Xander Bogaerts 8.00 20.00
TTRYD1 Yu Darvish 6.00 15.00
TTRYD2 Yu Darvish 6.00 15.00
TTRYD3 Yu Darvish 6.00 15.00
TTRYM1 Yadier Molina 10.00 25.00
TTRYM2 Yadier Molina 10.00 25.00
TTRYM3 Yadier Molina 10.00 25.00
TTRYP1 Yasiel Puig 6.00 15.00
TTRYP2 Yasiel Puig 6.00 15.00
TTRYV1 Yordano Ventura 5.00 12.00
TTRYV2 Yordano Ventura 5.00 12.00
TTRYV3 Yordano Ventura 5.00 12.00

2015 Topps Triple Threads Rookie Autographs

STATED ODDS 1:88 MINI BOX
STATED PRINT RUN 99 SER.#'d SETS
EXCHANGE DEADLINE 8/31/2017
RABBN Byron Buxton 20.00 50.00
RABFN Brandon Finnegan 4.00 10.00
RABS Blake Swihart 5.00 12.00
RACC Carlos Correa 40.00 100.00
RACR Carlos Rodon 10.00 25.00
RADT Devon Travis 4.00 10.00
RAFL Francisco Lindor 15.00 40.00
RAJGO Joey Gallo 20.00 50.00
RAJK Jung-Ho Kang 4.00 10.00
RAKB Kris Bryant 60.00 150.00
RAKP Kevin Plawecki 4.00 10.00
RAMFO Maikel Franco 12.00 30.00
RAMFZ Mike Foltynewicz 4.00 10.00
RAMJ Micah Johnson 4.00 10.00
RAMT Michael Taylor 4.00 10.00
RASM Steven Matz 10.00 25.00
RAYT Yasmany Tomas 5.00 12.00

2015 Topps Triple Threads Triple Threads

STATED ODDS 1:73 MINI BOX
STATED PRINT RUN 25 SER.#'d SETS
T3DAM Andrew McCutchen 60.00 150.00
T3DAP Albert Pujols 25.00 60.00
T3DBH Bryce Harper 60.00 150.00
T3DBP Buster Posey 60.00 150.00
T3DCB Craig Biggio 20.00 50.00
T3DCL Cliff Lee 15.00 40.00
T3DCR Cal Ripken Jr. 60.00 150.00
T3DDJ Derek Jeter 40.00 100.00
T3DDW David Wright 15.00 40.00
T3DJA Jose Abreu 12.00 30.00
T3DJB Jeff Bagwell 20.00 50.00
T3DJB Javier Baez 25.00 60.00
T3DJE Jacoby Ellsbury 15.00 40.00
T3DJPA Jorge Posada 20.00 50.00
T3DKG Ken Griffey Jr. 30.00 80.00
T3DMB Madison Bumgarner 25.00 60.00
T3DMC Miguel Cabrera 25.00 60.00
T3DMTA Masahiro Tanaka 15.00 40.00
T3DMTT Mike Trout 40.00 100.00
T3DRCA Rusney Castillo 15.00 40.00
T3DRCO Robinson Cano 15.00 40.00
T3DRJ Reggie Jackson 15.00 40.00
T3DSS Stephen Strasburg 12.00 30.00
T3DYD Yu Darvish 20.00 50.00
T3DYM Yadier Molina 25.00 60.00

2015 Topps Triple Threads Unity Relic Autographs

STATED ODDS 1:6 MINI BOX
STATED PRINT RUN 99 SER.#'d SETS
EXCHANGE DEADLINE 8/31/2017
*SEPIA/75: .4X TO 1X BASIC
*EMERALD/50: .5X TO 1.2X BASIC
*GOLD/25: .6X TO 1.5X BASIC
UAJRAA Arismendy Alcantara 4.00 10.00
UAJRAB Archie Bradley 4.00 10.00
UAJRAC Alex Colome 4.00 10.00
UAJRAG Adrian Gonzalez 8.00 20.00
UAJRAJ Adam Jones 6.00 15.00
UAJRAR Anthony Ranaudo 4.00 10.00
UAJRAS Aaron Sanchez 5.00 12.00
UAJRBBT Brandon Belt 5.00 12.00
UAJRBBZ Bryce Brentz 4.00 10.00
UAJRBC Brandon Crawford 5.00 12.00
UAJRBH Brock Holt 4.00 10.00
UAJRBS Blake Swihart 5.00 12.00
UAJRCC C.J. Cron 4.00 10.00
UAJRCG Carlos Gonzalez 6.00 15.00
UAJRCM Carlos Martinez 6.00 15.00
UAJRCSA CC Sabathia 8.00 20.00
UAJRCSE Chris Sale 8.00 20.00
UAJRCV Christian Vazquez 5.00 12.00
UAJRCY Christian Yelich 15.00 40.00
UAJRDB Dellin Betances 8.00 20.00
UAJRDF Dexter Fowler 5.00 12.00
UAJRDG Didi Gregorius 8.00 20.00
UAJRDM Devin Mesoraco 4.00 10.00
UAJRDN Daniel Norris 4.00 10.00
UAJRDNA Daniel Nava 4.00 10.00
UAJRDPA Dustin Pedroia 12.00 30.00
UAJRDPY Dalton Pompey 5.00 12.00
UAJREEN Edwin Encarnacion 6.00 15.00
UAJREER Edwin Escobar 4.00 10.00
UAJREG Evan Gattis 6.00 15.00
UAJRFF Freddie Freeman 6.00 15.00
UAJRGB Gary Brown 4.00 10.00
UAJRGR Garrett Richards 5.00 12.00
UAJRHR Hanley Ramirez 6.00 15.00
UAJRJA Jose Abreu 10.00 25.00
UAJRJB Javier Baez 10.00 25.00
UAJRJC Jarred Cosart 4.00 10.00
UAJRJD Jacob deGrom 30.00 80.00
UAJRJF Jose Fernandez 40.00 100.00
UAJRJHD Jason Heyward 5.00 12.00
UAJRJK Jung-Ho Kang 30.00 80.00
UAJRJLR Jon Lester 15.00 40.00
UAJRJLS Juan Lagares 4.00 10.00
UAJRJM James McCann 6.00 15.00
UAJRJP Joc Pederson 15.00 40.00
UAJRJPA Jose Pirela 4.00 10.00
UAJRJR Jason Rogers 4.00 10.00
UAJRJSR Jorge Soler 10.00 25.00
UAJRKG Kendall Graveman 4.00 10.00
UAJRKL Kyle Lobstein 4.00 10.00
UAJRKS Kyle Seager 4.00 10.00
UAJRKV Kennys Vargas 4.00 10.00
UAJRLG Luis Gonzalez 6.00 15.00
UAJRLS Luis Sardinas 4.00 10.00
UAJRMAS Matt Adams 4.00 10.00
UAJRMB Matt Barnes 4.00 10.00
UAJRMBS Matt Barnes 4.00 10.00
UAJRMCK Matt Clark 4.00 10.00
UAJRMCN Matt Cain 6.00 15.00
UAJRMCR Matt Carpenter 8.00 20.00
UAJRMG Mark Grace 10.00 25.00
UAJRMM Matt Moore 5.00 12.00
UAJRMS Matt Shoemaker 5.00 12.00
UAJRMSE Marcus Semien 6.00 15.00
UAJRMZ Mike Zunino 4.00 10.00
UAJROV Omar Vizquel 10.00 25.00
UAJRPG Paul Goldschmidt 10.00 25.00
UAJRRA R.J. Alvarez 4.00 10.00
UAJRRB Ryan Braun 8.00 20.00
UAJRRCA Robinson Cano 10.00 25.00
UAJRRCO Rusney Castillo 5.00 12.00
UAJRRL Rymer Liriano 4.00 10.00
UAJRROS Roberto Osuna 4.00 10.00
UAJRRP Rick Porcello 5.00 12.00
UAJRRZ Ryan Zimmerman 5.00 12.00
UAJRSG Sonny Gray 5.00 12.00
UAJRSGN Shane Greene 4.00 10.00
UAJRSMA Steven Moya 5.00 12.00
UAJRSMR Shelby Miller 6.00 15.00
UAJRSS Steven Souza Jr. 5.00 12.00
UAJRTW Taijuan Walker 4.00 10.00
UAJRWF Wilmer Flores 5.00 12.00
UAJRWP Wily Peralta 4.00 10.00
UAJRYT Yasmany Tomas 5.00 12.00
UAJRZW Zack Wheeler 5.00 12.00

2015 Topps Triple Threads Unity Relics

STATED ODDS 1:6 MINI BOX
STATED PRINT RUN 36 SER.#'d SETS
ALL VERSIONS EQUALLY PRICED
*SEPIA/27: .4X TO 1X BASIC
*EMERALD/18: .5X TO 1.2X BASIC
*GOLD/9: .6X TO 1.5X BASIC
UJRAB Adrian Beltre 5.00 12.00
UJRACA Aroldis Chapman 5.00 12.00
UJRACB Alex Cobb 3.00 8.00
UJRACH Aroldis Chapman 5.00 12.00
UJRAD Adam Dunn 4.00 10.00
UJRAEA Adam Eaton 3.00 8.00
UJRAEN Adam Eaton 3.00 8.00
UJRAGN Adrian Gonzalez 4.00 10.00
UJRAGO Adrian Gonzalez 4.00 10.00
UJRAGR Alex Gordon 4.00 10.00
UJRAGZ Adrian Gonzalez 4.00 10.00
UJRAJ Adam Jones 4.00 10.00
UJRAM Andrew McCutchen 5.00 12.00
UJRAPS Albert Pujols 6.00 15.00
UJRAPU Albert Pujols 6.00 15.00
UJRARO Anthony Rizzo 6.00 15.00
UJRASA Aaron Sanchez 4.00 10.00
UJRASZ Aaron Sanchez 4.00 10.00
UJRAWA Adam Wainwright 4.00 10.00
UJRAWD Alex Wood 3.00 8.00
UJRAWO Alex Wood 3.00 8.00
UJRAWT Adam Wainwright 4.00 10.00
UJRBD Brian Dozier 6.00 15.00
UJRBHN Billy Hamilton 4.00 10.00
UJRBMC Brian McCann 4.00 10.00
UJRBMN Brian McCann 4.00 10.00
UJRBPH Brandon Phillips 3.00 8.00
UJRBPP Brandon Phillips 3.00 8.00
UJRBPS Brandon Phillips 3.00 8.00
UJRBPY Buster Posey 6.00 15.00
UJRCBE Carlos Beltran 4.00 10.00
UJRCBL Charlie Blackmon 5.00 12.00
UJRCBN Carlos Beltran 4.00 10.00
UJRCBO Charlie Blackmon 5.00 12.00
UJRCC Chris Carter 3.00 8.00
UJRCDA Chris Davis 3.00 8.00
UJRCDN Corey Dickerson 3.00 8.00
UJRCDS Chris Davis 3.00 8.00
UJRCGO Carlos Gonzalez 4.00 10.00
UJRCGZ Carlos Gomez 3.00 8.00
UJRCH Cole Hamels 4.00 10.00
UJRCKL Craig Kimbrel 4.00 10.00
UJRCKR Corey Kluber 4.00 10.00
UJRCKW Clayton Kershaw 8.00 20.00
UJRCMA Carlos Martinez 4.00 10.00
UJRCMZ Carlos Martinez 4.00 10.00
UJRCOS Chris Owings 3.00 8.00
UJRCOW Chris Owings 3.00 8.00
UJRCSA Carlos Santana 4.00 10.00
UJRCSE Chris Sale 5.00 12.00
UJRCSL Chris Sale 5.00 12.00
UJRCU Chase Utley 4.00 10.00
UJRCYE Christian Yelich 6.00 15.00
UJRCYH Christian Yelich 6.00 15.00
UJRCYL Christian Yelich 6.00 15.00
UJRDBE Dellin Betances 4.00 10.00
UJRDBN Domonic Brown 4.00 10.00
UJRDBR Domonic Brown 4.00 10.00
UJRDBS Dellin Betances 4.00 10.00
UJRDF Doug Fister 3.00 8.00
UJRDHD Derek Holland 3.00 8.00
UJRDHO Derek Holland 3.00 8.00
UJRDJE Derek Jeter 25.00 60.00
UJRDJR Derek Jeter 25.00 60.00
UJRDJT Derek Jeter 25.00 60.00
UJRDNA Daniel Nava 3.00 8.00
UJRDNO Daniel Norris 3.00 8.00
UJRDNS Daniel Norris 3.00 8.00
UJRDNV Daniel Nava 3.00 8.00
UJRDO David Ortiz 5.00 12.00
UJRDPA Dustin Pedroia 5.00 12.00
UJRDPD Dustin Pedroia 5.00 12.00
UJRDPE David Price 4.00 10.00
UJRDPO Dalton Pompey 4.00 10.00
UJRDPY Dalton Pompey 4.00 10.00
UJRDWR David Wright 4.00 10.00
UJRDWT David Wright 4.00 10.00
UJREA Elvis Andrus 4.00 10.00
UJREEE Edwin Escobar 3.00 8.00
UJREEN Edwin Encarnacion 5.00 12.00
UJREER Edwin Escobar 3.00 8.00
UJREH Eric Hosmer 4.00 10.00
UJREL Evan Longoria 4.00 10.00
UJRFFN Freddie Freeman 6.00 15.00
UJRFFR Freddie Freeman 6.00 15.00
UJRFH Felix Hernandez 4.00 10.00
UJRGCE Gerrit Cole 5.00 12.00
UJRGCO Gerrit Cole 5.00 12.00
UJRGG Gio Gonzalez 4.00 10.00
UJRGSR George Springer 4.00 10.00
UJRGST Giancarlo Stanton 5.00 12.00
UJRHP Hunter Pence 6.00 15.00
UJRHRA Hanley Ramirez 4.00 10.00
UJRHRU Hyun-Jin Ryu 4.00 10.00
UJRHRY Hyun-Jin Ryu 4.00 10.00
UJRHRZ Hanley Ramirez 4.00 10.00
UJRID Ian Desmond 3.00 8.00
UJRIKI Ian Kinsler 4.00 10.00
UJRIKR Ian Kinsler 4.00 10.00
UJRJAE Jose Altuve 4.00 10.00
UJRJAU Jose Abreu 5.00 12.00
UJRJBA Javier Baez 25.00 60.00
UJRJBE Jay Bruce 4.00 10.00
UJRJBR Jay Bruce 4.00 10.00
UJRJBT Jose Bautista 4.00 10.00
UJRJBU Jay Bruce 4.00 10.00
UJRJBZ Javier Baez 25.00 60.00
UJRJC Johnny Cueto 4.00 10.00
UJRJD Josh Donaldson 10.00 25.00
UJRJDM Jacob deGrom 10.00 25.00
UJRJE Jacoby Ellsbury 4.00 10.00
UJRJF Jose Fernandez 5.00 12.00
UJRJGO Jedd Gyorko 3.00 8.00
UJRJGY Jedd Gyorko 3.00 8.00
UJRJHA Josh Hamilton 4.00 10.00
UJRJHD Jason Heyward 4.00 10.00
UJRJHE Jason Heyward 4.00 10.00
UJRJHN Josh Hamilton 4.00 10.00
UJRJHT Josh Hamilton 4.00 10.00
UJRJHY Jason Heyward 4.00 10.00
UJRJK Jason Kipnis 4.00 10.00
UJRJLA Juan Lagares 3.00 8.00
UJRJLR Jon Lester 5.00 12.00
UJRJLY Jonathan Lucroy 4.00 10.00
UJRJMA Joe Mauer 4.00 10.00
UJRJMC Jake McGee 4.00 10.00
UJRJME Jake McGee 4.00 10.00
UJRJMR Joe Mauer 4.00 10.00
UJRJR Jose Reyes 6.00 15.00
UJRJSA Jarrod Saltalamacchia 3.00 8.00
UJRJSG Jean Segura 4.00 10.00
UJRJSH Jonathan Schoop 3.00 8.00
UJRJSL Jarrod Saltalamacchia 3.00 8.00
UJRJSP Jonathan Schoop 3.00 8.00
UJRJSR Jorge Soler 5.00 12.00
UJRJSS James Shields 3.00 8.00
UJRJSU Jean Segura 4.00 10.00
UJRJTA Junichi Tazawa 3.00 8.00
UJRJTN Julio Teheran 4.00 10.00
UJRJTZ Junichi Tazawa 3.00 8.00
UJRJU Justin Upton 4.00 10.00
UJRJV Justin Verlander 5.00 12.00
UJRJVE Justin Verlander 5.00 12.00
UJRJVO Joey Votto 5.00 12.00
UJRJVR Justin Verlander 5.00 12.00
UJRJVT Joey Votto 5.00 12.00
UJRJZ Jordan Zimmermann 4.00 10.00
UJRKC Kole Calhoun 3.00 8.00
UJRKSE Kyle Seager 3.00 8.00
UJRKSR Kyle Seager 3.00 8.00
UJRKW Kolten Wong 4.00 10.00
UJRLD Lucas Duda 4.00 10.00
UJRLL Lance Lynn 3.00 8.00
UJRLMA Leonys Martin 3.00 8.00
UJRLMN Leonys Martin 3.00 8.00
UJRMAD Matt Adams 3.00 8.00
UJRMAS Matt Adams 3.00 8.00
UJRMBR Madison Bumgarner 8.00 20.00
UJRMBY Michael Brantley 4.00 10.00
UJRMCA Miguel Cabrera 6.00 15.00
UJRMCB Miguel Cabrera 6.00 15.00
UJRMCE Michael Choice 3.00 8.00
UJRMCH Michael Choice 3.00 8.00
UJRMCR Miguel Cabrera 6.00 15.00
UJRMHA Matt Harvey 4.00 10.00
UJRMHO Matt Holliday 5.00 12.00
UJRMHY Matt Holliday 5.00 12.00
UJRMK Matt Kemp 6.00 15.00
UJRMMI Mike Minor 3.00 8.00
UJRMMO Manny Machado 8.00 20.00
UJRMMR Mike Minor 3.00 8.00
UJRMMS Mike Moustakas 4.00 10.00
UJRMOA Marcell Ozuna 5.00 12.00
UJRMOL Mike Olt 3.00 8.00
UJRMOT Mike Olt 3.00 8.00
UJRMOZ Marcell Ozuna 5.00 12.00
UJRMPA Michael Pineda 3.00 8.00
UJRMPI Michael Pineda 3.00 8.00
UJRMS Max Scherzer 5.00 12.00
UJRMTA Mark Teixeira 6.00 15.00
UJRMTE Mark Teixeira 6.00 15.00
UJRMTT Mike Trout 20.00 50.00
UJRMW Michael Wacha 4.00 10.00
UJRMZO Mike Zunino 3.00 8.00
UJRMZU Mike Zunino 3.00 8.00
UJRNAI Norichika Aoki 10.00 25.00
UJRNAO Nolan Arenado 8.00 20.00
UJRNCA Nick Castellanos 5.00 12.00
UJRNCS Nick Castellanos 5.00 12.00
UJRNMA Nick Martinez 3.00 8.00
UJRNMZ Nick Martinez 3.00 8.00
UJRPAL Pedro Alvarez 3.00 8.00
UJRPAZ Pedro Alvarez 3.00 8.00
UJRPF Prince Fielder 4.00 10.00
UJRPG Paul Goldschmidt 5.00 12.00
UJRPS Pablo Sandoval 4.00 10.00
UJRRBA Ryan Braun 4.00 10.00
UJRRBN Ryan Braun 4.00 10.00
UJRRBR Ryan Braun 4.00 10.00
UJRRCA Robinson Cano 4.00 10.00
UJRRCL Rusney Castillo 5.00 12.00
UJRRCN Robinson Cano 4.00 10.00
UJRRCO Robinson Cano 4.00 10.00
UJRRCT Rusney Castillo 5.00 12.00
UJRRLI Rymer Liriano 3.00 8.00
UJRRLO Rymer Liriano 3.00 8.00
UJRRZI Ryan Zimmerman 4.00 10.00
UJRRZN Ryan Zimmerman 4.00 10.00
UJRSCA Starlin Castro 3.00 8.00
UJRSCO Shin-Soo Choo 4.00 10.00
UJRSG Sonny Gray 4.00 10.00
UJRSM Starling Marte 4.00 10.00
UJRSP Salvador Perez 4.00 10.00
UJRSS Stephen Strasburg 5.00 12.00
UJRSTA Sam Tuivailala 3.00 8.00
UJRSTU Sam Tuivailala 3.00 8.00
UJRTBA Trevor Bauer 6.00 15.00
UJRTBR Trevor Bauer 6.00 15.00
UJRTDA Travis d'Arnaud 4.00 10.00
UJRTDD Travis d'Arnaud 4.00 10.00
UJRTDR Travis d'Arnaud 4.00 10.00
UJRTF Todd Frazier 3.00 8.00
UJRTRO Tyson Ross 3.00 8.00
UJRTRS Tyson Ross 3.00 8.00
UJRTT Troy Tulowitzki 5.00 12.00
UJRTWA Taijuan Walker 3.00 8.00
UJRTWR Taijuan Walker 3.00 8.00
UJRVMA Victor Martinez 4.00 10.00
UJRVMT Victor Martinez 4.00 10.00
UJRVMZ Victor Martinez 4.00 10.00
UJRWFL Wilmer Flores 4.00 10.00
UJRWFS Wilmer Flores 4.00 10.00
UJRWPA Wily Peralta 3.00 8.00
UJRWPE Wily Peralta 3.00 8.00
UJRYC Yoenis Cespedes 4.00 10.00
UJRYD Yu Darvish 5.00 12.00
UJRYMA Yadier Molina 6.00 15.00
UJRYMO Yadier Molina 6.00 15.00
UJRYP Yasiel Puig 5.00 12.00
UJRYT Yasmany Tomas 5.00 12.00
UJRZG Zack Greinke 6.00 15.00
UJRZW Zack Wheeler 4.00 10.00

2016 Topps Triple Threads

COMP.SET w/o AU's (100) 75.00 200.00
JSY AU RC ODDS 1:12 MINI BOX
JSY AU RC PRINT RUN 99 SER.#'d SETS
JSY AU ODDS 1:12 MINI BOX
JSY AU PRINT RUN 99 SER.#'d SETS
EXCHANGE DEADLINE 8/31/2018
1-100 PLATE ODDS 1:115 MINI BOX
JSY AU PLATE ODDS 1:276 MINI BOX
PLATE PRINT RUN 1 SET PER COLOR
BLACK-CYAN-MAGENTA-YELLOW ISSUED
NO PLATE PRICING DUE TO SCARCITY
1 Ken Griffey Jr. 1.25 3.00
2 Frank Thomas .60 1.50
3 David Ortiz .60 1.50
4 Nolan Arenado 1.00 2.50
5 Mark McGwire 1.00 2.50
6 Albert Pujols .75 2.00
7 Satchel Paige .60 1.50
8 Ryan Braun .50 1.25
9 Hank Aaron 1.25 3.00
10 Blake Snell RC .75 2.00
11 David Wright .50 1.25
12 Justin Verlander .60 1.50
13 Honus Wagner .60 1.50
14 Paul Goldschmidt .60 1.50
15 Jose Fernandez .60 1.50
16 Jacob deGrom 1.25 3.00
17 Freddie Freeman .75 2.00
18 Chipper Jones .60 1.50
19 Lou Gehrig 1.25 3.00
20 Yasiel Puig .60 1.50
21 Reggie Jackson .50 1.25
22 Lorenzo Cain .40 1.00
23 Todd Frazier .40 1.00
24 Adam Jones .50 1.25
25 Eric Hosmer .50 1.25
26 Mookie Betts 1.25 3.00
27 Roberto Clemente 1.50 4.00
28 Kris Bryant .75 2.00
29 Ichiro Suzuki .75 2.00
30 Vladimir Guerrero .50 1.25
31 Wade Boggs .50 1.25
32 Kenta Maeda RC 1.25 3.00
33 Sandy Koufax 1.25 3.00
34 Willie Mays 1.25 3.00
35 Noah Syndergaard .50 1.25
36 Joey Votto .60 1.50
37 Clayton Kershaw 1.00 2.50
38 Cal Ripken Jr. 2.00 5.00
39 Sonny Gray .50 1.25
40 Miguel Cabrera .60 1.50
41 Max Scherzer .60 1.50
42 Nolan Ryan 2.00 5.00
43 Carl Yastrzemski 1.00 2.50
44 Prince Fielder .50 1.25
45 A.J. Reed RC .60 1.50
46 Zack Greinke .60 1.50
47 Ted Williams 1.25 3.00
48 Matt Harvey .50 1.25
49 Mike Piazza .60 1.50
50 Chris Archer .40 1.00
51 Buster Posey .75 2.00
52 Roger Clemens .75 2.00
53 George Brett 1.25 3.00
54 Manny Machado .60 1.50
55 Gerrit Cole .60 1.50
56 Bryce Harper 1.00 2.50
57 Randy Johnson .60 1.50
58 Aaron Nola RC 1.25 3.00
59 Dallas Keuchel .50 1.25
60 Jose Berrios RC 1.00 2.50
61 Jake Arrieta .50 1.25
62 Chris Sale .60 1.50
63 Edwin Encarnacion .60 1.50
64 Robinson Cano .50 1.25
65 Jose Abreu .60 1.50
66 Troy Tulowitzki .60 1.50
67 Stephen Strasburg .60 1.50
68 Giancarlo Stanton .60 1.50
69 Mike Trout 3.00 8.00
70 Felix Hernandez .50 1.25
71 Adrian Gonzalez .50 1.25
72 Lucas Giolito RC 1.00 2.50
73 Hunter Pence .50 1.25
74 Bo Jackson .60 1.50
75 Ozzie Smith .75 2.00
76 Justin Upton .50 1.25
77 Johnny Cueto .50 1.25
78 Jackie Robinson .60 1.50
79 Jason Heyward .50 1.25
80 Stan Musial 1.00 2.50
81 Yoenis Cespedes .60 1.50
82 John Smoltz .60 1.50
83 Andrew McCutchen .60 1.50
84 Matt Kemp .50 1.25
85 Josh Donaldson .50 1.25
86 Jose Altuve .50 1.25
87 George Springer .50 1.25
88 Carlos Gonzalez .50 1.25
89 Madison Bumgarner .50 1.25
90 David Price .50 1.25
91 Jose Bautista .50 1.25
92 Trevor Story RC 3.00 8.00
93 Carlos Correa .60 1.50
94 Anthony Rizzo .75 2.00
95 Nomar Mazara RC 1.00 2.50
96 Don Mattingly 1.25 3.00
97 Greg Maddux .75 2.00
98 Yu Darvish .60 1.50
99 Babe Ruth 1.50 4.00
100 Julio Urias RC 2.00 5.00
RFPBD Brandon Drury JSY AU RC 8.00 20.00
RFPBS Blake Swihart JSY AU 4.00 10.00
RFPCC Carlos Correa JSY AU 30.00 80.00
RFPCE Carl Edwards Jr. JSY AU RC 5.00 12.00
RFPCM Carlos Martinez JSY AU 4.00 10.00
RFPCR Carlos Rodon JSY AU 5.00 12.00
RFPCRE Colin Rea JSY AU RC 3.00 8.00
RFPCS Corey Seager JSY AU RC 25.00 60.00
RFPEI Ender Inciarte JSY AU 4.00 10.00
RFPER Eduardo Rodriguez JSY AU 3.00 8.00
RFPGB Greg Bird JSY AU RC 4.00 10.00
RFPGS George Springer JSY AU 6.00 15.00
RFPHO Hector Olivera JSY AU RC 4.00 10.00
RFPHOW Henry Owens JSY AU RC 4.00 10.00
RFPJB Justin Bour JSY AU 4.00 10.00
RFPJG Jon Gray JSY AU RC 3.00 8.00

RFPJH Jesse Hahn JSY AU 3.00 8.00
RFPJP Joc Pederson JSY AU 8.00 20.00
RFPJPA Joe Panik JSY AU 4.00 10.00
RFPJS Jorge Soler JSY AU 6.00 15.00
RFPKB Kris Bryant JSY AU 60.00 150.00
RFPKC Kaleb Cowart JSY AU RC 3.00 8.00
RFPKMA Ketel Marte JSY AU RC 6.00 15.00
RFPKP Kevin Plawecki JSY AU 3.00 8.00
RFPKS Kyle Schwarber JSY AU RC 30.00 80.00
RFPLS Luis Severino JSY AU RC 4.00 10.00
RFPMC Michael Conforto
JSY AU RC EXCH 15.00 40.00
RFPMD Matt Duffy JSY AU 3.00 8.00
RFPMF Maikel Franco JSY AU 4.00 10.00
RFPMS Miguel Sano JSY AU RC 5.00 12.00
RFPNS Noah Syndergaard JSY AU 15.00 40.00
RFPPO Peter O'Brien JSY AU RC 3.00 8.00
RFPRO Roberto Osuna JSY AU 3.00 8.00
RFPRR Rob Refsnyder JSY AU RC 4.00 10.00
RFPRS Richie Shaffer JSY AU RC 3.00 8.00
RFPSM Steven Matz JSY AU 3.00 8.00
RFPSP Stephen Piscotty JSY AU RC 5.00 12.00
RFPTT Trea Turner JSY AU RC 20.00 50.00

2016 Topps Triple Threads Amber

*AMBER VET: .75X TO 2X BASIC
*AMBER RC: .5X TO 1.2X BASIC RC
STATED ODDS 1:4 MINI BOX
STATED PRINT RUN 150 SER.#'d SETS

2016 Topps Triple Threads Amethyst

*AMETHYST VET: .6X TO 1.5X BASIC
*AMETHYST RC: .4X TO 1X BASIC RC
STATED ODDS 1:2 MINI BOX
STATED PRINT RUN 340 SER.#'d SETS

2016 Topps Triple Threads Emerald

*EMERALD VET: .6X TO 1.5X BASIC
*EMERALD RC: .4X TO 1X BASIC RC
*EMERALD JSY AU: .4X TO 1X BASIC RC
1-100 ODDS 1:2 MINI BOX
JSY AU ODDS 1:23 MINI BOX
1-100 PRINT RUN 250 SER.#'d SETS
JSY AU PRINT RUN 50 SER.#'d SETS
EXCHANGE DEADLINE 8/31/2018

2016 Topps Triple Threads Gold

*GOLD VET: 1X TO 2.5X BASIC
*GOLD RC: .6X TO 1.5X BASIC RC
STATED ODDS 1:5 MINI BOX
STATED PRINT RUN 99 SER.#'d SETS

2016 Topps Triple Threads Onyx

*ONYX VET: 2.5X TO 6X BASIC
*ONYX RC: 1.5X TO 4X BASIC RC
*ONYX JSY AU: .5X TO 1.2X BASIC RC
1-100 ODDS 1:10 MINI BOX
JSY AU ODDS 1:32 MINI BOX
1-100 PRINT RUN 50 SER.#'d SETS
JSY AU PRINT RUN 35 SER.#'d SETS
EXCHANGE DEADLINE 8/31/2018

2016 Topps Triple Threads Sapphire

*SAPPHIRE VET: 3X TO 8X BASIC
*SAPPHIRE RC: 2X TO 5X BASIC RC
STATED ODDS 1:19 MINI BOX
STATED PRINT RUN 25 SER.#'d SETS

2016 Topps Triple Threads Silver

*SILVER JSY AU: .4X TO 1X BASIC RC
STATED ODDS 1:15 MINI BOX
STATED PRINT RUN 75 SER.#'d SETS
EXCHANGE DEADLINE 8/31/2018

2016 Topps Triple Threads Autograph Relic Combos

STATED ODDS 1:82 MINI BOX
STATED PRINT RUN 36 SER.#'d SETS
EXCHANGE DEADLINE 8/31/2018
*SILVER/27: .4X TO 1X BASIC
*EMERALD/18: .5X TO 1.2 BASIC
TTARCBLR Ltr/Brynt/Rzzo 150.00 400.00
TTARCCAK Crra/Kchl/Altve 60.00 150.00
TTARCDCB Crwfrd/Belt/Dffy 20.00 50.00
TTARCHCI Cano/Iwkma/Hrnndz 30.00 80.00
TTARCHTS Hdly/Txra/Svrno 20.00 50.00
TTARCMPH Plnco/Hrrsn/Marte 25.00 60.00
TTARCOIF Inciarte/Freeman/Olivera 15.00 40.00
TTARCPSM Mda/Sger/Pdrsn 60.00 150.00
TTARCPTM Tms/Pllck/Mllr 15.00 40.00
TTARCPWM Wong/Mrtnz/Psctty 20.00 50.00
TTARCSHS Soler/Hywrd/Schwrbr 30.00 80.00
TTARCSMD deGrm/Syndrgrd/Mtz 100.00 250.00
TTARCSPP Prcllo/Pdra/Swhrt 25.00 60.00
TTARCTGG Trnr/Gnzlz/Grndl 25.00 60.00
TTARCTSE Encrncn/Strmn/Tlwtzki 25.00 60.00

2016 Topps Triple Threads Legend Relics

STATED ODDS 1:85 MINI BOX
STATED PRINT RUN 36 SER.#'d SETS
*SILVER/27: .4X TO 1X BASIC
*EMERALD/18: .4X TO 1X BASIC
TTRLBL Bob Lemon 10.00 25.00
TTRLCJ Chipper Jones 12.00 30.00
TTRLCR Cal Ripken Jr. 20.00 50.00
TTRLCY Carl Yastrzemski 30.00 80.00
TTRLEW Early Wynn 10.00 25.00
TTRLFT Frank Thomas 15.00 40.00
TTRLHA Hank Aaron 25.00 60.00
TTRLHN Hal Newhouser 8.00 20.00
TTRLHW Honus Wagner 50.00 120.00
TTRLJM Juan Marichal 8.00 20.00
TTRLJS John Smoltz 8.00 20.00
TTRLKG Ken Griffey Jr. 30.00 80.00
TTRLMP Mike Piazza 10.00 25.00
TTRLOS Ozzie Smith 12.00 30.00
TTRLPM Paul Molitor 8.00 20.00
TTRLRA Roberto Alomar 8.00 20.00
TTRLRC Roberto Clemente 60.00 150.00
TTRLRH Rickey Henderson 12.00 30.00
TTRLRS Ryne Sandberg 12.00 30.00
TTRLTW Ted Williams 50.00 120.00
TTRLWB Wade Boggs 8.00 20.00
TTRLWM Willie Mays 50.00 120.00
TTRLWS Willie Stargell 10.00 25.00

2016 Topps Triple Threads Relic Autographs

STATED ODDS 1:10 MINI BOX
STATED PRINT RUN 18 SER.#'d SETS
EXCHANGE DEADLINE 8/31/2018
*GOLD/9: .5X TO 1.2X BASIC
SOME GOLD NOT PRICED DUE TO SCARCITY
ALL VERSIONS EQUALLY PRICED
TTARAE1 Alcides Escobar 6.00 15.00
TTARAE2 Alcides Escobar 6.00 15.00
TTARAE3 Alcides Escobar 6.00 15.00
TTARAE4 Alcides Escobar 6.00 15.00
TTARAE5 Alcides Escobar 6.00 15.00
TTARAG1 Adrian Gonzalez 10.00 25.00
TTARAG2 Adrian Gonzalez 10.00 25.00
TTARAG3 Adrian Gonzalez 10.00 25.00
TTARAG4 Adrian Gonzalez 10.00 25.00
TTARAJ1 Adam Jones 15.00 40.00
TTARAJ2 Adam Jones 15.00 40.00
TTARAJ3 Adam Jones 15.00 40.00
TTARAJ4 Adam Jones 15.00 40.00
TTARAM1 Andrew Miller 12.00 30.00
TTARAM2 Andrew Miller 12.00 30.00
TTARAM3 Andrew Miller 12.00 30.00
TTARAM4 Andrew Miller 12.00 30.00
TTARAM5 Andrew Miller 12.00 30.00
TTARAP1 A.J. Pollock 10.00 25.00
TTARAP2 A.J. Pollock 10.00 25.00
TTARAP3 A.J. Pollock 10.00 25.00
TTARAP4 A.J. Pollock 10.00 25.00
TTARAP5 A.J. Pollock 10.00 25.00
TTARAR1 Anthony Rizzo 40.00 100.00
TTARAR2 Anthony Rizzo 40.00 100.00
TTARAR3 Anthony Rizzo 40.00 100.00
TTARAR4 Anthony Rizzo 40.00 100.00
TTARAR5 Anthony Rizzo 40.00 100.00
TTARAW1 Alex Wood 5.00 12.00
TTARAW2 Alex Wood 5.00 12.00
TTARAW3 Alex Wood 5.00 12.00
TTARAW4 Alex Wood 5.00 12.00
TTARAW5 Alex Wood 5.00 12.00
TTARBB1 Brandon Belt 10.00 25.00
TTARBC1 Brandon Crawford 15.00 40.00
TTARBC2 Brandon Crawford 15.00 40.00
TTARBC3 Brandon Crawford 15.00 40.00
TTARBC4 Brandon Crawford 15.00 40.00
TTARBC5 Brandon Crawford 15.00 40.00
TTARBH1 Bryce Harper 150.00 300.00
TTARBH2 Bryce Harper 150.00 300.00
TTARBHO1 Brock Holt 10.00 25.00
TTARBHO2 Brock Holt 10.00 25.00
TTARBHO3 Brock Holt 10.00 25.00
TTARBHO4 Brock Holt 10.00 25.00
TTARBHO5 Brock Holt 10.00 25.00
TTARBM1 Brian McCann 6.00 15.00
TTARBM2 Brian McCann 6.00 15.00
TTARBM3 Brian McCann 6.00 15.00
TTARBP1 Buster Posey 60.00 150.00
TTARCB1 Craig Biggio 25.00 60.00
TTARCD1 Kevin Costner 125.00 250.00
TTARCD2 Kevin Costner 125.00 250.00
TTARCDI1 Corey Dickerson 5.00 12.00
TTARCDI2 Corey Dickerson 5.00 12.00
TTARCDI3 Corey Dickerson 5.00 12.00
TTARCF1 Carlton Fisk 25.00 60.00
TTARCH1 Cole Hamels 10.00 25.00
TTARCK1 Clayton Kershaw 60.00 150.00
TTARCM1 Carlos Martinez 8.00 20.00
TTARCM2 Carlos Martinez 8.00 20.00
TTARCM3 Carlos Martinez 8.00 20.00
TTARCM4 Carlos Martinez 8.00 20.00
TTARCM5 Carlos Martinez 8.00 20.00
TTARCR1 Cal Ripken Jr. 75.00 200.00
TTARCS1 Curt Schilling 20.00 50.00
TTARCSA1 Chris Sale 10.00 25.00
TTARCSA2 Chris Sale 10.00 25.00
TTARCSA3 Chris Sale 10.00 25.00
TTARCSA4 Chris Sale 10.00 25.00
TTARCSH1 Curt Schilling 20.00 50.00
TTARCY1 Carl Yastrzemski 75.00 200.00
TTARCYE1 Christian Yelich 15.00 40.00
TTARCYE2 Christian Yelich 15.00 40.00
TTARCYE3 Christian Yelich 15.00 40.00
TTARCYE4 Christian Yelich 15.00 40.00
TTARCYE5 Christian Yelich 15.00 40.00
TTARDG1 Dee Gordon 8.00 20.00
TTARDG2 Dee Gordon 8.00 20.00
TTARDG3 Dee Gordon 8.00 20.00
TTARDG4 Dee Gordon 8.00 20.00
TTARDG5 Dee Gordon 8.00 20.00
TTARDK1 Dallas Keuchel 6.00 15.00
TTARDK2 Dallas Keuchel 6.00 15.00
TTARDK3 Dallas Keuchel 6.00 15.00
TTARDK4 Dallas Keuchel 6.00 15.00
TTARDK5 Dallas Keuchel 6.00 15.00
TTARDL1 Derrek Lee 8.00 20.00
TTARDL2 Derrek Lee 8.00 20.00
TTARDL3 Derrek Lee 8.00 20.00
TTARDL4 Derrek Lee 8.00 20.00
TTARDL5 Derrek Lee 8.00 20.00
TTARDO1 David Ortiz 75.00 200.00
TTAREE1 Edwin Encarnacion 12.00 30.00
TTAREI1 Ender Inciarte 8.00 20.00
TTAREI2 Ender Inciarte 8.00 20.00
TTAREI3 Ender Inciarte 8.00 20.00
TTAREI4 Ender Inciarte 8.00 20.00
TTAREI5 Ender Inciarte 8.00 20.00
TTAREL1 Evan Longoria 8.00 20.00
TTARFH1 Felix Hernandez 40.00 100.00
TTARGR1 Garrett Richards 6.00 15.00
TTARGR2 Garrett Richards 6.00 15.00
TTARGR3 Garrett Richards 6.00 15.00
TTARGR4 Garrett Richards 6.00 15.00
TTARGR5 Garrett Richards 6.00 15.00
TTARHA1 Hank Aaron 125.00 250.00
TTARI Ichiro Suzuki 200.00 400.00
TTARICH1 Ichiro Suzuki 200.00 400.00
TTARIS Ichiro Suzuki 200.00 400.00
TTARJA1 Jose Abreu 20.00 50.00
TTARJB1 Jeff Bagwell 30.00 80.00
TTARJB2 Jeff Bagwell 30.00 80.00
TTARJB3 Jeff Bagwell 30.00 80.00
TTARJB4 Jeff Bagwell 30.00 80.00
TTARJD1 Jacob deGrom 40.00 100.00
TTARJD2 Jacob deGrom 30.00 80.00
TTARJD3 Jacob deGrom 30.00 80.00
TTARJD4 Jacob deGrom 30.00 80.00
TTARJD5 Jacob deGrom 30.00 80.00
TTARJF1 Jeurys Familia 12.00 30.00
TTARJF2 Jeurys Familia 12.00 30.00
TTARJF3 Jeurys Familia 12.00 30.00
TTARJG1 Joey Gallo 20.00 50.00
TTARJH1 Jesse Hahn 5.00 12.00
TTARJH2 Jesse Hahn 5.00 12.00
TTARJHE1 Jason Heyward 12.00 30.00
TTARJHE2 Jason Heyward 12.00 30.00
TTARJHE3 Jason Heyward 12.00 30.00
TTARJHE4 Jason Heyward 12.00 30.00
TTARJHE5 Jason Heyward 12.00 30.00
TTARJL1 Jon Lester 40.00 100.00
TTARJL2 Jon Lester 40.00 100.00
TTARJM1 J.D. Martinez 20.00 50.00
TTARJM2 J.D. Martinez 20.00 50.00
TTARJM3 J.D. Martinez 20.00 50.00
TTARJM4 J.D. Martinez 20.00 50.00
TTARJM5 J.D. Martinez 20.00 50.00
TTARJR1 Jim Rice 12.00 30.00
TTARJR2 Jim Rice 12.00 30.00
TTARJRE1 J.T. Realmuto 20.00 50.00
TTARJRE2 J.T. Realmuto 20.00 50.00
TTARJRE3 J.T. Realmuto 20.00 50.00
TTARJS1 James Shields 5.00 12.00
TTARJS2 James Shields 5.00 12.00
TTARJS3 James Shields 5.00 12.00
TTARJS4 James Shields 5.00 12.00
TTARJS5 James Shields 5.00 12.00
TTARJSO1 Jorge Soler 10.00 25.00
TTARJSO2 Jorge Soler 10.00 25.00
TTARJSO3 Jorge Soler 10.00 25.00
TTARJSO4 Jorge Soler 10.00 25.00
TTARJSO5 Jorge Soler 10.00 25.00
TTARJT1 Justin Turner 25.00 60.00
TTARJT2 Justin Turner 25.00 60.00
TTARKC1 Kole Calhoun 5.00 12.00
TTARKC2 Kole Calhoun 5.00 12.00
TTARKC3 Kole Calhoun 5.00 12.00
TTARKC4 Kole Calhoun 5.00 12.00
TTARKC5 Kole Calhoun 5.00 12.00
TTARKGM Ken Griffey Jr. 125.00 300.00
TTARKGR Ken Griffey Jr. 125.00 300.00
TTARKM1 Kendrys Morales 8.00 20.00
TTARKM2 Kendrys Morales 8.00 20.00
TTARKM3 Kendrys Morales 8.00 20.00
TTARKM4 Kendrys Morales 8.00 20.00
TTARKM5 Kendrys Morales 8.00 20.00
TTARKS1 Kyle Seager 10.00 25.00
TTARKS2 Kyle Seager 10.00 25.00
TTARKS3 Kyle Seager 10.00 25.00
TTARKS4 Kyle Seager 10.00 25.00
TTARKS5 Kyle Seager 10.00 25.00
TTARKW1 Kolten Wong 6.00 15.00
TTARKW2 Kolten Wong 6.00 15.00
TTARKW3 Kolten Wong 6.00 15.00
TTARKW4 Kolten Wong 6.00 15.00
TTARKW5 Kolten Wong 6.00 15.00
TTARMC2 Matt Carpenter 10.00 25.00
TTARMG1 Mark Grace 20.00 50.00
TTARMG2 Mark Grace 20.00 50.00
TTARMG3 Mark Grace 20.00 50.00
TTARMG4 Mark Grace 20.00 50.00
TTARMGR1 Mark Grace 20.00 50.00
TTARMH1 Matt Harvey 25.00 60.00
TTARMM1 Manny Machado 40.00 100.00
TTARMM2 Manny Machado 40.00 100.00
TTARMM3 Manny Machado 40.00 100.00
TTARMM4 Manny Machado 40.00 100.00
TTARMMC1 Mark McGwire 60.00 150.00
TTARMMG1 Mark McGwire 60.00 150.00
TTARMP1 Mike Piazza 50.00 120.00
TTARMPI1 Michael Pineda 5.00 12.00
TTARMPI2 Michael Pineda 5.00 12.00
TTARMPI3 Michael Pineda 5.00 12.00
TTARMPI4 Michael Pineda 5.00 12.00
TTARMPI5 Michael Pineda 5.00 12.00
TTARMPIA1 Mike Piazza 50.00 120.00
TTARMR1 Matt Reynolds 5.00 12.00
TTARMR2 Matt Reynolds 5.00 12.00
TTARMR3 Matt Reynolds 5.00 12.00
TTARMR4 Matt Reynolds 5.00 12.00
TTARMR5 Matt Reynolds 5.00 12.00
TTARMS1 Matt Shoemaker 6.00 15.00
TTARMS2 Matt Shoemaker 6.00 15.00
TTARMS3 Matt Shoemaker 6.00 15.00
TTARMS4 Matt Shoemaker 6.00 15.00
TTARMS5 Matt Shoemaker 6.00 15.00
TTARMSE3 Marcus Semien
TTARMST1 Marcus Stroman 10.00 25.00
TTARMST2 Marcus Stroman 10.00 25.00
TTARMST3 Marcus Stroman 10.00 25.00
TTARMST4 Marcus Stroman 10.00 25.00
TTARMST5 Marcus Stroman 10.00 25.00
TTARMT1 Mike Trout 150.00 250.00
TTARMW1 Michael Wacha
TTARMW2 Michael Wacha
TTARMW3 Michael Wacha
TTARMW4 Michael Wacha
TTARMW5 Michael Wacha
TTARNA1 Nolan Arenado 30.00 80.00
TTARNA2 Nolan Arenado 30.00 80.00
TTARNA3 Nolan Arenado 30.00 80.00
TTARNA4 Nolan Arenado 30.00 80.00
TTARNR1 Nolan Ryan
TTARPF1 Prince Fielder 8.00 20.00
TTARPM1 Paul Molitor 15.00 40.00
TTARRB1 Ryan Braun 15.00 40.00
TTARRC1 Roger Clemens 30.00 80.00
TTARRCA1 Rusney Castillo 5.00 12.00
TTARRCAN Robinson Cano 20.00 50.00
TTARRH1 Rickey Henderson 40.00 100.00
TTARRHE1 Rickey Henderson 40.00 100.00
TTARRI1 Raisel Iglesias 6.00 15.00
TTARRI2 Raisel Iglesias 6.00 15.00
TTARRJO1 Randy Johnson 40.00 100.00
TTARROL1 Rollie Fingers 10.00 25.00
TTARROL2 Rollie Fingers 10.00 25.00
TTARROL3 Rollie Fingers 10.00 25.00
TTARROL4 Rollie Fingers 10.00 25.00
TTARROL5 Rollie Fingers 10.00 25.00
TTARRS1 Ryne Sandberg 25.00 60.00
TTARSC1 Steve Carlton 15.00 40.00
TTARSCA2 Starlin Castro 25.00 60.00
TTARSD1 Sean Doolittle 5.00 12.00
TTARSD2 Sean Doolittle 5.00 12.00
TTARSD3 Sean Doolittle 5.00 12.00
TTARSG1 Sonny Gray 6.00 15.00
TTARSG2 Sonny Gray 6.00 15.00
TTARSG3 Sonny Gray 6.00 15.00
TTARSG4 Sonny Gray 6.00 15.00
TTARSG5 Sonny Gray 6.00 15.00
TTARSM1 Starling Marte 10.00 25.00
TTARSM2 Starling Marte 10.00 25.00
TTARSM3 Starling Marte 10.00 25.00
TTARSM4 Starling Marte 10.00 25.00
TTARTEX1 Mark Teixeira 12.00 30.00
TTARTEX2 Mark Teixeira 12.00 30.00
TTARTEX3 Mark Teixeira 12.00 30.00
TTARTEX4 Mark Teixeira 12.00 30.00
TTARTT1 Troy Tulowitzki
TTARWD1 Wade Davis 8.00 20.00
TTARWD2 Wade Davis 8.00 20.00
TTARWD3 Wade Davis 8.00 20.00
TTARWD4 Wade Davis 8.00 20.00
TTARWD5 Wade Davis 8.00 20.00
TTARWM1 Wil Myers 10.00 25.00
TTARYD1 Yu Darvish 40.00 100.00
TTARYG1 Yasmani Grandal 10.00 25.00
TTARYG2 Yasmani Grandal 10.00 25.00
TTARYG3 Yasmani Grandal 10.00 25.00
TTARYG4 Yasmani Grandal 10.00 25.00
TTARYG5 Yasmani Grandal 10.00 25.00
TTARYT1 Yasmany Tomas 5.00 12.00

2016 Topps Triple Threads Relic Combos

STATED ODDS 1:26 MINI BOX
STATED PRINT RUN 36 SER.#'d SETS
*SILVER/27: .4X TO 1X BASIC
*EMERALD/18: .5X TO 1.2X BASIC
TTRCHG Ichiro/Giffy/Hrnndz 25.00 60.00
TTRCBLR Brnt/Rzzo/Lstr 10.00 25.00
TTRCBLS Santana/Braun/Lucroy 6.00 15.00
TTRCBPC Cain/Bmgrnr/Psy 10.00 25.00
TTRCBTE Encrncn/Tulo/Btsta 12.00 30.00
TTRCBVP Bruce/Phillips/Votto 8.00 20.00
TTRCCMB Mllr/Chpmn/Btncs 12.00 30.00
TTRCCMH Cole/McCutchen/Harrison 8.00 20.00
TTRCCTE Ellsbury/Teixeira/Castro 6.00 15.00
TTRCDBE Bggs/Ellsbry/Dmn 10.00 25.00
TTRCDCB Belt/Duffy/Crawford 8.00 20.00
TTRCFBA Beltre/Fielder/Andrus 8.00 20.00
TTRCFSG Stanton/Fernandez/Gordon 6.00 15.00
TTRCFSI Stntn/Szki/Frnndz 15.00 40.00
TTRCGBP Grdn/Prz/Brtt 15.00 40.00
TTRCGHC Granderson/Harvey/Conforto 6.00 15.00
TTRCHCC Hernandez/Cruz/Cano 8.00 20.00
TTRCHTS Teixeira/Headley/Severino 6.00 15.00
TTRCICH Ichiro Suzuki 30.00 80.00
TTRCKCU Uptn/Knslr/Cbrra 5.00 12.00
TTRCKKL Lndr/Kpns/Klbr 15.00 40.00
TTRCKPS Sgr/Krshw/Puig 12.00 30.00
TTRCLBG Gonzalez/LeMahieu/Blackmon 8.00 20.00
TTRCMCH Holliday/Molina/Carpenter 10.00 25.00
TTRCMDJ Davis/Machado/Jones 6.00 15.00
TTRCMGJ Gausman/Machado/Jones 8.00 20.00
TTRCMKH Kang/Marte/Harrison 6.00 15.00
TTRCMKS Kemp/Myers/Shields 5.00 12.00
TTRCMRP Mrry/Plmr/Rpkn 30.00 80.00
TTRCMSB Buxton/Mauer/Sano 8.00 20.00
TTRCMSN Norris/Shields/Myers 5.00 12.00
TTRCPBO Owens/Buchholz/Price 6.00 15.00
TTRCPPC Psy/Crwfrd/Pnk 10.00 25.00
TTRCPSP Pdrsn/Sgr/Puig 10.00 25.00
TTRCPVH Hmltn/Vtto/Phllps 10.00 25.00
TTRCPWM Piscotty/Martinez/Wong 20.00 50.00
TTRCRGV Reddick/Gray/Vogt 6.00 15.00
TTRCRRB Brnt/Rssll/Rzzo 30.00 80.00
TTRCRRH Hywrd/Rzzo/Rssll 10.00 25.00
TTRCRSA Sale/Rodon/Abreu 6.00 15.00
TTRCSHS Hrpr/Strsbrg/Schrzr 10.00 25.00
TTRCSMD Syndrgrd/Matz/dGrm 12.00 30.00
TTRCSPP Pedroia/Porcello/Swihart 8.00 20.00
TTRCSSB Brnt/Slr/Schwrbr 20.00 50.00
TTRCTPC Clhn/Pjls/Trt 12.00 30.00
TTRCTSE Stroman/Encarnacion
Tulowitzki 6.00 15.00
TTRCVCM Mrtnz/Vrlndr/Cbrra 12.00 30.00
TTRCVCP Ventura/Cain/Perez 6.00 15.00
TTRCVCU Cabrera/Verlander/Upton 8.00 20.00
TTRCWHC Harvey/Wright/Conforto 6.00 15.00

2016 Topps Triple Threads Relics

STATED ODDS 1:8 MINI BOX
STATED PRINT RUN 36 SER.#'d SETS
*SILVER/27: .4X TO 1X BASIC
*EMERALD/18: .5X TO 1.2X BASIC
*GOLD/9: .6X TO 1.5X BASIC
ALL VERSIONS EQUALLY PRICED
TTRI1 Ichiro Suzuki 6.00 15.00
TTRI2 Ichiro Suzuki 6.00 15.00
TTRAG1 Adrian Gonzalez 4.00 10.00
TTRAG2 Adrian Gonzalez 4.00 10.00
TTRAG3 Adrian Gonzalez 4.00 10.00
TTRAM1 Andrew McCutchen 6.00 15.00
TTRAM2 Andrew McCutchen 6.00 15.00
TTRAM3 Andrew McCutchen 6.00 15.00
TTRAP1 Albert Pujols 6.00 15.00
TTRAP2 Albert Pujols 6.00 15.00
TTRAP3 Albert Pujols 6.00 15.00
TTRAR1 Anthony Rizzo 6.00 15.00
TTRAR2 Anthony Rizzo 6.00 15.00
TTRAR3 Anthony Rizzo 6.00 15.00
TTRARU1 Addison Russell 5.00 12.00
TTRARU2 Addison Russell 5.00 12.00
TTRARU3 Addison Russell 5.00 12.00
TTRAW1 Adam Wainwright 4.00 10.00
TTRAW2 Adam Wainwright 4.00 10.00
TTRBG1 Brett Gardner 5.00 12.00
TTRBG2 Brett Gardner 5.00 12.00
TTRBH1 Bryce Harper 8.00 20.00
TTRBH2 Bryce Harper 8.00 20.00
TTRBM1 Brian McCann 4.00 10.00
TTRBM2 Brian McCann 4.00 10.00
TTRBP1 Brandon Phillips 3.00 8.00
TTRBP2 Brandon Phillips 3.00 8.00
TTRBP3 Brandon Phillips 3.00 8.00
TTRBPO1 Buster Posey 6.00 15.00
TTRBPO2 Buster Posey 6.00 15.00
TTRBPO3 Buster Posey 6.00 15.00
TTRCB1 Carlos Beltran 4.00 10.00
TTRCB2 Carlos Beltran 4.00 10.00
TTRCB3 Carlos Beltran 4.00 10.00
TTRCBI1 Craig Biggio 4.00 10.00
TTRCBI2 Craig Biggio 4.00 10.00
TTRCK1 Clayton Kershaw 8.00 20.00
TTRCK2 Clayton Kershaw 8.00 20.00
TTRCK3 Clayton Kershaw 8.00 20.00
TTRCM1 Carlos Martinez 4.00 10.00
TTRCM2 Carlos Martinez 4.00 10.00
TTRCR1 Cal Ripken Jr. 15.00 40.00
TTRCR2 Cal Ripken Jr. 15.00 40.00
TTRDL1 DJ LeMahieu 5.00 12.00
TTRDL2 DJ LeMahieu 5.00 12.00
TTRDO1 David Ortiz 8.00 20.00
TTRDO2 David Ortiz 8.00 20.00
TTRDO3 David Ortiz 8.00 20.00
TTRDP1 Dustin Pedroia 6.00 15.00
TTRDP2 Dustin Pedroia 6.00 15.00
TTRDP3 Dustin Pedroia 6.00 15.00
TTRDW1 David Wright 4.00 10.00
TTRDW2 David Wright 4.00 10.00
TTRDW3 David Wright 4.00 10.00
TTREL1 Evan Longoria 4.00 10.00
TTREL2 Evan Longoria 4.00 10.00
TTREL3 Evan Longoria 4.00 10.00
TTRFH1 Felix Hernandez 4.00 10.00
TTRFH2 Felix Hernandez 4.00 10.00
TTRFH3 Felix Hernandez 4.00 10.00
TTRGS1 Giancarlo Stanton 5.00 12.00
TTRGS2 Giancarlo Stanton 5.00 12.00
TTRGS3 Giancarlo Stanton 5.00 12.00
TTRHR1 Hanley Ramirez 4.00 10.00
TTRHR2 Hanley Ramirez 4.00 10.00
TTRHR3 Hanley Ramirez 4.00 10.00
TTRIR1 Ivan Rodriguez 6.00 15.00
TTRIR2 Ivan Rodriguez 6.00 15.00
TTRJA1 Jose Abreu 5.00 12.00
TTRJA2 Jose Abreu 5.00 12.00
TTRJA3 Jose Abreu 5.00 12.00
TTRJAL1 Jose Altuve 5.00 12.00
TTRJAL2 Jose Altuve 5.00 12.00
TTRJC1 Jose Canseco 10.00 25.00
TTRJC2 Jose Canseco 10.00 25.00
TTRJD1 Johnny Damon 4.00 10.00
TTRJD2 Johnny Damon 4.00 10.00
TTRJDE1 Jacob deGrom 10.00 25.00
TTRJDE2 Jacob deGrom 10.00 25.00
TTRJDE3 Jacob deGrom 10.00 25.00
TTRJF1 Jose Fernandez 6.00 15.00
TTRJF2 Jose Fernandez 6.00 15.00
TTRJF3 Jose Fernandez 6.00 15.00
TTRJH1 Josh Harrison 3.00 8.00
TTRJH2 Josh Harrison 3.00 8.00
TTRJK1 Jung Ho Kang 3.00 8.00
TTRJK2 Jung Ho Kang 3.00 8.00
TTRJL1 Jon Lester 4.00 10.00
TTRJL2 Jon Lester 4.00 10.00
TTRJL3 Jon Lester 4.00 10.00
TTRJLU1 Jonathan Lucroy 4.00 10.00
TTRJS1 Jorge Soler 5.00 12.00
TTRJS2 Jorge Soler 5.00 12.00
TTRJV1 Justin Verlander 5.00 12.00
TTRJV2 Justin Verlander 5.00 12.00
TTRJV3 Justin Verlander 5.00 12.00
TTRJVO1 Joey Votto 5.00 12.00
TTRJVO2 Joey Votto 5.00 12.00
TTRJVO3 Joey Votto 5.00 12.00
TTRKB1 Kris Bryant 25.00 60.00
TTRKB2 Kris Bryant 25.00 60.00
TTRKP1 Kevin Plawecki 3.00 8.00
TTRKS1 Kurt Suzuki 3.00 8.00
TTRKW1 Kolten Wong 4.00 10.00
TTRKW2 Kolten Wong 4.00 10.00
TTRLD1 Lucas Duda 4.00 10.00
TTRLD2 Lucas Duda 4.00 10.00
TTRMB1 Madison Bumgarner 4.00 10.00
TTRMC1 Miguel Cabrera 5.00 12.00
TTRMC2 Miguel Cabrera 5.00 12.00
TTRMC3 Miguel Cabrera 5.00 12.00
TTRMF1 Maikel Franco 4.00 10.00
TTRMF2 Maikel Franco 4.00 10.00
TTRMH1 Matt Harvey 4.00 10.00
TTRMH2 Matt Harvey 4.00 10.00
TTRMH3 Matt Harvey 4.00 10.00
TTRMM1 Manny Machado 6.00 15.00
TTRMM2 Manny Machado 6.00 15.00
TTRMM3 Manny Machado 6.00 15.00
TTRMMC1 Mark McGwire 8.00 20.00
TTRMMC2 Mark McGwire 8.00 20.00
TTRMP1 Mike Piazza 5.00 12.00
TTRMP2 Mike Piazza 5.00 12.00
TTRMS1 Max Scherzer 5.00 12.00
TTRMS2 Max Scherzer 5.00 12.00
TTRMT1 Masahiro Tanaka 4.00 10.00
TTRMT2 Masahiro Tanaka 4.00 10.00
TTRMT3 Masahiro Tanaka 4.00 10.00
TTRMTE1 Mark Teixeira 4.00 10.00
TTRMTE2 Mark Teixeira 4.00 10.00
TTRMTR1 Mike Trout 12.00 30.00
TTRMTR2 Mike Trout 12.00 30.00
TTRPF1 Prince Fielder 4.00 10.00
TTRPF2 Prince Fielder 4.00 10.00
TTRPF3 Prince Fielder 4.00 10.00
TTRPG1 Paul Goldschmidt 5.00 12.00
TTRPG2 Paul Goldschmidt 5.00 12.00
TTRPG3 Paul Goldschmidt 5.00 12.00
TTRPS1 Pablo Sandoval 4.00 10.00
TTRPS2 Pablo Sandoval 4.00 10.00
TTRPS3 Pablo Sandoval 4.00 10.00
TTRRC1 Robinson Cano 4.00 10.00
TTRRC2 Robinson Cano 4.00 10.00
TTRRC3 Robinson Cano 4.00 10.00
TTRRCA1 Rusney Castillo 3.00 8.00
TTRRCA2 Rusney Castillo 3.00 8.00
TTRRCA3 Rusney Castillo 3.00 8.00
TTRRCL1 Roger Clemens 6.00 15.00
TTRRH1 Ryan Howard 4.00 10.00
TTRRH2 Ryan Howard 4.00 10.00
TTRSC1 Shin-Soo Choo 4.00 10.00
TTRSC2 Shin-Soo Choo 4.00 10.00
TTRSM1 Steven Matz 3.00 8.00
TTRSM2 Steven Matz 3.00 8.00
TTRTD1 Travis d'Arnaud 4.00 10.00
TTRTD2 Travis d'Arnaud 4.00 10.00
TTRVG1 Vladimir Guerrero 4.00 10.00
TTRVM1 Victor Martinez 4.00 10.00
TTRVM2 Victor Martinez 4.00 10.00
TTRVM3 Victor Martinez 4.00 10.00
TTRYM1 Yadier Molina 6.00 15.00
TTRYM2 Yadier Molina 6.00 15.00
TTRYM3 Yadier Molina 6.00 15.00
TTRZW1 Zack Wheeler 4.00 10.00
TTRZW2 Zack Wheeler 4.00 10.00

2016 Topps Triple Threads Unity Jumbo Relic Autographs

STATED ODDS 1:6 MINI BOX
STATED PRINT RUN 99 SER.#'d SETS
EXCHANGE DEADLINE 8/31/2018
*SILVER/75: .4X TO 1X BASIC
*EMERALD/50: .5X TO 1.2X BASIC
*GOLD/25: .6X TO 1.5X BASIC
UAJRAC Alex Cobb 4.00 10.00
UAJRAE Alcides Escobar 5.00 12.00
UAJRAM Andrew Miller 8.00 20.00
UAJRAR Anthony Rizzo 30.00 80.00
UAJRARU Addison Russell 25.00 60.00
UAJRAW Alex Wood 4.00 10.00
UAJRBB Brandon Belt 5.00 12.00
UAJRBC Brandon Crawford 6.00 15.00
UAJRBDR Brandon Drury 6.00 15.00
UAJRBH Brock Holt 4.00 10.00
UAJRCD Corey Dickerson 4.00 10.00
UAJRCE Carl Edwards Jr. 6.00 15.00
UAJRCM Carlos Martinez 5.00 12.00
UAJRCR Colin Rea 4.00 10.00
UAJRCRO Carlos Rodon 6.00 15.00
UAJRCS Corey Seager 25.00 60.00
UAJRCY Christian Yelich 15.00 40.00
UAJRDA Dariel Alvarez 4.00 10.00
UAJRDK Dallas Keuchel 5.00 12.00
UAJRDL DJ LeMahieu 12.00 30.00
UAJRDLE DJ LeMahieu 12.00 30.00
UAJRDTR Devon Travis 4.00 10.00
UAJREI Ender Inciarte 4.00 10.00
UAJRFM Frankie Montas 5.00 12.00
UAJRGB Greg Bird 5.00 12.00
UAJRGHO Greg Holland
UAJRGS George Springer 5.00 12.00
UAJRGSP George Springer 5.00 12.00
UAJRHO Hector Olivera 5.00 12.00
UAJRHOE Henry Owens 5.00 12.00
UAJRHOW Henry Owens 5.00 12.00
UAJRJC Jose Canseco 10.00 25.00
UAJRJCA Jose Canseco 10.00 25.00
UAJRJF Jeurys Familia 5.00 12.00
UAJRJH Jesse Hahn 4.00 10.00
UAJRJP Joc Pederson 5.00 12.00
UAJRJPAN Joe Panik 5.00 12.00
UAJRJR J.T. Realmuto 20.00 50.00
UAJRJS Jorge Soler 6.00 15.00
UAJRJSH James Shields 4.00 10.00
UAJRJT Justin Turner 30.00 80.00
UAJRKC Kole Calhoun 4.00 10.00
UAJRKCA Kole Calhoun 4.00 10.00
UAJRKGI Ken Giles 4.00 10.00
UAJRKH Kelvin Herrera 4.00 10.00
UAJRKMA Ketel Marte 8.00 20.00
UAJRKW Kolten Wong 5.00 12.00
UAJRKWO Kolten Wong 5.00 12.00
UAJRLS Luis Severino 5.00 12.00
UAJRMCO Michael Conforto 8.00 20.00
UAJRMD1 Matt Duffy 4.00 10.00
UAJRMD2 Matt Duffy 4.00 10.00
UAJRMDU Matt Duffy 4.00 10.00
UAJRMF Maikel Franco 5.00 12.00
UAJRMP Michael Pineda 4.00 10.00
UAJRMR Matt Reynolds 4.00 10.00
UAJRMRE Michael Reed 4.00 10.00
UAJRMS Marcus Semien 6.00 15.00
UAJRMSA Miguel Sano 6.00 15.00
UAJRMSE Marcus Semien 6.00 15.00
UAJRMSH Matt Shoemaker 5.00 12.00
UAJRMW Matt Wisler 4.00 10.00
UAJRMWA Michael Wacha 6.00 15.00
UAJRNEO Nathan Eovaldi 5.00 12.00
UAJRNS Noah Syndergaard 10.00 25.00
UAJROV Omar Vizquel 6.00 15.00
UAJRRI Raisel Iglesias 5.00 12.00
UAJRRR Rob Refsnyder 5.00 12.00
UAJRSD Sean Doolittle 4.00 10.00
UAJRSDO Sean Doolittle 4.00 10.00
UAJRSM Steven Matz 4.00 10.00
UAJRSMA Starling Marte 5.00 12.00
UAJRSMT Steven Matz 4.00 10.00
UAJRYG Yasmani Grandal 4.00 10.00
UAJRYR Yadiel Rivera 4.00 10.00
UAJRZW Zack Wheeler 5.00 12.00

2016 Topps Triple Threads Unity Jumbo Relics

STATED ODDS 1:6 MINI BOX
STATED PRINT RUN 36 SER.#'d SETS
*SILVER/27: .4X TO 1X BASIC
*EMERALD/18: .5X TO 1.2X BASIC
*GOLD/9: .6X TO 1.5X BASIC
ALL VERSIONS EQUALLY PRICED
UJRABA Archie Bradley 3.00 8.00
UJRABD Archie Bradley 3.00 8.00
UJRABR Archie Bradley 3.00 8.00
UJRAGN Adrian Gonzalez 4.00 10.00
UJRAGO Adrian Gonzalez 4.00 10.00
UJRAGZ Adrian Gonzalez 4.00 10.00
UJRALP Albert Pujols 6.00 15.00
UJRALU Albert Pujols 6.00 15.00
UJRAMC Andrew McCutchen 6.00 15.00
UJRAMI Andrew Miller 4.00 10.00
UJRAML Andrew Miller 4.00 10.00
UJRAMR Andrew Miller 4.00 10.00
UJRAMU Andrew McCutchen 6.00 15.00
UJRANI Anthony Rizzo 6.00 15.00
UJRANR Anthony Rizzo 6.00 15.00
UJRAPJ Albert Pujols 6.00 15.00
UJRARE Addison Russell 5.00 12.00
UJRARI Anthony Rizzo 6.00 15.00
UJRARL Addison Russell 5.00 12.00
UJRARS Addison Russell 5.00 12.00
UJRARU Addison Russell 5.00 12.00
UJRARZ Anthony Rizzo 6.00 15.00
UJRAWA Adam Wainwright 4.00 10.00
UJRAWI Adam Wainwright 4.00 10.00
UJRBHA Bryce Harper 8.00 20.00
UJRBHL Brock Holt 3.00 8.00
UJRBHO Brock Holt 3.00 8.00
UJRBHT Brock Holt 3.00 8.00
UJRBMA Brian McCann 4.00 10.00
UJRBMC Brian McCann 4.00 10.00
UJRBMN Brian McCann 4.00 10.00
UJRBPH Brandon Phillips 3.00 8.00
UJRBPI Brandon Phillips 3.00 8.00
UJRBPL Brandon Phillips 3.00 8.00
UJRBPO Buster Posey 6.00 15.00
UJRBRA Bryce Harper 8.00 20.00
UJRBRH Bryce Harper 8.00 20.00
UJRBSH Blake Swihart 4.00 10.00
UJRBSI Blake Swihart 4.00 10.00
UJRBST Blake Swihart 4.00 10.00
UJRBSW Blake Swihart 4.00 10.00
UJRCBE Carlos Beltran 4.00 10.00
UJRCBL Carlos Beltran 4.00 10.00
UJRCDA Chris Davis 3.00 8.00
UJRCDV Chris Davis 3.00 8.00
UJRCGA Curtis Granderson 4.00 10.00
UJRCGN Carlos Gonzalez 4.00 10.00
UJRCGO Carlos Gonzalez 4.00 10.00
UJRCGR Curtis Granderson 4.00 10.00
UJRCKE Clayton Kershaw 8.00 20.00
UJRCMA Carlos Martinez 4.00 10.00
UJRCMR Carlos Martinez 4.00 10.00
UJRCSA Carlos Santana 4.00 10.00
UJRCSN Carlos Santana 4.00 10.00
UJRCST Carlos Santana 4.00 10.00
UJRCVA Christian Vazquez 4.00 10.00
UJRCVQ Christian Vazquez 4.00 10.00
UJRCVZ Christian Vazquez 4.00 10.00
UJRDAR David Wright 4.00 10.00
UJRDAW David Wright 4.00 10.00
UJRDBA Dellin Betances 4.00 10.00
UJRDBE Dellin Betances 4.00 10.00
UJRDBN Dellin Betances 4.00 10.00
UJRDBT Dellin Betances 4.00 10.00
UJRDKE Dallas Keuchel 4.00 10.00
UJRDOT David Ortiz 8.00 20.00
UJRDPD Dustin Pedroia 6.00 15.00
UJRDPE Dustin Pedroia 6.00 15.00
UJRDWR David Wright 4.00 10.00
UJRDWT David Wright 4.00 10.00
UJREAD Elvis Andrus 4.00 10.00
UJREAN Elvis Andrus 4.00 10.00
UJREAR Elvis Andrus 4.00 10.00
UJREEC Edwin Encarnacion 5.00 12.00
UJREEN Edwin Encarnacion 5.00 12.00
UJRELG Evan Longoria 4.00 10.00
UJRELN Evan Longoria 4.00 10.00
UJRELO Evan Longoria 4.00 10.00
UJRFHE Felix Hernandez 4.00 10.00
UJRGCE Gerrit Cole 5.00 12.00
UJRGCL Gerrit Cole 5.00 12.00
UJRGCO Gerrit Cole 5.00 12.00
UJRGGN Gio Gonzalez 4.00 10.00
UJRGGO Gio Gonzalez 4.00 10.00
UJRGGZ Gio Gonzalez 4.00 10.00
UJRGPA Gregory Polanco 4.00 10.00
UJRGPL Gregory Polanco 4.00 10.00
UJRGPO Gregory Polanco 4.00 10.00
UJRGSA Giancarlo Stanton 5.00 12.00
UJRGST Giancarlo Stanton 5.00 12.00
UJRHJR Hyun-Jin Ryu 4.00 10.00
UJRHRA Hanley Ramirez 4.00 10.00
UJRHRM Hanley Ramirez 4.00 10.00
UJRHRU Hyun-Jin Ryu 4.00 10.00
UJRHRY Hyun-Jin Ryu 4.00 10.00
UJRHRZ Hanley Ramirez 4.00 10.00
UJRICH Ichiro Suzuki 6.00 15.00
UJRICY Ichiro Suzuki 6.00 15.00
UJRIKI Ian Kinsler 4.00 10.00
UJRIKN Ian Kinsler 4.00 10.00
UJRIKS Ian Kinsler 4.00 10.00
UJRIRO Ivan Rodriguez 6.00 15.00
UJRJAB Javier Baez 6.00 15.00
UJRJAD Jacob deGrom 10.00 25.00
UJRJAE Jacob deGrom 10.00 25.00
UJRJBA Javier Baez 6.00 15.00
UJRJBE Javier Baez 6.00 15.00
UJRJBR Jay Bruce 4.00 10.00
UJRJBU Jay Bruce 4.00 10.00
UJRJBZ Javier Baez 6.00 15.00
UJRJDA Johnny Damon 4.00 10.00
UJRJDG Jacob deGrom 10.00 25.00
UJRJDM Johnny Damon 4.00 10.00
UJRJEB Jacoby Ellsbury 4.00 10.00
UJRJEL Jacoby Ellsbury 4.00 10.00
UJRJFE Jose Fernandez 6.00 15.00
UJRJFR Jose Fernandez 6.00 15.00
UJRJGA Joey Gallo 5.00 12.00
UJRJGL Joey Gallo 4.00 10.00
UJRJGO Joey Gallo 4.00 10.00
UJRJHA Josh Harrison 3.00 8.00
UJRJHR Josh Harrison 3.00 8.00
UJRJHS Josh Harrison 3.00 8.00
UJRJLA Juan Lagares 3.00 8.00
UJRJLE Jon Lester 4.00 10.00
UJRJLG Juan Lagares 3.00 8.00
UJRJLS Jon Lester 4.00 10.00
UJRJMA J.D. Martinez 5.00 12.00
UJRJMA Joe Mauer 4.00 10.00
UJRJMR J.D. Martinez 5.00 12.00
UJRJMT J.D. Martinez 5.00 12.00
UJRJMU Joe Mauer 4.00 10.00
UJRJVA Justin Verlander 5.00 12.00
UJRJVE Justin Verlander 5.00 12.00
UJRJVL Justin Verlander 5.00 12.00
UJRJVO Joey Votto 5.00 12.00
UJRJVR Justin Verlander 5.00 12.00
UJRJVT Joey Votto 5.00 12.00
UJRJYV Joey Votto 5.00 12.00
UJRKCA Kole Calhoun 3.00 8.00
UJRKCL Kole Calhoun 3.00 8.00
UJRKPA Kevin Plawecki 3.00 8.00
UJRKPL Kevin Plawecki 3.00 8.00
UJRKPW Kevin Plawecki 3.00 8.00
UJRKSE Kyle Seager 3.00 8.00
UJRKWG Kolten Wong 4.00 10.00
UJRKWN Kolten Wong 4.00 10.00
UJRKWO Kolten Wong 4.00 10.00
UJRKYS Kyle Seager 3.00 8.00
UJRLDA Lucas Duda 4.00 10.00
UJRLDD Lucas Duda 4.00 10.00
UJRLDU Lucas Duda 4.00 10.00
UJRLLN Lance Lynn 3.00 8.00
UJRLLY Lance Lynn 3.00 8.00
UJRMAA Matt Harvey 4.00 10.00
UJRMAC Manny Machado 6.00 15.00
UJRMAH Matt Harvey 4.00 10.00
UJRMAM Manny Machado 6.00 15.00
UJRMBE Mookie Betts 10.00 25.00
UJRMBM Madison Bumgarner 4.00 10.00
UJRMBT Mookie Betts 10.00 25.00
UJRMCA Matt Cain 4.00 10.00
UJRMCA Miguel Cabrera 5.00 12.00

UJRMCA Matt Carpenter 5.00 12.00
UJRMCB Miguel Cabrera 5.00 12.00
UJRMCE Miguel Cabrera 5.00 12.00
UJRMCI Matt Cain 4.00 10.00
UJRMCN Michael Conforto 4.00 10.00
UJRMCN Matt Cain 4.00 10.00
UJRMCO Michael Conforto 4.00 10.00
UJRMCP Matt Carpenter 5.00 12.00
UJRMCR Miguel Cabrera 5.00 12.00
UJRMCR Matt Carpenter 5.00 12.00
UJRMFA Maikel Franco 4.00 10.00
UJRMFR Maikel Franco 4.00 10.00
UJRMHA Matt Harvey 4.00 10.00
UJRMMC Mark Melancon 3.00 8.00
UJRMME Mark Melancon 3.00 8.00
UJRMML Mark Melancon 3.00 8.00
UJRMMY Mark McGwire 8.00 20.00
UJRMON Marcell Ozuna 5.00 12.00
UJRMOU Marcell Ozuna 5.00 12.00
UJRMOZ Marcell Ozuna 5.00 12.00
UJRMPD Michael Pineda 3.00 8.00
UJRMPI Michael Pineda 3.00 8.00
UJRMPN Michael Pineda 3.00 8.00
UJRMTA Masahiro Tanaka 4.00 10.00
UJRMTN Masahiro Tanaka 4.00 10.00
UJRMTR Mike Trout 12.00 30.00
UJRMZI Mike Zunino 3.00 8.00
UJRMZN Mike Zunino 3.00 8.00
UJRMZU Mike Zunino 3.00 8.00
UJRPFE Prince Fielder 4.00 10.00
UJRPFI Prince Fielder 4.00 10.00
UJRPSA Pablo Sandoval 4.00 10.00
UJRPSD Pablo Sandoval 4.00 10.00
UJRPSN Pablo Sandoval 4.00 10.00
UJRRCA Rusney Castillo 3.00 8.00
UJRRCS Rusney Castillo 3.00 8.00
UJRRCT Rusney Castillo 3.00 8.00
UJRRHO Ryan Howard 4.00 10.00
UJRRHW Ryan Howard 4.00 10.00
UJRSCH Shin-Soo Choo 4.00 10.00
UJRSCO Shin-Soo Choo 4.00 10.00
UJRSMA Starling Marte 4.00 10.00
UJRSMR Starling Marte 4.00 10.00
UJRSSC Shin-Soo Choo 4.00 10.00
UJRSSO Steven Souza Jr. 4.00 10.00
UJRSSU Steven Souza Jr. 4.00 10.00
UJRSSZ Steven Souza Jr. 4.00 10.00
UJRTLI Tim Lincecum 4.00 10.00
UJRTLN Tim Lincecum 4.00 10.00
UJRTRO Tyson Ross 3.00 8.00
UJRTRS Tyson Ross 3.00 8.00
UJRTWA Taijuan Walker 3.00 8.00
UJRTWK Taijuan Walker 3.00 8.00
UJRTWL Taijuan Walker 3.00 8.00
UJRTYR Tyson Ross 3.00 8.00
UJRVMA Victor Martinez 4.00 10.00
UJRVMR Victor Martinez 4.00 10.00
UJRVMT Victor Martinez 4.00 10.00
UJRVMZ Victor Martinez 4.00 10.00
UJRWFL Wilmer Flores 4.00 10.00
UJRWFO Wilmer Flores 4.00 10.00
UJRWFR Wilmer Flores 4.00 10.00
UJRWLM Wil Myers 4.00 10.00
UJRWME Wil Myers 4.00 10.00
UJRWMR Wil Myers 4.00 10.00
UJRWMS Wil Myers 4.00 10.00
UJRYCE Yoenis Cespedes 5.00 12.00
UJRYCS Yoenis Cespedes 5.00 12.00
UJRYGM Yan Gomes 3.00 8.00
UJRYGO Yan Gomes 3.00 8.00
UJRYML Yadier Molina 6.00 15.00
UJRYMN Yadier Molina 6.00 15.00
UJRYMO Yadier Molina 6.00 15.00
UJRYPG Yasiel Puig 5.00 12.00
UJRYPI Yasiel Puig 5.00 12.00
UJRYPU Yasiel Puig 5.00 12.00
UJRYVE Yordano Ventura 4.00 10.00
UJRYVN Yordano Ventura 4.00 10.00
UJRYVT Yordano Ventura 4.00 10.00
UJRZWE Zack Wheeler 4.00 10.00
UJRZWH Zack Wheeler 4.00 10.00
UJRZWL Zack Wheeler 4.00 10.00

2017 Topps Triple Threads

COMP.SET w/o AU's (100) 75.00 200.00
JSY AU RC ODDS 1:12 MINI BOX
JSY AU RC PRINT RUN 99 SER.#'d SETS
JSY AU ODDS 1:12 MINI BOX
JSY AU PRINT RUN 99 SER.#'d SETS
EXCHANGE DEADLINE 8/31/2019
1-100 PLATE ODDS 1:115 MINI BOX
JSY AU PLATE ODDS 1:278 MINI BOX
PLATE PRINT RUN 1 SET PER COLOR
BLACK-CYAN-MAGENTA-YELLOW ISSUED
NO PLATE PRICING DUE TO SCARCITY
1 Bryce Harper 1.00 2.50
2 Ken Griffey Jr. 1.25 3.00
3 Kris Bryant .75 2.00
4 Mike Trout 3.00 8.00
5 Paul Goldschmidt .60 1.50
6 Manny Machado .60 1.50
7 Mookie Betts 1.25 3.00
8 Anthony Rizzo .75 2.00
9 Kyle Schwarber .60 1.50
10 Joey Votto .60 1.50
11 Nolan Arenado 1.00 2.50
12 Miguel Cabrera .60 1.50
13 Justin Verlander .60 1.50
14 Carlos Correa .60 1.50
15 Eric Hosmer .50 1.25
16 Clayton Kershaw 1.00 2.50
17 Corey Seager .60 1.50
18 Julio Urias .60 1.50
19 Giancarlo Stanton .60 1.50
20 Ichiro .75 2.00
21 Noah Syndergaard .50 1.25
22 Masahiro Tanaka .50 1.25
23 Gary Sanchez .60 1.50
24 Buster Posey .75 2.00
25 Felix Hernandez .50 1.25
26 Robinson Cano .50 1.25
27 Aledmys Diaz .50 1.25
28 Yu Darvish .60 1.50
29 Josh Donaldson .50 1.25
30 Jose Bautista .50 1.25
31 Max Scherzer .60 1.50
32 Francisco Lindor .60 1.50
33 Chris Sale .60 1.50
34 Addison Russell .60 1.50
35 Javier Baez .75 2.00
36 Jacob deGrom 1.25 3.00
37 Andrew McCutchen .60 1.50
38 Wil Myers .50 1.25
39 Albert Pujols .75 2.00
40 Yoenis Cespedes .60 1.50
41 Jose Altuve .50 1.25
42 Jake Arrieta .50 1.25
43 Edwin Encarnacion .60 1.50
44 David Price .50 1.25
45 Ryan Braun .50 1.25
46 Freddie Freeman .75 2.00
47 Troy Tulowitzki .60 1.50
48 Matt Carpenter .60 1.50
49 Carlos Gonzalez .50 1.25
50 Adrian Beltre .60 1.50
51 Hunter Pence .50 1.25
52 Corey Kluber .50 1.25
53 Trea Turner .50 1.25
54 Kenta Maeda .50 1.25
55 Stephen Strasburg .60 1.50
56 Matt Kemp .50 1.25
57 David Wright .50 1.25
58 Xander Bogaerts .60 1.50
59 Adam Jones .50 1.25
60 Daniel Murphy .50 1.25
61 Roberto Clemente 1.50 4.00
62 Cal Ripken Jr. 2.00 5.00
63 Hank Aaron 1.25 3.00
64 Ted Williams 1.25 3.00
65 Jackie Robinson .60 1.50
66 Sandy Koufax 1.25 3.00
67 Babe Ruth 1.50 4.00
68 Ernie Banks .60 1.50
69 Derek Jeter 1.50 4.00
70 David Ortiz .60 1.50
71 Mark McGwire 1.00 2.50
72 Randy Johnson .60 1.50
73 Honus Wagner .60 1.50
74 Roger Maris .60 1.50
75 Ty Cobb 1.00 2.50
76 Lou Gehrig 1.25 3.00
77 Reggie Jackson .50 1.25
78 George Brett 1.25 3.00
79 Don Mattingly 1.25 3.00
80 Frank Thomas .60 1.50
81 Bo Jackson .60 1.50
82 Johnny Bench .60 1.50
83 Greg Maddux .75 2.00
84 Roger Clemens .75 2.00
85 Mike Piazza .60 1.50
86 Nolan Ryan 2.00 5.00
87 Brooks Robinson .50 1.25
88 Chipper Jones .60 1.50
89 Ozzie Smith .75 2.00
90 Carl Yastrzemski 1.00 2.50
91 George Springer .50 1.25
92 Zack Greinke .60 1.50
93 Pedro Martinez .50 1.25
94 Ryne Sandberg 1.25 3.00
95 Barry Larkin .50 1.25
96 Starling Marte .50 1.25
97 Chris Davis .40 1.00
98 Byron Buxton .60 1.50
99 Dustin Pedroia .60 1.50
100 John Smoltz .60 1.50
RPAAB Bregman JSY AU RC 20.00 50.00
RPAABE Bnntndi JSY AU RC EXCH 30.00 80.00
RPAAD Aledmys Diaz JSY AU 4.00 10.00
RPAAJ Judge JSY AU RC EXCH 75.00 200.00
RPAAN Nola JSY AU EXCH 10.00 25.00
RPAAR Alex Reyes JSY AU RC 6.00 15.00
RPAARU A.Russell JSY AU 10.00 25.00
RPAAT Andrew Toles JSY AU RC 3.00 8.00
RPABB Byron Buxton JSY AU 10.00 25.00
RPABS Blake Snell JSY AU 4.00 10.00
RPABSE Braden Shipley JSY AU RC 3.00 8.00
RPACF Carson Fulmer JSY AU RC 4.00 10.00
RPACS Seager JSY AU EXCH 20.00 50.00
RPADS Swnsn JSY AU RC EXCH 8.00 20.00
RPAGB Greg Bird JSY AU 4.00 10.00
RPAHD Hunter Dozier JSY AU RC 3.00 8.00
RPAHR Hunter Renfroe JSY AU RC 4.00 10.00
RPAJB Javier Baez JSY AU 15.00 40.00
RPAJC Jharel Cotton JSY AU RC 3.00 8.00
RPAJH Jeff Hoffman JSY AU RC 3.00 8.00
RPAJM Joe Musgrove JSY AU RC 10.00 25.00
RPAJT Jameson Taillon JSY AU 5.00 12.00
RPAJU Julio Urias JSY AU EXCH 5.00 12.00
RPAKS Kyle Schwarber JSY AU
RPALG Lucas Giolito JSY AU 15.00 40.00
RPALS Luis Severino JSY AU 10.00 25.00
RPAMF Michael Fulmer JSY AU 3.00 8.00
RPAMM Manny Margot JSY AU RC 4.00 10.00
RPAMS Miguel Sano JSY AU 4.00 10.00
RPARG Robert Gsellman JSY AU RC 3.00 8.00
RPARH Ryon Healy JSY AU RC 6.00 15.00
RPARQ Roman Quinn JSY AU RC 3.00 8.00
RPART Raimel Tapia JSY AU RC 4.00 10.00
RPASM Steven Matz JSY AU 3.00 8.00
RPASP Stephen Piscotty JSY AU 4.00 10.00
RPATA Tyler Austin JSY AU RC 8.00 20.00
RPATG Tyler Glasnow JSY AU RC 10.00 25.00
RPATS Trevor Story JSY AU 5.00 12.00
RPAWC W.Contreras JSY AU 10.00 25.00
RPAYG Gurriel JSY AU RC 10.00 25.00
RPAYM Moncada JSY AU RC 20.00 50.00

2017 Topps Triple Threads Amber

*AMBER VET: .75X TO 2X BASIC
STATED ODDS 1:4 MINI BOX
STATED PRINT RUN 150 SER.#'d SETS
69 Derek Jeter 5.00 12.00

2017 Topps Triple Threads Amethyst

*AMETHYST VET: .6X TO 1.5X BASIC
STATED ODDS 1:2 MINI BOX
STATED PRINT RUN 340 SER.#'d SETS
69 Derek Jeter 4.00 10.00

2017 Topps Triple Threads Emerald

*EMERALD VET: .6X TO 1.5X BASIC
*EMERALD JSY AU: .4X TO 1X BASIC RC
1-100 ODDS 1:2 MINI BOX
JSY AU ODDS 1:23 MINI BOX
1-100 PRINT RUN 250 SER.#'d SETS
JSY AU PRINT RUN 50 SER.#'d SETS
EXCHANGE DEADLINE 8/31/2019
69 Derek Jeter 4.00 10.00

2017 Topps Triple Threads Gold

*GOLD VET: 1X TO 2.5X BASIC
STATED ODDS 1:5 MINI BOX
STATED PRINT RUN 99 SER.#'d SETS
4 Mike Trout 6.00 15.00
61 Roberto Clemente 5.00 12.00
62 Cal Ripken Jr. 10.00 25.00
69 Derek Jeter 6.00 15.00
86 Nolan Ryan 8.00 20.00

2017 Topps Triple Threads Onyx

*ONYX VET: 1.5X TO 4X BASIC
*ONYX JSY AU: .5X TO 1.2X BASIC RC
1-100 ODDS 1:10 MINI BOX
JSY AU ODDS 1:32 MINI BOX
1-100 PRINT RUN 50 SER.#'d SETS
JSY AU PRINT RUN 35 SER.#'d SETS
EXCHANGE DEADLINE 8/31/2019
4 Mike Trout 10.00 25.00
61 Roberto Clemente 8.00 20.00
62 Cal Ripken Jr. 15.00 40.00
64 Ted Williams 8.00 20.00
69 Derek Jeter 12.00 30.00
78 George Brett 12.00 30.00
79 Don Mattingly 10.00 25.00
86 Nolan Ryan 12.00 30.00

2017 Topps Triple Threads Sapphire

*SAPPHIRE VET: 2.5X TO 6X BASIC
STATED ODDS 1:19 MINI BOX
STATED PRINT RUN 25 SER.#'d SETS
2 Ken Griffey Jr. 20.00 50.00
4 Mike Trout 20.00 50.00
61 Roberto Clemente 12.00 30.00
62 Cal Ripken Jr. 25.00 60.00
64 Ted Williams 12.00 30.00
69 Derek Jeter 50.00 120.00
78 George Brett 20.00 50.00
79 Don Mattingly 15.00 40.00
80 Frank Thomas 8.00 20.00
86 Nolan Ryan 20.00 50.00

2017 Topps Triple Threads Silver

*SILVER JSY AU: .4X TO 1X BASIC RC
STATED ODDS 1:16 MINI BOX
STATED PRINT RUN 75 SER.#'d SETS
EXCHANGE DEADLINE 8/31/2019

2017 Topps Triple Threads Autograph Relic Combos

STATED ODDS 1:82 HOBBY
STATED PRINT RUN 36 SER.#'d SETS
EXCHANGE DEADLINE 8/31/2019
*SILVER/27: .4X TO 1X BASIC
*EMERALD/18: .4X TO 1X BASIC
PRINTING PLATE ODDS 1:743 HOBBY
PLATE PRINT RUN 1 SET PER COLOR
BLACK-CYAN-MAGENTA-YELLOW ISSUED
NO PLATE PRICING DUE TO SCARCITY
ARCBBA Altve/Bgwll/Bggo EX 125.00 300.00
ARCBRS Schwrbr/Rssll/Baez EX 40.00 100.00
ARCBSK Bnntndi/Kmbrl/Sale EX 75.00 200.00
ARCBSU Urs/Bllngr/Sgr EX 125.00 300.00
ARCCAB Brgmn/Crra/Altve EX 75.00 200.00
ARCCAS Crra/Altve/Sprngr EX 60.00 150.00
ARCDSC dGrm/Sndrgrd/Cnfrto 75.00 200.00
ARCDSM Sndrgrd/Matz/dGrm 60.00 150.00
ARCJMM Mchdo/Jns/Mncni 30.00 80.00
ARCKSU Sgr/Urs/Krshw
ARCLGV Vtto/Grffy/Lrkn 125.00 300.00
ARCLKE Lndr/Klbr/Encrncn EX 50.00 120.00
ARCLKZ Zmmr/Lndr/Klbr
ARCPCD Psctty/Crpntr/Diaz 10.00 25.00
ARCRBS Rzzo/Schwrbr/Brnt EX 150.00 400.00
ARCRGB Grzlz/Rdrgz/Bltre 50.00 120.00
ARCRRM Mchdo/Rbnsn/Rpkn
ARCSAB Sprngr/Brgmn/Altve EX 60.00 150.00
ARCSJF Swnsn/Frmn/Jns EX 75.00 200.00
ARCSPB Bnntndi/Sale/Pdrla

2017 Topps Triple Threads Legend Relics

STATED ODDS 1:85 HOBBY
STATED PRINT RUN 36 SER.#'d SETS
*SILVER/27: .4X TO 1X BASIC
*EMERALD/18: .4X TO 1X BASIC
RLCCJ Chipper Jones 10.00 25.00
RLCCR Cal Ripken Jr. 25.00 60.00
RLCCY Carl Yastrzemski
RLCDJ Derek Jeter 40.00 100.00
RLCFT Frank Thomas 10.00 25.00
RLCGB George Brett 25.00 60.00
RLCGM Greg Maddux 12.00 30.00
RLCJB Johnny Bench 12.00 30.00
RLCJS John Smoltz 10.00 25.00
RLCKG Ken Griffey Jr. 30.00 80.00
RLCMP Mike Piazza 10.00 25.00
RLCNR Nolan Ryan 30.00 80.00
RLCOS Ozzie Smith 12.00 30.00
RLCPM Pedro Martinez 8.00 20.00
RLCRH Rickey Henderson 12.00 30.00
RLCRJ Reggie Jackson 8.00 20.00
RLCRL Roger Clemens 10.00 25.00
RLCRS Ryne Sandberg 12.00 30.00
RLCSC Steve Carlton 10.00 25.00
RLCTW Ted Williams 40.00 100.00

2017 Topps Triple Threads Relic Autographs

STATED ODDS 1:9 HOBBY
STATED PRINT RUN 18 SER.#'d SETS
EXCHANGE DEADLINE 8/31/2019
*GOLD/9: .5X TO 1.2X BASIC
SOME GOLD NOT PRICED DUE TO SCARCITY
ALL VERSIONS EQUALLY PRICED
TTARAB1 Adrian Beltre 50.00 120.00
TTARAB2 Adrian Beltre 50.00 120.00
TTARAD1 Aledmys Diaz 6.00 15.00
TTARAD2 Aledmys Diaz 6.00 15.00
TTARAD3 Aledmys Diaz 6.00 15.00
TTARAD4 Aledmys Diaz 6.00 15.00
TTARAD5 Aledmys Diaz 6.00 15.00
TTARAJ1 Adam Jones 12.00 30.00
TTARAJ2 Adam Jones 12.00 30.00
TTARAJ3 Adam Jones 12.00 30.00
TTARAJ4 Adam Jones 12.00 30.00
TTARAJ5 Adam Jones 12.00 30.00
TTARALO1 Roberto Alomar 15.00 40.00
TTARALO2 Roberto Alomar 15.00 40.00
TTARAR1 Anthony Rizzo 30.00 80.00
TTARAR2 Anthony Rizzo 30.00 80.00
TTARAR3 Anthony Rizzo 30.00 80.00
TTARAR4 Anthony Rizzo 30.00 80.00
TTARAR5 Anthony Rizzo 30.00 80.00
TTARBA1 Bobby Abreu 12.00 30.00
TTARBA2 Bobby Abreu 12.00 30.00
TTARBB1 Brandon Belt 10.00 25.00
TTARBB2 Brandon Belt 10.00 25.00
TTARBH1 Bryce Harper 100.00 250.00
TTARBH2 Bryce Harper 100.00 250.00
TTARBP1 Buster Posey
TTARBZ1 Ben Zobrist
TTARBZ2 Ben Zobrist
TTARBZ3 Ben Zobrist
TTARBZ4 Ben Zobrist
TTARCB1 Craig Biggio 12.00 30.00
TTARCBE1 Cody Bellinger 75.00 200.00
TTARCBE2 Cody Bellinger 75.00 200.00
TTARCBE3 Cody Bellinger 75.00 200.00
TTARCBE4 Cody Bellinger 75.00 200.00
TTARCBE5 Cody Bellinger 75.00 200.00
TTARCC1 Carlos Correa 40.00 100.00
TTARCC2 Carlos Correa 40.00 100.00
TTARCF1 Carlton Fisk 15.00 40.00
TTARCK1 Corey Kluber 15.00 40.00
TTARCK2 Corey Kluber 15.00 40.00
TTARCK3 Corey Kluber 15.00 40.00
TTARCK4 Corey Kluber 15.00 40.00
TTARCKE1 Clayton Kershaw 75.00 200.00
TTARCKI1 Craig Kimbrel 15.00 40.00
TTARCKI2 Craig Kimbrel 15.00 40.00
TTARCKI3 Craig Kimbrel 15.00 40.00
TTARCKI4 Craig Kimbrel 15.00 40.00
TTARCKI5 Craig Kimbrel 15.00 40.00
TTARCRJ1 Cal Ripken Jr. 60.00 150.00
TTARCS1 Corey Seager 25.00 60.00
TTARCS2 Corey Seager 25.00 60.00
TTARCS3 Corey Seager 25.00 60.00
TTARCS4 Chris Sale 20.00 50.00
TTARCS5 Chris Sale 20.00 50.00
TTARCSA1 Chris Sale 20.00 50.00
TTARCSA2 Chris Sale 20.00 50.00
TTARCSA3 Chris Sale 20.00 50.00
TTARCY1 Carl Yastrzemski 40.00 100.00
TTARDA1 Daniel Murphy EXCH 20.00 50.00
TTARDA2 Daniel Murphy EXCH 20.00 50.00
TTARDB1 Dellin Betances 6.00 15.00
TTARDB2 Dellin Betances 6.00 15.00
TTARDB3 Dellin Betances 6.00 15.00
TTARDB4 Dellin Betances 6.00 15.00
TTARDB5 Dellin Betances 6.00 15.00
TTARDJ1 Derek Jeter 600.00 800.00
TTARDL1 Derrek Lee 8.00 20.00
TTARDL2 Derrek Lee 8.00 20.00
TTARDL3 Derrek Lee 8.00 20.00
TTARDM1 Don Mattingly 50.00 120.00
TTARDM2 Don Mattingly 50.00 120.00
TTARDM3 Daniel Murphy EXCH 20.00 50.00
TTARDM4 Daniel Murphy EXCH 20.00 50.00
TTARDM5 Daniel Murphy EXCH 20.00 50.00
TTARDO1 David Ortiz 40.00 100.00
TTARDP1 David Price 10.00 25.00
TTARDP2 David Price 10.00 25.00
TTARDP3 David Price 10.00 25.00
TTARDPE1 Dustin Pedroia 20.00 50.00
TTARDPE2 Dustin Pedroia 20.00 50.00
TTARDW1 Dave Winfield 25.00 60.00
TTARDW2 Dave Winfield 25.00 60.00
TTAREE1 Edwin Encarnacion 15.00 40.00
TTAREE2 Edwin Encarnacion 15.00 40.00
TTAREE3 Edwin Encarnacion 15.00 40.00
TTAREE4 Edwin Encarnacion 15.00 40.00
TTARET1 Eric Thames 8.00 20.00
TTARET2 Eric Thames 8.00 20.00
TTARET3 Eric Thames 8.00 20.00
TTARET4 Eric Thames 8.00 20.00
TTARET5 Eric Thames 8.00 20.00
TTARFF1 Freddie Freeman 20.00 50.00
TTARFF2 Freddie Freeman 20.00 50.00
TTARFF3 Freddie Freeman 20.00 50.00
TTARFL1 Francisco Lindor 30.00 80.00
TTARFL2 Francisco Lindor 30.00 80.00
TTARFL3 Francisco Lindor 30.00 80.00
TTARFL4 Francisco Lindor 30.00 80.00
TTARFM1 Floyd Mayweather 250.00 500.00
TTARFM2 Floyd Mayweather 250.00 500.00
TTARFT1 Frank Thomas 50.00 120.00
TTARFT2 Frank Thomas 50.00 120.00
TTARGS1 George Springer 12.00 30.00
TTARGS2 George Springer 12.00 30.00
TTARGS3 George Springer 12.00 30.00
TTARGS4 George Springer 12.00 30.00
TTARGS5 George Springer 12.00 30.00
TTARHA1 Hank Aaron 150.00 300.00
TTARIR1 Ivan Rodriguez 25.00 60.00
TTARIR2 Ivan Rodriguez 25.00 60.00
TTARIR3 Ivan Rodriguez 25.00 60.00
TTARI3 Ichiro 200.00 400.00
TTARJA1 Jose Altuve 25.00 60.00
TTARJA2 Jose Altuve 25.00 60.00
TTARJA3 Jose Altuve 25.00 60.00
TTARJA4 Jose Altuve 25.00 60.00
TTARJA5 Jose Altuve 25.00 60.00
TTARJAB1 Jose Abreu 25.00 60.00
TTARJB1 Javier Baez 20.00 50.00
TTARJB2 Javier Baez 20.00 50.00
TTARJB3 Javier Baez 20.00 50.00
TTARJB4 Javier Baez 20.00 50.00
TTARJB5 Javier Baez 20.00 50.00
TTARJBA1 Jeff Bagwell 30.00 80.00
TTARJBA2 Jeff Bagwell 30.00 80.00
TTARJBA3 Jeff Bagwell 30.00 80.00
TTARJBA4 Jeff Bagwell 30.00 80.00
TTARJD1 Josh Donaldson 20.00 50.00
TTARJD2 Josh Donaldson 20.00 50.00
TTARJD3 Josh Donaldson 20.00 50.00
TTARJDA1 Johnny Damon 20.00 50.00
TTARJDA2 Johnny Damon 20.00 50.00
TTARJDE1 Jacob deGrom 25.00 60.00
TTARJDE2 Jacob deGrom 20.00 50.00
TTARJDE3 Jacob deGrom 20.00 50.00
TTARJDE4 Jacob deGrom 20.00 50.00
TTARJDE5 Jacob deGrom 20.00 50.00
TTARJDM1 J.D. Martinez 10.00 25.00
TTARJDM2 J.D. Martinez 10.00 25.00
TTARJDM3 J.D. Martinez 10.00 25.00
TTARJDM4 J.D. Martinez 10.00 25.00
TTARJDM5 J.D. Martinez 10.00 25.00
TTARJE1 Jim Edmonds 30.00 80.00
TTARJE2 Jim Edmonds 30.00 80.00
TTARJE3 Jim Edmonds 30.00 80.00
TTARJG1 Joey Gallo 12.00 30.00
TTARJG2 Joey Gallo 12.00 30.00
TTARJG3 Joey Gallo 12.00 30.00
TTARJG4 Joey Gallo 12.00 30.00
TTARJG5 Joey Gallo 12.00 30.00
TTARJM1 Juan Marichal 20.00 50.00
TTARJM2 Juan Marichal 20.00 50.00
TTARJP1 Jim Palmer 10.00 25.00
TTARJP2 Jim Palmer 10.00 25.00
TTARJT1 Jim Thome 60.00 150.00
TTARJT2 Jim Thome 60.00 150.00
TTARJU1 Julio Urias 8.00 20.00
TTARJU2 Julio Urias 8.00 20.00
TTARJU3 Julio Urias 8.00 20.00
TTARJU4 Julio Urias 8.00 20.00
TTARJU5 Julio Urias 8.00 20.00
TTARJV1 Joey Votto 40.00 100.00
TTARJV2 Joey Votto 40.00 100.00
TTARKB1 Kris Bryant 75.00 200.00
TTARKB2 Kris Bryant 75.00 200.00
TTARKB3 Kris Bryant 75.00 200.00
TTARKGJ1 Ken Griffey Jr. 100.00 250.00
TTARKGJ2 Ken Griffey Jr. 100.00 250.00
TTARKK1 Kevin Kiermaier 6.00 15.00
TTARKK2 Kevin Kiermaier 6.00 15.00
TTARKK3 Kevin Kiermaier 6.00 15.00
TTARKK4 Kevin Kiermaier 6.00 15.00
TTARKK5 Kevin Kiermaier 6.00 15.00
TTARKM1 Kenta Maeda 20.00 50.00
TTARKM2 Kenta Maeda 20.00 50.00
TTARKM3 Kendrys Morales 5.00 12.00
TTARKM4 Kendrys Morales 5.00 12.00
TTARKM5 Kendrys Morales 5.00 12.00
TTARKMO1 Kendrys Morales 5.00 12.00
TTARKMO2 Kendrys Morales 5.00 12.00
TTARKS1 Kyle Seager 8.00 20.00
TTARKS2 Kyle Seager 8.00 20.00
TTARKS3 Kyle Seager 8.00 20.00
TTARKS4 Kyle Seager 8.00 20.00
TTARKS5 Kyle Seager 8.00 20.00
TTARMC1 Matt Carpenter 8.00 20.00
TTARMC2 Matt Carpenter 8.00 20.00
TTARMC3 Matt Carpenter 8.00 20.00
TTARMC4 Matt Carpenter 8.00 20.00
TTARMC5 Matt Carpenter 8.00 20.00
TTARMF1 Michael Fulmer 10.00 25.00
TTARMF2 Michael Fulmer 10.00 25.00
TTARMF3 Michael Fulmer 10.00 25.00
TTARMF4 Michael Fulmer 10.00 25.00
TTARMF5 Michael Fulmer 10.00 25.00
TTARMIKE1 Mike Piazza 50.00 120.00
TTARMIKE2 Mike Piazza 50.00 120.00
TTARMM1 Manny Machado 50.00 120.00
TTARMM2 Manny Machado 50.00 120.00
TTARMM3 Manny Machado 50.00 120.00
TTARMM4 Manny Machado 50.00 120.00
TTARMM5 Manny Machado 50.00 120.00
TTARMMC1 Mark McGwire 60.00 150.00
TTARMMC2 Mark McGwire 60.00 150.00
TTARMPI1 Michael Pineda 5.00 12.00
TTARMPI2 Michael Pineda 5.00 12.00
TTARMSA1 Miguel Sano EXCH 12.00 30.00
TTARMSA2 Miguel Sano EXCH 12.00 30.00
TTARMSA3 Miguel Sano EXCH 12.00 30.00
TTARMSA4 Miguel Sano EXCH 12.00 30.00
TTARMSA5 Miguel Sano EXCH 12.00 30.00
TTARMST1 Marcus Stroman 8.00 20.00
TTARMST2 Marcus Stroman 8.00 20.00
TTARMST3 Marcus Stroman 8.00 20.00
TTARMST4 Marcus Stroman 8.00 20.00
TTARMT1 Mike Trout EXCH 200.00 400.00
TTARNG1 Nomar Garciaparra 25.00 60.00
TTARNR1 Nolan Ryan 75.00 200.00
TTARNS1 Noah Syndergaard 20.00 50.00
TTARNS2 Noah Syndergaard 20.00 50.00
TTARNS3 Noah Syndergaard 20.00 50.00
TTARPG1 Paul Goldschmidt EXCH 20.00 50.00
TTARPG2 Paul Goldschmidt EXCH 20.00 50.00
TTARPG3 Paul Goldschmidt EXCH 20.00 50.00
TTARPG4 Paul Goldschmidt EXCH 20.00 50.00
TTARPG5 Paul Goldschmidt EXCH 20.00 50.00
TTARPK1 Paul Konerko 12.00 30.00
TTARRB1 Ryan Braun 10.00 25.00
TTARRC1 Roger Clemens 30.00 80.00
TTARRC2 Roger Clemens 30.00 80.00
TTARRCA1 Rod Carew 20.00 50.00
TTARRCA2 Rod Carew 20.00 50.00
TTARRF1 Rollie Fingers 12.00 30.00
TTARRF2 Rollie Fingers 12.00 30.00
TTARRH1 Rickey Henderson 40.00 100.00
TTARRHA1 Roy Halladay EXCH 25.00 60.00
TTARRHA2 Roy Halladay EXCH 25.00 60.00
TTARRHA3 Roy Halladay EXCH 25.00 60.00
TTARRHA4 Roy Halladay EXCH 25.00 60.00
TTARRHA5 Roy Halladay EXCH 25.00 60.00
TTARRJO1 Randy Johnson 40.00 100.00
TTARRJO2 Randy Johnson 40.00 100.00
TTARRS1 Ryne Sandberg 30.00 80.00
TTARRY1 Robin Yount 30.00 80.00
TTARRY2 Robin Yount 30.00 80.00
TTARSG1 Sonny Gray 6.00 15.00
TTARSG2 Sonny Gray 6.00 15.00
TTARSG3 Sonny Gray 6.00 15.00
TTARSG4 Sonny Gray 6.00 15.00
TTARSMA1 Steven Matz 5.00 12.00
TTARSMA2 Steven Matz 5.00 12.00
TTARSMA3 Steven Matz 5.00 12.00
TTARSMA4 Steven Matz 5.00 12.00
TTARSMA5 Steven Matz 5.00 12.00
TTARSP1 Stephen Piscotty 6.00 15.00
TTARSP2 Stephen Piscotty 6.00 15.00
TTARSP3 Stephen Piscotty 6.00 15.00
TTARSP4 Stephen Piscotty 6.00 15.00
TTARSP5 Stephen Piscotty 6.00 15.00
TTARTE1 Theo Epstein 75.00 200.00
TTARTE2 Theo Epstein 75.00 200.00
TTARTE3 Theo Epstein 75.00 200.00
TTARTR1 Tim Raines 20.00 50.00
TTARTR2 Tim Raines 20.00 50.00
TTARTS1 Trevor Story 10.00 25.00
TTARTS2 Trevor Story 10.00 25.00
TTARTS3 Trevor Story 10.00 25.00
TTARTS4 Trevor Story 10.00 25.00
TTARTS5 Trevor Story 10.00 25.00
TTARTT1 Trea Turner 15.00 40.00
TTARTT2 Trea Turner 15.00 40.00
TTARTT3 Trea Turner 15.00 40.00
TTARTT4 Trea Turner 15.00 40.00
TTARTT5 Trea Turner 15.00 40.00
TTARVG1 Vladimir Guerrero 20.00 50.00
TTARVG2 Vladimir Guerrero 20.00 50.00
TTARVG3 Vladimir Guerrero 20.00 50.00
TTARVG4 Vladimir Guerrero 20.00 50.00

2017 Topps Triple Threads Relic Combos

STATED ODDS 1:37 HOBBY
STATED PRINT RUN 36 SER.#'d SETS
*SILVER/27: .4X TO 1X BASIC
*EMERALD/18: .5X TO 1.2X BASIC
TTRCACB Crra/Brgmn/Altuve 15.00 40.00
TTRCACS Sprngr/Crra/Altuve 15.00 40.00
TTRCBBA Bggo/Altve/Bgwll 15.00 40.00
TTRCBBB Brdly/Betts/Bnntndi 15.00 40.00
TTRCBPH Pedrola/Bogaerts/Ramirez 8.00 20.00
TTRCBRR Baez/Rssll/Rizzo 10.00 25.00
TTRCBRS Rssll/Baez/Schwrbr 10.00 25.00
TTRCCPP Posey/Crwfrd/Pence 10.00 25.00
TTRCCST Tnka/Chpmn/Sanchez 8.00 20.00
TTRCDSH deGrom/Syndergaard/Harvey 15.00 40.00
TTRCGAB Gonzalez/Blackmon/Arenado 12.00 30.00
TTRCGHP Grdn/Hsmr/Perez 10.00 25.00
TTRCGSY Gordon/Stanton/Yelich 8.00 20.00
TTRCHCC Cruz/Hernandez/Cano 8.00 20.00
TTRCHTB Hrpr/Brynt/Trout 30.00 80.00
TTRCHVD Duvall/Votto/Hamilton 8.00 20.00
TTRCIGH Grffy/Ichiro/Hrnndz 20.00 50.00
TTRCISY Ichiro/Stntn/Ylich 10.00 25.00
TTRCJMD Davis/Machado/Jones 8.00 20.00
TTRCKFS Kemp/Swanson/Freeman 8.00 20.00
TTRCLGV Votto/Griffey/Larkin 12.00 30.00
TTRCLKS Klbr/Lndr/Sntna 15.00 40.00
TTRCMCM Crpntr/Mlna/Mrtnz 10.00 25.00
TTRCMJJ Jtr/Jcksn/Mttngly 30.00 80.00
TTRCMKU Kershaw/Urias/Maeda 8.00 20.00
TTRCMMP Polanco/Marte/McCutchen 8.00 20.00
TTRCPGP Pollock/Greinke/Goldschmidt 8.00 20.00
TTRCPGP Pederson/Gonzalez/Puig 8.00 20.00
TTRCPSP Sale/Price/Porcello 8.00 20.00
TTRCRBS Rzzo/Schwrbr/Brnt 12.00 30.00
TTRCSAB Sprngr/Altve/Brgmn 10.00 25.00
TTRCSBM Mauer/Sano/Buxton 8.00 20.00
TTRCSFJ Frmn/Smoltz/Jones 12.00 30.00
TTRCSGA Gonzalez/Story/Arenado 12.00 30.00
TTRCSKU Krshw/Urias/Seager 10.00 25.00
TTRCSWC Syndergaard/Wright/Cespedes 8.00 20.00
TTRCTCG Cole/Glasnow/Taillon 20.00 50.00
TTRCUCM Cabrera/Upton/Martinez 8.00 20.00
TTRCVCU Verlander/Cabrera/Upton 6.00 15.00

2017 Topps Triple Threads Relics

STATED ODDS 1:9 MINI BOX
STATED PRINT RUN 36 SER.#'d SETS
*SILVER/27: .4X TO 1X BASIC
*EMERALD/18: .5X TO 1.2X BASIC
*GOLD/9: .6X TO 1.5X BASIC
ALL VERSIONS EQUALLY PRICED
TTRAC1 Aroldis Chapman 6.00 15.00
TTRAJ1 Adam Jones 3.00 8.00
TTRAJ2 Adam Jones 3.00 8.00
TTRAJ3 Adam Jones 3.00 8.00
TTRAM1 Andrew McCutchen 6.00 15.00
TTRAM2 Andrew McCutchen 6.00 15.00
TTRAM3 Andrew McCutchen 6.00 15.00
TTRAM4 Andrew McCutchen 6.00 15.00
TTRAM5 Andrew McCutchen 6.00 15.00
TTRAR1 Anthony Rizzo 6.00 15.00
TTRAR2 Anthony Rizzo 6.00 15.00
TTRAR3 Anthony Rizzo 6.00 15.00
TTRBH1 Bryce Harper 10.00 25.00
TTRBH2 Bryce Harper 10.00 25.00
TTRBP1 Buster Posey 8.00 20.00
TTRBP2 Buster Posey 8.00 20.00
TTRCA1 Corey Seager 6.00 15.00
TTRCA2 Corey Seager 6.00 15.00
TTRCA3 Corey Seager 6.00 15.00
TTRCC1 Carlos Correa 4.00 10.00
TTRCC2 Carlos Correa 4.00 10.00
TTRCC3 Carlos Correa 4.00 10.00
TTRCE1 Clayton Kershaw 8.00 20.00
TTRCE2 Clayton Kershaw 8.00 20.00
TTRCS1 Chris Sale 4.00 10.00
TTRCS2 Chris Sale 4.00 10.00
TTRCS3 Chris Sale 4.00 10.00
TTRCS4 Chris Sale 4.00 10.00
TTRCS5 Chris Sale 4.00 10.00
TTRDE1 Dustin Pedroia 5.00 12.00
TTRDE2 Dustin Pedroia 5.00 12.00
TTRDE3 Dustin Pedroia 5.00 12.00
TTRDJ1 Derek Jeter 40.00 100.00
TTRDJ2 Derek Jeter 40.00 100.00
TTRDO1 David Ortiz 6.00 15.00
TTRDO2 David Ortiz 6.00 15.00
TTRDW1 David Wright 3.00 8.00
TTRDW2 David Wright 3.00 8.00
TTRDW3 David Wright 3.00 8.00
TTREL1 Evan Longoria 3.00 8.00
TTREL2 Evan Longoria 3.00 8.00
TTREL3 Evan Longoria 3.00 8.00
TTRFF1 Freddie Freeman 5.00 12.00
TTRFF2 Freddie Freeman 5.00 12.00
TTRFF3 Freddie Freeman 5.00 12.00
TTRFH1 Felix Hernandez 5.00 12.00
TTRFH2 Felix Hernandez 5.00 12.00
TTRFH3 Felix Hernandez 5.00 12.00
TTRFH4 Felix Hernandez 5.00 12.00
TTRFH5 Felix Hernandez 5.00 12.00
TTRFL1 Francisco Lindor 6.00 15.00
TTRFL2 Francisco Lindor 6.00 15.00
TTRFL3 Francisco Lindor 6.00 15.00
TTRFL4 Francisco Lindor 6.00 15.00
TTRGP1 George Springer 5.00 12.00
TTRGP2 George Springer 5.00 12.00
TTRGP3 George Springer 5.00 12.00
TTRGS1 Gary Sanchez 4.00 10.00
TTRGS2 Gary Sanchez 4.00 10.00
TTRGS3 Gary Sanchez 4.00 10.00
TTRGT1 Giancarlo Stanton 4.00 10.00
TTRGT2 Giancarlo Stanton 4.00 10.00
TTRGT3 Giancarlo Stanton 4.00 10.00
TTRGT4 Giancarlo Stanton 4.00 10.00
TTRI1 Ichiro 8.00 20.00
TTRI2 Ichiro 8.00 20.00
TTRJD1 Josh Donaldson 6.00 15.00
TTRJD2 Josh Donaldson 6.00 15.00
TTRJD3 Josh Donaldson 6.00 15.00
TTRJE1 Jacob deGrom 8.00 20.00
TTRJE2 Jacob deGrom 8.00 20.00
TTRJE3 Jacob deGrom 8.00 20.00
TTRJE4 Jacob deGrom 8.00 20.00
TTRJE5 Jacob deGrom 8.00 20.00
TTRJL1 Jose Altuve 8.00 20.00
TTRJL2 Jose Altuve 8.00 20.00
TTRJL3 Jose Altuve 8.00 20.00
TTRJL4 Jose Altuve 8.00 20.00
TTRJL5 Jose Altuve 8.00 20.00
TTRJO1 Joey Votto 6.00 15.00
TTRJO2 Joey Votto 6.00 15.00
TTRJO3 Joey Votto 6.00 15.00
TTRJU1 Jose Bautista 4.00 10.00
TTRJU2 Jose Bautista 4.00 10.00
TTRJU3 Jose Bautista 4.00 10.00
TTRJV1 Justin Verlander 4.00 10.00
TTRJV2 Justin Verlander 4.00 10.00
TTRJV3 Justin Verlander 4.00 10.00
TTRJV4 Justin Verlander 4.00 10.00
TTRJV5 Justin Verlander 4.00 10.00
TTRJZ1 Javier Baez 5.00 12.00
TTRJZ2 Javier Baez 5.00 12.00
TTRJZ3 Javier Baez 5.00 12.00
TTRKB1 Kris Bryant 5.00 12.00
TTRKB2 Kris Bryant 5.00 12.00
TTRKB3 Kris Bryant 5.00 12.00
TTRKM1 Kenta Maeda 3.00 8.00
TTRKM2 Kenta Maeda 3.00 8.00
TTRMA1 Matt Carpenter 4.00 10.00
TTRMA2 Matt Carpenter 4.00 10.00
TTRMA3 Matt Carpenter 4.00 10.00
TTRMB1 Mookie Betts 8.00 20.00
TTRMB2 Mookie Betts 8.00 20.00
TTRMB3 Mookie Betts 8.00 20.00
TTRMB4 Mookie Betts 8.00 20.00
TTRMB5 Mookie Betts 8.00 20.00
TTRMC1 Miguel Cabrera 4.00 10.00
TTRMC2 Miguel Cabrera 4.00 10.00
TTRMC3 Miguel Cabrera 4.00 10.00
TTRMC4 Miguel Cabrera 4.00 10.00
TTRMC5 Miguel Cabrera 4.00 10.00
TTRMMA1 Manny Machado 5.00 12.00
TTRMMA2 Manny Machado 5.00 12.00
TTRMMA3 Manny Machado 5.00 12.00
TTRMMA4 Manny Machado 5.00 12.00
TTRMO1 Mike Trout 20.00 50.00
TTRMO2 Mike Trout 20.00 50.00
TTRMS1 Miguel Sano 3.00 8.00
TTRMS2 Miguel Sano 3.00 8.00
TTRMS3 Miguel Sano 3.00 8.00
TTRMS4 Miguel Sano 3.00 8.00
TTRMS5 Miguel Sano 3.00 8.00
TTRMT1 Masahiro Tanaka 3.00 8.00
TTRMT2 Masahiro Tanaka 3.00 8.00
TTRMT3 Masahiro Tanaka 3.00 8.00
TTRMT4 Masahiro Tanaka 3.00 8.00
TTRNA1 Nolan Arenado 6.00 15.00
TTRNA2 Nolan Arenado 6.00 15.00
TTRNA3 Nolan Arenado 6.00 15.00
TTRNA4 Nolan Arenado 6.00 15.00
TTRNA5 Nolan Arenado 6.00 15.00
TTRNS1 Noah Syndergaard 3.00 8.00
TTRNS2 Noah Syndergaard 3.00 8.00
TTRNS3 Noah Syndergaard 3.00 8.00
TTRNS4 Noah Syndergaard 3.00 8.00
TTRRC1 Robinson Cano 3.00 8.00
TTRRC2 Robinson Cano 3.00 8.00
TTRRC3 Robinson Cano 3.00 8.00
TTRRC4 Robinson Cano 3.00 8.00
TTRRC5 Robinson Cano 3.00 8.00
TTRWM1 Wil Myers 3.00 8.00
TTRXB1 Xander Bogaerts 4.00 10.00
TTRXB2 Xander Bogaerts 4.00 10.00
TTRXB3 Xander Bogaerts 4.00 10.00
TTRYC1 Yoenis Cespedes 5.00 12.00
TTRYC2 Yoenis Cespedes 5.00 12.00
TTRYC3 Yoenis Cespedes 5.00 12.00
TTRYC4 Yoenis Cespedes 5.00 12.00
TTRYC5 Yoenis Cespedes 5.00 12.00
TTRYM1 Yadier Molina 8.00 20.00
TTRYM2 Yadier Molina 8.00 20.00
TTRYM3 Yadier Molina 8.00 20.00
TTRYM4 Yadier Molina 8.00 20.00

2017 Topps Triple Threads Rookie Autographs

STATED ODDS 1:23 HOBBY
STATED PRINT RUN 99 SER.#'d SETS
EXCHANGE DEADLINE 8/31/2019
PRINTING PLATE ODDS 1:577 HOBBY
PLATE PRINT RUN 1 SET PER COLOR
BLACK-CYAN-MAGENTA-YELLOW ISSUED
NO PLATE PRICING DUE TO SCARCITY
*EMERALD/50: .4X TO 1X BASIC
*GOLD/25: .5X TO 1.2X BASIC
RAAG Amir Garrett 4.00 10.00
RABP Brett Phillips 5.00 12.00
RABZ Bradley Zimmer 6.00 15.00
RACA Christian Arroyo 6.00 15.00
RACB Cody Bellinger 60.00 150.00
RADF Derek Fisher 5.00 12.00
RADV Dan Vogelbach 5.00 12.00
RAFB Franklin Barreto 4.00 10.00
RAGC Gavin Cecchini 5.00 12.00
RAGM German Marquez 6.00 15.00
RAIH Ian Happ 8.00 20.00
RAJD Jose De Leon 4.00 10.00
RAJMO Jordan Montgomery 20.00 50.00
RAJW Jesse Winker 30.00 80.00
RALB Lewis Brinson 6.00 15.00
RALW Luke Weaver 5.00 12.00
RAMH Mitch Haniger 6.00 15.00
RASN Sean Newcomb 6.00 15.00
RATM Trey Mancini 12.00 30.00
RAYM Yoan Moncada 10.00 25.00

2017 Topps Triple Threads Unity Jumbo Relic Autographs

STATED ODDS 1:7 HOBBY
STATED PRINT RUN 99 SER.#'d SETS
EXCHANGE DEADLINE 8/31/2019
*SILVER/75: .4X TO 1X BASIC
*EMERALD/50: .5X TO 1.2X BASIC

*GOLD/25: .6X TO 1.5X BASIC
UAJRAB Aledmys Diaz 5.00 12.00
UAJRAD Adam Duvall 5.00 12.00
UAJRAG Amir Garrett 4.00 10.00
UAJRAI Andrew Benintendi 25.00 60.00
UAJRAM Alex Bregman 15.00 40.00
UAJRAO Alex Gordon 5.00 12.00
UAJRAR Anthony Rendon 8.00 20.00
UAJRAS Addison Russell 10.00 25.00
UAJRAU Adam Duvall 5.00 12.00
UAJRAZ Aledmys Diaz 5.00 12.00
UAJRCB Charlie Blackmon 8.00 20.00
UAJRCBL Charlie Blackmon 8.00 20.00
UAJRCI Corey Dickerson 4.00 10.00
UAJRCK Corey Kluber 10.00 25.00
UAJRCS Corey Seager 20.00 50.00
UAJRDB Dellin Betances 5.00 12.00
UAJRDF Dexter Fowler 5.00 12.00
UAJRDG Dee Gordon 4.00 10.00
UAJRDO Didi Gregorius 12.00 30.00
UAJRDP Drew Pomeranz 5.00 12.00
UAJRDR Didi Gregorius 12.00 30.00
UAJREN Ender Inciarte 8.00 20.00
UAJRGB Greg Bird 5.00 12.00
UAJRGD Greg Bird 5.00 12.00
UAJRGG Gary Sheffield 4.00 10.00
UAJRGH Gary Sheffield 4.00 10.00
UAJRGP George Springer 8.00 20.00
UAJRGS George Springer 8.00 20.00
UAJRHW Henry Owens 4.00 10.00
UAJRJA Jose Altuve EXCH 20.00 50.00
UAJRJB Justin Bour 5.00 12.00
UAJRJC Jose Canseco 10.00 25.00
UAJRJD Jacob deGrom 12.00 30.00
UAJRJE Jose Canseco 10.00 25.00
UAJRJF Jeurys Familia
UAJRJJ Javier Baez 12.00 30.00
UAJRJK Jameson Taillon 5.00 12.00
UAJRJM J.D. Martinez 6.00 15.00
UAJRJN Juan Gonzalez 5.00 12.00
UAJRJR Jon Gray 4.00 10.00
UAJRJS Jorge Soler 6.00 15.00
UAJRJU Joe Panik 5.00 12.00
UAJRJV Joe Panik 5.00 12.00
UAJRJY Joey Gallo 5.00 12.00
UAJRJZ Andrew Benintendi EXCH 25.00 60.00
UAJRKA Kenta Maeda 8.00 20.00
UAJRKD Khris Davis 6.00 15.00
UAJRKH Kelvin Herrera 4.00 10.00
UAJRKI Kevin Kiermaier 5.00 12.00
UAJRKK Kevin Kiermaier 5.00 12.00
UAJRKM Kendrys Morales 4.00 10.00
UAJRKR Kendall Graveman 4.00 10.00
UAJRKV Khris Davis 6.00 15.00
UAJRLS Luis Severino 10.00 25.00
UAJRMA Miguel Sano 5.00 12.00
UAJRMC Matt Carpenter 6.00 15.00
UAJRMD Matt Adams 4.00 10.00
UAJRMI Michael Fulmer 4.00 10.00
UAJRMM Michael Conforto 10.00 25.00
UAJRMR Maikel Franco 5.00 12.00
UAJRMU Michael Fulmer 4.00 10.00
UAJRNS Noah Syndergaard 12.00 30.00
UAJRRG Randal Grichuk 4.00 10.00
UAJRRR Randal Grichuk 4.00 10.00
UAJRSG Sonny Gray 5.00 12.00
UAJRSM Steven Matz 4.00 10.00
UAJRSP Stephen Piscotty 5.00 12.00
UAJRST Steven Matz 4.00 10.00
UAJRTM Trey Mancini 10.00 25.00
UAJRTR Trevor Story 6.00 15.00
UAJRTS Trevor Story 6.00 15.00
UAJRWC Willson Contreras 10.00 25.00
UAJRYG Yulieski Gurriel 8.00 20.00
UAJRZC Zack Cozart 4.00 10.00

2017 Topps Triple Threads Unity Jumbo Relics

STATED ODDS 1:6 HOBBY
STATED PRINT RUN 36 SER.#'d SETS
*SILVER/27: .4X TO 1X BASIC
*EMERALD/18: .5X TO 1.2X BASIC
*GOLD/9: .6X TO 1.5X BASIC
ALL VERSIONS EQUALLY PRICED
SJRAB Alex Bregman 5.00 12.00
SJRABI Andrew Benintendi 5.00 12.00
SJRABN Andrew Benintendi 5.00 12.00
SJRABR Alex Bregman 5.00 12.00
SJRAC Aroldis Chapman 6.00 15.00
SJRACH Aroldis Chapman 6.00 15.00
SJRADJ Adam Jones 3.00 8.00
SJRAG Adrian Gonzalez 3.00 8.00
SJRAJE Adam Jones 3.00 8.00
SJRAJO Adam Jones 3.00 8.00
SJRAMC Andrew McCutchen 6.00 15.00
SJRAMT Andrew McCutchen 6.00 15.00
SJRAMU Andrew McCutchen 6.00 15.00
SJRANR Anthony Rizzo 6.00 15.00
SJRAPJ Albert Pujols 5.00 12.00
SJRAPO Albert Pujols 5.00 12.00
SJRAPU Albert Pujols 5.00 12.00
SJRAR Alex Reyes 3.00 8.00
SJRARD Alex Rodriguez 8.00 20.00
SJRARE Alex Reyes 3.00 8.00
SJRARG Alex Rodriguez 8.00 20.00
SJRARI Anthony Rizzo 6.00 15.00
SJRARL Addison Russell 4.00 10.00
SJRARO Alex Rodriguez 8.00 20.00
SJRARR Addison Russell 4.00 10.00
SJRARU Addison Russell 4.00 10.00
SJRARZ Anthony Rizzo 6.00 15.00
SJRAW Adam Wainwright 3.00 8.00
SJRAWA Adam Wainwright 3.00 8.00
SJRAWI Adam Wainwright 3.00 8.00
SJRBB Byron Buxton 4.00 10.00
SJRBBU Byron Buxton 4.00 10.00
SJRBBX Byron Buxton 4.00 10.00
SJRBH Bryce Harper 10.00 25.00
SJRBP Buster Posey 8.00 20.00
SJRBPO Buster Posey 8.00 20.00
SJRBZ Ben Zobrist 3.00 8.00
SJRBZB Ben Zobrist 3.00 8.00
SJRBZO Ben Zobrist 3.00 8.00
SJRCC Carlos Correa 4.00 10.00
SJRCCO Carlos Correa 4.00 10.00
SJRCG Curtis Granderson 3.00 8.00
SJRCGN Carlos Gonzalez 3.00 8.00
SJRCGO Carlos Gonzalez 3.00 8.00
SJRCGR Curtis Granderson 3.00 8.00
SJRCGZ Carlos Gonzalez 3.00 8.00
SJRCH Cole Hamels 3.00 8.00
SJRCK Craig Kimbrel 3.00 8.00
SJRCKB Corey Kluber 3.00 8.00
SJRCKE Clayton Kershaw 8.00 20.00
SJRCKI Craig Kimbrel 3.00 8.00
SJRCKL Corey Kluber 3.00 8.00
SJRCKR Clayton Kershaw 8.00 20.00
SJRCKU Corey Kluber 3.00 8.00
SJRCO Carlos Correa 4.00 10.00
SJRCS Chris Sale 4.00 10.00
SJRCSA Chris Sale 4.00 10.00
SJRCSE Corey Seager 6.00 15.00
SJRCSL Chris Sale 4.00 10.00
SJRCY Christian Yelich 5.00 12.00
SJRCYE Christian Yelich 5.00 12.00
SJRDJ Derek Jeter 40.00 100.00
SJRDMP Daniel Murphy 3.00 8.00
SJRDMR Daniel Murphy 3.00 8.00
SJRDMU Daniel Murphy 3.00 8.00
SJRDO David Ortiz 6.00 15.00
SJRDOR David Ortiz 6.00 15.00
SJRDOT David Ortiz 6.00 15.00
SJRDP Dustin Pedroia 5.00 12.00
SJRDPC David Price 3.00 8.00
SJRDPD Dustin Pedroia 5.00 12.00
SJRDPE Dustin Pedroia 5.00 12.00
SJRDPI David Price 3.00 8.00
SJRDPO Dustin Pedroia 5.00 12.00
SJRDPR David Price 3.00 8.00
SJRDS Dansby Swanson 5.00 12.00
SJRDSW Dansby Swanson 5.00 12.00
SJRDW David Wright 3.00 8.00
SJRDWI David Wright 3.00 8.00
SJRDWR David Wright 3.00 8.00
SJREH Eric Hosmer 3.00 8.00
SJREHO Eric Hosmer 3.00 8.00
SJREHS Eric Hosmer 3.00 8.00
SJREL Evan Longoria 3.00 8.00
SJRELN Evan Longoria 3.00 8.00
SJRELO Evan Longoria 3.00 8.00
SJRFF Freddie Freeman 5.00 12.00
SJRFFE Freddie Freeman 5.00 12.00
SJRFFR Freddie Freeman 5.00 12.00
SJRFH Felix Hernandez 5.00 12.00
SJRFHE Felix Hernandez 5.00 12.00
SJRFHR Felix Hernandez 5.00 12.00
SJRFL Francisco Lindor 6.00 15.00
SJRFLI Francisco Lindor 6.00 15.00
SJRGAS Gary Sanchez 4.00 10.00
SJRGC Gerrit Cole 4.00 10.00
SJRGP Gregory Polanco 3.00 8.00
SJRGPO Gregory Polanco 3.00 8.00
SJRGRS Gary Sanchez 4.00 10.00
SJRGS Gary Sheffield 4.00 10.00
SJRGSA Giancarlo Stanton 4.00 10.00
SJRGSE Gary Sheffield 4.00 10.00
SJRGSF Gary Sheffield 4.00 10.00
SJRGSH Gary Sheffield 4.00 10.00
SJRGSI George Springer 5.00 12.00
SJRGSN Giancarlo Stanton 4.00 10.00
SJRGSP George Springer 5.00 12.00
SJRGSR George Springer 5.00 12.00
SJRGST Giancarlo Stanton 4.00 10.00
SJRGYS Gary Sanchez 4.00 10.00
SJRHP Hunter Pence 3.00 8.00
SJRHPE Hunter Pence 3.00 8.00
SJRHPN Hunter Pence 3.00 8.00
SJRHR Hanley Ramirez 3.00 8.00
SJRHRA Hanley Ramirez 3.00 8.00
SJRHRI Hanley Ramirez 3.00 8.00
SJRHRM Hanley Ramirez 3.00 8.00
SJRIK Ichiro 8.00 20.00
SJRIS Ichiro 8.00 20.00
SJRJA Jake Arrieta 3.00 8.00
SJRJAE Jake Arrieta 3.00 8.00
SJRJAL Jose Altuve 8.00 20.00
SJRJAR Jake Arrieta 3.00 8.00
SJRJAT Jose Altuve 8.00 20.00
SJRJAU Jose Altuve 8.00 20.00
SJRJB Jackie Bradley Jr. 4.00 10.00
SJRJBA Javier Baez 5.00 12.00
SJRJBE Javier Baez 5.00 12.00
SJRJBI Jose Bautista 4.00 10.00
SJRJBR Jackie Bradley Jr. 4.00 10.00
SJRJBT Jose Bautista 4.00 10.00
SJRJBU Jose Bautista 4.00 10.00
SJRJBZ Javier Baez 5.00 12.00
SJRJD Josh Donaldson 6.00 15.00
SJRJDE Jacob deGrom 8.00 20.00
SJRJDG Jacob deGrom 8.00 20.00
SJRJDN Josh Donaldson 6.00 15.00
SJRJDR Jacob deGrom 8.00 20.00
SJRJE Jacoby Ellsbury 6.00 15.00
SJRJEL Jacoby Ellsbury 6.00 15.00
SJRJH Jason Heyward 3.00 8.00
SJRJHE Jason Heyward 3.00 8.00
SJRJHY Jason Heyward 3.00 8.00
SJRJL Jon Lester 3.00 8.00
SJRJLL Jon Lester 3.00 8.00
SJRJM J.D. Martinez 6.00 15.00
SJRJMA J.D. Martinez 6.00 15.00
SJRJOV Joey Votto 6.00 15.00
SJRJS John Smoltz 8.00 20.00
SJRJT Jameson Taillon 3.00 8.00
SJRJU Julio Urias 4.00 10.00
SJRJUP Justin Upton 6.00 15.00
SJRJUT Justin Upton 6.00 15.00
SJRJV Justin Verlander 4.00 10.00
SJRJVA Justin Verlander 4.00 10.00
SJRJVE Justin Verlander 4.00 10.00
SJRJVL Justin Verlander 4.00 10.00
SJRJVO Joey Votto 6.00 15.00
SJRJVR Justin Verlander 4.00 10.00
SJRJVT Joey Votto 6.00 15.00
SJRKB Kris Bryant 5.00 12.00
SJRKBR Kris Bryant 5.00 12.00
SJRKM Kenta Maeda 3.00 8.00
SJRKMA Kenta Maeda 3.00 8.00
SJRKS Kyle Seager 2.50 6.00
SJRKSA Kyle Seager 2.50 6.00
SJRKSE Kyle Seager 2.50 6.00
SJRMB Mookie Betts 8.00 20.00
SJRMBE Mookie Betts 8.00 20.00
SJRMBS Mookie Betts 8.00 20.00
SJRMBT Mookie Betts 8.00 20.00
SJRMC Miguel Cabrera 4.00 10.00
SJRMCA Matt Carpenter 4.00 10.00
SJRMCB Miguel Cabrera 4.00 10.00
SJRMCE Miguel Cabrera 4.00 10.00
SJRMCP Matt Carpenter 4.00 10.00
SJRMCR Matt Carpenter 4.00 10.00
SJRMF Michael Fulmer 2.50 6.00
SJRMFU Michael Fulmer 2.50 6.00
SJRMGC Miguel Cabrera 4.00 10.00
SJRMH Matt Harvey 3.00 8.00
SJRMHA Matt Harvey 3.00 8.00
SJRMHR Matt Harvey 3.00 8.00
SJRMHV Matt Harvey 3.00 8.00
SJRMIC Miguel Cabrera 4.00 10.00
SJRMM Mark McGwire 10.00 25.00
SJRMMA Manny Machado 5.00 12.00
SJRMMC Manny Machado 5.00 12.00
SJRMMG Mark McGwire 10.00 25.00
SJRMS Miguel Sano 3.00 8.00
SJRMSA Miguel Sano 3.00 8.00
SJRMSN Miguel Sano 3.00 8.00
SJRMSR Marcus Stroman 3.00 8.00
SJRMST Marcus Stroman 3.00 8.00
SJRMT Mark Teixeira 3.00 8.00
SJRMTA Masahiro Tanaka 3.00 8.00
SJRMTE Mark Teixeira 3.00 8.00
SJRMTI Mark Teixeira 3.00 8.00
SJRMTK Masahiro Tanaka 3.00 8.00
SJRMTN Masahiro Tanaka 3.00 8.00
SJRMTR Mike Trout 20.00 50.00
SJRNA Nolan Arenado 6.00 15.00
SJRNAA Nolan Arenado 6.00 15.00
SJRNAR Nolan Arenado 6.00 15.00
SJRNC Nelson Cruz 4.00 10.00
SJRNCR Nelson Cruz 4.00 10.00
SJRNS Noah Syndergaard 3.00 8.00
SJRNSN Noah Syndergaard 3.00 8.00
SJRNSY Noah Syndergaard 3.00 8.00
SJRPG Paul Goldschmidt 5.00 12.00
SJRPGL Paul Goldschmidt 5.00 12.00
SJRPGO Paul Goldschmidt 5.00 12.00
SJRRB Ryan Braun 3.00 8.00
SJRRBA Ryan Braun 3.00 8.00
SJRRBR Ryan Braun 3.00 8.00
SJRRCA Robinson Cano 3.00 8.00
SJRRCN Robinson Cano 3.00 8.00
SJRRCO Robinson Cano 3.00 8.00
SJRRO Rougned Odor 3.00 8.00
SJRSM Starling Marte 6.00 15.00
SJRSMA Starling Marte 6.00 15.00
SJRSMR Starling Marte 6.00 15.00
SJRSP Salvador Perez 8.00 20.00
SJRSPC Stephen Piscotty 3.00 8.00
SJRSPI Stephen Piscotty 3.00 8.00
SJRSPS Stephen Piscotty 3.00 8.00
SJRTG Tyler Glasnow 10.00 25.00
SJRTGL Tyler Glasnow 10.00 25.00
SJRTL Tim Lincecum 3.00 8.00
SJRTS Trevor Story 4.00 10.00
SJRTSO Trevor Story 4.00 10.00
SJRTST Trevor Story 4.00 10.00
SJRTT Troy Tulowitzki 4.00 10.00
SJRVMA Victor Martinez 3.00 8.00
SJRVMR Victor Martinez 3.00 8.00
SJRVMT Victor Martinez 3.00 8.00
SJRWM Wil Myers 3.00 8.00
SJRWME Wil Myers 3.00 8.00
SJRWMY Wil Myers 3.00 8.00
SJRXB Xander Bogaerts 4.00 10.00
SJRXBG Xander Bogaerts 4.00 10.00
SJRXBO Xander Bogaerts 4.00 10.00
SJRYC Yoenis Cespedes 5.00 12.00
SJRYCE Yoenis Cespedes 5.00 12.00
SJRYCP Yoenis Cespedes 5.00 12.00
SJRYCS Yoenis Cespedes 5.00 12.00
SJRYG Yulieski Gurriel 4.00 10.00
SJRYGU Yulieski Gurriel 4.00 10.00
SJRYM Yadier Molina 8.00 20.00
SJRYML Yadier Molina 8.00 20.00
SJRYMO Yadier Molina 8.00 20.00

2017 Topps Triple Threads WBC Relic Combos

STATED ODDS 1:128 HOBBY
STATED PRINT RUN 36 SER.#'d SETS
*SILVER/27: .4X TO 1X BASIC
*EMERALD/18: .4X TO 1X BASIC
WBCACH Cbrra/Altve/Hrnndz 10.00 25.00
WBCBML Beltran/Lindor/Molina 10.00 25.00
WBCCAK Ian Kinsler 10.00 25.00
Brandon Crawford
Nolan Arenado
WBCGCA Altve/Gnzlz/Cbrra 10.00 25.00
WBCHPG Gldschmdt/Posey/Hsmr 8.00 20.00
WBCJSM Stntn/McCtchn/Jones 6.00 15.00
WBCLCB Correa/Lindor/Baez 15.00 40.00
WBCMCB Jose Bautista 6.00 15.00
Robinson Cano
Manny Machado
WBCPBG Grgrs/Bgrts/Prfr 15.00 40.00
WBCSYT Ymda/Skmto/Tstsgh 12.00 30.00

2017 Topps Triple Threads WBC Relics

STATED ODDS 1:64 HOBBY
STATED PRINT RUN 36 SER.#'d SETS
*SILVER/27: .4X TO 1X BASIC
*EMERALD/18: .4X TO 1X BASIC
WBCRAB Alex Bregman 8.00 20.00
WBCRAJ Adam Jones 6.00 15.00
WBCRAM Andrew McCutchen 12.00 30.00
WBCRBP Buster Posey 6.00 15.00
WBCRCC Carlos Correa 12.00 30.00
WBCRDG Didi Gregorius 10.00 25.00
WBCRFF Freddie Freeman 8.00 20.00
WBCRFH Felix Hernandez 4.00 10.00
WBCRGS Giancarlo Stanton 5.00 12.00
WBCRHS Hayato Sakamoto 12.00 30.00
WBCRJA Jose Altuve 4.00 10.00
WBCRJB Javier Baez 10.00 25.00
WBCRKT Kohsuke Tanaka 6.00 15.00
WBCRMC Miguel Cabrera 12.00 30.00
WBCRMM Manny Machado 8.00 20.00
WBCRNA Nolan Arenado 10.00 25.00
WBCRRC Robinson Cano 6.00 15.00
WBCRTY Tetsuto Yamada 6.00 15.00
WBCRYM Yadier Molina 10.00 25.00
WBCRYT Yoshitomo Tsutsugo 10.00 25.00

2018 Topps Triple Threads

COMP.SET w/o AU's (100) 75.00 200.00
JSY AU RC ODDS 1:13 MINI BOX
JSY AU RC PRINT RUN 99 SER.#'d SETS
JSY AU ODDS 1:13 MINI BOX
JSY AU PRINT RUN 99 SER.#'d SETS
EXCHANGE DEADLINE 8/31/2020
1-100 PLATE ODDS 1:116 MINI BOX
JSY AU PLATE ODDS 1:273 MINI BOX
PLATE PRINT RUN 1 SET PER COLOR
BLACK-CYAN-MAGENTA-YELLOW ISSUED
NO PLATE PRICING DUE TO SCARCITY
1 Bryce Harper 1.00 2.50
2 Charlie Blackmon .60 1.50
3 Kris Bryant .75 2.00
4 Mike Trout 3.00 8.00
5 Paul Goldschmidt .60 1.50
6 Manny Machado .60 1.50
7 Mookie Betts 1.25 3.00
8 Anthony Rizzo .75 2.00
9 Kyle Schwarber .60 1.50
10 Joey Votto .60 1.50
11 Nolan Arenado 1.00 2.50
12 Miguel Cabrera .60 1.50
13 Justin Verlander .60 1.50
14 Carlos Correa .60 1.50
15 Eric Hosmer .50 1.25
16 Clayton Kershaw 1.00 2.50
17 Corey Seager .60 1.50
18 Evan Longoria .50 1.25
19 Giancarlo Stanton .60 1.50
20 Ichiro .75 2.00
21 Noah Syndergaard .50 1.25
22 Masahiro Tanaka .50 1.25
23 Gary Sanchez .60 1.50
24 Buster Posey .75 2.00
25 Felix Hernandez .50 1.25
26 Robinson Cano .50 1.25
27 Nelson Cruz .60 1.50
28 Yu Darvish .60 1.50
29 Josh Donaldson .50 1.25
30 Andrew Benintendi .60 1.50
31 Max Scherzer .60 1.50
32 Francisco Lindor .60 1.50
33 Chris Sale .60 1.50
34 Addison Russell .50 1.25
35 Javier Baez .75 2.00
36 Jacob deGrom 1.25 3.00
37 Andrew McCutchen .60 1.50
38 Wil Myers .50 1.25
39 Albert Pujols .75 2.00
40 Michael Conforto .50 1.25
41 Jose Altuve .50 1.25
42 Justin Upton .50 1.25
43 Edwin Encarnacion .60 1.50
44 Cody Bellinger 1.25 3.00
45 Ryan Braun .50 1.25
46 Freddie Freeman .75 2.00
47 Marcus Stroman .50 1.25
48 Marcell Ozuna .60 1.50
49 Aaron Judge 1.50 4.00
50 Adrian Beltre .60 1.50
51 Luis Severino .50 1.25
52 Corey Kluber .50 1.25
53 Trea Turner .50 1.25
54 Byron Buxton .60 1.50
55 Stephen Strasburg .60 1.50
56 J.D. Martinez .60 1.50
57 Mariano Rivera .75 2.00
58 Xander Bogaerts .60 1.50
59 Adam Jones .50 1.25
60 Daniel Murphy .50 1.25
61 Roberto Clemente 1.50 4.00
62 Cal Ripken Jr. 2.00 5.00
63 Hank Aaron 1.25 3.00
64 Ted Williams 1.25 3.00
65 Jackie Robinson .60 1.50
66 Sandy Koufax 1.25 3.00
67 Babe Ruth 1.50 4.00
68 Ernie Banks .60 1.50
69 Derek Jeter 1.50 4.00
70 David Ortiz .60 1.50
71 Mark McGwire 1.00 2.50
72 Randy Johnson .60 1.50
73 Honus Wagner .60 1.50
74 Roger Maris .60 1.50
75 Ty Cobb 1.00 2.50
76 Lou Gehrig 1.25 3.00
77 Reggie Jackson .50 1.25
78 George Brett 1.25 3.00
79 Don Mattingly 1.25 3.00
80 Frank Thomas .60 1.50
81 Bo Jackson .60 1.50
82 Johnny Bench .60 1.50
83 Greg Maddux .75 2.00
84 Roger Clemens .75 2.00
85 Mike Piazza .60 1.50
86 Nolan Ryan 2.00 5.00
87 Bob Gibson .50 1.25
88 Chipper Jones .60 1.50
89 Ozzie Smith .75 2.00
90 Alex Bregman .60 1.50
91 George Springer .50 1.25
92 Zack Greinke .60 1.50
93 Pedro Martinez .50 1.25
94 Ryne Sandberg 1.25 3.00
95 Barry Larkin .50 1.25
96 Starling Marte .50 1.25
97 Chris Davis .40 1.00
98 Bartolo Colon .40 1.00
99 Dustin Pedroia .60 1.50
100 John Smoltz .60 1.50
RFPARAA Anthony Banda JSY AU RC 3.00 8.00
RFPARAB Bregman JSY AU EXCH 15.00 40.00
RFPARAV Verdugo JSY AU RC 10.00 25.00
RFPARBA Brian Anderson JSY AU RC 4.00 10.00
RFPARBB Byron Buxton JSY AU 5.00 12.00
RFPARBZ Bradley Zimmer JSY AU 3.00 8.00
RFPARCA Christian Arroyo JSY AU 3.00 8.00
RFPARCR Frazier JSY AU RC 6.00 15.00
RFPARCS Chance Sisco JSY AU RC 4.00 10.00
RFPARDF Derek Fisher JSY AU 3.00 8.00
RFPARFB Franklin Barreto JSY AU 3.00 8.00
RFPARFM Mejia JSY AU RC 6.00 15.00
RFPARGT Torres JSY AU RC 25.00 60.00
RFPARHR Hunter Renfroe JSY AU 4.00 10.00
RFPARIH Ian Happ JSY AU 4.00 10.00
RFPARJC J.P. Crawford JSY AU RC 5.00 12.00
RFPARJH Hader JSY AU 6.00 15.00
RFPARJL Flaherty JSY AU RC 20.00 50.00
RFPARJW Jesse Winker JSY AU 5.00 12.00
RFPARLB Lewis Brinson JSY AU EXCH 3.00 8.00
RFPARLS Lucas Sims JSY AU RC 4.00 10.00
RFPARMF Max Fried JSY AU RC 12.00 30.00
RFPARMH Haniger JSY AU 10.00 25.00
RFPARMM Manny Margot JSY AU 3.00 8.00
RFPARMO Matt Olson JSY AU 8.00 20.00
RFPARND Nicky Delmonico JSY AU RC 3.00 8.00
RFPAROA Albies JSY AU RC 15.00 40.00
RFPARPD DeJong JSY AU 6.00 15.00
RFPARRA Acuna Jr. JSY AU RC 125.00 300.00
RFPARRD Devers JSY AU RC EXCH 25.00 60.00
RFPARRH Hoskins JSY AU RC 12.00 30.00
RFPARRM Ryan McMahon JSY AU RC 8.00 20.00
RFPARSA Sandy Alcantara JSY AU RC 3.00 8.00
RFPARSN Sean Newcomb JSY AU 4.00 10.00
RFPARTA Tyler Mahle JSY AU RC 4.00 10.00
RFPARTT Story JSY AU EXCH 6.00 15.00
RFPARTW Tyler Wade JSY AU RC 4.00 10.00
RFPARVR Robles JSY AU RC 15.00 40.00
RFPARWM Whit Merrifield JSY AU 5.00 12.00
RFPARZG Zack Granite JSY AU RC 3.00 8.00

2018 Topps Triple Threads Amber

*AMBER VET: .75X TO 2X BASIC
STATED ODDS 1:3 MINI BOX
STATED PRINT RUN 199 SER.#'d SETS

2018 Topps Triple Threads Amethyst

*AMETHYST VET: .6X TO 1.5X BASIC
STATED ODDS 1:2 MINI BOX
STATED PRINT RUN 299 SER.#'d SETS

2018 Topps Triple Threads Emerald

*EMERALD VET: .6X TO 1.5X BASIC
*EMERALD JSY AU: .4X TO 1X BASIC RC
1-100 ODDS 1:2 MINI BOX
JSY AU ODDS 1:23 MINI BOX
1-100 PRINT RUN 259 SER.#'d SETS
JSY AU PRINT RUN 50 SER.#'d SETS
EXCHANGE DEADLINE 8/31/2020

2018 Topps Triple Threads Gold

*GOLD VET: 1X TO 2.5X BASIC
STATED ODDS 1:5 MINI BOX
STATED PRINT RUN 99 SER.#'d SETS
62 Cal Ripken Jr. 8.00 20.00
86 Nolan Ryan 10.00 25.00

2018 Topps Triple Threads Onyx

*ONYX VET: 1.5X TO 4X BASIC
*ONYX JSY AU: .5X TO 1.2X BASIC RC
1-100 ODDS 1:10 MINI BOX
JSY AU ODDS 1:31 MINI BOX
1-100 PRINT RUN 50 SER.#'d SETS
JSY AU PRINT RUN 35 SER.#'d SETS
EXCHANGE DEADLINE 8/31/2020
4 Mike Trout 12.00 30.00
62 Cal Ripken Jr. 12.00 30.00
69 Derek Jeter 12.00 30.00
79 Don Mattingly 10.00 25.00
86 Nolan Ryan 12.00 30.00
RFPARDM Dominic Smith 4.00 10.00
RFPARLW Luke Weaver 5.00 12.00

2018 Topps Triple Threads Sapphire

*SAPPHIRE VET: 3X TO 8X BASIC
STATED ODDS 1:19 MINI BOX
STATED PRINT RUN 25 SER.#'d SETS
4 Mike Trout 20.00 50.00
62 Cal Ripken Jr. 20.00 50.00
69 Derek Jeter 20.00 50.00
79 Don Mattingly 20.00 50.00
86 Nolan Ryan 30.00 80.00

2018 Topps Triple Threads Silver

*SILVER JSY AU: .4X TO 1X BASIC RC
STATED ODDS 1:15 MINI BOX
STATED PRINT RUN 75 SER.#'d SETS
EXCHANGE DEADLINE 8/31/2020

2018 Topps Triple Threads Autograph Relic Combos

STATED ODDS 1:62 HOBBY
STATED PRINT RUN 36 SER.#'d SETS
EXCHANGE DEADLINE 8/31/2020
*SILVER/27: .4X TO 1X BASIC
*EMERALD/18: .4X TO 1X BASIC
PRINTING PLATE ODDS 1:442 HOBBY
PLATE PRINT RUN 1 SET PER COLOR
BLACK-CYAN-MAGENTA-YELLOW ISSUED
NO PLATE PRICING DUE TO SCARCITY
ARCADM Pettitte/Jeter/Rivera
ARCAJA Acuna/Albies/Jones 125.00 300.00
ARCAJG Brgmn/Altve/Sprngr EXCH 50.00 120.00
ARCAMS Trout/Pujols/Ohtani
ARCAMT Mncni/Mchdo/Jns EXCH 30.00 80.00
ARCATV Dawson/Raines/Vlad 40.00 100.00
ARCBCM Brooks/Cal/Machado EXCH 75.00 200.00
ARCBKJ Larkin/Bench/Votto 125.00 300.00
ARCCGD Frazier/Gregorius/Bird 20.00 50.00
ARCCJJ Altuve/Bagwell/Biggio 60.00 150.00
ARCFCJ Kluber/Lindor/Ramirez EXCH 50.00 120.00
ARCHIS Ichiro/Matsui/Ohtani
ARCIJA Beltre/Gonzalez/Rodriguez 40.00 100.00
ARCJAK Schwrbr/Baez/Rssll EXCH 30.00 80.00
ARCJCD Smoltz/Jones/Murphy 75.00 200.00
ARCJNM Conforto/deGrom/Syndgrd 60.00 150.00
ARCLGD Svrno/Grgrs/Trrs 40.00 100.00
ARCLKT Thme/Lndr/Klbr EXCH 40.00 100.00
ARCLPJ Lamb/Gldschmdt/Gnzlz 20.00 50.00
ARCMKM Davis/Chapman/Olson 40.00 100.00
ARCMYM Wcha/Mlna/Ozna 40.00 100.00
ARCOFD Swanson/Albies/Freeman 40.00 100.00
ARCPAB Williams/Posada/Pettitte 60.00 150.00
ARCRAK Sandberg/Bryant/Rizzo 100.00 250.00
ARCRDC Sale/Pdria/Dvrs EXCH 40.00 100.00
ARCTCE Thames/Shaw/Yelich 30.00 80.00
ARCTCT Stry/Blckmn/Andrsn EXCH 20.00 50.00
ARCYAD Smith/Rosario/Cespedes

2018 Topps Triple Threads Autograph Relics

STATED ODDS 1:10 HOBBY
STATED PRINT RUN 18 SER.#'d SETS
EXCHANGE DEADLINE 8/31/2020
*GOLD/9: .5X TO 1.2X BASIC
SOME GOLD NOT PRICED DUE TO SCARCITY
ALL VERSIONS EQUALLY PRICED
TTARAB1 Adrian Beltre 30.00 80.00
TTARAB2 Adrian Beltre 30.00 80.00
TTARAB3 Adrian Beltre 30.00 80.00
TTARABR1 Alex Bregman EXCH 20.00 50.00
TTARABR2 Alex Bregman EXCH 20.00 50.00
TTARABR3 Alex Bregman EXCH 20.00 50.00
TTARABR4 Alex Bregman EXCH 20.00 50.00
TTARABR5 Alex Bregman EXCH 20.00 50.00
TTARAD1 Andre Dawson 15.00 40.00
TTARAD2 Andre Dawson 15.00 40.00
TTARAD3 Andre Dawson 15.00 40.00
TTARAJ1 Aaron Judge 60.00 150.00
TTARAJ2 Aaron Judge 60.00 150.00
TTARAM1 Andrew McCutchen 20.00 50.00
TTARAM2 Andrew McCutchen 20.00 50.00
TTARAM3 Andrew McCutchen 20.00 50.00
TTARAM4 Andrew McCutchen 20.00 50.00
TTARAP1 Andy Pettitte 20.00 50.00
TTARAP2 Andy Pettitte 20.00 50.00
TTARAP3 Andy Pettitte 20.00 50.00
TTARAP4 Andy Pettitte 20.00 50.00
TTARAR1 Addison Russell 6.00 15.00
TTARAR2 Addison Russell 6.00 15.00
TTARARI1 Anthony Rizzo 25.00 60.00
TTARARI2 Anthony Rizzo 25.00 60.00
TTARARI3 Anthony Rizzo 25.00 60.00
TTARARI4 Anthony Rizzo 25.00 60.00
TTARBB1 Byron Buxton 10.00 25.00
TTARBB2 Byron Buxton 10.00 25.00
TTARBB3 Byron Buxton 10.00 25.00
TTARBD1 Brian Dozier 10.00 25.00
TTARBD2 Brian Dozier 10.00 25.00
TTARBD3 Brian Dozier 10.00 25.00
TTARBH1 Bryce Harper 75.00 200.00
TTARBH2 Bryce Harper 75.00 200.00
TTARBL1 Barry Larkin 20.00 50.00
TTARBL2 Barry Larkin 20.00 50.00
TTARBP1 Buster Posey
TTARCBI1 Craig Biggio 15.00 40.00
TTARCBI2 Craig Biggio 15.00 40.00
TTARCBI3 Craig Biggio 15.00 40.00
TTARCBL1 Charlie Blackmon 8.00 20.00
TTARCBL2 Charlie Blackmon 8.00 20.00
TTARCBL3 Charlie Blackmon 8.00 20.00
TTARCBL4 Charlie Blackmon 8.00 20.00
TTARCBL5 Charlie Blackmon 8.00 20.00
TTARCF1 Carlton Fisk 20.00 50.00
TTARCF2 Carlton Fisk 20.00 50.00
TTARCF3 Carlton Fisk 20.00 50.00
TTARCJ1 Chipper Jones 75.00 200.00
TTARCJ2 Chipper Jones 75.00 200.00
TTARCKI1 Craig Kimbrel 15.00 40.00
TTARCKI2 Craig Kimbrel 15.00 40.00
TTARCKI3 Craig Kimbrel 15.00 40.00
TTARCKI4 Craig Kimbrel 15.00 40.00
TTARCKI5 Craig Kimbrel 15.00 40.00
TTARCKL1 Corey Kluber 10.00 25.00
TTARCKL2 Corey Kluber 10.00 25.00
TTARCKL3 Corey Kluber 10.00 25.00
TTARCKL4 Corey Kluber 10.00 25.00
TTARCKL5 Corey Kluber 10.00 25.00
TTARCR1 Cal Ripken Jr. 60.00 150.00
TTARCSA1 Chris Sale 20.00 50.00
TTARCSA2 Chris Sale 20.00 50.00
TTARCSA3 Chris Sale 20.00 50.00
TTARCSA4 Chris Sale 20.00 50.00
TTARCSA5 Chris Sale 20.00 50.00
TTARCY1 Christian Yelich 30.00 80.00
TTARCY2 Christian Yelich 30.00 80.00
TTARCY3 Christian Yelich 30.00 80.00
TTARCY4 Christian Yelich 30.00 80.00
TTARCY5 Christian Yelich 30.00 80.00
TTARDE1 Dennis Eckersley 12.00 30.00
TTARDE2 Dennis Eckersley 12.00 30.00
TTARDE3 Dennis Eckersley 12.00 30.00
TTARDE4 Dennis Eckersley 12.00 30.00
TTARDG1 Didi Gregorius 12.00 30.00
TTARDG2 Didi Gregorius 12.00 30.00
TTARDG3 Didi Gregorius 12.00 30.00
TTARDG4 Didi Gregorius 12.00 30.00
TTARDG5 Didi Gregorius 12.00 30.00
TTARDJ1 Derek Jeter 300.00 500.00
TTARDMA1 Don Mattingly 60.00 150.00
TTARDMA2 Don Mattingly 60.00 150.00
TTARDMU1 Dale Murphy 30.00 80.00
TTARDMU2 Dale Murphy 30.00 80.00
TTARDMU3 Dale Murphy 30.00 80.00
TTARDO1 David Ortiz 40.00 100.00
TTARDO2 David Ortiz 40.00 100.00
TTARFF1 Freddie Freeman 15.00 40.00
TTARFF2 Freddie Freeman 15.00 40.00
TTARFF3 Freddie Freeman 15.00 40.00
TTARFF4 Freddie Freeman 15.00 40.00
TTARFF5 Freddie Freeman 15.00 40.00
TTARFL1 Francisco Lindor 25.00 60.00
TTARFL2 Francisco Lindor 25.00 60.00
TTARFL3 Francisco Lindor 25.00 60.00
TTARFL4 Francisco Lindor 25.00 60.00
TTARFT1 Frank Thomas 40.00 100.00
TTARFT2 Frank Thomas 40.00 100.00
TTARFT3 Frank Thomas 40.00 100.00
TTARGS1 Gary Sanchez 20.00 50.00
TTARGS2 Gary Sanchez 20.00 50.00
TTARGS3 Gary Sanchez 20.00 50.00
TTARGS4 Gary Sanchez 20.00 50.00
TTARGS5 Gary Sanchez 20.00 50.00
TTARGSP1 George Springer 15.00 40.00
TTARGSP2 George Springer 15.00 40.00
TTARGSP3 George Springer 15.00 40.00
TTARGSP4 George Springer 15.00 40.00
TTARGSP5 George Springer 15.00 40.00
TTARHA1 Hank Aaron 200.00 400.00
TTARIH1 Ian Happ 6.00 15.00
TTARIH2 Ian Happ 6.00 15.00
TTARIH3 Ian Happ 6.00 15.00
TTARIH4 Ian Happ 6.00 15.00
TTARIH5 Ian Happ 6.00 15.00
TTARIR1 Ivan Rodriguez 15.00 40.00
TTARIR2 Ivan Rodriguez 15.00 40.00
TTARIR3 Ivan Rodriguez 15.00 40.00
TTARJA1 Jose Altuve 20.00 50.00
TTARJA2 Jose Altuve 20.00 50.00
TTARJA3 Jose Altuve 20.00 50.00
TTARJA4 Jose Altuve 20.00 50.00
TTARJA5 Jose Altuve 20.00 50.00
TTARJB1 Jeff Bagwell 25.00 60.00
TTARJB2 Jeff Bagwell 25.00 60.00
TTARJB3 Jeff Bagwell 25.00 60.00
TTARJB4 Jeff Bagwell 25.00 60.00
TTARJBA1 Javier Baez EXCH 20.00 50.00
TTARJBA2 Javier Baez EXCH 20.00 50.00
TTARJBA3 Javier Baez EXCH 20.00 50.00
TTARJBA4 Javier Baez EXCH 20.00 50.00
TTARJBA5 Javier Baez EXCH 20.00 50.00
TTARJC1 Jose Canseco 15.00 40.00
TTARJC2 Jose Canseco 15.00 40.00
TTARJC3 Jose Canseco 15.00 40.00
TTARJC4 Jose Canseco 15.00 40.00
TTARJD1 Jacob deGrom 40.00 100.00
TTARJD2 Jacob deGrom 30.00 80.00
TTARJD3 Jacob deGrom 30.00 80.00
TTARJD4 Jacob deGrom 30.00 80.00
TTARJD5 Jacob deGrom 30.00 80.00
TTARJDO1 Josh Donaldson 15.00 40.00
TTARJDO2 Josh Donaldson 15.00 40.00
TTARJDO3 Josh Donaldson 15.00 40.00
TTARJG1 Juan Gonzalez 20.00 50.00
TTARJG2 Juan Gonzalez 20.00 50.00
TTARJG3 Juan Gonzalez 20.00 50.00
TTARJR1 Jose Ramirez 20.00 50.00
TTARJR2 Jose Ramirez 20.00 50.00
TTARJR3 Jose Ramirez 20.00 50.00
TTARJR4 Jose Ramirez 20.00 50.00
TTARJS1 John Smoltz 25.00 60.00
TTARJS2 John Smoltz 25.00 60.00
TTARJS3 John Smoltz 25.00 60.00
TTARJT1 Jim Thome 25.00 60.00
TTARJT2 Jim Thome 25.00 60.00
TTARJT3 Jim Thome 25.00 60.00
TTARJU1 Justin Upton 6.00 15.00
TTARJU2 Justin Upton 6.00 15.00
TTARJU3 Justin Upton 6.00 15.00
TTARJU4 Justin Upton 6.00 15.00
TTARJV1 Joey Votto 30.00 80.00
TTARJV2 Joey Votto 30.00 80.00
TTARKB1 Kris Bryant 60.00 150.00
TTARKB2 Kris Bryant 60.00 150.00
TTARKB3 Kris Bryant 60.00 150.00
TTARKS1 Kyle Schwarber 12.00 30.00
TTARKS2 Kyle Schwarber 12.00 30.00
TTARKS3 Kyle Schwarber 12.00 30.00
TTARKS4 Kyle Schwarber 12.00 30.00
TTARKS5 Kyle Schwarber 12.00 30.00
TTARLS1 Luis Severino 12.00 30.00
TTARLS2 Luis Severino 12.00 30.00
TTARLS3 Luis Severino 12.00 30.00
TTARLS4 Luis Severino 12.00 30.00
TTARLS5 Luis Severino 12.00 30.00
TTARMM1 Mark McGwire 40.00 100.00
TTARMM2 Mark McGwire 40.00 100.00
TTARMMA1 Manny Machado 20.00 50.00
TTARMMA2 Manny Machado 20.00 50.00
TTARMMA3 Manny Machado 20.00 50.00
TTARMMA4 Manny Machado 20.00 50.00
TTARMP1 Mike Piazza 30.00 80.00
TTARMT1 Mike Trout 150.00 400.00
TTARMT2 Mike Trout 150.00 400.00
TTARNG1 Nomar Garciaparra 15.00 40.00
TTARNG2 Nomar Garciaparra 15.00 40.00
TTARNG3 Nomar Garciaparra 15.00 40.00
TTARNR1 Nolan Ryan 75.00 200.00
TTARNR2 Nolan Ryan 75.00 200.00
TTARNS1 Noah Syndergaard 12.00 30.00
TTARNS2 Noah Syndergaard 12.00 30.00
TTARNS3 Noah Syndergaard 12.00 30.00
TTARNS4 Noah Syndergaard 12.00 30.00
TTARNS5 Noah Syndergaard 12.00 30.00
TTAROS1 Ozzie Smith 25.00 60.00
TTAROS2 Ozzie Smith 25.00 60.00
TTAROS3 Ozzie Smith 25.00 60.00
TTARPG1 Paul Goldschmidt 20.00 50.00
TTARPG2 Paul Goldschmidt 20.00 50.00
TTARPG3 Paul Goldschmidt 20.00 50.00
TTARPG4 Paul Goldschmidt 20.00 50.00
TTARPG5 Paul Goldschmidt 20.00 50.00
TTARRA1 Roberto Alomar 20.00 50.00
TTARRA2 Roberto Alomar 20.00 50.00
TTARRA3 Roberto Alomar 20.00 50.00
TTARRC1 Rod Carew 15.00 40.00
TTARRC2 Rod Carew 15.00 40.00
TTARRC3 Rod Carew 15.00 40.00
TTARRFI1 Rollie Fingers 12.00 30.00
TTARRH1 Rickey Henderson 30.00 80.00
TTARRH2 Rickey Henderson 30.00 80.00
TTARRJ1 Randy Johnson 40.00 100.00
TTARRY1 Robin Yount 30.00 80.00
TTARRY2 Robin Yount 30.00 80.00
TTARSG1 Sonny Gray 6.00 15.00
TTARSG2 Sonny Gray 6.00 15.00
TTARSG3 Sonny Gray 6.00 15.00
TTARSM1 Starling Marte 10.00 25.00
TTARSM2 Starling Marte 10.00 25.00
TTARSM3 Starling Marte 10.00 25.00
TTARSM4 Starling Marte 10.00 25.00
TTARSM5 Starling Marte 10.00 25.00
TTARSO1 Shohei Ohtani 300.00 500.00
TTARSO2 Shohei Ohtani 300.00 500.00
TTARSP1 Salvador Perez 15.00 40.00
TTARSP2 Salvador Perez 15.00 40.00
TTARSP3 Salvador Perez 15.00 40.00
TTARSP4 Salvador Perez 15.00 40.00
TTARSP5 Salvador Perez 15.00 40.00
TTARTG1 Tom Glavine 20.00 50.00
TTARTG2 Tom Glavine 20.00 50.00
TTARTH1 Torii Hunter 12.00 30.00
TTARTH2 Torii Hunter 12.00 30.00
TTARTH3 Torii Hunter 12.00 30.00
TTARTH4 Torii Hunter 12.00 30.00
TTARTM1 Trey Mancini 10.00 25.00
TTARTM2 Trey Mancini 10.00 25.00
TTARTM3 Trey Mancini 10.00 25.00
TTARTM4 Trey Mancini 10.00 25.00
TTARTM5 Trey Mancini 10.00 25.00
TTARTR1 Tim Raines 10.00 25.00
TTARTR2 Tim Raines 10.00 25.00
TTARTR3 Tim Raines 10.00 25.00
TTARVG1 Vladimir Guerrero 30.00 80.00
TTARVG2 Vladimir Guerrero 30.00 80.00
TTARVG3 Vladimir Guerrero 30.00 80.00
TTARWC1 Will Clark 40.00 100.00
TTARWC2 Will Clark 40.00 100.00
TTARWC3 Will Clark 40.00 100.00
TTARWC4 Will Clark 40.00 100.00
TTARWCO1 Willson Contreras 12.00 30.00
TTARWCO2 Willson Contreras 12.00 30.00
TTARWCO3 Willson Contreras 12.00 30.00

TTARWCO4 Willson Contreras 12.00 30.00
TTARWCO5 Willson Contreras 12.00 30.00
TTARYM1 Yadier Molina 40.00 100.00
TTARYM2 Yadier Molina 40.00 100.00
TTARYM3 Yadier Molina 40.00 100.00
TTARYM4 Yadier Molina 40.00 100.00
TTARYM5 Yadier Molina 40.00 100.00

2018 Topps Triple Threads Legend Relics

STATED ODDS 1:68 HOBBY
STATED PRINT RUN 36 SER.#'d SETS
*SILVER/27: .4X TO 1X BASIC
*EMERALD/18: .4X TO 1X BASIC
RLCCF Carlton Fisk 8.00 20.00
RLCCJ Chipper Jones 10.00 25.00
RLCCR Cal Ripken Jr. 20.00 50.00
RLCDJ Derek Jeter 25.00 60.00
RLCEB Ernie Banks 20.00 50.00
RLCFT Frank Thomas 12.00 30.00
RLCGM Greg Maddux 10.00 25.00
RLCJB Johnny Bench 12.00 30.00
RLCJS John Smoltz 10.00 25.00
RLCMM Mark McGwire 12.00 30.00
RLCMP Mike Piazza 10.00 25.00
RLCMR Mariano Rivera 10.00 25.00
RLCNR Nolan Ryan 20.00 50.00
RLCOS Ozzie Smith 10.00 25.00
RLCPM Pedro Martinez 8.00 20.00
RLCRC Roger Clemens 8.00 20.00
RLCRE Roberto Clemente 75.00 200.00
RLCRH Rickey Henderson 10.00 25.00
RLCRK Reggie Jackson 8.00 20.00
RLCRS Ryne Sandberg 10.00 25.00
RLCTW Ted Williams 60.00 150.00
RLCWB Wade Boggs 10.00 25.00

2018 Topps Triple Threads Players Weekend Relics

STATED ODDS 1:142 HOBBY
STATED PRINT RUN 36 SER.#'d SETS
*SILVER/27: .4X TO 1X BASIC
*EMERALD/18: .4X TO 1X BASIC
PWAR Amed Rosario 5.00 12.00
PWBP Buster Posey 10.00 25.00
PWI Ichiro 20.00 50.00
PWKB Kris Bryant 20.00 50.00
PWKD Khris Davis 6.00 15.00
PWKS Kyle Schwarber 8.00 20.00
PWRB Ryan Braun 5.00 12.00
PWRD Rafael Devers 12.00 30.00
PWYM Yadier Molina 12.00 30.00

2018 Topps Triple Threads Relic Combos

STATED ODDS 1:33 HOBBY
STATED PRINT RUN 36 SER.#'d SETS
*SILVER/27: .4X TO 1X BASIC
*EMERALD/18: .5X TO 1.2X BASIC
RCCAGM Chapman/Sanchez/Tanaka 6.00 15.00
RCCAKK Rizzo/Schwrbr/Bryant 8.00 20.00
RCCAMT Mancini/Jones/Machado 6.00 15.00
RCCAPJ Goldschmidt/Lamb/Pollock 6.00 15.00
RCCAPZ Greinke/Pollock/Goldschmidt 6.00 15.00
RCCARJ Crawford/Nola/Hoskins 10.00 25.00
RCCBBE Lngria/Posey/Crawford 8.00 20.00
RCCBMK Harper/Bryant/Trout 30.00 80.00
RCCCAJ Hamels/Gallo/Beltre 6.00 15.00
RCCCCC Krshw/Bellinger/Seager 12.00 30.00
RCCCCK Krshw/Jansen/Seager 10.00 25.00
RCCCDC Sale/Price/Kimbrel 10.00 25.00
RCCCJJ Biggio/Bagwell/Altuve 10.00 25.00
RCCCMA Betts/Benintendi/Sale 20.00 50.00
RCCCNC Gonzalez/Blackmon/Arenado 10.00 25.00
RCCCYA Martinez/Reyes/Molina 8.00 20.00
RCCDDA Judge/Jeter/Mattingly 40.00 100.00
RCCDFO Albies/Frmn/Swanson 8.00 20.00
RCCDMA Bnntndi/Betts/Pedroia 15.00 40.00
RCCDYT Pham/Fowler/Molina 8.00 20.00
RCCFRN Hernandez/Cano/Cruz 6.00 15.00
RCCGAD Snchz/Grgrius/Judge 10.00 25.00
RCCIJA Gonzalez/Rodriguez/Beltre 6.00 15.00
RCCJAA Rizzo/Baez/Russell 8.00 20.00
RCCJBJ Votto/Larkin/Bench 10.00 25.00
RCCJCA Brgmn/Correa/Altuve 6.00 15.00
RCCJCJ Altuve/Vrlndr/Correa 6.00 15.00
RCCJGS Polanco/Marte/Bell 5.00 12.00
RCCJJA Sanchez/Smoak/Donaldson 5.00 12.00
RCCJMA Trout/Upton/Pujols 15.00 40.00
RCCJNS Sndrgrd/deGrom/Matz 10.00 25.00
RCCJWK Cntrra/Baez/Schwarber 8.00 20.00
RCCJYJ Turner/Puig/Pederson 6.00 15.00
RCCLMS Severino/Tanaka/Gray 5.00 12.00
RCCMBJ Buxton/Mauer/Sano 6.00 15.00
RCCMBS Schrzr/Harper/Strasburg 8.00 20.00
RCCNMM Cstllns/Cabrera/Fulmer 6.00 15.00
RCCSGJ Marte/Taillon/Polanco 5.00 12.00
RCCWMS Moustakas/Mrrfld/Perez 8.00 20.00
RCCYMA Conforto/Rosario/Cespedes 6.00 15.00

2018 Topps Triple Threads Relics

STATED ODDS 1:8 MINI BOX
STATED PRINT RUN 36 SER.#'d SETS
*SILVER/27: .4X TO 1X BASIC
*EMERALD/18: .5X TO 1.2X BASIC
*GOLD/9: .6X TO 1.5X BASIC
ALL VERSIONS EQUALLY PRICED
TTRAB1 Adrian Beltre 4.00 10.00
TTRAB2 Adrian Beltre 4.00 10.00
TTRABE1 Andrew Benintendi 10.00 25.00
TTRABE2 Andrew Benintendi 10.00 25.00
TTRAJE1 Adam Jones 3.00 8.00
TTRAJE2 Adam Jones 3.00 8.00
TTRAJE3 Adam Jones 3.00 8.00
TTRAJE4 Adam Jones 3.00 8.00
TTRAP1 Albert Pujols 5.00 12.00
TTRAP2 Albert Pujols 5.00 12.00
TTRAR1 Anthony Rizzo 5.00 12.00
TTRAR2 Anthony Rizzo 5.00 12.00
TTRAR3 Anthony Rizzo 5.00 12.00
TTRARU1 Addison Russell 3.00 8.00
TTRARU2 Addison Russell 3.00 8.00
TTRARU3 Addison Russell 3.00 8.00
TTRARU4 Addison Russell 3.00 8.00
TTRAW1 Adam Wainwright 3.00 8.00
TTRAW2 Adam Wainwright 3.00 8.00
TTRAW3 Adam Wainwright 3.00 8.00
TTRAW4 Adam Wainwright 3.00 8.00
TTRBB1 Byron Buxton 4.00 10.00
TTRBB2 Byron Buxton 4.00 10.00
TTRBB3 Byron Buxton 4.00 10.00
TTRBH1 Bryce Harper 6.00 15.00
TTRBH2 Bryce Harper 6.00 15.00
TTRBP1 Buster Posey 5.00 12.00
TTRBP2 Buster Posey 5.00 12.00
TTRCC1 Carlos Correa 4.00 10.00
TTRCC2 Carlos Correa 4.00 10.00
TTRCC3 Carlos Correa 4.00 10.00
TTRCG1 Carlos Gonzalez 3.00 8.00
TTRCG2 Carlos Gonzalez 3.00 8.00
TTRCG3 Carlos Gonzalez 3.00 8.00
TTRCKRS1 Clayton Kershaw 6.00 15.00
TTRCKRS2 Clayton Kershaw 6.00 15.00
TTRCR1 Cal Ripken Jr. 12.00 30.00
TTRCS1 Corey Seager 4.00 10.00
TTRCS2 Corey Seager 4.00 10.00
TTRCS3 Corey Seager 4.00 10.00
TTRCSA1 Chris Sale 4.00 10.00
TTRCSA2 Chris Sale 4.00 10.00
TTRCSA3 Chris Sale 4.00 10.00
TTRCSA4 Chris Sale 4.00 10.00
TTRCSA5 Chris Sale 4.00 10.00
TTRDJ1 Derek Jeter 20.00 50.00
TTRDJ2 Derek Jeter 20.00 50.00
TTRDO1 David Ortiz 6.00 15.00
TTRDO2 David Ortiz 6.00 15.00
TTRDP1 Dustin Pedroia 4.00 10.00
TTRDP2 Dustin Pedroia 4.00 10.00
TTRDP3 Dustin Pedroia 4.00 10.00
TTRDPR1 David Price 3.00 8.00
TTRDPR2 David Price 3.00 8.00
TTRDPR3 David Price 3.00 8.00
TTREL1 Evan Longoria 3.00 8.00
TTREL2 Evan Longoria 3.00 8.00
TTREL3 Evan Longoria 3.00 8.00
TTRFF1 Freddie Freeman 5.00 12.00
TTRFF2 Freddie Freeman 5.00 12.00
TTRFF3 Freddie Freeman 5.00 12.00
TTRGSA1 Gary Sanchez 4.00 10.00
TTRGSA2 Gary Sanchez 4.00 10.00
TTRGSA3 Gary Sanchez 4.00 10.00
TTRIK1 Ian Kinsler 3.00 8.00
TTRIK2 Ian Kinsler 3.00 8.00
TTRIK3 Ian Kinsler 3.00 8.00
TTRIK4 Ian Kinsler 3.00 8.00
TTRI1 Ichiro 6.00 15.00
TTRI2 Ichiro 6.00 15.00
TTRJAL1 Jose Altuve 3.00 8.00
TTRJAL2 Jose Altuve 3.00 8.00
TTRJAL3 Jose Altuve 3.00 8.00
TTRJAL4 Jose Altuve 3.00 8.00
TTRJAL5 Jose Altuve 3.00 8.00
TTRJBZ1 Javier Baez 8.00 20.00
TTRJBZ2 Javier Baez 8.00 20.00
TTRJBZ3 Javier Baez 8.00 20.00
TTRJBZ4 Javier Baez 8.00 20.00
TTRJBZ5 Javier Baez 8.00 20.00
TTRJD1 Josh Donaldson 3.00 8.00
TTRJD2 Josh Donaldson 3.00 8.00
TTRJD3 Josh Donaldson 3.00 8.00
TTRJDE1 Jacob deGrom 5.00 12.00
TTRJDE2 Jacob deGrom 5.00 12.00
TTRJDE3 Jacob deGrom 5.00 12.00
TTRJDE4 Jacob deGrom 5.00 12.00
TTRJDE5 Jacob deGrom 5.00 12.00
TTRJU1 Justin Upton 3.00 8.00
TTRJU2 Justin Upton 3.00 8.00
TTRJU3 Justin Upton 3.00 8.00
TTRJU4 Justin Upton 3.00 8.00
TTRJV1 Justin Verlander 4.00 10.00
TTRJV2 Justin Verlander 4.00 10.00
TTRJV3 Justin Verlander 4.00 10.00
TTRJV4 Justin Verlander 4.00 10.00
TTRJV5 Justin Verlander 4.00 10.00
TTRJVO1 Joey Votto 4.00 10.00
TTRJVO2 Joey Votto 4.00 10.00
TTRJVO3 Joey Votto 4.00 10.00
TTRKB1 Kris Bryant 8.00 20.00
TTRKB2 Kris Bryant 8.00 20.00
TTRKB3 Kris Bryant 8.00 20.00
TTRKM1 Kenta Maeda 3.00 8.00
TTRKM2 Kenta Maeda 3.00 8.00
TTRMB1 Mookie Betts 8.00 20.00
TTRMB2 Mookie Betts 8.00 20.00
TTRMB3 Mookie Betts 8.00 20.00
TTRMB4 Mookie Betts 8.00 20.00
TTRMB5 Mookie Betts 8.00 20.00
TTRMCB1 Miguel Cabrera 4.00 10.00
TTRMCB2 Miguel Cabrera 4.00 10.00
TTRMCB3 Miguel Cabrera 4.00 10.00
TTRMCB4 Miguel Cabrera 4.00 10.00
TTRMCB5 Miguel Cabrera 4.00 10.00
TTRMM1 Manny Machado 4.00 10.00
TTRMM2 Manny Machado 4.00 10.00
TTRMM3 Manny Machado 4.00 10.00
TTRMMG1 Mark McGwire 12.00 30.00
TTRMMG2 Mark McGwire 12.00 30.00
TTRMP1 Mike Piazza 6.00 15.00
TTRMS1 Marcus Stroman 3.00 8.00
TTRMS2 Marcus Stroman 3.00 8.00
TTRMS3 Marcus Stroman 3.00 8.00
TTRMS4 Marcus Stroman 3.00 8.00
TTRMSC1 Max Scherzer 4.00 10.00
TTRMSC2 Max Scherzer 4.00 10.00
TTRMSC3 Max Scherzer 4.00 10.00
TTRMTA1 Masahiro Tanaka 3.00 8.00
TTRMT1 Mike Trout 25.00 60.00
TTRMT2 Mike Trout 25.00 60.00
TTRMTA2 Masahiro Tanaka 3.00 8.00
TTRMTA3 Masahiro Tanaka 3.00 8.00
TTRMTA4 Masahiro Tanaka 3.00 8.00
TTRRB1 Ryan Braun 3.00 8.00
TTRRB2 Ryan Braun 3.00 8.00
TTRRB3 Ryan Braun 3.00 8.00
TTRSM1 Starling Marte 3.00 8.00
TTRSM2 Starling Marte 3.00 8.00
TTRSM3 Starling Marte 3.00 8.00
TTRSM4 Starling Marte 3.00 8.00
TTRSS1 Stephen Strasburg 4.00 10.00
TTRSS2 Stephen Strasburg 4.00 10.00
TTRSS3 Stephen Strasburg 4.00 10.00
TTRSS4 Stephen Strasburg 4.00 10.00
TTRSS5 Stephen Strasburg 4.00 10.00
TTRTST1 Trevor Story 4.00 10.00
TTRTST2 Trevor Story 4.00 10.00
TTRTST3 Trevor Story 4.00 10.00
TTRTST4 Trevor Story 4.00 10.00
TTRWM1 Wil Myers 3.00 8.00
TTRWM2 Wil Myers 3.00 8.00
TTRXB1 Xander Bogaerts 4.00 10.00
TTRXB2 Xander Bogaerts 4.00 10.00
TTRXB3 Xander Bogaerts 4.00 10.00
TTRYC1 Yoenis Cespedes 4.00 10.00
TTRYC2 Yoenis Cespedes 4.00 10.00
TTRYC3 Yoenis Cespedes 4.00 10.00
TTRYC4 Yoenis Cespedes 4.00 10.00
TTRYC5 Yoenis Cespedes 4.00 10.00
TTRYM1 Yadier Molina 6.00 15.00
TTRYM2 Yadier Molina 6.00 15.00
TTRYM3 Yadier Molina 6.00 15.00
TTRYM4 Yadier Molina 6.00 15.00

2018 Topps Triple Threads Rookie Autographs

STATED ODDS 1:29 MINI BOX
STATED PRINT RUN 99 SER.#'d SETS
EXCHANGE DEADLINE 8/31/2020
PRINTING PLATE ODDS 1:701 MINI BOX
PLATE PRINT RUN 1 SET PER COLOR
BLACK-CYAN-MAGENTA-YELLOW ISSUED
NO PLATE PRICING DUE TO SCARCITY
*EMERALD/50: .4X TO 1X BASIC
*GOLD/25: .5X TO 1.2X BASIC
RAAH Austin Hays 6.00 15.00
RAAM Austin Meadows EXCH 10.00 25.00
RACV Christian Villanueva 4.00 10.00
RADF Dustin Fowler 4.00 10.00
RAFR Fernando Romero 4.00 10.00
RAHB Harrison Bader 6.00 15.00
RAJH Jordan Hicks 8.00 20.00
RAJS Juan Soto 100.00 250.00
RALG Lourdes Gurriel Jr. 8.00 20.00
RAMA Miguel Andujar 20.00 50.00
RAMM Miles Mikolas 8.00 20.00
RAMS Mike Soroka 20.00 50.00
RANK Nick Kingham 4.00 10.00
RASK Scott Kingery 6.00 15.00
RASO Shohei Ohtani 250.00 500.00
RAWA Willy Adames 5.00 12.00
RAWB Walker Buehler 20.00 50.00

2018 Topps Triple Threads Unity Autograph Jumbo Relics

STATED ODDS 1:7 HOBBY
STATED PRINT RUN 99 SER.#'d SETS
EXCHANGE DEADLINE 8/31/2020
UAJRABR Alex Bregman EXCH 15.00 40.00
UAJRAD Adam Duvall 5.00 12.00
UAJRAE Alcides Escobar 5.00 12.00
UAJRAMED Amed Rosario 5.00 12.00
UAJRARO Amed Rosario 5.00 12.00
UAJRAV Adam Duvall 5.00 12.00
UAJRAW Alex Wood 4.00 10.00
UAJRBS Blake Snell 5.00 12.00
UAJRBSN Blake Snell 5.00 12.00
UAJRBZO Ben Zobrist 15.00 40.00
UAJRCA Christian Arroyo 4.00 10.00
UAJRCB Charlie Blackmon 6.00 15.00
UAJRCSA Chris Sale 15.00 40.00
UAJRCYH Christian Yelich 20.00 50.00
UAJRDB Dellin Betances EXCH 5.00 12.00
UAJRDE Dellin Betances EXCH 5.00 12.00
UAJRDG Didi Gregorius 6.00 15.00
UAJRDP Drew Pomeranz 4.00 10.00
UAJRDPR David Price 12.00 30.00
UAJRDT Darryl Strawberry 8.00 20.00
UAJRET Eric Thames 5.00 12.00
UAJRGB Greg Bird 5.00 12.00
UAJRGI Greg Bird 5.00 12.00
UAJRHOS Rhys Hoskins 15.00 40.00
UAJRIH Ian Happ 5.00 12.00
UAJRIHA Ian Happ 5.00 12.00
UAJRIKS Ian Kinsler 5.00 12.00
UAJRJB Javier Baez EXCH 20.00 50.00
UAJRJBO Justin Bour 4.00 10.00
UAJRJE Jose Berrios 5.00 12.00
UAJRJG Juan Gonzalez 4.00 10.00
UAJRJH Josh Harrison 4.00 10.00
UAJRJHA Josh Harrison 4.00 10.00
UAJRJL Jake Lamb 5.00 12.00
UAJRJP Joc Pederson 5.00 12.00
UAJRJSM Justin Smoak 4.00 10.00
UAJRJU Jay Bruce 5.00 12.00
UAJRJW Jesse Winker 6.00 15.00
UAJRKD Khris Davis 6.00 15.00
UAJRKS Kyle Schwarber 10.00 25.00
UAJRKV Khris Davis 6.00 15.00
UAJRLSE Luis Severino 10.00 25.00
UAJRMA Matt Carpenter 6.00 15.00
UAJRMAR Marcell Ozuna 6.00 15.00
UAJRMCF Michael Conforto 6.00 15.00
UAJRMC Matt Carpenter 6.00 15.00
UAJRMCO Michael Conforto 6.00 15.00
UAJRMF Michael Fulmer 4.00 10.00
UAJRMG Marwin Gonzalez 4.00 10.00
UAJRMGO Marwin Gonzalez 4.00 10.00
UAJRMH Matt Chapman 6.00 15.00
UAJRML Matt Olson 6.00 15.00
UAJRMO Matt Olson 6.00 15.00
UAJRMOZ Marcell Ozuna 6.00 15.00
UAJRRHY Rhys Hoskins 15.00 40.00
UAJRRI Raisel Iglesias 5.00 12.00
UAJRRP Rafael Palmeiro 5.00 12.00
UAJRSD Sean Doolittle 4.00 10.00
UAJRSMO Justin Smoak 4.00 10.00
UAJRSP Stephen Piscotty 4.00 10.00
UAJRSPE Salvador Perez 10.00 25.00
UAJRSPZ Salvador Perez 10.00 25.00
UAJRTH Tommy Pham 4.00 10.00
UAJRTM Trey Mancini 5.00 12.00
UAJRTMA Trey Mancini 5.00 12.00
UAJRTP Tommy Pham 4.00 10.00
UAJRTS Travis Shaw 4.00 10.00
UAJRTY Trevor Story EXCH 6.00 15.00
UAJRWC Willson Contreras 6.00 15.00
UAJRWE Whit Merrifield 6.00 15.00
UAJRWM Whit Merrifield 6.00 15.00
UAJRYA Yonder Alonso 4.00 10.00
UAJRYGL Yasmani Grandal 4.00 10.00
UAJRZC Zack Cozart 4.00 10.00

2018 Topps Triple Threads Unity Autograph Jumbo Relics Emerald

*EMERALD: .5X TO 1.2X BASIC
STATED ODDS 1:13 HOBBY
STATED PRINT RUN 50 SER.#'d SETS
EXCHANGE DEADLINE 8/31/2020
UAJRAB Archie Bradley 5.00 12.00
UAJRAR Anthony Rendon 10.00 25.00
UAJRDS Domingo Santana 6.00 15.00
UAJREI Ender Inciarte 5.00 12.00
UAJRGR Garrett Richards 6.00 15.00
UAJRGSP George Springer 10.00 25.00
UAJRKSG Kyle Seager 5.00 12.00
UAJRPG Paul Goldschmidt 15.00 40.00
UAJRRO Roy Oswalt 6.00 15.00
UAJRTB Tim Beckham 6.00 15.00

2018 Topps Triple Threads Unity Autograph Jumbo Relics Gold

*GOLD: .6X TO 1.5X BASIC
STATED ODDS 1:22 HOBBY
STATED PRINT RUN 25 SER.#'d SETS
EXCHANGE DEADLINE 8/31/2020
UAJRAB Archie Bradley 6.00 15.00
UAJRAR Anthony Rendon 12.00 30.00
UAJRDS Domingo Santana 8.00 20.00
UAJREI Ender Inciarte 6.00 15.00
UAJRGR Garrett Richards 8.00 20.00
UAJRGSP George Springer 12.00 30.00
UAJRJV Joey Votto 25.00 60.00
UAJRKSG Kyle Seager 6.00 15.00
UAJRPG Paul Goldschmidt 20.00 50.00
UAJRRO Roy Oswalt 8.00 20.00
UAJRTB Tim Beckham 8.00 20.00

2018 Topps Triple Threads Unity Autograph Jumbo Relics Silver

*SILVER: .4X TO 1X BASIC
STATED ODDS 1:8 HOBBY
STATED PRINT RUN 75 SER.#'d SETS
EXCHANGE DEADLINE 8/31/2020
UAJRGSP George Springer 8.00 20.00
UAJRKSG Kyle Seager 4.00 10.00
UAJRPG Paul Goldschmidt 12.00 30.00

2018 Topps Triple Threads Unity Single Jumbo Relics

STATED ODDS 1:6 HOBBY
STATED PRINT RUN 36 SER.#'d SETS
*SILVER/27: .4X TO 1X BASIC
*EMERALD/18: .5X TO 1.2X BASIC
*GOLD/9: .6X TO 1.5X BASIC
ALL VERSIONS EQUALLY PRICED
SJRAB1 Andrew Benintendi 10.00 25.00
SJRAB2 Andrew Benintendi 10.00 25.00
SJRABL1 Adrian Beltre 4.00 10.00
SJRABL2 Adrian Beltre 4.00 10.00
SJRABR1 Alex Bregman 4.00 10.00
SJRABR2 Alex Bregman 4.00 10.00
SJRAC1 Aroldis Chapman 4.00 10.00
SJRAJ1 Aaron Judge 15.00 40.00
SJRAJO1 Adam Jones 3.00 8.00
SJRAJO2 Adam Jones 3.00 8.00
SJRAMC1 Andrew McCutchen 4.00 10.00
SJRAMC2 Andrew McCutchen 4.00 10.00
SJRAP1 Albert Pujols 5.00 12.00
SJRAP2 Albert Pujols 5.00 12.00
SJRAP3 Albert Pujols 5.00 12.00
SJRAPT1 Andy Pettitte 3.00 8.00
SJRARO1 Alex Rodriguez 6.00 15.00
SJRARO2 Alex Rodriguez 6.00 15.00
SJRARO3 Alex Rodriguez 6.00 15.00
SJRARU1 Addison Russell 3.00 8.00
SJRARU2 Addison Russell 3.00 8.00
SJRARU3 Addison Russell 3.00 8.00
SJRARZ1 Anthony Rizzo 5.00 12.00
SJRARZ2 Anthony Rizzo 5.00 12.00
SJRARZ3 Anthony Rizzo 5.00 12.00
SJRAW1 Adam Wainwright 3.00 8.00
SJRAW2 Adam Wainwright 3.00 8.00
SJRAW3 Adam Wainwright 3.00 8.00
SJRBB1 Byron Buxton 4.00 10.00
SJRBB2 Byron Buxton 4.00 10.00
SJRBB3 Byron Buxton 4.00 10.00
SJRBC1 Brandon Crawford 3.00 8.00
SJRBC2 Brandon Crawford 3.00 8.00
SJRBC3 Brandon Crawford 3.00 8.00
SJRBH1 Bryce Harper 6.00 15.00
SJRBL1 Barry Larkin 3.00 8.00
SJRBP1 Buster Posey 5.00 12.00
SJRBP2 Buster Posey 5.00 12.00
SJRCA1 Chris Archer 2.50 6.00
SJRCB1 Craig Biggio 3.00 8.00
SJRCC1 Carlos Correa 4.00 10.00
SJRCC2 Carlos Correa 4.00 10.00
SJRCC3 Carlos Correa 4.00 10.00
SJRCG1 Carlos Gonzalez 3.00 8.00
SJRCG2 Carlos Gonzalez 3.00 8.00
SJRCG3 Carlos Gonzalez 3.00 8.00
SJRCH1 Cole Hamels 3.00 8.00
SJRCJ1 Chipper Jones 6.00 15.00
SJRCKE1 Clayton Kershaw 6.00 15.00
SJRCKE2 Clayton Kershaw 6.00 15.00
SJRCKI1 Craig Kimbrel 3.00 8.00
SJRCKI2 Craig Kimbrel 3.00 8.00
SJRCM1 Carlos Martinez 3.00 8.00
SJRCR1 Cal Ripken Jr. 12.00 30.00
SJRCS1 Chris Sale 4.00 10.00
SJRCS2 Chris Sale 4.00 10.00
SJRCS3 Chris Sale 4.00 10.00
SJRCSE1 Corey Seager 4.00 10.00
SJRCY1 Christian Yelich 5.00 12.00
SJRCY2 Christian Yelich 5.00 12.00
SJRDG1 Didi Gregorius 3.00 8.00
SJRDJ1 Derek Jeter 20.00 50.00
SJRDM1 Don Mattingly 20.00 50.00
SJRDMU1 Daniel Murphy 3.00 8.00
SJRDO1 David Ortiz 6.00 15.00
SJRDO2 David Ortiz 6.00 15.00
SJRDO3 David Ortiz 6.00 15.00
SJRDP1 David Price 3.00 8.00
SJRDP2 David Price 3.00 8.00
SJRDP3 David Price 3.00 8.00
SJRDPE1 Dustin Pedroia 4.00 10.00
SJRDPE2 Dustin Pedroia 4.00 10.00
SJRDPE3 Dustin Pedroia 4.00 10.00
SJRDPE4 Dustin Pedroia 4.00 10.00
SJRDS1 Dansby Swanson 4.00 10.00
SJRDS2 Dansby Swanson 4.00 10.00
SJREE1 Edwin Encarnacion 4.00 10.00
SJREH1 Eric Hosmer 3.00 8.00
SJREH2 Eric Hosmer 3.00 8.00
SJREH3 Eric Hosmer 3.00 8.00
SJREL1 Evan Longoria 3.00 8.00
SJREL2 Evan Longoria 3.00 8.00
SJRFF1 Freddie Freeman 5.00 12.00
SJRFF2 Freddie Freeman 5.00 12.00
SJRFF3 Freddie Freeman 5.00 12.00
SJRFT1 Frank Thomas 10.00 25.00
SJRGP1 Gregory Polanco 3.00 8.00
SJRGP2 Gregory Polanco 3.00 8.00
SJRGS1 Gary Sanchez 4.00 10.00
SJRGS2 Gary Sanchez 4.00 10.00
SJRGS3 Gary Sanchez 4.00 10.00
SJRGSP1 George Springer 3.00 8.00
SJRGSP2 George Springer 3.00 8.00
SJRGSP3 George Springer 3.00 8.00
SJRHR1 Hanley Ramirez 3.00 8.00
SJRHR2 Hanley Ramirez 3.00 8.00
SJRHR3 Hanley Ramirez 3.00 8.00
SJRHR4 Hanley Ramirez 3.00 8.00
SJRIK1 Ian Kinsler 3.00 8.00
SJRIK2 Ian Kinsler 3.00 8.00
SJRIK3 Ian Kinsler 3.00 8.00
SJRI1 Ichiro 6.00 15.00
SJRI2 Ichiro 6.00 15.00
SJRI3 Ichiro 6.00 15.00
SJRI4 Ichiro 6.00 15.00
SJRJA1 Jake Arrieta 3.00 8.00
SJRJA2 Jake Arrieta 3.00 8.00
SJRJA3 Jake Arrieta 3.00 8.00
SJRJAL1 Jose Altuve 3.00 8.00
SJRJAL2 Jose Altuve 3.00 8.00
SJRJAL3 Jose Altuve 3.00 8.00
SJRJB1 Jackie Bradley Jr. 4.00 10.00
SJRJB2 Jackie Bradley Jr. 4.00 10.00
SJRJBZ1 Javier Baez 8.00 20.00
SJRJBZ2 Javier Baez 8.00 20.00
SJRJBZ3 Javier Baez 8.00 20.00
SJRJD1 Josh Donaldson 3.00 8.00
SJRJD2 Josh Donaldson 3.00 8.00
SJRJDE1 Jacob deGrom 5.00 12.00
SJRJDE2 Jacob deGrom 5.00 12.00
SJRJDE3 Jacob deGrom 5.00 12.00
SJRJG1 Joey Gallo 3.00 8.00
SJRJH1 Jason Heyward 3.00 8.00
SJRJH2

Jason Heyward

3

2018 Topps Triple Threads Unity Single Jumbo Relics

SJRJH3 Jason Heyward 3.00 8.00
SJRJL1 Jon Lester 3.00 8.00
SJRJL2 Jon Lester 3.00 8.00
SJRJM1 J.D. Martinez 4.00 10.00
SJRJM2 J.D. Martinez 4.00 10.00
SJRJT1 Jameson Taillon 3.00 8.00
SJRJU1 Justin Upton 3.00 8.00
SJRJU2 Justin Upton 3.00 8.00
SJRJU3 Justin Upton 3.00 8.00
SJRJU4 Justin Upton 3.00 8.00
SJRJU5 Justin Upton 3.00 8.00
SJRJV1 Justin Verlander 4.00 10.00
SJRJV2 Justin Verlander 4.00 10.00
SJRJV3 Justin Verlander 4.00 10.00
SJRJV4 Justin Verlander 4.00 10.00
SJRJV5 Justin Verlander 4.00 10.00
SJRJVO1 Joey Votto 4.00 10.00
SJRJVO2 Joey Votto 4.00 10.00
SJRJVO3 Joey Votto 4.00 10.00
SJRKB1 Kris Bryant 8.00 20.00
SJRKB2 Kris Bryant 8.00 20.00
SJRKD1 Khris Davis 4.00 10.00
SJRKM1 Kenta Maeda 3.00 8.00
SJRKM2 Kenta Maeda 3.00 8.00
SJRKS1 Kyle Seager 2.50 6.00
SJRKS2 Kyle Seager 2.50 6.00
SJRKS3 Kyle Seager 2.50 6.00
SJRLS1 Luis Severino 3.00 8.00
SJRLS2 Luis Severino 3.00 8.00
SJRMB1 Mookie Betts 8.00 20.00
SJRMB2 Mookie Betts 8.00 20.00
SJRMB3 Mookie Betts 8.00 20.00
SJRMB4 Mookie Betts 8.00 20.00
SJRMC1 Michael Conforto 3.00 8.00
SJRMC2 Michael Conforto 3.00 8.00
SJRMC3 Michael Conforto 3.00 8.00
SJRMCA1 Matt Carpenter 4.00 10.00
SJRMCA2 Matt Carpenter 4.00 10.00
SJRMCA3 Matt Carpenter 4.00 10.00
SJRMCB1 Miguel Cabrera 4.00 10.00
SJRMCB2 Miguel Cabrera 4.00 10.00
SJRMCB3 Miguel Cabrera 4.00 10.00
SJRMCB4 Miguel Cabrera 4.00 10.00
SJRMCB5 Miguel Cabrera 4.00 10.00
SJRMF1 Michael Fulmer 2.50 6.00
SJRMF2 Michael Fulmer 2.50 6.00
SJRMM1 Mark McGwire 12.00 30.00
SJRMM2 Mark McGwire 12.00 30.00
SJRMMC1 Manny Machado 4.00 10.00
SJRMMC2 Manny Machado 4.00 10.00
SJRMO1 Marcell Ozuna 4.00 10.00
SJRMO2 Marcell Ozuna 4.00 10.00
SJRMO3 Marcell Ozuna 4.00 10.00
SJRMOL1 Matt Olson 4.00 10.00
SJRMP1 Mike Piazza 6.00 15.00
SJRMS1 Max Scherzer 4.00 10.00
SJRMS2 Max Scherzer 4.00 10.00
SJRMS3 Max Scherzer 4.00 10.00
SJRMSA1 Miguel Sano 3.00 8.00
SJRMSA2 Miguel Sano 3.00 8.00
SJRMSA3 Miguel Sano 3.00 8.00
SJRMST1 Marcus Stroman 3.00 8.00
SJRMST2 Marcus Stroman 3.00 8.00
SJRMT1 Masahiro Tanaka 3.00 8.00
SJRMT2 Masahiro Tanaka 3.00 8.00
SJRMT3 Masahiro Tanaka 3.00 8.00
SJRMTR1 Mike Trout 25.00 60.00
SJRNC1 Nelson Cruz 4.00 10.00
SJRNC2 Nelson Cruz 4.00 10.00
SJRNS1 Noah Syndergaard 3.00 8.00
SJRNS2 Noah Syndergaard 3.00 8.00
SJRNS3 Noah Syndergaard 3.00 8.00
SJRPG1 Paul Goldschmidt 4.00 10.00
SJRPG2 Paul Goldschmidt 4.00 10.00
SJRPG3 Paul Goldschmidt 4.00 10.00
SJRPM1 Pedro Martinez 3.00 8.00
SJRRA1 Roberto Alomar 8.00 20.00
SJRRB1 Ryan Braun 3.00 8.00
SJRRB2 Ryan Braun 3.00 8.00
SJRRB3 Ryan Braun 3.00 8.00
SJRRC1 Roger Clemens 5.00 12.00
SJRRD1 Rafael Devers 8.00 20.00
SJRRH1 Rhys Hoskins 5.00 12.00
SJRRH2 Rhys Hoskins 5.00 12.00
SJRRO1 Rougned Odor 3.00 8.00
SJRRZ1 Ryan Zimmerman 3.00 8.00
SJRRZ2 Ryan Zimmerman 3.00 8.00
SJRSM1 Starling Marte 3.00 8.00
SJRSM2 Starling Marte 3.00 8.00
SJRSM3 Starling Marte 3.00 8.00
SJRSP1 Salvador Perez 3.00 8.00
SJRSP2 Salvador Perez 3.00 8.00
SJRSS1 Stephen Strasburg 4.00 10.00
SJRSS2 Stephen Strasburg 4.00 10.00
SJRSS3 Stephen Strasburg 4.00 10.00
SJRSS4 Stephen Strasburg 4.00 10.00
SJRTM1 Trey Mancini 3.00 8.00
SJRTM2 Trey Mancini 3.00 8.00
SJRTM3 Trey Mancini 3.00 8.00
SJRTS1 Trevor Story 4.00 10.00
SJRTS2 Trevor Story 4.00 10.00
SJRTS3 Trevor Story 4.00 10.00
SJRTTU1 Troy Tulowitzki 4.00 10.00
SJRVM1

Victor Martinez

3

2018 Topps Triple Threads Unity Single Jumbo Relics

SJRVM2 Victor Martinez 3.00 8.00
SJRWB1 Wade Boggs 10.00 25.00
SJRWC1 Willson Contreras 4.00 10.00
SJRWC2 Willson Contreras 4.00 10.00
SJRWC3 Willson Contreras 4.00 10.00
SJRWM1 Wil Myers 3.00 8.00
SJRWM2 Wil Myers 3.00 8.00
SJRWM3 Wil Myers 3.00 8.00
SJRXB1 Xander Bogaerts 4.00 10.00
SJRXB2 Xander Bogaerts 4.00 10.00
SJRXB3 Xander Bogaerts 4.00 10.00
SJRYC1 Yoenis Cespedes 4.00 10.00
SJRYC2 Yoenis Cespedes 4.00 10.00
SJRYC3 Yoenis Cespedes 4.00 10.00
SJRYC4 Yoenis Cespedes 4.00 10.00
SJRYG1 Yuli Gurriel 3.00 8.00
SJRYG2 Yuli Gurriel 3.00 8.00
SJRYM1 Yadier Molina 6.00 15.00
SJRYM2 Yadier Molina 6.00 15.00
SJRYM3 Yadier Molina 6.00 15.00

2019 Topps Triple Threads

JSY AU RC ODDS 1:XX MINI BOX
JSY AU RC PRINT RUN 99 SER.#'d SETS
JSY AU ODDS 1:XX MINI BOX
JSY AU PRINT RUN 99 SER.#'d SETS
EXCHANGE DEADLINE 8/31/2020
1-100 PLATE ODDS 1:XXX MINI BOX
JSY AU PLATE ODDS 1:XXX MINI BOX
PLATE PRINT RUN 1 SET PER COLOR
BLACK-CYAN-MAGENTA-YELLOW ISSUED
NO PLATE PRICING DUE TO SCARCITY
1 Noah Syndergaard .50 1.25
2 Bryce Harper 1.00 2.50
3 Todd Helton .50 1.25
4 Clayton Kershaw 1.00 2.50
5 Randy Johnson .60 1.50
6 Alex Gordon .50 1.25
7 Trevor Story .60 1.50
8 Jose Berrios .50 1.25
9 Jose Abreu .60 1.50
10 Jose Altuve .50 1.25
11 Roy Halladay .50 1.25
12 Roberto Alomar .50 1.25
13 Christian Yelich .75 2.00
14 Khris Davis .60 1.50
15 Andrew Benintendi .60 1.50
16 George Springer .50 1.25
17 Cody Bellinger 1.25 3.00
18 Tom Seaver .50 1.25
19 Blake Snell .50 1.25
20 Tony Gwynn .60 1.50
21 Gerrit Cole .60 1.50
22 Cal Ripken Jr. 2.00 5.00
23 Nolan Ryan 2.00 5.00
24 Francisco Lindor .60 1.50
25 George Brett 1.25 3.00
26 Kris Bryant .75 2.00
27 Trevor Bauer .75 2.00
28 Stephen Strasburg .60 1.50
29 Ken Griffey Jr. 1.25 3.00
30 Robin Yount .60 1.50
31 Derek Jeter 1.50 4.00
32 Don Mattingly 1.25 3.00
33 Ronald Acuna Jr. 3.00 8.00
34 Max Scherzer .60 1.50
35 Manny Machado .60 1.50
36 Willie Stargell .50 1.25
37 Ryne Sandberg 1.25 3.00
38 Josh Hader .50 1.25
39 Frank Thomas .60 1.50
40 Jim Thome .50 1.25
41 Ichiro Suzuki .75 2.00
42 Chipper Jones .60 1.50
43 Al Kaline .60 1.50
44 Trey Mancini .50 1.25
45 Aaron Nola .50 1.25
46 Ted Williams 1.25 3.00
47 Mark McGwire 1.00 2.50
48 Sandy Koufax 1.25 3.00
49 Albert Pujols .75 2.00
50 Jackie Robinson .60 1.50
51 Rhys Hoskins .75 2.00
52 Roberto Clemente 1.50 4.00
53 Yadier Molina .75 2.00
54 Zack Greinke .60 1.50
55 Andres Galarraga .50 1.25
56 Alex Bregman .60 1.50
57 Babe Ruth 1.50 4.00
58 Javier Baez .75 2.00
59 Mariano Rivera .75 2.00
60 Josh Bell .50 1.25
61 Jim Palmer .50 1.25
62 Aaron Judge 1.50 4.00
63 Barry Larkin .50 1.25
64 Buster Posey .75 2.00
65 Jose Ramirez .50 1.25
66 Justin Verlander .60 1.50
67 Yoan Moncada .60 1.50
68 Eddie Rosario .50 1.25
69 Wade Boggs .50 1.25
70 Anthony Rizzo .75 2.00
71 Roger Clemens .75 2.00
72 Rafael Devers .75 2.00
73 Mike Trout 3.00 8.00
74 John Smoltz .60 1.50
75 Hunter Dozier .40 1.00
76 Hank Aaron 1.25 3.00
77 Mike Piazza .60 1.50
78 Byron Buxton .60 1.50
79 Joey Votto .60 1.50
80 Nolan Arenado 1.00 2.50
81 Paul Goldschmidt .60 1.50
82 Willie McCovey .50 1.25
83 Ozzie Smith .75 2.00
84 J.D. Martinez .60 1.50
85 Gleyber Torres 1.25 3.00
86 Mookie Betts 1.25 3.00
87 Shohei Ohtani 1.00 2.50
88 Reggie Jackson .50 1.25
89 Vladimir Guerrero .50 1.25
90 Johnny Bench .60 1.50
91 Miguel Cabrera .60 1.50
92 Pedro Martinez .50 1.25
93 Carlos Correa .60 1.50
94 Ivan Rodriguez .50 1.25
95 Willie Mays 1.25 3.00
96 Juan Soto 2.00 5.00
97 David Ortiz .60 1.50
98 Michael Conforto .50 1.25
99 Jacob deGrom 1.25 3.00
100 Rickey Henderson .60 1.50
RFPARAG Aramis Garcia JSY AU RC 3.00 8.00
RFPARBK Brad Keller JSY AU 3.00 8.00
RFPARBN Brandon Nimmo JSY AU 4.00 10.00
RFPARCA Chance Adams JSY AU RC 3.00 8.00
RFPARCB Corbin Burnes JSY AU RC 10.00 25.00
RFPARCMU Cedric Mullins JSY AU RC 10.00 25.00
RFPARCS Chris Shaw JSY AU RC 3.00 8.00
RFPARCST C.Stewart JSY AU RC 6.00 15.00
RFPARDB David Bote JSY AU 8.00 20.00
RFPARDC Dylan Cozens JSY AU 3.00 8.00
RFPARDH Dakota Hudson JSY AU RC 4.00 10.00
RFPARDJ Danny Jansen JSY AU RC 3.00 8.00
RFPARDP Daniel Ponce de Leon JSY AU RC 5.00 12.00
RFPARDR Dereck Rodriguez JSY AU 3.00 8.00
RFPARFT F.Tatis Jr. JSY AU RC 150.00 400.00
RFPARGT G.Torres JSY AU EXCH 40.00 100.00
RFPARGU Gio Urshela JSY AU EXCH 20.00 50.00
RFPARIK Isiah Kiner-Falefa JSY AU 4.00 10.00
RFPARJA Jesus Aguilar JSY AU 4.00 10.00
RFPARJC Johan Camargo JSY AU 6.00 15.00
RFPARJSO Juan Soto JSY AU 40.00 100.00
RFPARKA Kolby Allard JSY AU RC 5.00 12.00
RFPARKH Hiura JSY AU RC EXCH 40.00 100.00
RFPARKK Kevin Kramer JSY AU RC 4.00 10.00
RFPARKW Kyle Wright JSY AU RC 5.00 12.00
RFPARLU Luis Urias JSY AU RC 10.00 25.00
RFPARMA Miguel Andujar JSY AU 15.00 40.00
RFPARMK M.Kopech JSY AU RC 12.00 30.00
RFPARMM Miles Mikolas JSY AU 5.00 12.00
RFPARNC Nick Ciuffo JSY AU RC 3.00 8.00
RFPAROA Ozzie Albies JSY AU 10.00 25.00
RFPARPA Pete Alonso JSY AU RC 60.00 150.00
RFPARRB Ryan Borucki JSY AU RC 3.00 8.00
RFPARRD Rafael Devers JSY AU 15.00 40.00
RFPARRO Ryan O'Hearn JSY AU 3.00 8.00
RFPARRT Rowdy Tellez JSY AU RC 6.00 15.00
RFPARRY Ryan Yarbrough JSY AU 3.00 8.00
RFPARSK Scott Kingery JSY AU 10.00 25.00
RFPARTO Tyler O'Neill JSY AU 4.00 10.00
RFPARTT Touki Toussaint JSY AU RC 4.00 10.00
RFPARVG Guerrero Jr. JSY AU RC 60.00 150.00
RFPARWA Willy Adames JSY AU 3.00 8.00
RFPARWAS W.Astudillo JSY AU RC 6.00 15.00
RFPARYK Yusei Kikuchi JSY AU RC 8.00 20.00

2019 Topps Triple Threads Amber

*AMBER VET: .75X TO 2X BASIC
STATED ODDS 1:XX MINI BOX
STATED PRINT RUN 199 SER.#'d SETS

2019 Topps Triple Threads Amethyst

*AMETHYST VET: .6X TO 1.5X BASIC
*AMETHYST JSY AU: .4X TO 1X BASIC RC
STATED ODDS 1:XX MINI BOX
JSY AU ODDS 1:XX MINI BOX
1-100 PRINT RUN 299 SER.#'d SETS
JSY AU PRINT RUN 75 SER.#'d SETS
EXCHANGE DEADLINE 8/31/2021

2019 Topps Triple Threads Citrine

*CITRINE VET: 1X TO 2.5X BASIC
STATED ODDS 1:XX MINI BOX
STATED PRINT RUN 75 SER.#'d SETS

2019 Topps Triple Threads Emerald

*EMERALD VET: .6X TO 1.5X BASIC
*EMERALD JSY AU: .4X TO 1X BASIC RC
1-100 ODDS 1:XX MINI BOX
JSY AU ODDS 1:XX MINI BOX
1-100 PRINT RUN 259 SER.#'d SETS
JSY AU PRINT RUN 50 SER.#'d SETS
EXCHANGE DEADLINE 8/31/2021

2019 Topps Triple Threads Gold

*GOLD VET: 1X TO 2.5X BASIC
STATED ODDS 1:XX MINI BOX
STATED PRINT RUN 99 SER.#'d SETS

2019 Topps Triple Threads Onyx

*ONYX VET: 1.5X TO 4X BASIC
*ONYX JSY AU: .5X TO 1.2X BASIC RC
1-100 ODDS 1:XX MINI BOX
JSY AU ODDS 1:XX MINI BOX
1-100 PRINT RUN 50 SER.#'d SETS
JSY AU PRINT RUN 35 SER.#'d SETS
EXCHANGE DEADLINE 8/31/2021
RFPARSO Shohei Ohtani JSY AU 100.00 250.00

2019 Topps Triple Threads Sapphire

*SAPPHIRE VET: 2.5X TO 6X BASIC
STATED ODDS 1:XX MINI BOX
STATED PRINT RUN 25 SER.#'d SETS
29 Ken Griffey Jr. 20.00 50.00
31 Derek Jeter 25.00 60.00

2019 Topps Triple Threads Autograph Jumbo Relics

STATED ODDS 1:XX HOBBY
STATED PRINT RUN 99 SER.#'d SETS
EXCHANGE DEADLINE 8/31/2021
AUJRABE Andrew Benintendi 10.00 25.00
AUJRAG Andres Galarraga 5.00 12.00
AUJRAM Austin Meadows 6.00 15.00
AUJRAN Aaron Nola 8.00 20.00
AUJRAR Amed Rosario 5.00 12.00
AUJRBB Byron Buxton 8.00 20.00
AUJRBN Brandon Nimmo 5.00 12.00
AUJRBT Blake Treinen 4.00 10.00
AUJRCD Corey Dickerson 4.00 10.00
AUJRCF Clint Frazier 8.00 20.00
AUJRCK Corey Kluber 8.00 20.00
AUJRCM Charlie Morton 6.00 15.00
AUJRCSA Chris Sale 8.00 20.00
AUJRCV Christian Vazquez 5.00 12.00
AUJRCY Christian Yelich 30.00 80.00
AUJRDB David Bote 6.00 15.00
AUJRDC Dylan Cozens 4.00 10.00
AUJRDE Dennis Eckersley 12.00 30.00
AUJRDPR David Price 8.00 20.00
AUJRDR Dereck Rodriguez 4.00 10.00
AUJRET Eric Thames 4.00 10.00
AUJRFL Francisco Lindor 12.00 30.00
AUJRFV Felipe Vazquez 4.00 10.00
AUJRIH Ian Happ 20.00 50.00
AUJRJA Jesus Aguilar 5.00 12.00
AUJRJB Jose Berrios 5.00 12.00
AUJRJC Jose Canseco 6.00 15.00
AUJRJD Johnny Damon 10.00 25.00
AUJRJDM J.D. Martinez 10.00 25.00
AUJRJH Josh Hader 5.00 12.00
AUJRJHI Jordan Hicks 5.00 12.00
AUJRJJ Jeremy Jeffress 4.00 10.00
AUJRJM Jose Martinez 4.00 10.00
AUJRJR Jose Ramirez 5.00 12.00
AUJRJS Jean Segura 6.00 15.00
AUJRJT Jim Thome 20.00 50.00
AUJRKF Kyle Freeland 5.00 12.00
AUJRKS Kyle Schwarber 6.00 15.00
AUJRKW Kerry Wood 8.00 20.00
AUJRLG Luis Gonzalez 4.00 10.00
AUJRLGU Lourdes Gurriel Jr. 5.00 12.00
AUJRLM Lance McCullers Jr. 4.00 10.00
AUJRLS Luis Severino 8.00 20.00
AUJRLV Luke Voit 20.00 50.00
AUJRMA Miguel Andujar 6.00 15.00
AUJRMC Matt Chapman 6.00 15.00
AUJRMCL Mike Clevinger 5.00 12.00
AUJRMF Mike Foltynewicz 6.00 15.00
AUJRMH Mitch Haniger 5.00 12.00
AUJRMKE Max Kepler 5.00 12.00
AUJRMMI Miles Mikolas 6.00 15.00
AUJRMO Matt Olson 6.00 15.00
AUJRNW Nick Williams 4.00 10.00
AUJROA Ozzie Albies 10.00 25.00
AUJRPC Patrick Corbin 6.00 15.00
AUJRPD Paul DeJong 6.00 15.00
AUJRRA Ronald Acuna Jr. 75.00 200.00
AUJRRD Rafael Devers 15.00 40.00
AUJRRH Rhys Hoskins 10.00 25.00
AUJRRI Raisel Iglesias 4.00 10.00
AUJRSD Sean Doolittle 6.00 15.00
AUJRSG Scooter Gennett 6.00 15.00
AUJRSK Scott Kingery 8.00 20.00
AUJRSMA Steven Matz 4.00 10.00
AUJRTA Tim Anderson 6.00 15.00
AUJRTB Trevor Bauer 8.00 20.00
AUJRTO Tyler O'Neill 5.00 12.00
AUJRTP Tommy Pham 4.00 10.00
AUJRTS Travis Shaw 4.00 10.00
AUJRWA Willy Adames 4.00 10.00
AUJRWM Whit Merrifield 6.00 15.00
AUJRXB Xander Bogaerts 15.00 40.00
AUJRYG Yuli Gurriel 8.00 20.00
AUJRZW Zack Wheeler 5.00 12.00

2019 Topps Triple Threads Autograph Jumbo Relics Amethyst

*AMETHYST: .4X TO 1X BASIC
STATED ODDS 1:XX HOBBY
STATED PRINT RUN 75 SER.#'d SETS
EXCHANGE DEADLINE 8/31/2021
AUJRCS CC Sabathia 20.00 50.00
AUJRJL Jake Lamb 5.00 12.00

2019 Topps Triple Threads Autograph Jumbo Relics Emerald

*EMERALD: .5X TO 1.2X BASIC
STATED ODDS 1:XX HOBBY
STATED PRINT RUN 50 SER.#'d SETS
EXCHANGE DEADLINE 8/31/2021
AUJRCS CC Sabathia 25.00 60.00
AUJRFB Franklin Barreto 5.00 12.00
AUJRJL Jake Lamb 6.00 15.00

2019 Topps Triple Threads Autograph Jumbo Relics Gold

*GOLD: .6X TO 1.5X BASIC
STATED ODDS 1:XX HOBBY
STATED PRINT RUN 25 SER.#'d SETS
EXCHANGE DEADLINE 8/31/2021
AUJRCS CC Sabathia 30.00 80.00
AUJRFB Franklin Barreto 6.00 15.00
AUJRJL Jake Lamb 8.00 20.00

2019 Topps Triple Threads Autograph Relic Combos

STATED ODDS 1:XX HOBBY
STATED PRINT RUN 36 SER.#'d SETS
EXCHANGE DEADLINE 8/31/2021
PRINTING PLATE ODDS 1:XXX HOBBY
PLATE PRINT RUN 1 SET PER COLOR
BLACK-CYAN-MAGENTA-YELLOW ISSUED
NO PLATE PRICING DUE TO SCARCITY
*AMETHYST/27: .4X TO 1X BASIC
ARCBRB Rosario/Buxton/Berrios 20.00 50.00
ARCBRS Bryant/Rizzo/Schwrbr 60.00 150.00
ARCCHS Cbrra/Stwrt/Harrison 30.00 80.00
ARCDSW Syndrgrd/deGrom/Whlr 60.00 150.00
ARCFAA Albies/Freeman/Acuna 100.00 250.00
ARCHKS Haniger/Seager/Kikuchi 15.00 40.00
ARCHTG Hiura/Tatis/Guerrero 150.00 400.00
ARCLKR Lindor/Ramirez/Kluber 30.00 80.00
ARCMGC Mlna/Crpntr/Gldschmdt 60.00 150.00
ARCMTU Urias/Tatis/Machado 100.00 250.00
ARCPDB Dvrs/Pdra/Bgrts 40.00 100.00
ARCPMC Molina/Contreras/Perez 40.00 100.00
ARCPRB IRod/Bltre/Plmro 30.00 80.00
ARCRNA Nimmo/Rosario/Alonso 60.00 150.00
ARCSAP Adames/Snell/Mdws 25.00 60.00
ARCSJJ Jones/Jones/Smoltz 60.00 150.00
ARCSMP Price/Sale/Martinez 25.00 60.00
ARCSSR Robles/Soto/Scherzer 75.00 200.00
ARCSST Svrno/Sbtha/Sanchez 40.00 100.00
ARCTOP Pujols/Ohtani/Trout
ARCYHA Yelich/Aguilar/Hader 30.00 80.00

2019 Topps Triple Threads Autograph Relic Combos Emerald

*EMERALD: .4X TO 1X BASIC
STATED ODDS 1:XXX HOBBY
STATED PRINT RUN 18 SER.#'d SETS
EXCHANGE DEADLINE 8/31/2021
ARCHHN Hskns/Nola/Hrpr EXCH 150.00 400.00
ARCIOK Kikuchi/Ichiro/Ohtani 200.00 500.00

2019 Topps Triple Threads Autograph Relics

STATED ODDS 1:XX HOBBY
STATED PRINT RUN 18 SER.#'d SETS
EXCHANGE DEADLINE 8/31/2021
*GOLD/9: .5X TO 1.2X BASIC
SOME GOLD NOT PRICED DUE TO SCARCITY
ALL VERSIONS EQUALLY PRICED
TTARAB1 Adrian Beltre 25.00 60.00
TTARAB2 Adrian Beltre 25.00 60.00
TTARABE1 Andrew Benintendi 20.00 50.00
TTARABE2 Andrew Benintendi 20.00 50.00
TTARABE3 Andrew Benintendi 20.00 50.00
TTARABE4 Andrew Benintendi 20.00 50.00
TTARAJ1 Andruw Jones 12.00 30.00
TTARAJ2 Andruw Jones 12.00 30.00
TTARAJ3 Andruw Jones 12.00 30.00
TTARAJ4 Andruw Jones 12.00 30.00
TTARAJ5 Andruw Jones 12.00 30.00
TTARAJU1 Aaron Judge 75.00 200.00
TTARALR1 Alex Rodriguez 60.00 150.00
TTARAM1 Austin Meadows 10.00 25.00
TTARAM2 Austin Meadows 10.00 25.00
TTARAM3 Austin Meadows 10.00 25.00
TTARAM4 Austin Meadows 10.00 25.00
TTARAM5 Austin Meadows 10.00 25.00
TTARAP1 Andy Pettitte 25.00 60.00
TTARAP2 Andy Pettitte 25.00 60.00
TTARAR1 Anthony Rizzo 15.00 40.00
TTARAR2 Anthony Rizzo 15.00 40.00
TTARARO1 Amed Rosario 8.00 20.00
TTARARO2 Amed Rosario 8.00 20.00
TTARARO3 Amed Rosario 8.00 20.00
TTARARO4 Amed Rosario 8.00 20.00
TTARARO5 Amed Rosario 8.00 20.00
TTARBB1 Bert Blyleven 8.00 20.00
TTARBB2 Bert Blyleven 8.00 20.00
TTARBBU1 Byron Buxton 10.00 25.00
TTARBBU2 Byron Buxton 10.00 25.00
TTARBBU3 Byron Buxton 10.00 25.00
TTARBBU4 Byron Buxton 10.00 25.00
TTARBBU5 Byron Buxton 10.00 25.00
TTARBP1 Buster Posey 40.00 100.00
TTARBS1 Blake Snell 8.00 20.00
TTARBS2 Blake Snell 8.00 20.00
TTARBS3 Blake Snell 8.00 20.00
TTARBS4 Blake Snell 8.00 20.00
TTARBS5 Blake Snell 8.00 20.00
TTARCJ1 Chipper Jones 50.00 120.00
TTARCJ2 Chipper Jones 50.00 120.00
TTARCK1 Corey Kluber 10.00 25.00
TTARCK2 Corey Kluber 10.00 25.00
TTARCKE1 Clayton Kershaw 40.00 100.00
TTARCKE2 Clayton Kershaw 40.00 100.00
TTARCS1 Chris Sale 12.00 30.00
TTARCS2 Chris Sale 12.00 30.00
TTARCS3 Chris Sale 12.00 30.00
TTARCS4 Chris Sale 12.00 30.00
TTARCS5 Chris Sale 12.00 30.00
TTARCSA1 CC Sabathia 30.00 80.00
TTARCSA2 CC Sabathia 30.00 80.00
TTARCSA3 CC Sabathia 30.00 80.00
TTARCSA4 CC Sabathia 30.00 80.00
TTARCSA5 CC Sabathia 30.00 80.00
TTARDC1 David Cone 15.00 40.00
TTARDC2 David Cone 15.00 40.00
TTARDC3 David Cone 15.00 40.00
TTARDC4 David Cone 15.00 40.00
TTARDC5 David Cone 15.00 40.00
TTARDG1 Didi Gregorius 10.00 25.00
TTARDG2 Didi Gregorius 10.00 25.00
TTARDG3 Didi Gregorius 10.00 25.00
TTARDO1 David Ortiz 30.00 80.00
TTARDO2 David Ortiz 30.00 80.00
TTARDP1 Dustin Pedroia 20.00 50.00
TTARDP2 Dustin Pedroia 20.00 50.00
TTARDP3 Dustin Pedroia 20.00 50.00
TTARDPR1 David Price 8.00 20.00
TTARDPR2 David Price 8.00 20.00
TTARDPR3 David Price 8.00 20.00
TTARDS1 Dansby Swanson 15.00 40.00
TTARDS2 Dansby Swanson 15.00 40.00
TTARDS3 Dansby Swanson 15.00 40.00
TTAREM1 Edgar Martinez 20.00 50.00
TTAREM2 Edgar Martinez 20.00 50.00
TTAREM3 Edgar Martinez 20.00 50.00
TTAREM4 Edgar Martinez 20.00 50.00
TTARER1 Eddie Rosario 10.00 25.00
TTARER2 Eddie Rosario 10.00 25.00
TTARER3 Eddie Rosario 10.00 25.00
TTARER4 Eddie Rosario 10.00 25.00
TTARER5 Eddie Rosario 10.00 25.00
TTARFF1 Freddie Freeman 20.00 50.00
TTARFL1 Francisco Lindor 25.00 60.00
TTARFL2 Francisco Lindor 25.00 60.00
TTARFL3 Francisco Lindor 25.00 60.00
TTARFL4 Francisco Lindor 25.00 60.00
TTARFL5 Francisco Lindor 25.00 60.00
TTARFV1 Felipe Vazquez 5.00 12.00
TTARFV2 Felipe Vazquez 5.00 12.00
TTARFV3 Felipe Vazquez 5.00 12.00
TTARFV4 Felipe Vazquez 5.00 12.00
TTARGC1 Gerrit Cole 25.00 60.00
TTARGC2 Gerrit Cole 25.00 60.00
TTARGC3 Gerrit Cole 25.00 60.00
TTARGC4 Gerrit Cole 25.00 60.00
TTARGC5 Gerrit Cole 25.00 60.00
TTARGS1 George Springer 20.00 50.00
TTARGS2 George Springer 20.00 50.00
TTARGS3 George Springer 20.00 50.00
TTARI Ichiro Suzuki 125.00 300.00
TTARIR1 Ivan Rodriguez 15.00 40.00
TTARIR2 Ivan Rodriguez 15.00 40.00
TTARIR3 Ivan Rodriguez 15.00 40.00
TTARJAL1 Jose Altuve 25.00 60.00
TTARJAL2 Jose Altuve 25.00 60.00
TTARJAL3 Jose Altuve 25.00 60.00
TTARJB1 Jose Berrios 12.00 30.00
TTARJB2 Jose Berrios 12.00 30.00
TTARJB3 Jose Berrios 12.00 30.00
TTARJB4 Jose Berrios 12.00 30.00
TTARJD1 Jacob deGrom 25.00 60.00
TTARJD2 Jacob deGrom 20.00 50.00
TTARJD3 Jacob deGrom 20.00 50.00
TTARJD4 Jacob deGrom 20.00 50.00
TTARJD5 Jacob deGrom 20.00 50.00
TTARJDA1 Johnny Damon 10.00 25.00
TTARJDA2 Johnny Damon 10.00 25.00
TTARJDA3 Johnny Damon 10.00 25.00
TTARJDA4 Johnny Damon 10.00 25.00
TTARJH1 Josh Hader 10.00 25.00
TTARJH2 Josh Hader 10.00 25.00
TTARJH3 Josh Hader 10.00 25.00
TTARJH4 Josh Hader 10.00 25.00
TTARJH5 Josh Hader 10.00 25.00
TTARJM1 J.D. Martinez 10.00 25.00
TTARJM2 J.D. Martinez 10.00 25.00
TTARJM3 J.D. Martinez 10.00 25.00
TTARJM4 J.D. Martinez 10.00 25.00
TTARJM5 J.D. Martinez 10.00 25.00
TTARJP1 Joc Pederson 8.00 20.00
TTARJP2 Joc Pederson 8.00 20.00
TTARJP3 Joc Pederson 8.00 20.00
TTARJR1 Jose Ramirez 6.00 15.00
TTARJR2 Jose Ramirez 6.00 15.00
TTARJR3 Jose Ramirez 6.00 15.00
TTARJR4 Jose Ramirez 6.00 15.00
TTARJSM1 John Smoltz 20.00 50.00
TTARJSO1 Juan Soto 50.00 120.00
TTARJSO2 Juan Soto 50.00 120.00
TTARJSO3 Juan Soto 50.00 120.00
TTARJV1 Joey Votto 30.00 80.00
TTARJV2 Joey Votto 30.00 80.00
TTARKB1 Kris Bryant 40.00 100.00
TTARKG1 Ken Griffey Jr. 100.00 250.00
TTARKS1 Kyle Schwarber 10.00 25.00
TTARKS2 Kyle Schwarber 10.00 25.00
TTARKS3 Kyle Schwarber 10.00 25.00
TTARKS4 Kyle Schwarber 10.00 25.00
TTARKS5 Kyle Schwarber 10.00 25.00
TTARKSE1 Kyle Seager 5.00 12.00
TTARKSE2 Kyle Seager 5.00 12.00
TTARKSE3 Kyle Seager 5.00 12.00
TTARKSE4 Kyle Seager 5.00 12.00
TTARKSE5 Kyle Seager 5.00 12.00
TTARLM1 Lance McCullers Jr. 8.00 20.00
TTARLM2 Lance McCullers Jr. 8.00 20.00
TTARLM3 Lance McCullers Jr. 8.00 20.00
TTARLM4 Lance McCullers Jr. 8.00 20.00
TTARLS1 Luis Severino 10.00 25.00
TTARLS2 Luis Severino 10.00 25.00
TTARLS3 Luis Severino 10.00 25.00
TTARLS4 Luis Severino 10.00 25.00
TTARMA1 Miguel Andujar 12.00 30.00
TTARMA2 Miguel Andujar 12.00 30.00
TTARMA3 Miguel Andujar 12.00 30.00
TTARMC1 Miguel Cabrera 25.00 60.00
TTARMC2 Miguel Cabrera 25.00 60.00
TTARMCA1 Matt Carpenter 10.00 25.00
TTARMCA2 Matt Carpenter 10.00 25.00
TTARMCA3 Matt Carpenter 10.00 2.00
TTARMM1 Manny Machado 20.00 50.00
TTARMM2 Manny Machado 20.00 50.00
TTARMM3 Manny Machado 20.00 50.00
TTARMMU1 Max Muncy 6.00 15.00
TTARMMU2 Max Muncy 6.00 15.00
TTARMMU3 Max Muncy 6.00 15.00
TTARMO1 Matt Olson 10.00 25.00
TTARMO2 Matt Olson 10.00 25.00
TTARMO3 Matt Olson 10.00 25.00
TTARMO4 Matt Olson 10.00 25.00
TTARMO5 Matt Olson 10.00 25.00
TTARMS1 Max Scherzer 30.00 80.00
TTARMS2 Max Scherzer 30.00 80.00
TTARMS3 Max Scherzer 30.00 80.00
TTARMS4 Max Scherzer 30.00 80.00
TTARMT1 Mike Trout 200.00 500.00
TTARMT2 Mike Trout 200.00 500.00
TTARNA1 Nolan Arenado 50.00 120.00
TTARNA2 Nolan Arenado 50.00 120.00
TTARNA3 Nolan Arenado 50.00 120.00
TTARNS1 Noah Syndergaard 12.00 30.00
TTARNS2 Noah Syndergaard 12.00 30.00
TTARNS3 Noah Syndergaard 12.00 30.00
TTARNS4 Noah Syndergaard 12.00 30.00
TTARNS5 Noah Syndergaard 12.00 30.00
TTAROA1 Ozzie Albies 15.00 40.00
TTAROA2 Ozzie Albies 15.00 40.00
TTAROA3 Ozzie Albies 15.00 40.00
TTAROA4 Ozzie Albies 15.00 40.00
TTAROA5 Ozzie Albies 15.00 40.00
TTARPG1 Paul Goldschmidt 20.00 50.00
TTARPG2 Paul Goldschmidt 20.00 50.00
TTARPG3 Paul Goldschmidt 20.00 50.00
TTARPG4 Paul Goldschmidt 20.00 50.00
TTARRA1 Ronald Acuna Jr. 60.00 150.00
TTARRA2 Ronald Acuna Jr. 60.00 150.00
TTARRA3 Ronald Acuna Jr. 60.00 150.00
TTARRA4 Ronald Acuna Jr. 60.00 150.00
TTARRD1 Rafael Devers 20.00 50.00
TTARRD2 Rafael Devers 20.00 50.00
TTARRD3 Rafael Devers 20.00 50.00
TTARRD4 Rafael Devers 20.00 50.00
TTARRD5 Rafael Devers 20.00 50.00
TTARRH1 Rhys Hoskins 25.00 60.00
TTARRH2 Rhys Hoskins 25.00 60.00
TTARRH3 Rhys Hoskins 25.00 60.00
TTARRH4 Rhys Hoskins 25.00 60.00
TTARRHE Rickey Henderson 60.00 150.00
TTARSC1 Shin-Soo Choo 30.00 80.00
TTARSC2 Shin-Soo Choo 30.00 80.00
TTARSC3 Shin-Soo Choo 30.00 80.00
TTARSC4 Shin-Soo Choo 30.00 80.00
TTARSG1 Scooter Gennett 10.00 25.00
TTARSG2 Scooter Gennett 10.00 25.00
TTARSG3 Scooter Gennett 10.00 25.00
TTARSG4 Scooter Gennett 10.00 25.00
TTARSG5 Scooter Gennett 10.00 25.00
TTARSO1 Shohei Ohtani 75.00 200.00
TTARSO2 Shohei Ohtani 75.00 200.00
TTARSP1 Salvador Perez 12.00 30.00
TTARSP2 Salvador Perez 12.00 30.00
TTARSP3 Salvador Perez 12.00 30.00
TTARSP4 Salvador Perez 12.00 30.00
TTARSPI1 Stephen Piscotty 5.00 12.00
TTARSPI2 Stephen Piscotty 5.00 12.00
TTARSPI3 Stephen Piscotty 5.00 12.00
TTARSPI4 Stephen Piscotty 5.00 12.00
TTARSS1 Sammy Sosa 75.00 200.00
TTARTA1 Tim Anderson 8.00 20.00
TTARTA2 Tim Anderson 8.00 20.00
TTARTA3 Tim Anderson 8.00 20.00
TTARTA4 Tim Anderson 8.00 20.00
TTARTA5 Tim Anderson 8.00 20.00
TTARTB1 Trevor Bauer 10.00 25.00
TTARTB2 Trevor Bauer 10.00 25.00
TTARTB3 Trevor Bauer 10.00 25.00
TTARTB4 Trevor Bauer 10.00 25.00
TTARTG1 Tom Glavine 15.00 40.00
TTARTG2 Tom Glavine 15.00 40.00
TTARTG3 Tom Glavine 15.00 40.00
TTARTH1 Todd Helton 12.00 30.00
TTARTH2 Todd Helton 12.00 30.00
TTARTH3 Todd Helton 12.00 30.00
TTARTHU1 Torii Hunter 8.00 20.00
TTARTHU2 Torii Hunter 8.00 20.00
TTARTHU3 Torii Hunter 8.00 20.00
TTARTHU4 Torii Hunter 8.00 20.00
TTARTHU5 Torii Hunter 8.00 20.00
TTARTM1 Trey Mancini 6.00 15.00
TTARTM2 Trey Mancini 6.00 15.00
TTARTM3 Trey Mancini 6.00 15.00
TTARTM4 Trey Mancini 6.00 15.00
TTARTM5 Trey Mancini 6.00 15.00
TTARVR1 Victor Robles 10.00 25.00
TTARVR2 Victor Robles 10.00 25.00
TTARVR3 Victor Robles 10.00 25.00
TTARVR4 Victor Robles 10.00 25.00
TTARVR5 Victor Robles 10.00 25.00
TTARWB1 Walker Buehler 20.00 50.00
TTARWB2 Walker Buehler 20.00 50.00
TTARWB3 Walker Buehler 20.00 50.00
TTARWC1 Willson Contreras 10.00 25.00
TTARWC2 Willson Contreras 10.00 25.00
TTARWC3 Willson Contreras 10.00 25.00
TTARWC4 Willson Contreras 10.00 25.00
TTARWC5 Willson Contreras 10.00 25.00
TTARWM1 Whit Merrifield 10.00 25.00
TTARWM2 Whit Merrifield 10.00 25.00
TTARWM3 Whit Merrifield 10.00 25.00
TTARWM4 Whit Merrifield 10.00 25.00
TTARXB1 Xander Bogaerts 20.00 50.00
TTARXB2 Xander Bogaerts 20.00 50.00
TTARXB3 Xander Bogaerts 20.00 50.00
TTARXB4 Xander Bogaerts 20.00 50.00
TTARXB5 Xander Bogaerts 20.00 50.00

2019 Topps Triple Threads Legend Relics

STATED ODDS 1:XX HOBBY
STATED PRINT RUN 36 SER.#'d SETS
*SILVER/27: .4X TO 1X BASIC
*EMERALD/18: .4X TO 1X BASIC
RLCAD Andre Dawson 8.00 20.00
RLCBG Bob Gibson 15.00 40.00
RLCBL Barry Larkin 6.00 15.00
RLCCF Carlton Fisk 8.00 20.00
RLCCJ Chipper Jones 12.00 30.00
RLCCR Cal Ripken Jr. 12.00 30.00
RLCDJ Derek Jeter 25.00 60.00
RLCDO David Ortiz 8.00 20.00
RLCHA Hank Aaron
RLCI Ichiro Suzuki 15.00 40.00
RLCKG Ken Griffey Jr. 15.00 40.00
RLCMM Mark McGwire 12.00 30.00
RLCPM Pedro Martinez 6.00 15.00
RLCRA Roberto Alomar 10.00 25.00
RLCRC Rod Carew 6.00 15.00
RLCRCL Roberto Clemente
RLCRH Roy Halladay 15.00 40.00
RLCRJ Reggie Jackson 20.00 50.00
RLCRJO Randy Johnson 10.00 25.00
RLCSC Steve Carlton 8.00 20.00
RLCTG Tony Gwynn 12.00 30.00
RLCVG Vladimir Guerrero 6.00 15.00
RLCWB Wade Boggs 8.00 20.00

2019 Topps Triple Threads Pieces of the Game Autograph Relics

STATED ODDS 1:XX MINI BOX
STATED PRINT RUN 18 SER.#'d SETS
EXCHANGE DEADLINE 8/31/2021
PTGARAJ Aaron Judge 75.00 200.00
PTGARAR Anthony Rizzo 40.00 100.00
PTGARJA Jorge Alfaro 8.00 20.00
PTGARJD Jacob deGrom 40.00 100.00
PTGARJM J.D. Martinez 25.00 60.00
PTGARKB Kris Bryant 40.00 100.00
PTGAROA Ozzie Albies 20.00 50.00
PTGARPA Pete Alonso 60.00 150.00
PTGARRD Rafael Devers 20.00 50.00

2019 Topps Triple Threads Pieces of the Game Relics

STATED ODDS 1:XX MINI BOX
STATED PRINT RUN 18 SER.#'d SETS
PTGRAJ Aaron Judge 20.00 50.00
PTGRAR Anthony Rizzo 12.00 30.00
PTGRFT Fernando Tatis Jr. 25.00 60.00
PTGRJA Jorge Alfaro 3.00 8.00
PTGRJD Jacob deGrom 10.00 25.00
PTGRJM J.D. Martinez 10.00 25.00
PTGRKB Kris Bryant 15.00 40.00
PTGROA Ozzie Albies 10.00 25.00
PTGRPA Pete Alonso 50.00 120.00
PTGRRD Rafael Devers 12.00 30.00

2019 Topps Triple Threads Relic Combos

STATED ODDS 1:XX HOBBY
STATED PRINT RUN 36 SER.#'d SETS
*AMETHYST/27: .4X TO 1X BASIC
*EMERALD/18: .5X TO 1.2X BASIC
RCCAAF Acuna/Freeman/Albies 15.00 40.00
RCCAHN Nola/Hoskins/Arrieta 10.00 25.00
RCCBAC Bregman/Altuve/Correa 5.00 12.00
RCCBDP Pedroia/Devers/Bogaerts 6.00 15.00
RCCBMB Bnntndi/Mrtnz/Betts 10.00 25.00
RCCBRM Maeda/Buehler/Ryu 6.00 15.00
RCCCCF Cbrra/Fldr/Cstllns 8.00 20.00
RCCCDM Carpenter/DeJong/Martinez 5.00 12.00
RCCCSV McCllrs/Cole/Vrlndr 5.00 12.00
RCCDAS deGrom/Syndrgrd/Alonso 25.00 60.00
RCCDLP Davis/Laureano/Pinder 6.00 15.00
RCCFGH Frazier/Gardner/Hicks 6.00 15.00
RCCFMO Molina/Ozuna/Flaherty 6.00 15.00
RCCGIR Rodriguez/Griffey/Ichiro 20.00 50.00
RCCGLV Griffey/Votto/Larkin 25.00 60.00
RCCGPM Glavine/Mrtnz/Piazza 8.00 20.00
RCCHAS Story/Arenado/Helton 8.00 20.00
RCCHDW Hader/Woodruff/Davies 5.00 12.00
RCCHKF Harper/Franco/Kingery 25.00 60.00
RCCHSB Beckham/Santana/Haniger 4.00 10.00
RCCJSS Sanchez/Stanton/Judge 12.00 30.00
RCCKMP Meadows/Pham/Kiermaier 5.00 12.00
RCCLCH Contreras/Lester/Hamels 4.00 10.00
RCCLRS Lindor/Sntna/Ramirez 8.00 20.00
RCCMAG Mazara/Andrus/Gallo 4.00 10.00
RCCMMR Myers/Reyes/Margot 4.00 10.00
RCCMPD Dozier/Perez/Merrifield 5.00 12.00
RCCMPO Pedroia/Martinez/Ortiz 12.00 30.00
RCCMTH Tatis/Machado/Hosmer 12.00 30.00
RCCOTP Pujols/Ohtani/Trout 25.00 60.00
RCCPBV Vazquez/Bell/Polanco 4.00 10.00
RCCPCL Posey/Longoria/Crawford 6.00 15.00
RCCPJR Rivera/Pettitte/Jeter 30.00 80.00
RCCRBB Baez/Bryant/Rizzo 25.00 60.00
RCCRHB Buxton/Hunter/Rosario 5.00 12.00
RCCRMA Ripken/Alomar/Mancini 10.00 25.00
RCCRPR Plmro/ARod/IRod 8.00 20.00
RCCSAH Heyward/Schwarber/Almora Jr. 5.00 12.00
RCCSCR Conforto/Smith/Rosario 4.00 10.00
RCCSMG Glasnow/Morton/Snell 5.00 12.00
RCCSST Tanaka/Severino/Sabathia 4.00 10.00
RCCTGA Trrs/Andjr/Gregorius 10.00 25.00
RCCTGAL Alonso/Tatis/Guerrero 50.00 125.00
RCCTGM Griffey/McGwire/Thomas 30.00 80.00
RCCYCB Braun/Yelich/Cain 8.00 20.00

2019 Topps Triple Threads Relics

STATED ODDS 1:XX MINI BOX
STATED PRINT RUN 36 SER.#'d SETS
*SILVER/27: .4X TO 1X BASIC
*EMERALD/18: .5X TO 1.2X BASIC
*GOLD/9: .6X TO 1.5X BASIC
ALL VERSIONS EQUALLY PRICED
TTRAB Andrew Benintendi 5.00 12.00
TTRAB2 Andrew Benintendi 5.00 12.00
TTRAB3 Andrew Benintendi 5.00 12.00
TTRAB4 Andrew Benintendi 5.00 12.00
TTRABR Alex Bregman 4.00 10.00
TTRABR2 Alex Bregman 4.00 10.00
TTRABR3 Alex Bregman 4.00 10.00
TTRABR4 Alex Bregman 4.00 10.00
TTRAC Aroldis Chapman 4.00 10.00
TTRAC2 Aroldis Chapman 4.00 10.00
TTRAC3 Aroldis Chapman 4.00 10.00
TTRAJ Aaron Judge 10.00 25.00
TTRAM Austin Meadows 4.00 10.00
TTRAM2 Austin Meadows 4.00 10.00
TTRAM3 Austin Meadows 4.00 10.00
TTRAN Aaron Nola 3.00 8.00
TTRAN2 Aaron Nola 3.00 8.00
TTRAN3 Aaron Nola 3.00 8.00
TTRAR Anthony Rendon 4.00 10.00
TTRAR2 Anthony Rendon 4.00 10.00
TTRAR3 Anthony Rendon 4.00 10.00
TTRAR4 Anthony Rendon 4.00 10.00
TTRARO Amed Rosario 3.00 8.00
TTRARO2 Amed Rosario 3.00 8.00
TTRARO3 Amed Rosario 3.00 8.00
TTRARO4 Amed Rosario 3.00 8.00
TTRBB Byron Buxton 4.00 10.00
TTRBB2 Byron Buxton 4.00 10.00
TTRBB3 Byron Buxton 4.00 10.00
TTRBB4 Byron Buxton 4.00 10.00
TTRBP Buster Posey 5.00 12.00
TTRBP2 Buster Posey 5.00 12.00
TTRBP3 Buster Posey 5.00 12.00
TTRCB Cody Bellinger 8.00 20.00
TTRCC Carlos Correa 4.00 10.00
TTRCC2 Carlos Correa 4.00 10.00
TTRCC3 Carlos Correa 4.00 10.00
TTRCS CC Sabathia 3.00 8.00
TTRCS2 CC Sabathia 3.00 8.00
TTRDB Dellin Betances 3.00 8.00
TTRDB2 Dellin Betances 3.00 8.00
TTRDB3 Dellin Betances 3.00 8.00
TTRDB4 Dellin Betances 3.00 8.00
TTRDO David Ortiz 4.00 10.00
TTRDO2 David Ortiz 4.00 10.00
TTRDP Dustin Pedroia 4.00 10.00
TTRDP2 Dustin Pedroia 4.00 10.00
TTRDP3 Dustin Pedroia 4.00 10.00
TTRDP4 Dustin Pedroia 4.00 10.00
TTRDP5 Dustin Pedroia 4.00 10.00
TTRDPR David Price 3.00 8.00
TTRDPR2 David Price 3.00 8.00
TTRDPR3 David Price 3.00 8.00
TTREH Eric Hosmer 3.00 8.00
TTREH2 Eric Hosmer 3.00 8.00
TTREH3 Eric Hosmer 3.00 8.00
TTREL Evan Longoria 3.00 8.00
TTREL2 Evan Longoria 3.00 8.00
TTREL3 Evan Longoria 3.00 8.00
TTREL4 Evan Longoria 3.00 8.00
TTRER Eddie Rosario 3.00 8.00
TTRER2 Eddie Rosario 3.00 8.00
TTRER3 Eddie Rosario 3.00 8.00
TTRFL Francisco Lindor 6.00 15.00
TTRGC Gerrit Cole 4.00 10.00
TTRGC2 Gerrit Cole 4.00 10.00
TTRGC3 Gerrit Cole 4.00 10.00
TTRGP Gregory Polanco 3.00 8.00
TTRGP2 Gregory Polanco 3.00 8.00
TTRGP3 Gregory Polanco 3.00 8.00
TTRGP4 Gregory Polanco 3.00 8.00
TTRGP5 Gregory Polanco 3.00 8.00
TTRGS George Springer 3.00 8.00
TTRGS2 George Springer 3.00 8.00
TTRGST Giancarlo Stanton 4.00 10.00
TTRGST2 Giancarlo Stanton 4.00 10.00
TTRGST3 Giancarlo Stanton 4.00 10.00
TTRHD Hunter Dozier 2.50 6.00
TTRHD2 Hunter Dozier 2.50 6.00
TTRHD3 Hunter Dozier 2.50 6.00
TTRJA Jose Abreu 4.00 10.00
TTRJA2 Jose Abreu 4.00 10.00
TTRJA3 Jose Abreu 4.00 10.00
TTRJA4 Jose Abreu 4.00 10.00
TTRJA5 Jose Abreu 4.00 10.00
TTRJAL Jorge Alfaro 2.50 6.00
TTRJAL2 Jorge Alfaro 2.50 6.00
TTRJAL3 Jorge Alfaro 2.50 6.00
TTRJAR Jake Arrieta 3.00 8.00
TTRJAR2 Jake Arrieta 3.00 8.00
TTRJAR3 Jake Arrieta 3.00 8.00
TTRJAR4 Jake Arrieta 3.00 8.00
TTRJD Jacob deGrom 8.00 20.00
TTRJD2 Jacob deGrom 8.00 20.00
TTRJH Jason Heyward 3.00 8.00
TTRJH2 Jason Heyward 3.00 8.00
TTRJH3 Jason Heyward 3.00 8.00
TTRJL Jon Lester 3.00 8.00
TTRJL2 Jon Lester 3.00 8.00
TTRJL3 Jon Lester 3.00 8.00
TTRJLU Joey Lucchesi 2.50 6.00
TTRJLU2 Joey Lucchesi 2.50 6.00
TTRJLU3 Joey Lucchesi 2.50 6.00
TTRJOA Jose Altuve 3.00 8.00
TTRJOA2 Jose Altuve 3.00 8.00
TTRJOA3 Jose Altuve 3.00 8.00
TTRJOA4 Jose Altuve 3.00 8.00
TTRJS Juan Soto 6.00 15.00
TTRJS2 Juan Soto 6.00 15.00
TTRKG Ken Griffey Jr. 15.00 40.00
TTRKG2 Ken Griffey Jr. 15.00 40.00
TTRLC Luis Castillo 3.00 8.00
TTRLC2 Luis Castillo 3.00 8.00
TTRLC3 Luis Castillo 3.00 8.00
TTRLC4 Luis Castillo 3.00 8.00
TTRMA Miguel Andujar 4.00 10.00
TTRMA2 Miguel Andujar 4.00 10.00
TTRMB Mookie Betts 5.00 12.00
TTRMB2 Mookie Betts 5.00 12.00
TTRMB3 Mookie Betts 5.00 12.00
TTRMB4 Mookie Betts 5.00 12.00
TTRMB5 Mookie Betts 5.00 12.00
TTRMC Miguel Cabrera 4.00 10.00
TTRMC2 Miguel Cabrera 4.00 10.00
TTRMC3 Miguel Cabrera 4.00 10.00
TTRMC4 Miguel Cabrera 4.00 10.00
TTRMC5 Miguel Cabrera 4.00 10.00
TTRMM Manny Machado 4.00 10.00
TTRMM2 Manny Machado 4.00 10.00
TTRMO Matt Olson 4.00 10.00
TTRMO2 Matt Olson 4.00 10.00
TTRMO3 Matt Olson 4.00 10.00
TTRMOZ Marcell Ozuna 4.00 10.00
TTRMOZ2 Marcell Ozuna 4.00 10.00
TTRMOZ3 Marcell Ozuna 4.00 10.00
TTRMS Max Scherzer 4.00 10.00
TTRMS2 Max Scherzer 4.00 10.00
TTRNA Nolan Arenado 6.00 15.00
TTRNA2 Nolan Arenado 6.00 15.00
TTRNA3 Nolan Arenado 6.00 15.00
TTRNM Nomar Mazara 2.50 6.00
TTRNM2 Nomar Mazara 2.50 6.00
TTRNM3 Nomar Mazara 2.50 6.00
TTRNM4 Nomar Mazara 2.50 6.00
TTROA Ozzie Albies 4.00 10.00
TTROA2 Ozzie Albies 4.00 10.00
TTROA3 Ozzie Albies 4.00 10.00
TTROA4 Ozzie Albies 4.00 10.00
TTROA5 Ozzie Albies 4.00 10.00
TTRRA Roberto Alomar 8.00 20.00
TTRRA2 Roberto Alomar 8.00 20.00
TTRRB Ryan Braun 3.00 8.00
TTRRB2 Ryan Braun 3.00 8.00
TTRRB3 Ryan Braun 3.00 8.00
TTRRD Rafael Devers 5.00 12.00
TTRRD2 Rafael Devers 5.00 12.00
TTRRD3 Rafael Devers 5.00 12.00
TTRRD4 Rafael Devers 5.00 12.00
TTRRH Rhys Hoskins 6.00 15.00
TTRSK Scott Kingery 3.00 8.00
TTRSK2 Scott Kingery 3.00 8.00
TTRSK3 Scott Kingery 3.00 8.00
TTRSM Starling Marte 3.00 8.00
TTRSM2 Starling Marte 3.00 8.00
TTRSM3 Starling Marte 3.00 8.00
TTRSP Salvador Perez 3.00 8.00
TTRSP2 Salvador Perez 3.00 8.00
TTRSP3 Salvador Perez 3.00 8.00
TTRTM Trey Mancini 3.00 8.00
TTRTM2 Trey Mancini 3.00 8.00
TTRTM3 Trey Mancini 3.00 8.00
TTRWB Walker Buehler 5.00 12.00
TTRWB2 Walker Buehler 5.00 12.00
TTRWB3 Walker Buehler 5.00 12.00
TTRWC Willson Contreras 3.00 8.00
TTRWC2 Willson Contreras 3.00 8.00
TTRWM Wil Myers 3.00 8.00
TTRWM2 Wil Myers 3.00 8.00
TTRWM3 Wil Myers 3.00 8.00
TTRWM4 Wil Myers 3.00 8.00
TTRXB Xander Bogaerts 4.00 10.00
TTRXB2 Xander Bogaerts 4.00 10.00
TTRXB3 Xander Bogaerts 4.00 10.00
TTRXB4 Xander Bogaerts 4.00 10.00
TTRXB5 Xander Bogaerts 4.00 10.00

2019 Topps Triple Threads Rookie Autographs

STATED ODDS 1:XX MINI BOX
STATED PRINT RUN 99 SER.#'d SETS
EXCHANGE DEADLINE 8/31/2021
PRINTING PLATE ODDS 1:XXX MINI BOX
PLATE PRINT RUN 1 SET PER COLOR
BLACK-CYAN-MAGENTA-YELLOW ISSUED
NO PLATE PRICING DUE TO SCARCITY
*EMERALD/50: .4X TO 1X BASIC
*GOLD/25: .5X TO 1.2X BASIC
RAUAR Austin Riley 15.00 40.00
RAUBL Brandon Lowe 10.00 25.00
RAUCK Carter Kieboom 10.00 25.00
RAUDC Dylan Cozens 4.00 10.00
RAUDH Darwinzon Hernandez 4.00 10.00
RAUDJ Danny Jansen 4.00 10.00
RAUEJ Eloy Jimenez 20.00 50.00
RAUFT Fernando Tatis Jr. 125.00 300.00
RAUGH Garrett Hampson 6.00 15.00
RAUJD Jon Duplantier 4.00 10.00
RAUKS Kohl Stewart 5.00 12.00
RAULT Lane Thomas 6.00 15.00
RAUMS Myles Straw 6.00 15.00
RAUNL Nate Lowe 20.00 50.00
RAUNM Nick Margevicius 4.00 10.00
RAUNS Nick Senzel 15.00 40.00
RAUPA Pete Alonso 60.00 150.00
RAURB Ryan Borucki 4.00 10.00
RAURR Ronny Rodriguez 4.00 10.00
RAUSB Skye Bolt 5.00 12.00
RAUTB Ty Buttrey 4.00 10.00
RAUTE Thairo Estrada 8.00 20.00
RAUVG Vladimir Guerrero Jr. 50.00 120.00
RAUWA Willians Astudillo 4.00 10.00
RAUYK Yusei Kikuchi 6.00 15.00

2019 Topps Triple Threads Single Jumbo Relics

STATED ODDS 1:XX HOBBY
STATED PRINT RUN 36 SER.#'d SETS
*SILVER/27: .4X TO 1X BASIC
*EMERALD/18: .5X TO 1.2X BASIC
*GOLD/9: .6X TO 1.5X BASIC
ALL VERSIONS EQUALLY PRICED
SJRAB1 Andrew Benintendi 5.00 12.00
SJRAB2 Andrew Benintendi 5.00 12.00
SJRAB3 Andrew Benintendi 5.00 12.00
SJRABR1 Alex Bregman 4.00 10.00
SJRABR2 Alex Bregman 4.00 10.00
SJRABR3 Alex Bregman 4.00 10.00
SJRAC1 Aroldis Chapman 4.00 10.00
SJRAC2 Aroldis Chapman 4.00 10.00
SJRAC3 Aroldis Chapman 4.00 10.00
SJRAG1 Alex Gordon 3.00 8.00
SJRAG2 Alex Gordon 3.00 8.00
SJRAG3 Alex Gordon 3.00 8.00
SJRAJ1 Aaron Judge 10.00 25.00
SJRAJ2 Aaron Judge 10.00 25.00
SJRAM1 Adalberto Mondesi 3.00 8.00
SJRAM2 Adalberto Mondesi 3.00 8.00
SJRAN1 Aaron Nola 3.00 8.00
SJRAN2 Aaron Nola 3.00 8.00
SJRAP1 Albert Pujols 5.00 12.00
SJRAP2 Albert Pujols 5.00 12.00
SJRAP3 Albert Pujols 5.00 12.00
SJRAR1 Anthony Rendon 4.00 10.00
SJRAR2 Anthony Rendon 4.00 10.00
SJRARI1 Anthony Rizzo 5.00 12.00
SJRARI2 Anthony Rizzo 5.00 12.00
SJRARI3 Anthony Rizzo 5.00 12.00
SJRARI4 Anthony Rizzo 5.00 12.00
SJRARO1 Amed Rosario 3.00 8.00
SJRARO2 Amed Rosario 3.00 8.00
SJRARO3 Amed Rosario 3.00 8.00
SJRBB1 Byron Buxton 4.00 10.00
SJRBB2 Byron Buxton 4.00 10.00
SJRBB3 Byron Buxton 4.00 10.00
SJRBG1 Brett Gardner 3.00 8.00
SJRBG2 Brett Gardner 3.00 8.00
SJRBG3 Brett Gardner 3.00 8.00
SJRBP1 Buster Posey 5.00 12.00
SJRBP2 Buster Posey 5.00 12.00
SJRBP3 Buster Posey 5.00 12.00
SJRBP4 Buster Posey 5.00 12.00
SJRBS1 Blake Snell 3.00 8.00
SJRBS2 Blake Snell 3.00 8.00
SJRCB Cody Bellinger 12.00 30.00
SJRCC1 Carlos Carrasco 2.50 6.00
SJRCC2 Carlos Carrasco 2.50 6.00
SJRCCO1 Carlos Correa 4.00 10.00
SJRCCO2 Carlos Correa 4.00 10.00
SJRCCO3 Carlos Correa 4.00 10.00
SJRCF1 Clint Frazier 3.00 8.00
SJRCF2 Clint Frazier 3.00 8.00
SJRCH1 Cole Hamels 3.00 8.00
SJRCH2 Cole Hamels 3.00 8.00
SJRCS1 CC Sabathia 3.00 8.00
SJRCS2 CC Sabathia 3.00 8.00
SJRCS3 CC Sabathia 3.00 8.00
SJRCS4 CC Sabathia 3.00 8.00
SJRCSA1 Chris Sale 4.00 10.00
SJRCSA2 Chris Sale 4.00 10.00
SJRCSA3 Chris Sale 4.00 10.00
SJRCSA4 Chris Sale 4.00 10.00
SJRCY Christian Yelich 5.00 12.00
SJRDD1 David Dahl 2.50 6.00
SJRDD2 David Dahl 2.50 6.00
SJRDP1 Dustin Pedroia 4.00 10.00
SJRDP2 Dustin Pedroia 4.00 10.00
SJRDP3 Dustin Pedroia 4.00 10.00
SJRDP4 Dustin Pedroia 4.00 10.00
SJRDPR1 David Price 3.00 8.00
SJRDPR2 David Price 3.00 8.00
SJRDPR3 David Price 3.00 8.00
SJRDPR4 David Price 3.00 8.00
SJRDPR5 David Price 3.00 8.00
SJRDS1 Dominic Smith 2.50 6.00
SJRDS2 Dominic Smith 2.50 6.00
SJRDS3 Dominic Smith 2.50 6.00
SJRDS4 Dominic Smith 2.50 6.00
SJRDSW1 Dansby Swanson 4.00 10.00
SJRDSW2 Dansby Swanson 4.00 10.00
SJRDSW3 Dansby Swanson 4.00 10.00
SJREH1 Eric Hosmer 3.00 8.00
SJREH2 Eric Hosmer 3.00 8.00
SJREL1 Evan Longoria 3.00 8.00
SJREL2 Evan Longoria 3.00 8.00
SJREL3 Evan Longoria 3.00 8.00
SJRER1 Eddie Rosario 3.00 8.00
SJRER2 Eddie Rosario 3.00 8.00
SJRER3 Eddie Rosario 3.00 8.00
SJRES1 Eugenio Suarez 3.00 8.00
SJRES2 Eugenio Suarez 3.00 8.00
SJRES3 Eugenio Suarez 3.00 8.00
SJRFF1 Freddie Freeman 5.00 12.00
SJRFF2 Freddie Freeman 5.00 12.00
SJRFF3 Freddie Freeman 5.00 12.00
SJRFL1 Francisco Lindor 4.00 10.00
SJRFL2 Francisco Lindor 4.00 10.00
SJRFL3 Francisco Lindor 4.00 10.00
SJRFR1 Franmil Reyes 2.50 6.00
SJRFR2 Franmil Reyes 2.50 6.00
SJRGC1 Gerrit Cole 4.00 10.00
SJRGC2 Gerrit Cole 4.00 10.00
SJRGM1 German Marquez 2.50 6.00
SJRGM2 German Marquez 2.50 6.00

SJRGP1 Gregory Polanco 3.00 8.00
SJRGP2 Gregory Polanco 3.00 8.00
SJRGP3 Gregory Polanco 3.00 8.00
SJRGP4 Gregory Polanco 3.00 8.00
SJRGS1 Gary Sanchez 4.00 10.00
SJRGS2 Gary Sanchez 4.00 10.00
SJRGS3 Gary Sanchez 4.00 10.00
SJRGSP1 George Springer 3.00 8.00
SJRGSP2 George Springer 3.00 8.00
SJRGSP3 George Springer 3.00 8.00
SJRGSP4 George Springer 3.00 8.00
SJRGST1 Giancarlo Stanton 4.00 10.00
SJRGST2 Giancarlo Stanton 4.00 10.00
SJRGST3 Giancarlo Stanton 4.00 10.00
SJRHD1 Hunter Dozier 2.50 6.00
SJRHD2 Hunter Dozier 2.50 6.00
SJRJA1 Jose Abreu 4.00 10.00
SJRJA2 Jose Abreu 4.00 10.00
SJRJAL1 Jose Altuve 3.00 8.00
SJRJAL2 Jose Altuve 3.00 8.00
SJRJAR1 Jake Arrieta 3.00 8.00
SJRJAR2 Jake Arrieta 3.00 8.00
SJRJB1 Javier Baez 8.00 20.00
SJRJB2 Javier Baez 8.00 20.00
SJRJH1 Josh Hader 3.00 8.00
SJRJH2 Josh Hader 3.00 8.00
SJRJHE1 Jason Heyward 3.00 8.00
SJRJHE2 Jason Heyward 3.00 8.00
SJRJHE3 Jason Heyward 3.00 8.00
SJRJHI1 Jordan Hicks 3.00 8.00
SJRJHI2 Jordan Hicks 3.00 8.00
SJRJL1 Jon Lester 3.00 8.00
SJRJL2 Jon Lester 3.00 8.00
SJRJL3 Jon Lester 3.00 8.00
SJRJL4 Jon Lester 3.00 8.00
SJRJLU Joey Lucchesi 2.50 6.00
SJRJM1 J.D. Martinez 4.00 10.00
SJRJM2 J.D. Martinez 4.00 10.00
SJRJP1 Joc Pederson 3.00 8.00
SJRJP2 Joc Pederson 3.00 8.00
SJRJR1 Jose Ramirez 3.00 8.00
SJRJR2 Jose Ramirez 3.00 8.00
SJRJR3 Jose Ramirez 3.00 8.00
SJRJSO1 Juan Soto 6.00 15.00
SJRJSO2 Juan Soto 6.00 15.00
SJRJV Justin Verlander 4.00 10.00
SJRJV1 Joey Votto 4.00 10.00
SJRJV2 Joey Votto 4.00 10.00
SJRJV3 Joey Votto 4.00 10.00
SJRKB1 Kris Bryant 5.00 12.00
SJRKB2 Kris Bryant 5.00 12.00
SJRKD Khris Davis 4.00 10.00
SJRKM1 Kenta Maeda 3.00 8.00
SJRKM2 Kenta Maeda 3.00 8.00
SJRKS1 Kyle Schwarber 4.00 10.00
SJRKS2 Kyle Schwarber 4.00 10.00
SJRKS3 Kyle Schwarber 4.00 10.00
SJRKS4 Kyle Schwarber 4.00 10.00
SJRKSE1 Kyle Seager 2.50 6.00
SJRKSE2 Kyle Seager 2.50 6.00
SJRKSE3 Kyle Seager 2.50 6.00
SJRKW1 Kolten Wong 3.00 8.00
SJRKW2 Kolten Wong 3.00 8.00
SJRKW3 Kolten Wong 3.00 8.00
SJRLC1 Lorenzo Cain 2.50 6.00
SJRLC2 Lorenzo Cain 2.50 6.00
SJRLCA1 Luis Castillo 3.00 8.00
SJRLCA2 Luis Castillo 3.00 8.00
SJRLCA3 Luis Castillo 3.00 8.00
SJRLS1 Luis Severino 3.00 8.00
SJRLS2 Luis Severino 3.00 8.00
SJRLS3 Luis Severino 3.00 8.00
SJRLS4 Luis Severino 3.00 8.00
SJRMA1 Miguel Andujar 4.00 10.00
SJRMA2 Miguel Andujar 4.00 10.00
SJRMB1 Mookie Betts 5.00 12.00
SJRMB2 Mookie Betts 5.00 12.00
SJRMB3 Mookie Betts 5.00 12.00
SJRMC1 Miguel Cabrera 4.00 10.00
SJRMC2 Miguel Cabrera 4.00 10.00
SJRMC3 Miguel Cabrera 4.00 10.00
SJRMC4 Miguel Cabrera 4.00 10.00
SJRMC5 Miguel Cabrera 4.00 10.00
SJRMCO1 Michael Conforto 3.00 8.00
SJRMCO2 Michael Conforto 3.00 8.00
SJRMF1 Maikel Franco 3.00 8.00
SJRMF2 Maikel Franco 3.00 8.00
SJRMF3 Maikel Franco 3.00 8.00
SJRMFR1 Max Fried 4.00 10.00
SJRMFR2 Max Fried 4.00 10.00
SJRMFR3 Max Fried 4.00 10.00
SJRMM Manny Machado 4.00 10.00
SJRMO1 Marcell Ozuna 4.00 10.00
SJRMO2 Marcell Ozuna 4.00 10.00
SJRMS1 Max Scherzer 4.00 10.00
SJRMS2 Max Scherzer 4.00 10.00
SJRMS3 Max Scherzer 4.00 10.00
SJRMT1 Mike Trout 20.00 50.00
SJRMT2 Mike Trout 20.00 50.00
SJRNA1 Nolan Arenado 6.00 15.00
SJRNA2 Nolan Arenado 6.00 15.00
SJRNC1 Nicholas Castellanos 4.00 10.00
SJRNC2 Nicholas Castellanos 4.00 10.00
SJRNM1 Nomar Mazara 2.50 6.00
SJRNM2 Nomar Mazara 2.50 6.00
SJRNS1 Noah Syndergaard 3.00 8.00
SJRNS2 Noah Syndergaard 3.00 8.00
SJROA1 Ozzie Albies 4.00 10.00
SJROA2 Ozzie Albies 4.00 10.00
SJROA3 Ozzie Albies 4.00 10.00
SJRPG1 Paul Goldschmidt 4.00 10.00
SJRPG2 Paul Goldschmidt 4.00 10.00
SJRRA Ronald Acuna Jr. 15.00 40.00
SJRRB1 Ryan Braun 3.00 8.00
SJRRB2 Ryan Braun 3.00 8.00
SJRRD1 Rafael Devers 5.00 12.00
SJRRD2 Rafael Devers 5.00 12.00
SJRRD3 Rafael Devers 5.00 12.00
SJRRH1 Rhys Hoskins 6.00 15.00
SJRRH2 Rhys Hoskins 6.00 15.00
SJRRH3 Rhys Hoskins 6.00 15.00
SJRRP1 Rick Porcello 3.00 8.00
SJRRP2 Rick Porcello 3.00 8.00
SJRRP3 Rick Porcello 3.00 8.00
SJRRP4 Rick Porcello 3.00 8.00
SJRRT1 Raimel Tapia 2.50 6.00
SJRRT2 Raimel Tapia 2.50 6.00
SJRSK1 Scott Kingery 3.00 8.00
SJRSK2 Scott Kingery 3.00 8.00
SJRSK3 Scott Kingery 3.00 8.00
SJRSO Shohei Ohtani 6.00 15.00
SJRSP1 Salvador Perez 3.00 8.00
SJRSP2 Salvador Perez 3.00 8.00
SJRSP3 Salvador Perez 3.00 8.00
SJRSS1 Stephen Strasburg 4.00 10.00
SJRSS2 Stephen Strasburg 4.00 10.00
SJRTM1 Trey Mancini 3.00 8.00
SJRTM2 Trey Mancini 3.00 8.00
SJRTP1 Tommy Pham 2.50 6.00
SJRTP2 Tommy Pham 2.50 6.00
SJRTP3 Tommy Pham 2.50 6.00
SJRTS1 Trevor Story 4.00 10.00
SJRTS2 Trevor Story 4.00 10.00
SJRTS3 Trevor Story 4.00 10.00
SJRTT1 Trea Turner 3.00 8.00
SJRTT2 Trea Turner 3.00 8.00
SJRWB Walker Buehler 5.00 12.00
SJRWC1 Willson Contreras 3.00 8.00
SJRWC2 Willson Contreras 3.00 8.00
SJRWC3 Willson Contreras 3.00 8.00
SJRWM1 Whit Merrifield 4.00 10.00
SJRWM2 Whit Merrifield 4.00 10.00
SJRWM3 Whit Merrifield 4.00 10.00
SJRWMY1 Wil Myers 3.00 8.00
SJRWMY2 Wil Myers 3.00 8.00
SJRXB1 Xander Bogaerts 4.00 10.00
SJRXB2 Xander Bogaerts 4.00 10.00
SJRXB3 Xander Bogaerts 4.00 10.00
SJRXB4 Xander Bogaerts 4.00 10.00
SJRYM1 Yadier Molina 8.00 20.00
SJRYM2 Yadier Molina 8.00 20.00
SJRYP1 Yasiel Puig 4.00 10.00
SJRYP2 Yasiel Puig 4.00 10.00
SJRZD1 Zach Davies 2.50 6.00
SJRZD2 Zach Davies 2.50 6.00

2020 Topps Triple Threads

JSY AU RC ODDS 1:XX MINI BOX
JSY AU RC PRINT RUN 99 SER.#'d SETS
JSY AU ODDS 1:XX MINI BOX
JSY AU PRINT RUN 99 SER.#'d SETS
EXCHANGE DEADLINE 8/31/2022
1-100 PLATE ODDS 1:XXX MINI BOX
JSY AU PLATE ODDS 1:XXX MINI BOX
PLATE PRINT RUN 1 SET PER COLOR
BLACK-CYAN-MAGENTA-YELLOW ISSUED
NO PLATE PRICING DUE TO SCARCITY
1 Mike Trout 3.00 8.00
2 Albert Pujols .75 2.00
3 Shohei Ohtani 1.00 2.50
4 Anthony Rendon .60 1.50
5 Freddie Freeman .75 2.00
6 Yoshi Tsutsugo RC 1.50 4.00
7 Ronald Acuna Jr. 2.50 6.00
8 Chipper Jones .60 1.50
9 Cal Ripken Jr. 2.00 5.00
10 Hank Aaron 1.25 3.00
11 Rafael Devers .75 2.00
12 J.D. Martinez .60 1.50
13 Ted Williams 1.25 3.00
14 David Ortiz .60 1.50
15 Thurman Munson .60 1.50
16 Jackie Robinson .60 1.50
17 Nico Hoerner RC 2.50 6.00
18 Kris Bryant .75 2.00
19 Anthony Rizzo .75 2.00
20 Javier Baez .75 2.00
21 Ernie Banks .60 1.50
22 Ryne Sandberg 1.25 3.00
23 Frank Thomas .60 1.50
24 Luis Robert RC 10.00 25.00
25 Eloy Jimenez 1.25 3.00
26 Joey Votto .60 1.50
27 Johnny Bench .60 1.50
28 Barry Larkin .50 1.25
29 Aristides Aquino RC 1.50 4.00
30 Francisco Lindor .60 1.50
31 Shane Bieber .60 1.50
32 Nolan Arenado 1.00 2.50
33 Trevor Story .60 1.50
34 Miguel Cabrera .60 1.50
35 Justin Verlander .60 1.50
36 Jose Altuve .50 1.25
37 George Springer .50 1.25
38 Alex Bregman .60 1.50
39 Yordan Alvarez RC 6.00 15.00
40 Whit Merrifield .60 1.50
41 George Brett 1.25 3.00
42 Dave Winfield .50 1.25
43 Mookie Betts 1.25 3.00
44 Clayton Kershaw 1.00 2.50
45 Cody Bellinger 1.25 3.00
46 Sandy Koufax 1.25 3.00
47 Walker Buehler .75 2.00
48 Gavin Lux RC 3.00 8.00
49 Christian Yelich .75 2.00
50 Keston Hiura .75 2.00
51 Jacob deGrom 1.25 3.00
52 Pete Alonso 1.50 4.00
53 Robin Yount .60 1.50
54 Tom Seaver .50 1.25
55 Darryl Strawberry .40 1.00
56 Aaron Judge 1.50 4.00
57 Gleyber Torres 1.25 3.00
58 Derek Jeter 1.50 4.00
59 Don Mattingly 1.25 3.00
60 Mariano Rivera .75 2.00
61 Gerrit Cole 1.00 2.50
62 Babe Ruth 1.50 4.00
63 Lou Gehrig 1.25 3.00
64 Jesus Luzardo RC 1.25 3.00
65 Matt Chapman .60 1.50
66 Rickey Henderson .60 1.50
67 Mark McGwire 1.00 2.50
68 Rhys Hoskins .75 2.00
69 Andrew McCutchen .60 1.50
70 Bryce Harper 1.00 2.50
71 Mike Schmidt 1.00 2.50
72 Roberto Clemente 1.50 4.00
73 Ty Cobb 1.00 2.50
74 Honus Wagner .60 1.50
75 Manny Machado .60 1.50
76 Tony Gwynn .60 1.50
77 Fernando Tatis Jr. 3.00 8.00
78 Buster Posey .75 2.00
79 Will Clark .50 1.25
80 Willie Mays 1.25 3.00
81 Ichiro .75 2.00
82 Ken Griffey Jr. 1.25 3.00
83 Kyle Lewis RC 5.00 12.00
84 Randy Johnson .60 1.50
85 Paul Goldschmidt .60 1.50
86 Yadier Molina .75 2.00
87 Ozzie Smith .75 2.00
88 Shogo Akiyama RC 1.00 2.50
89 Brendan McKay RC 1.00 2.50
90 Nolan Ryan 2.00 5.00
91 Josh Donaldson .50 1.25
92 Bo Bichette RC 5.00 12.00
93 Roberto Alomar .50 1.25
94 Vladimir Guerrero Jr. 1.00 2.50
95 Max Scherzer .60 1.50
96 Stephen Strasburg .60 1.50
97 Juan Soto 2.00 5.00
98 Brooks Robinson .50 1.25
99 Mike Piazza .60 1.50
100 Reggie Jackson .50 1.25
RFPARAAQ A.Aquino JSY AU 12.00 30.00
RFPARAM Andres Munoz JSY AU RC 5.00 12.00
RFPARAN Austin Nola JSY AU RC 5.00 12.00
RFPARAP A.Puk JSY AU RC 5.00 12.00
RFPARAR A.Riley JSY AU 12.00 30.00
RFPARBBR Bobby Bradley JSY AU RC 5.00 12.00
RFPARBL B.Lowe JSY AU 8.00 20.00
RFPARBM B.McKay JSY AU 6.00 15.00
RFPARBR Brendan Rodgers JSY AU 5.00 12.00
RFPAREJ E.Jimenez JSY AU EXCH 20.00 50.00
RFPARGL G.Lux JSY AU EXCH 30.00 80.00
RFPARID I.Diaz JSY AU RC 8.00 20.00
RFPARJD Justin Dunn JSY AU RC 4.00 10.00
RFPARJDD J.Davis JSY AU 8.00 20.00
RFPARJL J.Luzardo JSY AU 10.00 25.00
RFPARJM J.McNeil JSY AU 12.00 30.00
RFPARJME J.Means JSY AU 40.00 100.00
RFPARJP Jorge Polanco JSY AU 4.00 10.00
RFPARJR Jake Rogers JSY AU RC 6.00 15.00
RFPARKN Kevin Newman JSY AU 5.00 12.00
RFPARLA L.Arraez JSY AU 8.00 20.00
RFPARLG L.Gurriel Jr. JSY AU 8.00 20.00
RFPARLR L.Robert JSY AU 100.00 250.00
RFPARLW L.Webb JSY AU RC 10.00 25.00
RFPARMC M.Chavis JSY AU 8.00 20.00
RFPARMG Mitch Garver JSY AU 5.00 12.00
RFPARMK M.King JSY AU RC 8.00 20.00
RFPARMS M.Soroka JSY AU 12.00 30.00
RFPARNL Nicky Lopez JSY AU 5.00 12.00
RFPARNS N.Senzel JSY AU 6.00 15.00
RFPARNSO N.Solak JSY AU RC 6.00 15.00
RFPARRL R.Laureano JSY AU 6.00 15.00
RFPARSB S.Brown JSY AU RC 6.00 15.00
RFPARSL Shed Long JSY AU 4.00 10.00
RFPARSM S.Murphy JSY AU RC 8.00 20.00
RFPARSN Sheldon Neuse JSY AU RC 4.00 10.00
RFPARTE T.Edman JSY AU 10.00 25.00
RFPARTES Thairo Estrada JSY AU 4.00 10.00
RFPARTZ T.J. Zeuch JSY AU RC 3.00 8.00
RFPARWS W.Smith JSY AU 10.00 25.00

2020 Topps Triple Threads Amber

*AMBER VET: .75X TO 2X BASIC
*AMBER RC: .5X TO 1.2X BASIC
STATED ODDS 1:XX MINI BOX
STATED PRINT RUN 199 SER.#'d SETS
24 Luis Robert 20.00 50.00

2020 Topps Triple Threads Amethyst

*AMETHYST VET: .75X TO 2X BASIC
*AMETHYST RC: .5X TO 1.2X BASIC
*AMETHYST JSY AU: .4X TO 1X BASIC RC
STATED ODDS 1:XX MINI BOX
JSY AU ODDS 1:XX MINI BOX
1-100 PRINT RUN 299 SER.#'d SETS
JSY AU PRINT RUN 75 SER.#'d SETS
EXCHANGE DEADLINE 8/31/2022
24 Luis Robert 20.00 50.00

2020 Topps Triple Threads Citrine

*CITRINE VET: 1X TO 2.5X BASIC
*CITRINE RC: .6X TO 1.5X BASIC
STATED ODDS 1:XX MINI BOX
STATED PRINT RUN 75 SER.#'d SETS
24 Luis Robert 25.00 60.00
72 Roberto Clemente 10.00 25.00
82 Ken Griffey Jr. 10.00 25.00
90 Nolan Ryan 8.00 20.00
92 Bo Bichette 15.00 40.00

2020 Topps Triple Threads Emerald

*EMERALD VET: .75X TO 2X BASIC
*EMERALD RC: .5X TO 1.2X BASIC
*EMERALD JSY AU: .4X TO 1X BASIC RC
1-100 ODDS 1:XX MINI BOX
JSY AU ODDS 1:XX MINI BOX
1-100 PRINT RUN 275 SER.#'d SETS
JSY AU PRINT RUN 50 SER.#'d SETS
EXCHANGE DEADLINE 8/31/2022
24 Luis Robert 20.00 50.00

2020 Topps Triple Threads Gold

*GOLD VET: 1X TO 2.5X BASIC
*GOLD RC: .6X TO 1.5X BASIC
STATED ODDS 1:XX MINI BOX
STATED PRINT RUN 99 SER.#'d SETS
24 Luis Robert 25.00 60.00
72 Roberto Clemente 10.00 25.00
82 Ken Griffey Jr. 10.00 25.00
90 Nolan Ryan 8.00 20.00
92 Bo Bichette 15.00 40.00

2020 Topps Triple Threads Onyx

*ONYX VET: 1.5X TO 4X BASIC
*ONYX RC: 1X TO 2.5X BASIC
*ONYX JSY AU: .5X TO 1.2X BASIC RC
1-100 ODDS 1:XX MINI BOX
JSY AU ODDS 1:XX MINI BOX
1-100 PRINT RUN 50 SER.#'d SETS
JSY AU PRINT RUN 35 SER.#'d SETS
EXCHANGE DEADLINE 8/31/2022
24 Luis Robert 40.00 100.00
72 Roberto Clemente 15.00 40.00
79 Will Clark 6.00 15.00
82 Ken Griffey Jr. 15.00 40.00
87 Ozzie Smith 8.00 20.00
90 Nolan Ryan 12.00 30.00
92 Bo Bichette 25.00 60.00

2020 Topps Triple Threads Sapphire

*SAPPHIRE VET: 2.5X TO 6X BASIC
*SAPPHIRE RC: 1.5X TO 4X BASIC
STATED ODDS 1:XX MINI BOX
STATED PRINT RUN 25 SER.#'d SETS
101-140 PRINT RUN 10 SER.#'d SETS
NO JSY AU PRICING DUE TO SCARCITY
EXCHANGE DEADLINE 8/31/2022
24 Luis Robert 60.00 150.00
58 Derek Jeter 20.00 50.00
66 Rickey Henderson 15.00 40.00
72 Roberto Clemente 25.00 60.00
79 Will Clark 10.00 25.00
82 Ken Griffey Jr. 25.00 60.00
87 Ozzie Smith 12.00 30.00
90 Nolan Ryan 20.00 50.00
92 Bo Bichette 40.00 100.00

2020 Topps Triple Threads Autograph Relic Combos

STATED ODDS 1:XX HOBBY
STATED PRINT RUN 36 SER.#'d SETS
EXCHANGE DEADLINE 8/31/2022
PRINTING PLATE ODDS 1:XXX HOBBY
PLATE PRINT RUN 1 SET PER COLOR
BLACK-CYAN-MAGENTA-YELLOW ISSUED
NO PLATE PRICING DUE TO SCARCITY
ARCBKB Brrs/Bxtn/Kplr 25.00 60.00
ARCBLM Bhlr/Lux/May 60.00 150.00

2020 Topps Triple Threads Autograph Relic Combos

ARCBRS Sndbrg/Brnt/Rzzo
ARCCOL Chpmn/Olsn/Lzrdo 30.00 80.00
ARCCPL Psy/Clrk/Lnccm
ARCDSW Alnso/Wight/dGom
ARCFAA Jns/Acna/Mrphy 100.00 250.00
ARCFTB Thms/Bhrle/Fsk 100.00 250.00
ARCGVD Dmn/Vrtk/Grcprra
ARCHNR Nola/Hskns/Rlmto 60.00 150.00
ARCKBB Bhlr/Blingr/Krshw
ARCMDB Bgrts/Dvrs/Mrtnz 40.00 100.00
ARCMGF Flhrty/Gldschmdt/Mlna 75.00 200.00
ARCMLP Puk/Lzrdo/Mrphy EXCH 40.00 100.00
ARCPMS Prz/Mrrfild/Slr 30.00 80.00
ARCPRB Andrs/Rdigz/Bltre
ARCPWP Pttte/Wllms/Psda 100.00 250.00
ARCSAP Snll/Lowe/Mdws 30.00 80.00
ARCSBA Sprngr/Brgmn/Alvrz 50.00 120.00
ARCSDG Dwsn/Sndbrg/Grce
ARCSJG Jns/Smltz/Glvne
ARCSJM Jstce/Smltz/McGrff 50.00 120.00
ARCSLM Lux/Sgr/Mncy 75.00 200.00
ARCSRC Soto/Grrro Jr./Acna Jr. 200.00 500.00
ARCSSC Strsbrg/Crbn/Soto
ARCSWA Alnso/Wrght/Stawbrry 75.00 200.00
ARCTBY Bllngr/Trt/Ylch
ARCVGS Snzl/Vtto/Gray 40.00 100.00
ARCWHA Hltn/Arndo/Wlkr
ARCYYH Hra/Ynt/Ylch EXCH

2020 Topps Triple Threads Autograph Relic Combos Amethyst

*AMETHYST: .4X TO 1X BASIC
STATED ODDS 1:XX HOBBY
STATED PRINT RUN 27 SER.#'d SETS
EXCHANGE DEADLINE 8/31/2022
ARCCPL Psy/Clrk/Lnccm 125.00 300.00
ARCDSW Alnso/Wight/dGom 200.00 500.00
ARCGVD Dmn/Vrtk/Grcprra 50.00 120.00
ARCPRB Andrs/Rdigz/Bltre 50.00 120.00
ARCSDG Dwsn/Sndbrg/Grce 125.00 300.00
ARCWHA Hltn/Arndo/Wlkr 125.00 300.00

2020 Topps Triple Threads Autograph Relic Combos Emerald

*EMERALD: .4X TO 1X BASIC
STATED ODDS 1:XXX HOBBY
STATED PRINT RUN 18 SER.#'d SETS
EXCHANGE DEADLINE 8/31/2022
ARCBRS Sndbrg/Brnt/Rzzo 75.00 200.00
ARCCPL Psy/Clrk/Lnccm 125.00 300.00
ARCDSW Alnso/Wight/dGom 200.00 500.00
ARCGVD Dmn/Vrtk/Grcprra 50.00 120.00
ARCKBB Bhlr/Blingr/Krshw 200.00 500.00
ARCPRB Andrs/Rdigz/Bltre 50.00 120.00
ARCSDG Dwsn/Sndbrg/Grce 125.00 300.00
ARCSJG Jns/Smltz/Glvne 100.00 250.00
ARCSSC Strsbrg/Crbn/Soto 100.00 250.00
ARCWHA Hltn/Arndo/Wlkr 125.00 300.00
ARCYYH Hra/Ynt/Ylch EXCH 100.00 250.00

2020 Topps Triple Threads Autograph Relics

STATED ODDS 1:XX HOBBY
STATED PRINT RUN 18 SER.#'d SETS
EXCHANGE DEADLINE 8/31/2022
ALL VERSIONS EQUALLY PRICED
TTARAB1 Adrian Beltre
TTARAB2 Adrian Beltre
TTARABE1 Andrew Benintendi 12.00 30.00
TTARABE2 Andrew Benintendi 12.00 30.00
TTARABE3 Andrew Benintendi 12.00 30.00
TTARABE4 Andrew Benintendi 12.00 30.00
TTARABR1 Alex Bregman 20.00 50.00
TTARABR2 Alex Bregman 20.00 50.00
TTARABR3 Alex Bregman 20.00 50.00
TTARABR4 Alex Bregman 20.00 50.00
TTARABR5 Alex Bregman 20.00 50.00
TTARAJ1 Andruw Jones 20.00 50.00
TTARAJ2 Andruw Jones 20.00 50.00
TTARAJ3 Andruw Jones 20.00 50.00
TTARAJ4 Andruw Jones 20.00 50.00
TTARAJU1 Aaron Judge
TTARAJU2 Aaron Judge
TTARAM1 Austin Meadows 10.00 25.00
TTARAM2 Austin Meadows 10.00 25.00
TTARAM3 Austin Meadows 10.00 25.00
TTARAM4 Austin Meadows 10.00 25.00
TTARAMC1 Andrew McCutchen 50.00 120.00
TTARAMC2 Andrew McCutchen 50.00 120.00
TTARAMC3 Andrew McCutchen 50.00 12.00
TTARAP1 Andy Pettitte 20.00 50.00
TTARAP2 Andy Pettitte 20.00 50.00
TTARAP3 Andy Pettitte 20.00 50.00
TTARAR1 Anthony Rizzo
TTARAR2 Anthony Rizzo
TTARAS1 Alfonso Soriano 15.00 40.00
TTARAS2 Alfonso Soriano 15.00 40.00
TTARAS3 Alfonso Soriano 15.00 40.00
TTARAS4 Alfonso Soriano 15.00 40.00
TTARBB1 Bert Blyleven 12.00 30.00
TTARBB2 Bert Blyleven 12.00 30.00
TTARBH1 Bryce Harper
TTARBH2 Bryce Harper
TTARBW1 Bernie Williams 25.00 60.00
TTARBW2 Bernie Williams 25.00 60.00
TTARBW3 Bernie Williams 25.00 60.00
TTARCB1 Cody Bellinger 75.00 200.00
TTARCB2 Cody Bellinger 75.00 200.00
TTARCB3 Cody Bellinger 75.00 200.00
TTARCF1 Carlton Fisk 25.00 60.00
TTARCF2 Carlton Fisk 25.00 60.00
TTARCF3 Carlton Fisk 25.00 60.00
TTARCFE1 Cecil Fielder 25.00 60.00
TTARCFE2 Cecil Fielder 25.00 60.00
TTARCFE3 Cecil Fielder 25.00 60.00
TTARCJ1 Chipper Jones
TTARCJ2 Chipper Jones
TTARCKE1 Clayton Kershaw
TTARCKE2 Clayton Kershaw
TTARCRJ1 Cal Ripken Jr. 100.00 250.00
TTARCRJ2 Cal Ripken Jr. 100.00 250.00
TTARCSA1 CC Sabathia 20.00 50.00
TTARCSA2 CC Sabathia 20.00 50.00
TTARCSA3 CC Sabathia 20.00 50.00
TTARCY1 Christian Yelich EXCH 50.00 120.00
TTARCY2 Christian Yelich EXCH 50.00 120.00
TTARCY3 Christian Yelich EXCH 50.00 120.00
TTARCY4 Christian Yelich EXCH 50.00 120.00
TTARDE1 Dennis Eckersley 15.00 40.00
TTARDE2 Dennis Eckersley 15.00 40.00
TTARDE3 Dennis Eckersley 15.00 40.00
TTARDJ2 Derek Jeter
TTARDJL1 DJ LeMahieu 40.00 100.00
TTARDJL2 DJ LeMahieu 40.00 100.00
TTARDJL3 DJ LeMahieu 40.00 100.00
TTARDJL4 DJ LeMahieu 40.00 100.00
TTARDL1 Derrek Lee 10.00 25.00
TTARDL2 Derrek Lee 10.00 25.00
TTARDL3 Derrek Lee 10.00 25.00
TTARDO1 David Ortiz
TTARDO2 David Ortiz
TTARDP1 Dustin Pedroia 20.00 50.00
TTARDP2 Dustin Pedroia 20.00 50.00
TTARDP3 Dustin Pedroia 20.00 50.00
TTARDS1 Dansby Swanson 12.00 30.00
TTARDS2 Dansby Swanson 12.00 30.00
TTARDS3 Dansby Swanson 12.00 30.00
TTARDST1 Darryl Strawberry 20.00 50.00
TTARDST2 Darryl Strawberry 20.00 50.00
TTARDST3 Darryl Strawberry 20.00 50.00
TTARDST4 Darryl Strawberry 20.00 50.00
TTARDW1 David Wright 25.00 60.00
TTARDW2 David Wright 25.00 60.00
TTAREA1 Elvis Andrus 10.00 25.00
TTAREA2 Elvis Andrus 10.00 25.00
TTAREA3 Elvis Andrus 10.00 25.00
TTAREA4 Elvis Andrus 10.00 25.00
TTAREH1 Eric Hosmer 12.00 30.00
TTAREH2 Eric Hosmer 12.00 30.00
TTAREH3 Eric Hosmer 12.00 30.00
TTAREH4 Eric Hosmer 12.00 30.00
TTAREH5 Eric Hosmer 12.00 30.00
TTAREJ1 Eloy Jimenez
TTAREJ2 Eloy Jimenez
TTAREJ3 Eloy Jimenez
TTAREJ4 Eloy Jimenez
TTAREM1 Edgar Martinez 25.00 60.00
TTAREM2 Edgar Martinez 25.00 60.00
TTAREM3 Edgar Martinez 25.00 60.00
TTAREM4 Edgar Martinez 25.00 60.00
TTARFF1 Freddie Freeman 40.00 100.00
TTARFF2 Freddie Freeman 40.00 100.00
TTARFF3 Freddie Freeman 40.00 100.00
TTARFF4 Freddie Freeman 40.00 100.00
TTARFF5 Freddie Freeman 40.00 100.00
TTARFM1 Fred McGriff 25.00 60.00
TTARFM2 Fred McGriff 25.00 60.00
TTARFT1 Frank Thomas 40.00 100.00
TTARFT2 Frank Thomas 40.00 100.00
TTARFTJ1 Fernando Tatis Jr. 100.00 250.00
TTARFTJ2 Fernando Tatis Jr. 100.00 250.00
TTARFTJ3 Fernando Tatis Jr. 100.00 250.00
TTARFTJ4 Fernando Tatis Jr. 100.00 250.00
TTARFTJ5 Fernando Tatis Jr. 100.00 250.00
TTARGS1 George Springer 25.00 60.00
TTARGS2 George Springer 25.00 60.00
TTARGS3 George Springer 25.00 60.00
TTARGT1 Gleyber Torres 50.00 120.00
TTARGT2 Gleyber Torres 50.00 120.00
TTARGT3 Gleyber Torres 50.00 120.00
TTARIR1 Ivan Rodriguez 25.00 60.00
TTARIR2 Ivan Rodriguez 25.00 60.00
TTARIR3 Ivan Rodriguez 25.00 60.00
TTARI Ichiro
TTARJAL1 Jose Altuve 15.00 40.00
TTARJAL2 Jose Altuve 15.00 40.00
TTARJAL3 Jose Altuve 15.00 40.00
TTARJDA1 Johnny Damon 20.00 50.00
TTARJDA2 Johnny Damon 20.00 50.00
TTARJDA3 Johnny Damon 20.00 50.00
TTARJF1 Jack Flaherty 12.00 30.00
TTARJF2 Jack Flaherty 12.00 30.00
TTARJF3 Jack Flaherty 12.00 30.00
TTARJF4 Jack Flaherty 12.00 30.00
TTARJF5 Jack Flaherty 12.00 30.00
TTARJG1 Joey Gallo
TTARJG2 Joey Gallo
TTARJG3 Joey Gallo
TTARJG4 Joey Gallo
TTARJM1 J.D. Martinez 15.00 40.00
TTARJM2 J.D. Martinez 15.00 40.00
TTARJM3 J.D. Martinez 15.00 40.00
TTARJM4 J.D. Martinez 15.00 40.00
TTARJMA1 Joe Mauer 30.00 80.00
TTARJMA2 Joe Mauer 30.00 80.00
TTARJMA3 Joe Mauer 30.00 80.00
TTARJS1 Jorge Soler 8.00 20.00
TTARJS2 Jorge Soler 8.00 20.00
TTARJS3 Jorge Soler 8.00 20.00
TTARJS4 Jorge Soler 8.00 20.00
TTARJSM1 John Smoltz 30.00 80.00
TTARJSM2 John Smoltz 30.00 80.00
TTARJSO1 Juan Soto 60.00 150.00
TTARJSO2 Juan Soto 60.00 150.00
TTARJSO3 Juan Soto 60.00 150.00
TTARJSO4 Juan Soto 60.00 150.00
TTARJSO5 Juan Soto 60.00 150.00
TTARJT1 Jim Thome 40.00 100.00
TTARJT2 Jim Thome 40.00 100.00
TTARJV1 Joey Votto
TTARJV2 Joey Votto
TTARKB1 Kris Bryant 30.00 80.00
TTARKB2 Kris Bryant 30.00 80.00
TTARKGJ1 Ken Griffey Jr.
TTARKGJ2 Ken Griffey Jr.
TTARKH1 Keston Hiura 12.00 30.00
TTARKH2 Keston Hiura 12.00 30.00
TTARKH3 Keston Hiura 12.00 30.00
TTARKH4 Keston Hiura 12.00 30.00
TTARKL1 Kenny Lofton 30.00 80.00
TTARKL2 Kenny Lofton 30.00 80.00
TTARKL3 Kenny Lofton 30.00 80.00
TTARKL4 Kenny Lofton 30.00 80.00
TTARKS1 Kyle Schwarber 15.00 40.00
TTARKS2 Kyle Schwarber 15.00 40.00
TTARKS3 Kyle Schwarber 15.00 40.00
TTARKS4 Kyle Schwarber 15.00 40.00
TTARKS5 Kyle Schwarber 15.00 40.00
TTARLW1 Larry Walker 40.00 100.00
TTARLW2 Larry Walker 40.00 100.00
TTARLW3 Larry Walker 40.00 100.00
TTARLW4 Larry Walker 40.00 100.00
TTARMC1 Miguel Cabrera
TTARMC2 Miguel Cabrera
TTARMCH1 Matt Chapman 12.00 30.00
TTARMCH2 Matt Chapman 12.00 30.00
TTARMCH3 Matt Chapman 12.00 30.00
TTARMCH4 Matt Chapman 12.00 30.00
TTARMG1 Mark Grace 20.00 50.00
TTARMG2 Mark Grace 20.00 50.00
TTARMG3 Mark Grace 20.00 50.00
TTARMMC Mark McGwire
TTARMMO1 Mike Moustakas 15.00 40.00
TTARMMO2 Mike Moustakas 15.00 40.00
TTARMMO3 Mike Moustakas 15.00 40.00
TTARMMO4 Mike Moustakas 15.00 40.00
TTARMMO5 Mike Moustakas 15.00 40.00
TTARMMU1 Max Muncy 10.00 25.00
TTARMMU2 Max Muncy 10.00 25.00
TTARMMU3 Max Muncy 10.00 25.00
TTARMMU4 Max Muncy 10.00 25.00
TTARMO1 Matt Olson 8.00 20.00
TTARMO2 Matt Olson 8.00 20.00
TTARMO3 Matt Olson 8.00 20.00
TTARMT1 Mike Trout 250.00 600.00
TTARMT2 Mike Trout 250.00 600.00
TTARMV1 Mo Vaughn 20.00 50.00
TTARMV2 Mo Vaughn 20.00 50.00
TTARMV3 Mo Vaughn 20.00 50.00
TTARNA1 Nolan Arenado 40.00 100.00
TTARNA2 Nolan Arenado 40.00 100.00
TTARNA3 Nolan Arenado 40.00 100.00
TTARNRY Nolan Ryan 75.00 200.00
TTAROS1 Ozzie Smith 30.00 80.00
TTAROS2 Ozzie Smith 30.00 80.00
TTAROS3 Ozzie Smith 30.00 80.00
TTARPA1 Pete Alonso 40.00 100.00
TTARPA2 Pete Alonso 40.00 100.00
TTARPA3 Pete Alonso 40.00 100.00
TTARPC1 Patrick Corbin 8.00 20.00
TTARPC2 Patrick Corbin 8.00 20.00
TTARPC3 Patrick Corbin 8.00 20.00
TTARPC4 Patrick Corbin 8.00 20.00
TTARPC5 Patrick Corbin 8.00 20.00
TTARPG1 Paul Goldschmidt 15.00 40.00
TTARPG2 Paul Goldschmidt 15.00 40.00
TTARPG3 Paul Goldschmidt 15.00 40.00
TTARPG4 Paul Goldschmidt 15.00 40.00
TTARRA1 Ronald Acuna Jr. 75.00 200.00
TTARRA2 Ronald Acuna Jr. 75.00 200.00
TTARRA3 Ronald Acuna Jr. 75.00 200.00
TTARRA4 Ronald Acuna Jr. 75.00 200.00
TTARRA5 Ronald Acuna Jr. 75.00 200.00
TTARRAL1 Roberto Alomar 40.00 100.00
TTARRAL2 Roberto Alomar 40.00 100.00
TTARRD1 Rafael Devers 12.00 30.00
TTARRD2 Rafael Devers 12.00 30.00
TTARRD3 Rafael Devers 12.00 30.00
TTARRD4 Rafael Devers 12.00 30.00
TTARRD5 Rafael Devers 12.00 30.00
TTARRH1 Rhys Hoskins 20.00 50.00
TTARRH2 Rhys Hoskins 20.00 50.00
TTARRH3 Rhys Hoskins 20.00 50.00
TTARRH4 Rhys Hoskins 20.00 50.00
TTARRHE Rickey Henderson 75.00 200.00
TTARRS1 Ryne Sandberg
TTARRS2 Ryne Sandberg
TTARRY1 Robin Yount 40.00 100.00
TTARRY2 Robin Yount 40.00 100.00
TTARRYN1 Ryan Howard 20.00 50.00
TTARRYN2 Ryan Howard 20.00 50.00
TTARRYN3 Ryan Howard 20.00 50.00
TTARSC1 Shin-Soo Choo 25.00 60.00
TTARSC2 Shin-Soo Choo 25.00 60.00
TTARSC3 Shin-Soo Choo 25.00 60.00
TTARSC4 Shin-Soo Choo 25.00 60.00
TTARSCA1 Steve Carlton 25.00 60.00
TTARSCA2 Steve Carlton 25.00 60.00
TTARSCA3 Steve Carlton 25.00 60.00
TTARSGR1 Sonny Gray 15.00 40.00
TTARSGR2 Sonny Gray 15.00 40.00
TTARSGR3 Sonny Gray 15.00 40.00
TTARSGR4 Sonny Gray 15.00 40.00
TTARSO1 Shohei Ohtani 75.00 200.00
TTARSO2 Shohei Ohtani 75.00 200.00
TTARSR1 Scott Rolen 20.00 50.00
TTARSR2 Scott Rolen 20.00 50.00
TTARSR3 Scott Rolen 20.00 50.00
TTARSST1 Stephen Strasburg 30.00 80.00
TTARSST2 Stephen Strasburg 30.00 80.00
TTARSST3 Stephen Strasburg 30.00 80.00
TTARSST4 Stephen Strasburg 30.00 80.00
TTARSST5 Stephen Strasburg 30.00 80.00
TTARTB1 Trevor Bauer 25.00 60.00
TTARTB2 Trevor Bauer 25.00 60.00
TTARTB3 Trevor Bauer 25.00 60.00
TTARTB4 Trevor Bauer 25.00 60.00
TTARTG1 Tom Glavine 25.00 60.00
TTARTG2 Tom Glavine 25.00 60.00
TTARTG3 Tom Glavine 25.00 60.00
TTARTH1 Todd Helton 20.00 50.00
TTARTH2 Todd Helton 20.00 50.00
TTARTH3 Todd Helton 20.00 50.00
TTARTHU1 Torii Hunter
TTARTHU2 Torii Hunter
TTARTL1 Tim Lincecum
TTARTL2 Tim Lincecum
TTARTL3 Tim Lincecum
TTARTL4 Tim Lincecum
TTARTS1 Trevor Story EXCH 30.00 80.00
TTARTS2 Trevor Story EXCH 30.00 80.00
TTARTS3 Trevor Story EXCH 30.00 80.00
TTARTS4 Trevor Story EXCH 30.00 80.00
TTARTS5 Trevor Story EXCH 30.00 80.00
TTARVGJ1 Vladimir Guerrero Jr. 40.00 100.00
TTARVGJ2 Vladimir Guerrero Jr. 40.00 100.00
TTARVGJ3 Vladimir Guerrero Jr. 40.00 100.00
TTARVGJ4 Vladimir Guerrero Jr. 40.00 100.00
TTARVGJ5 Vladimir Guerrero Jr. 40.00 100.00
TTARVR1 Victor Robles 10.00 25.00
TTARVR2 Victor Robles 10.00 25.00
TTARVR3 Victor Robles 10.00 25.00
TTARVR4 Victor Robles 10.00 25.00
TTARWC1 Willson Contreras 12.00 3.00
TTARWC2 Willson Contreras 12.00 30.00
TTARWC3 Willson Contreras 12.00 30.00
TTARWC4 Willson Contreras 12.00 30.00
TTARWCL1 Will Clark 30.00 80.00
TTARWCL2 Will Clark 30.00 80.00
TTARXB1 Xander Bogaerts 25.00 60.00
TTARXB2 Xander Bogaerts 25.00 60.00
TTARXB3 Xander Bogaerts 25.00 60.00
TTARXB4 Xander Bogaerts 25.00 60.00
TTARXB5 Xander Bogaerts 25.00 60.00
TTARYM1 Yadier Molina 60.00 150.00
TTARYM2 Yadier Molina 60.00 150.00
TTARYM3 Yadier Molina 60.00 150.00
TTARYM4 Yadier Molina 60.00 150.00

2020 Topps Triple Threads Autograph Relics Gold

*GOLD: .5X TO 1.2X BASIC
STATED ODDS 1:XX HOBBY
STATED PRINT RUN 9 SER.#'d SETS
SOME NOT PRICED DUE TO SCARCITY
EXCHANGE DEADLINE 8/31/2022
TTARAB1 Adrian Beltre 40.00 100.00
TTARAJU1 Aaron Judge 125.00 300.00
TTARAR1 Anthony Rizzo 40.00 100.00
TTARBH1 Bryce Harper 125.00 300.00
TTARCJ1 Chipper Jones
TTARCKE1 Clayton Kershaw 75.00 200.00
TTARDO1 David Ortiz 40.00 100.00
TTARJG1 Joey Gallo 20.00 50.00
TTARJV1 Joey Votto 30.00 80.00
TTARMC1 Miguel Cabrera 60.00 150.00
TTARRS1 Ryne Sandberg 75.00 200.00
TTARTHU1 Torii Hunter 12.00 3.00

2020 Topps Triple Threads Legend Relics

STATED ODDS 1:XX HOBBY
STATED PRINT RUN 36 SER.#'d SETS
*SILVER/27: .4X TO 1X BASIC
RLCAR Alex Rodriguez 20.00 50.00
RLCBL Barry Larkin 12.00 30.00
RLCCJ Chipper Jones 15.00 40.00
RLCCR Cal Ripken Jr. 20.00 50.00
RLCI Ichiro 30.00 80.00
RLCJB Johnny Bench 20.00 50.00
RLCKG Ken Griffey Jr. 30.00 80.00
RLCLB Lou Brock 12.00 30.00
RLCMM Mark McGwire 12.00 30.00
RLCMP Mike Piazza 10.00 25.00
RLCMS Mike Schmidt 12.00 30.00
RLCPM Pedro Martinez 6.00 15.00
RLCRC Rod Carew 6.00 15.00
RLCRJ Reggie Jackson 12.00 30.00
RLCRJO Randy Johnson 10.00 25.00
RLCRY Robin Yount 10.00 25.00
RLCSC Steve Carlton 12.00 30.00
RLCTG Tony Gwynn 12.00 30.00

2020 Topps Triple Threads Legend Relics Amethyst

*AMETHYST: .4X TO 1X BASIC
STATED ODDS 1:XX HOBBY
STATED PRINT RUN 27 SER.#'d SETS
RLCTM Thurman Munson 75.00 200.00
RLCVG Ted Williams 40.00 100.00
RLCWM Willie Mays 40.00 100.00

2020 Topps Triple Threads Legend Relics Emerald

*EMERALD: .4X TO 1X BASIC
STATED ODDS 1:XX HOBBY
STATED PRINT RUN 18 SER.#'d SETS
RLCBG Bob Gibson 15.00 40.00
RLCTM Thurman Munson 75.00 200.00
RLCVG Ted Williams 40.00 100.00
RLCWM Willie Mays 40.00 100.00

2020 Topps Triple Threads Relic Combos

STATED ODDS 1:XX HOBBY
STATED PRINT RUN 36 SER.#'d SETS
*AMETHYST/27: .4X TO 1X BASIC
*EMERALD/18: .5X TO 1.2X BASIC
RCCACA Alvarez/Altuve/Correa 12.00 30.00
RCCAFA Acuna Jr./Albies/Freeman 20.00 50.00
RCCAGC Gallo/Andrus/Calhoun 5.00 12.00
RCCATG Guerrero Jr./Tatis Jr./Acuna Jr. 40.00 100.00
RCCBAS Story/Arenado/Blackmon 8.00 20.00
RCCBDC Devers/Bogaerts/Chavis 10.00 25.00
RCCBGB Bichette/Guerrero Jr./Biggio 12.00 30.00
RCCBKR Rosario/Kepler/Berrios 8.00 20.00
RCCBMB Martinez/Benintendi/Bogaerts 6.00 15.00
RCCCJS Sanchez/Sabathia/Judge 15.00 40.00
RCCCOS Semien/Olson/Chapman 6.00 15.00
RCCCYH Hiura/Cain/Yelich 8.00 20.00
RCCDCL Davis/Chapman/Luzardo 6.00 15.00
RCCGIR Griffey Jr./Rodriguez/Ichiro 25.00 60.00
RCCGMF Molina/Flaherty/Goldschmidt 15.00 40.00
RCCGSM McKay/Snell/Glasnow 5.00 12.00
RCCGVB Gray/Bauer/Votto 15.00 40.00
RCCHHM Harper/McCutchen/Hoskins 20.00 50.00
RCCHNR Nola/Realmuto/Hoskins 20.00 50.00

RCCKBB Bellinger/Kershaw/Buehler 20.00 50.00
RCCLGV Votto/Griffey Jr./Larkin 25.00 60.00
RCCLMK Lowe/Kiermaier/Meadows 5.00 12.00
RCCLRS Lindor/Santana/Reyes 8.00 20.00
RCCMAJ Moncada/Jimenez/Abreu 15.00 40.00
RCCMCR Conforto/McNeil/Rosario 12.00 30.00
RCCMGT McGwire/Griffey Jr./Thomas 30.00 80.00
RCCMOP Pedroia/Martinez/Ortiz 15.00 40.00
RCCPBY Posey/Pence/Yaz 12.00 30.00
RCCPTO Trout/Ohtani/Pujols 30.00 80.00
RCCRBB Baez/Rizzo/Bryant 15.00 40.00
RCCRBC Rizzo/Baez/Contreras 12.00 30.00
RCCRRB Beltre/Rodriguez/Rodriguez 15.00 40.00
RCCRRM Ripken Jr./Murray/Robinson 15.00 40.00
RCCSHH Schwarber/Hoerner/Happ 12.00 30.00
RCCSJG Glavine/Jones/Smoltz 25.00 60.00
RCCSRO Riley/Soroka/Swanson 6.00 15.00
RCCSSS Scherzer/Strasburg/Corbin 8.00 20.00
RCCSTG Soto/Tatis Jr./Guerrero Jr. 25.00 60.00
RCCSVS Suarez/Senzel/Votto 10.00 25.00
RCCSWA Wright/Alonso/Strawberry 12.00 30.00
RCCTBY Trout/Bellinger/Yelich 30.00 80.00
RCCTJR Jimenez/Thomas/Robert 60.00 150.00
RCCTJS Stanton/Judge/Torres 20.00 50.00
RCCTSR Soto/Robles/Turner 10.00 25.00
RCCVBS Verlander/Springer/Bregman 8.00 20.00
RCCWHA Walker/Arenado/Helton 10.00 25.00

2020 Topps Triple Threads Relics

STATED ODDS 1:XX MINI BOX
STATED PRINT RUN 36 SER.#'d SETS
*SILVER/27: .4X TO 1X BASIC
*EMERALD/18: .5X TO 1.2X BASIC
*GOLD/9: .6X TO 1.5X BASIC
ALL VERSIONS EQUALLY PRICED
TTRAA1 Aristides Aquino 6.00 15.00
TTRAA2 Aristides Aquino 6.00 15.00
TTRAA3 Aristides Aquino 6.00 15.00
TTRAB Andrew Benintendi 4.00 10.00
TTRAB2 Andrew Benintendi 4.00 10.00
TTRAB3 Andrew Benintendi 4.00 10.00
TTRAB4 Andrew Benintendi 4.00 10.00
TTRABR Alex Bregman 4.00 10.00
TTRABR2 Alex Bregman 4.00 10.00
TTRABR3 Alex Bregman 4.00 10.00
TTRABR4 Alex Bregman 4.00 10.00
TTRAJ Aaron Judge 12.00 30.00
TTRAJ2 Aaron Judge 12.00 30.00
TTRAM Austin Meadows 4.00 10.00
TTRAM2 Austin Meadows 4.00 10.00
TTRAM3 Austin Meadows 4.00 10.00
TTRAN1 Aaron Nola 3.00 8.00
TTRAN2 Aaron Nola 3.00 8.00
TTRAN3 Aaron Nola 3.00 8.00
TTRARO Amed Rosario 3.00 8.00
TTRARO2 Amed Rosario 3.00 8.00
TTRARO3 Amed Rosario 3.00 8.00
TTRAUR1 Austin Riley 5.00 12.00
TTRAUR2 Austin Riley 5.00 12.00
TTRAUR3 Austin Riley 5.00 12.00
TTRBB1 Bo Bichette 10.00 25.00
TTRBB2 Bo Bichette 10.00 25.00
TTRBEL Josh Bell 3.00 8.00
TTRBEL2 Josh Bell 3.00 8.00
TTRBEL3 Josh Bell 3.00 8.00
TTRBH1 Bryce Harper 12.00 30.00
TTRBH2 Bryce Harper 12.00 30.00
TTRBL1 Brandon Lowe 3.00 8.00
TTRBL2 Brandon Lowe 3.00 8.00
TTRBL3 Brandon Lowe 3.00 8.00
TTRBP Buster Posey 5.00 12.00
TTRBP2 Buster Posey 5.00 12.00
TTRBP3 Buster Posey 5.00 12.00
TTRCB Cody Bellinger 6.00 15.00
TTRCB2 Cody Bellinger 6.00 15.00
TTRCB3 Cody Bellinger 6.00 15.00
TTRCB4 Cody Bellinger 6.00 15.00
TTRCS CC Sabathia 5.00 12.00
TTRCS2 CC Sabathia 5.00 12.00
TTRCS3 CC Sabathia 5.00 12.00
TTRCY Christian Yelich 6.00 15.00
TTRCY2 Christian Yelich 6.00 15.00
TTRCY3 Christian Yelich 6.00 15.00
TTRDD1 David Dahl 2.50 6.00
TTRDD2 David Dahl 2.50 6.00
TTRDD3 David Dahl 2.50 6.00
TTRDO David Ortiz 10.00 25.00
TTRDO2 David Ortiz 10.00 25.00
TTRDO3 David Ortiz 10.00 25.00
TTRDSW Dansby Swanson 6.00 15.00
TTRDSW2 Dansby Swanson 6.00 15.00
TTRDSW3 Dansby Swanson 6.00 15.00
TTRDSW4 Dansby Swanson 6.00 15.00
TTRFF1 Freddie Freeman 8.00 20.00
TTRFF2 Freddie Freeman 8.00 20.00
TTRFF3 Freddie Freeman 8.00 20.00
TTRFL Francisco Lindor 6.00 15.00
TTRFL2 Francisco Lindor 6.00 15.00
TTRFL3 Francisco Lindor 6.00 15.00
TTRFTJ Fernando Tatis Jr. 20.00 50.00
TTRFTJ2 Fernando Tatis Jr. 20.00 50.00
TTRFTJ3 Fernando Tatis Jr. 20.00 50.00
TTRGS George Springer 6.00 15.00
TTRGS2 George Springer 6.00 15.00
TTRGS3 George Springer 6.00 15.00
TTRGS4 George Springer 6.00 15.00
TTRGSA1 Gary Sanchez 5.00 12.00
TTRGSA2 Gary Sanchez 5.00 12.00
TTRGSA3 Gary Sanchez 5.00 12.00
TTRGSA4 Gary Sanchez 5.00 12.00
TTRGST Giancarlo Stanton 6.00 15.00
TTRGST2 Giancarlo Stanton 6.00 15.00
TTRGST3 Giancarlo Stanton 6.00 15.00
TTRJA Jose Abreu 6.00 15.00
TTRJA2 Jose Abreu 6.00 15.00
TTRJB1 Javier Baez 8.00 20.00
TTRJB2 Javier Baez 8.00 20.00
TTRJB3 Javier Baez 8.00 20.00
TTRJBE1 Jose Berrios 4.00 10.00
TTRJBE2 Jose Berrios 4.00 10.00
TTRJBE3 Jose Berrios 4.00 10.00
TTRJG1 Joey Gallo 4.00 10.00
TTRJG2 Joey Gallo 4.00 10.00
TTRJG3 Joey Gallo 4.00 10.00
TTRJMC1 Jeff McNeil 3.00 8.00
TTRJMC2 Jeff McNeil 3.00 8.00
TTRJMC3 Jeff McNeil 3.00 8.00
TTRJOA Jose Altuve 5.00 12.00
TTRJOA2 Jose Altuve 5.00 12.00
TTRJOA3 Jose Altuve 5.00 12.00
TTRJOA4 Jose Altuve 5.00 12.00
TTRJS Juan Soto 10.00 25.00
TTRJS2 Juan Soto 10.00 25.00
TTRJSO1 Jorge Soler 4.00 10.00
TTRJSO2 Jorge Soler 4.00 10.00
TTRJSO3 Jorge Soler 4.00 10.00
TTRJV1 Joey Votto 8.00 20.00
TTRJV2 Joey Votto 8.00 20.00
TTRJV3 Joey Votto 8.00 20.00
TTRKH Keston Hiura 5.00 12.00
TTRKH2 Keston Hiura 5.00 12.00
TTRKH3 Keston Hiura 5.00 12.00
TTRMC Miguel Cabrera 6.00 15.00
TTRMC2 Miguel Cabrera 6.00 15.00
TTRMC3 Miguel Cabrera 6.00 15.00
TTRMC4 Miguel Cabrera 6.00 15.00
TTRMCC1 Andrew McCutchen 6.00 15.00
TTRMCC2 Andrew McCutchen 10.00 25.00
TTRMCC3 Andrew McCutchen 6.00 15.00
TTRMCC4 Andrew McCutchen 6.00 15.00
TTRMCH1 Matt Chapman 6.00 15.00
TTRMCH2 Matt Chapman 6.00 15.00
TTRMCH3 Matt Chapman 6.00 15.00
TTRMCO1 Michael Conforto 5.00 12.00
TTRMCO2 Michael Conforto 5.00 12.00
TTRMCO3 Michael Conforto 5.00 12.00
TTRMK1 Max Kepler 6.00 15.00
TTRMK2 Max Kepler 6.00 15.00
TTRMK3 Max Kepler 6.00 15.00
TTRMO Matt Olson 4.00 10.00
TTRMO2 Matt Olson 4.00 10.00
TTRMO3 Matt Olson 4.00 10.00
TTRMS Max Scherzer 4.00 10.00
TTRMS2 Max Scherzer 4.00 10.00
TTRMSE1 Marcus Semien 4.00 10.00
TTRMSE2 Marcus Semien 4.00 10.00
TTRMSE3 Marcus Semien 4.00 10.00
TTRMT Mike Trout 40.00 100.00
TTRMT2 Mike Trout 40.00 100.00
TTRMT3 Mike Trout 40.00 100.00
TTRMT4 Mike Trout 40.00 100.00
TTRMTA1 Masahiro Tanaka 6.00 15.00
TTRMTA2 Masahiro Tanaka 6.00 15.00
TTRMTA3 Masahiro Tanaka 6.00 15.00
TTRNA Nolan Arenado 6.00 15.00
TTRNA2 Nolan Arenado 6.00 15.00
TTRNA3 Nolan Arenado 6.00 15.00
TTRNS1 Nick Senzel 4.00 10.00
TTRNS2 Nick Senzel 4.00 10.00
TTRNS3 Nick Senzel 4.00 10.00
TTROA Ozzie Albies 5.00 12.00
TTROA2 Ozzie Albies 5.00 12.00
TTROA3 Ozzie Albies 5.00 12.00
TTROA4 Ozzie Albies 5.00 12.00
TTRPD1 Paul DeJong 4.00 10.00
TTRPD2 Paul DeJong 4.00 10.00
TTRPD3 Paul DeJong 4.00 10.00
TTRRD Rafael Devers 5.00 12.00
TTRRD2 Rafael Devers 5.00 12.00
TTRRD3 Rafael Devers 5.00 12.00
TTRRD4 Rafael Devers 5.00 12.00
TTRRH Rhys Hoskins 5.00 12.00
TTRRH2 Rhys Hoskins 5.00 12.00
TTRRH3 Rhys Hoskins 5.00 12.00
TTRRIZ1 Anthony Rizzo 8.00 20.00
TTRRIZ2 Anthony Rizzo 8.00 20.00
TTRRIZ3 Anthony Rizzo 8.00 20.00
TTRSG1 Sonny Gray 3.00 8.00
TTRSG2 Sonny Gray 3.00 8.00
TTRSG3 Sonny Gray 3.00 8.00
TTRSTR1 Stephen Strasburg 5.00 12.00
TTRSTR2 Stephen Strasburg 5.00 12.00
TTRSTR3 Stephen Strasburg 5.00 12.00
TTRTS1 Trevor Story 4.00 10.00
TTRTS2 Trevor Story 4.00 10.00
TTRTS3 Trevor Story 4.00 10.00
TTRTS4 Trevor Story 4.00 10.00
TTRTT1 Trea Turner 3.00 8.00
TTRTT2 Trea Turner 3.00 8.00
TTRTT3 Trea Turner 5.00 12.00
TTRVGJ Vladimir Guerrero Jr. 6.00 15.00
TTRVGJ2 Vladimir Guerrero Jr. 6.00 15.00
TTRVGJ3 Vladimir Guerrero Jr. 6.00 15.00
TTRWC Willson Contreras 4.00 10.00
TTRWC2 Willson Contreras 4.00 10.00
TTRWC3 Willson Contreras 4.00 10.00
TTRXB Xander Bogaerts 6.00 15.00
TTRXB2 Xander Bogaerts 6.00 15.00
TTRXB3 Xander Bogaerts 6.00 15.00
TTRXB4 Xander Bogaerts 6.00 15.00
TTRYM1 Yadier Molina 15.00 40.00
TTRYM2 Yadier Molina 15.00 40.00
TTRYM3 Yadier Molina 15.00 40.00

2020 Topps Triple Threads Rookie Autographs

STATED ODDS 1:XXX HOBBY
STATED PRINT RUN 99 SER.#'d SETS
EXCHANGE DEADLINE 8/31/2022
PRINTING PLATE ODDS 1:XXX MINI BOX
PLATE PRINT RUN 1 SET PER COLOR
BLACK-CYAN-MAGENTA-YELLOW ISSUED
NO PLATE PRICING DUE TO SCARCITY
*EMERALD/50: .4X TO 1X BASIC
*GOLD/25: .5X TO 1.2X BASIC
RACAA Adbert Alzolay 6.00 15.00
RACAQ Aristides Aquino 10.00 25.00
RACAT Abraham Toro 5.00 12.00
RACBA Bryan Abreu 4.00 10.00
RACBB Bo Bichette EXCH 75.00 200.00
RACBM Brendan McKay 6.00 15.00
RACBQ Bobby Bradley 4.00 10.00
RACDC Dylan Cease 6.00 15.00
RACDM Dustin May 20.00 50.00
RACHH Hunter Harvey 6.00 15.00
RACJK James Karinchak 20.00 50.00
RACJS Josh Staumont 4.00 10.00
RACJU Jose Urquidy 5.00 12.00
RACJY Jordan Yamamoto 4.00 10.00
RACKH Kwang-Hyun Kim 15.00 40.00
RACLR Luis Robert 125.00 300.00
RACMB Mike Brosseau 8.00 20.00
RACMD Mauricio Dubon 6.00 15.00
RACMT Matt Thaiss 5.00 12.00
RACMZ Michel Baez 4.00 10.00
RACNH Nico Hoerner 15.00 40.00
RACNS Nick Solak 8.00 20.00
RACRA Randy Arozarena 75.00 200.00
RACRG Robel Garcia 4.00 10.00
RACSA Shogo Akiyama 8.00 20.00
RACSY Shun Yamaguchi 5.00 12.00
RACTGO Tony Gonsolin 10.00 25.00
RACYD Yonathan Daza 5.00 12.00
RACYT Yoshi Tsutsugo 10.00 25.00
RACZG Zac Gallen 8.00 20.00

2020 Topps Triple Threads Single Jumbo Relic Autographs

STATED ODDS 1:XX HOBBY
STATED PRINT RUN 99 SER.#'d SETS
EXCHANGE DEADLINE 8/31/2022
ASJRAA Aristides Aquino 12.00 30.00
ASJRAAL Adbert Alzolay 8.00 20.00
ASJRAB Andrew Benintendi 10.00 25.00
ASJRAC Aaron Civale 8.00 20.00
ASJRAN Aaron Nola 10.00 25.00
ASJRAR Austin Riley 12.00 30.00
ASJRAY Alex Young 4.00 10.00
ASJRBL Brandon Lowe 5.00 12.00
ASJRBM Brendan McKay 6.00 15.00
ASJRBR Bryan Reynolds 5.00 12.00
ASJRBRO Brendan Rodgers 6.00 15.00
ASJRBS Blake Snell 10.00 25.00
ASJRCB Cavan Biggio 8.00 20.00
ASJRCF Clint Frazier 10.00 25.00
ASJRCK Carter Kieboom 5.00 12.00
ASJRCP Chris Paddack 8.00 20.00
ASJRCS Corey Seager 25.00 60.00
ASJRDC Dylan Cease 6.00 15.00
ASJRDJ Danny Jansen 4.00 10.00
ASJRDP David Peralta 4.00 10.00
ASJRDS Dansby Swanson 20.00 50.00
ASJRDSM Dominic Smith 8.00 20.00
ASJRDV Daniel Vogelbach 4.00 10.00
ASJRES Eugenio Suarez 8.00 20.00
ASJRFT Fernando Tatis Jr. 75.00 200.00
ASJRGL Gavin Lux 20.00 50.00
ASJRIH Ian Happ 15.00 40.00
ASJRJF Jack Flaherty 12.00 30.00
ASJRJL Jesus Luzardo 8.00 20.00
ASJRJM Jeff McNeil 8.00 20.00
ASJRJR J.T. Realmuto 10.00 25.00
ASJRJRO Jake Rogers 4.00 10.00
ASJRJY Jordan Yamamoto 4.00 10.00
ASJRKN Kevin Newman 6.00 15.00
ASJRKT Kyle Tucker 8.00 20.00
ASJRLC Luis Castillo 5.00 12.00
ASJRLG Lourdes Gurriel Jr. 5.00 12.00
ASJRLV Luke Voit 10.00 25.00
ASJRMA Miguel Andujar 8.00 20.00
ASJRMCH Michael Chavis 8.00 20.00
ASJRMD Mauricio Dubon 10.00 25.00
ASJRMH Mitch Haniger 5.00 12.00
ASJRMK Max Kepler EXCH 8.00 20.00
ASJRMMI Miles Mikolas 4.00 10.00
ASJRMS Mike Soroka 12.00 30.00
ASJRMT Matt Thaiss 5.00 12.00
ASJRNH Nico Hoerner 10.00 25.00
ASJRNS Nick Solak 8.00 20.00
ASJRNSE Nick Senzel 8.00 20.00
ASJRNSY Noah Syndergaard 10.00 25.00
ASJRPd Paul DeJong 6.00 15.00
ASJRRD Rafael Devers 12.00 30.00
ASJRRH Rhys Hoskins 15.00 40.00
ASJRRL Ramon Laureano 8.00 20.00
ASJRRM Ryan McMahon 6.00 15.00
ASJRRO Ryan O'Hearn 4.00 10.00
ASJRSA Shogo Akiyama 8.00 20.00
ASJRSB Seth Brown 4.00 10.00
ASJRSK Scott Kingery 5.00 12.00
ASJRSY Shun Yamaguchi EXCH 5.00 12.00
ASJRTA Tim Anderson 12.00 30.00
ASJRVR Victor Robles 8.00 20.00
ASJRWC Willson Contreras 8.00 20.00
ASJRWS Will Smith 10.00 25.00
ASJRXB Xander Bogaerts 12.00 30.00
ASJRYA Yordan Alvarez 30.00 80.00
ASJRYG Yasmani Grandal 4.00 10.00

2020 Topps Triple Threads Single Jumbo Relic Autographs Amethyst

*AMETHYST: .4X TO 1X BASIC
STATED ODDS 1:XX HOBBY
STATED PRINT RUN 75 SER.#'d SETS
EXCHANGE DEADLINE 8/31/2022
ASJRABR Alex Bregman 20.00 50.00
ASJRKH Keston Hiura 10.00 25.00
ASJRKL Kyle Lewis 30.00 80.00
ASJRMKO Michael Kopech 8.00 20.00
ASJRMO Matt Olson 6.00 15.00
ASJRPG Paul Goldschmidt 15.00 40.00
ASJRRA Ronald Acuna Jr. 75.00 200.00
ASJRRD Rafael Devers 20.00 50.00
ASJRTG Trent Grisham 123.00

2020 Topps Triple Threads Single Jumbo Relic Autographs Emerald

*EMERALD: .5X TO 1.2X BASIC
STATED ODDS 1:XX HOBBY
STATED PRINT RUN 50 SER.#'d SETS
EXCHANGE DEADLINE 8/31/2022
ASJRABR Alex Bregman 25.00 60.00
ASJRJA Jose Altuve EXCH 12.00 30.00
ASJRJH Josh Hader 5.00 12.00
ASJRKH Keston Hiura 12.00 30.00
ASJRKL Kyle Lewis 40.00 100.00
ASJRMKO Michael Kopech 10.00 25.00
ASJRMO Matt Olson 8.00 20.00
ASJRPG Paul Goldschmidt 20.00 50.00
ASJRRA Ronald Acuna Jr. 100.00 250.00
ASJRRD Rafael Devers 25.00 60.00
ASJRTG Trent Grisham 15.00 40.00
ASJRTM Trey Mancini 8.00 20.00
ASJRVG Vladimir Guerrero Jr. 25.00 60.00

2020 Topps Triple Threads Single Jumbo Relic Autographs Gold

*GOLD: .6X TO 1.5X BASIC
STATED ODDS 1:XX HOBBY
STATED PRINT RUN 25 SER.#'d SETS
EXCHANGE DEADLINE 8/31/2022
ASJRAAL Adbert Alzolay 20.00 50.00
ASJRABR Alex Bregman 30.00 80.00
ASJRARO Amed Rosario 8.00
ASJRJA Jose Altuve EXCH 15.00 40.00
ASJRJH Josh Hader 6.00 15.00
ASJRKH Keston Hiura 15.00 40.00
ASJRKL Kyle Lewis 50.00 125.00
ASJRLR Luis Robert 125.00 300.00
ASJRMKO Michael Kopech 12.00 30.00
ASJRMO Matt Olson 10.00 25.00
ASJRPG Paul Goldschmidt 25.00 60.00
ASJRRA Ronald Acuna Jr. 125.00 300.00
ASJRRD Rafael Devers 30.00 80.00
ASJRTG Trent Grisham 20.00 50.00
ASJRTM Trey Mancini 10.00 25.00
ASJRVG Vladimir Guerrero Jr. 30.00 80.00

2020 Topps Triple Threads Single Jumbo Relics

STATED ODDS 1:XX HOBBY
STATED PRINT RUN 36 SER.#'d SETS
*SILVER/27: .4X TO 1X BASIC
*EMERALD/18: .5X TO 1.2X BASIC
*GOLD/9: .6X TO 1.5X BASIC
ALL VERSIONS EQUALLY PRICED
SJRAA Aristides Aquino 6.00 15.00
SJRAAL Adbert Alzolay 3.00 8.00
SJRAAQ Aristides Aquino 6.00 15.00
SJRAB Andrew Benintendi 4.00 10.00
SJRABE Alex Bregman 4.00 10.00
SJRABN Andrew Benintendi 4.00 10.00
SJRABR Alex Bregman 4.00 10.00
SJRAC Aroldis Chapman 4.00 10.00
SJRACH Aroldis Chapman 4.00 10.00
SJRAJ Aaron Judge 12.00 30.00
SJRAJU Aaron Judge 12.00 30.00
SJRAM Andrew McCutchen 6.00 15.00
SJRAMC Andrew McCutchen 6.00 15.00
SJRAME Austin Meadows 4.00 10.00
SJRAMU Andres Munoz 4.00 10.00
SJRAN Aaron Nola 3.00 8.00
SJRANO Aaron Nola 3.00 8.00
SJRAP A.J. Puk 4.00 10.00
SJRAPU A.J. Puk 4.00 10.00
SJRAR Anthony Rizzo 8.00 20.00
SJRARI Anthony Rizzo 8.00 20.00
SJRARL Austin Riley 5.00 12.00
SJRARO Amed Rosario 3.00 8.00
SJRARS Amed Rosario 3.00 8.00
SJRARY Austin Riley 5.00 12.00
SJRAV Alex Verdugo 6.00 15.00
SJRAVE Alex Verdugo 6.00 15.00
SJRBA Brian Anderson 2.50 6.00
SJRBB Bo Bichette 10.00 25.00
SJRBBI Bo Bichette 10.00 50.00
SJRBBR Bobby Bradley 2.50 6.00
SJRBH Bryce Harper 12.00 30.00
SJRBHA Bryce Harper 12.00 30.00
SJRBL Brandon Lowe 3.00 8.00
SJRBLO Brandon Lowe 3.00 8.00
SJRBM Brendan McKay 4.00 10.00
SJRBMC Brendan McKay 4.00 10.00
SJRBP Buster Posey 5.00 12.00
SJRBPO Buster Posey 5.00 12.00
SJRBR Bryan Reynolds 3.00 8.00
SJRBRD Brendan Rodgers 4.00 10.00
SJRBRE Bryan Reynolds 3.00 8.00
SJRBRO Brendan Rodgers 4.00 10.00
SJRBS Blake Snell 3.00 8.00
SJRBSN Blake Snell 3.00 8.00
SJRCB Cavan Biggio 5.00 12.00
SJRCBE Cody Bellinger 6.00 15.00
SJRCBI Cavan Biggio 5.00 12.00
SJRCC Carlos Correa 4.00 10.00
SJRCCO Carlos Correa 4.00 10.00
SJRCF Clint Frazier 3.00 8.00
SJRCFR Clint Frazier 3.00 8.00
SJRCK Clayton Kershaw 6.00 15.00
SJRCKB Carter Kieboom 3.00 8.00
SJRCKE Clayton Kershaw 6.00 15.00
SJRCKI Carter Kieboom 3.00 8.00
SJRCP Chris Paddack 4.00 10.00
SJRCPA Chris Paddack 4.00 10.00
SJRCS Chris Sale 4.00 10.00
SJRCSA Chris Sale 4.00 10.00
SJRCSE Corey Seager 6.00 15.00
SJRCSG Corey Seager 6.00 15.00
SJRCY Christian Yelich 6.00 15.00
SJRCYE Christian Yelich 6.00 15.00
SJRDC Dylan Cease 4.00 10.00
SJRDCE Dylan Cease 4.00 10.00
SJRDD David Dahl 2.50 6.00
SJRDDA David Dahl 2.50 6.00
SJRDL DJ LeMahieu 6.00 15.00
SJRDLE DJ LeMahieu 6.00 15.00
SJRDM Dustin May 8.00 20.00
SJRDMA Dustin May 8.00 20.00
SJRDP Dustin Pedroia 4.00 10.00
SJRDPE Dustin Pedroia 4.00 10.00
SJRDS Dansby Swanson 6.00 15.00
SJRDSW Dansby Swanson 6.00 15.00
SJRDV Daniel Vogelbach 2.50 6.00
SJREH Eric Hosmer 3.00 8.00
SJREHO Eric Hosmer 3.00 8.00
SJREJ Eloy Jimenez 5.00 12.00
SJREJI Eloy Jimenez 5.00 12.00
SJRER Eduardo Rodriguez 2.50 6.00
SJRERO Eduardo Rodriguez 2.50 6.00
SJRFF Freddie Freeman 8.00 20.00
SJRFFR Freddie Freeman 8.00 20.00
SJRFL Francisco Lindor 6.00 15.00
SJRFLI Francisco Lindor 6.00 15.00
SJRFT Fernando Tatis Jr. 20.00 50.00
SJRFTA Fernando Tatis Jr. 20.00 50.00
SJRGC Griffin Canning 4.00 10.00
SJRGL Gavin Lux 6.00 15.00
SJRGLU Gavin Lux 6.00 15.00
SJRGS George Springer 6.00 15.00
SJRGSA Gary Sanchez 5.00 12.00
SJRGSN Gary Sanchez 5.00 12.00
SJRGT Gleyber Torres 8.00 20.00
SJRGTO Gleyber Torres 8.00 20.00
SJRGU Gio Urshela 4.00 10.00
SJRHD Hunter Dozier 2.50 6.00
SJRHP Hunter Pence 3.00 8.00
SJRIH Ian Happ 6.00 15.00
SJRIHA Ian Happ 6.00 15.00
SJRIHH Ian Happ 6.00 15.00
SJRIHP Ian Happ 6.00 15.00
SJRJA Jose Altuve 5.00 12.00
SJRJAL Jose Altuve 5.00 12.00
SJRJB Javier Baez 8.00 20.00
SJRJBA Javier Baez 8.00 20.00
SJRJBE Jose Berrios 4.00 10.00
SJRJBR Jose Berrios 4.00 10.00
SJRJD Jacob deGrom 6.00 15.00
SJRJDE Jacob deGrom 6.00 15.00
SJRJDN Josh Donaldson 3.00 8.00
SJRJDO Josh Donaldson 3.00 8.00
SJRJF Jack Flaherty 6.00 15.00
SJRJFL Jack Flaherty 6.00 15.00
SJRJG Joey Gallo 4.00 10.00
SJRJH Josh Hader 3.00 8.00
SJRJHA Josh Hader 3.00 8.00
SJRJL Jesus Luzardo 5.00 12.00
SJRJLU Jesus Luzardo 5.00 12.00
SJRJM J.D. Martinez 4.00 10.00
SJRJMA J.D. Martinez 4.00 10.00
SJRJMC Jeff McNeil 3.00 8.00
SJRJMN Jeff McNeil 3.00 8.00
SJRJP Joc Pederson 4.00 10.00
SJRJPE Joc Pederson 4.00 10.00
SJRJR Jose Ramirez 3.00 8.00
SJRJRE J.T. Realmuto 6.00 15.00
SJRJSE Justus Sheffield 4.00 10.00
SJRJSH Justus Sheffield 4.00 10.00
SJRJSL Jorge Soler 4.00 10.00
SJRJT Jameson Taillon 3.00 8.00
SJRJU Julio Urias 8.00 20.00
SJRJUR Julio Urias 8.00 20.00
SJRKB Kris Bryant 5.00 12.00
SJRKBR Kris Bryant 5.00 12.00
SJRKD Khris Davis 4.00 10.00
SJRKDA Khris Davis 4.00 10.00
SJRKH Keston Hiura 5.00 12.00
SJRKHI Keston Hiura 5.00 12.00
SJRKL Kyle Lewis 10.00 25.00
SJRKLE Kyle Lewis 10.00 25.00
SJRKS Kyle Schwarber 4.00 10.00
SJRKSC Kyle Schwarber 4.00 10.00
SJRKT Kyle Tucker 4.00 10.00
SJRKTU Kyle Tucker 4.00 10.00
SJRLC Lorenzo Cain 2.50 6.00
SJRLCL Luis Castillo 3.00 8.00
SJRLCS Luis Castillo 3.00 8.00
SJRLG Lourdes Gurriel Jr. 3.00 8.00
SJRLGR Lourdes Gurriel Jr. 3.00 8.00
SJRLR Luis Robert 30.00 80.00
SJRLRO Luis Robert 30.00 80.00
SJRLS Luis Severino 3.00 8.00
SJRLSE Luis Severino 3.00 8.00
SJRLV Luke Voit 5.00 12.00
SJRLVO Luke Voit 5.00 12.00
SJRMA Miguel Andujar 4.00 10.00
SJRMAN Miguel Andujar 4.00 10.00
SJRMB Matt Boyd 5.00 12.00
SJRMC Mike Clevinger 3.00 8.00
SJRMCA Miguel Cabrera 6.00 15.00
SJRMCB Miguel Cabrera 6.00 15.00
SJRMCH Michael Chavis 3.00 8.00
SJRMCN Matt Chapman 6.00 15.00
SJRMCP Matt Chapman 6.00 15.00
SJRMCR Matt Carpenter 4.00 10.00
SJRMCT Matt Carpenter 4.00 10.00
SJRMCV Michael Chavis 3.00 8.00
SJRMD Mauricio Dubon 3.00 8.00
SJRMDU Mauricio Dubon 3.00 8.00
SJRMG Mitch Garver 2.50 6.00
SJRMH Mitch Haniger 3.00 8.00
SJRMHN Mitch Haniger 3.00 8.00
SJRMK Max Kepler 6.00 15.00
SJRMKE Max Kepler 6.00 15.00
SJRMKO Michael Kopech 5.00 12.00
SJRMKP Michael Kopech 5.00 12.00
SJRMM Max Muncy 3.00 8.00
SJRMMA Manny Machado 4.00 10.00
SJRMMN Manny Machado 4.00 10.00
SJRMMU Max Muncy 3.00 8.00
SJRMO Matt Olson 4.00 10.00
SJRMOL Matt Olson 4.00 10.00
SJRMSC Max Scherzer 4.00 10.00
SJRMSH Max Scherzer 4.00 10.00
SJRMSN Miguel Sano 3.00 8.00
SJRMSO Mike Soroka 4.00 10.00
SJRMSR Mike Soroka 4.00 10.00
SJRMSS Miguel Sano 3.00 8.00
SJRMT Mike Trout 40.00 100.00
SJRMTR Mike Trout 40.00 100.00
SJRNA Nolan Arenado 6.00 15.00
SJRNAR Nolan Arenado 6.00 15.00
SJRNH Nico Hoerner 6.00 15.00
SJRNHO Nico Hoerner 6.00 15.00
SJRNS Noah Syndergaard 3.00 8.00
SJRNSE Nick Senzel 4.00 10.00
SJRNSL Nick Solak 10.00 25.00
SJRNSN Nick Senzel 4.00 10.00
SJRNSO Nick Solak 10.00 25.00
SJRNSY Noah Syndergaard 3.00 8.00
SJROA Ozzie Albies 5.00 12.00
SJROAL Ozzie Albies 5.00 12.00
SJRPA Pete Alonso 6.00 15.00
SJRPAL Pete Alonso 6.00 15.00
SJRPC Patrick Corbin 3.00 8.00
SJRPCO Patrick Corbin 3.00 8.00
SJRPD Paul DeJong 4.00 10.00
SJRPDE Paul DeJong 4.00 10.00
SJRPG Paul Goldschmidt 5.00 12.00
SJRPGO Paul Goldschmidt 5.00 12.00
SJRRA Ronald Acuna Jr. 10.00 25.00
SJRRAC Ronald Acuna Jr. 10.00 25.00
SJRRD Rafael Devers 5.00 12.00
SJRRDE Rafael Devers 5.00 12.00
SJRRG Robel Garcia 2.50 6.00
SJRRGA Robel Garcia 2.50 6.00
SJRRH Rhys Hoskins 5.00 12.00
SJRRHO Rhys Hoskins 5.00 12.00
SJRRL Ramon Laureano 3.00 8.00
SJRRLA Ramon Laureano 3.00 8.00
SJRRM Ryan McMahon 4.00 10.00
SJRRMC Ryan McMahon 4.00 10.00
SJRSA Shogo Akiyama 4.00 10.00
SJRSAK Shogo Akiyama 4.00 10.00
SJRSB Seth Brown 2.50 6.00
SJRSG Sonny Gray 3.00 8.00
SJRSGR Sonny Gray 3.00 8.00
SJRSK Scott Kingery 3.00 8.00
SJRSKI Scott Kingery 3.00 8.00
SJRSM Sean Murphy 4.00 10.00
SJRSO Shohei Ohtani 6.00 15.00
SJRSOH Shohei Ohtani 6.00 15.00
SJRTA Tim Anderson 6.00 15.00
SJRTAN Tim Anderson 6.00 15.00
SJRTE Tommy Edman 4.00 10.00
SJRTED Tommy Edman 4.00 10.00
SJRTG Trent Grisham 6.00 15.00
SJRTGL Tyler Glasnow 4.00 10.00
SJRTGR Trent Grisham 6.00 15.00
SJRTM Trey Mancini 4.00 10.00
SJRTMA Trey Mancini 4.00 10.00
SJRTS Trevor Story 4.00 10.00
SJRTST Trevor Story 4.00 10.00
SJRTT Trea Turner 5.00 12.00
SJRTTU Trea Turner 5.00 12.00
SJRVG Vladimir Guerrero Jr. 6.00 15.00
SJRVR Victor Robles 5.00 12.00
SJRWA Willy Adames 2.50 6.00
SJRWB Walker Buehler 8.00 20.00
SJRWC Willson Contreras 4.00 10.00
SJRWM Whit Merrifield 4.00 10.00
SJRWS Will Smith 6.00 15.00
SJRXB Xander Bogaerts 6.00 15.00
SJRYA Yordan Alvarez 8.00 20.00
SJRYG Yasmani Grandal 2.50 6.00
SJRYM Yadier Molina 15.00 40.00
SJRYMC Yoan Moncada 4.00 10.00
SJRYMN Yoan Moncada 4.00 10.00
SJRYMO Yadier Molina 15.00 40.00
SJRVGU Vladimir Guerrero Jr. 6.00 15.00
SJRVRO Victor Robles 5.00 12.00
SJRWBU Walker Buehler 8.00 20.00
SJRWCN Willson Contreras 4.00 10.00
SJRWSM Will Smith 6.00 15.00
SJRXBO Xander Bogaerts 6.00 15.00
SJRYAL Yordan Alvarez 8.00 20.00
SJRYGI Yuli Gurriel 3.00 8.00
SJRYGR Yasmani Grandal 2.50 6.00
SJRYGU Yuli Gurriel 3.00 8.00

2020 Topps Triple Threads Touch 'Em All Relics

STATED ODDS 1:XX HOBBY
STATED PRINT RUN 18 SER.#'d SETS
TEARABB McKay/Meadows/Lowe 8.00 20.00
TEARAJE Gallo/Beltre/Andrus 12.00 30.00
TEARCNT Blckmn/Arndo/Stry 12.00 30.00
TEARDAM Txra/Rdrgz/Jeter 50.00 120.00
TEARGAJ Brgmn/Sprngr/Altve 15.00 40.00
TEARJVH Soto/Kndrck/Rbls 12.00 30.00
TEARMDK Vglbch/Hngr/Lws 15.00 40.00
TEARMMK Chapman/Olson/Davis 8.00 20.00
TEARXRA Bnntndi/Bgrts/Dvrs 15.00 40.00

2005 Topps Turkey Red

COMPLETE SET (330) 50.00 120.00
COMP.SET w/o SP's (275) 10.00 25.00
COMMON CARD (1-270) .15 .40
COMMON SP (1-270) 3.00 8.00
SP STATED ODDS 1:4 HOBBY/RETAIL
SP CL: 1A/5A/5B/10A/10B/16A/20/25/28/30
SP CL: 55/59/60/70/75A/75B/78/83B/85/87
SP CL: 90/100A/100B/102A/106/110/115/120A
SP CL: 120B/125B/130B/132/149/150/155
SP CL: 160A/160B/170/175/181/184/185/193
SP CL: 195/199/214/220/225A/225B/230A
SP CL: 230B/233/266/270A/270B
COMMON REPRINT .30 .75
REP MINORS .30 .75
REP SEMIS .50 1.25
REP UNLISTED .75 2.00
REP CL: 6/8/14/15/18
COMMON RC (271-300) .25 .60
COMMON RET (301-315) .30 .75
VAR CL: 1/5/10/16/75/83/100/102/120/125
VAR CL: 130/160/225/230/270
TWO VERSIONS OF EACH VARIATION EXIST
1A B.Bonds Grey Uni SP 6.00 15.00
1B B.Bonds White Uni .60 1.50
2 Michael Young .15 .40
3 Jim Edmonds .25 .60
4 Cliff Floyd .15 .40
5A R.Clemens Blue Sky SP 4.00 10.00
5B R.Clemens Yellow Sky SP 4.00 10.00
6 Hal Chase REP .30 .75
7 Shannon Stewart .15 .40
8 Fred Clarke REP .30 .75
9 Travis Hafner .15 .40
10A S.Sosa w/Name SP 3.00 8.00
10B S.Sosa w/o Name SP 3.00 8.00
11 Jermaine Dye .15 .40
12 Lyle Overbay .15 .40
13 Oliver Perez .15 .40
14 Red Dooin REP .30 .75
15 Kid Elberfeld REP .30 .75
16A M.Piazza Blue Uni SP 3.00 8.00
16B M.Piazza Pinstripe .40 1.00
17 Bret Boone .15 .40
18 Hughie Jennings REP .60 1.50
19 Jeff Francis .15 .40
20 Manny Ramirez SP 3.00 8.00
21 Russ Ortiz .15 .40
22 Carlos Zambrano .25 .60
23 Luis Castillo .15 .40
24 David DeJesus .15 .40
25 Carlos Beltran SP 3.00 8.00
26 Doug Davis .15 .40
27 Bobby Abreu .15 .40
28 Rich Harden SP 3.00 8.00
29 Brian Giles .15 .40
30 Richie Sexson SP 3.00 8.00
31 Nick Johnson .15 .40
32 Roy Halladay .25 .60
33 Andy Pettitte .25 .60
34 Miguel Cabrera .40 1.00
35 Jeff Kent .15 .40
36 Chone Figgins .15 .40
37 Carlos Lee .15 .40
38 Greg Maddux .50 1.25
39 Preston Wilson .15 .40
40 Chipper Jones .40 1.00
41 Coco Crisp .15 .40
42 Adam Dunn .25 .60
43 Out At Second M.Tejada CL .25 .60
44 Sheffield At Bat CL .15 .40
45 Play At the Plate J.Lopez CL .15 .40
46 Rolen Diggin' In CL .25 .60
47 Helton With the Slap Tag CL .25 .60
48 Clemens Bringing Heat CL .50 1.25
49 A Close Play J.Rollins CL .25 .60
50 Ichiro At Bat CL .50 1.25
51 Can of Corn C.Floyd CL .15 .40
52 Pulling String J.Santana CL .25 .60
53 Mark Teixeira .25 .60
54 Chris Carpenter .25 .60
55 Roy Oswalt SP 3.00 8.00
56 Casey Kotchman .15 .40
57 Torii Hunter .15 .40
58 Jose Reyes .25 .60
59 Wily Mo Pena SP 3.00 8.00
60 Magglio Ordonez SP 3.00 8.00
61 Aaron Miles .15 .40
62 Dallas McPherson .15 .40
63 Javy Lopez .15 .40
64 Luis Gonzalez .15 .40
65 David Ortiz .40 1.00
66 Jorge Posada .25 .60
67 Xavier Nady .15 .40
68 Larry Walker .25 .60
69 Mark Loretta .15 .40
70 Jim Thome SP 3.00 8.00
71 Livan Hernandez .15 .40
72 Garrett Atkins .15 .40
73 Milton Bradley .15 .40
74 B.J. Upton .25 .60
75A I.Suzuki w/Name SP 4.00 10.00
75B I.Suzuki w/o Name SP 4.00 10.00
76 Aramis Ramirez .15 .40
77 Eric Milton .15 .40
78 Troy Glaus SP 3.00 8.00
79 David Newhan .15 .40
80 Delmon Young .40 1.00
81 Justin Morneau .25 .60
82 Ramon Ortiz .15 .40
83A E.Chavez Blue Sky .15 .40
83B E.Chavez Purple Sky SP 3.00 8.00
84 Sean Burroughs .15 .40
85 Scott Rolen SP 3.00 8.00
86 Rocco Baldelli .15 .40
87 Joe Mauer SP 4.00 10.00
88 Tony Womack .15 .40
89 Ken Griffey Jr. .75 2.00
90 Alfonso Soriano SP 3.00 8.00
91 Paul Konerko .25 .60
92 Guillermo Mota .15 .40
93 Lance Berkman .25 .60
94 Mark Buehrle .25 .60
95 Matt Clement .15 .40
96 Melvin Mora .15 .40
97 Khalil Greene .15 .40
98 David Wright .30 .75
99 Jack Wilson .15 .40
100A A.Rodriguez w/Bat SP 4.00 10.00
100B A.Rodriguez w/Glove SP 4.00 10.00
101 Joe Nathan .15 .40
102A A.Beltre Grey Uni SP 3.00 8.00
102B A.Beltre White Uni .40 1.00
103 Mike Sweeney .15 .40
104 Brad Lidge .15 .40
105 Shawn Green .15 .40
106 Miguel Tejada SP 3.00 8.00
107 Derrek Lee .15 .40
108 Eric Hinske .15 .40
109 Eric Byrnes .15 .40
110 Hideki Matsui SP 3.00 8.00
111 Tom Glavine .25 .60
112 Jimmy Rollins .25 .60
113 Ryan Drese .15 .40
114 Josh Beckett .15 .40
115 Curt Schilling SP 3.00 8.00
116 Jeremy Bonderman .15 .40
117 Kazuo Matsui .15 .40
118 Chase Utley .25 .60
119 Troy Percival .15 .40
120A V.Guerrero w/Bat SP 3.00 8.00
120B V.Guerrero w/Glove SP 3.00 8.00
121 Gary Sheffield .15 .40
122 Jeromy Burnitz .15 .40
123 Javier Vazquez .15 .40
124 Kevin Millar .15 .40
125A R.Johnson Blue Sky .40 1.00
125B R.Johnson Purple Sky SP 3.00 8.00
126 Pat Burrell .15 .40
127 Jason Schmidt .15 .40
128 Jose Vidro .15 .40
129 Kip Wells .15 .40
130A I.Rodriguez w/Cap .25 .60
130B I.Rodriguez w/Helmet SP 3.00 8.00
131 C.C. Sabathia .25 .60
132 Carlos Delgado SP 3.00 8.00
133 Bartolo Colon .15 .40
134 Andruw Jones .15 .40
135 Kerry Wood .15 .40
136 Sidney Ponson .15 .40
137 Eric Gagne .15 .40
138 Rickie Weeks .15 .40
139 Mariano Rivera .50 1.25
140 Bobby Crosby .15 .40
141 Jamie Moyer .15 .40
142 Corey Koskie .15 .40
143 John Smoltz .40 1.00
144 Frank Thomas .40 1.00
145 Cristian Guzman .15 .40
146 Paul Lo Duca .15 .40
147 Geoff Jenkins .15 .40
148 Nick Swisher .25 .60
149 Jason Bay SP 3.00 8.00
150 Albert Pujols SP 6.00 15.00

151 Edwin Jackson .15 .40
152 Carl Crawford .25 .60
153 Mark Mulder .15 .40
154 Rafael Palmeiro .25 .60
155 Pedro Martinez SP 3.00 8.00
156 Jake Westbrook .15 .40
157 Sean Casey .15 .40
158 Aaron Rowand .15 .40
159 J.D. Drew .15 .40
160A J.Sant Glove on Knee SP 3.00 8.00
160B J.Santana Throwing SP 3.00 8.00
161 Gavin Floyd .15 .40
162 Vernon Wells .15 .40
163 Aubrey Huff .15 .40
164 Jeff Bagwell .25 .60
165 Boomer Wells .15 .40
166 Brad Penny .15 .40
167 Austin Kearns .15 .40
168 Mike Mussina .25 .60
169 Randy Wolf .15 .40
170 Tim Hudson SP 3.00 8.00
171 Casey Blake .15 .40
172 Edgar Renteria .15 .40
173 Ben Sheets .15 .40
174 Kevin Brown .15 .40
175 Nomar Garciaparra SP 3.00 8.00
176 Armando Benitez .15 .40
177 Jody Gerut .15 .40
178 Craig Biggio .25 .60
179 Omar Vizquel .25 .60
180 Jake Peavy .15 .40
181 Gustavo Chacin SP 3.00 8.00
182 Johnny Damon .25 .60
183 Mike Lieberthal .15 .40
184 Felix Hernandez SP 6.00 15.00
185 Zach Day SP 3.00 8.00
186 Matt Cain 1.00 2.50
187 Erubiel Durazo .15 .40
188 Zack Greinke .50 1.25
189 Matt Morris .15 .40
190 Billy Wagner .15 .40
191 Al Leiter .15 .40
192 Miguel Olivo .15 .40
193 Jose Capellan SP 3.00 8.00
194 Adam Eaton .15 .40
195 Steven White SP RC 3.00 8.00
196 Joe Randa .15 .40
197 Richard Hidalgo .15 .40
198 Orlando Cabrera .15 .40
199 Joel Guzman SP 3.00 8.00
200 Garret Anderson .15 .40
201 Endy Chavez .15 .40
202 Andy Marte .15 .40
203 Jose Guillen .15 .40
204 Victor Martinez .25 .60
205 Johnny Estrada .15 .40
206 Damian Miller .15 .40
207 Ken Harvey .15 .40
208 Ronnie Belliard .15 .40
209 Chan Ho Park .25 .60
210 Laynce Nix .15 .40
211 Lew Ford .15 .40
212 Moises Alou .15 .40
213 Kris Benson .15 .40
214 Mike Gonzalez SP 3.00 8.00
215 Chris Burke .15 .40
216 Juan Pierre .15 .40
217 Phil Nevin .15 .40
218 Jerry Hairston Jr. .15 .40
219 Jeremy Reed .15 .40
220 Scott Kazmir SP 3.00 8.00
221 Mike Maroth .15 .40
222 Alex Rios .15 .40
223 Esteban Loaiza .15 .40
224 Termel Sledge .15 .40
225A M.Prior Blue Sky SP 3.00 8.00
225B M.Prior Yellow Sky SP 3.00 8.00
226 Hank Blalock .15 .40
227 Craig Wilson .15 .40
228 Cesar Izturis .15 .40
229 Dmitri Young .15 .40
230A D.Jeter Blue Sky SP 6.00 15.00
230B D.Jeter Purple Sky SP 6.00 15.00
231 Mark Kotsay .15 .40
232 Darin Erstad .15 .40
233 Brandon Backe SP 3.00 8.00
234 Mike Lowell .15 .40
235 Scott Podsednik .15 .40
236 Michael Barrett .15 .40
237 Chad Tracy .15 .40
238 David Dellucci .15 .40
239 Brady Clark .15 .40
240 Jorge Cantu .15 .40
241 Wil Ledezma .15 .40
242 Morgan Ensberg .15 .40
243 Omar Infante .15 .40
244 Corey Patterson .15 .40
245 Matt Holliday .40 1.00
246 Vinny Castilla .15 .40
247 Jason Bartlett .15 .40
248 Noah Lowry .15 .40
249 Huston Street .15 .40
250 Russell Branyan .15 .40
251 Juan Uribe .15 .40
252 Larry Bigbie .15 .40
253 Grady Sizemore .25 .60
254 Pedro Feliz .15 .40
255 Brad Wilkerson .15 .40
256 Brandon Inge .15 .40
257 Dewon Brazelton .15 .40
258 Rodrigo Lopez .15 .40
259 Jacque Jones .15 .40
260 Jason Giambi .15 .40
261 Clint Barmes .15 .40
262 Willy Taveras .15 .40
263 Marcus Giles .15 .40
264 Joe Blanton .15 .40
265 John Thomson .15 .40
266 Steve Finley SP 3.00 8.00
267 Kevin Millwood .15 .40
268 David Eckstein .15 .40
269 Barry Zito .25 .60
270A T.Helton Purple Sky SP 3.00 8.00
270B T.Helton Yellow Sky SP 3.00 8.00
271 Landon Powell RC .25 .60
272 Justin Verlander RC 5.00 12.00
273 Wes Swackhamer RC .25 .60
274 Wladimir Balentien RC .40 1.00
275 Philip Humber RC .60 1.50
276 Kevin Melillo RC .25 .60
277 Billy Butler RC 1.25 3.00
278 Michael Rogers RC .25 .60
279 Bobby Livingston RC .25 .60
280 Glen Perkins RC .25 .60
281 Mike Bourn RC .60 1.50
282 Tyler Pelland RC .25 .60
283 Jeremy West RC .25 .60
284 Brandon McCarthy RC .40 1.00
285 Ian Kinsler RC 1.25 3.00
286 Chris Roberson RC .25 .60
287 Melky Cabrera RC .75 2.00
288 Ryan Sweeney RC .40 1.00
289 Chip Cannon RC .25 .60
290 Andy LaRoche RC .25 .60
291 Chuck Tiffany RC .60 1.50
292 Ian Bladergroen RC .25 .60
293 Bear Bay RC .25 .60
294 Hernan Iribarren RC .25 .60
295 Stuart Pomeranz RC .25 .60
296 Luke Scott RC .60 1.50
297 Chuck James RC .60 1.50
298 Kennard Bibbs RC .25 .60
299 Steven Bondurant RC .25 .60
300 Thomas Oldham RC .25 .60
301 Nolan Ryan RET 2.50 6.00
302 Reggie Jackson RET .50 1.25
303 Tom Seaver RET .50 1.25
304 Al Kaline RET .75 2.00
305 Cal Ripken RET 2.50 6.00
306 Josh Gibson RET .75 2.00
307 Frank Robinson RET .50 1.25
308 Duke Snider RET .50 1.25
309 Wade Boggs RET .50 1.25
310 Tony Gwynn RET 1.00 2.50
311 Carl Yastrzemski RET 1.00 2.50
312 Ryne Sandberg RET 1.50 4.00
313 Gary Carter RET .50 1.25
314 Brooks Robinson RET .50 1.25
315 Ernie Banks RET .75 2.00

2005 Topps Turkey Red Black

*BLACK 1-270: 5X TO 12X BASIC
*BLACK 1-270: .75X TO 2X BASIC SP
*BLACK 1-270: 4X TO 10X BASIC REP
*BLACK 271-300: 3X TO 8X BASIC
*BLACK 301-315: 2.5X TO 6X BASIC
STATED ODDS 1:20 HOBBY/RETAIL
STATED PRINT RUN 142 SETS
CARDS ARE NOT SERIAL-NUMBERED
PRINT RUN INFO PROVIDED BY TOPPS
THERE ARE NO SP'S IN THIS SET
1A Barry Bonds Grey Uni 20.00 50.00
1B Barry Bonds White Uni 20.00 50.00
5A Roger Clemens Blue Sky 8.00 20.00
10A Sammy Sosa w/Name 5.00 12.00
10B Sammy Sosa w/o Name 5.00 12.00
16A Mike Piazza Blue Uni 5.00 12.00
20 Manny Ramirez 3.00 8.00
25 Carlos Beltran 2.00 5.00
28 Rich Harden 2.00 5.00
30 Richie Sexson 2.00 5.00
52 Pulling String J.Santana CL 3.00 8.00
55 Roy Oswalt 2.00 5.00
59 Wily Mo Pena 2.00 5.00
60 Magglio Ordonez 2.00 5.00
70 Jim Thome 3.00 8.00
75A Ichiro Suzuki w/Name 10.00 25.00
75B Ichiro Suzuki w/o Name 10.00 25.00
78 Troy Glaus 2.00 5.00
83B Eric Chavez Purple Sky 2.00 5.00
85 Scott Rolen 3.00 8.00
87 Joe Mauer 3.00 8.00
90 Alfonso Soriano 2.00 5.00
102A Adrian Beltre Grey Uni 2.00 5.00
106 Miguel Tejada 2.00 5.00
110 Hideki Matsui 8.00 20.00
115 Curt Schilling 3.00 8.00
120A Vladimir Guerrero w/Bat 5.00 12.00
120B Vladimir Guerrero w/Glove 5.00 12.00
125B Randy Johnson Purple Sky 5.00 12.00
130B Ivan Rodriguez w/Helmet 3.00 8.00
132 Carlos Delgado 2.00 5.00
149 Jason Bay 2.00 5.00
150 Albert Pujols 10.00 25.00
155 Pedro Martinez 3.00 8.00
160A J.Santana Glove on Knee 5.00 12.00
160B J.Santana Throwing 5.00 12.00
170 Tim Hudson 2.00 5.00
175 Nomar Garciaparra 5.00 12.00
181 Gustavo Chacin 2.00 5.00
184 Felix Hernandez 8.00 20.00
185 Zach Day 2.00 5.00
193 Jose Capellan 2.00 5.00
195 Steven White 2.00 5.00
199 Joel Guzman 2.00 5.00
214 Mike Gonzalez 2.00 5.00
220 Scott Kazmir 2.00 5.00
225A Mark Prior Blue Sky 3.00 8.00
225B Mark Prior Yellow Sky 3.00 8.00
230A Derek Jeter Blue Sky 15.00 40.00
230B Derek Jeter Purple Sky 15.00 40.00
233 Brandon Backe 2.00 5.00
266 Steve Finley 2.00 5.00
270A Todd Helton Purple Sky 3.00 8.00
270B Todd Helton Yellow Sky 3.00 8.00

2005 Topps Turkey Red Gold

*GOLD 1-270: 12X TO 30X BASIC
*GOLD 1-270: 2X TO 5X BASIC SP
*GOLD 1-270: 10X TO 25X BASIC REP
*GOLD 271-300: 6X TO 15X BASIC
*GOLD 301-315: 5X TO 12X BASIC
STATED ODDS 1:59 HOBBY/RETAIL
STATED PRINT RUN 50 SERIAL #'d SETS
1A Barry Bonds Grey Uni 75.00 150.00
1B Barry Bonds White Uni 75.00 150.00
10A Sammy Sosa w/Name 12.50 30.00
10B Sammy Sosa w/o Name 12.50 30.00
16A Mike Piazza Blue Uni 12.50 30.00
20 Manny Ramirez 8.00 20.00
25 Carlos Beltran 5.00 12.00
28 Rich Harden 5.00 12.00
30 Richie Sexson 5.00 12.00
52 Pulling String J.Santana CL 8.00 20.00
55 Roy Oswalt 5.00 12.00
59 Wily Mo Pena 5.00 12.00
60 Magglio Ordonez 5.00 12.00
70 Jim Thome 8.00 20.00
75A Ichiro Suzuki w/Name 30.00 60.00
75B Ichiro Suzuki w/o Name 30.00 60.00
78 Troy Glaus 5.00 12.00
83B Eric Chavez Purple Sky 5.00 12.00
85 Scott Rolen 8.00 20.00
87 Joe Mauer 8.00 20.00
90 Alfonso Soriano 5.00 12.00
102A Adrian Beltre Grey Uni 5.00 12.00
106 Miguel Tejada 5.00 12.00
110 Hideki Matsui 20.00 50.00
115 Curt Schilling 8.00 20.00
120A Vladimir Guerrero w/Bat 12.50 30.00
120B Vladimir Guerrero w/Glove 12.50 30.00
125B Randy Johnson Purple Sky 12.50 30.00
130B Ivan Rodriguez w/Helmet 8.00 20.00
132 Carlos Delgado 5.00 12.00
149 Jason Bay 5.00 12.00
150 Albert Pujols 30.00 60.00
155 Pedro Martinez 8.00 20.00
160A J.Santana Glove on Knee 8.00 20.00
160B J.Santana Throwing 8.00 20.00
170 Tim Hudson 5.00 12.00
175 Nomar Garciaparra 12.50 30.00
181 Gustavo Chacin 5.00 12.00
184 Felix Hernandez 20.00 50.00
185 Zach Day 5.00 12.00
193 Jose Capellan 5.00 12.00
195 Steven White 5.00 12.00
199 Joel Guzman 5.00 12.00
214 Mike Gonzalez 5.00 12.00
220 Scott Kazmir 5.00 12.00
225A Mark Prior Blue Sky 8.00 20.00
225B Mark Prior Yellow Sky 8.00 20.00
230A Derek Jeter Blue Sky 50.00 100.00
230B Derek Jeter Purple Sky 50.00 100.00
233 Brandon Backe 5.00 12.00
270A Todd Helton Purple Sky 8.00 20.00
270B Todd Helton Yellow Sky 8.00 20.00
305 Cal Ripken RET 50.00 100.00

2005 Topps Turkey Red Red

*RED 1-270: 1X TO 2.5X BASIC
*RED 1-270: .2X TO .5X BASIC SP
*RED 1-270: .75X TO 2X BASIC REP
*RED 271-300: 1.2X TO 3X BASIC
*RED 301-315: .75X TO 2X BASIC
ONE RED OR OTHER PARALLEL PER PACK
THERE ARE NO SP'S IN THIS SET
10A Sammy Sosa w/Name 1.00 2.50
10B Sammy Sosa w/o Name 1.00 2.50
16A Mike Piazza Blue Uni 1.00 2.50
20 Manny Ramirez .60 1.50
25 Carlos Beltran .40 1.00
28 Rich Harden .40 1.00
30 Richie Sexson .40 1.00
52 Pulling String J.Santana CL 1.00 2.50
55 Roy Oswalt .40 1.00
59 Wily Mo Pena .40 1.00
60 Magglio Ordonez .40 1.00
70 Jim Thome .60 1.50
78 Troy Glaus .40 1.00
83B Eric Chavez Purple Sky .40 1.00
85 Scott Rolen .60 1.50
87 Joe Mauer 1.00 2.50
90 Alfonso Soriano .40 1.00
102B Adrian Beltre White Uni .40 1.00
106 Miguel Tejada .40 1.00
115 Curt Schilling .60 1.50
120A Vladimir Guerrero w/Bat 1.00 2.50
120B Vladimir Guerrero w/Glove 1.00 2.50
125B Randy Johnson Purple Sky 1.00 2.50
130B Ivan Rodriguez w/Helmet .60 1.50
132 Carlos Delgado .40 1.00
149 Jason Bay .40 1.00
155 Pedro Martinez .60 1.50
160A J.Santana Glove on Knee 1.00 2.50
160B J.Santana Throwing 1.00 2.50
170 Tim Hudson .40 1.00
175 Nomar Garciaparra 1.00 2.50
181 Gustavo Chacin .40 1.00
185 Zach Day .40 1.00
193 Jose Capellan .40 1.00
195 Steven White .40 1.00
199 Joel Guzman .40 1.00
214 Mike Gonzalez .40 1.00
220 Scott Kazmir .40 1.00
225A Mark Prior Blue Sky .60 1.50
225B Mark Prior Yellow Sky .60 1.50
233 Brandon Backe .40 1.00
266 Steve Finley .40 1.00
270A Todd Helton Purple Sky .60 1.50
270B Todd Helton Yellow Sky .60 1.50

2005 Topps Turkey Red Suede

STATED ODDS 1:2955 H, 1:3072 R
STATED PRINT RUN 1 SERIAL #'d SET
NO PRICING DUE TO SCARCITY

2005 Topps Turkey Red White

*WHITE 1-270: 2X TO 5X BASIC
*WHITE 1-270: .3X TO .8X BASIC SP
*WHITE 1-270: 1.5X TO 4X BASIC REP
*WHITE 271-300: 1X TO 2.5X BASIC
*WHITE 301-315: 1.5X TO 4X BASIC
STATED ODDS 1:4 HOBBY/RETAIL
THERE ARE NO SP'S IN THIS SET
10A Sammy Sosa w/Name 2.00 5.00
10B Sammy Sosa w/o Name 2.00 5.00
16A Mike Piazza Blue Uni 2.00 5.00
20 Manny Ramirez 1.25 3.00
25 Carlos Beltran .75 2.00
28 Rich Harden .75 2.00
30 Richie Sexson .75 2.00
52 Pulling String J.Santana CL 2.00 5.00
55 Roy Oswalt .75 2.00
59 Wily Mo Pena .75 2.00
60 Magglio Ordonez .75 2.00
70 Jim Thome 1.25 3.00
75A Ichiro Suzuki w/Name 4.00 10.00
75B Ichiro Suzuki w/o Name 4.00 10.00
78 Troy Glaus .75 2.00
83B Eric Chavez Purple Sky .75 2.00
85 Scott Rolen 1.25 3.00
87 Joe Mauer 2.00 5.00
90 Alfonso Soriano .75 2.00
102A Adrian Beltre Grey Uni .75 2.00
106 Miguel Tejada .75 2.00
110 Hideki Matsui 3.00 8.00
115 Curt Schilling 1.25 3.00
120A Vladimir Guerrero w/Bat 2.00 5.00
120B Vladimir Guerrero w/Glove 2.00 5.00
125B Randy Johnson Purple Sky 2.00 5.00
130B Ivan Rodriguez w/Helmet 1.25 3.00
132 Carlos Delgado .75 2.00
149 Jason Bay .75 2.00
150 Albert Pujols 4.00 10.00
155 Pedro Martinez 1.25 3.00
160A J.Santana Glove on Knee 2.00 5.00
160B J.Santana Throwing 2.00 5.00
170 Tim Hudson .75 2.00
175 Nomar Garciaparra 2.00 5.00
181 Gustavo Chacin .75 2.00
184 Felix Hernandez 4.00 10.00
185 Zach Day .75 2.00
193 Jose Capellan .75 2.00
195 Steven White .75 2.00
199 Joel Guzman .75 2.00
214 Mike Gonzalez .75 2.00
220 Scott Kazmir .75 2.00
225A Mark Prior Blue Sky 1.25 3.00
225B Mark Prior Yellow Sky 1.25 3.00
230A Derek Jeter Blue Sky 4.00 10.00
230B Derek Jeter Purple Sky 4.00 10.00
233 Brandon Backe .75 2.00
266 Steve Finley .75 2.00
270A Todd Helton Purple Sky 1.25 3.00
270B Todd Helton Yellow Sky 1.25 3.00

2005 Topps Turkey Red Autographs

GROUP A ODDS 1:6495 H, 1:6262 R
GROUP B ODDS 1:1280 H, 1:4372 R
GROUP C ODDS 1:106 H, 1:1037 R
GROUP D ODDS 1:270 H, 1:2714 R
GROUP E ODDS 1:816 H, 1:3024 R
GROUP A PRINT RUNS B/WN 17-67 PER
GROUP B PRINT RUNS B/WN 142-192 PER
GROUP A-B ARE NOT SERIAL-NUMBERED
A-B PRINT RUNS PROVIDED BY TOPPS
NO GROUP A PRICING DUE TO SCARCITY
EXCHANGE DEADLINE 08/31/07
AS A.Soriano B/142 * 10.00 25.00
BJ Blake Johnson C 4.00 10.00
CN Chris Nelson C 4.00 10.00
DO David Ortiz C 30.00 80.00
DP Dustin Pedroia C 12.00 30.00
EG Eric Gagne B/142 * 15.00 40.00
GS Gary Sheffield C 10.00 25.00
JF Josh Fields C 6.00 15.00
JG Jody Gerut D 4.00 10.00
JJ Jason Jaramillo C 6.00 15.00
JPH J.P. Howell C 4.00 10.00
JS Jeremy Sowers C 6.00 15.00
MRO Mike Rodriguez E 4.00 10.00
SE Scott Elbert C 6.00 15.00
ZJ Zach Jackson C 4.00 10.00
ZP Zach Parker C 4.00 10.00

2005 Topps Turkey Red Autographs Black

*GROUP B: .6X TO 1.5X BASIC
BONDS ODDS 1:344,256 H
GROUP A ODDS 1:18,119 H, 1:20,032 R
GROUP B ODDS 1:574 H, 1:1809 R
BONDS PRINT RUN 1 SERIAL #'d CARD
GROUP A PRINT RUN 5 SERIAL #'d SETS
GROUP B PRINT RUN 99 SERIAL #'d SETS
NO BONDS PRICING DUE TO SCARCITY
NO GROUP A PRICING DUE TO SCARCITY
EXCHANGE DEADLINE 08/31/07

2005 Topps Turkey Red Autographs Red

*GROUP B: .4X TO 1X BASIC
BONDS ODDS 1:344,256 H
GROUP A ODDS 1:5935 H, 1:6048 R
GROUP B ODDS 1:153 H, 1:1943R
BONDS PRINT RUN 1 SERIAL #'d CARD
GROUP A PRINT RUN 15 SERIAL #'d SETS
GROUP B PRINT RUN 25 SERIAL #'d SETS
NO BONDS PRICING DUE TO SCARCITY
NO GROUP A PRICING DUE TO SCARCITY
EXCHANGE DEADLINE 08/31/07

2005 Topps Turkey Red Autographs White

*GROUP B: .5X TO 1.2X BASIC
BONDS ODDS 1:344,256 H
GROUP A ODDS 1:9563 H, 1:9072 R
GROUP B ODDS 1:242 H, 1:1536 R
BONDS PRINT RUN 1 SERIAL #'d CARD
GROUP A PRINT RUN 10 SERIAL #'d SETS
GROUP B PRINT RUN 200 SERIAL #'d SETS
NO BONDS PRICING DUE TO SCARCITY
NO GROUP A PRICING DUE TO SCARCITY
EXCHANGE DEADLINE 08/31/07

2005 Topps Turkey Red B-18 Blankets

STATED ODDS 1:2 JUMBO
SP STATED ODDS 1:6 JUMBO
REPURCHASED ODDS 1:165 JUMBO
AR1 Alex Rodriguez Blue SP 10.00 25.00
AR2 Alex Rodriguez Green 6.00 15.00
AS1 Alfonso Soriano Red SP 6.00 15.00
AS2 Alfonso Soriano White 4.00 10.00
BB1 Barry Bonds Red SP 15.00 40.00
BB2 Barry Bonds White 10.00 25.00
CS1 Curt Schilling Red SP 6.00 15.00
CS2 Curt Schilling White 4.00 10.00
DJ1 Derek Jeter Blue SP 10.00 25.00
DJ2 Derek Jeter Green 6.00 15.00
IS1 Ichiro Suzuki Green SP 10.00 25.00
IS2 Ichiro Suzuki White 6.00 15.00
RC1 Roger Clemens Purple SP 10.00 25.00
RC2 Roger Clemens White 6.00 15.00
TH1 Todd Helton Green SP 6.00 15.00
TH2 Todd Helton White 4.00 10.00

2005 Topps Turkey Red Cabinet

STATED ODDS 1:2 JUMBO
SP STATED ODDS 1:30 JUMBO
SP STATED PRINT RUNS 118 COPIES PER
SP'S ARE NOT SERIAL-NUMBERED
SP PRINT RUNS PROVIDED BY TOPPS
SP'S HAVE ADVERTISEMENTS ON BACK
REPURCHASED ODDS 1:211 JUMBO
AP Albert Pujols 4.00 10.00
AR1 Alex Rodriguez w/Bat 4.00 10.00
AR2 A.Rod w/Glove SP/118 * 5.00 12.00
BB1 Barry Bonds At Bat SP/118 * 6.00 15.00
BB2 Barry Bonds On Steps 5.00 12.00
GB George W. Bush 3.00 8.00
GW George Washington 3.00 8.00
JS Johan Santana 2.00 5.00
JT Jim Thome 2.00 5.00
MP Mike Piazza 3.00 8.00
MR Manny Ramirez 3.00 8.00
MT Miguel Tejada 2.00 5.00
RJ Randy Johnson 3.00 8.00
SR Scott Rolen 2.00 5.00
SS Sammy Sosa 3.00 8.00
WT William Howard Taft 3.00 8.00

2005 Topps Turkey Red Cabinet Auto Relics

GROUP A ODDS 1:2869 JUMBO
GROUP B ODDS 1:202 JUMBO
GROUP C ODDS 1:67 JUMBO
GROUP D ODDS 1:101 JUMBO
GROUP E ODDS 1:9 JUMBO
GROUP A PRINT RUN 5 SERIAL #'d SETS
GROUP B PRINT RUN 25 SERIAL #'d SETS
GROUP C PRINT RUN 75 SERIAL #'d SETS
GROUP D PRINT RUN 150 SERIAL #'d SETS
GROUP E PRINT RUN 450 SERIAL #'d SETS
NO GROUP A-B PRICING DUE TO SCARCITY
EXCHANGE DEADLINE 08/31/07
BM Brett Myers Jsy D/150 15.00 40.00
CC Carl Crawford Bat E/450 10.00 25.00
DO David Ortiz Bat C/75 40.00 80.00
EG Eric Gagne Jsy C/75 60.00 120.00
JG Jody Gerut Bat E/450 6.00 15.00
MB Matt Bush Jsy E/450 10.00 25.00
MK Mark Kotsay Bat E/450 10.00 25.00

2005 Topps Turkey Red Relics

GROUP A ODDS 1:2550 H, 1:2560 R
GROUP B ODDS 1:1776 H, 1:1781 R
GROUP C ODDS 1:1383 H, 1:1398 R
GROUP D ODDS 1:349 H, 1:1202 R
GROUP E ODDS 1:208 H, 1:577 R
GROUP F ODDS 1:65 H, 1:200 R
GROUP G ODDS 1:172 H, 1:427 R
GROUP H ODDS 1:52 H, 1:102 R
AB Adrian Beltre Bat C 4.00 10.00
AP Albert Pujols Bat E 6.00 15.00
AR Alex Rodriguez Uni D 5.00 12.00
AR2 Alex Rodriguez Bat G 4.00 10.00
AS Alfonso Soriano Bat H 2.00 5.00
BB Barry Bonds Pants D 8.00 20.00
CB Carlos Beltran Bat E 3.00 8.00
CJ Chipper Jones Jsy H 3.00 8.00
CS Curt Schilling Jsy F 3.00 8.00
DO David Ortiz Jsy F 3.00 8.00
GS Gary Sheffield Bat H 2.00 5.00
HB Hank Blalock Bat F 2.00 5.00
JB Jeff Bagwell Uni H 3.00 8.00
JD Johnny Damon Bat G 3.00 8.00
JD2 Johnny Damon Jsy E 4.00 10.00
JT Jim Thome Bat F 3.00 8.00
LW Larry Walker Bat B 6.00 15.00
MC Miguel Cabrera Jsy H 3.00 8.00
ML Mike Lowell Jsy H 2.00 5.00
MM Mark Mulder Uni F 2.00 5.00
MO Magglio Ordonez Bat F 2.00 5.00
MP Mike Piazza Uni A 6.00 15.00
MPR Mark Prior Jsy B 6.00 15.00
MR Manny Ramirez Jsy D 4.00 10.00
MT Miguel Tejada Uni F 2.00 5.00
MTE Mark Teixeira Bat G 3.00 8.00
RC Roger Clemens Bat A 8.00 20.00
RC2 Roger Clemens Jsy E 5.00 12.00
RP Rafael Palmeiro Bat F 3.00 8.00
SS Sammy Sosa Bat C 6.00 15.00
TH Todd Helton Jsy H 3.00 8.00
VG Vladimir Guerrero Bat H 3.00 8.00

2005 Topps Turkey Red Relics Black

*BLACK: 1.25X TO 3X BASIC F-H
*BLACK: 1X TO 2.5X BASIC D-E
*BLACK: .6X TO 1.5X BASIC A-C
STATED ODDS 1:608 H, 1:614 R
STATED PRINT RUN 50 SERIAL #'d SETS

2005 Topps Turkey Red Relics Red

*RED: .75X TO 2X BASIC F-H
*RED: .6X TO 1.5X BASIC D-E
*RED: .4X TO 1X BASIC A-C
STATED ODDS 1:295 H, 1:341 R
STATED PRINT RUN 99 SERIAL #'d SETS

2005 Topps Turkey Red Relics White

*WHITE: 1X TO 2.5X BASIC F-H
*WHITE: .75X TO 2X BASIC D-E
*WHITE: .5X TO 1.2X BASIC A-C
STATED ODDS 1:377 H, 1:417 R
STATED PRINT RUN 75 SERIAL #'d SETS

2006 Topps Turkey Red

COMPLETE SET (330) 75.00 150.00
COMP.SET w/o SP's (275) 10.00 25.00
COMMON CARD (316-580) .15 .40
COMMON SP (316-580) 3.00 8.00
SP STATED ODDS 1:4 HOBBY, 1:4 RETAIL
SEE BECKETT.COM FOR SP CHECKLIST
COMMON CL (571-580) .07 .20
COMMON RET (581-590) .30 .75
COMMON RC (591-630) .40 1.00
OVERALL PLATE ODDS 1:477 H
PLATE PRINT RUN 1 SET PER COLOR
BLACK-CYAN-MAGENTA-YELLOW ISSUED
NO PLATE PRICING DUE TO SCARCITY
316A A.Rodriguez Yanks .50 1.25
316B A.Rodriguez Rangers SP 4.00 10.00
316C Alex Rodriguez M's SP 4.00 10.00
317 Jeff Francoeur SP 3.00 8.00
318 Shawn Green .15 .40
319 Daniel Cabrera .15 .40
320 Craig Biggio .25 .60
321 Jeremy Bonderman .15 .40
322 Mark Kotsay .15 .40
323 Cliff Floyd .15 .40
324 Jimmy Rollins .25 .60
325A M.Ordonez Tigers .25 .60
325B M.Ordonez W.Sox SP 3.00 8.00
326 C.C. Sabathia .25 .60
327 Oliver Perez .15 .40
328 Orlando Hudson .15 .40
329 Chris Ray .15 .40
330 Manny Ramirez .40 1.00
331 Paul Konerko .25 .60
332 Joe Mauer SP 3.00 8.00
333 Jorge Posada .25 .60
334 Mark Ellis .15 .40
335 A.J. Burnett .15 .40
336 Mike Sweeney .15 .40
337 Shannon Stewart .15 .40
338 Jake Peavy SP 3.00 8.00
339A C.Delgado Mets SP 3.00 8.00
339B C.Delgado B.Jays SP 3.00 8.00
340 Brian Roberts .15 .40
341 Dontrelle Willis .15 .40
342 Aaron Rowand .15 .40
343A R.Sexson M's .15 .40
343B R.Sexson Brewers SP 3.00 8.00
344 Chris Carpenter .25 .60
345 Carlos Zambrano .25 .60
346 Nomar Garciaparra .25 .60
347 Carlos Lee .15 .40
348A P.Wilson Astros .15 .40
348B P.Wilson Marlins SP 3.00 8.00
349 Mariano Rivera .50 1.25
350 Ichiro Suzuki SP 4.00 10.00
351A M.Piazza Padres .40 1.00
351B Mike Piazza Mets SP 3.00 8.00
352 Jason Schmidt .15 .40
353 Jeff Weaver .15 .40
354 Rocco Baldelli .15 .40
355 Adam Dunn .25 .60
356 Jeromy Burnitz .15 .40
357 Chris Shelton SP 3.00 8.00
358 Chone Figgins SP 3.00 8.00
359 Javier Vazquez .15 .40
360 Chipper Jones .40 1.00
361 Frank Thomas .40 1.00
362 Mark Loretta .15 .40
363 Hideki Matsui .40 1.00
364 J.J. Hardy SP 3.00 8.00
365 Todd Helton .25 .60
366 Reggie Sanders .15 .40
367 Jay Gibbons .15 .40
368 Johnny Estrada .15 .40
369 Grady Sizemore .25 .60
370 Jim Thome .25 .60
371 Ivan Rodriguez .25 .60
372 Jason Bay .15 .40
373 Carl Crawford .25 .60
374 Adrian Beltre .40 1.00
375 Derrek Lee SP 3.00 8.00
376 Miguel Olivo .15 .40
377 Roy Oswalt .25 .60
378 Coco Crisp .15 .40
379 Moises Alou .15 .40
380 Kevin Millwood .15 .40
381 Mark Grudzielanek .15 .40
382 Justin Morneau .25 .60
383 Austin Kearns .15 .40
384 Brad Penny .15 .40
385 Troy Glaus .15 .40
386 Cliff Lee .25 .60
387 Armando Benitez .15 .40
388 Clint Barmes .15 .40
389 Orlando Cabrera .15 .40
390 Jim Edmonds SP 3.00 8.00
391 Jermaine Dye .15 .40
392 Morgan Ensberg SP 3.00 8.00
393 Paul LoDuca .15 .40
394 Eric Chavez .15 .40
395 Greg Maddux SP 4.00 10.00
396 Jack Wilson .15 .40
397 Omar Vizquel .25 .60
398 Joe Nathan .15 .40
399 Bobby Abreu .15 .40
400 Barry Bonds SP 6.00 15.00
401 Gary Sheffield .15 .40
402 John Patterson .15 .40
403 J.D. Drew .15 .40
404 Bruce Chen .15 .40
405 Johnny Damon SP 3.00 8.00
406 Aubrey Huff .15 .40
407 Mark Mulder .15 .40
408 Jamie Moyer .15 .40
409 Carlos Guillen .15 .40
410 Andruw Jones SP 3.00 8.00
411 Jhonny Peralta SP 3.00 8.00
412 Doug Davis .15 .40
413 Aaron Miles .15 .40
414 Jon Lieber .15 .40
415 Aaron Hill .15 .40
416 Josh Beckett SP 3.00 8.00
417 Bobby Crosby .15 .40
418 Noah Lowry SP 3.00 8.00
419 Sidney Ponson .15 .40
420 Luis Castillo .15 .40
421 Brad Wilkerson .15 .40
422 Felix Hernandez SP 3.00 8.00
423 Vinny Castilla .15 .40
424 Tom Glavine .25 .60
425 Vladimir Guerrero .25 .60
426 Javy Lopez .15 .40
427 Ronnie Belliard .15 .40
428 Dmitri Young .15 .40
429 Johan Santana .25 .60
430A D.Ortiz Red Sox SP 3.00 8.00
430B D.Ortiz Twins SP 3.00 8.00
431 Ben Sheets .15 .40
432 Matt Holliday .40 1.00
433 Brian McCann .15 .40
434 Joe Blanton .15 .40
435 Sean Casey .15 .40
436 Brad Lidge .15 .40
437 Chad Tracy .15 .40
438 Brett Myers .15 .40
439 Matt Morris .15 .40
440 Brian Giles .15 .40
441 Zach Duke .15 .40
442 Jose Lopez .15 .40
443 Kris Benson .15 .40
444 Jose Reyes SP 3.00 8.00
445 Travis Hafner .15 .40
446 Orlando Hernandez .15 .40
447 Edgar Renteria .15 .40
448 Scott Podsednik .15 .40
449 Nick Swisher SP 3.00 8.00
450 Derek Jeter SP 6.00 15.00
451 Scott Kazmir SP 3.00 8.00
452 Hank Blalock .15 .40
453 Jake Westbrook .15 .40
454 Miguel Cabrera .40 1.00
455A K.Griffey Jr. Reds .75 2.00
455B K.Griffey Jr. M's SP 5.00 12.00
456 Rafael Furcal .15 .40
457 Lance Berkman .25 .60
458 Aramis Ramirez .15 .40
459A X.Nady Mets .15 .40
459B X.Nady Padres SP 3.00 8.00
460A R.Johnson Yanks .40 1.00
460B R.Johnson Astros SP 3.00 8.00
461 Khalil Greene .15 .40
462 Bartolo Colon .15 .40
463 Mike Lowell .15 .40
464 David DeJesus .15 .40
465 Ryan Howard SP 4.00 10.00
466 Tim Salmon SP 3.00 8.00
467 Mark Buehrle SP 3.00 8.00
468 Curtis Granderson .30 .75
469 Kerry Wood .15 .40
470 Miguel Tejada .25 .60
471 Geoff Jenkins .15 .40
472 Jeremy Reed .15 .40
473 David Eckstein .15 .40
474 Lyle Overbay .15 .40
475 Michael Young .15 .40
476A N.Johnson Nats SP 3.00 8.00
476B N.Johnson Yanks SP 3.00 8.00
477 Carlos Beltran .25 .60
478 Huston Street .15 .40
479 Brandon Webb .25 .60
480 Phil Nevin .15 .40
481 Ryan Madson SP 3.00 8.00
482 Jason Giambi .15 .40
483 Angel Berroa .15 .40
484 Casey Blake .15 .40
485 Pat Burrell .15 .40
486 B.J. Ryan .15 .40
487 Torii Hunter .15 .40
488 Garret Anderson .15 .40
489 Chase Utley SP 3.00 8.00
490 Matt Murton .15 .40
491 Rich Harden .15 .40
492 Garrett Atkins .15 .40
493 Tadahito Iguchi SP 3.00 8.00
494 Jarrod Washburn .15 .40
495 Carl Everett .15 .40
496 Kameron Loe .15 .40
497 Jorge Cantu SP 3.00 8.00
498 Chris Young .15 .40
499 Marcus Giles .15 .40
500 Albert Pujols .50 1.25
501A A.Soriano Nats SP 3.00 8.00
501B A.Soriano Yanks SP 3.00 8.00
502 Randy Winn .15 .40
503 Roy Halladay .25 .60
504 Victor Martinez .25 .60
505 Pedro Martinez .25 .60
506 Rickie Weeks .15 .40
507 Dan Johnson .15 .40
508A T.Hudson Braves .25 .60
508B T.Hudson A's SP 3.00 8.00
509 Mark Prior .25 .60
510 Melvin Mora .15 .40
511 Matt Clement .15 .40
512 Brandon Inge .15 .40
513 Mike Mussina .25 .60
514 Mike Cameron .15 .40
515 Barry Zito .25 .60
516 Luis Gonzalez .15 .40
517 Jose Castillo .15 .40
518 Andy Pettitte .25 .60
519 Wily Mo Pena .15 .40
520 Billy Wagner .15 .40
521 Ervin Santana SP 3.00 8.00
522 Juan Pierre .15 .40
523 Dan Haren .15 .40
524 Adrian Gonzalez SP 3.00 8.00
525 Robinson Cano .25 .60
526 Jeff Kent .15 .40
527 Cory Sullivan .15 .40
528 Joe Crede SP 3.00 8.00
529 John Smoltz .40 1.00
530 David Wright .30 .75
531 Chad Cordero .15 .40
532 Scott Rolen SP 3.00 8.00
533 Edwin Jackson .15 .40
534 Doug Mientkiewicz .15 .40
535 Mark Teixeira SP 3.00 8.00
536 Kelvim Escobar .15 .40
537 Alex Rios .15 .40
538 Jose Vidro .15 .40
539 Alex Gonzalez .15 .40
540 Yadier Molina .50 1.25
541 Ronny Cedeno SP 3.00 8.00
542 Mark Hendrickson .15 .40
543 Russ Adams .15 .40
544 Chris Capuano .15 .40
545 Raul Ibanez .25 .60
546 Vicente Padilla .15 .40
547 Chris Duffy .15 .40
548 Bengie Molina .15 .40
549 Chien-Ming Wang .25 .60
550 Curt Schilling .25 .60
551 Craig Wilson .15 .40
552 Mike Lieberthal .15 .40
553 Kazuo Matsui .15 .40
554 Jeff Francis .15 .40
555 Brady Clark .15 .40
556 Willy Taveras .15 .40
557 Mike Maroth .15 .40
558 Bernie Williams .25 .60
559 Edwin Encarnacion .40 1.00
560 Vernon Wells .15 .40
561A L.Hernandez Nats .15 .40

561B L.Hernandez Giants SP 3.00 8.00
562 Kenny Rogers .15 .40
563 Steve Finley .15 .40
564 Trot Nixon .15 .40
565 Jonny Gomes SP 3.00 8.00
566 Brandon Phillips .15 .40
567 Shawn Chacon .15 .40
568 Dave Bush .15 .40
569 Jose Guillen .15 .40
570 Gustavo Chacin .15 .40
571 A.Rod Safe at the Plate CL .25 .60
572 Pujols At Bat CL .25 .60
573 Bonds On Deck CL .30 .75
574 Breaking Up Two CL .07 .20
575 Conference On The Mound CL .20 .50
576 Touch Em All CL .15 .40
577 Avoiding The Runner CL .07 .20
578 Bunting The Runner Over CL .07 .20
579 In The Hole CL .12 .30
580 Jeter Steals Third CL .50 1.25
581 Nolan Ryan RET 2.50 6.00
582 Cal Ripken RET 2.50 6.00
583 Carl Yastrzemski RET 1.25 3.00
584 Duke Snider RET .50 1.25
585 Tom Seaver RET .50 1.25
586 Mickey Mantle RET 2.50 6.00
587 Jim Palmer RET .50 1.25
588 Gary Carter RET .50 1.25
589 Stan Musial RET 1.25 3.00
590 Luis Aparicio RET .50 1.25
591 Prince Fielder (RC) 2.00 5.00
592 Conor Jackson (RC) .60 1.50
593 Jeremy Hermida (RC) .40 1.00
594 Jeff Mathis (RC) .40 1.00
595 Alay Soler RC .40 1.00
596 Ryan Spilborghs (RC) .40 1.00
597 Chuck James (RC) .40 1.00
598 Josh Barfield (RC) .40 1.00
599 Ian Kinsler (RC) 1.25 3.00
600 Val Majewski (RC) .40 1.00
601 Brian Slocum (RC) .40 1.00
602 Matt Kemp (RC) 1.00 2.50
603 Nate McLouth (RC) .40 1.00
604 Sean Marshall (RC) .40 1.00
605 Brian Bannister (RC) .40 1.00
606 Ryan Zimmerman (RC) 1.25 3.00
607 Kendry Morales (RC) 1.00 2.50
608 Jonathan Papelbon (RC) 2.00 5.00
609 Matt Cain (RC) 2.50 6.00
610 Anderson Hernandez (RC) .40 1.00
611 Jose Capellan (RC) .40 1.00
612 Lastings Milledge (RC) .40 1.00
613 Francisco Liriano (RC) 1.00 2.50
614 Hanley Ramirez (RC) .60 1.50
615 Brian Anderson (RC) .40 1.00
616 Reggie Abercrombie (RC) .40 1.00
617 Erick Aybar (RC) .40 1.00
618 James Loney (RC) .60 1.50
619 Joel Zumaya (RC) 1.00 2.50
620 Travis Ishikawa (RC) .60 1.50
621 Jason Kubel (RC) .40 1.00
622 Drew Meyer (RC) .40 1.00
623 Kenji Johjima RC 1.00 2.50
624 Fausto Carmona (RC) .40 1.00
625 Nick Markakis (RC) .75 2.00
626 John Rheinecker (RC) .40 1.00
627 Melky Cabrera (RC) .60 1.50
628 Michael Pelfrey RC 1.00 2.50
629 Dan Uggla (RC) .60 1.50
630 Justin Verlander (RC) 3.00 8.00

2006 Topps Turkey Red Black

*BLACK 316-580: 4X TO 10X BASIC
*BLACK 316-580: .6X TO 1.5X BASIC SP
*BLACK 581-590: 2X TO 5X BASIC RET
*BLACK 591-630: 1.25X TO 3X BASIC ROOKIE
STATED ODDS 1:20 HOBBY/RETAIL
THERE ARE NO SP'S IN THIS SET

2006 Topps Turkey Red Gold

COMMON CARD (316-580) 5.00 12.00
COMMON CL (571-580) 3.00 8.00
COMMON RET (581-590) 5.00 12.00
COMMON ROOKIE (591-630) 6.00 15.00
STATED ODDS 1:60 HOBBY/RETAIL
THERE ARE NO SP'S IN THIS SET
316A A.Rodriguez Yanks 15.00 40.00
316B A.Rodriguez Rangers 15.00 40.00
316C Alex Rodriguez M's 15.00 40.00
317 Jeff Francoeur 12.00 30.00
318 Shawn Green 5.00 12.00
319 Daniel Cabrera 5.00 12.00
320 Craig Biggio 8.00 20.00
321 Jeremy Bonderman 5.00 12.00
322 Mark Kotsay 5.00 12.00
323 Cliff Floyd 5.00 12.00
324 Jimmy Rollins 8.00 20.00
325A M.Ordonez Tigers 8.00 20.00
325B M.Ordonez W.Sox 8.00 20.00
326 C.C. Sabathia 8.00 20.00
327 Oliver Perez 5.00 12.00
328 Orlando Hudson 5.00 12.00
329 Chris Ray 5.00 12.00
330 Manny Ramirez 12.00 30.00
331 Paul Konerko 8.00 20.00
332 Joe Mauer 8.00 20.00
333 Jorge Posada 8.00 20.00
334 Mark Ellis 5.00 12.00
335 A.J. Burnett 5.00 12.00
336 Mike Sweeney 5.00 12.00
337 Shannon Stewart 5.00 12.00
338 Jake Peavy 5.00 12.00
339A C.Delgado Mets 5.00 12.00
339B C.Delgado B.Jays 5.00 12.00
340 Brian Roberts 5.00 12.00
341 Dontrelle Willis 5.00 12.00
342 Aaron Rowand 5.00 12.00
343A R.Sexson M's 5.00 12.00
343B R.Sexson Brewers 5.00 12.00
344 Chris Carpenter 8.00 20.00
345 Carlos Zambrano 8.00 20.00
346 Nomar Garciaparra 8.00 20.00
347 Carlos Lee 5.00 12.00
348A P.Wilson Astros 5.00 12.00
348B P.Wilson Marlins 5.00 12.00
349 Mariano Rivera 15.00 40.00
350 Ichiro Suzuki 15.00 40.00
351A M.Piazza Padres 12.00 30.00
351B M.Piazza Mets 12.00 30.00
352 Jason Schmidt 5.00 12.00
353 Jeff Weaver 5.00 12.00
354 Rocco Baldelli 5.00 12.00
355 Adam Dunn 8.00 20.00
356 Jeromy Burnitz 5.00 12.00
357 Chris Shelton 5.00 12.00
358 Chone Figgins 5.00 12.00
359 Javier Vazquez 5.00 12.00
360 Chipper Jones 12.00 30.00
361 Frank Thomas 12.00 30.00
362 Mark Loretta 5.00 12.00
363 Hideki Matsui 12.00 30.00
364 J.J. Hardy 5.00 12.00
365 Todd Helton 8.00 20.00
366 Reggie Sanders 5.00 12.00
367 Jay Gibbons 5.00 12.00
368 Johnny Estrada 5.00 12.00
369 Grady Sizemore 8.00 20.00
370 Jim Thome 8.00 20.00
371 Ivan Rodriguez 8.00 20.00
372 Jason Bay 5.00 12.00
373 Carl Crawford 8.00 20.00
374 Adrian Beltre 12.00 30.00
375 Derrek Lee 5.00 12.00
376 Miguel Olivo 5.00 12.00
377 Roy Oswalt 8.00 20.00
378 Coco Crisp 5.00 12.00
379 Moises Alou 5.00 12.00
380 Kevin Millwood 5.00 12.00
381 Mark Grudzielanek 5.00 12.00
382 Justin Morneau 8.00 20.00
383 Austin Kearns 5.00 12.00
384 Brad Penny 5.00 12.00
385 Troy Glaus 5.00 12.00
386 Cliff Lee 8.00 20.00
387 Armando Benitez 5.00 12.00
388 Clint Barmes 5.00 12.00
389 Orlando Cabrera 5.00 12.00
390 Jim Edmonds 8.00 20.00
391 Jermaine Dye 5.00 12.00
392 Morgan Ensberg 5.00 12.00
393 Paul LoDuca 5.00 12.00
394 Eric Chavez 5.00 12.00
395 Greg Maddux 15.00 40.00
396 Jack Wilson 5.00 12.00
397 Omar Vizquel 8.00 20.00
398 Joe Nathan 5.00 12.00
399 Bobby Abreu 5.00 12.00
400 Barry Bonds 20.00 50.00
401 Gary Sheffield 5.00 12.00
402 John Patterson 5.00 12.00
403 J.D. Drew 5.00 12.00
404 Bruce Chen 5.00 12.00
405 Johnny Damon 8.00 20.00
406 Aubrey Huff 5.00 12.00
407 Mark Mulder 5.00 12.00
408 Jamie Moyer 5.00 12.00
409 Carlos Guillen 5.00 12.00
410 Andruw Jones 5.00 12.00
411 Jhonny Peralta 5.00 12.00
412 Doug Davis 5.00 12.00
413 Aaron Miles 5.00 12.00
414 Jon Lieber 5.00 12.00
415 Aaron Hill 5.00 12.00
416 Josh Beckett 5.00 12.00
417 Bobby Crosby 5.00 12.00
418 Noah Lowry 5.00 12.00
419 Sidney Ponson 5.00 12.00
420 Luis Castillo 5.00 12.00
421 Brad Wilkerson 5.00 12.00
422 Felix Hernandez 8.00 20.00
423 Vinny Castilla 5.00 12.00
424 Tom Glavine 8.00 20.00
425 Vladimir Guerrero 8.00 20.00
426 Javy Lopez 5.00 12.00
427 Ronnie Belliard 5.00 12.00
428 Dmitri Young 5.00 12.00
429 Johan Santana 8.00 20.00
430A D.Ortiz Red Sox 12.00 30.00
430B D.Ortiz Twins 12.00 30.00
431 Ben Sheets 5.00 12.00
432 Matt Holliday 12.00 30.00
433 Brian McCann 5.00 12.00
434 Joe Blanton 5.00 12.00
435 Sean Casey 5.00 12.00
436 Brad Lidge 5.00 12.00
437 Chad Tracy 5.00 12.00
438 Brett Myers 5.00 12.00
439 Matt Morris 5.00 12.00
440 Brian Giles 5.00 12.00
441 Zach Duke 5.00 12.00
442 Jose Lopez 5.00 12.00
443 Kris Benson 5.00 12.00
444 Jose Reyes 8.00 20.00
445 Travis Hafner 5.00 12.00
446 Orlando Hernandez 5.00 12.00
447 Edgar Renteria 5.00 12.00
448 Scott Podsednik 5.00 12.00
449 Nick Swisher 8.00 20.00
450 Derek Jeter 30.00 80.00
451 Scott Kazmir 8.00 20.00
452 Hank Blalock 5.00 12.00
453 Jake Westbrook 5.00 12.00
454 Miguel Cabrera 12.00 30.00
455A K.Griffey Jr. Reds 25.00 60.00
455B K.Griffey Jr. M's 25.00 60.00
456 Rafael Furcal 5.00 12.00
457 Lance Berkman 8.00 20.00
458 Aramis Ramirez 5.00 12.00
459A X.Nady Mets 5.00 12.00
459B X.Nady Padres 5.00 12.00
460A R.Johnson Yanks 12.00 30.00
460B R.Johnson Astros 12.00 30.00
461 Khalil Greene 5.00 12.00
462 Bartolo Colon 5.00 12.00
463 Mike Lowell 5.00 12.00
464 David DeJesus 5.00 12.00
465 Ryan Howard 10.00 25.00
466 Tim Salmon 5.00 12.00
467 Mark Buehrle 8.00 20.00
468 Curtis Granderson 10.00 25.00
469 Kerry Wood 5.00 12.00
470 Miguel Tejada 8.00 20.00
471 Geoff Jenkins 5.00 12.00
472 Jeremy Reed 5.00 12.00
473 David Eckstein 5.00 12.00
474 Lyle Overbay 5.00 12.00
475 Michael Young 5.00 12.00
476A N.Johnson Nats 5.00 12.00
476B N.Johnson Yanks 5.00 12.00
477 Carlos Beltran 8.00 20.00
478 Huston Street 5.00 12.00
479 Brandon Webb 8.00 20.00
480 Phil Nevin 5.00 12.00
481 Ryan Madson 5.00 12.00
482 Jason Giambi 5.00 12.00
483 Angel Berroa 5.00 12.00
484 Casey Blake 5.00 12.00
485 Pat Burrell 5.00 12.00
486 B.J. Ryan 5.00 12.00
487 Torii Hunter 5.00 12.00
488 Garret Anderson 5.00 12.00
489 Chase Utley 8.00 20.00
490 Matt Murton 5.00 12.00
491 Rich Harden 5.00 12.00
492 Garrett Atkins 5.00 12.00
493 Tadahito Iguchi 5.00 12.00
494 Jarrod Washburn 5.00 12.00
495 Carl Everett 5.00 12.00
496 Kameron Loe 5.00 12.00
497 Jorge Cantu 5.00 12.00
498 Chris Young 5.00 12.00
499 Marcus Giles 5.00 12.00
500 Albert Pujols 15.00 40.00
501A A.Soriano Nats 8.00 20.00
501B A.Soriano Yanks 8.00 20.00
502 Randy Winn 5.00 12.00
503 Roy Halladay 8.00 20.00
504 Victor Martinez 8.00 20.00
505 Pedro Martinez 8.00 20.00
506 Rickie Weeks 5.00 12.00
507 Dan Johnson 5.00 12.00
508A T.Hudson Braves 8.00 20.00
508B T.Hudson A's 8.00 20.00
509 Mark Prior 8.00 20.00
510 Melvin Mora 5.00 12.00
511 Matt Clement 5.00 12.00
512 Brandon Inge 5.00 12.00
513 Mike Mussina 8.00 20.00
514 Mike Cameron 5.00 12.00
515 Barry Zito 8.00 20.00
516 Luis Gonzalez 5.00 12.00
517 Jose Castillo 5.00 12.00
518 Andy Pettitte 8.00 20.00
519 Wily Mo Pena 5.00 12.00
520 Billy Wagner 5.00 12.00
521 Ervin Santana 5.00 12.00
522 Juan Pierre 5.00 12.00
523 Dan Haren 5.00 12.00
524 Adrian Gonzalez 10.00 25.00
525 Robinson Cano 8.00 20.00
526 Jeff Kent 5.00 12.00
527 Cory Sullivan 5.00 12.00
528 Joe Crede 5.00 12.00
529 John Smoltz 12.00 30.00
530 David Wright 10.00 25.00
531 Chad Cordero 5.00 12.00
532 Scott Rolen 8.00 20.00
533 Edwin Jackson 5.00 12.00
534 Doug Mientkiewicz 5.00 12.00
535 Mark Teixeira 8.00 20.00
536 Kelvim Escobar 5.00 12.00
537 Alex Rios 5.00 12.00
538 Jose Vidro 5.00 12.00
539 Alex Gonzalez 5.00 12.00
540 Yadier Molina 15.00 40.00
541 Ronny Cedeno 5.00 12.00
542 Mark Hendrickson 5.00 12.00
543 Russ Adams 5.00 12.00
544 Chris Capuano 5.00 12.00
545 Raul Ibanez 8.00 20.00
546 Vicente Padilla 5.00 12.00
547 Chris Duffy 5.00 12.00
548 Bengie Molina 5.00 12.00
549 Chien-Ming Wang 8.00 20.00
550 Curt Schilling 8.00 20.00
551 Craig Wilson 5.00 12.00
552 Mike Lieberthal 5.00 12.00
553 Kazuo Matsui 5.00 12.00
554 Jeff Francis 5.00 12.00
555 Brady Clark 5.00 12.00
556 Willy Taveras 5.00 12.00
557 Mike Maroth 5.00 12.00
558 Bernie Williams 8.00 20.00
559 Edwin Encarnacion 12.00 30.00
560 Vernon Wells 5.00 12.00
561A L.Hernandez Nats 5.00 12.00
561B L.Hernandez Giants 5.00 12.00
562 Kenny Rogers 5.00 12.00
563 Steve Finley 5.00 12.00
564 Trot Nixon 5.00 12.00
565 Jonny Gomes 5.00 12.00
566 Brandon Phillips 5.00 12.00
567 Shawn Chacon 5.00 12.00
568 Dave Bush 5.00 12.00
569 Jose Guillen 5.00 12.00
570 Gustavo Chacin 5.00 12.00
571 A.Rod Safe at the Plate CL 10.00 25.00
572 Pujols At Bat CL 10.00 25.00
573 Bonds On Deck CL 12.00 30.00
574 Breaking Up Two CL 3.00 8.00
575 Conference On The Mound CL 8.00 20.00
576 Touch Em All CL 6.00 15.00
577 Avoiding The Runner CL 3.00 8.00
578 Bunting The Runner Over CL 3.00 8.00
579 In The Hole CL 5.00 12.00
580 Jeter Steals Third CL 20.00 50.00
581 Nolan Ryan 40.00 100.00
582 Cal Ripken 40.00 100.00
583 Carl Yastrzemski 20.00 50.00
584 Duke Snider 8.00 20.00
585 Tom Seaver 8.00 20.00
586 Mickey Mantle 40.00 100.00
587 Jim Palmer 8.00 20.00
588 Gary Carter 8.00 20.00
589 Stan Musial 20.00 50.00
590 Luis Aparicio 8.00 20.00
591 Prince Fielder 30.00 80.00
592 Conor Jackson 10.00 25.00
593 Jeremy Hermida 6.00 15.00
594 Jeff Mathis 6.00 15.00
595 Alay Soler 6.00 15.00
596 Ryan Spilborghs 6.00 15.00
597 Chuck James 6.00 15.00
598 Josh Barfield 6.00 15.00
599 Ian Kinsler 20.00 50.00
600 Val Majewski 6.00 15.00
601 Brian Slocum 6.00 15.00
602 Matt Kemp 15.00 40.00
603 Nate McLouth 6.00 15.00
604 Sean Marshall 6.00 15.00
605 Brian Bannister 6.00 15.00
606 Ryan Zimmerman 20.00 50.00
607 Kendry Morales 15.00 40.00
608 Jonathan Papelbon 30.00 80.00
609 Matt Cain 40.00 100.00
610 Anderson Hernandez 6.00 15.00
611 Jose Capellan 6.00 15.00
612 Lastings Milledge 6.00 15.00
613 Francisco Liriano 15.00 40.00
614 Hanley Ramirez 10.00 25.00
615 Brian Anderson 6.00 15.00
616 Reggie Abercrombie 6.00 15.00
617 Erick Aybar 6.00 15.00
618 James Loney 10.00 25.00
619 Joel Zumaya 15.00 40.00
620 Travis Ishikawa 10.00 25.00
621 Jason Kubel 6.00 15.00
622 Drew Meyer 6.00 15.00
623 Kenji Johjima 15.00 40.00
624 Fausto Carmona 6.00 15.00
625 Nick Markakis 12.00 30.00
626 John Rheinecker 6.00 15.00
627 Melky Cabrera 10.00 25.00
628 Michael Pelfrey 15.00 40.00
629 Dan Uggla 10.00 25.00
630 Justin Verlander 50.00 125.00

2006 Topps Turkey Red Red

*RED 316-580: 1X TO 2X BASIC
*RED 316-580: .2X TO .5X BASIC SP
*RED 581-590: .5X TO 1.2X BASIC RET
*RED 591-630: .6X TO 1.5X BASIC ROOKIE
ONE RED OR OTHER PARALLEL PER PACK
THERE ARE NO SP'S IN THIS SET

2006 Topps Turkey Red White

*WHITE 316-580: 2X TO 5X BASIC
*WHITE 316-580: .25X TO .6X BASIC SP
*WHITE 581-590: .6X TO 1.5X BASIC RET
*WHITE 591-630: .75X TO 2X BASIC ROOKIE
STATED ODDS 1:4 HOBBY/RETAIL
THERE ARE NO SP'S IN THIS SET

2006 Topps Turkey Red Autographs

GROUP A ODDS 1:870 H, 1:880 R
GROUP B ODDS 1:165 H, 1:170 R
EXCHANGE DEADLINE 09/30/08
AR Alex Rodriguez 40.00 80.00
BM Brian McCann B 6.00 15.00
BMC Brandon McCarthy B 4.00 10.00
CB Clint Barmes B 4.00 10.00
CJ Chipper Jones A 40.00 80.00
CV Claudio Vargas B 4.00 10.00
DJ Dan Johnson B 4.00 10.00
DL Derrek Lee A 15.00 40.00
DW David Wright A 15.00 40.00
GA Garrett Atkins B 4.00 10.00
HS Huston Street A 6.00 15.00
JB Josh Barfield B 6.00 15.00
JG Jonny Gomes A 6.00 15.00
JS Johan Santana A 8.00 20.00
KJ Kenji Johjima A 12.50 30.00
MC Miguel Cabrera A 25.00 60.00
MM Mike Morse B 6.00 15.00
PL Paul LoDuca A 15.00 40.00
RC Robinson Cano A 30.00 60.00
RH Ryan Howard A 10.00 25.00
RO Roy Oswalt A 15.00 40.00

2006 Topps Turkey Red Autographs Black

*BLACK GROUP B: .6X TO 1.5X BASIC
GROUP A ODDS 1:6000 H, 1:6200 R
GROUP B ODDS 1:1185 H, 1:1200 R
GROUP A PRINT RUN 15 SERIAL #'d SETS
GROUP B PRINT RUN 99 SERIAL #'d SETS
NO GROUP A PRICING DUE TO SCARCITY
EXCHANGE DEADLINE 09/30/08

2006 Topps Turkey Red Autographs Red

*RED GROUP A: .4X TO 1X BASIC
*RED GROUP B: .4X TO 1X BASIC
GROUP A ODDS 1:1800 H, 1:1850 R
GROUP B ODDS 1:245 H, 1:250 R
GROUP A PRINT RUN 50 SERIAL #'d SETS
GROUP B PRINT RUN 475 SERIAL #'d SETS
EXCHANGE DEADLINE 09/30/08
DW David Wright A/50 15.00 40.00
KJ Kenji Johjima A/50 15.00 40.00
MC Miguel Cabrera A/50 30.00 60.00
PL Paul LoDuca A/50 12.50 30.00

2006 Topps Turkey Red Autographs White

*WHITE GROUP B: .5X TO 1.2X BASIC
GROUP A ODDS 1:3600 H, 1:3800 R
GROUP B ODDS 1:585 H, 1:600 R
GROUP A PRINT RUN 25 SERIAL #'d SETS
GROUP B PRINT RUN 200 SERIAL #'d SETS
NO GROUP A PRICING DUE TO SCARCITY
EXCHANGE DEADLINE 09/30/08

2006 Topps Turkey Red B-18 Blankets

STATED ODDS 1:2 JUMBO
REPURCHASED ODDS 1:159 JUMBO
AR1 Alex Rodriguez White 4.00 10.00
AR2 Alex Rodriguez Blue 4.00 10.00
BB1 Barry Bonds White 5.00 12.00
BB2 Barry Bonds Red 5.00 12.00
DL1 Derrek Lee White 1.25 3.00
DL2 Derrek Lee Red 1.25 3.00
DO1 David Ortiz White 3.00 8.00
DO2 David Ortiz Orange 3.00 8.00
HM1 Hideki Matsui White 3.00 8.00
HM2 Hideki Matsui Blue 3.00 8.00
IS1 Ichiro Suzuki White 4.00 10.00
IS2 Ichiro Suzuki Green 4.00 10.00
KJ1 Kenji Johjima White 3.00 8.00
KJ2 Kenji Johjima Green 3.00 8.00
MM1 Mickey Mantle White 10.00 25.00
MM2 Mickey Mantle Blue 10.00 25.00
MR1 Manny Ramirez White 3.00 8.00
MR2 Manny Ramirez Orange 3.00 8.00
VG1 Vladimir Guerrero White 2.00 5.00
VG2 Vladimir Guerrero Green 2.00 5.00
NNO Repurchased B-18 Blanket

2006 Topps Turkey Red Cabinet

STATED ODDS 1:2 JUMBO
REPURCHASED ODDS 1:4340 JUMBO
SUEDE ODDS 1:634 JUMBO
SUEDE PRINT RUN 1 SERIAL #'d SET
NO SUEDE PRICING DUE TO SCARCITY
AJ Andruw Jones 6.00 15.00
AP Albert Pujols 12.50 30.00
AR Alex Rodriguez 10.00 25.00
AS Alfonso Soriano 4.00 10.00
BB Barry Bonds 10.00 25.00
CC Carl Crawford 4.00 10.00
CCA Chris Carpenter 4.00 10.00
CD Carlos Delgado 4.00 10.00
CY Carl Yastrzemski 10.00 25.00
DJ Derek Jeter 12.50 30.00
DL Derrek Lee 4.00 10.00
DO David Ortiz 6.00 15.00
DS Duke Snider 6.00 15.00
DW David Wright 10.00 25.00
FL Francisco Liriano 6.00 15.00
GC Gary Carter 4.00 10.00
HM Hideki Matsui 6.00 15.00
IR Ivan Rodriguez 6.00 15.00
IS Ichiro Suzuki 10.00 25.00
JB Josh Barfield 4.00 10.00
JBE Josh Beckett 4.00 10.00
JC Jorge Cantu 4.00 10.00
JD Johnny Damon 6.00 15.00
JF Jeff Francoeur 6.00 15.00
JG Jonny Gomes 4.00 10.00
JP Jake Peavy 4.00 10.00
JPA Jonathan Papelbon 10.00 25.00
JR Jimmy Rollins 4.00 10.00
JS Johan Santana 6.00 15.00
JT Jim Thome 6.00 15.00
KG Ken Griffey Jr. 12.50 30.00
MM Mickey Mantle 30.00 60.00
MP Mike Piazza 6.00 15.00
NG Nomar Garciaparra 6.00 15.00
NJ Nick Johnson 4.00 10.00
NM Nick Markakis 6.00 15.00
NR Nolan Ryan 15.00 40.00
PF Prince Fielder 6.00 15.00
PM Pedro Martinez 6.00 15.00
RH Ryan Howard 10.00 25.00
RJ Randy Johnson 6.00 15.00
TG Troy Glaus 4.00 10.00
NNO Repurchased T-3 Cabinet

2006 Topps Turkey Red Relics

GROUP A ODDS 1:330 H, 1:335 R
GROUP B ODDS 1:205 H, 1:211 R
GROUP C-D ODDS 1:50 H, 1:54 R
GROUP E ODDS 1:88 H, 1:88 R
AJ Andruw Jones Jsy D 3.00 8.00
AP Albert Pujols Jsy D 8.00 20.00
APE Andy Pettitte Jsy B 3.00 8.00
AR Alex Rodriguez Jsy C 8.00 20.00
BL Brad Lidge Jsy C 3.00 8.00
BR Brian Roberts Jsy E 3.00 8.00
BW Bernie Williams Pants C 3.00 8.00
CB Carlos Beltran Jsy C 3.00 8.00
CBA Clint Barmes Jsy A 3.00 8.00
CC Chris Carpenter Jsy D 3.00 8.00
CD Carlos Delgado Bat A 3.00 8.00
CJ Chipper Jones Jsy C 5.00 12.00
DL Derrek Lee Jsy B 3.00 8.00
DO David Ortiz Jsy D 5.00 12.00
DW David Wright Jsy C 6.00 15.00
DWI Dontrelle Willis Jsy D 3.00 8.00
EC Eric Chavez Pants D 3.00 8.00
HB Hank Blalock Jsy D 3.00 8.00
HM Hideki Matsui Jsy C 5.00 12.00
IS Ichiro Suzuki Jsy A 8.00 20.00
JC Jose Contreras Jsy D 3.00 8.00
JD Johnny Damon Bat A 3.00 8.00
JE Jim Edmonds Jsy C 3.00 8.00
JF Jeff Francoeur Jsy E 5.00 12.00
JG Jon Garland Pants D 3.00 8.00
JH Jeremy Hermida Bat A 3.00 8.00
JM Joe Mauer Jsy E 3.00 8.00
JR Jose Reyes Jsy C 3.00 8.00
JS Johan Santana Jsy B 3.00 8.00
LB Lance Berkman Jsy D 3.00 8.00
MC Miguel Cabrera Jsy C 3.00 8.00
ME Morgan Ensberg Jsy E 3.00 8.00
MM Mike Mussina Pants B 3.00 8.00
MP Mike Piazza Bat A 5.00 12.00
MR Manny Ramirez Pants E 3.00 8.00
MRI Mariano Rivera Jsy C 6.00 15.00
MT Mark Teixeira Jsy D 3.00 8.00
MY Michael Young Jsy C 3.00 8.00
PK Paul Konerko Pants C 3.00 8.00
PL Paul LoDuca Jsy D 3.00 8.00
PM Pedro Martinez Jsy C 3.00 8.00
RC Robinson Cano Bat C 5.00 12.00
RH Ryan Howard Bat A 8.00 20.00
RHA Roy Halladay Jsy E 3.00 8.00
RIH Rich Harden Jsy C 3.00 8.00
RO Roy Oswalt Jsy B 3.00 8.00
TH Torii Hunter Jsy E 3.00 8.00
VG Vladimir Guerrero Jsy D 5.00 12.00

2006 Topps Turkey Red Relics Black

*BLACK: .75X TO 2X BASIC
STATED ODDS 1:485 H, 1:500 R
STATED PRINT RUN 50 SERIAL #'d SETS

2006 Topps Turkey Red Relics Red

*RED: .5X TO 1.2X BASIC
STATED ODDS 1:160 H, 1:170 R
STATED PRINT RUN 150 SERIAL #'d SETS

2006 Topps Turkey Red Relics White

*WHITE: .6X TO 1.5X BASIC
STATED ODDS 1:245 H, 1:250 R
STATED PRINT RUN 99 SERIAL #'d SETS

2007 Topps Turkey Red

COMPLETE SET (200) 150.00 200.00
COMP.SET w/o SP's (150) 12.50 30.00
COMMON CARD (1-186) .12 .30
COMMON RC (1-186) .15 .40
COMMON SP (1-186) 2.50 6.00
SP ODDS 1:4 HOBBY, 1:4 RETAIL
COMMON AD BACK (1-186) 2.50 6.00
AD BACK ODDS 1:4 HOBBY,1:4 RETAIL
1 Ryan Howard .25 .60
1b R.Howard Ad Back SP 4.00 10.00
2 Dontrelle Willis .12 .30
3 Matt Cain .20 .50
4 John Maine .12 .30
5 Cole Hamels .25 .60
6 Corey Patterson .12 .30
7 Mickey Mantle SP 10.00 25.00
8 Servin Up Strikes Joham Santana CL .20 .50
9 Josh Beckett .12 .30
10 Jimmy Rollins .20 .50
11 Kenji Johjima .30 .75
12 Orlando Hernandez .12 .30
13 Jorge Posada Play at the Plate CL .20 .50
14 Ivan Rodriguez .20 .50
15 Ichiro Suzuki .40 1.00
15b I.Suzuki Ad Back SP 4.00 10.00
16 Double Griffey CL .60 1.50
17 Stephen Drew .12 .30
18 B.J. Upton .12 .30
19 Mickey Mantle 1.00 2.50
20 Alex Rodriguez .40 1.00
20b A.Rod Ad Back SP 4.00 10.00
21 Adam Dunn .20 .50
22 Adam Lind SP (RC) 2.50 6.00
23 Adrian Gonzalez .25 .60
24 Akinori Iwamura RC .40 1.00
25 Albert Pujols .40 1.00
25b A.Pujols Ad Back SP 4.00 10.00
26 Frank Thomas .30 .75
27 Roy Halladay .20 .50
28 Alejandro De Aza RC .25 .60
29 Alex Gordon RC .50 1.25
30 Barry Bonds .50 1.25
31 Andrew Miller RC .60 1.50
32 Andruw Jones .12 .30
33 Kurt Suzuki SP (RC) 2.50 6.00
34 Mickey Mantle 1.00 2.50
35 Andy Pettitte .20 .50
36 Tadahito Iguchi .12 .30
37 Edgar Renteria .12 .30
38 Tim Hudson .20 .50
39 Micah Owings (RC) .15 .40
40 Chipper Jones .30 .75
40b C.Jones Ad Back SP 3.00 8.00
41 Barry Zito .20 .50
42 Dice-K CL .50 1.25
43 Jarrod Saltalamacchia SP (RC) 2.50 6.00
44 Bill Hall .12 .30
45 Billy Butler (RC) .25 .60
46 Billy Wagner .12 .30
47 Rich Harden SP 2.50 6.00
48 Prince Albert CL .40 1.00
49 Brandon Inge .12 .30
50 Jason Giambi .12 .30
51 Brandon Webb .20 .50
52 Brandon Wood (RC) .15 .40
53 Swiping Second Carl Crawford CL .20 .50
54 Brian Giles .12 .30
55 Josh Hamilton (RC) .50 1.25
56 C.Utley Ad Back SP 3.00 8.00
57 Miguel Montero (RC) .15 .40
58 Carl Crawford .20 .50
59 Carlos Beltran .20 .50
60 Mariano Rivera .40 1.00
61 Carlos Delgado .12 .30
62 Carlos Lee SP 2.50 6.00
63 Carlos Zambrano SP 2.50 6.00
64 Miguel Tejada .20 .50
65 Mike Cameron .12 .30
66 Chase Utley SP 3.00 8.00
67 Chase Wright RC .40 1.00
68 Chien-Ming Wang .20 .50
69 Nick Swisher .20 .50
70 David Wright .25 .60
71 Mike Piazza SP 3.00 8.00
72 Chris Carpenter .20 .50
73 Mark Buehrle SP 2.50 6.00
74 Torii Hunter SP 2.50 6.00
75 Tyler Clippard (RC) .25 .60
76 Nick Markakis .25 .60
77 Mickey Mantle 1.00 2.50
78 Curt Schilling .20 .50
79 Curtis Granderson .25 .60
80 Craig Biggio .20 .50
81 Juan Pierre .12 .30
82 Dallas Braden SP RC 2.50 6.00
83 Dan Haren SP 3.00 8.00
84 Dan Uggla .12 .30
85 Danny Putnam (RC) .15 .40
86 David DeJesus .12 .30
87 David Eckstein .12 .30
88 Tim Lincecum RC .75 2.00
89 Johnny Damon SP 2.50 6.00
90 Justin Morneau .20 .50
91 Delmon Young (RC) .25 .60
92 Homer Bailey (RC) .25 .60
93 Carlos Gomez RC .30 .75
94 Josh Fields SP (RC) 2.50 6.00
95 Derek Jeter .75 2.00
95b D.Jeter Ad Back SP 6.00 15.00
96 Derek Lee .12 .30
97 Don Kelly (RC) .15 .40
98 Doug Slaten RC .15 .40
99 Dustin Moseley .12 .30
100 Gary Sheffield .12 .30
101 Orlando Hudson SP 2.50 6.00
102 Elijah Dukes RC .25 .60
103 Eric Byrnes SP 2.50 6.00
104 Eric Chavez .12 .30
105 Phil Hughes (RC) .40 1.00
105b Hughes Ad Back SP (RC) 4.00 10.00
106 Felix Hernandez SP 2.50 6.00
106b Felix Hernandez Ad Back SP 2.50 6.00
107 Mickey Mantle 1.00 2.50
108 Felix Pie (RC) .15 .40
109 Captain Jeter CL .75 2.00
110 Daisuke Matsuzaka RC .60 1.50
110b Dice-K Ad Back SP RC 6.00 15.00
111 Francisco Rodriguez .20 .50
112 Ramon Hernandez .12 .30
113 Randy Johnson .30 .75
114 Gary Matthews .12 .30
115 Prince Fielder .20 .50
116 Vladdy Yard CL .20 .50
117 Mickey Mantle 1.00 2.50
118 Hideki Matsui .30 .75
119 Hideki Okajima RC .75 2.00
120 Manny Ramirez .30 .75
121 H.Pence SP (RC) 6.00 15.00
122 Roy Oswalt .20 .50
123 Josh Willingham SP 2.50 6.00
124 Tom Gordon SP 2.50 6.00
125 Michael Young .12 .30
126 J.D. Drew .12 .30
127 Ryan Zimmerman .20 .50
128 James Shields SP 3.00 8.00
129 Jack Wilson .12 .30
130 David Ortiz .30 .75
130b D.Ortiz Ad Back SP 3.00 8.00
131 Jose Reyes CL .20 .50
132 Jamie Vermilyea RC .15 .40
133 Jason Bay .20 .50
134 Scott Kazmir SP 2.50 6.00
135 Jason Isringhausen SP 3.00 8.00
136 Jason Marquis SP 2.50 6.00
137 Jason Schmidt .12 .30
138 Shawn Green .12 .30
139 Jeff Francoeur SP 3.00 8.00
140 Alfonso Soriano .20 .50
141 Kevin Kouzmanoff (RC) .15 .40
142 Jered Weaver .20 .50
143 Todd Helton SP 2.50 6.00
144 Jermaine Dye .12 .30
145 Jim Thome .20 .50
146 Tom Glavine SP 2.50 6.00
147 Joe Mauer .25 .60
148 Joe Nathan .12 .30
149 Joe Smith RC .15 .40
150 Ken Griffey Jr. .60 1.50
150b Griffey Ad Back SP 5.00 12.00
151 Grady Sizemore .20 .50
152 Sammy Sosa SP 3.00 8.00
153 Andy LaRoche (RC) .15 .40
154 Travis Buck (RC) .15 .40
155 Alex Rios .12 .30
156 Travis Hafner .12 .30
157 Jake Peavy .12 .30
158 Jeff Kent .12 .30
159 Johan Santana .20 .50
159b Johan Santana Ad Back SP 2.50 6.00
160 Ivan Rodriguez .20 .50
161 Trevor Hoffman .20 .50
162 Troy Glaus .12 .30
163 Troy Tulowitzki (RC) .50 1.25
164 Jorge Posada .20 .50
165 Kei Igawa SP RC 3.00 8.00
166 Jose Reyes .20 .50
167 Mickey Mantle 1.00 2.50
168 Utley Streak CL .20 .50
169 Justin Verlander .30 .75
170 Hanley Ramirez .20 .50
171 Kelly Johnson SP 2.50 6.00
172 Kelvin Jimenez RC .15 .40
173 Roger Clemens .40 1.00
174 Khalil Greene SP 2.50 6.00
175 Lance Berkman .20 .50
176 Turning Two Hanley Ramirez CL .20 .50
177 Kyle Kendrick RC .40 1.00
178 Magglio Ordonez .20 .50
179 Marcus Giles SP 2.50 6.00
180 Miguel Cabrera .30 .75
180b Miguel Cabrera Ad Back SP 2.50 6.00
181 Mark Teahen .12 .30
182 Mark Teixeira SP 2.50 6.00
183 Matt Chico SP (RC) 2.50 6.00
184 Matt Holliday .30 .75
185 Vladimir Guerrero .20 .50
185b V. Guerrero Ad Back SP 3.00 8.00
186 Yovani Gallardo (RC) .40 1.00

2007 Topps Turkey Red Chrome

STATED ODDS 1:4 HOBBY,1:7 RETAIL
STATED PRINT RUN 1999 SER.#'d SETS
SKIP NUMBERED SET
1 Ryan Howard 2.00 5.00
2 Dontrelle Willis 1.00 2.50
4 John Maine 1.00 2.50
5 Cole Hamels 2.00 5.00
9 Josh Beckett 1.00 2.50
11 Kenji Johjima 2.50 6.00
12 Orlando Hernandez 1.00 2.50
15 Ichiro Suzuki 3.00 8.00
17 Stephen Drew 1.00 2.50
20 Alex Rodriguez 3.00 8.00
21 Adam Dunn 1.50 4.00
24 Akinori Iwamura 2.50 6.00
25 Albert Pujols 3.00 8.00
29 Alex Gordon 3.00 8.00
30 Barry Bonds 4.00 10.00
31 Andrew Miller 4.00 10.00
32 Andruw Jones 1.00 2.50
34 Mickey Mantle 8.00 20.00
35 Andy Pettitte 1.50 4.00
36 Tadahito Iguchi 1.00 2.50
39 Micah Owings 1.00 2.50
40 Chipper Jones 2.50 6.00
41 Barry Zito 1.50 4.00
45 Billy Butler 1.50 4.00
46 Billy Wagner 1.00 2.50
51 Brandon Webb 1.50 4.00
52 Brandon Wood 1.00 2.50
55 Josh Hamilton 3.00 8.00
59 Carlos Beltran 1.50 4.00
60 Mariano Rivera 3.00 8.00
61 Carlos Delgado 1.00 2.50
64 Miguel Tejada 1.50 4.00
68 Chien-Ming Wang 1.50 4.00
70 David Wright 2.00 5.00
72 Chris Carpenter 1.50 4.00
75 Tyler Clippard 1.50 4.00
76 Nick Markakis 2.00 5.00
77 Mickey Mantle 8.00 20.00
81 Juan Pierre 1.00 2.50
84 Dan Uggla 1.00 2.50
85 Danny Putnam 1.00 2.50
87 David Eckstein 1.00 2.50
88 Tim Lincecum 5.00 12.00
90 Justin Morneau 1.50 4.00
91 Delmon Young 1.50 4.00
93 Carlos Gomez 2.00 5.00
95 Derek Jeter 6.00 15.00
96 Derek Lee 1.00 2.50
97 Don Kelly 1.00 2.50

98 Doug Slaten 1.00 2.50
99 Dustin Moseley 1.00 2.50
100 Gary Sheffield 1.00 2.50
102 Elijah Dukes 1.50 4.00
104 Eric Chavez 1.00 2.50
105 Phil Hughes 2.50 6.00
107 Mickey Mantle 8.00 20.00
108 Felix Pie 1.00 2.50
110 Daisuke Matsuzaka 4.00 10.00
111 Francisco Rodriguez 1.50 4.00
113 Randy Johnson 2.50 6.00
114 Gary Matthews 1.00 2.50
115 Prince Fielder 1.50 4.00
117 Mickey Mantle 8.00 20.00
119 Hideki Okajima 5.00 12.00
120 Manny Ramirez 2.50 6.00
122 Roy Oswalt 1.50 4.00
125 Michael Young 1.00 2.50
126 J.D. Drew 1.00 2.50
127 Ryan Zimmerman 1.50 4.00
130 David Ortiz 2.50 6.00
133 Jason Bay 1.50 4.00
137 Jason Schmidt 1.00 2.50
140 Alfonso Soriano 1.50 4.00
141 Kevin Kouzmanoff 1.00 2.50
142 Jered Weaver 1.50 4.00
144 Jermaine Dye 1.00 2.50
147 Joe Mauer 2.00 5.00
149 Joe Smith 1.00 2.50
150 Ken Griffey Jr. 5.00 12.00
151 Grady Sizemore 1.50 4.00
154 Travis Buck 1.00 2.50
155 Alex Rios 1.00 2.50
158 Jeff Kent 1.00 2.50
159 Johan Santana 1.50 4.00
160 Ivan Rodriguez 1.50 4.00
162 Troy Glaus 1.00 2.50
163 Troy Tulowitzki 3.00 8.00
166 Jose Reyes 1.50 4.00
167 Mickey Mantle 8.00 20.00
169 Justin Verlander 2.50 6.00
170 Hanley Ramirez 1.50 4.00
172 Kelvin Jimenez 1.00 2.50
173 Roger Clemens 3.00 8.00
175 Lance Berkman 1.50 4.00
177 Kyle Kendrick 2.50 6.00
178 Magglio Ordonez 1.50 4.00
180 Miguel Cabrera 2.50 6.00
181 Mark Teahen 1.00 2.50
185 Vladimir Guerrero 1.50 4.00
186 Yovani Gallardo 2.50 6.00

2007 Topps Turkey Red Chrome Refractors

*CHROME REF: .5X TO 1.2X BASIC CHROME
STATED ODDS 1:8 HOBBY,1:16 RETAIL
STATED PRINT RUN 999 SER.#'d SETS
SKIP NUMBERED SET

2007 Topps Turkey Red Chrome Black Refractors

*BLACK REF: 1X TO 2.5X BASIC CHROME
STATED ODDS 1:43 HOBBY
STATED PRINT RUN 99 SER.#'d SETS
SKIP NUMBERED SET

2007 Topps Turkey Red Cabinet

STATED ODDS 1:2 HOB.BOXLOADER
AD Adam Dunn 2.00 5.00
AG Alex Gordon 4.00 10.00
AI Akinori Iwamura 3.00 8.00
AJ Andruw Jones 1.25 3.00
AP Albert Pujols 4.00 10.00
AR Alex Rodriguez 4.00 10.00
AS Alfonso Soriano 2.00 5.00
BW Brandon Webb 2.00 5.00
BZ Barry Zito 2.00 5.00
CC Chris Carpenter 2.00 5.00
CL Carlos Lee 1.25 3.00
CU Chase Utley 2.00 5.00
CW Chien-Ming Wang 2.00 5.00
DJ Derek Jeter 8.00 20.00
DM Daisuke Matsuzaka 5.00 12.00
DO David Ortiz 3.00 8.00
DW David Wright 2.50 6.00
DY Delmon Young 2.00 5.00
ED Elijah Dukes 2.00 5.00
FH Felix Hernandez 2.00 5.00
FR Francisco Rodriguez 2.00 5.00
GS Grady Sizemore 2.00 5.00
HO Hideki Okajima 6.00 15.00
HR Hanley Ramirez 2.00 5.00
IR Ivan Rodrighuez 2.00 5.00
IS Ichiro Suzuki 4.00 10.00
JB Jason Bay 2.00 5.00
JD Jermaine Dye 1.25 3.00
JDS Jason Schmidt 1.25 3.00
JEM Justin Morneau 2.00 5.00
JF Jeff Francoeur 3.00 8.00
JM Joe Mauer 2.50 6.00
JR Jose Reyes 2.00 5.00
JS Johan Santana 2.00 5.00
JV Justin Verlander 3.00 8.00
KG Ken Griffey Jr. 6.00 15.00
LB Lance Berkman 2.00 5.00
MC Miguel Cabrera 3.00 8.00
MM Mickey Mantle 10.00 25.00
MP Mike Piazza 3.00 8.00
MR Manny Ramirez 3.00 8.00
MT Miguel Tejada 2.00 5.00
MY Michael Young 1.25 3.00
NM Nick Markakis 2.50 6.00
PF Prince Fielder 2.00 5.00
RC Roger Clemens 4.00 10.00
RH Ryan Howard 2.50 6.00
RZ Ryan Zimmerman 2.00 5.00
SD Stephen Drew 1.25 3.00
TT Troy Tulowitzki 4.00 10.00
VG Vladimir Guerrero 2.00 5.00

2007 Topps Turkey Red Chromographs

GROUP A ODDS 1:3700 HOBBY/RETAIL
GROUP B ODDS 1:292 HOBBY/RETAIL
GROUP C ODDS 1:194 HOBBY/RETAIL
GROUP D ODDS 1:177 HOBBY/RETAIL
NO GROUP A PRICING AVAILABLE
EXCH DEADLINE 9/30/2009
AG Alex Gordon D 12.00 30.00
AK Austin Kearns D 4.00 10.00
BJ Bobby Jenks C 8.00 20.00
BW Brad Wilkerson B 3.00 8.00
CAH Clay Hensley C 3.00 8.00
CG Curtis Granderson B 30.00 60.00
CH Cole Hamels C 6.00 15.00
CJ Chuck James B 4.00 10.00
DE Darin Erstad B 4.00 10.00
DU Dan Uggla D 3.00 8.00
EC Eric Chavez B 4.00 10.00
FP Felix Pie C 4.00 10.00
HCK Hong-Chih Kuo C 6.00 15.00
HR Hanley Ramirez C 6.00 15.00
JM John Maine C 10.00 25.00
JZ Joel Zumaya D 6.00 15.00
LM Lastings Milledge D 6.00 15.00
MC Melky Cabrera D 3.00 8.00
MG Mike Gonzalez C 3.00 8.00
NM Nick Markakis D 6.00 15.00
NR Nate Robertson C 6.00 15.00
PL Paul LoDuca B 4.00 10.00
RC Robinson Cano B 12.50 30.00
RJH Rich Hill D 4.00 10.00
RM Rob Mackowiak B 3.00 8.00
RNM Russell Martin D 5.00 12.00
SC Sean Casey B 6.00 15.00
SP Scott Podsednik B 3.00 8.00
SV Shane Victorino C 6.00 15.00
TG Tony Gwynn Jr. B 6.00 15.00
WN Wil Nieves B 6.00 15.00

2007 Topps Turkey Red Presidents

COMPLETE SET (43) 60.00 150.00
STATED ODDS 1:12 HOBBY, 1:12 RETAIL
TRP1 George Washington 2.00 5.00
TRP2 John Adams 1.50 4.00
TRP3 Thomas Jefferson 1.50 4.00
TRP4 James Madison 1.50 4.00
TRP5 James Monroe 1.50 4.00
TRP6 John Quincy Adams 1.50 4.00
TRP7 Andrew Jackson 1.50 4.00
TRP8 Martin Van Buren 1.50 4.00
TRP9 William H. Harrison 1.50 4.00
TRP10 John Tyler 1.50 4.00
TRP11 James K. Polk 1.50 4.00
TRP12 Zachary Taylor 1.50 4.00
TRP13 Millard Fillmore 1.50 4.00
TRP14 Franklin Pierce 1.50 4.00
TRP15 James Buchanan 1.50 4.00
TRP16 Abraham Lincoln 2.00 5.00
TRP17 Andrew Johnson 1.50 4.00
TRP18 Ulysses S. Grant 1.50 4.00
TRP19 Rutherford B. Hayes 1.50 4.00
TRP20 James Garfield 1.50 4.00
TRP21 Chester A. Arthur 1.50 4.00
TRP22 Grover Cleveland 1.50 4.00
TRP23 Benjamin Harrison 1.50 4.00
TRP24 Grover Cleveland 1.50 4.00
TRP25 William McKinley 1.50 4.00
TRP26 Theodore Roosevelt 1.50 4.00
TRP27 William H. Taft 1.50 4.00
TRP28 Woodrow Wilson 1.50 4.00
TRP29 Warren G. Harding 1.50 4.00
TRP30 Calvin Coolidge 1.50 4.00
TRP31 Herbert Hoover 1.50 4.00
TRP32 Franklin D. Roosevelt 1.50 4.00
TRP33 Harry S. Truman 1.50 4.00
TRP34 Dwight D. Eisenhower 1.50 4.00
TRP35 John F. Kennedy 2.00 5.00
TRP36 Lyndon B. Johnson 1.50 4.00
TRP37 Richard Nixon 1.50 4.00
TRP38 Gerald Ford 1.50 4.00
TRP39 Jimmy Carter 1.50 4.00
TRP40 Ronald Reagan 2.00 5.00
TRP41 George H. W. Bush 2.00 5.00
TRP42 Bill Clinton 2.00 5.00
TRP43 George W. Bush 2.00 5.00

2007 Topps Turkey Red Relics

GROUP A ODDS 1:13,000 HOBBY/RETAIL
GROUP B ODDS 1:211 HOBBY/RETAIL
GROUP C ODDS 1:58 HOBBY/RETAIL
GROUP D ODDS 1:155 HOBBY/RETAIL
GROUP E ODDS 1:85 HOBBY/RETAIL
GROUP F ODDS 1:80 HOBBY/RETAIL
GROUP G ODDS 1:53 HOBBY/RETAIL
AB Adrian Beltre Bat D 3.00 8.00
AD Adam Dunn Jsy C 3.00 8.00
AH Aaron Harang Bat D 3.00 8.00
AJ1 Andruw Jones Jsy B 4.00 10.00
AJ2 Andruw Jones Bat F 3.00 8.00
AM Andrew Miller Jsy G 3.00 8.00
ANB Angel Berroa Bat F 3.00 8.00
AS Alfonso Soriano Bat C 4.00 10.00
BB Barry Bonds Bat B 12.50 30.00
BC Bobby Crosby Pants C 3.00 8.00
BJR B.J. Ryan Jsy C 3.00 8.00
BR Brian Roberts B 5.00 12.00
BS Brian Stokes E 3.00 8.00
BT Brad Thompson E 3.00 8.00
BW Brandon Webb Pants B 5.00 12.00
BZ Ben Zobrist Bat B 4.00 10.00
CB1 Carlos Beltran Jsy G 3.00 8.00
CB2 Carlos Beltran Bat B 4.00 10.00
CC Coco Crisp Bat C 3.00 8.00
CD Carlos Delgado B 5.00 12.00
CH Cole Hamels D 5.00 12.00
CJ Chipper Jones C 4.00 10.00
CJC Chris Carpenter C 3.00 8.00
CL Carlos Lee B 4.00 10.00
CR Chris Ray E 3.00 8.00
CS C.C. Sabathia E 3.00 8.00
DN Dioner Navarro C 3.00 8.00
DO David Ortiz Bat C 4.00 10.00
DR Darrell Rasner E 3.00 8.00
DU Dan Uggla C 3.00 8.00
DW David Wright D 6.00 15.00
DWA Daryle Ward Bat G 3.00 8.00
DWW Dontrelle Willis G 3.00 8.00
DY Delmon Young Bat C 3.00 8.00
ES Ervin Santana C 3.00 8.00
GP Glen Perkins C 3.00 8.00
HB Hank Blalock C 3.00 8.00
HR Hanley Ramirez B 5.00 12.00
IR Ivan Rodriguez Pants D 4.00 10.00
IS Ichiro Suzuki Bat B 8.00 20.00
JB Josh Beckett Bat G 3.00 8.00
JC Jorge Cantu Bat C 3.00 8.00
JD Jermaine Dye Pants B 5.00 12.00
JE Jim Edmonds C 3.00 8.00
JF Jeff Francoeur Bat B 6.00 15.00
JG Jon Garland Pants G 3.00 8.00
JH Josh Hamilton Bat G 4.00 10.00
JK Jeff Kent Bat B 4.00 10.00
JM Justin Morneau Bat C 3.00 8.00
JP Josh Paul D 3.00 8.00
JPM Joe Mauer C 4.00 10.00
JR Jose Reyes E 3.00 8.00
JRB Jason Bay B 4.00 10.00
JS John Smoltz C 4.00 10.00
JV2 Jason Varitek Bat D 4.00 10.00
JW Jered Weaver B 5.00 12.00
JZ Joel Zumaya D 3.00 8.00
KM Kaz Matsui Bat D 3.00 8.00
LB Lance Berkman G 3.00 8.00
LC Luis Castillo Bat C 3.00 8.00
MC Melky Cabrera Bat C 3.00 8.00
ME Morgan Ensberg E 3.00 8.00
MG Marcus Giles F 3.00 8.00
MJC Miguel Cairo Bat C 3.00 8.00
MM Mickey Mantle Bat B 20.00 50.00
MP Mike Piazza Bat D 5.00 12.00
MR Manny Ramirez F 4.00 10.00
MT Miguel Tejada Pants C 3.00 8.00
MY Michael Young C 3.00 8.00
NM Nick Markakis Bat B 6.00 15.00
NP Neifi Perez Bat G 3.00 8.00
NS Nick Swisher Pants E 3.00 8.00
PM Pedro Martinez Bat C 3.00 8.00
PP Placido Polanco Bat D 3.00 8.00
RB1 Rocco Baldelli Jsy F 3.00 8.00
RB2 Rocco Baldelli Bat C 3.00 8.00
RH Ryan Howard B 10.00 25.00
RJH Rich Hill F 3.00 8.00
RK Ryan Klesko Bat C 3.00 8.00
RS Reggie Sanders Bat C 3.00 8.00
RZ Ryan Zimmerman Bat C 5.00 12.00
SR Scott Rolen F 3.00 8.00
SS Sammy Sosa Bat E 4.00 10.00
ST So Taguchi Bat C 3.00 8.00
TB Travis Buck F 3.00 8.00
TH Travis Hafner B 5.00 12.00
TI Tadahito Iguchi C 3.00 8.00
TJ Tyler Johnson Pants C 3.00 8.00
VG Vladimir Guerrero B 5.00 12.00
VW Vernon Wells B 5.00 12.00

2007 Topps Turkey Red Silks

STATED ODDS 1:85 HOBBY
STATED PRINT RUN 99 SER.#'d SETS
AD Adam Dunn 6.00 15.00
AI Akinori Iwamura 8.00 20.00
AIR Alex Rios 8.00 20.00
AP Albert Pujols 12.50 30.00
AR Alex Rodriguez 30.00 60.00
AS Alfonso Soriano 10.00 25.00
BB Billy Butler 12.50 30.00
BLB Barry Bonds 20.00 50.00
CH Cole Hamels 10.00 25.00
CJ Chipper Jones 12.50 30.00
CS C.C. Sabathia 8.00 20.00
CY Adrian Gonzalez 6.00 15.00
DH Dan Haren 6.00 15.00
DJ Derek Jeter 20.00 50.00
DM Daisuke Matsuzaka 12.50 30.00
DO David Ortiz 12.50 30.00
DU Dan Uggla 8.00 20.00
DW David Wright 12.50 30.00
DWW Dontrelle Willis 6.00 15.00
EB Erik Bedard 8.00 20.00
GS Grady Sizemore 10.00 25.00
HP Hunter Pence 15.00 40.00
HR Hanley Ramirez 8.00 20.00
IS Ichiro Suzuki 20.00 50.00
JAS John Smoltz 12.50 30.00
JB Josh Beckett 10.00 25.00
JBR Jose Reyes 12.50 30.00
JD Jermaine Dye 6.00 15.00
JH J.J. Hardy 6.00 15.00
JL John Lackey 6.00 15.00
JM Justin Morneau 6.00 15.00
JP Jake Peavy 10.00 25.00
JR Jimmy Rollins 12.50 30.00
JRB Jason Bay 6.00 15.00
JS Johan Santana 15.00 40.00
JV Justin Verlander 10.00 25.00
KG Ken Griffey Jr. 25.00 60.00
MAR Manny Ramirez 10.00 25.00
MH Matt Holliday 12.50 30.00
MM Mickey Mantle 60.00 120.00
MO Magglio Ordonez 15.00 40.00
MR Mark Reynolds 10.00 25.00
MT Mark Teixeira 8.00 20.00
NS Nick Swisher 8.00 20.00
PF Prince Fielder 15.00 40.00
RH Ryan Howard 20.00 50.00
RM Russell Martin 8.00 20.00
RZ Ryan Zimmerman 8.00 20.00
TH Torri Hunter 6.00 15.00
VG Vladimir Guerrero 8.00 20.00

2013 Topps Turkey Red

COMMON CARD (1-100) 1.00 2.50
COMMON RC (1-100) 1.00 2.50
1 R.A. Dickey 2.00 5.00
2 Derek Jeter 6.00 15.00
3 Mike Trout 20.00 50.00
4 Jose Altuve 2.00 5.00
5 David Wright 2.00 5.00
6 Manny Machado RC 40.00 80.00
7 Albert Pujols 3.00 8.00
8 Bryce Harper 10.00 25.00
9 Felix Hernandez 2.00 5.00
10 Adam Jones 2.00 5.00
11 Clayton Kershaw 4.00 10.00
12 Justin Morneau 2.00 5.00
13 Roy Halladay 2.00 5.00
14 Jimmy Rollins 2.00 5.00
15 Curtis Granderson 2.00 5.00
16 Andre Ethier 2.00 5.00
17 Jose Reyes 2.00 5.00
18 Matt Kemp 2.00 5.00
19 Yovani Gallardo 1.50 4.00
20 Fernando Rodney 1.50 4.00
21 Jonathan Papelbon 2.00 5.00
22 Robinson Cano 2.00 5.00
23 Ryan Braun 2.00 5.00
24 Joe Mauer 2.00 5.00
25 Gio Gonzalez 2.00 5.00
26 Pablo Sandoval 2.00 5.00
27 Yonder Alonso 1.50 4.00
28 Ryan Zimmerman 2.00 5.00
29 Yadier Molina 3.00 8.00
30 David Price 2.00 5.00
31 Adam Wainwright 2.00 5.00
32 Prince Fielder 2.00 5.00
33 Edwin Encarnacion 2.50 6.00
34 Yasmani Grandal 1.50 4.00
35 Chase Utley 2.00 5.00
36 Jose Bautista 2.00 5.00
37 Jake Peavy 1.50 4.00
38 Carlos Santana 2.00 5.00
39 Brian McCann 2.00 5.00
40 Starlin Castro 1.50 4.00
41 Brandon Phillips 1.50 4.00
42 Aroldis Chapman 2.50 6.00
43 Justin Upton 2.00 5.00
44 Joey Votto 2.50 6.00
45 Jon Lester 2.00 5.00
46 Wade Miley 1.50 4.00
47 Mark Trumbo 1.50 4.00
48 Adrian Beltre 2.50 6.00
49 Eric Hosmer 2.00 5.00
50 Andrew McCutchen 2.50 6.00
51 C.J. Wilson 1.50 4.00
52 Dustin Pedroia 2.50 6.00
53 Asdrubal Cabrera 2.00 5.00
54 Tim Lincecum 2.00 5.00
55 Tim Hudson 2.00 5.00
56 Freddie Freeman 3.00 8.00
57 Paul Konerko 2.00 5.00
58 CC Sabathia 2.00 5.00
59 Josh Hamilton 2.00 5.00
60 Buster Posey 3.00 8.00
61 Matt Cain 2.00 5.00
62 Ian Kinsler 2.00 5.00
63 Matt Holliday 2.50 6.00
64 Jesus Montero 1.50 4.00
65 Carlos Gonzalez 2.00 5.00
66 Austin Jackson 1.50 4.00
67 Mat Latos 2.00 5.00
68 Adam Dunn 2.00 5.00
69 Josh Reddick 1.50 4.00
70 Yoenis Cespedes 2.50 6.00
71 Hunter Pence 2.00 5.00
72 Cole Hamels 2.00 5.00
73 Yu Darvish 2.50 6.00
74 Johnny Cueto 2.00 5.00
75 Miguel Cabrera 2.50 6.00
76 Jean Segura 2.00 5.00
77 Anthony Rizzo 3.00 8.00
78 Tyler Skaggs RC 2.50 6.00
79 Ian Kennedy 1.50 4.00
80 Jered Weaver 2.00 5.00
81 Zack Greinke 2.50 6.00
82 Chris Sale 2.50 6.00
83 Craig Kimbrel 2.00 5.00
84 Jason Heyward 2.00 5.00
85 Evan Longoria 2.00 5.00
86 Ryan Howard 2.00 5.00
87 Giancarlo Stanton 2.50 6.00
88 Adrian Gonzalez 2.00 5.00
89 Cliff Lee 2.00 5.00
90 Carlos Beltran 2.00 5.00
91 Josh Beckett 1.50 4.00
92 Justin Verlander 2.50 6.00
93 Billy Butler 1.50 4.00
94 Colby Rasmus 2.00 5.00
95 Brett Wallace 1.50 4.00
96 Starling Marte 2.00 5.00
97 Troy Tulowitzki 2.50 6.00
98 Hanley Ramirez 2.00 5.00
99 James Shields 1.50 4.00
100 Stephen Strasburg 2.50 6.00

2013 Topps Turkey Red Autographs

ONE AUTOGRAPH PER BOX
PRINT RUNS B/WN 10-689 COPIES PER
AA Alexi Amarista/32 10.00 25.00
AC Andrew Carignan/620 3.00 8.00
BP Brad Peacock/64 3.00 8.00
CA Chris Archer/689 4.00 10.00
DH Drew Hutchison/389 3.00 8.00
DN Derek Norris/64 6.00 15.00
ES Eduardo Sanchez/39 10.00 25.00
JN Jeff Niemann/48 5.00 12.00
JSA Jerry Sands/139 3.00 8.00
JSE Jean Segura/30 10.00 25.00
KS Kyle Seager/29 12.50 30.00
MF Mike Fiers/689 3.00 8.00
MO Mike Olt/29 20.00 50.00
RW Rickie Weeks/48 12.50 30.00
SC Steve Cishek/689 3.00 8.00
SD Scott Diamond/689 4.00 10.00
TC Tyler Colvin/29 15.00 40.00

2014 Topps Turkey Red

COMPLETE SET (100) 150.00 250.00
PLATE PRINT RUN 1 SET PER COLOR
BLACK-CYAN-MAGENTA-YELLOW ISSUED
NO PLATE PRICING DUE TO SCARCITY
1 Mike Trout 10.00 25.00
2 Patrick Corbin 1.50 4.00
3 Paul Goldschmidt 2.00 5.00
4 Craig Kimbrel 1.50 4.00
5 Chris Davis 1.25 3.00
6 J.J. Hardy 1.25 3.00
7 Adam Jones 1.50 4.00
8 Manny Machado 2.00 5.00
9 David Ortiz 2.00 5.00
10 Clay Buchholz 1.25 3.00
11 Dustin Pedroia 2.00 5.00
12 Anthony Rizzo 2.50 6.00
13 Jake Peavy 1.25 3.00
14 Chris Sale 2.00 5.00
15 Joey Votto 2.00 5.00
16 Brandon Phillips 1.25 3.00
17 Aroldis Chapman 2.00 5.00
18 Justin Masterson 1.25 3.00
19 Jason Kipnis 1.50 4.00
20 Troy Tulowitzki 2.00 5.00
21 Carlos Gonzalez 1.50 4.00
22 Miguel Cabrera 2.00 5.00
23 Max Scherzer 2.00 5.00
24 Justin Verlander 2.00 5.00
25 Prince Fielder 1.50 4.00
26 Eric Hosmer 1.50 4.00
27 Torii Hunter 1.25 3.00
28 Jason Castro 1.25 3.00
29 Salvador Perez 1.50 4.00
30 Alex Gordon 1.50 4.00
31 Clayton Kershaw 3.00 8.00
32 Jose Fernandez 2.00 5.00
33 Jean Segura 1.50 4.00
34 Joe Mauer 1.50 4.00
35 Travis d'Arnaud RC 3.00 8.00
36 David Wright 1.50 4.00
37 Matt Harvey 1.50 4.00
38 Robinson Cano 1.50 4.00
39 Mariano Rivera 3.00 8.00
40 Bartolo Colon 1.25 3.00
41 Cliff Lee 1.50 4.00
42 Jason Grilli 1.25 3.00
43 Wil Myers 1.25 3.00
44 Pedro Alvarez 1.25 3.00
45 Domonic Brown 1.50 4.00
46 Yonder Alonso 1.25 3.00
47 Madison Bumgarner 1.50 4.00
48 Buster Posey 2.50 6.00
49 Marco Scutaro 1.50 4.00
50 Felix Hernandez 1.50 4.00
51 Hisashi Iwakuma 1.50 4.00
52 Yadier Molina 2.50 6.00
53 David Freese 1.25 3.00
54 Adam Wainwright 1.50 4.00
55 Allen Craig 1.50 4.00
56 Matt Carpenter 2.00 5.00
57 Matt Moore 1.50 4.00
58 Yu Darvish 2.00 5.00
59 Cole Hamels 1.50 4.00
60 Ian Kinsler 1.50 4.00
61 Jose Bautista 1.50 4.00
62 Jose Reyes 1.50 4.00
63 Edwin Encarnacion 2.00 5.00
64 Bryce Harper 3.00 8.00
65 Jordan Zimmermann 1.50 4.00
66 Albert Pujols 2.50 6.00
67 Josh Hamilton 1.50 4.00
68 Yoenis Cespedes 2.00 5.00
69 Evan Gattis 1.25 3.00
70 Carlos Gomez 1.25 3.00
71 Jose Altuve 1.50 4.00
72 Zack Greinke 2.00 5.00
73 Hyun-Jin Ryu 1.50 4.00
74 Hanley Ramirez 1.50 4.00
75 Matt Kemp 1.50 4.00
76 Yasiel Puig 2.00 5.00
77 Ryan Braun 1.50 4.00
78 Derek Jeter 8.00 20.00
79 Zack Wheeler 1.50 4.00
80 Andy Pettitte 1.50 4.00
81 CC Sabathia 1.50 4.00
82 Stephen Strasburg 2.00 5.00
83 Roy Halladay 1.50 4.00
84 Ryan Howard 1.50 4.00
85 Chase Utley 1.50 4.00
86 Matt Cain 1.50 4.00
87 Shelby Miller 1.50 4.00
88 Pablo Sandoval 1.50 4.00
89 Justin Upton 1.50 4.00
90 Jurickson Profar 1.50 4.00
91 Adrian Beltre 2.00 5.00
92 Andrew McCutchen 2.00 5.00
93 Gerrit Cole 2.00 5.00
94 David Price 1.50 4.00
95 Evan Longoria 1.50 4.00
96 Giancarlo Stanton 2.00 5.00
97 Nick Swisher 1.50 4.00
98 Xander Bogaerts RC 5.00 12.00
99 Mat Latos 1.50 4.00
100 Adrian Gonzalez 1.50 4.00

2014 Topps Turkey Red Autographs

PRINT RUNS B/WN 5-699 COPIES PER
NO PRICING ON QTY 5
TRA1 Matt Davidson/499 5.00 12.00
TRA2 Chad Bettis/699 4.00 10.00
TRA3 Onelki Garcia/699 4.00 10.00
TRA4 Matt Magill/499 4.00 10.00
TRA5 Alex Wood/35 20.00 50.00
TRA6 Kevin Gausman/499 6.00 15.00
TRA7 Yan Gomes/499 5.00 12.00
TRA8 Andre Rienzo/499 4.00 10.00
TRA9 Danny Salazar/182 8.00 20.00
TRA10 Chris Owings/599 4.00 10.00
TRA11 Jake Marisnick/299 4.00 10.00
TRA12 Taylor Jordan/499 5.00 12.00
TRA13 Michael Wacha/299 12.00 30.00
TRA15 Steve Delabar/99 5.00 12.00
TRA17 Jonathan Schoop/474 6.00 15.00
TRA18 Zoilo Almonte/99 10.00 25.00
TRA19 Casey Kelly/81 5.00 12.00
TRA20 Jake Odorizzi/99 5.00 12.00
TRA21 Joe Kelly/253 4.00 10.00
TRA22 Nate Eovaldi/99 5.00 12.00
TRA23 Zack Cozart/99 5.00 12.00
TRA24 Anthony Gose/64 10.00 25.00
TRA25 Glen Perkins/49 6.00 15.00
TRA26 Junior Lake/49 15.00 40.00
TRA27 Xander Bogaerts/49 15.00 40.00
TRA38 Luis Avilan/214 8.00 20.00

2009 Topps Uncirculated Autographs

ISSUED AS EXCHANGE REPLACEMENTS
1 Andre Dawson 8.00 20.00
2 Lou Piniella 8.00 20.00
3 Clay Buchholz 5.00 12.00
5 Adam Lind 5.00 12.00
6 Carlos Pena 5.00 12.00
7 Prince Fielder 8.00 20.00
8 Robinson Cano 12.50 30.00
9 Darryl Strawberry 8.00 20.00

2009 Topps Unique

COMP.SET w/o RC's (150) 12.50 30.00
COMMON CARD (1-150) .20 .50
COMMON ROOKIE (151-200) .75 2.00
RC PRINT RUN 2699 SER.#'d SETS
1 Nick Markakis .40 1.00
2 Geovany Soto .30 .75
3 Brandon Phillips .20 .50
4 Torii Hunter .20 .50
5 Jay Bruce .30 .75
6 Cliff Lee .30 .75
7 Jose Reyes .30 .75
8 Justin Masterson .20 .50
9 Jermaine Dye .20 .50
10 Ryan Braun .30 .75
11 Ubaldo Jimenez .20 .50
12 Carlos Lee .20 .50
13 Alex Rodriguez .60 1.50
14 Jon Lester .30 .75
15 Chipper Jones .50 1.25
16 Justin Morneau .30 .75
17 Dan Haren .20 .50
18 Andre Ethier .30 .75
19 Felix Hernandez .30 .75
20 Grady Sizemore .30 .75
21 Rick Ankiel .20 .50
22 Ryan Dempster .20 .50
23 Justin Verlander .50 1.25
24 Chase Utley .30 .75
25 David Wright .40 1.00
26 Matt Cain .30 .75
27 Brad Hawpe .20 .50
28 John Lackey .30 .75
29 Roy Oswalt .30 .75
30 Alfonso Soriano .30 .75
31 Braden Looper .20 .50
32 Jayson Werth .30 .75
33 Edinson Volquez .20 .50
34 Matt Kemp .40 1.00
35 Adam Jones .30 .75
36 Joba Chamberlain .20 .50
37 Jason Giambi .20 .50
38 Chris Carpenter .30 .75
39 Jim Thome .30 .75
40 Daisuke Matsuzaka .30 .75
41 Kevin Millwood .20 .50
42 Francisco Liriano .20 .50
43 Joey Votto .50 1.25
44 Aramis Ramirez .20 .50
45 Hanley Ramirez .30 .75
46 Johan Santana .30 .75
47 Hank Blalock .20 .50
48 Joe Saunders .20 .50
49 Carlos Quentin .20 .50
50 Ryan Howard .40 1.00
51 Aaron Rowand .20 .50
52 Aaron Cook .20 .50
53 Curtis Granderson .40 1.00
54 Max Scherzer .50 1.25
55 Manny Ramirez .50 1.25
56 Carlos Delgado .20 .50
57 Garrett Atkins .20 .50
58 Josh Johnson .30 .75
59 Gary Sheffield .20 .50
60 Victor Martinez .30 .75
61 Miguel Tejada .30 .75
62 Roy Halladay .30 .75
63 Kevin Kouzmanoff .20 .50
64 Javier Vazquez .20 .50
65 Joe Mauer .40 1.00
66 Lance Berkman .30 .75
67 Ryan Zimmerman .30 .75
68 Ryan Ludwick .30 .75
69 Randy Johnson .50 1.25
70 Jimmy Rollins .30 .75
71 A.J. Burnett .20 .50
72 Adrian Beltre .50 1.25
73 Nelson Cruz .50 1.25
74 Bobby Abreu .20 .50
75 Miguel Cabrera .50 1.25
76 Chad Billingsley .30 .75
77 Freddy Sanchez .20 .50
78 Scott Kazmir .20 .50
79 Magglio Ordonez .30 .75
80 Brandon Webb .30 .75
81 Hunter Pence .30 .75
82 Adam Dunn .30 .75
83 Dan Uggla .20 .50
84 Jair Jurrjens .20 .50
85 Prince Fielder .30 .75
86 Melvin Mora .20 .50
87 Jason Bay .30 .75
88 Clayton Kershaw .75 2.00
89 Akinori Iwamura .20 .50
90 Zack Greinke .50 1.25
91 Yunel Escobar .20 .50
92 Russell Martin .20 .50
93 Derrek Lee .20 .50
94 Mike Pelfrey .20 .50
95 Tim Lincecum .30 .75
96 Carlos Pena .30 .75
97 Justin Upton .30 .75
98 Denard Span .20 .50
99 Paul Konerko .30 .75
100 Albert Pujols .60 1.50
101 Kurt Suzuki .20 .50
102 Corey Hart .20 .50
103 Aubrey Huff .20 .50
104 Scott Rolen .30 .75
105 Ken Griffey Jr. 1.00 2.50
106 Stephen Drew .20 .50
107 Carlos Beltran .30 .75
108 Dustin Pedroia .50 1.25
109 Derek Jeter 1.25 3.00
110 Carl Crawford .30 .75
111 Carlos Zambrano .30 .75
112 Yovani Gallardo .20 .50
113 Raul Ibanez .30 .75
114 Vernon Wells .20 .50
115 Vladimir Guerrero .30 .75
116 Adam LaRoche .20 .50
117 Carlos Guillen .20 .50
118 Todd Helton .30 .75
119 Brian McCann .30 .75
120 Jake Peavy .20 .50
121 David Ortiz .50 1.25
122 Mark Buehrle .30 .75
123 CC Sabathia .30 .75
124 Jorge Cantu .20 .50
125 Ichiro Suzuki .60 1.50
126 Josh Hamilton .30 .75
127 Nate McLouth .20 .50
128 B.J. Upton .30 .75
129 Alex Gordon .30 .75
130 Cole Hamels .40 1.00
131 Josh Beckett .20 .50
132 James Shields .20 .50
133 Alexei Ramirez .30 .75
134 Kosuke Fukudome .30 .75
135 Adrian Gonzalez .40 1.00
136 Ian Kinsler .30 .75
137 Johnny Cueto .30 .75
138 Jacoby Ellsbury .40 1.00
139 Jorge Posada .30 .75
140 Alex Rios .20 .50
141 Matt Holliday .50 1.25
142 Michael Young .20 .50
143 Robinson Cano .30 .75
144 Mike Lowell .20 .50
145 Evan Longoria .30 .75
146 John Maine .20 .50
147 Jose Lopez .20 .50
148 Aaron Hill .20 .50
149 Garret Anderson .20 .50
150 Mark Teixeira .30 .75
151 Fernando Martinez RC 1.50 4.00
152 David Hernandez RC .60 1.50
153 Chris Coghlan RC 1.50 4.00
154 Brett Anderson RC 1.00 2.50
155 Tyler Greene (RC) .60 1.50
156 Michael Bowden (RC) .60 1.50
157 Wilkin Ramirez RC .60 1.50
158 Trevor Cahill RC 1.50 4.00
159 Dexter Fowler (RC) 1.00 2.50
160 Bud Norris RC .60 1.50
161 Francisco Cervelli RC 1.50 4.00
162 Brett Cecil RC .60 1.50
163 Mat Latos RC 2.00 5.00
164 Derek Holland RC 1.00 2.50
165 Mat Gamel RC 1.50 4.00
166 Kenshin Kawakami RC 1.00 2.50
167 Matt LaPorta RC 1.00 2.50
168 Kris Medlen RC 1.50 4.00
169 Gerardo Parra RC 1.00 2.50
170 Josh Outman RC 1.00 2.50
171 Trevor Crowe RC .60 1.50
172 Ryan Perry RC 1.50 4.00
173 Colby Rasmus (RC) 1.00 2.50
174 Rick Porcello RC 2.00 5.00
175 Nolan Reimold (RC) .60 1.50
176 David Price RC 1.25 3.00
177 Omir Santos RC .60 1.50
178 Ricky Romero (RC) 1.00 2.50
179 Jordan Schafer (RC) 1.00 2.50
180 Anthony Swarzak (RC) .60 1.50
181 Travis Snider RC 1.00 2.50
182 Koji Uehara RC 1.50 4.00
183 Jesus Guzman RC .60 1.50
184 Sean West (RC) 1.00 2.50
185 Neftali Feliz RC 1.00 2.50
186 Vin Mazzaro RC .60 1.50
187 Gordon Beckham RC 1.00 2.50
188 Jordan Zimmermann RC 1.50 4.00
189 Chris Tillman RC 1.00 2.50
190 Tommy Hanson RC 1.50 4.00
191 Josh Reddick RC 1.00 2.50
192 Michael Saunders RC 1.50 4.00
193 Alfredo Aceves RC 1.00 2.50
194 Kyle Blanks RC 1.00 2.50
195 Elvis Andrus RC 1.50 4.00
196 Andrew McCutchen (RC) 3.00 8.00
197 Will Venable RC .60 1.50
198 David Huff RC .60 1.50
199 Aaron Bates RC .60 1.50
200 Jhoulys Chacin RC 1.00 2.50

2009 Topps Unique Bronze

*BRONZE VET: 2X TO 5X BASIC VET
*BRONZE RC: .75X TO 2X BASIC RC
STATED PRINT RUN 99 SER.#'d SETS
187 Gordon Beckham 6.00 15.00

2009 Topps Unique Red

*RED VET: .75X TO 2X BASIC VET
*RED RC: .5X TO 1.2X BASIC RC
STATED PRINT RUN 1199 SER.#'d SETS

2009 Topps Unique Alone at the Top

*BRONZE: .6X TO 1.5X BASIC
BRONZE PRINT RUN 99 SER.#'d SETS
GOLD PRINT RUN 25 SER.#'d SETS
NO GOLD PRICING AVAILABLE
PLATINUM PRINT RUN 1 SER.#'d SET
NO PLATINUM PRICING AVAILABLE
AT01 Chipper Jones 1.00 2.50
AT02 Albert Pujols 1.25 3.00
AT03 Hanley Ramirez .60 1.50
AT04 Ryan Howard .75 2.00
AT05 Adam Dunn .60 1.50
AT06 Willy Taveras .40 1.00
AT07 Johan Santana .60 1.50
AT08 Tim Lincecum .60 1.50
AT09 Francisco Rodriguez .60 1.50
AT10 Roy Halladay .60 1.50

2009 Topps Unique Dual Distinction Relics

STATED PRINT RUN 99 SER.#'d SETS
BF R.Braun/P.Fielder 6.00 15.00
BP Lance Berkman 4.00 10.00
Hunter Pence
CL M.Cain/T.Lincecum 6.00 15.00
CP M.Cabrera/A.Pujols 6.00 15.00
EP J.Ellsbury/D.Pedroia 10.00 25.00
GH Vladimir Guerrero 4.00 10.00
Torii Hunter
GP A.Gonzalez/A.Pujols 8.00 20.00
HB Roy Halladay 4.00 10.00
Josh Beckett
HK Josh Hamilton 4.00 10.00
Ian Kinsler
HU R.Howard/C.Utley 8.00 20.00
IM I.Suzuki/D.Matsuzaka 12.00 30.00
JM C.Jones/B.McCann 6.00 15.00
KR Matt Kemp 5.00 12.00
Manny Ramirez
LC E.Longoria/C.Crawford 6.00 15.00

MJ N.Markakis/A.Jones 8.00 20.00
MM J.Mauer/J.Morneau 8.00 20.00
OY David Ortiz 4.00 10.00
Kevin Youkilis
PR J.Posada/M.Rivera 20.00 50.00
RU Hanley Ramirez 4.00 10.00
Dan Uggla
SH Johan Santana 5.00 12.00
Cole Hamels
SR Alfonso Soriano 4.00 10.00
Aramis Ramirez
SS G.Sizemore/I.Suzuki 8.00 20.00
TR M.Teixeira/A.Rodriguez 10.00 25.00
VP Justin Verlander 5.00 12.00
Rick Porcello
WR David Wright 4.00 10.00
Jose Reyes

2009 Topps Unique Jumbo Patches

PRINT RUNS B/WN 13-40 COPIES PER
NO PRICING ON QTY 22 OR LESS
PRICING FOR NON-PREMIUM PATCHES
BM Brian McCann/40 8.00 20.00
CL Che-Hsuan Lin/40 30.00 60.00
CS CC Sabathia/40 12.50 30.00
DE Damaso Espino/40 5.00 12.00
DU Dan Uggla/35 50.00 100.00
FC Francisco Cervelli/40 5.00 12.00
FH Felix Hernandez/40 40.00 80.00
JE Justin Erasmus/40 5.00 12.00
MT Mark Teixeira/40 15.00 40.00
RA Rick Ankiel/40 8.00 20.00
RJ Randy Johnson/30 20.00 50.00
RL Ryan Ludwick/40 50.00 100.00
CSM Curt Smith/40 8.00 20.00
HJR Hyun-Jin Ryu/40 5.00 12.00
JWE Jeff Weaver/40 10.00 25.00
MO2 Magglio Ordonez/40 30.00 60.00

2009 Topps Unique Presidential Plates

PLATINUM PRINT RUN 1 SER.#'d SET
NO PLATINUM PRICING AVAILABLE
PP1 George Washington 30.00 60.00
PP2 John Adams 20.00 50.00
PP3 Thomas Jefferson 20.00 50.00
PP4 James Madison 15.00 40.00
PP5 James Monroe 15.00 40.00
PP6 John Quincy Adams 15.00 40.00
PP7 Andrew Jackson 30.00 60.00
PP8 Martin Van Buren 15.00 40.00
PP9 William Henry Harrison 15.00 40.00
PP10 John Tyler 15.00 40.00
PP11 James K. Polk 15.00 40.00
PP12 Zachary Taylor 15.00 40.00
PP13 Millard Fillmore 15.00 40.00
PP14 Franklin Pierce 15.00 40.00
PP15 James Buchanan 15.00 40.00
PP16 Abraham Lincoln 60.00 120.00
PP17 Andrew Johnson 15.00 40.00
PP18 Ulysses S. Grant 20.00 50.00
PP19 Rutherford B. Hayes 15.00 40.00
PP20 James A. Garfield 15.00 40.00
PP21 Chester A. Arthur 10.00 25.00
PP22 Grover Cleveland 15.00 40.00
PP23 Benjamin Harrison 10.00 25.00
PP24 Grover Cleveland 15.00 40.00
PP25 William McKinley 15.00 40.00
PP26 Theodore Roosevelt 20.00 50.00
PP27 William Howard Taft 15.00 40.00
PP28 Woodrow Wilson 20.00 50.00
PP29 Warren G. Harding 30.00 60.00
PP30 Calvin Coolidge 15.00 40.00
PP32 Franklin D. Roosevelt 20.00 50.00
PP33 Harry S Truman 20.00 50.00
PP34 Dwight D. Eisenhower 20.00 50.00
PP35 John F. Kennedy 50.00 100.00
PP36 Lyndon B. Johnson 20.00 50.00
PP37 Richard Nixon 20.00 50.00
PP38 Gerald R. Ford 15.00 40.00
PP40 Ronald Reagan 20.00 50.00
PP41 George Bush 20.00 50.00
PP42 Bill Clinton 20.00 50.00
PP43 George W. Bush 20.00 50.00
PP44 Barack Obama 40.00 80.00

2009 Topps Unique Primetime Patches

PRINT RUNS B/WN 20-99 COPIES PER
NO PRICING ON QTY 25 OR LESS
PRICING FOR NON-PREMIUM PATCHES
PTP1 Adam Dunn/99 4.00 10.00
PTP2 Adrian Beltre/99 4.00 10.00
PTP3 Albert Pujols/99 12.50 30.00
PTP4 Alex Gordon/99 10.00 25.00
PTP6 Alex Rodriguez/99 8.00 20.00
PTP7 Andrew Miller/99 4.00 10.00
PTP8 Anthony Reyes/75 5.00 12.00
PTP10 Barry Zito/99 4.00 10.00
PTP11 Brad Lidge/99 4.00 10.00
PTP12 Brett Myers/99 4.00 10.00
PTP13 Carlos Beltran/99 6.00 15.00
PTP14 Carlos Delgado/75 8.00 20.00
PTP16 CC Sabathia/99 4.00 10.00
PTP17 Chase Utley/50 20.00 50.00
PTP18 Chipper Jones/99 12.50 30.00
PTP19 David Ortiz/99 4.00 10.00
PTP20 Edinson Volquez/99 4.00 10.00
PTP21 Ervin Santana/75 4.00 10.00
PTP22 Freddy Sanchez/99 4.00 10.00
PTP23 Hank Blalock/99 4.00 10.00
PTP24 Hideki Okajima/50 8.00 20.00
PTP25 Howie Kendrick/99 4.00 10.00
PTP26 Ian Kinsler/99 4.00 10.00
PTP27 Ivan Rodriguez/99 5.00 12.00
PTP28 J.D. Drew/50 4.00 10.00
PTP29 J.J. Hardy/75 4.00 10.00
PTP30 Jacoby Ellsbury/75 12.50 30.00
PTP31 Jason Giambi/75 4.00 10.00
PTP33 Jim Thome/75 5.00 12.00
PTP35 Joey Votto/99 8.00 20.00
PTP36 John Smoltz/99 5.00 12.00
PTP37 Johnny Damon/75 5.00 12.00
PTP38 Jorge Posada/75 10.00 25.00
PTP39 Jose Reyes/99 5.00 12.00
PTP40 Josh Hamilton/99 5.00 12.00
PTP41 Kevin Millwood/99 4.00 10.00
PTP42 Kevin Youkilis/75 6.00 15.00
PTP43 Lance Berkman/99 4.00 10.00
PTP44 Magglio Ordonez/99 6.00 15.00
PTP45 Manny Ramirez/99 10.00 25.00
PTP46 Mark Teixeira/75 8.00 20.00
PTP47 Matt Holliday/75 4.00 10.00
PTP48 Michael Young/99 6.00 15.00
PTP49 Miguel Cabrera/99 8.00 20.00
PTP50 Miguel Tejada/99 4.00 10.00
PTP51 Mike Lowell/99 4.00 10.00
PTP52 Mike Napoli/99 6.00 15.00
PTP53 Pablo Sandoval/75 30.00 60.00
PTP54 Pat Burrell/99 4.00 10.00
PTP55 Pedro Martinez/99 5.00 12.00
PTP56 Phil Hughes/75 5.00 12.00
PTP57 Prince Fielder/75 6.00 15.00
PTP58 Rafael Furcal/99 4.00 10.00
PTP59 Robinson Cano/50 6.00 15.00
PTP60 Rocco Baldelli/99 4.00 10.00
PTP61 Roy Oswalt/99 4.00 10.00
PTP62 Scott Rolen/99 5.00 12.00
PTP63 Todd Helton/99 4.00 10.00
PTP64 Torii Hunter/99 4.00 10.00
PTP65 Trevor Hoffman/75 4.00 10.00
PTP66 Vernon Wells/75 4.00 10.00
PTP67 Victor Martinez/99 5.00 12.00
PTP68 Vladimir Guerrero/99 4.00 10.00
PTP69 Wladimir Balentien/99 4.00 10.00
PTP70 Yovani Gallardo/99 5.00 12.00
PTP71 Anthony Reyes/50 5.00 12.00
PTP72 Carlos Delgado/50 10.00 25.00
PTP73 Jason Giambi/50 4.00 10.00
PTP74 Jim Thome/50 5.00 12.00
PTP76 Johnny Damon/50 5.00 12.00
PTP77 Mark Teixeira/50 8.00 20.00
PTP78 Pablo Sandoval/50 30.00 60.00
PTP79 Prince Fielder/50 6.00 15.00
PTP80 Albert Pujols/50 20.00 50.00
PTP81 Andrew Miller/50 5.00 12.00
PTP82 Brett Myers/50 5.00 12.00
PTP83 Carlos Beltran/50 8.00 20.00
PTP84 Edinson Volquez/50 5.00 12.00
PTP85 Freddy Sanchez/50 5.00 12.00
PTP86 Josh Hamilton/50 6.00 15.00
PTP87 Miguel Cabrera/50 6.00 15.00
PTP88 Mike Lowell/50 5.00 12.00
PTP89 Mike Napoli/50 8.00 20.00
PTP90 Vladimir Guerrero/50 5.00 12.00
PTP91 Adrian Beltre/99 4.00 10.00
PTP92 Barry Zito/99 4.00 10.00
PTP93 David Ortiz/99 4.00 10.00
PTP94 Hank Blalock/99 4.00 10.00
PTP95 Ivan Rodriguez/99 5.00 12.00
PTP96 Jose Reyes/99 5.00 12.00
PTP97 Magglio Ordonez/99 6.00 15.00
PTP98 Michael Young/99 6.00 15.00
PTP99 Miguel Tejada/99 4.00 10.00
PTP100 Pedro Martinez/99 5.00 12.00
PTP101 Rocco Baldelli/99 4.00 10.00
PTP102 Roy Oswalt/99 4.00 10.00
PTP103 Scott Rolen/99 5.00 12.00
PTP104 Wladimir Balentien/99 4.00 10.00
PTP105 Kevin Millwood/99 4.00 10.00
PTP106 Kevin Millwood/50 5.00 12.00
PTP107 Torii Hunter/99 4.00 10.00
PTP108 Torii Hunter/99 4.00 10.00
PTP109 Adam Dunn/99 4.00 10.00
PTP110 Adam Dunn/99 4.00 10.00
PTP111 Adam Dunn/99 4.00 10.00
PTP112 Chipper Jones/99 12.50 30.00
PTP113 Chipper Jones/99 12.50 30.00
PTP114 Chipper Jones/99 12.50 30.00
PTP115 Lance Berkman/99 4.00 10.00
PTP116 Lance Berkman/99 4.00 10.00
PTP117 Lance Berkman/99 4.00 10.00
PTP118 Todd Helton/99 4.00 10.00
PTP119 Todd Helton/99 4.00 10.00
PTP120 Todd Helton/99 4.00 10.00

2009 Topps Unique Solo Shot Relics

STATED PRINT RUN 275 SER.#'d SETS
AG Adrian Gonzalez 5.00 12.00
AP Albert Pujols 6.00 15.00
AR Alex Rodriguez 8.00 20.00
AS Alfonso Soriano 3.00 8.00
CJ Chipper Jones 4.00 10.00
CU Chase Utley 5.00 12.00
DO David Ortiz 3.00 8.00
DW David Wright 5.00 12.00
EL Evan Longoria 5.00 12.00
GS Grady Sizemore 3.00 8.00
HR Hanley Ramirez 4.00 10.00
IS Ichiro Suzuki 15.00 40.00
JH Josh Hamilton 3.00 8.00
JM Joe Mauer 4.00 10.00
JR Jimmy Rollins 4.00 10.00
MC Miguel Cabrera 3.00 8.00
MH Matt Holliday 5.00 12.00
MR Manny Ramirez 5.00 12.00
MT Mark Teixeira 10.00 25.00
NM Nick Markakis 5.00 12.00
PF Prince Fielder 3.00 8.00
RB Ryan Braun 4.00 10.00
RH Ryan Howard 6.00 15.00
VG Vladimir Guerrero 3.00 8.00
JMO Justin Morneau 3.00 8.00

2009 Topps Unique Solo Shots Autographs

AE Andre Ethier 6.00 15.00
AG Adrian Gonzalez 6.00 15.00
AL Adam Lind 3.00 8.00
CB Chad Billingsley 4.00 10.00
CG Curtis Granderson 6.00 15.00
DP David Price 8.00 20.00
DPE Dustin Pedroia 12.50 30.00
DU Dan Uggla 4.00 10.00
GB Gordon Beckham 20.00 50.00
JB Jay Bruce 6.00 15.00
JC Johnny Cueto 5.00 12.00
JCH Joba Chamberlain 6.00 15.00
JCU Jack Cust 3.00 8.00
JJ Josh Johnson 3.00 8.00
MB Milton Bradley 3.00 8.00
MC Melky Cabrera 8.00 20.00
MCA Matt Cain 6.00 15.00
MK Matt Kemp 5.00 12.00
MS Max Scherzer 15.00 40.00
NM Nick Markakis 5.00 12.00
PH Phil Hughes 3.00 8.00
RB Ryan Braun 8.00 20.00
RC Ryan Church 3.00 8.00
RH Rich Hill 3.00 8.00
RI Raul Ibanez 3.00 8.00
RP Rick Porcello 5.00 12.00
TL Tim Lincecum 60.00 120.00
ZG Zack Greinke 10.00 25.00

2009 Topps Unique Unique Unis

*BRONZE: .6X TO 1.5X BASIC
BRONZE PRINT RUN 99 SER.#'d SETS
GOLD PRINT RUN 25 SER.#'d SETS
NO GOLD PRICING AVAILABLE
PLATINUM PRINT RUN 1 SER.#'d SET
NO PLATINUM PRICING AVAILABLE
UU01 Chipper Jones 1.00 2.50
UU02 Ryan Braun .60 1.50
UU03 Alexei Ramirez .60 1.50
UU04 Andrew McCutchen 2.00 5.00
UU05 Ben Sheets .40 1.00
UU06 Jermaine Dye .40 1.00
UU07 Prince Fielder .60 1.50
UU08 Evan Longoria .60 1.50
UU09 Jason Giambi .40 1.00
UU10 Jose Reyes .60 1.50
UU11 Curtis Granderson .75 2.00
UU12 Jason Bay .60 1.50
UU13 Jimmy Rollins .60 1.50
UU14 Justin Verlander 1.00 2.50
UU15 Roy Halladay .60 1.50
UU16 David Wright .75 2.00
UU17 Carl Crawford .60 1.50
UU18 Gil Meche .40 1.00
UU19 Kevin Youkilis .40 1.00
UU20 Ryan Zimmerman .60 1.50

2009 Topps Unique Unparalleled Performances

*BRONZE: .6X TO 1.5X BASIC
BRONZE PRINT RUN 99 SER.#'d SETS
GOLD PRINT RUN 25 SER.#'d SETS
NO GOLD PRICING AVAILABLE
PLATINUM PRINT RUN 1 SER.#'d SET
NO PLATINUM PRICING AVAILABLE
UP01 Ian Kinsler .60 1.50
UP02 Carlos Delgado .40 1.00
UP03 Randy Johnson 1.00 2.50
UP04 Alex Rodriguez 1.25 3.00
UP05 Orlando Hudson .40 1.00
UP06 Carl Crawford .60 1.50
UP07 Mariano Rivera 1.25 3.00
UP08 Alfonso Soriano .60 1.50
UP09 Dexter Fowler .60 1.50
UP10 Fernando Tatis .40 1.00
UP11 Adam LaRoche .40 1.00
UP12 Raul Ibanez .60 1.50
UP13 Carlos Beltran .60 1.50
UP14 James Loney .40 1.00
UP15 Bronson Arroyo .40 1.00
UP16 Aaron Hill .40 1.00
UP17 Jeremy Hermida .40 1.00
UP18 Randy Johnson 1.00 2.50
UP19 Micah Owings .40 1.00
UP20 Johnny Cueto .60 1.50

2019 Topps Utz

1 Buster Posey 1.50 4.00
2 Yadier Molina 1.50 4.00
3 Brandon Crawford 1.00 2.50
4 Aaron Judge 3.00 8.00
5 Lorenzo Cain .75 2.00
6 Aaron Nola 1.00 2.50
7 Whit Merrifield 1.25 3.00
8 Wade LeBlanc .75 2.00
9 Jonathan Loaisiga 1.00 2.50
10 Adam Jones 1.00 2.50
11 Dansby Swanson 1.25 3.00
12 Gleyber Torres 2.50 6.00
13 Javier Baez 1.50 4.00
14 Steven Duggar 1.00 2.50
15 Kyle Tucker 2.00 5.00
16 Shin-Soo Choo 1.00 2.50
17 Jesus Aguilar 1.00 2.50
18 Sean Reid-Foley .75 2.00
19 Nick Markakis 1.00 2.50
20 Kohl Stewart 1.00 2.50
21 Francisco Arcia 1.25 3.00
22 Khris Davis 1.25 3.00
23 Shohei Ohtani 2.00 5.00
24 Ryan Zimmerman 1.00 2.50
25 Nolan Arenado 2.00 5.00
26 Kris Bryant 1.50 4.00
27 J.D. Martinez 1.25 3.00
28 Ramon Laureano 1.50 4.00
29 Byron Buxton 1.25 3.00
30 Joey Votto 1.25 3.00
31 Blake Snell 1.00 2.50
32 Clayton Kershaw 2.00 5.00
33 Carlos Correa 1.25 3.00
34 Todd Frazier .75 2.00
35 Corey Dickerson .75 2.00
36 Ronald Acuna Jr. 6.00 15.00
37 Chance Adams .75 2.00
38 Trea Turner 1.00 2.50
39 Mookie Betts 2.50 6.00
40 Paul DeJong 1.25 3.00
41 Austin Hedges .75 2.00
42 Aroldis Chapman 1.25 3.00
43 Josh Harrison .75 2.00
44 Rhys Hoskins 1.50 4.00
45 Max Scherzer 1.25 3.00
46 Willson Contreras 1.00 2.50
47 David Bote 1.00 2.50
48 Justin Turner 1.25 3.00
49 Miguel Cabrera 1.25 3.00
50 J.T. Realmuto 1.25 3.00
51 Robinson Cano 1.00 2.50
52 Starling Marte 1.00 2.50
53 Didi Gregorius 1.00 2.50
54 Miguel Andujar 1.25 3.00
55 Luis Severino 1.00 2.50
56 Jonathan Schoop .75 2.00
57 Jake Bauers 1.25 3.00
58 Trey Mancini 1.00 2.50
59 Kyle Schwarber 1.25 3.00
60 Salvador Perez 1.00 2.50
61 David Price 1.00 2.50
62 Dee Gordon .75 2.00
63 Nick Pivetta .75 2.00
64 Francisco Lindor 1.25 3.00
65 Joey Gallo 1.00 2.50
66 Corey Kluber 1.00 2.50
67 Jeff McNeil 2.00 5.00
68 Jake Arrieta 1.00 2.50
69 Freddie Freeman 1.50 4.00
70 Brad Keller .75 2.00
71 Jose Ramirez 1.00 2.50
72 Julio Teheran 1.00 2.50
73 Mike Clevinger 1.00 2.50
74 Cedric Mullins 1.50 4.00
75 Eric Hosmer 1.00 2.50
76 Matt Carpenter 1.25 3.00
77 Harrison Bader 1.00 2.50
78 Justin Verlander 1.25 3.00
79 Miles Mikolas 1.25 3.00
80 Mike Trout 6.00 15.00
81 Jacob deGrom 2.50 6.00
82 Corey Seager 1.25 3.00
83 Jose Altuve 1.00 2.50
84 Michael Conforto 1.00 2.50
85 Juan Soto 4.00 10.00
86 Charlie Blackmon 1.25 3.00
87 Johnny Cueto 1.00 2.50
88 George Springer 1.00 2.50
89 Marcus Stroman 1.00 2.50
90 Jose Quintana .75 2.00
91 Jake Lamb 1.00 2.50
92 Christian Yelich 1.50 4.00
93 Brian Anderson .75 2.00
94 Eddie Rosario 1.00 2.50
95 Matt Chapman 1.25 3.00
96 Edwin Diaz 1.00 2.50
97 Ryon Healy .75 2.00
98 Paul Goldschmidt 1.25 3.00
99 Ryan O'Hearn .75 2.00
100 Nicholas Castellanos 1.25 3.00

2020 Topps Utz

1 Mike Clevinger .75 2.00
2 Albert Pujols 1.25 3.00
3 Shane Bieber 1.00 2.50
4 Kyle Schwarber 1.00 2.50
5 Dan Vogelbach .60 1.50
6 Keston Hiura 1.25 3.00
7 Trevor Story 1.00 2.50
8 Mookie Betts 2.00 5.00
9 Matthew Boyd .60 1.50
10 Max Scherzer 1.00 2.50
11 Zac Gallen 1.50 4.00
12 Paul Goldschmidt 1.00 2.50
13 Anthony Rizzo 1.25 3.00
14 Xander Bogaerts 1.00 2.50
15 Miguel Cabrera 1.00 2.50
16 Juan Soto 3.00 8.00
17 Fernando Tatis Jr. 5.00 12.00
18 Jose Altuve .75 2.00
19 Shohei Ohtani 1.50 4.00
20 Eloy Jimenez 2.00 5.00
21 Tim Anderson 1.00 2.50
22 Javier Baez 1.25 3.00
23 J.T. Realmuto 1.00 2.50
24 Aristides Aquino 1.50 4.00
25 Dustin May 2.00 5.00
26 Ozzie Albies 1.00 2.50
27 Lorenzo Cain .60 1.50
28 Charlie Blackmon 1.00 2.50
29 Jorge Soler 1.00 2.50
30 Pete Alonso 2.50 6.00
31 Max Kepler .75 2.00
32 Christian Yelich 1.25 3.00
33 Francisco Lindor 1.00 2.50
34 Jordan Yamamoto .60 1.50
35 Cody Bellinger 2.00 5.00
36 J.D. Martinez 1.00 2.50
37 Clayton Kershaw 1.50 4.00
38 Jeff McNeil .75 2.00
39 Aaron Judge 2.50 6.00
40 Rafael Devers 1.25 3.00
41 Hunter Harvey 1.00 2.50
42 Nico Hoerner 2.50 6.00
43 Manny Machado 1.00 2.50
44 Nick Senzel 1.00 2.50
45 Jacob deGrom 2.00 5.00
46 Masahiro Tanaka 1.00 2.50
47 Rhys Hoskins 1.25 3.00
48 Bryan Reynolds .75 2.00
49 Aaron Nola .75 2.00
50 Gary Sanchez 1.00 2.50
51 Ronald Acuna Jr. 4.00 10.00
52 Eddie Rosario .75 2.00
53 Matt Chapman 1.00 2.50
54 Brian Anderson .60 1.50
55 Sean Murphy 1.00 2.50
56 Chris Sale 1.00 2.50
57 Trey Mancini 1.00 2.50
58 Nolan Arenado 1.50 4.00
59 Mike Trout 5.00 12.00
60 Jose Ramirez .75 2.00
61 Blake Snell .75 2.00
62 Brendan McKay 1.00 2.50
63 Kris Bryant 1.25 3.00
64 Jose Berrios .75 2.00
65 Freddie Freeman 1.25 3.00
66 Whit Merrifield 1.00 2.50
67 Giancarlo Stanton 1.00 2.50
68 Ketel Marte .75 2.00
69 Yadier Molina 1.25 3.00
70 Bo Bichette 5.00 12.00
71 Anthony Rendon 1.00 2.50
72 Joey Gallo 1.00 2.50
73 Buster Posey 1.25 3.00
74 Walker Buehler 1.25 3.00
75 Yordan Alvarez 6.00 15.00
76 Josh Bell .75 2.00
77 Matt Olson 1.00 2.50
78 George Springer .75 2.00
79 Elvis Andrus .75 2.00
80 Mike Yastrzemski 1.50 4.00
81 Austin Meadows 1.00 2.50
82 Willson Contreras 1.00 2.50
83 Jack Flaherty 1.00 2.50
84 Luis Castillo .75 2.00
85 Joey Votto 1.00 2.50
86 Zack Greinke 1.00 2.50
87 Trent Grisham 2.50 6.00
88 Yoan Moncada 1.00 2.50
89 Kyle Lewis 5.00 12.00
90 Mike Soroka 1.00 2.50
91 Justin Verlander 1.00 2.50
92 Jesus Luzardo 1.25 3.00
93 Gleyber Torres 2.00 5.00
94 Vladimir Guerrero Jr. 1.50 4.00
95 Nelson Cruz 1.00 2.50
96 Alex Bregman 1.00 2.50
97 Gavin Lux 3.00 8.00
98 Chris Paddack 1.00 2.50
99 Bryce Harper 1.50 4.00
100 Dylan Cease 1.00 2.50

2017 Topps Walmart Holiday Snowflake

COMPLETE SET (200) 15.00 40.00
HMW1 Kris Bryant .40 1.00
HMW2 Reynaldo Lopez RC .20 .50
HMW3 Sean Newcomb RC .25 .60
HMW4 Michael Pineda .20 .50
HMW5 Brian Dozier .30 .75
HMW6 Hunter Renfroe RC .25 .60
HMW7 Wil Myers .25 .60
HMW8 Eric Skoglund RC .20 .50
HMW9 Antonio Senzatela RC .20 .50
HMW10 Jose Berrios .25 .60
HMW11 Robbie Ray .20 .50
HMW12 Anthony Rizzo .40 1.00
HMW13 Manny Machado .30 .75
HMW14 Byron Buxton .30 .75
HMW15 Carson Fulmer RC .20 .50
HMW16 Alex Reyes RC .25 .60
HMW17 Jake Arrieta .25 .60
HMW18 Joe Mauer .25 .60
HMW19 Buster Posey .40 1.00
HMW20 Khris Davis .30 .75
HMW21 Bradley Zimmer .25 .60
HMW22 Christian Yelich .40 1.00
HMW23 Jeff Hoffman RC .20 .50
HMW24 Kyle Schwarber .30 .75
HMW25 Mike Trout 1.50 4.00
HMW26 Todd Frazier .20 .50
HMW27 Kyle Hendricks .30 .75
HMW28 Ian Kinsler .25 .60
HMW29 Yu Darvish .30 .75
HMW30 Kyle Freeland RC .25 .60
Missing snowflakes on top
HMW31 Edwin Encarnacion .30 .75
HMW32 Masahiro Tanaka .25 .60
HMW33 Carlos Martinez .25 .60
HMW34 Rougned Odor .25 .60
HMW35 Dansby Swanson RC .50 1.25
HMW36 Mark Trumbo .20 .50
HMW37 Christian Arroyo RC .30 .75
HMW38 Jason Kipnis .25 .60
HMW39 Corey Kluber .25 .60
HMW40 Justin Verlander .30 .75
HMW41 Joey Gallo .25 .60
HMW42 Yonder Alonso .20 .50
HMW43 Jake Thompson RC .20 .50
HMW44 Starling Marte .25 .60
HMW45 Ryan Braun .25 .60
HMW46 Joe Musgrove RC .60 1.50
HMW47 Alex Bregman RC 1.00 2.50
HMW48 Yasiel Puig .30 .75
HMW49 Jorge Bonifacio RC .20 .50
Missing snowflakes on top
HMW50 Zack Greinke .30 .75
HMW51 Daniel Murphy .25 .60
HMW52 Odubel Herrera .25 .60
HMW53 Matt Carpenter .30 .75
HMW54 Ender Inciarte .20 .50
HMW55 Jose Abreu .30 .75
HMW56 Javier Baez .40 1.00
HMW57 Johnny Cueto .25 .60
HMW58 Nolan Arenado .50 1.25
HMW59 Sonny Gray .25 .60
HMW60 Chris Sale .30 .75
HMW61 Curtis Granderson .25 .60
HMW62 Paul Goldschmidt .30 .75
HMW63 Aroldis Chapman .30 .75
HMW64 Jose Bautista .25 .60
HMW65 Felix Hernandez .25 .60
HMW66 Miguel Cabrera .30 .75
HMW67 Jesse Winker RC .75 2.00
Missing snowflakes on top
HMW68 David Wright .25 .60
HMW69 Marcus Stroman .25 .60
HMW70 Yoan Moncada RC .60 1.50
HMW71 Kole Calhoun .20 .50
HMW72 Adrian Beltre .30 .75
HMW73 Maikel Franco .25 .60
HMW74 Trevor Story .30 .75
HMW75 Clayton Kershaw .50 1.25
HMW76 Hanley Ramirez .25 .60
HMW77 Gregory Polanco .25 .60
HMW78 Ian Happ RC .40 1.00
HMW79 Salvador Perez .25 .60
HMW80 Giancarlo Stanton .30 .75
HMW81 Aaron Sanchez .25 .60
HMW82 Lewis Brinson RC .30 .75
HMW83 Sam Travis RC .25 .60
HMW84 Yulieski Gurriel RC .30 .75
HMW85 Stephen Piscotty .25 .60
HMW86 Josh Donaldson .25 .60
HMW87 Domingo Santana .25 .60
HMW88 Didi Gregorius .25 .60
HMW89 Alex Gordon .25 .60
HMW90 Trey Mancini RC .40 1.00
HMW91 Nelson Cruz .30 .75
HMW92 Michael Conforto .25 .60
HMW93 Robert Gsellman RC .20 .50
HMW94 Joey Votto .30 .75
HMW95 Seung-Hwan Oh .40 1.00
HMW96 Amir Garrett RC .20 .50
HMW97 Kevin Kiermaier .25 .60
HMW98 Robinson Cano .25 .60
HMW99 Aaron Judge RC 2.50 6.00
HMW100 Jose Altuve .25 .60
HMW101 Guillermo Heredia .30 .75
HMW102 Troy Tulowitzki .30 .75
HMW103 Billy Hamilton .25 .60
HMW104 Jake Lamb .25 .60
HMW105 Manny Margot RC .20 .50
HMW106 Albert Pujols .40 1.00
HMW107 Cole Hamels SP 25.00 60.00
HMW108 Jordan Montgomery RC .30 .75
HMW109 Miguel Sano .25 .60
HMW110 Corey Seager .30 .75
HMW111 Kenta Maeda .25 .60
HMW112 Tyler Austin RC .25 .60
HMW113 Adam Jones .25 .60
HMW114 Cameron Maybin .20 .50
HMW115 Luke Weaver RC .25 .60
HMW116 Yoenis Cespedes .30 .75
HMW117 Marco Estrada .20 .50
HMW118 Elvis Andrus .25 .60
HMW119 Eric Thames .25 .60
HMW120 Cody Bellinger RC 3.00 8.00
HMW121 Jay Bruce .25 .60
HMW122 Dinelson Lamet RC .20 .50
HMW123 Jharel Cotton RC .20 .50
HMW124 Dallas Keuchel .25 .60
HMW125 Mookie Betts .60 1.50
HMW126 David Dahl RC .25 .60
HMW127 Jon Lester .25 .60
HMW128 Aaron Nola .25 .60
HMW129 Mitch Haniger RC .30 .75
HMW130 A.J. Pollock .20 .50
HMW131 Yadier Molina .40 1.00
HMW132 Andrew McCutchen .30 .75
HMW133 Dustin Pedroia .30 .75
HMW134 Xander Bogaerts .30 .75
HMW135 Max Scherzer .30 .75
HMW136 Hunter Pence .25 .60
HMW137 Noah Syndergaard .25 .60
HMW138 Steven Matz .20 .50
HMW139 Orlando Arcia RC .30 .75
HMW140 Andrew Benintendi RC .60 1.50
HMW141 Freddie Freeman .40 1.00
HMW142 Dexter Fowler .25 .60
HMW143 Craig Kimbrel .25 .60
HMW144 Alex Wood .20 .50
HMW145 George Springer .25 .60
HMW146 Stephen Strasburg .30 .75
HMW147 Addison Russell .30 .75
HMW148 David Price .25 .60
HMW149 Evan Longoria .25 .60
HMW150 Francisco Lindor .30 .75
HMW151 Gary Sanchez .30 .75
HMW152 Adam Wainwright .25 .60
HMW153 Lance McCullers .20 .50
HMW154 Charlie Blackmon .30 .75
HMW155 German Marquez RC .30 .75
HMW156 Adam Duvall .25 .60
HMW157 J.D. Martinez .30 .75
HMW158 Carlos Rodon .30 .75
HMW159 Justin Upton .25 .60
HMW160 Andrew Toles RC .20 .50
HMW161 Ryon Healy RC .25 .60
HMW162 Brandon Phillips .20 .50
HMW163 Trea Turner .25 .60
HMW164 Danny Duffy .20 .50
HMW165 Michael Fulmer .20 .50
HMW166 Jean Segura .25 .60
HMW167 Franklin Barreto RC .20 .50
HMW168 Aledmys Diaz .25 .60
HMW169 Chris Archer .20 .50
HMW170 Ty Blach .20 .50
HMW171 Luis Severino .25 .60
HMW172 Tyler Glasnow RC .75 2.00
HMW173 Ryan Zimmerman .25 .60
HMW174 Carlos Gonzalez .25 .60
HMW175 Carlos Correa .30 .75
HMW176 Eric Hosmer .25 .60
HMW177 Jacob deGrom .60 1.50
HMW178 Derek Fisher RC .25 .60
HMW179 Gerrit Cole .30 .75
HMW180 Chris Davis .20 .50
HMW181 Jameson Taillon .25 .60
HMW182 Marcell Ozuna .30 .75
HMW183 Dee Gordon .20 .50
HMW184 Julio Urias .30 .75
HMW185 Josh Bell RC .50 1.25
HMW186 Ben Zobrist .25 .60
HMW187 Kyle Seager .20 .50
HMW188 Brandon Crawford .25 .60
HMW189 Lucas Giolito .25 .60
HMW190 Nomar Mazara .20 .50
HMW191 Travis Shaw .20 .50
HMW192 Matt Kemp .25 .60
HMW193 Corey Dickerson .20 .50
HMW194 Sean Manaea .20 .50
HMW195 Ichiro .40 1.00
HMW196 Jason Heyward .25 .60
HMW197 Carlos Santana .25 .60
HMW198 Kevin Gausman .30 .75
HMW199 Jose De Leon RC .20 .50
HMW200 Bryce Harper .50 1.25

2017 Topps Walmart Holiday Snowflake Metallic

*METALLIC: .6X TO 1.5X BASIC
STATED ODDS 1:2 PACKS

2017 Topps Walmart Holiday Snowflake Autographs

STATED ODDS 1:272 PACKS
EXCHANGE DEADLINE 10/31/2019
AAAM Albert Almora 8.00 20.00
AABE Andrew Benintendi EXCH 40.00 100.00
AAG Amir Garrett 4.00 10.00
AAJ Aaron Judge EXCH 75.00 200.00
AAR Anthony Rizzo
ABH Bryce Harper
ABP Brett Phillips 5.00 12.00
ACA Christian Arroyo
ACBE Cody Bellinger EXCH 60.00 150.00
ACBL Charlie Blackmon 8.00 20.00
ACC Carlos Correa
ACR Carlos Rodon 6.00 15.00
ACSA Chris Sale
ADF Derek Fisher 8.00 20.00
ADG Dee Gordon
ADL Dinelson Lamet
AEL Evan Longoria 6.00 15.00
AFB Franklin Barreto 4.00 10.00
AGM German Marquez 6.00 15.00
AIH Ian Happ 10.00 25.00
AJBE Jose Berrios
AJG Joey Gallo
AJH Josh Hader 5.00 12.00
AJM Jordan Montgomery 6.00 15.00
AJV Joey Votto 15.00 40.00
AKB Kris Bryant 60.00 150.00
AKD Khris Davis
AKM Ketel Marte 5.00 12.00
ALB Lewis Brinson 15.00 40.00
AMMA Manny Machado 20.00 50.00
AMMR Manny Margot 4.00 10.00
AMT Mike Trout 150.00 400.00
ANS Noah Syndergaard 50.00 120.00
ASN Sean Newcomb
ATM Trey Mancini 20.00 50.00
ATT Troy Tulowitzki 6.00 15.00
AYG Yulieski Gurriel 10.00 25.00
AYM Yoan Moncada

2017 Topps Walmart Holiday Snowflake Relics

STATED ODDS 1:11 PACKS
RAD Adam Duvall 2.50 6.00
RAG Adrian Gonzalez 2.50 6.00
RAW Adam Wainwright 2.50 6.00
RBP Buster Posey 4.00 10.00
RBZ Ben Zobrist 2.50 6.00
RCA Chris Archer 2.00 5.00
RCC Carlos Correa 3.00 8.00
RCG Curtis Granderson 2.50 6.00
RDB Dellin Betances 2.50 6.00
RDG Didi Gregorius 2.50 6.00
RDO David Ortiz 3.00 8.00
RDS Dansby Swanson 5.00 12.00
REL Evan Longoria 2.50 6.00
RFF Freddie Freeman 4.00 10.00
RGP Gregory Polanco 2.50 6.00
RHR Hanley Ramirez 2.50 6.00
RI Ichiro 4.00 10.00
RJD Jacob deGrom 6.00 15.00
RJG Jon Gray 2.00 5.00
RJH Jason Heyward 2.50 6.00
RJM J.D. Martinez 3.00 8.00
RJU Justin Upton 2.50 6.00
RKB Kris Bryant 4.00 10.00
RKK Kevin Kiermaier 2.50 6.00
RKM Kenta Maeda 2.50 6.00
RLS Luis Severino 2.50 6.00
RMF Michael Fulmer 2.00 5.00
RMM Manny Machado 3.00 8.00
RNA Nolan Arenado 5.00 12.00
RNC Nelson Cruz 3.00 8.00
RNS Noah Syndergaard 2.50 6.00
RSC Starlin Castro 2.00 5.00
RTG Tyler Glasnow 8.00 20.00
RVM Victor Martinez 2.50 6.00
RWC Willson Contreras 3.00 8.00
RXB Xander Bogaerts 3.00 8.00
RYC Yoenis Cespedes 3.00 8.00
RYP Yasiel Puig 3.00 8.00
RABE Andrew Benintendi 5.00 12.00
RABR Alex Bregman 10.00 25.00
RAJO Adam Jones 2.50 6.00
RARI Anthony Rizzo 4.00 10.00
RARU Addison Russell 3.00 8.00
RBHM Billy Hamilton 2.50 6.00
RBHR Bryce Harper 5.00 12.00
RCKE Clayton Kershaw 5.00 12.00
RCKI Craig Kimbrel 2.50 6.00
RCKL Corey Kluber 2.50 6.00
RCSA Chris Sale 3.00 8.00
RCSE Corey Seager 3.00 8.00
RDPE Dustin Pedroia 3.00 8.00
RDPR David Price 2.50 6.00
RGSP George Springer 2.50 6.00
RGST Giancarlo Stanton 3.00 8.00
RJBZ Javier Baez 4.00 10.00
RJTE Julio Teheran 2.50 6.00
RJVE Justin Verlander 3.00 8.00
RJVO Joey Votto 3.00 8.00
RMCA Miguel Cabrera 3.00 8.00
RMCO Michael Conforto 2.50 6.00
RMTA Masahiro Tanaka 2.50 6.00
RMTR Mike Trout 20.00 50.00
RMTX Mark Teixeira 2.50 6.00
RTTL Troy Tulowitzki 3.00 8.00
RYMN Yoan Moncada 4.00 10.00
RYMO Yadier Molina 4.00 10.00

2018 Topps Walmart Holiday Snowflake

COMPLETE SET (200) 15.00 40.00
HMW1 Bryce Harper .50 1.25
HMW2 Starlin Castro .20 .50
HMW3 Edwin Encarnacion .30 .75
HMW4 Chris Stratton RC .20 .50
HMW5 Anthony Rizzo .40 1.00
HMW6 Garrett Cooper RC .20 .50
HMW7 Tim Anderson .30 .75
HMW8 Jacob deGrom .60 1.50
HMW9 Chris Taylor .25 .60
HMW10 Amed Rosario RC .25 .60
HMW11 Nick Williams RC .25 .60
HMW12 Buster Posey .40 1.00
HMW13 Craig Kimbrel .25 .60
HMW14 Miguel Andujar RC .75 2.00
HMW15 Jose Ramirez .25 .60
HMW16 Michael Conforto .25 .60
HMW17 Shohei Ohtani RC 5.00 12.00
HMW18 Joey Gallo .25 .60
HMW19 Austin Hays RC .30 .75
HMW20 Justin Verlander .30 .75
HMW21 Blake Snell .25 .60
HMW22 Jon Gray .20 .50
HMW23 Jorge Soler .30 .75
HMW24 Mookie Betts .60 1.50
HMW25 Chris Sale .30 .75
HMW26 Odubel Herrera .25 .60
HMW27 Willie Calhoun RC .30 .75
HMW28 Masahiro Tanaka .25 .60
HMW29 Mike Soroka RC .60 1.50
HMW30 Corey Seager .30 .75
HMW31 Clayton Kershaw .50 1.25
HMW32 Ryan Braun .25 .60
HMW33 Gerrit Cole .30 .75
HMW34 Matt Chapman .30 .75
HMW35 Ichiro .40 1.00
HMW36 Trevor Bauer .40 1.00
HMW37 Manny Machado .30 .75
HMW38 Clint Frazier RC .40 1.00
HMW39 Alex Gordon .25 .60
HMW40 Joey Lucchesi RC .20 .50
HMW41 J.A. Happ .25 .60
HMW42 Daniel Murphy .25 .60
HMW43 Nicholas Castellanos .30 .75
HMW44 Jonathan Schoop .20 .50
HMW45 Yu Darvish .30 .75
HMW46 Max Scherzer .30 .75
HMW47 Miles Mikolas RC .25 .60
HMW48 Dustin Fowler RC .20 .50
HMW49 Stephen Strasburg .30 .75

HMW50 Ronald Acuna Jr. RC	10.00	25.00
HMW51 Christian Yelich	.40	1.00
HMW52 Manny Margot	.20	.50
HMW53 Lance McCullers	.20	.50
HMW54 Giancarlo Stanton	.30	.75
HMW55 Dallas Keuchel	.25	.60
HMW56 Luke Weaver	.25	.60
HMW57 Khris Davis	.30	.75
HMW58 Francisco Mejia RC	.25	.60
HMW59 Gary Sanchez	.30	.75
HMW60 Corey Dickerson	.20	.50
HMW61 Walker Buehler RC	1.00	2.50
HMW62 Nolan Arenado	.50	1.25
HMW63 Tommy Pham	.20	.50
HMW64 Byron Buxton	.30	.75
HMW65 Josh Hader	.25	.60
HMW66 Alex Bregman	.30	.75
HMW67 Rafael Devers RC	.60	1.50
HMW68 Zack Greinke	.30	.75
HMW69 Kris Bryant	.40	1.00
HMW70 Miguel Sano	.25	.60
HMW71 Chris Archer	.20	.50
HMW72 Jake Lamb	.25	.60
HMW73 Tyler Mahle RC	.25	.60
HMW74 Miguel Cabrera	.30	.75
HMW75 Freddie Freeman	.40	1.00
HMW76 Curtis Granderson	.25	.60
HMW77 Paul Goldschmidt	.30	.75
HMW78 Ian Kennedy	.20	.50
HMW79 Andrew McCutchen	.30	.75
HMW80 Willson Contreras	.30	.75
HMW81 Hunter Renfroe	.20	.50
HMW82 Jesse Winker	.30	.75
HMW83 Ryon Healy	.20	.50
HMW84 Albert Pujols	.40	1.00
HMW85 Joey Votto	.30	.75
HMW86 Andrew Benintendi	.30	.75
HMW87 George Springer	.25	.60
HMW88 Marcus Stroman	.25	.60
HMW89 Jose Berrios	.25	.60
HMW90 Jake Arrieta	.25	.60
HMW91 Yadier Molina	.40	1.00
HMW92 Kenta Maeda	.25	.60
HMW93 Michael Fulmer	.20	.50
HMW94 Josh Bell	.25	.60
HMW95 Kevin Gausman	.30	.75
HMW96 Brandon Crawford	.25	.60
HMW97 Sean Manaea	.20	.50
HMW98 Brian Anderson RC	.25	.60
HMW99 Aaron Judge	.75	2.00
HMW100 Mike Trout	1.50	4.00
HMW101 Tyler O'Neill RC	.30	.75
HMW102 Marcell Ozuna	.30	.75
HMW103 Xander Bogaerts	.30	.75
HMW104 Mitch Haniger	.25	.60
HMW105 Alex Verdugo RC	.30	.75
HMW106 Nelson Cruz	.30	.75
HMW107 Dee Gordon	.20	.50
HMW108 Lewis Brinson RC	.20	.50
HMW109 Joe Mauer	.25	.60
HMW110 Domingo Santana	.25	.60
HMW111 Carlos Martinez	.25	.60
HMW112 Jordan Hicks RC	.40	1.00
HMW113 Matt Kemp	.25	.60
HMW114 Michael Brantley	.25	.60
HMW115 Aaron Nola	.25	.60
HMW116 Noah Syndergaard	.25	.60
HMW117 Justin Bour	.20	.50
HMW118 Luis Severino	.25	.60
HMW119 Aroldis Chapman	.30	.75
HMW120 Nick Kingham RC	.20	.50
HMW121 Ian Happ	.25	.60
HMW122 Reynaldo Lopez	.25	.60
HMW123 Todd Frazier	.20	.50
HMW124 Jose Bautista	.25	.60
HMW125 Cody Bellinger	.60	1.50
HMW126 Jon Lester	.25	.60
HMW127 Kevin Kiermaier	.25	.60
HMW128 Trevor Story	.30	.75
HMW129 Javier Baez	.40	1.00
HMW130 Justin Upton	.25	.60
HMW131 Eugenio Suarez	.25	.60
HMW132 Felix Hernandez	.25	.60
HMW133 Elvis Andrus	.25	.60
HMW134 Jameson Taillon	.25	.60
HMW135 Kyle Seager	.20	.50
HMW136 Corey Kluber	.25	.60
HMW137 Cole Hamels	.25	.60
HMW138 David Dahl	.20	.50
HMW139 Kyle Schwarber	.30	.75
HMW140 Ozzie Albies RC	.60	1.50
HMW141 Carlos Correa	.30	.75
HMW142 Scott Kingery RC	.30	.75
HMW143 Evan Longoria	.25	.60
HMW144 Trey Mancini	.25	.60
HMW145 Jack Flaherty RC	.75	2.00
HMW146 Jay Bruce	.25	.60
HMW147 Jose Abreu	.30	.75
HMW148 Dansby Swanson	.30	.75
HMW149 Dustin Pedroia	.30	.75
HMW150 Yoan Moncada	.30	.75
HMW151 Matt Olson	.30	.75
HMW152 Sean Newcomb	.25	.60
HMW153 Adrian Beltre	.30	.75
HMW154 Francisco Lindor	.30	.75
HMW155 Whit Merrifield	.30	.75
HMW156 Carlos Santana	.25	.60
HMW157 Jean Segura	.20	.50
HMW158 Jose Altuve	.25	.60
HMW159 James Paxton	.25	.60
HMW160 J.D. Martinez	.30	.75
HMW161 Lorenzo Cain	.20	.50
HMW162 Anthony Rendon	.30	.75
HMW163 Billy Hamilton	.25	.60
HMW164 Wil Myers	.25	.60
HMW165 Adam Jones	.25	.60
HMW166 Starling Marte	.25	.60
HMW167 Chance Sisco RC	.25	.60
HMW168 Rougned Odor	.25	.60
HMW169 Ryan Zimmerman	.25	.60
HMW170 Robbie Ray	.20	.50
HMW171 Nomar Mazara	.20	.50
HMW172 Ian Kinsler	.25	.60
HMW173 Brian Dozier	.25	.60
HMW174 Fernando Romero RC	.20	.50
HMW175 J.P. Crawford RC	.20	.50
HMW176 Sean Doolittle	.20	.50
HMW177 A.J. Pollock	.20	.50
HMW178 J.D. Davis RC	.25	.60
HMW179 Salvador Perez	.25	.60
HMW180 Christian Villanueva RC	.20	.50
HMW181 Josh Donaldson	.25	.60
HMW182 Gleyber Torres RC	2.00	5.00
HMW183 Dominic Smith RC	.25	.60
HMW184 Charlie Blackmon	.30	.75
HMW185 Yoenis Cespedes	.30	.75
HMW186 Trea Turner	.25	.60
HMW187 Lourdes Gurriel Jr. RC	.40	1.00
HMW188 Justin Smoak	.20	.50
HMW189 Victor Robles RC	.50	1.25
HMW190 Didi Gregorius	.25	.60
HMW191 Dexter Fowler	.25	.60
HMW192 Matt Davidson	.25	.60
HMW193 Gregory Polanco	.25	.60
HMW194 Stephen Piscotty	.20	.50
HMW195 Robinson Cano	.25	.60
HMW196 Eric Hosmer	.25	.60
HMW197 Mike Moustakas	.25	.60
HMW198 Travis Shaw	.20	.50
HMW199 Rick Porcello	.25	.60
HMW200 Eric Thames	.25	.60

2018 Topps Walmart Holiday Snowflake Metallic

*METALLIC: .6X TO 1.5X BASIC
STATED ODDS 1:2 PACKS

HMW17 Shohei Ohtani	8.00	20.00

2018 Topps Walmart Holiday Snowflake Autographs

STATED ODDS 1:297 PACKS
PRINT RUNS B/WN 20-200 COPIES PER
MANY NOT PRICED DUE TO SCARCITY
EXCHANGE DEADLINE 10/31/2020

AAA Anthony Banda/160	3.00	8.00
AAB Adrian Beltre		
AAI A.J. Minter/200	4.00	10.00
AAM Austin Meadows/75	8.00	20.00
AAR Amed Rosario/20	15.00	40.00
AAZ Anthony Rizzo		
ABH Bryce Harper		
ACF Clint Frazier		
ACK Corey Kluber		
ACT Chris Stratton/200	3.00	8.00
ACV Christian Villanueva/200	5.00	12.00
ADC Dylan Cozens/115	3.00	8.00
ADM Daniel Mengden/200	10.00	25.00
AFR Fernando Romero/200	3.00	8.00
AFV Felipe Vazquez/200	4.00	10.00
AGA Gary Sanchez		
AGS George Springer		
AGT Gleyber Torres		
AIH Ian Happ		
AIK Ian Kinsler		
AJA Jose Altuve		
AJE Jose Berrios		
AJF Jack Flaherty		
AJH Jordan Hicks/200	8.00	20.00
AJR Jacob deGrom		
AJS Juan Soto		
AKB Kris Bryant		
ALW Luke Weaver/150	4.00	10.00
AMI Miles Mikolas/200	4.00	10.00
AMS Mike Soroka/150	10.00	25.00
AMT Mike Trout/4		
AOA Ozzie Albies EXCH		
ARA Ronald Acuna Jr.		
ARD Rafael Devers/15		
ARE Ryon Healy		
ARH Rhys Hoskins		
ASD Sean Doolittle/200	5.00	12.00
ASK Scott Kingery		
ASO Shohei Ohtani		
ATB Tyler Beede/200	3.00	8.00
AWA Willy Adames/75	10.00	25.00
AWB Walker Buehler/200	15.00	40.00
AWM Whit Merrifield/200	8.00	20.00
AZG Zack Godley		

2018 Topps Walmart Holiday Snowflake Relics

STATED ODDS 1:11 PACKS

RAB Adrian Beltre	2.50	6.00
RAP Albert Pujols	3.00	8.00
RAR Anthony Rizzo	3.00	8.00
RBG Brett Gardner	2.00	5.00
RBH Bryce Harper	4.00	10.00
RBP Buster Posey	3.00	8.00
RBZ Ben Zobrist	2.00	5.00
RCB Charlie Blackmon	2.50	6.00
RCC Carlos Correa	2.50	6.00
RCK Clayton Kershaw	4.00	10.00
RCM Carlos Martinez	2.00	5.00
RCS Chris Sale	2.50	6.00
RDG Didi Gregorius	2.00	5.00
RDK Dallas Keuchel	2.00	5.00
RDP Dustin Pedroia	2.50	6.00
REE Edwin Encarnacion	2.50	6.00
REH Eric Hosmer	2.00	5.00
REL Evan Longoria	2.00	5.00
RFL Francisco Lindor	2.50	6.00
RGP Gregory Polanco	2.00	5.00
RGS Gary Sanchez	2.50	6.00
RJA Jose Abreu	2.50	6.00
RJB Javier Baez	3.00	8.00
RJC Johnny Cueto	2.00	5.00
RJD Jacob deGrom	5.00	12.00
RJG Jon Gray	1.50	4.00
RJH Josh Harrison	1.50	4.00
RJM J.D. Martinez	2.50	6.00
RJS Jorge Soler	2.50	6.00
RKB Kris Bryant	3.00	8.00
RKD Khris Davis	2.50	6.00
RKS Kyle Schwarber	2.50	6.00
RLC Lorenzo Cain	1.50	4.00
RLS Luis Severino	2.00	5.00
RMB Mookie Betts	5.00	12.00
RMC Miguel Cabrera	2.50	6.00
RMS Miguel Sano	2.00	5.00
RMT Masahiro Tanaka	2.00	5,00
RMW Michael Wacha	2.00	5.00
RNA Nolan Arenado	4.00	10.00
RNC Nelson Cruz	2.50	6.00
RNS Noah Syndergaard	2.00	5.00
RPG Paul Goldschmidt	2.50	6.00
RRC Robinson Cano	2.00	5.00
RSG Sonny Gray	2.00	5.00
RSM Starling Marte	2.00	5.00
RSS Stephen Strasburg	2.50	6.00
RWC Willson Contreras	2.50	6.00
RXB Xander Bogaerts	2.50	6.00
RYC Yoenis Cespedes	2.50	6.00
RYM Yadier Molina	3.00	8.00
RABE Andrew Benintendi	2.50	6.00
RABR Alex Bregman	2.50	6.00
RAJU Aaron Judge	6.00	15.00
RBCR Brandon Crawford	2.00	5.00
RCKI Craig Kimbrel	2.00	5.00
RCSE Corey Seager	2.50	6.00
RDPR David Price	2.00	5.00
RGSP George Springer	2.00	5.00
RJAL Jose Altuve	2.00	5.00
RJBE Josh Bell	2.00	5.00
RJBR Jackie Bradley Jr.	2.50	6.00
RJHE Jason Heyward	2.00	5.00
RJVO Joey Votto	2.50	6.00
RMCO Michael Conforto	2.00	5.00
RMTR Mike Trout	12.00	30.00

2019 Topps Walmart Holiday

HW1 Trevor Bauer	.40	1.00
HW2 Charlie Morton	.30	.75
HW3 Nate Lowe RC	1.00	2.50
HW4 Adam Jones	.25	.60
HW5 Taylor Clarke RC	.20	.50
HW6 Whit Merrifield	.30	.75
HW7 JD Hammer RC	.25	.60
HW8 Juan Soto	1.00	2.50
HW9 Alex Verdugo	.25	.60
HW10 Eddie Rosario	.25	.60
HW11 Ryan Pressly	.20	.50
HW12 Nick Anderson RC	.20	.50
HW13 Hunter Renfroe	.20	.50
HW14 Mitch Haniger	.25	.60
HW15 Edwin Diaz	.25	.60
HW16 Shohei Ohtani	.50	1.25
HW17 Billy Hamilton	.25	.60
HW18 Dee Gordon	.20	.50
HW19 Yusei Kikuchi RC	.30	.75
HW20 Harold Ramirez RC	.30	.75
HW21 Pedro Avila RC	.20	.50
HW22 Michael Conforto	.25	.60
HW23 Michael Chavis RC	.30	.75
HW24 Stephen Strasburg	.30	.75
HW25 Joc Pederson	.25	.60
HW26 Anthony Rizzo	.40	1.00
HW27 Giancarlo Stanton	.30	.75
HW28 DJ LeMahieu	.30	.75
HW29 Mookie Betts	.60	1.50
HW30 Clayton Kershaw	.50	1.25
HW31 Mike Trout	2.00	5.00
HW32 Jose Abreu	.30	.75
HW33 Shohei Ohtani	.50	1.25
HW34 Austin Meadows	.30	.75
HW35 Alex Bregman	.30	.75
HW36 Rafael Devers	.40	1.00
HW37 Lucas Giolito	.25	.60
HW38 Luis Castillo	.25	.60
HW39 Kyle Schwarber	.30	.75
HW40 Dallas Keuchel	.25	.60
HW41 Max Muncy	.25	.60
HW42 Cody Bellinger	.60	1.50
HW43 Keston Hiura RC	.60	1.50
HW44 Derek Dietrich	.25	.60
HW45 Byron Buxton	.30	.75
HW46 Hunter Pence	.25	.60
HW47 Jake Arrieta	.25	.60
HW48 Domingo Santana	.25	.60
HW49 Spencer Turnbull RC	.30	.75
HW50 Max Scherzer	.30	.75
HW51 Oscar Mercado RC	.50	1.25
HW52 Clint Frazier	.25	.60
HW53 Shane Bieber	.30	.75
HW54 Rhys Hoskins	.40	1.00
HW55 Josh Bell	.25	.60
HW56 Trevor Story	.30	.75
HW57 Matt Chapman	.30	.75
HW58 Cole Hamels	.25	.60
HW59 Jose Peraza	.25	.60
HW60 Blake Snell	.25	.60
HW61 Orlando Arcia	.20	.50
HW62 Eduardo Escobar	.20	.50
HW63 Ryne Harper RC	.30	.75
HW64 Willson Contreras	.25	.60
HW65 Joey Votto	.30	.75
HW66 Griffin Canning RC	.30	.75
HW67 Max Kepler	.25	.60
HW68 David Price	.25	.60
HW69 Kevin Pillar	.20	.50
HW70 Maikel Franco	.25	.60
HW71 Pete Alonso RC	2.00	5.00
HW72 Christian Yelich	.40	1.00
HW73 Zack Greinke	.30	.75
HW74 Francisco Lindor	.30	.75
HW75 Zack Wheeler	.25	.60
HW76 Austin Riley RC	1.00	2.50
HW77 Patrick Corbin	.25	.60
HW78 Justin Smoak	.20	.50
HW79 Matthew Beaty RC	.40	1.00
HW80 Scott Kingery	.25	.60
HW81 Evan Longoria	.25	.60
HW82 Trea Turner	.25	.60
HW83 Paul Goldschmidt	.30	.75
HW84 Eric Hosmer	.25	.60
HW85 Ronald Acuna Jr.	2.00	5.00
HW86 Jeff McNeil RC	.50	1.25
HW87 Albert Pujols	.40	1.00
HW88 Pablo Sandoval	.25	.60
HW89 Cal Quantrill RC	.20	.50
HW90 Hyun-Jin Ryu	.25	.60
HW91 Brad Hand	.20	.50
HW92 Kevin Cron RC	.60	1.50
HW93 Josh Donaldson	.25	.60
HW94 C.J. Cron	.20	.50
HW95 Manny Machado	.30	.75
HW96 Buster Posey	.40	1.00
HW97 Jonathan Schoop	.20	.50
HW98 Darwinzon Hernandez RC	.20	.50
HW99 Will Smith RC	.50	1.25
HW100 Jason Heyward	.25	.60
HW101 Eloy Jimenez RC	.75	2.00
HW102 Miguel Sano	.25	.60
HW103 Yasiel Puig	.30	.75
HW104 Renato Nunez	.25	.60
HW105 Francisco Mejia	.25	.60
HW106 Andrew McCutchen	.30	.75
HW107 Miguel Cabrera	.30	.75
HW108 Lane Thomas RC	.30	.75
HW109 Javier Baez	.40	1.00
HW110 Anthony Rendon	.30	.75
HW111 Edwin Encarnacion	.30	.75
HW112 George Springer	.25	.60
HW113 Ozzie Albies	.30	.75
HW114 Thairo Estrada RC	.30	.75
HW115 Ryan Helsley RC	.25	.60
HW116 Elvis Andrus	.25	.60
HW117 Amed Rosario	.25	.60
HW118 Luke Weaver	.20	.50
HW119 Lorenzo Cain	.20	.50
HW120 Tim Beckham	.25	.60
HW121 Brandon Brennan RC	.20	.50
HW122 Andrew Benintendi	.30	.75
HW123 Xander Bogaerts	.30	.75
HW124 Franmil Reyes	.20	.50
HW125 Nick Senzel RC	.60	1.50
HW126 Fernando Tatis Jr. RC	5.00	12.00
HW127 J.D. Martinez	.30	.75
HW128 Khris Davis	.30	.75
HW129 Justin Verlander	.30	.75
HW130 Nomar Mazara	.20	.50
HW131 Tim Anderson	.30	.75
HW132 Bryan Reynolds RC	.60	1.50
HW133 Jose Berrios	.25	.60
HW134 Yasmani Grandal	.20	.50
HW135 Robinson Cano	.25	.60
HW136 Carlos Correa	.30	.75
HW137 Jacob deGrom	.60	1.50
HW138 Nicky Lopez RC	.30	.75
HW139 CC Sabathia	.25	.60
HW140 Josh Naylor RC	.25	.60
HW141 Merrill Kelly RC	.20	.50
HW142 J.T. Realmuto	.30	.75
HW143 Victor Robles	.40	1.00
HW144 Yadier Molina	.40	1.00
HW145 Kolten Wong	.25	.60
HW146 Mitch Keller RC	.25	.60
HW147 Adam Ottavino	.20	.50
HW148 Aaron Judge	.75	2.00
HW149 David Peralta	.20	.50
HW150 Gerrit Cole	.30	.75
HW151 Jorge Polanco	.25	.60
HW152 Aaron Nola	.25	.60
HW153 German Marquez	.20	.50
HW154 Chris Sale	.30	.75
HW155 Williams Astudillo RC	.20	.50
HW156 Michael Soroka	.30	.75
HW157 Mike Yastrzemski RC	1.25	3.00
HW158 Jorge Soler	.30	.75
HW159 Jose Altuve	.25	.60
HW160 Carter Kieboom RC	.30	.75
HW161 Aroldis Chapman	.30	.75
HW162 Dominic Smith	.20	.50
HW163 Hunter Dozier	.20	.50
HW164 Kirby Yates	.25	.60
HW165 Nolan Arenado	.50	1.25
HW166 Tommy La Stella	.20	.50
HW167 Vladimir Guerrero Jr. RC	2.00	5.00
HW168 Cole Tucker RC	.30	.75
HW169 Jon Duplantier RC	.20	.50
HW170 Yoan Moncada	.30	.75
HW171 Brendan Rodgers RC	.30	.75
HW172 Shaun Anderson RC	.20	.50
HW173 Trent Thornton RC	.20	.50
HW174 Corey Seager	.30	.75
HW175 Gary Sanchez	.30	.75
HW176 Freddie Freeman	.40	1.00
HW177 Luke Voit	.50	1.25
HW178 Austin Allen RC	.25	.60
HW179 Tyler O'Neill	.25	.60
HW180 Noah Syndergaard	.25	.60
HW181 Chris Paddack RC	.40	1.00
HW182 Gleyber Torres	.60	1.50
HW183 Devin Smeltzer RC	.30	.75
HW184 Jake Odorizzi	.20	.50
HW185 Joey Gallo	.25	.60
HW186 Jorge Alfaro RC	.20	.50
HW187 Walker Buehler RC	.40	1.00
HW188 David Dahl	.20	.50
HW189 Cavan Biggio RC	1.00	2.50
HW190 Corbin Martin RC	.30	.75
HW191 Luis Arraez RC	.75	2.00
HW192 Bryce Harper	.50	1.25
HW193 Josh Hader	.25	.60
HW194 Marcell Ozuna	.30	.75
HW195 Jose Iglesias	.25	.60
HW196 Charlie Blackmon	.30	.75
HW197 Kris Bryant	.40	1.00
HW198 Felipe Vazquez	.20	.50
HW199 Masahiro Tanaka	.25	.60
HW200 Craig Kimbrel	.25	.60

2019 Topps Walmart Holiday Metallic

*METALLIC: .6X TO 1.5X BASIC
STATED ODDS 1:2 PACKS

HW31 Mike Trout	5.00	12.00
HW85 Ronald Acuna Jr.	5.00	12.00

2019 Topps Walmart Holiday Photo Variations

STATED ODDS 1:7 PACKS

HW8 Juan Soto	3.00	8.00
HW16 Shohei Ohtani	1.50	4.00
HW23 Michael Chavis	1.00	2.50
HW26 Anthony Rizzo	1.25	3.00
HW29 Mookie Betts	2.00	5.00
HW30 Clayton Kershaw	1.50	4.00
HW31 Mike Trout	5.00	12.00
HW33 Shohei Ohtani	1.50	4.00
HW35 Alex Bregman	1.00	2.50
HW36 Rafael Devers	1.25	3.00
HW42 Cody Bellinger	2.00	5.00
HW43 Keston Hiura	2.00	5.00
HW50 Max Scherzer	1.00	2.50
HW54 Rhys Hoskins	1.25	3.00
HW56 Trevor Story	1.00	2.50
HW57 Matt Chapman	1.00	2.50
HW64 Willson Contreras	.75	2.00
HW65 Joey Votto	1.00	2.50
HW71 Pete Alonso	5.00	12.00
HW72 Christian Yelich	1.25	3.00
HW74 Francisco Lindor	1.00	2.50
HW76 Austin Riley	3.00	8.00
HW85 Ronald Acuna Jr.	5.00	12.00
HW87 Albert Pujols	1.25	3.00
HW95 Manny Machado	1.00	2.50
HW96 Buster Posey	1.25	3.00
HW101 Eloy Jimenez	2.50	6.00
HW109 Javier Baez	1.25	3.00
HW112 George Springer	.75	2.00
HW125 Nick Senzel	2.00	5.00
HW126 Fernando Tatis Jr.	12.00	30.00
HW127 J.D. Martinez	1.00	2.50
HW129 Justin Verlander	1.00	2.50
HW136 Carlos Correa	1.00	2.50
HW137 Jacob deGrom	2.00	5.00
HW144 Yadier Molina	1.25	3.00
HW148 Aaron Judge	2.50	6.00
HW152 Aaron Nola	.75	2.00
HW159 Jose Altuve	.75	2.00
HW160 Carter Kieboom	1.00	2.50
HW165 Nolan Arenado	1.50	4.00
HW167 Vladimir Guerrero Jr.	4.00	10.00
HW171 Brendan Rodgers	1.00	2.50
HW175 Gary Sanchez	1.00	2.50
HW182 Gleyber Torres	2.00	5.00
HW187 Walker Buehler	1.25	3.00
HW189 Cavan Biggio	3.00	8.00
HW192 Bryce Harper	1.50	4.00
HW197 Kris Bryant	1.25	3.00
HW199 Masahiro Tanaka	.75	2.00

2019 Topps Walmart Holiday Rare Photo Variations

STATED ODDS 1:20 PACKS

HW8 Juan Soto	8.00	20.00
HW16 Shohei Ohtani	4.00	10.00
HW26 Anthony Rizzo	3.00	8.00
HW30 Clayton Kershaw	4.00	10.00
HW31 Mike Trout	12.00	30.00
HW33 Shohei Ohtani	4.00	10.00
HW35 Alex Bregman	2.50	6.00
HW36 Rafael Devers	3.00	8.00
HW42 Cody Bellinger	5.00	12.00
HW54 Rhys Hoskins	3.00	8.00
HW72 Christian Yelich	3.00	8.00
HW74 Francisco Lindor	2.50	6.00
HW85 Ronald Acuna Jr.	12.00	30.00
HW87 Albert Pujols	3.00	8.00
HW95 Manny Machado	2.50	6.00
HW112 George Springer	2.00	5.00
HW127 J.D. Martinez	2.50	6.00
HW129 Justin Verlander	2.50	6.00
HW148 Aaron Judge	6.00	15.00
HW159 Jose Altuve	2.00	5.00
HW165 Nolan Arenado	4.00	10.00
HW182 Gleyber Torres	5.00	12.00
HW187 Walker Buehler	3.00	8.00
HW192 Bryce Harper	4.00	10.00
HW197 Kris Bryant	3.00	8.00

2019 Topps Walmart Holiday Super Rare Photo Variations

STATED ODDS 1:161 PACKS

HW16 Shohei Ohtani	12.00	30.00
HW26 Anthony Rizzo	10.00	25.00
HW29 Mookie Betts	15.00	40.00
HW30 Clayton Kershaw	12.00	30.00
HW31 Mike Trout	40.00	100.00
HW33 Shohei Ohtani	12.00	30.00
HW42 Cody Bellinger	15.00	40.00
HW54 Rhys Hoskins	10.00	25.00
HW71 Pete Alonso	40.00	100.00
HW72 Christian Yelich	10.00	25.00
HW74 Francisco Lindor	8.00	20.00
HW85 Ronald Acuna Jr.	40.00	100.00
HW87 Albert Pujols	10.00	25.00
HW95 Manny Machado	8.00	20.00
HW96 Buster Posey	10.00	25.00
HW109 Javier Baez	10.00	25.00
HW126 Fernando Tatis Jr.	80.00	200.00
HW129 Justin Verlander	8.00	20.00
HW136 Carlos Correa	8.00	20.00
HW144 Yadier Molina	10.00	25.00
HW148 Aaron Judge	20.00	50.00
HW159 Jose Altuve	6.00	15.00
HW167 Vladimir Guerrero Jr.	30.00	80.00
HW192 Bryce Harper	12.00	30.00
HW197 Kris Bryant	10.00	25.00

2019 Topps Walmart Holiday Autographs

STATED ODDS 1:334 PACKS
PRINT RUNS B/WN 35-200 COPIES PER
MANY NOT PRICED DUE TO SCARCITY
EXCHANGE DEADLINE 10/31/2021

WHAAN Aaron Nola		
WHABL Brandon Lowe/200	8.00	20.00
WHABR Brendan Rodgers/45	15.00	40.00
WHACM Charlie Morton/125	5.00	12.00
WHACY Christian Yelich		
WHAEJ Eloy Jimenez		
WHAFL Francisco Lindor		
WHAFT Fernando Tatis Jr./40	150.00	400.00
WHAGC Griffin Canning/181	5.00	12.00
WHAHR Hunter Renfroe/150	3.00	8.00
WHAJA Jose Altuve		
WHAJD Jon Duplantier/200	3.00	8.00
WHAJH JD Hammer/200	4.00	10.00
WHAJM Jeff McNeil/200	10.00	25.00
WHAJP Joc Pederson/45	10.00	25.00
WHAJV Joey Votto		
WHAKH Keston Hiura/200	15.00	40.00
WHAKN Kevin Newman/200	5.00	12.00
WHALT Lane Thomas/200	8.00	20.00
WHALV Luke Voit/200	15.00	40.00
WHAMC Michael Chavis/150	12.00	30.00
WHAMM Manny Machado		
WHAMS Max Scherzer		
WHAMT Mike Trout		
WHANA Nolan Arenado		
WHANS Nick Senzel EXCH		
WHAPA Pete Alonso/45	100.00	250.00
WHAPD Paul DeJong/50	10.00	25.00
WHARA Ronald Acuna Jr.		
WHARD Rafael Devers		
WHARH Ryan Helsley/200	4.00	10.00
WHASA Shaun Anderson/200	3.00	8.00
WHASO Shohei Ohtani		
WHATA Tim Anderson/185	5.00	12.00
WHATB Trevor Bauer/35	12.00	30.00
WHAVG Vladimir Guerrero Jr.		
WHAWA Willians Astudillo/185	3.00	8.00
WHAWC Willson Contreras		
WHAWS Will Smith/200	10.00	25.00
WHAYK Yusei Kikuchi/45	8.00	20.00
WHAMMU Max Muncy/194	4.00	10.00

2019 Topps Walmart Holiday Faux Relics

STATED ODDS 1:4782 PACKS
STATED PRINT RUN 25 SER.#'d SETS

WHFRES Ebenezer Scrooge		
WHFREW Workshop Elves		
WHFRFH Frosty The Snowman	25.00	60.00
WHFRMA Mrs. Claus	40.00	100.00
WHFRSG Santa Claus	40.00	100.00
WHFRSP Santa Claus	40.00	100.00
WHFRSR Santa Claus	40.00	100.00
WHFRSS Santa Claus	40.00	100.00
WHFREST Workshop Elf	20.00	50.00
WHFRSSU Santa Claus	40.00	100.00

2019 Topps Walmart Holiday Holiday Relics

STATED ODDS 1:638 PACKS
STATED PRINT RUN 75 SER.#'d SETS

WHHRAB Andrew Benintendi	8.00	20.00
WHHRAJ Aaron Judge	30.00	80.00
WHHRAM Andrew McCutchen	20.00	50.00
WHHRAR Anthony Rizzo	15.00	40.00
WHHRBS Blake Snell	8.00	20.00
WHHRCK Clayton Kershaw	15.00	40.00
WHHRCY Christian Yelich	15.00	40.00
WHHREJ Eloy Jimenez	20.00	50.00
WHHRFL Francisco Lindor	8.00	20.00
WHHRFT Fernando Tatis Jr.	80.00	200.00
WHHRGS Giancarlo Stanton	8.00	20.00
WHHRJA Jose Altuve	6.00	15.00
WHHRJB Javier Baez	10.00	25.00
WHHRJM J.D. Martinez	12.00	30.00
WHHRJS Juan Soto	25.00	60.00
WHHRKB Kris Bryant	15.00	40.00
WHHRMB Mookie Betts	15.00	40.00
WHHRMC Miguel Cabrera	15.00	40.00
WHHRMT Mike Trout	40.00	100.00
WHHRNA Nolan Arenado	12.00	30.00
WHHRRD Rafael Devers	12.00	30.00
WHHRSO Shohei Ohtani	25.00	60.00
WHHRWB Walker Buehler	10.00	25.00
WHHRJBE Josh Bell	6.00	15.00
WHHRJOB Jose Berrios	6.00	15.00

2019 Topps Walmart Holiday Relics

STATED ODDS 1:11 PACKS

WHRAA Albert Almora Jr.	2.00	5.00
WHRAB Andrew Benintendi	2.50	6.00
WHRAC Aroldis Chapman	2.50	6.00
WHRAH Aaron Hicks	2.00	5.00
WHRAM Adalberto Mondesi	2.00	5.00
WHRAR Anthony Rizzo	3.00	8.00
WHRBB Byron Buxton	2.50	6.00
WHRBP Buster Posey	3.00	8.00
WHRCB Cody Bellinger	5.00	12.00
WHRCC Carlos Correa	2.50	6.00
WHRCS CC Sabathia	2.00	5.00
WHRDG Didi Gregorius	2.00	5.00
WHRDP Dustin Pedroia	2.50	6.00
WHRDS Dominic Smith	1.50	4.00
WHREL Evan Longoria	2.00	5.00
WHRER Eddie Rosario	2.00	5.00
WHRES Eugenio Suarez	2.00	5.00
WHRFF Freddie Freeman	3.00	8.00
WHRFL Francisco Lindor	2.50	6.00
WHRFT Fernando Tatis Jr.	4.00	10.00
WHRGC Gerrit Cole	2.50	6.00
WHRGS Gary Sanchez	2.50	6.00
WHRHD Hunter Dozier	1.50	4.00
WHRHR Hyun-Jin Ryu	2.00	5.00
WHRJB Javier Baez	3.00	8.00
WHRJH Jason Heyward	2.00	5.00
WHRJL Jon Lester	2.00	5.00
WHRJM J.D. Martinez	2.50	6.00
WHRJP Joc Pederson	2.00	5.00
WHRJR Jose Ramirez	2.00	5.00
WHRJV Justin Verlander	2.50	6.00
WHRKB Kris Bryant	3.00	8.00
WHRKS Kyle Schwarber	2.50	6.00
WHRLS Luis Severino	2.00	5.00
WHRMA Miguel Andujar	2.50	6.00
WHRMB Mookie Betts	5.00	12.00
WHRMC Miguel Cabrera	2.50	6.00
WHRMF Max Fried	2.50	6.00
WHRMK Max Kepler	2.00	5.00
WHRMO Marcell Ozuna	2.50	6.00
WHRNA Nolan Arenado	4.00	10.00
WHRNM Nomar Mazara	1.50	4.00
WHROA Ozzie Albies	2.50	6.00
WHRRA Ronald Acuna Jr.	4.00	10.00
WHRRD Rafael Devers	3.00	8.00
WHRRH Rhys Hoskins	3.00	8.00
WHRSP Salvador Perez	2.00	5.00
WHRSS Stephen Strasburg	2.50	6.00
WHRTS Trevor Story	2.50	6.00
WHRTT Trea Turner	2.00	5.00
WHRWC Willson Contreras	2.00	5.00
WHRWM Whit Merrifield	2.50	6.00
WHRXB Xander Bogaerts	2.50	6.00
WHRZG Zack Greinke	2.50	6.00
WHRABR Alex Bregman	2.50	6.00
WHRARO Amed Rosario	2.00	5.00
WHRCSA Chris Sale	2.50	6.00
WHRDPR David Price	2.00	5.00
WHRDSW Dansby Swanson	2.50	6.00
WHRGSP George Springer	2.00	5.00
WHRJAR Jake Arrieta	2.00	5.00
WHRJRE J.T. Realmuto	2.50	6.00
WHRJVO Joey Votto	2.50	6.00
WHRMCO Michael Conforto	2.00	5.00

2020 Topps Walmart Holiday

HW1 Gavin Lux RC	1.25	3.00
HW2 Luis Robert RC	4.00	10.00
HW3 Travis Demeritte RC	.30	.75
HW4 Cavan Biggio	.40	1.00
HW5 Kyle Garlick RC	.30	.75
HW6 Xander Bogaerts	.30	.75
HW7 Rick Porcello	.25	.60
HW8 Stephen Strasburg	.30	.75
HW9 Kyle Tucker	.30	.75
HW10 Zack Greinke	.30	.75
HW11 Eric Hosmer	.25	.60
HW12 Jon Berti RC	.20	.50
HW13 Josh Bell	.25	.60
HW14 Kyle Schwarber	.30	.75
HW15 Tim Lopes RC	.25	.60
HW16 Mike Moustakas	.25	.60
HW17 Carter Kieboom	.25	.60
HW18 Lourdes Gurriel Jr.	.25	.60
HW19 Eugenio Suarez	.25	.60
HW20 Jaylin Davis RC	.30	.75
HW21 Kevin Kiermaier	.25	.60
HW22 Justin Turner	.30	.75
HW23 Yadier Molina	.40	1.00
HW24 Trea Turner	.25	.60
HW25 Oscar Mercado	.30	.75
HW26 Shohei Ohtani	.50	1.25
HW27 Joey Votto	.30	.75
HW28 Max Kepler	.25	.60
HW29 Brandon Crawford	.25	.60
HW30 Miguel Andujar	.30	.75
HW31 Zac Gallen RC	.50	1.25
HW32 Luis Arraez	.40	1.00
HW33 J.D. Martinez	.30	.75
HW34 Ketel Marte	.25	.60
HW35 Jesus Luzardo	.40	1.00
HW36 Corey Kluber	.25	.60
HW37 Max Scherzer	.30	.75
HW38 Aaron Judge	.75	2.00
HW39 Randy Dobnak RC	.40	1.00
HW40 Blake Snell	.25	.60
HW41 Brandon Lowe	.25	.60
HW42 Jake Odorizzi	.20	.50
HW43 Justin Verlander	.30	.75
HW44 Marcell Ozuna	.30	.75
HW45 Albert Pujols	.40	1.00
HW46 Matt Olson	.30	.75
HW47 Dansby Swanson	.30	.75
HW48 Nolan Arenado	.50	1.25
HW49 Vladimir Guerrero Jr.	.50	1.25
HW50 Alex Bregman	.30	.75
HW51 Brusdar Graterol RC	.30	.75
HW52 Ramon Laureano	.25	.60
HW53 Luis Urias	.25	.60
HW54 Randy Arozarena RC	2.00	5.00
HW55 Willi Castro RC	.30	.75
HW56 Rhys Hoskins	.40	1.00
HW57 Mallex Smith	.20	.50
HW58 Shogo Akiyama RC	.30	.75
HW59 Fernando Tatis Jr.	1.50	4.00
HW60 Luke Voit	.40	1.00
HW61 Dakota Hudson	.25	.60
HW62 Dustin May RC	.60	1.50
HW63 Kris Bryant	.40	1.00
HW64 Corey Seager	.30	.75
HW65 Gerrit Cole	.50	1.25
HW66 Cody Bellinger	.60	1.50
HW67 Javier Baez	.40	1.00
HW68 Shane Bieber	.30	.75
HW69 Jake Fraley RC	.25	.60
HW70 Nick Senzel	.30	.75
HW71 Evan Longoria	.25	.60
HW72 Max Fried	.30	.75
HW73 Aaron Nola	.25	.60
HW74 Michael Chavis	.25	.60
HW75 Wil Myers	.25	.60
HW76 Anthony Rendon	.30	.75
HW77 Whit Merrifield	.30	.75
HW78 Eddie Rosario	.25	.60
HW79 Robert Dugger RC	.20	.50
HW80 Willson Contreras	.30	.75
HW81 Paul DeJong	.30	.75
HW82 Clayton Kershaw	.50	1.25
HW83 Jose Ramirez	.25	.60
HW84 Isan Diaz RC	.30	.75
HW85 Jose Urena	.20	.50
HW86 Ryan McBroom RC	.25	.60
HW87 Rangel Ravelo RC	.25	.60
HW88 Giancarlo Stanton	.30	.75
HW89 Mookie Betts	.60	1.50
HW90 Rafael Devers	.40	1.00
HW91 Brendan McKay RC	.30	.75
HW92 Domingo Leyba RC	.25	.60
HW93 Shun Yamaguchi RC	.25	.60
HW94 Bo Bichette RC	1.50	4.00
HW95 Charlie Blackmon	.30	.75
HW96 Ronald Acuna Jr.	1.25	3.00
HW97 DJ LeMahieu	.30	.75
HW98 Aristides Aquino RC	.50	1.25
HW99 Dee Gordon	.20	.50
HW100 Jack Mayfield RC	.20	.50
HW101 Aroldis Chapman	.30	.75
HW102 Tony Gonsolin RC	.75	2.00
HW103 Gregory Polanco	.25	.60
HW104 Bryan Reynolds	.25	.60
HW105 Yordan Alvarez RC	1.25	3.00
HW106 Robinson Cano	.25	.60
HW107 Chris Sale	.30	.75
HW108 Nick Solak	.75	2.00
HW109 Matt Carpenter	.30	.75
HW110 Josh Hader	.25	.60
HW111 Nico Hoerner RC	.75	2.00
HW112 Sean Murphy RC	.30	.75
HW113 Kwang-Hyun Kim RC	.40	1.00
HW114 Walker Buehler	.40	1.00
HW115 Luis Severino	.25	.60
HW116 Noah Syndergaard	.25	.60
HW117 Yoan Moncada	.30	.75
HW118 Elvis Andrus	.25	.60
HW119 Matthew Boyd	.20	.50
HW120 Tony Kemp	.20	.50
HW121 Jake Rogers RC	.20	.50
HW122 Pete Alonso	.75	2.00
HW123 Mike Trout	1.50	4.00
HW124 George Springer	.25	.60
HW125 Brendan Rodgers	.30	.75
HW126 Ryan Zimmerman	.25	.60
HW127 Zack Collins RC	.25	.60
HW128 Chris Paddack	.30	.75
HW129 Miguel Cabrera	.30	.75
HW130 Gio Urshela	.30	.75
HW131 Carlos Correa	.30	.75
HW132 Anthony Rizzo	.40	1.00
HW133 Trevor Story	.30	.75
HW134 Marcus Stroman	.25	.60
HW135 Joc Pederson	.25	.60
HW136 Jorge Polanco	.25	.60
HW137 Buster Posey	.40	1.00
HW138 Jose Altuve	.25	.60
HW139 Gary Sanchez	.30	.75
HW140 Patrick Corbin	.25	.60
HW141 Christian Walker	.25	.60
HW142 Eloy Jimenez RC	.60	1.50
HW143 Willy Adames	.20	.50

HW144 Jake Arrieta .25 .60
HW145 Trent Grisham RC .75 2.00
HW146 Tommy Edman .30 .75
HW147 Trey Mancini .30 .75
HW148 Freddie Freeman .40 1.00
HW149 Nick Anderson RC .20 .50
HW150 Edwin Rios RC .50 1.25
HW151 Austin Riley .40 1.00
HW152 Francisco Lindor .30 .75
HW153 Kyle Seager .20 .50
HW154 Andrew McCutchen .30 .75
HW155 Christian Yelich .40 1.00
HW156 Paul Goldschmidt .30 .75
HW157 Nelson Cruz .30 .75
HW158 Jackie Bradley Jr. .30 .75
HW159 Victor Robles .40 1.00
HW160 Will Smith .30 .75
HW161 Jorge Soler .30 .75
HW162 Kevin Newman .30 .75
HW163 Alex Young RC .20 .50
HW164 Manny Machado .20 .50
HW165 Nick Castellanos .30 .75
HW166 Ryan Braun .25 .60
HW167 Ozzie Albies .30 .75
HW168 Jack Flaherty .30 .75
HW169 Kyle Lewis RC 2.00 5.00
HW170 Sam Hilliard RC .30 .75
HW171 Adbert Alzolay RC .25 .60
HW172 Masahiro Tanaka .25 .60
HW173 Mitch Haniger .25 .60
HW174 Andrew Benintendi .30 .75
HW175 Matt Thaiss RC .25 .60
HW176 J.T. Realmuto .30 .75
HW177 Mauricio Dubon RC .25 .60
HW178 Matt Chapman .30 .75
HW179 Ronny Rodriguez .20 .50
HW180 Gleyber Torres .60 1.50
HW181 Danny Mendick RC .25 .60
HW182 Jorge Alfaro .20 .50
HW183 Michael Brosseau RC .40 1.00
HW184 Mike Yastrzemski .50 1.25
HW185 Brandon Nimmo .25 .60
HW186 Mitch Garver .20 .50
HW187 Michael Conforto .25 .60
HW188 Kean Wong RC .20 .50
HW189 Aaron Barrett .20 .50
HW190 Bryce Harper .50 1.25
HW191 Griffin Canning .30 .75
HW192 Tim Anderson .30 .75
HW193 A.J. Puk RC .30 .75
HW194 Josh Donaldson .25 .60
HW195 Jeff McNeil .25 .60
HW196 Juan Soto 1.25 3.00
HW197 Keston Hiura .40 1.00
HW198 Mike Clevinger .25 .60
HW199 Jose Berrios .25 .60
HW200 John Means .30 .75

2020 Topps Walmart Holiday Metallic

*METALLIC: .6X TO 1.5X BASIC
STATED ODDS 1:2 HOBBY
HW2 Luis Robert 10.00 25.00
HW59 Fernando Tatis Jr. 3.00 8.00

2020 Topps Walmart Holiday Photo Variations

STATED ODDS 1:7 PACKS
*RARE VAR.: 3X TO 8X BASIC
HW2 Luis Robert 10.00 25.00
HW13 Josh Bell .75 2.00
HW26 Shohei Ohtani 1.50 4.00
HW35 Jesus Luzardo 1.25 3.00
HW37 Max Scherzer 1.00 2.50
HW38 Aaron Judge 2.50 6.00
HW40 Blake Snell .75 2.00
HW43 Justin Verlander 1.00 2.50
HW48 Nolan Arenado 1.50 4.00
HW49 Vladimir Guerrero Jr. 4.00 10.00
HW50 Alex Bregman 1.00 2.50
HW56 Rhys Hoskins 1.25 3.00
HW58 Shogo Akiyama 1.00 2.50
HW59 Fernando Tatis Jr. 5.00 12.00
HW62 Dustin May 2.00 5.00
HW63 Kris Bryant 1.25 3.00
HW65 Gerrit Cole 1.50 4.00
HW66 Cody Bellinger 2.00 5.00
HW67 Javier Baez 1.25 3.00
HW76 Anthony Rendon 1.00 2.50
HW82 Clayton Kershaw 1.50 4.00
HW89 Mookie Betts 2.00 5.00
HW90 Rafael Devers 1.25 3.00
HW91 Brendan McKay 1.00 2.50
HW93 Shun Yamaguchi .75 2.00
HW94 Bo Bichette 6.00 15.00
HW96 Ronald Acuna Jr. 4.00 10.00
HW98 Aristides Aquino 1.50 4.00
HW105 Yordan Alvarez 6.00 15.00
HW111 Nico Hoerner 2.50 6.00
HW113 Kwang-Hyun Kim 1.25 3.00
HW114 Walker Buehler 1.25 3.00
HW122 Pete Alonso 2.50 6.00
HW123 Mike Trout 5.00 12.00
HW129 Miguel Cabrera 1.00 2.50
HW131 Carlos Correa 1.00 2.50
HW133 Trevor Story 1.00 2.50
HW138 Jose Altuve .75 2.00
HW142 Eloy Jimenez 4.00 10.00
HW152 Francisco Lindor 1.00 2.50
HW155 Christian Yelich 1.25 3.00
HW156 Paul Goldschmidt 1.00 2.50
HW164 Manny Machado 1.00 2.50
HW169 Kyle Lewis 5.00 12.00
HW178 Matt Chapman 1.00 2.50
HW180 Gleyber Torres 3.00 8.00
HW190 Bryce Harper 1.50 4.00
HW194 Josh Donaldson .75 2.00
HW196 Juan Soto 2.50 6.00
HW199 Jose Berrios .75 2.00

2020 Topps Walmart Holiday Super Rare Photo Variations

*SUP.RARE VAR.: 8X TO 20X BASIC
STATED ODDS 1:161 HOBBY
HW2 Luis Robert 75.00 200.00
HW59 Fernando Tatis Jr. 40.00 100.00
HW94 Bo Bichette 50.00 120.00
HW123 Mike Trout 50.00 120.00

2020 Topps Walmart Holiday Die Cut Ornaments

WHOAJ Aaron Judge 2.00 5.00
WHOBB Bo Bichette 4.00 10.00
WHOBM Brendan McKay .75 2.00
WHOCK Clayton Kershaw 1.25 3.00
WHOFL Francisco Lindor 2.00 5.00
WHOGC Gerrit Cole 1.25 3.00
WHOGS George Springer .60 1.50
WHOGT Gleyber Torres 1.50 4.00
WHOJB Javier Baez 1.00 2.50
WHOJS Juan Soto 2.50 6.00
WHOKB Kris Bryant 1.00 2.50
WHOKH Keston Hiura 1.00 2.50
WHOLR Luis Robert 4.00 10.00
WHOMB Mookie Betts 1.50 4.00
WHOMK Max Kepler .60 1.50
WHOMT Mike Trout 4.00 10.00
WHONA Nolan Arenado 1.25 3.00
WHONH Nico Hoerner 2.00 5.00
WHOPA Pete Alonso 2.00 5.00
WHOSO Shohei Ohtani 1.25 3.00

2020 Topps Walmart Holiday Faux Relics

STATED ODDS 1:6990 PACKS
STATED PRINT RUN 25 SER.#'d SETS
WHFREL Workshop Elf 20.00 50.00
WHFRES Ebenezer Scrooge 12.00 30.00
WHFRFT Frosty The Snowman
WHFRMC Mrs. Claus 25.00 60.00
WHFRSC Santa Claus 50.00 120.00
WHFRSG Santa Claus 50.00 120.00
WHFRSN Santa Claus 50.00 120.00
WHFRSR Santa Claus 50.00 120.00
WHFRSS Santa Claus 50.00 120.00
WHFRWE Workshop Elf 20.00 50.00

2020 Topps Walmart Holiday Relics

STATED ODDS 1:7 PACKS
WHRAA Aristides Aquino 4.00 10.00
WHRAB Alex Bregman 2.50 6.00
WHRAH Adam Haseley 2.00 5.00
WHRAI Austin Riley 3.00 8.00
WHRAJ Aaron Judge 8.00 20.00
WHRAN Andrew Benintendi 2.50 6.00
WHRAP Albert Pujols 3.00 8.00
WHRAR Anthony Rizzo 3.00 8.00
WHRBB Bo Bichette 15.00 40.00
WHRBC Brandon Crawford 2.00 5.00
WHRBH Bryce Harper 5.00 12.00
WHRBP Buster Posey 3.00 8.00
WHRBZ Ben Zobrist 2.00 5.00
WHRCF Clint Frazier 2.00 5.00
WHRCK Clayton Kershaw 4.00 10.00
WHRCT Cole Tucker 2.50 6.00
WHRCY Christian Yelich 3.00 8.00
WHRDJ Danny Jansen 1.50 4.00
WHRGA Gary Sanchez 2.50 6.00
WHRGS George Springer 2.00 5.00
WHRGT Gleyber Torres 5.00 12.00
WHRHD Hunter Dozier 1.50 4.00
WHRID Isan Diaz 2.50 6.00
WHRIH Ian Happ 2.00 5.00
WHRJA Jose Altuve 2.00 5.00
WHRJB Javier Baez 3.00 8.00
WHRJC Jake Cave 2.00 5.00
WHRJd Jacob deGrom 5.00 12.00
WHRJE Josh Bell 2.00 5.00
WHRJG Joey Gallo 2.50 6.00
WHRJH Josh Hader 2.00 5.00
WHRJJ Jackie Bradley Jr. 2.50 6.00
WHRJL Joey Lucchesi 1.50 4.00
WHRJP James Paxton 2.00 5.00
WHRJR J.T. Realmuto 2.50 6.00
WHRJV Joey Votto 2.50 6.00
WHRJY Jason Heyward 2.00 5.00
WHRKB Kris Bryant 3.00 8.00
WHRKW Kolten Wong 2.00 5.00
WHRLC Luis Castillo 2.00 5.00
WHRLS Luis Severino 2.00 5.00
WHRLV Luke Voit 3.00 8.00
WHRLW Logan Webb 2.50 6.00
WHRMA Matt Chapman 2.50 6.00
WHRMB Matthew Boyd 1.50 4.00
WHRMC Michael Chavis 2.00 5.00
WHRMF Michael Fulmer 1.50 4.00
WHRMH Mitch Haniger 2.00 5.00
WHRMI Miguel Cabrera 2.50 6.00
WHRMK Mike King 2.50 6.00
WHRMM Max Muncy 2.00 5.00
WHRMN Miguel Sano 2.00 5.00
WHRMT Mike Trout 12.00 30.00
WHRNA Nolan Arenado 4.00 10.00
WHRNS Nick Senzel 2.50 6.00
WHRPA Pete Alonso 8.00 20.00
WHRPG Paul Goldschmidt 2.50 6.00
WHRRA Ronald Acuna Jr. 10.00 25.00
WHRRD Rafael Devers 3.00 8.00
WHRRH Rhys Hoskins 3.00 8.00
WHRRO Randy Dobnak 3.00 8.00
WHRRT Rowdy Tellez 2.00 5.00
WHRTS Trevor Story 2.50 6.00
WHRTT Trea Turner 2.00 5.00
WHRVG Vladimir Guerrero Jr. 4.00 10.00
WHRWC Willson Contreras 2.50 6.00
WHRXB Xander Bogaerts 2.50 6.00
WHRYA Yordan Alvarez 5.00 12.00
WHRYG Yuli Gurriel 2.00 5.00
WHRYM Yadier Molina 3.00 8.00
WHRAHA Oscar Mercado 2.50 6.00
WHRBBE Brandon Belt 2.00 5.00
WHRJSM Jeff Samardzija 1.50 4.00
WHRJVM Josh VanMeter 2.50 6.00
WHRMBR Mike Brosseau 3.00 8.00

2016 Topps WalMart Marketside Pizza

1 Mike Trout 5.00 12.00
2 Freddie Freeman 1.25 3.00
3 Nolan Arenado 1.50 4.00
4 Adam Jones .75 2.00
5 Manny Machado 1.00 2.50
6 Carlos Correa 1.00 2.50
7 Michael Wacha .75 2.00
8 Miguel Cabrera 1.00 2.50
9 Jacob deGrom 1.00 2.50
10 David Ortiz 1.00 2.50
11 Evan Longoria .75 2.00
12 Dustin Pedroia 1.00 2.50
13 Troy Tulowitzki 1.00 2.50
14 Miguel Sano 1.00 2.50
15 Robinson Cano .75 2.00
16 Phillie Phanatic .75 2.00
17 Chris Sale 1.00 2.50
18 Francisco Lindor 1.00 2.50
19 Buster Posey 1.25 3.00
20 Jacoby Ellsbury .75 2.00
21 Luis Severino .75 2.00
22 Noah Syndergaard .75 2.00
23 Prince Fielder .75 2.00
24 Bryce Harper 1.50 4.00
25 Alex Gordon .75 2.00
26 Madison Bumgarner .75 2.00
27 Paul Goldschmidt 1.00 2.50
28 Sonny Gray .75 2.00
29 Yadier Molina 1.25 3.00
30 Josh Donaldson .75 2.00
31 Giancarlo Stanton 1.00 2.50
32 Hector Olivera .75 2.00
33 Aaron Nola 1.25 3.00
34 Andrew McCutchen 1.00 2.50
35 Tyson Ross .60 1.50
36 Salvador Perez .75 2.00
37 Todd Frazier .60 1.50
38 A.J. Pollock .60 1.50
39 Jose Abreu 1.00 2.50
40 George Springer .75 2.00
41 Kris Bryant 1.25 3.00
42 Joe Mauer .75 2.00
43 Dee Gordon .60 1.50
44 Albert Pujols 1.25 3.00
45 Clayton Kershaw 1.50 4.00
46 Kyle Schwarber 2.00 5.00
47 Corey Seager 6.00 15.00
48 Ryan Braun .75 2.00
49 Mr. Met .75 2.00
50 Justin Verlander 1.00 2.50

2017 Topps Walmart Online Exclusive

WM1 Buster Posey .75 2.00
WM2 Clayton Kershaw 1.00 2.50
WM3 Carlos Correa .60 1.50
WM4 Kris Bryant .75 2.00
WM5 Miguel Cabrera .60 1.50

2009 Topps World Baseball Classic Box Set

COMPLETE SET (55) 10.00 25.00
1 Yu Darvish .75 2.00
2 Derek Jeter 1.25 3.00
3 Ryan Braun .30 .75
4 Michel Enriquez .20 .50
5 Phillippe Aumont .30 .75
6 Yulieski Gourriel .60 1.50
7 Shinnosuke Abe .30 .75
8 Hanley Ramirez .30 .75
9 Daisuke Matsuzaka .30 .75
10 Justin Erasmus .20 .50
11 Frank Catalanotto .20 .50
12 Travis Blackley .20 .50
13 Alex Rodriguez .60 1.50
14 Brian McCann .30 .75
15 Arquimedes Nieto .20 .50
16 Joakim Soria .20 .50
17 Justin Morneau .30 .75
18 Geovany Soto .30 .75
19 Alex Liddi .30 .75
20 Cheng-Min Peng .30 .75
21 Luke Hughes .20 .50
22 Manuel Corpas .20 .50
23 Chipper Jones .50 1.25
24 Drew Naylor .20 .50
25 Jimmy Rollins .30 .75
26 Kosuke Fukudome .30 .75
27 Jose Reyes .30 .75
28 David Wright .40 1.00
29 Ichiro Suzuki .60 1.50
30 Carlos Lee .20 .50
31 Joey Votto .50 1.25
32 Jin Young Lee .20 .50
33 Jonathan Sanchez .20 .50
34 Lenny DiNardo .20 .50
35 Miguel Cabrera .50 1.25
36 Rick VanDenHurk .20 .50
37 David Ortiz .50 1.25
38 Jason Bay .30 .75
39 Dylan Lindsay .30 .75
40 Chris Denorfia .30 .75
41 Bernie Williams .30 .75
42 Akinori Iwamura .20 .50
43 Pedro Martinez .30 .75
44 Gift Ngoepe .20 .50
45 Chenhao Li .20 .50
46 Roy Oswalt .30 .75
47 Dustin Pedroia .50 1.25
48 Tao Bu .20 .50
49 Greg Halman .30 .75
50 Adrian Gonzalez .40 1.00
51 Carlos Beltran .30 .75
52 Pedro Lazo .20 .50
53 Jorge Cantu .20 .50
54 Kenji Johjima .30 .75
55 Fu-Te Ni .30 .75

2000 Topps Honus Wagner Reprint

1 Honus Wagner .40 1.00

2020 Topps X Steve Aoki

PRINT RUNS B/WN 8076-15556 COPIES PER
1 Mike Trout/15566* 4.00 10.00
2 Cody Bellinger/15566* 1.50 4.00
3 Vladimir Guerrero Jr./15566* 1.25 3.00
4 Shane Bieber/15566* .75 2.00
5 Alex Bregman/15566* .75 2.00
6 Yadier Molina/15566* 1.00 2.50
7 Freddie Freeman/15566* 1.00 2.50
8 Gerrit Cole/15566* 1.25 3.00
9 Bryce Harper/15566* 1.25 3.00
10 Rafael Devers/15566* 1.00 2.50
11 Trea Turner/15566* .60 1.50
12 Nolan Ryan/15566* 2.50 6.00
13 Dave Winfield/15566* .60 1.50
14 Greg Maddux/15566* 1.00 2.50
15 Reggie Jackson/15566* .60 1.50
16 Roger Clemens/15566* 1.00 2.50
17 Hideki Matsui/15566* .75 2.00
18 Ken Griffey Jr./15566* 1.50 4.00
19 Cal Ripken Jr./15566* 2.50 6.00
20 Gavin Lux/15566* 2.50 6.00
21 Jesus Luzardo/15566* 1.00 2.50
22 Bo Bichette/15566* 4.00 10.00
23 Mike Brosseau/15566* 1.00 2.50
24 Brendan McKay/15566* .75 2.00
25 James Karinchak/15566* .75 2.00
26 Juan Soto/8956* 2.50 6.00
27 Fernando Tatis Jr./8956* 4.00 10.00
28 Corey Seager/8956* .75 2.00
29 Nolan Arenado/8956* 1.25 3.00
30 Yu Darvish/8956* .75 2.00
31 Andrew Benintendi/8956* .75 2.00
32 Francisco Lindor/8956* .75 2.00
33 Gleyber Torres/8956* 1.50 4.00
34 Keston Hiura/8956* 1.00 2.50
35 Byron Buxton/8956* .75 2.00
36 Manny Machado/8956* .75 2.00
37 Chipper Jones/8956* .75 2.00
38 Ichiro/8956* 1.00 2.50
39 Hank Aaron/8956* 1.50 4.00
40 George Brett/8956* 1.50 4.00
41 Mariano Rivera/8956* 1.00 2.50
42 Frank Thomas/8956* .75 2.00
43 Ozzie Smith/8956* 1.00 2.50
44 Randy Johnson/8956* .75 2.00
45 Kyle Lewis/8956* 4.00 10.00
46 Dustin May/8956* 1.50 4.00
47 Aristides Aquino/8956* 1.25 3.00
48 Jordan Yamamoto/8956* .50 1.25
49 A.J. Puk/8956* .75 2.00
50 Randy Arozarena/8956* 4.00 10.00
51 Mookie Betts/8076* 1.50 4.00
52 Ronald Acuna Jr./8076* 3.00 8.00
53 Eloy Jimenez/8076* 1.50 4.00
54 Pete Alonso/8076* 2.00 5.00
55 Kris Bryant/8076* 1.00 2.50
56 Max Scherzer/8076* .75 2.00
57 DJ LeMahieu/8076* .75 2.00
58 Lucas Giolito/8076* .60 1.50
59 Mike Yastrzemski/8076* 1.25 3.00
60 Jacob deGrom/8076* 1.50 4.00
61 Tim Anderson/8076* .75 2.00
62 Mike Piazza/8076* .75 2.00
63 Rickey Henderson/8076* .75 2.00
64 Ryne Sandberg/8076* 1.50 4.00
65 Bernie Williams/8076* .60 1.50
66 Nomar Garciaparra/8076* .60 1.50
67 Johnny Bench/8076* .75 2.00
68 Don Mattingly/8076* 1.50 4.00
69 David Ortiz/8076* .75 2.00
70 Yordan Alvarez/8076* 5.00 12.00
71 Zac Gallen/8076* 1.25 3.00
72 Tony Gonsolin/8076* 2.00 5.00
73 Isan Diaz/8076* .75 2.00
74 Nick Solak/8076* 2.00 5.00
75 Dylan Cease/8076* .75 2.00
76 Aaron Judge/8158* 2.00 5.00
77 Clayton Kershaw/8158* 1.25 3.00
78 Jose Abreu/8158* .75 2.00
79 Jose Altuve/8158* .60 1.50
80 Matt Chapman/8158* .75 2.00
81 Anthony Rizzo/8158* 1.00 2.50
82 Max Fried/8158* .75 2.00
83 Blake Snell/8158* .60 1.50
84 Shohei Ohtani/8158* 1.25 3.00
85 Christian Yelich/8158* 1.00 2.50
86 Trevor Bauer/8158* 1.00 2.50
87 Mark McGwire/8158* 1.25 3.00
88 Ivan Rodriguez/8158* .60 1.50
89 Jackie Robinson/8158* .75 2.00
90 Andre Dawson/8158* .60 1.50
91 Jose Canseco/8158* .60 1.50
92 Carl Yastrzemski/8158* 1.25 3.00
93 Derek Jeter/8158* 2.00 5.00
94 Willie Mays/8158* 1.50 4.00
95 Devin Williams/8158* 1.25 3.00
96 Justin Dunn/8158* .60 1.50
97 Kwang-Hyun Kim/8158* 1.00 2.50
98 Aaron Civale/8158* 1.00 2.50
99 Nico Hoerner/8158* 2.00 5.00
100 Luis Robert/8158* 4.00 10.00

2020 Topps X Steve Aoki Holo Blue Frosting

*HOLO BLUE: 2X TO 5X BASIC
RANDOM INSERTS IN PACKS
STATED PRINT RUN 77 SER.#'d SETS
1 Mike Trout 75.00 200.00
12 Nolan Ryan 20.00 50.00
18 Ken Griffey Jr. 40.00 100.00
22 Bo Bichette 25.00 60.00
27 Fernando Tatis Jr. 50.00 120.00
38 Ichiro 30.00 80.00
39 Hank Aaron 15.00 40.00
50 Randy Arozarena 30.00 80.00
52 Ronald Acuna Jr. 20.00 50.00
76 Aaron Judge 30.00 80.00
93 Derek Jeter 20.00 50.00
94 Willie Mays 20.00 50.00
100 Luis Robert 75.00 200.00

2020 Topps X Steve Aoki Rainbow Foilboard

*RAINBOW: .75X TO 2X BASIC
1 Mike Trout 15.00 40.00
100 Luis Robert 30.00 80.00

2020 Topps X Steve Aoki Autograph Relics

RANDOM INSERTS IN PACKS
STATED PRINT RUN 150 SER.#'d SETS
*HOLO BLUE: .6X TO 1.5X BASIC
SA1 Steve Aoki 75.00 200.00
SA2 Steve Aoki 75.00 200.00
SA3 Steve Aoki 75.00 200.00
SA4 Steve Aoki 75.00 200.00

2020 Topps X Super 70s Sports

ANNCD PRINT RUN 8971 SER.#'d SETS
1 Al Oliver .50 1.25
2 Andre Dawson .60 1.50
3 Bert Blyleven .60 1.50
4 Bob Gibson .60 1.50
5 Cody Bellinger 1.50 4.00
6 Dale Murphy .75 2.00
7 Eddie Murray .60 1.50
8 Ernie Banks .75 2.00
9 Frank Robinson .60 1.50
10 Gary Carter .60 1.50
11 George Brett 1.50 4.00
12 Hank Aaron 1.50 4.00
13 Jacob deGrom 1.50 4.00
14 Jim Palmer .60 1.50
15 Jim Rice .60 1.50
16 Joe Morgan .60 1.50
17 Johnny Bench .75 2.00
18 Mookie Betts 1.50 4.00
19 Reggie Jackson .60 1.50
20 Rickey Henderson .75 2.00
21 Roberto Clemente 2.00 5.00
22 Rod Carew .60 1.50
23 Sandy Koufax 1.50 4.00
24 Nolan Ryan 2.50 6.00
25 J.R. Richard .50 1.25
26 Alan Trammell .60 1.50
27 Babe Ruth 2.00 5.00
28 Cal Ripken Jr. 2.50 6.00
29 Christian Yelich 1.00 2.50
30 Darryl Strawberry .50 1.25
31 Dave Kingman .50 1.25
32 Dave Parker .50 1.25
33 David Ortiz .75 2.00
34 Derek Jeter 2.00 5.00
35 Dusty Baker .50 1.25
36 Dwight Gooden .50 1.25
37 Eric Davis .50 1.25
38 Fergie Jenkins .60 1.50
39 Frank Thomas .75 2.00
40 George Foster .50 1.25
41 Harmon Killebrew .75 2.00
42 Ichiro 1.00 2.50
43 Ken Griffey Jr. 1.50 4.00
44 Mike Piazza .75 2.00
45 Mike Schmidt 1.25 3.00
46 Mike Trout 4.00 10.00
47 Robin Yount .75 2.00
48 Ryne Sandberg 1.50 4.00
49 Steve Carlton .60 1.50
50 Steve Garvey .50 1.25
51 Ted Williams 1.50 4.00
52 Tim Raines .60 1.50
53 Tom Seaver .60 1.50
54 Tony Gwynn .75 2.00
55 Ty Cobb 1.25 3.00
56 Willie Mays 1.50 4.00
57 Willie McCovey .60 1.50
58 Carl Yastrzemski 1.25 3.00
59 Don Sutton .60 1.50
60 Jackie Robinson .75 2.00
61 Don Mattingly 1.50 4.00
62 Brooks Robinson .60 1.50
63 Al Kaline .75 2.00
64 Paul Molitor .75 2.00
65 Fred McGriff .60 1.50
66 Dave Concepcion .50 1.25
67 Carlton Fisk .60 1.50
68 Ronald Acuna Jr. 3.00 8.00
69 Bryce Harper 1.25 3.00
70 Vladimir Guerrero Jr. 1.25 3.00
71 Nolan Arenado 1.25 3.00
72 Francisco Lindor .75 2.00
73 Max Scherzer .75 2.00
74 Pete Alonso 2.00 5.00
75 Gerrit Cole 1.25 3.00
76 Fernando Tatis Jr. 4.00 10.00
77 Juan Soto 2.50 6.00
78 Javier Baez 1.00 2.50
79 Albert Pujols 1.00 2.50
80 Manny Machado .75 2.00
81 Clayton Kershaw 1.25 3.00
82 Alex Bregman .75 2.00
83 Aaron Judge 2.00 5.00
84 Shohei Ohtani 1.25 3.00
85 Giancarlo Stanton .75 2.00
86 Trevor Bauer 1.00 2.50
87 Matt Olson .75 2.00
88 Anthony Rizzo 1.00 2.50
89 Justin Verlander .75 2.00
90 Justin Turner .75 2.00

2020 Topps X Super 70s Sports Autographs

RANDOM INSERTS IN PACKS
EXCHANGE DEADLINE XX/XX/XXXX
1A Al Oliver 8.00 20.00
3A Bert Blyleven 12.00 30.00
15A Jim Rice 25.00 60.00
17A Johnny Bench
19A Reggie Jackson
20A Rickey Henderson
25A J.R. Richard 10.00 25.00
31A Dave Kingman 8.00 20.00
32A Dave Parker 15.00 40.00
35A Dusty Baker 10.00 25.00
36A Dwight Gooden
40A George Foster 10.00 25.00
45A Mike Schmidt
58A Carl Yastrzemski
59A Don Sutton 15.00 40.00
66A Dave Concepcion
67A Carlton Fisk

2020 Topps X Super 70s Sports Happening Hairdos

RANDOM INSERTS IN PACKS
HH1 Ozzie Smith 1.25 3.00
HH2 Randy Johnson 1.00 2.50
HH3 Bruce Sutter .75 2.00
HH4 Phil Niekro .75 2.00
HH5 Harold Baines .75 2.00

2020 Topps X Super 70s Sports Magnificent Mustaches

RANDOM INSERTS IN PACKS
MM1 Dennis Eckersley .75 2.00
MM2 Gorman Thomas .60 1.50
MM3 Luis Tiant .60 1.50
MM4 Rollie Fingers .75 2.00
MM5 Wade Boggs .75 2.00

2020 Topps X Super 70s Sports Magnificent Mustaches Autographs

RANDOM INSERTS IN PACKS
EXCHANGE DEADLINE XX/XX/XXXX
MM2A Gorman Thomas 8.00 20.00
MM3A Luis Tiant 15.00 40.00
MM4A Rollie Fingers 12.00 30.00
MM5A Wade Boggs 30.00 80.00

2020 Topps X Super 70s Sports Memorable Managers

RANDOM INSERTS IN PACKS
MMGR1 Earl Weaver .75 2.00
MMGR2 Frank Robinson .75 2.00
MMGR3 Sparky Anderson .75 2.00
MMGR4 Ted Williams 2.00 5.00
MMGR5 Tommy Lasorda .75 2.00

2020 Topps X Super 70s Sports Ricky Cobb Autographs

RANDOM INSERTS IN PACKS
S70ARC Ricky Cobb 15.00 40.00

2020 Topps X Super 70s Sports Spectacular Spectacles

RANDOM INSERTS IN PACKS
SPS1 Jeff Burroughs .60 1.50
SPS2 Kent Tekulve .60 1.50
SPS3 Lou Brock .75 2.00
SPS4 Mario Mendoza .60 1.50
SPS5 Reggie Jackson .75 2.00

2020 Topps X Super 70s Sports Spectacular Spectacles Autographs

RANDOM INSERTS IN PACKS
EXCHANGE DEADLINE XX/XX/XXXX
SPS2A Kent Tekulve 8.00 20.00
SPS3A Lou Brock 30.00 80.00
SPS5A Reggie Jackson

2020 Topps X Super 70s Sports Ultimate Uniforms

RANDOM INSERTS IN PACKS
UU1 Dave Winfield .75 2.00
UU2 Goose Gossage .75 2.00
UU3 Nolan Ryan 3.00 8.00
UU4 Vida Blue .60 1.50
UU5 Willie Stargell .75 2.00

2020 Topps X Super 70s Sports Ultimate Uniforms Autographs

UU3A Nolan Ryan/20 75.00 200.00

1976 Towne Club Discs

This set, also is another version of the 76 Crane Discs. These discs have the Towne Club back and are a multiple of the Crane issue.

COMPLETE SET (70) 10.00 25.00
1 Hank Aaron 1.25 3.00
2 Johnny Bench .75 2.00
3 Vida Blue .12 .30
4 Larry Bowa .12 .30
5 Lou Brock .75 2.00
6 Jeff Burroughs .08 .20
7 John Candelaria .08 .20
8 Jose Cardenal .08 .20
9 Rod Carew .75 2.00
10 Steve Carlton .75 2.00
11 Dave Cash .08 .20
12 Cesar Cedeno .12 .30
13 Ron Cey .12 .30
14 Carlton Fisk 1.50 4.00
15 Tito Fuentes .08 .20
16 Steve Garvey .75 2.00
17 Ken Griffey .12 .30
18 Don Gullett .08 .20
19 Willie Horton .08 .20
20 Al Hrabosky .08 .20
21 Catfish Hunter 1.25 3.00
22A Reggie Jackson Oakland Athletics 4.00 10.00
22B Reggie Jackson Baltimore Orioles 1.25 3.00
23 Randy Jones .08 .20
24 Jim Kaat .25 .60
25 Don Kessinger .08 .20
26 Dave Kingman .25 .60
27 Jerry Koosman .12 .30
28 Mickey Lolich .12 .30
29 Greg Luzinski .25 .60
30 Fred Lynn .25 .60
31 Bill Madlock .12 .30
32A Carlos May Chicago White Sox .75 2.00
32B Carlos May New York Yankees .08 .20
33 John Mayberry .08 .20
34 Bake McBride .08 .20
35 Doc Medich .08 .20
36A Andy Messersmith Los Angeles Dodgers .75 2.00
36B Andy Messersmith Atlanta Braves .08 .20
37 Rick Monday .08 .20
38 John Montefusco .08 .20
39 Jerry Morales .08 .20
40 Joe Morgan 1.25 3.00
41 Thurman Munson .75 2.00
42 Bobby Murcer .25 .60
43 Al Oliver .25 .60
44 Jim Palmer 1.25 3.00
45 Dave Parker .40 1.00
46 Tony Perez .75 2.00
47 Jerry Reuss .08 .20
48 Brooks Robinson 1.25 3.00
49 Frank Robinson 1.25 3.00
50 Steve Rogers .08 .20
51 Pete Rose 1.50 4.00
52 Nolan Ryan 3.00 8.00
53 Manny Sanguillen .08 .20
54 Mike Schmidt 2.00 5.00
55 Tom Seaver 1.50 4.00
56 Ted Simmons .25 .60
57 Reggie Smith .12 .30
58 Willie Stargell 1.25 3.00
59 Rusty Staub .25 .60
60 Rennie Stennett .08 .20
61 Don Sutton 1.25 3.00
62A Andre Thornton Chicago Cubs .75 2.00
62B Andre Thornton Montreal Expos .08 .20
63 Luis Tiant .25 .60
64 Joe Torre .40 1.00
65 Mike Tyson .08 .20
66 Bob Watson .08 .20
67 Wilbur Wood .08 .20
68 Jimmy Wynn .08 .20
69 Carl Yastrzemski 1.25 3.00
70 Richie Zisk .08 .20

1987 Toys R Us Rookies

COMP.FACT.SET (33) 6.00 15.00
DISTRIBUTED IN FACTORY SET FORM
1 Andy Allanson .05 .15
2 Paul Assenmacher .05 .15
3 Scott Bailes .05 .15
4 Barry Bonds 3.00 8.00
5 Jose Canseco .40 1.00
6 John Cerutti .05 .15
7 Will Clark .60 1.50
8 Kal Daniels .05 .15
9 Jim Deshaies .05 .15
10 Mark Eichhorn .05 .15
11 Ed Hearn .05 .15
12 Pete Incaviglia .08 .25
13 Bo Jackson 1.50 4.00
14 Wally Joyner .15 .40
15 Charlie Kerfeld .05 .15
16 Eric King .05 .15
17 John Kruk .25 .60
18 Barry Larkin .60 1.50
19 Mike LaValliere .05 .15
20 Greg Mathews .05 .15
21 Kevin Mitchell .08 .25
22 Dan Plesac .05 .15
23 Bruce Ruffin .05 .15
24 Ruben Sierra .25 .60
25 Cory Snyder .05 .15
26 Kurt Stillwell .05 .15
27 Dale Sveum .05 .15
28 Danny Tartabull .05 .15
29 Andres Thomas .05 .15
30 Robby Thompson .08 .25
31 Jim Traber .05 .15
32 Mitch Williams .08 .25
33 Todd Worrell .08 .25

1988 Toys'R'Us Rookies

Topps produced this 33-card boxed standard-size set for Toys'R'Us stores. The set is subtitled "Baseball Rookies" and features predominantly younger players. The cards feature a high-gloss, full-color photo of the player inside a blue border. The card backs are printed in pink and blue on white card stock. The checklist for the set is found on the back panel of the small collector box. The statistics provided on the card backs cover only three lines, Minor League totals, last season, and Major League totals. The set numbering is in alphabetical order by player's name.

COMPLETE SET (33) 2.50 6.00
1 Todd Benzinger .01 .05
2 Bob Brower .01 .05
3 Jerry Browne .01 .05
4 DeWayne Buice .01 .05
5 Ellis Burks .20 .50
6 Ken Caminiti .40 1.00
7 Casey Candaele .01 .05
8 Dave Cone (David) .10 .30
9 Kelly Downs .01 .05
10 Mike Dunne .01 .05
11 Ken Gerhart .01 .05
12 Mike Greenwell .01 .05
13 Mike Henneman .02 .10
14 Sam Horn .01 .05
15 Joe Magrane .01 .05
16 Fred Manrique .01 .05
17 John Marzano .01 .05
18 Fred McGriff .30 .75
19 Mark McGwire .75 2.00
20 Jeff Musselman .01 .05
21 Randy Myers .07 .20
22 Matt Nokes .01 .05
23 Al Pedrique .01 .05
24 Luis Polonia .01 .05
25 Billy Ripken .01 .05
26 Benito Santiago .02 .10
27 Kevin Seitzer .01 .05
28 John Smiley .01 .05
29 Mike Stanley .01 .05
30 Terry Steinbach .01 .05
31 B.J. Surhoff .02 .10
32 Bobby Thigpen .01 .05
33 Devon White .01 .05

1989 Toys'R'Us Rookies

The 1989 Toys'R'Us Rookies set contains 33 standard-size glossy cards. The fronts are yellow and magenta. The horizontally oriented backs are sky blue and red, and feature 1988 and career stats. The cards were distributed through Toys'R'Us stores as a boxed set. The subjects are numbered alphabetically. The set checklist is printed on the back panel of the set's custom box.

COMPLETE SET (33) 1.50 4.00
1 Roberto Alomar .30 .75
2 Brady Anderson .07 .20
3 Tim Belcher .01 .05
4 Damon Berryhill .01 .05
5 Jay Buhner .07 .20
6 Sherman Corbett .01 .05
7 Kevin Elster .01 .05
8 Cecil Espy .01 .05
9 Dave Gallagher .01 .05
10 Ron Gant .02 .10
11 Paul Gibson .01 .05
12 Mark Grace .30 .75
13 Bryan Harvey .01 .05
14 Darrin Jackson .01 .05
15 Gregg Jefferies .01 .05
16 Ron Jones .01 .05
17 Ricky Jordan .01 .05
18 Roberto Kelly .01 .05
19 Al Leiter .07 .20
20 Jack McDowell .01 .05
21 Melido Perez .01 .05
22 Jeff Pico .01 .05
23 Jody Reed .01 .05
24 Chris Sabo .01 .05
25 Nelson Santovenia .01 .05
26 Mackey Sasser .01 .05
27 Mike Schooler .01 .05
28 Gary Sheffield .60 1.50
29 Pete Smith .01 .05
30 Pete Stanicek .01 .05
31 Jeff Treadway .01 .05

32 Walt Weiss	.01	.05
33 Dave West	.01	.05

1990 Toys R Us Rookies

The 1990 Toys'R'Us Rookies set is a 33-card standard-size set of young prospects issued by Topps. For the fourth consecutive year Topps issued a rookie set for Toys'R'Us. There are several players in the set which were on Topps cards for the second time in 1990, i.e., not rookies even for the Topps Company. These players included Gregg Jefferies and Gregg Olson. This set might be more appropriately called the Young Stars set. The cards are numbered, with the numbering being essentially in alphabetical order by player's name. The set checklist is printed on the back panel of the set's custom box.

COMPLETE SET (33)	2.50	6.00
1 Jim Abbott	.08	.25
2 Eric Anthony	.01	.05
3 Joey Belle	.30	.75
4 Andy Benes	.01	.05
5 Greg Briley	.01	.05
6 Kevin Brown	.07	.20
7 Mark Carreon	.01	.05
8 Mike Devereaux	.01	.05
9 Junior Felix	.01	.05
10 Mark Gardner	.01	.05
11 Bob Geren	.01	.05
12 Tom Gordon	.05	.15
13 Ken Griffey Jr.	1.25	3.00
14 Pete Harnisch	.01	.05
15 Ken Hill	.01	.05
16 Gregg Jefferies	.01	.05
17 Derek Lilliquist	.01	.05
18 Carlos Martinez	.01	.05
19 Ramon Martinez	.01	.05
20 Bob Milacki	.01	.05
21 Gregg Olson	.01	.05
22 Kenny Rogers	.05	.15
23 Alex Sanchez	.01	.05
24 Gary Sheffield	.20	.50
25 Dwight Smith	.01	.05
26 Billy Spiers	.01	.05
27 Greg Vaughn	.07	.20
28 Robin Ventura	.07	.20
29 Jerome Walton	.01	.05
30 Dave West	.01	.05
31 John Wetteland	.07	.20
32 Craig Worthington	.01	.05
33 Todd Zeile	.02	.10

1991 Toys'R'Us Rookies

For the fifth year in a row this 33-card standard-size set was produced by Topps for Toys'R'Us, and the sponsor's logo adorns the top of the card front. The front design features glossy color action player photos with yellow borders on a black card face. The words "Topps 1991 Collectors' Edition" appear in a yellow stripe above the picture. The horizontally oriented backs are printed in brown and yellow, and present biographical information, career highlights, and statistics.

COMPLETE SET (33)	1.50	4.00
1 Sandy Alomar Jr.	.02	.10
2 Kevin Appier	.02	.10
3 Steve Avery	.01	.05
4 Carlos Baerga	.01	.05
5 Alex Cole	.01	.05
6 Pat Combs	.01	.05
7 Delino DeShields	.01	.05
8 Travis Fryman	.07	.20
9 Marquis Grissom	.02	.10
10 Mike Harkey	.01	.05
11 Glenallen Hill	.01	.05
12 Jeff Huson	.01	.05
13 Felix Jose	.01	.05
14 Dave Justice	.10	.30
15 Dana Kiecker	.01	.05
16 Kevin Maas	.01	.05
17 Ben McDonald	.01	.05
18 Brian McRae	.01	.05
19 Kent Mercker	.01	.05
20 Hal Morris	.01	.05
21 Chris Nabholz	.01	.05
22 Tim Naehring	.01	.05
23 Jose Offerman	.01	.05
24 John Olerud	.07	.20
25 Scott Radinsky	.01	.05
26 Bill Sampen	.01	.05
27 Frank Thomas	.30	.75
28 Randy Tomlin	.01	.05
29 Greg Vaughn	.10	.30
30 Robin Ventura	.10	.30
31 Larry Walker	.20	.50
32 Wally Whitehurst	.01	.05
33 Todd Zeile	.02	.10

1993 Toys'R'Us

This 100-card standard-size set produced by Topps Stadium Club for Toys'R'Us features 100 young stars, rookie stars, and future stars. The cards carry glossy, full-bleed color photos with the Toys'R'Us logo in an upper corner. In silver lettering on a blue bar near the bottom of the photo, are the words Future Star, Rookie Star, or Young Star. The player's name is printed on a red bar below. The horizontal backs display a player close-up superimposed on a blue sky with clouds background. Also included are player biography, statistics and some career highlights. The cards were distributed through Toys'R'Us in a molded plastic box designed to resemble a store. 7,500 cases of this product was produced.

COMPLETE SET (100)	3.00	8.00
1 Ken Griffey Jr.	.75	2.00
2 Chad Curtis	.01	.05
3 Mike Bordick	.01	.05
4 Ryan Klesko	.05	.15
5 Pat Listach	.01	.05
6 Jim Bullinger	.01	.05
7 Tim Laker	.01	.05
8 Mike Devereaux	.01	.05
9 Kevin Young	.01	.05
10 John Valentin	.01	.05
11 Pat Mahomes	.01	.05
12 Todd Hundley	.05	.15
13 Roberto Alomar	.07	.20
14 David Justice	.07	.20
15 Mike Perez	.01	.05
16 Royce Clayton	.01	.05
17 Ryan Thompson	.01	.05
18 Dave Hollins	.01	.05
19 Brien Taylor	.01	.05
20 Melvin Nieves	.01	.05
21 Rheal Cormier	.01	.05
22 Mike Piazza	.60	1.50
23 Larry Walker	.20	.50
24 Tim Wakefield	.15	.40
25 Tim Costo	.01	.05
26 Pedro Munoz	.01	.05
27 Reggie Sanders	.02	.10
28 Arthur Rhodes	.01	.05
29 Scott Cooper	.01	.05
30 Marquis Grissom	.05	.15
31 Dave Nilsson	.01	.05
32 John Patterson	.01	.05
33 Ivan Rodriguez	.30	.75
34 Andy Stankiewicz	.01	.05
35 Bret Boone	.05	.15
36 Gerald Williams	.01	.05
37 Mike Mussina	.10	.30
38 Henry Rodriguez	.01	.05
39 Chuck Knoblauch	.07	.20
40 Bob Wickman	.01	.05
41 Donovan Osborne	.01	.05
42 Mike Timlin	.01	.05
43 Damion Easley	.02	.10
44 Pedro Astacio	.01	.05
45 David Segui	.01	.05
46 Willie Greene	.01	.05
47 Mike Trombley	.01	.05
48 Bernie Williams	.08	.25
49 Eric Anthony	.01	.05
50 Tim Naehring	.01	.05
51 Carlos Baerga	.01	.05
52 Brady Anderson	.02	.10
53 Mo Vaughn	.07	.20
54 Willie Banks	.01	.05
55 Mark Wohlers	.01	.05
56 Jeff Bagwell	.20	.50
57 Frank Seminara	.01	.05
58 Robin Ventura	.02	.10
59 Alan Embree	.01	.05
60 Rey Sanchez	.01	.05
61 Delino DeShields	.01	.05
62 Todd Van Poppel	.01	.05
63 Eric Karros	.05	.15
64 Gary Sheffield	.15	.40
65 Dan Wilson	.02	.10
66 Frank Thomas	.25	.60
67 Tim Salmon	.07	.20
68 Dan Smith	.01	.05
69 Kenny Lofton	.02	.10
70 Carlos Garcia	.01	.05
71 Scott Livingstone	.01	.05
72 Sam Militello	.01	.05
73 Juan Guzman	.01	.05
74 Greg Colbrunn	.01	.05
75 David Hulse	.01	.05
76 Rusty Meacham	.01	.05
77 Dave Fleming	.01	.05
78 Rene Arocha	.01	.05
79 Derrick May	.01	.05
80 Cal Eldred	.01	.05
81 Bernard Gilkey	.01	.05
82 Deion Sanders	.08	.25
83 Reggie Jefferson	.01	.05
84 Jeff Kent	.08	.25
85 Juan Gonzalez	.15	.40
86 Billy Ashley	.01	.05
87 Travis Fryman	.02	.10
88 Roberto Hernandez	.02	.10
89 Hipolito Pichardo	.01	.05
90 Wilfredo Cordero	.01	.05
91 John Jaha	.01	.05
92 Javier Lopez	.15	.40
93 Derek Bell	.01	.05
94 Jeff Juden	.01	.05
95 Steve Avery	.01	.05
96 Moises Alou	.02	.10
97 Brian Jordan	.02	.10
98 Brian Williams	.01	.05
99 Bob Zupcic	.01	.05
100 Ray Lankford	.02	.10

1993 Toys'R'Us Master Photos

COMPLETE SET (12)	1.50	4.00
1 Moises Alou	.07	.20
2 Eric Anthony	.02	.10
3 Carlos Baerga	.02	.10
4 Willie Greene	.02	.10
5 Ken Griffey Jr.	.60	1.50
6 Marquis Grissom	.07	.20
7 Chuck Knoblauch	.15	.40
8 Scott Livingstone	.02	.10
9 Sam Militello	.02	.10
10 Ivan Rodriguez	.20	.50
11 Gary Sheffield	.25	.60
12 Frank Thomas	.30	.75

1969 Transogram Statues Cards

The reverse of the 1969 Transogram statue box contains a full color, blank-backed card corresponding to the statue inside. All prices are for just the cards. If a box is included, please use a 2X multiplier.

COMPLETE SET (60)	750.00	1500.00
1 Joe Azcue	2.50	6.00
2 Willie Horton	3.00	8.00
3 Luis Tiant	4.00	10.00
4 Denny McLain	4.00	10.00
5 Jose Cardenal	2.50	6.00
6 Al Kaline	20.00	50.00
7 Tony Oliva	4.00	10.00
8 Blue Moon Odom	2.50	6.00
9 Cesar Tovar	2.50	6.00
10 Rick Monday	3.00	8.00
11 Harmon Killebrew	15.00	40.00
12 Danny Cater	2.50	6.00
13 Brooks Robinson	20.00	50.00
14 Jim Fregosi	4.00	10.00
15 Dave McNally	3.00	8.00
16 Frank Robinson	20.00	50.00
17 Bobby Knoop	2.50	6.00
18 Rick Reichardt	2.50	6.00
19 Carl Yastrzemski	20.00	50.00
20 Pete Ward	2.50	6.00
21 Rico Petrocelli	3.00	8.00
22 Tommy John	4.00	10.00
23 Ken Harrelson	4.00	10.00
24 Luis Aparicio	12.50	30.00
25 Mike Epstein	2.50	6.00
26 Roy White	3.00	8.00
27 Camilo Pascual	3.00	8.00
28 Mel Stottlemyre	3.00	8.00
29 Frank Howard	4.00	10.00
30 Mickey Mantle	150.00	300.00
31 Lou Brock	15.00	40.00
32 Juan Marichal	15.00	40.00
33 Bob Gibson	15.00	40.00
34 Willie Mays	75.00	150.00
35 Tim McCarver	6.00	15.00
36 Willie McCovey	15.00	40.00
37 Don Wilson	2.50	6.00
38 Billy Williams	12.50	30.00
39 Rusty Staub	4.00	10.00
40 Ernie Banks	20.00	50.00
41 Jim Wynn	3.00	8.00
42 Ron Santo	4.00	10.00
43 Tom Haller	3.00	8.00
44 Ron Swoboda	4.00	10.00
45 Willie Davis	2.50	6.00
46 Jerry Koosman	4.00	10.00
47 Jim Lefebvre	2.50	6.00
48 Tom Seaver	40.00	80.00
49 Joe Torre	4.00	10.00
50 Tony Perez	8.00	20.00
51 Felipe Alou	4.00	10.00
52 Lee May	3.00	8.00
53 Hank Aaron	60.00	120.00
54 Pete Rose	60.00	120.00
55 Cookie Rojas	2.50	6.00
56 Roberto Clemente	100.00	200.00
57 Richie Allen	6.00	15.00
58 Matty Alou	3.00	8.00
59 John Callison	3.00	8.00
60 Bill Mazeroski	6.00	15.00

1970 Mets Transogram Statues Cards

The reverse of each 1970 Transogram Mets box features blank backed, unnumbered cards issued in three card panels corresponding to the three small plastic statues honoring the 1969 Mets. The listed prices are for the single cards cut from the box. If the box is included, please use a 1.5X multiplier.

COMPLETE SET	200.00	400.00
21A Ed Kranepool	3.00	8.00
21B Al Weis	1.50	4.00
21C Tom Seaver	75.00	150.00
22A Ken Boswell	1.50	4.00
22B Jerry Koosman	4.00	10.00
22C Jerry Grote	2.00	5.00
23A Art Shamsky	1.50	4.00
23B Gary Gentry	1.50	4.00
23C Tommie Agee	2.00	5.00
24A Nolan Ryan	150.00	300.00
24B Tug McGraw	8.00	20.00
24C Cleon Jones	1.50	4.00
25A Ron Swoboda	1.50	4.00
25B Bud Harrelson	2.50	6.00
25C Donn Clendenon	1.50	4.00

1993 Treadway Boy Scouts of America

This single standard-size card was distributed by the Flint River Council of the Boy Scouts of America (Griffin, Georgia) to boys who were in scouting as of October 1992. Only 7,000 were produced. The front features a color action photo of Jeff Treadway. The card has black borders. Hot pink lettering sets off the player's name at the bottom and the words "Collector's Edition" at the top. The phrase "Official B.S.A. Baseball Card" is printed in blue just above the player's head. The Flint River Council logo appears in the bottom right corner. The back is white and displays a light blue panel containing personal and career information. Sponsor logos appear at the bottom. The player's name, team logo and the words "Limited Edition" and "National League Champs" are at the top. The bottom has advertisements for Willis Oil Company and Willis Tire and Auto.

1 Jeff Treadway	.75	2.00

1992 Triple Play Previews

COMPLETE SET (8)	60.00	120.00
1 Ken Griffey Jr.	20.00	50.00
2 Darryl Strawberry	2.00	5.00
3 Andy Van Slyke	3.00	8.00
4 Don Mattingly	15.00	40.00
5 Gary Carter	2.00	5.00
Steve Finley		
6 Frank Thomas	6.00	15.00
7 Kirby Puckett	8.00	20.00
8 David Cone	2.00	5.00
John Franco		
Jeff Innis		
Fun at the Ballpark		

1992 Triple Play

The 1992 Triple Play set contains 264 standard-size cards. Cards were distributed in 15-card foil packs and jumbo packs. Each 15-card foil pack came with one rub off game card. The Triple Play set was created especially for children ages 5-12, featuring bright color borders, player quotes, fun facts. Subsets include Little Hotshots (picturing some players when they were kids) and Awesome Action.

COMPLETE SET (264)	4.00	10.00
1 SkyDome	.02	.10
2 Tom Foley	.02	.10
3 Scott Erickson	.02	.10
4 Matt Williams	.07	.20
5 David Valle	.02	.10
6 Andy Van Slyke LH	.07	.20
7 Tom Glavine	.10	.30
8 Kevin Appier	.07	.20
9 Pedro Guerrero	.07	.20
10 Terry Steinbach	.02	.10
11 Terry Mulholland	.02	.10
12 Mike Boddicker	.02	.10
13 Gregg Olson	.02	.10
14 Tim Burke	.02	.10
15 Candy Maldonado	.02	.10
16 Orlando Merced	.02	.10
17 Robin Ventura	.07	.20
18 Eric Anthony	.02	.10
19 Greg Maddux	.30	.75
20 Erik Hanson	.02	.10
21 Bobby Ojeda	.02	.10
22 Nolan Ryan	.60	1.50
23 Dave Righetti	.07	.20
24 Reggie Jefferson	.02	.10
25 Jody Reed	.02	.10
26 S.Finley/G.Carter AA	.02	.10
27 Chili Davis	.07	.20
28 Hector Villanueva	.02	.10
29 Cecil Fielder	.07	.20
30 Hal Morris	.02	.10
31 Barry Larkin	.10	.30
32 Bobby Thigpen	.02	.10
33 Andy Benes	.02	.10
34 Harold Baines	.07	.20
35 David Cone	.07	.20
36 Mark Langston	.02	.10
37 Bryan Harvey	.02	.10
38 John Kruk	.07	.20
39 Scott Sanderson	.02	.10
40 Lonnie Smith	.02	.10
41 Rex Hudler AA	.02	.10
42 George Bell	.02	.10
43 Steve Finley	.07	.20
44 Mickey Tettleton	.02	.10
45 Robby Thompson	.02	.10
46 Pat Kelly	.02	.10
47 Marquis Grissom	.07	.20
48 Tony Pena	.02	.10
49 Alex Cole	.02	.10
50 Steve Buechele	.02	.10
51 Ivan Rodriguez	.20	.50
52 John Smiley	.02	.10
53 Gary Sheffield	.07	.20
54 Greg Olson	.02	.10
55 Ramon Martinez	.02	.10
56 B.J. Surhoff	.07	.20
57 Bruce Hurst	.02	.10
58 Todd Stottlemyre	.02	.10
59 Brett Butler	.07	.20
60 Glenn Davis	.02	.10
61 Glenn Braggs	.02	.10
Kirt Manwaring AA		
62 Lee Smith	.07	.20
63 Rickey Henderson	.20	.50
64 Fun at the Ballpark	.07	.20
65 Rick Aguilera	.07	.20
66 Kevin Elster	.02	.10
67 Dwight Evans	.10	.30
68 Andujar Cedeno	.02	.10
69 Brian McRae	.02	.10
70 Benito Santiago	.07	.20
71 Randy Johnson	.20	.50
72 Roberto Kelly	.02	.10
73 Juan Samuel AA	.02	.10
74 Alex Fernandez	.02	.10
75 Felix Jose	.02	.10
76 Brian Harper	.02	.10
77 Scott Sanderson LH	.02	.10
78 Ken Caminiti	.07	.20
79 Mo Vaughn	.07	.20
80 Roger McDowell	.02	.10
81 Robin Yount	.30	.75
82 Dave Magadan	.02	.10
83 Julio Franco	.07	.20
84 Roberto Alomar	.10	.30
85 Steve Avery	.02	.10
86 Travis Fryman	.07	.20
87 Fred McGriff	.10	.30
88 Dave Stewart	.07	.20
89 Larry Walker	.10	.30
90 Chris Sabo	.02	.10
91 Chuck Finley	.07	.20
92 Dennis Martinez	.07	.20
93 Jeff Johnson	.02	.10
94 Len Dykstra	.07	.20
95 Mark Whiten	.02	.10
96 Wade Taylor	.02	.10
97 Lance Dickson	.02	.10
98 Kevin Tapani	.02	.10
99 Luis Polonia	.02	.10
Tony Phillips AA		
100 Milt Cuyler	.02	.10
101 Willie McGee	.07	.20
102 Tony Fernandez AA	.02	.10
103 Albert Belle	.07	.20
104 Todd Hundley	.02	.10
105 Ben McDonald	.02	.10
106 Doug Drabek	.02	.10
107 Tim Raines	.07	.20
108 Joe Carter	.07	.20
109 Reggie Sanders	.07	.20
110 John Olerud	.07	.20
111 Darren Lewis	.02	.10
112 Juan Gonzalez	.10	.30
113 Andre Dawson AA	.02	.10
114 Mark Grace	.10	.30
115 George Brett	.50	1.25
116 Barry Bonds	.60	1.50
117 Lou Whitaker	.07	.20
118 Jose Oquendo	.02	.10
119 Lee Stevens	.02	.10
120 Phil Plantier	.02	.10
121 Matt Merullo AA	.02	.10
122 Greg Vaughn	.02	.10
123 Royce Clayton	.02	.10
124 Bob Welch	.07	.20
125 Juan Samuel	.02	.10
126 Ron Gant	.07	.20
127 Edgar Martinez	.10	.30
128 Andy Ashby	.02	.10
129 Jack McDowell	.02	.10
130 D.Henderson	.02	.10
J.Browne AA		
131 Leo Gomez	.02	.10
132 Checklist 1-88	.02	.10
133 Phillie Phanatic	.07	.20
134 Bret Barberie	.02	.10
135 Kent Hrbek	.07	.20
136 Hall of Fame	.02	.10
137 Omar Vizquel	.10	.30
138 The Famous Chicken	.07	.20
139 Terry Pendleton	.07	.20
140 Jim Eisenreich	.02	.10
141 Todd Zeile	.07	.20
142 Todd Van Poppel	.02	.10
143 Darren Daulton	.07	.20
144 Mike Macfarlane	.02	.10
145 Luis Mercedes	.02	.10
146 Trevor Wilson	.02	.10
147 Dave Stieb	.07	.20
148 Andy Van Slyke	.10	.30
149 Carlton Fisk	.10	.30
150 Craig Biggio	.10	.30
151 Joe Girardi	.02	.10
152 Ken Griffey Jr.	.40	1.00
153 Jose Offerman	.02	.10
154 Bobby Witt	.02	.10
155 Will Clark	.10	.30
156 Steve Olin	.02	.10
157 Greg W. Harris	.02	.10
158 Dale Murphy LH	.10	.30
159 Don Mattingly	.50	1.25
160 Shawon Dunston	.02	.10
161 Bill Gullickson	.02	.10
162 Paul O'Neill	.10	.30
163 Norm Charlton	.02	.10
164 Bo Jackson	.20	.50
165 Tony Fernandez	.02	.10
166 Dave Henderson	.02	.10
167 Dwight Gooden	.07	.20
168 Junior Felix	.02	.10
169 Lance Parrish	.07	.20
170 Pat Combs	.02	.10
171 Chuck Knoblauch	.07	.20
172 John Smoltz	.10	.30
173 Wrigley Field	.07	.20
174 Andre Dawson	.07	.20
175 Pete Harnisch	.02	.10
176 Alan Trammell	.07	.20
177 Kirk Dressendorfer	.02	.10
178 Matt Nokes	.02	.10
179 Wil Cordero	.02	.10
180 Scott Cooper	.02	.10
181 Glenallen Hill	.02	.10
182 John Franco	.07	.20
183 Rafael Palmeiro	.10	.30
184 Jay Bell	.07	.20
185 Bill Wegman	.02	.10
186 Deion Sanders	.10	.30
187 Darryl Strawberry	.07	.20
188 Jaime Navarro	.02	.10
189 Darrin Jackson	.02	.10
190 Eddie Zosky	.02	.10
191 Mike Scioscia	.02	.10
192 Chito Martinez	.02	.10
193 Pat Kelly	.02	.10
Ron Tingley AA		
194 Ray Lankford	.07	.20
195 Dennis Eckersley	.07	.20
196 Ivan Calderon	.02	.10
Mike Maddux AA		
197 Shane Mack	.02	.10
198 Checklist 89-176	.02	.10
199 Cal Ripken	.60	1.50
200 Jeff Bagwell	.20	.50
201 Dave Howard	.02	.10
202 Kirby Puckett	.20	.50
203 Harold Reynolds	.07	.20
204 Jim Abbott	.10	.30
205 Mark Lewis	.02	.10
206 Frank Thomas	.20	.50
207 Rex Hudler	.02	.10
208 Vince Coleman	.02	.10
209 Delino DeShields	.02	.10
210 Luis Gonzalez	.07	.20
211 Wade Boggs	.10	.30
212 Orel Hershiser	.07	.20
213 Cal Eldred	.02	.10
214 Jose Canseco	.10	.30
215 Jose Guzman	.02	.10
216 Roger Clemens	.40	1.00
217 David Justice	.07	.20
218 Tony Phillips	.02	.10
219 Tony Gwynn	.25	.60
220 Mitch Williams	.02	.10
221 Bill Sampen	.02	.10
222 Billy Hatcher	.02	.10
223 Gary Gaetti	.07	.20
224 Tim Wallach	.02	.10
225 Kevin Maas	.02	.10
226 Kevin Brown	.07	.20
227 Sandy Alomar Jr.	.02	.10
228 John Habyan	.02	.10
229 Ryne Sandberg	.30	.75
230 Greg Gagne	.02	.10
231 Mark McGwire Signing	.25	.60
232 Mike LaValliere	.02	.10
233 Mark Gubicza	.02	.10
234 Lance Parrish LH	.02	.10
235 Carlos Baerga	.02	.10
236 Howard Johnson	.02	.10
237 Mike Mussina	.20	.50
238 Ruben Sierra	.07	.20
239 Lance Johnson	.02	.10
240 Devon White	.07	.20
241 Dan Wilson	.02	.10
242 Kelly Gruber	.02	.10
243 Brett Butler LH	.02	.10
244 Ozzie Smith	.30	.75
245 Chuck McElroy	.02	.10
246 Shawn Boskie	.02	.10
247 Mark Davis	.02	.10
248 Bill Landrum	.02	.10
249 Frank Tanana	.07	.20
250 Darryl Hamilton	.02	.10
251 Gary DiSarcina	.02	.10
252 Mike Greenwell	.02	.10
253 Cal Ripken LH	.30	.75
254 Paul Molitor	.07	.20
255 Tim Teufel	.02	.10
256 Chris Hoiles	.02	.10
257 Rob Dibble	.07	.20
258 Sid Bream	.02	.10
259 Tino Martinez	.10	.30
260 Dale Murphy	.10	.30
261 Greg Hibbard	.02	.10
262 Mark McGwire	.50	1.25
263 Oriole Park	.02	.10
264 Checklist 177-264	.02	.10

1992 Triple Play Gallery

COMPLETE FOIL SET (6)	1.00	2.50
COMMON FOIL (GS1-GS6)	.20	.50
COMPLETE JUMBO SET (6)	5.00	12.00
1-6: RANDOM INSERTS IN FOIL PACKS		
7-12: ONE PER JUMBO PACK		
GS1 Bobby Bonilla	.20	.50
GS2 Wally Joyner	.20	.50
GS3 Jack Morris	.20	.50
GS4 Steve Sax	.20	.50
GS5 Danny Tartabull	.20	.50
GS6 Frank Viola	.20	.50
GS7 Jeff Bagwell	.50	1.25
GS8 Ken Griffey Jr.	1.25	3.00
GS9 Dave Justice	.20	.50
GS10 Ryan Klesko	.20	.50
GS11 Cal Ripken	2.00	5.00
GS12 Frank Thomas	.50	1.25

1993 Triple Play Previews

COMPLETE SET (12)	75.00	150.00
1 Ken Griffey Jr.	10.00	25.00
2 Roberto Alomar	4.00	10.00
3 Cal Ripken	20.00	50.00
4 Eric Karros	2.50	6.00
5 Cecil Fielder	1.50	4.00
6 Gary Sheffield	5.00	12.00
7 Darren Daulton	1.50	4.00
8 Andy Van Slyke	.75	2.00
9 Dennis Eckersley	5.00	12.00
10 Ryne Sandberg	8.00	20.00
11 Mark Grace	4.00	10.00
12 David Segui	.75	2.00
Luis Polonia		

1993 Triple Play

The 1993 Triple Play baseball set consists of 264 standard-size cards. Approximately eight players from each of the 28 teams is represented in the set. Each pack also included one of thirty Triple Play Action Baseball game cards. Scattered throughout the set are seven Little Hotshot (11, 77, 97, 143, 209, 229, 245) and eight Awesome Action (12, 61, 64, 68, 144, 193, 196, 200) cards. There are no key Rookie Cards in this set, however the set does feature the first card of President Bill Clinton.

COMPLETE SET (264)	6.00	15.00
1 Ken Griffey Jr.	.40	1.00
2 Roberto Alomar	.10	.30
3 Cal Ripken	.60	1.50
4 Eric Karros	.07	.20
5 Cecil Fielder	.07	.20
6 Gary Sheffield	.07	.20
7 Darren Daulton	.07	.20
8 Andy Van Slyke	.10	.30
9 Dennis Eckersley	.07	.20
10 Ryne Sandberg	.30	.75
11 Mark Grace LH	.07	.20
12 David Segui	.02	.10
Luis Polonia AA		
13 Mike Mussina	.10	.30
14 Vince Coleman	.02	.10
15 Rafael Belliard	.02	.10
16 Ivan Rodriguez	.10	.30
17 Eddie Taubensee	.02	.10
18 Cal Eldred	.02	.10
19 Rick Wilkins	.02	.10
20 Edgar Martinez	.10	.30
21 Brian McRae	.02	.10
22 Darren Holmes	.02	.10
23 Mark Whiten	.02	.10
24 Todd Zeile	.07	.20
25 Scott Cooper	.02	.10
26 Frank Thomas	.20	.50
27 Wil Cordero	.02	.10
28 Juan Guzman	.02	.10
29 Pedro Astacio	.02	.10
30 Steve Avery	.02	.10
31 Barry Larkin	.10	.30
32 President Bill Clinton	2.00	5.00
33 Scott Erickson	.02	.10
34 Mike Devereaux	.02	.10
35 Tino Martinez	.10	.30
36 Brent Mayne	.02	.10
37 Tim Salmon	.10	.30
38 Dave Hollins	.02	.10
39 Royce Clayton	.02	.10
40 Shawon Dunston	.02	.10
41 Eddie Murray	.20	.50
42 Larry Walker	.07	.20
43 Jeff Bagwell	.10	.30
44 Milt Cuyler	.02	.10
45 Mike Bordick	.07	.20
46 Mike Greenwell	.02	.10
47 Steve Sax	.02	.10
48 Chuck Knoblauch	.07	.20
49 Charles Nagy	.02	.10
50 Tim Wakefield	.20	.50
51 Tony Gwynn	.25	.60
52 Rob Dibble	.07	.20
53 Mickey Morandini	.02	.10
54 Steve Hosey	.02	.10
55 Mike Piazza	.75	2.00
56 Bill Wegman	.02	.10
57 Kevin Maas	.02	.10
58 Gary DiSarcina	.02	.10
59 Travis Fryman	.07	.20
60 Ruben Sierra	.07	.20
61 Ken Caminiti AA	.02	.10
62 Brian Jordan	.07	.20
63 Scott Chiamparino	.02	.10
64 George Brett	.25	.60
Mike Bordick AA		
65 Carlos Garcia	.02	.10
66 Checklist	.02	.10
67 John Smoltz	.10	.30
68 Mark McGwire	.25	.60
Brian Harper AA		
69 Kurt Stillwell	.02	.10
70 Chad Curtis	.02	.10
71 Rafael Palmeiro	.10	.30
72 Kevin Young	.02	.10
73 Glenn Davis	.02	.10
74 Dennis Martinez	.07	.20
75 Sam Militello	.02	.10
76 Mike Morgan	.02	.10
77 Frank Thomas LH	.10	.30
78 Staying Fit	.02	.10
79 Steve Buechele	.02	.10
80 Carlos Baerga	.02	.10
81 Robby Thompson	.02	.10
82 Kirk McCaskill	.02	.10
83 Lee Smith	.07	.20
84 Gary Scott	.02	.10
85 Tony Pena	.02	.10
86 Howard Johnson	.02	.10
87 Mark McGwire	.50	1.25
88 Bip Roberts	.02	.10
89 Devon White	.07	.20
90 John Franco	.07	.20
91 Tom Browning	.02	.10
92 Mickey Tettleton	.02	.10
93 Jeff Conine	.07	.20
94 Albert Belle	.07	.20
95 Fred McGriff	.10	.30
96 Nolan Ryan	.60	1.50
97 Paul Molitor LH	.02	.10
98 Juan Bell	.02	.10
99 Dave Fleming	.02	.10
100 Craig Biggio	.10	.30
101A Andy Stankiewicz ERR	.02	.10
Name on front in white		
101B Andy Stankiewicz COR	.02	.10
Name on front in red		
102 Delino DeShields	.02	.10
103 Damion Easley	.02	.10
104 Kevin McReynolds	.02	.10
105 David Nied	.02	.10
106 Rick Sutcliffe	.07	.20
107 Will Clark	.10	.30
108 Tim Raines	.07	.20
109 Eric Anthony	.02	.10
110 Mike LaValliere	.02	.10
111 Dean Palmer	.07	.20
112 Eric Davis	.07	.20
113 Damon Berryhill	.02	.10
114 Felix Jose	.02	.10
115 Ozzie Guillen	.07	.20
116 Pat Listach	.02	.10
117 Tom Glavine	.10	.30
118 Roger Clemens	.40	1.00
119 Dave Henderson	.02	.10
120 Don Mattingly	.50	1.25
121 Orel Hershiser	.07	.20
122 Ozzie Smith	.30	.75
123 Joe Carter	.07	.20
124 Bret Saberhagen	.07	.20
125 Mitch Williams	.02	.10
126 Jerald Clark	.02	.10
127 Mile High Stadium	.07	.20
128 Kent Hrbek	.07	.20
129 Equipment	.02	.10
Curt Schilling		
130 Gregg Jefferies	.02	.10
131 John Orton	.02	.10
132 Checklist	.02	.10
133 Bret Boone	.07	.20
134 Pat Borders	.02	.10
135 Gregg Olson	.02	.10
136 Brett Butler	.07	.20
137 Rob Deer	.02	.10
138 Darrin Jackson	.02	.10
139 John Kruk	.07	.20
140 Jay Bell	.07	.20
141 Bobby Witt	.02	.10
142 Dan Plesac	.02	.10
Randy Myers		
Jose Guzman		
143 Wade Boggs LH	.07	.20
144 Ken Lofton AA	.02	.10
145 Ben McDonald	.02	.10
146 Dwight Gooden	.07	.20
147 Terry Pendleton	.07	.20
148 Julio Franco	.07	.20
149 Ken Caminiti	.07	.20
150 Greg Vaughn	.02	.10
151 Sammy Sosa	.20	.50
152 David Valle	.02	.10
153 Wally Joyner	.07	.20
154 Dante Bichette	.07	.20
155 Mark Lewis	.02	.10
156 Bob Tewksbury	.02	.10
157 Billy Hatcher	.02	.10
158 Jack McDowell	.02	.10
159 Marquis Grissom	.07	.20
160 Jack Morris	.07	.20
161 Ramon Martinez	.02	.10
162 Deion Sanders	.10	.30
163 Tim Belcher	.02	.10
164 Mascots	.02	.10
Pirate Parrot		
165 Scott Leius	.02	.10
166 Brady Anderson	.07	.20
167 Randy Johnson	.20	.50
168 Mark Gubicza	.02	.10
169 Chuck Finley	.07	.20
170 Terry Mulholland	.02	.10
171 Matt Williams	.07	.20
172 Dwight Smith	.02	.10
173 Bobby Bonilla	.07	.20
174 Ken Hill	.02	.10
175 Doug Jones	.02	.10
176 Tony Phillips	.02	.10
177 Terry Steinbach	.02	.10
178 Frank Viola	.07	.20
179 Robin Ventura	.07	.20
180 Shane Mack	.02	.10
181 Kenny Lofton	.07	.20
182 Jeff King	.02	.10
183 Tim Teufel	.02	.10
184 Chris Sabo	.02	.10
185 Len Dykstra	.07	.20
186 Trevor Wilson	.02	.10
187 Darryl Strawberry	.07	.20
188 Robin Yount	.30	.75
189 Bob Wickman	.02	.10
190 Luis Polonia	.02	.10
191 Alan Trammell	.07	.20
192 Bob Welch	.07	.20
193 Omar Vizquel AA	.07	.20
194 Tom Pagnozzi	.02	.10
195 Bret Barberie	.02	.10
196 Mike Scioscia AA	.02	.10

Card	Low	High
197 Randy Tomlin	.02	.10
198 Checklist	.02	.10
199 Ron Gant	.07	.20
200 Roberto Alomar AA	.07	.20
201 Andy Benes	.02	.10
202 Pirates Pepper	.02	.10
203 Steve Finley	.07	.20
204 Steve Olin	.02	.10
205 Chris Hoiles	.02	.10
206 John Wetteland	.07	.20
207 Danny Tartabull	.02	.10
208 Bernard Gilkey	.02	.10
209 Tom Glavine LH	.07	.20
210 Benito Santiago	.07	.20
211 Mark Grace	.10	.30
212 Glenallen Hill	.02	.10
213 Jeff Brantley	.02	.10
214 George Brett	.50	1.25
215 Mark Lemke	.02	.10
216 Ron Karkovice	.02	.10
217 Tom Brunansky	.02	.10
218 Todd Hundley	.02	.10
219 Rickey Henderson	.20	.50
220 Joe Oliver	.02	.10
221 Juan Gonzalez	.07	.20
222 John Olerud	.07	.20
223 Hal Morris	.02	.10
224 Lou Whitaker	.07	.20
225 Bryan Harvey	.02	.10
226 Mike Gallego	.02	.10
227 Willie McGee	.07	.20
228 Jose Oquendo	.02	.10
229 Darren Daulton LH	.02	.10
230 Curt Schilling	.07	.20
231 Jay Buhner	.07	.20
232 Doug Drabek	.02	.10
Greg Swindell		
233 Jaime Navarro	.02	.10
234 Kevin Appier	.07	.20
235 Mark Langston	.02	.10
236 Jeff Montgomery	.02	.10
237 Joe Girardi	.02	.10
238 Ed Sprague	.02	.10
239 Dan Walters	.02	.10
240 Kevin Tapani	.02	.10
241 Pete Harnisch	.02	.10
242 Al Martin	.02	.10
243 Jose Canseco	.10	.30
244 Moises Alou	.07	.20
245 Mark McGwire LH	.25	.60
246 Luis Rivera	.02	.10
247 George Bell	.02	.10
248 B.J. Surhoff	.07	.20
249 David Justice	.07	.20
250 Brian Harper	.02	.10
251 Sandy Alomar Jr.	.02	.10
252 Kevin Brown	.07	.20
253 Tim Wallach	.02	.10
Todd Worrell		
Jody Reed		
254 Ray Lankford	.07	.20
255 Derek Bell	.02	.10
256 Joe Grahe	.02	.10
257 Charlie Hayes	.02	.10
258 Wade Boggs	.10	.30
Jim Abbott		
259A Joe Robbie Stadium ERR (Misnumbered 129)	.07	.20
259B Joe Robbie Stadium COR	.07	.20
260 Kirby Puckett	.20	.50
261 Jay Bell	.07	.20
262 Bill Swift	.02	.10
263 Roger McDowell	.02	.10
264 Checklist	.02	.10

1993 Triple Play Action

Card	Low	High
COMPLETE SET (30)	4.00	10.00
ONE PER PACK		
1 Andy Van Slyke	.15	.40
2 Bobby Bonilla	.08	.25
3 Ozzie Smith	.40	1.00
4 Ryne Sandberg	.40	1.00
5 Darren Daulton	.08	.25
6 Larry Walker	.08	.25
7 Eric Karros	.08	.25
8 Barry Larkin	.15	.40
9 Deion Sanders	.15	.40
10 Gary Sheffield	.08	.25
11 Will Clark	.15	.40
12 Jeff Bagwell	.15	.40
13 Roberto Alomar	.15	.40
14 Roger Clemens	.50	1.25
15 Cecil Fielder	.08	.25
16 Robin Yount	.40	1.00
17 Cal Ripken	.75	2.00
18 Carlos Baerga	.05	.15
19 Don Mattingly	.60	1.50
20 Kirby Puckett	.25	.60
21 Frank Thomas	.25	.60
22 Juan Gonzalez	.08	.25
23 Mark McGwire	.60	1.50
24 Ken Griffey Jr.	.50	1.25
25 Wally Joyner	.08	.25
26 Chad Curtis	.05	.15
27 Rockies vs. Marlins	.05	.15
28 Juan Guzman	.05	.15
29 David Justice	.08	.25
30 Joe Carter	.08	.25

1993 Triple Play Gallery

Card	Low	High
COMPLETE SET (10)	8.00	20.00
ONE PER JUMBO PACK		
GS1 Barry Bonds	4.00	10.00
GS2 Andre Dawson	.60	1.50
GS3 Wade Boggs	1.00	2.50
GS4 Greg Maddux	3.00	8.00
GS5 Dave Winfield	.60	1.50
GS6 Paul Molitor	.60	1.50
GS7 Jim Abbott	1.00	2.50
GS8 J.T. Snow	1.00	2.50
GS9 Benito Santiago	.60	1.50
GS10 David Nied	.40	1.00

1993 Triple Play League Leaders

Card	Low	High
COMPLETE SET (6)	8.00	20.00
RANDOM INSERTS IN RETAIL PACKS		
L1 B.Bonds/D.Eckersley	4.00	10.00
L2 G.Maddux/D.Eckersley	2.50	6.00
L3 E.Karros/P.Listach ROY	.60	1.50
L4 F.McGriff/J.Gonzalez	1.00	2.50
L5 D.Daulton/C.Fielder	.60	1.50
L6 G.Sheffield/E.Martinez	1.00	2.50

1993 Triple Play Nicknames

Card	Low	High
COMPLETE SET (10)	8.00	20.00
RANDOM INSERTS IN HOBBY PACKS		
1 Frank Thomas Big Hurt	.75	2.00
2 Roger Clemens Rocket	1.50	4.00
3 Ryne Sandberg Ryno	1.50	4.00
4 Will Clark Thrill	.50	1.25
5 Ken Griffey Jr. Junior	1.50	4.00
6 Dwight Gooden Dr. K	.30	.75
7 Nolan Ryan Express	2.50	6.00
8 Deion Sanders Prime Time	.50	1.25
9 Ozzie Smith Wizard	1.25	3.00
10 Fred McGriff Crime Dog	.50	1.25

1994 Triple Play Promos

Card	Low	High
COMPLETE SET (10)	6.00	15.00
1 Juan Gonzalez	.30	.75
2 Frank Thomas	.40	1.00
3 Barry Bonds	.75	2.00
4 Ken Griffey Jr.	1.25	3.00
5 Paul Molitor	.40	1.00
6 Mike Piazza	1.00	2.50
7 Tim Salmon	.08	.25
8 Lenny Dykstra	.08	.25
9 Don Mattingly	1.00	2.50
10 Greg Maddux	1.25	3.00

1994 Triple Play

The 1994 Triple Play set consists of 300 standard-size cards, featuring ten players from each team along with a 17-card Rookie Review set. Triple Play game cards, redeemable for various prizes, were inserted one per pack.

Card	Low	High
COMPLETE SET (300)	10.00	25.00
1 Mike Bordick	.07	.20
2 Dennis Eckersley	.07	.20
3 Brent Gates	.02	.10
4 Rickey Henderson	.20	.50
5 Mark McGwire	.50	1.25
6 Troy Neel	.02	.10
7 Craig Paquette	.02	.10
8 Ruben Sierra	.07	.20
9 Terry Steinbach	.02	.10
10 Bobby Witt	.02	.10
11 Chad Curtis	.02	.10
12 Chili Davis	.07	.20
13 Gary DiSarcina	.02	.10
14 Damion Easley	.02	.10
15 Chuck Finley	.07	.20
16 Joe Grahe	.02	.10
17 Mark Langston	.02	.10
18 Eduardo Perez	.02	.10
19 Tim Salmon	.10	.30
20 J.T. Snow	.07	.20
21 Jeff Bagwell	.10	.30
22 Craig Biggio	.10	.30
23 Ken Caminiti	.07	.20
24 Andujar Cedeno	.02	.10
25 Doug Drabek	.02	.10
26 Steve Finley	.07	.20
27 Luis Gonzalez	.07	.20
28 Pete Harnisch	.02	.10
29 Darryl Kile	.07	.20
30 Mitch Williams	.02	.10
31 Roberto Alomar	.10	.30
32 Joe Carter	.07	.20
33 Juan Guzman	.02	.10
34 Pat Hentgen	.02	.10
35 Paul Molitor	.07	.20
36 John Olerud	.07	.20
37 Ed Sprague	.02	.10
38 Dave Stewart	.07	.20
39 Duane Ward	.02	.10
40 Devon White	.07	.20
41 Steve Avery	.02	.10
42 Jeff Blauser	.02	.10
43 Ron Gant	.07	.20
44 Tom Glavine	.10	.30
45 David Justice	.07	.20
46 Greg Maddux	.30	.75
47 Fred McGriff	.10	.30
48 Terry Pendleton	.07	.20
49 Deion Sanders	.10	.30
50 John Smoltz	.10	.30
51 Ricky Bones	.02	.10
52 Cal Eldred	.02	.10
53 Darryl Hamilton	.02	.10
54 John Jaha	.02	.10
55 Pat Listach	.02	.10
56 Jaime Navarro	.02	.10
57 Dave Nilsson	.02	.10
58 B.J. Surhoff	.07	.20
59 Greg Vaughn	.02	.10
60 Robin Yount	.30	.75
61 Bernard Gilkey	.02	.10
62 Gregg Jefferies	.02	.10
63 Brian Jordan	.07	.20
64 Ray Lankford	.07	.20
65 Tom Pagnozzi	.02	.10
66 Ozzie Smith	.30	.75
67 Bob Tewksbury	.02	.10
68 Allen Watson	.02	.10
69 Mark Whiten	.02	.10
70 Todd Zeile	.07	.20
71 Steve Buechele	.02	.10
72 Mark Grace	.10	.30
73 Jose Guzman	.02	.10
74 Derrick May	.02	.10
75 Mike Morgan	.02	.10
76 Randy Myers	.07	.20
77 Ryne Sandberg	.30	.75
78 Sammy Sosa	.20	.50
79 Jose Vizcaino	.02	.10
80 Rick Wilkins	.02	.10
81 Pedro Astacio	.02	.10
82 Brett Butler	.07	.20
83 Delino DeShields	.02	.10
84 Orel Hershiser	.07	.20
85 Eric Karros	.07	.20
86 Ramon Martinez	.02	.10
87 Jose Offerman	.02	.10
88 Mike Piazza	.30	.75
89 Darryl Strawberry	.07	.20
90 Tim Wallach	.02	.10
91 Moises Alou	.07	.20
92 Wil Cordero	.02	.10
93 Jeff Fassero	.02	.10
94 Darrin Fletcher	.02	.10
95 Marquis Grissom	.07	.20
96 Ken Hill	.02	.10
97 Mike Lansing	.02	.10
98 Kirk Rueter	.02	.10
99 Larry Walker	.07	.20
100 John Wetteland	.07	.20
101 Rod Beck	.02	.10
102 Barry Bonds	.60	1.50
103 John Burkett	.02	.10
104 Royce Clayton	.02	.10
105 Darren Lewis	.02	.10
106 Kirt Manwaring	.02	.10
107 Willie McGee	.07	.20
108 Bill Swift	.02	.10
109 Robby Thompson	.02	.10
110 Matt Williams	.07	.20
111 Sandy Alomar Jr.	.02	.10
112 Carlos Baerga	.02	.10
113 Albert Belle	.07	.20
114 Wayne Kirby	.02	.10
115 Kenny Lofton	.07	.20
116 Jose Mesa	.02	.10
117 Eddie Murray	.20	.50
118 Charles Nagy	.02	.10
119 Paul Sorrento	.02	.10
120 Jim Thome	.10	.30
121 Rich Amaral	.02	.10
122 Eric Anthony	.02	.10
123 Mike Blowers	.02	.10
124 Chris Bosio	.02	.10
125 Jay Buhner	.07	.20
126 Dave Fleming	.02	.10
127 Ken Griffey Jr.	.40	1.00
128 Randy Johnson	.20	.50
129 Edgar Martinez	.10	.30
130 Tino Martinez	.10	.30
131 Bret Barberie	.02	.10
132 Ryan Bowen	.02	.10
133 Chuck Carr	.02	.10
134 Jeff Conine	.07	.20
135 Orestes Destrade	.02	.10
136 Chris Hammond	.02	.10
137 Bryan Harvey	.02	.10
138 Dave Magadan	.02	.10
139 Benito Santiago	.07	.20
140 Gary Sheffield	.07	.20
141 Bobby Bonilla	.07	.20
142 Jeromy Burnitz	.07	.20
143 Dwight Gooden	.07	.20
144 Todd Hundley	.02	.10
145 Bobby Jones	.02	.10
146 Jeff Kent	.10	.30
147 Joe Orsulak	.02	.10
148 Bret Saberhagen	.07	.20
149 Pete Schourek	.02	.10
150 Ryan Thompson	.02	.10
151 Brady Anderson	.07	.20
152 Harold Baines	.07	.20
153 Mike Devereaux	.02	.10
154 Chris Hoiles	.02	.10
155 Ben McDonald	.02	.10
156 Mark McLemore	.02	.10
157 Mike Mussina	.10	.30
158 Rafael Palmeiro	.10	.30
159 Cal Ripken	.60	1.50
160 Chris Sabo	.02	.10
161 Brad Ausmus	.10	.30
162 Derek Bell	.02	.10
163 Andy Benes	.02	.10
164 Doug Brocail	.02	.10
165 Archi Cianfrocco	.02	.10
166 Ricky Gutierrez	.02	.10
167 Tony Gwynn	.25	.60
168 Gene Harris	.02	.10
169 Pedro Martinez RC	.60	1.50
170 Phil Plantier	.02	.10
171 Darren Daulton	.07	.20
172 Mariano Duncan	.02	.10
173 Lenny Dykstra	.07	.20
174 Tommy Greene	.02	.10
175 Dave Hollins	.02	.10
176 Danny Jackson	.02	.10
177 John Kruk	.07	.20
178 Terry Mulholland	.02	.10
179 Curt Schilling	.07	.20
180 Kevin Stocker	.02	.10
181 Jay Bell	.07	.20
182 Steve Cooke	.02	.10
183 Carlos Garcia	.02	.10
184 Joel Johnston	.02	.10
185 Jeff King	.02	.10
186 Al Martin	.02	.10
187 Orlando Merced	.02	.10
188 Don Slaught	.02	.10
189 Andy Van Slyke	.10	.30
190 Kevin Young	.02	.10
191 Kevin Brown	.07	.20
192 Jose Canseco	.10	.30
193 Will Clark	.10	.30
194 Juan Gonzalez	.07	.20
195 Tom Henke	.02	.10
196 David Hulse	.02	.10
197 Dean Palmer	.07	.20
198 Roger Pavlik	.02	.10
199 Ivan Rodriguez	.10	.30
200 Kenny Rogers	.07	.20
201 Roger Clemens	.40	1.00
202 Scott Cooper	.02	.10
203 Andre Dawson	.07	.20
204 Mike Greenwell	.02	.10
205 Billy Hatcher	.02	.10
206 Jeff Russell	.02	.10
207 Aaron Sele	.02	.10
208 John Valentin	.02	.10
209 Mo Vaughn	.07	.20
210 Frank Viola	.07	.20
211 Rob Dibble	.07	.20
212 Willie Greene	.02	.10
213 Roberto Kelly	.02	.10
214 Barry Larkin	.10	.30
215 Kevin Mitchell	.02	.10
216 Hal Morris	.02	.10
217 Joe Oliver	.02	.10
218 Jose Rijo	.02	.10
219 Reggie Sanders	.07	.20
220 John Smiley	.02	.10
221 Dante Bichette	.07	.20
222 Ellis Burks	.07	.20
223 Andres Galarraga	.07	.20
224 Joe Girardi	.02	.10
225 Charlie Hayes	.02	.10
226 Darren Holmes	.02	.10
227 Howard Johnson	.02	.10
228 Roberto Mejia	.02	.10
229 David Nied	.02	.10
230 Armando Reynoso	.02	.10
231 Kevin Appier	.07	.20
232 David Cone	.07	.20
233 Greg Gagne	.02	.10
234 Tom Gordon	.02	.10
235 Felix Jose	.02	.10
236 Wally Joyner	.07	.20
237 Jose Lind	.02	.10
238 Brian McRae	.02	.10
239 Mike Macfarlane	.02	.10
240 Jeff Montgomery	.02	.10
241 Eric Davis	.07	.20
242 John Doherty	.02	.10
243 Cecil Fielder	.07	.20
244 Travis Fryman	.07	.20
245 Bill Gullickson	.02	.10
246 Mike Henneman	.02	.10
247 Tony Phillips	.02	.10
248 Mickey Tettleton	.02	.10
249 Alan Trammell	.07	.20
250 Lou Whitaker	.07	.20
251 Rick Aguilera	.02	.10
252 Scott Erickson	.02	.10
253 Kent Hrbek	.07	.20
254 Chuck Knoblauch	.07	.20
255 Shane Mack	.02	.10
256 Dave McCarty	.02	.10
257 Pat Meares	.02	.10
258 Kirby Puckett	.20	.50
259 Kevin Tapani	.02	.10
260 Dave Winfield	.07	.20
261 Wilson Alvarez	.02	.10
262 Jason Bere	.02	.10
263 Alex Fernandez	.02	.10
264 Ozzie Guillen	.07	.20
265 Roberto Hernandez	.02	.10
266 Lance Johnson	.02	.10
267 Jack McDowell	.02	.10
268 Tim Raines	.07	.20
269 Frank Thomas	.20	.50
270 Robin Ventura	.07	.20
271 Jim Abbott	.10	.30
272 Wade Boggs	.10	.30
273 Mike Gallego	.02	.10
274 Pat Kelly	.02	.10
275 Jimmy Key	.07	.20
276 Don Mattingly	.50	1.25
277 Paul O'Neill	.10	.30
278 Mike Stanley	.02	.10
279 Danny Tartabull	.02	.10
280 Bernie Williams	.10	.30
281 Chipper Jones	.20	.50
282 Ryan Klesko	.07	.20
283 Javier Lopez	.07	.20
284 Jeffrey Hammonds	.07	.20
285 Jeff McNeely	.02	.10
286 Manny Ramirez	.20	.50
287 Billy Ashley	.02	.10
288 Raul Mondesi	.07	.20
289 Cliff Floyd	.07	.20
290 Rondell White	.07	.20
291 Steve Karsay	.02	.10
292 Midre Cummings	.02	.10
293 Salomon Torres	.02	.10
294 J.R. Phillips	.02	.10
295 Marc Newfield	.02	.10
296 Carlos Delgado	.10	.30
297 Butch Huskey	.02	.10
298 Frank Thomas Checklist	.10	.25
299 Barry Bonds Checklist	.15	.40
300 Juan Gonzalez Checklist	.06	.15

1994 Triple Play Bomb Squad

Card	Low	High
COMPLETE SET (10)	6.00	15.00
STATED ODDS 1:18, 1:8 JUMBO		
1 Frank Thomas	.75	2.00
2 Cecil Fielder	.30	.75
3 Juan Gonzalez	.30	.75
4 Barry Bonds	2.00	5.00
5 David Justice	.30	.75
6 Fred McGriff	.50	1.25
7 Ron Gant	.30	.75
8 Ken Griffey Jr.	1.50	4.00
9 Albert Belle	.30	.75
10 Matt Williams	.30	.75

1994 Triple Play Medalists

Card	Low	High
COMPLETE SET (15)	8.00	20.00
STATED ODDS 1:12, 1:6 JUMBO		
1 Hoiles/Tettleton/Harper	.30	.75
2 Daulton/Wilkins/Manwaring	.30	.75
3 Thomas/Palmeiro/Olerud	.75	2.00
4 Grace/McGriff/Bagwell	.50	1.25
5 Alomar/Baerga/Whitaker	.50	1.25
6 Sandberg/Biggio/Thompson	1.50	4.00
7 Ripken/Trammell/Fern	2.50	6.00
8 Larkin/Bell/Blauser	.50	1.25
9 Ventura/Fryman/Boggs	.50	1.25
10 Pendleton/Hollins/Sheffield	.30	.75
11 Griffey/Puckett/Belle	1.50	4.00
12 Bonds/Van Slyke/Dykstra	2.00	5.00
13 McDowell/Brown/R.Johnson	.75	2.00
14 Maddux/Rijo/Swift	1.25	3.00
15 Molitor/Winfield/Baines	.30	.75

1994 Triple Play Nicknames

Card	Low	High
COMPLETE SET (8)	12.00	30.00
STATED ODDS 1:36, 1:12 JUMBO		
1 Cecil Fielder	.75	2.00
2 Ryne Sandberg	4.00	10.00
3 Gary Sheffield	.75	2.00
4 Joe Carter	.75	2.00
5 John Olerud	.75	2.00
6 Cal Ripken	6.00	15.00
7 Mark McGwire	5.00	12.00
8 Gregg Jefferies	.75	2.00

2012 Triple Play

Card	Low	High
1 Ian Kennedy	.20	.50
2 Miguel Montero	.20	.50
3 Paul Goldschmidt	.30	.75
4 Brian McCann	.25	.60
5 Chipper Jones	.30	.75
6 Dan Uggla	.25	.60
7 Adam Jones	.25	.60
8 Brian Matusz	.20	.50
9 Matt Wieters	.30	.75
10 Adrian Gonzalez	.25	.60
11 Dustin Pedroia	.30	.75
12 Jacoby Ellsbury	.25	.60
13 Alfonso Soriano	.25	.60
14 Geovany Soto	.25	.60
15 Matt Garza	.20	.50
16 A.J. Pierzynski	.20	.50
17 John Danks	.20	.50
18 Paul Konerko	.25	.60
19 Brandon Phillips	.20	.50
20 Joey Votto	.30	.75
21 Mat Latos	.25	.60
22 Asdrubal Cabrera	.25	.60
23 Carlos Santana	.25	.60
24 Grady Sizemore	.25	.60
25 Carlos Gonzalez	.25	.60
26 Todd Helton	.25	.60
27 Troy Tulowitzki	.30	.75
28 Justin Verlander	.30	.75
29 Miguel Cabrera	.30	.75
30 Prince Fielder	.25	.60
31 Brett Myers	.20	.50
32 Brett Wallace	.20	.50
33 Carlos Lee	.20	.50
34 Alex Gordon	.20	.50
35 Billy Butler	.20	.50
36 Eric Hosmer	.25	.60
37 Albert Pujols	.40	1.00
38 Dan Haren	.20	.50
39 Jered Weaver	.25	.60
40 Clayton Kershaw	.50	1.25
41 James Loney	.20	.50
42 Matt Kemp	.25	.60
43 Giancarlo Stanton	.30	.75
44 Jose Reyes	.20	.50
45 Josh Johnson	.20	.50
46 Rickie Weeks	.20	.50
47 Ryan Braun	.20	.50
48 Yovani Gallardo	.20	.50
49 Francisco Liriano	.20	.50
50 Joe Mauer	.25	.60
51 Justin Morneau	.25	.60
52 David Wright	.25	.60
53 Ike Davis	.20	.50
54 Johan Santana	.25	.60
55 Alex Rodriguez	.40	1.00
56 Curtis Granderson	.25	.60
57 Derek Jeter	.75	2.00
58 Jemile Weeks	.20	.50
59 Kurt Suzuki	.20	.50
60 Yoenis Cespedes	.50	1.25
61 Chase Utley	.25	.60
62 Roy Halladay	.25	.60
63 Ryan Howard	.25	.60
64 Andrew McCutchen	.30	.75
65 Joel Hanrahan	.20	.50
66 Pedro Alvarez	.20	.50
67 Carlos Quentin	.20	.50
68 Chase Headley	.20	.50
69 Orlando Hudson	.20	.50
70 Brian Wilson	.30	.75
71 Buster Posey	.40	1.00
72 Tim Lincecum	.25	.60
73 Dustin Ackley	.20	.50
74 Felix Hernandez	.25	.60
75 Ichiro Suzuki	.40	1.00
76 Carlos Beltran	.25	.60
77 Lance Berkman	.25	.60
78 Matt Holliday	.30	.75
79 B.J. Upton	.25	.60
80 David Price	.25	.60
81 Evan Longoria	.25	.60
82 Ian Kinsler	.25	.60
83 Josh Hamilton	.25	.60
84 Yu Darvish	.50	1.25
85 Brett Lawrie	.25	.60
86 Jose Bautista	.25	.60
87 Ricky Romero	.20	.50
88 Mike Morse	.20	.50
89 Ryan Zimmerman	.25	.60
90 Stephen Strasburg	.30	.75
91 Justin Upton Puzzle	.25	.60
92 Justin Upton Puzzle	.25	.60
93 Justin Upton Puzzle	.25	.60
94 Justin Upton Puzzle	.25	.60
95 Justin Upton Puzzle	.25	.60
96 Justin Upton Puzzle	.25	.60
97 Justin Upton Puzzle	.25	.60
98 Justin Upton Puzzle	.25	.60
99 Justin Upton Puzzle	.25	.60
100 Starlin Castro Puzzle	.25	.60
101 Starlin Castro Puzzle	.25	.60
102 Starlin Castro Puzzle	.25	.60
103 Starlin Castro Puzzle	.25	.60
104 Starlin Castro Puzzle	.25	.60
105 Starlin Castro Puzzle	.25	.60
106 Starlin Castro Puzzle	.25	.60
107 Starlin Castro Puzzle	.25	.60
108 Starlin Castro Puzzle	.25	.60
109 Carlos Lee Puzzle	.20	.50
110 Carlos Lee Puzzle	.20	.50
111 Carlos Lee Puzzle	.20	.50
112 Carlos Lee Puzzle	.20	.50
113 Carlos Lee Puzzle	.20	.50
114 Carlos Lee Puzzle	.20	.50
115 Carlos Lee Puzzle	.20	.50
116 Carlos Lee Puzzle	.20	.50
117 Carlos Lee Puzzle	.20	.50
118 A.Pujols Puzzle	.40	1.00
119 Albert Pujols Puzzle	.40	1.00
120 Albert Pujols Puzzle	.40	1.00
121 Albert Pujols Puzzle	.40	1.00
122 Albert Pujols Puzzle	.40	1.00
123 Albert Pujols Puzzle	.40	1.00
124 Albert Pujols Puzzle	.40	1.00
125 Albert Pujols Puzzle	.40	1.00
126 Albert Pujols Puzzle	.40	1.00
127 Jose Reyes Puzzle	.20	.50
128 Jose Reyes Puzzle	.20	.50
129 Jose Reyes Puzzle	.20	.50
130 Jose Reyes Puzzle	.20	.50
131 Jose Reyes Puzzle	.20	.50
132 Jose Reyes Puzzle	.20	.50
133 Jose Reyes Puzzle	.20	.50
134 Jose Reyes Puzzle	.20	.50
135 Jose Reyes Puzzle	.20	.50
136 A.Rodriguez Puzzle	.40	1.00
137 Alex Rodriguez Puzzle	.40	1.00
138 Alex Rodriguez Puzzle	.40	1.00
139 Alex Rodriguez Puzzle	.40	1.00
140 Alex Rodriguez Puzzle	.40	1.00
141 Alex Rodriguez Puzzle	.40	1.00
142 Alex Rodriguez Puzzle	.40	1.00
143 Alex Rodriguez Puzzle	.40	1.00
144 Alex Rodriguez Puzzle	.40	1.00
145 Y.Cespedes Puzzle	.50	1.25
146 Yoenis Cespedes Puzzle	.50	1.25
147 Yoenis Cespedes Puzzle	.50	1.25
148 Yoenis Cespedes Puzzle	.50	1.25
149 Yoenis Cespedes Puzzle	.50	1.25
150 Yoenis Cespedes Puzzle	.50	1.25
151 Yoenis Cespedes Puzzle	.50	1.25
152 Yoenis Cespedes Puzzle	.50	1.25
153 Yoenis Cespedes Puzzle	.50	1.25
154 Roy Halladay Puzzle	.25	.60
155 Roy Halladay Puzzle	.25	.60
156 Roy Halladay Puzzle	.25	.60
157 Roy Halladay Puzzle	.25	.60
158 Roy Halladay Puzzle	.25	.60
159 Roy Halladay Puzzle	.25	.60
160 Roy Halladay Puzzle	.25	.60
161 Roy Halladay Puzzle	.25	.60
162 Roy Halladay Puzzle	.25	.60
163 Andrew McCutchen Puzzle	.30	.75
164 Andrew McCutchen Puzzle	.30	.75
165 Andrew McCutchen Puzzle	.30	.75
166 Andrew McCutchen Puzzle	.30	.75
167 Andrew McCutchen Puzzle	.30	.75
168 Andrew McCutchen Puzzle	.30	.75
169 Andrew McCutchen Puzzle	.30	.75
170 Andrew McCutchen Puzzle	.30	.75
171 Andrew McCutchen Puzzle	.30	.75
172 Orlando Hudson Puzzle	.20	.50
173 Orlando Hudson Puzzle	.20	.50
174 Orlando Hudson Puzzle	.20	.50
175 Orlando Hudson Puzzle	.20	.50
176 Orlando Hudson Puzzle	.20	.50
177 Orlando Hudson Puzzle	.20	.50
178 Orlando Hudson Puzzle	.20	.50
179 Orlando Hudson Puzzle	.20	.50
180 Orlando Hudson Puzzle	.20	.50
181 B.Posey Puzzle	.40	1.00
182 Buster Posey Puzzle	.40	1.00
183 Buster Posey Puzzle	.40	1.00
184 Buster Posey Puzzle	.40	1.00
185 Buster Posey Puzzle	.40	1.00
186 Buster Posey Puzzle	.40	1.00
187 Buster Posey Puzzle	.40	1.00
188 Buster Posey Puzzle	.40	1.00
189 Buster Posey Puzzle	.40	1.00
190 I.Suzuki Puzzle	.40	1.00
191 Ichiro Suzuki Puzzle	.40	1.00
192 Ichiro Suzuki Puzzle	.40	1.00
193 Ichiro Suzuki Puzzle	.40	1.00
194 Ichiro Suzuki Puzzle	.40	1.00
195 Ichiro Suzuki Puzzle	.40	1.00
196 Ichiro Suzuki Puzzle	.40	1.00
197 Ichiro Suzuki Puzzle	.40	1.00
198 Ichiro Suzuki Puzzle	.40	1.00
199 Matt Holliday Puzzle	.30	.75
200 Matt Holliday Puzzle	.30	.75
201 Matt Holliday Puzzle	.30	.75
202 Matt Holliday Puzzle	.30	.75
203 Matt Holliday Puzzle	.30	.75
204 Matt Holliday Puzzle	.30	.75
205 Matt Holliday Puzzle	.30	.75
206 Matt Holliday Puzzle	.30	.75
207 Matt Holliday Puzzle	.30	.75
208 E.Longoria Puzzle	.25	.60
209 Evan Longoria Puzzle	.25	.60
210 Evan Longoria Puzzle	.25	.60
211 Evan Longoria Puzzle	.25	.60
212 Evan Longoria Puzzle	.25	.60
213 Evan Longoria Puzzle	.25	.60
214 Evan Longoria Puzzle	.25	.60
215 Evan Longoria Puzzle	.25	.60
216 Evan Longoria Puzzle	.25	.60
217 Josh Hamilton Puzzle	.25	.60
218 Josh Hamilton Puzzle	.25	.60
219 Josh Hamilton Puzzle	.25	.60
220 Josh Hamilton Puzzle	.25	.60
221 Josh Hamilton Puzzle	.25	.60
222 Josh Hamilton Puzzle	.25	.60
223 Josh Hamilton Puzzle	.25	.60
224 Josh Hamilton Puzzle	.25	.60
225 Josh Hamilton Puzzle	.25	.60
226 Jose Bautista Puzzle	.25	.60
227 Jose Bautista Puzzle	.25	.60
228 Jose Bautista Puzzle	.25	.60
229 Jose Bautista Puzzle	.25	.60
230 Jose Bautista Puzzle	.25	.60
231 Jose Bautista Puzzle	.25	.60
232 Jose Bautista Puzzle	.25	.60
233 Jose Bautista Puzzle	.25	.60
234 Jose Bautista Puzzle	.25	.60
235 Ian Kennedy FOC	.20	.50
236 Brian McCann FOC	.25	.60
237 Adam Jones FOC	.25	.60
238 Dustin Pedroia FOC	.30	.75
239 Matt Garza FOC	.20	.50
240 John Danks FOC	.20	.50
241 Joey Votto FOC	.30	.75
242 Asdrubal Cabrera FOC	.25	.60
243 Carlos Gonzalez FOC	.25	.60
244 Miguel Cabrera FOC	.30	.75
245 Brett Wallace FOC	.20	.50
246 Eric Hosmer FOC	.25	.60
247 Jered Weaver FOC	.25	.60
248 Matt Kemp FOC	.25	.60
249 Giancarlo Stanton FOC	.30	.75
250 Ryan Braun FOC	.20	.50
251 Justin Morneau FOC	.25	.60
252 Johan Santana FOC	.25	.60
253 Derek Jeter FOC	.75	2.00
254 Jemile Weeks FOC	.20	.50
255 Ryan Howard FOC	.25	.60
256 Joel Hanrahan FOC	.20	.50
257 Chase Headley FOC	.20	.50
258 Tim Lincecum FOC	.25	.60
259 Felix Hernandez FOC	.25	.60
260 Lance Berkman FOC	.25	.60
261 B.J. Upton FOC	.25	.60
262 Yu Darvish FOC	.50	1.25
263 Ricky Romero FOC	.20	.50
264 Stephen Strasburg FOC	.30	.75
265 Batter's Box	.07	.20
266 Diamond	.07	.20
267 Double Play	.07	.20
268 Home Run	.07	.20
269 Pitcher's Mound	.07	.20
270 Scoring Runs	.07	.20
271 Stealing	.07	.20
272 Tag Play	.07	.20
273 Cal Ripken Jr. HOF	1.00	2.50
274 George Brett HOF	.60	1.50
275 Nolan Ryan HOF	1.00	2.50
276 Wade Boggs HOF	.20	.50
277 Willie Stargell HOF	.20	.50
278 Bob Feller HOF	.20	.50
279 Tony Gwynn HOF	.30	.75
280 Reggie Jackson HOF	.20	.50
281 Al Kaline HOF	.30	.75
282 Willie McCovey HOF	.20	.50
283 Paul Molitor HOF	.30	.75
284 Joe Morgan HOF	.20	.50
285 Albert Pujols KID	.40	1.00
286 Derek Jeter KID	.75	2.00
287 Tim Lincecum KID	.25	.60
288 Josh Hamilton KID	.25	.60
289 Matt Kemp KID	.25	.60
290 Roy Halladay KID	.25	.60
291 Justin Verlander KID	.30	.75
292 Jacoby Ellsbury KID	.25	.60
293 Ichiro Suzuki KID	.40	1.00
294 Chipper Jones KID	.30	.75
295 Base	4.00	10.00
296 Bat	2.50	6.00
297 Pants	2.50	6.00
298 Fld Glove	4.00	10.00
299 Bat Glove	6.00	15.00
300 Jersey	2.50	6.00

2012 Triple Play Eye Black

Card	Low	High
COMMON CARD	.20	.50
APPROXIMATE ODDS 1:6		

2012 Triple Play Stickers

Card	Low	High
1 Flaming Baseball	.15	.40
2 Flaming Bats	.15	.40
3 Smiling Baseball	.15	.40
4 Catcher's Mask	.15	.40
5 Line Drive at Pitcher	.15	.40
6 Diving Catch	.15	.40
7 Yer Out	.15	.40
8 Arguing	.15	.40
9 Crash Trough Wall	.15	.40
10 Hit By Pitch	.15	.40
11 Slugger	.15	.40
12 Home Run	.15	.40
13 Grand Slam	.15	.40
14 Power Hitter	.15	.40
15 Stolen Base	.15	.40
16 Great Catch	.15	.40
17 Chipper Jones	.40	1.00
18 Brian Matusz	.25	.60
19 Adrian Gonzalez	.30	.75
20 Paul Konerko	.25	.60
21 Brandon Phillips	.25	.60
22 Grady Sizemore	.30	.75
23 Troy Tulowitzki	.40	1.00
24 Justin Verlander	.40	1.00
25 Alex Gordon	.30	.75
26 Clayton Kershaw	.60	1.50
27 Rickie Weeks	.25	.60
28 Joe Mauer	.30	.75
29 David Wright	.30	.75
30 Ryan Zimmerman	.30	.75

2012 Triple Play Tattoos

Card	Low	High
COMMON CARD	.20	.50
APPROXIMATE ODDS 1:4		

2013 Triple Play

Card	Low	High
1 Aaron Hill	.12	.30
2 Wade Miley	.12	.30
3 Paul Goldschmidt	.20	.50
4 Freddie Freeman	.25	.60
5 Craig Kimbrel	.15	.40
6 Jason Heyward	.15	.40
7 Adam Jones	.15	.40
8 Manny Machado	.75	2.00

9 Matt Wieters .20 .50
10 Will Middlebrooks .12 .30
11 Dustin Pedroia .20 .50
12 David Ortiz .20 .50
13 Starlin Castro .12 .30
14 Anthony Rizzo .25 .60
15 Alfonso Soriano .15 .40
16 Kevin Youkilis .12 .30
17 Chris Sale .20 .50
18 Alex Rios .15 .40
19 Aroldis Chapman .20 .50
20 Jay Bruce .15 .40
21 Johnny Cueto .15 .40
22 Shin-Soo Choo .15 .40
23 Chris Perez .12 .30
24 Carlos Gonzalez .15 .40
25 Dexter Fowler .15 .40
26 Troy Tulowitzki .20 .50
27 Austin Jackson .12 .30
28 Miguel Cabrera .20 .50
29 Prince Fielder .15 .40
30 Justin Verlander .20 .50
31 Jose Altuve .15 .40
32 Matt Dominguez .12 .30
33 Alex Gordon .15 .40
34 Eric Hosmer .15 .40
35 Billy Butler .12 .30
36 Mike Trout 1.50 4.00
37 Jered Weaver .15 .40
38 Albert Pujols .25 .60
39 Mark Trumbo .12 .30
40 Adrian Gonzalez .15 .40
41 Andre Ethier .15 .40
42 Clayton Kershaw .30 .75
43 Matt Kemp .15 .40
44 Giancarlo Stanton .20 .50
45 Josh Johnson .15 .40
46 Jose Reyes .15 .40
47 Ryan Braun .15 .40
48 Yovani Gallardo .12 .30
49 Aramis Ramirez .12 .30
50 Josh Willingham .15 .40
51 Joe Mauer .15 .40
52 R.A. Dickey .15 .40
53 David Wright .15 .40
54 Matt Harvey .15 .40
55 Ichiro Suzuki .25 .60
56 Derek Jeter .50 1.25
57 Robinson Cano .15 .40
58 Nick Swisher .15 .40
59 Jarrod Parker .12 .30
60 Yoenis Cespedes .20 .50
61 Josh Reddick .12 .30
62 Cole Hamels .15 .40
63 Ryan Howard .15 .40
64 Carlos Ruiz .12 .30
65 Andrew McCutchen .20 .50
66 Pedro Alvarez .12 .30
67 Carlos Quentin .12 .30
68 Chase Headley .12 .30
69 Buster Posey .25 .60
70 Matt Cain .15 .40
71 Hunter Pence .15 .40
72 Blake Beavan .12 .30
73 Felix Hernandez .15 .40
74 Jesus Montero .12 .30
75 Carlos Beltran .15 .40
76 David Freese .12 .30
77 Allen Craig .15 .40
78 David Price .15 .40
79 Evan Longoria .15 .40
80 James Shields .12 .30
81 Jurickson Profar .15 .40
82 Yu Darvish .20 .50
83 Adrian Beltre .20 .50
84 Brett Lawrie .15 .40
85 Jose Bautista .15 .40
86 Edwin Encarnacion .20 .50
87 Stephen Strasburg .20 .50
88 Gio Gonzalez .15 .40
89 Bryce Harper .30 .75
90 Jayson Werth .15 .40
91 Mike Trout KID 3.00 8.00
92 Miguel Cabrera KID .40 1.00
93 Buster Posey KID .50 1.25
94 Bryce Harper KID .60 1.50
95 Felix Hernandez KID .30 .75
96 Clayton Kershaw KID .60 1.50
97 Andrew McCutchen KID .40 1.00
98 Stephen Strasburg KID .40 1.00
99 Giancarlo Stanton KID .40 1.00
100 Yu Darvish KID .40 1.00

2013 Triple Play All-Stars

1 Adam Jones .40 1.00
2 Adrian Gonzalez .40 1.00
3 Albert Pujols .60 1.50
4 Andrew McCutchen .50 1.25
5 Bryce Harper .75 2.00
6 Buster Posey .60 1.50
7 Carlos Beltran .40 1.00
8 Carlos Gonzalez .40 1.00
9 David Ortiz .50 1.25
10 David Price .40 1.00
11 David Wright .40 1.00
12 Derek Jeter 1.25 3.00
13 Dustin Pedroia .50 1.25
14 Evan Longoria .40 1.00
15 Felix Hernandez .40 1.00
16 Giancarlo Stanton .50 1.25
17 Ichiro Suzuki .60 1.50
18 Joe Mauer .40 1.00
19 Jose Bautista .40 1.00
20 Justin Verlander .50 1.25
21 Matt Kemp .40 1.00
22 Miguel Cabrera .50 1.25
23 Mike Trout 4.00 10.00
24 Prince Fielder .40 1.00
25 Robinson Cano .40 1.00
26 Ryan Braun .40 1.00
27 Ryan Howard .40 1.00
28 Stephen Strasburg .50 1.25
29 Yoenis Cespedes .50 1.25
30 Yu Darvish .50 1.25

2013 Triple Play Baseball 101

1 Fastball .20 .50
2 Knuckleball .20 .50
3 Triple Play .20 .50
4 Bullpen .20 .50
5 Outfield .20 .50
6 Infield .20 .50
7 Strike Zone .20 .50
8 Sacrifice Fly .20 .50

2013 Triple Play Cartoon Stickers

1 Bullpen .20 .50
2 Fastball .20 .50
3 Infield .20 .50
4 Knuckleball .20 .50
5 Outfield .20 .50
6 Sacrifice Fly .20 .50
7 Strike Zone .20 .50
8 Triple Play .20 .50
9 Sticker .20 .50
10 Sticker .20 .50

2013 Triple Play Eye Black

1 Derek Jeter .20 .50
2 Mike Trout .20 .50
3 Josh Hamilton .20 .50
4 Bryce Harper .20 .50
5 Albert Pujols .20 .50
6 Miguel Cabrera .20 .50
7 Jose Bautista .20 .50
8 Justin Verlander .20 .50
9 Felix Hernandez .20 .50
10 Clayton Kershaw .20 .50
11 Triple Crown Logo .20 .50
12 Rated Rookie Logo .20 .50

2013 Triple Play Real Feel

COMMON CARD 2.50 6.00
1 Batting Gloves 2.50 6.00
1 Fielding Gloves 2.50 6.00
1 Game Base 2.50 6.00
1 Game Bat 2.50 6.00
1 Game Jersey 2.50 6.00
1 Game Pants 2.50 6.00

2013 Triple Play Stickers Blue

1 Jason Heyward .40 1.00
2 Adam Jones .40 1.00
3 Carlos Gonzalez .40 1.00
4 Austin Jackson .30 .75
5 Miguel Cabrera .50 1.25
6 Jered Weaver .40 1.00
7 Adrian Gonzalez .40 1.00
8 Clayton Kershaw .75 2.00
9 Jose Reyes .40 1.00
10 David Wright .40 1.00
11 Derek Jeter 1.25 3.00
12 Ryan Howard .40 1.00
13 Hunter Pence .40 1.00
14 Felix Hernandez .40 1.00
15 Carlos Beltran .40 1.00
16 Evan Longoria .40 1.00
17 Jose Bautista .40 1.00
18 Gio Gonzalez .40 1.00
19 Justin Verlander .50 1.25
20 Matt Wieters .50 1.25

2013 Triple Play Stickers Red

1 Freddie Freeman .60 1.50
2 Manny Machado 2.00 5.00
3 Dustin Pedroia .50 1.25
4 Starlin Castro .30 .75
5 Kevin Youkilis .30 .75
6 Aroldis Chapman .50 1.25
7 Chris Perez .30 .75
8 Prince Fielder .40 1.00
9 Jose Altuve .40 1.00
10 Alex Gordon .40 1.00
11 Mike Trout 4.00 10.00
12 Matt Kemp .40 1.00
13 Giancarlo Stanton .50 1.25
14 Ryan Braun .40 1.00
15 Joe Mauer .40 1.00
16 R.A. Dickey .40 1.00
17 Ichiro Suzuki .60 1.50
18 Yoenis Cespedes .50 1.25
19 Cole Hamels .40 1.00
20 Andrew McCutchen .50 1.25
21 Buster Posey .60 1.50
22 Blake Beavan .30 .75
23 Jarrod Parker .30 .75
24 David Price .40 1.00
25 Yu Darvish .50 1.25
26 Brett Lawrie .40 1.00
27 Stephen Strasburg .50 1.25
28 Bryce Harper .75 2.00
29 Aaron Hill .30 .75
30 Albert Pujols .60 1.50

2013 Triple Play Tattoos

1 MLBPA Logo .20 .50
2 Rated Rookie Logo .20 .50
3 Bryce Harper .20 .50
4 Miguel Cabrera .20 .50
5 Joe Mauer .20 .50
6 Yu Darvish .20 .50
7 Matt Kemp .20 .50
8 Buster Posey .20 .50
9 Derek Jeter .20 .50
10 Mike Trout .20 .50

2013 Triple Play Traditions

1 The Wave .20 .50
2 Seventh Inning Stretch .20 .50
3 Fireworks .20 .50
4 Hot Dogs .20 .50
5 First Pitch .20 .50
6 National Anthem .20 .50
7 Father Son .20 .50
8 Flyover .20 .50

1996 Tropicana Hall of Fame Chips

These chips, all have a $5 demoniation and are numbered 1 of 1000. The fronts have a player photo while the back have a photo of the Tropicana casino. Since these are unnumbered, we have sequenced them in in alphabetical order.

COMPLETE SET 12.50 30.00
1 Ernie Banks 4.00 10.00
2 Brooks Robinson 4.00 10.00
3 Willie Stargell 4.00 10.00

1867 Troy Haymakers CdV's

These six cards represent one of the earliest known team sets. The Troy Haymakers were among the best known traveling squads of the tme. These photos were taken at a studio in Lansingburg, N.Y. Since these cards are unnumbered, we have sequenced them in alphabetical order.

COMPLETE SET 12000.00 24000.00
1 Thomas Abrams 2000.00 4000.00
2 William Craver 2000.00 4000.00
3 Steve King 2000.00 4000.00
4 Michael McAtee 2000.00 4000.00
5 Peter McKeon 2000.00 4000.00
6 Andrew McQuide 2000.00 4000.00

1986 True Value

The 1986 True Value set consists of 30 cards, each measuring 2 1/2" by 3 1/2", which were printed as panels of four although one of the cards in the panel only pictures a featured product. The complete panel measures approximately 10 3/8" by 3 1/2". The True Value logo is in the upper left corner of the obverse of each card. Supposedly the cards were distributed to customers purchasing 5.00 or more at the store. Cards are frequently found with perforations intact and still in the closed form where only the top card in the folded panel is visible. The card number appears at the bottom of the reverse. Team logos have been surgically removed (airbrushed) from the photos. A Don Mattingly card was recently discovered to have the words infield as his position.

COMPLETE SET (30) 4.00 10.00
1 Pedro Guerrero .02 .10
2 Steve Garvey .07 .20
3 Eddie Murray .30 .75
4 Pete Rose .30 .75
5 Don Mattingly .60 1.50
5A Don Mattingly
Position listed as infield
6 Fernando Valenzuela .07 .20
7 Jim Rice .07 .20
8 Kirk Gibson .07 .20
9 Ozzie Smith .50 1.25
10 Dale Murphy .15 .40
11 Robin Yount .30 .75
12 Tom Seaver .30 .75
13 Reggie Jackson .30 .75
14 Ryne Sandberg .60 1.50
15 Bruce Sutter .30 .75
16 Gary Carter .30 .75
17 George Brett .60 1.50
18 Rick Sutcliffe .02 .10
19 Dave Stieb .02 .10
20 Buddy Bell .02 .10
21 Alvin Davis .02 .10
22 Cal Ripken 1.25 3.00
23 Bill Madlock .02 .10
24 Kent Hrbek .07 .20
25 Lou Whitaker .07 .20
26 Nolan Ryan 1.25 3.00
27 Dwayne Murphy .02 .10
28 Mike Schmidt .30 .75
29 Andre Dawson .25 .60
30 Wade Boggs .60 1.50

1910-11 Turkey Red T3

The cards in this 126-card set measure approximately 5 3/4" by 8". The 1911 Turkey Red set of color cabinet style cards, designated T3 in the American Card Catalog, is named after the brand of cigarettes with which it was offered as a premium. Cards 1-50 and 77-126 depict baseball players while the middle series (51-76) portrays boxers. The cards themselves are not numbered but were assigned numbers for ordering purposes by the manufacturer. This list appears on the backs of cards in the 77-126 sub-series and has been used in the checklist below. At one time the boxers (51-76) were assigned a separate catalog number (T9) but were later returned to the classification to which they properly belong. This attractive set has been reprinted in 2 1/2" by 3 1/2" form. A small number of proofs were found in the early 1970's. Approximately 70 of the cards in the set have been discovered in proof form.

1 Mordecai Brown 600.00 1000.00
2 Bill Bergen 250.00 400.00
3 Fred Leach 250.00 400.00
4 Roger Bresnahan 350.00 600.00
5 Sam Crawford 500.00 800.00
6 Hal Chase 350.00 600.00
7 Howie Camnitz 250.00 400.00
8 Fred Clarke 500.00 800.00
9 Ty Cobb 3500.00 6000.00
10 Art Devlin 250.00 400.00
11 Bill Dahlen 250.00 400.00
12 Bill Donovan 250.00 400.00
13 Larry Doyle 250.00 400.00
14 Red Dooin 250.00 400.00
15 Kid Elberfeld 250.00 400.00
16 Johnny Evers 500.00 800.00
17 Clark Griffith 500.00 800.00
18 Hughie Jennings 500.00 800.00
19 Addie Joss 600.00 1000.00
20 Tim Jordan 250.00 400.00
21 Red Kleinow 250.00 400.00
22 Harry Krause 250.00 400.00
23 Napoleon Lajoie 700.00 1200.00
24 Mike Mitchell 250.00 400.00
25 Matty McIntyre 250.00 400.00
26 John McGraw 500.00 800.00
27 Christy Mathewson 2500.00 4000.00
28 Harry McIntire 250.00 400.00
29 Amby McConnell 250.00 400.00
30 George Mullin 250.00 400.00
31 Sherry Magee 300.00 500.00
32 Orval Overall 250.00 400.00
33 Jack Pfeister 250.00 400.00
34 Nap Rucker 250.00 400.00
35 Joe Tinker 500.00 800.00
36 Tris Speaker 900.00 1500.00
37 Slim Sallee 250.00 400.00
38 Jake Stahl 250.00 400.00
39 Rube Waddell 500.00 800.00
40 Vic Willis 350.00 600.00
41 Hooks Wiltse 250.00 400.00
42 Cy Young 1500.00 2500.00
43 Out At Third 250.00 400.00
44 Trying to Catch Him Napping 250.00 400.00
45 Tim Jordan Buck Herzog 250.00 400.00
46 Safe At Third 250.00 400.00
47 Frank Chance At Bat 600.00 1000.00
48 Jack Murray At Bat 300.00 500.00
49 Close Play At Second 300.00 500.00
50 Chief Myers At Bat UER 300.00 500.00
77 Red Ames 250.00 400.00
78 Frank Baker 500.00 800.00
79 George Bell 250.00 400.00
80 Chief Bender 500.00 800.00
81 Bob Bescher 250.00 400.00
82 Kitty Bransfield 250.00 400.00
83 Al Bridwell 250.00 400.00
84 George Browne 250.00 400.00
85 Bill Burns 250.00 400.00
86 Bill Carrigan 250.00 400.00
87 Eddie Collins 500.00 800.00
88 Harry Coveleski 250.00 400.00
89 Lou Criger 250.00 400.00
90 Mickey Doolan 250.00 400.00
91 Tom Downey 250.00 400.00
92 Jimmy Dygert 250.00 400.00
93 Art Fromme 250.00 400.00
94 George Gibson 250.00 400.00
95 Peaches Graham 250.00 400.00
96 Bob Groom 250.00 400.00
97 Bob Hoblitzel 300.00 500.00
98 Doc Hofman 250.00 400.00
99 Walter Johnson 1500.00 2500.00
100 Davy Jones 250.00 400.00
101 Willie Keeler 500.00 800.00
102 Johnny Kling 250.00 400.00
103 Ed Konetchy 250.00 400.00
104 Ed Lennox 250.00 400.00
105 Hans Lobert 250.00 400.00
106 Bris Lord 250.00 400.00
107 Rube Manning 250.00 400.00
108 Fred Merkle 250.00 400.00
109 Pat Moran 250.00 400.00
110 George McBride 250.00 400.00
111 Harry Niles 250.00 400.00
112 Dode Paskert 250.00 400.00
113 Bugs Raymond 250.00 400.00
114 Bob Rhoads 900.00 1500.00
115 Admiral Schlei 250.00 400.00
116 Boss Schmidt 250.00 400.00
117 Frank Schulte 250.00 400.00
118 Charlie Smith 250.00 400.00
119 George Stone 250.00 400.00
120 Gabby Street 250.00 400.00
121 Billy Sullivan 250.00 400.00
122 Fred Tenney 700.00 1200.00
123 Ira Thomas 250.00 400.00
124 Bobby Wallace 350.00 600.00
125 Ed Walsh 500.00 800.00
126 Chief Wilson 350.00 600.00
C1 Turkey Red Coupon 20.00 50.00
1-75 on back
C2 Turkey Red Coupon 20.00 50.00
1-76 on back
C3 Fez Coupon
C4 Old Mill Coupon

1989 TV Sports Mailbags

This 140-card set features glossy 8" by 10" color player photos and was distributed in packs with four pictures to a pack at the suggested retail price of $4.95. The backs carry the player's name, playing position, and team name.

COMPLETE SET (140) 30.00 80.00
1 Darryl Strawberry .20 .50
2 Ron Darling .08 .25
3 Dwight Gooden .20 .50
4 Keith Hernandez .20 .50
5 Kevin McReynolds .08 .25
6 David Cone .30 .75
7 Randy Myers .08 .25
8 Gregg Jefferies .08 .25
9 Andy Van Slyke .08 .25
10 Bobby Bonilla .20 .50
11 Doug Drabek .08 .25
12 Barry Bonds .75 2.00
13 Tim Raines .08 .25
14 Andres Galarraga .40 1.00
15 Hubie Brooks .08 .25
16 Tim Wallach .08 .25
17 Mark Grace .40 1.00
18 Ryne Sandberg .75 2.00
19 Shawon Dunston .08 .25
20 Mitch Webster .08 .25
21 Andre Dawson .40 1.00
22 Damon Berryhill .08 .25
23 Greg Maddux 1.25 3.00
24 Vance Law .08 .25
25 Ozzie Smith 1.00 2.50
26 Tom Brunansky .08 .25
27 Padro Guerrero .08 .25
28 Vince Coleman .08 .25
29 Juan Samuel .08 .25
30 Von Hayes .08 .25
31 Ricky Jordan .08 .25
32 Mike Schmidt .40 1.25
33 Kirk Gibson .30 .75
34 Orel Hershiser .20 .50
35 Mike Marshall .08 .25
36 Mike Scioscia .20 .50
37 Eric Davis .20 .50
38 Chris Sabo .08 .25
39 Barry Larkin .40 1.00
40 Danny Jackson .08 .25
41 Tom Browning .08 .25
42 Kal Daniels .08 .25
43 John Franco .20 .50
44 Paul O'Neill .40 1.00
45 Tony Gwynn 1.00 2.50
46 Benito Santiago .20 .50
47 Roberto Alomar .75 2.00
48 John Kruk .20 .50
49 Will Clark .60 1.50
50 Rick Reuschel .08 .25
51 Kevin Mitchell .08 .25
52 Robby Thompson .08 .25
53 Mike Scott .08 .25
54 Glenn Davis .08 .25
55 Billy Hatcher .08 .25
56 Gerald Young .08 .25
57 Gerald Perry .08 .25
58 Dale Murphy .30 .75
59 Ron Gant .30 .75
60 Jodie Davis .08 .25
61 Mike Greenwell .08 .25
62 Ellis Burks .20 .50
63 Roger Clemens 1.00 2.50
64 Wade Boggs .40 1.00
65 Dwight Evans .20 .50
66 Marty Barrett .08 .25
67 Mike Boddicker .08 .25
68 Lee Smith .20 .50
69 Alan Trammell .30 .75
70 Matt Nokes .08 .25
71 Jack Morris .20 .50
72 Jeff Robinson .08 .25
73 Paul Molitor .40 1.25
74 Robin Yount .30 1.25
75 Ted Higuera .08 .25
76 Jim Gantner .08 .25
77 Fred McGriff .40 1.00
78 Dave Stieb .08 .25
79 George Bell .08 .25
80 Tony Fernandez .08 .25
81 Dave Winfield .50 1.25
82 Don Mattingly 1.00 2.50
83 Rickey Henderson .60 1.50
84 Dave Righetti .08 .25
85 Joe Carter .30 .75
86 Mel Hall .08 .25
87 Cory Snyder .08 .25
88 Greg Swindell .08 .25
89 Cal Ripken 2.00 5.00
90 Brady Anderson .40 1.00
91 Larry Sheets .08 .25
92 Billy Ripken .08 .25
93 Jose Canseco .50 1.25
94 Walt Weiss .08 .25
95 Dave Stewart .08 .25
96 Dennis Eckersley .50 1.25
97 Terry Steinback .08 .25
98 Mark McGwire 1.00 2.50
99 Carney Lansford .08 .25
100 Dave Henderson .08 .25
101 Kent Hrbek .08 .25
102 Kirby Puckett .60 1.50
103 Frank Viola .08 .25
104 Gary Gaetti .20 .50
105 George Brett 1.00 2.50
15-Apr Kevin Seitzer .08 .25
16-Apr Danny Tartabull .08 .25
17-Apr Bo Jackson .40 1.00
18-Apr Wally Joyner .20 .50
19-Apr Devon White .08 .25
20-Apr Johnny Ray .08 .25
21-Apr Mike Witt .08 .25
22-Apr Harold Baines .20 .50
23-Apr Ozzie Guillen .30 .75
24-Apr Bobby Thigpen .08 .25
25-Apr Dan Pasqua .08 .25
26-Apr Ruben Sierra .20 .50
27-Apr Pete Incaviglia .08 .25
28-Apr Charlie Hough .08 .25
29-Apr Scott Fletcher .08 .25
30-Apr Mark Langston .08 .25
01-May Alvin Davis .08 .25
02-May Harold Reynolds .20 .50
03-May Jay Buhner .40 1.00
04-May Jose Canseco .50 1.25
05-May Wade Boggs .50 1.25
06-May Rickey Henderson .60 1.50
07-May Mike Greenwell .08 .25
08-May Darryl Strawberry .20 .50
09-May Tony Gwynn 1.00 2.50
10-May Will Clark .60 1.50
11-May Vince Coleman .08 .25
12-May Jose Canseco .50 1.25
13-May Frank Viola .08 .25
14-May Orel Hershiser .20 .50
15-May Kirk Gibson .30 .75
16-May Mark McGwire 1.00 2.50
17-May Benito Santiago .20 .50
18-May Chris Sabo .08 .25
19-May Walt Weiss .08 .25

1992 TV Sports Mailbag/Photo File 500 Home Run Club

This 15-piece set features horizontal, blank-backed, oversized (10" X 8") cards.They are color action shots (except Ruth, Ott, and Foxx, which are black-and-white) on left side. Player's name, biography, teams, and key home run information are printed on the right side. The cards are unnumbered and checklisted below in alphabetical order.

COMPLETE SET (15) 12.50 30.00
1 Hank Aaron 1.50 4.00
2 Ernie Banks .75 2.00
3 Jimmie Foxx .75 2.00
4 Reggie Jackson 1.00 2.50
5 Harmon Killebrew .60 1.50
6 Mickey Mantle 2.00 5.00
7 Eddie Mathews .60 1.50
8 Willie Mays 1.50 4.00
9 Willie McCovey .60 1.50
10 Mel Ott .60 1.50
11 Frank Robinson .60 1.50
12 Babe Ruth 2.00 5.00
13 Mike Schmidt .75 2.00
14 Ted Williams 1.50 4.00
15 Header card .40 1.00

1961 Twins Universal Match Corp.

The Farmers and Mechanics Savings Bank of Minneapolis sponsored this issue produced by the Universal Match Corp. of Minneapolis, MN. Each cover carries a player photo on the outside and a brief bio for each player appears on the covers inside. Players are shown wearing Washington Senators hats. Complete matchbooks carry a fifty percent premium.

COMPLETE SET (13) 75.00 150.00
1 Bob Allison 6.00 15.00
2 Earl Battey 4.00 10.00
3 Reno Bertoia 4.00 10.00
4 Billy Gardner 4.00 10.00
5 Lenny Green 4.00 10.00
6 Jim Kaat/(With Twins cap) 8.00 20.00
7 Harmon Killebrew 10.00 25.00
8 Jack Kralick/(With Twins cap) 4.00 10.00
9 Cookie Lavagetto 6.00 15.00
10 Jim Lemon 4.00 10.00
11 Camilo Pascual 4.00 10.00
12 Pedro Ramos 4.00 10.00
13 Zoilo Versalles/(With Twins cap) 6.00 15.00

1961 Twins Peter's Meats

The cards in this 26 card set measure 3 1/2" by 4 5/8". The 1961 Peter's Meats set of full color numbered cards depicts Minnesota Twins players only. The individual cards served as partial packaging for various meat products and are blank backed and heavily waxed. Complete boxes are sometimes available and are valued approximately 50 percent more than single cards. The catalog designation is F173.

COMPLETE SET (26) 500.00 1000.00
1 Zoilo Versalles 20.00 50.00
2 Ed Lopat 12.50 30.00
3 Pedro Ramos 10.00 25.00
4 Chuck Stobbs 10.00 25.00
5 Don Mincher 12.50 30.00
6 Jack Kralick 10.00 25.00
7 Jim Kaat 60.00 120.00
8 Hal Naragon 10.00 25.00
9 Don Lee 10.00 25.00
10 Cookie Lavagetto 12.50 30.00
11 Pete Whisenant 10.00 25.00
12 Elmer Valo 10.00 25.00
13 Ray Moore 10.00 25.00
14 Billy Gardner 10.00 25.00
15 Lenny Green 10.00 25.00
16 Sam Mele 10.00 25.00
17 Jim Lemon 10.00 25.00
18 Harmon Killebrew 150.00 300.00
19 Paul Giel 10.00 25.00
20 Reno Bertoia 10.00 25.00
21 Clyde McCullough 10.00 25.00
22 Earl Battey 10.00 25.00
23 Camilo Pascual 12.50 30.00
24 Dan Dobbek 10.00 25.00
25 Jose Valdivielso 10.00 25.00
26 Billy Consolo 10.00 25.00

1961 Twins Postcards

These postcards, most of which measure 4" by 5" and are in black and white and are blank-backed, feature members of the 1961 Minnesota Twins, the first year they were in Minnesota. These cards have black and white photograph along with a fascimile autograph. A couple of cards measure 5" by 4" instead. Since these cards are not numbered, we have sequenced them in alphabetical order. Some collectors refer to these as the type 1 postcards for the Twins.

COMPLETE SET 60.00 120.00
1 Bob Allison 1.50 4.00
2 Floyd Baker CO 1.50 4.00
3 Earl Battey 1.50 4.00
4 Reno Bertoia 1.50 4.00
5 Fred Bruckbauer 1.50 4.00
6 Billy Consolo 1.50 4.00
7 Dan Dobbek 1.50 4.00
8 Billy Gardner 1.50 4.00
9 Lenny Green 1.50 4.00
10 Calvin Griffith PRES 1.50 4.00
11 Ron Henry 1.50 4.00
12 Jim Kaat 3.00 8.00
13 Harmon Killebrew 6.00 15.00
14 Jack Kralick 1.50 4.00
15 Cookie Lavagetto MG 1.50 4.00
16 Don Lee 1.50 4.00
17 Jim Lemon 1.50 4.00
18 Ed Lopat CO 1.50 4.00
19 Clyde McCullough CO 1.50 4.00
20 Sam Mele CO 1.50 4.00
21 Don Mincher 1.50 4.00
22 Ray Moore 1.50 4.00
23 Hal Naragon 1.50 4.00
24 Ed Palmquist 1.50 4.00
25 Camilo Pascual 2.00 5.00
26 Bill Pleis 1.50 4.00
27 Pedro Ramos 1.50 4.00
28 Ted Sadowski 1.50 4.00
29 Lee Stange 1.50 4.00
30 Chuck Stobbs 1.50 4.00
31 Jose Valdivielso 1.50 4.00
32 Elmer Valo 1.50 4.00
33 Zoilo Versalles 2.00 5.00

1961-62 Twins Cloverleaf Dairy

These large (3 3/4" by 7 3/4") cards are unnumbered; they made up the side of a Cloverleaf Dairy milk carton. Cards still on the carton are valued double the listed price below. The last two digits of the year of issue for each player is given in parentheses. However those players appearing both (BOTH) years are indistinguishable (as to which year they were produced) when cut from the carton. There were 16 cards produced in 1961 and 24 cards produced in 1962. These unnumbered cards are sequenced in alphabetical order. The catalog designation for this set is F103.

COMPLETE SET (31) 1250.00 2500.00
1 Bernie Allen 62 40.00 80.00
2 George Banks 62 40.00 80.00
3 Earl Battey BOTH 30.00 60.00
4 Joe Bonikowski 62 40.00 80.00
5 Billy Gardner 61 50.00 100.00
6 Paul Giel 61 40.00 80.00
7 John Goryl 62 40.00 80.00
8 Lenny Green BOTH 30.00 60.00
9 Jim Kaat BOTH 60.00 120.00
10 Harmon Killebrew 61 200.00 400.00
11 Jack Kralick BOTH 30.00 60.00
12 Don Lee 61 40.00 80.00
13 Jim Lemon BOTH 30.00 60.00
14 Manager 40.00 80.00
Coaches 62
15 Georges Maranda 62 40.00 80.00
16 Orlando Martinez 62 40.00 80.00
17 Don Mincher BOTH 40.00 80.00
18 Ray Moore 62 40.00 80.00
19 Hal Naragon 62 40.00 80.00
20 Camilo Pascual BOTH 40.00 80.00
21 Vic Power 62 40.00 80.00
22 Pedro Ramos 61 50.00 100.00
23 Rich Rollins 62 50.00 100.00
24 Theodore Sadowski 62 40.00 80.00
25 Albert Stange 62 40.00 80.00
26 Dick Stigman 62 40.00 80.00
27 Chuck Stobbs 61 50.00 100.00
28 Bill Tuttle BOTH 30.00 60.00
29 Jose Valdivielso 61 40.00 80.00
30 Zoilo Versalles BOTH 30.00 60.00
31 Gerald Zimmerman 62 40.00 80.00

1962 Twins Jay Publishing

This 12-card set of the Minnesota Twins measures approximately 5" by 7". The fronts feature black-and-white posed player photos with the player's and team name printed below in the white border. These cards were packaged 12 to a packet. The backs are blank. The cards are unnumbered and checklisted below in alphabetical order.

COMPLETE SET (12) 15.00 40.00
1 Bob Allison 1.50 4.00
2 Earl Battey 1.00 2.50
3 Lenny Green 1.00 2.50
4 Jim Kaat 2.00 5.00
5 Harmon Killebrew 5.00 12.00
6 John Kralick 1.00 2.50
7 Don Lee 1.00 2.50
8 Jim Lemon 1.00 2.50
9 Sam Mele MG 1.00 2.50
10 Camilo Pascual 1.25 3.00
11 Jose Valdivielso 1.00 2.50
12 Zoilo Versalles 1.50 4.00

1963 Twins Jay Publishing

This 12-card set of the Minnesota Twins measures approximately 5" by 7". The fronts feature black-and-white posed player photos with the player's and team name printed below in the white border. These cards were packaged 12 to a packet. The backs are blank. The cards are unnumbered and checklisted below in alphabetical order.

COMPLETE SET (12) 20.00 50.00
1 Bernie Allen .75 2.00
2 Bob Allison .75 2.00
3 Earl Battey .75 2.00
4 Jim Kaat 1.50 4.00
5 Harmon Killebrew 5.00 12.00
6 Jack Kralick .75 2.00
7 Jim Lemon .75 2.00
8 Sam Mele MG .75 2.00
9 Camilo Pascual 1.00 2.50
10 Vic Power .75 2.00
11 Rich Rollins 1.00 2.50
12 Zoilo Versalles 1.00 2.50

1963 Twins Volpe

Sponsored by Western Oil and Fuel Company, these 24 portraits of the 1963 Minnesota Twins by noted artist Nicholas Volpe measure approximately 8 1/2" by 11". Each white-bordered color reproduction of pastel chalk on bordered color reproduction features a larger portrait and a smaller action drawing. The player's name appears in black lettering within the white margin at bottom, and also as a white fascimile autograph on the black background. The white back carries the player's name, position and biography at the top, followed below by career highlights and statistics. Artist information and the sponsor's logo at the bottom round out the backs. The drawings are unnumbered and checklisted in alphabetical order.

COMPLETE SET (24) 100.00 200.00
1 Bernie Allen 3.00 8.00
2 Bob Allison 4.00 10.00
3 George Banks 3.00 8.00
4 Earl Battey 4.00 10.00
5 Bill Dailey 3.00 8.00
6 John Goryl 3.00 8.00
7 Lenny Green 3.00 8.00
8 Jimmie Hall 3.00 8.00
9 Jim Kaat 6.00 15.00
10 Harmon Killebrew 10.00 25.00
11 Sam Mele MG 4.00 10.00
12 Don Mincher 4.00 10.00
13 Ray Moore 3.00 8.00
14 Camilio Pascual 4.00 10.00
15 Jim Perry 5.00 12.00
16 Bill Pleis 3.00 8.00
17 Vic Power 4.00 10.00
18 Gary Roggenburk 3.00 8.00
19 Jim Roland 3.00 8.00
20 Rich Rollins 4.00 10.00
21 Lee Stange 3.00 8.00
22 Dick Stigman
23 Zoilo Versalles 4.00 10.00
24 Jerry Zimmerman 3.00 8.00

1964 Twins Jay Publishing

The 1964 Twins Jay set consists of 12 cards produced by Jay Publishing. The Henry and Oliva cards establish the year of the set, since 1964 was Henry's last year and Oliva's first year with the Twins. The cards measure approximately 5" by 7" and are printed on photographic paper stock. The white fronts feature a black-and-white player portrait with the player's name and the team name below. The backs are blank. The cards are packaged 12 to a packet. The cards are unnumbered and checklisted below in alphabetical order.

COMPLETE SET (12) 15.00 40.00
1 Bob Allison 1.25 3.00
2 Earl Battey .75 2.00
3 Jim Grant .75 2.00
4 Jimmie Hall .75 2.00
5 Ron Henry .75 2.00
6 Jim Kaat 1.50 4.00
7 Harmon Killebrew 5.00 12.00
8 Tony Oliva 1.50 4.00
9 Camilo Pascual 1.00 2.50
10 Rich Rollins .75 2.00
11 Dick Stigman .75 2.00
12 Zorro Versalles 1.00 2.50

1964 Twins Volpe

This 15 drawings, which measure 8" by 11", feature members of the 1964 Minnesota Twins. The fronts feature two drawings of the players while the backs have biographical information, a blurb about the player as well as career statistics. Since these are unnumbered, we have sequenced them in alphabetical order.

COMPLETE SET 75.00 150.00
1 Bernie Allen 3.00 8.00
2 Bob Allison 4.00 10.00
3 Earl Battey 3.00 8.00
4 Bill Dailey 3.00 8.00
5 Jim Hall 3.00 8.00
6 Jim Kaat 6.00 15.00
7 Harmon Killebrew 10.00 25.00
8 Don Mincher 4.00 10.00
9 Tony Oliva 8.00 20.00
10 Camilo Pascual 4.00 10.00

11 Bill Pleis	3.00	8.00
12 Jim Roland	3.00	8.00
13 Rich Rollins	3.00	8.00
14 Dick Stigman	3.00	8.00
15 Zoilo Versalles	3.00	8.00

1965 Twins Jay Publishing

This 12-card set of the Minnesota Twins measures approximately 5" by 7". The fronts feature black-and-white posed player photos with the player's and team name printed below in the white border. These cards were packaged 12 to a packet. The backs are blank. The cards are unnumbered and checklisted below in alphabetical order.

COMPLETE SET (12)	12.50	30.00
1 Bernie Allen	.75	2.00
2 Bob Allison	1.25	3.00
3 Earl Battey	.75	2.00
4 Bill Dailey	.75	2.00
5 Jim Kaat	1.50	4.00
6 Harmon Killebrew	5.00	12.00
7 Sam Mele MG	1.00	2.50
8 Camilo Pascual	1.25	3.00
9 Vic Power	.75	2.00
10 Rich Rollins	.75	2.00
11 Dick Stigman	.75	2.00
12 Zoilo Versalles	1.00	2.50

1965 Twins Postcards

This 10-card set of the Minnesota Twins features color player portraits measuring approximately 4 3/4" by 7" with the player's name in the wide bottom margin. The backs display a postcard format. The cards are unnumbered and checklisted below in alphabetical order.

COMPLETE SET (10)	50.00	100.00
1 Bob Allison	4.00	10.00
2 Earl Battey	3.00	8.00
3 Jimmie Hall	3.00	8.00
4 Jim Kaat	6.00	15.00
5 Harmon Killebrew	10.00	25.00
6 Sam Mele	3.00	8.00
7 Tony Oliva	6.00	15.00
8 Camilo Pascual	4.00	10.00
9 Rich Rollins	3.00	8.00
10 Zoilo Versalles	4.00	10.00

1966 Twins Fairway Grocery

This 17-card set features 8" by 10" color player portraits of the Minnesota Twins with player information and statistics on the backs. The cards are unnumbered and checklisted below in alphabetical order.

COMPLETE SET (17)	50.00	100.00
1 Bernie Allen	2.00	5.00
2 Bob Allison	3.00	8.00
3 Earl Battey	2.00	5.00
4 Jim Grant	2.50	6.00
5 Jimmie Hall	2.00	5.00
6 Jim Kaat	3.00	8.00
7 Harmon Killebrew	8.00	20.00
8 Jim Merritt	2.00	5.00
9 Don Mincher	2.00	5.00
10 Tony Oliva	4.00	10.00
11 Camilo Pascual	2.50	6.00
12 Jim Perry	2.50	6.00
13 Frank Quilici	2.00	5.00
14 Rich Rollins	2.50	6.00
15 Sandy Valdespino	2.00	5.00
16 Zoilo Versalles	2.50	6.00
17 Al Worthington	2.00	5.00

1967 Twins Team Issue

This 26-card set of the 1967 Minnesota Twins measures approximately 4" by 5" and features black-and-white facsimile autographed player portraits with white borders. The backs are blank. The cards are unnumbered and checklisted below in alphabetical order. A card of Rod Carew is featured in his Rookie Card year.

COMPLETE SET (26)	30.00	60.00
1 Bob Allison	1.00	2.50
2 Earl Battey	.75	2.00
3 Rod Carew	6.00	15.00
4 Dean Chance Pitching	1.00	2.50
5 Dean Chance Portrait	1.00	2.50
6 Ron Clark	.75	2.00
7 Harmon Killebrew	4.00	10.00
8 Ron Kline	.75	2.00
9 Jim Lemon CO	.75	2.00
10 Billy Martin CO	1.50	4.00
11 Jim Merritt	.75	2.00
12 Tony Oliva Portrait	1.50	4.00
13 Tony Oliva Batting)	1.50	4.00
14 Jim Ollom	.75	2.00
15 Jim Perry	1.00	2.50
16 Frank Quilici	.75	2.00
17 Rich Reese	.75	2.00
18 Jim Roland	.75	2.00
19 Rich Rollins	.75	2.00
20 Cesar Tovar	.75	2.00
21 Cesar Tovar Closeup	.75	2.00
22 Ted Uhlaender	.75	2.00
23 Sandy Valdespino	.75	2.00
24 Zoilo Versalles	1.00	2.50
25 Early Wynn CO	1.50	4.00
26 Jerry Zimmerman	.75	2.00

1969 Twins Team Issue Color

This 13-card set of the Minnesota Twins measures approximately 7" by 8 3/4" with the fronts featuring white-bordered color player photos. The player's name and team is printed in black in the white margin below the picture. The backs are blank. The cards are unnumbered and checklisted below in alphabetical order.

COMPLETE SET (13)	30.00	60.00
1 Bob Allison	1.50	4.00
2 Leo Cardenas	1.50	4.00
3 Rod Carew	4.00	10.00
4 Dean Chance	1.50	4.00
5 Jim Kaat	2.00	5.00
6 Harmon Killebrew	3.00	8.00
7 Billy Martin MG	3.00	8.00
8 Tony Oliva	2.50	6.00
9 Ron Perranoski	1.25	3.00
10 Jim Perry	1.50	4.00
11 Rich Reese	1.25	3.00
12 Cesar Tovar	1.50	4.00
13 Ted Uhlaender	1.25	3.00

1970 Twins Super Valu

This 12-card set features color player drawings in white borders and measures approximately 7 3/4" by 9 3/8". The cards feature both an action player drawing and a head drawing with a facsimile autograph. The player's name is printed in the bottom margin. The backs are blank. The cards are unnumbered and checklisted below in alphabetical order.

COMPLETE SET (12)	20.00	50.00
1 Brant Alyea	1.25	3.00
2 Leo Cardenas	1.25	3.00
3 Rod Carew	6.00	15.00
4 Jim Kaat	1.50	4.00
5 Harmon Killebrew	4.00	10.00
6 George Mitterwald	1.25	3.00
7 Tony Oliva	2.50	6.00
8 Ron Perranoski	1.50	4.00
9 Jim Perry	2.00	5.00
10 Rich Reese	1.25	3.00
11 Luis Tiant	2.50	6.00
12 Cesar Tovar	1.25	3.00

1970 Twins Team Issue

This 14-card set features black-and-white player portraits with white borders and a facsimile autograph printed on the front. The backs are blank. The cards are unnumbered and checklisted below in alphabetical order.

COMPLETE SET (14)	6.00	15.00
1 Brant Alyea	.40	1.00
2 Steve Barber	.40	1.00
3 Frank Crosetti CO	.75	2.00
4 Marv Grissom	.40	1.00
5 Minnie Mendoza	.40	1.00
6 Paul Ratliff	.40	1.00
7 Rich Reese	.40	1.00
8 Bill Rigney MG	.40	1.00
9 Bob Rodgers Co	.40	1.00
10 Luis Tiant	1.00	2.50
11 Cesar Tovar	.40	1.00
12 Stan Williams	.40	1.00
13 Bill Zepp	.40	1.00
14 Metropolitan Stadium	.40	1.00

1972 Twins Team Issue

This 25-card set of the Minnesota Twins features black-and-white player portraits in white borders with facsimile autographs and measures approximately 4" by 5 1/8". The backs are blank. The cards are unnumbered and checklisted below in alphabetical order.

COMPLETE SET (25)	40.00	80.00
1 Bert Blyleven	2.50	6.00
2 Steve Braun	1.25	3.00
3 Ray Corbin	1.25	3.00
4 Rick Dempsey	2.00	5.00
5 Bob Gebhard	1.25	3.00
6 Wayne Granger	1.25	3.00
7 Jim Kaat	2.50	6.00
8 Harmon Killebrew	4.00	10.00
9 Dave Laroche	1.25	3.00
10 George Mitterwald	1.25	3.00
11 Dan Monzon	1.25	3.00
12 Vern Morgan	1.25	3.00
13 Jim Nettles	1.25	3.00
14 Tom Norton	1.25	3.00
15 Tony Oliva	2.50	6.00
16 Jim Perry	2.00	5.00
17 Frank Quilici	1.25	3.00
18 Rich Reese	1.25	3.00
19 Phil Roof	1.25	3.00
20 Ralph Rowe CO	1.25	3.00
21 Eric Soderholm	1.25	3.00
22 Danny Thompson	1.25	3.00
23 Cesar Tovar	1.50	4.00
24 Dick Woodson	1.25	3.00
25 Al Worthington CO	1.25	3.00

1975 Twins Postcards

This 24-card set of the Minnesota Twins features player photos on postcard-size cards. The cards are unnumbered and checklisted below in alphabetical order.

COMPLETE SET (24)	5.00	12.00
1 Vic Albury	.20	.50
2 Bert Blyleven	.60	1.50
3 Glenn Borgmann	.20	.50
4 Steve Braun	.20	.50
5 Steve Brye	.20	.50
6 Bill Campbell	.20	.50
7 Rod Carew	1.50	4.00
8 Ray Corbin	.20	.50
9 Bobby Darwin	.20	.50
10 Joe Decker	.20	.50
11 Dan Ford	.20	.50
12 Dave Goltz	.20	.50
13 Luis Gomez	.20	.50
14 Larry Hisle	.30	.75
15 Craig Kusick	.20	.50
16 Tom Lundstedt	.20	.50
17 Vern Morgan CO	.20	.50
18 Tony Oliva	.40	1.00
19 Frank Quilici MG	.20	.50
20 Phil Roof	.20	.50
21 Ralph Rowe CO	.20	.50
22 Eric Soderholm	.20	.50
23 Lee Stange CO	.20	.50
24 Jerry Terrell	.20	.50

1975 Twins Team Issue

These photos feature members of the 1975 Minnesota Twins. They are unnumbered and we have sequenced them in alphabetical order.

COMPLETE SET	10.00	25.00
1 Vic Albury	.40	1.00
2 Bert Blyleven	1.00	2.50
3 Glen Borgmann	.40	1.00
4 Lyman Bostock	1.00	2.50
5 Steve Braun	.40	1.00
6 John Briggs	.40	1.00
7 Steve Brye	.40	1.00
8 Tom Burgmeier	.40	1.00
9 Bill Butler	.40	1.00
10 Bill Campbell	.40	1.00
11 Ray Corbin	.40	1.00
12 Joe Decker	.40	1.00
13 Dan Ford	.40	1.00
14 Dave Goltz	.40	1.00
15 Luis Gomez	.40	1.00
16 Larry Hisle	.40	1.00
17 Jim Hughes	.40	1.00
18 Tom Johnson	.40	1.00
19 Craig Kusick	.40	1.00
20 Tom Lundstedt	.40	1.00
21 Tony Oliva	1.00	2.50
22 Frank Quilici MG	.40	1.00
23 Phil Roof	.40	1.00
24 Eric Soderholm	.40	1.00
25 Lee Strange	.40	1.00
26 Jerry Terrell	.40	1.00
27 Danny Thompson	.40	1.00
28 Mark Wiley	.40	1.00

1976 Twins Postcards

This 18-card set of the Minnesota Twins features player photos on postcard-size cards. The cards are unnumbered and checklisted below in alphabetical order.

COMPLETE SET (18)	4.00	10.00
1 Bert Blyleven	.60	1.50
2 Lyman Bostock	.40	1.00
3 Steve Brye	.20	.50
4 Bill Campbell	.20	.50
5 Rod Carew	1.50	4.00
6 Mike Cubbage	.20	.50
7 Dan Ford	.20	.50
8 Dave Goltz	.20	.50
9 Larry Hisle	.20	.50
10 Craig Kusick	.20	.50
11 Dave McKay	.20	.50
12 Bob Randall	.20	.50
13 Pete Redfern	.20	.50
14 Phil Roof	.20	.50
15 Bill Singer	.20	.50
16 Roy Smalley	.30	.75
17 Jerry Terrell	.20	.50
18 Danny Thompson	.20	.50

1977 Twins Postcards

These black and white postcards, which measure approximately 4" by 5" feature members of the 1977 Minnesota Twins. As these postcards were issued over a series of years, most of these years look alike and this grouping appears to be players who were fairly new to the Twins in 1977. Since these photos are not numbered, we have sequenced them in alphabetical order.

COMPLETE SET (17)	4.00	10.00
1 Glenn Adams	.20	.50
2 Rich Chiles	.20	.50
3 Mike Cubbage	.20	.50
4 Bob Gorinski	.20	.50
5 Jeff Holly	.20	.50
6 Dave Johnson	.20	.50
7 Tom Johnson	.20	.50
8 Karl Kuehl CO	.20	.50
9 Don McMahon CO	.20	.50
10 Willie Norwood	.20	.50
11 Tony Oliva CO	1.00	2.50
12 Ron Schueler	.20	.50
13 Roy Smalley	.40	1.00
14 Paul Thormodsgard	.20	.50
15 Rob Wilfong	.20	.50
16 Geoff Zahn	.20	.50
17 Jerry Zimmerman CO	.20	.50

1978 Twins Frisz

Manufactured by Barry R. Frisz and issued by the Twins in two 25-card series, these cards measure approximately 2 1/2" by 3 3/4" and feature on their fronts white-bordered posed color photos of retired Twins players. The white and gray horizontal back carries the player's name, biography, position, statistics, and career highlights. The cards are numbered on the back.

COMPLETE SET (50)	10.00	25.00
1 Bob Allison	.60	1.50
2 Earl Battey	.20	.50
3 Dave Boswell	.20	.50
4 Dean Chance	.60	1.50
5 Jim Grant	.40	1.00
6 Calvin Griffith PRES	.20	.50
7 Jimmie Hall	.20	.50
8 Harmon Killebrew	1.00	2.50
9 Jim Lemon	.20	.50
10 Billy Martin MG	.60	1.50
11 Gene Mauch MG	.30	.75
12 Sam Mele MG	.20	.50
13 Metropolitan Stadium	.60	1.50
14 Don Mincher	.20	.50
15 Tony Oliva	.40	1.00
16 Camilo Pascual	.30	.75
17 Jim Perry	.20	.50
18 Frank Quilici MG	.20	.50
19 Rich Reese	.20	.50
20 Bill Rigney MG	.20	.50
21 Cesar Tovar	.30	.75
22 Zoilo Versalles	.30	.75
23 Al Worthington	.20	.50
24 Jerry Zimmerman	.20	.50
25 Checklist 1-25	.20	.50
26 Bernie Allen	.20	.50
27 Leo Cardenas	.40	1.00
28 Ray Corbin	.20	.50
29 Joe Decker	.20	.50
30 Johnny Goryl	.20	.50
31 Tom Hall	.20	.50
32 Bill Hands	.20	.50
33 Jim Holt	.20	.50
34 Randy Hundley	.40	1.00
35 Jerry Kindall	.20	.50
36 Johnny Klippstein	.20	.50
37 Jack Kralick	.20	.50
38 Jim Merritt	.20	.50
39 Joe Nossek	.20	.50
40 Ron Perranoski	.30	.75
41 Bill Pleis	.20	.50
42 Rick Renick	.20	.50
43 Jim Roland	.20	.50
44 Lee Stange	.20	.50
45 Dick Stigman	.20	.50
46 Danny Thompson	.20	.50
47 Ted Uhlaender	.20	.50
48 Sandy Valdespino	.30	.75
49 Dick Woodson	.20	.50
50 Checklist 25-50	.20	.50

1978 Twins Frisz Postcards

Manufactured by Barry R. Frisz and issued by the Twins, these 25 postcards measure 3 1/2" by 5 1/2" and feature on their fronts borderless color posed-on-field photos of then-current Twins. The back carries the player's name, position, and height and weight at the upper left. Below is a ghosted cartoon logo that carries the words "Win, Twins." The year of the set appears in the vertical lettering bisecting the postcard. The postcards are unnumbered and checklisted below in alphabetical order.

COMPLETE SET (25)	8.00	20.00
1 Glenn Adams	.30	.75
2 Glenn Borgmann	.30	.75
3 Rod Carew	1.50	4.00
4 Rich Chiles	.30	.75
5 Mike Cubbage	.30	.75
6 Roger Erickson	.30	.75
7 Dan Ford	.30	.75
8 Dave Goltz	.30	.75
9 Dave Johnson	.30	.75
10 Tom Johnson	.30	.75
11 Craig Kusick	.30	.75
12 Jose Morales	.30	.75
13 Willie Norwood	.30	.75
14 Hosken Powell	.30	.75
15 Bob Randall	.30	.75
16 Pete Redfern	.30	.75
17 Bombo Rivera	.30	.75
18 Gary Serum	.30	.75
19 Roy Smalley	.60	1.50
20 Greg Thayer	.30	.75
21 Paul Thormodsgard	.30	.75
22 Rob Wilfong	.30	.75
23 Larry Wolfe	.30	.75
24 Butch Wynegar	.30	.75
25 Geoff Zahn	.30	.75

1979 Twins Frisz Postcards

Manufactured by Barry R. Frisz and issued by the Twins, these 30 postcards measure 3 1/2" by 5 1/2" and feature on their fronts borderless color posed-on-field photos of then-current Twins. The back carries the player's name, position, and height and weight at the upper left. Below is a ghosted cartoon logo that carries the words "Win, Twins." The year of the set appears in the vertical lettering bisecting the postcard. The postcards are unnumbered and checklisted below in alphabetical order.

COMPLETE SET (30)	6.00	15.00
1 Glenn Adams	.20	.50
2 Glenn Borgmann	.20	.50
3 John Castino	.20	.50
4 Mike Cubbage	.20	.50
5 Dave Edwards	.20	.50
6 Roger Erickson	.20	.50
7 Dave Goltz	.20	.50
8 John Goryl CO	.20	.50
9 Paul Hartzell	.20	.50
10 Jeff Holly	.20	.50
11 Ron Jackson	.20	.50
12 Jerry Koosman	.60	1.50
13 Karl Kuehl CO	.20	.50
14 Craig Kusick	.20	.50
15 Ken Landreaux	.20	.50
16 Mike Marshall	.40	1.00
17 Gene Mauch MG	.40	1.00
18 Jose Morales	.20	.50
19 Willie Norwood	.20	.50
20 Camilo Pascual CO	.40	1.00
21 Hosken Powell	.20	.50
22 Bobby Randall	.20	.50
23 Pete Redfern	.20	.50
24 Bombo Rivera	.20	.50
25 Gary Serum	.20	.50
26 Roy Smalley	.40	1.00
27 Rob Wilfong	.20	.50
28 Butch Wynegar	.20	.50
29 Geoff Zahn	.20	.50
30 Jerry Zimmerman CO	.20	.50

1980 Twins Postcards

This 33-card set features photos of the 1980 Minnesota Twins on postcard-size cards. A facsimile autograph is printed on some of the cards. The cards are unnumbered and checklisted below in alphabetical order.

COMPLETE SET (33)	6.00	15.00
1 Glenn Adams	.20	.50
2 Sal Butera	.20	.50
3 John Castino	.20	.50
4 Doug Corbett	.20	.50
5 Mike Cubbage	.20	.50
6 Dave Edwards	.20	.50
7 Roger Erickson	.20	.50
8 Terry Felton	.20	.50
9 Danny Goodwin	.20	.50
10 Johnny Goryl CO	.20	.50
11 Darrell Jackson	.20	.50
12 Ron Jackson	.20	.50
13 Harmon Killebrew CO	1.25	3.00
14 Jerry Koosman	.40	1.00
15 Karl Kuehl CO	.20	.50
16 Ken Landreaux	.20	.50
17 Pete Mackanin	.20	.50
18 Mike Marshall	.30	.75
19 Gene Mauch MG	.20	.50
20 Jose Morales	.20	.50
21 Willie Norwood	.20	.50
22 Camilo Pascual CO	.30	.75
23 Hosken Powell	.20	.50
24 Bobby Randall CO	.20	.50
25 Pete Redfern	.20	.50
26 Bombo Rivera	.20	.50
27 Roy Smalley	.20	.50
28 Rich Sofield	.20	.50
29 John Verhoeven	.20	.50
30 Rob Wilfong	.20	.50
31 Butch Wynegar	.20	.50
32 Geoff Zahn	.20	.50
33 Jerry Zimmerman CO	.20	.50

1981 Twins Postcards

This 33-card set of the Minnesota Twins measures approximately 3 1/2" by 5 7/16" and features borderless color player photos with a facsimile autograph. The backs display a postcard format. The cards are unnumbered and checklisted below in alphabetical order. This set could be obtained from the Twins upon release for $2.50 postpaid.

COMPLETE SET (33)	6.00	15.00
1 Glenn Adams	.20	.50
2 Fernando Arroyo	.20	.50
3 Chuck Baker	.20	.50
4 Sal Butera	.20	.50
5 John Castino	.20	.50
6 Don Cooper	.20	.50
7 Doug Corbett	.20	.50
8 Dave Engle	.20	.50
9 Roger Erickson	.20	.50
10 Billy Gardner CO	.20	.50
11 Danny Goodwin	.20	.50
12 Johnny Goryl MG	.20	.50
13 Mickey Hatcher	.20	.50
14 Darrell Jackson	.20	.50
15 Ron Jackson	.20	.50
16 Greg Johnston	.20	.50
17 Jerry Koosman	.40	1.00
18 Karl Kuehl CO	.20	.50
19 Pete Mackanin	.20	.50
20 Jack O'Connor	.20	.50
21 Johnny Podres CO	.30	.75
22 Hosken Powell	.20	.50
23 Pete Redfern	.20	.50
24 Roy Smalley	.20	.50
25 Ray Smith	.20	.50
26 Rick Sofield	.20	.50
27 Rick Stelmaszek CO	.20	.50
28 John Verhoeven	.20	.50
29 Gary Ward	.20	.50
30 Rob Wilfong	.20	.50
31 Al Williams	.20	.50
32 Butch Wynegar	.20	.50
33 Metropolitan Stadium	.20	.50

1982 Twins Postcards

This 34-postcard set features the 1982 Minnesota Twins Baseball Team and features borderless color player photos with a simulated autograph. The backs display a postcard format. The cards are unnumbered and checklisted below in alphabetical order.

COMPLETE SET (34)	4.00	10.00
1 Fernando Arroyo	.08	.25
2 Sal Butera	.08	.25
3 Bobby Castillo	.08	.25
4 John Castino	.08	.25
5 Doug Corbett	.08	.25
6 Ron Davis	.08	.25
7 Jim Eisenreich	.40	1.00
8 Dave Engle	.08	.25
9 Roger Erickson	.08	.25
10 Lenny Faedo	.08	.25
11 Terry Felton	.08	.25
12 Gary Gaetti	1.00	2.50
13 Billy Gardner MG	.08	.25
14 Mickey Hatcher	.08	.25
15 Brad Havens	.08	.25
16 Kent Hrbek	.75	2.00
17 Darrell Jackson	.08	.25
18 Randy Johnson	.08	.25
19 Karl Kuehl CO	.08	.25
20 Jim Lemon CO	.08	.25
21 Bobby Mitchell	.08	.25
22 Jack O'Connor	.08	.25
23 Johnny Podres CO	.20	.50
24 Pete Redfern	.08	.25
25 Rick Stelmaszek CO	.08	.25
26 Jesus Vega	.08	.25
27 Gary Ward	.08	.25
28 Ron Washington	.08	.25
29 Rob Wilfong	.08	.25
30 Al Williams	.08	.25
31 Butch Wynegar	.08	.25
32 Hubert H. Humphrey Metrodome/	.08	.25
33 Hubert H. Humphrey Metrodome/	.08	.25
34 Team Picture	.08	.25

1983 Twins Team Issue

This 36-card set measures the standard size. The fronts feature borderless color player photos with a miniature representation of the player's jersey superimposed on the picture at the bottom. On a white background, biographical information and statistics are printed in red and blue.

COMPLETE SET (36)	2.50	6.00
1 John Castino	.02	.10
2 Jim Eisenreich	.30	.75
3 Ray Smith	.02	.10
4 Scott Ullger	.02	.10
5 Gary Gaetti	.60	1.50
6 Mickey Hatcher	.08	.25
7 Bobby Mitchell	.02	.10
8 Len Faedo	.02	.10
9 Kent Hrbek	.30	.75
10 Tim Laudner	.02	.10
11 Frank Viola	.30	.75
12 Bryan Oelkers	.02	.10
13 Rick Lysander	.02	.10
14 Dave Engle	.02	.10
15 Len Whitehouse	.02	.10
16 Pete Filson	.02	.10
17 Tom Brunansky	.08	.25
18 Randy Bush	.02	.10
19 Brad Havens	.02	.10
20 Al Williams	.02	.10
21 Gary Ward	.02	.10
22 Jack O'Connor	.02	.10
23 Robert Castillo	.02	.10
24 Ron Washington	.02	.10
25 Ron Davis	.02	.10
26 Tom Kelly CO	.08	.25
27 Billy Gardner MG	.02	.10
28 Rich Stelmaszek CO	.02	.10
29 Jim Lemon CO	.02	.10
30 Johnny Podres CO	.08	.25
31 Native Sons	.20	.50
Tim Laudner		
Jim Eisenreich		
Kent Hrb		
32 Twins Catchers	.02	.10
Ray Smith		
Dave Engle		
Tim Laudner		
33 Lumber Company	.08	.25
Tom Brunansky		
Gary Gaetti		
Gary W		
34 Twins Coaches	.02	.10
Tom Kelly		
Rick Stelmaszek		
Billy G		
35 Team Photo	.02	.10
36 Metrodome Checklist	.02	.10

1984 Twins Postcards

This 34-postcard set features the 1984 Minnesota Twins Baseball Team and features borderless color player photos with a simulated autograph. The backs display a postcard format. The cards are unnumbered and checklisted below in alphabetical order.

COMPLETE SET (34)	4.00	10.00
1 Darrell Brown	.08	.25
2 Tom Brunansky	.20	.50
3 Randy Bush	.08	.25
4 John Butcher	.08	.25
5 Bobby Castillo	.08	.25
6 John Castino	.08	.25
7 Keith Comstock	.08	.25
8 Ron Davis	.08	.25
9 Jim Eisenreich	.40	1.00
10 Dave Engle	.08	.25
11 Lenny Faedo	.08	.25
12 Pete Filson	.08	.25
13 Gary Gaetti	.40	1.00
14 Billy Gardner	.08	.25
15 Mickey Hatcher	.08	.25
16 Kent Hrbek	.20	.50
17 Houston Jimenez	.08	.25
18 Tim Laudner	.08	.25
19 Tom Kelly CO	.20	.50
20 Jim Lemon CO	.08	.25
21 Dave Meier	.08	.25
22 Larry Pashnick	.08	.25
23 Johnny Podres	.20	.50
24 Jeff Reed	.08	.25
25 Ken Schrom	.08	.25
26 Mike Smithson	.08	.25
27 Rick Stelmaszek	.08	.25
28 Tim Teufel	.20	.50
29 Frank Viola	.30	.75
30 Mike Walters	.08	.25
31 Ron Washington	.08	.25
32 Al Williams	.08	.25
33 Hubert H. Humphrey Metrodome	.08	.25
34 Team Picture	.08	.25

1984 Twins Team Issue

This 36-card set features borderless color player photos of the Minnesota Twins with a small jersey replica in the bottom right displaying the player's jersey number. The backs carry player information and statistics.

COMPLETE SET (36)	2.50	6.00
1 John Castino	.02	.10
2 Jim Eisenreich	.20	.50
3 Houston Jimenez	.02	.10
4 Dave Meier	.02	.10
5 Gary Gaetti	.30	.75
6 Mickey Hatcher	.02	.10
7 Jeff Reed	.02	.10
8 Tim Teufel	.02	.10
9 Lenny Faedo	.02	.10
10 Kent Hrbek	.08	.25
11 Tim Laudner	.02	.10
12 Frank Viola	.20	.50
13 Ken Schrom	.02	.10
14 Larry Pashnick	.02	.10
15 Dave Engle	.02	.10
16 Keith Comstock	.02	.10
17 Pete Filson	.02	.10
18 Tom Brunansky	.08	.25
19 Randy Bush	.02	.10
20 Darrell Brown	.02	.10
21 Al Williams	.02	.10
22 Mike Walters	.02	.10
23 John Butcher	.02	.10
24 Bobby Castillo	.02	.10
25 Ron Washington	.02	.10
26 Ron Davis	.02	.10
27 Tom Kelly CO	.08	.25
28 Billy Gardner MG	.02	.10
29 Rick Stelmaszek CO	.02	.10
30 Jim Lemon CO	.02	.10
31 Johnny Podres CO	.08	.25
32 Mike Smithson	.02	.10
33 Harmon Killebrew	.40	1.00
34 1984 Minnesota Twins Team Picture	.02	.10
35 Twins Logo Card	.02	.10
36 Metrodome CL	.02	.10

1985 Twins Postcards

This 33-card set features photos of the Minnesota Twins on postcard-size cards. The All-Star Game logo appears in the upper right. The cards are unnumbered and checklisted below in alphabetical order. Kirby Puckett appears in his Rookie Card year.

COMPLETE SET (33)	8.00	20.00
1 Tom Brunansky	.30	.75
2 Randy Bush	.20	.50
3 John Butcher	.20	.50
4 Andre David	.20	.50
5 Ron Davis	.20	.50
6 Dave Engle	.20	.50
7 Alvaro Espinoza	.20	.50
8 Pete Filson	.20	.50
9 Gary Gaetti	.40	1.00
10 Greg Gagne	.20	.50
11 Billy Gardner MG	.20	.50
12 Mickey Hatcher	.20	.50
13 Kent Hrbek	.30	.75
14 Tom Kelly CO	.20	.50
15 Tom Klawitter	.20	.50
16 Tim Laudner	.20	.50
17 Rick Lysander	.20	.50
18 Dave Meier	.20	.50
19 Tony Oliva CO	.60	1.50
20 Johnny Podres CO	.30	.75
21 Kirby Puckett	5.00	12.00
22 Mark Salas	.20	.50
23 Ken Schrom	.20	.50
24 Roy Smalley	.20	.50
25 Mike Smithson	.20	.50
26 Rick Stelmaszek CO	.20	.50
27 Mike Stenhouse	.20	.50
28 Tim Teufel	.20	.50
29 Frank Viola	.30	.75
30 Curt Wardle	.20	.50
31 Ron Washington	.20	.50
32 Len Whitehouse	.20	.50
33 Rich Yett	.20	.50

1985 Twins 7-Eleven

This 13-card set of Minnesota Twins was produced and distributed by the Twins in conjunction with the 7-Eleven stores and the Fire Marshall's Association. The cards measure approximately 2 1/2" by 3 1/2" and are in full color. Supposedly 20,000 sets of cards were distributed during the promotion which began on June 2nd and lasted throughout the month of July. The card backs have some statistics and a fire safety tip. The set features an early Kirby Puckett card.

COMPLETE SET (13)	5.00	12.00
1 Kirby Puckett	4.00	10.00
2 Frank Viola	.30	.75
3 Mickey Hatcher	.20	.50
4 Kent Hrbek	.40	1.00
5 John Butcher	.20	.50
6 Roy Smalley	.30	.75
7 Tom Brunansky	.30	.75
8 Ron Davis	.20	.50
9 Gary Gaetti	.60	1.50
10 Tim Teufel	.20	.50
11 Mike Smithson	.20	.50
12 Tim Laudner	.20	.50
NNO Checklist Card	.20	.50

1985 Twins Team Issue

This 36-card set measures the standard size. The fronts feature borderless color player photos with a miniature representation of the player's jersey superimposed on the picture at the lower right corner. The "1985 All-Star Game" logo in the lower left corner rounds out the card face. On a white background, the horizontally oriented backs carry biographical information and statistics printed in red and blue. Kirby Puckett appears in his Rookie Card year.

COMPLETE SET (36)	8.00	20.00
1 Alvaro Espinoza	.02	.10
2 Roy Smalley	.08	.25
3 Tony Oliva CO	.20	.50
4 Dave Meier	.02	.10
5 Gary Gaetti	.30	.75
6 Mickey Hatcher	.08	.25
7 Jeff Reed	.02	.10
8 Tim Teufel	.02	.10
9 Mark Salas	.02	.10
10 Kent Hrbek	.20	.50
11 Tim Laudner	.02	.10
12 Frank Viola	.20	.50
13 Ken Schrom	.02	.10
14 Rick Lysander	.02	.10
15 Dave Engle	.02	.10
16 Andre David	.02	.10
17 Len Whitehouse	.02	.10
18 Pete Filson	.02	.10
19 Tom Brunansky	.08	.25
20 Randy Bush	.02	.10
21 Greg Gagne	.02	.10
22 John Butcher	.02	.10
23 Mike Stenhouse	.02	.10
24 Kirby Puckett	1.50	4.00
25 Tom Klawitter	.02	.10
26 Curt Wardle	.02	.10
27 Rich Yett	.02	.10
28 Ron Washington	.02	.10
29 Ron Davis	.02	.10
30 Tom Kelly CO	.08	.25
31 Bill Gardner MG	.02	.10
32 Rick Stelmaszek CO	.02	.10
33 Johnny Podres CO	.08	.25
34 Mike Smithson	.02	.10
35 All-Star Game Logo	.02	.10
36 Twins Logo Checklist	.02	.10

1986 Twins Greats TCMA

This 12-card standard-size set features some of the best Minnesota Twins from their first 25 seasons. These cards have player photos on the front and player information on the back.

COMPLETE SET (12)	2.00	5.00
1 Harmon Killebrew	.40	1.00
2 Rod Carew	.60	1.50
3 Zoilo Versalles	.08	.25
4 Cesar Tovar	.08	.25
5 Bob Allison	.20	.50
6 Larry Hisle	.08	.25
7 Tony Oliva	.30	.75
8 Earl Battey	.08	.25
9 Jim Perry	.20	.50
10 Jim Kaat	.30	.75
11 Al Worthington	.08	.25
12 Sam Mele MG	.08	.25

1986 Twins Team Issue

These cards feature members of the 1986 Minnesota Twins. Players, coaches and the manager are included in this set. The 25th anniversary logo is in the upper right hand corner of each card. Billy Beane appears in his Rookie Card year.

COMPLETE SET (36)	2.50	6.00
1 Chris Pittaro	.02	.10

2 Steve Lombardozzi .02 .10
3 Roy Smalley .08 .25
4 Tony Oliva CO .20 .50
5 Gary Gaetti .30 .75
6 Mickey Hatcher .08 .25
7 Jeff Reed .02 .10
8 Mark Salas .02 .10
9 Kent Hrbek .20 .50
10 Tim Laudner .02 .10
11 Frank Viola .08 .25
12 Dennis Burtt .02 .10
13 Alex Sanchez .02 .10
14 Roy Smith .02 .10
15 Billy Beane .60 1.50
16 Pete Filson .02 .10
17 Tom Brunansky .08 .25
18 Randy Bush .02 .10
19 Frank Eufemia .02 .10
20 Mark Davidson .02 .10
21 Bert Blyleven .20 .50
22 Greg Gagne .08 .25
23 John Butcher .02 .10
24 Kirby Puckett .60 1.50
25 Bill Latham .02 .10
26 Ron Washington .02 .10
27 Ron Davis .02 .10
28 Tom Kelly CO .08 .25
29 Dick Such CO .02 .10
30 Rick Stelmaszek CO .02 .10
31 Ray Miller MG .02 .10
32 Wayne Terwilliger CO .02 .10
33 Mike Smithson .02 .10
34 Al Woods .02 .10
35 Team Photo .08 .25
36 Twins Logo .02 .10
Checklist

1987 Twins Postcards

This 32-card set features photos of the 1987 Minnesota Twins on postcard-size cards. The cards are unnumbered and checklisted below in alphabetical order.

COMPLETE SET (32) 6.00 15.00
1 Keith Atherton .20 .50
2 Juan Berenguer .20 .50
3 Bert Blyleven .40 1.00
4 Tom Brunansky .30 .75
5 Randy Bush .20 .50
6 Mark Davidson .20 .50
7 George Frazier .20 .50
8 Gary Gaetti .40 1.00
9 Greg Gagne .20 .50
10 Dan Gladden .20 .50
11 Kent Hrbek .30 .75
12 Tom Kelly MG .30 .75
13 Joe Klink .20 .50
14 Tim Laudner .20 .50
15 Steve Lombardozzi .20 .50
16 Al Newman .20 .50
17 Tom Nieto .20 .50
18 Tony Oliva CO .40 1.00
19 Mark Portugal .20 .50
20 Kirby Puckett 1.00 2.50
21 Jeff Reardon .30 .75
22 Rick Renick .20 .50
23 Mark Salas .20 .50
24 Roy Smalley .30 .75
25 Mike Smithson .20 .50
26 Rick Stelmaszek CO .20 .50
27 Dick Such CO .20 .50
28 Les Straker .20 .50
29 Wayne Terwilliger CO .20 .50
30 Frank Viola .30 .75
31 Team Photo .20 .50
32 Team Logo .20 .50

1987 Twins Team Issue

This 33-card standard-size set features borderless color player photos of the 1987 Minnesota Twins World Championship Team. There are two versions of this set. One features the 1987 World Championship Logo, the other does not. We have priced the version with the logo which was pulled from circulation shortly after released. The backs carry player information and season statistics. The cards were pulled from distribution after a dispute with the Commissioner's office.

COMMON PLAYER (33) 15.00 40.00
1 Steve Lombardozzi .40 1.00
2 Roy Smalley .40 1.00
3 Tony Oliva 1.00 2.50
4 Greg Gagne .40 1.00
5 Gary Gaetti 1.00 2.50
6 Gene Larkin .60 1.50
7 Tom Kelly MG .75 2.00
8 Kent Hrbek .40 1.00
9 Tim Laudner .40 1.00
10 Frank Viola .60 1.50
11 Les Straker .40 1.00
12 Don Baylor .75 2.00
13 George Frazier .40 1.00
14 Keith Atherton .40 1.00
15 Tom Brunansky .60 1.50
16 Randy Bush .40 1.00
17 Al Newman .40 1.00
18 Mark Davidson .40 1.00
19 Bert Blyleven .75 2.00
20 Dan Schatzeder .40 1.00
21 Dan Gladden .40 1.00
22 Sal Butera .40 1.00
23 Kirby Puckett 6.00 15.00
24 Joe Niekro .60 1.50
25 Juan Berenguer .40 1.00
26 Jeff Reardon .60 1.50
27 Dick Such CO .40 1.00
28 Rick Stelmaszek CO .40 1.00
29 Rick Renick CO .40 1.00
30 Wayne Terwilliger CO .40 1.00
31 1987 Team Photo .40 1.00
32 Twins Championship Logo .40 1.00
33 Twins Logo .40 1.00
Checklist

1988 Twins Master Bread Discs

Master Bread introduced a set of 12 discs produced in conjunction with the Major League Baseball Players Association and Mike Schechter Associates. The set commemorates the Minnesota Twins' World Championship the year before and features only Twins players. A single disc was inserted inside each loaf of bread. The discs are numbered on the back and have a medium blue border on the front. Discs are approximately 2 3/4" in diameter. The disc backs contain very sparse personal or statistical information about the player and are printed in blue on white stock.

COMPLETE SET (12) 3.00 8.00
1 Bert Blyleven .40 1.00
2 Frank Viola .40 1.00
3 Juan Berenguer .20 .50
4 Jeff Reardon .30 .75
5 Tim Laudner .20 .50
6 Steve Lombardozzi .20 .50
7 Randy Bush .20 .50
8 Kirby Puckett 1.50 4.00
9 Gary Gaetti .30 .75
10 Kent Hrbek .60 1.50
11 Greg Gagne .20 .50
12 Tom Brunansky .20 .50

1988 Twins Smokey Colorgrams

These cards are actually pages of a booklet featuring members of the Minnesota Twins and Smokey's fire safety tips. The booklet has 12 pages each containing a black and white photo card (approximately 2 1/2" by 3 3/4") and a black and white player caricature (oversized head) postcard (approximately 3 3/4" by 5 5/8"). The cards are unnumbered but they have biographical information and a fire-prevention cartoon on the back of the card.

COMPLETE SET (12) 6.00 15.00
1 Frank Viola .60 1.50
2 Gary Gaetti .75 2.00
3 Kent Hrbek .60 1.50
4 Jeff Reardon .60 1.50
5 Gene Larkin .40 1.00
6 Bert Blyleven .60 1.50
7 Tim Laudner .40 1.00
8 Greg Gagne .50 1.25
9 Randy Bush .40 1.00
10 Dan Gladden .40 1.00
11 Al Newman .40 1.00
12 Kirby Puckett 3.00 8.00

1992 Twins Photos

These photos feature members of the 1991 World Champion Minnesota Twins.

COMPLETE SET 4.00 10.00
1 Tom Kelly MG .08 .25
2 Minnesota Twins .08 .25
3 Terry Crowley CO .08 .25
4 Ron Gardenhire CO .08 .25
5 Tony Oliva CO .40 1.00
6 Dick Such CO .08 .25
7 Wayne Terrwilliger CO .08 .25
8 Rick Aguilera .20 .50
9 Steve Bedrosian .08 .25
10 Allen Anderson .08 .25
11 Randy Bush .08 .25
12 Chili Davis .30 .75
13 Scott Erickson .20 .50
14 Dan Gladden .08 .25
15 Brian Harper .08 .25
16 Greg Gagne .08 .25
17 Chuck Knoblauch .40 1.00
18 Terry Leach .08 .25
19 Gene Larkin .08 .25
20 Kent Hrbek .30 .75
21 Al Newman .08 .25
22 Shane Mack .08 .25
23 Jack Morris .40 1.00
24 Scott Leius .08 .25
25 Junior Ortiz .06 .25
26 Kevin Tapani .08 .25
27 Kirby Puckett 1.25 3.00
28 Carl Willis .08 .25
29 Gene Larkin WS .08 .25

1993 Twins Puckett Library Association Bookmark

This one-card bookmark set features Kirby Puckett sitting in the stands along with a group of young fans. The back features standard information about local libraries.

1 Kirby Puckett

2002 Twins Police

COMPLETE SET (8) 2.50 6.00
COMMON CARD .20 .50
1 Eddie Guardado .40 1.00
2 Cristian Guzman .30 .75
3 Torii Hunter .60 1.50
4 Jacque Jones .40 1.00
5 Corey Koskie .30 .75
6 Doug Mientkiewicz .20 .50
7 A.J. Pierzynski .60 1.50
8 Luis Rivas .20 .50

2003 Twins Police

COMPLETE SET (8) 3.00 8.00
1 Eddie Guardado .40 1.00
2 Torii Hunter .60 1.50
3 Jacque Jones .40 1.00
4 Corey Koskie .30 .75
5 Doug Mientkiewicz .20 .50
6 Eric Milton .20 .50
7 A.J. Pierzynski .60 1.50
8 Brad Radke .60 1.50
9 McGruff the Crime Dog .20 .50

2003 Twins Team Issue

COMPLETE SET 5.00 12.00
73 Cristian Guzman .30 .75
74 Torii Hunter .60 1.50
75 Corey Koskie .30 .75
76 Joe Mauer 2.00 5.00
77 Doug Mientkiewicz .20 .50
78 A.J. Pierzynski .60 1.50
79 Kirby Puckett 1.00 2.50
80 Brad Radke .60 1.50
81 J.C. Romero .40 1.00
82 Johan Santana 1.50 4.00
83 T.C. (The Bear Mascot) .20 .50

2004 Twins Donruss Joe Mauer Card Night

COMPLETE SET (1) 2.00 5.00
1 Joe Mauer 2.50 6.00

2004 Twins Police

COMPLETE SET (9) 3.00 8.00
1 Cristian Guzman .30 .75
2 Torii Hunter .60 1.50
3 Corey Koskie .30 .75
4 Kyle Lohse .30 .75
5 Doug Mientkiewicz .20 .50
6 Brad Radke .60 1.50
7 Johan Santana 1.00 2.50
8 Shannon Stewart .60 1.50
XX McGruff the Crime Dog .20 .50

2004 Twins Team Issue Colla

COMPLETE SET
33 Ron Gardenhire MG .25 .50
34 Torii Hunter .60 1.50
35 Jacque Jones .40 1.00
36 Corey Koskie .25 .50
37 Kyle Lohse .25 .50
38 Doug Mientkiewicz .25 .50
40 Joe Mauer .75 2.00
41 Shannon Stewart .40 1.00
42 Rod Carew .75 2.00

2004 Twins TwinFest

COMPLETE SET
1 Rick Anderson .20 .50
2 Bert Blyleven .60 1.50
3 Rod Carew .75 2.00
4 Michael Cuddyer .30 .75
5 Ron Gardenhire MG .20 .50
6 Dan Gladden .20 .50
7 Kent Hrbek .60 1.50
8 Jacque Jones .20 .50
9 Harmon Killebrew .75 2.00
10 Corey Koskie .20 .50
11 Matt LeCroy .20 .50
12 Al Newman CO .20 .50
13 Tony Oliva .60 1.50
14 Michael Restovich .20 .50
15 Michael Ryan .20 .50
16 Johan Santana 1.00 2.50

2005 Twins Donruss

COMPLETE SET (30)
1 Dave Boswell .10 .25
2 Jim Kaat .40 1.00
3 Jim Merritt .10 .25
4 Mel Nelson .10 .25
5 Bill Pleis .10 .25
6 Dick Stigman .10 .25
7 Earl Battey .10 .25
8 Jerry Kindall .10 .25
9 Frank Quilici .10 .25
10 Zoilo Versalles .20 .50
11 Bob Allison .20 .50
12 Joe Nossek .10 .25
13 Tony Oliva .40 1.00
14 Sam Mele MG .10 .25
15 John Sain CO .10 .25
16 Jim Grant .10 .25
17 John Klippstein .10 .25
18 Camilo Pascual .30 .75
19 Jim Perry .20 .50
20 Al Worthington .10 .25
21 John Sevcik .10 .25
22 Jerry Zimmerman .10 .25
23 Harmon Killebrew .75 2.00
24 Don Mincher .10 .25
25 Rich Rollins .10 .25
26 Billy Martin CO .20 .50
27 Jimmie Hall .10 .25
28 Sandy Valdespino .10 .25
29 Hal Naragon CO .10 .25
30 Jim Lemon CO .10 .25

2005 Twins Police

COMPLETE SET (8) 2.00 5.00
1 Joe Nathan .20 .50
2 Joe Mauer .50 1.25
3 Johan Santana .50 1.25
4 Brad Radke .20 .50
5 Kyle Lohse .20 .50
6 Torii Hunter .20 .50
7 Shannon Stewart .20 .50
8 McGruff the Crime Dog .20 .50

2005 Twins UPN 29

COMPLETE SET (30) 6.00 15.00
1 Bob Allison .20 .50
2 Rod Carew .30 .75
3 Scott Erickson .20 .50
4 Gary Gaetti .20 .50
5 Dan Gladden .20 .50
6 Kent Hrbek .20 .50
7 Kent Hrbek .20 .50
8 Kent Hrbek .20 .50
9 Torii Hunter .20 .50
10 Harmon Killebrew .50 1.25
11 Harmon Killebrew .50 1.25
12 Gene Larkin .20 .50
13 Eric Milton .20 .50
14 Paul Molitor .20 .50
15 Jack Morris .20 .50
16 Tony Oliva .20 .50
17 Tony Oliva .20 .50
18 A.J. Pierzynski .20 .50
19 Kirby Puckett .50 1.25
20 Kirby Puckett .50 1.25
21 Kirby Puckett/Dave Winfield .50 1.25
22 Johan Santana .30 .75
23 Homer Simpson .20 .50
24 Shannon Stewart .20 .50
25 World Series Tropy .20 .50
26 Ticker Tape Parade .20 .50
27 1965 World Series .20 .50
28 1965 All-Star Game .20 .50
29 Frank Viola .20 .50
30 Dave Winfield .20 .50

2006 Twins Topps

COMPLETE SET (14) 3.00 8.00
MIN1 Torii Hunter .12 .30
MIN2 Michael Cuddyer .12 .30
MIN3 Joe Mauer .20 .50
MIN4 Lew Ford .12 .30
MIN5 Shannon Stewart .12 .30
MIN6 Justin Morneau .20 .50
MIN7 Jesse Crain .12 .30
MIN8 Juan Rincon .12 .30
MIN9 Brad Radke .12 .30
MIN10 Joe Nathan .12 .30
MIN11 Johan Santana .20 .50
MIN12 Jason Bartlett .12 .30
MIN13 Rondell White .12 .30
MIN14 Luis Castillo .12 .30

2006 Twins Police

COMPLETE SET (9) 2.00 5.00
1 Justin Morneau .50 1.25
2 Carlos Silva .20 .50
3 Brad Radke .20 .50
4 Joe Nathan .20 .50
5 Joe Mauer .50 1.25
6 Shannon Stewart .20 .50
7 Torii Hunter .20 .50
8 Johan Santana .50 1.25
9 McGruff the Crime Dog .20 .50

2007 Twins Topps

COMPLETE SET (14) 3.00 8.00
MIN1 Joe Mauer .25 .60
MIN2 Nick Punto .12 .30
MIN3 Jason Kubel .12 .30
MIN4 Johan Santana .20 .50
MIN5 Pat Neshek .25 .60
MIN6 Boof Bonser .12 .30
MIN7 Jason Bartlett .12 .30
MIN8 Torii Hunter .12 .30
MIN9 Carlos Silva .12 .30
MIN10 Michael Cuddyer .12 .30
MIN11 Glen Perkins .12 .30
MIN12 Justin Morneau .20 .50
MIN13 Joe Nathan .12 .30
MIN14 Francisco Liriano .12 .30

2007 Twins Upper Deck 1987 20th Anniversary

COMPLETE SET (30) 5.00 12.00
1 Frank Viola .20 .50
2 Al Newman .20 .50
3 Kent Hrbek .20 .50
4 Dan Gladden .20 .50
5 Dan Schatzeder .20 .50
6 Don Baylor .20 .50
7 Gary Gaetti .20 .50
8 Gene Larkin .20 .50
9 George Frazier .20 .50
10 Greg Gagne .20 .50
11 Jeff Reardon .20 .50
12 Joe Niekro .20 .50
13 Bert Blyleven .20 .50
14 Les Straker .20 .50
15 Kirby Puckett .50 1.25
16 Randy Bush .20 .50
17 Sal Butera .20 .50
18 Steve Lombardozzi .20 .50
19 Roy Smalley .20 .50
20 Keith Atherton .20 .50
21 Mark Davidson .20 .50
22 Tim Laudner .20 .50
23 Tom Brunansky .20 .50
24 Juan Berenguer .20 .50
25 Tom Kelly MG .20 .50
26 Dick Such CO .20 .50
27 Wayne Terwilliger CO .20 .50
28 Rick Stelmaszek CO .20 .50
29 Tony Oliva CO .20 .50
30 Rick Renick CO .20 .50

2007 Twins Upper Deck Awards

COMPLETE SET (17) 3.00 8.00

2008 Twins Topps

COMPLETE SET (14) 3.00 8.00
MIN1 Joe Mauer .25 .60
MIN2 Craig Monroe .12 .30
MIN3 Jason Kubel .12 .30
MIN4 Phil Humber
MIN5 Pat Neshek .20 .50
MIN6 Boof Bonser .12 .30
MIN7 Mike Lamb .12 .30
MIN8 Delmon Young .20 .50
MIN9 Mike Redmond
MIN10 Michael Cuddyer .12 .30
MIN11 Kevin Slowey
MIN12 Justin Morneau .20 .50
MIN13 Joe Nathan .12 .30
MIN14 Francisco Liriano .12 .30

2009 Twins Topps

MIN1 Joe Mauer .30 .75
MIN2 Francisco Liriano .15 .40
MIN3 Justin Morneau .25 .60
MIN4 Glen Perkins .15 .40
MIN5 Delmon Young .25 .60
MIN6 Alexi Casilla .15 .40
MIN7 Kevin Slowey .25 .60
MIN8 Michael Cuddyer .15 .40
MIN9 Joe Nathan .15 .40
MIN10 Jason Kubel .15 .40
MIN11 Nick Blackburn .15 .40
MIN12 Carlos Gomez .15 .40
MIN13 Scott Baker .15 .40
MIN14 Denard Span .15 .40
MIN15 HHH Metrodome .15 .40

2010 Twins Topps

MIN1 Joe Mauer .30 .75
MIN2 Pat Neshek .15 .40
MIN3 Anthony Swarzak .15 .40
MIN4 J.J. Hardy .15 .40
MIN5 Scott Baker .15 .40
MIN6 Denard Span .15 .40
MIN7 Jason Kubel .15 .40
MIN8 Carl Pavano .15 .40
MIN9 Joe Nathan .15 .40
MIN10 Nick Blackburn .15 .40
MIN11 Michael Cuddyer .15 .40
MIN12 Glen Perkins .15 .40
MIN13 Delmon Young .25 .60
MIN14 Nick Punto .15 .40
MIN15 Francisco Liriano .15 .40
MIN16 Alexi Casilla .15 .40
MIN17 Justin Morneau .25 .60

2011 Twins Topps

MIN1 Joe Mauer .30 .75
MIN2 Justin Morneau .25 .60
MIN3 Michael Cuddyer .15 .40
MIN4 Brian Duensing .15 .40
MIN5 Tsuyoshi Nishioka .50 1.25
MIN6 Scott Baker .15 .40
MIN7 Jason Kubel .15 .40
MIN8 Francisco Liriano .15 .40
MIN9 Joe Nathan .15 .40
MIN10 Kevin Slowey .15 .40
MIN11 Carl Pavano .15 .40
MIN12 Delmon Young .25 .60
MIN13 Trevor Plouffe .15 .40
MIN14 Danny Valencia .25 .60
MIN15 Denard Span .15 .40
MIN16 Jim Thome .25 .60
MIN17 Target Field .15 .40

2012 Twins Topps

MIN1 Joe Mauer .30 .75
MIN2 Danny Valencia .30 .75
MIN3 Ben Revere .30 .75
MIN4 Trevor Plouffe .25 .60
MIN5 Ryan Doumit .25 .60
MIN6 Carl Pavano .25 .60
MIN7 Denard Span .25 .60
MIN8 Nick Blackburn .25 .60
MIN9 Tsuyoshi Nishioka .30 .75
MIN10 Josh Willingham .30 .75
MIN11 Scott Baker .25 .60
MIN12 Chris Parmelee .25 .60
MIN13 Justin Morneau .30 .75
MIN14 Francisco Liriano .25 .60
MIN15 Matt Capps .25 .60
MIN16 Joe Benson .25 .60
MIN17 Target Field .15 .40

2013 Twins Topps

COMPLETE SET (17) 3.00 8.00
MIN1 Joe Mauer .30 .75
MIN2 Justin Morneau .20 .50
MIN3 Josh Willingham .20 .50
MIN4 Darin Mastroianni .15 .40
MIN5 Chris Parmelee .25 .60
MIN6 Ryan Doumit .15 .40
MIN7 Jamey Carroll .15 .40
MIN8 Brian Dozier .20 .50
MIN9 Scott Diamond .15 .40
MIN10 Trevor Plouffe .15 .40
MIN11 Glen Perkins .25 .60
MIN12 Vance Worley .20 .50
MIN13 Liam Hendriks .25 .60
MIN14 Pedro Florimon .25 .60
MIN15 Kevin Correia .15 .40
MIN16 Mike Pelfrey .25 .60
MIN17 Target Field .15 .40

2014 Twins Topps

COMPLETE SET (17) 3.00 8.00
MIN1 Joe Mauer .20 .50
MIN2 Oswaldo Arcia .15 .40
MIN3 Josh Willingham .20 .50
MIN4 Alex Presley .15 .40
MIN5 Chris Parmelee .15 .40
MIN6 Phil Hughes .15 .40
MIN7 Aaron Hicks .20 .50
MIN8 Brian Dozier .20 .50
MIN9 Samuel Deduno .15 .40
MIN10 Trevor Plouffe .15 .40
MIN11 Glen Perkins .15 .40
MIN12 Ricky Nolasco .15 .40
MIN13 Kurt Suzuki .15 .40
MIN14 Pedro Florimon .15 .40
MIN15 Kevin Correia .15 .40
MIN16 Mike Pelfrey .15 .40
MIN17 Target Field .15 .40

2015 Twins Topps

COMPLETE SET (17) 3.00 8.00
MT1 Torii Hunter .15 .40
MT2 Brian Dozier .20 .50
MT3 Brian Duensing .15 .40
MT4 Eduardo Escobar .15 .40
MT5 Phil Hughes .15 .40
MT6 Ricky Nolasco .15 .40
MT7 Joe Mauer .20 .50
MT8 Glen Perkins .15 .40
MT9 Kurt Suzuki .15 .40
MT10 Trevor May .15 .40
MT11 Kennys Vargas .15 .40
MT12 Danny Santana .15 .40
MT13 Trevor Plouffe .15 .40
MT14 Josmil Pinto .15 .40
MT15 Aaron Hicks .20 .50
MT16 Oswaldo Arcia .15 .40
MT17 Ervin Santana .15 .40

2016 Twins Topps

COMPLETE SET (17) 3.00 8.00
MIN1 Miguel Sano .25 .60
MIN2 Kurt Suzuki .15 .40
MIN3 Joe Mauer .20 .50
MIN4 Brian Dozier .20 .50
MIN5 Eduardo Escobar .15 .40
MIN6 Trevor Plouffe .15 .40
MIN7 Eddie Rosario .20 .50
MIN8 Byron Buxton .25 .60
MIN9 Phil Hughes .15 .40
MIN10 Ervin Santana .15 .40
MIN11 Glen Perkins .15 .40
MIN12 Eduardo Nunez .15 .40
MIN13 Kennys Vargas .15 .40
MIN14 Kyle Gibson .20 .50
MIN15 Tyler Duffey .15 .40
MIN16 Max Kepler .25 .60
MIN17 Danny Santana .15 .40

2017 Twins Topps

COMPLETE SET (17) 3.00 8.00
MIN1 Miguel Sano .20 .50
MIN2 Byron Buxton .25 .60
MIN3 Joe Mauer .20 .50
MIN4 Jose Berrios .20 .50
MIN5 Kyle Gibson .20 .50
MIN6 Eddie Rosario .20 .50
MIN7 Glen Perkins .15 .40
MIN8 Danny Santana .15 .40
MIN9 Ervin Santana .15 .40
MIN10 Byung-Ho Park .15 .40
MIN11 Jason Castro .15 .40
MIN12 Eduardo Escobar .15 .40
MIN13 Hector Santiago .15 .40
MIN14 Robbie Grossman .15 .40
MIN15 Max Kepler .20 .50
MIN16 Brian Dozier .25 .60
MIN17 Phil Hughes .15 .40

2018 Twins Topps

COMPLETE SET (17) 2.00 5.00
MT1 Byron Buxton .25 .60
MT2 Brian Dozier .20 .50
MT3 Joe Mauer .20 .50
MT4 Eddie Rosario .25 .60
MT5 Miguel Sano .20 .50
MT6 Ervin Santana .15 .40
MT7 Robbie Grossman .15 .40
MT8 Jorge Polanco .20 .50
MT9 Eduardo Escobar .15 .40
MT10 Kennys Vargas .15 .40
MT11 Kyle Gibson .20 .50
MT12 Jason Castro .15 .40
MT13 Jose Berrios .20 .50
MT14 Adalberto Mejia .15 .40
MT15 Max Kepler .20 .50
MT16 Ehire Adrianza .15 .40
MT17 Trevor Hildenberger .15 .40

2019 Twins Topps

COMPLETE SET (17) 2.00 5.00
MT1 Jose Berrios .20 .50
MT2 Jorge Polanco .20 .50
MT3 Miguel Sano .20 .50
MT4 Jake Odorizzi .15 .40
MT5 Max Kepler .20 .50
MT6 Tyler Austin .25 .60
MT7 Jake Cave .20 .50
MT8 Kyle Gibson .20 .50
MT9 Addison Reed .15 .40
MT10 Jonathan Schoop .15 .40
MT11 Eddie Rosario .20 .50
MT12 Willans Astudillo .15 .40
MT13 Ehire Adrianza .15 .40
MT14 Nelson Cruz .25 .60
MT15 Jason Castro .15 .40
MT16 Adalberto Mejia .15 .40
MT17 C.J. Cron .15 .40

2020 Twins Topps

MIN1 Nelson Cruz .25 .60
MIN2 Max Kepler .20 .50
MIN3 Jorge Polanco .20 .50
MIN4 Jake Odorizzi .15 .40
MIN5 Randy Dobnak .30 .75
MIN6 Eddie Rosario .20 .50
MIN7 Miguel Sano .20 .50
MIN8 Byron Buxton .25 .60
MIN9 Jose Berrios .20 .50
MIN10 Jake Cave .20 .50
MIN11 Luis Arraez .30 .75
MIN12 Marwin Gonzalez .15 .40
MIN13 Mitch Garver .15 .40
MIN14 Taylor Rogers .15 .40
MIN15 Michael Pineda .15 .40
MIN16 Ehire Adrianza .15 .40
MIN17 Willians Astudillo .15 .40

2017 Twins Topps National Baseball Card Day

COMPLETE SET (10) 5.00 12.00
MIN1 Byron Buxton 1.00 2.50
MIN2 Max Kepler .75 2.00
MIN3 Joe Mauer .75 2.00
MIN4 Eddie Rosario .75 2.00
MIN5 Miguel Sano .75 2.00
MIN6 Phil Hughes .60 1.50
MIN7 Jason Castro .60 1.50
MIN8 Eduardo Escobar .60 1.50
MIN9 Jorge Polanco .75 2.00
MIN10 Rod Carew .75 2.00

1932 U.S. Caramel

The cards in this 32-card set measure 2 1/2" by 3". The U.S. Caramel set of "Famous Athletes" was issued in 1932. The cards contain black and white bust shots set against an attractive red background. Boxers and golfers are included in the set. The existence of card number 16, Fred Lindstrom has only recently been verified. The set price does not include the Lindstrom card.

1 Eddie Collins 200.00 400.00
2 Paul Waner 200.00 400.00
4 Bill Terry 200.00 400.00
5 Earl Combs 200.00 400.00
6 Bill Dickey 200.00 400.00
7 Joe Cronin 200.00 400.00
8 Chick Hafey 150.00 300.00
10 Rabbit Maranville 150.00 300.00
11 Rogers Hornsby 250.00 500.00
12 Mickey Cochrane 200.00 400.00
13 Lloyd Waner 150.00 300.00
14 Ty Cobb 500.00 1000.00
16 Fred Lindstrom 75000.00 125000.00
17 Al Simmons 200.00 400.00
18 Tony Lazzeri 150.00 300.00
19 Wally Berger 125.00 250.00
20 Red Ruffing 150.00 300.00
21 Chuck Klein 200.00 400.00
23 Jimmie Foxx 1500.00 2500.00
24 Lefty O'Doul 100.00 200.00
26 Lou Gehrig 5000.00 10000.00
27 Lefty Grove 250.00 500.00
28 Edward Brandt 100.00 200.00
29 George Earnshaw 100.00 200.00
30 Frankie Frisch 200.00 400.00
31 Lefty Gomez 200.00 400.00
32 Babe Ruth 8000.00 12000.00

1994 U.S. Department of Transportation

These strip of three cards was co-sponsored by the U.S. Department of Transportation and the National Highway Traffic Safety Administration. The cards were reportedly given out at the Little League World Series. The 8" by 3 1/2" strip is not perforated, but if the cards were cut along the dotted lines, they would measure the standard size. The cards are unnumbered and checklisted below in alphabetical order.

COMPLETE SET (6) 6.00 15.00
1 Mike Piazza 1.50 4.00
2 Cal Ripken 2.50 6.00
3 Mo Vaughn .60 1.50
4 Orel Hershiser .60 1.50
5 Don Mattingly 1.25 3.00
6 Mike Mussina 1.00 2.50

1991 U.S. Game Systems Baseball Legends

These cards feature leading all time greats. Each player is given one card (Ace, Queen, etc.) in all four suits. This set was issued in its own card box and we have used 1 for Ace, 11 for Jacks, 12 for Queens and 13 for Kings.

COMP. FACT SET (56) 2.00 5.00
1C Ty Cobb .20 .50
1D Ty Cobb .20 .50
1H Ty Cobb .20 .50
1S Ty Cobb .20 .50
2C Babe Ruth .30 .75
2D Babe Ruth .30 .75
2H Babe Ruth .30 .75
2S Babe Ruth .30 .75
3C Lou Gehrig .20 .50
3D Lou Gehrig .20 .50
3H Lou Gehrig .20 .50
3S Lou Gehrig .20 .50
4C Hank Aaron .20 .50
4D Hank Aaron .20 .50
4H Hank Aaron .20 .50
4S Hank Aaron .20 .50
5C Satchel Paige .10 .30
5D Satchel Paige .10 .30
5H Satchel Paige .10 .30
5S Satchel Paige .10 .30
6C Jimmie Foxx .07 .20
6D Jimmie Foxx .07 .20
6H Jimmie Foxx .07 .20
6S Jimmie Foxx .07 .20
7C Rogers Hornsby .07 .20
7D Rogers Hornsby .07 .20
7H Rogers Hornsby .07 .20
7S Rogers Hornsby .07 .20
8C Stan Musial .20 .50
8D Stan Musial .20 .50
8H Stan Musial .20 .50
8S Stan Musial .20 .50
9C Walter Johnson .07 .20
9D Walter Johnson .07 .20
9H Walter Johnson .07 .20
9S Walter Johnson .07 .20
10C Honus Wagner .07 .20
10D Honus Wagner .07 .20
10H Honus Wagner .07 .20
10S Honus Wagner .07 .20
11C Roberto Clemente .20 .50
11D Roberto Clemente .20 .50
11H Roberto Clemente .20 .50
11S Roberto Clemente .20 .50
12C Christy Mathewson .07 .20
12D Christy Mathewson .07 .20
12H Christy Mathewson .07 .20
12S Christy Mathewson .07 .20
13A Cy Young .07 .20
13C Cy Young .07 .20
13D Cy Young .07 .20
13H Cy Young .07 .20
NNO Title Card .02 .10

1990 U.S. Playing Cards All-Stars

Thse 56 playing standard-size cards have rounded corners and feature color posed and action player photos on white-bordered fronts. The cards are checklisted in playing card order by suits and assigned numbers to aces (1), jacks (11), queens (12), and kings (13). A limited Silver Series parallel set was produced distinguished from the regular set by the silver foil on the cards' edges.

COMP. FACT SET (56) 2.50 6.00
1C Bob Welch .01 .05
1D Frank Viola .01 .05
1H Ramon Martinez .01 .05
1S Roger Clemens .40 1.00
2C Lance Parrish .01 .05
2D Greg Olson .01 .05
2H Mike Scioscia .02 .10
2S Sandy Alomar .02 .10
3C Bret Saberhagen .01 .05
3D Dennis Martinez .02 .10
3H Jeff Brantley .02 .10
3S Randy Johnson .20 .50
4C Gregg Olson .01 .05
4D Roberto Alomar .08 .25
4H Ryne Sandberg .20 .50
4S Steve Sax .01 .05
5C Brook Jacoby .01 .05
5D Tim Wallach .01 .05
5H Chris Sabo .01 .05
5S Kelly Gruber .01 .05
6C Ozzie Guillen .05 .15
6D Barry Larkin .08 .25
6H Ozzie Smith .30 .75
6S Cal Ripken .75 2.00
7C Ellis Burks .05 .15
7D Neal Heaton .01 .05
7H John Franco .02 .10
7S Doug Jones .01 .05
8C Dennis Eckersley .15 .40
8D Dave Smith .01 .05
8H Matt Williams .05 .15
8S Kirby Puckett .25 .60
9C Bobby Thigpen .01 .05
9D Lenny Dykstra .01 .05
9H Andre Dawson .05 .15
9S Chuck Finley .02 .10
10C Dave Stieb .01 .05
10D Shawon Dunston .01 .05
10H Benito Santiago .02 .10
10S Alan Trammell .05 .15
11C Wade Boggs .20 .50
11D Tony Gwynn .40 1.00
11H Bobby Bonilla .01 .05
11S Ken Griffey Jr. .50 1.25
12C George Bell .01 .05
12D Will Clark .15 .40
12H Kevin Mitchell .01 .05
12S Dave Parker .01 .05
13C Rickey Henderson .20 .50
13D Barry Bonds .30 .75
13H Darryl Strawberry .02 .10
13S Cecil Fielder .02 .10

JKO Joker .01 .05
Jack Armstrong
JKO Joker .02 .10
Julio Franco
WCO Wild Card .30 .75
Mark McGwire
Jose Canseco
WCO Wild Card .01 .05
Rob Dibble
Randy Myers

1991 U.S. Playing Cards All-Stars

Thse 56 playing standard-size cards have rounded corners and feature color posed and action player photos on white-bordered fronts. The cards are checklisted in playing card order by suits and assigned numbers to aces (1), jacks (11), queens (12), and kings (13). A limited Silver Series parallel set was produced distinguished from the regular set by the silver foil on the cards' edges.

COMP. FACT SET (56) 2.50 6.00
1C Tony Gwynn .40 1.00
1D Ken Griffey Jr. .40 1.00
1H Jack Morris .02 .10
1S Tom Glavine .15 .40
2C Paul O'Neill .08 .25
2D Carlton Fisk .20 .50
2H Ozzie Guillen .05 .15
2S Eddie Murray .20 .50
3C John Smiley .01 .05
3D Scott Sanderson .01 .05
3H Jack McDowell .01 .05
3S Pete Harnisch .01 .05
4C Howard Johnson .01 .05
4D Kirby Puckett .25 .60
4H Joe Carter .05 .15
4S John Kruk .02 .10
5C Mike Morgan .01 .05
5D Jeff Reardon .01 .05
5H Mark Langston .01 .05
5S Tom Browning .01 .05
6C Barry Larkin .08 .25
6D Rafael Palmeiro .15 .40
6H Julio Franco .02 .10
6S George Bell .01 .05
7C Frank Viola .01 .05
7D Bryan Harvey .01 .05
7H Rick Aguilera .02 .10
7S Dennis Martinez .02 .10
8C Juan Samuel .01 .05
8D Jimmy Key .01 .05
8H Paul Molitor .15 .40
8S Brett Butler .01 .05
9C Craig Biggio .08 .25
9D Harold Baines .02 .10
9H Ruben Sierra .02 .10
9S Felix Jose .01 .05
10C Lee Smith .02 .10
10D Dennis Eckersley .15 .40
10H Roger Clemens .40 1.00
10S Rob Dibble .01 .05
11C Andre Dawson .08 .25
11D Sandy Alomar .01 .05
11H Rickey Henderson .30 .75
11S Benito Santiago .02 .10
12C Chris Sabo .01 .05
12D Cecil Fielder .02 .10
12H Roberto Alomar .08 .25
12S Ryne Sandberg .25 .60
13C Ivan Calderon .01 .05
13D Cal Ripken .75 2.00
13H Dave Henderson .01 .05
13S Ozzie Smith .25 .60
JKO Joker .01 .05
Bobby Bonilla
JKO Joker .01 .05
Danny Tartabull
WCO Wild Card .15 .40
Wade Boggs
WCO Wild Card .08 .25
Will Clark

1992 U.S. Playing Cards All-Stars

hse 54 playing standard-size cards have rounded orners and feature color posed and action player hotos on white-bordered fronts. The cards are hecklisted in playing card order by suits and assigned umbers to aces (1), jacks (11), queens (12), and ngs (13).

OMP. FACT SET (54) 2.00 5.00
C Jose Canseco .20 .50
D Julio Franco .02 .10
H Cecil Fielder .02 .10
S Denny Martinez .02 .10
C Chili Davis .02 .10
D Danny Tartabull .01 .05
H Juan Gonzalez UER .15 .40
Card spelled Gonzales
S Mike Moore .01 .05
C Mickey Tettleton .01 .05
D Tony Gwynn .40 1.00
H Andre Dawson .10 .30
S Nolan Ryan .75 2.00
C Danny Tartabull .01 .05
D Frank Thomas .20 .50
H Ron Gant .02 .10
S Jim Abbott .01 .05
C Fred McGriff .07 .20
D Hal Morris .01 .05
H Fred McGriff .07 .20
S Bill Wegman .01 .05
C Andre Dawson .10 .30
D Kirby Puckett .20 .50
H Joe Carter .02 .10
S Mike Morgan .01 .05
C Frank Thomas .15 .40
D Terry Pendleton .01 .05
H Frank Thomas .15 .40
S Jose DeLeon .01 .05
C Ron Gant .01 .05
D Rafael Palmeiro .10 .30
Cal Ripken Jr UER .75 2.00
Spelled Ripkin
Pete Harnisch .01 .05
Joe Carter .01 .05
Cal Ripken Jr UER .75 2.00
Spelled Ripkin

9H Ruben Sierra .02 .10
9S Tom Candiotti .01 .05
10C Matt Williams .07 .20
10D Paul Molitor .15 .40
10H Barry Bonds .30 .75
10S Roger Clemens .40 1.00
11C Cal Ripken Jr UER .75 2.00
Spelled Ripkin
11D Ken Griffey Jr .50 1.25
11H Will Clark .10 .30
11S Tim Belcher .01 .05
12C Howard Johnson .01 .05
12D Willie Randolph .02 .10
12H Howard Johnson .01 .05
12S Tom Glavine .15 .40
13C Cecil Fielder .02 .10
13D Wade Boggs .25 .60
13H Jose Canseco .15 .40
13S Jose Rijo .01 .05
JKA Roger Clemens .40 1.00
JKN Tom Glavine .15 .40

1993 U.S. Playing Cards Aces

This 55-card standard-size set features the top 13 players in four categories according to suits: lowest ERA's, (spades) Most Stolen Bases, (hearts) Most Home Runs, (clubs) and Highest Batting Average (diamonds). Since this set is similar to a playing card set, the set is checklisted as if it were a playing card deck. In the checklist C means Clubs, D means Diamonds, H means Hearts, S means Spades, and JK means Joker. The cards are checklisted in playing order by suits and numbers are assigned to Aces, (1) Jacks, (11) Queens, (12) and Kings (13). The Jokers, Wild Card, and the title card are unnumbered and listed at the end. A few players signed some limited cards for this set. Due to market scarcity, those cards are unpriced but more information is greatly appreciated.

COMP. FACT SET (56) 2.50 6.00
1C Juan Gonzalez .10 .30
1D Edgar Martinez .05 .15
1H Marquis Grissom .02 .10
1S Bill Swift .01 .05
2C Dave Hollins .01 .05
2D Roberto Alomar .08 .25
2H Chad Curtis .01 .05
2S Tom Glavine .15 .40
3C Darren Daulton .02 .10
3D Terry Pendleton .01 .05
3H Ozzie Smith .30 .75
3S Sid Fernandez .01 .05
4C Ken Griffey Jr. .50 1.25
4D Carlos Baerga .01 .05
4H Bip Roberts .01 .05
4S Greg Swindell .01 .05
5C Rob Deer .01 .05
5D Shane Mack .01 .05
5H Steve Finley .05 .15
5S Juan Guzman .01 .05
6C Mickey Tettleton .01 .05
6D Tony Gwynn .40 1.00
6H Tim Raines .02 .10
6S Jose Rijo .01 .05
7C Gary Sheffield .20 .50
7D Paul Molitor .15 .40
7H Delino DeShields .01 .05
7S Mike Morgan .01 .05
8C Joe Carter .05 .15
8D Frank Thomas .15 .40
8H Rickey Henderson .25 .60
8S Mike Mussina .08 .25
9C Albert Belle .02 .10
9D Bip Roberts .01 .05
9H Roberto Alomar .08 .25
9S Dennis Martinez .02 .10
10C Barry Bonds .30 .75
10D John Kruk .01 .05
10H Luis Polonia .01 .05
10S Kevin Appier .01 .05
11C Fred McGriff .05 .15
11D Andy Van Slyke .01 .05
11H Brady Anderson .02 .10
11S Roger Clemens .40 1.00
12C Cecil Fielder .02 .10
12D Kirby Puckett .25 .60
12H Pat Listach .01 .05
12S Curt Schilling .20 .50
13C Mark McGwire .40 1.00
13D Gary Sheffield .20 .50
13H Kenny Lofton .02 .10
13S Greg Maddux .50 1.25
WCO Wild Card .75 2.00
Cal Ripken
JKO American League Logo .01 .05
WCOA Cal Ripken AU
AU1 Terry Pendleton AU/3 Diamonds Auto
AU2 Fred McGriff AU(Jack of Clubs autographed
NNO Title Card .01 .05

1993 U.S. Playing Cards Rookies

These 56 playing cards from the Bicycle Sports Collection feature outstanding 1992 rookies. The set is checklisted in playing card order by suits and assigned numbers to Aces (1), Jacks (11), Queens (12), Kings (13), and Jokers (JK).

COMP. FACT SET (56) 2.00 5.00
1C Kenny Lofton .30 .75
1D Dave Fleming .01 .05
1H Pat Listach .01 .05
1S Eric Karros .20 .50
2C Eric Fox .01 .05
2D Reggie Jefferson .01 .05
2H Pat Mahomes .01 .05
2S Butch Henry .01 .05
3C Mark Wohlers .01 .05
3D Anthony Young .01 .05
3H Greg Colbrunn .01 .05
3S Wilfredo Cordero .01 .05
4C John Patterson .01 .05
4D Kevin Koslofski .01 .05
4H Dan Walters .01 .05
4S Pedro Astacio .01 .05
5C Eric Young .02 .10
5D Brian Williams .01 .05
5H John Vander Wal .01 .05
5S Derek Bell .01 .05
6C Arthur Rhodes .01 .05
6D Brian Jordan .15 .40

6H Jeff Branson .01 .05
6S David Nied .01 .05
7C Jeff Frye .01 .05
7D John Doherty .01 .05
7H Monty Fariss .01 .05
7S Jeff Kent .40 1.00
8C Scott Servais .01 .05
8D Lenny Webster .01 .05
8H Rey Sanchez .01 .05
8S David Haas .01 .05
9C Ruben Amaro .01 .05
9D Roberto Hernandez .08 .25
9H Robert Wickman .01 .05
9S Eddie Taubensee .01 .05
10C Reggie Sanders .02 .10
10D Frank Seminara .01 .05
10H Derrick May .01 .05
10S Royce Clayton .01 .05
11C Alan Mills .01 .05
11D Scott Cooper .01 .05
11H Donovan Osborne .01 .05
11S Moises Alou .08 .25
12C Bob Zupcic .01 .05
12D Andy Stankiewicz .01 .05
12H Scott Livingstone .01 .05
12S Rusty Meacham .01 .05
13C Cal Eldred .01 .05
13D Tim Wakefield .05 .15
13H Gary DiSarcina .01 .05
13S Chad Curtis .01 .05
JK Pat Listach AL ROY .01 .05
NNO Alphabetical Checklist .01 .05

1994 U.S. Playing Cards Aces

These 56 playing standard-size cards have rounded corners, and feature borderless color posed and action player photos on their fronts. The set is checklisted in playing card order by suits and assigned numbers to aces (1), jacks (11), queens (12), and kings (13).

COMP. FACT SET (56) 2.50 6.00
1C Barry Bonds .30 .75
1D Andres Galarraga .08 .25
1H Kenny Lofton .02 .10
1S Greg Maddux .50 1.25
2C Phil Plantier .01 .05
2D John Kruk .01 .05
2H Brett Butler .01 .05
2S Tom Candiotti .01 .05
3C Bobby Bonilla .02 .10
3D Frank Thomas .15 .40
3H Eric Young .02 .10
3S Jimmy Key .01 .05
4C Mike Piazza .50 1.25
4D Mike Piazza .50 1.25
4H Delino DeShields .01 .05
4S Jack McDowell .01 .05
5C Ron Gant .02 .10
5D Jeff Bagwell .20 .50
5H Darren Lewis .01 .05
5S John Burkett .01 .05
6C Rafael Palmeiro .15 .40
6D Carlos Baerga .01 .05
6H Gregg Jefferies .01 .05
6S Tom Glavine .15 .40
7C Fred McGriff .05 .15
7D Mark Grace .08 .25
7H Otis Nixon .01 .05
7S Pete Harnisch .01 .05
8C Matt Williams .02 .10
8D Kenny Lofton .02 .10
8H Chad Curtis .01 .05
8S Wilson Alvarez .01 .05
9C Albert Belle .02 .10
9D Roberto Alomar .08 .25
9H Rickey Henderson .25 .60
9S Steve Avery .01 .05
10C David Justice .08 .25
10D Paul Molitor .15 .40
10H Marquis Grissom .02 .10
10S Bill Swift .01 .05
11C Frank Thomas .15 .40
11D Barry Bonds .30 .75
11H Luis Polonia .01 .05
11S Mark Portugal .01 .05
12C Ken Griffey Jr. .40 1.00
12D Gregg Jefferies .01 .05
12H Roberto Alomar .08 .25
12S Kevin Appier .01 .05
13C Juan Gonzalez .10 .30
13D John Olerud .02 .10
13H Chuck Carr .01 .05
13S Jose Rijo .01 .05
NNO Featured Players .01 .05

1994 U.S. Playing Cards Rookies

These 56 playing standard-size cards have rounded corners, and feature color posed and action player photos on their white-bordered fronts. The set is checklisted in playing card order by suits and assigned numbers to aces (1), jacks (11), queens (12), and kings (13).

COMP. FACT SET (56) 2.00 5.00
1C Mike Piazza .60 1.50
1D Chuck Carr .01 .05
1H Kevin Stocker .01 .05
1S Greg McMichael .01 .05
2C Vinny Castilla .08 .25
2D Jeff McNeely .01 .05
2H Alex Arias .01 .05
2S Paul Quantrill .01 .05
3C Wil Cordero .01 .05
3D Joe Kmak .01 .05
3H Carlos Garcia .01 .05
3S Steve Reed .01 .05
4C Ryan Thompson .01 .05
4D Phil Hiatt .01 .05

4H Erik Pappas .01 .05
4S Trevor Hoffman .08 .25
5C Craig Paquette .01 .05
5D Brent Gates .01 .05
5H Al Martin .01 .05
5S Tim Pugh .01 .05
6C Carlos Garcia .01 .05
6D Wil Cordero .01 .05
6H Tim Salmon .20 .50
6S Angel Miranda .01 .05
7C Jeff Conine .02 .10
7D Al Martin .01 .05
7H Mike Lansing .01 .05
7S Steve Cooke .01 .05
8C Bret Boone .08 .25
8D Wayne Kirby .01 .05
8H Rich Amaral .01 .05
8S Aaron Sele .01 .05
9C Jeromy Burnitz .08 .25
9D Lou Frazier .01 .05
9H Brent Gates .01 .05
9S Kirk Rueter .01 .05
10C J.T. Snow .08 .25
10D Carlos Garcia .01 .05
10H David Hulse .01 .05
10S Rene Arocha .01 .05
11C Al Martin .01 .05
11D Rich Amaral .01 .05
11H Troy Neel .01 .05
11S Pedro Martinez .30 .75
12C Troy Neel .01 .05
12D Mike Lansing .01 .05
12H Jeff Conine .02 .10
12S Armando Reynoso .01 .05
13C Tim Salmon .20 .50
13D David Hulse .01 .05
13H Mike Piazza .60 1.50
13S Jason Bere .01 .05
JK Mike Piazza NL ROY .30 .75
JK Tim Salmon AL ROY .08 .25
NNO Rookie Qualification .01 .05

1995 U.S. Playing Cards Aces

This 52 standard-size card set features leading major league players. The fronts of these rounded-corner cards feature borderless full-color posed and action player shots while the backs have the 1995 Major League Baseball Aces design on a silver and black background. The team logo appears in the lower left of each picture. The player's name and position appear in a reddish-brown stripe to the right of the team logo. Since this set is similar to a playing card set, the set is checklisted as if it were a playing card deck. In the checklist C means Clubs, D means Diamonds, H means Hearts and S means Spades. The cards are checklisted in playing order by suits and numbers are assigned to Aces (1), Jacks (11), Queens (12) and Kings (13).

COMP. FACT SET (52) 2.50 6.00
1C Matt Williams .05 .15
1D Tony Gwynn .30 .75
1H Kenny Lofton .02 .10
1S Greg Maddux .50 1.25
2C Joe Carter .05 .15
2D Gregg Jefferies .01 .05
2H Brian McRae .01 .05
2S Steve Trachsel .01 .05
3C Dante Bichette .02 .10
3D Kevin Mitchell .01 .05
3H Alex Cole .01 .05
3S Randy Johnson .25 .60
4C Cecil Fielder .02 .10
4D Will Clark .08 .25
4H Barry Bonds .40 1.00
4S Bobby Jones .01 .05
5C Kevin Mitchell* .01 .05
5D Hal Morris .01 .05
5H Darren Lewis .01 .05
5S Jose Rijo .01 .05
6C Andres Galarraga .08 .25
6D Moises Alou .02 .10
6H Brady Anderson .02 .10
6S Mike Mussina .08 .25
7C Jose Canseco .15 .40
7D Paul Molitor .15 .40
7H Chuck Carr .01 .05
7S Shane Reynolds .01 .05
8C Fred McGriff .05 .15
8D Wade Boggs .25 .60
8H Chuck Knoblauch .02 .10
8S Jeff Fassero .01 .05
9C Albert Belle .02 .10
9D Kenny Lofton .02 .10
9H Marquis Grissom .02 .10
9S David Cone .02 .10
10C Barry Bonds .30 .75
10D Frank Thomas .20 .50
10H Deion Sanders .08 .25
10S Roger Clemens .40 1.00
11C Frank Thomas .15 .40
11D Albert Belle .02 .10
11H Craig Biggio .05 .15
11S Doug Drabek .01 .05
12C Jeff Bagwell .20 .50
12D Paul O'Neill .05 .15
12H Otis Nixon .01 .05
12S Bret Saberhagen .01 .05
13C Ken Griffey Jr. .60 1.50
13D Jeff Bagwell .20 .50
13H Vince Coleman .01 .05
13S Steve Ontiveros .01 .05

2000 U.S. Playing Card All Century Team

COMP.FACT SET 6.00 15.00
1C Willie Keeler .10 .25
1D Eddie Collins .15 .40
1H Bob Gibson .25 .60
1S Babe Ruth .60 1.50
2C Bob Feller .10 .25
2D Robin Roberts .10 .25
2H Whitey Ford .25 .60
2S Satchel Paige .25 .60
3C Luke Appling .10 .25
3D Honus Wagner .40 1.00
3H Christy Mathewson .40 1.00
3S Willie McCovey .25 .60
4C Dizzy Dean .25 .60
4D Warren Spahn .15 .40

4H Ralph Kiner .10 .25
4S Joe Morgan .15 .40
5C Johnny Bench .25 .60
5D Mickey Mantle .60 1.50
5H Juan Marichal .25 .60
5S Mel Ott .30 .75
6C Lou Brock .10 .25
6D Brooks Robinson .10 .25
6H Lefty Grove .25 .60
6S Jim Palmer .15 .40
7C Joe Cronin .10 .25
7D Hank Aaron .50 1.25
7H Carl Hubbell .10 .25
7S Frank Robinson .25 .60
8C Mickey Cochrane .10 .25
8D Rollie Fingers .10 .25
8H Al Kaline .25 .60
8S Mike Schmidt .30 .75
9C Rod Carew .25 .60
9D Dennis Eckersley .15 .40
9H Rogers Hornsby .30 .75
9S George Sisler .10 .25
10C Bill Dickey .15 .40
10D Ty Cobb .50 1.25
10H Harmon Killebrew .25 .60
10S Al Simmons .10 .25
11C Josh Gibson .40 1.00
11D Joe Medwick .10 .25
11H Walter Johnson .40 1.00
11S Cy Young .40 1.00
12C Lou Gehrig .50 1.25
12D Ernie Banks .30 .75
12H Jimmie Foxx .40 1.00
12S Ozzie Smith .40 1.00
13C Jackie Robinson .60 1.50
13D Grover Alexander .30 .75
13H Carlton Fisk .25 .60
13S Tris Speaker .25 .60

1995 UC3

This 147-card standard-size set was issued by Pinnacle Brands. The cards were issued in 16-box cases with 36 packs per box and five cards per pack. The fronts feature a mix of horizontal and vertical designs. The player's photo is shown against a computer generated background. According to Pinnacle, this is the first set issued as an all-3D product. The key Rookie Card in this set is Hideo Nomo.

COMPLETE SET (147) 8.00 20.00
SUBSET CARDS HALF VALUE OF BASE CARDS
1 Frank Thomas .30 .75
2 Wil Cordero .05 .15
3 John Olerud .10 .30
4 Deion Sanders .20 .50
5 Mike Mussina .20 .50
6 Mo Vaughn .10 .30
7 Will Clark .20 .50
8 Chili Davis .10 .30
9 Jimmy Key .10 .30
10 John Valentin .05 .15
11 Tony Tarasco .05 .15
12 Alan Trammell .10 .30
13 David Cone .10 .30
14 Tim Salmon .20 .50
15 Danny Tartabull .05 .15
16 Aaron Sele .05 .15
17 Alex Fernandez .05 .15
18 Barry Bonds .75 2.00
19 Andres Galarraga .10 .30
20 Don Mattingly .75 2.00
21 Kevin Appier .10 .30
22 Paul Molitor .10 .30
23 Omar Vizquel .20 .50
24 Andy Benes .05 .15
25 Rafael Palmeiro .20 .50
26 Barry Larkin .20 .50
27 Bernie Williams .20 .50
28 Gary Sheffield .10 .30
29 Wally Joyner .10 .30
30 Wade Boggs .20 .50
31 Rico Brogna .05 .15
32 Ken Caminiti .10 .30
33 Kirby Puckett .30 .75
34 Bobby Bonilla .10 .30
35 Hal Morris .05 .15
36 Moises Alou .10 .30
37 Jim Thome .20 .50
38 Chuck Knoblauch .10 .30
39 Mike Piazza .50 1.25
40 Travis Fryman .10 .30
41 Rickey Henderson .30 .75
42 Jack McDowell .05 .15
43 Carlos Baerga .05 .15
44 Gregg Jefferies .05 .15
45 Kirk Gibson .10 .30
46 Bret Saberhagen .10 .30
47 Cecil Fielder .10 .30
48 Manny Ramirez .20 .50
49 Marquis Grissom .10 .30
50 Dave Winfield .10 .30
51 Mark McGwire .75 2.00
52 Dennis Eckersley .10 .30
53 Robin Ventura .10 .30
54 Ryan Klesko .10 .30
55 Jeff Bagwell .20 .50
56 Ozzie Smith .50 1.25
57 Brian McRae .05 .15
58 Albert Belle .10 .30
59 Darren Daulton .10 .30
60 Jose Canseco .20 .50
61 Greg Maddux .50 1.25
62 Ben McDonald .05 .15
63 Lenny Dykstra .10 .30
64 Randy Johnson .30 .75
65 Fred McGriff .20 .50
66 Ray Lankford .10 .30
67 David Justice .10 .30
68 Paul O'Neill .20 .50
69 Tony Gwynn .40 1.00
70 Matt Williams .10 .30
71 Dante Bichette .10 .30
72 Craig Biggio .20 .50
73 Ken Griffey Jr. .60 1.50
74 Juan Gonzalez .10 .30
75 Cal Ripken 1.00 2.50
76 Jay Bell .10 .30
77 Joe Carter .10 .30
78 Roberto Alomar .20 .50

79 Mark Langston .05 .15
80 Dave Hollins .05 .15
81 Tom Glavine .20 .50
82 Ivan Rodriguez .20 .50
83 Mark Whiten .05 .15
84 Raul Mondesi .10 .30
85 Kenny Lofton .10 .30
86 Ruben Sierra .10 .30
87 Mark Grace .20 .50
88 Royce Clayton .05 .15
89 Billy Ashley .05 .15
90 Larry Walker .10 .30
91 Sammy Sosa .30 .75
92 Jason Bere .05 .15
93 Bob Hamelin .05 .15
94 Greg Vaughn .05 .15
95 Roger Clemens .60 1.50
96 Scott Ruffcorn .05 .15
97 Hideo Nomo RC 1.00 2.50
98 Michael Tucker .05 .15
99 J.R. Phillips .05 .15
100 Roberto Petagine .05 .15
101 Chipper Jones .30 .75
102 Armando Benitez .05 .15
103 Orlando Miller .05 .15
104 Carlos Delgado .10 .30
105 Jeff Cirillo .05 .15
106 Shawn Green .10 .30
107 Joe Randa .10 .30
108 Vaughn Eshelman .05 .15
109 Frank Rodriguez .05 .15
110 Russ Davis .05 .15
111 Todd Hollandsworth .05 .15
112 Mark Grudzielanek RC .20 .50
113 Jose Oliva .05 .15
114 Ray Durham .10 .30
115 Alex Rodriguez .75 2.00
116 Alex Gonzalez .05 .15
117 Midre Cummings .05 .15
118 Marty Cordova .05 .15
119 John Mabry .05 .15
120 Jason Jacome .05 .15
121 Joe Vitiello .05 .15
122 Charles Johnson .10 .30
123 Cal Ripken ID .50 1.25
124 Ken Griffey Jr. ID .40 1.00
125 Frank Thomas ID .20 .50
126 Mike Piazza ID .30 .75
127 Matt Williams ID .05 .15
128 Barry Bonds ID .40 1.00
129 Greg Maddux ID .30 .75
130 Randy Johnson ID .20 .50
131 Albert Belle ID .10 .30
132 Will Clark ID .10 .30
133 Tony Gwynn ID .20 .50
134 Manny Ramirez ID .10 .30
135 Raul Mondesi ID .05 .15
136 Mo Vaughn ID .05 .15
137 Mark McGwire ID .40 1.00
138 Kirby Puckett ID .20 .50
139 Don Mattingly ID .40 1.00
140 Carlos Baerga ID .05 .15
141 Roger Clemens ID .30 .75
142 Fred McGriff ID .10 .30
143 Kenny Lofton ID .05 .15
144 Jeff Bagwell ID .10 .30
145 Larry Walker ID .05 .15
146 Joe Carter ID .05 .15
147 Rafael Palmeiro ID .10 .30

1995 UC3 Artist's Proofs

COMPLETE SET (147) 500.00 1000.00
*STARS: 8X TO 20X BASIC CARDS
*ROOKIES: 6X TO 15X BASIC CARDS
STATED ODDS 1:36

1995 UC3 Clear Shots

COMPLETE SET (12) 15.00 40.00
STATED ODDS 1:24
CS1 Alex Rodriguez 5.00 12.00
CS2 Shawn Green 1.00 2.50
CS3 Hideo Nomo 2.50 6.00
CS4 Charles Johnson 1.00 2.50
CS5 Orlando Miller .60 1.50
CS6 Billy Ashley .60 1.50
CS7 Carlos Delgado 1.00 2.50
CS8 Cliff Floyd 1.00 2.50
CS9 Chipper Jones 2.00 5.00
CS10 Alex Gonzalez .60 1.50
CS11 J.R. Phillips .60 1.50
CS12 Michael Tucker .60 1.50
PCS8 Cliff Floyd Promo .40 1.00
PCS10 Alex Gonzalez Promo .40 1.00

1995 UC3 Cyclone Squad

COMPLETE SET (20) 8.00 20.00
STATED ODDS 1:4
CS1 Frank Thomas .40 1.00
CS2 Ken Griffey Jr. .75 2.00
CS3 Jeff Bagwell .25 .60
CS4 Cal Ripken 1.25 3.00
CS5 Barry Bonds 1.00 2.50
CS6 Mike Piazza .60 1.50
CS7 Matt Williams .15 .40
CS8 Kirby Puckett .40 1.00
CS9 Jose Canseco .25 .60
CS10 Will Clark .25 .60
CS11 Don Mattingly 1.00 2.50
CS12 Albert Belle .15 .40
CS13 Tony Gwynn .50 1.25
CS14 Raul Mondesi .15 .40
CS15 Bobby Bonilla .15 .40
CS16 Rafael Palmeiro .25 .60
CS17 Fred McGriff .25 .60
CS18 Tim Salmon .25 .60
CS19 Kenny Lofton .15 .40
CS20 Joe Carter .15 .40

1995 UC3 In Motion

COMPLETE SET (10) 12.50 30.00
STATED ODDS 1:18
IM1 Cal Ripken 2.50 6.00
IM2 Ken Griffey Jr. 1.50 4.00
IM3 Frank Thomas .75 2.00
IM4 Mike Piazza 1.25 3.00
IM5 Barry Bonds 2.00 5.00
IM6 Matt Williams .30 .75
IM7 Kirby Puckett .75 2.00
IM8 Greg Maddux 1.25 3.00
IM9 Don Mattingly 2.00 5.00
IM10 Will Clark .50 1.25

1997 UD3

This 60-card standard-size super premium set was released by Upper Deck exclusively to retail outlets in mid-April,1997. Packs carried a suggested retail price of $3.99. Each pack contained three cards, one from each of the subsets. Boxes contained 24 packs. The set is broken up into three distinct 20-card subsets: Homerun Heroes (1-20) featuring Electric Wood technology, Pro-Motion (21-40) featuring Light F/X technology and Future Impact (41-60) featuring Cel Chrome technology.

COMPLETE SET (60) 15.00 40.00
1 Mark McGwire 1.50 4.00
2 Brady Anderson .25 .60
3 Ken Griffey Jr. 1.25 3.00
4 Albert Belle .25 .60
5 Andres Galarraga .25 .60
6 Juan Gonzalez .25 .60
7 Jay Buhner .25 .60
8 Mo Vaughn .25 .60
9 Barry Bonds 1.50 4.00
10 Gary Sheffield .25 .60
11 Todd Hundley .25 .60
12 Ellis Burks .25 .60
13 Ken Caminiti .25 .60
14 Vinny Castilla .25 .60
15 Sammy Sosa .60 1.50
16 Frank Thomas .60 1.50
17 Rafael Palmeiro .40 1.00
18 Mike Piazza 1.00 2.50
19 Matt Williams .25 .60
20 Eddie Murray .60 1.50
21 Roger Clemens 1.25 3.00
22 Tim Salmon .40 1.00
23 Robin Ventura .25 .60
24 Ron Gant .25 .60
25 Cal Ripken 2.00 5.00
26 Bernie Williams .40 1.00
27 Hideo Nomo .60 1.50
28 Ivan Rodriguez .40 1.00
29 John Smoltz .40 1.00
30 Paul Molitor .25 .60
31 Greg Maddux 1.00 2.50
32 Raul Mondesi .25 .60
33 Roberto Alomar .40 1.00
34 Barry Larkin .40 1.00
35 Tony Gwynn .75 2.00
36 Jim Thome .40 1.00
37 Kenny Lofton .25 .60
38 Jeff Bagwell .40 1.00
39 Ozzie Smith 1.00 2.50
40 Kirby Puckett .60 1.50
41 Andruw Jones .40 1.00
42 Vladimir Guerrero .60 1.50
43 Edgar Renteria .25 .60
44 Luis Castillo .25 .60
45 Darin Erstad .25 .60
46 Nomar Garciaparra 1.00 2.50
47 Todd Greene .25 .60
48 Jason Kendall .25 .60
49 Rey Ordonez .25 .60
50 Alex Rodriguez 1.00 2.50
51 Manny Ramirez .40 1.00
52 Todd Walker .25 .60
53 Ruben Rivera .25 .60
54 Andy Pettitte .40 1.00
55 Derek Jeter 1.50 4.00
56 Todd Hollandsworth .25 .60
57 Rocky Coppinger .25 .60
58 Scott Rolen .40 1.00
59 Jermaine Dye .25 .60
60 Chipper Jones .60 1.50

1997 UD3 Generation Next

COMPLETE SET (20) 40.00 100.00
STATED ODDS 1:11
GN1 Alex Rodriguez 5.00 12.00
GN2 Vladimir Guerrero 3.00 8.00
GN3 Luis Castillo 1.25 3.00
GN4 Rey Ordonez 1.25 3.00
GN5 Andruw Jones 2.00 5.00
GN6 Darin Erstad 1.25 3.00
GN7 Edgar Renteria 1.25 3.00
GN8 Jason Kendall 1.25 3.00
GN9 Jermaine Dye 1.25 3.00
GN10 Chipper Jones 3.00 8.00
GN11 Rocky Coppinger 1.25 3.00
GN12 Andy Pettitte 2.00 5.00
GN13 Todd Greene 1.25 3.00
GN14 Todd Hollandsworth 1.25 3.00
GN15 Derek Jeter 8.00 20.00
GN16 Ruben Rivera 1.25 3.00
GN17 Todd Walker 1.25 3.00
GN18 Nomar Garciaparra 5.00 12.00
GN19 Scott Rolen 2.00 5.00
GN20 Manny Ramirez 2.00 5.00

1997 UD3 Marquee Attraction

COMPLETE SET (10) 75.00 150.00
STATED ODDS 1:144
MA1 Ken Griffey Jr. 10.00 25.00
MA2 Mark McGwire 12.50 30.00
MA3 Juan Gonzalez 2.00 5.00
MA4 Barry Bonds 12.50 30.00
MA5 Frank Thomas 5.00 12.00
MA6 Albert Belle 2.00 5.00
MA7 Mike Piazza 8.00 20.00
MA8 Cal Ripken 15.00 40.00
MA9 Mo Vaughn 2.00 5.00
MA10 Alex Rodriguez 8.00 20.00

1997 UD3 Superb Signatures

STATED ODDS 1:1500
1 Ken Caminiti 20.00 50.00
2 Ken Griffey Jr. 100.00 175.00
3 Vladimir Guerrero 20.00 50.00
4 Derek Jeter 200.00 300.00

1998 UD3

The 1998 UD3 set (made by Upper Deck) consists of 270 cards. The three-card packs retailed for a suggested price of $3.99 each. The set contains the subsets: Future Impact-Light FX (1-30) seeded 1:12, Power Corps-Light FX (31-60) seeded 1:1, The Establishment-Light FX (61-90) seeded 1:6, Future Impact-Embossed (91-120) seeded 1:6, Power Corps-Embossed (121-150) seeded 1:4, The Establishment-Embossed (151-180) seeded 1:1,

Future Impact-Rainbow (181-210) seeded 1:1, Power Corps-Rainbow (211-240) seeded 1:12, and The Establishment-Rainbow (241-270) seeded 1:24. A Ken Griffey Jr. Power Corps Embossed Sample card was distributed to dealers prior to release. The card is easily differentiated by the bold red "SAMPLE" text running diagonally across it's back.

COMP.FUTURE FX SET (30) 25.00 60.00
COMMON FUTURE FX (1-30) .60 1.50
FUTURE IMPACT FX ODDS 1:12
COMP.POWER FX SET (30) 12.50 30.00
COMMON POWER FX (31-60) .20 .50
POWER CORPS FX ODDS 1:1
COMP.EST.FX SET (30) 20.00 50.00
COMMON EST.FX (61-90) .50 1.25
ESTABLISHMENT FX ODDS 1:6
COMP.FUTURE EMB.SET (30) 15.00 40.00
COM.FUTURE EMB. (91-120) .40 1.00
FUTURE IMPACT EMBOSSED ODDS 1:6
COMP.POWER EMB.SET (30) 20.00 50.00
COM.POWER EMB. (121-150) .30 .75
POWER CORPS EMBOSSED ODDS 1:4
COMP.EST.EMB.SET (30) 6.00 15.00
COMMON EST.EMB. (151-180) .15 .40
ESTABLISHMENT EMBOSSED ODDS 1:1
COMP.FUTURE RBW.SET (30) 8.00 20.00
COM.FUTURE RBW (181-210) .20 .50
FUTURE IMPACT RAINBOW ODDS 1:1
COMP.POWER RBW.SET (30) 40.00 100.00
COM.POWER RBW (211-240) .75 2.00
POWER CORPS RAINBOW ODDS 1:12
COMP.EST.RBW.SET (30) 50.00 120.00
COMMON EST.RBW (241-270) 1.25 3.00
ESTABLISHMENT RAINBOW ODDS 1:24
1 Travis Lee FF .60 1.50
2 A.J. Hinch FF .60 1.50
3 Mike Caruso FF .60 1.50
4 Miguel Tejada FF 1.50 4.00
5 Brad Fullmer FF .60 1.50
6 Eric Milton FF .60 1.50
7 Mark Kotsay FF .60 1.50
8 Darin Erstad FF .60 1.50
9 Magglio Ordonez FF 5.00 12.00
10 Ben Grieve FF .60 1.50
11 Brett Tomko FF .60 1.50
12 Mike Kinkade FF 1.50 4.00
13 Rolando Arrojo FF 1.50 4.00
14 Todd Helton FF 1.00 2.50
15 Scott Rolen FF 1.00 2.50
16 Bruce Chen FF .60 1.50
17 Daryle Ward FF .60 1.50
18 Jaret Wright FF .60 1.50
19 Sean Casey FF .60 1.50
20 Paul Konerko FF .60 1.50
21 Kerry Wood FF .75 2.00
22 Russell Branyan FF .60 1.50
23 Gabe Alvarez FF .60 1.50
24 Juan Encarnacion FF .60 1.50
25 Andruw Jones FF 1.00 2.50
26 Vladimir Guerrero FF 1.50 4.00
27 Eli Marrero FF .60 1.50
28 Matt Clement FF .60 1.50
29 Gary Matthews Jr. FF 2.50 6.00
30 Derrek Lee FF 1.00 2.50
31 Ken Caminiti PF .20 .50
32 Gary Sheffield PF .20 .50
33 Jay Buhner PF .20 .50
34 Ryan Klesko PF .20 .50
35 Nomar Garciaparra PF .75 2.00
36 Vinny Castilla PF .20 .50
37 Tony Clark PF .20 .50
38 Sammy Sosa PF .50 1.25
39 Tino Martinez PF .30 .75
40 Mike Piazza PF .75 2.00
41 Manny Ramirez PF .30 .75
42 Larry Walker PF .20 .50
43 Jose Cruz Jr. PF .20 .50
44 Matt Williams PF .20 .50
45 Frank Thomas PF .50 1.25
46 Jim Edmonds PF .20 .50
47 Raul Mondesi PF .20 .50
48 Alex Rodriguez PF .75 2.00
49 Albert Belle PF .20 .50
50 Mark McGwire PF 1.25 3.00
51 Tim Salmon PF .30 .75
52 Andres Galarraga PF .20 .50
53 Jeff Bagwell PF .30 .75
54 Jim Thome PF .30 .75
55 Barry Bonds PF 1.25 3.00
56 Carlos Delgado PF .20 .50
57 Mo Vaughn PF .20 .50
58 Chipper Jones PF .50 1.25
59 Juan Gonzalez PF .20 .50
60 Ken Griffey Jr. PF 1.00 2.50
61 David Cone EF .50 1.25
62 Hideo Nomo EF 1.25 3.00
63 Edgar Martinez EF .75 2.00
64 Fred McGriff EF .75 2.00
65 Cal Ripken EF 4.00 10.00
66 Todd Hundley EF .50 1.25
67 Barry Larkin EF .75 2.00
68 Dennis Eckersley EF .50 1.25
69 Randy Johnson EF 1.25 3.00
70 Paul Molitor EF .50 1.25
71 Eric Karros EF .50 1.25
72 Rafael Palmeiro EF .75 2.00
73 Chuck Knoblauch EF .50 1.25
74 Ivan Rodriguez EF .75 2.00
75 Greg Maddux EF 2.00 5.00
76 Dante Bichette EF .50 1.25
77 Brady Anderson EF .50 1.25
78 Craig Biggio EF .75 2.00
79 Derek Jeter EF 3.00 8.00
80 Roger Clemens EF 2.50 6.00
81 Roberto Alomar EF .75 2.00
82 Wade Boggs EF .75 2.00
83 Charles Johnson EF .50 1.25
84 Mark Grace EF .75 2.00
85 Kenny Lofton EF .50 1.25
86 Mike Mussina EF .75 2.00
87 Pedro Martinez EF .75 2.00
88 Curt Schilling EF .50 1.25
89 Bernie Williams EF .75 2.00
90 Tony Gwynn EF 1.50 4.00
91 Travis Lee FE .40 1.00
92 A.J. Hinch FE .40 1.00
93 Mike Caruso FE .40 1.00
94 Miguel Tejada FE 1.00 2.50
95 Brad Fullmer FE .40 1.00
96 Eric Milton FE .40 1.00
97 Mark Kotsay FE .40 1.00
98 Darin Erstad FE .40 1.00
99 Magglio Ordonez FE 3.00 8.00
100 Ben Grieve FE .40 1.00
101 Brett Tomko FE .40 1.00
102 Mike Kinkade FE 1.00 2.50
103 Rolando Arrojo FE 1.00 2.50
104 Todd Helton FE .60 1.50
105 Scott Rolen FE .60 1.50
106 Bruce Chen FE .40 1.00
107 Daryle Ward FE .40 1.00
108 Jaret Wright FE .40 1.00
109 Sean Casey FE .40 1.00
110 Paul Konerko FE .40 1.00
111 Kerry Wood FE .50 1.25
112 Russell Branyan FE .40 1.00
113 Gabe Alvarez FE .40 1.00
114 Juan Encarnacion FE .40 1.00
115 Andruw Jones FE .60 1.50
116 Vladimir Guerrero FE 1.00 2.50
117 Eli Marrero FE .40 1.00
118 Matt Clement FE .40 1.00
119 Gary Matthews Jr. FE 1.50 4.00
120 Derrek Lee FE .60 1.50
121 Ken Caminiti PE .30 .75
122 Gary Sheffield PE .30 .75
123 Jay Buhner PE .30 .75
124 Ryan Klesko PE .30 .75
125 Nomar Garciaparra PE 1.25 3.00
126 Vinny Castilla PE .30 .75
127 Tony Clark PE .30 .75
128 Sammy Sosa PE .75 2.00
129 Tino Martinez PE .50 1.25
130 Mike Piazza PE 1.25 3.00
131 Manny Ramirez PE .50 1.25
132 Larry Walker PE .30 .75
133 Jose Cruz Jr. PE .30 .75
134 Matt Williams PE .30 .75
135 Frank Thomas PE .75 2.00
136 Jim Edmonds PE .30 .75
137 Raul Mondesi PE .30 .75
138 Alex Rodriguez PE 1.25 3.00
139 Albert Belle PE .30 .75
140 Mark McGwire PE 2.00 5.00
141 Tim Salmon PE .50 1.25
142 Andres Galarraga PE .30 .75
143 Jeff Bagwell PE .50 1.25
144 Jim Thome PE .50 1.25
145 Barry Bonds PE 2.00 5.00
146 Carlos Delgado PE .30 .75
147 Mo Vaughn PE .30 .75
148 Chipper Jones PE .75 2.00
149 Juan Gonzalez PE .30 .75
150 Ken Griffey Jr. PE 1.50 4.00
151 David Cone EE .15 .40
152 Hideo Nomo EE .40 1.00
153 Edgar Martinez EE .25 .60
154 Fred McGriff EE .25 .60
155 Cal Ripken EE 1.25 3.00
156 Todd Hundley EE .15 .40
157 Barry Larkin EE .25 .60
158 Dennis Eckersley EE .15 .40
159 Randy Johnson EE .40 1.00
160 Paul Molitor EE .15 .40
161 Eric Karros EE .15 .40
162 Rafael Palmeiro EE .25 .60
163 Chuck Knoblauch EE .15 .40
164 Ivan Rodriguez EE .50 1.25
165 Greg Maddux EE .60 1.50
166 Dante Bichette EE .15 .40
167 Brady Anderson EE .15 .40
168 Craig Biggio EE .25 .60
169 Derek Jeter EE 1.00 2.50
170 Roger Clemens EE .75 2.00
171 Roberto Alomar EE .25 .60
172 Wade Boggs EE .25 .60
173 Charles Johnson EE .15 .40
174 Mark Grace EE .25 .60
175 Kenny Lofton EE .15 .40
176 Mike Mussina EE .25 .60
177 Pedro Martinez EE .25 .60
178 Curt Schilling EE .15 .40
179 Bernie Williams EE .25 .60
180 Tony Gwynn EE .50 1.25
181 Travis Lee FR .20 .50
182 A.J. Hinch FR .20 .50
183 Mike Caruso FR .20 .50
184 Miguel Tejada FR .50 1.25
185 Brad Fullmer FR .20 .50
186 Eric Milton FR .20 .50
187 Mark Kotsay FR .20 .50
188 Darin Erstad FR .20 .50
189 Magglio Ordonez FR RC 2.00 5.00
190 Ben Grieve FR .20 .50
191 Brett Tomko FR .20 .50
192 Mike Kinkade FR RC .20 .50
193 Rolando Arrojo FR RC .20 .50
194 Todd Helton FR .30 .75
195 Scott Rolen FR .30 .75
196 Bruce Chen FR .20 .50
197 Daryle Ward FR .20 .50
198 Jaret Wright FR .20 .50
199 Sean Casey FR .20 .50
200 Paul Konerko FR .20 .50
201 Kerry Wood FR .25 .60
202 Russell Branyan FR .20 .50
203 Gabe Alvarez FR .20 .50
204 Juan Encarnacion FR .20 .50
205 Andruw Jones FR .30 .75
206 Vladimir Guerrero FR .50 1.25
207 Eli Marrero FR .20 .50
208 Matt Clement FR .20 .50
209 Gary Matthews Jr. FR RC .30 .75
210 Derrek Lee FR .30 .75
211 Ken Caminiti PR .75 2.00
212 Gary Sheffield PR .75 2.00
213 Jay Buhner PR .75 2.00
214 Ryan Klesko PR .75 2.00
215 Nomar Garciaparra PR 3.00 8.00
216 Vinny Castilla PR .75 2.00
217 Tony Clark PR .75 2.00
218 Sammy Sosa PR 2.00 5.00
219 Tino Martinez PR 1.25 3.00
220 Mike Piazza PR 3.00 8.00
221 Manny Ramirez PR 1.25 3.00
222 Larry Walker PR .75 2.00
223 Jose Cruz Jr. PR .75 2.00
224 Matt Williams PR .75 2.00
225 Frank Thomas PR 2.00 5.00
226 Jim Edmonds PR .75 2.00
227 Raul Mondesi PR .75 2.00
228 Alex Rodriguez PR 3.00 8.00
229 Albert Belle PR .75 2.00
230 Mark McGwire PR 5.00 12.00
231 Tim Salmon PR 1.25 3.00
232 Andres Galarraga PR .75 2.00
233 Jeff Bagwell PR 1.25 3.00
234 Jim Thome PR 1.25 3.00
235 Barry Bonds PR 5.00 12.00
236 Carlos Delgado PR .75 2.00
237 Mo Vaughn PR .75 2.00
238 Chipper Jones PR 2.00 5.00
239 Juan Gonzalez PR .75 2.00
240 Ken Griffey Jr. PR 4.00 10.00
241 David Cone ER 1.25 3.00
242 Hideo Nomo ER 3.00 8.00
243 Edgar Martinez ER 2.00 5.00
244 Fred McGriff ER 2.00 5.00
245 Cal Ripken ER 10.00 25.00
246 Todd Hundley ER 1.25 3.00
247 Barry Larkin ER 2.00 5.00
248 Dennis Eckersley ER 1.25 3.00
249 Randy Johnson ER 3.00 8.00
250 Paul Molitor ER 1.25 3.00
251 Eric Karros ER 1.25 3.00
252 Rafael Palmeiro ER 2.00 5.00
253 Chuck Knoblauch ER 1.25 3.00
254 Ivan Rodriguez ER 2.00 5.00
255 Greg Maddux ER 5.00 12.00
256 Dante Bichette ER 1.25 3.00
257 Brady Anderson ER 1.25 3.00
258 Craig Biggio ER 2.00 5.00
259 Derek Jeter ER 8.00 20.00
260 Roger Clemens ER 6.00 15.00
261 Roberto Alomar ER 2.00 5.00
262 Wade Boggs ER 2.00 5.00
263 Charles Johnson ER 1.25 3.00
264 Mark Grace ER 2.00 5.00
265 Kenny Lofton ER 1.25 3.00
266 Mike Mussina ER 2.00 5.00
267 Pedro Martinez ER 2.00 5.00
268 Curt Schilling ER 1.25 3.00
269 Bernie Williams ER 2.00 5.00
270 Tony Gwynn ER 4.00 10.00
S1 Ken Griffey Jr. PE Sample 1.00 2.50

1998 UD3 Die Cuts

COMP.FX SET (90) 200.00 400.00
*DC'S 1-30: .5X TO 1.2X BASIC 1-30
*DC'S 31-60: 2.5X TO 6X BASIC 31-60
*DC'S 61-90: 1.25X TO 3X BASIC 61-90
1-90 PRINT RUN 2000 SERIAL #'d SETS
*DC'S 91-120: 1X TO 2.5X BASIC 91-120
*DC'S 121-150: 2.5X TO 6X BASIC 121-150
*DC'S 151-180: 5X TO 12X BASIC 151-180
91-180 PRINT RUN 1000 SERIAL #'d SETS
*DC'S 181-210: 6X TO 15X BASIC 181-210
*RC'S 181-210: 4X TO 10X BASE 181-210
*DC'S 211-240: 2X TO 5X BASIC 211-240
*DC'S 241-270: 1.25X TO 3X BASIC 241-270
181-270 PRINT RUN 100 SERIAL #'d SETS
RANDOM INSERTS IN PACKS

1998 UD3 Power Corps Blowups

COMPLETE SET (10) 25.00 60.00
35 Nomar Garciaparra 4.00 10.00
38 Sammy Sosa 2.00 5.00
40 Mike Piazza 5.00 12.00
45 Frank Thomas 2.00 5.00
48 Alex Rodriguez 4.00 10.00
50 Mark McGwire 4.00 10.00
55 Barry Bonds 2.50 6.00
58 Chipper Jones 4.00 8.00
59 Juan Gonzalez 1.50 4.00
60 Ken Griffey Jr. 3.00 8.00

1995-97 UDA Commemorative Cards

Upper Deck Authenticated, in addition to its line of certified autograph products, has produced a series of double-size (3 1/2 by 5 inch) unsigned cards commemorating various events, players and teams. These are often referred to as "C-Cards." These cards typically are serially numbered out of limited editions of 10,000, 5,000 or less, and encased in clear plastic holders. This limited edition number is noted at the end of the card description. Most of these cards are unnumbered. No complete set price is given since most of these cards are one-offs.

CR1 1995 Cal Ripken SP Champ. 2131/2131 10.00 25.00
NH1 1996 Ken Griffey Jr. National Hero/5000 8.00 20.00
NH2 1996 Cal Ripken National Hero/5000 6.00 15.00
NNO 1997 Tony Gwynn 8 bat.titles/2500 10.00 25.00
NNO 1996 Ken Griffey Jr. AS Game/2500 12.50 30.00
NNO 1996 Hideo Nomo '95 ROY/5000 6.00 15.00
NNO 1997 Ken Griffey Jr. Gold Glove/5000 8.00 20.00
NNO 1997 Jackie Robinson debut/5000 6.00 15.00
NNO 1997 Florida Marlins Champs/5000 6.00 15.00

1998 UDA Mark McGwire Die-Cuts

These two cards were sold on the Upper Deck Website. This set features two die-cut oversized Mark McGwire cards encapsulated in "PKK" snap-tite holders. One card features his 62nd homerun, while the other pictures his 70th homerun of the season.

COMPLETE SET (2) 6.00 15.00
COMMON CARD (1-2) 3.00 8.00

2000 Upper Deck 22K Gold Ken Griffey Jr.

1 Ken Griffey Jr. 15.00 40.00

2008 UD A Piece of History

COMPLETE SET (200) 15.00 40.00
COMMON CARD (1-100) .20 .50
COMMON ROOKIE (101-150) .40 1.00
COMMON HM (151-200) .20 .50
1 Brandon Webb .30 .75
2 Dan Haren .20 .50
3 Justin Upton .30 .75
4 Chris B. Young .20 .50
5 Mark Teixeira .30 .75
6 Jeff Francoeur .30 .75
7 John Smoltz .50 1.25
8 Tom Glavine .30 .75
9 Brian McCann .30 .75
10 Chipper Jones .50 1.25
11 Erik Bedard .20 .50
12 Nick Markakis .40 1.00
13 Josh Beckett .20 .50
14 David Ortiz .50 1.25
15 Manny Ramirez .50 1.25
16 Dustin Pedroia .50 1.25
17 Grady Sizemore .30 .75
18 Jonathan Papelbon .30 .75
19 Daisuke Matsuzaka .30 .75
20 Curt Schilling .30 .75
21 Alfonso Soriano .30 .75
22 Aramis Ramirez .20 .50
23 Carlos Zambrano .30 .75
24 Nick Swisher .30 .75
25 Jim Thome .30 .75
26 Ken Griffey Jr. 1.00 2.50
27 Adam Dunn .30 .75
28 Aaron Harang .20 .50
29 Matt Holliday .50 1.25
30 Troy Tulowitzki .50 1.25
31 Todd Helton .30 .75
32 Magglio Ordonez .30 .75
33 Justin Verlander .50 1.25
34 Miguel Cabrera .50 1.25
35 Gary Sheffield .20 .50
36 Ivan Rodriguez .30 .75
37 Dontrelle Willis .20 .50
38 Hanley Ramirez .30 .75
39 Andrew Miller .30 .75
40 Lance Berkman .30 .75
41 Roy Oswalt .30 .75
42 Carlos Lee .20 .50
43 Hunter Pence .30 .75
44 Alex Gordon .30 .75
45 Mark Teahen .20 .50
46 Torii Hunter .20 .50
47 Vladimir Guerrero .30 .75
48 Victor Martinez .30 .75
49 Andruw Jones .20 .50
50 James Loney .20 .50
51 Russell Martin .20 .50
52 Jeff Kent .20 .50
53 Ryan Braun .30 .75
54 Prince Fielder .30 .75
55 Joe Mauer .40 1.00
56 Justin Morneau .30 .75
57 Delmon Young .30 .75
58 Jose Reyes .30 .75
59 David Wright .30 .75
60 Carlos Beltran .30 .75
61 Johan Santana .30 .75
62 Pedro Martinez .30 .75
63 Alex Rodriguez .60 1.50
64 Derek Jeter 1.25 3.00
65 Hideki Matsui .50 1.25
66 Robinson Cano .30 .75
67 Joba Chamberlain .20 .50
68 Phil Hughes .20 .50
69 Mariano Rivera .60 1.50
70 Rich Harden .20 .50
71 Joe Blanton .20 .50
72 Cole Hamels .40 1.00
73 Ryan Howard .30 .75
74 Jimmy Rollins .30 .75
75 Chase Utley .30 .75
76 Jason Bay .30 .75
77 Freddy Sanchez .20 .50
78 Jake Peavy .20 .50
79 Greg Maddux .60 1.50
80 Trevor Hoffman .30 .75
81 Barry Zito .30 .75
82 Tim Lincecum .30 .75
83 Travis Hafner .20 .50
84 C.C. Sabathia .30 .75
85 Felix Hernandez .30 .75
86 Ichiro Suzuki .60 1.50
87 Troy Glaus .30 .75
88 Albert Pujols .60 1.50
89 Chris Carpenter .30 .75
90 Scott Kazmir .30 .75
91 Carl Crawford .30 .75
92 B.J. Upton .30 .75
93 Michael Young .20 .50
94 Josh Hamilton .30 .75
95 Vernon Wells .20 .50
96 Alex Rios .20 .50
97 Scott Rolen .30 .75
98 Frank Thomas .50 1.25
99 Chad Cordero .20 .50
100 Ryan Zimmerman .30 .75
101 Emilio Bonifacio RC 1.00 2.50
102 Bill Murphy (RC) .40 1.00
103 Billy Buckner (RC) .40 1.00
104 Brandon Jones RC 1.00 2.50
105 Clint Sammons (RC) .40 1.00
106 Clay Buchholz (RC) .60 1.50
107 Kevin Hart (RC) .40 1.00
108 Lance Broadway (RC) .40 1.00
109 Donny Lucy (RC) .40 1.00
110 Heath Phillips RC .60 1.50
111 Ryan Hanigan RC .60 1.50
112 Joey Votto (RC) 3.00 8.00
113 Joe Koshansky (RC) .40 1.00
114 Josh Newman RC .60 1.50
115 Seth Smith (RC) .40 1.00
116 Harvey Garcia (RC) .40 1.00
117 Chris Seddon (RC) .40 1.00
118 Josh Anderson (RC) .40 1.00
119 Troy Patton (RC) .40 1.00
120 Felipe Paulino RC .60 1.50
121 J.R. Towles RC .60 1.50
122 Luke Hochevar RC .60 1.50
123 Chin-Lung Hu (RC) .40 1.00
124 Jonathan Meloan RC .60 1.50
125 Sam Fuld RC 1.25 3.00
126 Mitch Stetter RC .60 1.50
127 Jose Morales (RC) .40 1.00
128 Carlos Muniz RC .60 1.50
129 Alberto Gonzalez RC .60 1.50
130 Ian Kennedy RC 1.00 2.50
131 Ross Ohlendorf RC .60 1.50
132 Jonathan Albaladejo RC .60 1.50
133 Daric Barton (RC) .40 1.00
134 Jerry Blevins RC .60 1.50
135 Dave Davidson RC .60 1.50
136 Nyjer Morgan (RC) .40 1.00
137 Steve Pearce RC 2.00 5.00
138 Colt Morton RC .60 1.50
139 Eugenio Velez RC .40 1.00
140 Erick Threets (RC) .40 1.00
141 Bronson Sardinha (RC) .40 1.00
142 Wladimir Balentien (RC) .40 1.00
143 Jeff Clement (RC) .60 1.50
144 Rob Johnson (RC) .40 1.00
145 Jeff Ridgway RC .60 1.50
146 Justin Ruggiano RC .60 1.50
147 Luis Mendoza (RC) .40 1.00
148 Bill White RC .40 1.00
149 Ross Detwiler RC .60 1.50
150 Justin Maxwell RC .40 1.00
151 Fall of the Berlin Wall .20 .50
152 Wright Brothers 1st Flight .20 .50
153 Signing of Declaration of Independence .20 .50
154 Columbus Discovers America .20 .50
155 First Space Shuttle launch .20 .50
156 Hawaii becomes 50th state .20 .50
157 Statue of Liberty given to U.S. .20 .50
158 Gettysburg Address .20 .50
159 Completion of Transcontinental Railroad .20 .50
160 Opening of Panama Canal .20 .50
161 U.S. enters World War 1 .20 .50
162 Treaty of Versailles .20 .50
163 Television invented .20 .50
164 Geneva Summit .20 .50
165 Woodstock .20 .50
166 Invention of Cotton Gin .20 .50
167 Eiffel Tower .20 .50
168 Suez Canal opens .20 .50
169 New York City Subway opens .20 .50
170 Polio Vaccine invented .20 .50
171 Bell X-1 Breaks Sound Barrier .20 .50
172 USS Enterprise Carrier launched .20 .50
173 Hubble Telescope launches .20 .50
174 N.A.T.O. created .20 .50
175 Sputnik launched by Russia .20 .50
176 U.S.S.R. Crumbles .20 .50
177 Boston Tea Party .20 .50
178 Paul Revere's Ride .20 .50
179 Civil Rights Act Passes .20 .50
180 Hindenburg blows up .20 .50
181 Franklin discovers electricity .20 .50
182 Creation of the Internet .20 .50
183 1st World's Fair - 1851 London .20 .50
184 Pope John Paul II .20 .50
185 1st Heart Transplant .20 .50
186 California Gold Rush .20 .50
187 Creation of the personal computer .20 .50
188 Louisiana Purchase .20 .50
189 1st Dictionary published .20 .50
190 Steam Engine invented .20 .50
191 History of Nobel Prize .20 .50
192 Liberty Bell .20 .50
193 International Space Station .20 .50
194 Human Genome Project .20 .50
195 The Supreme Court .20 .50
196 Lewis and Clark .20 .50
197 Battle of the Alamo .20 .50
198 The creation of baseball .20 .50
199 Juan Ponce De Leon .20 .50
200 Jamestown - 1607 .20 .50

2008 UD A Piece of History Gold

*GOLD 1-100: 1.5X TO 4X BASIC 1-100
*GOLD RC 101-150: 1.5X TO 4X BASIC RC
*GOLD HM 151-200: 1.5X TO 4X BASIC HM
RANDOM INSERTS IN PACKS
STATED PRINT RUN 75 SER.#'d SETS

2008 UD A Piece of History Red

*RED 1-100: 1X TO 2.5X BASIC 1-100
*RED RC 101-150: 1X TO 2.5X BASIC RC
*RED HM 151-200: 1X TO 2.5X BASIC HM
RANDOM INSERTS IN PACKS
STATED PRINT RUN 149 SER.#'d SETS

2008 UD A Piece of History Silver

*SILVER 1-100: .6X TO 1.5X BASIC 1-100
*SILVER RC 101-150: .6X TO 1.5X BASIC RC
*SILVER HM 151-200: .6X TO 1.5X BASIC HM
RANDOM INSERTS IN PACKS

2008 UD A Piece of History Rookie Autographs

OVERALL AU ODDS 1:16
PRINT RUNS B/W 50-499 COPIES PER
101 Emilio Bonifacio/499 15.00 40.00
102 Bill Murphy/499 3.00 8.00
103 Billy Buckner/149 4.00 10.00
104 Brandon Jones/499 3.00 8.00
105 Clint Sammons/499 3.00 8.00
106 Clay Buchholz/199 8.00 20.00
107 Kevin Hart/499 3.00 8.00
108 Lance Broadway/99 4.00 10.00
111 Ryan Hanigan/499 3.00 8.00
112 Joey Votto/50 25.00 60.00
113 Joe Koshansky/499 3.00 8.00
114 Josh Newman/499 3.00 8.00
115 Seth Smith/499 3.00 8.00
116 Harvey Garcia/499 3.00 8.00
117 Chris Seddon/459 3.00 8.00
118 Josh Anderson/499 3.00 8.00
119 Troy Patton/499 4.00 10.00
120 Felipe Paulino/499 3.00 8.00
121 J.R. Towles/499 4.00 10.00
123 Chin-Lung Hu/99 4.00 10.00
127 Jose Morales/499 3.00 8.00
129 Alberto Gonzalez/499 4.00 10.00
130 Ian Kennedy/199 3.00 8.00
131 Ross Ohlendorf/499 4.00 10.00
132 Jonathan Albaladejo/499 3.00 8.00
133 Daric Barton/99 4.00 10.00
134 Jerry Blevins/499 3.00 8.00
135 Dave Davidson/499 3.00 8.00
136 Nyjer Morgan/499 3.00 8.00
137 Steve Pearce/499 6.00 15.00
138 Colt Morton/499 3.00 8.00
139 Eugenio Velez/499 3.00 8.00
141 Bronson Sardinha/499 3.00 8.00
142 Wladimir Balentien/199 4.00 10.00
144 Rob Johnson/499 3.00 8.00
146 Justin Ruggiano/499 3.00 8.00
147 Luis Mendoza/499 3.00 8.00
148 Bill White/499 3.00 8.00
149 Ross Detwiler/499 3.00 8.00
150 Justin Maxwell/499 4.00 10.00

2008 UD A Piece of History Rookie Autographs Blue

*BLUE: .6X TO 1.5X BASIC
OVERALL AU ODDS 1:16
PRINT RUNS B/WN 15-50 COPIES PER
NO PRICING ON QTY 25 OR LESS

2008 UD A Piece of History Rookie Autographs Gold

*GOLD: .6X TO 1.5X BASIC
OVERALL AU ODDS 1:16
PRINT RUNS B/WN 20-75 COPIES PER
NO PRICING ON QTY 25 OR LESS
106 Clay Buchholz/50 15.00 40.00

2008 UD A Piece of History Rookie Autographs Red

*RED: .6X TO 1.5X BASIC
OVERALL AU ODDS 1:16
PRINT RUNS B/WN 25-99 COPIES PER
NO PRICING ON QTY 25 OR LESS

2008 UD A Piece of History A Piece of Hollywood Memorablia

STATED ODDS 1:16
1 Amanda Bynes Costume 6.00 15.00
2 Mel Gibson Shirt 5.00 12.00
3 Brad Pitt Shirt 5.00 12.00
4 George Clooney Jacket 4.00 10.00
5 Denzell Washington Jacket 4.00 10.00
6 Jamie Foxx Shirt 4.00 10.00
7 Kevin Costner Shirt 5.00 12.00
8 Jack Nicholson Shirt 5.00 12.00
9 Mike Myers Pants 6.00 15.00
10 Dana Carvey Jersey 6.00 15.00
11 Phillip Seymour Hoffman Sweater 4.00 10.00
12 Jim Carrey Shirt 4.00 10.00
13 Scarlett Johanson T-Shirt 6.00 15.00
14 Demi Moore Jacket 4.00 10.00
15 C.Reeve Cape 12.50 30.00
16 M.Gibson Shoe SP 20.00 50.00
17 D.Washington Hat SP 10.00 25.00
18 Jim Carrey Pants 4.00 10.00
19 George Clooney Pants 4.00 10.00
20 S.Johanson U-Shirt SP 10.00 25.00
21 Phillip Seymour Hoffman Jacket 12.50 30.00
22 Denzell Washington Pants 4.00 10.00
23 Mel Gibson Pants 5.00 12.00
24 Woody Harrelson Jackey 4.00 10.00
25 Robin Williams Shirt 4.00 10.00
26 Jennifer Garner Pajamas 5.00 12.00
27 Tom Cruise Shirt 6.00 15.00

2008 UD A Piece of History Box Score Memories

RANDOM INSERTS IN PACKS
STATED PRINT RUN 699 SER.#'d SETS
*BLUE: .6X TO 1.5X BASIC
BLUE RANDOMLY INSERTED
BLUE PRINT RUN 75 SER.#'d SETS
*COPPER: .6X TO 1.5X BASIC
COPPER RANDOMLY INSERTED
COPPER PRINT RUN 99 SER.#'d SETS
*RED: .5X TO 1.2X BASIC
RED RANDOMLY INSERTED
RED PRINT RUN 149 SER.#'d SETS
SILVER RANDOMLY INSERTED
SILVER PRINT RUN 25 SER.#'d SETS
NO SILVER PRICING DUE TO SCARCITY
BSM1 Chris B. Young .50 1.25
BSM2 Stephen Drew .50 1.25
BSM3 Chipper Jones 1.25 3.00
BSM4 Mark Teixeira .75 2.00
BSM5 Jeff Francoeur .75 2.00
BSM6 David Ortiz 1.25 3.00
BSM7 Dustin Pedroia 1.25 3.00
BSM8 Manny Ramirez 1.25 3.00
BSM9 Mike Lowell .50 1.25
BSM10 Alfonso Soriano .75 2.00
BSM11 Aramis Ramirez .50 1.25
BSM12 Jim Thome .75 2.00
BSM13 Ken Griffey Jr. 2.50 6.00
BSM14 Adam Dunn .75 2.00
BSM15 Grady Sizemore .75 2.00
BSM16 Travis Hafner .50 1.25
BSM17 Victor Martinez .75 2.00
BSM18 Matt Holliday 1.25 3.00
BSM19 Todd Helton .75 2.00
BSM20 Troy Tulowitzki 1.25 3.00
BSM21 Ivan Rodriguez .75 2.00
BSM22 Miguel Cabrera 1.50 4.00
BSM23 Magglio Ordonez .75 2.00
BSM24 Hanley Ramirez .75 2.00
BSM25 Hunter Pence .75 2.00
BSM26 Lance Berkman .75 2.00
BSM27 Carlos Lee .50 1.25
BSM28 Alex Gordon .75 2.00
BSM29 Vladimir Guerrero .75 2.00
BSM30 Andruw Jones .50 1.25
BSM31 Jeff Kent .50 1.25
BSM32 Ryan Braun .75 2.00
BSM33 Prince Fielder .75 2.00
BSM34 Joe Mauer 1.00 2.50
BSM35 Justin Morneau .75 2.00
BSM36 David Wright .75 2.00
BSM37 Carlos Beltran .75 2.00
BSM38 Jose Reyes .75 2.00
BSM39 Derek Jeter 1.50 4.00
BSM40 Alex Rodriguez 1.50 4.00
BSM41 Hideki Matsui 1.25 3.00
BSM42 Bobby Abreu .50 1.25
BSM43 Chase Utley .75 2.00
BSM44 Ryan Howard .75 2.00
BSM45 Jimmy Rollins .75 2.00
BSM46 Jason Bay .75 2.00
BSM47 Khalil Greene .50 1.25
BSM48 Ichiro Suzuki 1.50 4.00
BSM49 Albert Pujols 1.50 4.00
BSM50 Frank Thomas 1.25 3.00

2008 UD A Piece of History Box Score Memories Jersey Red

OVERALL GU ODDS 1:8
BSM1 Chris B. Young 3.00 8.00
BSM2 Stephen Drew 3.00 8.00
BSM3 Chipper Jones 3.00 8.00
BSM4 Mark Teixeira 3.00 8.00
BSM5 Jeff Francoeur 3.00 8.00
BSM6 David Ortiz 4.00 10.00
BSM7 Dustin Pedroia 3.00 8.00
BSM8 Manny Ramirez 3.00 8.00
BSM10 Alfonso Soriano 3.00 8.00
BSM11 Aramis Ramirez 3.00 8.00
BSM12 Jim Thome 3.00 8.00
BSM16 Travis Hafner 3.00 8.00
BSM17 Victor Martinez 3.00 8.00
BSM18 Matt Holliday 3.00 8.00
BSM19 Todd Helton 3.00 8.00
BSM20 Troy Tulowitzki 3.00 8.00
BSM21 Ivan Rodriguez 3.00 8.00
BSM23 Magglio Ordonez 3.00 8.00
BSM24 Hanley Ramirez 3.00 8.00
BSM25 Hunter Pence 4.00 10.00
BSM26 Lance Berkman 3.00 8.00
BSM27 Carlos Lee 3.00 8.00
BSM28 Alex Gordon 4.00 10.00
BSM29 Vladimir Guerrero 3.00 8.00
BSM31 Jeff Kent 3.00 8.00
BSM33 Prince Fielder 4.00 10.00
BSM34 Joe Mauer 3.00 8.00
BSM35 Justin Morneau 3.00 8.00
BSM37 Carlos Beltran 3.00 8.00
BSM38 Jose Reyes 3.00 8.00
BSM39 Derek Jeter 8.00 20.00
BSM40 Alex Rodriguez 6.00 15.00
BSM42 Bobby Abreu 3.00 8.00
BSM45 Jimmy Rollins 3.00 8.00
BSM46 Jason Bay 3.00 8.00
BSM47 Khalil Greene 3.00 8.00
BSM49 Albert Pujols 6.00 15.00
BSM50 Frank Thomas 4.00 10.00

2008 UD A Piece of History Box Score Memories Jersey Gold

*GOLD: .5X TO 1.2X BASIC
OVERALL GU ODDS 1:8
STATED PRINT RUN 75 SER.#'d SETS
BSM14 Adam Dunn 4.00 10.00
BSM15 Grady Sizemore 4.00 10.00
BSM22 Miguel Cabrera 4.00 10.00
BSM32 Ryan Braun 6.00 15.00
BSM43 Chase Utley 4.00 10.00

2008 UD A Piece of History Box Score Memories Jersey Autographs

OVERALL AUTO ODDS 1:16
PRINT RUNS B/WN 10-99 COPIES PER
NO PRICING ON QTY 25 OR LESS
BSM5 Jeff Francoeur/99 12.50 30.00
BSM11 Aramis Ramirez/99 10.00 25.00
BSM16 Travis Hafner/50 6.00 15.00
BSM17 Victor Martinez/99 6.00 15.00
BSM20 Troy Tulowitzki/99 10.00 25.00
BSM24 Hanley Ramirez/50 12.50 30.00
BSM27 Carlos Lee/99 10.00 25.00
BSM46 Jason Bay/99 6.00 15.00

2008 UD A Piece of History Cut From the Same Cloth

RANDOM INSERTS IN PACKS
STATED PRINT RUN 799 SER.#'d SETS
BLUE RANDOMLY INSERTED
BLUE PRINT RUN 25 SER.#'d SETS
NO BLUE PRICING DUE TO SCARCITY
*PEWTER: .6X TO 1.5X BASIC
PEWTER RANDOMLY INSERTED
PEWTER PRINT RUN 75 SER.#'d SETS
*RED: .6X TO 1.5X BASIC
RED RANDOMLY INSERTED
RED PRINT RUN 99 SER.#'d SETS
*SILVER: .5X TO 1.2X BASIC
SILVER RANDOMLY INSERTED
SILVER PRINT RUN 149 SER.#'d SETS
BB Jeremy Bonderman/Joe Blanton .40 1.00
BP A.J. Burnett/Jake Peavy .40 1.00
BR Carlos Beltran/Jose Reyes .60 1.50
BS Mark Buehrle/Johan Santana .60 1.50
BV Buehrle/Verlander 1.00 2.50
BZ R.Zimmerman/R.Braun .60 1.50
CB Carlos Beltran/Carlos Beltran .60 1.50
CH Trevor Hoffman/Chad Cordero .60 1.50
CS Curt Schilling/Curt Schilling .60 1.50
DD Johnny Damon/Johnny Damon .60 1.50
FT Frank Thomas/Frank Thomas 1.00 2.50
GD K.Griffey Jr./A.Dunn 2.00 5.00
GM G.Maddux/G.Maddux 1.25 3.00
GO Magglio Ordonez/Curtis Granderson .60 1.50
GT K.Griffey Jr./F.Thomas 2.00 5.00
HH Todd Helton/Matt Holliday 1.00 2.50
HJ Matt Holliday/Andruw Jones 1.00 2.50
HL Francisco Liriano/Cole Hamels .75 2.00
HM G.Maddux/T.Hudson 1.25 3.00
HP Jake Peavy/Dan Haren .40 1.00
HS John Smoltz/Tim Hudson 1.00 2.50
HY Michael Young/J.J. Hardy .40 1.00
HZ Carlos Zambrano/Felix Hernandez .60 1.50
JB Josh Beckett/Josh Beckett .40 1.00
JD J.Varitek/D.Matsuzaka 1.00 2.50
JH Andruw Jones/Torii Hunter .40 1.00
JS Randy Johnson/Johan Santana 1.00 2.50
JT Jim Thome/Jim Thome .60 1.50
JY D.Jeter/M.Young 2.50 6.00
JZ Chipper Jones/Ryan Zimmerman 1.00 2.50
KS Johan Santana/Scott Kazmir .60 1.50
LF Derrek Lee/Prince Fielder .60 1.50
MA Joe Mauer/Russell Martin .75 2.00
MJ M.Rivera/J.Papelbon 1.25 3.00
MK Justin Morneau/Jason Kubel .60 1.50
MM Victor Martinez/Joe Mauer .75 2.00

MS C.Schilling/D.Matsuzaka .60 1.50
OF David Ortiz/Prince Fielder 1.00 2.50
OG Carlos Guillen/Magglio Ordonez .60 1.50
OP D.Ortiz/A.Pujols 1.25 3.00
OR Manny Ramirez/David Ortiz 1.00 2.50
OV Jason Varitek/David Ortiz 1.00 2.50
PG V.Guerrero/A.Pujols 1.25 3.00
PH Roy Halladay/Jake Peavy .60 1.50
PM Pedro Martinez/Pedro Martinez .60 1.50
PO Roy Oswalt/Jake Peavy .60 1.50
PS Curt Schilling/Jonathan Papelbon .60 1.50
PV Jason Varitek/Jorge Posada 1.00 2.50
RJ Randy Johnson/Randy Johnson 1.00 2.50
RL Derrek Lee/Aramis Ramirez .40 1.00
RP BJ Ryan/Jonathan Papelbon .60 1.50
RR Jose Reyes/Hanley Ramirez .60 1.50
RU Jimmy Rollins/Chase Utley .60 1.50
SH Travis Hafner/Grady Sizemore .60 1.50
SL Francisco Liriano/Johan Santana .60 1.50
SM Pedro Martinez/Curt Schilling .60 1.50
TR Roy Halladay/Tim Hudson .60 1.50
UU Chase Utley/Dan Uggla .60 1.50
VR Manny Ramirez/Jason Varitek 1.00 2.50
WS C.C. Sabathia/Dontrelle Willis .60 1.50

2008 UD A Piece of History Cut From the Same Cloth Dual Jersey

OVERALL GU ODDS 1:8
PRINT RUNS B/WN 33-99 COPIES PER
BB Jeremy Bonderman 4.00 10.00
Joe Blanton/99
BP A.J. Burnett 5.00 12.00
Jake Peavy/99
BR Carlos Beltran 5.00 12.00
Jose Reyes/99
BS Mark Buehrle 6.00 15.00
Johan Santana/99
BV Mark Buehrle 6.00 15.00
Justin Verlander/33
BZ Zimmerman/Braun/99 8.00 20.00
CB Carlos Beltran 4.00 10.00
Carlos Beltran/70
CH Trevor Hoffman 4.00 10.00
Chad Cordero/99
CS Curt Schilling 5.00 12.00
Curt Schilling/99
DD Johnny Damon 4.00 10.00
Johnny Damon/99
FT Frank Thomas 6.00 15.00
Frank Thomas/99
GM Maddux/Maddux/99 8.00 20.00
GO Magglio Ordonez 5.00 12.00
Curtis Granderson/99
HH Todd Helton 5.00 12.00
Matt Holliday/99
HJ Matt Holliday 5.00 12.00
Andruw Jones/99
HL Francisco Liriano 5.00 12.00
Cole Hamels/99
HM Maddux/Hudson/99 8.00 20.00
HP Jake Peavy 5.00 12.00
Dan Haren/99
HS John Smoltz 5.00 12.00
Tim Hudson/99
HY Michael Young 4.00 10.00
J.J. Hardy/99
HZ Carlos Zambrano 5.00 12.00
Felix Hernandez/99
JB Josh Beckett 5.00 12.00
Josh Beckett/99
JD Varitek/Matsuzaka/99 10.00 25.00
JH Andruw Jones 4.00 10.00
Torii Hunter/99
JS Randy Johnson 6.00 15.00
Johan Santana/99
JT Jim Thome 5.00 12.00
Jim Thome/99
JY Jeter/Young/99 12.50 30.00
JZ Chipper Jones 5.00 12.00
Ryan Zimmerman/99
LF Derrek Lee 6.00 15.00
Prince Fielder/99
MA Joe Mauer 5.00 12.00
Russell Martin/99
MJ Rivera/Papelbon/99 8.00 20.00
MK Justin Morneau 5.00 12.00
Jason Kubel/99
MM Victor Martinez 5.00 12.00
Joe Mauer/99
MS Schilling/Matsuzaka/99 10.00 25.00
OF David Ortiz 6.00 15.00
Prince Fielder/99
OG Carlos Guillen 5.00 12.00
Magglio Ordonez/99
OP Ortiz/Pujols/99 12.50 30.00
OR Manny/Ortiz/99 8.00 20.00
OV Varitek/Ortiz/99 8.00 20.00
PG Vlad/Pujols/99 10.00 25.00
PH Roy Halladay 5.00 12.00
Jake Peavy/99
PM Pedro Martinez 5.00 12.00
Pedro Martinez/99
PO Roy Oswalt 5.00 12.00
Jake Peavy/99
PS Curt Schilling 5.00 12.00
Jonathan Papelbon/99
PV Jason Varitek 6.00 15.00
Jorge Posada/99
RJ Randy Johnson 6.00 15.00
Randy Johnson/99
RL Derrek Lee 4.00 10.00
Aramis Ramirez/99
RP BJ Ryan 5.00 12.00
Jonathan Papelbon/99
RR Jose Reyes 5.00 12.00
Hanley Ramirez/99
RU Jimmy Rollins 5.00 12.00
Chase Utley/99
SH Travis Hafner 5.00 12.00
Grady Sizemore/99
SL Francisco Liriano 6.00 15.00
Johan Santana/99
SM Pedro Martinez 5.00 12.00
Curt Schilling/99
TR Tim Hudson 4.00 10.00
Roy Halladay/99
UU Chase Utley 5.00 12.00
Dan Uggla/99
VR Manny/Varitek/99 8.00 20.00
WS C.C. Sabathia 4.00 10.00
Dontrelle Willis/99

2008 UD A Piece of History Franchise History

RANDOM INSERTS IN PACKS
STATED PRINT RUN 699 SER.#'d SETS
*BLUE: .6X TO 1.5X BASIC
BLUE RANDOMLY INSERTED
BLUE PRINT RUN 75 SER.#'d SETS
*COPPER: .6X TO 1.5X BASIC
COPPER RANDOMLY INSERTED
COPPER PRINT RUN 99 SER.#'d SETS
*RED: .5X TO 1.2X BASIC
RED RANDOMLY INSERTED
RED PRINT RUN 149 SER.#'d SETS
SILVER RANDOMLY INSERTED
SILVER PRINT RUN 25 SER.#'d SETS
NO SILVER PRICING DUE TO SCARCITY
FH1 Justin Upton .75 2.00
FH2 Randy Johnson 1.25 3.00
FH3 Mark Teixeira .75 2.00
FH4 John Smoltz 1.25 3.00
FH5 Chipper Jones 1.25 3.00
FH6 Jonathan Papelbon .75 2.00
FH7 Manny Ramirez 1.25 3.00
FH8 Daisuke Matsuzaka .75 2.00
FH9 Josh Beckett .50 1.25
FH10 David Ortiz 1.25 3.00
FH11 Alfonso Soriano .75 2.00
FH12 Jim Thome .75 2.00
FH13 Adam Dunn .75 2.00
FH14 Ken Griffey Jr. 2.50 6.00
FH15 C.C. Sabathia .75 2.00
FH16 Grady Sizemore .75 2.00
FH17 Travis Hafner .50 1.25
FH18 Matt Holliday 1.25 3.00
FH19 Troy Tulowitzki 1.25 3.00
FH20 Magglio Ordonez .75 2.00
FH21 Ivan Rodriguez .75 2.00
FH22 Miguel Cabrera 1.25 3.00
FH23 Hanley Ramirez .75 2.00
FH24 Hunter Pence .75 2.00
FH25 Lance Berkman .75 2.00
FH26 Vladimir Guerrero .75 2.00
FH27 Andruw Jones .50 1.25
FH28 Prince Fielder .75 2.00
FH29 Ryan Braun .75 2.00
FH30 Joe Mauer 1.00 2.50
FH31 Carlos Beltran .75 2.00
FH32 Pedro Martinez .75 2.00
FH33 Johan Santana .75 2.00
FH34 Jose Reyes .75 2.00
FH35 David Wright .75 2.00
FH36 Joba Chamberlain .50 1.25
FH37 Hideki Matsui 1.25 3.00
FH38 Alex Rodriguez 1.50 4.00
FH39 Derek Jeter 3.00 8.00
FH40 Jimmy Rollins .75 2.00
FH41 Ryan Howard .75 2.00
FH42 Chase Utley .75 2.00
FH43 Greg Maddux 1.50 4.00
FH44 Jake Peavy .50 1.25
FH45 Trevor Hoffman .75 2.00
FH46 Ichiro Suzuki 1.50 4.00
FH47 Felix Hernandez .75 2.00
FH48 Albert Pujols 1.50 4.00
FH49 Frank Thomas 1.25 3.00
FH50 Vernon Wells .50 1.25

2008 UD A Piece of History Franchise History Jersey Red

OVERALL GU ODDS 1:8
FH1 Justin Upton 4.00 10.00
FH2 Randy Johnson 4.00 10.00
FH3 Mark Teixeira 3.00 8.00
FH4 John Smoltz 3.00 8.00
FH5 Chipper Jones 3.00 8.00
FH6 Jonathan Papelbon 3.00 8.00
FH7 Manny Ramirez 3.00 8.00
FH8 Daisuke Matsuzaka 6.00 15.00
FH9 Josh Beckett 3.00 8.00
FH10 David Ortiz 4.00 10.00
FH11 Alfonso Soriano 3.00 8.00
FH12 Jim Thome 3.00 8.00
FH13 Adam Dunn 3.00 8.00
FH14 Ken Griffey Jr. 5.00 12.00
FH15 C.C. Sabathia 3.00 8.00
FH16 Grady Sizemore 3.00 8.00
FH17 Travis Hafner 3.00 8.00
FH18 Matt Holliday 3.00 8.00
FH19 Troy Tulowitzki 3.00 8.00
FH20 Magglio Ordonez 3.00 8.00
FH21 Ivan Rodriguez 3.00 8.00
FH22 Miguel Cabrera 3.00 8.00
FH23 Hanley Ramirez 3.00 8.00
FH24 Hunter Pence 4.00 10.00
FH25 Lance Berkman 3.00 8.00
FH26 Vladimir Guerrero 3.00 8.00
FH27 Andruw Jones 3.00 8.00
FH28 Prince Fielder 4.00 10.00
FH29 Ryan Braun 5.00 12.00
FH30 Joe Mauer 3.00 8.00
FH31 Carlos Beltran 3.00 8.00
FH32 Pedro Martinez 3.00 8.00
FH33 Johan Santana 4.00 10.00
FH34 Jose Reyes 3.00 8.00
FH36 Joba Chamberlain 3.00 8.00
FH38 Alex Rodriguez 6.00 15.00
FH39 Derek Jeter 8.00 20.00
FH40 Jimmy Rollins 3.00 8.00
FH42 Chase Utley 3.00 8.00
FH43 Greg Maddux 5.00 12.00
FH44 Jake Peavy 3.00 8.00
FH45 Trevor Hoffman 3.00 8.00
FH47 Felix Hernandez 3.00 8.00
FH48 Albert Pujols 6.00 15.00
FH49 Frank Thomas 4.00 10.00
FH50 Vernon Wells 3.00 8.00

2008 UD A Piece of History Franchise History Jersey Gold

*GOLD: .5X TO 1.2X BASIC
OVERALL GU ODDS 1:8
STATED PRINT RUN 99 SER.#'d SETS

2008 UD A Piece of History Franchise History Jersey Autographs

OVERALL AUTO ODDS 1:16
PRINT RUNS B/WN 5-99 COPIES PER
NO PRICING ON QTY 25 OR LESS
FH6 Jonathan Papelbon/99 6.00 15.00
FH17 Travis Hafner/50 6.00 15.00
FH19 Troy Tulowitzki/50 12.50 30.00
FH23 Hanley Ramirez/50 12.50 30.00
FH47 Felix Hernandez/75 12.50 30.00

2008 UD A Piece of History Franchise Members Triple

RANDOM INSERTS IN PACKS
STATED PRINT RUN 799 SER.#'d SETS
BLUE RANDOMLY INSERTED
BLUE PRINT RUN 25 SER.#'d SETS
NO BLUE PRICING DUE TO SCARCITY
*PEWTER: .6X TO 1.5X BASIC
PEWTER RANDOMLY INSERTED
PEWTER PRINT RUN 75 SER.#'d SETS
*RED: .6X TO 1.5X BASIC
RED RANDOMLY INSERTED
RED PRINT RUN 99 SER.#'d SETS
*SILVER: .5X TO 1.2X BASIC
SILVER RANDOMLY INSERTED
SILVER PRINT RUN 149 SER.#'d SETS
1 John Smoltz 1.00 2.50
Tim Hudson
Tom Glavine
2 Josh Beckett .60 1.50
Daisuke Matsuzaka
Curt Schilling
3 David Ortiz 1.00 2.50
Manny Ramirez
Jason Varitek
4 Griffey/F.Thomas/Thome 2.00 5.00
5 Grady Sizemore .60 1.50
Travis Hafner
Victor Martinez
6 Matt Holliday 1.00 2.50
Carlos Lee
Jason Bay
7 Guillen/Ordonez/Cabrera 1.00 2.50
8 Roy Oswalt .60 1.50
Jake Peavy
Dan Haren
9 Jered Weaver .60 1.50
Vladimir Guerrero
Casey Kotchman
10 Russell Martin .75 2.00
Joe Mauer
Brian McCann
11 Fielder/Braun/Hardy .60 1.50
12 Joe Mauer .75 2.00
Justin Morneau
Joe Nathan
13 Johan Santana .60 1.50
Pedro Martinez
Billy Wagner
14 Jeter/Reyes/Hanley 2.50 6.00
15 Jeter/Cano/Giambi 2.50 6.00
16 Peavy/Maddux/Hoffman 1.25 3.00
17 King Felix/Verlander/Harden 1.00 2.50
18 Chris Carpenter 1.00 2.50
Randy Johnson
Cole Hamels
19 Pujols/Glaus/Duncan 1.25 3.00
20 Roy Halladay .60 1.50
A.J. Burnett
Vernon Wells

2008 UD A Piece of History Franchise Members Triple Jersey

OVERALL GU ODDS 1:8
STATED PRINT RUN 99 SER.#'d SETS
1 John Smoltz 5.00 12.00
Tim Hudson
Tom Glavine
2 Beckett/Matsuzaka/Schilling 12.50 30.00
3 Ortiz/Manny/Varitek 10.00 25.00
5 Grady Sizemore 5.00 12.00
Travis Hafner
Victor Martinez
6 Matt Holliday 5.00 12.00
Carlos Lee
Jason Bay
7 Carlos Guillen 5.00 12.00
Magglio Ordonez
Miguel Cabrera
8 Roy Oswalt 5.00 12.00
Jake Peavy
Dan Haren
9 Jered Weaver 5.00 12.00
Vladimir Guerrero
Casey Kotchman
10 Russell Martin 5.00 12.00
Joe Mauer
Brian McCann
11 Fielder/Braun/Hardy 8.00 20.00
12 Joe Mauer 5.00 12.00
Justin Morneau
Joe Nathan
13 Johan Santana 6.00 15.00
Pedro Martinez
Billy Wagner
14 Jeter/Reyes/Hanley 12.50 30.00
15 Jeter/Cano/Giambi 15.00 40.00
16 Peavy/Maddux/Hoffman 8.00 20.00
17 Felix Hernandez 5.00 12.00
Justin Verlander
Rich Harden
18 Chris Carpenter 6.00 15.00
Randy Johnson
Cole Hamels
19 Pujols/Glaus/Duncan 10.00 25.00
20 Roy Halladay 4.00 10.00
A.J. Burnett
Vernon Wells

2008 UD A Piece of History Franchise Members Quad

RANDOM INSERTS IN PACKS
STATED PRINT RUN 799 SER.#'d SETS
BLUE RANDOMLY INSERTED
BLUE PRINT RUN 25 SER.#'d SETS
NO BLUE PRICING DUE TO SCARCITY
*PEWTER: .6X TO 1.5X BASIC
PEWTER RANDOMLY INSERTED
PEWTER PRINT RUN 75 SER.#'d SETS
*RED: .6X TO 1.5X BASIC
RED RANDOMLY INSERTED
RED PRINT RUN 99 SER.#'d SETS
*SILVER: .5X TO 1.2X BASIC
SILVER RANDOMLY INSERTED
SILVER PRINT RUN 149 SER.#'d SETS
1 Jeter/Damon/Posada/Giambi 2.50 6.00
2 Dice-K/Beckett/Papel/Schilling .60 1.50
3 Jose Reyes/Carlos Beltran
Carlos Delgado/Johan Santana .60 1.50
4 Jeff Francoeur/Brian McCann
Mark Teixeira/Chipper Jones 1.00 2.50
5 Fielder/Weeks/Braun/Hardy .40 1.00
6 Griffey/Dunn/Phillips/Harang 2.00 5.00
7 Verlan/Zum/Bond/Willis 1.00 2.50
8 Jim Thome/David Ortiz/Frank Thomas
Gary Sheffield 1.00 2.50
9 Peavy/Maddux/Prior/Young 1.25 3.00
10 Brandon Webb/Dan Haren
Randy Johnson/Conor Jackson 1.00 2.50
11 Eric Chavez/Bobby Crosby
Rich Harden/Huston Street .60 1.50
12 Felix Hernandez/Erik Bedard
Adrian Beltre/Kenji Johjima 1.00 2.50
13 Chone Figgins/Vladimir Guerrero
Torii Hunter/Garret Anderson .60 1.50
14 Reyes/Furcal/Jeter/Peralta 2.50 6.00
15 Griffey/Edmonds/A.Jones/Beltran 2.00 5.00
16 Ivan Rodriguez/Jason Varitek
Joe Mauer/Jorge Posada 1.00 2.50
17 Hanley Ramirez/Dan Uggla/Josh
Willingham/Jeremy Hermida .60 1.50
18 Johan Santana/Cole Hamels/C.C.
Sabathia/Francisco Liriano .75 2.00
19 Prince Fielder/Lance Berkman
Derrek Lee/Conor Jackson .60 1.50
20 Rafael Furcal/Matt Kemp
Andruw Jones/Jeff Kent .75 2.00

2008 UD A Piece of History Franchise Members Quad Jersey

OVERALL GU ODDS 1:8
STATED PRINT RUN 99 SER.#'d SETS
1 Jeter/Damon/Posada/Giambi 20.00 50.00
2 Dice-K/Beckett/Papel/Schilling 15.00 40.00
3 Jose Reyes/Carlos Beltran
Carlos Delgado/Johan Santana 6.00 15.00
4 Jeff Francoeur/Brian McCann
Mark Teixeira/Chipper Jones 5.00 12.00
5 Fielder/Weeks/Braun/Hardy 8.00 20.00
7 Justin Verlander/Joel Zumaya/Jeremy
Bonderman/Dontrelle Willis 5.00 12.00
8 Jim Thome/David Ortiz/Frank Thomas
Gary Sheffield 6.00 15.00
9 Peavy/Maddux/Prior/Young 8.00 20.00
10 Brandon Webb/Dan Haren
Randy Johnson/Conor Jackson 6.00 15.00
11 Eric Chavez/Bobby Crosby
Rich Harden/Huston Street 4.00 10.00
12 Felix Hernandez/Erik Bedard
Adrian Beltre/Kenji Johjima 5.00 12.00
13 Chone Figgins/Vladimir Guerrero
Torii Hunter/Garret Anderson 5.00 12.00
14 Reyes/Furcal/Jeter/Peralta 12.50 30.00
16 Ivan Rodriguez/Jason Varitek
Joe Mauer/Jorge Posada 6.00 15.00
18 Johan Santana/Cole Hamels/C.C.
Sabathia/Francisco Liriano 6.00 15.00
19 Prince Fielder/Lance Berkman
Derrek Lee/Conor Jackson 6.00 15.00
20 Rafael Furcal/Matt Kemp
Andruw Jones/Jeff Kent 4.00 10.00

2008 UD A Piece of History Stadium Scenes

RANDOM INSERTS IN PACKS
STATED PRINT RUN 699 SER.#'d SETS
*BLUE: .6X TO 1.5X BASIC
BLUE RANDOMLY INSERTED
BLUE PRINT RUN 75 SER.#'d SETS
*COPPER: .6X TO 1.5X BASIC
COPPER RANDOMLY INSERTED
COPPER PRINT RUN 99 SER.#'d SETS
*RED: .5X TO 1.2X BASIC
RED RANDOMLY INSERTED
RED PRINT RUN 149 SER.#'d SETS
SILVER RANDOMLY INSERTED
SILVER PRINT RUN 25 SER.#'d SETS
NO SILVER PRICING DUE TO SCARCITY
SS1 Randy Johnson 1.25 3.00
SS2 Justin Upton .75 2.00
SS3 Mark Teixeira .75 2.00
SS4 Chipper Jones 1.25 3.00
SS5 John Smoltz 1.25 3.00
SS6 David Ortiz 1.25 3.00
SS7 Josh Beckett .50 1.25
SS8 Daisuke Matsuzaka .75 2.00
SS9 Manny Ramirez 1.25 3.00
SS10 Jonathan Papelbon .75 2.00
SS11 Alfonso Soriano .75 2.00
SS12 Kerry Wood .50 1.25
SS13 Derrek Lee .50 1.25
SS14 Jim Thome .75 2.00
SS15 Ken Griffey Jr. 2.50 6.00
SS16 Adam Dunn .75 2.00
SS17 Grady Sizemore .75 2.00
SS18 Travis Hafner .50 1.25
SS19 Victor Martinez .75 2.00
SS20 C.C. Sabathia .75 2.00
SS21 Miguel Cabrera 1.25 3.00
SS22 Justin Verlander 1.25 3.00
SS23 Ivan Rodriguez .75 2.00
SS24 Magglio Ordonez .75 2.00
SS25 Lance Berkman .75 2.00
SS26 Roy Oswalt .75 2.00
SS27 Vladimir Guerrero .75 2.00
SS28 Andruw Jones .50 1.25
SS29 Rickie Weeks .50 1.25
SS30 Ryan Braun .75 2.00
SS31 Prince Fielder .75 2.00
SS32 Joe Mauer 1.00 2.50
SS33 Pedro Martinez .75 2.00
SS34 Jose Reyes .75 2.00
SS35 David Wright .75 2.00
SS36 Johan Santana .75 2.00
SS37 Derek Jeter 3.00 8.00
SS38 Alex Rodriguez 1.50 4.00
SS39 Hideki Matsui 1.25 3.00
SS40 Joba Chamberlain .50 1.25
SS41 Cole Hamels 1.00 2.50
SS42 Chase Utley .75 2.00
SS43 Ryan Howard .75 2.00
SS44 Jimmy Rollins .75 2.00
SS45 Jake Peavy .50 1.25
SS46 Greg Maddux 1.50 4.00
SS47 Felix Hernandez .75 2.00
SS48 Ichiro Suzuki 1.50 4.00
SS49 Albert Pujols 1.50 4.00
SS50 Frank Thomas 1.25 3.00

2008 UD A Piece of History Stadium Scenes Button

OVERALL GU ODDS 1:8
STATED PRINT RUN 5 SER.#'d SETS
NO PRICING DUE TO SCARCITY

2008 UD A Piece of History Stadium Scenes Jersey Red

OVERALL GU ODDS 1:8
SS1 Randy Johnson 4.00 10.00
SS2 Justin Upton 4.00 10.00
SS3 Mark Teixeira 3.00 8.00
SS4 Chipper Jones 3.00 8.00
SS5 John Smoltz 3.00 8.00
SS6 David Ortiz 4.00 10.00
SS7 Josh Beckett 3.00 8.00
SS8 Daisuke Matsuzaka 6.00 15.00
SS9 Manny Ramirez 3.00 8.00
SS10 Jonathan Papelbon 3.00 8.00
SS11 Alfonso Soriano 3.00 8.00
SS12 Kerry Wood 3.00 8.00
SS13 Derrek Lee 3.00 8.00
SS14 Jim Thome 3.00 8.00
SS15 Ken Griffey Jr. 5.00 12.00
SS16 Adam Dunn 3.00 8.00
SS18 Travis Hafner 3.00 8.00
SS19 Victor Martinez 3.00 8.00
SS20 C.C. Sabathia 3.00 8.00
SS21 Miguel Cabrera 3.00 8.00
SS22 Justin Verlander 3.00 8.00
SS23 Ivan Rodriguez 3.00 8.00
SS24 Magglio Ordonez 3.00 8.00
SS25 Lance Berkman 3.00 8.00
SS26 Roy Oswalt 3.00 8.00
SS27 Vladimir Guerrero 3.00 8.00
SS28 Andruw Jones 3.00 8.00
SS29 Rickie Weeks 3.00 8.00
SS30 Ryan Braun 5.00 12.00
SS31 Prince Fielder 4.00 10.00
SS32 Joe Mauer 3.00 8.00
SS33 Pedro Martinez 3.00 8.00
SS34 Jose Reyes 3.00 8.00
SS36 Johan Santana 4.00 10.00
SS37 Derek Jeter 8.00 20.00
SS38 Alex Rodriguez 6.00 15.00
SS40 Joba Chamberlain 8.00 20.00
SS41 Cole Hamels 3.00 8.00
SS42 Chase Utley 3.00 8.00
SS44 Jimmy Rollins 3.00 8.00
SS45 Jake Peavy 3.00 8.00
SS46 Greg Maddux 5.00 12.00
SS47 Felix Hernandez 3.00 8.00
SS49 Albert Pujols 6.00 15.00
SS50 Frank Thomas 4.00 10.00

2008 UD A Piece of History Stadium Scenes Jersey Gold

*GOLD: .5X TO 1.2X BASIC
OVERALL GU ODDS 1:8
STATED PRINT RUN 99 SER.#'d SETS

2008 UD A Piece of History Stadium Scenes Jersey Autographs

OVERALL AUTO ODDS 1:16
PRINT RUNS B/WN 10-99 COPIES PER
NO PRICING ON QTY 25 OR LESS
SS10 Jonathan Papelbon/99 6.00 15.00
SS12 Kerry Wood/99 6.00 15.00
SS18 Travis Hafner/50 6.00 15.00
SS19 Victor Martinez/99 6.00 15.00
SS29 Rickie Weeks/50 6.00 15.00
SS47 Felix Hernandez/75 8.00 20.00

2008 UD A Piece of History Timeless Moments

RANDOM INSERTS IN PACKS
STATED PRINT RUN 699 SER.#'d SETS
*BLUE: .6X TO 1.5X BASIC
BLUE RANDOMLY INSERTED
BLUE PRINT RUN 75 SER.#'d SETS
*COPPER: .6X TO 1.5X BASIC
COPPER RANDOMLY INSERTED
COPPER PRINT RUN 99 SER.#'d SETS
*RED: .5X TO 1.2X BASIC
RED RANDOMLY INSERTED
RED PRINT RUN 149 SER.#'d SETS
SILVER RANDOMLY INSERTED
SILVER PRINT RUN 25 SER.#'d SETS
NO SILVER PRICING DUE TO SCARCITY
1 Randy Johnson 1.25 3.00
2 Dan Haren .50 1.25
3 John Smoltz 1.25 3.00
4 Chipper Jones 1.25 3.00
5 Mark Teixeira .75 2.00
6 David Ortiz 1.25 3.00
7 Dustin Pedroia 1.25 3.00
8 Josh Beckett .50 1.25
9 Curt Schilling .75 2.00
10 Daisuke Matsuzaka .75 2.00
11 Alfonso Soriano .75 2.00
12 Carlos Zambrano .75 2.00
13 Jim Thome .75 2.00
14 Ken Griffey Jr. 2.50 6.00
15 Adam Dunn .75 2.00
16 Grady Sizemore .75 2.00
17 C.C. Sabathia .75 2.00
18 Troy Tulowitzki 1.25 3.00
19 Matt Holliday 1.25 3.00
20 Justin Verlander 1.25 3.00
21 Ivan Rodriguez .75 2.00
22 Hanley Ramirez .75 2.00
23 Alex Gordon .75 2.00
24 Vladimir Guerrero .75 2.00
25 Jeff Kent .50 1.25
26 Nomar Garciaparra .75 2.00
27 Prince Fielder .75 2.00
28 Joe Mauer 1.00 2.50
29 Justin Morneau .75 2.00
30 Jose Reyes .75 2.00
31 David Wright .75 2.00
32 Pedro Martinez .75 2.00
33 Johan Santana .75 2.00
34 Joba Chamberlain .50 1.25
35 Derek Jeter 3.00 8.00
36 Alex Rodriguez 1.50 4.00
37 Hideki Matsui 1.25 3.00
38 Ryan Howard .75 2.00
39 Chase Utley .75 2.00
40 Jimmy Rollins .75 2.00
41 Cole Hamels 1.00 2.50
42 Jake Peavy .50 1.25
43 Greg Maddux 1.50 4.00
44 Phil Hughes .50 1.25
45 Felix Hernandez .75 2.00
46 Ichiro Suzuki 1.50 4.00
47 Albert Pujols 1.50 4.00
48 Chris Carpenter .75 2.00
49 Frank Thomas 1.25 3.00
50 Vernon Wells .50 1.25

2008 UD A Piece of History Timeless Moments Red

RANDOM INSERTS IN PACKS

2008 UD A Piece of History Timeless Moments Silver

RANDOM INSERTS IN PACKS

2008 UD A Piece of History Timeless Moments Jersey

OVERALL GU ODDS 1:8
1 Randy Johnson 4.00 10.00
2 Dan Haren 3.00 8.00
3 John Smoltz 3.00 8.00
5 Mark Teixeira 3.00 8.00
6 David Ortiz 4.00 10.00
7 Dustin Pedroia 3.00 8.00
8 Josh Beckett 3.00 8.00
9 Curt Schilling 3.00 8.00
10 Daisuke Matsuzaka 6.00 15.00
11 Alfonso Soriano 3.00 8.00
12 Carlos Zambrano 3.00 8.00
13 Jim Thome 3.00 8.00
17 C.C. Sabathia 3.00 8.00
18 Troy Tulowitzki 3.00 8.00
19 Matt Holliday 3.00 8.00
20 Justin Verlander 3.00 8.00
21 Ivan Rodriguez 3.00 8.00
22 Hanley Ramirez 3.00 8.00
23 Alex Gordon 4.00 10.00
24 Vladimir Guerrero 3.00 8.00
25 Jeff Kent 3.00 8.00
27 Prince Fielder 4.00 10.00
28 Joe Mauer 3.00 8.00
29 Justin Morneau 3.00 8.00
30 Jose Reyes 3.00 8.00
32 Pedro Martinez 3.00 8.00
33 Johan Santana 4.00 10.00
34 Joba Chamberlain 8.00 20.00
35 Derek Jeter 8.00 20.00
36 Alex Rodriguez 6.00 15.00
39 Chase Utley 3.00 8.00
40 Jimmy Rollins 3.00 8.00
41 Cole Hamels 3.00 8.00
42 Jake Peavy 3.00 8.00
43 Greg Maddux 5.00 12.00
44 Phil Hughes 4.00 10.00
45 Felix Hernandez 3.00 8.00
47 Albert Pujols 6.00 15.00
48 Chris Carpenter 3.00 8.00
49 Frank Thomas 4.00 10.00
50 Vernon Wells 3.00 8.00

2008 UD A Piece of History Timeless Moments Jersey Gold

*GOLD: .5X TO 1.2X BASIC
OVERALL GU ODDS 1:8
STATED PRINT RUN 99 SER.#'d SETS

2008 UD A Piece of History Timeless Moments Jersey Autographs

OVERALL AUTO ODDS 1:16
PRINT RUNS B/WN 5-75 COPIES PER
NO PRICING ON QTY 25 OR LESS
2 Dan Haren/50 6.00 15.00
18 Troy Tulowitzki/50 12.50 30.00
34 Joba Chamberlain/50 100.00 150.00
44 Phil Hughes/50 15.00 40.00
45 Felix Hernandez/75 12.50 30.00

2009 UD A Piece of History

COMPLETE SET (200) 20.00 50.00
COMMON CARD .20 .50
COMMON ROOKIE .40 1.00
1 Brandon Webb .30 .75
2 Randy Johnson .50 1.25
3 Dan Haren .20 .50
4 Adam Dunn .30 .75
5 Chipper Jones .50 1.25
6 John Smoltz .50 1.25
7 Tom Glavine .30 .75
8 Brian Roberts .20 .50
9 Nick Markakis .40 1.00
10 Josh Beckett .20 .50
11 David Ortiz .50 1.25
12 Daisuke Matsuzaka .30 .75
13 Jacoby Ellsbury .40 1.00
14 Jonathan Papelbon .30 .75
15 Alfonso Soriano .30 .75
16 Derrek Lee .20 .50
17 Kosuke Fukudome .30 .75
18 Carlos Zambrano .30 .75
19 Aramis Ramirez .20 .50
20 Rich Harden .20 .50
21 Carlos Quentin .20 .50
22 Jim Thome .30 .75
23 Ken Griffey Jr. 1.00 2.50
24 Jay Bruce .30 .75
25 Edinson Volquez .20 .50
26 Brandon Phillips .20 .50
27 Victor Martinez .30 .75
28 Grady Sizemore .30 .75
29 Travis Hafner .20 .50
30 Matt Holliday .50 1.25
31 Troy Tulowitzki .50 1.25
32 Garrett Atkins .20 .50
33 Miguel Cabrera .50 1.25
34 Magglio Ordonez .30 .75
35 Justin Verlander .50 1.25
36 Hanley Ramirez .30 .75
37 Dan Uggla .20 .50
38 Lance Berkman .30 .75
39 Carlos Lee .20 .50
40 Kevin Youkilis .20 .50
41 Miguel Tejada .30 .75
42 Alex Gordon .30 .75
43 Zack Greinke .50 1.25
44 Mark Teixeira .30 .75
45 Vladimir Guerrero .30 .75
46 Torii Hunter .20 .50
47 Manny Ramirez .50 1.25
48 Russell Martin .20 .50
49 Matt Kemp .40 1.00
50 Clayton Kershaw .75 2.00
51 CC Sabathia .30 .75
52 Corey Hart .20 .50
53 Prince Fielder .30 .75
54 Ryan Braun .30 .75
55 Joe Mauer .40 1.00
56 Justin Morneau .30 .75
57 Jose Reyes .30 .75
58 David Wright .40 1.00
59 Johan Santana .30 .75
60 Carlos Beltran .30 .75
61 Pedro Martinez .30 .75
62 Alex Rodriguez .60 1.50
63 Derek Jeter 1.25 3.00
64 Chien-Ming Wang .30 .75
65 Hideki Matsui .50 1.25
66 Joba Chamberlain .20 .50
67 Mariano Rivera .60 1.50
68 Xavier Nady .20 .50
69 Frank Thomas .50 1.25
70 Jason Giambi .20 .50
71 Chase Utley .30 .75
72 Ryan Howard .40 1.00
73 Jimmy Rollins .30 .75
74 Ryan Doumit .20 .50
75 Nate McLouth .20 .50
76 Adrian Gonzalez .40 1.00
78 Jake Peavy .20 .50
79 Brian Giles .20 .50
80 Tim Lincecum .30 .75
81 Matt Cain .30 .75
82 Felix Hernandez .30 .75
83 Ichiro Suzuki .60 1.50
84 Erik Bedard .20 .50
85 Ryan Ludwick .30 .75
86 Albert Pujols .60 1.50
87 Chris Carpenter .30 .75
88 Rick Ankiel .20 .50
89 B.J. Upton .30 .75
90 Evan Longoria .30 .75
91 Scott Kazmir .20 .50
92 Carl Crawford .30 .75
93 Josh Hamilton .30 .75
94 Ian Kinsler .30 .75
95 Michael Young .20 .50
96 Roy Halladay .30 .75
97 Vernon Wells .20 .50
98 Alex Rios .20 .50
99 Ryan Zimmerman .30 .75
100 Lastings Milledge .20 .50
101 David Price RC .75 2.00
102 Conor Gillaspie RC 1.00 2.50
103 Josh Roenicke RC .40 1.00
104 Jeff Baisley RC .40 1.00
105 Alfredo Aceves RC .60 1.50
106 Matt Antonelli (RC) .60 1.50
107 Michael Bowden (RC) .40 1.00
108 Josh Whitesell RC .60 1.50
109 Wilkin Castillo RC .40 1.00
110 Francisco Cervelli RC 1.00 2.50
111 Phil Coke RC .60 1.50
112 Luis Cruz RC .40 1.00
113 Jesus Delgado RC .60 1.50
114 Scott Elbert (RC) .40 1.00
115 Alcides Escobar RC .60 1.50
116 Dexter Fowler (RC) .60 1.50
117 Mat Gamel RC 1.00 2.50
118 Josh Geer (RC) .40 1.00
119 Greg Golson (RC) .40 1.00
120 Kila Ka'aihue (RC) .60 1.50
121 Chris Lambert (RC) .40 1.00
122 Wade LeBlanc RC .60 1.50
123 Scott Lewis (RC) .40 1.00
124 Lou Marson (RC) .40 1.00
125 Shairon Martis RC .60 1.50
126 James McDonald RC 1.00 2.50
127 Juan Miranda RC .60 1.50
128 Luke Montz RC .40 1.00
129 Jonathon Niese RC .60 1.50
130 Josh Outman RC .60 1.50
131 James Parr (RC) .40 1.00
132 Dusty Ryan RC .40 1.00
133 Angel Salome (RC) .40 1.00
134 Travis Snider RC .60 1.50
135 Matt Tuiasosopo (RC) .40 1.00
136 Will Venable RC .40 1.00
137 Aaron Cunningham RC .40 1.00
138 George Kottaras (RC) .40 1.00
139 Devon Lowery (RC) .40 1.00
140 Jose Mijares RC 1.00 2.50
141 Jason Motte (RC) .60 1.50
142 Bobby Parnell RC .60 1.50
143 Fernando Perez (RC) .40 1.00
144 Jason Pridie (RC) .40 1.00
145 Ramon Ramirez (RC) .40 1.00
146 Justin Thomas (RC) .40 1.00
147 Luis Valbuena RC .60 1.50
148 Gaby Sanchez RC .60 1.50
149 Mike Hinckley (RC) .40 1.00
150 Mitch Talbot (RC) .40 1.00
151 Star Spangled Banner .20 .50
152 Dwight D. Eisenhower .20 .50
153 First Atomic Submarine Launched .20 .50
154 Alaska Becomes 49th State .20 .50
155 I Have A Dream Speech .20 .50
156 18th Amendment Adopted .20 .50
157 Discovery of Penicilin .20 .50
158 Germany Leaves League of Nations .20 .50
159 Attack on Pearl Harbor .20 .50
160 U.S.A. Enters World War II .20 .50

161 D-Day Invasion .20 .50
162 NATO Organized .20 .50
163 1970 Earth Day .20 .50
164 1989 San Francisco Earthquake .20 .50
165 Warsaw Pact .20 .50
166 NAFTA .20 .50
167 Boy Scouts of America Launches .20 .50
168 New Zealand Pioneers Women's Voting Rights .20 .50
169 First Moving Assembly Line .20 .50
170 Hollywood Sign Debuts .20 .50
171 Taj Mahal Completed .20 .50
172 United States Constitution Signed .20 .50
173 Empire State Building Built .20 .50
174 Golden Gate Bridge Completed .20 .50
175 Smallpox Eradicated .20 .50
176 Elevator Invented .20 .50
177 Microwave Oven Invented .20 .50
178 E-Mail Invented .20 .50
179 Eiffel Tower Erected .20 .50
180 Pilgrims Land at Plymouth Rock .20 .50
181 First Photograph Taken .20 .50
182 First Anesthetic Used .20 .50
183 First Kentucky Derby .20 .50
184 Brooklyn Bridge Completed .20 .50
185 X-Ray Invented .20 .50
186 Pluto Recategorized as Dwarf Planet .20 .50
187 Mount Rushmore Finished .20 .50
188 Thanksgiving Adopted as Holiday .20 .50
189 Chicago Cubs .20 .50
190 Baseball Hall of Fame Opens .20 .50
191 National League Established .20 .50
192 Olympic Games Begin .20 .50
193 Voyager 2 .20 .50
194 New Orleans Founded .20 .50
195 Discovery of New York .20 .50
196 Debut of New York Times .20 .50
197 Republican Party Founded .20 .50
198 City of Boston Founded .20 .50
199 Introduction of EURO Currency .20 .50
200 Czechoslovakia Splits in Two .20 .50

2009 UD A Piece of History Blue

*BLUE VET 1-100: .75X TO 2X BASIC
*BLUE RC 101-150: .6X TO 1.5X BASIC
*BLUE HIST.151-200: .75X TO 2X BASIC
RANDOM INSERTS IN PACKS
STATED PRINT RUN 299 SER.#'d SETS

2009 UD A Piece of History Gold

*GOLD VET 1-100: 2X TO 5X BASIC
*GOLD RC 101-150: 1X TO 2.5X BASIC
*GOLD HIST.151-200: 1.2X TO 3X BASIC
RANDOM INSERTS IN PACKS
STATED PRINT RUN 50 SER.#'d SETS

2009 UD A Piece of History Green

*GRN VET 1-100: 1.5X TO 4X BASIC
*GRN RC 101-150: .75X TO 2X BASIC
*GRN.HIST.151-200: 1X TO 2.5X BASIC
RANDOM INSERTS IN PACKS
STATED PRINT RUN 150 SER.#'d SETS

2009 UD A Piece of History Red

*RED VET 1-100: .6X TO 1.5X BASIC
*RED RC 101-150: .5X TO 1.2X BASIC
*RED.HIST.151-200: .6X TO 1.5X BASIC
RANDOM INSERTS IN PACKS

2009 UD A Piece of History Rookie Autographs Blue

*BLUE: .5X TO 1.2X BASIC
OVERALL AUTO ODDS 1:16
STATED PRINT RUN 99 SER.#'d SETS
EXCHANGE DEADLINE 3/16/2011
125 Shairon Martis 5.00 12.00

2009 UD A Piece of History Rookie Autographs Violet

OVERALL AUTO ODDS 1:16
RANDOM INSERTS IN PACKS
101 David Price 6.00 15.00
102 Conor Gillaspie 10.00 25.00
104 Jeff Baisley 3.00 8.00
106 Matt Antonelli 3.00 8.00
107 Michael Bowden 10.00 25.00
110 Francisco Cervelli 6.00 15.00
111 Phil Coke 5.00 12.00
112 Luis Cruz 3.00 8.00
113 Jesus Delgado 3.00 8.00
116 Dexter Fowler 10.00 25.00
117 Mat Gamel 8.00 20.00
118 Josh Geer 4.00 10.00
119 Greg Golson 3.00 8.00
120 Kila Ka'aihue 4.00 10.00
121 Chris Lambert 3.00 8.00
122 Wade LeBlanc 3.00 8.00
124 Lou Marson 5.00 12.00
125 Shairon Martis 3.00 8.00
126 James McDonald 5.00 12.00
127 Juan Miranda 5.00 12.00
128 Luke Montz 3.00 8.00
130 Josh Outman 3.00 8.00
131 James Parr 3.00 8.00
133 Angel Salome 4.00 10.00
134 Travis Snider 15.00 40.00
135 Matt Tuiasosopo 4.00 10.00
137 Aaron Cunningham 3.00 8.00
143 Fernando Perez 4.00 10.00
148 Gaby Sanchez 5.00 12.00

2009 UD A Piece of History A Piece of Hollywood

STATED ODDS 1:16
POHAS Arnold Schwarzenegger 20.00 50.00
POHBA Ben Affleck 3.00 8.00
POHBL Bruce Lee 30.00 60.00
POHBS Ben Stiller 3.00 8.00
POHDB Drew Barrymore 6.00 15.00
POHDW Denzel Washington 6.00 15.00
POHHJ John Hurt 3.00 8.00
POHHL Heath Ledger 12.50 30.00
POHHU John Hurt 3.00 8.00
POHJH John Hurt 3.00 8.00
POHMM Mike Myers 3.00 8.00
POHRM Rachel McAdams 8.00 20.00
POHSA Adam Sandler 4.00 10.00
POHSB Ben Stiller 3.00 8.00
POHSG Sidney Greenstreet 5.00 12.00
POHSP Sean Penn 4.00 10.00
POHST Ben Stiller 3.00 8.00
POHTH Tom Hanks 5.00 12.00
POHWD Denzel Washington 6.00 15.00
POHWF Will Ferrell 4.00 10.00
POHWS Will Smith 30.00 60.00

2009 UD A Piece of History Box Score Memories

RANDOM INSERTS IN PACKS
STATED PRINT RUN 999 SER.#'d SETS
*BLACK: .5X TO 1.2X BASIC
BLACK RANDOMLY INSERTED
BLACK PRINT RUN 149 SER.#'d SETS
*BLUE: 1.5X TO 4X BASIC
BLUE RANDOMLY INSERTED
BLUE PRINT RUN 25 SER.#'d SETS
*RED: .75X TO 2X BASIC
RED RANDOMLY INSERTED
RED PRINT RUN 75 SER.#'d SETS
*TURQUOISE: .6X TO 1.5X BASIC
TURQUOISE RANDOMLY INSERTED
TURQUOISE PRINT RUN 99 SER.#'d SETS
BSMCD Carlos Delgado .40 1.00
BSMCF Chone Figgins .40 1.00
BSMCJ Chipper Jones 1.00 2.50
BSMCL Carlos Lee .40 1.00
BSMDL Derrek Lee .40 1.00
BSMDO David Ortiz 1.00 2.50
BSMDU Dan Uggla .40 1.00
BSMGS Gary Sheffield .40 1.00
BSMHR Hanley Ramirez .60 1.50
BSMJD Johnny Damon .60 1.50
BSMJF Jeff Francoeur .60 1.50
BSMJH Jeremy Hermida .40 1.00
BSMJM Justin Morneau .60 1.50
BSMKG Khalil Greene .40 1.00
BSMMM Melvin Mora .40 1.00
BSMMR Manny Ramirez 1.00 2.50
BSMNM Nick Markakis .75 2.00
BSMPB Pat Burrell .40 1.00
BSMPK Paul Konerko .60 1.50
BSMRB Ryan Braun .60 1.50
BSMRF Rafael Furcal .40 1.00
BSMRW Rickie Weeks .40 1.00
BSMTH Travis Hafner .40 1.00
BSMVM Victor Martinez .60 1.50
BSMYE Yunel Escobar .40 1.00

2009 UD A Piece of History Box Score Memories Jersey

OVERALL MEM ODDS 1:16
BSMCD Carlos Delgado 3.00 8.00
BSMCF Chone Figgins 3.00 8.00
BSMCJ Chipper Jones 4.00 10.00
BSMCL Carlos Lee 3.00 8.00
BSMDL Derrek Lee 3.00 8.00
BSMDO David Ortiz 3.00 8.00
BSMDU Dan Uggla 3.00 8.00
BSMGS Gary Sheffield 3.00 8.00
BSMHR Hanley Ramirez 4.00 10.00
BSMJD Johnny Damon 3.00 8.00
BSMJF Jeff Francoeur 3.00 8.00
BSMJH Jeremy Hermida 3.00 8.00
BSMJM Justin Morneau 3.00 8.00
BSMKG Khalil Greene 3.00 8.00
BSMMM Melvin Mora 3.00 8.00
BSMMR Manny Ramirez 4.00 10.00
BSMNM Nick Markakis 4.00 10.00
BSMPB Pat Burrell 4.00 10.00
BSMPK Paul Konerko 3.00 8.00
BSMRB Ryan Braun 4.00 10.00
BSMRF Rafael Furcal 3.00 8.00
BSMRW Rickie Weeks 3.00 8.00
BSMTH Travis Hafner 3.00 8.00
BSMVM Victor Martinez 3.00 8.00
BSMYE Yunel Escobar 3.00 8.00

2009 UD A Piece of History Box Score Memories Jersey Red

*RED: .4X TO 1X BASIC
OVERALL MEM ODDS 1:16
STATED PRINT RUN 180 SER.#'d SETS

2009 UD A Piece of History Cut From The Same Cloth

RANDOM INSERTS IN PACKS
STATED PRINT RUN 999 SER.#'d SETS
*GOLD: .75X TO 2X BASIC
GOLD RANDOMLY INSERTED
GOLD PRINT RUN 75 SER.#'d SETS
*GREEN: .5X TO 1.2X BASIC
GREEN RANDOMLY INSERTED
GREEN PRINT RUN 149 SER.#'d SETS
*PURPLE: 1.5X TO 4X BASIC
PURPLE RANDOMLY INSERTED
PURPLE PRINT RUN 25 SER.#'d SETS
*RED: .6X TO 1.5X BASIC
RED RANDOMLY INSERTED
RED PRINT RUN 99 SER.#'d SETS
CSCAH Josh Hamilton/Rick Ankiel .60 1.50
CSCBC J.Beckett/J.Chamberlain .40 1.00
CSCBH Lance Berkman/Josh Hamilton .60 1.50
CSCBS Carlos Beltran/Grady Sizemore .60 1.50
CSCGB K.Griffey/J.Bruce 2.00 5.00
CSCGO Vladimir Guerrero/David Ortiz 1.00 2.50
CSCHF R.Howard/P.Fielder .75 2.00
CSCHV Felix Hernandez/Edinson Volquez .60 1.50
CSCIC I.Suzuki/C.Crawford 1.25 3.00
CSCJK Randy Johnson/Scott Kazmir 1.00 2.50
CSCJT D.Jeter/T.Tulowitzki 2.50 6.00
CSCMG Justin Morneau/Adrian Gonzalez .75 2.00
CSCMM Joe Mauer/Russell Martin .75 2.00
CSCMS Pedro Martinez/Johan Santana .60 1.50
CSCOL Roy Oswalt/Tim Lincecum .60 1.50
CSCPC A.Pujols/M.Cabrera 1.25 3.00
CSCPE D.Pedroia/J.Ellsbury 1.00 2.50
CSCPW Jake Peavy/Brandon Webb .60 1.50
CSCQB C.Quentin/R.Braun .60 1.50
CSCRH Manny Ramirez/Matt Holliday 1.00 2.50
CSCRP Francisco Rodriguez Jonathan Papelbon .60 1.50
CSCRR Jose Reyes/Jimmy Rollins .60 1.50
CSCRW A.Rodriguez/D.Wright 1.25 3.00
CSCSR Alfonso Soriano/Hanley Ramirez .60 1.50
CSCTJ Mark Teixeira/Chipper Jones 1.00 2.50
CSCUK Chase Utley/Ian Kinsler .60 1.50
CSCUU B.J. Upton/Justin Upton .60 1.50
CSCWL D.Wright/E.Longoria .75 2.00
CSCWM C.Wang/D.Matsuzaka .60 1.50
CSCZS Carlos Zambrano/CC Sabathia .60 1.50

2009 UD A Piece of History Franchise History

RANDOM INSERTS IN PACKS
STATED PRINT RUN 999 SER.#'d SETS
*BLACK: .5X TO 1.2X BASIC
BLACK RANDOMLY INSERTED
BLACK PRINT RUN 149 SER.#'d SETS
*BLUE: 1.5X TO 4X BASIC
BLUE RANDOMLY INSERTED
BLUE PRINT RUN 25 SER.#'d SETS
*RED: .75X TO 2X BASIC
RED RANDOMLY INSERTED
RED PRINT RUN 75 SER.#'d SETS
*TURQUOISE: .6X TO 1.5X BASIC
TURQUOISE RANDOMLY INSERTED
TURQUOISE PRINT RUN 99 SER.#'d SETS
FHAP Albert Pujols 1.25 3.00
FHBC Bobby Crosby .40 1.00
FHBM Brian McCann .60 1.50
FHBR Brian Roberts .40 1.00
FHCH Cole Hamels .75 2.00
FHCL Carlos Lee .40 1.00
FHDJ Derek Jeter 2.50 6.00
FHDL Derrek Lee .40 1.00
FHDU Dan Uggla .40 1.00
FHFL Francisco Liriano .40 1.00
FHHE Todd Helton .60 1.50
FHJH Josh Hamilton .60 1.50
FHJR Jose Reyes .60 1.50
FHJV Jason Varitek 1.00 2.50
FHKG Khalil Greene .40 1.00
FHMO Magglio Ordonez .60 1.50
FHPF Prince Fielder .60 1.50
FHPK Paul Konerko .60 1.50
FHRH Roy Halladay .60 1.50
FHRJ Randy Johnson 1.00 2.50
FHRM Russell Martin .40 1.00
FHSK Scott Kazmir .40 1.00
FHTH Travis Hafner .40 1.00
FHTL Tim Lincecum .60 1.50
FHZG Zack Greinke 1.00 2.50

2009 UD A Piece of History Franchise History Jersey

OVERALL MEM ODDS 1:16
FHAP Albert Pujols 6.00 15.00
FHBC Bobby Crosby 3.00 8.00
FHBM Brian McCann 3.00 8.00
FHBR Brian Roberts 3.00 8.00
FHCH Cole Hamels 6.00 15.00
FHCL Carlos Lee 3.00 8.00
FHDJ Derek Jeter 8.00 20.00
FHDL Derrek Lee 3.00 8.00
FHDU Dan Uggla 3.00 8.00
FHFL Francisco Liriano 3.00 8.00
FHHE Todd Helton 4.00 10.00
FHJR Jose Reyes 4.00 10.00
FHJV Jason Varitek 3.00 8.00
FHKG Khalil Greene 3.00 8.00
FHMO Magglio Ordonez 3.00 8.00
FHPF Prince Fielder 3.00 8.00
FHPK Paul Konerko 3.00 8.00
FHRH Roy Halladay 3.00 8.00
FHRM Russell Martin 3.00 8.00
FHSK Scott Kazmir 3.00 8.00
FHTH Travis Hafner 3.00 8.00
FHTL Tim Lincecum 5.00 12.00
FHZG Zack Greinke 4.00 10.00

2009 UD A Piece of History Franchise History Jersey Red

*RED: .4X TO 1X BASIC
OVERALL MEM ODDS 1:16
STATED PRINT RUN 180 SER.#'d SETS

2009 UD A Piece of History Franchise Members Quad

RANDOM INSERTS IN PACKS
STATED PRINT RUN 999 SER.#'d SETS
*GOLD: .75X TO 2X BASIC
GOLD RANDOMLY INSERTED
GOLD PRINT RUN 75 SER.#'d SETS
*GREEN: .5X TO 1.2X BASIC
GREEN RANDOMLY INSERTED
GREEN PRINT RUN 149 SER.#'d SETS
*PURPLE: 1.5X TO 4X BASIC
PURPLE RANDOMLY INSERTED
PURPLE PRINT RUN 25 SER.#'d SETS
*RED: .6X TO 1.5X BASIC
RED RANDOMLY INSERTED
RED PRINT RUN 99 SER.#'d SETS
FMBLTO Lance Berkman/Carlos Lee/Miguel Tejada/Roy Oswalt .60 1.50
FMFGHW Chone Figgins/Vladimir Guerrero/Torii Hunter/Reggie Willits .60 1.50
FMGTDQ Gavin Floyd/Jim Thome/Jermaine Dye/Carlos Quentin .60 1.50
FMJRCR Jeter/ARod/Joba/Rivera 2.50 6.00
FMKCLU Kaz/Craw/Longoria/Upton .60 1.50
FMOCGG Ordon/Cabrera/Guillen/Grand 1.00 2.50
FMOYPD Papi/Youk/Pedroia/Drew 1.00 2.50
FMRWBS Reyes/Wright/Beltran/Johan .75 2.00
FMSHMG Grady Sizemore/Travis Hafner/Victor Martinez/Ryan Garko .60 1.50
FMSLRS Alfonso Soriano/Derrek Lee/Aramis Ramirez/Geovany Soto .60 1.50

2009 UD A Piece of History Franchise Members Trio

RANDOM INSERTS IN PACKS
STATED PRINT RUN 999 SER.#'d SETS
*GOLD: .75X TO 2X BASIC
GOLD RANDOMLY INSERTED
GOLD PRINT RUN 75 SER.#'d SETS
*GREEN: .5X TO 1.2X BASIC
GREEN RANDOMLY INSERTED
GREEN PRINT RUN 149 SER.#'d SETS
*PURPLE: 1.5X TO 4X BASIC
PURPLE RANDOMLY INSERTED
PURPLE PRINT RUN 25 SER.#'d SETS
*RED: .6X TO 1.5X BASIC
RED RANDOMLY INSERTED
RED PRINT RUN 99 SER.#'d SETS
FMBML Beckett/Dice-K/Lester .60 1.50
FMFBS Fielder/Braun/Suppan .60 1.50
FMGYG Brian Giles/Chris Young Adrian Gonzalez .75 2.00
FMHKY Josh Hamilton/Ian Kinsler Michael Young .60 1.50
FMJEM Chipper Jones Yunel Escobar/Brian McCann 1.00 2.50
FMJRM Jeter/A-Rod/Matsui 2.50 6.00
FMPAL Pujols/Ankiel/Ludwick 1.25 3.00
FMRUH Hanley Ramirez Dan Uggla/Jeremy Hermida .60 1.50
FMRWB Reyes/Wright/Beltran .75 2.00
FMURH Utley/Rollins/Howard .75 2.00

2009 UD A Piece of History Hair Cuts

RANDOM INSERTS IN PACKS
EXCHANGE DEADLINE 3/16/2011
NNO EXCH Card 800.00 1200.00

2009 UD A Piece of History Stadium Scenes

RANDOM INSERTS IN PACKS
STATED PRINT RUN 999 SER.#'d SETS
*BLACK: .5X TO 1.2X BASIC
BLACK RANDOMLY INSERTED
BLACK PRINT RUN 149 SER.#'d SETS
*BLUE: 1.5X TO 4X BASIC
BLUE RANDOMLY INSERTED
BLUE PRINT RUN 25 SER.#'d SETS
*RED: .75X TO 2X BASIC
RED RANDOMLY INSERTED
RED PRINT RUN 75 SER.#'d SETS
*TURQUOISE: .6X TO 1.5X BASIC
TURQUOISE RANDOMLY INSERTED
TURQUOISE PRINT RUN 99 SER.#'d SETS
SSAL Adam LaRoche .40 1.00
SSCC Chris Carpenter .60 1.50
SSCD Carlos Delgado .40 1.00
SSCG Curtis Granderson .75 2.00
SSCO Chad Cordero .40 1.00
SSCY Chris Young .40 1.00
SSDL Derrek Lee .40 1.00
SSDM Daisuke Matsuzaka .60 1.50
SSEC Eric Chavez .40 1.00
SSJC Johnny Cueto .60 1.50
SSJF Jeff Francoeur .60 1.50
SSJM Joe Mauer .75 2.00
SSJP Jorge Posada .60 1.50
SSLB Lance Berkman .60 1.50
SSMB Mark Buehrle .60 1.50
SSMR Mark Reynolds .40 1.00
SSNM Nick Markakis .75 2.00
SSRB Rocco Baldelli .40 1.00
SSRG Ryan Garko .40 1.00
SSRH Roy Halladay .60 1.50
SSRM Russell Martin .40 1.00
SSRW Rickie Weeks .40 1.00
SSTL Tim Lincecum .60 1.50
SSVG Vladimir Guerrero .60 1.50
SSZG Zack Greinke 1.00 2.50

2009 UD A Piece of History Stadium Scenes Jersey

OVERALL MEM ODDS 1:16
SSAL Adam LaRoche 3.00 8.00
SSCC Chris Carpenter 3.00 8.00
SSCD Carlos Delgado 3.00 8.00
SSCG Curtis Granderson 3.00 8.00
SSCO Chad Cordero 3.00 8.00
SSCY Chris Young 3.00 8.00
SSDL Derrek Lee 3.00 8.00
SSDM Daisuke Matsuzaka 6.00 15.00
SSEC Eric Chavez 3.00 8.00
SSJC Johnny Cueto 3.00 8.00
SSJF Jeff Francoeur 3.00 8.00
SSJM Joe Mauer 3.00 8.00
SSJP Jorge Posada 3.00 8.00
SSLB Lance Berkman 3.00 8.00
SSMB Mark Buehrle 3.00 8.00
SSMR Mark Reynolds 3.00 8.00
SSNM Nick Markakis 4.00 10.00
SSRB Rocco Baldelli 3.00 8.00
SSRH Roy Halladay 3.00 8.00
SSRM Russell Martin 3.00 8.00
SSRW Rickie Weeks 3.00 8.00
SSTL Tim Lincecum 5.00 12.00
SSVG Vladimir Guerrero 3.00 8.00
SSZG Zack Greinke 4.00 10.00

2009 UD A Piece of History Stadium Scenes Jersey Red

*RED: .4X TO 1X BASIC
OVERALL MEM ODDS 1:16
STATED PRINT RUN 180 SER.#'d SETS

2009 UD A Piece of History Stadium Scenes Patch

STATED PRINT RUN 35 SER.#'d SETS
SSAL Adam LaRoche 6.00 15.00
SSCC Chris Carpenter 6.00 15.00
SSCD Carlos Delgado 6.00 15.00
SSCO Chad Cordero 6.00 15.00
SSCY Chris Young 6.00 15.00
SSDL Derrek Lee 10.00 25.00
SSEC Eric Chavez 6.00 15.00
SSJF Jeff Francoeur 12.50 30.00
SSMB Mark Buehrle 6.00 15.00
SSMR Mark Reynolds 6.00 15.00
SSNM Nick Markakis 15.00 40.00
SSRH Roy Halladay 15.00 40.00
SSRM Russell Martin 10.00 25.00
SSRW Rickie Weeks 6.00 15.00
SSZG Zack Greinke 6.00 15.00

2009 UD A Piece of History Timeless Moments

RANDOM INSERTS IN PACKS
STATED PRINT RUN 999 SER.#'d SETS
*BLACK: .5X TO 1.2X BASIC
BLACK RANDOMLY INSERTED
BLACK PRINT RUN 149 SER.#'d SETS
*BLUE: 1.5X TO 4X BASIC
BLUE RANDOMLY INSERTED
BLUE PRINT RUN 25 SER.#'d SETS
*RED: .75X TO 2X BASIC
RED RANDOMLY INSERTED
RED PRINT RUN 75 SER.#'d SETS
*TURQUOISE: .6X TO 1.5X BASIC
TURQUOISE RANDOMLY INSERTED
TURQUOISE PRINT RUN 99 SER.#'d SETS
TMAP Albert Pujols 1.25 3.00
TMBR Brian Roberts .40 1.00
TMCH Cole Hamels .75 2.00
TMDL Derek Lowe .40 1.00
TMDO David Ortiz 1.00 2.50
TMDW Dontrelle Willis .40 1.00
TMEL Evan Longoria .60 1.50
TMEV Edinson Volquez .40 1.00
TMFT Frank Thomas 1.00 2.50
TMJB Jay Bruce .60 1.50
TMJD Jermaine Dye .40 1.00
TMJH Josh Hamilton .60 1.50
TMJL Jon Lester .60 1.50
TMJP Jonathan Papelbon .60 1.50
TMJV Joey Votto 1.00 2.50
TMKG Ken Griffey Jr. 2.00 5.00
TMMB Mark Buehrle .60 1.50
TMML Mike Lowell .40 1.00
TMPE Jake Peavy .40 1.00
TMRB Ryan Braun .60 1.50
TMRJ Randy Johnson 1.00 2.50
TMSK Scott Kazmir .40 1.00
TMSM John Smoltz 1.00 2.50
TMTG Tom Glavine .60 1.50

2009 UD A Piece of History Timeless Moments Jersey

OVERALL MEM ODDS 1:16
TMAP Albert Pujols 6.00 15.00
TMBR Brian Roberts 3.00 8.00
TMCH Cole Hamels 6.00 15.00
TMDO David Ortiz 3.00 8.00
TMEL Evan Longoria 10.00 25.00
TMEV Edinson Volquez 3.00 8.00
TMFT Frank Thomas 8.00 20.00
TMJB Jay Bruce 5.00 12.00
TMJD Jermaine Dye 3.00 8.00
TMJH Josh Hamilton 4.00 10.00
TMJL Jon Lester 3.00 8.00
TMJP Jonathan Papelbon 4.00 10.00
TMJV Joey Votto 4.00 10.00
TMKG Ken Griffey Jr. 6.00 15.00
TMMB Mark Buehrle 3.00 8.00
TMML Mike Lowell 3.00 8.00
TMPE Jake Peavy 3.00 8.00
TMRB Ryan Braun 4.00 10.00
TMRJ Randy Johnson 3.00 8.00
TMSK Scott Kazmir 3.00 8.00
TMSM John Smoltz 3.00 8.00
TMTG Tom Glavine 4.00 10.00

2009 UD A Piece of History Timeless Moments Jersey Red

*RED: .4X TO 1X BASIC
OVERALL MEM ODDS 1:16
STATED PRINT RUN 180 SER.#'d SETS

2009 UD A Piece of History Timeless Moments Patch

RANDOM INSERTS IN PACKS
STATED PRINT RUN 25 SER.#'d SETS
NO PRICING DUE TO SCARCITY

2009 UD A Piece of History Timeless Moments Jersey Autograph

RANDOM INSERTS IN PACKS
PRINT RUNS B/WN 10-25 COPIES PER
NO PRICING DUE TO SCARCITY
EXCHANGE DEADLINE 3/16/2011

2005 UD All-Star Classics

COMPLETE SET (100) 10.00 25.00
COMMON CARD (1-50) .10 .30
COMMON CARD (51-75) .10 .30
COMMON CARD (76-100) .10 .30
51-100 ARE NOT SHORT PRINTS
1 Albert Pujols .40 1.00
2 Alex Rodriguez .40 1.00
3 Alfonso Soriano .20 .50
4 Barry Zito .20 .50
5 Bobby Abreu .12 .30
6 Carlos Beltran .20 .50
7 Carlos Delgado .12 .30
8 Chipper Jones .30 .75
9 Curt Schilling .20 .50
10 David Ortiz .30 .75
11 Derek Jeter .75 2.00
12 Edgar Renteria .12 .30
13 Eric Gagne .12 .30
14 Frank Thomas .30 .75
15 Gary Sheffield .12 .30
16 Greg Maddux .40 1.00
17 Hank Blalock .12 .30
18 Hideki Matsui .50 1.25
19 Ichiro Suzuki .40 1.00
20 Ivan Rodriguez .20 .50
21 Jason Schmidt .12 .30
22 Jason Varitek .30 .75
23 Jeff Kent .12 .30
24 Jim Thome .20 .50
25 Jorge Posada .20 .50
26 Ken Griffey Jr. .60 1.50
27 Kerry Wood .12 .30
28 Lance Berkman .20 .50
29 Manny Ramirez .30 .75
30 Mariano Rivera .40 1.00
31 Mark Mulder .12 .30
32 Mark Prior .20 .50
33 Miguel Cabrera .30 .75
34 Miguel Tejada .20 .50
35 Mike Piazza .30 .75
36 Nomar Garciaparra .20 .50
37 Pedro Martinez .20 .50
38 Randy Johnson .30 .75
39 Richie Sexson .12 .30
40 Roger Clemens .40 1.00
41 Roy Halladay .20 .50
42 Sammy Sosa .30 .75
43 Scott Rolen .20 .50
44 Sean Casey .12 .30
45 Tim Hudson .20 .50
46 Todd Helton .20 .50
47 Tom Glavine .20 .50
48 Torii Hunter .12 .30
49 Troy Glaus .12 .30
50 Vladimir Guerrero .20 .50
51 Adrian Beltre FUT .30 .75
52 Alexis Rios FUT .12 .30
53 Aubrey Huff FUT .12 .30
54 Brandon Webb FUT .12 .30
55 Dallas McPherson FUT .12 .30
56 David Wright FUT .25 .60
57 Edwin Jackson FUT .12 .30
58 Grady Sizemore FUT .20 .50
59 Tadahito Iguchi FUT RC .20 .50
60 Jake Peavy FUT .12 .30
61 Jake Westbrook FUT .12 .30
62 Jason Bay FUT .12 .30
63 Jeff Francis FUT .12 .30
64 Jeremy Reed FUT .12 .30
65 Joe Mauer FUT .25 .60
66 Johan Santana FUT .20 .50
67 Jose Capellan FUT .12 .30
68 Jose Reyes FUT .20 .50
69 Justin Morneau FUT .20 .50
70 Mark Teixeira FUT .20 .50
71 Oliver Perez FUT .12 .30
72 Rich Harden FUT .12 .30
73 Rickie Weeks FUT .12 .30
74 Ryan Howard FUT .25 .60
75 Scott Kazmir FUT .30 .75
76 Al Kaline LGD .30 .75
77 Bill Mazeroski LGD .20 .50
78 Bob Feller LGD .20 .50
79 Bob Gibson LGD .20 .50
80 Brooks Robinson LGD .20 .50
81 Cal Ripken LGD 1.00 2.50
82 Carlton Fisk LGD .20 .50
83 Eddie Murray LGD .20 .50
84 Gaylord Perry LGD .20 .50
85 Harmon Killebrew LGD .30 .75
86 Jim Palmer LGD .20 .50
87 Joe DiMaggio LGD .60 1.50
88 Joe Morgan LGD .20 .50
89 Johnny Bench LGD .30 .75
90 Juan Marichal LGD .20 .50
91 Lou Brock LGD .20 .50
92 Mike Schmidt LGD .50 1.25
93 Nolan Ryan LGD 1.00 2.50
94 Ozzie Smith LGD .40 1.00
95 Phil Niekro LGD .20 .50
96 Robin Yount LGD .30 .75
97 Rollie Fingers LGD .20 .50
98 Tom Seaver LGD .20 .50
99 Willie McCovey LGD .20 .50
100 Yogi Berra LGD .30 .75

2005 UD All-Star Classics Gold

*GOLD 1-50: 2.5X TO 6X BASIC
*GOLD 51-75: 2.5X TO 6X BASIC
*GOLD 76-100: 2.5X TO 6X BASIC
STATED ODDS 1:24
STATED PRINT RUN 499 SERIAL #'d SETS

2005 UD All-Star Classics Box Scores

STATED ODDS 1:24
1 Juan Marichal .60 1.50
2 Brooks Robinson .60 1.50
3 Tony Perez .60 1.50
4 Willie McCovey .60 1.50
5 Harmon Killebrew 1.00 2.50
6 Johnny Bench 1.00 2.50
7 Joe Morgan .60 1.50
8 Lou Brock .60 1.50
9 Jim Palmer .60 1.50
10 Mike Schmidt 1.50 4.00
11 Ozzie Smith 1.25 3.00
12 Roger Clemens 1.25 3.00
13 Cal Ripken 3.00 8.00
14 Ken Griffey Jr. 2.00 5.00
15 Greg Maddux 1.25 3.00
16 Alex Rodriguez 1.25 3.00
17 Derek Jeter 2.50 6.00
18 Johnny Damon .60 1.50
19 Garret Anderson .40 1.00
20 Alfonso Soriano .60 1.50

2005 UD All-Star Classics Matchups

STATED ODDS 1:24
1 H.Blalock E.Gagne .40 1.00
2 C.Schilling A.Rodriguez 1.25 3.00
3 M.Ramirez R.Clemens 1.25 3.00
4 K.Griffey Jr. G.Maddux 2.00 5.00
5 B.Robinson F.Jenkins .60 1.50
6 H.Killebrew F.Jenkins 1.00 2.50
7 C.Yastrzemski T.Seaver 1.25 3.00
8 C.Ripken C.Park 3.00 8.00
9 T.Hoffman J.Posada .60 1.50
10 E.Gagne A.Soriano .60 1.50
11 A.Soriano R.Clemens 1.25 3.00
12 D.Ortiz C.Pavano 1.00 2.50
13 A.Jones M.Mulder .40 1.00
14 G.Anderson W.Williams .40 1.00
15 M.Ordonez J.Leiber .60 1.50
16 D.Jeter J.Lieber 2.50 6.00
17 C.Jones J.Baldwin 1.00 2.50
18 R.Alomar T.Hoffman .60 1.50
19 M.Piazza K.Rogers 1.00 2.50
20 A.Rodriguez A.Ashby 1.25 3.00

2005 UD All-Star Classics Midsummer Classics

STATED ODDS 1:24
1 Derek Jeter 2.50 6.00
2 Pedro Martinez .60 1.50
3 Mike Piazza 1.00 2.50
4 Randy Johnson 1.00 2.50
5 Gary Sheffield .40 1.00
6 Albert Pujols 1.25 3.00
7 David Ortiz 1.00 2.50
8 Manny Ramirez 1.00 2.50
9 Garret Anderson .40 1.00
10 Andruw Jones .40 1.00
11 Todd Helton .60 1.50
12 Paul Konerko .60 1.50
13 Alfonso Soriano .60 1.50
14 Magglio Ordonez .60 1.50
15 Cal Ripken 3.00 8.00
16 Ken Griffey Jr. 2.00 5.00
17 Harmon Killebrew 1.00 2.50
18 Mike Schmidt 1.50 4.00
19 Frank Thomas 1.00 2.50
20 Alex Rodriguez 1.25 3.00

2005 UD All-Star Classics Midsummer Swatches

STATED ODDS 1:12
PATCHES RANDOM INSERTS IN PACKS
PATCH PRINT RUN 25 SERIAL #'d SETS
NO PATCH PRICING DUE TO SCARCITY
AJ Andruw Jones Pants 4.00 10.00
BB Bret Boone Jsy 3.00 8.00
BS Ben Sheets Jsy 3.00 8.00
CB Carlos Beltran Jsy 3.00 8.00
CC C.C. Sabathia Jsy 3.00 8.00
CD Carlos Delgado Jsy 3.00 8.00
CI Craig Biggio Jsy 4.00 10.00
CJ Chipper Jones Jsy 4.00 10.00
CR Cal Ripken Pants 10.00 25.00
DO David Ortiz Pants 4.00 10.00
DW Dontrelle Willis Jsy 3.00 8.00
EG Eric Gagne Jsy 3.00 8.00
ER Edgar Renteria Jsy 3.00 8.00
FT Frank Thomas Jsy 4.00 10.00
GS Gary Sheffield Jsy 3.00 8.00
IS Ichiro Suzuki Jsy 10.00 25.00
JB Jeff Bagwell Jsy 4.00 10.00
JE Jim Edmonds Jsy 3.00 8.00
JK Jeff Kent Jsy 3.00 8.00
JL Javy Lopez Jsy 3.00 8.00
JS John Smoltz Jsy 4.00 10.00
JT Jim Thome Jsy 4.00 10.00
KF Keith Foulke Jsy 3.00 8.00
KG Ken Griffey Jr. Jsy 8.00 20.00
MA Moises Alou Jsy 3.00 8.00
ML Matt Lawton Jsy 3.00 8.00
MP Mike Piazza Jsy 4.00 10.00
MS Mike Sweeney Jsy 3.00 8.00
MT Miguel Tejada Jsy 3.00 8.00
OM Omar Vizquel Jsy 4.00 10.00
PL Paul LoDuca Jsy 3.00 8.00
PM Pedro Martinez Jsy 4.00 10.00
RF Rafael Furcal Jsy 3.00 8.00
RK Ryan Klesko Jsy 3.00 8.00
RP Rafael Palmeiro Jsy 4.00 10.00
SC Jason Schmidt Jsy 3.00 8.00
SG Shawn Green Jsy 3.00 8.00
SS Sammy Sosa Jsy 4.00 10.00
TH Todd Helton Jsy 4.00 10.00
TI Torii Hunter Jsy 3.00 8.00
VM Victor Martinez Jsy 3.00 8.00
WE David Wells Jsy 3.00 8.00

2005 UD All-Star Classics MVPs

STATED ODDS 1:24
1 Alfonso Soriano .60 1.50
2 Ken Griffey Sr. .40 1.00
3 Brooks Robinson .60 1.50
4 Cal Ripken 3.00 8.00
5 Cal Ripken 3.00 8.00
6 Derek Jeter 2.50 6.00
7 Carl Yastrzemski 1.25 3.00
8 Garret Anderson .40 1.00
9 Jeff Conine .40 1.00
10 Joe Morgan .60 1.50
11 Juan Marichal .60 1.50
12 Julio Franco .40 1.00
13 Ken Griffey Jr. 2.00 5.00
14 Mike Piazza 1.00 2.50
15 Pedro Martinez .60 1.50
16 Roberto Alomar .60 1.50
17 Roger Clemens 1.25 3.00
18 Sandy Alomar Jr. .40 1.00
19 Tony Perez .60 1.50
20 Willie McCovey .60 1.50

2005 UD All-Star Classics Perennial All-Stars

STATED ODDS 1:24
1 Albert Pujols 1.25 3.00
2 Alex Rodriguez 1.25 3.00
3 Alfonso Soriano .60 1.50
4 Curt Schilling .60 1.50
5 Derek Jeter 2.50 6.00
6 Eric Gagne .40 1.00
7 Greg Maddux 1.25 3.00
8 Ichiro Suzuki 1.25 3.00
9 Ivan Rodriguez .60 1.50
10 Jim Thome .60 1.50
11 Ken Griffey Jr. 2.00 5.00
12 Mariano Rivera 1.25 3.00
13 Miguel Tejada .60 1.50
14 Mike Piazza 1.00 2.50
15 Randy Johnson 1.00 2.50
16 Roger Clemens 1.25 3.00
17 Sammy Sosa 1.00 2.50
18 Scott Rolen .60 1.50
19 Todd Helton .60 1.50
20 Vladimir Guerrero .60 1.50

2002 UD Authentics

COMPLETE SET (200) 20.00 50.00
COMMON CARD (1-170) .20 .50
COMMON CARD (171-200) .50 1.25
SR CARDS 171-200 ARE NOT SP'S
1 Brad Fullmer .20 .50
2 Garret Anderson .20 .50
3 Darin Erstad .20 .50
4 Jarrod Washburn .20 .50
5 Troy Glaus .20 .50
6 Barry Zito .20 .50

7 David Justice .20 .50
8 Eric Chavez .20 .50
9 Tim Hudson .20 .50
10 Miguel Tejada .20 .50
11 Jermaine Dye .20 .50
12 Mark Mulder .20 .50
13 Carlos Delgado .20 .50
14 Jose Cruz Jr. .20 .50
16 Shannon Stewart .20 .50
17 Raul Mondesi .20 .50
18 Tanyon Sturtze .20 .50
19 Toby Hall .20 .50
20 Greg Vaughn .20 .50
21 Aubrey Huff .20 .50
22 Ben Grieve .20 .50
23 Brent Abernathy .20 .50
24 Jim Thome .30 .75
25 C.C. Sabathia .20 .50
26 Matt Lawton .20 .50
27 Omar Vizquel .30 .75
28 Ellis Burks .20 .50
29 Russ Branyan .20 .50
30 Bartolo Colon .20 .50
31 Ichiro Suzuki 1.00 2.50
32 John Olerud .20 .50
33 Freddy Garcia .20 .50
34 Mike Cameron .20 .50
35 Jeff Cirillo .20 .50
36 Kazuhiro Sasaki .20 .50
37 Edgar Martinez .30 .75
38 Bret Boone .20 .50
39 Jeff Conine .20 .50
40 Melvin Mora .20 .50
41 Jason Johnson .20 .50
42 Chris Richard .20 .50
43 Tony Batista .20 .50
44 Ivan Rodriguez .30 .75
45 Gabe Kapler .20 .50
46 Rafael Palmeiro .30 .75
47 Alex Rodriguez .60 1.50
48 Juan Gonzalez .20 .50
49 Carl Everett .20 .50
50 Nomar Garciaparra .75 2.00
51 Trot Nixon .20 .50
52 Manny Ramirez .30 .75
53 Pedro Martinez .30 .75
54 Johnny Damon Sox .30 .75
55 Shea Hillenbrand .20 .50
56 Mike Sweeney .20 .50
57 Mark Quinn .20 .50
58 Joe Randa .20 .50
59 Carlos Beltran .20 .50
60 Chuck Knoblauch .20 .50
61 Robert Fick .20 .50
62 Jeff Weaver .20 .50
63 Bobby Higginson .20 .50
64 Dean Palmer .20 .50
65 Dmitri Young .20 .50
66 Corey Koskie .20 .50
67 Doug Mientkiewicz .20 .50
68 Joe Mays .20 .50
69 Torii Hunter .20 .50
70 Cristian Guzman .20 .50
71 Jacque Jones .20 .50
72 Magglio Ordonez .20 .50
73 Paul Konerko .20 .50
74 Carlos Lee .20 .50
75 Mark Buehrle .20 .50
76 Jose Canseco .30 .75
77 Frank Thomas .50 1.25
78 Roger Clemens 1.00 2.50
79 Derek Jeter 1.25 3.00
80 Jason Giambi Yankees .20 .50
81 Rondell White .20 .50
82 Bernie Williams .30 .75
83 Jorge Posada .30 .75
84 Mike Mussina .30 .75
85 Alfonso Soriano .20 .50
86 Wade Miller .20 .50
87 Jeff Bagwell .30 .75
88 Craig Biggio .30 .75
89 Roy Oswalt .20 .50
90 Lance Berkman .20 .50
91 Daryle Ward .20 .50
92 Chipper Jones .50 1.25
93 Greg Maddux .75 2.00
94 Marcus Giles .20 .50
95 Gary Sheffield .20 .50
96 Tom Glavine .30 .75
97 Andruw Jones .30 .75
98 Rafael Furcal .20 .50
99 Richie Sexson .20 .50
100 Ben Sheets .20 .50
101 Jose Hernandez .20 .50
102 Geoff Jenkins .20 .50
103 Jeffrey Hammonds .20 .50
104 Edgar Renteria .20 .50
105 Matt Morris .20 .50
106 Tino Martinez .30 .75
107 Jim Edmonds .20 .50
108 Albert Pujols 1.00 2.50
109 J.D. Drew .20 .50
110 Fernando Vina .20 .50
111 Darryl Kile .20 .50
112 Sammy Sosa .50 1.25
113 Fred McGriff .30 .75
114 Kerry Wood .20 .50
115 Moises Alou .20 .50
116 Jon Lieber .20 .50
117 Mark Grace .30 .75
118 Randy Johnson .50 1.25
119 Curt Schilling .20 .50
120 Luis Gonzalez .20 .50
121 Steve Finley .20 .50
122 Matt Williams .20 .50
123 Shawn Green .20 .50
124 Kevin Brown .20 .50
125 Adrian Beltre .20 .50
126 Paul LoDuca .20 .50
127 Hideo Nomo .50 1.25
128 Brian Jordan .20 .50
129 Vladimir Guerrero .50 1.25
130 Javier Vazquez .20 .50
131 Jose Vidro .20 .50
132 Orlando Cabrera .20 .50
133 Jeff Kent .20 .50
134 Rich Aurilia .20 .50
135 Russ Ortiz .20 .50
136 Barry Bonds 1.25 3.00
137 Preston Wilson .20 .50
138 Ryan Dempster .20 .50
139 Cliff Floyd .20 .50
140 Josh Beckett .20 .50
141 Mike Lowell .20 .50
142 Mike Piazza .75 2.00
143 Roberto Alomar .30 .75
144 Al Leiter .20 .50
145A Edgardo Alfonzo .20 .50
145B Mo Vaughn .20 .50
146 Roger Cedeno .20 .50
147 Jeromy Burnitz .20 .50
148 Phil Nevin .20 .50
149 Mark Kotsay .20 .50
150 Ryan Klesko .20 .50
151 Trevor Hoffman .20 .50
152 Bobby Abreu .20 .50
153 Scott Rolen .30 .75
154 Jimmy Rollins .20 .50
155 Robert Person .20 .50
156 Pat Burrell .20 .50
157 Randy Wolf .20 .50
158 Brian Giles .20 .50
159 Aramis Ramirez .20 .50
160 Kris Benson .20 .50
161 Jason Kendall .20 .50
162 Ken Griffey Jr. 1.00 2.50
163 Sean Casey .20 .50
164 Adam Dunn .20 .50
165 Barry Larkin .30 .75
166 Todd Helton .30 .75
167 Mike Hampton .20 .50
168 Larry Walker .20 .50
169 Juan Pierre .20 .50
170 Juan Uribe .20 .50
171 So Taguchi SR RC .75 2.00
172 Brendan Donnelly SR RC .50 1.25
173 Chris Baker SR RC .50 1.25
174 John Ennis SR RC .50 1.25
175 Francis Beltran SR RC .50 1.25
176 Danny Wright SR .50 1.25
177 Brandon Backe SR RC .75 2.00
178 Mark Corey SR RC .50 1.25
179 Kazuhisa Ishii SR RC .75 2.00
180 Ron Calloway SR RC .50 1.25
181 Kevin Frederick SR RC .50 1.25
182 Jaime Cerda SR RC .50 1.25
183 Doug Devore SR RC .50 1.25
184 Brandon Puffer SR RC .50 1.25
185 Andy Pratt SR RC .50 1.25
186 Adrian Burnside SR RC .50 1.25
187 Josh Hancock SR RC .60 1.50
188 Jorge Nunez SR RC .50 1.25
189 Tyler Yates SR RC .50 1.25
190 Kyle Kane SR RC .50 1.25
191 Jose Valverde SR RC .50 1.25
192 Matt Thornton SR RC .50 1.25
193 Ben Howard SR RC .50 1.25
194 Reed Johnson SR RC .60 1.50
195 Rene Reyes SR RC .50 1.25
196 Jeremy Ward SR RC .50 1.25
197 Steve Bechler SR RC .50 1.25
198 Cam Esslinger SR RC .50 1.25
199 Michael Crudale SR RC .50 1.25
200 Todd Donovan SR RC .50 1.25

2002 UD Authentics Reverse Negatives

*REV.NEG 1-170: 2.5X TO 6X BASIC
*REV.NEG 171-200: 1X TO 2.5X BASIC
STATED ODDS 1:9
CARDS FEATURE AIRBRUSHED IMAGES

2002 UD Authentics 1989 Flashbacks

COMPLETE SET (12) 20.00 50.00
RANDOM INSERTS IN PACKS
STATED PRINT RUN 4225 SERIAL #'d SETS
F1 Ken Griffey Jr. 3.00 8.00
F2 Gary Sheffield 1.25 3.00
F3 Randy Johnson 1.50 4.00
F4 Roger Clemens 3.00 8.00
F5 Greg Maddux 2.50 6.00
F6 Mark Grace 1.25 3.00
F7 Barry Bonds 4.00 10.00
F8 Roberto Alomar 1.25 3.00
F9 Sammy Sosa 1.50 4.00
F10 Rafael Palmeiro 1.25 3.00
F11 Edgar Martinez 1.25 3.00
F12 Jose Canseco 1.25 3.00

2002 UD Authentics Heroes of Baseball

COMP.GRIFFEY SET (10) 25.00 60.00
COMMON GRIFFEY (G1-G10) 3.00 8.00
COMP.ICHIRO SET (10) 25.00 60.00
COMMON ICHIRO (I1-I10) 3.00 8.00
COMP.A.ROD SET (10) 25.00 60.00
COMMON A.ROD (R1-R10) 3.00 8.00
STATED PRINT RUN 1989 SERIAL #'d SETS

2002 UD Authentics Heroes of Baseball Autographs

RANDOM INSERTS IN PACKS
STATED PRINT RUNS LISTED BELOW
SHBG Ken Griffey Jr./185 60.00 120.00
SHBI Ichiro Suzuki/125 250.00 400.00
SHBR Alex Rodriguez/185 30.00 60.00

2002 UD Authentics Reverse Negative Jerseys

STATED ODDS 1:16
RAJ Andruw Jones 6.00 15.00
RAR Alex Rodriguez 6.00 15.00
RBW Bernie Williams 6.00 15.00
RBZ Barry Zito 4.00 10.00
RCD Carlos Delgado 4.00 10.00
RCJ Chipper Jones 6.00 15.00
RDE Darin Erstad 4.00 10.00
REC Eric Chavez 4.00 10.00
RFT Frank Thomas 6.00 15.00
RGM Greg Maddux 6.00 15.00
RIR Ivan Rodriguez 6.00 15.00
RJB Jeff Bagwell 6.00 15.00
RJD J.D. Drew 4.00 10.00
RJE Jim Edmonds 4.00 10.00
RJG Jason Giambi 4.00 10.00
RKB Kevin Brown 4.00 10.00
RKG Ken Griffey Jr. 6.00 15.00
RLG Luis Gonzalez 4.00 10.00
RMP Mike Piazza 6.00 15.00
RMR Manny Ramirez 6.00 15.00
RMS Mike Sweeney 4.00 10.00
RRC Roger Clemens SP 15.00 40.00
RRF Rafael Furcal 4.00 10.00
RRJ Randy Johnson 6.00 15.00
RSS Sammy Sosa SP 6.00 15.00
RTG Tom Glavine 6.00 15.00
RTH Todd Helton 6.00 15.00

2002 UD Authentics Retro Star Rookie Jerseys

STATED ODDS 1:16
*GOLD: .5X TO 1.2X BASIC
SRAP Albert Pujols 6.00 15.00
SRAR Alex Rodriguez 4.00 10.00
SRBG Brian Giles 1.25 3.00
SRCB Craig Biggio 2.00 5.00
SRCJ Chipper Jones 3.00 8.00
SRDJ David Justice 1.25 3.00
SRGK Gabe Kapler SP 1.25 3.00
SRGS Gary Sheffield 1.25 3.00
SRHN Hideo Nomo 3.00 8.00
SRI Ichiro Suzuki 4.00 10.00
SRIR Ivan Rodriguez 2.00 5.00
SRJG Juan Gonzalez 1.25 3.00
SRJO John Olerud 1.25 3.00
SRJT Jim Thome 2.00 5.00
SRKG Ken Griffey Jr. 6.00 15.00
SRKL Kenny Lofton 1.25 3.00
SRKS Kazuhiro Sasaki 1.25 3.00
SRLG Luis Gonzalez 1.25 3.00
SRLW Larry Walker 2.00 5.00
SRMO Magglio Ordonez 2.00 5.00
SRMR Manny Ramirez SP 2.00 5.00
SRPB Pat Burrell 1.25 3.00
SRPM Pedro Martinez 2.00 5.00
SRRJ Randy Johnson 3.00 8.00
SRRK Ryan Klesko 1.25 3.00
SRRP Robert Person 1.25 3.00
SRSG Shawn Green 1.25 3.00
SRSS Sammy Sosa SP 3.00 8.00

2002 UD Authentics Retro Star Rookie Jerseys Autographs

RANDOM INSERTS IN PACKS
STATED PRINT RUN 40 SERIAL #'d SETS
SSRAR Alex Rodriguez 100.00 175.00
SSRJT Jim Thome 40.00 80.00
SSRKG Ken Griffey Jr. 75.00 150.00

2002 UD Authentics Stars of '89 Jerseys

STATED ODDS 1:16
SLAG Andres Galarraga 4.00 10.00
SLAL Al Leiter 4.00 10.00
SLBL Barry Larkin SP 6.00 15.00
SLCS Curt Schilling 4.00 10.00
SLDC David Cone 4.00 10.00
SLDJ David Justice 4.00 10.00
SLEB Ellis Burks 4.00 10.00
SLEM Edgar Martinez 6.00 15.00
SLFM Fred McGriff 6.00 15.00
SLGM Greg Maddux 6.00 15.00
SLGS Gary Sheffield 4.00 10.00
SLJC Jose Canseco 6.00 15.00
SLJG Juan Gonzalez 4.00 10.00
SLJO John Olerud 4.00 10.00
SLKB Kevin Brown 4.00 10.00
SLKG Ken Griffey Jr. 8.00 20.00
SLLW Larry Walker 4.00 10.00
SLMG Mark Grace 6.00 15.00
SLMW Matt Williams 4.00 10.00
SLPO Paul O'Neill 6.00 15.00
SLRA Roberto Alomar 6.00 15.00
SLRC Roger Clemens 10.00 25.00
SLRH Rickey Henderson 6.00 15.00
SLRJ Randy Johnson 6.00 15.00
SLRP Rafael Palmeiro 6.00 15.00
SLRV Robin Ventura 4.00 10.00
SLSS Sammy Sosa 6.00 15.00
SLTG Tom Glavine 6.00 15.00

2003 UD Authentics

COMP.SET w/o SP's (100) 15.00 40.00
COMMON ACTIVE (1-100) .15 .40
COMMON RETIRED (1-100) .15 .40
COMMON CARD (101-130) .75 2.00
101-130 RANDOM INSERTS IN PACKS
101-130 PRINT RUN 999 SERIAL #'d SETS
COMMON CARD (131-140) 1.25 3.00
131-140 RANDOM IN FINITE BONUS PACKS
131-140 PRINT RUN 150 SERIAL #'d SETS
1 Pee Wee Reese .25 .60
2 Richie Ashburn .25 .60
3 Derek Jeter 1.00 2.50
4 Alex Rodriguez .50 1.25
5 Jose Vidro .15 .40
6 Miguel Tejada .25 .60
7 Nomar Garciaparra .25 .60
8 Pat Burrell .15 .40
9 Albert Pujols .50 1.25
10 Jeff Bagwell .25 .60
11 Stan Musial .60 1.50
12 Mickey Mantle 1.25 3.00
13 J.D. Drew .15 .40
14 Ivan Rodriguez .25 .60
15 Joe Morgan .25 .60
16 Ted Williams .75 2.00
17 Travis Hafner .15 .40
18 Chipper Jones .40 1.00
19 Hideo Nomo .40 1.00
20 Gary Sheffield .15 .40
21 Jacque Jones .15 .40
22 Alfonso Soriano .25 .60
23 Roberto Alomar .25 .60
24 Jeff Kent .15 .40
25 Omar Vizquel .25 .60
26 Ernie Banks .40 1.00
27 Shawn Green .15 .40
28 Tim Hudson .25 .60
29 Jim Edmonds .25 .60
30 Brandon Larson .15 .40
31 Doug Mientkiewicz .15 .40
32 Darin Erstad .15 .40
33 Bobby Hill .15 .40
34 Todd Helton .25 .60
35 Kazuhisa Ishii .15 .40
36 Lance Berkman .25 .60
37 Eric Hinske .15 .40
38 Jason Kendall .15 .40
39 Bob Feller .25 .60
40 Luis Gonzalez .15 .40
41 Sammy Sosa .40 1.00
42 Mike Piazza .40 1.00
43 Roger Clemens .50 1.25
44 Jose Cruz Jr. .15 .40
45 Mark Prior .25 .60
46 Mark Teixeira .25 .60
47 Phil Nevin .15 .40
48 Lyle Overbay .15 .40
49 Manny Ramirez .40 1.00
50 Brian Giles .15 .40
51 Preston Wilson .15 .40
52 Jermaine Dye .15 .40
53 Troy Glaus .15 .40
54 Frank Thomas .40 1.00
55 Jim Thome .25 .60
56 Barry Bonds .60 1.50
57 Carlos Delgado .15 .40
58 Jason Giambi .15 .40
59 Joe Mays .15 .40
60 Andruw Jones .15 .40
61 Billy Williams .25 .60
62 Vladimir Guerrero .25 .60
63 Scott Rolen .25 .60
64 Juan Marichal .25 .60
65 Austin Kearns .15 .40
66 Kerry Wood .15 .40
67 Bret Boone .15 .40
68 Shea Hillenbrand .15 .40
69 Mike Sweeney .15 .40
70 Rocco Baldelli .15 .40
71 Ken Griffey Jr. .75 2.00
72 Cliff Floyd .15 .40
73 Greg Maddux .50 1.25
74 Mike Hampton .15 .40
75 Larry Walker .25 .60
76 Nolan Ryan 1.25 3.00
77 Rollie Fingers .25 .60
78 Mike Mussina .25 .60
79 Matt Morris .15 .40
80 Robin Roberts .25 .60
81 Barry Zito .25 .60
82 Curt Schilling .25 .60
83 Ken Harvey .15 .40
84 Troy Percival .15 .40
85 Tom Seaver .25 .60
86 Mariano Rivera .50 1.25
87 Raul Mondesi .15 .40
88 Adam Dunn .25 .60
89 Roy Oswalt .25 .60
90 Pedro Martinez .25 .60
91 Andy Pettitte .25 .60
92 Tom Glavine .25 .60
93 Torii Hunter .15 .40
94 Joe Thurston .15 .40
95 Runelvys Hernandez .15 .40
96 Randy Johnson .40 1.00
97 Bernie Williams .25 .60
98 Ichiro Suzuki .50 1.25
99 C.C. Sabathia .25 .60
100 Bobby Abreu .15 .40
101 Jose Contreras RH RC 2.00 5.00
102 Hideki Matsui RH RC 4.00 10.00
103 Chris Capuano RH RC .75 2.00
104 Willie Eyre RH RC .75 2.00
105 Lew Ford RH RC .75 2.00
106 Shane Bazzell RH RC .75 2.00
107 Guillermo Quiroz RH RC .75 2.00
108 Fernando Cabrera RH RC .75 2.00
109 Francisco Cruceta RH RC .75 2.00
110 Jhonny Peralta RH .75 2.00
111 Bobby Madritsch RH RC .75 2.00
112 Diego Markwell RH RC .75 2.00
113 Matt Bruback RH RC .75 2.00
114 Matt Kata RH RC .75 2.00
115 Rob Hammock RH RC .75 2.00
116 Brandon Webb RH RC 2.50 6.00
117 Jon Leicester RH RC .75 2.00
118 Josh Willingham RH RC 2.50 6.00
119 Prentice Redman RH RC .75 2.00
120 Jeff Duncan RH RC .75 2.00
121 Craig Brazell RH RC .75 2.00
122 Jeremy Griffiths RH RC .75 2.00
123 Phil Seibel RH RC .75 2.00
124 Luis Ayala RH RC .75 2.00
125 Miguel Ojeda RH RC .75 2.00
126 Jeremy Wedel RH RC .75 2.00
127 Josh Hall RH RC .75 2.00
128 Oscar Villarreal RH RC .75 2.00
129 Clint Barmes RH RC 2.00 5.00
130 Nook Logan RH RC .75 2.00
131 Dan Haren RH RC 6.00 15.00
132 Delmon Young RH RC 8.00 20.00
133 Dontrelle Willis RH 1.25 3.00
134 Edwin Jackson RH RC 2.00 5.00
135 Jeremy Bonderman RH RC 5.00 12.00
136 Khalil Greene RH 2.00 5.00
137 Rich Harden RH 2.00 5.00
138 Rickie Weeks RH RC 4.00 10.00
139 Rosman Garcia RH RC 1.25 3.00
140 Ryan Wagner RH RC 1.25 3.00

2003 UD Authentics Rookie Hype Gold

*RH GOLD: 1X TO 2.5X BASIC
RANDOM INSERTS IN PACKS
STATED PRINT RUN 50 SERIAL #'d SETS

2003 UD Authentics Autograph Frames

PRINT RUNS B/WN 1-350 COPIES PER
NO PRICING ON QTY OF 25 OR LESS
MCGWIRE FRAME AVAIL.VIA MAIL EXCH.
AK1 Austin Kearns 28/175 15.00 40.00
AK2 Austin Kearns 28/200 15.00 40.00
AK3 Austin Kearns 28/325 15.00 40.00
AK4 Austin Kearns Mascot/300 15.00 40.00
AK5 Austin Kearns TL Jsy/28 40.00 80.00
BG1 Bob Gibson 45/200 30.00 60.00
BG2 Bob Gibson Cap/50 60.00 120.00
BG3 Bob Gibson TL Jsy/45 60.00 120.00
CF1 Carlton Fisk 27/250 30.00 60.00
CF2 Carlton Fisk B/70 40.00 80.00
CF3 Carlton Fisk Socks/125 30.00 60.00
CF4 Carlton Fisk TL Jsy/27 100.00 200.00
CJ1 Chipper Jones 10/350 40.00 80.00
CJ2 Chipper Jones A/200 40.00 80.00
CJ3 Chipper Jones MVP/100 50.00 100.00
CR1 Cal Ripken 8/125 100.00 200.00
CR2 Cal Ripken Mascot/50 150.00 250.00
DH1 Drew Henson 57/100 20.00 50.00
DH2 Drew Henson 57/250 15.00 40.00
DH3 Drew Henson 57/350 15.00 40.00
DH4 Drew Henson NY/300 15.00 40.00
DS1 Duke Snider 4/150 30.00 60.00
DS2 Duke Snider 55 WS/50 60.00 120.00
GC1 Gary Carter 8/225 20.00 50.00
GC2 Gary Carter 86 WS/75 30.00 60.00
HB1 Hank Blalock 9/175 15.00 40.00
HB2 Hank Blalock 9/200 15.00 40.00
HB3 Hank Blalock 9/325 15.00 40.00
HB4 Hank Blalock Flag/300 15.00 40.00
HM1 Hideki Matsui 55/75 175.00 300.00
HM2 Hideki Matsui NY/75 175.00 300.00
HM3 H.Matsui TL Jsy/55 175.00 300.00
IS1 Ichiro Suzuki 51/75 300.00 500.00
IS2 Ichiro Suzuki S/75 300.00 500.00
IS3 Ichiro Suzuki TL Jsy/51 1000.00 2000.00
JC1 Jose Contreras 52/350 15.00 40.00
JC2 Jose Contreras NY/120 15.00 40.00
JG1 J.Giambi A's Cap/75 20.00 50.00
JG2 J.Giambi A's Mascot/150 15.00 40.00
JG3 J.Giambi Yanks 25/100 20.00 50.00
JG4 J.Giambi Yanks 25/200 15.00 40.00
JG5 J.Giambi Yanks 25/300 15.00 40.00
JG6 J.Giambi Yanks NY/350 15.00 40.00
KG1 K.Griffey M's MVP/75 60.00 120.00
KG2 K.Griffey Reds 30/325 50.00 100.00
KG3 K.Griffey Reds Mascot/200 50.00 100.00
KG4 K.Griffey Reds TL Jsy/30 75.00 150.00
LB1 Lance Berkman 17/150 20.00 50.00
LB2 Lance Berkman Cap/50 40.00 80.00
MP2 Mark Prior 22/175 15.00 40.00
MP3 Mark Prior 22/250 15.00 40.00
MP4 Mark Prior C/300 15.00 40.00
MP5 Mark Prior Mascot/100 20.00 50.00
MT1 Mark Teixeira 23/175 15.00 40.00
MT2 Mark Teixeira 23/200 15.00 40.00
MT3 Mark Teixeira 23/325 15.00 40.00
MT4 Mark Teixeira Flag/150 15.00 40.00
NG1 N.Garciaparra 5/250 50.00 100.00
NG2 N.Garciaparra B/150 50.00 100.00
NG3 N.Garciaparra Socks/75 60.00 120.00
NR1 Nolan Ryan Angels A/100 100.00 200.00
NR2 Nolan Ryan Mets TL/50 150.00 250.00
NR3 Nolan Ryan Rgr 34/150 75.00 150.00
NR4 Nolan Ryan Rgr TL Jsy/34 175.00 300.00
OS1 Ozzie Smith 1/150 15.00 40.00
OS2 Ozzie Smith Cap/50 30.00 60.00
PB1 Pat Burrell 5/330 15.00 40.00
PB2 Pat Burrell Comm/150 15.00 40.00
PB3 Pat Burrell P/240 15.00 40.00
PR1 Phil Rizzuto 10/350 30.00 60.00
PR2 Phil Rizzuto 51 WS/100 40.00 80.00
PR3 Phil Rizzuto NY/200 30.00 60.00
SR1 Scott Rolen 27/300 20.00 50.00
SR2 Scott Rolen STL/100 30.00 60.00
SR3 Scott Rolen TL Jsy/27 50.00 100.00
TGL1 Tom Glavine 47/275 30.00 60.00
TGL2 Tom Glavine Mascot/150 20.00 50.00
TGL3 Tom Glavine TL Jsy/47 40.00 80.00
TG1 Troy Glaus 25/350 20.00 50.00
TG2 Troy Glaus 02 WS/100 40.00 80.00
TG3 Troy Glaus A/200 20.00 50.00
TS1 Tom Seaver 41/100 40.00 100.00
TS2 Tom Seaver Mascot/50 60.00 150.00
TS3 Tom Seaver NY/50 60.00 150.00
TS4 Tom Seaver TL Jsy/41 60.00 150.00
VG1 Vladimir Guerrero 27/150 50.00 100.00
VG2 Vlad Guerrero TL Jsy/27 125.00 250.00

2003 UD Authentics Star Quality Memorabilia

PRINT RUNS B/WN 130-350 COPIES PER
ALL COPIES ARE #'d TO 350 UNLESS NOTED
*GOLD: .75X TO 2X BASIC
GOLD PRINT RUNS B/WN 10-50 COPIES PER
NO GOLD PRICING ON QTY OF 25 OR LESS
AD Adam Dunn Jsy 3.00 8.00
AK Austin Kearns Jsy 3.00 8.00
AP Albert Pujols Jsy 10.00 25.00
AS Alfonso Soriano Jsy 3.00 8.00
BW Bernie Williams Jsy 4.00 10.00
CD Carlos Delgado Jsy 3.00 8.00
CJ Chipper Jones Jsy 4.00 10.00
CR Cal Ripken Jsy/250 10.00 25.00
CS Casey Stengel Pants 8.00 20.00
GS Gary Sheffield Jsy 3.00 8.00
HM Hideki Matsui Jsy/250 12.50 30.00
HN Hideo Nomo Jsy 6.00 15.00
JB Jeff Bagwell Jsy 4.00 10.00
JD J.D. Drew Jsy 3.00 8.00
JG Jason Giambi Jsy 3.00 8.00
JK Jeff Kent Jsy 3.00 8.00
JO Josh Beckett Jsy 3.00 8.00
JT Jim Thome Jsy 4.00 10.00
KG Ken Griffey Jr. Jsy/250 6.00 15.00
KW Kerry Wood Jsy 3.00 8.00
LB Lance Berkman Jsy 3.00 8.00
MM Mickey Mantle Pants/250 30.00 60.00
MP Mark Prior Jsy 4.00 10.00
MU Mike Mussina Jsy 4.00 10.00
NR Nolan Ryan Jsy/130 20.00 50.00
PM Paul Molitor Pants/250 4.00 10.00
RA Roberto Alomar Jsy 4.00 10.00
RC Roger Clemens White Jsy 6.00 15.00
RC1 Roger Clemens Blue Jsy 6.00 15.00
RO Roy Oswalt Jsy 3.00 8.00
RP Rafael Palmeiro Jsy 4.00 10.00
SG Shawn Green Jsy 3.00 8.00
SS Sammy Sosa Jsy/250 4.00 10.00
TB Eric Hinske Jsy 3.00 8.00
TG Tom Glavine Jsy/250 4.00 10.00
TH Todd Helton PT Jsy 4.00 10.00
TR Troy Glaus Jsy 3.00 8.00
TS Tom Seaver Pants 6.00 15.00
TW Ted Williams Pants/250 10.00 25.00
VG Vladimir Guerrero PT Jsy 4.00 10.00

2003 UD Authentics Threads of Time

PRINT RUNS B/WN 250-350 COPIES PER
ALL COPIES ARE #'d TO 350 UNLESS NOTED
*GOLD ACTIVE: .75X TO 2X BASIC
*GOLD RETIRED: 1.25X TO 3X BASIC
GOLD PRINT RUNS B/WN 10-50 COPIES PER
NO GOLD PRICING ON QTY OF 25 OR LESS
APE Andy Pettitte Jsy 4.00 10.00
APU Albert Pujols Jsy 10.00 25.00
AR Alex Rodriguez Jsy 6.00 15.00
CJ Chipper Jones Jsy 4.00 10.00
CR Cal Ripken Jsy 10.00 25.00
DD Don Drysdale Pants 6.00 15.00
DE Dennis Eckersley Jsy 4.00 10.00
DM Don Mattingly Jsy 10.00 25.00
DW Dave Winfield Jsy/250 4.00 10.00
FR Frank Robinson Jsy 6.00 15.00
FT Frank Thomas Jsy 4.00 10.00
GC Gary Carter Jsy 4.00 10.00
GM Greg Maddux Jsy 6.00 15.00
HK Harmon Killebrew Jsy 6.00 15.00
HM Hideo Nomo Jsy 6.00 15.00
HW Honus Wagner Pants 30.00 60.00
IR Ivan Rodriguez Jsy 4.00 10.00
IS Ichiro Suzuki Jsy/250 10.00 25.00
JB Johnny Bench Pants 6.00 15.00
JGI Jason Giambi Jsy/250 3.00 8.00
JGO Juan Gonzalez Jsy 3.00 8.00
JT Jim Thome Jsy 4.00 10.00
KG Ken Griffey Jr. Jsy/250 6.00 15.00
LG Lou Gehrig Jsy/250 50.00 100.00
MM Mickey Mantle Pants/250 40.00 100.00
MP Mike Piazza Jsy 6.00 15.00
MW Maury Wills Jsy 4.00 10.00
NR Nolan Ryan Pants 15.00 40.00
OS Ozzie Smith Jsy 10.00 25.00
PM Pedro Martinez Jsy 4.00 10.00
RC Roger Clemens Jsy 6.00 15.00
RF Rollie Fingers Jsy 4.00 10.00
RJ Randy Johnson Jsy 4.00 10.00
RM Roger Maris Pants 20.00 50.00
RS Ryne Sandberg Jsy 10.00 25.00
SS Sammy Sosa Jsy/250 4.00 10.00
TC Ty Cobb Pants 50.00 100.00
TM Tom Seaver Pants 6.00 15.00
TW Ted Williams Pants/250 15.00 40.00
VG Vladimir Guerrero PT Jsy 4.00 10.00

2007 UD Black

1-42 PRINT RUNS B/WN 16-75 COPIES PER
NO PRICING ON QTY 25 OR LESS
COMMON AU RC (43-72) 6.00 15.00
43-72 PRINT RUN 99 SER.#'d SETS
EXCHANGE DEADLINE 11/26/2009
AUTO PRINTING PLATES RANDOMLY INSERTED
PLATE PRINT RUN 1 SET PER COLOR
BLACK-CYAN-MAGENTA-YELLOW ISSUED
NO PLATE PRICING DUE TO SCARCITY
1 B.Webb Jsy AU/75 6.00 15.00
2 T.Hudson Jsy AU/75 20.00 50.00
3 C.Ripken Jsy AU/75 100.00 175.00
4 N.Markakis Jsy AU/35 30.00 60.00
5 D.Ortiz Jsy AU/52 40.00 100.00
6 J.Papelbon Jsy AU/75 6.00 15.00
7 C.Crisp Jsy AU/43 6.00 15.00
8 D.Lee Jsy AU/75 10.00 25.00
9 P.Konerko Jsy AU/75 15.00 40.00
10 A.Dunn Jsy AU/75 10.00 25.00
11 K.Griffey Jr. Jsy AU/75 100.00 175.00
12 T.Hafner Jsy AU/75 6.00 15.00
13 V.Martinez Jsy AU/75 15.00 40.00
14 Garrett Atkins Jsy AU/75 6.00 15.00
15 J.Verlander Jsy AU/75 40.00 80.00
16 Jeremy Bonderman Jsy AU/75 6.00 15.00
17 C.Grand Jsy AU/75 6.00 15.00
18 H.Ramirez Jsy AU/75 12.50 30.00
19 Dan Uggla Jsy AU/75 10.00 25.00
20 L.Berkman Jsy AU/75 12.00 30.00
21 Mark Teahen Jsy AU/75 6.00 15.00
22 John Lackey Jsy AU/75 6.00 15.00
23 H.Kendrick Jsy AU/75 8.00 20.00
24 R.Martin Jsy AU/75 20.00 50.00
25 P.Fielder Jsy AU/75 6.00 15.00
26 Torii Hunter Jsy AU/75 12.00 30.00
27 J.Morneau Jsy AU/75 40.00 80.00
28 J.Maine Jsy AU/75 6.00 15.00
30 Dan Haren Jsy AU/75 6.00 15.00
31 Eric Chavez Jsy AU/75 6.00 15.00
32 C.Hamels Jsy AU/75 15.00 40.00
33 J.Bay Jsy AU/75 15.00 40.00
34 Adrian Gonzalez Jsy AU/75 6.00 15.00
35 C.Young Jsy AU/75 15.00 40.00
36 M.Cain Jsy AU/75 15.00 40.00
37 F.Hernandez Jsy AU/75 40.00 80.00
38 C.Duncan Jsy AU/75 6.00 15.00
39 B.Upton Jsy AU/75 6.00 15.00
40 Ian Kinsler Jsy AU/75 6.00 15.00
41 R.Halladay Jsy AU/75 20.00 50.00
42a Chad Cordero Jsy AU/75 6.00 15.00
42b Chad Cordero Jsy AU/52 6.00 15.00
43 Adam Lind AU (RC) 10.00 25.00
44 A.Iwamura AU RC 50.00 100.00
45 Alex Gordon AU RC 10.00 25.00
46 A.LaRoche AU (RC) 6.00 15.00
47 Billy Butler AU (RC) 8.00 20.00
48 David Murphy AU (RC) 10.00 25.00
49 B.Wood AU (RC) 6.00 15.00
50 Carlos Gomez AU RC 6.00 15.00
51 Chase Headley AU (RC) 6.00 15.00
52 Curtis Thigpen AU (RC) 6.00 15.00
53 J.Chamberlain AU RC 12.00 30.00
54 Delmon Young AU (RC) 6.00 15.00
55 Felix Pie AU (RC) 6.00 15.00
56 Homer Bailey AU (RC) 6.00 15.00
57 Hunter Pence AU (RC) 12.50 30.00
58 Josh Hamilton AU (RC) 10.00 25.00
59 Kei Igawa AU RC 6.00 15.00
60 Kevin Slowey AU (RC) 20.00 50.00
61 Kurt Suzuki AU (RC) 6.00 15.00
62 Mark Reynolds AU RC 6.00 15.00
63 D.Matsuzaka AU RC 60.00 150.00
64 Justin Upton AU RC 10.00 25.00
65 Phil Hughes AU (RC) 4.00 10.00
66 Ryan Braun AU (RC) 12.00 30.00
67 Ryan Sweeney AU (RC) 6.00 15.00
68 Sean Gallagher AU (RC) 6.00 15.00
69 Tim Lincecum AU RC 60.00 120.00
70 Travis Buck AU (RC) 6.00 15.00
71 T.Tulowitzki AU (RC) 12.00 30.00
72 Y.Gallardo AU (RC) 6.00 15.00

2007 UD Black Bat Barrel Autographs

RANDOM INSERTS IN PACKS
PRINT RUNS B/WN 25-50 COPIES PER
GOLD SPEC.PRINT RUN 10 SER.#'d SETS
NO GOLD PRICING DUE TO SCARCITY
NAT.PEARL PRINT RUN 1 SER.#'d SET
NO PEARL PRICING DUE TO SCARCITY
EXCHANGE DEADLINE 11/26/2009
AD Adam Dunn 10.00 25.00
AE Andre Ethier 30.00 60.00
AI Akinori Iwamura 10.00 25.00
AL Andy LaRoche 10.00 25.00
BO Jeremy Bonderman 12.50 30.00
BU B.J. Upton 10.00 25.00
CC Carl Crawford 10.00 25.00
CL Carlos Lee 10.00 25.00
DJ Derek Jeter 100.00 200.00
DL Derrek Lee 15.00 40.00
DY Delmon Young 10.00 25.00
GA Garrett Atkins 10.00 25.00
HB Homer Bailey 15.00 40.00
HK Howie Kendrick 12.50 30.00
HR Hanley Ramirez 15.00 40.00
HU Torii Hunter 12.50 30.00
IK Ian Kinsler 20.00 50.00
JB Jason Bay 40.00 80.00
JH Josh Hamilton 50.00 100.00
JL John Lackey 12.50 30.00
JM Joe Mauer 40.00 80.00
KG Ken Griffey Jr. 100.00 200.00
KJ Kelly Johnson 12.50 30.00
MO Justin Morneau 15.00 40.00
MT Mark Teixeira 15.00 40.00
RB Ryan Braun 15.00 40.00
RM Russell Martin 10.00 25.00
TH Travis Hafner 20.00 50.00
TT Troy Tulowitzki 30.00 60.00

2007 UD Black Game Day Box Score Autographs

RANDOM INSERTS IN PACKS
STATED PRINT RUN 50 SER.#'d SETS
GOLD SPEC. PRINT RUN 10 SER.#'d SETS
NO GOLD PRICING DUE TO SCARCITY
NAT.PEARL PRINT RUN 1 SER.#'d SET
NO PEARL PRICING DUE TO SCARCITY
EXCHANGE DEADLINE 11/26/2009
AE Andre Ethier 15.00 40.00
AG Adrian Gonzalez 8.00 20.00
AH Aaron Harang 6.00 15.00
AI Akinori Iwamura 20.00 50.00
AL Adam LaRoche 6.00 15.00
AM Andrew Miller 10.00 25.00
AR Aaron Rowand 6.00 15.00
BA Bronson Arroyo 10.00 25.00
BB Billy Butler 10.00 25.00
BP Brandon Phillips 6.00 15.00
BS Ben Sheets 6.00 15.00
CC Coco Crisp 6.00 15.00
CG Curtis Granderson 10.00 25.00
CH Cole Hamels 12.50 30.00
CY Chris Young 6.00 15.00
DH Dan Haren 8.00 20.00
DL Derrek Lee 10.00 25.00
DW Dontrelle Willis 6.00 15.00
DY Delmon Young 10.00 25.00
FC Fausto Carmona 10.00 25.00
FL Fred Lewis 6.00 15.00
GM Greg Maddux 40.00 80.00
GO Alex Gordon 10.00 25.00
HP Hunter Pence 30.00 60.00
JB Joe Blanton 6.00 15.00
JM John Maine 10.00 25.00
JN Joe Nathan 6.00 15.00
JV Justin Verlander 30.00 60.00
KG Ken Griffey Jr. 40.00 80.00
KI Kei Igawa 15.00 40.00
KJ Kelly Johnson 6.00 15.00
LI Francisco Liriano 6.00 15.00
MC Matt Cain 6.00 15.00
MH Matt Holliday 20.00 50.00
MM Melvin Mora 6.00 15.00
NS Nick Swisher 10.00 25.00
PH Phil Hughes 6.00 15.00
RB Ryan Braun 10.00 25.00
RZ Ryan Zimmerman 15.00 40.00
TB Travis Buck 6.00 15.00
TH Tim Hudson 10.00 25.00
TL Tim Lincecum 60.00 120.00

2007 UD Black Game Day Lineup Autographs

RANDOM INSERTS IN PACKS
STATED PRINT RUN 50 SER.#'d SETS
GOLD SPEC. PRINT RUN 10 SER.#'d SETS
NO GOLD PRICING DUE TO SCARCITY
NAT.PEARL PRINT RUN 1 SER.#'d SET
NO PEARL PRICING DUE TO SCARCITY
EXCHANGE DEADLINE 11/26/2009
AE Andre Ethier 15.00 40.00
AG Adrian Gonzalez 8.00 20.00
AH Aaron Harang 6.00 15.00
AI Akinori Iwamura 20.00 50.00
AL Adam LaRoche 6.00 15.00
AM Andrew Miller 10.00 25.00
AR Aaron Rowand 6.00 15.00
BA Bronson Arroyo 10.00 25.00
BB Billy Butler 10.00 25.00
BP Brandon Phillips 6.00 15.00
BS Ben Sheets 6.00 15.00
CC Coco Crisp 6.00 15.00
CG Curtis Granderson 6.00 15.00
CH Cole Hamels 6.00 15.00
CY Chris Young 6.00 15.00
DH Dan Haren 8.00 20.00
DL Derrek Lee 10.00 25.00
DW Dontrelle Willis 6.00 15.00
DY Delmon Young 10.00 25.00
FC Fausto Carmona 10.00 25.00
FL Fred Lewis 6.00 15.00
GM Greg Maddux 40.00 80.00

GO Alex Gordon 10.00 25.00
HP Hunter Pence 30.00 60.00
JB Joe Blanton 6.00 15.00
JM John Maine 10.00 25.00
JN Joe Nathan 6.00 15.00
JV Justin Verlander 30.00 60.00
KG Ken Griffey Jr. 50.00 100.00
KI Kei Igawa 15.00 40.00
KJ Kelly Johnson 6.00 15.00
LI Francisco Liriano 6.00 15.00
MC Matt Cain 6.00 15.00
MH Matt Holliday 20.00 50.00
MM Melvin Mora 6.00 15.00
NS Nick Swisher 6.00 25.00
PH Phil Hughes 30.00 60.00
RB Ryan Braun 20.00 50.00
RZ Ryan Zimmerman 15.00 40.00
TB Travis Buck 6.00 15.00
TH Tim Hudson 10.00 25.00
TL Tim Lincecum 60.00 120.00

2007 UD Black Game Day Ticket Autographs

RANDOM INSERTS IN PACKS
PRINT RUNS B/WN 15-50 COPIES PER
NO PRICING ON QTY OF 15
GOLD SPEC. PRINT RUN 10 SER.#'d SETS
NO GOLD PRICING DUE TO SCARCITY
NAT.PEARL PRINT RUN 1 SER.#'d SET
NO PEARL PRICING DUE TO SCARCITY
EXCHANGE DEADLINE 11/26/2009
AE Andre Ethier 15.00 40.00
AG Adrian Gonzalez 10.00 25.00
AH Aaron Harang 6.00 15.00
AI Akinori Iwamura 10.00 25.00
AL Adam LaRoche 6.00 15.00
AM Andrew Miller 10.00 25.00
AR Aaron Rowand 6.00 15.00
BA Bronson Arroyo 10.00 25.00
BB Billy Butler 10.00 25.00
BP Brandon Phillips 6.00 15.00
BS Ben Sheets 6.00 15.00
CC Coco Crisp 6.00 15.00
CG Curtis Granderson 10.00 25.00
CH Cole Hamels 6.00 15.00
CY Chris Young 6.00 15.00
DH Dan Haren 8.00 20.00
DL Derrek Lee 10.00 25.00
DW Dontrelle Willis 6.00 15.00
DY Delmon Young 10.00 25.00
FC Fausto Carmona 10.00 25.00
FL Fred Lewis 6.00 15.00
GM Greg Maddux 40.00 80.00
GO Alex Gordon 10.00 25.00
HP Hunter Pence 30.00 60.00
JB Joe Blanton 6.00 15.00
JN Joe Nathan 6.00 15.00
JV Justin Verlander 30.00 60.00
KI Kei Igawa 15.00 40.00
KJ Kelly Johnson 6.00 15.00
LI Francisco Liriano 6.00 15.00
MC Matt Cain 6.00 15.00
MH Matt Holliday 20.00 50.00
MM Melvin Mora 6.00 15.00
NS Nick Swisher 6.00 25.00
PH Phil Hughes 30.00 60.00
RB Ryan Braun 20.00 50.00
RZ Ryan Zimmerman 15.00 40.00
TB Travis Buck 6.00 15.00
TH Tim Hudson 10.00 25.00
TL Tim Lincecum 60.00 120.00

2007 UD Black Illustrious Dual Materials Autographs

RANDOM INSERTS IN PACKS
PRINT RUNS B/WN 15-50 COPIES PER
NO PRICING ON QTY 15
EXCHANGE DEADLINE 11/26/2009
CI E.Chavez/A.Iwamura 12.00 30.00
CK C.Crawford/S.Kazmir 12.00 30.00
CP C.Crisp/J.Papelbon 20.00 50.00
GB A.Gordon/R.Braun 20.00 50.00
GC C.Granderson/C.Crisp 20.00 50.00
GY A.Gonzalez/C.Young 12.00 30.00
HH D.Haren/R.Harden 12.00 30.00
HM A.Harang/J.Maine 12.00 30.00
HW J.Hermida/D.Willis 12.00 30.00
JJ J.Morneau/J.Bay 12.00 30.00
LC T.Lincecum/M.Cain 12.00 30.00
LK J.Lackey/H.Kendrick 20.00 50.00
LP C.Lee/H.Pence 30.00 60.00
MM R.Martin/V.Martinez 12.00 20.00
NH J.Nathan/T.Hunter 12.00 30.00
NM N.Markakis/M.Mora 12.00 30.00
RG A.Rowand/B.Giles 12.00 30.00
SB H.Street/J.Blanton 12.00 30.00
TA T.Tulowitzki/G.Atkins 12.00 30.00
UW D.Uggla/J.Willingham 12.00 30.00
UY B.Upton/D.Young 12.00 30.00
ZB J.Zumaya/J.Bonderman 15.00 40.00

2007 UD Black Lustrous Autographs

RANDOM INSERTS IN PACKS
PRINT RUNS B/WN 15-50 COPIES PER
NO PRICING ON QTY 15
GOLD SPEC. PRINT RUN 10 SER.#'d SETS
NO GOLD PRICING DUE TO SCARCITY
NAT.PEARL PRINT RUN 1 SER.#'d SET
NO PEARL PRICING DUE TO SCARCITY
EXCHANGE DEADLINE 11/26/2009
AG Alex Gordon/50 12.00 30.00
BB Billy Butler/50 10.00 25.00
BU B.J. Upton/50 6.00 15.00
CC Carl Crawford/50 6.00 15.00
CH Cole Hamels/50 6.00 15.00
DJ Derek Jeter/50 75.00 150.00
DL Derrek Lee/50 10.00 25.00
DU Dan Uggla/50 6.00 15.00
DW Dontrelle Willis/50 6.00 15.00
GA Garrett Atkins/50 6.00 15.00
GR Khalil Greene/50 10.00 25.00
HA Josh Hamilton/50 8.00 20.00
HP Hunter Pence/50 15.00 40.00
HR Hanley Ramirez/50 10.00 25.00
HS Huston Street/50 6.00 15.00
IK Ian Kinsler/50 6.00 15.00
JB Jason Bay/50 10.00 25.00
JF Jeff Francis/50 6.00 15.00
JH Jeremy Hermida/50 6.00 15.00
JL Jon Lester/50 6.00 15.00
JN Joe Nathan/50 6.00 15.00
JV Justin Verlander/50 30.00 60.00
KE Howie Kendrick/50 6.00 15.00
KG Ken Griffey Jr./50 50.00 100.00
KI Kei Igawa/50 6.00 15.00
LA John Lackey/50 6.00 15.00
MO Justin Morneau/50 10.00 25.00
MY Michael Young/50 6.00 15.00
PA Jonathan Papelbon/50 20.00 50.00
PF Prince Fielder/50 20.00 50.00
PH Phil Hughes/50 30.00 60.00
PK Paul Konerko/50 10.00 25.00
RM Russell Martin/50 10.00 25.00
RO Roy Oswalt/50 5.00 12.00
RT Ryan Theriot/50 10.00 25.00
RW Rickie Weeks/50 6.00 15.00
RZ Ryan Zimmerman/50 8.00 20.00
SA Jarrod Saltalamacchia/50 4.00 10.00
SK Scott Kazmir/50 8.00 20.00
TH Torii Hunter/50 6.00 15.00
VW Vernon Wells/50 6.00 15.00

2007 UD Black Lustrous Materials Autographs

RANDOM INSERTS IN PACKS
PRINT RUNS B/WN 33-50 COPIES PER
GOLD SPEC. PRINT RUN 10 SER.#'d SETS
NO GOLD PRICING DUE TO SCARCITY
NAT.PEARL PRINT RUN 1 SER.#'d SET
NO PEARL PRICING DUE TO SCARCITY
EXCHANGE DEADLINE 11/26/2009
AD Adam Dunn/50 6.00 15.00
AE Andre Ethier/50 15.00 40.00
BO Jeremy Bonderman/50 10.00 25.00
BU B.J. Upton/50 10.00 25.00
CA Melky Cabrera/50 6.00 15.00
CC Carl Crawford/50 6.00 15.00
CL Carlos Lee/50 6.00 15.00
CO Chad Cordero/50 6.00 15.00
CP Coco Crisp/50 6.00 15.00
CR Cal Ripken Jr./50 40.00 100.00
DH Dan Haren/50 8.00 20.00
DJ Derek Jeter/50 100.00 200.00
DL Derrek Lee/50 10.00 25.00
DU Dan Uggla/50 6.00 15.00
DW Dontrelle Willis/50 6.00 15.00
DY Delmon Young/50 10.00 25.00
FH Felix Hernandez/50 20.00 50.00
GR Khalil Greene/50 6.00 15.00
HR Hanley Ramirez/33 10.00 25.00
HS Huston Street/50 6.00 15.00
IK Ian Kinsler/50 10.00 25.00
JB Jason Bay/50 12.00 30.00
JH Jeremy Hermida/50 6.00 15.00
JM Joe Mauer/50 30.00 60.00
JN Joe Nathan/50 6.00 15.00
JV Justin Verlander/50 30.00 60.00
JW Josh Willingham/50 6.00 15.00
JZ Joel Zumaya/50 10.00 25.00
KE Howie Kendrick/50 10.00 25.00
KG Ken Griffey Jr./50 60.00 120.00
KM Kendry Morales/50 6.00 15.00
MC Matt Cain/50 12.00 30.00
MM Melvin Mora/50 6.00 15.00
MP Mike Pelfrey/50 6.00 15.00
NM Nick Markakis/50 8.00 20.00
PA Jonathan Papelbon/50 10.00 25.00
PF Prince Fielder/50 30.00 60.00
RW Rickie Weeks/50 6.00 15.00
RZ Ryan Zimmerman/50 15.00 40.00
SD Stephen Drew/50 10.00 25.00
TH Torii Hunter/50 10.00 25.00
VW Vernon Wells/50 3.00 8.00

2007 UD Black Pride of a Nation Autographs

RANDOM INSERTS IN PACKS
PRINT RUNS B/WN 25-75 COPIES PER
NO PRICING ON QTY 25
GOLD SPEC.PRINT RUN 10 SER.#'d SETS
NO GOLD PRICING DUE TO SCARCITY
NAT.PEARL PRINT RUN 1 SER.#'d SET
NO PEARL PRICING DUE TO SCARCITY
PRINTING PLATES RANDOMLY INSERTED
PLATE PRINT RUN 1 SET PER COLOR
BLACK-CYAN-MAGENTA-YELLOW ISSUED
NO PLATE PRICING DUE TO SCARCITY
EXCHANGE DEADLINE 11/26/2009
AH Aaron Harang 10.00 25.00
AL Adam LaRoche 10.00 25.00
AR Aaron Rowand 10.00 25.00
BO Jeremy Bonderman 6.00 15.00
BP Brandon Phillips 10.00 25.00
CA Carl Crawford 6.00 15.00
CC Coco Crisp 10.00 25.00
CG Curtis Granderson 20.00 50.00
CL Carlos Lee 10.00 25.00
DH Dan Haren 10.00 25.00
DL Derrek Lee 6.00 15.00
DU Dan Uggla 10.00 25.00
DW Dontrelle Willis 12.50 30.00
EC Eric Chavez 12.50 30.00
FH Felix Hernandez 30.00 60.00
FT Frank Thomas 50.00 100.00
HR Hanley Ramirez 6.00 15.00
JB Jason Bay 6.00 15.00
JL John Lackey 6.00 15.00
JM John Maine 10.00 25.00
LB Lance Berkman 10.00 25.00
MM Melvin Mora 10.00 25.00
MO Justin Morneau 6.00 15.00
PF Prince Fielder 10.00 25.00
RM Russell Martin 12.50 30.00
RO Roy Oswalt 15.00 40.00
SK Scott Kazmir 12.50 30.00
VM Victor Martinez 6.00 15.00

2007 UD Black Prodigious Autographs

RANDOM INSERTS IN PACKS
PRINT RUNS B/WN 50-75 COPIES PER
GOLD SPEC. PRINT RUN 25 SER.#'d SETS
NO GOLD PRICING DUE TO SCARCITY
NAT.PEARL PRINT RUN 1 SER.#'d SET
NO PEARL PRICING DUE TO SCARCITY
EXCHANGE DEADLINE 11/26/2009
AE Andre Ethier/75 5.00 12.00
AG Adrian Gonzalez/75 6.00 15.00
AH Aaron Harang/75 5.00 12.00
AI Akinori Iwamura/75 20.00 50.00
AL Adam LaRoche/75 5.00 12.00
AR Aaron Rowand/50 5.00 12.00
BB Billy Butler/75 6.00 15.00
BE Josh Beckett/50 5.00 12.00
BP Brandon Phillips/50 5.00 12.00
BS Ben Sheets/50 5.00 12.00
BU B.J. Upton/75 5.00 12.00
CA Carl Crawford/75 6.00 15.00
CC Coco Crisp/50 5.00 12.00
CG Curtis Granderson/50 6.00 15.00
CH Cole Hamels/50 8.00 20.00
CO Chad Cordero/50 5.00 12.00
CR Cal Ripken Jr./75 30.00 80.00
CY Chris Young/50 5.00 12.00
DH Dan Haren/75 5.00 12.00
DM Daisuke Matsuzaka/75 30.00 80.00
DU Dan Uggla/75 5.00 12.00
DY Delmon Young/75 5.00 12.00
FP Felix Pie/75 5.00 12.00
GA Garrett Atkins/75 5.00 12.00
GO Alex Gordon/75 6.00 15.00
GP Glen Perkins/75 5.00 12.00
HB Homer Bailey/75 5.00 12.00
HK Howie Kendrick/50 12.00 30.00
HP Hunter Pence/75 8.00 20.00
HS Huston Street/50 5.00 12.00
JB Jeremy Bonderman/75 6.00 15.00
JE Johnny Estrada/75 5.00 12.00
JH Josh Hamilton/50 8.00 20.00
JL John Lackey/50 5.00 12.00
JM John Maine/50 6.00 15.00
JP Jonathan Papelbon/75 5.00 12.00
JS Joakim Soria/75 6.00 15.00
JV Justin Verlander/50 30.00 60.00
JW Josh Willingham/50 5.00 12.00
KE Kelvim Escobar/50 5.00 12.00
KI Kei Igawa/75 8.00 20.00
KJ Kelly Johnson/50 5.00 12.00
LE Jon Lester/75 6.00 15.00
MC Matt Cain/75 6.00 15.00
MH Matt Holliday/75 5.00 12.00
MM Melvin Mora/50 5.00 12.00
MO Justin Morneau/75 6.00 15.00
NM Nick Markakis/75 6.00 15.00
NS Nick Swisher/75 6.00 15.00
PK Paul Konerko/50 6.00 15.00
RB Ryan Braun/75 10.00 25.00
RH Rich Harden/50 5.00 12.00
RM Russell Martin/75 6.00 15.00
RZ Ryan Zimmerman/75 5.00 12.00
SK Scott Kazmir/75 5.00 12.00
SM Sergio Mitre/50 5.00 12.00
TH Tim Hudson/75 6.00 15.00
TL Tim Lincecum/75 20.00 50.00
VM Victor Martinez/75 6.00 15.00
YG Yovani Gallardo/50 6.00 15.00

2007 UD Black Prodigious Materials Autographs

RANDOM INSERTS IN PACKS
PRINT RUNS B/WN 35-50 COPIES PER
GOLD SPEC. PRINT RUN 10 SER.#'d SETS
NO GOLD PRICING DUE TO SCARCITY
NAT.PEARL PRINT RUN 1 SER.#'d SET
NO PEARL PRICING DUE TO SCARCITY
EXCHANGE DEADLINE 11/26/2009
AD Adam Dunn 10.00 25.00
AE Andre Ethier 8.00 20.00
AL Adam LaRoche 10.00 25.00
AR Aaron Rowand 10.00 25.00
BO Jeremy Bonderman 10.00 25.00
BP Brandon Phillips 6.00 15.00
BU B.J. Upton 6.00 15.00
CC Coco Crisp 6.00 15.00
CD Chris Duncan 6.00 15.00
CH Cole Hamels 20.00 50.00
CL Cliff Lee 12.50 30.00
CR Carl Crawford 6.00 15.00
CY Chris Young 6.00 15.00
DH Dan Haren 6.00 15.00
DU Dan Uggla 10.00 25.00
DW Dontrelle Willis 10.00 25.00
FH Felix Hernandez 20.00 50.00
GA Garrett Atkins 6.00 15.00
HA Josh Hamilton 12.00 30.00
HK Hong-Chih Kuo 40.00 80.00
HR Hanley Ramirez 6.00 15.00
HS Huston Street 6.00 15.00
IK Ian Kinsler 10.00 25.00
JB Joe Blanton 6.00 15.00
JH Jeremy Hermida 6.00 15.00
JL Jon Lester 20.00 50.00
JN Joe Nathan 6.00 15.00
JS Johan Santana 20.00 50.00
JV Justin Verlander 30.00 60.00
JZ Joel Zumaya 10.00 25.00
KE Howie Kendrick 10.00 25.00
KW Kerry Wood 10.00 25.00
MO Justin Morneau 15.00 40.00
MT Mark Teixeira 15.00 40.00
PA Jonathan Papelbon 8.00 20.00
RI Cal Ripken Jr./35 50.00 100.00
RW Rickie Weeks 6.00 15.00
SK Scott Kazmir 6.00 15.00
SR Scott Rolen 10.00 25.00
TE Miguel Tejada 10.00 25.00
TG Tom Glavine 20.00 50.00
VW Vernon Wells 10.00 25.00

2007 UD Black Prominent Numbers Autographs

RANDOM INSERTS IN PACKS
PRINT RUNS B/WN 1-58 COPIES PER
NO PRICING ON QTY 25 OR LESS
GOLD SPEC. PRINT RUN 10 SER.#'d SETS
NO GOLD PRICING DUE TO SCARCITY
NAT.PEARL PRINT RUN 1 SER.#'d SET
NO PEARL PRICING DUE TO SCARCITY
EXCHANGE DEADLINE 11/26/2009
AH Aaron Harang/39 6.00 15.00
BL Joe Blanton/55 6.00 15.00
CG C.Granderson/28 20.00 50.00
CH Cole Hamels/35 10.00 25.00
CY Chris Young/32 10.00 25.00
DY Delmon Young/26 10.00 25.00
FH Felix Hernandez/34 20.00 50.00
GA Garrett Atkins/27 10.00 25.00
HK Howie Kendrick/47 6.00 15.00
JB Jason Bay/38 10.00 25.00
JE Johnny Estrada/33 6.00 15.00
JM Justin Morneau/33 10.00 25.00
JN Joe Nathan/36 6.00 15.00
JP J.Papelbon/58 6.00 15.00
JV Justin Verlander/35 30.00 60.00
JZ Joel Zumaya/54 6.00 15.00
MA John Maine/33 10.00 25.00
MB Michael Bourn/45 6.00 15.00
RH Rich Harden/40 6.00 15.00
RM Russell Martin/55 15.00 40.00

2013-14 UD Black

1-45 PRINT RUN 175 SER.#'d SETS
46-67 PRINT RUNS 199 SER.#'d SETS
68-72 PRINT RUNS 99 SER.#'d SETS
EXCHANGE DEADLINE 2/24/2016
9 Tony Gwynn/175 2.00 5.00

2013-14 UD Black Gold Spectrum

1-44 PRINT RUN 1 SER.#'d SET
NO 1-44 PRICING DUE TO SCARCITY
*GOLD 46-67: .75X TO 2X BASIC
*GOLD 68-73: .75X TO 2X BASIC
46-73 PRINT RUN 25 SER.#'d SETS
EXCHANGE DEADLINE 2/24/2016

2013-14 UD Black Legendary Lustrous Signatures

STATED PRINT RUN 25 SER.#'d SETS
EXCHANGE DEADLINE 2/24/2016
LLTG Tony Gwynn 30.00 60.00

2013-14 UD Black Logo Signatures

STATED PRINT RUN 40 SER.#'d SETS
EXCHANGE DEADLINE 2/24/2016
LSTG Tony Gwynn 20.00 50.00

2013-14 UD Black Old School Signatures

PRINT RUNS B/WN 23-75 COPIES PER
EXCHANGE DEADLINE 2/24/2016
OSTG Tony Gwynn/75 20.00 50.00

2013-14 UD Black Signatures

PRINT RUNS B/WN 23-75 COPIES PER
EXCHANGE DEADLINE 2/24/2016
STG Tony Gwynn/75 20.00 50.00

1999 UD Choice Preview

COMPLETE SET (55) 6.00 15.00
46 Tim Salmon .07 .20
48 Chuck Finley .07 .20
50 Matt Williams .10 .30
52 Travis Lee .07 .20
54 Andres Galarraga .15 .40
56 Greg Maddux .50 1.25
58 Cal Ripken Jr. .75 2.00
60 Rafael Palmeiro .15 .40
62 Nomar Garciaparra .40 1.00
64 Pedro Martinez .20 .50
66 Kerry Wood .15 .40
67 Sammy Sosa .25 .60
70 Albert Belle .07 .20
72 Frank Thomas .30 .75
74 Pete Harnisch .02 .10
76 Manny Ramirez .20 .50
78 Travis Fryman .07 .20
80 Kenny Lofton .07 .20
82 Larry Walker .15 .40
84 Gabe Alvarez .02 .10
86 Damion Easley .02 .10
88 Mark Kotsay .02 .10
90 Jeff Bagwell .20 .50
93 Craig Biggio .15 .40
94 Larry Sutton .02 .10
96 Johnny Damon .20 .50
98 Gary Sheffield .20 .50
100 Mark Grudzielanek .02 .10
102 Jeff Cirillo .02 .10
104 Mark Loretta .02 .10
106 David Ortiz .40 1.00
108 Brad Fullmer .07 .20
110 Vladimir Guerrero .30 .75
112 Brian McRae .02 .10
114 Rey Ordonez .02 .10
115 Derek Jeter .75 2.00
118 Paul O'Neill .15 .40
120 A.J. Hinch .02 .10
122 Miguel Tejada .20 .50
124 Scott Rolen .20 .50
126 Bob Abreu .20 .50
128 Jason Kendall .07 .20
130 Mark McGwire .40 1.00
132 Eli Marrero .02 .10
136 Kevin Brown .10 .30
137 Tony Gwynn .40 1.00
138 Bill Mueller .02 .10
140 Barry Bonds .30 .75
142 Ken Griffey Jr .50 1.25
143 Alex Rodriguez .40 1.00
146 Rolando Arrojo .02 .10
148 Quinton McCracken .02 .10
150 Will Clark .15 .40
152 Juan Gonzalez .15 .40
154 Carlos Delgado .15 .40

1999 UD Choice

This 155-card set features color action player photos in white borders. The backs carry player information. The set contains the following subsets: Rookie Class (1-27) and Cover Glory (28-45). Approximately 350 Eddie Murray A Piece of History 500 Club bat cards were randomly seeded into packs. Pricing for this card can be referenced under 1999 Upper Deck A Piece of History 500 Club.

COMPLETE SET (155) 8.00 20.00
MURRAY BAT LISTED W/UD APH 500 CLUB
1 Gabe Kapler .07 .20
2 Jin Ho Cho .07 .20
3 Matt Anderson .07 .20
4 Ricky Ledee .07 .20
5 Bruce Chen .07 .20
6 Alex Gonzalez .07 .20
7 Ryan Minor .07 .20
8 Michael Barrett .07 .20
9 Carlos Beltran .10 .30
10 Ramon E.Martinez RC .07 .20
11 Dermal Brown .07 .20
12 Robert Fick .07 .20
13 Preston Wilson .07 .20
14 Orlando Hernandez .07 .20
15 Troy Glaus .10 .30
16 Calvin Pickering .07 .20
17 Corey Koskie .07 .20
18 Fernando Seguignol .07 .20
19 Carlos Guillen .07 .20
20 Kevin Witt .07 .20
21 Mike Kinkade .07 .20
22 Eric Chavez .07 .20
23 Mike Lowell .07 .20
24 Adrian Beltre .07 .20
25 George Lombard .07 .20
26 Jeremy Giambi .07 .20
27 J.D. Drew .07 .20
28 Mark McGwire CG .25 .60
29 Kerry Wood CG .07 .20
30 David Wells CG .07 .20
31 Juan Gonzalez CG .07 .20
32 Randy Johnson CG .10 .30
33 Derek Jeter CG .25 .60
34 Tony Gwynn CG .10 .30
35 Greg Maddux CG .20 .50
36 Cal Ripken CG .30 .75
37 Ken Griffey Jr. CG .25 .60
38 Bartolo Colon CG .07 .20
39 Troy Glaus CG .07 .20
40 Ben Grieve CG .07 .20
41 Roger Clemens CG .20 .50
42 Chipper Jones CG .10 .30
43 Scott Rolen CG .07 .20
44 Nomar Garciaparra CG .20 .50
45 Sammy Sosa CG .10 .30
46 Tim Salmon .10 .30
47 Darin Erstad .07 .20
48 Chuck Finley .07 .20
49 Garret Anderson .07 .20
50 Matt Williams .07 .20
51 Jay Bell .07 .20
52 Travis Lee .07 .20
53 Andruw Jones .10 .30
54 Andres Galarraga .07 .20
55 Chipper Jones .20 .50
56 Greg Maddux .30 .75
57 Javy Lopez .07 .20
58 Cal Ripken .60 1.50
59 Brady Anderson .07 .20
60 Rafael Palmeiro .10 .30
61 B.J. Surhoff .07 .20
62 Nomar Garciaparra .30 .75
63 Troy O'Leary .07 .20
64 Pedro Martinez .10 .30
65 Jason Varitek .20 .50
66 Kerry Wood .07 .20
67 Sammy Sosa .20 .50
68 Mark Grace .10 .30
69 Mickey Morandini .07 .20
70 Albert Belle .07 .20
71 Mike Caruso .07 .20
72 Frank Thomas .20 .50
73 Sean Casey .07 .20
74 Pete Harnisch .07 .20
75 Dmitri Young .07 .20
76 Manny Ramirez .10 .30
77 Omar Vizquel .10 .30
78 Travis Fryman .07 .20
79 Jim Thome .10 .30
80 Kenny Lofton .07 .20
81 Todd Helton .10 .30
82 Larry Walker .07 .20
83 Vinny Castilla .07 .20
84 Gabe Alvarez .07 .20
85 Tony Clark .07 .20
86 Damion Easley .07 .20
87 Livan Hernandez .07 .20
88 Mark Kotsay .07 .20
89 Cliff Floyd .07 .20
90 Jeff Bagwell .10 .30
91 Moises Alou .07 .20
92 Randy Johnson .20 .50
93 Craig Biggio .10 .30
94 Larry Sutton .07 .20
95 Dean Palmer .07 .20
96 Johnny Damon .10 .30
97 Charles Johnson .07 .20
98 Gary Sheffield .07 .20
99 Raul Mondesi .07 .20
100 Mark Grudzielanek .07 .20
101 Jeromy Burnitz .07 .20
102 Jeff Cirillo .07 .20
103 Jose Valentin .07 .20
104 Mark Loretta .07 .20
105 Todd Walker .07 .20
106 David Ortiz .20 .50
107 Brad Radke .07 .20
108 Brad Fullmer .07 .20
109 Rondell White .07 .20
110 Vladimir Guerrero .20 .50
111 Mike Piazza .30 .75
112 Brian McRae .07 .20
113 John Olerud .07 .20
114 Rey Ordonez .07 .20
115 Derek Jeter .50 1.25
116 Bernie Williams .10 .30
117 David Wells .07 .20
118 Paul O'Neill .10 .30
119 Tino Martinez .10 .30
120 A.J. Hinch .07 .20
121 Jason Giambi .07 .20
122 Miguel Tejada .07 .20
123 Ben Grieve .07 .20
124 Scott Rolen .10 .30
125 Desi Relaford .07 .20
126 Bob Abreu .07 .20
127 Jose Guillen .07 .20
128 Jason Kendall .07 .20
129 Aramis Ramirez .07 .20
130 Mark McGwire .50 1.25
131 Ray Lankford .07 .20
132 Eli Marrero .07 .20
133 Wally Joyner .07 .20
134 Greg Vaughn .07 .20
135 Trevor Hoffman .07 .20
136 Kevin Brown .10 .30
137 Tony Gwynn .25 .60
138 Bill Mueller .07 .20
139 Ellis Burks .07 .20
140 Barry Bonds .60 1.50
141 Robb Nen .07 .20
142 Ken Griffey Jr. .40 1.00
143 Alex Rodriguez .30 .75
144 Jay Buhner .07 .20
145 Edgar Martinez .10 .30
146 Rolando Arrojo .07 .20
147 Robert Smith .07 .20
148 Quinton McCracken .07 .20
149 Ivan Rodriguez .10 .30
150 Will Clark .10 .30
151 Mark McLemore .07 .20
152 Juan Gonzalez .07 .20
153 Jose Cruz Jr. .07 .20
154 Carlos Delgado .07 .20
155 Roger Clemens .40 1.00

1999 UD Choice Prime Choice Reserve

*STARS: 20X TO 40X BASIC CARDS
RANDOM INSERTS IN PACKS
STATED PRINT RUN 100 SERIAL #'d SETS

1999 UD Choice Blow Up

COMPLETE SET (10) 8.00 20.00
STATED ODDS
1 Ken Griffey Jr. .75 2.00
2 Sammy Sosa .50 1.25
3 Mark McGwire .75 2.00
4 Cal Ripken 1.50 4.00
5 Roger Clemens .75 2.00
6 Derek Jeter 1.50 4.00
7 Kerry Wood .20 .50
8 Alex Rodriguez .75 2.00
9 Nomar Garciaparra .75 2.00
10 Greg Maddux 1.00 2.50

1999 UD Choice Blow Up Cover Glory

COMPLETE SET (10) 8.00 20.00
STATED ODDS
1 Mark McGwire .75 2.00
2 Kerry Wood .30 .75
3 Juan Gonzalez .30 .75
4 Derek Jeter 1.50 4.00
5 Tony Gwynn .75 2.00
6 Cal Ripken 1.50 4.00
7 Ken Griffey Jr. 1.25 3.00
8 Roger Clemens .75 2.00
9 Nomar Garciaparra .75 2.00
10 Sammy Sosa .50 1.25

1999 UD Choice Homerun Heroes

COMPLETE SET 4.00 10.00
H1 Ken Griffey Jr .60 1.50
H2 Mark McGwire .50 1.25
H3 Sammy Sosa .50 1.25
H4 Troy Glaus .40 1.00
H5 Mike Piazza .75 2.00
H6 Chipper Jones .60 1.50
H7 Vladimir Guerrero .40 1.00
H8 Frank Thomas .50 1.25
H9 Juan Gonzalez .40 1.00
H10 Alex Rodriguez .60 1.50

1999 UD Choice Mini Bobbing Head

COMPLETE SET (30) 10.00 25.00
STATED ODDS 1:5
B1 Randy Johnson .50 1.25
B2 Troy Glaus .30 .75
B3 Chipper Jones .50 1.25
B4 Cal Ripken 1.50 4.00
B5 Nomar Garciaparra .75 2.00
B6 Pedro Martinez .30 .75
B7 Kerry Wood .20 .50
B8 Sammy Sosa .50 1.25
B9 Frank Thomas .50 1.25
B10 Paul Konerko .20 .50
B11 Omar Vizquel .30 .75
B12 Kenny Lofton .20 .50
B13 Gabe Kapler .20 .50
B14 Adrian Beltre .20 .50
B15 Orlando Hernandez .20 .50
B16 Derek Jeter 1.25 3.00
B17 Mike Piazza .75 2.00
B18 Tino Martinez .30 .75
B19 Ben Grieve .20 .50
B20 Rickey Henderson .50 1.25
B21 Scott Rolen .30 .75
B22 Aramis Ramirez .20 .50
B23 Greg Vaughn .20 .50
B24 Tony Gwynn .60 1.50
B25 Barry Bonds 1.50 4.00
B26 Alex Rodriguez .75 2.00
B27 Ken Griffey Jr. 1.00 2.50
B28 Mark McGwire 1.25 3.00
B29 J.D. Drew .20 .50
B30 Juan Gonzalez .20 .50

1999 UD Choice Rookie Class

COMPLETE SEI 3.00 8.00
STATED ODDS 1:TBD
R1 J.D. Drew .40 1.00
R2 Gabe Kapler .08 .25
R3 Eric Chavez 1.00 2.50
R4 Troy Glaus .75 2.00
R5 Ryan Minor .08 .25
R6 Corey Koskie .40 1.00
R7 Jeremy Giambi .08 .25
R8 Carlos Beltran 1.25 3.00
R9 Carlos Guillen .20 .50
R10 Mike Kinkade .08 .25

1999 UD Choice StarQuest

COMP.BLUE SET (30) 8.00 20.00
ONE BLUE PER PACK
*GREEN: 1X TO 2.5X BASIC BLUE STARQUEST
GREEN STATED ODDS 1:8
*RED: 2.5X TO 6X BASIC BLUE STARQUEST
RED STATED ODDS 1:23
*GOLD: 30X TO 80X BASIC BLUE STARQUEST
GOLD RANDOM INSERTS IN PACKS
GOLD PRINT RUN 100 SERIAL #'d SETS
1 Ken Griffey Jr. .60 1.50
2 Sammy Sosa .30 .75
3 Alex Rodriguez .50 1.25
4 Derek Jeter .75 2.00
5 Troy Glaus .20 .50
6 Mike Piazza .50 1.25
7 Barry Bonds 1.00 2.50
8 Tony Gwynn .40 1.00
9 Juan Gonzalez .10 .30
10 Chipper Jones .30 .75
11 Greg Maddux .50 1.25
12 Randy Johnson .30 .75
13 Roger Clemens .60 1.50
14 Ben Grieve .10 .30
15 Nomar Garciaparra .50 1.25
16 Travis Lee .10 .30
17 Frank Thomas .30 .75
18 Vladimir Guerrero .30 .75
19 Scott Rolen .20 .50
20 Ivan Rodriguez .20 .50
21 Cal Ripken 1.00 2.50
22 Mark McGwire .75 2.00
23 Jeff Bagwell .20 .50
24 Tony Clark .10 .30
25 Kerry Wood .10 .30
26 Kenny Lofton .10 .30
27 Adrian Beltre .10 .30
28 Larry Walker .10 .30
29 Curt Schilling .10 .30
30 Jim Thome .20 .50

1999 UD Choice Superstars

COMPLETE SET 4.00 10.00
S1 Ken Griffey Jr .60 1.50
S2 Mark McGwire .50 1.25
S3 Sammy Sosa .50 1.25
S4 Cal Ripken Jr 1.25 3.00
S5 Nomar Garciaparra .60 1.50
S6 Alex Rodriguez .60 1.50
S7 Kerry Wood .40 1.00
S8 Juan Gonzalez .40 1.00
S9 Derek Jeter 1.25 3.00
S10 Greg Maddux .75 2.00

1999 UD Choice Yard Work

COMPLETE SET (30) 25.00 60.00
STATED ODDS 1:13
Y1 Andres Galarraga .40 1.00
Y2 Chipper Jones -1.00 2.50
Y3 Rafael Palmeiro .60 1.50
Y4 Nomar Garciaparra 1.50 4.00
Y5 Sammy Sosa 1.00 2.50
Y6 Frank Thomas 1.00 2.50
Y7 J.D. Drew .40 1.00
Y8 Albert Belle .40 1.00
Y9 Jim Thome .60 1.50
Y10 Manny Ramirez .60 1.50
Y11 Larry Walker .40 1.00
Y12 Vinny Castilla .40 1.00
Y13 Tony Clark .40 1.00
Y14 Jeff Bagwell .60 1.50
Y15 Moises Alou .40 1.00
Y16 Dean Palmer .40 1.00
Y17 Gary Sheffield .40 1.00
Y18 Vladimir Guerrero 1.00 2.50
Y19 Mike Piazza 1.50 4.00
Y20 Tino Martinez .60 1.50
Y21 Ben Grieve .40 1.00
Y22 Greg Vaughn .40 1.00
Y23 Ken Caminiti .40 1.00
Y24 Barry Bonds 3.00 8.00
Y25 Ken Griffey Jr. 2.00 5.00
Y26 Alex Rodriguez 1.50 4.00
Y27 Mark McGwire 2.50 6.00
Y28 Juan Gonzalez .40 1.00
Y29 Jose Canseco 1.00 2.50
Y30 Jose Cruz Jr. .40 1.00

2004 UD Diamond All-Star

COMP.SET w/o SP's (90) 10.00 25.00
COMMON CARD (1-90) .10 .30
COMMON CARD (91-120) .40 1.00
91-120 STATED ODDS 1:6
1 Garret Anderson .12 .30
2 Darin Erstad .12 .30
3 Troy Glaus .12 .30
4 Curt Schilling .20 .50
5 Brandon Webb .12 .30
6 Randy Johnson .30 .75
7 Andruw Jones .12 .30
8 Chipper Jones .30 .75
9 Gary Sheffield .12 .30
10 Jay Gibbons .12 .30
11 Miguel Tejada .20 .50
12 Tony Batista .12 .30
13 Nomar Garciaparra .20 .50
14 Manny Ramirez .30 .75
15 Pedro Martinez .20 .50
16 Mark Prior .20 .50
17 Kerry Wood .12 .30
18 Sammy Sosa .30 .75
19 Bartolo Colon .12 .30
20 Magglio Ordonez .20 .50
21 Frank Thomas .30 .75
22 Adam Dunn .20 .50
23 Austin Kearns .12 .30
24 Ken Griffey Jr. .60 1.50
25 Brandon Phillips .12 .30
26 Milton Bradley .12 .30
27 Jody Gerut .12 .30
28 Todd Helton .20 .50
29 Larry Walker .20 .50
30 Preston Wilson .12 .30
31 Jeremy Bonderman .12 .30
32 Carlos Pena .20 .50
33 Dmitri Young .12 .30
34 Dontrelle Willis .12 .30
35 Miguel Cabrera .30 .75
36 Mike Lowell .12 .30
37 Jeff Bagwell .20 .50
38 Roy Oswalt .20 .50
39 Lance Berkman .20 .50
40 Carlos Beltran .20 .50
41 Mike Sweeney .12 .30
42 Rondell White .12 .30

43 Hideo Nomo .30 .75
44 Kevin Brown .12 .30
45 Shawn Green .12 .30
46 Ben Sheets .12 .30
47 Geoff Jenkins .12 .30
48 Richie Sexson .12 .30
49 Jacque Jones .12 .30
50 Johan Santana .20 .50
51 Torii Hunter .12 .30
52 Javier Vazquez .12 .30
53 Jose Vidro .12 .30
54 Vladimir Guerrero .20 .50
55 Cliff Floyd .12 .30
56 Mike Piazza .30 .75
57 Jose Reyes .20 .50
58 Derek Jeter .75 2.00
59 Jason Giambi .12 .30
60 Alfonso Soriano .20 .50
61 Eric Chavez .12 .30
62 Barry Zito .20 .50
63 Tim Hudson .20 .50
64 Bobby Abreu .12 .30
65 Jim Thome .20 .50
66 Kevin Millwood .12 .30
67 Roger Clemens .40 1.00
68 Jason Kendall .12 .30
69 Reggie Sanders .12 .30
70 Phil Nevin .12 .30
71 Ryan Klesko .12 .30
72 Brian Giles .12 .30
73 A.J. Pierzynski .12 .30
74 Jason Schmidt .12 .30
75 Sidney Ponson .12 .30
76 Edgar Martinez .20 .50
77 Ichiro Suzuki .40 1.00
78 Bret Boone .12 .30
79 Albert Pujols .40 1.00
80 Scott Rolen .20 .50
81 Jim Edmonds .20 .50
82 Aubrey Huff .12 .30
83 Delmon Young .20 .50
84 Rocco Baldelli .12 .30
85 Alex Rodriguez .40 1.00
86 Mark Teixeira .20 .50
87 Rafael Palmeiro .20 .50
88 Carlos Delgado .12 .30
89 Vernon Wells .12 .30
90 Roy Halladay .20 .50
91 Brandon Medders FC RC .40 1.00
92 Colby Miller FC RC .40 1.00
93 Dave Crouthers FC RC .40 1.00
94 Dennis Sarfate FC RC .40 1.00
95 Donald Kelly FC RC .60 1.50
96 Alec Zumwalt FC RC .40 1.00
97 Frank Brooks FC RC .40 1.00
98 Greg Dobbs FC RC .40 1.00
99 Ian Snell FC RC .40 1.00
100 Jake Woods FC RC .40 1.00
101 Jamie Brown FC RC .40 1.00
102 Jason Frasor FC RC .40 1.00
103 Jerome Gamble FC RC .40 1.00
104 Jesse Harper FC RC .40 1.00
105 Josh Labandeira FC RC .40 1.00
106 Justin Hampson FC RC .40 1.00
107 Justin Huisman FC RC .40 1.00
108 Justin Leone FC RC .40 1.00
109 Chris Aguila FC RC .40 1.00
110 Lincoln Holdzkom FC RC .40 1.00
111 Mike Bumatay FC RC .40 1.00
112 Mike Gosling FC RC .40 1.00
113 Mike Johnston FC RC .40 1.00
114 Mike Rouse FC RC .40 1.00
115 Nick Regilio FC RC .40 1.00
116 Ryan Meaux FC RC .40 1.00
117 Scott Dohmann FC RC .40 1.00
118 Sean Henn FC RC .40 1.00
119 Tim Bausher FC RC .40 1.00
120 Tim Bittner FC RC .40 1.00

2004 UD Diamond All-Star Gold Honors

*GOLD 1-90: 6X TO 15X BASIC
*GOLD 91-120: 2X TO 5X BASIC
RANDOM INSERTS IN PACKS
STATED PRINT RUN 50 SERIAL #'d SETS

2004 UD Diamond All-Star Silver Honors

*SILVER 1-90: 2X TO 5X BASIC
*SILVER 91-120: .6X TO 1.5X BASIC
1-90 STATED ODDS 1:6
91-120 STATED ODDS 1:48

2004 UD Diamond All-Star Class of 2004 Autographs

STATED ODDS 1:5800
PRINT RUNS B/WN 50-100 COPIES PER
BZ Barry Zito/100 10.00 25.00
DW Dontrelle Willis/100 6.00 15.00
HM Hideki Matsui/100 175.00 300.00
JR Jose Reyes/100 6.00 15.00
KG Ken Griffey Jr./100 50.00 120.00
MC Miguel Cabrera/50 15.00 40.00
MP Mark Prior/100 4.00 10.00
RH Rich Harden/100 6.00 15.00
VG Vladimir Guerrero/100 15.00 40.00

2004 UD Diamond All-Star Dean's List Jersey

STATED ODDS 1:72
AP Albert Pujols 6.00 15.00
AR Alex Rodriguez 4.00 10.00
AS Alfonso Soriano 3.00 8.00
BA Jeff Bagwell 4.00 10.00
CS Curt Schilling 4.00 10.00
DW Dontrelle Willis 4.00 10.00
GL Troy Glaus 3.00 8.00
GM Greg Maddux 4.00 10.00
HB Hank Blalock 3.00 8.00
HM Hideki Matsui 15.00 40.00
HN Hideo Nomo 4.00 10.00
IS Ichiro Suzuki 10.00 25.00
JG Jason Giambi 3.00 8.00
JT Jim Thome 4.00 10.00
KG Ken Griffey Jr. 6.00 15.00
LG Luis Gonzalez 3.00 8.00
MP Mark Prior 4.00 10.00
PI Mike Piazza 4.00 10.00
SG Shawn Green 3.00 8.00
SS Sammy Sosa 4.00 10.00
VG Vladimir Guerrero 4.00 10.00

2004 UD Diamond All-Star Future Gems Jersey

STATED ODDS 1:72
AE Adam Eaton 3.00 8.00
AH Aaron Heilman 3.00 8.00
BA Josh Bard 3.00 8.00
BO Jeremy Bonderman 3.00 8.00
BS Ben Sheets 3.00 8.00
DS David Sanders 3.00 8.00
EM Eric Milton 3.00 8.00
GU Jeremy Guthrie 3.00 8.00
IS Kazuhisa Ishii 3.00 8.00
JB Josh Beckett 3.00 8.00
JJ Jason Jennings 3.00 8.00
JL Jon Leicester 3.00 8.00
JR Jose Reyes 3.00 8.00
KA Matt Kata 3.00 8.00
LF Lew Ford 3.00 8.00
MC Mike Cameron 3.00 8.00
MK Mark Kotsay 3.00 8.00
MT Mark Teixeira 4.00 10.00
PS Phil Seibel 3.00 8.00
RH Roy Halladay 3.00 8.00
RR Rick Roberts 3.00 8.00
SB Sean Burroughs 3.00 8.00
TH Travis Hafner 3.00 8.00
TW Todd Wellemeyer 3.00 8.00
WE Willie Eyre 3.00 8.00
WI Josh Willingham 3.00 8.00

2004 UD Diamond All-Star Premium Stars

STATED ODDS 1:4 MASS BLASTER
AP Albert Pujols 2.00 5.00
AR Alex Rodriguez 2.00 5.00
AS Alfonso Soriano 1.00 2.50
CD Carlos Delgado .60 1.50
DJ Derek Jeter 4.00 10.00
GS Gary Sheffield .60 1.50
HM Hideki Matsui 2.50 6.00
IS Ichiro Suzuki 2.00 5.00
JG Jason Giambi .60 1.50
KG Ken Griffey Jr. 3.00 8.00
MP Mike Piazza 1.50 4.00
NG Nomar Garciaparra 1.00 2.50
SG Shawn Green .60 1.50
SS Sammy Sosa 1.50 4.00
VG Vladimir Guerrero 1.00 2.50

2004 UD Diamond All-Star Promo

ONE PER PACK
AD Adam Dunn .60 1.50
AJ Andruw Jones .40 1.00
AK Austin Kearns .40 1.00
BA Bobby Abreu .40 1.00
BC Bartolo Colon .40 1.00
BE Josh Beckett .40 1.00
BO Bret Boone .40 1.00
BZ Barry Zito .60 1.50
CB Carlos Beltran .60 1.50
CJ Chipper Jones 1.00 2.50
CS Curt Schilling .60 1.50
DJ Derek Jeter 2.50 6.00
DW Dontrelle Willis .40 1.00
EC Eric Chavez .40 1.00
ER Edgar Renteria .40 1.00
FT Frank Thomas 1.00 2.50
GA Garret Anderson .40 1.00
GS Gary Sheffield .40 1.00
HB Hank Blalock .40 1.00
HM Hideki Matsui 1.50 4.00
HU Tim Hudson .60 1.50
IR Ivan Rodriguez .60 1.50
JB Jeff Bagwell .60 1.50
JD Johnny Damon .60 1.50
JE Jim Edmonds .60 1.50
JG Jason Giambi .40 1.00
JJ Jacque Jones .40 1.00
JK Jeff Kent .40 1.00
JL Javy Lopez .40 1.00
JP Jorge Posada .60 1.50
JS Jason Schmidt .40 1.00
JT Jim Thome .60 1.50
JV Jason Varitek 1.00 2.50
KG Ken Griffey Jr. 2.00 5.00
KW Kerry Wood .40 1.00
MG Marcus Giles .40 1.00
ML Mike Lowell .40 1.00
MM Mark Mulder .40 1.00
MO Magglio Ordonez .60 1.50
MP Mark Prior .60 1.50
MR Manny Ramirez 1.00 2.50
MS Mike Sweeney .40 1.00
MT Mark Teixeira .60 1.50
MU Mike Mussina .60 1.50
OC Orlando Cabrera .40 1.00
PI Mike Piazza 1.00 2.50
PM Pedro Martinez .60 1.50
PW Preston Wilson .40 1.00
RF Rafael Furcal .40 1.00
RH Roy Halladay .60 1.50
RJ Randy Johnson 1.00 2.50
RP Rafael Palmeiro .60 1.50
RS Richie Sexson .40 1.00
SG Shawn Green .40 1.00
SR Scott Rolen .60 1.50
TE Miguel Tejada .60 1.50
TG Troy Glaus .40 1.00
TH Torii Hunter .40 1.00
VI Jose Vidro .40 1.00
VW Vernon Wells .40 1.00

2004 UD Diamond All-Star Promo e-Card

STATED ODDS 1:12
AP Albert Pujols 1.25 3.00
AR Alex Rodriguez 1.25 3.00
AS Alfonso Soriano .60 1.50
CD Carlos Delgado .40 1.00
IS Ichiro Suzuki 1.25 3.00
NG Nomar Garciaparra .60 1.50
SS Sammy Sosa 1.00 2.50
TH Todd Helton .60 1.50
VG Vladimir Guerrero .60 1.50

2004 UD Diamond Pro Sigs

COMP.SET w/o SP's (90) 6.00 15.00
COMMON CARD (1-90) .10 .30
COMMON CARD (91-150) 1.50 4.00
91-150 STATED ODDS 1:6
COMMON CARD (151-240) 4.00 10.00
151-240 STATED ODDS 1:24
CARDS 160/169/174-175/177 DO NOT EXIST
CARDS 220/224/226-228 DO NOT EXIST
INSTANT WIN EXCH.ODDS 1:60,000
1 Alfonso Soriano .20 .50
2 Josh Beckett .12 .30
3 Kerry Wood .12 .30
4 Brandon Webb .12 .30
5 Shannon Stewart .12 .30
6 Larry Walker .20 .50
7 Tim Hudson .20 .50
8 Carlos Lee .12 .30
9 Austin Kearns .12 .30
10 Vernon Wells .12 .30
11 Jeff Bagwell .20 .50
12 Hideo Nomo .30 .75
13 Jerome Williams .12 .30
14 Kevin Brown .12 .30
15 Jose Vidro .12 .30
16 Rocco Baldelli .12 .30
17 Frank Thomas .30 .75
18 Albert Pujols .40 1.00
19 Bartolo Colon .12 .30
20 C.C. Sabathia .20 .50
21 Andruw Jones .12 .30
22 Reggie Sanders .12 .30
23 Carlos Beltran .20 .50
24 Curt Schilling .20 .50
25 Miguel Tejada .20 .50
26 Barry Zito .20 .50
27 Pedro Martinez .20 .50
28 Sean Burroughs .12 .30
29 Sammy Sosa .30 .75
30 Eric Chavez .12 .30
31 Roy Halladay .20 .50
32 Todd Helton .20 .50
33 Mark Prior .20 .50
34 Mike Mussina .20 .50
35 Alex Rodriguez Yanks .40 1.00
36 Ivan Rodriguez .20 .50
37 Mike Piazza .30 .75
38 Angel Berroa .12 .30
39 Orlando Cabrera .12 .30
40 Jim Thome .20 .50
42 Ichiro Suzuki .40 1.00
43 Edgar Renteria .12 .30
44 Eric Gagne .12 .30
45 Gary Sheffield .12 .30
46 Torii Hunter .12 .30
47 Roger Clemens .40 1.00
48 Scott Rolen .20 .50
49 Johan Santana .20 .50
50 Jacque Jones .12 .30
51 Hank Blalock .12 .30
52 Rafael Palmeiro .20 .50
53 Dmitri Young .12 .30
54 Ryan Klesko .12 .30
55 Mark Teixeira .20 .50
56 Nomar Garciaparra .20 .50
57 Jose Reyes .20 .50
58 Vladimir Guerrero .20 .50
59 Mike Sweeney .12 .30
60 Jorge Posada .20 .50
61 Derek Jeter .75 2.00
62 Milton Bradley .12 .30
63 Bobby Abreu .12 .30
64 Greg Maddux .40 1.00
65 Adam Dunn .20 .50
66 Troy Glaus .12 .30
67 Luis Gonzalez .12 .30
68 Shawn Green .12 .30
69 Bret Boone .12 .30
70 Mark Mulder .12 .30
71 Lance Berkman .20 .50
72 Preston Wilson .12 .30
73 Phil Nevin .12 .30
74 Chipper Jones .30 .75
75 Garret Anderson .12 .30
76 Jason Giambi .12 .30
77 Magglio Ordonez .20 .50
78 Jeff Kent .12 .30
79 Richie Sexson .12 .30
80 Mike Lowell .12 .30
81 Ben Sheets .12 .30
82 Randy Johnson .30 .75
83 Dontrelle Willis .12 .30
84 Javier Vazquez .12 .30
85 Geoff Jenkins .12 .30
86 Manny Ramirez .30 .75
87 Jim Edmonds .20 .50
88A Roy Oswalt .20 .50
88B Brian Giles .20 .50
89 Edgar Martinez .20 .50
90 Carlos Delgado .12 .30
91 Chris Saenz FC RC .40 1.00
92 Justin Leone FC RC .40 1.00
93 Shawn Hill FC RC .40 1.00
94 Chad Bentz FC RC .40 1.00
95 Jesse Harper FC RC .40 1.00
96 Dave Crouthers FC RC .40 1.00
97 Justin Germano FC RC .40 1.00
98 Tim Bausher FC RC .40 1.00
99 Greg Dobbs FC RC .40 1.00
100 Enemencio Pacheco FC RC .40 1.00
101 Dennis Sarfate FC RC .40 1.00
102 Edwin Moreno FC RC .40 1.00
103 Colby Miller FC RC .40 1.00
104 Mike Rouse FC RC .40 1.00
105 Fernando Nieve FC RC .40 1.00
106 Tim Hamulack FC RC .40 1.00
107 Jason Frasor FC RC .40 1.00
108 Jose Capellan FC RC .40 1.00
109 Jamie Brown FC RC .40 1.00
110 Mariano Gomez FC RC .40 1.00
111 Mike Vento FC RC .40 1.00
112 Josh Labandeira FC RC .40 1.00
113 Mike Gosling FC RC .40 1.00
114 Shingo Takatsu FC RC .40 1.00
115 Justin Hampson FC RC .40 1.00
116 Tim Bittner FC RC .40 1.00
117 Jerry Gil FC RC .40 1.00
118 Carlos Vasquez FC RC .40 1.00
119 Lincoln Holdzkom FC RC .40 1.00
120 Mike Johnston FC RC .40 1.00
121 William Bergolla FC RC .40 1.00
122 Luis A. Gonzalez FC RC .40 1.00
123 Ivan Ochoa FC RC .40 1.00
124 Roman Colon FC RC .40 1.00
125 Renyel Pinto FC RC .40 1.00
126 Donnie Kelly FC RC .60 1.50
127 Chris Oxspring FC RC .40 1.00
128 Sean Henn FC RC .40 1.00
129 Ryan Meaux FC RC .40 1.00
130 Shawn Camp FC RC .40 1.00
131 Brandon Medders FC RC .40 1.00
132 Rusty Tucker FC RC .40 1.00
133 Kazuo Matsui FC RC .60 1.50
134 Jorge Sequea FC RC .40 1.00
135 Hector Gimenez FC RC .40 1.00
136 Casey Daigle FC RC .40 1.00
137 Ian Snell FC RC .40 1.00
138 Scott Dohmann FC RC .40 1.00
139 Ronny Cedeno FC RC .40 1.00
140 Jorge Vasquez FC RC .40 1.00
141 David Aardsma FC RC .40 1.00
142 Carlos Hines FC RC .40 1.00
143 Scott Proctor FC RC .40 1.00
144 Jerome Gamble FC RC .40 1.00
145 Jason Bartlett FC RC 1.25 3.00
146 Akinori Otsuka FC RC .40 1.00
147 Merkin Valdez FC RC .40 1.00
148 Jake Woods FC RC .40 1.00
149 Chris Aguila FC RC .40 1.00
150 John Gall FC RC .40 1.00
151 Aaron Miles AU 4.00 10.00
152 Aquilino Lopez AU 4.00 10.00
153 Bill Hall AU 4.00 10.00
154 Billy Traber AU 4.00 10.00
155 Brad Lidge AU 6.00 15.00
156 Brady Clark AU 6.00 15.00
157 Brandon Duckworth AU 4.00 10.00
158 Brett Tomko AU 4.00 10.00
159 Brian Fuentes AU 4.00 10.00
161 Brooks Kieshnick AU 4.00 10.00
162 Carlos Rivera AU 4.00 10.00
163 Chad Cordero AU 6.00 15.00
164 Chad Tracy AU 4.00 10.00
165 Claudio Vargas AU 4.00 10.00
166 D.J. Carrasco AU 4.00 10.00
167 Damian Rolls AU 4.00 10.00
168 David Sanders AU 4.00 10.00
170 Derrick Turnbow AU 4.00 10.00
171 Desi Relaford AU 4.00 10.00
172 Doug Davis AU 4.00 10.00
173 Dustan Mohr AU 4.00 10.00
176 Frank Catalanotto AU 4.00 10.00
178 Franklyn German AU 4.00 10.00
179 Ron Belliard AU 4.00 10.00
180 Geoff Geary AU 4.00 10.00
181 Greg Colbrunn AU 4.00 10.00
182 Henry Mateo AU 4.00 10.00
183 Brent Mayne AU 4.00 10.00
184 Horacio Ramirez AU 4.00 10.00
185 J.C. Romero AU 4.00 10.00
186 J.J. Putz AU 4.00 10.00
187 Ferdin Tejeda AU 4.00 10.00
188 Jaime Cerda AU 4.00 10.00
189 Jason Michaels AU 4.00 10.00
190 Jason Simontacchi AU 4.00 10.00
191 Jay Witasick AU 4.00 10.00
192 Joe Valentine AU 4.00 10.00
193 Joey Eischen AU 4.00 10.00
194 Johnny Estrada AU 4.00 10.00
195 Jon Garland AU 15.00 40.00
196 Jon Switzer AU 4.00 10.00
197 Jorge Julio AU 4.00 10.00
198 Jorge Sosa AU 4.00 10.00
199 Jose Castillo AU 4.00 10.00
200 Jose Macias AU 4.00 10.00
201 Josh Bard AU 4.00 10.00
202 Juan Cruz AU 4.00 10.00
203 Juan Rivera AU 4.00 10.00
204 Ken Griffey Jr. AU 30.00 60.00
205 Kevin Hooper AU 4.00 10.00
206 Kiko Calero AU 4.00 10.00
207 Chad Gaudin AU 4.00 10.00
208 Luis Rivas AU 4.00 10.00
209 Mark Corey AU 4.00 10.00
210 Matt Ford AU 4.00 10.00
211 Matt Herges AU 4.00 10.00
212 Miguel Cairo AU 4.00 10.00
213 Fernando Cabrera AU 4.00 10.00
214 Mike MacDougal AU 4.00 10.00
215 Mike Neu AU 4.00 10.00
216 Lew Ford AU 4.00 10.00
217 Mike Wood AU 4.00 10.00
218 Nate Robertson AU 10.00 25.00
219 Nick Punto AU 4.00 10.00
221 Oscar Villarreal AU 4.00 10.00
222 Ramon Vazquez AU 4.00 10.00
223 Randall Simon AU 4.00 10.00
225 Ricky Stone AU 4.00 10.00
229 Ryan Drese AU 4.00 10.00
230 Ryan Ludwick AU 15.00 40.00
231 Scot Shields AU 4.00 10.00
232 Shane Nance AU 4.00 10.00
233 Steve Colyer AU 4.00 10.00
234 Tony Armas Jr. AU 4.00 10.00
235 Robby Hammock AU 4.00 10.00
236 Travis Hafner AU 6.00 15.00
237 Victor Martinez AU 6.00 15.00
238 Wilfredo Ledezma AU 4.00 10.00
239 Willie Bloomquist AU 4.00 10.00
240 Yorvit Torrealba AU 4.00 10.00

2004 UD Diamond Pro Sigs Gold

*GOLD: 3X TO 8X BASIC
OVERALL PARALLEL ODDS 1:6

2004 UD Diamond Pro Sigs Silver

*SILVER: 1.5X TO 4X BASIC
OVERALL PARALLEL ODDS 1:6

2004 UD Diamond Pro Sigs Signature Blue Ink

STATED PRINT RUN 25 SERIAL #'d SETS
RED INK PRINT RUN 10 SERIAL #'d SETS
OVERALL AU ODDS 1:24
NO PRICING DUE TO SCARCITY

2004 UD Diamond Pro Sigs Hall of Famers

ONE PER SEALED STARTER BOX
1 Al Kaline 2.50 6.00
2 Billy Williams 1.50 4.00
3 Bob Feller 1.50 4.00
4 Bob Gibson 1.50 4.00
5 Brooks Robinson 1.50 4.00
6 Catfish Hunter 1.50 4.00
7 Eddie Mathews 2.50 6.00
8 Ernie Banks 2.50 6.00
9 Ferguson Jenkins 1.50 4.00
10 Harmon Killebrew 2.50 6.00
11 Joe DiMaggio 5.00 12.00
12 Joe Morgan 1.50 4.00
13 Juan Marichal 1.50 4.00
14 Lou Brock 1.50 4.00
15 Mickey Mantle 8.00 20.00
16 Mike Schmidt 4.00 10.00
17 Nolan Ryan 8.00 20.00
18 Pee Wee Reese 1.50 4.00
19 Phil Rizzuto 1.50 4.00
20 Ralph Kiner 1.50 4.00
21 Robin Yount 2.50 6.00
22 Rollie Fingers 1.50 4.00
23 Stan Musial 4.00 10.00
24 Ted Williams 5.00 12.00
25 Tom Seaver 1.50 4.00
26 Warren Spahn 1.50 4.00
27 Whitey Ford 1.50 4.00
28 Willie McCovey 1.50 4.00
29 Willie Stargell 1.50 4.00
30 Yogi Berra 2.50 6.00

1999 UD Ionix

This 90-card set (produced by Upper Deck) was distributed in four-card packs with a suggested retail price of $4.99. The set features color action photos of top MLB players printed on super-thick, double-laminated, metalized cards. The set contains a 30-card short-printed subset, Techno (61-90), of which cards were randomly inserted in packs at the rate of one in four. A game-used bat from Hall of Fame slugger Frank Robinson was cut up and incorporated into 370 special 500 Home Run Bat Cards. Robinson signed 20 of these cards. Pack odds for these cards was not officially released, but suffice to say, they're few and far between. Pricing for these bat cards can be referenced under 1999 Upper Deck A Piece of History 500 Club. In addition, a Ken Griffey Jr. sample card was distributed to dealers and hobby media several weeks prior to the product's release. The card can be readily identified by the bold "SAMPLE" text running diagonally across the back.

COMPLETE SET (90) 60.00 120.00
COMP.SET w/o SP's (60) 8.00 20.00
COMMON CARD (1-60) .15 .40
COMMON TECH (61-90) .75 2.00
TECH STATED ODDS 1:4
F.ROB BAT LISTED W/UD APH 500 CLUB
1 Troy Glaus .25 .60
2 Darin Erstad .15 .40
3 Travis Lee .15 .40
4 Matt Williams .15 .40
5 Chipper Jones .40 1.00
6 Greg Maddux .60 1.50
7 Andruw Jones .25 .60
8 Andres Galarraga .15 .40
9 Tom Glavine .25 .60
10 Cal Ripken 1.25 3.00
11 Ryan Minor .15 .40
12 Nomar Garciaparra .60 1.50
13 Mo Vaughn .15 .40
14 Pedro Martinez .25 .60
15 Sammy Sosa .40 1.00
16 Kerry Wood .15 .40
17 Albert Belle .15 .40
18 Frank Thomas .40 1.00
19 Sean Casey .15 .40
20 Kenny Lofton .15 .40
21 Manny Ramirez .25 .60
22 Jim Thome .25 .60
23 Bartolo Colon .15 .40
24 Jaret Wright .15 .40
25 Larry Walker .15 .40
26 Tony Clark .15 .40
27 Gabe Kapler .15 .40
28 Edgar Renteria .15 .40
29 Randy Johnson .40 1.00
30 Craig Biggio .25 .60
31 Jeff Bagwell .25 .60
32 Moises Alou .15 .40
33 Johnny Damon .25 .60
34 Adrian Beltre .15 .40
35 Jeromy Burnitz .15 .40
36 Todd Walker .15 .40
37 Corey Koskie .15 .40
38 Vladimir Guerrero .40 1.00
39 Mike Piazza .60 1.50
40 Hideo Nomo .40 1.00
41 Derek Jeter 1.00 2.50
42 Tino Martinez .25 .60
43 Orlando Hernandez .15 .40
44 Ben Grieve .15 .40
45 Rickey Henderson .40 1.00
46 Scott Rolen .25 .60
47 Curt Schilling .15 .40
48 Aramis Ramirez .15 .40
49 Tony Gwynn .50 1.25
50 Kevin Brown .15 .40
51 Barry Bonds 1.00 2.50
52 Ken Griffey Jr. .75 2.00
53 Alex Rodriguez .60 1.50
54 Mark McGwire 1.00 2.50
55 J.D. Drew .15 .40
56 Rolando Arrojo .15 .40
57 Ivan Rodriguez .25 .60
58 Juan Gonzalez .15 .40
59 Roger Clemens .75 2.00
60 Jose Cruz Jr. .15 .40
61 Travis Lee TECH .75 2.00
62 Andres Galarraga TECH .75 2.00
63 Andruw Jones TECH 1.00 2.50
64 Chipper Jones TECH 1.50 4.00
65 Greg Maddux TECH 2.50 6.00
66 Cal Ripken TECH 5.00 12.00
67 Nomar Garciaparra TECH 2.50 6.00
68 Mo Vaughn TECH .75 2.00
69 Sammy Sosa TECH 1.50 4.00
70 Frank Thomas TECH 1.50 4.00
71 Kerry Wood TECH .75 2.00
72 Kenny Lofton TECH .75 2.00
73 Manny Ramirez TECH 1.00 2.50
74 Larry Walker TECH .75 2.00
75 Jeff Bagwell TECH 1.00 2.50
76 Randy Johnson TECH 1.50 4.00
77 Paul Molitor TECH .75 2.00
78 Derek Jeter TECH 4.00 10.00
79 Tino Martinez TECH 1.00 2.50
80 Mike Piazza TECH 2.50 6.00
81 Ben Grieve TECH .75 2.00
82 Scott Rolen TECH 1.00 2.50
83 Mark McGwire TECH 4.00 10.00
84 Tony Gwynn TECH 2.00 5.00
85 Barry Bonds TECH 4.00 10.00
86 Ken Griffey Jr. TECH 3.00 8.00
87 Alex Rodriguez TECH 2.50 6.00
88 Juan Gonzalez TECH .75 2.00
89 Roger Clemens TECH 3.00 8.00
90 J.D. Drew TECH .75 2.00
S100 Ken Griffey Jr. Sample 1.00 2.50

1999 UD Ionix Reciprocal

*RECIP.1-60: 4X TO 10X BASIC 1-60
RECIP.1-60 PRINT RUN 750 SERIAL #'d SETS
*TECH RECIP: 3X TO 8X BASIC TECH
TECH RECIP.PRINT RUN 100 SERIAL #'d SETS
RANDOM INSERTS IN PACKS

1999 UD Ionix Cyber

STATED ODDS 1:53
C1 Ken Griffey Jr. 10.00 25.00
C2 Cal Ripken 20.00 50.00
C3 Frank Thomas 6.00 15.00
C4 Greg Maddux 10.00 25.00
C5 Mike Piazza 10.00 25.00
C6 Alex Rodriguez 10.00 25.00
C7 Chipper Jones 6.00 15.00
C8 Derek Jeter 15.00 40.00
C9 Mark McGwire 15.00 40.00
C10 Juan Gonzalez 2.50 6.00
C11 Kerry Wood 2.50 6.00
C12 Tony Gwynn 8.00 20.00
C13 Scott Rolen 4.00 10.00
C14 Nomar Garciaparra 10.00 25.00
C15 Roger Clemens 12.50 30.00
C16 Sammy Sosa 6.00 15.00
C17 Travis Lee 2.50 6.00
C18 Ben Grieve 2.50 6.00
C19 Jeff Bagwell 4.00 10.00
C20 Ivan Rodriguez 4.00 10.00
C21 Barry Bonds 15.00 40.00
C22 J.D. Drew 2.50 6.00
C23 Kenny Lofton 2.50 6.00
C24 Andruw Jones 4.00 10.00
C25 Vladimir Guerrero 6.00 15.00

1999 UD Ionix HoloGrFX

STATED ODDS 1:1500
HG1 Ken Griffey Jr. 75.00 200.00
HG2 Cal Ripken 40.00 100.00
HG3 Frank Thomas 40.00 100.00
HG4 Greg Maddux 25.00 60.00
HG5 Mike Piazza 30.00 80.00
HG6 Alex Rodriguez 20.00 50.00
HG7 Chipper Jones 20.00 50.00
HG8 Derek Jeter 30.00 80.00
HG9 Mark McGwire 40.00 100.00
HG10 Juan Gonzalez 12.00 30.00

1999 UD Ionix Hyper

COMPLETE SET (20) 75.00 150.00
STATED ODDS 1:9
H1 Ken Griffey Jr. 4.00 10.00
H2 Cal Ripken 6.00 15.00
H3 Frank Thomas 2.00 5.00
H4 Greg Maddux 3.00 8.00
H5 Mike Piazza 3.00 8.00
H6 Alex Rodriguez 3.00 8.00
H7 Chipper Jones 2.00 5.00
H8 Derek Jeter 5.00 12.00
H9 Mark McGwire 5.00 12.00
H10 Juan Gonzalez .75 2.00
H11 Kerry Wood .75 2.00
H12 Tony Gwynn 2.50 6.00
H13 Scott Rolen 1.25 3.00
H14 Nomar Garciaparra 3.00 8.00
H15 Roger Clemens 4.00 10.00
H16 Sammy Sosa 2.00 5.00
H17 Travis Lee .75 2.00
H18 Ben Grieve .75 2.00
H19 Jeff Bagwell 1.25 3.00
H20 J.D. Drew .75 2.00

1999 UD Ionix Nitro

COMPLETE SET (10) 30.00 80.00
STATED ODDS 1:18
N1 Ken Griffey Jr. 4.00 10.00
N2 Cal Ripken 6.00 15.00
N3 Frank Thomas 2.00 5.00
N4 Greg Maddux 3.00 8.00
N5 Mike Piazza 3.00 8.00
N6 Alex Rodriguez 3.00 8.00
N7 Chipper Jones 2.00 5.00
N8 Derek Jeter 5.00 12.00
N9 Mark McGwire 5.00 12.00
N10 J.D. Drew .75 2.00

1999 UD Ionix Warp Zone

COMPLETE SET (15) 50.00 100.00
STATED ODDS 1:216
WZ1 Ken Griffey Jr. 6.00 15.00
WZ2 Cal Ripken 10.00 25.00
WZ3 Frank Thomas 3.00 8.00
WZ4 Greg Maddux 4.00 10.00
WZ5 Mike Piazza 3.00 8.00
WZ6 Alex Rodriguez 4.00 10.00
WZ7 Chipper Jones 3.00 8.00
WZ8 Derek Jeter 8.00 20.00
WZ9 Mark McGwire 5.00 12.00
WZ10 Juan Gonzalez 1.25 3.00
WZ11 Kerry Wood 1.25 3.00
WZ12 Tony Gwynn 3.00 8.00
WZ13 Scott Rolen 2.00 5.00
WZ14 Nomar Garciaparra 2.00 5.00
WZ15 J.D. Drew 1.25 3.00

2000 UD Ionix

COMPLETE SET (90) 30.00 60.00
COMP.SET w/o SP's (60) 8.00 *20.00
COMMON CARD (1-60) .15 .40
COMMON FUTURE (61-90) .60 1.50
FUTURE UNLISTED STARS 1.50 4.00
FUTURE STATED ODDS 1:4
CLEMENTE 3K LISTED W/UD 3000 CLUB
1 Mo Vaughn .15 .40
2 Troy Glaus .15 .40
3 Jeff Bagwell .25 .60
4 Craig Biggio .25 .60
5 Jose Lima .15 .40
6 Jason Giambi .15 .40
7 Tim Hudson .25 .60
8 Shawn Green .15 .40
9 Carlos Delgado .15 .40
10 Chipper Jones .40 1.00
11 Andruw Jones .15 .40
12 Greg Maddux .50 1.25
13 Jeromy Burnitz .15 .40
14 Mark McGwire .60 1.50
15 J.D. Drew .15 .40
16 Sammy Sosa .40 1.00
17 Jose Canseco .25 .60
18 Fred McGriff .25 .60
19 Randy Johnson .40 1.00
20 Matt Williams .15 .40
21 Kevin Brown .15 .40
22 Gary Sheffield .15 .40
23 Vladimir Guerrero .25 .60
24 Barry Bonds .60 1.50
25 Jim Thome .25 .60
26 Manny Ramirez .40 1.00
27 Roberto Alomar .25 .60
28 Kenny Lofton .15 .40
29 Ken Griffey Jr. .75 2.00
30 Alex Rodriguez .50 1.25
31 Alex Gonzalez .15 .40
32 Preston Wilson .15 .40
33 Mike Piazza .40 1.00
34 Robin Ventura .15 .40
35 Cal Ripken 1.25 3.00
36 Albert Belle .15 .40
37 Tony Gwynn .40 1.00
38 Scott Rolen .25 .60
39 Curt Schilling .25 .60
40 Brian Giles .15 .40
41 Juan Gonzalez .15 .40
42 Ivan Rodriguez .25 .60
43 Rafael Palmeiro .25 .60
44 Pedro Martinez .25 .60
45 Nomar Garciaparra .25 .60
46 Sean Casey .15 .40
47 Aaron Boone .15 .40
48 Barry Larkin .25 .60
49 Larry Walker .25 .60
50 Vinny Castilla .15 .40
51 Carlos Beltran .25 .60
52 Gabe Kapler .15 .40
53 Dean Palmer .15 .40
54 Eric Milton .15 .40
55 Corey Koskie .15 .40
56 Frank Thomas .40 1.00
57 Magglio Ordonez .25 .60
58 Roger Clemens .50 1.25
59 Bernie Williams .25 .60
60 Derek Jeter 1.00 2.50
61 Josh Beckett FUT 1.25 3.00
62 Eric Munson FUT .60 1.50
63 Rick Ankiel FUT 1.00 2.50
64 Matt Riley FUT .60 1.50
65 Rob Ramsay FUT .60 1.50
66 Vernon Wells FUT .60 1.50
67 Eric Gagne FUT .60 1.50
68 Robert Fick FUT .60 1.50
69 Mark Quinn FUT .60 1.50
70 Kip Wells FUT .60 1.50
71 Peter Bergeron FUT .60 1.50
72 Ed Yarnall FUT .60 1.50
73 Jorge Toca FUT .60 1.50
74 Alfonso Soriano FUT 1.50 4.00
75 Calvin Murray FUT .60 1.50
76 Ramon Ortiz FUT .60 1.50
77 Chad Meyers FUT .60 1.50
78 Jason LaRue FUT .60 1.50
79 Pat Burrell FUT .60 1.50
80 Chad Hermansen FUT .60 1.50
81 Lance Berkman FUT 1.00 2.50
82 Erubiel Durazo FUT .60 1.50
83 Juan Pena FUT .60 1.50
84 Adam Kennedy FUT .60 1.50
85 Ben Petrick FUT .60 1.50
86 Kevin Barker FUT .60 1.50
87 Bruce Chen FUT .60 1.50
88 Jerry Hairston Jr. FUT .60 1.50
89 A.J. Burnett FUT .60 1.50
90 Gary Matthews Jr. FUT .60 1.50

2000 UD Ionix Reciprocal

*STARS 1-60: 1.5X TO 4X BASIC 1-60
1-60 STATED ODDS 1:4
*FUTURE 61-90: .75X TO 2X BASIC 61-90
FUTURE STATED ODDS 1:11

2000 UD Ionix Atomic

COMPLETE SET (15) 12.50 30.00
STATED ODDS 1:8
A1 Pedro Martinez .60 1.50
A2 Mark McGwire 1.50 4.00
A3 Ken Griffey Jr. 2.00 5.00
A4 Jeff Bagwell .60 1.50
A5 Greg Maddux 1.25 3.00
A6 Derek Jeter 2.50 6.00
A7 Cal Ripken 3.00 8.00
A8 Manny Ramirez 1.00 2.50
A9 Randy Johnson 1.00 2.50
A10 Nomar Garciaparra .60 1.50
A11 Tony Gwynn 1.00 2.50
A12 Bernie Williams .60 1.50
A13 Mike Piazza 1.00 2.50
A14 Roger Clemens 1.25 3.00
A15 Alex Rodriguez 1.25 3.00

2000 UD Ionix Awesome Powers

COMPLETE SET (15)	12.50	30.00
STATED ODDS 1:23		
AP1 Ken Griffey Jr.	2.00	5.00
AP2 Mike Piazza	1.00	2.50
AP3 Carlos Delgado	.40	1.00
AP4 Mark McGwire	1.50	4.00
AP5 Chipper Jones	1.00	2.50
AP6 Scott Rolen	.60	1.50
AP7 Cal Ripken	3.00	8.00
AP8 Alex Rodriguez	1.25	3.00
AP9 Larry Walker	.60	1.50
AP10 Sammy Sosa	1.00	2.50
AP11 Barry Bonds	1.50	4.00
AP12 Nomar Garciaparra	.60	1.50
AP13 Jose Canseco	.60	1.50
AP14 Manny Ramirez	1.00	2.50
AP15 Jeff Bagwell	.60	1.50

2000 UD Ionix BIOrhythm

COMPLETE SET (15)	12.50	30.00
STATED ODDS 1:11		
B1 Randy Johnson	1.00	2.50
B2 Derek Jeter	2.50	6.00
B3 Sammy Sosa	1.00	2.50
B4 Jose Lima	.40	1.00
B5 Chipper Jones	1.00	2.50
B6 Barry Bonds	1.50	4.00
B7 Ken Griffey Jr.	2.00	5.00
B8 Nomar Garciaparra	.60	1.50
B9 Frank Thomas	1.00	2.50
B10 Pedro Martinez	.60	1.50
B11 Larry Walker	.60	1.50
B12 Greg Maddux	1.25	3.00
B13 Alex Rodriguez	1.25	3.00
B14 Mark McGwire	1.50	4.00
B15 Cal Ripken	3.00	8.00

2000 UD Ionix Pyrotechnics

COMPLETE SET (15)	40.00	80.00
STATED ODDS 1:72		
P1 Roger Clemens	2.50	6.00
P2 Chipper Jones	2.00	5.00
P3 Alex Rodriguez	2.50	6.00
P4 Jeff Bagwell	1.25	3.00
P5 Mark McGwire	3.00	8.00
P6 Pedro Martinez	1.25	3.00
P7 Manny Ramirez	2.00	5.00
P8 Cal Ripken	6.00	15.00
P9 Mike Piazza	2.00	5.00
P10 Derek Jeter	5.00	12.00
P11 Ken Griffey Jr.	4.00	10.00
P12 Frank Thomas	2.00	5.00
P13 Sammy Sosa	2.00	5.00
P14 Nomar Garciaparra	1.25	3.00
P15 Greg Maddux	2.50	6.00

2000 UD Ionix Shockwave

COMPLETE SET (15)	5.00	12.00
STATED ODDS 1:4		
S1 Mark McGwire	.75	2.00
S2 Sammy Sosa	.50	1.25
S3 Manny Ramirez	.50	1.25
S4 Ken Griffey Jr.	1.00	2.50
S5 Vladimir Guerrero	.30	.75
S6 Barry Bonds	.75	2.00
S7 Albert Belle	.20	.50
S8 Ivan Rodriguez	.30	.75
S9 Chipper Jones	.50	1.25
S10 Mo Vaughn	.20	.50
S11 Jose Canseco	.30	.75
S12 Jeff Bagwell	.30	.75
S13 Matt Williams	.20	.50
S14 Alex Rodriguez	.60	1.50
S15 Carlos Delgado	.20	.50

2000 UD Ionix UD Authentics

STATED ODDS 1:144		
EXCH.DEADLINE 09/20/00		
AB Adrian Beltre	15.00	40.00
BD Ben Davis	4.00	10.00
DJ Derek Jeter	100.00	250.00
JC Jose Canseco	10.00	25.00
JR Ken Griffey Jr.	75.00	200.00
MR Manny Ramirez	12.00	30.00
PB Pat Burrell	6.00	15.00
RM Ruben Mateo	4.00	10.00
SC Sean Casey	6.00	15.00
SG Shawn Green	6.00	15.00
SR Scott Rolen	4.00	10.00
VG Vladimir Guerrero	12.00	30.00
CBE Carlos Beltran	8.00	20.00

2000 UD Ionix Warp Zone

STATED ODDS 1:288		
WZ1 Cal Ripken	15.00	40.00
WZ2 Barry Bonds	8.00	20.00
WZ3 Ken Griffey Jr.	10.00	25.00
WZ4 Nomar Garciaparra	3.00	8.00
WZ5 Chipper Jones	5.00	12.00
WZ6 Ivan Rodriguez	3.00	8.00
WZ7 Greg Maddux	6.00	15.00
WZ8 Derek Jeter	12.00	30.00
WZ9 Mike Piazza	5.00	12.00
WZ10 Sammy Sosa	5.00	12.00
WZ11 Roger Clemens	6.00	15.00
WZ12 Alex Rodriguez	6.00	15.00
WZ13 Vladimir Guerrero	3.00	8.00
WZ14 Pedro Martinez	3.00	8.00
WZ15 Mark McGwire	8.00	20.00

2004 UD Legends Timeless Teams

COMPLETE SET (300)	20.00	50.00
COMMON CARD (1-300)	.15	.40
1 Bob Gibson 64	.25	.60
2 Lou Brock MM 64	.25	.60
3 Ray Washburn 64	.15	.40
4 Tim McCarver 64	.15	.40
5 Harmon Killebrew 65	.40	1.00
6 Jim Kaat 65	.15	.40
7 Jim Perry 65	.15	.40
8 Mudcat Grant 65	.15	.40
9 Boog Powell 66	.15	.40
10 Brooks Robinson 66	.25	.60
11 Frank Robinson MM 66	.25	.60
12 Jim Palmer 66	.25	.60
13 Carl Yastrzemski MM 67	.40	1.00
14 Jim Lonborg 67	.15	.40
15 George Scott 67	.15	.40
16 Sparky Lyle 67	.15	.40
17 Rico Petrocelli 67	.15	.40
18 Bob Gibson 67	.25	.60
19 Julian Javier 67	.15	.40
20 Lou Brock 67	.25	.60
21 Orlando Cepeda 67	.25	.60
22 Ray Washburn 67	.15	.40
23 Steve Carlton 67	.25	.60
24 Tim McCarver 67	.15	.40
25 Al Kaline 68	.40	1.00
26 Bill Freehan 68	.15	.40
27 Denny McLain MM 68	.15	.40
28 Dick McAuliffe 68	.15	.40
29 Jim Northrup 68	.15	.40
30 John Hiller 68	.15	.40
31 Mickey Lolich MM 68	.15	.40
32 Mickey Stanley 68	.15	.40
33 Willie Horton 68	.15	.40
34 Bob Gibson MM 68	.25	.60
35 Julian Javier 68	.15	.40
36 Lou Brock 68	.25	.60
37 Orlando Cepeda 68	.25	.60
38 Steve Carlton 68	.25	.60
39 Boog Powell 69	.15	.40
40 Brooks Robinson 69	.25	.60
41 Davey Johnson 69	.15	.40
42 Merv Rettenmund 69	.15	.40
43 Eddie Watt 69	.15	.40
44 Frank Robinson 69	.25	.60
45 Jim Palmer 69	.25	.60
46 Mike Cuellar 69	.15	.40
47 Paul Blair 69	.15	.40
48 Pete Richert 69	.15	.40
49 Ellie Hendricks 69	.15	.40
50 Billy Williams 69	.25	.60
51 Randy Hundley 69	.15	.40
52 Ernie Banks 69	.40	1.00
53 Fergie Jenkins 69	.25	.60
54 Jim Hickman 69	.15	.40
55 Ken Holtzman 69	.15	.40
56 Ron Santo MM 69	.25	.60
57 Ed Kranepool 69	.15	.40
58 Jerry Koosman MM 69	.15	.40
59 Nolan Ryan 69	1.25	3.00
60 Tom Seaver 69	.25	.60
61 Boog Powell 70	.15	.40
62 Brooks Robinson MM 70	.25	.60
63 Davey Johnson 70	.15	.40
64 Merv Rettenmund 70	.15	.40
65 Eddie Watt 70	.15	.40
66 Frank Robinson 70	.25	.60
67 Jim Palmer 70	.25	.60
68 Mike Cuellar 70	.15	.40
69 Paul Blair 70	.15	.40
70 Pete Richert 70	.15	.40
71 Ellie Hendricks 70	.15	.40
72 Al Kaline 72	.40	1.00
73 Bill Freehan 72	.15	.40
74 Dick McAuliffe 72	.15	.40
75 Jim Northrup 72	.15	.40
76 John Hiller 72	.15	.40
77 Mickey Lolich 72	.15	.40
78 Mickey Stanley 72	.15	.40
79 Willie Horton 72	.15	.40
80 Bert Campaneris 72	.15	.40
81 Blue Moon Odom MM 72	.15	.40
82 Sal Bando 72	.15	.40
83 Joe Rudi 72	.15	.40
84 Ken Holtzman 72	.15	.40
85 Billy North 73	.15	.40
86 Blue Moon Odom 73	.15	.40
87 Gene Tenace 73	.15	.40
88 Manny Trillo 73	.15	.40
89 Dick Green 73	.15	.40
90 Rollie Fingers 73	.25	.60
91 Sal Bando 73	.15	.40
92 Vida Blue 73	.15	.40
93 Bill Buckner 74	.15	.40
94 Davey Lopes 74	.15	.40
95 Don Sutton 74	.25	.60
96 Al Downing MM 74	.15	.40
97 Ron Cey 74	.15	.40
98 Steve Garvey 74	.15	.40
99 Tommy John 74	.15	.40
100 Bert Campaneris 74	.15	.40
101 Billy North 74	.15	.40
102 Joe Rudi MM 74	.15	.40
103 Sal Bando 74	.15	.40
104 Vida Blue 74	.15	.40
105 Carl Yastrzemski 75	.40	1.00
106 Carlton Fisk MM 75	.25	.60
107 Cecil Cooper 75	.15	.40
108 Dwight Evans 75	.15	.40
109 Fred Lynn 75	.15	.40
110 Jim Rice 75	.25	.60
111 Luis Tiant 75	.15	.40
112 Rick Burleson 75	.15	.40
113 Rico Petrocelli 75	.15	.40
114 Pedro Borbon 75	.15	.40
115 Dave Concepcion 75	.15	.40
116 Don Gullett 75	.15	.40
117 George Foster 75	.15	.40
118 Joe Morgan MM 75	.25	.60
119 Johnny Bench 75	.40	1.00
120 Rawly Eastwick 75	.15	.40
121 Sparky Anderson 75	.25	.60
122 Tony Perez 75	.25	.60
123 Billy Williams 75	.25	.60
124 Gene Tenace 75	.15	.40
125 Jim Perry 75	.15	.40
126 Vida Blue 75	.15	.40
127 Pedro Borbon 76	.15	.40
128 Dave Concepcion 76	.15	.40
129 Don Gullett 76	.15	.40
130 George Foster 76	.15	.40
131 Joe Morgan 76	.25	.60
132 Johnny Bench MM 76	.40	1.00
133 Ken Griffey Sr. 76	.15	.40
134 Rawly Eastwick 76	.15	.40
135 Tony Perez 76	.25	.60
136 Bill Russell 77	.15	.40
137 Burt Hooton 77	.15	.40
138 Davey Lopes 77	.15	.40
139 Don Sutton 77	.25	.60
140 Dusty Baker 77	.15	.40
141 Steve Yeager 77	.15	.40
142 Ron Cey 77	.15	.40
143 Steve Garvey MM 77	.15	.40
144 Tommy John 77	.15	.40
145 Bucky Dent 77	.15	.40
146 Chris Chambliss 77	.15	.40
147 Ed Figueroa 77	.15	.40
148 Graig Nettles 77	.15	.40
149 Lou Piniella 77	.15	.40
150 Roy White 77	.15	.40
151 Don Gullett 77	.15	.40
152 Sparky Lyle 77	.15	.40
153 Brian Doyle 78	.15	.40
154 Bucky Dent MM 78	.15	.40
155 Chris Chambliss 78	.15	.40
156 Ed Figueroa 78	.15	.40
157 Graig Nettles 78	.15	.40
158 Lou Piniella 78	.15	.40
159 Roy White 78	.15	.40
160 Rich Gossage 78	.25	.60
161 Sparky Lyle 78	.15	.40
162 Bobby Grich 79	.15	.40
163 Brian Downing 79	.15	.40
164 Dan Ford 79	.15	.40
165 Nolan Ryan 79	1.25	3.00
166 Dave Concepcion 79	.15	.40
167 George Foster 79	.15	.40
168 Johnny Bench 79	.40	1.00
169 Ray Knight 79	.15	.40
170 Tom Seaver 79	.25	.60
171 Bert Blyleven 79	.25	.60
172 Bill Madlock 79	.15	.40
173 Dave Parker MM 79	.15	.40
174 Phil Garner 79	.15	.40
175 Bill Russell 80	.15	.40
176 Steve Yeager 80	.15	.40
177 Don Sutton 80	.25	.60
178 Dusty Baker 80	.15	.40
179 Jerry Reuss 80	.15	.40
180 Mickey Hatcher 80	.15	.40
181 Pedro Guerrero 80	.15	.40
182 Ron Cey 80	.15	.40
183 Steve Garvey 80	.15	.40
184 Rudy May 80	.15	.40
185 Brian Doyle 80	.15	.40
186 Bucky Dent 80	.15	.40
187 Jim Kaat 80	.15	.40
188 Lou Piniella 80	.15	.40
189 Luis Tiant 80	.15	.40
190 Tommy John 80	.15	.40
191 Bake McBride 80	.15	.40
192 Bob Boone 80	.15	.40
193 Dickie Noles MM 80	.15	.40
194 Manny Trillo 80	.15	.40
195 Mike Schmidt 80	.60	1.50
196 Sparky Lyle 80	.15	.40
197 Steve Carlton 80	.25	.60
198 Steve Yeager 81	.15	.40
199 Burt Hooton 81	.15	.40
200 Dusty Baker 81	.15	.40
201 Jerry Reuss 81	.15	.40
202 Mike Scioscia 81	.15	.40
203 Pedro Guerrero 81	.15	.40
204 Ron Cey 81	.15	.40
205 Steve Garvey 81	.15	.40
206 Alejandro Pena 81	.15	.40
207 Steve Sax 81	.15	.40
208 Cecil Cooper 81	.15	.40
209 Gorman Thomas 81	.15	.40
210 Paul Molitor 81	.40	1.00
211 Robin Yount 81	.40	1.00
212 Rollie Fingers 81	.25	.60
213 Don Money 81	.15	.40
214 Rudy May 81	.15	.40
215 Bucky Dent 81	.15	.40
216 Dave Winfield 81	.25	.60
217 Lou Piniella 81	.15	.40
218 Rich Gossage 81	.25	.60
219 Tommy John 81	.15	.40
220 Cecil Cooper 82	.15	.40
221 Gorman Thomas 82	.15	.40
222 Paul Molitor MM 82	.40	1.00
223 Robin Yount 82	.40	1.00
224 Don Money 82	.15	.40
225 Cal Ripken MM 83	1.25	3.00
226 Dan Ford 83	.15	.40
227 Jim Palmer 83	.25	.60
228 John Shelby 83	.15	.40
229 Alan Trammell 84	.25	.60
230 Chet Lemon 84	.15	.40
231 Howard Johnson 84	.15	.40
232 Jack Morris MM 84	.25	.60
233 Kirk Gibson 84	.15	.40
234 Lou Whitaker 84	.15	.40
235 Sparky Anderson 84	.25	.60
236 Dave Winfield 85	.25	.60
237 Don Mattingly 85	.75	2.00
238 Ken Griffey Sr. 85	.15	.40
239 Phil Niekro 85	.25	.60
240 Yogi Berra 85	.40	1.00
241 Bill Buckner MM 86	.15	.40
242 Bruce Hurst 86	.15	.40
243 Dave Henderson 86	.15	.40
244 Dwight Evans 86	.15	.40
245 Jim Rice 86	.25	.60
246 Tom Seaver 86	.25	.60
247 Wade Boggs 86	.25	.60
248 Bob Boone 86	.15	.40
249 Bobby Grich 86	.15	.40
250 Brian Downing 86	.15	.40
251 Don Sutton 86	.25	.60
252 Terry Forster 86	.15	.40
253 Rick Burleson 86	.15	.40
254 Wally Joyner MM 86	.15	.40
255 Darryl Strawberry 86	.15	.40
256 Dwight Gooden 86	.15	.40
257 Gary Carter 86	.25	.60
258 Jesse Orosco MM 86	.15	.40
259 Keith Hernandez 86	.15	.40
260 Lenny Dykstra 86	.15	.40
261 Mookie Wilson 86	.15	.40
262 Ray Knight 86	.15	.40
263 Wally Backman 86	.15	.40
264 Sid Fernandez 86	.15	.40
265 Alan Trammell 87	.25	.60
266 Dan Petry 87	.15	.40
267 Chet Lemon 87	.15	.40
268 Sparky Anderson 87	.25	.60
269 Jack Morris 87	.25	.60
270 Kirk Gibson 87	.15	.40
271 Lou Whitaker 87	.15	.40
272 Bert Blyleven 87	.25	.60
273 Kent Hrbek MM 87	.15	.40
274 Kirby Puckett 87	.40	1.00
275 Alejandro Pena 88	.15	.40
276 Jesse Orosco 88	.15	.40
277 John Shelby 88	.15	.40
278 Kirk Gibson MM 88	.15	.40
279 Mickey Hatcher 88	.15	.40
280 Mike Scioscia 88	.15	.40
281 Steve Sax 88	.15	.40
282 Darryl Strawberry 88	.15	.40
283 Dwight Gooden 88	.15	.40
284 Gary Carter 88	.25	.60
285 Howard Johnson 88	.15	.40
286 Keith Hernandez 88	.15	.40
287 Lenny Dykstra 88	.15	.40
288 Mookie Wilson 88	.15	.40
289 Wally Backman 88	.15	.40
290 Sid Fernandez 88	.15	.40
291 Jack Morris 91	.25	.60
292 Kent Hrbek 91	.15	.40
293 Kirby Puckett MM 91	.40	1.00
294 Dave Winfield MM 92	.25	.60
295 Jack Morris 92	.25	.60
296 Joe Carter 92	.15	.40
297 Don Mattingly MM 95	.75	2.00
298 Paul O'Neill 95	.25	.60
299 Jack McDowell 95	.15	.40
300 Wade Boggs 95	.25	.60

2004 UD Legends Timeless Teams Bronze

*BRONZE: X TO X BASIC
RANDOM INSERTS IN RETAIL PACKS
STATED PRINT RUN 50 SERIAL #'d SETS

2004 UD Legends Timeless Teams Autographs

OVERALL AU PARALLEL ODDS 1:9		
SP PRINT RUNS B/WN 25-100 COPIES PER		
SP'S ARE NOT SERIAL-NUMBERED		
SP PRINT RUNS PROVIDED BY UD		
EXCHANGE DEADLINE 08/19/07		
ASTERISK ='s SOME LIVE/SOME EXCH		
1 Bob Gibson 64 SP/50	12.50	30.00
2 Lou Brock MM 64 SP/75 *	10.00	25.00
3 Ray Washburn 64	4.00	10.00
4 Tim McCarver 64	6.00	15.00
5 Harmon Killebrew 65	10.00	25.00
6 Jim Kaat 65	6.00	15.00
7 Jim Perry 65	6.00	15.00
8 Mudcat Grant 65	8.00	20.00
9 Boog Powell 66	6.00	15.00
10 Brooks Robinson 66	10.00	25.00
11 F.Robinson MM 66 SP/35	15.00	40.00
12 Jim Palmer 66 SP/50	12.50	30.00
13 C.Yastrzemski MM 67 SP/25	40.00	80.00
14 Jim Lonborg 67	6.00	15.00
15 George Scott 67	6.00	15.00
16 Sparky Lyle 67 *	4.00	10.00
17 Rico Petrocelli 67	4.00	10.00
18 Bob Gibson 67 SP/35	15.00	40.00
19 Julian Javier 67	6.00	15.00
20 Lou Brock 67 SP/60	12.50	30.00
21 Orlando Cepeda 67 SP/50	8.00	20.00
22 Ray Washburn 67	4.00	10.00
23 Steve Carlton 67 SP/25	12.50	30.00
24 Tim McCarver 67	6.00	15.00
25 Al Kaline 68 *	15.00	40.00
26 Bill Freehan 68	6.00	15.00
27 Denny McLain MM 68	8.00	20.00
28 Dick McAuliffe 68	6.00	15.00
29 Jim Northrup 68	10.00	25.00
30 John Hiller 68	8.00	20.00
31 Mickey Lolich MM 68	6.00	15.00
32 Mickey Stanley 68	8.00	20.00
33 Willie Horton 68	4.00	10.00
34 Bob Gibson MM 68 SP/25	8.00	20.00
35 Julian Javier 68	4.00	10.00
36 Lou Brock 68 SP/50	12.50	30.00
37 Orlando Cepeda 68 SP/25	10.00	25.00
38 Steve Carlton 68 SP/35	10.00	25.00
39 Boog Powell 69	10.00	25.00
40 Brooks Robinson 69 SP/100	10.00	25.00
41 Davey Johnson 69	4.00	10.00
42 Merv Rettenmund 69	4.00	10.00
43 Eddie Watt 69	4.00	10.00
44 Frank Robinson 69 SP/25	15.00	40.00
45 Jim Palmer 69 SP/25	15.00	40.00
46 Mike Cuellar 69	6.00	15.00
47 Paul Blair 69	4.00	10.00
48 Pete Richert 69	4.00	10.00
49 Ellie Hendricks 69	6.00	15.00
50 Billy Williams 69 SP/75	10.00	25.00
51 Randy Hundley 69	6.00	15.00
52 Ernie Banks 69 SP/50	30.00	60.00
53 Fergie Jenkins 69	6.00	15.00
54 Jim Hickman 69	8.00	20.00
55 Ken Holtzman 69	6.00	15.00
56 Ron Santo MM 69	12.50	30.00
57 Ed Kranepool 69	4.00	10.00
58 Jerry Koosman MM 69	6.00	15.00
60 Tom Seaver 69 SP/50	25.00	60.00
61 Boog Powell 70	6.00	15.00
62 B.Robinson MM 70 SP/35	15.00	40.00
63 Davey Johnson 70	6.00	15.00
64 Merv Rettenmund 70	12.50	30.00
65 Eddie Watt 70	4.00	10.00
66 Frank Robinson 70 SP/50	12.50	30.00
67 Jim Palmer 70 SP/75	10.00	25.00
68 Mike Cuellar 70	4.00	10.00
69 Paul Blair 70	4.00	10.00
70 Pete Richert 70	10.00	25.00
71 Ellie Hendricks 70	8.00	20.00
72 Al Kaline 72 *	15.00	40.00
73 Bill Freehan 72	6.00	15.00
74 Dick McAuliffe 72	4.00	10.00
75 Jim Northrup 72	6.00	15.00
76 John Hiller 72	4.00	10.00
77 Mickey Lolich 72	8.00	20.00
78 Mickey Stanley 72	4.00	10.00
79 Willie Horton 72	6.00	15.00
80 Bert Campaneris 72	6.00	15.00
81 Blue Moon Odom MM 72	4.00	10.00
82 Sal Bando 72	8.00	20.00
83 Joe Rudi 72	6.00	15.00
84 Ken Holtzman 72	6.00	15.00
85 Billy North 73	4.00	10.00
86 Blue Moon Odom 73	6.00	15.00
87 Gene Tenace 73	4.00	10.00
88 Manny Trillo 73	6.00	15.00
89 Dick Green 73	6.00	15.00
90 Rollie Fingers 73	6.00	15.00
91 Sal Bando 73	4.00	10.00
92 Vida Blue 73	4.00	10.00
93 Bill Buckner 74 *	8.00	20.00
94 Davey Lopes 74	4.00	10.00
95 Don Sutton 74	6.00	15.00
96 Al Downing MM 74	4.00	10.00
97 Ron Cey 74 SP/25	6.00	15.00
98 Steve Garvey 74 SP/25	15.00	40.00
99 Tommy John 74 SP/25	6.00	15.00
100 Bert Campaneris 74	6.00	15.00
101 Billy North 74	6.00	15.00
102 Joe Rudi MM 74	4.00	10.00
103 Sal Bando 74	4.00	10.00
104 Vida Blue 74 SP/100 *	4.00	10.00
105 Carl Yastrzemski 75 SP/50	30.00	60.00
106 Carlton Fisk MM 75 SP/100	10.00	25.00
107 Cecil Cooper 75 SP/75	6.00	15.00
108 Dwight Evans 75 SP/75	10.00	25.00
109 Fred Lynn 75	6.00	15.00
112 Rick Burleson 75	4.00	10.00
113 Rico Petrocelli 75	5.00	12.00
114 Pedro Borbon 75	8.00	20.00
116 Don Gullett 75	4.00	10.00
117 George Foster 75 SP/50	12.50	30.00
118 Joe Morgan MM 75 SP/25	12.00	30.00
119 Johnny Bench 75 SP/85	40.00	80.00
120 Rawly Eastwick 75	6.00	15.00
121 Sparky Anderson 75	6.00	15.00
122 Tony Perez 75	10.00	25.00
123 Billy Williams 75 SP/50	12.50	30.00
124 Gene Tenace 75	4.00	10.00
125 Jim Perry 75	5.00	12.00
126 Vida Blue 75 SP/75	4.00	10.00
127 Pedro Borbon 76	8.00	20.00
128 Dave Concepcion 76	8.00	20.00
129 Don Gullett 76	6.00	15.00
130 George Foster 76 SP/35	12.50	30.00
131 Joe Morgan 76 SP/50	8.00	20.00
132 J.Bench MM 76 SP/50	30.00	60.00
133 Ken Griffey Sr. 76	6.00	15.00
134 Rawly Eastwick 76	4.00	10.00
135 Tony Perez 76	10.00	25.00
136 Bill Russell 77	4.00	10.00
137 Burt Hooton 77	4.00	10.00
138 Davey Lopes 77	5.00	12.00
139 Don Sutton 77	6.00	15.00
140 Dusty Baker 77	4.00	10.00
141 Steve Yeager 77 SP/75	5.00	12.00
142 Ron Cey 77 SP/35	6.00	15.00
143 Steve Garvey MM 77 SP/35	15.00	40.00
144 Tommy John 77 SP/35	6.00	15.00
145 Bucky Dent 77 SP/75	8.00	20.00
146 Chris Chambliss 77	4.00	10.00
147 Ed Figueroa 77	4.00	10.00
148 Graig Nettles 77	6.00	15.00
149 Lou Piniella 77 SP/25	10.00	25.00
150 Roy White 77	4.00	10.00
151 Don Gullett 77	4.00	10.00
152 Sparky Lyle 77 *	4.00	10.00
153 Brian Doyle 78	4.00	10.00
154 Bucky Dent MM 78 SP/75	6.00	15.00
155 Chris Chambliss 78	6.00	15.00
156 Ed Figueroa 78	4.00	10.00
157 Graig Nettles 78	6.00	15.00
158 Lou Piniella 78 SP/35	12.50	30.00
159 Roy White 78	6.00	15.00
160 Rich Gossage 78	10.00	25.00
161 Sparky Lyle 78 *	6.00	15.00
162 Bobby Grich 79	4.00	10.00
163 Brian Downing 79	6.00	15.00
164 Dan Ford 79	4.00	10.00
165 Nolan Ryan 79 SP/25	75.00	150.00
167 George Foster 79 SP/25	15.00	40.00
168 Johnny Bench 79 SP/25	40.00	80.00
169 Ray Knight 79	4.00	10.00
170 Tom Seaver 79 SP/35	25.00	60.00
171 Bert Blyleven 79 *	12.50	30.00
172 Bill Madlock 79	6.00	15.00
173 Dave Parker MM 79	6.00	15.00
174 Phil Garner 79	6.00	15.00
175 Bill Russell 80	8.00	20.00
176 Steve Yeager 80	4.00	10.00
177 Don Sutton 80 SP/50	8.00	20.00
178 Dusty Baker 80	6.00	15.00
179 Jerry Reuss 80	4.00	10.00
180 Mickey Hatcher 80	4.00	10.00
181 Pedro Guerrero 80	4.00	10.00
182 Ron Cey 80 SP/50	6.00	15.00
183 Steve Garvey 80 SP/50	12.50	30.00
184 Rudy May 80	4.00	10.00
185 Brian Doyle 80	4.00	10.00
186 Bucky Dent 80 SP/60	8.00	20.00
187 Jim Kaat 80	6.00	15.00
188 Lou Piniella 80 SP/50	10.00	25.00
189 Luis Tiant 80	4.00	10.00
190 Tommy John 80 SP/50	6.00	15.00
191 Bake McBride 80	6.00	15.00
192 Bob Boone 80	6.00	15.00
193 Dickie Noles MM 80	4.00	10.00
194 Manny Trillo 80	4.00	10.00
196 Sparky Lyle 80	4.00	10.00
197 Steve Carlton 80 SP/50	12.50	30.00
198 Steve Yeager 81	4.00	10.00
199 Burt Hooton 81	4.00	10.00
200 Dusty Baker 81	10.00	25.00
201 Jerry Reuss 81	4.00	10.00
202 Mike Scioscia 81	10.00	25.00
203 Pedro Guerrero 81	4.00	10.00
204 Ron Cey 81 SP/75	12.50	30.00
205 Steve Garvey 81 SP/75	10.00	25.00
206 Alejandro Pena 81	4.00	10.00
207 Steve Sax 81 SP/100	6.00	15.00
208 Cecil Cooper 81 SP/85	6.00	15.00
210 Paul Molitor 81 SP/25	10.00	25.00
212 Rollie Fingers 81	6.00	15.00
213 Don Money 81	6.00	15.00
214 Rudy May 81	4.00	10.00
215 Bucky Dent 81 SP/25	10.00	25.00
216 Dave Winfield 81 SP/50	12.50	30.00
217 Lou Piniella 81 SP/75	12.50	30.00
218 Rich Gossage 81	10.00	25.00
219 Tommy John 81 SP/75	6.00	15.00
220 Cecil Cooper 82	6.00	15.00
221 Gorman Thomas 82	8.00	20.00
222 Paul Molitor MM 82 SP/50	40.00	80.00
223 Robin Yount 82 SP/50	30.00	60.00
224 Don Money 82	4.00	10.00
225 Cal Ripken MM 83 SP/50	75.00	150.00
226 Dan Ford 83	4.00	10.00
227 Jim Palmer 83 SP/35	15.00	40.00
228 John Shelby 83	4.00	10.00
229 Alan Trammell 84	8.00	20.00
230 Chet Lemon 84	4.00	10.00
231 Howard Johnson 84	4.00	10.00
232 Jack Morris MM 84 SP/35	10.00	25.00
233 Kirk Gibson 84	6.00	15.00
234 Lou Whitaker 84 SP/100	8.00	20.00
235 Sparky Anderson 84 *	8.00	20.00
236 Dave Winfield 85 SP/25	15.00	40.00
237 Don Mattingly 85 SP/50	30.00	60.00
238 Ken Griffey Sr. 85	6.00	15.00
239 Phil Niekro 85	6.00	15.00
240 Yogi Berra 85 SP/47 UER	30.00	80.00
241 Bill Buckner MM 86	8.00	20.00
242 Bruce Hurst 86	8.00	20.00
243 Dave Henderson 86	6.00	15.00
244 Dwight Evans 86 SP/50	12.50	30.00
245 Jim Rice 86 SP/75	10.00	25.00
246 Tom Seaver 86 SP/25	25.00	60.00
247 Wade Boggs 86 SP/50	15.00	40.00
248 Bob Boone 86	6.00	15.00
249 Bobby Grich 86	4.00	10.00
250 Brian Downing 86	8.00	20.00
251 Don Sutton 86 SP/75	6.00	15.00
252 Terry Forster 86	4.00	10.00
253 Rick Burleson 86	4.00	10.00
254 Wally Joyner MM 86	4.00	10.00
255 Darryl Strawberry 86	10.00	25.00
256 Dwight Gooden 86	6.00	15.00
257 Gary Carter 86 SP/75	15.00	40.00
258 Jesse Orosco MM 86	4.00	10.00
259 Keith Hernandez 86	6.00	15.00
260 Lenny Dykstra 86	6.00	15.00
261 Mookie Wilson 86	6.00	15.00
262 Ray Knight 86	4.00	10.00
263 Wally Backman 86	6.00	15.00
264 Sid Fernandez 86	6.00	15.00
265 Alan Trammell 87	8.00	20.00
266 Dan Petry 87	6.00	15.00
267 Chet Lemon 87	8.00	20.00
268 Sparky Anderson 87	12.00	30.00
269 Jack Morris 87 SP/25	10.00	25.00
270 Kirk Gibson 87	6.00	15.00
271 Lou Whitaker 87 SP/50	30.00	60.00
272 Bert Blyleven 87 *	4.00	10.00
273 Kent Hrbek MM 87	6.00	15.00
274 Kirby Puckett 87 SP/25	125.00	250.00
275 Alejandro Pena 88	4.00	10.00
276 Jesse Orosco 88	4.00	10.00
277 John Shelby 88	4.00	10.00
278 Kirk Gibson MM 88 SP/50	10.00	25.00
279 Mickey Hatcher 88	4.00	10.00
280 Mike Scioscia 88	6.00	15.00
281 Steve Sax 88	8.00	20.00
282 Darryl Strawberry 88	10.00	25.00
283 Dwight Gooden 88	6.00	15.00
284 Gary Carter 88 SP/50	20.00	50.00
285 Howard Johnson 88	8.00	20.00
286 Keith Hernandez 88	6.00	15.00
287 Lenny Dykstra 88	8.00	20.00
288 Mookie Wilson 88	8.00	20.00
289 Wally Backman 88	6.00	15.00
291 Jack Morris 91 SP/50	8.00	20.00
292 Kent Hrbek 91	6.00	15.00
293 Kirby Puckett MM 91 SP/50	60.00	120.00
294 D.Winfield MM 92 SP/35	15.00	40.00
295 Jack Morris 92 SP/75	6.00	15.00
296 Joe Carter 92 SP/100	10.00	25.00
297 Don Mattingly MM 95 SP/25	40.00	80.00
298 Paul O'Neill 95 *	10.00	25.00
299 Jack McDowell 95	10.00	25.00
300 Wade Boggs 95 SP/75	12.50	30.00

2004 UD Legends Timeless Teams Legendary Signatures Dual

OVERALL DUAL/TRIPLE SIG ODDS 1:90		
PRINT RUNS B/WN 25-150 COPIES PER		
EXCHANGE DEADLINE 08/19/07		
BC L.Brock/O.Cepeda/75	20.00	50.00
BJ L.Brock/J.Javier/150	15.00	40.00
BM W.Boggs/D.Mattingly/50	75.00	150.00
BO V.Blue/B.Odom/150	12.00	30.00
BW E.Banks/B.Williams/25	60.00	120.00
CB S.Carlton/B.Boone/150	15.00	40.00
CG R.Cey/S.Garvey/150	15.00	40.00
CH G.Carter/K.Hernandez/150	20.00	50.00
CM D.Conc/J.Morgan/75 EXCH	15.00	40.00
CW J.Carter/D.Winfield/25	30.00	80.00
DD B.Dent/B.Doyle/150	12.00	30.00
FR F.Lynn/J.Rice/150	20.00	50.00
GA K.Gibson/S.Anderson/150	25.00	60.00
GB B.Gibson/L.Brock/50	40.00	80.00
GC D.Gooden/G.Carter/150	25.00	60.00
GL Gossage/Lyle/150 EXCH	20.00	50.00
GM B.Gibson/T.McCarver/50	30.00	80.00
HJ K.Holtzman/F.Jenkins/150	20.00	50.00
HK K.Hernandez/R.Knight/150	10.00	25.00
JH F.Jenkins/R.Hundley/150	10.00	25.00
JS T.John/D.Sutton/150	12.00	30.00
KH A.Kaline/W.Horton/150	30.00	80.00
KK H.Killebrew/J.Kaat/150	12.00	30.00
LM M.Lolich/D.McLain/75	25.00	60.00
MB J.Morgan/J.Bench/25	50.00	100.00
MF D.McLain/B.Freehan/150	15.00	40.00
NC G.Nettles/C.Chambliss/150	12.00	30.00
OM P.O'Neill/D.Mattingly/75	30.00	80.00
PC J.Palmer/M.Cuellar/150	10.00	25.00
PF T.Perez/G.Foster/150	12.00	30.00
PN L.Piniella/G.Nettles/150	15.00	40.00
PR J.Palmer/M.R'mund/150	10.00	25.00
RL B.Russell/D.Lopes/150	12.00	30.00
RR B.Robinson/F.Robinson/50	40.00	80.00
RS N.Ryan/T.Seaver/25	100.00	250.00
SD S.Garvey/D.Lopes/150	12.00	30.00
SG D.Straw/D.Gooden/150	20.00	50.00
SY D.Sutton/S.Yeager/150	10.00	25.00
TF L.Tiant/C.Fisk/50	30.00	60.00
TM Gorman/Molitor/150 EXCH	12.00	30.00
WB M.Wilson/B.Buckner/150	30.00	80.00
WT L.Whitaker/A.Trammell/75	75.00	150.00
YM R.Yount/P.Molitor/50	75.00	150.00
YP C.Yaz/R.Petrocelli/50	40.00	100.00

2004 UD Legends Timeless Teams Legendary Signatures Triple

OVERALL DUAL/TRIPLE AU ODDS 1:90		
PRINT RUNS B/WN 25-75 COPIES PER		
EXCHANGE DEADLINE 08/19/07		
BCM Bench/Con/Morg/25 EX	60.00	120.00
BOM Boggs/O'Neill/Matt/50	50.00	100.00
BRB Bando/Rudi/Blue/75	25.00	60.00
BSW Banks/Santo/B.Will/25	125.00	200.00
CDK G.Cart/Dyks/Knight/50	50.00	100.00
CND Chamb/Nett/Dent/50	20.00	50.00
ERL Evans/Rice/Lynn/50	50.00	100.00
GBC Garvey/Baker/Cey/50	40.00	80.00
GBM Gibs/Brock/McCar/25	50.00	100.00
GDR Grich/Down/Ryan/25	100.00	200.00
GHS K.Gib/Hatch/Scios/75	20.00	50.00
GMP Garn/Madl/Parker/50	30.00	60.00
HHS Hick/Holtz/Santo/75	40.00	80.00
HSJ Hoot/Sutton/John/50	40.00	80.00
JHH Jenk/Hundley/Holtz/75	30.00	60.00
KKP Killebrew/Kaat/Perry/50	50.00	100.00
KPG Kaat/Perry/Grant/75 EX	30.00	60.00
KSR Koos/Seaver/Ryan/25	200.00	500.00
MHP Morris/Hrbek/Puckett/50	100.00	250.00
MLF McLain/Lolich/Free/50	40.00	80.00
NKH Northrup/Kaline/Hort/75	50.00	120.00
PBH Puckett/Blylev/Hrbek/50	100.00	250.00
PCR Palmer/Cuel/Richert/75	20.00	50.00
PPW Palmer/Boog/Weaver/75	30.00	60.00
RPR F.Rob/Boog/Brooks/50	50.00	100.00
RWP Ripken/Weav/Palm/25	150.00	250.00
SCB Schmidt/Carlt/Boone/50	100.00	175.00
SGS Sax/Guerrero/Scios/75	30.00	60.00
STM Schmidt/Trillo/McBr/50	20.00	50.00
TWA Tram/Whit/Sparky/50	100.00	200.00
YCT Yount/Coop/Gorm/50 EX	60.00	120.00
YFT Yaz/Fisk/Tiant/25	100.00	175.00
YMT Yount/Moll/Gorm/75 EX	75.00	150.00

2004 UD Legends Timeless Teams Team Terrific GU Team Logo

PRINT RUNS B/WN 30-100 COPIES PER		
*BRAND LOGO p/r 35-41: .5X TO 1.2X TEAM		
BRAND LOGO PRINT RUN B/WN 10-41 PER		
NO BRAND LOGO PRICING ON QTY OF 10		
*HAT LOGO p/r 82: .4X TO 1X TEAM		
*HAT LOGO p/r 50: .5X TO 1.2X TEAM		
HAT LOGO PRINT RUN B/WN 15-82 PER		
NO HAT LOGO PRICING ON QTY OF 15		
LEAGUE LOGO PRINT RUN B/WN 5-15 PER		
NO LEAGUE LOGO PRICING AVAILABLE		
STATS PRINT RUN B/WN 1-5 COPIES PER		
NO STATS PRICING AVAILABLE		
OVERALL FOLD-OPEN CARD ODDS 1:360		
BO Baltimore Orioles/85	50.00	100.00
BR Boston Red Sox/85	40.00	80.00
CR Cincinnati Reds/85	50.00	100.00
LD Los Angeles Dodgers/85	30.00	60.00
MB Milwaukee Brewers/100	20.00	50.00
NM New York Mets/85	20.00	50.00
NY New York Yankees/30		
OA Oakland A's/100	15.00	40.00
SC St. Louis Cardinals/100	40.00	80.00

2007 UD Masterpieces

COMPLETE SET (90)	15.00	40.00
COMMON CARD (1-90)	.25	.60
COMMON ROOKIE (1-90)	.25	.60
PRINTING PLATES RANDOMLY INSERTED		
PLATE PRINT RUN 1 SET PER COLOR		
BLACK-CYAN-MAGENTA-YELLOW ISSUED		
NO PLATE PRICING DUE TO SCARCITY		
1 Babe Ruth	1.50	4.00
2 Babe Ruth	1.50	4.00
3 Bobby Thomson	.40	1.00
4 Bill Mazeroski	.40	1.00
5 Carlton Fisk	.40	1.00
6 Kirk Gibson	.25	.60
7 Don Larsen	.25	.60
8 Lou Gehrig	1.25	3.00
9 Roger Maris	.60	1.50
10 Cal Ripken Jr.	2.00	5.00
11 Bucky Dent	.25	.60
12 Ryan Howard	.50	1.25
13 Brooks Robinson	.40	1.00
14 David Ortiz	.60	1.50
15 Hideki Matsui	.60	1.50
16 Roger Clemens	.75	2.00
17 Sandy Koufax	1.25	3.00
18 Reggie Jackson	.40	1.00
19 Ozzie Smith	.75	2.00
20 Ty Cobb	1.00	2.50
21 Walter Johnson	.60	1.50
22 Babe Ruth	1.50	4.00
23 Roy Campanella	.60	1.50
24 Jackie Robinson	.60	1.50
25 Carl Yastrzemski	1.00	2.50
26 Sandy Koufax	1.25	3.00
27 Daisuke Matsuzaka RC	1.00	2.50
28 Kei Igawa RC	.60	1.50
29 Ken Griffey Jr.	1.25	3.00
30 Derek Jeter	1.50	4.00
31 David Ortiz	.60	1.50
32 Vladimir Guerrero	.40	1.00
33 Chase Utley	.40	1.00
34 Troy Tulowitzki (RC)	.75	2.00
35 Joe Mauer	.50	1.25
36 Travis Hafner	.25	.60
37 Miguel Cabrera	.60	1.50
38 Albert Pujols	.75	2.00
39 Frank Thomas	.60	1.50
40 Mike Piazza	.60	1.50
41 Josh Hamilton	.75	2.00
42 T.Gwynn/C.Ripken Jr.	2.00	5.00

43 Ichiro Suzuki .75 2.00
44 Hideki Matsui .60 1.50
45 Ken Griffey Jr. 1.25 3.00
46 Michael Jordan 1.50 4.00
47 John F. Kennedy 1.00 2.50
48 Randy Johnson .60 1.50
49 Albert Pujols .75 2.00
50 Carlos Beltran .40 1.00
51 Delmon Young (RC) .40 1.00
52 Johan Santana .40 1.00
53 Cal Ripken Jr. 2.00 5.00
54 Y.Berra/J.Robinson .60 1.50
55 Cal Ripken Jr. 2.00 5.00
56 Hanley Ramirez .40 1.00
57 Victor Martinez .40 1.00
58 Cole Hamels .50 1.25
59 Bobby Doerr .40 1.00
60 Bruce Sutter .40 1.00
61 Jason Bay .40 1.00
62 Luis Aparicio .40 1.00
63 Stephen Drew .25 .60
64 Jered Weaver .40 1.00
65 Alex Gordon RC .75 2.00
66 Howie Kendrick .25 .60
67 Ryan Zimmerman .40 1.00
68 Akinori Iwamura RC .60 1.50
69 Chien-Ming Wang .40 1.00
70 David Wright .50 1.25
71 Ryan Howard .50 1.25
72 Alex Rodriguez .75 2.00
73 Justin Morneau .40 1.00
74 Andrew Miller RC 1.00 2.50
75 Richard Nixon .60 1.50
76 Bill Clinton 1.00 2.50
77 Phil Hughes (RC) .60 1.50
78 Tom Glavine .40 1.00
79 Chipper Jones .60 1.50
80 Craig Biggio .40 1.00
81 Chris Chambliss .25 .60
82 Tim Lincecum RC 1.25 3.00
83 Billy Butler (RC) .40 1.00
84 Andy LaRoche (RC) .25 .60
85 1969 New York Mets .25 .60
86 2004 Boston Red Sox 1.00 2.50
87 Roberto Clemente 1.50 4.00
88 Chase Utley .40 1.00
89 Reggie Jackson .40 1.00
90 Curt Schilling .40 1.00

2007 UD Masterpieces Black Linen

*BLACK VET: 1.5X TO 4X BASIC
*BLACK RC: 1.5X TO 4X BASIC
RANDOM INSERTS IN PACKS
STATED PRINT RUN 99 SER.#'d SETS
1 Babe Ruth 5.00 12.00
2 Babe Ruth 5.00 12.00
10 Cal Ripken Jr. 15.00 40.00
17 Sandy Koufax 12.50 30.00
22 Babe Ruth 5.00 12.00
26 Sandy Koufax 12.50 30.00
27 Daisuke Matsuzaka 12.50 30.00
29 Ken Griffey Jr. 8.00 20.00
30 Derek Jeter 15.00 40.00
40 Mike Piazza 6.00 15.00
42 T.Gwynn/C.Ripken Jr. 15.00 40.00
43 Ichiro Suzuki 6.00 15.00
45 Ken Griffey Jr. 8.00 20.00
46 Michael Jordan 15.00 40.00
53 Cal Ripken Jr. 15.00 40.00
55 Cal Ripken Jr. 15.00 40.00
69 Chien-Ming Wang 12.50 30.00

2007 UD Masterpieces Blue Steel

*BLUE STEEL VET: 1.5X TO 4X BASIC
*BLUE STEEL RC: 1.5X TO 4X BASIC
RANDOM INSERTS IN PACKS
STATED PRINT RUN 50 SER.#'d SETS
1 Babe Ruth 5.00 12.00
2 Babe Ruth 5.00 12.00
10 Cal Ripken Jr. 15.00 40.00
17 Sandy Koufax 12.50 30.00
22 Babe Ruth 5.00 12.00
26 Sandy Koufax 12.50 30.00
27 Daisuke Matsuzaka 12.50 30.00
29 Ken Griffey Jr. 8.00 20.00
30 Derek Jeter 15.00 40.00
40 Mike Piazza 6.00 15.00
42 T.Gwynn/C.Ripken Jr. 15.00 40.00
43 Ichiro Suzuki 6.00 15.00
45 Ken Griffey Jr. 8.00 20.00
46 Michael Jordan 15.00 40.00
53 Cal Ripken Jr. 15.00 40.00
55 Cal Ripken Jr. 15.00 40.00
69 Chien-Ming Wang 12.50 30.00

2007 UD Masterpieces Deep Blue Linen

*DEEP BLUE VET: 1.5X TO 4X BASIC
*DEEP BLUE RC: 1.5X TO 4X BASIC
RANDOM INSERTS IN PACKS
STATED PRINT RUN 75 SER.#'d SETS
1 Babe Ruth 5.00 12.00
2 Babe Ruth 5.00 12.00
10 Cal Ripken Jr. 15.00 40.00
17 Sandy Koufax 12.50 30.00
22 Babe Ruth 5.00 12.00
26 Sandy Koufax 12.50 30.00
27 Daisuke Matsuzaka 12.50 30.00
29 Ken Griffey Jr. 8.00 20.00
30 Derek Jeter 15.00 40.00
40 Mike Piazza 6.00 15.00
42 T.Gwynn/C.Ripken Jr. 15.00 40.00
43 Ichiro Suzuki 6.00 15.00
45 Ken Griffey Jr. 8.00 20.00
46 Michael Jordan 15.00 40.00
53 Cal Ripken Jr. 15.00 40.00
55 Cal Ripken Jr. 15.00 40.00
69 Chien-Ming Wang 12.50 30.00

2007 UD Masterpieces Glossy

*GLOSSY: .5X TO 1.2X BASIC

2007 UD Masterpieces Green Linen

*GREEN VET: .75X TO 2X BASIC
*GREEN RC: .75X TO 2X BASIC
STATED ODDS 1:6 H, 1:48 R, 1:48 BLASTER

2007 UD Masterpieces Hades

*HADES VET: 1.5X TO 4X BASIC
*HADES RC: 1.5X TO 4X BASIC
RANDOM INSERTS IN PACKS
STATED PRINT RUN 50 SER.#'d SETS
1 Babe Ruth 5.00 12.00
2 Babe Ruth 5.00 12.00
10 Cal Ripken Jr. 15.00 40.00
17 Sandy Koufax 12.50 30.00
22 Babe Ruth 5.00 12.00
26 Sandy Koufax 12.50 30.00
29 Ken Griffey Jr. 8.00 20.00
30 Derek Jeter 15.00 40.00
40 Mike Piazza 6.00 15.00
42 T.Gwynn/C.Ripken Jr. 15.00 40.00
43 Ichiro Suzuki 6.00 15.00
45 Ken Griffey Jr. 8.00 20.00
46 Michael Jordan 15.00 40.00
53 Cal Ripken Jr. 15.00 40.00
55 Cal Ripken Jr. 15.00 40.00
69 Chien-Ming Wang 12.50 30.00

2007 UD Masterpieces Ionised

*IONISED VET: 1.5X TO 4X BASIC
*IONISED RC: 1.5X TO 4X BASIC
RANDOM INSERTS IN PACKS
STATED PRINT RUN 50 SER.#'d SETS
1 Babe Ruth 5.00 12.00
2 Babe Ruth 5.00 12.00
10 Cal Ripken Jr. 15.00 40.00
17 Sandy Koufax 12.50 30.00
22 Babe Ruth 5.00 12.00
26 Sandy Koufax 12.50 30.00
29 Ken Griffey Jr. 8.00 20.00
30 Derek Jeter 15.00 40.00
40 Mike Piazza 6.00 15.00
42 T.Gwynn/C.Ripken Jr. 15.00 40.00
43 Ichiro Suzuki 6.00 15.00
45 Ken Griffey Jr. 8.00 20.00
46 Michael Jordan 15.00 40.00
53 Cal Ripken Jr. 15.00 40.00
55 Cal Ripken Jr. 15.00 40.00
69 Chien-Ming Wang 12.50 30.00

2007 UD Masterpieces Pinot Red

*PINOT RED VET: 1.5X TO 4X BASIC
*PINOT RED RC: 1.5X TO 4X BASIC
RANDOM INSERTS IN PACKS
STATED PRINT RUN 75 SER.#'d SETS
1 Babe Ruth 5.00 12.00
2 Babe Ruth 5.00 12.00
10 Cal Ripken Jr. 15.00 40.00
17 Sandy Koufax 12.50 30.00
22 Babe Ruth 5.00 12.00
26 Sandy Koufax 12.50 30.00
29 Ken Griffey Jr. 8.00 20.00
30 Derek Jeter 15.00 40.00
40 Mike Piazza 6.00 15.00
42 T.Gwynn/C.Ripken Jr. 15.00 40.00
43 Ichiro Suzuki 6.00 15.00
45 Ken Griffey Jr. 8.00 20.00
46 Michael Jordan 15.00 40.00
53 Cal Ripken Jr. 15.00 40.00
55 Cal Ripken Jr. 15.00 40.00
69 Chien-Ming Wang 12.50 30.00

2007 UD Masterpieces Rusted

*RUSTED VET: 1.5X TO 4X BASIC
*RUSTED RC: 1.5X TO 4X BASIC
RANDOM INSERTS IN PACKS
STATED PRINT RUN 50 SER.#'d SETS
1 Babe Ruth 5.00 12.00
2 Babe Ruth 5.00 12.00
17 Sandy Koufax 12.50 30.00
22 Babe Ruth 5.00 12.00
26 Sandy Koufax 12.50 30.00
29 Ken Griffey Jr. 8.00 20.00
30 Derek Jeter 15.00 40.00
40 Mike Piazza 6.00 15.00
42 T.Gwynn/C.Ripken Jr. 15.00 40.00
43 Ichiro Suzuki 6.00 15.00
45 Ken Griffey Jr. 8.00 20.00
46 Michael Jordan 15.00 40.00
53 Cal Ripken Jr. 15.00 40.00
55 Cal Ripken Jr. 15.00 40.00
69 Chien-Ming Wang 12.50 30.00

2007 UD Masterpieces Serious Black

*SER.BLACK VET: 1.5X TO 4X BASIC
*SER.BLACK RC: 1.5X TO 4X BASIC
RANDOM INSERTS IN PACKS
STATED PRINT RUN 99 SER.#'d SETS
1 Babe Ruth 5.00 12.00
2 Babe Ruth 5.00 12.00
10 Cal Ripken Jr. 15.00 40.00
17 Sandy Koufax 12.50 30.00
22 Babe Ruth 5.00 12.00
26 Sandy Koufax 12.50 30.00
29 Ken Griffey Jr. 8.00 20.00
30 Derek Jeter 15.00 40.00
40 Mike Piazza 6.00 15.00
42 T.Gwynn/C.Ripken Jr. 15.00 40.00
43 Ichiro Suzuki 6.00 15.00
45 Ken Griffey Jr. 8.00 20.00
46 Michael Jordan 15.00 40.00
53 Cal Ripken Jr. 15.00 40.00
55 Cal Ripken Jr. 15.00 40.00
69 Chien-Ming Wang 12.50 30.00

2007 UD Masterpieces Windsor Green

*WIN.GREEN VET: .75X TO 2X BASIC
*WIN.GREEN RC: .75X TO 2X BASIC
STATED ODDS 1:9 H, 1:72 R, 1:750 BLASTER

2007 UD Masterpieces 5x7 Box Topper

STATED ODDS ONE PER HOBBY BOX
MP1 Cal Ripken Jr. 6.00 15.00
MP2 Ken Griffey Jr. 6.00 15.00
MP3 Derek Jeter 6.00 15.00
MP4 Sandy Koufax 6.00 15.00
MP5 Babe Ruth 6.00 15.00
MP6 Lou Gehrig 6.00 15.00
MP7 Travis Hafner 3.00 8.00
MP8 Victor Martinez 3.00 8.00
MP9 Jered Weaver 3.00 8.00
MP10 Phil Hughes 4.00 10.00
MP11 Bobby Doerr 4.00 10.00
MP12 Billy Butler 3.00 8.00
MP13 Andy LaRoche 3.00 8.00
MP14 Josh Hamilton 6.00 15.00
MP15 Reggie Jackson 4.00 10.00
MP16 Hanley Ramirez 3.00 8.00
MP17 Don Larsen 4.00 10.00
MP18 Ken Griffey Jr. 6.00 15.00
MP19 Jason Bay 3.00 8.00
MP20 Daisuke Matsuzaka 5.00 12.00

2007 UD Masterpieces Captured on Canvas

STATED ODDS 1:6 H, 1:24 R, 1:1500 BLAST
BRONZE RANDOMLY INSERTED
BRONZE PRINT RUN 1 SER.#'d SET
NO BRONZE PRICING AVAILABLE
FOR.GREEN RANDOMLY INSERTED
FOR.GREEN PRINT RUN 1 SER.#'d SET
NO FOR.GREEN PRICING AVAILABLE
AB Adrian Beltre 3.00 8.00
AD Adam Dunn 3.00 8.00
AI Akinori Iwamura 4.00 10.00
AJ Andruw Jones 3.00 8.00
AP Albert Pujols 6.00 15.00
BA Bobby Abreu 3.00 8.00
BC Bobby Crosby 3.00 8.00
BE Carlos Beltran 3.00 8.00
BG Brian Giles 3.00 8.00
BL Brad Lidge 3.00 8.00
BO Jeremy Bonderman 3.00 8.00
BR Brian Roberts 3.00 8.00
BS Ben Sheets 3.00 8.00
CA Chris Carpenter 3.00 8.00
CB Craig Biggio 4.00 10.00
CC Carl Crawford 3.00 8.00
CD Carlos Delgado 3.00 8.00
CF Carlton Fisk 4.00 10.00
CJ Chipper Jones 4.00 10.00
CL Carlos Lee 3.00 8.00
CR Coco Crisp 3.00 8.00
CS C.C. Sabathia 4.00 10.00
CU Chase Utley 4.00 10.00
CY Carl Yastrzemski 4.00 10.00
DJ Derek Jeter 8.00 20.00
DL Derrek Lee 3.00 8.00
DM Don Mattingly 6.00 15.00
DO David Ortiz 4.00 10.00
DR J.D. Drew 3.00 8.00
DW Dontrelle Willis 3.00 8.00
EB Erik Bedard 3.00 8.00
EC Eric Chavez 3.00 8.00
EG Eric Gagne 3.00 8.00
FH Felix Hernandez 3.00 8.00
FL Francisco Liriano 4.00 10.00
GA Garrett Atkins 3.00 8.00
GL Tom Glavine 4.00 10.00
GR Khalil Greene 4.00 10.00
GS Grady Sizemore 4.00 10.00
HA Roy Halladay 3.00 8.00
HB Hank Blalock 3.00 8.00
HE Todd Helton 3.00 8.00
HR Hanley Ramirez 3.00 8.00
HS Huston Street 3.00 8.00
IR Ivan Rodriguez 3.00 8.00
JA Jason Bay 3.00 8.00
JB Josh Beckett 3.00 8.00
JH J.J. Hardy 4.00 10.00
JK Jason Kendall 3.00 8.00
JM Joe Mauer 3.00 8.00
JN Joe Nathan 3.00 8.00
JP Jake Peavy 3.00 8.00
JR Jose Reyes 4.00 10.00
JS John Smoltz 4.00 10.00
JV Jason Varitek 4.00 10.00
JW Jered Weaver 3.00 8.00
KG Ken Griffey Jr. 6.00 15.00
LB Lance Berkman 3.00 8.00
MA Daisuke Matsuzaka 8.00 20.00
MC Miguel Cabrera 3.00 8.00
MG Marcus Giles 3.00 8.00
MH Matt Holliday 6.00 15.00
MO Magglio Ordonez 3.00 8.00
MR Mariano Rivera 4.00 10.00
MT Miguel Tejada 3.00 8.00
MY Michael Young 3.00 8.00
PA Jonathan Papelbon 6.00 15.00
RA Manny Ramirez 3.00 8.00
RB Rocco Baldelli 3.00 8.00
RC Roger Clemens 6.00 15.00
RH Rich Harden 3.00 8.00
RI Cal Ripken Jr. 8.00 20.00
RJ Randy Johnson 3.00 8.00
RO Roy Oswalt 4.00 10.00
RW Rickie Weeks 3.00 8.00
RZ Ryan Zimmerman 4.00 10.00
SA Johan Santana 4.00 10.00
SC Curt Schilling 3.00 8.00
SH Gary Sheffield 4.00 10.00
SK Scott Kazmir 3.00 8.00
SR Scott Rolen 4.00 10.00
TE Mark Teixeira 4.00 10.00
TG Tony Gwynn 4.00 10.00
TH Tim Hudson 3.00 8.00
TR Travis Hafner 3.00 8.00
VG Vladimir Guerrero 4.00 10.00
VM Victor Martinez 3.00 8.00
WC Will Clark 6.00 15.00

2007 UD Masterpieces Stroke of Genius Signatures

STATED ODDS 1:18 H, 1:2500 R, 1:2500 BLAST
WIN.GREEN RANDOMLY INSERTED
WIN.GREEN PRINT RUN 1 SER.#'d SET
NO WIN.GREEN PRICING AVAILABLE
PRINTING PLATES RANDOMLY INSERTED
PLATE PRINT RUN 1 SET PER COLOR
BLACK-CYAN-MAGENTA-YELLOW ISSUED
NO PLATE PRICING DUE TO SCARCITY
EXCHANGE DEADLINE 10/10/2009
AD Adam Dunn 15.00 40.00
AG Adrian Gonzalez 6.00 15.00
AJ Andruw Jones 8.00 20.00
AK Al Kaline 15.00 40.00
AL Andy LaRoche 4.00 10.00
BA Bronson Arroyo 6.00 15.00
BB Billy Butler 5.00 12.00
BO Boof Bonser 3.00 8.00
BR Brooks Robinson 10.00 25.00
BS Ben Sheets 3.00 8.00
BU B.J. Upton 4.00 10.00
CD Chris Duffy 3.00 8.00
CF Chone Figgins 3.00 8.00
CH Cole Hamels 10.00 25.00
CQ Carlos Quentin 6.00 15.00
CR Cal Ripken Jr. 200.00 300.00
DH Dan Haren 6.00 15.00
DJ Derek Jeter 125.00 250.00
DO David Ortiz 20.00 50.00
DU Dan Uggla 3.00 8.00
DW Dontrelle Willis 6.00 15.00
EC Eric Chavez 3.00 8.00
GO Alex Gordon 8.00 20.00
GP Glen Perkins 3.00 8.00
HA Justin Hampson 3.00 8.00
HI Rich Hill 4.00 10.00
HK Howie Kendrick 4.00 10.00
HP Hunter Pence 4.00 10.00
HR Hanley Ramirez 6.00 15.00
HS Huston Street 4.00 10.00
HU Torii Hunter 8.00 20.00
IK Ian Kinsler 6.00 15.00
JA Jason Bay 5.00 12.00
JB Jeff Baker 3.00 8.00
JH Josh Hamilton 30.00 60.00
JP Jonathan Papelbon 15.00 40.00
JT Jim Thome 30.00 60.00
JU Justin Morneau 6.00 15.00
JV Justin Verlander 20.00 50.00
JW Jered Weaver 8.00 20.00
JZ Joel Zumaya 4.00 10.00
KE Austin Kearns 3.00 8.00
KG Ken Griffey Jr. 50.00 120.00
KK Kevin Kouzmanoff 4.00 10.00
LE Cliff Lee 6.00 15.00
LI Adam Lind 3.00 8.00
MB Michael Bourn 3.00 8.00
MC Matt Cain 12.50 30.00
MO Micah Owings 4.00 10.00
MS Mike Schmidt 20.00 50.00
PS Phil Hughes 8.00 20.00
RA Aramis Ramirez 4.00 10.00
RC Roger Clemens 30.00 60.00
RH Rich Harden 3.00 8.00
RO Roy Oswalt 6.00 15.00
RZ Ryan Zimmerman 6.00 15.00
SD Stephen Drew 6.00 15.00
SH Sean Henn 3.00 8.00
SK Scott Kazmir 12.50 30.00
SO Jeremy Sowers 3.00 8.00
TI Tim Hudson 5.00 12.00
TL Tim Lincecum 15.00 40.00
TR Travis Hafner 10.00 25.00
TT Troy Tulowitzki 10.00 25.00
VM Victor Martinez 5.00 12.00
XN Xavier Nady 3.00 8.00

2008 UD Masterpieces

COMPLETE SET (120) 30.00 60.00
COMP.SET w/o SPs (90) 8.00 20.00
COMMON CARD (1-90) .20 .50
COMMON ROOKIE (1-90) .40 1.00
COMMON SP (91-120) .50 1.25
SP ODDS 1:2 HOBBY
1 Brandon Webb .30 .75
2 Justin Upton .30 .75
3 Randy Johnson .50 1.25
4 Chipper Jones .50 1.25
5 Max Scherzer RC 4.00 10.00
6 Mark Teixeira .30 .75
7 Evan Longoria RC 2.00 5.00
8 Jim Palmer .30 .75
9 Brooks Robinson .30 .75
10 Nick Markakis .40 1.00
11 Carl Yastrzemski .75 2.00
12 Wade Boggs .30 .75
13 Curt Schilling .30 .75
14 Daisuke Matsuzaka .30 .75
15 David Ortiz .50 1.25
16 Jonathan Papelbon .30 .75
17 Manny Ramirez .50 1.25
18 Alfonso Soriano .30 .75
19 Ryne Sandberg 1.00 2.50
20 Carlos Zambrano .30 .75
21 Derrek Lee .20 .50
22 Kosuke Fukudome RC 1.25 3.00
23 Jim Thome .30 .75
24 Adam Dunn .30 .75
25 Joe Morgan .30 .75
26 Grady Sizemore .30 .75
27 Victor Martinez .30 .75
28 Travis Hafner .20 .50
29 Troy Tulowitzki .50 1.25
30 Matt Holliday .50 1.25
31 Todd Helton .30 .75
32 Justin Verlander .50 1.25
33 Asdrubal Cabrera .30 .75
34 Gary Sheffield .20 .50
35 Magglio Ordonez .30 .75
36 Miguel Cabrera .50 1.25
37 Hanley Ramirez .30 .75
38 Lance Berkman .30 .75
39 Roy Oswalt .30 .75
40 Alex Gordon .30 .75
41 Vladimir Guerrero .30 .75
42 Andruw Jones .20 .50
43 Chin-Lung Hu (RC) .40 1.00
44 James Loney .20 .50
45 Hunter Pence .30 .75
46 Robin Yount .50 1.25
47 Prince Fielder .30 .75
48 Ryan Braun .30 .75
49 Harmon Killebrew .50 1.25
50 Joe Mauer .40 1.00
51 Justin Morneau .30 .75
52 Ken Griffey Jr. 1.00 2.50
53 Carlos Beltran .30 .75
54 David Wright .30 .75
55 Johan Santana .30 .75
56 Jose Reyes .30 .75
57 Pedro Martinez .30 .75
58 Ian Kennedy RC 1.00 2.50
59 Jay Bruce (RC) 1.25 3.00
60 Whitey Ford .30 .75
61 Mariano Rivera .60 1.50
62 Alex Rodriguez .60 1.50
63 Hideki Matsui .50 1.25
64 Joba Chamberlain .30 .75
65 Jorge Posada .30 .75
66 Robinson Cano .30 .75
67 Eric Chavez .20 .50
68 Rich Harden .20 .50
69 Chase Utley .30 .75
70 Jimmy Rollins .30 .75
71 Ryan Howard .30 .75
72 Bill Mazeroski .30 .75
73 Freddy Sanchez .20 .50
74 Luke Hochevar RC .60 1.50
75 Tony Gwynn .50 1.25
76 Greg Maddux .60 1.50
77 Jake Peavy .20 .50
78 Barry Zito .30 .75
79 Russell Martin .20 .50
80 Tim Lincecum .30 .75
81 Ichiro Suzuki .60 1.50
82 Felix Hernandez .30 .75
83 Ozzie Smith .60 1.50
84 Jason Varitek .50 1.25
85 Chris Carpenter .30 .75
86 Carl Crawford .30 .75
87 Michael Young .20 .50
88 Frank Thomas .50 1.25
89 Roy Halladay .30 .75
90 Ryan Zimmerman .30 .75
91 Eddie Murray SP .75 2.00
92 Cal Ripken Jr. SP 4.00 10.00
93 Frank Robinson SP .75 2.00
94 Ryne Sandberg SP 2.50 6.00
95 Warren Spahn SP .75 2.00
96 Ernie Banks SP 1.25 3.00
97 Carlton Fisk SP .75 2.00
98 Johnny Bench SP 1.25 3.00
99 Ken Griffey Jr. SP 2.50 6.00
100 Al Kaline SP 1.25 3.00
101 Cal Ripken Jr. SP 4.00 10.00
102 Nolan Ryan SP 4.00 10.00
103 Jack Morris SP .75 2.00
104 Rod Carew SP .75 2.00
105 Tom Seaver SP .75 2.00
106 Don Mattingly SP 2.50 6.00
107 Lou Brock SP .75 2.00
108 Joe DiMaggio SP 2.50 6.00
109 Derek Jeter SP 3.00 8.00
110 Yogi Berra SP 1.25 3.00
111 Reggie Jackson SP .75 2.00
112 Mike Schmidt SP 2.00 5.00
113 Steve Carlton SP .75 2.00
114 Willie Stargell SP .75 2.00
115 Roberto Clemente SP 3.00 8.00
116 Albert Pujols SP 1.50 4.00
117 Stan Musial SP 2.00 5.00
118 Bob Gibson SP .75 2.00
119 Dave Winfield SP .75 2.00
120 Joe Carter SP .50 1.25

2008 UD Masterpieces Framed Black

*BLK 1-90: 1X TO 2.5X BASIC
*BLK RC 1-90: .5X TO 1.2X BASIC
*BLK SP 91-120: .5X TO 1.2X BASIC
APPX.ODDS 1:3 HOBBY

2008 UD Masterpieces Framed Blue 125

*BLUE 1-90: 2X TO 5X BASIC
*BLUE RC 1-90: 1X TO 2.5X BASIC
*BLUE SP 91-120: 1X TO 2.5X BASIC
RANDOM INSERTS IN PACKS
PRINT RUN 125 SER.#'d SETS

2008 UD Masterpieces Framed Blue 50

*BLUE 1-90: 4X TO 10X BASIC
*BLUE RC 1-90: 2X TO 5X BASIC
*BLUE SP 91-120: 1.2X TO 3X BASIC
RANDOM INSERTS IN PACKS
PRINT RUN 50 SER.#'d SETS

2008 UD Masterpieces Framed Brown 100

*BRN 1-90: 2X TO 5X BASIC
*BRN RC 1-90: 1X TO 2.5X BASIC
*BRN SP 91-120: 1X TO 2.5X BASIC
RANDOM INSERTS IN PACKS
PRINT RUN 100 SER.#'d SETS

2008 UD Masterpieces Framed Green 75

*GRN 1-90: 3X TO 8X BASIC
*GRN RC 1-90: 1.5X TO 4X BASIC
*GRN SP 91-120: 1X TO 2.5X BASIC
RANDOM INSERTS IN PACKS
PRINT RUN 75 SER.#'d SETS

2008 UD Masterpieces Framed Red

*RED 1-90: 1.2X TO 3X BASIC
*RED RC 1-90: .6X TO 1.5X BASIC
*RED SP 91-120: .6X TO 1.5X BASIC
APPX.ODDS 1:12 HOBBY
7 Evan Longoria 4.00 10.00
92 Cal Ripken Jr. 8.00 20.00
101 Cal Ripken Jr. 8.00 20.00
102 Nolan Ryan 8.00 20.00

2008 UD Masterpieces Captured on Canvas

OVERALL MEM ODDS 1:12
AJ Andruw Jones 3.00 8.00
AP Albert Pujols 6.00 15.00
AR Alex Rodriguez 8.00 20.00
BE Carlos Beltran 3.00 8.00
BH Bill Hall 3.00 8.00
BM Brian McCann 3.00 8.00
BP Brandon Phillips 4.00 10.00
BR Brian Roberts 5.00 12.00
BS Ben Sheets 3.00 8.00
BU B.J. Upton 3.00 8.00
CA Matt Cain 3.00 8.00
CB Chad Billingsley 3.00 8.00
CC Chris Carpenter 3.00 8.00
CD Chris Duncan 3.00 8.00
CF Carlton Fisk 3.00 8.00
CH Cole Hamels 3.00 8.00
CJ Chipper Jones 3.00 8.00
CL Carlos Lee 3.00 8.00
CR Cal Ripken Jr. 40.00 80.00
CS C.C. Sabathia 4.00 10.00
CW Rod Carew 3.00 8.00
CZ Carlos Zambrano 3.00 8.00
DJ Derek Jeter 10.00 25.00
DL Derrek Lee 3.00 8.00
DM Don Mattingly 6.00 15.00
DO David Ortiz 3.00 8.00
DU Dan Uggla 3.00 8.00
DW Dontrelle Willis 3.00 8.00
EB Erik Bedard 3.00 8.00
EC Eric Chavez 3.00 8.00
EM Eddie Murray 3.00 8.00
FH Felix Hernandez 3.00 8.00
FR Francisco Rodriguez 3.00 8.00
FS Freddy Sanchez 3.00 8.00
FT Frank Thomas 4.00 10.00
GA Garrett Atkins 3.00 8.00
GL Tom Glavine 5.00 12.00
GM Greg Maddux 8.00 20.00
GR Ken Griffey Jr. 6.00 15.00
GS Gary Sheffield 3.00 8.00
HK Howie Kendrick 3.00 8.00
HR Hanley Ramirez 3.00 8.00
HU Torii Hunter 3.00 8.00
IR Ivan Rodriguez 3.00 8.00
JB Josh Beckett 3.00 8.00
JE Derek Jeter 10.00 25.00
JF Jeff Francoeur 3.00 8.00
JL John Lackey 3.00 8.00
JM Joe Mauer 3.00 8.00
JO Kelly Johnson 3.00 8.00
JP Jake Peavy 3.00 8.00
JR Jose Reyes 4.00 10.00
JS Johan Santana 3.00 8.00
JT Jim Thome 3.00 8.00
JV Jason Varitek 5.00 12.00
JW Jered Weaver 3.00 8.00
KG Khalil Greene 3.00 8.00
KJ Kenji Johjima 3.00 8.00
KY Kevin Youkilis 3.00 8.00
LB Lance Berkman 3.00 8.00
MC Miguel Cabrera 3.00 8.00
MM Mark Mulder 3.00 8.00
MO Justin Morneau 3.00 8.00
MR Manny Ramirez 4.00 10.00
MT Mark Teixeira 3.00 8.00
MY Michael Young 3.00 8.00
NM Nick Markakis 6.00 15.00
NR Nolan Ryan 6.00 15.00
PA Jonathan Papelbon 4.00 10.00
PF Prince Fielder 3.00 8.00
PM Pedro Martinez 3.00 8.00
PO Jorge Posada 3.00 8.00
RA Aramis Ramirez 3.00 8.00
RB Ryan Braun 10.00 25.00
RC Roger Clemens 20.00 50.00
RH Rich Harden 3.00 8.00
RJ Randy Johnson 3.00 8.00
RO Roy Oswalt 3.00 8.00
RY Nolan Ryan 12.00 30.00
RZ Ryan Zimmerman 3.00 8.00
SC Curt Schilling 3.00 8.00
TG Tony Gwynn 15.00 40.00
TH Travis Hafner 3.00 8.00
VE Justin Verlander 3.00 8.00
VG Vladimir Guerrero 3.00 8.00
VM Victor Martinez 3.00 8.00
VW Vernon Wells 3.00 8.00
WI Josh Willingham 3.00 8.00
YB Yogi Berra 8.00 20.00

2008 UD Masterpieces Captured on Canvas Autographs

OVERALL AUTO ODDS 1:12
EXCH DEADLINE 9/15/2010
BH Bill Hall 4.00 10.00
BM Brian McCann 6.00 15.00
BP Brandon Phillips 8.00 20.00
BR Brian Roberts
BU B.J. Upton 5.00 12.00
CA Matt Cain 8.00 20.00
CB Chad Billingsley 6.00 15.00
CF Carlton Fisk
CH Cole Hamels 40.00 80.00
CJ Chipper Jones 40.00 80.00
CL Carlos Lee 8.00 20.00
CR Cal Ripken Jr. 90.00 150.00
CW Rod Carew 10.00 25.00
DJ Derek Jeter 150.00 250.00
DL Derrek Lee 6.00 15.00
DM Don Mattingly 50.00 100.00
DU Dan Uggla 6.00 15.00
FH Felix Hernandez 15.00 40.00
GR Ken Griffey Jr. 90.00 150.00
HR Hanley Ramirez 8.00 20.00
HU Torii Hunter
JB Josh Beckett 20.00 50.00
JE Derek Jeter 150.00 250.00
JF Jeff Francoeur 8.00 20.00
JO Kelly Johnson 4.00 10.00
KY Kevin Youkilis 6.00 15.00
LB Lance Berkman 10.00 25.00
MC Miguel Cabrera 50.00 100.00
NR Nolan Ryan 90.00 150.00
PA Jonathan Papelbon 12.50 30.00
PF Prince Fielder 30.00 60.00
RA Aramis Ramirez 4.00 10.00
RH Rich Harden 4.00 10.00
RZ Ryan Zimmerman 8.00 20.00
TG Tony Gwynn 30.00 60.00
TG Tom Glavine 30.00 60.00
WI Josh Willingham 4.00 10.00

2008 UD Masterpieces Stroke of Genius Signatures

OVERALL AUTO ODDS 1:12
EXCH DEADLINE 9/15/2010
AE Andre Ethier 8.00 20.00
AG Adrian Gonzalez 10.00 25.00
AL Adam LaRoche 3.00 8.00
AR Aramis Ramirez 6.00 15.00
BC Clay Buchholz 8.00 20.00
BH Bill Hall 4.00 10.00
BM Brian McCann 10.00 25.00
BP Brandon Phillips 3.00 8.00
BS Bill Skowron 6.00 15.00
BU B.J. Upton 10.00 25.00
CB Chad Billingsley 8.00 20.00
CF Chone Figgins 4.00 10.00
CH Cole Hamels 20.00 50.00
CR Cal Ripken Jr. 100.00 175.00
CY Chris B. Young 6.00 15.00
DC Daniel Cabrera 3.00 8.00
EE Edwin Encarnacion 8.00 20.00
EL Evan Longoria 40.00 80.00
EV Edinson Volquez 8.00 20.00
FC Fausto Carmona 4.00 10.00
GF Gavin Floyd 5.00 12.00
GJ Geoff Jenkins 6.00 15.00
GL Tom Glavine 30.00 60.00
GN Graig Nettles 5.00 12.00
GP Glen Perkins 3.00 8.00
HR Hanley Ramirez 10.00 25.00
HU Chin-Lung Hu 12.00 30.00
IA Ian Kinsler 6.00 15.00
JA James Loney 6.00 15.00
JB Joe Blanton 3.00 8.00
JC Jack Cust 3.00 8.00
JF Jeff Francoeur 12.00 30.00
JG Jeremy Guthrie 10.00 25.00
JK John Kruk 10.00 25.00
JN Joe Nathan 4.00 10.00
JO Josh Hamilton 10.00 25.00
JT J.R. Towles 6.00 15.00
JW Josh Willingham 4.00 10.00
KJ Kelly Johnson 3.00 8.00
KY Kevin Youkilis 8.00 20.00
LE Jon Lester 10.00 25.00
LH Luke Hochevar 5.00 12.00
MA John Maine 4.00 10.00
MC Matt Cain 4.00 10.00
MK Matt Kemp 12.00 30.00
MS Max Scherzer 30.00 80.00
NA Nick Adenhart 10.00 25.00
NB Nick Blackburn 8.00 20.00
NL Noah Lowry 3.00 8.00
NS Nick Swisher 5.00 12.00
PK Paul Konerko 20.00 50.00
RH Rich Hill 3.00 8.00
RM R.Martin EXCH 8.00 20.00
TG Tom Gorzelanny 3.00 8.00
TT Troy Tulowitzki 20.00 50.00
WB Wladimir Balentien 8.00 20.00
XN Xavier Nady 5.00 12.00
YG Yovani Gallardo 3.00 8.00

2005 UD Mini Jersey Collection

COMMON CARD (1-70) .30 .75
COMMON CARD (71-85) .30 .75
COMMON CARD (86-100) .30 .75
1 Garret Anderson .30 .75
2 Vladimir Guerrero .50 1.25
3 Luis Gonzalez .30 .75
4 Shawn Green .30 .75
5 Troy Glaus .30 .75
6 Andruw Jones .30 .75
7 Chipper Jones .75 2.00
8 John Smoltz .75 2.00
9 Tim Hudson .30 .75
10 Miguel Tejada .50 1.25
11 Sammy Sosa .75 2.00
12 Curt Schilling .50 1.25
13 David Ortiz .75 2.00
14 Johnny Damon .50 1.25
15 Manny Ramirez .75 2.00
16 Greg Maddux 1.00 2.50
17 Kerry Wood .30 .75
18 Mark Prior .50 1.25
19 Nomar Garciaparra .50 1.25
20 Frank Thomas .75 2.00
21 Adam Dunn .50 1.25
22 Ken Griffey Jr. 1.50 4.00
23 Travis Hafner .30 .75
24 Victor Martinez .50 1.25
25 Todd Helton .50 1.25
26 Ivan Rodriguez .50 1.25
27 Magglio Ordonez .50 1.25
28 Carlos Delgado .30 .75
29 Miguel Cabrera .75 2.00
30 Jeff Bagwell .50 1.25
31 Lance Berkman .50 1.25
32 Roger Clemens 1.00 2.50
33 Roy Oswalt .50 1.25
34 Mike Sweeney .30 .75
35 Eric Gagne .30 .75
36 J.D. Drew .30 .75
37 Ben Sheets .30 .75
38 Johan Santana .50 1.25
39 Torii Hunter .30 .75
40 Carlos Beltran .50 1.25
41 Mike Piazza .75 2.00
42 Pedro Martinez .50 1.25
43 Alex Rodriguez 1.00 2.50
44 Derek Jeter 2.00 5.00
45 Hideki Matsui 1.25 3.00
46 Mike Mussina .50 1.25
47 Randy Johnson .75 2.00
48 Bobby Crosby .30 .75
49 Eric Chavez .30 .75
50 Bobby Abreu .30 .75
51 Jim Thome .50 1.25
52 Jason Bay .30 .75
53 Oliver Perez .30 .75
54 Jake Peavy .30 .75
55 Khalil Greene .30 .75
56 Jason Schmidt .30 .75
57 Moises Alou .30 .75
58 Adrian Beltre .75 2.00
59 Ichiro Suzuki 1.00 2.50
60 Albert Pujols 1.00 2.50
61 Jim Edmonds .50 1.25
62 Mark Mulder .30 .75
63 Scott Rolen .50 1.25
64 Aubrey Huff .30 .75
65 Alfonso Soriano .50 1.25
66 Hank Blalock .30 .75
67 Mark Teixeira .50 1.25
68 Roy Halladay .30 .75
69 Jose Vidro .30 .75
70 Livan Hernandez .30 .75
71 Andruw Jones JE .30 .75
72 Mark Prior JE .50 1.25
73 Frank Thomas JE .75 2.00
74 Ken Griffey Jr. JE 1.50 4.00
75 C.C. Sabathia JE .50 1.25
76 Jeff Bagwell JE .50 1.25
77 Garret Anderson JE .30 .75
78 Eric Gagne JE .30 .75
79 Derek Jeter JE 2.00 5.00
80 Eric Chavez JE .30 .75
81 Bobby Abreu JE .30 .75
82 Jason Bay JE .30 .75

83 Khalil Greene JE .30 .75
84 Jason Schmidt JE .30 .75
85 Michael Young JE .30 .75
86 Cal Ripken MCM 2.50 6.00
87 Derek Jeter MCM 2.00 5.00
88 Hank Blalock MCM .30 .75
89 Hideo Nomo MCM .75 2.00
90 Joe DiMaggio MCM 1.50 4.00
91 Joe Morgan MCM .50 1.25
92 Ken Griffey Jr. MCM 1.50 4.00
93 Larry Doby MCM .50 1.25
94 Pedro Martinez MCM .50 1.25
95 Randy Johnson MCM .75 2.00
96 Rick Ferrell MCM .30 .75
97 Roger Clemens MCM 1.00 2.50
98 Stan Musial MCM 1.25 3.00
99 Ted Williams MCM 1.50 4.00
100 Torii Hunter MCM .30 .75

2005 UD Mini Jersey Collection Replica Jerseys

ONE PER PACK
AP Albert Pujols 2.50 6.00
AR Alex Rodriguez 2.50 6.00
CB Carlos Beltran 1.25 3.00
CJ Chipper Jones 2.00 5.00
CS Curt Schilling 1.25 3.00
DJ Derek Jeter 5.00 12.00
EG Eric Gagne .75 2.00
HM Hideki Matsui 3.00 8.00
IS Ichiro Suzuki 2.50 6.00
JD Johnny Damon 1.25 3.00
JS Johan Santana 1.25 3.00
JT Jim Thome 1.25 3.00
KG Ken Griffey Jr. 4.00 10.00
KW Kerry Wood .75 2.00
MC Miguel Cabrera 2.00 5.00
MP Mike Piazza 2.00 5.00
MR Manny Ramirez 2.00 5.00
NG Nomar Garciaparra 1.25 3.00
PM Pedro Martinez 1.25 3.00
RC Roger Clemens 2.50 6.00
RJ Randy Johnson 2.00 5.00
VG Vladimir Guerrero 1.25 3.00

2005 UD Mini Jersey Collection Replica Legends Jerseys

STATED ODDS 1:18
BR Babe Ruth 12.00 30.00
JD Joe DiMaggio 10.00 25.00
JR Jackie Robinson 3.00 8.00
LG Lou Gehrig 10.00 25.00
MM Mickey Mantle 15.00 40.00
RC Roberto Clemente 12.00 30.00
SP Satchel Paige 5.00 12.00
TC Ty Cobb 8.00 20.00
TW Ted Williams 10.00 25.00

2005 UD Past Time Pennants

COMPLETE SET (90) 10.00 25.00
COMMON CARD (1-90) .20 .50
1 Al Kaline .50 1.25
2 Al Rosen .20 .50
3 Bert Blyleven .30 .75
4 Bill Mazeroski .30 .75
5 Billy Williams .30 .75
6 Bob Feller .30 .75
7 Bob Gibson .30 .75
8 Bob Lemon .30 .75
9 Bobby Doerr .30 .75
10 Brooks Robinson .30 .75
11 Bruce Sutter .30 .75
12 Bucky Dent .20 .50
13 Cal Ripken 1.50 4.00
14 Carl Yastrzemski .60 1.50
15 Carlton Fisk .30 .75
16 Catfish Hunter .30 .75
17 Dale Murphy .50 1.25
18 Dave Parker .20 .50
19 Don Larsen .20 .50
20 Don Mattingly 1.00 2.50
21 Don Newcombe .20 .50
22 Duke Snider .30 .75
23 Early Wynn .30 .75
24 Eddie Mathews .50 1.25
25 Eddie Murray .30 .75
26 Enos Slaughter .30 .75
27 Ernie Banks .50 1.25
28 Fergie Jenkins .30 .75
29 Frank Howard .20 .50
30 Frank Robinson .30 .75
31 Fred Lynn .20 .50
32 Gary Carter .30 .75
33 Gaylord Perry .30 .75
34 George Brett 1.00 2.50
35 George Kell .30 .75
36 Goose Gossage .30 .75
37 Graig Nettles .20 .50
38 Harmon Killebrew .50 1.25
39 Jack Morris .30 .75
40 Jim Bunning .30 .75
41 Felipe Alou .20 .50
42 Jim Palmer .30 .75
43 Jim Rice .30 .75
44 Joe DiMaggio 1.00 2.50
45 Joe Morgan .30 .75
46 Johnny Bench .50 1.25
47 Johnny Podres .20 .50
48 Juan Marichal .30 .75
49 Keith Hernandez .20 .50
50 Kirby Puckett .50 1.25
51 Larry Doby .30 .75
52 Lou Brock .30 .75
53 Luis Aparicio .30 .75
54 Luis Tiant .20 .50
55 Maury Wills .20 .50
56 Mickey Mantle 1.50 4.00
57 Mike Schmidt .75 2.00
58 Monte Irvin .30 .75
59 Nolan Ryan 1.50 4.00
60 Orlando Cepeda .30 .75
61 Ozzie Smith .60 1.50
62 Paul Molitor .50 1.25
63 Pee Wee Reese .30 .75
64 Phil Niekro .30 .75
65 Phil Rizzuto .30 .75
66 Ralph Kiner .30 .75
67 Richie Ashburn .30 .75
68 Rico Petrocelli .20 .50
69 Robin Roberts .30 .75
70 Robin Yount .50 1.25
71 Rocky Colavito .30 .75
72 Rod Carew .30 .75
73 Rollie Fingers .30 .75
74 Ron Guidry .20 .50
75 Ron Santo .30 .75
76 Tony Gwynn .60 1.50
77 Sparky Lyle .20 .50
78 Stan Musial .75 2.00
79 Steve Carlton .30 .75
80 Rick Ferrell .20 .50
81 Tom Seaver .30 .75
82 Tommy John .20 .50
83 Tony Perez .30 .75
84 Wade Boggs .30 .75
85 Warren Spahn .30 .75
86 Whitey Ford .30 .75
87 Will Clark .30 .75
88 Willie McCovey .30 .75
89 Willie Stargell .30 .75
90 Yogi Berra .50 1.25

2005 UD Past Time Pennants Gold

*GOLD: 4X TO 10X BASIC
STATED ODDS 1:110 HOBBY
STATED PRINT RUN 50 SERIAL #'d SETS

2005 UD Past Time Pennants Silver

*SILVER: 2.5X TO 6X BASIC
RANDOM INSERTS IN RETAIL PACKS
STATED PRINT RUN 100 SERIAL #'d SETS

2005 UD Past Time Pennants Signatures Bronze

TIER 3 PRINT RUNS 325 OR MORE PER
TIER 2 PRINT RUNS B/WN 75-150 PER
TIER 1 PRINT RUNS B/WN 3-25 PER
NO TIER 1 PRICING DUE TO SCARCITY
OVERALL AUTO ODDS 1:10
TIER 1-3 ARE NOT SERIAL-NUMBERED
TIER 1-3 PRINT RUNS PROVIDED BY UD
EXCHANGE DEADLINE 04/08/08
AR Al Rosen T2 8.00 20.00
BF Bill Freehan T3 6.00 15.00
BH Burt Hooton T3 6.00 15.00
BM Bill Madlock T3 6.00 15.00
BO Bobby Murcer T3 12.50 30.00
BP Boog Powell T2 6.00 15.00
DC David Cone T2 8.00 20.00
DG Dwight Gooden T2 8.00 20.00
DK Dave Kingman T3 6.00 15.00
DL Don Larsen T1 8.00 20.00
FA Felipe Alou T3 6.00 15.00
FH Frank Howard T2 8.00 20.00
GU Don Gullett T3 4.00 10.00
HO Ken Holtzman T3 6.00 15.00
HR Kent Hrbek T3 6.00 15.00
KG Ken Griffey Sr. T3 6.00 15.00
KN Ray Knight T3 6.00 15.00
LD Lenny Dykstra T3 6.00 15.00
PG Pedro Guerrero T3 6.00 15.00
RB Rick Burleson T3 6.00 15.00
RH Randy Hundley T3 6.00 15.00
RP Rico Petrocelli T3 6.00 15.00
SF Sid Fernandez T3 6.00 15.00
SL Sparky Lyle T3 6.00 15.00
SS Steve Sax T2 5.00 12.00
WI Mookie Wilson T2 8.00 20.00
WJ Wally Joyner T2 8.00 20.00

2005 UD Past Time Pennants Signatures Gold

*GOLD T3: .5X TO 1.2X BRONZE T3
TIER 3 PRINT RUN 90 OR MORE PER
TIER 2 PRINT RUN 10 COPIES PER
NO TIER 2 PRICING DUE TO SCARCITY
TIER 1 PRINT RUN 1 COPY PER
NO TIER 1 PRICING DUE TO SCARCITY
OVERALL AUTO ODDS 1:10
TIER 1-3 ARE NOT SERIAL-NUMBERED
TIER 1-3 PRINT RUNS PROVIDED BY UD
EXCHANGE DEADLINE 04/08/08

2005 UD Past Time Pennants Signatures Silver

*SILVER T4: .4X TO 1X BRONZE T3
T4 PRINT RUNS 399 OR MORE PER
*SILVER T3: .4X TO 1X BRONZE T2
T3 PRINT RUNS B/WN 101-268 PER
T2 PRINT RUNS B/WN 40-83 PER
T1 PRINT RUNS B/WN 7-20 PER
NO TIER 1 PRICING DUE TO SCARCITY
TIER 1-3 ARE NOT SERIAL-NUMBERED
TIER 1-3 PRINT RUNS PROVIDED BY UD
EXCHANGE DEADLINE 04/08/08
AK Al Kaline T2 30.00 80.00
BB Bert Blyleven T3 8.00 20.00
BD Bobby Doerr T3 8.00 20.00
BR Lou Brock T2 15.00 40.00
BS Bill Skowron T3 8.00 20.00
CC Chris Chambliss T3 8.00 20.00
DE Bucky Dent T3 8.00 20.00
DN Don Newcombe T3 8.00 20.00
DP Dave Parker T2 20.00 50.00
EV Dwight Evans T2 15.00 40.00
FE Bob Feller T2 10.00 25.00
FJ Fergie Jenkins T2 10.00 25.00
FL Fred Lynn T2 10.00 25.00
GC Gary Carter T2 25.00 60.00
GG Goose Gossage T3 8.00 20.00
GK George Kell T3 12.50 30.00
GN Graig Nettles T3 10.00 25.00
GP Gaylord Perry T3 8.00 20.00
HK Harmon Killebrew T2 20.00 50.00
JM Jack Morris T3 8.00 20.00
JP Jim Palmer T2 10.00 25.00
JR Jim Rice T2 10.00 25.00
KH Keith Hernandez T3 8.00 20.00
LA Luis Aparicio T2 10.00 25.00
LT Luis Tiant T3 8.00 20.00
MA Bill Mazeroski T2 12.00 30.00
MI Monte Irvin T3 12.00 30.00
MO Joe Morgan T2 12.00 30.00
MU Dale Murphy T3 12.50 30.00
MW Maury Wills T2 10.00 25.00
OC Orlando Cepeda T2 10.00 25.00
OS Ozzie Smith T2 30.00 60.00
PM Paul Molitor T2 15.00 40.00
PO Johnny Podres T2 10.00 25.00
RC Rocky Colavito T2 30.00 60.00
RF Rollie Fingers T2 6.00 15.00
RK Ralph Kiner T2 10.00 25.00
RO Brooks Robinson T2 30.00 60.00
RS Ron Santo T3 12.50 30.00
SC Mike Scioscia T3 15.00 40.00
ST Steve Carlton T2 10.00 25.00
SU Bruce Sutter T3 12.50 30.00
TP Tony Perez T2 15.00 40.00
WC Will Clark T2 15.00 40.00
WH Willie Horton T4 8.00 20.00

2005 UD Past Time Pennants Mitchell and Ness Pennants

ONE PER SEALED HOBBY BOX
STATED ODDS 1:40 RETAIL EXCH
STATED PRINT RUNS B/WN 100-500 PER
PENNANTS ARE NOT SERIAL-NUMBERED
PRINT RUN INFO PROVIDED BY UD
1903 1903 Bost. Americans/100 * 8.00 20.00
1905 1905 N.Y. Giants/100 * 8.00 20.00
1906 1906 Chic. White Sox/100 * 8.00 20.00
1907 1907 Detroit Tigers/100 * 8.00 20.00
1908 1908 Chic. Cubs/105 * 8.00 20.00
1909 1909 Pittsburgh Pirates/125 * 8.00 20.00
1910 1910 Philad. A's/125 * 8.00 20.00
1912 1912 Boston Red Sox/125 * 8.00 20.00
1914 1914 Boston Braves/125 * 8.00 20.00
1915 1915 Philad. Phillies/125 * 8.00 20.00
1916 1916 Brook. Robins/200 * 8.00 20.00
1917 1917 N.Y. Giants/200 * 8.00 20.00
1918 1918 Boston Red Sox/200 * 8.00 20.00
1919 1919 Chic. White Sox/200 * 8.00 20.00
1920 1920 Cleveland Indians/200 * 8.00 20.00
1921 1921 N.Y. Yankees/200 * 10.00 25.00
1922 1922 N.Y. Giants/200 * 8.00 20.00
1924 1924 Wash. Senators/200 * 8.00 20.00
1925 1925 Pittsburgh Pirates/200 * 8.00 20.00
1926 1926 Stl. Cardinals/200 * 8.00 20.00
1927 1927 N.Y. Yankees/500 * 10.00 25.00
1928 1928 N.Y. Yankees/500 * 10.00 25.00
1929 1929 Chic. Cubs/337 * 8.00 20.00
1930 1930 Philad. A's/337 * 8.00 20.00
1931 1931 Stl. Cardinals/337 * 8.00 20.00
1932 1932 Chic. Cubs/337 * 8.00 20.00
1934 1934 Detroit Tigers/337 * 8.00 20.00
1935 1935 Chic. Cubs/337 * 8.00 20.00
1936 1936 N.Y. Yankees/337 * 10.00 25.00
1937 1937 N.Y. Giants/337 * 8.00 20.00
1938 1938 N.Y. Yankees/337 * 10.00 25.00
1939 1939 Cincinnati Reds/337 * 8.00 20.00
1940 1940 Cincinnati Reds/337 * 8.00 20.00
1941 1941 Brook. Dodgers/337 * 10.00 25.00
1942 1942 Stl. Cardinals/337 * 8.00 20.00
1943 1943 N.Y. Yankees/500 * 10.00 25.00
1944 1944 Stl. Browns/337 * 8.00 20.00
1945 1945 Chic. Cubs/337 * 8.00 20.00
1946 1946 Boston Red Sox/337 * 8.00 20.00
1947 1947 Brook. Dodgers/337 * 10.00 25.00
1948 1948 Boston Braves/337 * 8.00 20.00
1949 1949 N.Y. Yankees/337 * 10.00 25.00
1950 1950 Philad. Phillies/337 * 8.00 20.00
1951 1951 N.Y. Giants/337 * 8.00 20.00
1952 1952 Brook. Dodgers/500 * 10.00 25.00
1953 1953 N.Y. Yankees/337 * 10.00 25.00
1954 1954 Cleveland Indians/337 * 8.00 20.00
1955 1955 Brook. Dodgers/337 * 15.00 40.00
1956 1956 Brook. Dodgers/500 * 10.00 25.00
1957 1957 Milw. Braves/337 * 8.00 20.00
1958 1958 N.Y. Yankees/500 * 10.00 25.00
1959 1959 L.A. Dodgers/337 * 8.00 20.00
1960 1960 Pittsburgh Pirates/337 * 8.00 20.00
1961 1961 Cincinnati Reds/337 * 8.00 20.00
1962 1962 S.F. Giants/337 * 8.00 20.00
1963 1963 L.A. Dodgers/337 * 8.00 20.00
1964 1964 Stl. Cardinals/337 * 8.00 20.00
1965 1965 Minnesota Twins/337 * 8.00 20.00
1966 1966 Baltimore Orioles/337 * 8.00 20.00
1967 1967 Boston Red Sox/337 * 8.00 20.00
1968 1968 Detroit Tigers/337 * 8.00 20.00
1969 1969 N.Y. Mets/337 * 20.00 50.00
1970 1970 Baltimore Orioles/337 * 8.00 20.00
1971 1971 Pittsburgh Pirates/337 * 8.00 20.00
1972 1972 Oakland A's/337 * 8.00 20.00
1973 1973 Oakland A's/337 * 8.00 20.00
1974 1974 L.A. Dodgers/337 * 8.00 20.00
1975B 1975 Boston R.Sox/337 * 15.00 40.00
1975C 1975 Cincinnati Reds/337 * 10.00 25.00
1977 1977 N.Y. Yankees/337 * 10.00 25.00
1978 1978 L.A. Dodgers/337 * 8.00 20.00
1979 1979 Pittsburgh Pirates/337 * 8.00 20.00
1980 1980 Philad. Phillies/337 * 8.00 20.00
1981 1981 L.A. Dodgers/337 * 8.00 20.00
1982 1982 Milw. Brewers/337 * 8.00 20.00
1983 1983 Baltimore Orioles/337 * 8.00 20.00
1984 1984 San Diego Padres/337 * 8.00 20.00
1985 1985 K.C. Royals/337 * 8.00 20.00
1986 1986 Boston R.Sox/337 * 15.00 40.00
1988 1988 L.A. Dodgers/337 * 8.00 20.00

2005 UD Past Time Pennants Mitchell and Ness Pennants Autograph

STATED ODDS 1:400 H, 1:800 R EXCH
PRINT RUNS B/WN 86-87 COPIES PER
PENNANTS ARE NOT SERIAL-NUMBERED
PRINT RUN INFO PROVIDED BY UD
AK Al Kaline 68/87 * 50.00 120.00
BR Brooks Robinson 66/87 * 50.00 100.00
CF Carlton Fisk 75/87 * 40.00 80.00
CY Carl Yastrzemski 67/86 * 50.00 100.00
DN Don Newcombe 55/87 * 20.00 50.00
GN Graig Nettles 77/87 * 40.00 80.00
JB Johnny Bench 75/87 * 50.00 100.00
PM Paul Molitor 82/87 * 20.00 50.00
RF Rollie Fingers 73/87 * 20.00 50.00
SC Steve Carlton 80/87 * 20.00 50.00
SG Steve Garvey 84/87 * 20.00 50.00
TS Tom Seaver 69/87 * 50.00 120.00

2005 UD Past Time Pennants Mitchell and Ness Jersey Redemption

STATED ODDS 1:400 HOBBY, 1:648 RETAIL
STATED PRINT RUN 36-37 COPIES PER
PRINT RUNS = 24 HOME & 12-13 AWAY PER
EXCH.CARDS ARE NOT SERIAL-NUMBERED
PRINT RUN INFO PROVIDED BY UD
EXCHANGE DEADLINE 04/08/08
NO PRICING DUE TO SCARCITY

2003 UD Patch Collection

COMP.SET w/o SP's (90) 10.00 25.00
COMMON CARD (1-120) .20 .50
COMMON RC .20 .50
COMMON SP (1-120) .75 2.00
SP 1-120 STATED ODDS 1:4
SP: 5/6/9/10/17/19/21/22/28/37/42-44/51
SP: 54/55/59/61/66/69-71/73/80-82/86/91
SP: 104/118
COMMON CARD (121-135) 1.00 2.50
121-135 STATED ODDS 1:40
COMMON CARD (136-150) 1.00 2.50
136-150 STATED ODDS 1:40
COMMON CARD (151-161) .75 2.00
151-161 STATED ODDS 1:20
1 Darin Erstad .20 .50
2 Troy Glaus .20 .50
3 Robby Hammock RC .20 .50
4 Luis Gonzalez .20 .50
5 Randy Johnson SP 2.00 5.00
6 Curt Schilling SP 1.25 3.00
7 Oscar Villarreal RC .20 .50
8 Gary Sheffield .20 .50
9 Mike Hampton SP .75 2.00
10 Greg Maddux SP 2.50 6.00
11 Chipper Jones .50 1.25
12 Tony Batista .20 .50
13 Rodrigo Lopez .20 .50
14 Jay Gibbons .20 .50
15 Shea Hillenbrand .20 .50
16 Johnny Damon .30 .75
17 Derek Lowe SP .75 2.00
18 Nomar Garciaparra .30 .75
19 Pedro Martinez SP 1.25 3.00
20 Manny Ramirez .50 1.25
21 Mark Prior SP 1.25 3.00
22 Kerry Wood SP .75 2.00
23 Corey Patterson .20 .50
24 Sammy Sosa .50 1.25
25 Troy O'Leary .20 .50
26 Frank Thomas .50 1.25
27 Magglio Ordonez .30 .75
28 Bartolo Colon SP .75 2.00
29 Austin Kearns .20 .50
30 Aaron Boone .20 .50
31 Ken Griffey Jr. 1.00 2.50
32 Adam Dunn .30 .75
33 C.C. Sabathia .30 .75
34 Karim Garcia .20 .50
35 Larry Walker .30 .75
36 Preston Wilson .20 .50
37 Jason Jennings SP .75 2.00
38 Todd Helton .30 .75
39 Carlos Pena .30 .75
40 Eric Munson .20 .50
41 Ivan Rodriguez .30 .75
42 Josh Beckett SP .75 2.00
43 A.J. Burnett SP .75 2.00
44 Roy Oswalt SP 1.25 3.00
45 Craig Biggio .30 .75
46 Jeff Bagwell .30 .75
47 Lance Berkman .30 .75
48 Jeff Kent .20 .50
49 Carlos Beltran .30 .75
50 Mike Sweeney .20 .50
51 Hideo Nomo SP 2.00 5.00
52 Adrian Beltre .50 1.25
53 Shawn Green .20 .50
54 Kazuhisa Ishii SP .75 2.00
55 Ben Sheets SP .75 2.00
56 Richie Sexson .20 .50
57 Torii Hunter .20 .50
58 Doug Mientkiewicz .20 .50
59 Eric Milton SP .75 2.00
60 Corey Koskie .20 .50
61 Joe Mays SP .75 2.00
62 Jose Vidro .20 .50
63 Vladimir Guerrero .30 .75
64 Luis Ayala RC .20 .50
65 Cliff Floyd .20 .50
66 Tom Glavine SP 1.25 3.00
67 Mike Piazza .50 1.25
68 Roberto Alomar .30 .75
69 Al Leiter SP .75 2.00
70 Mike Mussina SP 1.25 3.00
71 Mariano Rivera SP 2.50 6.00
72 Drew Henson .20 .50
73 Roger Clemens SP 2.50 6.00
74 Jason Giambi .20 .50
75 Bernie Williams .30 .75
76 Alfonso Soriano .30 .75
77 Derek Jeter 1.25 3.00
78 Miguel Tejada .30 .75
79 Jermaine Dye .20 .50
80 Tim Hudson SP 1.25 3.00
81 Barry Zito SP 1.25 3.00
82 Mark Mulder SP .75 2.00
83 Pat Burrell .20 .50
84 Jim Thome .30 .75
85 Bobby Abreu .20 .50
86 Kevin Millwood SP .75 2.00
87 Jason Kendall .20 .50
88 Brian Giles .20 .50
89 Phil Nevin .20 .50
90 Sean Burroughs .20 .50
91 Oliver Perez SP .75 2.00
92 Jose Cruz Jr. .20 .50
93 Rich Aurilia .20 .50
94 Edgardo Alfonzo .20 .50
95 Barry Bonds .75 2.00
96 J.T. Snow .20 .50
97 Mike Cameron .20 .50
98 John Olerud .20 .50
99 Bret Boone .20 .50
100 Ichiro Suzuki .60 1.50
101 J.D. Drew .20 .50
102 Jim Edmonds .30 .75
103 Scott Rolen .30 .75
104 Matt Morris SP .75 2.00
105 Tino Martinez .20 .50
106 Albert Pujols .60 1.50
107 Rocco Baldelli .20 .50
108 Carl Crawford .30 .75
109 Mark Teixeira .30 .75
110 Rafael Palmeiro .30 .75
111 Hank Blalock .20 .50
112 Alex Rodriguez .60 1.50
113 Kevin Mench .20 .50
114 Juan Gonzalez .20 .50
115 Shannon Stewart .20 .50
116 Vernon Wells .20 .50
117 Josh Phelps .20 .50
118 Eric Hinske SP .75 2.00
119 Orlando Hudson .20 .50
120 Carlos Delgado .20 .50
121 Alex Rodriguez AS 3.00 8.00
122 Nomar Garciaparra AS 1.50 4.00
123 Miguel Tejada AS 1.50 4.00
124 Jim Thome AS 1.50 4.00
125 Alfonso Soriano AS 1.50 4.00
126 Vladimir Guerrero AS 1.50 4.00
127 Derek Jeter AS 6.00 15.00
128 Mike Piazza AS 2.50 6.00
129 Ichiro Suzuki AS 3.00 8.00
130 Pedro Martinez AS 1.50 4.00
131 Luis Gonzalez AS 1.00 2.50
132 Adam Dunn AS 1.50 4.00
133 Shawn Green AS 1.00 2.50
134 Barry Zito AS 1.50 4.00
135 Torii Hunter AS 1.00 2.50
136 Ted Williams HOF 5.00 12.00
137 Mickey Mantle HOF 8.00 20.00
138 Ernie Banks HOF 2.50 6.00
139 Yogi Berra HOF 2.50 6.00
140 Rollie Fingers HOF 1.50 4.00
141 Catfish Hunter HOF 1.50 4.00
142 Juan Marichal HOF 1.50 4.00
143 Eddie Mathews HOF 2.50 6.00
144 Willie McCovey HOF 1.50 4.00
145 Joe Morgan HOF 1.50 4.00
146 Stan Musial HOF 4.00 10.00
147 Pee Wee Reese HOF 1.50 4.00
148 Phil Rizzuto HOF 1.50 4.00
149 Nolan Ryan HOF 8.00 20.00
150 Tom Seaver HOF 1.50 4.00
151 Hideki Matsui RI RC 4.00 10.00
152 Jose Contreras RI RC 2.00 5.00
153 Lew Ford RI RC .75 2.00
154 Jeremy Griffiths RI RC .75 2.00
155 Guillermo Quiroz RI RC .75 2.00
156 Ryan Cameron RI RC .75 2.00
157 Jon Leicester RI RC .75 2.00
158 Josh Willingham RI RC 2.50 6.00
159 Shane Bazzell RI RC .75 2.00
160 Willie Eyre RI RC .75 2.00
161 Prentice Redman RI RC .75 2.00
IS Ichiro Suzuki SAMPLE 1.00 2.50

2003 UD Patch Collection All-Star Game Patches

COMMON CARD (1-27) 6.00 15.00
COMMON CARD (28-73) 4.00 10.00
TWO PER SEALED BOX-TOPPER PACK
1 Chicago White Sox 1933 6.00 15.00
2 New York Giants 1934 6.00 15.00
3 Cleveland Indians 1935 6.00 15.00
4 Boston Braves 1936 6.00 15.00
5 Washington Senators 1937 6.00 15.00
6 Cincinnati Reds 1938 6.00 15.00
7 New York Yankees 1939 10.00 25.00
8 St. Louis Cardinals 1940 6.00 15.00
9 Detroit Tigers 1941 6.00 15.00
10 New York Giants 1942 6.00 15.00
11 Philadelphia A's 1943 6.00 15.00
12 Pittsburgh Pirates 1944 6.00 15.00
13 Boston Red Sox 1946 6.00 15.00
14 Chicago Cubs 1947 8.00 20.00
15 St. Louis Browns 1948 8.00 20.00
16 Brooklyn Dodgers 1949 8.00 20.00
17 Chicago White Sox 1950 6.00 15.00
18 Detroit Tigers 1951 6.00 15.00
19 Philadelphia Phillies 1952 8.00 20.00
20 Cincinnati Reds 1953 6.00 15.00
21 Cleveland Indians 1954 6.00 15.00
22 Milwaukee Braves 1955 6.00 15.00
23 Washington Senators 1956 6.00 15.00
24 St. Louis Cardinals 1957 8.00 20.00
25 Baltimore Orioles 1958 6.00 15.00
26 Pittsburgh Pirates 1959 6.00 15.00
27 Los Angeles Dodgers 1959 6.00 15.00
28 Kansas City A's 1960 4.00 10.00
29 New York Yankees 1960 10.00 25.00
30 San Francisco Giants 1961 4.00 10.00
31 Boston Red Sox 1961 6.00 15.00
32 Washington Senators 1962 4.00 10.00
33 Chicago Cubs 1962 4.00 10.00
34 Cleveland Indians 1963 4.00 10.00
35 New York Mets 1964 6.00 15.00
36 Minnesota Twins 1965 4.00 10.00
37 St. Louis Cardinals 1966 6.00 15.00
38 Anaheim Angels 1967 4.00 10.00
39 Houston Astros 1968 4.00 10.00
40 Washington Senators 1969 4.00 10.00
41 Cincinnati Reds 1970 4.00 10.00
42 Detroit Tigers 1971 6.00 15.00
43 Atlanta Braves 1972 4.00 10.00
44 Kansas City Royals 1973 4.00 10.00
45 Pittsburgh Pirates 1974 4.00 10.00
46 Milwaukee Brewers 1975 4.00 10.00
47 Philadelphia Phillies 1976 4.00 10.00
48 New York Yankees 1977 10.00 25.00
49 San Diego Padres 1978 4.00 10.00
50 Seattle Mariners 1979 4.00 10.00
51 Los Angeles Dodgers 1980 4.00 10.00
52 Cleveland Indians 1981 4.00 10.00
53 Montreal Expos 1982 4.00 10.00
54 Chicago White Sox 1983 4.00 10.00
55 San Francisco Giants 1984 4.00 10.00
56 Minnesota Twins 1985 4.00 10.00
57 Houston Astros 1986 4.00 10.00
58 Oakland A's 1987 4.00 10.00
59 Cincinnati Reds 1988 4.00 10.00
60 Anaheim Angels 1989 4.00 10.00
61 Chicago Cubs 1990 4.00 10.00
62 Toronto Blue Jays 1991 4.00 10.00
63 San Diego Padres 1992 4.00 10.00
64 Baltimore Orioles 1993 4.00 10.00
65 Pittsburgh Pirates 1994 4.00 10.00
66 Texas Rangers 1995 4.00 10.00
67 Philadelphia Phillies 1996 4.00 10.00
68 Cleveland Indians 1997 4.00 10.00
69 Colorado Rockies 1998 4.00 10.00
70 Boston Red Sox 1999 6.00 15.00
71 Atlanta Braves 2000 4.00 10.00
72 Seattle Mariners 2001 4.00 10.00
73 Milwaukee Brewers 2002 4.00 10.00

2003 UD Patch Collection MVP's

STATED ODDS 1:20
MVP1 Derek Jeter 00 WS 6.00 15.00
MVP2 Randy Johnson 01 WS 2.50 6.00
MVP3 Curt Schilling 01 WS 1.50 4.00
MVP4 Troy Glaus 02 WS 1.00 2.50
MVP5 Ted Williams 46 MVP 5.00 12.00
MVP6 Ted Williams 49 MVP 5.00 12.00
MVP7 Mickey Mantle 56 MVP 8.00 20.00
MVP8 Mickey Mantle 57 MVP 8.00 20.00
MVP9 Phil Rizzuto 50 MVP 1.50 4.00
MVP10 Roger Clemens 86 MVP 3.00 8.00
MVP11 Ken Griffey Jr. 97 MVP 5.00 12.00
MVP12 Jason Giambi 00 MVP 1.00 2.50
MVP13 Ichiro Suzuki 01 MVP 3.00 8.00
MVP14 Roger Clemens AS MVP 3.00 8.00
MVP15 Yogi Berra 54 MVP 2.50 6.00
MVP16 Sammy Sosa 98 MVP 2.50 6.00
MVP17 Derek Jeter 00 AS MVP 6.00 15.00
MVP18 Mike Piazza 96 AS MVP 2.50 6.00
MVP19 Barry Bonds 02 MVP 4.00 10.00
MVP20 Stan Musial 46 MVP 4.00 10.00
MVP21 Joe Morgan 75 MVP 1.50 4.00

2003 UD Patch Collection Signature Patches

STATED ODDS 1:320
EXCHANGE DEADLINE 06/19/06
AD Adam Dunn 8.00 20.00
BZ Barry Zito 12.50 30.00
CS Curt Schilling 12.50 30.00
DH Drew Henson 8.00 20.00
EH Eric Hinske 8.00 20.00
FG Freddy Garcia 10.00 25.00
GS Gary Sheffield 8.00 20.00
JB Jeff Bagwell 30.00 60.00
KG Ken Griffey Jr. 50.00 100.00
LB Lance Berkman 30.00 60.00
LG Luis Gonzalez 10.00 25.00
MT Miguel Tejada 30.00 60.00
RC Roger Clemens SP 60.00 120.00
SR Scott Rolen 30.00 60.00
SS Sammy Sosa SP 50.00 100.00
TP Troy Percival 8.00 20.00

2002 UD Piece of History

COMP.SET w/SP'S (90) 75.00 150.00
COMP.SET w/o SP'S (80) 8.00 20.00
COMMON CARD (1-90) .10 .30
COMMON CARD (91A-132P) 3.00 8.00
91A-132P RANDOM INSERTS IN PACKS
91A-132P PRINT RUN 625 SERIAL #'d SETS
91-132 ACTION & PORTRAIT EQUAL VALUE
1 Troy Glaus .10 .30
2 Darin Erstad .10 .30
3 Reggie Jackson .20 .50
4 Miguel Tejada .10 .30
5 Tim Hudson .10 .30
6 Catfish Hunter .20 .50
7 Joe Carter .10 .30
8 Carlos Delgado .10 .30
9 Greg Vaughn .10 .30
10 Early Wynn .10 .30
11 Omar Vizquel .20 .50
12 Jim Thome .20 .50
13 Ichiro Suzuki .60 1.50
14 Edgar Martinez .20 .50
15 Freddy Garcia .10 .30
16 Cal Ripken SP 10.00 25.00
17 Jeff Conine .10 .30
18 Juan Gonzalez .10 .30
19 Nolan Ryan SP 8.00 20.00
20 Alex Rodriguez SP 5.00 12.00
21 Rafael Palmeiro .20 .50
22 Ivan Rodriguez .20 .50
23 Carlton Fisk .20 .50
24 Wade Boggs .20 .50
25 Pedro Martinez .20 .50
26 Nomar Garciaparra .50 1.25
27 Manny Ramirez .20 .50
28 Mike Sweeney .10 .30
29 Bobby Higginson .10 .30
30 Kirby Puckett .30 .75
31 Doug Mientkiewicz .10 .30
32 Corey Koskie .10 .30
33 Joe Mays .10 .30
34 Frank Thomas .30 .75
35 Magglio Ordonez .10 .30
36 Jason Giambi SP 6.00 15.00
37 Derek Jeter SP 8.00 20.00
38 Mickey Mantle SP 12.50 30.00
39 Joe DiMaggio .60 1.50
40 Roger Maris .30 .75
41 Roger Clemens .60 1.50
42 Bernie Williams .20 .50
43 Jeff Bagwell .20 .50
44 Lance Berkman .10 .30
45 Eddie Mathews .30 .75
46 Andruw Jones .20 .50
47 Phil Niekro .10 .30
48 Gary Sheffield .10 .30
49 Chipper Jones .30 .75
50 Greg Maddux .50 1.25
51 Robin Yount .30 .75
52 Richie Sexson .10 .30
53 Jim Edmonds .10 .30
54 J.D. Drew .10 .30
55 Albert Pujols .60 1.50
56 Andre Dawson .10 .30
57 Billy Williams .10 .30
58 Ernie Banks .30 .75
59 Sammy Sosa SP 6.00 15.00
60 Randy Johnson .30 .75
61 Curt Schilling .10 .30
62 Luis Gonzalez .10 .30
63 Kirk Gibson .10 .30
64 Steve Garvey .10 .30
65 Sandy Koufax SP 8.00 20.00
66 Shawn Green .10 .30
67 Hideo Nomo .30 .75
68 Kevin Brown .10 .30
69 Vladimir Guerrero .30 .75
70 Tim Raines .10 .30
71 Gaylord Perry .10 .30
72 Mel Ott .20 .50
73 Willie McCovey .10 .30
74 Barry Bonds SP 4.00 10.00
75 Jeff Kent .10 .30
76 Cliff Floyd .10 .30
77 Dwight Gooden .10 .30
78 Tom Seaver .20 .50
79 Mike Piazza .50 1.25
80 Roberto Alomar .20 .50
81 Dave Winfield .10 .30
82 Tony Gwynn .40 1.00
83 Scott Rolen .20 .50
84 Bill Mazeroski .10 .30
85 Willie Stargell .20 .50
86 Brian Giles .10 .30
87 Ken Griffey Jr. SP 8.00 20.00
88 Sean Casey .10 .30
89 Todd Helton .20 .50
90 Larry Walker .10 .30
91A Brendan Donnelly 21CP RC 3.00 8.00
91P Brendan Donnelly 21CP RC 3.00 8.00
92A Tom Shearn 21CP RC 3.00 8.00
92P Tom Shearn 21CP RC 3.00 8.00
93A Brandon Puffer 21CP RC 3.00 8.00
93P Brandon Puffer 21CP RC 3.00 8.00
94A Corey Thurman 21CP RC 3.00 8.00
94P Corey Thurman 21CP RC 3.00 8.00
95A Reed Johnson 21CP RC 3.00 8.00
95P Reed Johnson 21CP RC 3.00 8.00
96A Gustavo Chacin 21CP RC 3.00 8.00
96P Gustavo Chacin 21CP RC 3.00 8.00
97A Chris Baker 21CP RC 3.00 8.00
97P Chris Baker 21CP RC 3.00 8.00
98A John Ennis 21CP RC 3.00 8.00
98P John Ennis 21CP RC 3.00 8.00
99A So Taguchi 21CP RC 4.00 10.00
99P So Taguchi 21CP RC 4.00 10.00
100A Michael Crudale 21CP RC 3.00 8.00
100P Michael Crudale 21CP RC 3.00 8.00
101A Francis Beltran 21CP RC 3.00 8.00
101P Francis Beltran 21CP RC 3.00 8.00
102A Jose Valverde 21CP RC 3.00 8.00
102P Jose Valverde 21CP RC 3.00 8.00
103A Doug Devore 21CP RC 3.00 8.00
103P Doug Devore 21CP RC 3.00 8.00
104A Jeremy Ward 21CP RC 3.00 8.00
104P Jeremy Ward 21CP RC 3.00 8.00
105A P.J. Bevis 21CP RC 3.00 8.00
105P P.J. Bevis 21CP RC 3.00 8.00
106A Steve Kent 21CP RC 3.00 8.00
106P Steve Kent 21CP RC 3.00 8.00
107A Brandon Backe 21CP RC 4.00 10.00
107P Brandon Backe 21CP RC 4.00 10.00
108A Jorge Nunez 21CP RC 3.00 8.00
108P Jorge Nunez 21CP RC 3.00 8.00
109A Kazuhisa Ishii 21CP RC 4.00 10.00
109P Kazuhisa Ishii 21CP RC 6.00 15.00
110A Ron Calloway 21CP RC 3.00 8.00
110P Ron Calloway 21CP RC 3.00 8.00
111A Val Pascucci 21CP 3.00 8.00
111P Val Pascucci 21CP 3.00 8.00
112A J.J. Putz 21CP RC 3.00 8.00
112P J.J. Putz 21CP RC 3.00 8.00
113A Matt Thornton 21CP RC 3.00 8.00
113P Matt Thornton 21CP RC 3.00 8.00
114A Allan Simpson 21CP RC 3.00 8.00
114P Allan Simpson 21CP RC 3.00 8.00
115A Jaime Cerda 21CP RC 3.00 8.00
115P Jaime Cerda 21CP RC 3.00 8.00
116A Mark Corey 21CP RC 3.00 8.00
116P Mark Corey 21CP RC 3.00 8.00
117A Tyler Yates 21CP RC 3.00 8.00
117P Tyler Yates 21CP RC 3.00 8.00
118A Steve Bechler 21CP RC 3.00 8.00
118P Steve Bechler 21CP RC 3.00 8.00
119A Ben Howard 21CP RC 3.00 8.00
119P Ben Howard 21CP RC 3.00 8.00
120A Cliff Bartosh 21CP RC 3.00 8.00
120P Cliff Bartosh 21CP RC 3.00 8.00
121A Todd Donovan 21CP RC 3.00 8.00
121P Todd Donovan 21CP RC 3.00 8.00
122A Eric Junge 21CP RC 3.00 8.00
122P Eric Junge 21CP RC 3.00 8.00
123A Adrian Burnside 21CP RC 3.00 8.00
123P Adrian Burnside 21CP RC 3.00 8.00
124A Andy Pratt 21CP RC 3.00 8.00
124P Andy Pratt 21CP RC 3.00 8.00
125A Josh Hancock 21CP RC 4.00 10.00
125P Josh Hancock 21CP RC 4.00 10.00
126A Rene Reyes 21CP RC 3.00 8.00
126P Rene Reyes 21CP RC 3.00 8.00
127A Cam Esslinger 21CP RC 3.00 8.00
127P Cam Esslinger 21CP RC 3.00 8.00
128A Colin Young 21CP RC 3.00 8.00
128P Colin Young 21CP RC 3.00 8.00
129A Kevin Frederick 21CP RC 3.00 8.00
129P Kevin Frederick 21CP RC 3.00 8.00
130A Kyle Kane 21CP RC 3.00 8.00
130P Kyle Kane 21CP RC 3.00 8.00
131A Mitch Wylie 21CP RC 3.00 8.00
131P Mitch Wylie 21CP RC 3.00 8.00
132A Danny Wright 21CP 3.00 8.00
132P Danny Wright 21CP 3.00 8.00

2002 UD Piece of History 21st Century Phenoms 950

*21ST CP 950: .25X TO .6X BASIC CARDS
RANDOM INSERTS IN RETAIL PACKS
STATED PRINT RUN 950 SERIAL #'d SETS
ONLY PORTRAIT VERSION MADE IN RETAIL

2002 UD Piece of History 300 Game Winners

COMPLETE SET (6) 12.50 30.00
STATED ODDS 1:50
GW1 Nolan Ryan 5.00 12.00
GW2 Tom Seaver 1.25 3.00
GW3 Cy Young 2.00 5.00
GW4 Gaylord Perry 1.25 3.00
GW5 Early Wynn 1.25 3.00
GW6 Phil Niekro 1.25 3.00

2002 UD Piece of History 300 Game Winners Jersey

STATED ODDS 1:576
WGP Gaylord Perry Pants 6.00 15.00
WNR Nolan Ryan SP 20.00 50.00
WPN Phil Niekro 6.00 15.00
WTS Tom Seaver SP 10.00 25.00

2002 UD Piece of History 500 Home Run Club

COMPLETE SET (9) 25.00 60.00
STATED ODDS 1:30
HR1 Harmon Killebrew 3.00 8.00
HR2 Jimmie Foxx 3.00 8.00
HR3 Reggie Jackson 2.00 5.00
HR4 Mickey Mantle 8.00 20.00
HR5 Ernie Banks 3.00 8.00
HR6 Eddie Mathews 3.00 8.00
HR7 Mark McGwire 6.00 15.00
HR8 Willie McCovey 2.00 5.00
HR9 Mel Ott 3.00 8.00

2002 UD Piece of History 500 Home Run Club Jersey

STATED ODDS 1:336
EB Ernie Banks SP 15.00 40.00
EM Eddie Mathews 10.00 25.00
HA Hank Aaron 10.00 25.00
JF Jimmie Foxx 20.00 50.00
MO Mel Ott 20.00 50.00
RJ Reggie Jackson 15.00 40.00
WM Willie McCovey 10.00 25.00
MMA M.Mantle Pants SP/50 150.00 250.00

2002 UD Piece of History Batting Champs

COMPLETE SET (10) 20.00 50.00
STATED ODDS 1:30
B1 Tony Gwynn 2.50 6.00
B2 Frank Thomas 2.00 5.00
B3 Billy Williams .75 2.00
B4 Edgar Martinez 1.25 3.00
B5 Bernie Williams 1.25 3.00
B6 Mickey Mantle 6.00 15.00
B7 Larry Walker .75 2.00
B8 Gary Sheffield .75 2.00
B9 Wade Boggs 1.25 3.00
B10 Alex Rodriguez 2.50 6.00

2002 UD Piece of History Batting Champs Jersey

STATED ODDS 1:96
AG Andres Galarraga 4.00 10.00
AR Alex Rodriguez 6.00 15.00
BEW Bernie Williams 6.00 15.00
EM Edgar Martinez 6.00 15.00
FT Frank Thomas 6.00 15.00
GS Gary Sheffield SP 4.00 10.00
JO John Olerud 4.00 10.00
LW Larry Walker SP 4.00 10.00
MM M.Mantle Pants SP/50 150.00 250.00
PO Paul O'Neill 6.00 15.00
TG Tony Gwynn 6.00 15.00
TR Tim Raines 4.00 10.00
WB Wade Boggs 6.00 15.00

2002 UD Piece of History ERA Leaders

COMPLETE SET (10) 20.00 50.00
STATED ODDS 1:30
E1 Greg Maddux 3.00 8.00
E2 Pedro Martinez 1.25 3.00
E3 Freddy Garcia .75 2.00
E4 Randy Johnson 2.00 5.00
E5 Tom Seaver 1.25 3.00
E6 Early Wynn .75 2.00
E7 Dwight Gooden .75 2.00
E8 Kevin Brown .75 2.00
E9 Roger Clemens 4.00 10.00
E10 Nolan Ryan 5.00 12.00

2002 UD Piece of History ERA Leaders Jersey

STATED ODDS 1:96
ELCH Catfish Hunter SP 6.00 15.00
ELDG Dwight Gooden 1.25 3.00
ELFG Freddy Garcia 1.25 3.00
ELGM Greg Maddux 5.00 12.00
ELKB Kevin Brown 1.25 3.00
ELNR Nolan Ryan SP 12.50 30.00
ELPM Pedro Martinez 2.00 5.00
ELPN Phil Niekro 2.00 5.00
ELRC Roger Clemens 4.00 10.00
ELRJ Randy Johnson 3.00 8.00
ELSK Sandy Koufax SP 30.00 60.00
ELTS Tom Seaver 2.00 5.00

2002 UD Piece of History Hitting for the Cycle

COMPLETE SET (20) 30.00 80.00
STATED ODDS 1:15
H1 Alex Rodriguez 2.50 6.00
H2 Andre Dawson .75 2.00
H3 Cal Ripken 6.00 15.00
H4 Carlton Fisk 1.25 3.00
H5 Dante Bichette .75 2.00
H6 Dave Winfield .75 2.00
H7 Eric Chavez .75 2.00
H8 Robin Yount 2.00 5.00
H9 Jason Kendall .75 2.00
H10 Jay Buhner .75 2.00
H11 Jeff Kent .75 2.00
H12 Joe DiMaggio 3.00 8.00
H13 John Olerud .75 2.00
H14 Kirby Puckett 2.00 5.00
H15 Luis Gonzalez .75 2.00
H16 Mark Grace 1.25 3.00
H17 Mickey Mantle 6.00 15.00
H18 Miguel Tejada .75 2.00
H19 Rondell White .75 2.00
H20 Todd Helton 1.25 3.00

2002 UD Piece of History Hitting for the Cycle Bats

STATED ODDS 1:576
HCAD Andre Dawson 6.00 15.00
HCAR Alex Rodriguez 10.00 25.00
HCCF Carlton Fisk 10.00 25.00
HCCR Cal Ripken SP 40.00 80.00
HCDB Dante Bichette 6.00 15.00
HCDW Dave Winfield 6.00 15.00
HCEC Eric Chavez 6.00 15.00
HCJB Jay Buhner 6.00 15.00
HCLG Luis Gonzalez 6.00 15.00
HCMM Mickey Mantle SP/50 60.00 120.00

2002 UD Piece of History MVP Club

COMPLETE SET (14) 30.00 80.00
STATED ODDS 1:22
M1 Jason Giambi .75 2.00
M2 Sammy Sosa 2.00 5.00
M3 Cal Ripken 6.00 15.00
M4 Robin Yount 2.00 5.00
M5 Ken Griffey Jr. 4.00 10.00
M6 Kirk Gibson .75 2.00
M7 Mickey Mantle 6.00 15.00
M8 Barry Bonds 5.00 12.00
M9 Frank Thomas 2.00 5.00
M10 Reggie Jackson 1.25 3.00
M11 Jeff Bagwell 1.25 3.00
M12 Roger Clemens 4.00 10.00
M13 Steve Garvey .75 2.00
M14 Chipper Jones 2.00 5.00

2002 UD Piece of History MVP Club Jersey

STATED ODDS 1:96
MBL Barry Larkin SP 10.00 25.00
MCJ Chipper Jones 6.00 15.00
MCR Cal Ripken 15.00 40.00
MFT Frank Thomas 6.00 15.00
MIR Ivan Rodriguez 6.00 15.00
MJB Jeff Bagwell 6.00 15.00
MJGI Jason Giambi 4.00 10.00
MJGO Juan Gonzalez 4.00 10.00
MJK Jeff Kent 4.00 10.00
MKGI Kirk Gibson 4.00 10.00
MKGR Ken Griffey Jr. 6.00 15.00
MMM M.Mantle Pants SP/50 125.00 250.00
MRC Roger Clemens 6.00 15.00
MRJ Reggie Jackson 6.00 15.00
MRY Robin Yount Pants SP 10.00 25.00
MSG Steve Garvey 4.00 10.00
MSS Sammy Sosa 6.00 15.00

2002 UD Piece of History Tape Measure Heroes

COMPLETE SET (30) 60.00 150.00
STATED ODDS 1:10
TM1 Joe Carter .75 2.00
TM2 Cal Ripken 6.00 15.00
TM3 Mike Piazza 3.00 8.00
TM4 Shawn Green .75 2.00
TM5 Mark McGwire 5.00 12.00
TM6 Reggie Jackson 1.25 3.00
TM7 Mickey Mantle 6.00 15.00
TM8 Manny Ramirez 1.25 3.00
TM9 Mo Vaughn .75 2.00
TM10 Jeff Bagwell 1.25 3.00
TM11 Sammy Sosa 2.00 5.00
TM12 Tony Gwynn 2.50 6.00
TM13 Bill Mazeroski 1.25 3.00
TM14 Jose Canseco 1.25 3.00
TM15 Brian Giles .75 2.00
TM16 Kirk Gibson .75 2.00
TM17 Kirby Puckett 2.00 5.00
TM18 Wade Boggs 1.25 3.00
TM19 Albert Pujols 4.00 10.00
TM20 David Justice .75 2.00
TM21 Steve Garvey .75 2.00
TM22 Luis Gonzalez .75 2.00
TM23 Derek Jeter 5.00 12.00
TM24 Robin Yount 2.00 5.00
TM25 Barry Bonds 5.00 12.00
TM26 Alex Rodriguez 2.50 6.00
TM27 Willie Stargell 1.25 3.00
TM28 Carlton Fisk 1.25 3.00
TM29 Carlos Delgado .75 2.00
TM30 Ken Griffey Jr. 4.00 10.00

2002 UD Piece of History Tape Measure Heroes Jersey

STATED ODDS 1:96
AR Alex Rodriguez 6.00 15.00
BG Brian Giles 4.00 10.00
BM Bill Mazeroski 6.00 15.00
CD Carlos Delgado 4.00 10.00
CF Carlton Fisk 6.00 15.00
CR Cal Ripken 15.00 40.00
JB Jeff Bagwell 6.00 15.00
JCA Jose Canseco 6.00 15.00
JOC Joe Carter 4.00 10.00
KGI Kirk Gibson 4.00 10.00
MMA M.Mantle Pants SP/50 150.00 250.00
MP Mike Piazza 6.00 15.00
MR Manny Ramirez 6.00 15.00
SGA Steve Garvey 4.00 10.00
SGR Shawn Green 4.00 10.00
SS Sammy Sosa 6.00 15.00
WB Wade Boggs 6.00 15.00
WS Willie Stargell 6.00 15.00

2005 UD Portraits

COMMON CARD (1-100) .40 1.00
COMMON RC YR .40 1.00
COMMON RETIRED .40 1.00
1 Dallas McPherson .40 1.00
2 Steve Finley .40 1.00
3 Vladimir Guerrero .60 1.50
4 Troy Glaus .40 1.00
5 Andruw Jones .40 1.00
6 Chipper Jones 1.00 2.50
7 John Smoltz 1.00 2.50
8 Marcus Giles .40 1.00
9 Tim Hudson .60 1.50
10 Cal Ripken 3.00 8.00
11 Miguel Tejada .60 1.50
12 Curt Schilling .60 1.50
13 David Ortiz 1.00 2.50
14 Edgar Renteria .40 1.00
15 Jason Varitek 1.00 2.50
16 Jim Rice .60 1.50
17 Johnny Damon .60 1.50
18 Matt Clement .40 1.00
19 Wade Boggs .60 1.50
20 Aramis Ramirez .40 1.00
21 Carlos Zambrano .60 1.50
22 Corey Patterson .40 1.00
23 Fergie Jenkins .60 1.50
24 Greg Maddux 1.25 3.00
25 Kerry Wood .40 1.00
26 Mark Prior .60 1.50
27 Nomar Garciaparra .60 1.50
28 Ryne Sandberg 2.00 5.00
29 Frank Thomas 1.00 2.50
30 Adam Dunn .60 1.50
31 Barry Larkin .60 1.50
32 Ken Griffey Jr. 2.00 5.00
33 Sean Casey .40 1.00
34 Travis Hafner .40 1.00
35 Victor Martinez .60 1.50
36 Todd Helton .60 1.50
37 Ivan Rodriguez .60 1.50
38 Magglio Ordonez .60 1.50
39 Josh Beckett .40 1.00
40 Miguel Cabrera 1.00 2.50
41 Mike Lowell .40 1.00
42 Craig Biggio .60 1.50
43 Jeff Bagwell .60 1.50
44 Roger Clemens 1.25 3.00
45 Roy Oswalt .60 1.50
46 Bo Jackson 1.00 2.50
47 Prince Fielder RC 2.00 5.00
48 Eric Gagne .40 1.00
49 J.D. Drew .40 1.00
50 Ben Sheets .40 1.00
51 Robin Yount 1.00 2.50
52 Jacque Jones .40 1.00
53 Joe Mauer .75 2.00
54 Johan Santana .60 1.50
55 Justin Morneau .60 1.50
56 Torii Hunter .40 1.00
57 Dontrelle Willis .40 1.00
58 David Wright .75 2.00
59 Gary Carter .60 1.50
60 Jose Reyes .60 1.50
61 Keith Hernandez .40 1.00
62 Mike Piazza 1.00 2.50
63 Pedro Martinez .60 1.50
64 Tom Glavine .60 1.50
65 Carl Pavano .40 1.00
66 Derek Jeter 2.50 6.00
67 Don Mattingly 2.00 5.00
68 Mike Mussina .60 1.50
69 Randy Johnson 1.00 2.50
70 Bobby Crosby .40 1.00
71 Eric Chavez .40 1.00
72 Rich Harden .40 1.00
73 Bobby Abreu .40 1.00
74 Mike Schmidt 1.50 4.00
75 Jason Bay .40 1.00
76 Oliver Perez .40 1.00
77 Brian Giles .40 1.00
78 Jake Peavy .40 1.00
79 Khalil Greene .40 1.00
80 Tony Gwynn 1.25 3.00
81 Jason Schmidt .40 1.00
82 Will Clark .60 1.50
83 Adrian Beltre 1.00 2.50
84 Justin Verlander RC 8.00 20.00
85 Albert Pujols 1.25 3.00
86 Jim Edmonds .60 1.50
87 Mark Mulder .40 1.00
88 Scott Rolen .60 1.50
89 Aubrey Huff .40 1.00
90 B.J. Upton .60 1.50
91 Carl Crawford .60 1.50
92 Tadahito Iguchi RC .60 1.50
93 Scott Kazmir 1.00 2.50
94 Alfonso Soriano .60 1.50
95 Hank Blalock .40 1.00
96 Mark Teixeira .60 1.50
97 Michael Young .40 1.00
98 Nolan Ryan 3.00 8.00
99 Roy Halladay .60 1.50
100 Jose Vidro .40 1.00

2005 UD Portraits Jersey Emerald

STATED PRINT RUN 99 SERIAL #'d SETS
*BLUE: .6X TO 1.5X BASIC
BLUE PRINT RUN 25 SERIAL #'d SETS
*GOLD: .75X TO 2X BASIC
GOLD PRINT RUN 15 SERIAL #'d SETS
OVERALL GU PARALLEL ODDS 1:1
1 Dallas McPherson 3.00 8.00
2 Steve Finley 3.00 8.00
3 Vladimir Guerrero 4.00 10.00
4 Troy Glaus 3.00 8.00
5 Andruw Jones 4.00 10.00
6 Chipper Jones 4.00 10.00
7 John Smoltz 4.00 10.00
8 Marcus Giles 3.00 8.00
9 Tim Hudson 3.00 8.00
10 Cal Ripken 10.00 25.00
11 Miguel Tejada 3.00 8.00
12 Curt Schilling 4.00 10.00
13 David Ortiz 4.00 10.00
14 Edgar Renteria 3.00 8.00
15 Jason Varitek 4.00 10.00
16 Jim Rice 3.00 8.00
17 Johnny Damon 4.00 10.00
18 Matt Clement 3.00 8.00
19 Wade Boggs 4.00 10.00
20 Aramis Ramirez 3.00 8.00
21 Carlos Zambrano 3.00 8.00
22 Corey Patterson 3.00 8.00
23 Fergie Jenkins 3.00 8.00
24 Greg Maddux 4.00 10.00
25 Kerry Wood 3.00 8.00
26 Mark Prior 4.00 10.00
27 Nomar Garciaparra 4.00 10.00
28 Ryne Sandberg 6.00 15.00
29 Frank Thomas 4.00 10.00
30 Adam Dunn 3.00 8.00
31 Barry Larkin 4.00 10.00
32 Ken Griffey Jr. 6.00 15.00
33 Sean Casey 3.00 8.00
34 Travis Hafner 3.00 8.00
35 Victor Martinez 3.00 8.00
36 Todd Helton 4.00 10.00
37 Ivan Rodriguez 4.00 10.00
38 Magglio Ordonez 3.00 8.00
39 Josh Beckett 3.00 8.00
40 Miguel Cabrera 4.00 10.00
41 Mike Lowell 3.00 8.00
42 Craig Biggio 4.00 10.00
43 Jeff Bagwell 4.00 10.00
44 Roger Clemens Pants 4.00 10.00
45 Roy Oswalt 3.00 8.00
46 Bo Jackson 4.00 10.00
48 Eric Gagne 3.00 8.00
49 J.D. Drew 3.00 8.00
50 Ben Sheets 3.00 8.00
51 Robin Yount 4.00 10.00
52 Jacque Jones 3.00 8.00
53 Joe Mauer 4.00 10.00
54 Johan Santana 4.00 10.00
55 Justin Morneau 3.00 8.00
56 Torii Hunter 3.00 8.00
57 Dontrelle Willis 3.00 8.00
58 David Wright 4.00 10.00
59 Gary Carter 3.00 8.00
60 Jose Reyes 3.00 8.00
61 Keith Hernandez 3.00 8.00
62 Mike Piazza 4.00 10.00
63 Pedro Martinez 4.00 10.00
64 Tom Glavine 4.00 10.00
65 Carl Pavano 3.00 8.00
66 Derek Jeter 10.00 25.00
67 Don Mattingly 6.00 15.00
68 Mike Mussina 4.00 10.00
69 Randy Johnson 4.00 10.00
70 Bobby Crosby 3.00 8.00
71 Eric Chavez 3.00 8.00
72 Rich Harden 3.00 8.00
73 Bobby Abreu 3.00 8.00
74 Mike Schmidt 6.00 15.00
75 Jason Bay 3.00 8.00
76 Oliver Perez 3.00 8.00
77 Brian Giles 3.00 8.00
78 Jake Peavy 3.00 8.00
79 Khalil Greene 4.00 10.00
80 Tony Gwynn 4.00 10.00
81 Jason Schmidt 3.00 8.00
82 Will Clark 4.00 10.00
83 Adrian Beltre 3.00 8.00
85 Albert Pujols 6.00 15.00
86 Jim Edmonds 3.00 8.00
87 Mark Mulder 3.00 8.00
88 Scott Rolen 4.00 10.00
89 Aubrey Huff 3.00 8.00
90 B.J. Upton 3.00 8.00
91 Carl Crawford 3.00 8.00
92 Tadahito Iguchi 6.00 15.00
93 Scott Kazmir 3.00 8.00
94 Alfonso Soriano 3.00 8.00
95 Hank Blalock 3.00 8.00
96 Mark Teixeira 4.00 10.00
97 Michael Young 3.00 8.00
98 Nolan Ryan Pants 6.00 15.00
99 Roy Halladay 3.00 8.00
100 Jose Vidro 3.00 8.00

2005 UD Portraits Scrapbook Materials

STATED ODDS ONE PER PACK
AB Adrian Beltre Jsy 2.00 5.00
AJ Andruw Jones Jsy 3.00 8.00
AP Albert Pujols Jsy 6.00 15.00
BA Bobby Abreu Jsy 2.00 5.00
BC Bobby Crosby Jsy 2.00 5.00
BE Josh Beckett Jsy 2.00 5.00
BG Brian Giles Jsy 2.00 5.00
BI Craig Biggio Jsy 3.00 8.00
BJ Bo Jackson Jsy 4.00 10.00
BL Barry Larkin Jsy 3.00 8.00
BU B.J. Upton Jsy 2.00 5.00
CA Miguel Cabrera Jsy 3.00 8.00
CJ Chipper Jones Jsy 3.00 8.00
CL Matt Clement Jsy 2.00 5.00
CP Carl Pavano Jsy 2.00 5.00
CR Cal Ripken Jsy 8.00 20.00
CZ Carlos Zambrano Jsy 2.00 5.00
DJ Derek Jeter Jsy 8.00 20.00
DM Dale Murphy Jsy 3.00 8.00
DO David Ortiz Jsy 3.00 8.00
DW David Wright Jsy 4.00 10.00
FT Frank Thomas Jsy 3.00 8.00
GR Khalil Greene Jsy 3.00 8.00
HU Torii Hunter Jsy 2.00 5.00
JB Jeff Bagwell 3.00 8.00
JE Jim Edmonds Jsy 2.00 5.00
JJ Jacque Jones Jsy 2.00 5.00
JM Joe Mauer Jsy 3.00 8.00
JP Jake Peavy Jsy 2.00 5.00
JR Jim Rice Jsy 2.00 5.00
JS Jason Schmidt Jsy 2.00 5.00
JV Jose Vidro Jsy 2.00 5.00
KG Ken Griffey Jr. Jsy 6.00 15.00
KH Keith Hernandez Jsy 2.00 5.00
MA Don Mattingly Jsy 6.00 15.00
MC Dallas McPherson Jsy 2.00 5.00
ML Mike Lowell Jsy 2.00 5.00
MM Mike Mussina Jsy 3.00 8.00
MO Justin Morneau Jsy 2.00 5.00
MP Mark Prior Jsy 3.00 8.00
MS Mike Schmidt Jsy 6.00 15.00
MT Mark Teixeira Jsy 3.00 8.00
NR Nolan Ryan Pants 6.00 15.00
OP Oliver Perez Jsy 2.00 5.00
OR Magglio Ordonez Jsy 2.00 5.00
PA Corey Patterson Jsy 2.00 5.00
RH Roy Halladay Jsy 2.00 5.00
RS Ryne Sandberg Jsy 6.00 15.00
SA Johan Santana Jsy 3.00 8.00
SF Steve Finley Jsy 2.00 5.00
SK Scott Kazmir Jsy 2.00 5.00
SM John Smoltz Jsy 3.00 8.00
TG Tony Gwynn Jsy 4.00 10.00
TH Todd Helton Jsy 3.00 8.00
VM Victor Martinez Jsy 2.00 5.00
WC Will Clark Jsy 3.00 8.00
WI Dontrelle Willis Jsy 2.00 5.00

2005 UD Portraits Scrapbook Moments

STATED ODDS ONE PER PACK
STATED PRINT RUN 250 SERIAL #'d SET
AB Adrian Beltre 2.00 5.00
AJ Andruw Jones .75 2.00
AP Albert Pujols 2.50 6.00
BA Bobby Abreu .75 2.00
BC Bobby Crosby .75 2.00
BE Josh Beckett .75 2.00
BG Brian Giles .75 2.00
BI Craig Biggio 1.25 3.00
BJ Bo Jackson 2.00 5.00
BL Barry Larkin 1.25 3.00
BU B.J. Upton 1.25 3.00
CA Miguel Cabrera 2.00 5.00
CJ Chipper Jones 2.00 5.00
CL Matt Clement .75 2.00
CP Carl Pavano .75 2.00
CR Cal Ripken 6.00 15.00
CZ Carlos Zambrano 1.25 3.00
DJ Derek Jeter 5.00 12.00
DM Dale Murphy 2.00 5.00
DO David Ortiz 2.00 5.00
DW David Wright 1.50 4.00
FT Frank Thomas 2.00 5.00
GR Khalil Greene .75 2.00
HU Torii Hunter .75 2.00
JB Jeff Bagwell 1.25 3.00
JE Jim Edmonds 1.25 3.00
JJ Jacque Jones .75 2.00
JM Joe Mauer 1.50 4.00
JP Jake Peavy .75 2.00
JR Jim Rice 1.25 3.00
JS Jason Schmidt .75 2.00
JV Jose Vidro .75 2.00
KG Ken Griffey Jr. 4.00 10.00
KH Keith Hernandez .75 2.00
MA Don Mattingly 4.00 10.00
MC Dallas McPherson .75 2.00
ML Mike Lowell .75 2.00
MM Mike Mussina 1.25 3.00
MO Justin Morneau 1.25 3.00
MP Mark Prior 1.25 3.00
MS Mike Schmidt 3.00 8.00
MT Mark Teixeira 1.25 3.00
NR Nolan Ryan 6.00 15.00
OP Oliver Perez .75 2.00
OR Magglio Ordonez 1.25 3.00
PA Corey Patterson .75 2.00
PF Prince Fielder 4.00 10.00
RC Roger Clemens 2.50 6.00
RH Roy Halladay 1.25 3.00
RS Ryne Sandberg 4.00 10.00
SA Johan Santana 1.25 3.00
SF Steve Finley .75 2.00
SK Scott Kazmir 2.00 5.00
SM John Smoltz 2.00 5.00
TG Tony Gwynn 2.50 6.00
TH Todd Helton 1.25 3.00
VE Justin Verlander 15.00 40.00
VM Victor Martinez 1.25 3.00
WC Will Clark 1.25 3.00
WI Dontrelle Willis .75 2.00

2005 UD Portraits Signature Portraits Auto 8 x 10

OVERALL 8 X 10 AUTO ODDS 1:1
SP PRINT RUNS PROVIDED BY UD
SP'S ARE NOT SERIAL-NUMBERED
NO PRICING ON QTY OF 25
BR Brooks Robinson 15.00 40.00
BS Ben Sheets 10.00 25.00
BU B.J. Upton 10.00 25.00
CA Miguel Cabrera 40.00 80.00
CR Cal Ripken SP/50 * 100.00 175.00
DB Dusty Baker SP/100 * 10.00 25.00
DJ Derek Jeter SP/150 * 75.00 150.00
DM Dale Murphy 12.50 30.00
DS Duke Snider SP/150 * 15.00 40.00
DW David Wright 10.00 25.00
GR Khalil Greene 15.00 40.00
HB Hank Blalock 10.00 25.00
JB Jason Bay 10.00 25.00
JD Johnny Damon SP/99 * 30.00 60.00
JM Joe Mauer 15.00 40.00
JN Jeff Niemann 6.00 15.00
KH Keith Hernandez 10.00 25.00
MA Don Mattingly 30.00 60.00
MS Mike Schmidt 20.00 50.00
MT Mark Teixeira 12.50 30.00
OS Ozzie Smith 20.00 50.00
PI Mike Piazza SP/35 * 90.00 150.00
RO Roy Oswalt 10.00 25.00
RS Ryne Sandberg SP/99 * 40.00 80.00
SK Scott Kazmir 10.00 25.00
SM Stan Musial SP/40 * 60.00 120.00
VE Justin Verlander 50.00 100.00
VG Vladimir Guerrero SP/40 * 40.00 80.00
VM Victor Martinez 10.00 25.00
WB Wade Boggs SP/40 * 30.00 60.00

2005 UD Portraits Signature Portraits Auto Dual 8 x 10

OVERALL 8 X 10 AUTO ODDS 1:1
PRINT RUNS B/WN 25-99 COPIES PER
NO PRICING ON QTY OF 25
EXCHANGE DEADLINE 10/25/08
BT H.Blalock/M.Teixeira/99 10.00 25.00
HS B.Sheets/R.Harden/99 20.00 50.00
NV J.Niemann/J.Verlander/99 30.00 60.00
SH J.Smoltz/T.Hudson/75 40.00 80.00
WP K.Wood/M.Prior/99 40.00 80.00
WR D.Wright/J.Reyes/99 100.00 150.00

2001 UD Reserve

COMP.SET w/o SP's (180) 10.00 25.00
COMMON CARD (1-180) .10 .30
COMMON CARD (181-210) 1.50 4.00
181-210 RANDOM INSERTS IN PACKS
181-210 PRINT RUN 2500 SERIAL #'d SETS
1 Darin Erstad .10 .30
2 Tim Salmon .20 .50
3 Bengie Molina .10 .30
4 Troy Glaus .10 .30
5 Glenallen Hill .10 .30
6 Garret Anderson .10 .30
7 Jason Giambi .10 .30
8 Johnny Damon .20 .50
9 Eric Chavez .10 .30
10 Tim Hudson .10 .30
11 Miguel Tejada .10 .30
12 Barry Zito .20 .50
13 Jose Ortiz .10 .30
14 Tony Batista .10 .30
15 Carlos Delgado .10 .30
16 Shannon Stewart .10 .30
17 Raul Mondesi .10 .30
18 Ben Grieve .10 .30
19 Aubrey Huff .10 .30
20 Greg Vaughn .10 .30
21 Fred McGriff .20 .50
22 Gerald Williams .10 .30
23 Bartolo Colon .10 .30
24 Roberto Alomar .20 .50
25 Jim Thome .20 .50
26 Omar Vizquel .20 .50
27 Juan Gonzalez .10 .30
28 Ellis Burks .10 .30
29 Edgar Martinez .20 .50
30 Aaron Sele .10 .30
31 Jay Buhner .10 .30
32 Mike Cameron .10 .30
33 Kazuhiro Sasaki .10 .30
34 John Olerud .10 .30
35 Cal Ripken 1.00 2.50
36 Brady Anderson .10 .30
37 Pat Hentgen .10 .30
38 Chris Richard .10 .30
39 Jerry Hairston Jr. .10 .30
40 Mike Bordick .10 .30
41 Ivan Rodriguez .20 .50
42 Rick Helling .10 .30
43 Rafael Palmeiro .20 .50
44 Alex Rodriguez .40 1.00
45 Andres Galarraga .10 .30
46 Rusty Greer .10 .30
47 Ruben Mateo .10 .30
48 Ken Caminiti .10 .30
49 Nomar Garciaparra .50 1.25
50 Pedro Martinez .20 .50
51 Manny Ramirez Sox .20 .50
52 Carl Everett .10 .30
53 Dante Bichette .10 .30
54 Hideo Nomo .30 .75
55 Mike Sweeney .10 .30
56 Carlos Beltran .10 .30
57 Jeff Suppan .10 .30
58 Jermaine Dye .10 .30
59 Mark Quinn .10 .30
60 Joe Randa .10 .30
61 Bobby Higginson .10 .30
62 Tony Clark .10 .30
63 Brian Moehler .10 .30
64 Dean Palmer .10 .30
65 Brandon Inge .10 .30
66 Damion Easley .10 .30
67 Brad Radke .10 .30
68 Corey Koskie .10 .30
69 Cristian Guzman .10 .30
70 Eric Milton .10 .30
71 Jacque Jones .10 .30
72 Matt Lawton .10 .30
73 Frank Thomas .30 .75
74 David Wells .10 .30
75 Magglio Ordonez .10 .30
76 Paul Konerko .10 .30
77 Sandy Alomar Jr. .10 .30
78 Ray Durham .10 .30
79 Roger Clemens .60 1.50
80 Bernie Williams .20 .50
81 Derek Jeter .75 2.00
82 David Justice .10 .30
83 Paul O'Neill .20 .50
84 Mike Mussina .20 .50
85 Jorge Posada .20 .50
86 Jeff Bagwell .20 .50
87 Richard Hidalgo .10 .30
88 Craig Biggio .20 .50
89 Scott Elarton .10 .30
90 Moises Alou .10 .30
91 Greg Maddux .50 1.25
92 Rafael Furcal .10 .30
93 Andruw Jones .20 .50
94 Tom Glavine .20 .50
95 Chipper Jones .30 .75
96 Javy Lopez .10 .30
97 Richie Sexson .10 .30
98 Jeromy Burnitz .10 .30
99 Jeff D'Amico .10 .30
100 Jeffrey Hammonds .10 .30
101 Geoff Jenkins .10 .30
102 Ben Sheets .20 .50
103 Mark McGwire .75 2.00
104 Rick Ankiel .10 .30
105 Darryl Kile .10 .30
106 Edgar Renteria .10 .30
107 Jim Edmonds .10 .30
108 J.D. Drew .10 .30
109 Sammy Sosa .30 .75
110 Corey Patterson .10 .30
111 Kerry Wood .10 .30
112 Todd Hundley .10 .30
113 Rondell White .10 .30
114 Matt Stairs .10 .30
115 Randy Johnson .30 .75
116 Mark Grace .20 .50
117 Steve Finley .10 .30
118 Luis Gonzalez .10 .30
119 Matt Williams .10 .30
120 Curt Schilling .10 .30
121 Gary Sheffield .10 .30
122 Kevin Brown .10 .30
123 Shawn Green .10 .30
124 Eric Karros .10 .30
125 Chan Ho Park .10 .30
126 Adrian Beltre .10 .30
127 Vladimir Guerrero .30 .75
128 Fernando Tatis .10 .30
129 Lee Stevens .10 .30
130 Jose Vidro .10 .30
131 Peter Bergeron .10 .30
132 Michael Barrett .10 .30
133 Jeff Kent .10 .30
134 Russ Ortiz .10 .30
135 Barry Bonds .75 2.00
136 J.T. Snow .10 .30
137 Livan Hernandez .10 .30
138 Rich Aurilia .10 .30
139 Preston Wilson .10 .30
140 Mike Lowell .10 .30
141 Ryan Dempster .10 .30
142 Charles Johnson .10 .30
143 Matt Clement .10 .30
144 Luis Castillo .10 .30
145 Mike Piazza .50 1.25
146 Al Leiter .10 .30
147 Robin Ventura .10 .30
148 Jay Payton .10 .30
149 Todd Zeile .10 .30
150 Edgardo Alfonzo .10 .30
151 Tony Gwynn .40 1.00
152 Ryan Klesko .10 .30
153 Phil Nevin .10 .30
154 Mark Kotsay .10 .30
155 Trevor Hoffman .10 .30
156 Damian Jackson .10 .30
157 Scott Rolen .20 .50
158 Mike Lieberthal .10 .30
159 Bruce Chen .10 .30
160 Bobby Abreu .10 .30
161 Pat Burrell .10 .30
162 Travis Lee .10 .30
163 Jason Kendall .10 .30
164 Derek Bell .10 .30
165 Kris Benson .10 .30
166 Kevin Young .10 .30
167 Brian Giles .10 .30
168 Pat Meares .10 .30
169 Sean Casey .10 .30
170 Pokey Reese .10 .30
171 Pete Harnisch .10 .30
172 Barry Larkin .20 .50
173 Ken Griffey Jr. .60 1.50
174 Dmitri Young .10 .30
175 Mike Hampton .10 .30
176 Todd Helton .20 .50
177 Jeff Cirillo .10 .30
178 Denny Neagle .10 .30
179 Larry Walker .10 .30
180 Todd Hollandsworth .10 .30
181 Ichiro Suzuki SP RC 10.00 25.00
182 Wilson Betemit SP RC 2.00 5.00
183 Adrian Hernandez SP RC 1.50 4.00
184 Travis Hafner SP RC 4.00 10.00
185 Sean Douglass SP RC 1.50 4.00
186 Juan Diaz SP RC 1.50 4.00
187 Horacio Ramirez SP RC 2.00 5.00
188 Morgan Ensberg SP RC 2.00 5.00
189 Brandon Duckworth SP RC 1.50 4.00
190 Jack Wilson SP RC 2.00 5.00
191 Erick Almonte SP RC 1.50 4.00
192 Ricardo Rodriguez SP RC 1.50 4.00
193 Elpidio Guzman SP RC 1.50 4.00
194 Juan Uribe SP RC 2.00 5.00
195 Ryan Freel SP RC 2.00 5.00
196 Christian Parker SP RC 1.50 4.00
197 Jackson Melian SP RC 1.50 4.00
198 Jose Mieses SP RC 1.50 4.00
199 Andres Torres SP RC 1.50 4.00
200 Jason Smith SP RC 1.50 4.00
201 Johnny Estrada SP RC 2.00 5.00
202 Cesar Crespo SP RC 1.50 4.00
203 Carlos Valderrama SP RC 1.50 4.00
204 Albert Pujols SP RC 25.00 60.00
205 Wilkin Ruan SP RC 1.50 4.00
206 Josh Fogg SP RC 1.50 4.00
207 Bert Snow SP RC 1.50 4.00
208 Brian Lawrence SP RC 1.50 4.00
209 Esix Snead SP RC 1.50 4.00
210 Tsuyoshi Shinjo SP RC 2.00 5.00

2001 UD Reserve Ball-Base Duos

STATED ODDS 1:240
BBH B.Bonds/T.Helton 15.00 40.00
BCR R.Clemens/A.Rodriguez 12.00 30.00
BGD V.Guerrero/C.Delgado 8.00 20.00
BGJ K.Griffey Jr./D.Jeter 8.00 20.00
BGR N.Garciaparra/A.Rodriguez 12.00 30.00
BGS K.Griffey Jr./S.Sosa 12.00 30.00
BJN C.Jones/N.Garciaparra 10.00 25.00
BJP D.Jeter/M.Piazza 10.00 25.00
BJR D.Jeter/A.Rodriguez 10.00 25.00
BMG M.McGwire/K.Griffey Jr. 20.00 50.00
BMJ M.McGwire/D.Jeter 30.00 60.00
BMP M.McGwire/M.Piazza 10.00 25.00
BNJ N.Garciaparra/D.Jeter 15.00 40.00
BRM A.Rodriguez/M.McGwire 15.00 40.00
BST S.Sosa/F.Thomas 8.00 20.00

2001 UD Reserve Ball-Base Quads

STATED PRINT RUN 50 SERIAL #'d SETS
GBJE Griffey/Bonds/Jones/Edm 15.00 40.00
GPJG Vlad/Piazza/Chipper/Nomar 40.00 80.00
PMJR Piazza/McGwire/Jeter/Arod 75.00 150.00
SGRM Arod/Griffey/Sosa/McGwire 30.00 60.00
THMJ Thomas/Helt/McGire/Jeter 60.00 120.00

2001 UD Reserve Ball-Base Trios

STATED ODDS 1:480
BSH Bonds/Sheffield/Helton 10.00 25.00
CMJ Clemens/Pedro/Jeter 30.00 60.00
GPJ Guerrero/Piazza/Chipper 12.00 30.00
GSG Griffey/Sosa/Guerrero 10.00 25.00
JGS Jeter/Griffey/Sosa 15.00 40.00
JRG Jeter/A-Rod/Garciaparra 15.00 40.00
MJR McGwire/Jeter/A-Rod 50.00 100.00
PRS Piazza/A-Rod/Sosa 30.00 60.00
SGM Sosa/Griffey/McGwire 20.00 50.00
THM Thomas/Helton/McGwire 10.00 25.00

2001 UD Reserve Big Game

COMPLETE SET (10) 20.00 50.00
STATED ODDS 1:24
BG1 Alex Rodriguez 1.50 4.00
BG2 Ken Griffey Jr. 2.50 6.00
BG3 Mark McGwire 3.00 8.00
BG4 Derek Jeter 3.00 8.00
BG5 Sammy Sosa 1.25 3.00
BG6 Pedro Martinez .75 2.00
BG7 Jason Giambi .75 2.00
BG8 Todd Helton .75 2.00
BG9 Carlos Delgado .75 2.00
BG10 Mike Piazza 2.00 5.00

2001 UD Reserve Game Jersey Duos

STATED ODDS 1:240
JBK B.Bonds/J.Kent 12.00 30.00
JDG C.Delgado/J.Giambi 6.00 15.00
JGE T.Glaus/D.Erstad 6.00 15.00
JGK J.Giambi/J.Kent 6.00 15.00
JGW B.Giles/B.Williams 10.00 25.00
JHE T.Helton/D.Erstad 10.00 25.00
JHG T.Hudson/J.Giambi 6.00 15.00
JJG C.Jones/T.Glaus 10.00 25.00
JJJ A.Jones/C.Jones 10.00 25.00
JJW R.Johnson/D.Wells 10.00 25.00
JRB A.Rodriguez/T.Batista 15.00 40.00
JSB G.Sheffield/B.Bonds 10.00 25.00
JSG S.Sosa/T.Glaus 10.00 25.00
JWE B.Williams/J.Edmonds 10.00 25.00
JWO D.Wells/M.Ordonez 6.00 15.00

2001 UD Reserve Game Jersey Quads

STATED ODDS 1:480
RGS Delg/Arod/Glaus/Sosa 40.00 80.00
WBG Giambi/Williams/Bonds/Giles 30.00 60.00
HKEJ Helt/Kent/Edm/Jones 20.00 50.00
JRSB Jones/Arod/Sosa/Bonds 20.00 50.00
SOEB Sheff/Ordnz/Erst/Batist 10.00 25.00

2001 UD Reserve Game Jersey Trios

STATED ODDS 1:480
JBSH Bonds/Sheffield/Helton 10.00 25.00
JBWD Batista/Bernie/Delg 15.00 40.00
JEKE Erstad/Kent/Edmonds 10.00 25.00
JGGR Giambi/Glaus/A-Rod 15.00 40.00
JGHD Giambi/Helton/Delg 15.00 40.00
JHJW Huds/R.John/Wells 15.00 40.00
JRSS A-Rod/Sosa/Sheff 20.00 50.00
JSOD Sosa/M.Ord/Delg 15.00 40.00
JWEJ Bernie/Edm/Andruw 15.00 40.00
JWSH D.Wells/Sosa/Helt 15.00 40.00

2001 UD Reserve New Order

COMPLETE SET (10) 20.00 50.00
STATED ODDS 1:24
NO1 Vladimir Guerrero 1.25 3.00
NO2 Andruw Jones .75 2.00
NO3 Corey Patterson .50 1.25
NO4 Derek Jeter 3.00 8.00
NO5 Alex Rodriguez 1.50 4.00
NO6 Pat Burrell .50 1.25
NO7 Ichiro Suzuki 10.00 25.00
NO8 Barry Zito .75 2.00
NO9 Rafael Furcal .50 1.25
NO10 Troy Glaus .50 1.25

2001 UD Reserve Royalty

COMPLETE SET (10) 20.00 50.00
STATED ODDS 1:24
R1 Ken Griffey Jr. 2.50 6.00
R2 Derek Jeter 3.00 8.00
R3 Alex Rodriguez 1.50 4.00
R4 Sammy Sosa 1.25 3.00
R5 Mark McGwire 3.00 8.00
R6 Mike Piazza 2.00 5.00
R7 Vladimir Guerrero 1.25 3.00
R8 Chipper Jones 1.25 3.00
R9 Frank Thomas 1.25 3.00
R10 Nomar Garciaparra 2.00 5.00

2004 UD Rivals

COMP.FACT.SET (32) 15.00 25.00
COMMON CARD (1-15) .20 .50
COMMON DUAL (16-30) .20 .50
ONE 5-PLAYER JUMBO CARD PER BOX
ONE WHAT IF CARD PER BOX
ISSUED ONLY IN FACTORY SET FORM
1 Alex Rodriguez .60 1.50
2 Bobby Doerr .30 .75
3 Don Mattingly 1.00 2.50
4 Dwight Evans .20 .50
5 Fred Lynn .20 .50
6 Jason Giambi .20 .50
7 Jim Rice .30 .75
8 Lou Gehrig 1.00 2.50
9 Luis Tiant .20 .50
10 Manny Ramirez .50 1.25
11 Mike Mussina .30 .75
12 Pedro Martinez .30 .75
13 Phil Rizzuto .30 .75
14 Whitey Ford .30 .75
15 Yogi Berra .50 1.25
16 A.Boone .30 .75
T.Wakefield
17 B.Martin .30 .75
D.Zimmer
18 B.Dent .20 .50
M.Torrez
19 D.Jeter 1.25 3.00
N.Garciaparra
20 G.Sheffield .30 .75
C.Schilling
21 J.DiMaggio 1.00 2.50
D.Newsome
22 J.DiMaggio 1.00 2.50
L.Grove
23 J.DiMaggio 1.00 2.50
T.Williams
24 J.Posada .50 1.25
J.Varitek
25 M.Mantle 1.50 4.00
C.Yastrzemski
26 R.Maris .50 1.25
T.Stallard
27 T.Munson .50 1.25
C.Fisk
28 Babe Ruth Sox-Yanks 1.25 3.00
29 Roger Clemens Sox-Yanks .60 1.50
30 Wade Boggs Sox-Yanks .30 .75
NNO 5-Player Jumbo 1.50 4.00

2004 UD Rivals What If Peter Gammons

ONE PER SEALED FACTORY SET
STATED PRINT RUN 2150 SERIAL #'d SETS
1 A.Boone .50 1.25
P.Gammons
2 A.Rodriguez 1.50 4.00
P.Gammons
3 B.Ruth 3.00 8.00
P.Gammons
4 B.Ruth 3.00 8.00
P.Gammons
5 B.Martin MG .75 2.00
P.Gammons
6 B.Dent .50 1.25
P.Gammons
7 C.Yastrzemski 1.25 3.00
P.Gammons
8 C.Fisk .75 2.00
P.Gammons
9 D.Jeter 3.00 8.00
P.Gammons
10 H.Matsui 2.00 5.00
P.Gammons
11 J.DiMaggio 2.50 6.00
P.Gammons
12 J.Torre MG .75 2.00
P.Gammons
13 M.Mantle 4.00 10.00
P.Gammons
14 P.Martinez .75 2.00
P.Gammons
15 P.Reese .75 2.00
P.Gammons
16 R.Clemens 1.50 4.00
P.Gammons
17 R.Maris 1.25 3.00
P.Gammons
18 T.Williams 2.50 6.00
P.Gammons
19 T.Williams 2.50 6.00
P.Gammons
20 C.Yastrzemski 3.00 8.00
P.Gammons

2002-03 UD SuperStars

COMPLETE SET (300) 30.00 80.00
2 Troy Glaus .15 .40
3 Darin Erstad .15 .40
4 Garret Anderson .15 .40
5 Jarrod Washburn .15 .40
7 Randy Johnson .25 .60
8 Curt Schilling .20 .50
9 Luis Gonzalez .15 .40
14 Tom Glavine .25 .60
15 Chipper Jones .40 1.00
16 Greg Maddux .60 1.50
17 Andruw Jones .20 .50
18 John Smoltz .25 .60
19 Gary Sheffield .15 .40
23 Cal Ripken 1.25 3.00
24 Jay Gibbons .15 .40
25 Tony Batista .15 .40
27 Nomar Garciaparra .25 .60
28 Pedro Martinez .20 .50
29 Manny Ramirez .25 .60
30 Derek Lowe .15 .40
31 Cliff Floyd .15 .40
32 Shea Hillenbrand .15 .40
33 Johnny Damon .25 .60
42 Sammy Sosa .40 1.00
43 Mark Prior .15 .40
44 Kerry Wood .20 .50
45 Fred McGriff .25 .60
46 Corey Patterson .15 .40
47 Paul Konerko .15 .40
48 Frank Thomas .25 .60
49 Magglio Ordonez .15 .40
50 Carlos Lee .15 .40
51 Mark Buehrle .15 .40
55 Ken Griffey Jr. .75 2.00
56 Austin Kearns .15 .40
57 Adam Dunn .15 .40
58 Aaron Boone .15 .40
59 Sean Casey .15 .40
61 C.C. Sabathia .20 .50
62 Omar Vizquel .20 .50
64 Todd Helton .25 .60
65 Larry Walker .15 .40
66 Juan Pierre .15 .40
76 Alex Rodriguez .60 1.50
77 Ivan Rodriguez .25 .60
78 Juan Gonzalez .15 .40
79 Rafael Palmeiro .20 .50
80 Hank Blalock .25 .60
85 Preston Wilson .15 .40
86 Josh Beckett .25 .60
87 Luis Castillo .15 .40
88 A.J. Burnett .15 .40
89 Mike Lowell .20 .50
94 Richie Sexson .15 .40
95 Geoff Jenkins .15 .40
96 Ben Sheets .15 .40
98 Roy Oswalt .20 .50
99 Richard Hidalgo .15 .40
100 Jeff Bagwell .25 .60
101 Lance Berkman .20 .50
102 Craig Biggio .25 .60
109 Mike Sweeney .15 .40
110 Carlos Beltran .20 .50
113 Hideo Nomo .25 .60
114 Shawn Green .15 .40
115 Kevin Brown .15 .40
116 Brian Jordan .15 .40
117 Eric Gagne .15 .40
118 Adrian Beltre .15 .40
127 Torii Hunter .15 .40
128 Corey Koskie .15 .40
129 Doug Mientkiewicz .15 .40
130 Eric Milton .15 .40
131 Jacque Jones .15 .40
135 Vladimir Guerrero .25 .60
136 Bartolo Colon .15 .40
137 Jose Vidro .15 .40
145 Derek Jeter 1.00 2.50
146 Alfonso Soriano .20 .50
147 Mike Mussina .25 .60
148 Jason Giambi .20 .50
149 Robin Ventura .15 .40
150 Roger Clemens .25 .60
151 Bernie Williams .20 .50
152 Mickey Mantle 1.50 4.00
153 Joe DiMaggio .75 2.00
154 Raul Mondesi .15 .40
155 Mariano Rivera .25 .60
156 Hideki Matsui 2.00 5.00
157 Mike Piazza .25 .60
158 Roberto Alomar .25 .60
159 Edgardo Alfonzo .15 .40
160 Jeromy Burnitz .15 .40
161 Armando Benitez .15 .40
162 Mo Vaughn .15 .40
168 Eric Chavez .15 .40
169 Miguel Tejada .20 .50
170 Tim Hudson .15 .40
171 Jermaine Dye .15 .40
172 David Justice .15 .40
173 Mark Mulder .15 .40
174 Ray Durham .15 .40
175 Barry Zito .15 .40
181 Carl Crawford .25 .60
182 Bobby Abreu .15 .40
183 Pat Burrell .15 .40
184 Jimmy Rollins .20 .50
185 Marlon Byrd .15 .40
186 Mike Lieberthal .15 .40
192 Jason Kendall .15 .40
193 Brian Giles .15 .40
194 Aramis Ramirez .15 .40
202 Ryan Klesko .15 .40
203 Sean Burroughs .15 .40
204 Trevor Hoffman .15 .40
205 Phil Nevin .15 .40
208 Kenny Lofton .15 .40
209 J.T. Snow .15 .40
210 Barry Bonds 1.00 2.50
211 Rich Aurilia .15 .40
212 Reggie Sanders .15 .40
213 Robb Nen .15 .40
217 Ichiro Suzuki .60 1.50
218 Bret Boone .15 .40
219 John Olerud .15 .40
220 Freddy Garcia .15 .40
221 Edgar Martinez .25 .60
226 Scott Rolen .25 .60
227 Tino Martinez .25 .60
228 Jim Edmonds .15 .40
229 Albert Pujols 1.00 2.50
230 Mark McGwire .60 1.50
231 J.D. Drew .15 .40
232 Matt Morris .15 .40
236 Shannon Stewart .15 .40
237 Jose Cruz Jr. .15 .40
238 Carlos Delgado .15 .40
239 Vernon Wells .15 .40
240 Josh Phelps .15 .40
241 Roy Halladay .20 .50
242 Eric Hinske .15 .40
251 J.McCown .30 .75
J.Valverde
252 D.Devore .20 .50
W.Bryant
255 D.Heatley .40 1.00
J.Ennis
256 F.Sanchez .75 2.00
R.Davey
258 J.Williams .50 1.25
F.Beltran
259 K.Kane .20 .50
R.Mason Jr.
260 E.Almonte .30 .75
A.Peterson
263 C.Esslinger 1.50 4.00
C.Portis
265 A.Lelie .75 2.00
R.Reyes
271 B.Puffer .20 .50
J.Gaffney
274 J.Brito .20 .50
R.Sims
275 K.Ishii .30 .75
K.Rush
277 L.Martinez .20 .50
C.Nall
279 K.Frederick .50 1.25
S.Hill
280 D.Stallworth .60 1.50
C.Borchardt
281 T.Yates 1.00 2.50
J.Shockey
282 J.Cerda .20 .50
T.Carter
284 A.Machado .40 1.00
J.Salmons
285 A.Stoudemire 1.50 4.00
J.Ward
286 A.Burnside .60 1.50
A.Randle El
287 B.Howard .20 .50
R.Caldwell
288 O.Perez .40 1.00
Q.Jammer
289 L.Ugueto .20 .50
J.Stevens
290 M.Morris .20 .50
M.Thornton
291 S.Taguchi .30 .75
L.Gordon
292 J.Simontacchi .20 .50
R.Thomas
293 F.Escalona .20 .50
M.Walker
294 B.Backe .30 .75
T.Stephens
295 R.Johnson .20 .50
C.Jefferies
297 J.Jeffries .20 .50
S.Bechler

2002-03 UD SuperStars Gold

*GOLD 1-250: 2.5X TO 6X BASIC
*GOLD MATSUI: 6X TO 12X BASIC
*GOLD 251-300: 2X TO 5X BASIC

2002-03 UD SuperStars Benchmarks

B1 J.DiMaggio 3.00 8.00
W.Gretzky
B2 B.Bonds 2.50 6.00
J.Rice
B3 M.Faulk 1.00 2.50
T.Gwynn
B4 B.Russell 4.00 10.00
M.Mantle
B6 N.Garciaparra 2.00 5.00
T.Brady
B8 S.Sosa 1.25 3.00
A.Thomas
B9 M.McGwire 2.50 6.00
K.Warner
B10 K.Bryant 3.00 8.00
D.Jeter

2002-03 UD SuperStars City All-Stars Dual Jersey

ABZP A.Beltre/Z.Palffy 4.00 10.00
ADPW A.Dunn/P.Warrick 4.00 10.00
CDMS C.Delgado/M.Sundin 6.00 15.00
DBTH D.Brees/T.Hoffman 6.00 15.00
DCTO D.Culpepper/T.Hunter 8.00 20.00
ECRG E.Chavez/R.Gannon 6.00 15.00
FPPL F.Potvin/P.Lo Duca 6.00 15.00
GAPK G.Anderson/P.Kariya 6.00 15.00
GSSA G.Sheffield/S.Abdur-Rahim 4.00 10.00
IRMF I.Rodriguez/M.Finley 6.00 15.00
JBJF J.Fiedler/J.Beckett 4.00 10.00
JGCB J.Gaffney/C.Biggio 6.00 15.00
JGJS J.Garcia/J.Snow 6.00 15.00
JPLG J.Plummer/L.Gonzalez 4.00 10.00
KPBA K.Primeau/B.Abreu 4.00 10.00
LTRK L.Tomlinson/R.Klesko 6.00 15.00
MFJD M.Faulk/J.Drew 6.00 15.00
MLBG M.Lemieux/B.Giles Pants 15.00 40.00
MMAR M.Modano/A.Rodriguez 6.00 15.00
MPEL M.Piazza/E.Lindros 6.00 15.00
MRPP M.Ramirez/P.Pierce 6.00 15.00
MVAJ M.Vick/A.Jones 10.00 25.00
PHMS P.Holmes/M.Sweeney 6.00 15.00
PLAM P.Lo Duca/A.Miller 6.00 15.00
RACP R.Alomar/C.Pennington 6.00 15.00
RCPB R.Clemens/P.Bure 8.00 20.00
RDBW R.Dayne/B.Williams 6.00 15.00
RJSM R.Johnson/S.Marbury 6.00 15.00
SAEM S.Alexander/E.Martinez 6.00 15.00
TCMO T.Chandler/M.Ordonez 6.00 15.00
THJD T.Holt/J.Drew 5.00 12.00
THRB T.Helton/R.Blake 6.00 15.00
TORA T.Owens/R.Aurilia 6.00 15.00
WGJG W.Gretzky/J.Giambi 10.00 25.00

2002-03 UD SuperStars City All-Stars Triple Jersey

CVT Chipper 12.00 30.00
Vick
Terry
DPE Erstad 10.00 25.00
Kariya
Brand
IGS Ichiro 10.00 25.00
Payton
Alexander
IMD I.Rod 15.00 40.00
Modano
Nowitzki
JCK Griffey 10.00 25.00
Dillon
K.Martin
JDW Jacque 10.00 25.00
Culp
Szczerbiak
JDY Bagwell 15.00 40.00
Carr
Ming
JKA Kendall/Stewart/Kovalev 15.00 30.00
JLP Giambi 6.00 15.00
Sprewell
Bure
JMK Drew/Faulk/Tkachuk 10.00 25.00
MJA Prior 5.00 12.00
J.Will
A.Thomas
MJC Piazza 10.00 25.00
Kidd
C.Martin
MJJ Tejada 10.00 25.00
J.Rich
Rice
OTD Vizquel 10.00 25.00
Couch
D.Wag
PTP Pedro 10.00 25.00
Brady
Pierce
REA Clemens 15.00 30.00
Lind
Houston
RSS R.Johnson 6.00 15.00
Marion
Doan
SWK Green 40.00 80.00
Gretzky
Kobe

2002-03 UD SuperStars Keys to the City

COMPLETE SET (10) 10.00 25.00
K1 C.Delgado .75 2.00
V.Carter
K2 K.Bryant 2.00 5.00
K.Ishii
K3 M.McGwire 1.50 4.00
K.Warner
K4 B.Urlacher 1.00 2.50
S.Sosa
K5 P.Martinez 1.00 2.50
T.Brady
K6 P.Roy 1.25 3.00
T.Helton
K7 M.Piazza .75 2.00
C.Martin
K8 J.Bagwell 1.50 4.00
D.Carr
K10 A.Rodriguez 1.25 3.00
E.Smith

2002-03 UD SuperStars Legendary Leaders Dual Jersey

DCJB D.Carr/J.Bagwell 6.00 15.00
ESAR E.Smith/A.Rodriguez 15.00 40.00
ISDB I.Suzuki/D.Beckham 12.00 30.00
JGKC J.Giambi/K.Collins 4.00 10.00
JRCD K.Griffey Jr./C.Dillon 6.00 15.00
JSTG J.Seau/T.Gwynn 6.00 15.00
KWMM K.Warner/M.McGwire 20.00 50.00
PMTB P.Martinez/T.Brady 30.00 80.00
SMRJ S.Marion/R.Johnson 6.00 15.00
SSBU S.Sosa/B.Urlacher 8.00 20.00
TCOV T.Couch/O.Vizquel 4.00 10.00
ZPSG Z.Palffy/S.Green 6.00 15.00

2002-03 UD SuperStars Legendary Leaders Triple Jersey

AEM A.Rod/Emmitt/Modano 20.00 50.00
CJS Ripken/Jagr/Davis 12.50 30.00
GMS Maddux 12.50 30.00
Vick
A-Rahim
IDK Ichiro 75.00 150.00
Beckham
Bryant
IKD Ichiro 40.00 80.00
Garnett
Beckham
JDM Giambi/Bledsoe/Messier 10.00 25.00
JWL DiMaggio 60.00 120.00
Gretzky
Bird
KJT Malone 10.00 25.00
Rice
Gwynn
LBP Walker/Griese/Roy 15.00 40.00
MCA Piazza/C.Penn/Yashin 10.00 25.00
MPS McGwire/Manning/Yzer 30.00 80.00
PPT Pedro 20.00 50.00
Pierce
Brady
RJM Clemens/Rice/Lemieux 30.00 60.00
SEB Sosa/Daze/Urlacher 10.00 25.00
SKM Sosa 15.00 40.00
Kobe
Faulk
SWK Green 40.00 80.00
Gretzky
Kobe
TEM Gwynn/Emmitt/Lemieux 12.50 30.00

2002-03 UD SuperStars Magic Moments

COMPLETE SET (20) 10.00 25.00
MM1 Barry Bonds 1.50 4.00
MM2 Mark McGwire 1.50 4.00
MM3 Roger Clemens 1.25 3.00
MM4 Joe DiMaggio 1.25 3.00
MM5 Cal Ripken 2.00 5.00
MM6 Ichiro Suzuki 1.00 2.50
MM7 Mickey Mantle 2.00 5.00
MM8 Sammy Sosa 1.00 2.50
MM9 Ken Griffey Jr. 1.25 3.00
MM10 Derek Jeter 1.50 4.00

2002-03 UD SuperStars Rookie Review

R1 M.Messier 2.00 5.00
O.Smith
R2 I.Suzuki 2.00 5.00
M.Vick
R3 J.Beckett 1.00 2.50
S.Francis
R5 E.Smith 2.00 5.00
S.Sosa
R6 M.Prior .75 2.00
D.Brees
R7 J.Kidd 1.00 2.50
A.Rodriguez
R8 A.Soriano 1.00 2.50
S.Marion
R9 K.Griffey Jr. 1.50 4.00
D.Robinson
R10 D.Jeter 1.50 4.00
J.Bettis

2002-03 UD SuperStars Spokesmen

*BLACK: 1.25X TO 3X BASIC SPOKESMEN
BLACK/GOLD INSERTS IN SPOKESMEN PACKS
BLACK PRINT RUN 250 SERIAL #'d SETS
*GOLD/25: 3X TO 8X BASIC INSERTS
GOLD PRINT RUN 25 SERIAL #'d SETS
UD1 Ken Griffey Jr. 1.50 4.00
UD2 Ichiro Suzuki 1.50 4.00
UD3 Sammy Sosa 1.25 3.00
UD4 Jason Giambi 1.25 3.00
UD5 Joe DiMaggio 1.00 2.50
UD6 Mark McGwire 2.00 5.00
UD16 Ken Griffey Jr. 1.50 4.00
UD17 Ichiro Suzuki 1.50 4.00
UD18 Sammy Sosa 1.25 3.00
UD19 Jason Giambi 1.25 3.00
UD20 Joe DiMaggio 1.00 2.50
UD21 Mark McGwire 2.00 5.00

2004 UD Yankees Classics

COMPLETE SET (90) 10.00 25.00
COMMON CARD (1-85) .15 .40
COMMON CARD 86-90 .40 1.00
1 Bill Skowron .15 .40
2 Bob Cerv .15 .40
3 Bobby Murcer .15 .40
4 Bobby Richardson .15 .40
5 Brian Doyle .15 .40
6 Bucky Dent .15 .40
7 Chris Chambliss .15 .40
8 Clete Boyer .15 .40
9 Dave Kingman .15 .40
10 Dave Righetti .15 .40
11 Dave Winfield .25 .60
12 David Cone .15 .40
13 Red Ruffing .15 .40
14 Dock Ellis .15 .40
15 Don Baylor .15 .40
16 Don Larsen .15 .40
17 Don Mattingly .75 2.00
18 Dwight Gooden .15 .40
19 Ed Figueroa .15 .40
20 Joe Torre .25 .60
21 Darryl Strawberry .15 .40
22 Horace Clarke .15 .40
23 Gaylord Perry .25 .60
24 Phil Linz .15 .40
25 Gil McDougald .15 .40
26 Goose Gossage .25 .60
27 Graig Nettles .15 .40
28 Hank Bauer .15 .40
29 Jack Clark .15 .40
30 Don Gullett .15 .40
31 Jim Abbott .15 .40
32 Jim Bouton .15 .40
33 Jim Kaat .15 .40
34 Jim Leyritz .15 .40
35 Jim Wynn .15 .40
36 Jimmy Key .15 .40
37 Joe Niekro .15 .40
38 Joe Pepitone .15 .40
39 John Wetteland .15 .40
40 Ken Griffey Sr. .15 .40
41 Felipe Alou .15 .40
42 Kevin Maas .15 .40
43 Lindy McDaniel .15 .40
44 Lou Piniella .15 .40
45 Luis Tiant .15 .40
46 Mel Stottlemyre .15 .40
47 Mickey Rivers .15 .40
48 Oscar Gamble .15 .40
49 Pat Dobson .15 .40
50 Paul O'Neil .25 .60
51 Phil Niekro .25 .60
52 Phil Rizzuto .25 .60
53 Doc Medich .15 .40
54 Rick Cerone .15 .40
55 Ron Blomberg .15 .40
56 Ron Guidry .15 .40
57 Roy White .15 .40
58 Rudy May .15 .40
59 Sam McDowell .15 .40
60 Sparky Lyle .15 .40
61 Steve Balboni .15 .40
62 Steve Sax .15 .40
63 Jerry Coleman .15 .40
64 Tom Tresh .15 .40
65 Tommy John .15 .40
66 Tony Kubek .15 .40
67 Wade Boggs .25 .60
68 Whitey Ford .25 .60
69 Willie Randolph .15 .40
70 Yogi Berra .40 1.00
71 Babe Ruth 1.00 2.50
72 Bill Dickey .15 .40
73 Billy Martin .25 .60
74 Bob Meusel .15 .40
75 Casey Stengel .25 .60
76 Elston Howard .15 .40
77 Catfish Hunter .25 .60
78 Joe DiMaggio .75 2.00
79 Lefty Gomez .15 .40
80 Lou Gehrig .75 2.00
81 Mickey Mantle 1.25 3.00
82 Miller Huggins .15 .40
83 Roger Maris .40 1.00
84 Thurman Munson .40 1.00
85 Tony Lazzeri .25 .60
86 Yankee Stadium .40 1.00
87 Times Square .40 1.00
88 Central Park .40 1.00
89 Empire State Building .40 1.00
90 Statue of Liberty .40 1.00

2004 UD Yankees Classics Bronze

*BRONZE: 4X TO 10X BASIC
OVERALL PARALLEL ODDS 1:78 HOBBY
STATED PRINT RUN 99 SERIAL #'d SETS

2004 UD Yankees Classics Gold

*GOLD: 8X TO 20X BASIC
OVERALL PARALLEL ODDS 1:78 HOBBY
STATED PRINT RUN 30 SERIAL #'d SETS

2004 UD Yankees Classics UD Promos

*PROMO: .6X TO 1.5X BASIC

2004 UD Yankees Classics Mitchell and Ness Jersey Redemption

STATED ODDS 1:384
PRINT RUNS B/WN 40-99 COPIES PER
EXCHANGE DEADLINE 01/05/08
1 Babe Ruth/40 250.00 400.00
2 Bill Dickey/75 75.00 150.00
3 Billy Martin/99 125.00 200.00
4 Bobby Murcer/99 125.00 200.00
5 Bucky Dent/92 60.00 120.00
6 Casey Stengel/65 75.00 150.00
7 Catfish Hunter/92 75.00 150.00
8 Chris Chambliss/99 60.00 120.00
9 Don Larsen/75 75.00 150.00
10 Don Mattingly/92 125.00 200.00
11 Elston Howard/88 60.00 120.00
12 Goose Gossage/92 60.00 120.00
13 Graig Nettles/99 60.00 120.00
14 Joe DiMaggio/55 150.00 250.00
15 Lefty Gomez/81 60.00 120.00
16 Lou Gehrig/40 150.00 250.00
17 Lou Piniella/92 60.00 120.00
18 Mickey Mantle/50 175.00 300.00
19 Moose Skowron/85 60.00 120.00
20 Phil Rizzuto/40 75.00 150.00
21 Roy White/50 60.00 120.00
22 Roger Maris/92 150.00 250.00
23 Ron Guidry/99 60.00 120.00
24 Sparky Lyle/99 60.00 120.00
25 Thurman Munson/91 125.00 200.00
26 Tony Kubek/75
27 Tony Lazzeri/79 60.00 120.00
28 Whitey Ford/43 125.00 200.00
29 Willie Randolph/92 60.00 120.00
30 Yogi Berra/50 125.00 200.00

2004 UD Yankees Classics Mitchell and Ness Pennants

ONE PER BOX W/CARD
PRINT RUNS B/WN 1-2000 COPIES PER
ITEMS ARE NOT SERIAL-NUMBERED
QTY PRODUCED LISTED ON CARD BACK
NO PRICING ON QTY OF 23 OR LESS
LISTED PRICES = PENNANT/CARD COMBO
*SEPARATE CARD: .08X TO .2X COMBO
*SEPARATE PENNANT: .3X TO .8X COMBO
1 1923 World Series/23
1D 1923 World Series/1
2 1927 World Series/1927 10.00 25.00
2D 1927 World Series/96 15.00 40.00
3 1928 World Series/1928 10.00 25.00
3D 1928 World Series/96 15.00 40.00
4 1932 World Series/1932 10.00 25.00
4D 1932 World Series/96 15.00 40.00
5 1936 World Series/36 20.00 50.00
5D 1936 World Series/1
6 1937 World Series/1937 10.00 25.00
6D 1937 World Series/96 15.00 40.00
7 1938 World Series/38 20.00 50.00
7D 1938 World Series/1
8 1939 World Series/1939 10.00 25.00
8D 1939 World Series/96 15.00 40.00
9 1941 World Series/41 20.00 50.00
9D 1941 World Series/2
10 1943 World Series/1943 10.00 25.00
10D 1943 World Series/97 15.00 40.00
11 1947 World Series/1947 10.00 25.00
11D 1947 World Series/97 15.00 40.00
12 1949 World Series/49 20.00 50.00
12D 1949 World Series/2
13 1950 World Series/1950 10.00 25.00
13D 1950 World Series/97 15.00 40.00
14 1951 World Series/51 20.00 50.00
14D 1951 World Series/2
15 1952 World Series/1952 10.00 25.00
15D 1952 World Series/97 15.00 40.00
16 1953 World Series/53 20.00 50.00
16D 1953 World Series/2
17 1956 World Series/1956 10.00 25.00
17D 1956 World Series/97 15.00 40.00
18 1958 World Series/1958 10.00 25.00
18D 1958 World Series/97 15.00 40.00
19 1961 World Series/61 20.00 50.00
19D 1961 World Series/3
20 1962 World Series/62 20.00 50.00
20D 1962 World Series/3
21 1977 World Series/77 15.00 40.00
21D 1977 World Series/3
22 1978 World Series/78 15.00 40.00
22D 1978 World Series/3
23 1996 World Series/1996 10.00 25.00
23D 1996 World Series/99 15.00 40.00
24 1998 World Series/1998 10.00 25.00
24D 1998 World Series/99 15.00 40.00
25 1999 World Series/1999 10.00 25.00
25D 1999 World Series/99 15.00 40.00
26 2000 World Series/2000 10.00 25.00
26D 2000 World Series/100 15.00 40.00
MM56 Mickey Mantle 56 MVP/7
MM56D Mickey Mantle 56 MVP/1
MM57 Mickey Mantle 57 MVP/1957 15.00 40.00
MM57D Mickey Mantle 57 MVP/97 30.00 60.00
MM62 Mickey Mantle 62 MVP/1962 15.00 40.00
MM62D Mickey Mantle 62 MVP/98 15.00 40.00

2004 UD Yankees Classics Scripts

OVERALL AUTO ODDS 1:8
SP INFO PROVIDED BY UPPER DECK
1 Bill Skowron 6.00 15.00
2 Bob Cerv 4.00 10.00
3 Bobby Murcer 12.00 30.00
4 Bobby Richardson 4.00 10.00
5 Brian Doyle 4.00 10.00
6 Bucky Dent 6.00 15.00
7 Chris Chambliss 6.00 15.00
8 Clete Boyer 8.00 20.00
9 Dave Kingman 6.00 15.00
10 Dave Righetti 6.00 15.00
11 Dave Winfield SP 12.00 30.00
12 David Cone 6.00 15.00
14 Dock Ellis 6.00 15.00
15 Don Baylor SP 15.00 40.00
16 Don Larsen SP 6.00 15.00
17 Don Mattingly SP 30.00 60.00
18 Dwight Gooden 6.00 15.00
19 Ed Figueroa 4.00 10.00
20 Joe Torre SP 60.00 120.00
21 Darryl Strawberry 8.00 20.00
23 Gaylord Perry 8.00 20.00
24 Phil Linz 6.00 15.00
25 Gil McDougald 6.00 15.00
26 Goose Gossage 10.00 25.00
27 Graig Nettles 4.00 10.00
28 Hank Bauer 6.00 15.00
29 Jack Clark 6.00 15.00
31 Jim Abbott 4.00 10.00
32 Jim Bouton 6.00 15.00
33 Jim Kaat 10.00 25.00
34 Jim Leyritz SP 12.00 30.00
35 Jim Wynn 4.00 10.00
36 Jimmy Key 6.00 15.00
37 Joe Niekro 6.00 15.00
38 Joe Pepitone 6.00 15.00
39 John Wetteland 6.00 15.00
40 Ken Griffey Sr. 6.00 15.00
42 Kevin Maas 6.00 15.00
43 Lindy McDaniel 6.00 15.00
44 Lou Piniella SP 10.00 25.00
45 Luis Tiant 6.00 15.00
46 Mel Stottlemyre 6.00 15.00
47 Mickey Rivers 6.00 15.00
48 Oscar Gamble 4.00 10.00
49 Pat Dobson 6.00 15.00
50 Paul O'Neil SP 15.00 40.00
51 Phil Niekro 6.00 15.00
52 Phil Rizzuto SP 20.00 50.00
53 Doc Medich 4.00 10.00
54 Rick Cerone 6.00 15.00
55 Ron Blomberg 4.00 10.00
56 Ron Guidry 8.00 20.00
57 Roy White 6.00 15.00
58 Rudy May 4.00 10.00
59 Sam McDowell 4.00 10.00
60 Sparky Lyle 6.00 15.00
61 Steve Balboni 6.00 15.00
62 Steve Sax 4.00 10.00
63 Jerry Coleman 6.00 15.00
64 Tom Tresh 6.00 15.00
65 Tommy John 6.00 15.00
66 Tony Kubek SP/70 * 400.00 550.00
67 Wade Boggs SP 10.00 25.00
68 Whitey Ford SP 20.00 50.00

69 Willie Randolph SP 20.00 50.00
70 Yogi Berra SP 40.00 100.00

2004 UD Yankees Classics Scripts Dual

OVERALL AUTO ODDS 1:8
STATED PRINT RUN 100 SERIAL #'d SETS
EXCHANGE DEADLINE 01/06/08
AK J.Abbott/J.Kaat 20.00 50.00
BF Y.Berra/W.Ford 75.00 200.00
BG D.Baylor/K.Griffey Sr. 20.00 50.00
BH Y.Berra/J.Torre 60.00 150.00
BL Y.Berra/D.Larsen 75.00 200.00
BM D.Mattingly/W.Boggs 100.00 175.00
BN C.Boyer/G.Nettles 20.00 50.00
CB C.Chambliss/R.Blomberg 20.00 50.00
CG D.Cone/D.Gooden 40.00 80.00
CL D.Cone/D.Larsen 20.00 50.00
CN C.Chambliss/G.Nettles 20.00 50.00
DN B.Dent/G.Nettles 20.00 50.00
ED D.Ellis/P.Dobson 20.00 50.00
FG E.Figueroa/R.Guidry 20.00 50.00
FL W.Ford/D.Larsen 75.00 150.00
GL G.Gossage/S.Lyle 20.00 50.00
KA J.Key/J.Abbott 20.00 50.00
KC D.Kingman/J.Clark 20.00 50.00
KJ J.Kaat/T.John 20.00 50.00
KR T.Kubek/B.Richardson 60.00 120.00
MB B.Murcer/H.Bauer 40.00 80.00
MC D.Mattingly/J.Clark 50.00 100.00
MM K.Maas/D.Mattingly 50.00 100.00
MP B.Murcer/L.Piniella 40.00 80.00
MW D.Mattingly/D.Winfield 75.00 150.00
NB G.Nettles/W.Boggs 40.00 80.00
OL P.O'Neill/J.Leyritz 40.00 80.00
PS J.Pepitone/B.Skowron 20.00 50.00
RC D.Righetti/R.Cerone 20.00 50.00
RM P.Rizzuto/G.McDougald 60.00 120.00
RW M.Rivers/R.White 20.00 50.00
SC B.Skowron/B.Cerv 20.00 50.00
SD S.Sax/B.Doyle 20.00 50.00
SG D.Strawberry/D.Gooden 40.00 80.00
WM B.Murcer/R.White 20.00 50.00

1988 Uecker Blue Shield

This one card set features former baseball player, actor and longtime Milwaukee Brewer announcer Bob Uecker. The front of the card is a replica of his 1963 Topps card while the back gives information on Uecker's run for the Arts on June 5, 1988.

1 Bob Uecker 2.00 5.00

1985 Ultimate Baseball Card

This 15-card set by the Decathlon Corporation measures approximately 4" by 5 5/8". The fronts display color artwork of great players by Gerry Dvorak. The white backs carry the card name, player's name and career information.

COMPLETE SET (15) 15.00 40.00
1 Ty Cobb 3.00 8.00
2 Honus Wagner 1.00 2.50
3 Babe Ruth 4.00 10.00
4 Lou Gehrig 3.00 8.00
5 Frank Baker .60 1.50
6 Casey Stengel .75 2.00
7 Moses Walker .40 1.00
8 Cy Young 1.00 2.50
9 Joe DiMaggio 3.00 8.00
10 John McGraw .75 2.00
11 Josh Gibson 2.00 5.00
12 Johnny Mize .60 1.50
13 Walter Johnson 1.00 2.50
14 Walter Alston .40 1.00
15 Enos Slaughter .60 1.50

2001 Ultimate Collection

COMMON CARD (1-90) 1.50 4.00
COMMON CARD (91-100) 4.00 10.00
91-100 PRINT RUN 1000 SERIAL #'d SETS
COMMON CARD (101-110) 4.00 10.00
101-110 PRINT RUN 750 SERIAL #'d SETS
COMMON CARD (111-120) 6.00 15.00
111-120 PRINT RUN 250 SERIAL #'d SETS
91-120 RANDOM INSERTS IN PACKS
1 Troy Glaus 1.50 4.00
2 Darin Erstad 1.50 4.00
3 Jason Giambi 1.50 4.00
4 Barry Zito 1.50 4.00
5 Tim Hudson 1.50 4.00
6 Miguel Tejada 1.50 4.00
7 Carlos Delgado 1.50 4.00
8 Shannon Stewart 1.50 4.00
9 Greg Vaughn 1.50 4.00
10 Toby Hall 1.50 4.00
11 Roberto Alomar 1.50 4.00
12 Juan Gonzalez 1.50 4.00
13 Jim Thome 1.50 4.00
14 Edgar Martinez 1.50 4.00
15 Freddy Garcia 1.50 4.00
16 Bret Boone 1.50 4.00
17 Kazuhiro Sasaki 1.50 4.00
18 Cal Ripken 8.00 20.00
19 Tim Raines Jr. 1.50 4.00
20 Alex Rodriguez 3.00 8.00
21 Ivan Rodriguez 1.50 4.00
22 Rafael Palmeiro 1.50 4.00
23 Pedro Martinez 1.50 4.00
24 Nomar Garciaparra 4.00 10.00
25 Manny Ramirez Sox 1.50 4.00
26 Hideo Nomo 2.50 6.00
27 Mike Sweeney 1.50 4.00
28 Carlos Beltran 1.50 4.00
29 Tony Clark 1.50 4.00
30 Dean Palmer 1.50 4.00
31 Doug Mientkiewicz 1.50 4.00
32 Cristian Guzman 1.50 4.00
33 Corey Koskie 1.50 4.00
34 Frank Thomas 2.50 6.00
35 Magglio Ordonez 1.50 4.00
36 Jose Canseco 1.50 4.00
37 Roger Clemens 5.00 12.00
38 Derek Jeter 6.00 15.00
39 Bernie Williams 1.50 4.00
40 Mike Mussina 1.50 4.00
41 Tino Martinez 1.50 4.00
42 Jeff Bagwell 1.50 4.00
43 Lance Berkman 1.50 4.00
44 Roy Oswalt 2.50 6.00
45 Chipper Jones 2.50 6.00
46 Greg Maddux 4.00 10.00
47 Andruw Jones 1.50 4.00
48 Tom Glavine 1.50 4.00
49 Richie Sexson 1.50 4.00
50 Jeromy Burnitz 1.50 4.00
51 Ben Sheets 1.50 4.00
52 Mark McGwire 6.00 15.00
53 Matt Morris 1.50 4.00
54 Jim Edmonds 1.50 4.00
55 J.D. Drew 1.50 4.00
56 Sammy Sosa 2.50 6.00
57 Fred McGriff 1.50 4.00
58 Kerry Wood 1.50 4.00
59 Randy Johnson 2.50 6.00
60 Luis Gonzalez 1.50 4.00
61 Curt Schilling 1.50 4.00
62 Shawn Green 1.50 4.00
63 Kevin Brown 1.50 4.00
64 Gary Sheffield 1.50 4.00
65 Vladimir Guerrero 2.50 6.00
66 Barry Bonds 6.00 15.00
67 Jeff Kent 1.50 4.00
68 Rich Aurilia 1.50 4.00
69 Cliff Floyd 1.50 4.00
70 Charles Johnson 1.50 4.00
71 Josh Beckett 1.50 4.00
72 Mike Piazza 4.00 10.00
73 Edgardo Alfonzo 1.50 4.00
74 Robin Ventura 1.50 4.00
75 Tony Gwynn 3.00 8.00
76 Ryan Klesko 1.50 4.00
77 Phil Nevin 1.50 4.00
78 Scott Rolen 1.50 4.00
79 Bobby Abreu 1.50 4.00
80 Jimmy Rollins 1.50 4.00
81 Brian Giles 1.50 4.00
82 Jason Kendall 1.50 4.00
83 Aramis Ramirez 1.50 4.00
84 Ken Griffey Jr. 5.00 12.00
85 Adam Dunn 1.50 4.00
86 Sean Casey 1.50 4.00
87 Barry Larkin 1.50 4.00
88 Larry Walker 1.50 4.00
89 Mike Hampton 1.50 4.00
90 Todd Helton 1.50 4.00
91 Ken Harvey T1 4.00 10.00
92 Bill Ortega T1 RC 4.00 10.00
93 Juan Diaz T1 RC 4.00 10.00
94 Greg Miller T1 RC 4.00 10.00
95 Brandon Berger T1 RC 4.00 10.00
96 Brandon Lyon T1 RC 4.00 10.00
97 Jay Gibbons T1 RC 6.00 15.00
98 Rob Mackowiak T1 RC 6.00 15.00
99 Erick Almonte T1 RC 4.00 10.00
100 Jason Middlebrook T1 RC 4.00 10.00
101 Johnny Estrada T2 RC 6.00 15.00
102 Juan Uribe T2 RC 6.00 15.00
103 Travis Hafner T2 RC 10.00 25.00
104 Morgan Ensberg T2 RC 6.00 15.00
105 Mike Rivera T2 RC 4.00 10.00
106 Josh Towers T2 RC 6.00 15.00
107 Adrian Hernandez T2 RC 4.00 10.00
108 Rafael Soriano T2 RC 4.00 10.00
109 Jackson Melian T2 RC 4.00 10.00
110 Wilkin Ruan T2 RC 4.00 10.00
111 Albert Pujols T3 RC 300.00 800.00
112 Tsuyoshi Shinjo T3 RC 10.00 25.00
113 Brandon Duckworth T3 RC 6.00 15.00
114 Juan Cruz T3 RC 6.00 15.00
115 Dewon Brazelton T3 RC 6.00 15.00
116 Mark Prior T3 AU RC 20.00 50.00
117 Mark Teixeira T3 AU RC 200.00 300.00
118 Wilson Betemit T3 RC 10.00 25.00
119 Bud Smith T3 RC 6.00 15.00
120 Ichiro Suzuki T3 AU RC 1250.00 3000.00

2001 Ultimate Collection Game Jersey

GAME JERSEY CUMULATIVE ODDS 1:2
STATED PRINT RUN 150 SERIAL #'d SETS
COPPER RANDOM INSERTS IN PACKS
COPPER PRINT RUN 24 SERIAL #'d SETS
NO COPPER PRICING DUE TO SCARCITY
GOLD RANDOM INSERTS IN PACKS
GOLD PRINT RUN 15 SERIAL #'d SETS
NO GOLD PRICING DUE TO SCARCITY
SILVER RANDOM INSERTS IN PACKS
SILVER PRINT RUN 20 SERIAL #'d SETS
NO SILVER PRICING DUE TO SCARCITY
UAJ Andruw Jones 10.00 25.00
UAP Albert Pujols 30.00 80.00
UAR Alex Rodriguez 10.00 25.00
UBB Barry Bonds 15.00 40.00
UBW Bernie Williams 10.00 25.00
UCD Carlos Delgado 6.00 15.00
UCJ Chipper Jones 10.00 25.00
UCR Cal Ripken 10.00 25.00
UDE Darin Erstad 6.00 15.00
UFT Frank Thomas 10.00 25.00
UGM Greg Maddux 10.00 25.00
UGS Gary Sheffield 6.00 15.00
UIR Ivan Rodriguez 10.00 25.00
UJAG Jason Giambi 6.00 15.00
UJB Jeff Bagwell 10.00 25.00
UJC Jose Canseco 10.00 25.00
UJG Juan Gonzalez 6.00 15.00
UKG Ken Griffey Jr. 10.00 25.00
ULG Luis Gonzalez 6.00 15.00
ULW Larry Walker 6.00 15.00
UMO Magglio Ordonez 6.00 15.00
UMP Mike Piazza 10.00 25.00
URA Roberto Alomar 10.00 25.00
URC Roger Clemens 10.00 25.00
URJ Randy Johnson 10.00 25.00
USG Shawn Green 6.00 15.00
USR Scott Rolen 10.00 25.00
USS Sammy Sosa 10.00 25.00
UTG Tony Gwynn 10.00 25.00
UTH Todd Helton 10.00 25.00

2001 Ultimate Collection Ichiro Ball

ICHIRO GAME-USED CUMULATIVE ODDS 1:4
STATED PRINT RUNS LISTED BELOW
NO PRICING ON QTY OF 25 OR LESS
IA Ichiro Suzuki SP 20.00 50.00
IH Ichiro Suzuki Copper/150 30.00 80.00
IS Ichiro Suzuki Silver/50 40.00 100.00

2001 Ultimate Collection Ichiro Base

ICHIRO GAME-USED CUMULATIVE ODDS 1:4
STATED PRINT RUNS LISTED BELOW
UIA Ichiro Suzuki 10.00 25.00
UIC Ichiro Suzuki Copper/150 40.00 100.00
UIS Ichiro Suzuki Silver/50 30.00 80.00

2001 Ultimate Collection Ichiro Bat

ICHIRO GAME-USED CUMULATIVE ODDS 1:4
STATED PRINT RUNS LISTED BELOW
BIA Ichiro Suzuki Away SP 15.00 40.00
BIC Ichiro Suzuki Home SP 20.00 50.00
BIG Ichiro Suzuki Gold/200 30.00 80.00
BIS Ichiro Suzuki Silver/250 30.00 80.00
SBI Ichiro Suzuki AU/50 1500.00 4000.00

2001 Ultimate Collection Ichiro Batting Glove

ICHIRO GAME-USED CUMULATIVE ODDS 1:4
STATED PRINT RUNS LISTED BELOW
BGI Ichiro Suzuki/75 150.00 400.00

2001 Ultimate Collection Ichiro Fielders Glove

ICHIRO GAME-USED CUMULATIVE ODDS 1:4
STATED PRINT RUNS LISTED BELOW
FGI Ichiro Suzuki/75 150.00 400.00

2001 Ultimate Collection Ichiro Jersey

ICHIRO GAME-USED CUMULATIVE ODDS 1:4
STATED PRINT RUNS LISTED BELOW
JIA Ichiro Suzuki Away 15.00 40.00
JIG Ichiro Suzuki Gold/200 50.00 120.00
JIH Ichiro Suzuki Home SP 20.00 50.00
JIS Ichiro Suzuki Silver/250 25.00 60.00
SJI Ichiro Suzuki AU/50 1500.00 4000.00

2001 Ultimate Collection Magic Numbers Game Jersey

GAME JERSEY CUMULATIVE ODDS 1:2
STATED PRINT RUN 150 SERIAL #'d SETS
*RED: .75X TO 2X BASIC MAGIC NUMBERS
RED RANDOM INSERTS IN PACKS
RED PRINT RUN 30 SERIAL #'d SETS
NO RED PUJOLS PRICING AVAILABLE
COPPER RANDOM INSERTS IN PACKS
COPPER PRINT RUN 24 SERIAL #'d SETS
NO COPPER PRICING DUE TO SCARCITY
SILVER RANDOM INSERTS IN PACKS
SILVER PRINT RUN 20 SERIAL #'d SETS
NO SILVER PRICING DUE TO SCARCITY
GOLD RANDOM INSERTS IN PACKS
GOLD PRINT RUN 15 SERIAL #'d SETS
NO GOLD PRICING DUE TO SCARCITY
MNG Tony Gwynn 10.00 25.00
MNAJ Andruw Jones 10.00 25.00
MNAP Albert Pujols 60.00 150.00
MNAR Alex Rodriguez 10.00 25.00
MNBB Barry Bonds 15.00 40.00
MNBW Bernie Williams 10.00 25.00
MNCD Carlos Delgado 6.00 15.00
MNCJ Chipper Jones 10.00 25.00
MNCR Cal Ripken 20.00 50.00
MNDE Darin Erstad 6.00 15.00
MNFT Frank Thomas 10.00 25.00
MNGM Greg Maddux 10.00 25.00
MNGS Gary Sheffield 6.00 15.00
MNIR Ivan Rodriguez 10.00 25.00
MNJAG Jason Giambi 6.00 15.00
MNJB Jeff Bagwell 10.00 25.00
MNJC Jose Canseco 10.00 25.00
MNJG Juan Gonzalez 6.00 15.00
MNKG Ken Griffey Jr. 10.00 25.00
MNLG Luis Gonzalez 6.00 15.00
MNLW Larry Walker 6.00 15.00
MNMO Magglio Ordonez 6.00 15.00
MNMP Mike Piazza 10.00 25.00
MNRA Roberto Alomar 10.00 25.00
MNRC Roger Clemens 10.00 25.00
MNRJ Randy Johnson 10.00 25.00
MNSG Shawn Green 6.00 15.00
MNSR Scott Rolen 10.00 25.00
MNSS Sammy Sosa 10.00 25.00
MNTH Todd Helton 10.00 25.00

2001 Ultimate Collection Signatures

STATED PRINT RUN 150 SERIAL #'d SETS
*COPPER: .75X TO 1.5X BASIC SIG
COPPER PRINT RUN 70 SERIAL #'d SETS
GOLD PRINT RUN 15 SERIAL #'d SETS
NO GOLD PRICING DUE TO SCARCITY
SILVER PRINT RUN 24 SERIAL #'d SETS
NO SILVER PRICING DUE TO SCARCITY
SIGNATURES CUMULATIVE ODDS 1:4
AR Alex Rodriguez 50.00 100.00
BAB Barry Bonds 60.00 120.00
CD Carlos Delgado 10.00 25.00
CF Carlton Fisk 15.00 40.00
CR Cal Ripken 75.00 150.00
DS Duke Snider 15.00 40.00
EB Ernie Banks 20.00 50.00
EM Edgar Martinez 10.00 25.00
FT Frank Thomas 20.00 50.00
GS Gary Sheffield 15.00 40.00
IR Ivan Rodriguez 20.00 50.00
JAG Jason Giambi 10.00 25.00
JT Jim Thome 20.00 50.00
KG Ken Griffey Jr. 60.00 120.00
KP Kirby Puckett 50.00 100.00
LG Luis Gonzalez 10.00 25.00
RA Roberto Alomar 15.00 40.00
RC Roger Clemens 30.00 60.00
RK Ryan Klesko 10.00 25.00
RY Robin Yount 30.00 60.00
SK Sandy Koufax 200.00 350.00
SS Sammy Sosa 50.00 100.00
TG Tony Gwynn 40.00 80.00
TGL Tom Glavine 20.00 50.00
TP Tony Perez 10.00 25.00
TS Tom Seaver 20.00 50.00

2002 Ultimate Collection

COMMON CARD (1-60) 1.50 4.00
1-60 ODDS APPX.TWO PER PACK
1-60 PRINT RUN 799 SERIAL #'d SETS
COMMON CARD (61-110) 4.00 10.00
61-110 ODDS APPX.ONE PER PACK
61-110 PRINT RUN 550 SERIAL #'d SETS
COMMON CARD (111-113) 6.00 15.00
111-113 PRINT RUN 330 SERIAL #'d SETS
COMMON CARD (114-120) 6.00 15.00
114-120 PRINT RUN 550 SERIAL #'d SETS
111-120 AU'S RANDOM INSERTS IN PACKS
MCGWIRE PRIORITY SIG EXCH.ODDS 1:1000
1 Troy Glaus 1.50 4.00
2 Luis Gonzalez 1.50 4.00
3 Curt Schilling 1.50 4.00
4 Randy Johnson 2.50 6.00
5 Andruw Jones 1.50 4.00
6 Greg Maddux 4.00 10.00
7 Chipper Jones 2.50 6.00
8 Gary Sheffield 1.50 4.00
9 Cal Ripken 8.00 20.00
10 Manny Ramirez 1.50 4.00
11 Pedro Martinez 1.50 4.00
12 Nomar Garciaparra 4.00 10.00
13 Sammy Sosa 2.50 6.00
14 Kerry Wood 1.50 4.00
15 Mark Prior 2.50 6.00
16 Magglio Ordonez 1.50 4.00
17 Frank Thomas 2.50 6.00
18 Adam Dunn 1.50 4.00
19 Ken Griffey Jr. 5.00 12.00
20 Jim Thome 1.50 4.00
21 Larry Walker 1.50 4.00
22 Todd Helton 1.50 4.00
23 Nolan Ryan 6.00 15.00
24 Jeff Bagwell 1.50 4.00
25 Roy Oswalt 1.50 4.00
26 Lance Berkman 1.50 4.00
27 Mike Sweeney 1.50 4.00
28 Shawn Green 1.50 4.00
29 Hideo Nomo 2.50 6.00
30 Torii Hunter 1.50 4.00
31 Vladimir Guerrero 2.50 6.00
32 Tom Seaver 1.50 4.00
33 Mike Piazza 4.00 10.00
34 Roberto Alomar 1.50 4.00
35 Derek Jeter 6.00 15.00
36 Alfonso Soriano 1.50 4.00
37 Jason Giambi 1.50 4.00
38 Roger Clemens 5.00 12.00
39 Mike Mussina 1.50 4.00
40 Bernie Williams 1.50 4.00
41 Joe DiMaggio 5.00 12.00
42 Mickey Mantle 10.00 25.00
43 Miguel Tejada 1.50 4.00
44 Eric Chavez 1.50 4.00
45 Barry Zito 1.50 4.00
46 Pat Burrell 1.50 4.00
47 Jason Kendall 1.50 4.00
48 Brian Giles 1.50 4.00
49 Barry Bonds 6.00 15.00
50 Ichiro Suzuki 5.00 12.00
51 Stan Musial 4.00 10.00
52 J.D. Drew 1.50 4.00
53 Scott Rolen 1.50 4.00
54 Albert Pujols 5.00 12.00
55 Mark McGwire 6.00 15.00
56 Alex Rodriguez 3.00 8.00
57 Ivan Rodriguez 1.50 4.00
58 Juan Gonzalez 1.50 4.00
59 Rafael Palmeiro 1.50 4.00
60 Carlos Delgado 1.50 4.00
61 Jose Valverde UR RC 4.00 10.00
62 Doug Devore UR RC 4.00 10.00
63 John Ennis UR RC 4.00 10.00
64 Joey Dawley UR RC 4.00 10.00
65 Trey Hodges UR RC 4.00 10.00
66 Mike Mahoney UR 4.00 10.00
67 Aaron Cook UR RC 4.00 10.00
68 Rene Reyes UR RC 4.00 10.00
69 Mark Corey UR RC 4.00 10.00
70 Hansel Izquierdo UR RC 4.00 10.00
71 Brandon Puffer UR RC 4.00 10.00
72 Jeriome Robertson UR RC 4.00 10.00
73 Jose Diaz UR RC 4.00 10.00
74 David Ross UR RC 4.00 10.00
75 Jayson Durocher UR RC 4.00 10.00
76 Eric Good UR RC 4.00 10.00
77 Satoru Komiyama UR RC 4.00 10.00
78 Tyler Yates UR RC 4.00 10.00
79 Eric Junge UR RC 4.00 10.00
80 Anderson Machado UR RC 4.00 10.00
81 Adrian Burnside UR RC 4.00 10.00
82 Ben Howard UR RC 4.00 10.00
83 Clay Condrey UR RC 4.00 10.00
84 Nelson Castro UR RC 4.00 10.00
85 So Taguchi UR RC 6.00 15.00
86 Mike Crudale UR RC 4.00 10.00
87 Scotty Layfield UR RC 4.00 10.00
88 Steve Bechler UR RC 4.00 10.00
89 Travis Driskill UR RC 4.00 10.00
90 Howie Clark UR RC 4.00 10.00
91 Josh Hancock UR RC 5.00 12.00
92 Jorge De La Rosa UR RC 4.00 10.00
93 Anastacio Martinez UR RC 4.00 10.00
94 Brian Tallet UR RC 4.00 10.00
95 Carl Sadler UR RC 4.00 10.00
96 Cliff Lee UR RC 6.00 15.00
97 Josh Bard UR RC 4.00 10.00
98 Wes Obermueller UR RC 4.00 10.00
99 Juan Brito UR RC 4.00 10.00
100 Aaron Guiel UR RC 4.00 10.00
101 Jeremy Hill UR RC 4.00 10.00
102 Kevin Frederick UR RC 4.00 10.00
103 Nate Field UR RC 4.00 10.00
104 Julio Mateo UR RC 4.00 10.00
105 Chris Snelling UR RC 5.00 12.00
106 Felix Escalona UR RC 4.00 10.00
107 Reynaldo Garcia UR RC 4.00 10.00
108 Mike Smith UR RC 4.00 10.00
109 Ken Huckaby UR RC 4.00 10.00
110 Kevin Cash UR RC 4.00 10.00
111 Kazuhisa Ishii UR AU RC 10.00 25.00
112 Freddy Sanchez UR AU RC 6.00 15.00
113 Jas Simontacchi UR AU RC 6.00 15.00
114 Jorge Padilla UR AU RC 6.00 15.00
115 Kirk Saarloos UR AU RC 6.00 15.00
116 Rodrigo Rosario UR AU RC 6.00 15.00
117 Oliver Perez UR AU RC 6.00 15.00
118 Miguel Asencio UR AU RC 6.00 15.00
119 Franklyn German UR AU RC 6.00 15.00
120 Jaime Cerda UR AU RC 6.00 15.00

2002 Ultimate Collection Game Jersey Tier 1

RANDOM INSERTS IN PACKS
STATED PRINT RUN 99 SERIAL #'d SETS
AD Adam Dunn 6.00 15.00
AJ Andruw Jones 10.00 25.00
AR Alex Rodriguez 10.00 25.00
AS Alfonso Soriano 6.00 15.00
CJ Chipper Jones 10.00 25.00
CR Cal Ripken 10.00 25.00
IR Ivan Rodriguez 10.00 25.00
IS Ichiro Suzuki 20.00 50.00
JD Joe DiMaggio 20.00 50.00
JG Jason Giambi 6.00 15.00
KG Ken Griffey Jr. 10.00 25.00
KI Kazuhisa Ishii 10.00 25.00
MC Mark McGwire 10.00 25.00
MM Mickey Mantle 30.00 80.00
MP Mike Piazza 10.00 25.00
MR Manny Ramirez 10.00 25.00
PM Pedro Martinez 10.00 25.00
PR Mark Prior 6.00 15.00
RC Roger Clemens 10.00 25.00
RJ Randy Johnson 10.00 25.00
SS Sammy Sosa 10.00 25.00

2002 Ultimate Collection Game Jersey Tier 1 Gold

*TIER 1 GOLD: .75X TO 1.5X TIER 1 JSY
RANDOM INSERTS IN PACKS
STATED PRINT RUN 50 SERIAL #'d SETS

2002 Ultimate Collection Game Jersey Tier 2

*TIER 2: .4X TO 1X TIER 1 JSY
RANDOM INSERTS IN PACKS
STATED PRINT RUN 99 SERIAL #'d SETS

2002 Ultimate Collection Game Jersey Tier 2 Gold

*TIER 2 GOLD: .75X TO 2X TIER JSY
RANDOM INSERTS IN PACKS
STATED PRINT RUN 30 SERIAL #'d SETS

2002 Ultimate Collection Game Jersey Tier 3

*TIER 3: .3X TO .8X TIER 1 JSY
RANDOM INSERTS IN PACKS
STATED PRINT RUN 199 SERIAL #'d SETS

2002 Ultimate Collection Game Jersey Tier 4

*TIER 4: .3X TO .8X TIER 1 JSY
RANDOM INSERTS IN PACKS
STATED PRINT RUN 199 SERIAL #'d SETS

2002 Ultimate Collection Patch Card

RANDOM INSERTS IN PACKS
STATED PRINT RUN 100 SERIAL #'d SETS
PRICES LISTED FOR 1 OR 2-COLOR PATCH
*3-COLOR PATCH: 1X TO 1.5X HI COLUMN
CJ Chipper Jones 20.00 50.00
IR Ivan Rodriguez 20.00 50.00
IS Ichiro Suzuki 75.00 150.00
KI Kazuhisa Ishii 20.00 50.00
LG Luis Gonzalez 15.00 40.00
MM Mark McGwire 15.00 40.00
MP Mark Prior 12.50 30.00
SG Shawn Green 15.00 40.00
SS Sammy Sosa 20.00 50.00
TH Todd Helton 20.00 50.00

2002 Ultimate Collection Patch Card Double

RANDOM INSERTS IN PACKS
STATED PRINT RUN 100 SERIAL #'d SETS
DE J.Drew/J.Edmonds 10.00 25.00
GC J.Giambi/R.Clemens 10.00 25.00
IG I.Suzuki/K.Griffey Jr. 75.00 150.00
JS R.Johnson/C.Schilling 40.00 80.00
MG G.Maddux/T.Glavine 20.00 50.00
MS M.McGwire/S.Sosa 50.00 100.00
PA M.Piazza/R.Alomar 50.00 100.00
RG A.Rodriguez/J.Gonzalez 50.00 100.00
RM M.Ramirez/P.Martinez 20.00 50.00

2002 Ultimate Collection Patch Card Double Gold

*GOLD: .75X TO 1.5X BASIC PATCH
RANDOM INSERTS IN PACKS
STATED PRINT RUN 50 SERIAL #'d SETS
MANTLE/DIMAGGIO PRINT 13 #'d CARDS
MANTLE/DIMAGGIO AVAIL.ONLY IN GOLD
MANTLE/DIMAGGIO TOO SCARCE TO PRICE

2002 Ultimate Collection Signatures Tier 1

PRINT RUNS B/WN 75-329 COPIES PER
GOLD PRINT RUN 25 SERIAL #'d SETS
NO GOLD PRICING DUE TO SCARCITY
AD1 Adam Dunn/125 8.00 20.00
AR1 Alex Rodriguez/329 30.00 60.00
BG1 Brian Giles/220 8.00 20.00
BZ1 Barry Zito/199 8.00 20.00
CD1 Carlos Delgado/95 12.00 30.00
CR1 Cal Ripken/75 100.00 200.00
GS1 Gary Sheffield/95 10.00 25.00
JD1 J.D. Drew/220 8.00 20.00
JG1 Jason Giambi/295 8.00 20.00
JK1 Jason Kendall/220 8.00 20.00
JT1 Jim Thome/90 30.00 80.00
KG1 Ken Griffey Jr./195 60.00 120.00
LB1 Lance Berkman/179 8.00 20.00
LG1 Luis Gonzalez/199 8.00 20.00
MP1 Mark Prior/160 10.00 25.00
PB1 Pat Burrell/95 12.00 30.00
RA1 Roberto Alomar/155 10.00 25.00
RC1 Roger Clemens/320 25.00 60.00
SR1 Scott Rolen/160 12.00 30.00

2002 Ultimate Collection Signatures Tier 2

PRINT RUNS B/WN 30-85 COPIES PER
GOLD PRINT RUN 10 SERIAL #'d SETS
NO GOLD PRICING DUE TO SCARCITY
AJ2 Andruw Jones/51 30.00 60.00
AR2 Alex Rodriguez/75 25.00 60.00
BZ2 Barry Zito/70 20.00 50.00
DS2 Duke Snider/51 30.00 60.00
FT2 Frank Thomas/51 40.00 80.00
JB2 Jeff Bagwell/51 20.00 50.00
JG2 Jason Giambi/50 20.00 50.00
KG2 Ken Griffey Jr./30 75.00 150.00
KP2 Kirby Puckett/75 60.00 120.00
KW2 Kerry Wood/51 30.00 60.00
LB2 Lance Berkman/85 12.50 30.00
LG2 Luis Gonzalez/70 12.50 30.00
MP2 Mark Prior/60 15.00 40.00
SR2 Scott Rolen/60 30.00 60.00
TG2 Tony Gwynn/51 50.00 100.00
TH2 Todd Helton/51 30.00 60.00

2002 Ultimate Collection Signed Excellence

*MCGWIRE 583 HR: 1X TO 1.5X HI COLUMN
STATED PRINT RUNS LISTED BELOW
LESS THAN 100 PER NON-SERIAL #'d MADE
I1 Ichiro Suzuki/56 1000.00 2000.00
I2 Ichiro Suzuki/51 1000.00 2000.00
I5 Ichiro Suzuki Batting 400.00 600.00
I6 Ichiro Suzuki Throwing 400.00 600.00
MM1 Mark McGwire/70 75.00 200.00
MM2 Mark McGwire/65 125.00 300.00
MM3 Mark McGwire A's/49 125.00 300.00
MM5 Mark McGwire Standing 75.00 200.00
MM6 Mark McGwire Waving 75.00 200.00
MM7 Mark McGwire A's Fldg 75.00 200.00
SS1 Sammy Sosa/66 40.00 100.00
SS2 Sammy Sosa/64 40.00 100.00
SS3 Sammy Sosa/54 40.00 100.00
SS5 Sammy Sosa Running 25.00 60.00
SS6 Sammy Sosa Holding Bat 25.00 60.00
SS7 Sammy Sosa Throwing 25.00 60.00

2003 Ultimate Collection

COMMON CARD (1-84) .60 1.50
1-84 STATED ODDS TWO PER PACK
1-84 PRINT RUN 850 SERIAL #'d SETS
COMMON CARD (85-117) 1.00 2.50
85-117 PRINT RUN 625 SERIAL #'d SETS
COMMON CARD (118-140) 1.00 2.50
118-140 PRINT RUN 399 SERIAL #'d SETS
COMMON CARD (141-158) 1.25 3.00
141-158 PRINT RUN 250 SERIAL #'d SETS
COMMON CARD (159-168) 2.00 5.00
159-168 PRINT RUN 100 SERIAL #'d SETS
85-168 STATED ODDS ONE PER PACK
COMMON CARD (169-174) 6.00 15.00
169-174 & ULT.SIG.OVERALL ODDS 1:4
COMMON CARD (175-180) 6.00 15.00
175-180 & BUYBACK OVERALL ODDS 1:8
169-180 PRINT RUN 250 SERIAL #'d SETS
MATSUI PART LIVE/ PART EXCH
EXCHANGE DEADLINE 12/17/06
1 Ichiro Suzuki 2.00 5.00
2 Ken Griffey Jr. 3.00 8.00
3 Sammy Sosa 1.50 4.00
4 Jason Giambi .60 1.50
5 Mike Piazza 1.50 4.00
6 Derek Jeter 4.00 10.00
7 Randy Johnson 1.50 4.00
8 Barry Bonds 2.50 6.00
9 Carlos Delgado .60 1.50
10 Mark Prior 1.00 2.50
11 Vladimir Guerrero 1.00 2.50
12 Alfonso Soriano 1.00 2.50
13 Jim Thome 1.00 2.50
14 Pedro Martinez 1.00 2.50
15 Nomar Garciaparra 1.00 2.50
16 Chipper Jones 1.50 4.00
17 Rocco Baldelli .60 1.50
18 Dontrelle Willis .60 1.50
19 Garret Anderson .60 1.50
20 Jeff Bagwell 1.00 2.50
21 Jim Edmonds 1.00 2.50
22 Rickey Henderson 1.50 4.00
23 Torii Hunter .60 1.50
24 Tom Glavine 1.00 2.50
25 Hideo Nomo 1.50 4.00
26 Luis Gonzalez .60 1.50
27 Alex Rodriguez 2.00 5.00
28 Albert Pujols 2.00 5.00
29 Manny Ramirez 1.50 4.00
30 Rafael Palmeiro 1.00 2.50
31 Bernie Williams 1.00 2.50
32 Curt Schilling 1.00 2.50
33 Roger Clemens 2.00 5.00
34 Andruw Jones .60 1.50
35 J.D. Drew .60 1.50
36 Kerry Wood .60 1.50
37 Scott Rolen 1.00 2.50
38 Darin Erstad .60 1.50
39 Joe DiMaggio 3.00 8.00
40 Magglio Ordonez 1.00 2.50
41 Todd Helton 1.00 2.50
42 Barry Zito 1.00 2.50
43 Mickey Mantle 5.00 12.00
44 Miguel Tejada 1.00 2.50
45 Troy Glaus .60 1.50
46 Kazuhisa Ishii .60 1.50
47 Adam Dunn 1.00 2.50
48 Ted Williams 3.00 8.00
49 Mike Mussina 1.00 2.50
50 Ivan Rodriguez 1.00 2.50
51 Jacque Jones .60 1.50
52 Stan Musial 2.50 6.00
53 Mariano Rivera 2.00 5.00
54 Larry Walker 1.00 2.50
55 Aaron Boone .60 1.50
56 Hank Blalock .60 1.50
57 Rich Harden 1.00 2.50
58 Lance Berkman 1.00 2.50
59 Eric Chavez .60 1.50
60 Carlos Beltran 1.00 2.50
61 Roy Oswalt 1.00 2.50
62 Moises Alou .60 1.50
63 Nolan Ryan 5.00 12.00
64 Jeff Kent .60 1.50
65 Roberto Alomar 1.00 2.50
66 Runelvys Hernandez .60 1.50
67 Roy Halladay 1.00 2.50
68 Tim Hudson 1.00 2.50
69 Tom Seaver 1.00 2.50
70 Edgardo Alfonzo .60 1.50
71 Andy Pettitte 1.00 2.50
72 Preston Wilson .60 1.50
73 Frank Thomas 1.50 4.00
74 Jerome Williams .60 1.50
75 Shawn Green .60 1.50
76 David Wells .60 1.50
77 John Smoltz 1.50 4.00
78 Jorge Posada 1.00 2.50
79 Marlon Byrd .60 1.50
80 Austin Kearns .60 1.50
81 Bret Boone .60 1.50
82 Rafael Furcal .60 1.50
83 Jay Gibbons .60 1.50
84 Shane Reynolds .60 1.50
85 Nate Bland UR T1 RC 1.00 2.50
86 Willie Eyre UR T1 RC 1.00 2.50
87 Jeremy Guthrie UR T1 1.00 2.50
88 Jeremy Wedel UR T1 RC 1.00 2.50
89 Jhonny Peralta UR T1 1.00 2.50
90 Luis Ayala UR T1 RC 1.00 2.50
91 Michael Hessman UR T1 RC 1.00 2.50
92 Michael Nakamura UR T1 RC 1.00 2.50
93 Nook Logan UR T1 RC 1.00 2.50
94 Rett Johnson UR T1 RC 1.00 2.50
95 Josh Hall UR T1 RC 1.00 2.50
96 Julio Manon UR T1 RC 1.00 2.50
97 Heath Bell UR T1 RC 1.50 4.00
98 Ian Ferguson UR T1 RC 1.00 2.50
99 Jason Gilfillan UR T1 RC 1.00 2.50
100 Jason Roach UR T1 RC 1.00 2.50
101 Jason Shiell UR T1 RC 1.00 2.50
102 Termel Sledge UR T1 RC 1.00 2.50
103 Phil Seibel UR T1 RC 1.00 2.50
104 Jeff Duncan UR T1 RC 1.00 2.50
105 Mike Neu UR T1 RC 1.00 2.50
106 Colin Porter UR T1 RC 1.00 2.50
107 David Matranga UR T1 RC 1.00 2.50
108 Aaron Looper UR T1 RC 1.00 2.50
109 Jeremy Bonderman UR T1 RC 4.00 10.00
110 Miguel Ojeda UR T1 RC 1.00 2.50
111 Chad Cordero UR T1 RC 1.00 2.50
112 Shane Bazzell UR T1 RC 1.00 2.50
113 Tim Olson UR T1 RC 1.00 2.50
114 Michel Hernandez UR T1 RC 1.00 2.50
115 Chien-Ming Wang UR T1 RC 4.00 10.00
116 Josh Stewart UR T1 RC 1.00 2.50
117 Clint Barmes UR T1 RC 2.50 6.00
118 Craig Brazell UR T2 RC 1.00 2.50
119 Josh Willingham UR T2 RC 3.00 8.00
120 Brent Hoard UR T2 RC 1.00 2.50
121 Francisco Rosario UR T2 RC 1.00 2.50
122 Rick Roberts UR T2 RC 1.00 2.50
123 Geoff Geary UR T2 RC 1.00 2.50
124 Edgar Gonzalez UR T2 RC 1.00 2.50
125 Kevin Correia UR T2 RC 1.00 2.50
126 Ryan Cameron UR T2 RC 1.00 2.50
127 Beau Kemp UR T2 RC 1.00 2.50
128 Tommy Phelps UR T2 1.00 2.50
129 Mark Malaska UR T2 RC 1.00 2.50
130 Kevin Ohme UR T2 RC 1.00 2.50
131 Humberto Quintero UR T2 RC 1.00 2.50
132 Aquilino Lopez UR T2 RC 1.00 2.50
133 Andrew Brown UR T2 RC 1.00 2.50
134 Wilfredo Ledezma UR T2 RC 1.00 2.50
135 Luis De Los Santos UR T2 1.00 2.50
136 Garrett Atkins UR T2 1.00 2.50
137 Fernando Cabrera UR T2 RC 1.00 2.50
138 D.J. Carrasco UR T2 RC 1.00 2.50
139 Alfredo Gonzalez UR T2 RC 1.00 2.50
140 Alex Prieto UR T2 RC 1.00 2.50
141 Matt Kata UR T3 RC 1.25 3.00
142 Chris Capuano UR T3 RC 1.25 3.00
143 Bobby Madritsch UR T3 RC 1.25 3.00
144 Greg Jones UR T3 RC 1.25 3.00
145 Pete Zoccolillo UR T3 RC 1.25 3.00
146 Chad Gaudin UR T3 RC 1.25 3.00
147 Rosman Garcia UR T3 RC 1.25 3.00
148 Gerald Laird UR T3 1.25 3.00
149 Danny Garcia UR T3 RC 1.25 3.00
150 Stephen Randolph UR T3 RC 1.25 3.00
151 Pete LaForest UR T3 RC 1.25 3.00
152 Brian Sweeney UR T3 RC 1.25 3.00
153 Aaron Miles UR T3 RC 1.25 3.00
154 Jorge DePaula UR T3 UER 1.25 3.00
155 Graham Koonce UR T3 RC 1.25 3.00
156 Tom Gregorio UR T3 RC 1.25 3.00
157 Javier A. Lopez UR T3 RC 1.25 3.00
158 Oscar Villarreal UR T3 RC 1.25 3.00
159 Prentice Redman UR T4 RC 2.00 5.00
160 Francisco Cruceta UR T4 RC 2.00 5.00
161 Guillermo Quiroz UR T4 RC 2.00 5.00
162 Jeremy Griffiths UR T4 RC 2.00 5.00
163 Lew Ford UR T4 RC 2.00 5.00
164 Rob Hammock UR T4 RC 2.00 5.00
165 Todd Wellemeyer UR T4 RC 2.00 5.00
166 Ryan Wagner UR T4 RC 2.00 5.00
167 Edwin Jackson UR T4 RC 3.00 8.00
168 Dan Haren UR T4 RC 10.00 25.00
169 Hideki Matsui AU RC 250.00 350.00
170 Jose Contreras AU RC 10.00 25.00
171 Delmon Young AU RC 25.00 60.00
172 Rickie Weeks AU RC 10.00 25.00
173 Brandon Webb AU RC 10.00 25.00
174 Bo Hart AU RC 6.00 15.00
175 Rocco Baldelli YS AU 6.00 15.00
176 Jose Reyes YS AU 10.00 25.00
177 Dontrelle Willis YS AU 6.00 15.00
178 Bobby Hill YS AU 6.00 15.00
179 Jae Weong Seo YS AU 10.00 25.00
180 Jesse Foppert YS AU 6.00 15.00

2003 Ultimate Collection Gold

*GOLD ACTIVE 1-84: 2.5X TO 6X BASIC
*GOLD RETIRED 1-84: 2.5X TO 6X BASIC
1-84 PRINT RUN 50 SERIAL #'d SETS
*GOLD 84-117: 1.5X TO 4X BASIC
84-117 PRINT RUN 50 SERIAL #'d SETS
*GOLD 118-140: 1.5X TO 4X BASIC
118-140 PRINT RUN 35 SERIAL #'d SETS
*GOLD 141-158: 1.5X TO 4X BASIC
141-158 PRINT RUN 25 SERIAL #'d SETS
159-168 PRINT RUN 10 SERIAL #'d SETS
159-168 NO PRICING DUE TO SCARCITY
169-174 AU PRINT RUN 25 SERIAL #'d SETS
169-174 AU NO PRICING DUE TO SCARCITY
175-180 AU PRINT RUN 25 SERIAL #'d SETS
175-180 AU NO PRICING DUE TO SCARCITY

2003 Ultimate Collection Buybacks
BUYBACKS & YS 175-180 OVERALL ODDS 1:8
PRINT RUNS B/WN 1-75 COPIES PER
NO PRICING ON QTY OF 15 OR LESS
4 Hank Blalock 02-3 SUP/35 15.00 40.00
5 Hank Blalock 03 40M/25 20.00 50.00
6 Hank Blalock 03 GF/25 20.00 50.00
8 Hank Blalock 03 Patch/25 20.00 50.00
9 Hank Blalock 03 SPA/20 20.00 50.00
10 Hank Blalock 03 SPA/25 20.00 50.00
12 Hank Blalock 03 VIN/25 20.00 50.00
61 Luis Gonzalez 03 40M HR/25 20.00 50.00
66 Luis Gonzalez 03 Patch/17 20.00 50.00
68 Luis Gonzalez 03 SPA/25 20.00 50.00
71 Luis Gonzalez 03 VIN/25 20.00 50.00
72 K.Griffey Jr. 02-3 SUP/75 30.00 60.00
73 K.Griffey 02-3 SUP Spok/50 30.00 60.00
74 K.Griffey Jr. 03 40M/50 30.00 60.00
75 K.Griffey 03 40M HR624/50 30.00 60.00
76 K.Griffey 03 40M HR825/50 30.00 60.00
77 K.Griffey 03 40M HR829/50 30.00 60.00
78 K.Griffey Jr. 03 40M T40/50 30.00 60.00
79 K.Griffey Jr. 03 GF/50 30.00 60.00
82 K.Griffey Jr. 03 HON/50 40.00 80.00
83 K.Griffey Jr. 03 HON SP/30 40.00 80.00
84 K.Griffey Jr. 03 Patch/75 40.00 80.00
85 K.Griffey Jr. 03 PB/75 40.00 80.00
86 K.Griffey Jr. 03 SPA/50 40.00 80.00
87 K.Griffey Jr. 03 SPA/75 40.00 80.00
88 K.Griffey Jr. 03 SPx/75 40.00 80.00
89 K.Griffey Jr. 03 SWS/75 40.00 80.00
94 K.Griffey Jr. 03 UDA/75 40.00 80.00
95 K.Griffey Jr. 03 VIN/50 40.00 80.00
96 Torii Hunter 03 40M/18 8.00 20.00
99 Torii Hunter 03 Patch/25 8.00 20.00
100 Torii Hunter 03 PB/50 8.00 20.00
105 Torii Hunter 03 VIN/25 8.00 20.00
118 Austin Kearns 03 40M/33 15.00 40.00
126 Matsui 03 40M NR/20 200.00 400.00
127 H.Mat 03 40M FlagNR/20 200.00 400.00
128 H.Mat 03 GFw Pedro/18 200.00 400.00
130 Hideki Matsui 03 PB/17 250.00 500.00
132 Hideki Matsui 03 UD/25 250.00 500.00
135 Hideki Matsui 03 VIN/25 250.00 500.00
143 Stan Musial 02 SPLC/30 40.00 80.00
145 Stan Musial 03 PB/50 30.00 60.00
147 Stan Musial 03 SWSC/37 40.00 80.00
150 Stan Musial 03 VIN/50 30.00 60.00
186 Sammy Sosa 02-3 SUP/25 50.00 100.00
194 Sammy Sosa 03 PB/25 50.00 100.00
195 Sammy Sosa 03 SPA/25 50.00 100.00
199 Sammy Sosa 03 UDA/17 50.00 100.00
202 Sammy Sosa 03 VIN/25 50.00 100.00
203 Mark Teixeira 03 40M/50 15.00 40.00
205 Mark Teixeira 03 Patch/50 15.00 40.00
206 Mark Teixeira 03 SPA RA/25 20.00 50.00
207 Mark Teixeira 03 SWS/23 20.00 50.00
208 Mark Teixeira 03 UD/25 20.00 50.00
210 Mark Teixeira 03 VIN/25 20.00 50.00

2003 Ultimate Collection Double Barrel
PRINT RUNS B/WN 1-3 COPIES PER
NO PRICING DUE TO SCARCITY

2003 Ultimate Collection Dual Jersey
STATED PRINT RUN 50 SERIAL #'d SETS
*GOLD: .75X TO 1.5X BASIC
GOLD PRINT RUN 25 SERIAL #'d SETS
OVERALL GU ODDS 3:4
ALL ARE DUAL JSY UNLESS NOTED
AH A.Soriano/H.Matsui 20.00 50.00
AI A.Pujols I.Suzuki 30.00 60.00
BK J.Bagwell J.Kent 10.00 25.00
CA C.Jones A.Jones 10.00 25.00
CJ C.Delgado J.Giambi 6.00 15.00
DE J.Drew J.Edmonds 6.00 15.00
DG C.Delgado V.Guerrero 10.00 25.00
DM DiMag Pant Mantle J-P 125.00 250.00
DP C.Delgado R.Palmeiro 10.00 25.00
DW DiMag J-P T.Williams 100.00 175.00
GB S.Green K.Brown 6.00 15.00
GD K.Griffey Jr. A.Dunn 15.00 40.00
GE T.Glaus D.Erstad 6.00 15.00
GP K.Griffey Jr. R.Palmeiro 15.00 40.00
GR N.Garciaparra A.Rodriguez 15.00 40.00
GS V.Guerrero S.Sosa 10.00 25.00
HJ T.Hunter J.Jones 6.00 15.00
HZ R.Halladay B.Zito 6.00 15.00
IG I.Suzuki K.Griffey Jr. 30.00 60.00
IN I.Suzuki H.Nomo 40.00 80.00
IS I.Suzuki S.Sosa 30.00 60.00
JF A.Jones R.Furcal 10.00 25.00
JM J.Posada M.Piazza 15.00 40.00
MC G.Maddux R.Clemens 15.00 40.00
MW Mantle J-P T.Williams 150.00 250.00
NI H.Nomo K.Ishii 15.00 40.00
NM H.Nomo H.Matsui 30.00 60.00
PC P.Martinez R.Clemens 15.00 40.00
PM A.Pettitte M.Mussina 10.00 25.00
PS M.Prior S.Sosa 10.00 25.00
RM M.Ramirez P.Martinez 10.00 25.00
RP A.Rodriguez R.Palmeiro 12.50 30.00
SA S.Rolen A.Pujols 20.00 50.00
SB A.Soriano B.Williams 10.00 25.00
SJ C.Schilling R.Johnson 10.00 25.00
SM J.Smoltz G.Maddux 15.00 40.00
TB M.Teixeira H.Blalock 10.00 25.00
TH J.Thome T.Helton 10.00 25.00
TR M.Tejada A.Rodriguez 10.00 25.00
WL D.Willis M.Lowell 10.00 25.00
YW D.Young Pants R.Weeks 15.00 40.00

2003 Ultimate Collection Dual Patch
OVERALL GU ODDS 3:4
PRINT RUNS B/WN 14-99 COPIES PER
NO PRICING ON QTY OF 14 OR LESS
AI A.Pujols/I.Suzuki/99 125.00 200.00
AM A.Pettitte/M.Mussina/99 30.00 60.00
BK J.Bagwell/J.Kent/99 20.00 50.00
CA C.Jones/A.Jones/99 20.00 50.00
CV C.Delgado/V.Guerrero/99 20.00 50.00
DE J.Drew/J.Edmonds/99 15.00 40.00
DG C.Delgado/J.Giambi/99 15.00 40.00
GB S.Green/K.Brown/99 15.00 40.00
GD K.Griffey Jr./A.Dunn/99 30.00 60.00
GE T.Glaus/D.Erstad/99 15.00 40.00
GR N.Garciaparra/A.Rod/99 50.00 100.00
GS V.Guerrero/S.Sosa/99 15.00 40.00
HJ T.Hunter/J.Jones/83 15.00 40.00
HZ R.Halladay/B.Zito/99 15.00 40.00
IG I.Suzuki/K.Griffey Jr./99 60.00 120.00
IN I.Suzuki/H.Nomo/99 75.00 150.00
IS I.Suzuki/S.Sosa/99 60.00 120.00
JF A.Jones/R.Furcal/99 20.00 50.00
JG J.Smoltz/G.Maddux/99 20.00 50.00
MC G.Maddux/R.Clemens/75 12.00 30.00
NI H.Nomo/K.Ishii/63 50.00 100.00
PM J.Posada/M.Piazza/73 30.00 60.00
PS M.Prior/S.Sosa/99 20.00 50.00
RM M.Ramirez/P.Martinez/99 20.00 50.00
SA S.Rolen/A.Pujols/99 50.00 100.00
SB A.Soriano/B.Williams/21 40.00 80.00
SJ C.Schilling/R.Johnson/99 20.00 50.00
SM A.Soriano/H.Matsui/99 40.00 80.00
TB M.Teixeira/H.Blalock/99 15.00 40.00
TH J.Thome/T.Helton/99 15.00 40.00
TR M.Tejada/A.Rodriguez/99 30.00 60.00
WL D.Willis/M.Lowell/85 20.00 50.00
YW D.Young/R.Weeks/28 50.00 100.00

2003 Ultimate Collection Dual Patch Gold
*GOLD: .6X TO 1.2X BASIC PATCH p/r 63-99
*GOLD: .5X TO 1X BASIC PATCH p/r 21-28
OVERALL GU ODDS 3:4
STATED PRINT RUN 35 SERIAL #'d SETS
DIMAGGIO/WILLIAMS PRINT RUN 1 #'d CARD
SORIANO/MATSUI PRINT RUN 15 #'d CARDS
NO PRICING ON QTY OF 15 OR LESS
DP C.Delgado/R.Palmeiro 30.00 60.00
GP K.Griffey Jr./R.Palmeiro 40.00 80.00
NM H.Nomo/H.Matsui 125.00 200.00
PR P.Martinez/R.Clemens 40.00 80.00
RP A.Rodriguez/R.Palmeiro 40.00 80.00

2003 Ultimate Collection Signatures
ULT.SIG. & AU RC OVERALL ODDS 1:4
PRINT RUNS B/WN 30-350 COPIES PER
GRIFFEY/MATSUI PART LIVE/ PART EXCH.
EXCHANGE DEADLINE 12/17/06
AP1 Albert Pujols w/Glove/40 175.00 250.00
AP2 Albert Pujols w/Bat/35 175.00 250.00
AR1 Alex Rodriguez/75 30.00 60.00
AR2 Alex Rodriguez/60 30.00 60.00
BG1 Bob Gibson Arm Up/299 10.00 25.00
BG2 Bob Gibson Stance/199 12.50 30.00
CD1 Carlos Delgado Hitting/150 10.00 25.00
CR1 Cal Ripken w/Helmet/85 75.00 150.00
CR2 Cal Ripken Fielding/85 75.00 150.00
CY1 Carl Yastrzemski w/Bat/199 40.00 80.00
DY1 Delmon Young Run/300 10.00 25.00
DY2 Delmon Young w/Bat/300 10.00 25.00
EG1 Eric Gagne Arm Down/350 20.00 50.00
GC1 Gary Carter Hitting/199 12.00 30.00
GM1 Greg Maddux New Uni/250 60.00 120.00
GM2 G.Maddux Retro Uni/140 50.00 100.00
HM1 H.Matsui w/Glove/250 175.00 300.00
HM2 H.Matsui Throwing/240 175.00 300.00
IS1 I.Suzuki w/Shades/199 500.00 600.00
IS2 Ichiro Suzuki Running/99 500.00 600.00
JG1 Jason Giambi Torso/35 10.00 25.00
JG2 J.Giambi Open Swing/35 10.00 25.00
KG1 Ken Griffey Jr. Hitting/350 40.00 80.00
KG2 Ken Griffey Jr. w/Bat/350 40.00 80.00
KW1 K.Wood Black Glv/170 10.00 25.00
KW2 K.Wood Brown Glv/85 10.00 25.00
MP1 Mark Prior w/Glove/299 10.00 25.00
MP2 Mark Prior Arm Up/225 10.00 25.00
NG1 N.Garciaparra/125 12.00 30.00
NG2 N.Garciaparra Hitting/180 12.00 30.00
NR1 Nolan Ryan Blue Uni/85 50.00 100.00
NR2 Nolan Ryan White Uni/75 50.00 100.00
OS1 Ozzie Smith Hitting/199 15.00 40.00
RC1 R.Clemens Glove Out/70 75.00 150.00
RC2 R.Clemens Arm Up/30 100.00 175.00
RJ1 R.Johnson Stripe Uni/75 75.00 150.00
RJ2 R.Johnson Black Uni/50 75.00 150.00
RS1 R.Sandberg Blue Uni/240 20.00 50.00
RS2 R.Sandberg Stripe Uni/200 20.00 50.00
RW1 R.Weeks White Uni/300 10.00 25.00
RW2 R.Weeks Red Uni/300 10.00 25.00
TS1 Tom Seaver Arm Up/50 40.00 100.00
TS2 Tom Seaver Arm Down/60 40.00 100.00
VG1 V.Guerrero Smiling/75 30.00 60.00
VG2 V.Guerrero Hitting/50 40.00 80.00

2003 Ultimate Collection Signatures Gold
ULT.SIG. & AU RC OVERALL ODDS 1:4
STATED PRINT RUN 25 SERIAL #'d SETS
AP Albert Pujols w/Glove 175.00 250.00
AR Alex Rodriguez 50.00 100.00
BG Bob Gibson Arm Up 15.00 40.00
CD Carlos Delgado Hitting 15.00 40.00
CR Cal Ripken w/Helmet 175.00 300.00
CY Carl Yastrzemski w/Bat 75.00 150.00
EG Eric Gagne Arm Down 50.00 100.00
GC Gary Carter Hitting 50.00 100.00
GM Greg Maddux New Uni 150.00 250.00
HM H.Matsui w/Glove 175.00 300.00
IS Ichiro Suzuki w/Shades 600.00 1200.00
JG Jason Giambi Torso 15.00 40.00
KG Ken Griffey Jr. Hitting 60.00 120.00
KW K.Wood Black Glv 15.00 40.00
MP Mark Prior w/Glove 15.00 40.00
NG N.Garciaparra 15.00 40.00
NR Nolan Ryan Blue Uni 60.00 120.00
OS Ozzie Smith Hitting 75.00 150.00
RC R.Clemens Glove Out 150.00 250.00
RJ R.Johnson Stripe Uni 100.00 200.00
RS R.Sandberg Blue Uni 75.00 150.00
RW R.Weeks White Uni 40.00 80.00
TS Tom Seaver Arms Up 20.00 50.00
VG V.Guerrero Smiling 50.00 100.00

2003 Ultimate Collection Game Jersey Tier 1
STATED PRINT RUN 99 SERIAL #'d SETS
COPPER PRINT RUN 10 SERIAL #'d SETS
NO COPPER PRICING DUE TO SCARCITY
*GOLD p/r 75: .4X TO 1X BASIC
*GOLD MATSUI p/r 55: .6X TO 1.5X BASIC
*GOLD p/r 51: .6X TO 1.5X BASIC
*GOLD p/r 44-48: .75X TO 2X BASIC
*GOLD p/r 25-35: 1X TO 2.5X BASIC
*GOLD p/r 17-24: 1.25X TO 3X BASIC
GOLD PRINT RUNS B/WN 1-75 COPIES PER
NO GOLD PRICING ON QTY OF 15 OR LESS
OVERALL GU ODDS 3:4
AD Adam Dunn Red Jsy 4.00 10.00
AJ Andruw Jones w/Bat 6.00 15.00
AP Albert Pujols Running 10.00 25.00
AR Alex Rodriguez Throw 8.00 20.00
AS Alfonso Soriano No Glv 4.00 10.00
BW Bernie Williams White Jsy 6.00 15.00
BZ Barry Zito Green Jsy 4.00 10.00
CD Carlos Delgado Blue Jsy 4.00 10.00
CJ Chipper Jones No Bat 6.00 15.00
CS Curt Schilling Arm Up 4.00 10.00
DW Dontrelle Willis Black Jsy 6.00 15.00
DY Delmon Young Throw 6.00 15.00
FT Frank Thomas Black Jsy 6.00 15.00
GM Greg Maddux White Jsy 8.00 20.00
GS Gary Sheffield Throw 4.00 10.00
HM Hideki Matsui Ball Toss 20.00 50.00
HN Hideo Nomo Gray Jsy 10.00 25.00
IS Ichiro Suzuki Gray Jsy 12.50 30.00
JE Jim Edmonds White Jsy 4.00 10.00
JG Jason Giambi No Bat 4.00 10.00
JR Jose Reyes Throw 4.00 10.00
JT Jim Thome Red Jsy 6.00 15.00
KG Ken Griffey Jr. Gray Jsy 10.00 25.00
KI Kazuhisa Ishii Arms Up 4.00 10.00
KW Kerry Wood Pitching 4.00 10.00
MI Mike Piazza Mask On 8.00 20.00
MM Mike Mussina Blue Jsy 6.00 15.00
MP Mark Prior Pitching 6.00 15.00
MR Manny Ramirez Red Jsy 6.00 15.00
MT Miguel Tejada White Jsy 4.00 10.00
PB Pat Burrell Running 4.00 10.00
RB Rocco Baldelli Batting 4.00 10.00
RC Roger Clemens White Jsy 10.00 25.00
RF Rafael Furcal Fielding 4.00 10.00
RJ Randy Johnson White Jsy 6.00 15.00
RW Rickie Weeks Bat Up 5.00 12.00
SG Shawn Green White Jsy 4.00 10.00
SS Sammy Sosa Running 6.00 15.00
TG Tom Glavine Black Jsy 6.00 15.00
TH Torii Hunter Running 4.00 10.00
TR Troy Glaus Dirty Jsy 4.00 10.00
VG Vladimir Guerrero w/Bat 6.00 15.00

2003 Ultimate Collection Game Jersey Tier 2
STATED PRINT RUN 75 SERIAL #'d SETS
COPPER PRINT RUN 10 SERIAL #'d SETS
NO COPPER PRICING DUE TO SCARCITY
*GOLD p/r 75: .4X TO 1X BASIC
*GOLD MATSUI p/r 55: .6X TO 1.5X BASIC
*GOLD p/r 51: .6X TO 1.5X BASIC
*GOLD p/r 44-48: .75X TO 2X BASIC
*GOLD p/r 25-35: 1X TO 2.5X BASIC
*GOLD p/r 17-24: 1.25X TO 3X BASIC
GOLD PRINT RUNS B/WN 1-75 COPIES PER
NO GOLD PRICING ON QTY OF 15 OR LESS
OVERALL GU ODDS 3:4
AD2 Adam Dunn Swing 4.00 10.00
AJ2 Andruw Jones w/Glv 6.00 15.00
AP2 Albert Pujols Batting 10.00 25.00
AR2 Alex Rodriguez Running 8.00 20.00
AS2 Alfonso Soriano w/Glv 4.00 10.00
BW2 Bernie Williams Gray Jsy 6.00 15.00
BZ2 Barry Zito Gray Jsy 4.00 10.00
CD2 Carlos Delgado Gray Jsy 4.00 10.00
CJ2 Chipper Jones w/Bat 6.00 15.00
CS2 Curt Schilling Arm Down 4.00 10.00
DW Dontrelle Willis Gray Jsy 6.00 15.00
DY2 Delmon Young w/Ball 8.00 20.00
FT2 Frank Thomas White Jsy 6.00 15.00
GM2 Greg Maddux Blue Jsy 8.00 20.00
GS2 Gary Sheffield Batting 4.00 10.00
HM2 Hideki Matsui w/Bat 20.00 50.00
HN2 Hideo Nomo Blue Jsy 10.00 25.00
IS2 Ichiro Suzuki w/Bat 10.00 25.00
JE2 Jim Edmonds Gray Jsy 4.00 10.00
JG2 Jason Giambi w/Bat 4.00 10.00
JR2 Jose Reyes Walking 4.00 10.00
JT2 Jim Thome White Jsy 6.00 15.00
KG2 Ken Griffey Jr. Red Jsy 10.00 25.00
KI2 Kazuhisa Ishii Arms Down 4.00 10.00
KW2 Kerry Wood Standing 4.00 10.00
MI2 Mike Piazza w/Bat 8.00 20.00
MM2 Mike Mussina Gray Jsy 6.00 15.00
MP2 Mark Prior Hitting 6.00 15.00
MR2 Manny Ramirez Gray Jsy 6.00 15.00
MT2 Miguel Tejada Green Jsy 4.00 10.00
PB2 Pat Burrell Swinging 4.00 10.00
RB2 Rocco Baldelli Running 4.00 10.00
RC2 Roger Clemens Blue Jsy 10.00 25.00
RF2 Rafael Furcal Running 4.00 10.00
RJ2 Randy Johnson Black Jsy 6.00 15.00
RW2 Rickie Weeks Bat Forward 5.00 12.00
SG2 Shawn Green Gray Jsy 4.00 10.00
SS2 Sammy Sosa Batting 6.00 15.00
TG2 Tom Glavine Orange Jsy 6.00 15.00
TH2 Torii Hunter Swinging 4.00 10.00
TR2 Troy Glaus Clean Jsy 4.00 10.00
VG2 Vladimir Guerrero Point Up 6.00 15.00

2003 Ultimate Collection Game Patch
STATED PRINT RUN 99 SERIAL #'d SETS
SORIANO PRINT RUN 42 SERIAL #'d CARDS
*COPPER: .6X TO 1.2X BASIC p/r 99
*COPPER: .6X TO 1.2X BASIC p/r 42
COPPER PRINT RUN 35 SERIAL #'d SETS
*GOLD: .75X TO 1.5X BASIC p/r 99
*GOLD: .75X TO 1.5X BASIC p/r 42
GOLD PRINT RUN 25 SERIAL #'d SETS
OVERALL GU ODDS 3:4
AD Adam Dunn 10.00 25.00
AJ Andruw Jones 15.00 40.00
AP Albert Pujols 15.00 40.00
AR Alex Rodriguez 20.00 50.00
AS Alfonso Soriano/42 10.00 25.00
BW Bernie Williams 15.00 40.00
BZ Barry Zito 10.00 25.00
CD Carlos Delgado 10.00 25.00
CJ Chipper Jones 15.00 40.00
CS Curt Schilling 10.00 25.00
DW Dontrelle Willis 10.00 25.00
DY Delmon Young 10.00 25.00
FT Frank Thomas 20.00 50.00
GM Greg Maddux 20.00 50.00
HM Hideki Matsui 40.00 100.00
HN Hideo Nomo 20.00 50.00
IS Ichiro Suzuki 75.00 200.00
JE Jim Edmonds 10.00 25.00
JG Jason Giambi 10.00 25.00
JR Jose Reyes 10.00 25.00
JT Jim Thome 15.00 40.00
KG Ken Griffey Jr. 25.00 60.00
KI Kazuhisa Ishii 10.00 25.00
KW Kerry Wood 10.00 25.00
MI Mike Piazza 20.00 50.00
MM Mike Mussina 15.00 40.00
MP Mark Prior 15.00 40.00
MR Manny Ramirez 15.00 40.00
MT Miguel Tejada 10.00 25.00
PB Pat Burrell 10.00 25.00
RB Rocco Baldelli 10.00 25.00
RC Roger Clemens 25.00 60.00
RF Rafael Furcal 10.00 25.00
RH Roy Halladay 10.00 25.00
RJ Randy Johnson 15.00 40.00
RW Rickie Weeks 15.00 40.00
SG Shawn Green 10.00 25.00
SS Sammy Sosa 15.00 40.00
TG Tom Glavine 15.00 40.00
TH Torii Hunter 10.00 25.00
TR Troy Glaus 10.00 25.00
VG Vladimir Guerrero 15.00 40.00

2003 Ultimate Collection Ultimate Signatures Koufax
STATED PRINT RUN 75 SERIAL #'d SETS
GOLD PRINT RUN 5 SER.#'d SETS
NO GOLD PRICING DUE TO SCARCITY
PLATINUM PRINT RUN 25 SER.#'d SETS
NO PLATINUM PRICING AVAILABLE
SK Sandy Koufax 125.00 300.00

2004 Ultimate Collection
COMMON CARD (1-42) .75 2.00
COMMON CARD (43-126) .75 2.00
1-126 STATED ODDS TWO PER PACK
1-126 PRINT RUN 675 SERIAL #'d CARDS
COMMON CARD (127-168) 1.00 2.50
127-168 PRINT RUN 525 SERIAL #'d SETS
COMMON CARD (169-194) 1.50 4.00
169-194 PRINT RUN 299 SERIAL #'d SETS
COMMON (195-209/222) 2.00 5.00
195-209/222 PRINT RUN 199 SER.#'d SETS
COMMON AUTO (210-221) 10.00 25.00
210-221 STATED ODDS 1:10
210-221 PRINT RUN 75 SERIAL #'d SETS
EXCHANGE DEADLINE 12/28/07
1 Al Kaline 2.00 5.00
2 Billy Williams 1.25 3.00
3 Bob Feller 1.25 3.00
4 Bob Gibson 1.25 3.00
5 Bob Lemon 1.25 3.00
6 Bobby Doerr 1.25 3.00
7 Brooks Robinson 1.25 3.00
8 Cal Ripken 6.00 15.00
9 Catfish Hunter 1.25 3.00
10 Eddie Mathews 2.00 5.00
11 Enos Slaughter 1.25 3.00
12 Ernie Banks 2.00 5.00
13 Fergie Jenkins 1.25 3.00
14 Gaylord Perry 1.25 3.00
15 Harmon Killebrew 2.00 5.00
16 Jim Bunning 1.25 3.00
17 Joe DiMaggio 4.00 10.00
18 Joe Morgan 1.25 3.00
19 Juan Marichal 1.25 3.00
20 Lou Brock 1.25 3.00
21 Luis Aparicio 1.25 3.00
22 Mickey Mantle 6.00 15.00
23 Mike Schmidt 3.00 8.00
24 Monte Irvin 1.25 3.00
25 Nolan Ryan 6.00 15.00
26 Pee Wee Reese 1.25 3.00
27 Phil Niekro 1.25 3.00
28 Phil Rizzuto 1.25 3.00
29 Ralph Kiner 1.25 3.00
30 Richie Ashburn 1.25 3.00
31 Robin Roberts 1.25 3.00
32 Robin Yount 2.00 5.00
33 Rod Carew 1.25 3.00
34 Rollie Fingers 1.25 3.00
35 Stan Musial 3.00 8.00
36 Ted Williams 4.00 10.00
37 Tom Seaver 1.25 3.00
38 Warren Spahn 1.25 3.00
39 Whitey Ford 1.25 3.00
40 Willie McCovey 1.25 3.00
41 Willie Stargell 1.25 3.00
42 Yogi Berra 2.00 5.00
43 Adrian Beltre 2.00 5.00
44 Albert Pujols 2.50 6.00
45 Alex Rodriguez 2.50 6.00
46 Alfonso Soriano 1.25 3.00
47 Andruw Jones .75 2.00
48 Andy Pettitte 1.25 3.00
49 Aubrey Huff .75 2.00
50 Barry Larkin 1.25 3.00
51 Ben Sheets .75 2.00
52 Bernie Williams 1.25 3.00
53 Bobby Abreu .75 2.00
54 Brad Penny .75 2.00
55 Bret Boone .75 2.00
56 Brian Giles .75 2.00
57 Carlos Beltran 1.25 3.00
58 Carlos Delgado .75 2.00
59 Carlos Guillen .75 2.00
60 Carlos Lee .75 2.00
61 Carlos Zambrano 1.25 3.00
62 Chipper Jones 2.00 5.00
63 Craig Biggio 1.25 3.00
64 Craig Wilson .75 2.00
65 Curt Schilling 1.25 3.00
66 David Ortiz 2.00 5.00
67 Derek Jeter 5.00 12.00
68 Eric Chavez .75 2.00
69 Eric Gagne .75 2.00
70 Frank Thomas 2.00 5.00
71 Garret Anderson .75 2.00
72 Gary Sheffield .75 2.00
73 Greg Maddux 2.50 6.00
74 Hank Blalock .75 2.00
75 Hideki Matsui 3.00 8.00
76 Ichiro Suzuki 2.50 6.00
77 Ivan Rodriguez 1.25 3.00
78 J.D. Drew .75 2.00
79 Jake Peavy .75 2.00
80 Jason Schmidt .75 2.00
81 Jeff Bagwell 1.25 3.00
82 Jeff Kent .75 2.00
83 Jim Thome 1.25 3.00
84 Joe Mauer 1.50 4.00
85 Johan Santana 1.25 3.00
86 Jose Reyes 1.25 3.00
87 Jose Vidro .75 2.00
88 Ken Griffey Jr. 4.00 10.00
89 Kerry Wood .75 2.00
90 Larry Walker Cards 1.25 3.00
91 Luis Gonzalez .75 2.00
92 Lyle Overbay .75 2.00
93 Magglio Ordonez 1.25 3.00
94 Manny Ramirez 2.00 5.00
95 Mark Mulder .75 2.00
96 Mark Prior 1.25 3.00
97 Mark Teixeira 1.25 3.00
98 Melvin Mora .75 2.00
99 Michael Young .75 2.00
100 Miguel Cabrera 2.00 5.00
101 Miguel Tejada 1.25 3.00
102 Mike Lowell .75 2.00
103 Mike Piazza 2.00 5.00
104 Mike Sweeney .75 2.00
105 Nomar Garciaparra 1.25 3.00
106 Oliver Perez .75 2.00
107 Pedro Martinez 1.25 3.00
108 Preston Wilson .75 2.00
109 Rafael Palmeiro 1.25 3.00
110 Randy Johnson 2.00 5.00
111 Roger Clemens 2.50 6.00
112 Roy Halladay 1.25 3.00
113 Roy Oswalt 1.25 3.00
114 Sammy Sosa 2.00 5.00
115 Scott Podsednik .75 2.00
116 Scott Rolen 1.25 3.00
117 Shawn Green .75 2.00
118 Tim Hudson 1.25 3.00
119 Todd Helton 1.25 3.00
120 Tom Glavine 1.25 3.00
121 Torii Hunter .75 2.00
122 Travis Hafner .75 2.00
123 Troy Glaus .75 2.00
124 Vernon Wells .75 2.00
125 Victor Martinez 1.25 3.00
126 Vladimir Guerrero 1.25 3.00
127 Aarom Baldiris UR T1 RC 1.00 2.50
128 Alfredo Simon UR T1 RC 1.50 4.00
129 Andres Blanco UR T1 RC 1.00 2.50
130 Jeff Bajenaru UR T1 RC 1.00 2.50
131 Bart Fortunato UR T1 RC 1.00 2.50
132 B.Medders UR T1 RC 1.00 2.50
133 Brian Dallimore UR T1 RC 1.00 2.50
134 Carlos Hines UR T1 RC 1.00 2.50
135 Carlos Vasquez UR T1 RC 1.00 2.50
136 Casey Daigle UR T1 RC 1.00 2.50
137 Chad Bentz UR T1 RC 1.00 2.50
138 Chris Aguila UR T1 RC 1.00 2.50
139 Chris Saenz UR T1 RC 1.00 2.50
140 Chris Shelton UR T1 RC 1.00 2.50
141 Colby Miller UR T1 RC 1.00 2.50
142 Dave Crouthers UR T1 RC 1.00 2.50
143 David Aardsma UR T1 RC 1.00 2.50
144 Dennis Sarfate UR T1 RC 1.00 2.50
145 Donnie Kelly UR T1 RC 1.50 4.00
146 Eddy Rodriguez UR T1 RC 1.00 2.50
147 Eduardo Villacis UR T1 RC 1.00 2.50
148 Edwardo Sierra UR T1 RC 1.00 2.50
149 Edwin Moreno UR T1 RC 1.00 2.50
150 Kyle Denney UR T1 RC 1.00 2.50
151 Evan Rust UR T1 RC 1.00 2.50
152 Fernando Nieve UR T1 RC 1.00 2.50
153 Frank Francisco UR T1 RC 1.00 2.50
154 Frank Gracesqui UR T1 RC 1.00 2.50
155 Freddy Guzman UR T1 RC 1.00 2.50
156 Greg Dobbs UR T1 RC 1.00 2.50
157 Hector Gimenez UR T1 RC 1.00 2.50
158 Jason Alfaro UR T1 RC 1.00 2.50
159 Jake Woods UR T1 RC 1.00 2.50
160 Andy Green UR T1 RC 1.00 2.50
161 Jason Bartlett UR T1 RC 3.00 8.00
162 Jason Frasor UR T1 RC 1.00 2.50
163 Jeff Bennett UR T1 RC 1.00 2.50
164 Jerome Gamble UR T1 RC 1.00 2.50
165 Jerry Gil UR T1 RC 1.00 2.50
166 Joe Hietpas UR T1 RC 1.00 2.50
167 Jorge Sequea UR T1 RC 1.00 2.50
168 Jorge Vasquez UR T1 RC 1.00 2.50
169 Josh Labandeira UR T2 RC 1.50 4.00
170 Justin Germano UR T2 RC 1.50 4.00
171 Justin Hampson UR T2 RC 1.50 4.00
172 Chris Young UR T2 RC 10.00 25.00
173 Justin Knoedler UR T2 RC 1.50 4.00
174 Justin Lehr UR T2 RC 1.50 4.00
175 Justin Leone UR T2 RC 1.50 4.00
176 Kaz Tadano UR T2 RC 1.50 4.00
177 Kevin Cave UR T2 RC 1.50 4.00
178 Linc Holdzkom UR T2 RC 1.50 4.00
179 Mike Rose UR T2 RC 1.50 4.00
180 Luis Gonzalez UR T2 RC 1.50 4.00
181 Mariano Gomez UR T2 RC 1.50 4.00
182 Rene Rivera UR T2 RC 1.50 4.00
183 Michael Wuertz UR T2 RC 1.50 4.00
184 Mike Gosling UR T2 RC 1.50 4.00
185 Mike Johnston UR T2 RC 1.50 4.00
186 Mike Rouse UR T2 RC 1.50 4.00
187 Nick Regilio UR T2 RC 1.50 4.00
188 Onil Joseph UR T2 RC 1.50 4.00
189 Orl Rodriguez UR T2 RC 1.50 4.00
190 Phil Stockman UR T2 RC 1.50 4.00
191 Renyel Pinto UR T2 RC 1.50 4.00
192 Roberto Novoa UR T2 RC 1.50 4.00
193 Roman Colon UR T2 RC 1.50 4.00
194 Ronald Belisario UR T2 RC 1.50 4.00
195 Ronny Cedeno UR T3 RC 2.00 5.00
196 Ryan Meaux UR T3 RC 2.00 5.00
197 Ryan Wing UR T3 RC 2.00 5.00
198 Scott Dohmann UR T3 RC 2.00 5.00
199 Joey Gathright UR T3 RC 2.00 5.00
200 Shawn Camp UR T3 RC 2.00 5.00
201 Shawn Hill UR T3 RC 2.00 5.00
202 Steve Andrade UR T3 RC 2.00 5.00
203 Tim Bausher UR T3 RC 2.00 5.00
204 Tim Bittner UR T3 RC 2.00 5.00
205 Brad Halsey UR T3 RC 2.00 5.00
206 William Bergolla UR T3 RC 2.00 5.00
207 Kameron Loe UR T3 RC 2.00 5.00
208 Jesse Crain UR T3 RC 3.00 8.00
209 Scott Kazmir UR T3 RC 10.00 25.00
210 Akinori Otsuka AU RC 20.00 50.00
211 Chris Oxspring AU RC 10.00 25.00
212 Ian Snell AU RC 15.00 40.00
213 John Gall AU RC 15.00 40.00
214 Jose Capellan AU RC 10.00 25.00
215 Yadier Molina AU RC 300.00 800.00
216 Merkin Valdez AU RC 10.00 25.00
218 Rusty Tucker AU RC 15.00 40.00
219 Scott Proctor AU RC 15.00 40.00
220 Sean Henn AU RC 10.00 25.00
221 Shingo Takatsu AU RC 8.00 20.00
222 Kazuo Matsui UR T3 RC 3.00 8.00

2004 Ultimate Collection Gold
*GOLD 1-42: 1.25X TO 3X BASIC
*GOLD 43-126: 1.25X TO 3X BASIC
*GOLD 127-168: 1X TO 2.5X BASIC
*GOLD 169-194: .6X TO 1.5X BASIC
OVERALL PARALLEL ODDS 1:4
1-194 PRINT RUN 50 SERIAL #'d SETS
195-209/222 PRINT RUN 25 SER.#'d SETS
AU 210-221 PRINT RUN 15 SERIAL #'d SETS
195-222 NO PRICING DUE TO SCARCITY
EXCHANGE DEADLINE 12/28/07

2004 Ultimate Collection Achievement Materials
OVERALL GAME-USED ODDS 1:4
PRINT RUNS B/WN 9-99 COPIES PER
NO PRICING ON QTY OF 9
BG Bob Gibson Jsy/68 6.00 15.00
BR Brooks Robinson Jsy/64 8.00 20.00
CA Roy Campanella Pants/51 10.00 25.00
CL Roger Clemens Jsy/63 12.50 30.00
CR Cal Ripken Pants/82 12.50 30.00
CY Carl Yastrzemski Jsy/67 12.50 30.00
DD Don Drysdale Pants/51 10.00 25.00
DJ Derek Jeter Jsy/96 12.50 30.00
DM Don Mattingly Jsy/85 10.00 25.00
EB Ernie Banks Jsy/58 10.00 25.00
EM Eddie Murray Jsy/77 6.00 15.00
FR Frank Robinson Pants/66 4.00 10.00
GB George Brett Jsy/80 10.00 25.00
GM Greg Maddux Jsy/92 10.00 25.00
HK Harmon Killebrew Jsy/69 6.00 15.00
JB Johnny Bench Jsy/68 6.00 15.00
JD Joe DiMaggio Pants/39 30.00 80.00
JP Jim Palmer Jsy/34 6.00 15.00
JR Jackie Robinson Jsy/47 30.00 60.00
KG Ken Griffey Jr. Jsy/97 10.00 25.00
MA Mickey Mantle Pants/56 60.00 120.00
MC Willie McCovey Jsy/59 8.00 20.00
MP Mike Piazza Jsy/93 10.00 25.00
MS Mike Schmidt Jsy/80 10.00 25.00
OC Orlando Cepeda Jsy/58 5.00 12.00
PM Pedro Martinez Jsy/87 6.00 15.00
RC Rob Clemente Pants/66 50.00 100.00
RJ Randy Johnson Jsy/57 6.00 15.00
RM Roger Maris Jsy/61 20.00 50.00
RO Rod Carew Jsy/49 8.00 20.00
RS Ryne Sandberg Jsy/84 8.00 20.00
RY Robin Yount Jsy/82 6.00 15.00
SC Steve Carlton Pants/72 4.00 10.00
SS Sammy Sosa Jsy/75 6.00 15.00
TM Thurman Munson Pants/70 6.00 15.00
TS Tom Seaver Jsy/69 6.00 15.00
TW Ted Williams Jsy/42 40.00 80.00
YB Yogi Berra Jsy/51 10.00 25.00

2004 Ultimate Collection All-Stars Signatures
OVERALL AU ODDS 1:4
PRINT RUNS B/WN 1-24 COPIES PER
NO PRICING ON QTY OF 12 OR LESS
EXCHANGE DEADLINE 12/28/07
BR Brooks Robinson/15 30.00 60.00
CR Cal Ripken/19 100.00 250.00
CY Carl Yastrzemski/18 40.00 80.00
OS Ozzie Smith/15 40.00 80.00
RC Rod Carew/18 20.00 50.00
SM Stan Musial/24 50.00 100.00

2004 Ultimate Collection Dual Game Patch
*OVERALL 4-COLOR: ADD 20% PREMIUM
*OVERALL 5+ COLOR: ADD 50% PREMIUM
*LOGO PATCH: ADD 50% PREMIUM
OVERALL PATCH ODDS 1:4
STATED PRINT RUN 25 SERIAL #'d SETS
BB C.Beltran/J.Bagwell 20.00 50.00
BC J.Beckett/M.Cabrera 20.00 50.00
BG L.Brock/T.Gwynn 40.00 80.00
BS G.Brett/M.Schmidt 60.00 120.00
BT H.Blalock/M.Teixeira 20.00 50.00
CG R.Carew/T.Gwynn 20.00 50.00
CP G.Carter/M.Piazza 20.00 50.00
CR E.Chavez/S.Rolen 20.00 40.00
FB C.Fisk/J.Bench 20.00 50.00
FR B.Feller/N.Ryan 50.00 100.00
GC M.Grace/W.Clark 20.00 50.00
GG K.Griffey Jr./K.Griffey Sr. 40.00 80.00
GM B.Gibson/S.Musial 40.00 80.00
GS M.Grace/R.Sandberg 75.00 150.00
HF C.Hunter/R.Fingers 20.00 50.00
JC R.Johnson/R.Clemens 20.00 50.00
JJ A.Jones/C.Jones 20.00 50.00
JM D.Jeter/H.Matsui 75.00 150.00
KC H.Killebrew/R.Carew 30.00 60.00
KM H.Killebrew/W.McCovey 30.00 60.00
KS K.Griffey Jr./S.Sosa 40.00 80.00
LS F.Lynn/I.Suzuki 60.00 120.00
MG G.Maddux/T.Glavine 20.00 50.00
MJ E.Mathews/C.Jones 40.00 80.00
MY P.Molitor/R.Yount 20.00 50.00
PC R.Palmeiro/W.Clark 20.00 50.00
PR A.Pujols/S.Rolen 30.00 60.00
RC N.Ryan/R.Clemens 50.00 100.00
RM C.Ripken/E.Murray 125.00 200.00
RP C.Ripken/J.Palmer 75.00 150.00
RR J.Robinson/P.Reese 150.00 250.00
RS N.Ryan/T.Seaver 50.00 100.00
RT C.Ripken/M.Tejada 40.00 80.00
SB J.Bunning/M.Schmidt 40.00 80.00
SM C.Schilling/P.Martinez 30.00 60.00
ST M.Schmidt/J.Thome 40.00 80.00
WM D.Winfield/D.Mattingly 40.00 80.00
WP K.Wood/M.Prior 15.00 40.00
WS B.Williams/S.Sosa 20.00 50.00
YR C.Yastrzemski/J.Rice 40.00 80.00

2004 Ultimate Collection Dual Legendary Materials
OVERALL GAME-USED ODDS 1:4
STATED PRINT RUN 50 SERIAL #'d SETS
BM Banks Jsy/McCovey Jsy 20.00 50.00
BR Ruth Pants/Maris Jsy 250.00 400.00
CB Campy Pants/Berra Jsy 40.00 80.00
CM Clemente Pnts/Muns Pnts 60.00 120.00
CS Campy Pants/Snider Pants 20.00 50.00
DM DiMag Pants/Mant Pants 150.00 250.00
DW DiMag Pants/T.Will Jsy 90.00 180.00
FD Feller Jsy/Drysdale Pants 20.00 50.00
MB Munson Pants/Berra Jsy 20.00 50.00
MC Mant Pants/Clemente Pnts 200.00 400.00
MM Mantle Pants/Maris Jsy 150.00 250.00
MW Mantle Pants/T.Will Jsy 150.00 250.00
RB Banks Jsy/Jackie Jsy 40.00 80.00
RC Jackie Jsy/Campy Pants 40.00 80.00
RD Ruth Pants/DiMag Pants 250.00 400.00
RM Ruth Pants/Mantle Pants 300.00 500.00
RP Jackie Jsy/Paige Pants 50.00 100.00
RW Clemente Pnts/McCov Jsy 60.00 120.00
WM Mathews Pants/T.Will Jsy 75.00 150.00

2004 Ultimate Collection Dual Materials
OVERALL GAME-USED ODDS 1:4
STATED PRINT RUN 60 SERIAL #'d SETS
BC Brooks Jsy/Ripken Pants 40.00 80.00
BP Bench Jsy/Piazza Jsy 15.00 40.00
BS Brett Jsy/Schmidt Jsy 15.00 40.00
CK Carew Jsy/Killebrew Jsy 15.00 40.00
CM Clark Jsy/McCovey Jsy 15.00 40.00
ER Banks Jsy/Sandberg Jsy 15.00 40.00
GS Sosa Jsy/Griffey Jr. Jsy 10.00 25.00
JC Randy Jsy/Clemens Jsy 20.00 50.00
JM Jeter Jsy/Mattingly Jsy 30.00 60.00
MC Mattingly Jsy/Clark Jsy 20.00 50.00
MP Mauer Jsy/Prior Jsy 10.00 25.00
MR Mazeroski Jsy/Jackie Jsy 40.00 80.00
MT K.Matsui Jsy/Takatsu Jsy 15.00 40.00
MY Molitor Jsy/Yount Jsy 15.00 40.00
PR Pujols Jsy/Manny Jsy 10.00 25.00
RC Ryan Jsy/Clemens Jsy 30.00 60.00
RP I.Rod Jsy/Piazza Jsy 10.00 25.00
RR Brooks Jsy/F.Rob Pants 15.00 40.00
RT Campy Pants/Muns Pants 15.00 40.00
SG Ichiro Jsy/Griffey Jr. Jsy 30.00 60.00
SP Sheets Jsy/Prior Jsy 6.00 15.00
SR Snider Pants/Reese Jsy 15.00 40.00
SS Sosa Jsy/Sandberg Jsy 30.00 60.00
TS Thome Jsy/Schmidt Jsy 20.00 50.00
WM Winf Jsy/Mattingly Jsy 15.00 40.00
WP Wood Jsy/Prior Jsy 6.00 15.00
WR Wood Jsy/Ryan Jsy 20.00 50.00
YR Yaz Jsy/Manny Jsy 20.00 50.00

2004 Ultimate Collection Dual Materials Signature
OVERALL AUTO ODDS 1:4
STATED PRINT RUN 25 SERIAL #'d SETS
BANKS/SANTO PRINT RUN 12 #'d CARDS
NO BANKS/SANTO PRICING AVAILABLE
EXCHANGE DEADLINE 12/28/07
AB Aparicio Jsy/Banks Jsy 50.00 100.00
BB Blalock Jsy/Boggs Jsy 40.00 80.00
BC Brooks Jsy/Ripken Jsy 175.00 300.00
BF Fisk Jsy/Bench Jsy 50.00 100.00
BG Beltran Jsy/Griffey Jr. Jsy 60.00 120.00

BJ Jeter Jsy/Berra Jsy 200.00 400.00
BM B.Giles Jsy/M.Giles Jsy 30.00 60.00
BP Bench Jsy/Piazza Jsy 125.00 200.00
BR Bunning Jsy/Roberts Jsy 30.00 80.00
BT Blalock Jsy/Teixeira Jsy 40.00 80.00
CB Chavez Jsy/Blalock Jsy 20.00 50.00
CC Clem Jsy/Carlt Pants EX 50.00 100.00
CJ Randy Jsy/Clemens Jsy 250.00 400.00
CK Carew Jsy/Killebrew Jsy 60.00 120.00
CL Cabrera Jsy/Lowell Jsy 50.00 100.00
CM Beltran Jsy/Cabrera Jsy 50.00 100.00
CR Chavez Jsy/Rolen Jsy 10.00 25.00
DD Jeter Jsy/Mattingly Jsy 200.00 350.00
DG Sutton Jsy/Perry Jsy 30.00 60.00
DJ Parker Jsy/Rice Jsy 20.00 50.00
DS Dawson Jsy/Sandberg Jsy 60.00 120.00
DW Dawson Pants/B.Will Jsy 30.00 60.00
ER Banks Jsy/Sandberg Jsy 125.00 200.00
FC Feller Jsy/Colavito Jsy 40.00 80.00
FR Feller Jsy/Ryan Jsy 125.00 200.00
GB Brooks Jsy/Brett Jsy 75.00 150.00
GG Grif Sr. Jsy/Grif Jr. Jsy 125.00 200.00
GM Brett Jsy/Schmidt Jsy 125.00 200.00
GP Grif Jr. Jsy/Palmeiro Jsy 125.00 200.00
GR Maddux Jsy/Clemens Jsy 200.00 350.00
GS Gagne Jsy/Smoltz Jsy 40.00 80.00
JB Jenkins Pants/Banks Pants 60.00 120.00
JC Randy Jsy/Carlt Pants EX 75.00 150.00
JD Podres Jsy/Sutton Jsy 30.00 60.00
JG Randy Jsy/Griffey Jr. Jsy 175.00 300.00
JM Chipper Jsy/Murphy Jsy 100.00 175.00
JP Jenkins Pants/Palmer Jsy 30.00 60.00
JR Jeter Jsy/Ripken Jsy 300.00 600.00
KG Killebrew Jsy/Grif Jr. Jsy 125.00 250.00
KN Wood Jsy/Ryan Jsy 75.00 150.00
KT Kazmir Jsy/Takatsu Jsy 10.00 25.00
LB Larsen Pants/Berra Pants 150.00 300.00
MB Morgan Jsy/Bench Jsy 50.00 100.00
MC Mattingly Jsy/Clark Jsy 75.00 150.00
MH Mulder Jsy/Hudson Jsy 15.00 40.00
MP Mauer Jsy/Prior Jsy 75.00 150.00
MS Mazeroski Jsy/Ryno Jsy 75.00 150.00
MW Grace Jsy/Clark Jsy 40.00 80.00
MY Molitor Jsy/Yount Jsy 75.00 150.00
NR Ryan Jsy/Clemens Jsy 250.00 400.00
OR Ortiz Jsy/Manny Jsy 125.00 200.00
OS Ozzie Jsy/Musial Jsy 100.00 250.00
PC Palmeiro Jsy/Clark Jsy 50.00 100.00
PN Perry Jsy/Niekro Jsy 30.00 60.00
PS Snider Pants/Podres Jsy 40.00 80.00
RB Mazeroski Jsy/Carew Jsy 40.00 80.00
RC Brooks Jsy/Chavez Jsy 20.00 50.00
RM Ripken Jsy/Murray Jsy 100.00 200.00
RP Brooks Jsy/Palmer Jsy 40.00 80.00
RR Brooks Jsy/F.Rob Jsy 40.00 80.00
RS Roberts Jsy/Carlt Pants EX 30.00 60.00
RT Ripken Pants/Tejada Jsy 175.00 300.00
SC Schm Jsy/Carlt Pants EX 75.00 150.00
SF Sheets Jsy/Feller Jsy 30.00 60.00
SG Sutter Jsy/Gagne Jsy 40.00 80.00
SO Sheets Jsy/Oswalt Jsy 30.00 60.00
SP Sheets Jsy/Prior Jsy 30.00 60.00
SR Brooks Jsy/Schmidt Jsy 125.00 200.00
SS Sheets Jsy/Seaver Jsy 50.00 120.00
TB Giles Jsy/Gwynn Jsy 40.00 80.00
TC Teixeira Jsy/Cabrera Jsy 50.00 100.00
WM Winf Jsy/Mattingly Jsy 40.00 80.00
WO McCovey Jsy/Cepeda Jsy 40.00 80.00
WW Clark Jsy/McCovey Jsy 75.00 150.00
YR Yaz Jsy/Manny Jsy 100.00 175.00

2004 Ultimate Collection Game Materials

OVERALL GAME-USED ODDS 1:4
STATED PRINT RUN 99 SERIAL #'d SETS
AK Al Kaline Jsy 6.00 15.00
AP Albert Pujols Jsy 10.00 25.00
BF Bob Feller Jsy 4.00 10.00
BG Bob Gibson Jsy 4.00 10.00
BM Bill Mazeroski Jsy 4.00 10.00
BR Brooks Robinson Jsy 4.00 10.00
CF Carlton Fisk Pants 4.00 10.00
CL Roger Clemens Jsy 8.00 20.00
CR Cal Ripken Jsy 10.00 25.00
CY Carl Yastrzemski Jsy 10.00 25.00
DD Don Drysdale Pants 4.00 10.00
DJ Derek Jeter Jsy 15.00 40.00
DM Don Mattingly Jsy 10.00 25.00
DS Duke Snider Pants 4.00 10.00
DW Dave Winfield Jsy 4.00 10.00
EB Ernie Banks Jsy 6.00 15.00
ED Eddie Mathews Pants 6.00 15.00
EM Eddie Murray Jsy 4.00 10.00
FR Frank Robinson Pants 4.00 10.00
GB George Brett Jsy 10.00 25.00
HK Harmon Killebrew Jsy 6.00 15.00
IS Ichiro Suzuki Jsy 25.00 60.00
JB Johnny Bench Jsy 6.00 15.00
JP Jim Palmer Jsy 4.00 10.00
JR Jackie Robinson Jsy 15.00 40.00
KG Ken Griffey Jr. Jsy 10.00 25.00
KW Kerry Wood Jsy 2.50 6.00
LB Lou Brock Jsy 4.00 10.00
MA Juan Marichal Jsy 4.00 10.00
MP Mark Prior Jsy 4.00 10.00
MS Mike Schmidt Jsy 10.00 25.00
OS Ozzie Smith Jsy 8.00 20.00
PI Mike Piazza Jsy 6.00 15.00
PM Paul Molitor Jsy 6.00 15.00
RC Rod Carew Jsy 4.00 10.00
RJ Randy Johnson Jsy 6.00 15.00
RM Roger Maris Jsy 20.00 50.00
RS Ryne Sandberg Jsy 10.00 25.00
RY Robin Yount Jsy 6.00 15.00
SC Steve Carlton Pants 4.00 10.00
SM Stan Musial Jsy 10.00 25.00
TC Ty Cobb Pants 30.00 80.00
TG Tony Gwynn Jsy 6.00 15.00
TM Thurman Munson Pants 6.00 15.00
TS Tom Seaver Jsy 4.00 10.00
WB Wade Boggs Jsy 4.00 10.00
WC Will Clark Jsy 4.00 10.00
WM Willie McCovey Jsy 4.00 10.00
WS Warren Spahn Jsy 4.00 10.00
WS Willie Stargell Jsy 4.00 10.00

2004 Ultimate Collection Game Materials Signatures

OVERALL AUTO/GAME-USED ODDS 1:4
STATED PRINT RUN 50 SERIAL #'d SETS
TEJADA A's PRINT RUN 34 SER.#'d CARDS
EXCHANGE DEADLINE 12/28/07
AD Andre Dawson Cubs Jsy 10.00 25.00
AD1 Andre Dawson Expos Jsy 10.00 25.00
AK Al Kaline Jsy 30.00 80.00
AS Alfonso Soriano Jsy 6.00 15.00
BE Josh Beckett Jsy 10.00 25.00
BF Bob Feller Jsy 10.00 25.00
BG Bob Gibson Jsy 20.00 50.00
BM Bill Mazeroski Jsy 12.00 30.00
BR Brooks Robinson Jsy 10.00 25.00
BS Ben Sheets Blue Jsy 6.00 15.00
BS1 Ben Sheets White Jsy 6.00 15.00
BU Jim Bunning Jsy 10.00 25.00
BW Billy Williams Jsy 10.00 25.00
CA Miguel Cabrera Jsy 30.00 60.00
CB Carlos Beltran Jsy 10.00 25.00
CF Carlton Fisk R.Sox Jsy 20.00 50.00
CF1 Carlton Fisk W.Sox Jsy 20.00 50.00
CJ Chipper Jones Jsy 40.00 80.00
CL R.Clemens Astros Jsy 30.00 60.00
CL1 R.Clemens Yanks Jsy 30.00 60.00
CL2 R.Clemens Sox Jsy 30.00 60.00
CO R.Colavito Tigers Jsy 40.00 80.00
CO1 R.Colavito Indians Jsy 40.00 80.00
CR Cal Ripken Jsy 75.00 150.00
CY Carl Yastrzemski Jsy 40.00 80.00
DE Dennis Eckersley Sox Jsy 10.00 25.00
DE1 Dennis Eckersley A's Jsy 10.00 25.00
DJ Derek Jeter Jsy 125.00 200.00
DM Dale Murphy Jsy 20.00 50.00
DO Don Mattingly Jsy 40.00 80.00
DS Don Sutton Jsy 10.00 25.00
DW D.Winfield Yanks Jsy 10.00 25.00
DW1 D.Winfield Padres Jsy 10.00 25.00
DY Delm Young D-Rays Jsy 6.00 15.00
DY1 Delmon Young USA Jsy 6.00 15.00
EB Ernie Banks Jsy 30.00 60.00
EC Eric Chavez Jsy 6.00 15.00
EG Eric Gagne Jsy 20.00 50.00
EM Eddie Murray O's Jsy 20.00 50.00
FJ Fergie Jenkins Pants 10.00 25.00
FR Frank Robinson O's Jsy 20.00 50.00
FR1 Frank Robinson Reds Jsy 20.00 50.00
FT Frank Thomas Jsy 40.00 80.00
GB George Brett Jsy 60.00 150.00
GC Gary Carter Expos Jsy 12.00 30.00
GC1 Gary Carter Mets Jsy 10.00 25.00
GM Greg Maddux Cubs Jsy 75.00 150.00
GM1 Greg Maddux Braves Jsy 75.00 150.00
GP Gaylord Perry Indians Jsy 10.00 25.00
GP1 Gaylord Perry Giants Jsy 10.00 25.00
HB Hank Blalock Jsy 6.00 15.00
HE Todd Helton Jsy 20.00 50.00
HK Harmon Killebrew Jsy 40.00 80.00
IR Ivan Rodriguez Jsy EXCH 15.00 40.00
JB Johnny Bench Jsy 30.00 60.00
JC Joe Carter Pants 10.00 25.00
JE Jeff Bagwell Jsy 40.00 80.00
JM Joe Mauer Blue Jsy 40.00 80.00
JM1 Joe Mauer White Jsy 40.00 80.00
JP Jim Palmer Jsy 10.00 25.00
JR Jim Rice Jsy 10.00 25.00
JS John Smoltz Jsy 30.00 60.00
JU Juan Marichal Jsy 10.00 25.00
KG Ken Griffey Jr. Reds Jsy 60.00 150.00
KG1 Ken Griffey Jr. M's Jsy 60.00 150.00
KW Kerry Wood Jsy 20.00 50.00
LB Lou Brock Cards Jsy 15.00 40.00
LB1 Lou Brock Cubs Jsy 12.50 30.00
MC Willie McCovey Jsy 40.00 80.00
MG Mark Grace Jsy 20.00 50.00
ML Mike Lowell Jsy 10.00 25.00
MO Joe Morgan Jsy 10.00 25.00
MP Mark Prior Cubs Jsy 6.00 15.00
MP1 Mark Prior USA Jsy 6.00 15.00
MR Manny Ramirez Jsy 40.00 80.00
MS Mike Schmidt Jsy 50.00 100.00
MT Mark Teixeira Jsy 12.50 30.00
MU Mark Mulder Jsy 6.00 15.00
NG N.Garciaparra Cubs Jsy 20.00 50.00
NG1 N. Garciaparra Sox Jsy 20.00 50.00
NR Nolan Ryan Rgr Jsy 40.00 80.00
NR1 Nolan Ryan Angels Jsy 40.00 80.00
NR2 Nolan Ryan Astros Jsy 40.00 80.00
NR3 Nolan Ryan Mets Jsy 40.00 80.00
OC Orl Cepeda Giants Jsy 10.00 25.00
OC1 Orl Cepeda Cards Jsy 10.00 25.00
OS Ozzie Smith Jsy 30.00 60.00
PI Mike Piazza Mets Jsy 75.00 150.00
PI1 Mike Piazza Dodgers Jsy 75.00 150.00
PM Paul Molitor Brewers Jsy 10.00 25.00
PM1 Paul Molitor Twins Jsy 10.00 25.00
PM2 Paul Molitor Jays Jsy 10.00 25.00
PO Johnny Podres Jsy 10.00 25.00
RC Rod Carew Twins Jsy 20.00 50.00
RC1 Rod Carew Angels Pants 20.00 50.00
RF R.Fingers Brewers Pants 10.00 25.00
RF1 Rollie Fingers A's Pants 10.00 25.00
RG Ron Guidry Jsy 20.00 50.00
RJ R.Johnson D'backs Jsy 60.00 120.00
RJ1 Randy Johnson M's Jsy 60.00 120.00
RO Roy Oswalt Jsy 10.00 25.00
RP Rafael Palmeiro Jsy 30.00 60.00
RR Robin Roberts Jsy 10.00 25.00
RS Red Schoendienst Jsy 10.00 25.00
RW Rickie Weeks Brewers Jsy 6.00 15.00
RW1 Rickie Weeks USA Jsy 6.00 15.00
SA Ryne Sandberg Jsy 50.00 100.00
SC1 S.Carlt Cards Pants 12.00 30.00
SN D.Snider Brooklyn Pants 20.00 50.00
TE1 Miguel Tejada A's Jsy/34 20.00 50.00
TG Tony Gwynn Jsy 15.00 40.00
TH Tim Hudson Jsy 10.00 25.00
TP Tony Perez Jsy 20.00 50.00
TS Tom Seaver Mets Jsy 30.00 80.00
TS1 Tom Seaver Reds Jsy 30.00 80.00
VG Vladimir Guerrero Jsy 40.00 80.00
WB Wade Boggs Sox Jsy 30.00 60.00
WB1 Wade Boggs Yanks Jsy 30.00 60.00
WC Will Clark Giants Jsy 25.00 60.00
WC1 Will Clark Cards Jsy 25.00 60.00
WC2 Will Clark Rgr Jsy 25.00 60.00
WC3 Will Clark O's Jsy 25.00 60.00

2004 Ultimate Collection Game Patch

*3-COLOR PATCH: ADD 20% PREMIUM
*4-COLOR PATCH: ADD 50% PREMIUM
*5+ COLOR PATCH: ADD 100% PREMIUM
*LOGO PATCH: ADD 150% PREMIUM
OVERALL PATCH ODDS 1:4
PRINT RUNS B/WN 10-75 COPIES PER
NO PRICING ON QTY OF 10
AK Al Kaline/21 40.00 80.00
AP Albert Pujols/75 20.00 50.00
AS Alfonso Soriano/75 6.00 15.00
BA Jeff Bagwell/75 10.00 25.00
BE Josh Beckett/75 6.00 15.00
BF Bob Feller/75 12.00 30.00
BM Bill Mazeroski/55 20.00 50.00
BR Brooks Robinson/75 15.00 40.00
BS Ben Sheets/75 6.00 15.00
BU Jim Bunning/66 15.00 40.00
BW Bernie Williams/75 10.00 25.00
CA Miguel Cabrera/75 12.50 30.00
CB Carlos Beltran/75 6.00 15.00
CF Carlton Fisk R.Sox/18 30.00 60.00
CH Catfish Hunter/75 15.00 40.00
CJ Chipper Jones/75 10.00 25.00
CL Roger Clemens/75 15.00 40.00
CO1 Rocky Colavito/75 50.00 100.00
CR Cal Ripken/75 30.00 60.00
CS Curt Schilling/75 10.00 25.00
CY Carl Yastrzemski/75 30.00 60.00
DJ Derek Jeter/75 20.00 50.00
DM Don Mattingly/75 20.00 50.00
DW Dave Winfield/75 10.00 25.00
EC Eric Chavez/75 6.00 15.00
EM Eddie Mathews/17 40.00 80.00
GB George Brett/75 20.00 50.00
GC Gary Carter/75 10.00 25.00
GL Troy Glaus/75 6.00 15.00
GM Greg Maddux Cubs/75 12.50 30.00
GM1 Greg Maddux Braves/75 12.50 30.00
GS Gary Sheffield/75 6.00 15.00
HB Hank Blalock/75 6.00 15.00
HK Harmon Killebrew/75 15.00 40.00
HM Hideki Matsui/44 50.00 100.00
IR Ivan Rodriguez/75 10.00 25.00
IS Ichiro Suzuki/75 60.00 120.00
JB Johnny Bench/75 15.00 40.00
JD Joe DiMaggio/75 150.00 300.00
JM Joe Mauer/75 8.00 20.00
JP Jim Palmer/75 10.00 25.00
KG Ken Griffey Jr./75 15.00 40.00
KM Kazuo Matsui/75 15.00 40.00
KW Kerry Wood/75 6.00 15.00
LB Lou Brock/75 15.00 40.00
MA Juan Marichal/75 10.00 25.00
MO Joe Morgan/75 10.00 25.00
MP Mark Prior/75 10.00 25.00
MR Manny Ramirez/75 10.00 25.00
MS Mike Schmidt/75 20.00 50.00
MT Mark Teixeira/75 10.00 25.00
MU Eddie Murray/75 15.00 40.00
NF Nellie Fox/55 60.00 120.00
NR Nolan Ryan Rgr/51 20.00 50.00
NR1 Nolan Ryan Astros/75 20.00 50.00
NR2 Nolan Ryan Angels/75 20.00 50.00
OS Ozzie Smith/75 15.00 40.00
PE Pedro Martinez/75 10.00 25.00
PI Mike Piazza/75 12.50 30.00
PM Paul Molitor/75 10.00 25.00
PO Johnny Podres/75 15.00 40.00
RB Roberto Clemente/75 125.00 200.00
RC Rod Carew Angels/75 15.00 40.00
RG Ron Guidry/75 15.00 40.00
RJ Randy Johnson D'backs/75 10.00 25.00
RJ1 Randy Johnson M's/75 10.00 25.00
RO Rod Carew Twins/75 15.00 40.00
RP Rafael Palmeiro/75 10.00 25.00
RS Ryne Sandberg/75 20.00 50.00
RY Robin Yount/75 10.00 25.00
SM Stan Musial/75 40.00 80.00
SP Warren Spahn/62 30.00 60.00
SR Scott Rolen/75 10.00 25.00
SS Sammy Sosa/75 10.00 25.00
TE Miguel Tejada/75 6.00 15.00
TG Tony Gwynn/75 12.50 30.00
TH Todd Helton/75 10.00 25.00
TM Thurman Munson/75 15.00 40.00
TS Tom Seaver/75 10.00 25.00
VG Vladimir Guerrero/75 10.00 25.00
WB Wade Boggs/75 10.00 25.00
WC Will Clark Giants/75 15.00 40.00
WC1 Will Clark Rgr/75 15.00 40.00
WI Billy Williams/75 10.00 25.00
WM Willie McCovey/75 15.00 40.00
WS Willie Stargell/75 20.00 50.00
YB Yogi Berra/75 15.00 40.00

2004 Ultimate Collection Game Patch Signature

*4-COLOR PATCH: ADD 20% PREMIUM
*5+ COLOR PATCH: ADD 50% PREMIUM
*LOGO PATCH: ADD 100% PREMIUM
OVERALL AUTO/GAME-USED ODDS 1:4
STATED PRINT RUN 30 SERIAL #'d SETS
C.FISK PRINT RUN 10 SERIAL #'d CARDS
NO C.FISK PRICING DUE TO SCARCITY
EXCHANGE DEADLINE 12/28/07
AD Andre Dawson 12.50 30.00
AK Al Kaline 75.00 200.00
BG Bob Gibson 30.00 60.00
BR Brooks Robinson 30.00 60.00
BS Ben Sheets 12.50 30.00
CB Carlos Beltran 12.50 30.00
CR Cal Ripken 150.00 250.00
CY Carl Yastrzemski 50.00 100.00
DJ Derek Jeter 200.00 500.00
DM Don Mattingly 50.00 100.00
EB Ernie Banks 60.00 120.00
EC Eric Chavez 12.50 30.00
EM Eddie Murray 40.00 80.00
FR Frank Robinson 60.00 120.00
GB George Brett 60.00 120.00
GM Greg Maddux 100.00 200.00
HB Hank Blalock 12.50 30.00
HK Harmon Killebrew 50.00 100.00
JB Johnny Bench 60.00 120.00
JM Joe Mauer 50.00 100.00
JP Jim Palmer 12.50 30.00
JR Jim Rice 50.00 100.00
KG Ken Griffey Jr. 100.00 200.00
MA Juan Marichal 12.50 30.00
MC Miguel Cabrera 100.00 200.00
MP Mark Prior 12.50 30.00
MS Mike Schmidt 60.00 120.00
MT Mark Teixeira 30.00 60.00
MU Mark Mulder 12.50 30.00
NR Nolan Ryan 40.00 80.00
OS Ozzie Smith 40.00 80.00
PI Mike Piazza 100.00 175.00
PM Paul Molitor 12.50 30.00
RC Rod Carew 30.00 60.00
RJ Randy Johnson 75.00 150.00
RO Roy Oswalt 12.50 30.00
RS Ryne Sandberg 75.00 150.00
RY Robin Yount 20.00 50.00
SC Red Schoendienst 12.50 30.00
SM Stan Musial 75.00 150.00
TG Tony Gwynn 40.00 80.00
TS Tom Seaver 40.00 100.00
WB Wade Boggs 40.00 80.00
WC Will Clark 30.00 60.00

2004 Ultimate Collection Legendary Materials

OVERALL GAME-USED ODDS 1:4
STATED PRINT RUN 50 SERIAL #'d SETS
LMBF Bob Feller Jsy 5.00 12.00
LMBR Babe Ruth Pants 250.00 500.00
LMCA Roy Campanella Pants 10.00 25.00
LMDD Don Drysdale Pants 10.00 25.00
LMDS Duke Snider Jsy 8.00 20.00
LMEB Ernie Banks Jsy 10.00 25.00
LMEM Eddie Mathews Pants 10.00 25.00
LMJD Joe DiMaggio Pants 50.00 100.00
LMJR Jackie Robinson Jsy 30.00 60.00
LMMM Mickey Mantle Pants 75.00 200.00
LMRC Roberto Clemente Jsy 75.00 150.00
LMRM Roger Maris Jsy 30.00 60.00
LMRM Stan Musial Jsy 15.00 40.00
LMSP Satchel Paige Pants 30.00 60.00
LMTC Ty Cobb Pants 60.00 120.00
LMTM Thurman Munson Pants 10.00 25.00
LMTW Ted Williams Jsy 20.00 50.00
LMWM Willie McCovey Jsy 8.00 20.00
LMYB Yogi Berra Jsy 12.50 30.00

2004 Ultimate Collection Loyalty Signature Materials

OVERALL AUTO/GAME-USED ODDS 1:4
PRINT RUNS B/WN 17-23 COPIES PER
BR Brooks Robinson Jsy/23 30.00 60.00
CR Cal Ripken Pants/21 150.00 250.00
CY Carl Yastrzemski Jsy/23 50.00 100.00
EB Ernie Banks Jsy/19 50.00 100.00
GB George Brett Jsy/21 60.00 120.00
HK Harmon Killebrew Jsy/21 50.00 100.00
MS Mike Schmidt Jsy/18 60.00 120.00
RY Robin Yount Jsy/20 40.00 80.00
TG Tony Gwynn Jsy/20 40.00 100.00

2004 Ultimate Collection Signature Numbers Patch

*4-COLOR PATCH: ADD 20% PREMIUM
*5+ COLOR PATCH: ADD 50% PREMIUM
*LOGO PATCH: ADD 100% PREMIUM
OVERALL AUTO/GAME-USED ODDS 1:4
PRINT RUNS B/WN 1-51 COPIES PER
NO PRICING ON QTY OF 14 OR LESS
EXCHANGE DEADLINE 12/28/07
BF Bob Feller/19 30.00 60.00
BW Billy Williams/26 20.00 50.00
DM Don Mattingly/23 60.00 120.00
DW Dave Winfield/31 30.00 60.00
EG Eric Gagne/38 20.00 50.00
JP Jim Palmer/22 20.00 50.00
KG Ken Griffey Jr./30 100.00 200.00
LB Lou Brock/20 30.00 60.00
MC Miguel Cabrera/24 40.00 80.00
MP Mark Prior/22 20.00 50.00
MS Mike Schmidt/20 60.00 120.00
MT Mark Teixeira/23 30.00 60.00
PI Mike Piazza/31 100.00 175.00
RJ Randy Johnson/51 60.00 120.00
RO Roy Oswalt/44 15.00 40.00
RS Ryne Sandberg/23 75.00 150.00
RY Robin Yount/19 50.00 100.00
VG Vladimir Guerrero/27 25.00 60.00
WB Wade Boggs/26 40.00 80.00
WM Willie McCovey/44 20.00 50.00

2004 Ultimate Collection Signatures

PRINT RUNS B/WN 6-99 COPIES PER
NO PRICING ON QTY OF 6
*GOLD p/r 25: .6X TO 1.5X BASIC p/r 69-99
GOLD PRINT RUNS B/WN 10-25 PER
NO GOLD PRICING ON QTY OF 10
OVERALL AUTO ODDS 1:4
PLATINUM: PREMIUM AU ODDS 1:20
PLATINUM PRINT RUN 1 SERIAL #'d SET
NO PLATINUM PRICING DUE TO SCARCITY
EXCHANGE DEADLINE 12/28/07
AD Andre Dawson/25 10.00 25.00
AK Al Kaline/25 25.00 50.00
AO Akinori Otsuka/99 15.00 40.00
AR Al Rosen/99 6.00 15.00
BD Bobby Doerr/99 10.00 25.00
BF Bob Feller/25 15.00 40.00
BG Brian Giles/99 6.00 15.00
BI Craig Biggio/25 20.00 50.00
BL Bert Blyleven/99 10.00 25.00
BM Bill Mazeroski/25 12.00 30.00
BR Brooks Robinson Btg/25 15.00 40.00
BS Ben Sheets/99 10.00 25.00
BW Billy Williams/25 15.00 40.00
CB Carlos Beltran/25 15.00 40.00
CC Carl Crawford/99 6.00 15.00
CP Corey Patterson/99 6.00 15.00
CR Cal Ripken/25 75.00 200.00
CW Rod Carew/25 20.00 50.00
CY Carl Yastrzemski/25 30.00 80.00
DC David Cone/99 10.00 25.00
DE Dennis Eckersley/25 15.00 40.00
DG Dwight Gooden/99 6.00 15.00
DM Dale Murphy/99 12.00 30.00
DN Don Newcombe/25 6.00 15.00
DP Dave Parker/25 10.00 25.00
DW Dave Winfield/25 15.00 40.00
DY Delmon Young/99 12.00 30.00
EC Eric Chavez/25 10.00 25.00
EG Eric Gagne/25 20.00 50.00
FH Frank Howard/99 12.00 30.00
FL Fred Lynn/25 10.00 25.00
GF George Foster/25 10.00 25.00
GG Goose Gossage/99 6.00 15.00
GI Bob Gibson/25 25.00 60.00
GK George Kell/99 10.00 25.00
GM Greg Maddux/25 75.00 200.00
GN Graig Nettles/99 10.00 25.00
GP Gaylord Perry/25 10.00 25.00
GR Mark Grace/99 15.00 40.00
HB Hank Blalock/25 15.00 40.00
HK H.Killebrew w Bat/25 30.00 80.00
HK1 H.Killebrew Swing/25 30.00 80.00
JB Jim Bunning/99 10.00 25.00
JK Jim Kaat/99 10.00 25.00
JM Joe Mauer/99 25.00 60.00
JP Jim Palmer Knee Up/99 10.00 25.00
JP1 Jim Palmer Thigh Up/25 10.00 25.00
JS Jason Schmidt/99 10.00 25.00
KG Ken Griffey Sr./69 10.00 25.00
KH Keith Hernandez/99 10.00 25.00
KP Kirby Puckett/25 75.00 200.00
LA Luis Aparicio R.Sox/25 10.00 25.00
LA1 Luis Aparicio W.Sox/25 10.00 25.00
LT Luis Tiant/99 6.00 15.00
MC M.Cabrera Swing/99 15.00 40.00
MC1 M.Cabrera Drop Bat/25 25.00 60.00
MG Marcus Giles/99 6.00 15.00
MI Monte Irvin/25 10.00 25.00
ML Mike Lowell/99 6.00 15.00
MM Mark Mulder/99 10.00 25.00
MO Joe Morgan/25 15.00 40.00
MP Mark Prior/25 10.00 25.00
MT Mark Teixeira/25 12.00 30.00
MU Stan Musial/25 20.00 50.00
MW Maury Wills/25 10.00 25.00
NG Nomar Garciaparra/25 30.00 80.00
OC Orlando Cepeda/25 10.00 25.00
OS Ozzie Smith/25 15.00 40.00
PI Mike Piazza/25 40.00 100.00
PO Johnny Podres/99 10.00 25.00
RC Rocky Colavito/99 20.00 50.00
RF Rollie Fingers Brewers/25 10.00 25.00
RF1 Rollie Fingers A's/25 10.00 25.00
RG Ron Guidry/25 20.00 50.00
RJ Randy Johnson/25 75.00 200.00
RK Ralph Kiner B W/25 10.00 25.00
RK1 Ralph Kiner Color/25 10.00 25.00
RO Roy Oswalt/99 10.00 25.00
RR Robin Roberts/25 15.00 40.00
RS Red Schoendienst/25 15.00 40.00
RW Rickie Weeks/99 10.00 25.00
RY Ryne Sandberg/25 20.00 50.00
SA Ron Santo/99 15.00 40.00
SC Sean Casey/99 10.00 25.00
SL Sparky Lyle/99 6.00 15.00
SM John Smoltz/25 25.00 60.00
SN Duke Snider/25 20.00 50.00
ST Shingo Takatsu/99 10.00 25.00
SU Bruce Sutter/99 12.00 30.00
TH Travis Hafner/99 10.00 25.00
TP Tony Perez/25 20.00 50.00
TS Tom Seaver/25 25.00 60.00
VG Vladimir Guerrero/25 15.00 40.00
VM Victor Martinez/99 10.00 25.00
WB Wade Boggs/25 25.00 60.00
WC Will Clark/25 20.00 50.00
WF Whitey Ford/25 30.00 80.00
YB Yogi Berra/25 30.00 80.00

2004 Ultimate Collection Signatures Dual

OVERALL AUTO ODDS 1:4
STATED PRINT RUN 25 SERIAL #'d SETS
EXCHANGE DEADLINE 12/28/07
BB H.Blalock/W.Boggs 40.00 80.00
BC C.Beltran/M.Cabrera 100.00 150.00
BS G.Brett/M.Schmidt 125.00 200.00
BT H.Blalock/M.Teixeira 40.00 80.00
CB E.Chavez/H.Blalock 10.00 25.00
CJ R.Johnson/R.Clemens 250.00 400.00
CL M.Cabrera/M.Lowell 50.00 100.00
CR B.Robinson/E.Chavez 40.00 80.00
DW A.Dawson/B.Williams 30.00 60.00
EF D.Eckersley/R.Fingers 12.00 30.00
FR B.Feller/N.Ryan 125.00 200.00
GC M.Grace/W.Clark 40.00 80.00
GG B.Giles/M.Giles 10.00 25.00
GK H.Killebrew/K.Griffey Jr. 125.00 250.00
GS E.Gagne/J.Smoltz 60.00 120.00
IC M.Irvin/O.Cepeda 30.00 60.00
JC R.Johnson/S.Carlton 75.00 150.00
JM D.Jeter/D.Mattingly 250.00 400.00
JP F.Jenkins/J.Palmer 30.00 60.00
JT F.Jenkins/L.Tiant 10.00 25.00
KG K.Griffey Sr./K.Griffey Jr. 100.00 200.00
KK A.Kaline/H.Killebrew 60.00 150.00
MC D.Mattingly/W.Clark 75.00 150.00
MH M.Mulder/T.Hudson 40.00 80.00
MP J.Mauer/M.Prior 50.00 100.00
NS D.Newcombe/D.Sutton 30.00 60.00
PN G.Perry/P.Niekro 10.00 25.00
PR D.Parker/J.Rice 40.00 80.00
PS B.Sheets/M.Prior 10.00 25.00
RJ C.Ripken/D.Jeter 350.00 600.00
RP B.Robinson/J.Palmer 50.00 100.00
SF B.Sheets/B.Feller 30.00 60.00
SG B.Sutter/E.Gagne 40.00 80.00
SO B.Sheets/R.Oswalt 30.00 60.00
SP D.Sutton/G.Perry 10.00 25.00
TC M.Teixeira/M.Cabrera 50.00 100.00
VM V.Guerrero/M.Cabrera 60.00 120.00
WS B.Williams/R.Santo 15.00 40.00

2004 Ultimate Collection Stat Patch

*3-COLOR PATCH: ADD 20% PREMIUM
*4-COLOR PATCH: ADD 50% PREMIUM
*5+ COLOR PATCH: ADD 100% PREMIUM
*LOGO PATCH: ADD 150% PREMIUM
OVERALL PATCH ODDS 1:4
PRINT RUNS B/WN 4-66 COPIES PER
NO PRICING ON QTY OF 14 OR LESS
AP Albert Pujols/43 30.00 60.00
AP1 Albert Pujols/51 20.00 50.00
AS Alfonso Soriano/39 8.00 20.00
AS1 Alfonso Soriano/43 8.00 20.00
BE Johnny Bench/45 30.00 60.00
CB Carlos Beltran/29 10.00 25.00
CB1 Carlos Beltran/41 8.00 20.00
CF Carlton Fisk/17 15.00 40.00
CJ Chipper Jones/45 12.50 30.00
CL1 Roger Clemens Sox/24 20.00 50.00
CR Cal Ripken/34 50.00 100.00
CR1 Cal Ripken/47 40.00 80.00
CY Carl Yastrzemski/44 20.00 50.00
DD Don Drysdale/25 40.00 80.00
DJ Derek Jeter/32 40.00 80.00
DJ1 Derek Jeter/24 40.00 80.00
DM Don Mattingly/35 40.00 80.00
DW Dave Winfield/37 12.50 30.00
EG Eric Gagne/55 8.00 20.00
GB George Brett/20 40.00 80.00
GM1 Greg Maddux Cubs/20 20.00 50.00
GM2 Greg Maddux Cubs/49 10.00 25.00
HB Hank Blalock/29 10.00 25.00
HK Harmon Killebrew/49 30.00 60.00
HM Hideki Matsui/31 60.00 120.00
IR Ivan Rodriguez/35 15.00 40.00
IR1 Ivan Rodriguez/25 15.00 40.00
IS Ichiro Suzuki/56 60.00 120.00
JB Jeff Bagwell/47 12.50 30.00
JM Juan Marichal/26 30.00 60.00
JP1 Jim Palmer/23 15.00 40.00
JR Jim Rice/15 15.00 40.00
JR1 Jim Rice/46 12.50 30.00
JS John Smoltz/24 15.00 40.00
JS1 John Smoltz/55 12.50 30.00
JT Jim Thome/52 30.00 60.00
KG Ken Griffey Jr./56 30.00 60.00
KW1 Kerry Wood/20 10.00 25.00
MA Pedro Martinez/23 15.00 40.00
MP Mark Prior/18 20.00 50.00
MR Manny Ramirez/45 12.50 30.00
MS Mike Schmidt/48 30.00 60.00
MT Miguel Tejada/34 10.00 25.00
PI Mike Piazza/40 15.00 40.00
PM Paul Molitor/39 12.50 30.00
PN Phil Niekro Wins/23 15.00 40.00
PN1 Phil Niekro CG/23 15.00 40.00
RJ Randy Johnson/20 15.00 40.00
RO Jackie Robinson/19 150.00 250.00
RP Rafael Palmeiro/47 12.50 30.00
RS Ryne Sandberg/40 30.00 60.00
RS1 Ryne Sandberg/19 50.00 100.00
SR Scott Rolen/31 15.00 40.00
SS1 Sammy Sosa/66 10.00 25.00
TG Tony Gwynn/56 15.00 40.00
TG1 Tony Gwynn/25 20.00 50.00
TM Thurman Munson/20 40.00 80.00
TS Tom Seaver/25 30.00 60.00
VG Vladimir Guerrero/44 12.50 30.00
VG1 Vladimir Guerrero/40 12.50 30.00
WC Will Clark/35 30.00 60.00
WS Willie Stargell/48 20.00 50.00

2004 Ultimate Collection Super Patch

*3-COLOR PATCH: ADD 20% PREMIUM
*4-COLOR PATCH: ADD 50% PREMIUM
*5+ COLOR PATCH: ADD 100% PREMIUM
*LOGO PATCH: ADD 150% PREMIUM
OVERALL PATCH ODDS 1:4
PRINT RUNS B/WN 4-20 COPIES PER
NO PRICING ON QTY OF 4
AP Albert Pujols/20 60.00 120.00
CL Roger Clemens/20 30.00 60.00
CR Cal Ripken/20 75.00 150.00
CY Carl Yastrzemski/15 50.00 100.00
DM Don Mattingly/20 50.00 100.00
DW Dave Winfield/20 15.00 40.00
EM Eddie Murray/20 75.00 150.00
GB George Brett/20 50.00 100.00
GM Greg Maddux/20 40.00 80.00
HK Harmon Killebrew/20 40.00 80.00
HM Hideki Matsui/20 60.00 120.00
IS Ichiro Suzuki/20 125.00 200.00
JB Johnny Bench/20 40.00 80.00
JP Jim Palmer/20 40.00 80.00
KG Ken Griffey Jr./20 75.00 150.00
KW Kerry Wood/20 12.50 30.00
LB Lou Brock/20 30.00 60.00
MP Mark Prior/20 20.00 50.00
MS Mike Schmidt/20 50.00 100.00
NR Nolan Ryan/20 50.00 100.00
OS Ozzie Smith/20 40.00 80.00
PI Mike Piazza/20 40.00 80.00
PM Paul Molitor/20 15.00 40.00
RC Rod Carew/20 30.00 60.00
RS Ryne Sandberg/20 50.00 100.00
RY Robin Yount/20 60.00 120.00
SC Red Schoendienst/20 60.00 120.00
SS Sammy Sosa/20 20.00 50.00
TG Tony Gwynn/20 40.00 80.00
TS Tom Seaver/20 30.00 60.00
VG Vladimir Guerrero/20 30.00 60.00
WC Will Clark Giants/20 30.00 60.00

2005 Ultimate Collection

COMMON CARD (1-100) .75 2.00
1-100 APPX ODDS 3:2 PACKS
1-100 PRINT RUN 475 SERIAL #'d SETS
COMMON CARD (101-142) 1.00 2.50
101-142 APPX. ODDS 1:3
101-142 PRINT RUN 275 SERIAL #'d SETS
COMMON CARD (143-237) 1.00 2.50
COMMON RC (143-237) 1.00 2.50
143-237 STATED ODDS 3:4 PACKS
143-237 PRINT RUN 275 SERIAL #'d SETS
COMMON AU (238-242) 6.00 15.00
238-242 OVERALL AU ODDS 1:4
238-242 PRINT RUN 99 SERIAL #'d SETS
1 A.J. Burnett .75 2.00
2 Adam Dunn 1.25 3.00
3 Adrian Beltre 2.00 5.00
4 Albert Pujols 2.50 6.00
5 Alex Rodriguez 2.50 6.00
6 Alfonso Soriano 1.25 3.00
7 Andruw Jones .75 2.00
8 Andy Pettitte 1.25 3.00
9 Aramis Ramirez .75 2.00
10 Aubrey Huff .75 2.00
11 Ben Sheets .75 2.00
12 Bobby Abreu .75 2.00
13 Bobby Crosby .75 2.00
14 Chris Carpenter 1.25 3.00
15 Brian Giles .75 2.00
16 Brian Roberts .75 2.00
17 Carl Crawford 1.25 3.00
18 Carlos Beltran 1.25 3.00
19 Carlos Delgado .75 2.00
20 Carlos Zambrano 1.25 3.00
21 Chipper Jones 2.00 5.00
22 Corey Patterson .75 2.00
23 Craig Biggio 1.25 3.00
24 Curt Schilling 1.25 3.00
25 Dallas McPherson .75 2.00
26 David Ortiz 2.00 5.00
27 David Wright 1.50 4.00
28 Delmon Young 2.00 5.00
29 Derek Jeter 5.00 12.00
30 Derrek Lee .75 2.00
31 Dontrelle Willis .75 2.00
32 Eric Chavez .75 2.00
33 Eric Gagne .75 2.00
34 Francisco Rodriguez 1.25 3.00
35 Gary Sheffield .75 2.00
36 Greg Maddux 2.50 6.00
37 Hank Blalock .75 2.00
38 Hideki Matsui 3.00 8.00
39 Ichiro Suzuki 2.50 6.00
40 Ivan Rodriguez 1.25 3.00
41 J.D. Drew .75 2.00
42 Jake Peavy .75 2.00
43 Jason Bay .75 2.00
44 Jason Schmidt .75 2.00
45 Jeff Bagwell 1.25 3.00
46 Jeff Kent .75 2.00
47 Jeremy Bonderman .75 2.00
48 Jim Edmonds 1.25 3.00
49 Jim Thome 1.25 3.00
50 Joe Mauer 1.50 4.00
51 Johan Santana 1.25 3.00
52 John Smoltz 2.00 5.00
53 Johnny Damon 1.25 3.00
54 Jose Reyes 1.25 3.00
55 Jose Vidro .75 2.00
56 Josh Beckett .75 2.00
57 Justin Morneau 1.25 3.00
58 Ken Griffey Jr. 4.00 10.00
59 Kerry Wood .75 2.00
60 Khalil Greene .75 2.00
61 Lance Berkman 1.25 3.00
62 Larry Walker 1.25 3.00
63 Luis Gonzalez .75 2.00
64 Manny Ramirez 2.00 5.00
65 Mark Buehrle 1.25 3.00
66 Mark Mulder .75 2.00
67 Mark Prior 1.25 3.00
68 Mark Teixeira 1.25 3.00
69 Michael Young .75 2.00
70 Miguel Cabrera 2.00 5.00
71 Miguel Tejada 1.25 3.00
72 Mike Mussina 1.25 3.00
73 Mike Piazza 2.00 5.00
74 Moises Alou .75 2.00
75 Nomar Garciaparra 1.25 3.00
76 Oliver Perez .75 2.00
77 Pat Burrell .75 2.00
78 Paul Konerko 1.25 3.00
79 Pedro Feliz .75 2.00
80 Pedro Martinez 1.25 3.00
81 Randy Johnson 2.00 5.00
82 Richie Sexson .75 2.00
83 Rickie Weeks .75 2.00
84 Roger Clemens 2.50 6.00
85 Roy Halladay 1.25 3.00
86 Roy Oswalt 1.25 3.00
87 Sammy Sosa 2.00 5.00
88 Scott Kazmir 2.00 5.00
89 Scott Rolen 1.25 3.00
90 Shawn Green .75 2.00
91 Tim Hudson 1.25 3.00
92 Todd Helton 1.25 3.00
93 Tom Glavine 1.25 3.00
94 Torii Hunter .75 2.00
95 Travis Hafner .75 2.00
96 Troy Glaus .75 2.00
97 Vernon Wells .75 2.00
98 Victor Martinez 1.25 3.00
99 Vladimir Guerrero 1.25 3.00
100 Zack Greinke 2.50 6.00
101 Al Kaline RET 2.50 6.00
102 Babe Ruth RET 6.00 15.00
103 Bo Jackson RET 2.50 6.00
104 Bob Gibson RET 1.50 4.00
105 Brooks Robinson RET 1.50 4.00
106 Cal Ripken RET 8.00 20.00
107 Carl Yastrzemski RET 3.00 8.00
108 Carlton Fisk RET 1.50 4.00
109 Catfish Hunter RET 1.50 4.00
110 Christy Mathewson RET 2.50 6.00
111 Cy Young RET 1.50 4.00
112 Don Mattingly RET 5.00 12.00
113 Eddie Mathews RET 2.50 6.00
114 Eddie Murray RET 1.50 4.00
115 Gary Carter RET 1.50 4.00
116 Harmon Killebrew RET 2.50 6.00
117 Jim Palmer RET 1.50 4.00
118 Jimmie Foxx RET 1.50 4.00
119 Joe DiMaggio RET 5.00 12.00
120 Johnny Bench RET 2.50 6.00
121 Lefty Grove RET 1.50 4.00
122 Lou Gehrig RET 5.00 12.00
123 Mel Ott RET 2.50 6.00
124 Reggie Jackson RET 1.50 4.00
125 Mike Schmidt RET 4.00 10.00
126 Nolan Ryan RET 8.00 20.00
127 Ozzie Smith RET 3.00 8.00
128 Paul Molitor RET 2.50 6.00
129 Pee Wee Reese RET 1.50 4.00

130 Robin Yount RET 2.50 6.00
131 Ryne Sandberg RET 5.00 12.00
132 Ted Williams RET 5.00 12.00
133 Thurman Munson RET 1.50 4.00
134 Tom Seaver RET 1.50 4.00
135 Tony Gwynn RET 3.00 8.00
136 Wade Boggs RET 1.50 4.00
137 Walter Johnson RET 1.50 4.00
138 Warren Spahn RET 1.50 4.00
139 Will Clark RET 1.50 4.00
140 Willie McCovey RET 1.50 4.00
141 Willie Stargell RET 1.50 4.00
142 Yogi Berra RET 2.50 6.00
143 Ambiorix Burgos UP RC 1.00 2.50
144 Ambiorix Concepcion UP RC 1.00 2.50
145 Anibal Sanchez UP RC 4.00 10.00
146 Bill McCarthy UP RC 1.00 2.50
147 Brian Burres UP RC 1.00 2.50
148 Carlos Ruiz UP RC 1.50 4.00
149 Casey Rogowski UP RC 1.50 4.00
150 Chris Resop UP RC 1.00 2.50
151 Chris Roberson UP RC 1.00 2.50
152 Chris Seddon UP RC 1.00 2.50
153 Colter Bean UP RC 1.00 2.50
154 Dae-Sung Koo UP RC 1.00 2.50
155 Danny Rueckel UP RC 1.00 2.50
156 Dave Gassner UP RC 1.00 2.50
157 Ryan Howard UP 2.00 5.00
158 D.J. Houlton UP RC 1.00 2.50
159 Derek Wathan UP RC 1.00 2.50
160 Devon Lowery UP RC 1.00 2.50
161 Enrique Gonzalez UP RC 1.00 2.50
162 Erick Threets UP RC 1.00 2.50
163 Eude Brito UP RC 1.00 2.50
164 Francisco Butto UP RC 1.00 2.50
165 Franquelis Osoria UP RC 1.00 2.50
166 Garrett Jones UP RC 1.50 4.00
167 Geovany Soto UP RC 5.00 12.00
168 Ismael Ramirez UP RC 1.00 2.50
169 Jared Gothreaux UP RC 1.00 2.50
170 Jason Hammel UP RC 2.50 6.00
171 Jeff Housman UP RC 1.00 2.50
172 Jeff Miller UP RC 1.00 2.50
173 Jeff Francoeur UP 2.50 6.00
174 John Hattig UP RC 1.00 2.50
175 Jorge Campillo UP RC 1.00 2.50
176 Juan Morillo UP RC 1.00 2.50
177 Justin Wechsler UP RC 1.00 2.50
178 Keiichi Yabu UP RC 1.00 2.50
179 Kendry Morales UP RC 2.50 6.00
180 Luis Hernandez UP RC 1.00 2.50
181 Luis Mendoza UP RC 1.00 2.50
182 Luis Pena UP RC 1.00 2.50
183 Luis O.Rodriguez UP RC 1.00 2.50
184 Luke Scott UP RC 2.50 6.00
185 Marcos Carvajal UP RC 1.00 2.50
186 Mark Woodyard UP RC 1.00 2.50
187 Matt Smith UP RC 1.00 2.50
188 Matthew Lindstrom UP RC 1.00 2.50
189 Miguel Negron UP RC 1.50 4.00
190 Mike Morse UP RC 3.00 8.00
191 Nate McLouth UP RC 1.50 4.00
192 Nick Masset UP RC 1.00 2.50
193 Paulino Reynoso UP RC 1.00 2.50
194 Pedro Lopez UP RC 1.00 2.50
195 Pete Orr UP RC 1.50 4.00
196 Randy Messenger UP RC 1.00 2.50
197 Randy Williams UP RC 1.00 2.50
198 Raul Tablado UP RC 1.00 2.50
199 Ronny Paulino UP RC 1.50 4.00
200 Russ Rohlicek UP RC 1.00 2.50
201 Russell Martin UP RC 3.00 8.00
202 Scott Baker UP RC 1.50 4.00
203 Scott Munter UP RC 1.00 2.50
204 Sean Thompson UP RC 1.00 2.50
205 Sean Tracey UP RC 1.00 2.50
206 Steve Schmoll UP RC 1.00 2.50
207 Tony Pena UP RC 1.00 2.50
208 Travis Bowyer UP RC 1.00 2.50
209 Ubaldo Jimenez UP RC 2.50 6.00
210 Wladimir Balentien UP RC 1.50 4.00
211 Yorman Bazardo UP RC 1.00 2.50
212 Yuniesky Betancourt UP RC 4.00 10.00
213 Adam Shabala UP RC 1.00 2.50
214 Brandon McCarthy UP RC 1.50 4.00
215 Chad Orvella UP RC 1.00 2.50
216 Jermaine Van Buren UP 1.00 2.50
217 Anthony Reyes UP RC 1.50 4.00
218 Dana Eveland UP RC 1.00 2.50
219 Brian Anderson UP RC 1.50 4.00
220 Hayden Penn UP RC 1.00 2.50
221 Chris Denorfia UP RC 1.00 2.50
222 Joel Peralta UP RC 1.00 2.50
223 Ryan Garko UP RC 1.00 2.50
224 Felix Hernandez UP 3.00 8.00
225 Mark McLemore UP RC 1.00 2.50
226 Melky Cabrera UP RC 3.00 8.00
227 Nelson Cruz UP RC 12.00 30.00
228 Norihiro Nakamura UP RC 1.00 2.50
229 Oscar Robles UP RC 1.00 2.50
230 Rick Short UP RC 1.00 2.50
231 Ryan Zimmerman UP RC 5.00 12.00
232 Ryan Speier UP RC 1.00 2.50
233 Ryan Spilborghs UP RC 2.50 6.00
234 Shane Costa UP RC 1.00 2.50
235 Zach Duke UP 1.00 2.50
236 Tony Giarratano UP RC 1.00 2.50
237 Jeff Niemann UP RC 2.50 6.00
238 Stephen Drew AU RC 6.00 15.00
239 Justin Verlander AU RC 125.00 300.00
240 Prince Fielder AU RC 15.00 40.00
241 Philip Humber AU RC 6.00 15.00
242 Tadahito Iguchi AU RC 40.00 100.00

2005 Ultimate Collection Silver

*SILVER 1-100: .75X TO 2X BASIC
*SILVER 101-142: 1X TO 2.5X BASIC
*SILVER 143-237: .75X TO 2X BASIC
*SILVER 143-237: .75X TO 2X BASIC RC
APPROXIMATE ODDS 1:3 PACKS
ACT/RC PRINT RUN 50 SERIAL #'d SETS
RET PRINT RUN 25 SER.#'d SETS

2005 Ultimate Collection Baseball Stars Signatures

OVERALL AUTO ODDS 1:4
PRINT RUNS B/WN 5-25 COPIES PER
NO PRICING ON QTY OF 10 OR LESS
NO RC YR PRICING ON QTY OF 25 OR LESS
EXCHANGE DEADLINE 01/10/09
AB Adrian Beltre/15 12.50 30.00
AR Aramis Ramirez/20 10.00 25.00
BC Bobby Crosby/15 12.50 30.00
BG Brian Giles/15 12.50 30.00
BL Barry Larkin/15 40.00 80.00
BO Jeremy Bonderman/25 10.00 25.00
BR Brian Roberts/25 10.00 25.00
BS Ben Sheets/15 12.50 30.00
BU B.J. Upton/25 10.00 25.00
CB Craig Biggio/15 20.00 50.00
CC Carl Crawford/25 10.00 25.00
CO Coco Crisp/25 10.00 25.00
CZ Carlos Zambrano/20 10.00 25.00
DA Andre Dawson/15 12.50 30.00
DG Dwight Gooden/25 10.00 25.00
DW Dontrelle Willis/15 20.00 50.00
EC Eric Chavez/15 12.50 30.00
GR Khalil Greene/15 20.00 50.00
HB Hank Blalock/15 12.50 30.00
HU Torii Hunter/15 12.50 30.00
JB Jason Bay/25 10.00 25.00
JM Justin Morneau/25 10.00 25.00
JO Joe Mauer/15 40.00 80.00
JP Jake Peavy/20 10.00 25.00
JR Jose Reyes/20 10.00 25.00
JV Jose Vidro/20 6.00 15.00
KG Ken Griffey Jr./25 50.00 100.00
KH Keith Hernandez/15 12.50 30.00
MC Miguel Cabrera/15 30.00 60.00
MM Mark Mulder/15 12.50 30.00
MT Mark Teixeira/15 20.00 50.00
MY Michael Young/20 10.00 25.00
PM Paul Molitor/15 12.50 30.00
RF Rafael Furcal/20 10.00 25.00
RH Rich Harden/25 10.00 25.00
RO Roy Oswalt/15 12.50 30.00
RW Rickie Weeks/15 12.50 30.00
SK Scott Kazmir/25 10.00 25.00
SM John Smoltz/15 40.00 80.00
SP Scott Podsednik/25 15.00 40.00
TH Tim Hudson/15 15.00 40.00
TR Travis Hafner/25 10.00 25.00
VM Victor Martinez/25 10.00 25.00
WC Will Clark/15 20.00 50.00
WP Wily Mo Pena/25 10.00 25.00
WR David Wright/15 50.00 100.00
ZG Zack Greinke/25 8.00 20.00

2005 Ultimate Collection Hurlers Materials

OVERALL GAME-USED ODDS 1:4
STATED PRINT RUN 20 SERIAL #'d SETS
*PATCH p/r 21-25: .6X TO 1.5X BASIC
OVERALL PATCH ODDS 1:4
PATCH PRINT RUN B/WN 2-25 PER
NO PATCH PRICING ON QTY OF 12 OR LESS
AB A.J. Burnett Jsy 4.00 10.00
BE Josh Beckett Jsy 4.00 10.00
BL Brad Lidge Jsy 4.00 10.00
BM Brett Myers Jsy 4.00 10.00
BO Jeremy Bonderman Jsy 4.00 10.00
BS Ben Sheets Jsy 4.00 10.00
CA Chris Carpenter Jsy 6.00 15.00
CC C.C. Sabathia Jsy 4.00 10.00
CP Carl Pavano Jsy 4.00 10.00
CS Curt Schilling Jsy 6.00 15.00
CZ Carlos Zambrano Jsy 4.00 10.00
DG Dwight Gooden Jsy 4.00 10.00
DH Danny Haren Jsy 4.00 10.00
DL Derek Lowe Jsy 4.00 10.00
DW Dontrelle Willis Jsy 4.00 10.00
EG Eric Gagne Jsy 4.00 10.00
FH Felix Hernandez Jsy 12.50 30.00
FR Francisco Rodriguez Jsy 4.00 10.00
GF Gavin Floyd Jsy 4.00 10.00
GM Greg Maddux Jsy 12.50 30.00
GP Gaylord Perry Jsy 4.00 10.00
HA Roy Halladay Jsy 4.00 10.00
HO Trevor Hoffman Jsy 6.00 15.00
JB Joe Blanton Jsy 4.00 10.00
JF Jeff Francis Jsy 4.00 10.00
JP Jake Peavy Jsy 4.00 10.00
JS Johan Santana Jsy 6.00 15.00
JW Jake Westbrook Jsy 4.00 10.00
KF Keith Foulke Jsy 4.00 10.00
KW Kerry Wood Jsy 4.00 10.00
LH Livan Hernandez Jsy 4.00 10.00
MA Matt Cain Jsy 15.00 40.00
MC Matt Clement Jsy 4.00 10.00
MM Mark Mulder Jsy 4.00 10.00
MP Mark Prior Jsy 6.00 15.00
MU Mike Mussina Jsy 6.00 15.00
NR1 Nolan Ryan Angels Jsy 30.00 60.00
NR2 Nolan Ryan Rgr Jsy 30.00 60.00
OP Odalis Perez Jsy 4.00 10.00
PE Oliver Perez Jsy 4.00 10.00
PM Pedro Martinez Jsy 6.00 15.00
RC Roger Clemens Jsy 12.50 30.00
RH Rich Harden Jsy 4.00 10.00
RJ Randy Johnson Jsy 8.00 20.00
RO Roy Oswalt Jsy 4.00 10.00
SK Scott Kazmir Jsy 4.00 10.00
SM John Smoltz Jsy 8.00 20.00
TG Tom Glavine Jsy 6.00 15.00
TH Tim Hudson Jsy 4.00 10.00
TW Tim Wakefield Jsy 10.00 25.00

2005 Ultimate Collection Hurlers Signature Materials

STATED PRINT RUN 20 SERIAL #'d SETS
PATCH PRINT RUN 10 SERIAL #'d SETS
NO PATCH PRICING DUE TO SCARCITY
OVERALL AU-GU ODDS 1:4
EXCHANGE DEADLINE 01/12/09
BE Josh Beckett Jsy 20.00 50.00
BL Brad Lidge Jsy 15.00 40.00
BM Brett Myers Jsy 6.00 15.00
BO Jeremy Bonderman Jsy 6.00 15.00
BS Ben Sheets Jsy 10.00 25.00
CA Chris Carpenter Jsy 20.00 50.00
CZ Carlos Zambrano Jsy 10.00 25.00
DH Danny Haren Jsy 15.00 40.00
DW Dontrelle Willis Jsy 6.00 15.00
EG Eric Gagne Jsy 10.00 25.00
FH Felix Hernandez Jsy 60.00 120.00
FR Francisco Rodriguez Jsy 10.00 25.00
GF Gavin Floyd Jsy 6.00 15.00
GP Gaylord Perry Jsy 10.00 25.00
HA Roy Halladay Jsy 12.50 30.00
JB Joe Blanton Jsy 6.00 15.00
JF Jeff Francis Jsy 6.00 15.00
JP Jake Peavy Jsy 10.00 25.00
JW Jake Westbrook Jsy 6.00 15.00
KW Kerry Wood Jsy 15.00 40.00
LH Livan Hernandez Jsy 10.00 25.00
MC Matt Clement Jsy 10.00 25.00
MM Mark Mulder Jsy 10.00 25.00
MP Mark Prior Jsy 12.50 30.00
MU Mike Mussina Jsy 20.00 50.00
NR1 Nolan Ryan Angels Jsy 60.00 120.00
NR2 Nolan Ryan Rgr Jsy 60.00 120.00
RO Roy Oswalt Jsy 6.00 15.00
SK Scott Kazmir Jsy 10.00 25.00
SM John Smoltz Jsy 30.00 60.00
TH Tim Hudson Jsy 15.00 40.00
TW Tim Wakefield Jsy 50.00 100.00

2005 Ultimate Collection Materials

OVERALL GAME-USED ODDS 1:4
STATED PRINT RUN 25 SERIAL #'d SETS
*PATCH p/r 25: .6X TO 1.5X BASIC
*PATCH p/r 15: .75X TO 2X BASIC
OVERALL PATCH ODDS 1:4
PATCH PRINT RUN B/WN 5-25 PER
NO PATCH PRICING ON QTY OF 10 OR LESS
AB Adrian Beltre Jsy 4.00 10.00
AD Adam Dunn Jsy 4.00 10.00
AH Aubrey Huff Jsy 4.00 10.00
AJ Andruw Jones Jsy 6.00 15.00
AP Albert Pujols Jsy 12.50 30.00
AR Aaron Rowand Jsy 4.00 10.00
BA Bobby Abreu Jsy 4.00 10.00
BC Bobby Crosby Jsy 4.00 10.00
BE Josh Beckett Jsy 4.00 10.00
BG Brian Giles Jsy 4.00 10.00
BJ B.J. Upton Jsy 4.00 10.00
BL Brad Lidge Jsy 4.00 10.00
BO Jeremy Bonderman Jsy 4.00 10.00
BR Brian Roberts Jsy 4.00 10.00
BS Ben Sheets Jsy 4.00 10.00
BU A.J. Burnett Jsy 4.00 10.00
CA Miguel Cabrera Jsy 6.00 15.00
CB Craig Biggio Jsy 6.00 15.00
CC C.C. Sabathia Jsy 4.00 10.00
CO Coco Crisp Jsy 4.00 10.00
CP Carl Pavano Jsy 4.00 10.00
CR Carl Crawford Jsy 4.00 10.00
CS Curt Schilling Jsy 6.00 15.00
CU Chase Utley Jsy 10.00 25.00
CW Rod Carew Jsy 6.00 15.00
CZ Carlos Zambrano Jsy 4.00 10.00
DJ Derek Jeter Jsy 15.00 40.00
DL Derek Lowe Jsy 4.00 10.00
DO David Ortiz Jsy 6.00 15.00
DW Dontrelle Willis Jsy 4.00 10.00
EC Eric Chavez Jsy 4.00 10.00
EG Eric Gagne Jsy 4.00 10.00
ER Edgar Renteria Jsy 4.00 10.00
ES Johnny Estrada Jsy 4.00 10.00
FH Felix Hernandez Jsy 12.50 30.00
FR Francisco Rodriguez Jsy 4.00 10.00
GF Gavin Floyd Jsy 4.00 10.00
GM Greg Maddux Jsy 12.50 30.00
GR Khalil Greene Jsy 6.00 15.00
GS Gary Sheffield Jsy 4.00 10.00
HA Roy Halladay Jsy 4.00 10.00
HB Hank Blalock Jsy 4.00 10.00
HO Trevor Hoffman Jsy 6.00 15.00
HU Torii Hunter Jsy 4.00 10.00
JA Jason Bay Jsy 4.00 10.00
JB Jeff Bagwell Jsy 8.00 20.00
JD J.D. Drew Jsy 4.00 10.00
JF Jeff Francis Jsy 4.00 10.00
JK Jeff Kent Jsy 4.00 10.00
JM Joe Mauer Jsy 8.00 20.00
JP Jake Peavy Jsy 4.00 10.00
JR Jeremy Reed Jsy 4.00 10.00
JV Jose Vidro Jsy 4.00 10.00
JW Jake Westbrook Jsy 4.00 10.00
KF Keith Foulke Jsy 4.00 10.00
KG Ken Griffey Jr. Jsy 12.50 30.00
LE Derrek Lee Jsy 6.00 15.00
MA Matt Cain Jsy 15.00 40.00
MC Matt Clement Jsy 4.00 10.00
MG Marcus Giles Jsy 4.00 10.00
ML Mark Loretta Jsy 4.00 10.00
MM Mark Mulder Jsy 4.00 10.00
MO Justin Morneau Jsy 4.00 10.00
MP Mark Prior Jsy 6.00 15.00
MS Mike Schmidt Jsy 15.00 40.00
MT Mark Teixeira Jsy 6.00 15.00
MY Michael Young Jsy 4.00 10.00
NR Nolan Ryan Jsy 15.00 40.00
OP Oliver Perez Jsy 4.00 10.00
OS Roy Oswalt Jsy 4.00 10.00
PA Corey Patterson Jsy 4.00 10.00
PF Prince Fielder Jsy 15.00 40.00
PM Pedro Martinez Jsy 6.00 15.00
RA Aramis Ramirez Jsy 4.00 10.00
RC Roger Clemens Jsy 12.50 30.00
RE Jose Reyes Jsy 4.00 10.00
RF Rafael Furcal Jsy 4.00 10.00
RH Rich Harden Jsy 4.00 10.00
RI Cal Ripken Jsy 30.00 60.00
RJ Randy Johnson Jsy 8.00 20.00
RP Rafael Palmeiro Jsy 6.00 15.00
RS Ryne Sandberg Jsy 15.00 40.00
RW Rickie Weeks Jsy 4.00 10.00
SA Johan Santana Jsy 8.00 20.00
SC Sean Casey Jsy 4.00 10.00
SK Scott Kazmir Jsy 4.00 10.00
SM John Smoltz Jsy 8.00 20.00
SP Scott Podsednik Jsy 6.00 15.00
SR Scott Rolen Jsy 6.00 15.00
TE Miguel Tejada Jsy 4.00 10.00
TH Tim Hudson Jsy 4.00 10.00
TI Tadahito Iguchi Jsy 12.50 30.00
TR Travis Hafner Jsy 4.00 10.00
TW Tim Wakefield Jsy 10.00 25.00
VG Vladimir Guerrero Jsy 8.00 20.00
VM Victor Martinez Jsy 4.00 10.00
WP Wily Mo Pena Jsy 4.00 10.00
WR David Wright Jsy 12.50 30.00
ZG Zack Greinke Jsy 4.00 10.00

2005 Ultimate Collection Materials Signature

STATED PRINT RUN 25 SERIAL #'d SETS
NO RC YR PRICING DUE TO SCARCITY
PATCH PRINT RUN 10 SERIAL #'d SETS
NO PATCH PRICING DUE TO SCARCITY
OVERALL AU-GU ODDS 1:4
EXCHANGE DEADLINE 01/10/09
AB Adrian Beltre Jsy 10.00 25.00
AD Adam Dunn Jsy 10.00 25.00
AH Aubrey Huff Jsy 6.00 15.00
AJ Andruw Jones Jsy 20.00 50.00
BC Bobby Crosby Jsy 10.00 25.00
BE Josh Beckett Jsy 15.00 40.00
BG Brian Giles Jsy 10.00 25.00
BJ B.J. Upton Jsy 12.00 30.00
BL Brad Lidge Jsy 10.00 25.00
BO Jeremy Bonderman Jsy 10.00 25.00
BR Brian Roberts Jsy 10.00 25.00
BS Ben Sheets Jsy 10.00 25.00
CA Miguel Cabrera Jsy 20.00 50.00
CA Rod Carew Jsy 15.00 40.00
CB Craig Biggio Jsy 20.00 50.00
CR Carl Crawford Jsy 10.00 25.00
CU Chase Utley Jsy 25.00 60.00
CZ Carlos Zambrano Jsy 10.00 25.00
DJ Derek Jeter Jsy 150.00 250.00
DO David Ortiz Jsy 25.00 60.00
DW Dontrelle Willis Jsy 15.00 40.00
EG Eric Gagne Jsy 10.00 25.00
ES Johnny Estrada Jsy 6.00 15.00
FH Felix Hernandez Jsy 60.00 120.00
FR Francisco Rodriguez Jsy 10.00 25.00
GF Gavin Floyd Jsy 6.00 15.00
GR Khalil Greene Jsy 15.00 40.00
GS Gary Sheffield Jsy 15.00 40.00
HA Roy Halladay Jsy 10.00 25.00
HB Hank Blalock Jsy 10.00 25.00
HU Torii Hunter Jsy 10.00 25.00
JA Jason Bay Jsy 10.00 25.00
JB Jeff Bagwell Jsy 30.00 80.00
JD J.D. Drew Jsy 10.00 25.00
JF Jeff Francis Jsy 6.00 15.00
JM Joe Mauer Jsy 25.00 60.00
JP Jake Peavy Jsy 10.00 25.00
JR Jeremy Reed Jsy 6.00 15.00
JV Jose Vidro Jsy 6.00 15.00
JW Jake Westbrook Jsy 6.00 15.00
KG Ken Griffey Jr. Jsy 75.00 150.00
LA Barry Larkin Jsy 25.00 60.00
LE Derrek Lee Jsy 15.00 40.00
MC Matt Clement Jsy 10.00 25.00
ML Mark Loretta Jsy 6.00 15.00
MM Mark Mulder Jsy 10.00 25.00
MO Justin Morneau Jsy 10.00 25.00
MP Mark Prior Jsy 6.00 15.00
MS Mike Schmidt Jsy 30.00 80.00
MT Mark Teixeira Jsy 12.00 30.00
MY Michael Young Jsy 10.00 25.00
NR Nolan Ryan Jsy 60.00 120.00
OS Roy Oswalt Jsy 10.00 25.00
RA Aramis Ramirez Jsy 10.00 25.00
RE Jose Reyes Jsy 10.00 25.00
RF Rafael Furcal Jsy 10.00 25.00
RP Rafael Palmeiro Jsy 20.00 50.00
RS Ryne Sandberg Jsy 20.00 50.00
RW Rickie Weeks Jsy 10.00 25.00
SK Scott Kazmir Jsy 10.00 25.00
SM John Smoltz Jsy 25.00 60.00
SP Scott Podsednik Jsy 15.00 40.00
TE Miguel Tejada Jsy 20.00 50.00
TH Tim Hudson Jsy 15.00 40.00
TR Travis Hafner Jsy 10.00 25.00
TW Tim Wakefield Jsy 50.00 100.00
VG Vladimir Guerrero Jsy 25.00 60.00
VM Victor Martinez Jsy 10.00 25.00
WP Wily Mo Pena Jsy 10.00 25.00
WR David Wright Jsy 50.00 100.00
ZG Zack Greinke Jsy 8.00 20.00

2005 Ultimate Collection Signatures

PRINT RUNS B/WN 10-99 COPIES PER
NO PRICING ON QTY OF 10
PLATINUM PRINT RUN 5 SERIAL #'d SETS
NO PLATINUM PRICING DUE TO SCARCITY
OVERALL AUTO ODDS 1:4
EXCHANGE DEADLINE 01/10/09
AB Adrian Beltre/69 10.00 25.00
AD Adam Dunn/35 10.00 25.00
AR Aramis Ramirez/69 10.00 25.00
BA Jason Bay/69 10.00 25.00
BC Bobby Crosby/69 10.00 25.00
BE Josh Beckett/35 15.00 40.00
BJ Bo Jackson/35 30.00 60.00
BL Barry Larkin/69 30.00 60.00
BR Brian Roberts/35 10.00 25.00
BS Ben Sheets/69 10.00 25.00
BU B.J. Upton/69 10.00 25.00
CB Craig Biggio/69 15.00 40.00
CF Carlton Fisk/15 20.00 50.00
CO Coco Crisp/69 20.00 50.00
CW Rod Carew/35 10.00 25.00
CZ Carlos Zambrano/69 10.00 25.00
DO David Ortiz/35 20.00 50.00
DW Dontrelle Willis/69 15.00 40.00
EC Eric Chavez/52 10.00 25.00
EG Eric Gagne/35 10.00 25.00
FH Felix Hernandez/69 50.00 100.00
GC Gary Carter/35 15.00 40.00
GR Khalil Greene/69 15.00 40.00
GS Gary Sheffield/25 15.00 40.00
GW Tony Gwynn/25 30.00 60.00
HA Roy Halladay/35 10.00 25.00
HB Hank Blalock/69 10.00 25.00
HU Torii Hunter/69 10.00 25.00
JB Johnny Bench/15 30.00 60.00
JD J.D. Drew/29 10.00 25.00
JE Jeff Bagwell/15 40.00 80.00
JM Joe Mauer/69 2.00 50.00
JN Jeff Niemann/69 6.00 15.00
JO Andruw Jones/35 20.00 50.00
JP Jake Peavy/69 10.00 25.00
JR Jose Reyes/69 10.00 25.00
JV Justin Verlander/69 25.00 60.00
KG Ken Griffey Jr./69 40.00 100.00
KM Kendry Morales/69 6.00 15.00
KW Kerry Wood/15 20.00 50.00
MA Don Mattingly/25 50.00 100.00
MC Miguel Cabrera/69 15.00 40.00
MM Mark Mulder/69 10.00 25.00
MP Mark Prior/15 15.00 40.00
MS Mike Schmidt/25 30.00 60.00
MT Mark Teixeira/99 12.00 30.00
MU Mike Mussina/15 30.00 60.00
MY Michael Young/69 10.00 25.00
OS Ozzie Smith/35 20.00 50.00
PF Prince Fielder/35 75.00 150.00
PH Philip Humber/69 12.00 30.00
PM Paul Molitor/49 10.00 25.00
RH Rich Harden/69 10.00 25.00
RO Roy Oswalt/69 10.00 25.00
RP Rafael Palmeiro/25 20.00 50.00
RS Ryne Sandberg/15 50.00 100.00
RW Rickie Weeks/30 10.00 25.00
RY Robin Yount/15 30.00 80.00
SK Scott Kazmir/69 10.00 25.00
SM John Smoltz/49 15.00 40.00
TH Tim Hudson/69 15.00 40.00
TI Tadahito Iguchi/69 50.00 100.00
TR Travis Hafner/69 10.00 25.00
VM Victor Martinez/69 10.00 25.00
WB Wade Boggs/15 20.00 50.00
WC Will Clark/69 15.00 40.00
WR David Wright/69 30.00 60.00
ZG Zack Greinke/69 20.00 50.00

2005 Ultimate Collection Sluggers Materials

OVERALL GAME-USED ODDS 1:4
STATED PRINT RUN 20 SERIAL #'d SETS
*PATCH p/r 25: .6X TO 1.5X BASIC
*PATCH p/r 19: .75X TO 2X BASIC
OVERALL PATCH ODDS 1:4
PATCH PRINT RUN B/WN 19-25 PER
AB Adrian Beltre Jsy 4.00 10.00
AD Adam Dunn Jsy 4.00 10.00
AH Aubrey Huff Jsy 4.00 10.00
AP Albert Pujols Jsy 12.50 30.00
AR Aramis Ramirez Jsy 4.00 10.00
BA Bobby Abreu Jsy 4.00 10.00
BC Bobby Crosby Jsy 4.00 10.00
BG Brian Giles Jsy 4.00 10.00
BR Brian Roberts Jsy 4.00 10.00
CA Rod Carew Jsy 6.00 15.00
CB Craig Biggio Jsy 6.00 15.00
CC Carl Crawford Jsy 4.00 10.00
CJ Chipper Jones Jsy 8.00 20.00
CO Coco Crisp Jsy 4.00 10.00
CP Corey Patterson Jsy 4.00 10.00
DJ Derek Jeter Jsy 10.00 25.00
DL Derrek Lee Jsy 6.00 15.00
DO David Ortiz Jsy 6.00 15.00
DW David Wright Jsy 12.50 30.00
EC Eric Chavez Jsy 4.00 10.00
ER Edgar Renteria Jsy 4.00 10.00
ES Johnny Estrada Jsy 4.00 10.00
GR Khalil Greene Jsy 6.00 15.00
GS Gary Sheffield Jsy 4.00 10.00
HA Travis Hafner Jsy 4.00 10.00
HB Hank Blalock Jsy 4.00 10.00
JA Jason Bay Jsy 4.00 10.00
JB Jeff Bagwell Jsy 8.00 20.00
JD J.D. Drew Jsy 4.00 10.00
JK Jeff Kent Jsy 4.00 10.00
JM Justin Morneau Jsy 4.00 10.00
JR Jose Reyes Jsy 4.00 10.00
JV Jose Vidro Jsy 4.00 10.00
KG Ken Griffey Jr. Jsy 12.50 30.00
MA Joe Mauer Jsy 8.00 20.00
MC Miguel Cabrera Jsy 6.00 15.00
MG Marcus Giles Jsy 4.00 10.00
ML Mark Loretta Jsy 4.00 10.00
MT Mark Teixeira Jsy 6.00 15.00
MY Michael Young Jsy 4.00 10.00
RF Rafael Furcal Jsy 4.00 10.00
RH Ryan Howard Jsy 15.00 40.00
RP Rafael Palmeiro Jsy 6.00 15.00
SC Sean Casey Jsy 4.00 10.00
SR Scott Rolen Jsy 6.00 15.00
TH Torii Hunter Jsy 4.00 10.00
VG Vladimir Guerrero Jsy 8.00 20.00
VM Victor Martinez Jsy 4.00 10.00
WP Wily Mo Pena Jsy 4.00 10.00

2005 Ultimate Collection Sluggers Signature Materials

STATED PRINT RUN 20 SERIAL #'d SETS
PATCH PRINT RUN B/WN 3-10 COPIES PER
NO PATCH PRICING DUE TO SCARCITY
OVERALL AU-GU ODDS 1:4
AB Adrian Beltre Jsy 10.00 25.00
AD Adam Dunn Jsy 10.00 25.00
AH Aubrey Huff Jsy 6.00 15.00
AR Aramis Ramirez Jsy 10.00 25.00
BC Bobby Crosby Jsy 10.00 25.00
BG Brian Giles Jsy 10.00 25.00
BR Brian Roberts Jsy 10.00 25.00
CA Rod Carew Jsy 15.00 40.00
CB Craig Biggio Jsy 20.00 50.00
CJ Chipper Jones Jsy 30.00 60.00
DJ Derek Jeter Jsy 150.00 250.00
DL Derrek Lee Jsy 15.00 40.00
DO David Ortiz Jsy 30.00 60.00
DW David Wright Jsy 50.00 100.00
EC Eric Chavez Jsy 10.00 25.00
ES Johnny Estrada Jsy 6.00 15.00
GR Khalil Greene Jsy 15.00 40.00
GS Gary Sheffield Jsy 15.00 40.00
HA Travis Hafner Jsy 10.00 25.00
HB Hank Blalock Jsy 10.00 25.00
JA Jason Bay Jsy 10.00 25.00
JB Jeff Bagwell Jsy 40.00 80.00
JD J.D. Drew Jsy 6.00 15.00
JM Justin Morneau Jsy 10.00 25.00
JR Jose Reyes Jsy 10.00 25.00
JV Jose Vidro Jsy 6.00 15.00
KG Ken Griffey Jr. Jsy 75.00 150.00
MA Joe Mauer Jsy 30.00 60.00
MC Miguel Cabrera Jsy 20.00 50.00
ML Mark Loretta Jsy 6.00 15.00
MT Mark Teixeira Jsy 20.00 50.00
MY Michael Young Jsy 10.00 25.00
RF Rafael Furcal Jsy 10.00 25.00
RH Ryan Howard Jsy 50.00 100.00
RP Rafael Palmeiro Jsy 20.00 50.00
TH Torii Hunter Jsy 10.00 25.00
VM Victor Martinez Jsy 10.00 25.00
WP Wily Mo Pena Jsy 10.00 25.00

2005 Ultimate Collection Veteran Materials

OVERALL GAME-USED ODDS 1:4
STATED PRINT RUN 20 SERIAL #'d SETS
*PATCH p/r 30: .6X TO 1.5X BASIC
*PATCH p/r 15-16: .75X TO 2X BASIC
OVERALL PATCH ODDS 1:4
PATCH PRINT RUN B/WN 7-30 PER
NO PATCH PRICING ON QTY OF 7
AB Adrian Beltre Jsy 4.00 10.00
AD Adam Dunn Jsy 4.00 10.00
AH Aubrey Huff Jsy 4.00 10.00
AJ Andruw Jones Jsy 6.00 15.00
AR Aramis Ramirez Jsy 4.00 10.00
AS Alfonso Soriano Jsy 4.00 10.00
BA Bobby Abreu Jsy 4.00 10.00
BE Josh Beckett Jsy 4.00 10.00
BG Brian Giles Jsy 4.00 10.00
BM Brett Myers Jsy 4.00 10.00
CA Rod Carew Jsy 6.00 15.00
CB Craig Biggio Jsy 6.00 15.00
CR Cal Ripken Jsy 30.00 60.00
CS C.C. Sabathia Jsy 4.00 10.00
DJ Derek Jeter Jsy 15.00 40.00
DL Derek Lowe Jsy 4.00 10.00
DO David Ortiz Jsy 6.00 15.00
DW Dontrelle Willis Jsy 4.00 10.00
EC Eric Chavez Jsy 4.00 10.00
EG Eric Gagne Jsy 4.00 10.00
ER Edgar Renteria Jsy 4.00 10.00
GM Greg Maddux Jsy 12.50 30.00
HB Hank Blalock Jsy 4.00 10.00
HO Trevor Hoffman Jsy 6.00 15.00
HU Torii Hunter Jsy 4.00 10.00
JB Jeff Bagwell Jsy 8.00 20.00
JD J.D. Drew Jsy 4.00 10.00
JK Jeff Kent Jsy 4.00 10.00
JV Jose Vidro Jsy 4.00 10.00
KF Keith Foulke Jsy 4.00 10.00
KG Ken Griffey Jr. Jsy 12.50 30.00
LE Derrek Lee Jsy 6.00 15.00
LH Livan Hernandez Jsy 4.00 10.00
MC Matt Clement Jsy 4.00 10.00
ML Mark Loretta Jsy 4.00 10.00
MM Mark Mulder Jsy 4.00 10.00
MP Mark Prior Jsy 6.00 15.00
MT Miguel Tejada Jsy 4.00 10.00
NR Nolan Ryan Jsy 15.00 40.00
OP Odalis Perez Jsy 4.00 10.00
RC Roger Clemens Jsy 12.50 30.00
RH Roy Halladay Jsy 4.00 10.00
RJ Randy Johnson Jsy 8.00 20.00
RO Roy Oswalt Jsy 4.00 10.00
SC Sean Casey Jsy 4.00 10.00
SM John Smoltz Jsy 8.00 20.00
SR Scott Rolen Jsy 6.00 15.00
TH Tim Hudson Jsy 4.00 10.00
TW Tim Wakefield Jsy 10.00 25.00
VG Vladimir Guerrero Jsy 8.00 20.00

2005 Ultimate Collection Veteran Materials Signature

STATED PRINT RUN 20 SERIAL #'d SETS
PATCH PRINT RUN 10 SERIAL #'d SETS
NO PATCH PRICING DUE TO SCARCITY
OVERALL AU-GU ODDS 1:4
EXCHANGE DEADLINE 01/10/09
AB Adrian Beltre Jsy 6.00 15.00
AD Adam Dunn Jsy 10.00 25.00
AH Aubrey Huff Jsy 6.00 15.00
AJ Andruw Jones Jsy 20.00 50.00
AR Aramis Ramirez Jsy 10.00 25.00
BE Josh Beckett Jsy 15.00 40.00
BG Brian Giles Jsy 10.00 25.00
BM Brett Myers Jsy 6.00 15.00
CA Rod Carew Jsy 15.00 40.00
CB Craig Biggio Jsy 20.00 50.00
DJ Derek Jeter Jsy 150.00 250.00
DO David Ortiz Jsy 30.00 60.00
DW Dontrelle Willis Jsy 15.00 40.00
EC Eric Chavez Jsy 10.00 25.00
EG Eric Gagne Jsy 10.00 25.00
HB Hank Blalock Jsy 10.00 25.00
HU Torii Hunter Jsy 10.00 25.00
JB Jeff Bagwell Jsy 40.00 80.00
JD J.D. Drew Jsy 10.00 25.00
JV Jose Vidro Jsy 6.00 15.00
KG Ken Griffey Jr. Jsy 75.00 150.00
LE Derrek Lee Jsy 15.00 40.00
LH Livan Hernandez Jsy 10.00 25.00
MC Matt Clement Jsy 10.00 25.00
ML Mark Loretta Jsy 6.00 15.00
MM Mark Mulder Jsy 10.00 25.00
MP Mark Prior Jsy 12.50 30.00
MT Miguel Tejada Jsy 20.00 50.00
NR Nolan Ryan Jsy 60.00 120.00
RH Roy Halladay Jsy 12.50 30.00
RO Roy Oswalt Jsy 10.00 25.00
SM John Smoltz Jsy 30.00 60.00
TH Tim Hudson Jsy 15.00 40.00
TW Tim Wakefield Jsy 50.00 100.00
VG Vladimir Guerrero Jsy 20.00 50.00

2005 Ultimate Collection Young Stars Materials

OVERALL GAME-USED ODDS 1:4
STATED PRINT RUN 20 SERIAL #'d SETS
*PATCH p/r 30: .6X TO 1.5X BASIC
*PATCH p/r 15: .75X TO 2X BASIC
OVERALL PATCH ODDS 1:4
PATCH PRINT RUN B/WN 6-30 PER
NO PATCH PRICING ON QTY OF 6
AB A.J. Burnett Jsy 4.00 10.00
AR Aaron Rowand Jsy 4.00 10.00
BA Jason Bay Jsy 4.00 10.00
BC Bobby Crosby Jsy 4.00 10.00
BL Brad Lidge Jsy 4.00 10.00
BO Jeremy Bonderman Jsy 4.00 10.00
BR Brian Roberts Jsy 4.00 10.00
BS Ben Sheets Jsy 4.00 10.00
BU B.J. Upton Jsy 4.00 10.00
CC Carl Crawford Jsy 4.00 10.00
CO Coco Crisp Jsy 4.00 10.00
CP Carl Pavano Jsy 4.00 10.00
CU Chase Utley Jsy 10.00 25.00
CZ Carlos Zambrano Jsy 4.00 10.00
DH Danny Haren Jsy 4.00 10.00
DW David Wright Jsy 12.50 30.00
FH Felix Hernandez Jsy 12.50 30.00
FR Francisco Rodriguez Jsy 4.00 10.00
GF Gavin Floyd Jsy 4.00 10.00
HO Ryan Howard Jsy 15.00 40.00
JB Joe Blanton Jsy 4.00 10.00
JE Johnny Estrada Jsy 4.00 10.00
JF Jeff Francis Jsy 4.00 10.00
JM Joe Mauer Jsy 6.00 15.00
JP Jake Peavy Jsy 4.00 10.00
JR Jeremy Reed Jsy 4.00 10.00
JS Johan Santana Jsy 6.00 15.00
JW Jake Westbrook Jsy 4.00 10.00
KG Khalil Greene Jsy 6.00 15.00
MA Matt Cain Jsy 6.00 15.00
MC Miguel Cabrera Jsy 6.00 15.00
MG Marcus Giles Jsy 4.00 10.00
MO Justin Morneau Jsy 4.00 10.00
MT Mark Teixeira Jsy 6.00 15.00
MY Michael Young Jsy 4.00 10.00
OP Oliver Perez Jsy 4.00 10.00
PA Corey Patterson Jsy 4.00 10.00
PF Prince Fielder Jsy 15.00 40.00
RE Jose Reyes Jsy 4.00 10.00
RF Rafael Furcal Jsy 4.00 10.00
RH Rich Harden Jsy 4.00 10.00
RW Rickie Weeks Jsy 4.00 10.00
SK Scott Kazmir Jsy 4.00 10.00
SP Scott Podsednik Jsy 6.00 15.00
TH Travis Hafner Jsy 4.00 10.00
TI Tadahito Iguchi Jsy 12.50 30.00
VM Victor Martinez Jsy 4.00 10.00
WP Wily Mo Pena Jsy 4.00 10.00
ZG Zack Greinke Jsy 4.00 10.00

2005 Ultimate Collection Young Stars Signature Materials

STATED PRINT RUN 20 SERIAL #'d SETS
NO RC YR PRICING DUE TO SCARCITY
PATCH PRINT RUN 10 SERIAL #'d SETS
NO PATCH PRICING DUE TO SCARCITY
OVERALL AU-GU ODDS 1:4
AR Aaron Rowand Jsy 10.00 25.00
BA Jason Bay Jsy 6.00 15.00
BC Bobby Crosby Jsy 10.00 25.00
BL Brad Lidge Jsy 15.00 40.00
BO Jeremy Bonderman Jsy 10.00 25.00
BR Brian Roberts Jsy 10.00 25.00
BS Ben Sheets Jsy 10.00 25.00
BU B.J. Upton Jsy 10.00 25.00
CC Carl Crawford Jsy 6.00 15.00
CZ Carlos Zambrano Jsy 15.00 40.00
DH Danny Haren Jsy 6.00 15.00
DW David Wright Jsy 30.00 60.00
FR Francisco Rodriguez Jsy 10.00 25.00
GF Gavin Floyd Jsy 6.00 15.00
JB Joe Blanton Jsy 6.00 15.00
JE Johnny Estrada Jsy 6.00 15.00
JF Jeff Francis Jsy 6.00 15.00
JM Joe Mauer Jsy 30.00 60.00
JP Jake Peavy Jsy 10.00 25.00
JR Jeremy Reed Jsy 6.00 15.00
JW Jake Westbrook Jsy 6.00 15.00
KG Khalil Greene Jsy 15.00 40.00
MA Matt Cain Jsy 75.00 150.00
MG Marcus Giles Jsy 10.00 25.00
MT Mark Teixeira Jsy 10.00 25.00
MY Michael Young Jsy 10.00 25.00
OP Oliver Perez Jsy 6.00 15.00
RE Jose Reyes Jsy 10.00 25.00
RF Rafael Furcal Jsy 10.00 25.00
RW Rickie Weeks Jsy 10.00 25.00
SK Scott Kazmir Jsy 10.00 25.00
SP Scott Podsednik Jsy 15.00 40.00
TH Travis Hafner Jsy 10.00 25.00
VM Victor Martinez Jsy 10.00 25.00
WP Wily Mo Pena Jsy 10.00 25.00
ZG Zack Greinke Jsy 10.00 25.00

2005 Ultimate Collection Dual Materials

OVERALL GAME-USED ODDS 1:4
STATED PRINT RUN 15 SERIAL #'d SETS
NO RC YR PRICING DUE TO SCARCITY
OVERALL PATCH ODDS 1:4
PATCH PRINT RUN 10 SERIAL #'d SETS
NO PATCH PRICING DUE TO SCARCITY
AC A.Jones/C.Jones 12.50 30.00
AE A.Beltre/E.Chavez 6.00 15.00
AH A.Beltre/H.Blalock 6.00 15.00
AJ A.Burnett/J.Beckett 6.00 15.00
AM A.Pujols/M.Cabrera 20.00 50.00
AP B.Abreu/C.Patterson 6.00 15.00
AU B.Abreu/C.Utley 15.00 40.00
BC J.Beckett/M.Cabrera 10.00 25.00
BG J.Bay/V.Guerrero 12.50 30.00
BH A.Beltre/F.Hernandez 15.00 40.00
BJ B.Sheets/J.Peavy 6.00 15.00
BK B.Crosby/K.Greene 10.00 25.00
BM J.Bonderman/M.Cain 30.00 60.00
BS R.Sandberg/W.Boggs 20.00 50.00
BT H.Blalock/M.Teixeira 10.00 25.00
BY H.Blalock/M.Young 6.00 15.00
CB B.Crosby/J.Bay 6.00 15.00
CC B.Crosby/E.Chavez 6.00 15.00
CG M.Cabrera/V.Guerrero 12.50 30.00
CJ C.Biggio/J.Bagwell 12.50 30.00
CO R.Clemens/R.Oswalt 15.00 40.00
CP C.Crawford/S.Podsednik 10.00 25.00
CR E.Chavez/S.Rolen 10.00 25.00
CT C.Ripken/T.Gwynn 50.00 100.00
CW E.Chavez/D.Wright 15.00 40.00
DG A.Dunn/K.Griffey Jr. 15.00 40.00
DJ D.Wright/J.Reyes 15.00 40.00
DP A.Dunn/W.Pena 6.00 15.00
DR D.Jeter/R.Johnson 30.00 60.00
GC K.Griffey Jr./M.Cabrera 15.00 40.00
GF M.Giles/R.Furcal 6.00 15.00

GG B.Giles/M.Giles 6.00 15.00
GH K.Griffey Jr./T.Hunter 15.00 40.00
GJ D.Jeter/K.Griffey Jr. 30.00 60.00
GL K.Greene/M.Loretta 10.00 25.00
GP K.Griffey Jr./W.Pena 15.00 40.00
GR E.Gagne/F.Rodriguez 6.00 15.00
HC F.Hernandez/M.Cain 40.00 80.00
HH D.Haren/R.Harden 6.00 15.00
HM T.Hafner/V.Martinez 6.00 15.00
HO R.Harden/R.Oswalt 6.00 15.00
HS B.Sheets/R.Harden 6.00 15.00
JC R.Johnson/R.Clemens 20.00 50.00
JF J.Santana/F.Hernandez 15.00 40.00
JG A.Jones/K.Griffey Jr. 15.00 40.00
JH A.Jones/T.Hunter 10.00 25.00
JJ D.Jeter/R.Jackson 40.00 80.00
JL D.Jeter/B.Larkin 30.00 60.00
JO J.Santana/O.Perez 10.00 25.00
JR D.Jeter/J.Reyes 30.00 60.00
JV J.Mauer/V.Martinez 10.00 25.00
LG B.Lidge/E.Gagne 6.00 15.00
LO B.Lidge/R.Oswalt 6.00 15.00
LR B.Lidge/F.Rodriguez 6.00 15.00
ME J.Mauer/J.Estrada 10.00 25.00
MG G.Maddux/M.Prior 15.00 40.00
MH M.Mulder/T.Hudson 6.00 15.00
MJ P.Martinez/R.Johnson 12.50 30.00
MM J.Mauer/J.Morneau 10.00 25.00
MP J.Mauer/M.Prior 10.00 25.00
MR M.Mussina/R.Johnson 12.50 30.00
NR N.Ryan/R.Johnson 30.00 60.00
PC M.Prior/R.Clemens 15.00 40.00
PD D.Gooden/P.Martinez 10.00 25.00
PG A.Pujols/K.Griffey Jr. 30.00 60.00
PH J.Peavy/R.Harden 6.00 15.00
PJ A.Pujols/D.Jeter 30.00 60.00
PL A.Pujols/D.Lee 20.00 50.00
PM M.Piazza/P.Martinez 12.50 30.00
PS B.Sheets/M.Prior 10.00 25.00
RB A.Ramirez/H.Blalock 6.00 15.00
RC N.Ryan/R.Clemens 30.00 60.00
RE A.Ramirez/E.Chavez 6.00 15.00
RF J.Reyes/R.Furcal 6.00 15.00
RG B.Roberts/M.Giles 6.00 15.00
RJ C.Ripken/D.Jeter 60.00 120.00
RL A.Ramirez/D.Lee 10.00 25.00
RP A.Rowand/S.Podsednik 10.00 25.00
RR A.Rowand/J.Reed 6.00 15.00
RS M.Schmidt/C.Ripken 50.00 100.00
RT C.Ripken/M.Tejada 15.00 40.00
RU J.Reyes/B.Upton 6.00 15.00
RW A.Ramirez/D.Wright 15.00 40.00
SB M.Schmidt/W.Boggs 20.00 50.00
SC J.Santana/R.Clemens 15.00 40.00
SH J.Smoltz/T.Hudson 12.50 30.00
SJ C.Schilling/R.Johnson 12.50 30.00
SM J.Mauer/J.Santana 10.00 25.00
SO C.Schilling/D.Ortiz 10.00 25.00
SP J.Santana/M.Prior 10.00 25.00
SR M.Schmidt/S.Rolen 20.00 50.00
TC M.Teixeira/M.Cabrera 10.00 25.00
UJ B.Upton/D.Jeter 30.00 60.00
WR D.Wright/S.Rolen 15.00 40.00
ZH C.Zambrano/R.Harden 6.00 15.00
ZO C.Zambrano/R.Oswalt 6.00 15.00
ZP C.Zambrano/O.Perez 6.00 15.00

2005 Ultimate Collection Dual Signatures

OVERALL AUTO ODDS 1:4
STATED PRINT RUN 25 SERIAL #'d SETS
NO RC YR PRICING DUE TO SCARCITY
EXCHANGE DEADLINE 01/10/09
BB C.Biggio/J.Bagwell 60.00 120.00
BC A.Beltre/E.Chavez 10.00 25.00
BH A.Beltre/F.Hernandez 75.00 150.00
BJ B.Crosby/J.Bay 10.00 25.00
BT H.Blalock/M.Teixeira 30.00 60.00
BY H.Blalock/M.Young 10.00 25.00
CC B.Crosby/E.Chavez 10.00 25.00
CG B.Crosby/K.Greene 30.00 60.00
CP C.Crawford/S.Podsednik 30.00 60.00
CY C.Crawford/D.Young 30.00 60.00
DG A.Dunn/K.Griffey Jr. 60.00 120.00
DJ D.Jeter/J.Reyes 100.00 175.00
DK D.Jeter/K.Griffey Jr. 150.00 250.00
DM D.Wright/M.Schmidt 60.00 120.00
DP A.Dawson/C.Patterson 12.50 30.00
FF G.Floyd/J.Francis 10.00 25.00
GC K.Griffey Jr./M.Cabrera 100.00 150.00
GH K.Griffey Jr./T.Hunter 60.00 120.00
GJ A.Jones/K.Griffey Jr. 75.00 150.00
GL K.Greene/M.Loretta 10.00 25.00
GP K.Griffey Jr./W.Pena 60.00 120.00
GR E.Gagne/F.Rodriguez 30.00 60.00
HH D.Haren/R.Harden 10.00 25.00
HM T.Hafner/V.Martinez 10.00 25.00
HO R.Harden/R.Oswalt 10.00 25.00
HS B.Sheets/R.Harden 10.00 25.00
JB B.Sheets/J.Peavy 10.00 25.00
JG D.Jeter/N.Garciaparra 125.00 200.00
JH A.Jones/T.Hunter 30.00 60.00
JJ A.Jones/C.Jones 75.00 150.00
JM D.Jeter/D.Mattingly 200.00 300.00
JV J.Mauer/V.Martinez 50.00 100.00
KH S.Kazmir/F.Hernandez 75.00 150.00
LO B.Lidge/R.Oswalt 15.00 40.00
LR B.Lidge/F.Rodriguez 30.00 60.00
MC D.Mattingly/W.Clark 50.00 100.00
MG G.Maddux/T.Glavine 125.00 200.00
MH J.Morneau/T.Hafner 10.00 25.00
MM J.Mauer/J.Morneau 50.00 100.00
MP J.Mauer/M.Prior 20.00 50.00
MT M.Mulder/T.Hudson 10.00 25.00
PH J.Peavy/R.Harden 10.00 25.00
PJ A.Pujols/D.Jeter 500.00 700.00
PP G.Perry/J.Peavy 10.00 25.00
RB A.Ramirez/H.Blalock 10.00 25.00
RC N.Ryan/R.Clemens 150.00 250.00
RE A.Ramirez/E.Chavez 10.00 25.00
RF J.Reyes/R.Furcal 10.00 25.00
RJ C.Ripken/D.Jeter 250.00 400.00
RL A.Ramirez/D.Lee 30.00 60.00
RP A.Rowand/C.Patterson 10.00 25.00
RP A.Rowand/S.Podsednik 30.00 60.00
RR A.Rowand/J.Reed 10.00 25.00
RW R.Sandberg/W.Boggs 50.00 100.00
RW A.Ramirez
D.Wright 50.00 100.00

SH J.Smoltz/T.Hudson 40.00 80.00
SO C.Schilling/D.Ortiz 40.00 80.00
SP B.Sheets/M.Prior 10.00 25.00
SW B.Sheets/R.Weeks 10.00 25.00
TC M.Teixeira/M.Cabrera 50.00 100.00
UJ B.Upton/D.Jeter 100.00 175.00
UW B.Upton/R.Weeks 10.00 25.00
WR D.Wright/J.Reyes 60.00 120.00
YU D.Young/B.Upton 30.00 60.00
YW D.Young/R.Weeks 30.00 60.00
ZH C.Zambrano/R.Harden 10.00 25.00
ZO C.Zambrano/R.Oswalt 10.00 25.00

2006 Ultimate Collection

COMMON CARD (1-274) 1.00 2.50
VETERAN PRINT RUN 799 SER.#'d SETS
COMMON RC (1-274) 1.00 2.50
RC PRINT RUN 799 SERIAL #'d SETS
COMMON AU RC (101-175) 4.00 10.00
AU RC MINORS 4.00 10.00
OVERALL AU ODDS 1:2
AU RC PRINT RUNS B/WN 150-180
EXCHANGE DEADLINE 12/20/09
PLATE ODDS APPX. 7:10 BONUS PACKS
PLATE PRINT RUN 1 SET PER COLOR
BLACK-CYAN-MAGENTA-YELLOW ISSUED
NO PLATE PRICING DUE TO SCARCITY
1 Babe Ruth 6.00 15.00
2 Chad Tracy 1.00 2.50
3 Brandon Webb 1.50 4.00
4 Andruw Jones 1.00 2.50
5 Chipper Jones 2.50 6.00
6 John Smoltz 2.50 6.00
7 Eddie Mathews 2.50 6.00
8 Miguel Tejada 1.50 4.00
9 Brian Roberts 1.00 2.50
10 Mickey Cochrane 1.50 4.00
11 Curt Schilling 1.50 4.00
12 David Ortiz 2.50 6.00
13 Manny Ramirez 2.50 6.00
14 Johnny Bench 2.50 6.00
15 Cy Young 2.50 6.00
16 Greg Maddux 3.00 8.00
17 Derrek Lee 1.00 2.50
18 Yogi Berra 2.50 6.00
19 Walter Johnson 2.50 6.00
20 Jim Thome 1.50 4.00
21 Paul Konerko 1.50 4.00
22 Lou Gehrig 5.00 12.00
23 Jose Contreras 1.00 2.50
24 Ken Griffey Jr. 5.00 12.00
25 Adam Dunn 1.50 4.00
26 Reggie Jackson 1.50 4.00
27 Travis Hafner 1.00 2.50
28 Victor Martinez 1.50 4.00
29 Grady Sizemore 1.50 4.00
30 Casey Stengel 1.50 4.00
31 Todd Helton 1.50 4.00
32 Nolan Ryan 8.00 20.00
33 Clint Barmes 1.00 2.50
34 Ivan Rodriguez 1.50 4.00
35 Chris Shelton 1.00 2.50
36 Ty Cobb 4.00 10.00
37 Miguel Cabrera 2.50 6.00
38 Dontrelle Willis 1.00 2.50
39 Lance Berkman 1.50 4.00
40 Tom Seaver 1.50 4.00
41 Roy Oswalt 1.50 4.00
42 Christy Mathewson 2.50 6.00
43 Luis Aparicio 1.50 4.00
44 Vladimir Guerrero 1.50 4.00
45 Bartolo Colon 1.00 2.50
46 Roy Campanella 2.50 6.00
47 George Sisler 1.50 4.00
48 Jeff Kent 1.00 2.50
49 J.D. Drew 1.00 2.50
50 Carlos Lee 1.00 2.50
51 Willie Stargell 1.50 4.00
52 Rickie Weeks 1.00 2.50
53 Johan Santana 1.50 4.00
54 Torii Hunter 1.00 2.50
55 Joe Mauer 1.50 4.00
56 Pedro Martinez 1.50 4.00
57 David Wright 2.00 5.00
58 Carlos Beltran 1.50 4.00
59 Jimmie Foxx 2.50 6.00
60 Jose Reyes 1.50 4.00
61 Derek Jeter 6.00 15.00
62 Alex Rodriguez 3.00 8.00
63 Randy Johnson 2.50 6.00
64 Hideki Matsui 2.50 6.00
65 Thurman Munson 2.50 6.00
66 Rich Harden 1.00 2.50
67 Eric Chavez 1.00 2.50
68 Don Drysdale 1.50 4.00
69 Bobby Crosby 1.00 2.50
70 Pee Wee Reese 1.50 4.00
71 Ryan Howard 2.00 5.00
72 Chase Utley 1.50 4.00
73 Jackie Robinson 2.50 6.00
74 Jason Bay 1.00 2.50
75 Honus Wagner 2.50 6.00
76 Lefty Grove 1.50 4.00
77 Jake Peavy 1.00 2.50
78 Brian Giles 1.00 2.50
79 Eddie Murray 1.50 4.00
80 Omar Vizquel 1.50 4.00
81 Jason Schmidt 1.00 2.50
82 Ichiro Suzuki 3.00 8.00
83 Felix Hernandez 1.50 4.00
84 Kenji Johjima RC 2.50 6.00
85 Albert Pujols 3.00 8.00
86 Chris Carpenter 1.50 4.00
87 Brooks Robinson 1.50 4.00
88 Dizzy Dean 1.50 4.00
89 Carl Crawford 1.50 4.00
90 Rogers Hornsby 1.50 4.00
91 Scott Kazmir 1.50 4.00
92 Mark Teixeira 1.50 4.00
93 Michael Young 1.00 2.50
94 Johnny Mize 1.50 4.00
95 Vernon Wells 1.00 2.50
96 Roy Halladay 1.50 4.00
97 Mel Ott 1.00 2.50
98 Alfonso Soriano 1.50 4.00
99 Joe Morgan 1.50 4.00
100 Satchel Paige 2.50 6.00
101 A.Wainwright AU/180 (RC) 20.00 50.00
102 A.Hernandez AU/180 (RC) 4.00 10.00
103 A.Ethier AU/180 (RC) 8.00 20.00
104 B.Johnson AU/180 (RC) 4.00 10.00
105 B.Bonser AU/180 (RC) 6.00 15.00
106 B.Logan AU/180 RC 4.00 10.00
107 B.Anderson AU/180 (RC) 4.00 10.00
108 B.Bannister AU/180 (RC) 20.00 50.00
109 C.Demaria AU/180 RC 4.00 10.00
110 C.Denorfia AU/180 (RC) 4.00 10.00
111 C.Ross AU/180 (RC) 5.00 12.00
112 C.Hamels AU/180 (RC) 10.00 25.00
113 C.Jackson AU/180 (RC) 6.00 15.00
114 D.Uggla AU/180 (RC) 6.00 15.00
115 D.Gassner AU/180 (RC) 4.00 10.00
116 E.Reed AU/180 (RC) 4.00 10.00
117 F.Carmona AU/180 (RC) 4.00 10.00
118 F.Nieve AU/180 (RC) 4.00 10.00
119 F.Liriano AU/180 (RC) 4.00 10.00
120 F.Bynum AU/180 (RC) 4.00 10.00
121 H.Ramirez AU/180 (RC) 6.00 15.00
123 I.Kinsler AU/180 (RC) 15.00 40.00
124 J.Hammel AU/180 (RC) 4.00 10.00
125 J.Kubel AU/180 (RC) 4.00 10.00
126 J.Harris AU/180 RC 4.00 10.00
127 J.Weaver AU/150 (RC) 15.00 40.00
128 J.Accardo AU/180 (RC) 4.00 10.00
129 J.Hermida AU/180 (RC) 6.00 15.00
130 J.Zumaya AU/180 (RC) 8.00 20.00
131 J.Devine AU/180 RC 4.00 10.00
132 J.Koronka AU/180 (RC) 4.00 10.00
133 J.Van Benschoten AU/180 (RC) 4.00 10.00
134 J.Papelbon AU/180 (RC) 6.00 15.00
135 J.Capellan AU/180 (RC) 4.00 10.00
136 J.Johnson AU/180 (RC) 6.00 15.00
137 J.Rupe AU/180 (RC) 4.00 10.00
138 J.Willingham AU/180 (RC) 8.00 20.00
139 J.Wilson AU/180 (RC) 4.00 10.00
140 J.Verlander AU/180 (RC) 20.00 50.00
141 K.Shoppach AU/180 (RC) 4.00 10.00
142 K.Morales AU/180 (RC) 6.00 15.00
143 M.McBride AU/180 (RC) 4.00 10.00
144 M.Prado AU/180 (RC) 4.00 10.00
145 M.Cain AU/180 (RC) 12.00 30.00
146 M.Jacobs AU/180 (RC) 4.00 10.00
147 M.Thompson AU/180 RC 4.00 10.00
148 N.McLouth AU/180 (RC) 8.00 20.00
149 P.Maholm AU/180 (RC) 4.00 10.00
150 P.Fielder AU/180 (RC) 12.00 30.00
151 R.Abercrombie AU/180 (RC) 4.00 10.00
152 R.Hill AU/180 (RC) 6.00 15.00
153 R.Flores AU/180 RC 4.00 10.00
154 R.Lugo AU/180 (RC) 4.00 10.00
155 R.Zimmerman AU/180 (RC) 12.00 30.00
156 S.Marshall AU/180 (RC) 10.00 25.00
157 T.Saito AU/180 RC 10.00 25.00
158 T.Buchholz AU/180 (RC) 4.00 10.00
159 T.Pena Jr. AU/180 (RC) 4.00 10.00
160 W.Nieves AU/180 (RC) 4.00 10.00
161 J.Shields AU/180 RC 10.00 25.00
162 J.Lester AU/180 RC 15.00 40.00
163 C.Hansen AU/180 RC 4.00 10.00
164 A.Rakers AU/180 (RC) 4.00 10.00
166 B.Livingston AU/180 (RC) 4.00 10.00
167 B.Harris AU/180 (RC) 4.00 10.00
169 C.Ruiz AU/180 (RC) 6.00 15.00
170 C.Britton AU/180 RC 4.00 10.00
171 H.Kendrick AU/180 (RC) 4.00 10.00
172 J.Van Buren AU/180 (RC) 4.00 10.00
173 K.Frandsen AU/180 (RC) 6.00 15.00
174 M.Capps AU/180 (RC) 6.00 15.00
175 P.Moylan AU/180 RC 4.00 10.00
191 Richie Ashburn 1.50 4.00
192 Lou Brock 1.50 4.00
193 Lou Boudreau 1.50 4.00
194 Orlando Cepeda 1.50 4.00
195 Bobby Doerr 1.00 2.50
196 Dennis Eckersley 1.50 4.00
197 Bob Feller 1.50 4.00
198 Rollie Fingers 1.50 4.00
199 Carlton Fisk 1.50 4.00
200 Bob Gibson 1.50 4.00
201 Catfish Hunter 1.50 4.00
202 Fergie Jenkins 1.50 4.00
203 Al Kaline 2.50 6.00
204 Harmon Killebrew 2.50 6.00
205 Ralph Kiner 1.50 4.00
206 Buck Leonard 1.00 2.50
207 Juan Marichal 1.50 4.00
208 Bill Mazeroski 1.50 4.00
209 Willie McCovey 1.50 4.00
210 Jim Palmer 1.50 4.00
211 Tony Perez 1.50 4.00
212 Gaylord Perry 1.50 4.00
213 Phil Rizzuto 1.50 4.00
214 Robin Roberts 1.50 4.00
215 Mike Schmidt 4.00 10.00
216 Enos Slaughter 1.50 4.00
217 Ozzie Smith 3.00 8.00
218 Billy Williams 1.50 4.00
219 Robin Yount 2.50 6.00
220 Carlos Quentin (RC) 1.50 4.00
221 Jeff Francoeur 2.50 6.00
222 Brian McCann 1.00 2.50
223 Nick Markakis (RC) 2.00 5.00
224 Josh Beckett 1.00 2.50
225 Jason Varitek 2.50 6.00
226 Mark Prior 1.50 4.00
227 Aramis Ramirez 1.00 2.50
228 Jermaine Dye 1.00 2.50
229 Tadahito Iguchi 1.00 2.50
230 Bobby Jenks 1.00 2.50
231 C.C. Sabathia 1.50 4.00
232 Jeff Francis 1.00 2.50
233 Matt Holliday 2.50 6.00
234 Magglio Ordonez 1.50 4.00
235 Kenny Rogers 1.00 2.50
236 Roger Clemens 3.00 8.00
237 Andy Pettitte 1.50 4.00
238 Craig Biggio 1.50 4.00
239 Chone Figgins 1.00 2.50
240 John Lackey 1.50 4.00
241 Nomar Garciaparra 1.50 4.00
242 Prince Fielder 5.00 12.00
243 Ben Sheets 1.00 2.50
244 Bill Hall 1.00 2.50
245 Justin Morneau 1.50 4.00
246 Joe Nathan 1.00 2.50
247 Carlos Delgado 1.00 2.50
248 Shawn Green 1.00 2.50
249 Billy Wagner 1.00 2.50
250 Jason Giambi 1.00 2.50
251 Mike Mussina 1.50 4.00
252 Mariano Rivera 3.00 8.00
253 Robinson Cano 1.50 4.00
254 Bobby Abreu 1.00 2.50
255 Huston Street 1.00 2.50
256 Frank Thomas 2.50 6.00
257 Danny Haren 1.00 2.50
258 Jason Kendall 1.00 2.50
259 Nick Swisher 1.50 4.00
260 Pat Burrell 1.00 2.50
261 Tom Gordon 1.00 2.50
262 Freddy Sanchez 1.00 2.50
263 Trevor Hoffman 1.50 4.00
264 Khalil Greene 1.00 2.50
265 Adrian Gonzalez 2.00 5.00
266 Moises Alou 1.00 2.50
267 Matt Morris 1.00 2.50
268 Pedro Feliz 1.00 2.50
269 Richie Sexson 1.00 2.50
270 Hoyt Wilhelm 1.50 4.00
271 Adrian Beltre 2.50 6.00
272 Jim Edmonds 1.50 4.00
273 Scott Rolen 1.50 4.00
274 Jason Isringhausen 1.00 2.50
275 Jorge Cantu 1.00 2.50
276 Hank Blalock 1.00 2.50
277 Kevin Millwood 1.00 2.50
278 Alex Rios 1.00 2.50
279 Troy Glaus 1.00 2.50
280 B.J. Ryan 1.00 2.50
281 Nick Johnson 1.00 2.50
282 Chad Cordero 1.00 2.50
283 Austin Kearns 1.00 2.50
284 Ricky Nolasco (RC) 1.00 2.50
285 Travis Ishikawa (RC) 1.50 4.00
286 Lastings Milledge (RC) 1.00 2.50
287 James Loney (RC) 1.50 4.00
288 Red Schoendienst 1.50 4.00
289 Warren Spahn 1.50 4.00
290 Early Wynn 1.50 4.00

2006 Ultimate Collection Ensemble Signatures Triple

OVERALL AU ODDS 1:2
STATED PRINT RUN 50 SER.#'d SETS
TRIPLE 15 PRINT RUN 15 SER.#'d SETS
NO TRI 15 PRICING DUE TO SCARCITY
TRIPLE 1 PRINT RUN 1 SER.#'d SET
NO TRI 1 PRICING DUE TO SCARCITY
EXCHANGE DEADLINE 12/20/09
AHW Willing/Abercrom/Hermida 15.00 40.00
BBW Buch/Wain/B.Bann 10.00 25.00
BDD Dawson/Davis/Bell 30.00 60.00
BKM Maz/Kiner/Bay 15.00 40.00
BNO Oswalt/Buch/Nieve 15.00 40.00
BSH Sheets/Harden/Burnett 10.00 25.00
BUK Biggio/Utley/Kinsler 40.00 80.00
BWC Wain/Cain/Bannister 15.00 40.00
BWV Bonser/Verland/Weaver 30.00 60.00
CBP Casey/Perez/Bay 15.00 40.00
CBS Cey/Sutton/Baker 20.00 50.00
CBZ Bonser/Cain/Zumaya 20.00 50.00
CDV Van Slyke/Davis/Clark 15.00 40.00
CHK Kubel/Cabrera/Hermida 20.00 50.00
CHO Carpenter/Oswalt/Harden 10.00 25.00
CKH Kendall/Crosby/Harden 15.00 40.00
CKS Crawford/Kazmir/Shields 20.00 50.00
CLH Liriano/Carmona/Hamels 10.00 25.00
CMH Hafner/Martinez/Carmona 15.00 40.00
CNS Santo/Nettles/Cey 30.00 60.00
CPC Crawford/Crisp/Podsednik 15.00 40.00
CSS Clemens/Smoltz/Schilling 100.00 200.00
CWW Cabrera/Willingham/Willis 15.00 40.00
CZC Chavez/Cabrera/Zimmerman 30.00 60.00
DJH Jeter/Reyes/Hanley 150.00 250.00
DPA Dye/Anderson/Podsednik 20.00 50.00
DPI Dye/Podsednik/Iguchi 30.00 60.00
FGC Cone/Gooden/Fernandez 40.00 80.00
FJM Jackson/Fielder/Morales 30.00 60.00
FWL Lee/Weeks/Fielder 12.50 30.00
GCN Gossage/Nettles/Chambliss 30.00 60.00
GCS Cone/Gooden/Saberhag 15.00 40.00
GJB Griffey/Jeter/Bay 250.00 500.00
GJP Griffey /Jeter/Pujols 700.00 800.00
GLK Liriano/Kubel/Gassner 20.00 50.00
GPN Gagne/Nathan/Papelbon 20.00 50.00
GRS Vlad/Soriano/Rios 15.00 40.00
HBS Swisher/Harden/Blanton 10.00 25.00
HKP Kruk/Hrbek/Powell 20.00 50.00
HMK Mulder/Kazmir/Hamels 15.00 40.00
HNP Hoffman/Nathan/Papelbon 15.00 40.00
HOT Hafner/Ortiz/Teixeira 15.00 40.00
HWU Willingham/Hermida/Uggla 10.00 25.00
IKU Iguchi/Kinsler/Uggla 30.00 60.00
JCN Jeter/Nieves/Cabrera 150.00 200.00
JGS Griffey/Andruw/Soriano 60.00 120.00
JRR Jeter/Reyes/Hanley 125.00 200.00
JWV Johnson/Verlan/Weaver 50.00 100.00
KGJ Joyner/Grace/Kruk 50.00 100.00
KLB Bonser/Liriano/Kubel 10.00 25.00
KUU Utley/Kinsler/Uggla 30.00 60.00
KWM Kendall/Martinez/Willing 15.00 40.00
LGB Bonser/Liriano/Gassner 20.00 50.00
LHC Liriano/Carmona/Hernan 20.00 50.00
LPO Lee/Ortiz/Pujols 150.00 250.00
MCN Nettles/Madlock/Cey 20.00 50.00
MMK Kendall/Martinez/Mauer 15.00 40.00
MNL Nathan/Mauer/Liriano 30.00 60.00
MWC Mulder/Carpen/Wain 40.00 80.00
MWP Willing/Martin/Paulino 15.00 40.00
NLP Nathan/Lidge/Papelbon 20.00 50.00
OBL Oswalt/Lidge/Buchholz 15.00 40.00
PCL Perez/Liriano/Carmona 30.00 60.00
PHL Perez/Liriano/Hamels 10.00 25.00
PSO Sheets/Oswalt/Peavy 10.00 25.00
PVW Verland/Papel/Weaver 40.00 80.00
RHW Ross/Willingham/Hermida 15.00 40.00
RMM Rodriguez/Martinez/Mauer 30.00 60.00
RRB Reyes/Ramirez/Betancourt 30.00 60.00
SGM Maddux/Glavine/Smoltz 125.00 250.00
SJF Fielder/Shelton/Jacobs 10.00 25.00
SKM Kuo/Martin/Saito 100.00 200.00
SWB Buch/Weaver/Shields 40.00 80.00
TGB Griffey/Bagwell/Thomas 150.00 250.00
TKY Young/Teixeira/Kinsler 15.00 40.00
UHC Cabrera/Hermida/Uggla 40.00 80.00
URC Cabrera/Hanley/Uggla 30.00 60.00
URW Willingham/Hanley/Uggla 20.00 50.00
VBZ Bonder/Verland/Zumaya 30.00 60.00
VWL Liriano/Verlan/Weaver 30.00 60.00
WJC Johnson/Cain/Weaver 20.00 50.00
WJO Johnson/Willis/Olsen 30.00 60.00
WSV Verland/Weaver/Shields 50.00 100.00
ZBC Bonser/Cain/Zumaya 15.00 40.00
ZHZ Zambran/Hernan/Zumaya 10.00 25.00

2006 Ultimate Collection Game Materials

OVERALL GAME-USED ODDS 1:2
STATED PRINT RUN 50 SERIAL #'d SETS
PLATE ODDS APPX. 7:10 BONUS PACKS
PLATE PRINT RUN 1 SET PER COLOR
BLACK-CYAN-MAGENTA-YELLOW ISSUED
NO PLATE PRICING DUE TO SCARCITY
AB A.J. Burnett Jsy 4.00 10.00
AD Adam Dunn Jsy 4.00 10.00
AJ Andruw Jones Jsy 5.00 12.00
AP Albert Pujols Jsy 12.50 30.00
AR Alex Rios Jsy 4.00 10.00
AS Alfonso Soriano Jsy 4.00 10.00
BA Brian Bannister Jsy 4.00 10.00
BG Brian Giles Jsy 4.00 10.00
BM Bill Mazeroski Bat 5.00 12.00
BO Jeremy Bonderman Jsy 4.00 10.00
BR Brian Roberts Jsy 4.00 10.00
CA Melky Cabrera Jsy 6.00 15.00
CC Carl Crawford Jsy 4.00 10.00
CH Chris Carpenter Jsy 4.00 10.00
CJ Conor Jackson Jsy 5.00 12.00
CL Carlos Lee Jsy 4.00 10.00
CR Coco Crisp Jsy 4.00 10.00
CS Chris Shelton Jsy 4.00 10.00
CU Chase Utley Jsy 6.00 15.00
CZ Carlos Zambrano Jsy 4.00 10.00
DJ Derek Jeter Jsy 12.50 30.00
DJ2 Derek Jeter Jsy 20.00 50.00
DL Derrek Lee Jsy 4.00 10.00
DU Dan Uggla Jsy 6.00 15.00
DW Dontrelle Willis Jsy 4.00 10.00
FH Felix Hernandez Jsy 5.00 12.00
FL Francisco Liriano Jsy 4.00 10.00
GA Garrett Atkins Jsy 4.00 10.00
GP Gaylord Perry Jsy 5.00 12.00
HA Cole Hamels Jsy 6.00 15.00
HB Hank Blalock Jsy 4.00 10.00
HC Craig Hansen Jsy 6.00 15.00
HO Trevor Hoffman Jsy 4.00 10.00
HR Hanley Ramirez Jsy 6.00 15.00
HT Tim Hudson Jsy 4.00 10.00
HU Torii Hunter Jsy 4.00 10.00
HY Roy Halladay Jsy 4.00 10.00
IK Ian Kinsler Jsy 5.00 12.00
IR Ivan Rodriguez Jsy 5.00 12.00
JB Jason Bay Jsy 4.00 10.00
JD Jermaine Dye Jsy 4.00 10.00
JH Jeremy Hermida Jsy 4.00 10.00
JJ Josh Johnson Jsy 5.00 12.00
JK Jason Kendall Jsy 4.00 10.00
JM Joe Mauer Jsy 5.00 12.00
JN Joe Nathan Jsy 4.00 10.00
JP Jake Peavy Jsy 4.00 10.00
JR Jose Reyes Jsy 4.00 10.00
JS Johan Santana Jsy 5.00 12.00
JV Justin Verlander Jsy 6.00 15.00
JW Jered Weaver Jsy 6.00 15.00
JZ Joel Zumaya Jsy 6.00 15.00
KG Ken Griffey Jr. Jsy 10.00 25.00
KG2 Ken Griffey Jr. Jsy 10.00 25.00
KH Khalil Greene Jsy 5.00 12.00
KJ Kenji Johjima Jsy 8.00 20.00
KM Kendry Morales Jsy 5.00 12.00
KU Jason Kubel Jsy 4.00 10.00
KY Kevin Youkilis Jsy 4.00 10.00
LA Luis Aparicio Jsy 5.00 12.00
LM Lastings Milledge Jsy 5.00 12.00
LY Fred Lynn Jsy 5.00 12.00
MA Matt Cain Jsy 5.00 12.00
MC Miguel Cabrera Jsy 5.00 12.00
MG Marcus Giles Jsy 4.00 10.00
MH Matt Holliday Jsy 8.00 20.00
ML Mark Loretta Jsy 4.00 10.00
MM Melvin Mora Jsy 4.00 10.00
MO Justin Morneau Jsy 5.00 12.00
MS Mike Schmidt Jsy 8.00 20.00
MT Mark Teixeira Jsy 5.00 12.00
MU Mark Mulder Jsy 4.00 10.00
MY Michael Young Jsy 4.00 10.00
NS Nick Swisher Jsy 4.00 10.00
PA Jonathan Papelbon Jsy 8.00 20.00
PF Prince Fielder Jsy 6.00 15.00
PM Paul Molitor Jsy 5.00 12.00
RC Cal Ripken Jsy 20.00 50.00
RH Rich Harden Jsy 4.00 10.00
RI Jim Rice Jsy 5.00 12.00
RO Roy Oswalt Jsy 4.00 10.00
RW Rickie Weeks Jsy 4.00 10.00
RZ Ryan Zimmerman Jsy 8.00 20.00
SK Scott Kazmir Jsy 5.00 12.00
SP Scott Podsednik Jsy 4.00 10.00
TE Miguel Tejada Jsy 4.00 10.00
TG Tony Gwynn Jsy 6.00 15.00
TH Travis Hafner Jsy 4.00 10.00
TI Tadahito Iguchi Jsy 4.00 10.00
TP Tony Perez Jsy 5.00 12.00
VM-Victor Martinez Jsy 4.00 10.00
WC Will Clark Pants 5.00 12.00
WI Josh Willingham Jsy 4.00 10.00
YB Yuniesky Betancourt Jsy 4.00 10.00

2006 Ultimate Collection Game Materials Signatures

STATED PRINT RUN 35 SERIAL #'d SETS
EXCHANGE DEADLINE 12/20/09
AB A.J. Burnett Jsy 10.00 25.00
AD Adam Dunn Jsy 10.00 15.00
AJ Andruw Jones Jsy 10.00 25.00
AR Alex Rios Jsy 10.00 25.00
AS Alfonso Soriano Jsy 30.00 60.00
BA Brian Bannister Jsy 10.00 25.00
BG Brian Giles Jsy 10.00 25.00
BM Bill Mazeroski Jsy 20.00 50.00
BO Jeremy Bonderman Jsy 15.00 40.00
BR Brian Roberts Jsy 10.00 25.00
CA Melky Cabrera Jsy 15.00 40.00
CC Carl Crawford Jsy 10.00 25.00
CH Chris Carpenter Jsy 10.00 25.00
CJ Conor Jackson Jsy 15.00 40.00
CL Carlos Lee Jsy 10.00 25.00
CR Coco Crisp Jsy 12.50 30.00
CS Chris Shelton Jsy 10.00 25.00
CU Chase Utley Jsy 30.00 60.00
CZ Carlos Zambrano Jsy 15.00 40.00
DJ Derek Jeter Jsy 200.00 300.00
DJ2 Derek Jeter Jsy 200.00 300.00
DL Derrek Lee Jsy 12.50 30.00
DU Dan Uggla Jsy 10.00 25.00
DW Dontrelle Willis Jsy 12.50 30.00
FH Felix Hernandez Jsy 15.00 40.00
FL Francisco Liriano Jsy 10.00 25.00
GA Garrett Atkins Jsy 10.00 25.00
GP Gaylord Perry Pants 10.00 25.00
HA Cole Hamels Jsy 30.00 60.00
HB Hank Blalock Jsy 10.00 25.00
HC Craig Hansen Jsy 15.00 40.00
HO Trevor Hoffman Jsy 15.00 40.00
HR Hanley Ramirez Jsy 30.00 60.00
HT Tim Hudson Jsy 10.00 25.00
HU Torii Hunter Jsy 10.00 25.00
HY Roy Halladay Jsy 30.00 60.00
IK Ian Kinsler Jsy 20.00 50.00
IR Ivan Rodriguez Jsy 15.00 40.00
JB Jason Bay Jsy 10.00 25.00
JD Jermaine Dye Jsy 10.00 25.00
JH Jeremy Hermida Jsy 10.00 25.00
JJ Josh Johnson Jsy 10.00 25.00
JK Jason Kendall Jsy 10.00 25.00
JM Joe Mauer Jsy 30.00 60.00
JN Joe Nathan Jsy 10.00 25.00
JP Jake Peavy Jsy 10.00 25.00
JR Jose Reyes Jsy 15.00 40.00
JS Johan Santana Jsy 10.00 25.00
JV Justin Verlander Jsy 40.00 80.00
JW Jered Weaver Jsy 15.00 40.00
JZ Joel Zumaya Jsy 12.50 30.00
KG Ken Griffey Jr. Jsy 60.00 120.00
KG2 Ken Griffey Jr. Jsy 60.00 120.00
KH Khalil Greene Jsy 12.50 30.00
KM Kendry Morales Jsy 15.00 40.00
KU Jason Kubel Jsy 10.00 25.00
KY Kevin Youkilis Jsy 10.00 25.00
LA Luis Aparicio Jsy 10.00 25.00
LY Fred Lynn Jsy 10.00 25.00
MA Matt Cain Jsy 20.00 50.00
MC Miguel Cabrera Jsy 40.00 80.00
MG Marcus Giles Jsy 10.00 25.00
MH Matt Holliday Jsy 8.00 20.00
ML Mark Loretta Jsy 10.00 25.00
MM Melvin Mora Jsy 10.00 25.00
MO Justin Morneau Jsy 8.00 20.00
MS Mike Schmidt Jsy 30.00 60.00
MU Mark Mulder Jsy 10.00 25.00
MY Michael Young Jsy 10.00 25.00
NS Nick Swisher Jsy 10.00 25.00
PA Jonathan Papelbon Jsy 10.00 25.00
PM Paul Molitor Jsy 12.50 30.00
RC Cal Ripken Jsy 50.00 100.00
RH Rich Harden Jsy 12.50 30.00
RI Jim Rice Jsy 12.50 30.00
RO Roy Oswalt Jsy 10.00 25.00
RW Rickie Weeks Jsy 10.00 25.00
RZ Ryan Zimmerman Jsy 12.00 30.00
SK Scott Kazmir Jsy 10.00 25.00
SP Scott Podsednik Jsy 10.00 25.00
TE Miguel Tejada Jsy 10.00 25.00
TG Tony Gwynn Jsy 30.00 60.00
TH Travis Hafner Jsy 10.00 25.00
TI Tadahito Iguchi Jsy 15.00 40.00
TP Tony Perez Jsy 10.00 25.00
VM Victor Martinez Jsy 10.00 25.00
WC Will Clark Pants 30.00 60.00
WI Josh Willingham Jsy 10.00 25.00
YB Yuniesky Betancourt Jsy 10.00 25.00

2006 Ultimate Collection Game Patches

*PATCH p/r 40-50: .6X TO 1.5X BASIC
*PATCH p/r 27-31: .6X TO 1.5X BASIC
OVERALL GAME-USED ODDS 1:2
PATCH PRINT RUN B/WN 3-50 PER
NO PRICING ON QTY 25 OR LESS
OVERALL AU-GU ODDS 1:4
PATCH SIG PRINT RUN 10 SER.#'d SETS
NO PATCH SIG PRICING
EXCHANGE DEADLINE 12/20/09
PLATE ODDS APPX. 7:10 BONUS PACKS
PLATE PRINT RUN 1 SET PER COLOR
BLACK-CYAN-MAGENTA-YELLOW ISSUED
NO PLATE PRICING DUE TO SCARCITY
AP Albert Pujols 30.00 60.00
AS Alfonso Soriano 12.50 30.00
BO Jeremy Bonderman 10.00 25.00
CU Chase Utley 15.00 40.00
JM Joe Mauer 15.00 40.00
JR Jose Reyes 12.50 30.00
JV Justin Verlander 20.00 50.00
KG Ken Griffey Jr. 20.00 50.00
KG2 Ken Griffey Jr. 20.00 50.00
KJ Kenji Johjima 20.00 50.00
MA Matt Cain 10.00 25.00
MC Miguel Cabrera 12.50 30.00
MO Justin Morneau 10.00 25.00
RZ Ryan Zimmerman 20.00 50.00
TI Tadahito Iguchi 10.00 25.00

2006 Ultimate Collection Legendary Materials

ODDS APPX. 3:10 BONUS PACKS
PRINT RUNS B/WN 5-55 PER
NO PRICING ON QTY 25 OR LESS
PLATE ODDS APPX. 7:10 BONUS PACKS
PLATE PRINT RUN 1 SET PER COLOR
BLACK-CYAN-MAGENTA-YELLOW ISSUED
NO PLATE PRICING DUE TO SCARCITY
AR Al Rosen Pants/55 6.00 15.00
BD Bill Dickey Jsy/55 12.50 30.00
BD2 Bill Dickey Jsy/55 12.50 30.00
BO Bo Jackson Bat/55 8.00 20.00
BO2 Bo Jackson Bat/55 8.00 20.00
CF Carlton Fisk Pants/55 4.00 10.00
CF2 Carlton Fisk Pants/55 4.00 10.00
CW Rod Carew Jsy/55 4.00 10.00
CW2 Rod Carew Jsy/55 4.00 10.00
GP Gaylord Perry Jsy/55 4.00 10.00
GP2 Gaylord Perry Jsy/55 4.00 10.00
JB Johnny Bench Jsy/55 8.00 20.00
JO Joe Morgan Jsy/55 4.00 10.00
JO2 Joe Morgan Jsy/55 4.00 10.00
JU Juan Marichal Jsy/55 4.00 10.00
KI Kirk Gibson Jsy/55 4.00 10.00
KP Kirby Puckett Jsy/55 12.50 30.00
KP2 Kirby Puckett Jsy/55 12.50 30.00
MA Don Mattingly Pants/55 10.00 25.00
MA2 Don Mattingly Jsy/55 10.00 25.00
MW Maury Wills Bat/41 4.00 10.00
NR Nolan Ryan Jkt/55 15.00 40.00
OS Ozzie Smith Jsy/55 12.50 30.00
OS2 Ozzie Smith Jsy/55 12.50 30.00
PM Paul Molitor Bat/55 4.00 10.00
PM2 Paul Molitor Bat/55 4.00 10.00
PN Phil Niekro Jsy/55 4.00 10.00
PN2 Phil Niekro Jsy/55 4.00 10.00
RJ2 Reggie Jackson Jsy/35 6.00 15.00
RO Brooks Robinson Pants/35 6.00 15.00
RO2 Brooks Robinson Jsy/35 6.00 15.00
RS Ryne Sandberg Bat/35 10.00 25.00
SC Steve Carlton Bat/55 4.00 10.00
SC2 Steve Carlton Bat/47 4.00 10.00
SU Don Sutton Jsy/55 4.00 10.00
SU2 Don Sutton Jsy/55 4.00 10.00
TG Tony Gwynn Jsy/55 10.00 25.00
TG2 Tony Gwynn Jsy/55 10.00 25.00
TP Tony Perez Pants/55 4.00 10.00
TP2 Tony Perez Jsy/55 4.00 10.00
WB Wade Boggs Jsy/55 4.00 10.00
WB2 Wade Boggs Pants/55 4.00 10.00
WC Will Clark Pants/45 6.00 15.00
WC2 Will Clark Pants/45 6.00 15.00

2006 Ultimate Collection Ultimate Numbers Materials

OVERALL GAME-USED ODDS 1:2
STATED PRINT RUN 35 SER.#'d SETS
PLATE ODDS APPX. 7:10 BONUS PACKS
PLATE PRINT RUN 1 SET PER COLOR
BLACK-CYAN-MAGENTA-YELLOW ISSUED
NO PLATE PRICING DUE TO SCARCITY
AB A.J. Burnett Jsy 5.00 12.00
AD Adam Dunn Jsy 5.00 12.00
AJ Andruw Jones Jsy 6.00 15.00
AP Albert Pujols Jsy 20.00 50.00
AR Alex Rios Jsy 5.00 12.00
AS Alfonso Soriano Jsy 5.00 12.00
BA Brian Bannister Jsy 6.00 15.00
BG Brian Giles Jsy 5.00 12.00
BM Bill Mazeroski Bat 6.00 15.00
BO Jeremy Bonderman Jsy 5.00 12.00
BR Brian Roberts Jsy 5.00 12.00
CA Melky Cabrera Jsy 8.00 20.00
CC Carl Crawford Jsy 5.00 12.00
CH Chris Carpenter Jsy 5.00 12.00
CJ Conor Jackson Jsy 6.00 15.00
CL Carlos Lee Jsy 5.00 12.00
CR Coco Crisp Jsy 5.00 12.00
CS Chris Shelton Jsy 5.00 12.00
CU Chase Utley Jsy 8.00 20.00
CZ Carlos Zambrano Jsy 5.00 12.00
DJ Derek Jeter Jsy 30.00 60.00
DJ2 Derek Jeter Jsy 30.00 60.00
DL Derrek Lee Jsy 5.00 12.00
DU Dan Uggla Jsy 8.00 20.00
DW Dontrelle Willis Jsy 5.00 12.00
FH Felix Hernandez Jsy 6.00 15.00
FL Francisco Liriano Jsy 8.00 20.00
GA Garrett Atkins Jsy 5.00 12.00
GP Gaylord Perry Pants 6.00 15.00
HA Cole Hamels Jsy 8.00 20.00
HB Hank Blalock Jsy 5.00 12.00
HC Craig Hansen Jsy 8.00 20.00
HO Trevor Hoffman Jsy 5.00 12.00
HR Hanley Ramirez Jsy 8.00 20.00
HT Tim Hudson Jsy 5.00 12.00
HU Torii Hunter Jsy 5.00 12.00
HY Roy Halladay Jsy 5.00 12.00
IK Ian Kinsler Jsy 5.00 12.00
IR Ivan Rodriguez Jsy 6.00 15.00
JB Jason Bay Jsy 5.00 12.00
JD Jermaine Dye Jsy 5.00 12.00
JH Jeremy Hermida Jsy 5.00 12.00
JJ Josh Johnson Jsy 6.00 15.00
JK Jason Kendall Jsy 5.00 12.00
JM Joe Mauer Jsy 6.00 15.00
JN Joe Nathan Jsy 5.00 12.00
JP Jake Peavy Jsy 5.00 12.00
JR Jose Reyes Jsy 5.00 12.00
JS Johan Santana Jsy 6.00 15.00
JV Justin Verlander Jsy 8.00 20.00
JW Jered Weaver Jsy 8.00 20.00
JZ Joel Zumaya Jsy 8.00 20.00
KG Ken Griffey Jr. Jsy 15.00 40.00
KG2 Ken Griffey Jr. Jsy 15.00 40.00
KH Khalil Greene Jsy 6.00 15.00
KJ Kenji Johjima Jsy 12.50 30.00
KM Kendry Morales Jsy 6.00 15.00
KU Jason Kubel Jsy 5.00 12.00
KY Kevin Youkilis Jsy 5.00 12.00
LA Luis Aparicio Jsy 6.00 15.00
LM Lastings Milledge Jsy 6.00 15.00
LY Fred Lynn Jsy 6.00 15.00
MA Matt Cain Jsy 6.00 15.00
MC Miguel Cabrera Jsy 8.00 20.00
MG Marcus Giles Jsy 5.00 12.00
MH Matt Holliday Jsy 6.00 15.00
ML Mark Loretta Jsy 5.00 12.00
MM Melvin Mora Jsy 5.00 12.00
MO Justin Morneau Jsy 6.00 15.00
MS Mike Schmidt Jsy 12.50 30.00
MT Mark Teixeira Jsy 6.00 15.00
MU Mark Mulder Jsy 5.00 12.00
MY Michael Young Jsy 5.00 12.00
NS Nick Swisher Jsy 5.00 12.00
PA Jonathan Papelbon Jsy 12.50 30.00

PF Prince Fielder Jsy	8.00	20.00
PM Paul Molitor Jsy	6.00	15.00
RC Cal Ripken Jsy	50.00	100.00
RH Rich Harden Jsy	5.00	12.00
RI Jim Rice Jsy	6.00	15.00
RO Roy Oswalt Jsy	5.00	12.00
RW Rickie Weeks Jsy	5.00	12.00
RZ Ryan Zimmerman Jsy	12.50	30.00
SK Scott Kazmir Jsy	6.00	15.00
SP Scott Podsednik Jsy	5.00	12.00
TE Miguel Tejada Jsy	5.00	12.00
TG Tony Gwynn Jsy	8.00	20.00
TH Travis Hafner Jsy	5.00	12.00
TI Tadahito Iguchi Jsy	5.00	12.00
TP Tony Perez Jsy	6.00	15.00
VM Victor Martinez Jsy	5.00	12.00
WC Will Clark Jsy	6.00	15.00
WI Josh Willingham Jsy	5.00	12.00
YB Yuniesky Betancourt Jsy	5.00	12.00

2006 Ultimate Collection Ultimate Numbers Patches

*PATCH p/r 35: .6X TO 1.5X BASIC
OVERALL GAME-USED ODDS 1:2
PATCH PRINT RUN B/WN 5-35 PER
NO PRICING ON QTY 25 OR LESS

AP Albert Pujols/35	50.00	100.00
AS Alfonso Soriano/35	10.00	25.00
BO Jeremy Bonderman/35	10.00	25.00
CU Chase Utley/35	15.00	40.00
DJ Derek Jeter/35	40.00	80.00
DJ2 Derek Jeter/35	40.00	80.00
IK Ian Kinsler/35	8.00	20.00
JV Justin Verlander/35	15.00	40.00
KG Ken Griffey Jr./35	20.00	50.00
KG2 Ken Griffey Jr./35	20.00	50.00
KJ Kenji Johjima/35	20.00	50.00
KY Kevin Youkilis/35	8.00	20.00
RC Cal Ripken/35	60.00	120.00
RZ Ryan Zimmerman/35	15.00	40.00
TI Tadahito Iguchi/35	10.00	25.00

2006 Ultimate Collection Tandem Materials Patch

OVERALL GAME-USED ODDS 1:2
STATED PRINT RUN 35 SERIAL #'d SETS

AA A.Soriano/A.Rios	6.00	15.00
AH G.Atkins/M.Holliday	8.00	20.00
AJ D.Jeter/L.Aparicio	15.00	40.00
BH F.Hernandez/Y.Betancourt	8.00	20.00
BM L.Milledge/B.Bannister	8.00	20.00
BR H.Ramirez/Y.Betancourt	6.00	15.00
BV J.Bonderman/J.Verlander	10.00	25.00
CH M.Cabrera/J.Hermida	8.00	20.00
CL M.Loretta/C.Crisp	6.00	15.00
CM L.Milledge/M.Cabrera	10.00	25.00
CO R.Clemens/R.Oswalt	12.00	30.00
CP C.Crawford/S.Podsednik	6.00	15.00
CR M.Cabrera/H.Ramirez	8.00	20.00
CS S.Kazmir/C.Hamels	20.00	50.00
CV J.Verlander/M.Cain	10.00	25.00
CW C.Carpenter/D.Willis	15.00	40.00
CZ M.Cabrera/R.Zimmerman	15.00	40.00
DH D.Jeter/H.Ramirez	20.00	50.00
FW R.Weeks/P.Fielder	12.50	30.00
GD K.Griffey Jr./A.Dunn	15.00	40.00
GG T.Gwynn/B.Giles	15.00	40.00
GP K.Griffey Jr./A.Pujols	40.00	80.00
GR K.Griffey Jr./A.Rios	15.00	40.00
GT K.Griffey Jr./F.Thomas	20.00	50.00
HB M.Holliday/J.Bay	10.00	25.00
HF T.Hafner/P.Fielder	12.50	30.00
HG B.Giles/T.Hoffman	6.00	15.00
HJ A.Jones/T.Hunter	12.50	30.00
HK J.Kubel/J.Hermida	6.00	15.00
HM T.Hafner/V.Martinez	8.00	20.00
HN T.Hoffman/J.Nathan	6.00	15.00
HO R.Oswalt/R.Harden	6.00	15.00
HP T.Hoffman/J.Papelbon	12.50	30.00
HR H.Ramirez/J.Hermida	10.00	25.00
HW J.Willingham/J.Hermida	6.00	15.00
ID J.Dye/T.Iguchi	12.50	30.00
JC D.Jeter/M.Cabrera	30.00	60.00
JG K.Griffey Jr./D.Jeter	40.00	80.00
JJ D.Jeter/R.Jackson	30.00	60.00
JK K.Morales/J.Weaver	10.00	25.00
JM V.Martinez/K.Johjima	12.50	30.00
JR C.Ripken/D.Jeter	50.00	100.00
KB B.Giles/K.Greene	12.50	30.00
KC C.Crawford/S.Kazmir	6.00	15.00
KM J.Kendall/J.Mauer	10.00	25.00
KU I.Kinsler/D.Uggla	10.00	25.00
KY M.Young/I.Kinsler	8.00	20.00
LC F.Lynn/C.Crisp	6.00	15.00
LF C.Lee/P.Fielder	8.00	20.00
LH F.Liriano/C.Hamels	12.50	30.00
MF P.Fielder/K.Morales	10.00	25.00
MH L.Hernandez/K.Morales	8.00	20.00
ML J.Mauer/F.Liriano	15.00	40.00
MM V.Martinez/J.Mauer	10.00	25.00
MR M.Mora/B.Roberts	6.00	15.00
MW P.Molitor/R.Weeks	8.00	20.00
NJ J.Nathan/J.Mauer	8.00	20.00
NL J.Nathan/F.Liriano	12.50	30.00
NM J.Nathan/J.Mauer	12.50	30.00
NP J.Nathan/J.Papelbon	12.50	30.00
PC G.Perry/M.Cain	12.50	30.00
PH J.Papelbon/C.Hansen	20.00	50.00
PO R.Oswalt/J.Peavy	6.00	15.00
PP G.Perry/J.Peavy	10.00	25.00
RC C.Crisp/A.Rios	6.00	15.00
RM J.Reyes/L.Milledge	10.00	25.00
RR J.Reyes/H.Ramirez	12.50	30.00
RS C.Ripken/M.Schmidt	40.00	80.00
RU H.Ramirez/D.Uggla	15.00	40.00
RV I.Rodriguez/J.Verlander	10.00	25.00
SH N.Swisher/R.Harden	6.00	15.00
SJ C.Jackson/C.Shelton	12.50	30.00
SZ M.Schmidt/R.Zimmerman	20.00	50.00
TY M.Young/M.Teixeira	8.00	20.00
UK C.Utley/I. Kinsler	20.00	50.00
UM J.Morgan/C.Utley	20.00	50.00
UR B.Roberts/D.Uggla	6.00	15.00
VM J.Morris/J.Verlander	30.00	60.00
VZ J.Verlander/J.Zumaya	10.00	25.00
WM J.Mauer/J.Willingham	12.50	30.00
WR J.Willingham/H.Ramirez	6.00	15.00
WV J.Verlander/J.Weaver	10.00	25.00
YL M.Loretta/K.Youkilis	6.00	15.00
ZA G.Atkins/R.Zimmerman	15.00	40.00
ZC M.Cabrera/R.Zimmerman	15.00	40.00
ZJ J.Johnson/J.Zumaya	8.00	20.00
ZZ C.Zambrano/J.Zumaya	10.00	25.00

2007 Ultimate Collection

COMMON CARD (1-100)	.75	2.00
1-100 PRINT RUN 450 SER.#'d SETS		
COMMON AU RC (101-141)	3.00	8.00
OVERALL AU ODDS ONE PER PACK		
AU RC PRINT RUNS B/WN 289-299 COPIES PER		
EXCHANGE DEADLINE 9/24/2009		
1 Chipper Jones	2.00	5.00
2 Andruw Jones	.75	2.00
3 Tim Hudson	1.25	3.00
4 Stephen Drew	.75	2.00
5 Randy Johnson	2.00	5.00
6 Brandon Webb	1.25	3.00
7 Alfonso Soriano	1.25	3.00
8 Derrek Lee	.75	2.00
9 Aramis Ramirez	.75	2.00
10 Carlos Zambrano	1.25	3.00
11 Ken Griffey Jr.	4.00	10.00
12 Adam Dunn	1.25	3.00
13 Ryan Freel	.75	2.00
14 Todd Helton	1.25	3.00
15 Garrett Atkins	.75	2.00
16 Matt Holliday	2.00	5.00
17 Hanley Ramirez	1.25	3.00
18 Dontrelle Willis	.75	2.00
19 Miguel Cabrera	2.00	5.00
20 Lance Berkman	1.25	3.00
21 Roy Oswalt	1.25	3.00
22 Carlos Lee	.75	2.00
23 Nomar Garciaparra	1.25	3.00
24 Jason Schmidt	.75	2.00
25 Juan Pierre	.75	2.00
26 Russell Martin	.75	2.00
27 Rickie Weeks	.75	2.00
28 Prince Fielder	1.25	3.00
29 Ben Sheets	.75	2.00
30 David Wright	1.50	4.00
31 Jose Reyes	1.25	3.00
32 Pedro Martinez	1.25	3.00
33 Carlos Beltran	1.25	3.00
34 Brett Myers	.75	2.00
35 Jimmy Rollins	1.25	3.00
36 Ryan Howard	1.50	4.00
37 Jason Bay	1.25	3.00
38 Freddy Sanchez	.75	2.00
39 Ian Snell	.75	2.00
40 Jake Peavy	.75	2.00
41 Greg Maddux	2.50	6.00
42 Brian Giles	.75	2.00
43 Matt Cain	1.25	3.00
44 Barry Zito	1.25	3.00
45 Ray Durham	.75	2.00
46 Albert Pujols	2.50	6.00
47 Chris Carpenter	1.25	3.00
48 Chris Duncan	.75	2.00
49 Scott Rolen	1.25	3.00
50 Ryan Zimmerman	1.25	3.00
51 Chad Cordero	.75	2.00
52 Ryan Church	.75	2.00
53 Miguel Tejada	1.25	3.00
54 Erik Bedard	.75	2.00
55 Brian Roberts	.75	2.00
56 David Ortiz	2.00	5.00
57 Josh Beckett	.75	2.00
58 Manny Ramirez	2.00	5.00
59 Daisuke Matsuzaka RC	3.00	8.00
60 Jim Thome	1.25	3.00
61 Paul Konerko	1.25	3.00
62 Jermaine Dye	.75	2.00
63 Grady Sizemore	1.25	3.00
64 Victor Martinez	1.25	3.00
65 C.C. Sabathia	1.25	3.00
66 Ivan Rodriguez	1.25	3.00
67 Justin Verlander	2.00	5.00
68 Gary Sheffield	.75	2.00
69 Jeremy Bonderman	.75	2.00
70 Gil Meche	.75	2.00
71 Mike Sweeney	.75	2.00
72 Mark Teahen	.75	2.00
73 Vladimir Guerrero	1.25	3.00
74 Howie Kendrick	.75	2.00
75 Francisco Rodriguez	1.25	3.00
76 Johan Santana	1.25	3.00
77 Justin Morneau	1.25	3.00
78 Joe Mauer	1.50	4.00
79 Michael Cuddyer	.75	2.00
80 Alex Rodriguez	2.50	6.00
81 Derek Jeter	5.00	12.00
82 Johnny Damon	1.25	3.00
83 Roger Clemens	2.50	6.00
84 Rich Harden	.75	2.00
85 Mike Piazza	2.00	5.00
86 Huston Street	.75	2.00
87 Ichiro Suzuki	2.50	6.00
88 Felix Hernandez	1.25	3.00
89 Kenji Johjima	2.00	5.00
90 Adrian Beltre	2.00	5.00
91 Carl Crawford	1.25	3.00
92 Scott Kazmir	1.25	3.00
93 B.J. Upton	.75	2.00
94 Michael Young	.75	2.00
95 Mark Teixeira	1.25	3.00
96 Sammy Sosa	2.00	5.00
97 Hank Blalock	.75	2.00
98 Vernon Wells	.75	2.00
99 Roy Halladay	1.25	3.00
100 Frank Thomas	2.00	5.00
101 Adam Lind AU (RC)	3.00	8.00
102 Akinori Iwamura AU RC	8.00	20.00
103 Andrew Miller AU RC	12.00	30.00
104 Michael Bourn AU (RC)	5.00	12.00
105 Kory Casto AU (RC)	3.00	8.00
106 Ryan Braun AU (RC)	15.00	40.00
107 Sean Gallagher AU (RC)	3.00	8.00
108 Billy Butler AU (RC)	5.00	12.00
109 Alexi Casilla AU RC	5.00	12.00
110 Chris Stewart AU RC	3.00	8.00
111 Matt DeSalvo AU (RC)	3.00	8.00
112 Chase Headley AU (RC)	3.00	8.00
113 D.Young AU/292 (RC)	5.00	12.00
114 Homer Bailey AU (RC)	5.00	12.00
115 Kurt Suzuki AU (RC)	3.00	8.00
116 A.Gordon AU/297 RC	10.00	25.00
117 Josh Hamilton AU (RC)	10.00	25.00
118 Fred Lewis AU (RC)	5.00	12.00
119 Glen Perkins AU (RC)	3.00	8.00
120 Hector Gimenez AU (RC)	3.00	8.00
121 Phil Hughes AU (RC)	8.00	20.00
122 Jeff Baker AU (RC)	3.00	8.00
123 Andy LaRoche AU (RC)	3.00	8.00
124 Tim Lincecum AU RC	15.00	40.00
125 Joaquin Arias AU (RC)	3.00	8.00
126 D.Matsuzaka AU	12.00	30.00
127 Micah Owings AU (RC)	3.00	8.00
128 H.Pence AU/297 (RC)	10.00	25.00
129 Matt Chico AU (RC)	3.00	8.00
130 Kei Igawa AU RC	8.00	20.00
131 Kevin Kouzmanoff AU (RC)	3.00	8.00
132 M.Montero AU/289 (RC)	3.00	8.00
133 Mike Rabelo AU RC	3.00	8.00
134 Felix Pie AU (RC)	3.00	8.00
135 Curtis Thigpen AU (RC)	3.00	8.00
136 Ryan Z. Braun AU RC	3.00	8.00
137 Ryan Sweeney AU (RC)	3.00	8.00
138 Brandon Wood AU (RC)	3.00	8.00
139 Troy Tulowitzki AU (RC)	10.00	25.00
140 Justin Upton AU RC	10.00	25.00
141 J.Chamberlain AU RC EXCH	5.00	12.00

2007 Ultimate Collection Jerseys

OVERALL GU ODDS TWO PER PACK
STATED PRINT RUN 50 SER.#'d SETS

1 Chipper Jones/50	4.00	10.00
2 Andruw Jones/50	4.00	10.00
3 Tim Hudson/50	3.00	8.00
4 Stephen Drew/50	4.00	10.00
5 Randy Johnson/50	4.00	10.00
6 Brandon Webb/50	4.00	10.00
7 Alfonso Soriano/50	3.00	8.00
8 Derrek Lee/50	3.00	8.00
9 Aramis Ramirez/50	3.00	8.00
10 Carlos Zambrano/50	3.00	8.00
11 Ken Griffey Jr./50	8.00	20.00
12 Adam Dunn/50	3.00	8.00
13 Ryan Freel/50	3.00	8.00
14 Todd Helton/50	4.00	10.00
15 Garrett Atkins/50	3.00	8.00
16 Matt Holliday/50	4.00	10.00
17 Hanley Ramirez/50	4.00	10.00
18 Dontrelle Willis/50	3.00	8.00
19 Miguel Cabrera/50	4.00	10.00
20 Lance Berkman/50	3.00	8.00
21 Roy Oswalt/50	3.00	8.00
22 Carlos Lee/50	3.00	8.00
24 Jason Schmidt/50	3.00	8.00
25 Juan Pierre/50	3.00	8.00
26 Russell Martin/50	3.00	8.00
27 Rickie Weeks/50	3.00	8.00
28 Prince Fielder/50	4.00	10.00
29 Ben Sheets/50	3.00	8.00
31 Jose Reyes/50	4.00	10.00
32 Pedro Martinez/50	4.00	10.00
33 Carlos Beltran/50	3.00	8.00
34 Brett Myers/50	3.00	8.00
35 Jimmy Rollins/50	6.00	15.00
37 Jason Bay/50	3.00	8.00
38 Freddy Sanchez/50	3.00	8.00
39 Ian Snell/50	3.00	8.00
40 Jake Peavy/50	3.00	8.00
41 Greg Maddux/50	6.00	15.00
42 Brian Giles/50	3.00	8.00
43 Matt Cain/50	4.00	10.00
44 Barry Zito/50	3.00	8.00
45 Ray Durham/50	3.00	8.00
46 Albert Pujols/50	15.00	40.00
47 Chris Carpenter/50	3.00	8.00
48 Chris Duncan/50	4.00	10.00
49 Scott Rolen/50	4.00	10.00
50 Ryan Zimmerman/50	4.00	10.00
51 Chad Cordero/50	3.00	8.00
52 Ryan Church/50	3.00	8.00
53 Miguel Tejada/50	3.00	8.00
54 Erik Bedard/50	3.00	8.00
55 Brian Roberts/50	3.00	8.00
56 David Ortiz/50	4.00	10.00
57 Josh Beckett/50	4.00	10.00
58 Manny Ramirez/50	4.00	10.00
59 Daisuke Matsuzaka/50	20.00	50.00
60 Jim Thome/50	4.00	10.00
61 Paul Konerko/50	3.00	8.00
62 Jermaine Dye/50	3.00	8.00
63 Grady Sizemore/50	4.00	10.00
64 Victor Martinez/50	3.00	8.00
65 C.C. Sabathia/50	3.00	8.00
66 Ivan Rodriguez/50	4.00	10.00
67 Justin Verlander/50	4.00	10.00
68 Gary Sheffield/50	3.00	8.00
69 Jeremy Bonderman/50	3.00	8.00
70 Gil Meche/50	3.00	8.00
71 Mike Sweeney/50	3.00	8.00
72 Mark Teahen/50	3.00	8.00
73 Vladimir Guerrero/50	4.00	10.00
74 Howie Kendrick/50	3.00	8.00
75 Francisco Rodriguez/50	3.00	8.00
76 Johan Santana/50	4.00	10.00
77 Justin Morneau/50	3.00	8.00
78 Joe Mauer/50	4.00	10.00
79 Michael Cuddyer/50	3.00	8.00
81 Derek Jeter/50	10.00	25.00
83 Roger Clemens/50	8.00	20.00
84 Rich Harden/50	3.00	8.00
85 Mike Piazza/50	6.00	15.00
86 Huston Street/50	3.00	8.00
88 Felix Hernandez/50	4.00	10.00
89 Kenji Johjima/50	4.00	10.00
90 Adrian Beltre/50	3.00	8.00
91 Carl Crawford/50	3.00	8.00
92 Scott Kazmir/50	4.00	10.00
93 B.J. Upton/50	3.00	8.00
94 Michael Young/50	3.00	8.00
95 Mark Teixeira/50	4.00	10.00
97 Hank Blalock/50	3.00	8.00
98 Vernon Wells/50	3.00	8.00
99 Roy Halladay/50	3.00	8.00
100 Frank Thomas/50	6.00	15.00

2007 Ultimate Collection America's Pastime Memorabilia

OVERALL GU ODDS TWO PER PACK
PRINT RUNS B/WN 25-75 COPIES PER
NO PRICING ON QTY 25 OR LESS

AB Adrian Beltre/75	3.00	8.00
AJ Andruw Jones/75	4.00	10.00
AP Andy Pettitte/75	4.00	10.00
AS Alfonso Soriano/75	3.00	8.00
BA Bobby Abreu/75	3.00	8.00
BE Josh Beckett/75	4.00	10.00
BG Brian Giles/75	3.00	8.00
BJ Jeff Bagwell/75	4.00	10.00
BR Brian Roberts/75	3.00	8.00
BS Ben Sheets/75	3.00	8.00
BW Brandon Webb/75	4.00	10.00
CA Chris Carpenter/75	3.00	8.00
CB Carlos Beltran/75	3.00	8.00
CC Carl Crawford/75	3.00	8.00
CF Carlton Fisk/75	4.00	10.00
CF2 Carlton Fisk/75	4.00	10.00
CJ Chipper Jones/75	4.00	10.00
CL Carlos Lee/75	3.00	8.00
CR Cal Ripken Jr./75	15.00	40.00
CS Curt Schilling/75	4.00	10.00
CU Chase Utley/75	4.00	10.00
DJ Derek Jeter/75	100.00	250.00
DL Derrek Lee/75	3.00	8.00
DO David Ortiz/75	4.00	10.00
DW Dontrelle Willis/75	3.00	8.00
FH Felix Hernandez/75	4.00	10.00
FL Francisco Liriano/75	4.00	10.00
FR Francisco Rodriguez/64	3.00	8.00
GA Garrett Atkins/75	3.00	8.00
GM Greg Maddux/75	6.00	15.00
GS Gary Sheffield/75	3.00	8.00
GW Tony Gwynn/75	4.00	10.00
GW2 Tony Gwynn/75	4.00	10.00
HA Rich Harden/75	3.00	8.00
HB Hank Blalock/75	3.00	8.00
HR Hanley Ramirez/75	4.00	10.00
JA Jason Bay/75	3.00	8.00
JB Jeremy Bonderman/75	3.00	8.00
JE Jim Edmonds/75	4.00	10.00
JG Jason Giambi/75	3.00	8.00
JM Justin Morneau/75	3.00	8.00
JN Joe Nathan/75	3.00	8.00
JO Randy Johnson/75	4.00	10.00
JP Jonathan Papelbon/75	4.00	10.00
JR Jim Rice/75	3.00	8.00
JS Johan Santana/75	4.00	10.00
JT Jim Thome/75	4.00	10.00
JV Justin Verlander/75	4.00	10.00
JW Josh Willingham/75	3.00	8.00
KG Ken Griffey Jr./75	8.00	20.00
KP Kirby Puckett/75	12.00	30.00
KY Kevin Youkilis/75	4.00	10.00
LB Lance Berkman/75	3.00	8.00
MA Joe Mauer/75	4.00	10.00
MC Matt Cain/75	4.00	10.00
MH Matt Holliday/75	4.00	10.00
MI Miguel Cabrera/75	4.00	10.00
MM Mike Mussina/75	4.00	10.00
MR Manny Ramirez/75	4.00	10.00
MR2 Manny Ramirez/75	4.00	10.00
MS Mike Schmidt/75	6.00	15.00
MT Miguel Tejada/75	3.00	8.00
MY Michael Young/75	3.00	8.00
MZ Pedro Martinez/75	4.00	10.00
NR Nolan Ryan/75	12.50	30.00
OR Magglio Ordonez/75	3.00	8.00
OS Ozzie Smith/75	10.00	25.00
PE Jake Peavy/75	3.00	8.00
PF Prince Fielder/75	4.00	10.00
PM Paul Molitor/75	3.00	8.00
PU Albert Pujols/75	8.00	20.00
RB Rocco Baldelli/75	3.00	8.00
RC Roger Clemens/75	6.00	15.00
RE Jose Reyes/75	4.00	10.00
RE2 Jose Reyes/75	4.00	10.00
RH Roy Halladay/75	3.00	8.00
RJ Reggie Jackson/75	6.00	15.00
RO Roy Oswalt/75	3.00	8.00
RS Ryne Sandberg/75	6.00	15.00
RW Rickie Weeks/75	3.00	8.00
RZ Ryan Zimmerman/75	4.00	10.00
SC Steve Carlton/75	3.00	8.00
SE Richie Sexson/75	3.00	8.00
SI Grady Sizemore/75	4.00	10.00
SI2 Grady Sizemore/75	4.00	10.00
SK Scott Kazmir/75	4.00	10.00
SM John Smoltz/75	4.00	10.00
TE Mark Teixeira/75	4.00	10.00
TG Troy Glaus/75	3.00	8.00
TH Todd Helton/75	4.00	10.00
TR Travis Hafner/75	3.00	8.00
TR2 Travis Hafner/75	3.00	8.00
VA Jason Varitek/75	4.00	10.00
VG Vladimir Guerrero/75	4.00	10.00
VG2 Vladimir Guerrero/75	4.00	10.00
VM Victor Martinez/75	3.00	8.00
WC Will Clark/75	4.00	10.00

2007 Ultimate Collection America's Pastime Memorabilia Patches

OVERALL GU ODDS TWO PER PACK
PRINT RUNS B/WN 5-50 COPIES PER
NO PRICING ON QTY 25 OR LESS

AB Adrian Beltre/50	5.00	12.00
AJ Andruw Jones/50	6.00	15.00
AP Andy Pettitte/50	6.00	15.00
AS Alfonso Soriano/50	6.00	15.00
BA Bobby Abreu/50	5.00	12.00
BE Josh Beckett/50	10.00	25.00
BG Brian Giles/50	5.00	12.00
BJ Jeff Bagwell/50	10.00	25.00
BR Brian Roberts/50	6.00	15.00
BS Ben Sheets/50	5.00	12.00
BW Brandon Webb/50	6.00	15.00
CA Chris Carpenter/50	5.00	12.00
CB Carlos Beltran/50	6.00	15.00
CC Carl Crawford/50	6.00	15.00
CF Carlton Fisk/50	5.00	12.00
CF2 Carlton Fisk/50	5.00	12.00
CJ Chipper Jones/50	12.50	30.00
CL Carlos Lee/50	5.00	12.00
CR Cal Ripken Jr./32	12.50	30.00
CS Curt Schilling/50	6.00	15.00
CU Chase Utley/50	6.00	15.00
DL Derrek Lee/50	5.00	12.00
DO David Ortiz/50	10.00	25.00
DW Dontrelle Willis/50	5.00	12.00
FH Felix Hernandez/50	6.00	15.00
FL Francisco Liriano/50	6.00	15.00
FR Francisco Rodriguez/50	5.00	12.00
GA Garrett Atkins/50	5.00	12.00
GS Gary Sheffield/50	5.00	12.00
GW Tony Gwynn/50	10.00	25.00
GW2 Tony Gwynn/50	10.00	25.00
HA Rich Harden/50	5.00	12.00
HB Hank Blalock/50	5.00	12.00
HR Hanley Ramirez/50	6.00	15.00
JA Jason Bay/50	5.00	12.00
JB Jeremy Bonderman/50	5.00	12.00
JE Jim Edmonds/50	6.00	15.00
JG Jason Giambi/50	5.00	12.00
JM Justin Morneau/50	6.00	15.00
JN Joe Nathan/50	5.00	12.00
JO Randy Johnson/50	6.00	15.00
JP Jonathan Papelbon/50	10.00	25.00
JS Johan Santana/50	6.00	15.00
JT Jim Thome/50	5.00	12.00
JW Josh Willingham/50	5.00	12.00
KG Ken Griffey Jr./50	10.00	25.00
KP Kirby Puckett/50	30.00	60.00
KY Kevin Youkilis/50	10.00	25.00
LB Lance Berkman/50	6.00	15.00
LO Lou Brock/50	10.00	25.00
MA Joe Mauer/40	6.00	15.00
MC Matt Cain/50	5.00	12.00
MH Matt Holliday/50	10.00	25.00
MI Miguel Cabrera/50	5.00	12.00
MM Mike Mussina/50	10.00	25.00
MP Mike Piazza/50	10.00	25.00
MR Manny Ramirez/30	6.00	15.00
MR2 Manny Ramirez/28	6.00	15.00
MS Mike Schmidt/50	8.00	20.00
MT Miguel Tejada/50	5.00	12.00
MY Michael Young/50	5.00	12.00
MZ Pedro Martinez/50	6.00	15.00
NR Nolan Ryan/50	12.00	30.00
OR Magglio Ordonez/50	6.00	15.00
PE Jake Peavy/50	5.00	12.00
PF Prince Fielder/50	10.00	25.00
PM Paul Molitor/50	10.00	25.00
RB Rocco Baldelli/50	5.00	12.00
RC Roger Clemens/50	10.00	25.00
RE Jose Reyes/50	10.00	25.00
RE2 Jose Reyes/50	10.00	25.00
RH Roy Halladay/50	5.00	12.00
RJ Reggie Jackson/50	10.00	25.00
RO Roy Oswalt/50	5.00	12.00
RS Ryne Sandberg/50	15.00	40.00
RY Robin Yount/50	15.00	40.00
RZ Ryan Zimmerman/50	10.00	25.00
SC Steve Carlton/50	5.00	12.00
SE Richie Sexson/50	5.00	12.00
SI Grady Sizemore/50	10.00	25.00
SI2 Grady Sizemore/50	10.00	25.00
SK Scott Kazmir/50	6.00	15.00
SM John Smoltz/50	6.00	15.00
TE Mark Teixeira/50	6.00	15.00
TG Troy Glaus/50	6.00	15.00
TH Todd Helton/50	6.00	15.00
TR Travis Hafner/50	5.00	12.00
TR2 Travis Hafner/50	5.00	12.00
VA Jason Varitek/50	10.00	25.00
VM Victor Martinez/50	5.00	12.00
WC Will Clark/50	6.00	15.00

2007 Ultimate Collection America's Pastime Signatures

OVERALL AU ODDS ONE PER PACK
EXCHANGE DEADLINE 9/24/2009

AD Adam Dunn	4.00	10.00
AE Andre Ethier	5.00	12.00
AG Adrian Gonzalez	4.00	10.00
AJ A.J. Burnett	4.00	10.00
AK Al Kaline	12.00	30.00
AL Adam LaRoche	4.00	10.00
AP Albert Pujols	100.00	150.00
AV Andy Van Slyke	8.00	20.00
BB Boof Bonser	4.00	10.00
BE Johnny Bench	10.00	25.00
BJ B.J. Upton	4.00	10.00
BM Bill Mazeroski	20.00	50.00
CB Chad Billingsley	6.00	15.00
CC Chad Cordero	4.00	10.00
CH Cole Hamels	5.00	12.00
CK Casey Kotchman	4.00	10.00
CQ Carlos Quentin	6.00	15.00
CR Craig Biggio	12.00	30.00
CT Curtis Thigpen	4.00	10.00
CW Chien-Ming Wang	10.00	25.00
CY Chris Young	4.00	10.00
DH Dan Haren	4.00	10.00
DJ Derek Jeter	100.00	200.00
DM Don Mattingly	30.00	60.00
DS Don Sutton	6.00	15.00
DU Dan Uggla	4.00	10.00
DY Delmon Young	6.00	15.00
FH Felix Hernandez	12.00	30.00
FR Frank Robinson	10.00	25.00
GA Garrett Atkins	4.00	10.00
GP Gaylord Perry	4.00	10.00
GR Khalil Greene	6.00	15.00
GW Tony Gwynn	30.00	80.00
HA Travis Hafner	4.00	10.00
HB Homer Bailey	8.00	20.00
HE Chase Headley	4.00	10.00
HO Howie Kendrick	4.00	10.00
HR Hanley Ramirez	4.00	10.00
HS Huston Street	4.00	10.00
HU Torii Hunter	6.00	15.00
IK Ian Kinsler	8.00	20.00
JB Jason Bay	4.00	10.00
JE Jeremy Bonderman	4.00	10.00
JI Jim Rice	6.00	10.00
JL James Loney	4.00	10.00
JM Jack Morris	4.00	10.00
JN Joe Nathan	4.00	10.00
JO Joe Blanton	4.00	10.00
JT Jim Thome	12.50	30.00
JV Justin Verlander	20.00	50.00
JZ Joel Zumaya	6.00	15.00
KI Kei Igawa	4.00	10.00
KJ Kelly Johnson	4.00	10.00
KM Kendry Morales	4.00	10.00
LA Andy LaRoche	4.00	10.00
LE Jon Lester	8.00	20.00
LY John Lackey	4.00	10.00
MA Daisuke Matsuzaka	30.00	60.00
MB Matt Brown	4.00	10.00
MC Matt Cain	5.00	12.00
MH Matt Holliday	4.00	10.00
MM Melvin Mora	4.00	10.00
MS Mike Schmidt	15.00	40.00
MT Mark Teixeira	6.00	15.00
NM Nick Markakis	8.00	20.00
NW Nick Swisher	4.00	10.00
OS Ozzie Smith	20.00	50.00
PA Jim Palmer	4.00	10.00
PB Jonathan Papelbon	8.00	20.00
PK Paul Konerko	6.00	15.00
RA Aramis Ramirez	6.00	15.00
RB Ryan Braun	10.00	25.00
RF Rafael Furcal	4.00	10.00
RG Ryan Garko	4.00	10.00
RH Rich Harden	4.00	10.00
RI Rich Hill	4.00	10.00
RT Ryan Theriot	4.00	10.00
RW Rickie Weeks	4.00	10.00
RZ Ryan Zimmerman	6.00	15.00
SD Stephen Drew	10.00	25.00
SG Sean Gallagher	4.00	10.00
SK Scott Kazmir	8.00	20.00
SM Stan Musial	50.00	100.00
SO Joakim Soria	4.00	10.00
TG Tom Glavine	10.00	25.00
TP Tony Perez	6.00	15.00
TR Tim Raines	6.00	15.00
TT Troy Tulowitzki	6.00	15.00
VM Victor Martinez	4.00	10.00
VW Vernon Wells	4.00	10.00
WC Will Clark	10.00	25.00
WI Josh Willingham	4.00	10.00
WM Willie McCovey	15.00	40.00
XN Xavier Nady	4.00	10.00

2007 Ultimate Collection Ultimate Ensemble Dual Swatches

OVERALL GU ODDS TWO PER PACK
PRINT RUNS B/WN 52-75 COPIES PER

BD Bay/J.Drew/75	4.00	10.00
BH Bonderman/Harden/75	4.00	10.00
BZ Boggs/Zimmerman/75	5.00	12.00
CG M.Cabrera/Vlad/75	5.00	12.00
CJ Schilling/Beckett/75	6.00	15.00
CR Clemens/Ryan/75	12.50	30.00
CW Cain/Jer.Weaver/75	4.00	10.00
FT Prince/Teixeira/75	5.00	12.00
GD Griffey Jr./Dunn/75	8.00	20.00
GM Glavine/Pedro/75	4.00	10.00
GP Gwynn/Peavy/75	10.00	25.00
GR Gwynn/Ripken/75	15.00	40.00
HH Helton/Holliday/75	5.00	12.00
HJ F.Hernandez/Johjima/75	5.00	12.00
HR Hardy/Reyes/75	5.00	12.00
HW Halladay/Wells/75	4.00	10.00
IK Iguchi/Konerko/75	4.00	10.00
JJ Chipper/Andruw/75	5.00	12.00
JR Jeter/Rivera/75	30.00	60.00
JV Mauer/V.Martinez/75	4.00	10.00
KY Kazmir/Delmon/75	4.00	10.00
LS Lee/Soriano/75	4.00	10.00
MB Schmidt/Brooks/75	8.00	20.00
MC Morneau/Cuddyer/75	4.00	10.00
MM Morneau/Mauer/75	5.00	12.00
NR Nathan/Rivera/75	5.00	12.00
OB Oswalt/Berkman/75	5.00	12.00
PC Pujols/Carpenter/75	8.00	20.00
PO Pujols/Ortiz/75	8.00	20.00
RB I.Rodriguez/Dench/75	5.00	12.00
SB Sizemore/Beltran/75	5.00	12.00
SC Soriano/Crawford/52	5.00	12.00
SL Johan/Liriano/75	6.00	15.00
SP Smoltz/Peavy/75	5.00	12.00
SR Sandberg/Ripken/63	20.00	50.00
SW Santana/Webb/75	5.00	12.00
TR Tejada/Ripken/75	6.00	15.00
WU Weeks/Utley/75	5.00	12.00
YR Young/Reyes/75	5.00	12.00

2007 Ultimate Collection Ultimate Ensemble Triple Swatches

OVERALL GU ODDS TWO PER PACK
STATED PRINT RUN 50 SER.#'d SETS

BCG Blalock/Chavez/Glaus	6.00	15.00
CBG Clark/Boggs/Gwynn	10.00	25.00
CRS Carlton/Ryan/Sutton	10.00	25.00
CSK Carlton/Johan/Kazmir	6.00	15.00
FHS Prince/Hardy/Sheets	6.00	15.00
GRR Greene/Reyes/Hanley	10.00	25.00
HTP Hafner/F.Thomas/Piazza	6.00	15.00
LPD Larkin/Perez/Dunn	6.00	15.00
LRS Larkin/Ripken/Ozzie	12.50	30.00
MCS Pedro/Clemens/Sutton	10.00	25.00
MJG Mauer/Chipper/Griffey	12.50	30.00
MMP Mauer/V.MartPosada	6.00	15.00
MSB Dice-K/Schilling/Beckett	40.00	80.00
MSU Mazeroski/Sandberg/Utley	10.00	25.00
OCZ Oswalt/Carpenter/Zambrano	6.00	15.00
ODH Ortiz/Dye/Hafner	6.00	15.00
OMT Ortiz/Morneau/Teixeira	6.00	15.00
OPR Ortiz/Pujols/Reyes	10.00	25.00
PJL Pujols/Andruw/Lee	10.00	25.00
RDB Pudge/Delgado/Beltran	6.00	15.00
RJG Ripken/Jeter/Griffey	20.00	50.00
RPJ Rice/Puckett/Reggie	40.00	80.00
RPS Manny/Pujols/Soriano	10.00	25.00
RSB Brooks/Schmidt/Boggs	10.00	25.00
SHS Santana/Halladay/Beckett	6.00	15.00
UWG Utley/Weeks/M.Giles	10.00	25.00
YBO Yaz/Boggs/Ortiz	10.00	25.00
YJT M.Young/Jeter/Tejada	10.00	25.00
YTS M.Young/Teixeira/Sosa	10.00	25.00
ZAJ Zimmerman/Atkins/Chipper	6.00	15.00

2007 Ultimate Collection Ultimate Iron Man Signatures

COMMON CARD	125.00	250.00
OVERALL AU ODDS ONE PER PACK		
STATED PRINT RUN 8 SER.#'d SETS		

2007 Ultimate Collection Ultimate Numbers Match Signatures

OVERALL AU ODDS ONE PER PACK
PRINT RUNS B/WN 2-48 COPIES PER
NO PRICING ON QTY 25 OR LESS
EXCHANGE DEADLINE 9/24/2009

AR Atkins/Reynolds/27	6.00	15.00
BW Bonderman/Wright/38	6.00	15.00
BZ Bay/Zambrano/38	6.00	15.00
FG Fisk/Vlad/27	40.00	80.00
HH Hafner/Hunter/48	12.50	30.00
HR F.Hernandez/Ryan/34	100.00	200.00
HV Hamels/Verlander/35	30.00	60.00
HW Harden/Wang/40	10.00	25.00
JD Reggie/Dunn/44	30.00	60.00
WH Willis/Hamels/35	12.50	30.00

2007 Ultimate Collection Ultimate Numbers Materials

OVERALL GU ODDS TWO PER PACK
PRINT RUNS B/WN 1-75 COPIES PER
NO PRICING ON QTY 25 OR LESS

AB A.J. Burnett/34	4.00	10.00
AD Adam Dunn/44	4.00	10.00
AG Alex Gordon/7		
AJ Andruw Jones/25		
AN Andy Pettitte/46	5.00	12.00
AS Alfonso Soriano/12		
BA Bobby Abreu/53	4.00	10.00
BE Adrian Beltre/29	4.00	10.00
BG Brian Giles/24		
BI Craig Biggio/7		
BK Brooks Robinson/5		
BR Brian Roberts/1		
BS Ben Sheets/15		
BT Carlos Beltran/15		
BU B.J. Upton/2		
BZ Barry Zito/75	4.00	10.00
CA Carl Crawford/13		
CC Chris Carpenter/29	4.00	10.00
CF Carlton Fisk/27	5.00	12.00
CF2 Carlton Fisk/72	5.00	12.00
CJ Chipper Jones/10		
CL Carlos Lee/45	4.00	10.00
CS Curt Schilling/38	5.00	12.00
CU Chase Utley/26	5.00	12.00
CY Carl Yastrzemski/8		
DJ Derek Jeter/2		
DJ2 Derek Jeter/2		
DL Derrek Lee/25		
DL2 Derrek Lee/25		
DM Don Mattingly/23		
DO David Ortiz/34	6.00	15.00
DO2 David Ortiz/25		
DY Delmon Young/26	5.00	12.00
EC Eric Chavez/3		
FH Felix Hernandez/34	6.00	15.00
FL Francisco Liriano/47	5.00	12.00
GA Garrett Atkins/27	4.00	10.00
GJ Geoff Jenkins/5		
GL Troy Glaus/25		
GP Gaylord Perry/36	4.00	10.00
GR Grady Sizemore/24		
GW Tony Gwynn/19		
HA Roy Halladay/32	4.00	10.00
HE Todd Helton/17		
HF Travis Hafner/48	4.00	10.00
HP Hunter Pence/9		
HU Torii Hunter/48	4.00	10.00
JB Jeff Bagwell/5		
JE Jeremy Bonderman/38	4.00	10.00
JH Josh Hamilton/33	20.00	50.00
JJ J.J. Hardy/7		
JM Joe Mauer/7		
JR Jim Rice/14		
JS Johan Santana/57	5.00	12.00
JT Jim Thome/25		
JV Jason Varitek/33	12.50	30.00
KG Ken Griffey Jr./3		
KG2 Ken Griffey Jr./3		
KI Kirk Gibson/23		
KJ Kenji Johjima/2		
LD Lenny Dykstra/4		
MA Daisuke Matsuzaka/18		
MA2 Daisuke Matsuzaka/18		
MO Magglio Ordonez/30	4.00	10.00
MR Manny Ramirez/24		
MR2 Manny Ramirez/24		
NR Nolan Ryan/34	20.00	50.00
OS Roy Oswalt/44	4.00	10.00
PF Prince Fielder/28	5.00	12.00
PU Albert Pujols/5		
PU2 Albert Pujols/5		
RC Rod Carew/29	6.00	15.00
RH Rich Harden/40	4.00	10.00
RI Cal Ripken Jr./8		
RJ Randy Johnson/51	5.00	12.00
RO Roger Clemens/22		
RS Ryne Sandberg/23		
RW Rickie Weeks/23		
RY Robin Yount/19		
SA C.C. Sabathia/52	4.00	10.00
SC Steve Carlton/32	4.00	10.00
SK Scott Kazmir/19		
SR Scott Rolen/27	5.00	12.00
TG Tom Glavine/47	6.00	15.00
TP Tony Perez/24		
TR Tim Raines/30	4.00	10.00
TV Trevor Hoffman/51	4.00	10.00

VG Vladimir Guerrero/27 6.00 15.00
VM Victor Martinez/41 4.00 10.00
WB Wade Boggs/12
WB2 Wade Boggs/12
WC Will Clark/22
WI Dontrelle Willis/35 4.00 10.00

2007 Ultimate Collection Ultimate Star Materials

OVERALL GU ODDS TWO PER PACK
AD Adam Dunn 3.00 8.00
AG Alex Gordon 6.00 15.00
AG2 Alex Gordon 6.00 15.00
AK Austin Kearns 3.00 8.00
AK2 Austin Kearns 3.00 8.00
AP Albert Pujols 6.00 15.00
BG Brian Giles 3.00 8.00
BI Craig Biggio 4.00 10.00
BO Jeremy Bonderman 3.00 8.00
BS Ben Sheets 3.00 8.00
BU B.J. Upton 3.00 8.00
CA Chris Carpenter 3.00 8.00
CF Carlton Fisk 4.00 10.00
CL Carlos Lee 3.00 8.00
CL2 Carlos Lee 3.00 8.00
CR Cal Ripken Jr. 8.00 20.00
CR2 Cal Ripken Jr. 8.00 20.00
CY Carl Yastrzemski 4.00 10.00
CZ Carlos Zambrano 3.00 8.00
DH Dan Haren 3.00 8.00
DJ Derek Jeter 8.00 20.00
DJ2 Derek Jeter 8.00 20.00
DL Derrek Lee 3.00 8.00
DM Don Mattingly 5.00 12.00
DO David Ortiz 4.00 10.00
DW Dontrelle Willis 3.00 8.00
DW2 Dontrelle Willis 3.00 8.00
EC Eric Chavez 3.00 8.00
FH Felix Hernandez 4.00 10.00
FH2 Felix Hernandez 4.00 10.00
FL Francisco Liriano 4.00 10.00
FR Francisco Rodriguez 3.00 8.00
FT Frank Thomas 5.00 12.00
GA Garrett Atkins 3.00 8.00
GA2 Garrett Atkins 3.00 8.00
GR Khalil Greene 4.00 10.00
GW Tony Gwynn 4.00 10.00
HA Roy Halladay 3.00 8.00
HP Hunter Pence 3.00 8.00
HR Hanley Ramirez 4.00 10.00
HS Huston Street 3.00 8.00
HU Torii Hunter 3.00 8.00
JA Jason Bay 3.00 8.00
JB Josh Beckett 3.00 8.00
JH Jeremy Hermida 3.00 8.00
JL John Lackey 3.00 8.00
JM Joe Mauer 4.00 10.00
JN Joe Nathan 3.00 8.00
JP Jonathan Papelbon 4.00 10.00
JR Jim Rice 3.00 8.00
JS John Smoltz 4.00 10.00
JT Jim Thome 4.00 10.00
JT2 Jim Thome 4.00 10.00
JU Justin Morneau 3.00 8.00
JU2 Justin Morneau 3.00 8.00
KG Ken Griffey Jr. 8.00 20.00
MA Matt Cain 3.00 8.00
MA2 Matt Cain 3.00 8.00
MC Miguel Cabrera 4.00 10.00
MH Matt Holliday 4.00 10.00
MH2 Matt Holliday 4.00 10.00
MS Mike Schmidt 5.00 12.00
MT Mark Teixeira 4.00 10.00
MT2 Mark Teixeira 4.00 10.00
MY Michael Young 3.00 8.00
MY2 Michael Young 3.00 8.00
NM Nick Markakis 4.00 10.00
NR Nolan Ryan 6.00 15.00
NS Nick Swisher 3.00 8.00
OR Roy Oswalt 3.00 8.00
OS Ozzie Smith 5.00 12.00
PA Jim Palmer 3.00 8.00
PE Jake Peavy 3.00 8.00
PE2 Jake Peavy 3.00 8.00
PF Prince Fielder 4.00 10.00
PK Paul Konerko 3.00 8.00
PM Paul Molitor 3.00 8.00
PM2 Paul Molitor 3.00 8.00
RA Roberto Alomar 4.00 10.00
RC Roger Clemens 5.00 12.00
RF Rollie Fingers 3.00 8.00
RH Rich Harden 3.00 8.00
RJ Randy Johnson 4.00 10.00
RO Rod Carew 4.00 10.00
RW Rickie Weeks 3.00 8.00
RY Robin Yount 4.00 10.00
RZ Ryan Zimmerman 4.00 10.00
RZ2 Ryan Zimmerman 4.00 10.00
SK Scott Kazmir 4.00 10.00
TG Tom Glavine 4.00 10.00
TH Travis Hafner 3.00 8.00
TH2 Travis Hafner 3.00 8.00
TI Tim Hudson 3.00 8.00
TT Troy Tulowitzki 4.00 10.00
VM Victor Martinez 3.00 8.00
VW Vernon Wells 3.00 8.00
WB Wade Boggs 4.00 10.00
WI Josh Willingham 3.00 8.00

2007 Ultimate Collection Ultimate Team Marks

OVERALL AU ODDS ONE PER PACK
PRINT RUNS B/WN 5-60 COPIES PER
NO PRICING ON QTY 25 OR LESS
EXCHANGE DEADLINE 9/24/2009
BG Bob Gibson/60 15.00 40.00
CC Carl Crawford/60 6.00 15.00
CL Carlos Lee/57 10.00 25.00
CY Carl Yastrzemski/58 30.00 60.00
DJ Derek Jeter/60 150.00 300.00
DL Derrek Lee/58 4.00 10.00
DO David Ortiz/60 40.00 80.00
DW Dontrelle Willis/56 4.00 10.00
FH Felix Hernandez/60 12.00 30.00
JM Joe Mauer/60 15.00 40.00
MO Justin Morneau/60 10.00 25.00
MT Mark Teixeira/60 6.00 15.00
PF Prince Fielder/60 6.00 15.00
VM Victor Martinez/60 10.00 25.00
VW Vernon Wells/60 4.00 10.00

2007 Ultimate Collection Ultimate Team Materials

OVERALL GU ODDS TWO PER PACK
PRINT RUNS B/WN 25-50 COPIES PER
NO PRICING ON QTY 25 OR LESS
AD Adam Dunn/50 3.00 8.00
AK Austin Kearns/50 3.00 8.00
AN Garret Anderson/50 3.00 8.00
AP Albert Pujols/50 8.00 20.00
BE Josh Beckett/50 4.00 10.00
BG Brian Giles/50 3.00 8.00
BS Ben Sheets/50 3.00 8.00
BU B.J. Upton/50 3.00 8.00
CA Rod Carew/50 4.00 10.00
CF Carlton Fisk/50 4.00 10.00
CH Chris Carpenter/50 3.00 8.00
CL Carlos Lee/50 3.00 8.00
CR Bobby Crosby/50 3.00 8.00
CY Carl Yastrzemski/50 6.00 15.00
DH Dan Haren/50 3.00 8.00
DJ Derek Jeter/50 10.00 25.00
DL Derrek Lee/50 3.00 8.00
DM Don Mattingly/50 6.00 15.00
DO David Ortiz/50 4.00 10.00
DW Dontrelle Willis/50 3.00 8.00
DW2 Dontrelle Willis/50 3.00 8.00
EC Eric Chavez/50 3.00 8.00
EC2 Eric Chavez/50 3.00 8.00
FH Felix Hernandez/50 4.00 10.00
FJ Fergie Jenkins/50 3.00 8.00
FL Francisco Liriano/50 4.00 10.00
FR Francisco Rodriguez/50 3.00 8.00
FT Frank Thomas/50 10.00 25.00
GA Garrett Atkins/50 3.00 8.00
GA2 Garrett Atkins/50 3.00 8.00
GR Khalil Greene/50 4.00 10.00
GW Tony Gwynn/50 4.00 10.00
HA Rich Harden/50 3.00 8.00
HP Hunter Pence/50 6.00 15.00
HR Hanley Ramirez/50 4.00 10.00
HS Huston Street/50 3.00 8.00
HS2 Huston Street/50 3.00 8.00
HU Tim Hudson/50 3.00 8.00
JA Jason Bay/50 3.00 8.00
JE Jeremy Bonderman/50 3.00 8.00
JG Jonny Gomes/50 3.00 8.00
JH Jeremy Hermida/50 3.00 8.00
JI Jim Palmer/50 4.00 10.00
JL John Lackey/50 3.00 8.00
JM Joe Mauer/50 4.00 10.00
JN Joe Nathan/50 3.00 8.00
JP Jake Peavy/50 3.00 8.00
JR Jim Rice/50 3.00 8.00
JS John Smoltz/50 4.00 10.00
JT Jim Thome/50 4.00 10.00
KG Ken Griffey Jr./50 8.00 20.00
KG2 Ken Griffey Jr./50 8.00 20.00
KM Kendry Morales/50 4.00 10.00
MA Daisuke Matsuzaka/50 30.00 60.00
MC Matt Cain/50 4.00 10.00
MH Matt Holliday/50 4.00 10.00
MH2 Matt Holliday/50 4.00 10.00
MI Miguel Cabrera/50 4.00 10.00
MI2 Miguel Cabrera/50 4.00 10.00
MO Justin Morneau/50 3.00 8.00
MO2 Justin Morneau/50 3.00 8.00
MS Mike Schmidt/50 6.00 15.00
MT Mark Teixeira/50 4.00 10.00
MY Michael Young/50 3.00 8.00
NM Nick Markakis/50 4.00 10.00
NR Nolan Ryan/50 12.50 30.00
OS Ozzie Smith/50 10.00 25.00
OS2 Ozzie Smith/50 10.00 25.00
PA Jonathan Papelbon/50 4.00 10.00
PF Prince Fielder/50 4.00 10.00
PK Paul Konerko/50 3.00 8.00
PM Paul Molitor/50 3.00 8.00
PN Phil Niekro/50 3.00 8.00
RA Roberto Alomar/50 6.00 15.00
RC Roger Clemens/50 6.00 15.00
RF Rollie Fingers/50 3.00 8.00
RH Roy Halladay/50 3.00 8.00
RI Cal Ripken Jr./50 10.00 25.00
RI2 Cal Ripken Jr./50 10.00 25.00
RJ Randy Johnson/50 4.00 10.00
RO Roy Oswalt/50 3.00 8.00
RS Ryne Sandberg/50 10.00 25.00
RW Rickie Weeks/50 3.00 8.00
RY Robin Yount/25
RZ Ryan Zimmerman/50 4.00 10.00
RZ2 Ryan Zimmerman/50 4.00 10.00
SK Scott Kazmir/50 4.00 10.00
SK2 Scott Kazmir/50 4.00 10.00
TG Tom Glavine/50 4.00 10.00
TH Torii Hunter/50 3.00 8.00
TR Travis Hafner/50 3.00 8.00
TR2 Travis Hafner/50 3.00 8.00
TT Troy Tulowitzki/50 4.00 10.00
VM Victor Martinez/50 3.00 8.00
WI Josh Willingham/50 3.00 8.00
WI2 Josh Willingham/50 3.00 8.00

2007 Ultimate Collection Ultimate Write of Passage

OVERALL AU ODDS ONE PER PACK
STATED PRINT RUN 60 SER.#'d SETS
NO PRICING DUE TO SCARCITY
EXCHANGE DEADLINE 9/24/2009
BH Baker AU/Holliday/60 4.00 10.00
BR Braun AU/Rolen/60 20.00 50.00
GR Gordon AU/ARodr/60 20.00 50.00
HS Hamels AU/Santana/60 15.00 40.00
IC Kei Igawa AU/60 15.00 40.00
IR Iwamura AU/A.Ramirez/60 8.00 20.00
KB H.Kendrick AU/Biggio/60 4.00 10.00
KJ Kouzmanoff AU/Chipper/60 4.00 10.00
LZ Lincecum AU/Zito/60 60.00 120.00
MS A.Miller AU/Sabathia/60 12.50 30.00
PG Pence AU/Griffey/60 30.00 60.00
PK Perkins AU/Kazmir/60 4.00 10.00
QC Quentin AU/Crawford/60 4.00 10.00
RF Hanley AU/Furcal/60 10.00 25.00
SD Sweeney AU/Dye/60 4.00 10.00
SS Sowers AU/Sabathia/60 4.00 10.00
TD Thigpen AU/Delgado/60 4.00 10.00
TJ Tulowitzki AU/Jeter/60 30.00 60.00
UU B.Upton AU/Utley/60 4.00 10.00
YG Delmon AU/Vlad/60 6.00 15.00

2008 Ultimate Collection

COMMON CARD (1-100) 1.00 2.50
1-100 PRINT RUN 350 SER.#'d SETS
OVERALL AUTO/MEM ODDS 1 PER PACK
101-108 PRINT RUN 99 SER.#'d SETS
EXCHANGE DEADLINE 12/12/2010
1 Jose Reyes 1.50 4.00
2 David Wright 1.50 4.00
3 Carlos Beltran 1.50 4.00
4 Johan Santana 1.50 4.00
5 Pedro Martinez 1.50 4.00
6 Jeff Francoeur 1.50 4.00
7 John Smoltz 2.50 6.00
8 Brian McCann 1.50 4.00
9 Chipper Jones 2.50 6.00
10 Cole Hamels 2.00 5.00
11 Ryan Howard 1.50 4.00
12 Jimmy Rollins 1.50 4.00
13 Chase Utley 1.50 4.00
14 Hanley Ramirez 1.50 4.00
15 Dan Uggla 1.00 2.50
16 Lastings Milledge 1.00 2.50
17 Ryan Zimmerman 1.50 4.00
18 Ryan Ludwick 1.00 2.50
19 Troy Glaus 1.50 4.00
20 Albert Pujols 3.00 8.00
21 Rick Ankiel 1.00 2.50
22 Ryan Doumit 1.00 2.50
23 Nate McLouth 1.00 2.50
24 Lance Berkman 1.50 4.00
25 Carlos Lee 1.00 2.50
26 Miguel Tejada 1.50 4.00
27 CC Sabathia 1.50 4.00
28 Ryan Braun 1.50 4.00
29 Prince Fielder 1.50 4.00
30 Alfonso Soriano 1.50 4.00
31 Derrek Lee 1.00 2.50
32 Carlos Zambrano 1.50 4.00
33 Aramis Ramirez 1.00 2.50
34 Rich Harden 1.00 2.50
35 Edinson Volquez 1.00 2.50
36 Brandon Phillips 1.00 2.50
37 Brandon Webb 1.50 4.00
38 Dan Haren 1.00 2.50
39 Chris B. Young 1.00 2.50
40 Randy Johnson 2.50 6.00
41 Adam Dunn 1.50 4.00
42 Matt Holliday 2.50 6.00
43 Troy Tulowitzki 2.50 6.00
44 Garrett Atkins 1.00 2.50
45 Manny Ramirez 2.50 6.00
46 Greg Maddux 3.00 8.00
47 Matt Kemp 2.00 5.00
48 Russell Martin 1.00 2.50
49 Aaron Rowand 1.00 2.50
50 Tim Lincecum 1.50 4.00
51 Adrian Gonzalez 1.50 4.00
52 Jake Peavy 1.00 2.50
53 Trevor Hoffman 1.50 4.00
54 Ivan Rodriguez 1.50 4.00
55 Alex Rodriguez 3.00 8.00
56 Derek Jeter 6.00 15.00
57 Hideki Matsui 2.50 6.00
58 Robinson Cano 1.50 4.00
59 Joba Chamberlain 1.00 2.50
60 Chien-Ming Wang 1.50 4.00
61 Mariano Rivera 3.00 8.00
62 Xavier Nady 1.00 2.50
63 Josh Beckett 1.00 2.50
64 David Ortiz 2.50 6.00
65 Dustin Pedroia 2.50 6.00
66 Jonathan Papelbon 1.50 4.00
67 Daisuke Matsuzaka 1.50 4.00
68 Kevin Youkilis 1.00 2.50
69 Jason Bay 1.50 4.00
70 Nick Markakis 2.00 5.00
71 Brian Roberts 1.00 2.50
72 Scott Kazmir 1.50 4.00
73 Carl Crawford 1.50 4.00
74 B.J. Upton 1.50 4.00
75 Vernon Wells 1.00 2.50
76 Roy Halladay 1.50 4.00
77 Jermaine Dye 1.00 2.50
78 Jim Thome 1.50 4.00
79 Ken Griffey Jr. 5.00 12.00
80 Carlos Quentin 1.00 2.50
81 Magglio Ordonez 1.50 4.00
82 Justin Verlander 2.50 6.00
83 Miguel Cabrera 2.50 6.00
84 Alex Gordon 1.50 4.00
85 Billy Butler 1.00 2.50
86 Grady Sizemore 1.50 4.00
87 Victor Martinez 1.50 4.00
88 Travis Hafner 1.00 2.50
89 Joe Mauer 2.00 5.00
90 Justin Morneau 1.50 4.00
91 Erik Bedard 1.00 2.50
92 Felix Hernandez 1.50 4.00
93 Ichiro Suzuki 3.00 8.00
94 Ian Kinsler 1.50 4.00
95 Josh Hamilton 1.50 4.00
96 Frank Thomas 2.50 6.00
97 Jack Cust 1.00 2.50
98 Torii Hunter 1.00 2.50
99 Vladimir Guerrero 1.50 4.00
100 Mark Teixeira 1.50 4.00
101 E.Longoria Jsy AU/99 RC 15.00 40.00
102 M.Scherzer Jsy AU/99 RC 100.00 250.00
103 K.Fukudome Jsy/99 RC 8.00 20.00
104 I.Kennedy Jsy AU/99 RC 6.00 15.00
105 C.Buchholz Jsy AU/99 (RC) 6.00 15.00
106 J.Bruce Jsy AU/99 (RC) 12.50 30.00
107 C.Kershaw Jsy AU/99 RC 150.00 250.00
108 C.Hu Jsy AU/99 (RC) 20.00 50.0

2008 Ultimate Collection Autographs Dual

OVERALL AUTO/MEM ODDS 1 PER PACK
PRINT RUNS B/WN 10-50 COPIES PER
NO PRICING ON QTY 25 OR LESS
EXCHANGE DEADLINE 12/12/2010
FE Chone Figgins 6.00 15.00
Edwin Encarnacion/50 -
GG Griffey Jr./Griffey Sr./50 75.00 200.00
IN M.Irvin/D.Newcombe/35 15.00 40.00
JR D.Jeter/H.Ramirez/50 100.00 175.00
KG A.Kaline/C.Granderson/35 30.00 80.00
RB J.Richard/D.Boyd/50 15.00 40.00
TK J.R. Towles 6.00 15.00
Ian Kennedy/50

2008 Ultimate Collection Autographs Triple

OVERALL AUTO/MEM ODDS 1 PER PACK
PRINT RUNS B/WN 10-50 COPIES PER
NO PRICING ON QTY 25 OR LESS
EXCHANGE DEADLINE 12/12/2010
AJK Allen/Jenkins/Kruk/35 10.00 25.00
PNW Papel/Nathan/Wagner/50 30.00 60.00
RHT Hanley/Hu/Tulo/50 10.00 25.00

2008 Ultimate Collection Barrel Autographs

OVERALL AUTO/MEM ODDS 1 PER PACK
PRINT RUNS B/WN 10-140 COPIES PER
NO PRICING ON QTY 25 OR LESS
EXCHANGE DEADLINE 12/12/2010
AR Aramis Ramirez/35 12.50 30.00
CH Chin-Lung Hu/68 40.00 80.00
DJ Derek Jeter/99 150.00 300.00
DL Derrek Lee/50 15.00 40.00
JR Jim Rice/140 12.50 30.00
KG Ken Griffey Jr./75 75.00 150.00
KY Kevin Youkilis/50 10.00 25.00

2008 Ultimate Collection Dual Memorabilia Autographs

OVERALL AUTO/MEM ODDS 1 PER PACK
PRINT RUNS B/WN 5-99 COPIES PER
NO PRICING ON QTY 25 OR LESS
EXCHANGE DEADLINE 12/12/2010
BP Brandon Phillips/75 8.00 20.00
CH Chin-Lung Hu/75 15.00 40.00
DJ Derek Jeter/50 150.00 300.00
DO Don Mattingly/99 30.00 60.00
KG Ken Griffey Jr./50 60.00 120.00
KJ Kelly Johnson/75 4.00 10.00
NM Nick Markakis/75 5.00 12.00
TT Troy Tulowitzki/50 10.00 25.00

2008 Ultimate Collection Dual Memorabilia Autographs Prime

OVERALL AUTO/MEM ODDS 1 PER PACK
PRINT RUNS B/WN 5-15 COPIES PER
NO PRICING DUE TO SCARCITY
EXCHANGE DEADLINE 12/12/2010

2008 Ultimate Collection Home Jersey Autographs

OVERALL AUTO/MEM ODDS 1 PER PACK
PRINT RUNS B/WN 5-99 COPIES PER
NO PRICING ON QTY 25 OR LESS
EXCHANGE DEADLINE 12/12/2010
DJ Derek Jeter/99 125.00 250.00
JF Jeff Francoeur/99 10.00 25.00
JI Jim Rice/50 15.00 40.00
JM Jack Morris/50 8.00 20.00
JO John Maine/50 8.00 20.00
JW Josh Willingham/99 5.00 12.00
KG Ken Griffey Jr./99 40.00 80.00
KY Kevin Youkilis/50 12.50 30.00
PA Jonathan Papelbon/50 12.50 30.00
RS Ron Santo/35 30.00 60.00
TT Troy Tulowitzki/99 8.00 20.00
WI Josh Willingham/99 5.00 12.00

2008 Ultimate Collection Pants Autographs

OVERALL AUTO/MEM ODDS 1 PER PACK
PRINT RUNS B/WN 10-99 COPIES PER
NO PRICING ON QTY 25 OR LESS
EXCHANGE DEADLINE 12/12/2010
BP Brandon Phillips/99 8.00 20.00
DJ Derek Jeter/99 125.00 250.00
JF Jeff Francoeur/99 10.00 25.00
JI Jim Rice/50 15.00 40.00
JM Jack Morris/50 8.00 20.00
JO John Maine/50 8.00 20.00
KG Ken Griffey Jr./99 50.00 100.00
KY Kevin Youkilis/50 8.00 20.00
PA Jonathan Papelbon/50 12.50 30.00
RS Ron Santo/50 30.00 60.00
TT Troy Tulowitzki/99 10.00 25.00

2008 Ultimate Collection Quad Memorabilia Autographs

OVERALL AUTO/MEM ODDS 1 PER PACK
PRINT RUNS B/WN 5-75 COPIES PER
NO PRICING ON QTY 25 OR LESS
EXCHANGE DEADLINE 12/12/2010
BP Brandon Phillips/75 6.00 15.00
CH Chin-Lung Hu/75 20.00 50.00
DJ Derek Jeter/50 150.00 300.00
JO John Maine/75 8.00 20.00
KG Ken Griffey Jr./50 75.00 150.00
TT Troy Tulowitzki/50 10.00 25.00

2008 Ultimate Collection Road Jersey Autographs

OVERALL AUTO/MEM ODDS 1 PER PACK
PRINT RUNS B/WN 10-99 COPIES PER
NO PRICING ON QTY 25 OR LESS
EXCHANGE DEADLINE 12/12/2010
AR Aramis Ramirez/50 12.50 30.00
BP Brandon Phillips/99 10.00 25.00
DJ Derek Jeter/99 125.00 250.00
JF Jeff Francoeur/99 10.00 25.00
JI Jim Rice/50 15.00 40.00
JM Jack Morris/50 8.00 20.00
JO John Maine/75 6.00 15.00
KG Ken Griffey Jr./99 40.00 80.00
KY Kevin Youkilis/50 12.50 30.00
PH Phil Hughes/35 8.00 20.00
RS Ron Santo/50 15.00 40.00

2008 Ultimate Collection Triple Memorabilia Autographs

OVERALL AUTO/MEM ODDS 1 PER PACK
PRINT RUNS B/WN 5-99 COPIES PER
NO PRICING ON QTY 25 OR LESS
EXCHANGE DEADLINE 12/12/2010
BP Brandon Phillips/99 10.00 25.00
CH Chin-Lung Hu/99 20.00 50.00
DJ Derek Jeter/50 150.00 300.00
JO John Maine/99 8.00 20.00
KG Ken Griffey Jr./50 75.00 150.00
TT Troy Tulowitzki/50 10.00 25.00

2008 Ultimate Collection Triple Memorabilia Autographs Prime

OVERALL AUTO/MEM ODDS 1 PER PACK
PRINT RUNS B/WN 5-10 COPIES PER
NO PRICING DUE TO SCARCITY
EXCHANGE DEADLINE 12/12/2010

2009 Ultimate Collection

COMMON CARD (1-55) .75 2.00
1-55 PRINT RUN 599 SER.#'d SETS
COMMON CARD (56-100) 1.25 3.00
56-100 PRINT RUN 599 SER.#'d SETS
COMMON AUTO (101-109) 4.00 10.00
APPX. ROOKIE AU ODDS 1:8 HOBBY PACKS
101-109 PRINT RUNS B/WN 15-175 COPIES PER
NO D.PRICE PRICING AVAILABLE
1 Stephen Drew .75 2.00
2 Chipper Jones 2.00 5.00
3 Brian McCann 1.25 3.00
4 Nick Markakis 1.50 4.00
5 Adam Jones 1.25 3.00
6 Dustin Pedroia 2.00 5.00
7 Josh Beckett .75 2.00
8 Kevin Youkilis .75 2.00
9 Victor Martinez 1.25 3.00
10 Daisuke Matsuzaka 1.25 3.00
11 Kosuke Fukudome 1.25 3.00
12 Carlos Zambrano 1.25 3.00
13 Alfonso Soriano 1.25 3.00
14 Jim Thome 1.25 3.00
15 Joey Votto 2.00 5.00
16 Grady Sizemore 1.25 3.00
17 Todd Helton 1.25 3.00
18 Miguel Cabrera 2.00 5.00
19 Curtis Granderson 1.50 4.00
20 Hanley Ramirez 1.25 3.00
21 Josh Johnson 1.25 3.00
22 Lance Berkman 1.25 3.00
23 Roy Oswalt 1.25 3.00
24 Zack Greinke 2.00 5.00
25 Vladimir Guerrero 1.25 3.00
26 Clayton Kershaw 3.00 8.00
27 Manny Ramirez 2.00 5.00
28 Russell Martin .75 2.00
29 Prince Fielder 1.25 3.00
30 Ryan Braun 1.25 3.00
31 Joe Mauer 1.50 4.00
32 Justin Morneau 1.25 3.00
33 Francisco Liriano .75 2.00
34 Johan Santana 1.25 3.00
35 David Wright 1.50 4.00
36 Jose Reyes 1.25 3.00
37 Derek Jeter 5.00 12.00
38 CC Sabathia 1.25 3.00
39 Hideki Matsui 2.00 5.00
40 Alex Rodriguez 2.50 6.00
41 Chase Utley 1.25 3.00
42 Cole Hamels 1.50 4.00
43 Ryan Howard 1.50 4.00
44 Jimmy Rollins 1.25 3.00
45 Cliff Lee 1.25 3.00
46 Adrian Gonzalez 1.50 4.00
47 Randy Johnson 2.00 5.00
48 Ken Griffey Jr. 4.00 10.00
49 Ichiro Suzuki 2.50 6.00
50 Albert Pujols 2.50 6.00
51 Evan Longoria 1.25 3.00
52 B.J. Upton 1.25 3.00
53 Josh Hamilton 1.25 3.00
54 Roy Halladay 1.25 3.00
55 Adam Dunn 1.25 3.00
56 Brett Anderson RC 2.00 5.00
57 Elvis Andrus RC 3.00 8.00
58 Alex Avila RC 4.00 10.00
59 Andrew Bailey RC 3.00 8.00
60 Daniel Bard RC 1.25 3.00
61 Brad Bergesen (RC) 1.25 3.00
62 Kyle Blanks RC 2.00 5.00
63 Michael Bowden (RC) 1.25 3.00
64 Everth Cabrera RC 2.00 5.00
65 Trevor Cahill RC 3.00 8.00
66 Brett Cecil RC 1.25 3.00
67 Jhoulys Chacin RC 2.00 5.00
68 Aaron Cunningham RC 1.25 3.00
69 Travis Snider RC 2.00 5.00
70 Dexter Fowler (RC) 2.00 5.00
71 Lucas French (RC) 1.25 3.00
72 Mat Gamel RC 3.00 8.00
73 David Hernandez RC 1.25 3.00
74 Derek Holland RC 2.00 5.00
75 Tommy Hunter RC 2.00 5.00
76 Mat Latos RC 4.00 10.00
77 Fernando Martinez RC 3.00 8.00
78 Vin Mazzaro RC 1.25 3.00
79 Andrew McCutchen (RC) 6.00 15.00
80 Kris Medlen RC 3.00 8.00
81 Fu-Te Ni RC 2.00 5.00
82 Bud Norris RC 1.25 3.00
83 Gerardo Parra RC 2.00 5.00
84 Ryan Perry RC 3.00 8.00
85 Aaron Poreda RC 1.25 3.00
86 Sean O'Sullivan RC 1.25 3.00
87 Wilkin Ramirez RC 1.25 3.00
88 Josh Reddick RC 2.00 5.00
89 Nolan Reimold (RC) 1.25 3.00
90 Ricky Romero (RC) 2.00 5.00
91 Marc Rzepczynski RC 2.00 5.00
92 Pablo Sandoval 2.50 6.00
93 Michael Saunders RC 3.00 8.00
94 Jordan Schafer (RC) 2.00 5.00
95 Daniel Schlereth RC 1.25 3.00
96 Anthony Swarzak (RC) 1.25 3.00
97 Junichi Tazawa RC 4.00 10.00
98 Chris Tillman RC 2.00 5.00
99 Sean West (RC) 2.00 5.00
100 Trevor Bell (RC) 1.25 3.00
101 Uehara AU/175 RC 20.00 50.00
102 Rasmus AU/135 (RC) 4.00 10.00
103 Wieters AU/135 RC 6.00 15.00
104 Kenshin Kawakami AU/135 RC 8.00 20.00
106 Hanson AU/135 RC 4.00 10.00
107 LaPorta AU/160 RC 4.00 10.00
108 Feliz AU/135 RC 20.00 50.00
109 Beckham AU/135 RC 5.00 12.00
110 Porcello AU/135 RC 6.00 15.00

2009 Ultimate Collection Gold Rookie Signatures

ONE AU,MEM, OR AU MEM PER PACK
PRINT RUNS B/WN 5-75 COPIES PER
NO D.PRICE PRICING AVAILABLE
ALL VARIATIONS PRICED EQUALLY
101a Koji Uehara/75 12.50 30.00
101b Koji Uehara/75 12.50 30.00
102a Colby Rasmus/45 8.00 20.00
102b Colby Rasmus/45 8.00 20.00
103a Matt Wieters/45 50.00 100.00
103b Matt Wieters/45 50.00 100.00
106a Tommy Hanson/45 10.00 25.00
106b Tommy Hanson/45 10.00 25.00
107a Matt LaPorta/45 5.00 12.00
107b Matt LaPorta/45 5.00 12.00
108a Neftali Feliz/45 5.00 12.00
108b Neftali Feliz/45 5.00 12.00
109a Gordon Beckham/45 6.00 15.00
109b Gordon Beckham/45 6.00 15.00
110a Rick Porcello/45 10.00 25.00
110b Rick Porcello/45 10.00 25.00

2009 Ultimate Collection Career Highlight Signatures

ONE AU,MEM, OR AU MEM PER PACK
PRINT RUNS B/WN 1-40 COPIES PER
NO PRICING ON QTY 25 OR LESS
DJ4 Derek Jeter/30 100.00 200.00
DJ5 Derek Jeter/40 100.00 200.00
HR1 Hanley Ramirez/26 30.00 60.00
JL2 Jon Lester/31 15.00 40.00
JR7 Ken Griffey Jr./40 40.00 80.00
JR8 Ken Griffey Jr./40 40.00 80.00
KG4 Ken Griffey Sr./30 6.00 15.00
KG5 Ken Griffey Sr./40 12.50 30.00

2009 Ultimate Collection Generations Eight Memorabilia

ONE AU,MEM, OR AU MEM PER PACK
STATED PRINT RUN 35 SER.#'d SETS
G8M3 B/D/P/M/B/D/J/J/35 50.00 100.00
G8M4 J/L/H/R/J/D/B/F/35 60.00 120.00
G8M5 B/D/P/J/R/W/J/C/35 60.00 120.00
G8M8 P/P/J/R/R/S/N/M/35 50.00 100.00
G8M9 M/M/G/J/S/V/M/J/P/35 12.50 30.00
G8M13 S/R/J/R/R/T/D/R/35 20.00 50.00
G8M14 W/J/W/L/F/M/P/D/35 30.00 60.00
G8M15 V/F/M/R/W/M/C/J/35 30.00 60.00

2009 Ultimate Collection Generations Six Memorabilia

ONE AU,MEM, OR AU MEM PER PACK
PRINT RUNS B/WN 25-50 COPIES PER
NO PRICING ON QTY 25 OR LESS
G6M2 Je/Wi/Va/Fi/Pe/Or/50 20.00 50.00
G6M3 Po/Be/Di/Je/Wa/Ja/40 30.00 60.00
G6M7 Ch/Di/Cr/Wi/Ja/Ki/50 20.00 50.00
G6M9 Je/Da/Po/Fo/Ja/Ca/50 15.00 40.00
G6M10 Ma/El/Le/Ma/Wi/Ma/50 30.00 60.00
G6M12 Sc/Su/Sl/Pu/Br/Sm/50 30.00 60.00
G6M17 Si/Ma/Pa/Ha/Ec/Fe/50 20.00 50.00
G6M19 Ja/Di/Be/Be/Mu/Je/50 30.00 60.00

2009 Ultimate Collection Jumbo Bat Signatures

ONE AU,MEM, OR AU MEM PER PACK
PRINT RUNS B/WN 5-50 COPIES PER
NO PRICING ON QTY 25 OR LESS
DJ Derek Jeter/50 100.00 175.00
RC Rod Carew/29 20.00 50.00

2009 Ultimate Collection Jumbo Jersey

ONE AU,MEM, OR AU MEM PER PACK
PRINT RUNS B/WN 5-35 COPIES PER
NO PRICING ON QTY 25 OR LESS
JA Reggie Jackson/44 10.00 25.00
SP Satchel Paige/29 100.00 -200.00

2009 Ultimate Collection Jumbo Jersey Signatures

ONE AU,MEM, OR AU MEM PER PACK
PRINT RUNS B/WN 8-50 COPIES PER
NO PRICING ON QTY 25 OR LESS
BF Bob Feller/28 15.00 40.00
BM Brian McCann/35 20.00 50.00
BU B.J. Upton/40 12.50 30.00
CF Carlton Fisk/27 30.00 60.00
DJ Derek Jeter/50 100.00 175.00
GP Gaylord Perry/36 12.50 30.00
HR Hanley Ramirez/50 10.00 25.00
JL Jon Lester/31 20.00 50.00
JP Jim Palmer/50 15.00 40.00
JS James Shields/50 5.00 12.00
KG Ken Griffey Jr./50 60.00 150.00
MK Matt Kemp/50 15.00 40.00
NM Nick Markakis/49 15.00 40.00
PA Jonathan Papelbon/50 10.00 25.00
WF Whitey Ford/40 30.00 60.00
ZG Zack Greinke/35 15.00 40.00

2009 Ultimate Collection Legendary Dual Patch Signature

OVERALL AU-MEM CARDS 1:5 HOBBY PACKS
PRINT RUNS B/WN 5-30 COPIES PER
NO PRICING ON QTY 25 OR LESS
TR Tim Raines/30 15.00 40.00

2009 Ultimate Collection Legendary Eight Memorabilia

ONE AU,MEM, OR AU MEM PER PACK
PRINT RUNS B/WN 25-35 COPIES PER
L8M1 R/H/L/J/D/F/B/D/35 40.00 80.00
L8M4 S/M/N/S/S/F/Y/J/35 40.00 80.00
L8M5 P/R/S/D/B/W/B/F/35 60.00 120.00
L8M6 C/M/R/B/P/B/K/J/35 40.00 80.00
L8M7 W/J/B/B/D/B/W/S/35 50.00 100.00
L8M8 S/C/B/P/B/B/S/W/35 40.00 80.00

2009 Ultimate Collection Legendary Eight Memorabilia Gold

ONE AU,MEM, OR AU MEM PER PACK
PRINT RUNS B/WN 5-20 COPIES PER
NO PRICING DUE TO SCARCITY

2009 Ultimate Collection Legendary Signatures

ONE AU,MEM, OR AU MEM PER PACK
PRINT RUNS B/WN 2-35 COPIES PER
NO PRICING ON QTY 25 OR LESS
BF1 Bob Feller/35 12.50 30.00
DE1 Dennis Eckersley/35 10.00 25.00
DE4 Dennis Eckersley/35 10.00 25.00
NR2 Nolan Ryan/35 75.00 150.00

2009 Ultimate Collection Legendary Six Memorabilia

ONE AU,MEM, OR AU MEM PER PACK
PRINT RUNS B/WN 25-50 COPIES PER
NO PRICING ON QTY 25 OR LESS
L6M1 Ja/Hu/Le/Di/Be/Ni 30.00 60.00
L6M2 Ni/Wi/Fi/Hu/Ja/Ce 20.00 50.00
L6M3 Wi/Mo/Be/Sa/Bo/Se 20.00 50.00
L6M4 Sm/Ri/Sa/Fi/Ry/An 20.00 50.00
L6M6 Ni/Br/Be/Mo/Sc/Su/ 15.00 40.00
L6M7 Ja/Ry/Sa/Sc/Ri/Sm 30.00 60.00
L6M8 Bo/Wi/Di/Be/Ri/Ma 50.00 100.00
L6M9 Wi/Ja/Di/Cl/Ja/Wi 60.00 120.00

2009 Ultimate Collection Signature Moments

ONE AU,MEM, OR AU MEM PER PACK
PRINT RUNS B/WN 3-40 COPIES PER
NO PRICING ON QTY 25 OR LESS
DJ Derek Jeter/40 100.00 175.00
JC Joba Chamberlain/30 20.00 50.00
JL Jon Lester/31 12.50 30.00
KG Ken Griffey Jr./40 60.00 120.00

2009 Ultimate Collection Ultimate Dual Patch Signature

OVERALL AU-MEM CARDS 1:5 HOBBY PACKS
PRINT RUNS B/WN 4-34 COPIES PER
NO PRICING ON QTY 25 OR LESS
CJ Chipper Jones/34 100.00 175.00
DJ Derek Jeter/34 400.00 600.00
JP Jonathan Papelbon/31 20.00 50.00
MK Matt Kemp/29 30.00 60.00
NM Nick Markakis/33 30.00 60.00

2009 Ultimate Collection Ultimate Dual Signatures

ONE AU,MEM, OR AU MEM PER PACK
PRINT RUNS B/WN 19-75 COPIES PER
UDS1 C.Ripken/B.Robinson/39 100.00 175.00
UDS2 B.Robinson/N.Markakis/37 40.00 80.00
UDS3 J.Chamberlain/D.Jeter/38 100.00 175.00
UDS4 B.Jackson/Z.Greinke/33 40.00 80.00
UDS8 Kevin Youkilis 10.00 25.00
Dennis Eckersley/39
UDS11 Dennis Eckersley 30.00 60.00
Ozzie Smith/42
UDS12 D.Jeter/B.Dent/50 100.00 175.00
UDS14 Griffey Jr./Griffey Sr./75 60.00 120.00
UDS15 Griffey Jr./Griffey Sr./70 60.00 120.00
UDS16 J.Lester/K.Youkilis/46 20.00 50.00
UDS18 Papelbon/Joba/35 40.00 80.00
UDS24 B.Jackson/Griffey Jr./72 125.00 250.00
UDS25 D.Jeter/Hanley/72 75.00 150.00

2009 Ultimate Collection Ultimate Eight Memorabilia

ONE AU,MEM, OR AU MEM PER PACK
PRINT RUNS B/WN 25-35 COPIES PER
U8M2 B/R/F/R/F/J/M/S/35 40.00 80.00
U8M7 G/B/G/S/P/J/B/S/35 20.00 50.00
U8M9 J/S/M/G/M/R/W/T/35 40.00 80.00
U8M12 M/J/G/P/M/H/J/B/35 30.00 60.00
U8M14 S/G/B/C/P/S/S/S/35 15.00 40.00

2009 Ultimate Collection Ultimate Inscriptions

ONE AU,MEM, OR AU MEM PER PACK
PRINT RUNS B/WN 3-35 COPIES PER
NO PRICING ON QTY 25 OR LESS
BU B.J. Upton/27 10.00 25.00
NM Nick Markakis/28 10.00 25.00
TR Tim Raines/30 10.00 25.00
MK2 Matt Kemp/35 12.00 30.00

2009 Ultimate Collection Ultimate Patch

ONE AU,MEM, OR AU MEM PER PACK
PRINT RUNS B/WN 5-35 COPIES PER
NO PRICING ON QTY 25 OR LESS
PRICING FOR NON-PREMIUM PATCHES
AN Rick Ankiel/35 30.00 60.00
BE Josh Beckett/35 20.00 50.00
BH Johnny Bench/35 75.00 150.00
BI Chad Billingsley/35 20.00 50.00
BP Brandon Phillips/35 15.00 40.00
CC Chris Carpenter/35 50.00 100.00
CD Carlos Delgado/35 30.00 60.00
CF Carl Crawford/35 30.00 60.00
CG Curtis Granderson/35 15.00 40.00
CH Cole Hamels/35 40.00 80.00
CJ Chipper Jones/35 75.00 150.00
CK Clayton Kershaw/35 50.00 100.00
CL Carlos Lee/35 10.00 25.00
CU Chase Utley/35 75.00 150.00
CW Chien-Ming Wang/35 50.00 100.00
CY Chris B. Young/35 30.00 60.00
DL Derrek Lee/35 60.00 120.00
DO David Ortiz/35 50.00 100.00
DS Don Sutton/35 40.00 80.00
EC Eric Chavez/35 15.00 40.00
EL Evan Longoria/35 75.00 150.00
EM Edgar Martinez/35 100.00 175.00
FC Carlton Fisk/35 15.00 40.00
FH Felix Hernandez/35 40.00 80.00
FI Carlton Fisk/35 20.00 50.00
GA Garrett Atkins/35 10.00 30.00
GR Ken Griffey Sr./35 20.00 50.00
GS Grady Sizemore/35 15.00 40.00
HR Hanley Ramirez/35 50.00 100.00
IK Ian Kinsler/35 30.00 60.00
JH Josh Hamilton/35 40.00 80.00
JL James Loney/35 15.00 40.00
JM Joe Mauer/35 100.00 200.00
JP Jorge Posada/35 100.00 200.00
JR Ken Griffey Jr./35 150.00 250.00
JT Jim Thome/35 40.00 80.00
JU Justin Upton/35 20.00 50.00
JV Jason Varitek/35 40.00 80.00
JW Jered Weaver/35 30.00 60.00
KG Ken Griffey Jr./35 150.00 250.00

KY Kevin Youkilis/35 30.00 60.00
LA Lance Berkman/35 20.00 50.00
LB Lou Brock/35 50.00 100.00
MB Mark Buehrle/35 40.00 80.00
MJ Joe Morgan/35 30.00 60.00
MO Justin Morneau/35 30.00 60.00
MP Pedro Martinez/35 60.00 120.00
MR Mariano Rivera/35 150.00 300.00
MU Eddie Murray/35 60.00 120.00
MY Michael Young/35 15.00 40.00
NI Nick Markakis/35 15.00 40.00
NK Phil Niekro/35 40.00 80.00
NP Phil Niekro/35 40.00 80.00
NR Nolan Ryan/35 125.00 250.00
OM Magglio Ordonez/35 20.00 50.00
OS Ozzie Smith/35 100.00 200.00
OZ Ozzie Smith/35 100.00 200.00
PA Jonathan Papelbon/35 10.00 25.00
PE Jhonny Peralta/35 15.00 40.00
PF Prince Fielder/35 30.00 60.00
PK Paul Konerko/35 40.00 80.00
PN Phil Niekro/35 40.00 80.00
PR Pedro Martinez/35 15.00 40.00
RA Aramis Ramirez/35 20.00 50.00
RB Ryan Braun/35 60.00 120.00
RC Roberto Clemente/35 800.00 1000.00
RD Rod Carew/35 20.00 50.00
RE Jose Reyes/35 30.00 60.00
RF Rafael Furcal/35 15.00 40.00
RJ Reggie Jackson/35 50.00 100.00
RO Roy Oswalt/35 20.00 50.00
RW Rickie Weeks/35 20.00 50.00
RY Robin Yount/35 50.00 100.00
RZ Ryan Zimmerman/35 30.00 60.00
SA Ryne Sandberg/35 100.00 175.00
SM Mike Schmidt/35 75.00 150.00
SP Sparky Anderson/35 50.00 100.00
ST Tom Seaver/35 60.00 120.00
TH Todd Helton/35 30.00 60.00
TL Tim Lincecum/35 150.00 300.00
TR Tim Raines/35 15.00 40.00
TS Tom Seaver/35 20.00 50.00
TT Troy Tulowitzki/35 40.00 80.00
VG Vladimir Guerrero/35 30.00 60.00
VO Joey Votto/35 30.00 60.00
YM Yadier Molina/35 75.00 200.00

2009 Ultimate Collection Ultimate Quad Materials Signature

ONE AU,MEM, OR AU MEM PER PACK
PRINT RUNS B/WN 6-36 COPIES PER
NO PRICING ON QTY 25 OR LESS
BR Jay Bruce/32 15.00 40.00
JL Jon Lester/35 15.00 40.00
JP Jonathan Papelbon/36 10.00 25.00

2009 Ultimate Collection Ultimate Signatures

ONE AU,MEM, OR AU MEM PER PACK
PRINT RUNS B/WN 2-50 COPIES PER
NO PRICING ON QTY 25 OR LESS
BM Brian McCann/46 10.00 25.00
BU B.J. Upton/35 6.00 15.00
JC Joba Chamberlain/27 20.00 50.00
KU Koji Uehara/50 20.00 50.00
DJ1 Derek Jeter/50 100.00 200.00
DJ2 Derek Jeter/50 100.00 200.00
DJ3 Derek Jeter/50 100.00 200.00
DJ4 Derek Jeter/50 100.00 200.00
HR1 Hanley Ramirez/26 15.00 40.00
HR2 Hanley Ramirez/50 12.50 30.00
KG1 Ken Griffey Jr./50 60.00 120.00
KG5 Ken Griffey Jr./30 60.00 120.00
KG6 Ken Griffey Jr./30 60.00 120.00
KG7 Ken Griffey Jr./50 60.00 120.00
KG9 Ken Griffey Jr./50 60.00 120.00
KG10 Ken Griffey Jr./50 60.00 120.00
NM1 Nick Markakis/39 12.50 30.00

2009 Ultimate Collection Ultimate Six Memorabilia

ONE AU,MEM, OR AU MEM PER PACK
PRINT RUNS B/WN 20-50 COPIES PER
NO PRICING ON QTY 25 OR LESS
U6M4 Bo/Sm/Ri/Je/Ri/Yo 30.00 60.00
U6M11 Ja/Pu/Sm/Je/Sa/Le 30.00 60.00
U6M14 Pe/Wi/Ri/Ro/Ma/Yo 15.00 40.00
U6M15 Bi/Ki/Jo/Gr/Pe/Ry 15.00 40.00
U6M21 Ro/Ri/We/Yo/Ca/Ri 12.50 30.00
U6M22 Ri/Bo/Yo/Ri/Mo/Ca 15.00 40.00
U6M23 Bu/Ma/Wi/Je/Di/Cl 50.00 100.00
U6M25 Si/Je/Pa/El/Fe/Va 30.00 60.00

2009 Ultimate Collection Ultimate Triple Patch Signature

OVERALL AU-MEM CARDS 1:5 HOBBY PACKS
PRINT RUNS B/WN 2-29 COPIES PER
NO PRICING ON QTY 25 OR LESS
HP Hunter Pence/26 20.00 50.00
HR Hanley Ramirez/28 20.00 50.00
MK Matt Kemp/29 50.00 100.00
NM Nick Markakis/27 12.00 30.00

2009 Ultimate Collection Ultimate Triple Signatures

OVERALL AU ODDS 1:15 HOBBY PACKS
PRINT RUNS B/WN 5-30 COPIES PER
NO PRICING ON QTY 25 OR LESS
UTS3 Joba/Jeter/Dent/30 150.00 250.00
UTS4 Grif Jr./Braun/Markakis/26 75.00 150.00
UTS11 Griff Jr./Bo/B.Upton/26 100.00 175.00

2005 Ultimate Signature

COMMON CARD (1-50) .75 2.00
COMMON CARD (51-100) .75 2.00
1-100 PRINT RUN 825 SERIAL #'d SETS
COMMON AUTO (101-110) 4.00 10.00
COMMON AU RC (101-110) 4.00 10.00
101-110 STATED ODDS 1:20
101-110 PRINT RUN 225 SERIAL #'d SETS
COMMON AUTO (111-193) 4.00 10.00
111-193 ODDS APPX 1:8 '05 UD UPDATE
111-193 PRINT RUN 125 SERIAL #'d SETS
113, 123, 126-127, 150, 163 DO NOT EXIST
170, 189 DO NOT EXIST
1 Al Kaline 2.00 5.00
2 Babe Ruth 5.00 12.00
3 Billy Williams 1.25 3.00
4 Bob Feller 1.25 3.00
5 Bob Gibson 1.25 3.00
6 Brooks Robinson 1.25 3.00
7 Carlton Fisk 1.25 3.00
8 Cy Young 1.25 3.00
9 Dizzy Dean 1.25 3.00
10 Don Drysdale 1.25 3.00
11 Eddie Mathews 2.00 5.00
12 Enos Slaughter 1.25 3.00
13 Ernie Banks 2.00 5.00
14 Fergie Jenkins 1.25 3.00
15 Eddie Murray 1.25 3.00
16 Harmon Killebrew 2.00 5.00
17 Honus Wagner 1.25 3.00
18 Jackie Robinson 1.25 3.00
19 Jimmie Foxx 1.25 3.00
20 Joe DiMaggio 4.00 10.00
21 Joe Morgan 1.25 3.00
22 Juan Marichal 1.25 3.00
23 Larry Doby 1.25 3.00
24 Jim Palmer 1.25 3.00
25 Johnny Bench 2.00 5.00
26 Lou Brock 1.25 3.00
27 Lou Gehrig 4.00 10.00
28 Mel Ott 2.00 5.00
29 Mickey Cochrane 1.25 3.00
30 Mickey Mantle 6.00 15.00
31 Mike Schmidt 3.00 8.00
32 Nolan Ryan 6.00 15.00
33 Pee Wee Reese 1.25 3.00
34 Phil Rizzuto 1.25 3.00
35 Ralph Kiner 1.25 3.00
36 Robin Yount 2.00 5.00
37 Ozzie Smith 2.50 6.00
38 Roy Campanella 1.25 3.00
39 Satchel Paige 2.00 5.00
40 Stan Musial 3.00 8.00
41 Ted Williams 4.00 10.00
42 Thurman Munson 1.25 3.00
43 Tom Seaver 1.25 3.00
44 Ty Cobb 3.00 8.00
45 Walter Johnson 1.25 3.00
46 Warren Spahn 1.25 3.00
47 Whitey Ford 1.25 3.00
48 Willie McCovey 1.25 3.00
49 Willie Stargell 1.25 3.00
50 Yogi Berra 2.00 5.00
51 Adrian Beltre 2.00 5.00
52 Albert Pujols 2.50 6.00
53 Alex Rodriguez 2.50 6.00
54 Alfonso Soriano 1.25 3.00
55 Andruw Jones .75 2.00
56 B.J. Upton 1.25 3.00
57 Ben Sheets .75 2.00
58 Bret Boone .75 2.00
59 Brian Giles .75 2.00
60 Carlos Beltran 1.25 3.00
61 Carlos Delgado .75 2.00
62 Chipper Jones 2.00 5.00
63 Curt Schilling 1.25 3.00
64 David Ortiz 2.00 5.00
65 Derek Jeter 5.00 12.00
66 Eric Chavez .75 2.00
67 Frank Thomas 2.00 5.00
68 Gary Sheffield .75 2.00
69 Greg Maddux 2.50 6.00
70 Hank Blalock .75 2.00
71 Hideki Matsui 3.00 8.00
72 Ichiro Suzuki 2.50 6.00
73 Ivan Rodriguez 1.25 3.00
74 Jason Schmidt .75 2.00
75 Jeff Bagwell 1.25 3.00
76 Jim Thome 1.25 3.00
77 Johnny Damon 1.25 3.00
78 Jose Vidro .75 2.00
79 Ken Griffey Jr. 4.00 10.00
80 Kerry Wood .75 2.00
81 Manny Ramirez 2.00 5.00
82 Mark Prior 1.25 3.00
83 Mark Teixeira 1.25 3.00
84 Miguel Cabrera 2.00 5.00
85 Miguel Tejada 1.25 3.00
86 Mike Mussina 1.25 3.00
87 Mike Piazza 2.00 5.00
88 Mike Sweeney .75 2.00
89 Oliver Perez .75 2.00
90 Pedro Martinez 2.00 5.00
91 Rafael Palmeiro 1.25 3.00
92 Randy Johnson 2.00 5.00
93 Roger Clemens 2.50 6.00
94 Sammy Sosa 2.00 5.00
95 Scott Rolen 1.25 3.00
96 Tim Hudson 1.25 3.00
97 Todd Helton 1.25 3.00
98 Torii Hunter .75 2.00
99 Victor Martinez 1.25 3.00
100 Vladimir Guerrero 1.25 3.00
101 Adrian Gonzalez AU 15.00 40.00
102 Ambiorix Burgos AU RC 4.00 10.00
103 Ambiorix Concepcion AU RC 4.00 10.00
104 Dan Meyer AU 4.00 10.00
105 Ervin Santana AU 6.00 15.00
106 Gavin Floyd AU 4.00 10.00
107 Joe Blanton AU 4.00 10.00
108 Eric Crozier AU 4.00 10.00
109 Mark Teahen AU 4.00 10.00
110 Ryan Howard AU 12.50 30.00
111 Adam Shabala AU RC 4.00 10.00
112 Anibal Sanchez AU RC 10.00 25.00
114 Brandon McCarthy AU RC 12.50 30.00
115 Brian Burres AU RC 4.00 10.00
116 Carlos Ruiz AU RC 10.00 25.00
117 Casey Rogowski AU RC 6.00 15.00
118 Chad Orvella AU RC 4.00 10.00
119 Chris Resop AU RC 6.00 15.00
120 Chris Roberson AU RC 4.00 10.00
121 Chris Seddon AU RC 4.00 10.00
122 Colter Bean AU RC 6.00 15.00
124 Dave Gassner AU RC 4.00 10.00
125 Brian Anderson AU RC 15.00 40.00
128 Devon Lowery AU RC 4.00 10.00
129 Enrique Gonzalez AU RC 6.00 15.00
130 Eude Brito AU RC 4.00 10.00
131 Francisco Butto AU RC 4.00 10.00
132 Franquelis Osoria AU RC 4.00 10.00
133 Garrett Jones AU RC 6.00 15.00
134 Geovany Soto AU RC 10.00 25.00
135 Hayden Penn AU RC 8.00 20.00
136 Ismael Ramirez AU RC 4.00 10.00
137 Jared Gothreaux AU RC 4.00 10.00
138 Jason Hammel AU RC 10.00 25.00
139 Jeff Miller AU RC 4.00 10.00
140 Jeff Niemann AU RC 8.00 20.00
141 Joel Peralta AU RC 4.00 10.00
142 John Hattig AU RC 4.00 10.00
143 Jorge Campillo AU RC 4.00 10.00
144 Juan Morillo AU RC 4.00 10.00
145 Justin Verlander AU RC 75.00 150.00
146 Ryan Garko AU RC 12.50 30.00
147 Keiichi Yabu AU RC 6.00 15.00
148 Kendry Morales AU RC 6.00 15.00
149 Luis Hernandez AU RC 4.00 10.00
151 Luis O.Rodriguez AU RC 4.00 10.00
152 Luke Scott AU RC 12.50 30.00
153 Marcos Carvajal AU RC 4.00 10.00
154 Mark Woodyard AU RC 4.00 10.00
155 Matt A.Smith AU RC 4.00 10.00
156 Matthew Lindstrom AU RC 4.00 10.00
157 Miguel Negron AU RC 6.00 15.00
158 Mike Morse AU RC 6.00 15.00
159 Nate McLouth AU RC 8.00 20.00
160 Nelson Cruz AU RC 60.00 150.00
161 Nick Masset AU RC 4.00 10.00
162 Mark McLemore AU RC 4.00 10.00
164 Paulino Reynoso AU RC 4.00 10.00
165 Pedro Lopez AU RC 4.00 10.00
166 Pete Orr AU RC 4.00 10.00
167 Philip Humber AU RC 4.00 10.00
168 Prince Fielder AU RC 30.00 60.00
169 Randy Messenger AU RC 4.00 10.00
171 Raul Tablado AU RC 4.00 10.00
172 Ronny Paulino AU RC 6.00 15.00
173 Russ Rohlicek AU RC 4.00 10.00
174 Russell Martin AU RC 10.00 25.00
175 Scott Baker AU RC 6.00 15.00
176 Scott Munter AU RC 4.00 10.00
177 Sean Thompson AU RC 4.00 10.00
178 Sean Tracey AU RC 4.00 10.00
179 Shane Costa AU RC 4.00 10.00
180 Stephen Drew AU RC 8.00 20.00
181 Steve Schmoll AU RC 4.00 10.00
182 Tadahito Iguchi AU RC 30.00 60.00
183 Tony Giarratano AU RC 4.00 10.00
184 Tony Pena AU RC 4.00 10.00
185 Travis Bowyer AU RC 4.00 10.00
186 Ubaldo Jimenez AU RC 20.00 50.00
187 Wladimir Balentien AU RC 8.00 20.00
188 Yorman Bazardo AU RC 4.00 10.00
190 Ryan Zimmerman AU RC 12.50 30.00
191 Chris Denorfia AU RC 6.00 15.00
192 Ryan Speier AU RC 4.00 10.00
193 Jermaine Van Buren AU 4.00 10.00

2005 Ultimate Signature Cy Young Dual Autograph

OVERALL DUAL AU ODDS 1:4
PRINT RUNS B/WN 15-250 COPIES PER
NO PRICING ON QTY OF 25 OR LESS
EXCHANGE DEADLINE 06/07/08
EG D.Eckersley/E.Gagne/200 15.00 40.00
ES D.Eck/B.Sutter/250 12.50 30.00
GF R.Guidry/W.Ford/175 30.00 60.00
GM B.Gibson/D.McLain/175 20.00 50.00
LC S.Lyle/S.Carlton/250 15.00 40.00
MS D.McLain/T.Seaver/100 30.00 80.00
NF D.Newcombe/W.Ford/125 50.00 100.00
PC G.Perry/S.Carlton/250 12.50 30.00
PS J.Palmer/T.Seaver/100 40.00 100.00

2005 Ultimate Signature Decades

TIER 3 PRINT RUNS 350+ PER
TIER 2 PRINT RUNS B/WN 225-275 PER
TIER 1 PRINT RUNS B/WN 100-175 PER
SERIAL #'d PRINT RUNS B/WN 10-99 PER
NO PRICING ON #'d QTY OF 25 OR LESS
TIER 1-3 PRINT RUN INFO PROVIDED BY UD
TIER 1-3 ARE NOT SERIAL-NUMBERED
STATED ODDS 3:5 TINS
PLATINUM OVERALL PREMIUM AU ODDS 1:5
PLATINUM PRINT RUN 1 SERIAL #'d SET
NO PLATINUM PRICING DUE TO SCARCITY
EXCHANGE DEADLINE 06/07/08
AD Andre Dawson T2 12.50 30.00
AK Al Kaline/99 25.00 50.00
AR Al Rosen T3 6.00 15.00
BD Bobby Doerr T3 8.00 20.00
BF Bob Feller T1 10.00 25.00
BJ Bo Jackson/50 40.00 80.00
BM Bill Mazeroski/99 15.00 40.00
BR Brooks Robinson T2 10.00 25.00
BS Ben Sheets T3 6.00 15.00
BU B.J. Upton T3 6.00 15.00
BW Billy Williams T2 8.00 20.00
CB Carlos Beltran/99 8.00 20.00
DE Dennis Eckersley T1 8.00 20.00
DJ Derek Jeter/99 125.00 200.00
DL Don Larsen/99 EXCH 6.00 15.00
DN Don Newcombe/99 10.00 25.00
DO David Ortiz T1 20.00 50.00
FJ Fergie Jenkins/50 12.50 30.00
FL Fred Lynn T2 8.00 20.00
GC Gary Carter/50 12.50 30.00
GK George Kell T3 8.00 20.00
GP Gaylord Perry Giants T3 8.00 20.00
GP1 Gaylord Perry Rgr T3 8.00 20.00
HK Harmon Killebrew/99 20.00 50.00
JB Jim Bunning T2 6.00 15.00
JC Jose Canseco/99 20.00 50.00
JM Juan Marichal/99 10.00 25.00
JP Jim Palmer T2 6.00 15.00
JR Jim Rice T2 6.00 15.00
JS Johan Santana T1 10.00 25.00
KG Ken Griffey Jr. T1 60.00 150.00
KH Keith Hernandez Cards T3 6.00 15.00
KH1 Keith Hernandez Mets T3 6.00 15.00
LA Luis Aparicio W.Sox T1 8.00 20.00
LA1 Luis Aparicio R.Sox T1 8.00 20.00
LB Lou Brock/50 20.00 50.00
LT Luis Tiant Twins T3 8.00 20.00
LT1 Luis Tiant Sox T3 8.00 20.00
MC Miguel Cabrera T2 25.00 60.00
MI Monte Irvin T3 8.00 20.00
MG Joe Morgan/50 12.50 30.00
MT Mark Teixeira T3 6.00 15.00
MU Dale Murphy T3 10.00 25.00
MW Maury Wills T2 6.00 15.00
OC Orlando Cepeda T2 6.00 15.00
PM Paul Molitor/99 10.00 25.00
PN Phil Niekro T2 6.00 15.00
RC Rocky Colavito Indians T1 30.00 60.00
RC1 Rocky Colavito Tigers T1 30.00 60.00
RF Rollie Fingers T2 6.00 15.00
RG Ron Guidry T3 10.00 25.00
RK Ralph Kiner/99 15.00 40.00
RO Roy Oswalt T3 6.00 15.00
RS Ron Santo T2 15.00 40.00
RW Rickie Weeks T3 6.00 15.00
SC Steve Carlton Cards T1 12.50 30.00
SC1 Steve Carlton Phils T1 12.50 30.00
SU Don Sutton T1 6.00 15.00
TP Tony Perez T2 8.00 20.00
WC Will Clark/99 12.00 30.00

2005 Ultimate Signature Hits Dual Autograph

OVERALL DUAL AU ODDS 1:4
PRINT RUNS B/WN 15-125 COPIES PER
NO PRICING ON QTY OF 15
EXCHANGE DEADLINE 06/07/08
BM L.Brock/S.Musial/35 75.00 150.00
MY P.Molitor/R.Yount/125 40.00 80.00
WG D.Winfield/T.Gwynn/35 50.00 100.00
YB C.Yastrzemski/W.Boggs/35 75.00 150.00

2005 Ultimate Signature Home Runs Dual Autograph

OVERALL DUAL AU ODDS 1:4
PRINT RUNS B/WN 15-250 COPIES PER
NO PRICING ON QTY OF 25 OR LESS
EXCHANGE DEADLINE 06/07/08
GM K.Grif Jr./W.McCovey/250 60.00 120.00
RG F.Robinson/K.Griffey Jr./250 75.00 150.00

2005 Ultimate Signature Immortal Inscriptions

OVERALL PREMIUM SINGLE AU 1:5
PRINT RUNS B/WN 10-99 COPIES PER
NO PRICING ON QTY OF 25 OR LESS
PLATINUM OVERALL PREMIUM AU ODDS 1:5
PLATINUM PRINT RUN 1 SERIAL #'d SET
NO PLATINUM PRICING DUE TO SCARCITY
BR B.Robinson Hoover/99 40.00 80.00
DM D.Matt Donnie Baseball/75 150.00 250.00
EG E.Gagne Game Over/99 40.00 80.00
FT F.Thomas Big Hurt/50 100.00 200.00
JB J.Bunning Senator/99 40.00 80.00
KG K.Griffey Jr. Junior/99 400.00 500.00
OS O.Smith The Wizard/75 50.00 100.00
SC S.Carlton Lefty/99 20.00 50.00
TG T.Gwynn The Tiger/50 60.00 120.00
WB W.Boggs Chicken Man/75 50.00 120.00
WC W.Clark The Thrill/99 40.00 80.00

2005 Ultimate Signature MVP's Dual Autograph

OVERALL DUAL AU ODDS 1:4
PRINT RUNS B/WN 15-250 COPIES PER
NO PRICING ON QTY OF 25 OR LESS
EXCHANGE DEADLINE 06/07/08
BM D.Mattingly 60.00 150.00
Y.Berra/175
CM O.Cepeda/S.Musial/100 50.00 100.00
DS A.Dawson/R.Sandberg/175 60.00 120.00
EF D.Eckersley/R.Fingers/250 15.00 40.00
GM K.Grif Jr./J.Morg/250 60.00 100.00
HY K.Hernandez/R.Yount/200 20.00 50.00
JR C.Jones/I.Rodriguez/35 100.00 175.00
KC H.Killebrew/R.Carew/100 60.00 120.00
LM F.Lynn/J.Morgan/200 20.00 50.00
LW B.Larkin/M.Wills/250 20.00 50.00
MG B.Gibson/D.McLain/175 20.00 50.00
PR D.Parker/J.Rice/250 20.00 50.00
SF M.Schmidt/R.Fingers/175 30.00 60.00
SS M.Schmidt/R.Sandberg/75 100.00 175.00
TB F.Thomas/J.Bagwell/50 175.00 350.00
YC C.Yaz/O.Cepeda/100 40.00 80.00
YS C.Yastrzemski/J.Rice/100 40.00 80.00

2005 Ultimate Signature No-Hitters Dual Autograph

OVERALL DUAL AU ODDS 1:4
PRINT RUNS B/WN 15-250 COPIES PER
NO PRICING ON QTY OF 25 OR LESS
EXCHANGE DEADLINE 06/07/08
BG J.Bunning/B.Gibson/125 20.00 50.00
CL D.Cone/D.Larsen/250 20.00 50.00
GP B.Gibson/J.Palmer/125 30.00 60.00

2005 Ultimate Signature Numbers

OVERALL PREMIUM SINGLE AU 1:5
PRINT RUNS B/WN 1-49 COPIES PER
NO PRICING ON QTY OF 24 OR LESS
PLATINUM OVERALL PREMIUM AU ODDS 1:5
PLATINUM PRINT RUN 1 SERIAL #'d SET
NO PLATINUM PRICING DUE TO SCARCITY
EXCHANGE DEADLINE 06/07/08
BG Bob Gibson/45 12.00 30.00
BW Billy Williams/26 12.00 30.00
CA Rod Carew/29 20.00 50.00
CF Carlton Fisk/27 20.00 50.00
DO David Ortiz/34 30.00 60.00
DW Dave Winfield/31 20.00 50.00
EM Eddie Murray/33 20.00 50.00
FJ Fergie Jenkins/31 12.00 30.00
FT Frank Thomas/35 40.00 80.00
GL Tom Glavine/47 20.00 50.00
JC Jose Canseco/33 30.00 60.00
JS John Smoltz/29 20.00 50.00
KG Ken Griffey Jr./30 75.00 150.00
KP Kirby Puckett/34 50.00 100.00
KW Kerry Wood/34 6.00 15.00
MA Juan Marichal/27 12.00 30.00
NR Nolan Ryan/34 125.00 250.00
OC Orlando Cepeda/30 12.00 30.00
PI Mike Piazza/31 60.00 120.00
RF Rollie Fingers/34 12.00 30.00
RG Ron Guidry/49 20.00 50.00
RJ Randy Johnson/41 50.00 100.00
RO Roy Oswalt/44 12.00 30.00
SC Steve Carlton/32 15.00 40.00
SR Scott Rolen/27 6.00 15.00
TS Tom Seaver/41 30.00 80.00
VG Vladimir Guerrero/27 12.00 30.00
WB Wade Boggs/26 20.00 50.00
WM Willie McCovey/44 20.00 50.00

2005 Ultimate Signature ROY Dual Autograph

OVERALL DUAL AU ODDS 1:4
PRINT RUNS B/WN 15-250 COPIES PER
NO PRICING ON QTY OF 25 OR LESS
EXCHANGE DEADLINE 06/07/08
CM O.Cepeda/W.McCovey/75 30.00 60.00
FB C.Fisk/J.Bench/35 50.00 100.00
FL C.Fisk/F.Lynn/125 40.00 80.00
GR N.Garc/S.Rolen/200 10.00 25.00
JG D.Jeter/N.Garciaparra/75 200.00 400.00
RA F.Robinson/L.Aparicio/125 20.00 50.00
RJ C.Ripken/D.Jeter/75 250.00 500.00
SG D.Straw/D.Gooden/250 15.00 40.00
WD B.Williams/A.Dawson/250 15.00 40.00

2005 Ultimate Signature Signs of October Dual Autograph

OVERALL DUAL AU ODDS 1:4
PRINT RUNS B/WN 15-250 COPIES PER
NO PRICING ON QTY OF 25 OR LESS
EXCHANGE DEADLINE 06/07/08
BW B.Buckr/M.Wils/250 40.00 100.00
CS J.Cart/J.Smoltz/250 30.00 60.00
EG D.Eckersley/K.Gibson/200 50.00 100.00
FM C.Fisk/J.Morgan/100 20.00 50.00
GB B.Gibson/L.Brock/100 50.00 100.00
GG S.Garvey/R.Guidry/250 20.00 50.00
GL B.Gibson/M.Lolich/100 40.00 80.00
JG D.Jeter/T.Gwynn/250 150.00 300.00
LB D.Larsen/Y.Berra/250 50.00 120.00
MP J.Morris/K.Puckett/100 150.00 250.00
PS K.Puckett/O.Smith/35 150.00 300.00
RR B.Robinson/F.Rob/250 40.00 100.00
SY O.Smith/R.Yount/100 40.00 80.00
TG A.Trammell/K.Gibson/250 12.50 30.00

2005 Ultimate Signature Supremacy

OVERALL PREMIUM SINGLE AU 1:5
PRINT RUNS B/WN 15-99 COPIES PER
NO PRICING ON QTY 25 OR LESS
EXCHANGE DEADLINE 06/07/08
AD Andre Dawson/99 6.00 15.00
AK Al Kaline/50 30.00 80.00
AR Al Rosen/99 6.00 15.00
BD Bobby Doerr/99 6.00 15.00
BF Bob Feller/99 15.00 40.00
BM Bill Mazeroski/50 6.00 15.00
BR Brooks Robinson/99 15.00 40.00
BS Ben Sheets/99 6.00 15.00
BU Jim Bunning/99 6.00 15.00
BW Billy Williams/99 6.00 15.00
DJ Derek Jeter/50 150.00 250.00
DM Dale Murphy/99 15.00 40.00
DN Don Newcombe/99 6.00 15.00
DO David Ortiz/99 20.00 50.00
EC Eric Chavez/99 6.00 15.00
EG Eric Gagne/50 20.00 50.00
GK George Kell/99 15.00 40.00
HB Hank Blalock/50 15.00 40.00
HK Harmon Killebrew/50 40.00 80.00
JP Jim Palmer/99 6.00 15.00
JR Jim Rice/99 6.00 15.00
JS Johan Santana/99 6.00 15.00
KG Ken Griffey Jr./99 50.00 100.00
LA Luis Aparicio/50 15.00 40.00
MC Miguel Cabrera/99 20.00 50.00
MI Monte Irvin/99 6.00 15.00
MM Mark Mulder/99 6.00 15.00
MT Mark Teixeira/99 15.00 40.00
OC Orlando Cepeda/99 6.00 15.00
PM Paul Molitor/50 12.00 30.00
RF Rollie Fingers/99 6.00 15.00
RG Ron Guidry/99 8.00 20.00
RO Roy Oswalt/99 6.00 15.00
RR Robin Roberts/99 6.00 15.00
RS Ron Santo/99 15.00 40.00
SC Steve Carlton/99 12.00 30.00
SM John Smoltz/50 20.00 50.00
TH Tim Hudson/50 20.00 50.00
TP Tony Perez/99 6.00 15.00
WC Will Clark/50 20.00 50.00

1999 Ultimate Victory

The 1999 Upper Deck Ultimate Victory Product was issued late in 1999. The cards were distributed in five card packs with a SRP of $2.99 per pack and each box had 24 packs in it. The set, consisting of 180 cards has 120 cards printed in normal quantities and 60 short prints. The cards from 121 through 150 feature players in their rookie campaign and cards numbered 151 through 180 all feature Mark McGwire in a set entitled "McGwire's Magic". Cards 121-180 were all released at a rate of one in four. Rookie Cards of Rick Ankiel, Josh Beckett, Pat Burrell, Freddy Garcia, Tim Hudson, Eric Munson, and Alfonso Soriano are all included in this set.

COMPLETE SET (180) 75.00 150.00
COMP.SET w/o SP's (120) 10.00 25.00
COMMON CARD (1-120) .10 .30
COMMON SP (121-150) .75 2.00
121-150 STATED ODDS 1:4
COMMON MCGWIRE (151-180) .75 2.00
151-180 STATED ODDS 1:4
CONDITION SENSITIVE SET
1 Troy Glaus .20 .50
2 Tim Salmon .20 .50
3 Mo Vaughn .10 .30
4 Garret Anderson .10 .30
5 Darin Erstad .10 .30
6 Randy Johnson .30 .75
7 Matt Williams .10 .30
8 Travis Lee .10 .30
9 Jay Bell .10 .30
10 Steve Finley .10 .30
11 Luis Gonzalez .10 .30
12 Greg Maddux .50 1.25
13 Chipper Jones .30 .75
14 Javy Lopez .10 .30
15 Tom Glavine .20 .50
16 John Smoltz .20 .50
17 Cal Ripken 1.00 2.50
18 Charles Johnson .10 .30
19 Albert Belle .10 .30
20 Mike Mussina .20 .50
21 Pedro Martinez .20 .50
22 Nomar Garciaparra .50 1.25
23 Jose Offerman .10 .30
24 Sammy Sosa .30 .75
25 Mark Grace .20 .50
26 Kerry Wood .10 .30
27 Frank Thomas .30 .75
28 Ray Durham .10 .30
29 Paul Konerko .10 .30
30 Pete Harnisch .10 .30
31 Greg Vaughn .10 .30
32 Sean Casey .10 .30
33 Manny Ramirez .20 .50
34 Jim Thome .20 .50
35 Sandy Alomar Jr. .10 .30
36 Roberto Alomar .20 .50
37 Travis Fryman .10 .30
38 Kenny Lofton .10 .30
39 Omar Vizquel .20 .50
40 Larry Walker .10 .30
41 Todd Helton .20 .50
42 Vinny Castilla .10 .30
43 Tony Clark .10 .30
44 Juan Encarnacion .10 .30
45 Dean Palmer .10 .30
46 Damion Easley .10 .30
47 Mark Kotsay .10 .30
48 Cliff Floyd .10 .30
49 Jeff Bagwell .20 .50
50 Ken Caminiti .10 .30
51 Craig Biggio .20 .50
52 Moises Alou .10 .30
53 Johnny Damon .20 .50
54 Larry Sutton .10 .30
55 Kevin Brown .20 .50
56 Adrian Beltre .10 .30
57 Raul Mondesi .10 .30
58 Gary Sheffield .10 .30
59 Jeromy Burnitz .10 .30
60 Sean Berry .10 .30
61 Jeff Cirillo .10 .30
62 Brad Radke .10 .30
63 Todd Walker .10 .30
64 Matt Lawton .10 .30
65 Vladimir Guerrero .30 .75
66 Rondell White .10 .30
67 Dustin Hermanson .10 .30
68 Mike Piazza .50 1.25
69 Rickey Henderson .30 .75
70 Robin Ventura .10 .30
71 John Olerud .10 .30
72 Derek Jeter .75 2.00
73 Roger Clemens .60 1.50
74 Orlando Hernandez .10 .30
75 Paul O'Neill .20 .50
76 Bernie Williams .20 .50
77 Chuck Knoblauch .10 .30
78 Tino Martinez .20 .50
79 Jason Giambi .10 .30
80 Ben Grieve .10 .30
81 Matt Stairs .10 .30
82 Scott Rolen .20 .50
83 Ron Gant .10 .30
84 Bobby Abreu .10 .30
85 Curt Schilling .10 .30
86 Brian Giles .10 .30
87 Jason Kendall .10 .30
88 Kevin Young .10 .30
89 Mark McGwire .75 2.00
90 Fernando Tatis .10 .30
91 Ray Lankford .10 .30
92 Eric Davis .10 .30
93 Tony Gwynn .40 1.00
94 Reggie Sanders .10 .30
95 Wally Joyner .10 .30
96 Trevor Hoffman .10 .30
97 Robb Nen .10 .30
98 Barry Bonds .75 2.00
99 Jeff Kent .10 .30
100 J.T. Snow .10 .30
101 Ellis Burks .10 .30
102 Ken Griffey Jr. .60 1.50
103 Alex Rodriguez .50 1.25
104 Jay Buhner .10 .30
105 Edgar Martinez .20 .50
106 David Bell .10 .30
107 Bobby Smith .10 .30
108 Wade Boggs .20 .50
109 Fred McGriff .20 .50
110 Rolando Arrojo .10 .30
111 Jose Canseco .20 .50
112 Ivan Rodriguez .20 .50
113 Juan Gonzalez .10 .30
114 Rafael Palmeiro .20 .50
115 Rusty Greer .10 .30
116 Todd Zeile .10 .30
117 Jose Cruz Jr. .10 .30
118 Carlos Delgado .10 .30
119 Shawn Green .10 .30
120 David Wells .10 .30
121 Eric Munson SP RC 1.25 3.00
122 Lance Berkman SP 1.25 3.00
123 Ed Yarnall SP .75 2.00
124 Jacque Jones SP 1.25 3.00
125 Kyle Farnsworth SP RC 1.25 3.00
126 Ryan Rupe SP RC .75 2.00
127 Jeff Weaver SP RC 1.25 3.00
128 Gabe Kapler SP 1.25 3.00
129 Alex Gonzalez SP .75 2.00
130 Randy Wolf SP .75 2.00
131 Ben Davis SP .75 2.00
132 Carlos Beltran SP 2.00 5.00
133 Jim Morris SP RC 2.00 5.00
134 Jeff Zimmerman SP RC 1.25 3.00
135 Bruce Aven SP .75 2.00
136 Alfonso Soriano SP RC 6.00 15.00
137 Tim Hudson SP RC 5.00 12.00
138 Josh Beckett SP RC 6.00 15.00
139 Michael Barrett SP .75 2.00
140 Eric Chavez SP 1.25 3.00
141 Pat Burrell SP RC 5.00 12.00
142 Kris Benson SP .75 2.00
143 J.D. Drew SP 1.25 3.00
144 Matt Clement SP 1.25 3.00
145 Rick Ankiel SP RC 5.00 12.00
146 Vernon Wells SP 1.25 3.00
147 Ruben Mateo SP UER .75 2.00
148 Roy Halladay SP 3.00 8.00
149 Joe McEwing SP RC 1.25 3.00
150 Freddy Garcia SP RC 3.00 8.00
151 Mark McGwire MM .75 2.00
152 Mark McGwire MM .75 2.00
153 Mark McGwire MM .75 2.00
154 Mark McGwire MM .75 2.00
155 Mark McGwire MM .75 2.00
156 Mark McGwire MM .75 2.00
157 Mark McGwire MM .75 2.00
158 Mark McGwire MM .75 2.00
159 Mark McGwire MM .75 2.00
160 Mark McGwire MM .75 2.00
161 Mark McGwire MM .75 2.00
162 Mark McGwire MM .75 2.00
163 Mark McGwire MM .75 2.00
164 Mark McGwire MM .75 2.00
165 Mark McGwire MM .75 2.00
166 Mark McGwire MM .75 2.00
167 Mark McGwire MM .75 2.00
168 Mark McGwire MM .75 2.00
169 Mark McGwire MM .75 2.00
170 Mark McGwire MM .75 2.00
171 Mark McGwire MM .75 2.00
172 Mark McGwire MM .75 2.00
173 Mark McGwire MM .75 2.00
174 Mark McGwire MM .75 2.00
175 Mark McGwire MM .75 2.00
176 Mark McGwire MM .75 2.00
177 Mark McGwire MM .75 2.00
178 Mark McGwire MM .75 2.00
179 Mark McGwire MM .75 2.00
180 Mark McGwire MM .75 2.00

1999 Ultimate Victory Parallel

*PARALLEL 1-120: 2X TO 5X BASIC
*PARALLEL 121-150: .6X TO 1.5X BASIC
*PARALLEL 121-150: .6X TO 1.5X BASIC RC
*MCGWIRE 151-180: 2X TO 5X BASIC
STATED ODDS 1:12
136 Alfonso Soriano 40.00 80.00
138 Josh Beckett 10.00 25.00
145 Rick Ankiel 100.00 200.00

1999 Ultimate Victory Parallel 100

*PAR.100 1-120: 5X TO 12X BASIC
*PAR.100 121-150: 1.5X TO 4X BASIC
*PAR.100 121-150: 2X TO 4X BASIC RC
*MCGWIRE 151-180: 3X TO 8X BASIC
RANDOM INSERTS IN PACKS
STATED PRINT RUN 100 SERIAL #'d SETS
136 Alfonso Soriano 100.00 200.00
138 Josh Beckett 30.00 60.00
145 Rick Ankiel 200.00 300.00

1999 Ultimate Victory Bleacher Reachers

COMPLETE SET (11) 20.00 50.00
STATED ODDS 1:23
BR1 Ken Griffey Jr. 2.00 5.00
BR2 Mark McGwire 2.50 6.00
BR3 Sammy Sosa 1.00 2.50
BR4 Barry Bonds 2.50 6.00
BR5 Nomar Garciaparra 1.50 4.00
BR6 Juan Gonzalez .40 1.00
BR7 Jose Canseco .60 1.50
BR8 Manny Ramirez .60 1.50
BR9 Mike Piazza 1.50 4.00
BR10 Jeff Bagwell .60 1.50
BR11 Alex Rodriguez 1.50 4.00

1999 Ultimate Victory Fame-Used Memorabilia

RANDOM INSERTS IN PACKS
350 OF EACH CARD EXCEPT HOF CARD
HOF PRINT RUN 99 SERIAL #'d CARDS
GB George Brett 10.00 25.00
NR Nolan Ryan 15.00 40.00
OC Orlando Cepeda 4.00 10.00
RY Robin Yount 6.00 15.00
HOF Ryan/Brett/Yount/Cepeda 60.00 120.00

1999 Ultimate Victory Frozen Ropes

COMPLETE SET (10) 20.00 50.00
STATED ODDS 1:23
F1 Ken Griffey Jr. 2.00 5.00
F2 Mark McGwire 2.50 6.00
F3 Sammy Sosa 1.00 2.50
F4 Derek Jeter 2.50 6.00
F5 Tony Gwynn 1.25 3.00
F6 Nomar Garciaparra 1.50 4.00
F7 Alex Rodriguez 1.50 4.00
F8 Mike Piazza 1.50 4.00
F9 Mo Vaughn .40 1.00
F10 Craig Biggio .60 1.50

1999 Ultimate Victory STATure

COMPLETE SET (15) 10.00 25.00
STATED ODDS 1:6
S1 Ken Griffey Jr. .60 1.50
S2 Mark McGwire .75 2.00
S3 Sammy Sosa .30 .75
S4 Nomar Garciaparra .50 1.25
S5 Roger Clemens .60 1.50
S6 Greg Maddux .50 1.25
S7 Alex Rodriguez .50 1.25
S8 Derek Jeter .75 2.00
S9 Juan Gonzalez .10 .30
S10 Manny Ramirez .20 .50
S11 Mike Piazza .50 1.25
S12 Tony Gwynn .40 1.00
S13 Chipper Jones .30 .75
S14 Pedro Martinez .20 .50
S15 Frank Thomas .30 .75

1999 Ultimate Victory Tribute 1999

COMPLETE SET (4) 6.00 15.00
STATED ODDS 1:11
T1 Nolan Ryan 2.50 6.00
T2 Robin Yount 1.50 4.00
T3 George Brett 2.50 6.00
T4 Orlando Cepeda .60 1.50

1999 Ultimate Victory Ultimate Competitors

COMPLETE SET (12) 25.00 60.00
STATED ODDS 1:23
U1 Ken Griffey Jr. 2.50 6.00
U2 Roger Clemens 2.50 6.00
U3 Scott Rolen .75 2.00
U4 Greg Maddux 2.00 5.00
U5 Mark McGwire 3.00 8.00
U6 Derek Jeter 3.00 8.00
U7 Randy Johnson 1.25 3.00
U8 Cal Ripken 4.00 10.00
U9 Craig Biggio .75 2.00
U10 Kevin Brown .75 2.00
U11 Chipper Jones 1.25 3.00
U12 Vladimir Guerrero 1.25 3.00

1999 Ultimate Victory Ultimate Hit Men

COMPLETE SET (8) 12.50 30.00
STATED ODDS 1:23
H1 Tony Gwynn 1.00 2.50
H2 Cal Ripken 2.50 6.00
H3 Wade Boggs .50 1.25
H4 Larry Walker .30 .75
H5 Alex Rodriguez 1.25 3.00
H6 Derek Jeter 2.00 5.00
H7 Ivan Rodriguez .50 1.25
H8 Ken Griffey Jr. 1.50 4.00

2000 Ultimate Victory

COMP.SET w/o SP's (90) 10.00 25.00
COMMON CARD (1-90) .12 .30
COMMON RC/1000 .75 2.00
RC/1000 PRINT RUN 1000 SERIAL #'d SETS
COMMON RC/2500 .50 1.25
RC/2500 PRINT RUN 2500 SERIAL #'d SETS
COMMON RC/3500 .40 1.00
RC/3500 PRINT RUN 3500 SERIAL #'d SETS
91-120 RANDOM INSERTS IN PACKS
1 Mo Vaughn .12 .30
2 Darin Erstad .12 .30
3 Troy Glaus .12 .30
4 Adam Kennedy .12 .30
5 Jason Giambi .12 .30
6 Ben Grieve .12 .30
7 Terrence Long .12 .30
8 Tim Hudson .20 .50
9 David Wells .12 .30
10 Carlos Delgado .12 .30
11 Shannon Stewart .12 .30
12 Greg Vaughn .12 .30
13 Gerald Williams .12 .30
14 Manny Ramirez .30 .75
15 Roberto Alomar .20 .50
16 Jim Thome .20 .50
17 Edgar Martinez .20 .50
18 Alex Rodriguez .40 1.00
19 Matt Riley .12 .30
20 Cal Ripken 1.00 2.50
21 Mike Mussina .20 .50
22 Albert Belle .12 .30
23 Ivan Rodriguez .20 .50
24 Rafael Palmeiro .20 .50
25 Nomar Garciaparra .20 .50
26 Pedro Martinez .20 .50
27 Carl Everett .12 .30
28 Tomokazu Ohka RC .12 .30
29 Jermaine Dye .12 .30
30 Johnny Damon .20 .50
31 Dean Palmer .12 .30
32 Juan Gonzalez .12 .30
33 Eric Milton .12 .30
34 Matt Lawton .12 .30
35 Frank Thomas .30 .75
36 Paul Konerko .12 .30
37 Magglio Ordonez .20 .50
38 Jon Garland .12 .30
39 Derek Jeter .75 2.00
40 Roger Clemens .40 1.00
41 Bernie Williams .20 .50
42 Nick Johnson .12 .30
43 Julio Lugo .12 .30
44 Jeff Bagwell .20 .50
45 Richard Hidalgo .12 .30
46 Chipper Jones .30 .75
47 Greg Maddux .40 1.00
48 Andruw Jones .12 .30
49 Andres Galarraga .20 .50
50 Rafael Furcal .20 .50
51 Jeromy Burnitz .12 .30
52 Geoff Jenkins .12 .30
53 Mark McGwire .50 1.25
54 Jim Edmonds .12 .30
55 Rick Ankiel .20 .50
56 Sammy Sosa .30 .75
57 Julio Zuleta RC .12 .30
58 Kerry Wood .12 .30
59 Randy Johnson .30 .75
60 Matt Williams .12 .30
61 Steve Finley .12 .30
62 Gary Sheffield .12 .30
63 Kevin Brown .12 .30
64 Shawn Green .12 .30
65 Milton Bradley .12 .30
66 Vladimir Guerrero .20 .50
67 Jose Vidro .12 .30
68 Barry Bonds .50 1.25
69 Jeff Kent .12 .30
70 Preston Wilson .12 .30
71 Mike Lowell .12 .30
72 Mike Piazza .30 .75
73 Robin Ventura .12 .30
74 Edgardo Alfonzo .12 .30
75 Jay Payton .12 .30
76 Tony Gwynn .30 .75
77 Adam Eaton .12 .30
78 Phil Nevin .12 .30
79 Scott Rolen .20 .50
80 Bob Abreu .12 .30
81 Pat Burrell .12 .30
82 Brian Giles .12 .30
83 Jason Kendall .12 .30
84 Kris Benson .12 .30
85 Gookie Dawkins .12 .30
86 Ken Griffey Jr. .60 1.50
87 Barry Larkin .20 .50
88 Larry Walker .20 .50
89 Todd Helton .20 .50
90 Ben Petrick .12 .30
91 Alex Cabrera/3500 RC .40 1.00
92 Matt Wheatland/1000 RC .75 2.00
93 Joe Torres/1000 RC .75 2.00
94 Xavier Nady/1000 RC 2.00 5.00
95 Kenny Kelly/3500 RC .40 1.00
96 Matt Ginter/3500 RC .40 1.00
97 Ben Diggins/1000 RC .75 2.00
98 Danys Baez/3500 RC .40 1.00
99 Daylan Holt/2500 RC .50 1.25
100 Kazuhiro Sasaki/3500 RC 1.00 2.50
101 Dane Artman/2500 RC .50 1.25
102 Mike Tonis/1000 RC .75 2.00
103 Timo Perez/2500 RC .75 2.00
104 Barry Zito/2500 RC 4.00 10.00
105 Koyie Hill/2500 RC .50 1.25
106 Brad Wilkerson/2500 RC 1.25 3.00
107 Juan Pierre/3500 RC 2.00 5.00
108 Aaron McNeal/3500 RC .40 1.00
109 Jay Spurgeon/3500 RC .40 1.00
110 Sean Burnett/1000 RC .75 2.00
111 Luis Matos/3500 RC .40 1.00
112 Dave Krynzel/1000 RC .75 2.00
113 Scott Heard/1000 RC .75 2.00
114 Ben Sheets/2500 RC 1.25 3.00
115 Dane Sardinha/1000 RC .75 2.00
116 David Espinosa/1000 RC .75 2.00
117 Leo Estrella/3500 RC .40 1.00
118 Kurt Ainsworth/2500 RC .50 1.25
119 Jon Rauch/2500 RC .50 1.25
120 Ryan Franklin/2500 RC .50 1.25

2000 Ultimate Victory Parallel 25

*PAR.25 1-90: 15X TO 40X BASIC 1-90
STATED PRINT RUN 25 SERIAL #'d SETS
NO ROOKIE PRICING DUE TO SCARCITY

2000 Ultimate Victory Parallel 100

*PAR.100 1-90: 8X TO 20X BASIC 1-90
*TIER 1 91-120: .6X TO 1.5X BASIC 1000
*TIER 2 91-120: 1X TO 2.5X BASIC 2500
*TIER 3 91-120: 1.25X TO 3X BASIC 3500
STATED PRINT RUN 100 SERIAL #'d SETS

2000 Ultimate Victory Parallel 250

*PAR.250 1-90: 3X TO 8X BASIC 1-90
*TIER 1 91-120: .4X TO 1X BASIC 1000
*TIER 2 91-120: .6X TO 1.5X BASIC 2500
*TIER 3 91-120: .75X TO 2X BASIC 3500
STATED PRINT RUN 250 SERIAL #'d SETS

2000 Ultimate Victory Diamond Dignitaries

COMPLETE SET (10) 10.00 25.00
STATED ODDS 1:23
D1 Ken Griffey Jr. 2.00 5.00
D2 Nomar Garciaparra .60 1.50
D3 Chipper Jones 1.00 2.50
D4 Ivan Rodriguez .60 1.50
D5 Mark McGwire 1.50 4.00
D6 Cal Ripken 3.00 8.00
D7 Vladimir Guerrero .60 1.50
D8 Alex Rodriguez 1.25 3.00
D9 Sammy Sosa 1.00 2.50
D10 Derek Jeter 2.50 6.00

2000 Ultimate Victory Hall of Fame Game Jersey

STATED PRINT RUN 500 SETS
TRI-COMBO PRINT RUN 100 #'d CARDS
CF Carlton Fisk 6.00 15.00
SA Sparky Anderson 6.00 15.00
TP Tony Perez 6.00 15.00
HOF Fisk/Anderson/Perez/100 30.00 60.00

2000 Ultimate Victory Lasting Impressions

COMPLETE SET (10) 8.00 20.00
STATED ODDS 1:11
L1 Barry Bonds 1.50 4.00
L2 Mike Piazza 1.00 2.50
L3 Manny Ramirez 1.00 2.50
L4 Pedro Martinez .60 1.50
L5 Mark McGwire 1.50 4.00
L6 Ken Griffey Jr. 2.00 5.00
L7 Ivan Rodriguez .60 1.50
L8 Jeff Bagwell .60 1.50
L9 Randy Johnson 1.00 2.50
L10 Alex Rodriguez 1.25 3.00

2000 Ultimate Victory Starstruck

COMPLETE SET (10) 10.00 25.00
STATED ODDS 1:11
S1 Alex Rodriguez 1.25 3.00
S2 Frank Thomas 1.00 2.50
S3 Derek Jeter 2.50 6.00
S4 Mark McGwire 1.50 4.00
S5 Nomar Garciaparra .60 1.50
S6 Chipper Jones 1.00 2.50
S7 Cal Ripken 3.00 8.00
S8 Sammy Sosa 1.00 2.50
S9 Vladimir Guerrero .60 1.50
S10 Ken Griffey Jr. 2.00 5.00

1991 Ultra

This 400-card standard-size set marked Fleer's first entry into the premium card market. The cards were distributed exclusively in foil-wrapped packs. Fleer claimed in their original press release that there would only be 15 percent the amount of Ultra issued as there was of the regular 1991 Fleer issue. The cards feature full color action photography on the fronts and three full-color photos on the backs. Fleer also issued the sets in their now traditional alphabetical order as well as the teams in alphabetical order. Subsets include Major League Prospects (373-390), Elite Performance (391-396), and Checklists (397-400). Rookie Cards include Eric Karros and Denny Neagle.

COMPLETE SET (400) 8.00 20.00
1 Steve Avery .02 .10
2 Jeff Blauser .02 .10
3 Francisco Cabrera .02 .10
4 Ron Gant .07 .20
5 Tom Glavine .10 .30
6 Tommy Gregg .02 .10
7 Dave Justice .07 .20
8 Oddibe McDowell .02 .10
9 Greg Olson .02 .10
10 Terry Pendleton .07 .20
11 Lonnie Smith .02 .10
12 John Smoltz .10 .30
13 Jeff Treadway .02 .10
14 Glenn Davis .02 .10
15 Mike Devereaux .02 .10
16 Leo Gomez .02 .10
17 Chris Hoiles .02 .10
18 Dave Johnson .02 .10
19 Ben McDonald .02 .10
20 Randy Milligan .02 .10
21 Gregg Olson .02 .10
22 Joe Orsulak .02 .10
23 Bill Ripken .02 .10
24 Cal Ripken .60 1.50
25 David Segui .02 .10
26 Craig Worthington .02 .10
27 Wade Boggs .10 .30
28 Tom Bolton .02 .10
29 Tom Brunansky .02 .10
30 Ellis Burks .07 .20
31 Roger Clemens .60 1.50
32 Mike Greenwell .02 .10
33 Greg A. Harris .02 .10
34 Daryl Irvine RC .02 .10
35 Mike Marshall UER .02 .10
1990 in stats is
shown as 990
36 Tim Naehring .02 .10
37 Tony Pena .02 .10
38 Phil Plantier RC .05 .15
39 Carlos Quintana .02 .10
40 Jeff Reardon .07 .20
41 Jody Reed .02 .10
42 Luis Rivera .02 .10
43 Jim Abbott .10 .30
44 Chuck Finley .07 .20
45 Bryan Harvey .02 .10
46 Donnie Hill .02 .10
47 Jack Howell .02 .10
48 Wally Joyner .07 .20
49 Mark Langston .02 .10
50 Kirk McCaskill .02 .10
51 Lance Parrish .07 .20
52 Dick Schofield .02 .10
53 Lee Stevens .02 .10
54 Dave Winfield .07 .20
55 George Bell .02 .10
56 Damon Berryhill .02 .10
57 Mike Bielecki .02 .10
58 Andre Dawson .07 .20
59 Shawon Dunston .02 .10
60 Joe Girardi UER .02 .10
Bats right, LH hitter
shown is Doug Dascenzo
61 Mark Grace .10 .30
62 Mike Harkey .02 .10
63 Les Lancaster .02 .10
64 Greg Maddux .30 .75
65 Derrick May .02 .10
66 Ryne Sandberg .30 .75
67 Luis Salazar .02 .10
68 Dwight Smith .02 .10
69 Hector Villanueva .02 .10
70 Jerome Walton .02 .10
71 Mitch Williams .02 .10
72 Carlton Fisk .10 .30
73 Scott Fletcher .02 .10
74 Ozzie Guillen .07 .20
75 Greg Hibbard .02 .10
76 Lance Johnson .02 .10
77 Steve Lyons .02 .10
78 Jack McDowell .02 .10
79 Dan Pasqua .02 .10
80 Melido Perez .02 .10
81 Tim Raines .07 .20
82 Sammy Sosa .20 .50
83 Cory Snyder .02 .10
84 Bobby Thigpen .02 .10
85 Frank Thomas .20 .50
Card says he is
an outfielder
86 Robin Ventura .07 .20
87 Todd Benzinger .02 .10
88 Glenn Braggs .02 .10
89 Tom Browning UER .02 .10
Front photo actually
Norm Charlton
90 Norm Charlton .02 .10
91 Eric Davis .07 .20
92 Rob Dibble .07 .20
93 Bill Doran .02 .10
94 Mariano Duncan UER .02 .10
Right back photo
is Billy Hatcher
95 Billy Hatcher .02 .10
96 Barry Larkin .10 .30
97 Randy Myers .02 .10
98 Hal Morris .02 .10
99 Joe Oliver .02 .10
100 Paul O'Neill .10 .30
101 Jeff Reed .02 .10
See also 104
102 Jose Rijo .02 .10
103 Chris Sabo .02 .10
See also 106
104 Beau Allred UER .02 .10
Card number is 101
105 Sandy Alomar Jr. .02 .10
106 Carlos Baerga UER .02 .10
Card number is 103
107 Albert Belle .07 .20
108 Jerry Browne .02 .10
109 Tom Candiotti .02 .10
110 Alex Cole .02 .10
111 John Farrell .02 .10
See also 114
112 Felix Fermin .02 .10
113 Brook Jacoby .02 .10
114 Chris James UER .02 .10
Card number is 111
115 Doug Jones .02 .10
116 Steve Olin .02 .10
See also 119
117 Greg Swindell .02 .10
118 Turner Ward RC .05 .15
119 Mitch Webster UER .02 .10
Card number is 116
120 Dave Bergman .02 .10
121 Cecil Fielder .07 .20
122 Travis Fryman .07 .20
123 Mike Henneman .02 .10
124 Lloyd Moseby .02 .10
125 Dan Petry .02 .10
126 Tony Phillips .02 .10
127 Mark Salas .02 .10
128 Frank Tanana .02 .10
129 Alan Trammell .07 .20
130 Lou Whitaker .07 .20
131 Eric Anthony .02 .10
132 Craig Biggio .10 .30
133 Ken Caminiti .07 .20
134 Casey Candaele .02 .10
135 Andujar Cedeno .02 .10
136 Mark Davidson .02 .10
137 Jim Deshaies .02 .10
138 Mark Portugal .02 .10
139 Rafael Ramirez .02 .10
140 Mike Scott .02 .10
141 Eric Yelding .02 .10
142 Gerald Young .02 .10
143 Kevin Appier .07 .20
144 George Brett .50 1.25
145 Jeff Conine RC .20 .50
146 Jim Eisenreich .02 .10
147 Tom Gordon .02 .10
148 Mark Gubicza .02 .10
149 Bo Jackson .20 .50
150 Brent Mayne .02 .10
151 Mike Macfarlane .02 .10
152 Brian McRae RC .15 .40
153 Jeff Montgomery .02 .10
154 Bret Saberhagen .07 .20
155 Kevin Seitzer .02 .10
156 Terry Shumpert .02 .10
157 Kurt Stillwell .02 .10
158 Danny Tartabull .02 .10
159 Tim Belcher .02 .10
160 Kal Daniels .02 .10
161 Alfredo Griffin .02 .10
162 Lenny Harris .02 .10
163 Jay Howell .02 .10
164 Ramon Martinez .02 .10
165 Mike Morgan .02 .10
166 Eddie Murray .20 .50
167 Jose Offerman .02 .10
168 Juan Samuel .02 .10
169 Mike Scioscia .02 .10
170 Mike Sharperson .02 .10
171 Darryl Strawberry .07 .20
172 Greg Brock .02 .10
173 Chuck Crim .02 .10
174 Jim Gantner .02 .10
175 Ted Higuera .02 .10
176 Mark Knudson .02 .10
177 Tim McIntosh .02 .10
178 Paul Molitor .07 .20
179 Dan Plesac .02 .10
180 Gary Sheffield .07 .20
181 Bill Spiers .02 .10
182 B.J. Surhoff .07 .20
183 Greg Vaughn .02 .10
184 Robin Yount .30 .75
185 Rick Aguilera .07 .20
186 Greg Gagne .02 .10
187 Dan Gladden .02 .10
188 Brian Harper .02 .10
189 Kent Hrbek .07 .20
190 Gene Larkin .02 .10
191 Shane Mack .02 .10
192 Pedro Munoz RC .05 .15
193 Al Newman .02 .10
194 Junior Ortiz .02 .10
195 Kirby Puckett .20 .50
196 Kevin Tapani .02 .10
197 Dennis Boyd .02 .10
198 Tim Burke .02 .10
199 Ivan Calderon .02 .10
200 Delino DeShields .07 .20
201 Mike Fitzgerald .02 .10
202 Steve Frey .02 .10
203 Andres Galarraga .07 .20
204 Marquis Grissom .07 .20
205 Dave Martinez .02 .10
206 Dennis Martinez .07 .20
207 Junior Noboa .02 .10
208 Spike Owen .02 .10
209 Scott Ruskin .02 .10
210 Tim Wallach .02 .10
211 Daryl Boston .02 .10
212 Vince Coleman .02 .10
213 David Cone .07 .20
214 Ron Darling .02 .10
215 Kevin Elster .02 .10
216 Sid Fernandez .02 .10
217 John Franco .07 .20
218 Dwight Gooden .07 .20
219 Tom Herr .02 .10
220 Todd Hundley .02 .10
221 Gregg Jefferies .02 .10
222 Howard Johnson .02 .10
223 Dave Magadan .02 .10
224 Kevin McReynolds .02 .10
225 Keith Miller .02 .10
226 Mackey Sasser .02 .10
227 Frank Viola .07 .20
228 Jesse Barfield .02 .10
229 Greg Cadaret .02 .10
230 Alvaro Espinoza .02 .10
231 Bob Geren .02 .10
232 Lee Guetterman .02 .10
233 Mel Hall .02 .10
234 Andy Hawkins UER .02 .10
Back center photo
is not him
235 Roberto Kelly .02 .10
236 Tim Leary .02 .10
237 Jim Leyritz .02 .10
238 Kevin Maas .02 .10
239 Don Mattingly .50 1.25
240 Hensley Meulens .02 .10
241 Eric Plunk .02 .10
242 Steve Sax .02 .10
243 Todd Burns .02 .10
244 Jose Canseco .10 .30
245 Dennis Eckersley .07 .20
246 Mike Gallego .02 .10
247 Dave Henderson .02 .10
248 Rickey Henderson .20 .50
249 Rick Honeycutt .02 .10
250 Carney Lansford .07 .20
251 Mark McGwire .60 1.50
252 Mike Moore .02 .10
253 Terry Steinbach .02 .10
254 Dave Stewart .07 .20
255 Walt Weiss .02 .10
256 Bob Welch .02 .10
257 Curt Young .02 .10
258 Wes Chamberlain RC .15 .40
259 Pat Combs .02 .10
260 Darren Daulton .07 .20
261 Jose DeJesus .02 .10
262 Len Dykstra .07 .20
263 Charlie Hayes .02 .10
264 Von Hayes .02 .10
265 Ken Howell .02 .10
266 John Kruk .07 .20
267 Roger McDowell .02 .10
268 Mickey Morandini .02 .10
269 Terry Mulholland .02 .10
270 Dale Murphy .10 .30
271 Randy Ready .02 .10
272 Dickie Thon .02 .10
273 Stan Belinda .02 .10
274 Jay Bell .07 .20
275 Barry Bonds .60 1.50
276 Bobby Bonilla .07 .20
277 Doug Drabek .02 .10
278 Carlos Garcia RC .05 .15
279 Neal Heaton .02 .10
280 Jeff King .02 .10
281 Bill Landrum .02 .10
282 Mike LaValliere .02 .10
283 Jose Lind .02 .10
284 Orlando Merced RC .05 .15
285 Gary Redus .02 .10
286 Don Slaught .02 .10
287 Andy Van Slyke .10 .30
288 Jose DeLeon .02 .10
289 Pedro Guerrero .07 .20
290 Ray Lankford .07 .20
291 Joe Magrane .02 .10
292 Jose Oquendo .02 .10
293 Tom Pagnozzi .02 .10
294 Bryn Smith .02 .10
295 Lee Smith .07 .20
296 Ozzie Smith UER .30 .75
Born 12-26, 54,
should have hyphen
297 Milt Thompson .02 .10
298 Craig Wilson RC .02 .10
299 Todd Zeile .02 .10
300 Shawn Abner .02 .10
301 Andy Benes .02 .10
302 Paul Faries RC .02 .10
303 Tony Gwynn .25 .60
304 Greg W. Harris .02 .10
305 Thomas Howard .02 .10
306 Bruce Hurst .02 .10
307 Craig Lefferts .02 .10
308 Fred McGriff .10 .30
309 Dennis Rasmussen .02 .10
310 Bip Roberts .02 .10
311 Benito Santiago .07 .20
312 Garry Templeton .02 .10
313 Ed Whitson .02 .10
314 Dave Anderson .02 .10
315 Kevin Bass .02 .10
316 Jeff Brantley .02 .10
317 John Burkett .02 .10
318 Will Clark .10 .30
319 Steve Decker RC .02 .10
320 Scott Garrelts .02 .10
321 Terry Kennedy .02 .10
322 Mark Leonard RC .02 .10
323 Darren Lewis .02 .10
324 Greg Litton .02 .10
325 Willie McGee .07 .20
326 Kevin Mitchell .02 .10
327 Don Robinson .02 .10
328 Andres Santana .02 .10
329 Robby Thompson .02 .10
330 Jose Uribe .02 .10
331 Matt Williams .07 .20
332 Scott Bradley .02 .10
333 Henry Cotto .02 .10
334 Alvin Davis .02 .10
335 Ken Griffey Sr. .07 .20
336 Ken Griffey Jr. .50 1.25
337 Erik Hanson .02 .10
338 Brian Holman .02 .10
339 Randy Johnson .25 .60
340 Edgar Martinez UER .10 .30
Listed as playing SS
341 Tino Martinez .20 .50
342 Pete O'Brien .02 .10
343 Harold Reynolds .07 .20
344 Dave Valle .02 .10
345 Omar Vizquel .10 .30
346 Brad Arnsberg .02 .10
347 Kevin Brown .07 .20
348 Julio Franco .07 .20
349 Jeff Huson .02 .10
350 Rafael Palmeiro .10 .30
351 Geno Petralli .02 .10
352 Gary Pettis .02 .10
353 Kenny Rogers .07 .20
354 Jeff Russell .02 .10
355 Nolan Ryan .75 2.00
356 Ruben Sierra .07 .20
357 Bobby Witt .02 .10
358 Roberto Alomar .10 .30
359 Pat Borders .02 .10
360 Joe Carter UER .07 .20
Reverse negative
on back photo
361 Kelly Gruber .02 .10
362 Tom Henke .02 .10
363 Glenallen Hill .02 .10
364 Jimmy Key .07 .20
365 Manny Lee .02 .10
366 Rance Mulliniks .02 .10
367 John Olerud UER .07 .20
Throwing left on card;
back has throws right;
he does throw lefty
368 Dave Stieb .02 .10
369 Duane Ward .02 .10
370 David Wells .07 .20
371 Mark Whiten .02 .10
372 Mookie Wilson .07 .20
373 Willie Banks MLP .02 .10
374 Steve Carter MLP .02 .10
375 Scott Chiamparino MLP .02 .10
376 Steve Chitren RC .02 .10
377 Darrin Fletcher MLP .02 .10
378 Rich Garces RC .05 .15
379 Reggie Jefferson MLP .02 .10
380 Eric Karros RC .30 .75
381 Pat Kelly RC .05 .15
382 Chuck Knoblauch MLP .07 .20
383 Denny Neagle RC .15 .40
384 Dan Opperman RC .02 .10
385 John Ramos RC .02 .10
386 Henry Rodriguez RC .15 .40
387 Mo Vaughn MLP .07 .20
388 Gerald Williams RC .15 .40
389 Mike York RC .02 .10
390 Eddie Zosky MLP .02 .10
391 Barry Bonds EP .30 .75
392 Cecil Fielder EP .02 .10
393 Rickey Henderson EP .10 .30
394 Dave Justice EP .02 .10
395 Nolan Ryan EP .40 1.00
396 Bobby Thigpen EP .02 .10
397 Gregg Jefferies CL .02 .10
398 Von Hayes CL .02 .10
399 Terry Kennedy CL .02 .10
400 Nolan Ryan CL .20 .50

1991 Ultra Gold

COMPLETE SET (10) 4.00 10.00
RANDOM INSERTS IN FOIL PACKS
1 Barry Bonds 1.25 3.00
2 Will Clark .25 .60
3 Doug Drabek .07 .20
4 Ken Griffey Jr. 1.00 2.50
5 Rickey Henderson .40 1.00
6 Bo Jackson .40 1.00
7 Ramon Martinez .07 .20
8 Kirby Puckett .40 1.00
9 Chris Sabo .07 .20
10 Ryne Sandberg .60 1.50

1991 Ultra Update

The 120-card set was distributed exclusively in factory set form along with 20 team logo stickers through hobby dealers. The set includes the year's hottest rookies and important veteran players traded after the original Ultra series was produced. Card design is identical to regular issue 1991 cards except for the U-prefixed numbering on back. Cards are ordered alphabetically within and according to teams for each league. Rookie Cards in this set include Jeff Bagwell, Mike Mussina, and Ivan Rodriguez.

COMP.FACT.SET (120) 10.00 25.00
U PREFIX ON CARD NUMBER
1 Dwight Evans .30 .75
2 Chito Martinez RC .08 .25
3 Bob Melvin .08 .25
4 Mike Mussina RC 2.50 6.00
5 Jack Clark .20 .50
6 Dana Kiecker .08 .25
7 Steve Lyons .08 .25
8 Gary Gaetti .20 .50
9 Dave Gallagher .08 .25
10 Dave Parker .20 .50
11 Luis Polonia .08 .25
12 Luis Sojo .08 .25
13 Wilson Alvarez .08 .25
14 Alex Fernandez .08 .25
15 Craig Grebeck .08 .25
16 Ron Karkovice .08 .25
17 Warren Newson RC .08 .25
18 Scott Radinsky .08 .25
19 Glenallen Hill .08 .25
20 Charles Nagy .08 .25
21 Mark Whiten .08 .25
22 Milt Cuyler .08 .25
23 Paul Gibson .08 .25
24 Mickey Tettleton .08 .25
25 Todd Benzinger .08 .25
26 Storm Davis .08 .25
27 Kirk Gibson .20 .50
28 Bill Pecota .08 .25
29 Gary Thurman .08 .25
30 Darryl Hamilton .08 .25
31 Jaime Navarro .08 .25
32 Willie Randolph .20 .50
33 Bill Wegman .08 .25
34 Randy Bush .08 .25
35 Chili Davis .20 .50
36 Scott Erickson .08 .25
37 Chuck Knoblauch .20 .50
38 Scott Leius .08 .25
39 Jack Morris .20 .50
40 John Habyan .08 .25
41 Pat Kelly .08 .25
42 Matt Nokes .08 .25
43 Scott Sanderson .08 .25
44 Bernie Williams .75 2.00
45 Harold Baines .20 .50
46 Brook Jacoby .08 .25
47 Earnest Riles .08 .25
48 Willie Wilson .08 .25
49 Jay Buhner .20 .50
50 Rich DeLucia RC .08 .25
51 Mike Jackson .08 .25
52 Bill Krueger .08 .25
53 Bill Swift .08 .25
54 Brian Downing .08 .25
55 Juan Gonzalez .60 1.50
56 Dean Palmer .20 .50
57 Kevin Reimer .08 .25
58 Ivan Rodriguez RC 4.00 10.00
59 Tom Candiotti .08 .25
60 Juan Guzman RC .20 .50
61 Bob MacDonald RC .08 .25
62 Greg Myers .08 .25
63 Ed Sprague .08 .25
64 Devon White .20 .50
65 Rafael Belliard .08 .25
66 Juan Berenguer .08 .25
67 Brian R.Hunter RC .20 .50
68 Kent Mercker .08 .25
69 Otis Nixon .08 .25
70 Danny Jackson .08 .25
71 Chuck McElroy .08 .25
72 Gary Scott RC .08 .25
73 Heathcliff Slocumb RC .08 .25
74 Chico Walker .08 .25
75 Rick Wilkins RC .08 .25
76 Chris Hammond .08 .25
77 Luis Quinones .08 .25
78 Herm Winningham .08 .25
79 Jeff Bagwell RC 2.50 6.00
80 Jim Corsi .08 .25
81 Steve Finley .20 .50
82 Luis Gonzalez RC .60 1.50
83 Pete Harnisch .08 .25
84 Darryl Kile .20 .50
85 Brett Butler .20 .50
86 Gary Carter .20 .50
87 Tim Crews .08 .25
88 Orel Hershiser .20 .50
89 Bob Ojeda .08 .25
90 Bret Barberie RC .08 .25
91 Barry Jones .08 .25
92 Gilberto Reyes .08 .25
93 Larry Walker .60 1.50
94 Hubie Brooks .08 .25
95 Tim Burke .08 .25
96 Rick Cerone .08 .25
97 Jeff Innis .08 .25
98 Wally Backman .08 .25
99 Tommy Greene .08 .25
100 Ricky Jordan .08 .25
101 Mitch Williams .08 .25
102 John Smiley .08 .25
103 Randy Tomlin RC .08 .25
104 Gary Varsho .08 .25
105 Cris Carpenter .08 .25
106 Ken Hill .08 .25
107 Felix Jose .08 .25
108 Omar Olivares RC .08 .25
109 Gerald Perry .08 .25
110 Jerald Clark .08 .25
111 Tony Fernandez .08 .25
112 Darrin Jackson .08 .25
113 Mike Maddux .08 .25
114 Tim Teufel .08 .25
115 Bud Black .08 .25
116 Kelly Downs .08 .25
117 Mike Felder .08 .25
118 Willie McGee .20 .50
119 Trevor Wilson .08 .25
120 Checklist 1-120 .08 .25

1992 Ultra

Consisting of 600 standard-size cards, the 1992 Ultra set was issued in two series of 300 cards each. Cards were distributed exclusively in foil packs. The cards are numbered on the back and ordered below alphabetically within and according to teams for each league with AL preceding NL. Some cards have been found without the word Fleer on the front.

COMPLETE SET (600) 12.50 30.00
COMPLETE SERIES 1 (300) 8.00 20.00
COMPLETE SERIES 2 (300) 4.00 10.00
1 Glenn Davis .02 .10
2 Mike Devereaux .02 .10
3 Dwight Evans .10 .30
4 Leo Gomez .02 .10
5 Chris Hoiles .02 .10
6 Sam Horn .02 .10
7 Chito Martinez .02 .10
8 Randy Milligan .02 .10
9 Mike Mussina .20 .50
10 Billy Ripken .02 .10
11 Cal Ripken .60 1.50
12 Tom Brunansky .02 .10
13 Ellis Burks .07 .20
14 Jack Clark .07 .20
15 Roger Clemens .40 1.00
16 Mike Greenwell .02 .10
17 Joe Hesketh .02 .10
18 Tony Pena .02 .10
19 Carlos Quintana .02 .10
20 Jeff Reardon .07 .20
21 Jody Reed .02 .10
22 Luis Rivera .02 .10
23 Mo Vaughn .07 .20
24 Gary DiSarcina .02 .10
25 Chuck Finley .07 .20
26 Gary Gaetti .07 .20
27 Bryan Harvey .02 .10
28 Lance Parrish .07 .20
29 Luis Polonia .02 .10
30 Dick Schofield .02 .10
31 Luis Sojo .02 .10
32 Wilson Alvarez .02 .10
33 Carlton Fisk .10 .30
34 Craig Grebeck .02 .10
35 Ozzie Guillen .07 .20
36 Greg Hibbard .02 .10
37 Charlie Hough .07 .20
38 Lance Johnson .02 .10
39 Ron Karkovice .02 .10
40 Jack McDowell .02 .10
41 Donn Pall .02 .10
42 Melido Perez .02 .10
43 Tim Raines .07 .20
44 Frank Thomas .20 .50
45 Sandy Alomar Jr. .02 .10
46 Carlos Baerga .02 .10
47 Albert Belle .07 .20
48 Jerry Browne UER .02 .10
Reversed negative
on card back

49 Felix Fermin .02 .10
50 Reggie Jefferson UER .02 .10
Born 1968, not 1966
51 Mark Lewis .02 .10
52 Carlos Martinez .02 .10
53 Steve Olin .02 .10
54 Jim Thome .20 .50
55 Mark Whiten .02 .10
56 Dave Bergman .02 .10
57 Milt Cuyler .02 .10
58 Rob Deer .02 .10
59 Cecil Fielder .07 .20
60 Travis Fryman .07 .20
61 Scott Livingstone .02 .10
62 Tony Phillips .02 .10
63 Mickey Tettleton .02 .10
64 Alan Trammell .07 .20
65 Lou Whitaker .07 .20
66 Kevin Appier .07 .20
67 Mike Boddicker .02 .10
68 George Brett .50 1.25
69 Jim Eisenreich .02 .10
70 Mark Gubicza .02 .10
71 David Howard .02 .10
72 Joel Johntson .02 .10
73 Mike Macfarlane .02 .10
74 Brent Mayne .02 .10
75 Brian McRae .02 .10
76 Jeff Montgomery .02 .10
77 Terry Shumpert .02 .10
78 Don August .02 .10
79 Dante Bichette .07 .20
80 Ted Higuera .02 .10
81 Paul Molitor .07 .20
82 Jaime Navarro .02 .10
83 Gary Sheffield .07 .20
84 Bill Spiers .02 .10
85 B.J. Surhoff .07 .20
86 Greg Vaughn .02 .10
87 Robin Yount .30 .75
88 Rick Aguilera .07 .20
89 Chili Davis .07 .20
90 Scott Erickson .02 .10
91 Brian Harper .02 .10
92 Kent Hrbek .07 .20
93 Chuck Knoblauch .07 .20
94 Scott Leius .02 .10
95 Shane Mack .02 .10
96 Mike Pagliarulo .02 .10
97 Kirby Puckett .20 .50
98 Kevin Tapani .02 .10
99 Jesse Barfield .02 .10
100 Alvaro Espinoza .02 .10
101 Mel Hall .02 .10
102 Pat Kelly .02 .10
103 Roberto Kelly .02 .10
104 Kevin Maas .02 .10
105 Don Mattingly .50 1.25
106 Hensley Meulens .02 .10
107 Matt Nokes .02 .10
108 Steve Sax .02 .10
109 Harold Baines .07 .20
110 Jose Canseco .10 .30
111 Ron Darling .02 .10
112 Mike Gallego .02 .10
113 Dave Henderson .02 .10
114 Rickey Henderson .20 .50
115 Mark McGwire .50 1.25
116 Terry Steinbach .02 .10
117 Dave Stewart .07 .20
118 Todd Van Poppel .02 .10
119 Bob Welch .02 .10
120 Greg Briley .02 .10
121 Jay Buhner .07 .20
122 Rick DeLucia .02 .10
123 Ken Griffey Jr. .40 1.00
124 Erik Hanson .02 .10
125 Randy Johnson .20 .50
126 Edgar Martinez .10 .30
127 Tino Martinez .10 .30
128 Pete O'Brien .02 .10
129 Harold Reynolds .07 .20
130 Dave Valle .02 .10
131 Julio Franco .07 .20
132 Juan Gonzalez .10 .30
133 Jeff Huson .07 .20
134 Mike Jeffcoat .02 .10
135 Terry Mathews .02 .10
136 Rafael Palmeiro .10 .30
137 Dean Palmer .07 .20
138 Geno Petralli .02 .10
139 Ivan Rodriguez .20 .50
140 Jeff Russell .02 .10
141 Nolan Ryan .75 2.00
142 Ruben Sierra .07 .20
143 Roberto Alomar .10 .30
144 Pat Borders .02 .10
145 Joe Carter .07 .20
146 Kelly Gruber .02 .10
147 Jimmy Key .07 .20
148 Manny Lee .02 .10
149 Rance Mulliniks .02 .10
150 Greg Myers .02 .10
151 John Olerud .07 .20
152 Dave Stieb .02 .10
153 Todd Stottlemyre .02 .10
154 Duane Ward .02 .10
155 Devon White .07 .20
156 Eddie Zosky .02 .10
157 Steve Avery .02 .10
158 Rafael Belliard .02 .10
159 Jeff Blauser .02 .10
160 Sid Bream .02 .10
161 Ron Gant .07 .20
162 Tom Glavine .10 .30
163 Brian Hunter .02 .10
164 Dave Justice .07 .20
165 Mark Lemke .02 .10
166 Greg Olson .02 .10
167 Terry Pendleton .07 .20
168 Lonnie Smith .02 .10
169 John Smoltz .10 .30
170 Mike Stanton .02 .10
171 Jeff Treadway .02 .10
172 Paul Assenmacher .02 .10
173 George Bell .02 .10
174 Shawon Dunston .02 .10
175 Mark Grace .10 .30
176 Danny Jackson .02 .10
177 Les Lancaster .02 .10
178 Greg Maddux .30 .75
179 Luis Salazar .02 .10
180 Rey Sanchez RC .08 .25
181 Ryne Sandberg .30 .75
182 Jose Vizcaino .02 .10
183 Chico Walker .02 .10
184 Jerome Walton .02 .10
185 Glenn Braggs .02 .10
186 Tom Browning .02 .10
187 Rob Dibble .07 .20
188 Bill Doran .02 .10
189 Chris Hammond .02 .10
190 Billy Hatcher .02 .10
191 Barry Larkin .10 .30
192 Hal Morris .02 .10
193 Joe Oliver .02 .10
194 Paul O'Neill .10 .30
195 Jeff Reed .02 .10
196 Jose Rijo .02 .10
197 Chris Sabo .02 .10
198 Jeff Bagwell .20 .50
199 Craig Biggio .10 .30
200 Ken Caminiti .07 .20
201 Andujar Cedeno .02 .10
202 Steve Finley .07 .20
203 Luis Gonzalez .07 .20
204 Pete Harnisch .02 .10
205 Xavier Hernandez .02 .10
206 Darryl Kile .07 .20
207 Al Osuna .02 .10
208 Curt Schilling .10 .30
209 Brett Butler .07 .20
210 Kal Daniels .02 .10
211 Lenny Harris .02 .10
212 Stan Javier .02 .10
213 Ramon Martinez .02 .10
214 Roger McDowell .02 .10
215 Jose Offerman .02 .10
216 Juan Samuel .02 .10
217 Mike Scioscia .02 .10
218 Mike Sharperson .02 .10
219 Darryl Strawberry .07 .20
220 Delino DeShields .02 .10
221 Tom Foley .02 .10
222 Steve Frey .02 .10
223 Dennis Martinez .07 .20
224 Spike Owen .02 .10
225 Gilberto Reyes .02 .10
226 Tim Wallach .02 .10
227 Daryl Boston .02 .10
228 Tim Burke .02 .10
229 Vince Coleman .02 .10
230 David Cone .07 .20
231 Kevin Elster .02 .10
232 Dwight Gooden .07 .20
233 Todd Hundley .02 .10
234 Jeff Innis .02 .10
235 Howard Johnson .02 .10
236 Dave Magadan .02 .10
237 Mackey Sasser .02 .10
238 Anthony Young .02 .10
239 Wes Chamberlain .02 .10
240 Darren Daulton .07 .20
241 Len Dykstra .07 .20
242 Tommy Greene .02 .10
243 Charlie Hayes .02 .10
244 Dave Hollins .02 .10
245 Ricky Jordan .02 .10
246 John Kruk .07 .20
247 Mickey Morandini .02 .10
248 Terry Mulholland .02 .10
249 Dale Murphy .10 .30
250 Jay Bell .07 .20
251 Barry Bonds .60 1.50
252 Steve Buechele .02 .10
253 Doug Drabek .02 .10
254 Mike LaValliere .02 .10
255 Jose Lind .02 .10
256 Lloyd McClendon .02 .10
257 Orlando Merced .02 .10
258 Don Slaught .02 .10
259 John Smiley .02 .10
260 Zane Smith .02 .10
261 Randy Tomlin .02 .10
262 Andy Van Slyke .10 .30
263 Pedro Guerrero .07 .20
264 Felix Jose .02 .10
265 Ray Lankford .07 .20
266 Omar Olivares .02 .10
267 Jose Oquendo .02 .10
268 Tom Pagnozzi .02 .10
269 Bryn Smith .02 .10
270 Lee Smith UER .07 .20
1991 record listed
as 61-61
271 Ozzie Smith UER .30 .75
272 Milt Thompson .02 .10
273 Todd Zeile .02 .10
274 Andy Benes .02 .10
275 Jerald Clark .02 .10
276 Tony Fernandez .02 .10
277 Tony Gwynn .25 .60
278 Greg W. Harris .02 .10
279 Thomas Howard .02 .10
280 Bruce Hurst .02 .10
281 Mike Maddux .02 .10
282 Fred McGriff .10 .30
283 Benito Santiago .07 .20
284 Kevin Bass .02 .10
285 Jeff Brantley .02 .10
286 John Burkett .02 .10
287 Will Clark .10 .30
288 Royce Clayton .02 .10
289 Steve Decker .02 .10
290 Kelly Downs .02 .10
291 Mike Felder .02 .10
292 Darren Lewis .02 .10
293 Kirt Manwaring .02 .10
294 Willie McGee .07 .20
295 Robby Thompson .02 .10
296 Matt Williams .07 .20
297 Trevor Wilson .02 .10
298 Checklist 1-100 .02 .10
299 Checklist 101-200 .02 .10
300 Nolan Ryan CL .02 .10
301 Brady Anderson .07 .20
302 Todd Frohwirth .02 .10
303 Ben McDonald .02 .10
304 Mark McLemore .02 .10
305 Jose Mesa .02 .10
306 Bob Milacki .02 .10
307 Gregg Olson .02 .10
308 David Segui .02 .10
309 Rick Sutcliffe .07 .20
310 Jeff Tackett .02 .10
311 Wade Boggs .10 .30
312 Scott Cooper .02 .10
313 John Flaherty RC .02 .10
314 Wayne Housie .02 .10
315 Peter Hoy .02 .10
316 John Marzano .02 .10
317 Tim Naehring .02 .10
318 Phil Plantier .02 .10
319 Frank Viola .07 .20
320 Matt Young .02 .10
321 Jim Abbott .10 .30
322 Hubie Brooks .02 .10
323 Chad Curtis RC .08 .25
324 Alvin Davis .02 .10
325 Junior Felix .02 .10
326 Von Hayes .02 .10
327 Mark Langston .02 .10
328 Scott Lewis .02 .10
329 Don Robinson .02 .10
330 Bobby Rose .02 .10
331 Lee Stevens .02 .10
332 George Bell .02 .10
333 Esteban Beltre .02 .10
334 Joey Cora .02 .10
335 Alex Fernandez .02 .10
336 Roberto Hernandez .02 .10
337 Mike Huff .02 .10
338 Kirk McCaskill .02 .10
339 Dan Pasqua .02 .10
340 Scott Radinsky .02 .10
341 Steve Sax .02 .10
342 Bobby Thigpen .02 .10
343 Robin Ventura .07 .20
344 Jack Armstrong .02 .10
345 Alex Cole .02 .10
346 Dennis Cook .02 .10
347 Glenallen Hill .02 .10
348 Thomas Howard .02 .10
349 Brook Jacoby .02 .10
350 Kenny Lofton .10 .30
351 Charles Nagy .02 .10
352 Rod Nichols .02 .10
353 Junior Ortiz .02 .10
354 Dave Otto .02 .10
355 Tony Perezchica .02 .10
356 Scott Scudder .02 .10
357 Paul Sorrento .02 .10
358 Skeeter Barnes .02 .10
359 Mark Carreon .02 .10
360 John Doherty RC .02 .10
361 Dan Gladden .02 .10
362 Bill Gullickson .02 .10
363 Shawn Hare RC .02 .10
364 Mike Henneman .02 .10
365 Chad Kreuter .02 .10
366 Mark Leiter .02 .10
367 Mike Munoz .02 .10
368 Kevin Ritz .02 .10
369 Mark Davis .02 .10
370 Tom Gordon .02 .10
371 Chris Gwynn .02 .10
372 Gregg Jefferies .02 .10
373 Wally Joyner .07 .20
374 Kevin McReynolds .02 .10
375 Keith Miller .02 .10
376 Rico Rossy .02 .10
377 Curtis Wilkerson .02 .10
378 Ricky Bones .02 .10
379 Chris Bosio .02 .10
380 Cal Eldred .02 .10
381 Scott Fletcher .02 .10
382 Jim Gantner .02 .10
383 Darryl Hamilton .02 .10
384 Doug Henry RC .08 .25
385 Pat Listach RC .08 .25
386 Tim McIntosh .02 .10
387 Edwin Nunez .02 .10
388 Dan Plesac .02 .10
389 Kevin Seitzer .02 .10
390 Franklin Stubbs .02 .10
391 William Suero .02 .10
392 Bill Wegman .02 .10
393 Willie Banks .02 .10
394 Jarvis Brown .02 .10
395 Greg Gagne .02 .10
396 Mark Guthrie .02 .10
397 Bill Krueger .02 .10
398 Pat Mahomes RC .08 .25
399 Pedro Munoz .02 .10
400 John Smiley .02 .10
401 Gary Wayne .02 .10
402 Lenny Webster .02 .10
403 Carl Willis .02 .10
404 Greg Cadaret .02 .10
405 Steve Farr .02 .10
406 Mike Gallego .02 .10
407 Charlie Hayes .02 .10
408 Steve Howe .02 .10
409 Dion James .02 .10
410 Jeff Johnson .02 .10
411 Tim Leary .02 .10
412 Jim Leyritz .02 .10
413 Melido Perez .02 .10
414 Scott Sanderson .02 .10
415 Andy Stankiewicz .02 .10
416 Mike Stanley .02 .10
417 Danny Tartabull .02 .10
418 Lance Blankenship .02 .10
419 Mike Bordick .02 .10
420 Scott Brosius RC .15 .40
421 Dennis Eckersley .07 .20
422 Scott Hemond .02 .10
423 Carney Lansford .07 .20
424 Henry Mercedes .02 .10
425 Mike Moore .02 .10
426 Gene Nelson .02 .10
427 Randy Ready .02 .10
428 Bruce Walton .02 .10
429 Willie Wilson .02 .10
430 Rich Amaral .02 .10
431 Dave Cochrane .02 .10
432 Henry Cotto .02 .10
433 Calvin Jones .02 .10
434 Kevin Mitchell .02 .10
435 Clay Parker .02 .10
436 Omar Vizquel .10 .30
437 Floyd Bannister .02 .10
438 Kevin Brown .07 .20
439 John Cangelosi .02 .10
440 Brian Downing .02 .10
441 Monty Fariss .02 .10
442 Jose Guzman .02 .10
443 Donald Harris .02 .10
444 Kevin Reimer .02 .10
445 Kenny Rogers .07 .20
446 Wayne Rosenthal .02 .10
447 Dickie Thon .02 .10
448 Derek Bell .07 .20
449 Juan Guzman .02 .10
450 Tom Henke .02 .10
451 Candy Maldonado .02 .10
452 Jack Morris .07 .20
453 David Wells .07 .20
454 Dave Winfield .07 .20
455 Juan Berenguer .02 .10
456 Damon Berryhill .02 .10
457 Mike Bielecki .02 .10
458 Marvin Freeman .02 .10
459 Charlie Leibrandt .02 .10
460 Kent Mercker .02 .10
461 Otis Nixon .02 .10
462 Alejandro Pena .02 .10
463 Ben Rivera .02 .10
464 Deion Sanders .10 .30
465 Mark Wohlers .02 .10
466 Shawn Boskie .02 .10
467 Frank Castillo .02 .10
468 Andre Dawson .07 .20
469 Joe Girardi .02 .10
470 Chuck McElroy .02 .10
471 Mike Morgan .02 .10
472 Ken Patterson .02 .10
473 Bob Scanlan .02 .10
474 Gary Scott .02 .10
475 Dave Smith .02 .10
476 Sammy Sosa .20 .50
477 Hector Villanueva .02 .10
478 Scott Bankhead .02 .10
479 Tim Belcher .02 .10
480 Freddie Benavides .02 .10
481 Jacob Brumfield .02 .10
482 Norm Charlton .02 .10
483 Dwayne Henry .02 .10
484 Dave Martinez .02 .10
485 Bip Roberts .02 .10
486 Reggie Sanders .07 .20
487 Greg Swindell .02 .10
488 Ryan Bowen .02 .10
489 Casey Candaele .02 .10
490 Juan Guerrero UER .02 .10
photo on front is Andujar Cedeno
491 Pete Incaviglia .02 .10
492 Jeff Juden .02 .10
493 Rob Murphy .02 .10
494 Mark Portugal .02 .10
495 Rafael Ramirez .02 .10
496 Scott Servais .02 .10
497 Ed Taubensee RC .08 .25
498 Brian Williams RC .02 .10
499 Todd Benzinger .02 .10
500 John Candelaria .02 .10
501 Tom Candiotti .02 .10
502 Tim Crews .02 .10
503 Eric Davis .07 .20
504 Jim Gott .02 .10
505 Dave Hansen .02 .10
506 Carlos Hernandez .02 .10
507 Orel Hershiser .07 .20
508 Eric Karros .07 .20
509 Bob Ojeda .02 .10
510 Steve Wilson .02 .10
511 Moises Alou .07 .20
512 Bret Barberie .02 .10
513 Ivan Calderon .02 .10
514 Gary Carter .07 .20
515 Archi Cianfrocco RC .02 .10
516 Jeff Fassero .02 .10
517 Darrin Fletcher .02 .10
518 Marquis Grissom .07 .20
519 Chris Haney .02 .10
520 Ken Hill .02 .10
521 Chris Nabholz .02 .10
522 Bill Sampen .02 .10
523 John Vander Wal .02 .10
524 Dave Wainhouse .02 .10
525 Larry Walker .10 .30
526 John Wetteland .07 .20
527 Bobby Bonilla .07 .20
528 Sid Fernandez .02 .10
529 John Franco .07 .20
530 Dave Gallagher .02 .10
531 Paul Gibson .02 .10
532 Eddie Murray .20 .50
533 Junior Noboa .02 .10
534 Charlie O'Brien .02 .10
535 Bill Pecota .02 .10
536 Willie Randolph .07 .20
537 Bret Saberhagen .07 .20
538 Dick Schofield .02 .10
539 Pete Schourek .02 .10
540 Ruben Amaro .02 .10
541 Andy Ashby .02 .10
542 Kim Batiste .02 .10
543 Cliff Brantley .02 .10
544 Mariano Duncan .02 .10
545 Jeff Grotewold .02 .10
546 Barry Jones .02 .10
547 Julio Peguero .02 .10
548 Curt Schilling .10 .30
549 Mitch Williams .02 .10
550 Stan Belinda .02 .10
551 Scott Bullett RC .02 .10
552 Cecil Espy .02 .10
553 Jeff King .02 .10
554 Roger Mason .02 .10
555 Paul Miller .02 .10
556 Denny Neagle .07 .20
557 Vicente Palacios .02 .10
558 Bob Patterson .02 .10
559 Tom Prince .02 .10
560 Gary Redus .02 .10
561 Gary Varsho .02 .10
562 Juan Agosto .02 .10
563 Cris Carpenter .02 .10
564 Mark Clark RC .08 .25
565 Jose DeLeon .02 .10
566 Rich Gedman .02 .10
567 Bernard Gilkey .02 .10
568 Rex Hudler .02 .10
569 Tim Jones .02 .10
570 Donovan Osborne .02 .10
571 Mike Perez .02 .10
572 Gerald Perry .02 .10
573 Bob Tewksbury .02 .10
574 Todd Worrell .02 .10
575 Dave Eiland .02 .10
576 Jeremy Hernandez RC .02 .10
577 Craig Lefferts .02 .10
578 Jose Melendez .02 .10
579 Randy Myers .02 .10
580 Gary Pettis .02 .10
581 Rich Rodriguez .02 .10
582 Gary Sheffield .07 .20
583 Craig Shipley .02 .10
584 Kurt Stillwell .02 .10
585 Tim Teufel .02 .10
586 Rod Beck RC .15 .40
587 Dave Burba .02 .10
588 Craig Colbert .02 .10
589 Bryan Hickerson RC .02 .10
590 Mike Jackson .02 .10
591 Mark Leonard .02 .10
592 Jim McNamara .02 .10
593 John Patterson RC .02 .10
594 Dave Righetti .07 .20
595 Cory Snyder .02 .10
596 Bill Swift .02 .10
597 Ted Wood .02 .10
598 Checklist 301-400 .02 .10
599 Checklist 401-500 .02 .10
600 Checklist 501-600 .02 .10

1992 Ultra All-Rookies

COMPLETE SET (10) 2.50 6.00
COMMON CARD (1-10) .20 .50
SER.2 STATED ODDS 1:13
1 Eric Karros .40 1.00
2 Andy Stankiewicz .20 .50
3 Gary DiSarcina .20 .50
4 Archi Cianfrocco .20 .50
5 Jim McNamara .20 .50
6 Chad Curtis .50 1.25
7 Kenny Lofton .60 1.50
8 Reggie Sanders .40 1.00
9 Pat Mahomes .50 1.25
10 Donovan Osborne .20 .50

1992 Ultra All-Stars

COMPLETE SET (20) 10.00 25.00
COMMON CARD (1-20) .15 .30
SER.2 STATED ODDS 1:6.5
1 Mark McGwire 1.50 4.00
2 Roberto Alomar .40 1.00
3 Cal Ripken 2.00 5.00
4 Wade Boggs .40 1.00
5 Mickey Tottloton .10 .30
6 Ken Griffey Jr. 1.25 3.00
7 Roberto Kelly .10 .30
8 Kirby Puckett .60 1.50
9 Frank Thomas .60 1.50
10 Jack McDowell .10 .30
11 Will Clark .40 1.00
12 Ryne Sandberg 1.00 2.50
13 Barry Larkin .40 1.00
14 Gary Sheffield .25 .60
15 Tom Pagnozzi .10 .30
16 Barry Bonds 2.00 5.00
17 Deion Sanders .40 1.00
18 Darryl Strawberry .25 .60
19 David Cone .25 .60
20 Tom Glavine .40 1.00

1992 Ultra Award Winners

COMPLETE SET (25) 15.00 40.00
COMMON CARD (1-25) .20 .50
RANDOM INSERTS IN SER.1 PACKS
1 Jack Morris .40 1.00
2 Chuck Knoblauch .40 1.00
3 Jeff Bagwell 1.00 2.50
4 Terry Pendleton .40 1.00
5 Cal Ripken 3.00 8.00
6 Roger Clemens 2.00 5.00
7 Tom Glavine .60 1.50
8 Tom Pagnozzi .20 .50
9 Ozzie Smith 1.50 4.00
10 Andy Van Slyke .60 1.50
11 Barry Bonds 3.00 8.00
12 Tony Gwynn 1.25 3.00
13 Matt Williams .40 1.00
14 Will Clark .60 1.50
15 Robin Ventura .40 1.00
16 Mark Langston .20 .50
17 Tony Pena .20 .50
18 Devon White .40 1.00
19 Don Mattingly 2.50 6.00
20 Roberto Alomar .60 1.50
21A Cal Ripken RevNeg 3.00 8.00
21B Cal Ripken COR 3.00 8.00
22 Ken Griffey Jr. 2.00 5.00
23 Kirby Puckett 1.00 2.50
24 Greg Maddux 1.50 4.00
25 Ryne Sandberg 1.50 4.00

1992 Ultra Gwynn

COMPLETE SET (10) 4.00 10.00
COMMON GWYNN (1-10) .40 1.00
RANDOM INSERTS IN SER.1 PACKS
COMMON MAIL-IN (S1-S2) .40 1.00
MAIL-IN CARDS AVAIL.VIA WRAPPER EXCH.
1AU Tony Gwynn AU 25.00 60.00

1993 Ultra

The 1993 Ultra baseball set was issued in two series and totaled 650 standard-size cards. The cards are numbered on the back, grouped alphabetically within teams, with NL teams preceding AL. The first series closes with checklist cards (298-300). The second series features 83 Ultra Rookies, 51 Rockies and Marlins, traded veteran players, and other major league veterans not included in the first series. The Rookie cards show a gold foil stamped Rookie "flag" as part of the card design. The key Rookie Card in this set is Jim Edmonds.

COMPLETE SET (650) 12.50 30.00
COMPLETE SERIES 1 (300) 6.00 15.00
COMPLETE SERIES 2 (350) 6.00 15.00
1 Steve Avery .05 .15
2 Rafael Belliard .05 .15
3 Damon Berryhill .05 .15
4 Sid Bream .05 .15
5 Ron Gant .10 .30
6 Tom Glavine .20 .50
7 Ryan Klesko .10 .30
8 Mark Lemke .05 .15
9 Javier Lopez .20 .50
10 Greg Olson .05 .15
11 Terry Pendleton .10 .30
12 Deion Sanders .20 .50
13 Mike Stanton .05 .15
14 Paul Assenmacher .05 .15
15 Steve Buechele .05 .15
16 Frank Castillo .05 .15
17 Shawon Dunston .05 .15
18 Mark Grace .20 .50
19 Derrick May .05 .15
20 Chuck McElroy .05 .15
21 Mike Morgan .05 .15
22 Bob Scanlan .05 .15
23 Dwight Smith .05 .15
24 Sammy Sosa .30 .75
25 Rick Wilkins .05 .15
26 Tim Belcher .05 .15
27 Jeff Branson .05 .15
28 Bill Doran .05 .15
29 Chris Hammond .05 .15
30 Barry Larkin .20 .50
31 Hal Morris .05 .15
32 Joe Oliver .05 .15
33 Jose Rijo .05 .15
34 Bip Roberts .05 .15
35 Chris Sabo .05 .15
36 Reggie Sanders .10 .30
37 Craig Biggio .20 .50
38 Ken Caminiti .10 .30
39 Steve Finley .10 .30
40 Luis Gonzalez .10 .30
41 Juan Guerrero .05 .15
42 Pete Harnisch .05 .15
43 Xavier Hernandez .05 .15
44 Doug Jones .05 .15
45 Al Osuna .05 .15
46 Eddie Taubensee .05 .15
47 Scooter Tucker .05 .15
48 Brian Williams .05 .15
49 Pedro Astacio .05 .15
50 Rafael Bournigal .05 .15
51 Brett Butler .10 .30
52 Tom Candiotti .05 .15
53 Eric Davis .10 .30
54 Lenny Harris .05 .15
55 Orel Hershiser .10 .30
56 Eric Karros .10 .30
57 Pedro Martinez .60 1.50
58 Roger McDowell .05 .15
59 Jose Offerman .05 .15
60 Mike Piazza 1.25 3.00
61 Moises Alou .10 .30
62 Kent Bottenfield .05 .15
63 Archi Cianfrocco .05 .15
64 Greg Colbrunn .05 .15
65 Wil Cordero .05 .15
66 Delino DeShields .05 .15
67 Darrin Fletcher .05 .15
68 Ken Hill .05 .15
69 Chris Nabholz .05 .15
70 Mel Rojas .05 .15
71 Larry Walker .10 .30
72 Sid Fernandez .05 .15
73 John Franco .10 .30
74 Dave Gallagher .05 .15
75 Todd Hundley .05 .15
76 Howard Johnson .05 .15
77 Jeff Kent .30 .75
78 Eddie Murray .30 .75
79 Bret Saberhagen .10 .30
80 Chico Walker .05 .15
81 Anthony Young .05 .15
82 Kyle Abbott .05 .15
83 Ruben Amaro .05 .15
84 Juan Bell .05 .15
85 Wes Chamberlain .05 .15
86 Darren Daulton .10 .30
87 Mariano Duncan .05 .15
88 Dave Hollins .05 .15
89 Ricky Jordan .05 .15
90 John Kruk .10 .30
91 Mickey Morandini .05 .15
92 Terry Mulholland .05 .15
93 Ben Rivera .05 .15
94 Mike Williams .05 .15
95 Stan Belinda .05 .15
96 Jay Bell .10 .30
97 Jeff King .05 .15
98 Mike LaValliere .05 .15
99 Lloyd McClendon .05 .15
100 Orlando Merced .05 .15
101 Zane Smith .05 .15
102 Randy Tomlin .05 .15
103 Andy Van Slyke .20 .50
104 Tim Wakefield .30 .75
105 John Wehner .05 .15
106 Bernard Gilkey .05 .15
107 Brian Jordan .10 .30
108 Ray Lankford .10 .30
109 Donovan Osborne .05 .15
110 Tom Pagnozzi .05 .15
111 Mike Perez .05 .15
112 Lee Smith .10 .30
113 Ozzie Smith .50 1.25
114 Bob Tewksbury .05 .15
115 Todd Zeile .05 .15
116 Andy Benes .05 .15
117 Greg W. Harris .05 .15
118 Darrin Jackson .05 .15
119 Fred McGriff .20 .50
120 Rich Rodriguez .05 .15
121 Frank Seminara .05 .15
122 Gary Sheffield .10 .30
123 Craig Shipley .05 .15
124 Kurt Stillwell .05 .15
125 Dan Walters .05 .15
126 Rod Beck .05 .15
127 Mike Benjamin .05 .15
128 Jeff Brantley .05 .15
129 John Burkett .05 .15
130 Will Clark .20 .50
131 Royce Clayton .05 .15
132 Steve Hosey .05 .15
133 Mike Jackson .05 .15
134 Darren Lewis .05 .15
135 Kirt Manwaring .05 .15
136 Bill Swift .05 .15
137 Robby Thompson .05 .15
138 Brady Anderson .10 .30
139 Glenn Davis .05 .15
140 Leo Gomez .05 .15
141 Chito Martinez .05 .15
142 Ben McDonald .05 .15
143 Alan Mills .05 .15
144 Mike Mussina .20 .50
145 Gregg Olson .05 .15
146 David Segui .05 .15
147 Jeff Tackett .05 .15
148 Jack Clark .10 .30
149 Scott Cooper .05 .15
150 Danny Darwin .05 .15
151 John Dopson .05 .15
152 Mike Greenwell .05 .15
153 Tim Naehring .05 .15
154 Tony Pena .05 .15
155 Paul Quantrill .05 .15
156 Mo Vaughn .10 .30
157 Frank Viola .10 .30
158 Bob Zupcic .05 .15
159 Chad Curtis .05 .15
160 Gary DiSarcina .05 .15
161 Damion Easley .05 .15
162 Chuck Finley .10 .30
163 Tim Fortugno .05 .15
164 Rene Gonzales .05 .15
165 Joe Grahe .05 .15
166 Mark Langston .05 .15
167 John Orton .05 .15
168 Luis Polonia .05 .15
169 Julio Valera .05 .15
170 Wilson Alvarez .05 .15
171 George Bell .05 .15
172 Joey Cora .05 .15
173 Alex Fernandez .05 .15
174 Lance Johnson .05 .15
175 Ron Karkovice .05 .15
176 Jack McDowell .05 .15
177 Scott Radinsky .05 .15
178 Tim Raines .10 .30
179 Steve Sax .05 .15
180 Bobby Thigpen .05 .15
181 Frank Thomas .30 .75
182 Sandy Alomar Jr. .05 .15
183 Carlos Baerga .05 .15
184 Felix Fermin .05 .15
185 Thomas Howard .05 .15
186 Mark Lewis .05 .15
187 Derek Lilliquist .05 .15
188 Carlos Martinez .05 .15
189 Charles Nagy .05 .15
190 Scott Scudder .05 .15
191 Paul Sorrento .05 .15
192 Jim Thome .20 .50
193 Mark Whiten .05 .15
194 Milt Cuyler UER .05 .15
Reversed negative
on card front
195 Rob Deer .05 .15
196 John Doherty .05 .15
197 Travis Fryman .10 .30
198 Dan Gladden .05 .15
199 Mike Henneman .05 .15
200 John Kiely .05 .15
201 Chad Kreuter .05 .15
202 Scott Livingstone .05 .15
203 Tony Phillips .05 .15
204 Alan Trammell .10 .30
205 Mike Boddicker .05 .15
206 George Brett .75 2.00
207 Tom Gordon .05 .15
208 Mark Gubicza .05 .15
209 Gregg Jefferies .05 .15
210 Wally Joyner .10 .30
211 Kevin Koslofski .05 .15
212 Brent Mayne .05 .15
213 Brian McRae .05 .15
214 Kevin McReynolds .05 .15
215 Rusty Meacham .05 .15
216 Steve Shifflett .05 .15
217 Jim Austin .05 .15
218 Cal Eldred .05 .15
219 Darryl Hamilton .05 .15
220 Doug Henry .05 .15
221 John Jaha .05 .15
222 Dave Nilsson .05 .15
223 Jesse Orosco .05 .15
224 B.J. Surhoff .10 .30
225 Greg Vaughn .05 .15
226 Bill Wegman .05 .15
227 Robin Yount UER .50 1.25
Born in Illinois,
not in Virginia
228 Rick Aguilera .05 .15
229 J.T. Bruett .05 .15

230 Scott Erickson .05 .15
231 Kent Hrbek .10 .30
232 Terry Jorgensen .05 .15
233 Scott Leius .05 .15
234 Pat Mahomes .05 .15
235 Pedro Munoz .05 .15
236 Kirby Puckett .30 .75
237 Kevin Tapani .05 .15
238 Lenny Webster .05 .15
239 Carl Willis .05 .15
240 Mike Gallego .05 .15
241 John Habyan .05 .15
242 Pat Kelly .05 .15
243 Kevin Maas .05 .15
244 Don Mattingly .75 2.00
245 Hensley Meulens .05 .15
246 Sam Militello .05 .15
247 Matt Nokes .05 .15
248 Melido Perez .05 .15
249 Andy Stankiewicz .05 .15
250 Randy Velarde .05 .15
251 Bob Wickman .05 .15
252 Bernie Williams .20 .50
253 Lance Blankenship .05 .15
254 Mike Bordick .05 .15
255 Jerry Browne .05 .15
256 Ron Darling .05 .15
257 Dennis Eckersley .10 .30
258 Rickey Henderson .30 .75
259 Vince Horsman .05 .15
260 Troy Neel .05 .15
261 Jeff Parrett .05 .15
262 Terry Steinbach .05 .15
263 Bob Welch .05 .15
264 Bobby Witt .05 .15
265 Rich Amaral .05 .15
266 Bret Boone .10 .30
267 Jay Buhner .10 .30
268 Dave Fleming .05 .15
269 Randy Johnson .30 .75
270 Edgar Martinez .20 .50
271 Mike Schooler .05 .15
272 Russ Swan .05 .15
273 Dave Valle .05 .15
274 Omar Vizquel .20 .50
275 Kerry Woodson .05 .15
276 Kevin Brown .10 .30
277 Julio Franco .10 .30
278 Jeff Frye .05 .15
279 Juan Gonzalez .10 .30
280 Jeff Huson .05 .15
281 Rafael Palmeiro .20 .50
282 Dean Palmer .10 .30
283 Roger Pavlik .05 .15
284 Ivan Rodriguez .20 .50
285 Kenny Rogers .10 .30
286 Derek Bell .05 .15
287 Pat Borders .05 .15
288 Joe Carter .10 .30
289 Bob MacDonald .05 .15
290 Jack Morris .10 .30
291 John Olerud .10 .30
292 Ed Sprague .05 .15
293 Todd Stottlemyre .05 .15
294 Mike Timlin .05 .15
295 Duane Ward .05 .15
296 David Wells .10 .30
297 Devon White .10 .30
298 Ray Lankford CL .05 .15
299 Bobby Witt CL .05 .15
300 Mike Piazza CL .30 .75
301 Steve Bedrosian .05 .15
302 Jeff Blauser .05 .15
303 Francisco Cabrera .05 .15
304 Marvin Freeman .05 .15
305 Brian Hunter .05 .15
306 David Justice .10 .30
307 Greg Maddux .50 1.25
308 Greg McMichael RC .10 .30
309 Kent Mercker .05 .15
310 Otis Nixon .05 .15
311 Pete Smith .05 .15
312 John Smoltz .20 .50
313 Jose Guzman .05 .15
314 Mike Harkey .05 .15
315 Greg Hibbard .05 .15
316 Candy Maldonado .05 .15
317 Randy Myers .05 .15
318 Dan Plesac .05 .15
319 Rey Sanchez .05 .15
320 Ryne Sandberg .50 1.25
321 Tommy Shields .05 .15
322 Jose Vizcaino .05 .15
323 Matt Walbeck RC .10 .30
324 Willie Wilson .05 .15
325 Tom Browning .05 .15
326 Tim Costo .05 .15
327 Rob Dibble .10 .30
328 Steve Foster .05 .15
329 Roberto Kelly .05 .15
330 Randy Milligan .05 .15
331 Kevin Mitchell .05 .15
332 Tim Pugh RC .10 .30
333 Jeff Reardon .10 .30
334 John Roper .05 .15
335 Juan Samuel .05 .15
336 John Smiley .05 .15
337 Dan Wilson .10 .30
338 Scott Aldred .05 .15
339 Andy Ashby .05 .15
340 Freddie Benavides .05 .15
341 Dante Bichette .10 .30
342 Willie Blair .05 .15
343 Daryl Boston .05 .15
344 Vinny Castilla .30 .75
345 Jerald Clark .05 .15
346 Alex Cole .05 .15
347 Andres Galarraga .10 .30
348 Joe Girardi .05 .15
349 Ryan Hawblitzel .05 .15
350 Charlie Hayes .05 .15
351 Butch Henry .05 .15
352 Darren Holmes .05 .15
353 Dale Murphy .20 .50
354 David Nied .05 .15
355 Jeff Parrett .05 .15
356 Steve Reed RC .10 .30
357 Bruce Ruffin .05 .15
358 Danny Sheaffer RC .10 .30
359 Bryn Smith .05 .15
360 Jim Tatum RC .10 .30
361 Eric Young .05 .15
362 Gerald Young .05 .15
363 Luis Aquino .05 .15
364 Alex Arias .05 .15
365 Jack Armstrong .05 .15
366 Bret Barberie .05 .15
367 Ryan Bowen .05 .15
368 Greg Briley .05 .15
369 Cris Carpenter .05 .15
370 Chuck Carr .05 .15
371 Jeff Conine .10 .30
372 Steve Decker .05 .15
373 Orestes Destrade .05 .15
374 Monty Fariss .05 .15
375 Junior Felix .05 .15
376 Chris Hammond .05 .15
377 Bryan Harvey .05 .15
378 Trevor Hoffman .30 .75
379 Charlie Hough .10 .30
380 Joe Klink .05 .15
381 Richie Lewis RC .10 .30
382 Dave Magadan .05 .15
383 Bob McClure .05 .15
384 Scott Pose RC .10 .30
385 Rich Renteria .05 .15
386 Benito Santiago .10 .30
387 Walt Weiss .05 .15
388 Nigel Wilson .05 .15
389 Eric Anthony .05 .15
390 Jeff Bagwell .20 .50
391 Andujar Cedeno .05 .15
392 Doug Drabek .05 .15
393 Darryl Kile .10 .30
394 Mark Portugal .05 .15
395 Karl Rhodes .05 .15
396 Scott Servais .05 .15
397 Greg Swindell .05 .15
398 Tom Goodwin .05 .15
399 Kevin Gross .05 .15
400 Carlos Hernandez .05 .15
401 Ramon Martinez .05 .15
402 Raul Mondesi .10 .30
403 Jody Reed .05 .15
404 Mike Sharperson .05 .15
405 Cory Snyder .05 .15
406 Darryl Strawberry .10 .30
407 Rick Trlicek .05 .15
408 Tim Wallach .05 .15
409 Todd Worrell .05 .15
410 Tavo Alvarez .05 .15
411 Sean Berry .05 .15
412 Frank Bolick .05 .15
413 Cliff Floyd .10 .30
414 Mike Gardiner .05 .15
415 Marquis Grissom .10 .30
416 Tim Laker RC .10 .30
417 Mike Lansing RC .20 .50
418 Dennis Martinez .10 .30
419 John Vander Wal .05 .15
420 John Wetteland .10 .30
421 Rondell White .10 .30
422 Bobby Bonilla .10 .30
423 Jeromy Burnitz .10 .30
424 Vince Coleman .05 .15
425 Mike Draper .05 .15
426 Tony Fernandez .05 .15
427 Dwight Gooden .10 .30
428 Jeff Innis .05 .15
429 Bobby Jones .10 .30
430 Mike Maddux .05 .15
431 Charlie O'Brien .05 .15
432 Joe Orsulak .05 .15
433 Pete Schourek .05 .15
434 Frank Tanana .05 .15
435 Ryan Thompson .05 .15
436 Kim Batiste .05 .15
437 Mark Davis .05 .15
438 Jose DeLeon .05 .15
439 Len Dykstra .10 .30
440 Jim Eisenreich .05 .15
441 Tommy Greene .05 .15
442 Pete Incaviglia .05 .15
443 Danny Jackson .05 .15
444 Todd Pratt RC .20 .50
445 Curt Schilling .10 .30
446 Milt Thompson .05 .15
447 David West .05 .15
448 Mitch Williams .05 .15
449 Steve Cooke .05 .15
450 Carlos Garcia .05 .15
451 Al Martin .10 .30
452 Blas Minor .05 .15
453 Dennis Moeller .05 .15
454 Denny Neagle .10 .30
455 Don Slaught .05 .15
456 Lonnie Smith .05 .15
457 Paul Wagner .05 .15
458 Bob Walk .05 .15
459 Kevin Young .10 .30
460 Rene Arocha RC .20 .50
461 Brian Barber .10 .30
462 Rheal Cormier .05 .15
463 Gregg Jefferies .05 .15
464 Joe Magrane .05 .15
465 Omar Olivares .05 .15
466 Geronimo Pena .05 .15
467 Allen Watson .05 .15
468 Mark Whiten .05 .15
469 Derek Bell .05 .15
470 Phil Clark .05 .15
471 Pat Gomez RC .10 .30
472 Tony Gwynn .40 1.00
473 Jeremy Hernandez .05 .15
474 Bruce Hurst .05 .15
475 Phil Plantier .05 .15
476 Scott Sanders RC .10 .30
477 Tim Scott .05 .15
478 Darrell Sherman RC .10 .30
479 Guillermo Velasquez .05 .15
480 Tim Worrell RC .10 .30
481 Todd Benzinger .05 .15
482 Bud Black .05 .15
483 Barry Bonds .75 2.00
484 Dave Burba .05 .15
485 Bryan Hickerson .05 .15
486 Dave Martinez .05 .15
487 Willie McGee .10 .30
488 Jeff Reed .05 .15
489 Kevin Rogers .05 .15
490 Matt Williams .10 .30
491 Trevor Wilson .05 .15
492 Harold Baines .10 .30
493 Mike Devereaux .05 .15
494 Todd Frohwirth .05 .15
495 Chris Hoiles .05 .15
496 Luis Mercedes .05 .15
497 Sherman Obando RC .10 .30
498 Brad Pennington .05 .15
499 Harold Reynolds .10 .30
500 Arthur Rhodes .05 .15
501 Cal Ripken 1.00 2.50
502 Rick Sutcliffe .10 .30
503 Fernando Valenzuela .10 .30
504 Mark Williamson .05 .15
505 Scott Bankhead .05 .15
506 Greg Blosser .05 .15
507 Ivan Calderon .05 .15
508 Roger Clemens .60 1.50
509 Andre Dawson .10 .30
510 Scott Fletcher .05 .15
511 Greg A. Harris .05 .15
512 Billy Hatcher .05 .15
513 Bob Melvin .05 .15
514 Carlos Quintana .05 .15
515 Luis Rivera .05 .15
516 Jeff Russell .05 .15
517 Ken Ryan RC .10 .30
518 Chili Davis .10 .30
519 Jim Edmonds RC 2.00 5.00
520 Gary Gaetti .10 .30
521 Torey Lovullo .05 .15
522 Troy Percival .20 .50
523 Tim Salmon .20 .50
524 Scott Sanderson .05 .15
525 J.T. Snow RC .30 .75
526 Jerome Walton .05 .15
527 Jason Bere .05 .15
528 Rod Bolton .05 .15
529 Ellis Burks .10 .30
530 Carlton Fisk .20 .50
531 Craig Grebeck .05 .15
532 Ozzie Guillen .10 .30
533 Roberto Hernandez .05 .15
534 Bo Jackson .30 .75
535 Kirk McCaskill .05 .15
536 Dave Stieb .05 .15
537 Robin Ventura .10 .30
538 Albert Belle .10 .30
539 Mike Bielecki .05 .15
540 Glenallen Hill .05 .15
541 Reggie Jefferson .05 .15
542 Kenny Lofton .10 .30
543 Jeff Mutis .05 .15
544 Junior Ortiz .05 .15
545 Manny Ramirez .50 1.25
546 Jeff Treadway .05 .15
547 Kevin Wickander .05 .15
548 Cecil Fielder .10 .30
549 Kirk Gibson .10 .30
550 Greg Gohr .05 .15
551 David Haas .05 .15
552 Bill Krueger .05 .15
553 Mike Moore .05 .15
554 Mickey Tettleton .05 .15
555 Lou Whitaker .10 .30
556 Kevin Appier .10 .30
557 Billy Brewer .05 .15
558 David Cone .10 .30
559 Greg Gagne .05 .15
560 Mark Gardner .05 .15
561 Phil Hiatt .05 .15
562 Felix Jose .05 .15
563 Jose Lind .05 .15
564 Mike Macfarlane .05 .15
565 Keith Miller .05 .15
566 Jeff Montgomery .05 .15
567 Hipolito Pichardo .05 .15
568 Ricky Bones .05 .15
569 Tom Brunansky .05 .15
570 Joe Kmak .05 .15
571 Pat Listach .05 .15
572 Graeme Lloyd RC .20 .50
573 Carlos Maldonado .05 .15
574 Josias Manzanillo .05 .15
575 Matt Mieske .05 .15
576 Kevin Reimer .05 .15
577 Bill Spiers .05 .15
578 Dickie Thon .05 .15
579 Willie Banks .05 .15
580 Jim Deshaies .05 .15
581 Mark Guthrie .05 .15
582 Brian Harper .05 .15
583 Chuck Knoblauch .10 .30
584 Gene Larkin .05 .15
585 Shane Mack .05 .15
586 David McCarty .05 .15
587 Mike Pagliarulo .05 .15
588 Mike Trombley .05 .15
589 Dave Winfield .10 .30
590 Jim Abbott .20 .50
591 Wade Boggs .20 .50
592 Russ Davis RC .10 .30
593 Steve Farr .05 .15
594 Steve Howe .05 .15
595 Mike Humphreys .05 .15
596 Jimmy Key .10 .30
597 Jim Leyritz .05 .15
598 Bobby Munoz .05 .15
599 Paul O'Neill .20 .50
600 Spike Owen .05 .15
601 Mike Stanley .05 .15
602 Danny Tartabull .05 .15
603 Scott Brosius .10 .30
604 Storm Davis .05 .15
605 Eric Fox .05 .15
606 Rich Gossage .10 .30
607 Scott Hemond .05 .15
608 Dave Henderson .05 .15
609 Mark McGwire .75 2.00
610 Mike Mohler RC .10 .30
611 Edwin Nunez .05 .15
612 Kevin Seitzer .05 .15
613 Ruben Sierra .10 .30
614 Chris Bosio .05 .15
615 Norm Charlton .05 .15
616 Jim Converse RC .10 .30
617 John Cummings RC .10 .30
618 Mike Felder .05 .15
619 Ken Griffey Jr. .60 1.50
620 Mike Hampton .10 .30
621 Erik Hanson .05 .15
622 Bill Haselman .05 .15
623 Tino Martinez .20 .50
624 Lee Tinsley .05 .15
625 Fernando Vina RC .20 .50
626 David Wainhouse .05 .15
627 Jose Canseco .20 .50
628 Benji Gil .05 .15
629 Tom Henke .05 .15
630 David Hulse RC .10 .30
631 Manuel Lee .05 .15
632 Craig Lefferts .05 .15
633 Robb Nen .10 .30
634 Gary Redus .05 .15
635 Bill Ripken .05 .15
636 Nolan Ryan 1.25 3.00
637 Dan Smith .05 .15
638 Matt Whiteside RC .10 .30
639 Roberto Alomar .20 .50
640 Juan Guzman .05 .15
641 Pat Hentgen .05 .15
642 Darrin Jackson .05 .15
643 Randy Knorr .05 .15
644 Domingo Martinez RC .10 .30
645 Paul Molitor .10 .30
646 Dick Schofield .05 .15
647 Dave Stewart .10 .30
648 Rey Sanchez CL .05 .15
649 Jeremy Hernandez CL .05 .15
650 Junior Ortiz CL .05 .15

1993 Ultra All-Rookies

COMPLETE SET (10) 6.00 15.00
SER.2 STATED ODDS 1:18
1 Rene Arocha .75 2.00
2 Jeff Conine .50 1.25
3 Phil Hiatt .25 .60
4 Mike Lansing .75 2.00
5 Al Martin .25 .60
6 David Nied .25 .60
7 Mike Piazza 5.00 12.00
8 Tim Salmon .75 2.00
9 J.T. Snow 1.25 3.00
10 Kevin Young .50 1.25

1993 Ultra All-Stars

COMPLETE SET (20) 15.00 40.00
SER.2 STATED ODDS 1:9
1 Darren Daulton .50 1.25
2 Will Clark .75 2.00
3 Ryne Sandberg 2.00 5.00
4 Barry Larkin .75 2.00
5 Gary Sheffield .50 1.25
6 Barry Bonds 3.00 8.00
7 Ray Lankford .50 1.25
8 Larry Walker .50 1.25
9 Greg Maddux 2.00 5.00
10 Lee Smith .50 1.25
11 Ivan Rodriguez .75 2.00
12 Mark McGwire 3.00 8.00
13 Carlos Baerga .25 .60
14 Cal Ripken 4.00 10.00
15 Edgar Martinez .75 2.00
16 Juan Gonzalez .50 1.25
17 Ken Griffey Jr. 2.50 6.00
18 Kirby Puckett 1.25 3.00
19 Frank Thomas 1.25 3.00
20 Mike Mussina .75 2.00

1993 Ultra Award Winners

COMPLETE SET (25) 15.00 40.00
RANDOM INSERTS IN SER.1 PACKS
1 Greg Maddux 2.00 5.00
2 Tom Pagnozzi .25 .60
3 Mark Grace .75 2.00
4 Jose Lind .25 .60
5 Terry Pendleton .50 1.25
6 Ozzie Smith 2.00 5.00
7 Barry Bonds 3.00 8.00
8 Andy Van Slyke .75 2.00
9 Larry Walker .50 1.25
10 Mark Langston .25 .60
11 Ivan Rodriguez .75 2.00
12 Don Mattingly 3.00 8.00
13 Roberto Alomar .75 2.00
14 Robin Ventura .50 1.25
15 Cal Ripken 4.00 10.00
16 Ken Griffey Jr. 2.50 6.00
17 Kirby Puckett 1.25 3.00
18 Devon White .50 1.25
19 Pat Listach .25 .60
20 Eric Karros .50 1.25
21 Pat Borders .25 .60
22 Greg Maddux 2.00 5.00
23 Dennis Eckersley .50 1.25
24 Barry Bonds 3.00 8.00
25 Gary Sheffield .50 1.25

1993 Ultra Eckersley

COMPLETE SET (10) 1.50 4.00
COMMON CARD (1-10) .20 .50
RANDOM INSERTS IN SER.1 PACKS
COMMON MAIL-IN (11-12) .40 1.00
MAIL-IN CARDS. DIST.VIA WRAPPER EXCH.
P1 D.Eckersley 1.50 4.00
P.Mullan Promo
AU Dennis Eckersley AU 20.00 50.00

1993 Ultra Home Run Kings

COMPLETE SET (10) 8.00 20.00
RANDOM INSERTS IN PACKS
1 Juan Gonzalez .60 1.50
2 Mark McGwire 4.00 10.00
3 Cecil Fielder .60 1.50
4 Fred McGriff 1.00 2.50
5 Albert Belle .60 1.50
6 Barry Bonds 4.00 10.00
7 Joe Carter .60 1.50
8 Gary Sheffield .60 1.50
9 Darren Daulton .60 1.50
10 Dave Hollins .30 .75

1993 Ultra Performers

COMPLETE SET (10) 8.00 20.00
SETS DISTRIBUTED VIA MAIL-IN OFFER
1 Barry Bonds 2.00 5.00
2 Juan Gonzalez .30 .75
3 Ken Griffey Jr. 1.50 4.00
4 Eric Karros .30 .75
5 Pat Listach .15 .40
6 Greg Maddux 1.25 3.00
7 David Nied .15 .40
8 Gary Sheffield .30 .75
9 J.T.Snow .75 2.00
10 Frank Thomas .75 2.00

1993 Ultra Strikeout Kings

COMPLETE SET (5) 5.00 12.00
SER.2 STATED ODDS 1:37
1 Roger Clemens 1.50 4.00
2 Juan Guzman .50 1.25
3 Randy Johnson 1.25 3.00
4 Nolan Ryan 4.00 10.00
5 John Smoltz .75 2.00

1994 Ultra

The 1994 Ultra baseball set consists of 600 standard-size cards that were issued in two series of 300. Each pack contains at least one insert card, while "Hot Packs" have nothing but insert cards in them. The cards are numbered on the back, grouped alphabetically within teams, and checklisted below alphabetically according to teams for each league with AL preceding NL. Rookie Cards include Ray Durham and Chan Ho Park.

COMPLETE SET (600) 12.50 30.00
COMPLETE SERIES 1 (300) 6.00 15.00
COMPLETE SERIES 2 (300) 6.00 15.00
1 Jeffrey Hammonds .05 .15
2 Chris Hoiles .05 .15
3 Ben McDonald .05 .15
4 Mark McLemore .05 .15
5 Alan Mills .05 .15
6 Jamie Moyer .10 .30
7 Brad Pennington .05 .15
8 Jim Poole .05 .15
9 Cal Ripken 1.00 2.50
10 Jack Voigt .05 .15
11 Roger Clemens .60 1.50
12 Danny Darwin .05 .15
13 Andre Dawson .10 .30
14 Scott Fletcher .05 .15
15 Greg A. Harris .05 .15
16 Billy Hatcher .05 .15
17 Jeff Russell .05 .15
18 Aaron Sele .05 .15
19 Mo Vaughn .10 .30
20 Mike Butcher .05 .15
21 Rod Correia .05 .15
22 Steve Frey .05 .15
23 Phil Leftwich RC .05 .15
24 Torey Lovullo .05 .15
25 Ken Patterson .05 .15
26 Eduardo Perez .05 .15
27 Tim Salmon .20 .50
28 J.T.Snow .10 .30
29 Chris Turner .05 .15
30 Wilson Alvarez .05 .15
31 Jason Bere .05 .15
32 Joey Cora .05 .15
33 Alex Fernandez .05 .15
34 Roberto Hernandez .05 .15
35 Lance Johnson .05 .15
36 Ron Karkovice .05 .15
37 Kirk McCaskill .05 .15
38 Jeff Schwarz .05 .15
39 Frank Thomas .30 .75
40 Sandy Alomar Jr. .05 .15
41 Albert Belle .10 .30
42 Felix Fermin .05 .15
43 Wayne Kirby .05 .15
44 Tom Kramer .05 .15
45 Kenny Lofton .10 .30
46 Jose Mesa .05 .15
47 Eric Plunk .05 .15
48 Paul Sorrento .05 .15
49 Jim Thome .20 .50
50 Bill Wertz .05 .15
51 John Doherty .05 .15
52 Cecil Fielder .10 .30
53 Travis Fryman .10 .30
54 Chris Gomez .05 .15
55 Mike Henneman .05 .15
56 Chad Kreuter .05 .15
57 Bob MacDonald .05 .15
58 Mike Moore .05 .15
59 Tony Phillips .05 .15
60 Lou Whitaker .10 .30
61 Kevin Appier .10 .30
62 Greg Gagne .05 .15
63 Chris Gwynn .05 .15
64 Bob Hamelin .05 .15
65 Chris Haney .05 .15
66 Phil Hiatt .05 .15
67 Felix Jose .05 .15
68 Jose Lind .05 .15
69 Mike Macfarlane .05 .15
70 Jeff Montgomery .05 .15
71 Hipolito Pichardo .05 .15
72 Juan Bell .05 .15
73 Cal Eldred .05 .15
74 Darryl Hamilton .05 .15
75 Doug Henry .05 .15
76 Mike Ignasiak .05 .15
77 John Jaha .05 .15
78 Graeme Lloyd .05 .15
79 Angel Miranda .05 .15
80 Dave Nilsson .05 .15
81 Troy O'Leary .05 .15
82 Kevin Reimer .05 .15
83 Willie Banks .05 .15
84 Larry Casian .05 .15
85 Scott Erickson .05 .15
86 Eddie Guardado .10 .30
87 Kent Hrbek .10 .30
88 Terry Jorgensen .05 .15
89 Chuck Knoblauch .10 .30
90 Pat Meares .05 .15
91 Mike Trombley .05 .15
92 Dave Winfield .10 .30
93 Wade Boggs .20 .50
94 Scott Kamieniecki .05 .15
95 Pat Kelly .05 .15
96 Jimmy Key .10 .30
97 Jim Leyritz .05 .15
98 Bobby Munoz .05 .15
99 Paul O'Neill .20 .50
100 Melido Perez .05 .15
101 Mike Stanley .05 .15
102 Danny Tartabull .05 .15
103 Bernie Williams .20 .50
104 Kurt Abbott RC .05 .15
105 Mike Bordick .05 .15
106 Ron Darling .05 .15
107 Brent Gates .05 .15
108 Miguel Jimenez .05 .15
109 Steve Karsay .05 .15
110 Scott Lydy .05 .15
111 Mark McGwire .75 2.00
112 Troy Neel .05 .15
113 Craig Paquette .05 .15
114 Bob Welch .05 .15
115 Bobby Witt .05 .15
116 Rich Amaral .05 .15
117 Mike Blowers .05 .15
118 Jay Buhner .10 .30
119 Dave Fleming .05 .15
120 Ken Griffey Jr. .60 1.50
121 Tino Martinez .20 .50
122 Marc Newfield .05 .15
123 Ted Power .05 .15
124 Mackey Sasser .05 .15
125 Omar Vizquel .20 .50
126 Kevin Brown .10 .30
127 Juan Gonzalez .10 .30
128 Tom Henke .05 .15
129 David Hulse .05 .15
130 Dean Palmer .10 .30
131 Roger Pavlik .05 .15
132 Ivan Rodriguez .20 .50
133 Kenny Rogers .10 .30
134 Doug Strange .05 .15
135 Pat Borders .05 .15
136 Joe Carter .10 .30
137 Darnell Coles .05 .15
138 Pat Hentgen .05 .15
139 Al Leiter .10 .30
140 Paul Molitor .10 .30
141 John Olerud .10 .30
142 Ed Sprague .05 .15
143 Dave Stewart .10 .30
144 Mike Timlin .05 .15
145 Duane Ward .05 .15
146 Devon White .10 .30
147 Steve Avery .05 .15
148 Steve Bedrosian .05 .15
149 Damon Berryhill .05 .15
150 Jeff Blauser .05 .15
151 Tom Glavine .20 .50
152 Chipper Jones .30 .75
153 Mark Lemke .05 .15
154 Fred McGriff .20 .50
155 Greg McMichael .05 .15
156 Deion Sanders .20 .50
157 John Smoltz .20 .50
158 Mark Wohlers .05 .15
159 Jose Bautista .05 .15
160 Steve Buechele .05 .15
161 Mike Harkey .05 .15
162 Greg Hibbard .05 .15
163 Chuck McElroy .05 .15
164 Mike Morgan .05 .15
165 Kevin Roberson .05 .15
166 Ryne Sandberg .50 1.25
167 Jose Vizcaino .05 .15
168 Rick Wilkins .05 .15
169 Willie Wilson .05 .15
170 Willie Greene .05 .15
171 Roberto Kelly .05 .15
172 Larry Luebbers RC .05 .15
173 Kevin Mitchell .05 .15
174 Joe Oliver .05 .15
175 John Roper .05 .15
176 Johnny Ruffin .05 .15
177 Reggie Sanders .10 .30
178 John Smiley .05 .15
179 Jerry Spradlin RC .05 .15
180 Freddie Benavides .05 .15
181 Dante Bichette .10 .30
182 Willie Blair .05 .15
183 Kent Bottenfield .05 .15
184 Jerald Clark .05 .15
185 Joe Girardi .05 .15
186 Roberto Mejia .05 .15
187 Steve Reed .05 .15
188 Armando Reynoso .05 .15
189 Bruce Ruffin .05 .15
190 Eric Young .05 .15
191 Luis Aquino .05 .15
192 Bret Barberie .05 .15
193 Ryan Bowen .05 .15
194 Chuck Carr .05 .15
195 Orestes Destrade .05 .15
196 Richie Lewis .05 .15
197 Dave Magadan .05 .15
198 Bob Natal .05 .15
199 Gary Sheffield .10 .30
200 Matt Turner .05 .15
201 Darrell Whitmore .05 .15
202 Eric Anthony .05 .15
203 Jeff Bagwell .20 .50
204 Andujar Cedeno .05 .15
205 Luis Gonzalez .10 .30
206 Xavier Hernandez .05 .15
207 Doug Jones .05 .15
208 Darryl Kile .10 .30
209 Scott Servais .05 .15
210 Greg Swindell .05 .15
211 Brian Williams .05 .15
212 Pedro Astacio .05 .15
213 Brett Butler .10 .30
214 Omar Daal .05 .15
215 Jim Gott .05 .15
216 Raul Mondesi .10 .30
217 Jose Offerman .05 .15
218 Mike Piazza .60 1.50
219 Cory Snyder .05 .15
220 Tim Wallach .05 .15
221 Todd Worrell .05 .15
222 Moises Alou .10 .30
223 Sean Berry .05 .15
224 Wil Cordero .05 .15
225 Jeff Fassero .05 .15
226 Darrin Fletcher .05 .15
227 Cliff Floyd .10 .30
228 Marquis Grissom .10 .30
229 Ken Hill .05 .15
230 Mike Lansing .05 .15
231 Kirk Rueter .05 .15
232 John Wetteland .10 .30
233 Rondell White .10 .30
234 Tim Bogar .05 .15
235 Jeromy Burnitz .10 .30
236 Dwight Gooden .10 .30
237 Todd Hundley .05 .15
238 Jeff Kent .20 .50
239 Josias Manzanillo .05 .15
240 Joe Orsulak .05 .15
241 Ryan Thompson .05 .15
242 Kim Batiste .05 .15
243 Darren Daulton .10 .30
244 Tommy Greene .05 .15
245 Dave Hollins .05 .15
246 Pete Incaviglia .05 .15
247 Danny Jackson .05 .15
248 Ricky Jordan .05 .15
249 John Kruk .10 .30
250 Mickey Morandini .05 .15
251 Terry Mulholland .05 .15
252 Ben Rivera .05 .15
253 Kevin Stocker .05 .15
254 Jay Bell .10 .30
255 Steve Cooke .05 .15
256 Jeff King .05 .15
257 Al Martin .05 .15
258 Danny Miceli .05 .15
259 Blas Minor .05 .15
260 Don Slaught .05 .15
261 Paul Wagner .05 .15
262 Tim Wakefield .20 .50
263 Kevin Young .05 .15
264 Rene Arocha .05 .15
265 Rich Batchelor RC .05 .15
266 Gregg Jefferies .05 .15
267 Brian Jordan .10 .30
268 Jose Oquendo .05 .15
269 Donovan Osborne .05 .15
270 Erik Pappas .05 .15
271 Mike Perez .05 .15
272 Bob Tewksbury .05 .15
273 Mark Whiten .05 .15
274 Todd Zeile .05 .15
275 Andy Ashby .05 .15
276 Brad Ausmus .20 .50
277 Phil Clark .05 .15
278 Jeff Gardner .05 .15
279 Ricky Gutierrez .05 .15
280 Tony Gwynn .40 1.00
281 Tim Mauser .05 .15
282 Scott Sanders .05 .15
283 Frank Seminara .05 .15
284 Wally Whitehurst .05 .15
285 Rod Beck .05 .15
286 Barry Bonds .75 2.00
287 Dave Burba .05 .15
288 Mark Carreon .05 .15
289 Royce Clayton .05 .15
290 Mike Jackson .05 .15
291 Darren Lewis .05 .15
292 Kirt Manwaring .05 .15
293 Dave Martinez .05 .15
294 Billy Swift .05 .15
295 Salomon Torres .05 .15
296 Matt Williams .10 .30
297 Checklist 1-75 .05 .15
298 Checklist 76-150 .05 .15
299 Checklist 151-225 .05 .15
300 Checklist 226-300 .05 .15
301 Brady Anderson .10 .30
302 Harold Baines .10 .30
303 Damon Buford .05 .15
304 Mike Devereaux .05 .15
305 Sid Fernandez .05 .15
306 Rick Krivda RC .05 .15
307 Mike Mussina .20 .50
308 Rafael Palmeiro .20 .50
309 Arthur Rhodes .05 .15
310 Chris Sabo .05 .15
311 Lee Smith .10 .30
312 Gregg Zaun RC .08 .25
313 Scott Cooper .05 .15
314 Mike Greenwell .05 .15
315 Tim Naehring .05 .15
316 Otis Nixon .05 .15
317 Paul Quantrill .05 .15
318 John Valentin .05 .15
319 Dave Valle .05 .15
320 Frank Viola .10 .30
321 Brian Anderson RC .15 .40
322 Garret Anderson .30 .75
323 Chad Curtis .05 .15
324 Chili Davis .10 .30
325 Gary DiSarcina .05 .15
326 Damion Easley .05 .15
327 Jim Edmonds .30 .75
328 Chuck Finley .10 .30
329 Joe Grahe .05 .15
330 Bo Jackson .30 .75
331 Mark Langston .05 .15
332 Harold Reynolds .10 .30
333 James Baldwin .05 .15
334 Ray Durham RC .40 1.00
335 Julio Franco .10 .30
336 Craig Grebeck .05 .15
337 Ozzie Guillen .10 .30
338 Joe Hall RC .05 .15
339 Darrin Jackson .05 .15
340 Jack McDowell .05 .15

341 Tim Raines .10 .30
342 Robin Ventura .10 .30
343 Carlos Baerga .05 .15
344 Derek Lilliquist .05 .15
345 Dennis Martinez .10 .30
346 Jack Morris .10 .30
347 Eddie Murray .30 .75
348 Chris Nabholz .05 .15
349 Charles Nagy .05 .15
350 Chad Ogea .05 .15
351 Manny Ramirez .30 .75
352 Omar Vizquel .20 .50
353 Tim Belcher .05 .15
354 Eric Davis .10 .30
355 Kirk Gibson .10 .30
356 Rick Greene .05 .15
357 Mickey Tettleton .05 .15
358 Alan Trammell .10 .30
359 David Wells .10 .30
360 Stan Belinda .05 .15
361 Vince Coleman .05 .15
362 David Cone .10 .30
363 Gary Gaetti .10 .30
364 Tom Gordon .05 .15
365 Dave Henderson .05 .15
366 Wally Joyner .10 .30
367 Brent Mayne .05 .15
368 Brian McRae .05 .15
369 Michael Tucker .05 .15
370 Ricky Bones .05 .15
371 Brian Harper .05 .15
372 Tyrone Hill .05 .15
373 Mark Kiefer .05 .15
374 Pat Listach .05 .15
375 Mike Matheny RC .30 .75
376 Jose Mercedes RC .05 .15
377 Jody Reed .05 .15
378 Kevin Seitzer .05 .15
379 B.J. Surhoff .10 .30
380 Greg Vaughn .05 .15
381 Turner Ward .05 .15
382 Wes Weger RC .05 .15
383 Bill Wegman .05 .15
384 Rick Aguilera .05 .15
385 Rich Becker .05 .15
386 Alex Cole .05 .15
387 Steve Dunn .05 .15
388 Keith Garagozzo RC .05 .15
389 LaTroy Hawkins RC .15 .40
390 Shane Mack .05 .15
391 David McCarty .05 .15
392 Pedro Munoz .05 .15
393 Derek Parks .05 .15
394 Kirby Puckett .30 .75
395 Kevin Tapani .05 .15
396 Matt Walbeck .05 .15
397 Jim Abbott .20 .50
398 Mike Gallego .05 .15
399 Xavier Hernandez .05 .15
400 Don Mattingly .75 2.00
401 Terry Mulholland .05 .15
402 Matt Nokes .05 .15
403 Luis Polonia .05 .15
404 Bob Wickman .05 .15
405 Mark Acre RC .05 .15
406 Fausto Cruz RC .05 .15
407 Dennis Eckersley .05 .15
408 Rickey Henderson .30 .75
409 Stan Javier .05 .15
410 Carlos Reyes RC .05 .15
411 Ruben Sierra .10 .30
412 Terry Steinbach .05 .15
413 Bill Taylor RC .05 .15
414 Todd Van Poppel .05 .15
415 Eric Anthony .05 .15
416 Bobby Ayala .05 .15
417 Chris Bosio .05 .15
418 Tim Davis .05 .15
419 Randy Johnson .30 .75
420 Kevin King RC .05 .15
421 Anthony Manahan RC .05 .15
422 Edgar Martinez .20 .50
423 Keith Mitchell .05 .15
424 Roger Salkeld .05 .15
425 Mac Suzuki RC .15 .40
426 Dan Wilson .05 .15
427 Duff Brumley RC .05 .15
428 Jose Canseco .20 .50
429 Will Clark .20 .50
430 Steve Dreyer RC .05 .15
431 Rick Helling .05 .15
432 Chris James .05 .15
433 Matt Whiteside .05 .15
434 Roberto Alomar .20 .50
435 Scott Brow .05 .15
436 Domingo Cedeno .05 .15
437 Carlos Delgado .20 .50
438 Juan Guzman .05 .15
439 Paul Spoljaric .05 .15
440 Todd Stottlemyre .05 .15
441 Woody Williams .05 .15
442 David Justice .10 .30
443 Mike Kelly .05 .15
444 Ryan Klesko .10 .30
445 Javier Lopez .10 .30
446 Greg Maddux .50 1.25
447 Kent Mercker .05 .15
448 Charlie O'Brien .05 .15
449 Terry Pendleton .10 .30
450 Mike Stanton .05 .15
451 Tony Tarasco .05 .15
452 Terrell Wade RC .05 .15
453 Willie Banks .05 .15
454 Shawon Dunston .05 .15
455 Mark Grace .20 .50
456 Jose Guzman .05 .15
457 Jose Hernandez .05 .15
458 Glenallen Hill .05 .15
459 Blaise Ilsley RC .05 .15
460 Brooks Kieschnick RC .05 .15
461 Derrick May .05 .15
462 Randy Myers .05 .15
463 Karl Rhodes .05 .15
464 Sammy Sosa .30 .75
465 Steve Trachsel .05 .15
466 Anthony Young .05 .15
467 Eddie Zambrano RC .05 .15
468 Bret Boone .10 .30
469 Tom Browning .05 .15
470 Hector Carrasco .05 .15
471 Rob Dibble .10 .30
472 Erik Hanson .05 .15
473 Thomas Howard .05 .15
474 Barry Larkin .20 .50
475 Hal Morris .05 .15
476 Jose Rijo .05 .15
477 John Burke .05 .15
478 Ellis Burks .10 .30
479 Marvin Freeman .05 .15
480 Andres Galarraga .10 .30
481 Greg W. Harris .05 .15
482 Charlie Hayes .05 .15
483 Darren Holmes .05 .15
484 Howard Johnson .05 .15
485 Marcus Moore .05 .15
486 David Nied .05 .15
487 Mark Thompson .05 .15
488 Walt Weiss .05 .15
489 Kurt Abbott .05 .15
490 Matias Carrillo RC .05 .15
491 Jeff Conine .10 .30
492 Chris Hammond .05 .15
493 Bryan Harvey .05 .15
494 Charlie Hough .10 .30
495 Yorkis Perez .05 .15
496 Pat Rapp .05 .15
497 Benito Santiago .10 .30
498 David Weathers .05 .15
499 Craig Biggio .20 .50
500 Ken Caminiti .10 .30
501 Doug Drabek .05 .15
502 Tony Eusebio .05 .15
503 Steve Finley .10 .30
504 Pete Harnisch .05 .15
505 Brian L. Hunter .05 .15
506 Domingo Jean .05 .15
507 Todd Jones .05 .15
508 Orlando Miller .05 .15
509 James Mouton .05 .15
510 Roberto Petagine .05 .15
511 Shane Reynolds .05 .15
512 Mitch Williams .05 .15
513 Billy Ashley .05 .15
514 Tom Candiotti .05 .15
515 Delino DeShields .05 .15
516 Kevin Gross .05 .15
517 Orel Hershiser .10 .30
518 Eric Karros .10 .30
519 Ramon Martinez .05 .15
520 Chan Ho Park RC .30 .75
521 Henry Rodriguez .05 .15
522 Joey Eischen .05 .15
523 Rod Henderson .05 .15
524 Pedro Martinez .30 .75
525 Mel Rojas .05 .15
526 Larry Walker .10 .30
527 Gabe White .05 .15
528 Bobby Bonilla .10 .30
529 Jonathan Hurst .05 .15
530 Bobby Jones .05 .15
531 Kevin McReynolds .05 .15
532 Bill Pulsipher .10 .30
533 Bret Saberhagen .10 .30
534 David Segui .05 .15
535 Pete Smith .05 .15
536 Kelly Stinnett RC .15 .40
537 Dave Telgheder .05 .15
538 Quilvio Veras .05 .15
539 Jose Vizcaino .05 .15
540 Pete Walker RC .05 .15
541 Ricky Bottalico RC .05 .15
542 Wes Chamberlain .05 .15
543 Mariano Duncan .05 .15
544 Lenny Dykstra .10 .30
545 Jim Eisenreich .05 .15
546 Phil Geisler RC .05 .15
547 Wayne Gomes RC .15 .40
548 Doug Jones .05 .15
549 Jeff Juden .05 .15
550 Mike Lieberthal .10 .30
551 Tony Longmire .05 .15
552 Tom Marsh .05 .15
553 Bobby Munoz .05 .15
554 Curt Schilling .10 .30
555 Carlos Garcia .05 .15
556 Ravelo Manzanillo RC .05 .15
557 Orlando Merced .05 .15
558 Will Pennyfeather .05 .15
559 Zane Smith .05 .15
560 Andy Van Slyke .20 .50
561 Rick White .05 .15
562 Luis Alicea .05 .15
563 Brian Barber .05 .15
564 Clint Davis RC .05 .15
565 Bernard Gilkey .05 .15
566 Ray Lankford .10 .30
567 Tom Pagnozzi .05 .15
568 Ozzie Smith .50 1.25
569 Rick Sutcliffe .10 .30
570 Allen Watson .05 .15
571 Dmitri Young .10 .30
572 Derek Bell .05 .15
573 Andy Benes .05 .15
574 Archi Cianfrocco .05 .15
575 Joey Hamilton .05 .15
576 Gene Harris .05 .15
577 Trevor Hoffman .20 .50
578 Tim Hyers RC .05 .15
579 Brian Johnson RC .05 .15
580 Keith Lockhart RC .15 .40
581 Pedro A.Martinez RC .05 .15
582 Ray McDavid .05 .15
583 Phil Plantier .05 .15
584 Bip Roberts .05 .15
585 Dave Staton .05 .15
586 Todd Benzinger .05 .15
587 John Burkett .05 .15
588 Bryan Hickerson .05 .15
589 Willie McGee .10 .30
590 John Patterson .05 .15
591 Mark Portugal .05 .15
592 Kevin Rogers .05 .15
593 Joe Rosselli .05 .15
594 Steve Soderstrom RC .05 .15
595 Robby Thompson .05 .15
596 125th Anniversary .05 .15
597 Jaime Navarro CL .05 .15
598 Andy Van Slyke CL .10 .30
599 Checklist .05 .15
600 Bryan Harvey CL .05 .15
P243 Darren Daulton Promo .75 2.00
P249 John Kruk Promo .75 2.00

1994 Ultra All-Rookies

COMPLETE SET (10) 3.00 8.00
SER.2 STATED ODDS 1:10
*JUMBOS: .75X TO 2X BASIC ALL-ROOK.
ONE JUMBO SET PER HOBBY CASE
1 Kurt Abbott .20 .50
2 Carlos Delgado .40 1.00
3 Cliff Floyd .40 1.00
4 Jeffrey Hammonds .20 .50
5 Ryan Klesko .40 1.00
6 Javier Lopez .40 1.00
7 Raul Mondesi .40 1.00
8 James Mouton .20 .50
9 Chan Ho Park .40 1.00
10 Dave Staton .20 .50

1994 Ultra All-Stars

COMPLETE SET (20) 6.00 15.00
SER.2 STATED ODDS 1:3
1 Chris Hoiles .08 .25
2 Frank Thomas .50 1.25
3 Roberto Alomar .30 .75
4 Cal Ripken 1.50 4.00
5 Robin Ventura .20 .50
6 Albert Belle .20 .50
7 Juan Gonzalez .20 .50
8 Ken Griffey Jr. 1.00 2.50
9 John Olerud .20 .50
10 Jack McDowell .08 .25
11 Mike Piazza 1.00 2.50
12 Fred McGriff .30 .75
13 Ryne Sandberg .75 2.00
14 Jay Bell .20 .50
15 Matt Williams .20 .50
16 Barry Bonds 1.25 3.00
17 Lenny Dykstra .20 .50
18 David Justice .20 .50
19 Tom Glavine .30 .75
20 Greg Maddux .75 2.00

1994 Ultra Award Winners

COMPLETE SET (25) 6.00 15.00
SER.1 STATED ODDS 1:3
1 Ivan Rodriguez .30 .75
2 Don Mattingly 1.25 3.00
3 Roberto Alomar .30 .75
4 Robin Ventura .20 .50
5 Omar Vizquel .30 .75
6 Ken Griffey Jr. 1.00 2.50
7 Kenny Lofton .20 .50
8 Devon White .20 .50
9 Mark Langston .08 .25
10 Kirt Manwaring .08 .25
11 Mark Grace .30 .75
12 Robby Thompson .08 .25
13 Matt Williams .20 .50
14 Jay Bell .20 .50
15 Barry Bonds 1.25 3.00
16 Marquis Grissom .20 .50
17 Larry Walker .20 .50
18 Greg Maddux .75 2.00
19 Frank Thomas .50 1.25
20 Barry Bonds 1.25 3.00
21 Paul Molitor .20 .50
22 Jack McDowell .08 .25
AL POY
23 Greg Maddux .75 2.00
24 Tim Salmon .30 .75
25 Mike Piazza 1.00 2.50

1994 Ultra Career Achievement

COMPLETE SET (5) 4.00 10.00
SER.2 STATED ODDS 1:21
1 Joe Carter .40 1.00
2 Paul Molitor .40 1.00
3 Cal Ripken 3.00 8.00
4 Ryne Sandberg 1.50 4.00
5 Dave Winfield .40 1.00

1994 Ultra Firemen

COMPLETE SET (10) 2.00 5.00
SER.1 STATED ODDS 1:11
1 Jeff Montgomery .20 .50
2 Duane Ward .20 .50
3 Tom Henke .20 .50
4 Roberto Hernandez .20 .50
5 Dennis Eckersley .40 1.00
6 Randy Myers .20 .50
7 Rod Beck .20 .50
8 Bryan Harvey .20 .50
9 John Wetteland .40 1.00
10 Mitch Williams .20 .50

1994 Ultra Hitting Machines

COMPLETE SET (10) 4.00 10.00
SER.2 STATED ODDS 1:5
1 Roberto Alomar .30 .75
2 Carlos Baerga .08 .25
3 Barry Bonds 1.25 3.00
4 Andres Galarraga .20 .50
5 Juan Gonzalez .20 .50
6 Tony Gwynn .60 1.50
7 Paul Molitor .20 .50
8 John Olerud .20 .50
9 Mike Piazza 1.00 2.50
10 Frank Thomas .50 1.25

1994 Ultra Home Run Kings

COMPLETE SET (12) 15.00 40.00
SER.1 FOIL STATED ODDS 1:36
1 Juan Gonzalez 1.50 4.00
2 Ken Griffey Jr. 5.00 12.00
3 Frank Thomas 2.50 6.00
4 Albert Belle 1.00 2.50
5 Rafael Palmeiro 1.50 4.00
6 Joe Carter 1.50 4.00
7 Barry Bonds 5.00 12.00
8 David Justice 1.00 2.50
9 Matt Williams 1.00 2.50
10 Fred McGriff 1.50 4.00
11 Ron Gant 1.00 2.50
12 Mike Piazza 2.50 6.00

1994 Ultra League Leaders

COMPLETE SET (10) 2.00 5.00
SER.1 STATED ODDS 1:11
1 John Olerud .30 .75
2 Rafael Palmeiro .50 1.25
3 Kenny Lofton .30 .75
4 Jack McDowell .15 .40
5 Randy Johnson .75 2.00
6 Andres Galarraga .30 .75
7 Lenny Dykstra .30 .75
8 Chuck Carr .15 .40
9 Tom Glavine .50 1.25
10 Jose Rijo .15 .40

1994 Ultra On-Base Leaders

COMPLETE SET (12) 40.00 100.00
SER.2 JUMBO STATED ODDS 1:36
1 Roberto Alomar 3.00 8.00
2 Barry Bonds 12.50 30.00
3 Lenny Dykstra 2.00 5.00
4 Andres Galarraga 2.00 5.00
5 Mark Grace 3.00 8.00
6 Ken Griffey Jr. 10.00 25.00
7 Gregg Jefferies 1.00 2.50
8 Orlando Merced 1.00 2.50
9 Paul Molitor 2.00 5.00
10 John Olerud 2.00 5.00
11 Tony Phillips 1.00 2.50
12 Frank Thomas 5.00 12.00

1994 Ultra Phillies Finest

COMPLETE SET (20) 4.00 10.00
COMPLETE SERIES 1 (10) 2.00 5.00
COMPLETE SERIES 2 (10) 2.00 5.00
COMMON DAULTON (1-5/11-15) .20 .50
COMMON KRUK (6-10/16-20) .20 .50
SER.1 STATED ODDS 1:6
SER.2 STATED ODDS 1:10
COMMON MAIL-IN (M1-M4) .40 1.00
MAIL-IN CARDS DIST.VIA WRAPPER EXCH.
AU1 Darren Daulton AU/1000 60.00 150.00
AU2 John Kruk AU/1000 30.00 60.00

1994 Ultra RBI Kings

COMPLETE SET (12) 25.00 60.00
SER.1 JUMBO STATED ODDS 1:36
1 Albert Belle 1.25 3.00
2 Frank Thomas 3.00 8.00
3 Joe Carter 1.25 3.00
4 Juan Gonzalez 1.25 3.00
5 Cecil Fielder 1.25 3.00
6 Carlos Baerga .60 1.50
7 Barry Bonds 8.00 20.00
8 David Justice 1.25 3.00
9 Ron Gant .60 1.50
10 Mike Piazza 6.00 15.00
11 Matt Williams 1.25 3.00
12 Darren Daulton 1.25 3.00

1994 Ultra Rising Stars

COMPLETE SET (12) 25.00 60.00
SER.2 FOIL STATED ODDS 1:36
1 Carlos Baerga .75 2.00
2 Jeff Bagwell 2.50 6.00
3 Albert Belle 1.50 4.00
4 Cliff Floyd 1.50 4.00
5 Travis Fryman 1.50 4.00
6 Marquis Grissom 1.50 4.00
7 Kenny Lofton 1.50 4.00
8 John Olerud 1.50 4.00
9 Mike Piazza 6.00 15.00
10 Kirk Rueter .75 2.00
11 Tim Salmon 2.50 6.00
12 Aaron Sele .75 2.00

1994 Ultra Second Year Standouts

COMPLETE SET (10) 4.00 10.00
SER.1 STATED ODDS 1:11
1 Jason Bere .25 .60
2 Brent Gates .25 .60
3 Jeffrey Hammonds .25 .60
4 Tim Salmon .75 2.00
5 Aaron Sele .25 .60
6 Chuck Carr .25 .60
7 Jeff Conine .50 1.25
8 Greg McMichael .25 .60
9 Mike Piazza 2.50 6.00
10 Kevin Stocker .25 .60

1994 Ultra Strikeout Kings

COMPLETE SET (5) 1.50 4.00
SER.2 STATED ODDS 1:7
1 Randy Johnson .50 1.25
2 Mark Langston .08 .25
3 Greg Maddux .75 2.00
4 Jose Rijo .08 .25
5 John Smoltz .30 .75

1995 Ultra

This 450-card standard-size set was issued in two series. The first series contained 250 cards while the second series consisted of 200 cards. They were issued in 12-card packs (either hobby or retail) with a suggested retail price of $1.99. Also, 15-card pre-priced packs with a suggested retail of $2.69. Each pack contained two inserts: one is a Gold Medallion parallel while the other is from one of Ultra's many insert sets. "Hot Packs" contained nothing but insert cards. The full-bleed fronts feature the player's photo with the team name and player's name at the bottom. The "95 Fleer Ultra" logo is in the upper right corner. The backs have a two-photo design; one of which is a full-size duotone shot with the other being a full-color action shot. In each series the cards were grouped alphabetically within teams and checklisted alphabetically according to teams for each league with AL preceding NL.

COMPLETE SET (450) 12.50 30.00
COMPLETE SERIES 1 (250) 8.00 20.00
COMPLETE SERIES 2 (200) 5.00 12.00
1 Brady Anderson .10 .30
2 Sid Fernandez .05 .15
3 Jeffrey Hammonds .05 .15
4 Chris Hoiles .05 .15
5 Ben McDonald .05 .15
6 Mike Mussina .20 .50
7 Rafael Palmeiro .20 .50
8 Jack Voigt .05 .15
9 Wes Chamberlain .05 .15
10 Roger Clemens .60 1.50
11 Chris Howard .05 .15
12 Tim Naehring .05 .15
13 Otis Nixon .05 .15
14 Rich Rowland .05 .15
15 Ken Ryan .05 .15
16 John Valentin .05 .15
17 Mo Vaughn .10 .30
18 Brian Anderson .05 .15
19 Chili Davis .10 .30
20 Damion Easley .05 .15
21 Jim Edmonds .20 .50
22 Mark Langston .05 .15
23 Tim Salmon .20 .50
24 J.T. Snow .10 .30
25 Chris Turner .05 .15
26 Wilson Alvarez .05 .15
27 Joey Cora .05 .15
28 Alex Fernandez .05 .15
29 Roberto Hernandez .05 .15
30 Lance Johnson .05 .15
31 Ron Karkovice .05 .15
32 Kirk McCaskill .05 .15
33 Tim Raines .10 .30
34 Frank Thomas .30 .75
35 Sandy Alomar Jr. .05 .15
36 Albert Belle .10 .30
37 Mark Clark .05 .15
38 Kenny Lofton .10 .30
39 Eddie Murray .30 .75
40 Eric Plunk .05 .15
41 Manny Ramirez .20 .50
42 Jim Thome .20 .50
43 Omar Vizquel .20 .50
44 Danny Bautista .05 .15
45 Junior Felix .05 .15
46 Cecil Fielder .10 .30
47 Chris Gomez .05 .15
48 Chad Kreuter .05 .15
49 Mike Moore .05 .15
50 Tony Phillips .05 .15
51 Alan Trammell .10 .30
52 David Wells .10 .30
53 Kevin Appier .10 .30
54 Billy Brewer .05 .15
55 David Cone .10 .30
56 Greg Gagne .05 .15
57 Bob Hamelin .05 .15
58 Jose Lind .05 .15
59 Brent Mayne .05 .15
60 Brian McRae .05 .15
61 Terry Shumpert .05 .15
62 Ricky Bones .05 .15
63 Mike Fetters .05 .15
64 Darryl Hamilton .05 .15
65 John Jaha .05 .15
66 Graeme Lloyd .05 .15
67 Matt Mieske .05 .15
68 Kevin Seitzer .05 .15
69 Jose Valentin .05 .15
70 Turner Ward .05 .15
71 Rick Aguilera .05 .15
72 Rich Becker .05 .15
73 Alex Cole .05 .15
74 Scott Leius .05 .15
75 Pat Meares .05 .15
76 Kirby Puckett .30 .75
77 Dave Stevens .05 .15
78 Kevin Tapani .05 .15
79 Matt Walbeck .05 .15
80 Wade Boggs .20 .50
81 Scott Kamieniecki .05 .15
82 Pat Kelly .05 .15
83 Jimmy Key .10 .30
84 Paul O'Neill .20 .50
85 Luis Polonia .05 .15
86 Mike Stanley .05 .15
87 Danny Tartabull .05 .15
88 Bob Wickman .05 .15
89 Mark Acre .05 .15
90 Geronimo Berroa .05 .15
91 Mike Bordick .05 .15
92 Ron Darling .05 .15
93 Stan Javier .05 .15
94 Mark McGwire .75 2.00
95 Troy Neel .05 .15
96 Ruben Sierra .10 .30
97 Terry Steinbach .05 .15
98 Eric Anthony .05 .15
99 Chris Bosio .05 .15
100 Dave Fleming .05 .15
101 Ken Griffey Jr. .60 1.50
102 Reggie Jefferson .05 .15
103 Randy Johnson .30 .75
104 Edgar Martinez .20 .50
105 Bill Risley .05 .15
106 Dan Wilson .05 .15
107 Cris Carpenter .05 .15
108 Will Clark .20 .50
109 Juan Gonzalez .10 .30
110 Rusty Greer .10 .30
111 David Hulse .05 .15
112 Roger Pavlik .05 .15
113 Ivan Rodriguez .20 .50
114 Doug Strange .05 .15
115 Matt Whiteside .05 .15
116 Roberto Alomar .20 .50
117 Brad Cornett .05 .15
118 Carlos Delgado .10 .30
119 Alex Gonzalez .05 .15
120 Darren Hall .05 .15
121 Pat Hentgen .05 .15
122 Paul Molitor .10 .30
123 Ed Sprague .05 .15
124 Devon White .10 .30
125 Tom Glavine .20 .50
126 David Justice .10 .30
127 Roberto Kelly .05 .15
128 Mark Lemke .05 .15
129 Greg Maddux .50 1.25
130 Greg McMichael .05 .15
131 Kent Mercker .05 .15
132 Charlie O'Brien .05 .15
133 John Smoltz .20 .50
134 Willie Banks .05 .15
135 Steve Buechele .05 .15
136 Kevin Foster .05 .15
137 Glenallen Hill .05 .15
138 Rey Sanchez .05 .15
139 Sammy Sosa .30 .75
140 Steve Trachsel .05 .15
141 Rick Wilkins .05 .15
142 Jeff Brantley .05 .15
143 Hector Carrasco .05 .15
144 Kevin Jarvis .05 .15
145 Barry Larkin .20 .50
146 Chuck McElroy .05 .15
147 Jose Rijo .05 .15
148 Johnny Ruffin .05 .15
149 Deion Sanders .20 .50
150 Eddie Taubensee .05 .15
151 Dante Bichette .10 .30
152 Ellis Burks .10 .30
153 Joe Girardi .05 .15
154 Charlie Hayes .05 .15
155 Mike Kingery .05 .15
156 Steve Reed .05 .15
157 Kevin Ritz .05 .15
158 Bruce Ruffin .05 .15
159 Eric Young .05 .15
160 Kurt Abbott .05 .15
161 Chuck Carr .05 .15
162 Chris Hammond .05 .15
163 Bryan Harvey .05 .15
164 Terry Mathews .05 .15
165 Yorkis Perez .05 .15
166 Pat Rapp .05 .15
167 Gary Sheffield .10 .30
168 Dave Weathers .05 .15
169 Jeff Bagwell .20 .50
170 Ken Caminiti .10 .30
171 Doug Drabek .05 .15
172 Steve Finley .10 .30
173 John Hudek .05 .15
174 Todd Jones .05 .15
175 James Mouton .05 .15
176 Shane Reynolds .05 .15
177 Scott Servais .05 .15
178 Tom Candiotti .05 .15
179 Omar Daal .05 .15
180 Darren Dreifort .05 .15
181 Eric Karros .10 .30
182 Ramon J.Martinez .05 .15
183 Raul Mondesi .10 .30
184 Henry Rodriguez .05 .15
185 Todd Worrell .05 .15
186 Moises Alou .10 .30
187 Sean Berry .05 .15
188 Wil Cordero .05 .15
189 Jeff Fassero .05 .15
190 Darrin Fletcher .05 .15
191 Butch Henry .05 .15
192 Ken Hill .05 .15
193 Mel Rojas .05 .15
194 John Wetteland .10 .30
195 Bobby Bonilla .10 .30
196 Rico Brogna .05 .15
197 Bobby Jones .05 .15
198 Jeff Kent .10 .30
199 Josias Manzanillo .05 .15
200 Kelly Stinnett .05 .15
201 Ryan Thompson .05 .15
202 Jose Vizcaino .05 .15
203 Lenny Dykstra .10 .30
204 Jim Eisenreich .05 .15
205 Dave Hollins .05 .15
206 Mike Lieberthal .10 .30
207 Mickey Morandini .05 .15
208 Bobby Munoz .05 .15
209 Curt Schilling .10 .30
210 Heathcliff Slocumb .05 .15
211 David West .05 .15
212 Dave Clark .05 .15
213 Steve Cooke .05 .15
214 Midre Cummings .05 .15
215 Carlos Garcia .05 .15
216 Jeff King .05 .15
217 Jon Lieber .05 .15
218 Orlando Merced .05 .15
219 Don Slaught .05 .15
220 Rick White .05 .15
221 Rene Arocha .05 .15
222 Bernard Gilkey .05 .15
223 Brian Jordan .10 .30
224 Tom Pagnozzi .05 .15
225 Vicente Palacios .05 .15
226 Geronimo Pena .05 .15
227 Ozzie Smith .50 1.25
228 Allen Watson .05 .15
229 Mark Whiten .05 .15
230 Brad Ausmus .10 .30
231 Derek Bell .05 .15
232 Andy Benes .05 .15
233 Tony Gwynn .40 1.00
234 Joey Hamilton .05 .15
235 Luis Lopez .05 .15
236 Pedro A.Martinez .05 .15
237 Scott Sanders .05 .15
238 Eddie Williams .05 .15
239 Rod Beck .05 .15
240 Dave Burba .05 .15
241 Darren Lewis .05 .15
242 Kirt Manwaring .05 .15
243 Mark Portugal .05 .15
244 Darryl Strawberry .10 .30
245 Robby Thompson .05 .15
246 Wm.VanLandingham .05 .15
247 Matt Williams .10 .30
248 Checklist .05 .15
249 Checklist .05 .15
250 Checklist .05 .15
251 Harold Baines .10 .30
252 Bret Barberie .05 .15
253 Armando Benitez .05 .15
254 Mike Devereaux .05 .15
255 Leo Gomez .05 .15
256 Jamie Moyer .10 .30
257 Arthur Rhodes .05 .15
258 Cal Ripken 1.00 2.50
259 Luis Alicea .05 .15
260 Jose Canseco .20 .50
261 Scott Cooper .05 .15
262 Andre Dawson .10 .30
263 Mike Greenwell .05 .15
264 Aaron Sele .05 .15
265 Garret Anderson .10 .30
266 Chad Curtis .05 .15
267 Gary DiSarcina .05 .15
268 Chuck Finley .10 .30
269 Rex Hudler .05 .15
270 Andrew Lorraine .05 .15
271 Spike Owen .05 .15
272 Lee Smith .10 .30
273 Jason Bere .05 .15
274 Ozzie Guillen .10 .30
275 Norberto Martin .05 .15
276 Scott Ruffcorn .05 .15
277 Robin Ventura .10 .30
278 Carlos Baerga .05 .15
279 Jason Grimsley .05 .15
280 Dennis Martinez .10 .30
281 Charles Nagy .05 .15
282 Paul Sorrento .05 .15
283 Dave Winfield .10 .30
284 John Doherty .05 .15
285 Travis Fryman .10 .30
286 Kirk Gibson .10 .30
287 Lou Whitaker .10 .30
288 Gary Gaetti .10 .30
289 Tom Gordon .05 .15
290 Mark Gubicza .05 .15
291 Wally Joyner .10 .30
292 Mike Macfarlane .05 .15
293 Jeff Montgomery .05 .15
294 Jeff Cirillo .05 .15
295 Cal Eldred .05 .15
296 Pat Listach .05 .15
297 Jose Mercedes .05 .15
298 Dave Nilsson .05 .15
299 Duane Singleton .05 .15
300 Greg Vaughn .05 .15
301 Scott Erickson .05 .15
302 Denny Hocking .05 .15
303 Chuck Knoblauch .10 .30
304 Pat Mahomes .05 .15
305 Pedro Munoz .05 .15
306 Erik Schullstrom .05 .15
307 Jim Abbott .20 .50
308 Tony Fernandez .05 .15
309 Sterling Hitchcock .05 .15
310 Jim Leyritz .05 .15
311 Don Mattingly .75 2.00
312 Jack McDowell .05 .15
313 Melido Perez .05 .15
314 Bernie Williams .20 .50
315 Scott Brosius .10 .30
316 Dennis Eckersley .10 .30
317 Brent Gates .05 .15
318 Rickey Henderson .30 .75
319 Steve Karsay .05 .15
320 Steve Ontiveros .05 .15
321 Bill Taylor .05 .15
322 Todd Van Poppel .05 .15
323 Bob Welch .05 .15
324 Bobby Ayala .05 .15
325 Mike Blowers .05 .15
326 Jay Buhner .10 .30
327 Felix Fermin .05 .15
328 Tino Martinez .20 .50
329 Marc Newfield .05 .15
330 Greg Pirkl .05 .15
331 Alex Rodriguez .75 2.00
332 Kevin Brown .10 .30
333 John Burkett .05 .15
334 Jeff Frye .05 .15
335 Kevin Gross .05 .15
336 Dean Palmer .10 .30
337 Joe Carter .10 .30
338 Shawn Green .10 .30
339 Juan Guzman .05 .15
340 Mike Huff .05 .15
341 Al Leiter .10 .30
342 John Olerud .10 .30
343 Dave Stewart .10 .30
344 Todd Stottlemyre .05 .15
345 Steve Avery .05 .15
346 Jeff Blauser .05 .15
347 Chipper Jones .30 .75
348 Mike Kelly .05 .15
349 Ryan Klesko .10 .30
350 Javier Lopez .10 .30
351 Fred McGriff .20 .50
352 Jose Oliva .05 .15
353 Terry Pendleton .10 .30
354 Mike Stanton .05 .15
355 Tony Tarasco .05 .15
356 Mark Wohlers .05 .15
357 Jim Bullinger .05 .15
358 Shawon Dunston .05 .15
359 Mark Grace .20 .50
360 Derrick May .05 .15
361 Randy Myers .05 .15
362 Karl Rhodes .05 .15
363 Bret Boone .10 .30
364 Brian Dorsett .05 .15
365 Ron Gant .10 .30
366 Brian R.Hunter .05 .15
367 Hal Morris .05 .15
368 Jack Morris .10 .30
369 John Roper .05 .15
370 Reggie Sanders .10 .30
371 Pete Schourek .05 .15
372 John Smiley .05 .15
373 Marvin Freeman .05 .15
374 Andres Galarraga .10 .30
375 Mike Munoz .05 .15
376 David Nied .05 .15
377 Walt Weiss .05 .15
378 Greg Colbrunn .05 .15
379 Jeff Conine .10 .30
380 Charles Johnson .10 .30
381 Kurt Miller .05 .15
382 Robb Nen .10 .30
383 Benito Santiago .10 .30
384 Craig Biggio .20 .50
385 Tony Eusebio .05 .15

386 Luis Gonzalez .10 .30
387 Brian L.Hunter .05 .15
388 Darryl Kile .10 .30
389 Orlando Miller .05 .15
390 Phil Plantier .05 .15
391 Greg Swindell .05 .15
392 Billy Ashley .05 .15
393 Pedro Astacio .05 .15
394 Brett Butler .10 .30
395 Delino DeShields .05 .15
396 Orel Hershiser .10 .30
397 Garey Ingram .05 .15
398 Chan Ho Park .10 .30
399 Mike Piazza .50 1.25
400 Ismael Valdes .05 .15
401 Tim Wallach .05 .15
402 Cliff Floyd .10 .30
403 Marquis Grissom .10 .30
404 Mike Lansing .05 .15
405 Pedro Martinez .20 .50
406 Kirk Rueter .05 .15
407 Tim Scott .05 .15
408 Jeff Shaw .05 .15
409 Larry Walker .10 .30
410 Rondell White .10 .30
411 John Franco .10 .30
412 Todd Hundley .05 .15
413 Jason Jacome .05 .15
414 Joe Orsulak .05 .15
415 Bret Saberhagen .10 .30
416 David Segui .05 .15
417 Darren Daulton .10 .30
418 Mariano Duncan .05 .15
419 Tommy Greene .05 .15
420 Gregg Jefferies .05 .15
421 John Kruk .10 .30
422 Kevin Stocker .05 .15
423 Jay Bell .10 .30
424 Al Martin .05 .15
425 Denny Neagle .10 .30
426 Zane Smith .05 .15
427 Andy Van Slyke .20 .50
428 Paul Wagner .05 .15
429 Tom Henke .05 .15
430 Danny Jackson .05 .15
431 Ray Lankford .10 .30
432 John Mabry .05 .15
433 Bob Tewksbury .05 .15
434 Todd Zeile .05 .15
435 Andy Ashby .05 .15
436 Andujar Cedeno .05 .15
437 Donnie Elliott .05 .15
438 Bryce Florie .05 .15
439 Trevor Hoffman .10 .30
440 Melvin Nieves .05 .15
441 Bip Roberts .05 .15
442 Barry Bonds .75 2.00
443 Royce Clayton .05 .15
444 Mike Jackson .05 .15
445 John Patterson .05 .15
446 J.R. Phillips .05 .15
447 Bill Swift .05 .15
448 Checklist .05 .15
449 Checklist .05 .15
450 Checklist .05 .15

1995 Ultra Gold Medallion

COMPLETE SET (450) 60.00 120.00
COMPLETE SERIES 1 (250) 30.00 60.00
COMPLETE SERIES 2 (200) 20.00 50.00
*STARS: 1.25X TO 3X BASIC CARDS
ONE PER PACK

1995 Ultra All-Rookies

COMPLETE SET (10) 2.00 5.00
SER.2 STATED ODDS 1:5
*GOLD MEDAL: .75X TO 2X BASIC AR
GM SER.2 STATED ODDS 1:50
1 Cliff Floyd .30 .75
2 Chris Gomez .15 .40
3 Rusty Greer .30 .75
4 Bob Hamelin .15 .40
5 Joey Hamilton .15 .40
6 John Hudek .15 .40
7 Ryan Klesko .30 .75
8 Raul Mondesi .30 .75
9 Manny Ramirez .50 1.25
10 Steve Trachsel .15 .40

1995 Ultra All-Stars

COMPLETE SET (20) 6.00 15.00
SER.2 STATED ODDS 1:4
*GOLD MEDAL: .75X TO 2X BASIC ALL-STARS
GM SER.2 STATED ODDS 1:40
1 Moises Alou .20 .50
2 Albert Belle .20 .50
3 Craig Biggio .30 .75
4 Wade Boggs .30 .75
5 Barry Bonds 1.25 3.00
6 David Cone .20 .50
7 Ken Griffey Jr. 1.00 2.50
8 Tony Gwynn .60 1.50
9 Chuck Knoblauch .20 .50
10 Barry Larkin .30 .75
11 Kenny Lofton .20 .50
12 Greg Maddux .75 2.00
13 Fred McGriff .30 .75
14 Paul O'Neill .30 .75
15 Mike Piazza .75 2.00
16 Kirby Puckett .50 1.25
17 Cal Ripken 1.50 4.00
18 Ivan Rodriguez .30 .75
19 Frank Thomas .50 1.25
20 Matt Williams .20 .50

1995 Ultra Award Winners

COMPLETE SET (25) 8.00 20.00
SER.1 STATED ODDS 1:4
*GOLD MEDAL: .75X TO 2X BASIC BASIC AW
GM SER.1 STATED ODDS 1:40
1 Ivan Rodriguez .30 .75
2 Don Mattingly 1.25 3.00
3 Roberto Alomar .30 .75
4 Wade Boggs .30 .75
5 Omar Vizquel .30 .75
6 Ken Griffey Jr. 1.00 2.50
7 Kenny Lofton .20 .50
8 Devon White .20 .50
9 Mark Langston .08 .25
10 Tom Pagnozzi .08 .25
11 Jeff Bagwell .30 .75
12 Craig Biggio .30 .75
13 Matt Williams .20 .50
14 Barry Larkin .30 .75
15 Barry Bonds 1.25 3.00
16 Marquis Grissom .20 .50
17 Darren Lewis .08 .25
18 Greg Maddux .75 2.00
19 Frank Thomas .50 1.25
20 Jeff Bagwell .30 .75
21 David Cone .20 .50
22 Greg Maddux .75 2.00
23 Bob Hamelin .08 .25
24 Raul Mondesi .20 .50
25 Moises Alou .20 .50

1995 Ultra Gold Medallion Rookies

COMPLETE SET (20) 3.00 8.00
SET DIST.VIA MAIL-IN WRAPPER OFFER
M1 Manny Alexander .08 .25
M2 Edgardo Alfonzo .08 .25
M3 Jason Bates .08 .25
M4 Andres Berumen .08 .25
M5 Darren Bragg .08 .25
M6 Jamie Brewington .08 .25
M7 Jason Christiansen .08 .25
M8 Brad Clontz .08 .25
M9 Marty Cordova .08 .25
M10 Johnny Damon .30 .75
M11 Vaughn Eshelman .08 .25
M12 Chad Fonville .08 .25
M13 Curtis Goodwin .08 .25
M14 Tyler Green .08 .25
M15 Bobby Higginson .30 .75
M16 Jason Isringhausen .20 .50
M17 Hideo Nomo 1.00 2.50
M18 Jon Nunnally .08 .25
M19 Carlos Perez .20 .50
M20 Julian Tavarez .08 .25

1995 Ultra Golden Prospects

COMPLETE SET (10) 4.00 10.00
SER.1 STATED ODDS 1:8 HOBBY
*GOLD MED: .75X TO 2X BASIC PROSPECTS
GM SER.1 STATED ODDS 1:80
1 James Baldwin .20 .50
2 Alan Benes .20 .50
3 Armando Benitez .20 .50
4 Ray Durham .40 1.00
5 LaTroy Hawkins .20 .50
6 Brian L.Hunter .20 .50
7 Derek Jeter 8.00 20.00
8 Charles Johnson .40 1.00
9 Alex Rodriguez 1.50 4.00
10 Michael Tucker .20 .50

1995 Ultra Hitting Machines

COMPLETE SET (10) 5.00 12.00
SER.2 STATED ODDS 1:8 RETAIL
*GOLD MEDAL: .75X TO 2X BASIC HIT.MACH.
GM SER.2 STATED ODDS 1:80 RETAIL
1 Jeff Bagwell .30 .75
2 Albert Belle .20 .50
3 Dante Bichette .20 .50
4 Barry Bonds 1.25 3.00
5 Jose Canseco .30 .75
6 Ken Griffey Jr. 1.00 2.50
7 Tony Gwynn .60 1.50
8 Fred McGriff .30 .75
9 Mike Piazza .75 2.00
10 Frank Thomas .50 1.25

1995 Ultra Home Run Kings

COMPLETE SET (10) 12.50 30.00
SER.1 STATED ODDS 1:8 RETAIL
*GOLD MEDAL: .75X TO 2X BASIC HR KINGS
GM SER.1 STATED ODDS 1:80 RETAIL
1 Ken Griffey Jr. 2.50 6.00
2 Frank Thomas 1.25 3.00
3 Albert Belle .50 1.25
4 Jose Canseco .75 2.00
5 Cecil Fielder .50 1.25
6 Matt Williams .50 1.25
7 Jeff Bagwell .75 2.00
8 Barry Bonds 3.00 8.00
9 Fred McGriff .75 2.00
10 Andres Galarraga .50 1.25
S8 Barry Bonds Sample .75 2.00

1995 Ultra League Leaders

COMPLETE SET (10) 2.50 6.00
SER.1 STATED ODDS 1:3
*GOLD MEDAL: .75X TO 2X BASIC LL
GM SER.1 STATED ODDS 1:30
1 Paul O'Neill .30 .75
2 Kenny Lofton .20 .50
3 Jimmy Key .20 .50
4 Randy Johnson .50 1.25
5 Lee Smith .20 .50
6 Tony Gwynn .60 1.50
7 Craig Biggio .30 .75
8 Greg Maddux .75 2.00
9 Andy Benes .08 .25
10 John Franco .20 .50

1995 Ultra On-Base Leaders

COMPLETE SET (10) 15.00 40.00
SER.2 STATED ODDS 1:8 JUMBO
*GOLD MEDAL: .75X TO 2X BASIC OBL
GM SER.2 STATED ODDS 1:80 JUMBO
1 Jeff Bagwell 1.25 3.00
2 Albert Belle .75 2.00
3 Craig Biggio 1.25 3.00
4 Wade Boggs 1.25 3.00
5 Barry Bonds 5.00 12.00
6 Will Clark 1.25 3.00
7 Tony Gwynn 2.50 6.00
8 David Justice .75 2.00
9 Paul O'Neill 1.25 3.00
10 Frank Thomas 2.00 5.00

1995 Ultra Power Plus

COMPLETE SET (6) 10.00 25.00
SER.1 STATED ODDS 1:37
*GOLD MEDAL: .75X TO 2X BASIC PLUS
GM SER.1 STATED ODDS 1:370
1 Albert Belle .60 1.50
2 Ken Griffey Jr. 3.00 8.00
3 Frank Thomas 1.50 4.00
4 Jeff Bagwell 1.00 2.50
5 Barry Bonds 4.00 10.00
6 Matt Williams .60 1.50

1995 Ultra RBI Kings

COMPLETE SET (10) 12.50 30.00
SER.1 STATED ODDS 1:11 JUMBO
*GOLD MEDAL: .75X TO 2X BASIC RBI KINGS
GM SER.1 STATED ODDS 1:110 JUMBO
1 Kirby Puckett 2.00 5.00
2 Joe Carter .75 2.00
3 Albert Belle .75 2.00
4 Frank Thomas 2.00 5.00
5 Julio Franco .40 1.00
6 Jeff Bagwell 1.25 3.00
7 Matt Williams .75 2.00
8 Dante Bichette .75 2.00
9 Fred McGriff 1.25 3.00
10 Mike Piazza 3.00 8.00

1995 Ultra Rising Stars

COMPLETE SET (9) 15.00 40.00
SER.2 STATED ODDS 1:37
*GOLD MEDAL: .75X TO 2X BASIC RISING
GM SER.2 STATED ODDS 1:370
1 Moises Alou 1.25 3.00
2 Jeff Bagwell 2.00 5.00
3 Albert Belle 1.25 3.00
4 Juan Gonzalez 1.25 3.00
5 Chuck Knoblauch 1.25 3.00
6 Kenny Lofton 1.25 3.00
7 Raul Mondesi 1.25 3.00
8 Mike Piazza 5.00 12.00
9 Frank Thomas 3.00 8.00

1995 Ultra Second Year Standouts

COMPLETE SET (15) 3.00 8.00
SER.1 STATED ODDS 1:6
*GOLD MEDAL: .75X TO 2X BASIC 2YS
GM SER.1 STATED ODDS 1:60
1 Cliff Floyd .50 1.25
2 Chris Gomez .25 .60
3 Rusty Greer .50 1.25
4 Darren Hall .25 .60
5 Bob Hamelin .25 .60
6 Joey Hamilton .25 .60
7 Jeffrey Hammonds .25 .60
8 John Hudek .25 .60
9 Ryan Klesko .50 1.25
10 Raul Mondesi .50 1.25
11 Manny Ramirez .75 2.00
12 Bill Risley .25 .60
13 Steve Trachsel .25 .60
14 W.VanLandingham .25 .60
15 Rondell White .50 1.25

1995 Ultra Strikeout Kings

COMPLETE SET (6) 2.00 5.00
SER.2 STATED ODDS 1:5
*GOLD MEDAL: .75X TO 2X BASIC K KINGS
GM SER.2 STATED ODDS 1:50
1 Andy Benes .08 .25
2 Roger Clemens 1.00 2.50
3 Randy Johnson .50 1.25
4 Greg Maddux .75 2.00
5 Pedro Martinez .30 .75
6 Jose Rijo .08 .25

1996 Ultra Promos

COMPLETE SET (6) 3.00 8.00
SC2 Tony Gwynn Season Crown .60 1.50
SC4 Kenny Lofton Season Crown .30 .75
NNO Roberto Alomar Prime Leather .30 .75
NNO Ken Griffey Jr. .75 2.00
NNO Cal Ripken Prime Leather 1.25 3.00
NNO Barry Bonds HR King .50 1.25

1996 Ultra

The 1996 Ultra set, produced by Fleer, contains 600 standard-size cards. The cards were distributed in packs that included two inserts. One insert is a Gold Medallion parallel while the other insert comes from one of the many Ultra insert sets. The cards are thicker than their 1995 counterparts and the fronts feature the player in an action shot in full-bleed color. The cards are sequenced in alphabetical order within league and team order.

COMPLETE SET (600) 20.00 50.00
COMPLETE SERIES 1 (300) 10.00 25.00
COMPLETE SERIES 2 (300) 10.00 25.00
SUBSET CARDS HALF VALUE OF BASE CARDS
RIPKEN DUST AVAIL.VIA MAIL EXCHANGE
1 Manny Alexander .10 .30
2 Brady Anderson .10 .30
3 Bobby Bonilla .10 .30
4 Scott Erickson .10 .30
5 Curtis Goodwin .10 .30
6 Chris Hoiles .10 .30
7 Doug Jones .10 .30
8 Jeff Manto .10 .30
9 Mike Mussina .20 .50
10 Rafael Palmeiro .20 .50
11 Cal Ripken 1.00 2.50
12 Rick Aguilera .10 .30
13 Luis Alicea .10 .30
14 Stan Belinda .10 .30
15 Jose Canseco .20 .50
16 Roger Clemens .60 1.50
17 Mike Greenwell .10 .30
18 Mike Macfarlane .10 .30
19 Tim Naehring .10 .30
20 Troy O'Leary .10 .30
21 John Valentin .10 .30
22 Mo Vaughn .10 .30
23 Tim Wakefield .10 .30
24 Brian Anderson .10 .30
25 Garret Anderson .10 .30
26 Chili Davis .10 .30
27 Gary DiSarcina .10 .30
28 Jim Edmonds .10 .30
29 Jorge Fabregas .10 .30
30 Chuck Finley .10 .30
31 Mark Langston .10 .30
32 Troy Percival .10 .30
33 Tim Salmon .20 .50
34 Lee Smith .10 .30
35 Wilson Alvarez .10 .30
36 Ray Durham .10 .30
37 Alex Fernandez .10 .30
38 Ozzie Guillen .10 .30
39 Roberto Hernandez .10 .30
40 Lance Johnson .10 .30
41 Ron Karkovice .10 .30
42 Lyle Mouton .10 .30
43 Tim Raines .10 .30
44 Frank Thomas .30 .75
45 Carlos Baerga .10 .30
46 Albert Belle .10 .30
47 Orel Hershiser .10 .30
48 Kenny Lofton .10 .30
49 Dennis Martinez .10 .30
50 Jose Mesa .10 .30
51 Eddie Murray .30 .75
52 Chad Ogea .10 .30
53 Manny Ramirez .20 .50
54 Jim Thome .20 .50
55 Omar Vizquel .20 .50
56 Dave Winfield .10 .30
57 Chad Curtis .10 .30
58 Cecil Fielder .10 .30
59 John Flaherty .10 .30
60 Travis Fryman .10 .30
61 Chris Gomez .10 .30
62 Bob Higginson .10 .30
63 Felipe Lira .10 .30
64 Brian Maxcy .10 .30
65 Alan Trammell .10 .30
66 Lou Whitaker .10 .30
67 Kevin Appier .10 .30
68 Gary Gaetti .10 .30
69 Tom Goodwin .10 .30
70 Tom Gordon .10 .30
71 Jason Jacome .10 .30
72 Wally Joyner .10 .30
73 Brent Mayne .10 .30
74 Jeff Montgomery .10 .30
75 Jon Nunnally .10 .30
76 Joe Vitiello .10 .30
77 Ricky Bones .10 .30
78 Jeff Cirillo .10 .30
79 Mike Fetters .10 .30
80 Darryl Hamilton .10 .30
81 David Hulse .10 .30
82 Dave Nilsson .10 .30
83 Kevin Seitzer .10 .30
84 Steve Sparks .10 .30
85 B.J. Surhoff .10 .30
86 Jose Valentin .10 .30
87 Greg Vaughn .10 .30
88 Marty Cordova .10 .30
89 Chuck Knoblauch .10 .30
90 Pat Meares .10 .30
91 Pedro Munoz .10 .30
92 Kirby Puckett .30 .75
93 Brad Radke .10 .30
94 Scott Stahoviak .10 .30
95 Dave Stevens .10 .30
96 Mike Trombley .10 .30
97 Matt Walbeck .10 .30
98 Wade Boggs .20 .50
99 Russ Davis .10 .30
100 Jim Leyritz .10 .30
101 Don Mattingly .75 2.00
102 Jack McDowell .10 .30
103 Paul O'Neill .20 .50
104 Andy Pettitte .20 .50
105 Mariano Rivera 2.00 5.00
106 Ruben Sierra .10 .30
107 Darryl Strawberry .10 .30
108 John Wetteland .10 .30
109 Bernie Williams .20 .50
110 Geronimo Berroa .10 .30
111 Scott Brosius .10 .30
112 Dennis Eckersley .10 .30
113 Brent Gates .10 .30
114 Rickey Henderson .30 .75
115 Mark McGwire .75 2.00
116 Ariel Prieto .10 .30
117 Terry Steinbach .10 .30
118 Todd Stottlemyre .10 .30
119 Todd Van Poppel .10 .30
120 Steve Wojciechowski .10 .30
121 Rich Amaral .10 .30
122 Bobby Ayala .10 .30
123 Mike Blowers .10 .30
124 Chris Bosio .10 .30
125 Joey Cora .10 .30
126 Ken Griffey Jr. .60 1.50
127 Randy Johnson .30 .75
128 Edgar Martinez .20 .50
129 Tino Martinez .20 .50
130 Alex Rodriguez .60 1.50
131 Dan Wilson .10 .30
132 Will Clark .20 .50
133 Jeff Frye .10 .30
134 Benji Gil .10 .30
135 Juan Gonzalez .10 .30
136 Rusty Greer .10 .30
137 Mark McLemore .10 .30
138 Roger Pavlik .10 .30
139 Ivan Rodriguez .20 .50
140 Kenny Rogers .10 .30
141 Mickey Tettleton .10 .30
142 Roberto Alomar .20 .50
143 Joe Carter .10 .30
144 Tony Castillo .10 .30
145 Alex Gonzalez .10 .30
146 Shawn Green .10 .30
147 Pat Hentgen .10 .30
148 Sandy Martinez .10 .30
149 Paul Molitor .10 .30
150 John Olerud .10 .30
151 Ed Sprague .10 .30
152 Jeff Blauser .10 .30
153 Brad Clontz .10 .30
154 Tom Glavine .20 .50
155 Marquis Grissom .10 .30
156 Chipper Jones .30 .75
157 David Justice .10 .30
158 Ryan Klesko .10 .30
159 Javier Lopez .10 .30
160 Greg Maddux .50 1.25
161 John Smoltz .20 .50
162 Mark Wohlers .10 .30
163 Jim Bullinger .10 .30
164 Frank Castillo .10 .30
165 Shawon Dunston .10 .30
166 Kevin Foster .10 .30
167 Luis Gonzalez .10 .30
168 Mark Grace .20 .50
169 Rey Sanchez .10 .30
170 Scott Servais .10 .30
171 Sammy Sosa .30 .75
172 Ozzie Timmons .10 .30
173 Steve Trachsel .10 .30
174 Bret Boone .10 .30
175 Jeff Branson .10 .30
176 Jeff Brantley .10 .30
177 Dave Burba .10 .30
178 Ron Gant .10 .30
179 Barry Larkin .20 .50
180 Darren Lewis .10 .30
181 Mark Portugal .10 .30
182 Reggie Sanders .10 .30
183 Pete Schourek .10 .30
184 John Smiley .10 .30
185 Jason Bates .10 .30
186 Dante Bichette .10 .30
187 Ellis Burks .10 .30
188 Vinny Castilla .10 .30
189 Andres Galarraga .10 .30
190 Darren Holmes .10 .30
191 Armando Reynoso .10 .30
192 Kevin Ritz .10 .30
193 Bill Swift .10 .30
194 Larry Walker .10 .30
195 Kurt Abbott .10 .30
196 John Burkett .10 .30
197 Greg Colbrunn .10 .30
198 Jeff Conine .10 .30
199 Andre Dawson .10 .30
200 Chris Hammond .10 .30
201 Charles Johnson .10 .30
202 Robb Nen .10 .30
203 Terry Pendleton .10 .30
204 Quilvio Veras .10 .30
205 Jeff Bagwell .20 .50
206 Derek Bell .10 .30
207 Doug Drabek .10 .30
208 Tony Eusebio .10 .30
209 Mike Hampton .10 .30
210 Brian L. Hunter .10 .30
211 Todd Jones .10 .30
212 Orlando Miller .10 .30
213 James Mouton .10 .30
214 Shane Reynolds .10 .30
215 Dave Veres .10 .30
216 Billy Ashley .10 .30
217 Brett Butler .10 .30
218 Chad Fonville .10 .30
219 Todd Hollandsworth .10 .30
220 Eric Karros .10 .30
221 Ramon Martinez .10 .30
222 Raul Mondesi .10 .30
223 Hideo Nomo .30 .75
224 Mike Piazza .50 1.25
225 Kevin Tapani .10 .30
226 Ismael Valdes .10 .30
227 Todd Worrell .10 .30
228 Moises Alou .10 .30
229 Wil Cordero .10 .30
230 Jeff Fassero .10 .30
231 Darrin Fletcher .10 .30
232 Mike Lansing .10 .30
233 Pedro Martinez .20 .50
234 Carlos Perez .10 .30
235 Mel Rojas .10 .30
236 David Segui .10 .30
237 Tony Tarasco .10 .30
238 Rondell White .10 .30
239 Edgardo Alfonzo .10 .30
240 Rico Brogna .10 .30
241 Carl Everett .10 .30
242 Todd Hundley .10 .30
243 Butch Huskey .10 .30
244 Jason Isringhausen .10 .30
245 Bobby Jones .10 .30
246 Jeff Kent .10 .30
247 Bill Pulsipher .10 .30
248 Jose Vizcaino .10 .30
249 Ricky Bottalico .10 .30
250 Darren Daulton .10 .30
251 Jim Eisenreich .10 .30
252 Tyler Green .10 .30
253 Charlie Hayes .10 .30
254 Gregg Jefferies .10 .30
255 Tony Longmire .10 .30
256 Michael Mimbs .10 .30
257 Mickey Morandini .10 .30
258 Paul Quantrill .10 .30
259 Heathcliff Slocumb .10 .30
260 Jay Bell .10 .30
261 Jacob Brumfield .10 .30
262 Angelo Encarnacion RC .10 .30
263 John Ericks .10 .30
264 Mark Johnson .10 .30
265 Esteban Loaiza .10 .30
266 Al Martin .10 .30
267 Orlando Merced .10 .30
268 Dan Miceli .10 .30
269 Denny Neagle .10 .30
270 Brian Barber .10 .30
271 Scott Cooper .10 .30
272 Tripp Cromer .10 .30
273 Bernard Gilkey .10 .30
274 Tom Henke .10 .30
275 Brian Jordan .10 .30
276 John Mabry .10 .30
277 Tom Pagnozzi .10 .30
278 Mark Petkovsek .10 .30
279 Ozzie Smith .50 1.25
280 Andy Ashby .10 .30
281 Brad Ausmus .10 .30
282 Ken Caminiti .10 .30
283 Glenn Dishman .10 .30
284 Tony Gwynn .40 1.00
285 Joey Hamilton .10 .30
286 Trevor Hoffman .10 .30
287 Phil Plantier .10 .30
288 Jody Reed .10 .30
289 Eddie Williams .10 .30
290 Barry Bonds .75 2.00
291 Jamie Brewington RC .10 .30
292 Mark Carreon .10 .30
293 Royce Clayton .10 .30
294 Glenallen Hill .10 .30
295 Mark Leiter .10 .30
296 Kirt Manwaring .10 .30
297 J.R. Phillips .10 .30
298 Deion Sanders .20 .50
299 Wm. VanLandingham .10 .30
300 Matt Williams .10 .30
301 Roberto Alomar .20 .50
302 Armando Benitez .10 .30
303 Mike Devereaux .10 .30
304 Jeffrey Hammonds .10 .30
305 Jimmy Haynes .10 .30
306 Scott McClain .10 .30
307 Kent Mercker .10 .30
308 Randy Myers .10 .30
309 B.J. Surhoff .10 .30
310 Tony Tarasco .10 .30
311 David Wells .10 .30
312 Wil Cordero .10 .30
313 Alex Delgado .10 .30
314 Tom Gordon .10 .30
315 Dwayne Hosey .10 .30
316 Jose Malave .10 .30
317 Kevin Mitchell .10 .30
318 Jamie Moyer .10 .30
319 Aaron Sele .10 .30
320 Heathcliff Slocumb .10 .30
321 Mike Stanley .10 .30
322 Jeff Suppan .10 .30
323 Jim Abbott .20 .50
324 George Arias .10 .30
325 Todd Greene .10 .30
326 Bryan Harvey .10 .30
327 J.T. Snow .10 .30
328 Randy Velarde .10 .30
329 Tim Wallach .10 .30
330 Harold Baines .10 .30
331 Jason Bere .10 .30
332 Darren Lewis .10 .30
333 Norberto Martin .10 .30
334 Tony Phillips .10 .30
335 Bill Simas .10 .30
336 Chris Snopek .10 .30
337 Kevin Tapani .10 .30
338 Danny Tartabull .10 .30
339 Robin Ventura .10 .30
340 Sandy Alomar Jr. .10 .30
341 Julio Franco .10 .30
342 Jack McDowell .10 .30
343 Charles Nagy .10 .30
344 Julian Tavarez .10 .30
345 Kimera Bartee .10 .30
346 Greg Keagle .10 .30
347 Mark Lewis .10 .30
348 Jose Lima .10 .30
349 Melvin Nieves .10 .30
350 Mark Parent .10 .30
351 Eddie Williams .10 .30
352 Johnny Damon .20 .50
353 Sal Fasano .10 .30
354 Mark Gubicza .10 .30
355 Bob Hamelin .10 .30
356 Chris Haney .10 .30
357 Keith Lockhart .10 .30
358 Mike Macfarlane .10 .30
359 Jose Offerman .10 .30
360 Bip Roberts .10 .30
361 Michael Tucker .10 .30
362 Chuck Carr .10 .30
363 Bobby Hughes .10 .30
364 John Jaha .10 .30
365 Mark Loretta .10 .30
366 Mike Matheny .10 .30
367 Ben McDonald .10 .30
368 Matt Mieske .10 .30
369 Angel Miranda .10 .30
370 Fernando Vina .10 .30
371 Rick Aguilera .10 .30
372 Rich Becker .10 .30
373 LaTroy Hawkins .10 .30
374 Dave Hollins .10 .30
375 Roberto Kelly .10 .30
376 Matt Lawton RC .15 .40
377 Paul Molitor .10 .30
378 Dan Naulty RC .10 .30
379 Rich Robertson .10 .30
380 Frank Rodriguez .10 .30
381 David Cone .10 .30
382 Mariano Duncan .10 .30
383 Andy Fox .10 .30
384 Joe Girardi .10 .30
385 Dwight Gooden .10 .30
386 Derek Jeter 1.00 2.50
387 Pat Kelly .10 .30
388 Jimmy Key .10 .30
389 Matt Luke .10 .30
390 Tino Martinez .20 .50
391 Jeff Nelson .10 .30
392 Melido Perez .10 .30
393 Tim Raines .10 .30
394 Ruben Rivera .10 .30
395 Kenny Rogers .10 .30
396 Tony Batista RC .25 .60
397 Allen Battle .10 .30
398 Mike Bordick .10 .30
399 Steve Cox .10 .30
400 Jason Giambi .10 .30
401 Doug Johns .10 .30
402 Pedro Munoz .10 .30
403 Phil Plantier .10 .30
404 Scott Spiezio .10 .30
405 George Williams .10 .30
406 Ernie Young .10 .30
407 Darren Bragg .10 .30
408 Jay Buhner .10 .30
409 Norm Charlton .10 .30
410 Russ Davis .10 .30
411 Sterling Hitchcock .10 .30
412 Edwin Hurtado .10 .30
413 Raul Ibanez RC .75 2.00
414 Mike Jackson .10 .30
415 Luis Sojo .10 .30
416 Paul Sorrento .10 .30
417 Bob Wolcott .10 .30
418 Damon Buford .10 .30
419 Kevin Gross .10 .30
420 Darryl Hamilton UER .10 .30
421 Mike Henneman .10 .30
422 Ken Hill .10 .30
423 Dean Palmer .10 .30
424 Bobby Witt .10 .30
425 Tilson Brito RC .10 .30
426 Giovanni Carrara RC .10 .30
427 Domingo Cedeno .10 .30
428 Felipe Crespo .10 .30
429 Carlos Delgado .10 .30
430 Juan Guzman .10 .30
431 Erik Hanson .10 .30
432 Marty Janzen .10 .30
433 Otis Nixon .10 .30
434 Robert Perez .10 .30
435 Paul Quantrill .10 .30
436 Bill Risley .10 .30
437 Steve Avery .10 .30
438 Jermaine Dye .10 .30
439 Mark Lemke .10 .30
440 Marty Malloy RC .10 .30
441 Fred McGriff .20 .50
442 Greg McMichael .10 .30
443 Wonderful Monds RC .10 .30
444 Eddie Perez .10 .30
445 Jason Schmidt .20 .50
446 Terrell Wade .10 .30
447 Terry Adams .10 .30
448 Scott Bullett .10 .30
449 Robin Jennings .10 .30
450 Doug Jones .10 .30
451 Brooks Kieschnick .10 .30
452 Dave Magadan .10 .30
453 Jason Maxwell RC .10 .30
454 Brian McRae .10 .30
455 Rodney Myers RC .10 .30
456 Jaime Navarro .10 .30
457 Ryne Sandberg .50 1.25
458 Vince Coleman .10 .30
459 Eric Davis .10 .30
460 Steve Gibralter .10 .30
461 Thomas Howard .10 .30
462 Mike Kelly .10 .30
463 Hal Morris .10 .30
464 Eric Owens .10 .30
465 Jose Rijo .10 .30
466 Chris Sabo .10 .30
467 Eddie Taubensee .10 .30
468 Trenidad Hubbard .10 .30
469 Curt Leskanic .10 .30
470 Quinton McCracken .10 .30
471 Jayhawk Owens .10 .30
472 Steve Reed .10 .30
473 Bryan Rekar .10 .30
474 Bruce Ruffin .10 .30
475 Bret Saberhagen .10 .30
476 Walt Weiss .10 .30
477 Eric Young .10 .30
478 Kevin Brown .10 .30
479 Al Leiter .10 .30
480 Pat Rapp .10 .30
481 Gary Sheffield .10 .30
482 Devon White .10 .30
483 Bob Abreu .30 .75
484 Sean Berry .10 .30
485 Craig Biggio .20 .50
486 Jim Dougherty .10 .30
487 Richard Hidalgo .10 .30
488 Darryl Kile .10 .30
489 Derrick May .10 .30
490 Greg Swindell .10 .30
491 Rick Wilkins .10 .30
492 Mike Blowers .10 .30
493 Tom Candiotti .10 .30
494 Roger Cedeno .10 .30
495 Delino DeShields .10 .30
496 Greg Gagne .10 .30
497 Karim Garcia .10 .30
498 Wilton Guerrero RC .10 .30
499 Chan Ho Park .10 .30
500 Israel Alcantara .10 .30
501 Shane Andrews .10 .30
502 Yamil Benitez .10 .30
503 Cliff Floyd .10 .30
504 Mark Grudzielanek .10 .30
505 Ryan McGuire .10 .30
506 Sherman Obando .10 .30
507 Jose Paniagua .10 .30
508 Henry Rodriguez .10 .30
509 Kirk Rueter .10 .30
510 Juan Acevedo .10 .30
511 John Franco .10 .30
512 Bernard Gilkey .10 .30
513 Lance Johnson .10 .30
514 Rey Ordonez .10 .30
515 Robert Person .10 .30
516 Paul Wilson .10 .30
517 Toby Borland .10 .30
518 David Doster RC .10 .30
519 Lenny Dykstra .10 .30
520 Sid Fernandez .10 .30
521 Mike Grace RC .10 .30
522 Rich Hunter .10 .30
523 Benito Santiago .10 .30
524 Gene Schall .10 .30
525 Curt Schilling .10 .30
526 Kevin Sefcik RC .10 .30
527 Lee Tinsley .10 .30
528 David West .10 .30
529 Mark Whiten .10 .30
530 Todd Zeile .10 .30
531 Carlos Garcia .10 .30
532 Charlie Hayes .10 .30
533 Jason Kendall .10 .30
534 Jeff King .10 .30
535 Mike Kingery .10 .30
536 Nelson Liriano .10 .30

537 Dan Plesac	.10	.30
538 Paul Wagner	.10	.30
539 Luis Alicea	.10	.30
540 David Bell	.10	.30
541 Alan Benes	.10	.30
542 Andy Benes	.10	.30
543 Mike Busby RC	.10	.30
544 Royce Clayton	.10	.30
545 Dennis Eckersley	.10	.30
546 Gary Gaetti	.10	.30
547 Ron Gant	.10	.30
548 Aaron Holbert	.10	.30
549 Ray Lankford	.10	.30
550 T.J. Mathews	.10	.30
551 Willie McGee	.10	.30
552 Miguel Mejia	.10	.30
553 Todd Stottlemyre	.10	.30
554 Sean Bergman	.10	.30
555 Willie Blair	.10	.30
556 Andujar Cedeno	.10	.30
557 Steve Finley	.10	.30
558 Rickey Henderson	.30	.75
559 Wally Joyner	.10	.30
560 Scott Livingstone	.10	.30
561 Marc Newfield	.10	.30
562 Bob Tewksbury	.10	.30
563 Fernando Valenzuela	.10	.30
564 Rod Beck	.10	.30
565 Doug Creek	.10	.30
566 Shawon Dunston	.10	.30
567 Osvaldo Fernandez RC	.10	.30
568 Stan Javier	.10	.30
569 Marcus Jensen	.10	.30
570 Steve Scarsone	.10	.30
571 Robby Thompson	.10	.30
572 Allen Watson	.10	.30
573 Roberto Alomar STA	.10	.30
574 Jeff Bagwell STA	.10	.30
575 Albert Belle STA	.10	.30
576 Wade Boggs STA	.10	.30
577 Barry Bonds STA	.40	1.00
578 Juan Gonzalez STA	.10	.30
579 Ken Griffey Jr. STA	.40	1.00
580 Tony Gwynn STA	.20	.50
581 Randy Johnson STA	.20	.50
582 Chipper Jones STA	.20	.50
583 Barry Larkin STA	.10	.30
584 Kenny Lofton STA	.10	.30
585 Greg Maddux STA	.30	.75
586 Raul Mondesi STA	.10	.30
587 Mike Piazza STA	.30	.75
588 Cal Ripken STA	.50	1.25
589 Tim Salmon STA	.10	.30
590 Frank Thomas STA	.20	.50
591 Mo Vaughn STA	.10	.30
592 Matt Williams STA	.10	.30
593 Marty Cordova RAW	.10	.30
594 Jim Edmonds RAW	.10	.30
595 Cliff Floyd RAW	.10	.30
596 Chipper Jones RAW	.20	.50
597 Ryan Klesko RAW	.10	.30
598 Raul Mondesi RAW	.10	.30
599 Manny Ramirez RAW	.10	.30
600 Ruben Rivera RAW	.10	.30
DD1 Cal Ripken Diam.Dust/2131	12.50	30.00
DD2 Cal Ripken Diam.Dust	6.00	15.00

1996 Ultra Gold Medallion

COMPLETE SET (600)	100.00	200.00
COMPLETE SERIES 1 (300)	40.00	100.00
COMPLETE SERIES 2 (300)	40.00	100.00

*STARS: 1.25X TO 3X BASIC CARDS
*ROOKIES: 1.25X TO 3X BASIC CARDS
ONE PER PACK

1996 Ultra Call to the Hall

COMPLETE SET (10)	25.00	60.00
SER.2 STATED ODDS 1:24		
*GOLD MEDAL: .75X TO 2X BASIC CALL		
GM SER.2 STATED ODDS 1:240		
1 Barry Bonds	5.00	12.00
2 Ken Griffey Jr.	4.00	10.00
3 Tony Gwynn	2.50	6.00
4 Rickey Henderson	2.00	5.00
5 Greg Maddux	3.00	8.00
6 Eddie Murray	2.00	5.00
7 Cal Ripken	6.00	15.00
8 Ryne Sandberg	3.00	8.00
9 Ozzie Smith	3.00	8.00
10 Frank Thomas	2.00	5.00

1996 Ultra Checklists

COMPLETE SERIES 1 (10)	4.00	10.00
COMPLETE SERIES 2 (10)	3.00	8.00
STATED ODDS 1:4		
*GOLD MEDAL: .75X TO 2X BASIC CL		
GM STATED ODDS 1:40		
A1 Jeff Bagwell	.25	.60
A2 Barry Bonds	1.00	2.50
A3 Juan Gonzalez	.15	.40
A4 Ken Griffey Jr.	.75	2.00
A5 Chipper Jones	.40	1.00
A6 Mike Piazza	.60	1.50
A7 Manny Ramirez	.25	.60
A8 Cal Ripken	1.25	3.00
A9 Frank Thomas	.40	1.00
A10 Matt Williams	.15	.40
B1 Albert Belle	.15	.40
B2 Cecil Fielder	.15	.40
B3 Ken Griffey Jr.	.75	2.00
B4 Tony Gwynn	.50	1.25
B5 Derek Jeter	1.00	2.50
B6 Jason Kendall	.15	.40
B7 Ryan Klesko	.15	.40
B8 Greg Maddux	.60	1.50
B9 Cal Ripken	1.25	3.00
B10 Frank Thomas	.40	1.00

1996 Ultra Diamond Producers

COMPLETE SET (12)	25.00	60.00
SER.1 STATED ODDS 1:20		
*GOLD MEDAL: .75X TO 2X BASIC DIAMOND		
GM SER.1 STATED ODDS 1:200		
1 Albert Belle	.60	1.50
2 Barry Bonds	4.00	10.00
3 Ken Griffey Jr.	3.00	8.00
4 Tony Gwynn	2.00	5.00
5 Greg Maddux	2.50	6.00
6 Hideo Nomo	1.50	4.00
7 Mike Piazza	2.50	6.00
8 Kirby Puckett	1.50	4.00
9 Cal Ripken	5.00	12.00
10 Frank Thomas	1.50	4.00
11 Mo Vaughn	.60	1.50
12 Matt Williams	.60	1.50

1996 Ultra Fresh Foundations

COMPLETE SET (10)	1.25	3.00
SER.1 STATED ODDS 1:3		
*GOLD MEDAL: .75X TO 2X BASIC FRESH		
GM SER.1 STATED ODDS 1:30		
1 Garret Anderson	.10	.30
2 Marty Cordova	.10	.30
3 Jim Edmonds	.10	.30
4 Brian L.Hunter	.10	.30
5 Chipper Jones	.30	.75
6 Ryan Klesko	.10	.30
7 Raul Mondesi	.10	.30
8 Hideo Nomo	.30	.75
9 Manny Ramirez	.20	.50
10 Rondell White	.10	.30

1996 Ultra Golden Prospects

COMPLETE SET (10)	2.00	5.00
SER.1 STATED ODDS 1:5 HOBBY		
*GOLD MEDAL: .75X TO 2X BASIC GOLDEN		
GM SER.1 STATED ODDS 1:50 HOBBY		
1 Yamil Benitez	.25	.60
2 Alberto Castillo	.25	.60
3 Roger Cedeno	.25	.60
4 Johnny Damon	.40	1.00
5 Micah Franklin	.25	.60
6 Jason Giambi	.25	.60
7 Jose Herrera	.25	.60
8 Derek Jeter	1.50	4.00
9 Kevin Jordan	.25	.60
10 Ruben Rivera	.25	.60

1996 Ultra Golden Prospects Hobby

COMPLETE SET (15)	40.00	100.00
SER.2 STATED ODDS 1:72 HOBBY		
*GOLD MED: .75X TO 2X BASIC GOLD.HOB		
GM SER.2 STATED ODDS 1:720 HOBBY		
1 Bob Abreu	3.00	8.00
2 Israel Alcantara	1.50	4.00
3 Tony Batista	2.00	5.00
4 Mike Cameron	2.00	5.00
5 Steve Cox	1.50	4.00
6 Jermaine Dye	1.50	4.00
7 Wilton Guerrero	1.50	4.00
8 Richard Hidalgo	1.50	4.00
9 Raul Ibanez	2.50	6.00
10 Marty Janzen	1.50	4.00
11 Robin Jennings	1.50	4.00
12 Jason Maxwell	1.50	4.00
13 Scott McClain	1.50	4.00
14 Wonderful Monds	1.50	4.00
15 Chris Singleton	1.50	4.00

1996 Ultra Hitting Machines

COMPLETE SET (10)	30.00	80.00
SER.2 STATED ODDS 1:288		
*GOLD MEDAL: 1 TO 2.5X BASIC HIT.MACH.		
GM SER.2 STATED ODDS 1:2880		
1 Albert Belle	1.25	3.00
2 Barry Bonds	5.00	12.00
3 Juan Gonzalez	1.25	3.00
4 Ken Griffey Jr.	25.00	60.00
5 Edgar Martinez	2.00	5.00
6 Rafael Palmeiro	2.00	5.00
7 Mike Piazza	3.00	8.00
8 Tim Salmon	1.25	3.00
9 Frank Thomas	3.00	8.00
10 Matt Williams	1.25	3.00

1996 Ultra Home Run Kings

COMPLETE SET (12)	20.00	50.00
SER.1 STATED ODDS 1:75		
*GOLD MEDAL: 2.5X TO 6X BASIC HR KINGS		
GM SER.1 STATED ODDS 1:750		
*REDEMPTION: .4X TO 1X BASIC HR KINGS		
ONE RDMP.CARD VIA MAIL PER HR CARD		
1 Albert Belle	1.25	3.00
2 Dante Bichette	1.25	3.00
3 Barry Bonds	5.00	12.00
4 Jose Canseco	2.00	5.00
5 Juan Gonzalez	1.25	3.00
6 Ken Griffey Jr.	6.00	15.00
7 Mark McGwire	5.00	12.00
8 Manny Ramirez	2.00	5.00
9 Tim Salmon	1.25	3.00
10 Frank Thomas	3.00	8.00
11 Mo Vaughn	1.25	3.00
12 Matt Williams	1.25	3.00

1996 Ultra Home Run Kings Redemption Gold Medallion

*REDEMPTION CARDS: 1X BASIC CARDS

1996 Ultra On-Base Leaders

COMPLETE SET (10)	2.00	5.00
SER.2 STATED ODDS 1:4		
*GOLD MEDAL: .75X TO 2X BASIC OBL		
GM SER.2 STATED ODDS 1:40		
1 Wade Boggs	.25	.60
2 Barry Bonds	1.00	2.50
3 Tony Gwynn	.50	1.25
4 Rickey Henderson	.40	1.00
5 Chuck Knoblauch	.15	.40
6 Edgar Martinez	.25	.60
7 Mike Piazza	.60	1.50
8 Tim Salmon	.25	.60
9 Frank Thomas	.40	1.00
10 Jim Thome	.25	.60

1996 Ultra Power Plus

COMPLETE SET (12)	10.00	25.00
SER.1 STATED ODDS 1:10		
*GOLD MEDAL: .75X TO 2X BASIC PLUS		
GM SER.1 STATED ODDS 1:100		
1 Jeff Bagwell	.60	1.50
2 Barry Bonds	2.50	6.00
3 Ken Griffey Jr.	2.00	5.00
4 Raul Mondesi	.40	1.00
5 Rafael Palmeiro	.60	1.50
6 Mike Piazza	1.50	4.00
7 Manny Ramirez	.60	1.50
8 Tim Salmon	.60	1.50
9 Reggie Sanders	.40	1.00
10 Frank Thomas	1.00	2.50
11 Larry Walker	.40	1.00
12 Matt Williams	.40	1.00

1996 Ultra Prime Leather

COMPLETE SET (18)	10.00	25.00
SER.1 STATED ODDS 1:8		
*GOLD MEDAL: .75X TO 2X BASIC LEATHER		
GM SER.1 STATED ODDS 1:80		
1 Ivan Rodriguez	.60	1.50
2 Will Clark	.60	1.50
3 Roberto Alomar	.60	1.50
4 Cal Ripken	3.00	8.00
5 Wade Boggs	.60	1.50
6 Ken Griffey Jr.	2.00	5.00
7 Kenny Lofton	.40	1.00
8 Kirby Puckett	1.00	2.50
9 Tim Salmon	.60	1.50
10 Mike Piazza	1.50	4.00
11 Mark Grace	.60	1.50
12 Craig Biggio	.60	1.50
13 Barry Larkin	.60	1.50
14 Matt Williams	.40	1.00
15 Barry Bonds	2.50	6.00
16 Tony Gwynn	1.25	3.00
17 Brian McRae	.40	1.00
18 Raul Mondesi	.40	1.00
S4 Cal Ripken Jr Promo	3.00	8.00

1996 Ultra Rawhide

COMPLETE SET (10)	6.00	15.00
SER.2 STATED ODDS 1:8		
*GOLD MEDAL: .75X TO 2X BASIC RAWHIDE		
GM SER.2 STATED ODDS 1:80		
1 Roberto Alomar	.40	1.00
2 Barry Bonds	1.50	4.00
3 Mark Grace	.40	1.00
4 Ken Griffey Jr.	1.25	3.00
5 Kenny Lofton	.25	.60
6 Greg Maddux	1.00	2.50
7 Raul Mondesi	.25	.60
8 Mike Piazza	1.00	2.50
9 Cal Ripken	2.00	5.00
10 Matt Williams	.25	.60

1996 Ultra RBI Kings

COMPLETE SET (10)	12.50	30.00
SER.1 STATED ODDS 1:5 RETAIL		
*GOLD MEDAL: .75X TO 2X BASIC RBI KINGS		
GM SER.1 STATED ODDS 1:50 RETAIL		
1 Derek Bell	.75	2.00
2 Albert Belle	.75	2.00
3 Dante Bichette	.75	2.00
4 Barry Bonds	5.00	12.00
5 Jim Edmonds	.75	2.00
6 Manny Ramirez	1.25	3.00
7 Reggie Sanders	.75	2.00
8 Sammy Sosa	2.00	5.00
9 Frank Thomas	2.00	5.00
10 Mo Vaughn	.75	2.00

1996 Ultra Respect

COMPLETE SET (10)	20.00	50.00
SER.2 STATED ODDS 1:18		
*GOLD MEDAL: .75X TO 2X BASIC RESPECT		
GM SER.2 STATED ODDS 1:180		
1 Joe Carter	.60	1.50
2 Ken Griffey Jr.	3.00	8.00
3 Tony Gwynn	2.00	5.00
4 Greg Maddux	2.50	6.00
5 Eddie Murray	1.50	4.00
6 Kirby Puckett	1.50	4.00
7 Cal Ripken	5.00	12.00
8 Ryne Sandberg	2.50	6.00
9 Frank Thomas	1.50	4.00
10 Mo Vaughn	.60	1.50

1996 Ultra Rising Stars

COMPLETE SET (10)	1.50	4.00
SER.2 STATED ODDS 1:4		
*GOLD MEDAL: .75X TO 2X BASIC RISING		
GM SER.2 STATED ODDS 1:40		
1 Garret Anderson	.10	.30
2 Marty Cordova	.10	.30
3 Jim Edmonds	.10	.30
4 Cliff Floyd	.10	.30
5 Brian L.Hunter	.10	.30
6 Chipper Jones	.30	.75
7 Ryan Klesko	.10	.30
8 Hideo Nomo	.30	.75
9 Manny Ramirez	.20	.50
10 Rondell White	.10	.30

1996 Ultra Season Crowns

COMPLETE SET (10)	12.50	30.00
SER.1 STATED ODDS 1:10		
*GOLD MEDAL: .75X TO 2X BASIC CROWNS		
GM SER.1 STATED ODDS 1:100		
1 Barry Bonds	2.50	6.00
2 Tony Gwynn	1.25	3.00
3 Randy Johnson	1.00	2.50
4 Kenny Lofton	.40	1.00
5 Greg Maddux	1.50	4.00
6 Edgar Martinez	.60	1.50
7 Hideo Nomo	1.00	2.50
8 Cal Ripken	3.00	8.00
9 Frank Thomas	1.00	2.50
10 Tim Wakefield	.40	1.00

1996 Ultra Thunderclap

COMPLETE SET (20)	50.00	100.00
SER.2 STATED ODDS 1:72 RETAIL		
*GOLD MEDAL: 1.25X TO 3X BASIC THUNDER		
GM SER.2 STATED ODDS 1:720 RETAIL		
1 Albert Belle	1.00	2.50
2 Barry Bonds	6.00	15.00
3 Bobby Bonilla	1.00	2.50
4 Jose Canseco	1.50	4.00
5 Joe Carter	1.00	2.50
6 Will Clark	1.50	4.00
7 Andre Dawson	1.00	2.50
8 Cecil Fielder	1.00	2.50
9 Andres Galarraga	1.00	2.50
10 Juan Gonzalez	1.00	2.50
11 Ken Griffey Jr.	5.00	12.00
12 Fred McGriff	1.50	4.00
13 Mark McGwire	6.00	15.00
14 Eddie Murray	2.50	6.00
15 Rafael Palmeiro	1.50	4.00
16 Kirby Puckett	2.50	6.00
17 Cal Ripken	8.00	20.00
18 Ryne Sandberg	5.00	12.00
19 Frank Thomas	2.50	6.00
20 Matt Williams	1.00	2.50

1997 Ultra

The 1997 Ultra was issued in two series totalling 553 cards. The first series consisted of 300 cards with the second containing 253. The 10-card packs had a suggested retail price of 2.49 each. Each pack had two insert cards, with one insert being a gold medallion parallel and the other insert being from one of serveral other insert sets. The fronts features borderless color action player photos with career statistics on the backs. As in most Fleer produced sets, the cards are arranged in alphabetical order by league, player and team. Second series retail packs contained only cards 301-450 while second series hobby packs contained all cards from 301-553. Rookie Cards include Jose Cruz Jr., Brian Giles and Fernando Tatis.

COMPLETE SET (553)	30.00	60.00
COMPLETE SERIES 1 (300)	8.00	20.00
COMPLETE SERIES 2 (253)	15.00	40.00
COMMON CARD (1-553)	.10	.30
COMMON RC	.15	.40
1 Roberto Alomar	.20	.50
2 Brady Anderson	.10	.30
3 Rocky Coppinger	.10	.30
4 Jeffrey Hammonds	.10	.30
5 Chris Hoiles	.10	.30
6 Eddie Murray	.30	.75
7 Mike Mussina	.20	.50
8 Jimmy Myers	.10	.30
9 Randy Myers	.10	.30
10 Arthur Rhodes	.10	.30
11 Cal Ripken	1.00	2.50
12 Jose Canseco	.20	.50
13 Roger Clemens	.60	1.50
14 Tom Gordon	.10	.30
15 Jose Malave	.10	.30
16 Tim Naehring	.10	.30
17 Troy O'Leary	.10	.30
18 Bill Selby	.10	.30
19 Heathcliff Slocumb	.10	.30
20 Mike Stanley	.10	.30
21 Mo Vaughn	.10	.30
22 Garret Anderson	.10	.30
23 George Arias	.10	.30
24 Chili Davis	.10	.30
25 Jim Edmonds	.10	.30
26 Darin Erstad	.10	.30
27 Chuck Finley	.10	.30
28 Todd Greene	.10	.30
29 Troy Percival	.10	.30
30 Tim Salmon	.20	.50
31 Jeff Schmidt	.10	.30
32 Randy Velarde	.10	.30
33 Shad Williams	.10	.30
34 Wilson Alvarez	.10	.30
35 Harold Baines	.10	.30
36 James Baldwin	.10	.30
37 Mike Cameron	.10	.30
38 Ray Durham	.10	.30
39 Ozzie Guillen	.10	.30
40 Roberto Hernandez	.10	.30
41 Darren Lewis	.10	.30
42 Jose Munoz	.10	.30
43 Tony Phillips	.10	.30
44 Frank Thomas	.30	.75
45 Sandy Alomar Jr.	.10	.30
46 Albert Belle	.10	.30
47 Mark Carreon	.10	.30
48 Julio Franco	.10	.30
49 Orel Hershiser	.10	.30
50 Kenny Lofton	.10	.30
51 Jack McDowell	.10	.30
52 Jose Mesa	.10	.30
53 Charles Nagy	.10	.30
54 Manny Ramirez	.20	.50
55 Julian Tavarez	.10	.30
56 Omar Vizquel	.20	.50
57 Raul Casanova	.10	.30
58 Tony Clark	.10	.30
59 Travis Fryman	.10	.30
60 Bob Higginson	.10	.30
61 Melvin Nieves	.10	.30
62 Curtis Pride	.10	.30
63 Justin Thompson	.10	.30
64 Alan Trammell	.10	.30
65 Kevin Appier	.10	.30
66 Johnny Damon	.20	.50
67 Keith Lockhart	.10	.30
68 Jeff Montgomery	.10	.30
69 Jose Offerman	.10	.30
70 Bip Roberts	.10	.30
71 Jose Rosado	.10	.30
72 Chris Stynes	.10	.30
73 Mike Sweeney	.10	.30
74 Jeff Cirillo	.10	.30
75 Jeff D'Amico	.10	.30
76 John Jaha	.10	.30
77 Scott Karl	.10	.30
78 Mike Matheny	.10	.30
79 Ben McDonald	.10	.30
80 Matt Mieske	.10	.30
81 Marc Newfield	.10	.30
82 Dave Nilsson	.10	.30
83 Jose Valentin	.10	.30
84 Fernando Vina	.10	.30
85 Rick Aguilera	.10	.30
86 Marty Cordova	.10	.30
87 Chuck Knoblauch	.10	.30
88 Matt Lawton	.10	.30
89 Pat Meares	.10	.30
90 Paul Molitor	.10	.30
91 Greg Myers	.10	.30
92 Dan Naulty	.10	.30
93 Kirby Puckett	.30	.75
94 Frank Rodriguez	.10	.30
95 Wade Boggs	.20	.50
96 Cecil Fielder	.10	.30
97 Joe Girardi	.10	.30
98 Dwight Gooden	.10	.30
99 Derek Jeter	.75	2.00
100 Tino Martinez	.20	.50
101 Ramiro Mendoza RC	.10	.30
102 Andy Pettitte	.20	.50
103 Mariano Rivera	.30	.75
104 Ruben Rivera	.10	.30
105 Kenny Rogers	.10	.30
106 Darryl Strawberry	.10	.30
107 Bernie Williams	.20	.50
108 Tony Batista	.10	.30
109 Geronimo Berroa	.10	.30
110 Bobby Chouinard	.10	.30
111 Brent Gates	.10	.30
112 Jason Giambi	.10	.30
113 Damon Mashore	.10	.30
114 Mark McGwire	.75	2.00
115 Scott Spiezio	.10	.30
116 John Wasdin	.10	.30
117 Steve Wojciechowski	.10	.30
118 Ernie Young	.10	.30
119 Norm Charlton	.10	.30
120 Joey Cora	.10	.30
121 Ken Griffey Jr.	.60	1.50
122 Sterling Hitchcock	.10	.30
123 Raul Ibanez	.10	.30
124 Randy Johnson	.30	.75
125 Edgar Martinez	.20	.50
126 Alex Rodriguez	.50	1.25
127 Matt Wagner	.10	.30
128 Bob Wells	.10	.30
129 Dan Wilson	.10	.30
130 Will Clark	.20	.50
131 Kevin Elster	.10	.30
132 Juan Gonzalez	.10	.30
133 Rusty Greer	.10	.30
134 Darryl Hamilton	.10	.30
135 Mike Henneman	.10	.30
136 Ken Hill	.10	.30
137 Mark McLemore	.10	.30
138 Dean Palmer	.10	.30
139 Roger Pavlik	.10	.30
140 Ivan Rodriguez	.20	.50
141 Joe Carter	.10	.30
142 Carlos Delgado	.10	.30
143 Alex Gonzalez	.10	.30
144 Juan Guzman	.10	.30
145 Pat Hentgen	.10	.30
146 Marty Janzen	.10	.30
147 Otis Nixon	.10	.30
148 Charlie O'Brien	.10	.30
149 John Olerud	.10	.30
150 Robert Perez	.10	.30
151 Jermaine Dye	.10	.30
152 Tom Glavine	.20	.50
153 Andruw Jones	.20	.50
154 Chipper Jones	.30	.75
155 Ryan Klesko	.10	.30
156 Javier Lopez	.10	.30
157 Greg Maddux	.50	1.25
158 Fred McGriff	.20	.50
159 Wonderful Monds	.10	.30
160 John Smoltz	.20	.50
161 Terrell Wade	.10	.30
162 Mark Wohlers	.10	.30
163 Brant Brown	.10	.30
164 Mark Grace	.20	.50
165 Tyler Houston	.10	.30
166 Robin Jennings	.10	.30
167 Jason Maxwell	.10	.30
168 Ryne Sandberg	.50	1.25
169 Sammy Sosa	.30	.75
170 Amaury Telemaco	.10	.30
171 Steve Trachsel	.10	.30
172 Pedro Valdes RC	.10	.30
173 Tim Belk	.10	.30
174 Bret Boone	.10	.30
175 Jeff Brantley	.10	.30
176 Eric Davis	.10	.30
177 Barry Larkin	.20	.50
178 Chad Mottola	.10	.30
179 Mark Portugal	.10	.30
180 Reggie Sanders	.10	.30
181 John Smiley	.10	.30
182 Eddie Taubensee	.10	.30
183 Dante Bichette	.10	.30
184 Ellis Burks	.10	.30
185 Andres Galarraga	.10	.30
186 Curt Leskanic	.10	.30
187 Quinton McCracken	.10	.30
188 Jeff Reed	.10	.30
189 Kevin Ritz	.10	.30
190 Walt Weiss	.10	.30
191 Jamey Wright	.10	.30
192 Eric Young	.10	.30
193 Kevin Brown	.10	.30
194 Luis Castillo	.10	.30
195 Jeff Conine	.10	.30
196 Andre Dawson	.10	.30
197 Charles Johnson	.10	.30
198 Al Leiter	.10	.30
199 Ralph Milliard	.10	.30
200 Robb Nen	.10	.30
201 Edgar Renteria	.10	.30
202 Gary Sheffield	.10	.30
203 Bob Abreu	.20	.50
204 Jeff Bagwell	.20	.50
205 Derek Bell	.10	.30
206 Sean Berry	.10	.30
207 Richard Hidalgo	.10	.30
208 Todd Jones	.10	.30
209 Darryl Kile	.10	.30
210 Orlando Miller	.10	.30
211 Shane Reynolds	.10	.30
212 Billy Wagner	.10	.30
213 Donne Wall	.10	.30
214 Roger Cedeno	.10	.30
215 Greg Gagne	.10	.30
216 Karim Garcia	.10	.30
217 Wilton Guerrero	.10	.30
218 Todd Hollandsworth	.10	.30
219 Ramon Martinez	.10	.30
220 Raul Mondesi	.10	.30
221 Hideo Nomo	.30	.75
222 Chan Ho Park	.10	.30
223 Mike Piazza	.50	1.25
224 Ismael Valdes	.10	.30
225 Moises Alou	.10	.30
226 Derek Aucoin	.10	.30
227 Yamil Benitez	.10	.30
228 Jeff Fassero	.10	.30
229 Darrin Fletcher	.10	.30
230 Mark Grudzielanek	.10	.30
231 Barry Manuel	.10	.30
232 Pedro Martinez	.20	.50
233 Henry Rodriguez	.10	.30
234 Ugueth Urbina	.10	.30
235 Rondell White	.10	.30
236 Carlos Baerga	.10	.30
237 John Franco	.10	.30
238 Bernard Gilkey	.10	.30
239 Todd Hundley	.10	.30
240 Butch Huskey	.10	.30
241 Jason Isringhausen	.10	.30
242 Lance Johnson	.10	.30
243 Bobby Jones	.10	.30
244 Alex Ochoa	.10	.30
245 Rey Ordonez	.10	.30
246 Paul Wilson	.10	.30
247 Ron Blazier	.10	.30
248 David Doster	.10	.30
249 Jim Eisenreich	.10	.30
250 Mike Grace	.10	.30
251 Mike Lieberthal	.10	.30
252 Wendell Magee	.10	.30
253 Mickey Morandini	.10	.30
254 Ricky Otero	.10	.30
255 Scott Rolen	.20	.50
256 Curt Schilling	.10	.30
257 Todd Zeile	.10	.30
258 Jermaine Allensworth	.10	.30
259 Trey Beamon	.10	.30
260 Carlos Garcia	.10	.30
261 Mark Johnson	.10	.30
262 Jason Kendall	.10	.30
263 Jeff King	.10	.30
264 Al Martin	.10	.30
265 Denny Neagle	.10	.30
266 Matt Ruebel	.10	.30
267 Marc Wilkins	.10	.30
268 Alan Benes	.10	.30
269 Dennis Eckersley	.10	.30
270 Ron Gant	.10	.30
271 Aaron Holbert	.10	.30
272 Brian Jordan	.10	.30
273 Ray Lankford	.10	.30
274 John Mabry	.10	.30
275 T.J. Mathews	.10	.30
276 Ozzie Smith	.50	1.25
277 Todd Stottlemyre	.10	.30
278 Mark Sweeney	.10	.30
279 Andy Ashby	.10	.30
280 Steve Finley	.10	.30
281 John Flaherty	.10	.30
282 Chris Gomez	.10	.30
283 Tony Gwynn	.40	1.00
284 Joey Hamilton	.10	.30
285 Rickey Henderson	.30	.75
286 Trevor Hoffman	.10	.30
287 Jason Thompson	.10	.30
288 Fernando Valenzuela	.10	.30
289 Greg Vaughn	.10	.30
290 Barry Bonds	.75	2.00
291 Jay Canizaro	.10	.30
292 Jacob Cruz	.10	.30
293 Shawon Dunston	.10	.30
294 Shawn Estes	.10	.30
295 Mark Gardner	.10	.30
296 Marcus Jensen	.10	.30
297 Bill Mueller RC	.50	1.25
298 Chris Singleton	.10	.30
299 Allen Watson	.10	.30
300 Matt Williams	.10	.30
301 Rod Beck	.10	.30
302 Jay Bell	.10	.30
303 Shawon Dunston	.10	.30
304 Reggie Jefferson	.10	.30
305 Darren Oliver	.10	.30
306 Benito Santiago	.10	.30
307 Gerald Williams	.10	.30
308 Damon Buford	.10	.30
309 Jeromy Burnitz	.10	.30
310 Sterling Hitchcock	.10	.30
311 Dave Hollins	.10	.30
312 Mel Rojas	.10	.30
313 Robin Ventura	.10	.30
314 David Wells	.10	.30
315 Cal Eldred	.10	.30
316 Gary Gaetti	.10	.30
317 John Hudek	.10	.30
318 Brian Johnson	.10	.30
319 Denny Neagle	.10	.30
320 Larry Walker	.10	.30
321 Russ Davis	.10	.30
322 Delino DeShields	.10	.30
323 Charlie Hayes	.10	.30
324 Jermaine Dye	.10	.30
325 John Ericks	.10	.30
326 Jeff Fassero	.10	.30
327 Nomar Garciaparra	.50	1.25
328 Willie Greene	.10	.30
329 Greg McMichael	.10	.30
330 Damion Easley	.10	.30
331 Ricky Bones	.10	.30
332 John Burkett	.10	.30
333 Royce Clayton	.10	.30
334 Greg Colbrunn	.10	.30
335 Tony Eusebio	.10	.30
336 Gregg Jefferies	.10	.30
337 Wally Joyner	.10	.30
338 Jim Leyritz	.10	.30
339 Paul O'Neill	.20	.50
340 Bruce Ruffin	.10	.30
341 Michael Tucker	.10	.30
342 Andy Benes	.10	.30
343 Craig Biggio	.20	.50
344 Rex Hudler	.10	.30
345 Brad Radke	.10	.30
346 Deion Sanders	.20	.50
347 Moises Alou	.10	.30
348 Brad Ausmus	.10	.30
349 Armando Benitez	.10	.30
350 Mark Gubicza	.10	.30
351 Terry Steinbach	.10	.30
352 Mark Whiten	.10	.30
353 Ricky Bottalico	.10	.30
354 Brian Giles RC	.60	1.50
355 Eric Karros	.10	.30
356 Jimmy Key	.10	.30
357 Carlos Perez	.10	.30
358 Alex Fernandez	.10	.30
359 J.T. Snow	.10	.30
360 Bobby Bonilla	.10	.30
361 Scott Brosius	.10	.30
362 Greg Swindell	.10	.30
363 Jose Vizcaino	.10	.30
364 Matt Williams	.10	.30
365 Darren Daulton	.10	.30
366 Shane Andrews	.10	.30
367 Jim Eisenreich	.10	.30
368 Ariel Prieto	.10	.30
369 Bob Tewksbury	.10	.30
370 Mike Bordick	.10	.30
371 Rheal Cormier	.10	.30
372 Cliff Floyd	.10	.30
373 David Justice	.10	.30
374 John Wetteland	.10	.30
375 Mike Blowers	.10	.30
376 Jose Canseco	.20	.50
377 Roger Clemens	.60	1.50
378 Kevin Mitchell	.10	.30
379 Todd Zeile	.10	.30
380 Jim Thome	.20	.50
381 Turk Wendell	.10	.30
382 Rico Brogna	.10	.30
383 Eric Davis	.10	.30
384 Mike Lansing	.10	.30
385 Devon White	.10	.30
386 Marquis Grissom	.10	.30
387 Todd Worrell	.10	.30
388 Jeff Kent	.10	.30
389 Mickey Tettleton	.10	.30
390 Steve Avery	.10	.30
391 David Cone	.10	.30
392 Scott Cooper	.10	.30
393 Lee Stevens	.10	.30
394 Kevin Elster	.10	.30
395 Tom Goodwin	.10	.30
396 Shawn Green	.10	.30
397 Pete Harnisch	.10	.30
398 Eddie Murray	.30	.75
399 Joe Randa	.10	.30
400 Scott Sanders	.10	.30
401 John Valentin	.10	.30
402 Todd Jones	.10	.30
403 Terry Adams	.10	.30
404 Brian Hunter	.10	.30
405 Pat Listach	.10	.30
406 Kenny Lofton	.10	.30
407 Hal Morris	.10	.30
408 Ed Sprague	.10	.30
409 Rich Becker	.10	.30
410 Edgardo Alfonzo	.10	.30
411 Albert Belle	.10	.30
412 Jeff King	.10	.30
413 Kirt Manwaring	.10	.30
414 Jason Schmidt	.10	.30
415 Allen Watson	.10	.30
416 Lee Tinsley	.10	.30
417 Brett Butler	.10	.30
418 Carlos Garcia	.10	.30
419 Mark Lemke	.10	.30
420 Jaime Navarro	.10	.30
421 David Segui	.10	.30
422 Ruben Sierra	.10	.30
423 B.J. Surhoff	.10	.30
424 Julian Tavarez	.10	.30
425 Billy Taylor	.10	.30
426 Ken Caminiti	.10	.30
427 Chuck Carr	.10	.30
428 Benji Gil	.10	.30
429 Terry Mulholland	.10	.30
430 Mike Stanton	.10	.30
431 Wil Cordero	.10	.30
432 Chili Davis	.10	.30
433 Mariano Duncan	.10	.30
434 Orlando Merced	.10	.30
435 Kent Mercker	.10	.30
436 John Olerud	.10	.30
437 Quilvio Veras	.10	.30
438 Mike Fetters	.10	.30
439 Glenallen Hill	.10	.30
440 Bill Swift	.10	.30
441 Tim Wakefield	.10	.30
442 Pedro Astacio	.10	.30
443 Vinny Castilla	.10	.30
444 Doug Drabek	.10	.30
445 Alan Embree	.10	.30
446 Lee Smith	.10	.30
447 Darryl Hamilton	.10	.30
448 Brian McRae	.10	.30
449 Mike Timlin	.10	.30
450 Bob Wickman	.10	.30
451 Jason Dickson	.10	.30
452 Chad Curtis	.10	.30
453 Mark Leiter	.10	.30
454 Damon Berryhill	.10	.30
455 Kevin Orie	.10	.30
456 Dave Burba	.10	.30
457 Chris Holt	.10	.30
458 Ricky Ledee RC	.15	.40
459 Mike Devereaux	.10	.30
460 Pokey Reese	.10	.30
461 Tim Raines	.10	.30
462 Ryan Jones	.10	.30
463 Shane Mack	.10	.30
464 Darren Dreifort	.10	.30
465 Mark Parent	.10	.30
466 Mark Portugal	.10	.30
467 Dante Powell	.10	.30
468 Craig Grebeck	.10	.30
469 Ron Villone	.10	.30
470 Dmitri Young	.10	.30
471 Shannon Stewart	.10	.30
472 Rick Helling	.10	.30
473 Bill Haselman	.10	.30
474 Albie Lopez	.10	.30
475 Glendon Rusch	.10	.30
476 Derrick May	.10	.30
477 Chad Ogea	.10	.30
478 Kirk Rueter	.10	.30
479 Chris Hammond	.10	.30
480 Russ Johnson	.10	.30
481 James Mouton	.10	.30

482 Mike Macfarlane .10 .30
483 Scott Ruffcorn .10 .30
484 Jeff Frye .10 .30
485 Richie Sexson .10 .30
486 Emil Brown RC .15 .40
487 Desi Wilson .10 .30
488 Brent Gates .10 .30
489 Tony Graffanino .10 .30
490 Dan Miceli .10 .30
491 Orlando Cabrera RC .40 1.00
492 Tony Womack RC .15 .40
493 Jerome Walton .10 .30
494 Mark Thompson .10 .30
495 Jose Guillen .10 .30
496 Willie Blair .10 .30
497 T.J. Staton RC .15 .40
498 Scott Kamieniecki .10 .30
499 Vince Coleman .10 .30
500 Jeff Abbott .10 .30
501 Chris Widger .10 .30
502 Kevin Tapani .10 .30
503 Carlos Castillo RC .15 .40
504 Luis Gonzalez .10 .30
505 Tim Belcher .10 .30
506 Armando Reynoso .10 .30
507 Jamie Moyer .10 .30
508 Randall Simon RC .15 .40
509 Vladimir Guerrero .30 .75
510 Wady Almonte RC .15 .40
511 Dustin Hermanson .10 .30
512 Deivi Cruz RC .15 .40
513 Luis Alicea .10 .30
514 Felix Heredia RC .15 .40
515 Don Slaught .10 .30
516 Shigetoshi Hasegawa RC .25 .60
517 Matt Walbeck .10 .30
518 David Arias-Ortiz RC 60.00 150.00
519 Brady Raggio RC .15 .40
520 Rudy Pemberton .10 .30
521 Wayne Kirby .10 .30
522 Calvin Maduro .10 .30
523 Mark Lewis .10 .30
524 Mike Jackson .10 .30
525 Sid Fernandez .10 .30
526 Mike Bielecki .10 .30
527 Bubba Trammell RC .15 .40
528 Brent Brede RC .15 .40
529 Matt Morris .10 .30
530 Joe Borowski RC .15 .40
531 Orlando Miller .10 .30
532 Jim Bullinger .10 .30
533 Robert Person .10 .30
534 Doug Glanville .10 .30
535 Terry Pendleton .10 .30
536 Jorge Posada .20 .50
537 Marc Sagmoen RC .15 .40
538 Fernando Tatis RC .15 .40
539 Aaron Sele .10 .30
540 Brian Banks .10 .30
541 Derrek Lee .20 .50
542 John Wasdin .10 .30
543 Justin Towle RC .15 .40
544 Pat Cline .10 .30
545 Dave Magadan .10 .30
546 Jeff Blauser .10 .30
547 Phil Nevin .10 .30
548 Todd Walker .10 .30
549 Eli Marrero .10 .30
550 Bartolo Colon .10 .30
551 Jose Cruz Jr. RC .15 .40
552 Todd Dunwoody .10 .30
553 Hideki Irabu RC .15 .40
P11 C.Ripken Promo Strip .75 2.00

1997 Ultra Gold Medallion

COMPLETE SET (553) 150.00 300.00
COMPLETE SERIES 1 (300) 60.00 150.00
COMPLETE SERIES 2 (253) 50.00 120.00
*STARS: 1.25X TO 3X BASIC CARDS
*ROOKIES: .75X TO 2X BASIC
ONE PER PACK
G.MED HAS DIFT.PHOTO THAN BASE CARD
518 David Arias-Ortiz 100.00 250.00

1997 Ultra Platinum Medallion

*STARS 1-450: 12.5X TO 30X BASIC CARDS
*STARS 451-553: 10X TO 25X BASIC CARDS
*ROOKIES 1-450: 6X TO 15X BASIC
*ROOKIES: 451-553: 5X TO 12X BASIC
STATED ODDS 1:100
STATED PRINT RUN LESS THAN 200 SETS
PLAT.HAS DIFT.PHOTO THAN BASE CARD
518 David Arias-Ortiz 600.00 1500.00

1997 Ultra Autographstix Emeralds

RANDOM INSERTS IN SER.2 HOBBY PACKS
STATED PRINT RUN 25 SETS
EXCHANGE DEADLINE: 07/01/98
NO PRICING DUE TO SCARCITY
1 Alex Ochoa
2 Todd Walker
3 Scott Rolen
4 Darin Erstad
5 Alex Rodriguez
6 Todd Hollandsworth

1997 Ultra Baseball Rules

COMPLETE SET (10) 60.00 120.00
SER.1 STATED ODDS 1:36 RETAIL
1 Barry Bonds 6.00 15.00
2 Ken Griffey Jr. 5.00 12.00
3 Derek Jeter 6.00 15.00
4 Chipper Jones 2.50 6.00
5 Greg Maddux 4.00 10.00
6 Mark McGwire 6.00 15.00
7 Troy Percival 1.00 2.50
8 Mike Piazza 4.00 10.00
9 Cal Ripken 8.00 20.00
10 Frank Thomas 2.50 6.00

1997 Ultra Checklists

COMPLETE SERIES 1 (10) 3.00 8.00
COMPLETE SERIES 2 (10) 5.00 12.00
STATED ODDS 1:4 HOBBY
A1 Dante Bichette .10 .30
A2 Barry Bonds .75 2.00
A3 Ken Griffey Jr. .60 1.50
A4 Greg Maddux .50 1.25
A5 Mark McGwire .75 2.00
A6 Mike Piazza .50 1.25
A7 Cal Ripken 1.00 2.50
A8 John Smoltz .20 .50
A9 Sammy Sosa .30 .75
A10 Frank Thomas .30 .75
B1 Andruw Jones .20 .50
B2 Ken Griffey Jr. .60 1.50
B3 Frank Thomas .30 .75
B4 Alex Rodriguez .50 1.25
B5 Cal Ripken 1.00 2.50
B6 Mike Piazza .50 1.25
B7 Greg Maddux .50 1.25
B8 Chipper Jones .30 .75
B9 Derek Jeter .75 2.00
B10 Juan Gonzalez .10 .30

1997 Ultra Diamond Producers

COMPLETE SET (12) 40.00 80.00
SER.1 STATED ODDS 1:288
1 Jeff Bagwell 2.00 5.00
2 Barry Bonds 8.00 20.00
3 Ken Griffey Jr. 12.00 30.00
4 Chipper Jones 3.00 8.00
5 Kenny Lofton 1.25 3.00
6 Greg Maddux 5.00 12.00
7 Mark McGwire 8.00 20.00
8 Mike Piazza 5.00 12.00
9 Cal Ripken 10.00 25.00
10 Alex Rodriguez 5.00 12.00
11 Frank Thomas 3.00 8.00
12 Matt Williams 1.25 3.00

1997 Ultra Double Trouble

COMPLETE SET (20) 4.00 10.00
SER.1 STATED ODDS 1:4
1 C.Ripken 1.00 2.50
R.Alomar
2 J.Canseco .10 .30
M.Vaughn
3 J.Edmonds .10 .30
T.Salmon
4 F.Thomas .30 .75
H.Baines
5 K.Lofton .10 .30
A.Belle
6 M.Cordova .10 .30
C.Knoblauch
7 D.Jeter .75 2.00
A.Pettitte
8 M.McGwire .75 2.00
J.Giambi
9 K.Griffey Jr. .60 1.50
A.Rodriguez
10 J.Gonzalez .10 .30
W.Clark
11 G.Maddux .50 1.25
C.Jones
12 S.Sosa .30 .75
M.Grace
13 D.Bichette .10 .30
A.Galarraga
14 J.Bagwell .20 .50
D.Bell
15 M.Piazza .50 1.25
H.Nomo
16 H.Rodriguez .10 .30
M.Alou
17 R.Ordonez .10 .30
A.Ochoa
18 R.Lankford .10 .30
R.Gant
19 T.Gwynn .40 1.00
R.Henderson
20 B.Bonds .75 2.00
M.Williams

1997 Ultra Fame Game

COMPLETE SET (18) 25.00 60.00
SER.2 STATED ODDS 1:8 HOBBY
1 Ken Griffey Jr. 2.50 6.00
2 Frank Thomas 1.25 3.00
3 Alex Rodriguez 2.00 5.00
4 Cal Ripken 4.00 10.00
5 Mike Piazza 2.00 5.00
6 Greg Maddux 2.00 5.00
7 Derek Jeter 3.00 8.00
8 Jeff Bagwell .75 2.00
9 Juan Gonzalez .50 1.25
10 Albert Belle .50 1.25
11 Tony Gwynn 1.50 4.00
12 Mark McGwire 3.00 8.00
13 Andy Pettitte .75 2.00
14 Kenny Lofton .50 1.25
15 Roberto Alomar .75 2.00
16 Ryne Sandberg 2.00 5.00
17 Barry Bonds 3.00 8.00
18 Eddie Murray 1.25 3.00

1997 Ultra Fielder's Choice

COMPLETE SET (18) 20.00 50.00
SER.1 STATED ODDS 1:144
1 Roberto Alomar 1.25 3.00
2 Jeff Bagwell 1.25 3.00
3 Wade Boggs 1.25 3.00
4 Barry Bonds 3.00 8.00
5 Mark Grace 1.25 3.00
6 Ken Griffey Jr. 6.00 15.00
7 Marquis Grissom .75 2.00
8 Charles Johnson .75 2.00
9 Chuck Knoblauch .75 2.00
10 Barry Larkin 1.25 3.00
11 Kenny Lofton .75 2.00
12 Greg Maddux 3.00 8.00
13 Raul Mondesi .75 2.00
14 Rey Ordonez .75 2.00
15 Cal Ripken 6.00 15.00
16 Alex Rodriguez 2.50 6.00
17 Ivan Rodriguez 1.25 3.00
18 Matt Williams .75 2.00

1997 Ultra Golden Prospects

COMPLETE SET (10) 2.00 5.00
SER.2 STATED ODDS 1:4 HOBBY
1 Andruw Jones .20 .50
2 Vladimir Guerrero .30 .75
3 Todd Walker .10 .30
4 Karim Garcia .10 .30
5 Kevin Orie .10 .30
6 Brian Giles .60 1.50
7 Jason Dickson .10 .30
8 Jose Guillen .10 .30
9 Ruben Rivera .10 .30
10 Derrek Lee .20 .50

1997 Ultra Hitting Machines

COMPLETE SET (18) 20.00 50.00
SER.2 STATED ODDS 1:36 HOBBY
1 Andruw Jones .50 1.25
2 Ken Griffey Jr. 8.00 20.00
3 Frank Thomas 1.25 3.00
4 Alex Rodriguez 1.50 4.00
5 Cal Ripken 4.00 10.00
6 Mike Piazza 1.25 3.00
7 Derek Jeter 3.00 8.00
8 Albert Belle .50 1.25
9 Tony Gwynn 1.25 3.00
10 Jeff Bagwell .75 2.00
11 Mark McGwire 2.00 5.00
12 Kenny Lofton .50 1.25
13 Manny Ramirez .75 2.00
14 Roberto Alomar .75 2.00
15 Ryne Sandberg 2.00 5.00
16 Eddie Murray .75 2.00
17 Sammy Sosa .75 2.00
18 Ken Caminiti .50 1.25

1997 Ultra Home Run Kings

COMPLETE SET (12) 30.00 80.00
SER.1 STATED ODDS 1:36 HOBBY
1 Albert Belle 1.00 2.50
2 Barry Bonds 6.00 15.00
3 Juan Gonzalez 1.00 2.50
4 Ken Griffey Jr. 5.00 12.00
5 Todd Hundley 1.00 2.50
6 Ryan Klesko 1.00 2.50
7 Mark McGwire 6.00 15.00
8 Mike Piazza 4.00 10.00
9 Sammy Sosa 2.50 6.00
10 Frank Thomas 2.50 6.00
11 Mo Vaughn 1.00 2.50
12 Matt Williams 1.00 2.50

1997 Ultra Irabu Commemorative

COMPLETE SET (7) 6.00 15.00
COMMON 5 x 7 (C1-C3) .80 2.00
COMMON CARD (C4-C7) 1.20 3.00

1997 Ultra Leather Shop

COMPLETE SET (12) 6.00 15.00
SER.2 STATED ODDS 1:6 HOBBY
1 Ken Griffey Jr. .75 2.00
2 Alex Rodriguez .60 1.50
3 Cal Ripken 1.25 3.00
4 Derek Jeter 1.00 2.50
5 Juan Gonzalez .15 .40
6 Tony Gwynn .50 1.25
7 Jeff Bagwell .25 .60
8 Roberto Alomar .25 .60
9 Ryne Sandberg .60 1.50
10 Ken Caminiti .15 .40
11 Kenny Lofton .15 .40
12 John Smoltz .25 .60

1997 Ultra Power Plus

COMPLETE SERIES 1 (12) 30.00 80.00
SER.1 STATED ODDS 1:24
COMPLETE SERIES 2 (12) 1.50 4.00
SER.2 STATED ODDS 1:8 HOBBY
A1 Jeff Bagwell 1.00 2.50
A2 Barry Bonds 4.00 10.00
A3 Juan Gonzalez .60 1.50
A4 Ken Griffey Jr. 3.00 8.00
A5 Chipper Jones 1.50 4.00
A6 Mark McGwire 4.00 10.00
A7 Mike Piazza 2.50 6.00
A8 Cal Ripken 5.00 12.00
A9 Alex Rodriguez 2.50 6.00
A10 Sammy Sosa 1.50 4.00
A11 Frank Thomas 1.50 4.00
A12 Matt Williams .60 1.50
B1 Ken Griffey Jr. 1.25 3.00
B2 Frank Thomas .60 1.50
B3 Alex Rodriguez 1.00 2.50
B4 Cal Ripken 2.00 5.00
B5 Mike Piazza 1.00 2.50
B6 Chipper Jones .60 1.50
B7 Albert Belle .25 .60
B8 Juan Gonzalez .25 .60
B9 Jeff Bagwell .40 1.00
B10 Mark McGwire 1.50 4.00
B11 Mo Vaughn .25 .60
B12 Barry Bonds 1.50 4.00

1997 Ultra RBI Kings

COMPLETE SET (10) 12.50 30.00
SER.1 STATED ODDS 1:18
1 Jeff Bagwell 1.00 2.50
2 Albert Belle .60 1.50
3 Dante Bichette .60 1.50
4 Barry Bonds 4.00 10.00
5 Jay Buhner .60 1.50
6 Juan Gonzalez .60 1.50
7 Ken Griffey Jr. 3.00 8.00
8 Sammy Sosa 1.50 4.00
9 Frank Thomas 1.50 4.00
10 Mo Vaughn .60 1.50

1997 Ultra Rookie Reflections

COMPLETE SET (10) 1.50 4.00
SER.1 STATED ODDS 1:4
1 James Baldwin .15 .40
2 Jermaine Dye .15 .40
3 Darin Erstad .15 .40
4 Todd Hollandsworth .15 .40
5 Derek Jeter 1.00 2.50
6 Jason Kendall .15 .40
7 Alex Ochoa .15 .40
8 Rey Ordonez .15 .40
9 Edgar Renteria .15 .40
10 Scott Rolen .25 .60

1997 Ultra Season Crowns

COMPLETE SET (12) 4.00 10.00
SER.1 STATED ODDS 1:8
1 Albert Belle .15 .40
2 Dante Bichette .15 .40
3 Barry Bonds 1.00 2.50
4 Kenny Lofton .15 .40
5 Edgar Martinez .25 .60
6 Mark McGwire 1.00 2.50
7 Andy Pettitte .25 .60
8 Mike Piazza .60 1.50
9 Alex Rodriguez .60 1.50
10 John Smoltz .25 .60
11 Sammy Sosa .40 1.00
12 Frank Thomas .40 1.00

1997 Ultra Starring Role

COMPLETE SET (12) 125.00 250.00
SER.2 STATED ODDS 1:288 HOBBY
1 Andruw Jones 5.00 12.00
2 Ken Griffey Jr. 25.00 60.00
3 Frank Thomas 12.00 30.00
4 Alex Rodriguez 15.00 40.00
5 Cal Ripken 20.00 50.00
6 Mike Piazza 12.00 30.00
7 Greg Maddux 20.00 50.00
8 Chipper Jones 12.00 30.00
9 Derek Jeter 30.00 80.00
10 Juan Gonzalez 5.00 12.00
11 Albert Belle 5.00 12.00
12 Tony Gwynn 12.00 30.00

1997 Ultra Thunderclap

COMPLETE SET (10) 25.00 60.00
SER.2 STATED ODDS 1:18 HOBBY
1 Barry Bonds 4.00 10.00
2 Mo Vaughn .60 1.50
3 Mark McGwire 4.00 10.00
4 Jeff Bagwell 1.00 2.50
5 Juan Gonzalez .60 1.50
6 Alex Rodriguez 2.50 6.00
7 Chipper Jones 1.50 4.00
8 Ken Griffey Jr. 3.00 8.00
9 Mike Piazza 2.50 6.00
10 Frank Thomas 1.50 4.00

1997 Ultra Top 30

COMPLETE SET (30) 15.00 40.00
SER.2 STATED ODDS 1:1 RETAIL
*GOLD MED: 2.5X TO 6X BASIC TOP 30
G.MED SER.2 STATED ODDS 1:18 RETAIL
1 Andruw Jones .30 .75
2 Ken Griffey 1.00 2.50
3 Frank Thomas .50 1.25
4 Alex Rodriguez .75 2.00
5 Cal Ripken 1.50 4.00
6 Mike Piazza .75 2.00
7 Greg Maddux .75 2.00
8 Chipper Jones .50 1.25
9 Derek Jeter 1.25 3.00
10 Juan Gonzalez .20 .50
11 Albert Belle .20 .50
12 Tony Gwynn .60 1.50
13 Jeff Bagwell .30 .75
14 Mark McGwire 1.25 3.00
15 Andy Pettitte .30 .75
16 Mo Vaughn .20 .50
17 Kenny Lofton .20 .50
18 Manny Ramirez .30 .75
19 Roberto Alomar .30 .75
20 Ryne Sandberg .75 2.00
21 Hideo Nomo .50 1.25
22 Barry Bonds 1.25 3.00
23 Eddie Murray .50 1.25
24 Ken Caminiti .20 .50
25 John Smoltz .30 .75
26 Pat Hentgen .20 .50
27 Todd Hollandsworth .20 .50
28 Matt Williams .20 .50
29 Bernie Williams .30 .75
30 Brady Anderson .20 .50

1998 Ultra

The complete 1998 Ultra set features 501 cards and was distributed in 10-card first and second series packs with a suggested retail price of $2.59. The fronts carry UV coated color action player photos printed on 20 pt. card stock. The backs display another player photo with player information and career statistics. The set contains the following subsets: Season's Crown (211-220) seeded 1:12 packs, Prospects (221-245) seeded 1:4 packs, Checklists (246-250), and Checklists (473-475) seeded 1:4 packs and Pizzazz (476-500) seeded 1:4 packs. Rookie Cards include Kevin Millwood and Magglio Ordonez. Though not confirmed by the manufacturer, it's believed that several cards within the Prospects subset are in shorter supply than others - most notably number 238 Ricky Ledee and number 243 Jorge Velandia. Also, seeded one in every pack, was one of 50 Million Dollar Moment cards which pictured some of the greatest moments in baseball histroy and gave the collector a chance to win a million dollars. As a special last minute promotion, Fleer/SkyBox got Alex Rodriguez to autograph 750 of his 1998 Fleer Promo cards. Each card is serial-numbered by hand on the card front. The signed cards were randomly seeded into Ultra Series two hobby packs.

COMPLETE SET (501) 25.00 60.00
COMPLETE SERIES 1 (250) 15.00 40.00
COMPLETE SERIES 2 (251) 10.00 25.00
COMP.SER.1 w/o SP's (210) 5.00 12.00
COMP.SER.2 w/o SP's (226) 5.00 12.00
COMMON 1 (1-220/246-250) .10 .30
COMMON 2 (251-475/501) .10 .30
246-250 CHECKLIST ODDS 1:4
COMMON SC (211-220) .75 2.00
211-220 SEASON CROWN ODDS 1:12
COMMON PROS (221-245) 1.25 3.00
221-245 PROSPECTS ODDS 1:4
COMMON PZ (476-500) .40 1.00
476-500 PIZZAZZ ODDS 1:4
1 Ken Griffey Jr. .60 1.50
2 Matt Morris .10 .30
3 Roger Clemens .60 1.50
4 Matt Williams .10 .30
5 Roberto Hernandez .10 .30
6 Rondell White .10 .30
7 Tim Salmon .20 .50
8 Brad Radke .10 .30
9 Brett Butler .10 .30
10 Carl Everett .10 .30
11 Chili Davis .10 .30
12 Chuck Finley .10 .30
13 Darryl Kile .10 .30
14 Deivi Cruz .10 .30
15 Gary Gaetti .10 .30
16 Matt Stairs .10 .30
17 Pat Meares .10 .30
18 Will Cunnane .10 .30
19 Steve Woodard .10 .30
20 Andy Ashby .10 .30
21 Bobby Higginson .10 .30
22 Brian Jordan .10 .30
23 Craig Biggio .20 .50
24 Jim Edmonds .10 .30
25 Ryan McGuire .10 .30
26 Scott Hatteberg .10 .30
27 Willie Greene .10 .30
28 Albert Belle .10 .30
29 Ellis Burks .10 .30
30 Hideo Nomo .30 .75
31 Jeff Bagwell .20 .50
32 Kevin Brown .20 .50
33 Nomar Garciaparra .50 1.25
34 Pedro Martinez .20 .50
35 Raul Mondesi .10 .30
36 Ricky Bottalico .10 .30
37 Shawn Estes .10 .30
38 Otis Nixon .10 .30
39 Terry Steinbach .10 .30
40 Tom Glavine .20 .50
41 Todd Dunwoody .10 .30
42 Deion Sanders .20 .50
43 Gary Sheffield .10 .30
44 Mike Lansing .10 .30
45 Mike Lieberthal .10 .30
46 Paul Sorrento .10 .30
47 Paul O'Neill .20 .50
48 Tom Goodwin .10 .30
49 Andruw Jones .20 .50
50 Barry Bonds .75 2.00
51 Bernie Williams .20 .50
52 Jeremi Gonzalez .10 .30
53 Mike Piazza .50 1.25
54 Russ Davis .10 .30
55 Vinny Castilla .10 .30
56 Rod Beck .10 .30
57 Andres Galarraga .10 .30
58 Ben McDonald .10 .30
59 Billy Wagner .10 .30
60 Charles Johnson .10 .30
61 Fred McGriff .20 .50
62 Dean Palmer .10 .30
63 Frank Thomas .30 .75
64 Ismael Valdes .10 .30
65 Mark Bellhorn .10 .30
66 Jeff King .10 .30
67 John Wetteland .10 .30
68 Mark Grace .20 .50
69 Mark Kotsay .10 .30
70 Scott Rolen .20 .50
71 Todd Hundley .10 .30
72 Todd Worrell .10 .30
73 Wilson Alvarez .10 .30
74 Bobby Jones .10 .30
75 Jose Canseco .20 .50
76 Kevin Appier .10 .30
77 Neifi Perez .10 .30
78 Paul Molitor .10 .30
79 Quilvio Veras .10 .30
80 Randy Johnson .30 .75
81 Glendon Rusch .10 .30
82 Curt Schilling .10 .30
83 Alex Rodriguez .50 1.25
84 Rey Ordonez .10 .30
85 Jeff Juden .10 .30
86 Mike Cameron .10 .30
87 Ryan Klesko .10 .30
88 Trevor Hoffman .10 .30
89 Chuck Knoblauch .10 .30
90 Larry Walker .10 .30
91 Mark McLemore .10 .30
92 B.J. Surhoff .10 .30
93 Darren Daulton .10 .30
94 Ray Durham .10 .30
95 Sammy Sosa .30 .75
96 Eric Young .10 .30
97 Gerald Williams .10 .30
98 Javy Lopez .10 .30
99 John Smiley .10 .30
100 Juan Gonzalez .10 .30
101 Shawn Green .10 .30
102 Charles Nagy .10 .30
103 David Justice .10 .30
104 Joey Hamilton .10 .30
105 Pat Hentgen .10 .30
106 Raul Casanova .10 .30
107 Tony Phillips .10 .30
108 Tony Gwynn .40 1.00
109 Will Clark .20 .50
110 Jason Giambi .10 .30
111 Jay Bell .10 .30
112 Johnny Damon .20 .50
113 Alan Benes .10 .30
114 Jeff Suppan .10 .30
115 Kevin Polcovich .10 .30
116 Shigetoshi Hasegawa .10 .30
117 Steve Finley .10 .30
118 Tony Clark .10 .30
119 David Cone .10 .30
120 Jose Guillen .10 .30
121 Kevin Millwood RC .40 1.00
122 Greg Maddux .50 1.25
123 Dave Nilsson .10 .30
124 Hideki Irabu .10 .30
125 Jason Kendall .10 .30
126 Jim Thome .20 .50
127 Delino DeShields .10 .30
128 Edgar Renteria .10 .30
129 Edgardo Alfonzo .10 .30
130 J.T. Snow .10 .30
131 Jeff Abbott .10 .30
132 Jeffrey Hammonds .10 .30
133 Todd Greene .10 .30
134 Vladimir Guerrero .30 .75
135 Jay Buhner .10 .30
136 Jeff Cirillo .10 .30
137 Jeromy Burnitz .10 .30
138 Mickey Morandini .10 .30
139 Tino Martinez .20 .50
140 Jeff Shaw .10 .30
141 Rafael Palmeiro .20 .50
142 Bobby Bonilla .10 .30
143 Cal Ripken 1.00 2.50
144 Chad Fox RC .10 .30
145 Dante Bichette .10 .30
146 Dennis Eckersley .10 .30
147 Mariano Rivera .30 .75
148 Mo Vaughn .10 .30
149 Reggie Sanders .10 .30
150 Derek Jeter .75 2.00
151 Rusty Greer .10 .30
152 Brady Anderson .10 .30
153 Brett Tomko .10 .30
154 Jaime Navarro .10 .30
155 Kevin Orie .10 .30
156 Roberto Alomar .20 .50
157 Edgar Martinez .20 .50
158 John Olerud .10 .30
159 John Smoltz .20 .50
160 Ryne Sandberg .50 1.25
161 Billy Taylor .10 .30
162 Chris Holt .10 .30
163 Damion Easley .10 .30
164 Darin Erstad .10 .30
165 Joe Carter .10 .30
166 Kelvim Escobar .10 .30
167 Ken Caminiti .10 .30
168 Pokey Reese .10 .30
169 Ray Lankford .10 .30
170 Livan Hernandez .10 .30
171 Steve Kline .10 .30
172 Tom Gordon .10 .30
173 Travis Fryman .10 .30
174 Al Martin .10 .30
175 Andy Pettitte .20 .50
176 Jeff Kent .10 .30
177 Jimmy Key .10 .30
178 Mark Grudzielanek .10 .30
179 Tony Saunders .10 .30
180 Barry Larkin .20 .50
181 Bubba Trammell .10 .30
182 Carlos Delgado .10 .30
183 Carlos Baerga .10 .30
184 Derek Bell .10 .30
185 Henry Rodriguez .10 .30
186 Jason Dickson .10 .30
187 Ron Gant .10 .30
188 Tony Womack .10 .30
189 Justin Thompson .10 .30
190 Fernando Tatis .10 .30
191 Mark Wohlers .10 .30
192 Takashi Kashiwada .10 .30
193 Garret Anderson .10 .30
194 Jose Cruz Jr. .10 .30
195 Ricardo Rincon .10 .30
196 Tim Naehring .10 .30
197 Moises Alou .10 .30
198 Eric Karros .10 .30
199 John Jaha .10 .30
200 Marty Cordova .10 .30
201 Ken Hill .10 .30
202 Chipper Jones .30 .75
203 Kenny Lofton .10 .30
204 Mike Mussina .20 .50
205 Manny Ramirez .20 .50
206 Todd Hollandsworth .10 .30
207 Cecil Fielder .10 .30
208 Mark McGwire .75 2.00
209 Jim Leyritz .10 .30
210 Ivan Rodriguez .20 .50
211 Jeff Bagwell SC .75 2.00
212 Barry Bonds SC 3.00 8.00
213 Roger Clemens SC 2.50 6.00
214 Nomar Garciaparra SC 2.00 5.00
215 Ken Griffey Jr. SC 2.50 6.00
216 Tony Gwynn SC 1.50 4.00
217 Randy Johnson SC 1.25 3.00
218 Mark McGwire SC 3.00 8.00
219 Scott Rolen SC .75 2.00
220 Frank Thomas SC 1.25 3.00
221 Matt Perisho PROS 1.25 3.00
222 Wes Helms PROS 1.25 3.00
223 Dave Dellucci PROS RC 1.25 3.00
224 Todd Helton PROS 1.25 3.00
225 Brian Rose PROS 1.25 3.00
226 Aaron Boone PROS 1.25 3.00
227 Keith Foulke PROS 1.25 3.00
228 Homer Bush PROS 1.25 3.00
229 Shannon Stewart PROS 1.25 3.00
230 Richard Hidalgo PROS 1.25 3.00
231 Russ Johnson PROS 1.25 3.00
232 Henry Blanco PROS RC 1.25 3.00
233 Paul Konerko PROS 1.25 3.00
234 Antone Williamson PROS 1.25 3.00
235 Shane Bowers PROS RC 1.25 3.00
236 Jose Vidro PROS 1.25 3.00
237 Derek Wallace PROS 1.25 3.00
238 Ricky Ledee PROS SP 2.00 5.00
239 Ben Grieve PROS 1.25 3.00
240 Lou Collier PROS 1.25 3.00
241 Derrek Lee PROS 1.25 3.00
242 Ruben Rivera PROS 1.25 3.00
243 Jorge Velandia PROS SP 2.00 5.00
244 Andrew Vessel PROS 1.25 3.00
245 Chris Carpenter PROS 1.25 3.00
246 Ken Griffey Jr. CL .40 1.00
247 Alex Rodriguez CL .30 .75
248 Diamond Ink CL .10 .30
249 Frank Thomas CL .20 .50
250 Cal Ripken CL .50 1.25
251 Carlos Perez .10 .30
252 Larry Sutton .10 .30
253 Gary Sheffield .10 .30
254 Wally Joyner .10 .30
255 Todd Stottlemyre .10 .30
256 Nerio Rodriguez .10 .30
257 Charles Johnson .10 .30
258 Pedro Astacio .10 .30
259 Cal Eldred .10 .30
260 Chili Davis .10 .30
261 Freddy Garcia .10 .30
262 Bobby Witt .10 .30
263 Michael Coleman .10 .30
264 Mike Caruso .10 .30
265 Mike Lansing .10 .30
266 Dennis Reyes .10 .30
267 F.P. Santangelo .10 .30
268 Darryl Hamilton .10 .30
269 Mike Fetters .10 .30
270 Charlie Hayes .10 .30
271 Royce Clayton .10 .30
272 Doug Drabek .10 .30
273 James Baldwin .10 .30
274 Brian Hunter .10 .30
275 Chan Ho Park .10 .30
276 John Franco .10 .30
277 David Wells .10 .30
278 Eli Marrero .10 .30
279 Kerry Wood .15 .40
280 Donnie Sadler .10 .30
281 Scott Winchester RC .10 .30
282 Hal Morris .10 .30
283 Brad Fullmer .10 .30
284 Bernard Gilkey .10 .30
285 Ramiro Mendoza .10 .30
286 Kevin Brown .20 .50
287 David Segui .10 .30
288 Willie McGee .10 .30
289 Darren Oliver .10 .30
290 Antonio Alfonseca .10 .30
291 Eric Davis .10 .30
292 Mickey Morandini .10 .30
293 Frank Catalanotto RC .25 .60
294 Derrek Lee .20 .50
295 Todd Zeile .10 .30
296 Chuck Knoblauch .10 .30
297 Wilson Delgado .10 .30
298 Bobby Bonilla .10 .30
299 Orel Hershiser .10 .30
300 Ozzie Guillen .10 .30
301 Aaron Sele .10 .30
302 Joe Carter .10 .30
303 Darryl Kile .10 .30
304 Shane Reynolds .10 .30
305 Todd Dunn .10 .30
306 Bob Abreu .10 .30
307 Doug Strange .10 .30
308 Jose Canseco .20 .50
309 Lance Johnson .10 .30
310 Harold Baines .10 .30
311 Todd Pratt .10 .30
312 Greg Colbrunn .10 .30
313 Masato Yoshii RC .15 .40
314 Felix Heredia .10 .30
315 Dennis Martinez .10 .30
316 Geronimo Berroa .10 .30
317 Darren Lewis .10 .30
318 Bill Ripken .10 .30
319 Enrique Wilson .10 .30
320 Alex Ochoa .10 .30
321 Doug Glanville .10 .30
322 Mike Stanley .10 .30
323 Gerald Williams .10 .30
324 Pedro Martinez .20 .50
325 Jaret Wright .10 .30
326 Terry Pendleton .10 .30
327 LaTroy Hawkins .10 .30
328 Emil Brown .10 .30
329 Walt Weiss .10 .30
330 Omar Vizquel .20 .50
331 Carl Everett .10 .30
332 Fernando Vina .10 .30
333 Mike Blowers .10 .30
334 Dwight Gooden .10 .30
335 Mark Lewis .10 .30
336 Jim Leyritz .10 .30
337 Kenny Lofton .10 .30
338 John Halama RC .15 .40
339 Jose Valentin .10 .30
340 Desi Relaford .10 .30
341 Dante Powell .10 .30
342 Ed Sprague .10 .30
343 Reggie Jefferson .10 .30
344 Mike Hampton .10 .30
345 Marquis Grissom .10 .30
346 Heathcliff Slocumb .10 .30
347 Francisco Cordova .10 .30
348 Ken Cloude .10 .30
349 Benito Santiago .10 .30
350 Denny Neagle .10 .30
351 Sean Casey .10 .30
352 Robb Nen .10 .30
353 Orlando Merced .10 .30
354 Adrian Brown .10 .30
355 Gregg Jefferies .10 .30
356 Otis Nixon .10 .30
357 Michael Tucker .10 .30
358 Eric Milton .10 .30
359 Travis Fryman .10 .30
360 Gary DiSarcina .10 .30
361 Mario Valdez .10 .30
362 Craig Counsell .10 .30
363 Jose Offerman .10 .30
364 Tony Fernandez .10 .30
365 Jason McDonald .10 .30
366 Sterling Hitchcock .10 .30
367 Donovan Osborne .10 .30
368 Troy Percival .10 .30
369 Henry Rodriguez .10 .30
370 Dmitri Young .10 .30
371 Jay Powell .10 .30
372 Jeff Conine .10 .30
373 Orlando Cabrera .10 .30
374 Butch Huskey .10 .30
375 Mike Lowell RC .60 1.50
376 Kevin Young .10 .30
377 Jamie Moyer .10 .30
378 Jeff D'Amico .10 .30
379 Scott Erickson .10 .30
380 Magglio Ordonez RC 1.25 3.00
381 Melvin Nieves .10 .30
382 Ramon Martinez .10 .30
383 A.J. Hinch .10 .30
384 Jeff Brantley .10 .30
385 Kevin Elster .10 .30
386 Allen Watson .10 .30
387 Moises Alou .10 .30
388 Jeff Blauser .10 .30
389 Pete Harnisch .10 .30
390 Shane Andrews .10 .30
391 Rico Brogna .10 .30
392 Stan Javier .10 .30
393 David Howard .10 .30
394 Darryl Strawberry .10 .30
395 Kent Mercker .10 .30

396 Juan Encarnacion .10 .30
397 Sandy Alomar Jr. .10 .30
398 Al Leiter .10 .30
399 Tony Graffanino .10 .30
400 Terry Adams .10 .30
401 Bruce Aven .10 .30
402 Derrick Gibson .10 .30
403 Jose Cabrera RC .10 .30
404 Rich Becker .10 .30
405 David Ortiz .40 1.00
406 Brian McRae .10 .30
407 Bobby Estalella .10 .30
408 Bill Mueller .10 .30
409 Dennis Eckersley .10 .30
410 Sandy Martinez .10 .30
411 Jose Vizcaino .10 .30
412 Jermaine Allensworth .10 .30
413 Miguel Tejada .30 .75
414 Turner Ward .10 .30
415 Glenallen Hill .10 .30
416 Lee Stevens .10 .30
417 Cecil Fielder .10 .30
418 Ruben Sierra .10 .30
419 Jon Nunnally .10 .30
420 Rod Myers .10 .30
421 Dustin Hermanson .10 .30
422 James Mouton .10 .30
423 Dan Wilson .10 .30
424 Roberto Kelly .10 .30
425 Antonio Osuna .10 .30
426 Jacob Cruz .10 .30
427 Brent Mayne .10 .30
428 Matt Karchner .10 .30
429 Damian Jackson .10 .30
430 Roger Cedeno .10 .30
431 Rickey Henderson .30 .75
432 Joe Randa .10 .30
433 Greg Vaughn .10 .30
434 Andres Galarraga .10 .30
435 Rod Beck .10 .30
436 Curtis Goodwin .10 .30
437 Brad Ausmus .10 .30
438 Bob Hamelin .10 .30
439 Todd Walker .10 .30
440 Scott Brosius .10 .30
441 Len Dykstra .10 .30
442 Abraham Nunez .10 .30
443 Brian Johnson .10 .30
444 Randy Myers .10 .30
445 Bret Boone .10 .30
446 Oscar Henriquez .10 .30
447 Mike Sweeney .10 .30
448 Kenny Rogers .10 .30
449 Mark Langston .10 .30
450 Luis Gonzalez .10 .30
451 John Burkett .10 .30
452 Bip Roberts .10 .30
453 Travis Lee .10 .30
454 Felix Rodriguez .10 .30
455 Andy Benes .10 .30
456 Willie Blair .10 .30
457 Brian Anderson .10 .30
458 Jay Bell .10 .30
459 Matt Williams .10 .30
460 Devon White .10 .30
461 Karim Garcia .10 .30
462 Jorge Fabregas .10 .30
463 Wilson Alvarez .10 .30
464 Roberto Hernandez .10 .30
465 Tony Saunders .10 .30
466 Rolando Arrojo RC .15 .40
467 Wade Boggs .30 .75
468 Fred McGriff .20 .50
469 Paul Sorrento .10 .30
470 Kevin Stocker .10 .30
471 Bubba Trammell .10 .30
472 Quinton McCracken .10 .30
473 Ken Griffey Jr. CL .40 1.00
474 Cal Ripken CL .50 1.25
475 Frank Thomas CL .20 .50
476 Ken Griffey Jr. PZ 2.00 5.00
477 Cal Ripken PZ 3.00 8.00
478 Frank Thomas PZ 1.00 2.50
479 Alex Rodriguez PZ 1.50 4.00
480 Nomar Garciaparra PZ 1.50 4.00
481 Derek Jeter PZ 2.50 6.00
482 Andruw Jones PZ .60 1.50
483 Chipper Jones PZ 1.00 2.50
484 Greg Maddux PZ 1.50 4.00
485 Mike Piazza PZ 1.50 4.00
486 Juan Gonzalez PZ .40 1.00
487 Jose Cruz Jr. PZ .40 1.00
488 Jaret Wright PZ .40 1.00
489 Hideo Nomo PZ 1.00 2.50
490 Scott Rolen PZ .60 1.50
491 Tony Gwynn PZ 1.25 3.00
492 Roger Clemens PZ 2.00 5.00
493 Darin Erstad PZ .40 1.00
494 Mark McGwire PZ 2.50 6.00
495 Jeff Bagwell PZ .60 1.50
496 Mo Vaughn PZ .40 1.00
497 Albert Belle PZ .40 1.00
498 Kenny Lofton PZ .40 1.00
499 Ben Grieve PZ .40 1.00
500 Barry Bonds PZ 2.50 6.00
501 Mike Piazza .50 1.25
S100 A.Rodriguez AU/750 50.00 100.00

1998 Ultra Gold Medallion

COMPLETE SET (501) 100.00 200.00
COMPLETE SERIES 1 (250) 40.00 100.00
COMPLETE SERIES 2 (251) 40.00 100.00
*STARS: 1.25X TO 3X BASIC CARDS
*ROOKIES: .75X TO 2X BASIC CARDS
*SEASON CROWNS: .3X TO .8X BASIC SC
*PROSPECTS: .25X TO .6X BASIC PROSPECTS
*CHECKLISTS: 1.25X TO 3X BASIC CL'S
*PIZZAZZ: .4X TO 1X BASIC PIZZAZZ
ONE PER HOBBY PACK
SUBSETS ARE NOT SP'S IN G.MED SET

1998 Ultra Platinum Medallion

*STARS: 10X TO 25X BASIC CARDS
*ROOKIES: 10X TO 25X BASIC CARDS
*SEASON CROWNS: 1.5X TO 4X BASIC SC
*PROSPECTS: 2.5X TO 6X BASIC PROSP.
*CHECKLISTS: 12.5X TO 30X BASIC CL'S
*PIZZAZZ: 2X TO 5X BASIC PIZZAZZ
RANDOM INSERTS IN HOBBY PACKS
SER.1 PRINT RUN 100 SERIAL #'d SETS
SER.2 PRINT RUN 98 SERIAL #'d SETS
SUBSETS ARE NOT SP'S IN PLAT.MED SET
CARDS 473-475 DO NOT EXIST

1998 Ultra Artistic Talents

COMPLETE SET (18) 20.00 50.00
SER.1 STATED ODDS 1:8
1 Ken Griffey Jr. 2.00 5.00
2 Andruw Jones .60 1.50
3 Alex Rodriguez 1.50 4.00
4 Frank Thomas 1.00 2.50
5 Cal Ripken 3.00 8.00
6 Derek Jeter 2.50 6.00
7 Chipper Jones 1.00 2.50
8 Greg Maddux 1.50 4.00
9 Mike Piazza 1.50 4.00
10 Albert Belle .40 1.00
11 Darin Erstad .40 1.00
12 Juan Gonzalez .40 1.00
13 Jeff Bagwell .60 1.50
14 Tony Gwynn 1.25 3.00
15 Mark McGwire 2.50 6.00
16 Scott Rolen .60 1.50
17 Barry Bonds 2.50 6.00
18 Kenny Lofton .40 1.00

1998 Ultra Back to the Future

COMPLETE SET (15) 5.00 12.00
SER.1 STATED ODDS 1:6
1 Andruw Jones .30 .75
2 Alex Rodriguez .75 2.00
3 Derek Jeter 1.25 3.00
4 Darin Erstad .20 .50
5 Mike Cameron .20 .50
6 Scott Rolen .30 .75
7 Nomar Garciaparra .75 2.00
8 Hideki Irabu .20 .50
9 Jose Cruz Jr. .20 .50
10 Vladimir Guerrero .50 1.25
11 Mark Kotsay .20 .50
12 Tony Womack .20 .50
13 Jason Dickson .20 .50
14 Jose Guillen .20 .50
15 Tony Clark .20 .50

1998 Ultra Big Shots

COMPLETE SET (15) 4.00 10.00
SER.1 STATED ODDS 1:4
1 Ken Griffey Jr. .75 2.00
2 Frank Thomas .40 1.00
3 Chipper Jones .40 1.00
4 Albert Belle .15 .40
5 Juan Gonzalez .15 .40
6 Jeff Bagwell .25 .60
7 Mark McGwire 1.00 2.50
8 Barry Bonds 1.00 2.50
9 Manny Ramirez .25 .60
10 Mo Vaughn .15 .40
11 Matt Williams .15 .40
12 Jim Thome .25 .60
13 Tino Martinez .25 .60
14 Mike Piazza .60 1.50
15 Tony Clark .15 .40

1998 Ultra Diamond Immortals

SER.2 STATED ODDS 1:288
1 Ken Griffey Jr. 75.00 200.00
2 Frank Thomas 15.00 40.00
3 Alex Rodriguez 30.00 80.00
4 Cal Ripken 30.00 80.00
5 Mike Piazza 10.00 25.00
6 Mark McGwire 15.00 40.00
7 Greg Maddux 12.00 30.00
8 Andruw Jones 4.00 10.00
9 Chipper Jones 10.00 25.00
10 Derek Jeter 75.00 200.00
11 Tony Gwynn 10.00 25.00
12 Juan Gonzalez 10.00 25.00
13 Jose Cruz Jr. 4.00 10.00
14 Roger Clemens 12.00 30.00
15 Barry Bonds 15.00 40.00

1998 Ultra Diamond Producers

COMPLETE SET (15) 75.00 150.00
SER.1 STATED ODDS 1:288
1 Ken Griffey Jr. 8.00 20.00
2 Andruw Jones 1.50 4.00
3 Alex Rodriguez 5.00 12.00
4 Frank Thomas 4.00 10.00
5 Cal Ripken 12.00 30.00
6 Derek Jeter 10.00 25.00
7 Chipper Jones 4.00 10.00
8 Greg Maddux 5.00 12.00
9 Mike Piazza 4.00 10.00
10 Juan Gonzalez 1.50 4.00
11 Jeff Bagwell 2.50 6.00
12 Tony Gwynn 4.00 10.00
13 Mark McGwire 6.00 15.00
14 Barry Bonds 6.00 15.00
15 Jose Cruz Jr. 1.50 4.00

1998 Ultra Double Trouble

COMPLETE SET (20) 6.00 15.00
SER.1 STATED ODDS 1:4
1 K.Griffey Jr. / A.Rodriguez .75 2.00
2 V.Guerrero / P.Martinez .40 1.00
3 A.Jones / K.Lofton .40 1.00
4 C.Jones / G.Maddux .60 1.50
5 D.Jeter / T.Martinez .75 2.00
6 F.Thomas / A.Belle .40 1.00
7 C.Ripken / R.Alomar 1.25 3.00
8 M.Piazza / H.Nomo .60 1.50
9 D.Erstad / J.Dickson .30 .75
10 J.Gonzalez / I.Rodriguez .40 1.00
11 J.Bagwell / D.Kile UER .40 1.00
12 T.Gwynn / S.Finley .50 1.25
13 M.McGwire / R.Lankford 1.00 2.50
14 B.Bonds / J.Kent 1.00 2.50
15 A.Pettitte / B.Williams .40 1.00
16 N.Garciaparra / M.Vaughn .60 1.50
17 M.Williams / J.Thome .40 1.00
18 H.Irabu / M.Rivera .40 1.00
19 R.Clemens / J.Cruz Jr. .75 2.00
20 M.Ramirez / D.Justice .40 1.00

1998 Ultra Fall Classics

COMPLETE SET (15) 40.00 100.00
SER.1 STATED ODDS 1:18
1 Ken Griffey Jr. 4.00 10.00
2 Andruw Jones 1.25 3.00
3 Alex Rodriguez 3.00 8.00
4 Frank Thomas 2.00 5.00
5 Cal Ripken 6.00 15.00
6 Derek Jeter 5.00 12.00
7 Chipper Jones 2.00 5.00
8 Greg Maddux 3.00 8.00
9 Mike Piazza 3.00 8.00
10 Albert Belle .75 2.00
11 Juan Gonzalez .75 2.00
12 Jeff Bagwell 1.25 3.00
13 Tony Gwynn 2.50 6.00
14 Mark McGwire 5.00 12.00
15 Barry Bonds 5.00 12.00

1998 Ultra Kid Gloves

COMPLETE SET (12) 6.00 15.00
SER.1 STATED ODDS 1:8
1 Andruw Jones .40 1.00
2 Alex Rodriguez 1.00 2.50
3 Derek Jeter 1.50 4.00
4 Chipper Jones .60 1.50
5 Darin Erstad .25 .60
6 Todd Walker .25 .60
7 Scott Rolen .40 1.00
8 Nomar Garciaparra 1.00 2.50
9 Jose Cruz Jr. .25 .60
10 Charles Johnson .25 .60
11 Rey Ordonez .25 .60
12 Vladimir Guerrero .60 1.50

1998 Ultra Millennium Men

COMPLETE SET (15) 60.00 120.00
SER.2 STATED ODDS 1:35 HOBBY
1 Jose Cruz Jr. 1.00 2.50
2 Ken Griffey Jr. 5.00 12.00
3 Cal Ripken 8.00 20.00
4 Derek Jeter 6.00 15.00
5 Andruw Jones 1.50 4.00
6 Alex Rodriguez 4.00 10.00
7 Chipper Jones 2.50 6.00
8 Scott Rolen 1.50 4.00
9 Nomar Garciaparra 4.00 10.00
10 Frank Thomas 2.50 6.00
11 Mike Piazza 4.00 10.00
12 Greg Maddux 4.00 10.00
13 Juan Gonzalez 1.00 2.50
14 Ben Grieve 1.00 2.50
15 Jaret Wright 1.00 2.50

1998 Ultra Notables

COMPLETE SET (20) 10.00 25.00
SER.2 STATED ODDS 1:4
1 Frank Thomas .50 1.25
2 Ken Griffey Jr. 1.00 2.50
3 Edgar Renteria .20 .50
4 Albert Belle .20 .50
5 Juan Gonzalez .20 .50
6 Jeff Bagwell .30 .75
7 Mark McGwire 1.25 3.00
8 Barry Bonds 1.25 3.00
9 Scott Rolen .30 .75
10 Mo Vaughn .20 .50
11 Andruw Jones .30 .75
12 Chipper Jones .50 1.25
13 Tino Martinez .30 .75
14 Mike Piazza .75 2.00
15 Tony Clark .20 .50
16 Jose Cruz Jr. .20 .50
17 Nomar Garciaparra .75 2.00
18 Cal Ripken 1.50 4.00
19 Alex Rodriguez .75 2.00
20 Derek Jeter 1.25 3.00

1998 Ultra Power Plus

COMPLETE SET (10) 25.00 60.00
SER.1 STATED ODDS 1:36
1 Ken Griffey Jr. 6.00 15.00
2 Andruw Jones 2.00 5.00
3 Alex Rodriguez 5.00 12.00
4 Frank Thomas 3.00 8.00
5 Mike Piazza 5.00 12.00
6 Albert Belle 1.25 3.00
7 Juan Gonzalez 1.25 3.00
8 Jeff Bagwell 2.00 5.00
9 Barry Bonds 8.00 20.00
10 Jose Cruz Jr. 1.25 3.00

1998 Ultra Prime Leather

SER.1 STATED ODDS 1:144
1 Ken Griffey Jr. 8.00 20.00
2 Andruw Jones 1.50 4.00
3 Alex Rodriguez 5.00 12.00
4 Frank Thomas 4.00 10.00
5 Cal Ripken 12.00 30.00
6 Derek Jeter 10.00 25.00
7 Chipper Jones 4.00 10.00
8 Greg Maddux 5.00 12.00
9 Mike Piazza 4.00 10.00
10 Albert Belle 1.50 4.00
11 Darin Erstad 1.50 4.00
12 Juan Gonzalez 1.50 4.00
13 Jeff Bagwell 2.50 6.00
14 Tony Gwynn 4.00 10.00
15 Roberto Alomar 2.50 6.00
16 Barry Bonds 6.00 15.00
17 Kenny Lofton 1.50 4.00
18 Jose Cruz Jr. 1.50 4.00

1998 Ultra Rocket to Stardom

COMPLETE SET (15) 12.50 30.00
SER.2 STATED ODDS 1:20
1 Ben Grieve .75 2.00
2 Magglio Ordonez 2.50 6.00
3 Travis Lee .75 2.00
4 Mike Caruso .75 2.00
5 Brian Rose .75 2.00
6 Brad Fullmer .75 2.00
7 Michael Coleman .75 2.00
8 Juan Encarnacion .75 2.00
9 Karim Garcia .75 2.00
10 Todd Helton 1.25 3.00
11 Richard Hidalgo .75 2.00
12 Paul Konerko .75 2.00
13 Rod Myers .75 2.00
14 Jaret Wright .75 2.00
15 Miguel Tejada 2.00 5.00

1998 Ultra Ticket Studs

COMPLETE SET (15) 20.00 50.00
SER.2 STATED ODDS 1:144
1 Travis Lee .75 2.00
2 Tony Gwynn 2.00 5.00
3 Scott Rolen 1.25 3.00
4 Nomar Garciaparra 1.25 3.00
5 Mike Piazza 2.00 5.00
6 Mark McGwire 3.00 8.00
7 Ken Griffey Jr. 4.00 10.00
8 Juan Gonzalez .75 2.00
9 Jose Cruz Jr. .75 2.00
10 Frank Thomas 2.00 5.00
11 Derek Jeter 5.00 12.00
12 Chipper Jones 2.00 5.00
13 Cal Ripken 6.00 15.00
14 Andruw Jones .75 2.00
15 Alex Rodriguez 2.50 6.00

1998 Ultra Top 30

COMPLETE SET (30) 10.00 25.00
1 Barry Bonds 1.00 2.50
2 Ivan Rodriguez .25 .60
3 Kenny Lofton .15 .40
4 Albert Belle .15 .40
5 Mo Vaughn .15 .40
6 Jeff Bagwell .25 .60
7 Mark McGwire 1.00 2.50
8 Darin Erstad .15 .40
9 Roger Clemens .75 2.00
10 Tony Gwynn .50 1.25
11 Scott Rolen .25 .60
12 Hideo Nomo .40 1.00
13 Juan Gonzalez .15 .40
14 Mike Piazza .60 1.50
15 Greg Maddux .60 1.50
16 Chipper Jones .40 1.00
17 Andruw Jones .25 .60
18 Derek Jeter 1.00 2.50
19 Nomar Garciaparra .60 1.50
20 Alex Rodriguez .60 1.50
21 Frank Thomas .40 1.00
22 Cal Ripken 1.25 3.00
23 Ken Griffey Jr. .75 2.00
24 Jose Cruz Jr. .15 .40
25 Jaret Wright .15 .40
26 Travis Lee .15 .40
27 Wade Boggs .40 1.00
28 Chuck Knoblauch .15 .40
29 Joe Carter .15 .40
30 Ben Grieve .15 .40

1998 Ultra Win Now

COMPLETE SET (20) 20.00 50.00
SER.2 STATED ODDS 1:72
1 Alex Rodriguez 2.00 5.00
2 Andruw Jones .60 1.50
3 Cal Ripken 5.00 12.00
4 Chipper Jones 1.50 4.00
5 Darin Erstad .60 1.50
6 Derek Jeter 4.00 10.00
7 Frank Thomas 1.50 4.00
8 Greg Maddux 2.00 5.00
9 Hideo Nomo 1.50 4.00
10 Jeff Bagwell 1.00 2.50
11 Jose Cruz Jr. .60 1.50
12 Juan Gonzalez .60 1.50
13 Ken Griffey Jr. 3.00 8.00
14 Mark McGwire 2.50 6.00
15 Mike Piazza 1.50 4.00
16 Mo Vaughn .60 1.50
17 Nomar Garciaparra 1.00 2.50
18 Roger Clemens 2.00 5.00
19 Scott Rolen 1.00 2.50
20 Tony Gwynn 1.50 4.00

1999 Ultra Promo Sheet

NNO 99 Ultra 1 Promo Sheet 2.00 5.00

1999 Ultra

This 250-card single-series set was distributed in 10-card packs with a suggested retail price of $2.69 and features color player photos on the fronts with stats by year in 15 categories and career highlights on the backs for 210 veterans. The set contains the following subsets: Prospects (25 rookie cards seeded 1:4 packs), Season Crowns (10 1998 statistical leaders seeded 1:8) and five checklist cards.

COMPLETE SET (250) 30.00 80.00
COMP.SET w/o SP's (215) 10.00 25.00
COMMON CARD (1-215) .10 .30
COMMON SC (216-225) .30 .75
SEASON CROWN STATED ODDS 1:8
COMMON PROSPECT (226-250) .75 2.00
PROSPECT STATED ODDS 1:4
1 Greg Maddux .50 1.25
2 Greg Vaughn .10 .30
3 John Wetteland .10 .30
4 Tino Martinez .20 .50
5 Todd Walker .10 .30
6 Troy O'Leary .10 .30
7 Barry Larkin .20 .50
8 Mike Lansing .10 .30
9 Delino DeShields .10 .30
10 Brett Tomko .10 .30
11 Carlos Perez .10 .30
12 Mark Langston .10 .30
13 Jamie Moyer .10 .30
14 Jose Guillen .10 .30
15 Bartolo Colon .10 .30
16 Brady Anderson .10 .30
17 Walt Weiss .10 .30
18 Shane Reynolds .10 .30
19 David Segui .10 .30
20 Vladimir Guerrero .30 .75
21 Freddy Garcia .10 .30
22 Carl Everett .10 .30
23 Jose Cruz Jr. .10 .30
24 David Ortiz .30 .75
25 Andruw Jones .20 .50
26 Darren Lewis .10 .30
27 Ray Lankford .10 .30
28 Wally Joyner .10 .30
29 Charles Johnson .10 .30
30 Derek Jeter .75 2.00
31 Sean Casey .10 .30
32 Bobby Bonilla .10 .30
33 Todd Zeile .10 .30
34 Todd Helton .20 .50
35 David Wells .10 .30
36 Darin Erstad .10 .30
37 Ivan Rodriguez .20 .50
38 Antonio Osuna .10 .30
39 Mickey Morandini .10 .30
40 Rusty Greer .10 .30
41 Rod Beck .10 .30
42 Larry Sutton .10 .30
43 Edgar Renteria .10 .30
44 Otis Nixon .10 .30
45 Eli Marrero .10 .30
46 Reggie Jefferson .10 .30
47 Trevor Hoffman .10 .30
48 Andres Galarraga .10 .30
49 Scott Brosius .10 .30
50 Vinny Castilla .10 .30
51 Bret Boone .10 .30
52 Masato Yoshii .10 .30
53 Matt Williams .10 .30
54 Robin Ventura .10 .30
55 Jay Powell .10 .30
56 Dean Palmer .10 .30
57 Eric Milton .10 .30
58 Willie McGee .10 .30
59 Tony Gwynn .40 1.00
60 Tom Gordon .10 .30
61 Dante Bichette .10 .30
62 Jaret Wright .10 .30
63 Devon White .10 .30
64 Frank Thomas .30 .75
65 Mike Piazza .50 1.25
66 Jose Offerman .10 .30
67 Pat Meares .10 .30
68 Brian Meadows .10 .30
69 Nomar Garciaparra .50 1.25
70 Mark McGwire .75 2.00
71 Tony Graffanino .10 .30
72 Ken Griffey Jr. .60 1.50
73 Ken Caminiti .10 .30
74 Todd Jones .10 .30
75 A.J. Hinch .10 .30
76 Marquis Grissom .10 .30
77 Jay Buhner .10 .30
78 Albert Belle .10 .30
79 Brian Anderson .10 .30
80 Quinton McCracken .10 .30
81 Omar Vizquel .20 .50
82 Todd Stottlemyre .10 .30
83 Cal Ripken 1.00 2.50
84 Magglio Ordonez .10 .30
85 John Olerud .10 .30
86 Hal Morris .10 .30
87 Derrek Lee .20 .50
88 Doug Glanville .10 .30
89 Marty Cordova .10 .30
90 Kevin Brown .10 .30
91 Kevin Young .10 .30
92 Rico Brogna .10 .30
93 Wilson Alvarez .10 .30
94 Bob Wickman .10 .30
95 Jim Thome .20 .50
96 Mike Mussina .20 .50
97 Al Leiter .10 .30
98 Travis Lee .10 .30
99 Jeff King .10 .30
100 Kerry Wood .10 .30
101 Cliff Floyd .10 .30
102 Jose Valentin .10 .30
103 Manny Ramirez .20 .50
104 Butch Huskey .10 .30
105 Scott Erickson .10 .30
106 Ray Durham .10 .30
107 Johnny Damon .20 .50
108 Craig Counsell .10 .30
109 Rolando Arrojo .10 .30
110 Bob Abreu .10 .30
111 Tony Womack .10 .30
112 Mike Stanley .10 .30
113 Kenny Lofton .10 .30
114 Eric Davis .10 .30
115 Jeff Conine .10 .30
116 Carlos Baerga .10 .30
117 Rondell White .10 .30
118 Billy Wagner .10 .30
119 Ed Sprague .10 .30
120 Jason Schmidt .10 .30
121 Edgar Martinez .20 .50
122 Travis Fryman .10 .30
123 Armando Benitez .10 .30
124 Matt Stairs .10 .30
125 Roberto Hernandez .10 .30
126 Jay Bell .10 .30
127 Justin Thompson .10 .30
128 John Jaha .10 .30
129 Mike Caruso .10 .30
130 Miguel Tejada .10 .30
131 Geoff Jenkins .10 .30
132 Wade Boggs .20 .50
133 Andy Benes .10 .30
134 Aaron Sele .10 .30
135 Bret Saberhagen .10 .30
136 Mariano Rivera .30 .75
137 Neifi Perez .10 .30
138 Paul Konerko .10 .30
139 Barry Bonds .75 2.00
140 Garret Anderson .10 .30
141 Bernie Williams .20 .50
142 Gary Sheffield .10 .30
143 Rafael Palmeiro .20 .50
144 Orel Hershiser .10 .30
145 Craig Biggio .20 .50
146 Dmitri Young .10 .30
147 Damion Easley .10 .30
148 Henry Rodriguez .10 .30
149 Brad Radke .10 .30
150 Pedro Martinez .20 .50
151 Mike Lieberthal .10 .30
152 Jim Leyritz .10 .30
153 Chuck Knoblauch .10 .30
154 Darryl Kile .10 .30
155 Brian Jordan .10 .30
156 Chipper Jones .30 .75
157 Pete Harnisch .10 .30
158 Moises Alou .10 .30
159 Ismael Valdes .10 .30
160 Stan Javier .10 .30
161 Mark Grace .20 .50
162 Jason Giambi .10 .30
163 Chuck Finley .10 .30
164 Juan Encarnacion .10 .30
165 Chan Ho Park .10 .30
166 Randy Johnson .30 .75
167 J.T. Snow .10 .30
168 Tim Salmon .20 .50
169 Brian L.Hunter .10 .30
170 Rickey Henderson .30 .75
171 Cal Eldred .10 .30
172 Curt Schilling .10 .30
173 Alex Rodriguez .50 1.25
174 Dustin Hermanson .10 .30
175 Mike Hampton .10 .30
176 Shawn Green .10 .30
177 Roberto Alomar .20 .50
178 Sandy Alomar Jr. .10 .30
179 Larry Walker .10 .30
180 Mo Vaughn .10 .30
181 Raul Mondesi .10 .30
182 Hideki Irabu .10 .30
183 Jim Edmonds .10 .30
184 Shawn Estes .10 .30
185 Tony Clark .10 .30
186 Dan Wilson .10 .30
187 Michael Tucker .10 .30
188 Jeff Shaw .10 .30
189 Mark Grudzielanek .10 .30
190 Roger Clemens .60 1.50
191 Juan Gonzalez .10 .30
192 Sammy Sosa .30 .75
193 Troy Percival .10 .30
194 Robb Nen .10 .30
195 Bill Mueller .10 .30
196 Ben Grieve .10 .30
197 Luis Gonzalez .10 .30
198 Will Clark .20 .50
199 Jeff Cirillo .10 .30
200 Scott Rolen .20 .50
201 Reggie Sanders .10 .30
202 Fred McGriff .20 .50
203 Denny Neagle .10 .30
204 Brad Fullmer .10 .30
205 Royce Clayton .10 .30
206 Jose Canseco .20 .50
207 Jeff Bagwell .20 .50
208 Hideo Nomo .30 .75
209 Karim Garcia .10 .30
210 Kenny Rogers .10 .30
211 Kerry Wood CL .10 .30
212 Alex Rodriguez CL .30 .75
213 Cal Ripken CL .50 1.25
214 Frank Thomas CL .20 .50
215 Ken Griffey Jr. CL .40 1.00
216 Alex Rodriguez SC 1.25 3.00
217 Greg Maddux SC 1.25 3.00
218 Juan Gonzaloz SC .30 .75
219 Ken Griffey Jr. SC 1.50 4.00
220 Kerry Wood SC .30 .75
221 Mark McGwire SC 2.00 5.00
222 Mike Piazza SC 1.25 3.00
223 Rickey Henderson SC .75 2.00
224 Sammy Sosa SC .75 2.00
225 Travis Lee SC .30 .75
226 Gabe Alvarez PROS .75 2.00
227 Matt Anderson PROS .75 2.00
228 Adrian Beltre PROS .75 2.00
229 Orlando Cabrera PROS .75 2.00
230 Orlando Hernandez PROS .75 2.00
231 Aramis Ramirez PROS .75 2.00
232 Troy Glaus PROS 1.25 3.00
233 Gabe Kapler PROS .75 2.00
234 Jeremy Giambi PROS .75 2.00
235 Derrick Gibson PROS .75 2.00
236 Carlton Loewer PROS .75 2.00
237 Mike Frank PROS .75 2.00
238 Carlos Guillen PROS .75 2.00
239 Alex Gonzalez PROS .75 2.00
240 Enrique Wilson PROS .75 2.00
241 J.D. Drew PROS .75 2.00
242 Bruce Chen PROS .75 2.00
243 Ryan Minor PROS .75 2.00
244 Preston Wilson PROS .75 2.00
245 Josh Booty PROS .75 2.00
246 Luis Ordaz PROS .75 2.00
247 George Lombard PROS .75 2.00
248 Matt Clement PROS .75 2.00
249 Eric Chavez PROS .75 2.00
250 Corey Koskie PROS .75 2.00

1999 Ultra Gold Medallion

*GOLD: 1.25X TO 3X BASIC CARDS
1-215 ONE PER HOBBY PACK
*GOLD SC: 2X TO 5X BASIC SC
SEASON CROWN ODDS 1:80 HOBBY
*GOLD PROS: 1X TO 2.5X BASIC PROS
PROSPECT ODDS 1:40 HOBBY

1999 Ultra Platinum Medallion

*PLAT: 15X TO 40X BASIC CARDS
1-215 PRINT RUN 99 SERIAL #'d SETS
*PLAT SC: 12.5X TO 30X BASIC SC
SEASON CROWN PRINT RUN 50 #'d SETS
*PLAT PROS: 2.5X TO 6X BASIC PROS
PROSPECT PRINT RUN 65 SERIAL #'d SETS
RANDOM INSERTS IN HOBBY PACKS

1999 Ultra The Book On

COMPLETE SET (20) 20.00 50.00
SER.1 STATED ODDS 1:6
1 Kerry Wood .30 .75
2 Ken Griffey Jr. 1.50 4.00
3 Frank Thomas .75 2.00
4 Albert Belle .30 .75
5 Juan Gonzalez .30 .75
6 Jeff Bagwell .50 1.25
7 Mark McGwire 2.00 5.00
8 Barry Bonds 2.00 5.00
9 Andruw Jones .50 1.25
10 Mo Vaughn .30 .75
11 Scott Rolen .50 1.25
12 Travis Lee .30 .75
13 Tony Gwynn 1.00 2.50
14 Greg Maddux 1.25 3.00
15 Mike Piazza 1.25 3.00
16 Chipper Jones .75 2.00
17 Nomar Garciaparra 1.25 3.00
18 Cal Ripken 2.50 6.00
19 Derek Jeter 2.00 5.00
20 Alex Rodriguez 1.25 3.00

1999 Ultra Damage Inc.

COMPLETE SET (15) 20.00 50.00
SER.1 STATED ODDS 1:72
1 Alex Rodriguez 2.00 5.00
2 Greg Maddux 2.00 5.00
3 Cal Ripken 5.00 12.00
4 Chipper Jones 1.50 4.00
5 Derek Jeter 4.00 10.00
6 Frank Thomas 1.50 4.00
7 Juan Gonzalez .60 1.50
8 Ken Griffey Jr. 3.00 8.00
9 Kerry Wood .60 1.50
10 Mark McGwire 2.50 6.00
11 Mike Piazza 1.50 4.00
12 Nomar Garciaparra 1.00 2.50
13 Scott Rolen 1.00 2.50
14 Tony Gwynn 1.50 4.00
15 Travis Lee .60 1.50

1999 Ultra Diamond Producers

COMPLETE SET (10) 150.00 300.00
SER.1 STATED ODDS 1:288
1 Ken Griffey Jr. 10.00 25.00
2 Frank Thomas 5.00 12.00
3 Alex Rodriguez 8.00 20.00
4 Cal Ripken 15.00 40.00
5 Mike Piazza 8.00 20.00
6 Mark McGwire 12.50 30.00
7 Greg Maddux 8.00 20.00
8 Kerry Wood 2.00 5.00
9 Chipper Jones 5.00 12.00
10 Derek Jeter 12.50 30.00

1999 Ultra RBI Kings

COMPLETE SET (30) 12.50 30.00
ONE PER RETAIL PACK
1 Rafael Palmeiro .25 .60
2 Mo Vaughn .15 .40
3 Ivan Rodriguez .25 .60
4 Barry Bonds 1.00 2.50
5 Albert Belle .15 .40
6 Jeff Bagwell .25 .60
7 Mark McGwire 1.00 2.50
8 Darin Erstad .15 .40
9 Manny Ramirez .25 .60
10 Chipper Jones .40 1.00
11 Jim Thome .25 .60
12 Scott Rolen .25 .60
13 Tony Gwynn .50 1.25
14 Juan Gonzalez .15 .40
15 Mike Piazza .60 1.50
16 Sammy Sosa .40 1.00
17 Andruw Jones .25 .60
18 Derek Jeter 1.00 2.50
19 Nomar Garciaparra .60 1.50
20 Alex Rodriguez .60 1.50
21 Frank Thomas .40 1.00
22 Cal Ripken 1.25 3.00
23 Ken Griffey Jr. .75 2.00
24 Travis Lee .15 .40
25 Paul O'Neill .15 .40
26 Greg Vaughn .15 .40
27 Andres Galarraga .15 .40
28 Tino Martinez .25 .60
29 Jose Canseco .25 .60
30 Ben Grieve .15 .40

1999 Ultra Thunderclap

COMPLETE SET (15) 12.00 30.00
SER.1 STATED ODDS 1:36
1 Alex Rodriguez 1.50 4.00
2 Andruw Jones .50 1.25
3 Cal Ripken 4.00 10.00
4 Chipper Jones 1.25 3.00
5 Darin Erstad .50 1.25
6 Derek Jeter 3.00 8.00
7 Frank Thomas 1.25 3.00
8 Jeff Bagwell .75 2.00
9 Juan Gonzalez .50 1.25
10 Ken Griffey Jr. 2.50 6.00
11 Mark McGwire 2.00 5.00
12 Mike Piazza 1.25 3.00
13 Travis Lee .50 1.25
14 Nomar Garciaparra .75 2.00
15 Scott Rolen .75 2.00

1999 Ultra World Premiere

COMPLETE SET (15) 8.00 20.00
SER.1 STATED ODDS 1:18
1 Gabe Alvarez .50 1.25
2 Kerry Wood .75 2.00
3 Orlando Hernandez .50 1.25
4 Mike Caruso .75 2.00
5 Matt Anderson .50 1.25

6 Randall Simón .75 2.00
7 Adrian Beltre .50 1.25
8 Scott Elarton .75 2.00
9 Karim Garcia .75 2.00
10 Mike Frank .50 1.25
11 Richard Hidalgo .75 2.00
12 Paul Konerko .75 2.00
13 Travis Lee .75 2.00
14 J.D. Drew .75 2.00
15 Miguel Tejada .75 2.00

2000 Ultra

COMPLETE SET (300) 40.00 100.00
COMP.SET w/o SP's (250) 10.00 25.00
COMMON CARD (1-250) .12 .30
COMMON PROSPECT (251-300) 1.50 4.00
PROSPECT STATED ODDS 1:4
CLUB 3000 CARDS LISTED UNDER FLEER
1 Alex Rodriguez .40 1.00
2 Shawn Green .12 .30
3 Magglio Ordonez .20 .50
4 Tony Gwynn .30 .75
5 Joe McEwing .12 .30
6 Jose Rosado .12 .30
7 Sammy Sosa .30 .75
8 Gary Sheffield .12 .30
9 Mickey Morandini .12 .30
10 Mo Vaughn .12 .30
11 Todd Hollandsworth .12 .30
12 Tom Gordon .12 .30
13 Charles Johnson .12 .30
14 Derek Bell .12 .30
15 Kevin Young .12 .30
16 Jay Buhner .12 .30
17 J.T. Snow .12 .30
18 Jay Bell .12 .30
19 John Rocker .12 .30
20 Ivan Rodriguez .20 .50
21 Pokey Reese .12 .30
22 Paul O'Neill .20 .50
23 Ronnie Belliard .12 .30
24 Ryan Rupe .12 .30
25 Travis Fryman .12 .30
26 Trot Nixon .12 .30
27 Wally Joyner .12 .30
28 Andy Pettitte .20 .50
29 Dan Wilson .12 .30
30 Orlando Hernandez .12 .30
31 Dmitri Young .12 .30
32 Edgar Renteria .12 .30
33 Eric Karros .12 .30
34 Fernando Seguignol .12 .30
35 Jason Kendall .12 .30
36 Jeff Shaw .12 .30
37 Matt Lawton .12 .30
38 Robin Ventura .12 .30
39 Scott Williamson .12 .30
40 Ben Grieve .12 .30
41 Billy Wagner .12 .30
42 Javy Lopez .12 .30
43 Joe Randa .12 .30
44 Neifi Perez .12 .30
45 David Justice .12 .30
46 Ray Durham .12 .30
47 Dustin Hermanson .12 .30
48 Andres Galarraga .20 .50
49 Brad Fullmer .12 .30
50 Nomar Garciaparra .20 .50
51 David Cone .12 .30
52 David Nilsson .12 .30
53 David Wells .12 .30
54 Miguel Tejada .20 .50
55 Ismael Valdes .12 .30
56 Jose Lima .12 .30
57 Juan Encarnacion .12 .30
58 Fred McGriff .20 .50
59 Kenny Rogers .12 .30
60 Vladimir Guerrero .20 .50
61 Benito Santiago .12 .30
62 Chris Singleton .12 .30
63 Carlos Lee .12 .30
64 Sean Casey .12 .30
65 Tom Goodwin .12 .30
66 Todd Hundley .12 .30
67 Ellis Burks .12 .30
68 Tim Hudson .20 .50
69 Matt Stairs .12 .30
70 Chipper Jones .30 .75
71 Craig Biggio .20 .50
72 Brian Rose .12 .30
73 Carlos Delgado .12 .30
74 Eddie Taubensee .12 .30
75 John Smoltz .30 .75
76 Ken Caminiti .12 .30
77 Rafael Palmeiro .20 .50
78 Sidney Ponson .12 .30
79 Todd Helton .20 .50
80 Juan Gonzalez .12 .30
81 Bruce Aven .12 .30
82 Desi Relaford .12 .30
83 Johnny Damon .20 .50
84 Albert Belle .12 .30
85 Mark McGwire .50 1.25
86 Rico Brogna .12 .30
87 Tom Glavine .20 .50
88 Harold Baines .20 .50
89 Chad Allen .12 .30
90 Barry Bonds .50 1.25
91 Mark Grace .20 .50
92 Paul Byrd .12 .30
93 Roberto Alomar .20 .50
94 Roberto Hernandez .12 .30
95 Steve Finley .12 .30
96 Bret Boone .12 .30
97 Charles Nagy .12 .30
98 Eric Chavez .12 .30
99 Jamie Moyer .12 .30
100 Ken Griffey Jr. .60 1.50
101 J.D. Drew .12 .30
102 Todd Stottlemyre .12 .30
103 Tony Fernandez .12 .30
104 Jeromy Burnitz .12 .30
105 Jeremy Giambi .12 .30
106 Livan Hernandez .12 .30
107 Marlon Anderson .12 .30
108 Troy Glaus .12 .30
109 Troy O'Leary .12 .30
110 Scott Rolen .20 .50
111 Bernard Gilkey .12 .30
112 Brady Anderson .12 .30
113 Chuck Knoblauch .12 .30
114 Jeff Weaver .12 .30
115 B.J. Surhoff .12 .30
116 Alex Gonzalez .12 .30
117 Vinny Castilla .12 .30
118 Tim Salmon .12 .30
119 Brian Jordan .12 .30
120 Corey Koskie .12 .30
121 Dean Palmer .12 .30
122 Gabe Kapler .12 .30
123 Jim Edmonds .12 .30
124 John Jaha .12 .30
125 Mark Grudzielanek .12 .30
126 Mike Bordick .12 .30
127 Mike Lieberthal .12 .30
128 Pete Harnisch .12 .30
129 Russ Ortiz .12 .30
130 Kevin Brown .12 .30
131 Troy Percival .12 .30
132 Alex Gonzalez .12 .30
133 Bartolo Colon .12 .30
134 John Valentin .12 .30
135 Jose Hernandez .12 .30
136 Marquis Grissom .12 .30
137 Wade Boggs .20 .50
138 Dante Bichette .12 .30
139 Bobby Higginson .12 .30
140 Frank Thomas .30 .75
141 Geoff Jenkins .12 .30
142 Jason Giambi .12 .30
143 Jeff Cirillo .12 .30
144 Sandy Alomar Jr. .12 .30
145 Luis Gonzalez .12 .30
146 Preston Wilson .12 .30
147 Carlos Beltran .20 .50
148 Greg Vaughn .12 .30
149 Carlos Febles .12 .30
150 Jose Canseco .20 .50
151 Kris Benson .12 .30
152 Chuck Finley .12 .30
153 Michael Barrett .12 .30
154 Rey Ordonez .12 .30
155 Adrian Beltre .30 .75
156 Andruw Jones .12 .30
157 Barry Larkin .20 .50
158 Brian Giles .12 .30
159 Carl Everett .12 .30
160 Manny Ramirez .30 .75
161 Darryl Kile .12 .30
162 Edgar Martinez .20 .50
163 Jeff Kent .12 .30
164 Matt Williams .12 .30
165 Mike Piazza .30 .75
166 Pedro Martinez .20 .50
167 Ray Lankford .12 .30
168 Roger Cedeno .12 .30
169 Ron Coomer .12 .30
170 Cal Ripken 1.00 2.50
171 Jose Offerman .12 .30
172 Kenny Lofton .12 .30
173 Kent Bottenfield .12 .30
174 Kevin Millwood .12 .30
175 Omar Daal .12 .30
176 Orlando Cabrera .12 .30
177 Pat Hentgen .12 .30
178 Tino Martinez .12 .30
179 Tony Clark .12 .30
180 Roger Clemens .40 1.00
181 Brad Radke .12 .30
182 Darin Erstad .12 .30
183 Jose Jimenez .12 .30
184 Jim Thome .20 .50
185 John Wetteland .12 .30
186 Justin Thompson .12 .30
187 John Halama .12 .30
188 Lee Stevens .12 .30
189 Miguel Cairo .12 .30
190 Mike Mussina .20 .50
191 Raul Mondesi .12 .30
192 Armando Rios .12 .30
193 Trevor Hoffman .20 .50
194 Tony Batista .12 .30
195 Will Clark .20 .50
196 Brad Ausmus .12 .30
197 Chili Davis .12 .30
198 Cliff Floyd .12 .30
199 Curt Schilling .20 .50
200 Derek Jeter .75 2.00
201 Henry Rodriguez .12 .30
202 Jose Cruz Jr. .12 .30
203 Omar Vizquel .20 .50
204 Randy Johnson .30 .75
205 Reggie Sanders .12 .30
206 Al Leiter .12 .30
207 Damion Easley .12 .30
208 David Bell .12 .30
209 Fernando Tatis .12 .30
210 Kerry Wood .12 .30
211 Kevin Appier .12 .30
212 Mariano Rivera .40 1.00
213 Mike Caruso .12 .30
214 Moises Alou .12 .30
215 Randy Winn .12 .30
216 Roy Halladay .20 .50
217 Shannon Stewart .12 .30
218 Todd Walker .12 .30
219 Jim Parque .12 .30
220 Travis Lee .12 .30
221 Andy Ashby .12 .30
222 Ed Sprague .12 .30
223 Larry Walker .20 .50
224 Rick Helling .12 .30
225 Rusty Greer .12 .30
226 Todd Zeile .12 .30
227 Freddy Garcia .12 .30
228 Hideo Nomo .30 .75
229 Marty Cordova .12 .30
230 Greg Maddux .40 1.00
231 Rondell White .12 .30
232 Paul Konerko .12 .30
233 Warren Morris .12 .30
234 Bernie Williams .20 .50
235 Bob Abreu .12 .30
236 John Olerud .12 .30
237 Doug Glanville .12 .30
238 Eric Young .12 .30
239 Robb Nen .12 .30
240 Jeff Bagwell .20 .50
241 Sterling Hitchcock .12 .30
242 Todd Greene .12 .30
243 Bill Mueller .12 .30
244 Rickey Henderson .30 .75
245 Chan Ho Park .20 .50
246 Jason Schmidt .12 .30
247 Jeff Zimmerman .12 .30
248 Jermaine Dye .12 .30
249 Randall Simon .12 .30
250 Richie Sexson .12 .30
251 Micah Bowie PROS .75 2.00
252 Joe Nathan PROS .75 2.00
253 Chris Woodward PROS .75 2.00
254 Lance Berkman PROS 1.25 3.00
255 Ruben Mateo PROS .75 2.00
256 Russell Branyan PROS .75 2.00
257 Randy Wolf PROS .75 2.00
258 A.J. Burnett PROS .75 2.00
259 Mark Quinn PROS .75 2.00
260 Buddy Carlyle PROS .75 2.00
261 Ben Davis PROS .75 2.00
262 Yamid Haad PROS .75 2.00
263 Mike Colangelo PROS .75 2.00
264 Rick Ankiel PROS 1.25 3.00
265 Jacque Jones PROS .75 2.00
266 Kelly Dransfeldt PROS .75 2.00
267 Matt Riley PROS .75 2.00
268 Adam Kennedy PROS .75 2.00
269 Octavio Dotel PROS .75 2.00
270 Francisco Cordero PROS .75 2.00
271 Wilton Veras PROS .75 2.00
272 Calvin Pickering PROS .75 2.00
273 Alex Sanchez PROS .75 2.00
274 Tony Armas Jr. PROS .75 2.00
275 Pat Burrell PROS .75 2.00
276 Chad Meyers PROS .75 2.00
277 Ben Petrick PROS .75 2.00
278 Ramon Hernandez PROS .75 2.00
279 Ed Yarnall PROS .75 2.00
280 Erubiel Durazo PROS .75 2.00
281 Vernon Wells PROS .75 2.00
282 Gary Matthews Jr. PROS .75 2.00
283 Kip Wells PROS .75 2.00
284 Peter Bergeron PROS .75 2.00
285 Travis Dawkins PROS .75 2.00
286 Jorge Toca PROS .75 2.00
287 Cole Liniak PROS .75 2.00
288 Chad Hermansen PROS .75 2.00
289 Eric Gagne PROS .75 2.00
290 Chad Hutchinson PROS .75 2.00
291 Eric Munson PROS .75 2.00
292 Wiki Gonzalez PROS .75 2.00
293 Alfonso Soriano PROS 2.00 5.00
294 Trent Durrington PROS .75 2.00
295 Ben Molina PROS .75 2.00
296 Aaron Myette PROS .75 2.00
297 Wily Pena PROS .75 2.00
298 Kevin Barker PROS .75 2.00
299 Geoff Blum PROS .75 2.00
300 Josh Beckett PROS 1.50 4.00
P1 ARod Promo .50 1.25
P2 ARod Promo 3-D 1.50 4.00

2000 Ultra Gold Medallion

*GOLD 1-250: 1.25X TO 3X BASIC CARDS
1-250 ONE PER HOBBY PACK
*GOLD PROS: .75X TO 2X BASIC CARDS
GOLD PROSPECT ODDS 1:24 HOBBY

2000 Ultra Platinum Medallion

*PLAT 1-250: 15X TO 40X BASIC CARDS
1-250 PRINT RUN 50 SERIAL #'d SETS
*PROSPECTS: 4X TO 10X BASIC CARDS
PLAT PROS PRINT RUN 25 SERIAL #'d SETS
251-300 NO PRICING DUE TO SCARCITY
RANDOM INSERTS IN HOBBY PACKS

2000 Ultra Crunch Time

COMPLETE SET (15) 20.00 50.00
STATED ODDS 1:72
1 Nomar Garciaparra 1.00 2.50
2 Ken Griffey Jr. 3.00 8.00
3 Mark McGwire 2.50 6.00
4 Alex Rodriguez 2.00 5.00
5 Derek Jeter 4.00 10.00
6 Sammy Sosa 1.50 4.00
7 Mike Piazza 1.50 4.00
8 Cal Ripken 5.00 12.00
9 Frank Thomas 1.50 4.00
10 Juan Gonzalez .60 1.50
11 J.D. Drew .60 1.50
12 Greg Maddux 2.00 5.00
13 Tony Gwynn 1.50 4.00
14 Vladimir Guerrero 1.00 2.50
15 Ben Grieve .60 1.50

2000 Ultra Diamond Mine

COMPLETE SET (15) 12.50 30.00
STATED ODDS 1:6
1 Greg Maddux 1.25 3.00
2 Mark McGwire 1.50 4.00
3 Ken Griffey Jr. 2.00 5.00
4 Cal Ripken 3.00 8.00
5 Nomar Garciaparra .60 1.50
6 Mike Piazza 1.00 2.50
7 Alex Rodriguez 1.25 3.00
8 Frank Thomas 1.00 2.50
9 Juan Gonzalez .40 1.00
10 Derek Jeter 2.50 6.00
11 Tony Gwynn 1.00 2.50
12 Chipper Jones 1.00 2.50
13 Sammy Sosa 1.00 2.50
14 Roger Clemens 1.25 3.00
15 Vladimir Guerrero .60 1.50

2000 Ultra Feel the Game

STATED ODDS 1:168
1 Alex Rodriguez Jsy 4.00 10.00
2 Chipper Jones Jsy 3.00 8.00
3 Rob Alomar Btg Glv SP 20.00 50.00
4 Greg Maddux Jsy 4.00 10.00
5 Pedro Martinez Jsy 2.00 5.00
6 Cal Ripken Jsy 10.00 25.00
7 Robin Ventura Jsy 1.25 3.00
8 J.D. Drew Jsy 1.25 3.00
9 Randy Johnson Jsy 3.00 8.00
10 Scott Rolen Jsy 2.00 5.00
11 Kevin Millwood Jsy 1.25 3.00
12 Frank Thomas Btg Glv SP 40.00 80.00
13 Tony Gwynn Btg Glv SP 20.00 50.00
14 Curt Schilling Jsy 2.00 5.00
15 Edgar Martinez Btg Glv 2.00 5.00

2000 Ultra Fresh Ink

RANDOM INSERTS IN PACKS
PRINT RUNS B/WN 95-1000 COPIES PER
1 Bob Abreu/200 10.00 25.00
2 Chad Allen/975 3.00 8.00
3 Marlon Anderson/975 3.00 8.00
4 Rick Ankiel/500 10.00 25.00
5 Glen Barker/975 3.00 8.00
6 Michael Barrett/975 3.00 8.00
7 Carlos Beltran/975 5.00 12.00
8 Adrian Beltre/900 8.00 20.00
9 Peter Bergeron/1000 3.00 8.00
10 Wade Boggs/250 8.00 20.00
11 Barry Bonds/250 40.00 80.00
12 Pat Burrell/600 3.00 8.00
13 Roger Cedeno/500 3.00 8.00
14 Eric Chavez/800 3.00 8.00
15 Bruce Chen/600 3.00 8.00
16 Johnny Damon/750 5.00 12.00
17 Ben Davis/1000 3.00 8.00
18 Carlos Delgado/275 10.00 25.00
19 Einar Diaz/975 3.00 8.00
20 Octavio Dotel/950 3.00 8.00
21 J.D. Drew/600 3.00 8.00
22 Scott Elarton/1000 3.00 8.00
23 Freddy Garcia/500 3.00 8.00
24 Jeremy Giambi/975 3.00 8.00
25 Troy Glaus/500 10.00 25.00
26 Shawn Green/350 6.00 15.00
27 Tony Gwynn/250 40.00 100.00
28 Richard Hidalgo/500 3.00 8.00
29 Bobby Higginson/975 3.00 8.00
30 Tim Hudson/975 5.00 12.00
31 Norm Hutchins/1000 3.00 8.00
32 Derek Jeter/95 200.00 400.00
33 Randy Johnson/240 40.00 80.00
34 Gabe Kapler/725 3.00 8.00
35 Jason Kendall/375 10.00 25.00
36 Paul Konerko/500 10.00 25.00
37 Matt Lawton/1000 3.00 8.00
38 Carlos Lee/900 3.00 8.00
39 Jose Macias/1000 3.00 8.00
40 Greg Maddux/225 60.00 120.00
41 Kevin Millwood/500 3.00 8.00
42 Warren Morris/1000 3.00 8.00
43 Eric Munson/900 3.00 8.00
44 Heath Murray/925 3.00 8.00
45 Joe Nathan/1000 3.00 8.00
46 Magglio Ordonez/335 6.00 15.00
47 Angel Pena/1000 3.00 8.00
48 Cal Ripken/350 40.00 80.00
49 Alex Rodriguez/350 30.00 80.00
50 Scott Rolen/250 15.00 40.00
51 Ryan Rupe/1000 3.00 8.00
52 Curt Schilling/375 10.00 25.00
53 Randall Simon/1000 3.00 8.00
54 Alfonso Soriano/975 8.00 20.00
55 Shannon Stewart/275 10.00 25.00
56 Miguel Tejada/1000 5.00 12.00
57 Frank Thomas/150 50.00 100.00
58 Jeff Weaver/1000 3.00 8.00
59 Randy Wolf/1000 3.00 8.00
60 Ed Yarnall/1000 3.00 8.00
61 Kevin Young/1000 3.00 8.00
62 Boggs/Gwynn/Ryan/100 250.00 450.00

2000 Ultra Fresh Ink Gold

NO PRICING DUE TO SCARCITY

2000 Ultra Swing Kings

COMPLETE SET (10) 10.00 25.00
STATED ODDS 1:24
1 Cal Ripken 3.00 8.00
2 Nomar Garciaparra .60 1.50
3 Frank Thomas 1.00 2.50
4 Tony Gwynn 1.00 2.50
5 Ken Griffey Jr. 2.00 5.00
6 Chipper Jones 1.00 2.50
7 Mark McGwire 1.50 4.00
8 Sammy Sosa 1.00 2.50
9 Derek Jeter 2.50 6.00
10 Alex Rodriguez 1.25 3.00

2000 Ultra Talented

STATED PRINT RUN 99 SERIAL #'d SETS
1 Sammy Sosa 20.00 50.00
2 Derek Jeter 50.00 125.00
3 Alex Rodriguez 25.00 60.00
4 Mike Piazza 20.00 50.00
5 Ken Griffey Jr. 40.00 100.00
6 Nomar Garciaparra 12.00 30.00
7 Mark McGwire 30.00 80.00
8 Cal Ripken 60.00 150.00
9 Frank Thomas 20.00 50.00
10 J.D. Drew 8.00 20.00

2000 Ultra World Premiere

COMPLETE SET (10) 3.00 8.00
STATED ODDS 1:12
1 Ruben Mateo .40 1.00
2 Lance Berkman .60 1.50
3 Octavio Dotel .40 1.00
4 Ben Davis .40 1.00
5 Warren Morris .40 1.00
6 Carlos Beltran .60 1.50
7 Rick Ankiel .60 1.50
8 Adam Kennedy .40 1.00
9 Tim Hudson .60 1.50
10 Jorge Toca .40 1.00

2001 Ultra

COMPLETE SET (275) 40.00 80.00
COMP.SET w/o SP's (250) 10.00 25.00
COMMON CARD (1-250) .10 .30
COMMON CARD (251-275) 1.25 3.00
251-275 STATED ODDS 1:4
COMMON CARD (276-280) 2.00 5.00
276-280 DIST.IN FLEER PLAT.RC HOB/RET
276-280 PRINT RUN 1499 SERIAL #'d SETS
1 Pedro Martinez .20 .50
2 Derek Jeter .75 2.00
3 Cal Ripken 1.00 2.50
4 Alex Rodriguez .40 1.00
5 Vladimir Guerrero .30 .75
6 Troy Glaus .10 .30
7 Sammy Sosa .30 .75
8 Mike Piazza .50 1.25
9 Tony Gwynn .40 1.00
10 Tim Hudson .10 .30
11 John Flaherty .10 .30
12 Jeff Cirillo .10 .30
13 Ellis Burks .10 .30
14 Carlos Lee .10 .30
15 Carlos Beltran .10 .30
16 Ruben Rivera .10 .30
17 Richard Hidalgo .10 .30
18 Omar Vizquel .20 .50
19 Michael Barrett .10 .30
20 Jose Canseco .20 .50
21 Jason Giambi .10 .30
22 Greg Maddux .50 1.25
23 Charles Johnson .10 .30
24 Sandy Alomar Jr. .10 .30
25 Rick Ankiel .10 .30
26 Richie Sexson .10 .30
27 Matt Williams .10 .30
28 Joe Girardi .10 .30
29 Jason Kendall .10 .30
30 Brad Fullmer .10 .30
31 Alex Gonzalez .10 .30
32 Rick Helling .10 .30
33 Mike Mussina .20 .50
34 Joe Randa .10 .30
35 J.T. Snow .10 .30
36 Edgardo Alfonzo .10 .30
37 Dante Bichette .10 .30
38 Brad Ausmus .10 .30
39 Bobby Abreu .10 .30
40 Warren Morris .10 .30
41 Tony Womack .10 .30
42 Russell Branyan .10 .30
43 Mike Lowell .10 .30
44 Mark Grace .20 .50
45 Jeromy Burnitz .10 .30
46 J.D. Drew .10 .30
47 David Justice .10 .30
48 Alex Gonzalez .10 .30
49 Tino Martinez .20 .50
50 Raul Mondesi .10 .30
51 Rafael Furcal .10 .30
52 Marquis Grissom .10 .30
53 Kevin Young .10 .30
54 Jon Lieber .10 .30
55 Henry Rodriguez .10 .30
56 Dave Burba .10 .30
57 Shannon Stewart .10 .30
58 Preston Wilson .10 .30
59 Paul O'Neill .20 .50
60 Jimmy Haynes .10 .30
61 Darryl Kile .10 .30
62 Bret Boone .10 .30
63 Bartolo Colon .10 .30
64 Andres Galarraga .10 .30
65 Trot Nixon .10 .30
66 Steve Finley .10 .30
67 Shawn Green .10 .30
68 Robert Person .10 .30
69 Kenny Rogers .10 .30
70 Bobby Higginson .10 .30
71 Barry Larkin .20 .50
72 Al Martin .10 .30
73 Tom Glavine .20 .50
74 Rondell White .10 .30
75 Ray Lankford .10 .30
76 Moises Alou .10 .30
77 Matt Clement .10 .30
78 Geoff Jenkins .10 .30
79 David Wells .10 .30
80 Chuck Finley .10 .30
81 Andy Pettitte .20 .50
82 Travis Fryman .10 .30
83 Ron Coomer .10 .30
84 Mark McGwire .75 2.00
85 Kerry Wood .10 .30
86 Jorge Posada .20 .50
87 Jeff Bagwell .20 .50
88 Andruw Jones .20 .50
89 Ryan Klesko .10 .30
90 Mariano Rivera .30 .75
91 Lance Berkman .10 .30
92 Kenny Lofton .10 .30
93 Jacque Jones .10 .30
94 Eric Young .10 .30
95 Edgar Renteria .10 .30
96 Chipper Jones .30 .75
97 Todd Helton .20 .50
98 Shawn Estes .10 .30
99 Mark Mulder .10 .30
100 Lee Stevens .10 .30
101 Jermaine Dye .10 .30
102 Greg Vaughn .10 .30
103 Chris Singleton .10 .30
104 Brady Anderson .10 .30
105 Terrence Long .10 .30
106 Quilvio Veras .10 .30
107 Magglio Ordonez .10 .30
108 Johnny Damon .20 .50
109 Jeffrey Hammonds .10 .30
110 Fred McGriff .20 .50
111 Carl Pavano .10 .30
112 Bobby Estalella .10 .30
113 Todd Hundley .10 .30
114 Scott Rolen .20 .50
115 Robin Ventura .10 .30
116 Pokey Reese .10 .30
117 Luis Gonzalez .10 .30
118 Jose Offerman .10 .30
119 Edgar Martinez .20 .50
120 Dean Palmer .10 .30
121 David Segui .10 .30
122 Troy O'Leary .10 .30
123 Tony Batista .10 .30
124 Todd Zeile .10 .30
125 Randy Johnson .30 .75
126 Luis Castillo .10 .30
127 Kris Benson .10 .30
128 John Olerud .10 .30
129 Eric Karros .10 .30
130 Eddie Taubensee .10 .30
131 Neifi Perez .10 .30
132 Matt Stairs .10 .30
133 Luis Alicea .10 .30
134 Jeff Kent .10 .30
135 Javier Vazquez .10 .30
136 Garret Anderson .10 .30
137 Frank Thomas .30 .75
138 Carlos Febles .10 .30
139 Albert Belle .10 .30
140 Tony Clark .10 .30
141 Pat Burrell .10 .30
142 Mike Sweeney .10 .30
143 Jay Buhner .10 .30
144 Gabe Kapler .10 .30
145 Derek Bell .10 .30
146 B.J. Surhoff .10 .30
147 Adam Kennedy .10 .30
148 Aaron Boone .10 .30
149 Todd Stottlemyre .10 .30
150 Roberto Alomar .20 .50
151 Orlando Hernandez .10 .30
152 Jason Varitek .30 .75
153 Gary Sheffield .10 .30
154 Cliff Floyd .10 .30
155 Chad Hermansen .10 .30
156 Carlos Delgado .10 .30
157 Aaron Sele .10 .30
158 Sean Casey .10 .30
159 Ruben Mateo .10 .30
160 Mike Bordick .10 .30
161 Mike Cameron .10 .30
162 Doug Glanville .10 .30
163 Damion Easley .10 .30
164 Carl Everett .10 .30
165 Bengie Molina .10 .30
166 Adrian Beltre .10 .30
167 Tom Goodwin .10 .30
168 Rickey Henderson .30 .75
169 Mo Vaughn .10 .30
170 Mike Lieberthal .10 .30
171 Ken Griffey Jr. .60 1.50
172 Juan Gonzalez .10 .30
173 Ivan Rodriguez .20 .50
174 Al Leiter .10 .30
175 Vinny Castilla .10 .30
176 Peter Bergeron .10 .30
177 Pedro Astacio .10 .30
178 Paul Konerko .10 .30
179 Mitch Meluskey .10 .30
180 Kevin Millwood .10 .30
181 Ben Grieve .10 .30
182 Barry Bonds .75 2.00
183 Rusty Greer .10 .30
184 Miguel Tejada .10 .30
185 Mark Quinn .10 .30
186 Larry Walker .10 .30
187 Jose Valentin .10 .30
188 Jose Vidro .10 .30
189 Delino DeShields .10 .30
190 Darin Erstad .10 .30
191 Bill Mueller .10 .30
192 Ray Durham .10 .30
193 Ken Caminiti .10 .30
194 Jim Thome .20 .50
195 Javy Lopez .10 .30
196 Fernando Vina .10 .30
197 Eric Chavez .10 .30
198 Eric Owens .10 .30
199 Brad Radke .10 .30
200 Travis Lee .10 .30
201 Tim Salmon .20 .50
202 Rafael Palmeiro .20 .50
203 Nomar Garciaparra .50 1.25
204 Mike Hampton .10 .30
205 Kevin Brown .10 .30
206 Juan Encarnacion .10 .30
207 Danny Graves .10 .30
208 Carlos Guillen .10 .30
209 Phil Nevin .10 .30
210 Matt Lawton .10 .30
211 Manny Ramirez .20 .50
212 James Baldwin .10 .30
213 Fernando Tatis .10 .30
214 Craig Biggio .20 .50
215 Brian Jordan .10 .30
216 Bernie Williams .20 .50
217 Ryan Dempster .10 .30
218 Roger Clemens .60 1.50
219 Jose Cruz Jr. .10 .30
220 John Valentin .10 .30
221 Dmitri Young .10 .30
222 Curt Schilling .10 .30
223 Jim Edmonds .10 .30
224 Chan Ho Park .10 .30
225 Brian Giles .10 .30
226 J.Anderson .10 .30
T.Redman
227 A.Piatt .10 .30
J.Ortiz
228 K.Kelly .10 .30
A.Huff
229 R.Choate .10 .30
C.Dingman
230 E.Cammack .10 .30
G.Roberts
231 Y.Lara .10 .30
A.Tracy
232 W.Franklin .10 .30
S.Linebrink
233 C.Cairncross .10 .30
C.Perry
234 J.Romero .10 .30
M.LeCroy
235 G.Guzman .10 .30
J.Conti
236 M.Burkhart .10 .30
P.Crawford
237 P.Coco .10 .30
L.Estrella
238 J.Parrish .10 .30
F.Lunar
239 K.McDonald .10 .30
J.Brunette
240 C.Casimiro .10 .30
I.Coffie
241 D.Garibay .10 .30
R.Quevedo
242 S.Lee .10 .30
T.Ohka
243 H.Ortiz .10 .30
J.D'Amico
244 J.Sparks .10 .30
T.Harper
245 J.Boyd .10 .30
D.Coggin
246 M.Buehrle .20 .50
L.Barcelo
247 A.Melhuse .10 .30
B.Petrick
248 K.Davis .10 .30
P.Rigdon
249 M.Darr .10 .30
K.DeHaan
250 V.Padilla 1.25 3.00
M.Brownson
251 Barry Zito PROS 2.00 5.00
252 Tim Drew PROS 1.25 3.00
253 Luis Matos PROS 1.25 3.00
254 Alex Cabrera PROS 1.25 3.00
255 Jon Garland PROS 1.25 3.00
256 Milton Bradley PROS 1.25 3.00
257 Juan Pierre PROS 1.25 3.00
258 Ismael Villegas PROS 1.25 3.00
259 Eric Munson PROS 1.25 3.00
260 Tomas De la Rosa PROS 1.25 3.00
261 Chris Richard PROS 1.25 3.00
262 Jason Tyner PROS 1.25 3.00
263 B.J. Waszgis PROS 1.25 3.00
264 Jason Marquis PROS 1.25 3.00
265 Dusty Allen PROS 1.25 3.00
266 Corey Patterson PROS 1.25 3.00
267 Eric Byrnes PROS 1.25 3.00
268 Xavier Nady PROS 1.25 3.00
269 George Lombard PROS 1.25 3.00
270 Timo Perez PROS 1.25 3.00
271 Gary Matthews Jr. PROS 1.25 3.00
272 Chad Durbin PROS 1.25 3.00
273 Tony Armas Jr. PROS 1.25 3.00
274 Francisco Cordero PROS 1.25 3.00
275 Alfonso Soriano PROS 2.00 5.00
276 J.Spivey RC 3.00 8.00
J.Uribe RC
277 A.Pujols RC 20.00 50.00
B.Smith RC
278 I.Suzuki RC 15.00 40.00
T.Shinjo RC
279 D.Henson RC 3.00 8.00
J.Melian RC
280 M.White RC 2.00 5.00
A.Hernandez RC

2001 Ultra Gold Medallion

*STARS 1-225: 1.25X TO 3X BASIC CARDS
*PROSPECTS 226-250: 1.25X TO 3X BASIC
CARDS 1-250 ONE PER HOBBY PACK
*PROSPECTS 251-275: .75X TO 2X BASIC
PROSPECTS 251-275 ODDS 1:24

2001 Ultra Platinum Medallion

*PLATINUM 1-225: 15X TO 40X BASIC
CARDS 1-250 PRINT RUN 50 SERIAL #'d SETS
*PLATINUM 251-275: 3X TO 8X BASIC
251-275 PRINT RUN 25 SERIAL #'d SETS

2001 Ultra Decade of Dominance

COMPLETE SET (15) 12.50 30.00
STATED ODDS 1:8
PLATINUM PRINT RUN 10 SERIAL #'d SETS
PLATINUM NO PRICING DUE TO SCARCITY
1 Barry Bonds 1.50 4.00
2 Mark McGwire 1.50 4.00
3 Sammy Sosa .60 1.50
4 Ken Griffey Jr. 1.25 3.00
5 Cal Ripken 2.00 5.00
6 Tony Gwynn .75 2.00
7 Albert Belle .30 .75
8 Frank Thomas .60 1.50
9 Randy Johnson .60 1.50
10 Juan Gonzalez .30 .75
11 Greg Maddux 1.00 2.50
12 Craig Biggio .40 1.00
13 Edgar Martinez .40 1.00
14 Roger Clemens 1.25 3.00
15 Andres Galarraga .30 .75

2001 Ultra Fall Classics

STATED ODDS 1:20
1 Jackie Robinson 2.00 5.00
2 Enos Slaughter 1.25 3.00
3 Mariano Rivera 2.00 5.00
4 Hank Bauer 1.25 3.00
5 Cal Ripken 6.00 15.00
6 Babe Ruth 6.00 15.00
7 Thurman Munson 2.00 5.00
8 Tom Glavine 1.25 3.00
9 Fred Lynn 1.25 3.00
10 Johnny Bench 2.00 5.00
11 Tony Lazzeri 1.25 3.00
12 Al Kaline 2.00 5.00
13 Reggie Jackson 1.25 3.00
14 Derek Jeter 5.00 12.00
15 Willie Stargell 1.25 3.00
16 Roy Campanella 2.00 5.00
17 Phil Rizzuto 2.00 5.00
18 Roberto Clemente 6.00 15.00
19 Carlton Fisk 1.25 3.00
20 Duke Snider 1.25 3.00
21 Ted Williams 5.00 12.00
22 Bill Skowron 1.25 3.00
23 Bucky Dent 1.25 3.00
24 Mike Schmidt 4.00 10.00
25 Lou Brock 1.25 3.00
26 Whitey Ford 1.25 3.00
27 Brooks Robinson 1.25 3.00
28 Roberto Alomar 1.25 3.00
29 Yogi Berra 2.00 5.00
30 Joe Carter 1.25 3.00
31 Bill Mazeroski 1.25 3.00
32 Bob Gibson 1.25 3.00
33 Hank Greenberg 2.50 6.00
34 Andruw Jones 1.25 3.00
35 Bernie Williams 1.25 3.00
36 Don Larsen 1.25 3.00
37 Billy Martin 1.25 3.00

2001 Ultra Fall Classics Memorabilia

STATED ODDS 1:288
1 Hank Bauer Bat 6.00 15.00
2 Johnny Bench Jsy 10.00 25.00
3 Lou Brock Jsy 10.00 25.00
4 Roy Campanella Bat 20.00 50.00
5 Roberto Clemente Bat 50.00 100.00
6 Bucky Dent Bat 6.00 15.00
7 Carlton Fisk Jsy 10.00 25.00

8 Tom Glavine Jsy 10.00 25.00
9 Reggie Jackson Jsy 10.00 25.00
10 Derek Jeter Jsy 10.00 25.00
11 Al Kaline Jsy 10.00 25.00
12 Tony Lazzeri Bat 6.00 15.00
13 Fred Lynn Bat 6.00 15.00
14 Thurman Munson Bat 12.00 30.00
15 Cal Ripken Jsy 15.00 40.00
16 Mariano Rivera Jsy 10.00 25.00
17 Phil Rizzuto Bat 10.00 25.00
18 Brooks Robinson Bat 10.00 25.00
19 Jackie Robinson Pants 30.00 60.00
20 Babe Ruth Bat 125.00 200.00
21 Mike Schmidt Jsy 10.00 25.00
22 Bill Skowron Bat 6.00 15.00
23 Enos Slaughter Bat 6.00 15.00
24 Duke Snider Bat 10.00 25.00
25 Willie Stargell Bat 10.00 25.00
26 Ted Williams Bat 50.00 100.00

2001 Ultra Fall Classics Memorabilia Autograph

PRINT RUNS B/WN 2-44 COPIES PER
NO PRICING ON QTY OF 40 OR LESS
NNO CARDS LISTED IN ALPH.ORDER
3 Reggie Jackson Jsy AU/44 60.00 120.00

2001 Ultra Greatest Hits

COMPLETE SET (10) 10.00 25.00
STATED ODDS 1:12
PLATINUM PRINT RUN 10 SERIAL #'d SETS
PLATINUM NO PRICING DUE TO SCARCITY
1 Mark McGwire 1.50 4.00
2 Alex Rodriguez .75 2.00
3 Ken Griffey Jr. 1.25 3.00
4 Ivan Rodriguez .40 1.00
5 Cal Ripken 2.00 5.00
6 Todd Helton .40 1.00
7 Derek Jeter 1.50 4.00
8 Pedro Martinez .40 1.00
9 Tony Gwynn .75 2.00
10 Jim Edmonds .40 1.00

2001 Ultra Power Plus

COMPLETE SET (10) 15.00 40.00
STATED ODDS 1:24
PLATINUM PRINT RUN 10 SERIAL #'d SETS
PLATINUM NO PRICING DUE TO SCARCITY
1 Vladimir Guerrero 1.00 2.50
2 Mark McGwire 2.50 6.00
3 Mike Piazza 1.50 4.00
4 Derek Jeter 2.50 6.00
5 Chipper Jones 1.00 2.50
6 Carlos Delgado .60 1.50
7 Sammy Sosa 1.00 2.50
8 Ken Griffey Jr. 2.00 5.00
9 Nomar Garciaparra 1.50 4.00
10 Alex Rodriguez 1.25 3.00

2001 Ultra Tomorrow's Legends

COMPLETE SET (15) 6.00 15.00
STATED ODDS 1:4
PLATINUM PRINT RUN 10 SERIAL #'d SETS
PLATINUM NO PRICING DUE TO SCARCITY
1 Rick Ankiel .20 .50
2 J.D. Drew .20 .50
3 Carlos Delgado .20 .50
4 Todd Helton .30 .75
5 Andruw Jones .30 .75
6 Troy Glaus .20 .50
7 Jermaine Dye .20 .50
8 Vladimir Guerrero .50 1.25
9 Brian Giles .20 .50
10 Scott Rolen .30 .75
11 Darin Erstad .20 .50
12 Derek Jeter 1.25 3.00
13 Alex Rodriguez .60 1.50
14 Pat Burrell .20 .50
15 Nomar Garciaparra .75 2.00

2002 Ultra

COMPLETE SET (285) 80.00 200.00
COMP.SET w/o SP's (200) 10.00 25.00
COMMON CARD (1-200) .10 .30
COMMON CARD (201-220) .40 1.00
201-220 STATED ODDS 1:4
COMMON CARD (221-250) .40 1.00
221-250 STATED ODDS 1:4
COMMON CARD (251-285) 1.25 3.00
251-285 STATED ODDS 1:4 HOB, 1:10 RET
1 Jeff Bagwell .20 .50
2 Derek Jeter .75 2.00
3 Alex Rodriguez .40 1.00
4 Eric Chavez .10 .30
5 Tsuyoshi Shinjo .10 .30
6 Chris Stynes .10 .30
7 Ivan Rodriguez .20 .50
8 Cal Ripken 1.00 2.50
9 Freddy Garcia .10 .30
10 Chipper Jones .30 .75
11 Hideo Nomo .30 .75
12 Rafael Furcal .10 .30
13 Preston Wilson .10 .30
14 Jimmy Rollins .10 .30
15 Cristian Guzman .10 .30
16 Garret Anderson .10 .30
17 Todd Helton .20 .50
18 Moises Alou .10 .30
19 Tony Gwynn .40 1.00
20 Jorge Posada .20 .50
21 Sean Casey .10 .30
22 Kazuhiro Sasaki .10 .30
23 Ray Lankford .10 .30
24 Manny Ramirez .20 .50
25 Barry Bonds .75 2.00
26 Fred McGriff .20 .50
27 Vladimir Guerrero .30 .75
28 Jermaine Dye .10 .30
29 Adrian Beltre .10 .30
30 Ken Griffey Jr. .60 1.50
31 Ramon Hernandez .10 .30
32 Kerry Wood .10 .30
33 Greg Maddux .50 1.25
34 Rondell White .10 .30
35 Mike Mussina .20 .50
36 Jim Edmonds .20 .50
37 Scott Rolen .20 .50
38 Mike Lowell .10 .30
39 Al Leiter .10 .30
40 Tony Clark .10 .30
41 Joe Mays .10 .30
42 Mo Vaughn .10 .30
43 Geoff Jenkins .10 .30
44 Curt Schilling .10 .30
45 Pedro Martinez .20 .50
46 Andy Pettitte .20 .50
47 Tim Salmon .20 .50
48 Carl Everett .10 .30
49 Lance Berkman .10 .30
50 Troy Glaus .10 .30
51 Ichiro Suzuki .60 1.50
52 Alfonso Soriano .10 .30
53 Tomo Ohka .10 .30
54 Dean Palmer .10 .30
55 Kevin Brown .10 .30
56 Albert Pujols .60 1.50
57 Homer Bush .10 .30
58 Tim Hudson .10 .30
59 Frank Thomas .30 .75
60 Joe Randa .10 .30
61 Chan Ho Park .10 .30
62 Bobby Higginson .10 .30
63 Bartolo Colon .10 .30
64 Aramis Ramirez .10 .30
65 Jeff Cirillo .10 .30
66 Roberto Alomar .20 .50
67 Mark Kotsay .10 .30
68 Mike Cameron .10 .30
69 Mike Hampton .10 .30
70 Trot Nixon .10 .30
71 Juan Gonzalez .10 .30
72 Damian Rolls .10 .30
73 Brad Fullmer .10 .30
74 David Ortiz .30 .75
75 Brandon Inge .10 .30
76 Orlando Hernandez .10 .30
77 Matt Stairs .10 .30
78 Jay Gibbons .10 .30
79 Greg Vaughn .10 .30
80 Brady Anderson .10 .30
81 Jim Thome .20 .50
82 Ben Sheets .10 .30
83 Rafael Palmeiro .20 .50
84 Edgar Renteria .10 .30
85 Doug Mientkiewicz .10 .30
86 Raul Mondesi .10 .30
87 Shane Reynolds .10 .30
88 Steve Finley .10 .30
89 Jose Cruz Jr. .10 .30
90 Edgardo Alfonzo .10 .30
91 Jose Valentin .10 .30
92 Mark McGwire .75 2.00
93 Mark Grace .20 .50
94 Mike Lieberthal .10 .30
95 Barry Larkin .20 .50
96 Chuck Knoblauch .10 .30
97 Deivi Cruz .10 .30
98 Jeromy Burnitz .10 .30
99 Shannon Stewart .10 .30
100 David Wells .10 .30
101 Brook Fordyce .10 .30
102 Rusty Greer .10 .30
103 Andruw Jones .20 .50
104 Jason Kendall .10 .30
105 Nomar Garciaparra .50 1.25
106 Shawn Green .10 .30
107 Craig Biggio .20 .50
108 Masato Yoshii .10 .30
109 Ben Petrick .10 .30
110 Gary Sheffield .10 .30
111 Travis Lee .10 .30
112 Matt Williams .10 .30
113 Billy Wagner .10 .30
114 Robin Ventura .10 .30
115 Jerry Hairston .10 .30
116 Paul LoDuca .10 .30
117 Darin Erstad .10 .30
118 Ruben Sierra .10 .30
119 Ricky Gutierrez .10 .30
120 Bret Boone .10 .30
121 John Rocker .10 .30
122 Roger Clemens .60 1.50
123 Eric Karros .10 .30
124 J.D. Drew .10 .30
125 Carlos Delgado .10 .30
126 Jeffrey Hammonds .10 .30
127 Jeff Kent .10 .30
128 David Justice .10 .30
129 Cliff Floyd .10 .30
130 Omar Vizquel .20 .50
131 Matt Morris .10 .30
132 Rich Aurilia .10 .30
133 Larry Walker .10 .30
134 Miguel Tejada .10 .30
135 Eric Young .10 .30
136 Aaron Sele .10 .30
137 Eric Milton .10 .30
138 Travis Fryman .10 .30
139 Magglio Ordonez .10 .30
140 Sammy Sosa .30 .75
141 Pokey Reese .10 .30
142 Adam Eaton .10 .30
143 Adam Kennedy .10 .30
144 Mike Piazza .50 1.25
145 Larry Barnes .10 .30
146 Darryl Kile .10 .30
147 Tom Glavine .20 .50
148 Ryan Klesko .10 .30
149 Jose Vidro .10 .30
150 Joe Kennedy .10 .30
151 Bernie Williams .20 .50
152 C.C. Sabathia .10 .30
153 Alex Ochoa .10 .30
154 A.J. Pierzynski .10 .30
155 Johnny Damon .20 .50
156 Omar Daal .10 .30
157 A.J. Burnett .10 .30
158 Eric Munson .10 .30
159 Fernando Vina .10 .30
160 Chris Singleton .10 .30
161 Juan Pierre .10 .30
162 John Olerud .10 .30
163 Randy Johnson .30 .75
164 Paul Konerko .10 .30
165 Tino Martinez .20 .50
166 Richard Hidalgo .10 .30
167 Luis Gonzalez .10 .30
168 Ben Grieve .10 .30
169 Matt Lawton .10 .30
170 Gabe Kapler .10 .30
171 Mariano Rivera .30 .75
172 Kenny Lofton .10 .30
173 Brian Jordan .10 .30
174 Brian Giles .10 .30
175 Mark Quinn .10 .30
176 Neifi Perez .10 .30
177 Ellis Burks .10 .30
178 Bobby Abreu .10 .30
179 Jeff Weaver .10 .30
180 Andres Galarraga .10 .30
181 Javy Lopez .10 .30
182 Todd Walker .10 .30
183 Fernando Tatis .10 .30
184 Charles Johnson .10 .30
185 Pat Burrell .10 .30
186 Jay Bell .10 .30
187 Aaron Boone .10 .30
188 Jason Giambi .10 .30
189 Jay Payton .10 .30
190 Carlos Lee .10 .30
191 Phil Nevin .10 .30
192 Mike Sweeney .10 .30
193 J.T. Snow .10 .30
194 Dmitri Young .10 .30
195 Richie Sexson .10 .30
196 Derrek Lee .20 .50
197 Corey Koskie .10 .30
198 Edgar Martinez .20 .50
199 Wade Miller .10 .30
200 Tony Batista .10 .30
201 John Olerud AS .40 1.00
202 Bret Boone AS .40 1.00
203 Cal Ripken AS 2.00 5.00
204 Alex Rodriguez AS .75 2.00
205 Ichiro Suzuki AS 1.25 3.00
206 Manny Ramirez AS .20 .50
207 Juan Gonzalez AS .40 1.00
208 Ivan Rodriguez AS .60 1.50
209 Roger Clemens AS 1.25 3.00
210 Edgar Martinez AS .60 1.50
211 Todd Helton AS .60 1.50
212 Jeff Kent AS .40 1.00
213 Chipper Jones AS .60 1.50
214 Rich Aurilia AS .40 1.00
215 Barry Bonds AS 1.50 4.00
216 Sammy Sosa AS .60 1.50
217 Luis Gonzalez AS .40 1.00
218 Mike Piazza AS 1.00 2.50
219 Randy Johnson AS .60 1.50
220 Larry Walker AS .40 1.00
221 T.Helton .40 1.00
J.Uribe
222 P.Burrell .40 1.00
E.Valent
223 E.Martinez 1.25 3.00
I.Suzuki
224 B.Grieve .40 1.00
J.Tyner
225 M.Quinn .40 1.00
D.Brown
226 C.Ripken 2.00 5.00
B.Roberts
227 C.Floyd .40 1.00
A.Nunez
228 J.Bagwell .40 1.00
A.Everett
229 M.McGwire 1.50 4.00
A.Pujols
230 D.Mientkewicz .40 1.00
L.Rivas
231 J.Gonzalez .40 1.00
D.Peoples
232 K.Brown .40 1.00
L.Prokopec
233 R.Sexson .40 1.00
B.Sheets
234 J.Giambi .40 1.00
J.Hart
235 B.Bonds 1.50 4.00
C.Valderrama
236 T.Gwynn .75 2.00
C.Crespo
237 K.Griffey Jr. 1.25 3.00
A.Dunn
238 F.Thomas .60 1.50
J.Crede
239 D.Jeter 1.50 4.00
D.Henson
240 C.Jones .60 1.50
W.Betemit
241 L.Gonzalez .40 1.00
J.Spivey
242 B.Higginson .40 1.00
A.Torres
243 C.Delgado .40 1.00
V.Wells
244 S.Sosa .60 1.50
C.Patterson
245 N.Garciaparra 1.00 2.50
S.Hillenbrand
246 A.Rodriguez .75 2.00
J.Romano
247 T.Glaus .40 1.00
D.Eckstein
248 M.Piazza 1.00 2.50
A.Escobar
249 B.Giles .40 1.00
J.Wilson
250 V.Guerrero .60 1.50
S.Hodges
251 Bud Smith PROS 1.25 3.00
252 Juan Diaz PROS 1.25 3.00
253 Wilkin Ruan PROS 1.25 3.00
254 Chris Spurling PROS RC 1.25 3.00
255 Toby Hall PROS 1.25 3.00
256 Jason Jennings PROS 1.25 3.00
257 George Perez PROS 1.25 3.00
258 D'Angelo Jimenez PROS 1.25 3.00
259 Jose Acevedo PROS 1.25 3.00
260 Josue Perez PROS 1.25 3.00
261 Brian Rogers PROS 1.25 3.00
262 Carlos Maldonado PROS RC 1.25 3.00
263 Travis Phelps PROS 1.25 3.00
264 Rob Mackowiak PROS 1.25 3.00
265 Ryan Drese PROS 1.25 3.00
266 Carlos Garcia PROS 1.25 3.00
267 Alexis Gomez PROS 1.25 3.00
268 Jeremy Affeldt PROS 1.25 3.00
269 Scott Podsednik PROS 1.50 4.00
270 Adam Johnson PROS 1.25 3.00
271 Pedro Santana PROS 1.25 3.00
272 Les Walrond PROS 1.25 3.00
273 Jackson Melian PROS 1.25 3.00
274 Carlos Hernandez PROS 1.25 3.00
275 Mark Nussbeck PROS RC 1.25 3.00
276 Cory Aldridge PROS 1.25 3.00
277 Troy Mattes PROS 1.25 3.00
278 Brent Abernathy PROS 1.25 3.00
279 J.J. Davis PROS 1.25 3.00
280 Brandon Duckworth PROS 1.25 3.00
281 Kyle Lohse PROS 1.25 3.00
282 Justin Kaye PROS 1.25 3.00
283 Cody Ransom PROS 1.25 3.00
284 Dave Williams PROS 1.25 3.00
285 Luis Lopez PROS 1.25 3.00

2002 Ultra Gold Medallion

COMP.SET w/o SP's (200) 60.00 150.00
*GOLD 1-200: 1.25X TO 3X BASIC
1-200 STATED ODDS 1:1
*GOLD 201-220: .75X TO 2X BASIC
201-220 STATED ODDS 1:24
*GOLD 221-250: 1X TO 2.5X BASIC
221-250 STATED ODDS 1:24
*GOLD 251-285: 3X TO 8X BASIC
251-285 RANDOM INSERTS IN PACKS
251-285 PRINT RUN 100 SERIAL #'d SETS

2002 Ultra Fall Classic

COMPLETE SET (36) 100.00 200.00
STATED ODDS 1:20 HOBBY
1 Ty Cobb 4.00 10.00
2 Lou Gehrig 4.00 10.00
3 Babe Ruth 8.00 20.00
4 Stan Musial 4.00 10.00
5 Ted Williams 5.00 12.00
6 Dizzy Dean 3.00 8.00
7 Mickey Cochrane 2.00 5.00
8 Jimmie Foxx 3.00 8.00
9 Mel Ott 3.00 8.00
10 Rogers Hornsby 3.00 8.00
12 Clete Boyer 2.00 5.00
13 George Brett 6.00 15.00
14 Bob Gibson 3.00 8.00
15 Carlton Fisk 3.00 8.00
16 Johnny Bench 3.00 8.00
18 Willie McCovey 2.00 5.00
19 Paul Molitor 2.00 5.00
20 Jim Palmer 2.00 5.00
21 Frank Robinson 3.00 8.00
22 Derek Jeter 5.00 12.00
23 Earl Weaver 2.00 5.00
24 Lefty Grove 2.00 5.00
25 Tony Perez 2.00 5.00
26 Reggie Jackson 3.00 8.00
27 Sparky Anderson 2.00 5.00
28 Casey Stengel 2.00 5.00
29 Roy Campanella 3.00 8.00
31 Don Drysdale 3.00 8.00
32 Joe Morgan 2.00 5.00
33 Eddie Murray 3.00 8.00
34 Nolan Ryan 6.00 15.00
35 Tom Seaver 3.00 8.00
36 Bill Mazeroski 2.00 5.00
37 Jackie Robinson 3.00 8.00
38 Kirk Gibson 2.00 5.00
39 Robin Yount 3.00 8.00

2002 Ultra Fall Classic Autographs

STATED ODDS 1:240
ALL EXCEPT SPARKY & WEAVER WERE EXCH
1 Sparky Anderson 15.00 40.00
2 Johnny Bench SP 20.00 50.00
3 George Brett SP 50.00 100.00
4 Carlton Fisk 10.00 25.00
5 Bob Gibson 10.00 25.00
6 Kirk Gibson 8.00 20.00
7 Reggie Jackson SP 20.00 50.00
8 Bill Mazeroski 8.00 20.00
10 Willie McCovey SP 15.00 40.00
11 Joe Morgan 6.00 15.00
12 Eddie Murray SP 20.00 50.00
14 Jim Palmer 6.00 15.00
15 Tony Perez 8.00 20.00
16 Frank Robinson 12.50 30.00
17 Nolan Ryan SP 125.00 250.00
18 Tom Seaver SP 20.00 50.00
19 Earl Weaver 6.00 15.00
20 Robin Yount SP 30.00 60.00

2002 Ultra Fall Classic Memorabilia

STATED ODDS 1:113 HOBBY, 1:400 RETAIL
SP PRINT RUNS LISTED BELOW
1 Sparky Anderson Pants 4.00 10.00
2 Johnny Bench Pants 6.00 15.00
3 Johnny Bench Jsy 6.00 15.00
4 George Brett White Jsy 10.00 25.00
5 George Brett Bat 10.00 25.00
8 Carlton Fisk Jsy 8.00 20.00
9 Carlton Fisk Bat/42 * 20.00 50.00
10 Jimmie Foxx Bat 20.00 50.00
11 Bob Gibson Jsy 6.00 15.00
12 Kirk Gibson Bat 4.00 10.00
13 Reggie Jackson Bat 6.00 15.00
16 Derek Jeter Pants 10.00 25.00
17 Willie McCovey Jsy 4.00 10.00
18 Paul Molitor Bat 4.00 10.00
20 Joe Morgan Bat 4.00 10.00
22 Eddie Murray Bat 6.00 15.00
23 Eddie Murray Jsy/91 * 20.00 50.00
24 Jim Palmer White Jsy 4.00 10.00
25 Jim Palmer Gray Jsy/85 * 15.00 40.00
26 Tony Perez Bat 4.00 10.00
27 Frank Robinson Bat/40 * 15.00 40.00
28 Jackie Robinson Pants 30.00 60.00
29 Babe Ruth Bat/44 * 100.00 200.00
30 Nolan Ryan Pants 20.00 50.00
31 Tom Seaver Jsy 6.00 15.00
32 Earl Weaver Jsy 4.00 10.00
33 Ted Williams Jsy 20.00 50.00
37 Robin Yount Bat 6.00 15.00

2002 Ultra Glove Works

COMPLETE SET (15) 20.00 50.00
STATED ODDS 1:20 HOBBY, 1:36 RETAIL
1 Andruw Jones 1.25 3.00
2 Derek Jeter 3.00 8.00
3 Cal Ripken 4.00 10.00
4 Larry Walker 1.25 3.00
5 Chipper Jones 1.50 4.00
6 Barry Bonds 3.00 8.00
7 Scott Rolen 1.25 3.00
8 Jim Edmonds 1.25 3.00
9 Robin Ventura 1.25 3.00
10 Darin Erstad 1.25 3.00
11 Barry Larkin 1.25 3.00
12 Raul Mondesi 1.25 3.00
13 Mark Grace 1.25 3.00
14 Bernie Williams 1.25 3.00
15 Ivan Rodriguez 1.25 3.00

2002 Ultra Glove Works Memorabilia

RANDOM INSERTS IN PACKS
STATED PRINT RUN 450 #'d SETS
PLATINUM PRINT RUN 25 SERIAL #'d SETS
PLATINUM NO PRICING DUE TO SCARCITY
1 Derek Jeter/450 12.50 30.00
3 Cal Ripken/450 10.00 25.00
6 Barry Bonds/450 10.00 25.00
8 Robin Ventura/450 6.00 15.00
9 Barry Larkin/375 6.00 15.00
10 Raul Mondesi/450 6.00 15.00
11 Ivan Rodriguez/450 6.00 15.00

2002 Ultra Hitting Machines

COMPLETE SET (25) 60.00 120.00
STATED ODDS 1:20 RETAIL
1 Frank Thomas 2.00 5.00
2 Derek Jeter 5.00 12.00
3 Vladimir Guerrero 2.00 5.00
4 Jim Edmonds 1.00 2.50
5 Mike Piazza 3.00 8.00
6 Ivan Rodriguez 1.25 3.00
7 Chipper Jones 2.00 5.00
8 Tony Gwynn 2.50 6.00
9 Manny Ramirez 1.25 3.00
10 Andruw Jones 1.25 3.00
11 Carlos Delgado 1.00 2.50
12 Bernie Williams 1.25 3.00
13 Larry Walker 1.00 2.50
14 Juan Gonzalez 1.00 2.50
15 Ichiro Suzuki 4.00 10.00
16 Albert Pujols 4.00 10.00
17 Barry Bonds 5.00 12.00
18 Cal Ripken 6.00 15.00
19 Edgar Martinez 1.25 3.00
20 Luis Gonzalez 1.00 2.50
21 Moises Alou 1.00 2.50
22 Roberto Alomar 1.25 3.00
23 Todd Helton 1.25 3.00
24 Rafael Palmeiro 1.25 3.00
25 Bobby Abreu 1.00 2.50

2002 Ultra Hitting Machines Game Bat

STATED ODDS 1:81 HOBBY, 1:102 RETAIL
PLATINUM PRINT RUN 25 SERIAL #'d SETS
PLATINUM: NO PRICING DUE TO SCARCITY
1 Bobby Abreu 1.50 4.00
2 Roberto Alomar 2.50 6.00
3 Moises Alou 1.50 4.00
4 Barry Bonds 10.00 25.00
5 Carlos Delgado 1.50 4.00
6 Jim Edmonds 2.50 6.00
7 Juan Gonzalez 1.50 4.00
8 Luis Gonzalez 1.50 4.00
9 Tony Gwynn 4.00 10.00
10 Todd Helton 2.50 6.00
11 Derek Jeter 10.00 25.00
12 Andruw Jones 1.50 4.00
13 Chipper Jones 4.00 10.00
14 Edgar Martinez 2.50 6.00
15 Rafael Palmeiro 2.50 6.00
16 Mike Piazza 4.00 10.00
17 Albert Pujols 8.00 20.00
18 Manny Ramirez 2.50 6.00
19 Cal Ripken 12.00 30.00
20 Ivan Rodriguez 2.50 6.00
21 Frank Thomas 4.00 10.00
22 Larry Walker 2.50 6.00
23 Bernie Williams 2.50 6.00

2002 Ultra On the Road Game Jersey

STATED ODDS 1:93 HOBBY, 1:268 RETAIL
PLATINUM PRINT RUN 25 SERIAL #'d SETS
PLATINUM: NO PRICING DUE TO SCARCITY
1 Derek Jeter 10.00 25.00
2 Ivan Rodriguez 8.00 20.00
3 Carlos Delgado 6.00 15.00
4 Larry Walker 6.00 15.00
5 Roberto Alomar 8.00 20.00
6 Tony Gwynn 8.00 20.00
7 Greg Maddux 8.00 20.00
8 Barry Bonds 15.00 40.00
9 Todd Helton 8.00 20.00
10 Kazuhiro Sasaki 6.00 15.00
11 Jeff Bagwell 8.00 20.00
12 Omar Vizquel 8.00 20.00
13 Chan Ho Park 6.00 15.00
14 Tom Glavine 8.00 20.00

2002 Ultra Rising Stars

COMPLETE SET (15) 12.50 30.00
STATED ODDS 1:12 HOBBY, 1:20 RETAIL
1 Ichiro Suzuki 2.00 5.00
2 Derek Jeter 2.50 6.00
3 Albert Pujols 2.00 5.00
4 Jimmy Rollins .75 2.00
5 Adam Dunn .75 2.00
6 Sean Casey .75 2.00
7 Kerry Wood .75 2.00
8 Tsuyoshi Shinjo .75 2.00
9 Shea Hillenbrand .75 2.00
10 Pat Burrell .75 2.00
11 Ben Sheets .75 2.00
12 Alfonso Soriano .75 2.00
13 J.D. Drew .75 2.00
14 Kazuhiro Sasaki .75 2.00
15 Corey Patterson .75 2.00

2002 Ultra Rising Stars Game Hat

RANDOM INSERTS IN PACKS
STATED PRINT RUN 100 SERIAL #'d SETS
PLATINUM PRINT RUN 25 SERIAL #'d SETS
PLATINUM NO PRICING DUE TO SCARCITY
1 Derek Jeter 40.00 80.00
2 Albert Pujols 20.00 50.00
3 Tsuyoshi Shinjo 15.00 40.00
4 Alfonso Soriano 15.00 40.00
5 J.D. Drew 15.00 40.00
6 Kazuhiro Sasaki 15.00 40.00

2003 Ultra

COMP.LO SET (250) 40.00 100.00
COMP.LO SET w/o SP's (200) 10.00 25.00
COMMON CARD (1-200) .12 .30
COMMON CARD (201-220) .25 .60
201-220 STATED ODDS 1:4
COMMON CARD (221-250) .40 1.00
221-250 STATED ODDS 1:2
COMMON CARD (251-265) .60 1.50
251-265 RANDOM IN FLEER R/G PACKS
251-265 PRINT RUN 1500 SERIAL #'d SETS
1 Barry Bonds .50 1.25
2 Derek Jeter .75 2.00
3 Ichiro Suzuki .40 1.00
4 Mike Lowell .12 .30
5 Hideo Nomo .30 .75
6 Javier Vazquez .12 .30
7 Jeremy Giambi .12 .30
8 Jamie Moyer .12 .30
9 Rafael Palmeiro .20 .50
10 Magglio Ordonez .20 .50
11 Trot Nixon .12 .30
12 Luis Castillo .12 .30
13 Paul Byrd .12 .30
14 Adam Kennedy .12 .30
15 Trevor Hoffman .20 .50
16 Matt Morris .12 .30
17 Nomar Garciaparra .20 .50
18 Matt Lawton .12 .30
19 Carlos Beltran .20 .50
20 Jason Giambi .12 .30
21 Brian Giles .12 .30
22 Jim Edmonds .20 .50
23 Garret Anderson .12 .30
24 Tony Batista .12 .30
25 Aaron Boone .12 .30
26 Mike Hampton .12 .30
27 Billy Wagner .12 .30
28 Kazuhisa Ishii .12 .30
29 Al Leiter .12 .30
30 Pat Burrell .12 .30
31 Jeff Kent .12 .30
32 Randy Johnson .30 .75
33 Ray Durham .12 .30
34 Josh Beckett .12 .30
35 Cristian Guzman .12 .30
36 Roger Clemens .40 1.00
37 Freddy Garcia .12 .30
38 Roy Halladay .20 .50
39 David Eckstein .12 .30
40 Jerry Hairston .12 .30
41 Barry Larkin .20 .50
42 Larry Walker .20 .50
43 Craig Biggio .20 .50
44 Edgardo Alfonzo .12 .30
45 Marlon Byrd .12 .30
46 J.T. Snow .12 .30
47 Juan Gonzalez .12 .30
48 Ramon Ortiz .12 .30
49 Jay Gibbons .12 .30
50 Adam Dunn .20 .50
51 Juan Pierre .12 .30
52 Jeff Bagwell .20 .50
53 Kevin Brown .12 .30
54 Pedro Astacio .12 .30
55 Mike Lieberthal .12 .30
56 Johnny Damon .20 .50
57 Tim Salmon .12 .30
58 Mike Bordick .12 .30
59 Ken Griffey Jr. .60 1.50
60 Jason Jennings .12 .30
61 Lance Berkman .20 .50
62 Jeromy Burnitz .12 .30
63 Jimmy Rollins .20 .50
64 Tsuyoshi Shinjo .12 .30
65 Alex Rodriguez .40 1.00
66 Greg Maddux .40 1.00
67 Mark Prior .20 .50
68 Mike Maroth .12 .30
69 Geoff Jenkins .12 .30
70 Tony Armas Jr. .12 .30
71 Jermaine Dye .12 .30
72 Albert Pujols .40 1.00
73 Shannon Stewart .12 .30
74 Troy Glaus .12 .30
75 Brook Fordyce .12 .30
76 Juan Encarnacion .12 .30
77 Todd Hollandsworth .12 .30
78 Roy Oswalt .20 .50
79 Paul Lo Duca .12 .30
80 Mike Piazza .30 .75
81 Bobby Abreu .12 .30
82 Sean Burroughs .12 .30
83 Randy Winn .12 .30
84 Curt Schilling .20 .50
85 Chris Singleton .12 .30
86 Sean Casey .12 .30
87 Todd Zeile .12 .30
88 Richard Hidalgo .20 .50
89 Roberto Alomar .20 .50
90 Tim Hudson .20 .50
91 Ryan Klesko .12 .30
92 Greg Vaughn .12 .30
93 Tony Womack .12 .30
94 Fred McGriff .20 .50
95 Tom Glavine .20 .50
96 Todd Walker .12 .30
97 Travis Fryman .12 .30
98 Shane Reynolds .12 .30
99 Shawn Green .12 .30
100 Mo Vaughn .12 .30
101 Adam Platt .12 .30
102 Deivi Cruz .12 .30
103 Steve Cox .12 .30
104 Luis Gonzalez .12 .30
105 Russell Branyan .12 .30
106 Daryle Ward .12 .30
107 Mariano Rivera .40 1.00
108 Phil Nevin .12 .30
109 Ben Grieve .12 .30
110 Moises Alou .12 .30
111 Omar Vizquel .20 .50
112 Joe Randa .12 .30
113 Jorge Posada .20 .50
114 Mark Kotsay .12 .30
115 Ryan Rupe .12 .30
116 Javy Lopez .12 .30
117 Corey Patterson .12 .30
118 Bobby Higginson .12 .30
119 Jose Vidro .12 .30
120 Barry Zito .20 .50
121 Scott Rolen .20 .50
122 Gary Sheffield .12 .30
123 Kerry Wood .12 .30
124 Brandon Inge .12 .30
125 Jose Hernandez .12 .30
126 Michael Barrett .12 .30
127 Miguel Tejada .20 .50
128 Edgar Renteria .12 .30
129 Junior Spivey .12 .30
130 Jose Valentin .12 .30
131 Derrek Lee .12 .30
132 A.J. Pierzynski .12 .30
133 Mike Mussina .20 .50
134 Bret Boone .12 .30
135 Chan Ho Park .20 .50
136 Steve Finley .12 .30
137 Mark Buehrle .20 .50
138 A.J. Burnett .12 .30
139 Ben Sheets .12 .30
140 David Ortiz .30 .75
141 Nick Johnson .12 .30
142 Randall Simon .12 .30
143 Carlos Delgado .12 .30
144 Darin Erstad .12 .30
145 Shea Hillenbrand .12 .30
146 Todd Helton .20 .50
147 Preston Wilson .12 .30
148 Eric Gagne .12 .30
149 Vladimir Guerrero .20 .50
150 Brandon Duckworth .12 .30
151 Rich Aurilia .12 .30
152 Ivan Rodriguez .20 .50
153 Andruw Jones .12 .30
154 Carlos Lee .12 .30
155 Robert Fick .12 .30
156 Jacque Jones .12 .30
157 Bernie Williams .20 .50
158 John Olerud .12 .30
159 Eric Hinske .12 .30
160 Matt Clement .12 .30
161 Dmitri Young .12 .30
162 Torii Hunter .12 .30
163 Carlos Pena .20 .50
164 Mike Cameron .12 .30
165 Raul Mondesi .12 .30
166 Pedro Martinez .20 .50
167 Bob Wickman .12 .30
168 Mike Sweeney .12 .30
169 David Wells .12 .30
170 Jason Kendall .12 .30
171 Tino Martinez .12 .30
172 Matt Williams .12 .30
173 Frank Thomas .30 .75
174 Cliff Floyd .12 .30
175 Corey Koskie .12 .30
176 Orlando Hernandez .12 .30
177 Edgar Martinez .20 .50
178 Richie Sexson .12 .30
179 Manny Ramirez .30 .75
180 Jim Thome .20 .50
181 Andy Pettitte .20 .50
182 Aramis Ramirez .12 .30
183 J.D. Drew .12 .30
184 Brian Jordan .12 .30
185 Sammy Sosa .30 .75
186 Jeff Weaver .12 .30
187 Jeffrey Hammonds .12 .30
188 Eric Milton .12 .30
189 Eric Chavez .12 .30
190 Kazuhiro Sasaki .12 .30
191 Jose Cruz Jr. .12 .30
192 Derek Lowe .12 .30
193 C.C. Sabathia .12 .30
194 Adrian Beltre .30 .75
195 Alfonso Soriano .20 .50
196 Jack Wilson .12 .30
197 Fernando Vina .12 .30
198 Chipper Jones .30 .75
199 Paul Konerko .20 .50
200 Rusty Greer .12 .30
201 Jason Giambi AS .25 .60
202 Alfonso Soriano AS .40 1.00
203 Shea Hillenbrand AS .25 .60
204 Alex Rodriguez AS .75 2.00
205 Jorge Posada AS .40 1.00
206 Ichiro Suzuki AS .75 2.00
207 Manny Ramirez AS .60 1.50
208 Torii Hunter AS .25 .60
209 Todd Helton AS .40 1.00
210 Jose Vidro AS .25 .60
211 Scott Rolen AS .40 1.00
212 Jimmy Rollins AS .40 1.00
213 Mike Piazza AS .60 1.50
214 Barry Bonds AS 1.00 2.50
215 Sammy Sosa AS .60 1.50
216 Vladimir Guerrero AS .40 1.00
217 Lance Berkman AS .40 1.00
218 Derek Jeter AS 1.50 4.00
219 Nomar Garciaparra AS .40 1.00
220 Luis Gonzalez AS .25 .60
221 Kazuhisa Ishii 02R .40 1.00
222 Satoru Komiyama 02R .40 1.00
223 So Taguchi 02R .40 1.00
224 Jorge Padilla 02R .40 1.00

225 Ben Howard 02R	.40	1.00
226 Jason Simontacchi 02R	.40	1.00
227 Barry Wesson 02R	.40	1.00
228 Howie Clark 02R	.40	1.00
229 Aaron Guiel 02R	.40	1.00
230 Oliver Perez 02R	.40	1.00
231 David Ross 02R	.40	1.00
232 Julius Matos 02R	.40	1.00
233 Chris Snelling 02R	.40	1.00
234 Rodrigo Lopez 02R	.40	1.00
235 Will Nieves 02R	.40	1.00
236 Joe Borchard 02R	.40	1.00
237 Aaron Cook 02R	.40	1.00
238 Anderson Machado 02R	.40	1.00
239 Corey Thurman 02R	.40	1.00
240 Tyler Yates 02R	.40	1.00
241 Coco Crisp 03R	.40	1.00
242 Andy Van Hekken 03R	.40	1.00
243 Jim Rushford 03R	.40	1.00
244 Jeriome Robertson 03R	.40	1.00
245 Shane Nance 03R	.40	1.00
246 Kevin Cash 03R	.40	1.00
247 Kirk Saarloos 03R	.40	1.00
248 Josh Bard 03R	.40	1.00
249 Dave Pember 03R RC	.40	1.00
250 Freddy Sanchez 03R	.40	1.00
251 Chien-Ming Wang PROS RC	2.50	6.00
252 Rickie Weeks PROS RC	2.00	5.00
253 Brandon Webb PROS RC	2.00	5.00
254 Hideki Matsui PROS RC	3.00	8.00
255 Michael Hessman PROS RC	.60	1.50
256 Ryan Wagner PROS RC	.60	1.50
257 Matt Kata PROS RC	.60	1.50
258 Edwin Jackson PROS RC	1.00	2.50
259 Jose Contreras PROS RC	1.50	4.00
260 Delmon Young PROS RC	4.00	10.00
261 Bo Hart PROS RC	.60	1.50
262 Jeff Duncan PROS RC	.60	1.50
263 Robby Hammock PROS RC	.60	1.50
264 Jeremy Bonderman PROS RC	2.50	6.00
265 Clint Barmes PROS RC	1.50	4.00

2003 Ultra Gold Medallion

*GOLD MED 1-200: 1.25X TO 3X BASIC
1-200 STATED ODDS 1:1
*GOLD MED 201-220: 1X TO 2.5X BASIC
201-220 STATED ODDS 1:24
*GOLD MED 221-250: 1X TO 2.5X BASIC
221-250 STATED ODDS 1:24

2003 Ultra Back 2 Back

RANDOM INSERTS IN PACKS
STATED PRINT RUN 1000 SERIAL #'d SETS

1 Derek Jeter	4.00	10.00
2 Barry Bonds	2.50	6.00
3 Mike Piazza	1.50	4.00
4 Alex Rodriguez	2.00	5.00
5 Todd Helton	1.00	2.50
6 Edgar Martinez	1.00	2.50
7 Chipper Jones	1.50	4.00
8 Shawn Green	.60	1.50
9 Chan Ho Park	1.00	2.50
10 Preston Wilson	.60	1.50
11 Manny Ramirez	1.50	4.00
12 Aramis Ramirez	.60	1.50
13 Pedro Martinez	1.00	2.50
14 Ivan Rodriguez	1.00	2.50
15 Ichiro Suzuki	2.00	5.00
16 Sammy Sosa	1.50	4.00
17 Jason Giambi	.60	1.50

2003 Ultra Back 2 Back Memorabilia

STATED PRINT RUN 500 SERIAL #'d SETS
*GOLD: 1.25X TO 3X BASIC B2B MEMORABILIA
GOLD PRINT RUN 50 SERIAL #'d SETS

AR Aramis Ramirez Pants	4.00	10.00
AR1 Alex Rodriguez Jsy	8.00	20.00
BB Barry Bonds Bat	10.00	25.00
CJ Chipper Jones Jsy	6.00	15.00
CP Chan Ho Park Bat	4.00	10.00
DJ Derek Jeter Jsy	10.00	25.00
EM Edgar Martinez Jsy	6.00	15.00
IR Ivan Rodriguez Jsy	6.00	15.00
IS Ichiro Suzuki Base	8.00	20.00
JG Jason Giambi Base	4.00	10.00
MP Mike Piazza Jsy	6.00	15.00
MR Manny Ramirez Jsy	6.00	15.00
PM Pedro Martinez Jsy	6.00	15.00
PW Preston Wilson Jsy	4.00	10.00
SG Shawn Green Jsy	4.00	10.00
SS Sammy Sosa Base	6.00	15.00
TH Todd Helton Jsy	6.00	15.00

2003 Ultra Double Up

COMPLETE SET (16)	12.50	30.00
STATED ODDS 1:8		
1 D.Jeter M.Piazza	2.50	6.00
2 A.Rodriguez R.Palmeiro	1.25	3.00
3 C.Jones A.Jones	1.00	2.50
4 D.Jeter A.Rodriguez	2.50	6.00
5 N.Garciaparra D.Jeter	2.50	6.00
6 B.Bonds J.Giambi	1.50	4.00
7 I.Suzuki H.Nomo	1.25	3.00
8 R.Johnson C.Schilling	1.00	2.50
9 P.Martinez N.Garciaparra	.60	1.50
10 R.Clemens K.Brown	1.25	3.00
11 N.Garciaparra M.Ramirez	1.00	2.50
12 K.Sasaki H.Nomo	1.00	2.50
13 M.Piazza I.Rodriguez	1.00	2.50
14 I.Suzuki K.Griffey Jr	2.00	5.00
15 B.Bonds S.Sosa	1.50	4.00
16 A.Soriano R.Alomar	.60	1.50

2003 Ultra Double Up Memorabilia

RANDOM INSERTS IN PACKS
STATED PRINT RUN 100 SERIAL #'d SETS

1 Jeter Jsy/Piazza Jsy	25.00	60.00
2 A.Rod Jsy/Palmeiro Jsy	15.00	40.00
3 C.Jones Bat/A.Jones Jsy	10.00	25.00
4 Jeter Jsy/A.Rod Jsy	25.00	60.00
5 Garciaparra Jsy/Jeter Jsy	25.00	60.00
6 Bonds Bat/Giambi Base	15.00	40.00
7 Ichiro Base/Nomo Jsy	50.00	120.00
8 Johnson Jsy/Schilling Jsy	10.00	25.00
9 Martinez Jsy/Garciaparra Jsy	15.00	40.00
10 Clemens Jsy/K.Brown Jsy	15.00	40.00
11 Garciaparra Jsy/Ramirez Jsy	15.00	40.00
12 Sasaki Jsy/Nomo Jsy	25.00	60.00
13 Piazza Jsy/I.Rodriguez Jsy	15.00	40.00
14 Ichiro Base/Griffey Jr. Base	30.00	80.00
15 Bonds Bat/Sosa Base	25.00	60.00
16 Soriano Pants/Alomar Jsy	10.00	25.00

2003 Ultra Moonshots

STATED ODDS 1:12

1 Mike Piazza	1.00	2.50
2 Alex Rodriguez	1.25	3.00
3 Manny Ramirez	1.00	2.50
4 Ivan Rodriguez	.60	1.50
5 Luis Gonzalez	.40	1.00
6 Shawn Green	.40	1.00
7 Barry Bonds	1.50	4.00
8 Jason Giambi	.40	1.00
9 Nomar Garciaparra	.60	1.50
10 Edgar Martinez	.60	1.50
11 Mo Vaughn	.40	1.00
12 Chipper Jones	1.00	2.50
13 Todd Helton	.60	1.50
14 Raul Mondesi	.40	1.00
15 Preston Wilson	.40	1.00
16 Rafael Palmeiro	.60	1.50
17 Jim Edmonds	.60	1.50
18 Bernie Williams	.60	1.50
19 Vladimir Guerrero	.60	1.50
20 Alfonso Soriano	.60	1.50

2003 Ultra Moonshots Memorabilia

STATED ODDS 1:20

AR Alex Rodriguez Jsy	6.00	15.00
AS Alfonso Soriano Pants	3.00	8.00
BB Barry Bonds Jsy	6.00	15.00
BW Bernie Williams Jsy	4.00	10.00
CG Vladimir Guerrero Base	4.00	10.00
CJ Chipper Jones Jsy	4.00	10.00
EM Edgar Martinez Jsy	4.00	10.00
IR Ivan Rodriguez Jsy	4.00	10.00
JE Jim Edmonds Jsy	3.00	8.00
JG Jason Giambi Base	3.00	8.00
LG Luis Gonzalez Jsy	3.00	8.00
MP Mike Piazza Jsy	6.00	15.00
MR Manny Ramirez Jsy	4.00	10.00
MV Mo Vaughn Jsy	3.00	8.00
NG Nomar Garciaparra Jsy	6.00	15.00
PW Preston Wilson Jsy	3.00	8.00
RM Raul Mondesi Jsy	3.00	8.00
RP Rafael Palmeiro Jsy	4.00	10.00
SG Shawn Green Jsy	3.00	8.00
TH Todd Helton Jsy	4.00	10.00

2003 Ultra Photo Effex

STATED ODDS 1:12
GOLD RANDOM INSERTS IN PACKS
GOLD PRINT RUN 25 SERIAL #'d SETS
GOLD NO PRICING DUE TO SCARCITY

1 Derek Jeter	2.50	6.00
2 Barry Bonds	1.50	4.00
3 Sammy Sosa	1.00	2.50
4 Troy Glaus	.40	1.00
5 Albert Pujols	1.25	3.00
6 Alex Rodriguez	1.25	3.00
7 Ichiro Suzuki	1.25	3.00
8 Greg Maddux	1.25	3.00
9 Nomar Garciaparra	.60	1.50
10 Jeff Bagwell	.60	1.50
11 Chipper Jones	1.00	2.50
12 Mike Piazza	1.00	2.50
13 Randy Johnson	1.00	2.50
14 Vladimir Guerrero	.60	1.50
15 Alfonso Soriano	.60	1.50
16 Lance Berkman	.60	1.50
17 Todd Helton	.60	1.50
18 Mike Lowell	.40	1.00
19 Carlos Delgado	.40	1.00
20 Jason Giambi	.40	1.00

2003 Ultra When It Was A Game

STATED ODDS 1:20

1 Derek Jeter	4.00	10.00
2 Barry Bonds	2.50	6.00
3 Luis Aparicio	.60	1.50
4 Richie Ashburn	1.00	2.50
5 Ernie Banks	1.50	4.00
6 Enos Slaughter	1.00	2.50
7 Yogi Berra	1.50	4.00
8 Lou Boudreau	1.00	2.50
9 Lou Brock	1.00	2.50
10 Jim Bunning	1.00	2.50
11 Rod Carew	1.00	2.50
12 Orlando Cepeda	1.00	2.50
13 Larry Doby	1.00	2.50
14 Bobby Doerr	1.00	2.50
15 Bob Feller	1.00	2.50
16 Brooks Robinson	1.00	2.50
17 Rollie Fingers	1.00	2.50
18 Whitey Ford	1.00	2.50
19 Bob Gibson	1.00	2.50
20 Catfish Hunter	1.00	2.50
21 Nolan Ryan	5.00	12.00
22 Reggie Jackson	1.00	2.50
23 Fergie Jenkins	1.00	2.50
24 Al Kaline	1.00	2.50
25 Mike Schmidt	2.50	6.00
26 Harmon Killebrew	1.50	4.00
27 Ralph Kiner	1.00	2.50
28 Willie Stargell	1.00	2.50
29 Billy Williams	1.00	2.50
30 Tom Seaver	1.00	2.50
31 Juan Marichal	1.00	2.50
32 Eddie Mathews	1.50	4.00
33 Willie McCovey	1.00	2.50
34 Joe Morgan	1.00	2.50
35 Stan Musial	2.50	6.00
36 Robin Roberts	1.00	2.50
37 Robin Yount	1.50	4.00
38 Jim Palmer	1.00	2.50
39 Phil Rizzuto	1.00	2.50
40 Pee Wee Reese	1.00	2.50

2003 Ultra When It Was A Game Used

STATED PRINT RUNS B/WN 100-300 PER

1 Yogi Berra Pants/100	20.00	50.00
2 Barry Bonds Bat/200	15.00	40.00
3 Larry Doby Bat/150	8.00	20.00
4 Catfish Hunter Jsy/200	8.00	20.00
5 Reggie Jackson Bat/300	8.00	20.00
6 Derek Jeter Jsy/200	15.00	40.00
7 Juan Marichal Jsy/300	6.00	15.00
8 Eddie Mathews Bat/300	10.00	25.00
9 Willie McCovey Jsy/150	8.00	20.00
10 Joe Morgan Pants/200	6.00	15.00
11 Jim Palmer Pants/300	6.00	15.00
12 Tom Seaver Pants/100	10.00	25.00

2004 Ultra

COMPLETE SERIES 1 (220)	30.00	60.00
COMP.SERIES 1 w/o SP's (200)	10.00	25.00
COMP.SERIES 2 w/o SP's (75)	10.00	25.00
COMP.SERIES 2 w/o L13 (162)	50.00	100.00
COMMON CARD (1-200)	.10	.30
COMMON CARD (201-220)	.40	1.00
201-220 APPROXIMATE ODDS 1:2 HOBBY		
201-220 RANDOM IN RETAIL PACKS		
COMMON CARD (221-295)	.20	.50
COMMON CARD (296-382)	.40	1.00
296-382 ODDS TWO PER HOBBY/RETAIL		
COMMON CARD (383-395)	2.50	6.00
COMMON RC (383-395)	2.50	6.00
383-395 ODDS 1:28 HOBBY, 1:2000 RETAIL		
383-395 PRINT RUN 500 SERIAL #'d SETS		
1 Magglio Ordonez	.20	.50
2 Bobby Abreu	.12	.30
3 Eric Munson	.12	.30
4 Eric Byrnes	.12	.30
5 Bartolo Colon	.12	.30
6 Juan Encarnacion	.12	.30
7 Jody Gerut	.12	.30
8 Eddie Guardado	.12	.30
9 Shea Hillenbrand	.12	.30
10 Andruw Jones	.12	.30
11 Carlos Lee	.12	.30
12 Pedro Martinez	.20	.50
13 Barry Larkin	.20	.50
14 Angel Berroa	.12	.30
15 Edgar Martinez	.20	.50
16 Sidney Ponson	.12	.30
17 Mariano Rivera	.40	1.00
18 Richie Sexson	.12	.30
19 Frank Thomas	.30	.75
20 Jerome Williams	.12	.30
21 Barry Zito	.20	.50
22 Roberto Alomar	.20	.50
23 Rocky Biddle	.12	.30
24 Orlando Cabrera	.12	.30
25 Placido Polanco	.12	.30
26 Morgan Ensberg	.12	.30
27 Jason Giambi	.12	.30
28 Jim Thome	.20	.50
29 Vladimir Guerrero	.20	.50
30 Tim Hudson	.20	.50
31 Jacque Jones	.12	.30
32 Derrek Lee	.12	.30
33 Rafael Palmeiro	.20	.50
34 Mike Mussina	.20	.50
35 Corey Patterson	.12	.30
36 Mike Cameron	.12	.30
37 Ivan Rodriguez	.20	.50
38 Ben Sheets	.12	.30
39 Woody Williams	.12	.30
40 Ichiro Suzuki	.40	1.00
41 Moises Alou	.12	.30
42 Craig Biggio	.20	.50
43 Jorge Posada	.20	.50
44 Craig Monroe	.12	.30
45 Darin Erstad	.12	.30
46 Jay Gibbons	.12	.30
47 Aaron Guiel	.12	.30
48 Travis Lee	.12	.30
49 Jorge Julio	.12	.30
50 Torii Hunter	.12	.30
51 Luis Matos	.12	.30
52 Brett Myers	.12	.30
53 Sean Casey	.12	.30
54 Mark Prior	.20	.50
55 Alex Rodriguez	.40	1.00
56 Gary Sheffield	.12	.30
57 Jason Varitek	.30	.75
58 Dontrelle Willis	.12	.30
59 Garret Anderson	.12	.30
60 Casey Blake	.12	.30
61 Jay Payton	.12	.30
62 Carl Crawford	.20	.50
63 Carl Everett	.12	.30
64 Marcus Giles	.12	.30
65 Jose Guillen	.12	.30
66 Eric Karros	.12	.30
67 Mike Lieberthal	.12	.30
68 Hideki Matsui	.50	1.25
69 Xavier Nady	.12	.30
70 Hank Blalock	.12	.30
71 Albert Pujols	.40	1.00
72 Jose Cruz Jr.	.12	.30
73 Randall Simon	.12	.30
74 Javier Vazquez	.12	.30
75 Preston Wilson	.12	.30
76 Danys Baez	.12	.30
77 Alex Cintron	.12	.30
78 Jake Peavy	.12	.30
79 Scott Rolen	.20	.50
80 Robert Fick	.12	.30
81 Brian Giles	.12	.30
82 Roy Halladay	.20	.50
83 Kazuhisa Ishii	.12	.30
84 Austin Kearns	.12	.30
85 Paul Lo Duca	.12	.30
86 Darrell May	.12	.30
87 Phil Nevin	.12	.30
88 Carlos Pena	.20	.50
89 Manny Ramirez	.30	.75
90 C.C. Sabathia	.20	.50
91 John Smoltz	.30	.75
92 Jose Vidro	.12	.30
93 Randy Wolf	.12	.30
94 Jeff Bagwell	.20	.50
95 Barry Bonds	.50	1.25
96 Frank Catalanotto	.12	.30
97 Zach Day	.12	.30
98 David Ortiz	.30	.75
99 Troy Glaus	.12	.30
100 Bo Hart	.12	.30
101 Geoff Jenkins	.12	.30
102 Jason Kendall	.12	.30
103 Esteban Loaiza	.12	.30
104 Doug Mientkiewicz	.12	.30
105 Trot Nixon	.12	.30
106 Troy Percival	.12	.30
107 Aramis Ramirez	.12	.30
108 Alex Sanchez	.12	.30
109 Alfonso Soriano	.20	.50
110 Omar Vizquel	.20	.50
111 Kerry Wood	.12	.30
112 Rocco Baldelli	.12	.30
113 Bret Boone	.12	.30
114 Shawn Chacon	.12	.30
115 Carlos Delgado	.12	.30
116 Shawn Green	.12	.30
117 Tim Worrell	.12	.30
118 Tom Glavine	.20	.50
119 Shigetoshi Hasegawa	.12	.30
120 Derek Jeter	.75	2.00
121 Jeff Kent	.12	.30
122 Braden Looper	.12	.30
123 Kevin Millwood	.12	.30
124 Hideo Nomo	.30	.75
125 Jason Phillips	.12	.30
126 Tim Redding	.12	.30
127 Reggie Sanders	.12	.30
128 Sammy Sosa	.30	.75
129 Billy Wagner	.12	.30
130 Miguel Batista	.12	.30
131 Milton Bradley	.12	.30
132 Eric Chavez	.12	.30
133 J.D. Drew	.12	.30
134 Keith Foulke	.12	.30
135 Luis Gonzalez	.12	.30
136 LaTroy Hawkins	.12	.30
137 Randy Johnson	.30	.75
138 Byung-Hyun Kim	.12	.30
139 Javy Lopez	.12	.30
140 Melvin Mora	.12	.30
141 Aubrey Huff	.12	.30
142 Mike Piazza	.30	.75
143 Mark Redman	.12	.30
144 Kazuhiro Sasaki	.12	.30
145 Shannon Stewart	.12	.30
146 Larry Walker	.20	.50
147 Dmitri Young	.12	.30
148 Josh Beckett	.12	.30
149 Jae Weong Seo	.12	.30
150 Hee Seop Choi	.12	.30
151 Adam Dunn	.20	.50
152 Rafael Furcal	.12	.30
153 Juan Gonzalez	.12	.30
154 Todd Helton	.20	.50
155 Carlos Zambrano	.20	.50
156 Ryan Klesko	.12	.30
157 Mike Lowell	.12	.30
158 Jamie Moyer	.12	.30
159 Russ Ortiz	.12	.30
160 Juan Pierre	.12	.30
161 Edgar Renteria	.12	.30
162 Curt Schilling	.20	.50
163 Mike Sweeney	.12	.30
164 Brandon Webb	.12	.30
165 Michael Young	.12	.30
166 Carlos Beltran	.20	.50
167 Sean Burroughs	.12	.30
168 Luis Castillo	.12	.30
169 David Eckstein	.12	.30
170 Eric Gagne	.12	.30
171 Chipper Jones	.30	.75
172 Livan Hernandez	.12	.30
173 Nick Johnson	.12	.30
174 Corey Koskie	.12	.30
175 Jason Schmidt	.12	.30
176 Bill Mueller	.12	.30
177 Steve Finley	.12	.30
178 A.J. Pierzynski	.12	.30
179 Rene Reyes	.12	.30
180 Jason Johnson	.12	.30
181 Mark Teixeira	.20	.50
182 Kip Wells	.12	.30
183 Mike MacDougal	.12	.30
184 Lance Berkman	.20	.50
185 Victor Zambrano	.12	.30
186 Roger Clemens	.40	1.00
187 Jim Edmonds	.20	.50
188 Nomar Garciaparra	.20	.50
189 Ken Griffey Jr.	.60	1.50
190 Richard Hidalgo	.12	.30
191 Cliff Floyd	.12	.30
192 Greg Maddux	.40	1.00
193 Mark Mulder	.12	.30
194 Roy Oswalt	.20	.50
195 Marlon Byrd	.12	.30
196 Jose Reyes	.20	.50
197 Kevin Brown	.12	.30
198 Miguel Tejada	.20	.50
199 Vernon Wells	.12	.30
200 Joel Pineiro	.12	.30
201 Rickie Weeks AR	.40	1.00
202 Chad Gaudin AR	.40	1.00
203 Ryan Wagner AR	.40	1.00
204 Chris Bootcheck AR	.40	1.00
205 Koyie Hill AR	.40	1.00
206 Jeff Duncan AR	.40	1.00
207 Rich Harden AR	.40	1.00
208 Edwin Jackson AR	.40	1.00
209 Robby Hammock AR	.40	1.00
210 Khalil Greene AR	.60	1.50
211 Chien-Ming Wang AR	1.50	4.00
212 Prentice Redman AR	.40	1.00
213 Todd Wellemeyer AR	.40	1.00
214 Clint Barmes AR	.60	1.50
215 Matt Kata AR	.40	1.00
216 Jon Leicester AR	.40	1.00
217 Jeremy Guthrie AR	.40	1.00
218 Chin-Hui Tsao AR	.40	1.00
219 Dan Haren AR	.40	1.00
220 Delmon Young AR	.60	1.50
221 Vladimir Guerrero	.30	.75
222 Andy Pettitte	.30	.75
223 Gary Sheffield	.20	.50
224 Javier Vazquez	.20	.50
225 Alex Rodriguez	.60	1.50
226 Billy Wagner	.20	.50
227 Miguel Tejada	.30	.75
228 Greg Maddux	.60	1.50
229 Ivan Rodriguez	.30	.75
230 Roger Clemens	.60	1.50
231 Alfonso Soriano	.30	.75
232 Miguel Cabrera	.50	1.25
233 Javy Lopez	.20	.50
234 David Wells	.20	.50
235 Eric Milton	.20	.50
236 Armando Benitez	.20	.50
237 Mike Cameron	.20	.50
238 J.D. Drew	.20	.50
239 Carlos Beltran	.30	.75
240 Bartolo Colon	.20	.50
241 Jose Guillen	.20	.50
242 Kevin Brown	.20	.50
243 Carlos Guillen	.20	.50
244 Kenny Lofton	.20	.50
245 Pokey Reese	.20	.50
246 Rafael Palmeiro	.30	.75
247 Nomar Garciaparra	.30	.75
248 Hee Seop Choi	.20	.50
249 Juan Uribe	.20	.50
250 Nick Johnson	.20	.50
251 Scott Podsednik	.20	.50
252 Richie Sexson	.20	.50
253 Keith Foulke Sox	.20	.50
254 Jaret Wright	.20	.50
255 Johnny Estrada	.20	.50
256 Michael Barrett	.20	.50
257 Bernie Williams	.30	.75
258 Octavio Dotel	.20	.50
259 Jeromy Burnitz	.20	.50
260 Kevin Youkilis	.20	.50
261 Derrek Lee	.20	.50
262 Jack Wilson	.20	.50
263 Craig Wilson	.20	.50
264 Richard Hidalgo	.20	.50
265 Royce Clayton	.20	.50
266 Curt Schilling	.30	.75
267 Joe Mauer	.40	1.00
268 Bobby Crosby	.20	.50
269 Zack Greinke	.75	2.00
270 Victor Martinez	.30	.75
271 Pedro Feliz	.20	.50
272 Tony Batista	.20	.50
273 Casey Kotchman	.20	.50
274 Freddy Garcia	.20	.50
275 Adam Everett	.20	.50
276 Alexis Rios	.20	.50
277 Lew Ford	.20	.50
278 Adam LaRoche	.20	.50
279 Lyle Overbay	.20	.50
280 Juan Gonzalez	.20	.50
281 A.J. Pierzynski	.20	.50
282 Scott Hairston	.20	.50
283 Danny Bautista	.20	.50
284 Brad Penny	.20	.50
285 Paul Konerko	.30	.75
286 Matt Lawton	.20	.50
287 Carl Pavano	.20	.50
288 Pat Burrell	.20	.50
289 Kenny Rogers	.20	.50
290 Laynce Nix	.20	.50
291 Johnny Damon	.30	.75
292 Paul Wilson	.20	.50
293 Vinny Castilla	.20	.50
294 Aaron Miles	.20	.50
295 Ken Harvey	.20	.50
296 Onil Joseph RC	.40	1.00
297 Kazuhito Tadano RC	.40	1.00
298 Jeff Bennett RC	.40	1.00
299 Chad Bentz RC	.40	1.00
300 Akinori Otsuka RC	.40	1.00
301 Jon Knott RC	.40	1.00
302 Ian Snell RC	.40	1.00
303 Fernando Nieve RC	.40	1.00
304 Mike Rouse RC	.40	1.00
305 Dennis Sarfate RC	.40	1.00
306 Josh Labandeira RC	.40	1.00
307 Chris Oxspring RC	.40	1.00
308 Alfredo Simon RC	.60	1.50
309 Rusty Tucker RC	.40	1.00
310 Lincoln Holdzkom RC	.40	1.00
311 Justin Leone RC	.40	1.00
312 Jorge Sequea RC	.40	1.00
313 Brian Dallimore RC	.40	1.00
314 Tim Bittner RC	.40	1.00
315 Ronny Cedeno RC	.40	1.00
316 Justin Hampson RC	.40	1.00
317 Ryan Wing RC	.40	1.00
318 Mariano Gomez RC	.40	1.00
319 Carlos Vasquez RC	.40	1.00
320 Casey Daigle RC	.40	1.00
321 Renyel Pinto RC	.40	1.00
322 Chris Shelton RC	.40	1.00
323 Mike Gosling RC	.40	1.00
324 Aarom Baldiris RC	.40	1.00
325 Ramon Ramirez RC	.40	1.00
326 Roberto Novoa RC	.40	1.00
327 Sean Henn RC	.40	1.00
328 Nick Regilio RC	.40	1.00
329 Dave Crouthers RC	.40	1.00
330 Greg Dobbs RC	.40	1.00
331 Angel Chavez RC	.40	1.00
332 Luis A. Gonzalez RC	.40	1.00
333 Justin Knoedler RC	.40	1.00
334 Jason Frasor RC	.40	1.00
335 Jerry Gil RC	.40	1.00
336 Carlos Hines RC	.40	1.00
337 Ivan Ochoa RC	.40	1.00
338 Jose Capellan RC	.40	1.00
339 Hector Gimenez RC	.40	1.00
340 Shawn Hill RC	.40	1.00
341 Freddy Guzman RC	.40	1.00
342 Scott Proctor RC	.40	1.00
343 Frank Francisco RC	.40	1.00
344 Brandon Medders RC	.40	1.00
345 Andy Green RC	.40	1.00
346 Eddy Rodriguez RC	.40	1.00
347 Tim Hamulack RC	.40	1.00
348 Michael Wuertz RC	.40	1.00
349 Arnie Munoz	.40	1.00
350 Enemencio Pacheco RC	.40	1.00
351 Dusty Bergman RC	.40	1.00
352 Charles Thomas RC	.40	1.00
353 William Bergolla RC	.40	1.00
354 Ramon Castro RC	.40	1.00
355 Justin Lehr RC	.40	1.00
356 Lino Urdaneta RC	.40	1.00
357 Donnie Kelly RC	.60	1.50
358 Kevin Cave RC	.40	1.00
359 Franklyn Gracesqui RC	.40	1.00
360 Chris Aguila RC	.40	1.00
361 Jorge Vasquez RC	.40	1.00
362 Andres Blanco RC	.40	1.00
363 Orlando Rodriguez RC	.40	1.00
364 Colby Miller RC	.40	1.00
365 Shawn Camp RC	.40	1.00
366 Jake Woods RC	.40	1.00
367 George Sherrill RC	.40	1.00
368 Justin Huisman RC	.40	1.00
369 Jimmy Serrano RC	.40	1.00
370 Mike Johnston RC	.40	1.00
371 Ryan Meaux RC	.40	1.00
372 Scott Dohmann RC	.40	1.00
373 Brad Halsey RC	.40	1.00
374 Joey Gathright RC	.40	1.00
375 Yadier Molina RC	30.00	80.00
376 Travis Blackley RC	.40	1.00
377 Steve Andrade RC	.40	1.00
378 Phil Stockman RC	.40	1.00
379 Roman Colon RC	.40	1.00
380 Jesse Crain RC	.60	1.50
381 Edwardo Sierra RC	.40	1.00
382 Justin Germano RC	.40	1.00
383 Kaz Matsui L13 RC	4.00	10.00
384 Shingo Takatsu L13 RC	2.50	6.00
385 John Gall L13 RC	2.50	6.00
386 Chris Saenz L13 RC	2.50	6.00
387 Merkin Valdez L13 RC	2.50	6.00
388 Jamie Brown L13 RC	2.50	6.00
389 Jason Bartlett L13 RC	8.00	20.00
390 David Aardsma L13 RC	2.50	6.00
391 Scott Kazmir L13 RC	12.00	30.00
392 David Wright L13	5.00	12.00
393 Dioner Navarro L13 RC	4.00	10.00
394 B.J. Upton L13	4.00	10.00
395 Gavin Floyd L13	2.50	6.00

2004 Ultra Gold Medallion

*GOLD 1-200: 1.25X TO 3X BASIC
1-200 SERIES 1 ODDS 1:1
*GOLD 201-220: 1X TO 2.5X BASIC
201-220 SERIES 1 ODDS 1:8
*GOLD 221-295: .75X TO 2X BASIC
221-295 SERIES 2 ODDS 1:1 H, 1:3 R
*GOLD 296-382: 1X TO 2.5X BASIC
*GOLD 383-395: .15X TO .4X BASIC
296-395 SERIES 2 ODDS 1:4 H, 1:12 R

2004 Ultra Platinum Medallion

*PLATINUM 1-200: 8X TO 20X BASIC
*PLATINUM 201-220: 2.5X TO 6X BASIC
1-220 SERIES 1 ODDS 1:36
1-220 PRINT RUN 66 SERIAL #'d SETS
*PLATINUM 221-295: 5X TO 12X BASIC
*PLATINUM 296-382: 2.5X TO 6X BASIC
221-382 PRINT RUN 100 SERIAL #'d SETS
383-395 PRINT RUN 13 SERIAL #'d SETS
383-395 NO PRICING DUE TO SCARCITY
221-395 SER.2 ODDS 1:12 HOB, 1:145 RET
CARDS KNOWN TO EXIST W/O SER.#

2004 Ultra Season Crowns Autograph

STATED PRINT RUN 150 SERIAL #'d SETS
GOLD PRINT RUN 25 SERIAL #'d SETS
NO GOLD PRICING DUE TO SCARCITY
SERIES 1 AUTO PARALLEL ODDS 1:192
EXCHANGE DEADLINE INDEFINITE

35 Corey Patterson	5.00	12.00
58 Dontrelle Willis	12.50	30.00
70 Hank Blalock	8.00	20.00
79 Scott Rolen	12.50	30.00
84 Austin Kearns	5.00	12.00
88 Carlos Pena	5.00	12.00
100 Bo Hart	5.00	12.00
112 Rocco Baldelli	8.00	20.00
141 Aubrey Huff	8.00	20.00
151 Mike Lowell	8.00	20.00
164 Brandon Webb	5.00	12.00
171 Chipper Jones	30.00	60.00
196 Jose Reyes	8.00	20.00
198 Miguel Tejada	5.00	12.00

2004 Ultra Season Crowns Game Used

STATED PRINT RUN 399 SERIAL #'d SETS
*GOLD: .5X TO 1.2X BASIC
GOLD PRINT RUN 99 SERIAL #'d SETS
*PLATINUM: .75X TO 2X BASIC
PLATINUM PRINT RUN 25 SERIAL #'d SETS
SERIES 1 GU PARALLEL ODDS 1:24

10 Andruw Jones Bat	4.00	10.00
12 Pedro Martinez Jsy	4.00	10.00
14 Angel Berroa Jsy	3.00	8.00
19 Frank Thomas Jsy	4.00	10.00
22 Roberto Alomar Bat	4.00	10.00
27 Jason Giambi Jsy	3.00	8.00
28 Jim Thome Jsy	4.00	10.00
29 Vladimir Guerrero Jsy	4.00	10.00
30 Tim Hudson Jsy	3.00	8.00
40 Ichiro Suzuki Base	10.00	25.00
50 Torii Hunter Bat	3.00	8.00
53 Sean Casey Bat	3.00	8.00
55 Alex Rodriguez Jsy	6.00	15.00
56 Gary Sheffield Bat	3.00	8.00
58 Dontrelle Willis Jsy	4.00	10.00
68 Hideki Matsui Base	10.00	25.00
70 Hank Blalock Bat	3.00	8.00
71 Albert Pujols Jsy	8.00	20.00
79 Scott Rolen Bat	4.00	10.00
84 Austin Kearns Bat	3.00	8.00
88 Carlos Pena Bat	3.00	8.00
89 Manny Ramirez Jsy	4.00	10.00
94 Jeff Bagwell Pants	4.00	10.00
95 Barry Bonds Base	8.00	20.00
99 Troy Glaus Jsy	3.00	8.00
102 Jason Kendall Jsy	3.00	8.00
109 Alfonso Soriano Bat	3.00	8.00
110 Omar Vizquel Jsy	4.00	10.00
112 Rocco Baldelli Jsy	3.00	8.00
115 Carlos Delgado Jsy	3.00	8.00
116 Shawn Green Jsy	3.00	8.00
118 Tom Glavine Bat	4.00	10.00
120 Derek Jeter Jsy	10.00	25.00
124 Hideo Nomo Jsy	4.00	10.00
128 Sammy Sosa Jsy	4.00	10.00
137 Randy Johnson Jsy	4.00	10.00
142 Mike Piazza Bat	6.00	15.00
144 Kazuhiro Sasaki Jsy	3.00	8.00
146 Larry Walker Jsy	3.00	8.00
151 Adam Dunn Bat	3.00	8.00
154 Todd Helton Jsy	4.00	10.00
164 Brandon Webb Jsy	3.00	8.00
166 Carlos Beltran Jsy	3.00	8.00
167 Sean Burroughs Jsy	3.00	8.00
171 Chipper Jones Jsy	4.00	10.00
184 Lance Berkman Bat	3.00	8.00
186 Roger Clemens Jsy	6.00	15.00
192 Greg Maddux Jsy	6.00	15.00
193 Mark Mulder Jsy	3.00	8.00
196 Jose Reyes Jsy	3.00	8.00

2004 Ultra Diamond Producers

SERIES 1 STATED ODDS 1:144

1 Greg Maddux	8.00	20.00
2 Dontrelle Willis	2.50	6.00
3 Jim Thome	4.00	10.00
4 Alfonso Soriano	4.00	10.00
5 Alex Rodriguez	8.00	20.00
6 Sammy Sosa	6.00	15.00
7 Nomar Garciaparra	4.00	10.00
8 Derek Jeter	15.00	40.00
9 Adam Dunn	4.00	10.00
10 Mark Prior	4.00	10.00

2004 Ultra Diamond Producers Game Used

SERIES 1 GU INSERT ODDS 1:12
STATED PRINT RUN 1000 SERIAL #'d SETS

1 Greg Maddux Jsy	4.00	10.00
2 Dontrelle Willis Jsy	4.00	10.00
3 Jim Thome Jsy	4.00	10.00
4 Alfonso Soriano Bat	3.00	8.00
5 Alex Rodriguez Jsy	6.00	15.00
6 Sammy Sosa Jsy	4.00	10.00
7 Nomar Garciaparra Jsy	6.00	15.00
8 Derek Jeter Jsy	10.00	25.00
9 Adam Dunn Bat	3.00	8.00
10 Mark Prior Jsy	4.00	10.00

2004 Ultra Hitting Machines

SERIES 2 ODDS 1:12 HOBBY, 1:24 RETAIL
*DIE CUT: .75X TO 2X BASIC
DC RANDOM IN SER.2 VINTAGE/MVP

1 Albert Pujols	1.25	3.00
2 Ken Griffey Jr.	2.00	5.00
3 Vladimir Guerrero	.60	1.50
4 Mike Piazza	1.00	2.50
5 Ichiro Suzuki	1.25	3.00
6 Miguel Cabrera	1.00	2.50
7 Hideki Matsui	1.50	4.00
8 Nomar Garciaparra	.60	1.50
9 Derek Jeter	2.50	6.00
10 Chipper Jones	1.00	2.50

2004 Ultra Hitting Machines Jersey Silver

*GOLD: 1.25X TO 3X SILVER
GOLD PRINT RUN 50 SERIAL #'d SETS
PLATINUM PRINT RUN 10 SERIAL #'d SETS
NO PLATINUM PRICING DUE TO SCARCITY
SER.2 OVERALL GU ODDS 1:6 H, 1:48 R

AD Adam Dunn	2.00	5.00
AP Albert Pujols	6.00	15.00
CJ Chipper Jones	3.00	8.00
FT Frank Thomas	3.00	8.00
HM Hideki Matsui	8.00	20.00
JB Jeff Bagwell	3.00	8.00
MC Miguel Cabrera	3.00	8.00
MP Mike Piazza	4.00	10.00
TH Todd Helton	3.00	8.00
VG Vladimir Guerrero	3.00	8.00

2004 Ultra HR Kings

SERIES 1 HR/K/RBI KING ODDS 1:12
*GOLD: 2X TO 5X BASIC
GOLD SER.1 HR/K/RBI KING ODDS 1:350
GOLD PRINT RUN 50 SERIAL #'d SETS

1 Barry Bonds	1.50	4.00
2 Albert Pujols	1.25	3.00
3 Jason Giambi	.40	1.00
4 Jeff Bagwell	.60	1.50
5 Ken Griffey Jr.	2.00	5.00
6 Alex Rodriguez	1.25	3.00
7 Sammy Sosa	1.00	2.50
8 Alfonso Soriano	.60	1.50
9 Chipper Jones	1.00	2.50
10 Mike Piazza	1.00	2.50

2004 Ultra K Kings

SERIES 1 HR/K/RBI KING ODDS 1:12
*GOLD: 2X TO 5X BASIC
GOLD SER.1 HR/K/RBI KING ODDS 1:350
GOLD PRINT RUN 50 SERIAL #'d SETS

1 Randy Johnson	1.00	2.50
2 Pedro Martinez	.60	1.50
3 Curt Schilling	.60	1.50
4 Roger Clemens	1.25	3.00
5 Mike Mussina	.60	1.50
6 Roy Halladay	.60	1.50
7 Kerry Wood	.40	1.00
8 Dontrelle Willis	.40	1.00
9 Greg Maddux	1.25	3.00
10 Mark Prior	.60	1.50

2004 Ultra Legendary 13 Dual Game Used Autograph Platinum
STATED PRINT RUN 3 SERIAL #'d SETS
MASTERPIECE PRINT RUN 1 #'d SET
SER.2 OVERALL LGD 13 ODDS 1:192 HOBBY
NO PRICING DUE TO SCARCITY

2004 Ultra Legendary 13 Single Game Used Gold
PRINT RUNS B/WN 5-72 COPIES PER
NO PRICING ON QTY OF 9 OR LESS
MASTERPIECE PRINT RUN 1 #'d SET
NO M'PIECE PRICING DUE TO SCARCITY
SER.2 OVERALL LGD 13 ODDS 1:192 HOBBY
CF Carlton Fisk Jsy/72 6.00 15.00
DM Don Mattingly Patch/23 40.00 80.00
MP Mark Prior Patch/22 10.00 25.00
MS Mike Schmidt Patch/20 50.00 100.00
NR Nolan Ryan Jsy/34 15.00 40.00
RC Roger Clemens Patch/22 20.00 50.00

2004 Ultra Legendary 13 Single Game Used Autograph Platinum
STATED PRINT RUN 5 SERIAL #'d SETS
MASTERPIECE PRINT RUN 1 #'d SET
SER.2 OVERALL LGD 13 ODDS 1:192 HOBBY
NO PRICING DUE TO SCARCITY

2004 Ultra Performers
COMPLETE SET (15) 10.00 25.00
SERIES 1 STATED ODDS 1:6
1 Ichiro Suzuki 1.25 3.00
2 Albert Pujols 1.25 3.00
3 Barry Bonds 1.50 4.00
4 Hideki Matsui 1.50 4.00
5 Randy Johnson 1.00 2.50
6 Jason Giambi .40 1.00
7 Pedro Martinez .60 1.50
8 Hank Blalock .40 1.00
9 Chipper Jones 1.00 2.50
10 Mike Piazza 1.00 2.50
11 Derek Jeter 2.50 6.00
12 Vladimir Guerrero .60 1.50
13 Barry Zito .60 1.50
14 Rocco Baldelli .40 1.00
15 Hideo Nomo 1.00 2.50

2004 Ultra Performers Game Used
SERIES 1 GU INSERT ODDS 1:12
STATED PRINT RUN 500 SERIAL #'d SETS
1 Albert Pujols Jsy 8.00 20.00
2 Barry Bonds Base 8.00 20.00
3 Randy Johnson Jsy 4.00 10.00
4 Jason Giambi Jsy 3.00 8.00
5 Pedro Martinez Jsy 4.00 10.00
6 Hank Blalock Bat 3.00 8.00
7 Chipper Jones Jsy 4.00 10.00
8 Mike Piazza Bat 4.00 10.00
9 Derek Jeter Jsy 10.00 25.00
10 Vladimir Guerrero Jsy 4.00 10.00
11 Rocco Baldelli Jsy 3.00 8.00
12 Hideo Nomo Jsy 4.00 10.00

2004 Ultra Performers Game Used UltraSwatch
SERIES 1 GU INSERT ODDS 1:12
PRINT RUNS B/WN 2-51 COPIES PER
NO PRICING DUE TO SCARCITY

2004 Ultra RBI Kings
OVERALL HR/K/RBI KING ODDS 1:12
*GOLD: 2X TO 5X BASIC
GOLD SER.1 HR/K/RBI KING ODDS 1:350
GOLD PRINT RUN 50 SERIAL #'d SETS
1 Hideki Matsui 1.50 4.00
2 Albert Pujols 1.25 3.00
3 Todd Helton .60 1.50
4 Jim Thome .60 1.50
5 Carlos Delgado .40 1.00
6 Alex Rodriguez 1.25 3.00
7 Barry Bonds 1.50 4.00
8 Manny Ramirez 1.00 2.50
9 Vladimir Guerrero .60 1.50
10 Nomar Garciaparra .60 1.50

2004 Ultra Turn Back the Clock
SERIES 2 ODDS 1:6 HOBBY, 1:12 RETAIL
1 Roger Clemens Sox 1.25 3.00
2 Alex Rodriguez Rgr 1.25 3.00
3 Randy Johnson M's 1.00 2.50
4 Pedro Martinez Expos .60 1.50
5 Alfonso Soriano Yanks .60 1.50
6 Curt Schilling Phils .60 1.50
7 Miguel Tejada A's .60 1.50
8 Scott Rolen Phils .60 1.50
9 Jim Thome Indians .60 1.50
10 Manny Ramirez Indians 1.00 2.50
11 Vladimir Guerrero Expos .60 1.50
12 Tom Glavine Braves .60 1.50
13 Andy Pettitte Yanks .60 1.50
14 Ivan Rodriguez Marlins .60 1.50
15 Jason Giambi A's .40 1.00
16 Rafael Palmeiro Rgr .60 1.50
17 Greg Maddux Braves 1.25 3.00
18 Hideo Nomo Sox 1.00 2.50
19 Mike Mussina O's .60 1.50
20 Sammy Sosa Sox 1.00 2.50

2004 Ultra Turn Back the Clock Jersey Copper
STATED PRINT RUN 399 SERIAL #'d SETS
*GOLD: .6X TO 1.5X COPPER
GOLD PRINT RUN 99 SERIAL #'d SETS
*SILVER: .5X TO 1.2X COPPER
SILVER PRINT RUN 199 SERIAL #'d SETS
*PATCH PLAT: 1.5X TO 4X COPPER
PATCH PLATINUM PRINT RUN 29 #'d SETS
SER.2 OVERALL GU ODDS 1:6 H, 1:48 R
AP Andy Pettitte Yanks 4.00 10.00
AR Alex Rodriguez Rgr 5.00 12.00
AS Alfonso Soriano Yanks 3.00 8.00
CS Curt Schilling Phils 3.00 8.00
GM Greg Maddux Braves 5.00 12.00
HM Hideo Nomo Sox 4.00 10.00
IR Ivan Rodriguez Marlins 4.00 10.00
JG Jason Giambi A's 3.00 8.00
JT Jim Thome Indians 4.00 10.00
MM Mike Mussina O's 4.00 10.00
MR Manny Ramirez Indians 4.00 10.00
MT Miguel Tejada A's 3.00 8.00
PR Pedro Martinez Expos 4.00 10.00
RC Roger Clemens Sox 5.00 12.00
RJ Randy Johnson M's 4.00 10.00
RP Rafael Palmeiro Rgr 4.00 10.00
SR Scott Rolen Phils 4.00 10.00
SS Sammy Sosa Sox 4.00 10.00
TG Tom Glavine Braves 4.00 10.00
VG Vladimir Guerrero Expos 4.00 10.00

2005 Ultra
COMPLETE SET (220) 12.00 30.00
COMP.SET w/o SP's (200) 5.00 12.00
COMMON CARD (1-200) .10 .30
COMMON CARD (201-220) .40 1.00
201-220 ODDS 1:4 HOBBY, 1:5 RETAIL
1 Andy Pettitte .20 .50
2 Jose Cruz Jr. .12 .30
3 Cliff Floyd .12 .30
4 Paul Konerko .20 .50
5 Joe Mauer .25 .60
6 Scott Spiezio .12 .30
7 Ben Sheets .12 .30
8 Kerry Wood .12 .30
9 Carl Pavano .12 .30
10 Matt Morris .12 .30
11 Kaz Matsui .12 .30
12 Ivan Rodriguez .20 .50
13 Victor Martinez .20 .50
14 Justin Morneau .20 .50
15 Adam Everett .12 .30
16 Carl Crawford .20 .50
17 David Ortiz .30 .75
18 Jason Giambi .12 .30
19 Derrek Lee .12 .30
20 Magglio Ordonez .20 .50
21 Bobby Abreu .12 .30
22 Milton Bradley .12 .30
23 Jeff Bagwell .20 .50
24 Jim Edmonds .20 .50
25 Garret Anderson .12 .30
26 Jacque Jones .12 .30
27 Ted Lilly .12 .30
28 Greg Maddux .40 1.00
29 Jermaine Dye .12 .30
30 Bill Mueller .12 .30
31 Roy Oswalt .20 .50
32 Tony Womack .12 .30
33 Andruw Jones .12 .30
34 Tom Glavine .20 .50
35 Mariano Rivera .40 1.00
36 Sean Casey .12 .30
37 Edgardo Alfonzo .12 .30
38 Brad Penny .12 .30
39 Johan Santana .20 .50
40 Mark Teixeira .20 .50
41 Manny Ramirez .30 .75
42 Gary Sheffield .12 .30
43 Matt Lawton .12 .30
44 Troy Percival .12 .30
45 Rocco Baldelli .12 .30
46 Doug Mientkiewicz .12 .30
47 Corey Patterson .12 .30
48 Austin Kearns .12 .30
49 Edgar Martinez .20 .50
50 Brad Radke .12 .30
51 Barry Larkin .20 .50
52 Chone Figgins .12 .30
53 Alexis Rios .12 .30
54 Alex Rodriguez .40 1.00
55 Vinny Castilla .12 .30
56 Javier Vazquez .12 .30
57 Javy Lopez .12 .30
58 Mike Cameron .12 .30
59 Brian Giles .12 .30
60 Dontrelle Willis .12 .30
61 Rafael Furcal .12 .30
62 Trot Nixon .12 .30
63 Mark Mulder .12 .30
64 Josh Beckett .12 .30
65 J.D. Drew .12 .30
66 Brandon Webb .20 .50
67 Wade Miller .12 .30
68 Lyle Overbay .12 .30
69 Pedro Martinez .20 .50
70 Rich Harden .12 .30
71 Al Leiter .12 .30
72 Adam Eaton .12 .30
73 Mike Sweeney .12 .30
74 Steve Finley .12 .30
75 Kris Benson .12 .30
76 Jim Thome .20 .50
77 Juan Pierre .12 .30
78 Bartolo Colon .12 .30
79 Carlos Delgado .12 .30
80 Jack Wilson .12 .30
81 Ken Harvey .12 .30
82 Nomar Garciaparra .20 .50
83 Paul Lo Duca .12 .30
84 Cesar Izturis .12 .30
85 Adrian Beltre .30 .75
86 Brian Roberts .12 .30
87 David Eckstein .12 .30
88 Jimmy Rollins .20 .50
89 Roger Clemens .40 1.00
90 Randy Johnson .30 .75
91 Orlando Hudson .12 .30
92 Tim Hudson .20 .50
93 Dmitri Young .12 .30
94 Chipper Jones .30 .75
95 John Smoltz .30 .75
96 Billy Wagner .12 .30
97 Hideo Nomo .30 .75
98 Sammy Sosa .30 .75
99 Darin Erstad .12 .30
100 Todd Helton .20 .50
101 Aubrey Huff .12 .30
102 Alfonso Soriano .20 .50
103 Jose Vidro .12 .30
104 Carlos Lee .12 .30
105 Corey Koskie .12 .30
106 Bret Boone .12 .30
107 Torii Hunter .12 .30
108 Aramis Ramirez .12 .30
109 Chase Utley .20 .50
110 Reggie Sanders .12 .30
111 Livan Hernandez .12 .30
112 Jeromy Burnitz .12 .30
113 Carlos Zambrano .20 .50
114 Hank Blalock .12 .30
115 Sidney Ponson .12 .30
116 Zack Greinke .40 1.00
117 Trevor Hoffman .20 .50
118 Jeff Kent .12 .30
119 Richie Sexson .12 .30
120 Melvin Mora .12 .30
121 Eric Chavez .12 .30
122 Miguel Cabrera .30 .75
123 Ryan Freel .12 .30
124 Russ Ortiz .12 .30
125 Craig Wilson .12 .30
126 Craig Biggio .20 .50
127 Curt Schilling .20 .50
128 Kaz Ishii .12 .30
129 Marquis Grissom .12 .30
130 Bernie Williams .20 .50
131 Travis Hafner .12 .30
132 Hee Seop Choi .12 .30
133 Scott Rolen .20 .50
134 Tony Batista .12 .30
135 Frank Thomas .30 .75
136 Jason Varitek .30 .75
137 Ichiro Suzuki .40 1.00
138 Junior Spivey .12 .30
139 Adam Dunn .20 .50
140 Jorge Posada .20 .50
141 Edgar Renteria .12 .30
142 Hideki Matsui .50 1.25
143 Carlos Guillen .12 .30
144 Jody Gerut .12 .30
145 Wily Mo Pena .12 .30
146 Derek Jeter .75 2.00
147 C.C. Sabathia .20 .50
148 Geoff Jenkins .12 .30
149 Albert Pujols .40 1.00
150 Eric Munson .12 .30
151 Moises Alou .12 .30
152 Jerry Hairston .12 .30
153 Ray Durham .12 .30
154 Mike Piazza .30 .75
155 Omar Vizquel .20 .50
156 A.J. Pierzynski .12 .30
157 Michael Young .12 .30
158 Jason Bay .12 .30
159 Mark Loretta .12 .30
160 Shawn Green .12 .30
161 Luis Gonzalez .12 .30
162 Johnny Damon .20 .50
163 Eric Milton .12 .30
164 Mike Lowell .12 .30
165 Jose Guillen .12 .30
166 Eric Hinske .12 .30
167 Jason Kendall .12 .30
168 Carlos Beltran .20 .50
169 Johnny Estrada .12 .30
170 Scott Hatteberg .12 .30
171 Laynce Nix .12 .30
172 Eric Gagne .12 .30
173 Richard Hidalgo .12 .30
174 Bobby Crosby .12 .30
175 Woody Williams .12 .30
176 Justin Leone .12 .30
177 Orlando Cabrera .12 .30
178 Mark Prior .20 .50
179 Jorge Julio .12 .30
180 Jamie Moyer .12 .30
181 Jose Reyes .20 .50
182 Ken Griffey Jr. .60 1.50
183 Mike Lieberthal .12 .30
184 Kenny Rogers .12 .30
185 Mike Mussina .20 .50
186 Preston Wilson .12 .30
187 Khalil Greene .12 .30
188 Angel Berroa .12 .30
189 Miguel Tejada .20 .50
190 Freddy Garcia .12 .30
191 Pat Burrell .12 .30
192 Luis Castillo .12 .30
193 Vladimir Guerrero .20 .50
194 Roy Halladay .20 .50
195 Barry Zito .20 .50
196 Lance Berkman .20 .50
197 Rafael Palmeiro .20 .50
198 Nate Robertson .12 .30
199 Jason Schmidt .12 .30
200 Scott Podsednik .12 .30
201 Casey Kotchman AR .40 1.00
202 Scott Kazmir AR 1.00 2.50
203 Bucky Jacobsen AR .40 1.00
204 Jeff Keppinger AR .40 1.00
205 Dave Bush AR .40 1.00
206 Gavin Floyd AR .40 1.00
207 David Wright AR .75 2.00
208 B.J. Upton AR .60 1.50
209 David Aardsma AR .40 1.00
210 Jason Bartlett AR .40 1.00
211 Dioner Navarro AR .40 1.00
212 Jason Kubel AR .40 1.00
213 Ryan Howard AR .75 2.00
214 Charles Thomas AR .40 1.00
215 Freddy Guzman AR .40 1.00
216 Brad Halsey AR .40 1.00
217 Joey Gathright AR .40 1.00
218 Jeff Francis AR .40 1.00
219 Terry Tiffee AR .40 1.00
220 Nick Swisher AR .60 1.50

2005 Ultra Gold Medallion
*GOLD 1-200: 1.25X TO 3X BASIC
*GOLD 201-220: .6X TO 1.5X BASIC
STATED ODDS 1:1 HOBBY, 1:3 RETAIL

2005 Ultra Platinum Medallion
*PLATINUM 1-200: 8X TO 20X BASIC
*PLATINUM 201-220: 2X TO 5X BASIC
RANDOM INSERTS IN HOBBY PACKS
STATED PRINT RUN 50 SERIAL #'d SETS

2005 Ultra Season Crown Autographs Copper
OVERALL SC AU ODDS 1:192 HOBBY
STATED PRINT RUN 199 SERIAL #'d SETS
UER'S #'d OF 199 BUT 22-199 PER MADE
ACTUAL UER QTY PROVIDED BY FLEER
31 Roy Oswalt/50 UER 10.00 25.00
80 Jack Wilson/199 8.00 20.00
125 Craig Wilson/130 UER 5.00 12.00
157 Michael Young/150 UER 8.00 20.00
200 Scott Podsednik/22 UER 20.00 50.00

2005 Ultra Season Crown Autographs Gold
OVERALL SC AU ODDS 1:192 HOBBY
STATED PRINT RUN 99 SERIAL #'d SETS
UER'S ARE #'d OF 99 BUT 13-99 PER MADE
ACTUAL UER QTY PROVIDED BY FLEER
NO PRICING ON QTY OF 13 OR LESS
31 Roy Oswalt/99 8.00 20.00
40 Mark Teixeira/25 UER 20.00 50.00
50 Brad Radke/89 UER 8.00 20.00
51 Barry Larkin/99 15.00 40.00
62 Trot Nixon/37 UER 10.00 25.00
70 Rich Harden/41 UER 10.00 25.00
80 Jack Wilson/99 8.00 20.00
88 Jimmy Rollins/45 UER 15.00 40.00
121 Eric Chavez/69 UER 8.00 20.00
125 Craig Wilson/99 5.00 12.00
157 Michael Young/99 8.00 20.00
200 Scott Podsednik/99 12.50 30.00
201 Casey Kotchman AR/21 UER 12.50 30.00

2005 Ultra Season Crown Autographs Masterpiece
OVERALL SC AU ODDS 1:192 HOBBY
STATED PRINT RUN 1 SERIAL #'d SET
NO PRICING DUE TO SCARCITY

2005 Ultra Season Crown Autographs Platinum
OVERALL SC AU ODDS 1:192 HOBBY
STATED PRINT RUN 50 SERIAL #'d SETS
UER'S ARE #'d OF 50 BUT 7-50 PER MADE
ACTUAL UER QTY PROVIDED BY FLEER
NO PRICING ON QTY OF 10 OR LESS
12 Ivan Rodriguez/25 UER 30.00 60.00
20 Magglio Ordonez/50 10.00 25.00
25 Garret Anderson/50 10.00 25.00
31 Roy Oswalt/50 10.00 25.00
35 Mariano Rivera/25 UER 30.00 60.00
40 Mark Teixeira/50 15.00 40.00
41 Manny Ramirez/25 UER 30.00 60.00
50 Brad Radke/50 10.00 25.00
51 Barry Larkin/50 20.00 50.00
62 Trot Nixon/50 10.00 25.00
65 J.D. Drew/19 UER 15.00 40.00
70 Rich Harden/50 10.00 25.00
80 Jack Wilson/50 10.00 25.00
87 David Eckstein/45 UER 20.00 50.00
88 Jimmy Rollins/50 15.00 40.00
94 Chipper Jones/19 UER 40.00 80.00
95 John Smoltz/23 UER 30.00 60.00
96 Billy Wagner/50 15.00 40.00
116 Zack Greinke/49 UER 12.50 30.00
121 Eric Chavez/50 10.00 25.00
125 Craig Wilson/50 6.00 15.00
130 Bernie Williams/15 UER 40.00 80.00
136 Jason Varitek/19 UER 40.00 80.00
157 Michael Young/50 10.00 25.00
161 Luis Gonzalez/50 10.00 25.00
185 Mike Mussina/50 15.00 40.00
195 Barry Zito/50 10.00 25.00
199 Jason Schmidt/50 10.00 25.00
200 Scott Podsednik/50 15.00 40.00
201 Casey Kotchman AR/50 10.00 25.00

2005 Ultra Season Crowns Game Used Copper
STATED PRINT RUN 399 SERIAL #'d SETS
*GOLD: .5X TO 1.2X COPPER
GOLD PRINT RUN 99 SERIAL #'d SETS
*PLATINUM: .75X TO 2X COPPER
*PLATINUM PATCH: ADD 100% PREMIUM
PLATINUM PRINT RUN 25 SERIAL #'d SETS
OVERALL SC GU 1:24 HOBBY
1 Andy Pettitte Jsy 4.00 10.00
3 Cliff Floyd Jsy 3.00 8.00
7 Ben Sheets Jsy 3.00 8.00
8 Kerry Wood Jsy 3.00 8.00
11 Kaz Matsui Bat 6.00 15.00
13 Victor Martinez Jsy 3.00 8.00
17 David Ortiz Jsy 4.00 10.00
20 Magglio Ordonez Bat 3.00 8.00
21 Bobby Abreu Bat 3.00 8.00
24 Jim Edmonds Jsy 3.00 8.00
31 Roy Oswalt Jsy 3.00 8.00
33 Andruw Jones Jsy 4.00 10.00
34 Tom Glavine Bat 4.00 10.00
36 Sean Casey Jsy 3.00 8.00
37 Edgardo Alfonzo Bat 3.00 8.00
41 Manny Ramirez Bat 4.00 10.00
42 Gary Sheffield Bat 3.00 8.00
45 Rocco Baldelli Jsy 3.00 8.00
48 Austin Kearns Jsy 3.00 8.00
49 Edgar Martinez Jsy 4.00 10.00
60 Dontrelle Willis Jsy 3.00 8.00
65 J.D. Drew Jsy 3.00 8.00
70 Rich Harden Jsy 3.00 8.00
71 Al Leiter Jsy 3.00 8.00
80 Jack Wilson Bat 3.00 8.00
93 Dmitri Young Bat 3.00 8.00
94 Chipper Jones Bat 4.00 10.00
97 Hideo Nomo Jsy 4.00 10.00
98 Sammy Sosa Bat 4.00 10.00
100 Todd Helton Bat 4.00 10.00
102 Alfonso Soriano Bat 3.00 8.00
107 Torii Hunter Jsy 3.00 8.00
114 Hank Blalock Bat 3.00 8.00
119 Richie Sexson Jsy 3.00 8.00
121 Eric Chavez Jsy 3.00 8.00
130 Bernie Williams Bat 4.00 10.00
135 Frank Thomas Bat 4.00 10.00
139 Adam Dunn Bat 3.00 8.00
142 Hideki Matsui Bat 10.00 25.00
144 Jody Gerut Bat 3.00 8.00
154 Mike Piazza Bat 4.00 10.00
158 Jason Bay Bat 3.00 8.00
162 Johnny Damon Jsy 4.00 10.00
168 Carlos Beltran Bat 3.00 8.00
173 Richard Hidalgo Jsy 3.00 8.00
181 Jose Reyes Bat 3.00 8.00
187 Khalil Greene Jsy 4.00 10.00
191 Pat Burrell Bat 3.00 8.00
193 Vladimir Guerrero Bat 4.00 10.00
197 Rafael Palmeiro Jsy 4.00 10.00

2005 Ultra 3 Kings Jersey Triple Swatch
OVERALL GU ODDS 1:12 HOB, 1:48 RET
PRINT RUN 33 SERIAL #'d SETS
BCB Bagwell/Clemens/Berk 20.00 50.00
BCR Beckett/Cabrera/I.Rod 15.00 40.00
JMM Randy/Maddux/Pedro 15.00 40.00
MPW Maddux/Prior/Wood 20.00 50.00
PDC Pujols/Dunn/Cabrera 20.00 50.00
RJB Rolen/Chipper/Beltre 15.00 40.00
SMP Shef/Hideki/Piazza 20.00 50.00
SMR Schilling/Pedro/Manny 30.00 60.00
TBS Teixeira/Blalock/Soriano 15.00 40.00
TBW Thome/Burrell/Wagner 15.00 40.00

2005 Ultra Follow the Leader
COMPLETE SET (15) 10.00 25.00
STATED ODDS 1:6 HOBBY, 1:8 RETAIL
*DIE CUT: .6X TO 1.5X BASIC
DIE CUT RANDOM IN EXCEL/MVP RETAIL
1 Roger Clemens 1.25 3.00
2 Albert Pujols 1.25 3.00
3 Sammy Sosa 1.00 2.50
4 Manny Ramirez 1.00 2.50
5 Vladimir Guerrero .60 1.50
6 Ivan Rodriguez .60 1.50
7 Mike Piazza 1.00 2.50
8 Scott Rolen .60 1.50
9 Ichiro Suzuki 1.25 3.00
10 Randy Johnson 1.00 2.50
11 Mark Prior .60 1.50
12 Jim Thome .60 1.50
13 Greg Maddux 1.25 3.00
14 Pedro Martinez .60 1.50
15 Miguel Cabrera 1.00 2.50

2005 Ultra Follow the Leader Jersey Copper
COPPER ISSUED ONLY IN HOBBY PACKS
*GOLD: .4X TO 1X COPPER
GOLD PRINT RUN 250 SERIAL #'d SETS
*PLATINUM: .5X TO 1.2X COPPER
*PLATINUM PATCH: ADD 100% PREMIUM
PLATINUM PRINT RUN 99 SERIAL #'d SETS
PLATINUM ISSUED ONLY IN HOBBY PACKS
*RED: .4X TO 1X COPPER
RED STATED ODDS 1:48 RETAIL
RED RANDOM IN HOBBY HOT PACKS
*ULTRA p/r 45-51: .75X TO 2X COPPER
*ULTRA p/r 21-31: 1X TO 2.5X COPPER
ULTRA PRINT RUNS B/WN 5-51 PER
NO ULTRA PRICING ON QTY OF 7 OR LESS
OVERALL GU ODDS 1:12 HOB, 1:48 RET
AP Albert Pujols 6.00 15.00
GM Greg Maddux 6.00 15.00
IR Ivan Rodriguez 4.00 10.00
JT Jim Thome 4.00 10.00
MC Miguel Cabrera 4.00 10.00
MPI Mike Piazza 4.00 10.00
MPR Mark Prior 4.00 10.00
MR Manny Ramirez 4.00 10.00
PM Pedro Martinez 4.00 10.00
RC Roger Clemens 6.00 15.00
RJ Randy Johnson 4.00 10.00
SR Scott Rolen 3.00 8.00
SS Sammy Sosa 4.00 10.00
VG Vladimir Guerrero 4.00 10.00

2005 Ultra Kings
OVERALL KINGS ODDS 1:12 HOB, 1:24 RET
K PERCEIVED 3X TOUGHER THAN HR-RBI
*GOLD: 2X TO 5X BASIC HR-RBI
*GOLD: 1.25X TO 3X BASIC K
GOLD RANDOM INSERTS IN HOBBY PACKS
GOLD PRINT RUN 50 SERIAL #'d SETS
H1 Jim Thome HR .60 1.50
H2 David Ortiz HR 1.00 2.50
H3 Adam Dunn HR .60 1.50
H4 Albert Pujols HR 1.25 3.00
H5 Manny Ramirez HR 1.00 2.50
H6 Vladimir Guerrero HR .60 1.50
H7 Miguel Tejada HR .60 1.50
H8 Rafael Palmeiro HR .60 1.50
H9 Mark Teixeira HR .60 1.50
H10 Sammy Sosa HR 1.00 2.50
H11 Frank Thomas HR 1.00 2.50
H12 Pat Burrell HR .40 1.00
H13 Adrian Beltre HR 1.00 2.50
H14 Miguel Cabrera HR 1.00 2.50
H15 Gary Sheffield HR .40 1.00
K1 Pedro Martinez K 1.00 2.50
K2 Randy Johnson K 1.50 4.00
K3 Mark Mulder K .60 1.50
K4 Barry Zito K 1.00 2.50
K5 Roger Clemens K 2.00 5.00
K6 Mark Prior K 1.00 2.50
K7 Ben Sheets K .60 1.50
K8 Curt Schilling K 1.00 2.50
K9 Billy Wagner K .60 1.50
K10 Eric Gagne K .60 1.50
K11 Josh Beckett K .60 1.50
K12 Kerry Wood K .60 1.50
K13 Jason Schmidt K .60 1.50
K14 Roy Halladay K 1.00 2.50
K15 Greg Maddux K 2.00 5.00
R1 Sean Casey RBI .40 1.00
R2 Ivan Rodriguez RBI .60 1.50
R3 Mike Piazza RBI 1.00 2.50
R4 Todd Helton RBI .60 1.50
R5 Scott Rolen RBI .60 1.50
R6 Hideki Matsui RBI 1.50 4.00
R7 Gary Sheffield RBI .40 1.00
R8 Alfonso Soriano RBI .60 1.50
R9 Bobby Abreu RBI .40 1.00
R10 Lance Berkman RBI .60 1.50
R11 Miguel Tejada RBI .60 1.50
R12 Travis Hafner RBI .40 1.00
R13 Hank Blalock RBI .40 1.00
R14 Jeff Bagwell RBI .60 1.50
R15 Chipper Jones RBI 1.00 2.50

2005 Ultra Kings Jersey Gold
STATED PRINT RUN 150 SERIAL #'d SETS
*ULTRA p/r 75: .5X TO 1.2X GOLD
*ULTRA p/r 38-55: .6X TO 1.5X GOLD
*ULTRA p/r 20-34: .75X TO 2X GOLD
*ULTRA p/r 15-17: 1X TO 2.5X GOLD
ULTRA PRINT RUN B/WN 5-75 #'d PER
NO ULTRA PRICING ON QTY 13 OR LESS
*PLATINUM: .6X TO 1.5X COPPER
*PLATINUM PATCH: ADD 100% PREMIUM
PLATINUM PRINT RUN 25 SERIAL #'d SETS
PLATINUM ISSUED ONLY IN HOBBY PACKS
OVERALL GU ODDS 1:12 HOB, 1:48 RET
AB Adrian Beltre HR 4.00 10.00
AD Adam Dunn HR 4.00 10.00
AP Albert Pujols HR 8.00 20.00
AS Alfonso Soriano RBI 4.00 10.00
BA Bobby Abreu RBI 4.00 10.00
BS Ben Sheets K 4.00 10.00
BW Billy Wagner K 4.00 10.00
BZ Barry Zito K 4.00 10.00
CJ Chipper Jones RBI 5.00 12.00
CS Curt Schilling K 5.00 12.00
DO David Ortiz HR 5.00 12.00
EG Eric Gagne K 4.00 10.00
FT Frank Thomas HR 5.00 12.00
GM Greg Maddux K 8.00 20.00
GSH Gary Sheffield HR 4.00 10.00
GSR Gary Sheffield RBI 4.00 10.00
HB Hank Blalock RBI 4.00 10.00
HM Hideki Matsui RBI 12.50 30.00
IR Ivan Rodriguez RBI 5.00 12.00
JBA Jeff Bagwell RBI 5.00 12.00
JBE Josh Beckett K 4.00 10.00
JS Jason Schmidt K 4.00 10.00
JT Jim Thome HR 5.00 12.00
KW Kerry Wood K 4.00 10.00
LB Lance Berkman RBI 4.00 10.00
MC Miguel Cabrera HR 5.00 12.00
MM Mark Mulder K 4.00 10.00
MPI Mike Piazza RBI 5.00 12.00
MPR Mark Prior K 5.00 12.00
MR Manny Ramirez HR 5.00 12.00
MTH Miguel Tejada HR 4.00 10.00
MTR Miguel Tejada RBI 4.00 10.00
MTX Mark Teixeira HR 5.00 12.00
PB Pat Burrell HR 4.00 10.00
PM Pedro Martinez K 5.00 12.00
RC Roger Clemens K 8.00 20.00
RH Roy Halladay K 4.00 10.00
RJ Randy Johnson K 5.00 12.00
RP Rafael Palmeiro HR 5.00 12.00
SC Sean Casey RBI 4.00 10.00
SR Scott Rolen RBI 5.00 12.00
SS Sammy Sosa HR 5.00 12.00
THA Travis Hafner RBI 4.00 10.00
THE Todd Helton RBI 5.00 12.00
VG Vladimir Guerrero HR 5.00 12.00

2006 Ultra
COMP.SET w/o RL13 (200) 15.00 40.00
COMMON CARD (1-180) .15 .40
RL13 201-250 ODDS 1:4 HOBBY, 1:4 RETAIL
251 PRINT RUN 5000 CARDS
251 JOHJIMA IS NOT SERIAL NUMBERED
251 PRINT RUN INFO PROVIDED BY UD
251 JOHJIMA EXCH. DEADLINE 05/25/08
1 Vladimir Guerrero .25 .60
2 Bartolo Colon .15 .40
3 Francisco Rodriguez .25 .60
4 Darin Erstad .15 .40
5 Chone Figgins .15 .40
6 Bengie Molina .15 .40
7 Roger Clemens .50 1.25
8 Lance Berkman .25 .60
9 Morgan Ensberg .15 .40
10 Roy Oswalt .25 .60
11 Andy Pettitte .25 .60
12 Craig Biggio .25 .60
13 Eric Chavez .15 .40
14 Barry Zito .25 .60
15 Huston Street .15 .40
16 Bobby Crosby .15 .40
17 Nick Swisher .25 .60
18 Rich Harden .15 .40
19 Vernon Wells .15 .40
20 Roy Halladay .25 .60
21 Alex Rios .15 .40
22 Orlando Hudson .15 .40
23 Shea Hillenbrand .15 .40
24 Gustavo Chacin .15 .40
25 Chipper Jones .40 1.00
26 Andruw Jones .15 .40
27 Jeff Francoeur .40 1.00
28 John Smoltz .40 1.00
29 Tim Hudson .25 .60
30 Marcus Giles .15 .40
31 Carlos Lee .15 .40
32 Ben Sheets .15 .40
33 Rickie Weeks .15 .40
34 Chris Capuano .15 .40
35 Geoff Jenkins .15 .40
36 Brady Clark .15 .40
37 Albert Pujols .50 1.25
38 Jim Edmonds .25 .60
39 Chris Carpenter .25 .60
40 Mark Mulder .15 .40
41 Yadier Molina .50 1.25
42 Scott Rolen .25 .60
43 Derrek Lee .15 .40
44 Mark Prior .25 .60
45 Aramis Ramirez .15 .40
46 Carlos Zambrano .25 .60
47 Greg Maddux .50 1.25
48 Nomar Garciaparra .25 .60
49 Jonny Gomes .15 .40
50 Carl Crawford .25 .60
51 Scott Kazmir .25 .60
52 Jorge Cantu .15 .40
53 Julio Lugo .15 .40
54 Aubrey Huff .15 .40
55 Luis Gonzalez .15 .40
56 Brandon Webb .25 .60
57 Troy Glaus .15 .40
58 Shawn Green .15 .40
59 Craig Counsell .15 .40
60 Conor Jackson (RC) .60 1.50
61 Jeff Kent .15 .40
62 Eric Gagne .15 .40
63 J.D. Drew .15 .40
64 Milton Bradley .15 .40
65 Jeff Weaver .15 .40
66 Cesar Izturis .15 .40
67 Jason Schmidt .15 .40
68 Moises Alou .15 .40
69 Pedro Feliz .15 .40
70 Randy Winn .15 .40
71 Omar Vizquel .25 .60
72 Noah Lowry .15 .40
73 Travis Hafner .15 .40
74 Victor Martinez .25 .60
75 C.C. Sabathia .25 .60
76 Grady Sizemore .25 .60
77 Coco Crisp .15 .40
78 Cliff Lee .25 .60
79 Raul Ibañez .25 .60
80 Ichiro Suzuki .50 1.25
81 Richie Sexson .15 .40
82 Felix Hernandez .25 .60
83 Adrian Beltre .40 1.00
84 Jamie Moyer .15 .40
85 Miguel Cabrera .40 1.00
86 A.J. Burnett .15 .40
87 Juan Pierre .15 .40
88 Carlos Delgado .15 .40
89 Dontrelle Willis .15 .40
90 Juan Encarnacion .15 .40
91 Carlos Beltran .25 .60
92 Jose Reyes .25 .60
93 David Wright .30 .75
94 Tom Glavine .25 .60
95 Mike Piazza .40 1.00
96 Pedro Martinez .25 .60
97 Ryan Zimmerman (RC) 1.25 3.00
98 Nick Johnson .15 .40
99 Jose Vidro .15 .40
100 Jose Guillen .15 .40
101 Livan Hernandez .15 .40
102 John Patterson .15 .40
103 Miguel Tejada .25 .60
104 Melvin Mora .15 .40
105 Brian Roberts .15 .40
106 Erik Bedard .15 .40
107 Javy Lopez .15 .40
108 Rodrigo Lopez .15 .40
109 Jake Peavy .15 .40
110 Mike Cameron .15 .40
111 Mark Loretta .15 .40
112 Brian Giles .15 .40
113 Trevor Hoffman .25 .60
114 Ramon Hernandez .15 .40
115 Bobby Abreu .15 .40
116 Chase Utley .25 .60
117 Pat Burrell .15 .40
118 Jimmy Rollins .25 .60
119 Ryan Howard .30 .75
120 Billy Wagner .15 .40
121 Jason Bay .15 .40
122 Oliver Perez .15 .40
123 Jack Wilson .15 .40
124 Zach Duke .15 .40
125 Rob Mackowiak .15 .40
126 Freddy Sanchez .15 .40
127 Mark Teixeira .25 .60
128 Michael Young .15 .40
129 Alfonso Soriano .25 .60
130 Hank Blalock .15 .40
131 Kenny Rogers .15 .40
132 Kevin Mench .15 .40
133 Manny Ramirez .40 1.00
134 Josh Beckett .15 .40
135 David Ortiz .40 1.00
136 Johnny Damon .25 .60
137 Edgar Renteria .15 .40
138 Curt Schilling .25 .60
139 Ken Griffey Jr. .75 2.00
140 Adam Dunn .25 .60
141 Felipe Lopez .15 .40
142 Wily Mo Pena .15 .40
143 Aaron Harang .15 .40
144 Sean Casey .15 .40
145 Todd Helton .25 .60
146 Garrett Atkins .15 .40
147 Matt Holliday .40 1.00
148 Jeff Francis .15 .40
149 Clint Barmes .15 .40
150 Luis Gonzalez .15 .40
151 Mike Sweeney .15 .40
152 Zack Greinke .40 1.00
153 Angel Berroa .15 .40
154 Emil Brown .15 .40
155 David DeJesus .15 .40
156 Ivan Rodriguez .25 .60
157 Jeremy Bonderman .15 .40
158 Brandon Inge .15 .40
159 Craig Monroe .15 .40
160 Chris Shelton .15 .40
161 Dmitri Young .15 .40
162 Johan Santana .25 .60
163 Joe Mauer .25 .60
164 Torii Hunter .15 .40
165 Shannon Stewart .15 .40
166 Scott Baker .15 .40
167 Brad Radke .15 .40
168 Jon Garland .15 .40
169 Tadahito Iguchi .15 .40
170 Paul Konerko .25 .60
171 Scott Podsednik .15 .40
172 Mark Buehrle .25 .60
173 Joe Crede .15 .40
174 Derek Jeter 1.00 2.50
175 Alex Rodriguez .50 1.25
176 Hideki Matsui .40 1.00
177 Randy Johnson .40 1.00
178 Gary Sheffield .15 .40
179 Mariano Rivera .50 1.25
180 Jason Giambi .15 .40
181 Joey Devine RC .40 1.00
182 Alejandro Freire RC .40 1.00
183 Craig Hansen RC .75 2.00
184 Robert Andino RC .40 1.00
185 Ryan Jorgensen RC .40 1.00
186 Chris Demaria RC .40 1.00
187 Jonah Bayliss RC .40 1.00
188 Ryan Theriot RC 1.00 2.50
189 Steve Stemle RC .40 1.00
190 Brian Myrow RC .40 1.00
191 Chris Heintz RC .40 1.00
192 Ron Flores RC .40 1.00
193 Danny Sandoval RC .40 1.00

194 Craig Breslow RC .40 1.00
195 Jeremy Accardo RC .40 1.00
196 Jeff Harris RC .40 1.00
197 Tim Corcoran RC .40 1.00
198 Scott Feldman RC .40 1.00
199 Robinson Cano .25 .60
200 Jason Bergmann RC .40 1.00
201 Ken Griffey Jr. RL13 4.00 10.00
202 Frank Thomas RL13 2.00 5.00
203 Chipper Jones RL13 2.00 5.00
204 Tony Clark RL13 .75 2.00
205 Mike Lieberthal RL13 .75 2.00
206 Manny Ramirez RL13 2.00 5.00
207 Phil Nevin RL13 .75 2.00
208 Derek Jeter RL13 5.00 12.00
209 Preston Wilson RL13 .75 2.00
210 Billy Wagner RL13 .75 2.00
211 Alex Rodriguez RL13 2.50 6.00
212 Trot Nixon RL13 .75 2.00
213 Jaret Wright RL13 .75 2.00
214 Nomar Garciaparra RL13 1.25 3.00
215 Paul Konerko RL13 1.25 3.00
216 Paul Wilson RL13 .75 2.00
217 Dustin Hermanson RL13 .75 2.00
218 Todd Walker RL13 .75 2.00
219 Matt Morris RL13 .75 2.00
220 Darin Erstad RL13 .75 2.00
221 Todd Helton RL13 1.25 3.00
222 Geoff Jenkins RL13 .75 2.00
223 Eric Chavez RL13 .75 2.00
224 Kris Benson RL13 .75 2.00
225 Jon Garland RL13 .75 2.00
226 Troy Glaus RL13 .75 2.00
227 Vernon Wells RL13 .75 2.00
228 Michael Cuddyer RL13 .75 2.00
229 Justin Verlander RL13 6.00 15.00
230 Pat Burrell RL13 .75 2.00
231 Mark Mulder RL13 .75 2.00
232 Corey Patterson RL13 .75 2.00
233 J.D. Drew RL13 .75 2.00
234 Austin Kearns RL13 .60 1.50
235 Felipe Lopez RL13 .75 2.00
236 Sean Burroughs RL13 .75 2.00
237 Ben Sheets RL13 .75 2.00
238 Brett Myers RL13 .75 2.00
239 Josh Beckett RL13 .75 2.00
240 Barry Zito RL13 1.25 3.00
241 Adrian Gonzalez RL13 1.50 4.00
242 Rocco Baldelli RL13 .75 2.00
243 Chris Burke RL13 .75 2.00
244 Joe Mauer RL13 1.25 3.00
245 Mark Prior RL13 1.25 3.00
246 Mark Teixiera RL13 1.25 3.00
247 Khalil Greene RL13 .75 2.00
248 Zack Greinke RL13 2.00 5.00
249 Prince Fielder RL13 4.00 10.00
250 Rickie Weeks RL13 .75 2.00
251 Kenji Johjima 4.00 10.00

2006 Ultra Gold Medallion

COMP.SET w/o RL13 (200) 60.00 120.00
*GOLD 1-180: 1X TO 2.5X BASIC
*GOLD 60/97/181-198/200: .6X TO 1.5X BASIC
GOLD 1-200 ODDS 1:1 HOBBY/RETAIL
*GOLD 201-250: .5X TO 1.2X BASIC
GOLD 201-250 ODDS 1:24 HOB, 1:72 RET

2006 Ultra Autographics

STATED ODDS 1:576 HOBBY, 1:1920 RETAIL
NO PRICING DUE TO SCARCITY

2006 Ultra Diamond Producers

COMPLETE SET (25) 10.00 25.00
OVERALL INSERT ODDS 1:1 HOBBY/RETAIL
DP1 Derek Jeter 2.50 6.00
DP2 Chipper Jones .75 2.00
DP3 Jim Edmonds .60 1.50
DP4 Ken Griffey Jr. 2.00 5.00
DP5 David Ortiz 1.00 2.50
DP6 Manny Ramirez 1.00 2.50
DP7 Mark Teixeira .60 1.50
DP8 Alex Rodriguez 1.25 3.00
DP9 Jeff Kent .40 1.00
DP10 Albert Pujols 1.25 3.00
DP11 Todd Helton .60 1.50
DP12 Miguel Cabrera 1.00 2.50
DP13 Hideki Matsui 1.00 2.50
DP14 Derrek Lee .40 1.00
DP15 Vladimir Guerrero .60 1.50
DP16 Miguel Tejada .60 1.50
DP17 Jorge Cantu .40 1.00
DP18 Travis Hafner .40 1.00
DP19 Pat Burrell .40 1.00
DP20 Bobby Abreu .40 1.00
DP21 David Wright .75 2.00
DP22 Jason Bay .40 1.00
DP23 Adam Dunn .60 1.50
DP24 Eric Chavez .40 1.00
DP25 Paul Konerko .60 1.50

2006 Ultra Feel the Game

STATED ODDS 1:36 HOBBY, 1:72 RETAIL
AB Adrian Beltre Jsy 3.00 8.00
AJ Andruw Jones Jsy 4.00 10.00
AP Albert Pujols Jsy 8.00 20.00
AS Alfonso Soriano Jsy 3.00 8.00
BA Bobby Abreu Jsy 3.00 8.00
BG Brian Giles Jsy 3.00 8.00
CB Carlos Beltran Jsy 3.00 8.00
CD Carlos Delgado Jsy 3.00 8.00
CJ Chipper Jones Jsy 4.00 10.00
DJ Derek Jeter Jsy 10.00 25.00
DW David Wright Jsy 4.00 10.00
EC Eric Chavez Jsy 3.00 8.00
FH Felix Hernandez Jsy 4.00 10.00
FT Frank Thomas Jsy SP 4.00 10.00
GM Greg Maddux Jsy 4.00 10.00
IR Ivan Rodriguez Jsy 4.00 10.00
JB Josh Beckett Jsy 3.00 8.00
JR Jose Reyes Jsy SP 3.00 8.00
KG Ken Griffey Jr. Jsy 8.00 20.00
MC Matt Clement Jsy SP 3.00 8.00
MO Maggio Ordonez Jsy 3.00 8.00
MP Mike Piazza Jsy 4.00 10.00
MR Manny Ramirez Jsy 4.00 10.00
MT Miguel Tejada Jsy 3.00 8.00
PW Preston Wilson Jsy 3.00 8.00
RJ Randy Johnson Pants SP 4.00 10.00
RS Richie Sexson Jsy 3.00 8.00
SG Shawn Green Jsy 3.00 8.00
TG Troy Glaus Jsy 3.00 8.00
VG Vladimir Guerrero Jsy 4.00 10.00

2006 Ultra Fine Fabrics

STATED ODDS 1:18 HOBBY, 1:36 RETAIL
AB Adrian Beltre Jsy 3.00 8.00
AD Adam Dunn Jsy 2.00 5.00
AJ Andruw Jones Jsy 1.25 3.00
AP Albert Pujols Jsy 4.00 10.00
AS Alfonso Soriano Jsy 2.00 5.00
BA Bobby Abreu Jsy 1.25 3.00
BC Bobby Crosby Jsy 1.25 3.00
BG Brian Giles Jsy 1.25 3.00
BR Brian Roberts Jsy 1.25 3.00
BW Bernie Williams Jsy 2.00 5.00
BZ Barry Zito Jsy 2.00 5.00
CB Carlos Beltran Jsy 2.00 5.00
CD Carlos Delgado Jsy 1.25 3.00
CJ Chipper Jones Jsy 3.00 8.00
CP Corey Patterson Jsy 1.25 3.00
CU Chase Utley Jsy 2.00 5.00
DJ Derek Jeter Jsy 8.00 20.00
DL Derrek Lee Jsy 1.25 3.00
DO David Ortiz Jsy 3.00 8.00
DW David Wright Jsy 2.50 6.00
EC Eric Chavez Jsy 1.25 3.00
FH Felix Hernandez Jsy 2.00 5.00
FT Frank Thomas Jsy 3.00 8.00
GM Greg Maddux Jsy 4.00 10.00
HB Hank Blalock Jsy 1.25 3.00
HS Huston Street Jsy 1.25 3.00
IR Ivan Rodriguez Jsy 2.00 5.00
JB Josh Beckett Jsy 1.25 3.00
JD J.D. Drew Jsy 1.25 3.00
JG Jason Giambi Jsy 1.25 3.00
JK Jeff Kent Jsy 1.25 3.00
JP Jorge Posada Jsy 2.00 5.00
JR Jose Reyes Jsy 2.00 5.00
JS John Smoltz Jsy 3.00 8.00
KG Ken Griffey Jr. Jsy 6.00 15.00
KH Khalil Greene Jsy SP 1.25 3.00
KW Kerry Wood Jsy 1.25 3.00
MC Matt Clement Jsy 1.25 3.00
MO Magglio Ordonez Jsy 2.00 5.00
MP Mike Piazza Jsy 3.00 8.00
MR Manny Ramirez Jsy 3.00 8.00
MT Miguel Tejada Jsy 2.00 5.00
PW Preston Wilson Jsy 1.25 3.00
RC Roger Clemens Jsy SP 4.00 10.00
RH Ramon Hernandez Jsy 1.25 3.00
RJ Randy Johnson Pants SP 3.00 8.00
RK Ryan Klesko Jsy 1.25 3.00
RS Richie Sexson Jsy 1.25 3.00
RY Ryan Howard Jsy 2.50 6.00
SB Sean Burroughs Jsy 1.25 3.00
SF Steve Finley Jsy 1.25 3.00
SG Shawn Green Jsy 1.25 3.00
SR Scott Rolen Jsy 2.00 5.00
SS Sammy Sosa Jsy 3.00 8.00
TG Troy Glaus Jsy 1.25 3.00
TH Travis Hafner Jsy 1.25 3.00
TX Mark Teixeira Jsy 2.00 5.00
VG Vladimir Guerrero Jsy 2.00 5.00
VW Vernon Wells Jsy 1.25 3.00
WI Dontrelle Willis Jsy 1.25 3.00

2006 Ultra Home Run Kings

COMPLETE SET (15) 8.00 20.00
OVERALL INSERT ODDS 1:1 HOBBY/RETAIL
HRK1 Albert Pujols 1.25 3.00
HRK2 Ken Griffey Jr. 2.00 5.00
HRK3 Andruw Jones .40 1.00
HRK4 Alex Rodriguez 1.25 3.00
HRK5 David Ortiz 1.00 2.50
HRK6 Manny Ramirez 1.00 2.50
HRK7 Derrek Lee .40 1.00
HRK8 Mark Teixeira .60 1.50
HRK9 Adam Dunn .60 1.50
HRK10 Paul Konerko .60 1.50
HRK11 Richie Sexson .40 1.00
HRK12 Alfonso Soriano .60 1.50
HRK13 Vladimir Guerrero .60 1.50
HRK14 Gary Sheffield .40 1.00
HRK15 Mike Piazza 1.00 2.50

2006 Ultra Midsummer Classic Kings

COMPLETE SET (10) 6.00 15.00
OVERALL INSERT ODDS 1:1 HOBBY/RETAIL
MCK1 Ken Griffey Jr. 2.00 5.00
MCK2 Mike Piazza 1.00 2.50
MCK3 Derek Jeter 2.50 6.00
MCK4 Roger Clemens 1.25 3.00
MCK5 Randy Johnson 1.00 2.50
MCK6 Miguel Tejada .60 1.50
MCK7 Alfonso Soriano .60 1.50
MCK8 Garret Anderson .40 1.00
MCK9 Pedro Martinez .60 1.50
MCK10 Ivan Rodriguez .60 1.50

2006 Ultra RBI Kings

COMPLETE SET (20) 8.00 20.00
OVERALL INSERT ODDS 1:1 HOBBY/RETAIL
RBI1 Ken Griffey Jr. 2.00 5.00
RBI2 David Ortiz 1.00 2.50
RBI3 Manny Ramirez 1.00 2.50
RBI4 Mark Teixeira .60 1.50
RBI5 Alex Rodriguez 1.25 3.00
RBI6 Andruw Jones .40 1.00
RBI7 Jeff Bagwell .60 1.50
RBI8 Gary Sheffield .40 1.00
RBI9 Richie Sexson .40 1.00
RBI10 Jeff Kent .40 1.00
RBI11 Albert Pujols 1.25 3.00
RBI12 Todd Helton .60 1.50
RBI13 Miguel Cabrera 1.00 2.50
RBI14 Hideki Matsui 1.00 2.50
RBI15 Carlos Delgado .40 1.00
RBI16 Carlos Lee .40 1.00
RBI17 Derrek Lee .40 1.00
RBI18 Vladimir Guerrero .60 1.50
RBI19 Luis Gonzalez .40 1.00
RBI20 Mike Piazza 1.00 2.50

2006 Ultra Rising Stars

COMPLETE SET (10) 6.00 15.00
OVERALL INSERT ODDS 1:1 HOBBY/RETAIL
URS1 Ryan Howard .75 2.00
URS2 Huston Street .40 1.00
URS3 Jeff Francoeur 1.00 2.50
URS4 Felix Hernandez .60 1.50
URS5 Chase Utley .60 1.50
URS6 Robinson Cano .60 1.50
URS7 Zach Duke .40 1.00
URS8 Scott Kazmir .60 1.50
URS9 Willy Taveras .40 1.00
URS10 Tadahito Iguchi .40 1.00

2006 Ultra Star

OVERALL ODDS 2:1 FAT PACKS
1 Ken Griffey Jr. 2.00 5.00
2 Derek Jeter 2.50 6.00
3 Albert Pujols 1.25 3.00
4 Alex Rodriguez 1.25 3.00
5 Vladimir Guerrero .60 1.50
6 Roger Clemens 1.25 3.00
7 Derrek Lee .40 1.00
8 David Ortiz 1.00 2.50
9 Miguel Cabrera 1.00 2.50
10 Bobby Abreu .40 1.00
11 Mark Teixeira .60 1.50
12 Johan Santana .60 1.50
13 Hideki Matsui 1.00 2.50
14 Ichiro Suzuki 1.25 3.00
15 Andruw Jones .40 1.00
16 Eric Chavez .40 1.00
17 Roy Oswalt .60 1.50
18 Curt Schilling .60 1.50
19 Randy Johnson 1.00 2.50
20 Ivan Rodriguez .60 1.50
21 Chipper Jones 1.00 2.50
22 Mark Prior .60 1.50
23 Jason Bay .40 1.00
24 Pedro Martinez .60 1.50
25 David Wright .75 2.00
26 Carlos Beltran .60 1.50
27 Jim Edmonds .60 1.50
28 Chris Carpenter .60 1.50
29 Roy Halladay .60 1.50
30 Jake Peavy .40 1.00
31 Paul Konerko .60 1.50
32 Travis Hafner .40 1.00
33 Barry Zito .60 1.50
34 Miguel Tejada .60 1.50
35 Josh Beckett .40 1.00
36 Todd Helton .60 1.50
37 Dontrelle Willis .40 1.00
38 Manny Ramirez 1.00 2.50
39 Mariano Rivera 1.25 3.00
40 Jeff Kent .40 1.00

2006 Ultra Strikeout Kings

COMPLETE SET (10) 6.00 15.00
OVERALL INSERT ODDS 1:1 HOBBY/RETAIL
SOK1 Roger Clemens 1.25 3.00
SOK2 Johan Santana .60 1.50
SOK3 Jake Peavy .40 1.00
SOK4 Randy Johnson 1.00 2.50
SOK5 Curt Schilling .60 1.50
SOK6 Chris Carpenter .60 1.50
SOK7 Pedro Martinez .60 1.50
SOK8 Mark Prior .60 1.50
SOK9 Carlos Zambrano .60 1.50
SOK10 John Smoltz 1.00 2.50

2007 Ultra

COMP.SET w/o RC's (200) 20.00 50.00
COMMON CARD .20 .50
COMMON ROOKIE .50 1.25
COMMON L13 .50 1.25
PRINTING PLATE ODDS 1:1252 HOB/RET
PLATE PRINT RUN 1 SET PER COLOR
BLACK-CYAN-MAGENTA-YELLOW ISSUED
NO PLATE PRICING DUE TO SCARCITY
1 Brandon Webb .30 .75
2 Randy Johnson .50 1.25
3 Conor Jackson .20 .50
4 Stephen Drew .20 .50
5 Eric Byrnes .20 .50
6 Carlos Quentin .20 .50
7 Andruw Jones .20 .50
8 Chipper Jones .50 1.25
9 Jeff Francoeur .50 1.25
10 Tim Hudson .30 .75
11 John Smoltz .50 1.25
12 Edgar Renteria .20 .50
13 Erik Bedard .20 .50
14 Kris Benson .20 .50
15 Miguel Tejada .30 .75
16 Nick Markakis .40 1.00
17 Brian Roberts .20 .50
18 Melvin Mora .20 .50
19 Aubrey Huff .20 .50
20 Curt Schilling .30 .75
21 Jonathan Papelbon .50 1.25
22 Josh Beckett .20 .50
23 Jason Varitek .50 1.25
24 David Ortiz .50 1.25
25 Manny Ramirez .50 1.25
26 J.D. Drew .20 .50
27 Carlos Zambrano .30 .75
28 Derrek Lee .20 .50
29 Aramis Ramirez .20 .50
30 Alfonso Soriano .30 .75
31 Rich Hill .20 .50
32 Jacque Jones .20 .50
33 A.J. Pierzynski .20 .50
34 Jermaine Dye .20 .50
35 Paul Konerko .30 .75
36 Bobby Jenks .20 .50
37 Jon Garland .20 .50
38 Mark Buehrle .30 .75
39 Tadahito Iguchi .20 .50
40 Adam Dunn .30 .75
41 Ken Griffey Jr. 1.00 2.50
42 Aaron Harang .20 .50
43 Bronson Arroyo .20 .50
44 Ryan Freel .20 .50
45 Brandon Phillips .20 .50
46 Grady Sizemore .30 .75
47 Travis Hafner .20 .50
48 Victor Martinez .30 .75
49 Jhonny Peralta .20 .50
50 C.C. Sabathia .30 .75
51 Jeremy Sowers .20 .50
52 Ryan Garko .20 .50
53 Garrett Atkins .20 .50
54 Willy Taveras .20 .50
55 Todd Helton .30 .75
56 Jeff Francis .20 .50
57 Brad Hawpe .20 .50
58 Matt Holliday .50 1.25
59 Justin Verlander .50 1.25
60 Jeremy Bonderman .20 .50
61 Magglio Ordonez .30 .75
62 Ivan Rodriguez .30 .75
63 Gary Sheffield .20 .50
64 Kenny Rogers .20 .50
65 Brandon Inge .20 .50
66 Anibal Sanchez .20 .50
67 Scott Olsen .20 .50
68 Dontrelle Willis .20 .50
69 Dan Uggla .20 .50
70 Hanley Ramirez .30 .75
71 Miguel Cabrera .50 1.25
72 Jeremy Hermida .20 .50
73 Roy Oswalt .30 .75
74 Brad Lidge .20 .50
75 Lance Berkman .30 .75
76 Carlos Lee .20 .50
77 Morgan Ensberg .20 .50
78 Craig Biggio .30 .75
79 Reggie Sanders .20 .50
80 Mike Sweeney .20 .50
81 Mark Teahen .20 .50
82 John Buck .20 .50
83 Mark Grudzielanek .20 .50
84 Gary Matthews .20 .50
85 Vladimir Guerrero .30 .75
86 Garret Anderson .20 .50
87 Howie Kendrick .20 .50
88 Jered Weaver .30 .75
89 Chone Figgins .20 .50
90 Bartolo Colon .20 .50
91 Francisco Rodriguez .30 .75
92 Nomar Garciaparra .30 .75
93 Andre Ethier .30 .75
94 Rafael Furcal .20 .50
95 Jeff Kent .20 .50
96 Derek Lowe .20 .50
97 Jason Schmidt .20 .50
98 Takashi Saito .20 .50
99 Ben Sheets .20 .50
100 Prince Fielder .30 .75
101 Bill Hall .20 .50
102 Rickie Weeks .20 .50
103 Francisco Cordero .20 .50
104 J.J. Hardy .20 .50
105 Johan Santana .30 .75
106 Justin Morneau .30 .75
107 Joe Mauer .40 1.00
108 Joe Nathan .20 .50
109 Torii Hunter .20 .50
110 Michael Cuddyer .20 .50
111 Boof Bonser .20 .50
112 Tom Glavine .30 .75
113 Pedro Martinez .30 .75
114 Billy Wagner .20 .50
115 Jose Reyes .30 .75
116 David Wright .40 1.00
117 Carlos Delgado .20 .50
118 Carlos Beltran .30 .75
119 Alex Rodriguez .60 1.50
120 Chien-Ming Wang .30 .75
121 Mariano Rivera .60 1.50
122 Bobby Abreu .20 .50
123 Hideki Matsui .50 1.25
124 Johnny Damon .30 .75
125 Robinson Cano .30 .75
126 Derek Jeter 1.25 3.00
127 Nick Swisher .30 .75
128 Eric Chavez .20 .50
129 Jason Kendall .20 .50
130 Bobby Crosby .20 .50
131 Huston Street .20 .50
132 Dan Haren .20 .50
133 Rich Harden .20 .50
134 Mike Piazza .50 1.25
135 Chase Utley .30 .75
136 Jimmy Rollins .30 .75
137 Aaron Rowand .20 .50
138 Jamie Moyer .20 .50
139 Cole Hamels .40 1.00
140 Pat Burrell .20 .50
141 Ryan Howard .40 1.00
142 Freddy Sanchez .20 .50
143 Zach Duke .20 .50
144 Ian Snell .20 .50
145 Jack Wilson .20 .50
146 Jason Bay .30 .75
147 Albert Pujols .60 1.50
148 Scott Rolen .30 .75
149 Jim Edmonds .30 .75
150 Chris Carpenter .30 .75
151 Yadier Molina .60 1.50
152 Adam Wainwright .30 .75
153 David Eckstein .20 .50
154 Trevor Hoffman .30 .75
155 Brian Giles .20 .50
156 Adrian Gonzalez .40 1.00
157 Jake Peavy .20 .50
158 Khalil Greene .20 .50
159 Chris Young .20 .50
160 Greg Maddux .60 1.50
161 Mike Cameron .20 .50
162 Matt Cain .30 .75
163 Matt Morris .20 .50
164 Pedro Feliz .20 .50
165 Omar Vizquel .30 .75
166 Randy Winn .20 .50
167 Barry Zito .30 .75
168 Adrian Beltre .50 1.25
169 Yuniesky Betancourt .20 .50
170 Richie Sexson .20 .50
171 Raul Ibanez .30 .75
172 Kenji Johjima .50 1.25
173 Ichiro Suzuki .60 1.50
174 Felix Hernandez .30 .75
175 Scott Kazmir .30 .75
176 Carl Crawford .30 .75
177 B.J. Upton .20 .50
178 James Shields .20 .50
179 Rocco Baldelli .20 .50
180 Jorge Cantu .20 .50
181 Ty Wigginton .20 .50
182 Mark Teixeira .30 .75
183 Hank Blalock .20 .50
184 Ian Kinsler .30 .75
185 Michael Young .20 .50
186 Vicente Padilla .20 .50
187 Akinori Otsuka .20 .50
188 Kenny Lofton .20 .50
189 A.J. Burnett .20 .50
190 Roy Halladay .30 .75
191 B.J. Ryan .20 .50
192 Vernon Wells .20 .50
193 Alex Rios .20 .50
194 Troy Glaus .20 .50
195 Frank Thomas .50 1.25
196 Ryan Zimmerman .30 .75
197 Michael O'Connor .20 .50
198 Chad Cordero .20 .50
199 Nick Johnson .20 .50
200 Felipe Lopez .20 .50
201 Miguel Montero (RC) .50 1.25
202 Doug Slaten RC .50 1.25
203 Joseph Bisenius RC .50 1.25
204 Jared Burton RC .50 1.25
205 Kevin Cameron RC .50 1.25
206 Matt Chico (RC) .50 1.25
207 Chris Stewart RC .50 1.25
208 Joe Smith RC .50 1.25
209 Zack Segovia (RC) .50 1.25
210 John Danks RC .75 2.00
211 Lee Gardner (RC) .50 1.25
212 Jeff Baker (RC) .50 1.25
213 Jamie Burke (RC) .50 1.25
214 Phil Hughes (RC) 1.25 3.00
215 Mike Rabelo RC .50 1.25
216 Jose Garcia RC .50 1.25
217 Hector Gimenez (RC) .50 1.25
218 Jesus Flores RC .50 1.25
219 Brandon Morrow RC 2.50 6.00
220 Hideki Okajima RC 2.50 6.00
221 Jay Marshall RC .50 1.25
222 Matt Lindstrom (RC) .50 1.25
223 Juan Salas (RC) .50 1.25
224 Juan Perez RC .50 1.25
225 Sean Henn (RC) .50 1.25
226 Travis Buck (RC) .50 1.25
227 Gustavo Molina RC .50 1.25
228 Hunter Pence (RC) 1.50 4.00
229 Michael Bourn (RC) .75 2.00
230 Brian Barden RC .50 1.25
231 Don Kelly (RC) .50 1.25
232 Joakim Soria RC .50 1.25
233 Cesar Jimenez RC .50 1.25
234 Levale Speigner RC .50 1.25
235 Micah Owings (RC) .50 1.25
236 Brian Stokes (RC) .50 1.25
237 Joaquin Arias (RC) .50 1.25
238 Josh Hamilton L13 (RC) 1.50 4.00
239 Daisuke Matsuzaka L13 RC 2.00 5.00
240 Alejandro De Aza L13 RC .75 2.00
241 Kory Casto L13 (RC) .50 1.25
242 Troy Tulowitzki L13 (RC) 1.50 4.00
243 Akinori Iwamura L13 RC 1.25 3.00
244 Angel Sanchez L13 RC .50 1.25
245 Ryan Braun L13 (RC) 2.50 6.00
246 Alex Gordon L13 RC 1.50 4.00
247 Elijah Dukes L13 RC .75 2.00
248 Kei Igawa L13 RC 1.25 3.00
249 Kevin Kouzmanoff L13 (RC) .50 1.25
250 Delmon Young L13 (RC) .75 2.00

2007 Ultra Gold

*GOLD 1-200: 1.5X TO 3X BASIC
*GOLD RC 201-237: .5X TO 1.2X BASIC RC
*GOLD L13 238-250: .5X TO 1.2X BASIC L13
STATED ODDS 1:10 HOBBY
239 Daisuke Matsuzaka L13 5.00 12.00
245 Ryan Braun L13 5.00 12.00

2007 Ultra Retail

*RETAIL 1-200: .25X TO .6X BASIC
*RETAIL RC 201-237: .3X TO .8X BASIC RC
*RETAIL L13 238-250: .3X TO .8X BASIC L13

2007 Ultra Retail Gold

*RETAIL GLD 1-200: 1.5X TO 4X BASIC
*RET.RC GLD 201-237: .6X TO 1.5X BASIC RC
*RET.L13 GLD 238-250: .6X TO 1.5X BASIC L13
STATED ODDS 2:1 FAT PACK
STATED PRINT RUN 999 SER.#'d SETS
239 Daisuke Matsuzaka L13 6.00 15.00
245 Ryan Braun L13 5.00 12.00

2007 Ultra Autographics

RANDOM INSERTS IN PACKS
PRINT RUNS B/WN 49-499 COPIES PER
AG Alex Gordon/499 4.00 10.00
AH Aaron Harang/499 4.00 10.00
BM Brandon McCarthy/499 3.00 8.00
CC Chad Cordero/499 3.00 8.00
CH Clay Hensley/499 3.00 8.00
CI Cesar Izturis/122 4.00 10.00
JA Jason Bay/499 4.00 10.00
JB Joe Blanton/299 3.00 8.00
JE Johnny Estrada/132 6.00 15.00
JS Johan Santana/173 3.00 8.00
KG Khalil Greene/299 3.00 8.00
KI Kei Igawa/199 6.00 15.00

2007 Ultra Autographics Retail

STATED ODDS 1:1440 RETAIL
NO PRICING DUE TO SCARCITY

2007 Ultra Dual Materials

RANDOM INSERTS IN PACKS
PRINT RUNS B/WN 81-160 COPIES PER
GOLD p/r 39-75: .5X TO 1.2X BASIC
GOLD p/r 20-25: .6X TO 1.5X BASIC
GOLD RANDOMLY INSERTED
GOLD PRINT RUN B/WN 20-75 PER
PATCH: .75X TO 2X BASIC
PATCHES RANDOMLY INSERTED
PATCH PRINT RUN B/WN 1-25 PER
NO PATCH PRICING ON QTY 16 OR LESS
AB A.J. Burnett 3.00 8.00
AE Andre Ethier 3.00 8.00
AJ Andruw Jones 3.00 8.00
AK Austin Kearns 3.00 8.00
AL Adam LaRoche 3.00 8.00
AN Garret Anderson 3.00 8.00
AP Albert Pujols 6.00 15.00
AS Anibal Sanchez 3.00 8.00
BA Bobby Abreu 3.00 8.00
BC Bobby Crosby 3.00 8.00
BE Adrian Beltre 3.00 8.00
BG Brian Giles 3.00 8.00
BI Craig Biggio 3.00 8.00
BJ Bobby Jenks 3.00 8.00
BL Brad Lidge 3.00 8.00
BM Brandon McCarthy 3.00 8.00
BR Brian Roberts 3.00 8.00
BS Ben Sheets 3.00 8.00
BW Brandon Webb 3.00 8.00
CA Carlos Beltran 3.00 8.00
CB Chris Burke 3.00 8.00
CC Carl Crawford 3.00 8.00
CF Chone Figgins 3.00 8.00
CH Chris Carpenter/81 4.00 10.00
CJ Conor Jackson 3.00 8.00
CK Casey Kotchman 3.00 8.00
CL Carlos Lee 3.00 8.00
CP Corey Patterson 3.00 8.00
CR Coco Crisp 3.00 8.00
CS C.C. Sabathia/154 3.00 8.00
CU Curt Schilling 3.00 8.00
DJ Derek Jeter 8.00 20.00
DL Derek Lowe 3.00 8.00
DO David Ortiz 4.00 10.00
DR J.D. Drew 3.00 8.00
DU Dan Uggla 3.00 8.00
DW David Wells 3.00 8.00
ED Jim Edmonds 3.00 8.00
ES Ervin Santana 3.00 8.00
FG Freddy Garcia 3.00 8.00
FH Felix Hernandez 3.00 8.00
GA Garrett Atkins 3.00 8.00
GJ Geoff Jenkins 3.00 8.00
GM Greg Maddux 4.00 10.00
GS Gary Sheffield 3.00 8.00
HE Todd Helton 3.00 8.00
HO Trevor Hoffman 3.00 8.00
HR Hanley Ramirez 3.00 8.00
HU Torii Hunter 3.00 8.00
IS Ian Snell 3.00 8.00
JB Jeremy Bonderman 3.00 8.00
JC Chipper Jones 4.00 10.00
JD Jermaine Dye 3.00 8.00
JG Jonny Gomes 3.00 8.00
JH J.J. Hardy 4.00 10.00
JJ Josh Johnson 3.00 8.00
JK Jeff Kent 3.00 8.00
JM Justin Morneau 3.00 8.00
JN Joe Nathan 3.00 8.00
JO Josh Beckett 3.00 8.00
JP Jorge Posada 3.00 8.00
JS James Shields 3.00 8.00
JV Jason Varitek 4.00 10.00
JW Josh Willingham 3.00 8.00
KG Kahlil Greene 3.00 8.00
KW Kerry Wood 3.00 8.00
LB Lance Berkman 3.00 8.00
LE Derrek Lee 3.00 8.00
LG Luis Gonzalez 3.00 8.00
LM Lastings Milledge 3.00 8.00
LS Luke Scott 3.00 8.00
MC Matt Cain 3.00 8.00
ME Melky Cabrera 3.00 8.00
MH Matt Holliday 4.00 10.00
MI Mike Mussina 3.00 8.00
MM Melvin Mora 3.00 8.00
MO Magglio Ordonez 3.00 8.00
MR Manny Ramirez 3.00 8.00
MS Mike Sweeney 3.00 8.00
MT Miguel Tejada 3.00 8.00
MU Mark Mulder 3.00 8.00
PE Andy Pettitte 3.00 8.00
PF Prince Fielder 4.00 10.00
PJ Jhonny Peralta 3.00 8.00
RH Rich Harden 3.00 8.00
SC Jason Schmidt 3.00 8.00
SI Grady Sizemore 3.00 8.00
SO Scott Olsen 3.00 8.00
TE Mark Teixeira 3.00 8.00
TH Travis Hafner 3.00 8.00
TW Tim Wakefield 3.00 8.00
VG Vladimir Guerrero 3.00 8.00
VM Victor Martinez 3.00 8.00
VW Vernon Wells 3.00 8.00
WI Dontrelle Willis 3.00 8.00
ZD Zach Duke 3.00 8.00

2007 Ultra Faces of the Game

STATED ODDS 1:10 HOBBY/RETAIL
PRINTING PLATE ODDS 1:1252 HOB/RET
PLATE PRINT RUN 1 SET PER COLOR
BLACK-CYAN-MAGENTA-YELLOW ISSUED
NO PLATE PRICING DUE TO SCARCITY
AB Adrian Beltre 1.25 3.00
AJ Andruw Jones .50 1.25
BS Ben Sheets .50 1.25
CJ Chipper Jones 1.25 3.00
CS C.C. Sabathia .75 2.00
CU Chase Utley .75 2.00
DJ Derek Jeter 3.00 8.00
FR Francisco Rodriguez .75 2.00
GM Greg Maddux 1.50 4.00
HU Torii Hunter .50 1.25
JB Jason Bay .75 2.00
JG Jason Giambi .50 1.25
KG Ken Griffey Jr. 2.50 6.00
LG Luis Gonzalez .50 1.25
MC Miguel Cabrera 1.25 3.00
MP Mike Piazza 1.25 3.00
MR Mariano Rivera 1.50 4.00
OV Omar Vizquel .75 2.00
TG Tom Glavine .75 2.00
HO Trevor Hoffman .75 2.00

2007 Ultra Faces of the Game Materials

APPX.ODDS 1:8 HOBBY/RETAIL
AB Adrian Beltre 2.50 6.00
AJ Andruw Jones 3.00 8.00
BS Ben Sheets 2.50 6.00
CJ Chipper Jones 3.00 8.00
CS C.C. Sabathia 2.50 6.00
CU Chase Utley 4.00 10.00
DJ Derek Jeter 8.00 20.00
FR Francisco Rodriguez 2.50 6.00
GM Greg Maddux 4.00 10.00
HO Trevor Hoffman 2.50 6.00
JB Jason Bay 2.50 6.00
JG Jason Giambi 2.50 6.00
KG Ken Griffey Jr. 6.00 15.00
LG Luis Gonzalez 2.50 6.00
MC Miguel Cabrera 3.00 8.00
MP Mike Piazza 4.00 10.00
MR Mariano Rivera 4.00 10.00
OV Omar Vizquel 3.00 8.00
TG Tom Glavine 3.00 8.00
TH Torii Hunter 2.50 6.00

2007 Ultra Feel the Game

APPX.ODDS 1:7 HOBBY/RETAIL
PRINTING PLATE ODDS 1:1252 HOB/RET
PLATE PRINT RUN 1 SET PER COLOR
BLACK-CYAN-MAGENTA-YELLOW ISSUED
NO PLATE PRICING DUE TO SCARCITY
AP Albert Pujols 1.50 4.00
BA Bobby Abreu .50 1.25
BR Brian Roberts .50 1.25
BW Brandon Webb .75 2.00
CC Chris Carpenter .75 2.00
CJ Chipper Jones 1.25 3.00
CR Carl Crawford .75 2.00
CS Curt Schilling .75 2.00
CU Chase Utley .75 2.00
CZ Carlos Zambrano .75 2.00
DJ Derek Jeter 3.00 8.00
DW Dontrelle Willis .50 1.25
EC Eric Chavez .50 1.25
GS Grady Sizemore .75 2.00
HR Hanley Ramirez .75 2.00
IR Ivan Rodriguez .75 2.00
JM Justin Morneau .75 2.00
JP Jonathan Papelbon 1.25 3.00
JR Jose Reyes .75 2.00
JS John Smoltz 1.25 3.00
KG Ken Griffey Jr. 2.50 6.00
KJ Kenji Johjima 1.25 3.00
LB Lance Berkman .75 2.00
LG Luis Gonzalez .50 1.25
MC Miguel Cabrera 1.25 3.00
RC Robinson Cano .75 2.00
RJ Randy Johnson 1.25 3.00
SA Johan Santana .75 2.00
SC Jason Schmidt .50 1.25
VG Vladimir Guerrero .75 2.00

2007 Ultra Feel the Game Materials

APPX.ODDS 1:7 HOBBY/RETAIL
AP Albert Pujols 8.00 20.00
BA Bobby Abreu 2.50 6.00
BR Brian Roberts 3.00 8.00
BW Brandon Webb 2.50 6.00
CC Chris Carpenter 2.50 6.00
CJ Chipper Jones 3.00 8.00
CR Carl Crawford 2.50 6.00
CS Curt Schilling 3.00 8.00
CZ Carlos Zambrano 2.50 6.00
DJ Derek Jeter 8.00 20.00
DW Dontrelle Willis 2.50 6.00
EC Eric Chavez 2.50 6.00
GS Grady Sizemore 3.00 8.00
HR Hanley Ramirez 3.00 8.00
IR Ivan Rodriguez 3.00 8.00
JM Justin Morneau 2.50 6.00
JP Jonathan Papelbon 4.00 10.00
JR Jose Reyes 4.00 10.00
JS John Smoltz 3.00 8.00
KG Ken Griffey Jr. 6.00 15.00
KJ Kenji Johjima 4.00 10.00
LB Lance Berkman 2.50 6.00
LG Luis Gonzalez 2.50 6.00
MC Miguel Cabrera 3.00 8.00
RC Robinson Cano 4.00 10.00
RJ Randy Johnson 4.00 10.00
SA Johan Santana 3.00 8.00
SC Jason Schmidt 2.50 6.00
VG Vladimir Guerrero 3.00 8.00

2007 Ultra Hitting Machines

APPX.ODDS 1:13 HOBBY/RETAIL
PRINTING PLATE ODDS 1:1252 HOB/RET
PLATE PRINT RUN 1 SET PER COLOR
BLACK-CYAN-MAGENTA-YELLOW ISSUED
NO PLATE PRICING DUE TO SCARCITY
AR Aramis Ramirez .50 1.25
AS Alfonso Soriano .75 2.00
BI Craig Biggio .75 2.00
CB Carlos Beltran .75 2.00
DO David Ortiz 1.25 3.00
FS Freddy Sanchez .50 1.25
FT Frank Thomas 1.25 3.00
JK Jeff Kent .50 1.25
JM Joe Mauer 1.00 2.50
JT Jim Thome .75 2.00
MT Mark Teixeira .75 2.00
NS Nick Swisher .75 2.00
TE Miguel Tejada .75 2.00
TG Troy Glaus .50 1.25
TH Todd Helton .75 2.00

2007 Ultra Hitting Machines Materials

APPX.ODDS 1:12 HOBBY/RETAIL
AR Aramis Ramirez 2.50 6.00
AS Alfonso Soriano 2.50 6.00
BI Craig Biggio 3.00 8.00
CB Carlos Beltran 2.50 6.00
DO David Ortiz 4.00 10.00
FS Freddy Sanchez 2.50 6.00
FT Frank Thomas 4.00 10.00
JK Jeff Kent 2.50 6.00
JM Joe Mauer 3.00 8.00
JT Jim Thome 3.00 8.00
MT Mark Teixeira 3.00 8.00
NS Nick Swisher 2.50 6.00
TE Miguel Tejada 2.50 6.00
TG Troy Glaus 2.50 6.00
TH Todd Helton 3.00 8.00

2007 Ultra Iron Man

COMMON CARD 1.25 3.00
APPX.ODDS 1:3 HOBBY/RETAIL

2007 Ultra Iron Man Signatures

COMMON CARD 40.00 80.00
RANDOM INSERTS IN PACKS
STATED PRINT RUN 10 SER.#'d SETS

2007 Ultra Rookie Autographs

RANDOM INSERTS IN PACKS
PRINT RUNS B/WN 23-499 COPIES PER
NO PRICING ON QTY 38 OR LESS
201a Miguel Montero/299 3.00 8.00
201b Miguel Montero/149 4.00 10.00
202a Doug Slaten/299 3.00 8.00
202b Doug Slaten/349 3.00 8.00
203a Joseph Bisenius/299 3.00 8.00
203b Joseph Bisenius/349 3.00 8.00
204a Jared Burton/299 5.00 12.00
204b Jared Burton/349 5.00 12.00
205a Kevin Cameron/299 3.00 8.00
205b Kevin Cameron/349 3.00 8.00
206a Matt Chico/299 3.00 8.00
206b Matt Chico/349 3.00 8.00
207a Chris Stewart/299 3.00 8.00
207b Chris Stewart/349 3.00 8.00
209a Zack Segovia/299 4.00 10.00
209b Zack Segovia/149 5.00 12.00
210 John Danks/299 3.00 8.00
213a Jamie Burke/299 5.00 12.00
213b Jamie Burke/349 5.00 12.00
215a Mike Rabelo/299 3.00 8.00
215b Mike Rabelo/349 3.00 8.00
217a Hector Gimenez/299 3.00 8.00
217b Hector Gimenez/349 3.00 8.00
219a Brandon Morrow/299 3.00 8.00
219b Brandon Morrow/349 3.00 8.00
221a Jay Marshall/299 6.00 15.00
221b Jay Marshall/349 6.00 15.00
225a Sean Henn/299 3.00 8.00
225b Sean Henn/349 3.00 8.00
226a Travis Buck/299 4.00 10.00
226b Travis Buck/99 6.00 15.00
227a Gustavo Molina/299 4.00 10.00
227b Gustavo Molina/349 4.00 10.00
229a Michael Bourn/299 4.00 10.00
229b Michael Bourn/349 4.00 10.00
232a Joakim Soria/299 4.00 10.00
232b Joakim Soria/349 4.00 10.00
234a Levale Speigner/299 3.00 8.00
234b Levale Speigner/349 3.00 8.00
236a Brian Stokes/299 3.00 8.00
236b Brian Stokes/349 3.00 8.00
237a Joaquin Arias/299 3.00 8.00
237b Joaquin Arias/349 3.00 8.00
238a Josh Hamilton L13/499 5.00 12.00
238b Josh Hamilton L13/99 15.00 40.00
241 Kory Casto L13/499 5.00 12.00
242 Troy Tulowitzki L13/499 6.00 15.00
243 Akinori Iwamura L13/99 30.00 60.00
245 Ryan Braun L13/499 5.00 12.00
246a Alex Gordon L13/499 8.00 20.00
246b Alex Gordon L13/99 12.00 30.00
248a Kei Igawa L13/299 3.00 8.00
248b Kei Igawa L13/99 20.00 50.00
249a Kevin Kouzmanoff L13/499 4.00 10.00
249b Kevin Kouzmanoff L13/199 5.00 12.00

2007 Ultra Rookie Autographs Retail

STATED ODDS 1:1440 RETAIL
NO PRICING DUE TO SCARCITY

2007 Ultra Strike Zone

STATED ODDS 1:20 HOBBY/RETAIL
PRINTING PLATE ODDS 1:1252 HOB/RET
PLATE PRINT RUN 1 SET PER COLOR
BLACK-CYAN-MAGENTA-YELLOW ISSUED
NO PLATE PRICING DUE TO SCARCITY
BZ Barry Zito .75 2.00
CC C.C. Sabathia .75 2.00
CZ Carlos Zambrano .75 2.00
DW Dontrelle WIllls .50 1.25
JS Johan Santana .75 2.00
JV Justin Verlander 1.25 3.00
MM Mike Mussina .75 2.00
PM Pedro Martinez .75 2.00
RH Roy Halladay .75 2.00
RO Roy Oswalt .75 2.00

2007 Ultra Strike Zone Materials

APPX.ODDS 1:14 HOBBY/RETAIL
BZ Barry Zito 2.50 6.00
CC C.C. Sabathia 2.50 6.00
CZ Carlos Zambrano 2.50 6.00
DW Dontrelle Willis 2.50 6.00
JS Johan Santana 3.00 8.00
JV Justin Verlander 4.00 10.00
MM Mike Mussina 3.00 8.00
PM Pedro Martinez 3.00 8.00
RH Roy Halladay 2.50 6.00
RO Roy Oswalt 2.50 6.00

2007 Ultra Swing Kings

STATED ODDS 1:8 HOBBY/RETAIL
PRINTING PLATE ODDS 1:1252 HOB/RET
PLATE PRINT RUN 1 SET PER COLOR
BLACK-CYAN-MAGENTA-YELLOW ISSUED
NO PLATE PRICING DUE TO SCARCITY
AD Adam Dunn .75 2.00
AJ Andruw Jones .50 1.25
AP Albert Pujols 1.50 4.00
AR Aramis Ramirez .50 1.25
AS Alfonso Soriano .75 2.00
CB Carlos Beltran .75 2.00
CL Carlos Lee .50 1.25
DJ Derek Jeter 3.00 8.00
DO David Ortiz 1.25 3.00
FT Frank Thomas 1.25 3.00
GS Gary Sheffield .50 1.25
HE Todd Helton .75 2.00
JM Joe Mauer 1.00 2.50
JR Jose Reyes .75 2.00
JT Jim Thome .75 2.00
KG Ken Griffey Jr. 2.50 6.00
MC Miguel Cabrera 1.25 3.00
MR Manny Ramirez 1.25 3.00
MT Miguel Tejada .75 2.00
NG Nomar Garciaparra .75 2.00
PB Pat Burrell .50 1.25
TE Mark Teixeira .75 2.00
TH Travis Hafner .50 1.25
VG Vladimir Guerrero .75 2.00
VW Vernon Wells .50 1.25

2007 Ultra Swing Kings Materials

APPX ODDS 1:7 HOBBY/RETAIL
AD Adam Dunn 2.50 6.00
AJ Andruw Jones 3.00 8.00
AP Albert Pujols 6.00 15.00
AR Aramis Ramirez 2.50 6.00
AS Alfonso Soriano 2.50 6.00
CB Carlos Beltran 2.50 6.00
CL Carlos Lee 2.50 6.00
DJ Derek Jeter 8.00 20.00
DO David Ortiz 4.00 10.00
FT Frank Thomas 4.00 10.00
GS Gary Sheffield 2.50 6.00
HE Todd Helton 3.00 8.00
JM Joe Mauer 3.00 8.00
JR Jose Reyes 4.00 10.00
JT Jim Thome 3.00 8.00
KG Ken Griffey Jr. 6.00 15.00
MC Miguel Cabrera 3.00 8.00
MR Manny Ramirez 3.00 8.00
MT Miguel Tejada 2.50 6.00
NG Nomar Garciaparra 4.00 10.00
PB Pat Burrell 2.50 6.00
TE Mark Teixeira 3.00 8.00
TH Travis Hafner 2.50 6.00
VG Vladimir Guerrero 4.00 10.00
VW Vernon Wells 2.50 6.00

2007 Ultra Ultragraphs

RANDOM INSERTS IN PACKS
PRINT RUNS B/WN 49-499 COPIES PER
AK Austin Kearns/399 3.00 8.00
AL Adam LaRoche/499 3.00 8.00
AN Garret Anderson/499 3.00 8.00
BB Boof Bonser/499 3.00 8.00
GA Garrett Atkins/499 3.00 8.00
JJ Jorge Julio/499 3.00 8.00
JN Joe Nathan/299 4.00 10.00
JW Jered Weaver/150 10.00 25.00
MM Mark Mulder/319 3.00 8.00
RW Rickie Weeks/68 6.00 15.00
TH Travis Hafner/499 4.00 10.00
ZG Zack Greinke/199 10.00 25.00

2007 Ultra Ultragraphs Retail

STATED ODDS 1:1440 RETAIL
NO PRICING DUE TO SCARCITY

1991 Ultra Pro Dave Justice Promo

COMPLETE SET (1) .40 1.00
NNO David Justice .40 1.00

1925 Universal Toy and Novelty W-504

Issued in uncut sheet form, by Universal Toy and Novelty, this "Strip card" series appears to have been issued early in the 1925 season. Presently, examples of individual players representing four teams are accounted for. Three of the checklists appear to be complete (Brooklyn, Giants, Yankees - as listed below). The cards are numbered on the fronts, although the number is sometimes cut off when being separated from the sheet. The backs are blank. Like all "Strip cards" these were cut down by hand, after they were marketed. As such, size variances may very well exist. Approximate size is 1 3/8" x 2 1/4".

COMPLETE SET (58) 750.00 1500.00
101 Eddie Brown 10.00 20.00
102 Hank DeBerry 10.00 20.00
103 Bill Doak 10.00 20.00
104 Rube Ehrhardt 10.00 20.00
105 Jake Fournier 12.50 25.00
106 Tommy Griffith 10.00 20.00
107 Burleigh Grimes 20.00 40.00
108 Charlie Hargreaves 10.00 20.00
109 Andy High 10.00 20.00
110 Jimmy Johnston 10.00 20.00
111 John Mitchell 10.00 20.00
112 Tiny Osborne 10.00 20.00
113 Milt Stock 10.00 20.00
114 Zack Taylor 10.00 20.00
115 Dazzy Vance 20.00 40.00
116 Zach Wheat 20.00 40.00
117 Bennie Bengough 10.00 20.00
118 Joe Dugan 10.00 20.00
119 Waite Hoyt 20.00 40.00
120 Sam Jones 12.50 25.00
121 Bob Meusel 15.00 30.00
122 Wally Pipp 10.00 20.00
123 Babe Ruth 50.00 150.00
124 Wally Schang 10.00 20.00
125 Bob Shawkey 12.50 25.00
126 Everett Scott 10.00 20.00
127 Urban Shocker 10.00 20.00
128 Aaron Ward 10.00 20.00
129 Whitey Witt 10.00 20.00
130 Carl Mays 10.00 20.00
131 Miller Huggins 20.00 40.00
132 Ben. Paschal 10.00 20.00
133 Virgil Barnes 10.00 20.00
134 Jack Bentley 10.00 20.00
135 Frank Frisch 20.00 40.00
136 Hank Gowdy 10.00 20.00
137 Heinie Groh 12.50 25.00
138 Travis Jackson 20.00 40.00
139 George Kelly 20.00 40.00
140 Emil Meusel 10.00 20.00
141 Hugh McQuillan 10.00 20.00
142 Arthur Nehf 10.00 20.00
143 Rosy Ryan 10.00 20.00
144 Pancho Snyder 10.00 20.00
145 Hack Wilson 20.00 40.00
146 Ross Youngs 20.00 40.00
147 Hugh Jennings 20.00 40.00
148 John J. McGraw 25.00 50.00
149 Joe Judge 12.50 25.00
151 R. Peckinpaugh 12.50 25.00
152 Ossie Bluege 10.00 20.00
153 Mike McNally 10.00 20.00
154 Sam Rice 20.00 40.00
159 Pinky Hargrave 10.00 20.00
162 Muddy Ruel 10.00 20.00
164 George Mogridge 10.00 20.00
NNO Brooklyn Dodgers Team Photo 20.00 40.00
NNO New York Yankees Team Photo 20.00 40.00
NNO New York Giants Team Photo 20.00 40.00

1933 Uncle Jack

These blank-backed cards, which measure approximately 1 7/8" by 2 7/8" feauture the leading players in baseball at this time. The fronts feature a blue duotone photo with the players name on the bottom. Since the cards are unnumbered, they are sequenced in alphabetical order. The cards were issued in one-card packs along with a coupon for a "World Series trip" contest and a piece of gum.

COMPLETE SET (30) 1800.00 3600.00
1 Earl Averill 200.00 400.00
2 James Bottomley 200.00 400.00
3 Ed Brandt 100.00 200.00
4 Ben Chapman 100.00 200.00
5 Gordon Cochrane 200.00 400.00
6 Joe Cronin 200.00 400.00
7 Kiki Cuyler 200.00 400.00
8 George Earnshaw 100.00 200.00
9 Wes Ferrell 150.00 300.00
10 Jimmie Foxx 300.00 600.00
11 Frank Frisch 200.00 400.00
12 Burleigh Grimes 200.00 400.00
13 Lefty Grove 300.00 600.00
14 Wild Bill Hallahan 125.00 250.00
15 Gabby Hartnett 200.00 400.00
16 Babe Herman 150.00 300.00
17 Rogers Hornsby 500.00 1000.00
18 Charles Klein 200.00 400.00
19 Tony Lazzeri 200.00 400.00
20 Fred Lindstrom 200.00 400.00
21 Ted Lyons 200.00 400.00
22 Pepper Martin 150.00 300.00
23 Herb Pennock 200.00 400.00
24 Babe Ruth 750.00 1500.00
25 Al Simmons 200.00 400.00
26 Bill Terry 200.00 400.00
27 Dazzy Vance 200.00 400.00
28 Lloyd Waner 200.00 400.00
29 Paul Waner 200.00 400.00
30 Hack Wilson 200.00 400.00

1988 Upper Deck Promos

The first two cards were test issues given away as samples during the summer of 1988 in anticipation of Upper Deck obtaining licenses from Major League Baseball and the Major League Baseball Players Association. Not many were produced (probably less than 25,000 of each) but few were thrown away as they were distributed basically only to those who would hold on to them. There are three versions based on where the hologram is located. Type A, the most common variety, has a hologram on the bottom that extends as far as the photo. On Type B, the hologram is on the bottom but extends to the edge of the card. Type C, by far the scarcest, has the hologram at the top. Joyner and Buice were supposedly interested in investing in Upper Deck (conflict of interest prohibited them) and apparently were helpful in getting Upper Deck the necessary licenses. Cards were passed out freely to every dealer at the National Sports Collectors Convention in Atlantic City, New Jersey in August 1988.

A1 DeWayne Buice 4.00 10.00
A700 Wally Joyner 20.00 50.00
B1 DeWayne Buice 8.00 20.00
B700 Wally Joyner 40.00 100.00
C1 DeWayne Buice 20.00 50.00
C700 Wally Joyner 100.00 250.00

1989 Upper Deck

This attractive 800-card standard-size set was introduced in 1989 as the premier issue by the then-fledgling Upper Deck company. Unlike other 1989 major releases, this set was issued in two separate series - a low series numbered 1-700 and a high series numbered 701-800. Cards were primarily issued in fin-wrapped low and high series foil packs, complete 800-card factory sets and 100-card high series factory sets. High series packs contained a mixture of both low and high series cards. Collectors should also note that many dealers consider that Upper Deck's "planned" production of 1,000,000 of each player was increased (perhaps even doubled) later in the year due to the explosion in popularity of the product. The cards feature slick paper stock, full color on both the front and the back and carry a hologram on the reverse to protect against counterfeiting. Subsets include Rookie Stars (1-26) and Collector's Choice art cards (668-693). The more significant variations involving changed photos or changed type are listed below. According to the company, the Murphy and Sheridan cards were corrected very early, after only two percent of the cards had been produced. Similarly, the Sheffield was corrected after 15 percent had been printed; Varsho, Gallego, and Schroeder were corrected after 20 percent; and Holton, Manrique, and Winningham were corrected 30 percent of the way through. Rookie Cards in the set include Jim Abbott, Sandy Alomar Jr., Dante Bichette, Craig Biggio, Steve Finley, Ken Griffey Jr., Randy Johnson, Gary Sheffield, John Smoltz and Todd Zeile. Cards with missing or duplicate holograms appear to be relatively common and are generally considered to be flawed copies that sell for substantial discounts.

COMPLETE SET (800) 25.00 60.00
COMP.FACT.SET (800) 25.00 60.00
COMPLETE LO SET (700) 15.00 40.00
COMPLETE HI SET (100) 6.00 15.00
COMP.HI FACT.SET (100) 6.00 15.00
1 Ken Griffey Jr. RC 50.00 120.00
2 Luis Medina RC .08 .25
3 Tony Chance RC .08 .25
4 Dave Otto .08 .25
5 Sandy Alomar Jr. RC UER .40 1.00
Born 6/16/66
should be 6/18/66
6 Rolando Roomes RC .08 .25
7 Dave West RC .08 .25
8 Cris Carpenter RC .08 .25
9 Gregg Jefferies .08 .25
10 Doug Dascenzo RC .08 .25
11 Ron Jones RC .08 .25
12 Luis DeLosSantos RC .08 .25
13 Gary Sheffield COR RC 2.00 5.00
13A Gary Sheffield ERR 2.00 5.00
14 Mike Harkey RC .08 .25
15 Lance Blankenship RC .08 .25
16 William Brennan RC .08 .25
17 John Smoltz RC 3.00 8.00
18 Ramon Martinez RC .20 .50
19 Mark Lemke RC .40 1.00
20 Juan Bell RC .08 .25
21 Rey Palacios RC .08 .25
22 Felix Jose RC .08 .25
23 Van Snider RC .08 .25
24 Dante Bichette RC .40 1.00
25 Randy Johnson RC 5.00 12.00
26 Carlos Quintana RC .08 .25
27 Star Rookie CL .08 .25
28 Mike Schooler .08 .25
29 Randy St.Claire .08 .25
30 Jerald Clark RC .08 .25
31 Kevin Gross .08 .25
32 Dan Firova .08 .25
33 Jeff Calhoun .08 .25
34 Tommy Hinzo .08 .25
35 Ricky Jordan RC .20 .50
36 Larry Parrish .08 .25
37 Bret Saberhagen UER .15 .40
38 Mike Smithson .08 .25
39 Dave Dravecky .08 .25
40 Ed Romero .08 .25
41 Jeff Musselman .08 .25
42 Ed Hearn .08 .25
43 Rance Mulliniks .08 .25
44 Jim Eisenreich .08 .25
45 Sil Campusano .08 .25
46 Mike Krukow .08 .25
47 Paul Gibson .08 .25
48 Mike LaCoss .08 .25
49 Larry Herndon .08 .25
50 Scott Garrelts .08 .25
51 Dwayne Henry .08 .25
52 Jim Acker .08 .25
53 Steve Sax .08 .25
54 Pete O'Brien .08 .25
55 Paul Runge .08 .25
56 Rick Rhoden .08 .25
57 John Dopson .08 .25
58 Casey Candaele UER .08 .25
No stats for Astros
for '88 season
59 Dave Righetti .15 .40
60 Joe Hesketh .08 .25
61 Frank DiPino .08 .25
62 Tim Laudner .08 .25
63 Jamie Moyer .15 .40
64 Fred Toliver .08 .25
65 Mitch Webster .08 .25
66 John Tudor .15 .40
67 John Cangelosi .08 .25
68 Mike Devereaux .08 .25
69 Brian Fisher .08 .25
70 Mike Marshall .08 .25
71 Zane Smith .08 .25
72A Brian Holton ERR .40 1.00
Photo actually
Shawn Hillegas
72B Brian Holton COR .15 .40
73 Jose Guzman .08 .25
74 Rick Mahler .08 .25
75 John Shelby .08 .25
76 Jim Deshaies .08 .25
77 Bobby Meacham .08 .25
78 Bryn Smith .08 .25
79 Joaquin Andujar .15 .40
80 Richard Dotson .08 .25
81 Charlie Lea .08 .25
82 Calvin Schiraldi .08 .25
83 Les Straker .08 .25
84 Les Lancaster .08 .25
85 Allan Anderson .08 .25
86 Junior Ortiz .08 .25
87 Jesse Orosco .08 .25
88 Felix Fermin .08 .25
89 Dave Anderson .08 .25
90 Rafael Belliard UER .08 .25
Born '61 not '51
91 Franklin Stubbs .08 .25
92 Cecil Espy .08 .25
93 Albert Hall .08 .25
94 Tim Leary .08 .25
95 Mitch Williams .08 .25
96 Tracy Jones .08 .25
97 Danny Darwin .08 .25
98 Gary Ward .08 .25
99 Neal Heaton .08 .25
100 Jim Pankovits .08 .25
101 Bill Doran .08 .25
102 Tim Wallach .08 .25
103 Joe Magrane .08 .25
104 Ozzie Virgil .08 .25
105 Alvin Davis .08 .25
106 Tom Brookens .08 .25
107 Shawon Dunston .08 .25
108 Tracy Woodson .08 .25
109 Nelson Liriano .08 .25
110 Devon White UER .15 .40
Doubles total 46
should be 56
111 Steve Balboni .08 .25
112 Buddy Bell .15 .40
113 German Jimenez .08 .25
114 Ken Dayley .08 .25
115 Andres Galarraga .15 .40
116 Mike Scioscia .15 .40
117 Gary Pettis .08 .25
118 Ernie Whitt .08 .25
119 Bob Boone .15 .40
120 Ryne Sandberg .60 1.50
121 Bruce Benedict .08 .25
122 Hubie Brooks .08 .25
123 Mike Moore .08 .25
124 Wallace Johnson .08 .25
125 Bob Horner .15 .40
126 Chili Davis .15 .40
127 Manny Trillo .08 .25
128 Chet Lemon .15 .40
129 John Cerutti .08 .25
130 Orel Hershiser .15 .40
131 Terry Pendleton .15 .40
132 Jeff Blauser .08 .25
133 Mike Fitzgerald .08 .25
134 Henry Cotto .08 .25
135 Gerald Young .08 .25
136 Luis Salazar .08 .25
137 Alejandro Pena .08 .25
138 Jack Howell .08 .25
139 Tony Fernandez .08 .25
140 Mark Grace .40 1.00
141 Ken Caminiti .25 .60
142 Mike Jackson .08 .25
143 Larry McWilliams .08 .25
144 Andres Thomas .08 .25
145 Nolan Ryan 3X 1.50 4.00
146 Mike Davis .08 .25
147 DeWayne Buice .08 .25
148 Jody Davis .08 .25
149 Jesse Barfield .15 .40
150 Matt Nokes .08 .25
151 Jerry Reuss .08 .25
152 Rick Cerone .08 .25
153 Storm Davis .08 .25
154 Marvell Wynne .08 .25
155 Will Clark .25 .60
156 Luis Aguayo .08 .25
157 Willie Upshaw .08 .25
158 Randy Bush .08 .25
159 Ron Darling .15 .40
160 Kal Daniels .08 .25
161 Spike Owen .08 .25
162 Luis Polonia .08 .25
163 Kevin Mitchell UER .15 .40
'88 total HR should be 19
164 Dave Gallagher .08 .25
165 Benito Santiago .15 .40
166 Greg Gagne .08 .25
167 Ken Phelps .08 .25
168 Sid Fernandez .08 .25
169 Bo Diaz .08 .25
170 Cory Snyder .08 .25
171 Eric Show .08 .25
172 Robby Thompson .08 .25
173 Marty Barrett .08 .25
174 Dave Henderson .08 .25
175 Ozzie Guillen .15 .40
176 Barry Lyons .08 .25
177 Kelvin Torve .08 .25
178 Don Slaught .08 .25
179 Steve Lombardozzi .08 .25
180 Chris Sabo RC .40 1.00
181 Jose Uribe .08 .25
182 Shane Mack .08 .25
183 Ron Karkovice .08 .25
184 Todd Benzinger .08 .25
185 Dave Stewart .15 .40
186 Julio Franco .15 .40
187 Ron Robinson .08 .25
188 Wally Backman .08 .25
189 Randy Velarde .08 .25
190 Joe Carter .15 .40
191 Bob Welch .15 .40
192 Kelly Paris .08 .25
193 Chris Brown .08 .25
194 Rick Reuschel .15 .40
195 Roger Clemens .75 2.00
196 Dave Concepcion .15 .40
197 Al Newman .08 .25
198 Brook Jacoby .08 .25
199 Mookie Wilson .15 .40
200 Don Mattingly 1.00 2.50
201 Dick Schofield .08 .25
202 Mark Gubicza .08 .25
203 Gary Gaetti .15 .40
204 Dan Pasqua .08 .25
205 Andre Dawson .15 .40
206 Chris Speier .08 .25
207 Kent Tekulve .08 .25
208 Rod Scurry .08 .25
209 Scott Bailes .08 .25
210 R.Henderson UER .40 1.00
Throws Right
211 Harold Baines .15 .40
212 Tony Armas .15 .40
213 Kent Hrbek .15 .40
214 Darrin Jackson .08 .25
215 George Brett 1.00 2.50
216 Rafael Santana .08 .25
217 Andy Allanson .08 .25
218 Brett Butler .15 .40
219 Steve Jeltz .08 .25
220 Jay Buhner .15 .40
221 Bo Jackson .40 1.00
222 Angel Salazar .08 .25
223 Kirk McCaskill .08 .25
224 Steve Lyons .08 .25
225 Bert Blyleven .15 .40
226 Scott Bradley .08 .25
227 Bob Melvin .08 .25
228 Ron Kittle .08 .25
229 Phil Bradley .08 .25
230 Tommy John .15 .40
231 Greg Walker .08 .25
232 Juan Berenguer .08 .25
233 Pat Tabler .08 .25
234 Terry Clark .08 .25
235 Rafael Palmeiro .40 1.00
236 Paul Zuvella .08 .25
237 Willie Randolph .15 .40
238 Bruce Fields .08 .25
239 Mike Aldrete .08 .25
240 Lance Parrish .15 .40
241 Greg Maddux 1.00 2.50
242 John Moses .08 .25
243 Melido Perez .08 .25
244 Willie Wilson .15 .40
245 Mark McLemore .08 .25
246 Von Hayes .08 .25
247 Matt Williams .40 1.00
248 John Candelaria UER
(Listed as Yankee for/part o .08 .25
249 Harold Reynolds .15 .40
250 Greg Swindell .08 .25
251 Juan Agosto .08 .25
252 Mike Felder .08 .25
253 Vince Coleman .08 .25
254 Larry Sheets .08 .25
255 George Bell .15 .40
256 Terry Steinbach .15 .40
257 Jack Armstrong RC .20 .50
258 Dickie Thon .08 .25
259 Ray Knight .15 .40
260 Darryl Strawberry .15 .40
261 Doug Sisk .08 .25
262 Alex Trevino .08 .25
263 Jeffrey Leonard .08 .25
264 Tom Henke .08 .25
265 Ozzie Smith .60 1.50
266 Dave Bergman .08 .25
267 Tony Phillips .08 .25
268 Mark Davis .08 .25
269 Kevin Elster .08 .25
270 Barry Larkin .25 .60
271 Manny Lee .08 .25
272 Tom Brunansky .08 .25
273 Craig Biggio RC 2.50 6.00
274 Jim Gantner .08 .25
275 Eddie Murray .40 1.00
276 Jeff Reed .08 .25
277 Tim Teufel .08 .25
278 Rick Honeycutt .08 .25
279 Guillermo Hernandez .08 .25
280 John Kruk .15 .40
281 Luis Alicea RC .20 .50
282 Jim Clancy .08 .25
283 Billy Ripken .08 .25
284 Craig Reynolds .08 .25
285 Robin Yount .60 1.50
286 Jimmy Jones .08 .25
287 Ron Oester .08 .25
288 Terry Leach .08 .25
289 Dennis Eckersley .25 .60
290 Alan Trammell .15 .40
291 Jimmy Key .15 .40
292 Chris Bosio .08 .25
293 Jose DeLeon .08 .25
294 Jim Traber .08 .25
295 Mike Scott .15 .40
296 Roger McDowell .08 .25
297 Garry Templeton .15 .40
298 Doyle Alexander .08 .25
299 Nick Esasky .08 .25
300 Mark McGwire UER 2.00 5.00
301 Darryl Hamilton RC .20 .50
302 Dave Smith .08 .25
303 Rick Sutcliffe .15 .40
304 Dave Stapleton .08 .25
305 Alan Ashby .08 .25
306 Pedro Guerrero .15 .40
307 Ron Guidry .15 .40
308 Steve Farr .08 .25
309 Curt Ford .08 .25
310 Claudell Washington .08 .25
311 Tom Prince .08 .25
312 Chad Kreuter RC .20 .50
313 Ken Oberkfell .08 .25
314 Jerry Browne .08 .25
315 R.J. Reynolds .08 .25
316 Scott Bankhead .08 .25
317 Milt Thompson .08 .25
318 Mario Diaz .08 .25
319 Bruce Ruffin .08 .25
320 Dave Valle .08 .25
321A Gary Varsho ERR .75 2.00
321B Gary Varsho COR .08 .25
In road uniform
322 Paul Mirabella .08 .25
323 Chuck Jackson .08 .25
324 Drew Hall .08 .25
325 Don August .08 .25
326 Israel Sanchez .08 .25
327 Denny Walling .08 .25
328 Joel Skinner .08 .25
329 Danny Tartabull .08 .25
330 Tony Pena .08 .25
331 Jim Sundberg .15 .40
332 Jeff D. Robinson .08 .25
333 Oddibe McDowell .08 .25
334 Jose Lind .08 .25
335 Paul Kilgus .08 .25
336 Juan Samuel .08 .25
337 Mike Campbell .08 .25
338 Mike Maddux .08 .25
339 Darnell Coles .08 .25
340 Bob Dernier .08 .25
341 Rafael Ramirez .08 .25
342 Scott Sanderson .08 .25
343 B.J. Surhoff .15 .40
344 Billy Hatcher .08 .25
345 Pat Perry .08 .25
346 Jack Clark .15 .40
347 Gary Thurman .08 .25
348 Tim Jones .08 .25
349 Dave Winfield .15 .40
350 Frank White .15 .40
351 Dave Collins .08 .25
352 Jack Morris .15 .40
353 Eric Plunk .08 .25
354 Leon Durham .08 .25
355 Ivan DeJesus .08 .25
356 Brian Holman RC .08 .25
357A Dale Murphy ERR 12.50 30.00
357B Dale Murphy COR .25 .60
358 Mark Portugal .08 .25
359 Andy McGaffigan .08 .25
360 Tom Glavine .40 1.00
361 Keith Moreland .08 .25
362 Todd Stottlemyre .08 .25
363 Dave Leiper .08 .25
364 Cecil Fielder .15 .40
365 Carmelo Martinez .08 .25
366 Dwight Evans .25 .60
367 Kevin McReynolds .08 .25
368 Rich Gedman .08 .25
369 Len Dykstra .15 .40
370 Jody Reed .08 .25
371 Jose Canseco UER .40 1.00
Strikeout total 391
should be 491
372 Rob Murphy .08 .25
373 Mike Henneman .08 .25
374 Walt Weiss .08 .25
375 Rob Dibble RC .40 1.00
376 Kirby Puckett .40 1.00
Mark McGwire
in background
377 Dennis Martinez .15 .40
378 Ron Gant .15 .40
379 Brian Harper .08 .25
380 Nelson Santovenia .08 .25
381 Lloyd Moseby .08 .25
382 Lance McCullers .08 .25
383 Dave Stieb .15 .40
384 Tony Gwynn .50 1.25
385 Mike Flanagan .08 .25
386 Bob Ojeda .08 .25
387 Bruce Hurst .08 .25
388 Dave Magadan .08 .25
389 Wade Boggs .25 .60
390 Gary Carter .15 .40
391 Frank Tanana .15 .40
392 Curt Young .08 .25
393 Jeff Treadway .08 .25
394 Darrell Evans .15 .40
395 Glenn Hubbard .08 .25
396 Chuck Cary .08 .25
397 Frank Viola .15 .40
398 Jeff Parrett .08 .25
399 Terry Blocker .08 .25
400 Dan Gladden .08 .25
401 Louie Meadows RC .08 .25
402 Tim Raines .15 .40
403 Joey Meyer .08 .25
404 Larry Andersen .08 .25
405 Rex Hudler .08 .25
406 Mike Schmidt .75 2.00
407 John Franco .15 .40
408 Brady Anderson RC .40 1.00
409 Don Carman .08 .25
410 Eric Davis .15 .40
411 Bob Stanley .08 .25
412 Pete Smith .08 .25
413 Jim Rice .15 .40
414 Bruce Sutter .15 .40
415 Oil Can Boyd .08 .25
416 Ruben Sierra .15 .40
417 Mike LaValliere .08 .25
418 Steve Buechele .08 .25
419 Gary Redus .08 .25
420 Scott Fletcher .08 .25
421 Dale Sveum .08 .25
422 Bob Knepper .08 .25
423 Luis Rivera .08 .25
424 Ted Higuera .08 .25
425 Kevin Bass .08 .25
426 Ken Gerhart .08 .25
427 Shane Rawley .08 .25
428 Paul O'Neill .25 .60
429 Joe Orsulak .08 .25
430 Jackie Gutierrez .08 .25
431 Gerald Perry .08 .25
432 Mike Greenwell .08 .25
433 Jerry Royster .08 .25
434 Ellis Burks .15 .40
435 Ed Olwine .08 .25
436 Dave Rucker .08 .25
437 Charlie Hough .15 .40
438 Bob Walk .08 .25
439 Bob Brower .08 .25
440 Barry Bonds 2.00 5.00
441 Tom Foley .08 .25
442 Rob Deer .08 .25
443 Glenn Davis .08 .25
444 Dave Martinez .08 .25
445 Bill Wegman .08 .25
446 Lloyd McClendon .08 .25
447 Dave Schmidt .08 .25
448 Darren Daulton .15 .40
449 Frank Williams .08 .25
450 Don Aase .08 .25
451 Lou Whitaker .15 .40
452 Rich Gossage .15 .40
453 Ed Whitson .08 .25
454 Jim Walewander .08 .25
455 Damon Berryhill .08 .25
456 Tim Burke .08 .25
457 Barry Jones .08 .25
458 Joel Youngblood .08 .25
459 Floyd Youmans .08 .25
460 Mark Salas .08 .25
461 Jeff Russell .08 .25
462 Darrell Miller .08 .25
463 Jeff Kunkel .08 .25
464 Sherman Corbett RC .08 .25
465 Curtis Wilkerson .08 .25
466 Bud Black .08 .25
467 Cal Ripken 1.25 3.00
468 John Farrell .08 .25
469 Terry Kennedy .08 .25
470 Tom Candiotti .08 .25
471 Roberto Alomar .40 1.00
472 Jeff M. Robinson .08 .25
473 Vance Law .08 .25
474 Randy Ready UER .08 .25
Strikeout total 136
should be 115
475 Walt Terrell .08 .25
476 Kelly Downs .08 .25
477 Johnny Paredes .08 .25
478 Shawn Hillegas .08 .25
479 Bob Brenly .08 .25
480 Otis Nixon .08 .25
481 Johnny Ray .08 .25
482 Geno Petralli .08 .25
483 Stu Cliburn .08 .25
484 Pete Incaviglia .08 .25
485 Brian Downing .15 .40
486 Jeff Stone .08 .25
487 Carmen Castillo .08 .25
488 Tom Niedenfuer .08 .25
489 Jay Bell .15 .40
490 Rick Schu .08 .25
491 Jeff Pico .08 .25

492 Mark Parent RC .08 .25
493 Eric King .08 .25
494 Al Nipper .08 .25
495 Andy Hawkins .08 .25
496 Daryl Boston .08 .25
497 Ernie Riles .08 .25
498 Pascual Perez .08 .25
499 Bill Long UER/(Games started total
70& should be .08 .25
500 Kirt Manwaring .08 .25
501 Chuck Crim .08 .25
502 Candy Maldonado .08 .25
503 Dennis Lamp .08 .25
504 Glenn Braggs .08 .25
505 Joe Price .08 .25
506 Ken Williams .08 .25
507 Bill Pecota .08 .25
508 Rey Quinones .08 .25
509 Jeff Bittiger .08 .25
510 Kevin Seitzer .08 .25
511 Steve Bedrosian .08 .25
512 Todd Worrell .08 .25
513 Chris James .08 .25
514 Jose Oquendo .08 .25
515 David Palmer .08 .25
516 John Smiley .08 .25
517 Dave Clark .08 .25
518 Mike Dunne .08 .25
519 Ron Washington .08 .25
520 Bob Kipper .08 .25
521 Lee Smith .15 .40
522 Juan Castillo .08 .25
523 Don Robinson .08 .25
524 Kevin Romine .08 .25
525 Paul Molitor .15 .40
526 Mark Langston .08 .25
527 Donnie Hill .08 .25
528 Larry Owen .08 .25
529 Jerry Reed .08 .25
530 Jack McDowell .15 .40
531 Greg Mathews .08 .25
532 John Russell .08 .25
533 Dan Quisenberry .08 .25
534 Greg Gross .08 .25
535 Danny Cox .08 .25
536 Terry Francona .15 .40
537 Andy Van Slyke .25 .60
538 Mel Hall .08 .25
539 Jim Gott .08 .25
540 Doug Jones .08 .25
541 Craig Lefferts .08 .25
542 Mike Boddicker .08 .25
543 Greg Brock .08 .25
544 Atlee Hammaker .08 .25
545 Tom Bolton .08 .25
546 Mike Macfarlane RC .20 .50
547 Rich Renteria .08 .25
548 John Davis .08 .25
549 Floyd Bannister .08 .25
550 Mickey Brantley .08 .25
551 Duane Ward .08 .25
552 Dan Petry .08 .25
553 Mickey Tettleton UER .08 .25
Walks total 175
should be 136
554 Rick Leach .08 .25
555 Mike Witt .08 .25
556 Sid Bream .08 .25
557 Bobby Witt .08 .25
558 Tommy Herr .08 .25
559 Randy Milligan .08 .25
560 Jose Cecena .08 .25
561 Mackey Sasser .08 .25
562 Carney Lansford .15 .40
563 Rick Aguilera .08 .25
564 Ron Hassey .08 .25
565 Dwight Gooden .15 .40
566 Paul Assenmacher .08 .25
567 Neil Allen .08 .25
568 Jim Morrison .08 .25
569 Mike Pagliarulo .08 .25
570 Ted Simmons .15 .40
571 Mark Thurmond .08 .25
572 Fred McGriff .25 .60
573 Wally Joyner .15 .40
574 Jose Bautista RC .08 .25
575 Kelly Gruber .08 .25
576 Cecilio Guante .08 .25
577 Mark Davidson .08 .25
578 Bobby Bonilla UER .15 .40
Total steals 2 in '87
should be 3
579 Mike Stanley .08 .25
580 Gene Larkin .08 .25
581 Stan Javier .08 .25
582 Howard Johnson .15 .40
583A Mike Gallego ERR .40 1.00
Front reversed
negative
583B Mike Gallego COR .40 1.00
584 David Cone .15 .40
585 Doug Jennings RC .08 .25
586 Charles Hudson .08 .25
587 Dion James .08 .25
588 Al Leiter .40 1.00
589 Charlie Puleo .08 .25
590 Roberto Kelly .08 .25
591 Thad Bosley .08 .25
592 Pete Stanicek .08 .25
593 Pat Borders RC .20 .50
594 Bryan Harvey RC .20 .50
595 Jeff Ballard .08 .25
596 Jeff Reardon .15 .40
597 Doug Drabek .08 .25
598 Edwin Correa .08 .25
599 Keith Atherton .08 .25
600 Dave LaPoint .08 .25
601 Don Baylor .15 .40
602 Tom Pagnozzi .08 .25
603 Tim Flannery .08 .25
604 Gene Walter .08 .25
605 Dave Parker .15 .40
606 Mike Diaz .08 .25
607 Chris Gwynn .08 .25
608 Odell Jones .08 .25
609 Carlton Fisk .25 .60
610 Jay Howell .08 .25
611 Tim Crews .08 .25
612 Keith Hernandez .15 .40
613 Willie Fraser .08 .25
614 Jim Eppard .08 .25
615 Jeff Hamilton .08 .25
616 Kurt Stillwell .08 .25
617 Tom Browning .08 .25
618 Jeff Montgomery .08 .25
619 Jose Rijo .15 .40
620 Jamie Quirk .08 .25
621 Willie McGee .15 .40
622 Mark Grant UER .08 .25
Glove on wrong hand
623 Bill Swift .08 .25
624 Orlando Mercado .08 .25
625 John Costello RC .08 .25
626 Jose Gonzalez .08 .25
627A Bill Schroeder ERR .25 .60
Back photo actually
Ronn Reynolds buckling
shin guards
627B Bill Schroeder COR .25 .60
628A Fred Manrique ERR .25 .60
Back photo actually
Ozzie Guillen throwing
628B Fred Manrique COR .08 .25
Swinging bat on back
629 Ricky Horton .08 .25
630 Dan Plesac .08 .25
631 Alfredo Griffin .08 .25
632 Chuck Finley .15 .40
633 Kirk Gibson .15 .40
634 Randy Myers .15 .40
635 Greg Minton .08 .25
636A Herm Winningham .40 1.00
ERR W1nningham
on back
636B Herm Winningham COR .08 .25
637 Charlie Leibrandt .08 .25
638 Tim Birtsas .08 .25
639 Bill Buckner .15 .40
640 Danny Jackson .08 .25
641 Greg Booker .08 .25
642 Jim Presley .08 .25
643 Gene Nelson .08 .25
644 Rod Booker .08 .25
645 Dennis Rasmussen .08 .25
646 Juan Nieves .08 .25
647 Bobby Thigpen .08 .25
648 Tim Belcher .08 .25
649 Mike Young .08 .25
650 Ivan Calderon .08 .25
651 Oswald Peraza RC .08 .25
652A Pat Sheridan ERR 6.00 15.00
652B Pat Sheridan COR .08 .25
653 Mike Morgan .08 .25
654 Mike Heath .08 .25
655 Jay Tibbs .08 .25
656 Fernando Valenzuela .15 .40
657 Lee Mazzilli .15 .40
658 Frank Viola AL CY .08 .25
659A Jose Canseco AL MVP .25 .60
Eagle logo in black
659B Jose Canseco AL MVP .25 .60
Eagle logo in blue
660 Walt Weiss AL ROY .08 .25
661 Orel Hershiser NL CY .08 .25
662 Kirk Gibson NL MVP .15 .40
663 Chris Sabo NL ROY .15 .40
664 Dennis Eckersley .15 .40
ALCS MVP
665 Orel Hershiser .15 .40
NLCS MVP
666 Kirk Gibson WS .40 1.00
667 Orel Hershiser WS MVP .08 .25
668 Wally Joyner TC .08 .25
669 Nolan Ryan TC .50 1.25
670 Jose Canseco TC .25 .60
671 Fred McGriff TC .15 .40
672 Dale Murphy TC .15 .40
673 Paul Molitor TC .08 .25
674 Ozzie Smith TC .40 1.00
675 Ryne Sandberg TC .40 1.00
676 Kirk Gibson TC .15 .40
677 Andres Galarraga TC .08 .25
678 Will Clark TC .15 .40
679 Cory Snyder TC .08 .25
680 Alvin Davis TC .08 .25
681 Darryl Strawberry TC .08 .25
682 Cal Ripken TC .40 1.00
683 Tony Gwynn TC .25 .60
684 Mike Schmidt TC .40 1.00
685 Andy Van Slyke TC
Pittsburgh Pirates/UER (96 Jun .15 .40
686 Ruben Sierra TC .08 .25
687 Wade Boggs TC .15 .40
688 Eric Davis TC .08 .25
689 George Brett TC .40 1.00
690 Alan Trammell TC .08 .25
691 Frank Viola TC .08 .25
692 Harold Baines TC .08 .25
Chicago White Sox
693 Don Mattingly TC .40 1.00
694 Checklist 1-100 .08 .25
695 Checklist 101-200 .08 .25
696 Checklist 201-300 .08 .25
697 Checklist 301-400 .08 .25
698 CL 401-500 UER .08 .25
467 Cal Ripkin Jr.
699 CL 501-600 UER .08 .25
543 Greg Booker
700 Checklist 601-700 .08 .25
701 Checklist 701-800 .08 .25
702 Jesse Barfield .15 .40
703 Walt Terrell .08 .25
704 Dickie Thon .08 .25
705 Al Leiter .40 1.00
706 Dave LaPoint .08 .25
707 Charlie Hayes RC .20 .50
708 Andy Hawkins .08 .25
709 Mickey Hatcher .08 .25
710 Lance McCullers .08 .25
711 Ron Kittle .08 .25
712 Bert Blyleven .15 .40
713 Rick Dempsey .08 .25
714 Ken Williams .08 .25
715 Steve Rosenberg .08 .25
716 Joe Skalski .08 .25
717 Spike Owen .08 .25
718 Todd Burns .08 .25
719 Kevin Gross .08 .25
720 Tommy Herr .08 .25
721 Rob Ducey .08 .25
722 Gary Green .08 .25
723 Gregg Olson RC .20 .50
724 Greg W. Harris RC .08 .25
725 Craig Worthington .08 .25
726 Tom Howard RC .08 .25
727 Dale Mohorcic .08 .25
728 Rich Yett .08 .25
729 Mel Hall .08 .25
730 Floyd Youmans .08 .25
731 Lonnie Smith .08 .25
732 Wally Backman .08 .25
733 Trevor Wilson RC .08 .25
734 Jose Alvarez RC .08 .25
735 Bob Milacki .08 .25
736 Tom Gordon RC .60 1.50
737 Wally Whitehurst RC .08 .25
738 Mike Aldrete .08 .25
739 Keith Miller .08 .25
740 Randy Milligan .08 .25
741 Jeff Parrett .08 .25
742 Steve Finley RC .75 2.00
743 Junior Felix RC .08 .25
744 Pete Harnisch RC .20 .50
745 Bill Spiers RC .20 .50
746 Hensley Meulens RC .08 .25
747 Juan Bell RC .08 .25
748 Steve Sax .08 .25
749 Phil Bradley .08 .25
750 Rey Quinones .08 .25
751 Tommy Gregg .08 .25
752 Kevin Brown .40 1.00
753 Derek Lilliquist RC .08 .25
754 Todd Zeile RC .40 1.00
755 Jim Abbott RC .75 2.00
756 Ozzie Canseco .08 .25
757 Nick Esasky .08 .25
758 Mike Moore .08 .25
759 Rob Murphy .08 .25
760 Rick Mahler .08 .25
761 Fred Lynn .15 .40
762 Kevin Blankenship .08 .25
763 Eddie Murray .40 1.00
764 Steve Searcy .08 .25
765 Jerome Walton RC .20 .50
766 Erik Hanson RC .20 .50
767 Bob Boone .15 .40
768 Edgar Martinez .40 1.00
769 Jose DeJesus .08 .25
770 Greg Briley .08 .25
771 Steve Peters .08 .25
772 Rafael Palmeiro .40 1.00
773 Jack Clark .15 .40
774 Nolan Ryan 1.50 4.00
775 Lance Parrish .15 .40
776 Joe Girardi RC .40 1.00
777 Willie Randolph .15 .40
778 Mitch Williams .08 .25
779 Dennis Cook RC .20 .50
780 Dwight Smith RC .20 .50
781 Lenny Harris RC .20 .50
782 Torey Lovullo RC .08 .25
783 Norm Charlton RC .20 .50
784 Chris Brown .08 .25
785 Todd Benzinger .08 .25
786 Shane Rawley .08 .25
787 Omar Vizquel RC 1.25 3.00
788 LaVel Freeman .08 .25
789 Jeffrey Leonard .08 .25
790 Eddie Williams .08 .25
791 Jamie Moyer .15 .40
792 Bruce Hurst UER .08 .25
World Series
793 Julio Franco .15 .40
794 Claudell Washington .08 .25
795 Jody Davis .08 .25
796 Oddibe McDowell .08 .25
797 Paul Kilgus .08 .25
798 Tracy Jones .08 .25
799 Steve Wilson .08 .25
800 Pete O'Brien .08 .25

1989 Upper Deck Sheets

These blank-backed, 8 1/2" by 11" sheets feature pictures of Upper Deck baseball cards and were distributed at conventions in Chicago and Washington, D.C. The sheets carried a production run number but not the total number produced. The sheets are listed below in chronological order.

COMPLETE SET (3) 15.00 40.00
1 10th National Sports Collectors Convention Chica 4.00 10.00
2 National Candy Wholesalers Expo Washington& D.C. 10.00 25.00
3 Sun-Times Card Show Chicago& Illinois Dec. 16-17 5.00 12.00

1990 Upper Deck

Kevin Maas

The 1990 Upper Deck set contains 800 standard-size cards issued in two series, low numbers (1-700) and high numbers (701-800). Cards were distributed in fin-wrapped low and high series foil packs, complete 800-card factory sets and 100-card high series factory sets. High series foil packs contained a mixture of low and high series cards. The front and back borders are white, and both sides feature full-color photos. The horizontally oriented backs have recent stats and anti-counterfeiting holograms. Team checklist cards are mixed in with the first 100 cards of the set. Rookie Cards in the set include Juan Gonzalez, David Justice, Ray Lankford, Dean Palmer, Sammy Sosa and Larry Walker. The high series contains a Nolan Ryan variation; all cards produced before August 12th only discuss Ryan's sixth no-hitter while the later-issue cards include a stripe honoring Ryan's 300th victory. Card 702 (Rookie Threats) was originally scheduled to be Mike Witt. A few Witt cards with 702 on back and checklist cards showing Witt as 702 escaped into early packs; they are characterized by a black rectangle covering much of the card's back.

COMPLETE SET (800) 10.00 25.00
COMP.FACT.SET (800) 10.00 25.00
COMPLETE LO SET (700) 10.00 25.00
COMPLETE HI SET (100) 2.00 5.00
COMP.HI FACT.SET (100) 2.00 4.00
1 Star Rookie Checklist .02 .10
2 Randy Nosek RC .02 .10
3 Tom Drees RC .02 .10
4 Curt Young .02 .10
5 Devon White TC .02 .10
6 Luis Salazar .02 .10
7 Von Hayes TC .02 .10
8 Jose Bautista .02 .10
9 Marquis Grissom RC .20 .50
10 Orel Hershiser TC .02 .10
11 Rick Aguilera .07 .20
12 Benito Santiago TC .02 .10
13 Deion Sanders .20 .50
14 Marvell Wynne .02 .10
15 Dave West .02 .10
16 Bobby Bonilla TC .02 .10
17 Sammy Sosa RC 1.25 3.00
18 Steve Sax TC .02 .10
19 Jack Howell .02 .10
20 Mike Schmidt SPEC .40 1.00
21 Robin Ventura .20 .50
22 Brian Meyer .02 .10
23 Blaine Beatty RC .02 .10
24 Ken Griffey Jr. TC .30 .75
25 Greg Vaughn .02 .10
26 Xavier Hernandez RC .02 .10
27 Jason Grimsley RC .02 .10
28 Eric Anthony RC .02 .10
29 Tim Raines TC UER .02 .10
30 David Wells .07 .20
31 Hal Morris .02 .10
32 Bo Jackson TC .07 .20
33 Kelly Mann RC .02 .10
34 Nolan Ryan SPEC .40 1.00
35 Scott Service UER
(Born Cincinnati on/7/27/67& s .02 .10
36 Mark McGwire TC .30 .75
37 Tino Martinez .40 1.00
38 Chili Davis .07 .20
39 Scott Sanderson .02 .10
40 Kevin Mitchell TC .02 .10
41 Lou Whitaker TC .02 .10
42 Scott Coolbaugh RC .02 .10
43 Jose Cano RC .02 .10
44 Jose Vizcaino RC .08 .25
45 Bob Hamelin RC .08 .25
46 Jose Offerman RC .08 .25
47 Kevin Blankenship .02 .10
48 Kirby Puckett TC .10 .30
49 Tommy Greene UER RC .02 .10
50 Will Clark SPEC .07 .20
51 Rob Nelson .02 .10
52 Chris Hammond UER RC .02 .10
53 Joe Carter TC .02 .10
54A Ben McDonald ERR 2.00 5.00
54B Ben McDonald COR RC .08 .25
55 Andy Benes UER .07 .20
56 John Olerud RC .30 .75
57 Roger Clemens TC .30 .75
58 Tony Armas .02 .10
59 George Canale RC .02 .10
60A Mickey Tettleton TC ERR .75 2.00
60B Mickey Tettleton TC COR .02 .10
61 Mike Stanton RC .08 .25
62 Dwight Gooden TC .02 .10
63 Kent Mercker RC .08 .25
64 Francisco Cabrera .02 .10
65 Steve Avery .02 .10
66 Jose Canseco .10 .30
67 Matt Merullo .02 .10
68 Vince Coleman TC UER .02 .10
69 Ron Karkovice .02 .10
70 Kevin Maas RC .08 .25
71 Dennis Cook UER
(Shown with righty/glove on card .02 .10
72 Juan Gonzalez RC .60 1.50
73 Andre Dawson TC .02 .10
74 Dean Palmer RC .08 .25
75 Bo Jackson SPEC .07 .20
76 Rob Richie RC .02 .10
77 Bobby Rose UER
(Pickin& should/be pick in) .02 .10
78 Brian DuBois UER RC .02 .10
79 Ozzie Guillen TC .02 .10
80 Gene Nelson .02 .10
81 Bob McClure .02 .10
82 Julio Franco TC .02 .10
83 Greg Minton .02 .10
84 John Smoltz TC UER .10 .30
85 Willie Fraser .02 .10
86 Neal Heaton .02 .10
87 Kevin Tapani RC .08 .25
88 Mike Scott TC .02 .10
89A Jim Gott ERR .75 2.00
89B Jim Gott COR .02 .10
90 Lance Johnson .02 .10
91 Robin Yount TC UER .20 .50
92 Jeff Parrett .02 .10
93 Julio Machado RC .02 .10
94 Ron Jones .02 .10
95 George Bell TC .02 .10
96 Jerry Reuss .02 .10
97 Brian Fisher .02 .10
98 Kevin Ritz RC .02 .10
99 Barry Larkin TC .07 .20
100 Checklist 1-100 .02 .10
101 Gerald Perry .02 .10
102 Kevin Appier .07 .20
103 Julio Franco .07 .20
104 Craig Biggio .20 .50
105 Bo Jackson UER .20 .50
106 Junior Felix .02 .10
107 Mike Harkey .02 .10
108 Fred McGriff .20 .50
109 Rick Sutcliffe .07 .20
110 Pete O'Brien .02 .10
111 Kelly Gruber .02 .10
112 Dwight Evans .10 .30
113 Pat Borders .02 .10
114 Dwight Gooden .07 .20
115 Kevin Batiste RC .02 .10
116 Eric Davis .07 .20
117 Kevin Mitchell UER
(Career HR total 99&/should b .02 .10
118 Ron Oester .02 .10
119 Brett Butler .07 .20
120 Danny Jackson .02 .10
121 Tommy Gregg .02 .10
122 Ken Caminiti .07 .20
123 Kevin Brown .07 .20
124 George Brett .50 1.25
125 Mike Scott .02 .10
126 Cory Snyder .02 .10
127 George Bell .02 .10
128 Mark Grace .10 .30
129 Devon White .07 .20
130 Tony Fernandez .02 .10
131 Don Aase .02 .10
132 Rance Mulliniks .02 .10
133 Marty Barrett .02 .10
134 Nelson Liriano .02 .10
135 Mark Carreon .02 .10
136 Candy Maldonado .02 .10
137 Tim Birtsas .02 .10
138 Tom Brookens .02 .10
139 John Franco .07 .20
140 Mike LaCoss .02 .10
141 Jeff Treadway .02 .10
142 Pat Tabler .02 .10
143 Darrell Evans .07 .20
144 Rafael Ramirez .02 .10
145 Oddibe McDowell UER
(Misspelled Odibbe) .02 .10
146 Brian Downing .02 .10
147 Curt Wilkerson .02 .10
148 Ernie Whitt .02 .10
149 Bill Schroeder .02 .10
150 Domingo Ramos UER
(Says throws right&/but shows .02 .10
151 Rick Honeycutt .02 .10
152 Don Slaught .02 .10
153 Mitch Webster .02 .10
154 Tony Phillips .02 .10
155 Paul Kilgus .02 .10
156 Ken Griffey Jr. .75 2.00
157 Gary Sheffield .20 .50
158 Wally Backman .02 .10
159 B.J. Surhoff .07 .20
160 Louie Meadows .02 .10
161 Paul O'Neill .10 .30
162 Jeff McKnight RC .02 .10
163 Alvaro Espinoza .02 .10
164 Scott Scudder .02 .10
165 Jeff Reed .02 .10
166 Gregg Jefferies .07 .20
167 Barry Larkin .10 .30
168 Gary Carter .07 .20
169 Robby Thompson .02 .10
170 Rolando Roomes .02 .10
171 Mark McGwire .60 1.50
172 Steve Sax .02 .10
173 Mark Williamson .02 .10
174 Mitch Williams .02 .10
175 Brian Holton .02 .10
176 Rob Deer .02 .10
177 Tim Raines .07 .20
178 Mike Felder .02 .10
179 Harold Reynolds .07 .20
180 Terry Francona .07 .20
181 Chris Sabo .02 .10
182 Darryl Strawberry .07 .20
183 Willie Randolph .07 .20
184 Bill Ripken .02 .10
185 Mackey Sasser .02 .10
186 Todd Benzinger .02 .10
187 Kevin Elster UER
(16 homers in 1989&/should be 1 .02 .10
188 Jose Uribe .02 .10
189 Tom Browning .02 .10
190 Keith Miller .02 .10
191 Don Mattingly .50 1.25
192 Dave Parker .07 .20
193 Roberto Kelly UER .02 .10
194 Phil Bradley .02 .10
195 Ron Hassey .02 .10
196 Gerald Young .02 .10
197 Hubie Brooks .02 .10
198 Bill Doran .02 .10
199 Al Newman .02 .10
200 Checklist 101-200 .02 .10
201 Terry Puhl .02 .10
202 Frank DiPino .02 .10
203 Jim Clancy .02 .10
204 Bob Ojeda .02 .10
205 Alex Trevino .02 .10
206 Dave Henderson .02 .10
207 Henry Cotto .02 .10
208 Rafael Belliard UER
(Born 1961& not 1951) .02 .10
209 Stan Javier .02 .10
210 Jerry Reed .02 .10
211 Doug Dascenzo .02 .10
212 Andres Thomas .02 .10
213 Greg Maddux .30 .75
214 Mike Schooler .02 .10
215 Lonnie Smith .02 .10
216 Jose Rijo .02 .10
217 Greg Gagne .02 .10
218 Jim Gantner .02 .10
219 Allan Anderson .02 .10
220 Rick Mahler .02 .10
221 Jim Deshaies .02 .10
222 Keith Hernandez .07 .20
223 Vince Coleman .02 .10
224 David Cone .07 .20
225 Ozzie Smith .30 .75
226 Matt Nokes .02 .10
227 Barry Bonds .60 1.50
228 Felix Jose .02 .10
229 Dennis Powell .02 .10
230 Mike Gallego .02 .10
231 Shawon Dunston UER
('89 stats are/Andre Dawson's .02 .10
232 Ron Gant .07 .20
233 Omar Vizquel .20 .50
234 Derek Lilliquist .02 .10
235 Erik Hanson .02 .10
236 Kirby Puckett .20 .50
237 Bill Spiers .02 .10
238 Dan Gladden .02 .10
239 Bryan Clutterbuck .02 .10
240 John Moses .02 .10
241 Ron Darling .02 .10
242 Joe Magrane .02 .10
243 Dave Magadan .02 .10
244 Pedro Guerrero UER .02 .10
Misspelled Guerrero
245 Glenn Davis .02 .10
246 Terry Steinbach .02 .10
247 Fred Lynn .02 .10
248 Gary Redus .02 .10
249 Ken Williams .02 .10
250 Sid Bream .02 .10
251 Bob Welch UER/(2587 career strike-
outs& should .02 .10
252 Bill Buckner .02 .10
253 Carney Lansford .07 .20
254 Paul Molitor .07 .20
255 Jose DeJesus .02 .10
256 Orel Hershiser .07 .20
257 Tom Brunansky .02 .10
258 Mike Davis .02 .10
259 Jeff Ballard .02 .10
260 Scott Terry .02 .10
261 Sid Fernandez .02 .10
262 Mike Marshall .02 .10
263 Howard Johnson UER
(192 SO& should be 592) .02 .10
264 Kirk Gibson UER .07 .20
265 Kevin McReynolds .02 .10
266 Cal Ripken .60 1.50
267 Ozzie Guillen UER .07 .20
268 Jim Traber .02 .10
269 Bobby Thigpen UER
(31 saves in 1989&/should be 3 .02 .10
270 Joe Orsulak .02 .10
271 Bob Boone .07 .20
272 Dave Stewart UER .07 .20
273 Tim Wallach .02 .10
274 Luis Aquino UER
(Says throws lefty&/but shows hi .02 .10
275 Mike Moore .02 .10
276 Tony Pena .02 .10
277 Eddie Murray .20 .50
278 Milt Thompson .02 .10
279 Alejandro Pena .02 .10
280 Ken Dayley .02 .10
281 Carmelo Castillo .02 .10
282 Tom Henke .02 .10
283 Mickey Hatcher .02 .10
284 Roy Smith .02 .10
285 Manny Lee .02 .10
286 Dan Pasqua .02 .10
287 Larry Sheets .02 .10
288 Garry Templeton .02 .10
289 Eddie Williams .02 .10
290 Brady Anderson .07 .20
291 Spike Owen .02 .10
292 Storm Davis .02 .10
293 Chris Bosio .02 .10
294 Jim Eisenreich .02 .10
295 Don August .02 .10
296 Jeff Hamilton .02 .10
297 Mickey Tettleton .02 .10
298 Mike Scioscia .02 .10
299 Kevin Hickey .02 .10
300 Checklist 201-300 .02 .10
301 Shawn Abner .02 .10
302 Kevin Bass .02 .10
303 Bip Roberts .02 .10
304 Joe Girardi .10 .30
305 Danny Darwin .02 .10
306 Mike Heath .02 .10
307 Mike Macfarlane .02 .10
308 Ed Whitson .02 .10
309 Tracy Jones .02 .10
310 Scott Fletcher .02 .10
311 Darnell Coles .02 .10
312 Mike Brumley .02 .10
313 Bill Swift .02 .10
314 Charlie Hough .07 .20
315 Jim Presley .02 .10
316 Luis Polonia .02 .10
317 Mike Morgan .02 .10
318 Lee Guetterman .02 .10
319 Jose Oquendo .02 .10
320 Wayne Tolleson .02 .10
321 Jody Reed .02 .10
322 Damon Berryhill .02 .10
323 Roger Clemens .60 1.50
324 Ryne Sandberg .30 .75
325 Benito Santiago UER .07 .20
326 Bret Saberhagen UER
(1140 hits& should be/1240; .07 .20
327 Lou Whitaker .07 .20
328 Dave Gallagher .02 .10
329 Mike Pagliarulo .02 .10
330 Doyle Alexander .02 .10
331 Jeffrey Leonard .02 .10
332 Torey Lovullo .02 .10
333 Pete Incaviglia .02 .10
334 Rickey Henderson .20 .50
335 Rafael Palmeiro .10 .30
336 Ken Hill .07 .20
337 Dave Winfield UER .07 .20
338 Alfredo Griffin .02 .10
339 Andy Hawkins .02 .10
340 Ted Power .02 .10
341 Steve Wilson .02 .10
342 Jack Clark UER
(916 BB& should be/1006; 1142 SO& .07 .20
343 Ellis Burks .10 .30
344 Tony Gwynn .25 .60
345 Jerome Walton UER
(Total At Bats 476&/should be .02 .10
346 Roberto Alomar .10 .30
347 Carlos Martinez UER
(Born 8/11/64& should/be 8/1 .02 .10
348 Chet Lemon .02 .10
349 Willie Wilson .02 .10
350 Greg Walker .02 .10
351 Tom Bolton .02 .10
352 German Gonzalez .02 .10
353 Harold Baines .07 .20
354 Mike Greenwell .02 .10
355 Ruben Sierra .07 .20
356 Andres Galarraga .07 .20
357 Andre Dawson .07 .20
358 Jeff Brantley .02 .10
359 Mike Bielecki .02 .10
360 Ken Oberkfell .02 .10
361 Kurt Stillwell .02 .10
362 Brian Holman .02 .10
363 Kevin Seitzer UER
(Career triples total/does not .02 .10
364 Alvin Davis .02 .10
365 Tom Gordon .07 .20
366 Bobby Bonilla UER
(Two steals in 1987&/should be .07 .20
367 Carlton Fisk .10 .30
368 Steve Carter UER .02 .10
Charlotesville
369 Joel Skinner .02 .10
370 John Cangelosi .02 .10
371 Cecil Espy .02 .10
372 Gary Wayne .02 .10
373 Jim Rice .07 .20
374 Mike Dyer RC .02 .10
375 Joe Carter .07 .20
376 Dwight Smith .02 .10
377 John Wetteland .20 .50
378 Ernie Riles .02 .10
379 Otis Nixon .02 .10
380 Vance Law .02 .10
381 Dave Bergman .02 .10
382 Frank White .07 .20
383 Scott Bradley .02 .10
384 Israel Sanchez UER
(Totals don't in-/clude '89 s .02 .10
385 Gary Pettis .02 .10
386 Donn Pall .02 .10
387 John Smiley .02 .10
388 Tom Candiotti .02 .10
389 Junior Ortiz .02 .10
390 Steve Lyons .02 .10
391 Brian Harper .02 .10
392 Fred Manrique .02 .10
393 Lee Smith .07 .20
394 Jeff Kunkel .02 .10
395 Claudell Washington .02 .10
396 John Tudor .02 .10
397 Terry Kennedy UER .02 .10
Career totals all
wrong
398 Lloyd McClendon .02 .10
399 Craig Lefferts .02 .10
400 Checklist 301-400 .02 .10
401 Keith Moreland .02 .10
402 Rich Gedman .02 .10
403 Jeff D. Robinson .02 .10
404 Randy Ready .02 .10
405 Rick Cerone .02 .10
406 Jeff Blauser .02 .10
407 Larry Andersen .02 .10
408 Joe Boever .02 .10
409 Felix Fermin .02 .10
410 Glenn Wilson .02 .10
411 Rex Hudler .02 .10
412 Mark Grant .02 .10
413 Dennis Martinez .07 .20
414 Darrin Jackson .02 .10
415 Mike Aldrete .02 .10
416 Roger McDowell .02 .10
417 Jeff Reardon .07 .20
418 Darren Daulton .07 .20
419 Tim Laudner .02 .10
420 Don Carman .02 .10
421 Lloyd Moseby .02 .10
422 Doug Drabek .02 .10
423 Lenny Harris UER
(Walks 2 in '89&/should be 20) .02 .10
424 Jose Lind .02 .10
425 Dave Wayne Johnson RC .02 .10
426 Jerry Browne .02 .10
427 Eric Yelding RC .02 .10
428 Brad Komminsk .02 .10
429 Jody Davis .02 .10
430 Mariano Duncan .02 .10
431 Mark Davis .02 .10
432 Nelson Santovenia .02 .10
433 Bruce Hurst .02 .10
434 Jeff Huson RC .02 .10
435 Chris James .02 .10
436 Mark Guthrie RC .02 .10
437 Charlie Hayes .02 .10
438 Shane Rawley .02 .10
439 Dickie Thon .02 .10
440 Juan Berenguer .02 .10
441 Kevin Romine .02 .10
442 Bill Landrum .02 .10
443 Todd Frohwirth .02 .10
444 Craig Worthington .02 .10
445 Fernando Valenzuela .07 .20
446 Albert Belle .20 .50
447 Ed Whited UER RC .02 .10
448 Dave Smith .02 .10
449 Dave Clark .02 .10
450 Juan Agosto .02 .10
451 Dave Valle .02 .10
452 Kent Hrbek .07 .20
453 Von Hayes .02 .10
454 Gary Gaetti .07 .20
455 Greg Briley .02 .10
456 Glenn Braggs .02 .10
457 Kirt Manwaring .02 .10
458 Mel Hall .02 .10
459 Brook Jacoby .02 .10
460 Pat Sheridan .02 .10
461 Rob Murphy .02 .10
462 Jimmy Key .07 .20
463 Nick Esasky .02 .10
464 Rob Ducey .02 .10
465 Carlos Quintana UER .02 .10
International
466 Larry Walker RC .60 1.50
467 Todd Worrell .02 .10
468 Kevin Gross .02 .10

469 Terry Pendleton .07 .20
470 Dave Martinez .02 .10
471 Gene Larkin .02 .10
472 Len Dykstra UER .07 .20
473 Barry Lyons .02 .10
474 Terry Mulholland .02 .10
475 Chip Hale RC .02 .10
476 Jesse Barfield .02 .10
477 Dan Plesac .02 .10
478A Scott Garrelts ERR .75 2.00
478B Scott Garrelts COR .02 .10
479 Dave Righetti .02 .10
480 Gus Polidor UER
(Wearing 14 on front&/but 10 on .02 .10
481 Mookie Wilson .07 .20
482 Luis Rivera .02 .10
483 Mike Flanagan .02 .10
484 Dennis Boyd .02 .10
485 John Cerutti .02 .10
486 John Costello .02 .10
487 Pascual Perez .02 .10
488 Tommy Herr .02 .10
489 Tom Foley .02 .10
490 Curt Ford .02 .10
491 Steve Lake .02 .10
492 Tim Teufel .02 .10
493 Randy Bush .02 .10
494 Mike Jackson .02 .10
495 Steve Jeltz .02 .10
496 Paul Gibson .02 .10
497 Steve Balboni .02 .10
498 Bud Black .02 .10
499 Dale Sveum .02 .10
500 Checklist 401-500 .02 .10
501 Tim Jones .02 .10
502 Mark Portugal .02 .10
503 Ivan Calderon .02 .10
504 Rick Rhoden .02 .10
505 Willie McGee .07 .20
506 Kirk McCaskill .02 .10
507 Dave LaPoint .02 .10
508 Jay Howell .02 .10
509 Johnny Ray .02 .10
510 Dave Anderson .02 .10
511 Chuck Crim .02 .10
512 Joe Hesketh .02 .10
513 Dennis Eckersley .07 .20
514 Greg Brock .02 .10
515 Tim Burke .02 .10
516 Frank Tanana .02 .10
517 Jay Bell .07 .20
518 Guillermo Hernandez .02 .10
519 Randy Kramer UER
(Codiroli misspelled/as Codorol .02 .10
520 Charles Hudson .02 .10
521 Jim Corsi .02 .10
522 Steve Rosenberg .02 .10
523 Cris Carpenter .02 .10
524 Matt Winters RC .02 .10
525 Melido Perez .02 .10
526 Chris Gwynn UER .02 .10
Albeguergue
527 Bert Blyleven UER .07 .20
528 Chuck Cary .02 .10
529 Daryl Boston .02 .10
530 Dale Mohorcic .02 .10
531 Geronimo Berroa .02 .10
532 Edgar Martinez .10 .30
533 Dale Murphy .10 .30
534 Jay Buhner .07 .20
535 John Smoltz .20 .50
536 Andy Van Slyke .10 .30
537 Mike Henneman .02 .10
538 Miguel Garcia .02 .10
539 Frank Williams .02 .10
540 R.J. Reynolds .02 .10
541 Shawn Hillegas .02 .10
542 Walt Weiss .02 .10
543 Greg Hibbard RC .02 .10
544 Nolan Ryan .75 2.00
545 Todd Zeile .07 .20
546 Hensley Meulens .02 .10
547 Tim Belcher .02 .10
548 Mike Witt .02 .10
549 Greg Cadaret UER
(Aquiring& should/be Acquiring) .02 .10
550 Franklin Stubbs .02 .10
551 Tony Castillo .02 .10
552 Jeff M. Robinson .02 .10
553 Steve Olin RC .08 .25
554 Alan Trammell .07 .20
555 Wade Boggs 4X .10 .30
556 Will Clark .10 .30
557 Jeff King .02 .10
558 Mike Fitzgerald .02 .10
559 Ken Howell .02 .10
560 Bob Kipper .02 .10
561 Scott Bankhead .02 .10
562A Jeff Innis ERR .75 2.00
562B Jeff Innis COR RC .02 .10
563 Randy Johnson .40 1.00
564 Wally Whitehurst .02 .10
565 Gene Harris .02 .10
566 Norm Charlton .02 .10
567 Robin Yount UER .30 .75
568 Joe Oliver .02 .10
569 Mark Parent .02 .10
570 John Farrell UER .02 .10
Loss total added wrong
571 Tom Glavine .10 .30
572 Rod Nichols .02 .10
573 Jack Morris .07 .20
574 Greg Swindell .02 .10
575 Steve Searcy .02 .10
576 Ricky Jordan .02 .10
577 Matt Williams .07 .20
578 Mike LaValliere .02 .10
579 Bryn Smith .02 .10
580 Bruce Ruffin .02 .10
581 Randy Myers .07 .20
582 Rick Wrona .02 .10
583 Juan Samuel .02 .10
584 Les Lancaster .02 .10
585 Jeff Musselman .02 .10
586 Rob Dibble .07 .20
587 Eric Show .02 .10
588 Jesse Orosco .02 .10
589 Herm Winningham .02 .10
590 Andy Allanson .02 .10
591 Dion James .02 .10
592 Carmelo Martinez .02 .10
593 Luis Quinones .02 .10
594 Dennis Rasmussen .02 .10
595 Rich Yett .02 .10
596 Bob Walk .02 .10
597A Andy McGaffigan ERR
(Photo actually/Rich Thompso .75 2.00
597B Andy McGaffigan COR .02 .10
598 Billy Hatcher .02 .10
599 Bob Knepper .02 .10
600 Checklist 501-600 UER
(599 Bob Kneppers) .02 .10
601 Joey Cora .07 .20
602 Steve Finley .07 .20
603 Kal Daniels UER
(12 hits in '87& should/be 123; .02 .10
604 Gregg Olson .07 .20
605 Dave Stieb .07 .20
606 Kenny Rogers .07 .20
607 Zane Smith .02 .10
608 Bob Geren UER .02 .10
Origionally
609 Chad Kreuter .02 .10
610 Mike Smithson .02 .10
611 Jeff Wetherby RC .02 .10
612 Gary Mielke RC .02 .10
613 Pete Smith .02 .10
614 Jack Daugherty RC .02 .10
615 Lance McCullers .02 .10
616 Don Robinson .02 .10
617 Jose Guzman .02 .10
618 Steve Bedrosian .02 .10
619 Jamie Moyer .07 .20
620 Atlee Hammaker .02 .10
621 Rick Luecken RC .02 .10
622 Greg W. Harris .02 .10
623 Pete Harnisch .02 .10
624 Jerald Clark .02 .10
625 Jack McDowell .02 .10
626 Frank Viola .02 .10
627 Teddy Higuera .02 .10
628 Marty Pevey RC .02 .10
629 Bill Wegman .02 .10
630 Eric Plunk .02 .10
631 Drew Hall .02 .10
632 Doug Jones .02 .10
633 Geno Petralli UER .02 .10
Sacremento
634 Jose Alvarez .02 .10
635 Bob Milacki .02 .10
636 Bobby Witt .02 .10
637 Trevor Wilson .02 .10
638 Jeff Russell UER .02 .10
Shutout stats wrong
639 Mike Krukow .02 .10
640 Rick Leach .02 .10
641 Dave Schmidt .02 .10
642 Terry Leach .02 .10
643 Calvin Schiraldi .02 .10
644 Bob Melvin .02 .10
645 Jim Abbott .10 .30
646 Jaime Navarro .02 .10
647 Mark Langston UER
(Several errors in/stats total .02 .10
648 Juan Nieves .02 .10
649 Damaso Garcia .02 .10
650 Charlie O'Brien .02 .10
651 Eric King .02 .10
652 Mike Boddicker .02 .10
653 Duane Ward .02 .10
654 Bob Stanley .02 .10
655 Sandy Alomar Jr. .07 .20
656 Danny Tartabull UER .02 .10
657 Randy McCament RC .02 .10
658 Charlie Leibrandt .02 .10
659 Dan Quisenberry .02 .10
660 Paul Assenmacher .02 .10
661 Walt Terrell .02 .10
662 Tim Leary .02 .10
663 Randy Milligan .02 .10
664 Bo Diaz .02 .10
665 Mark Lemke UER
(Richmond misspelled/as Richomond.02 .10
666 Jose Gonzalez .02 .10
667 Chuck Finley UER
(Born 11/16/62& should/be 11/26 .07 .20
668 John Kruk .07 .20
669 Dick Schofield .02 .10
670 Tim Crews .02 .10
671 John Dopson .02 .10
672 John Orton RC .02 .10
673 Eric Hetzel .02 .10
674 Lance Parrish .02 .10
675 Ramon Martinez .02 .10
676 Mark Gubicza .02 .10
677 Greg Litton .02 .10
678 Greg Mathews .02 .10
679 Dave Dravecky .07 .20
680 Steve Farr .02 .10
681 Mike Devereaux .02 .10
682 Ken Griffey Sr. .07 .20
683A Jamie Weston ERR .75 2.00
683B Mickey Weston COR RC .02 .10
684 Jack Armstrong .02 .10
685 Steve Buechele .02 .10
686 Bryan Harvey .02 .10
687 Lance Blankenship .02 .10
688 Dante Bichette .07 .20
689 Todd Burns .02 .10
690 Dan Petry .02 .10
691 Kent Anderson .02 .10
692 Todd Stottlemyre .07 .20
693 Wally Joyner UER .07 .20
Several stats errors
694 Mike Rochford .02 .10
695 Floyd Bannister .02 .10
696 Rick Reuschel .02 .10
697 Jose DeLeon .02 .10
698 Jeff Montgomery .07 .20
699 Kelly Downs .02 .10
700A CL 601-700 ERR .75 2.00
700B Checklist 601-700 .02 .10
683 Mickey Weston
701 Jim Gott .02 .10
702 L.Walker/Grissom/DeSh .20 .50
703 Alejandro Pena .02 .10
704 Willie Randolph .07 .20
705 Tim Leary .02 .10
706 Chuck McElroy RC .02 .10
707 Gerald Perry .02 .10
708 Tom Brunansky .02 .10
709 John Franco .07 .20
710 Mark Davis .02 .10
711 David Justice RC .30 .75
712 Storm Davis .02 .10
713 Scott Ruskin RC .02 .10
714 Glenn Braggs .02 .10
715 Kevin Bearse RC .02 .10
716 Jose Nunez .02 .10
717 Tim Layana RC .02 .10
718 Greg Myers .02 .10
719 Pete O'Brien .02 .10
720 John Candelaria .02 .10
721 Craig Grebeck RC .02 .10
722 Shawn Boskie RC .02 .10
723 Jim Leyritz RC .08 .25
724 Bill Sampen RC .02 .10
725 Scott Radinsky RC .02 .10
726 Todd Hundley RC .08 .25
727 Scott Hemond RC .02 .10
728 Lenny Webster RC .02 .10
729 Jeff Reardon .07 .20
730 Mitch Webster .02 .10
731 Brian Bohanon RC .02 .10
732 Rick Parker RC .02 .10
733 Terry Shumpert RC .02 .10
734A Nolan Ryan 6th 1.25 3.00
734B Nolan Ryan 6th/300 .40 1.00
735 John Burkett .02 .10
736 Derrick May RC .02 .10
737 Carlos Baerga RC .08 .25
738 Greg Smith RC .02 .10
739 Scott Sanderson .02 .10
740 Joe Kraemer RC .02 .10
741 Hector Villanueva RC .02 .10
742 Mike Fetters RC .08 .25
743 Mark Gardner RC .02 .10
744 Matt Nokes .02 .10
745 Dave Winfield .07 .20
746 Delino DeShields RC .08 .25
747 Dann Howitt RC .02 .10
748 Tony Pena .02 .10
749 Oil Can Boyd .02 .10
750 Mike Benjamin RC .02 .10
751 Alex Cole RC .02 .10
752 Eric Gunderson RC .02 .10
753 Howard Farmer RC .02 .10
754 Joe Carter .07 .20
755 Ray Lankford RC .20 .50
756 Sandy Alomar Jr. .07 .20
757 Alex Sanchez .02 .10
758 Nick Esasky .02 .10
759 Stan Belinda RC .02 .10
760 Jim Presley .02 .10
761 Gary DiSarcina RC .08 .25
762 Wayne Edwards RC .02 .10
763 Pat Combs .02 .10
764 Mickey Pina RC .02 .10
765 Wilson Alvarez RC .08 .25
766 Dave Parker .07 .20
767 Mike Blowers RC .02 .10
768 Tony Phillips .02 .10
769 Pascual Perez .02 .10
770 Gary Pettis .02 .10
771 Fred Lynn .02 .10
772 Mel Rojas RC .02 .10
773 David Segui RC .20 .50
774 Gary Carter .07 .20
775 Rafael Valdez RC .02 .10
776 Glenallen Hill .02 .10
777 Keith Hernandez .07 .20
778 Billy Hatcher .02 .10
779 Marty Clary .02 .10
780 Candy Maldonado .02 .10
781 Mike Marshall .02 .10
782 Billy Joe Robidoux .02 .10
783 Mark Langston .02 .10
784 Paul Sorrento RC .08 .25
785 Dave Hollins RC .08 .25
786 Cecil Fielder .07 .20
787 Matt Young .02 .10
788 Jeff Huson .02 .10
789 Lloyd Moseby .02 .10
790 Ron Kittle .02 .10
791 Hubie Brooks .02 .10
792 Craig Lefferts .02 .10
793 Kevin Bass .02 .10
794 Bryn Smith .02 .10
795 Juan Samuel .02 .10
796 Sam Horn .02 .10
797 Randy Myers .07 .20
798 Chris James .02 .10
799 Bill Gullickson .02 .10
800 Checklist 701-800 .02 .10

1990 Upper Deck Jackson Heroes

COMPLETE SET (10) 6.00 15.00
COMMON REGGIE (1-9) .60 1.50
RANDOM INSERTS IN HI SERIES
NNO Reggie Jackson Header 1.25 3.00
AU1 Reggie Jackson AU/2500 75.00 200.00

1990 Upper Deck Sheets

These blank-backed, 8 1/2" by 11" sheets feature pictures of Upper Deck baseball cards and were distributed at various specific events and times around the country. The sheets carried a production run number but not necessarily a total number produced. There were four regionally-issued sheets bound inside Street and Smith's 1990 Baseball Annual magazines to celebrate its 50th anniversary. The top five 1990 Upper Deck cards featured on all four sheets were the same: Carlton Fisk, Tim Raines, Jose Canseco and Will Clark. The Street and Smith sheets are listed below by their regions and regional players. The sheets are listed below in chronological order.

COMPLETE SET (5) 15.00 40.00
1 11th Annual National 3.00 8.00
Sports Collectors
Conventio
2 San Francisco 3.00 8.00
Conv. Center Show
Aug. 31-Sept. 3&
3 Street 8.00 20.00
Smith: West
Ken Griffey Jr.
Roberto Aloma
4 Street 3.00 8.00
Smith: East
Gregg Olson
Wade Boggs
Gregg
5 Street 3.00 8.00
Smith: Midwest
Tom Gordon
Pedro Guerrero#

1991 Upper Deck

This set marked the third year Upper Deck issued a 800-card standard-size set in two separate series of 700 and 100 cards respectively. Cards were distributed in low and high series foil packs and factory sets. The 100-card extended or high-number series was issued by Upper Deck several months after the release of their first series. For the first time in Upper Deck's three-year history, they did not issue a factory Extended set. The basic cards are made on the typical Upper Deck slick, white card stock and features full-color photos on both the front and the back. Subsets include Star Rookies (1-26), Team Cards (28-34, 43-49, 77-82, 95-99) and Top Prospects (50-76). Several other special achievement cards are seeded throughout the set. The team checklist (TC) cards in the set feature an attractive Vernon Wells drawing of a featured player for that particular team. Rookie Cards in this set include Jeff Bagwell, Luis Gonzalez, Chipper Jones, Eric Karros, and Mike Mussina. A special Michael Jordan card (numbered SP1) was randomly included in packs on a somewhat limited basis. The Hank Aaron hologram card was randomly inserted in the 1991 Upper Deck high number foil packs. Neither card is included in the price of the regular issue set though both are listed at the end of our checklist.

COMPLETE SET (800) 6.00 15.00
COMP.FACT.SET (800) 8.00 20.00
COMPLETE LO SET (700) 6.00 15.00
COMPLETE HI SET (100) 2.00 5.00
1 Star Rookie Checklist .01 .05
2 Phil Plantier RC .02 .10
3 D.J. Dozier .01 .05
4 Dave Hansen .01 .05
5 Maurice Vaughn .02 .10
6 Leo Gomez .01 .05
7 Scott Aldred .01 .05
8 Scott Chiamparino .01 .05
9 Lance Dickson RC .02 .10
10 Sean Berry RC .02 .10
11 Bernie Williams .08 .25
12 Brian Barnes UER RC .02 .10
13 Narciso Elvira RC .01 .05
14 Mike Gardiner RC .01 .05
15 Greg Colbrunn RC .08 .25
16 Bernard Gilkey .01 .05
17 Mark Lewis .01 .05
18 Mickey Morandini .01 .05
19 Charles Nagy .01 .05
20 Geronimo Pena .01 .05
21 Henry Rodriguez RC .08 .25
22 Scott Cooper .01 .05
23 Andujar Cedeno UER .01 .05
Shown batting left
back says right
24 Eric Karros RC .30 .75
25 Steve Decker UER RC .01 .05
26 Kevin Belcher RC .01 .05
27 Jeff Conine RC .20 .50
28 Dave Stewart TC .01 .05
29 Carlton Fisk TC .02 .10
30 Rafael Palmeiro TC .02 .10
31 Chuck Finley TC .01 .05
32 Harold Reynolds TC .01 .05
33 Bret Saberhagen TC .01 .05
34 Gary Gaetti TC .01 .05
35 Scott Leius .01 .05
36 Neal Heaton .01 .05
37 Terry Lee RC .01 .05
38 Gary Redus .01 .05
39 Barry Jones .01 .05
40 Chuck Knoblauch .02 .10
41 Larry Andersen .01 .05
42 Darryl Hamilton .01 .05
43 Mike Greenwell TC .01 .05
44 Kelly Gruber TC .01 .05
45 Jack Morris TC .01 .05
46 Sandy Alomar Jr. TC .01 .05
47 Gregg Olson TC .01 .05
48 Dave Parker TC .01 .05
49 Roberto Kelly TC .01 .05
50 Top Prospect Checklist .01 .05
51 Kyle Abbott .01 .05
52 Jeff Juden .01 .05
53 Todd Van Poppel UER RC .08 .25
54 Steve Karsay RC .08 .25
55 Chipper Jones RC 2.50 6.00
56 Chris Johnson UER RC .02 .10
57 John Ericks .01 .05
58 Gary Scott RC .01 .05
59 Kiki Jones .01 .05
60 Wil Cordero RC .02 .10
61 Royce Clayton .01 .05
62 Tim Costo RC .02 .10
63 Roger Salkeld .01 .05
64 Brook Fordyce RC .08 .25
65 Mike Mussina RC 1.00 2.50
66 Dave Staton RC .02 .10
67 Mike Lieberthal RC .20 .50
68 Kurt Miller RC .01 .05
69 Dan Peltier RC .02 .10
70 Greg Blosser .01 .05
71 Reggie Sanders RC .30 .75
72 Brent Mayne .01 .05
73 Rico Brogna .01 .05
74 Willie Banks .01 .05
75 Len Brutcher RC .01 .05
76 Pat Kelly RC .02 .10
77 Chris Sabo TC .01 .05
78 Ramon Martinez TC .01 .05
79 Matt Williams TC .01 .05
80 Roberto Alomar TC .02 .10
81 Glenn Davis TC .01 .05
82 Ron Gant TC .01 .05
83 Cecil Fielder FEAT .01 .05
84 Orlando Merced RC .02 .10
85 Domingo Ramos .01 .05
86 Tom Bolton .01 .05
87 Andres Santana .01 .05
88 John Dopson .01 .05
89 Kenny Williams .01 .05
90 Marty Barrett .01 .05
91 Tom Pagnozzi .01 .05
92 Carmelo Martinez .01 .05
93 Bobby Thigpen SAVE .01 .05
94 Barry Bonds TC .20 .50
95 Gregg Jefferies TC .01 .05
96 Tim Wallach TC .01 .05
97 Len Dykstra TC .01 .05
98 Pedro Guerrero TC .01 .05
99 Mark Grace TC .02 .10
100 Checklist 1-100 .01 .05
101 Kevin Elster .01 .05
102 Tom Brookens .01 .05
103 Mackey Sasser .01 .05
104 Felix Fermin .01 .05
105 Kevin McReynolds .01 .05
106 Dave Stieb .01 .05
107 Jeffrey Leonard .01 .05
108 Dave Henderson .01 .05
109 Sid Bream .01 .05
110 Henry Cotto .01 .05
111 Shawon Dunston .01 .05
112 Mariano Duncan .01 .05
113 Joe Girardi .01 .05
114 Billy Hatcher .01 .05
115 Greg Maddux .15 .40
116 Jerry Browne .01 .05
117 Juan Samuel .01 .05
118 Steve Olin .01 .05
119 Alfredo Griffin .01 .05
120 Mitch Webster .01 .05
121 Joel Skinner .01 .05
122 Frank Viola .02 .10
123 Cory Snyder .01 .05
124 Howard Johnson .01 .05
125 Carlos Baerga .01 .05
126 Tony Fernandez .01 .05
127 Dave Stewart .02 .10
128 Jay Buhner .02 .10
129 Mike LaValliere .01 .05
130 Scott Bradley .01 .05
131 Tony Phillips .01 .05
132 Ryne Sandberg .15 .40
133 Paul O'Neill .05 .15
134 Mark Grace .05 .15
135 Chris Sabo .01 .05
136 Ramon Martinez .01 .05
137 Brook Jacoby .01 .05
138 Candy Maldonado .01 .05
139 Mike Scioscia .01 .05
140 Chris James .01 .05
141 Craig Worthington .01 .05
142 Manny Lee .01 .05
143 Tim Raines .02 .10
144 Sandy Alomar Jr. .01 .05
145 John Olerud .02 .10
146 Ozzie Canseco .02 .10
With Jose
147 Pat Borders .01 .05
148 Harold Reynolds .02 .10
149 Tom Henke .01 .05
150 R.J. Reynolds .01 .05
151 Mike Gallego .01 .05
152 Bobby Bonilla .02 .10
153 Terry Steinbach .01 .05
154 Barry Bonds .40 1.00
155 Jose Canseco .05 .15
156 Gregg Jefferies .01 .05
157 Matt Williams .02 .10
158 Craig Biggio .05 .15
159 Daryl Boston .01 .05
160 Ricky Jordan .01 .05
161 Stan Belinda .01 .05
162 Ozzie Smith .15 .40
163 Tom Brunansky .01 .05
164 Todd Zeile .01 .05
165 Mike Greenwell .01 .05
166 Kal Daniels .01 .05
167 Kent Hrbek .02 .10
168 Franklin Stubbs .01 .05
169 Dick Schofield .01 .05
170 Junior Ortiz .01 .05
171 Hector Villanueva .01 .05
172 Dennis Eckersley .02 .10
173 Mitch Williams .01 .05
174 Mark McGwire .30 .75
175 Fernando Valenzuela 3X .02 .10
176 Gary Carter .02 .10
177 Dave Magadan .01 .05
178 Robby Thompson .01 .05
179 Bob Ojeda .01 .05
180 Ken Caminiti .02 .10
181 Don Slaught .01 .05
182 Luis Rivera .01 .05
183 Jay Bell .02 .10
184 Jody Reed .01 .05
185 Wally Backman .01 .05
186 Dave Martinez .01 .05
187 Luis Polonia .01 .05
188 Shane Mack .01 .05
189 Spike Owen .01 .05
190 Scott Bailes .01 .05
191 John Russell .01 .05
192 Walt Weiss .01 .05
193 Jose Oquendo .01 .05
194 Carney Lansford .02 .10
195 Jeff Huson .01 .05
196 Keith Miller .01 .05
197 Eric Yelding .01 .05
198 Ron Darling .01 .05
199 John Kruk .02 .10
200 Checklist 101-200 .01 .05
201 John Shelby .01 .05
202 Bob Geren .01 .05
203 Lance McCullers .01 .05
204 Alvaro Espinoza .01 .05
205 Mark Salas .01 .05
206 Mike Pagliarulo .01 .05
207 Jose Uribe .01 .05
208 Jim Deshaies .01 .05
209 Ron Karkovice .01 .05
210 Rafael Ramirez .01 .05
211 Donnie Hill .01 .05
212 Brian Harper .01 .05
213 Jack Howell .01 .05
214 Wes Gardner .01 .05
215 Tim Burke .01 .05
216 Doug Jones .01 .05
217 Hubie Brooks .01 .05
218 Tom Candiotti .01 .05
219 Gerald Perry .01 .05
220 Jose DeLeon .01 .05
221 Wally Whitehurst .01 .05
222 Alan Mills .01 .05
223 Alan Trammell .02 .10
224 Dwight Gooden .02 .10
225 Travis Fryman .02 .10
226 Joe Carter .02 .10
227 Julio Franco .02 .10
228 Craig Lefferts .01 .05
229 Gary Pettis .01 .05
230 Dennis Rasmussen .01 .05
231A Brian Downing ERR .01 .05
No position on front
231B Brian Downing COR .08 .25
DH on front
232 Carlos Quintana .01 .05
233 Gary Gaetti .02 .10
234 Mark Langston .01 .05
235 Tim Wallach .01 .05
236 Greg Swindell .01 .05
237 Eddie Murray .08 .25
238 Jeff Manto .01 .05
239 Lenny Harris .01 .05
240 Jesse Orosco .01 .05
241 Scott Lusader .01 .05
242 Sid Fernandez .01 .05
243 Jim Leyritz .01 .05
244 Cecil Fielder .02 .10
245 Darryl Strawberry .02 .10
246 Frank Thomas UER .08 .25
Comiskey Park
misspelled Comisky
247 Kevin Mitchell .01 .05
248 Lance Johnson .01 .05
249 Rick Reuschel .01 .05
250 Mark Portugal .01 .05
251 Derek Lilliquist .01 .05
252 Brian Holman .01 .05
253 Rafael Valdez UER .01 .05
Born 4/17/68
should be 12/17/67
254 B.J. Surhoff .02 .10
255 Tony Gwynn .10 .30
256 Andy Van Slyke .05 .15
257 Todd Stottlemyre .01 .05
258 Jose Lind .01 .05
259 Greg Myers .01 .05
260 Jeff Ballard .01 .05
261 Bobby Thigpen .01 .05
262 Jimmy Kremers .01 .05
263 Robin Ventura .02 .10
264 John Smoltz .05 .15
265 Sammy Sosa .08 .25
266 Gary Sheffield .02 .10
267 Len Dykstra .02 .10
268 Bill Spiers .01 .05
269 Charlie Hayes .01 .05
270 Brett Butler .02 .10
271 Bip Roberts .01 .05
272 Rob Deer .01 .05
273 Fred Lynn .01 .05
274 Dave Parker .02 .10
275 Andy Benes .01 .05
276 Glenallen Hill .01 .05
277 Steve Howard .01 .05
278 Doug Drabek .01 .05
279 Joe Oliver .01 .05
280 Todd Benzinger .01 .05
281 Eric King .01 .05
282 Jim Presley .01 .05
283 Ken Patterson .01 .05
284 Jack Daugherty .01 .05
285 Ivan Calderon .01 .05
286 Edgar Diaz .01 .05
287 Kevin Bass .01 .05
288 Don Carman .01 .05
289 Greg Brock .01 .05
290 John Franco .02 .10
291 Joey Cora .01 .05
292 Bill Wegman .01 .05
293 Eric Show .01 .05
294 Scott Bankhead .01 .05
295 Garry Templeton .01 .05
296 Mickey Tettleton .01 .05
297 Luis Sojo .01 .05
298 Jose Rijo .01 .05
299 Dave Johnson .01 .05
300 Checklist 201-300 .01 .05
301 Mark Grant .01 .05
302 Pete Harnisch .01 .05
303 Greg Olson .01 .05
304 Anthony Telford RC .01 .05
305 Lonnie Smith .01 .05
306 Chris Hoiles .01 .05
307 Bryn Smith .01 .05
308 Mike Devereaux .01 .05
309A Milt Thompson ERR .08 .25
Under yr information
has print dot
309B Milt Thompson COR .01 .05
Under yr information
says 86
310 Bob Melvin .01 .05
311 Luis Salazar .01 .05
312 Ed Whitson .01 .05
313 Charlie Hough .02 .10
314 Dave Clark .01 .05
315 Eric Gunderson .01 .05
316 Dan Petry .01 .05
317 Dante Bichette UER .02 .10
Assists misspelled
as assissts
318 Mike Heath .01 .05
319 Damon Berryhill .01 .05
320 Walt Terrell .01 .05
321 Scott Fletcher .01 .05
322 Dan Plesac .01 .05
323 Jack McDowell .01 .05
324 Paul Molitor .02 .10
325 Ozzie Guillen .02 .10
326 Gregg Olson .01 .05
327 Pedro Guerrero .02 .10
328 Bob Milacki .01 .05
329 John Tudor UER .01 .05
'90 Cardinals
should be '90 Dodgers
330 Steve Finley UER .02 .10
Born 3/12/65
should be 5/12
331 Jack Clark .02 .10
332 Jerome Walton .01 .05
333 Andy Hawkins .01 .05
334 Derrick May .01 .05
335 Roberto Alomar .05 .15
336 Jack Morris .02 .10
337 Dave Winfield .02 .10
338 Steve Searcy .01 .05
339 Chili Davis .02 .10
340 Larry Sheets .01 .05
341 Ted Higuera .01 .05
342 David Segui .01 .05
343 Greg Cadaret .01 .05
344 Robin Yount .15 .40
345 Nolan Ryan .40 1.00
346 Ray Lankford .02 .10
347 Cal Ripken .30 .75
348 Lee Smith .02 .10
349 Brady Anderson .02 .10
350 Frank DiPino .01 .05
351 Hal Morris .01 .05
352 Deion Sanders .05 .15
353 Barry Larkin .05 .15
354 Don Mattingly .25 .60
355 Eric Davis .02 .10
356 Jose Offerman .01 .05
357 Mel Rojas .01 .05
358 Rudy Seanez .01 .05
359 Oil Can Boyd .01 .05
360 Nelson Liriano .01 .05
361 Ron Gant .02 .10
362 Howard Farmer .01 .05
363 David Justice .02 .10
364 Delino DeShields .02 .10
365 Steve Avery .01 .05
366 David Cone .02 .10
367 Lou Whitaker .02 .10
368 Von Hayes .01 .05
369 Frank Tanana .01 .05
370 Tim Teufel .01 .05
371 Randy Myers .01 .05
372 Roberto Kelly .01 .05
373 Jack Armstrong .01 .05
374 Kelly Gruber .01 .05
375 Kevin Maas .01 .05
376 Randy Johnson .10 .30
377 David West .01 .05
378 Brent Knackert .01 .05
379 Rick Honeycutt .01 .05
380 Kevin Gross .01 .05
381 Tom Foley .01 .05
382 Jeff Blauser .01 .05
383 Scott Ruskin .01 .05
384 Andres Thomas .01 .05
385 Dennis Martinez .02 .10
386 Mike Henneman .01 .05
387 Felix Jose .01 .05
388 Alejandro Pena .01 .05
309 Chet Lemon .01 .05
390 Craig Wilson RC .01 .05
391 Chuck Crim .01 .05
392 Mel Hall .01 .05
393 Mark Knudson .01 .05
394 Norm Charlton .01 .05
395 Mike Felder .01 .05
396 Tim Layana .01 .05
397 Steve Frey .01 .05
398 Bill Doran .01 .05
399 Dion James .01 .05
400 Checklist 301-400 .01 .05
401 Ron Hassey .01 .05
402 Don Robinson .01 .05
403 Gene Nelson .01 .05
404 Terry Kennedy .01 .05
405 Todd Burns .01 .05
406 Roger McDowell .01 .05
407 Bob Kipper .01 .05
408 Darren Daulton .02 .10
409 Chuck Cary .01 .05
410 Bruce Ruffin .01 .05
411 Juan Berenguer .01 .05
412 Gary Ward .01 .05
413 Al Newman .01 .05
414 Danny Jackson .01 .05
415 Greg Gagne .01 .05
416 Tom Herr .01 .05
417 Jeff Parrett .01 .05
418 Jeff Reardon .02 .10
419 Mark Lemke .01 .05
420 Charlie O'Brien .01 .05
421 Willie Randolph .02 .10
422 Steve Bedrosian .01 .05
423 Mike Moore .01 .05
424 Jeff Brantley .01 .05
425 Bob Welch .01 .05
426 Terry Mulholland .01 .05
427 Willie Blair .01 .05
428 Darrin Fletcher .01 .05
429 Mike Witt .01 .05
430 Joe Boever .01 .05
431 Tom Gordon .01 .05
432 Pedro Munoz RC .02 .10
433 Kevin Seitzer .01 .05
434 Kevin Tapani .01 .05
435 Bret Saberhagen .02 .10
436 Ellis Burks .02 .10

437 Chuck Finley .02 .10
438 Mike Boddicker .01 .05
439 Francisco Cabrera .01 .05
440 Todd Hundley .01 .05
441 Kelly Downs .01 .05
442 Dann Howitt .01 .05
443 Scott Garrelts .01 .05
444 Rickey Henderson 3X .08 .25
445 Will Clark .05 .15
446 Ben McDonald .01 .05
447 Dale Murphy .05 .15
448 Dave Righetti .02 .10
449 Dickie Thon .01 .05
450 Ted Power .01 .05
451 Scott Coolbaugh .01 .05
452 Dwight Smith .01 .05
453 Pete Incaviglia .01 .05
454 Andre Dawson .02 .10
455 Ruben Sierra .02 .10
456 Andres Galarraga .02 .10
457 Alvin Davis .01 .05
458 Tony Castillo .01 .05
459 Pete O'Brien .01 .05
460 Charlie Leibrandt .01 .05
461 Vince Coleman .01 .05
462 Steve Sax .01 .05
463 Omar Olivares RC .02 .10
464 Oscar Azocar .01 .05
465 Joe Magrane .01 .05
466 Karl Rhodes .01 .05
467 Benito Santiago .02 .10
468 Joe Klink .01 .05
469 Sil Campusano .01 .05
470 Mark Parent .01 .05
471 Shawn Boskie UER .01 .05
Depleted misspelled
as depleated
472 Kevin Brown .02 .10
473 Rick Sutcliffe .02 .10
474 Rafael Palmeiro .05 .15
475 Mike Harkey .01 .05
476 Jaime Navarro .01 .05
477 Marquis Grissom UER .02 .10
DeShields misspelled
as DeSheilds
478 Marty Clary .01 .05
479 Greg Briley .01 .05
480 Tom Glavine .05 .15
481 Lee Guetterman .01 .05
482 Rex Hudler .01 .05
483 Dave LaPoint .01 .05
484 Terry Pendleton .02 .10
485 Jesse Barfield .01 .05
486 Jose DeJesus .01 .05
487 Paul Abbott RC .02 .10
488 Ken Howell .01 .05
489 Greg W. Harris .01 .05
490 Roy Smith .01 .05
491 Paul Assenmacher .01 .05
492 Geno Petralli .01 .05
493 Steve Wilson .01 .05
494 Kevin Reimer .01 .05
495 Bill Long .01 .05
496 Mike Jackson .01 .05
497 Oddibe McDowell .01 .05
498 Bill Swift .01 .05
499 Jeff Treadway .01 .05
500 Checklist 401-500 .01 .05
501 Gene Larkin .01 .05
502 Bob Boone .02 .10
503 Allan Anderson .01 .05
504 Luis Aquino .01 .05
505 Mark Guthrie .01 .05
506 Joe Orsulak .01 .05
507 Dana Kiecker .01 .05
508 Dave Gallagher .01 .05
509 Greg A. Harris .01 .05
510 Mark Williamson .01 .05
511 Casey Candaele .01 .05
512 Mookie Wilson .02 .10
513 Dave Smith .01 .05
514 Chuck Carr .01 .05
515 Glenn Wilson .01 .05
516 Mike Fitzgerald .01 .05
517 Devon White .02 .10
518 Dave Hollins .01 .05
519 Mark Eichhorn .01 .05
520 Otis Nixon .01 .05
521 Terry Shumpert .01 .05
522 Scott Erickson .01 .05
523 Danny Tartabull .01 .05
524 Orel Hershiser .02 .10
525 George Brett .25 .60
526 Greg Vaughn .01 .05
527 Tim Naehring .01 .05
528 Curt Schilling .08 .25
529 Chris Bosio .01 .05
530 Sam Horn .01 .05
531 Mike Scott .01 .05
532 George Bell .01 .05
533 Eric Anthony .01 .05
534 Julio Valera .01 .05
535 Glenn Davis .01 .05
536 Larry Walker UER .08 .25
Should have comma
after Expos in text
537 Pat Combs .01 .05
538 Chris Nabholz .01 .05
539 Kirk McCaskill .01 .05
540 Randy Ready .01 .05
541 Mark Gubicza .01 .05
542 Rick Aguilera .02 .10
543 Brian McRae RC .08 .25
544 Kirby Puckett .08 .25
545 Bo Jackson .08 .25
546 Wade Boggs .05 .15
547 Tim McIntosh .01 .05
548 Randy Milligan .01 .05
549 Dwight Evans .05 .15
550 Billy Ripken .01 .05
551 Erik Hanson .01 .05
552 Lance Parrish .02 .10
553 Tino Martinez .08 .25
554 Jim Abbott .05 .15
555 Ken Griffey Jr. UER .25 .60
556 Milt Cuyler .01 .05
557 Mark Leonard RC .01 .05
558 Jay Howell .01 .05
559 Lloyd Moseby .01 .05
560 Chris Gwynn .01 .05
561 Mark Whiten .01 .05
562 Harold Baines .02 .10
563 Junior Felix .01 .05
564 Darren Lewis .01 .05
565 Fred McGriff .05 .15
566 Kevin Appier .02 .10
567 Luis Gonzalez RC .30 .75
568 Frank White .02 .10
569 Juan Agosto .01 .05
570 Mike Macfarlane .01 .05
571 Bert Blyleven .02 .10
572 Ken Griffey Sr. .10 .30
Ken Griffey Jr.
573 Lee Stevens .01 .05
574 Edgar Martinez .05 .15
575 Wally Joyner .02 .10
576 Tim Belcher .01 .05
577 John Burkett .01 .05
578 Mike Morgan .01 .05
579 Paul Gibson .01 .05
580 Jose Vizcaino .01 .05
581 Duane Ward .01 .05
582 Scott Sanderson .01 .05
583 David Wells .02 .10
584 Willie McGee .02 .10
585 John Cerutti .01 .05
586 Danny Darwin .01 .05
587 Kurt Stillwell .01 .05
588 Rich Gedman .01 .05
589 Mark Davis .01 .05
590 Bill Gullickson .01 .05
591 Matt Young .01 .05
592 Bryan Harvey .01 .05
593 Omar Vizquel .05 .15
594 Scott Lewis RC .02 .10
595 Dave Valle .01 .05
596 Tim Crews .01 .05
597 Mike Bielecki .01 .05
598 Mike Sharperson .01 .05
599 Dave Bergman .01 .05
600 Checklist 501-600 .01 .05
601 Steve Lyons .01 .05
602 Bruce Hurst .01 .05
603 Donn Pall .01 .05
604 Jim Vatcher RC .01 .05
605 Dan Pasqua .01 .05
606 Kenny Rogers .02 .10
607 Jeff Schulz RC .01 .05
608 Brad Arnsberg .01 .05
609 Willie Wilson .01 .05
610 Jamie Moyer .02 .10
611 Ron Oester .01 .05
612 Dennis Cook .01 .05
613 Rick Mahler .01 .05
614 Bill Landrum .01 .05
615 Scott Scudder .01 .05
616 Tom Edens RC .01 .05
617 1917 Revisited .02 .10
White Sox vintage uniforms
618 Jim Gantner .01 .05
619 Darrel Akerfelds .01 .05
620 Ron Robinson .01 .05
621 Scott Radinsky .01 .05
622 Pete Smith .01 .05
623 Melido Perez .01 .05
624 Jerald Clark .01 .05
625 Carlos Martinez .01 .05
626 Wes Chamberlain RC .08 .25
627 Bobby Witt .01 .05
628 Ken Dayley .01 .05
629 John Barfield .01 .05
630 Bob Tewksbury .01 .05
631 Glenn Braggs .01 .05
632 Jim Neidlinger RC .01 .05
633 Tom Browning .01 .05
634 Kirk Gibson .02 .10
635 Rob Dibble .02 .10
636 Rickey Henderson SB .08 .25
Lou Brock
May 1 1991 on front
636A R.Henderson SB .08 .25
Lou Brock
no date on card
637 Jeff Montgomery .01 .05
638 Mike Schooler .01 .05
639 Storm Davis .01 .05
640 Rich Rodriguez RC .01 .05
641 Phil Bradley .01 .05
642 Kent Mercker .01 .05
643 Carlton Fisk .05 .15
644 Mike Bell RC .01 .05
645 Alex Fernandez .01 .05
646 Juan Gonzalez .08 .25
647 Ken Hill .01 .05
648 Jeff Russell .01 .05
649 Chuck Malone .01 .05
650 Steve Buechele .01 .05
651 Mike Benjamin .01 .05
652 Tony Pena .01 .05
653 Trevor Wilson .01 .05
654 Alex Cole .01 .05
655 Roger Clemens .30 .75
656 Mark McGwire BASH .15 .40
657 Joe Grahe RC .02 .10
658 Jim Eisenreich .01 .05
659 Dan Gladden .01 .05
660 Steve Farr .01 .05
661 Bill Sampen .01 .05
662 Dave Rohde .01 .05
663 Mark Gardner .01 .05
664 Mike Simms RC .01 .05
665 Moises Alou .01 .05
666 Mickey Hatcher .01 .05
667 Jimmy Key .02 .10
668 John Wetteland .02 .10
669 John Smiley .01 .05
670 Jim Acker .01 .05
671 Pascual Perez .01 .05
672 Reggie Harris UER .01 .05
Opportunity misspelled
as oppurtinty
673 Matt Nokes .01 .05
674 Rafael Novoa RC .01 .05
675 Hensley Meulens .01 .05
676 Jeff M. Robinson .01 .05
677 Ground Breaking .02 .10
New Comiskey Park;
Carlton Fisk and
Robin Ventura
678 Johnny Ray .01 .05
679 Greg Hibbard .01 .05
680 Paul Sorrento .01 .05
681 Mike Marshall .01 .05
682 Jim Clancy .01 .05
683 Rob Murphy .01 .05
684 Dave Schmidt .01 .05
685 Jeff Gray RC .01 .05
686 Mike Hartley .01 .05
687 Jeff King .01 .05
688 Stan Javier .01 .05
689 Bob Walk .01 .05
690 Jim Gott .01 .05
691 Mike LaCoss .01 .05
692 John Farrell .01 .05
693 Tim Leary .01 .05
694 Mike Walker .01 .05
695 Eric Plunk .01 .05
696 Mike Fetters .01 .05
697 Wayne Edwards .01 .05
698 Tim Drummond .01 .05
699 Willie Fraser .01 .05
700 Checklist 601-700 .01 .05
701 Mike Heath .01 .05
702 Gonzalez/Rhodes/Bagwell .40 1.00
703 Jose Mesa .01 .05
704 Dave Smith .01 .05
705 Danny Darwin .01 .05
706 Rafael Belliard .01 .05
707 Rob Murphy .01 .05
708 Terry Pendleton .02 .10
709 Mike Pagliarulo .01 .05
710 Sid Bream .01 .05
711 Junior Felix .01 .05
712 Dante Bichette .02 .10
713 Kevin Gross .01 .05
714 Luis Sojo .01 .05
715 Bob Ojeda .01 .05
716 Julio Machado .01 .05
717 Steve Farr .01 .05
718 Franklin Stubbs .01 .05
719 Mike Boddicker .01 .05
720 Willie Randolph .02 .10
721 Willie McGee .02 .10
722 Chili Davis .02 .10
723 Danny Jackson .01 .05
724 Cory Snyder .01 .05
725 Andre Dawson .08 .25
George Bell
Ryne Sandberg
726 Rob Deer .01 .05
727 Rich DeLucia RC .01 .05
728 Mike Perez RC .02 .10
729 Mickey Tettleton .01 .05
730 Mike Blowers .01 .05
731 Gary Gaetti .02 .10
732 Brett Butler .02 .10
733 Dave Parker .02 .10
734 Eddie Zosky .02 .10
735 Jack Clark .02 .10
736 Jack Morris .02 .10
737 Kirk Gibson .02 .10
738 Steve Bedrosian .01 .05
739 Candy Maldonado .01 .05
740 Matt Young .01 .05
741 Rich Garces RC .02 .10
742 George Bell .02 .10
743 Deion Sanders .05 .15
744 Bo Jackson .08 .25
745 Luis Mercedes RC .02 .10
746 Reggie Jefferson UER .01 .05
Throwing left on card;
back has throws right
747 Pete Incaviglia .01 .05
748 Chris Hammond .01 .05
749 Mike Stanton .01 .05
750 Scott Sanderson .01 .05
751 Paul Faries RC .01 .05
752 Al Osuna RC .01 .05
753 Steve Chitren RC .01 .05
754 Tony Fernandez .01 .05
755 Jeff Bagwell UER RC .60 1.50
756 Kirk Dressendorfer RC .02 .10
757 Glenn Davis .01 .05
758 Gary Carter .02 .10
759 Zane Smith .01 .05
760 Vance Law .01 .05
761 Denis Boucher RC .02 .10
762 Turner Ward RC .02 .10
763 Roberto Alomar .05 .15
764 Albert Belle .02 .10
765 Joe Carter .02 .10
766 Pete Schourek RC .02 .10
767 Heathcliff Slocumb RC .02 .10
768 Vince Coleman .01 .05
769 Mitch Williams .01 .05
770 Brian Downing .01 .05
771 Dana Allison RC .01 .05
772 Pete Harnisch .01 .05
773 Tim Raines .02 .10
774 Darryl Kile .05 .15
775 Fred McGriff .05 .15
776 Dwight Evans .05 .15
777 Joe Slusarski RC .01 .05
778 Dave Righetti .02 .10
779 Jeff Hamilton .01 .05
780 Ernest Riles .01 .05
781 Ken Dayley .01 .05
782 Eric King .01 .05
783 Devon White .02 .10
784 Beau Allred .01 .05
785 Mike Timlin RC .08 .25
786 Ivan Calderon .01 .05
787 Hubie Brooks .01 .05
788 Juan Agosto .01 .05
789 Barry Jones .01 .05
790 Wally Backman .01 .05
791 Jim Presley .01 .05
792 Charlie Hough .02 .10
793 Larry Andersen .01 .05
794 Steve Finley .02 .10
795 Shawn Abner .01 .05
796 Jeff M. Robinson .01 .05
797 Joe Bitker RC .01 .05
798 Eric Show .01 .05
799 Bud Black .01 .05
800 Checklist 701-800 .01 .05
HH1 Hank Aaron Hologram .60 1.50
SP1 Michael Jordan SP 20.00 50.00
SP2 R.Henderson/N.Ryan .75 2.00

1991 Upper Deck Aaron Heroes

COMPLETE SET (10) 2.00 5.00
COMMON AARON (19-27) .20 .50
RANDOM INSERTS IN HI SERIES
NNO Hank Aaron Header SP .40 1.00
AU3 Hank Aaron AU/2500 75.00 200.00

1991 Upper Deck Heroes of Baseball

COMPLETE SET (4) 10.00 25.00
RANDOM INSERTS IN HEROES FOIL
H1 Harmon Killebrew 3.00 8.00
H2 Gaylord Perry 2.00 5.00
H3 Fergie Jenkins 2.00 5.00
H4 Header 3.00 8.00
Art Card
AU1 Harmon Killebrew AU/3000 20.00 50.00
AU2 Gaylord Perry AU/3000 20.00 50.00
AU3 Fergie Jenkins AU/3000 12.00 30.00

1991 Upper Deck Ryan Heroes

COMPLETE SET (10) 2.00 5.00
COMMON RYAN (10-18) .20 .50
RANDOM INSERTS IN LO SERIES
NNO Nolan Ryan Header SP .40 1.00
AU2 Nolan Ryan AU/2500 100.00 200.00

1991 Upper Deck Silver Sluggers

COMPLETE SET (18) 6.00 15.00
ONE PER LO OR HI JUMBO PACK
SS1 Julio Franco .30 .75
SS2 Alan Trammell .30 .75
SS3 Rickey Henderson .75 2.00
SS4 Jose Canseco .50 1.25
SS5 Barry Bonds 3.00 8.00
SS6 Eddie Murray .75 2.00
SS7 Kelly Gruber .15 .40
SS8 Ryne Sandberg 1.25 3.00
SS9 Darryl Strawberry .30 .75
SS10 Ellis Burks .30 .75
SS11 Lance Parrish .30 .75
SS12 Cecil Fielder .30 .75
SS13 Matt Williams .30 .75
SS14 Dave Parker .30 .75
SS15 Bobby Bonilla .30 .75
SS16 Don Robinson .15 .40
SS17 Benito Santiago .30 .75
SS18 Barry Larkin .50 1.25

1991 Upper Deck Final Edition

The 1991 Upper Deck Final Edition boxed set contains 100 standard-size cards and showcases players who made major contributions during their team's late-season pennant drive. In addition to the late season traded and impact rookie cards (22-78), the set includes two special subsets: Diamond Skills cards (1-21), depicting the best Minor League prospects, and All-Star cards (80-99). Six assorted team logo hologram cards were issued with each set. The cards are numbered on the back with an F suffix. Among the outstanding Rookie Cards in this set are Ryan Klesko, Kenny Lofton, Pedro Martinez, Ivan Rodriguez, Jim Thome, Rondell White, and Dmitri Young.

COMP.FACT.SET (100) 3.00 8.00
1F R.Klesko .08 .25
R.Sanders CL
2F Pedro Martinez RC 4.00 10.00
3F Lance Dickson .01 .05
4F Royce Clayton .01 .05
5F Scott Bryant .01 .05
6F Dan Wilson RC .08 .25
7F Dmitri Young RC .30 .75
8F Ryan Klesko RC .30 .75
9F Tom Goodwin .01 .05
10F Rondell White RC .20 .50
11F Reggie Sanders .20 .50
12F Todd Van Poppel .01 .05
13F Arthur Rhodes RC .08 .25
14F Eddie Zosky .01 .05
15F Gerald Williams RC .08 .25
16F Robert Eenhoorn RC .02 .10
17F Jim Thome RC 4.00 10.00
18F Marc Newfield RC .02 .10
19F Kerwin Moore RC .02 .10
20F Jeff McNeely RC .02 .10
21F Frank Rodriguez RC .02 .10
22F Andy Mota RC .01 .05
23F Chris Haney RC .02 .10
24F Kenny Lofton RC .30 .75
25F Dave Nilsson RC .08 .25
26F Derek Bell .02 .10
27F Frank Castillo RC .08 .25
28F Candy Maldonado .01 .05
29F Chuck McElroy .01 .05
30F Chito Martinez RC .01 .05
31F Steve Howe .01 .05
32F Freddie Benavides RC .01 .05
33F Scott Kamieniecki RC .02 .10
34F Denny Neagle RC .08 .25
35F Mike Humphreys RC .02 .10
36F Mike Remlinger .01 .05
37F Scott Coolbaugh .01 .05
38F Darren Lewis .01 .05
39F Thomas Howard .01 .05
40F John Candelaria .01 .05
41F Todd Benzinger .01 .05
42F Wilson Alvarez .02 .10
43F Patrick Lennon RC .02 .10
44F Rusty Meacham RC .02 .10
45F Ryan Bowen RC .02 .10
46F Rick Wilkins RC .02 .10
47F Ed Sprague .01 .05
48F Bob Scanlan RC .01 .05
49F Tom Candiotti .01 .05
50F Dennis Martinez Perfect .02 .10
51F Oil Can Boyd .01 .05
52F Glenallen Hill .01 .05
53F Scott Livingstone RC .02 .10
54F Brian R.Hunter RC .08 .25
55F Ivan Rodriguez RC .75 2.00
56F Keith Mitchell RC .02 .10
57F Roger McDowell .01 .05
58F Otis Nixon .01 .05
59F Juan Bell .01 .05
60F Bill Krueger .01 .05
61F Chris Donnels RC .01 .05
62F Tommy Greene .01 .05
63F Doug Simons RC .01 .05
64F Andy Ashby RC .08 .25
65F Anthony Young RC .02 .10
66F Kevin Morton RC .01 .05
67F Bret Barberie RC .02 .10
68F Scott Servais RC .08 .25
69F Ron Darling .01 .05
70F Tim Burke .01 .05
71F Vicente Palacios .01 .05
72F Gerald Alexander RC .01 .05
73F Reggie Jefferson .01 .05
74F Dean Palmer .02 .10
75F Mark Whiten .01 .05
76F Randy Tomlin RC .02 .10
77F Mark Wohlers RC .08 .25
78F Brook Jacoby .01 .05
79F K.Griffey Jr. .20 .50
R.Sandberg CL
80F Jack Morris AS .01 .05
81F Sandy Alomar Jr. AS .01 .05
82F Cecil Fielder AS .01 .05
83F Roberto Alomar AS .02 .10
84F Wade Boggs AS .02 .10
85F Cal Ripken AS .15 .40
86F Rickey Henderson AS .05 .15
87F Ken Griffey Jr. AS .10 .30
88F Dave Henderson AS .01 .05
89F Danny Tartabull AS .01 .05
90F Tom Glavine AS .02 .10
91F Benito Santiago AS .01 .05
92F Will Clark AS .02 .10
93F Ryne Sandberg AS .08 .25
94F Chris Sabo AS .01 .05
95F Ozzie Smith AS .08 .25
96F Ivan Calderon AS .01 .05
97F Tony Gwynn AS .05 .15
98F Andre Dawson AS .01 .05
99F Bobby Bonilla AS .01 .05
100F Checklist 1-100 .01 .05

1991 Upper Deck Comic Ball 2 Promos

COMPLETE SET (4) 5.00 12.00
1 The National 7/4/91 2.00 5.00
Nolan Ryan
(with Daffy and Bugs Bunny)
2 The National 7/5/91 1.00 2.50
Reggie Jackson
(with Taz)
3 The National 7/6/91 2.00 5.00
Nolan Ryan
(with Speedy Gonzales)
4 The National 7/7/91 1.00 2.50
Reggie Jackson
(with Elmer Fudd/Sylvester)

1991 Upper Deck Heroes of Baseball 5x7

1 Date sheet 5x7 8.00 20.00
Reggie Jackson
Lou Brock
Harmon

1991 Upper Deck Sheets

These 23 commemorative sheets were issued in 1991 to fans attending old-timers games preceding major league games. The sheets measure 8 1/2" by 11" and feature artist renderings of players from the teams recreated for the old-timers game. The front carries the individual production number out of the total number produced, but otherwise the sheets are unnumbered and so listed below in chronological order. The cover sheet was produced in two different versions, one numbered to 10,000, the other to 20,000. After the original 10,000 were produced, another 10,000 were needed for promotions.

COMPLETE SET (23) 75.00 150.00
1 Cover sheet 2.00 5.00
Reggie Jackson/(20&000)
Dates and s
2 Philadelphia Scholars 6.00 15.00
Fund Sports Show
Oct. 17&
3 Tribute to Baltimore 4.00 10.00
Orioles Heroes
April 21& 19
4 Tribute to Joe 4.00 10.00
DiMaggio and Ted
Williams in cele
5 Heroes of the '70s 4.00 10.00
May 18& 1991 (22&000)
Clevela
6 Atlanta Braves Heroes 4.00 10.00
vs. National League
Heroes
7 Oakland A's 4.00 10.00
June 9& 1991 (22&000)
Oakland Colise
8 World Series Heroes 2.50 6.00
June 15& 1991 (47&000)
Shea
9 Cincinnati Reds Heroes 6.00 15.00
vs. World Series Heroes
J
10 1981 American League 2.50 6.00
Divisional Playoff Heroes
J
11 A Tribute to All-Star 2.00 5.00
Heroes
Toronto
July 8& 19
12 Tribute to Home 2.50 6.00
Run Heroes
July 14& 1991 (44&000
13 Pittsburgh Pirates 4.00 10.00
July 20& 1991 (18&000)
Three
14 Battle of Missouri 4.00 10.00
July 21, 1991 (17,000)
Busch
15 David vs. Goliath 4.00 10.00
July 27& 1991 (17&000)
Astrodo
16 45th Annual Old-Timer's 2.50 6.00
Day Classic
July 27& 199
17 1971 Phillies vs. 2.50 6.00
Upper Deck Heroes
Aug. 10& 199
18 Tribute to Hall 4.00 10.00
of Famers
Aug. 10& 1991 (17&000)
19 All-Star Joes vs. 3.00 8.00
All-Star Bobs
Aug. 16& 1991 (2
20 Giants Reunion with 2.50 6.00
Newest Hall of Famer
Aug. 18
21 American League vs. 4.00 10.00
National League
Aug. 24& 199
22 Tribute to 1971 Heroes 3.00 8.00
Aug. 25& 1991 (32&000)
Ti
23 10th Anniversary of 2.50 6.00
Expos' Divisional
Championship

1992 Upper Deck

The 1992 Upper Deck set contains 800 standard-size cards issued in two separate series of 700 and 100 cards respectively. The cards were distributed in low and high series foil packs in addition to factory sets. Factory sets feature a unique gold-foil hologram on the card backs (in contrast to the silver hologram on foil pack cards). Special subsets included in the set are Star Rookies (1-27), Team Checklists (29-40/86-99), with player portraits by Vernon Wells Sr.; Top Prospects (52-77); Bloodlines (79-85), Diamond Skills (640-650/711-721) and Diamond Debuts (771-780). Rookie Cards in the set include Shawn Green, Brian Jordan and Manny Ramirez. A special card picturing Tom Selleck and Frank Thomas, commemorating the forgettable movie "Mr. Baseball", was randomly inserted into high series packs. A standard-size Ted Williams hologram card was randomly inserted into low series packs. By mailing in 15 low series foil wrappers, a completed order form, and a handling fee, the collector could receive an 8 1/2" by 11" numbered, black and white lithograph picturing Ted Williams in his batting swing.

COMPLETE SET (800) 10.00 25.00
COMPLETE LO SET (700) 8.00 20.00
COMPLETE HI SET (100) 2.00 5.00
1 J.Thome .08 .25
R.Klesko CL
2 Royce Clayton SR .01 .05
3 Brian Jordan RC .20 .50
4 Dave Fleming .01 .05
5 Jim Thome .08 .25
6 Jeff Juden SR .01 .05
7 Roberto Hernandez SR .01 .05
8 Kyle Abbott SR .01 .05
9 Chris George SR .01 .05
10 Rob Maurer SR RC .01 .05
11 Donald Harris SR .01 .05
12 Ted Wood SR .01 .05
13 Patrick Lennon SR .01 .05
14 Willie Banks SR .01 .05
15 Roger Salkeld SR UER/(Bill was his grand- .01
.05
father
16 Wil Cordero SR .01 .05
17 Arthur Rhodes SR .01 .05
18 Pedro Martinez .40 1.00
19 Andy Ashby SR .01 .05
20 Tom Goodwin SR .01 .05
21 Braulio Castillo SR .01 .05
22 Todd Van Poppel .01 .05
23 Brian Williams RC .01 .05
24 Ryan Klesko .02 .10
25 Kenny Lofton .05 .15
26 Derek Bell .02 .10
27 Reggie Sanders .02 .10
28 Dave Winfield's 400th .01 .05
29 David Justice TC .01 .05
30 Rob Dibble TC .01 .05
Cincinnati Reds
31 Craig Biggio TC .02 .10
32 Eddie Murray TC .05 .15
33 Fred McGriff TC .02 .10
34 Willie McGee TC .01 .05
San Francisco Giants
35 Shawon Dunston TC .01 .05
Chicago Cubs
36 Delino DeShields TC .01 .05
37 Howard Johnson TC .01 .05
New York Mets
38 John Kruk TC .01 .05
39 Doug Drabek TC .01 .05
Pittsburgh Pirates
40 Todd Zeile TC .01 .05
41 Steve Avery Playoff .01 .05
42 Jeremy Hernandez RC .01 .05
43 Doug Henry RC .02 .10
44 Chris Donnels .01 .05
45 Mo Sanford .01 .05
46 Scott Kamieniecki .01 .05
47 Mark Lemke .01 .05
48 Steve Farr .01 .05
49 Francisco Oliveras .01 .05
50 Ced Landrum .01 .05
51 R.White .02 .10
M.Newfield CL
52 Eduardo Perez RC .08 .25
53 Tom Nevers TP .01 .05
54 David Zancanaro TP .01 .05
55 Shawn Green RC .40 1.00
56 Mark Wohlers TP .01 .05
57 Dave Nilsson .01 .05
58 Dmitri Young .02 .10
59 Ryan Hawblitzel RC .02 .10
60 Raul Mondesi .02 .10
61 Rondell White .02 .10
62 Steve Hosey .01 .05
63 Manny Ramirez RC 1.50 4.00
64 Marc Newfield .01 .05
65 Jeromy Burnitz .02 .10
66 Mark Smith RC .02 .10
67 Joey Hamilton RC .02 .10
68 Tyler Green RC .02 .10
69 Jon Farrell RC .02 .10
70 Kurt Miller TP .01 .05
71 Jeff Plympton TP .01 .05
72 Dan Wilson TP .01 .05
73 Joe Vitiello RC .02 .10
74 Rico Brogna TP .01 .05
75 David McCarty RC .08 .25
76 Bob Wickman .08 .25
77 Carlos Rodriguez TP .01 .05
78 Jim Abbott .02 .10
Stay In School
79 P.Martinez .08 .25
R.Martinez
80 Kevin Mitchell .01 .05
Keith Mitchell
81 Sandy .02 .10
Roberto Alomar
82 Ripken Brothers .20 .50
83 Tony .05 .15
Chris Gwynn
84 D.Gooden .02 .10
G.Sheffield
85 K.Griffey Jr. w .10 .30
Family
86 Jim Abbott TC .02 .10
California Angels
87 Frank Thomas TC .05 .15
88 Danny Tartabull TC .01 .05
Kansas City Royals
89 Scott Erickson TC .01 .05
Minnesota Twins
90 Rickey Henderson TC .05 .15
91 Edgar Martinez TC .02 .10
92 Nolan Ryan TC .20 .50
93 Ben McDonald TC .01 .05
Baltimore Orioles
94 Ellis Burks TC .01 .05
Boston Red Sox
95 Greg Swindell TC .01 .05
Cleveland Indians
96 Cecil Fielder TC .01 .05
97 Greg Vaughn TC .01 .05
98 Kevin Maas TC .01 .05
New York Yankees
99 Dave Stieb TC .01 .05
Toronto Blue Jays
100 Checklist 1-100 .01 .05
101 Joe Oliver .01 .05
102 Hector Villanueva .01 .05
103 Ed Whitson .01 .05
104 Danny Jackson .01 .05
105 Chris Hammond .01 .05
106 Ricky Jordan .01 .05
107 Kevin Bass .01 .05
108 Darrin Fletcher .01 .05
109 Junior Ortiz .01 .05
110 Tom Bolton .01 .05
111 Jeff King .01 .05
112 Dave Magadan .01 .05
113 Mike LaValliere .01 .05
114 Hubie Brooks .01 .05
115 Jay Bell .02 .10
116 David Wells .02 .10
117 Jim Leyritz .01 .05
118 Manuel Lee .01 .05
119 Alvaro Espinoza .01 .05
120 B.J. Surhoff .02 .10
121 Hal Morris .01 .05
122 Shawon Dunston .01 .05
123 Chris Sabo .01 .05
124 Andre Dawson .02 .10
125 Eric Davis .02 .10
126 Chili Davis .02 .10
127 Dale Murphy .05 .15
128 Kirk McCaskill .01 .05
129 Terry Mulholland .01 .05
130 Rick Aguilera .02 .10
131 Vince Coleman .01 .05
132 Andy Van Slyke .05 .15
133 Gregg Jefferies .01 .05
134 Barry Bonds .40 1.00
135 Dwight Gooden .02 .10
136 Dave Stieb .01 .05
137 Albert Belle .02 .10
138 Teddy Higuera .01 .05
139 Jesse Barfield .01 .05
140 Pat Borders .01 .05
141 Bip Roberts .01 .05
142 Rob Dibble .02 .10
143 Mark Grace .05 .15
144 Barry Larkin .05 .15
145 Ryne Sandberg .15 .40
146 Scott Erickson .01 .05
147 Luis Polonia .01 .05
148 John Burkett .01 .05
149 Luis Sojo .01 .05
150 Dickie Thon .01 .05
151 Walt Weiss .01 .05
152 Mike Scioscia .01 .05
153 Mark McGwire .25 .60
154 Matt Williams .02 .10
155 Rickey Henderson .08 .25
156 Sandy Alomar Jr. .01 .05
157 Brian McRae .01 .05
158 Harold Baines .02 .10
159 Kevin Appier .02 .10
160 Felix Fermin .01 .05

161 Leo Gomez .01 .05
162 Craig Biggio .05 .15
163 Ben McDonald .01 .05
164 Randy Johnson .08 .25
165 Cal Ripken .30 .75
166 Frank Thomas .08 .25
167 Delino DeShields .01 .05
168 Greg Gagne .01 .05
169 Ron Karkovice .01 .05
170 Charlie Leibrandt .01 .05
171 Dave Righetti .02 .10
172 Dave Henderson .01 .05
173 Steve Decker .01 .05
174 Darryl Strawberry .02 .10
175 Will Clark .05 .15
176 Ruben Sierra .02 .10
177 Ozzie Smith .15 .40
178 Charles Nagy .01 .05
179 Gary Pettis .01 .05
180 Kirk Gibson .02 .10
181 Randy Milligan .01 .05
182 Dave Valle .01 .05
183 Chris Hoiles .01 .05
184 Tony Phillips .01 .05
185 Brady Anderson .02 .10
186 Scott Fletcher .01 .05
187 Gene Larkin .01 .05
188 Lance Johnson .01 .05
189 Greg Olson .01 .05
190 Melido Perez .01 .05
191 Lenny Harris .01 .05
192 Terry Kennedy .01 .05
193 Mike Gallego .01 .05
194 Willie McGee .02 .10
195 Juan Samuel .01 .05
196 Jeff Huson .02 .10
197 Alex Cole .01 .05
198 Ron Robinson .01 .05
199 Joel Skinner .01 .05
200 Checklist 101-200 .01 .05
201 Kevin Reimer .01 .05
202 Stan Belinda .01 .05
203 Pat Tabler .01 .05
204 Jose Guzman .01 .05
205 Jose Lind .01 .05
206 Spike Owen .01 .05
207 Joe Orsulak .01 .05
208 Charlie Hayes .01 .05
209 Mike Devereaux .01 .05
210 Mike Fitzgerald .01 .05
211 Willie Randolph .02 .10
212 Rod Nichols .01 .05
213 Mike Boddicker .01 .05
214 Bill Spiers .01 .05
215 Steve Olin .01 .05
216 David Howard .01 .05
217 Gary Varsho .01 .05
218 Mike Harkey .01 .05
219 Luis Aquino .01 .05
220 Chuck McElroy .01 .05
221 Doug Drabek .01 .05
222 Dave Winfield .02 .10
223 Rafael Palmeiro .05 .15
224 Joe Carter .02 .10
225 Bobby Bonilla .02 .10
226 Ivan Calderon .01 .05
227 Gregg Olson .01 .05
228 Tim Wallach .01 .05
229 Terry Pendleton .02 .10
230 Gilberto Reyes .01 .05
231 Carlos Baerga .01 .05
232 Greg Vaughn .01 .05
233 Bret Saberhagen .02 .10
234 Gary Sheffield .02 .10
235 Mark Lewis .01 .05
236 George Bell .01 .05
237 Danny Tartabull .01 .05
238 Willie Wilson .01 .05
239 Doug Dascenzo .01 .05
240 Bill Pecota .01 .05
241 Julio Franco .02 .10
242 Ed Sprague .01 .05
243 Juan Gonzalez .05 .15
244 Chuck Finley .02 .10
245 Ivan Rodriguez .08 .25
246 Len Dykstra .02 .10
247 Deion Sanders .05 .15
248 Dwight Evans .05 .15
249 Larry Walker .05 .15
250 Billy Ripken .01 .05
251 Mickey Tettleton .01 .05
252 Tony Pena .01 .05
253 Benito Santiago .02 .10
254 Kirby Puckett .08 .25
255 Cecil Fielder .02 .10
256 Howard Johnson .01 .05
257 Andujar Cedeno .01 .05
258 Jose Rijo .01 .05
259 Al Osuna .01 .05
260 Todd Hundley .01 .05
261 Orel Hershiser .02 .10
262 Ray Lankford .02 .10
263 Robin Ventura .02 .10
264 Felix Jose .01 .05
265 Eddie Murray .08 .25
266 Kevin Mitchell .01 .05
267 Gary Carter .02 .10
268 Mike Benjamin .01 .05
269 Dick Schofield .01 .05
270 Jose Uribe .01 .05
271 Pete Incaviglia .01 .05
272 Tony Fernandez .01 .05
273 Alan Trammell .02 .10
274 Tony Gwynn .10 .30
275 Mike Greenwell .01 .05
276 Jeff Bagwell .08 .25
277 Frank Viola .02 .10
278 Randy Myers .01 .05
279 Ken Caminiti .02 .10
280 Bill Doran .01 .05
281 Dan Pasqua .01 .05
282 Alfredo Griffin .01 .05
283 Jose Oquendo .01 .05
284 Kal Daniels .01 .05
285 Bobby Thigpen .01 .05
286 Robby Thompson .01 .05
287 Mark Eichhorn .01 .05
288 Mike Felder .01 .05
289 Dave Gallagher .01 .05
290 Dave Anderson .01 .05
291 Mel Hall .01 .05
292 Jerald Clark .01 .05
293 Al Newman .01 .05
294 Rob Deer .01 .05
295 Matt Nokes .01 .05
296 Jack Armstrong .01 .05
297 Jim Deshaies .01 .05
298 Jeff Innis .01 .05
299 Jeff Reed .01 .05
300 Checklist 201-300 .01 .05
301 Lonnie Smith .01 .05
302 Jimmy Key .02 .10
303 Junior Felix .01 .05
304 Mike Heath .01 .05
305 Mark Langston .01 .05
306 Greg W. Harris .01 .05
307 Brett Butler .02 .10
308 Luis Rivera .01 .05
309 Bruce Ruffin .01 .05
310 Paul Faries .01 .05
311 Terry Leach .01 .05
312 Scott Brosius RC .20 .50
313 Scott Leius .01 .05
314 Harold Reynolds .02 .10
315 Jack Morris .02 .10
316 David Segui .01 .05
317 Bill Gullickson .01 .05
318 Todd Frohwirth .01 .05
319 Mark Leiter .01 .05
320 Jeff M. Robinson .01 .05
321 Gary Gaetti .02 .10
322 John Smoltz .05 .15
323 Andy Benes .01 .05
324 Kelly Gruber .01 .05
325 Jim Abbott .05 .15
326 John Kruk .02 .10
327 Kevin Seitzer .01 .05
328 Darrin Jackson .01 .05
329 Kurt Stillwell .01 .05
330 Mike Maddux .01 .05
331 Dennis Eckersley .02 .10
332 Dan Gladden .01 .05
333 Jose Canseco .05 .15
334 Kent Hrbek .02 .10
335 Ken Griffey Sr. .02 .10
336 Greg Swindell .01 .05
337 Trevor Wilson .01 .05
338 Sam Horn .01 .05
339 Mike Henneman .01 .05
340 Jerry Browne .01 .05
341 Glenn Braggs .01 .05
342 Tom Glavine .05 .15
343 Wally Joyner .02 .10
344 Fred McGriff .05 .15
345 Ron Gant .02 .10
346 Ramon Martinez .01 .05
347 Wes Chamberlain .01 .05
348 Terry Shumpert .01 .05
349 Tim Teufel .01 .05
350 Wally Backman .01 .05
351 Joe Girardi .01 .05
352 Devon White .02 .10
353 Greg Maddux .15 .40
354 Ryan Bowen .01 .05
355 Roberto Alomar .05 .15
356 Don Mattingly .25 .60
357 Pedro Guerrero .02 .10
358 Steve Sax .01 .05
359 Joey Cora .01 .05
360 Jim Gantner .01 .05
361 Brian Barnes .01 .05
362 Kevin McReynolds .01 .05
363 Bret Barberie .01 .05
364 David Cone .02 .10
365 Dennis Martinez .02 .10
366 Brian Hunter .01 .05
367 Edgar Martinez .05 .15
368 Steve Finley .02 .10
369 Greg Briley .01 .05
370 Jeff Blauser .01 .05
371 Todd Stottlemyre .01 .05
372 Luis Gonzalez .02 .10
373 Rick Wilkins .01 .05
374 Darryl Kile .02 .10
375 John Olerud .02 .10
376 Lee Smith .02 .10
377 Kevin Maas .01 .05
378 Dante Bichette .02 .10
379 Tom Pagnozzi .01 .05
380 Mike Flanagan .01 .05
381 Charlie O'Brien .01 .05
382 Dave Martinez .01 .05
383 Keith Miller .01 .05
384 Scott Ruskin .01 .05
385 Kevin Elster .01 .05
386 Alvin Davis .01 .05
387 Casey Candaele .01 .05
388 Pete O'Brien .01 .05
389 Jeff Treadway .01 .05
390 Scott Bradley .01 .05
391 Mookie Wilson .02 .10
392 Jimmy Jones .01 .05
393 Candy Maldonado .01 .05
394 Eric Yelding .01 .05
395 Tom Henke .01 .05
396 Franklin Stubbs .01 .05
397 Milt Thompson .01 .05
398 Mark Carreon .01 .05
399 Randy Velarde .01 .05
400 Checklist 301-400 .01 .05
401 Omar Vizquel .05 .15
402 Joe Boever .01 .05
403 Bill Krueger .01 .05
404 Jody Reed .01 .05
405 Mike Schooler .01 .05
406 Jason Grimsley .01 .05
407 Greg Myers .01 .05
408 Randy Ready .01 .05
409 Mike Timlin .01 .05
410 Mitch Williams .01 .05
411 Garry Templeton .01 .05
412 Greg Cadaret .01 .05
413 Donnie Hill .01 .05
414 Wally Whitehurst .01 .05
415 Scott Sanderson .01 .05
416 Thomas Howard .01 .05
417 Neal Heaton .01 .05
418 Charlie Hough .02 .10
419 Jack Howell .01 .05
420 Greg Hibbard .01 .05
421 Carlos Quintana .01 .05
422 Kim Batiste .01 .05
423 Paul Molitor .02 .10
424 Ken Griffey Jr. .20 .50
425 Phil Plantier .01 .05
426 Denny Neagle .02 .10
427 Von Hayes .01 .05
428 Shane Mack .01 .05
429 Darren Daulton .02 .10
430 Dwayne Henry .01 .05
431 Lance Parrish .02 .10
432 Mike Humphreys .01 .05
433 Tim Burke .01 .05
434 Bryan Harvey .01 .05
435 Pat Kelly .01 .05
436 Ozzie Guillen .02 .10
437 Bruce Hurst .01 .05
438 Sammy Sosa .08 .25
439 Dennis Rasmussen .01 .05
440 Ken Patterson .01 .05
441 Jay Buhner .02 .10
442 Pat Combs .01 .05
443 Wade Boggs .05 .15
444 George Brett .25 .60
445 Mo Vaughn .02 .10
446 Chuck Knoblauch .02 .10
447 Tom Candiotti .01 .05
448 Mark Portugal .01 .05
449 Mickey Morandini .01 .05
450 Duane Ward .01 .05
451 Otis Nixon .01 .05
452 Bob Welch .01 .05
453 Rusty Meacham .01 .05
454 Keith Mitchell .01 .05
455 Marquis Grissom .02 .10
456 Robin Yount .15 .40
457 Harvey Pulliam .01 .05
458 Jose DeLeon .01 .05
459 Mark Gubicza .01 .05
460 Darryl Hamilton .01 .05
461 Tom Browning .01 .05
462 Monty Fariss .01 .05
463 Jerome Walton .01 .05
464 Paul O'Neill .05 .15
465 Dean Palmer .02 .10
466 Travis Fryman .02 .10
467 John Smiley .01 .05
468 Lloyd Moseby .01 .05
469 John Wehner .01 .05
470 Skeeter Barnes .01 .05
471 Steve Chitren .01 .05
472 Kent Mercker .01 .05
473 Terry Steinbach .01 .05
474 Andres Galarraga .02 .10
475 Steve Avery .01 .05
476 Tom Gordon .01 .05
477 Cal Eldred .01 .05
478 Omar Olivares .01 .05
479 Julio Machado .01 .05
480 Bob Milacki .01 .05
481 Les Lancaster .01 .05
482 John Candelaria .01 .05
483 Brian Downing .01 .05
484 Roger McDowell .01 .05
485 Scott Scudder .01 .05
486 Zane Smith .01 .05
487 John Cerutti .01 .05
488 Steve Buechele .01 .05
489 Paul Gibson .01 .05
490 Curtis Wilkerson .01 .05
491 Marvin Freeman .01 .05
492 Tom Foley .01 .05
493 Juan Berenguer .01 .05
494 Ernest Riles .01 .05
495 Sid Bream .01 .05
496 Chuck Crim .01 .05
497 Mike Macfarlane .01 .05
498 Dale Sveum .01 .05
499 Storm Davis .01 .05
500 Checklist 401-500 .01 .05
501 Jeff Reardon .02 .10
502 Shawn Abner .01 .05
503 Tony Fossas .01 .05
504 Cory Snyder .01 .05
505 Matt Young .01 .05
506 Allan Anderson .01 .05
507 Mark Lee .01 .05
508 Gene Nelson .01 .05
509 Mike Pagliarulo .01 .05
510 Rafael Belliard .01 .05
511 Jay Howell .01 .05
512 Bob Tewksbury .01 .05
513 Mike Morgan .01 .05
514 John Franco .02 .10
515 Kevin Gross .01 .05
516 Lou Whitaker .02 .10
517 Orlando Merced .01 .05
518 Todd Benzinger .01 .05
519 Gary Redus .01 .05
520 Walt Terrell .01 .05
521 Jack Clark .02 .10
522 Dave Parker .02 .10
523 Tim Naehring .01 .05
524 Mark Whiten .01 .05
525 Ellis Burks .02 .10
526 Frank Castillo .01 .05
527 Brian Harper .01 .05
528 Brook Jacoby .01 .05
529 Rick Sutcliffe .02 .10
530 Joe Klink .01 .05
531 Terry Bross .01 .05
532 Jose Offerman .01 .05
533 Todd Zeile .01 .05
534 Eric Karros .05 .15
535 Anthony Young .01 .05
536 Milt Cuyler .01 .05
537 Randy Tomlin .01 .05
538 Scott Livingstone .01 .05
539 Jim Eisenreich .01 .05
540 Don Slaught .01 .05
541 Scott Cooper .01 .05
542 Joe Grahe .01 .05
543 Tom Brunansky .01 .05
544 Eddie Zosky .01 .05
545 Roger Clemens .20 .50
546 David Justice .02 .10
547 Dave Stewart .02 .10
548 David West .01 .05
549 Dave Smith .01 .05
550 Dan Plesac .01 .05
551 Alex Fernandez .01 .05
552 Bernard Gilkey .01 .05
553 Jack McDowell .01 .05
554 Tino Martinez .05 .15
555 Bo Jackson .08 .25
556 Bernie Williams .05 .15
557 Mark Gardner .01 .05
558 Glenallen Hill .01 .05
559 Oil Can Boyd .01 .05
560 Chris James .01 .05
561 Scott Servais .01 .05
562 Rey Sanchez RC .08 .25
563 Paul McClellan .01 .05
564 Andy Mota .01 .05
565 Darren Lewis .01 .05
566 Jose Melendez .01 .05
567 Tommy Greene .01 .05
568 Rich Rodriguez .01 .05
569 Heathcliff Slocumb .01 .05
570 Joe Hesketh .01 .05
571 Carlton Fisk .05 .15
572 Erik Hanson .01 .05
573 Wilson Alvarez .01 .05
574 Rheal Cormier .01 .05
575 Tim Raines .02 .10
576 Bobby Witt .01 .05
577 Roberto Kelly .01 .05
578 Kevin Brown .02 .10
579 Chris Nabholz .01 .05
580 Jesse Orosco .01 .05
581 Jeff Brantley .01 .05
582 Rafael Ramirez .01 .05
583 Kelly Downs .01 .05
584 Mike Simms .01 .05
585 Mike Remlinger .01 .05
586 Dave Hollins .01 .05
587 Larry Andersen .01 .05
588 Mike Gardiner .01 .05
589 Craig Lefferts .01 .05
590 Paul Assenmacher .01 .05
591 Bryn Smith .01 .05
592 Donn Pall .01 .05
593 Mike Jackson .01 .05
594 Scott Radinsky .01 .05
595 Brian Holman .01 .05
596 Geronimo Pena .01 .05
597 Mike Jeffcoat .01 .05
598 Carlos Martinez .01 .05
599 Geno Petralli .01 .05
600 Checklist 501-600 .01 .05
601 Jerry Don Gleaton .01 .05
602 Adam Peterson .01 .05
603 Craig Grebeck .01 .05
604 Mark Guthrie .01 .05
605 Frank Tanana .01 .05
606 Hensley Meulens .01 .05
607 Mark Davis .01 .05
608 Eric Plunk .01 .05
609 Mark Williamson .01 .05
610 Lee Guetterman .01 .05
611 Bobby Rose .01 .05
612 Bill Wegman .01 .05
613 Mike Hartley .01 .05
614 Chris Beasley .01 .05
615 Chris Bosio .01 .05
616 Henry Cotto .01 .05
617 Chico Walker .01 .05
618 Russ Swan .01 .05
619 Bob Walk .01 .05
620 Bill Swift .01 .05
621 Warren Newson .01 .05
622 Steve Bedrosian .01 .05
623 Ricky Bones .01 .05
624 Kevin Tapani .01 .05
625 Juan Guzman .01 .05
626 Jeff Johnson .01 .05
627 Jeff Montgomery .01 .05
628 Ken Hill .01 .05
629 Gary Thurman .01 .05
630 Steve Howe .01 .05
631 Jose DeJesus .01 .05
632 Kirk Dressendorfer .01 .05
633 Jaime Navarro .01 .05
634 Lee Stevens .01 .05
635 Pete Harnisch .01 .05
636 Bill Landrum .01 .05
637 Rich DeLucia .01 .05
638 Luis Salazar .01 .05
639 Rob Murphy .01 .05
640 J.Canseco
R.Henderson CL .05 .15
641 Roger Clemens DS .08 .25
642 Jim Abbott DS .02 .10
643 Travis Fryman DS .01 .05
644 Jesse Barfield DS .01 .05
645 Cal Ripken DS .15 .40
646 Wade Boggs DS .02 .10
647 Cecil Fielder DS .01 .05
648 Rickey Henderson DS .05 .15
649 Jose Canseco DS .02 .10
650 Ken Griffey Jr. DS .10 .30
651 Kenny Rogers .02 .10
652 Luis Mercedes .01 .05
653 Mike Stanton .01 .05
654 Glenn Davis .01 .05
655 Nolan Ryan .40 1.00
656 Reggie Jefferson .01 .05
657 Javier Ortiz .01 .05
658 Greg A. Harris .01 .05
659 Mariano Duncan .01 .05
660 Jeff Shaw .01 .05
661 Mike Moore .01 .05
662 Chris Haney .01 .05
663 Joe Slusarski .01 .05
664 Wayne Housie .01 .05
665 Carlos Garcia .01 .05
666 Bob Ojeda .01 .05
667 Bryan Hickerson RC .02 .10
668 Tim Belcher .01 .05
669 Ron Darling .01 .05
670 Rex Hudler .01 .05
671 Sid Fernandez .01 .05
672 Chito Martinez .01 .05
673 Pete Schourek .01 .05
674 Armando Reynoso RC .08 .25
675 Mike Mussina .08 .25
676 Kevin Morton .01 .05
677 Norm Charlton .01 .05
678 Danny Darwin .01 .05
679 Eric King .01 .05
680 Ted Power .01 .05
681 Barry Jones .01 .05
682 Carney Lansford .02 .10
683 Mel Rojas .01 .05
684 Rick Honeycutt .01 .05
685 Jeff Fassero .01 .05
686 Cris Carpenter .01 .05
687 Tim Crews .01 .05
688 Scott Terry .01 .05
689 Chris Gwynn .01 .05
690 Gerald Perry .01 .05
691 John Barfield .01 .05
692 Bob Melvin .01 .05
693 Juan Agosto .01 .05
694 Alejandro Pena .01 .05
695 Jeff Russell .01 .05
696 Carmelo Martinez .01 .05
697 Bud Black .01 .05
698 Dave Otto .01 .05
699 Billy Hatcher .01 .05
700 Checklist 601-700 .01 .05
701 Clemente Nunez RC .01 .05
702 M.Clark
Osborne
Jordan .01 .05
703 Mike Morgan .01 .05
704 Keith Miller .01 .05
705 Kurt Stillwell .01 .05
706 Damon Berryhill .01 .05
707 Von Hayes .01 .05
708 Rick Sutcliffe .02 .10
709 Hubie Brooks .01 .05
710 Ryan Turner RC .02 .10
711 B.Bonds
A.Van Slyke CL .20 .50
712 Jose Rijo DS .01 .05
713 Tom Glavine DS .02 .10
714 Shawon Dunston DS .01 .05
715 Andy Van Slyke DS .02 .10
716 Ozzie Smith DS .08 .25
717 Tony Gwynn DS .05 .15
718 Will Clark DS .02 .10
719 Marquis Grissom DS .01 .05
720 Howard Johnson DS .01 .05
721 Barry Bonds DS .20 .50
722 Kirk McCaskill .01 .05
723 Sammy Sosa Cubs .30 .75
724 George Bell .01 .05
725 Gregg Jefferies .01 .05
726 Gary DiSarcina .01 .05
727 Mike Bordick .01 .05
728 Eddie Murray 400 HR .05 .15
729 Rene Gonzales .01 .05
730 Mike Bielecki .01 .05
731 Calvin Jones .01 .05
732 Jack Morris .02 .10
733 Frank Viola .02 .10
734 Dave Winfield .02 .10
735 Kevin Mitchell .01 .05
736 Bill Swift .01 .05
737 Dan Gladden .01 .05
738 Mike Jackson .01 .05
739 Mark Carreon .01 .05
740 Kirt Manwaring .01 .05
741 Randy Myers .01 .05
742 Kevin McReynolds .01 .05
743 Steve Sax .01 .05
744 Wally Joyner .02 .10
745 Gary Sheffield .02 .10
746 Danny Tartabull .01 .05
747 Julio Valera .01 .05
748 Denny Neagle .02 .10
749 Lance Blankenship .01 .05
750 Mike Gallego .01 .05
751 Bret Saberhagen .02 .10
752 Ruben Amaro .01 .05
753 Eddie Murray .08 .25
754 Kyle Abbott .01 .05
755 Bobby Bonilla .02 .10
756 Eric Davis .02 .10
757 Eddie Taubensee RC .08 .25
758 Andres Galarraga .02 .10
759 Pete Incaviglia .01 .05
760 Tom Candiotti .01 .05
761 Tim Belcher .01 .05
762 Ricky Bones .01 .05
763 Bip Roberts .01 .05
764 Pedro Munoz .01 .05
765 Greg Swindell .01 .05
766 Kenny Lofton .05 .15
767 Gary Carter .02 .10
768 Charlie Hayes .01 .05
769 Dickie Thon .01 .05
770 Donovan Osborne DD CL .01 .05
771 Bret Boone .05 .15
772 Archi Cianfrocco RC .02 .10
773 Mark Clark RC .02 .10
774 Chad Curtis RC .08 .25
775 Pat Listach RC .08 .25
776 Pat Mahomes RC .08 .25
777 Donovan Osborne .01 .05
778 John Patterson RC .02 .10
779 Andy Stankiewicz DD .01 .05
780 Turk Wendell RC .08 .25
781 Bill Krueger .01 .05
782 Rickey Henderson 1000 .05 .15
783 Kevin Seitzer .01 .05
784 Dave Martinez .01 .05
785 John Smiley .01 .05
786 Matt Stairs RC .08 .25
787 Scott Scudder .01 .05
788 John Wetteland .02 .10
789 Jack Armstrong .01 .05
790 Ken Hill .01 .05
791 Dick Schofield .01 .05
792 Mariano Duncan .01 .05
793 Bill Pecota .01 .05
794 Mike Kelly RC .02 .10
795 Willie Randolph .02 .10
796 Butch Henry .01 .05
797 Carlos Hernandez .01 .05
798 Doug Jones .01 .05
799 Melido Perez .01 .05
800 Checklist 701-800 .01 .05
HH2 Ted Williams Holo .75 2.00
SP3 Deion Sanders FB/BB .40 1.00
SP4 F.Thomas
T.Selleck .40 1.00

1992 Upper Deck Gold Hologram

COMP.FACT.SET (800) 10.00 25.00
*STARS: .4X TO 1X BASIC CARDS
*ROOKIES: .4X TO 1X BASIC
ALL FACTORY CARDS FEATURE GOLD HOLO
DISTRIBUTED ONLY IN FACT.SET FORM

1992 Upper Deck Bench/Morgan Heroes

COMPLETE SET (10) 6.00 15.00
COMMON BENCH/MORG (37-45) .60 1.50
RANDOM INSERTS IN HI SERIES PACKS
NNO Bench
Morgan Hdr SP 1.00 2.50
AU5 Bench/Morgan AU/2500 40.00 80.00

1992 Upper Deck College POY Holograms

COMPLETE SET (3) .75 2.00
RANDOM INSERTS IN HI SERIES
CP1 David McCarty .40 1.00
CP2 Mike Kelly .40 1.00
CP3 Ben McDonald .40 1.00

1992 Upper Deck Heroes of Baseball

RANDOM INSERTS IN HEROES FOIL
H5 Vida Blue .75 2.00
H6 Lou Brock .75 2.00
H7 Rollie Fingers .75 2.00
H8 L.Brock
Blue
Fingers .75 2.00
AU5 Vida Blue AU/3000 8.00 20.00
AU6 Lou Brock AU/3000 15.00 40.00
AU7 R.Fingers AU/3000 10.00 25.00

1992 Upper Deck Heroes Highlights

COMPLETE SET (10) 6.00 15.00
HI1 Bobby Bonds .20 .50
HI2 Lou Brock 1.25 3.00
HI3 Rollie Fingers .75 2.00
HI4 Bob Gibson 1.25 3.00
HI5 Reggie Jackson 1.50 4.00
HI6 Gaylord Perry .75 2.00
HI7 Robin Roberts .75 2.00
HI8 Brooks Robinson 1.50 4.00
HI9 Billy Williams .75 2.00
HI10 Ted Williams 2.50 6.00

1992 Upper Deck Home Run Heroes

COMPLETE SET (26) 5.00 12.00
ONE PER LO SERIES JUMBO
HR1 Jose Canseco .20 .50
HR2 Cecil Fielder .10 .30
HR3 Howard Johnson .05 .15
HR4 Cal Ripken 1.00 2.50
HR5 Matt Williams .10 .30
HR6 Joe Carter .10 .30
HR7 Ron Gant .10 .30
HR8 Frank Thomas .30 .75
HR9 Andre Dawson .10 .30
HR10 Fred McGriff .20 .50
HR11 Danny Tartabull .05 .15
HR12 Chili Davis .10 .30
HR13 Albert Belle .10 .30
HR14 Jack Clark .10 .30
HR15 Paul O'Neill .20 .50
HR16 Darryl Strawberry .10 .30
HR17 Dave Winfield .10 .30
HR18 Jay Buhner .10 .30
HR19 Juan Gonzalez .20 .50
HR20 Greg Vaughn .05 .15
HR21 Barry Bonds 1.25 3.00
HR22 Matt Nokes .05 .15
HR23 John Kruk .10 .30
HR24 Ivan Calderon .05 .15
HR25 Jeff Bagwell .30 .75
HR26 Todd Zeile .05 .15

1992 Upper Deck Scouting Report

COMPLETE SET (25) 8.00 20.00
COMMON CARD (SR1-SR25) .40 1.00
ONE PER HI SERIES JUMBO
CONDITION SENSITIVE SET
SR1 Andy Ashby .40 1.00
SR2 Willie Banks .40 1.00
SR3 Kim Batiste .40 1.00
SR4 Derek Bell .40 1.00
SR5 Archi Cianfrocco .40 1.00
SR6 Royce Clayton .40 1.00
SR7 Gary DiSarcina .40 1.00
SR8 Dave Fleming .40 1.00
SR9 Butch Henry .40 1.00
SR10 Todd Hundley .40 1.00
SR11 Brian Jordan .40 1.00
SR12 Eric Karros .40 1.00
SR13 Pat Listach .40 1.00
SR14 Scott Livingstone .40 1.00
SR15 Kenny Lofton .40 1.00
SR16 Pat Mahomes .40 1.00
SR17 Denny Neagle .40 1.00
SR18 Dave Nilsson .40 1.00
SR19 Donovan Osborne .40 1.00
SR20 Reggie Sanders .40 1.00
SR21 Andy Stankiewicz .40 1.00
SR22 Jim Thome .75 2.00
SR23 Julio Valera .40 1.00
SR24 Mark Wohlers .40 1.00
SR25 Anthony Young .40 1.00

1992 Upper Deck Williams Best

COMPLETE SET (20) 8.00 20.00
COMMON CARD (T1-T20) .10 .25
RANDOM INSERTS IN HI SERIES
CONDITION SENSITIVE SET
T1 Wade Boggs .30 .75
T2 Barry Bonds 2.00 5.00
T3 Jose Canseco .30 .75
T4 Will Clark .30 .75
T5 Cecil Fielder .20 .50
T6 Tony Gwynn .60 1.50
T7 Rickey Henderson .50 1.25
T8 Fred McGriff .30 .75
T9 Kirby Puckett .50 1.25
T10 Ruben Sierra .20 .50
T11 Roberto Alomar .30 .75
T12 Jeff Bagwell .50 1.25
T13 Albert Belle .20 .50
T14 Juan Gonzalez .30 .75
T15 Ken Griffey Jr. 1.00 2.50
T16 Chris Hoiles .08 .25
T17 David Justice .20 .50
T18 Phil Plantier .08 .25
T19 Frank Thomas .50 1.25
T20 Robin Ventura .20 .50

1992 Upper Deck Williams Heroes

COMPLETE SET (10) 3.00 8.00
COMMON T.WILLIAMS (28-36) .20 .50
RANDOM INSERTS IN LO SERIES PACKS
NNO Ted Williams Header SP .75 2.00
AU4 Ted Williams AU/2500 300.00 500.00

1992 Upper Deck Williams Wax Boxes

COMMON PLAYER (28-35) .20 .50

1992 Upper Deck FanFest

As a title sponsor of the 1992 All-Star FanFest in San Diego, Upper Deck produced this 54-card standard size set to commemorate past, present, and future All-Stars Heroes of Major League Baseball. Sixty sets were packaged in a case, and each case had at least one gold foil set. Cards 1-10 feature ten Future Heroes that are, in Upper Deck's opinion, sure bets to make an upcoming team; cards 11-44 present active All-Star alumni; and cards 45-54 salute All-Star Heroes of the past with ten fan favorites.

COMP.FACT SET (54) 4.00 10.00
1 Steve Avery .02 .10
2 Ivan Rodriguez .30 .75
3 Jeff Bagwell .30 .75
4 Delino DeShields .07 .20
5 Royce Clayton .02 .10
6 Robin Ventura .20 .50
7 Phil Plantier .02 .10
8 Ray Lankford .07 .20
9 Juan Gonzalez .25 .60
10 Frank Thomas .30 .75
11 Roberto Alomar .20 .50
12 Sandy Alomar Jr. .07 .20
13 Wade Boggs .30 .75
14 Barry Bonds .50 1.25
15 Bobby Bonilla .02 .10
16 George Brett .60 1.50
17 Jose Canseco .25 .60
18 Will Clark .20 .50
19 Roger Clemens .60 1.50
20 Eric Davis .07 .20
21 Rob Dibble .07 .20
22 Cecil Fielder .07 .20
23 Dwight Gooden .07 .20
24 Ken Griffey Jr. .75 2.00
25 Tony Gwynn .60 1.50
26 Bryan Harvey .02 .10
27 Rickey Henderson .40 1.00
28 Howard Johnson .02 .10
29 Wally Joyner .07 .20
30 Barry Larkin .20 .50
31 Don Mattingly .60 1.50
32 Mark McGwire .60 1.50
33 Dale Murphy .20 .50
34 Rafael Palmeiro .20 .50
35 Kirby Puckett .40 1.00
36 Cal Ripken 1.25 3.00
37 Nolan Ryan 1.25 3.00
38 Chris Sabo .02 .10
39 Ryne Sandberg .60 1.50
40 Benito Santiago .07 .20
41 Ruben Sierra .07 .20
42 Ozzie Smith .60 1.50
43 Darryl Strawberry .07 .20
44 Robin Yount .30 .75
45 Rollie Fingers .07 .20
46 Reggie Jackson .20 .50
47 Billy Williams .20 .50
48 Lou Brock .20 .50
49 Gaylord Perry .07 .20
50 Ted Williams 1.25 3.00
51 Brooks Robinson .20 .50
52 Bob Gibson .20 .50
53 Bobby Bonds .07 .20
54 Robin Roberts .07 .20

1992 Upper Deck Heroes of Baseball 5x7

1 Ted Williams 20.00 50.00

1992 Upper Deck Sheets

The 35 commemorative sheets listed below in chronological order were issued by Upper Deck in 1992. The Upper Deck Heroes of Baseball made stops in all 26 MLB ballparks, as well as Mile High Stadium in Denver. They sponsored old-timer baseball games and donated $10,000 to the Baseball Assistance Team, a group dedicated to helping members of the baseball family that have fallen upon hard times. At each game a limited edition commemorative sheet was distributed. Four other commemorative sheets were produced in honor of other events. When the Orioles moved to Oriole Park at Camden Yards on April 6, Upper Deck distributed 17,000 individually numbered sheets free to fans. These sheets feature four artistic views of the new stadium. The first 1992 sheet listed below was issued at the Yankee Fan Festival held at the Jacob Javits Convention Center in New York Jan. 31-Feb. 2. Sheets 17 and 18 were issued at the All-Star Game in San Diego. Sheets 31 and 32 were inserted into retail repacks of eight 1992 Upper Deck foil packs. Displaying different player cards, sheets 33-34 are two different versions of the same sheet and list dates and locations of collectors shows. All the sheets measure 8 1/2" by 11" and most feature artist renderings of players from the teams recreated for the old-timers games. The front carries the individual production number out of the total number produced, but otherwise the sheets are unnumbered.

COMPLETE SET (35) 125.00 250.00
1 Yankee Fan Festival 6.00 15.00

Jan. 31-Feb. 2, 1992/12,500
Pictures regular-issue/1992 Upper Deck cards
Don Mattingly
Mel Hall
Pat Kelly
Matt Nokes
Alvaro Espinoza
Bernie Williams
2 Opening of Oriole Park 12.50 30.00
at Camden Yards
April 6, 1992 (17,000)
Features four artist
renderings of the Park
3 Toronto Blue Jays 2.00 5.00
April 25, 1992/52,000)
SkyDome
Bob Bailor
John Mayberry
Rick Bosetti
Balor Moore
Garth Iorg
4 '72 Upper Deck Heroes 3.00 8.00
vs. Atlanta Braves Heroes
May 1, 1992 (22,000)
Fulton County
Coliseum
Bruce Benedict
Darrell Evans
Glenn Hubbard
Dave Johnson
Reggie Jackson
5 Rangers Heroes vs. 2.50 6.00
White Sox Heroes
May 3, 1992 (22,000)
Comiskey Park
Bill Melton
Dick Allen
Wilbur Wood
Carlos May
Chuck Tanner MG
6 Silver Anniversary of 2.50 6.00
the Impossible Dream
May 16, 1992 (38,000)
Fenway Park
Jim Lonborg
George Scott
Carl Yastrzemski
Tony Conigliaro
Dick Williams MG
7 Nickname Heroes at 2.50 6.00
the 'Stick
May 17, 1992 (37,000)
Candlestick Park
Orlando Cepeda
Jim Davenport
Juan Marichal
Dave Kingman
John Montefusco
8 American League Heroes 3.00 8.00
vs. National League Heroes
May 30, 1992 (17,000)
Astrodome
Tony Oliva
Joe Niekro
Jose Cruz
Mark Fidrych
Jim Wynn
9 Harvey's Wallbangers 2.50 6.00
May 30, 1992 (32,000)
County Stadium
Ben Oglivie
Harvey Kuenn
Cecil Cooper
Gorman Thomas
10 30 Years of Mets 2.00 5.00
Baseball
June 13, 1992 (47,000)
Shea Stadium
Cleon Jones
Bud Harrelson
Rusty Staub
Jerry Koosman
Ed Kranepool
11 Cardinals' 100th 4.00 10.00
Anniversary
June 14, 1992 (22,000)
Busch Stadium
Red Schoendeinst
Bob Gibson
Enos Slaughter
Lou Brock
12 N.L. Heroes 2.00 5.00
vs. American
League Heroes
June 20. 1992 (47.000)
Arlington Stadium
former Texas Rangers
Jim Sundberg
Toby Harrah
Jim Kern
Al Oliver
Jim Spencer
13 Record Setters 6.00 15.00
June 21, 1992 (52,000)
Anaheim Stadium
Nolan Ryan
Jim Abbott
Jimmie Reese CO
14 Cubs Heroes vs. 3.00 8.00
Reds Heroes
June 28, 1992 (27,000)
Riverfront Stadium
George Foster
Gary Nolan
Pedro Borbon
Cesar Cedeno
Bernie Carbo
15 The Record-Setting 2.50 6.00
Infield
July 5, 1992 (62,000)
Dodger Stadium
Bill Russell
Davey Lopes
Steve Garvey
Ron Cey
16 46th Annual Old-Timers 2.50 6.00
Day Classic
July 11, 1992 (50,000)
Yankee Stadium
Phil Rizzuto
Bobby Brown
Allie Reynolds
Hank Bauer
Tom Henrich
17 Heroes of Baseball 3.00 8.00
All-Star Game
July 13, 1992 (67,000)
Jack Murphy Stadium
Reggie Jackson
Rollie Fingers
Steve Garvey
Brooks Robinson
Bob Feller
18 All-Star Fanfest 6.00 15.00
July 13, 1992 (12,000)
Jack Murphy Stadium
Larry Doby
Steve Garvey
Rollie Fingers
This card measures 5 1/2-in by 8 1/2-in
19 All-Star Game Heroes 3.00 8.00
July 18, 1992 (27,000)
Three Rivers Stadium
Kent Tekulve
Frank Thomas
Elroy Face
Bob Veale
Chuck Tanner
20 Royals HOF Inductees 2.00 5.00
July 18-19, 1992 (42,000)
Royal Stadium
Fred Patek
Joe Burke GM
Larry Gura
21 More Than 100 Years of 3.00 8.00
Baseball in Montreal
July 26, 1992 (22,000)
Olympic Stadium
Claude Raymond
Duke Snider
Jean-Pierre Roy ANN
Rusty Staub
Steve Rogers
22 Seattle Mariners 2.50 6.00
Heroes of Baseball
July 26, 1992
Kingdome
23 A Tribute to 3.00 8.00
Rocky Colavito
Aug. 1, 1992 (22,000)
Municipal Stadium
24 '70s A's vs./'76 Phillies 3.00 8.00
Aug. 8, 1992 (44,000)
Veterans Stadium
Tug McGraw
Steve Carlton
Greg Luzinski
Larry Bowa
Dick Allen
25 Rollie Fingers 2.50 6.00
Hall of Fame Day
Aug. 9, 1992 (32,000)
County Stadium
26 200 Club 3.00 8.00
Aug. 9, 1992 (50,000)
Camden Yards
Luis Aparicio
J.R. Richard
Brooks Robinson
Milt Pappas
Bill Buckner
27 25th Anniversary of 4.00 10.00
the Oakland Athletics
Aug. 15, 1992 (22,000)
Oakland-Alameda
County Stadium
Jim(Catfish) Hunter
Reggie Jackson
Rollie Fingers
Vida Blue
Bert Campaneris
28 Chicago Cubs 2.00 5.00
August 16, 1992
Ron Santo
Ernie Banks
Randy Hundley
Billy Williams
Don Kessinger
29 Minnesota Twins 3.00 8.00
World Series Heroes
Aug. 23, 1992 (22,000)
Metrodome
Maury Wills
Bob Gibson
Zoilo Versalles
Jim(Mudcat) Grant
Tony Oliva
30 1972 Division Winners 3.00 8.00
Detroit Tigers
Aug. 30, 1992 (32,000)
Bert Campaneris
Aurelio Rodriguez
Sparky Anderson MG
Al Oliver
31 Upper Deck Authenticated 2.00 5.00
Salutes The Legends
Past, Present and Future
Nov. 13-15, 1992 (18,000)
Midwest Sports Collectors Show
List of Tri-Star Sports, Inc. shows
32 50 Year Anniversary of 4.00 10.00
the 1942 Triple Crown
Season by Ted Williams/(Numbered, but without
total production number)
Ted Williams
33 Upper Deck Honors 3.00 8.00
Lou Brock
Vida Blue
Rollie Fingers/50,000
34 Upper Deck 2.00 5.00
Heroes of Baseball Shows
Rollie Fingers
Reggie Jackson
Gaylord Perry
Brooks Robinson
Ted Williams/76,400)
35 Upper Deck Heroes of 2.00 5.00
Baseball Shows
Bobby Bonds
Lou Brock
Bob Gibson
Robin Roberts
Billy Williams/76,400

1992 Upper Deck Team MVP Holograms

The 54 hologram cards in this standard size set feature the top offensive player and pitcher from each Major League team plus two checklist cards. Only 216,000 number sets were produced, and each set was packaged in a custom-designed box with protective sleeve and included a numbered certificate. To display the set, Upper Deck also made available a custom album through a mail-in offer for 10.00. Cards 1-2 feature the AL and NL MVPs (with checklists) while cards 3-54 are arranged in alphabetical order.

COMP. FACT SET (54) 6.00 15.00
1 Cal Ripken MVP .60 1.50
AL Checklist
2 Terry Pendleton MVP .02 .10
NL Checklist
3 Jim Abbott .07 .20
4 Roberto Alomar .20 .50
5 Kevin Appier .02 .10
6 Steve Avery .02 .10
7 Jeff Bagwell .30 .75
8 Albert Belle .07 .20
9 Andy Benes .02 .10
10 Wade Boggs .30 .75
11 Barry Bonds .50 1.25
12 George Brett .60 1.50
13 Ivan Calderon .02 .10
14 Jose Canseco .30 .75
15 Will Clark .20 .50
16 Roger Clemens .60 1.50
17 David Cone .10 .30
18 Doug Drabek .02 .10
19 Dennis Eckersley .25 .60
20 Scott Erickson .07 .20
21 Cecil Fielder .07 .20
22 Ken Griffey Jr. .75 2.00
23 Bill Gullickson .02 .10
24 Juan Guzman .02 .10
25 Pete Harnisch .02 .10
26 Howard Johnson .02 .10
27 Randy Johnson .30 .75
28 John Kruk .07 .20
29 Barry Larkin .20 .50
30 Greg Maddux .60 1.50
31 Dennis Martinez .07 .20
32 Ramon Martinez .02 .10
33 Don Mattingly .60 1.50
34 Jack McDowell .02 .10
35 Fred McGriff .10 .30
36 Paul Molitor .25 .60
37 Charles Nagy .02 .10
38 Gregg Olson .07 .20
39 Terry Pendleton .02 .10
40 Luis Polonia .02 .10
41 Kirby Puckett .25 .60
42 Dave Righetti .02 .10
43 Jose Rijo .02 .10
44 Cal Ripken 1.25 3.00
45 Nolan Ryan 1.25 3.00
46 Ryne Sandberg .60 1.50
47 Scott Sanderson .02 .10
48 Ruben Sierra .07 .20
49 Lee Smith .07 .20
50 Ozzie Smith .60 1.50
51 Darryl Strawberry .07 .20
52 Frank Thomas .30 .75
53 Bill Wegman .02 .10
54 Mitch Williams .02 .10

1993 Upper Deck

The 1993 Upper Deck set consists of two series of 420 standard-size cards. Special subsets featured include Star Rookies (1-29), Community Heroes (30-40), and American League Teammates (41-55), Top Prospects (421-449), Inside the Numbers (450-470), Team Stars (471-485), Award Winners (486-499), and Diamond Debuts (500-510). Derek Jeter is the only notable Rookie Card in this set. A special card (SP5) was randomly inserted in first series packs to commemorate the 3,000th hit of George Brett and Robin Yount. A special card (SP6) commemorating Nolan Ryan's last season was randomly inserted into second series packs. Both SP cards were inserted at a rate of one every 72 packs

COMPLETE SET (840) 15.00 40.00
COMP.FACT.SET (840) 20.00 50.00
COMPLETE SERIES 1 (420) 6.00 15.00
COMPLETE SERIES 2 (420) 10.00 25.00
SUBSET CARDS HALF VALUE OF BASE CARDS
SP CARDS STATED ODDS 1:72
1 Tim Salmon CL .07 .20
2 Mike Piazza 1.25 3.00
3 Rene Arocha RC .20 .50
4 Willie Greene .02 .10
5 Manny Alexander .02 .10
6 Dan Wilson .07 .20
7 Dan Smith .02 .10
8 Kevin Rogers .02 .10
9 Nigel Wilson .02 .10
10 Joe Vitko .02 .10
11 Tim Costo .02 .10
12 Alan Embree .02 .10
13 Jim Tatum RC .05 .15
14 Cris Colon .02 .10
15 Steve Hosey .02 .10
16 Sterling Hitchcock RC .20 .50
17 Dave Mlicki .02 .10
18 Jessie Hollins .02 .10
19 Bobby Jones .07 .20
20 Kurt Miller .02 .10
21 Melvin Nieves .02 .10
22 Billy Ashley .02 .10
23 J.T.Snow RC .30 .75
24 Chipper Jones .20 .50
25 Tim Salmon .10 .30
26 Tim Pugh RC .05 .15
27 David Nied .02 .10
28 Mike Trombley .02 .10
29 Javier Lopez .10 .30
30 Jim Abbott CH CL .07 .20
31 Jim Abbott CH .02 .10
32 Dale Murphy CH .10 .30
33 Tony Pena CH .02 .10
34 Kirby Puckett CH .10 .30
35 Harold Reynolds CH .02 .10
36 Cal Ripken CH .30 .75
37 Nolan Ryan CH .40 1.00
38 Ryne Sandberg CH .20 .50
39 Dave Stewart CH .02 .10
40 Dave Winfield CH .02 .10
41 M.McGwire .20 .50
J.Carter CL
42 R.Alomar .07 .20
J.Carter
43 Molitor .20 .50
Listach
Yount
44 C.Ripken .20 .50
B.Anderson
45 Belle .07 .20
Baerga
Thome
Lofton
46 C.Fielder .02 .10
M.Tettleton
47 R.Kelly .25 .60
D.Mattingly
48 R.Clemens .20 .50
F.Viola
49 R.Sierra .20 .50
M.McGwire
50 K.Puckett .10 .30
K.Hrbek
51 F.Thomas .10 .30
R.Ventura
52 Cans .10 .30
IRod
Gonz
Palmeiro
53 Lethal Lefties .07 .20
Mark Langston
Jim Abbott
Chuck F
54 Joyner .20 .50
Jefferies
Brett
55 K.Griffey .25 .60
Buhner
Mitchell
56 George Brett .50 1.25
57 Scott Cooper .02 .10
58 Mike Maddux .02 .10
59 Rusty Meacham .02 .10
60 Wil Cordero .02 .10
61 Tim Teufel .02 .10
62 Jeff Montgomery .02 .10
63 Scott Livingstone .02 .10
64 Doug Dascenzo .02 .10
65 Bret Boone .07 .20
66 Tim Wakefield .20 .50
67 Curt Schilling .07 .20
68 Frank Tanana .02 .10
69 Len Dykstra .07 .20
70 Derek Lilliquist .02 .10
71 Anthony Young .02 .10
72 Hipolito Pichardo .02 .10
73 Rod Beck .02 .10
74 Kent Hrbek .07 .20
75 Tom Glavine .10 .30
76 Kevin Brown .07 .20
77 Chuck Finley .07 .20
78 Bob Walk .02 .10
79 Rheal Cormier UER .02 .10
80 Rick Sutcliffe .07 .20
81 Harold Baines .07 .20
82 Lee Smith .07 .20
83 Geno Petralli .02 .10
84 Jose Oquendo .02 .10
85 Mark Gubicza .02 .10
86 Mickey Tettleton .02 .10
87 Bobby Witt .02 .10
88 Mark Lewis .02 .10
89 Kevin Appier .07 .20
90 Mike Stanton .02 .10
91 Rafael Belliard .02 .10
92 Kenny Rogers .07 .20
93 Randy Velarde .02 .10
94 Luis Sojo .02 .10
95 Mark Leiter .02 .10
96 Jody Reed .02 .10
97 Pete Harnisch .02 .10
98 Tom Candiotti .02 .10
99 Mark Portugal .02 .10
100 Dave Valle .02 .10
101 Shawon Dunston .02 .10
102 B.J. Surhoff .07 .20
103 Jay Bell .07 .20
104 Sid Bream .02 .10
105 Frank Thomas CL .10 .30
106 Mike Morgan .02 .10
107 Bill Doran .02 .10
108 Lance Blankenship .02 .10
109 Mark Lemke .02 .10
110 Brian Harper .02 .10
111 Brady Anderson .07 .20
112 Bip Roberts .02 .10
113 Mitch Williams .02 .10
114 Craig Biggio .10 .30
115 Eddie Murray .20 .50
116 Matt Nokes .02 .10
117 Lance Parrish .07 .20
118 Bill Swift .02 .10
119 Jeff Innis .02 .10
120 Mike LaValliere .02 .10
121 Hal Morris .02 .10
122 Walt Weiss .02 .10
123 Ivan Rodriguez .10 .30
124 Andy Van Slyke .10 .30
125 Roberto Alomar .10 .30
126 Robby Thompson .02 .10
127 Sammy Sosa .20 .50
128 Mark Langston .02 .10
129 Jerry Browne .02 .10
130 Chuck McElroy .02 .10
131 Frank Viola .07 .20
132 Leo Gomez .02 .10
133 Ramon Martinez .02 .10
134 Don Mattingly .50 1.25
135 Roger Clemens .40 1.00
136 Rickey Henderson .20 .50
137 Darren Daulton .07 .20
138 Ken Hill .02 .10
139 Ozzie Guillen .07 .20
140 Jerald Clark .02 .10
141 Dave Fleming .02 .10
142 Delino DeShields .02 .10
143 Matt Williams .07 .20
144 Larry Walker .07 .20
145 Ruben Sierra .07 .20
146 Ozzie Smith .30 .75
147 Chris Sabo .02 .10
148 Carlos Hernandez .02 .10
149 Pat Borders .02 .10
150 Orlando Merced .02 .10
151 Royce Clayton .02 .10
152 Kurt Stillwell .02 .10
153 Dave Hollins .02 .10
154 Mike Greenwell .02 .10
155 Nolan Ryan .75 2.00
156 Felix Jose .02 .10
157 Junior Felix .02 .10
158 Derek Bell .02 .10
159 Steve Buechele .02 .10
160 John Burkett .02 .10
161 Pat Howell .02 .10
162 Milt Cuyler .02 .10
163 Terry Pendleton .07 .20
164 Jack Morris .07 .20
165 Tony Gwynn .25 .60
166 Deion Sanders .10 .30
167 Mike Devereaux .02 .10
168 Ron Darling .02 .10
169 Orel Hershiser .07 .20
170 Mike Jackson .02 .10
171 Doug Jones .02 .10
172 Dan Walters .02 .10
173 Darren Lewis .02 .10
174 Carlos Baerga .02 .10
175 Ryne Sandberg .30 .75
176 Gregg Jefferies .02 .10
177 John Jaha .02 .10
178 Luis Polonia .02 .10
179 Kirt Manwaring .02 .10
180 Mike Magnante .02 .10
181 Billy Ripken .02 .10
182 Mike Moore .02 .10
183 Eric Anthony .02 .10
184 Lenny Harris .02 .10
185 Tony Pena .02 .10
186 Mike Felder .02 .10
187 Greg Olson .02 .10
188 Rene Gonzales .02 .10
189 Mike Bordick .02 .10
190 Mel Rojas .02 .10
191 Todd Frohwirth .02 .10
192 Darryl Hamilton .02 .10
193 Mike Fetters .02 .10
194 Omar Olivares .02 .10
195 Tony Phillips .02 .10
196 Paul Sorrento .02 .10
197 Trevor Wilson .02 .10
198 Kevin Gross .02 .10
199 Ron Karkovice .02 .10
200 Brook Jacoby .02 .10
201 Mariano Duncan .02 .10
202 Dennis Cook .02 .10
203 Daryl Boston .02 .10
204 Mike Perez .02 .10
205 Manuel Lee .02 .10
206 Steve Olin .02 .10
207 Charlie Hough .07 .20
208 Scott Scudder .02 .10
209 Charlie O'Brien .02 .10
210 Barry Bonds CL .30 .75
211 Jose Vizcaino .02 .10
212 Scott Leius .02 .10
213 Kevin Mitchell .02 .10
214 Brian Barnes .02 .10
215 Pat Kelly .02 .10
216 Chris Hammond .02 .10
217 Rob Deer .02 .10
218 Cory Snyder .02 .10
219 Gary Carter .07 .20
220 Danny Darwin .02 .10
221 Tom Gordon .02 .10
222 Gary Sheffield 2X .07 .20
223 Joe Carter .07 .20
224 Jay Buhner .07 .20
225 Jose Offerman .02 .10
226 Jose Rijo .02 .10
227 Mark Whiten .02 .10
228 Randy Milligan .02 .10
229 Bud Black .02 .10
230 Gary DiSarcina .02 .10
231 Steve Finley .07 .20
232 Dennis Martinez .07 .20
233 Mike Mussina .10 .30
234 Joe Oliver .02 .10
235 Chad Curtis .02 .10
236 Shane Mack .02 .10
237 Jaime Navarro .02 .10
238 Brian McRae .02 .10
239 Chili Davis .07 .20
240 Jeff King .02 .10
241 Dean Palmer .07 .20
242 Danny Tartabull .02 .10
243 Charles Nagy .02 .10
244 Ray Lankford .07 .20
245 Barry Larkin .10 .30
246 Steve Avery .02 .10
247 John Kruk .07 .20
248 Derrick May .02 .10
249 Stan Javier .02 .10
250 Roger McDowell .02 .10
251 Dan Gladden .02 .10
252 Wally Joyner .07 .20
253 Pat Listach .02 .10
254 Chuck Knoblauch .07 .20
255 Sandy Alomar Jr. .02 .10
256 Jeff Bagwell .10 .30
257 Andy Stankiewicz .02 .10
258 Darrin Jackson .02 .10
259 Brett Butler .07 .20
260 Joe Orsulak .02 .10
261 Andy Benes .02 .10
262 Kenny Lofton .07 .20
263 Robin Ventura .07 .20
264 Ron Gant .07 .20
265 Ellis Burks .07 .20
266 Juan Guzman .02 .10
267 Wes Chamberlain .02 .10
268 John Smiley .02 .10
269 Franklin Stubbs .02 .10
270 Tom Browning .02 .10
271 Dennis Eckersley .07 .20
272 Carlton Fisk .10 .30
273 Lou Whitaker .07 .20
274 Phil Plantier .02 .10
275 Bobby Bonilla .07 .20
276 Ben McDonald .02 .10
277 Bob Zupcic .02 .10
278 Terry Steinbach .02 .10
279 Terry Mulholland .02 .10
280 Lance Johnson .02 .10
281 Willie McGee .07 .20
282 Bret Saberhagen .07 .20
283 Randy Myers .02 .10
284 Randy Tomlin .02 .10
285 Mickey Morandini .02 .10
286 Brian Williams .02 .10
287 Tino Martinez .10 .30
288 Jose Melendez .02 .10
289 Jeff Huson .02 .10
290 Joe Grahe .02 .10
291 Mel Hall .02 .10
292 Otis Nixon .02 .10
293 Todd Hundley .02 .10
294 Casey Candaele .02 .10
295 Kevin Seitzer .02 .10
296 Eddie Taubensee .02 .10
297 Moises Alou .07 .20
298 Scott Radinsky .02 .10
299 Thomas Howard .02 .10
300 Kyle Abbott .02 .10
301 Omar Vizquel .10 .30
302 Keith Miller .02 .10
303 Rick Aguilera .02 .10
304 Bruce Hurst .02 .10
305 Ken Caminiti .07 .20
306 Mike Pagliarulo .02 .10
307 Frank Seminara .02 .10
308 Andre Dawson .07 .20
309 Jose Lind .02 .10
310 Joe Boever .02 .10
311 Jeff Parrett .02 .10
312 Alan Mills .02 .10
313 Kevin Tapani .02 .10
314 Darryl Kile .07 .20
315 Checklist 211-315 .07 .20
Will Clark
316 Mike Sharperson .02 .10
317 John Orton .02 .10
318 Bob Tewksbury .02 .10
319 Xavier Hernandez .02 .10
320 Paul Assenmacher .02 .10
321 John Franco .07 .20
322 Mike Timlin .02 .10
323 Jose Guzman .02 .10
324 Pedro Martinez .40 1.00
325 Bill Spiers .02 .10
326 Melido Perez .02 .10
327 Mike Macfarlane .02 .10
328 Ricky Bones .02 .10
329 Scott Bankhead .02 .10
330 Rich Rodriguez .02 .10
331 Geronimo Pena .02 .10
332 Bernie Williams .10 .30
333 Paul Molitor .07 .20
334 Carlos Garcia .02 .10
335 David Cone .07 .20
336 Randy Johnson .20 .50
337 Pat Mahomes .02 .10
338 Erik Hanson .02 .10
339 Duane Ward .02 .10
340 Al Martin .02 .10
341 Pedro Munoz .02 .10
342 Greg Colbrunn .02 .10
343 Julio Valera .02 .10
344 John Olerud .07 .20
345 George Bell .02 .10
346 Devon White .07 .20
347 Donovan Osborne .02 .10
348 Mark Gardner .02 .10
349 Zane Smith .02 .10
350 Wilson Alvarez .02 .10
351 Kevin Koslofski .02 .10
352 Roberto Hernandez .02 .10
353 Glenn Davis .02 .10
354 Reggie Sanders .07 .20
355 Ken Griffey Jr. .40 1.00
356 Marquis Grissom .07 .20
357 Jack McDowell .02 .10
358 Jimmy Key .07 .20
359 Stan Belinda .02 .10
360 Gerald Williams .02 .10
361 Sid Fernandez .02 .10
362 Alex Fernandez .02 .10
363 John Smoltz .10 .30
364 Travis Fryman .07 .20
365 Jose Canseco .10 .30
366 David Justice .07 .20
367 Pedro Astacio .02 .10
368 Tim Belcher .02 .10
369 Steve Sax .02 .10
370 Gary Gaetti .07 .20
371 Jeff Frye .02 .10
372 Bob Wickman .02 .10
373 Ryan Thompson .02 .10
374 David Hulse RC .05 .15
375 Cal Eldred .02 .10
376 Ryan Klesko .07 .20
377 Damion Easley .02 .10
378 John Kiely .02 .10
379 Jim Bullinger .02 .10
380 Brian Bohanon .02 .10
381 Rod Brewer .02 .10
382 Fernando Ramsey RC .05 .15
383 Sam Militello .02 .10
384 Arthur Rhodes .02 .10
385 Eric Karros .07 .20
386 Rico Brogna .02 .10
387 John Valentin .02 .10
388 Kerry Woodson .02 .10
389 Ben Rivera .02 .10
390 Matt Whiteside RC .05 .15
391 Henry Rodriguez .02 .10
392 John Wetteland .07 .20
393 Kent Mercker .02 .10
394 Bernard Gilkey .02 .10
395 Doug Henry .02 .10
396 Mo Vaughn .07 .20
397 Scott Erickson .02 .10
398 Bill Gullickson .02 .10
399 Mark Guthrie .02 .10
400 Dave Martinez .02 .10
401 Jeff Kent .20 .50
402 Chris Hoiles .02 .10
403 Mike Henneman .02 .10
404 Chris Nabholz .02 .10
405 Tom Pagnozzi .02 .10
406 Kelly Gruber .02 .10
407 Bob Welch .02 .10
408 Frank Castillo .02 .10
409 John Dopson .02 .10
410 Steve Farr .02 .10
411 Henry Cotto .02 .10
412 Bob Patterson .02 .10
413 Todd Stottlemyre .02 .10
414 Greg A. Harris .02 .10
415 Denny Neagle .07 .20
416 Bill Wegman .02 .10
417 Willie Wilson .02 .10
418 Terry Leach .02 .10
419 Willie Randolph .07 .20
420 Checklist 316-420 McGwire .10 .30
421 Calvin Murray CL .02 .10
422 Pete Janicki RC .05 .15
423 Todd Jones TP .07 .20
424 Mike Neill .02 .10
425 Carlos Delgado .20 .50
426 Jose Oliva .02 .10
427 Tyrone Hill .02 .10
428 Dmitri Young .07 .20
429 Derek Wallace RC .05 .15
430 Michael Moore RC .05 .15
431 Cliff Floyd .07 .20
432 Calvin Murray .02 .10
433 Manny Ramirez .30 .75
434 Marc Newfield .02 .10
435 Charles Johnson .07 .20
436 Butch Huskey .02 .10
437 Brad Pennington TP .02 .10
438 Ray McDavid RC .05 .15
439 Chad McConnell .02 .10
440 Midre Cummings RC .05 .15
441 Benji Gil .02 .10
442 Frankie Rodriguez .02 .10
443 Chad Mottola RC .05 .15
444 John Burke RC .05 .15
445 Michael Tucker .02 .10
446 Rick Greene .02 .10
447 Rich Becker .02 .10
448 Mike Robertson TP .02 .10
449 Derek Jeter RC ! 6.00 15.00
450 I.Rodriguez .10 .30
D.McCarty CL
451 Jim Abbott IN .07 .20
452 Jeff Bagwell IN .07 .20
453 Jason Bere IN .02 .10
454 Delino DeShields IN .02 .10
455 Travis Fryman IN .02 .10
456 Alex Gonzalez IN .02 .10
457 Phil Hiatt IN .02 .10
458 Dave Hollins IN .02 .10
459 Chipper Jones IN .10 .30
460 David Justice IN .02 .10
461 Ray Lankford IN .02 .10
462 David McCarty IN .02 .10
463 Mike Mussina IN .07 .20
464 Jose Offerman IN .02 .10
465 Dean Palmer IN .02 .10
466 Geronimo Pena IN .02 .10
467 Eduardo Perez IN .02 .10
468 Ivan Rodriguez IN .07 .20
469 Reggie Sanders IN .02 .10
470 Bernie Williams IN .07 .20
471 Bonds .30 .75
Williams
Clark CL
472 Madd .20 .50
Avery
Smolt
Glav
473 Red October .07 .20
Jose Rijo
Rob Dibble
Roberto Kelly#
474 Sheff .07 .20
Plant
Gwynn
McGrif
475 Biggio .07 .20
Drabek
Bagwell
476 Clark .30 .75
Bonds
Williams
477 Eric Davis .07 .20
Darryl Strawberry
478 Bich .07 .20
Nied
Galarraga
479 Maga .02 .10
Destr
Barbe
Conine
480 Wakefield .07 .20
Van Slyke
Bell

481 Griss .10 .30
DeSh
Mart
Walker
482 O.Smith .20 .50
Redbirds
483 Myers .20 .50
Sandberg
Grace
484 Big Apple Power Switch .10 .30
485 Kruk .02 .10
Holl
Dault
Dyks
486 Barry Bonds AW .30 .75
487 Dennis Eckersley AW .07 .20
488 Greg Maddux AW .20 .50
489 Dennis Eckersley AW .07 .20
490 Eric Karros AW .02 .10
491 Pat Listach AW .02 .10
492 Gary Sheffield AW .02 .10
493 Mark McGwire AW .25 .60
494 Gary Sheffield AW .02 .10
495 Edgar Martinez AW .07 .20
496 Fred McGriff AW .07 .20
497 Juan Gonzalez AW .02 .10
498 Darren Daulton AW .02 .10
499 Cecil Fielder AW .02 .10
500 Brent Gates CL .02 .10
501 Tavo Alvarez .02 .10
502 Rod Bolton .02 .10
503 John Cummings RC .05 .15
504 Brent Gates .02 .10
505 Tyler Green .02 .10
506 Jose Martinez RC .05 .15
507 Troy Percival .10 .30
508 Kevin Stocker .02 .10
509 Matt Walbeck RC .05 .15
510 Rondell White .07 .20
511 Billy Ripken .02 .10
512 Mike Moore .02 .10
513 Jose Lind .02 .10
514 Chito Martinez .02 .10
515 Jose Guzman .02 .10
516 Kim Batiste .02 .10
517 Jeff Tackett .02 .10
518 Charlie Hough .07 .20
519 Marvin Freeman .02 .10
520 Carlos Martinez .02 .10
521 Eric Young .02 .10
522 Pete Incaviglia .02 .10
523 Scott Fletcher .02 .10
524 Orestes Destrade .02 .10
525 Ken Griffey Jr. CL .25 .60
526 Ellis Burks .07 .20
527 Juan Samuel .02 .10
528 Dave Magadan .02 .10
529 Jeff Parrett .02 .10
530 Bill Krueger .02 .10
531 Frank Bolick .02 .10
532 Alan Trammell .07 .20
533 Walt Weiss .02 .10
534 David Cone .07 .20
535 Greg Maddux .30 .75
536 Kevin Young .07 .20
537 Dave Hansen .02 .10
538 Alex Cole .02 .10
539 Greg Hibbard .02 .10
540 Gene Larkin .02 .10
541 Jeff Reardon .07 .20
542 Felix Jose .02 .10
543 Jimmy Key .07 .20
544 Reggie Jefferson .02 .10
545 Gregg Jefferies .02 .10
546 Dave Stewart .07 .20
547 Tim Wallach .02 .10
548 Spike Owen .02 .10
549 Tommy Greene .02 .10
550 Fernando Valenzuela .07 .20
551 Rich Amaral .02 .10
552 Bret Barberie .02 .10
553 Edgar Martinez .10 .30
554 Jim Abbott .10 .30
555 Frank Thomas .20 .50
556 Wade Boggs .10 .30
557 Tom Henke .02 .10
558 Milt Thompson .02 .10
559 Lloyd McClendon .02 .10
560 Vinny Castilla .20 .50
561 Ricky Jordan .02 .10
562 Andujar Cedeno .02 .10
563 Greg Vaughn .02 .10
564 Cecil Fielder .07 .20
565 Kirby Puckett .20 .50
566 Mark McGwire .50 1.25
567 Barry Bonds .60 1.50
568 Jody Reed .02 .10
569 Todd Zeile .02 .10
570 Mark Carreon .02 .10
571 Joe Girardi .02 .10
572 Luis Gonzalez .07 .20
573 Mark Grace .10 .30
574 Rafael Palmeiro .10 .30
575 Darryl Strawberry .07 .20
576 Will Clark .10 .30
577 Fred McGriff .10 .30
578 Kevin Reimer .02 .10
579 Dave Righetti .07 .20
580 Juan Bell .02 .10
581 Jeff Brantley .02 .10
582 Brian Hunter .02 .10
583 Tim Naehring .02 .10
584 Glenallen Hill .02 .10
585 Cal Ripken .60 1.50
586 Albert Belle .07 .20
587 Robin Yount .30 .75
588 Chris Bosio .02 .10
589 Pete Smith .02 .10
590 Chuck Carr .02 .10
591 Jeff Blauser .02 .10
592 Kevin McReynolds .02 .10
593 Andres Galarraga .07 .20
594 Kevin Maas .02 .10
595 Eric Davis .07 .20
596 Brian Jordan .07 .20
597 Tim Raines .07 .20
598 Rick Wilkins .02 .10
599 Steve Cooke .02 .10
600 Mike Gallego .02 .10
601 Mike Munoz .02 .10
602 Luis Rivera .02 .10
603 Junior Ortiz .02 .10
604 Brent Mayne .02 .10
605 Luis Alicea .02 .10
606 Damon Berryhill .02 .10
607 Dave Henderson .02 .10
608 Kirk McCaskill .02 .10
609 Jeff Fassero .02 .10
610 Mike Harkey .02 .10
611 Francisco Cabrera .02 .10
612 Rey Sanchez .02 .10
613 Scott Servais .02 .10
614 Darrin Fletcher .02 .10
615 Felix Fermin .02 .10
616 Kevin Seitzer .02 .10
617 Bob Scanlan .02 .10
618 Billy Hatcher .02 .10
619 John Vander Wal .02 .10
620 Joe Hesketh .02 .10
621 Hector Villanueva .02 .10
622 Randy Milligan .02 .10
623 Tony Tarasco RC .05 .15
624 Russ Swan .02 .10
625 Willie Wilson .02 .10
626 Frank Tanana .02 .10
627 Pete O'Brien .02 .10
628 Lenny Webster .02 .10
629 Mark Clark .02 .10
630 Roger Clemens CL .20 .50
631 Alex Arias .02 .10
632 Chris Gwynn .02 .10
633 Tom Bolton .02 .10
634 Greg Briley .02 .10
635 Kent Bottenfield .02 .10
636 Kelly Downs .02 .10
637 Manuel Lee .02 .10
638 Al Leiter .07 .20
639 Jeff Gardner .02 .10
640 Mike Gardiner .02 .10
641 Mark Gardner .02 .10
642 Jeff Branson .02 .10
643 Paul Wagner .02 .10
644 Sean Berry .02 .10
645 Phil Hiatt .02 .10
646 Kevin Mitchell .02 .10
647 Charlie Hayes .02 .10
648 Jim Deshaies .02 .10
649 Dan Pasqua .02 .10
650 Mike Maddux .02 .10
651 Domingo Martinez RC .05 .15
652 Greg McMichael RC .05 .15
653 Eric Wedge RC .20 .50
654 Mark Whiten .02 .10
655 Roberto Kelly .02 .10
656 Julio Franco .07 .20
657 Gene Harris .02 .10
658 Pete Schourek .02 .10
659 Mike Bielecki .02 .10
660 Ricky Gutierrez .02 .10
661 Chris Hammond .02 .10
662 Tim Scott .02 .10
663 Norm Charlton .02 .10
664 Doug Drabek .02 .10
665 Dwight Gooden .07 .20
666 Jim Gott .02 .10
667 Randy Myers .02 .10
668 Darren Holmes .02 .10
669 Tim Spehr .02 .10
670 Bruce Ruffin .02 .10
671 Bobby Thigpen .02 .10
672 Tony Fernandez .02 .10
673 Darrin Jackson .02 .10
674 Gregg Olson .02 .10
675 Rob Dibble .07 .20
676 Howard Johnson .02 .10
677 Mike Lansing RC .20 .50
678 Charlie Leibrandt .02 .10
679 Kevin Bass .02 .10
680 Hubie Brooks .02 .10
601 Scott Drosius .07 .20
682 Randy Knorr .02 .10
683 Dante Bichette .07 .20
684 Bryan Harvey .02 .10
685 Greg Gohr .02 .10
686 Willie Banks .02 .10
687 Robb Nen .07 .20
688 Mike Scioscia .02 .10
689 John Farrell .02 .10
690 John Candelaria .02 .10
691 Damon Buford .02 .10
692 Todd Worrell .02 .10
693 Pat Hentgen .02 .10
694 John Smiley .02 .10
695 Greg Swindell .02 .10
696 Derek Bell .02 .10
697 Terry Jorgensen .02 .10
698 Jimmy Jones .02 .10
699 David Wells .07 .20
700 Dave Martinez .02 .10
701 Steve Bedrosian .02 .10
702 Jeff Russell .02 .10
703 Joe Magrane .02 .10
704 Matt Mieske .02 .10
705 Paul Molitor .07 .20
706 Dale Murphy .10 .30
707 Steve Howe .02 .10
708 Greg Gagne .02 .10
709 Dave Eiland .02 .10
710 David West .02 .10
711 Luis Aquino .02 .10
712 Joe Orsulak .02 .10
713 Eric Plunk .02 .10
714 Mike Felder .02 .10
715 Joe Klink .02 .10
716 Lonnie Smith .02 .10
717 Monty Fariss .02 .10
718 Craig Lefferts .02 .10
719 John Habyan .02 .10
720 Willie Blair .02 .10
721 Darnell Coles .02 .10
722 Mark Williamson .02 .10
723 Bryn Smith .02 .10
724 Greg W. Harris .02 .10
725 Graeme Lloyd RC .20 .50
726 Cris Carpenter .02 .10
727 Chico Walker .02 .10
728 Tracy Woodson .02 .10
729 Jose Uribe .02 .10
730 Stan Javier .02 .10
731 Jay Howell .02 .10
732 Freddie Benavides .02 .10
733 Jeff Reboulet .02 .10
734 Scott Sanderson .02 .10
735 Ryne Sandberg CL .20 .50
736 Archi Cianfrocco .02 .10
737 Daryl Boston .02 .10
738 Craig Grebeck .02 .10
739 Doug Dascenzo .02 .10
740 Gerald Young .02 .10
741 Candy Maldonado .02 .10
742 Joey Cora .02 .10
743 Don Slaught .02 .10
744 Steve Decker .02 .10
745 Blas Minor .02 .10
746 Storm Davis .02 .10
747 Carlos Quintana .02 .10
748 Vince Coleman .02 .10
749 Todd Burns .02 .10
750 Steve Frey .02 .10
751 Ivan Calderon .02 .10
752 Steve Reed RC .05 .15
753 Danny Jackson .02 .10
754 Jeff Conine .07 .20
755 Juan Gonzalez .07 .20
756 Mike Kelly .02 .10
757 John Doherty .02 .10
758 Jack Armstrong .02 .10
759 John Wehner .02 .10
760 Scott Bankhead .02 .10
761 Jim Tatum .02 .10
762 Scott Pose RC .05 .15
763 Andy Ashby .02 .10
764 Ed Sprague .02 .10
765 Harold Baines .07 .20
766 Kirk Gibson .07 .20
767 Troy Neel .02 .10
768 Dick Schofield .02 .10
769 Dickie Thon .02 .10
770 Butch Henry .02 .10
771 Junior Felix .02 .10
772 Ken Ryan RC .05 .15
773 Trevor Hoffman .20 .50
774 Phil Plantier .02 .10
775 Bo Jackson .20 .50
776 Benito Santiago .07 .20
777 Andre Dawson .07 .20
778 Bryan Hickerson .02 .10
779 Dennis Moeller .02 .10
780 Ryan Bowen .02 .10
781 Eric Fox .02 .10
782 Joe Kmak .02 .10
783 Mike Hampton .07 .20
784 Darrell Sherman RC .05 .15
785 J.T.Snow .10 .30
786 Dave Winfield .07 .20
787 Jim Austin .02 .10
788 Craig Shipley .02 .10
789 Greg Myers .02 .10
790 Todd Benzinger .02 .10
791 Cory Snyder .02 .10
792 David Segui .02 .10
793 Armando Reynoso .02 .10
794 Chili Davis .07 .20
795 Dave Nilsson .02 .10
796 Paul O'Neill .10 .30
797 Jerald Clark .02 .10
798 Jose Mesa .02 .10
799 Brain Holman .02 .10
800 Jim Eisenreich .02 .10
801 Mark McLemore .02 .10
802 Luis Sojo .02 .10
803 Harold Reynolds .07 .20
804 Dan Plesac .02 .10
805 Dave Stieb .02 .10
806 Tom Brunansky .02 .10
807 Kelly Gruber .02 .10
808 Bob Ojeda .02 .10
809 Dave Burba .02 .10
810 Joe Boever .02 .10
811 Jeremy Hernandez .02 .10
812 Tim Salmon TC .07 .20
813 Jeff Bagwell TC .07 .20
814 Dennis Eckersley TC .07 .20
815 Roberto Alomar TC .07 .20
816 Steve Avery TC .02 .10
817 Pat Listach TC .02 .10
818 Gregg Jefferies TC .02 .10
819 Sammy Sosa TC .20 .50
820 Darryl Strawberry TC .02 .10
821 Dennis Martinez TC .02 .10
822 Robby Thompson TC .02 .10
823 Albert Belle TC .07 .20
824 Randy Johnson TC .10 .30
825 Nigel Wilson TC .02 .10
826 Bobby Bonilla TC .02 .10
827 Glenn Davis TC .02 .10
828 Gary Sheffield TC .02 .10
829 Darren Daulton TC .02 .10
830 Jay Bell TC .02 .10
831 Juan Gonzalez TC .02 .10
832 Andre Dawson TC .02 .10
833 Hal Morris TC .02 .10
834 David Nied TC .02 .10
835 Felix Jose TC .02 .10
836 Travis Fryman TC .02 .10
837 Shane Mack TC .02 .10
838 Robin Ventura TC .02 .10
839 Danny Tartabull TC .02 .10
840 Roberto Alomar CL .07 .20
SP5 G.Brett .40 1.00
R.Yount
SP6 Nolan Ryan .75 2.00

1993 Upper Deck Gold Hologram

COMP.FACT.SET (840) 40.00 100.00
*STARS: 3X TO 8X BASIC CARDS
*ROOKIES: 3X TO 8X BASIC CARDS
ONE GOLD SET PER 15 CT FACT.SET CASE
ALL GOLD SETS MUST BE OPENED TO VERIFY
HOLOGRAM ON BACK IS GOLD
DISTRIBUTED ONLY IN FACT.SET FORM
449 Derek Jeter ! 75.00 200.00

1993 Upper Deck Clutch Performers

COMPLETE SET (20) 8.00 20.00
SER.2 STAT.ODDS 1:9 RET, 1:1 RED JUMBO
CONDITION SENSITIVE SET
R1 Roberto Alomar .30 .75
R2 Wade Boggs .30 .75
R3 Barry Bonds 1.50 4.00
R4 Jose Canseco .30 .75
R5 Joe Carter .20 .50
R6 Will Clark .30 .75
R7 Roger Clemens 1.00 2.50
R8 Dennis Eckersley .20 .50
R9 Cecil Fielder .20 .50
R10 Juan Gonzalez .20 .50
R11 Ken Griffey Jr. 1.00 2.50
R12 Rickey Henderson .50 1.25
R13 Barry Larkin .30 .75
R14 Don Mattingly 1.25 3.00
R15 Fred McGriff .30 .75
R16 Terry Pendleton .20 .50
R17 Kirby Puckett .50 1.25
R18 Ryne Sandberg .75 2.00
R19 John Smoltz .30 .75
R20 Frank Thomas .50 1.25

1993 Upper Deck Fifth Anniversary

COMPLETE SET (15) 6.00 15.00
SER.2 STATED ODDS 1:9 HOBBY
JUMBOS DISTRIBUTED IN RETAIL PACKS
CONDITION SENSITIVE SET
A1 Ken Griffey Jr. 1.00 2.50
A2 Gary Sheffield .20 .50
A3 Roberto Alomar .30 .75
A4 Jim Abbott .30 .75
A5 Nolan Ryan 2.00 5.00
A6 Juan Gonzalez .20 .50
A7 David Justice .20 .50
A8 Carlos Baerga .08 .25
A9 Reggie Jackson .30 .75
A10 Eric Karros .20 .50
A11 Chipper Jones .50 1.25
A12 Ivan Rodriguez .30 .75
A13 Pat Listach .08 .25
A14 Frank Thomas .50 1.25
A15 Tim Salmon .30 .75

1993 Upper Deck Future Heroes

COMPLETE SET (10) 5.00 12.00
SER.2 STATED ODDS 1:9
55 Roberto Alomar .30 .75
56 Barry Bonds 1.50 4.00
57 Roger Clemens 1.00 2.50
58 Juan Gonzalez .20 .50
59 Ken Griffey Jr. 1.00 2.50
60 Mark McGwire 1.25 3.00
61 Kirby Puckett .50 1.25
62 Frank Thomas .50 1.25
63 Art Card .20 .50
NNO Header Card SP .08 .25

1993 Upper Deck Home Run Heroes

COMPLETE SET (28) 6.00 15.00
ONE PER SER.1 JUMBO PACK
HR1 Juan Gonzalez .20 .50
HR2 Mark McGwire 1.25 3.00
HR3 Cecil Fielder .20 .50
HR4 Fred McGriff .30 .75
HR5 Albert Belle .20 .50
HR6 Barry Bonds 1.50 4.00
HR7 Joe Carter .20 .50
HR8 Darren Daulton .20 .50
HR9 Ken Griffey Jr. 1.00 2.50
HR10 Dave Hollins .08 .25
HR11 Ryne Sandberg .75 2.00
HR12 George Bell .08 .25
HR13 Danny Tartabull .08 .25
HR14 Mike Devereaux .08 .25
HR15 Greg Vaughn .08 .25
HR16 Larry Walker .20 .50
HR17 David Justice .20 .50
HR18 Terry Pendleton .20 .50
HR19 Eric Karros .20 .50
HR20 Ray Lankford .20 .50
HR21 Matt Williams .20 .50
HR22 Eric Anthony .08 .25
HR23 Bobby Bonilla .20 .50
HR24 Kirby Puckett .50 1.25
HR25 Mike Macfarlane .08 .25
HR26 Tom Brunansky .08 .25
HR27 Paul O'Neill .30 .75
HR28 Gary Gaetti .20 .50

1993 Upper Deck Iooss Collection

COMPLETE SET (27) 12.50 30.00
SER.1 STATED ODDS 1:9 RET, 1:5 JUM
CONDITION SENSITIVE SET
*JUMBO CARDS: 2X TO 5X BASIC IOOSS
JUMBOS DISTRIBUTED IN RETAIL PACKS
WI1 Tim Salmon .40 1.00
WI2 Jeff Bagwell .40 1.00
WI3 Mark McGwire 1.50 4.00
WI4 Roberto Alomar .40 1.00
WI5 Steve Avery .10 .30
WI6 Paul Molitor .25 .60
WI7 Ozzie Smith 1.00 2.50
WI8 Mark Grace .40 1.00
WI9 Eric Karros .25 .60
WI10 Delino DeShields .10 .30
WI11 Will Clark .40 1.00
WI12 Albert Belle .25 .60
WI13 Ken Griffey Jr. 1.25 3.00
WI14 Howard Johnson .10 .30
WI15 Cal Ripken 2.00 5.00
WI16 Fred McGriff .40 1.00
WI17 Darren Daulton .25 .60
WI18 Andy Van Slyke .40 1.00
WI19 Nolan Ryan 2.50 6.00
WI20 Wade Boggs .40 1.00
WI21 Barry Larkin .40 1.00
WI22 George Brett 1.50 4.00
WI23 Cecil Fielder .25 .60
WI24 Kirby Puckett .60 1.50
WI25 Frank Thomas .60 1.50
WI26 Don Mattingly 1.50 4.00
NNO Iooss Header .10 .30

1993 Upper Deck Mays Heroes

COMPLETE SET (10) 1.25 3.00
COMMON CARD (46-54/HDR) .20 .50
SER.1 STATED ODDS 1:9

1993 Upper Deck On Deck

COMPLETE SET (25) 8.00 20.00
SER.2 STAT.ODDS 1:1 RED/BLUE JUMBO
D1 Jim Abbott .30 .75
D2 Roberto Alomar .30 .75
D3 Carlos Baerga .08 .25
D4 Albert Belle .20 .50
D5 Wade Boggs .30 .75
D6 George Brett 1.25 3.00
D7 Jose Canseco .30 .75
D8 Will Clark .30 .75
D9 Roger Clemens 1.00 2.50
D10 Dennis Eckersley .20 .50
D11 Cecil Fielder .20 .50
D12 Juan Gonzalez .20 .50
D13 Ken Griffey Jr. 1.00 2.50
D14 Tony Gwynn .60 1.50
D15 Bo Jackson .50 1.25
D16 Chipper Jones .50 1.25
D17 Eric Karros .20 .50
D18 Mark McGwire 1.25 3.00
D19 Kirby Puckett .50 1.25
D20 Nolan Ryan 2.00 5.00
D21 Tim Salmon .30 .75
D22 Ryne Sandberg .75 2.00
D23 Darryl Strawberry .20 .50
D24 Frank Thomas .50 1.25
D25 Andy Van Slyke .30 .75

1993 Upper Deck Season Highlights

COMPLETE SET (20) 60.00 120.00
STATED ODDS 1:9 HOBBY SEASON HL
HI1 Roberto Alomar 2.00 5.00
HI2 Steve Avery .60 1.50
HI3 Harold Baines 1.25 3.00
HI4 Damon Berryhill .60 1.50
HI5 Barry Bonds 10.00 25.00
HI6 Bret Boone 1.25 3.00
HI7 George Brett 8.00 20.00
HI8 Francisco Cabrera .60 1.50
HI9 Ken Griffey Jr. 6.00 15.00
HI10 Rickey Henderson 3.00 8.00
HI11 Kenny Lofton 1.25 3.00
HI12 Mickey Morandini .60 1.50
HI13 Eddie Murray 3.00 8.00
HI14 David Nied .60 1.50
HI15 Jeff Reardon 1.25 3.00
HI16 Bip Roberts .60 1.50
HI17 Nolan Ryan 12.50 30.00
HI18 Ed Sprague .60 1.50
HI19 Dave Winfield 1.25 3.00
HI20 Robin Yount 5.00 12.00

1993 Upper Deck Then And Now

COMPLETE SET (18) 10.00 25.00
COMPLETE SERIES 1 (9) 4.00 10.00
COMPLETE SERIES 2 (9) 6.00 15.00
STATED ODDS 1:27 HOBBY
TN1 Wade Boggs .50 1.25
TN2 George Brett 2.00 5.00
TN3 Rickey Henderson .75 2.00
TN4 Cal Ripken 2.50 6.00
TN5 Nolan Ryan 3.00 8.00
TN6 Ryne Sandberg 1.25 3.00
TN7 Ozzie Smith 1.25 3.00
TN8 Darryl Strawberry .30 .75
TN9 Dave Winfield .30 .75
TN10 Dennis Eckersley .30 .75
TN11 Tony Gwynn 1.00 2.50
TN12 Howard Johnson .15 .40
TN13 Don Mattingly 2.00 5.00
TN14 Eddie Murray .75 2.00
TN15 Robin Yount 1.25 3.00
TN16 Reggie Jackson 1.00 2.50
TN17 Mickey Mantle 5.00 12.00
TN18 Willie Mays 2.50 6.00

1993 Upper Deck Triple Crown

COMPLETE SET (10) 5.00 12.00
STATED ODDS 1:15 HOBBY
TC1 Barry Bonds 1.50 4.00
TC2 Jose Canseco .30 .75
TC3 Will Clark .30 .75
TC4 Ken Griffey Jr. 1.00 2.50
TC5 Fred McGriff .30 .75
TC6 Kirby Puckett .50 1.25
TC7 Cal Ripken Jr. 1.50 4.00
TC8 Gary Sheffield .20 .50
TC9 Frank Thomas .50 1.25
TC10 Larry Walker .20 .50

1993 Upper Deck Adventures in Toon World

IT'S WAY COOLER! This new Upper Deck produced set definitely builds the success of the 'Comic Ball' series on. Indeed, nothing creates funnier stories than pairing Looney Tune characters with respected professional athletes. The base set is divided into 9-card subsets: 'Act 1' (A1S1-A1S9) through 'Act 10' (A10S1-A10S9); each of 18 scenes and with each card being double-sided with two different scenes.

COMPLETE SET (91) 10.00 25.00
COMMON CARD (1-90) .20 .50

1993 Upper Deck All-Time Heroes Preview

COMPLETE SET (4) 2.00 5.00
1 Ted Williams .60 1.50
Mickey Mantle
2 Reggie Jackson .60 1.50
Mickey Mantle
3 Ted Williams .60 1.50
Reggie Jackson
4 Reggie Jackson .60 1.50
Mickey Mantle
Ted Williams

1993 Upper Deck All-Time Heroes

This 165-card set of All-Time Heroes of Baseball is patterned after the T-202 Hassan Triple Folders cards, which first appeared in 1912. The cards measure approximately 2 1/4" by 5 1/4" and feature two side panels and a larger middle panel. The set consists of 130 regular cards and the Classic Combinations subset (131-165). The fronts feature candid or action photos of the featured player on the center panel, along with a portrait on one of the side panels and the B.A.T. (Baseball Assistance Team) logo on the other. The backs include player biographies and career highlights, as well as an explanation of the B.A.T. cause. The Classic Combinations subset have center panels that feature either artwork by Todd Reigle or a photograph of multiple greats. The side panels feature photos of two players. The backs include player biographies on the side panels, with the center panel detailing the association between the players. The foil packs contained 12 cards per pack. Each card is holographically enhanced. Reggie Jackson and Mickey Mantle were the spokespersons for this set and they are featured prominently on the front of the box. The grand prize for the set's mail-in contest was an actual, original set of T202 Hassan Triplefolders, which Upper Deck had purchased in the open hobby market expressly for the promotion.

COMPLETE SET (165) 10.00 25.00
1 Hank Aaron .75 2.00
2 Tommie Agee .02 .10
3 Bob Allison .02 .10
4 Matty Alou .02 .10
5 Sal Bando .02 .10
6 Hank Bauer .02 .10
7 Don Baylor .05 .15
8 Glenn Beckert .02 .10
9 Yogi Berra .40 1.00
10 Buddy Biancalana .02 .10
11 Jack Billingham .02 .10
12 Joe Black .05 .15
13 Paul Blair .02 .10
14 Steve Blass .02 .10
15 Ray Boone .02 .10
16 Lou Boudreau .08 .25
17 Ken Brett .02 .10
18 Nellie Briles .02 .10
19 Bobby Brown .05 .15
20 Bill Buckner .05 .15
21 Don Buford .02 .10
22 Al Bumbry .02 .10
23 Lew Burdette .05 .15
24 Jeff Burroughs .02 .10
25 Johnny Callison .02 .10
26 Bert Campaneris .02 .10
27 Rico Carty .02 .10
28 Dave Cash .02 .10
29 Cesar Cedeno .05 .15
30 Frank Chance .08 .25
31 Joe Charboneau .05 .15
32 Ty Cobb .75 2.00
33 Jerry Coleman .02 .10
34 Cecil Cooper .02 .10
35 Frankie Crosetti .02 .10
36 Alvin Dark .02 .10
37 Tommy Davis .02 .10
38 Dizzy Dean .20 .50
39 Doug DeCinces .02 .10
40 Bucky Dent .02 .10
41 Larry Dierker .02 .10
42 Larry Doby .15 .40
43 Moe Drabowsky .02 .10
44 Dave Dravecky .02 .10
45 Del Ennis .02 .10
46 Carl Erskine .05 .15
47 Johnny Evers .08 .25
48 Roy Face .02 .10
49 Rick Ferrell .08 .25
50 Mark Fidrych .05 .15
51 Curt Flood .05 .15
52 Whitey Ford .30 .75
53 George Foster .05 .15
54 Jimmie Foxx .20 .50
55 Jim Fregosi .02 .10
56 Phil Garner .05 .15
57 Ralph Garr .02 .10
58 Lou Gehrig 1.00 2.50
59 Bobby Grich .05 .15
60 Jerry Grote .02 .10
61 Harvey Haddix .02 .10
62 Toby Harrah .02 .10
63 Bud Harrelson .05 .15
64 Jim Hegan .02 .10
65 Gil Hodges .08 .25
66 Ken Holtzman .02 .10
67 Bob Horner .02 .10
68 Rogers Hornsby .20 .50
69 Carl Hubbell .15 .40
70 Ron Hunt .02 .10
71 Monte Irvin .07 .20
72 Reggie Jackson .30 .75
73 Larry Jansen .02 .10
74 Ferguson Jenkins .08 .25
75 Tommy John .05 .15
76 Cliff Johnson .02 .10
77 Davey Johnson .05 .15
78 Walter Johnson .20 .50
79 George Kell .07 .20
80 Don Kessinger .02 .10
81 Vern Law .02 .10
82 Dennis Leonard .02 .10
83 Johnny Logan .02 .10
84 Mickey Lolich .05 .15
85 Jim Lonborg .02 .10
86 Bill Madlock .02 .10
87 Mickey Mantle 2.00 5.00
88 Billy Martin .07 .20
89 Christy Mathewson .20 .50
90 Lee May .02 .10
91 Willie Mays .75 2.00
92 Bill Mazeroski .08 .25
93 Gil McDougald .05 .15
94 Sam McDowell .02 .10
95 Minnie Minoso .05 .15
96 Johnny Mize .07 .20
97 Rick Monday .02 .10
98 Wally Moon .02 .10
99 Manny Mota .02 .10
100 Bobby Murcer .02 .10
101 Ron Necciai .02 .10
102 Al Oliver .05 .15
103 Mel Ott .07 .20
104 Mel Parnell .02 .10
105 Jimmy Piersall .05 .15
106 Johnny Podres .02 .10
107 Bobby Richardson .05 .15
108 Robin Roberts .07 .20
109 Al Rosen .05 .15
110 Babe Ruth 2.00 5.00
111 Joe Sambito .02 .10
112 Manny Sanguillen .02 .10
113 Ron Santo .07 .20
114 Bill Skowron .02 .10
115 Enos Slaughter .08 .25
116 Warren Spahn .08 .25
117 Tris Speaker .08 .25
118 Frank Thomas .02 .10
119 Bobby Thomson .05 .15
120 Andre Thornton .02 .10
121 Marv Throneberry .02 .10
122 Luis Tiant .05 .15
123 Joe Tinker .08 .25
124 Honus Wagner .20 .50
125 Bill White .05 .15
126 Ted Williams 1.50 4.00
127 Earl Wilson .02 .10
128 Joe Wood .05 .15
129 Cy Young .20 .50
130 Richie Zisk .02 .10
131 Babe Ruth .75 2.00
Lou Gehrig
132 Ted Williams .40 1.00
Rogers Hornsby
133 Lou Gehrig .75 2.00
Babe Ruth
134 Babe Ruth .75 2.00
Mickey Mantle
135 Mickey Mantle .50 1.25
Reggie Jackson
136 Mel Ott .05 .15
Carl Hubbell
137 Mickey Mantle .60 1.50
Willie Mays
138 Cy Young .07 .20
Walter Johnson
139 Honus Wagner .07 .20
Rogers Hornsby
140 Mickey Mantle .50 1.25
Whitey Ford
141 Mickey Mantle .50 1.25
Billy Martin
142 Cy Young .07 .20
Walter Johnson
143 Christy Mathewson .07 .20
Walter Johnson
144 Warren Spahn .07 .20
Christy Mathewson
145 Honus Wagner .40 1.00
Ty Cobb
146 Babe Ruth .75 2.00
Ty Cobb
147 Joe Tinker .07 .20
Johnny Evers
148 Johnny Evers .07 .20
Frank Chance
149 Hank Aaron .75 2.00
Babe Ruth
150 Willie Mays .50 1.25
Hank Aaron
151 Babe Ruth .75 2.00
Willie Mays
152 Babe Ruth .50 1.25
Whitey Ford
153 Larry Doby .02 .10
Minnie Minoso
154 Joe Black .05 .15
Monte Irvin
155 Joe Wood .05 .15
Christy Mathewson
156 Christy Mathewson .07 .20
Cy Young
157 Cy Young .05 .15
Joe Wood
158 Cy Young .05 .15
Whitey Ford
159 Cy Young .05 .15
Ferguson Jenkins
160 Ty Cobb .40 1.00
Rogers Hornsby
161 Tris Speaker .40 1.00
Ted Williams
162 Rogers Hornsby .40 1.00
Ted Williams
163 Willie Mays .30 .75
Monte Irvin
164 Willie Mays .30 .75
Bobby Thomson
165 Reggie Jackson .60 1.50
Mickey Mantle

1993 Upper Deck All-Time Heroes T202 Reprints

COMPLETE SET (10) 6.00 15.00
1 Art Devlin .40 1.00
Christy Mathewson
2 Hugh Jennings 1.00 2.50
Ty Cobb
3 John Kling .40 1.00
Cy Young
4 Jack Knight .40 1.00
Walter Johnson
5 John McGraw .60 1.50
Hugh Jennings
6 George Moriarty .75 2.00
Ty Cobb
7 Charles O'Leary .75 2.00
Ty Cobb
8 Charles O'Leary .75 2.00
Ty Cobb
9 Joe Tinker 1.00 2.50
Frank Chance
10 Joe Wood .40 1.00
Tris Speaker

1993 Upper Deck Clark Reggie Jackson

Issued to promote the reintroduction of the Reggie bar by the Clark Candy Co., these three standard-size cards highlight Jackson's career and feature on their fronts white-bordered color photos of Jackson as an Athletic and as a Yankee, with all team logos airbrushed out. The cards are numbered on the back with a "C" prefix. One card was inserted in each Reggie bar and Jackson autographed 200 cards that were randomly inserted into the candy bar packages.

COMPLETE SET (3)	2.00	5.00
COMMON CARD (C1-C3)	.80	2.00
RJ Reggie Jackson AU Autograph card		

1993 Upper Deck Diamond Gallery

This 38-card standard-size boxed set features two player action photos on its horizontal fronts. One is a hologram, the other is a color action shot of the player, which is displayed on the left side projecting from a baseball diamond design. In the hologram, the player's uniform number appears behind him. Two subsets are present in this set; cards 29-31 are Gallery Heroes subset, and cards 32-36 are Diamonds in the Rough. Also included in the set are the checklist bearing the production number out of 123,600 sets produced, and a mail-away card for the Diamond Gallery card album.

COMPLETE SET (38)	6.00	15.00
1 Tim Salmon	.20	.50
2 Jeff Bagwell	.30	.75
3 Mark McGwire	.60	1.50
4 Roberto Alomar	.20	.50
5 Terry Pendleton	.02	.10
6 Robin Yount	.20	.50
7 Ray Lankford	.07	.20
8 Ryne Sandberg	.60	1.50
9 Darryl Strawberry	.07	.20
10 Marquis Grissom	.07	.20
11 Barry Bonds	.50	1.25
12 Carlos Baerga	.02	.10
13 Ken Griffey Jr.	.75	2.00
14 Benito Santiago	.07	.20
15 Dwight Gooden	.07	.20
16 Cal Ripken	1.25	3.00
17 Tony Gwynn	.60	1.50
18 Dave Hollins	.02	.10
19 Andy Van Slyke	.02	.10
20 Juan Gonzalez	.25	.60
21 Roger Clemens	.60	1.50
22 Barry Larkin	.20	.50
23 David Nied	.02	.10
24 George Brett	.60	1.50
25 Travis Fryman	.07	.20
26 Kirby Puckett	.40	1.00
27 Frank Thomas	.30	.75
28 Don Mattingly	.60	1.50
29 Rickey Henderson	.40	1.00
30 Nolan Ryan	1.25	3.00
31 Ozzie Smith	.60	1.50
32 Wil Cordero	.02	.10
33 Phil Hiatt	.02	.10
34 Mike Piazza	1.25	3.00
35 J.T. Snow	.20	.50
36 Kevin Young	.02	.10
NNO Checklist Card	.02	.10
NNO Album Offer Card	.02	.10

1993 Upper Deck Folder

This folder features four 1993 Upper Deck Triple Crown Contenders insert cards on the front. The back of the folder features the back of the cards involved. Inside the folder is room to place some of a collectors favorite cards.

1 Ken Griffey Jr. Will Clark Cal Ripken Jr Kirby	1.00	2.50

1993 Upper Deck Sheets

The 31 commemorative sheets listed below in chronological order were issued by Upper Deck in 1993. The Upper Deck Heroes of Baseball made stops in MLB ballparks and sponsored old-timer baseball games preceding major league games. At each game a limited edition commemorative sheet was distributed. Commemorative sheets were produced in honor of other events. Days prior to the All-Star Game, sheets 16 and 17 were issued to fans who were at Camden Yards to watch the All-Star Workout. Sheet 19 was issued at the National in Chicago. Sheet 21 commemorates the World Children's Baseball Fair. And sheet 29 was handed out at by Upper Deck to collectors at various shows during the year. All the sheets measure 8 1/2" by 11" and most feature artist renderings of players from the teams recreated for the old-timers games. The front of each sheet carries the individual production number out of the total number produced, but otherwise the sheets are unnumbered.

COMPLETE SET (31)	100.00	200.00
1 Blue Jays Heroes vs. Upper Deck Heroes April 25&	2.50	6.00
2 Atlanta Braves Heroes vs. Upper Deck Award Winne	2.50	6.00
3 Upper Deck Heroes of Baseball vs. St. Louis Card	2.50	6.00
4 '69 Royals vs./'69 Twins May 22& 1993 (42&600)/	2.50	6.00
5 Ewing M. Kauffman Induction into Royals Hall of	2.00	5.00
6 Upper Deck Heroes vs. Red Sox Heroes May 29& 199	3.00	8.00
7 Heroes of the '60s June 6& 1993 (31&600) Candles	2.50	6.00
8 125 Years of Cincinnati Baseball June 6& 1993 (5	1.50	4.00
9 Nickname Heroes Milwaukee County Stad. June 12&	2.50	6.00
10 20th Anniversary of the 1973 World Series June 1	2.50	6.00
11 Colorado Rockies Inaugural Season June 19& 1993	4.00	10.00
12 '83 Phillies vs./'83 Heroes June 19& 1993 (56&60	3.00	8.00
13 25 Years of Padres Baseball June 25& 1993 (41&60	2.50	6.00
14 White Sox 1983 Winning Ugly vs./1983 Baltimore O	2.50	6.00
15 All-Time Home Run Hitters July 4& 1993 (21&600)#	3.00	8.00
16 1993 Upper Deck All-Star FanFest Autograph Sheet	.75	2.00
17 A Celebration of Early Black Baseball July 10& 1	3.00	8.00
18 Upper Deck Heroes of Baseball All-Star Game Jul	2.50	6.00
19 The 1993 National Chicago Upper Deck Five Year/	2.00	5.00
20 1978 Yankees/22nd World Championship July 24& 19	2.50	6.00
21 Astros All-Star Heroes Game July 24, 1993 Fergus	.75	2.00
22 World Children's Baseball Fair July 31& 1993 (61	3.00	8.00
23 Reggie Jackson Hall of Fame Induction Aug. 1& 1	2.50	6.00
24 Seattle Mariners Salutes Heroes of the 70's/26,6	.75	2.00
25 A Tribute to Billy Ball Billy Martin Aug. 15& 1	2.50	6.00
26 25th Anniversary of the 1968 World Series August	4.00	10.00
27 The Expos' 25th Anniversary August 28& 1993 (41&	2.50	6.00
28 Florida Marlins Inaugural Season September 25& 1	3.00	8.00
29 Upper Deck Company Salutes the Heroes of Arlingt	1.50	4.00
30 Tribute to Cleveland Stadium October 2& 1993 (76	1.50	4.00
31 Upper Deck Heroes of Baseball Autograph Sheet N	.75	2.00

1994 Upper Deck

The 1994 Upper Deck set was issued in two series of 280 and 270 standard-size cards for a total of 550. There are number of topical subsets including Star Rookies (1-30), Fantasy Team (31-40), The Future is Now (41-55), Home Field Advantage (267-294), Upper Deck Classic Alumni (295-299), Diamond Debuts (511-522) and Top Prospects (523-550). Three autograph cards were randomly inserted into first series retail packs. They are Ken Griffey Jr. (KG), Mickey Mantle (MM) and a combo card with Griffey and Mantle (GM). Though they lack serial-numbering, all three cards have an announced print run of 1,000 copies per. An Alex Rodriguez (296A) autograph card was randomly inserted into second series retail packs but production quantities were never divulged by the manufacturer. Rookie Cards include Michael Jordan (as an baseball player), Chan Ho Park, Alex Rodriguez and Billy Wagner. Many cards have been found with a significant variation on the back. The player's name, the horizontal bar containing the biographical information and the vertical bar containing the stats header are normally printed in copper-gold color. On the variation cards, these areas are printed in silver. It is not known exactly how many of the 550 cards have silver versions, nor has any premium been established for them. Also, all of the American League Home Field Advantage subset cards (numbers 281-294) are minor uncorrected errors because the Upper Deck logos on the front are missing the year "1994".

COMPLETE SET (550)	15.00	40.00
COMPLETE SERIES 1 (280)	10.00	25.00
COMPLETE SERIES 2 (270)	6.00	15.00
SUBSET CARDS HALF VALUE OF BASE CARDS		
GRIFFEY/MANTLE AU INSERTS IN SER.1 RET.		
A.RODRIGUEZ AU INSERT IN SER.2 RET.		
1 Brian Anderson RC	.15	.40
2 Shane Andrews	.05	.15
3 James Baldwin	.05	.15
4 Rich Becker	.05	.15
5 Greg Blosser	.05	.15
6 Ricky Bottalico RC	.05	.15
7 Midre Cummings	.05	.15
8 Carlos Delgado	.20	.50
9 Steve Dreyer RC	.05	.15
10 Joey Eischen	.05	.15
11 Carl Everett	.10	.30
12 Cliff Floyd	.10	.30
13 Alex Gonzalez	.05	.15
14 Jeff Granger	.05	.15
15 Shawn Green	.30	.75
16 Brian L.Hunter	.05	.15
17 Butch Huskey	.05	.15
18 Mark Hutton	.05	.15
19 Michael Jordan RC	3.00	8.00
20 Steve Karsay	.05	.15
21 Jeff McNeely	.05	.15
22 Marc Newfield	.05	.15
23 Manny Ramirez	.30	.75
24 Alex Rodriguez RC	6.00	15.00
25 Scott Ruffcorn UER	.05	.15
26 Paul Spoljaric UER	.05	.15
27 Salomon Torres	.05	.15
28 Steve Trachsel	.05	.15
29 Chris Turner	.05	.15
30 Gabe White	.05	.15
31 Randy Johnson FT	.20	.50
32 John Wetteland FT	.05	.15
33 Mike Piazza FT	.30	.75
34 Rafael Palmeiro FT	.10	.30
35 Roberto Alomar FT	.10	.30
36 Matt Williams FT	.05	.15
37 Travis Fryman FT	.05	.15
38 Barry Bonds FT	.40	1.00
39 Marquis Grissom FT	.05	.15
40 Albert Belle FT	.10	.30
41 Steve Avery FUT	.05	.15
42 Jason Bere FUT	.05	.15
43 Alex Fernandez FUT	.05	.15
44 Mike Mussina FUT	.10	.30
45 Aaron Sele FUT	.05	.15
46 Rod Beck FUT	.05	.15
47 Mike Piazza FUT	.30	.75
48 John Olerud FUT	.05	.15
49 Carlos Baerga FUT	.05	.15
50 Gary Sheffield FUT	.05	.15
51 Travis Fryman FUT	.05	.15
52 Juan Gonzalez FUT	.05	.15
53 Ken Griffey Jr. FUT	.40	1.00
54 Tim Salmon FUT	.10	.30
55 Frank Thomas FUT	.20	.50
56 Tony Phillips	.05	.15
57 Julio Franco	.10	.30
58 Kevin Mitchell	.05	.15
59 Raul Mondesi	.10	.30
60 Rickey Henderson	.30	.75
61 Jay Buhner	.10	.30
62 Bill Swift	.05	.15
63 Brady Anderson	.10	.30
64 Ryan Klesko	.10	.30
65 Darren Daulton	.10	.30
66 Damion Easley	.05	.15
67 Mark McGwire	.75	2.00
68 John Roper	.05	.15
69 Dave Telgheder	.05	.15
70 David Nied	.05	.15
71 Mo Vaughn	.10	.30
72 Tyler Green	.05	.15
73 Dave Magadan	.05	.15
74 Chili Davis	.10	.30
75 Archi Cianfrocco	.05	.15
76 Joe Girardi	.05	.15
77 Chris Hoiles	.05	.15
78 Ryan Bowen	.05	.15
79 Greg Gagne	.05	.15
80 Aaron Sele	.05	.15
81 Dave Winfield	.10	.30
82 Chad Curtis	.05	.15
83 Andy Van Slyke	.20	.50
84 Kevin Stocker	.05	.15
85 Deion Sanders	.20	.50
86 Bernie Williams	.20	.50
87 John Smoltz	.20	.50
88 Ruben Santana	.05	.15
89 Dave Stewart	.10	.30
90 Don Mattingly	.75	2.00
91 Joe Carter	.10	.30
92 Ryne Sandberg	.50	1.25
93 Chris Gomez	.05	.15
94 Tino Martinez	.20	.50
95 Terry Pendleton	.10	.30
96 Andre Dawson	.10	.30
97 Wil Cordero	.05	.15
98 Kent Hrbek	.10	.30
99 John Olerud	.10	.30
100 Kirt Manwaring	.05	.15
101 Tim Bogar	.05	.15
102 Mike Mussina	.20	.50
103 Nigel Wilson	.05	.15
104 Ricky Gutierrez	.05	.15
105 Roberto Mejia	.05	.15
106 Tom Pagnozzi	.05	.15
107 Mike Macfarlane	.05	.15
108 Jose Bautista	.05	.15
109 Luis Ortiz	.05	.15
110 Brent Gates	.05	.15
111 Tim Salmon	.20	.50
112 Wade Boggs	.20	.50
113 Tripp Cromer	.05	.15
114 Denny Hocking	.05	.15
115 Carlos Baerga	.05	.15
116 J.R. Phillips	.05	.15
117 Bo Jackson	.30	.75
118 Lance Johnson	.05	.15
119 Bobby Jones	.05	.15
120 Bobby Witt	.05	.15
121 Ron Karkovice	.05	.15
122 Jose Vizcaino	.05	.15
123 Danny Darwin	.05	.15
124 Eduardo Perez	.05	.15
125 Brian Looney RC	.05	.15
126 Pat Hentgen	.05	.15
127 Frank Viola	.10	.30
128 Darren Holmes	.05	.15
129 Wally Whitehurst	.05	.15
130 Matt Walbeck	.05	.15
131 Albert Belle	.10	.30
132 Steve Cooke	.05	.15
133 Kevin Appier	.10	.30
134 Joe Oliver	.05	.15
135 Benji Gil	.05	.15
136 Steve Buechele	.05	.15
137 Devon White	.10	.30
138 Sterling Hitchcock UER	.05	.15
139 Phil Leftwich RC	.05	.15
140 Jose Canseco	.20	.50
141 Rick Aguilera	.05	.15
142 Rod Beck	.05	.15
143 Jose Rijo	.05	.15
144 Tom Glavine	.20	.50
145 Phil Plantier	.05	.15
146 Jason Bere	.05	.15
147 Jamie Moyer	.10	.30
148 Wes Chamberlain	.05	.15
149 Glenallen Hill	.05	.15
150 Mark Whiten	.05	.15
151 Bret Barberie	.05	.15
152 Chuck Knoblauch	.10	.30
153 Trevor Hoffman	.20	.50
154 Rick Wilkins	.05	.15
155 Juan Gonzalez	.10	.30
156 Ozzie Guillen	.10	.30
157 Jim Eisenreich	.05	.15
158 Pedro Astacio	.05	.15
159 Joe Magrane	.05	.15
160 Ryan Thompson	.05	.15
161 Jose Lind	.05	.15
162 Jeff Conine	.10	.30
163 Todd Benzinger	.05	.15
164 Roger Salkeld	.05	.15
165 Gary DiSarcina	.05	.15
166 Kevin Gross	.05	.15
167 Charlie Hayes	.05	.15
168 Tim Costo	.05	.15
169 Wally Joyner	.10	.30
170 Johnny Ruffin	.05	.15
171 Kirk Rueter	.05	.15
172 Lenny Dykstra	.10	.30
173 Ken Hill	.05	.15
174 Mike Bordick	.05	.15
175 Billy Hall	.05	.15
176 Rob Butler	.05	.15
177 Jay Bell	.10	.30
178 Jeff Kent	.20	.50
179 David Wells	.10	.30
180 Dean Palmer	.10	.30
181 Mariano Duncan	.05	.15
182 Orlando Merced	.05	.15
183 Brett Butler	.10	.30
184 Milt Thompson	.05	.15
185 Chipper Jones	.30	.75
186 Paul O'Neill	.20	.50
187 Mike Greenwell	.05	.15
188 Harold Baines	.10	.30
189 Todd Stottlemyre	.05	.15
190 Jeromy Burnitz	.10	.30
191 Rene Arocha	.05	.15
192 Jeff Fassero	.05	.15
193 Robby Thompson	.05	.15
194 Greg W. Harris	.05	.15
195 Todd Van Poppel	.05	.15
196 Jose Guzman	.05	.15
197 Shane Mack	.05	.15
198 Carlos Garcia	.05	.15
199 Kevin Roberson	.05	.15
200 David McCarty	.05	.15
201 Alan Trammell	.10	.30
202 Chuck Carr	.05	.15
203 Tommy Greene	.05	.15
204 Wilson Alvarez	.05	.15
205 Dwight Gooden	.10	.30
206 Tony Tarasco	.05	.15
207 Darren Lewis	.05	.15
208 Eric Karros	.10	.30
209 Chris Hammond	.05	.15
210 Jeffrey Hammonds	.05	.15
211 Rich Amaral	.05	.15
212 Danny Tartabull	.05	.15
213 Jeff Russell	.05	.15
214 Dave Staton	.05	.15
215 Kenny Lofton	.10	.30
216 Manuel Lee	.05	.15
217 Brian Koelling	.05	.15
218 Scott Lydy	.05	.15
219 Tony Gwynn	.40	1.00
220 Cecil Fielder	.10	.30
221 Royce Clayton	.05	.15
222 Reggie Sanders	.10	.30
223 Brian Jordan	.10	.30
224 Ken Griffey Jr.	.60	1.50
225 Fred McGriff	.20	.50
226 Felix Jose	.05	.15
227 Brad Pennington	.05	.15
228 Chris Bosio	.05	.15
229 Mike Stanley	.05	.15
230 Willie Greene	.05	.15
231 Alex Fernandez	.05	.15
232 Brad Ausmus	.20	.50
233 Darrell Whitmore	.05	.15
234 Marcus Moore	.05	.15
235 Allen Watson	.05	.15
236 Jose Offerman	.05	.15
237 Rondell White	.10	.30
238 Jeff King	.05	.15
239 Luis Alicea	.05	.15
240 Dan Wilson	.05	.15
241 Ed Sprague	.05	.15
242 Todd Hundley	.05	.15
243 Al Martin	.05	.15
244 Mike Lansing	.05	.15
245 Ivan Rodriguez	.20	.50
246 Dave Fleming	.05	.15
247 John Doherty	.05	.15
248 Mark McLemore	.05	.15
249 Bob Hamelin	.05	.15
250 Curtis Pride RC	.15	.40
251 Zane Smith	.05	.15
252 Eric Young	.05	.15
253 Brian McRae	.05	.15
254 Tim Raines	.10	.30
255 Javier Lopez	.10	.30
256 Melvin Nieves	.05	.15
257 Randy Myers	.05	.15
258 Willie McGee	.10	.30
259 Jimmy Key UER	.10	.30
260 Tom Candiotti	.05	.15
261 Eric Davis	.10	.30
262 Craig Paquette	.05	.15
263 Robin Ventura	.10	.30
264 Pat Kelly	.05	.15
265 Gregg Jefferies	.05	.15
266 Cory Snyder	.05	.15
267 David Justice HFA	.05	.15
268 Sammy Sosa HFA	.30	.75
269 Barry Larkin HFA	.10	.30
270 Andres Galarraga HFA	.05	.15
271 Gary Sheffield HFA	.05	.15
272 Jeff Bagwell HFA	.10	.30
273 Mike Piazza HFA	.30	.75
274 Larry Walker HFA	.05	.15
275 Bobby Bonilla HFA	.05	.15
276 John Kruk HFA	.05	.15
277 Jay Bell HFA	.05	.15
278 Ozzie Smith HFA	.30	.75
279 Tony Gwynn HFA	.20	.50
280 Barry Bonds HFA	.40	1.00
281 Cal Ripken HFA	.50	1.25
282 Mo Vaughn HFA	.05	.15
283 Tim Salmon HFA	.10	.30
284 Frank Thomas HFA	.20	.50
285 Albert Belle HFA	.10	.30
286 Cecil Fielder HFA	.05	.15
287 Wally Joyner HFA	.05	.15
288 Greg Vaughn HFA	.05	.15
289 Kirby Puckett HFA	.20	.50
290 Don Mattingly HFA	.40	1.00
291 Terry Steinbach HFA	.05	.15
292 Ken Griffey Jr. HFA	.40	1.00
293 Juan Gonzalez HFA	.05	.15
294 Paul Molitor HFA	.05	.15
295 Tavo Alvarez UDCA	.05	.15
296 Matt Brunson UDCA	.05	.15
297 Shawn Green UDCA	.10	.30
298 Alex Rodriguez UDCA	2.50	6.00
299 Shannon Stewart UDCA	.30	.75
300 Frank Thomas	.30	.75
301 Mickey Tettleton	.05	.15
302 Pedro Munoz	.05	.15
303 Jose Valentin	.05	.15
304 Orestes Destrade	.05	.15
305 Pat Listach	.05	.15
306 Scott Brosius	.10	.30
307 Kurt Miller	.05	.15
308 Rob Dibble	.10	.30
309 Mike Blowers	.05	.15
310 Jim Abbott	.20	.50
311 Mike Jackson	.05	.15
312 Craig Biggio	.20	.50
313 Kurt Abbott RC	.05	.15
314 Chuck Finley	.10	.30
315 Andres Galarraga	.10	.30
316 Mike Moore	.05	.15
317 Doug Strange	.05	.15
318 Pedro Martinez	.30	.75
319 Kevin McReynolds	.05	.15
320 Greg Maddux	.50	1.25
321 Mike Henneman	.05	.15
322 Scott Leius	.05	.15
323 John Franco	.10	.30
324 Jeff Blauser	.05	.15
325 Kirby Puckett	.30	.75
326 Darryl Hamilton	.05	.15
327 John Smiley	.05	.15
328 Derrick May	.05	.15
329 Jose Vizcaino	.05	.15
330 Randy Johnson	.30	.75
331 Jack Morris	.05	.15
332 Graeme Lloyd	.05	.15
333 Dave Valle	.05	.15
334 Greg Myers	.05	.15
335 John Wetteland	.05	.15
336 Jim Gott	.05	.15
337 Tim Naehring	.05	.15
338 Mike Kelly	.05	.15
339 Jeff Montgomery	.05	.15
340 Rafael Palmeiro	.20	.50
341 Eddie Murray	.30	.75
342 Xavier Hernandez	.05	.15
343 Bobby Munoz	.05	.15
344 Bobby Bonilla	.10	.30
345 Travis Fryman	.10	.30
346 Steve Finley	.10	.30
347 Chris Sabo	.05	.15
348 Armando Reynoso	.05	.15
349 Ramon Martinez	.05	.15
350 Will Clark	.20	.50
351 Moises Alou	.10	.30
352 Jim Thome	.20	.50
353 Bob Tewksbury	.05	.15
354 Andujar Cedeno	.05	.15
355 Orel Hershiser	.10	.30
356 Mike Devereaux	.05	.15
357 Mike Perez	.05	.15
358 Dennis Martinez	.10	.30
359 Dave Nilsson	.05	.15
360 Ozzie Smith	.50	1.25
361 Eric Anthony	.05	.15
362 Scott Sanders	.05	.15
363 Paul Sorrento	.05	.15
364 Tim Belcher	.05	.15
365 Dennis Eckersley	.10	.30
366 Mel Rojas	.05	.15
367 Tom Henke	.05	.15
368 Randy Tomlin	.05	.15
369 B.J. Surhoff	.10	.30
370 Larry Walker	.10	.30
371 Joey Cora	.05	.15
372 Mike Harkey	.05	.15
373 John Valentin	.05	.15
374 Doug Jones	.05	.15
375 David Justice	.10	.30
376 Vince Coleman	.05	.15
377 David Hulse	.05	.15
378 Kevin Seitzer	.05	.15
379 Pete Harnisch	.05	.15
380 Ruben Sierra	.10	.30
381 Mark Lewis	.05	.15
382 Bip Roberts	.05	.15
383 Paul Wagner	.05	.15
384 Stan Javier	.05	.15
385 Barry Larkin	.20	.50
386 Mark Portugal	.05	.15
387 Roberto Kelly	.05	.15
388 Andy Benes	.05	.15
389 Felix Fermin	.05	.15
390 Marquis Grissom	.10	.30
391 Troy Neel	.05	.15
392 Chad Kreuter	.05	.15
393 Gregg Olson	.05	.15
394 Charles Nagy	.05	.15
395 Jack McDowell	.05	.15
396 Luis Gonzalez	.10	.30
397 Benito Santiago	.10	.30
398 Chris James	.05	.15
399 Terry Mulholland	.05	.15
400 Barry Bonds	.75	2.00
401 Joe Grahe	.05	.15
402 Duane Ward	.05	.15
403 John Burkett	.05	.15
404 Scott Servais	.05	.15
405 Bryan Harvey	.05	.15
406 Bernard Gilkey	.05	.15
407 Greg McMichael	.05	.15
408 Tim Wallach	.05	.15
409 Ken Caminiti	.10	.30
410 John Kruk	.10	.30
411 Darrin Jackson	.05	.15
412 Mike Gallego	.05	.15
413 David Cone	.10	.30
414 Lou Whitaker	.10	.30
415 Sandy Alomar Jr.	.05	.15
416 Bill Wegman	.05	.15
417 Pat Borders	.05	.15
418 Roger Pavlik	.05	.15
419 Pete Smith	.05	.15
420 Steve Avery	.05	.15
421 David Segui	.05	.15
422 Rheal Cormier	.05	.15
423 Harold Reynolds	.10	.30
424 Edgar Martinez	.20	.50
425 Cal Ripken	1.00	2.50
426 Jaime Navarro	.05	.15
427 Sean Berry	.05	.15
428 Bret Saberhagen	.10	.30
429 Bob Welch	.05	.15
430 Juan Guzman	.05	.15
431 Cal Eldred	.05	.15
432 Dave Hollins	.05	.15
433 Sid Fernandez	.05	.15
434 Willie Banks	.05	.15
435 Darryl Kile	.10	.30
436 Henry Rodriguez	.05	.15
437 Tony Fernandez	.05	.15
438 Walt Weiss	.05	.15
439 Kevin Tapani	.05	.15
440 Mark Grace	.20	.50
441 Brian Harper	.05	.15
442 Kent Mercker	.05	.15
443 Anthony Young	.05	.15
444 Todd Zeile	.05	.15
445 Greg Vaughn	.05	.15
446 Ray Lankford	.10	.30
447 Dave Weathers	.05	.15
448 Bret Boone	.10	.30
449 Charlie Hough	.10	.30
450 Roger Clemens	.60	1.50
451 Mike Morgan	.05	.15
452 Doug Drabek	.05	.15
453 Danny Jackson	.05	.15
454 Dante Bichette	.10	.30
455 Roberto Alomar	.20	.50
456 Ben McDonald	.05	.15
457 Kenny Rogers	.10	.30
458 Bill Gullickson	.05	.15
459 Darrin Fletcher	.05	.15
460 Curt Schilling	.10	.30
461 Billy Hatcher	.05	.15
462 Howard Johnson	.05	.15
463 Mickey Morandini	.05	.15
464 Frank Castillo	.05	.15
465 Delino DeShields	.05	.15
466 Gary Gaetti	.10	.30
467 Steve Farr	.05	.15
468 Roberto Hernandez	.05	.15
469 Jack Armstrong	.05	.15
470 Paul Molitor	.10	.30
471 Melido Perez	.05	.15
472 Greg Hibbard	.05	.15
473 Jody Reed	.05	.15
474 Tom Gordon	.05	.15
475 Gary Sheffield	.10	.30
476 John Jaha	.05	.15
477 Shawon Dunston	.05	.15
478 Reggie Jefferson	.05	.15
479 Don Slaught	.05	.15
480 Jeff Bagwell	.20	.50
481 Tim Pugh	.05	.15
482 Kevin Young	.05	.15
483 Ellis Burks	.10	.30
484 Greg Swindell	.05	.15
485 Mark Langston	.05	.15
486 Omar Vizquel	.20	.50
487 Kevin Brown	.10	.30
488 Terry Steinbach	.05	.15
489 Mark Lemke	.05	.15
490 Matt Williams	.10	.30
491 Pete Incaviglia	.05	.15
492 Karl Rhodes	.05	.15
493 Shawn Green	.30	.75
494 Hal Morris	.05	.15
495 Derek Bell	.05	.15
496 Luis Polonia	.05	.15
497 Otis Nixon	.05	.15
498 Ron Darling	.05	.15
499 Mitch Williams	.05	.15
500 Mike Piazza	.60	1.50
501 Pat Meares	.05	.15
502 Scott Cooper	.05	.15
503 Scott Erickson	.05	.15
504 Jeff Juden	.05	.15
505 Lee Smith	.10	.30
506 Bobby Ayala	.05	.15
507 Dave Henderson	.05	.15
508 Erik Hanson	.05	.15
509 Bob Wickman	.05	.15
510 Sammy Sosa	.30	.75
511 Hector Carrasco	.05	.15
512 Tim Davis	.05	.15
513 Joey Hamilton	.20	.50
514 Robert Eenhoorn	.05	.15
515 Jorge Fabregas	.05	.15
516 Tim Hyers RC	.05	.15
517 John Hudek RC	.05	.15
518 James Mouton	.05	.15
519 Herbert Perry RC	.05	.15
520 Chan Ho Park RC	.30	.75
521 W.VanLandingham RC	.05	.15
522 Paul Shuey DD	.05	.15
523 Ryan Hancock RC	.05	.15
524 Billy Wagner RC	.75	2.00
525 Jason Giambi	.30	.75
526 Jose Silva RC	.05	.15
527 Terrell Wade RC	.05	.15
528 Todd Dunn	.05	.15
529 Alan Benes RC	.15	.40
530 Brooks Kieschnick RC	.05	.15
531 Todd Hollandsworth	.05	.15
532 Brad Fullmer RC	.15	.40
533 Steve Soderstrom RC	.05	.15
534 Daron Kirkreit	.05	.15
535 Arquimedez Pozo RC	.05	.15
536 Charles Johnson	.10	.30
537 Preston Wilson	.10	.30
538 Alex Ochoa	.05	.15
539 Derrek Lee RC	1.50	4.00
540 Wayne Gomes RC	.05	.15
541 Jermaine Allensworth RC	.05	.15
542 Mike Bell RC	.05	.15
543 Trot Nixon RC	.75	2.00
544 Pokey Reese	.05	.15
545 Neifi Perez RC	.15	.40
546 Johnny Damon	.30	.75
547 Matt Brunson RC	.05	.15
548 LaTroy Hawkins RC	.15	.40
549 Eddie Pearson RC	.05	.15
550 Derek Jeter	1.00	2.50
A298 Alex Rodriguez AU	40.00	100.00
P224 Ken Griffey Jr. Promo	1.00	2.50
GM1 Griff AU/Mant AU/1000	900.00	1200.00
KG1 K.Griffey Jr. AU/1000	75.00	150.00
MM1 M.Mantle AU/1000	450.00	650.00

1994 Upper Deck Electric Diamond

COMPLETE SET (550)	30.00	60.00
COMPLETE SERIES 1 (280)	15.00	40.00
COMPLETE SERIES 2 (270)	8.00	20.00
*STARS: .75X TO 2X BASIC CARDS		
*ROOKIES: .6X TO 1.5X BASIC CARDS		
ONE PER PACK/TWO PER MINI JUMBO		

1994 Upper Deck Electric Diamond Silver Back

*SILVER: .4X TO 1X ELECTRIC DIAMOND

1994 Upper Deck Diamond Collection

COMPLETE SET (30)	100.00	200.00
COMPLETE CENTRAL (10)	30.00	80.00
COMPLETE EAST (10)	15.00	40.00
COMPLETE WEST (10)	25.00	60.00
SER.1 STATED ODDS 1:18 HOBBY REGIONAL		
C1 Jeff Bagwell	1.50	4.00
C2 Michael Jordan	15.00	40.00
C3 Barry Larkin	1.50	4.00
C4 Kirby Puckett	2.50	6.00
C5 Manny Ramirez	2.50	6.00
C6 Ryne Sandberg	4.00	10.00
C7 Ozzie Smith	4.00	10.00
C8 Frank Thomas	2.50	6.00
C9 Andy Van Slyke	1.50	4.00
C10 Robin Yount	2.50	6.00
E1 Roberto Alomar	1.50	4.00
E2 Roger Clemens	5.00	12.00
E3 Len Dykstra	1.00	2.50
E4 Cecil Fielder	1.00	2.50
E5 Cliff Floyd	1.00	2.50
E6 Dwight Gooden	1.00	2.50
E7 David Justice	1.00	2.50
E8 Don Mattingly	6.00	15.00
E9 Cal Ripken	8.00	20.00
E10 Gary Sheffield	1.00	2.50
W1 Barry Bonds	6.00	15.00
W2 Andres Galarraga	1.00	2.50
W3 Juan Gonzalez	1.00	2.50
W4 Ken Griffey Jr.	5.00	12.00
W5 Tony Gwynn	3.00	8.00
W6 Rickey Henderson	2.50	6.00
W7 Bo Jackson	2.50	6.00
W8 Mark McGwire	6.00	15.00
W9 Mike Piazza	5.00	12.00
W10 Tim Salmon	1.50	4.00

1994 Upper Deck Griffey Jumbos

COMPLETE SET (4)	4.00	10.00
COMMON GRIFFEY (CL1-CL4)	1.25	3.00
ONE PER SEALED SER.1 HOBBY FOIL BOX		

1994 Upper Deck Mantle Heroes

COMPLETE SET (10)	15.00	40.00
COMMON CARD (64-72/HDR)	4.00	10.00
SER.2 STATED ODDS 1:35		

1994 Upper Deck Mantle's Long Shots

COMPLETE SET (21)	12.50	30.00
SER.1 STATED ODDS 1:18 RETAIL		
ONE SET VIA MAIL PER SILVER TRADE CARD		
*ED: .5X TO 1.2X BASIC MANTLE LS		
ONE ED SET VIA MAIL PER BLUE TRD.CARD		
MANTLE TRADES: RANDOM IN SER.1 HOB		
MM1 Jeff Bagwell	.60	1.50
MM2 Albert Belle	.40	1.00
MM3 Barry Bonds	2.50	6.00
MM4 Jose Canseco	.60	1.50
MM5 Joe Carter	.40	1.00
MM6 Carlos Delgado	.60	1.50
MM7 Cecil Fielder	.40	1.00
MM8 Cliff Floyd	.40	1.00
MM9 Juan Gonzalez	.40	1.00
MM10 Ken Griffey Jr.	2.00	5.00
MM11 David Justice	.40	1.00
MM12 Fred McGriff	.60	1.50
MM13 Mark McGwire	2.50	6.00
MM14 Dean Palmer	.40	1.00
MM15 Mike Piazza	2.00	5.00
MM16 Manny Ramirez	1.00	2.50
MM17 Tim Salmon	.60	1.50

MM18 Frank Thomas 1.00 2.50
MM19 Mo Vaughn .40 1.00
MM20 Matt Williams .40 1.00
MM21 Mickey Mantle 6.00 15.00
NNO M.Mantle Silver Trade 2.50 6.00
NNO M.Mantle Blue EDTrade 6.00 15.00

1994 Upper Deck Next Generation

COMPLETE SET (18) 40.00 100.00
SER.2 STATED ODDS 1:20 RETAIL
ONE SET VIA MAIL PER TRADE CARD
TRADES: RANDOM INSERTS IN SER.2 HOB
1 Roberto Alomar 1.25 3.00
2 Carlos Delgado 1.25 3.00
3 Cliff Floyd .75 2.00
4 Alex Gonzalez .40 1.00
5 Juan Gonzalez .75 2.00
6 Ken Griffey Jr. 4.00 10.00
7 Jeffrey Hammonds .40 1.00
8 Michael Jordan 6.00 15.00
9 David Justice .75 2.00
10 Ryan Klesko .75 2.00
11 Javier Lopez .75 2.00
12 Raul Mondesi .75 2.00
13 Mike Piazza 4.00 10.00
14 Kirby Puckett 2.00 5.00
15 Manny Ramirez 2.00 5.00
16 Alex Rodriguez 8.00 20.00
17 Tim Salmon 1.25 3.00
18 Gary Sheffield .75 2.00
NNO Expired NG Trade Card .40 1.00

1994 Upper Deck Next Generation Electric Diamond

COMPLETE SET (18) 60.00 120.00
*ELEC.DIAM: .5X TO 1.2X BASIC NEXT.GEN.
ONE ED SET VIA MAIL PER ED TRADE CARD
TRADES: RANDOM INSERTS IN SER.2 HOBBY
8 Michael Jordan 10.00 25.00
16 Alex Rodriguez 8.00 20.00

1994 Upper Deck All-Star Jumbos

This 48-card boxed set captures the photography of Walter Iooss Jr. Iooss shot 42 of the 49 cards in the set. The set included an order form for an album. The cards are oversized, measuring 3 1/2" by 5 1/4". The full-bleed color player photos are edged on one side by a green stripe carrying the player's name. A special green foil All-Star logo appears in one of the lower corners. One set per 40-box case uses gold foil in place of green. The horizontal back has a thick black stripe carrying a small color photo and Iooss' comments on the left, with a career summary and another closeup photo on the remainder of the back. The set closes with six cards commemorating historic events during the 125-year history of baseball (43-48). Some dealers believe that gold production was limited to 1,200 sets.

COMP.FACT SET (48) 6.00 15.00
1 Ken Griffey Jr. .75 2.00
2 Ruben Sierra .02 .10
Todd Van Poppel
3 Bryan Harvey .15 .40
Gary Sheffield
4 Gregg Jefferies .07 .20
Brian Jordan
5 Ryne Sandberg .30 .75
6 Matt Williams .10 .30
John Burkett
7 Darren Daulton .07 .20
John Kruk
8 Don Mattingly .40 1.00
Wade Boggs
9 Pat Listach .02 .10
Greg Vaughn
10 Tim Salmon .15 .40
Eduardo Perez
11 Fred McGriff .10 .30
Tom Glavine
12 Mo Vaughn .07 .20
Andre Dawson
13 Brian McRae .02 .10
Kevin Appier
14 Kirby Puckett .40 1.00
Kent Hrbek
15 Cal Ripken .75 2.00
16 Roberto Alomar .15 .40
Paul Molitor
17 Tony Gwynn .40 1.00
Phil Plantier
18 Greg Maddux .50 1.25
Steve Avery
19 Mike Mussina .15 .40
Chris Hoiles
20 Randy Johnson .15 .40
21 Roger Clemens .40 1.00
Aaron Sele
22 Will Clark .15 .40
Dean Palmer
23 Cecil Fielder .07 .20
Travis Fryman
24 John Olerud .07 .20
Joe Carter
25 Juan Gonzalez .15 .40
26 Jose Rijo .10 .30
Barry Larkin
27 Andy Van Slyke .07 .20
Jeff King
28 Larry Walker .07 .20
Marquis Grissom
29 Kenny Lofton .07 .20
Albert Belle
30 Mark Grace .50 1.25
Sammy Sosa
31 Mike Piazza .60 1.50
32 Ramon Martinez .20 .50
Pedro Martinez
Orel Hershiser
33 David Justice .15 .40
Terry Pendleton
34 Ivan Rodriguez .20 .50
Jose Canseco
35 Barry Bonds .40 1.00
36 Jeff Bagwell .30 .75
Craig Biggio
37 Jay Bell .02 .10
Orlando Merced
38 Jeff Kent .07 .20
Dwight Gooden
39 Andres Galarraga .15 .40
Charlie Hayes
40 Frank Thomas .30 .75
41 Bobby Bonilla .02 .10
42 Jack McDowell .02 .10
Tim Raines
43 1869 Red Stockings .02 .10
44 Ty Cobb 25th Ann. .30 .75
45 Babe Ruth 50th Ann. .75 2.00
46 Mickey Mantle 75th Ann. .75 2.00
47 Reggie Jackson 125th Ann. .30 .75
48 Ken Griffey Jr. 125th Ann. .60 1.50
P48 Ken Griffey Jr. Promo 2.50 6.00

1994 Upper Deck All-Time Heroes

This set consists of 225 standard-size cards. According to Upper Deck, production was limited to 4,015 numbered cases. Special subsets featured are Off The Wire (1-18), All-Time Heroes (101-125), Diamond Legends (151-177), and Heroes of Baseball (208-224). Mickey Mantle and three other superstars (Reggie Jackson, Tom Seaver, and George Brett) each autographed 1,000 cards that were randomly inserted into packs. (Nolan Ryan had been expected to sign cards for this product but did not. Instead, Brett signed an additional 1,000 cards). According to Upper Deck, a signed card would be found in one of every 385 packs. A Reggie Jackson Promo card was distributed to dealers and hobby media to preview the set.

COMPLETE SET (225) 8.00 20.00
1 Ted Williams OW .20 .50
2 Johnny Vander Meer OW .02 .10
3 Lou Brock OW .10 .30
4 Lou Gehrig OW .20 .50
5 Hank Aaron OW .20 .50
6 Tommie Agee OW .02 .10
7 Mickey Mantle OW .40 1.00
8 Bill Mazeroski OW .07 .20
9 Reggie Jackson OW .10 .30
10 W.Mays .40 1.00
M.Mantle OW
11 Roy Campanella OW .07 .20
12 Harvey Haddix OW .02 .10
13 Jimmy Piersall OW .02 .10
14 Enos Slaughter OW .02 .10
15 Nolan Ryan OW .30 .75
16 Bobby Thomson OW .02 .10
17 Willie Mays OW .20 .50
18 Bucky Dent OW .02 .10
19 Joe Garagiola .07 .20
20 George Brett .50 1.25
21 Cecil Cooper .07 .20
22 Ray Boone .02 .10
23 King Kelly .07 .20
24 Willie Mays .40 1.00
25 Napoleon Lajoie .10 .30
26 Gil McDougald .07 .20
27 Nelson Briles .02 .10
28 Bucky Dent .07 .20
29 Manny Sanguillen .02 .10
30 Ty Cobb .30 .75
31 Jim Grant .02 .10
32 Del Ennis .02 .10
33 Ron Hunt .02 .10
34 Nolan Ryan .60 1.50
35 Christy Mathewson .10 .30
36 Robin Roberts .07 .20
37 Frank Crosetti .02 .10
38 Johnny Vander Meer .02 .10
39 Virgil Trucks .02 .10
40 Lou Gehrig .40 1.00
41 Luke Appling .07 .20
42 Rico Petrocelli .02 .10
43 Harry Walker .02 .10
44 Reggie Jackson .10 .30
45 Mel Ott .10 .30
46 Phil Cavarretta .07 .20
47 Larry Doby .07 .20
48 Johnny Mize .07 .20
49 Ralph Kiner .10 .30
50 Ted Williams .40 1.00
51 Bobby Thomson .07 .20
52 Joe Black .07 .20
53 Monte Irvin .07 .20
54 Bill Virdon .07 .20
55 Honus Wagner .20 .50
56 Herb Score .07 .20
57 Jerry Coleman .02 .10
58 Jimmie Foxx .10 .30
59 Roy Face .02 .10
60 Babe Ruth .60 1.50
61 Jimmy Piersall .07 .20
62 Ed Charles .02 .10
63 Johnny Podres .07 .20
64 Charlie Neal .02 .10
65 Bill White .07 .20
66 Bill Skowron .10 .30
67 Al Rosen .07 .20
68 Eddie Lopat .02 .10
69 Bud Harrelson .07 .20
70 Steve Carlton .07 .20
71 Vida Blue .02 .10
72 Don Newcombe .07 .20
73 Al Bumbry .02 .10
74 Bill Madlock .07 .20
75 Hank Aaron CL .10 .30
76 Bill Mazeroski .10 .30
77 Ron Cey .07 .20
78 Tommy John .07 .20
79 Lou Brock .10 .30
80 Walter Johnson .20 .50
81 Harvey Haddix .07 .20
82 Al Oliver .07 .20
83 Johnny Logan .07 .20
84 Dave Dravecky .07 .20
85 Tony Oliva .07 .20
86 Dave Kingman .07 .20
87 Luis Tiant .07 .20
88 Sal Bando .07 .20
89 Cesar Cedeno .07 .20
90 Warren Spahn .10 .30
91 Mickey Lolich .02 .10
92 Lew Burdette .07 .20
93 Hank Bauer .07 .20
94 Marv Throneberry .02 .10
95 Willie Stargell .10 .30
96 George Kell .07 .20
97 Ferguson Jenkins .07 .20
98 Al Kaline .20 .50
99 Billy Martin .10 .30
100 Mickey Mantle .75 2.00
101 1869 Red Stockings ATH .02 .10
102 King Kelly ATH .02 .10
103 Nap Lajoie ATH .07 .20
104 Christy Mathewson ATH .07 .20
105 Cy Young ATH .07 .20
106 Ty Cobb ATH .20 .50
107 Reggie Jackson CL .07 .20
108 Rogers Hornsby ATH .07 .20
109 Walter Johnson ATH .07 .20
110 Babe Ruth ATH .30 .75
111 Hack Wilson ATH .07 .20
112 Lou Gehrig ATH .20 .50
113 Ted Williams ATH .20 .50
114 Yogi Berra ATH .10 .30
115 Bobby Thomson ATH .02 .10
116 Mickey Mantle ATH .40 1.00
117 Willie Mays ATH .20 .50
118 Bill Mazeroski ATH .07 .20
119 Bob Gibson ATH .07 .20
120 1969 Miracle Mets ATH .20 .50
121 Hank Aaron ATH .20 .50
122 Reggie Jackson ATH .10 .30
123 George Brett ATH .25 .60
124 Steve Carlton ATH .02 .10
125 Nolan Ryan ATH .30 .75
126 Frank Thomas .07 .20
127 Sam McDowell .07 .20
128 Jim Lonborg .02 .10
129 Bert Campaneris .02 .10
130 Bob Gibson .10 .30
131 Bobby Richardson .07 .20
132 Bobby Grich .07 .20
133 Billy Pierce .07 .20
134 Enos Slaughter .07 .20
135 Honus Wagner CL .07 .20
136 Orlando Cepeda .07 .20
137 Rennie Stennett .02 .10
138 Gene Alley .02 .10
139 Manny Mota .02 .10
140 Rogers Hornsby .10 .30
141 Joe Charboneau .02 .10
142 Rick Ferrell .07 .20
143 Toby Harrah .02 .10
144 Hank Aaron .40 1.00
145 Yogi Berra .20 .50
146 Whitey Ford .10 .30
147 Roy Campanella .20 .50
148 Graig Nettles .07 .20
149 Bobby Brown .02 .10
150 Willie Mays CL .10 .30
151 Cy Young LGD .07 .20
152 Walter Johnson LGD .07 .20
153 Christy Mathewson LGD .07 .20
154 Warren Spahn LGD .10 .30
155 Steve Carlton LGD .02 .10
156 Bob Gibson LGD .07 .20
157 Whitey Ford LGD .07 .20
158 Yogi Berra LGD .10 .30
159 Roy Campanella LGD .07 .20
160 Lou Gehrig LGD .20 .50
161 Johnny Mize LGD .02 .10
162 Rogers Hornsby LGD .07 .20
163 Honus Wagner LGD .07 .20
164 Hank Aaron LGD .20 .50
165 Babe Ruth LGD .30 .75
166 Willie Mays LGD .20 .50
167 Reggie Jackson LGD .10 .30
168 Mickey Mantle LGD .40 1.00
169 Jimmie Foxx LGD .07 .20
170 Ted Williams LGD .20 .50
171 Mel Ott LGD .07 .20
172 Willie Stargell LGD .07 .20
173 Al Kaline LGD .07 .20
174 Ty Cobb LGD .20 .50
175 Nap Lajoie LGD .07 .20
176 Lou Brock LGD .10 .30
177 Tom Seaver LGD .07 .20
178 Mark Fidrych .07 .20
179 Don Baylor .07 .20
180 Tom Seaver .10 .30
181 Jerry Grote .02 .10
182 George Foster .02 .10
183 Buddy Bell .07 .20
184 Ralph Garr .07 .20
185 Steve Garvey .07 .20
186 Joe Torre .07 .20
187 Carl Erskine .10 .30
188 Tommy Davis .02 .10
189 Bill Buckner .07 .20
190 Hack Wilson .10 .30
191 Steve Blass .02 .10
192 Ken Brett .02 .10
193 Lee May .02 .10
194 Bob Horner .07 .20
195 Boog Powell .07 .20
196 Darrell Evans .07 .20
197 Paul Blair .02 .10
198 Johnny Callison .07 .20
199 Jimmie Reese .02 .10
200 Cy Young .20 .50
201 Ron Santo .07 .20
202 Rico Carty .02 .10
203 Ron Necciai .02 .10
204 Lou Boudreau .07 .20
205 Minnie Minoso .07 .20
206 Eddie Yost .02 .10
207 Tommie Agee .07 .20
208 Dave Kingman HB .02 .10
209 Tony Oliva HB .07 .20
210 Reggie Jackson HB .10 .30
211 Paul Blair HB .02 .10
212 Ferguson Jenkins HB .02 .10
213 Steve Garvey HB .07 .20
214 Bert Campaneris HB .02 .10
215 Orlando Cepeda HB .07 .20
216 Bill Madlock HB .02 .10
217 Rennie Stennett HB .02 .10
218 Frank Thomas HB .02 .10
219 Bob Gibson HB .07 .20
220 Lou Brock HB .10 .30
221 Rico Carty HB .02 .10
222 Mickey Mantle HB .40 1.00
223 Robin Roberts HB .07 .20
224 Manny Sanguillen HB .02 .10
225 Mickey Mantle CL .20 .50
P44 Reggie Jackson Promo 1.25 3.00

1994 Upper Deck All-Time Heroes 125th Anniversary

COMPLETE SET (225) 20.00 50.00
*STARS: 1.5X TO 4X BASIC CARDS
ONE PER PACK

1994 Upper Deck All-Time Heroes 1954 Archives

STATED ODDS 1:30
1 Ted Williams 12.00 30.00
250 Ted Williams 12.00 30.00
259 Mickey Mantle 15.00 40.00

1994 Upper Deck All-Time Heroes Autographs

STATED ODDS 1:385
PRINT RUNS B/WN 1000-2000 COPIES PER
CARDS ARE NOT SERIAL-NUMBERED
1 George Brett/2000 * 20.00 50.00
2 Reggie Jackson/1000 * 25.00 60.00
3 Mickey Mantle/1000 * 400.00 800.00
4 Tom Seaver/1000 * 12.00 30.00

1994 Upper Deck All-Time Heroes Next In Line

COMPLETE SET (20) 20.00 50.00
STATED ODDS 1:39
1 Mike Bell .75 2.00
2 Alan Benes .75 2.00
3 D.J. Boston .75 2.00
4 Johnny Damon 2.00 5.00
5 Brad Fullmer 1.25 3.00
6 LaTroy Hawkins 1.25 3.00
7 Derek Jeter 40.00 100.00
8 Daron Kirkreit .75 2.00
9 Trot Nixon 2.00 5.00
10 Alex Ochoa .75 2.00
11 Kirk Presley .75 2.00
12 Jose Silva .75 2.00
13 Terrell Wade .75 2.00
14 Billy Wagner 2.00 5.00
15 Glenn Williams .75 2.00
16 Preston Wilson 1.25 3.00
17 Wayne Gomes .75 2.00
18 Ben Grieve 1.25 3.00
19 Dustin Hermanson .75 2.00
20 Paul Wilson .75 2.00

1994 Upper Deck: The American Epic

This 80-card boxed standard-size set recounts the story behind the PBS documentary "Baseball: The American Epic," produced by Ken Burns and sponsored by GM. The suggested retail price for the set, including the storage container, was 19.95. It was available from leading retail stores, the QVC television network, direct mail solicitation, and the Upper Deck Authenticated catalog. Like the documentary, the set is divided into "nine innings" and arranged chronologically as follows: 1st Inning (the 19th century [1-10], 2nd Inning (the 1900s [11-20], 3rd Inning (the 1910s [21-29], 4th Inning (the 1920s [30-39], 5th Inning (the 1930s [40-49], 6th Inning (the 1940s [50-56], 7th Inning (the 1950s [57-64], 8th Inning (the 1960s [65-71], and 9th Inning (1970-present [72-80]. Three insert cards were included with the set. A Michael Jordan card was available for direct mail customers, a Babe Ruth card for retail customers and a Mickey Mantle card for QVC customers. These cards are horizontal, full-bleed cards with black and white player photos. The backs are black and white with player information. The set price applies to either of the three versions and includes either of the three inserts. Recently, some autographs of Mickey Mantle from this set have surfaced on one of the home shopping channels. Since no information on how these cards were issued, or whether they were actually inserted into packs is available we are not pricing or listing this card at this point. Any further information on this card is appreciated.

COMP.FACT SET (81) 6.00 15.00
1 Our Game .01 .05
2 Alexander Cartwright .02 .10
3 Henry Chadwick .01 .05
4 The Fair Sex .01 .05
5 Harry Wright .01 .05
6 Albert Goodwill Spalding .02 .10
7 Cap Anson .05 .15
8 Moses Fleetwood Walker/1884 .02 .10
9 King Kelly .02 .10
10 John Montgomery Ward/1890 .02 .10
11 Ty Cobb .50 1.25
12 John McGraw .05 .15
13 Rube Waddell .02 .10
14 Christy Mathewson .07 .20
15 Walter Johnson .20 .50
16 Alta Weiss .01 .05
17 Fred Merkle .01 .05
18 Take Me Out To The .01 .05
Ballgame
19 John Henry(Pop) Lloyd .02 .10
20 Honus Wagner .30 .75
21 Woodrow Wilson .05 .15
22 Nap Lajoie .02 .10
23 Addie Joss .02 .10
24 Joe Wood .05 .15
25 Royal Rooters .01 .05
26 Ebbets Field .01 .05
27 Johnny Evers .02 .10
28 World War I .01 .05
29 Joe Jackson .40 1.00
30 Babe Ruth 1.25 3.00
31 George(Rube) Foster .01 .05
32 Ray Chapman .01 .05
33 Kenesaw M. Landis .02 .10
34 Yankee Stadium .01 .05
35 Rogers Hornsby .07 .20
36 Warren G. Harding .01 .05
37 Lou Gehrig .75 2.00
38 Grover C. Alexander .02 .10
39 House of David .01 .05
40 Satchel Paige .30 .75
41 Lefty Grove .02 .10
42 Jimmie Foxx .05 .15
43 Connie Mack .05 .15
44 Josh Gibson .07 .20
45 Dizzy Dean .02 .10
46 Carl Hubbell .02 .10
47 Franklin D. Roosevelt .05 .15
48 Bob Feller .02 .10
49 Cool Papa Bell .02 .10
50 Jackie Robinson .75 2.00
51 Ted Williams .75 2.00
52 Sym-phony Band .01 .05
53 Annabel Lee .01 .05
54 Hank Greenberg .02 .10
55 Branch Rickey .02 .10
56 Harry S. Truman .07 .20
57 Casey Stengel .07 .20
58 Bobby Thomson .02 .10
59 Dwight D. Eisenhower .05 .15
60 Mario Cuomo .02 .10
61 Buck O'Neil .02 .10
62 Yogi Berra .20 .50
63 Mickey Mantle 1.25 3.00
64 Don Larsen .02 .10
65 John F. Kennedy .60 1.50
66 Bill Mazeroski .02 .10
67 Roger Maris .07 .20
68 Frank Robinson .02 .10
69 Bob Gibson .02 .10
70 Tom Seaver/1969 .20 .50
71 Curt Flood .01 .05
72 Roberto Clemente .75 2.00
73 Luis Tiant .01 .05
74 Marvin Miller .01 .05
75 Reggie Jackson .20 .50
76 Willie(Pops) Stargell .02 .10
77 Pete Rose .20 .50
78 Bill Clinton .40 1.00
79 Nolan Ryan 1.00 2.50
80 George Brett .07 .20
BC1 Mickey Mantle 2.00 5.00
Home shopping insert
BC2 Michael Jordan 2.00 5.00
Direct mail insert
BC3 Babe Ruth 2.00 5.00
Retail insert

1994 Upper Deck: The American Epic GM

COMPLETE SET (9) 1.50 4.00
1 Hank Aaron .20 .50
2 Roberto Clemente .30 .75
3 Ty Cobb .20 .50
4 Hank Greenberg .02 .10
5 Mickey Mantle .50 1.25
6 Satchel Paige .08 .25
7 Jackie Robinson .30 .75
8 Babe Ruth .50 1.25
9 Ted Williams .30 .75

1994 Upper Deck: The American Epic Little Debbies

COMPLETE SET (15) 4.00 10.00
LD1 Our Game CL .02 .10
LD2 Alexander Cartwright .02 .10
LD3 King Kelly .02 .10
LD4 John McGraw .07 .20
LD5 Christy Mathewson .07 .20
LD6 Walter Johnson .10 .30
LD7 Ted Williams .60 1.50
LD8 Annabel Lee .02 .10
LD9 Jackie Robinson .40 1.00
LD10 Bobby Thomson .07 .20
LD11 Buck O'Neil .07 .20
LD12 Mickey Mantle .60 1.50
LD13 Bob Gibson .10 .30
LD14 Curt Flood .02 .10
LD15 Reggie Jackson .15 .40

1994 Upper Deck Commemorative Cards

1 1994 Launch Tour/2000 2.00 5.00
Wayne Gretzky
Reggie Jackson
Michael Jordan
Joe Montana

1994 Upper Deck Mantle Phone Cards

Upper Deck in conjunction with Global Telecommunication Solutions produced this set of 10 phone cards to honor Mickey Mantle, the greatest switch-hitter in baseball history. The set was issued in two five-card sets: series one in early October, and series two later that year. Each five-card set retailed for $59.95. Chronicling his career from 1951 until his 1974 Hall of Fame Induction, the set is a replica of the "Baseball Heroes" insert cards featured in the 1994 Upper Deck baseball series 2. Just 5,000 sets of series 1 were produced, with each card including a bonus one-minute Mantle highlight replay moment. As an added bonus, 500 1869 Cincinnati Red Stockings phone cards were randomly inserted in series two sets, while Upper Deck distributed its allotment to the first 450 orders received from hobby dealers. Only 2,000 Red Stocking cards were produced. The phone cards are unnumbered and checklisted below in chronological order.

COMPLETE SET (11) 25.00 60.00
COMMON CARD (1-10) 3.20 8.00
NNO0 1869 Cincinnati 4.00 10.00
Red Stockings

1994 Upper Deck Sheets

These ten 8 1/2" by 11" sheets were produced by Upper Deck. They were issued to commemorate various special events sponsored by Upper Deck. We have listed the production quantities when known.

COMPLETE SET (10) 15.00 40.00
1 Heroes of Baseball Day .75 2.00
The Ballpark in Arlington#
2 Tribute to the 1964 3.00 8.00
Season
June 4& 1994 (50&000)
3 Milwaukee Brewers .75 2.00
Silver Anniversary
June 25, 19
4 Hollywood Softball Game 2.50 6.00
26-Jun
5 Heroes of Baseball 2.50 6.00
All-Star Game
July 11& 1994 (
6 25th Anniversary of the
1969 Season and the 3.00 8.00
Mira
7 All-Time Homerun Kings 3.00 8.00
23-Jul
8 Baseball 125th Anniversary .75 2.00
August 6, 1994 (40,000
9 All Star Fanfest .75 2.00
Autograph Sheet/(Drawing of
ba
10 Upper Deck Authenticated .75 2.00
Triple Crown Winners/2,
11 UDA Ted Williams Career
Commemorative .75 2.00

1994 Upper Deck Top Ten Promo

This one-card Ken Griffey promo was issued to promote the never issued 1994 Upper Deck Top Ten set. The set which was supposed to honor the best players in baseball was never issued by Upper Deck due to the baseball strike in 1994.

P6 Ken Griffey Jr. 2.50 6.00

1995 Upper Deck

The 1995 Upper Deck baseball set was issued in two series of 225 cards for a total of 450. The cards were distributed in 12-card packs (36 per box) with a suggested retail price of $1.99. Subsets include Top Prospect (1-15, 251-265), 90's Midpoint (101-110), Star Rookie (211-240), and Diamond Debuts (241-250). Rookie Cards in this set include Hideo Nomo. Five randomly inserted Trade Cards were each redeemable for nine updated cards of new rookies or players who changed teams, comprising a 45-card Trade Redemption set. The Trade cards expired Feb 1, 1996. Autographed jumbo cards (Roger Clemens for series one, Alex Rodriguez for either series) were available through a wrapper redemption offer.

COMP.MASTER SET (495) 60.00 120.00
COMPLETE SET (450) 20.00 50.00
COMPLETE SERIES 1 (225) 10.00 25.00
COMPLETE SERIES 2 (225) 10.00 25.00
COMMON CARD (1-450) .05 .15
COMP.TRADE SET (45) 30.00 60.00
COMMON TRADE (451T-495T) .40 1.00
NINE TRADE CARDS PER TRADE EXCH.CARD
SUBSET CARDS HALF VALUE OF BASE CARDS
JUMBO AUS WERE REDEEMED W/WRAPPERS
1 Ruben Rivera .05 .15
2 Bill Pulsipher .05 .15
3 Ben Grieve .05 .15
4 Curtis Goodwin .05 .15
5 Damon Hollins .05 .15
6 Todd Greene .05 .15
7 Glenn Williams .05 .15
8 Bret Wagner .05 .15
9 Karim Garcia RC .05 .15
10 Nomar Garciaparra .75 2.00
11 Raul Casanova RC .05 .15
12 Matt Smith .05 .15
13 Paul Wilson .05 .15
14 Jason Isringhausen .10 .30
15 Reid Ryan .10 .30
16 Lee Smith .10 .30
17 Chili Davis .10 .30
18 Brian Anderson .05 .15
19 Gary DiSarcina .05 .15
20 Bo Jackson .30 .75
21 Chuck Finley .10 .30
22 Darryl Kile .10 .30
23 Shane Reynolds .05 .15
24 Tony Fusebio .05 .15
25 Craig Biggio .20 .50
26 Doug Drabek .05 .15
27 Brian L.Hunter .05 .15
28 James Mouton .05 .15
29 Geronimo Berroa .05 .15
30 Rickey Henderson .30 .75
31 Steve Karsay .05 .15
32 Steve Ontiveros .05 .15
33 Ernie Young .05 .15
34 Dennis Eckersley .10 .30
35 Mark McGwire .75 2.00
36 Dave Stewart .10 .30
37 Pat Hentgen .05 .15
38 Carlos Delgado .10 .30
39 Joe Carter .10 .30
40 Roberto Alomar .20 .50
41 John Olerud .10 .30
42 Devon White .10 .30
43 Roberto Kelly .05 .15
44 Jeff Blauser .05 .15
45 Fred McGriff .20 .50
46 Tom Glavine .20 .50
47 Mike Kelly .05 .15
48 Javier Lopez .10 .30
49 Greg Maddux .50 1.25
50 Matt Mieske .05 .15
51 Troy O'Leary .05 .15
52 Jeff Cirillo .05 .15
53 Cal Eldred .05 .15
54 Pat Listach .05 .15
55 Jose Valentin .05 .15
56 John Mabry .05 .15
57 Bob Tewksbury .05 .15
58 Brian Jordan .10 .30
59 Gregg Jefferies .05 .15
60 Ozzie Smith .50 1.25
61 Geronimo Pena .05 .15
62 Mark Whiten .05 .15
63 Rey Sanchez .05 .15
64 Willie Banks .05 .15
65 Mark Grace .20 .50
66 Randy Myers .05 .15
67 Steve Trachsel .05 .15
68 Derrick May .05 .15
69 Brett Butler .10 .30
70 Eric Karros .10 .30
71 Tim Wallach .05 .15
72 Delino DeShields .05 .15
73 Darren Dreifort .05 .15
74 Orel Hershiser .10 .30
75 Billy Ashley .05 .15
76 Sean Berry .05 .15
77 Ken Hill .05 .15
78 John Wetteland .10 .30
79 Moises Alou .10 .30
80 Cliff Floyd .10 .30
81 Marquis Grissom .10 .30
82 Larry Walker .10 .30
83 Rondell White .10 .30
84 William VanLandingham .05 .15
85 Matt Williams .10 .30
86 Rod Beck .05 .15
87 Darren Lewis .05 .15
88 Robby Thompson .05 .15
89 Darryl Strawberry .10 .30
90 Kenny Lofton .10 .30
91 Charles Nagy .05 .15
92 Sandy Alomar Jr. .05 .15
93 Mark Clark .05 .15
94 Dennis Martinez .10 .30
95 Dave Winfield .10 .30
96 Jim Thome .20 .50
97 Manny Ramirez .20 .50
98 Goose Gossage .10 .30
99 Tino Martinez .20 .50
100 Ken Griffey Jr. .60 1.50
101 Greg Maddux ANA .30 .75
102 Randy Johnson ANA .20 .50
103 Barry Bonds ANA .40 1.00
104 Juan Gonzalez ANA .05 .15
105 Frank Thomas ANA .20 .50
106 Matt Williams ANA .05 .15
107 Paul Molitor ANA .05 .15
108 Fred McGriff ANA .10 .30
109 Carlos Baerga ANA .05 .15
110 Ken Griffey Jr. ANA .40 1.00
111 Reggie Jefferson .05 .15
112 Randy Johnson .30 .75
113 Marc Newfield .05 .15
114 Robb Nen .10 .30
115 Jeff Conine .10 .30
116 Kurt Abbott .05 .15
117 Charlie Hough .10 .30
118 Dave Weathers .05 .15
119 Juan Castillo .05 .15
120 Bret Saberhagen .10 .30
121 Rico Brogna .05 .15
122 John Franco .10 .30
123 Todd Hundley .05 .15
124 Jason Jacome .05 .15
125 Bobby Jones .05 .15
126 Bret Barberie .05 .15
127 Ben McDonald .05 .15
128 Harold Baines .10 .30
129 Jeffrey Hammonds .05 .15
130 Mike Mussina .20 .50
131 Chris Hoiles .05 .15
132 Brady Anderson .10 .30
133 Eddie Williams .05 .15
134 Andy Benes .05 .15
135 Tony Gwynn .40 1.00
136 Bip Roberts .05 .15
137 Joey Hamilton .05 .15
138 Luis Lopez .05 .15
139 Ray McDavid .05 .15
140 Lenny Dykstra .10 .30
141 Mariano Duncan .05 .15
142 Fernando Valenzuela .10 .30
143 Bobby Munoz .05 .15
144 Kevin Stocker .05 .15
145 John Kruk .10 .30
146 Jon Lieber .05 .15
147 Zane Smith .05 .15
148 Steve Cooke .05 .15
149 Andy Van Slyke .20 .50
150 Jay Bell .10 .30
151 Carlos Garcia .05 .15
152 John Dettmer .05 .15
153 Darren Oliver .05 .15
154 Dean Palmer .10 .30
155 Otis Nixon .05 .15
156 Rusty Greer .10 .30
157 Rick Helling .05 .15
158 Jose Canseco .20 .50
159 Roger Clemens .60 1.50
160 Andre Dawson .10 .30
161 Mo Vaughn .10 .30
162 Aaron Sele .05 .15
163 John Valentin .05 .15
164 Brian R. Hunter .05 .15
165 Bret Boone .10 .30
166 Hector Carrasco .05 .15
167 Pete Schourek .05 .15
168 Willie Greene .05 .15
169 Kevin Mitchell .05 .15
170 Deion Sanders .20 .50
171 John Roper .05 .15
172 Charlie Hayes .05 .15
173 David Nied .05 .15
174 Ellis Burks .10 .30
175 Dante Bichette .10 .30
176 Marvin Freeman .05 .15
177 Eric Young .05 .15
178 David Cone .10 .30
179 Greg Gagne .05 .15
180 Bob Hamelin .05 .15
181 Wally Joyner .10 .30
182 Jeff Montgomery .05 .15
183 Jose Lind .05 .15
184 Chris Gomez .05 .15
185 Travis Fryman .10 .30
186 Kirk Gibson .10 .30
187 Mike Moore .05 .15
188 Lou Whitaker .10 .30
189 Sean Bergman .05 .15
190 Shane Mack .05 .15
191 Rick Aguilera .05 .15
192 Denny Hocking .05 .15
193 Chuck Knoblauch .10 .30
194 Kevin Tapani .05 .15
195 Kent Hrbek .10 .30
196 Ozzie Guillen .10 .30
197 Wilson Alvarez .05 .15
198 Tim Raines .10 .30
199 Scott Ruffcorn .05 .15

200 Michael Jordan 1.00 2.50
201 Robin Ventura .10 .30
202 Jason Bere .05 .15
203 Darrin Jackson .05 .15
204 Russ Davis .05 .15
205 Jimmy Key .10 .30
206 Jack McDowell .05 .15
207 Jim Abbott .20 .50
208 Paul O'Neill .20 .50
209 Bernie Williams .20 .50
210 Don Mattingly .75 2.00
211 Orlando Miller .05 .15
212 Alex Gonzalez .05 .15
213 Terrell Wade .05 .15
214 Jose Oliva .05 .15
215 Alex Rodriguez .75 2.00
216 Garret Anderson .10 .30
217 Alan Benes .05 .15
218 Armando Benitez .05 .15
219 Dustin Hermanson .05 .15
220 Charles Johnson .10 .30
221 Julian Tavarez .05 .15
222 Jason Giambi .20 .50
223 LaTroy Hawkins .05 .15
224 Todd Hollandsworth .05 .15
225 Derek Jeter .75 2.00
226 Hideo Nomo RC 1.00 2.50
227 Tony Clark .05 .15
228 Roger Cedeno .05 .15
229 Scott Stahoviak .05 .15
230 Michael Tucker .05 .15
231 Joe Rosselli .05 .15
232 Antonio Osuna .05 .15
233 Bob Higginson RC .30 .75
234 Mark Grudzielanek RC .30 .75
235 Ray Durham .10 .30
236 Frank Rodriguez .05 .15
237 Quilvio Veras .05 .15
238 Darren Bragg .05 .15
239 Ugueth Urbina .05 .15
240 Jason Bates .05 .15
241 David Bell .05 .15
242 Ron Villone .05 .15
243 Joe Randa .10 .30
244 Carlos Perez RC .15 .40
245 Brad Clontz .05 .15
246 Steve Rodriguez .05 .15
247 Joe Vitiello .05 .15
248 Ozzie Timmons .05 .15
249 Rudy Pemberton .05 .15
250 Marty Cordova .05 .15
251 Tony Graffanino .05 .15
252 Mark Johnson RC .15 .40
253 Tomas Perez RC .05 .15
254 Jimmy Hurst .05 .15
255 Edgardo Alfonzo .05 .15
256 Jose Malave .05 .15
257 Brad Radke RC .30 .75
258 Jon Nunnally .05 .15
259 Dilson Torres RC .05 .15
260 Esteban Loaiza .05 .15
261 Freddy Adrian Garcia RC .05 .15
262 Don Wengert .05 .15
263 Robert Person RC .15 .40
264 Tim Unroe RC .05 .15
265 Juan Acevedo RC .05 .15
266 Eduardo Perez .05 .15
267 Tony Phillips .05 .15
268 Jim Edmonds .20 .50
269 Jorge Fabregas .05 .15
270 Tim Salmon .20 .50
271 Mark Langston .05 .15
272 J.T. Snow .10 .30
273 Phil Plantier .05 .15
274 Derek Bell .05 .15
275 Jeff Bagwell .20 .50
276 Luis Gonzalez .10 .30
277 John Hudek .05 .15
278 Todd Stottlemyre .05 .15
279 Mark Acre .05 .15
280 Ruben Sierra .10 .30
281 Mike Bordick .05 .15
282 Ron Darling .05 .15
283 Brent Gates .05 .15
284 Todd Van Poppel .05 .15
285 Paul Molitor .10 .30
286 Ed Sprague .05 .15
287 Juan Guzman .05 .15
288 David Cone .10 .30
289 Shawn Green .10 .30
290 Marquis Grissom .10 .30
291 Kent Mercker .05 .15
292 Steve Avery .05 .15
293 Chipper Jones .30 .75
294 John Smoltz .20 .50
295 David Justice .10 .30
296 Ryan Klesko .10 .30
297 Joe Oliver .05 .15
298 Ricky Bones .05 .15
299 John Jaha .05 .15
300 Greg Vaughn .05 .15
301 Dave Nilsson .05 .15
302 Kevin Seitzer .05 .15
303 Bernard Gilkey .05 .15
304 Allen Battle .05 .15
305 Ray Lankford .10 .30
306 Tom Pagnozzi .05 .15
307 Allen Watson .05 .15
308 Danny Jackson .05 .15
309 Ken Hill .05 .15
310 Todd Zeile .05 .15
311 Kevin Roberson .05 .15
312 Steve Buechele .05 .15
313 Rick Wilkins .05 .15
314 Kevin Foster .05 .15
315 Sammy Sosa .30 .75
316 Howard Johnson .05 .15
317 Greg Hansell .05 .15
318 Pedro Astacio .05 .15
319 Rafael Bournigal .05 .15
320 Mike Piazza .50 1.25
321 Ramon Martinez .05 .15
322 Raul Mondesi .10 .30
323 Ismael Valdes .05 .15
324 Wil Cordero .05 .15
325 Tony Tarasco .05 .15
326 Roberto Kelly .05 .15
327 Jeff Fassero .05 .15
328 Mike Lansing .05 .15
329 Pedro Martinez .20 .50
330 Kirk Rueter .05 .15
331 Glenallen Hill .05 .15
332 Kirt Manwaring .05 .15
333 Royce Clayton .05 .15
334 J.R. Phillips .05 .15
335 Barry Bonds .75 2.00
336 Mark Portugal .05 .15
337 Terry Mulholland .05 .15
338 Omar Vizquel .20 .50
339 Carlos Baerga .05 .15
340 Albert Belle .10 .30
341 Eddie Murray .30 .75
342 Wayne Kirby .05 .15
343 Chad Ogea .05 .15
344 Tim Davis .05 .15
345 Jay Buhner .10 .30
346 Bobby Ayala .05 .15
347 Mike Blowers .05 .15
348 Dave Fleming .05 .15
349 Edgar Martinez .20 .50
350 Andre Dawson .10 .30
351 Darrell Whitmore .05 .15
352 Chuck Carr .05 .15
353 John Burkett .05 .15
354 Chris Hammond .05 .15
355 Gary Sheffield .10 .30
356 Pat Rapp .05 .15
357 Greg Colbrunn .05 .15
358 David Segui .05 .15
359 Jeff Kent .10 .30
360 Bobby Bonilla .10 .30
361 Pete Harnisch .05 .15
362 Ryan Thompson .05 .15
363 Jose Vizcaino .05 .15
364 Brett Butler .10 .30
365 Cal Ripken 1.00 2.50
366 Rafael Palmeiro .20 .50
367 Leo Gomez .05 .15
368 Andy Van Slyke .20 .50
369 Arthur Rhodes .05 .15
370 Ken Caminiti .10 .30
371 Steve Finley .10 .30
372 Melvin Nieves .05 .15
373 Andujar Cedeno .05 .15
374 Trevor Hoffman .10 .30
375 Fernando Valenzuela .10 .30
376 Ricky Bottalico .05 .15
377 Dave Hollins .05 .15
378 Charlie Hayes .05 .15
379 Tommy Greene .05 .15
380 Darren Daulton .10 .30
381 Curt Schilling .10 .30
382 Midre Cummings .05 .15
383 Al Martin .05 .15
384 Jeff King .05 .15
385 Orlando Merced .05 .15
386 Denny Neagle .10 .30
387 Don Slaught .05 .15
388 Dave Clark .05 .15
389 Kevin Gross .05 .15
390 Will Clark .20 .50
391 Ivan Rodriguez .20 .50
392 Benji Gil .05 .15
393 Jeff Frye .05 .15
394 Kenny Rogers .10 .30
395 Juan Gonzalez .10 .30
396 Mike Macfarlane .05 .15
397 Lee Tinsley .05 .15
398 Tim Naehring .05 .15
399 Tim Vanegmond .05 .15
400 Mike Greenwell .05 .15
401 Ken Ryan .05 .15
402 John Smiley .05 .15
403 Tim Pugh .05 .15
404 Reggie Sanders .10 .30
405 Barry Larkin .20 .50
406 Hal Morris .05 .15
407 Jose Rijo .05 .15
408 Lance Painter .05 .15
409 Joe Girardi .05 .15
410 Andres Galarraga .10 .30
411 Mike Kingery .05 .15
412 Roberto Mejia .05 .15
413 Walt Weiss .05 .15
414 Bill Swift .05 .15
415 Larry Walker .10 .30
416 Billy Brewer .05 .15
417 Pat Borders .05 .15
418 Tom Gordon .05 .15
419 Kevin Appier .10 .30
420 Gary Gaetti .10 .30
421 Greg Gohr .05 .15
422 Felipe Lira .05 .15
423 John Doherty .05 .15
424 Chad Curtis .05 .15
425 Cecil Fielder .10 .30
426 Alan Trammell .10 .30
427 David McCarty .05 .15
428 Scott Erickson .05 .15
429 Pat Mahomes .05 .15
430 Kirby Puckett .30 .75
431 Dave Stevens .05 .15
432 Pedro Munoz .05 .15
433 Chris Sabo .05 .15
434 Alex Fernandez .05 .15
435 Frank Thomas .30 .75
436 Roberto Hernandez .05 .15
437 Lance Johnson .05 .15
438 Jim Abbott .20 .50
439 John Wetteland .10 .30
440 Melido Perez .05 .15
441 Tony Fernandez .05 .15
442 Pat Kelly .05 .15
443 Mike Stanley .05 .15
444 Danny Tartabull .05 .15
445 Wade Boggs .20 .50
446 Robin Yount TRIB .50 1.25
447 Ryne Sandberg TRIB .50 1.25
448 Nolan Ryan TRIB 1.25 3.00
449 George Brett TRIB .75 2.00
450 Mike Schmidt TRIB .50 1.25
451 Jim Abbott TRADE .75 2.00
452 Danny Tartabull TRADE .40 1.00
453 Ariel Prieto TRADE .40 1.00
454 Scott Cooper TRADE .40 1.00
455 Tom Henke TRADE .40 1.00
456 Todd Zeile TRADE .40 1.00
457 Brian McRae TRADE .40 1.00
458 Luis Gonzalez TRADE .60 1.50
459 Jaime Navarro TRADE .40 1.00
460 Todd Worrell TRADE .40 1.00
461 Roberto Kelly TRADE .40 1.00
462 Chad Fonville TRADE .40 1.00
463 Shane Andrews TRADE .40 1.00
464 David Segui TRADE .40 1.00
465 Deion Sanders TRADE .75 2.00
466 Orel Hershiser TRADE .60 1.50
467 Ken Hill TRADE .40 1.00
468 Andy Benes TRADE .40 1.00
469 Terry Pendleton TRADE .60 1.50
470 Bobby Bonilla TRADE .60 1.50
471 Scott Erickson TRADE .40 1.00
472 Kevin Brown TRADE .60 1.50
473 Glenn Dishman TRADE .40 1.00
474 Phil Plantier TRADE .40 1.00
475 Gregg Jefferies TRADE .40 1.00
476 Tyler Green TRADE .40 1.00
477 Heathcliff Slocumb TRADE .40 1.00
478 Mark Whiten TRADE .40 1.00
479 Mickey Tettleton TRADE .40 1.00
480 Tim Wakefield TRADE .60 1.50
481 Vaughn Eshelman TRADE .40 1.00
482 Rick Aguilera TRADE .40 1.00
483 Erik Hanson TRADE .40 1.00
484 Willie McGee TRADE .60 1.50
485 Troy O'Leary TRADE .40 1.00
486 Benito Santiago TRADE .60 1.50
487 Darren Lewis TRADE .40 1.00
488 Dave Burba TRADE .40 1.00
489 Ron Gant TRADE .60 1.50
490 Bret Saberhagen TRADE .60 1.50
491 Vinny Castilla TRADE .60 1.50
492 Frank Rodriguez TRADE .40 1.00
493 Andy Pettitte TRADE .75 2.00
494 Ruben Sierra TRADE .60 1.50
495 David Cone TRADE .60 1.50
J159 R.Clemens Jumbo AU 15.00 40.00
J215 A.Rodriguez Jumbo AU 20.00 50.00
P100 Ken Griffey Jr. Promo 1.00 2.50

1995 Upper Deck Electric Diamond

COMPLETE SET (450) 50.00 100.00
COMPLETE SERIES 1 (225) 20.00 50.00
COMPLETE SERIES 2 (225) 25.00 60.00
*STARS: 1.25X TO 3X BASIC CARDS
*ROOKIES: 1X TO 2.5X BASIC CARDS
ONE PER RETAIL PACK/TWO PER MINI JUMBO

1995 Upper Deck Autographs

SER.2 STATED ODDS 1:72 HOBBY
AC1 Reggie Jackson 15.00 40.00
AC2 Willie Mays 75.00 200.00
AC3 Frank Robinson 8.00 20.00
AC4 Roger Clemens 15.00 40.00
AC5 Raul Mondesi 8.00 20.00

1995 Upper Deck Checklists

COMPLETE SET (10) 5.00 12.00
COMPLETE SERIES 1 (5) 1.50 4.00
COMPLETE SERIES 2 (5) 3.00 8.00
STATED ODDS 1:17 ALL PACKS
1A Montreal Expos .10 .30
2A Fred McGriff .40 1.00
3A John Valentin .10 .30
4A Kenny Rogers .25 .60
5A Greg Maddux 1.00 2.50
1B Cecil Fielder .25 .60
2B Tony Gwynn .75 2.00
3B Greg Maddux 1.00 2.50
4B Randy Johnson .60 1.50
5B Mike Schmidt 1.00 2.50

1995 Upper Deck Predictor Award Winners

COMPLETE SET (40) 15.00 40.00
COMPLETE SERIES 1 (20) 8.00 20.00
COMPLETE SERIES 2 (20) 8.00 20.00
STATED ODDS 1:30 HOBBY
*EXCH: .5X TO 1.2X BASIC PREDICTOR AW
ONE EXCH.SET VIA MAIL PER PRED.WINNER
H1 Albert Belle .50 1.25
H2 Juan Gonzalez .50 1.25
H3 Ken Griffey Jr. 2.50 6.00
H4 Kirby Puckett 1.25 3.00
H5 Frank Thomas 1.25 3.00
H6 Jeff Bagwell .75 2.00
H7 Barry Bonds 3.00 8.00
H8 Mike Piazza 2.00 5.00
H9 Matt Williams .50 1.25
H10 MVP Wild Card W .25 .60
H11 Armando Benitez .25 .60
H12 Alex Gonzalez .25 .60
H13 Shawn Green .50 1.25
H14 Derek Jeter 12.00 30.00
H15 Alex Rodriguez 3.00 8.00
H16 Alan Benes .25 .60
H17 Brian L.Hunter .25 .60
H18 Charles Johnson .50 1.25
H19 Jose Oliva .25 .60
H20 ROY Wild Card .25 .60
H21 Cal Ripken 4.00 10.00
H22 Don Mattingly 3.00 8.00
H23 Roberto Alomar .75 2.00
H24 Kenny Lofton .50 1.25
H25 Will Clark .75 2.00
H26 Mark McGwire 3.00 8.00
H27 Greg Maddux 2.00 5.00
H28 Fred McGriff .75 2.00
H29 Andres Galarraga .50 1.25
H30 Jose Canseco .75 2.00
H31 Ray Durham .50 1.25
H32 Mark Grudzielanek 1.25 3.00
H33 Scott Ruffcorn .25 .60
H34 Michael Tucker .25 .60
H35 Garret Anderson .50 1.25
H36 Darren Bragg .25 .60
H37 Quilvio Veras .25 .60
H38 Hideo Nomo W 4.00 10.00
H39 Chipper Jones 1.25 3.00
H40 Marty Cordova W .25 .60

1995 Upper Deck Predictor League Leaders

COMPLETE SET (60) 40.00 100.00
COMPLETE SERIES 1 (30) 25.00 60.00
COMPLETE SERIES 2 (30) 15.00 40.00
STATED ODDS 1:30 RET, 1:17 ANCO
*EXCH: .5X TO 1.2X BASIC PREDICTOR LL
ONE EXCH.SET VIA MAIL PER PRED.WINNER
R1 Albert Belle W .50 1.25
R2 Jose Canseco .75 2.00
R3 Juan Gonzalez .50 1.25
R4 Ken Griffey Jr. 2.50 6.00
R5 Frank Thomas 1.25 3.00
R6 Jeff Bagwell .75 2.00
R7 Barry Bonds 3.00 8.00
R8 Fred McGriff .75 2.00
R9 Matt Williams .50 1.25
R10 HR Wild Card W .25 .60
R11 Albert Belle W .50 1.25
R12 Joe Carter .50 1.25
R13 Cecil Fielder .50 1.25
R14 Kirby Puckett 1.25 3.00
R15 Frank Thomas 1.25 3.00
R16 Jeff Bagwell .75 2.00
R17 Barry Bonds 3.00 8.00
R18 Mike Piazza 2.00 5.00
R19 Matt Williams .50 1.25
R20 RBI Wild Card W .25 .60
R21 Wade Boggs .75 2.00
R22 Kenny Lofton .50 1.25
R23 Paul Molitor .50 1.25
R24 Paul O'Neill .75 2.00
R25 Frank Thomas 1.25 3.00
R26 Jeff Bagwell .75 2.00
R27 Tony Gwynn W 1.50 4.00
R28 Gregg Jefferies .25 .60
R29 Hal Morris .25 .60
R30 Bat Wild Card W .25 .60
R31 Joe Carter .50 1.25
R32 Cecil Fielder .50 1.25
R33 Rafael Palmeiro .75 2.00
R34 Larry Walker .50 1.25
R35 Manny Ramirez .75 2.00
R36 Tim Salmon .75 2.00
R37 Mike Piazza 2.00 5.00
R38 Andres Galarraga .50 1.25
R39 David Justice .50 1.25
R40 Gary Sheffield .50 1.25
R41 Juan Gonzalez .50 1.25
R42 Jose Canseco .75 2.00
R43 Will Clark .75 2.00
R44 Rafael Palmeiro .75 2.00
R45 Ken Griffey Jr. 2.50 6.00
R46 Ruben Sierra .50 1.25
R47 Larry Walker .50 1.25
R48 Fred McGriff .75 2.00
R49 Dante Bichette W .50 1.25
R50 Darren Daulton .50 1.25
R51 Will Clark .75 2.00
R52 Ken Griffey Jr. 2.50 6.00
R53 Don Mattingly 3.00 8.00
R54 John Olerud .50 1.25
R55 Kirby Puckett 1.25 3.00
R56 Raul Mondesi .50 1.25
R57 Moises Alou .50 1.25
R58 Bret Boone .50 1.25
R59 Albert Belle .50 1.25
R60 Mike Piazza 2.00 5.00

1995 Upper Deck Ruth Heroes

COMPLETE SET (10) 40.00 100.00
COMMON CARD (73-81/HDR) 6.00 15.00
SER.2 STATED ODDS 1:34 HOBBY/RETAIL

1995 Upper Deck Special Edition

COMPLETE SET (270) 25.00 60.00
COMPLETE SERIES 1 (135) 12.50 30.00
COMPLETE SERIES 2 (135) 12.50 30.00
ONE PER HOBBY PACK
*SE GOLD STARS: 3X TO 8X HI COLUMN
*SE GOLD RC's: 2X TO 5X HI
SE GOLD ODDS 1:35 HOBBY
1 Cliff Floyd .30 .75
2 Wil Cordero .15 .40
3 Pedro Martinez .50 1.25
4 Larry Walker .30 .75
5 Derek Jeter 10.00 25.00
6 Mike Stanley .15 .40
7 Melido Perez .15 .40
8 Jim Leyritz .15 .40
9 Danny Tartabull .15 .40
10 Wade Boggs .50 1.25
11 Ryan Klesko .30 .75
12 Steve Avery .15 .40
13 Damon Hollins .15 .40
14 Chipper Jones .75 2.00
15 David Justice .30 .75
16 Glenn Williams .15 .40
17 Jose Oliva .15 .40
18 Terrell Wade .15 .40
19 Alex Fernandez .15 .40
20 Frank Thomas .75 2.00
21 Ozzie Guillen .30 .75
22 Roberto Hernandez .15 .40
23 Albie Lopez .15 .40
24 Eddie Murray .75 2.00
25 Albert Belle .30 .75
26 Omar Vizquel .50 1.25
27 Carlos Baerga .15 .40
28 Jose Rijo .15 .40
29 Hal Morris .15 .40
30 Reggie Sanders .30 .75
31 Jack Morris .30 .75
32 Raul Mondesi .30 .75
33 Karim Garcia .15 .40
34 Todd Hollandsworth .15 .40
35 Mike Piazza 1.25 3.00
36 Chan Ho Park .30 .75
37 Ramon Martinez .15 .40
38 Kenny Rogers .30 .75
39 Will Clark .50 1.25
40 Juan Gonzalez .30 .75
41 Ivan Rodriguez .50 1.25
42 Orlando Miller .15 .40
43 John Hudek .15 .40
44 Luis Gonzalez .30 .75
45 Jeff Bagwell .50 1.25
46 Cal Ripken 2.50 6.00
47 Mike Oquist .15 .40
48 Armando Benitez .15 .40
49 Ben McDonald .15 .40
50 Rafael Palmeiro .50 1.25
51 Curtis Goodwin .15 .40
52 Vince Coleman .15 .40
53 Tom Gordon .15 .40
54 Mike Macfarlane .15 .40
55 Brian McRae .15 .40
56 Matt Smith .15 .40
57 David Segui .15 .40
58 Paul Wilson .15 .40
59 Bill Pulsipher .15 .40
60 Bobby Bonilla .30 .75
61 Jeff Kent .30 .75
62 Ryan Thompson .15 .40
63 Jason Isringhausen .30 .75
64 Ed Sprague .15 .40
65 Paul Molitor .30 .75
66 Juan Guzman .15 .40
67 Alex Gonzalez .15 .40
68 Shawn Green .30 .75
69 Mark Portugal .15 .40
70 Barry Bonds 2.00 5.00
71 Robby Thompson .15 .40
72 Royce Clayton .15 .40
73 Ricky Bottalico .15 .40
74 Doug Jones .15 .40
75 Darren Daulton .30 .75
76 Gregg Jefferies .15 .40
77 Scott Cooper .15 .40
78 Nomar Garciaparra 1.25 3.00
79 Ken Ryan .15 .40
80 Mike Greenwell .15 .40
81 LaTroy Hawkins .15 .40
82 Rich Becker .15 .40
83 Scott Erickson .15 .40
84 Pedro Munoz .15 .40
85 Kirby Puckett .75 2.00
86 Orlando Merced .15 .40
87 Jeff King .15 .40
88 Midre Cummings .15 .40
89 Bernard Gilkey .15 .40
90 Ray Lankford .30 .75
91 Todd Zeile .15 .40
92 Alan Benes .15 .40
93 Bret Wagner .15 .40
94 Rene Arocha .15 .40
95 Cecil Fielder .30 .75
96 Alan Trammell .30 .75
97 Tony Phillips .15 .40
98 Junior Felix .15 .40
99 Brian Harper .15 .40
100 Greg Vaughn .15 .40
101 Ricky Bones .15 .40
102 Walt Weiss .15 .40
103 Lance Painter .15 .40
104 Roberto Mejia .15 .40
105 Andres Galarraga .30 .75
106 Todd Van Poppel .15 .40
107 Ben Grieve .15 .40
108 Brent Gates .15 .40
109 Jason Giambi .50 1.25
110 Ruben Sierra .30 .75
111 Terry Steinbach .15 .40
112 Chris Hammond .15 .40
113 Charles Johnson .30 .75
114 Jesus Tavarez .15 .40
115 Gary Sheffield .30 .75
116 Chuck Carr .15 .40
117 Bobby Ayala .15 .40
118 Randy Johnson .75 2.00
119 Edgar Martinez .50 1.25
120 Alex Rodriguez 2.00 5.00
121 Kevin Foster .15 .40
122 Kevin Roberson .15 .40
123 Sammy Sosa .75 2.00
124 Steve Trachsel .15 .40
125 Eduardo Perez .15 .40
126 Tim Salmon .50 1.25
127 Todd Greene .15 .40
128 Jorge Fabregas .15 .40
129 Mark Langston .15 .40
130 Mitch Williams .15 .40
131 Raul Casanova .15 .40
132 Mel Nieves .15 .40
133 Andy Benes .15 .40
134 Dustin Hermanson .15 .40
135 Trevor Hoffman .30 .75
136 Mark Grudzielanek .50 1.25
137 Ugueth Urbina .15 .40
138 Moises Alou .30 .75
139 Roberto Kelly .15 .40
140 Rondell White .30 .75
141 Paul O'Neill .50 1.25
142 Jimmy Key .30 .75
143 Jack McDowell .15 .40
144 Ruben Rivera .15 .40
145 Don Mattingly 2.00 5.00
146 John Wetteland .30 .75
147 Tom Glavine .50 1.25
148 Marquis Grissom .30 .75
149 Javier Lopez .30 .75
150 Fred McGriff .50 1.25
151 Greg Maddux 1.25 3.00
152 Chris Sabo .15 .40
153 Ray Durham .30 .75
154 Robin Ventura .30 .75
155 Jim Abbott .50 1.25
156 Jimmy Hurst .15 .40
157 Tim Raines .30 .75
158 Dennis Martinez .30 .75
159 Kenny Lofton .30 .75
160 Dave Winfield .30 .75
161 Manny Ramirez .50 1.25
162 Jim Thome .50 1.25
163 Barry Larkin .50 1.25
164 Bret Boone .30 .75
165 Deion Sanders .50 1.25
166 Ron Gant .30 .75
167 Benito Santiago .30 .75
168 Hideo Nomo 2.00 5.00
169 Billy Ashley .15 .40
170 Roger Cedeno .15 .40
171 Ismael Valdes .15 .40
172 Eric Karros .30 .75
173 Rusty Greer .30 .75
174 Rick Helling .15 .40
175 Nolan Ryan TRIB 3.00 8.00
176 Dean Palmer .30 .75
177 Phil Plantier .15 .40
178 Darryl Kile .30 .75
179 Derek Bell .15 .40
180 Doug Drabek .15 .40
181 Craig Biggio .50 1.25
182 Kevin Brown .30 .75
183 Harold Baines .30 .75
184 Jeffrey Hammonds .15 .40
185 Chris Hoiles .15 .40
186 Mike Mussina .50 1.25
187 Bob Hamelin .15 .40
188 Jeff Montgomery .15 .40
189 Michael Tucker .15 .40
190 George Brett TRIB 2.00 5.00
191 Edgardo Alfonzo .15 .40
192 Brett Butler .30 .75
193 Bobby Jones .15 .40
194 Todd Hundley .15 .40
195 Bret Saberhagen .30 .75
196 Pat Hentgen .15 .40
197 Roberto Alomar .50 1.25
198 David Cone .30 .75
199 Carlos Delgado .30 .75
200 Joe Carter .30 .75
201 Wm. VanLandingham .15 .40
202 Rod Beck .15 .40
203 J.R. Phillips .15 .40
204 Darren Lewis .15 .40
205 Matt Williams .30 .75
206 Lenny Dykstra .30 .75
207 Dave Hollins .15 .40
208 Mike Schmidt TRIB 1.25 3.00
209 Charlie Hayes .15 .40
210 Mo Vaughn .30 .75
211 Jose Malave .15 .40
212 Roger Clemens 1.50 4.00
213 Jose Canseco .50 1.25
214 Mark Whiten .15 .40
215 Marty Cordova .15 .40
216 Rick Aguilera .15 .40
217 Kevin Tapani .15 .40
218 Chuck Knoblauch .30 .75
219 Al Martin .15 .40
220 Jay Bell .30 .75
221 Carlos Garcia .15 .40
222 Freddy Adrian Garcia .15 .40
223 Jon Lieber .15 .40
224 Danny Jackson .15 .40
225 Ozzie Smith 1.25 3.00
226 Brian Jordan .30 .75
227 Ken Hill .15 .40
228 Scott Cooper .15 .40
229 Chad Curtis .15 .40
230 Lou Whitaker .30 .75
231 Kirk Gibson .30 .75
232 Travis Fryman .30 .75
233 Jose Valentin .15 .40
234 Dave Nilsson .15 .40
235 Cal Eldred .15 .40
236 Matt Mieske .15 .40
237 Bill Swift .15 .40
238 Marvin Freeman .15 .40
239 Jason Bates .15 .40
240 Larry Walker .30 .75
241 Dave Nied .15 .40
242 Dante Bichette .30 .75
243 Dennis Eckersley .30 .75
244 Todd Stottlemyre .15 .40
245 Rickey Henderson .75 2.00
246 Geronimo Berroa .15 .40
247 Mark McGwire 2.00 5.00
248 Quilvio Veras .15 .40
249 Terry Pendleton .30 .75
250 Andre Dawson .30 .75
251 Jeff Conine .30 .75
252 Kurt Abbott .15 .40
253 Jay Buhner .30 .75
254 Darren Bragg .15 .40
255 Ken Griffey Jr. 1.50 4.00
256 Tino Martinez .50 1.25
257 Mark Grace .50 1.25
258 Ryne Sandberg TRIB 1.25 3.00
259 Randy Myers .15 .40
260 Howard Johnson .15 .40
261 Lee Smith .30 .75
262 J.T. Snow .30 .75
263 Chili Davis .30 .75
264 Chuck Finley .30 .75
265 Eddie Williams .15 .40
266 Joey Hamilton .15 .40
267 Ken Caminiti .30 .75
268 Andujar Cedeno .15 .40
269 Steve Finley .30 .75
270 Tony Gwynn 1.00 2.50

1995 Upper Deck Steal of a Deal

COMPLETE SET (15) 30.00 80.00
SER.1 STATED ODDS 1:34 ALL PACKS
SD1 Mike Piazza 5.00 12.00
SD2 Fred McGriff 2.00 5.00
SD3 Kenny Lofton 1.25 3.00
SD4 Jose Oliva .60 1.50
SD5 Jeff Bagwell 2.00 5.00
SD6 R.Alomar 2.00 5.00
J.Carter
SD7 Steve Karsay .60 1.50
SD8 Ozzie Smith 5.00 12.00
SD9 Dennis Eckersley 1.25 3.00
SD10 Jose Canseco 2.00 5.00
SD11 Carlos Baerga .60 1.50
SD12 Cecil Fielder 1.25 3.00
SD13 Don Mattingly 8.00 20.00
SD14 Bret Boone 1.25 3.00
SD15 Michael Jordan 8.00 20.00

1995 Upper Deck Trade Exchange

COMPLETE SET (5) 2.50 5.00
RANDOM INSERTS IN SERIES 2 PACKS
TC1 Orel Hershiser .60 1.50
TC2 Terry Pendleton .40 1.00
TC3 Benito Santiago .60 1.50
TC4 Kevin Brown .75 2.00
TC5 Gregg Jefferies .40 1.00

1995 Upper Deck/GTS Phone Cards

Upper Deck joined with GTS (Global Telecommunication Solutions Inc.) to produce a series of MLB player phone cards. Each card contained 15 minutes of long distance phone time and was priced at $12.00. Card numbers 1-5 were released March 1, April 15, and May 15, for a total of fifteen cards. Moreover, other cards were to be released later in the year. The cards are unnumbered and checklisted below in alphabetical order in two sections--the first five that were released (MLB1-MLB5) and then the other ten cards (MLB6-MLB15).

COMPLETE SET (15) 60.00 120.00
MLB1 Tony Gwynn 5.00 12.00
MLB2 Fred McGriff 1.25 3.00
MLB3 Frank Thomas 2.50 6.00
MLB4 Ken Griffey Jr. 6.00 15.00
MLB5 Cecil Fielder .75 2.00
MLB6 Roberto Alomar 2.00 5.00
MLB7 Jeff Bagwell 2.50 6.00
MLB8 Barry Bonds 4.00 10.00
MLB9 Roger Clemens 5.00 12.00
MLB10 David Justice 2.00 5.00
MLB11 Don Mattingly 5.00 12.00
MLB12 Kirby Puckett 3.00 8.00
MLB13 Cal Ripken 10.00 25.00
MLB14 Gary Sheffield 2.50 6.00
MLB15 Ozzie Smith 4.00 10.00

1995 Upper Deck Mantle Metallic Impressions

This eight-card set features vintage photos of career highlights of Mickey Mantle printed on metal cards. The backs carry information about the various stages of his career with a small stamp-like photo. The set was distributed in a collector's edition metal box containing a Certificate of Authenticity.

COMPLETE SET (10) 10.00 25.00
COMMON CARD (1-10) 1.25 3.00

1995 Upper Deck Sonic Heroes of Baseball

These standard-size cards were given out in three-card cello packs to customers who purchased a combo meal at participating Sonic Restaurants. The fronts feature black-and-white player photos with white borders. The words "Exclusive Edition" are printed in a blue bar at the top, with the player's name in a red bar directly below. The team name and the player's position appear on the bottom. The backs carry stats, career highlights, and sponsor and producer logos.

COMPLETE SET (20) 2.50 6.00
1 Whitey Ford .10 .30
2 Cy Young .15 .40
3 Babe Ruth .60 1.50
4 Lou Gehrig .30 .75
5 Mike Schmidt .15 .40
6 Nolan Ryan .60 1.50
7 Robin Yount .15 .40
8 Gary Carter .07 .20
9 Tom Seaver .10 .30
10 Reggie Jackson .10 .30
11 Bob Gibson .07 .20
12 Gil Hodges .10 .30
13 Monte Irvin .02 .10
14 Minnie Minoso .02 .10
15 Willie Stargell .07 .20
16 Al Kaline .07 .20
17 Joe Jackson .20 .50
18 Walter Johnson .15 .40
19 Ty Cobb .20 .50
20 Satchel Paige .10 .30

1995 Upper Deck Sports Drink Jackson

Upper Deck and Energy Foods have joined together to produce the Upper Deck Authentic Sports Drink. The drink was available in four flavors (lemon lime, madarin orange, fruit cooler and tropical berry), and each package included one of three Reggie Jackson Heroes cards. Six-bottle packages retail for $2.00. The cards are similar to those that were included with Reggie Candy Bars in 1993, and come with and without a gold facsimile autograph. The cards are numbered on the back "X of 3."

COMPLETE SET (3) 2.00 5.00
COMMON CARD (1-3) .80 2.00

1996 Upper Deck

The 1996 Upper Deck set was issued in two series of 240 cards, and a 30 card update set, for a total of 510 cards. The cards were distributed in 10-card packs with a suggested retail price of $1.99, and 28 packs were contained in each box. Upper Deck issued 15,000 factory sets (containing all 510 cards) at season's end. In addition to being included in factory sets, the 30-card Update sets (U481-U510) were also available via mail through a wrapper exchange program. The attractive fronts of each basic card feature a full-bleed photo above a bronze foil bar that includes the player's name, team and position in a white oval. Subsets include Young at Heart (100-117), Beat the Odds (145-153), Postseason Checklist (218-222), Best of a Generation (370-387), Strange But True (415-423) and Managerial Salute Checklists (476-480). The only Rookie Card of note is Livan Hernandez.

COMPLETE SET (480) 15.00 40.00
COMP.FACT.SET (510) 25.00 60.00
COMPLETE SERIES 1 (240) 8.00 20.00
COMPLETE SERIES 2 (240) 8.00 20.00
COMMON CARD (1-480) .10 .30
COMP.UPDATE SET (30) 10.00 20.00
COMMON UPDATE (481U-510U) .20 .50
ONE UPDATE SET PER FACTORY SET
ONE UPDATE SET VIA SER.2 WRAP.OFFER
FACTORY SET PRINT RUN 15,000 SETS
SUBSET CARDS HALF VALUE OF BASE CARDS
1 Cal Ripken 2131 1.50 4.00
2 Eddie Murray 3000 Hits .20 .50
3 Mark Wohlers .10 .30
4 David Justice .10 .30
5 Chipper Jones .30 .75
6 Javier Lopez .10 .30
7 Mark Lemke .10 .30
8 Marquis Grissom .10 .30

9 Tom Glavine .20 .50
10 Greg Maddux .50 1.25
11 Manny Alexander .10 .30
12 Curtis Goodwin .10 .30
13 Scott Erickson .10 .30
14 Chris Hoiles .10 .30
15 Rafael Palmeiro .20 .50
16 Rick Krivda .10 .30
17 Jeff Manto .10 .30
18 Mo Vaughn .10 .30
19 Tim Wakefield .10 .30
20 Roger Clemens .60 1.50
21 Tim Naehring .10 .30
22 Troy O'Leary .10 .30
23 Mike Greenwell .10 .30
24 Stan Belinda .10 .30
25 John Valentin .10 .30
26 J.T. Snow .10 .30
27 Gary DiSarcina .10 .30
28 Mark Langston .10 .30
29 Brian Anderson .10 .30
30 Jim Edmonds .10 .30
31 Garret Anderson .10 .30
32 Orlando Palmeiro .10 .30
33 Brian McRae .10 .30
34 Kevin Foster .10 .30
35 Sammy Sosa .30 .75
36 Todd Zeile .10 .30
37 Jim Bullinger .10 .30
38 Luis Gonzalez .10 .30
39 Lyle Mouton .10 .30
40 Ray Durham .10 .30
41 Ozzie Guillen .10 .30
42 Alex Fernandez .10 .30
43 Brian Keyser .10 .30
44 Robin Ventura .10 .30
45 Reggie Sanders .10 .30
46 Pete Schourek .10 .30
47 John Smiley .10 .30
48 Jeff Brantley .10 .30
49 Thomas Howard .10 .30
50 Bret Boone .10 .30
51 Kevin Jarvis .10 .30
52 Jeff Branson .10 .30
53 Carlos Baerga .10 .30
54 Jim Thome .20 .50
55 Manny Ramirez .20 .50
56 Omar Vizquel .20 .50
57 Jose Mesa .10 .30
58 Julian Tavarez UER .10 .30
59 Orel Hershiser .10 .30
60 Larry Walker .10 .30
61 Bret Saberhagen .10 .30
62 Vinny Castilla .10 .30
63 Eric Young .10 .30
64 Bryan Rekar .10 .30
65 Andres Galarraga .10 .30
66 Steve Reed .10 .30
67 Chad Curtis .10 .30
68 Bobby Higginson .10 .30
69 Phil Nevin .10 .30
70 Cecil Fielder .10 .30
71 Felipe Lira .10 .30
72 Chris Gomez .10 .30
73 Charles Johnson .10 .30
74 Quilvio Veras .10 .30
75 Jeff Conine .10 .30
76 John Burkett .10 .30
77 Grog Colbrunn .10 .30
78 Terry Pendleton .10 .30
79 Shane Reynolds .10 .30
80 Jeff Bagwell .20 .50
81 Orlando Miller .10 .30
82 Mike Hampton .10 .30
83 James Mouton .10 .30
84 Brian L. Hunter .10 .30
85 Derek Bell .10 .30
86 Kevin Appier .10 .30
87 Joe Vitiello .10 .30
88 Wally Joyner .10 .30
89 Michael Tucker .10 .30
90 Johnny Damon .20 .50
91 Jon Nunnally .10 .30
92 Jason Jacome .10 .30
93 Chad Fonville .10 .30
94 Chan Ho Park .10 .30
95 Hideo Nomo .30 .75
96 Ismael Valdes .10 .30
97 Greg Gagne .10 .30
98 Diamondbacks-Devil Rays .30 .75
99 Raul Mondesi .10 .30
100 Dave Winfield YH .10 .30
101 Dennis Eckersley YH .10 .30
102 Andre Dawson YH .10 .30
103 Dennis Martinez YH .10 .30
104 Lance Parrish YH .10 .30
105 Eddie Murray YH .20 .50
106 Alan Trammell YH .10 .30
107 Lou Whitaker YH .10 .30
108 Ozzie Smith YH .30 .75
109 Paul Molitor YH .10 .30
110 Rickey Henderson YH .20 .50
111 Tim Raines YH .10 .30
112 Harold Baines YH .10 .30
113 Lee Smith YH .10 .30
114 Fernando Valenzuela YH .10 .30
115 Cal Ripken YH .50 1.25
116 Tony Gwynn YH .20 .50
117 Wade Boggs .20 .50
118 Todd Hollandsworth .10 .30
119 Dave Nilsson .10 .30
120 Jose Valentin .10 .30
121 Steve Sparks .10 .30
122 Chuck Carr .10 .30
123 John Jaha .10 .30
124 Scott Karl .10 .30
125 Chuck Knoblauch .10 .30
126 Brad Radke .10 .30
127 Pat Meares .10 .30
128 Ron Coomer .10 .30
129 Pedro Munoz .10 .30
130 Kirby Puckett .30 .75
131 David Segui .10 .30
132 Mark Grudzielanek .10 .30
133 Mike Lansing .10 .30
134 Sean Berry .10 .30
135 Rondell White .10 .30
136 Pedro Martinez .20 .50
137 Carl Everett .10 .30
138 Dave Mlicki .10 .30
139 Bill Pulsipher .10 .30
140 Jason Isringhausen .10 .30
141 Rico Brogna .10 .30
142 Edgardo Alfonzo .10 .30
143 Jeff Kent .10 .30
144 Andy Pettitte .20 .50
145 Mike Piazza BO .30 .75
146 Cliff Floyd BO .10 .30
147 Jason Isringhausen BO .10 .30
148 Tim Wakefield BO .10 .30
149 Chipper Jones BO .20 .50
150 Hideo Nomo BO .20 .50
151 Mark McGwire BO .40 1.00
152 Ron Gant BO .10 .30
153 Gary Gaetti BO .10 .30
154 Don Mattingly .75 2.00
155 Paul O'Neill .20 .50
156 Derek Jeter .75 2.00
157 Joe Girardi .10 .30
158 Ruben Sierra .10 .30
159 Jorge Posada .20 .50
160 Geronimo Berroa .10 .30
161 Steve Ontiveros .10 .30
162 George Williams .10 .30
163 Doug Johns .10 .30
164 Ariel Prieto .10 .30
165 Scott Brosius .10 .30
166 Mike Bordick .10 .30
167 Tyler Green .10 .30
168 Mickey Morandini .10 .30
169 Darren Daulton .10 .30
170 Gregg Jefferies .10 .30
171 Jim Eisenreich .10 .30
172 Heathcliff Slocumb .10 .30
173 Kevin Stocker .10 .30
174 Esteban Loaiza .10 .30
175 Jeff King .10 .30
176 Mark Johnson .10 .30
177 Denny Neagle .10 .30
178 Orlando Merced .10 .30
179 Carlos Garcia .10 .30
180 Brian Jordan .10 .30
181 Mike Morgan .10 .30
182 Mark Petkovsek .10 .30
183 Bernard Gilkey .10 .30
184 John Mabry .10 .30
185 Tom Henke .10 .30
186 Glenn Dishman .10 .30
187 Andy Ashby .10 .30
188 Bip Roberts .10 .30
189 Melvin Nieves .10 .30
190 Ken Caminiti .10 .30
191 Brad Ausmus .10 .30
192 Deion Sanders .20 .50
193 Jamie Brewington RC .10 .30
194 Glenallen Hill .10 .30
195 Barry Bonds .75 2.00
196 Wm. Van Landingham .10 .30
197 Mark Carreon .10 .30
198 Royce Clayton .10 .30
199 Joey Cora .10 .30
200 Ken Griffey Jr. .60 1.50
201 Jay Buhner .10 .30
202 Alex Rodriguez .60 1.50
203 Norm Charlton .10 .30
204 Andy Benes .10 .30
205 Edgar Martinez .20 .50
206 Juan Gonzalez .10 .30
207 Will Clark .20 .50
208 Kevin Gross .10 .30
209 Roger Pavlik .10 .30
210 Ivan Rodriguez .20 .50
211 Rusty Greer .10 .30
212 Angel Martinez .10 .30
213 Tomas Perez .10 .30
214 Alex Gonzalez .10 .30
215 Joe Carter .10 .30
216 Shawn Green .10 .30
217 Edwin Hurtado .10 .30
218 E.Martinez .10 .30
T.Pena CL
219 C.Jones .20 .50
B.Larkin CL
220 Orel Hershiser CL .10 .30
221 Mike Devereaux CL .10 .30
222 Tom Glavine CL .10 .30
223 Karim Garcia .10 .30
224 Arquimedez Pozo .10 .30
225 Billy Wagner .10 .30
226 John Wasdin .10 .30
227 Jeff Suppan .10 .30
228 Steve Gibralter .10 .30
229 Jimmy Haynes .10 .30
230 Ruben Rivera .10 .30
231 Chris Snopek .10 .30
232 Alex Ochoa .10 .30
233 Shannon Stewart .10 .30
234 Quinton McCracken .10 .30
235 Trey Beamon .10 .30
236 Billy McMillon .10 .30
237 Steve Cox .10 .30
238 George Arias .10 .30
239 Yamil Benitez .10 .30
240 Todd Greene .10 .30
241 Jason Kendall .10 .30
242 Brooks Kieschnick .10 .30
243 Osvaldo Fernandez RC .10 .30
244 Livan Hernandez RC .40 1.00
245 Rey Ordonez .10 .30
246 Mike Grace RC .10 .30
247 Jay Canizaro .10 .30
248 Bob Wolcott .10 .30
249 Jermaine Dye .10 .30
250 Jason Schmidt .20 .50
251 Mike Sweeney RC .40 1.00
252 Marcus Jensen .10 .30
253 Mendy Lopez .10 .30
254 Wilton Guerrero RC .10 .30
255 Paul Wilson .10 .30
256 Edgar Renteria .10 .30
257 Richard Hidalgo .10 .30
258 Bob Abreu .30 .75
259 Robert Smith RC .10 .30
260 Sal Fasano .10 .30
261 Enrique Wilson .10 .30
262 Rich Hunter RC .10 .30
263 Sergio Nunez .10 .30
264 Dan Serafini .10 .30
265 David Doster .10 .30
266 Ryan McGuire .10 .30
267 Scott Spiezio .10 .30
268 Rafael Orellano .10 .30
269 Steve Avery .10 .30
270 Fred McGriff .20 .50
271 John Smoltz .20 .50
272 Ryan Klesko .10 .30
273 Jeff Blauser .10 .30
274 Brad Clontz .10 .30
275 Roberto Alomar .20 .50
276 B.J. Surhoff .10 .30
277 Jeffrey Hammonds .10 .30
278 Brady Anderson .10 .30
279 Bobby Bonilla .10 .30
280 Cal Ripken 1.00 2.50
281 Mike Mussina .20 .50
282 Wil Cordero .10 .30
283 Mike Stanley .10 .30
284 Aaron Sele .10 .30
285 Jose Canseco .20 .50
286 Tom Gordon .10 .30
287 Heathcliff Slocumb .10 .30
288 Lee Smith .10 .30
289 Troy Percival .10 .30
290 Tim Salmon .20 .50
291 Chuck Finley .10 .30
292 Jim Abbott .20 .50
293 Chili Davis .10 .30
294 Steve Trachsel .10 .30
295 Mark Grace .20 .50
296 Rey Sanchez .10 .30
297 Scott Servais .10 .30
298 Jaime Navarro .10 .30
299 Frank Castillo .10 .30
300 Frank Thomas .30 .75
301 Jason Bere .10 .30
302 Danny Tartabull .10 .30
303 Darren Lewis .10 .30
304 Roberto Hernandez .10 .30
305 Tony Phillips .10 .30
306 Wilson Alvarez .10 .30
307 Jose Rijo .10 .30
308 Hal Morris .10 .30
309 Mark Portugal .10 .30
310 Barry Larkin .20 .50
311 Dave Burba .10 .30
312 Eddie Taubensee .10 .30
313 Sandy Alomar Jr. .10 .30
314 Dennis Martinez .10 .30
315 Albert Belle .10 .30
316 Eddie Murray .30 .75
317 Charles Nagy .10 .30
318 Chad Ogea .10 .30
319 Kenny Lofton .10 .30
320 Dante Bichette .10 .30
321 Armando Reynoso .10 .30
322 Walt Weiss .10 .30
323 Ellis Burks .10 .30
324 Kevin Ritz .10 .30
325 Bill Swift .10 .30
326 Jason Bates .10 .30
327 Tony Clark .10 .30
328 Travis Fryman .10 .30
329 Mark Parent .10 .30
330 Alan Trammell .10 .30
331 C.J. Nitkowski .10 .30
332 Jose Lima .10 .30
333 Phil Plantier .10 .30
334 Kurt Abbott .10 .30
335 Andre Dawson .10 .30
336 Chris Hammond .10 .30
337 Robb Nen .10 .30
338 Pat Rapp .10 .30
339 Al Leiter .10 .30
340 Gary Sheffield .10 .30
341 Todd Jones .10 .30
342 Doug Drabek .10 .30
343 Greg Swindell .10 .30
344 Tony Eusebio .10 .30
345 Craig Biggio .20 .50
346 Darryl Kile .10 .30
347 Mike Macfarlane .10 .30
348 Jeff Montgomery .10 .30
349 Chris Haney .10 .30
350 Bip Roberts .10 .30
351 Tom Goodwin .10 .30
352 Mark Gubicza .10 .30
353 Joe Randa .10 .30
354 Ramon Martinez .10 .30
355 Eric Karros .10 .30
356 Delino DeShields .10 .30
357 Brett Butler .10 .30
358 Todd Worrell .10 .30
359 Mike Blowers .10 .30
360 Mike Piazza .50 1.25
361 Ben McDonald .10 .30
362 Ricky Bones .10 .30
363 Greg Vaughn .10 .30
364 Matt Mieske .10 .30
365 Kevin Seitzer .10 .30
366 Jeff Cirillo .10 .30
367 LaTroy Hawkins .10 .30
368 Frank Rodriguez .10 .30
369 Rick Aguilera .10 .30
370 Roberto Alomar BG .10 .30
371 Albert Belle BG .10 .30
372 Wade Boggs BG .10 .30
373 Barry Bonds BG .40 1.00
374 Roger Clemens BG .30 .75
375 Dennis Eckersley BG .10 .30
376 Ken Griffey Jr. BG .40 1.00
377 Tony Gwynn BG .20 .50
378 Rickey Henderson BG .20 .50
379 Greg Maddux BG .30 .75
380 Fred McGriff BG .10 .30
381 Paul Molitor BG .10 .30
382 Eddie Murray BG .20 .50
383 Mike Piazza BG .30 .75
384 Kirby Puckett BG .20 .50
385 Cal Ripken BG .50 1.25
386 Ozzie Smith BG .30 .75
387 Frank Thomas BG .20 .50
388 Matt Walbeck .10 .30
389 Dave Stevens .10 .30
390 Marty Cordova .10 .30
391 Darrin Fletcher .10 .30
392 Cliff Floyd .10 .30
393 Mel Rojas .10 .30
394 Shane Andrews .10 .30
395 Moises Alou .10 .30
396 Carlos Perez .10 .30
397 Jeff Fassero .10 .30
398 Bobby Jones .10 .30
399 Todd Hundley .10 .30
400 John Franco .10 .30
401 Jose Vizcaino .10 .30
402 Bernard Gilkey .10 .30
403 Pete Harnisch .10 .30
404 Pat Kelly .10 .30
405 David Cone .10 .30
406 Bernie Williams .20 .50
407 John Wetteland .10 .30
408 Scott Kamieniecki .10 .30
409 Tim Raines .10 .30
410 Wade Boggs .20 .50
411 Terry Steinbach .10 .30
412 Jason Giambi .10 .30
413 Todd Van Poppel .10 .30
414 Pedro Munoz .10 .30
415 Eddie Murray SBT .20 .50
416 Dennis Eckersley SBT .10 .30
417 Bip Roberts SBT .10 .30
418 Glenallen Hill SBT .10 .30
419 John Hudek SBT .10 .30
420 Derek Bell SBT .10 .30
421 Larry Walker SBT .10 .30
422 Greg Maddux SBT .30 .75
423 Ken Caminiti SBT .10 .30
424 Brent Gates .10 .30
425 Mark McGwire .75 2.00
426 Mark Whiten .10 .30
427 Sid Fernandez .10 .30
428 Ricky Bottalico .10 .30
429 Mike Mimbs .10 .30
430 Lenny Dykstra .10 .30
431 Todd Zeile .10 .30
432 Benito Santiago .10 .30
433 Danny Miceli .10 .30
434 Al Martin .10 .30
435 Jay Bell .10 .30
436 Charlie Hayes .10 .30
437 Mike Kingery .10 .30
438 Paul Wagner .10 .30
439 Tom Pagnozzi .10 .30
440 Ozzie Smith .50 1.25
441 Ray Lankford .10 .30
442 Dennis Eckersley .10 .30
443 Ron Gant .10 .30
444 Alan Benes .10 .30
445 Rickey Henderson .30 .75
446 Jody Reed .10 .30
447 Trevor Hoffman .10 .30
448 Andujar Cedeno .10 .30
449 Steve Finley .10 .30
450 Tony Gwynn .40 1.00
451 Joey Hamilton .10 .30
452 Mark Leiter .10 .30
453 Rod Beck .10 .30
454 Kirt Manwaring .10 .30
455 Matt Williams .10 .30
456 Robby Thompson .10 .30
457 Shawon Dunston .10 .30
458 Russ Davis .10 .30
459 Paul Sorrento .10 .30
460 Randy Johnson .30 .75
461 Chris Bosio .10 .30
462 Luis Sojo .10 .30
463 Sterling Hitchcock .10 .30
464 Benji Gil .10 .30
465 Mickey Tettleton .10 .30
466 Mark McLemore .10 .30
467 Darryl Hamilton .10 .30
468 Ken Hill .10 .30
469 Dean Palmer .10 .30
470 Carlos Delgado .10 .30
471 Ed Sprague .10 .30
472 Otis Nixon .10 .30
473 Pat Hentgen .10 .30
474 Juan Guzman .10 .30
475 John Olerud .10 .30
476 Buck Showalter CL .10 .30
477 Bobby Cox CL .10 .30
478 Tommy Lasorda CL .10 .30
479 Buck Showalter CL .10 .30
480 Sparky Anderson CL .10 .30
481U Randy Myers .20 .50
482U Kent Mercker .20 .50
483U David Wells .30 .75
484U Kevin Mitchell .20 .50
485U Randy Velarde .20 .50
486U Ryne Sandberg 1.50 4.00
487U Doug Jones .20 .50
488U Terry Adams .20 .50
489U Kevin Tapani .20 .50
490U Harold Baines .30 .75
491U Eric Davis .30 .75
492U Julio Franco .30 .75
493U Jack McDowell .20 .50
494U Devon White .30 .75
495U Kevin Brown .30 .75
496U Rick Wilkins .20 .50
497U Sean Berry .20 .50
498U Keith Lockhart .20 .50
499U Mark Loretta .20 .50
500U Paul Molitor .30 .75
501U Roberto Kelly .20 .50
502U Lance Johnson .20 .50
503U Tino Martinez .50 1.25
504U Kenny Rogers .30 .75
505U Todd Stottlemyre .20 .50
506U Gary Gaetti .30 .75
507U Royce Clayton .20 .50
508U Andy Benes .20 .50
509U Wally Joyner .30 .75
510U Erik Hanson .20 .50
P100 Ken Griffey Jr Promo 1.50 4.00

1996 Upper Deck Blue Chip Prospects

COMPLETE SET (20) 40.00 100.00
SER.1 STATED ODDS 1:72
BC1 Hideo Nomo 4.00 10.00
BC2 Johnny Damon 2.50 6.00
BC3 Jason Isringhausen 1.50 4.00
BC4 Bill Pulsipher 1.50 4.00
BC5 Marty Cordova 1.50 4.00
BC6 Michael Tucker 1.50 4.00
BC7 John Wasdin 1.50 4.00
BC8 Karim Garcia 1.50 4.00
BC9 Ruben Rivera 1.50 4.00
BC10 Chipper Jones 4.00 10.00
BC11 Billy Wagner 1.50 4.00
BC12 Brooks Kieschnick 1.50 4.00
BC13 Alan Benes 1.50 4.00
BC14 Roger Cedeno 1.50 4.00
BC15 Alex Rodriguez 8.00 20.00
BC16 Jason Schmidt 2.50 6.00
BC17 Derek Jeter 12.00 30.00
BC18 Brian L.Hunter 1.50 4.00
BC19 Garret Anderson 1.50 4.00
BC20 Manny Ramirez 2.50 6.00

1996 Upper Deck Diamond Destiny

COMPLETE SET (40) 25.00 60.00
ONE PER UD TECH RETAIL PACK
*GOLD: 3X TO 8X BASIC DESTINY
GOLD ODDS 1:143 UD TECH RETAIL PACKS
*SILVER: 1X TO 2.5X BASIC DESTINY
SILVER ODDS 1:35 UD TECH RETAIL PACKS
DD1 Chipper Jones 1.00 2.50
DD2 Fred McGriff .60 1.50
DD3 John Smoltz .60 1.50
DD4 Ryan Klesko .40 1.00
DD5 Greg Maddux 1.50 4.00
DD6 Cal Ripken 3.00 8.00
DD7 Roberto Alomar .60 1.50
DD8 Eddie Murray .60 1.50
DD9 Brady Anderson .40 1.00
DD10 Mo Vaughn .40 1.00
DD11 Roger Clemens 1.25 3.00
DD12 Darin Erstad .40 1.00
DD13 Sammy Sosa 1.00 2.50
DD14 Frank Thomas 1.00 2.50
DD15 Barry Larkin .60 1.50
DD16 Albert Belle .40 1.00
DD17 Manny Ramirez .60 1.50
DD18 Kenny Lofton .40 1.00
DD19 Dante Bichette .40 1.00
DD20 Gary Sheffield .40 1.00
DD21 Jeff Bagwell .60 1.50
DD22 Hideo Nomo 1.00 2.50
DD23 Mike Piazza 1.00 2.50
DD24 Kirby Puckett 1.00 2.50
DD25 Paul Molitor 1.00 2.50
DD26 Chuck Knoblauch .40 1.00
DD27 Wade Boggs .60 1.50
DD28 Derek Jeter 2.50 6.00
DD29 Rey Ordonez .40 1.00
DD30 Mark McGwire 1.50 4.00
DD31 Ozzie Smith 1.25 3.00
DD32 Tony Gwynn 1.00 2.50
DD33 Barry Bonds 1.50 4.00
DD34 Matt Williams .40 1.00
DD35 Ken Griffey Jr. 2.00 5.00
DD36 Jay Buhner .40 1.00
DD37 Randy Johnson 1.00 2.50
DD38 Alex Rodriguez 1.25 3.00
DD39 Juan Gonzalez .40 1.00
DD40 Joe Carter .40 1.00

1996 Upper Deck Future Stock Prospects

COMPLETE SET (20) 3.00 8.00
SER.1 STATED ODDS 1:6 HOB/RET
FS1 George Arias .40 1.00
FS2 Brian Barber .40 1.00
FS3 Trey Beamon .40 1.00
FS4 Yamil Benitez .40 1.00
FS5 Jamie Brewington .40 1.00
FS6 Tony Clark .40 1.00
FS7 Steve Cox .40 1.00
FS8 Carlos Delgado .40 1.00
FS9 Chad Fonville .40 1.00
FS10 Alex Ochoa .40 1.00
FS11 Curtis Goodwin .40 1.00
FS12 Todd Greene .40 1.00
FS13 Jimmy Haynes .40 1.00
FS14 Quinton McCracken .40 1.00
FS15 Billy McMillon .40 1.00
FS16 Chan Ho Park .40 1.00
FS17 Arquimedez Pozo .40 1.00
FS18 Chris Snopek .40 1.00
FS19 Shannon Stewart .40 1.00
FS20 Jeff Suppan .40 1.00

1996 Upper Deck Gameface

COMPLETE SET (10) 5.00 12.00
ONE PER SPECIAL SER.2 RETAIL PACK
GF1 Ken Griffey Jr. .60 1.50
GF2 Frank Thomas .30 .75
GF3 Barry Bonds .75 2.00
GF4 Albert Belle .10 .30
GF5 Cal Ripken 1.00 2.50
GF6 Mike Piazza .50 1.25
GF7 Chipper Jones .30 .75
GF8 Matt Williams .10 .30
GF9 Hideo Nomo .30 .75
GF10 Greg Maddux .50 1.25

1996 Upper Deck Hot Commodities

COMPLETE SET (20) 20.00 50.00
SER.2 STATED ODDS 1:36 HOB/RET/ANCO
HC1 Ken Griffey Jr. 5.00 12.00
HC2 Hideo Nomo 1.50 4.00
HC3 Roberto Alomar 1.00 2.50
HC4 Paul Wilson .60 1.50
HC5 Albert Belle .60 1.50
HC6 Manny Ramirez 1.00 2.50
HC7 Kirby Puckett 1.50 4.00
HC8 Johnny Damon 1.00 2.50
HC9 Randy Johnson 1.50 4.00
HC10 Greg Maddux 2.50 6.00
HC11 Chipper Jones 1.50 4.00
HC12 Barry Bonds 2.50 6.00
HC13 Mo Vaughn .60 1.50
HC14 Mike Piazza 1.50 4.00
HC15 Cal Ripken 5.00 12.00
HC16 Tim Salmon .60 1.50
HC17 Sammy Sosa 1.50 4.00
HC18 Kenny Lofton .60 1.50
HC19 Tony Gwynn 1.50 4.00
HC20 Frank Thomas 1.50 4.00

1996 Upper Deck V.J. Lovero Showcase

COMPLETE SET (19) 10.00 25.00
SER.2 STATED ODDS 1:6 HOB/RET,1:3 ANCO
VJ1 Jim Abbott .50 1.25
VJ2 Hideo Nomo .75 2.00
VJ3 Derek Jeter 2.00 5.00
VJ4 Barry Bonds 2.00 5.00
VJ5 Greg Maddux 1.25 3.00
VJ6 Mark McGwire 2.00 5.00
VJ7 Jose Canseco .50 1.25
VJ8 Ken Caminiti .30 .75
VJ9 Raul Mondesi .30 .75
VJ10 Ken Griffey Jr. 1.50 4.00
VJ11 Jay Buhner .30 .75
VJ12 Randy Johnson .75 2.00
VJ13 Roger Clemens 1.50 4.00
VJ14 Brady Anderson .30 .75
VJ15 Frank Thomas .75 2.00
VJ16 G.And .30 .75
Edmonds
Salmon
VJ17 Mike Piazza 1.25 3.00
VJ18 Dante Bichette .30 .75
VJ19 Tony Gwynn 1.00 2.50

1996 Upper Deck Nomo Highlights

COMPLETE SET (5) 8.00 20.00
COMMON CARD (1-5) 2.00 5.00
SER.2 STATED ODDS 1:24

1996 Upper Deck Power Driven

COMPLETE SET (20) 60.00 120.00
SER.1 STATED ODDS 1:36 HOB/RET
PD1 Albert Belle 1.25 3.00
PD2 Barry Bonds 8.00 20.00
PD3 Jay Buhner 1.25 3.00
PD4 Jose Canseco 2.00 5.00
PD5 Cecil Fielder 1.25 3.00
PD6 Juan Gonzalez 1.25 3.00
PD7 Ken Griffey Jr. 6.00 15.00
PD8 Eric Karros 1.25 3.00
PD9 Fred McGriff 2.00 5.00
PD10 Mark McGwire 8.00 20.00
PD11 Rafael Palmeiro 2.00 5.00
PD12 Mike Piazza 5.00 12.00
PD13 Manny Ramirez 2.00 5.00
PD14 Tim Salmon 2.00 5.00
PD15 Reggie Sanders 1.25 3.00
PD16 Sammy Sosa 3.00 8.00
PD17 Frank Thomas 3.00 8.00
PD18 Mo Vaughn 1.25 3.00
PD19 Larry Walker 1.25 3.00
PD20 Matt Williams 1.25 3.00

1996 Upper Deck Predictor Hobby

COMPLETE SET (60) 25.00 60.00
COMPLETE SERIES 1 (30) 12.50 30.00
COMPLETE SERIES 2 (30) 12.50 30.00
STATED ODDS 1:12 HOBBY
EXPIRATION DATE: 11/18/96
*EXCHANGE: .4X TO 1X BASIC PREDICTOR
ONE EXCH.SET VIA MAIL PER PRED.WINNER
H1 Albert Belle .25 .60
H2 Kenny Lofton .25 .60
H3 Rafael Palmeiro .40 1.00
H4 Ken Griffey Jr. 1.25 3.00
H5 Tim Salmon .40 1.00
H6 Cal Ripken 2.00 5.00
H7 Mark McGwire 1.50 4.00
H8 Frank Thomas .60 1.50
H9 Mo Vaughn .25 .60
H10 AL Player of Month LS W .25 .60
H11 Roger Clemens 1.25 3.00
H12 David Cone .25 .60
H13 Jose Mesa .25 .60
H14 Randy Johnson .60 1.50
H15 Chuck Finley .25 .60
H16 Mike Mussina .40 1.00
H17 Kevin Appier .25 .60
H18 Kenny Rogers .60 1.50
H19 Lee Smith .25 .60
H20 AL Pitcher of Month LS W .25 .60
H21 George Arias .25 .60
H22 Jose Herrera .25 .60
H23 Tony Clark .25 .60
H24 Todd Greene .25 .60
H25 Derek Jeter 1.50 4.00
H26 Arquimedez Pozo .25 .60
H27 Matt Lawton .25 .60
H28 Shannon Stewart .25 .60
H29 Chris Snopek .25 .60
H30 AL Most Rookie Hits LS .25 .60
H31 Jeff Bagwell .40 1.00
H32 Dante Bichette W .25 .60
H33 Barry Bonds 1.50 4.00
H34 Tony Gwynn .75 2.00
H35 Chipper Jones .60 1.50
H36 Eric Karros .25 .60
H37 Barry Larkin .40 1.00
H38 Mike Piazza 1.00 2.50
H39 Matt Williams .25 .60
H40 NL Player of Month LS W .25 .60
H41 Osvaldo Fernandez .25 .60
H42 Tom Glavine .40 1.00
H43 Jason Isringhausen .25 .60
H44 Greg Maddux 1.00 2.50
H45 Pedro Martinez .40 1.00
H46 Hideo Nomo .60 1.50
H47 Pete Schourek .25 .60
H48 Paul Wilson .25 .60
H49 Mark Wohlers .25 .60
H50 NL Pitcher of Month LS W .25 .60
H51 Bob Abreu .60 1.50
H52 Trey Beamon .25 .60
H53 Yamil Benitez .25 .60
H54 Roger Cedeno W .25 .60
H55 Todd Hollandsworth .25 .60
H56 Marvin Benard .25 .60
H57 Jason Kendall .25 .60
H58 Brooks Kieschnick .25 .60
H59 Rey Ordonez .25 .60
H60 NL Most Rookie Hits LS W .25 .60

1996 Upper Deck Predictor Retail

COMPLETE SET (60) 30.00 80.00
COMPLETE SERIES 1 (30) 15.00 40.00
COMPLETE SERIES 2 (30) 15.00 40.00
STATED ODDS 1:12 RETAIL
EXPIRATION DATE: 11/18/96
*EXCHANGE: .4X TO 1X BASIC PREDICTOR
ONE EXCH.SET VIA MAIL PER PRED.WINNER
R1 Albert Belle .25 .60
R2 Jay Buhner W .25 .60
R3 Juan Gonzalez .25 .60
R4 Ken Griffey Jr. 1.25 3.00
R5 Mark McGwire 1.50 4.00
R6 Rafael Palmeiro .40 1.00
R7 Tim Salmon .40 1.00
R8 Frank Thomas .60 1.50
R9 Mo Vaughn .25 .60
R10 AL Monthly HR LS W .25 .60
R11 Albert Belle .25 .60
R12 Jay Buhner .25 .60
R13 Jim Edmonds .25 .60
R14 Cecil Fielder .25 .60
R15 Ken Griffey Jr. 1.25 3.00
R16 Edgar Martinez .40 1.00
R17 Manny Ramirez .40 1.00
R18 Frank Thomas .60 1.50
R19 Mo Vaughn .25 .60
R20 AL Monthly RBI LS W .25 .60
R21 Roberto Alomar .40 1.00
R22 Carlos Baerga .25 .60
R23 Wade Boggs .40 1.00
R24 Ken Griffey Jr. 1.25 3.00
R25 Chuck Knoblauch .25 .60
R26 Kenny Lofton .25 .60
R27 Edgar Martinez .40 1.00
R28 Tim Salmon .40 1.00
R29 Frank Thomas .60 1.50
R30 AL Monthly Batting LS W .25 .60
R31 Dante Bichette .25 .60
R32 Barry Bonds 1.50 4.00
R33 Ron Gant .25 .60
R34 Chipper Jones .60 1.50
R35 Fred McGriff .40 1.00
R36 Mike Piazza 1.00 2.50
R37 Sammy Sosa W .60 1.50
R38 Larry Walker .25 .60
R39 Matt Williams .25 .60
R40 NL Monthly HR LS W .25 .60
R41 Jeff Bagwell .40 1.00
R42 Dante Bichette W .25 .60
R43 Barry Bonds 1.50 4.00
R44 Jeff Conine .25 .60
R45 Andres Galarraga .25 .60
R46 Mike Piazza 1.00 2.50
R47 Reggie Sanders .25 .60
R48 Sammy Sosa .60 1.50
R49 Matt Williams .25 .60
R50 NL Monthly RBI LS W .25 .60
R51 Jeff Bagwell .40 1.00
R52 Derek Bell .25 .60
R53 Dante Bichette .25 .60
R54 Craig Biggio .40 1.00
R55 Barry Bonds 1.50 4.00
R56 Bret Boone .25 .60
R57 Tony Gwynn .75 2.00
R58 Barry Larkin .40 1.00
R59 Mike Piazza 1.00 2.50
R60 NL Monthly Batting LS W .25 .60

1996 Upper Deck Ripken Collection

COMPLETE SET (23) 15.00 40.00
COMP.COLC SER.1 (5) 1.50 4.00
COMP.UD SER.1 (4) 3.00 8.00
COMP.COLC SER.2 (4) 1.25 3.00
COMP.UD SER.2 (5) 3.00 8.00
COMP.SP SET (5) 6.00 15.00
COMMON COLC (1-4/9-12) 1.25 3.00
COMMON UD (5-8/13-17) 2.50 6.00
COMMON SP (18-22) 4.00 10.00
CARDS 1-4 STATED ODDS 1:12 CC SER.1
CARDS 5-8 STATED ODDS 1:24 UD SER.1
CARDS 9-12 STATED ODDS 1:12 CC SER.2
CARDS 13-17 STATED ODDS 1:24 UD SER.2
CARDS 18-22 STATED ODDS 1:45 SP
NNO Cal Ripken Header COLC 1.25 3.00

1996 Upper Deck Ripken Collection Jumbos

COMP.FACT SET 8.00 20.00
COMMON CARD .40 1.00
1 Cal Ripken Jr. .75 2.00
after playing in 2130 consecutive
2 Cal Ripken Jr./13th consecutive year as American
1.00 2.50
6 Cal Ripken Jr. .60 1.50
Brian McRae sliding into second/1
22 Cal Ripken SP 1.00 2.50
Eddie Murray/1981

1996 Upper Deck Run Producers

COMPLETE SET (20) 75.00 150.00
SER.2 ODDS 1:72 HOB/RET, 1:36 ANCO
CONDITION SENSITIVE SET
THIS SET PRICED IN NRMT CONDITION
RP1 Albert Belle 1.50 4.00
RP2 Dante Bichette 1.50 4.00
RP3 Barry Bonds 10.00 25.00
RP4 Jay Buhner 1.50 4.00
RP5 Jose Canseco 2.50 6.00
RP6 Juan Gonzalez 1.50 4.00
RP7 Ken Griffey Jr. 8.00 20.00
RP8 Tony Gwynn 5.00 12.00
RP9 Kenny Lofton 1.50 4.00
RP10 Edgar Martinez 2.50 6.00
RP11 Fred McGriff 2.50 6.00
RP12 Mark McGwire 10.00 25.00
RP13 Rafael Palmeiro 2.50 6.00
RP14 Mike Piazza 6.00 15.00
RP15 Manny Ramirez 2.50 6.00
RP16 Tim Salmon 2.50 6.00
RP17 Sammy Sosa 4.00 10.00
RP18 Frank Thomas 4.00 10.00
RP19 Mo Vaughn 1.50 4.00
RP20 Matt Williams 1.50 4.00

1996 Upper Deck All-Stars Jumbos

This 18-card set measures approximately 3 1/2" by 5" with a suggested retail price of $19.95 a set. The fronts feature borderless color player photos and are foil stamped with the official 1996 Major League Baseball All-Star game logo. The backs carry another player photo with player information and statistics. The cards are checklisted below in alphabetical order.

1 Roberto Alomar .30 .75
2 Sandy Alomar Jr. .15 .40
3 Jeff Bagwell .40 1.00
4 Albert Belle .15 .40
5 Dante Bichette .15 .40
6 Craig Biggio .25 .60
7 Wade Boggs .40 1.00
8 Barry Bonds .60 1.50
9 Ken Griffey Jr. 1.00 2.50
10 Tony Gwynn .75 2.00
11 Barry Larkin .30 .75
12 Kenny Lofton .25 .60
13 Charles Nagy .07 .20
14 Mike Piazza 1.25 3.00
15 Cal Ripken Jr. 1.50 4.00
16 John Smoltz .15 .40
17 Frank Thomas .40 1.00
18 Matt Williams .25 .60

1996 Upper Deck Meet the Stars Griffey Redemption

This one-card set features a postcard-size action photo of Ken Griffey Jr. with a "Magic Moment" from a 1995 Post-Season game printed on one side of the three-sided black-and-aqua border. The back is blank.

1 Ken Griffey Jr/1995 Post-Season 1.50 4.00

1996 Upper Deck Nomo Collection Jumbos

This 16-card set measures approximately 3 1/2" by 5" and features color action photos of Hideo Nomo with a small black-and-white head photo in the upper left. The backs carry a smaller black-and-white version of the front photo with a continuing story highlighting Nomo's major league career.

COMPLETE SET (16) 6.00 15.00
COMMON CARD (1-16) .40 1.00

1996 Upper Deck Nomo ROY Japanese

Produced by Upper Deck, this 3 1/2" by 5" card commemorates Hideo Nomo being named the Rookie-of-the-Year of the National League for 1995. The front features a color action player photo while the back displays a blue-tinted player portrait with player information in Japanese.

1 Hideo Nomo 2.00 5.00

1996 Upper Deck Sheet

This one 8 1/2" by 11" sheet was issued so fans at Fan Fest could have an item for players to sign at the show. The sheet has very little on the front so more signatures can be signed and the back is blank.

1 All-Star Fanfest Autograph Sheet .75 2.00

1997 Upper Deck

The 1997 Upper Deck set was issued in two series (series one 1-240, series two 271-520). The 12-card packs retailed for $2.49 each. Many cards have dates on the front to identify when, and when possible, what significant event is pictured. The backs include a player photo, stats and a brief blurb to go with vital statistics. Subsets include Jackie Robinson Tribute (1-9), Strike Force (64-72), Defensive Gems (136-153), Global Impact (181-207), Season Highlight Checklists (214-222/316-324), Star Rookies (223-240/271-288), Capture the Flag (370-387), Griffey's Hot List (415-424) and Diamond Debuts (470-483). It's critical to note that the Griffey's Hot List subset cards (in an unannounced move by the manufacturer) were shortprinted (about 1:7 packs) in relation to other cards in the series two set. The comparatively low print run on these cards created a dramatic surge in demand amongst set collectors and the cards soared in value on the secondary market. A 30-card first series Update set (numbered 241-270) was available to collectors that mailed in 10 series one wrappers along with $3 for postage and handling. The Series One Update set is composed primarily of 1996 post-season highlights. An additional 30-card series two Trade set (numbered 521-550) was also released around the end of the season. It too was available to collectors that mailed in ten series two wrappers along with $3 for postage and handling. The Series Two Trade set is composed primarily of traded players pictured in their new uniforms and a selection of rookies and prospects highlighted by the inclusion of Jose Cruz Jr. and Hideki Irabu.

COMP.MASTER SET (550) 100.00 200.00
COMPLETE SET (490) 50.00 100.00
COMPLETE SERIES 1 (240) 15.00 40.00
COMPLETE SERIES 2 (250) 25.00 60.00
COMP.SER.2 w/o GHL (240) 10.00 25.00
COMMON (1-240/271-520) .10 .30
COMP.UPDATE SET (30) 40.00 80.00
COMMON UPDATE (241-270) .40 1.00
1 UPD.SET VIA MAIL PER 10 SER.1 WRAPS
COMMON GHL (415-424) .60 1.50
GHL 415-424 SER.2 ODDS APPROX. 1:7
COMP.TRADE SET (30) 8.00 20.00
COMMON TRADE (521-550) .20 .50
1 TRD.SET VIA MAIL PER 10 SER.2 WRAPS
COMP.SET (490) EXCLUDES UPD/TRD SETS
1 Jackie Robinson .20 .50
2 Jackie Robinson .20 .50
3 Jackie Robinson .20 .50
4 Jackie Robinson .20 .50
5 Jackie Robinson .20 .50
6 Jackie Robinson .20 .50
7 Jackie Robinson .20 .50
8 Jackie Robinson .20 .50
9 Jackie Robinson .20 .50
10 Chipper Jones .30 .75
11 Marquis Grissom .10 .30
12 Jermaine Dye .10 .30
13 Mark Lemke .10 .30
14 Terrell Wade .10 .30
15 Fred McGriff .20 .50
16 Tom Glavine .20 .50
17 Mark Wohlers .10 .30
18 Randy Myers .10 .30
19 Roberto Alomar .20 .50
20 Cal Ripken 1.00 2.50
21 Rafael Palmeiro .20 .50
22 Mike Mussina .20 .50
23 Brady Anderson .10 .30
24 Jose Canseco .20 .50
25 Mo Vaughn .10 .30
26 Roger Clemens .60 1.50
27 Tim Naehring .10 .30
28 Jeff Suppan .10 .30
29 Troy Percival .10 .30
30 Sammy Sosa .30 .75
31 Amaury Telemaco .10 .30
32 Rey Sanchez .10 .30
33 Scott Servais .10 .30
34 Steve Trachsel .10 .30
35 Mark Grace .20 .50
36 Wilson Alvarez .10 .30
37 Harold Baines .10 .30
38 Tony Phillips .10 .30
39 James Baldwin .10 .30
40 Frank Thomas UER .30 .75
41 Lyle Mouton .10 .30
42 Chris Snopek .10 .30
43 Hal Morris .10 .30
44 Eric Davis .10 .30
45 Barry Larkin .20 .50
46 Reggie Sanders .10 .30
47 Pete Schourek .10 .30
48 Lee Smith .10 .30
49 Charles Nagy .10 .30
50 Albert Belle .10 .30
51 Julio Franco .10 .30
52 Kenny Lofton .10 .30
53 Orel Hershiser .10 .30
54 Omar Vizquel .20 .50
55 Eric Young .10 .30
56 Curtis Leskanic .10 .30
57 Quinton McCracken .10 .30
58 Kevin Ritz .10 .30
59 Walt Weiss .10 .30
60 Dante Bichette .10 .30
61 Mark Lewis .10 .30
62 Tony Clark .10 .30
63 Travis Fryman .10 .30
64 John Smoltz SF .10 .30
65 Greg Maddux SF .30 .75
66 Tom Glavine SF .10 .30
67 Mike Mussina SF .10 .30
68 Andy Pettitte SF .10 .30
69 Mariano Rivera SF .20 .50
70 Hideo Nomo SF .10 .30
71 Kevin Brown SF .10 .30
72 Randy Johnson SF .20 .50
73 Felipe Lira .10 .30
74 Kimera Bartee .10 .30
75 Alan Trammell .10 .30
76 Kevin Brown .10 .30
77 Edgar Renteria .10 .30
78 Al Leiter .10 .30
79 Charles Johnson .10 .30
80 Andre Dawson .10 .30
81 Billy Wagner .10 .30
82 Donne Wall .10 .30
83 Jeff Bagwell .20 .50
84 Keith Lockhart .10 .30
85 Jeff Montgomery .10 .30
86 Tom Goodwin .10 .30
87 Tim Belcher .10 .30
88 Mike Macfarlane .10 .30
89 Joe Randa .10 .30
90 Brett Butler .10 .30
91 Todd Worrell .10 .30
92 Todd Hollandsworth .10 .30
93 Ismael Valdes .10 .30
94 Hideo Nomo .30 .75
95 Mike Piazza .50 1.25
96 Jeff Cirillo .10 .30
97 Ricky Bones .10 .30
98 Fernando Vina .10 .30
99 Ben McDonald .10 .30
100 John Jaha .10 .30
101 Mark Loretta .10 .30
102 Paul Molitor .10 .30
103 Rick Aguilera .10 .30
104 Marty Cordova .10 .30
105 Kirby Puckett .30 .75
106 Dan Naulty .10 .30
107 Frank Rodriguez .10 .30
108 Shane Andrews .10 .30
109 Henry Rodriguez .10 .30
110 Mark Grudzielanek .10 .30
111 Pedro Martinez .20 .50
112 Ugueth Urbina .10 .30
113 David Segui .10 .30
114 Rey Ordonez .10 .30
115 Bernard Gilkey .10 .30
116 Butch Huskey .10 .30
117 Paul Wilson .10 .30
118 Alex Ochoa .10 .30
119 John Franco .10 .30
120 Dwight Gooden .10 .30
121 Ruben Rivera .10 .30
122 Andy Pettitte .20 .50
123 Tino Martinez .20 .50
124 Bernie Williams .20 .50
125 Wade Boggs .20 .50
126 Paul O'Neill .20 .50
127 Scott Brosius .10 .30
128 Ernie Young .10 .30
129 Doug Johns .10 .30
130 Geronimo Berroa .10 .30
131 Jason Giambi .10 .30
132 John Wasdin .10 .30
133 Jim Eisenreich .10 .30
134 Ricky Otero .10 .30
135 Ricky Bottalico .10 .30
136 Mark Langston DG .10 .30
137 Greg Maddux DG .30 .75
138 Ivan Rodriguez DG .10 .30
139 Charles Johnson DG .10 .30
140 J.T. Snow DG .10 .30
141 Mark Grace DG .10 .30
142 Roberto Alomar DG .10 .30
143 Craig Biggio DG .10 .30
144 Ken Caminiti DG .10 .30
145 Matt Williams DG .10 .30
146 Omar Vizquel DG .10 .30
147 Cal Ripken DG .50 1.25
148 Ozzie Smith DG .30 .75
149 Rey Ordonez DG .10 .30
150 Ken Griffey Jr. DG .40 1.00
151 Devon White DG .10 .30
152 Barry Bonds DG .40 1.00
153 Kenny Lofton DG .10 .30
154 Mickey Morandini .10 .30
155 Gregg Jefferies .10 .30
156 Curt Schilling .10 .30
157 Jason Kendall .10 .30
158 Francisco Cordova .10 .30
159 Dennis Eckersley .10 .30
160 Ron Gant .10 .30
161 Ozzie Smith .50 1.25
162 Brian Jordan .10 .30
163 John Mabry .10 .30
164 Andy Ashby .10 .30
165 Steve Finley .10 .30
166 Fernando Valenzuela .10 .30
167 Archi Cianfrocco .10 .30
168 Wally Joyner .10 .30
169 Greg Vaughn .10 .30
170 Barry Bonds .75 2.00
171 William VanLandingham .10 .30
172 Marvin Benard .10 .30
173 Rich Aurilia .10 .30
174 Jay Canizaro .10 .30
175 Ken Griffey Jr. .60 1.50
176 Bob Wells .10 .30
177 Jay Buhner .10 .30
178 Sterling Hitchcock .10 .30
179 Edgar Martinez .20 .50
180 Rusty Greer .10 .30
181 Dave Nilsson GI .10 .30
182 Larry Walker GI .10 .30
183 Edgar Renteria GI .10 .30
184 Rey Ordonez GI .10 .30
185 Rafael Palmeiro GI .10 .30
186 Osvaldo Fernandez GI .10 .30
187 Raul Mondesi GI .10 .30
188 Manny Ramirez GI .10 .30
189 Sammy Sosa GI .20 .50
190 Robert Eenhoorn GI .10 .30
191 Devon White GI .10 .30
192 Hideo Nomo GI .10 .30
193 Mac Suzuki GI .10 .30
194 Chan Ho Park GI .10 .30
195 Fernando Valenzuela GI .10 .30
196 Andruw Jones GI .10 .30
197 Vinny Castilla GI .10 .30
198 Dennis Martinez GI .10 .30
199 Ruben Rivera GI .10 .30
200 Juan Gonzalez GI .10 .30
201 Roberto Alomar GI .10 .30
202 Edgar Martinez GI .10 .30
203 Ivan Rodriguez GI .10 .30
204 Carlos Delgado GI .10 .30
205 Andres Galarraga GI .10 .30
206 Ozzie Guillen GI .10 .30
207 Midre Cummings GI .10 .30
208 Roger Pavlik .10 .30
209 Darren Oliver .10 .30
210 Dean Palmer .10 .30
211 Ivan Rodriguez .20 .50
212 Otis Nixon .10 .30
213 Pat Hentgen .10 .30
214 Ozzie Dawson Puckett HL CL .20 .50
215 Bonds Sheff Brady HL CL .40 1.00
216 Ken Caminiti SH CL .10 .30
217 John Smoltz SH CL .10 .30
218 Eric Young SH CL .10 .30
219 Juan Gonzalez SH CL .10 .30
220 Eddie Murray SH CL .20 .50
221 Tommy Lasorda SH CL .10 .30
222 Paul Molitor SH CL .10 .30
223 Luis Castillo .10 .30
224 Justin Thompson .10 .30
225 Rocky Coppinger .10 .30
226 Jermaine Allensworth .10 .30
227 Jeff D'Amico .10 .30
228 Jamey Wright .10 .30
229 Scott Rolen .20 .50
230 Darin Erstad .10 .30
231 Marty Janzen .10 .30
232 Jacob Cruz .10 .30
233 Raul Ibanez .10 .30
234 Nomar Garciaparra .50 1.25
235 Todd Walker .10 .30
236 Brian Giles RC .60 1.50
237 Matt Beech .10 .30
238 Mike Cameron .10 .30
239 Jose Paniagua .10 .30
240 Andruw Jones .20 .50
241 Brant Brown UPD .40 1.00
242 Robin Jennings UPD .40 1.00
243 Willie Adams UPD .40 1.00
244 Ken Caminiti UPD .60 1.50
245 Brian Jordan UPD .60 1.50
246 Chipper Jones UPD 1.50 4.00
247 Juan Gonzalez UPD .60 1.50
248 Bernie Williams UPD 1.00 2.50
249 Roberto Alomar UPD 1.00 2.50
250 Bernie Williams UPD 1.00 2.50
251 David Wells UPD .60 1.50
252 Cecil Fielder UPD .60 1.50
253 Darryl Strawberry UPD .60 1.50
254 Andy Pettitte UPD 1.00 2.50
255 Javier Lopez UPD .60 1.50
256 Gary Gaetti UPD .60 1.50
257 Ron Gant UPD .60 1.50
258 Brian Jordan UPD .60 1.50
259 John Smoltz UPD 1.00 2.50
260 Greg Maddux UPD 3.00 8.00
261 Tom Glavine UPD 1.00 2.50
262 Andruw Jones UPD 1.00 2.50
263 Greg Maddux UPD 3.00 8.00
264 David Cone UPD .60 1.50
265 Jim Leyritz UPD .40 1.00
266 Andy Pettitte UPD 1.00 2.50
267 John Wetteland UPD .60 1.50
268 Dario Veras UPD .40 1.00
269 Neifi Perez UPD .40 1.00
270 Bill Mueller UPD 1.50 4.00
271 Vladimir Guerrero .30 .75
272 Dmitri Young .10 .30
273 Nerio Rodriguez RC .10 .30
274 Kevin Orie .10 .30
275 Felipe Crespo .10 .30
276 Danny Graves .10 .30
277 Rod Myers .10 .30
278 Felix Heredia RC .10 .30
279 Ralph Milliard .10 .30
280 Greg Norton .10 .30
281 Derek Wallace .10 .30
282 Trot Nixon .10 .30
283 Bobby Chouinard .10 .30
284 Jay Witasick .10 .30
285 Travis Miller .10 .30
286 Brian Bevil .10 .30
287 Bobby Estalella .10 .30
288 Steve Soderstrom .10 .30
289 Mark Langston .10 .30
290 Tim Salmon .20 .50
291 Jim Edmonds .10 .30
292 Garret Anderson .10 .30
293 George Arias .10 .30
294 Gary DiSarcina .10 .30
295 Chuck Finley .10 .30
296 Todd Greene .10 .30
297 Randy Velarde .10 .30
298 David Justice .10 .30
299 Ryan Klesko .10 .30
300 John Smoltz .20 .50
301 Javier Lopez .10 .30
302 Greg Maddux .50 1.25
303 Denny Neagle .10 .30
304 B.J. Surhoff .10 .30
305 Chris Hoiles .10 .30
306 Eric Davis .10 .30
307 Scott Erickson .10 .30
308 Mike Bordick .10 .30
309 John Valentin .10 .30
310 Heathcliff Slocumb .10 .30
311 Tom Gordon .10 .30
312 Mike Stanley .10 .30
313 Reggie Jefferson .10 .30
314 Darren Bragg .10 .30
315 Troy O'Leary .10 .30
316 John Mabry SH CL .10 .30
317 Mark Whiten SH CL .10 .30
318 Edgar Martinez SH CL .10 .30
319 Alex Rodriguez SH CL .30 .75
320 Mark McGwire SH CL .40 1.00
321 Hideo Nomo SH CL .10 .30
322 Todd Hundley SH CL .10 .30
323 Barry Bonds SH CL .40 1.00
324 Andruw Jones SH CL .10 .30
325 Ryne Sandberg .50 1.25
326 Brian McRae .10 .30
327 Frank Castillo .10 .30
328 Shawon Dunston .10 .30
329 Ray Durham .10 .30
330 Robin Ventura .10 .30
331 Ozzie Guillen .10 .30
332 Roberto Hernandez .10 .30
333 Albert Belle .10 .30
334 Dave Martinez .10 .30
335 Willie Greene .10 .30
336 Jeff Brantley .10 .30
337 Kevin Jarvis .10 .30
338 John Smiley .10 .30
339 Eddie Taubensee .10 .30
340 Bret Boone .10 .30
341 Kevin Seitzer .10 .30
342 Jack McDowell .10 .30
343 Sandy Alomar Jr. .10 .30
344 Chad Curtis .10 .30
345 Manny Ramirez .20 .50
346 Chad Ogea .10 .30
347 Jim Thome .20 .50
348 Mark Thompson .10 .30
349 Ellis Burks .10 .30
350 Andres Galarraga .10 .30
351 Vinny Castilla .10 .30
352 Kirt Manwaring .10 .30
353 Larry Walker .10 .30
354 Omar Olivares .10 .30
355 Bobby Higginson .10 .30
356 Melvin Nieves .10 .30
357 Brian Johnson .10 .30
358 Devon White .10 .30
359 Jeff Conine .10 .30
360 Gary Sheffield .10 .30
361 Robb Nen .10 .30
362 Mike Hampton .10 .30
363 Bob Abreu .20 .50
364 Luis Gonzalez .10 .30
365 Derek Bell .10 .30
366 Sean Berry .10 .30
367 Craig Biggio .20 .50
368 Darryl Kile .10 .30
369 Shane Reynolds .10 .30
370A Jeff Bagwell CF .10 .30
370B Jeff Bagwell CF White back .10 .30
371A Ron Gant CF .10 .30
371B Ron Gant CF White back .10 .30
372A Andy Benes CF .10 .30
372B Andy Benes CF White back .10 .30
373A Gary Gaetti CF .10 .30
373B Gary Gaetti CF White back .10 .30
374A Ramon Martinez CF .10 .30
374B Ramon Martinez CF White back .10 .30
375A Raul Mondesi CF .10 .30
375B Raul Mondesi CF White back .10 .30
376A Steve Finley CF .10 .30
376B Steve Finley CF White back .10 .30
377A Ken Caminiti CF .10 .30
377B Ken Caminiti CF White back .10 .30
378A Tony Gwynn CF .20 .50
378B Tony Gwynn CF White back .20 .50
379A Dario Veras RC .10 .30
379B Dario Veras RC White back .10 .30
380A Andy Pettitte CF .10 .30
380B Andy Pettitte CF White back .10 .30
381A Ruben Rivera CF .10 .30
381B Ruben Rivera CF White back .10 .30
382A David Cone CF .10 .30
382B David Cone CF White back .10 .30
383A Roberto Alomar CF .10 .30
383B Roberto Alomar CF White back .30 .30
384A Edgar Martinez CF .10 .30
384B Edgar Martinez CF White back .10 .30
385A Ken Griffey Jr. CF .40 1.00
385B Griffey Jr CF Wht Back .40 1.00
386A Mark McGwire CF .40 1.00
386B McGwire CF Wht Back .40 1.00
387A Rusty Greer CF .10 .30
387B Rusty Greer CF White back .10 .30
388 Jose Rosado .10 .30
389 Kevin Appier .10 .30
390 Johnny Damon .20 .50
391 Jose Offerman .10 .30
392 Michael Tucker .10 .30
393 Craig Paquette .10 .30
394 Bip Roberts .10 .30
395 Ramon Martinez .10 .30
396 Greg Gagne .10 .30
397 Chan Ho Park .10 .30
398 Karim Garcia .10 .30
399 Wilton Guerrero .10 .30
400 Eric Karros .10 .30
401 Raul Mondesi .10 .30
402 Matt Mieske .10 .30
403 Mike Fetters .10 .30
404 Dave Nilsson .10 .30
405 Jose Valentin .10 .30
406 Scott Karl .10 .30
407 Marc Newfield .10 .30
408 Cal Eldred .10 .30
409 Rich Becker .10 .30
410 Terry Steinbach .10 .30
411 Chuck Knoblauch .10 .30
412 Pat Meares .10 .30
413 Brad Radke .10 .30
414 Kirby Puckett UER .30 .75
415 Andruw Jones GHL SP .60 1.50
416 Chipper Jones GHL SP 1.00 2.50
417 Mo Vaughn GHL SP .60 1.50
418 Frank Thomas GHL SP 1.00 2.50
419 Albert Belle GHL SP .60 1.50
420 Mark McGwire GHL SP 3.00 8.00
421 Derek Jeter GHL SP 3.00 8.00
422 Alex Rodriguez GHL SP 2.00 5.00
423 Juan Gonzalez GHL SP .60 1.50
424 Ken Griffey Jr. GHL SP 2.50 6.00
425 Rondell White .10 .30
426 Darrin Fletcher .10 .30
427 Cliff Floyd .10 .30
428 Mike Lansing .10 .30
429 F.P. Santangelo .10 .30
430 Todd Hundley .10 .30
431 Mark Clark .10 .30
432 Pete Harnisch .10 .30
433 Jason Isringhausen .10 .30
434 Bobby Jones .10 .30
435 Lance Johnson .10 .30
436 Carlos Baerga .10 .30
437 Mariano Duncan .10 .30
438 David Cone .10 .30
439 Mariano Rivera .30 .75
440 Derek Jeter .75 2.00
441 Joe Girardi .10 .30
442 Charlie Hayes .10 .30
443 Tim Raines .10 .30
444 Darryl Strawberry .10 .30
445 Cecil Fielder .10 .30
446 Ariel Prieto .10 .30
447 Tony Batista .10 .30
448 Brent Gates .10 .30
449 Scott Spiezio .10 .30
450 Mark McGwire .75 2.00
451 Don Wengert .10 .30
452 Mike Lieberthal .10 .30
453 Lenny Dykstra .10 .30
454 Rex Hudler .10 .30
455 Darren Daulton .10 .30
456 Kevin Stocker .10 .30
457 Trey Beamon .10 .30
458 Midre Cummings .10 .30
459 Mark Johnson .10 .30
460 Al Martin .10 .30
461 Kevin Elster .10 .30
462 Jon Lieber .10 .30
463 Jason Schmidt .10 .30
464 Paul Wagner .10 .30
465 Andy Benes .10 .30
466 Alan Benes .10 .30
467 Royce Clayton .10 .30
468 Gary Gaetti .10 .30
469 Curt Lyons RC .10 .30
470 Eugene Kingsale DD .10 .30
471 Damian Jackson DD .10 .30
472 Wendell Magee DD .10 .30
473 Kevin L. Brown DD .10 .30
474 Raul Casanova DD .10 .30
475 Ramiro Mendoza RC .10 .30
476 Todd Dunn DD .10 .30
477 Chad Mottola DD .10 .30
478 Andy Larkin DD .10 .30
479 Jaime Bluma DD .10 .30
480 Mac Suzuki DD .10 .30
481 Brian Banks DD .10 .30
482 Desi Wilson DD .10 .30
483 Einar Diaz DD .10 .30
484 Tom Pagnozzi .10 .30
485 Ray Lankford .10 .30
486 Todd Stottlemyre .10 .30
487 Donovan Osborne .10 .30
488 Trevor Hoffman .10 .30
489 Chris Gomez .10 .30
490 Ken Caminiti .10 .30
491 John Flaherty .10 .30
492 Tony Gwynn .40 1.00
493 Joey Hamilton .10 .30
494 Rickey Henderson .30 .75
495 Glenallen Hill .10 .30
496 Rod Beck .10 .30
497 Osvaldo Fernandez .10 .30
498 Rick Wilkins .10 .30
499 Joey Cora .10 .30
500 Alex Rodriguez .50 1.25
501 Randy Johnson .30 .75
502 Paul Sorrento .10 .30
503 Dan Wilson .10 .30
504 Jamie Moyer .10 .30
505 Will Clark .20 .50
506 Mickey Tettleton .10 .30
507 John Burkett .10 .30
508 Ken Hill .10 .30
509 Mark McLemore .10 .30
510 Juan Gonzalez .10 .30
511 Bobby Witt .10 .30
512 Carlos Delgado .10 .30
513 Alex Gonzalez .10 .30
514 Shawn Green .10 .30
515 Joe Carter .10 .30
516 Juan Guzman .10 .30
517 Charlie O'Brien .10 .30
518 Ed Sprague .10 .30
519 Mike Timlin .10 .30
520 Roger Clemens .60 1.50
521 Eddie Murray TRADE .75 2.00
522 Jason Dickson TRADE .20 .50
523 Jim Leyritz TRADE .20 .50
524 Michael Tucker TRADE .20 .50
525 Kenny Lofton TRADE .30 .75
526 Jimmy Key TRADE .30 .75
527 Mel Rojas TRADE .20 .50
528 Deion Sanders TRADE .50 1.25
529 Bartolo Colon TRADE .30 .75
530 Matt Williams TRADE .30 .75
531 Marquis Grissom TRADE .30 .75
532 David Justice TRADE .30 .75
533 Bubba Trammell TRADE .30 .75
534 Moises Alou TRADE .30 .75
535 Bobby Bonilla TRADE .30 .75
536 Alex Fernandez TRADE .20 .50
537 Jay Bell TRADE .30 .75
538 Chili Davis TRADE .30 .75
539 Jeff King TRADE .20 .50
540 Todd Zeile TRADE .20 .50
541 John Olerud TRADE .30 .75
542 Jose Guillen TRADE .30 .75
543 Derrek Lee TRADE .50 1.25
544 Dante Powell TRADE .20 .50
545 J.T. Snow TRADE .30 .75
546 Jeff Kent TRADE .30 .75
547 Jose Cruz Jr. TRADE .30 .75
548 John Wetteland TRADE .30 .75
549 Orlando Merced TRADE .20 .50
550 Hideki Irabu TRADE .30 .75

1997 Upper Deck Amazing Greats

SER.1 STATED ODDS 1:69
AG1 Ken Griffey Jr. 5.00 12.00
AG2 Roberto Alomar 1.50 4.00
AG3 Alex Rodriguez 3.00 8.00
AG4 Paul Molitor 2.50 6.00
AG5 Chipper Jones 2.50 6.00
AG6 Tony Gwynn 2.50 6.00
AG7 Kenny Lofton 1.00 2.50
AG8 Albert Belle 1.00 2.50
AG9 Matt Williams 1.00 2.50
AG10 Frank Thomas 2.50 6.00
AG11 Greg Maddux 4.00 10.00
AG12 Sammy Sosa 1.50 4.00
AG13 Kirby Puckett 2.50 6.00
AG14 Jeff Bagwell 1.50 4.00
AG15 Cal Ripken 8.00 20.00
AG16 Manny Ramirez 1.50 4.00
AG17 Barry Bonds 4.00 10.00
AG18 Mo Vaughn 1.00 2.50
AG19 Eddie Murray 1.50 4.00
AG20 Mike Piazza 2.50 6.00

1997 Upper Deck Blue Chip Prospects

RANDOM INSERTS IN SER.2 PACKS
STATED PRINT RUN 500 SERIAL #'d SETS
BC1 Andruw Jones 15.00 40.00
BC2 Derek Jeter 40.00 80.00
BC3 Scott Rolen 15.00 40.00
BC4 Manny Ramirez 15.00 40.00
BC5 Todd Walker 10.00 25.00
BC6 Rocky Coppinger 6.00 15.00
BC7 Nomar Garciaparra 8.00 20.00
BC8 Darin Erstad 10.00 25.00
BC9 Jermaine Dye 10.00 25.00
BC10 Vladimir Guerrero 10.00 25.00
BC11 Edgar Renteria 10.00 25.00
BC12 Bob Abreu 15.00 40.00
BC13 Karim Garcia 6.00 15.00
BC14 Jeff D'Amico 6.00 15.00
BC15 Chipper Jones 10.00 25.00
BC16 Todd Hollandsworth 6.00 15.00
BC17 Andy Pettitte 15.00 40.00
BC18 Ruben Rivera 6.00 15.00
BC19 Jason Kendall 10.00 25.00
BC20 Alex Rodriguez 15.00 40.00

1997 Upper Deck Game Jersey

SER.1 STATED ODDS 1:800
GJ1 Ken Griffey Jr. 500.00 1000.00
GJ2 Tony Gwynn 25.00 60.00
GJ3 Rey Ordonez 10.00 25.00

1997 Upper Deck Hot Commodities

COMPLETE SET (20) 10.00 25.00
SER.2 STATED ODDS 1:13
HC1 Alex Rodriguez 1.00 2.50
HC2 Andruw Jones .30 .75
HC3 Derek Jeter 2.00 5.00
HC4 Frank Thomas .75 2.00
HC5 Ken Griffey Jr. 1.50 4.00
HC6 Chipper Jones .75 2.00
HC7 Juan Gonzalez .30 .75
HC8 Cal Ripken 2.50 6.00
HC9 John Smoltz .50 1.25
HC10 Mark McGwire 1.25 3.00
HC11 Barry Bonds 1.25 3.00
HC12 Albert Belle .30 .75
HC13 Mike Piazza .75 2.00
HC14 Manny Ramirez .50 1.25
HC15 Mo Vaughn .30 .75
HC16 Tony Gwynn .75 2.00
HC17 Vladimir Guerrero .50 1.25
HC18 Hideo Nomo .50 1.25
HC19 Greg Maddux 1.25 3.00
HC20 Kirby Puckett .75 2.00

1997 Upper Deck Long Distance Connection

COMPLETE SET (20) 15.00 40.00
SER.2 STATED ODDS 1:35
LD1 Mark McGwire 1.50 4.00
LD2 Brady Anderson .60 1.50
LD3 Ken Griffey Jr. 3.00 8.00
LD4 Albert Belle .60 1.50
LD5 Juan Gonzalez .60 1.50
LD6 Andres Galarraga 1.00 2.50
LD7 Jay Buhner .60 1.50
LD8 Mo Vaughn .60 1.50
LD9 Barry Bonds 2.50 6.00
LD10 Gary Sheffield .60 1.50
LD11 Todd Hundley .60 1.50
LD12 Frank Thomas 1.50 4.00
LD13 Sammy Sosa 1.00 2.50
LD14 Rafael Palmeiro .60 1.50
LD15 Alex Rodriguez 2.00 5.00
LD16 Mike Piazza 1.50 4.00
LD17 Ken Caminiti .60 1.50
LD18 Chipper Jones 1.50 4.00
LD19 Manny Ramirez 1.00 2.50
LD20 Andruw Jones .60 1.50

1997 Upper Deck Memorable Moments

COMPLETE SERIES 1 (10) 5.00 12.00
COMPLETE SERIES 2 (10) 5.00 12.00
A1 Andruw Jones .20 .50
A2 Chipper Jones .30 .75
A3 Cal Ripken 1.00 2.50
A4 Frank Thomas .30 .75
A5 Manny Ramirez .20 .50
A6 Mike Piazza .50 1.25
A7 Mark McGwire .75 2.00
A8 Barry Bonds .75 2.00
A9 Ken Griffey Jr. .60 1.50
A10 Alex Rodriguez .50 1.25
B1 Ken Griffey Jr. .60 1.50
B2 Albert Belle .10 .30
B3 Derek Jeter .75 2.00
B4 Greg Maddux .50 1.25
B5 Tony Gwynn .40 1.00
B6 Ryne Sandberg .50 1.25
B7 Juan Gonzalez .10 .30
B8 Roger Clemens .60 1.50
B9 Jose Cruz Jr. .10 .30
B10 Mo Vaughn .10 .30

1997 Upper Deck Power Package

COMPLETE SET (20) 30.00 80.00
SER.1 STATED ODDS 1:24
*JUMBOS: .2X TO .5X BASIC PP
JUMBOS ONE PER RETAIL JUMBO PACK
PP1 Ken Griffey Jr. 4.00 10.00
PP2 Joe Carter .75 2.00
PP3 Rafael Palmeiro 1.25 3.00
PP4 Jay Buhner .75 2.00
PP5 Sammy Sosa 2.00 5.00
PP6 Fred McGriff 1.25 3.00
PP7 Jeff Bagwell 1.25 3.00
PP8 Albert Belle .75 2.00
PP9 Matt Williams .75 2.00
PP10 Mark McGwire 5.00 12.00
PP11 Gary Sheffield .75 2.00
PP12 Tim Salmon 1.25 3.00
PP13 Ryan Klesko .75 2.00
PP14 Manny Ramirez 1.25 3.00
PP15 Mike Piazza 3.00 8.00
PP16 Barry Bonds 5.00 12.00
PP17 Mo Vaughn .75 2.00
PP18 Jose Canseco 1.25 3.00
PP19 Juan Gonzalez .75 2.00
PP20 Frank Thomas 2.00 5.00

1997 Upper Deck Predictor

COMPLETE SET (30) 12.50 30.00
*SCRATCH LOSER: .25X TO .6X UNSCRATCH
*EXCH.WIN: 1X TO 2.5X BASIC PREDICTOR
SER.2 STATED ODDS 1:5
1 Andruw Jones .25 .60
2 Chipper Jones .40 1.00
3 Greg Maddux .60 1.50
4 Fred McGriff .25 .60
5 John Smoltz .25 .60
6 Brady Anderson .15 .40
7 Cal Ripken 1.25 3.00
8 Mo Vaughn .15 .40
9 Sammy Sosa .40 1.00
10 Albert Belle .15 .40
11 Frank Thomas .40 1.00
12 Kenny Lofton .15 .40
13 Jim Thome .25 .60
14 Dante Bichette .15 .40
15 Andres Galarraga .15 .40
16 Gary Sheffield .15 .40
17 Hideo Nomo .40 1.00
18 Mike Piazza .60 1.50
19 Derek Jeter 1.00 2.50
20 Bernie Williams .25 .60
21 Mark McGwire 1.00 2.50
22 Ken Caminiti .15 .40
23 Tony Gwynn .50 1.25

24 Barry Bonds 1.00 2.50
25 Jay Buhner .15 .40
26 Ken Griffey Jr. .75 2.00
27 Alex Rodriguez .60 1.50
28 Juan Gonzalez .15 .40
29 Dean Palmer .15 .40
30 Roger Clemens .75 2.00

1997 Upper Deck Rock Solid Foundation

COMPLETE SET (20) 15.00 40.00
SER.1 STATED ODDS 1:7
RS1 Alex Rodriguez 2.50 6.00
RS2 Rey Ordonez .60 1.50
RS3 Derek Jeter 4.00 10.00
RS4 Darin Erstad .60 1.50
RS5 Chipper Jones 1.50 4.00
RS6 Johnny Damon 1.00 2.50
RS7 Ryan Klesko .60 1.50
RS8 Charles Johnson .60 1.50
RS9 Andy Pettitte 1.00 2.50
RS10 Manny Ramirez 1.00 2.50
RS11 Ivan Rodriguez 1.00 2.50
RS12 Jason Kendall .60 1.50
RS13 Rondell White .60 1.50
RS14 Alex Ochoa .60 1.50
RS15 Javier Lopez .60 1.50
RS16 Pedro Martinez 1.00 2.50
RS17 Carlos Delgado .60 1.50
RS18 Paul Wilson .60 1.50
RS19 Alan Benes .60 1.50
RS20 Raul Mondesi .60 1.50

1997 Upper Deck Run Producers

COMPLETE SET (24) 75.00 150.00
SER.2 STATED ODDS 1:69
RP1 Ken Griffey Jr. 8.00 20.00
RP2 Barry Bonds 10.00 25.00
RP3 Albert Belle 1.50 4.00
RP4 Mark McGwire 10.00 25.00
RP5 Frank Thomas 4.00 10.00
RP6 Juan Gonzalez 1.50 4.00
RP7 Brady Anderson 1.50 4.00
RP8 Andres Galarraga 1.50 4.00
RP9 Rafael Palmeiro 2.50 6.00
RP10 Alex Rodriguez 6.00 15.00
RP11 Jay Buhner 1.50 4.00
RP12 Gary Sheffield 1.50 4.00
RP13 Sammy Sosa 4.00 10.00
RP14 Dante Bichette 1.50 4.00
RP15 Mike Piazza 6.00 15.00
RP16 Manny Ramirez 2.50 6.00
RP17 Kenny Lofton 1.50 4.00
RP18 Mo Vaughn 1.50 4.00
RP19 Tim Salmon 2.50 6.00
RP20 Chipper Jones 4.00 10.00
RP21 Jim Thome 2.50 6.00
RP22 Ken Caminiti 1.50 4.00
RP23 Jeff Bagwell 2.50 6.00
RP24 Paul Molitor 1.50 4.00

1997 Upper Deck Star Attractions

COMPLETE SET (20) 10.00 25.00
1-10 ONE PER UD MADNESS RETAIL PACK
11-20 ONE PER CC MADNESS RETAIL PACK
*GOLD: 2X TO 5X BASIC STAR ATT.
GOLD INSERTS IN UD/CC MADNESS RETAIL
1 Ken Griffey Jr. .75 2.00
2 Barry Bonds 1.00 2.50
3 Jeff Bagwell .25 .60
4 Nomar Garciaparra .60 1.50
5 Tony Gwynn .50 1.25
6 Roger Clemens .75 2.00
7 Chipper Jones .40 1.00
8 Tino Martinez .25 .60
9 Albert Belle .15 .40
10 Kenny Lofton .15 .40
11 Alex Rodriguez .60 1.50
12 Mark McGwire 1.00 2.50
13 Cal Ripken 1.25 3.00
14 Larry Walker .15 .40
15 Mike Piazza .60 1.50
16 Frank Thomas .40 1.00
17 Juan Gonzalez .15 .40
18 Greg Maddux .60 1.50
19 Jose Cruz Jr. .40 1.00
20 Mo Vaughn .15 .40

1997 Upper Deck Ticket To Stardom

SER.1 STATED ODDS 1:34
TS1 Chipper Jones 2.50 6.00
TS2 Jermaine Dye 1.00 2.50
TS3 Rey Ordonez 1.00 2.50
TS4 Alex Ochoa 1.00 2.50
TS5 Derek Jeter 6.00 15.00
TS6 Ruben Rivera 1.00 2.50
TS7 Billy Wagner 1.00 2.50
TS8 Jason Kendall 1.00 2.50
TS9 Darin Erstad 1.00 2.50
TS10 Alex Rodriguez 4.00 10.00
TS11 Bob Abreu 1.50 4.00
TS12 Richard Hidalgo 2.50 6.00
TS13 Karim Garcia 1.00 2.50
TS14 Andruw Jones 1.50 4.00
TS15 Carlos Delgado 1.00 2.50
TS16 Rocky Coppinger 1.00 2.50
TS17 Jeff D'Amico 1.00 2.50
TS18 Johnny Damon 1.50 4.00
TS19 John Wasdin 1.00 2.50
TS20 Manny Ramirez 1.50 4.00

1997 Upper Deck Ticket To Stardom Combos

COMPLETE SET (10) 10.00 25.00
TS1 C.Jones 1.25 3.00
A.Jones
TS2 R.Ordonez/K.Orie .75 2.00
TS3 D.Jeter/N.Garciaparra 2.00 5.00
TS4 B.Wagner/J.Kendall .75 2.00
TS5 D.Erstad/A.Rodriguez 1.50 4.00
TS6 B.Abreu/J.Guillen 1.00 2.50
TS7 W.Guerrero/V.Guerrero 1.00 2.50
TS8 C.Delgado/R.Coppinger 1.00 2.50
TS9 J.Dickson/J.Damon .75 2.00
TS10 B.Colon/M.Ramirez 1.00 2.50

1997 Upper Deck 1996 Award Winner Jumbos

This 23-card set measures approximately 3 1/2" by 5" and features borderless color player photos with gold and silver foil highlights of both American and National League award winners. The backs carry another player photo and statistics with a sentence about winning his award. The set was issued through retail outlets and television promotions with a suggested retail set price of $19.95.

COMP.FACT SET (23) 4.00 10.00
1 Alex Rodriguez 1.25 3.00
American League
2 Tony Gwynn 1.00 2.50
National League
3 Mark McGwire 1.25 3.00
American League
4 Andres Galarraga .40 1.00
National League
5 Albert Belle .30 .75
6 Andres Galarraga .40 1.00
7 Kenny Lofton .20 .50
8 Eric Young .08 .25
9 Andy Pettitte .30 .75
10 John Smoltz .30 .75
11 Roger Clemens 1.00 2.50
12 John Smoltz .40 1.00
13 Juan Guzman .08 .25
14 Kevin Brown .30 .75
15 John Wetteland .20 .50
16 Jeff Brantley .08 .25
National League SAVE CoLeader
17 Todd Worrell .08 .25
18 Derek Jeter 2.00 5.00
19 Todd Hollandsworth .08 .25
National League
20 Juan Gonzalez .50 1.25
21 Ken Caminiti .40 1.00
22 Pat Hentgen .20 .50
23 John Smoltz .40 1.00

1997 Upper Deck Chris Berman Rock 'N Roll Hall of Fame

This one-card set features a borderless color picture of Chris Berman performing and was given away at the Rock 'N Roll Hall of Fame as part of the party Chris Berman hosted for ESPN. The back displays a small head shot of Berman along with a list of players and nicknames under the heading, "Baseball Nickname Hall of Fame."

1 Chris Berman .40 1.00

1997 Upper Deck Home Team Heroes

This 12-card set measures approximately 5" by 3 1/2" and features two color action embossed images of top players from the same team printed on a die-cut card with silver foil enhancements. The backs carry two small color action player photos with player information in paragraph form.

COMPLETE SET (12) 4.00 10.00
HT1 Alex Rodriguez 1.50 4.00
Ken Griffey Jr.
HT2 Bernie Williams .75 2.00
Derek Jeter
HT3 Bernard Gilkey .20 .50
Todd Hundley
HT4 Hideo Nomo .30 .75
Mike Piazza
HT5 Andruw Jones 1.00 2.50
Chipper Jones
HT6 John Smoltz 1.00 2.50
Greg Maddux
HT7 Mike Mussina 1.25 3.00
Cal Ripken Jr.
HT8 Andres Galarraga .30 .75
Dante Bichette
HT9 Juan Gonzalez .75 2.00
Ivan Rodriguez
HT10 Albert Belle .75 2.00
Frank Thomas
HT11 Kenny Lofton .30 .75
Manny Ramirez
HT12 Ken Caminiti .75 2.00
Tony Gwynn

1997 Upper Deck Ken Griffey Jr. Highlight Reels

This five-card hi-tech Diamond Vision set features actual MLB video footage of Ken Griffey Jr.'s most unbelievable plays. Each card was distributed in clamshell packaging for a suggested retail price of $9.99. The cards measure approximately 3.5" by 5" with each card containing over 20 frames of actual video footage of the player.

COMMON CARD (1-5) 4.00 10.00

1997 Upper Deck Shimano

This six-card set features color photos of top fishermen on a background of fish images with side and bottom aqua borders. The backs carry a smaller head photo and information about the pictured fisherman.

COMPLETE SET (6) 1.60 4.00
5 Jay Buhner .40 1.00
6 Tony Gwynn 1.20 3.00

1997 Upper Deck Sister Assumpta Trivia

This one-card set was introduced at the National in Cleveland, Ohio, on August 7, 1997, and is a tribute to Indians fan, Sister Mary Assumpta, who began baking chocolate chip cookies for the players in 1986. The front features the nun's picture holding a bat and a cookie. The back displays ten trivia questions with the answers printed upside down in a blue bar at the bottom.

1 Sister Mary Assumpta .20 .50

1998 Upper Deck

The 1998 Upper Deck set was issued in three series consisting of a 270-card first series, a 270-card second series and a 211-card third series. Each series was distributed in 12-card packs which carried a suggested retail price of $2.49. Card fronts feature game dated photographs of some of the season's most memorable moments. The following subsets are contained within the set: History in the Making (1-8/361-369), Griffey's Hot List (9-18), Define the Game (136-153), Season Highlights (244-252/532-540/748-750), Star Rookies (253-288/541-600), Postseason Headliners (415-432), Upper Echelon (451-459) and Eminent Prestige (601-630). The Eminent Prestige subset cards were slightly shortprinted (approximately 1:4 packs) and Upper Deck offered a free service to collectors trying to finish their Series three sets whereby Eminent Prestige cards were mailed to collectors who sent in proof of purchase of one-and-a-half boxes or more. The print run for Mike Piazza card number 681 was split exactly in half creating two shortprints: card number 681 (picturing Piazza as a New York Met) and card number 681A (picturing Piazza as a Florida Marlin). Both cards are exactly two times tougher to pull from packs than other regular issue Series three cards. The series three set is considered complete with both versions at 251 total cards. Notable Rookie Cards include Gabe Kapler and Magglio Ordonez.

COMPLETE SET (751) 100.00 200.00
COMPLETE SERIES 1 (270) 15.00 40.00
COMPLETE SERIES 2 (270) 15.00 40.00
COMPLETE SERIES 3 (211) 50.00 120.00
COMMON (1-600/631-750) .10 .30
COMMON EP (601-630) .75 2.00
EP SER.2 ODDS APPROXIMATELY 1:4
1 Tino Martinez HIST .10 .30
2 Jimmy Key HIST .10 .30
3 Jay Buhner HIST .10 .30
4 Mark Gardner HIST .10 .30
5 Greg Maddux HIST .30 .75
6 Pedro Martinez HIST .20 .50
7 Hideo Nomo HIST .20 .50
8 Sammy Sosa HIST .20 .50
9 Mark McGwire GHL .40 1.00
10 Ken Griffey Jr. GHL .40 1.00
11 Larry Walker GHL .10 .30
12 Tino Martinez GHL .10 .30
13 Mike Piazza GHL .30 .75
14 Jose Cruz Jr. GHL .10 .30
15 Tony Gwynn GHL .20 .50
16 Greg Maddux GHL .30 .75
17 Roger Clemens GHL .30 .75
18 Alex Rodriguez GHL .30 .75
19 Shigetoshi Hasegawa .10 .30
20 Eddie Murray .30 .75
21 Jason Dickson .10 .30
22 Darin Erstad .10 .30
23 Chuck Finley .10 .30
24 Dave Hollins .10 .30
25 Garret Anderson .10 .30
26 Michael Tucker .10 .30
27 Kenny Lofton .10 .30
28 Javier Lopez .10 .30
29 Fred McGriff .20 .50
30 Greg Maddux .50 1.25
31 Jeff Blauser .10 .30
32 John Smoltz .20 .50
33 Mark Wohlers .10 .30
34 Scott Erickson .10 .30
35 Jimmy Key .10 .30
36 Harold Baines .10 .30
37 Randy Myers .10 .30
38 B.J. Surhoff .10 .30
39 Eric Davis .10 .30
40 Rafael Palmeiro .20 .50
41 Jeffrey Hammonds .10 .30
42 Mo Vaughn .10 .30
43 Tom Gordon .10 .30
44 Tim Naehring .10 .30
45 Darren Bragg .10 .30
46 Aaron Sele .10 .30
47 Troy O'Leary .10 .30
48 John Valentin .10 .30
49 Doug Glanville .10 .30
50 Ryne Sandberg .50 1.25
51 Steve Trachsel .10 .30
52 Mark Grace .20 .50
53 Kevin Foster .10 .30
54 Kevin Tapani .10 .30
55 Kevin Orie .10 .30
56 Lyle Mouton .10 .30
57 Ray Durham .10 .30
58 Jaime Navarro .10 .30
59 Mike Cameron .10 .30
60 Albert Belle .10 .30
61 Doug Drabek .10 .30
62 Chris Snopek .10 .30
63 Eddie Taubensee .10 .30
64 Terry Pendleton .10 .30
65 Barry Larkin .20 .50
66 Willie Greene .10 .30
67 Deion Sanders .20 .50
68 Pokey Reese .10 .30
69 Jeff Shaw .10 .30
70 Jim Thome .20 .50
71 Orel Hershiser .10 .30
72 Omar Vizquel .20 .50
73 Brian Giles .10 .30
74 David Justice .10 .30
75 Bartolo Colon .10 .30
76 Sandy Alomar Jr. .10 .30
77 Neifi Perez .10 .30
78 Dante Bichette .10 .30
79 Vinny Castilla .10 .30
80 Eric Young .10 .30
81 Quinton McCracken .10 .30
82 Jamey Wright .10 .30
83 John Thomson .10 .30
84 Damion Easley .10 .30
85 Justin Thompson .10 .30
86 Willie Blair .10 .30
87 Raul Casanova .10 .30
88 Bobby Higginson .10 .30
89 Bubba Trammell .10 .30
90 Tony Clark .10 .30
91 Livan Hernandez .10 .30
92 Charles Johnson .10 .30
93 Edgar Renteria .10 .30
94 Alex Fernandez .10 .30
95 Gary Sheffield .10 .30
96 Moises Alou .10 .30
97 Tony Saunders .10 .30
98 Robb Nen .10 .30
99 Darryl Kile .10 .30
100 Craig Biggio .20 .50
101 Chris Holt .10 .30
102 Bob Abreu .10 .30
103 Luis Gonzalez .10 .30
104 Billy Wagner .10 .30
105 Brad Ausmus .10 .30
106 Chili Davis .10 .30
107 Tim Belcher .10 .30
108 Dean Palmer .10 .30
109 Jeff King .10 .30
110 Jose Rosado .10 .30
111 Mike Macfarlane .10 .30
112 Jay Bell .10 .30
113 Todd Worrell .10 .30
114 Chan Ho Park .10 .30
115 Raul Mondesi .10 .30
116 Brett Butler .10 .30
117 Greg Gagne .10 .30
118 Hideo Nomo .30 .75
119 Todd Zeile .10 .30
120 Eric Karros .10 .30
121 Cal Eldred .10 .30
122 Jeff D'Amico .10 .30
123 Antone Williamson .10 .30
124 Doug Jones .10 .30
125 Dave Nilsson .10 .30
126 Gerald Williams .10 .30
127 Fernando Vina .10 .30
128 Ron Coomer .10 .30
129 Matt Lawton .10 .30
130 Paul Molitor .10 .30
131 Todd Walker .10 .30
132 Rick Aguilera .10 .30
133 Brad Radke .10 .30
134 Bob Tewksbury .10 .30
135 Vladimir Guerrero .30 .75
136 Tony Gwynn DG .20 .50
137 Roger Clemens DG .30 .75
138 Dennis Eckersley DG .10 .30
139 Brady Anderson DG .10 .30
140 Ken Griffey Jr. DG .40 1.00
141 Derek Jeter DG .40 1.00
142 Ken Caminiti DG .10 .30
143 Frank Thomas DG .20 .50
144 Barry Bonds DG .40 1.00
145 Cal Ripken DG .50 1.25
146 Alex Rodriguez DG .30 .75
147 Greg Maddux DG .30 .75
148 Kenny Lofton DG .10 .30
149 Mike Piazza DG .30 .75
150 Mark McGwire DG .40 1.00
151 Andruw Jones DG .10 .30
152 Rusty Greer DG .10 .30
153 F.P. Santangelo DG .10 .30
154 Mike Lansing .10 .30
155 Lee Smith .10 .30
156 Carlos Perez .10 .30
157 Pedro Martinez .20 .50
158 Ryan McGuire .10 .30
159 F.P. Santangelo .10 .30
160 Rondell White .10 .30
161 Takashi Kashiwada RC .15 .40
162 Butch Huskey .10 .30
163 Edgardo Alfonzo .10 .30
164 John Franco .10 .30
165 Todd Hundley .10 .30
166 Rey Ordonez .10 .30
167 Armando Reynoso .10 .30
168 John Olerud .10 .30
169 Bernie Williams .20 .50
170 Andy Pettitte .20 .50
171 Wade Boggs .20 .50
172 Paul O'Neill .20 .50
173 Cecil Fielder .10 .30
174 Charlie Hayes .10 .30
175 David Cone .10 .30
176 Hideki Irabu .10 .30
177 Mark Bellhorn .10 .30
178 Steve Karsay .10 .30
179 Damon Mashore .10 .30
180 Jason McDonald .10 .30
181 Scott Spiezio .10 .30
182 Ariel Prieto .10 .30
183 Jason Giambi .10 .30
184 Wendell Magee .10 .30
185 Rico Brogna .10 .30
186 Garrett Stephenson .10 .30
187 Wayne Gomes .10 .30
188 Ricky Bottalico .10 .30
189 Mickey Morandini .10 .30
190 Mike Lieberthal .10 .30
191 Kevin Polcovich .10 .30
192 Francisco Cordova .10 .30
193 Kevin Young .10 .30
194 Jon Lieber .10 .30
195 Kevin Elster .10 .30
196 Tony Womack .10 .30
197 Lou Collier .10 .30
198 Mike Difelice RC .15 .40
199 Gary Gaetti .10 .30
200 Dennis Eckersley .10 .30
201 Alan Benes .10 .30
202 Willie McGee .10 .30
203 Ron Gant .10 .30
204 Fernando Valenzuela .10 .30
205 Mark McGwire .75 2.00
206 Archi Cianfrocco .10 .30
207 Andy Ashby .10 .30
208 Steve Finley .10 .30
209 Quilvio Veras .10 .30
210 Ken Caminiti .10 .30
211 Rickey Henderson .30 .75
212 Joey Hamilton .10 .30
213 Derrek Lee .20 .50
214 Bill Mueller .10 .30
215 Shawn Estes .10 .30
216 J.T. Snow .10 .30
217 Mark Gardner .10 .30
218 Terry Mulholland .10 .30
219 Dante Powell .10 .30
220 Jeff Kent .10 .30
221 Jamie Moyer .10 .30
222 Joey Cora .10 .30
223 Jeff Fassero .10 .30
224 Dennis Martinez .10 .30
225 Ken Griffey Jr. .60 1.50
226 Edgar Martinez .20 .50
227 Russ Davis .10 .30
228 Dan Wilson .10 .30
229 Will Clark .20 .50
230 Ivan Rodriguez .20 .50
231 Benji Gil .10 .30
232 Lee Stevens .10 .30
233 Mickey Tettleton .10 .30
234 Julio Santana .10 .30
235 Rusty Greer .10 .30
236 Bobby Witt .10 .30
237 Ed Sprague .10 .30
238 Pat Hentgen .10 .30
239 Kelvim Escobar .10 .30
240 Joe Carter .10 .30
241 Carlos Delgado .10 .30
242 Shannon Stewart .10 .30
243 Benito Santiago .10 .30
244 Tino Martinez SH .10 .30
245 Ken Griffey Jr. SH .40 1.00
246 Kevin Brown SH .10 .30
247 Ryne Sandberg SH .20 .50
248 Mo Vaughn SH .10 .30
249 Darryl Hamilton SH .10 .30
250 Randy Johnson SH .20 .50
251 Steve Finley SH .10 .30
252 Bobby Higginson SH .10 .30
253 Brett Tomko .10 .30
254 Mark Kotsay .10 .30
255 Jose Guillen .10 .30
256 Eli Marrero .10 .30
257 Dennis Reyes .10 .30
258 Richie Sexson .10 .30
259 Pat Cline .10 .30
260 Todd Helton .20 .50
261 Juan Melo .10 .30
262 Matt Morris .10 .30
263 Jeremi Gonzalez .10 .30
264 Jeff Abbott .10 .30
265 Aaron Boone .10 .30
266 Todd Dunwoody .10 .30
267 Jaret Wright .10 .30
268 Derrick Gibson .10 .30
269 Mario Valdez .10 .30
270 Fernando Tatis .10 .30
271 Craig Counsell .10 .30
272 Brad Rigby .10 .30
273 Danny Clyburn .10 .30
274 Brian Rose .10 .30
275 Miguel Tejada .30 .75
276 Jason Varitek .30 .75
277 Dave Dellucci RC .25 .60
278 Michael Coleman .10 .30
279 Adam Riggs .10 .30
280 Ben Grieve .10 .30
281 Brad Fullmer .10 .30
282 Ken Cloude .10 .30
283 Tom Evans .10 .30
284 Kevin Millwood RC .40 1.00
285 Paul Konerko .10 .30
286 Juan Encarnacion .10 .30
287 Chris Carpenter .10 .30
288 Tom Fordham .10 .30
289 Gary DiSarcina .10 .30
290 Tim Salmon .20 .50
291 Troy Percival .10 .30
292 Todd Greene .10 .30
293 Ken Hill .10 .30
294 Dennis Springer .10 .30
295 Jim Edmonds .10 .30
296 Allen Watson .10 .30
297 Brian Anderson .10 .30
298 Keith Lockhart .10 .30
299 Tom Glavine .20 .50
300 Chipper Jones .30 .75
301 Randall Simon .10 .30
302 Mark Lemke .10 .30
303 Ryan Klesko .10 .30
304 Denny Neagle .10 .30
305 Andruw Jones .20 .50
306 Mike Mussina .20 .50
307 Brady Anderson .10 .30
308 Chris Hoiles .10 .30
309 Mike Bordick .10 .30
310 Cal Ripken 1.00 2.50
311 Geronimo Berroa .10 .30
312 Armando Benitez .10 .30
313 Roberto Alomar .20 .50
314 Tim Wakefield .10 .30
315 Reggie Jefferson .10 .30
316 Jeff Frye .10 .30
317 Scott Hatteberg .10 .30
318 Steve Avery .10 .30
319 Robinson Checo .10 .30
320 Nomar Garciaparra .50 1.25
321 Lance Johnson .10 .30
322 Tyler Houston .10 .30
323 Mark Clark .10 .30
324 Terry Adams .10 .30
325 Sammy Sosa .30 .75
326 Scott Servais .10 .30
327 Manny Alexander .10 .30
328 Norberto Martin .10 .30
329 Scott Eyre .10 .30
330 Frank Thomas .30 .75
331 Robin Ventura .10 .30
332 Matt Karchner .10 .30
333 Keith Foulke .10 .30
334 James Baldwin .10 .30
335 Chris Stynes .10 .30
336 Bret Boone .10 .30
337 Jon Nunnally .10 .30
338 Dave Burba .10 .30
339 Eduardo Perez .10 .30
340 Reggie Sanders .10 .30
341 Mike Remlinger .10 .30
342 Pat Watkins .10 .30
343 Chad Ogea .10 .30
344 John Smiley .10 .30
345 Kenny Lofton .10 .30
346 Jose Mesa .10 .30
347 Charles Nagy .10 .30
348 Enrique Wilson .10 .30
349 Bruce Aven .10 .30
350 Manny Ramirez .20 .50
351 Jerry DiPoto .10 .30
352 Ellis Burks .10 .30
353 Kirt Manwaring .10 .30
354 Vinny Castilla .10 .30
355 Larry Walker .10 .30
356 Kevin Ritz .10 .30
357 Pedro Astacio .10 .30
358 Scott Sanders .10 .30
359 Deivi Cruz .10 .30
360 Brian L. Hunter .10 .30
361 Pedro Martinez HM .20 .50
362 Tom Glavine HM .10 .30
363 Willie McGee HM .10 .30
364 J.T. Snow HM .10 .30
365 Rusty Greer HM .10 .30
366 Mike Grace HM .10 .30
367 Tony Clark HM .10 .30
368 Ben Grieve HM .10 .30
369 Gary Sheffield HM .10 .30
370 Joe Oliver .10 .30
371 Todd Jones .10 .30
372 Frank Catalanotto RC .25 .60
373 Brian Moehler .10 .30
374 Cliff Floyd .10 .30
375 Bobby Bonilla .10 .30
376 Al Leiter .10 .30
377 Josh Booty .10 .30
378 Darren Daulton .10 .30
379 Jay Powell .10 .30
380 Felix Heredia .10 .30
381 Jim Eisenreich .10 .30
382 Richard Hidalgo .10 .30
383 Mike Hampton .10 .30
384 Shane Reynolds .10 .30
385 Jeff Bagwell .20 .50
386 Derek Bell .10 .30
387 Ricky Gutierrez .10 .30
388 Bill Spiers .10 .30
389 Jose Offerman .10 .30
390 Johnny Damon .20 .50
391 Jermaine Dye .10 .30
302 Jeff Montgomery .10 .30
393 Glendon Rusch .10 .30
394 Mike Sweeney .10 .30
395 Kevin Appier .10 .30
396 Joe Vitiello .10 .30
397 Ramon Martinez .10 .30
398 Darren Dreifort .10 .30
399 Wilton Guerrero .10 .30
400 Mike Piazza .50 1.25
401 Eddie Murray .30 .75
402 Ismael Valdes .10 .30
403 Todd Hollandsworth .10 .30
404 Mark Loretta .10 .30
405 Jeromy Burnitz .10 .30
406 Jeff Cirillo .10 .30
407 Scott Karl .10 .30
408 Mike Matheny .10 .30
409 Jose Valentin .10 .30
410 John Jaha .10 .30
411 Terry Steinbach .10 .30
412 Torii Hunter .10 .30
413 Pat Meares .10 .30
414 Marty Cordova .10 .30
415 Jaret Wright PH .10 .30
416 Mike Mussina PH .10 .30
417 John Smoltz PH .10 .30
418 Devon White PH .10 .30
419 Denny Neagle PH .10 .30
420 Livan Hernandez PH .10 .30
421 Kevin Brown PH .10 .30
422 Marquis Grissom PH .10 .30
423 Mike Mussina PH .10 .30
424 Eric Davis PH .10 .30
425 Tony Fernandez PH .10 .30
426 Moises Alou PH .10 .30
427 Sandy Alomar Jr. PH .10 .30
428 Gary Sheffield PH .10 .30
429 Jaret Wright PH .10 .30
430 Livan Hernandez PH .10 .30
431 Chad Ogea PH .10 .30
432 Edgar Renteria PH .10 .30
433 LaTroy Hawkins .10 .30
434 Rich Robertson .10 .30
435 Chuck Knoblauch .10 .30
436 Jose Vidro .10 .30
437 Dustin Hermanson .10 .30
438 Jim Bullinger .10 .30
439 Orlando Cabrera .10 .30
440 Vladimir Guerrero .30 .75
441 Ugueth Urbina .10 .30
442 Brian McRae .10 .30
443 Matt Franco .10 .30
444 Bobby Jones .10 .30
445 Bernard Gilkey .10 .30
446 Dave Mlicki .10 .30
447 Brian Bohanon .10 .30
448 Mel Rojas .10 .30
449 Tim Raines .10 .30
450 Derek Jeter .75 2.00
451 Roger Clemens UE .30 .75
452 Nomar Garciaparra UE .30 .75
453 Mike Piazza UE .30 .75
454 Mark McGwire UE .40 1.00
455 Ken Griffey Jr. UE .40 1.00
456 Larry Walker UE .10 .30
457 Alex Rodriguez UE .30 .75
458 Tony Gwynn UE .20 .50
459 Frank Thomas UE .20 .50
460 Tino Martinez .20 .50
461 Chad Curtis .10 .30
462 Ramiro Mendoza .10 .30
463 Joe Girardi .10 .30
464 David Wells .10 .30
465 Mariano Rivera .30 .75
466 Willie Adams .10 .30
467 George Williams .10 .30
468 Dave Telgheder .10 .30
469 Dave Magadan .10 .30
470 Matt Stairs .10 .30
471 Bill Taylor .10 .30
472 Jimmy Haynes .10 .30
473 Gregg Jefferies .10 .30
474 Midre Cummings .10 .30
475 Curt Schilling .10 .30
476 Mike Grace .10 .30
477 Mark Leiter .10 .30
478 Matt Beech .10 .30
479 Scott Rolen .20 .50
480 Jason Kendall .10 .30
481 Esteban Loaiza .10 .30
482 Jermaine Allensworth .10 .30
483 Mark Smith .10 .30
484 Jason Schmidt .10 .30
485 Jose Guillen .10 .30
486 Al Martin .10 .30
487 Delino DeShields .10 .30
488 Todd Stottlemyre .10 .30
489 Brian Jordan .10 .30
490 Ray Lankford .10 .30
491 Matt Morris .10 .30
492 Royce Clayton .10 .30
493 John Mabry .10 .30
494 Wally Joyner .10 .30
495 Trevor Hoffman .10 .30
496 Chris Gomez .10 .30
497 Sterling Hitchcock .10 .30
498 Pete Smith .10 .30
499 Greg Vaughn .10 .30
500 Tony Gwynn .40 1.00
501 Will Cunnane .10 .30
502 Darryl Hamilton .10 .30
503 Brian Johnson .10 .30
504 Kirk Rueter .10 .30
505 Barry Bonds .75 2.00
506 Osvaldo Fernandez .10 .30
507 Stan Javier .10 .30
508 Julian Tavarez .10 .30
509 Rich Aurilia .10 .30
510 Alex Rodriguez .50 1.25
511 David Segui .10 .30
512 Rich Amaral .10 .30
513 Raul Ibanez .10 .30
514 Jay Buhner .10 .30
515 Randy Johnson .30 .75
516 Heathcliff Slocumb .10 .30
517 Tony Saunders .10 .30
518 Kevin Elster .10 .30
519 John Burkett .10 .30
520 Juan Gonzalez .10 .30
521 John Wetteland .10 .30
522 Domingo Cedeno .10 .30
523 Darren Oliver .10 .30
524 Roger Pavlik .10 .30
525 Jose Cruz Jr. .10 .30
526 Woody Williams .10 .30
527 Alex Gonzalez .10 .30
528 Robert Person .10 .30
529 Juan Guzman .10 .30
530 Roger Clemens .60 1.50
531 Shawn Green .10 .30
532 F.Cordova .10 .30
R.Rincon
M.Smith SH
533 Nomar Garciaparra SH .30 .75
534 Roger Clemens SH .30 .75
535 Mark McGwire SH .40 1.00
536 Larry Walker SH .10 .30
537 Mike Piazza SH .30 .75
538 Curt Schilling SH .10 .30
539 Tony Gwynn SH .20 .50
540 Ken Griffey Jr. SH .40 1.00
541 Carl Pavano .10 .30
542 Shane Monahan .10 .30
543 Gabe Kapler RC .25 .60
544 Eric Milton .10 .30
545 Gary Matthews Jr. RC .25 .60
546 Mike Kinkade RC .10 .30
547 Ryan Christenson RC .10 .30
548 Corey Koskie RC .25 .60
549 Norm Hutchins .10 .30
550 Russell Branyan .10 .30
551 Masato Yoshii RC .15 .40
552 Jesus Sanchez RC .10 .30
553 Anthony Sanders .10 .30
554 Edwin Diaz .10 .30
555 Gabe Alvarez .10 .30
556 Carlos Lee RC .75 2.00
557 Mike Darr .10 .30
558 Kerry Wood .15 .40
550 Carlos Guillen .10 .30
560 Sean Casey .10 .30
561 Manny Aybar RC .10 .30
562 Octavio Dotel .10 .30
563 Jarrod Washburn .10 .30
564 Mark L. Johnson .10 .30
565 Ramon Hernandez .10 .30
566 Rich Butler RC .10 .30
567 Mike Caruso .10 .30
568 Cliff Politte .10 .30
569 Scott Elarton .10 .30
570 Magglio Ordonez RC 1.25 3.00
571 Adam Butler RC .10 .30
572 Marlon Anderson .10 .30
573 Julio Ramirez RC .10 .30
574 Darron Ingram RC .10 .30
575 Bruce Chen .10 .30
576 Steve Woodard .10 .30
577 Hiram Bocachica .10 .30
578 Kevin Witt .10 .30
579 Javier Vazquez .10 .30
580 Alex Gonzalez .10 .30
581 Brian Powell .10 .30
582 Wes Helms .10 .30
583 Ron Wright .10 .30
584 Rafael Medina .10 .30
585 Daryle Ward .10 .30
586 Geoff Jenkins .10 .30
587 Preston Wilson .10 .30
588 Jim Chamblee RC .10 .30
589 Mike Lowell RC .60 1.50
590 A.J. Hinch .10 .30
591 Francisco Cordero RC .25 .60
592 Rolando Arrojo RC .15 .40
593 Braden Looper .10 .30
594 Sidney Ponson .10 .30
595 Matt Clement .10 .30
596 Carlton Loewer .10 .30
597 Brian Meadows .10 .30
598 Danny Klassen .10 .30
599 Larry Sutton .10 .30
600 Travis Lee .10 .30
601 Randy Johnson EP 1.00 2.50
602 Greg Maddux EP 1.50 4.00
603 Roger Clemens EP 2.00 5.00
604 Jaret Wright EP .75 2.00
605 Mike Piazza EP 1.50 4.00
606 Tino Martinez EP .75 2.00

607 Frank Thomas EP 1.00 2.50
608 Mo Vaughn EP .75 2.00
609 Todd Helton EP .75 2.00
610 Mark McGwire EP 2.50 6.00
611 Jeff Bagwell EP .75 2.00
612 Travis Lee EP .75 2.00
613 Scott Rolen EP .75 2.00
614 Cal Ripken EP 3.00 8.00
615 Chipper Jones EP 1.00 2.50
616 Nomar Garciaparra EP 1.50 4.00
617 Alex Rodriguez EP 1.50 4.00
618 Derek Jeter EP 2.50 6.00
619 Tony Gwynn EP 1.25 3.00
620 Ken Griffey Jr. EP 2.00 5.00
621 Kenny Lofton EP .75 2.00
622 Juan Gonzalez EP .75 2.00
623 Jose Cruz Jr. EP .75 2.00
624 Larry Walker EP .75 2.00
625 Barry Bonds EP 2.50 6.00
626 Ben Grieve EP .75 2.00
627 Andruw Jones EP .75 2.00
628 Vladimir Guerrero EP 1.00 2.50
629 Paul Konerko EP .75 2.00
630 Paul Molitor EP .75 2.00
631 Cecil Fielder .10 .30
632 Jack McDowell .10 .30
633 Mike James .10 .30
634 Brian Anderson .10 .30
635 Jay Bell .10 .30
636 Devon White .10 .30
637 Andy Stankiewicz .10 .30
638 Tony Batista .10 .30
639 Omar Daal .10 .30
640 Matt Williams .10 .30
641 Brent Brede .10 .30
642 Jorge Fabregas .10 .30
643 Karim Garcia .10 .30
644 Felix Rodriguez .10 .30
645 Andy Benes .10 .30
646 Willie Blair .10 .30
647 Jeff Suppan .10 .30
648 Yamil Benitez .10 .30
649 Walt Weiss .10 .30
650 Andres Galarraga .10 .30
651 Doug Drabek .10 .30
652 Ozzie Guillen .10 .30
653 Joe Carter .10 .30
654 Dennis Eckersley .10 .30
655 Pedro Martinez .20 .50
656 Jim Leyritz .10 .30
657 Henry Rodriguez .10 .30
658 Rod Beck .10 .30
659 Mickey Morandini .10 .30
660 Jeff Blauser .10 .30
661 Ruben Sierra .10 .30
662 Mike Sirotka .10 .30
663 Pete Harnisch .10 .30
664 Damian Jackson .10 .30
665 Dmitri Young .10 .30
666 Steve Cooke .10 .30
667 Geronimo Berroa .10 .30
668 Shawon Dunston .10 .30
669 Mike Jackson .10 .30
670 Travis Fryman .10 .30
671 Dwight Gooden .10 .30
672 Paul Assenmacher .10 .30
673 Eric Plunk .10 .30
674 Mike Lansing .10 .30
675 Darryl Kile .10 .30
676 Luis Gonzalez .10 .30
677 Frank Castillo .10 .30
678 Joe Randa .10 .30
679 Bip Roberts .10 .30
680 Derrek Lee .20 .50
681 M.Piazza Mets SP 1.25 3.00
681A M.Piazza Marlins SP 1.25 3.00
682 Sean Berry .10 .30
683 Ramon Garcia .10 .30
684 Carl Everett .10 .30
685 Moises Alou .10 .30
686 Hal Morris .10 .30
687 Jeff Conine .10 .30
688 Gary Sheffield .10 .30
689 Jose Vizcaino .10 .30
690 Charles Johnson .10 .30
691 Bobby Bonilla .10 .30
692 Marquis Grissom .10 .30
693 Alex Ochoa .10 .30
694 Mike Morgan .10 .30
695 Orlando Merced .10 .30
696 David Ortiz .40 1.00
697 Brent Gates .10 .30
698 Otis Nixon .10 .30
699 Trey Moore .10 .30
700 Derrick May .10 .30
701 Rich Becker .10 .30
702 Al Leiter .10 .30
703 Chili Davis .10 .30
704 Scott Brosius .10 .30
705 Chuck Knoblauch .10 .30
706 Kenny Rogers .10 .30
707 Mike Blowers .10 .30
708 Mike Fetters .10 .30
709 Tom Candiotti .10 .30
710 Rickey Henderson .30 .75
711 Bob Abreu .10 .30
712 Mark Lewis .10 .30
713 Doug Glanville .10 .30
714 Desi Relaford .10 .30
715 Kent Mercker .10 .30
716 Kevin Brown .20 .50
717 James Mouton .10 .30
718 Mark Langston .10 .30
719 Greg Myers .10 .30
720 Orel Hershiser .10 .30
721 Charlie Hayes .10 .30
722 Robb Nen .10 .30
723 Glenallen Hill .10 .30
724 Tony Saunders .10 .30
725 Wade Boggs .20 .50
726 Kevin Stocker .10 .30
727 Wilson Alvarez .10 .30
728 Albie Lopez .10 .30
729 Dave Martinez .10 .30
730 Fred McGriff .20 .50
731 Quinton McCracken .10 .30
732 Bryan Rekar .10 .30
733 Paul Sorrento .10 .30
734 Roberto Hernandez .10 .30
735 Bubba Trammell .10 .30
736 Miguel Cairo .10 .30
737 John Flaherty .10 .30
738 Terrell Wade .10 .30
739 Roberto Kelly .10 .30
740 Mark McLemore .10 .30
741 Danny Patterson .10 .30
742 Aaron Sele .10 .30
743 Tony Fernandez .10 .30
744 Randy Myers .10 .30
745 Jose Canseco .20 .50
746 Darrin Fletcher .10 .30
747 Mike Stanley .10 .30
748 Marquis Grissom SH CL .10 .30
749 Fred McGriff SH CL .10 .30
750 Travis Lee SH CL .10 .30

1998 Upper Deck 3 x 5 Blow Ups

27 Kenny Lofton .30 .75
30 Greg Maddux 1.00 2.50
40 Rafael Palmeiro .50 1.25
50 Ryne Sandberg 1.25 3.00
60 Albert Belle .30 .75
65 Barry Larkin .50 1.25
67 Deion Sanders .50 1.25
95 Gary Sheffield .50 1.25
130 Paul Molitor .75 2.00
135 Vladimir Guerrero .50 1.25
176 Hideki Irabu .30 .75
205 Mark McGwire 1.25 3.00
211 Rickey Henderson .75 2.00
225 Ken Griffey Jr. 1.50 4.00
230 Ivan Rodriguez .50 1.25

1998 Upper Deck 5 x 7 Blow Ups

310 Cal Ripken 2.50 6.00
320 Nomar Garciaparra .50 1.25
330 Frank Thomas .75 2.00
355 Larry Walker .50 1.25
385 Jeff Bagwell .50 1.25
400 Mike Piazza .75 2.00
450 Derek Jeter 2.00 5.00
500 Tony Gwynn .75 2.00
510 Alex Rodriguez 1.00 2.50
530 Roger Clemens 1.00 2.50

1998 Upper Deck 10th Anniversary Preview

COMPLETE SET (60) 60.00 120.00
SER.1 STATED ODDS 1:5
COMP.RETAIL SET (60) 8.00 20.00
*RETAIL: .08X TO .2X BASIC 10TH ANN
RETAIL DISTRIBUTED AS FACTORY SET
1 Greg Maddux 2.00 5.00
2 Mike Mussina .75 2.00
3 Roger Clemens 2.50 6.00
4 Hideo Nomo 1.25 3.00
5 David Cone .50 1.25
6 Tom Glavine .75 2.00
7 Andy Pettitte .75 2.00
8 Jimmy Key .50 1.25
9 Randy Johnson 1.25 3.00
10 Dennis Eckersley .50 1.25
11 Lee Smith .50 1.25
12 John Franco .50 1.25
13 Randy Myers .50 1.25
14 Mike Piazza 2.00 5.00
15 Ivan Rodriguez .75 2.00
16 Todd Hundley .50 1.25
17 Sandy Alomar Jr. .50 1.25
18 Frank Thomas 1.25 3.00
19 Rafael Palmeiro .75 2.00
20 Mark McGwire 3.00 8.00
21 Mo Vaughn .50 1.25
22 Fred McGriff .75 2.00
23 Andres Galarraga .50 1.25
24 Mark Grace .75 2.00
25 Jeff Bagwell .75 2.00
26 Roberto Alomar .75 2.00
27 Chuck Knoblauch .50 1.25
28 Ryne Sandberg 2.00 5.00
29 Eric Young .50 1.25
30 Craig Biggio .75 2.00
31 Carlos Baerga .50 1.25
32 Robin Ventura .50 1.25
33 Matt Williams .50 1.25
34 Wade Boggs .75 2.00
35 Dean Palmer .50 1.25
36 Chipper Jones 1.25 3.00
37 Vinny Castilla .50 1.25
38 Ken Caminiti .50 1.25
39 Omar Vizquel .75 2.00
40 Cal Ripken 4.00 10.00
41 Derek Jeter 3.00 8.00
42 Alex Rodriguez 2.00 5.00
43 Barry Larkin .75 2.00
44 Mark Grudzielanek .50 1.25
45 Albert Belle .50 1.25
46 Manny Ramirez .75 2.00
47 Jose Canseco .75 2.00
48 Ken Griffey Jr. 2.50 6.00
49 Juan Gonzalez .50 1.25
50 Kenny Lofton .50 1.25
51 Sammy Sosa 1.25 3.00
52 Larry Walker .50 1.25
53 Gary Sheffield .50 1.25
54 Rickey Henderson 1.25 3.00
55 Tony Gwynn 1.50 4.00
56 Barry Bonds 3.00 8.00
57 Paul Molitor .75 2.00
58 Edgar Martinez .75 2.00
59 Chili Davis .50 1.25
60 Eddie Murray 1.25 3.00

1998 Upper Deck 10th Anniversary Preview Retail

COMPLETE SET (60) 8.00 20.00
*:STARS: .08X TO .2X BASIC CARDS

1998 Upper Deck A Piece of the Action 1

SER.1 STATED ODDS 1:2500
MULTI-COLOR PATCHES CARRY PREMIUMS
1 Jay Buhner Bat 10.00 25.00
2 Tony Gwynn Bat 15.00 40.00
3 Tony Gwynn Jersey 15.00 40.00
4 Todd Hollandsworth Bat 6.00 15.00
5 Todd Hollandsworth Jersey 6.00 15.00
6 Greg Maddux Jersey 30.00 60.00
7 Alex Rodriguez Bat 15.00 40.00
8 Alex Rodriguez Jersey 15.00 40.00
9 Gary Sheffield Bat 10.00 25.00
10 Gary Sheffield Jersey 10.00 25.00

1998 Upper Deck A Piece of the Action 2

SER.2 STATED ODDS 1:2500
STATED PRINT RUN 225 SETS
AJ Andruw Jones 30.00 60.00
GS Gary Sheffield 15.00 40.00
JB Jay Buhner 15.00 40.00
RA Roberto Alomar 30.00 60.00

1998 Upper Deck A Piece of the Action 3

RANDOM INSERTS IN SER.3 PACKS
PRINT RUNS B/WN 200-300 #'d COPIES PER
GRIFFEY AU PRINT RUN 24 #'d CARDS
NO GRIFFEY AU PRICE DUE TO SCARCITY
BG Ben Grieve/200 10.00 25.00
JC Jose Cruz Jr./200 10.00 25.00
KG Ken Griffey Jr./300 15.00 40.00
TL Travis Lee/200 10.00 25.00
KGS Ken Griffey Jr. AU/24

1998 Upper Deck All-Star Credentials

COMPLETE SET (30) 40.00 100.00
SER.3 STATED ODDS 1:9
AS1 Ken Griffey Jr. 2.50 6.00
AS2 Travis Lee .50 1.25
AS3 Ben Grieve .50 1.25
AS4 Jose Cruz Jr. .50 1.25
AS5 Andruw Jones .75 2.00
AS6 Craig Biggio .75 2.00
AS7 Hideo Nomo 1.25 3.00
AS8 Cal Ripken 4.00 10.00
AS9 Jaret Wright .50 1.25
AS10 Mark McGwire 3.00 8.00
AS11 Derek Jeter 3.00 8.00
AS12 Scott Rolen .75 2.00
AS13 Jeff Bagwell .75 2.00
AS14 Manny Ramirez .75 2.00
AS15 Alex Rodriguez 2.00 5.00
AS16 Chipper Jones 1.25 3.00
AS17 Larry Walker .50 1.25
AS18 Barry Bonds 3.00 8.00
AS19 Tony Gwynn 1.50 4.00
AS20 Mike Piazza 2.00 5.00
AS21 Roger Clemens 2.50 6.00
AS22 Greg Maddux 2.00 5.00
AS23 Jim Thome .75 2.00
AS24 Tino Martinez .75 2.00
AS25 Nomar Garciaparra 2.00 5.00
AS26 Juan Gonzalez .50 1.25
AS27 Kenny Lofton .50 1.25
AS28 Randy Johnson 1.25 3.00
AS29 Todd Helton .75 2.00
AS30 Frank Thomas 1.25 3.00

1998 Upper Deck Amazing Greats

COMPLETE SET (30) 200.00 400.00
STATED PRINT RUN 2000 SETS
*DIE CUTS: 1X TO 2.5X BASIC AMAZING
DIE CUT PRINT RUN 250 SERIAL #'d SETS
RANDOM INSERTS IN SER.1 PACKS
AG1 Ken Griffey Jr. 6.00 15.00
AG2 Derek Jeter 8.00 20.00
AG3 Alex Rodriguez 5.00 12.00
AG4 Paul Molitor 1.25 3.00
AG5 Jeff Bagwell 2.00 5.00
AG6 Larry Walker 1.25 3.00
AG7 Kenny Lofton 1.25 3.00
AG8 Cal Ripken 10.00 25.00
AG9 Juan Gonzalez 1.25 3.00
AG10 Chipper Jones 3.00 8.00
AG11 Greg Maddux 5.00 12.00
AG12 Roberto Alomar 2.00 5.00
AG13 Mike Piazza 5.00 12.00
AG14 Andres Galarraga 1.25 3.00
AG15 Barry Bonds 8.00 20.00
AG16 Andy Pettitte 2.00 5.00
AG17 Nomar Garciaparra 5.00 12.00
AG18 Tino Martinez 2.00 5.00
AG19 Tony Gwynn 4.00 10.00
AG20 Frank Thomas 3.00 8.00
AG21 Roger Clemens 6.00 15.00
AG22 Sammy Sosa 3.00 8.00
AG23 Jose Cruz Jr. 1.25 3.00
AG24 Manny Ramirez 2.00 5.00
AG25 Mark McGwire 8.00 20.00
AG26 Randy Johnson 3.00 8.00
AG27 Mo Vaughn 1.25 3.00
AG28 Gary Sheffield 1.25 3.00
AG29 Andruw Jones 2.00 5.00
AG30 Albert Belle 1.25 3.00

1998 Upper Deck Blue Chip Prospects

COMPLETE SET (30) 30.00 60.00
RANDOM INSERTS IN SER.2 PACKS
STATED PRINT RUN 2000 SERIAL #'d SETS
BC1 Nomar Garciaparra 2.00 5.00
BC2 Scott Rolen 2.00 5.00
BC3 Jason Dickson 1.25 3.00
BC4 Darin Erstad 1.25 3.00
BC5 Brad Fullmer 1.25 3.00
BC6 Jaret Wright 1.25 3.00
BC7 Justin Thompson 1.25 3.00
BC8 Matt Morris 1.25 3.00
BC9 Fernando Tatis 1.25 3.00
BC10 Alex Rodriguez 4.00 10.00
BC11 Todd Helton 2.00 5.00
BC12 Andy Pettitte 2.00 5.00
BC13 Jose Cruz Jr. 1.25 3.00
BC14 Mark Kotsay 1.25 3.00
BC15 Derek Jeter 8.00 20.00
BC16 Paul Konerko 1.25 3.00
BC17 Todd Dunwoody 1.25 3.00
BC18 Vladimir Guerrero 2.00 5.00
BC19 Miguel Tejada 3.00 8.00
BC20 Chipper Jones 3.00 8.00
BC21 Kevin Orie 1.25 3.00
BC22 Juan Encarnacion 1.25 3.00
BC23 Brian Rose 1.25 3.00
BC24 Livan Hernandez 1.25 3.00
BC25 Andruw Jones 1.25 3.00
BC26 Brian Giles 1.25 3.00
BC27 Brett Tomko 1.25 3.00
BC28 Jose Guillen 1.25 3.00
BC29 Aaron Boone 1.25 3.00
BC30 Ben Grieve 1.25 3.00

1998 Upper Deck Clearly Dominant

RANDOM INSERTS IN SER.2 PACKS
STATED PRINT RUN 250 SERIAL #'d SETS
CD1 Mark McGwire 20.00 50.00
CD2 Derek Jeter 30.00 80.00
CD3 Alex Rodriguez 15.00 40.00
CD4 Paul Molitor 12.00 30.00
CD5 Jeff Bagwell 8.00 20.00
CD6 Ivan Rodriguez 8.00 20.00
CD7 Kenny Lofton 5.00 12.00
CD8 Cal Ripken 40.00 100.00
CD9 Albert Belle 5.00 12.00
CD10 Chipper Jones 12.00 30.00
CD11 Gary Sheffield 5.00 12.00
CD12 Roberto Alomar 8.00 20.00
CD13 Mo Vaughn 5.00 12.00
CD14 Andres Galarraga 8.00 20.00
CD15 Nomar Garciaparra 8.00 20.00
CD16 Randy Johnson 12.00 30.00
CD17 Mike Mussina 8.00 20.00
CD18 Greg Maddux 15.00 40.00
CD19 Tony Gwynn 12.00 30.00
CD20 Frank Thomas 12.00 30.00
CD21 Roger Clemens 15.00 40.00
CD22 Dennis Eckersley 8.00 20.00
CD23 Juan Gonzalez 5.00 12.00
CD24 Tino Martinez 5.00 12.00
CD25 Andruw Jones 5.00 12.00
CD26 Larry Walker 8.00 20.00
CD27 Ken Caminiti 5.00 12.00
CD28 Mike Piazza 12.00 30.00
CD29 Barry Bonds 20.00 50.00
CD30 Ken Griffey Jr. 25.00 60.00

1998 Upper Deck Destination Stardom

COMPLETE SET (60) 40.00 100.00
SER.3 STATED ODDS 1:5
DS1 Travis Lee .40 1.00
DS2 Nomar Garciaparra 2.50 6.00
DS3 Alex Gonzalez .40 1.00
DS4 Richard Hidalgo .40 1.00
DS5 Jaret Wright .40 1.00
DS6 Mike Kinkade 1.25 3.00
DS7 Matt Morris .60 1.50
DS8 Gary Matthews Jr. 1.25 3.00
DS9 Brett Tomko .40 1.00
DS10 Todd Helton .75 2.00
DS11 Scott Elarton .40 1.00
DS12 Scott Rolen .75 2.00
DS13 Jose Cruz Jr. .40 1.00
DS14 Jarrod Washburn .40 1.00
DS15 Sean Casey .60 1.50
DS16 Magglio Ordonez 2.50 6.00
DS17 Gabe Alvarez .40 1.00
DS18 Todd Dunwoody .40 1.00
DS19 Kevin Witt .40 1.00
DS20 Ben Grieve .40 1.00
DS21 Daryle Ward .40 1.00
DS22 Matt Clement .60 1.50
DS23 Carlton Loewer .40 1.00
DS24 Javier Vazquez .60 1.50
DS25 Paul Konerko .60 1.50
DS26 Preston Wilson .60 1.50
DS27 Wes Helms .40 1.00
DS28 Derek Jeter 4.00 10.00
DS29 Corey Koskie 1.25 3.00
DS30 Russell Branyan .40 1.00
DS31 Vladimir Guerrero 1.25 3.00
DS32 Ryan Christenson .60 1.50
DS33 Carlos Lee 2.50 6.00
DS34 Dave Dellucci 1.25 3.00
DS35 Bruce Chen .40 1.00
DS36 Ricky Ledee .40 1.00
DS37 Ron Wright .40 1.00
DS38 Derrek Lee .75 2.00
DS39 Miguel Tejada 1.25 3.00
DS40 Brad Fullmer .40 1.00
DS41 Rich Butler .40 1.00
DS42 Chris Carpenter .60 1.50
DS43 Alex Rodriguez 2.50 6.00
DS44 Darron Ingram .60 1.50
DS45 Kerry Wood .60 1.50
DS46 Jason Varitek 1.25 3.00
DS47 Ramon Hernandez .40 1.00
DS48 Aaron Boone .60 1.50
DS49 Juan Encarnacion .40 1.00
DS50 A.J. Hinch .40 1.00
DS51 Mike Lowell 2.00 5.00
DS52 Fernando Tatis .40 1.00
DS53 Jose Guillen .60 1.50
DS54 Mike Caruso .40 1.00
DS55 Carl Pavano .60 1.50
DS56 Chris Clemens .40 1.00
DS57 Mark L. Johnson .40 1.00
DS58 Ken Cloude .40 1.00
DS59 Rolando Arrojo 1.25 3.00
DS60 Mark Kotsay .60 1.50

1998 Upper Deck Griffey Home Run Chronicles

COMPLETE SET (56) 20.00 50.00
COMPLETE SERIES 1 (30) 10.00 25.00
COMPLETE SERIES 2 (26) 10.00 25.00
COMMON GRIFFEY (1-56) .75 2.00
SER.1 AND 2 STATED ODDS 1:9

1998 Upper Deck National Pride

SER.1 STATED ODDS 1:23
NP1 Dave Nilsson 2.00 5.00
NP2 Larry Walker 2.00 5.00
NP3 Edgar Renteria 2.00 5.00
NP4 Jose Canseco 3.00 8.00
NP5 Rey Ordonez 2.00 5.00
NP6 Rafael Palmeiro 3.00 8.00
NP7 Livan Hernandez 2.00 5.00
NP8 Andruw Jones 3.00 8.00
NP9 Manny Ramirez 3.00 8.00
NP10 Sammy Sosa 5.00 12.00
NP11 Raul Mondesi 2.00 5.00
NP12 Moises Alou 2.00 5.00
NP13 Pedro Martinez 3.00 8.00
NP14 Vladimir Guerrero 5.00 12.00
NP15 Chili Davis 2.00 5.00
NP16 Hideo Nomo 5.00 12.00
NP17 Hideki Irabu 2.00 5.00
NP18 Shigetoshi Hasegawa 2.00 5.00
NP19 Takashi Kashiwada 2.50 6.00
NP20 Chan Ho Park 2.00 5.00
NP21 Fernando Valenzuela 2.00 5.00
NP22 Vinny Castilla 2.00 5.00
NP23 Armando Reynoso 2.00 5.00
NP24 Karim Garcia 2.00 5.00
NP25 Marvin Benard 2.00 5.00
NP26 Mariano Rivera 5.00 12.00
NP27 Juan Gonzalez 2.00 5.00
NP28 Roberto Alomar 3.00 8.00
NP29 Ivan Rodriguez 3.00 8.00
NP30 Carlos Delgado 2.00 5.00
NP31 Bernie Williams 3.00 8.00
NP32 Edgar Martinez 3.00 8.00
NP33 Frank Thomas 5.00 12.00
NP34 Barry Bonds 12.50 30.00
NP35 Mike Piazza 8.00 20.00
NP36 Chipper Jones 5.00 12.00
NP37 Cal Ripken 15.00 40.00
NP38 Alex Rodriguez 8.00 20.00
NP39 Ken Griffey Jr. 10.00 25.00
NP40 Andres Galarraga 2.00 5.00
NP41 Omar Vizquel 3.00 8.00
NP42 Ozzie Guillen 2.00 5.00

1998 Upper Deck Power Deck Audio Griffey

GREY STATED ODDS 1:46
BLUE STATED ODDS 1:500
TEAL STATED ODDS 1:2400
1 Ken Griffey Jr. Grey 1.00 2.50
2 Ken Griffey Jr. Blue 6.00 15.00
3 Ken Griffey Jr. Teal 20.00 50.00

1998 Upper Deck Prime Nine

COMPLETE SET (60) 40.00 100.00
COMMON GRIFFEY (1-7) .75 2.00
COMMON PIAZZA (8-14) .75 2.00
COMMON F.THOMAS (15-21) .50 1.25
COMMON MCGWIRE (22-28) 1.25 3.00
COMMON RIPKEN (29-35) 1.50 4.00
COMMON J.GONZALEZ (36-42) .20 .50
COMMON GWYNN (43-49) .60 1.50
COMMON BONDS (50-55) 1.25 3.00
COMMON MADDUX (56-60) .75 2.00
SER.2 STATED ODDS 1:5

1998 Upper Deck Retrospectives

SER.3 STATED ODDS 1:24 3.00 8.00
1 Dennis Eckersley 1.25 3.00
2 Rickey Henderson 3.00 8.00
3 Harold Baines 1.25 3.00
4 Cal Ripken 10.00 25.00
5 Tony Gwynn 4.00 10.00
6 Wade Boggs 2.00 5.00
7 Orel Hershiser 1.25 3.00
8 Joe Carter 1.25 3.00
9 Roger Clemens 6.00 15.00
10 Barry Bonds 8.00 20.00
11 Mark McGwire 8.00 20.00
12 Greg Maddux 5.00 12.00
13 Fred McGriff 2.00 5.00
14 Rafael Palmeiro 2.00 5.00
15 Craig Biggio 2.00 5.00
16 Brady Anderson 1.25 3.00
17 Randy Johnson 3.00 8.00
18 Gary Sheffield 1.25 3.00
19 Albert Belle 1.25 3.00
20 Ken Griffey Jr. 6.00 15.00
21 Juan Gonzalez 1.25 3.00
22 Larry Walker 1.25 3.00
23 Tino Martinez 2.00 5.00
24 Frank Thomas 3.00 8.00
25 Jeff Bagwell 2.00 5.00
26 Kenny Lofton 1.25 3.00
27 Mo Vaughn 1.25 3.00
28 Mike Piazza 5.00 12.00
29 Alex Rodriguez 5.00 12.00
30 Chipper Jones 3.00 8.00

1998 Upper Deck Rookie Edition Preview

COMPLETE SET (10) 2.50 6.00
1 Nomar Garciaparra .75 2.00
2 Scott Rolen .30 .75
3 Mark Kotsay .20 .50
4 Todd Helton .30 .75
5 Paul Konerko .20 .50
6 Juan Encarnacion .20 .50
7 Brad Fullmer .20 .50
8 Miguel Tejada .50 1.25
9 Richard Hidalgo .20 .50
10 Ben Grieve .20 .50

1998 Upper Deck Tape Measure Titans

COMPLETE SET (30) 75.00 150.00
SER.2 STATED ODDS 1:23
*GOLD: .4X TO 1X BASIC TITAN
GOLD: RANDOM IN RETAIL PACKS
GOLD PRINT RUN 2667 SERIAL #'d SETS
1 Mark McGwire 8.00 20.00
2 Andres Galarraga 1.25 3.00
3 Jeff Bagwell 2.00 5.00
4 Larry Walker 1.25 3.00
5 Frank Thomas 3.00 8.00
6 Rafael Palmeiro 2.00 5.00
7 Nomar Garciaparra 5.00 12.00
8 Mo Vaughn 1.25 3.00
9 Albert Belle 1.25 3.00
10 Ken Griffey Jr. 6.00 15.00
11 Manny Ramirez 2.00 5.00
12 Jim Thome 2.00 5.00
13 Tony Clark 1.25 3.00
14 Juan Gonzalez 1.25 3.00
15 Mike Piazza 5.00 12.00
16 Jose Canseco 2.00 5.00
17 Jay Buhner 1.25 3.00
18 Alex Rodriguez 5.00 12.00
19 Jose Cruz Jr. 1.25 3.00
20 Tino Martinez 2.00 5.00
21 Carlos Delgado 1.25 3.00
22 Andruw Jones 2.00 5.00
23 Chipper Jones 3.00 8.00
24 Fred McGriff 2.00 5.00
25 Matt Williams 1.25 3.00
26 Sammy Sosa 3.00 8.00
27 Vinny Castilla 1.25 3.00
28 Tim Salmon 2.00 5.00
29 Ken Caminiti 1.25 3.00
30 Barry Bonds 8.00 20.00

1998 Upper Deck Unparalleled

COMPLETE SET (20) 125.00 250.00
SER.3 STATED ODDS 1:72 HOBBY
1 Ken Griffey Jr. 8.00 20.00
2 Travis Lee 1.50 4.00
3 Ben Grieve 1.50 4.00
4 Jose Cruz Jr. 1.50 4.00
5 Nomar Garciaparra 6.00 15.00
6 Hideo Nomo 4.00 10.00
7 Kenny Lofton 1.50 4.00
8 Cal Ripken 12.50 30.00
9 Roger Clemens 8.00 20.00
10 Mike Piazza 6.00 15.00
11 Jeff Bagwell 2.50 6.00
12 Chipper Jones 4.00 10.00
13 Greg Maddux 6.00 15.00
14 Randy Johnson 4.00 10.00
15 Alex Rodriguez 6.00 15.00
16 Barry Bonds 10.00 25.00
17 Frank Thomas 4.00 10.00
18 Juan Gonzalez 1.50 4.00
19 Tony Gwynn 5.00 12.00
20 Mark McGwire 10.00 25.00

1998 Upper Deck Griffey Most Memorable Home Runs

This 10-card set features color action photos of Ken Griffey Jr. hitting the most memorable home runs of his career printed on cards measuring approximately 3 1/2" by 5" with gold foil highlights. The backs carry another photo of the home run along with the date and why the home run was important in his career. Limited Edition Ken Griffey Jr. Autograph cards were randomly inserted in the set boxes. Also inserted was a special redemption card to be redeemed for an exclusive Ken Griffey Jr. 300th HR Commemorative Card or a special oversized card of equal or geater value.
COMMON CARD (1-10) .50 1.25

1998 Upper Deck Griffey Most Memorable Home Runs Autographed

1 Ken Griffey Jr./4/10/89
2 Ken Griffey Jr./9/14/90
3 Ken Griffey Jr./7/14/92
4 Ken Griffey Jr./7/28/93
5 Ken Griffey Jr./6/30/94
6 Ken Griffey Jr./8/24/95
7 Ken Griffey Jr./10/8/95
8 Ken Griffey Jr./4/25/97
9 Ken Griffey Jr./9/7/97
10 Ken Griffey Jr./9/27/97

1998 Upper Deck Mark McGwire's Chase for 62

This 31-card set features color action photos of memorable moments in the 1998 season for Mark McGwire in his chase for 62 home runs. One oversized 3 1/2" by 5" commemorative card was included showing Big Mac's historical 61st and 62nd home runs. The set was distributed by the Home Shopping Network in a red box. The hobby box is yellow. The set carries a suggested retail price of $19.99. The oversize card is slightly different in each version (Home Shopping, Hobby and Retail) issued. However, there is no difference in the values of this card.
COMP.FACT SET (31) 6.00 15.00
COMMON CARD (1-30) .20 .50
4 Mark McGwire .40 1.00
Ken Griffey Jr.
NNO Mark McGwire/61st and 62nd homers 1.25
3.00

1998 Upper Deck McGwire Jumbo

This one-card set measuring 3 1/2" by 5" commemorates Mark McGwire's 62nd Home Run. The front features two action player photos with a reproduction of a ticket stub from the game in the center with a red border. The card was originally offered on the Home Shopping Network and then sold to Hobby dealers. Only 16,200 of this card were produced and sequentially numbered.
1 Mark McGwire 6.00 15.00

1998 Upper Deck Richie Ashburn

This one-card set was distributed as a wrapper redemption at SportsFest 98 held in Philadelphia. The front freatures a color action photo of Richie Ashburn with a white border. The back carries the top part of the photo with career statistics and player information.
1 Richie Ashburn .75 2.00

1999 Upper Deck

This 525-card set was distributed in two separate series. Series one packs contained cards 1-255 and series two contained 266-535. Cards 256-265 were never created. Subsets are as follows: Star Rookies (1-18, 266-292), Foreign Focus (229-246), Season Highlights Checklists (247-255, 527-535), and Arms Race '99 (518-526). The product was distributed in 10-card packs with a suggested retail price of $2.99. Though not confirmed by Upper Deck, it's widely believed by dealers that broke a good deal of product that these subset cards were slightly short-printed in comparison to other cards in the set. Notable Rookie Cards include Pat Burrell. 100 signed 1989 Upper Deck Ken Griffey Jr. RC's were randomly seeded into series one packs. These signed cards are real 89 RC's and they contain an additional diamond shaped hologram on back signifying that UD has verified Griffey's signature. Approximately 350 Babe Ruth A Piece of History cards were randomly seeded into all series one packs at a rate of one in 15,000. 50 Babe Ruth A Piece of History 500 Club bat cards were randomly seeded into second series packs. Pricing for these bat cards can be referenced under 1999 Upper Deck A Piece of History 500 Club.
COMPLETE SET (525) 30.00 60.00
COMPLETE SERIES 1 (255) 15.00 40.00
COMPLETE SERIES 2 (270) 10.00 25.00
COMMON (19-255/293-535) .10 .30
COMMON SER.1 SR (1-18) .20 .50
COMMON SER.2 SR (266-292) .20 .50
CARDS 256-265 DO NOT EXIST
GRIFFEY 89 AU RANDOM IN SER.1 PACKS
RUTH SER.1 BAT LISTED UNDER '99 APH
RUTH SER.2 BAT LISTED W/APH 500 CLUB
1 Troy Glaus SR .40 1.00
2 Adrian Beltre SR .25 .60
3 Matt Anderson SR .20 .50
4 Eric Chavez SR .25 .60
5 Jin Ho Cho SR .20 .50
6 Robert Smith SR .20 .50
7 George Lombard SR .20 .50
8 Mike Kinkade SR .20 .50
9 Seth Greisinger SR .20 .50
10 J.D. Drew SR .25 .60
11 Aramis Ramirez SR .25 .60
12 Carlos Guillen SR .25 .60
13 Justin Baughman SR .20 .50
14 Jim Parque SR .20 .50
15 Ryan Jackson SR .20 .50
16 Ramon E.Martinez SR RC .20 .50
17 Orlando Hernandez SR .25 .60
18 Jeremy Giambi SR .20 .50
19 Gary DiSarcina .10 .30
20 Darin Erstad .10 .30
21 Troy Glaus .20 .50
22 Chuck Finley .10 .30
23 Dave Hollins .10 .30
24 Troy Percival .10 .30
25 Tim Salmon .20 .50
26 Brian Anderson .10 .30
27 Jay Bell .10 .30
28 Andy Benes .10 .30
29 Brent Brede .10 .30
30 David Dellucci .10 .30
31 Karim Garcia .10 .30
32 Travis Lee .10 .30
33 Andres Galarraga .10 .30
34 Ryan Klesko .10 .30
35 Keith Lockhart .10 .30
36 Kevin Millwood .10 .30
37 Denny Neagle .10 .30
38 John Smoltz .20 .50
39 Michael Tucker .10 .30
40 Walt Weiss .10 .30
41 Dennis Martinez .10 .30
42 Javy Lopez .10 .30
43 Brady Anderson .10 .30
44 Harold Baines .10 .30
45 Mike Bordick .10 .30
46 Roberto Alomar .20 .50
47 Scott Erickson .10 .30
48 Mike Mussina .20 .50
49 Cal Ripken 1.00 2.50
50 Darren Bragg .10 .30
51 Dennis Eckersley .10 .30
52 Nomar Garciaparra .50 1.25
53 Scott Hatteberg .10 .30
54 Troy O'Leary .10 .30
55 Bret Saberhagen .10 .30
56 John Valentin .10 .30
57 Rod Beck .10 .30
58 Jeff Blauser .10 .30
59 Brant Brown .10 .30
60 Mark Clark .10 .30
61 Mark Grace .20 .50
62 Kevin Tapani .10 .30
63 Henry Rodriguez .10 .30
64 Mike Cameron .10 .30
65 Mike Caruso .10 .30
66 Ray Durham .10 .30
67 Jaime Navarro .10 .30
68 Magglio Ordonez .10 .30
69 Mike Sirotka .10 .30
70 Sean Casey .10 .30
71 Barry Larkin .20 .50
72 Jon Nunnally .10 .30
73 Paul Konerko .10 .30
74 Chris Stynes .10 .30
75 Brett Tomko .10 .30
76 Dmitri Young .10 .30
77 Sandy Alomar Jr. .10 .30
78 Bartolo Colon .10 .30
79 Travis Fryman .10 .30
80 Brian Giles .10 .30
81 David Justice .10 .30
82 Omar Vizquel .20 .50
83 Jaret Wright .10 .30
84 Jim Thome .20 .50
85 Charles Nagy .10 .30
86 Pedro Astacio .10 .30
87 Todd Helton .20 .50
88 Darryl Kile .10 .30
89 Mike Lansing .10 .30

90 Neifi Perez .10 .30
91 John Thomson .10 .30
92 Larry Walker .10 .30
93 Tony Clark .10 .30
94 Deivi Cruz .10 .30
95 Damion Easley .10 .30
96 Brian L.Hunter .10 .30
97 Todd Jones .10 .30
98 Brian Moehler .10 .30
99 Gabe Alvarez .10 .30
100 Craig Counsell .10 .30
101 Cliff Floyd .10 .30
102 Livan Hernandez .10 .30
103 Andy Larkin .10 .30
104 Derrek Lee .20 .50
105 Brian Meadows .10 .30
106 Moises Alou .10 .30
107 Sean Berry .10 .30
108 Craig Biggio .20 .50
109 Ricky Gutierrez .10 .30
110 Mike Hampton .10 .30
111 Jose Lima .10 .30
112 Billy Wagner .10 .30
113 Hal Morris .10 .30
114 Johnny Damon .20 .50
115 Jeff King .10 .30
116 Jeff Montgomery .10 .30
117 Glendon Rusch .10 .30
118 Larry Sutton .10 .30
119 Bobby Bonilla .10 .30
120 Jim Eisenreich .10 .30
121 Eric Karros .10 .30
122 Matt Luke .10 .30
123 Ramon Martinez .10 .30
124 Gary Sheffield .10 .30
125 Eric Young .10 .30
126 Charles Johnson .10 .30
127 Jeff Cirillo .10 .30
128 Marquis Grissom .10 .30
129 Jeromy Burnitz .10 .30
130 Bob Wickman .10 .30
131 Scott Karl .10 .30
132 Mark Loretta .10 .30
133 Fernando Vina .10 .30
134 Matt Lawton .10 .30
135 Pat Meares .10 .30
136 Eric Milton .10 .30
137 Paul Molitor .10 .30
138 David Ortiz .30 .75
139 Todd Walker .10 .30
140 Shane Andrews .10 .30
141 Brad Fullmer .10 .30
142 Vladimir Guerrero .30 .75
143 Dustin Hermanson .10 .30
144 Ryan McGuire .10 .30
145 Ugueth Urbina .10 .30
146 John Franco .10 .30
147 Butch Huskey .10 .30
148 Bobby Jones .10 .30
149 John Olerud .10 .30
150 Rey Ordonez .10 .30
151 Mike Piazza .50 1.25
152 Hideo Nomo .30 .75
153 Masato Yoshii .10 .30
154 Derek Jeter .75 2.00
155 Chuck Knoblauch .10 .30
156 Paul O'Neill .20 .50
157 Andy Pettitte .20 .50
158 Mariano Rivera .30 .75
159 Darryl Strawberry .10 .30
160 David Wells .10 .30
161 Jorge Posada .20 .50
162 Ramiro Mendoza .10 .30
163 Miguel Tejada .10 .30
164 Ryan Christenson .10 .30
165 Rickey Henderson .30 .75
166 A.J. Hinch .10 .30
167 Ben Grieve .10 .30
168 Kenny Rogers .10 .30
169 Matt Stairs .10 .30
170 Bob Abreu .10 .30
171 Rico Brogna .10 .30
172 Doug Glanville .10 .30
173 Mike Grace .10 .30
174 Desi Relaford .10 .30
175 Scott Rolen .20 .50
176 Jose Guillen .10 .30
177 Francisco Cordova .10 .30
178 Al Martin .10 .30
179 Jason Schmidt .10 .30
180 Turner Ward .10 .30
181 Kevin Young .10 .30
182 Mark McGwire .75 2.00
183 Delino DeShields .10 .30
184 Eli Marrero .10 .30
185 Tom Lampkin .10 .30
186 Ray Lankford .10 .30
187 Willie McGee .10 .30
188 Matt Morris .10 .30
189 Andy Ashby .10 .30
190 Kevin Brown .20 .50
191 Ken Caminiti .10 .30
192 Trevor Hoffman .10 .30
193 Wally Joyner .10 .30
194 Greg Vaughn .10 .30
195 Danny Darwin .10 .30
196 Shawn Estes .10 .30
197 Orel Hershiser .10 .30
198 Jeff Kent .10 .30
199 Bill Mueller .10 .30
200 Robb Nen .10 .30
201 J.T. Snow .10 .30
202 Ken Cloude .10 .30
203 Russ Davis .10 .30
204 Jeff Fassero .10 .30
205 Ken Griffey Jr. .60 1.50
206 Shane Monahan .10 .30
207 David Segui .10 .30
208 Dan Wilson .10 .30
209 Wilson Alvarez .10 .30
210 Wade Boggs .20 .50
211 Miguel Cairo .10 .30
212 Bubba Trammell .10 .30
213 Quinton McCracken .10 .30
214 Paul Sorrento .10 .30
215 Kevin Stocker .10 .30
216 Will Clark .20 .50
217 Rusty Greer .10 .30
218 Rick Helling .10 .30
219 Mark McLemore .10 .30
220 Ivan Rodriguez .20 .50
221 John Wetteland .10 .30
222 Jose Canseco .20 .50
223 Roger Clemens .60 1.50
224 Carlos Delgado .10 .30
225 Darrin Fletcher .10 .30
226 Alex Gonzalez .10 .30
227 Jose Cruz Jr. .10 .30
228 Shannon Stewart .10 .30
229 Rolando Arrojo FF .10 .30
230 Livan Hernandez FF .10 .30
231 Orlando Hernandez FF .10 .30
232 Raul Mondesi FF .10 .30
233 Moises Alou FF .10 .30
234 Pedro Martinez FF .20 .50
235 Sammy Sosa FF .20 .50
236 Vladimir Guerrero FF .30 .75
237 Bartolo Colon FF .10 .30
238 Miguel Tejada FF .10 .30
239 Ismael Valdes FF .10 .30
240 Mariano Rivera FF .20 .50
241 Jose Cruz Jr. FF .10 .30
242 Juan Gonzalez FF .10 .30
243 Ivan Rodriguez FF .20 .50
244 Sandy Alomar Jr. FF .10 .30
245 Roberto Alomar FF .20 .50
246 Magglio Ordonez FF .10 .30
247 Kerry Wood SH CL .10 .30
248 Mark McGwire SH CL .75 2.00
249 David Wells SH CL .10 .30
250 Rolando Arrojo SH CL .10 .30
251 Ken Griffey Jr. SH CL .60 1.50
252 Trevor Hoffman SH CL .10 .30
253 Travis Lee SH CL .10 .30
254 Roberto Alomar SH CL .10 .30
255 Sammy Sosa SH CL .20 .50
266 Pat Burrell SR RC 1.25 3.00
267 Shea Hillenbrand SR RC .60 1.50
268 Robert Fick SR .20 .50
269 Roy Halladay SR 2.00 5.00
270 Ruben Mateo SR .20 .50
271 Bruce Chen SR .20 .50
272 Angel Pena SR .20 .50
273 Michael Barrett SR .20 .50
274 Kevin Witt SR .20 .50
275 Damon Minor SR .20 .50
276 Ryan Minor SR .20 .50
277 A.J. Pierzynski SR .25 .60
278 A.J. Burnett SR RC .60 1.50
279 Dermal Brown SR .20 .50
280 Joe Lawrence SR .20 .50
281 Derrick Gibson SR .20 .50
282 Carlos Febles SR .20 .50
283 Chris Haas SR .20 .50
284 Cesar King SR .20 .50
285 Calvin Pickering SR .20 .50
286 Mitch Meluskey SR .20 .50
287 Carlos Beltran SR .40 1.00
288 Ron Belliard SR .20 .50
289 Jerry Hairston Jr. SR .20 .50
290 Fernando Seguignol SR .20 .50
291 Kris Benson SR .20 .50
292 Chad Hutchinson SR RC .25 .60
293 Jarrod Washburn .10 .30
294 Jason Dickson .10 .30
295 Mo Vaughn .10 .30
296 Garret Anderson .10 .30
297 Jim Edmonds .10 .30
298 Ken Hill .10 .30
299 Shigetoshi Hasegawa .10 .30
300 Todd Stottlemyre .10 .30
301 Randy Johnson .30 .75
302 Omar Daal .10 .30
303 Steve Finley .10 .30
304 Matt Williams .10 .30
305 Danny Klassen .10 .30
306 Tony Batista .10 .30
307 Brian Jordan .10 .30
308 Greg Maddux .50 1.25
309 Chipper Jones .30 .75
310 Bret Boone .10 .30
311 Ozzie Guillen .10 .30
312 John Rocker .10 .30
313 Tom Glavine .20 .50
314 Andruw Jones .20 .50
315 Albert Belle .10 .30
316 Charles Johnson .10 .30
317 Will Clark .20 .50
318 B.J. Surhoff .10 .30
319 Delino DeShields .10 .30
320 Heathcliff Slocumb .10 .30
321 Sidney Ponson .10 .30
322 Juan Guzman .10 .30
323 Reggie Jefferson .10 .30
324 Mark Portugal .10 .30
325 Tim Wakefield .10 .30
326 Jason Varitek .30 .75
327 Jose Offerman .10 .30
328 Pedro Martinez .20 .50
329 Trot Nixon .10 .30
330 Kerry Wood .10 .30
331 Sammy Sosa .30 .75
332 Glenallen Hill .10 .30
333 Gary Gaetti .10 .30
334 Mickey Morandini .10 .30
335 Benito Santiago .10 .30
336 Jeff Blauser .10 .30
337 Frank Thomas .30 .75
338 Paul Konerko .10 .30
339 Jaime Navarro .10 .30
340 Carlos Lee .10 .30
341 Brian Simmons .10 .30
342 Mark Johnson .10 .30
343 Jeff Abbott .10 .30
344 Steve Avery .10 .30
345 Mike Cameron .10 .30
346 Michael Tucker .10 .30
347 Greg Vaughn .10 .30
348 Hal Morris .10 .30
349 Pete Harnisch .10 .30
350 Denny Neagle .10 .30
351 Manny Ramirez .20 .50
352 Roberto Alomar .20 .50
353 Dwight Gooden .10 .30
354 Kenny Lofton .10 .30
355 Mike Jackson .10 .30
356 Charles Nagy .10 .30
357 Enrique Wilson .10 .30
358 Russ Branyan .10 .30
359 Richie Sexson .10 .30
360 Vinny Castilla .10 .30
361 Dante Bichette .10 .30
362 Kirt Manwaring .10 .30
363 Darryl Hamilton .10 .30
364 Jamey Wright .10 .30
365 Curtis Leskanic .10 .30
366 Jeff Reed .10 .30
367 Bobby Higginson .10 .30
368 Justin Thompson .10 .30
369 Brad Ausmus .10 .30
370 Dean Palmer .10 .30
371 Gabe Kapler .10 .30
372 Juan Encarnacion .10 .30
373 Karim Garcia .10 .30
374 Alex Gonzalez .10 .30
375 Braden Looper .10 .30
376 Preston Wilson .10 .30
377 Todd Dunwoody .10 .30
378 Alex Fernandez .10 .30
379 Mark Kotsay .10 .30
380 Matt Mantei .10 .30
381 Ken Caminiti .10 .30
382 Scott Elarton .10 .30
383 Jeff Bagwell .20 .50
384 Derek Bell .10 .30
385 Ricky Gutierrez .10 .30
386 Richard Hidalgo .10 .30
387 Shane Reynolds .10 .30
388 Carl Everett .10 .30
389 Scott Service .10 .30
390 Jeff Suppan .10 .30
391 Joe Randa .10 .30
392 Kevin Appier .10 .30
393 Shane Halter .10 .30
394 Chad Kreuter .10 .30
395 Mike Sweeney .10 .30
396 Kevin Brown .20 .50
397 Devon White .10 .30
398 Todd Hollandsworth .10 .30
399 Todd Hundley .10 .30
400 Chan Ho Park .10 .30
401 Mark Grudzielanek .10 .30
402 Raul Mondesi .10 .30
403 Ismael Valdes .10 .30
404 Rafael Roque RC .10 .30
405 Sean Berry .10 .30
406 Kevin Barker .10 .30
407 Dave Nilsson .10 .30
408 Geoff Jenkins .10 .30
409 Jim Abbott .20 .50
410 Bobby Hughes .10 .30
411 Corey Koskie .10 .30
412 Rick Aguilera .10 .30
413 LaTroy Hawkins .10 .30
414 Ron Coomer .10 .30
415 Denny Hocking .10 .30
416 Marty Cordova .10 .30
417 Terry Steinbach .10 .30
418 Rondell White .10 .30
419 Wilton Guerrero .10 .30
420 Shane Andrews .10 .30
421 Orlando Cabrera .10 .30
422 Carl Pavano .10 .30
423 Javier Vazquez .10 .30
424 Chris Widger .10 .30
425 Robin Ventura .10 .30
426 Rickey Henderson .30 .75
427 Al Leiter .10 .30
428 Bobby Jones .10 .30
429 Brian McRae .10 .30
430 Roger Cedeno .10 .30
431 Bobby Bonilla .10 .30
432 Edgardo Alfonzo .10 .30
433 Bernie Williams .20 .50
434 Ricky Ledee .10 .30
435 Chili Davis .10 .30
436 Tino Martinez .20 .50
437 Scott Brosius .10 .30
438 David Cone .10 .30
439 Joe Girardi .10 .30
440 Roger Clemens .60 1.50
441 Chad Curtis .10 .30
442 Hideki Irabu .10 .30
443 Jason Giambi .10 .30
444 Scott Spiezio .10 .30
445 Tony Phillips .10 .30
446 Ramon Hernandez .10 .30
447 Mike Macfarlane .10 .30
448 Tom Candiotti .10 .30
449 Billy Taylor .10 .30
450 Bobby Estalella .10 .30
451 Curt Schilling .10 .30
452 Carlton Loewer .10 .30
453 Marlon Anderson .10 .30
454 Kevin Jordan .10 .30
455 Ron Gant .10 .30
456 Chad Ogea .10 .30
457 Abraham Nunez .10 .30
458 Jason Kendall .10 .30
459 Pat Meares .10 .30
460 Brant Brown .10 .30
461 Brian Giles .10 .30
462 Chad Hermansen .10 .30
463 Freddy Adrian Garcia .10 .30
464 Edgar Renteria .10 .30
465 Fernando Tatis .10 .30
466 Eric Davis .10 .30
467 Darren Bragg .10 .30
468 Donovan Osborne .10 .30
469 Manny Aybar .10 .30
470 Jose Jimenez .10 .30
471 Kent Mercker .10 .30
472 Reggie Sanders .10 .30
473 Ruben Rivera .10 .30
474 Tony Gwynn .40 1.00
475 Jim Leyritz .10 .30
476 Chris Gomez .10 .30
477 Matt Clement .10 .30
478 Carlos Hernandez .10 .30
479 Sterling Hitchcock .10 .30
480 Ellis Burks .10 .30
481 Barry Bonds .75 2.00
482 Marvin Benard .10 .30
483 Kirk Rueter .10 .30
484 F.P. Santangelo .10 .30
485 Stan Javier .10 .30
486 Jeff Kent .10 .30
487 Alex Rodriguez .50 1.25
488 Tom Lampkin .10 .30
489 Jose Mesa .10 .30
490 Jay Buhner .10 .30
491 Edgar Martinez .20 .50
492 Butch Huskey .10 .30
493 John Mabry .10 .30
494 Jamie Moyer .10 .30
495 Roberto Hernandez .10 .30
496 Tony Saunders .10 .30
497 Fred McGriff .20 .50
498 Dave Martinez .10 .30
499 Jose Canseco .20 .50
500 Rolando Arrojo .10 .30
501 Esteban Yan .10 .30
502 Juan Gonzalez .10 .30
503 Rafael Palmeiro .20 .50
504 Aaron Sele .10 .30
505 Royce Clayton .10 .30
506 Todd Zeile .10 .30
507 Tom Goodwin .10 .30
508 Lee Stevens .10 .30
509 Esteban Loaiza .10 .30
510 Joey Hamilton .10 .30
511 Homer Bush .10 .30
512 Willie Greene .10 .30
513 Shawn Green .10 .30
514 David Wells .10 .30
515 Kelvim Escobar .10 .30
516 Tony Fernandez .10 .30
517 Pat Hentgen .10 .30
518 Mark McGwire AR .40 1.00
519 Ken Griffey Jr. AR .40 1.00
520 Sammy Sosa AR .20 .50
521 Juan Gonzalez AR .10 .30
522 J.D. Drew AR .10 .30
523 Chipper Jones AR .20 .50
524 Alex Rodriguez AR .30 .75
525 Mike Piazza AR .30 .75
526 Nomar Garciaparra AR .30 .75
527 Mark McGwire SH CL .40 1.00
528 Sammy Sosa SH CL .20 .50
529 Scott Brosius SH CL .10 .30
530 Cal Ripken SH CL .50 1.25
531 Barry Bonds SH CL .40 1.00
532 Roger Clemens SH CL .30 .75
533 Ken Griffey Jr. SH CL .40 1.00
534 Alex Rodriguez SH CL .30 .75
535 Curt Schilling SH CL .10 .30
NNO K.Griffey Jr. '89 AU/100 900.00 1200.00

1999 Upper Deck Exclusives Level 1

*STARS: 10X TO 25X BASIC CARDS
*SER.1 STAR ROOK: 4X TO 10X BASIC SR
*SER.2 STAR ROOK: 6X TO 15X BASIC SR
RANDOM INSERTS IN ALL HOBBY PACKS
STATED PRINT RUN 100 SERIAL #'d SETS
CARDS 256-265 DO NOT EXIST

1999 Upper Deck 10th Anniversary Team

COMPLETE SET (30) 20.00 50.00
SER.1 STATED ODDS 1:4
*DOUBLES: 1.25X TO 3X BASIC 10TH ANN.
DOUBLES RANDOM INSERTS IN SER.1 PACKS
DOUBLES PRINT RUN 4000 SERIAL #'d SETS
*TRIPLES: 8X TO 20X BASIC 10TH ANN
TRIPLES RANDOM INSERTS IN SER.1 PACKS
TRIPLES PRINT RUN 100 SERIAL #'d SETS
HR'S RANDOM INSERTS IN SER.1 PACKS
HOME RUN PRINT RUN 1 SERIAL #'d SET
HR'S NOT PRICED DUE TO SCARCITY
X1 Mike Piazza 1.00 2.50
X2 Mark McGwire 1.50 4.00
X3 Roberto Alomar .40 1.00
X4 Chipper Jones .60 1.50
X5 Cal Ripken 2.00 5.00
X6 Ken Griffey Jr. 1.25 3.00
X7 Barry Bonds 1.50 4.00
X8 Tony Gwynn .75 2.00
X9 Nolan Ryan 2.50 6.00
X10 Randy Johnson .60 1.50
X11 Dennis Eckersley .25 .60
X12 Ivan Rodriguez .40 1.00
X13 Frank Thomas .60 1.50
X14 Craig Biggio .40 1.00
X15 Wade Boggs .40 1.00
X16 Alex Rodriguez 1.00 2.50
X17 Albert Belle .25 .60
X18 Juan Gonzalez .25 .60
X19 Rickey Henderson .60 1.50
X20 Greg Maddux 1.00 2.50
X21 Tom Glavine .40 1.00
X22 Randy Myers .25 .60
X23 Sandy Alomar Jr. .25 .60
X24 Jeff Bagwell .40 1.00
X25 Derek Jeter 1.50 4.00
X26 Matt Williams .25 .60
X27 Kenny Lofton .25 .60
X28 Sammy Sosa .60 1.50
X29 Larry Walker .25 .60
X30 Roger Clemens 1.25 3.00

1999 Upper Deck A Piece of History

SER.1 STATED ODDS 1:15,000
PRINT RUN APPROXIMATELY 350 CARDS
B.RUTH AU RANDOM IN SER.1 PACKS
B.RUTH AU PRINT RUN 3 #'d CARDS
B.RUTH AU NOT PRICED DUE TO SCARCITY
PHLC Babe Ruth AU/3
PH Babe Ruth 750.00 1000.00

1999 Upper Deck A Piece of History 500 Club

RANDOM INSERTS IN 1999-2000 UD BRANDS
PRINT RUN APPROXIMATELY 350 SETS
BR Babe Ruth/50
EB Ernie Banks 50.00 120.00
EM Eddie Mathews 75.00 200.00
EM Eddie Murray 100.00 250.00
FR Frank Robinson 60.00 150.00
HA Hank Aaron 150.00 400.00
HK Harmon Killebrew 60.00 150.00
JF Jimmie Foxx 75.00 200.00
MM Mickey Mantle 300.00 600.00
MO Mel Ott 75.00 200.00
MS Mike Schmidt 60.00 150.00
RJ Reggie Jackson 50.00 120.00
TW Ted Williams 125.00 300.00
WM Willie Mays 125.00 300.00
WM Willie McCovey 60.00 150.00
ARM Aaron/Ruth/Mays SP

1999 Upper Deck A Piece of History 500 Club Autographs

RANDOM INSERTS IN 1999-2000 UD BRANDS
PRINT RUNS B/WN 3-44 COPIES PER
NO PRICING ON QTY OF 40 OR LESS
536HR Mickey Mantle/1
EBAU Ernie Banks/14
EMAU Eddie Mathews/41 500.00 800.00
FRAU Frank Robinson/20
HAAU Hank Aaron/44 1500.00 1800.00
HKAU Harmon Killebrew/3
MSAU Mike Schmidt/20
RJAU Reggie Jackson/44 600.00 900.00
TWAU Ted Williams/9
WMAU Willie Mays/24
WMAU Willie McCovey/44 500.00 800.00

1999 Upper Deck Crowning Glory

COMPLETE SET (3) 25.00 60.00
RANDOM INSERTS IN SER.1 PACKS
*DOUBLES: .6X TO 1.5X BASIC CROWN
DOUBLES RANDOM INSERTS IN SER.1 PACKS
DOUBLES PRINT RUN 1000 SERIAL #'d SETS
*TRIPLES: 4X TO 10X BASIC CROWN
TRIPLES RANDOM INSERTS IN SER.1 PACKS
TRIPLES PRINT RUN 25 SERIAL #'d SETS
HR'S RANDOM INSERTS IN SER.1 PACKS
HOME RUNS PRINT RUN 1 SERIAL #'d SET
HOME RUNS NOT PRICED DUE TO SCARCITY
CG1 R.Clemens 6.00 15.00
K.Wood
CG2 M.McGwire 8.00 20.00
B.Bonds
CG3 K.Griffey Jr. 8.00 20.00
M.McGwire

1999 Upper Deck Forte

COMPLETE SET (30) 20.00 50.00
SER.2 STATED ODDS 1:23
*DOUBLES: .6X TO 1.5X BASIC FORTE
DOUBLES RANDOM INSERTS IN SER.2 PACKS
DOUBLES PRINT RUN 2000 SERIAL #'d SETS
*TRIPLES: 2X TO 5X BASIC FORTE
TRIPLES RANDOM INSERTS IN SER.2 PACKS
TRIPLES PRINT RUN 100 SERIAL #'d SETS
QUADS RANDOM INSERTS IN SER.2 PACKS
QUADRUPLES PRINT RUN 10 SERIAL #'d SETS
QUADRUPLES NOT PRICED DUE TO SCARCITY
F1 Darin Erstad .40 1.00
F2 Troy Glaus .40 1.00
F3 Mo Vaughn .40 1.00
F4 Greg Maddux 1.25 3.00
F5 Andres Galarraga .60 1.50
F6 Chipper Jones 1.00 2.50
F7 Cal Ripken 3.00 8.00
F8 Albert Belle .40 1.00
F9 Nomar Garciaparra .60 1.50
F10 Sammy Sosa 1.00 2.50
F11 Kerry Wood .60 1.50
F12 Frank Thomas 1.00 2.50
F13 Jim Thome .60 1.50
F14 Jeff Bagwell .60 1.50
F15 Vladimir Guerrero .60 1.50
F16 Mike Piazza 1.00 2.50
F17 Derek Jeter 2.50 6.00
F18 Ben Grieve .40 1.00
F19 Eric Chavez .40 1.00
F20 Scott Rolen .60 1.50
F21 Mark McGwire 1.50 4.00
F22 J.D. Drew .40 1.00
F23 Tony Gwynn 1.00 2.50
F24 Barry Bonds 1.50 4.00
F25 Alex Rodriguez 1.25 3.00
F26 Ken Griffey Jr. 2.00 5.00
F27 Ivan Rodriguez .60 1.50
F28 Juan Gonzalez .40 1.00
F29 Roger Clemens 1.25 3.00
F30 Andruw Jones .40 1.00

1999 Upper Deck Game Jersey

H STATED ODDS 1:288 HOBBY
HR STATED ODDS 1:2500 HOBBY/RETAIL
H1 AND HR1 CARDS DIST.IN SER.1 PACKS
H2 AND HR2 CARDS DIST.IN SER.2 PACKS
AU'S RANDOM INSERTS IN PACKS
AU PRINT RUNS B/WN 24-34 COPIES PER
NO AU PRICING ON QTY OF 24 PER
COMP.SET DOES NOT INCLUDE AU CARDS
AB Adrian Beltre H1 4.00 10.00
AR Alex Rodriguez HR1 8.00 20.00
BF Brad Fullmer H2 4.00 10.00
BG Ben Grieve H1 4.00 10.00
BT Bubba Trammell H2 4.00 10.00
CJ Charles Johnson HR1 6.00 15.00
CJ Chipper Jones H2 8.00 20.00
DE Darin Erstad H1 6.00 15.00
EC Eric Chavez H2 6.00 15.00
FT Frank Thomas HR2 10.00 25.00
GM Greg Maddux HR2 12.50 30.00
IR Ivan Rodriguez H1 6.00 15.00
JD J.D. Drew H2 6.00 15.00
JG Juan Gonzalez HR1 6.00 15.00
JR Ken Griffey Jr. HR2 15.00 40.00
KG Ken Griffey Jr. H1 15.00 40.00
KW Kerry Wood HR1 6.00 15.00
MP Mike Piazza HR1 12.50 30.00
MR Manny Ramirez H2 6.00 15.00
NRA N.Ryan Astros H2 10.00 25.00
NRB N.Ryan Rangers HR2 10.00 25.00
SS Sammy Sosa H2 4.00 10.00
TH Todd Helton H2 6.00 15.00
TGW Tony Gwynn H2 6.00 15.00
TL Travis Lee H1 4.00 10.00
JDS J.Drew AU/8 H2
JRS Ken Griffey Jr. AU/24 HR2
KGAU Ken Griffey Jr. AU/24 H1
KWAU K.Wood AU/34 HR1 150.00 250.00
NRAS N.Ryan AU/34 H2 500.00 800.00

1999 Upper Deck Ken Griffey Jr. Box Blasters

COMPLETE SET (1-10) 20.00 50.00
COMMON CARD (1-10) 2.00 5.00

1999 Upper Deck Ken Griffey Jr. Box Blasters Autographs

COMMON CARD (90-99) 50.00 100.00
STATED ODDS 1:64 SPECIAL RETAIL BOXES
KG1989 Ken Griffey Jr. AU89 150.00 250.00

1999 Upper Deck Immaculate Perception

COMPLETE SET (27) 125.00 250.00
SER.1 STATED ODDS 1:23
*DOUBLES: .75X TO 2X BASIC IMM.PERC.
DOUBLES RANDOM INSERTS IN SER.1 PACKS
DOUBLES PRINT RUN 1000 SERIAL #'d SETS
*TRIPLES: 5X TO 12X BASIC IMM.PERC.
TRIPLES RANDOM INSERTS IN SER.1 PACKS
TRIPLES PRINT RUN 25 SERIAL #'d SETS
HR'S RANDOM INSERTS IN SER.1 PACKS
HOME RUNS PRINT RUN 1 SERIAL #'d SET
HOME RUNS NOT PRICED DUE TO SCARCITY
I1 Jeff Bagwell 2.00 5.00
I2 Craig Biggio 2.00 5.00
I3 Barry Bonds 8.00 20.00
I4 Roger Clemens 6.00 15.00
I5 Jose Cruz Jr. 1.25 3.00
I6 Nomar Garciaparra 5.00 12.00
I7 Tony Clark 1.25 3.00
I8 Ben Grieve 1.25 3.00
I9 Ken Griffey Jr. 6.00 15.00
I10 Tony Gwynn 4.00 10.00
I11 Randy Johnson 3.00 8.00
I12 Chipper Jones 3.00 8.00
I13 Travis Lee 1.25 3.00
I14 Kenny Lofton 1.25 3.00
I15 Greg Maddux 5.00 12.00
I16 Mark McGwire 8.00 20.00
I17 Hideo Nomo 3.00 8.00
I18 Mike Piazza 5.00 12.00
I19 Manny Ramirez 2.00 5.00
I20 Cal Ripken 10.00 25.00
I21 Alex Rodriguez 5.00 12.00
I22 Scott Rolen 2.00 5.00
I23 Frank Thomas 3.00 8.00
I24 Kerry Wood 1.25 3.00
I25 Larry Walker 1.25 3.00
I26 Vinny Castilla 1.25 3.00
I27 Derek Jeter 8.00 20.00

1999 Upper Deck Textbook Excellence

COMPLETE SET (30) 20.00 50.00
SER.2 STATED ODDS 1:4
*DOUBLES: 1.5X TO 4X BASIC TEXTBOOK
DOUBLES RANDOM INSERTS IN SER.2 PACKS
DOUBLES PRINT RUN 2000 SERIAL #'d SETS
*TRIPLES: 6X TO 15X BASIC TEXTBOOK
TRIPLES RANDOM INSERTS IN SER.2 PACKS
TRIPLES PRINT RUN 100 SERIAL #'d SETS
QUADS RANDOM INSERTS IN SER.2 PACKS
QUADRUPLES PRINT RUN 10 SERIAL #'d SETS
QUADRUPLES NOT PRICED DUE TO SCARCITY
T1 Mo Vaughn .30 .75
T2 Greg Maddux 1.25 3.00
T3 Chipper Jones .75 2.00
T4 Andruw Jones .50 1.25
T5 Cal Ripken 2.50 6.00
T6 Albert Belle .30 .75
T7 Roberto Alomar .50 1.25
T8 Nomar Garciaparra 1.25 3.00
T9 Kerry Wood .30 .75
T10 Sammy Sosa .75 2.00
T11 Greg Vaughn .30 .75
T12 Jeff Bagwell .50 1.25
T13 Kevin Brown .50 1.25
T14 Vladimir Guerrero .75 2.00
T15 Mike Piazza 1.25 3.00
T16 Bernie Williams .50 1.25
T17 Derek Jeter 2.00 5.00
T18 Ben Grieve .30 .75
T19 Eric Chavez .20 .50
T20 Scott Rolen .50 1.25
T21 Mark McGwire 2.00 5.00
T22 David Wells .30 .75
T23 J.D. Drew .20 .50
T24 Tony Gwynn 1.00 2.50
T25 Barry Bonds 2.00 5.00
T26 Alex Rodriguez 1.25 3.00
T27 Ken Griffey Jr. 1.50 4.00
T28 Juan Gonzalez .50 1.25
T29 Ivan Rodriguez .50 1.25
T30 Roger Clemens 1.50 4.00

1999 Upper Deck View to a Thrill

COMPLETE SET (30) 40.00 100.00
SER.2 STATED ODDS 1:7
*DOUBLES: 1X TO 2.5X BASIC VIEW
DOUBLES RANDOM INSERTS IN SER.2 PACKS
DOUBLES PRINT RUN 2000 SERIAL #'d SETS
*TRIPLES: 4X TO 10X BASIC VIEW
TRIPLES RANDOM INSERTS IN SER.2 PACKS
TRIPLES PRINT RUN 100 SERIAL #'d SETS
QUADS RANDOM INSERTS IN SER.2 PACKS
QUADRUPLES PRINT RUN 10 SERIAL #'d SETS
QUADRUPLES NOT PRICED DUE TO SCARCITY
V1 Mo Vaughn .50 1.25
V2 Darin Erstad .50 1.25
V3 Travis Lee .50 1.25
V4 Chipper Jones 1.25 3.00
V5 Greg Maddux 2.00 5.00
V6 Gabe Kapler .50 1.25
V7 Cal Ripken 4.00 10.00
V8 Nomar Garciaparra 2.00 5.00
V9 Kerry Wood .50 1.25
V10 Frank Thomas 1.25 3.00
V11 Manny Ramirez .75 2.00
V12 Larry Walker .50 1.25
V13 Tony Clark .50 1.25
V14 Jeff Bagwell .75 2.00
V15 Craig Biggio .75 2.00
V16 Vladimir Guerrero 1.25 3.00
V17 Mike Piazza 2.00 5.00
V18 Bernie Williams .75 2.00
V19 Derek Jeter 3.00 8.00
V20 Ben Grieve .50 1.25
V21 Eric Chavez .30 .75
V22 Scott Rolen .75 2.00
V23 Mark McGwire 3.00 8.00
V24 Tony Gwynn 1.50 4.00
V25 Barry Bonds 3.00 8.00
V26 Ken Griffey Jr. 2.50 6.00
V27 Alex Rodriguez 2.00 5.00
V28 J.D. Drew .30 .75
V29 Juan Gonzalez .50 1.25
V30 Roger Clemens 2.50 6.00

1999 Upper Deck Wonder Years

COMPLETE SET (30) 30.00 80.00
SER.1 STATED ODDS 1:7
*DOUBLES: 1X TO 2.5X BASIC WONDER
DOUBLES RANDOM INSERTS IN SER.1 PACKS
DOUBLES PRINT RUN 2000 SERIAL #'d SETS
*TRIPLES: 8X TO 20X BASIC WONDER
TRIPLES RANDOM INSERTS IN SER.1 PACKS
TRIPLES PRINT RUN 50 SERIAL #'d SETS
HR'S RANDOM INSERTS IN SER.1 PACKS
HOME RUNS PRINT RUN 1 SERIAL #'d SET
HOME RUNS NOT PRICED DUE TO SCARCITY
WY1 Kerry Wood .50 1.25
WY2 Travis Lee .50 1.25
WY3 Jeff Bagwell .75 2.00
WY4 Barry Bonds 3.00 8.00
WY5 Roger Clemens 2.50 6.00
WY6 Jose Cruz Jr. .50 1.25
WY7 Andres Galarraga .50 1.25
WY8 Nomar Garciaparra 2.00 5.00
WY9 Juan Gonzalez .50 1.25
WY10 Ken Griffey Jr. 2.50 6.00
WY11 Tony Gwynn 1.50 4.00
WY12 Derek Jeter 3.00 8.00
WY13 Randy Johnson 1.25 3.00
WY14 Andruw Jones .75 2.00
WY15 Chipper Jones 1.25 3.00
WY16 Kenny Lofton .50 1.25
WY17 Greg Maddux 2.00 5.00
WY18 Tino Martinez .75 2.00
WY19 Mark McGwire 3.00 8.00
WY20 Paul Molitor .50 1.25
WY21 Mike Piazza 2.00 5.00
WY22 Manny Ramirez .75 2.00
WY23 Cal Ripken 4.00 10.00
WY24 Alex Rodriguez 2.00 5.00
WY25 Sammy Sosa 1.25 3.00
WY26 Frank Thomas 1.25 3.00
WY27 Mo Vaughn .50 1.25
WY28 Larry Walker .50 1.25
WY29 Scott Rolen .75 2.00
WY30 Ben Grieve .50 1.25

1999 Upper Deck Employment Promo

This card was used as a promotional tool by Upper Deck to thank anyone who applied for a job there. The card features Upper Deck corporate spokesperson Ken Griffey Jr.

NNO Ken Griffey Jr. 1.00 2.50

1999 Upper Deck Ken Griffey Jr Santa

This one card was issued to Upper Deck employees as well as some of their guests. The card features a photo of Griffey on the front along a swatch of the "Santa" hat he wore for the shoot. The back has a congratulatory message from Upper Deck.

1 Ken Griffey Jr. 25.00 60.00

1999 Upper Deck Mark McGwire Tribute

This 30 card standard-size set was released by Upper Deck in 1999 to commemorate Mark McGwire's 70 home run season in 1998. The set was issued in a lunch box and each card features a highlight from the 1998 season. There is an action shot on the front of the card along with a little inset portrait photo. The back gives big play to the date along with a description of what happened on that day.

COMPLETE SET 6.00 15.00
COMMON CARD .30 .75

1999 Upper Deck McGwire 500 Home Run Set

This 30 card box set honors Mark McGwire hitting his 500th homer during the 1999 season. The cards were issued in a special box which also commemorated the feat.

COMPLETE SET (30) 8.00 20.00
COMMON CARD (1-30) .30 .75

1999 Upper Deck/Kodak

NNO Mark McGwire

2000 Upper Deck

COMPLETE SET (540) 20.00 50.00
COMPLETE SERIES 1 (270) 10.00 25.00
COMPLETE SERIES 2 (270) 10.00 25.00
COMMON CARD (1-540) .12 .30
COMMON SR (1-28/271-297) .20 .50
CARD 460 DOES NOT EXIST
1 Rick Ankiel SR .30 .75
2 Vernon Wells SR .20 .50
3 Ryan Anderson SR .20 .50
4 Ed Yarnall SR .20 .50
5 Brian McNichol SR .20 .50
6 Ben Petrick SR .20 .50
7 Kip Wells SR .20 .50
8 Eric Munson SR .20 .50

9 Matt Riley SR .20 .50
10 Peter Bergeron SR .20 .50
11 Eric Gagne SR .20 .50
12 Ramon Ortiz SR .20 .50
13 Josh Beckett SR .40 1.00
14 Alfonso Soriano SR .50 1.25
15 Jorge Toca SR .20 .50
16 Buddy Carlyle SR .20 .50
17 Chad Hermansen SR .20 .50
18 Matt Perisho SR .20 .50
19 Tomokazu Ohka SR RC .20 .50
20 Jacque Jones SR .20 .50
21 Josh Paul SR .20 .50
22 Dermal Brown SR .20 .50
23 Adam Kennedy SR .20 .50
24 Chad Harville SR .20 .50
25 Calvin Murray SR .20 .50
26 Chad Meyers SR .20 .50
27 Brian Cooper SR .20 .50
28 Troy Glaus .20 .50
29 Ben Molina .12 .30
30 Troy Percival .12 .30
31 Ken Hill .12 .30
32 Chuck Finley .12 .30
33 Todd Greene .12 .30
34 Tim Salmon .12 .30
35 Gary DiSarcina .12 .30
36 Luis Gonzalez .12 .30
37 Tony Womack .12 .30
38 Omar Daal .12 .30
39 Randy Johnson .30 .75
40 Erubiel Durazo .12 .30
41 Jay Bell .12 .30
42 Steve Finley .12 .30
43 Travis Lee .12 .30
44 Greg Maddux .40 1.00
45 Bret Boone .12 .30
46 Brian Jordan .12 .30
47 Kevin Millwood .12 .30
48 Odalis Perez .12 .30
49 Javy Lopez .12 .30
50 John Smoltz .30 .75
51 Bruce Chen .12 .30
52 Albert Belle .12 .30
53 Jerry Hairston Jr. .12 .30
54 Will Clark .20 .50
55 Sidney Ponson .12 .30
56 Charles Johnson .12 .30
57 Cal Ripken 1.00 2.50
58 Ryan Minor .12 .30
59 Mike Mussina .20 .50
60 Tom Gordon .12 .30
61 Jose Offerman .12 .30
62 Trot Nixon .12 .30
63 Pedro Martinez .20 .50
64 John Valentin .12 .30
65 Jason Varitek .30 .75
66 Juan Pena .12 .30
67 Troy O'Leary .12 .30
68 Sammy Sosa .30 .75
69 Henry Rodriguez .12 .30
70 Kyle Farnsworth .12 .30
71 Glenallen Hill .12 .30
72 Lance Johnson .12 .30
73 Mickey Morandini .12 .30
74 Jon Lieber .12 .30
75 Kevin Tapani .12 .30
76 Carlos Lee .12 .30
77 Ray Durham .12 .30
78 Jim Parque .12 .30
79 Bob Howry .12 .30
80 Magglio Ordonez .20 .50
81 Paul Konerko .12 .30
82 Mike Caruso .12 .30
83 Chris Singleton .12 .30
84 Sean Casey .12 .30
85 Barry Larkin .20 .50
86 Pokey Reese .12 .30
87 Eddie Taubensee .12 .30
88 Scott Williamson .12 .30
89 Jason LaRue .12 .30
90 Aaron Boone .12 .30
91 Jeffrey Hammonds .12 .30
92 Omar Vizquel .20 .50
93 Manny Ramirez .30 .75
94 Kenny Lofton .12 .30
95 Jaret Wright .12 .30
96 Einar Diaz .12 .30
97 Charles Nagy .12 .30
98 David Justice .12 .30
99 Richie Sexson .12 .30
100 Steve Karsay .12 .30
101 Todd Helton .20 .50
102 Dante Bichette .12 .30
103 Larry Walker .20 .50
104 Pedro Astacio .12 .30
105 Neifi Perez .12 .30
106 Brian Bohanon .12 .30
107 Edgard Clemente .12 .30
108 Dave Veres .12 .30
109 Gabe Kapler .12 .30
110 Juan Encarnacion .12 .30
111 Jeff Weaver .12 .30
112 Damion Easley .12 .30
113 Justin Thompson .12 .30
114 Brad Ausmus .12 .30
115 Frank Catalanotto .12 .30
116 Todd Jones .12 .30
117 Preston Wilson .12 .30
118 Cliff Floyd .12 .30
119 Mike Lowell .12 .30
120 Antonio Alfonseca .12 .30
121 Alex Gonzalez .12 .30
122 Braden Looper .12 .30
123 Bruce Aven .12 .30
124 Richard Hidalgo .12 .30
125 Mitch Meluskey .12 .30
126 Jeff Bagwell .20 .50
127 Jose Lima .12 .30
128 Derek Bell .12 .30
129 Billy Wagner .12 .30
130 Shane Reynolds .12 .30
131 Moises Alou .12 .30
132 Carlos Beltran .20 .50
133 Carlos Febles .12 .30
134 Jermaine Dye .12 .30
135 Jeremy Giambi .12 .30
136 Joe Randa .12 .30
137 Jose Rosado .12 .30
138 Chad Kreuter .12 .30
139 Jose Vizcaino .12 .30
140 Adrian Beltre .30 .75
141 Kevin Brown .12 .30
142 Ismael Valdes .12 .30
143 Angel Pena .12 .30
144 Chan Ho Park .20 .50
145 Mark Grudzielanek .12 .30
146 Jeff Shaw .12 .30
147 Geoff Jenkins .12 .30
148 Jeromy Burnitz .12 .30
149 Hideo Nomo .30 .75
150 Ron Belliard .12 .30
151 Sean Berry .12 .30
152 Mark Loretta .12 .30
153 Steve Woodard .12 .30
154 Joe Mays .12 .30
155 Eric Milton .12 .30
156 Corey Koskie .12 .30
157 Ron Coomer .12 .30
158 Brad Radke .12 .30
159 Terry Steinbach .12 .30
160 Cristian Guzman .12 .30
161 Vladimir Guerrero .20 .50
162 Wilton Guerrero .12 .30
163 Michael Barrett .12 .30
164 Chris Widger .12 .30
165 Fernando Seguignol .12 .30
166 Ugueth Urbina .12 .30
167 Dustin Hermanson .12 .30
168 Kenny Rogers .12 .30
169 Edgardo Alfonzo .12 .30
170 Orel Hershiser .12 .30
171 Robin Ventura .12 .30
172 Octavio Dotel .12 .30
173 Rickey Henderson .30 .75
174 Roger Cedeno .12 .30
175 John Olerud .12 .30
176 Derek Jeter .75 2.00
177 Tino Martinez .12 .30
178 Orlando Hernandez .12 .30
179 Chuck Knoblauch .12 .30
180 Bernie Williams .20 .50
181 Chili Davis .12 .30
182 David Cone .12 .30
183 Ricky Ledee .12 .30
184 Paul O'Neill .20 .50
185 Jason Giambi .12 .30
186 Eric Chavez .12 .30
187 Matt Stairs .12 .30
188 Miguel Tejada .20 .50
189 Olmedo Saenz .12 .30
190 Tim Hudson .20 .50
191 John Jaha .12 .30
192 Randy Velarde .12 .30
193 Rico Brogna .12 .30
194 Mike Lieberthal .12 .30
195 Marlon Anderson .12 .30
196 Bob Abreu .12 .30
197 Ron Gant .12 .30
198 Randy Wolf .12 .30
199 Desi Relaford .12 .30
200 Doug Glanville .12 .30
201 Warren Morris .12 .30
202 Kris Benson .12 .30
203 Kevin Young .12 .30
204 Brian Giles .12 .30
205 Jason Schmidt .12 .30
206 Ed Sprague .12 .30
207 Francisco Cordova .12 .30
208 Mark McGwire .50 1.25
209 Jose Jimenez .12 .30
210 Fernando Tatis .12 .30
211 Kent Bottenfield .12 .30
212 Eli Marrero .12 .30
213 Edgar Renteria .12 .30
214 Joe McEwing .12 .30
215 J.D. Drew .12 .30
216 Tony Gwynn .30 .75
217 Gary Matthews Jr. .12 .30
218 Eric Owens .12 .30
219 Damian Jackson .12 .30
220 Reggie Sanders .12 .30
221 Trevor Hoffman .20 .50
222 Ben Davis .12 .30
223 Shawn Estes .12 .30
224 F.P. Santangelo .12 .30
225 Livan Hernandez .12 .30
226 Ellis Burks .12 .30
227 J.T. Snow .12 .30
228 Jeff Kent .12 .30
229 Robb Nen .12 .30
230 Marvin Benard .12 .30
231 Ken Griffey Jr. .60 1.50
232 John Halama .12 .30
233 Gil Meche .12 .30
234 David Bell .12 .30
235 Brian Hunter .12 .30
236 Jay Buhner .12 .30
237 Edgar Martinez .20 .50
238 Jose Mesa .12 .30
239 Wilson Alvarez .12 .30
240 Wade Boggs .20 .50
241 Fred McGriff .20 .50
242 Jose Canseco .20 .50
243 Kevin Stocker .12 .30
244 Roberto Hernandez .12 .30
245 Bubba Trammell .12 .30
246 John Flaherty .12 .30
247 Ivan Rodriguez .20 .50
248 Rusty Greer .12 .30
249 Rafael Palmeiro .20 .50
250 Jeff Zimmerman .12 .30
251 Royce Clayton .12 .30
252 Todd Zeile .12 .30
253 John Wetteland .12 .30
254 Ruben Mateo .12 .30
255 Kelvim Escobar .12 .30
256 David Wells .12 .30
257 Shawn Green .12 .30
258 Homer Bush .12 .30
259 Shannon Stewart .12 .30
260 Carlos Delgado .12 .30
261 Roy Halladay .20 .50
262 Fernando Tatis SH CL .12 .30
263 Jose Jimenez SH CL .12 .30
264 Tony Gwynn SH CL .30 .75
265 Wade Boggs SH CL .20 .50
266 Cal Ripken SH CL 1.00 2.50
267 David Cone SH CL .12 .30
268 Mark McGwire SH CL .50 1.25
269 Pedro Martinez SH CL .20 .50
270 Nomar Garciaparra SH CL .20 .50
271 Nick Johnson SR .20 .50
272 Mark Quinn SR .20 .50
273 Roosevelt Brown SR .20 .50
274 Terrence Long SR .20 .50
275 Jason Marquis SR .20 .50
276 Kazuhiro Sasaki SR RC .50 1.25
277 Aaron Myette SR .20 .50
278 Danys Baez SR RC .20 .50
279 Travis Dawkins SR .20 .50
280 Mark Mulder SR .20 .50
281 Chris Haas SR .20 .50
282 Milton Bradley SR .20 .50
283 Brad Penny SR .20 .50
284 Rafael Furcal SR .30 .75
285 Luis Matos SR RC .20 .50
286 Victor Santos SR RC .20 .50
287 Rico Washington SR RC .20 .50
288 Rob Bell SR .20 .50
289 Joe Crede SR .20 .50
290 Pablo Ozuna SR .20 .50
291 Wascar Serrano SR RC .20 .50
292 Sang-Hoon Lee SR RC .20 .50
293 Chris Wakeland SR RC .20 .50
294 Luis Rivera SR RC .20 .50
295 Mike Lamb SR RC .20 .50
296 Wily Mo Pena SR .20 .50
297 Mike Meyers SR RC .30 .75
298 Mo Vaughn .12 .30
299 Darin Erstad .12 .30
300 Garret Anderson .12 .30
301 Tim Belcher .12 .30
302 Scott Spiezio .12 .30
303 Kent Bottenfield .12 .30
304 Orlando Palmeiro .12 .30
305 Jason Dickson .12 .30
306 Matt Williams .12 .30
307 Brian Anderson .12 .30
308 Hanley Frias .12 .30
309 Todd Stottlemyre .12 .30
310 Matt Mantei .12 .30
311 David Dellucci .12 .30
312 Armando Reynoso .12 .30
313 Bernard Gilkey .12 .30
314 Chipper Jones .30 .75
315 Tom Glavine .20 .50
316 Quilvio Veras .12 .30
317 Andruw Jones .12 .30
318 Bobby Bonilla .12 .30
319 Reggie Sanders .12 .30
320 Andres Galarraga .20 .50
321 George Lombard .12 .30
322 John Rocker .12 .30
323 Wally Joyner .12 .30
324 B.J. Surhoff .12 .30
325 Scott Erickson .12 .30
326 Delino DeShields .12 .30
327 Jeff Conine .12 .30
328 Mike Timlin .12 .30
329 Brady Anderson .12 .30
330 Mike Bordick .12 .30
331 Harold Baines .20 .50
332 Nomar Garciaparra .20 .50
333 Bret Saberhagen .12 .30
334 Ramon Martinez .12 .30
335 Donnie Sadler .12 .30
336 Wilton Veras .12 .30
337 Mike Stanley .12 .30
338 Brian Rose .12 .30
339 Carl Everett .12 .30
340 Tim Wakefield .20 .50
341 Mark Grace .20 .50
342 Kerry Wood .12 .30
343 Eric Young .12 .30
344 Jose Nieves .12 .30
345 Ismael Valdes .12 .30
346 Joe Girardi .20 .50
347 Damon Buford .12 .30
348 Ricky Gutierrez .12 .30
349 Frank Thomas .30 .75
350 Brian Simmons .12 .30
351 James Baldwin .12 .30
352 Brook Fordyce .12 .30
353 Jose Valentin .12 .30
354 Mike Sirotka .12 .30
355 Greg Norton .12 .30
356 Dante Bichette .12 .30
357 Deion Sanders .20 .50
358 Ken Griffey Jr. .60 1.50
359 Denny Neagle .12 .30
360 Dmitri Young .12 .30
361 Pete Harnisch .12 .30
362 Michael Tucker .12 .30
363 Roberto Alomar .20 .50
364 Dave Roberts .20 .50
365 Jim Thome .20 .50
366 Bartolo Colon .12 .30
367 Travis Fryman .12 .30
368 Chuck Finley .12 .30
369 Russell Branyan .12 .30
370 Alex Ramirez .12 .30
371 Jeff Cirillo .12 .30
372 Jeffrey Hammonds .12 .30
373 Scott Karl .12 .30
374 Brent Mayne .12 .30
375 Tom Goodwin .12 .30
376 Jose Jimenez .12 .30
377 Rolando Arrojo .12 .30
378 Terry Shumpert .12 .30
379 Juan Gonzalez .12 .30
380 Bobby Higginson .12 .30
381 Tony Clark .12 .30
382 Dave Mlicki .12 .30
383 Deivi Cruz .12 .30
384 Brian Moehler .12 .30
385 Dean Palmer .12 .30
386 Luis Castillo .12 .30
387 Mike Redmond .12 .30
388 Alex Fernandez .12 .30
389 Brant Brown .12 .30
390 Dave Berg .12 .30
391 A.J. Burnett .12 .30
392 Mark Kotsay .12 .30
393 Craig Biggio .20 .50
394 Daryle Ward .12 .30
395 Lance Berkman .20 .50
396 Roger Cedeno .12 .30
397 Scott Elarton .12 .30
398 Octavio Dotel .12 .30
399 Ken Caminiti .12 .30
400 Johnny Damon .20 .50
401 Mike Sweeney .12 .30
402 Jeff Suppan .12 .30
403 Rey Sanchez .12 .30
404 Blake Stein .12 .30
405 Ricky Bottalico .12 .30
406 Jay Witasick .12 .30
407 Shawn Green .12 .30
408 Orel Hershiser .12 .30
409 Gary Sheffield .12 .30
410 Todd Hollandsworth .12 .30
411 Terry Adams .12 .30
412 Todd Hundley .12 .30
413 Eric Karros .12 .30
414 F.P. Santangelo .12 .30
415 Alex Cora .20 .50
416 Marquis Grissom .12 .30
417 Henry Blanco .12 .30
418 Jose Hernandez .12 .30
419 Kyle Peterson .12 .30
420 John Snyder RC .12 .30
421 Bob Wickman .12 .30
422 Jamey Wright .12 .30
423 Chad Allen .12 .30
424 Todd Walker .12 .30
425 J.C. Romero RC .12 .30
426 Butch Huskey .12 .30
427 Jacque Jones .12 .30
428 Matt Lawton .12 .30
429 Rondell White .12 .30
430 Jose Vidro .12 .30
431 Hideki Irabu .12 .30
432 Javier Vazquez .12 .30
433 Lee Stevens .12 .30
434 Mike Thurman .12 .30
435 Geoff Blum .12 .30
436 Mike Hampton .12 .30
437 Mike Piazza .30 .75
438 Al Leiter .12 .30
439 Derek Bell .12 .30
440 Armando Benitez .12 .30
441 Rey Ordonez .12 .30
442 Todd Zeile .12 .30
443 Roger Clemens .40 1.00
444 Ramiro Mendoza .12 .30
445 Andy Pettitte .20 .50
446 Scott Brosius .12 .30
447 Mariano Rivera .40 1.00
448 Jim Leyritz .12 .30
449 Jorge Posada .20 .50
450 Omar Olivares .12 .30
451 Ben Grieve .12 .30
452 A.J. Hinch .12 .30
453 Gil Heredia .12 .30
454 Kevin Appier .12 .30
455 Ryan Christenson .12 .30
456 Ramon Hernandez .12 .30
457 Scott Rolen .20 .50
458 Alex Arias .12 .30
459 Andy Ashby .12 .30
461 Robert Person .12 .30
462 Paul Byrd .12 .30
463 Curt Schilling .20 .50
464 Mike Jackson .12 .30
465 Jason Kendall .12 .30
466 Pat Meares .12 .30
467 Bruce Aven .12 .30
468 Todd Ritchie .12 .30
469 Wil Cordero .12 .30
470 Aramis Ramirez .12 .30
471 Andy Benes .12 .30
472 Ray Lankford .12 .30
473 Fernando Vina .12 .30
474A Jim Edmonds .12 .30
474B Kevin Jordan .12 .30
475 Craig Paquette .12 .30
476 Pat Hentgen .12 .30
477 Darryl Kile .12 .30
478 Sterling Hitchcock .12 .30
479 Ruben Rivera .12 .30
480 Ryan Klesko .12 .30
481 Phil Nevin .12 .30
482 Woody Williams .12 .30
483 Carlos Hernandez .12 .30
484 Brian Meadows .12 .30
485 Bret Boone .12 .30
486 Barry Bonds .50 1.25
487 Russ Ortiz .12 .30
488 Bobby Estalella .12 .30
489 Rich Aurilia .12 .30
490 Bill Mueller .12 .30
491 Joe Nathan .12 .30
492 Russ Davis .12 .30
493 John Olerud .12 .30
494 Alex Rodriguez .40 1.00
495 Freddy Garcia .12 .30
496 Carlos Guillen .12 .30
497 Aaron Sele .12 .30
498 Brett Tomko .12 .30
499 Jamie Moyer .12 .30
500 Mike Cameron .12 .30
501 Vinny Castilla .12 .30
502 Gerald Williams .12 .30
503 Mike DiFelice .12 .30
504 Ryan Rupe .12 .30
505 Greg Vaughn .12 .30
506 Miguel Cairo .12 .30
507 Juan Guzman .12 .30
508 Jose Guillen .12 .30
509 Gabe Kapler .12 .30
510 Rick Helling .12 .30
511 David Segui .12 .30
512 Doug Davis .12 .30
513 Justin Thompson .12 .30
514 Chad Curtis .12 .30
515 Tony Batista .12 .30
516 Billy Koch .12 .30
517 Raul Mondesi .12 .30
518 Joey Hamilton .12 .30
519 Darrin Fletcher .12 .30
520 Brad Fullmer .12 .30
521 Jose Cruz Jr. .12 .30
522 Kevin Witt .12 .30
523 Mark McGwire AUT .50 1.25
524 Roberto Alomar AUT .20 .50
525 Chipper Jones AUT .30 .75
526 Derek Jeter AUT .75 2.00
527 Ken Griffey Jr. AUT .60 1.50
528 Sammy Sosa AUT .30 .75
529 Manny Ramirez AUT .30 .75
530 Ivan Rodriguez AUT .20 .50
531 Pedro Martinez AUT .20 .50
532 Mariano Rivera CL .40 1.00
533 Sammy Sosa CL .30 .75
534 Cal Ripken CL 1.00 2.50
535 Vladimir Guerrero CL .20 .50
536 Tony Gwynn CL .30 .75
537 Mark McGwire CL .50 1.25
538 Bernie Williams CL .20 .50
539 Pedro Martinez CL .20 .50
540 Ken Griffey Jr. CL .60 1.50

2000 Upper Deck Exclusives Gold

NO PRICING DUE TO SCARCITY

2000 Upper Deck Exclusives Silver

*EXC.SILV: 8X TO 20X BASIC CARDS
*SR: 5X TO 12X BASIC SR
STATED PRINT RUN 100 SERIAL #'d SETS
CARD 460 DOES NOT EXIST
JORDAN AND EDMONDS BOTH NUMBER 474

2000 Upper Deck 2K Plus

COMPLETE SET (12) 8.00 20.00
*SINGLES: 2X TO 5X BASE CARD HI
SER.1 STATED ODDS 1:23
*DIE CUTS: 2.5X TO 6X BASIC 2K PLUS
DIE CUTS RANDOM INSERTS IN SER.1 HOBBY
DIE CUTS PRINT RUN 100 SERIAL #'d SETS
GOLD DIE CUTS RANDOM IN SER.1 HOBBY
GOLD DIE CUT PRINT RUN 1 SERIAL #'d SET
GOLD DC NOT PRICED DUE TO SCARCITY
2K1 Ken Griffey Jr. 2.00 5.00
2K2 J.D. Drew .40 1.00
2K3 Derek Jeter 2.50 6.00
2K4 Nomar Garciaparra .60 1.50
2K5 Pat Burrell .40 1.00
2K6 Ruben Mateo .40 1.00
2K7 Carlos Beltran .60 1.50
2K8 Vladimir Guerrero .60 1.50
2K9 Scott Rolen .60 1.50
2K10 Chipper Jones 1.00 2.50
2K11 Alex Rodriguez 1.25 3.00
2K12 Magglio Ordonez .60 1.50

2000 Upper Deck A Piece of History 3000 Club

STATED PRINT RUNS LISTED BELOW
NO PRICING ON QTY OF 33 OR LESS
AKB A.Kaline Bat/400 12.00 30.00
BGB Boggs/Gwynn Bat/99 75.00 150.00
BYB Brett/Yount Bat/99 75.00 150.00
BYJ Brett/Yount Jersey/99 125.00 200.00
CRB C.Ripken Bat/350 12.00 30.00
CRJ C.Ripken Jersey/350 10.00 25.00
CRJB C.Ripken Bat-Jsy/100 30.00 60.00
CYB C.Yaz Bat/350 15.00 40.00
CYJ C.Yaz Jersey/350 10.00 25.00
CYJB C.Yaz Bat-Jsy/100 50.00 100.00
DWB D.Winf. Bat/350 10.00 25.00
DWJ D.Winf. Jersey/350 10.00 25.00
DWJB D.Winf. Bat-Jsy/100 40.00 80.00
EMB E.Murray Bat/350 12.00 30.00
EMJ E.Murray Jersey/350 20.00 50.00
EMJB E.Murray Bat-Jsy/100 12.50 30.00
GBB G.Brett Bat/350 25.00 60.00
GBJ G.Brett Jersey/350 20.00 50.00
HAB H.Aaron Bat/350 25.00 60.00
HABS H.Aaron Bat-Jsy AU/44 800.00 1200.00
HAJ H.Aaron Jersey/350 25.00 60.00
HAJB H.Aaron Bat-Jsy/100 125.00 250.00
LBB L.Brock Bat/350 15.00 40.00
LBJ L.Brock Jsy/350 15.00 40.00
LBJB L.Brock Bat-Jsy/100 40.00 80.00
PMB P.Molitor Bat/350 10.00 25.00
PWB P.Waner Bat/350 12.00 30.00
RCAB R.Carew Bat/350 12.50 30.00
RCAJ R.Carew Jsy/350 10.00 25.00
RCABJ R.Carew Bat-Jsy/100 30.00 60.00
RCLB R.Clemente Bat/350 40.00 80.00
RYB R.Yount Bat/350 20.00 50.00
RYJ R.Yount Jersey/350 20.00 50.00
SMB S.Musial Bat/350 12.00 30.00
SMJ S.Musial Jersey/350 15.00 40.00
SMJB S.Musial Bat-Jsy/100 75.00 150.00
TCB Ty Cobb Bat/350 60.00 150.00
TGB T.Gwynn Bat/350 12.00 30.00
TGBC T.Gwynn Bat-Cap/50 75.00 150.00
TSB T.Speaker Bat/350 15.00 40.00
WBB W.Boggs Bat/350 12.00 30.00
WBBC W.Boggs Bat-Cap/50 50.00 100.00
WMB W.Mays Bat/300 30.00 60.00
WMJ W.Mays Jersey/350 30.00 60.00
WMJB W.Mays Bat-Jsy/50 150.00 250.00

2000 Upper Deck Cooperstown Calling

COMPLETE SET (15) 15.00 40.00
SER.2 STATED ODDS 1:23
CC1 Roger Clemens 1.25 3.00
CC2 Cal Ripken 3.00 8.00
CC3 Ken Griffey Jr. 2.00 5.00
CC4 Mike Piazza 1.00 2.50
CC5 Tony Gwynn 1.00 2.50
CC6 Sammy Sosa 1.00 2.50
CC7 Jose Canseco .60 1.50
CC8 Larry Walker .60 1.50
CC9 Barry Bonds 1.50 4.00
CC10 Greg Maddux 1.25 3.00
CC11 Derek Jeter 2.50 6.00
CC12 Mark McGwire 1.50 4.00
CC13 Randy Johnson 1.00 2.50
CC14 Frank Thomas 1.00 2.50
CC15 Jeff Bagwell .60 1.50

2000 Upper Deck e-Card

COMPLETE SET (6) 4.00 10.00
TWO PER SER.2 BOX CHIPTOPPER
E1 Ken Griffey Jr. 1.25 3.00
E2 Alex Rodriguez .75 2.00
E3 Cal Ripken Jr. 2.00 5.00
E4 Jeff Bagwell .40 1.00
E5 Barry Bonds 1.00 2.50
E6 Manny Ramirez .60 1.50

2000 Upper Deck eVolve Autograph

EXCH.CARD AVAIL.VIA WEBSITE PROGRAM
STATED PRINT RUN 200 SERIAL #'d SETS
ES1 Ken Griffey Jr. 40.00 100.00
ES2 Alex Rodriguez 25.00 60.00
ES3 Cal Ripken 50.00 100.00
ES4 Jeff Bagwell 20.00 50.00
ES5 Barry Bonds 40.00 100.00
ES6 Manny Ramirez 12.00 50.00

2000 Upper Deck eVolve Game Jersey

EXCH.CARD AVAIL.VIA WEBSITE PROGRAM
STATED PRINT RUN 300 SERIAL #'d SETS
EJ1 Ken Griffey Jr. 10.00 25.00
EJ2 Alex Rodriguez 10.00 25.00
EJ3 Cal Ripken 10.00 25.00
EJ4 Jeff Bagwell 10.00 25.00
EJ5 Barry Bonds 10.00 25.00
EJ6 Manny Ramirez 10.00 25.00

2000 Upper Deck eVolve Game Jersey Autograph

EXCH.CARD AVAIL.VIA WEBSITE PROGRAM
STATED PRINT RUN 50 SERIAL #'d SETS
ESJ1 Ken Griffey Jr. 50.00 120.00
ESJ2 Alex Rodriguez 100.00 250.00
ESJ3 Cal Ripken 75.00 200.00
ESJ4 Jeff Bagwell 40.00 100.00
ESJ5 Barry Bonds 75.00 200.00
ESJ6 Manny Ramirez 60.00 150.00

2000 Upper Deck Faces of the Game

COMPLETE SET (20) 20.00 50.00
SER.1 STATED ODDS 1:11
*DIE CUTS: 3X TO 8X BASIC FACES
DIE CUTS RANDOM INSERTS IN SER.1 HOBBY
DIE CUTS PRINT RUN 100 SERIAL #'d SETS
GOLD DIE CUTS RANDOM IN SER.1 HOBBY
GOLD DIE CUT PRINT RUN 1 SERIAL #'d SET
GOLD DC NOT PRICED DUE TO SCARCITY
F1 Ken Griffey Jr. 2.00 5.00
F2 Mark McGwire 1.50 4.00
F3 Sammy Sosa 1.00 2.50
F4 Alex Rodriguez 1.25 3.00
F5 Manny Ramirez 1.00 2.50
F6 Derek Jeter 2.50 6.00
F7 Jeff Bagwell .60 1.50
F8 Roger Clemens 1.25 3.00
F9 Scott Rolen .60 1.50
F10 Tony Gwynn 1.00 2.50
F11 Nomar Garciaparra .60 1.50
F12 Randy Johnson 1.00 2.50
F13 Greg Maddux 1.25 3.00
F14 Mike Piazza 1.00 2.50
F15 Frank Thomas 1.00 2.50
F16 Cal Ripken 3.00 8.00
F17 Ivan Rodriguez .60 1.50
F18 Mo Vaughn .40 1.00
F19 Chipper Jones 1.00 2.50
F20 Sean Casey .40 1.00

2000 Upper Deck Five-Tool Talents

COMPLETE SET (15) 10.00 25.00
SER.2 STATED ODDS 1:11
FT1 Vladimir Guerrero .60 1.50
FT2 Barry Bonds 1.50 4.00
FT3 Jason Kendall .40 1.00
FT4 Derek Jeter 2.50 6.00
FT5 Ken Griffey Jr. 2.00 5.00
FT6 Andruw Jones .40 1.00
FT7 Bernie Williams .60 1.50
FT8 Jose Canseco .60 1.50
FT9 Scott Rolen .60 1.50
FT10 Shawn Green .40 1.00
FT11 Nomar Garciaparra .60 1.50
FT12 Jeff Bagwell .60 1.50
FT13 Larry Walker .60 1.50
FT14 Chipper Jones 1.00 2.50
FT15 Alex Rodriguez 1.25 3.00

2000 Upper Deck Game Ball

SER.2 STATED ODDS 1:287
BAJ Andruw Jones 4.00 10.00
BAR Alex Rodriguez 6.00 15.00
BBW Bernie Williams 4.00 10.00
BDJ Derek Jeter 15.00 40.00
BJB Jeff Bagwell 4.00 10.00
BKG Ken Griffey Jr. 15.00 40.00
BMM Mark McGwire 8.00 20.00
BRC Roger Clemens 6.00 15.00
BTG Tony Gwynn 6.00 15.00
BVG Vladimir Guerrero 4.00 10.00

2000 Upper Deck Game Jersey

H1 SER.1 STATED ODDS 1:288 HOBBY
HR1 SER.1 ODDS 1:2500 HOBBY/RETAIL
HR2 SER.2 ODDS 1:287 HOBBY/RETAIL
AJ Andruw Jones HR2 2.50 6.00
AR Alex Rodriguez H1 8.00 20.00
AR Alex Rodriguez HR2 8.00 20.00
BG Ben Grieve HR2 2.50 6.00
CJ Chipper Jones HR1 6.00 15.00
CR Cal Ripken HR1 8.00 20.00
CY Tom Glavine H1 4.00 10.00
DC David Cone HR2 2.50 6.00
DJ Derek Jeter H1 15.00 40.00
EC Eric Chavez HR2 2.50 6.00
EM Edgar Martinez HR2 4.00 10.00
FT Frank Thomas H1 6.00 15.00
FT Frank Thomas HR2 6.00 15.00
GK Gabe Kapler HR1 2.50 6.00
GM Greg Maddux HR1 8.00 20.00
GM Greg Maddux HR2 8.00 20.00
GV Greg Vaughn HR1 2.50 6.00
JB Jeff Bagwell H1 4.00 10.00
JC Jose Canseco HR1 4.00 10.00
JR Ken Griffey Jr. H1 12.00 30.00
KG Ken Griffey Jr. Reds HR2 12.00 30.00
KM Kevin Millwood HR2 2.50 6.00
MH Mike Hampton HR2 2.50 6.00
MP Mike Piazza H1 6.00 15.00
MR Manny Ramirez HR1 6.00 15.00
MV Mo Vaughn HR2 2.50 6.00
MW Matt Williams HR2 2.50 6.00
PM Pedro Martinez H1 4.00 10.00
RJ Randy Johnson HR2 6.00 15.00
RV Robin Ventura HR2 2.50 6.00
SA Sandy Alomar Jr. HR2 2.50 6.00
TG Tony Gwynn HR2 6.00 15.00
TH Todd Helton HR1 4.00 10.00
TH Todd Helton HR2 4.00 10.00
VG Vladimir Guerrero HR1 4.00 10.00
TGL Tom Glavine HR2 4.00 10.00
TRG Troy Glaus H1 2.50 6.00
TRG Troy Glaus HR2 2.50 6.00

2000 Upper Deck Game Jersey Autograph

EXCHANGE DEADLINE 03/06/01
HAR Alex Rodriguez 40.00 100.00
HBB Barry Bonds 60.00 150.00
HCR Cal Ripken 50.00 100.00
HDJ Derek Jeter 300.00 600.00
HIR Ivan Rodriguez 20.00 50.00
HJB Jeff Bagwell 25.00 60.00
HJC Jose Canseco 12.00 30.00
HJK Jason Kendall 6.00 15.00
HKG K.Griffey Jr. Reds 50.00 120.00
HMR Manny Ramirez 15.00 40.00
HPO Paul O'Neill 30.00 60.00
HSR Scott Rolen 6.00 15.00
HVG Vladimir Guerrero 15.00 40.00

2000 Upper Deck Game Jersey Autograph Numbered

H1 CARDS DIST.IN SER.1 HOBBY ONLY
HR1 CARDS DIST.IN SER.1 HOBBY & RETAIL
H2 CARDS DIST.IN SER.2 HOBBY ONLY
HR2 CARDS DIST.IN SER.2 HOBBY & RETAIL
PRINT RUNS B/WN 2-51 COPIES PER
NO PRICING ON QTY OF 25 OR LESS
SER.1 EXCHANGE DEADLINE 07/15/00
SER.2 EXCHANGE DEADLINE 03/06/01
FT Frank Thomas/35 HR2 75.00 200.00
GM Greg Maddux/31 HR2 100.00 200.00
JC Jose Canseco/33 H2 50.00 120.00
KG Ken Griffey Jr. Reds/30 H2 150.00 400.00
MV Mo Vaughn/42 HR2 30.00 60.00
RJ Randy Johnson/51 HR2 125.00 200.00
VG Vladimir Guerrero/27 H2 75.00 200.00
TGI Tom Glavine/47 HR2 50.00 100.00

2000 Upper Deck Game Jersey Patch

SER.1 STATED ODDS 1:10,000
SER.2 STATED ODDS 1:7500
1 OF 1 PATCH PRINT RUN 1 SERIAL #'d SET
NO 1 OF 1 PATCH PRICING AVAILABLE
PAJ Andruw Jones 2 50.00 100.00
PAR Alex Rodriguez 1 50.00 100.00
PAR Alex Rodriguez 2 50.00 100.00
PBB Barry Bonds 2 100.00 250.00
PBG Ben Grieve 2 20.00 50.00
PCJ Chipper Jones 1 50.00 100.00
PCR Cal Ripken 1 75.00 150.00
PCR Cal Ripken 2 75.00 150.00
PCY Tom Glavine 1 50.00 100.00
PDC David Cone 30.00 60.00
PDJ Derek Jeter 1 75.00 150.00
PDJ Derek Jeter 2 75.00 150.00
PEC Eric Chavez 1 30.00 60.00
PFT Frank Thomas 1 30.00 80.00
PGK Gabe Kapler 1 30.00 60.00
PGM Greg Maddux 1 60.00 120.00
PGM Greg Maddux 2 60.00 120.00
PGV Greg Vaughn 1 20.00 50.00
PIR Ivan Rodriguez 2 50.00 100.00
PJB Jeff Bagwell 1 60.00 150.00
PJC Jose Canseco 1 50.00 100.00
PJR Ken Griffey Jr. 1 75.00 150.00
PKG Ken Griffey Jr. Reds 2 75.00 150.00
PMP Mike Piazza 1 60.00 120.00
PMR Manny Ramirez 1 50.00 100.00
PMR Manny Ramirez 2 50.00 100.00
PMV Mo Vaughn 2 30.00 60.00
PMW Matt Williams 2 30.00 60.00
PPM Pedro Martinez 1 50.00 100.00
PRJ Randy Johnson 2 50.00 100.00
PSR Scott Rolen 2 50.00 100.00
PTG Tony Gwynn 2 50.00 100.00
PTH Todd Helton 1 50.00 100.00
PTRG Troy Glaus 1 30.00 60.00
PTRG Troy Glaus 2 30.00 60.00
PVG Vladimir Guerrero 1 60.00 120.00
PVG Vladimir Guerrero 2 60.00 120.00

2000 Upper Deck Hit Brigade

COMPLETE SET (15) 12.50 30.00
SER.1 STATED ODDS 1:8
*DIE CUTS: 3X TO 8X BASIC HIT BRIGADE
DIE CUTS RANDOM INSERTS IN SER.1 PACKS
DIE CUTS PRINT RUN 100 SERIAL #'d SETS
GOLD DIE CUTS RANDOM IN SER.1 PACKS
GOLD DIE CUT PRINT RUN 1 SERIAL #'d SET
GOLD DC NOT PRICED DUE TO SCARCITY
H1 Ken Griffey Jr. 2.00 5.00
H2 Tony Gwynn 1.00 2.50
H3 Alex Rodriguez 1.25 3.00
H4 Derek Jeter 2.50 6.00
H5 Mike Piazza 1.00 2.50
H6 Sammy Sosa 1.00 2.50
H7 Juan Gonzalez .40 1.00
H8 Scott Rolen .60 1.50
H9 Nomar Garciaparra .60 1.50
H10 Barry Bonds 1.50 4.00
H11 Craig Biggio .60 1.50
H12 Chipper Jones 1.00 2.50
H13 Frank Thomas 1.00 2.50
H14 Larry Walker .60 1.50
H15 Mark McGwire 1.50 4.00

2000 Upper Deck Hot Properties

COMPLETE SET (15) 2.00 5.00
SER.2 STATED ODDS 1:11
HP1 Carlos Beltran .30 .75
HP2 Rick Ankiel .30 .75
HP3 Sean Casey .20 .50
HP4 Preston Wilson .20 .50
HP5 Vernon Wells .20 .50
HP6 Pat Burrell .20 .50
HP7 Eric Chavez .20 .50
HP8 J.D. Drew .20 .50
HP9 Alfonso Soriano .50 1.25
HP10 Gabe Kapler .20 .50

HP11 Rafael Furcal .30 .75
HP12 Ruben Mateo .20 .50
HP13 Corey Koskie .20 .50
HP14 Kip Wells .20 .50
HP15 Ramon Ortiz .20 .50

2000 Upper Deck Legendary Cuts

NO PRICING DUE TO SCARCITY

2000 Upper Deck Pennant Driven

COMPLETE SET (10) 4.00 10.00
SER.2 STATED ODDS 1:4
PD1 Derek Jeter 1.25 3.00
PD2 Roberto Alomar .30 .75
PD3 Chipper Jones .50 1.25
PD4 Jeff Bagwell .30 .75
PD5 Roger Clemens .60 1.50
PD6 Nomar Garciaparra .30 .75
PD7 Manny Ramirez .50 1.25
PD8 Mike Piazza .50 1.25
PD9 Ivan Rodriguez .30 .75
PD10 Randy Johnson .50 1.25

2000 Upper Deck People's Choice

COMPLETE SET (15) 12.50 30.00
SER.2 STATED ODDS 1:23
PC1 Mark McGwire 1.50 4.00
PC2 Nomar Garciaparra .60 1.50
PC3 Derek Jeter 2.50 6.00
PC4 Shawn Green .40 1.00
PC5 Manny Ramirez 1.00 2.50
PC6 Pedro Martinez .60 1.50
PC7 Ivan Rodriguez .60 1.50
PC8 Alex Rodriguez 1.25 3.00
PC9 Juan Gonzalez .40 1.00
PC10 Ken Griffey Jr. 2.00 5.00
PC11 Sammy Sosa 1.00 2.50
PC12 Jeff Bagwell .60 1.50
PC13 Chipper Jones 1.00 2.50
PC14 Cal Ripken 3.00 8.00
PC15 Mike Piazza 1.00 2.50

2000 Upper Deck Power MARK

COMPLETE SET (10) 25.00 50.00
COMMON CARD (MC1-MC10) 2.50 6.00
SER.1 STATED ODDS 1:23
*DIE CUTS: 3X TO 8X BASIC POWER MARK
DIE CUTS RANDOM INSERTS IN SER.1 HOBBY
DIE CUTS PRINT RUN 100 SERIAL #'d SETS
GOLD DIE CUTS RANDOM IN SER.1 HOBBY
GOLD DIE CUT PRINT RUN 1 SERIAL #'d SET
GOLD DC NOT PRICED DUE TO SCARCITY

2000 Upper Deck Power Rally

COMPLETE SET (15) 10.00 25.00
SER.1 STATED ODDS 1:11
*DIE CUTS: 5X TO 12X BASIC POWER RALLY
DIE CUTS RANDOM INSERTS IN SER.1 PACKS
DIE CUTS PRINT RUN 100 SERIAL #'d SETS
GOLD DIE CUTS RANDOM IN SER.1 PACKS
GOLD DIE CUT PRINT RUN 1 SERIAL #'d SET
GOLD DC NOT PRICED DUE TO SCARCITY
P1 Ken Griffey Jr. 1.50 4.00
P2 Mark McGwire 1.25 3.00
P3 Sammy Sosa .75 2.00
P4 Jose Canseco .50 1.25
P5 Juan Gonzalez .30 .75
P6 Bernie Williams .50 1.25
P7 Jeff Bagwell .50 1.25
P8 Chipper Jones .75 2.00
P9 Vladimir Guerrero .50 1.25
P10 Mo Vaughn .30 .75
P11 Derek Jeter 2.00 5.00
P12 Mike Piazza .75 2.00
P13 Barry Bonds 1.25 3.00
P14 Alex Rodriguez 1.00 2.50
P15 Nomar Garciaparra .50 1.25

2000 Upper Deck PowerDeck Inserts

COMPLETE SET (11) 15.00 40.00
SER.1 1-8 STATED ODDS 1:23
SER.1 9-11 STATED ODDS 1:287
PD1 Ken Griffey Jr. 2.00 5.00
PD2 Cal Ripken 3.00 8.00
PD3 Mark McGwire 1.50 4.00
PD4 Tony Gwynn 1.00 2.50
PD5 Roger Clemens 1.25 3.00
PD6 Alex Rodriguez 1.25 3.00
PD7 Sammy Sosa 1.00 2.50
PD8 Derek Jeter 2.50 6.00
PD9 Ken Griffey Jr. SP 4.00 10.00
PD10 Mark McGwire SP 3.00 8.00
PD11 Reggie Jackson SP 1.25 3.00

2000 Upper Deck Prime Performers

COMPLETE SET (10) 2.50 6.00
SER.2 STATED ODDS 1:8
PP1 Manny Ramirez .40 1.00
PP2 Pedro Martinez .25 .60
PP3 Carlos Delgado .15 .40
PP4 Ken Griffey Jr. .75 2.00
PP5 Derek Jeter 1.00 2.50
PP6 Chipper Jones .40 1.00
PP7 Sean Casey .15 .40
PP8 Shawn Green .15 .40
PP9 Sammy Sosa .40 1.00
PP10 Alex Rodriguez .50 1.25

2000 Upper Deck Statitude

COMPLETE SET (30) 12.50 30.00
SER.1 STATED ODDS 1:4
*DIE CUTS: 6X TO 15X BASIC STATITUDE
DIE CUTS RANDOM INSERTS IN SER.1 RETAIL
DIE CUTS PRINT RUN 100 SERIAL #'d SETS
GOLD DIE CUTS RANDOM IN SER.1 RETAIL
GOLD DIE CUT PRINT RUN 1 SERIAL #'d SET
GOLD DC NOT PRICED DUE TO SCARCITY
S1 Mo Vaughn .25 .60
S2 Matt Williams .25 .60
S3 Travis Lee .25 .60
S4 Chipper Jones .60 1.50
S5 Greg Maddux .75 2.00
S6 Gabe Kapler .25 .60
S7 Cal Ripken 2.00 5.00
S8 Nomar Garciaparra .40 1.00
S9 Sammy Sosa .60 1.50
S10 Frank Thomas .60 1.50
S11 Manny Ramirez .60 1.50
S12 Larry Walker .40 1.00
S13 Ivan Rodriguez .40 1.00
S14 Jeff Bagwell .40 1.00
S15 Craig Biggio .40 1.00
S16 Vladimir Guerrero .40 1.00
S17 Mike Piazza .60 1.50
S18 Bernie Williams .40 1.00
S19 Derek Jeter 1.50 4.00
S20 Jose Canseco .40 1.00
S21 Eric Chavez .25 .60
S22 Scott Rolen .40 1.00
S23 Mark McGwire 1.00 2.50
S24 Tony Gwynn .60 1.50
S25 Barry Bonds 1.00 2.50
S26 Ken Griffey Jr. 1.25 3.00
S27 Alex Rodriguez .75 2.00
S28 J.D. Drew .25 .60
S29 Juan Gonzalez .25 .60
S30 Roger Clemens .75 2.00

2000 Upper Deck Subway Series

COMP. FACT SET (30) 6.00 15.00
NY1 Derek Jeter .50 1.25
NY2 Bernie Williams .12 .30
NY3 Roger Clemens .25 .60
NY4 Paul O'Neill .12 .30
NY5 Tino Martinez .07 .20
NY6 Jorge Posada .12 .30
NY7 David Justice .07 .20
NY8 Andy Pettitte .12 .30
NY9 Orlando Hernandez .07 .20
NY10 Mariano Rivera .25 .60
NY11 Scott Brosius .07 .20
NY12 Dwight Gooden .07 .20
NY13 Jose Canseco .12 .30
NY14 Mike Hampton .07 .20
NY15 Al Leiter .07 .20
NY16 Armando Benitez .07 .20
NY17 Bobby Jones .07 .20
NY18 Mike Piazza .20 .50
NY19 Todd Zeile .07 .20
NY20 Edgardo Alfonzo .07 .20
NY21 Mike Bordick .07 .20
NY22 Robin Ventura .07 .20
NY23 Jay Payton .07 .20
NY24 Timo Perez .12 .30
NY25 John Franco .07 .20
NY26 Turk Wendell .07 .20
NY27 Mickey Mantle .60 1.50
NY28 Don Larsen .07 .20
NY29 Jackie Robinson .20 .50
NY30 Pee Wee Reese .12 .30
NNO New York Yankees 3x5 .30 .60

2000 Upper Deck Hawaii

COMPLETE SET (6) 160.00 400.00
TS Tom Seaver AU 25.00 60.00
GAU Julius Erving AU/100 200.00 500.00
Gordie Howe AU
Joe Namath AU
Tom Seaver AU

2001 Upper Deck

COMPLETE SET (450) 90.00 150.00
COMPLETE SERIES 1 (270) 20.00 40.00
COMPLETE SERIES 2 (180) 60.00 100.00
COMMON (46-270/300-450) .10 .30
COMMON SR (1-45/271-300) .20 .50
1 Jeff DaVanon SR .20 .50
2 Aubrey Huff SR .20 .50
3 Pasqual Coco SR .20 .50
4 Barry Zito SR .25 .60
5 Augie Ojeda SR .20 .50
6 Chris Richard SR .20 .50
7 Josh Phelps SR .20 .50
8 Kevin Nicholson SR .20 .50
9 Juan Guzman SR .20 .50
10 Brandon Kolb SR .20 .50
11 Johan Santana SR 3.00 8.00
12 Josh Kalinowski SR .20 .50
13 Tike Redman SR .20 .50
14 Ivanon Coffie SR .20 .50
15 Chad Durbin SR .20 .50
16 Derrick Turnbow SR .20 .50
17 Scott Downs SR .20 .50
18 Jason Grilli SR .20 .50
19 Mark Buehrle SR .25 .60
20 Paxton Crawford SR .20 .50
21 Bronson Arroyo SR .40 1.00
22 Tomas De la Rosa SR .20 .50
23 Paul Rigdon SR .20 .50
24 Rob Ramsay SR .20 .50
25 Damian Rolls SR .20 .50
26 Jason Conti SR .20 .50
27 John Parrish SR .20 .50
28 Geraldo Guzman SR .20 .50
29 Tony Mota SR .20 .50
30 Luis Rivas SR .20 .50
31 Brian Tollberg SR .20 .50
32 Adam Bernero SR .20 .50
33 Michael Cuddyer SR .20 .50
34 Josue Espada SR .20 .50
35 Joe Lawrence SR .20 .50
36 Chad Moeller SR .20 .50
37 Nick Bierbrodt SR .20 .50
38 DeWayne Wise SR .20 .50
39 Javier Cardona SR .20 .50
40 Hiram Bocachica SR .20 .50
41 Giuseppe Chiaramonte SR .20 .50
42 Alex Cabrera SR .20 .50
43 Jimmy Rollins SR .20 .50
44 Pat Flury SR RC .20 .50
45 Leo Estrella SR .20 .50
46 Darin Erstad .10 .30
47 Seth Etherton .10 .30
48 Troy Glaus .10 .30
49 Brian Cooper .10 .30
50 Tim Salmon .20 .50
51 Adam Kennedy .10 .30
52 Bengie Molina .10 .30
53 Jason Giambi .10 .30
54 Miguel Tejada .10 .30
55 Tim Hudson .10 .30
56 Eric Chavez .10 .30
57 Terrence Long .10 .30
58 Jason Isringhausen .10 .30
59 Ramon Hernandez .10 .30
60 Raul Mondesi .10 .30
61 David Wells .10 .30
62 Shannon Stewart .10 .30
63 Tony Batista .10 .30
64 Brad Fullmer .10 .30
65 Chris Carpenter .10 .30
66 Homer Bush .10 .30
67 Gerald Williams .10 .30
68 Miguel Cairo .10 .30
69 Ryan Rupe .10 .30
70 Greg Vaughn .10 .30
71 John Flaherty .10 .30
72 Dan Wheeler .10 .30
73 Fred McGriff .20 .50
74 Roberto Alomar .20 .50
75 Bartolo Colon .10 .30
76 Kenny Lofton .10 .30
77 David Segui .10 .30
78 Omar Vizquel .20 .50
79 Russ Branyan .10 .30
80 Chuck Finley .10 .30
81 Manny Ramirez UER .20 .50
82 Alex Rodriguez .40 1.00
83 John Halama .10 .30
84 Mike Cameron .10 .30
85 David Bell .10 .30
86 Jay Buhner .10 .30
87 Aaron Sele .10 .30
88 Rickey Henderson .30 .75
89 Brook Fordyce .10 .30
90 Cal Ripken 1.00 2.50
91 Mike Mussina .20 .50
92 Delino DeShields .10 .30
93 Melvin Mora .10 .30
94 Sidney Ponson .10 .30
95 Brady Anderson .10 .30
96 Ivan Rodriguez .20 .50
97 Ricky Ledee .10 .30
98 Rick Helling .10 .30
99 Ruben Mateo .10 .30
100 Luis Alicea .10 .30
101 John Wetteland .10 .30
102 Mike Lamb .10 .30
103 Carl Everett .10 .30
104 Troy O'Leary .10 .30
105 Wilton Veras .10 .30
106 Pedro Martinez .20 .50
107 Rolando Arrojo .10 .30
108 Scott Hatteberg .10 .30
109 Jason Varitek .30 .75
110 Jose Offerman .10 .30
111 Carlos Beltran .10 .30
112 Johnny Damon .20 .50
113 Mark Quinn .10 .30
114 Rey Sanchez .10 .30
115 Mac Suzuki .10 .30
116 Jermaine Dye .10 .30
117 Chris Fussell .10 .30
118 Jeff Weaver .10 .30
119 Dean Palmer .10 .30
120 Robert Fick .10 .30
121 Brian Moehler .10 .30
122 Damion Easley .10 .30
123 Juan Encarnacion .10 .30
124 Tony Clark .10 .30
125 Cristian Guzman .10 .30
126 Matt LeCroy .10 .30
127 Eric Milton .10 .30
128 Jay Canizaro .10 .30
129 David Ortiz .30 .75
130 Brad Radke .10 .30
131 Jacque Jones .10 .30
132 Magglio Ordonez .10 .30
133 Carlos Lee .10 .30
134 Mike Sirotka .10 .30
135 Ray Durham .10 .30
136 Paul Konerko .10 .30
137 Charles Johnson .10 .30
138 James Baldwin .10 .30
139 Jeff Abbott .10 .30
140 Roger Clemens .60 1.50
141 Derek Jeter .75 2.00
142 David Justice .10 .30
143 Ramiro Mendoza .10 .30
144 Chuck Knoblauch .10 .30
145 Orlando Hernandez .10 .30
146 Alfonso Soriano .20 .50
147 Jeff Bagwell .20 .50
148 Julio Lugo .10 .30
149 Mitch Meluskey .10 .30
150 Jose Lima .10 .30
151 Richard Hidalgo .10 .30
152 Moises Alou .10 .30
153 Scott Elarton .10 .30
154 Andruw Jones .20 .50
155 Quilvio Veras .10 .30
156 Greg Maddux .50 1.25
157 Brian Jordan .10 .30
158 Andres Galarraga .10 .30
159 Kevin Millwood .10 .30
160 Rafael Furcal .10 .30
161 Jeromy Burnitz .10 .30
162 Jimmy Haynes .10 .30
163 Mark Loretta .10 .30
164 Ron Belliard .10 .30
165 Richie Sexson .10 .30
166 Kevin Barker .10 .30
167 Jeff D'Amico .10 .30
168 Rick Ankiel .10 .30
169 Mark McGwire .75 2.00
170 J.D. Drew .10 .30
171 Eli Marrero .10 .30
172 Darryl Kile .10 .30
173 Edgar Renteria .10 .30
174 Will Clark .20 .50
175 Eric Young .10 .30
176 Mark Grace .20 .50
177 Jon Lieber .10 .30
178 Damon Buford .10 .30
179 Kerry Wood .10 .30
180 Rondell White .10 .30
181 Joe Girardi .10 .30
182 Curt Schilling .10 .30
183 Randy Johnson .30 .75
184 Steve Finley .10 .30
185 Kelly Stinnett .10 .30
186 Jay Bell .10 .30
187 Matt Mantei .10 .30
188 Luis Gonzalez .10 .30
189 Shawn Green .10 .30
190 Todd Hundley .10 .30
191 Chan Ho Park .10 .30
192 Adrian Beltre .10 .30
193 Mark Grudzielanek .10 .30
194 Gary Sheffield .10 .30
195 Tom Goodwin .10 .30
196 Lee Stevens .10 .30
197 Javier Vazquez .10 .30
198 Milton Bradley .10 .30
199 Vladimir Guerrero .30 .75
200 Carl Pavano .10 .30
201 Orlando Cabrera .10 .30
202 Tony Armas Jr. .10 .30
203 Jeff Kent .10 .30
204 Calvin Murray .10 .30
205 Ellis Burks .10 .30
206 Barry Bonds .75 2.00
207 Russ Ortiz .10 .30
208 Marvin Benard .10 .30
209 Joe Nathan .10 .30
210 Preston Wilson .10 .30
211 Cliff Floyd .10 .30
212 Mike Lowell .10 .30
213 Ryan Dempster .10 .30
214 Brad Penny .10 .30
215 Mike Redmond .10 .30
216 Luis Castillo .10 .30
217 Derek Bell .10 .30
218 Mike Hampton .10 .30
219 Todd Zeile .10 .30
220 Robin Ventura .10 .30
221 Mike Piazza .50 1.25
222 Al Leiter .10 .30
223 Edgardo Alfonzo .10 .30
224 Mike Bordick .10 .30
225 Phil Nevin .10 .30
226 Ryan Klesko .10 .30
227 Adam Eaton .10 .30
228 Eric Owens .10 .30
229 Tony Gwynn .40 1.00
230 Matt Clement .10 .30
231 Wiki Gonzalez .10 .30
232 Robert Person .10 .30
233 Doug Glanville .10 .30
234 Scott Rolen .20 .50
235 Mike Lieberthal .10 .30
236 Randy Wolf .10 .30
237 Bob Abreu .10 .30
238 Pat Burrell .10 .30
239 Bruce Chen .10 .30
240 Kevin Young .10 .30
241 Todd Ritchie .10 .30
242 Adrian Brown .10 .30
243 Chad Hermansen .10 .30
244 Warren Morris .10 .30
245 Kris Benson .10 .30
246 Jason Kendall .10 .30
247 Pokey Reese .10 .30
248 Rob Bell .10 .30
249 Ken Griffey Jr. .60 1.50
250 Sean Casey .10 .30
251 Aaron Boone .10 .30
252 Pete Harnisch .10 .30
253 Barry Larkin .20 .50
254 Dmitri Young .10 .30
255 Todd Hollandsworth .10 .30
256 Pedro Astacio .10 .30
257 Todd Helton .20 .50
258 Terry Shumpert .10 .30
259 Neifi Perez .10 .30
260 Jeffrey Hammonds .10 .30
261 Ben Petrick .10 .30
262 Mark McGwire SH .40 1.00
263 Derek Jeter SH .40 1.00
264 Sammy Sosa SH .20 .50
265 Cal Ripken SH .50 1.25
266 Pedro Martinez SH .20 .50
267 Barry Bonds SH .40 1.00
268 Fred McGriff SH .10 .30
269 Randy Johnson SH .20 .50
270 Darin Erstad SH .10 .30
271 Ichiro Suzuki SR RC 8.00 20.00
272 Wilson Betemit SR RC .75 2.00
273 Corey Patterson SR .20 .50
274 Sean Douglass SR RC .20 .50
275 Mike Penney SR RC .20 .50
276 Nate Teut SR RC .20 .50
277 Ricardo Rodriguez SR RC .20 .50
278 Brandon Duckworth SR RC .20 .50
279 Rafael Soriano SR RC .20 .50
280 Juan Diaz SR RC .20 .50
281 Horacio Ramirez SR RC .25 .60
282 Tsuyoshi Shinjo SR RC .25 .60
283 Keith Ginter SR .20 .50
284 Esix Snead SR RC .20 .50
285 Erick Almonte SR RC .20 .50
286 Travis Hafner SR RC 2.00 5.00
287 Jason Smith SR RC .20 .50
288 Jackson Melian SR RC .20 .50
289 Tyler Walker SR RC .20 .50
290 Jason Standridge SR .20 .50
291 Juan Uribe SR RC .25 .60
292 Adrian Hernandez SR RC .20 .50
293 Jason Michaels SR RC .20 .50
294 Jason Hart SR .20 .50
295 Albert Pujols SR RC 40.00 100.00
296 Morgan Ensberg SR RC .75 2.00
297 Brandon Inge SR .20 .50
298 Jesus Colome SR .20 .50
299 Kyle Kessel SR RC .20 .50
300 Timo Perez SR .20 .50
301 Mo Vaughn .10 .30
302 Ismael Valdes .10 .30
303 Glenallen Hill .10 .30
304 Garret Anderson .10 .30
305 Johnny Damon .20 .50
306 Jose Ortiz .10 .30
307 Mark Mulder .10 .30
308 Adam Piatt .10 .30
309 Gil Heredia .10 .30
310 Mike Sirotka .10 .30
311 Carlos Delgado .10 .30
312 Alex Gonzalez .10 .30
313 Jose Cruz Jr. .10 .30
314 Darrin Fletcher .10 .30
315 Ben Grieve .10 .30
316 Vinny Castilla .10 .30
317 Wilson Alvarez .10 .30
318 Brent Abernathy .10 .30
319 Ellis Burks .10 .30
320 Jim Thome .20 .50
321 Juan Gonzalez .10 .30
322 Ed Taubensee .10 .30
323 Travis Fryman .10 .30
324 John Olerud .10 .30
325 Edgar Martinez .20 .50
326 Freddy Garcia .10 .30
327 Bret Boone .20 .50
328 Kazuhiro Sasaki .10 .30
329 Albert Belle .10 .30
330 Mike Bordick .10 .30
331 David Segui .10 .30
332 Pat Hentgen .10 .30
333 Alex Rodriguez .40 1.00
334 Andres Galarraga .10 .30
335 Gabe Kapler .10 .30
336 Ken Caminiti .10 .30
337 Rafael Palmeiro .20 .50
338 Manny Ramirez Sox .20 .50
339 David Cone .10 .30
340 Nomar Garciaparra .50 1.25
341 Trot Nixon .10 .30
342 Derek Lowe .10 .30
343 Roberto Hernandez .10 .30
344 Mike Sweeney .10 .30
345 Carlos Febles .10 .30
346 Jeff Suppan .10 .30
347 Roger Cedeno .10 .30
348 Bobby Higginson .10 .30
349 Deivi Cruz .10 .30
350 Mitch Meluskey .10 .30
351 Matt Lawton .10 .30
352 Mark Redman .10 .30
353 Jay Canizaro .10 .30
354 Corey Koskie .10 .30
355 Matt Kinney .10 .30
356 Frank Thomas .30 .75
357 Sandy Alomar Jr. .10 .30
358 David Wells .10 .30
359 Jim Parque .10 .30
360 Chris Singleton .10 .30
361 Tino Martinez .20 .50
362 Paul O'Neill .20 .50
363 Mike Mussina .20 .50
364 Bernie Williams .20 .50
365 Andy Pettitte .20 .50
366 Mariano Rivera .30 .75
367 Brad Ausmus .10 .30
368 Craig Biggio .20 .50
369 Lance Berkman .10 .30
370 Shane Reynolds .10 .30
371 Chipper Jones .30 .75
372 Tom Glavine .20 .50
373 B.J. Surhoff .10 .30
374 John Smoltz .20 .50
375 Rico Brogna .10 .30
376 Geoff Jenkins .10 .30
377 Jose Hernandez .10 .30
378 Tyler Houston .10 .30
379 Henry Blanco .10 .30
380 Jeffrey Hammonds .10 .30
381 Jim Edmonds .10 .30
382 Fernando Vina .10 .30
383 Andy Benes .10 .30
384 Ray Lankford .10 .30
385 Dustin Hermanson .10 .30
386 Todd Hundley .10 .30
387 Sammy Sosa .30 .75
388 Tom Gordon .10 .30
389 Bill Mueller .10 .30
390 Ron Coomer .10 .30
391 Matt Stairs .10 .30
392 Mark Grace .20 .50
393 Matt Williams .10 .30
394 Todd Stottlemyre .10 .30
395 Tony Womack .10 .30
396 Erubiel Durazo .10 .30
397 Reggie Sanders .10 .30
398 Andy Ashby .10 .30
399 Eric Karros .10 .30
400 Kevin Brown .10 .30
401 Darren Dreifort .10 .30
402 Fernando Tatis .10 .30
403 Jose Vidro .10 .30
404 Peter Bergeron .10 .30
405 Geoff Blum .10 .30
406 J.T. Snow .10 .30
407 Livan Hernandez .10 .30
408 Robb Nen .10 .30
409 Bobby Estalella .10 .30
410 Rich Aurilia .10 .30
411 Eric Davis .10 .30
412 Charles Johnson .10 .30
413 Alex Gonzalez .10 .30
414 A.J. Burnett .10 .30
415 Antonio Alfonseca .10 .30
416 Derrek Lee .20 .50
417 Jay Payton .10 .30
418 Kevin Appier .10 .30
419 Steve Trachsel .10 .30
420 Rey Ordonez .10 .30
421 Darryl Hamilton .10 .30
422 Ben Davis .10 .30
423 Damian Jackson .10 .30
424 Mark Kotsay .10 .30
425 Trevor Hoffman .10 .30
426 Travis Lee .10 .30
427 Omar Daal .10 .30
428 Paul Byrd .10 .30
429 Reggie Taylor .10 .30
430 Brian Giles .10 .30
431 Derek Bell .10 .30
432 Francisco Cordova .10 .30
433 Pat Meares .10 .30
434 Scott Williamson .10 .30
435 Jason LaRue .10 .30
436 Michael Tucker .10 .30
437 Wilton Guerrero .10 .30
438 Mike Hampton .10 .30
439 Ron Gant .10 .30
440 Jeff Cirillo .10 .30
441 Denny Neagle .10 .30
442 Larry Walker .10 .30
443 Juan Pierre .10 .30
444 Todd Walker .10 .30
445 Jason Giambi SH CL .10 .30
446 Jeff Kent SH CL .10 .30
447 Mariano Rivera SH CL .20 .50
448 Edgar Martinez SH CL .10 .30
449 Troy Glaus SH CL .10 .30
450 Alex Rodriguez SH CL .25 .60

2001 Upper Deck Exclusives Gold

*STARS: 30X TO 80X BASIC CARDS
*SR STARS: 15X TO 40X BASIC SR
*SR ROOKIES: 15X TO 40X BASIC SR
STATED PRINT RUN 25 SERIAL #'d SETS
11 Johan Santana SR 25.00 60.00

2001 Upper Deck Exclusives Silver

STARS: 12.5X TO 30X BASIC CARDS
*SR YNG.STARS: 6X TO 15X BASIC
*SR RC's: 6X TO 15X BASIC SR
STATED PRINT RUN 100 SERIAL #'d SETS
11 Johan Santana SR 10.00 25.00

2001 Upper Deck 1971 All-Star Game Salute

SER.2 STATED ODDS 1:288
ASBR Brooks Robinson Bat 8.00 20.00
ASFR Frank Robinson Jsy 6.00 15.00
ASHA Hank Aaron Bat 12.50 30.00
ASHA Hank Aaron Jsy 12.50 30.00
ASJB Johnny Bench Bat 8.00 20.00
ASJB Johnny Bench Jsy 8.00 20.00
ASLA Luis Aparicio Jsy 6.00 15.00
ASLB Lou Brock Bat 8.00 20.00
ASRC Roberto Clemente Jsy 25.00 60.00
ASRJ Reggie Jackson Jsy 8.00 20.00
ASTM Thurman Munson Jsy 25.00 60.00
ASTS Tom Seaver Jsy 8.00 20.00

2001 Upper Deck All-Star Heroes Memorabilia

PRINT RUNS B/WN 36-2000 COPIES PER
ASHAR A.Rodriguez Bat/1998 6.00 15.00
ASHBR Babe Ruth Bat/1933 75.00 150.00
ASHCR C.Ripken Bat/1991 10.00 25.00
ASHDJ D.Jeter Base/2000 10.00 25.00
ASHKG K.Griffey Jr. Bat/1992 15.00 40.00
ASHMM M.Mantle Jsy/54 150.00 400.00
ASHMP M.Piazza Base/1996 6.00 15.00
ASHRC R.Clemens Jsy/1986 4.00 15.00
ASHRJ R.Johnson Jsy/1993 6.00 15.00
ASHSS S.Sosa Jsy/2000 10.00 25.00
ASHTG T.Gwynn Jsy/1994 6.00 15.00
ASHTP T.Perez Bat/1967 4.00 10.00
ASHROC R.Clemente Bat/1961 20.00 50.00

2001 Upper Deck Big League Beat

COMPLETE SET (20) 8.00 20.00
SER.1 STATED ODDS 1:3
BB1 Barry Bonds .75 2.00
BB2 Nomar Garciaparra .50 1.25
BB3 Mark McGwire .75 2.00
BB4 Roger Clemens .60 1.50
BB5 Chipper Jones .30 .75
BB6 Jeff Bagwell .20 .50
BB7 Sammy Sosa .30 .75
BB8 Cal Ripken 1.00 2.50
BB9 Randy Johnson .30 .75
BB10 Carlos Delgado .20 .50
BB11 Manny Ramirez .20 .50
BB12 Derek Jeter .75 2.00
BB13 Tony Gwynn .40 1.00
BB14 Pedro Martinez .20 .50
BB15 Jose Canseco .20 .50
BB16 Frank Thomas .30 .75
BB17 Alex Rodriguez .40 1.00
BB18 Bernie Williams .20 .50
BB19 Greg Maddux .50 1.25
BB20 Rafael Palmeiro .20 .50

2001 Upper Deck Big League Challenge Game Jerseys

SER.2 STATED ODDS 1:288
BLCBB Barry Bonds 5.00 12.00
BLCFT Frank Thomas 3.00 8.00
BLCGS Gary Sheffield 1.25 3.00
BLCJC Jose Canseco 2.00 5.00
BLCJE Jim Edmonds 2.00 5.00
BLCMP Mike Piazza 3.00 8.00
BLCRH Richard Hidalgo 1.25 3.00
BLCRP Rafael Palmeiro 2.00 5.00
BLCSF Steve Finley 1.25 3.00
BLCTG Troy Glaus 1.25 3.00
BLCTH Todd Helton 2.00 5.00

2001 Upper Deck e-Card

COMPLETE SET (12) 7.50 15.00
COMPLETE SERIES 1 (6) 3.00 6.00
COMPLETE SERIES 2 (6) 5.00 10.00
STATED ODDS 1:12
E1 Andruw Jones .40 1.00
E2 Alex Rodriguez .50 1.25
E3 Frank Thomas .40 1.00
E4 Todd Helton .40 1.00
E5 Troy Glaus .40 1.00
E6 Barry Bonds 1.00 2.50
E7 Alex Rodriguez .50 1.25
E8 Ken Griffey Jr. .75 2.00
E9 Sammy Sosa .40 1.00
E10 Gary Sheffield .40 1.00
E11 Barry Bonds 1.00 2.50
E12 Andruw Jones .40 1.00

2001 Upper Deck eVolve Autograph

EXCH.CARD AVAIL.VIA WEBSITE PROGRAM
STATED PRINT RUN 200 SERIAL #'d SETS
ESAJ Andruw Jones S1 10.00 25.00
ESAJ Andruw Jones S2 10.00 25.00
ESAR Alex Rodriguez S1 20.00 50.00
ESAR Alex Rodriguez S2 20.00 50.00
ESBB Barry Bonds S1 60.00 120.00
ESBB Barry Bonds S2 60.00 120.00
ESFT Frank Thomas S1 30.00 60.00
ESGS Gary Sheffield S2 6.00 15.00
ESKG Ken Griffey Jr. S2 40.00 100.00
ESSS Sammy Sosa S2 30.00 60.00
ESTG Troy Glaus S1 6.00 15.00
ESTH Todd Helton S1 6.00 15.00

2001 Upper Deck eVolve Game Jersey

EXCH.CARD AVAIL.VIA WEBSITE PROGRAM
PRINT RUNS B/WN 200-300 COPIES PER
EJAJ Andruw Jones S1 6.00 15.00
EJAJ Andruw Jones S2 6.00 15.00
EJAR Alex Rodriguez S1 8.00 20.00
EJAR Alex Rodriguez S2 8.00 20.00
EJBB Barry Bonds S1 12.50 30.00
EJBB Barry Bonds S2 12.50 30.00
EJFT Frank Thomas S1 6.00 15.00
EJGS Gary Sheffield S2 4.00 10.00
EJKG Ken Griffey Jr. S2/300 10.00 25.00
EJSS Sammy Sosa S2 6.00 15.00
EJTG Troy Glaus S1 4.00 10.00
EJTH Todd Helton S1 6.00 15.00
EJKG Ken Griffey Jr. S1/200 10.00 25.00

2001 Upper Deck eVolve Game Jersey Autograph

EXCH.CARD AVAIL.VIA WEBSITE PROGRAM
STATED PRINT RUN 50 SERIAL #'d SETS
ESJAJ Andruw Jones S1 10.00 25.00
ESJAJ Andruw Jones S2 10.00 25.00
ESJAR Alex Rodriguez S1 15.00 40.00
ESJAR Alex Rodriguez S2 15.00 40.00
ESJBB Barry Bonds S1 125.00 250.00
ESJBB Barry Bonds S2 125.00 250.00
ESJFT Frank Thomas S1 40.00 80.00
ESJGS Gary Sheffield S2 10.00 25.00
ESJKG Ken Griffey Jr. S2 60.00 120.00
ESJSS Sammy Sosa S2 30.00 80.00
ESJTG Troy Glaus S1 30.00 60.00
ESJTH Todd Helton S1 30.00 60.00

2001 Upper Deck Franchise

COMPLETE SET (10) 25.00 60.00
SER.2 STATED ODDS 1:36
F1 Frank Thomas 1.50 4.00
F2 Mark McGwire 4.00 10.00
F3 Ken Griffey Jr. 3.00 8.00
F4 Manny Ramirez Sox 1.50 4.00
F5 Alex Rodriguez 2.00 5.00
F6 Greg Maddux 2.50 6.00
F7 Sammy Sosa 1.50 4.00
F8 Derek Jeter 4.00 10.00
F9 Mike Piazza 2.50 6.00
F10 Vladimir Guerrero 1.50 4.00

2001 Upper Deck Game Ball 1

STATED PRINT RUN 100 SERIAL #'d SETS
BAJ Andruw Jones 15.00 40.00
BAR Alex Rodriguez Mariners 30.00 60.00
BBB Barry Bonds 10.00 25.00
BDJ Derek Jeter 40.00 80.00
BIR Ivan Rodriguez 15.00 40.00
BJG Jason Giambi 10.00 25.00
BJG Jeff Bagwell 15.00 40.00
BKG Ken Griffey Jr. 10.00 25.00
BMM Mark McGwire 75.00 150.00
BMP Mike Piazza 30.00 60.00
BRA Rick Ankiel 10.00 25.00
BRJ Randy Johnson 15.00 40.00
BSG Shawn Green 10.00 25.00
BSS Sammy Sosa 15.00 40.00
BTH Todd Helton 15.00 40.00
BTOG Tony Gwynn 15.00 40.00
BTRG Troy Glaus 10.00 25.00
BVG Vladimir Guerrero 15.00 40.00

2001 Upper Deck Game Ball 2

SER.2 STATED ODDS 1:288
BAJ Andruw Jones 6.00 15.00
BAR Alex Rodriguez Rangers 10.00 25.00
BBB Barry Bonds 15.00 40.00
BBW Bernie Williams 6.00 15.00
BCJ Chipper Jones 6.00 15.00
BCR Cal Ripken 15.00 40.00
BDJ Derek Jeter 12.00 30.00
BGS Gary Sheffield 4.00 10.00
BJB Jeff Bagwell 6.00 15.00
BJK Jeff Kent 4.00 10.00
BKG Ken Griffey Jr. 10.00 25.00
BMM Mark McGwire 20.00 50.00
BMP Mike Piazza 10.00 25.00
BMR Mariano Rivera 6.00 15.00
BNG Nomar Garciaparra SP 15.00 40.00
BRC Roger Clemens 10.00 25.00
BSS Sammy Sosa 6.00 15.00
BVG Vladimir Guerrero 6.00 15.00

2001 Upper Deck Game Jersey

SER.1 STATED ODDS 1:288 HOB/RET
CAJ Andruw Jones 10.00 25.00
CAR Alex Rodriguez 10.00 25.00
CBW Bernie Williams 10.00 25.00
CCR Cal Ripken 20.00 50.00
CDJ Derek Jeter 12.50 30.00
CFT Fernando Tatis 6.00 15.00
CIR Ivan Rodriguez 10.00 25.00
CKG Ken Griffey Jr. 15.00 40.00
CMR Manny Ramirez 10.00 25.00
CMW Matt Williams 6.00 15.00
CNRA Nolan Ryan Astros 12.00 30.00
CNRR Nolan Ryan Rangers 12.00 30.00
CPO Paul O'Neill 10.00 25.00
CRV Robin Ventura 6.00 15.00
CSK Sandy Koufax 40.00 80.00
CTG Tony Gwynn 10.00 25.00
CTH Todd Helton 10.00 25.00
CTIH Tim Hudson 6.00 15.00

2001 Upper Deck Game Jersey Autograph 1

SER.1 STATED ODDS 1:288 HOBBY
HAR Alex Rodriguez 20.00 50.00
HBB Barry Bonds 60.00 120.00
HFT Frank Thomas 40.00 80.00
HGM Greg Maddux 75.00 150.00
HJB Jeff Bagwell 20.00 50.00
HJC Jose Canseco 20.00 50.00

HJD J.D. Drew 6.00 15.00
HJG Jason Giambi 6.00 15.00
HJL Javy Lopez 6.00 15.00
HKG Ken Griffey Jr. 50.00 100.00
HMH Mike Hampton 6.00 15.00
HNRA Nolan Ryan Angels 40.00 100.00
HNRM Nolan Ryan Mets 40.00 100.00
HRA Rick Ankiel 12.50 30.00
HRJ Randy Johnson 30.00 60.00
HRP Rafael Palmeiro 10.00 25.00
HSC Sean Casey 6.00 15.00
HSG Shawn Green 10.00 25.00

2001 Upper Deck Game Jersey Autograph 2

SER.2 STATED ODDS 1:288 HOBBY
EXCHANGE DEADLINE 06/26/06
AJ Andruw Jones 6.00 15.00
AR Alex Rodriguez 25.00 60.00
BB Barry Bonds 40.00 80.00
CJ Chipper Jones 40.00 80.00
CR Cal Ripken SP 60.00 120.00
GS Gary Sheffield 6.00 15.00
IR Ivan Rodriguez SP 15.00 40.00
JB Johnny Bench 20.00 50.00
JC Jose Canseco 20.00 50.00
KG Ken Griffey Jr. 60.00 120.00
NR Nolan Ryan 75.00 150.00
RC Roger Clemens 20.00 50.00
SS Sammy Sosa SP 15.00 40.00
TG Troy Glaus 20.00 50.00

2001 Upper Deck Game Jersey Autograph Numbered

PRINT RUNS LISTED BELOW
NO PRICING ON QTY OF 25 OR LESS
CKG Ken Griffey Jr./30 125.00 250.00
CNRA N.Ryan Astros/34 175.00 300.00
CNRR N.Ryan Rangers/34 175.00 300.00
CSK Sandy Koufax/32 600.00 1000.00
HFT Frank Thomas/35 75.00 150.00
HGM Greg Maddux/31 175.00 300.00
HJC Jose Canseco/33 50.00 100.00
HKG Ken Griffey Jr./30 125.00 250.00
HMH Mike Hampton/32 30.00 60.00
HNRA N.Ryan Angels/30 200.00 350.00
HNRM N.Ryan Mets/30 250.00 400.00
HRA Rick Ankiel/66 30.00 60.00
HRJ Randy Johnson/51 125.00 200.00

2001 Upper Deck Game Jersey Combo

STATED PRINT RUN 50 SERIAL #'d SETS
AJKG A.Jones 10.00 25.00
K.Griffey Jr.
BBJC B.Bonds 50.00 100.00
J.Canseco
BBKG B.Bonds 50.00 100.00
K.Griffey Jr.
DJAR D.Jeter 30.00 60.00
A.Rodriguez
FTJB F.Thomas 20.00 50.00
J.Bagwell
IRRP I.Rodriguez 20.00 50.00
R.Palmeiro
JDRA J.Drew 15.00 40.00
R.Ankiel
NRAR N.Ryan Astro-Rgr 60.00 120.00
NRMA N.Ryan Mets-Angels 60.00 120.00
RATH R.Ankiel 15.00 40.00
T.Hudson
RJGM R.Johnson 30.00 60.00
G.Maddux
TGCR T.Gwynn 50.00 100.00
C.Ripken
VGMR V.Guerrero 20.00 50.00
M.Ramirez

2001 Upper Deck Game Jersey Patch

SER.1 STATED ODDS 1:7500
SER.2 STATED ODDS 1:5000
PAR Alex Rodriguez S1 30.00 60.00
PAR Alex Rodriguez S2 30.00 60.00
PBB Barry Bonds S1 75.00 150.00
PBB Barry Bonds S2 75.00 150.00
PCJ Chipper Jones S2 50.00 100.00
PCR Cal Ripken S1 40.00 100.00
PCR Cal Ripken S2 40.00 100.00
PDJ Derek Jeter S1 75.00 150.00
PFT Frank Thomas S1 50.00 100.00
PIR Ivan Rodriguez S1 30.00 60.00
PIR Ivan Rodriguez S2 30.00 60.00
PJB Johnny Bench S2 50.00 100.00
PJB Jeff Bagwell S1 40.00 80.00
PJC Jose Canseco S1 40.00 80.00
PJG Jason Giambi S1 30.00 60.00
PKG Ken Griffey Jr. S1 30.00 60.00
PKG Ken Griffey Jr. S2 30.00 60.00
PNRA N.Ryan Astros S1 30.00 60.00
PNRR N.Ryan Rangers S1 30.00 60.00
PNRR N.Ryan Rangers S2 30.00 60.00
PRA Rick Ankiel S1 15.00 40.00
PRP Rafael Palmeiro S1 15.00 40.00
PSS Sammy Sosa S2 15.00 40.00
PTG Tony Gwynn S1 50.00 100.00

2001 Upper Deck Game Jersey Patch Autograph Numbered

PRINT RUNS B/WN 3-66 COPIES PER
SPKG Ken Griffey Jr./30 300.00 500.00
SPRA Rick Ankiel/66 40.00 80.00

2001 Upper Deck Home Run Derby Heroes

COMPLETE SET (10) 20.00 50.00
SER.2 STATED ODDS 1:36
HD1 Mark McGwire 99 4.00 10.00
HD2 Sammy Sosa 00 1.50 4.00
HD3 Frank Thomas 96 1.50 4.00
HD4 Cal Ripken 91 5.00 12.00
HD5 Tino Martinez 97 1.00 2.50
HD6 Ken Griffey Jr. 99 3.00 8.00
HD7 Barry Bonds 96 4.00 10.00
HD8 Albert Belle 95 .75 2.00
HD9 Mark McGwire 92 4.00 10.00
HD10 Juan Gonzalez 93 .75 2.00

2001 Upper Deck Home Run Explosion

COMPLETE SET (15) 15.00 40.00
SER.1 STATED ODDS 1:12
HR1 Mark McGwire 2.00 5.00
HR2 Chipper Jones .75 2.00
HR3 Jeff Bagwell .50 1.25
HR4 Carlos Delgado .40 1.00
HR5 Barry Bonds 2.00 5.00
HR6 Troy Glaus .40 1.00
HR7 Sammy Sosa .75 2.00
HR8 Alex Rodriguez 1.00 2.50
HR9 Mike Piazza 1.25 3.00
HR10 Vladimir Guerrero .75 2.00
HR11 Ken Griffey Jr. 1.50 4.00
HR12 Frank Thomas .75 2.00
HR13 Ivan Rodriguez .50 1.25
HR14 Jason Giambi .40 1.00
HR15 Carl Everett .40 1.00

2001 Upper Deck Midseason Superstar Summit

COMPLETE SET (15) 25.00 60.00
SER.2 STATED ODDS 1:24
MS1 Derek Jeter 4.00 10.00
MS2 Sammy Sosa 1.50 4.00
MS3 Jeff Bagwell 1.00 2.50
MS4 Tony Gwynn 2.00 5.00
MS5 Alex Rodriguez 2.00 5.00
MS6 Greg Maddux 2.50 6.00
MS7 Jason Giambi .75 2.00
MS8 Mark McGwire 4.00 10.00
MS9 Barry Bonds 4.00 10.00
MS10 Ken Griffey Jr. 3.00 8.00
MS11 Carlos Delgado .75 2.00
MS12 Troy Glaus .75 2.00
MS13 Todd Helton 1.00 2.50
MS14 Manny Ramirez Sox 1.00 2.50
MS15 Jeff Kent .75 2.00

2001 Upper Deck Midsummer Classic Moments

COMPLETE SET (20) 15.00 40.00
SER.2 STATED ODDS 1:12
CM1 Joe DiMaggio 36 1.25 3.00
CM2 Joe DiMaggio 51 1.25 3.00
CM3 Mickey Mantle 52 2.50 6.00
CM4 Mickey Mantle 68 2.50 6.00
CM5 Roger Clemens 86 1.50 4.00
CM6 Mark McGwire 87 2.00 5.00
CM7 Cal Ripken 91 2.50 6.00
CM8 Ken Griffey Jr. 92 1.50 4.00
CM9 Randy Johnson 93 .75 2.00
CM10 Tony Gwynn 94 1.00 2.50
CM11 Fred McGriff 94 .50 1.25
CM12 Hideo Nomo 95 .75 2.00
CM13 Jeff Conine 95 .40 1.00
CM14 Mike Piazza 96 1.25 3.00
CM15 Sandy Alomar Jr. 97 .40 1.00
CM16 Alex Rodriguez 98 .75 2.00
CM17 Roberto Alomar 98 .50 1.25
CM18 Pedro Martinez 99 .50 1.25
CM19 Andres Galarraga 00 .40 1.00
CM20 Derek Jeter 00 1.50 4.00

2001 Upper Deck People's Choice

COMPLETE SET (15) 30.00 80.00
SER.2 STATED ODDS 1:24
PC1 Alex Rodriguez 2.00 5.00
PC2 Ken Griffey Jr. 3.00 8.00
PC3 Mark McGwire 4.00 10.00
PC4 Todd Helton 1.00 2.50
PC5 Manny Ramirez 1.00 2.50
PC6 Mike Piazza 2.50 6.00
PC7 Vladimir Guerrero 1.50 4.00
PC8 Randy Johnson 1.50 4.00
PC9 Cal Ripken 5.00 12.00
PC10 Andruw Jones 1.00 2.50
PC11 Sammy Sosa 1.50 4.00
PC12 Derek Jeter 4.00 10.00
PC13 Pedro Martinez 1.00 2.50
PC14 Frank Thomas 1.50 4.00
PC15 Nomar Garciaparra 2.50 6.00

2001 Upper Deck Rookie Roundup

COMPLETE SET (10) 2.00 5.00
SER.1 STATED ODDS 1:6
RR1 Rick Ankiel .20 .50
RR2 Adam Kennedy .20 .50
RR3 Mike Lamb .20 .50
RR4 Adam Eaton .20 .50
RR5 Rafael Furcal .30 .75
RR6 Pat Burrell .30 .75
RR7 Adam Piatt .20 .50
RR8 Eric Munson .20 .50
RR9 Brad Penny .20 .50
RR10 Mark Mulder .30 .75

2001 Upper Deck Subway Series Game Jerseys

SER.2 STATED ODDS 1:144 HOBBY
CARDS ERRONEOUSLY STATE W.SERIES USE
SSAL Al Leiter 2.00 5.00
SSAP Andy Pettitte 3.00 8.00
SSBW Bernie Williams 3.00 8.00
SSEA Edgardo Alfonzo 2.00 5.00
SSJF John Franco 2.00 5.00
SSJP Jay Payton 2.00 5.00
SSOH Orlando Hernandez 2.00 5.00
SSPO Paul O'Neill 3.00 8.00
SSRC Roger Clemens 8.00 20.00
SSTP Timo Perez 2.00 5.00

2001 Upper Deck Superstar Summit

COMPLETE SET (15) 20.00 50.00
SER.1 STATED ODDS 1:12
SS1 Derek Jeter 2.00 5.00
SS2 Randy Johnson .75 2.00
SS3 Barry Bonds 2.00 5.00
SS4 Frank Thomas .75 2.00
SS5 Cal Ripken 2.50 6.00
SS6 Pedro Martinez .75 2.00
SS7 Ivan Rodriguez .75 2.00
SS8 Mike Piazza 1.25 3.00
SS9 Mark McGwire 2.00 5.00
SS10 Manny Ramirez Sox .75 2.00
SS11 Ken Griffey Jr. 1.50 4.00
SS12 Sammy Sosa .75 2.00
SS13 Alex Rodriguez 1.00 2.50
SS14 Chipper Jones .75 2.00
SS15 Nomar Garciaparra 1.25 3.00

2001 Upper Deck UD's Most Wanted

COMPLETE SET (15) 10.00 25.00
SER.1 STATED ODDS 1:14
MW1 Mark McGwire 1.50 4.00
MW2 Cal Ripken 3.00 8.00
MW3 Ivan Rodriguez .60 1.50
MW4 Pedro Martinez .60 1.50
MW5 Sammy Sosa .60 1.50
MW6 Tony Gwynn 1.00 2.50
MW7 Vladimir Guerrero 1.00 2.50
MW8 Derek Jeter 2.50 6.00
MW9 Mike Piazza 1.00 2.50
MW10 Chipper Jones 1.00 2.50
MW11 Alex Rodriguez 1.25 3.00
MW12 Barry Bonds 1.50 4.00
MW13 Jeff Bagwell .60 1.50
MW14 Frank Thomas 1.00 2.50
MW15 Nomar Garciaparra .60 1.50

2001 Upper Deck Pinstripe Exclusives DiMaggio

COMPLETE SET (56) 30.00 60.00
COMMON CARD (JD1-JD56) .60 1.50
ONE PACK PER SP BAT MILESTONE BOX
ONE PACK PER SP GAME-USED HOBBY BOX
ONE PACK PER SPX HOBBY BOX
ONE PACK PER UD DECADE 1970 HOBBY BOX
ONE PACK PER UD GOLD GLOVE HOBBY BOX
ONE PACK PER UD LEGENDS HOBBY BOX
ONE PACK PER UD OVATION HOBBY BOX
ONE PACK PER UD SWEET SPOT HOBBY BOX

2001 Upper Deck Pinstripe Exclusives DiMaggio Memorabilia

COMMON BAT (B1-B9) 30.00 60.00
COMMON JERSEY (J1-J9) 20.00 50.00
SUFFIX 1 CARDS DIST.IN SWEET SPOT
SUFFIX 2 CARDS DIST.IN OVATION
SUFFIX 3 CARDS DIST.IN SPX
SUFFIX 4 CARDS DIST.IN SP GAME USED
SUFFIX 5 CARDS DIST.IN LEGENDS
SUFFIX 6 CARDS DIST.IN DECADE 1970
SUFFIX 7 CARDS DIST.IN SP BAT MILE
SUFFIX 8 CARDS DIST.IN UD GOLD GLOVE
BAT 1-9 PRINT RUN 100 SERIAL #'d SETS
BAT-CUT 1-8 PRINT RUN 5 SERIAL #'d SETS
COMBO 1-6 PRINT RUN 50 SERIAL #'D SETS
CUT 1-8 PRINT RUN 5 SERIAL #'d SETS
JERSEY 1-8 PRINT RUN 100 SERIAL #'d SETS
CJ1 DiMag. 300.00 600.00
Gehrig Pants/50
CJ2 DiMag. 175.00 300.00
Mantle Jsy/50
CJ3 DiMag. 100.00 200.00
Griffey Jsy/50
CJ4 DiMag. 150.00 250.00
DiMag. Jsy/50
CJ5 DiMag. 150.00 300.00
Mantle Jsy/50
CJ6 DiMag. 150.00 300.00
Mantle Jsy/50

2001 Upper Deck Pinstripe Exclusives Mantle

COMPLETE SET (56) 50.00 100.00
COMMON CARD (MM1-MM56) 1.00 2.50
ONE PACK PER UD SER.2 HOBBY BOX
ONE PACK PER UD HOF'ers HOBBY BOX
ONE PACK PER UD MVP HOBBY BOX
ONE PACK PER UD VINTAGE HOBBY BOX

2001 Upper Deck Pinstripe Exclusives Mantle Memorabilia

COMMON BAT (B1-B4) 75.00 150.00
COMMON JERSEY (J1-J7) 100.00 200.00
COMMON BAT CUT (BC1-BC4)
COMMON CUT (C1-C4)
SUFFIX 1 CARDS DIST.IN UD VINTAGE
SUFFIX 2 CARDS DIST.IN UD HOF'ers
SUFFIX 3 CARDS DIST.IN UD MVP
SUFFIX 4 CARDS DIST.IN UD SER.2
SUFFIX 5 CARDS DIST. IN SP AUTH
SUFFIX 6 CARDS DIST. IN SP GAME BAT MILE
SUFFIX 7 CARDS DIST. IN UD LEG OF NY
BAT 1-9 PRINT RUN 100 SERIAL #'d SETS
BAT-CUT 1-4 PRINT RUN 7 SERIAL #'d SETS
COMBO 1-6 PRINT RUN 50 SERIAL #'d SETS
CUT 1-4 PRINT RUN 7 SERIAL #'D SETS
JERSEY 1-7 PRINT RUN 100 SERIAL #'d SETS
CJ1 Mantle 175.00 300.00
Maris Jsy/50
CJ2 Mantle 150.00 250.00
DiMag Jsy/50
CJ3 Mantle 75.00 150.00
Griffey Jsy/50
CJ4 Mantle 175.00 300.00
Maris Jsy/50
CJ5 Mantle 150.00 250.00
DiMag Jsy/50
CJ6 Mantle 150.00 250.00
DiMag Jsy 50
CJ7 Mantle 150.00 250.00
DiMag Jsy 50

2001 Upper Deck Gwynn

COMPLETE SET 10.00 25.00
COMMON CARD 2.00 5.00

2001 Upper Deck Collectibles Ichiro Tribute to 51

COMPLETE FACT. SET (26) 8.00 20.00
COMMON ICHIRO (I1-I25) .30 .75
XX Ichiro Suzuki/3 1/2 x 5
commemorative card 1.00 2.50

2001 Upper Deck DiMaggio Kit Young Game Bat

KYJD1 Joe DiMaggio Bat/450 25.00 60.00
KYJD2 Joe DiMaggio Bat/450 25.00 60.00

2001 Upper Deck Store Ichiro

COMPLETE SET

2001 Upper Deck Subway Series Heroes

COMPLETE SET (4) 50.00 100.00
KYSS1 Don Larsen 6.00 15.00
KYSS2 Whitey Ford 20.00 40.00
KYSS3 Johnny Podres 5.00 10.00
KYSS4 Duke Snider 20.00 40.00

2001 Upper Deck Twizzlers

COMPLETE SET (10)
COMMON CARD

2002 Upper Deck

COMPLETE SET (745) 50.00 100.00
COMPLETE SERIES 1 (500) 40.00 80.00
COMPLETE SERIES 2 (245) 10.00 25.00
COMMON (51-500/546-745) .10 .30
COMMON SR (1-50/501-545) .40 1.00
SR 501-545 ONE PER SER.2 PACK
1 Mark Prior SR .75 2.00
2 Mark Teixeira SR 3.00 8.00
3 Brian Roberts SR .75 2.00
4 Jason Romano SR .40 1.00
5 Dennis Stark SR .40 1.00
6 Oscar Salazar SR .40 1.00
7 John Patterson SR .40 1.00
8 Shane Loux SR .40 1.00
9 Marcus Giles SR .40 1.00
10 Juan Cruz SR .40 1.00
11 Jorge Julio SR .40 1.00
12 Adam Dunn SR .40 1.00
13 Delvin James SR .40 1.00
14 Jeremy Affeldt SR .40 1.00
15 Tim Raines Jr. SR .40 1.00
16 Luke Hudson SR .40 1.00
17 Todd Sears SR .40 1.00
18 George Perez SR .40 1.00
19 Wilmy Caceres SR .40 1.00
20 Abraham Nunez SR .40 1.00
21 Mike Amrhein SR RC .40 1.00
22 Carlos Hernandez SR .40 1.00
23 Scott Hodges SR .40 1.00
24 Brandon Knight SR .40 1.00
25 Geoff Goetz SR .40 1.00
26 Carlos Garcia SR .40 1.00
27 Luis Pineda SR .40 1.00
28 Chris Gissell SR .40 1.00
29 Jae Weong Seo SR .40 1.00
30 Paul Phillips SR .40 1.00
31 Cory Aldridge SR .40 1.00
32 Aaron Cook SR RC .40 1.00
33 Rendy Espina SR RC .40 1.00
34 Jason Phillips SR .40 1.00
35 Carlos Silva SR .40 1.00
36 Ryan Mills SR .40 1.00
37 Pedro Santana SR .40 1.00
38 John Grabow SR .40 1.00
39 Cody Ransom SR .40 1.00
40 Orlando Woodards SR .40 1.00
41 Bud Smith SR .40 1.00
42 Junior Guerrero SR .40 1.00
43 David Brous SR .40 1.00
44 Steve Green SR .40 1.00
45 Brian Rogers SR .40 1.00
46 Juan Figueroa SR RC .40 1.00
47 Nick Punto SR .40 1.00
48 Junior Herndon SR .40 1.00
49 Justin Kaye SR .40 1.00
50 Jason Karnuth SR .40 1.00
51 Troy Glaus .10 .30
52 Bengie Molina .10 .30
53 Ramon Ortiz .10 .30
54 Adam Kennedy .10 .30
55 Jarrod Washburn .10 .30
56 Troy Percival .10 .30
57 David Eckstein .10 .30
58 Ben Weber .10 .30
59 Larry Barnes .10 .30
60 Ismael Valdes .10 .30
61 Benji Gil .10 .30
62 Scott Schoeneweis .10 .30
63 Pat Rapp .10 .30
64 Jason Giambi .10 .30
65 Mark Mulder .10 .30
66 Ron Gant .10 .30
67 Johnny Damon .20 .50
68 Adam Piatt .10 .30
69 Jermaine Dye .10 .30
70 Jason Hart .10 .30
71 Eric Chavez .10 .30
72 Jim Mecir .10 .30
73 Barry Zito .10 .30
74 Jason Isringhausen .10 .30
75 Jeremy Giambi .10 .30
76 Olmedo Saenz .10 .30
77 Terrence Long .10 .30
78 Ramon Hernandez .10 .30
79 Chris Carpenter .10 .30
80 Raul Mondesi .10 .30
81 Carlos Delgado .10 .30
82 Billy Koch .10 .30
83 Vernon Wells .10 .30
84 Darrin Fletcher .10 .30
85 Homer Bush .10 .30
86 Pasqual Coco .10 .30
87 Shannon Stewart .10 .30
88 Chris Woodward .10 .30
89 Joe Lawrence .10 .30
90 Esteban Loaiza .10 .30
91 Cesar Izturis .10 .30
92 Kelvim Escobar .10 .30
93 Greg Vaughn .10 .30
94 Brent Abernathy .10 .30
95 Tanyon Sturtze .10 .30
96 Steve Cox .10 .30
97 Aubrey Huff .10 .30
98 Jesus Colome .10 .30
99 Ben Grieve .10 .30
100 Esteban Yan .10 .30
101 Joe Kennedy .10 .30
102 Felix Martinez .10 .30
103 Nick Bierbrodt .10 .30
104 Damian Rolls .10 .30
105 Russ Johnson .10 .30
106 Toby Hall .10 .30
107 Roberto Alomar .20 .50
108 Bartolo Colon .10 .30
109 John Rocker .10 .30
110 Juan Gonzalez .10 .30
111 Einar Diaz .10 .30
112 Chuck Finley .10 .30
113 Kenny Lofton .10 .30
114 Danys Baez .10 .30
115 Travis Fryman .10 .30
116 C.C. Sabathia .10 .30
117 Paul Shuey .10 .30
118 Marty Cordova .10 .30
119 Ellis Burks .10 .30
120 Bob Wickman .10 .30
121 Edgar Martinez .20 .50
122 Freddy Garcia .10 .30
123 Ichiro Suzuki .60 1.50
124 John Olerud .10 .30
125 Gil Meche .10 .30
126 Dan Wilson .10 .30
127 Aaron Sele .10 .30
128 Kazuhiro Sasaki .10 .30
129 Mark McLemore .10 .30
130 Carlos Guillen .10 .30
131 Al Martin .10 .30
132 David Bell .10 .30
133 Jay Buhner .10 .30
134 Stan Javier .10 .30
135 Tony Batista .10 .30
136 Jason Johnson .10 .30
137 Brook Fordyce .10 .30
138 Mike Kinkade .10 .30
139 Willis Roberts .10 .30
140 David Segui .10 .30
141 Josh Towers .10 .30
142 Jeff Conine .10 .30
143 Chris Richard .10 .30
144 Pat Hentgen .10 .30
145 Melvin Mora .10 .30
146 Jerry Hairston Jr. .10 .30
147 Calvin Maduro .10 .30
148 Brady Anderson .10 .30
149 Alex Rodriguez .40 1.00
150 Kenny Rogers .10 .30
151 Chad Curtis .10 .30
152 Ricky Ledee .10 .30
153 Rafael Palmeiro .20 .50
154 Rob Bell .10 .30
155 Rick Helling .10 .30
156 Doug Davis .10 .30
157 Mike Lamb .10 .30
158 Gabe Kapler .10 .30
159 Jeff Zimmerman .10 .30
160 Bill Haselman .10 .30
161 Tim Crabtree .10 .30
162 Carlos Pena .10 .30
163 Nomar Garciaparra .50 1.25
164 Shea Hillenbrand .10 .30
165 Hideo Nomo .30 .75
166 Manny Ramirez .20 .50
167 Jose Offerman .10 .30
168 Scott Hatteberg .10 .30
169 Trot Nixon .10 .30
170 Darren Lewis .10 .30
171 Derek Lowe .10 .30
172 Troy O'Leary .10 .30
173 Tim Wakefield .10 .30
174 Chris Stynes .10 .30
175 John Valentin .10 .30
176 David Cone .10 .30
177 Neifi Perez .10 .30
178 Brent Mayne .10 .30
179 Dan Reichert .10 .30
180 A.J. Hinch .10 .30
181 Chris George .10 .30
182 Mike Sweeney .10 .30
183 Jeff Suppan .10 .30
184 Roberto Hernandez .10 .30
185 Joe Randa .10 .30
186 Paul Byrd .10 .30
187 Luis Ordaz .10 .30
188 Kris Wilson .10 .30
189 Dee Brown .10 .30
190 Tony Clark .10 .30
191 Matt Anderson .10 .30
192 Robert Fick .10 .30
193 Juan Encarnacion .10 .30
194 Dean Palmer .10 .30
195 Victor Santos .10 .30
196 Damion Easley .10 .30
197 Jose Lima .10 .30
198 Deivi Cruz .10 .30
199 Roger Cedeno .10 .30
200 Jose Macias .10 .30
201 Jeff Weaver .10 .30
202 Brandon Inge .10 .30
203 Brian Moehler .10 .30
204 Brad Radke .10 .30
205 Doug Mientkiewicz .10 .30
206 Cristian Guzman .10 .30
207 Corey Koskie .10 .30
208 LaTroy Hawkins .10 .30
209 J.C. Romero .10 .30
210 Chad Allen .10 .30
211 Torii Hunter .10 .30
212 Travis Miller .10 .30
213 Joe Mays .10 .30
214 Todd Jones .10 .30
215 David Ortiz .30 .75
216 Brian Buchanan .10 .30
217 A.J. Pierzynski .10 .30
218 Carlos Lee .10 .30
219 Gary Glover .10 .30
220 Jose Valentin .10 .30
221 Aaron Rowand .10 .30
222 Sandy Alomar Jr. .10 .30
223 Herbert Perry .10 .30
224 Jon Garland .10 .30
225 Mark Buehrle .10 .30
226 Chris Singleton .10 .30
227 Kip Wells .10 .30
228 Ray Durham .10 .30
229 Joe Crede .10 .30
230 Keith Foulke .10 .30
231 Royce Clayton .10 .30
232 Andy Pettitte .20 .50
233 Derek Jeter .75 2.00
234 Jorge Posada .20 .50
235 Roger Clemens .60 1.50
236 Paul O'Neill .20 .50
237 Nick Johnson .10 .30
238 Gerald Williams .10 .30
239 Mariano Rivera .30 .75
240 Alfonso Soriano .10 .30
241 Ramiro Mendoza .10 .30
242 Mike Mussina .20 .50
243 Luis Sojo .10 .30
244 Scott Brosius .10 .30
245 David Justice .10 .30
246 Wade Miller .10 .30
247 Brad Ausmus .10 .30
248 Jeff Bagwell .20 .50
249 Daryle Ward .10 .30
250 Shane Reynolds .10 .30
251 Chris Truby .10 .30
252 Billy Wagner .10 .30
253 Craig Biggio .20 .50
254 Moises Alou .10 .30
255 Vinny Castilla .10 .30
256 Tim Redding .10 .30
257 Roy Oswalt .10 .30
258 Julio Lugo .10 .30
259 Chipper Jones .30 .75
260 Greg Maddux .50 1.25
261 Ken Caminiti .10 .30
262 Kevin Millwood .10 .30
263 Keith Lockhart .10 .30
264 Rey Sanchez .10 .30
265 Jason Marquis .10 .30
266 Brian Jordan .10 .30
267 Steve Karsay .10 .30
268 Wes Helms .10 .30
269 B.J. Surhoff .10 .30
270 Wilson Betemit .10 .30
271 John Smoltz .20 .50
272 Rafael Furcal .10 .30
273 Jeromy Burnitz .10 .30
274 Jimmy Haynes .10 .30
275 Mark Loretta .10 .30
276 Jose Hernandez .10 .30
277 Paul Rigdon .10 .30
278 Alex Sanchez .10 .30
279 Chad Fox .10 .30
280 Devon White .10 .30
281 Tyler Houston .10 .30
282 Ronnie Belliard .10 .30
283 Luis Lopez .10 .30
284 Ben Sheets .10 .30
285 Curtis Leskanic .10 .30
286 Henry Blanco .10 .30
287 Mark McGwire .75 2.00
288 Edgar Renteria .10 .30
289 Matt Morris .10 .30
290 Gene Stechschulte .10 .30
291 Dustin Hermanson .10 .30
292 Eli Marrero .10 .30
293 Albert Pujols .60 1.50
294 Luis Saturria .10 .30
295 Bobby Bonilla .10 .30
296 Garrett Stephenson .10 .30
297 Jim Edmonds .10 .30
298 Rick Ankiel .10 .30
299 Placido Polanco .10 .30
300 Dave Veres .10 .30
301 Sammy Sosa .30 .75
302 Eric Young .10 .30
303 Kerry Wood .10 .30
304 Jon Lieber .10 .30
305 Joe Girardi .10 .30
306 Fred McGriff .20 .50
307 Jeff Fassero .10 .30
308 Julio Zuleta .10 .30
309 Kevin Tapani .10 .30
310 Rondell White .10 .30
311 Julian Tavarez .10 .30
312 Tom Gordon .10 .30
313 Corey Patterson .10 .30
314 Bill Mueller .10 .30
315 Randy Johnson .30 .75
316 Chad Moeller .10 .30
317 Tony Womack .10 .30
318 Erubiel Durazo .10 .30
319 Luis Gonzalez .10 .30
320 Brian Anderson .10 .30
321 Reggie Sanders .10 .30
322 Greg Colbrunn .10 .30
323 Robert Ellis .10 .30
324 Jack Cust .10 .30
325 Bret Prinz .10 .30
326 Steve Finley .10 .30
327 Byung-Hyun Kim .10 .30
328 Albie Lopez .10 .30
329 Gary Sheffield .10 .30
330 Mark Grudzielanek .10 .30
331 Paul LoDuca .10 .30
332 Tom Goodwin .10 .30
333 Andy Ashby .10 .30
334 Hiram Bocachica .10 .30
335 Dave Hansen .10 .30
336 Kevin Brown .10 .30
337 Marquis Grissom .10 .30
338 Terry Adams .10 .30
339 Chan Ho Park .10 .30
340 Adrian Beltre .10 .30
341 Luke Prokopec .10 .30
342 Jeff Shaw .10 .30
343 Vladimir Guerrero .30 .75
344 Orlando Cabrera .10 .30
345 Tony Armas Jr. .10 .30
346 Michael Barrett .10 .30
347 Geoff Blum .10 .30
348 Ryan Minor .10 .30
349 Peter Bergeron .10 .30
350 Graeme Lloyd .10 .30
351 Jose Vidro .10 .30
352 Javier Vazquez .10 .30
353 Matt Blank .10 .30
354 Masato Yoshii .10 .30
355 Carl Pavano .10 .30
356 Barry Bonds .75 2.00
357 Shawon Dunston .10 .30
358 Livan Hernandez .10 .30
359 Felix Rodriguez .10 .30
360 Pedro Feliz .10 .30
361 Calvin Murray .10 .30
362 Robb Nen .10 .30
363 Marvin Benard .10 .30
364 Russ Ortiz .10 .30
365 Jason Schmidt .10 .30
366 Rich Aurilia .10 .30
367 John Vander Wal .10 .30
368 Benito Santiago .10 .30
369 Ryan Dempster .10 .30
370 Charles Johnson .10 .30
371 Alex Gonzalez .10 .30
372 Luis Castillo .10 .30
373 Mike Lowell .10 .30
374 Antonio Alfonseca .10 .30
375 A.J. Burnett .10 .30
376 Brad Penny .10 .30
377 Jason Grilli .10 .30
378 Derrek Lee .20 .50
379 Matt Clement .10 .30
380 Eric Owens .10 .30
381 Vladimir Nunez .10 .30
382 Cliff Floyd .10 .30
383 Mike Piazza .50 1.25
384 Lenny Harris .10 .30
385 Glendon Rusch .10 .30
386 Todd Zeile .10 .30
387 Al Leiter .10 .30
388 Armando Benitez .10 .30
389 Alex Escobar .10 .30
390 Kevin Appier .10 .30
391 Matt Lawton .10 .30
392 Bruce Chen .10 .30
393 John Franco .10 .30
394 Tsuyoshi Shinjo .10 .30
395 Rey Ordonez .10 .30
396 Joe McEwing .10 .30
397 Ryan Klesko .10 .30
398 Brian Lawrence .10 .30
399 Kevin Walker .10 .30
400 Phil Nevin .10 .30
401 Bubba Trammell .10 .30
402 Wiki Gonzalez .10 .30
403 D'Angelo Jimenez .10 .30
404 Rickey Henderson .30 .75
405 Mike Darr .10 .30
406 Trevor Hoffman .10 .30
407 Damian Jackson .10 .30
408 Santiago Perez .10 .30
409 Cesar Crespo .10 .30
410 Robert Person .10 .30
411 Travis Lee .10 .30
412 Scott Rolen .20 .50
413 Turk Wendell .10 .30
414 Randy Wolf .10 .30
415 Kevin Jordan .10 .30
416 Jose Mesa .10 .30
417 Mike Lieberthal .10 .30
418 Bobby Abreu .10 .30
419 Tomas Perez .10 .30
420 Doug Glanville .10 .30
421 Reggie Taylor .10 .30
422 Jimmy Rollins .10 .30
423 Brian Giles .10 .30
424 Rob Mackowiak .10 .30
425 Bronson Arroyo .10 .30
426 Kevin Young .10 .30
427 Jack Wilson .10 .30
428 Adrian Brown .10 .30
429 Chad Hermansen .10 .30
430 Jimmy Anderson .10 .30
431 Aramis Ramirez .10 .30
432 Todd Ritchie .10 .30
433 Pat Meares .10 .30
434 Warren Morris .10 .30
435 Derek Bell .10 .30
436 Ken Griffey Jr. .60 1.50
437 Elmer Dessens .10 .30
438 Ruben Rivera .10 .30
439 Jason LaRue .10 .30
440 Sean Casey .10 .30
441 Pete Harnisch .10 .30
442 Danny Graves .10 .30
443 Aaron Boone .10 .30
444 Dmitri Young .10 .30
445 Brandon Larson .10 .30
446 Pokey Reese .10 .30
447 Todd Walker .10 .30
448 Juan Castro .10 .30
449 Todd Helton .20 .50
450 Ben Petrick .10 .30
451 Juan Pierre .10 .30
452 Jeff Cirillo .10 .30
453 Juan Uribe .10 .30
454 Brian Bohanon .10 .30
455 Terry Shumpert .10 .30
456 Mike Hampton .10 .30
457 Shawn Chacon .10 .30
458 Adam Melhuse .10 .30
459 Greg Norton .10 .30
460 Gabe White .10 .30
461 Ichiro Suzuki WS .30 .75
462 Carlos Delgado WS .10 .30
463 Manny Ramirez WS .20 .50
464 Miguel Tejada WS .10 .30
465 Tsuyoshi Shinjo WS .10 .30
466 Bernie Williams WS .10 .30
467 Juan Gonzalez WS .10 .30
468 Andruw Jones WS .10 .30
469 Ivan Rodriguez WS .10 .30
470 Larry Walker WS .10 .30
471 Hideo Nomo WS .10 .30
472 Albert Pujols WS .30 .75
473 Pedro Martinez WS .20 .50
474 Vladimir Guerrero WS .20 .50
475 Tony Batista WS .10 .30
476 Kazuhiro Sasaki WS .10 .30
477 Richard Hidalgo WS .10 .30
478 Carlos Lee WS .10 .30
479 Roberto Alomar WS .10 .30
480 Rafael Palmeiro WS .10 .30
481 Ken Griffey Jr. GG .40 1.00
482 Ken Griffey Jr. GG .40 1.00
483 Ken Griffey Jr. GG .40 1.00
484 Ken Griffey Jr. GG .40 1.00
485 Ken Griffey Jr. GG .40 1.00

486 Ken Griffey Jr. GG .40 1.00
487 Ken Griffey Jr. GG .40 1.00
488 Ken Griffey Jr. GG .40 1.00
489 Ken Griffey Jr. GG .40 1.00
490 Ken Griffey Jr. GG .40 1.00
491 Barry Bonds CL .40 1.00
492 Hideo Nomo CL .10 .30
493 Ichiro Suzuki CL .30 .75
494 Cal Ripken CL .50 1.25
495 Tony Gwynn CL .20 .50
496 Randy Johnson CL .20 .50
497 A.J. Burnett CL .10 .30
498 Rickey Henderson CL .20 .50
499 Albert Pujols CL .30 .75
500 Luis Gonzalez CL .10 .30
501 Brandon Puffer SR RC .40 1.00
502 Rodrigo Rosario SR RC .40 1.00
503 Tom Shearn SR RC .40 1.00
504 Reed Johnson SR RC .60 1.50
505 Chris Baker SR RC .40 1.00
506 John Ennis SR RC .40 1.00
507 Luis Martinez SR RC .40 1.00
508 So Taguchi SR RC .60 1.50
509 Scotty Layfield SR RC .40 1.00
510 Francis Beltran SR RC .40 1.00
511 Brandon Backe SR RC .60 1.50
512 Doug Devore SR RC .40 1.00
513 Jeremy Ward SR RC .40 1.00
514 Jose Valverde SR RC 1.25 3.00
515 P.J. Bevis SR RC .40 1.00
516 Victor Alvarez SR RC .40 1.00
517 Kazuhisa Ishii SR RC .60 1.50
518 Jorge Nunez SR RC .40 1.00
519 Eric Good SR RC .40 1.00
520 Ron Calloway SR RC .40 1.00
521 Val Pascucci SR .40 1.00
522 Nelson Castro SR RC .40 1.00
523 Deivis Santos SR .40 1.00
524 Luis Ugueto SR RC .40 1.00
525 Matt Thornton SR RC .40 1.00
526 Hansel Izquierdo SR RC .40 1.00
527 Tyler Yates SR RC .40 1.00
528 Mark Corey SR RC .40 1.00
529 Jaime Cerda SR RC .40 1.00
530 Satoru Komiyama SR RC .40 1.00
531 Steve Bechler SR RC .40 1.00
532 Ben Howard SR RC .40 1.00
533 Anderson Machado SR RC .40 1.00
534 Jorge Padilla SR RC .40 1.00
535 Eric Junge SR RC .40 1.00
536 Adrian Burnside SR RC .40 1.00
537 Mike Gonzalez SR RC .40 1.00
538 Josh Hancock SR RC .50 1.25
539 Colin Young SR RC .40 1.00
540 Rene Reyes SR RC .40 1.00
541 Cam Esslinger SR RC .40 1.00
542 Tim Kalita SR RC .40 1.00
543 Kevin Frederick SR RC .40 1.00
544 Kyle Kane SR RC .40 1.00
545 Edwin Almonte SR RC .40 1.00
546 Aaron Sele .10 .30
547 Garret Anderson .10 .30
548 Darin Erstad .10 .30
549 Brad Fullmer .10 .30
550 Kevin Appier .10 .30
551 Tim Salmon .20 .50
552 David Justice .10 .30
553 Billy Koch .10 .30
554 Scott Hatteberg .10 .30
555 Tim Hudson .10 .30
556 Miguel Tejada .10 .30
557 Carlos Pena .10 .30
558 Mike Sirotka .10 .30
559 Jose Cruz Jr. .10 .30
560 Josh Phelps .10 .30
561 Brandon Lyon .10 .30
562 Luke Prokopec .10 .30
563 Felipe Lopez .10 .30
564 Jason Standridge .10 .30
565 Chris Gomez .10 .30
566 John Flaherty .10 .30
567 Jason Tyner .10 .30
568 Bobby Smith .10 .30
569 Wilson Alvarez .10 .30
570 Matt Lawton .10 .30
571 Omar Vizquel .20 .50
572 Jim Thome .20 .50
573 Brady Anderson .10 .30
574 Alex Escobar .10 .30
575 Russell Branyan .10 .30
576 Bret Boone .10 .30
577 Ben Davis .10 .30
578 Mike Cameron .10 .30
579 Jamie Moyer .10 .30
580 Ruben Sierra .10 .30
581 Jeff Cirillo .10 .30
582 Marty Cordova .10 .30
583 Mike Bordick .10 .30
584 Brian Roberts .10 .30
585 Luis Matos .10 .30
586 Geronimo Gil .10 .30
587 Jay Gibbons .10 .30
588 Carl Everett .10 .30
589 Ivan Rodriguez .20 .50
590 Chan Ho Park .10 .30
591 Juan Gonzalez .10 .30
592 Hank Blalock .20 .50
593 Todd Van Poppel .10 .30
594 Pedro Martinez .20 .50
595 Jason Varitek .30 .75
596 Tony Clark .10 .30
597 Johnny Damon Sox .20 .50
598 Dustin Hermanson .10 .30
599 John Burkett .10 .30
600 Carlos Beltran .10 .30
601 Mark Quinn .10 .30
602 Chuck Knoblauch .10 .30
603 Michael Tucker .10 .30
604 Carlos Febles .10 .30
605 Jose Rosado .10 .30
606 Dmitri Young .10 .30
607 Bobby Higginson .10 .30
608 Craig Paquette .10 .30
609 Mitch Meluskey .10 .30
610 Wendell Magee .10 .30
611 Mike Rivera .10 .30
612 Jacque Jones .10 .30
613 Luis Rivas .10 .30
614 Eric Milton .10 .30
615 Eddie Guardado .10 .30
616 Matt LeCroy .10 .30
617 Mike Jackson .10 .30
618 Magglio Ordonez .10 .30
619 Frank Thomas .30 .75
620 Rocky Biddle .10 .30
621 Paul Konerko .10 .30
622 Todd Ritchie .10 .30
623 Jon Rauch .10 .30
624 John Vander Wal .10 .30
625 Rondell White .10 .30
626 Jason Giambi .10 .30
627 Robin Ventura .10 .30
628 David Wells .10 .30
629 Bernie Williams .20 .50
630 Lance Berkman .10 .30
631 Richard Hidalgo .10 .30
632 Greg Zaun .10 .30
633 Jose Vizcaino .10 .30
634 Octavio Dotel .10 .30
635 Morgan Ensberg .10 .30
636 Andruw Jones .20 .50
637 Tom Glavine .20 .50
638 Gary Sheffield .10 .30
639 Vinny Castilla .10 .30
640 Javy Lopez .10 .30
641 Albie Lopez .10 .30
642 Geoff Jenkins .10 .30
643 Jeffrey Hammonds .10 .30
644 Alex Ochoa .10 .30
645 Richie Sexson .10 .30
646 Eric Young .10 .30
647 Glendon Rusch .10 .30
648 Tino Martinez .20 .50
649 Fernando Vina .10 .30
650 J.D. Drew .10 .30
651 Woody Williams .10 .30
652 Darryl Kile .10 .30
653 Jason Isringhausen .10 .30
654 Moises Alou .10 .30
655 Alex Gonzalez .10 .30
656 Delino DeShields .10 .30
657 Todd Hundley .10 .30
658 Chris Stynes .10 .30
659 Jason Bere .10 .30
660 Curt Schilling .10 .30
661 Craig Counsell .10 .30
662 Mark Grace .20 .50
663 Matt Williams .10 .30
664 Jay Bell .10 .30
665 Rick Helling .10 .30
666 Shawn Green .10 .30
667 Eric Karros .10 .30
668 Hideo Nomo .30 .75
669 Omar Daal .10 .30
670 Brian Jordan .10 .30
671 Cesar Izturis .10 .30
672 Fernando Tatis .10 .30
673 Lee Stevens .10 .30
674 Tomo Ohka .10 .30
675 Brian Schneider .10 .30
676 Brad Wilkerson .10 .30
677 Bruce Chen .10 .30
678 Tsuyoshi Shinjo .10 .30
679 Jeff Kent .10 .30
680 Kirk Rueter .10 .30
681 J.T. Snow .10 .30
682 David Bell .10 .30
683 Reggie Sanders .10 .30
684 Preston Wilson .10 .30
685 Vic Darensbourg .10 .30
686 Josh Beckett .10 .30
687 Pablo Ozuna .10 .30
688 Mike Redmond .10 .30
689 Scott Strickland .10 .30
690 Mo Vaughn .10 .30
691 Roberto Alomar .20 .50
692 Edgardo Alfonzo .10 .30
693 Shawn Estes .10 .30
694 Roger Cedeno .10 .30
695 Jeromy Burnitz .10 .30
696 Ray Lankford .10 .30
697 Mark Kotsay .10 .30
698 Kevin Jarvis .10 .30
699 Bobby Jones .10 .30
700 Sean Burroughs .10 .30
701 Ramon Vazquez .10 .30
702 Pat Burrell .10 .30
703 Marlon Byrd .10 .30
704 Brandon Duckworth .10 .30
705 Marlon Anderson .10 .30
706 Vicente Padilla .10 .30
707 Kip Wells .10 .30
708 Jason Kendall .10 .30
709 Pokey Reese .10 .30
710 Pat Meares .10 .30
711 Kris Benson .10 .30
712 Armando Rios .10 .30
713 Mike Williams .10 .30
714 Barry Larkin .20 .50
715 Adam Dunn .10 .30
716 Juan Encarnacion .10 .30
717 Scott Williamson .10 .30
718 Wilton Guerrero .10 .30
719 Chris Reitsma .10 .30
720 Larry Walker .10 .30
721 Denny Neagle .10 .30
722 Todd Zeile .10 .30
723 Jose Ortiz .10 .30
724 Jason Jennings .10 .30
725 Tony Eusebio .10 .30
726 Ichiro Suzuki YR .30 .75
727 Barry Bonds YR .40 1.00
728 Randy Johnson YR .20 .50
729 Albert Pujols YR .30 .75
730 Roger Clemens YR .30 .75
731 Sammy Sosa YR .20 .50
732 Alex Rodriguez YR .25 .60
733 Chipper Jones YR .20 .50
734 Rickey Henderson YR .20 .50
735 Ichiro Suzuki YR .30 .75
736 Luis Gonzalez SH CL .10 .30
737 Derek Jeter SH CL .40 1.00
738 Ichiro Suzuki SH CL .30 .75
739 Barry Bonds SH CL .40 1.00
740 Curt Schilling SH CL .10 .30
741 Shawn Green SH CL .10 .30
742 Jason Giambi SH CL .10 .30
743 Roberto Alomar SH CL .10 .30
744 Larry Walker SH CL .10 .30
745 Mark McGwire SH CL .40 1.00

2002 Upper Deck 2001 Greatest Hits

COMPLETE SET (10) 15.00 40.00
SER.1 STATED ODDS 1:14
GH1 Barry Bonds 2.50 6.00
GH2 Ichiro Suzuki 2.00 5.00
GH3 Albert Pujols 2.00 5.00
GH4 Mike Piazza 1.50 4.00
GH5 Alex Rodriguez 1.25 3.00
GH6 Mark McGwire 2.50 6.00
GH7 Manny Ramirez 1.00 2.50
GH8 Ken Griffey Jr. 2.00 5.00
GH9 Sammy Sosa 1.00 2.50
GH10 Derek Jeter 2.50 6.00

2002 Upper Deck A Piece of History 500 Club

RANDOM INSERTS IN SER.2 PACKS
STATED PRINT RUN 350 SETS
MMC Mark McGwire 150.00 300.00

2002 Upper Deck AL Centennial Memorabilia

SER.1 STATED ODDS 1:144
SP INFO PROVIDED BY UPPER DECK
ALBBR Babe Ruth Bat SP 30.00 80.00
ALBJD Joe DiMaggio Bat SP 40.00 80.00
ALBMM Mickey Mantle Bat SP 40.00 80.00
ALJAR Alex Rodriguez Jsy 6.00 15.00
ALJCR Cal Ripken Jsy 10.00 25.00
ALJFT Frank Thomas Jsy 6.00 15.00
ALJIR Ivan Rodriguez Jsy 6.00 15.00
ALJNR Nolan Ryan Jsy 10.00 25.00
ALJPM Pedro Martinez Jsy 6.00 15.00
ALJRA Roberto Alomar Jsy 6.00 15.00

2002 Upper Deck All-Star Home Run Derby Game Jersey

SER.1 STATED ODDS 1:288
HR DERBY SWATCHES UNLESS SPECIFIED
GOLD RANDOM INSERTS IN PACKS
GOLD PRINT RUN 25 SERIAL #'d SETS
NO GOLD PRICING DUE TO SCARCITY
ASAR Alex Rodriguez 10.00 25.00
ASBRB Bret Boone 6.00 15.00
ASJG1 Jason Giambi 6.00 15.00
ASJG2 Jason Giambi A's 6.00 15.00
ASSS1 Sammy Sosa 8.00 20.00
ASSS2 Sammy Sosa Cubs 8.00 20.00
ASTH Todd Helton 6.00 15.00

2002 Upper Deck All-Star Salute Game Jersey

SER.1 STATED ODDS 1:288
GOLD RANDOM INSERTS IN PACKS
GOLD PRINT RUN 25 SERIAL #'d SETS
NO GOLD PRICING DUE TO SCARCITY
SJAR1 Alex Rodriguez Mariners 10.00 25.00
SJAR2 Alex Rodriguez Rangers 10.00 25.00
SJDE Dennis Eckersley 6.00 15.00
SJDS Don Sutton 6.00 15.00
SJIS Ichiro Suzuki 20.00 50.00
SJKG Ken Griffey Jr. 12.50 30.00
SJLB Lou Boudreau 6.00 15.00
SJNF Nellie Fox 6.00 15.00
SJSA Sparky Anderson 6.00 15.00

2002 Upper Deck Authentic McGwire

RANDOM INSERTS IN SER.2 PACKS
STATED PRINT RUN 70 SERIAL #'d SETS
AMB Mark McGwire Bat 12.00 30.00
AMJ Mark McGwire Jsy 12.00 30.00

2002 Upper Deck Big Fly Zone

COMPLETE SET (10) 12.50 30.00
SER.1 STATED ODDS 1:14
Z1 Mark McGwire 2.50 6.00
Z2 Ken Griffey Jr. 2.00 5.00
Z3 Manny Ramirez .60 1.50
Z4 Sammy Sosa 1.00 2.50
Z5 Todd Helton .60 1.50
Z6 Barry Bonds 2.50 6.00
Z7 Luis Gonzalez .60 1.50
Z8 Alex Rodriguez 1.25 3.00
Z9 Carlos Delgado .60 1.50
Z10 Chipper Jones 1.00 2.50

2002 Upper Deck Breakout Performers

COMPLETE SET (10) 10.00 25.00
SER.1 STATED ODDS 1:14
BP1 Ichiro Suzuki 2.00 5.00
BP2 Albert Pujols 2.00 5.00
BP3 Doug Mientkiewicz .60 1.50
BP4 Lance Berkman .60 1.50
BP5 Tsuyoshi Shinjo .60 1.50
BP6 Ben Sheets .60 1.50
BP7 Jimmy Rollins .60 1.50
BP8 J.D. Drew .60 1.50
BP9 Bret Boone .60 1.50
BP10 Alfonso Soriano .60 1.50

2002 Upper Deck Championship Caliber

COMPLETE SET (6) 8.00 20.00
SER.1 STATED ODDS 1:23
CC1 Derek Jeter 2.50 6.00
CC2 Roberto Alomar .60 1.50
CC3 Chipper Jones 1.00 2.50
CC4 Gary Sheffield .60 1.50
CC5 Roger Clemens 2.00 5.00
CC6 Greg Maddux 1.50 4.00

2002 Upper Deck Championship Caliber Swatch

SER.2 STATED ODDS 1:288
SP INFO PROVIDED BY UPPER DECK
AP Andy Pettitte 6.00 15.00
BL Barry Larkin 6.00 15.00
BW Bernie Williams 6.00 15.00
CF Cliff Floyd 4.00 10.00
CHJ Charles Johnson 4.00 10.00
CS Curt Schilling 4.00 10.00
JO John Olerud 4.00 10.00
JP Jorge Posada 6.00 15.00
KB Kevin Brown SP 6.00 15.00
RJ Randy Johnson 6.00 15.00
TM Tino Martinez 6.00 15.00

2002 Upper Deck Chasing History

COMPLETE SET (15) 15.00 40.00
SER.2 STATED ODDS 1:11
CH1 Sammy Sosa 1.25 3.00
CH2 Ken Griffey Jr. 2.50 6.00
CH3 Roger Clemens 2.50 6.00
CH4 Barry Bonds 3.00 8.00
CH5 Rafael Palmeiro .75 2.00
CH6 Andres Galarraga .75 2.00
CH7 Juan Gonzalez .75 2.00
CH8 Roberto Alomar .75 2.00
CH9 Randy Johnson 1.25 3.00
CH10 Jeff Bagwell .75 2.00
CH11 Fred McGriff .75 2.00
CH12 Matt Williams .75 2.00
CH13 Greg Maddux 2.00 5.00
CH14 Robb Nen .75 2.00
CH15 Kenny Lofton .75 2.00

2002 Upper Deck Combo Memorabilia

SER.1 STATED ODDS 1:288
SP INFO PROVIDED BY UPPER DECK
GOLD RANDOM INSERTS IN PACKS
GOLD PRINT RUN 25 SERIAL #'d SETS
NO GOLD PRICING DUE TO SCARCITY
BDM DiMag Bat/Mantle Bat SP 40.00 100.00
BRG A.Rod Bat/Griffey Jr. Bat 10.00 25.00
JBS Bonds Jsy/S.Sosa Jsy 12.00 30.00
JHK Hasegawa Jsy/Kim Jsy 6.00 15.00
JRC Ryan Jsy/Clemens Jsy 10.00 25.00
JRM Ryan Jsy/Pedro Jsy 25.00 50.00
JRS A.Rod Jsy/Sosa Jsy 15.00 40.00

2002 Upper Deck Double Game Worn Gems

RANDOM INSERTS IN SERIES 2 RETAIL
STATED PRINT RUN 450 SERIAL #'d SETS
DGAP R.Alomar/M.Piazza 10.00 25.00
DGDF C.Delgado/S.Stewart 6.00 15.00
DGDH J.Dye/T.Hudson 6.00 15.00
DGGS L.Gonzalez/C.Schilling 6.00 15.00
DGKG J.Kendall/B.Giles 6.00 15.00
DGMM K.Millwood/G.Maddux 10.00 25.00
DGNK P.Nevin/R.Klesko 6.00 15.00
DGPL R.Person/M.Lieberthal 6.00 15.00
DGPN C.Park/H.Nomo 20.00 50.00
DGTO F.Thomas/M.Ordonez 8.00 20.00
DGVB O.Vizquel/R.Branyan 6.00 15.00

2002 Upper Deck Double Game Worn Gems Gold

RANDOM INSERTS IN SERIES 2 RETAIL
STATED PRINT RUN 100 SERIAL #'d SETS
DGAP R.Alomar/M.Piazza 20.00 50.00
DGDF C.Delgado/S.Stewart 12.50 30.00
DGDH J.Dye/T.Hudson 12.50 30.00
DGGS L.Gonzalez/C.Schilling 12.50 30.00
DGKG J.Kendall/B.Giles 12.50 30.00
DGMI E.Martinez/I.Suzuki SP/40 50.00 100.00
DGMM K.Millwood/G.Maddux 20.00 50.00
DGNK P.Nevin/R.Klesko 12.50 30.00
DGPL R.Person/M.Lieberthal 12.50 30.00
DGPN C.Park/H.Nomo 40.00 100.00
DGTO F.Thomas/M.Ordonez 15.00 40.00
DGVB O.Vizquel/R.Branyan 12.50 30.00

2002 Upper Deck First Timers Game Jersey

SER.1 STATED ODDS 1:288 HOBBY
FTAP Albert Pujols 20.00 50.00
FTCP Corey Patterson 4.00 10.00
FTEM Eric Milton 4.00 10.00
FTFG Freddy Garcia 4.00 10.00
FTJM Joe Mays 4.00 10.00
FTML Matt Lawton 4.00 10.00
FTOD Omar Daal 4.00 10.00
FTRB Russell Branyan 4.00 10.00
FTSS Shannon Stewart 4.00 10.00

2002 Upper Deck Game Base

SER.1 STATED ODDS 1:288
SP INFO PROVIDED BY UPPER DECK
BAJ Andruw Jones 6.00 15.00
BAR Alex Rodriguez 8.00 20.00
BBB Barry Bonds 12.50 30.00
BCD Carlos Delgado 4.00 10.00
BCJ Chipper Jones 6.00 15.00
BCR Cal Ripken 15.00 40.00
BDJ Derek Jeter 12.50 30.00
BIR Ivan Rodriguez 6.00 15.00
BIS Ichiro Suzuki 20.00 50.00
BJG Jason Giambi 4.00 10.00
BJG Juan Gonzalez 4.00 10.00
BKG Ken Griffey Jr. 8.00 20.00
BKS Kazuhiro Sasaki 4.00 10.00
BLG Luis Gonzalez 4.00 10.00
BMM Mark McGwire 20.00 50.00
BMP Mike Piazza 6.00 15.00
BRC Roger Clemens 10.00 25.00
BSG Shawn Green 4.00 10.00
BSS Sammy Sosa 6.00 15.00
BTG Troy Glaus 4.00 10.00
CBMJ McGwire Jeter SP 30.00 60.00
CBRG A.Rod Griffey Jr. SP 15.00 40.00

2002 Upper Deck Game Jersey

RANDOM INSERTS IN SER.2 HOBBY
STATED PRINT RUN 350 SERIAL #'d SETS
AB Adrian Beltre 4.00 10.00
CS Curt Schilling 4.00 10.00
FT Frank Thomas 6.00 15.00
JC Jeff Cirillo Pants 4.00 10.00
KG Ken Griffey Jr. 6.00 15.00
MP Mike Piazza Pants 6.00 15.00
PW Preston Wilson 4.00 10.00
SR Scott Rolen 4.00 10.00
SS Sammy Sosa 4.00 10.00
TB Tony Batista 4.00 10.00
TH Tim Hudson 4.00 10.00

2002 Upper Deck Game Jersey Autograph

RANDOM INSERTS IN SER.1 HOBBY PACKS
STATED PRINT RUN 200 SERIAL #'d SETS
EXCHANGE DEADLINE 11/19/04
JAJ Andruw Jones 20.00 50.00
JAP Albert Pujols 150.00 250.00
JBB Barry Bonds 40.00 80.00
JCD Carlos Delgado 8.00 20.00
JCR Cal Ripken 75.00 150.00
JGS Gary Sheffield 20.00 50.00
JIS Ichiro Suzuki 450.00 900.00
JJGI Jason Giambi 8.00 20.00
JKG Ken Griffey Jr. 60.00 120.00
JNR Nolan Ryan 75.00 150.00
JPW Preston Wilson 8.00 20.00
JRF Rafael Furcal 8.00 20.00

2002 Upper Deck Game Jersey Patch

LOGO SER.1 STATED ODDS 1:2500
NUMBER SER.1 STATED ODDS 1:2500
STRIPES SER.1 STATED ODDS 1:2500
PLAR Alex Rodriguez L 40.00 80.00
PLBB Barry Bonds L 40.00 80.00
PLCR Cal Ripken L 60.00 120.00
PLJG Jason Giambi L 20.00 50.00
PLKG Ken Griffey Jr. L 50.00 120.00
PLPM Pedro Martinez L 40.00 80.00
PLSS Sammy Sosa L 40.00 80.00
PNAR Alex Rodriguez N 40.00 80.00
PNBB Barry Bonds N 40.00 80.00
PNCR Cal Ripken N 60.00 120.00
PNJG Jason Giambi N 20.00 50.00
PNKG Ken Griffey Jr. N 50.00 120.00
PNPM Pedro Martinez N 40.00 80.00
PNSS Sammy Sosa N 40.00 80.00
PSAR Alex Rodriguez S 40.00 80.00
PSBB Barry Bonds S 40.00 80.00
PSCR Cal Ripken S 60.00 120.00
PSJG Jason Giambi S 20.00 50.00
PSKG Ken Griffey Jr. S 50.00 120.00
PSPM Pedro Martinez S 40.00 80.00
PSSS Sammy Sosa S 40.00 80.00

2002 Upper Deck Game Worn Gems

SER.2 STATED ODDS 1:48 RETAIL
SP INFO PROVIDED BY UPPER DECK
NO SP PRICING DUE TO SCARCITY
GAS Aaron Sele 4.00 10.00
GCD Carlos Delgado 4.00 10.00
GCJ Chipper Jones 6.00 15.00
GCR Cal Ripken 20.00 50.00
GCS Curt Schilling 4.00 10.00
GEC Eric Chavez 4.00 10.00
GEM Edgar Martinez 6.00 15.00
GEM Eric Milton 4.00 10.00
GFT Frank Thomas 6.00 15.00
GGM Greg Maddux 6.00 15.00
GIR Ivan Rodriguez 6.00 15.00
GJG Juan Gonzalez 4.00 10.00
GJK Jason Kendall 4.00 10.00
GJM Joe Mays 4.00 10.00
GPN Phil Nevin 4.00 10.00
GRA Roberto Alomar 6.00 15.00
GRP Robert Person 4.00 10.00
GRY Robin Yount 6.00 15.00
GSR Scott Rolen 6.00 15.00
GTG Tom Glavine 6.00 15.00
GTM Tino Martinez 6.00 15.00

2002 Upper Deck Global Swatch Game Jersey

SER.1 STATED ODDS 1:144
GSBK Byung-Hyun Kim 4.00 10.00
GSCD Carlos Delgado 4.00 10.00
GSCP Chan Ho Park 4.00 10.00
GSHN Hideo Nomo 10.00 25.00
GSIS Ichiro Suzuki 10.00 25.00
GSKS Kazuhiro Sasaki 4.00 10.00
GSMR Manny Ramirez 6.00 15.00
GSMY Masato Yoshii 4.00 10.00
GSSH Shigetoshi Hasegawa 4.00 10.00
GSTS Tsuyoshi Shinjo 4.00 10.00

2002 Upper Deck Peoples Choice Game Jersey

SER.2 STATED ODDS 1:24 HOBBY
SP INFO PROVIDED BY UPPER DECK
PJAG Andres Galarraga SP 6.00 15.00
PJAP Andy Pettitte 6.00 15.00
PJAR Alex Rodriguez 6.00 15.00
PJBG Brian Giles 4.00 10.00
PJBW Bernie Williams 6.00 15.00
PJCD Carlos Delgado 4.00 10.00
PJCJ Charles Johnson 4.00 10.00
PJCS Curt Schilling 4.00 10.00
PJDL Derek Lowe 4.00 10.00
PJDW David Wells 4.00 10.00
PJEB Ellis Burks SP 6.00 15.00
PJFT Frank Thomas 6.00 15.00
PJGM Greg Maddux 6.00 15.00
PJHI Hideki Irabu 4.00 10.00
PJJG Juan Gonzalez 4.00 10.00
PJJN Jeff Nelson 4.00 10.00
PJJS J.T. Snow 4.00 10.00
PJJBA Jeff Bagwell 6.00 15.00
PJJBU Jeromy Burnitz 4.00 10.00
PJKG Ken Griffey Jr. 8.00 20.00
PJMP Mike Piazza 6.00 15.00
PJMS Mike Stanton 4.00 10.00
PJMW Matt Williams SP 6.00 15.00
PJMRA Manny Ramirez 6.00 15.00
PJMRI Mariano Rivera 6.00 15.00
PJOD Omar Daal 4.00 10.00
PJOV Omar Vizquel 6.00 15.00
PJRF Rafael Furcal 4.00 10.00
PJRO Rey Ordonez 4.00 10.00
PJRP Rafael Palmeiro SP 10.00 25.00
PJRP Robert Person SP 6.00 15.00
PJRV Robin Ventura 4.00 10.00
PJSH Sterling Hitchcock 4.00 10.00
PJSS Sammy Sosa 6.00 15.00
PJTG Tony Gwynn 6.00 15.00
PJTM Tino Martinez 6.00 15.00
PJTR Tim Raines Sr. 4.00 10.00
PJTS Tim Salmon 6.00 15.00
PJTSh Tsuyoshi Shinjo 4.00 10.00

2002 Upper Deck Return of the Ace

COMPLETE SET (15) 12.50 30.00
SER.2 STATED ODDS 1:11
RA1 Randy Johnson 1.25 3.00
RA2 Greg Maddux 2.00 5.00
RA3 Pedro Martinez .75 2.00
RA4 Freddy Garcia .75 2.00
RA5 Matt Morris .75 2.00
RA6 Mark Mulder .75 2.00
RA7 Wade Miller .75 2.00
RA8 Kevin Brown .75 2.00
RA9 Roger Clemens 2.50 6.00
RA10 Jon Lieber .75 2.00
RA11 C.C. Sabathia .75 2.00
RA12 Tim Hudson .75 2.00
RA13 Curt Schilling .75 2.00
RA14 Al Leiter .75 2.00
RA15 Mike Mussina .75 2.00

2002 Upper Deck Sons of Summer Game Jersey

SER.2 STATED ODDS 1:288
SP INFO PROVIDED BY UPPER DECK
SSAR Alex Rodriguez 8.00 20.00
SSGM Greg Maddux 8.00 20.00
SSJB Jeff Bagwell 8.00 20.00
SSJG Juan Gonzalez 6.00 15.00
SSMP Mike Piazza 8.00 20.00
SSPM Pedro Martinez SP 10.00 25.00
SSRA Roberto Alomar 8.00 20.00
SSRC Roger Clemens 12.50 30.00

2002 Upper Deck Superstar Summit I

COMPLETE SET (6) 10.00 25.00
SER.1 STATED ODDS 1:23
SS1 Sammy Sosa 1.50 4.00
SS2 Alex Rodriguez 1.25 3.00
SS3 Mark McGwire 2.50 6.00
SS4 Barry Bonds 2.50 6.00
SS5 Mike Piazza 1.50 4.00
SS6 Ken Griffey Jr. 2.00 5.00

2002 Upper Deck Superstar Summit II

COMPLETE SET (15) 25.00 60.00
SER.2 STATED ODDS 1:11
SS1 Alex Rodriguez 1.50 4.00
SS2 Jason Giambi 1.25 3.00
SS3 Vladimir Guerrero 1.25 3.00
SS4 Randy Johnson 1.25 3.00
SS5 Chipper Jones 1.25 3.00
SS6 Ichiro Suzuki 2.50 6.00
SS7 Sammy Sosa 1.25 3.00
SS8 Greg Maddux 2.00 5.00
SS9 Ken Griffey Jr. 2.50 6.00
SS10 Todd Helton 1.25 3.00
SS11 Barry Bonds 3.00 8.00
SS12 Derek Jeter 3.00 8.00
SS13 Mike Piazza 2.00 5.00
SS14 Ivan Rodriguez 1.25 3.00
SS15 Frank Thomas 1.25 3.00

2002 Upper Deck UD Plus Hobby

ONE 2-CARD PACK PER SER.2 HOBBY BOX
STATED PRINT RUN 1125 SERIAL #'d SETS
COMP.SET CAN BE EXCH.FOR JSY CARD
HOBBY CARDS ARE SILVER
UD1 Darin Erstad 2.00 5.00
UD2 Troy Glaus 2.00 5.00
UD3 Tim Hudson 2.00 5.00
UD4 Jermaine Dye 2.00 5.00
UD5 Barry Zito 2.00 5.00
UD6 Carlos Delgado 2.00 5.00
UD7 Shannon Stewart 2.00 5.00
UD8 Greg Vaughn 2.00 5.00
UD9 Jim Thome 2.00 5.00
UD10 C.C. Sabathia 2.00 5.00
UD11 Ichiro Suzuki 5.00 12.00
UD12 Edgar Martinez 2.00 5.00
UD13 Bret Boone 2.00 5.00
UD14 Freddy Garcia 2.00 5.00
UD15 Matt Thornton 2.00 5.00
UD16 Jeff Conine 2.00 5.00
UD17 Steve Bechler 2.00 5.00
UD18 Rafael Palmeiro 2.00 5.00
UD19 Juan Gonzalez 2.00 5.00
UD20 Alex Rodriguez 3.00 8.00
UD21 Ivan Rodriguez 2.00 5.00
UD22 Carl Everett 2.00 5.00
UD23 Manny Ramirez 2.00 5.00
UD24 Nomar Garciaparra 4.00 10.00
UD25 Pedro Martinez 2.00 5.00
UD26 Mike Sweeney 2.00 5.00
UD27 Chuck Knoblauch 2.00 5.00
UD28 Dmitri Young 2.00 5.00
UD29 Bobby Higginson 2.00 5.00
UD30 Dean Palmer 2.00 5.00
UD31 Doug Mientkiewicz 2.00 5.00
UD32 Corey Koskie 2.00 5.00
UD33 Brad Radke 2.00 5.00
UD34 Cristian Guzman 2.00 5.00
UD35 Frank Thomas 2.50 6.00
UD36 Magglio Ordonez 2.00 5.00
UD37 Carlos Lee 2.00 5.00
UD38 Roger Clemens 5.00 12.00
UD39 Bernie Williams 2.00 5.00
UD40 Derek Jeter 6.00 15.00
UD41 Jason Giambi 2.00 5.00
UD42 Mike Mussina 2.00 5.00
UD43 Jeff Bagwell 2.00 5.00
UD44 Lance Berkman 2.00 5.00
UD45 Wade Miller 2.00 5.00
UD46 Greg Maddux 4.00 10.00
UD47 Chipper Jones 2.50 6.00
UD48 Andruw Jones 2.00 5.00
UD49 Gary Sheffield 2.00 5.00
UD50 Richie Sexson 2.00 5.00
UD51 Albert Pujols 5.00 12.00
UD52 J.D. Drew 2.00 5.00
UD53 Matt Morris 2.00 5.00
UD54 Jim Edmonds 2.00 5.00
UD55 So Taguchi 2.00 5.00
UD56 Sammy Sosa 2.50 6.00
UD57 Fred McGriff 2.00 5.00
UD58 Kerry Wood 2.00 5.00
UD59 Moises Alou 2.00 5.00
UD60 Randy Johnson 2.50 6.00
UD61 Luis Gonzalez 2.00 5.00
UD62 Mark Grace 2.00 5.00
UD63 Curt Schilling 2.00 5.00
UD64 Matt Williams 2.00 5.00
UD65 Kevin Brown 2.00 5.00
UD66 Brian Jordan 2.00 5.00
UD67 Shawn Green 2.00 5.00
UD68 Hideo Nomo 5.00 12.00
UD69 Kazuhisa Ishii 2.00 5.00
UD70 Vladimir Guerrero 2.50 6.00
UD71 Jose Vidro 2.00 5.00
UD72 Eric Good 2.00 5.00
UD73 Barry Bonds 6.00 15.00
UD74 Jeff Kent 2.00 5.00
UD75 Rich Aurilia 2.00 5.00
UD76 Deivis Santos 2.00 5.00
UD77 Preston Wilson 2.00 5.00
UD78 Cliff Floyd 2.00 5.00
UD79 Josh Beckett 2.00 5.00
UD80 Hansel Izquierdo 2.00 5.00
UD81 Mike Piazza 4.00 10.00
UD82 Roberto Alomar 2.00 5.00
UD83 Mo Vaughn 2.00 5.00
UD84 Jeromy Burnitz 2.00 5.00
UD85 Phil Nevin 2.00 5.00
UD86 Ryan Klesko 2.00 5.00
UD87 Bobby Abreu 2.00 5.00
UD88 Scott Rolen 2.00 5.00
UD89 Jimmy Rollins 2.00 5.00
UD90 Jason Kendall 2.00 5.00
UD91 Brian Giles 2.00 5.00
UD92 Aramis Ramirez 2.00 5.00
UD93 Ken Griffey Jr. 5.00 12.00
UD94 Sean Casey 2.00 5.00
UD95 Barry Larkin 2.00 5.00
UD96 Adam Dunn 2.00 5.00
UD97 Todd Helton 2.00 5.00
UD98 Larry Walker 2.00 5.00
UD99 Mike Hampton 2.00 5.00
UD100 Rene Reyes 2.00 5.00

2002 Upper Deck UD Plus Memorabilia Moments Game Uniform

COMMON DIMAGGIO (1-5) 60.00 120.00
COMMON MANTLE (1-5) 100.00 200.00
AVAILABLE VIA MAIL EXCHANGE
STATED PRINT RUN 25 SERIAL #'d SETS

2002 Upper Deck World Series Heroes Memorabilia

SER.1 STATED ODDS 1:288 HOBBY
SP INFO PROVIDED BY UPPER DECK
BDJ Derek Jeter Base SP 10.00 25.00
BES Enos Slaughter Bat 6.00 15.00
BJD Joe DiMaggio Bat SP 50.00 100.00
BKP Kirby Puckett Bat 10.00 25.00
BMM Mickey Mantle Bat 30.00 80.00
SBM Bill Mazeroski Jsy 15.00 40.00
SCF Carlton Fisk Jsy 8.00 20.00
SDL Don Larsen Jsy 8.00 20.00
SJC Joe Carter Jsy 6.00 15.00

2002 Upper Deck Yankee Dynasty Memorabilia

SER.1 STATED ODDS 1:144
SP INFO PROVIDED BY UPPER DECK
YBCJ Clemens/Jeter Base SP 75.00 150.00
YBJW Jeter/Bernie Base SP 30.00 60.00
YJBJ S.Brosius/D.Justice Jsy 10.00 25.00
YJBT W.Boggs/J.Torre Jsy 10.00 25.00
YJCP R.Clemens/J.Posada Jsy 10.00 25.00
YJDM J.DiMag/M.Mantle Jsy 75.00 150.00
YJGC J.Girardi/D.Cone Jsy 10.00 25.00
YJKR C.Knoblauch/T.Raines Jsy 10.00 25.00
YJOM P.O'Neill/T.Martinez Jsy 10.00 25.00
YJPR A.Pettitte/M.Rivera Jsy 12.00 30.00
YJRK W.Randolph/C.Knob Jsy 10.00 25.00
YJWG D.Wells/D.Gooden Jsy 10.00 25.00
YJWO B.Williams/P.O'Neill Jsy 10.00 25.00

2002 Upper Deck Ichiro Mini Playmaker

COMPLETE SET 8.00 20.00
COMMON CARD 1.50 4.00

2002 Upper Deck Mark McGwire Employee Game Jersey

UDCMM Mark McGwire 150.00

2002 Upper Deck Mark McGwire Holiday Card

1 Mark McGwire 2.00 5.00

2002 Upper Deck Twizzlers

3 Nomar Garciaparra 1.00 2.50
4 Nomar Garciaparra 1.00 2.50

2003 Upper Deck

COMPLETE SET (540) 25.00 50.00
COMPLETE SERIES 1 (270) 8.00 20.00
COMPLETE SERIES 2 (270) 8.00 20.00
COMP.UPDATE SET (60) 5.00 12.00
COMMON (31-500/531-600) .12 .30
COMMON (1-30/347/501-530) .40 1.00
COMMON RC (541-600) .20 .50
SR 1-30/501-530 ARE NOT SHORT PRINTS
CARD 19 DOES NOT EXIST
SCUTARO/NOMAR ARE BOTH CARD 96
541-600 ISSUED IN 04 UD1 HOBBY BOXES
UPDATE SET EXCH 1:240 '04 UD1 RETAIL
UPDATE SET EXCH.DEADLINE 11/10/06
1 John Lackey SR .60 1.50
2 Alex Cintron SR .40 1.00
3 Jose Leon SR .40 1.00
4 Bobby Hill SR .40 1.00
5 Brandon Larson SR .40 1.00
6 Raul Gonzalez SR .40 1.00
7 Ben Broussard SR .40 1.00
8 Earl Snyder SR .40 1.00
9 Ramon Santiago SR .40 1.00
10 Jason Lane SR .40 1.00
11 Keith Ginter SR .40 1.00
12 Kirk Saarloos SR .40 1.00
13 Juan Brito SR .40 1.00
14 Runelvys Hernandez SR .40 1.00
15 Shawn Sedlacek SR .40 1.00

16 Jayson Durocher SR .40 1.00
17 Kevin Frederick SR .40 1.00
18 Zach Day SR .40 1.00
20 Marcus Thames SR .40 1.00
21 Esteban German SR .40 1.00
22 Brett Myers SR .40 1.00
23 Oliver Perez SR .40 1.00
24 Dennis Tankersley SR .40 1.00
25 Julius Matos SR .40 1.00
26 Jake Peavy SR .40 1.00
27 Eric Cyr SR .40 1.00
28 Mike Crudale SR .40 1.00
29 Josh Pearce SR .40 1.00
30 Carl Crawford SR .60 1.50
31 Tim Salmon .12 .30
32 Troy Glaus .12 .30
33 Adam Kennedy .12 .30
34 David Eckstein .12 .30
35 Ben Molina .12 .30
36 Jarrod Washburn .12 .30
37 Ramon Ortiz .12 .30
38 Eric Chavez .12 .30
39 Miguel Tejada .20 .50
40 Adam Piatt .12 .30
41 Jermaine Dye .12 .30
42 Olmedo Saenz .12 .30
43 Tim Hudson .20 .50
44 Barry Zito .20 .50
45 Billy Koch .12 .30
46 Shannon Stewart .12 .30
47 Kelvim Escobar .12 .30
48 Jose Cruz Jr. .12 .30
49 Vernon Wells .12 .30
50 Roy Halladay .20 .50
51 Esteban Loaiza .12 .30
52 Eric Hinske .12 .30
53 Steve Cox .12 .30
54 Brent Abernathy .12 .30
55 Ben Grieve .12 .30
56 Aubrey Huff .12 .30
57 Jared Sandberg .12 .30
58 Paul Wilson .12 .30
59 Tanyon Sturtze .12 .30
60 Jim Thome .20 .50
61 Omar Vizquel .20 .50
62 C.C. Sabathia .20 .50
63 Chris Magruder .12 .30
64 Ricky Gutierrez .12 .30
65 Einar Diaz .12 .30
66 Danys Baez .12 .30
67 Ichiro Suzuki .40 1.00
68 Ruben Sierra .12 .30
69 Carlos Guillen .12 .30
70 Mark McLemore .12 .30
71 Dan Wilson .12 .30
72 Jamie Moyer .12 .30
73 Joel Pineiro .12 .30
74 Edgar Martinez .20 .50
75 Tony Batista .12 .30
76 Jay Gibbons .12 .30
77 Chris Singleton .12 .30
78 Melvin Mora .12 .30
79 Geronimo Gil .12 .30
80 Rodrigo Lopez .12 .30
81 Jorge Julio .12 .30
82 Rafael Palmeiro .20 .50
83 Juan Gonzalez .12 .30
84 Mike Young .12 .30
85 Hideki Irabu .12 .30
86 Chan Ho Park .20 .50
87 Kevin Mench .12 .30
88 Doug Davis .12 .30
89 Pedro Martinez .20 .50
90 Shea Hillenbrand .12 .30
91 Derek Lowe .12 .30
92 Jason Varitek .30 .75
93 Tony Clark .12 .30
94 John Burkett .12 .30
95 Frank Castillo .12 .30
96A Nomar Garciaparra .20 .50
96B Marcos Scutaro SR 2.50 6.00
97 Rickey Henderson .30 .75
98 Mike Sweeney .12 .30
99 Carlos Febles .12 .30
100 Mark Quinn .12 .30
101 Raul Ibanez .20 .50
102 A.J. Hinch .12 .30
103 Paul Byrd .12 .30
104 Chuck Knoblauch .12 .30
105 Dmitri Young .12 .30
106 Randall Simon .12 .30
107 Brandon Inge .12 .30
108 Damion Easley .12 .30
109 Carlos Pena .20 .50
110 George Lombard .12 .30
111 Juan Acevedo .12 .30
112 Torii Hunter .12 .30
113 Doug Mientkiewicz .12 .30
114 David Ortiz .30 .75
115 Eric Milton .12 .30
116 Eddie Guardado .12 .30
117 Cristian Guzman .12 .30
118 Corey Koskie .12 .30
119 Maggio Ordonez .20 .50
120 Mark Buehrle .20 .50
121 Todd Ritchie .12 .30
122 Jose Valentin .12 .30
123 Paul Konerko .20 .50
124 Carlos Lee .12 .30
125 Jon Garland .12 .30
126 Jason Giambi .12 .30
127 Derek Jeter .75 2.00
128 Roger Clemens .40 1.00
129 Raul Mondesi .12 .30
130 Jorge Posada .20 .50
131 Rondell White .12 .30
132 Robin Ventura .12 .30
133 Mike Mussina .20 .50
134 Jeff Bagwell .20 .50
135 Craig Biggio .20 .50
136 Morgan Ensberg .12 .30
137 Richard Hidalgo .12 .30
138 Brad Ausmus .12 .30
139 Roy Oswalt .20 .50
140 Carlos Hernandez .12 .30
141 Shane Reynolds .12 .30
142 Gary Sheffield .12 .30
143 Andruw Jones .12 .30
144 Tom Glavine .20 .50
145 Rafael Furcal .12 .30
146 Javy Lopez .12 .30
147 Vinny Castilla .12 .30
148 Marcus Giles .12 .30
149 Kevin Millwood .12 .30
150 Jason Marquis .12 .30
151 Ruben Quevedo .12 .30
152 Ben Sheets .12 .30
153 Geoff Jenkins .12 .30
154 Jose Hernandez .12 .30
155 Glendon Rusch .12 .30
156 Jeffrey Hammonds .12 .30
157 Alex Sanchez .12 .30
158 Jim Edmonds .20 .50
159 Tino Martinez .12 .30
160 Albert Pujols .40 1.00
161 Eli Marrero .12 .30
162 Woody Williams .12 .30
163 Fernando Vina .12 .30
164 Jason Isringhausen .12 .30
165 Jason Simontacchi .12 .30
166 Kerry Robinson .12 .30
167 Sammy Sosa .30 .75
168 Juan Cruz .12 .30
169 Fred McGriff .20 .50
170 Antonio Alfonseca .12 .30
171 Jon Lieber .12 .30
172 Mark Prior .20 .50
173 Moises Alou .12 .30
174 Matt Clement .12 .30
175 Mark Bellhorn .12 .30
176 Randy Johnson .30 .75
177 Luis Gonzalez .12 .30
178 Tony Womack .12 .30
179 Mark Grace .20 .50
180 Junior Spivey .12 .30
181 Byung Hyun Kim .12 .30
182 Danny Bautista .12 .30
183 Brian Anderson .12 .30
184 Shawn Green .12 .30
185 Brian Jordan .12 .30
186 Eric Karros .12 .30
187 Andy Ashby .12 .30
188 Cesar Izturis .12 .30
189 Dave Roberts .20 .50
190 Eric Gagne .12 .30
191 Kazuhisa Ishii .12 .30
192 Adrian Beltre .30 .75
193 Vladimir Guerrero .20 .50
194 Tony Armas Jr. .12 .30
195 Bartolo Colon .12 .30
196 Troy O'Leary .12 .30
197 Tomo Ohka .12 .30
198 Brad Wilkerson .12 .30
199 Orlando Cabrera .12 .30
200 Barry Bonds .50 1.25
201 David Bell .12 .30
202 Tsuyoshi Shinjo .12 .30
203 Benito Santiago .12 .30
204 Livan Hernandez .12 .30
205 Jason Schmidt .12 .30
206 Kirk Rueter .12 .30
207 Ramon E. Martinez .12 .30
208 Mike Lowell .12 .30
209 Luis Castillo .12 .30
210 Derrek Lee .12 .30
211 Andy Fox .12 .30
212 Eric Owens .12 .30
213 Charles Johnson .12 .30
214 Brad Penny .12 .30
215 A.J. Burnett .12 .30
216 Edgardo Alfonzo .12 .30
217 Roberto Alomar .20 .50
218 Rey Ordonez .12 .30
219 Al Leiter .12 .30
220 Roger Cedeno .12 .30
221 Timo Perez .12 .30
222 Jeromy Burnitz .12 .30
223 Pedro Astacio .12 .30
224 Joe McEwing .12 .30
225 Ryan Klesko .12 .30
226 Ramon Vazquez .12 .30
227 Mark Kotsay .12 .30
228 Bubba Trammell .12 .30
229 Wiki Gonzalez .12 .30
230 Trevor Hoffman .20 .50
231 Ron Gant .12 .30
232 Bob Abreu .12 .30
233 Marlon Anderson .12 .30
234 Jeremy Giambi .12 .30
235 Jimmy Rollins .20 .50
236 Mike Lieberthal .12 .30
237 Vicente Padilla .12 .30
238 Randy Wolf .12 .30
239 Pokey Reese .12 .30
240 Brian Giles .12 .30
241 Jack Wilson .12 .30
242 Mike Williams .12 .30
243 Kip Wells .12 .30
244 Rob Mackowiak .12 .30
245 Craig Wilson .12 .30
246 Adam Dunn .20 .50
247 Sean Casey .12 .30
248 Todd Walker .12 .30
249 Corky Miller .12 .30
250 Ryan Dempster .12 .30
251 Reggie Taylor .12 .30
252 Aaron Boone .12 .30
253 Larry Walker .20 .50
254 Jose Ortiz .12 .30
255 Todd Zeile .12 .30
256 Bobby Estalella .12 .30
257 Juan Pierre .12 .30
258 Terry Shumpert .12 .30
259 Mike Hampton .12 .30
260 Denny Stark .12 .30
261 Shawn Green SH CL .12 .30
262 Derek Lowe SH CL .12 .30
263 Barry Bonds SH CL .50 1.25
264 Mike Cameron SH CL .12 .30
265 Luis Castillo SH CL .12 .30
266 Vladimir Guerrero SH CL .20 .50
267 Jason Giambi SH CL .12 .30
268 Eric Gagne SH CL .12 .30
269 Maggio Ordonez SH CL .20 .50
270 Jim Thome SH CL .20 .50
271 Garret Anderson .12 .30
272 Troy Percival .12 .30
273 Brad Fullmer .12 .30
274 Scott Spiezio .12 .30
275 Darin Erstad .12 .30
276 Francisco Rodriguez .20 .50
277 Kevin Appier .12 .30
278 Shawn Wooten .12 .30
279 Eric Owens .12 .30
280 Scott Hatteberg .12 .30
281 Terrence Long .12 .30
282 Mark Mulder .12 .30
283 Ramon Hernandez .12 .30
284 Ted Lilly .12 .30
285 Erubiel Durazo .12 .30
286 Mark Ellis .12 .30
287 Carlos Delgado .12 .30
288 Orlando Hudson .12 .30
289 Chris Woodward .12 .30
290 Mark Hendrickson .12 .30
291 Josh Phelps .12 .30
292 Ken Huckaby .12 .30
293 Justin Miller .12 .30
294 Travis Lee .12 .30
295 Jorge Sosa .12 .30
296 Joe Kennedy .12 .30
297 Carl Crawford .20 .50
298 Toby Hall .12 .30
299 Rey Ordonez .12 .30
300 Brandon Phillips .12 .30
301 Matt Lawton .12 .30
302 Ellis Burks .12 .30
303 Bill Selby .12 .30
304 Travis Hafner .12 .30
305 Milton Bradley .12 .30
306 Karim Garcia .12 .30
307 Cliff Lee .75 2.00
308 Jeff Cirillo .12 .30
309 John Olerud .12 .30
310 Kazuhiro Sasaki .12 .30
311 Freddy Garcia .12 .30
312 Bret Boone .12 .30
313 Mike Cameron .12 .30
314 Ben Davis .12 .30
315 Randy Winn .12 .30
316 Gary Matthews Jr. .12 .30
317 Jeff Conine .12 .30
318 Sidney Ponson .12 .30
319 Jerry Hairston .12 .30
320 David Segui .12 .30
321 Scott Erickson .12 .30
322 Marty Cordova .12 .30
323 Hank Blalock .12 .30
324 Herbert Perry .12 .30
325 Alex Rodriguez .40 1.00
326 Carl Everett .12 .30
327 Einar Diaz .12 .30
328 Ugueth Urbina .12 .30
329 Mark Teixeira .20 .50
330 Manny Ramirez .30 .75
331 Johnny Damon .20 .50
332 Trot Nixon .12 .30
333 Tim Wakefield .20 .50
334 Casey Fossum .12 .30
335 Todd Walker .12 .30
336 Jeremy Giambi .12 .30
337 Bill Mueller .12 .30
338 Ramiro Mendoza .12 .30
339 Carlos Beltran .20 .50
340 Jason Grimsley .12 .30
341 Brent Mayne .12 .30
342 Angel Berroa .12 .30
343 Albie Lopez .12 .30
344 Michael Tucker .12 .30
345 Bobby Higginson .12 .30
346 Shane Halter .12 .30
347 Jeremy Bonderman RC 1.50 4.00
348 Eric Munson .12 .30
349 Andy Van Hekken .12 .30
350 Matt Anderson .12 .30
351 Jacque Jones .12 .30
352 A.J. Pierzynski .12 .30
353 Joe Mays .12 .30
354 Brad Radke .12 .30
355 Dustan Mohr .12 .30
356 Bobby Kielty .12 .30
357 Michael Cuddyer .12 .30
358 Luis Rivas .12 .30
359 Frank Thomas .30 .75
360 Joe Borchard .12 .30
361 D'Angelo Jimenez .12 .30
362 Bartolo Colon .12 .30
363 Joe Crede .12 .30
364 Miguel Olivo .12 .30
365 Billy Koch .12 .30
366 Bernie Williams .20 .50
367 Nick Johnson .12 .30
368 Andy Pettitte .20 .50
369 Mariano Rivera .40 1.00
370 Alfonso Soriano .20 .50
371 David Wells .12 .30
372 Drew Henson .12 .30
373 Juan Rivera .12 .30
374 Steve Karsay .12 .30
375 Jeff Kent .12 .30
376 Lance Berkman .20 .50
377 Octavio Dotel .12 .30
378 Julio Lugo .12 .30
379 Jason Lane .12 .30
380 Wade Miller .12 .30
381 Billy Wagner .12 .30
382 Brad Ausmus .12 .30
383 Mike Hampton .12 .30
384 Chipper Jones .30 .75
385 John Smoltz .30 .75
386 Greg Maddux .40 1.00
387 Javy Lopez .12 .30
388 Robert Fick .12 .30
389 Mark DeRosa .12 .30
390 Russ Ortiz .12 .30
391 Julio Franco .12 .30
392 Richie Sexson .12 .30
393 Eric Young .12 .30
394 Robert Machado .12 .30
395 Mike DeJean .12 .30
396 Todd Ritchie .12 .30
397 Royce Clayton .12 .30
398 Nick Neugebauer .12 .30
399 J.D. Drew .12 .30
400 Edgar Renteria .12 .30
401 Scott Rolen .20 .50
402 Matt Morris .12 .30
403 Garrett Stephenson .12 .30
404 Eduardo Perez .12 .30
405 Mike Matheny .12 .30
406 Miguel Cairo .12 .30
407 Brett Tomko .12 .30
408 Bobby Hill .12 .30
409 Troy O'Leary .12 .30
410 Corey Patterson .12 .30
411 Kerry Wood .12 .30
412 Eric Karros .12 .30
413 Hee Seop Choi .12 .30
414 Alex Gonzalez .12 .30
415 Matt Clement .12 .30
416 Mark Grudzielanek .12 .30
417 Curt Schilling .20 .50
418 Steve Finley .12 .30
419 Craig Counsell .12 .30
420 Matt Williams .12 .30
421 Quinton McCracken .12 .30
422 Chad Moeller .12 .30
423 Lyle Overbay .12 .30
424 Miguel Batista .12 .30
425 Paul Lo Duca .12 .30
426 Kevin Brown .12 .30
427 Hideo Nomo .30 .75
428 Fred McGriff .20 .50
429 Joe Thurston .12 .30
430 Odalis Perez .12 .30
431 Darren Dreifort .12 .30
432 Todd Hundley .12 .30
433 Dave Roberts .20 .50
434 Jose Vidro .12 .30
435 Javier Vazquez .12 .30
436 Michael Barrett .12 .30
437 Fernando Tatis .12 .30
438 Peter Bergeron .12 .30
439 Endy Chavez .12 .30
440 Orlando Hernandez .12 .30
441 Marvin Benard .12 .30
442 Rich Aurilia .12 .30
443 Pedro Feliz .12 .30
444 Robb Nen .12 .30
445 Ray Durham .12 .30
446 Marquis Grissom .12 .30
447 Damian Moss .12 .30
448 Edgardo Alfonzo .12 .30
449 Juan Pierre .12 .30
450 Braden Looper .12 .30
451 Alex Gonzalez .12 .30
452 Justin Wayne .12 .30
453 Josh Beckett .12 .30
454 Juan Encarnacion .12 .30
455 Ivan Rodriguez .20 .50
456 Todd Hollandsworth .12 .30
457 Cliff Floyd .12 .30
458 Rey Sanchez .12 .30
459 Mike Piazza .30 .75
460 Mo Vaughn .12 .30
461 Armando Benitez .12 .30
462 Tsuyoshi Shinjo .12 .30
463 Tom Glavine .20 .50
464 David Cone .12 .30
465 Phil Nevin .12 .30
466 Sean Burroughs .12 .30
467 Jake Peavy .12 .30
468 Brian Lawrence .12 .30
469 Mark Loretta .12 .30
470 Dennis Tankersley .12 .30
471 Jesse Orosco .12 .30
472 Jim Thome .20 .50
473 Kevin Millwood .12 .30
474 David Bell .12 .30
475 Pat Burrell .12 .30
476 Brandon Duckworth .12 .30
477 Jose Mesa .12 .30
478 Marlon Byrd .12 .30
479 Reggie Sanders .12 .30
480 Jason Kendall .12 .30
481 Aramis Ramirez .12 .30
482 Kris Benson .12 .30
483 Matt Stairs .12 .30
484 Kevin Young .12 .30
485 Kenny Lofton .12 .30
486 Austin Kearns .12 .30
487 Barry Larkin .20 .50
488 Jason LaRue .12 .30
489 Ken Griffey Jr. .60 1.50
490 Danny Graves .12 .30
491 Russell Branyan .12 .30
492 Reggie Taylor .12 .30
493 Jimmy Haynes .12 .30
494 Charles Johnson .12 .30
495 Todd Helton .20 .50
496 Juan Uribe .12 .30
497 Preston Wilson .12 .30
498 Chris Stynes .12 .30
499 Jason Jennings .12 .30
500 Jay Payton .12 .30
501 Hideki Matsui SR RC 2.00 5.00
502 Jose Contreras SR RC 1.00 2.50
503 Brandon Webb SR RC 1.25 3.00
504 Robby Hammock SR RC .40 1.00
505 Matt Kata SR RC .40 1.00
506 Tim Olson SR RC .40 1.00
507 Michael Hessman SR RC .40 1.00
508 Jon Leicester SR RC .40 1.00
509 Todd Wellemeyer SR RC .40 1.00
510 David Sanders SR RC .40 1.00
511 Josh Stewart SR RC .40 1.00
512 Luis Ayala SR RC .40 1.00
513 Clint Barmes SR RC 1.00 2.50
514 Josh Willingham SR RC 1.25 3.00
515 Alejandro Machado SR RC .40 1.00
516 Felix Sanchez SR RC .40 1.00
517 Willie Eyre SR RC .40 1.00
518 Brent Hoard SR RC .40 1.00
519 Lew Ford SR RC .40 1.00
520 Termel Sledge SR RC .40 1.00
521 Jeremy Griffiths SR RC .40 1.00
522 Phil Seibel SR RC .40 1.00
523 Craig Brazell SR RC .40 1.00
524 Prentice Redman SR RC .40 1.00
525 Jeff Duncan SR RC .40 1.00
526 Shane Bazzell SR RC .40 1.00
527 Bernie Castro SR RC .40 1.00
528 Rett Johnson SR RC .40 1.00
529 Bobby Madritsch SR RC .40 1.00
530 Rocco Baldelli SR .40 1.00
531 Alex Rodriguez SH CL .40 1.00
532 Eric Chavez SH CL .12 .30
533 Miguel Tejada SH CL .20 .50
534 Ichiro Suzuki SH CL .40 1.00
535 Sammy Sosa SH CL .30 .75
536 Barry Zito SH CL .20 .50
537 Darin Erstad SH CL .12 .30
538 Alfonso Soriano SH CL .20 .50
539 Troy Glaus SH CL .12 .30
540 Nomar Garciaparra SH CL .20 .50
541 Bo Hart RC .20 .50
542 Dan Haren RC 1.00 2.50
543 Ryan Wagner RC .20 .50
544 Rich Harden .20 .50
545 Dontrelle Willis .12 .30
546 Jerome Williams .12 .30
547 Bobby Crosby .12 .30
548 Greg Jones RC .20 .50
549 Todd Linden .12 .30
550 Byung-Hyun Kim .12 .30
551 Rickie Weeks RC .60 1.50
552 Jason Roach RC .20 .50
553 Oscar Villarreal RC .20 .50
554 Justin Duchscherer .12 .30
555 Chris Capuano RC .20 .50
556 Josh Hall RC .12 .30
557 Luis Matos .12 .30
558 Miguel Ojeda RC .20 .50
559 Kevin Ohme RC .20 .50
560 Julio Manon RC .20 .50
561 Kevin Correia RC .20 .50
562 Delmon Young RC 1.25 3.00
563 Aaron Boone .12 .30
564 Aaron Looper RC .20 .50
565 Mike Neu RC .20 .50
566 Aquilino Lopez RC .20 .50
567 Jhonny Peralta .12 .30
568 Duaner Sanchez .12 .30
569 Stephen Randolph RC .20 .50
570 Nate Bland RC .20 .50
571 Chin-Hui Tsao .12 .30
572 Michel Hernandez RC .12 .30
573 Rocco Baldelli .12 .30
574 Robb Quinlan .12 .30
575 Aaron Heilman .12 .30
576 Jae Weong Seo .12 .30
577 Joe Borowski .12 .30
578 Chris Bootcheck .12 .30
579 Michael Ryan RC .20 .50
580 Mark Malaska RC .20 .50
581 Jose Guillen .12 .30
582 Josh Towers .12 .30
583 Tom Gregorio RC .20 .50
584 Edwin Jackson RC .30 .75
585 Jason Anderson .12 .30
586 Jose Reyes .30 .75
587 Miguel Cabrera 1.50 4.00
588 Nate Bump .12 .30
589 Jeromy Burnitz .12 .30
590 David Ross .12 .30
591 Chase Utley .20 .50
592 Brandon Webb .40 1.00
593 Masao Kida .12 .30
594 Jimmy Journell .12 .30
595 Eric Young .12 .30
596 Tony Womack .12 .30
597 Amaury Telemaco .12 .30
598 Rickey Henderson .30 .75
599 Esteban Loaiza .12 .30
600 Sidney Ponson .12 .30

2003 Upper Deck Gold

COMP.FACT.SET (60) 15.00 40.00
*GOLD: 2X TO 5X BASIC
*GOLD: 1.25X TO 3X BASIC RC'S
ONE GOLD SET PER 12 CT HOBBY CASE

2003 Upper Deck A Piece of History 500 Club

RANDOM INSERT IN SERIES 2 PACKS
STATED PRINT RUN 350 CARDS
SS Sammy Sosa 30.00 60.00

2003 Upper Deck AL All-Star Swatches

SERIES 1 STATED ODDS 1:144 RETAIL
AP Andy Pettitte 6.00 15.00
AS Aaron Sele 4.00 10.00
CE Carl Everett 4.00 10.00
CF Chuck Finley 4.00 10.00
JG Juan Gonzalez 4.00 10.00
JM Joe Mays 4.00 10.00
JP Jorge Posada 6.00 15.00
MC Mike Cameron 4.00 10.00
MO Maggio Ordonez 4.00 10.00
MR Mariano Rivera 6.00 15.00
MS Mike Sweeney 4.00 10.00
RD Ray Durham 4.00 10.00
TF Travis Fryman 4.00 10.00

2003 Upper Deck Big League Breakdowns

COMPLETE SET (15) 10.00 25.00
SERIES 1 STATED ODDS 1:8
BL1 Troy Glaus .40 1.00
BL2 Miguel Tejada .60 1.50
BL3 Chipper Jones 1.00 2.50
BL4 Torii Hunter .40 1.00
BL5 Nomar Garciaparra .60 1.50
BL6 Sammy Sosa 1.00 2.50
BL7 Todd Helton .60 1.50
BL8 Lance Berkman .60 1.50
BL9 Shawn Green .40 1.00
BL10 Vladimir Guerrero .60 1.50
BL11 Jason Giambi .40 1.00
BL12 Derek Jeter 2.50 6.00
BL13 Barry Bonds 1.50 4.00
BL14 Ichiro Suzuki 1.25 3.00
BL15 Alex Rodriguez 1.25 3.00

2003 Upper Deck Chase for 755

COMPLETE SET (15) 8.00 20.00
SERIES 1 STATED ODDS 1:8
C1 Troy Glaus .40 1.00
C2 Andruw Jones .40 1.00
C3 Manny Ramirez 1.00 2.50
C4 Sammy Sosa 1.00 2.50
C5 Ken Griffey Jr. 2.00 5.00
C6 Adam Dunn .60 1.50
C7 Todd Helton .60 1.50
C8 Lance Berkman .60 1.50
C9 Jeff Bagwell .60 1.50
C10 Shawn Green .40 1.00
C11 Vladimir Guerrero .60 1.50
C12 Barry Bonds 1.50 4.00
C13 Alex Rodriguez 1.25 3.00
C14 Juan Gonzalez .40 1.00
C15 Carlos Delgado .40 1.00

2003 Upper Deck Game Swatches

SERIES 1 STATED ODDS 1:72 HOBBY/RETAIL
HJAR Alex Rodriguez 6.00 15.00
HJBW Bernie Williams 4.00 10.00
HJCC C.C. Sabathia 3.00 8.00
HJCD Carlos Delgado SP 6.00 15.00
HJCP Carlos Pena 3.00 8.00
HJCS Curt Schilling SP/100 6.00 15.00
HJGM Greg Maddux 4.00 10.00
HJMM Mike Mussina 4.00 10.00
HJMO Maggio Ordonez 3.00 8.00
HJMP Mike Piazza SP 10.00 25.00
HJSB Sean Burroughs SP 6.00 15.00
HJSS Sammy Sosa 4.00 10.00
RJAD Adam Dunn 3.00 8.00
RJDE Darin Erstad 3.00 8.00
RJEM Edgar Martinez 4.00 10.00
RJFT Frank Thomas 4.00 10.00
RJIR Ivan Rodriguez 4.00 10.00
RJJD J.D. Drew 3.00 8.00
RJJE Jim Edmonds 3.00 8.00
RJJG Jason Giambi 3.00 8.00
RJJK Jeff Kent 3.00 8.00
RJKG Ken Griffey Jr. 6.00 15.00
RJRC Roger Clemens 8.00 20.00
RJRJ Randy Johnson 4.00 10.00
RJTH Tim Hudson 3.00 8.00

2003 Upper Deck Leading Swatches

SERIES 2 STATED ODDS 1:24 HOB/1:48 RET
SP INFO PROVIDED BY UPPER DECK
SP'S ARE NOT SERIAL-NUMBERED
*GOLD: .75X TO 2X BASIC SWATCHES
*GOLD: .6X TO 1.5X BASIC SP SWATCHES
*GOLD MATSUI HR: .75X TO 1.5X BASIC HR
*GOLD MATSUI RBI: .6X TO 1.2X BASIC RBI
GOLD RANDOM INSERTS IN SER.2 PACKS
GOLD PRINT RUN 100 SERIAL #'d SETS
AB Adrian Beltre GM 3.00 8.00
AD Adam Dunn RUN 3.00 8.00
AD1 Adam Dunn BB SP 4.00 10.00
AJ Andruw Jones HR 4.00 10.00
AJ1 Andruw Jones AB SP 6.00 15.00
AP Andy Pettitte WIN SP 6.00 15.00
AR Alex Rodriguez HR 6.00 15.00
AR1 Alex Rodriguez RBI 6.00 15.00
AS Alfonso Soriano SB 3.00 8.00
AS1 Alfonso Soriano RUN 3.00 8.00
AS2 Aaron Sele WIN 3.00 8.00
BA Bobby Abreu 2B 3.00 8.00
BG Brian Giles HR 3.00 8.00
BG1 Brian Giles OBP 3.00 8.00
BW Bernie Williams 333 AVG 4.00 10.00
BW1 Bernie Williams 339 AVG 4.00 10.00
BZ Barry Zito WIN 3.00 8.00
CD Carlos Delgado RBI 3.00 8.00
CJ Chipper Jones AVG-RBI 4.00 10.00
CP Corey Patterson HR 3.00 8.00
CS Curt Schilling WIN 3.00 8.00
EC Eric Chavez HR 3.00 8.00
GA Garret Anderson RBI 3.00 8.00
GM Greg Maddux 2.62 ERA 4.00 10.00
GM1 Greg Maddux 1.56 ERA SP 6.00 15.00
GO Juan Gonzalez RBI 3.00 8.00
HM Hideki Matsui HR 15.00 40.00
HM1 Hideki Matsui RBI SP 20.00 50.00
HN Hideo Nomo WIN 6.00 15.00
IR Ivan Rodriguez AVG 4.00 10.00
IS Ichiro Suzuki HIT 10.00 25.00
IS1 Ichiro Suzuki SB SP 10.00 25.00
JB Jeff Bagwell RBI 4.00 10.00
JB1 Jeff Bagwell SLG SP 6.00 15.00
JD J.D. Drew RBI 3.00 8.00
JE Jim Edmonds RUN 3.00 8.00
JG Jason Giambi HR 3.00 8.00
JG1 Jason Giambi SLG 3.00 8.00
JL Javy Lopez NLCS 3.00 8.00
JP Jay Payton 3B 3.00 8.00
JS J.T. Snow GLV 3.00 8.00
JT Jim Thome HR 4.00 10.00
JT1 Jim Thome SLG 4.00 10.00
KE Jason Kendall RUN 3.00 8.00
KG Ken Griffey Jr. 40 HR 6.00 15.00
KG1 Ken Griffey Jr. 56 HR SP 8.00 20.00
KI Kazuhisa Ishii K 3.00 8.00
KS Kazuhiro Sasaki SV 3.00 8.00
KW Kerry Wood K 3.00 8.00
LB Lance Berkman HR 3.00 8.00
LG Luis Gonzalez RUN 3.00 8.00
LW Larry Walker AVG 3.00 8.00
MP Mike Piazza HR 6.00 15.00
MP1 Mike Piazza SLG 6.00 15.00
MR Manny Ramirez AVG 4.00 10.00
MSL Mike Sweeney AVG 3.00 8.00
MSW Mike Stanton Pants GM 3.00 8.00
MT Miguel Tejada RBI 3.00 8.00
MT1 Miguel Tejada GM SP 4.00 10.00
OV Omar Vizquel SAC 4.00 10.00
PB Pat Burrell HR 3.00 8.00
PB1 Pat Burrell RBI 3.00 8.00
PM Pedro Martinez K 4.00 10.00
RC Roger Clemens K 6.00 15.00
RC1 Roger Clemens ERA 6.00 15.00
RJ Randy Johnson K 4.00 10.00
RJ1 Randy Johnson ERA 4.00 10.00
RO Roy Oswalt WIN 3.00 8.00
RO1 Roy Oswalt PCT SP 4.00 10.00
RP Rafael Palmeiro RBI 4.00 10.00
RP1 Rafael Palmeiro 2B 4.00 10.00
SG Shawn Green HR 3.00 8.00
SG1 Shawn Green TB 3.00 8.00
SR Scott Rolen HR 4.00 10.00
SS Sammy Sosa 49 HR 4.00 10.00
SS1 Sammy Sosa 50 HR SP/170 6.00 15.00
TB Tony Batista HR 3.00 8.00
TG Troy Glaus HR 3.00 8.00
THE Todd Helton RBI 4.00 10.00
THU Tim Hudson IP 3.00 8.00
THU1 Tim Hudson GM SP 4.00 10.00
TP Troy Percival SV 3.00 8.00
VG Vladimir Guerrero HIT 4.00 10.00

2003 Upper Deck Lineup Time Jerseys

SERIES 1 STATED ODDS 1:96 HOBBY
BW Bernie Williams 4.00 10.00
CD Carlos Delgado 3.00 8.00
GM Greg Maddux 4.00 10.00
IS Ichiro Suzuki 10.00 25.00
JD J.D. Drew 3.00 8.00
JT Jim Thome 4.00 10.00
RC Roger Clemens SP 10.00 25.00
RJ Randy Johnson SP 8.00 20.00
SG Shawn Green 3.00 8.00
TH Todd Helton 4.00 10.00

2003 Upper Deck Magical Performances

SERIES 2 STATED ODDS 1:96 HOBBY
*GOLD: .6X TO 1.5X BASIC MAGIC
GOLD RANDOM INSERTS IN SER.2 PACKS
GOLD PRINT RUN 50 SERIAL #'d SETS
DUPE STARS EQUALLY VALUED
MP1 Hideki Matsui 6.00 15.00
MP2 Ken Griffey Jr. 6.00 15.00
MP3 Ichiro Suzuki 4.00 10.00
MP4 Ken Griffey Jr. 6.00 15.00
MP5 Hideo Nomo 3.00 8.00
MP6 Mickey Mantle 10.00 25.00
MP7 Ken Griffey Jr. 6.00 15.00
MP8 Barry Bonds 5.00 12.00
MP9 Mickey Mantle 10.00 25.00
MP10 Tom Seaver 2.00 5.00
MP11 Mike Piazza 3.00 8.00
MP12 Roger Clemens 4.00 10.00
MP13 Nolan Ryan 10.00 25.00
MP14 Nomar Garciaparra 2.00 5.00
MP15 Ernie Banks 3.00 8.00
MP16 Stan Musial 5.00 12.00
MP17 Mickey Mantle 10.00 25.00
MP18 Nolan Ryan 10.00 25.00
MP19 Nolan Ryan 10.00 25.00
MP20 Mickey Mantle 10.00 25.00
MP21 Ichiro Suzuki 4.00 10.00
MP22 Nolan Ryan 10.00 25.00
MP23 Tom Seaver 2.00 5.00
MP24 Ken Griffey Jr. 6.00 15.00
MP25 Hideo Nomo 3.00 8.00
MP26 Ken Griffey Jr. 6.00 15.00
MP27 Mark McGwire 5.00 12.00
MP28 Barry Bonds 5.00 12.00
MP29 Alex Rodriguez 4.00 10.00
MP30 Nolan Ryan 10.00 25.00
MP31 Mark McGwire 5.00 12.00
MP32 Nolan Ryan 10.00 25.00
MP33 Sammy Sosa 3.00 8.00
MP34 Ichiro Suzuki 4.00 10.00
MP35 Barry Bonds 5.00 12.00
MP36 Derek Jeter 8.00 20.00
MP37 Roger Clemens 4.00 10.00
MP38 Jason Giambi 1.25 3.00
MP39 Mickey Mantle 10.00 25.00
MP40 Ted Williams 6.00 15.00
MP41 Ted Williams 6.00 15.00
MP42 Ted Williams 6.00 15.00

2003 Upper Deck Mark of Greatness Autograph Jerseys

RANDOM INSERTS IN SERIES 1 PACKS
STATED PRINT RUNS LISTED BELOW
CARD MOG IS NOT SERIAL NUMBERED
MOG M.McGwire/400 * 125.00 250.00
MOGS M.McGwire Silver/70 250.00 400.00

2003 Upper Deck Masters with the Leather

COMPLETE SET (12) 8.00 20.00
SERIES 2 STATED ODDS 1:12
L1 Darin Erstad .40 1.00
L2 Andruw Jones .40 1.00
L3 Greg Maddux 1.25 3.00
L4 Nomar Garciaparra .60 1.50
L5 Torii Hunter .40 1.00
L6 Roberto Alomar .60 1.50
L7 Derek Jeter 2.50 6.00
L8 Eric Chavez .40 1.00
L9 Ichiro Suzuki 1.25 3.00
L10 Jim Edmonds .60 1.50
L11 Scott Rolen .60 1.50
L12 Alex Rodriguez 1.25 3.00

2003 Upper Deck Matsui Mania

COMMON CARD (HM1-HM18) 2.00 5.00
NO MANIA 25 PRICING AVAILABLE
HM1 Hideki Matsui 2.00 5.00
HM2 Hideki Matsui 2.00 5.00
HM3 Hideki Matsui 2.00 5.00
HM4 Hideki Matsui 2.00 5.00
HM5 Hideki Matsui 2.00 5.00
HM6 Hideki Matsui 2.00 5.00
HM7 Hideki Matsui 2.00 5.00
HM8 Hideki Matsui 2.00 5.00
HM9 Hideki Matsui 2.00 5.00
HM10 Hideki Matsui 2.00 5.00
HM11 Hideki Matsui 2.00 5.00
HM12 Hideki Matsui 2.00 5.00
HM13 Hideki Matsui 2.00 5.00
HM14 Hideki Matsui 2.00 5.00
HM15 Hideki Matsui 2.00 5.00
HM16 Hideki Matsui 2.00 5.00
HM17 Hideki Matsui 2.00 5.00
HM18 Hideki Matsui 2.00 5.00

2003 Upper Deck Mid-Summer Stars Swatches

SERIES 1 STATED ODDS 1:72
AJ Andruw Jones 4.00 10.00
AR Alex Rodriguez 6.00 15.00
BZ Barry Zito 3.00 8.00
CD Carlos Delgado 3.00 8.00
CS Curt Schilling 3.00 8.00
DE Darin Erstad 3.00 8.00
DW David Wells 3.00 8.00
EM Edgar Martinez 4.00 10.00
FG Freddy Garcia 3.00 8.00
FT Frank Thomas 4.00 10.00
HN Hideo Nomo 8.00 20.00

IS Ichiro Suzuki Turtleneck SP 20.00 50.00
JE Jim Edmonds SP * 4.00 10.00
JG Juan Gonzalez Pants 3.00 8.00
KS Kazuhiro Sasaki 3.00 8.00
MP Mike Piazza 6.00 15.00
MR Manny Ramirez 4.00 10.00
RC Roger Clemens 6.00 15.00
RJ Randy Johnson Shirt 4.00 10.00
RV Robin Ventura 4.00 10.00
SG Shawn Green SP 4.00 10.00
SS Sammy Sosa 4.00 10.00
TG Tom Glavine 4.00 10.00

2003 Upper Deck NL All-Star Swatches

SERIES 1 STATED ODDS 1:72 HOBBY
AL Al Leiter 3.00 8.00
CF Cliff Floyd 3.00 8.00
CS Curt Schilling 3.00 8.00
FM Fred McGriff 4.00 10.00
JV Jose Vidro 3.00 8.00
MH Mike Hampton 3.00 8.00
MM Matt Morris 3.00 8.00
RK Ryan Klesko 3.00 8.00
SC Sean Casey 3.00 8.00
TG Tom Glavine 4.00 10.00
TG Tony Gwynn 6.00 15.00
TH Trevor Hoffman 3.00 8.00

2003 Upper Deck National Pride Memorabilia

SERIES 2 ODDS 1:24 HOBBY/1:48 RETAIL
SP PRINT RUNS PROVIDED BY UPPER DECK
SP'S ARE NOT SERIAL-NUMBERED
ALL FEATURE PANTS UNLESS NOTED
AA Abe Alvarez 1.50 4.00
AH Aaron Hill 5.00 12.00
AJ A.J. Hinch Jsy 1.50 4.00
AK A.Kearns Right Jsy 1.50 4.00
AK1 A.Kearns Left Jsy SP/250 6.00 15.00
BH Bobby Hill Field Jsy 1.50 4.00
BH1 Bobby Hill Run Jsy SP/100 8.00 20.00
BS Brad Sullivan Wind Up 1.50 4.00
BS1 Brad Sullivan Throw SP/250 6.00 15.00
BZ Bob Zimmermann 1.50 4.00
CC Chad Cordero 1.50 4.00
CJ Conor Jackson 5.00 12.00
CQ Carlos Quentin 5.00 12.00
CS Clint Sammons 1.50 4.00
DP Dustin Pedroia 5.00 12.00
EM Eric Milton White Jsy 1.50 4.00
EM1 Eric Milton Blue Jsy SP/50 8.00 20.00
EP Eric Patterson 1.50 4.00
GJ Grant Johnson 1.50 4.00
HS Huston Street 2.50 6.00
JJ0 J.Jones White Jsy 1.50 4.00
JJ1 J.Jones Blue Jsy SP/250 6.00 15.00
JJE Jason Jennings Jsy 1.50 4.00
KB Kyle Bakker 1.50 4.00
KSA K.Saarloos Red Jsy 1.50 4.00
KSL Kyle Sleeth 1.50 4.00
KSA1 K.Saarloos Grey Jsy SP/250 6.00 15.00
LP Landon Powell 1.50 4.00
MA Michael Aubrey 4.00 10.00
MJ Mark Jurich 1.50 4.00
MP Mark Prior Pinstripes Jsy 2.50 6.00
MP1 Mark Prior Grey Jsy SP/100 10.00 25.00
PH Philip Humber 1.50 4.00
RF Robert Fick Jsy 1.50 4.00
RO R.Oswall Behind Jsy 2.50 6.00
RO1 R.Oswalt Beside Jsy SP/100 8.00 20.00
RW R.Weeks Glove-Chest 5.00 12.00
SB Sean Burroughs 1.50 4.00
SC Shane Costa 1.50 4.00
SF Sam Fuld 1.50 4.00
WL Wes Littleton 1.50 4.00

2003 Upper Deck Piece of the Action Game Ball

SERIES 2 ODDS 1:288 HOBBY/1:576 RETAIL
PRINT RUNS B/WN 10-175 COPIES PER
PRINT RUNS PROVIDED BY UPPER DECK
CARDS ARE NOT SERIAL-NUMBERED
NO PRICING ON QTY OF 25 OR LESS
AB Adrian Beltre/100 4.00 10.00
ARA Aramis Ramirez/100 4.00 10.00
ARO Alex Rodriguez/100 10.00 25.00
BA Bobby Abreu/125 4.00 10.00
BB Barry Bonds/125 15.00 40.00
BG Brian Giles/100 4.00 10.00
BW Bernie Williams/125 6.00 15.00
CJ Chipper Jones/62 10.00 25.00
CS Curt Schilling/100 4.00 10.00
DE Darin Erstad/125 4.00 10.00
DJ Derek Jeter/65 15.00 40.00
EM Edgar Martinez/125 6.00 15.00
FG Freddy Garcia/100 4.00 10.00
FT Frank Thomas/150 6.00 15.00
GA Garret Anderson/150 4.00 10.00
GS Gary Sheffield/100 4.00 10.00
HN Hideo Nomo/100 15.00 40.00
JG Juan Gonzalez/100 4.00 10.00
JK Jason Kendall/100 4.00 10.00
JT Jim Thome/125 6.00 15.00
JV Jose Vidro/100 4.00 10.00
KB Kevin Brown/100 4.00 10.00
KE Jeff Kent/150 4.00 10.00
KS Kazuhiro Sasaki/100 4.00 10.00
LG Luis Gonzalez/100 4.00 10.00
LW Larry Walker/150 4.00 10.00
MP Mike Piazza/150 10.00 25.00
PB Pat Burrell/150 4.00 10.00
PM Pedro Martinez/150 6.00 15.00
PN Phil Nevin/75 6.00 15.00
RJ Randy Johnson/100 6.00 15.00
RK Ryan Klesko/75 6.00 15.00
RP Rafael Palmeiro/150 6.00 15.00
RS Richie Sexson/160 4.00 10.00
SG Shawn Green/175 4.00 10.00
SS Sammy Sosa/85 10.00 25.00
TG Troy Glaus/150 4.00 10.00
THE Todd Helton/100 6.00 15.00
THO Trevor Hoffman/150 4.00 10.00
VG Vladimir Guerrero/50 10.00 25.00

2003 Upper Deck Piece of the Action Game Ball Gold

*GOLD: 1X TO 2.5X GAME BALL p/r 150-175
*GOLD: 1X TO 2.5X GAME BALL p/r 100-125
*GOLD: .6X TO 1.5X GAME BALL p/r 50-85

RANDOM INSERTS IN SERIES 2 PACKS
STATED PRINT RUN 50 SERIAL #'d SETS
IR Ivan Rodriguez 15.00 40.00

2003 Upper Deck Signed Game Jerseys

PRINT RUNS B/WN 150-350 COPIES PER
AR Alex Rodriguez/350 40.00 80.00
CR Cal Ripken/350 30.00 80.00
JG Jason Giambi/350 20.00 50.00
KG Ken Griffey Jr./350 40.00 80.00
MM Mark McGwire/150 250.00 400.00
RC Roger Clemens/350 25.00 60.00
SS Sammy Sosa/150 40.00 80.00

2003 Upper Deck Signed Game Jerseys Silver

RANDOM INSERTS IN SER.1 HOBBY PACKS
STATED PRINT RUN 75 SERIAL #'d SETS
JG Jason Giambi 30.00 60.00

2003 Upper Deck Slammin Sammy Autograph Jerseys

RANDOM INSERTS IN SERIES 1 PACKS
PRINT RUNS B/WN 25-384 COPIES PER
NO PRICING ON QTY OF 25 OR LESS
SST Sammy Sosa/384 40.00 80.00
SSTS Sammy Sosa Silver/66 125.00 200.00

2003 Upper Deck Star-Spangled Swatches

SERIES 1 STATED ODDS 1:72
AH Aaron Hill H 3.00 8.00
BS Brad Sullivan H 3.00 8.00
CC Chad Cordero H 3.00 8.00
CJ Conor Jackson Pants R 4.00 10.00
CQ Carlos Quentin H 4.00 10.00
DP Dustin Pedroia R 4.00 20.00
EP Eric Patterson H 3.00 8.00
GJ Grant Johnson H 3.00 8.00
HS Huston Street R 3.00 8.00
KB Kyle Bakker R 2.00 5.00
KS Kyle Sleeth R 3.00 8.00
LP Landon Powell R 3.00 8.00
MA Michael Aubrey H 3.00 8.00
PH Philip Humber R 3.00 8.00
RW Rickie Weeks H 6.00 15.00
SC Shane Costa R 2.00 5.00

2003 Upper Deck Superior Sluggers

COMPLETE SET (18) 12.50 30.00
SERIES 2 STATED ODDS 1:8
S1 Troy Glaus .40 1.00
S2 Chipper Jones 1.00 2.50
S3 Manny Ramirez 1.00 2.50
S4 Ken Griffey Jr. 2.00 5.00
S5 Jim Thome .60 1.50
S6 Todd Helton .60 1.50
S7 Lance Berkman .60 1.50
S8 Derek Jeter 2.50 6.00
S9 Vladimir Guerrero .60 1.50
S10 Mike Piazza 1.00 2.50
S11 Hideki Matsui 2.00 5.00
S12 Barry Bonds 1.50 4.00
S13 Mickey Mantle 3.00 8.00
S14 Alex Rodriguez 1.25 3.00
S15 Ted Williams 2.00 5.00
S16 Carlos Delgado .40 1.00
S17 Frank Thomas 1.00 2.50
S18 Adam Dunn .60 1.50

2003 Upper Deck Triple Game Jersey

GROUP A 150 SERIAL #'d SETS
GROUP B 75 SERIAL #'d SETS
GROUP C 25 SERIAL #'d SETS
NO GROUP C PRICING DUE TO SCARCITY
ARZ Johnson/Schilling/L.Gonz A 20.00 50.00
ATL Chipper/Maddux/Sheff B 12.00 30.00
CHC Sosa/Alou/Wood B 20.00 50.00
CIN Griffey/Casey/Dunn A 10.00 25.00
HOU Bagwell/Berkman/Biggio A 20.00 50.00
NYM Piazza/Alomar/Vaughn B 20.00 50.00
SEA Ichiro/Garcia/Boone B 60.00 120.00
TEX Palmeiro/A-Rod/Gonzalez A 20.00 50.00

2003 Upper Deck UD Bonus

SER.2 STATED ODDS 1:288 HOBBY
PRINT RUNS B/WN 2-201 COPIES PER
NO PRICING ON QTY OF 40 OR LESS
2 Josh Beckett 01 TP AU/55 12.50 30.00
3 C.Beltran 00 SPA AU/118 6.00 15.00
6 Barry Bonds 01 P 10.00 25.00
P Jsy/117
7 Lou Brock 00 LGD AU/198 10.00 25.00
8 Gary Carter 00 LGD AU/63 20.00 50.00
12 Roger Clemens 01 P 6.00 15.00
P Jsy/117
13 A.Dawson 00 LGD AU/140 6.00 15.00
14 J.D. Drew 00 SPA AU/55 8.00 20.00
15 Rollie Fingers 00 LGD AU/116 6.00 15.00
16 Rafael Furcal 00 SPA AU/87 6.00 15.00
18 Jason Giambi 00 SPA AU/106 6.00 15.00
20 Jason Giambi 01 P 4.00 10.00
P Jsy/97
21 Troy Glaus 00 SPA AU/110 10.00 25.00
28 Brandon Inge 01 TP AU/113 4.00 10.00
43 D.Mientkiewicz 00 BD Jsy/57 4.00 10.00
44 Dale Murphy 00 LGD AU/91 12.00 30.00
46 Jim Palmer 00 LGD AU/121 6.00 15.00
47 P.Reese 01 HOF Jsy/46 6.00 15.00
53 C.C. Sabathia 01 TP AU/64 8.00 20.00
56 Ben Sheets 01 TP AU/60 8.00 20.00
58 Alf Soriano 00 SPA AU/80 10.00 25.00
59 Sammy Sosa 01 P 6.00 15.00
P Jsy/77
63 Dave Winfield 00 YL Bat/53 4.00 10.00
64 B.Will/Ichiro 01 P/P Bat/87 20.00 50.00
65 Sosa/L.Gonz 01 P/P Bat/61 6.00 15.00

2003 Upper Deck UD Patch Logos

CJ Chipper Jones/52 50.00 120.00
FT Frank Thomas/52 50.00 120.00
GM Greg Maddux/50 60.00 150.00
KI Kazuhisa Ishii/54 20.00 50.00
RJ Randy Johnson/50 50.00 120.00

2003 Upper Deck UD Patch Logos Exclusives

KG Ken Griffey Jr./50 75.00 150.00
MP Mike Piazza/61 60.00 120.00
SS Sammy Sosa/60 15.00 40.00

2003 Upper Deck UD Patch Numbers

SERIES 1 STATED ODDS 1:7500
PRINT RUNS B/WN 27-91 COPIES PER
CARDS ARE NOT SERIAL-NUMBERED
NO PRICING ON QTY OF 40 OR LESS
BW Bernie Williams/66 40.00 80.00
FT Frank Thomas/91 40.00 80.00
KI Kazuhisa Ishii/63 30.00 60.00
RJ Randy Johnson/90 40.00 80.00

2003 Upper Deck UD Patch Numbers Exclusives

SERIES 1 STATED ODDS 1:7500
PRINT RUNS B/WN 56-100 COPIES PER
CARDS ARE NOT SERIAL-NUMBERED
AR Alex Rodriguez/56 75.00 150.00
JG Jason Giambi/68 30.00 60.00
KG Ken Griffey Jr./97 50.00 100.00
MG Mark McGwire/60 150.00 250.00
SS Sammy Sosa/100 40.00 80.00

2003 Upper Deck UD Patch Stripes

SERIES 1 STATED ODDS 1:7500
PRINT RUNS B/WN 43-73 COPIES PER
CARDS ARE NOT SERIAL-NUMBERED
BW Bernie Williams/58 40.00 80.00
CJ Chipper Jones/58 40.00 80.00
FT Frank Thomas/58 40.00 80.00
JB Jeff Bagwell/73 40.00 80.00
KI Kazuhisa Ishii/58 30.00 60.00
RJ Randy Johnson/58 40.00 80.00

2003 Upper Deck UD Patch Stripes Exclusives

SERIES 1 STATED ODDS 1:7500
PRINT RUNS B/WN 63-66 COPIES PER
CARDS ARE NOT SERIAL-NUMBERED
AR Alex Rodriguez/63 60.00 120.00
IS Ichiro Suzuki/63 150.00 250.00
JG Jason Giambi/66 30.00 60.00
KG Ken Griffey Jr./63 60.00 120.00
MG Mark McGwire/63 150.00 250.00
SS Sammy Sosa/63 60.00 120.00

2003 Upper Deck UD Superstar Slam Jerseys

SERIES 1 STATED ODDS 1:48 HOBBY
AR Alex Rodriguez 6.00 15.00
CJ Chipper Jones 4.00 10.00
FT Frank Thomas 4.00 10.00
JB Jeff Bagwell 4.00 10.00
JG Jason Giambi 3.00 8.00
KG Ken Griffey Jr. 6.00 15.00
LG Luis Gonzalez 3.00 8.00
MP Mike Piazza 6.00 15.00
SS Sammy Sosa 4.00 10.00
JGO Juan Gonzalez 3.00 8.00

2003 Upper Deck Gary Carter Hawaii Autograph

DISTRIBUTED AT 2003 HAWAII CONFERENCE
GC Gary Carter 20.00 50.00

2003 Upper Deck Star Rookie Hawaii

HM Hideki Matsui 30.00 80.00

2003 Upper Deck Star Rookie Sportsfest

COMPLETE SET 2.50 6.00
AM Alejandro Machado .40 1.00
HB Hank Blalock .40 1.00
HC Hee Seop Choi .40 1.00
HM Hideki Matsui 2.00 5.00
RB Rocco Baldelli .40 1.00
RH Runelvys Hernandez .40 1.00

2003 Upper Deck Magazine

COMPLETE SET (9) 8.00 20.00
UD2 Hideki Matsui 1.50 4.00
UD4 Ichiro Suzuki 1.25 3.00
UD7 Mickey Mantle 1.50 4.00

2004 Upper Deck

COMPLETE SERIES 1 (270) 20.00 50.00
COMPLETE SERIES 2 (270) 20.00 50.00
COMP.UPDATE SET (50) 7.50 15.00
COMMON (31-480/541-565) .10 .30
COMMON (1-30/481-540) .40 1.00
1-30/481-540 ARE NOT SHORT PRINTS
COMMON CARD (566-590) .20 .50
541-590 ONE SET PER '05 UD1 HOBBY BOX
UPDATE SET EXCH 1:480 '05 UD1 RETAIL
UPDATE SET EXCH.DEADLINE TBD
1 Dontrelle Willis SR .40 1.00
2 Edgar Gonzalez SR .40 1.00
3 Jose Reyes SR .60 1.50
4 Jae Weong Seo SR .40 1.00
5 Miguel Cabrera SR 1.00 2.50
6 Jesse Foppert SR .40 1.00
7 Mike Neu SR .40 1.00
8 Michael Nakamura SR .40 1.00
9 Luis Ayala SR .40 1.00
10 Jared Sandberg SR .40 1.00
11 Jhonny Peralta SR .40 1.00
12 Wil Ledezma SR .40 1.00
13 Jason Roach SR .40 1.00
14 Kirk Saarloos SR .40 1.00
15 Cliff Lee SR .60 1.50
16 Bobby Hill SR .40 1.00
17 Lyle Overbay SR .40 1.00
18 Josh Hall SR .40 1.00
19 Joe Thurston SR .40 1.00
20 Matt Kata SR .40 1.00
21 Jeremy Bonderman SR .40 1.00
22 Julio Manon SR .40 1.00
23 Rodrigo Rosario SR .40 1.00
24 Robby Hammock SR .40 1.00
25 David Sanders SR .40 1.00
26 Miguel Ojeda SR .40 1.00
27 Mark Teixeira SR .60 1.50
28 Franklyn German SR .40 1.00
29 Ken Harvey SR .40 1.00
30 Xavier Nady SR .40 1.00
31 Tim Salmon .12 .30
32 Troy Glaus .12 .30
33 Adam Kennedy .12 .30
34 David Eckstein .12 .30
35 Ben Molina .12 .30
36 Jarrod Washburn .12 .30
37 Ramon Ortiz .12 .30
38 Eric Chavez .12 .30
39 Miguel Tejada .20 .50
40 Chris Singleton .12 .30
41 Jermaine Dye .12 .30
42 John Halama .12 .30
43 Tim Hudson .20 .50
44 Barry Zito .20 .50
45 Ted Lilly .12 .30
46 Bobby Kielty .12 .30
47 Kelvim Escobar .12 .30
48 Josh Phelps .12 .30
49 Vernon Wells .12 .30
50 Roy Halladay .20 .50
51 Orlando Hudson .12 .30
52 Eric Hinske .12 .30
53 Brandon Backe .12 .30
54 Dewon Brazelton .12 .30
55 Ben Grieve .12 .30
56 Aubrey Huff .12 .30
57 Toby Hall .12 .30
58 Rocco Baldelli .12 .30
59 Al Martin .12 .30
60 Brandon Phillips .12 .30
61 Omar Vizquel .20 .50
62 C.C. Sabathia .20 .50
63 Milton Bradley .12 .30
64 Ricky Gutierrez .12 .30
65 Matt Lawton .12 .30
66 Danys Baez .12 .30
67 Ichiro Suzuki .40 1.00
68 Randy Winn .12 .30
69 Carlos Guillen .12 .30
70 Mark McLemore .12 .30
71 Dan Wilson .12 .30
72 Jamie Moyer .12 .30
73 Joel Pineiro .12 .30
74 Edgar Martinez .20 .50
75 Tony Batista .12 .30
76 Jay Gibbons .12 .30
77 Jeff Conine .12 .30
78 Melvin Mora .12 .30
79 Geronimo Gil .12 .30
80 Rodrigo Lopez .12 .30
81 Jorge Julio .12 .30
82 Rafael Palmeiro .20 .50
83 Juan Gonzalez .12 .30
84 Mike Young .12 .30
85 Alex Rodriguez .40 1.00
86 Einar Diaz .12 .30
87 Kevin Mench .12 .30
88 Hank Blalock .12 .30
89 Pedro Martinez .20 .50
90 Byung-Hyun Kim .12 .30
91 Derek Lowe .12 .30
92 Jason Varitek .30 .75
93 Manny Ramirez .30 .75
94 John Burkett .12 .30
95 Todd Walker .12 .30
96 Nomar Garciaparra .20 .50
97 Trot Nixon .12 .30
98 Mike Sweeney .12 .30
99 Carlos Febles .12 .30
100 Mike MacDougal .12 .30
101 Raul Ibanez .20 .50
102 Jason Grimsley .12 .30
103 Chris George .12 .30
104 Brent Mayne .12 .30
105 Dmitri Young .12 .30
106 Eric Munson .12 .30
107 A.J. Hinch .12 .30
108 Andres Torres .12 .30
109 Bobby Higginson .12 .30
110 Shane Halter .12 .30
111 Matt Walbeck .12 .30
112 Torii Hunter .12 .30
113 Doug Mientkiewicz .12 .30
114 Lew Ford .12 .30
115 Eric Milton .12 .30
116 Eddie Guardado .12 .30
117 Cristian Guzman .12 .30
118 Corey Koskie .12 .30
119 Magglio Ordonez .20 .50
120 Mark Buehrle .20 .50
121 Billy Koch .12 .30
122 Jose Valentin .12 .30
123 Paul Konerko .20 .50
124 Carlos Lee .12 .30
125 Jon Garland .12 .30
126 Jason Giambi .12 .30
127 Derek Jeter .75 2.00
128 Roger Clemens .40 1.00
129 Andy Pettitte .20 .50
130 Jorge Posada .20 .50
131 David Wells .12 .30
132 Hideki Matsui .50 1.25
133 Mike Mussina .20 .50
134 Jeff Bagwell .20 .50
135 Craig Biggio .20 .50
136 Morgan Ensberg .12 .30
137 Richard Hidalgo .12 .30
138 Brad Ausmus .12 .30
139 Roy Oswalt .20 .50
140 Billy Wagner .12 .30
141 Octavio Dotel .12 .30
142 Gary Sheffield .12 .30
143 Andruw Jones .12 .30
144 John Smoltz .30 .75
145 Rafael Furcal .12 .30
146 Javy Lopez .12 .30
147 Shane Reynolds .12 .30
148 Horacio Ramirez .12 .30
149 Mike Hampton .12 .30
150 Jung Bong .12 .30
151 Ruben Quevedo .12 .30
152 Ben Sheets .12 .30
153 Geoff Jenkins .12 .30
154 Royce Clayton .12 .30
155 Glendon Rusch .12 .30
156 John Vander Wal .12 .30
157 Scott Podsednik .12 .30
158 Jim Edmonds .20 .50
159 Tino Martinez .20 .50
160 Albert Pujols .40 1.00
161 Matt Morris .12 .30
162 Woody Williams .12 .30
163 Edgar Renteria .12 .30
164 Jason Isringhausen .12 .30
165 Jason Simontacchi .12 .30
166 Kerry Robinson .12 .30
167 Sammy Sosa .30 .75
168 Joe Borowski .12 .30
169 Tony Womack .12 .30
170 Antonio Alfonseca .12 .30
171 Corey Patterson .12 .30
172 Mark Prior .20 .50
173 Moises Alou .12 .30
174 Matt Clement .12 .30
175 Randall Simon .12 .30
176 Randy Johnson .30 .75
177 Luis Gonzalez .12 .30
178 Craig Counsell .12 .30
179 Miguel Batista .12 .30
180 Steve Finley .12 .30
181 Brandon Webb .12 .30
182 Danny Bautista .12 .30
183 Oscar Villarreal .12 .30
184 Shawn Green .12 .30
185 Brian Jordan .12 .30
186 Fred McGriff .12 .30
187 Andy Ashby .12 .30
188 Rickey Henderson .30 .75
189 Dave Roberts .20 .50
190 Eric Gagne .12 .30
191 Kazuhisa Ishii .12 .30
192 Adrian Beltre .30 .75
193 Vladimir Guerrero .20 .50
194 Livan Hernandez .12 .30
195 Ron Calloway .12 .30
196 Sun Woo Kim .12 .30
197 Wil Cordero .12 .30
198 Brad Wilkerson .12 .30
199 Orlando Cabrera .12 .30
200 Barry Bonds .50 1.25
201 Ray Durham .12 .30
202 Andres Galarraga .20 .50
203 Benito Santiago .12 .30
204 Jose Cruz Jr. .12 .30
205 Jason Schmidt .12 .30
206 Kirk Rueter .12 .30
207 Felix Rodriguez .12 .30
208 Mike Lowell .12 .30
209 Luis Castillo .12 .30
210 Derrek Lee .12 .30
211 Andy Fox .12 .30
212 Tommy Phelps .12 .30
213 Todd Hollandsworth .12 .30
214 Brad Penny .12 .30
215 Juan Pierre .12 .30
216 Mike Piazza .30 .75
217 Jae Weong Seo .12 .30
218 Ty Wigginton .12 .30
219 Al Leiter .12 .30
220 Roger Cedeno .12 .30
221 Timo Perez .12 .30
222 Aaron Heilman .12 .30
223 Pedro Astacio .12 .30
224 Joe McEwing .12 .30
225 Ryan Klesko .12 .30
226 Brian Giles .12 .30
227 Mark Kotsay .12 .30
228 Brian Lawrence .12 .30
229 Rod Beck .12 .30
230 Trevor Hoffman .20 .50
231 Sean Burroughs .12 .30
232 Bob Abreu .12 .30
233 Jim Thome .20 .50
234 David Bell .12 .30
235 Jimmy Rollins .20 .50
236 Mike Lieberthal .12 .30
237 Vicente Padilla .12 .30
238 Randy Wolf .12 .30
239 Reggie Sanders .12 .30
240 Jason Kendall .12 .30
241 Jack Wilson .12 .30
242 Jose Hernandez .12 .30
243 Kip Wells .12 .30
244 Carlos Rivera .12 .30
245 Craig Wilson .12 .30
246 Adam Dunn .20 .50
247 Sean Casey .12 .30
248 Danny Graves .12 .30
249 Ryan Dempster .12 .30
250 Barry Larkin .20 .50
251 Reggie Taylor .12 .30
252 Wily Mo Pena .12 .30
253 Larry Walker .20 .50
254 Mark Sweeney .12 .30
255 Preston Wilson .12 .30
256 Jason Jennings .12 .30
257 Charles Johnson .12 .30
258 Jay Payton .12 .30
259 Chris Stynes .12 .30
260 Juan Uribe .12 .30
261 Hideki Matsui SH CL .50 1.25
262 Barry Bonds SH CL .50 1.25
263 Dontrelle Willis SH CL .12 .30
264 Kevin Millwood SH CL .12 .30
265 Billy Wagner SH CL .12 .30
266 Rocco Baldelli SH CL .12 .30
267 Roger Clemens SH CL .40 1.00
268 Rafael Palmeiro SH CL .20 .50
269 Miguel Cabrera SH CL .30 .75
270 Jose Contreras SH CL .12 .30
271 Aaron Sele .12 .30
272 Bartolo Colon .12 .30
273 Darin Erstad .12 .30
274 Francisco Rodriguez .20 .50
275 Garret Anderson .12 .30
276 Jose Guillen .12 .30
277 Troy Percival .12 .30
278 Alex Cintron .12 .30
279 Casey Fossum .12 .30
280 Elmer Dessens .12 .30
281 Jose Valverde .12 .30
282 Matt Mantei .12 .30
283 Richie Sexson .12 .30
284 Roberto Alomar .20 .50
285 Shea Hillenbrand .12 .30
286 Chipper Jones .30 .75
287 Greg Maddux .40 1.00
288 J.D. Drew .12 .30
289 Marcus Giles .12 .30
290 Mike Hessman .12 .30
291 John Thomson .12 .30
292 Russ Ortiz .12 .30
293 Adam Loewen .12 .30
294 Jack Cust .12 .30
295 Jerry Hairston Jr. .12 .30
296 Kurt Ainsworth .12 .30
297 Luis Matos .12 .30
298 Marty Cordova .12 .30
299 Sidney Ponson .12 .30
300 Bill Mueller .12 .30
301 Curt Schilling .20 .50
302 David Ortiz .30 .75
303 Johnny Damon .20 .50
304 Keith Foulke Sox .12 .30
305 Pokey Reese .12 .30
306 Scott Williamson .12 .30
307 Tim Wakefield .20 .50
308 Alex S. Gonzalez .12 .30
309 Aramis Ramirez .12 .30
310 Carlos Zambrano .20 .50
311 Juan Cruz .12 .30
312 Kerry Wood .12 .30
313 Kyle Farnsworth .12 .30
314 Aaron Rowand .12 .30
315 Esteban Loaiza .12 .30
316 Frank Thomas .30 .75
317 Joe Borchard .12 .30
318 Joe Crede .12 .30
319 Miguel Olivo .12 .30
320 Willie Harris .12 .30
321 Aaron Harang .12 .30
322 Austin Kearns .12 .30
323 Brandon Claussen .12 .30
324 Brandon Larson .12 .30
325 Ryan Freel .12 .30
326 Ken Griffey Jr. .60 1.50
327 Ryan Wagner .12 .30
328 Alex Escobar .12 .30
329 Coco Crisp .12 .30
330 David Riske .12 .30
331 Jody Gerut .12 .30
332 Josh Bard .12 .30
333 Travis Hafner .12 .30
334 Chin-Hui Tsao .12 .30
335 Denny Stark .12 .30
336 Jeromy Burnitz .12 .30
337 Shawn Chacon .12 .30
338 Todd Helton .20 .50
339 Vinny Castilla .12 .30
340 Alex Sanchez .12 .30
341 Carlos Pena .20 .50
342 Fernando Vina .12 .30
343 Jason Johnson .12 .30
344 Matt Anderson .12 .30
345 Mike Maroth .12 .30
346 Rondell White .12 .30
347 A.J. Burnett .12 .30
348 Alex Gonzalez .12 .30
349 Armando Benitez .12 .30
350 Carl Pavano .12 .30
351 Hee Seop Choi .12 .30
352 Ivan Rodriguez .20 .50
353 Josh Beckett .12 .30
354 Josh Willingham .20 .50
355 Adam Everett .12 .30
356 Brandon Duckworth .12 .30
357 Jason Lane .12 .30
358 Jeff Kent .12 .30
359 Joriomo Robertson .12 .30
360 Lance Berkman .20 .50
361 Wade Miller .12 .30
362 Aaron Guiel .12 .30
363 Angel Berroa .12 .30
364 Carlos Beltran .20 .50
365 David DeJesus .12 .30
366 Desi Relaford .12 .30
367 Joe Randa .12 .30
368 Runelvys Hernandez .12 .30
369 Edwin Jackson .12 .30
370 Hideo Nomo .30 .75
371 Jeff Weaver .12 .30
372 Juan Encarnacion .12 .30
373 Odalis Perez .12 .30
374 Paul Lo Duca .12 .30
375 Robin Ventura .12 .30
376 Bill Hall .12 .30
377 Chad Moeller .12 .30
378 Chris Capuano .12 .30
379 Junior Spivey .12 .30
380 Rickie Weeks .12 .30
381 Wes Helms .12 .30
382 Brad Radke .12 .30
383 Jacque Jones .12 .30
384 Joe Mays .12 .30
385 Joe Nathan .12 .30
386 Johan Santana .20 .50
387 Nick Punto .12 .30
388 Shannon Stewart .12 .30
389 Carl Everett .12 .30
390 Claudio Vargas .12 .30
391 Jose Vidro .12 .30
392 Nick Johnson .12 .30
393 Rocky Biddle .12 .30
394 Tony Armas Jr. .12 .30
395 Braden Looper .12 .30
396 Cliff Floyd .12 .30
397 Jason Phillips .12 .30
398 Mike Cameron .12 .30
399 Tom Glavine .20 .50
400 Kenny Lofton .12 .30
401 Alfonso Soriano .20 .50
402 Bernie Williams .20 .50
403 Javier Vazquez .12 .30
404 Jon Lieber .12 .30
405 Jose Contreras .12 .30
406 Kevin Brown .12 .30
407 Mariano Rivera .40 1.00
408 Arthur Rhodes .12 .30
409 Eric Byrnes .12 .30
410 Erubiel Durazo .12 .30
411 Graham Koonce .12 .30
412 Marco Scutaro .20 .50
413 Mark Mulder .12 .30
414 Mark Redman .12 .30
415 Rich Harden .12 .30
416 Brett Myers .12 .30
417 Chase Utley .20 .50
418 Kevin Millwood .12 .30
419 Marlon Byrd .12 .30
420 Pat Burrell .12 .30
421 Placido Polanco .12 .30
422 Tim Worrell .12 .30
423 Jason Bay .20 .50
424 Josh Fogg .12 .30
425 Kris Benson .12 .30
426 Mike Gonzalez .12 .30
427 Oliver Perez .12 .30
428 Tike Redman .12 .30
429 Adam Eaton .12 .30
430 Ismael Valdes .12 .30
431 Jake Peavy .12 .30
432 Khalil Greene .20 .50
433 Mark Loretta .12 .30
434 Phil Nevin .12 .30
435 Ramon Hernandez .12 .30
436 A.J. Pierzynski .12 .30
437 Edgardo Alfonzo .12 .30
438 J.T. Snow .12 .30
439 Jerome Williams .12 .30
440 Marquis Grissom .12 .30
441 Robb Nen .12 .30
442 Bret Boone .12 .30
443 Freddy Garcia .12 .30
444 Gil Meche .12 .30
445 John Olerud .12 .30
446 Rich Aurilia .12 .30
447 Shigetoshi Hasegawa .12 .30
448 Bo Hart .12 .30
449 Danny Haren .12 .30
450 Jason Marquis .12 .30
451 Marlon Anderson .12 .30
452 Scott Rolen .20 .50
453 So Taguchi .12 .30
454 Carl Crawford .20 .50
455 Delmon Young .20 .50
456 Geoff Blum .12 .30
457 Jesus Colome .12 .30
458 Jonny Gomes .12 .30
459 Lance Carter .12 .30
460 Robert Fick .12 .30
461 Chan Ho Park .20 .50
462 Francisco Cordero .12 .30
463 Jeff Nelson .12 .30
464 Jeff Zimmerman .12 .30
465 Kenny Rogers .12 .30
466 Aquilino Lopez .12 .30
467 Carlos Delgado .12 .30
468 Frank Catalanotto .12 .30
469 Reed Johnson .12 .30
470 Pat Hentgen .12 .30
471 Curt Schilling SH CL .20 .50
472 Gary Sheffield SH CL .12 .30
473 Javier Vazquez SH CL .12 .30
474 Kazuo Matsui SH CL .20 .50
475 Kevin Brown SH CL .12 .30
476 Rafael Palmeiro SH CL .20 .50
477 Richie Sexson SH CL .12 .30
478 Roger Clemens SH CL .40 1.00
479 Vladimir Guerrero SH CL .20 .50
480 Alex Rodriguez SH CL .40 1.00
481 Jake Woods SR RC .40 1.00
482 Tim Bittner SR RC .40 1.00
483 Brandon Medders SR RC .40 1.00
484 Casey Daigle SR RC .40 1.00
485 Jerry Gil SR RC .40 1.00
486 Mike Gosling SR RC .40 1.00
487 Jose Capellan SR RC .40 1.00
488 Onil Joseph SR RC .40 1.00
489 Roman Colon SR RC .40 1.00
490 Dave Crouthers SR RC .40 1.00
491 Eddy Rodriguez SR RC .40 1.00
492 Franklyn Gracesqui SR RC .40 1.00
493 Jamie Brown SR RC .40 1.00
494 Jerome Gamble SR RC .40 1.00
495 Tim Hamulack SR RC .40 1.00
496 Carlos Vasquez SR RC .40 1.00
497 Renyel Pinto SR RC .40 1.00
498 Ronny Cedeno SR RC .40 1.00
499 Enemencio Pacheco SR RC .40 1.00
500 Ryan Meaux SR RC .40 1.00
501 Ryan Wing SR RC .40 1.00
502 Shingo Takatsu SR RC .40 1.00
503 William Bergolla SR RC .40 1.00
504 Ivan Ochoa SR RC .40 1.00
505 Mariano Gomez SR RC .40 1.00
506 Justin Hampson SR RC .40 1.00
507 Justin Huisman SR RC .40 1.00
508 Scott Dohmann SR RC .40 1.00
509 Donnie Kelly SR RC .60 1.50
510 Chris Aguila SR RC .40 1.00
511 Lincoln Holdzkom SR RC .40 1.00
512 Freddy Guzman SR RC .40 1.00
513 Hector Gimenez SR RC .40 1.00
514 Jorge Vasquez SR RC .40 1.00
515 Jason Frasor SR RC .40 1.00
516 Chris Saenz SR RC .40 1.00
517 Dennis Sarfate SR RC .40 1.00
518 Colby Miller SR RC .40 1.00
519 Jason Bartlett SR RC 1.25 3.00
520 Chad Bentz SR RC .40 1.00
521 Josh Labandeira SR RC .40 1.00
522 Shawn Hill SR RC .40 1.00
523 Kazuo Matsui SR RC .60 1.50
524 Carlos Hines SR RC .40 1.00
525 Mike Vento SR RC .40 1.00
526 Scott Proctor SR RC .40 1.00
527 Sean Henn SR RC .40 1.00
528 David Aardsma SR RC .40 1.00
529 Ian Snell SR RC .40 1.00
530 Mike Johnston SR RC .40 1.00
531 Akinori Otsuka SR RC .40 1.00
532 Rusty Tucker SR RC .40 1.00
533 Justin Knoedler SR RC .40 1.00
534 Merkin Valdez SR RC .40 1.00

535 Greg Dobbs SR RC .40 1.00
536 Justin Leone SR RC .40 1.00
537 Shawn Camp SR RC .40 1.00
538 Edwin Moreno SR RC .40 1.00
539 Angel Chavez SR RC .40 1.00
540 Jesse Harper SR RC .40 1.00
541 Alex Rodriguez .40 1.00
542 Roger Clemens .40 1.00
543 Andy Pettitte .20 .50
544 Vladimir Guerrero .20 .50
545 David Wells .12 .30
546 Derrek Lee .12 .30
547 Carlos Beltran .20 .50
548 Orlando Cabrera Sox .12 .30
549 Paul Lo Duca .12 .30
550 Dave Roberts .20 .50
551 Guillermo Mota .12 .30
552 Steve Finley .12 .30
553 Juan Encarnacion .12 .30
554 Larry Walker .20 .50
555 Ty Wigginton .12 .30
556 Doug Mientkiewicz .12 .30
557 Roberto Alomar .20 .50
558 B.J. Upton .20 .50
559 Brad Penny .12 .30
560 Hee Seop Choi .12 .30
561 David Wright .25 .60
562 Nomar Garciaparra .20 .50
563 Felix Rodriguez .12 .30
564 Victor Zambrano .12 .30
565 Kris Benson .12 .30
566 Aarom Baldiris SR RC .20 .50
567 Joey Gathright SR RC .20 .50
568 Charles Thomas SR RC .20 .50
569 Brian Dallimore SR RC .20 .50
570 Chris Oxspring SR RC .20 .50
571 Chris Shelton SR RC .20 .50
572 Dioner Navarro SR RC .30 .75
573 Edwardo Sierra SR RC .20 .50
574 Fernando Nieve SR RC .20 .50
575 Frank Francisco SR RC .20 .50
576 Jeff Bennett SR RC .20 .50
577 Justin Lehr SR RC .20 .50
578 John Gall SR RC .20 .50
579 Jorge Sequea SR RC .20 .50
580 Justin Germano SR RC .20 .50
581 Kazuhito Tadano SR RC .20 .50
582 Kevin Cave SR RC .20 .50
583 Jesse Crain SR RC .30 .75
584 Luis A. Gonzalez SR RC .20 .50
585 Michael Wuertz SR RC .20 .50
586 Orlando Rodriguez SR RC .20 .50
587 Phil Stockman SR RC .20 .50
588 Ramon Ramirez SR RC .20 .50
589 Roberto Novoa SR RC .20 .50
590 Scott Kazmir SR RC 1.00 2.50

2004 Upper Deck Glossy
COMP.FACT.SET (590) 70.00 100.00
*GLOSSY: .75X TO 2X BASIC
ISSUED ONLY IN FACTORY SET FORM

2004 Upper Deck A Piece of History 500 Club
SERIES 1 STATED ODDS 1:8700
STATED PRINT RUN 350 SERIAL #'D CARDS
504HR Rafael Palmeiro 150.00 300.00

2004 Upper Deck Authentic Stars Jersey
SERIES 1 ODDS 1:48 HOBBY, 1:96 RETAIL
*GOLD: .75X TO 2X BASIC AS JSY
GOLD RANDOM INSERTS IN SERIES 1 PACKS
GOLD PRINT RUN 100 SERIAL #'d SETS
AJ Andruw Jones 4.00 10.00
AP Albert Pujols 6.00 15.00
AR Alex Rodriguez 4.00 10.00
AS Alfonso Soriano 3.00 8.00
BA Bob Abreu 3.00 8.00
BW Bernie Williams 4.00 10.00
BZ Barry Zito 3.00 8.00
CD Carlos Delgado 3.00 8.00
CJ Chipper Jones 4.00 10.00
CS Curt Schilling 3.00 8.00
DE Darin Erstad 3.00 8.00
EC Eric Chavez 3.00 8.00
FT Frank Thomas 4.00 10.00
GM Greg Maddux 4.00 10.00
HB Hank Blalock 3.00 8.00
HM Hideki Matsui 8.00 20.00
IR Ivan Rodriguez 4.00 10.00
IS Ichiro Suzuki 10.00 25.00
JB Jeff Bagwell 4.00 10.00
JD J.D. Drew 3.00 8.00
JG Jason Giambi 3.00 8.00
JH Josh Beckett 3.00 8.00
JK Jeff Kent 3.00 8.00
KG Ken Griffey Jr. 6.00 15.00
LW Larry Walker 3.00 8.00
MI Mike Piazza 4.00 10.00
MP Mark Prior 4.00 10.00
MT Mark Teixeira 4.00 10.00
PM Pedro Martinez 4.00 10.00
PN Phil Nevin 3.00 8.00
RB Rocco Baldelli 3.00 8.00
RC Roger Clemens 6.00 15.00
RJ Randy Johnson 4.00 10.00
RO Roberto Alomar 4.00 10.00
SG Shawn Green 3.00 8.00
SS Sammy Sosa 4.00 10.00
TG Troy Glaus 3.00 8.00
TH Todd Helton 4.00 10.00
TL Tom Glavine 4.00 10.00
TM Tino Martinez 4.00 10.00
TO Torii Hunter 3.00 8.00
VG Vladimir Guerrero 4.00 10.00

2004 Upper Deck Authentic Stars Jersey Update
UPDATE GU ODDS 1:12 '04 UPDATE SETS
STATED PRINT RUN 75 SERIAL #'d SETS
AK Austin Kearns 4.00 10.00
CB Carlos Beltran 4.00 10.00
DJ Derek Jeter 8.00 20.00
HA Roy Halladay 4.00 10.00
HN Hideo Nomo 10.00 25.00
HU Tim Hudson 4.00 10.00
JE Jim Edmonds 4.00 10.00
JR Jose Reyes 4.00 10.00
JT Jim Thome 6.00 15.00
KW Kerry Wood 4.00 10.00
LB Lance Berkman 4.00 10.00
MO Magglio Ordonez 4.00 10.00
MR Manny Ramirez 6.00 15.00
OS Roy Oswalt 4.00 10.00
PW Preston Wilson 4.00 10.00
RF Rafael Furcal 4.00 10.00
RH Rich Harden 4.00 10.00
RP Rafael Palmeiro 6.00 15.00
SR Scott Rolen 6.00 15.00
TE Miguel Tejada 4.00 10.00
VW Vernon Wells 4.00 10.00
WE Brandon Webb 4.00 10.00

2004 Upper Deck Awesome Honors
COMPLETE SET (10) 8.00 20.00
SERIES 2 STATED ODDS 1:12 H/R
1 Albert Pujols 1.25 3.00
2 Alex Rodriguez 1.25 3.00
3 Angel Berroa .40 1.00
4 Dontrelle Willis .40 1.00
5 Eric Gagne .40 1.00
6 Garret Anderson .40 1.00
7 Ivan Rodriguez .60 1.50
8 Josh Beckett .40 1.00
9 Mariano Rivera 1.25 3.00
10 Roy Halladay .60 1.50

2004 Upper Deck Awesome Honors Jersey
*GOLD: .6X TO 1.5X BASIC
GOLD PRINT RUN 165 SERIAL #'d SETS
OVERALL SER.2 GU ODDS 1:12 H, 1:24 R
AJ Andruw Jones GG 3.00 8.00
AP Albert Pujols PC 6.00 15.00
AP1 Albert Pujols HA 6.00 15.00
AP2 Albert Pujols POM 6.00 15.00
AR Alex Rodriguez MVP 5.00 12.00
AR1 Alex Rodriguez GG 5.00 12.00
AR2 Alex Rodriguez HA 5.00 12.00
AR3 Alex Rodriguez POM 5.00 12.00
AS Alfonso Soriano POM 2.00 5.00
BB Bret Boone GG 2.00 5.00
BM Ben Molina GG 2.00 5.00
DL Derrek Lee GG 3.00 8.00
DW Dontrelle Willis ROY 3.00 8.00
EC Eric Chavez GG 2.00 5.00
EG Eric Gagne CY 2.00 5.00
EG1 Eric Gagne RA 2.00 5.00
EM Edgar Martinez POM 3.00 8.00
GA Garret Anderson AS MVP 2.00 5.00
HU Torii Hunter GG 2.00 5.00
IR Ivan Rodriguez NLCS MVP 3.00 8.00
IS Ichiro Suzuki GG 10.00 25.00
JB Josh Beckett WS MVP 2.00 5.00
JE Jim Edmonds GG 2.00 5.00
JG Jason Giambi POM 2.00 5.00
JM Jamie Moyer MAN 2.00 5.00
JO John Olerud GG 2.00 5.00
JS John Smoltz MAN 3.00 8.00
JT Jim Thome POM 3.00 8.00
LC Luis Castillo GG 2.00 5.00
MC Mike Cameron GG 2.00 5.00
MH Mike Hampton GG 2.00 5.00
MO Magglio Ordonez POM 2.00 5.00
MR Mariano Rivera ALCS MVP 3.00 8.00
MU Mike Mussina GG 3.00 8.00
RH Roy Halladay CY 2.00 5.00
SR Scott Rolen GG 3.00 8.00
TH Todd Helton POM 3.00 8.00
VG Vladimir Guerrero POM 3.00 8.00

2004 Upper Deck Awesome Honors Jersey Update
UPDATE GU ODDS 1:12 '04 UPDATE SETS
STATED PRINT RUN 75 SERIAL #'d SETS
AB Angel Berroa 4.00 10.00
AP Albert Pujols 10.00 25.00
AS Alfonso Soriano 4.00 10.00
BE Adrian Beltre 4.00 10.00
BG Brian Giles 4.00 10.00
DL Derrek Lee 6.00 15.00
EG Eric Gagne 4.00 10.00
GS Gary Sheffield 4.00 10.00
IR Ivan Rodriguez 6.00 15.00
JM Joe Mauer 4.00 10.00
KB Kevin Brown 4.00 10.00
KM Kazuo Matsui 4.00 10.00
MC Miguel Cabrera 6.00 15.00
PE Andy Pettitte 6.00 15.00
RC Roger Clemens 10.00 25.00
RS Richie Sexson 4.00 10.00
SC Curt Schilling 6.00 15.00
SP Scott Podsednik 4.00 10.00
VA Javier Vazquez 4.00 10.00

2004 Upper Deck First Pitch Inserts
SERIES 1 STATED ODDS 1:72
CARD SP9 DOES NOT EXIST
SP7 LeBron James 10.00 25.00
SP8 Gordie Howe 4.00 10.00
SP10 Ernie Banks 4.00 10.00
SP11 General Tommy Franks 2.00 5.00
SP12 Ben Affleck 4.00 10.00
SP13 Halle Berry UER 4.00 10.00
SP14 George H.W. Bush 2.00 5.00
SP15 George W. Bush 4.00 10.00

2004 Upper Deck Game Winners Bat
*GOLD: .6X TO 1.5X BASIC
GOLD PRINT RUN 50 SERIAL #'d SETS
OVERALL SER.2 GU ODDS 1:12 H, 1:24 R
AG Alex Gonzalez 3.00 8.00
AJ Andruw Jones 4.00 10.00
AP Albert Pujols 8.00 20.00
AS Alfonso Soriano 3.00 8.00
BA Bobby Abreu 3.00 8.00
BW Bernie Williams 4.00 10.00
CJ Chipper Jones 4.00 10.00
CP Corey Patterson 3.00 8.00
DE Darin Erstad 3.00 8.00
DJ Derek Jeter 10.00 25.00
GS Gary Sheffield 3.00 8.00
HB Hank Blalock 3.00 8.00
HM Hideki Matsui 12.50 30.00
HU Torii Hunter 3.00 8.00
IR Ivan Rodriguez 4.00 10.00
JB Jeff Bagwell 4.00 10.00
JE Jim Edmonds 3.00 8.00
JG Jason Giambi 3.00 8.00
JP Jorge Posada 4.00 10.00
JT Jim Thome 4.00 10.00
MC Miguel Cabrera 4.00 10.00
ML Mike Lowell 3.00 8.00
MO Magglio Ordonez 3.00 8.00
MP Mike Piazza 6.00 15.00
MT Mark Teixeira 4.00 10.00
RF Rafael Furcal 3.00 8.00
RH Ramon Hernandez 3.00 8.00
RK Ryan Klesko 3.00 8.00
SG Shawn Green 3.00 8.00
SR Scott Rolen 4.00 10.00
TE Miguel Tejada 3.00 8.00
TG Troy Glaus 3.00 8.00
TH Todd Helton 4.00 10.00
TN Trot Nixon 3.00 8.00
VG Vladimir Guerrero 4.00 10.00

2004 Upper Deck Going Deep Bat
SERIES 1 ODDS 1:288 HOB, 1:576 RET
SP PRINT RUNS B/WN 12-123 COPIES PER
SP PRINT RUNS PROVIDED BY UPPER DECK
NO PRICING ON QTY OF 41 OR LESS
GOLD RANDOM INSERTS IN PACKS
GOLD PRINT RUN 50 SERIAL #'d SETS
NO GOLD PRICING DUE TO SCARCITY
AP Albert Pujols 10.00 25.00
AS Alfonso Soriano SP/53 4.00 10.00
BA Bob Abreu SP/110 4.00 10.00
BW Bernie Williams SP/56 6.00 15.00
CB Craig Biggio SP/89 6.00 15.00
CJ Chipper Jones SP/69 6.00 15.00
CS Curt Schilling SP/57 4.00 10.00
DE Darin Erstad 4.00 10.00
DM Doug Mientkiewicz SP/123 4.00 10.00
GA Garret Anderson 4.00 10.00
HM Hideki Matsui SP/70 15.00 40.00
HN Hideo Nomo 6.00 15.00
JB Jeff Bagwell SP/92 6.00 15.00
JE Jim Edmonds SP 4.00 10.00
JL Javy Lopez SP/77 4.00 10.00
JPA Jorge Posada 6.00 15.00
JPO Jay Payton SP/100 4.00 10.00
JT Jim Thome 6.00 15.00
KG Ken Griffey Jr. SP 12.00 30.00
KW Kerry Wood SP/108 4.00 10.00
MO Magglio Ordonez 4.00 10.00
MP Mike Piazza 6.00 15.00
OV Omar Vizquel SP/115 6.00 15.00
RA Rich Aurilia SP/102 4.00 10.00
RB Rocco Baldelli SP 4.00 10.00
RF Rafael Furcal SP 4.00 10.00
RH Rickey Henderson SP/77 6.00 15.00
RO Roberto Alomar 6.00 15.00
SC Sandy Alomar Jr. SP/95 4.00 10.00
SG Shawn Green SP/100 4.00 10.00
SR Scott Rolen SP/77 6.00 15.00
TG Troy Glaus SP/113 4.00 10.00
TH Torii Hunter SP/115 4.00 10.00

2004 Upper Deck Headliners Jersey
SERIES 1 ODDS 1:48 HOBBY, 1:96 RETAIL
SP PRINT RUNS B/WN 97-153 COPIES PER
SP PRINT RUNS PROVIDED BY UPPER DECK
*GOLD: .75X TO 2X BASIC
*GOLD: .4X TO 1X BASIC SP p/r 97-153
GOLD RANDOM INSERTS IN SERIES 1 PACKS
GOLD PRINT RUN 100 SERIAL #'d SETS
AD Adam Dunn 2.50 6.00
BK Byung-Hyun Kim AS 1.50 4.00
BS Benito Santiago AS 1.50 4.00
CS Curt Schilling 2.50 6.00
GM Greg Maddux 5.00 12.00
HM Hideki Matsui 6.00 15.00
IS Ichiro Suzuki SP/153 15.00 40.00
JB Josh Beckett 1.50 4.00
JD Joe DiMaggio SP/153 20.00 50.00
JE Jim Edmonds 2.50 6.00
JH Jose Hernandez AS 1.50 4.00
JR Jimmy Rollins AS 2.50 6.00
JS Junior Spivey AS 1.50 4.00
JT Jim Thome 2.50 6.00
JV Jose Vidro AS 1.50 4.00
KG Ken Griffey Jr. 8.00 20.00
LB Lance Berkman 2.50 6.00
LC Luis Castillo AS 1.50 4.00
LG Luis Gonzalez 1.50 4.00
MA Mariano Rivera 5.00 12.00
MB Mark Buehrle AS 1.50 4.00
ML Mike Lowell AS 1.50 4.00
MM Mickey Mantle SP/97 30.00 80.00
MO Magglio Ordonez 2.50 6.00
MR Manny Ramirez 2.50 6.00
MS Matt Morris AS 1.50 4.00
MT Miguel Tejada 2.50 6.00
MU Mike Mussina 2.50 6.00
MY Mike Sweeney AS 1.50 4.00
PK Paul Konerko AS 1.50 4.00
PM Pedro Martinez 2.50 6.00
RF Robert Fick AS 1.50 4.00
RH Roy Halladay AS 2.50 6.00
RK Ryan Klesko 1.50 4.00
RO Roy Oswalt 2.50 6.00
SG Shawn Green 1.50 4.00
TB Tony Batista AS 1.50 4.00
TG Tom Glavine 2.50 6.00
TH Trevor Hoffman AS 2.50 6.00
TW Ted Williams SP/153 20.00 50.00
VG Vladimir Guerrero SP/153 6.00 15.00

2004 Upper Deck Derek Jeter Bonus
COMMON CARD (1-25) 2.00 5.00
1-25 THREE PER JETER BONUS PACK
COMMON JSY (26-32) 15.00 40.00
26-32 JSY PRINT RUN 99 #'d SETS
COMMON AU (33-37) 100.00 175.00
33-37 AU PRINT RUN 50 #'d SETS
38-42 AU JSY PRINT RUN 10 #'d SETS
AU JSY NO PRICING DUE TO SCARCITY
26-42 RANDOM IN JETER BONUS PACKS
ONE JETER BONUS PACK PER FACT.SET

2004 Upper Deck Magical Performances
SERIES 1 STATED ODDS 1:96 HOBBY
GOLD RANDOM INSERTS IN SER.1 HOBBY
GOLD STATED ODDS 1:1300 RETAIL
GOLD PRINT RUN 50 SERIAL #'d SETS
NO GOLD PRICING DUE TO SCARCITY
1 Mickey Mantle USC HR 12.00 30.00
2 Mickey Mantle 56 Triple Crown 12.00 30.00
3 Joe DiMaggio 56th Game 8.00 20.00
4 Joe DiMaggio Slides Home 8.00 20.00
5 Derek Jeter The Flip 10.00 25.00
6 Derek Jeter 00 AS MVP 10.00 25.00
7 R.Clemens 300 Win/4000 K 5.00 12.00
8 Roger Clemens 20-1 5.00 12.00
9 Alfonso Soriano Walkoff 2.50 6.00
10 Andy Pettitte 96 2.50 6.00
11 Hideki Matsui Grand Slam 6.00 15.00
12 Mike Mussina 1-Hitter 2.50 6.00
13 Jorge Posada ALDS HR 2.50 6.00
14 Jason Giambi Grand Slam 1.50 4.00
15 David Wells Perfect 1.50 4.00
16 Mariano Rivera 99 WS MVP 5.00 12.00
17 Yogi Berra 12 K's 4.00 10.00
18 Phil Rizzuto 50 MVP 2.50 6.00
19 Whitey Ford 61 CY 2.50 6.00
20 Jose Contreras 1st Win 1.50 4.00
21 Catfish Hunter Free Agent 2.50 6.00
22 Mickey Mantle Cycle 12.00 30.00
23 M.Mantle HR's Both Sides 12.00 30.00
24 Joe DiMaggio 3-Time MVP 8.00 20.00
25 Joe DiMaggio Cycle 8.00 20.00
26 Derek Jeter 7 Seasons 10.00 25.00
27 Derek Jeter Mr. November 10.00 25.00
28 Roger Clemens 1-Hitter 5.00 12.00
29 Roger Clemens 01 CY 5.00 12.00
30 Alfonso Soriano HR Record 2.50 6.00
31 Andy Pettitte ALCS 2.50 6.00
32 Hideki Matsui 4 Hits 6.00 15.00
33 Mike Mussina 1st Postseason 2.50 6.00
34 Jorge Posada 40 Doubles 2.50 6.00
35 Jason Giambi 200th HR 1.50 4.00
36 David Wells 3-Hitter 1.50 4.00
37 Mariano Rivera Saves 3 5.00 12.00
38 Yogi Berra 3-Time MVP 4.00 10.00
39 Phil Rizzuto Broadcasting 2.50 6.00
40 Whitey Ford 10 WS Wins 2.50 6.00
41 Jose Contreras 2 Hits 1.50 4.00
42 Catfish Hunter 200th Win 2.50 6.00

2004 Upper Deck Matsui Chronicles
COMPLETE SET (60) 30.00 60.00
COMMON CARD (HM1-HM60) .75 2.00
ONE PER SERIES 1 RETAIL PACK

2004 Upper Deck National Pride
SERIES 1 STATED ODDS 1:6
1 Justin Orenduff .40 1.00
2 Micah Owings .25 .60
3 Steven Register .25 .60
4 Huston Street .40 1.00
5 Justin Verlander 2.50 6.00
6 Jered Weaver 1.00 2.50
7 Matt Campbell .25 .60
8 Stephen Head .25 .60
9 Mark Romanczuk .25 .60
10 Jeff Clement .40 1.00
11 Mike Nickeas .25 .60
12 Tyler Greene .25 .60
13 Paul Janish .40 1.00
14 Jeff Larish .25 .60
15 Eric Patterson .25 .60
16 Dustin Pedroia 1.50 4.00
17 Michael Griffin .25 .60
18 Brent Lillibridge .25 .60
19 Danny Putnam .25 .60
20 Seth Smith .40 1.00

2004 Upper Deck National Pride Jersey 1
SERIES 1 ODDS 1:24 HOBBY, 1:48 RETAIL
1 Justin Orenduff 2.00 5.00
2 Micah Owings 2.00 5.00
3 Steven Register 2.00 5.00
4 Huston Street 2.50 6.00
5 Justin Verlander 10.00 25.00
6 Jered Weaver 5.00 12.00
7 Matt Campbell 2.00 5.00
8 Stephen Head 2.00 5.00
9 Mark Romanczuk 2.00 5.00
10 Jeff Clement 4.00 10.00
11 Mike Nickeas 2.00 5.00
12 Tyler Greene 2.00 5.00
13 Paul Janish 2.00 5.00
14 Jeff Larish 2.00 5.00
15 Eric Patterson 2.00 5.00
16 Dustin Pedroia 6.00 15.00
17 Michael Griffin 2.00 5.00
18 Brent Lillibridge 2.00 5.00
19 Danny Putnam 2.00 5.00
20 Seth Smith 3.00 8.00
21 Justin Orenduff SP 3.00 8.00
22 Micah Owings SP 3.00 8.00
23 Steven Register SP 3.00 8.00
24 Huston Street SP 3.00 8.00
25 Justin Verlander SP 10.00 25.00
26 Jered Weaver SP 6.00 15.00
27 Matt Campbell SP 3.00 8.00
28 Stephen Head SP 3.00 8.00
29 Mark Romanczuk SP 3.00 8.00
30 Jeff Clement SP 5.00 12.00
31 Mike Nickeas SP 3.00 8.00
32 Tyler Greene SP 3.00 8.00
33 Paul Janish SP 3.00 8.00
34 Jeff Larish SP 3.00 8.00
35 Eric Patterson SP 3.00 8.00
36 Dustin Pedroia SP 3.00 8.00
37 Michael Griffin SP 3.00 8.00
38 Brent Lillibridge SP 3.00 8.00
39 Danny Putnam SP 3.00 8.00
40 Seth Smith SP 4.00 10.00
41 Delmon Young SP 6.00 15.00
42 Rickie Weeks SP 3.00 8.00

2004 Upper Deck National Pride Memorabilia 2
OVERALL SER.2 GU ODDS 1:12 H, 1:24 R
BBJ Brian Bruney Jsy 2.00 5.00
CBJ Chris Burke Jsy 2.00 5.00
CBP Chris Burke Pants 2.00 5.00
DUJ Justin Duchscherer Jsy 2.00 5.00
DUP Justin Duchscherer Pants 2.00 5.00
ERJ Eddie Rodriguez CO Jsy 2.00 5.00
ERP Eddie Rodriguez CO Pants 2.00 5.00
EYJ Ernie Young Jsy 2.00 5.00
GGJ Gabe Gross Jsy 2.00 5.00
GKJ Graham Koonce Jsy 2.00 5.00
GKP Graham Koonce Pants 2.00 5.00
GLJ Gerald Laird Jsy 2.00 5.00
GSJ Grady Sizemore Jsy 3.00 8.00
GSP Grady Sizemore Pants 3.00 8.00
HRJ Horacio Ramirez Jsy 2.00 5.00
HRP Horacio Ramirez Pants 2.00 5.00
JBJ John Van Benschoten Jsy 2.00 5.00
JBP John Van Benschoten Pants 2.00 5.00
JCJ Jesse Crain Jsy 3.00 8.00
JCP Jesse Crain Pants 3.00 8.00
JDJ J.D. Durbin Jsy 2.00 5.00
JGJ John Grabow Jsy 2.00 5.00
JHJ J.J. Hardy Jsy 2.00 5.00
JLJ Justin Leone Jsy 3.00 8.00
JLP Justin Leone Pants 3.00 8.00
JMJ Joe Mauer Jsy 6.00 15.00
JMP Joe Mauer Pants 6.00 15.00
JRJ Jeremy Reed Jsy 4.00 10.00
JSJ Jason Stanford Jsy 2.00 5.00
JSP Jason Stanford Pants 2.00 5.00
MLJ Mike Lamb Jsy 2.00 5.00
MRJ Mike Rouse Jsy 2.00 5.00
MRP Mike Rouse Pants 2.00 5.00
RMP Ryan Madson Pants 2.00 5.00
RRJ Royce Ring Jsy 2.00 5.00
RRP Royce Ring Pants 2.00 5.00
TBJ Thad Bosley CO Jsy 2.00 5.00
TWJ Todd Williams Jsy 2.00 5.00

2004 Upper Deck Peak Performers Jersey
*GOLD: .6X TO 1.5X BASIC
GOLD PRINT RUN 165 SERIAL #'d SETS
OVERALL SER.2 GU ODDS 1:12 H, 1:24 R
AP Albert Pujols 6.00 15.00
AS Alfonso Soriano 2.00 5.00
BE Josh Beckett 2.00 5.00
BP Brandon Phillips 2.00 5.00
CB Craig Biggio 3.00 8.00
CD Carlos Delgado 2.00 5.00
CS Curt Schilling 3.00 8.00
EG Eric Gagne 2.00 5.00
FT Frank Thomas 3.00 8.00
HB Hank Blalock 2.00 5.00
HM Hideki Matsui 10.00 25.00
HN Hideo Nomo 3.00 8.00
IR Ivan Rodriguez 3.00 8.00
IS Ichiro Suzuki 10.00 25.00
JB Jeff Bagwell 3.00 8.00
JR Jose Reyes 2.00 5.00
JT Jim Thome 3.00 8.00
KG Ken Griffey Jr. 6.00 15.00
KW Kerry Wood 2.00 5.00
LB Lance Berkman 2.00 5.00
LC Luis Castillo 2.00 5.00
MM Mike Mussina 3.00 8.00
MO Magglio Ordonez 2.00 5.00
MP Mark Prior 3.00 8.00
MT Miguel Tejada 2.00 5.00
OV Omar Vizquel 3.00 8.00
PB Pat Burrell 2.00 5.00
PE Andy Pettitte 3.00 8.00
PL Paul Lo Duca 2.00 5.00
PM Pedro Martinez 3.00 8.00
RF Rafael Furcal 2.00 5.00
RP Rafael Palmeiro 3.00 8.00
SA C.C. Sabathia 2.00 5.00
SG Shawn Green 2.00 5.00
SR Scott Rolen 3.00 8.00
TH Todd Helton 3.00 8.00
VG Vladimir Guerrero 3.00 8.00
VW Vernon Wells 2.00 5.00

2004 Upper Deck Famous Quotes
COMPLETE SET (20) 15.00 40.00
SERIES 2 STATED ODDS 1:6 H/R
1 Al Lopez .40 1.00
2 Bob Feller .60 1.50
3 Bob Gibson .60 1.50
4 Brooks Robinson .60 1.50
5 Cal Ripken 3.00 8.00
6 Carl Yastrzemski 1.00 2.50
7 Earl Weaver .60 1.50
8 Eddie Mathews 1.00 2.50
9 Ernie Banks 1.00 2.50
10 Greg Maddux 1.25 3.00
11 Joe DiMaggio 2.00 5.00
12 Mickey Mantle 3.00 8.00
13 Nolan Ryan 3.00 8.00
14 Stan Musial 1.50 4.00
15 Ted Williams 2.00 5.00
16 Tom Seaver .60 1.50
17 Tommy Lasorda .60 1.50
18 Warren Spahn .60 1.50
19 Whitey Ford .60 1.50
20 Yogi Berra 1.00 2.50

2004 Upper Deck Signature Stars Black Ink 1
SER.1 ODDS 1:288 H,1:24 UPD BOX, 1:1800 R
PRINT RUNS B/WN 18-479 COPIES PER
NO PRICING ON QTY OF 25 OR LESS
EXCHANGE DEADLINE 11/10/06
AG Andres Galarraga/248 6.00 15.00
AH Aaron Heilman/49 10.00 25.00
BK Billy Koch/429 4.00 10.00
CR Cal Ripken/69 125.00 200.00
DR1 Dave Roberts/278 5.00 12.00
JRA Joe Randa/271 6.00 15.00
KI Kazuhisa Ishii/58 10.00 25.00
MO Magglio Ordonez/377 6.00 15.00
MU Mike Mussina/68 15.00 40.00
NG Nomar Garciaparra/69 60.00 120.00
NR1 Nolan Ryan/69 75.00 150.00
RA Rich Aurilia/479 4.00 10.00
RH1 Rich Harden/163 6.00 15.00
TH Torii Hunter/374 6.00 15.00
VG Vladimir Guerrero/68 30.00 60.00

2004 Upper Deck Signature Stars Black Ink 2
OVERALL SER.2 SIG ODDS 1:288 H, 1:1500 R
PRINT RUNS B/WN 43-450 COPIES PER
BB Bret Boone/43 15.00 40.00
BW Brandon Webb/60 6.00 15.00
DB Dewon Brazelton/96 4.00 10.00
DR2 Dave Roberts/450 5.00 12.00
DS Darryl Strawberry/160 10.00 25.00
DW Dontrelle Willis/160 10.00 25.00
EC Eric Chavez/60 10.00 25.00
EG Eric Gagne/160 10.00 25.00
JC Jose Canseco/160 15.00 40.00
JV Javier Vazquez/60 10.00 25.00
KG Ken Griffey Jr./450 40.00 80.00
MT Mark Teixeira/200 6.00 15.00
RH2 Rich Harden/65 10.00 25.00
RW Rickie Weeks/65 10.00 25.00

2004 Upper Deck Signature Stars Blue Ink 1
SER.1 ODDS 1:288 H,1:24 UPD BOX, 1:1800 R
STATED PRINT RUN 25 SERIAL #'d SETS
MATSUI PRINT RUN 324 SERIAL #'d CARDS
NO PRICING ON QTY OF 25 OR LESS
EXCHANGE DEADLINE 11/10/06
HM Hideki Matsui/324 175.00 300.00

2004 Upper Deck Signature Stars Blue Ink 2
OVERALL SER.2 SIG ODDS 1:288 H, 1:1500 R
PRINT RUNS B/WN 20-95 COPIES PER
NO PRICING ON QTY OF 25 OR LESS
NR2 Nolan Ryan/95 40.00 80.00

2004 Upper Deck Signature Stars Gold
SER.1 ODDS 1:288 H, 1:24 MINI, 1:1800 R
STATED PRINT RUN 99 SERIAL #'d SETS
ALL EXCEPT MATSUI FEATURE BLUE INK
NO PRICING DUE TO SCARCITY
EXCHANGE DEADLINE 11/10/06

2004 Upper Deck Super Patch Logos 2
OVERALL SERIES 2 ODDS 1:2500 H/R
PRINT RUNS B/WN 8-34 COPIES PER
PRINT RUNS PROVIDED BY UPPER DECK
CARDS ARE NOT SERIAL-NUMBERED
NO PRICING DUE TO SCARCITY

2004 Upper Deck Super Patches Logos 1
OVERALL PATCH SERIES 1 ODDS 1:7500
PRINT RUNS B/WN 8-25 COPIES PER
PRINT RUNS PROVIDED BY UPPER DECK
NO PRICING DUE TO SCARCITY

2004 Upper Deck Super Patch Numbers 2
OVERALL SERIES 2 ODDS 1:2500 H/R
PRINT RUNS B/WN 2-45 COPIES PER
PRINT RUNS PROVIDED BY UPPER DECK
CARDS ARE NOT SERIAL-NUMBERED
NO PRICING DUE TO SCARCITY

2004 Upper Deck Super Patches Numbers 1
OVERALL PATCH SERIES 1 ODDS 1:7500
PRINT RUNS B/WN 10-25 COPIES PER
PRINT RUNS PROVIDED BY UPPER DECK
NO PRICING DUE TO SCARCITY

2004 Upper Deck Super Patch Stripes 2
OVERALL SERIES 2 ODDS 1:2500 H/R
PRINT RUNS B/WN 6-65 COPIES PER
PRINT RUNS PROVIDED BY UPPER DECK
CARDS ARE NOT SERIAL-NUMBERED
NO PRICING DUE TO SCARCITY

2004 Upper Deck Super Patches Stripes 1
OVERALL PATCH SERIES 1 ODDS 1:7500
PRINT RUNS B/WN 25-40 COPIES PER
PRINT RUNS PROVIDED BY UPPER DECK
NO PRICING DUE TO SCARCITY

2004 Upper Deck Super Sluggers
COMPLETE SET (30) 10.00 25.00
ONE PER SERIES 2 RETAIL PACK
1 Albert Pujols 1.00 2.50
2 Alex Rodriguez 1.00 2.50
3 Alfonso Soriano .50 1.25
4 Andruw Jones .30 .75
5 Bret Boone .30 .75
6 Carlos Delgado .30 .75
7 Edgar Renteria .30 .75
8 Eric Chavez .30 .75
9 Frank Thomas .75 2.00
10 Garret Anderson .30 .75
11 Gary Sheffield .30 .75
12 Jason Giambi .30 .75
13 Javy Lopez .30 .75
14 Jeff Bagwell .50 1.25
15 Jim Edmonds .50 1.25
16 Jim Thome .50 1.25
17 Jorge Posada .50 1.25
18 Lance Berkman .50 1.25
19 Magglio Ordonez .50 1.25
20 Manny Ramirez .75 2.00
21 Mike Lowell .30 .75
22 Nomar Garciaparra .50 1.25
23 Preston Wilson .30 .75
24 Rafael Palmeiro .50 1.25
25 Richie Sexson .30 .75
26 Sammy Sosa .75 2.00
27 Shawn Green .30 .75
28 Todd Helton .50 1.25
29 Vernon Wells .30 .75
30 Vladimir Guerrero .50 1.25

2004 Upper Deck Twenty-Five Salute
COMPLETE SET (10) 4.00 10.00
SERIES 1 STATED ODDS 1:12
1 Barry Bonds 1.50 4.00
2 Troy Glaus .40 1.00
3 Andruw Jones .40 1.00
4 Jay Gibbons .40 1.00
5 Jeremy Giambi .40 1.00
6 Jason Giambi .40 1.00
7 Jim Thome .60 1.50
8 Rafael Palmeiro .60 1.50
9 Carlos Delgado .40 1.00
10 Dmitri Young .40 1.00

2004 Upper Deck Chevron
COMPLETE SET .75 2.00
1 Andruw Jones .10 .25
2 Hank Blalock .10 .25
3 Jeff Bagwell .15 .40
4 Vladimir Guerrero .15 .40
5 Shawn Green .10 .25
6 Mike Lowell .10 .25
7 Aubrey Huff .10 .25
8 Richie Sexson .10 .25
9 Brian Giles .10 .25
10 Bret Boone .10 .25
11 A.J. Pierzynski .10 .25
12 Eric Chavez .10 .25

2004 Upper Deck Holiday Card
HH4 Babe Ruth 5.00 12.00
Lou Gehrig
Joe DiMaggio
Mickey Mantle
Derek Jeter

2004 Upper Deck Pepsi Get Out There and Play
NNO Sammy Sosa 1.25 3.00

2004 Upper Deck Sportsfest
STATED PRINT RUN 500 SER.#'d SETS
SF4 Ken Griffey Jr. 2.00 5.00
SF5 Ichiro Suzuki 1.50 4.00
SF6 Derek Jeter 4.00 10.00
SF7 Mickey Mantle 2.50 6.00
SF8 Joe DiMaggio 2.00 5.00

2005 Upper Deck Sportsfest
STATED PRINT RUN 750 SER.#'d SETS
MLB1 Ken Griffey Jr. 2.00 5.00
MLB2 Mark Prior .60 1.50
MLB3 Derek Jeter 2.50 6.00
MLB4 Carlos Beltran .60 1.50
MLB5 Albert Pujols 1.25 3.00
MLB6 Curt Schilling .60 1.50

2006 Upper Deck Sportsfest
MLB1 Ken Griffey Jr. 1.50 4.00
MLB2 Derek Jeter 2.00 5.00
MLB3 Albert Pujols 1.00 2.50
MLB4 Miguel Cabrera .75 2.00
MLB5 Scott Podsednik .30 .75
MLB6 Derrek Lee .30 .75

2007 Upper Deck Sportsfest
UNPRICED AUTO PRINT RUN 3 TO 5 SETS
SF1 Cal Ripken Jr. 3.00 8.00
SF2 Ken Griffey Jr. 1.50 4.00
SF3 Derek Jeter 2.00 5.00
SF4 Kei Igawa .75 2.00
SF5 Daisuke Matsuzaka 1.25 3.00
SF6 Derrek Lee .30 .75

2004 Upper Deck Sunkist
COMPLETE SET (6) 1.25 3.00
1 Rollie Fingers .30 .75
2 Gary Carter .30 .75
3 Mark McGwire .75 2.00
4 Mickey Morandini
5 Paul O'Neill .30 .75
6 Dave Stieb .20 .50

2005 Upper Deck

COMPLETE SET (500) 20.00 50.00
COMPLETE SERIES 1 (300) 10.00 25.00
COMPLETE SERIES 2 (200) 10.00 25.00
COMMON CARD (1-500) .10 .30
COMMON (211-250/426-450) .25 .60
OVERALL PLATES SER.1 ODDS 1:1080 H
PLATES PRINT RUN 1 #'d SET PER COLOR
BLACK-CYAN-MAGENTA-YELLOW ISSUED
NO PLATES PRICING DUE TO SCARCITY
1 Casey Kotchman .12 .30
2 Chone Figgins .12 .30
3 David Eckstein .12 .30
4 Jarrod Washburn .12 .30
5 Robb Quinlan .12 .30
6 Troy Glaus .12 .30
7 Vladimir Guerrero .20 .50
8 Brandon Webb .20 .50
9 Danny Bautista .12 .30
10 Luis Gonzalez .12 .30
11 Matt Kata .12 .30
12 Randy Johnson .30 .75
13 Robby Hammock .12 .30
14 Shea Hillenbrand .12 .30
15 Adam LaRoche .12 .30
16 Andruw Jones .12 .30
17 Horacio Ramirez .12 .30
18 John Smoltz .30 .75
19 Johnny Estrada .12 .30
20 Mike Hampton .12 .30
21 Rafael Furcal .12 .30
22 Brian Roberts .12 .30
23 Javy Lopez .12 .30
24 Jay Gibbons .12 .30
25 Jorge Julio .12 .30
26 Melvin Mora .12 .30

27 Miguel Tejada .20 .50
28 Rafael Palmeiro .20 .50
29 Derek Lowe .12 .30
30 Jason Varitek .30 .75
31 Kevin Youkilis .12 .30
32 Manny Ramirez .30 .75
33 Curt Schilling .20 .50
34 Pedro Martinez .20 .50
35 Trot Nixon .12 .30
36 Corey Patterson .12 .30
37 Derrek Lee .12 .30
38 LaTroy Hawkins .12 .30
39 Mark Prior .20 .50
40 Matt Clement .12 .30
41 Moises Alou .12 .30
42 Sammy Sosa .30 .75
43 Aaron Rowand .12 .30
44 Carlos Lee .12 .30
45 Jose Valentin .12 .30
46 Juan Uribe .12 .30
47 Magglio Ordonez .20 .50
48 Mark Buehrle .20 .50
49 Paul Konerko .20 .50
50 Adam Dunn .20 .50
51 Barry Larkin .20 .50
52 D'Angelo Jimenez .12 .30
53 Danny Graves .12 .30
54 Paul Wilson .12 .30
55 Sean Casey .12 .30
56 Wily Mo Pena .12 .30
57 Ben Broussard .12 .30
58 C.C. Sabathia .20 .50
59 Casey Blake .12 .30
60 Cliff Lee .20 .50
61 Matt Lawton .12 .30
62 Omar Vizquel .20 .50
63 Victor Martinez .20 .50
64 Charles Johnson .12 .30
65 Joe Kennedy .12 .30
66 Jeromy Burnitz .12 .30
67 Matt Holliday .30 .75
68 Preston Wilson .12 .30
69 Royce Clayton .12 .30
70 Shawn Estes .12 .30
71 Bobby Higginson .12 .30
72 Brandon Inge .12 .30
73 Carlos Guillen .12 .30
74 Dmitri Young .12 .30
75 Eric Munson .12 .30
76 Jeremy Bonderman .12 .30
77 Ugueth Urbina .12 .30
78 Josh Beckett .12 .30
79 Dontrelle Willis .12 .30
80 Jeff Conine .12 .30
81 Juan Pierre .12 .30
82 Luis Castillo .12 .30
83 Miguel Cabrera .30 .75
84 Mike Lowell .12 .30
85 Andy Pettitte .20 .50
86 Brad Lidge .12 .30
87 Carlos Beltran .20 .50
88 Craig Biggio .20 .50
89 Jeff Bagwell .20 .50
90 Roger Clemens .40 1.00
91 Roy Oswalt .20 .50
92 Benito Santiago .12 .30
93 Jeremy Affeldt .12 .30
94 Juan Gonzalez .12 .30
95 Ken Harvey .12 .30
96 Mike MacDougal .12 .30
97 Mike Sweeney .12 .30
98 Zack Greinke .40 1.00
99 Adrian Beltre .30 .75
100 Alex Cora .20 .50
101 Cesar Izturis .12 .30
102 Eric Gagne .12 .30
103 Kazuhisa Ishii .12 .30
104 Milton Bradley .12 .30
105 Shawn Green .12 .30
106 Danny Kolb .12 .30
107 Ben Sheets .12 .30
108 Brooks Kieschnick .12 .30
109 Craig Counsell .12 .30
110 Geoff Jenkins .12 .30
111 Lyle Overbay .12 .30
112 Scott Podsednik .12 .30
113 Corey Koskie .12 .30
114 Johan Santana .20 .50
115 Joe Mauer .25 .60
116 Justin Morneau .20 .50
117 Lew Ford .12 .30
118 Matt LeCroy .12 .30
119 Torii Hunter .12 .30
120 Brad Wilkerson .12 .30
121 Chad Cordero .12 .30
122 Livan Hernandez .12 .30
123 Jose Vidro .12 .30
124 Termel Sledge .12 .30
125 Tony Batista .12 .30
126 Zach Day .12 .30
127 Al Leiter .12 .30
128 Jae Weong Seo .12 .30
129 Jose Reyes .20 .50
130 Kazuo Matsui .12 .30
131 Mike Piazza .30 .75
132 Todd Zeile .12 .30
133 Cliff Floyd .12 .30
134 Alex Rodriguez .40 1.00
135 Derek Jeter .75 2.00
136 Gary Sheffield .12 .30
137 Hideki Matsui .50 1.25
138 Jason Giambi .12 .30
139 Jorge Posada .20 .50
140 Mike Mussina .20 .50
141 Barry Zito .20 .50
142 Bobby Crosby .12 .30
143 Octavio Dotel .12 .30
144 Eric Chavez .12 .30
145 Jermaine Dye .12 .30
146 Mark Kotsay .12 .30
147 Tim Hudson .20 .50
148 Billy Wagner .12 .30
149 Bobby Abreu .12 .30
150 David Bell .12 .30
151 Jim Thome .20 .50
152 Jimmy Rollins .20 .50
153 Mike Lieberthal .12 .30
154 Randy Wolf .12 .30
155 Craig Wilson .12 .30
156 Daryle Ward .12 .30
157 Jack Wilson .12 .30
158 Jason Kendall .12 .30
159 Kip Wells .12 .30
160 Oliver Perez .12 .30
161 Rob Mackowiak .12 .30
162 Brian Giles .12 .30
163 Brian Lawrence .12 .30
164 David Wells .12 .30
165 Jay Payton .12 .30
166 Ryan Klesko .12 .30
167 Sean Burroughs .12 .30
168 Trevor Hoffman .20 .50
169 Brett Tomko .12 .30
170 J.T. Snow .12 .30
171 Jason Schmidt .12 .30
172 Kirk Rueter .12 .30
173 A.J. Pierzynski .12 .30
174 Pedro Feliz .12 .30
175 Ray Durham .12 .30
176 Eddie Guardado .12 .30
177 Edgar Martinez .20 .50
178 Ichiro Suzuki .40 1.00
179 Jamie Moyer .12 .30
180 Joel Pineiro .12 .30
181 Randy Winn .12 .30
182 Raul Ibanez .20 .50
183 Albert Pujols .40 1.00
184 Edgar Renteria .12 .30
185 Jason Isringhausen .12 .30
186 Jim Edmonds .20 .50
187 Matt Morris .12 .30
188 Reggie Sanders .12 .30
189 Tony Womack .12 .30
190 Aubrey Huff .12 .30
191 Danys Baez .12 .30
192 Carl Crawford .20 .50
193 Jose Cruz Jr. .12 .30
194 Rocco Baldelli .12 .30
195 Tino Martinez .20 .50
196 Dewon Brazelton .12 .30
197 Alfonso Soriano .20 .50
198 Brad Fullmer .12 .30
199 Gerald Laird .12 .30
200 Hank Blalock .12 .30
201 Laynce Nix .12 .30
202 Mark Teixeira .20 .50
203 Michael Young .12 .30
204 Alexis Rios .12 .30
205 Eric Hinske .12 .30
206 Miguel Batista .12 .30
207 Orlando Hudson .12 .30
208 Roy Halladay .20 .50
209 Ted Lilly .12 .30
210 Vernon Wells .12 .30
211 Aarom Baldiris SR .25 .60
212 B.J. Upton SR .40 1.00
213 Dallas McPherson SR .25 .60
214 Brian Dallimore SR .25 .60
215 Chris Oxspring SR .25 .60
216 Chris Shelton SR .25 .60
217 David Wright SR .50 1.25
218 Edwardo Sierra SR .25 .60
219 Fernando Nieve SR .25 .60
220 Frank Francisco SR .25 .60
221 Jeff Bennett SR .25 .60
222 Justin Lehr SR .25 .60
223 John Gall SR .25 .60
224 Jorge Sequea SR .25 .60
225 Justin Germano SR .25 .60
226 Kazuhito Tadano SR .25 .60
227 Kevin Cave SR .25 .60
228 Joe Blanton SR .25 .60
229 Luis A. Gonzalez SR .25 .60
230 Michael Wuertz SR .25 .60
231 Mike Rouse SR .25 .60
232 Nick Regilio SR .25 .60
233 Orlando Rodriguez SR .25 .60
234 Phil Stockman SR .25 .60
235 Ramon Ramirez SR .25 .60
236 Roberto Novoa SR .25 .60
237 Dioner Navarro SR .25 .60
238 Tim Bausher SR .25 .60
239 Logan Kensing SR .25 .60
240 Andy Green SR .25 .60
241 Brad Halsey SR .25 .60
242 Charles Thomas SR .25 .60
243 George Sherrill SR .25 .60
244 Jesse Crain SR .25 .60
245 Jimmy Serrano SR .25 .60
246 Joe Horgan SR .25 .60
247 Chris Young SR .40 1.00
248 Joey Gathright SR .25 .60
249 Gavin Floyd SR .25 .60
250 Ryan Howard SR .50 1.25
251 Lance Cormier SR .25 .60
252 Matt Treanor SR .25 .60
253 Jeff Francis SR .25 .60
254 Nick Swisher SR .40 1.00
255 Scott Atchison SR .25 .60
256 Travis Blackley SR .25 .60
257 Travis Smith SR .25 .60
258 Yadier Molina SR 2.50 6.00
259 Jeff Keppinger SR .25 .60
260 Scott Kazmir SR .60 1.50
261 G.Anderson .20 .50
V.Guerrero TL
262 L.Gonzalez .30 .75
R.Johnson TL
263 A.Jones .30 .75
C.Jones TL
264 M.Tejada .20 .50
R.Palmeiro TL
265 C.Schilling .30 .75
M.Ramirez TL
266 M.Prior .30 .75
S.Sosa TL
267 F.Thomas .30 .75
M.Ordonez TL
268 B.Larkin .60 1.50
K.Griffey Jr. TL
269 C.Sabathia .20 .50
V.Martinez TL
270 J.Burnitz .20 .50
T.Helton TL
271 D.Young .20 .50
I.Rodriguez TL
272 J.Beckett .30 .75
M.Cabrera TL
273 J.Bagwell .40 1.00
R.Clemens TL
274 K.Harvey .12 .30
M.Sweeney TL
275 A.Beltre .30 .75
E.Gagne TL
276 B.Sheets .12 .30
G.Jenkins TL
277 J.Mauer .25 .60
T.Hunter TL
278 J.Vidro .12 .30
L.Hernandez TL
279 K.Matsui .30 .75
M.Piazza TL
280 A.Rodriguez .75 2.00
D.Jeter TL
281 E.Chavez .20 .50
T.Hudson TL
282 B.Abreu .20 .50
J.Thome TL
283 C.Wilson .12 .30
J.Kendall TL
284 B.Giles .12 .30
P.Nevin TL
285 A.Pierzynski .12 .30
J.Schmidt TL
286 B.Boone .40 1.00
I.Suzuki TL
287 A.Pujols .40 1.00
S.Rolen TL
288 A.Huff .20 .50
T.Martinez TL
289 H.Blalock .20 .50
M.Teixeira TL
290 C.Delgado .20 .50
R.Halladay TL
291 Vladimir Guerrero PR .20 .50
292 Curt Schilling PR .20 .50
293 Mark Prior PR .20 .50
294 Josh Beckett PR .12 .30
295 Roger Clemens PR .40 1.00
296 Derek Jeter PR .75 2.00
297 Eric Chavez PR .12 .30
298 Jim Thome PR .20 .50
299 Albert Pujols PR .40 1.00
300 Hank Blalock PR .12 .30
301 Bartolo Colon .12 .30
302 Darin Erstad .12 .30
303 Garret Anderson .12 .30
304 Orlando Cabrera .12 .30
305 Steve Finley .12 .30
306 Javier Vazquez .12 .30
307 Russ Ortiz .12 .30
308 Chipper Jones .30 .75
309 Marcus Giles .12 .30
310 Raul Mondesi .12 .30
311 B.J. Ryan .12 .30
312 Luis Matos .12 .30
313 Sidney Ponson .12 .30
314 Bill Mueller .12 .30
315 David Ortiz .30 .75
316 Johnny Damon .20 .50
317 Keith Foulke .12 .30
318 Mark Bellhorn .12 .30
319 Wade Miller .12 .30
320 Aramis Ramirez .12 .30
321 Carlos Zambrano .20 .50
322 Greg Maddux .40 1.00
323 Kerry Wood .12 .30
324 Nomar Garciaparra .20 .50
325 Todd Walker .12 .30
326 Frank Thomas .30 .75
327 Freddy Garcia .12 .30
328 Joe Crede .12 .30
329 Jose Contreras .12 .30
330 Orlando Hernandez .12 .30
331 Shingo Takatsu .12 .30
332 Austin Kearns .12 .30
333 Eric Milton .12 .30
334 Ken Griffey Jr. .60 1.50
335 Aaron Boone .12 .30
336 David Riske .12 .30
337 Jake Westbrook .12 .30
338 Kevin Millwood .12 .30
339 Travis Hafner .12 .30
340 Aaron Miles .12 .30
341 Jeff Baker .12 .30
342 Todd Helton .20 .50
343 Garrett Atkins .12 .30
344 Carlos Pena .20 .50
345 Ivan Rodriguez .20 .50
346 Rondell White .12 .30
347 Troy Percival .12 .30
348 A.J. Burnett .12 .30
349 Carlos Delgado .12 .30
350 Guillermo Mota .12 .30
351 Paul Lo Duca .12 .30
352 Jason Lane .12 .30
353 Lance Berkman .20 .50
354 Angel Berroa .12 .30
355 David DeJesus .12 .30
356 Ruben Gotay .12 .30
357 Jose Lima .12 .30
358 Brad Penny .12 .30
359 J.D. Drew .12 .30
360 Jayson Werth .20 .50
361 Jeff Kent .12 .30
362 Odalis Perez .12 .30
363 Brady Clark .12 .30
364 Junior Spivey .12 .30
365 Rickie Weeks .12 .30
366 Jacque Jones .12 .30
367 Joe Nathan .12 .30
368 Nick Punto .12 .30
369 Shannon Stewart .12 .30
370 Doug Mientkiewicz .12 .30
371 Kris Benson .12 .30
372 Tom Glavine .20 .50
373 Victor Zambrano .12 .30
374 Bernie Williams .20 .50
375 Carl Pavano .12 .30
376 Jaret Wright .12 .30
377 Kevin Brown .12 .30
378 Mariano Rivera .40 1.00
379 Danny Haren .12 .30
380 Eric Byrnes .12 .30
381 Erubiel Durazo .12 .30
382 Rich Harden .12 .30
383 Brett Myers .12 .30
384 Chase Utley .20 .50
385 Marlon Byrd .12 .30
386 Pat Burrell .12 .30
387 Placido Polanco .12 .30
388 Freddy Sanchez .12 .30
389 Jason Bay .12 .30
390 Josh Fogg .12 .30
391 Adam Eaton .12 .30
392 Jake Peavy .12 .30
393 Khalil Greene .12 .30
394 Mark Loretta .12 .30
395 Phil Nevin .12 .30
396 Ramon Hernandez .12 .30
397 Woody Williams .12 .30
398 Armando Benitez .12 .30
399 Edgardo Alfonzo .12 .30
400 Marquis Grissom .12 .30
401 Mike Matheny .12 .30
402 Richie Sexson .12 .30
403 Bret Boone .12 .30
404 Gil Meche .12 .30
405 Chris Carpenter .20 .50
406 Jeff Suppan .12 .30
407 Larry Walker .20 .50
408 Mark Grudzielanek .12 .30
409 Mark Mulder .12 .30
410 Scott Rolen .20 .50
411 Josh Phelps .12 .30
412 Jonny Gomes .12 .30
413 Francisco Cordero .12 .30
414 Kenny Rogers .12 .30
415 Richard Hidalgo .12 .30
416 Dave Bush .12 .30
417 Frank Catalanotto .12 .30
418 Gabe Gross .12 .30
419 Guillermo Quiroz .12 .30
420 Reed Johnson .12 .30
421 Cristian Guzman .12 .30
422 Esteban Loaiza .12 .30
423 Jose Guillen .12 .30
424 Nick Johnson .12 .30
425 Vinny Castilla .12 .30
426 Pete Orr SR RC .40 1.00
427 Tadahito Iguchi SR RC .40 1.00
428 Jeff Baker SR .25 .60
429 Marcos Carvajal SR RC .25 .60
430 Justin Verlander SR RC 5.00 12.00
431 Luke Scott SR RC .60 1.50
432 Willy Taveras SR .25 .60
433 Ambiorix Burgos SR RC .25 .60
434 Andy Sisco SR .25 .60
435 Denny Bautista SR .25 .60
436 Mark Teahen SR .25 .60
437 Ervin Santana SR .25 .60
438 Dennis Houlton SR RC .25 .60
439 Philip Humber SR RC .60 1.50
440 Steve Schmoll SR RC .25 .60
441 J.J. Hardy SR .25 .60
442 Ambiorix Concepcion SR RC .25 .60
443 Dae-Sung Koo SR RC .25 .60
444 Andy Phillips SR .25 .60
445 Dan Meyer SR .25 .60
446 Huston Street SR .25 .60
447 Keiichi Yabu SR RC .25 .60
448 Jeff Niemann SR RC .60 1.50
449 Jeremy Reed SR .25 .60
450 Tony Blanco SR .25 .60
451 Albert Pujols BG .40 1.00
452 Alex Rodriguez BG .40 1.00
453 Curt Schilling BG .20 .50
454 Derek Jeter BG .75 2.00
455 Greg Maddux BG .40 1.00
456 Ichiro Suzuki BG .40 1.00
457 Ivan Rodriguez BG .20 .50
458 Jeff Bagwell BG .20 .50
459 Jim Thome BG .20 .50
460 Ken Griffey Jr. BG .60 1.50
461 Manny Ramirez BG .30 .75
462 Mike Mussina BG .20 .50
463 Mike Piazza BG .30 .75
464 Pedro Martinez BG .20 .50
465 Rafael Palmeiro BG .20 .50
466 Randy Johnson BG .30 .75
467 Roger Clemens BG .40 1.00
468 Sammy Sosa BG .30 .75
469 Todd Helton BG .20 .50
470 Vladimir Guerrero BG .20 .50
471 Vladimir Guerrero TC .20 .50
472 Shawn Green TC .12 .30
473 John Smoltz TC .30 .75
474 Miguel Tejada TC .20 .50
475 Curt Schilling TC .20 .50
476 Mark Prior TC .20 .50
477 Frank Thomas TC .30 .75
478 Ken Griffey Jr. TC .60 1.50
479 C.C. Sabathia TC .20 .50
480 Todd Helton TC .20 .50
481 Ivan Rodriguez TC .20 .50
482 Miguel Cabrera TC .30 .75
483 Roger Clemens TC .40 1.00
484 Mike Sweeney TC .12 .30
485 Eric Gagne TC .12 .30
486 Ben Sheets TC .12 .30
487 Johan Santana TC .20 .50
488 Mike Piazza TC .30 .75
489 Derek Jeter TC .75 2.00
490 Eric Chavez TC .12 .30
491 Jim Thome TC .20 .50
492 Craig Wilson TC .12 .30
493 Jake Peavy TC .12 .30
494 Jason Schmidt TC .12 .30
495 Ichiro Suzuki TC .40 1.00
496 Albert Pujols TC .40 1.00
497 Carl Crawford TC .20 .50
498 Mark Teixeira TC .20 .50
499 Vernon Wells TC .12 .30
500 Jose Vidro TC .12 .30

2005 Upper Deck Blue

*BLUE 300-425/451-500: 4X TO 10X BASIC
*BLUE 426-450: 2.5X TO 6X BASIC
OVERALL SER.2 PARALLEL ODDS 1:12 H
STATED PRINT RUN 150 SERIAL #'d SETS

2005 Upper Deck Emerald

*EMER 300-425/451-500: 12.5X TO 30X BASIC
OVERALL SER.2 PARALLEL ODDS 1:12 H
STATED PRINT RUN 25 SERIAL #'d SETS
NO PRICING AVAILABLE ON 426-450

2005 Upper Deck Gold

*GOLD 300-425/451-500: 5X TO 12X BASIC
*GOLD 426-450: 3X TO 8X BASIC
OVERALL SER.2 PARALLEL ODDS 1:12 H
STATED PRINT RUN 99 SERIAL #'d SETS

2005 Upper Deck Retro

*RETRO: 1.25X TO 3X BASIC
ONE RETRO BOX PER SER.1 HOBBY CASE
SER.1 HOBBY CASES CONTAIN 12 BOXES
10 Josh Beckett .12 .30
OVERALL PLATES SER.1 ODDS 1:1080 H
PLATES PRINT RUN 1 #'d SET PER COLOR
BLACK-CYAN-MAGENTA-YELLOW ISSUED
NO PLATES PRICING DUE TO SCARCITY

2005 Upper Deck 4000 Strikeout

RANDOM INSERTS IN SERIES 1 PACKS
STATED PRINT RUN 4000 SERIAL #'d SETS
CRCJ Carlton 8.00 20.00
Ryan
Clem
Randy

2005 Upper Deck Baseball Heroes Jeter

COMPLETE SET (10) 12.50 30.00
COMMON CARD (91-99) 1.50 4.00
SERIES 1 STATED ODDS 1:6 H/R

2005 Upper Deck Flyball

ONE PER '05 PRO SIGS PACK
1 Johan Santana .15 .40
2 Randy Johnson .25 .60
3 Pedro Martinez .15 .40
4 Jason Schmidt .10 .25
5 Curt Schilling .15 .40
6 Roger Clemens .30 .75
7 Eric Gagne .10 .25
8 Mariano Rivera .30 .75
9 Mike Piazza .25 .60
11 Ivan Rodriguez .15 .40
13 Albert Pujols .30 .75
14 Todd Helton .15 .40
15 Jim Thome .15 .40
16 Alfonso Soriano .15 .40
17 Jeff Kent .10 .25
18 Bret Boone .10 .25
19 Scott Rolen .15 .40
20 Alex Rodriguez .30 .75
21 Adrian Beltre .25 .60
22 Nomar Garciaparra .15 .40
23 Derek Jeter .60 1.50
24 Miguel Tejada .15 .40
25 Manny Ramirez .25 .60
26 Adam Dunn .15 .40
27 Miguel Cabrera .25 .60
29 Jim Edmonds .15 .40
30 Ken Griffey Jr. .50 1.25
31 Vladimir Guerrero .15 .40
32 Ichiro Suzuki .30 .75
34 Sammy Sosa .25 .60
35 Gary Sheffield .10 .25
37 Roy Oswalt .15 .40
38 Carlos Zambrano .15 .40
40 Mark Prior .15 .40
42 Tim Hudson .15 .40
43 Kerry Wood .10 .25
44 Joe Nathan .10 .25
45 Brad Lidge .10 .25
46 Jason Isringhausen .10 .25
47 Armando Benitez .10 .25
48 Keith Foulke .10 .25
49 Octavio Dotel .10 .25
50 Trevor Hoffman .15 .40
51 Johnny Estrada .10 .25
52 Victor Martinez .15 .40
53 Jason Varitek .25 .60
54 Paul Lo Duca .10 .25
55 Jason Kendall .10 .25
56 Michael Barrett .10 .25
57 Mike Lieberthal .10 .25
58 Carlos Delgado .10 .25
59 Derrek Lee .10 .25
60 Jason Giambi .10 .25
61 Rafael Palmeiro .15 .40
62 David Ortiz .25 .60
63 Jeff Bagwell .15 .40
64 Paul Konerko .15 .40
65 Mark Loretta .10 .25
66 Ray Durham .10 .25
67 Luis Castillo .10 .25
68 Marcus Giles .10 .25
69 Adam Kennedy .10 .25
70 Jose Vidro .10 .25
72 Eric Chavez .10 .25
74 Vinny Castilla .10 .25
75 Hank Blalock .10 .25
77 Michael Young .10 .25
78 Carlos Guillen .10 .25
79 Jimmy Rollins .15 .40
80 Rafael Furcal .10 .25
81 Edgar Renteria .10 .25
82 Alex Gonzalez .10 .25
83 Carlos Lee .10 .25
84 Hideki Matsui .40 1.00
86 Craig Biggio .15 .40
87 Moises Alou .10 .25
88 Chipper Jones .25 .60
89 Andruw Jones .10 .25
90 Corey Patterson .10 .25
91 Torii Hunter .10 .25
92 Carl Crawford .15 .40
93 Steve Finley .10 .25
95 J.D. Drew .10 .25
96 Brian Giles .10 .25
97 Lance Berkman .15 .40
98 Shawn Green .10 .25
99 Larry Walker .15 .40
100 Magglio Ordonez .15 .40
101 Mark Mulder .10 .25
103 Oliver Perez .10 .25
104 Carl Pavano .10 .25
105 Matt Clement .10 .25
106 Bartolo Colon .10 .25
107 Roy Halladay .15 .40
109 Javier Vazquez .10 .25
110 Josh Beckett .10 .25
111 Tom Gordon .10 .25
112 Francisco Rodriguez .15 .40
113 Guillermo Mota .10 .25
114 Juan Rincon .10 .25
115 Steve Kline .10 .25
116 Ray King .10 .25
117 Giovanni Carrara .10 .25
118 Akinori Otsuka .10 .25
119 Kyle Farnsworth .10 .25
121 Brandon Inge .10 .25
123 Yadier Molina 1.00 2.50
124 Miguel Olivo .10 .25
125 Joe Mauer .20 .50
126 Rod Barajas .10 .25
127 Aubrey Huff .10 .25
128 Travis Hafner .10 .25
129 Phil Nevin .10 .25
130 Pedro Feliz .10 .25
131 Lyle Overbay .10 .25
132 Carlos Pena .15 .40
133 Craig Wilson .10 .25
134 Brad Wilkerson .10 .25
135 Mike Sweeney .10 .25
138 Todd Walker .10 .25
139 D'Angelo Jimenez .10 .25
140 Jose Reyes .15 .40
141 Juan Uribe .10 .25
142 Mark Bellhorn .10 .25
143 Orlando Hudson .10 .25
144 Tony Womack .10 .25
146 Aaron Miles .10 .25
147 Miguel Cairo .10 .25
148 Ken Griffey Jr. .50 1.25
149 Casey Blake .10 .25
150 Chone Figgins .10 .25
151 Mike Lowell .10 .25
152 Shea Hillenbrand .10 .25
153 Corey Koskie .10 .25
154 David Bell .10 .25
155 Eric Hinske .10 .25
157 Morgan Ensberg .10 .25
158 Cesar Izturis .10 .25
159 Julio Lugo .10 .25
160 Jose Valentin .10 .25
161 Omar Vizquel .15 .40
162 Bobby Crosby .10 .25
163 Khalil Greene .10 .25
164 Angel Berroa .10 .25
165 David Eckstein .10 .25
166 Christian Guzman .10 .25
167 Kaz Matsui .10 .25
168 Lew Ford .10 .25
169 Geoff Jenkins .10 .25
171 Jason Bay .10 .25
173 Reggie Sanders .10 .25
174 Pat Burrell .10 .25
176 Cliff Floyd .10 .25
177 Ryan Klesko .10 .25
178 Luis Gonzalez
179 Jose Guillen .10 .25
180 Mike Cameron .10 .25
181 Vernon Wells .10 .25
182 Aaron Rowand .10 .25
183 Scott Podsednik .10 .25
186 Bernie Williams .15 .40
187 Mark Kotsay .10 .25
188 Milton Bradley .10 .25
189 Garret Anderson .10 .25
190 Preston Wilson
191 Wily Mo Pena .10 .25
192 Jeromy Burnitz .10 .25
193 Jermaine Dye .10 .25
194 Jose Cruz Jr. .10 .25
195 Richard Hidalgo .10 .25
196 Derek Jeter .60 1.50
197 Juan Encarnacion .10 .25
198 Bobby Higginson .10 .25
199 Alex Rios .10 .25
200 Austin Kearns .10 .25
201 Yogi Berra .25 .60
202 Harmon Killebrew .25 .60
203 Joe Morgan .15 .40
204 Ernie Banks .25 .60
205 Mike Schmidt .40 1.00
206 Mickey Mantle .75 2.00
207 Ted Williams .50 1.25
208 Babe Ruth .50 1.25
209 Nolan Ryan .75 2.00
210 Bob Gibson .15 .40

2005 Upper Deck Game Jersey

SERIES 2 OVERALL GU ODDS 1:8
SP INFO PROVIDED BY UPPER DECK
AB Adrian Beltre 3.00 8.00
AP Albert Pujols 6.00 15.00
AS Alfonso Soriano 3.00 8.00
CB Carlos Beltran SP 3.00 8.00
CJ Chipper Jones 4.00 10.00
CS Curt Schilling 4.00 10.00
DJ Derek Jeter 8.00 20.00
DO David Ortiz SP 4.00 10.00
DW David Wright 6.00 15.00
EC Eric Chavez 3.00 8.00
EG Eric Gagne 3.00 8.00
FT Frank Thomas 4.00 10.00
GM Greg Maddux SP 4.00 10.00
HB Hank Blalock 3.00 8.00
HE Todd Helton 4.00 10.00
HU Torii Hunter 3.00 8.00
IR Ivan Rodriguez 4.00 10.00
JB Jeff Bagwell SP 4.00 10.00
JK Jeff Kent 3.00 8.00
JS Johan Santana SP 4.00 10.00
JT Jim Thome SP 4.00 10.00
KG Ken Griffey Jr. SP 6.00 15.00
KW Kerry Wood 3.00 8.00
LB Lance Berkman 3.00 8.00
MC Miguel Cabrera 4.00 10.00
MM Mark Mulder 3.00 8.00
MP Mark Prior 4.00 10.00
MR Manny Ramirez SP 4.00 10.00
MT Mark Teixeira SP 4.00 10.00
PI Mike Piazza 4.00 10.00
PM Pedro Martinez 4.00 10.00
RC Roger Clemens 4.00 10.00
RJ Randy Johnson SP 4.00 10.00
SM John Smoltz 4.00 10.00
SR Scott Rolen 4.00 10.00
SS Sammy Sosa 4.00 10.00
TE Miguel Tejada 3.00 8.00
TG Troy Glaus 3.00 8.00
TH Tim Hudson 3.00 8.00
VG Vladimir Guerrero 4.00 10.00

2005 Upper Deck Hall of Fame Plaques

SERIES 1 STATED ODDS 1:36 H/R
16 Ernie Banks 2.50 6.00
17 Yogi Berra 2.50 6.00
18 Whitey Ford 1.50 4.00
19 Bob Gibson 1.50 4.00
20 Willie McCovey 1.50 4.00
21 Stan Musial 4.00 10.00
22 Nolan Ryan 8.00 20.00
23 Mike Schmidt 4.00 10.00
24 Tom Seaver 1.50 4.00
25 Robin Yount 2.50 6.00

2005 Upper Deck Marquee Attractions Jersey

SER.1 OVERALL GU ODDS 1:12 H
AD Adam Dunn 3.00 8.00
AJ Andruw Jones 4.00 10.00
AP Albert Pujols 6.00 15.00
BE Josh Beckett 3.00 8.00
BG Brian Giles 3.00 8.00
BW Billy Wagner 3.00 8.00
CD Carlos Delgado 3.00 8.00
CJ Chipper Jones 4.00 10.00
CS Curt Schilling 4.00 10.00
DJ Derek Jeter 8.00 20.00
DW Dontrelle Willis 3.00 8.00
EG Eric Gagne 3.00 8.00
GM Greg Maddux 5.00 12.00
HM Hideki Matsui 10.00 25.00
HN Hideo Nomo 4.00 10.00
HO Trevor Hoffman 3.00 8.00
IR Ivan Rodriguez 4.00 10.00
IS Ichiro Suzuki 10.00 25.00
JB Jeff Bagwell 4.00 10.00
JG Jason Giambi 3.00 8.00
JM Joe Mauer 4.00 10.00
JS Jason Schmidt 3.00 8.00
JT Jim Thome 4.00 10.00
KB Kevin Brown 3.00 8.00
KM Kazuo Matsui 3.00 8.00
KW Kerry Wood 3.00 8.00
MC Miguel Cabrera 4.00 10.00
MP Mark Prior 4.00 10.00
MT Miguel Tejada 3.00 8.00
PE Andy Pettitte 4.00 10.00
PI Mike Piazza 4.00 10.00
PM Pedro Martinez 4.00 10.00
PW Preston Wilson 3.00 8.00
RC Roger Clemens 5.00 12.00
RJ Randy Johnson 4.00 10.00
SG Shawn Green 3.00 8.00
SS Sammy Sosa 4.00 10.00
TH Todd Helton 4.00 10.00
VG Vladimir Guerrero 4.00 10.00

2005 Upper Deck Marquee Attractions Jersey Gold

*GOLD: .6X TO 1.5X BASIC
SER.1 OVERALL GU ODDS 1:12 H
GA Garret Anderson 5.00 12.00
RO Roy Oswalt 5.00 12.00

2005 Upper Deck Matinee Idols Jersey

SER.1 OVERALL GU ODDS 1:12 H, 1:24 R
SP INFO PROVIDED BY UPPER DECK
BB Bret Boone SP 4.00 10.00
BE Josh Beckett 3.00 8.00
BW Billy Wagner 3.00 8.00
BZ Barry Zito 3.00 8.00
CD Carlos Delgado 3.00 8.00
CJ Chipper Jones 4.00 10.00
CR Cal Ripken 15.00 40.00
CS Curt Schilling 4.00 10.00
DJ Derek Jeter 8.00 20.00
DW Dontrelle Willis 3.00 8.00
EC Eric Chavez 3.00 8.00
GS Gary Sheffield 3.00 8.00
HB Hank Blalock 3.00 8.00
HU Torii Hunter 3.00 8.00
JB Jeff Bagwell 4.00 10.00
JE Jim Edmonds 3.00 8.00
JG Jason Giambi 3.00 8.00
JT Jim Thome 4.00 10.00
KG Ken Griffey Jr. 6.00 15.00
KW Kerry Wood 3.00 8.00
ML Mike Lowell 4.00 10.00
MM Mike Mussina 4.00 10.00
MP Mark Prior 4.00 10.00
MT Mark Teixeira 4.00 10.00
NR Nolan Ryan 15.00 40.00
PB Pat Burrell 3.00 8.00
PI Mike Piazza 4.00 10.00
RB Rocco Baldelli 3.00 8.00
RC Roger Clemens 5.00 12.00
RH Roy Halladay 3.00 8.00
RJ Randy Johnson 4.00 10.00
RW Rickie Weeks 3.00 8.00
SG Shawn Green 3.00 8.00
SR Scott Rolen 4.00 10.00
SS Sammy Sosa 4.00 10.00
TG Troy Glaus 3.00 8.00
TH Todd Helton 4.00 10.00
TS Tom Seaver 6.00 15.00
VG Vladimir Guerrero 4.00 10.00
VW Vernon Wells 3.00 8.00

2005 Upper Deck Milestone Materials

SERIES 2 OVERALL GU ODDS 1:8
AP Albert Pujols 6.00 15.00
BA Jeff Bagwell 4.00 10.00
BC Bobby Crosby 3.00 8.00
CB Carlos Beltran 3.00 8.00
CS Curt Schilling 4.00 10.00
DO David Ortiz 4.00 10.00
EG Eric Gagne 3.00 8.00
GM Greg Maddux 4.00 10.00
JB Jason Bay 3.00 8.00
JP Jake Peavy 3.00 8.00
JS Johan Santana 4.00 10.00
JT Jim Thome 4.00 10.00
KG Ken Griffey Jr. 6.00 15.00
MR Manny Ramirez 4.00 10.00
MT Mark Teixeira 4.00 10.00
RJ Randy Johnson 4.00 10.00
RP Rafael Palmeiro 4.00 10.00
TE Miguel Tejada 3.00 8.00
VG Vladimir Guerrero 4.00 10.00

2005 Upper Deck Origins Jersey

SER.1 OVERALL GU ODDS 1:12 H, 1:24 R
AB Adrian Beltre 4.00 10.00
AJ Andruw Jones 1.50 4.00
AP Albert Pujols 5.00 12.00
AS Alfonso Soriano 2.50 6.00
BG Brian Giles 1.50 4.00
BU B.J. Upton 2.50 6.00
CB Carlos Beltran 2.50 6.00
EG Eric Gagne 1.50 4.00
GA Garret Anderson 1.50 4.00
GM Greg Maddux 5.00 12.00
HM Hideki Matsui 6.00 15.00
HN Hideo Nomo 4.00 10.00
IR Ivan Rodriguez 2.50 6.00
IS Ichiro Suzuki 5.00 12.00
JG Juan Gonzalez 1.50 4.00
JK Jeff Kent 1.50 4.00
JL Javy Lopez 1.50 4.00
JP Jorge Posada 2.50 6.00
JR Jose Reyes 2.50 6.00
JS Jason Schmidt 1.50 4.00
JV Javier Vazquez 1.50 4.00
KM Kazuo Matsui 1.50 4.00
LB Lance Berkman 2.50 6.00
LG Luis Gonzalez 1.50 4.00
MC Miguel Cabrera 4.00 10.00
MM Mark Mulder 1.50 4.00
MO Magglio Ordonez 2.50 6.00
MR Manny Ramirez 4.00 10.00
MT Miguel Tejada 2.50 6.00
PE Jake Peavy 1.50 4.00
PM Pedro Martinez 2.50 6.00
PW Preston Wilson 1.50 4.00
RF Rafael Furcal 1.50 4.00
RP Rafael Palmeiro 2.50 6.00
RS Richie Sexson 1.50 4.00
SS Sammy Sosa 4.00 10.00
TH Tim Hudson 2.50 6.00
VG Vladimir Guerrero 2.50 6.00

2005 Upper Deck Rewind to 1997 Jersey

SER.2 STATED ODDS 1:288 H, 1:480 R
PRINT RUNS B/WN 100-150 COPIES PER
CARDS ARE NOT SERIAL-NUMBERED
PRINT RUN INFO PROVIDED BY UD
AJ Andruw Jones 15.00 40.00
CJ Chipper Jones 15.00 40.00
CR Cal Ripken 20.00 50.00
CS Curt Schilling Phils 10.00 25.00
DJ Derek Jeter 20.00 50.00
FT Frank Thomas 15.00 40.00
GM Greg Maddux Braves 15.00 40.00
IR Ivan Rodriguez Rgr 15.00 40.00
JB Jeff Bagwell 15.00 40.00
JS John Smoltz 15.00 40.00
JT Jim Thome Indians 15.00 40.00
KG Ken Griffey Jr. M's 60.00 120.00
MP Mike Piazza Dgr 15.00 40.00
MR Manny Ramirez Indians 15.00 40.00
PM Pedro Martinez Expos 15.00 40.00
RJ Randy Johnson M's 15.00 40.00
SR Scott Rolen Phils Pants 15.00 40.00
TG Tony Gwynn 15.00 40.00
VG Vladimir Guerrero Expos 15.00 40.00
WC Will Clark Rgr 15.00 40.00

2005 Upper Deck Season Opener MLB Game-Worn Jersey Collection

STATED ODDS 1:8
AB Angel Berroa 2.00 5.00
AD Adam Dunn 2.00 5.00
AJ Andruw Jones 3.00 8.00
CD Carlos Delgado 2.00 5.00
CP Corey Patterson 2.00 5.00
DJ Derek Jeter 10.00 25.00
EB Eric Byrnes 2.00 5.00
EH Eric Hinske 2.00 5.00
JB Josh Beckett 2.00 5.00
JG Jody Gerut 2.00 5.00
JT Jim Thome 3.00 8.00
MO Magglio Ordonez 2.00 5.00
MT Michael Tucker 2.00 5.00
PM Pedro Martinez 3.00 8.00
RB Rocco Baldelli 2.00 5.00
RK Ryan Klesko 2.00 5.00
SG Shawn Green 2.00 5.00
SR Scott Rolen 3.00 8.00

2005 Upper Deck Signature Stars Hobby

SERIES 1 STATED ODDS 1:288 HOBBY
SP INFO PROVIDED BY UPPER DECK
BC Bobby Crosby 6.00 15.00
BS Ben Sheets 6.00 15.00
CR Cal Ripken SP 60.00 150.00
DW Dontrelle Willis 6.00 15.00
DY Delmon Young 10.00 25.00
HB Hank Blalock 6.00 15.00
JL Javy Lopez 6.00 15.00
JM Joe Mauer 20.00 50.00
KG Ken Griffey Jr. 60.00 150.00
KW Kerry Wood 10.00 25.00
LF Lew Ford 4.00 10.00
MC Miguel Cabrera 20.00 50.00

2005 Upper Deck Signature Stars Retail

NO PRICING DUE TO SCARCITY
SERIES 1 STATED ODDS 1:480 RETAIL
SP INFO PROVIDED BY UPPER DECK

2005 Upper Deck Super Patch Logo

SER.1 OVERALL GU ODDS 1:12 H, 1:24 R
PRINT RUNS B/WN 8-34 COPIES PER
CARDS ARE NOT SERIAL-NUMBERED
PRINT RUNS PROVIDED BY UPPER DECK

2005 Upper Deck Wingfield Collection

COMPLETE SET (20) 15.00 40.00
SERIES 1 STATED ODDS 1:9 H/R
1 Eddie Mathews 1.25 3.00
2 Ernie Banks 1.25 3.00
3 Joe DiMaggio 2.50 6.00
4 Mickey Mantle 4.00 10.00
5 Pee Wee Reese .75 2.00
6 Phil Rizzuto .75 2.00
7 Stan Musial 2.00 5.00
8 Ted Williams 2.50 6.00
9 Bob Feller .75 2.00
10 Whitey Ford .75 2.00
11 Willie Stargell .75 2.00
12 Yogi Berra 1.25 3.00
13 Roy Campanella .75 2.00
14 Franklin D. Roosevelt .50 1.25
15 Harry Truman .50 1.25
16 Dwight D. Eisenhower .50 1.25
17 John F. Kennedy 1.25 3.00
18 Lyndon Johnson .50 1.25
19 Richard Nixon .50 1.25
20 Thurman Munson .75 2.00

2005 Upper Deck World Series Heroes

COMPLETE SET (45) 10.00 25.00
SERIES 1 STATED ODDS 1:1 RETAIL
1 Garret Anderson .20 .50
2 Troy Glaus .20 .50
3 Vladimir Guerrero .30 .75
4 Andruw Jones .20 .50
5 Chipper Jones .50 1.25
6 Curt Schilling .30 .75
7 Keith Foulke .20 .50
8 Manny Ramirez .50 1.25
9 Nomar Garciaparra .30 .75
10 Pedro Martinez .30 .75
11 Kerry Wood .20 .50
12 Mark Prior .30 .75
13 Sammy Sosa .50 1.25
14 Frank Thomas .50 1.25
15 Magglio Ordonez .30 .75
16 Dontrelle Willis .20 .50
17 Josh Beckett .20 .50
18 Miguel Cabrera .50 1.25
19 Jeff Bagwell .30 .75
20 Lance Berkman .30 .75
21 Roger Clemens .60 1.50
22 Eric Gagne .20 .50
23 Torii Hunter .20 .50
24 Mike Piazza .50 1.25
25 Alex Rodriguez .60 1.50
26 Derek Jeter 1.25 3.00
27 Gary Sheffield .20 .50
28 Hideki Matsui .75 2.00
29 Jason Giambi .20 .50
30 Jorge Posada .30 .75
31 Kevin Brown .20 .50
32 Mariano Rivera .60 1.50
33 Mike Mussina .30 .75
34 Eric Chavez .20 .50
35 Mark Mulder .20 .50
36 Tim Hudson .30 .75
37 Billy Wagner .20 .50
38 Jim Thome .30 .75
39 Brian Giles .20 .50
40 Jason Schmidt .20 .50
41 Albert Pujols .60 1.50
42 Scott Rolen .30 .75
43 Alfonso Soriano .30 .75
44 Hank Blalock .20 .50
45 Mark Teixeira .30 .75

2005 Upper Deck Chicago National

COMPLETE SET (6) 2.50 6.00
DISTRIBUTED AT '05 CHICAGO NSCC
STATED PRINT RUN 750 SERIAL #'d SETS
MLB1 Mark Prior .60 1.50
MLB2 Greg Maddux 1.25 3.00
MLB3 Derrek Lee .40 1.00
MLB4 Kerry Wood .40 1.00
MLB5 Tadahito Iguchi .60 1.50
MLB6 Paul Konerko .60 1.50

2005 Upper Deck Sunkist

COMPLETE SET (5) 2.50 6.00
1 Mickey Mantle 1.50 4.00
2 Stan Musial .75 2.00
3 Roger Maris .50 1.25
4 Roberto Clemente 1.25 3.00
5 Bob Gibson .30 .75

2006 Upper Deck

COMPLETE SET (1250) 375.00 600.00
COMPLETE SERIES 1 (500) 125.00 200.00
COMPLETE SERIES 2 (500) 125.00 200.00
COMPLETE UPDATE (250) 125.00 200.00
COMP.UPDATE w/o SP's (200) 30.00 50.00
COMMON CARD (1-1250) .15 .40
1-500 ISSUED IN SERIES 1 PACKS
501-1000 ISSUED IN SERIES 2 PACKS
1001-1250 ISSUED IN UPDATE PACKS
BAKER & REPKO BOTH CARD 283
1001-1250 SP STATED ODDS 1:2
SP: 1005/1013/1021/1037/1045/1061/1069
SP: 1077/1093/1101/1117/1125/1133/1149
SP: 1157/1173/1181/1189/1205/1213
SP: 1221-1250
4 MATCHED PLATES 1:2 SER.2 HOBBY CASES
PLATE PRINT RUN 1 SET PER COLOR
BLACK-CYAN-MAGENTA-YELLOW ISSUED
NO PLATE PRICING DUE TO SCARCITY
EXQUISITE EXCH 1 PER SER.2 HOBBY CASE
EXQUISITE EXCH RANDOM IN UPD.CASES
EXQUISITE EXCH DEADLINE 07/27/07
1 Adam Kennedy .15 .40
2 Bartolo Colon .15 .40
3 Bengie Molina .15 .40
4 Casey Kotchman .15 .40
5 Chone Figgins .15 .40
6 Dallas McPherson .15 .40
7 Darin Erstad .15 .40
8 Ervin Santana .15 .40
9 Francisco Rodriguez .25 .60
10 Garret Anderson .15 .40
11 Jarrod Washburn .15 .40
12 John Lackey .25 .60
13 Juan Rivera .15 .40
14 Orlando Cabrera .15 .40
15 Paul Byrd .15 .40
16 Steve Finley .15 .40
17 Vladimir Guerrero .25 .60
18 Alex Cintron .15 .40
19 Brandon Lyon .15 .40
20 Brandon Webb .25 .60
21 Chad Tracy .15 .40
22 Chris Snyder .15 .40
23 Claudio Vargas .15 .40
24 Conor Jackson .25 .60
25 Craig Counsell .15 .40
26 Javier Vazquez .15 .40
27 Jose Valverde .15 .40
28 Luis Gonzalez .15 .40
29 Royce Clayton .15 .40
30 Russ Ortiz .15 .40
31 Shawn Green .15 .40
32 Dustin Nippert (RC) .30 .75
33 Tony Clark .15 .40
34 Troy Glaus .15 .40
35 Adam LaRoche .15 .40
36 Andruw Jones .15 .40
37 Craig Hansen RC .75 2.00
38 Chipper Jones .40 1.00
39 Horacio Ramirez .15 .40
40 Jeff Francoeur .40 1.00
41 John Smoltz .40 1.00
42 Joey Devine RC .30 .75
43 Johnny Estrada .15 .40
44 Anthony Lerew (RC) .30 .75
45 Julio Franco .15 .40
46 Kyle Farnsworth .15 .40
47 Marcus Giles .15 .40
48 Mike Hampton .15 .40
49 Rafael Furcal .15 .40
50 Chuck James (RC) .30 .75
51 Tim Hudson .25 .60
52 B.J. Ryan .15 .40
53 Bernie Castro (RC) .30 .75
54 Brian Roberts .15 .40
55 Walter Young (RC) .30 .75
56 Daniel Cabrera .15 .40
57 Eric Byrnes .15 .40
58 Alejandro Freire RC .30 .75
59 Erik Bedard .15 .40
60 Javy Lopez .15 .40
61 Jay Gibbons .15 .40
62 Jorge Julio .15 .40
63 Luis Matos .15 .40
64 Melvin Mora .15 .40
65 Miguel Tejada .25 .60
66 Rafael Palmeiro .25 .60
67 Rodrigo Lopez .15 .40
68 Sammy Sosa .40 1.00
69 Alejandro Machado (RC) .30 .75
70 Bill Mueller .15 .40
71 Bronson Arroyo .15 .40
72 Curt Schilling .25 .60
73 David Ortiz .40 1.00
74 David Wells .15 .40
75 Edgar Renteria .15 .40
76 Ryan Jorgensen RC .30 .75
77 Jason Varitek .40 1.00
78 Johnny Damon .25 .60
79 Keith Foulke .15 .40
80 Kevin Youkilis .15 .40
81 Manny Ramirez .40 1.00
82 Matt Clement .15 .40
83 Hanley Ramirez (RC) .50 1.25
84 Tim Wakefield .25 .60
85 Trot Nixon .15 .40
86 Wade Miller .15 .40
87 Aramis Ramirez .15 .40
88 Carlos Zambrano .25 .60
89 Corey Patterson .15 .40
90 Derrek Lee .15 .40
91 Geovany Soto (RC) .75 2.00
92 Greg Maddux .50 1.25
93 Jeromy Burnitz .15 .40
94 Jerry Hairston .15 .40
95 Kerry Wood .15 .40
96 Mark Prior .25 .60
97 Matt Murton .15 .40
98 Michael Barrett .15 .40
99 Neifi Perez .15 .40
100 Nomar Garciaparra .25 .60
101 Rich Hill .40 1.00
102 Ryan Dempster .15 .40
103 Todd Walker .15 .40
104 A.J. Pierzynski .15 .40
105 Aaron Rowand .15 .40
106 Bobby Jenks .15 .40
107 Carl Everett .15 .40
108 Dustin Hermanson .15 .40
109 Frank Thomas .40 1.00
110 Freddy Garcia .15 .40
111 Jermaine Dye .15 .40
112 Joe Crede .15 .40
113 Jon Garland .15 .40
114 Jose Contreras .15 .40
115 Juan Uribe .15 .40
116 Mark Buehrle .25 .60
117 Orlando Hernandez .15 .40
118 Paul Konerko .25 .60
119 Scott Podsednik .15 .40
120 Tadahito Iguchi .15 .40
121 Aaron Harang .15 .40
122 Adam Dunn .25 .60
123 Austin Kearns .15 .40
124 Brandon Claussen .15 .40
125 Chris Denorfia (RC) .30 .75
126 Edwin Encarnacion .40 1.00
127 Miguel Perez (RC) .30 .75
128 Felipe Lopez .15 .40
129 Jason LaRue .15 .40
130 Ken Griffey Jr. .75 2.00
131 Chris Booker (RC) .30 .75
132 Luke Hudson .15 .40
133 Jason Bergmann RC .30 .75
134 Ryan Freel .15 .40
135 Sean Casey .15 .40
136 Wily Mo Pena .15 .40
137 Aaron Boone .15 .40
138 Ben Broussard .15 .40
139 Ryan Garko (RC) .30 .75
140 C.C. Sabathia .25 .60
141 Casey Blake .15 .40
142 Cliff Lee .25 .60
143 Coco Crisp .15 .40
144 David Riske .15 .40
145 Grady Sizemore .25 .60
146 Jake Westbrook .15 .40
147 Jhonny Peralta .15 .40
148 Josh Bard .15 .40
149 Kevin Millwood .15 .40
150 Ronnie Belliard .15 .40
151 Scott Elarton .15 .40
152 Travis Hafner .15 .40
153 Victor Martinez .25 .60
154 Aaron Cook .15 .40
155 Aaron Miles .15 .40
156 Brad Hawpe .15 .40
157 Mike Esposito (RC) .30 .75
158 Chin-Hui Tsao .15 .40
159 Clint Barmes .15 .40
160 Cory Sullivan .15 .40
161 Garrett Atkins .15 .40
162 J.D. Closser .15 .40
163 Jason Jennings .15 .40
164 Jeff Baker .15 .40
165 Jeff Francis .15 .40
166 Luis A. Gonzalez .15 .40
167 Matt Holliday .40 1.00
168 Todd Helton .25 .60
169 Bradon Inge .15 .40
170 Carlos Guillen .15 .40
171 Carlos Pena .25 .60
172 Chris Shelton .15 .40
173 Craig Monroe .15 .40
174 Curtis Granderson .30 .75
175 Dmitri Young .15 .40
176 Ivan Rodriguez .25 .60
177 Jason Johnson .15 .40
178 Jeremy Bonderman .15 .40
179 Magglio Ordonez .25 .60
180 Mark Woodyard (RC) .30 .75
181 Nook Logan .15 .40
182 Omar Infante .15 .40
183 Placido Polanco .15 .40
184 Chris Heintz RC .30 .75
185 A.J. Burnett .15 .40
186 Alex Gonzalez .15 .40
187 Josh Johnson (RC) .75 2.00
188 Carlos Delgado .15 .40
189 Dontrelle Willis .15 .40
190 Josh Wilson (RC) .30 .75
191 Jason Vargas .15 .40
192 Jeff Conine .15 .40
193 Jeremy Hermida .15 .40
194 Josh Beckett .15 .40
195 Juan Encarnacion .15 .40
196 Juan Pierre .15 .40
197 Luis Castillo .15 .40
198 Miguel Cabrera .40 1.00
199 Mike Lowell .15 .40
200 Paul Lo Duca .15 .40
201 Todd Jones .15 .40
202 Adam Everett .15 .40
203 Andy Pettitte .25 .60
204 Brad Ausmus .15 .40
205 Brad Lidge .15 .40
206 Brandon Backe .15 .40
207 Charlton Jimerson (RC) .30 .75
208 Chris Burke .15 .40
209 Craig Biggio .25 .60
210 Dan Wheeler .15 .40
211 Jason Lane .15 .40
212 Jeff Bagwell .25 .60
213 Lance Berkman .25 .60
214 Luke Scott .15 .40
215 Morgan Ensberg .15 .40
216 Roger Clemens .50 1.25
217 Roy Oswalt .25 .60
218 Willy Taveras .15 .40
219 Andres Blanco .15 .40
220 Angel Berroa .15 .40
221 Ruben Gotay .15 .40
222 David DeJesus .15 .40
223 Emil Brown .15 .40
224 J.P. Howell .15 .40
225 Jeremy Affeldt .15 .40
226 Jimmy Gobble .15 .40
227 John Buck .15 .40
228 Jose Lima .15 .40
229 Mark Teahen .15 .40
230 Matt Stairs .15 .40
231 Mike MacDougal .15 .40
232 Mike Sweeney .15 .40
233 Runelvys Hernandez .15 .40
234 Terrence Long .15 .40
235 Zack Greinke .40 1.00
236 Ron Flores RC .30 .75
237 Brad Penny .15 .40
238 Cesar Izturis .15 .40
239 D.J. Houlton .15 .40
240 Derek Lowe .15 .40
241 Eric Gagne .15 .40
242 Hee Seop Choi .15 .40
243 J.D. Drew .15 .40
244 Jason Phillips .15 .40
245 Jason Repko .15 .40
246 Jayson Werth .25 .60
247 Jeff Kent .15 .40
248 Jeff Weaver .15 .40
249 Milton Bradley .15 .40
250 Odalis Perez .15 .40
251 Hong-Chih Kuo (RC) .75 2.00
252 Oscar Robles .15 .40
253 Ben Sheets .15 .40
254 Bill Hall .15 .40
255 Brady Clark .15 .40
256 Carlos Lee .15 .40
257 Chris Capuano .15 .40
258 Nelson Cruz (RC) 1.25 3.00
259 Derrick Turnbow .15 .40
260 Doug Davis .15 .40
261 Geoff Jenkins .15 .40
262 J.J. Hardy .15 .40
263 Lyle Overbay .15 .40
264 Prince Fielder .75 2.00
265 Rickie Weeks .15 .40
266 Russell Branyan .15 .40
267 Tomo Ohka .15 .40
268 Jonah Bayliss RC .30 .75
269 Brad Radke .15 .40
270 Carlos Silva .15 .40
271 Francisco Liriano (RC) .75 2.00
272 Jacque Jones .15 .40
273 Joe Mauer .25 .60
274 Travis Bowyer (RC) .30 .75
275 Joe Nathan .15 .40
276 Johan Santana .25 .60
277 Justin Morneau .25 .60
278 Kyle Lohse .15 .40
279 Lew Ford .15 .40
280 Matt LeCroy .15 .40
281 Michael Cuddyer .15 .40
282 Nick Punto .15 .40
283a Scott Baker .15 .40
283b Jason Repko UER .15 .40
284 Shannon Stewart .15 .40
285 Torii Hunter .15 .40
286 Braden Looper .15 .40
287 Carlos Beltran .25 .60
288 Cliff Floyd .15 .40
289 David Wright .30 .75
290 Doug Mientkiewicz .15 .40
291 Anderson Hernandez (RC) .30 .75
292 Jose Reyes .25 .60
293 Kazuo Matsui .15 .40
294 Kris Benson .15 .40
295 Miguel Cairo .15 .40
296 Mike Cameron .15 .40
297 Robert Andino RC .30 .75
298 Mike Piazza .40 1.00
299 Pedro Martinez .25 .60
300 Tom Glavine .25 .60
301 Victor Diaz .15 .40
302 Tim Hamulack (RC) .30 .75
303 Alex Rodriguez .50 1.25
304 Bernie Williams .25 .60
305 Carl Pavano .15 .40
306 Chien-Ming Wang .25 .60
307 Derek Jeter 1.00 2.50
308 Gary Sheffield .15 .40
309 Hideki Matsui .40 1.00
310 Jason Giambi .15 .40
311 Jorge Posada .25 .60
312 Kevin Brown .15 .40
313 Mariano Rivera .50 1.25
314 Matt Lawton .15 .40
315 Mike Mussina .25 .60
316 Randy Johnson .40 1.00
317 Robinson Cano .25 .60
318 Mike Vento (RC) .30 .75
319 Tino Martinez .15 .40
320 Tony Womack .15 .40
321 Barry Zito .25 .60
322 Bobby Crosby .15 .40
323 Bobby Kielty .15 .40
324 Dan Johnson .15 .40
325 Danny Haren .15 .40
326 Eric Chavez .15 .40
327 Erubiel Durazo .15 .40
328 Huston Street .15 .40
329 Jason Kendall .15 .40
330 Jay Payton .15 .40
331 Joe Blanton .15 .40
332 Joe Kennedy .15 .40
333 Kirk Saarloos .15 .40
334 Mark Kotsay .15 .40
335 Nick Swisher .25 .60
336 Rich Harden .15 .40
337 Scott Hatteberg .15 .40
338 Billy Wagner .15 .40
339 Bobby Abreu .15 .40
340 Brett Myers .15 .40
341 Chase Utley .25 .60
342 Danny Sandoval RC .30 .75
343 David Bell .15 .40
344 Gavin Floyd .15 .40
345 Jim Thome .25 .60
346 Jimmy Rollins .25 .60
347 Jon Lieber .15 .40
348 Kenny Lofton .15 .40
349 Mike Lieberthal .15 .40
350 Pat Burrell .15 .40
351 Randy Wolf .15 .40
352 Ryan Howard .30 .75
353 Vicente Padilla .15 .40
354 Bryan Bullington (RC) .30 .75
355 J.J. Furmaniak (RC) .30 .75
356 Craig Wilson .15 .40
357 Matt Capps (RC) .30 .75
358 Tom Gorzelanny (RC) .30 .75
359 Jack Wilson .15 .40
360 Jason Bay .15 .40
361 Jose Mesa .15 .40
362 Josh Fogg .15 .40
363 Kip Wells .15 .40
364 Steve Stemle RC .30 .75
365 Oliver Perez .15 .40
366 Rob Mackowiak .15 .40
367 Ronny Paulino (RC) .30 .75
368 Tike Redman .15 .40
369 Zach Duke .15 .40
370 Adam Eaton .15 .40
371 Scott Feldman RC .30 .75
372 Brian Giles .15 .40
373 Brian Lawrence .15 .40
374 Damian Jackson .15 .40
375 Dave Roberts .25 .60
376 Jake Peavy .15 .40
377 Joe Randa .15 .40
378 Khalil Greene .15 .40
379 Mark Loretta .15 .40
380 Ramon Hernandez .15 .40
381 Robert Fick .15 .40
382 Ryan Klesko .15 .40
383 Trevor Hoffman .25 .60
384 Woody Williams .15 .40
385 Xavier Nady .15 .40
386 Armando Benitez .15 .40
387 Brad Hennessey .15 .40
388 Brian Myrow RC .30 .75
389 Edgardo Alfonzo .15 .40
390 J.T. Snow .15 .40
391 Jeremy Accardo RC .30 .75
392 Jason Schmidt .15 .40
393 Lance Niekro .15 .40
394 Matt Cain 1.00 2.50
395 Dan Ortmeier (RC) .30 .75
396 Moises Alou .15 .40
397 Doug Clark (RC) .30 .75
398 Omar Vizquel .25 .60
399 Pedro Feliz .15 .40
400 Randy Winn .15 .40
401 Ray Durham .15 .40
402 Adrian Beltre .40 1.00
403 Eddie Guardado .15 .40
404 Felix Hernandez .25 .60
405 Gil Meche .15 .40
406 Ichiro Suzuki .50 1.25
407 Jamie Moyer .15 .40
408 Jeff Nelson .15 .40
409 Jeremy Reed .15 .40
410 Joel Pineiro .15 .40
411 Jaime Bubela (RC) .30 .75
412 Raul Ibanez .25 .60
413 Rickie Sexson .15 .40
414 Ryan Franklin .15 .40
415 Willie Bloomquist .15 .40
416 Yorvit Torrealba .15 .40
417 Yuniesky Betancourt .15 .40
418 Jeff Harris RC .30 .75
419 Albert Pujols .50 1.25
420 Chris Carpenter .25 .60
421 David Eckstein .15 .40
422 Jason Isringhausen .15 .40
423 Jason Marquis .15 .40
424 Adam Wainwright (RC) .50 1.25
425 Jim Edmonds .25 .60
426 Ryan Theriot RC 1.00 2.50
427 Chris Duncan (RC) .50 1.25
428 Mark Grudzielanek .15 .40
429 Mark Mulder .15 .40
430 Matt Morris .15 .40
431 Reggie Sanders .15 .40
432 Scott Rolen .25 .60
433 Tyler Johnson (RC) .30 .75
434 Yadier Molina .50 1.25
435 Alex S. Gonzalez .15 .40
436 Aubrey Huff .15 .40
437 Tim Corcoran RC .30 .75
438 Carl Crawford .25 .60
439 Casey Fossum .15 .40
440 Danys Baez .15 .40
441 Edwin Jackson .15 .40
442 Joey Gathright .15 .40
443 Jonny Gomes .15 .40
444 Jorge Cantu .15 .40
445 Julio Lugo .15 .40
446 Nick Green .15 .40
447 Rocco Baldelli .15 .40
448 Scott Kazmir .25 .60
449 Seth McClung .15 .40
450 Toby Hall .15 .40
451 Travis Lee .15 .40
452 Craig Breslow RC .30 .75
453 Alfonso Soriano .25 .60
454 Chris R. Young .15 .40
455 David Dellucci .15 .40
456 Francisco Cordero .15 .40
457 Gary Matthews .15 .40
458 Hank Blalock .15 .40
459 Juan Dominguez .15 .40
460 Josh Rupe (RC) .30 .75
461 Kenny Rogers .15 .40
462 Kevin Mench .15 .40
463 Laynce Nix .15 .40
464 Mark Teixeira .25 .60
465 Michael Young .15 .40
466 Richard Hidalgo .15 .40
467 Jason Botts (RC) .30 .75
468 Aaron Hill .15 .40
469 Alex Rios .15 .40
470 Corey Koskie .15 .40
471 Chris Demaria RC .30 .75
472 Eric Hinske .15 .40
473 Frank Catalanotto .15 .40
474 John-Ford Griffin (RC) .30 .75
475 Gustavo Chacin .15 .40
476 Josh Towers .15 .40
477 Miguel Batista .15 .40
478 Orlando Hudson .15 .40
479 Reed Johnson .15 .40
480 Roy Halladay .25 .60
481 Shaun Marcum (RC) .30 .75
482 Shea Hillenbrand .15 .40
483 Ted Lilly .15 .40
484 Vernon Wells .15 .40
485 Brad Wilkerson .15 .40
486 Darrell Rasner (RC) .30 .75
487 Chad Cordero .15 .40
488 Cristian Guzman .15 .40
489 Esteban Loaiza .15 .40
490 John Patterson .15 .40
491 Jose Guillen .15 .40
492 Jose Vidro .15 .40
493 Livan Hernandez .15 .40
494 Marlon Byrd .15 .40
495 Nick Johnson .15 .40
496 Preston Wilson .15 .40
497 Ryan Church .15 .40
498 Ryan Zimmerman (RC) 1.00 2.50
499 Tony Armas Jr. .15 .40
500 Vinny Castilla .15 .40
501 Andy Green .15 .40
502 Damion Easley .15 .40
503 Eric Byrnes .15 .40
504 Jason Grimsley .15 .40
505 Jeff DaVanon .15 .40
506 Johnny Estrada .15 .40
507 Luis Vizcaino .15 .40
508 Miguel Batista .15 .40
509 Orlando Hernandez .15 .40
510 Orlando Hudson .15 .40
511 Terry Mulholland .15 .40
512 Chris Reitsma .15 .40
513 Edgar Renteria .15 .40
514 John Thomson .15 .40
515 Jorge Sosa .15 .40
516 Oscar Villarreal .15 .40
517 Pete Orr .15 .40
518 Ryan Langerhans .15 .40
519 Todd Pratt .15 .40
520 Wilson Betemit .15 .40
521 Brian Jordan .15 .40
522 Lance Cormier .15 .40
523 Matt Diaz .15 .40
524 Mike Remlinger .15 .40
525 Bruce Chen .15 .40
526 Chris Gomez .15 .40
527 Chris Ray .15 .40
528 Corey Patterson .15 .40
529 David Newhan .15 .40
530 Ed Rogers (RC) .30 .75
531 John Halama .15 .40
532 Kris Benson .15 .40
533 LaTroy Hawkins .15 .40
534 Raul Chavez .15 .40
535 Alex Cora .25 .60
536 Alex Gonzalez .15 .40
537 Coco Crisp .15 .40
538 David Riske .15 .40
539 Doug Mirabelli .15 .40
540 Josh Beckett .15 .40
541 J.T. Snow .15 .40
542 Mike Timlin .15 .40
543 Julian Tavarez .15 .40
544 Rudy Seanez .15 .40
545 Wily Mo Pena .15 .40
546 Bob Howry .15 .40
547 Glendon Rusch .15 .40
548 Henry Blanco .15 .40
549 Jacque Jones .15 .40
550 Jerome Williams .15 .40
551 John Mabry .15 .40
552 Juan Pierre .15 .40
553 Scott Eyre .15 .40
554 Scott Williamson .15 .40
555 Wade Miller .15 .40
556 Will Ohman .15 .40
557 Alex Cintron .15 .40
558 Rob Mackowiak .15 .40
559 Brandon McCarthy .15 .40
560 Chris Widger .15 .40
561 Cliff Politte .15 .40
562 Javier Vazquez .15 .40
563 Jim Thome .25 .60
564 Matt Thornton .15 .40
565 Neal Cotts .15 .40
566 Pablo Ozuna .15 .40
567 Ross Gload .15 .40
568 Brandon Phillips .15 .40
569 Bronson Arroyo .15 .40
570 Dave Williams .15 .40
571 David Ross .15 .40
572 David Weathers .15 .40
573 Eric Milton .15 .40
574 Javier Valentin .15 .40
575 Kent Mercker .15 .40
576 Matt Belisle .15 .40
577 Paul Wilson .15 .40
578 Rich Aurilia .15 .40
579 Rick White .15 .40
580 Scott Hatteberg .15 .40
581 Todd Coffey .15 .40
582 Bob Wickman .15 .40
583 Danny Graves .15 .40
584 Eduardo Perez .15 .40
585 Guillermo Mota .15 .40
586 Jason Davis .15 .40
587 Jason Johnson .15 .40
588 Jason Michaels .15 .40
589 Rafael Betancourt .15 .40
590 Ramon Vazquez .15 .40
591 Scott Sauerbeck .15 .40
592 Todd Hollandsworth .15 .40
593 Brian Fuentes .15 .40
594 Danny Ardoin .15 .40
595 David Cortes .15 .40
18-Aug Eli Marrero .15 .40
597 Jamey Carroll .15 .40
598 Jason Smith .15 .40
599 Josh Fogg .15 .40
600 Miguel Ojeda .15 .40
601 Mike DeJean .15 .40
602 Ray King .15 .40
603 Omar Quintanilla (RC) .30 .75
604 Zach Day .15 .40
605 Fernando Rodney .15 .40
606 Kenny Rogers .15 .40
607 Mike Maroth .15 .40
608 Nate Robertson .15 .40
609 Todd Jones .15 .40
610 Vance Wilson .15 .40
611 Bobby Seay .15 .40
612 Chris Spurling .15 .40
613 Roman Colon .15 .40
614 Jason Grilli .15 .40
615 Marcus Thames .15 .40
616 Ramon Santiago .15 .40
617 Alfredo Amezaga .15 .40
618 Brian Moehler .15 .40
619 Chris Aguila .15 .40
620 Franklyn German .15 .40
621 Joe Borowski .15 .40
622 Logan Kensing (RC) .30 .75
623 Matt Treanor .15 .40
624 Miguel Olivo .15 .40
625 Sergio Mitre .15 .40
626 Todd Wellemeyer .15 .40
627 Wes Helms .15 .40
628 Chad Qualls .15 .40
629 Eric Bruntlett .15 .40
630 Mike Gallo .15 .40
631 Mike Lamb .15 .40
632 Orlando Palmeiro .15 .40
633 Russ Springer .15 .40
634 Dan Wheeler .15 .40
635 Eric Munson .15 .40
636 Preston Wilson .15 .40
637 Trever Miller .15 .40
638 Ambiorix Burgos .15 .40
639 Andy Sisco .15 .40

640 Denny Bautista .15 .40
641 Doug Mientkiewicz .15 .40
642 Elmer Dessens .15 .40
643 Esteban German .15 .40
644 Joe Nelson (RC) .30 .75
645 Mark Grudzielanek .15 .40
646 Mark Redman .15 .40
647 Mike Wood .15 .40
648 Paul Bako .15 .40
649 Reggie Sanders .15 .40
650 Scott Elarton .15 .40
651 Shane Costa .15 .40
652 Tony Graffanino .15 .40
653 Jason Bulger (RC) .30 .75
654 Chris Bootcheck (RC) .30 .75
655 Esteban Yan .15 .40
656 Hector Carrasco .15 .40
657 J.C. Romero .15 .40
658 Jeff Weaver .15 .40
659 Jose Molina .15 .40
660 Kelvim Escobar .15 .40
661 Maicer Izturis .15 .40
662 Robb Quinlan .15 .40
663 Scot Shields .15 .40
664 Tim Salmon .15 .40
665 Bill Mueller .15 .40
666 Brett Tomko .15 .40
667 Dioner Navarro .15 .40
668 Jae Seo .15 .40
669 Jose Cruz Jr. .15 .40
670 Kenny Lofton .15 .40
671 Lance Carter .15 .40
672 Nomar Garciaparra .25 .60
673 Olmedo Saenz .15 .40
674 Rafael Furcal .15 .40
675 Ramon Martinez .15 .40
676 Ricky Ledee .15 .40
677 Sandy Alomar Jr. .15 .40
678 Yhency Brazoban .15 .40
679 Corey Koskie .15 .40
680 Dan Kolb .15 .40
681 Gabe Gross .15 .40
682 Jeff Cirillo .15 .40
683 Matt Wise .15 .40
684 Rick Helling .15 .40
685 Chad Moeller .15 .40
686 Dave Bush .15 .40
687 Jorge De La Rosa .15 .40
688 Justin Lehr .15 .40
689 Jason Bartlett .15 .40
690 Jesse Crain .15 .40
691 Juan Rincon .15 .40
692 Luis Castillo .15 .40
693 Mike Redmond .15 .40
694 Rondell White .15 .40
695 Tony Batista .15 .40
696 Juan Castro .15 .40
697 Luis Rodriguez .15 .40
698 Matt Guerrier .15 .40
699 Willie Eyre (RC) .30 .75
700 Aaron Heilman .15 .40
701 Billy Wagner .15 .40
702 Carlos Delgado .15 .40
703 Chad Bradford .15 .40
704 Chris Woodward .15 .40
705 Darren Oliver .15 .40
706 Duaner Sanchez .15 .40
707 Endy Chavez .15 .40
708 Jorge Julio .15 .40
709 Jose Valentin .15 .40
710 Julio Franco .15 .40
711 Paul Lo Duca .15 .40
712 Ramon Castro .15 .40
713 Steve Trachsel .15 .40
714 Victor Zambrano .15 .40
715 Xavier Nady .15 .40
716 Andy Phillips .15 .40
717 Bubba Crosby .15 .40
718 Jaret Wright .15 .40
719 Kelly Stinnett .15 .40
720 Kyle Farnsworth .15 .40
721 Mike Myers .15 .40
722 Octavio Dotel .15 .40
723 Ron Villone .15 .40
724 Scott Proctor .15 .40
725 Shawn Chacon .15 .40
726 Tanyon Sturtze .15 .40
727 Adam Melhuse .15 .40
728 Brad Halsey .15 .40
729 Esteban Loaiza .15 .40
730 Frank Thomas .40 1.00
731 Jay Witasick .15 .40
732 Justin Duchscherer .15 .40
733 Kiko Calero .15 .40
734 Marco Scutaro .25 .60
735 Mark Ellis .15 .40
736 Milton Bradley .15 .40
737 Aaron Fultz .15 .40
738 Aaron Rowand .15 .40
739 Geoff Geary .15 .40
740 Arthur Rhodes .15 .40
741 Chris Coste RC .75 2.00
742 Rheal Cormier .15 .40
743 Ryan Franklin .15 .40
744 Ryan Madson .15 .40
745 Sal Fasano .15 .40
746 Tom Gordon .15 .40
747 Abraham Nunez .15 .40
748 David Dellucci .15 .40
749 Julio Santana .15 .40
750 Shane Victorino .15 .40
751 Damaso Marte .15 .40
752 Freddy Sanchez .15 .40
753 Humberto Cota .15 .40
754 Jeromy Burnitz .15 .40
755 Joe Randa .15 .40
756 Jose Castillo .15 .40
757 Mike Gonzalez .15 .40
758 Ryan Doumit .15 .40
759 Sean Burnett .15 .40
760 Sean Casey .15 .40
761 Ian Snell .15 .40
762 John Grabow .15 .40
763 Jose Hernandez .15 .40
764 Roberto Hernandez .15 .40
765 Ryan Vogelsong .15 .40
766 Victor Santos .15 .40
767 Adrian Gonzalez .30 .75
768 Alan Embree .15 .40
769 Brian Sweeney (RC) .30 .75
770 Chan Ho Park .25 .60
771 Clay Hensley .15 .40
772 Dewon Brazelton .15 .40
773 Doug Brocail .15 .40
774 Eric Young .15 .40
775 Geoff Blum .15 .40
776 Josh Bard .15 .40
777 Mark Bellhorn .15 .40
778 Mike Cameron .15 .40
779 Mike Piazza .40 1.00
780 Rob Bowen .15 .40
781 Scott Cassidy .15 .40
782 Scott Linebrink .15 .40
783 Shawn Estes .15 .40
784 Terrmel Sledge .15 .40
785 Vinny Castilla .15 .40
786 Jeff Fassero .15 .40
787 Jose Vizcaino .15 .40
788 Mark Sweeney .15 .40
789 Matt Morris .15 .40
790 Steve Finley .15 .40
791 Tim Worrell .15 .40
792 Jamey Wright .15 .40
793 Jason Ellison .15 .40
794 Noah Lowry .15 .40
795 Steve Kline .15 .40
796 Todd Greene .15 .40
797 Carl Everett .15 .40
798 George Sherrill .15 .40
799 J.J. Putz .15 .40
800 Jake Woods .15 .40
801 Jose Lopez .15 .40
802 Julio Mateo .15 .40
803 Mike Morse .15 .40
804 Rafael Soriano .15 .40
805 Roberto Petagine .15 .40
806 Aaron Miles .15 .40
807 Braden Looper .15 .40
808 Gary Bennett .15 .40
809 Hector Luna .15 .40
810 Jeff Suppan .15 .40
811 John Rodriguez .15 .40
812 Josh Hancock .15 .40
813 Juan Encarnacion .15 .40
814 Larry Bigbie .15 .40
815 Scott Spiezio .15 .40
816 Sidney Ponson .15 .40
817 So Taguchi .15 .40
818 Brian Meadows .15 .40
819 Damon Hollins .15 .40
820 Dan Miceli .15 .40
821 Doug Waechter .15 .40
822 Jason Childers RC .30 .75
823 Josh Paul .15 .40
824 Julio Lugo .15 .40
825 Mark Hendrickson .15 .40
826 Sean Burroughs .15 .40
827 Shawn Camp .15 .40
828 Travis Harper .15 .40
829 Ty Wigginton .15 .40
830 Adam Eaton .15 .40
831 Adrian Brown .15 .40
832 Akinori Otsuka .15 .40
833 Antonio Alfonseca .15 .40
834 Brad Wilkerson .15 .40
835 D'Angelo Jimenez .15 .40
836 Gerald Laird .15 .40
837 Joaquin Benoit .15 .40
838 Kameron Loe .15 .40
839 Kevin Millwood .15 .40
840 Mark DeRosa .15 .40
841 Phil Nevin .15 .40
842 Rod Barajas .15 .40
843 Vicente Padilla .15 .40
844 A.J. Burnett .15 .40
845 Bengie Molina .15 .40
846 Gregg Zaun .15 .40
847 John McDonald .15 .40
848 Lyle Overbay .15 .40
849 Russ Adams .15 .40
850 Troy Glaus .15 .40
851 Vinny Chulk .15 .40
852 B.J. Ryan .15 .40
853 Justin Speier .15 .40
854 Pete Walker .15 .40
855 Scott Downs .15 .40
856 Scott Schoeneweis .15 .40
857 Alfonso Soriano .25 .60
858 Brian Schneider .15 .40
859 Daryle Ward .15 .40
860 Felix Rodriguez .15 .40
861 Gary Majewski .15 .40
862 Joey Eischen .15 .40
863 Jon Rauch .15 .40
864 Marlon Anderson .15 .40
865 Matt LeCroy .15 .40
866 Mike Stanton .15 .40
867 Ramon Ortiz .15 .40
868 Robert Fick .15 .40
869 Royce Clayton .15 .40
870 Ryan Drese .15 .40
871 Vladimir Guerrero CL .25 .60
872 Craig Biggio CL .25 .60
873 Barry Zito CL .25 .60
874 Vernon Wells CL .15 .40
875 Chipper Jones CL .40 1.00
876 Prince Fielder CL .75 2.00
877 Albert Pujols CL .50 1.25
878 Greg Maddux CL .50 1.25
879 Carl Crawford CL .25 .60
880 Brandon Webb CL .25 .60
881 J.D. Drew CL .15 .40
882 Jason Schmidt CL .15 .40
883 Victor Martinez CL .25 .60
884 Ichiro Suzuki CL .50 1.25
885 Miguel Cabrera CL .40 1.00
886 David Wright CL .30 .75
887 Alfonso Soriano CL .25 .60
888 Miguel Tejada CL .25 .60
889 Khalil Greene CL .15 .40
890 Ryan Howard CL .30 .75
891 Jason Bay CL .15 .40
892 Mark Teixeira CL .25 .60
893 Manny Ramirez CL .40 1.00
894 Ken Griffey Jr. CL .75 2.00
895 Todd Helton CL .25 .60
896 Angel Berroa CL .15 .40
897 Ivan Rodriguez CL .25 .60
898 Johan Santana CL .25 .60
899 Paul Konerko CL .25 .60
900 Derek Jeter CL 1.00 2.50
901 Macay McBride (RC) .30 .75
902 Tony Pena (RC) .30 .75
903 Peter Moylan RC .30 .75
904 Aaron Rakers (RC) .30 .75
905 Chris Britton RC .30 .75
906 Nick Markakis (RC) .60 1.50
907 Sendy Rleal RC .30 .75
908 Val Majewski (RC) .30 .75
909 Jermaine Van Buren (RC) .30 .75
910 Jonathan Papelbon (RC) 1.50 4.00
911 Angel Pagan (RC) .30 .75
912 David Aardsma (RC) .30 .75
913 Sean Marshall (RC) .30 .75
914 Brian Anderson (RC) .30 .75
915 Freddie Bynum (RC) .30 .75
916 Fausto Carmona (RC) .30 .75
917 Kelly Shoppach (RC) .30 .75
918 Choo Freeman (RC) .30 .75
919 Ryan Shealy (RC) .30 .75
920 Joel Zumaya (RC) .75 2.00
921 Jordan Tata RC .30 .75
922 Justin Verlander (RC) 2.50 6.00
923 Carlos Martinez RC .30 .75
924 Chris Resop (RC) .30 .75
925 Dan Uggla (RC) .50 1.25
926 Eric Reed (RC) .30 .75
927 Hanley Ramirez .50 1.25
928 Yusmeiro Petit (RC) .30 .75
929 Josh Willingham (RC) .50 1.25
930 Mike Jacobs (RC) .30 .75
931 Reggie Abercrombie (RC) .30 .75
932 Ricky Nolasco (RC) .30 .75
933 Scott Olsen (RC) .30 .75
934 Fernando Nieve (RC) .30 .75
935 Taylor Buchholz (RC) .30 .75
936 Cody Ross (RC) .75 2.00
937 James Loney (RC) .50 1.25
938 Takashi Saito RC .50 1.25
939 Tim Hamulack .30 .75
940 Chris Demaria .30 .75
941 Jose Capellan (RC) .30 .75
942 David Gassner (RC) .30 .75
943 Jason Kubel (RC) .30 .75
944 Brian Bannister (RC) .30 .75
945 Mike Thompson RC .30 .75
946 Cole Hamels (RC) 1.00 2.50
947 Paul Maholm (RC) .30 .75
948 John Van Benschoten (RC) .30 .75
949 Nate McLouth (RC) .30 .75
950 Ben Johnson (RC) .30 .75
951 Josh Barfield (RC) .30 .75
952 Travis Ishikawa (RC) .50 1.25
953 Jack Taschner (RC) .30 .75
954 Kenji Johjima RC .75 2.00
955 Skip Schumaker (RC) .30 .75
956 Ruddy Lugo (RC) .30 .75
957 Jason Hammel (RC) .75 2.00
958 Chris Roberson (RC) .30 .75
959 Fabio Castro RC .30 .75
960 Ian Kinsler (RC) 1.00 2.50
961 John Koronka (RC) .30 .75
962 Brandon Watson (RC) .30 .75
963 Jon Lester RC 1.25 3.00
964 Ben Hendrickson (RC) .30 .75
965 Martin Prado (RC) .50 1.25
966 Erick Aybar (RC) .30 .75
967 Bobby Livingston (RC) .30 .75
968 Ryan Spilborghs (RC) .30 .75
969 Tommy Murphy (RC) .30 .75
970 Howie Kendrick (RC) .60 1.50
971 Casey Janssen RC .30 .75
972 Michael O'Connor RC .30 .75
973 Conor Jackson (RC) .50 1.25
974 Jeremy Hermida (RC) .30 .75
975 Renyel Pinto (RC) .30 .75
976 Prince Fielder (RC) 1.50 4.00
977 Kevin Frandsen (RC) .30 .75
978 Ty Taubenheim RC .50 1.25
979 Rich Hill (RC) .75 2.00
980 Jonathan Broxton (RC) .30 .75
981 Jamie Shields RC 1.00 2.50
982 Carlos Villanueva RC .30 .75
983 Boone Logan RC .30 .75
984 Brian Wilson RC 5.00 12.00
985 Andre Ethier (RC) 1.00 2.50
986 Mike Napoli RC .50 1.25
987 Agustin Montero (RC) .30 .75
988 Jack Hannahan RC .30 .75
989 Boof Bonser (RC) .50 1.25
990 Carlos Ruiz (RC) .30 .75
991 Jason Botts .30 .75
992 Kendry Morales (RC) .75 2.00
993 Alay Soler RC .30 .75
994 Santiago Ramirez (RC) .30 .75
995 Saul Rivera (RC) .30 .75
996 Anthony Reyes (RC) .30 .75
997 Matt Kemp (RC) .75 2.00
998 Jae Kuk Ryu RC .30 .75
999 Lastings Milledge (RC) .30 .75
NNO Exquisite Redemption
1000 Jered Weaver (RC) 1.00 2.50
1001 Stephen Drew (RC) .60 1.50
1002 Carlos Quentin (RC) .50 1.25
1003 Livan Hernandez .15 .40
1004 Chris B. Young (RC) .75 2.00
1005 Alberto Callaspo SP (RC) 1.25 3.00
1006 Enrique Gonzalez (RC) .30 .75
1007 Tony Pena (RC) .30 .75
1008 Bob Melvin MG .15 .40
1009 Fernando Tatis .15 .40
1010 Willy Aybar (RC) .30 .75
1011 Ken Ray (RC) .30 .75
1012 Scott Thorman (RC) .30 .75
1013 Eric Hinske SP 1.25 3.00
1014 Kevin Barry (RC) .30 .75
1015 Bobby Cox MG .15 .40
1016 Phil Stockman (RC) .30 .75
1017 Brayan Pena (RC) .30 .75
1018 Adam Loewen (RC) .30 .75
1019 Brandon Fahey RC .30 .75
1020 Jim Hoey RC .30 .75
1021 Kurt Birkins SP RC 1.25 3.00
1022 Jim Johnson RC 1.25 3.00
1023 Sam Perlozzo MG .15 .40
1024 Cory Morris RC .30 .75
1025 Hayden Penn (RC) .30 .75
1026 Javy Lopez .15 .40
1027 Dustin Pedroia (RC) 10.00 25.00
1028 Kason Gabbard (RC) .30 .75
1029 David Pauley (RC) .30 .75
1030 Kyle Snyder .30 .75
1031 Terry Francona MG .15 .40
1032 Craig Breslow .30 .75
1033 Bryan Corey (RC) .30 .75
1034 Manny Delcarmen (RC) .30 .75
1035 Carlos Marmol RC 1.00 2.50
1036 Buck Coats (RC) .30 .75
1037 Ryan O'Malley SP RC 1.25 3.00
1038 Angel Guzman (RC) .30 .75
1039 Ronny Cedeno .15 .40
1040 Juan Mateo RC .30 .75
1041 Cesar Izturis .15 .40
1042 Les Walrond (RC) .30 .75
1043 Geovany Soto .75 2.00
1044 Sean Tracey (RC) .30 .75
1045 Ozzie Guillen MG SP 1.25 3.00
1046 Royce Clayton .15 .40
1047 Norris Hopper RC .30 .75
1048 Bill Bray (RC) .30 .75
1049 Jerry Narron MG .15 .40
1050 Brendan Harris (RC) .30 .75
1051 Brian Shackelford .30 .75
1052 Jeremy Sowers (RC) .30 .75
1053 Joe Inglett RC .30 .75
1054 Brian Slocum (RC) .30 .75
1055 Andrew Brown (RC) .30 .75
1056 Rafael Perez RC .30 .75
1057 Edward Mujica RC .30 .75
1058 Andy Marte (RC) .30 .75
1059 Shin-Soo Choo (RC) .50 1.25
1060 Jeremy Guthrie (RC) .30 .75
1061 Franklin Gutierrez SP (RC) 1.25 3.00
1062 Kazuo Matsui .15 .40
1063 Chris Iannetta RC .30 .75
1064 Manny Corpas RC .30 .75
1065 Clint Hurdle MG .15 .40
1066 Ramon Ramirez (RC) .30 .75
1067 Sean Casey .15 .40
1068 Zach Miner (RC) .30 .75
1069 Brent Clevlen SP (RC) 2.00 5.00
1070 Bob Wickman .15 .40
1071 Jim Leyland MG .15 .40
1072 Alexis Gomez (RC) .30 .75
1073 Anibal Sanchez (RC) .30 .75
1074 Taylor Tankersley (RC) .30 .75
1075 Eric Wedge MG .15 .40
1076 Jonah Bayliss .30 .75
1077 Paul Hoover SP (RC) 1.25 3.00
1078 Eddie Guardado .15 .40
1079 Cody Ross .75 2.00
1080 Aubrey Huff .15 .40
1081 Jason Hirsh (RC) .30 .75
1082 Brandon League .15 .40
1083 Matt Albers (RC) .30 .75
1084 Chris Sampson RC .30 .75
1085 Phil Garner MG .15 .40
1086 J.R. House (RC) .30 .75
1087 Ryan Shealy .30 .75
1088 Stephen Andrade (RC) .30 .75
1089 Bob Keppel (RC) .30 .75
1090 Buddy Bell MG .15 .40
1091 Justin Huber (RC) .30 .75
1092 Paul Phillips (RC) .30 .75
1093 Greg Jones SP (RC) 1.25 3.00
1094 Jeff Mathis (RC) .30 .75
1095 Dustin Moseley (RC) .30 .75
1096 Joe Saunders (RC) .30 .75
1097 Reggie Willits RC .75 2.00
1098 Mike Scioscia MG .15 .40
1099 Greg Maddux .50 1.25
1100 Wilson Betemit .15 .40
1101 Chad Billingsley SP (RC) 2.00 5.00
1102 Russell Martin (RC) .50 1.25
1103 Grady Little MG .15 .40
1104 David Bell .15 .40
1105 Kevin Mench .15 .40
1106 Laynce Nix .15 .40
1107 Chris Barnwell RC .30 .75
1108 Tony Gwynn Jr. (RC) .30 .75
1109 Corey Hart (RC) .30 .75
1110 Zach Jackson (RC) .30 .75
1111 Francisco Cordero .15 .40
1112 Joe Winkelsas (RC) .30 .75
1113 Ned Yost MG .15 .40
1114 Matt Garza (RC) .30 .75
1115 Chris Heintz .15 .40
1116 Pat Neshek RC 3.00 8.00
1117 Josh Rabe SP RC 1.25 3.00
1118 Mike Rivera .15 .40
1119 Ron Gardenhire MG .15 .40
1120 Shawn Green .15 .40
1121 Oliver Perez .15 .40
1122 Heath Bell .15 .40
1123 Bartolome Fortunato (RC) .30 .75
1124 Anderson Garcia RC .30 .75
1125 John Maine SP (RC) 2.00 5.00
1126 Henry Owens RC .30 .75
1127 Mike Pelfrey RC .75 2.00
1128 Royce Ring (RC) .30 .75
1129 Willie Randolph MG .15 .40
1130 Bobby Abreu .15 .40
1131 Craig Wilson .15 .40
1132 T.J. Beam (RC) .30 .75
1133 Colter Bean SP (RC) 1.25 3.00
1134 Melky Cabrera (RC) .50 1.25
1135 Mitch Jones (RC) .30 .75
1136 Jeffrey Karstens RC .30 .75
1137 Wil Nieves (RC) .30 .75
1138 Kevin Reese (RC) .30 .75
1139 Kevin Thompson (RC) .30 .75
1140 Jose Veras RC .30 .75
1141 Joe Torre MG .25 .60
1142 Jeremy Brown (RC) .30 .75
1143 Santiago Casilla (RC) .30 .75
1144 Shane Komine RC .50 1.25
1145 Mike Rouse (RC) .30 .75
1146 Jason Windsor (RC) .30 .75
1147 Ken Macha MG .15 .40
1148 Jamie Moyer .15 .40
1149 Phil Nevin SP 1.25 3.00
1150 Eude Brito (RC) .30 .75
1151 Fabio Castro .15 .40
1152 Jeff Conine .15 .40
1153 Scott Mathieson (RC) .30 .75
1154 Brian Sanches (RC) .30 .75
1155 Matt Smith RC .30 .75
1156 Joe Thurston (RC) .30 .75
1157 Marlon Anderson SP 1.25 3.00
1158 Xavier Nady .15 .40
1159 Shawn Chacon .15 .40
1160 Rajai Davis (RC) .30 .75
1161 Yurendell DeCaster (RC) .30 .75
1162 Marty McLeary (RC) .30 .75
1163 Chris Duffy .15 .40
1164 Josh Sharpless RC .30 .75
1165 Jim Tracy MG .15 .40
1166 David Wells .15 .40
1167 Russell Branyan .15 .40
1168 Todd Walker .15 .40
1169 Paul McAnulty (RC) .30 .75
1170 Bruce Bochy MG .25 .60
1171 Shea Hillenbrand .15 .40
1172 Eliezer Alfonzo RC .30 .75
1173 Justin Knoedler SP (RC) 1.25 3.00
1174 Jonathan Sanchez (RC) .75 2.00
1175 Travis Smith (RC) .30 .75
1176 Cha-Seung Baek .15 .40
1177 T.J. Bohn (RC) .30 .75
1178 Emiliano Fruto RC .30 .75
1179 Sean Green RC .30 .75
1180 Jon Huber RC .30 .75
1181 Adam Jones SP RC 6.00 15.00
1182 Mark Lowe (RC) .30 .75
1183 Eric O'Flaherty RC .30 .75
1184 Preston Wilson .15 .40
1185 Mike Hargrove MG .15 .40
1186 Jeff Weaver .15 .40
1187 Ronnie Belliard .15 .40
1188 John Gall (RC) .30 .75
1189 Josh Kinney SP RC 1.25 3.00
1190 Tony LaRussa MG .25 .60
1191 Scott Dunn (RC) .30 .75
1192 B.J. Upton .15 .40
1193 Jon Switzer (RC) .30 .75
1194 Ben Zobrist (RC) 1.50 4.00
1195 Joe Maddon .15 .40
1196 Carlos Lee .15 .40
1197 Matt Stairs .15 .40
1198 Nick Masset (RC) .30 .75
1199 Nelson Cruz 1.25 3.00
1200 Francisco Rosario (RC) .30 .75
1201 Wes Littleton (RC) .30 .75
1202 Drew Meyer (RC) .30 .75
1203 John Rheinecker (RC) .30 .75
1204 Robinson Tejeda .15 .40
1205 Jeremy Accardo SP 1.25 3.00
1206 Luis Figueroa RC .30 .75
1207 John Hattig (RC) .30 .75
1208 Dustin McGowan (RC) .30 .75
1209 Ryan Roberts RC .30 .75
1210 Davis Romero (RC) .30 .75
1211 Ty Taubenheim .50 1.25
1212 John Gibbons MG .15 .40
1213 Shawn Hill SP (RC) 1.25 3.00
1214 Brandon Harper RC .30 .75
1215 Travis Hughes (RC) .30 .75
1216 Chris Schroder RC .30 .75
1217 Austin Kearns .15 .40
1218 Felipe Lopez .15 .40
1219 Roy Corcoran RC .30 .75
1220 Melvin Dorta RC .30 .75
1221 Brandon Webb CL SP 1.25 3.00
1222 Andruw Jones CL SP .75 2.00
1223 Miguel Tejada CL SP 1.25 3.00
1224 David Ortiz CL SP 2.00 5.00
1225 Derrek Lee CL SP .75 2.00
1226 Jim Thome CL SP 1.25 3.00
1227 Ken Griffey Jr. CL SP 4.00 10.00
1228 Travis Hafner CL SP .75 2.00
1229 Todd Helton CL SP .50 1.25
1230 Magglio Ordonez CL SP 1.25 3.00
1231 Miguel Cabrera CL SP 2.00 5.00
1232 Lance Berkman CL SP 2.00 5.00
1233 Mike Sweeney CL SP .75 2.00
1234 Vladimir Guerrero CL SP 1.25 3.00
1235 Nomar Garciaparra CL SP 1.25 3.00
1236 Prince Fielder CL SP 4.00 10.00
1237 Johan Santana CL SP 1.25 3.00
1238 Pedro Martinez CL SP 1.25 3.00
1239 Derek Jeter CL SP 5.00 12.00
1240 Barry Zito CL SP .75 2.00
1241 Ryan Howard CL SP 1.50 4.00
1242 Jason Bay CL SP .75 2.00
1243 Trevor Hoffman CL SP 1.25 3.00
1244 Jason Schmidt CL SP .75 2.00
1245 Ichiro Suzuki CL SP 2.50 6.00
1246 Albert Pujols CL SP 2.50 6.00
1247 Carl Crawford CL SP 1.25 3.00
1248 Mark Teixeira CL SP 1.25 3.00
1249 Vernon Wells CL SP .75 2.00
1250 Alfonso Soriano CL SP 1.25 3.00

2006 Upper Deck Gold

*GOLD 1-1000: 2X TO 5X BASIC
*GOLD 1-1000: 1X TO 2.5X BASIC RC's
*GOLD 1001-1250: 3X TO 8X BASIC
*GOLD 1001-1250: 1.5X TO 4X BASIC RC'S
*GOLD 1001-1250: .15X TO .4X BASIC SP
COMMON (1221-1250) 1.25 3.00
SEMIS 1221-1250 2.00 5.00
UNLISTED 1221-1250 3.00 8.00
1-500 FIVE #'d INSERTS PER SER.1 HOB.BOX
501-1000 SER.2 ODDS 1:8 H, RANDOM IN RET
1001-1250 UPDATE ODDS 1:24 RET
1-1000 PRINT RUN 299 SERIAL #'d SETS
1001-1250 PRINT RUN 99 SERIAL #'d SETS
984 Brian Wilson 20.00 50.00
1181 Adam Jones 8.00 20.00

2006 Upper Deck Silver Spectrum

*501-1000: 3X TO 8X BASIC
*501-1000: 1.5X TO 4X BASIC RC's
1-500 FIVE #'d INSERTS PER SER.1 HOB.BOX
501-1000 SER.2 ODDS 1:24 H,RANDOM IN RET
1-500 PRINT RUN 25 SERIAL #'d SETS
501-1000 PRINT RUN 99 SERIAL #'d SETS
1-500 NO PRICING DUE TO SCARCITY

2006 Upper Deck Ozzie Smith SABR San Diego

1 Ozzie Smith 1.25 3.00

2006 Upper Deck Rookie Foil Silver

*SILVER: 1X TO 2.5X BASIC
2-3 PER SER.2 RC PACK
ONE RC PACK PER SER.2 HOBBY BOX
3-CARDS PER SEALED RC PACK
STATED PRINT RUN 399 SERIAL #'d SETS
*GOLD: 1.5X TO 4X BASIC
GOLD RANDOM IN SER.2 RC PACKS
GOLD PRINT RUN 99 SERIAL #'d SETS
PLAT.RANDOM IN SER.2 RC PACKS
PLATINUM PRINT RUN 15 #'d SETS
NO PLATINUM PRICING DUE TO SCARCITY
AU PLATES RANDOM IN RC PACKS
AU PLATE PRINT RUN 1 SET PER COLOR
BLACK-CYAN-MAGENTA-YELLOW ISSUED
NO AU PLATE PRICING DUE TO SCARCITY
AU PLATES ISSUED FOR 28 OF 100 FOILS
SEE BECKETT.COM FOR AU PLATE CL

2006 Upper Deck All-Time Legends

TWO PER SERIES 2 FAT PACK
AT1 Ty Cobb 1.50 4.00
AT2 Lou Gehrig 2.00 5.00
AT3 Babe Ruth 2.50 6.00
AT4 Jimmie Foxx 1.00 2.50
AT5 Honus Wagner 1.00 2.50
AT6 Lou Brock .60 1.50
AT7 Joe Morgan .60 1.50
AT8 Christy Mathewson 1.00 2.50
AT9 Walter Johnson 1.00 2.50
AT10 Mike Schmidt 1.50 4.00
AT11 Al Kaline 1.00 2.50
AT12 Robin Yount 1.00 2.50
AT13 Johnny Bench 1.00 2.50
AT14 Yogi Berra 1.00 2.50
AT15 Rod Carew .60 1.50
AT16 Bob Feller .60 1.50
AT17 Carlton Fisk .60 1.50
AT18 Bob Gibson .60 1.50
AT19 Cy Young 1.00 2.50
AT20 Reggie Jackson .60 1.50
AT21 Jackie Robinson 1.00 2.50
AT22 Harmon Killebrew 1.00 2.50
AT23 Mickey Cochrane .60 1.50
AT24 Eddie Mathews 1.00 2.50
AT25 Bill Mazeroski .60 1.50
AT26 Willie McCovey .60 1.50
AT27 Eddie Murray .60 1.50
AT28 Lefty Grove .60 1.50
AT29 Jim Palmer .60 1.50
AT30 Pee Wee Reese .60 1.50
AT31 Phil Rizzuto .60 1.50
AT32 Brooks Robinson .60 1.50
AT33 Nolan Ryan 3.00 8.00
AT34 Tom Seaver .60 1.50
AT35 Ozzie Smith 1.25 3.00
AT36 Roy Campanella 1.00 2.50
AT37 Thurman Munson 1.00 2.50
AT38 Mel Ott .40 1.00
AT39 Satchel Paige 1.00 2.50
AT40 Rogers Hornsby .60 1.50

2006 Upper Deck All-Upper Deck Team

TWO PER SERIES 1 FAT PACK
UD1 Ken Griffey Jr. 2.00 5.00
UD2 Derek Jeter 2.50 6.00
UD3 Albert Pujols 1.25 3.00
UD4 Alex Rodriguez 1.25 3.00
UD5 Vladimir Guerrero .60 1.50
UD6 Roger Clemens 1.25 3.00
UD7 Derrek Lee .40 1.00
UD8 David Ortiz 1.00 2.50
UD9 Miguel Cabrera 1.00 2.50
UD10 Bobby Abreu .40 1.00
UD11 Mark Teixeira .60 1.50
UD12 Johan Santana .60 1.50
UD13 Hideki Matsui 1.00 2.50
UD14 Ichiro Suzuki 1.25 3.00
UD15 Andruw Jones .40 1.00
UD16 Eric Chavez .40 1.00
UD17 Roy Oswalt .60 1.50
UD18 Curt Schilling .60 1.50
UD19 Randy Johnson 1.00 2.50
UD20 Ivan Rodriguez .60 1.50
UD21 Chipper Jones 1.00 2.50
UD22 Mark Prior .60 1.50
UD23 Jason Bay .40 1.00
UD24 Pedro Martinez .60 1.50
UD25 David Wright .75 2.00
UD26 Carlos Beltran .60 1.50
UD27 Jim Edmonds .60 1.50
UD28 Chris Carpenter .60 1.50
UD29 Roy Halladay .60 1.50
UD30 Jake Peavy .40 1.00
UD31 Paul Konerko .60 1.50
UD32 Travis Hafner .40 1.00
UD33 Barry Zito .60 1.50
UD34 Miguel Tejada .60 1.50
UD35 Josh Beckett .40 1.00
UD36 Todd Helton .60 1.50
UD37 Dontrelle Willis .40 1.00
UD38 Manny Ramirez 1.00 2.50
UD39 Mariano Rivera 1.25 3.00
UD40 Jeff Kent .40 1.00

2006 Upper Deck Amazing Greats

SER.1 ODDS 1:6 HOBBY, 1:12 RETAIL
*GOLD: .6X TO 1.5X BASIC
FIVE #'d INSERTS PER SER.1 HOBBY BOX
GOLD STATED PRINT RUN 699 SERIAL #'d SETS
AB Adrian Beltre 1.25 3.00
AJ Andruw Jones .75 2.00
AP Albert Pujols 1.50 4.00
AS Alfonso Soriano .75 2.00
BA Bobby Abreu .50 1.25
CB Carlos Beltran .75 2.00
CC Carl Crawford .75 2.00
CJ Chipper Jones 1.25 3.00
CL Carlos Lee .50 1.25
CP Corey Patterson .50 1.25
CS Curt Schilling .75 2.00
DJ Derek Jeter 3.00 8.00
DO David Ortiz 1.25 3.00
DW Dontrelle Willis .50 1.25
EG Eric Gagne .50 1.25
FT Frank Thomas 1.25 3.00
GM Greg Maddux 1.50 4.00
GS Gary Sheffield .50 1.25
HE Todd Helton .75 2.00
IR Ivan Rodriguez .75 2.00
JB Jeff Bagwell .75 2.00
JD Johnny Damon .75 2.00
JE Jim Edmonds .75 2.00
JG Jason Giambi .75 2.00
JJ Jacque Jones .50 1.25
JL Javy Lopez .50 1.25
JR Jose Reyes .75 2.00
JS Johan Santana .75 2.00
JT Jim Thome .75 2.00
KG Ken Griffey Jr. 2.50 6.00
KW Kerry Wood .50 1.25
MC Miguel Cabrera 1.25 3.00
MP Mike Piazza 1.25 3.00
MR Manny Ramirez 1.25 3.00
MT Mark Teixeira .75 2.00
PK Paul Konerko .75 2.00
PM Pedro Martinez .75 2.00
PR Mark Prior .75 2.00
RC Roger Clemens 1.50 4.00
RF Rafael Furcal .50 1.25
RJ Randy Johnson 1.25 3.00
RO Roy Oswalt .75 2.00
RP Rafael Palmeiro .75 2.00
SM John Smoltz 1.25 3.00
SR Scott Rolen .75 2.00
SS Sammy Sosa 1.25 3.00
TE Miguel Tejada .75 2.00
TG Tom Glavine .75 2.00
TH Tim Hudson .75 2.00
WR David Wright 1.00 2.50

2006 Upper Deck Amazing Greats Materials

SER.1 ODDS 1:48 HOBBY, 1:288 RETAIL
AB Adrian Beltre Jsy 3.00 8.00
AJ Andruw Jones Jsy 4.00 10.00
AP Albert Pujols Jsy 6.00 15.00
AS Alfonso Soriano Jsy 3.00 8.00
BA Bobby Abreu Jsy 3.00 8.00
CB Carlos Beltran Jsy 3.00 8.00
CC Carl Crawford Jsy 3.00 8.00
CJ Chipper Jones Jsy 4.00 10.00
CL Carlos Lee Jsy 3.00 8.00
CP Corey Patterson Jsy 3.00 8.00
CS Curt Schilling Jsy 4.00 10.00
DJ Derek Jeter Jsy 10.00 25.00
DO David Ortiz Jsy 4.00 10.00
DW Dontrelle Willis Jsy 3.00 8.00
EG Eric Gagne Jsy 3.00 8.00
FT Frank Thomas Jsy 4.00 10.00
GM Greg Maddux Jsy 4.00 10.00
GS Gary Sheffield Jsy 3.00 8.00
HE Todd Helton Jsy 4.00 10.00
IR Ivan Rodriguez Jsy 4.00 10.00
JB Jeff Bagwell Jsy 4.00 10.00
JD Johnny Damon Jsy 4.00 10.00
JE Jim Edmonds Jsy 3.00 8.00
JG Jason Giambi Jsy 3.00 8.00
JJ Jacque Jones Jsy 3.00 8.00
JL Javy Lopez Jsy 3.00 8.00
JR Jose Reyes Jsy 3.00 8.00
JS Johan Santana Jsy 4.00 10.00
JT Jim Thome Jsy 4.00 10.00
KG Ken Griffey Jr. Jsy 6.00 15.00
KW Kerry Wood Jsy 3.00 8.00
MC Miguel Cabrera Jsy 4.00 10.00
MP Mike Piazza Jsy 4.00 10.00
MR Manny Ramirez Jsy 4.00 10.00
MT Mark Teixeira Jsy 4.00 10.00
PK Paul Konerko Jsy 3.00 8.00
PM Pedro Martinez Jsy 4.00 10.00
PR Mark Prior Jsy 3.00 8.00
RC Roger Clemens Jsy 6.00 15.00
RF Rafael Furcal Jsy 3.00 8.00
RJ Randy Johnson Pants 4.00 10.00
RO Roy Oswalt Jsy 3.00 8.00
RP Rafael Palmeiro Jsy 4.00 10.00
SM John Smoltz Jsy 4.00 10.00
SR Scott Rolen Jsy 4.00 10.00
SS Sammy Sosa Jsy 4.00 10.00
TE Miguel Tejada Jsy 3.00 8.00
TG Tom Glavine Jsy 4.00 10.00
TH Tim Hudson Jsy 3.00 8.00
WR David Wright Jsy 4.00 10.00

2006 Upper Deck Diamond Collection

SER.1 ODDS 1:6 HOBBY, 1:12 RETAIL
*GOLD: .6X TO 1.5X BASIC
FIVE #'d INSERTS PER SER.1 HOBBY BOX
GOLD PRINT RUN 699 SERIAL #'d SETS
AE Adam Eaton .50 1.25
AH Aubrey Huff .50 1.25
AK Adam Kennedy .50 1.25
AL Moises Alou .50 1.25
AO Akinori Otsuka .50 1.25
BC Bobby Crosby .50 1.25
BR Brad Radke .50 1.25
CC C.C. Sabathia .75 2.00
CK Casey Kotchman .50 1.25
CO Jose Contreras .50 1.25
CP Carl Pavano .50 1.25
CS Chris Shelton .50 1.25
DJ Derek Jeter 3.00 8.00
DO David Ortiz 1.25 3.00
EC Eric Chavez .50 1.25
EJ Edwin Jackson .50 1.25
FG Freddy Garcia .50 1.25

GM Greg Maddux 1.50 4.00
GO Juan Gonzalez .50 1.25
IR Ivan Rodriguez .75 2.00
JB Jeff Bagwell .75 2.00
JC Jesse Crain .50 1.25
JD Johnny Damon .75 2.00
JE Jim Edmonds .75 2.00
JG Jose Guillen .50 1.25
JJ Jacque Jones .50 1.25
JK Jason Kendall .50 1.25
JP Jorge Posada .75 2.00
JS John Smoltz 1.25 3.00
JT Jim Thome .75 2.00
JW Jayson Werth .75 2.00
KE Austin Kearns .50 1.25
KG Ken Griffey Jr. 2.50 6.00
KL Kenny Lofton .50 1.25
KM Kevin Millwood .50 1.25
LA Matt Lawton .50 1.25
LO Mike Lowell .50 1.25
MA Kazuo Matsui .50 1.25
MC Mike Cameron .50 1.25
MH Mike Hampton .50 1.25
ML Mike Lieberthal .50 1.25
NJ Nick Johnson .50 1.25
OC Orlando Cabrera .50 1.25
PL Paul Lo Duca .50 1.25
PW Preston Wilson .50 1.25
RB Rocco Baldelli .50 1.25
RJ Randy Johnson 1.25 3.00
SF Steve Finley .50 1.25
SK Scott Kazmir .75 2.00
SS Shannon Stewart .50 1.25

2006 Upper Deck Diamond Collection Materials

SER.1 ODDS 1:48 HOBBY, 1:288 RETAIL
AE Adam Eaton Jsy 3.00 8.00
AH Aubrey Huff Jsy 3.00 8.00
AK Adam Kennedy Jsy 3.00 8.00
AL Moises Alou Jsy 3.00 8.00
AO Akinori Otsuka Jsy 3.00 8.00
BC Bobby Crosby Jsy 3.00 8.00
BR Brad Radke Jsy 3.00 8.00
CC C.C. Sabathia Jsy 3.00 8.00
CK Casey Kotchman Jsy 3.00 8.00
CO Jose Contreras Jsy 3.00 8.00
CP Carl Pavano Jsy 3.00 8.00
CS Chris Shelton Jsy 4.00 10.00
DJ Derek Jeter Jsy 10.00 25.00
DO David Ortiz Jsy 4.00 10.00
EC Eric Chavez Jsy 3.00 8.00
EJ Edwin Jackson Jsy 3.00 8.00
FG Freddy Garcia Jsy 3.00 8.00
GM Greg Maddux Jsy 4.00 10.00
GO Juan Gonzalez Jsy 3.00 8.00
IR Ivan Rodriguez Jsy 4.00 10.00
JB Jeff Bagwell Jsy 4.00 10.00
JC Jesse Crain Jsy 3.00 8.00
JD Johnny Damon Jsy 4.00 10.00
JE Jim Edmonds Jsy 3.00 8.00
JG Jose Guillen Jsy 3.00 8.00
JJ Jacque Jones Jsy 3.00 8.00
JK Jason Kendall Jsy 3.00 8.00
JP Jorge Posada Jsy 4.00 10.00
JS John Smoltz Jsy 4.00 10.00
JT Jim Thome Jsy 4.00 10.00
JW Jayson Werth Jsy 3.00 8.00
KE Austin Kearns Jsy 3.00 8.00
KG Ken Griffey Jr. Jsy 6.00 15.00
KL Kenny Lofton Jsy 3.00 8.00
KM Kevin Millwood Jsy 3.00 8.00
LA Matt Lawton Jsy 3.00 8.00
LO Mike Lowell Jsy 3.00 8.00
MA Kazuo Matsui Jsy 3.00 8.00
MC Mike Cameron Jsy 3.00 8.00
MH Mike Hampton Jsy 3.00 8.00
ML Mike Lieberthal Jsy 3.00 8.00
NJ Nick Johnson Jsy 3.00 8.00
OC Orlando Cabrera Jsy 3.00 8.00
PL Paul Lo Duca Jsy 3.00 8.00
PW Preston Wilson Jsy 3.00 8.00
RB Rocco Baldelli Jsy 3.00 8.00
RJ Randy Johnson Pants 4.00 10.00
SF Steve Finley Jsy 3.00 8.00
SK Scott Kazmir Jsy 3.00 8.00
SS Shannon Stewart Jsy 3.00 8.00

2006 Upper Deck Diamond Debut

STATED ODDS 1:4 WAL MART PACKS
1-40 ISSUED IN SERIES 1 PACKS
41-82 ISSUED IN SERIES 2 PACKS
DD1 Tadahito Iguchi .60 1.50
DD2 Huston Street .60 1.50
DD3 Norihiro Nakamura .60 1.50
DD4 Chien-Ming Wang 1.00 2.50
DD5 Pedro Lopez
DD6 Robinson Cano 1.00 2.50
DD7 Tim Stauffer .60 1.50
DD8 Ervin Santana .60 1.50
DD9 Brandon McCarthy .60 1.50
DD10 Hayden Penn .60 1.50
DD11 Derek Jeter 4.00 10.00
DD12 Ken Griffey Jr. 3.00 8.00
DD13 Prince Fielder 3.00 8.00
DD14 Edwin Encarnacion 1.50 4.00
DD15 Scott Olsen .60 1.50
DD16 Chris Resop .60 1.50
DD17 Justin Verlander 5.00 12.00
DD18 Melky Cabrera 1.00 2.50
DD19 Jeff Francoeur 1.50 4.00
DD20 Yuniesky Betancourt .60 1.50
DD21 Conor Jackson 1.00 2.50
DD22 Felix Hernandez 1.00 2.50
DD23 Anthony Reyes .60 1.50
DD24 John-Ford Griffin .60 1.50
DD25 Adam Wainwright 1.00 2.50
DD26 Ryan Garko .60 1.50
DD27 Ryan Zimmerman 2.00 5.00
DD28 Tom Seaver 1.00 2.50
DD29 Johnny Bench 1.50 4.00
DD30 Reggie Jackson 1.00 2.50
DD31 Rod Carew 1.00 2.50
DD32 Nolan Ryan 5.00 12.00
DD33 Richie Ashburn 1.00 2.50
DD34 Yogi Berra 1.50 4.00
DD35 Lou Brock 1.00 2.50
DD36 Carlton Fisk 1.00 2.50
DD37 Joe Morgan 1.00 2.50
DD38 Bob Gibson 1.00 2.50
DD39 Willie McCovey 1.00 2.50
DD40 Harmon Killebrew 1.50 4.00
DD41 Takashi Saito 1.00 2.50
DD42 Kenji Johjima 1.50 4.00
DD43 Joel Zumaya 1.50 4.00
DD44 Dan Uggla 1.00 2.50
DD45 Taylor Buchholz .60 1.50
DD46 Josh Barfield .60 1.50
DD47 Brian Bannister .60 1.50
DD48 Nick Markakis 1.25 3.00
DD49 Carlos Martinez .60 1.50
DD50 Macay McBride .60 1.50
DD51 Brian Anderson .60 1.50
DD52 Freddie Bynum .60 1.50
DD53 Kelly Shoppach .60 1.50
DD54 Choo Freeman .60 1.50
DD55 Ryan Shealy .60 1.50
DD56 Chris Resop .60 1.50
DD57 Hanley Ramirez 1.00 2.50
DD58 Mike Jacobs .60 1.50
DD59 Cody Ross 1.50 4.00
DD60 Jose Capellan .60 1.50
DD61 David Gassner .60 1.50
DD62 Jason Kubel .60 1.50
DD63 Jered Weaver 2.00 5.00
DD64 Paul Maholm .60 1.50
DD65 Nate McLouth .60 1.50
DD66 Ben Johnson .60 1.50
DD67 Jack Taschner .60 1.50
DD68 Skip Schumaker .60 1.50
DD69 Brandon Watson .60 1.50
DD70 David Wright 1.25 3.00
DD71 David Ortiz 1.50 4.00
DD72 Alex Rodriguez 2.00 5.00
DD73 Johan Santana 1.00 2.50
DD74 Greg Maddux 2.00 5.00
DD75 Ichiro Suzuki 2.00 5.00
DD76 Albert Pujols 2.00 5.00
DD77 Hideki Matsui 1.50 4.00
DD78 Vladimir Guerrero 1.00 2.50
DD79 Pedro Martinez 1.00 2.50
DD80 Mike Schmidt 2.50 6.00
DD81 Al Kaline 1.50 4.00
DD82 Robin Yount 1.50 4.00

2006 Upper Deck First Class Cuts

RANDOM INSERTS IN SERIES 1 PACKS
STATED PRINT RUN 1 SERIAL #'d SET
NO PRICING DUE TO SCARCITY

2006 Upper Deck First Class Legends

COMMON RUTH (1-20) 1.25 3.00
COMMON COBB (21-40) .75 2.00
COMMON WAGNER (41-60 .40 1.00
COMMON MATHEWSON (61-80) .40 1.00
COMMON W.JOHNSON (81-100) .40 1.00
SER.1 STATED ODDS: 1:6 HOBBY
SER.2 ODDS APPROX. 1:12 HOBBY
*GOLD: .75X TO 2X BASIC
GOLD PRINT RUN 699 SERIAL #'d SETS
*SILVER SPECTRUM: 1.25X TO 3X BASIC
SILVER SPEC. PRINT RUN 99 SERIAL #'d SETS
FIVE #'d INSERTS PER SER.1 HOBBY BOX
GOLD-SILVER AVAIL ONLY IN SER.1 PACKS

2006 Upper Deck Collect the Mascots

COMPLETE SET (3) .40 1.00
ISSUED IN 06 UD 1 AND 2 FAT PACKS
MLB1 Wally the Green Monster .20 .50
MLB2 Phillie Phanatic .20 .50
MLB3 Mr. Met .20 .50

2006 Upper Deck Inaugural Images

SER.2 ODDS 1:8 H, RANDOM IN RETAIL
II1 Sung-Heon Hong .75 2.00
II2 Yulieski Gourriel 1.50 4.00
II3 Tsuyoshi Nishioka 3.00 8.00
II4 Miguel Cabrera 1.25 3.00
II5 Yung Chi Chen .75 2.00
II6 Ormari Romero .50 1.25
II7 Ken Griffey Jr. 2.50 6.00
II8 Bernie Williams .75 2.00
II9 Daniel Cabrera .50 1.25
II10 David Ortiz 1.25 3.00
II11 Alex Rodriguez 1.50 4.00
II12 Frederich Cepeda .50 1.25
II13 Derek Jeter 3.00 8.00
II14 Jorge Cantu .50 1.25
II15 Alexi Ramirez 3.00 8.00
II16 Yoandy Garlobo .50 1.25
II17 Koji Uehara 1.50 4.00
II18 Nobuhiko Matsunaka .75 2.00
II19 Tomoya Satozaki .75 2.00
II20 Seung Yeop Lee .75 2.00
II21 Yulieski Gourriel 1.50 4.00
II22 Adrian Beltre 1.25 3.00
II23 Ken Griffey Jr. 2.50 6.00
II24 Jong Beom Lee .50 1.25
II25 Ichiro Suzuki 1.50 4.00
II26 Yoandy Garlobo .50 1.25
II27 Daisuke Matsuzaka 1.50 4.00
II28 Yadel Marti .50 1.25
II29 Chan Ho Park .75 2.00
II30 Daisuke Matsuzaka 1.50 4.00

2006 Upper Deck INKredible

SER.2 ODDS 1:288 H, RANDOM IN RETAIL
UPDATE ODDS 1:24 RETAIL
SP INFO/PRINT RUNS PROVIDED BY UD
SP * INFO PROVIDED BY BECKETT
SP's ARE NOT SERIAL-NUMBERED
NO PRICING ON QTY OF 36 OR LESS
AB Ambiorix Burgos UPD SP * 6.00 15.00
AH Aaron Harang UPD 4.00 10.00
AJ Adam Jones UPD 12.00 30.00
AP Angel Pagan UPD 6.00 15.00
AR2 Alex Rios UPD SP 15.00 40.00
AR Alexis Rios 6.00 15.00
BA Brandon Backe UPD 4.00 10.00
BB Ben Broussard UPD 6.00 15.00
BC Brandon Claussen UPD 4.00 10.00
BM Brandon McCarthy UPD SP 6.00 15.00
BM Brett Myers SP/72 * 6.00 15.00
BR Brian Roberts 6.00 15.00
BR2 Brian Roberts UPD 6.00 15.00
BW Brian Wilson UPD 10.00 25.00
CA Miguel Cabrera 20.00 50.00
CB Colter Bean UPD 4.00 10.00
CC Coco Crisp UPD 5.00 12.00
CC Carl Crawford 6.00 15.00
CC2 Carl Crawford UPD 6.00 15.00
CD Chris Duffy UPD 4.00 10.00
CI Cesar Izturis UPD SP * 6.00 15.00
CK Casey Kotchman 4.00 10.00
CK2 Casey Kotchman UPD 4.00 10.00
CL Cliff Lee UPD 4.00 10.00
CO Chad Cordero 6.00 15.00
CO2 Chad Cordero UPD SP 6.00 15.00
CW C.J. Wilson UPD 6.00 15.00
DJ Derek Jeter 75.00 150.00
DJ2 Derek Jeter UPD SP 125.00 250.00
DR Darrell Rasner UPD 4.00 10.00
DW David Wright SP/91 * 8.00 20.00
EA Erick Aybar UPD 4.00 10.00
EB Eude Brito UPD 6.00 15.00
EG Eric Gagne UPD SP 30.00 60.00
GC Gustavo Chacin UPD 4.00 10.00
GF Gavin Floyd UPD 4.00 10.00
JB Joe Blanton 6.00 15.00
JC Jesse Crain 4.00 10.00
JD Jermaine Dye UPD 6.00 15.00
JH John Hattig UPD 4.00 10.00
JH J.J. Hardy 4.00 10.00
JJ Jorge Julio UPD SP 6.00 15.00
JM Joe Mauer SP/91 * 15.00 40.00
JO Jacque Jones UPD 6.00 15.00
JP Jhonny Peralta UPD 4.00 10.00
JR Juan Rivera UPD SP 10.00 25.00
JR Jeremy Reed 4.00 10.00
JV Justin Verlander SP/91 * 12.50 30.00
KG Ken Griffey Jr. 40.00 80.00
KG2 Ken Griffey Jr. UPD SP 40.00 80.00
KR Ken Ray UPD 4.00 10.00
KY Kevin Youkilis 6.00 15.00
KY2 Kevin Youkilis UPD 6.00 15.00
LN Leo Nunez UPD 4.00 10.00
LO Lyle Overbay SP/91 * 6.00 15.00
MH Matt Holliday UPD 8.00 20.00
MM Matt Murton UPD 10.00 25.00
MO Justin Morneau 10.00 25.00
MR Mike Rouse UPD 4.00 10.00
MT Mark Teahen UPD 6.00 15.00
MT Mark Teixeira 10.00 25.00
MV Mike Vento UPD 4.00 10.00
NG Nomar Garciaparra 30.00 60.00
NL Noah Lowry UPD 6.00 15.00
NS Nick Swisher UPD 6.00 15.00
PA John Patterson UPD 4.00 10.00
PE Joel Peralta UPD 4.00 10.00
PI Joel Pineiro UPD 4.00 10.00
RE Jose Reyes SP/91 * 8.00 20.00
RF Ryan Freel UPD 6.00 15.00
RG Ryan Garko UPD 4.00 10.00
RP Ronny Paulino UPD 6.00 15.00
RS Ryan Shealy UPD 6.00 15.00
RZ Ryan Zimmerman SP/91 * 10.00 25.00
SK Scott Kazmir 8.00 20.00
TH Travis Hafner 10.00 25.00
TI Tadahito Iguchi SP/91 * 20.00 50.00
TI2 Tadahito Iguchi UPD SP 30.00 60.00
VM Victor Martinez 6.00 15.00
WI Dontrelle Willis 10.00 25.00
YB Yuniesky Betancourt UPD 4.00 10.00
YM Yadier Molina UPD 20.00 50.00
ZM Zach Miner UPD 4.00 10.00

2006 Upper Deck Derek Jeter Spell and Win

COMPLETE SET (5) 6.00 15.00
COMMON CARD (1-5) 1.25 3.00
RANDOM IN SER.2 WAL-MART PACKS

2006 Upper Deck Player Highlights

SER.2 ODDS 1:6 H, RANDOM IN RETAIL
PH1 Andruw Jones .40 1.00
PH2 Manny Ramirez 1.00 2.50
PH3 Travis Hafner .40 1.00
PH4 Johnny Damon .60 1.50
PH5 Miguel Cabrera 1.00 2.50
PH6 Chris Carpenter .60 1.50
PH7 Derrek Lee .40 1.00
PH8 Jason Bay .40 1.00
PH9 Jason Varitek 1.00 2.50
PH10 Ryan Howard .75 2.00
PH11 Mark Teixeira .60 1.50
PH12 Carlos Delgado .40 1.00
PH13 Bartolo Colon .40 1.00
PH14 David Wright .75 2.00
PH15 Miguel Tejada .60 1.50
PH16 Mike Piazza 1.00 2.50
PH17 Paul Konerko .60 1.50
PH18 Jermaine Dye .40 1.00
PH19 Ichiro Suzuki 1.25 3.00
PH20 Brad Wilkerson .40 1.00
PH21 Hideki Matsui 1.00 2.50
PH22 Albert Pujols 1.25 3.00
PH23 Chris Burke .40 1.00
PH24 Derek Jeter 2.50 6.00
PH25 Brian Roberts .40 1.00
PH26 David Ortiz 1.00 2.50
PH27 Alex Rodriguez 1.25 3.00
PH28 Ken Griffey Jr. 2.00 5.00
PH29 Prince Fielder 2.00 5.00
PH30 Bobby Abreu .40 1.00
PH31 Vladimir Guerrero .60 1.50
PH32 Tadahito Iguchi .40 1.00
PH33 Jose Reyes .60 1.50
PH34 Scott Podsednik .40 1.00
PH35 Gary Sheffield .40 1.00

2006 Upper Deck Run Producers

SER.2 ODDS 1:8 H, RANDOM IN RETAIL
RP1 Ty Cobb 1.50 4.00
RP2 Derrek Lee .40 1.00
RP3 Andruw Jones .40 1.00
RP4 David Ortiz 1.00 2.50
RP5 Lou Gehrig 2.00 5.00
RP6 Ken Griffey Jr. 2.00 5.00
RP7 Albert Pujols 1.25 3.00
RP8 Derek Jeter 2.50 6.00
RP9 Manny Ramirez 1.00 2.50
RP10 Alex Rodriguez 1.25 3.00
RP11 Gary Sheffield .40 1.00
RP12 Miguel Cabrera 1.00 2.50
RP13 Hideki Matsui 1.00 2.50
RP14 Vladimir Guerrero .60 1.50
RP15 David Wright .75 2.00
RP16 Mike Schmidt 1.50 4.00
RP17 Mark Teixeira .60 1.50
RP18 Babe Ruth 2.50 6.00
RP19 Jimmie Foxx 1.00 2.50
RP20 Honus Wagner 1.00 2.50

2006 Upper Deck Season Highlights

ISSUED IN 06 UD 1 AND 2 FAT PACKS
SH1 Albert Pujols 1.25 3.00
SH2 Ken Griffey Jr. 2.00 5.00
SH3 Travis Hafner .40 1.00
SH4 David Ortiz 1.00 2.50
SH5 David Ortiz 1.00 2.50
SH6 Ryan Howard .75 2.00
SH7 Chase Utley .60 1.50
SH8 Manny Ramirez 1.00 2.50
SH9 Barry Zito .60 1.50
SH10 Roger Clemens 1.25 3.00
SH11 Francisco Liriano 1.00 2.50
SH12 Jered Weaver 1.25 3.00
SH13 Roy Halladay .60 1.50
SH14 Johan Santana .60 1.50
SH15 Tom Glavine .60 1.50
SH16 Pedro Martinez .60 1.50
SH17 Mike Piazza 1.00 2.50
SH18 Alfonso Soriano .60 1.50
SH19 Miguel Cabrera 1.00 2.50
SH20 Vladimir Guerrero .60 1.50
SH21 Joe Mauer .60 1.50
SH22 Ryan Zimmerman 1.25 3.00
SH23 Carlos Delgado .40 1.00
SH24 Jim Thome .60 1.50
SH25 Jermaine Dye .40 1.00
SH26 Derek Jeter 2.50 6.00
SH27 Ivan Rodriguez .60 1.50
SH28 Bobby Abreu .40 1.00
SH29 Greg Maddux 1.25 3.00
SH30 Alex Rodriguez 1.25 3.00

2006 Upper Deck Signature Sensations

SER.1 ODDS 1:288 HOBBY, 1:1920 RETAIL
SP INFO PROVIDED BY UPPER DECK
AL Al Leiter 6.00 15.00
AM Aaron Miles 4.00 10.00
AR Aaron Rowand 6.00 15.00
BA Bronson Arroyo 6.00 15.00
CS Cory Sullivan 4.00 10.00
GA Garrett Atkins 4.00 10.00
JE Johnny Estrada 4.00 10.00
JJ Josh Johnson 4.00 10.00
JS Jeff Suppan 4.00 10.00
JV Joe Valentine 4.00 10.00
KC Kiko Calero 4.00 10.00
NP Nick Punto 6.00 15.00
SB Scott Baker 6.00 15.00
TR Travis Hafner 6.00 15.00
YM Yadier Molina 20.00 50.00

2006 Upper Deck Speed To Burn

SER.2 ODDS 1:12 H, RANDOM IN RETAIL
CARDS 2/10/13 DO NOT EXIST
SB1 Lou Brock .60 1.50
SB3 Alfonso Soriano .60 1.50
SB4 Carl Crawford .60 1.50
SB5 Chone Figgins .40 1.00
SB6 Ichiro Suzuki 1.25 3.00
SB7 Jose Reyes .60 1.50
SB8 Juan Pierre .40 1.00
SB9 Scott Podsednik .40 1.00
SB11 Alex Rodriguez 1.25 3.00
SB12 David Wright .75 2.00
SB14 Bobby Abreu .40 1.00
SB15 Brian Roberts .40 1.00

2006 Upper Deck Star Attractions

COMPLETE UPDATE (50) 20.00 50.00
SER.1 MINORS .50 1.25
SER.1 SEMIS .75 2.00
SER.1 UNLISTED 1.25 3.00
SER.1 ODDS 1:6 HOBBY, 1:12 RETAIL
UPDATE ODDS 1:2 RETAIL
*GOLD: .6X TO 1.5X BASIC
FIVE #'d INSERTS PER SER.1 HOBBY BOX
GOLD PRINT RUN 699 SERIAL #'d SETS
*SILVER: 1.25X TO 3X BASIC
ONE #'d INSERT PER UPDATE BOX
SILVER PRINT RUN 99 SERIAL #'d SETS
AB Adrian Beltre 1.00 2.50
AE Andre Ethier UPD 1.25 3.00
AH Aubrey Huff .40 1.00
AJ Andruw Jones .40 1.00
AJ Adam Jones UPD 4.00 10.00
AL Adam Loewen UPD .40 1.00
AM Andy Marte UPD .40 1.00
AN Anibal Sanchez UPD .40 1.00
AP Andy Pettitte .60 1.50
AR Anthony Reyes UPD .40 1.00
AS Alfonso Soriano .60 1.50
AW Adam Wainwright UPD .60 1.50
BA Bobby Abreu .40 1.00
BI Chad Billingsley UPD .60 1.50
BR Brian Anderson UPD .40 1.00
BZ Barry Zito .60 1.50
CB Carlos Beltran .60 1.50
CD Carlos Delgado .40 1.00
CH Cole Hamels UPD 1.25 3.00
CJ Chipper Jones 1.00 2.50
CL Carlos Lee .40 1.00
CO Conor Jackson UPD .60 1.50
CQ Carlos Quentin UPD .60 1.50
CS Curt Schilling .60 1.50
CY Chris Young UPD 1.00 2.50
DJ Derek Jeter 2.50 6.00
DL Derrek Lee .40 1.00
DM Dustin McGowan UPD .40 1.00
DO David Ortiz 1.00 2.50
DP Dustin Pedroia UPD 12.00 30.00
DU Dan Uggla UPD .60 1.50
DW Dontrelle Willis .40 1.00
EA Erick Aybar UPD .40 1.00
EG Eric Gagne .40 1.00
FL Francisco Liriano UPD 1.00 2.50
FT Frank Thomas 1.00 2.50
GA Garret Anderson .40 1.00
GM Greg Maddux 1.25 3.00
GR Khalil Greene .40 1.00
GS Gary Sheffield .40 1.00
GU Jose Guillen .40 1.00
HI Jason Hirsh UPD .40 1.00
HK Howie Kendrick UPD .75 2.00
HP Hayden Penn UPD .40 1.00
HR Hanley Ramirez UPD .60 1.50
HU Justin Huber UPD .40 1.00
JA Chuck James UPD .40 1.00
JB Josh Beckett .40 1.00
JC Jose Contreras .40 1.00
JD Johnny Damon .60 1.50
JE Jim Edmonds .60 1.50
JG Jason Giambi .40 1.00
JH Jeremy Hermida UPD .40 1.00
JJ Josh Johnson UPD 1.00 2.50
JJ Jacque Jones .40 1.00
JK Jason Kubel UPD .40 1.00
JL Javy Lopez .40 1.00
JM Joe Mauer .60 1.50
JO Josh Barfield UPD .40 1.00
JP Jorge Posada .60 1.50
JR Jose Reyes .60 1.50
JS Jason Schmidt .40 1.00
JV Justin Verlander UPD 3.00 8.00
JW Jered Weaver UPD 1.25 3.00
JZ Joel Zumaya UPD 1.00 2.50
KG Ken Griffey Jr. 2.00 5.00
KJ Kenji Johjima UPD 1.00 2.50
KM Kendry Morales UPD 1.00 2.50
KW Kerry Wood .40 1.00
LB Lance Berkman .60 1.50
LE Jon Lester UPD 1.50 4.00
LM Lastings Milledge UPD .40 1.00
MA Jeff Mathis UPD .40 1.00
MC Matt Cain UPD 2.50 6.00
MK Matt Kemp UPD 1.00 2.50
MM Mark Mulder .40 1.00
MO Magglio Ordonez .60 1.50
MP Mark Prior .60 1.50
MR Manny Ramirez 1.00 2.50
MT Mark Teixeira .60 1.50
NM Nick Markakis UPD .75 2.00
PA Jonathan Papelbon UPD 2.00 5.00
PE Mike Pelfrey UPD 1.00 2.50
PF Prince Fielder UPD 2.00 5.00
PM Pedro Martinez .60 1.50
PU Albert Pujols 1.25 3.00
RC Ronny Cedeno UPD .40 1.00
RH Rich Harden .40 1.00
RM Russell Martin UPD .60 1.50
RZ Ryan Zimmerman UPD 1.25 3.00
SD Stephen Drew UPD .75 2.00
SG Shawn Green .40 1.00
SM John Smoltz 1.00 2.50
SO Scott Olsen UPD .40 1.00
SW Jeremy Sowers UPD .40 1.00
TG Tony Gwynn Jr. UPD .40 1.00
TH Torii Hunter .40 1.00
TI Tadahito Iguchi .40 1.00
WA Willy Aybar UPD .40 1.00
WR David Wright .75 2.00

2006 Upper Deck Star Attractions Swatches

SER.1 ODDS 1:48 HOBBY, 1:288 RETAIL
AB Adrian Beltre Jsy 3.00 8.00
AH Aubrey Huff Jsy 3.00 8.00
AJ Andruw Jones Jsy 4.00 10.00
AP Andy Pettitte Jsy 4.00 10.00
AS Alfonso Soriano Jsy 3.00 8.00
BA Bobby Abreu Jsy 3.00 8.00
BZ Barry Zito Jsy 3.00 8.00
CB Carlos Beltran Jsy 3.00 8.00
CD Carlos Delgado Jsy 3.00 8.00
CJ Chipper Jones Jsy 4.00 10.00
CL Carlos Lee Jsy 3.00 8.00
CS Curt Schilling Jsy 4.00 10.00
DJ Derek Jeter Jsy 10.00 25.00
DL Derrek Lee Jsy 4.00 10.00
DO David Ortiz Jsy 4.00 10.00
DW Dontrelle Willis Jsy 3.00 8.00
EG Eric Gagne Jsy 3.00 8.00
FT Frank Thomas Jsy 4.00 10.00
GA Garret Anderson Jsy 3.00 8.00
GM Greg Maddux Jsy 4.00 10.00
GR Khalil Greene Jsy 4.00 10.00
GS Gary Sheffield Jsy 3.00 8.00
GU Jose Guillen Jsy 3.00 8.00
JB Josh Beckett Jsy 3.00 8.00
JC Jose Contreras Jsy 3.00 8.00
JD Johnny Damon Jsy 4.00 10.00
JE Jim Edmonds Jsy 3.00 8.00
JG Jason Giambi Jsy 3.00 8.00
JJ Jacque Jones Jsy 3.00 8.00
JL Javy Lopez Jsy 3.00 8.00
JM Joe Mauer Jsy 4.00 10.00
JP Jorge Posada Jsy 4.00 10.00
JR Jose Reyes Jsy 3.00 8.00
JS Jason Schmidt Jsy 3.00 8.00
KG Ken Griffey Jr. Jsy 6.00 15.00
KW Kerry Wood Jsy 3.00 8.00
LB Lance Berkman Jsy 3.00 8.00
MM Mark Mulder Jsy 3.00 8.00
MO Magglio Ordonez Jsy 3.00 8.00
MP Mark Prior Jsy 3.00 8.00
MR Manny Ramirez Jsy 4.00 10.00
MT Mark Teixeira Jsy 4.00 10.00
PM Pedro Martinez Jsy 4.00 10.00
PU Albert Pujols Jsy 6.00 15.00
RH Rich Harden Jsy 3.00 8.00
SG Shawn Green Jsy 3.00 8.00
SM John Smoltz Jsy 4.00 10.00
TH Torii Hunter Jsy 3.00 8.00
TI Tadahito Iguchi Jsy 4.00 10.00
WR David Wright Jsy 4.00 10.00

2006 Upper Deck Team Pride

SER.1 ODDS 1:6 HOBBY, 1:12 RETAIL
*GOLD: .6X TO 1.5X BASIC
FIVE #'d INSERTS PER SER.1 HOBBY BOX
GOLD PRINT RUN 699 SERIAL #'d SETS
AH Aubrey Huff .50 1.25
AJ Andruw Jones .50 1.25
AP Albert Pujols 1.50 4.00
BA Bobby Abreu .50 1.25
BW Bernie Williams .75 2.00
BZ Barry Zito .75 2.00
CC C.C. Sabathia .75 2.00
CD Carlos Delgado .50 1.25
CJ Chipper Jones 1.25 3.00
CK Casey Kotchman .50 1.25
CS Curt Schilling .75 2.00
DJ Derek Jeter 3.00 8.00
DO David Ortiz 1.25 3.00
DW Dontrelle Willis .50 1.25
EC Eric Chavez .50 1.25
EG Eric Gagne .50 1.25
FT Frank Thomas 1.25 3.00
GA Garret Anderson .50 1.25
GM Greg Maddux 1.50 4.00
GR Khalil Greene .50 1.25
IR Ivan Rodriguez .75 2.00
JB Jeff Bagwell .75 2.00
JD Johnny Damon .75 2.00
JE Jim Edmonds .75 2.00
JM Jamie Moyer .50 1.25
JP Jorge Posada .75 2.00
JR Jose Reyes .75 2.00
JS John Smoltz 1.25 3.00
JT Jim Thome .75 2.00
JV Jose Vidro .50 1.25
KF Keith Foulke .50 1.25
KG Ken Griffey Jr. 2.50 6.00
KW Kerry Wood .50 1.25
LC Luis Castillo .50 1.25
LG Luis Gonzalez .50 1.25
LO Mike Lowell .50 1.25
MA Joe Mauer .75 2.00
ME Morgan Ensberg .50 1.25
ML Mike Lieberthal .50 1.25
MP Mark Prior .75 2.00
MS Mike Sweeney .50 1.25
MY Michael Young .50 1.25
NJ Nick Johnson .50 1.25
PE Andy Pettitte .75 2.00
RB Rocco Baldelli .50 1.25
RH Rich Harden .50 1.25
RK Ryan Klesko .50 1.25
SC Sean Casey .50 1.25
TH Trevor Hoffman .75 2.00
VA Jason Varitek 1.25 3.00

2006 Upper Deck Team Pride Materials

SER.1 ODDS 1:48 HOBBY, 1:288 RETAIL
AH Aubrey Huff Jsy 3.00 8.00
AJ Andruw Jones Jsy 4.00 10.00
AP Albert Pujols Jsy 6.00 15.00
BA Bobby Abreu Jsy 3.00 8.00
BW Bernie Williams Jsy 4.00 10.00
BZ Barry Zito Jsy 3.00 8.00
CC C.C. Sabathia Jsy 3.00 8.00
CD Carlos Delgado Jsy 3.00 8.00
CJ Chipper Jones Jsy 4.00 10.00
CK Casey Kotchman Jsy 3.00 8.00
CS Curt Schilling Jsy 4.00 10.00
DJ Derek Jeter Jsy 10.00 25.00
DO David Ortiz Jsy 4.00 10.00
DW Dontrelle Willis Jsy 3.00 8.00
EC Eric Chavez Jsy 3.00 8.00
EG Eric Gagne Jsy 3.00 8.00
FT Frank Thomas Jsy 4.00 10.00
GA Garret Anderson Jsy 3.00 8.00
GM Greg Maddux Jsy 4.00 10.00
GR Khalil Greene Jsy 4.00 10.00
IR Ivan Rodriguez Jsy 4.00 10.00
JB Jeff Bagwell Jsy 4.00 10.00
JD Johnny Damon Jsy 4.00 10.00
JE Jim Edmonds Jsy 3.00 8.00
JM Jamie Moyer Jsy 3.00 8.00
JP Jorge Posada Jsy 4.00 10.00
JR Jose Reyes Jsy 3.00 8.00
JS John Smoltz Jsy 4.00 10.00
JT Jim Thome Jsy 4.00 10.00
JV Jose Vidro Jsy 3.00 8.00
KF Keith Foulke Jsy 3.00 8.00
KG Ken Griffey Jr. Jsy 6.00 15.00
KW Kerry Wood Jsy 3.00 8.00
LC Luis Castillo Jsy 3.00 8.00
LG Luis Gonzalez Jsy 3.00 8.00
LO Mike Lowell Jsy 3.00 8.00
MA Joe Mauer Jsy 4.00 10.00
ME Morgan Ensberg Jsy 3.00 8.00
ML Mike Lieberthal Jsy 3.00 8.00
MP Mark Prior Jsy 3.00 8.00
MS Mike Sweeney Jsy 3.00 8.00
MY Michael Young Jsy 3.00 8.00
NJ Nick Johnson Jsy 3.00 8.00
PE Andy Pettitte Jsy 4.00 10.00
RB Rocco Baldelli Jsy 3.00 8.00
RH Rich Harden Jsy 3.00 8.00
RK Ryan Klesko Jsy 3.00 8.00
SC Sean Casey Jsy 3.00 8.00
TH Trevor Hoffman Jsy 3.00 8.00
VA Jason Varitek Jsy 4.00 10.00

2006 Upper Deck UD Game Materials

SER.1 ODDS 1:24 HOBBY, 1:24 RETAIL
SER.2 GU ODDS 1:24 H, RANDOM IN RETAIL
SP INFO PROVIDED BY UPPER DECK
SER.1 PATCH ODDS 1:288 H, 1:1500 R
SER.2 PATCH RANDOM IN HOBBY/RETAIL
SER.2 PATCH PRINT RUN 11 SETS
SER.2 PATCH PRINT RUN PROVIDED BY UD
NO PATCH PRICING DUE TO SCARCITY
AB Adrian Beltre Bat S2 5.00 12.00
AD Adam Dunn Jsy S2 3.00 8.00
AJ Andruw Jones Pants S1 2.00 5.00
AP1 Andy Pettitte Jsy S2 3.00 8.00
AP2 Albert Pujols Pants S1 6.00 15.00
AS Alfonso Soriano Jsy S1 3.00 8.00
BA Bobby Abreu Jsy S2 2.00 5.00
BI Craig Biggio Jsy S2 3.00 8.00
BR Brian Roberts Jsy S1 2.00 5.00
BZ Barry Zito Jsy S2 3.00 8.00
CB Carlos Beltran Jsy S2 3.00 8.00
CD Carlos Delgado Jsy S2 2.00 5.00
CJ Chipper Jones Pants S1 5.00 12.00
CL Carlos Lee Jsy S2 2.00 5.00
CP Corey Patterson Jsy S1 2.00 5.00
CS Curt Schilling Jsy S1 3.00 8.00
DJ1 Derek Jeter Jsy S1 10.00 25.00
DJ2 Derek Jeter Jsy S2 10.00 25.00
DL Derrek Lee Pants S1 2.00 5.00
DO David Ortiz Jsy S1 5.00 12.00
DW Dontrelle Willis Jsy S1 2.00 5.00
EC Eric Chavez Jsy S1 2.00 5.00
EG Eric Gagne Jsy S1 2.00 5.00
FT Frank Thomas Jsy S1 5.00 12.00
GA Garrett Atkins Jsy S2 2.00 5.00
GM Greg Maddux Jsy S1 6.00 15.00
GR Khalil Greene Jsy S2 2.00 5.00
GS Gary Sheffield Jsy S2 2.00 5.00
HA Travis Hafner Jsy S2 2.00 5.00
HB Hank Blalock Jsy S2 2.00 5.00
IR Ivan Rodriguez Jsy S1 3.00 8.00
JB1 Jeff Bagwell Pants S1 3.00 8.00
JB2 Josh Beckett Jsy S2 2.00 5.00
JD1 Johnny Damon Jsy S1 3.00 8.00
JD2 Johnny Damon Jsy S2 3.00 8.00
JE Jim Edmonds Jsy S1 3.00 8.00
JG Jason Giambi Jsy S1 2.00 5.00
JJ Jacque Jones Jsy S1 2.00 5.00
JL Javy Lopez Jsy S2 2.00 5.00
JM Joe Mauer Jsy S2 3.00 8.00
JP Jake Peavy Jsy S1 2.00 5.00
JR Jose Reyes Jsy S2 3.00 8.00
JS Johan Santana Pants S1 3.00 8.00
JT Jim Thome Jsy S1 3.00 8.00
JV Jason Varitek Jsy S2 5.00 12.00
KG1 Ken Griffey Jr. Jsy S1 6.00 15.00
KG2 Ken Griffey Jr. Jsy S2 6.00 15.00
KW Kerry Wood Jsy S2 2.00 5.00
MC Miguel Cabrera Pants S1 6.00 15.00
MM Mike Mussina Pants S2 3.00 8.00
MO Magglio Ordonez Jsy S2 3.00 8.00
MP1 Mike Piazza Jsy S1 5.00 12.00
MP2 Mike Piazza Bat S2 5.00 12.00
MR Manny Ramirez Jsy S1 5.00 12.00
MT Mark Teixeira Jsy S1 3.00 8.00
MY Michael Young Jsy S2 2.00 5.00
PF Prince Fielder Jsy S2 6.00 15.00
PK Paul Konerko Jsy S2 3.00 8.00
PM Pedro Martinez Pants S1 3.00 8.00
PO Jorge Posada Jsy S1 3.00 8.00
PR Mark Prior Jsy S1 3.00 8.00
RC Roger Clemens Jsy S1 6.00 15.00
RF Rafael Furcal Jsy S1 2.00 5.00
RH1 Roy Halladay Jsy S1 3.00 8.00
RH2 Ryan Howard Jsy S2 4.00 10.00
RO Roy Oswalt Jsy S2 3.00 8.00
RP Rafael Palmeiro Jsy S1 3.00 8.00
RW Rickie Weeks Jsy S2 2.00 5.00
RZ Ryan Zimmerman Jsy S2 6.00 15.00
SC Sean Casey Jsy S2 2.00 5.00
SI Grady Sizemore Jsy S2 3.00 8.00
SM John Smoltz Jsy S1 5.00 12.00
SR Scott Rolen Jsy S1 3.00 8.00
TE Miguel Tejada Pants S1 3.00 8.00
TG Tom Glavine Jsy S2 3.00 8.00
TH Todd Helton Jsy S2 3.00 8.00
TI Tadahito Iguchi Jsy S2 2.00 5.00
VG Vladimir Guerrero Jsy S1 3.00 8.00
VM Victor Martinez Jsy S2 3.00 8.00
WR David Wright Pants S1 4.00 10.00

2006 Upper Deck WBC Collection Jersey

SER.2 GU ODDS 1:24 H, RANDOM IN RETAIL
SER.2 PATCH RANDOM IN HOBBY/RETAIL
PATCH PRINT RUN 8 SETS
PATCH PRINT RUN PROVIDED BY UD
NO PATCH PRICING DUE TO SCARCITY
AI Akinori Iwamura 8.00 20.00
AJ Andruw Jones 8.00 20.00
AP Albert Pujols 15.00 40.00
AR Alex Rodriguez 20.00 50.00
AS Alfonso Soriano 6.00 15.00
CB Carlos Beltran 6.00 15.00
CD Carlos Delgado 6.00 15.00
CH Chin-Lung Hu 50.00 100.00
CL Carlos Lee 4.00 10.00
DL Derrek Lee 6.00 15.00
DM Daisuke Matsuzaka 10.00 25.00
DO David Ortiz 10.00 25.00
EB Erik Bedard 6.00 15.00
EP Eduardo Paret 10.00 25.00
FC Frederich Cepeda 10.00 25.00
FG Freddy Garcia 6.00 15.00
FR Jeff Francoeur 15.00 40.00
GL Guangbiao Liu 6.00 15.00
GY Guogan Yang 6.00 15.00
HS Chia-Hsien Hseih 40.00 80.00
HT Hitoshi Tamura 20.00 50.00
IR Ivan Rodriguez 8.00 20.00
IS Ichiro Suzuki 125.00 250.00
JB Jason Bay 6.00 15.00
JD Johnny Damon 6.00 15.00
JF Jeff Francis 6.00 15.00
JG Jason Grilli 4.00 10.00
JH Justin Huber 6.00 15.00
JL Jong Beom Lee 6.00 15.00
JM Justin Morneau 4.00 10.00
JP Jin Man Park 6.00 15.00
JS Johan Santana 10.00 25.00
JV Jason Varitek 10.00 25.00
KG Ken Griffey Jr. 15.00 40.00
KU Koji Uehara 6.00 15.00
MC Miguel Cabrera 6.00 15.00
ME Michel Enriquez 10.00 25.00
MF Maikel Folch 10.00 25.00
MK Munenori Kawasaki 20.00 50.00
MO Michihiro Ogasawara 20.00 50.00
MP Mike Piazza 20.00 50.00
MS Min Han Son 6.00 15.00
MT Mark Teixeira 6.00 15.00
NM Nobuhiko Matasunaka 30.00 60.00
OP Oliver Perez 4.00 10.00
PE Ariel Pestano 10.00 25.00
PL Pedro Lazo 10.00 25.00
RC Roger Clemens 12.50 30.00

SW Shunsuke Watanabe 30.00 60.00
TC Tai-San Chang 10.00 25.00
TE Miguel Tejada 6.00 15.00
TN Tsuyoshi Nishioka 30.00 60.00
TW Tsuyoshi Wada 30.00 60.00
VC Vinny Castilla 6.00 15.00
VM Victor Martinez 6.00 15.00
WL Wei-Chu Lin 75.00 150.00
WP Wei-Lun Pan 10.00 25.00
WW Wei Wang 6.00 15.00
YG Yuliesky Gourriel 15.00 40.00
YM Yunieski Maya 10.00 25.00

2006 Upper Deck Employee Quad Jerseys

LJDJSCRB James/Jeter/Crosby/Bush 20.00 40.00

2006 Upper Deck Tuff Stuff

5 Derek Jeter 1.25 3.00
6 Ken Griffey Jr. 1.00 2.50
7 Albert Pujols 1.25 3.00
8 Ichiro Suzuki .75 2.00
9 Pedro Martinez .30 .75
10 Derrek Lee .20 .50
11 Mark Teixeira .50 1.25
12 Kenji Johjima .20 .50
21 Francisco Liriano .20 .50
22 Justin Verlander .30 .75
23 Ryan Howard .60 1.50
24 David Wright .60 1.50
24 Jered Weaver .20 .50
25 Stephen Drew .20 .50
26 David Ortiz .30 .75
27 Chase Utley .50 1.25
37 Chien-Ming Wang .50 1.25
38 Jose Reyes .30 .75
39 Roger Clemens .60 1.50
40 Ryan Zimmerman .30 .75
45 Justin Morneau .50 1.25
46 Brandon Webb .30 .75
47 Hanley Ramirez .50 1.25
48 Johan Santana .50 1.25

2006 Upper Deck World Baseball Classic Box Set

COMP.FACT.SET (50) 10.00 15.00
COMMON CARD (1-50) .20 .50
UNLISTED STARS .50 1.25
ISSUED ONLY IN FACTORY SET FORMAT
DISTRIBUTED IN U.S.A. AND ASIA
1 Derek Jeter 1.25 3.00
2 Ken Griffey Jr. 1.00 2.50
3 Derrek Lee .20 .50
4 Dontrelle Willis .20 .50
5 Alex Rodriguez .60 1.50
6 Jeff Francoeur .50 1.25
7 Roger Clemens .60 1.50
8 Johnny Damon .30 .75
9 Chipper Jones .50 1.25
10 Mark Teixeira .30 .75
11 Chase Utley .30 .75
12 Jake Peavy .20 .50
13 Michael Collins .20 .50
14 Justin Huber .20 .50
15 Jason Bay .20 .50
16 Jeff Francis .20 .50
17 Justin Morneau .30 .75
18 Guogang Yang .20 .50
19 Wei Wang .20 .50
20 Chia-Hsien Hseih .50 1.25
21 Chin-Lung Hu .20 .50
22 Wei-Lun Pan .50 1.25
23 Yung Chi Chen .30 .75
24 Mike Piazza .50 1.25
25 Albert Pujols .60 1.50
26 David Ortiz .50 1.25
27 Jose Reyes .30 .75
28 Miguel Tejada .30 .75
29 Ichiro Suzuki .60 1.50
30 Nobuhiko Matsunaka .30 .75
31 Toshiaki Imae .20 .50
32 Kazuhiro Wada .20 .50
33 Shunsuke Watanabe .30 .75
34 Jung Bong .20 .50
35 Jong Beom Lee .20 .50
36 Seung-Yeop Lee .30 .75
37 Vinny Castilla .20 .50
38 Oliver Perez .20 .50
39 Jorge Cantu .20 .50
40 Andruw Jones .20 .50
41 Carlos Lee .20 .50
42 Carlos Beltran .30 .75
43 Carlos Delgado .20 .50
44 Ivan Rodriguez .30 .75
45 Bernie Williams .30 .75
46 Bobby Abreu .20 .50
47 Miguel Cabrera .50 1.25
48 Johan Santana .30 .75
49 Victor Martinez .30 .75
50 Omar Vizquel .30 .75

2007 Upper Deck

COMPLETE SET (1020) 200.00 300.00
COMP.SET w/o RC EXCH (1000) 120.00 200.00
COMP.SER.1 w/o RC EXCH (500) 40.00 80.00
COMP.SER.2 w/o RC EXCH (500) 80.00 120.00
COMMON CARD (1-1020) .15 .40
STATED PRINT RUN X SER.#'d SETS
COMMON ROOKIE .30 .75
COMMON ROOKIE (501-520) 1.00 2.50
1-500 ISSUED IN SERIES 1 PACKS
501-1020 ISSUED IN SERIES 2 PACKS
MATSUZAKA JSY RANDOMLY INSERTED
NO MATSUZAKA JSY PRICING AVAILABLE
OVERALL PLATE SER.1 ODDS 1:192 H
OVERALL PLATE SER.2 ODDS 1:96 H
PLATE PRINT RUN 1 SET PER COLOR
BLACK-CYAN-MAGENTA-YELLOW ISSUED
NO PLATE PRICING DUE TO SCARCITY
ROOKIE EXCH APPX. 1-2 PER CASE
ROOKIE EXCH DEADLINE 02/27/2010
1 Doug Slaten RC .30 .75
2 Miguel Montero (RC) .30 .75
3 Brian Burres (RC) .30 .75
4 Devern Hansack RC .30 .75
5 David Murphy (RC) .30 .75
6 Jose Reyes RC .30 .75
7 Scott Moore (RC) .30 .75
8 Josh Fields (RC) .30 .75
9 Chris Stewart RC .30 .75
10 Jerry Owens (RC) .30 .75
11 Ryan Sweeney (RC) .30 .75
12 Kevin Kouzmanoff (RC) .30 .75
13 Jeff Baker (RC) .30 .75
14 Justin Hampson (RC) .30 .75
15 Jeff Salazar (RC) .30 .75
16 Alvin Colina RC .75 2.00
17 Troy Tulowitzki (RC) 1.00 2.50
18 Andrew Miller RC 1.25 3.00
19 Mike Rabelo RC .30 .75
20 Jose Diaz (RC) .30 .75
21 Angel Sanchez RC .30 .75
22 Ryan Braun RC .30 .75
23 Delwyn Young (RC) .30 .75
24 Drew Anderson RC .30 .75
25 Dennis Sarfate (RC) .30 .75
26 Vinny Rottino (RC) .30 .75
27 Glen Perkins (RC) .30 .75
28 Alexi Casilla RC .50 1.25
29 Philip Humber (RC) .30 .75
30 Andy Cannizaro RC .30 .75
31 Jeremy Brown .15 .40
32 Sean Henn (RC) .30 .75
33 Brian Rogers .15 .40
34 Carlos Maldonado (RC) .30 .75
35 Juan Morillo (RC) .30 .75
36 Fred Lewis (RC) .50 1.25
37 Patrick Misch (RC) .30 .75
38 Billy Sadler (RC) .30 .75
39 Ryan Feierabend (RC) .30 .75
40 Cesar Jimenez RC .30 .75
41 Oswaldo Navarro RC .30 .75
42 Travis Chick (RC) .30 .75
43 Delmon Young (RC) .75 2.00
44 Shawn Riggans (RC) .30 .75
45 Brian Stokes (RC) .30 .75
46 Juan Salas (RC) .30 .75
47 Joaquin Arias (RC) .30 .75
48 Adam Lind (RC) .30 .75
49 Beltran Perez (RC) .30 .75
50 Brett Campbell RC .30 .75
51 Brian Roberts .15 .40
52 Miguel Tejada .25 .60
53 Brandon Fahey .15 .40
54 Jay Gibbons .15 .40
55 Corey Patterson .15 .40
56 Nick Markakis .30 .75
57 Ramon Hernandez .15 .40
58 Kris Benson .15 .40
59 Adam Loewen .15 .40
60 Erik Bedard .15 .40
61 Chris Ray .15 .40
62 Chris Britton .15 .40
63 Daniel Cabrera .15 .40
64 Sendy Rleal .15 .40
65 Manny Ramirez .40 1.00
66 David Ortiz .40 1.00
67 Gabe Kapler .15 .40
68 Alex Cora .25 .60
69 Dustin Pedroia .40 1.00
70 Trot Nixon .15 .40
71 Doug Mirabelli .15 .40
72 Mark Loretta .15 .40
73 Curt Schilling .25 .60
74 Jonathan Papelbon .40 1.00
75 Tim Wakefield .25 .60
76 Jon Lester .25 .60
77 Craig Hansen .15 .40
78 Keith Foulke .15 .40
79 Jermaine Dye .15 .40
80 Jim Thome .25 .60
81 Tadahito Iguchi .15 .40
82 Rob Mackowiak .15 .40
83 Brian Anderson .15 .40
84 Juan Uribe .15 .40
85 A.J. Pierzynski .15 .40
86 Alex Cintron .15 .40
87 Jon Garland .15 .40
88 Jose Contreras .15 .40
89 Neal Cotts .15 .40
90 Bobby Jenks .15 .40
91 Mike MacDougal .15 .40
92 Javier Vazquez .15 .40
93 Travis Hafner .15 .40
94 Jhonny Peralta .15 .40
95 Ryan Garko .15 .40
96 Victor Martinez .25 .60
97 Hector Luna .15 .40
98 Casey Blake .15 .40
99 Jason Michaels .15 .40
100 Shin-Soo Choo .25 .60
101 C.C. Sabathia .25 .60
102 Paul Byrd .15 .40
103 Jeremy Sowers .15 .40
104 Cliff Lee .25 .60
105 Rafael Betancourt .15 .40
106 Francisco Cruceta .15 .40
107 Sean Casey .15 .40
108 Brandon Inge .15 .40
109 Placido Polanco .15 .40
110 Omar Infante .15 .40
111 Ivan Rodriguez .25 .60
112 Magglio Ordonez .25 .60
113 Craig Monroe .15 .40
114 Marcus Thames .15 .40
115 Justin Verlander .40 1.00
116 Todd Jones .15 .40
117 Kenny Rogers .15 .40
118 Joel Zumaya .15 .40
119 Jeremy Bonderman .15 .40
120 Nate Robertson .15 .40
121 Mark Teahen .15 .40
122 Ryan Shealy .15 .40
123 Mitch Maier RC .30 .75
124 Doug Mientkiewicz .15 .40
125 Mark Grudzielanek .15 .40
126 Shane Costa .15 .40
127 John Buck .15 .40
128 Reggie Sanders .15 .40
129 Mike Sweeney .15 .40
130 Mark Redman .15 .40
131 Todd Wellemeyer .15 .40
132 Scott Elarton .15 .40
133 Ambiorix Burgos .15 .40
134 Joe Nelson .15 .40
135 Howie Kendrick .15 .40
136 Chone Figgins .15 .40
137 Orlando Cabrera .15 .40
138 Maicer Izturis .15 .40
139 Jose Molina .15 .40
140 Vladimir Guerrero .25 .60
141 Darin Erstad .15 .40
142 Juan Rivera .15 .40
143 Jered Weaver .25 .60
144 John Lackey .25 .60
145 Joe Saunders .15 .40
146 Bartolo Colon .15 .40
147 Scot Shields .15 .40
148 Francisco Rodriguez .25 .60
149 Justin Morneau .25 .60
150 Jason Bartlett .15 .40
151 Luis Castillo .15 .40
152 Nick Punto .15 .40
153 Shannon Stewart .15 .40
154 Michael Cuddyer .15 .40
155 Jason Kubel .15 .40
156 Joe Mauer .30 .75
157 Francisco Liriano .15 .40
158 Joe Nathan .15 .40
159 Dennys Reyes .15 .40
160 Brad Radke .15 .40
161 Boof Bonser .15 .40
162 Juan Rincon .15 .40
163 Derek Jeter 1.00 2.50
164 Jason Giambi .15 .40
165 Robinson Cano .25 .60
166 Andy Phillips .15 .40
167 Bobby Abreu .15 .40
168 Gary Sheffield .15 .40
169 Bernie Williams .25 .60
170 Melky Cabrera .15 .40
171 Mike Mussina .25 .60
172 Chien-Ming Wang .25 .60
173 Mariano Rivera .50 1.25
174 Scott Proctor .15 .40
175 Jaret Wright .15 .40
176 Kyle Farnsworth .15 .40
177 Eric Chavez .15 .40
178 Bobby Crosby .15 .40
179 Frank Thomas .40 1.00
180 Dan Johnson .15 .40
181 Marco Scutaro .25 .60
182 Nick Swisher .25 .60
183 Milton Bradley .15 .40
184 Jay Payton .15 .40
185 Joe Blanton .15 .40
186 Barry Zito .25 .60
187 Rich Harden .15 .40
188 Esteban Loaiza .15 .40
189 Huston Street .15 .40
190 Chad Gaudin .15 .40
191 Richie Sexson .15 .40
192 Yuniesky Betancourt .15 .40
193 Willie Bloomquist .15 .40
194 Ben Broussard .15 .40
195 Kenji Johjima .40 1.00
196 Ichiro Suzuki .50 1.25
197 Raul Ibanez .25 .60
198 Chris Snelling .15 .40
199 Felix Hernandez .25 .60
200 Cha-Seung Baek .15 .40
201 Joel Pineiro .15 .40
202 Julio Mateo .15 .40
203 J.J. Putz .15 .40
204 Rafael Soriano .15 .40
205 Jorge Cantu .15 .40
206 B.J. Upton .15 .40
207 Ty Wigginton .15 .40
208 Greg Norton .15 .40
209 Dioner Navarro .15 .40
210 Carl Crawford .25 .60
211 Jonny Gomes .15 .40
212 Damon Hollins .15 .40
213 Scott Kazmir .25 .60
214 Casey Fossum .15 .40
215 Ruddy Lugo .15 .40
216 James Shields .15 .40
217 Tyler Walker .15 .40
218 Shawn Camp .15 .40
219 Mark Teixeira .25 .60
220 Hank Blalock .15 .40
221 Ian Kinsler .25 .60
222 Jerry Hairston Jr. .15 .40
223 Gerald Laird .15 .40
224 Carlos Lee .15 .40
225 Gary Matthews .15 .40
226 Mark DeRosa .15 .40
227 Kip Wells .15 .40
228 Akinori Otsuka .15 .40
229 Vicente Padilla .15 .40
230 John Koronka .15 .40
231 Kevin Millwood .15 .40
232 Wes Littleton .15 .40
233 Troy Glaus .15 .40
234 Lyle Overbay .15 .40
235 Aaron Hill .15 .40
236 John McDonald .15 .40
237 Bengie Molina .15 .40
238 Vernon Wells .15 .40
239 Reed Johnson .15 .40
240 Frank Catalanotto .15 .40
241 Roy Halladay .25 .60
242 B.J. Ryan .15 .40
243 Gustavo Chacin .15 .40
244 Scott Downs .15 .40
245 Casey Janssen .15 .40
246 Justin Speier .15 .40
247 Stephen Drew .15 .40
248 Conor Jackson .15 .40
249 Orlando Hudson .15 .40
250 Chad Tracy .15 .40
251 Johnny Estrada .15 .40
252 Luis Gonzalez .15 .40
253 Eric Byrnes .15 .40
254 Carlos Quentin .15 .40
255 Brandon Webb .25 .60
256 Claudio Vargas .15 .40
257 Juan Cruz .15 .40
258 Jorge Julio .15 .40
259 Luis Vizcaino .15 .40
260 Livan Hernandez .15 .40
261 Chipper Jones .40 1.00
262 Edgar Renteria .15 .40
263 Adam LaRoche .15 .40
264 Willy Aybar .15 .40
265 Brian McCann .15 .40
266 Ryan Langerhans .15 .40
267 Jeff Francoeur .40 1.00
268 Matt Diaz .15 .40
269 Tim Hudson .25 .60
270 John Smoltz .40 1.00
271 Oscar Villarreal .15 .40
272 Horacio Ramirez .15 .40
273 Bob Wickman .15 .40
274 Chad Paronto .15 .40
275 Derrek Lee .15 .40
276 Ryan Theriot .15 .40
277 Cesar Izturis .15 .40
278 Ronny Cedeno .15 .40
279 Michael Barrett .15 .40
280 Juan Pierre .15 .40
281 Jacque Jones .15 .40
282 Matt Murton .15 .40
283 Carlos Zambrano .25 .60
284 Mark Prior .25 .60
285 Rich Hill .15 .40
286 Sean Marshall .15 .40
287 Ryan Dempster .15 .40
288 Ryan O'Malley .15 .40
289 Scott Hatteberg .15 .40
290 Brandon Phillips .15 .40
291 Edwin Encarnacion .40 1.00
292 Rich Aurilia .15 .40
293 David Ross .15 .40
294 Ken Griffey Jr. .75 2.00
295 Ryan Freel .15 .40
296 Chris Denorfia .15 .40
297 Bronson Arroyo .15 .40
298 Aaron Harang .15 .40
299 Brandon Claussen .15 .40
300 Todd Coffey .15 .40
301 David Weathers .15 .40
302 Eric Milton .15 .40
303 Todd Helton .25 .60
304 Clint Barmes .15 .40
305 Kazuo Matsui .15 .40
306 Jamey Carroll .15 .40
307 Yorvit Torrealba .15 .40
308 Matt Holliday .40 1.00
309 Choo Freeman .15 .40
310 Brad Hawpe .15 .40
311 Jason Jennings .15 .40
312 Jeff Francis .15 .40
313 Josh Fogg .15 .40
314 Aaron Cook .15 .40
315 Ubaldo Jimenez (RC) 1.00 2.50
316 Manny Corpas .15 .40
317 Miguel Cabrera .40 1.00
318 Dan Uggla .15 .40
319 Hanley Ramirez .25 .60
320 Wes Helms .15 .40
321 Miguel Olivo .15 .40
322 Jeremy Hermida .15 .40
323 Cody Ross .15 .40
324 Josh Willingham .25 .60
325 Dontrelle Willis .15 .40
326 Anibal Sanchez .15 .40
327 Josh Johnson .40 1.00
328 Jose Garcia RC .30 .75
329 Joe Borowski .15 .40
330 Taylor Tankersley .15 .40
331 Lance Berkman .25 .60
332 Craig Biggio .25 .60
333 Aubrey Huff .15 .40
334 Adam Everett .15 .40
335 Brad Ausmus .15 .40
336 Willy Taveras .15 .40
337 Luke Scott .15 .40
338 Chris Burke .15 .40
339 Roger Clemens .50 1.25
340 Andy Pettitte .25 .60
341 Brandon Backe .15 .40
342 Hector Gimenez (RC) .30 .75
343 Brad Lidge .15 .40
344 Dan Wheeler .15 .40
345 Nomar Garciaparra .25 .60
346 Rafael Furcal .15 .40
347 Wilson Betemit .15 .40
348 Julio Lugo .15 .40
349 Russell Martin .25 .60
350 Andre Ethier .25 .60
351 Matt Kemp .30 .75
352 Kenny Lofton .15 .40
353 Brad Penny .15 .40
354 Derek Lowe .15 .40
355 Chad Billingsley .25 .60
356 Greg Maddux .50 1.25
357 Takashi Saito .15 .40
358 Jonathan Broxton .15 .40
359 Prince Fielder .25 .60
360 Rickie Weeks .15 .40
361 Bill Hall .15 .40
362 J.J. Hardy .15 .40
363 Jeff Cirillo .15 .40
364 Tony Gwynn Jr. .15 .40
365 Corey Hart .15 .40
366 Laynce Nix .15 .40
367 Doug Davis .15 .40
368 Ben Sheets .15 .40
369 Chris Capuano .15 .40
370 Dave Bush .15 .40
371 Derrick Turnbow .15 .40
372 Francisco Cordero .15 .40
373 Jose Reyes .25 .60
374 Carlos Delgado .15 .40
375 Julio Franco .15 .40
376 Jose Valentin .15 .40
377 Paul LoDuca .15 .40
378 Carlos Beltran .25 .60
379 Shawn Green .15 .40
380 Lastings Milledge .25 .60
381 Endy Chavez .15 .40
382 Pedro Martinez .25 .60
383 John Maine .15 .40
384 Orlando Hernandez .15 .40
385 Steve Trachsel .15 .40
386 Billy Wagner .15 .40
387 Ryan Howard .30 .75
388 Chase Utley .25 .60
389 Jimmy Rollins .25 .60
390 Chris Coste .15 .40
391 Jeff Conine .15 .40
392 Aaron Rowand .15 .40
393 Shane Victorino .15 .40
394 David Dellucci .15 .40
395 Cole Hamels .30 .75
396 Jamie Moyer .15 .40
397 Ryan Madson .15 .40
398 Brett Myers .15 .40
399 Tom Gordon .15 .40
400 Geoff Geary .15 .40
401 Freddy Sanchez .15 .40
402 Xavier Nady .15 .40
403 Jose Castillo .15 .40
404 Joe Randa .15 .40
405 Jason Bay .25 .60
406 Chris Duffy .15 .40
407 Jose Bautista .25 .60
408 Ronny Paulino .15 .40
409 Ian Snell .15 .40
410 Zach Duke .15 .40
411 Tom Gorzelanny .15 .40
412 Shane Youman RC .30 .75
413 Mike Gonzalez .15 .40
414 Matt Capps .15 .40
415 Adrian Gonzalez .30 .75
416 Josh Barfield .15 .40
417 Todd Walker .15 .40
418 Khalil Greene .15 .40
419 Mike Piazza .40 1.00
420 Dave Roberts .25 .60
421 Mike Cameron .15 .40
422 Geoff Blum .15 .40
423 Jake Peavy .15 .40
424 Chris R. Young .15 .40
425 Woody Williams .15 .40
426 Clay Hensley .15 .40
427 Cla Meredith .15 .40
428 Trevor Hoffman .25 .60
429 Shea Hillenbrand .15 .40
430 Pedro Feliz .15 .40
431 Ray Durham .15 .40
432 Mark Sweeney .15 .40
433 Eliezer Alfonzo .15 .40
434 Moises Alou .15 .40
435 Steve Finley .15 .40
436 Todd Linden .15 .40
437 Jason Schmidt .15 .40
438 Matt Cain .25 .60
439 Noah Lowry .15 .40
440 Brad Hennessey .15 .40
441 Armando Benitez .15 .40
442 Jonathan Sanchez .15 .40
443 Albert Pujols .50 1.25
444 Ronnie Belliard .15 .40
445 David Eckstein .15 .40
446 Aaron Miles .15 .40
447 Yadier Molina .50 1.25
448 Jim Edmonds .25 .60
449 Chris Duncan .15 .40
450 Juan Encarnacion .15 .40
451 Chris Carpenter .25 .60
452 Jeff Suppan .15 .40
453 Jason Marquis .15 .40
454 Jeff Weaver .15 .40
455 Jason Isringhausen .15 .40
456 Braden Looper .15 .40
457 Ryan Zimmerman .25 .60
458 Nick Johnson .15 .40
459 Felipe Lopez .15 .40
460 Brian Schneider .15 .40
461 Alfonso Soriano .25 .60
462 Austin Kearns .15 .40
463 Ryan Church .15 .40
464 Alex Escobar .15 .40
465 Ramon Ortiz .15 .40
466 Tony Armas .15 .40
467 Michael O'Connor .15 .40
468 Chad Cordero .15 .40
469 Jon Rauch .15 .40
470 Pedro Astacio .15 .40
471 Miguel Tejada CL .25 .60
472 David Ortiz CL .40 1.00
473 Jermaine Dye CL .15 .40
474 Travis Hafner CL .15 .40
475 Magglio Ordonez CL .25 .60
476 Mark Teahen CL .15 .40
477 Vladimir Guerrero CL .25 .60
478 Justin Morneau CL .25 .60
479 Derek Jeter CL 1.00 2.50
480 Nick Swisher CL .25 .60
481 Ichiro Suzuki CL .50 1.25
482 Scott Kazmir CL .25 .60
483 Mark Teixeira CL .25 .60
484 Vernon Wells CL .15 .40
485 Brandon Webb CL .25 .60
486 Andruw Jones CL .15 .40
487 Carlos Zambrano CL .25 .60
488 Adam Dunn CL .25 .60
489 Matt Holliday CL .40 1.00
490 Miguel Cabrera CL .40 1.00
491 Lance Berkman CL .25 .60
492 Nomar Garciaparra CL .25 .60
493 Prince Fielder CL .25 .60
494 Carlos Beltran CL .25 .60
495 Ryan Howard CL .30 .75
496 Jason Bay CL .25 .60
497 Adrian Gonzalez CL .30 .75
498 Matt Cain CL .25 .60
499 Albert Pujols CL .50 1.25
500 Ryan Zimmerman CL .25 .60
501a D.Matsuzaka Suit RC 20.00 50.00
501b D.Matsuzaka Throwing RC 6.00 15.00
502 Kei Igawa RC 1.50 4.00
503 Akinori Iwamura RC 2.50 6.00
504 Alex Gordon RC 6.00 15.00
505 Matt Chico (RC) 1.00 2.50
506 John Danks RC 1.00 2.50
507 Elijah Dukes RC 1.00 2.50
508 Gustavo Molina RC 1.00 2.50
509 Joakim Soria RC 2.50 6.00
510 Jay Marshall RC 2.50 6.00
511 Travis Buck (RC) 1.00 2.50
512 Brandon Wood (RC) 1.00 2.50
513 Kevin Cameron RC 1.00 2.50
514 Jared Burton RC 2.50 6.00
515 Kory Casto (RC) 1.00 2.50
516 Joe Smith RC 1.00 2.50
517 Jose Garcia 1.00 2.50
518 Hunter Pence (RC) 6.00 15.00
519 Felix Pie (RC) 1.00 2.50
520 Zach Segovia (RC) 1.00 2.50
521 Randy Johnson .40 1.00
522 Brandon Lyon .15 .40
523 Robby Hammock .15 .40
524 Micah Owings (RC) .30 .75
525 Doug Davis .15 .40
526 Brian Barden RC .30 .75
527 Alberto Callaspo .15 .40
528 Stephen Drew .15 .40
529 Chris Young .15 .40
530 Edgar Gonzalez .15 .40
531 Brandon Medders .15 .40
532 Tony Pena .15 .40
533 Jose Valverde .15 .40
534 Chris Snyder .15 .40
535 Tony Clark .15 .40
536 Scott Hairston .15 .40
537 Jeff DaVanon .15 .40
538 Randy Johnson CL .40 1.00
539 Mark Redman .15 .40
540 Andruw Jones .15 .40
541 Rafael Soriano .15 .40
542 Scott Thorman .15 .40
543 Chipper Jones .40 1.00
544 Mike Gonzalez .15 .40
545 Lance Cormier .15 .40
546 Kyle Davies .15 .40
547 Mike Hampton .15 .40
548 Chuck James .15 .40
549 Macay McBride .15 .40
550 Tanyon Sturtze .15 .40
551 Tyler Yates .15 .40
552 Pete Orr .15 .40
553 Craig Wilson .15 .40
554 Chris Woodward .15 .40
555 Kelly Johnson .15 .40
556 Chipper Jones CL .40 1.00
557 Chad Bradford .15 .40
558 John Parrish .15 .40
559 Jeremy Guthrie .15 .40
560 Steve Trachsel .15 .40
561 Scott Williamson .15 .40
562 Jaret Wright .15 .40
563 Paul Bako .15 .40
564 Chris Gomez .15 .40
565 Melvin Mora .15 .40
566 Freddie Bynum .15 .40
567 Aubrey Huff .15 .40
568 Jay Payton .15 .40
569 Miguel Tejada .25 .60
570 Kurt Birkins .15 .40
571 Danys Baez .15 .40
572 Brian Roberts CL .15 .40
573 Josh Beckett .15 .40
574 Matt Clement .15 .40
575 Hideki Okajima RC 2.00 5.00
576 Javier Lopez .15 .40
577 Joel Pineiro .15 .40
578 J.C. Romero .15 .40
579 Kyle Snyder .15 .40
580 Julian Tavarez .15 .40
581 Mike Timlin .15 .40
582 Jason Varitek .40 1.00
583 Mike Lowell .15 .40
584 Kevin Youkilis .15 .40
585 Coco Crisp .15 .40
586 J.D. Drew .15 .40
587 Eric Hinske .15 .40
588 Wily Mo Pena .15 .40
589 Julio Lugo .15 .40
590 David Ortiz .40 1.00
591 Manny Ramirez .40 1.00
592 Daisuke Matsuzaka CL 1.50 4.00
593 Scott Eyre .15 .40
594 Angel Guzman .15 .40
595 Bob Howry .15 .40
596 Ted Lilly .15 .40
597 Juan Mateo .15 .40
598 Wade Miller .15 .40
599 Carlos Zambrano .25 .60
600 Will Ohman .15 .40
601 Michael Wuertz .15 .40
602 Henry Blanco .15 .40
603 Aramis Ramirez .15 .40
604 Cliff Floyd .15 .40
605 Kerry Wood .15 .40
606 Alfonso Soriano .25 .60
607 Daryle Ward .15 .40
608 Jason Marquis .15 .40
609 Mark DeRosa .15 .40
610 Neal Cotts .15 .40
611 Derrek Lee .15 .40
612 Aramis Ramirez CL .15 .40
613 David Aardsma .15 .40
614 Mark Buehrle .25 .60
615 Nick Masset .15 .40
616 Andrew Sisco .15 .40
617 Matt Thornton .15 .40
618 Toby Hall .15 .40
619 Joe Crede .15 .40
620 Paul Konerko .25 .60
621 Darin Erstad .15 .40
622 Pablo Ozuna .15 .40
623 Scott Podsednik .15 .40
624 Jim Thome .25 .60
625 Jermaine Dye .15 .40
626 Jim Thome CL .25 .60
627 Adam Dunn .25 .60
628 Bill Bray .15 .40
629 Alex Gonzalez .15 .40
630 Josh Hamilton (RC) 4.00 10.00
631 Matt Belisle .15 .40
632 Rheal Cormier .15 .40
633 Kyle Lohse .15 .40
634 Eric Milton .15 .40
635 Kirk Saarloos .15 .40
636 Mike Stanton .15 .40
637 Javier Valentin .15 .40
638 Juan Castro .15 .40
639 Jeff Conine .15 .40
640 Jon Coutlangus (RC) .30 .75
641 Ken Griffey Jr. .75 2.00
642 Ken Griffey Jr. CL .75 2.00
643 Fernando Cabrera .15 .40
644 Fausto Carmona .15 .40
645 Jason Davis .15 .40
646 Aaron Fultz .15 .40
647 Roberto Hernandez .15 .40
648 Jake Westbrook .15 .40
649 Kelly Shoppach .15 .40
650 Josh Barfield .15 .40
651 Andy Marte .15 .40
652 Joe Inglett .15 .40
653 David Dellucci .15 .40
654 Joe Borowski .15 .40
655 Franklin Gutierrez .15 .40
656 Trot Nixon .15 .40
657 Grady Sizemore .25 .60
658 Mike Rouse .15 .40
659 Travis Hafner .15 .40
660 Victor Martinez .25 .60
661 C.C. Sabathia .25 .60
662 Grady Sizemore CL .25 .60
663 Jeremy Affeldt .15 .40
664 Taylor Buchholz .15 .40
665 Brian Fuentes .15 .40
666 LaTroy Hawkins .15 .40
667 Byung-Hyun Kim .15 .40
668 Brian Lawrence .15 .40
669 Rodrigo Lopez .15 .40
670 Jeff Francis .15 .40
671 Chris Ianetta .15 .40
672 Garrett Atkins .15 .40
673 Todd Helton .25 .60
674 Steve Finley .15 .40
675 John Mabry .15 .40
676 Willy Taveras .15 .40
677 Jason Hirsh .15 .40
678 Ramon Ramirez .15 .40
679 Matt Holliday .40 1.00
680 Todd Helton CL .25 .60
681 Roman Colon .15 .40
682 Chad Durbin .15 .40
683 Jason Grilli .15 .40
684 Wilfredo Ledezma .15 .40
685 Mike Maroth .15 .40
686 Jose Mesa .15 .40
687 Justin Verlander .40 1.00
688 Fernando Rodney .15 .40
689 Vance Wilson .15 .40
690 Carlos Guillen .15 .40
691 Neifi Perez .15 .40
692 Curtis Granderson .30 .75
693 Gary Sheffield .15 .40
694 Justin Verlander CL .40 1.00
695 Kevin Gregg .15 .40
696 Logan Kensing .15 .40
697 Randy Messenger .15 .40
698 Sergio Mitre .15 .40
699 Ricky Nolasco .15 .40
700 Scott Olsen .15 .40
701 Renyel Pinto .15 .40
702 Matt Treanor .15 .40
703 Alfredo Amezaga .15 .40
704 Aaron Boone .15 .40
705 Mike Jacobs .15 .40
706 Miguel Cabrera .40 1.00
707 Joe Borchard .15 .40
708 Jorge Julio .15 .40
709 Rick Vanden Hurk RC .30 .75
710 Lee Gardner (RC) .30 .75
711 Matt Lindstrom (RC) .30 .75
712 Henry Owens .15 .40
713 Hanley Ramirez .25 .60
714 Alejandro De Aza RC .50 1.25
715 Hanley Ramirez CL .25 .60
716 Dave Borkowski .15 .40
717 Jason Jennings .15 .40
718 Trever Miller .15 .40
719 Roy Oswalt .25 .60
720 Wandy Rodriguez .15 .40
721 Humberto Quintero .15 .40
722 Morgan Ensberg .15 .40
723 Mike Lamb .15 .40
724 Mark Loretta .15 .40
725 Jason Lane .15 .40
726 Carlos Lee .15 .40
727 Orlando Palmeiro .15 .40
728 Woody Williams .15 .40
729 Chad Qualls .15 .40
730 Lance Berkman .25 .60
731 Rick White .15 .40
732 Chris Sampson .15 .40
733 Carlos Lee CL .15 .40
734 Jorge De La Rosa .15 .40
735 Octavio Dotel .15 .40
736 Jimmy Gobble .15 .40
737 Zack Greinke .40 1.00
738 Luke Hudson .15 .40
739 Gil Meche .15 .40
740 Joel Peralta .15 .40
741 Odalis Perez .15 .40
742 David Riske .15 .40
743 Jason LaRue .15 .40
744 Tony Pena .15 .40
745 Esteban German .15 .40
746 Ross Gload .15 .40
747 Emil Brown .15 .40
748 David DeJesus .15 .40
749 Brandon Duckworth .15 .40
750 Alex Gordon CL .50 1.25
751 Jered Weaver .25 .60
752 Vladimir Guerrero .25 .60
753 Hector Carrasco .15 .40
754 Kelvim Escobar .15 .40
755 Darren Oliver .15 .40
756 Dustin Moseley .15 .40
757 Ervin Santana .15 .40
758 Mike Napoli .15 .40
759 Shea Hillenbrand .15 .40
760 Casey Kotchman .15 .40
761 Reggie Willits .15 .40
762 Robb Quinlan .15 .40
763 Garret Anderson .15 .40
764 Gary Matthews .15 .40
765 Justin Speier .15 .40
766 Jered Weaver CL .25 .60
767 Joe Beimel .15 .40
768 Yhency Brazoban .15 .40
769 Elmer Dessens .15 .40
770 Mark Hendrickson .15 .40
771 Hong-Chih Kuo .15 .40
772 Jason Schmidt .15 .40
773 Brett Tomko .15 .40
774 Randy Wolf .15 .40
775 Mike Lieberthal .15 .40
776 Marlon Anderson .15 .40

777 Jeff Kent .15 .40
778 Ramon Martinez .15 .40
779 Olmedo Saenz .15 .40
780 Luis Gonzalez .15 .40
781 Juan Pierre .15 .40
782 Jason Repko .15 .40
783 Nomar Garciaparra .25 .60
784 Wilson Valdez .15 .40
785 Jason Schmidt CL .15 .40
786 Greg Aquino .15 .40
787 Brian Shouse .15 .40
788 Jeff Suppan .15 .40
789 Carlos Villanueva .15 .40
790 Matt Wise .15 .40
791 Johnny Estrada .15 .40
792 Craig Counsell .15 .40
793 Tony Graffanino .15 .40
794 Corey Koskie .15 .40
795 Claudio Vargas .15 .40
796 Brady Clark .15 .40
797 Gabe Gross .15 .40
798 Geoff Jenkins .15 .40
799 Kevin Mench .15 .40
800 Bill Hall CL .15 .40
801 Sidney Ponson .15 .40
802 Jesse Crain .15 .40
803 Matt Guerrier .15 .40
804 Pat Neshek .30 .75
805 Ramon Ortiz .15 .40
806 Johan Santana .25 .60
807 Carlos Silva .15 .40
808 Mike Redmond .15 .40
809 Jeff Cirillo .15 .40
810 Luis Rodriguez .15 .40
811 Lew Ford .15 .40
812 Torii Hunter .15 .40
813 Jason Tyner .15 .40
814 Rondell White .15 .40
815 Justin Morneau .25 .60
816 Joe Mauer .30 .75
817 Johan Santana CL .25 .60
818 David Newhan .15 .40
819 Aaron Sele .15 .40
820 Ambiorix Burgos .15 .40
821 Pedro Feliciano .15 .40
822 Tom Glavine .25 .60
823 Aaron Heilman .15 .40
824 Guillermo Mota .15 .40
825 Jose Reyes .25 .60
826 Oliver Perez .15 .40
827 Duaner Sanchez .15 .40
828 Scott Schoeneweis .15 .40
829 Ramon Castro .15 .40
830 Damion Easley .15 .40
831 David Wright .30 .75
832 Moises Alou .15 .40
833 Carlos Beltran .25 .60
834 Dave Williams .15 .40
835 David Wright CL .30 .75
836 Brian Bruney .15 .40
837 Mike Myers .15 .40
838 Carl Pavano .15 .40
839 Andy Pettitte .25 .60
840 Luis Vizcaino .15 .40
841 Jorge Posada .25 .60
842 Miguel Cairo .15 .40
843 Doug Mientkiewicz .15 .40
844 Derek Jeter 1.00 2.50
845 Alex Rodriguez .50 1.25
846 Johnny Damon .25 .60
847 Hideki Matsui .40 1.00
848 Josh Phelps .15 .40
849 Phil Hughes (RC) 1.50 4.00
850 Roger Clemens .50 1.25
851 Jason Giambi CL .15 .40
852 Kiko Calero .15 .40
853 Justin Duchscherer .15 .40
854 Alan Embree .15 .40
855 Todd Walker .15 .40
856 Rich Harden .15 .40
857 Dan Haren .15 .40
858 Joe Kennedy .15 .40
859 Jason Kendall .15 .40
860 Adam Melhuse .15 .40
861 Mark Ellis .15 .40
862 Bobby Kielty .15 .40
863 Mark Kotsay .15 .40
864 Shannon Stewart .15 .40
865 Mike Piazza .40 1.00
866 Mike Piazza CL .40 1.00
867 Antonio Alfonseca .15 .40
868 Carlos Ruiz .15 .40
869 Adam Eaton .15 .40
870 Freddy Garcia .15 .40
871 Jon Lieber .15 .40
872 Matt Smith .15 .40
873 Rod Barajas .15 .40
874 Wes Helms .15 .40
875 Abraham Nunez .15 .40
876 Pat Burrell .15 .40
877 Jayson Werth .25 .60
878 Greg Dobbs .15 .40
879 Joseph Bisenius RC .30 .75
880 Michael Bourn (RC) .50 1.25
881 Chase Utley .25 .60
882 Ryan Howard .30 .75
883 Chase Utley CL .25 .60
884 Tony Armas .15 .40
885 Shawn Chacon .15 .40
886 John Grabow .15 .40
887 Paul Maholm .15 .40
888 Damaso Marte .15 .40
889 Salomon Torres .15 .40
890 Humberto Cota .15 .40
891 Ryan Doumit .15 .40
892 Adam LaRoche .15 .40
893 Jack Wilson .15 .40
894 Nate McLouth .15 .40
895 Brad Eldred .15 .40
896 Jonah Bayliss .15 .40
897 Juan Perez RC .30 .75
898 Jason Bay .25 .60
899 Adam LaRoche CL .15 .40
900 Doug Brocail .15 .40
901 Scott Cassidy .15 .40
902 Scott Linebrink .15 .40
903 Greg Maddux .50 1.25
904 Jake Peavy .15 .40
905 Mike Thompson .15 .40
906 David Wells .15 .40
907 Josh Bard .15 .40
908 Rob Bowen .15 .40
909 Marcus Giles .15 .40
910 Russell Branyan .15 .40
911 Jose Cruz .15 .40
912 Termel Sledge .15 .40
913 Trevor Hoffman .25 .60
914 Brian Giles .15 .40
915 Trevor Hoffman CL .25 .60
916 Vinnie Chulk .15 .40
917 Kevin Correia .15 .40
918 Tim Lincecum RC 5.00 12.00
919 Matt Morris .15 .40
920 Russ Ortiz .15 .40
921 Barry Zito .25 .60
922 Bengie Molina .15 .40
923 Rich Aurilia .15 .40
924 Omar Vizquel .25 .60
925 Jason Ellison .15 .40
926 Ryan Klesko .15 .40
927 Dave Roberts .25 .60
928 Randy Winn .15 .40
929 Barry Zito CL .25 .60
930 Miguel Batista .15 .40
931 Horacio Ramirez .15 .40
932 Chris Reitsma .15 .40
933 George Sherrill .15 .40
934 Jarrod Washburn .15 .40
935 Jeff Weaver .15 .40
936 Jake Woods .15 .40
937 Adrian Beltre .40 1.00
938 Jose Lopez .15 .40
939 Ichiro Suzuki .50 1.25
940 Jose Vidro .15 .40
941 Jose Guillen .15 .40
942 Sean White RC .30 .75
943 Brandon Morrow RC 1.50 4.00
944 Felix Hernandez .25 .60
945 Felix Hernandez CL .25 .60
946 Randy Flores .15 .40
947 Ryan Franklin .15 .40
948 Kelvin Jimenez RC .30 .75
949 Tyler Johnson .15 .40
950 Mark Mulder .15 .40
951 Anthony Reyes .15 .40
952 Russ Springer .15 .40
953 Brad Thompson .15 .40
954 Adam Wainwright .25 .60
955 Kip Wells .15 .40
956 Gary Bennett .15 .40
957 Adam Kennedy .15 .40
958 Scott Rolen .25 .60
959 Scott Spiezio .15 .40
960 So Taguchi .15 .40
961 Preston Wilson .15 .40
962 Skip Schumaker .15 .40
963 Albert Pujols .50 1.25
964 Chris Carpenter .25 .60
965 Chris Carpenter CL .25 .60
966 Edwin Jackson .15 .40
967 Jae Kuk Ryu .15 .40
968 Jae Seo .15 .40
969 Jon Switzer .15 .40
970 Josh Paul .15 .40
971 Ben Zobrist .25 .60
972 Rocco Baldelli .15 .40
973 Scott Kazmir .25 .60
974 Carl Crawford .25 .60
975 Delmon Young CL .25 .60
976 Bruce Chen .15 .40
977 Joaquin Benoit .15 .40
978 Scott Feldman .25 .60
979 Eric Gagne .15 .40
980 Kameron Loe .15 .40
981 Brandon McCarthy .15 .40
982 Robinson Tejeda .15 .40
983 C.J. Wilson .25 .60
984 Mark Teixeira .25 .60
985 Michael Young .15 .40
986 Kenny Lofton .15 .40
987 Brad Wilkerson .15 .40
988 Nelson Cruz .40 1.00
989 Sammy Sosa .40 1.00
990 Michael Young CL .15 .40
991 Vernon Wells .15 .40
992 Matt Stairs .15 .40
993 Jeremy Accardo .15 .40
994 A.J. Burnett .15 .40
995 Jason Frasor .15 .40
996 Roy Halladay .25 .60
997 Shaun Marcum .15 .40
998 Tomo Ohka .15 .40
999 Josh Towers .15 .40
1000 Gregg Zaun .15 .40
1001 Royce Clayton .15 .40
1002 Jason Smith .15 .40
1003 Alex Rios .15 .40
1004 Frank Thomas .40 1.00
1005 Roy Halladay CL .25 .60
1006 Jesus Flores RC .30 .75
1007 Dmitri Young .15 .40
1008 Ray King .15 .40
1009 Micah Bowie .15 .40
1010 Shawn Hill .15 .40
1011 John Patterson .15 .40
1012 Levale Speigner RC .30 .75
1013 Ryan Wagner .15 .40
1014 Jerome Williams .15 .40
1015 Ryan Zimmerman .25 .60
1016 Cristian Guzman .15 .40
1017 Nook Logan .15 .40
1018 Chris Snelling .15 .40
1019 Ronnie Belliard .15 .40
1020 Nick Johnson CL .15 .40

2007 Upper Deck Gold

*GOLD: 3X TO 8X BASIC
*GOLD RC: 2.5X TO 6X BASIC RC
RANDOM INSERTS IN RETAIL PACKS
STATED PRINT RUN 75 SER.#'d SETS
18 Andrew Miller 10.00 25.00
163 Derek Jeter 10.00 25.00
172 Chien-Ming Wang 10.00 25.00
196 Ichiro Suzuki 6.00 15.00
443 Albert Pujols 10.00 25.00
479 Derek Jeter CL 10.00 25.00
481 Ichiro Suzuki CL 6.00 15.00
499 Albert Pujols CL 10.00 25.00

2007 Upper Deck 1989 Reprints

COMPLETE SET (26) 20.00 50.00
STATED ODDS 1:4 HOBBY
AK Al Kaline 1.25 3.00
BF Bob Feller .75 2.00
BR Babe Ruth 3.00 8.00
CA Rod Carew .75 2.00
CF Carlton Fisk .75 2.00
CM Christy Mathewson 1.25 3.00
CS Casey Stengel .75 2.00
CY Cy Young 1.25 3.00
DR Don Drysdale .75 2.00
FR Frank Robinson .75 2.00
GE Lou Gehrig 2.50 6.00
HW Honus Wagner 1.25 3.00
JB Johnny Bench 1.25 3.00
JF Jimmie Foxx 1.25 3.00
JR Jackie Robinson 1.25 3.00
LG Lefty Grove .75 2.00
MO Mel Ott .75 2.00
RC Roy Campanella 1.25 3.00
RH Rogers Hornsby .75 2.00
RJ Reggie Jackson .75 2.00
RO Brooks Robinson .75 2.00
SM Stan Musial 2.00 5.00
SP Satchel Paige 1.25 3.00
TC Ty Cobb 2.00 5.00
TM Thurman Munson 1.25 3.00
WJ Walter Johnson 1.25 3.00

2007 Upper Deck 1989 Rookie Reprints

STATED ODDS 1:4 HOBBY
OVERALL PRINTING PLATE ODDS 1:96 H
PLATE PRINT RUN 1 SET PER COLOR
BLACK-CYAN-MAGENTA-YELLOW ISSUED
NO PLATE PRICING DUE TO SCARCITY
AD Alejandro De Aza 1.00 2.50
AG Alex Gordon 2.00 5.00
AI Akinori Iwamura 1.50 4.00
AS Angel Sanchez .60 1.50
BB Brian Barden .60 1.50
BI Joseph Bisenius .60 1.50
BM Brandon Morrow 3.00 8.00
BN Jared Burton .60 1.50
BU Jamie Burke .60 1.50
CJ Cesar Jimenez .60 1.50
CS Chris Stewart .60 1.50
CW Chase Wright 1.50 4.00
DK Don Kelly .60 1.50
DM Daisuke Matsuzaka 2.50 6.00
DY Delmon Young 1.00 2.50
ED Elijah Dukes 1.00 2.50
FP Felix Pie .60 1.50
GM Gustavo Molina .60 1.50
HG Hector Gimenez .60 1.50
HO Hideki Okajima 3.00 8.00
JA Joaquin Arias .60 1.50
JB Jeff Baker .60 1.50
JD John Danks 1.00 2.50
JF Jesus Flores .60 1.50
JG Jose Garcia .60 1.50
JH Josh Hamilton 2.00 5.00
JM Jay Marshall .60 1.50
JP Juan Perez .60 1.50
JS Joe Smith .60 1.50
KC Kevin Cameron .60 1.50
KI Kei Igawa 1.50 4.00
KK Kevin Kouzmanoff .60 1.50
KO Kory Casto .60 1.50
LG Lee Gardner .60 1.50
LS Levale Speigner .60 1.50
MB Michael Bourn 1.00 2.50
MC Matt Chico .60 1.50
ML Matt Lindstrom .60 1.50
MM Miguel Montero .60 1.50
MO Micah Owings .60 1.50
MR Mike Rabelo .60 1.50
RB Ryan Z. Braun .60 1.50
SA Juan Salas .60 1.50
SH Sean Henn .60 1.50
SL Doug Slaten .60 1.50
SO Joakim Soria .60 1.50
ST Brian Stokes .60 1.50
TB Travis Buck .60 1.50
TT Troy Tulowitzki 2.00 5.00
ZS Zack Segovia .60 1.50

2007 Upper Deck 1989 Rookie Reprints Signatures

RANDOM INSERTS IN PACKS
STATED PRINT RUN 5 SERIAL #'d SETS
NO PRICING DUE TO SCARCITY

2007 Upper Deck Cal Ripken Jr. Chronicles

COMMON RIPKEN 2.50 6.00
STATED ODDS 1:8 H, 1:72 R
PRINTING PLATE ODDS 1:192 H
PLATE PRINT RUN 1 SET PER COLOR
BLACK-CYAN-MAGENTA-YELLOW ISSUED
NO PLATE PRICING DUE TO SCARCITY

2007 Upper Deck Cooperstown Calling

COMMON CARD 2.50 6.00
STATED ODDS 1:4 WAL MART PACKS
OVERALL PRINTING PLATE ODDS 1:96 H
PLATE PRINT RUN 1 SET PER COLOR
BLACK-CYAN-MAGENTA-YELLOW ISSUED
NO PLATE PRICING DUE TO SCARCITY

2007 Upper Deck Cooperstown Calling Signatures

STATED ODDS 1:1440 WAL-MART PACKS
NO PRICING DUE TO SCARCITY

2007 Upper Deck Iron Men

COMMON CARD (1-50) 2.50 6.00
IM1 C.Ripken Jr./L.Gehrig 2.00 5.00
IM2 C.Ripken Jr./L.Gehrig 2.00 5.00
IM3 C.Ripken Jr./L.Gehrig 2.00 5.00
IM4 C.Ripken Jr./L.Gehrig 2.00 5.00
IM5 C.Ripken Jr./L.Gehrig 2.00 5.00
IM6 C.Ripken Jr./L.Gehrig 2.00 5.00
IM7 C.Ripken Jr./L.Gehrig 2.00 5.00
IM8 C.Ripken Jr./L.Gehrig 2.00 5.00
IM9 C.Ripken Jr./L.Gehrig 2.00 5.00
IM10 C.Ripken Jr./L.Gehrig 2.00 5.00
IM11 C.Ripken Jr./L.Gehrig 2.00 5.00
IM12 C.Ripken Jr./L.Gehrig 2.00 5.00
IM13 C.Ripken Jr./L.Gehrig 2.00 5.00
IM14 C.Ripken Jr./L.Gehrig 2.00 5.00
IM15 C.Ripken Jr./L.Gehrig 2.00 5.00
IM16 C.Ripken Jr./L.Gehrig 2.00 5.00
IM17 C.Ripken Jr./L.Gehrig 2.00 5.00
IM18 C.Ripken Jr./L.Gehrig 2.00 5.00
IM19 C.Ripken Jr./L.Gehrig 2.00 5.00
IM20 C.Ripken Jr./L.Gehrig 2.00 5.00
IM21 C.Ripken Jr./L.Gehrig 2.00 5.00
IM22 C.Ripken Jr./L.Gehrig 2.00 5.00
IM23 C.Ripken Jr./L.Gehrig 2.00 5.00
IM24 C.Ripken Jr./L.Gehrig 2.00 5.00
IM25 C.Ripken Jr./L.Gehrig 2.00 5.00
IM26 C.Ripken Jr./L.Gehrig 2.00 5.00
IM27 C.Ripken Jr./L.Gehrig 2.00 5.00
IM28 C.Ripken Jr./L.Gehrig 2.00 5.00
IM29 C.Ripken Jr./L.Gehrig 2.00 5.00
IM30 C.Ripken Jr./L.Gehrig 2.00 5.00
IM31 C.Ripken Jr./L.Gehrig 2.00 5.00
IM32 C.Ripken Jr./L.Gehrig 2.00 5.00
IM33 C.Ripken Jr./L.Gehrig 2.00 5.00
IM34 C.Ripken Jr./L.Gehrig 2.00 5.00
IM35 C.Ripken Jr./L.Gehrig 2.00 5.00
IM36 C.Ripken Jr./L.Gehrig 2.00 5.00
IM37 C.Ripken Jr./L.Gehrig 2.00 5.00
IM38 C.Ripken Jr./L.Gehrig 2.00 5.00
IM39 C.Ripken Jr./L.Gehrig 2.00 5.00
IM40 C.Ripken Jr./L.Gehrig 2.00 5.00
IM41 C.Ripken Jr./L.Gehrig 2.00 5.00
IM42 C.Ripken Jr./L.Gehrig 2.00 5.00
IM43 C.Ripken Jr./L.Gehrig 2.00 5.00
IM44 C.Ripken Jr./L.Gehrig 2.00 5.00
IM45 C.Ripken Jr./L.Gehrig 2.00 5.00
IM46 C.Ripken Jr./L.Gehrig 2.00 5.00
IM47 C.Ripken Jr./L.Gehrig 2.00 5.00
IM48 C.Ripken Jr./L.Gehrig 2.00 5.00
IM49 C.Ripken Jr./L.Gehrig 2.00 5.00
IM50 C.Ripken Jr./L.Gehrig 2.00 5.00

2007 Upper Deck Ken Griffey Jr. Chronicles

COMMON GRIFFEY 2.00 5.00
STATED ODDS 1:8 H, 1:72 R
PRINTING PLATE ODDS 1:192 H
PLATE PRINT RUN 1 SET PER COLOR
BLACK-CYAN-MAGENTA-YELLOW ISSUED
NO PLATE PRICING DUE TO SCARCITY

2007 Upper Deck MLB Rookie Card of the Month

COMPLETE SET (9) 8.00 20.00
ROM1 Daisuke Matsuzaka 1.00 2.50
ROM2 Fred Lewis .40 1.00
ROM3 Hunter Pence .75 2.00
ROM4 Ryan Braun 1.25 3.00
ROM5 Tim Lincecum 1.25 3.00
ROM6 Joba Chamberlain .40 1.00
ROM7 Troy Tulowitzki .75 2.00
ROMAL Dustin Pedroia .60 1.50
ROMNL Ryan Braun 1.25 3.00

2007 Upper Deck MVP Potential

STATED ODDS 2:1 FAT PACKS
MVP1 Stephen Drew .40 1.00
MVP2 Brian McCann .40 1.00
MVP3 Adam LaRoche .40 1.00
MVP4 Brian Roberts .40 1.00
MVP5 Manny Ramirez 1.00 2.50
MVP6 David Ortiz 1.00 2.50
MVP7 J.D. Drew .40 1.00
MVP8 Alfonso Soriano .60 1.50
MVP9 Aramis Ramirez .40 1.00
MVP10 Derrek Lee .40 1.00
MVP11 Jermaine Dye .40 1.00
MVP12 Paul Konerko .60 1.50
MVP13 Jim Thome .60 1.50
MVP14 Adam Dunn .60 1.50
MVP15 Travis Hafner .40 1.00
MVP16 Victor Martinez .60 1.50
MVP17 Grady Sizemore .60 1.50
MVP18 Garrett Atkins .40 1.00
MVP19 Matt Holliday 1.00 2.50
MVP20 Magglio Ordonez .60 1.50
MVP21 Miguel Cabrera 1.00 2.50
MVP22 Hanley Ramirez .60 1.50
MVP23 Dan Uggla .40 1.00
MVP24 Lance Berkman .60 1.50
MVP25 Carlos Lee .40 1.00
MVP26 Jered Weaver .60 1.50
MVP27 Nomar Garciaparra .60 1.50
MVP28 Rafael Furcal .40 1.00
MVP29 Prince Fielder .60 1.50
MVP30 Joe Mauer .75 2.00
MVP31 Johan Santana .60 1.50
MVP32 David Wright .75 2.00
MVP33 Jose Reyes .60 1.50
MVP34 Carlos Beltran .60 1.50
MVP35 Robinson Cano .60 1.50
MVP36 Derek Jeter 2.50 6.00
MVP37 Bobby Abreu .40 1.00
MVP38 Johnny Damon .60 1.50
MVP39 Nick Swisher .60 1.50
MVP40 Chase Utley .60 1.50
MVP41 Jason Bay .60 1.50
MVP42 Adrian Gonzalez .75 2.00
MVP43 Adrian Beltre 1.00 2.50
MVP44 Scott Rolen .60 1.50
MVP45 Carl Crawford .60 1.50
MVP46 Mark Teixeira .60 1.50
MVP47 Michael Young .40 1.00
MVP48 Vernon Wells .40 1.00
MVP49 Roy Halladay .60 1.50
MVP50 Ryan Zimmerman .60 1.50

2007 Upper Deck MVP Predictors

STATED ODDS 1:16 H, 1:240 R
MVP1 Miguel Tejada 2.00 5.00
MVP2 David Ortiz 4.00 10.00
MVP3 Manny Ramirez 2.00 5.00
MVP4 Jermaine Dye 2.00 5.00
MVP5 Jim Thome 2.00 5.00
MVP6 Paul Konerko 2.00 5.00
MVP7 Travis Hafner 2.00 5.00
MVP8 Grady Sizemore 2.00 5.00
MVP9 Victor Martinez 2.00 5.00
MVP10 Magglio Ordonez 2.00 5.00
MVP11 Justin Verlander 2.00 5.00
MVP12 Vladimir Guerrero 4.00 10.00
MVP13 Jered Weaver 2.00 5.00
MVP14 Justin Morneau 2.00 5.00
MVP15 Joe Mauer 2.00 5.00
MVP16 Johan Santana 2.00 5.00
MVP17 Alex Rodriguez 6.00 15.00
MVP18 Derek Jeter 12.50 30.00
MVP19 Jason Giambi 2.00 5.00
MVP20 Johnny Damon 3.00 8.00
MVP21 Bobby Abreu 2.00 5.00
MVP22 American League Field 6.00 15.00
MVP23 Frank Thomas 3.00 8.00
MVP24 Eric Chavez 2.00 5.00
MVP25 Ichiro Suzuki 2.00 5.00
MVP26 Adrian Beltre 2.00 5.00
MVP27 Carl Crawford 2.00 5.00
MVP28 Scott Kazmir 2.00 5.00
MVP29 Mark Teixeira 2.00 5.00
MVP30 Michael Young 2.00 5.00
MVP31 Carlos Lee 2.00 5.00
MVP32 Vernon Wells 2.00 5.00
MVP33 Roy Halladay 2.00 5.00
MVP34 Troy Glaus 2.00 5.00
MVP35 Stephen Drew 2.00 5.00
MVP36 Chipper Jones 2.00 5.00
MVP37 Andruw Jones 2.00 5.00
MVP38 Adam LaRoche 2.00 5.00
MVP39 Derrek Lee 3.00 8.00
MVP40 Aramis Ramirez 2.00 5.00
MVP41 Adam Dunn 2.00 5.00
MVP42 Ken Griffey Jr. 15.00 40.00
MVP43 Matt Holliday 2.50 6.00
MVP44 Garrett Atkins 2.00 5.00
MVP45 Miguel Cabrera 2.00 5.00
MVP46 Hanley Ramirez 2.00 5.00
MVP47 Dan Uggla 2.00 5.00
MVP48 Lance Berkman 2.00 5.00
MVP49 Roy Oswalt 2.00 5.00
MVP50 Nomar Garciaparra 2.00 5.00
MVP51 J.D. Drew 2.00 5.00
MVP52 Rafael Furcal 2.00 5.00
MVP53 Prince Fielder 15.00 40.00
MVP54 Bill Hall 3.00 8.00
MVP55 Jose Reyes 4.00 10.00
MVP56 Carlos Beltran 2.00 5.00
MVP57 Carlos Delgado 2.00 5.00
MVP58 David Wright 4.00 10.00
MVP59 National League Field 6.00 15.00
MVP60 Chase Utley 3.00 8.00
MVP61 Ryan Howard 6.00 15.00
MVP62 Jimmy Rollins 2.00 5.00
MVP63 Jason Bay 2.00 5.00
MVP64 Freddy Sanchez 2.00 5.00
MVP65 Adrian Gonzalez 2.00 5.00
MVP66 Albert Pujols 10.00 25.00
MVP67 Scott Rolen 2.00 5.00
MVP68 Chris Carpenter 2.00 5.00
MVP69 Alfonso Soriano 4.00 10.00
MVP70 Ryan Zimmerman 2.00 5.00

2007 Upper Deck Postseason Predictors

STATED ODDS 1:16 H, 1:240 R
PP1 Arizona Diamondbacks 2.00 5.00
PP2 Atlanta Braves 4.00 10.00
PP3 Baltimore Orioles 2.00 5.00
PP4 Boston Red Sox 10.00 25.00
PP5 Chicago Cubs 6.00 15.00
PP6 Chicago White Sox 4.00 10.00
PP7 Cincinnati Reds 2.00 5.00
PP8 Cleveland Indians 4.00 10.00
PP9 Colorado Rockies 2.00 5.00
PP10 Detroit Tigers 6.00 15.00
PP11 Florida Marlins 2.00 5.00
PP12 Houston Astros 2.00 5.00
PP13 Kansas City Royals 2.00 5.00
PP14 Los Angeles Angels 6.00 15.00
PP15 Los Angeles Dodgers 4.00 10.00
PP16 Milwaukee Brewers 2.00 5.00
PP17 Minnesota Twins 6.00 15.00
PP18 New York Mets 10.00 25.00
PP19 New York Yankees 12.50 30.00
PP20 Oakland Athletics 4.00 10.00
PP21 Philadelphia Phillies 4.00 10.00
PP22 Pittsburgh Pirates 2.00 5.00
PP23 San Diego Padres 4.00 10.00
PP24 San Francisco Giants 4.00 10.00
PP25 Seattle Mariners 2.00 5.00
PP26 St. Louis Cardinals 6.00 15.00
PP27 Tampa Bay Devil Rays 2.00 5.00
PP28 Texas Rangers 2.00 5.00
PP29 Toronto Blue Jays 2.00 5.00
PP30 Washington Nationals 2.00 5.00

2007 Upper Deck Rookie of the Year Predictor

STATED ODDS 1:16 HOBBY, 1:96 RETAIL
OVERALL PRINTING PLATE ODDS 1:96 H
PLATE PRINT RUN 1 SET PER COLOR
BLACK-CYAN-MAGENTA-YELLOW ISSUED
NO PLATE PRICING DUE TO SCARCITY
ROY1 Doug Slaten 1.25 3.00
ROY2 Miguel Montero 1.25 3.00
ROY3 Joseph Bisenius 1.25 3.00
ROY4 Kory Casto 1.25 3.00
ROY5 Jesus Flores 1.25 3.00
ROY6 John Danks 1.25 3.00
ROY7 Daisuke Matsuzaka 12.50 30.00
ROY8 Matt Lindstrom 1.25 3.00
ROY9 Chris Stewart 1.25 3.00
ROY10 Kevin Cameron 1.25 3.00
ROY11 Hideki Okajima 6.00 15.00
ROY12 Levale Speigner 1.25 3.00
ROY13 Kevin Kouzmanoff 1.25 3.00
ROY14 Jeff Baker 1.25 3.00
ROY15 Don Kelly 1.25 3.00
ROY16 Troy Tulowitzki 4.00 10.00
ROY17 Felix Pie 4.00 10.00
ROY18 Cesar Jimenez 1.25 3.00
ROY19 Alejandro De Aza 1.25 3.00
ROY20 Jose Garcia 1.25 3.00
ROY21 Micah Owings 1.25 3.00
ROY22 Josh Hamilton 30.00 60.00
ROY23 Brian Barden 1.25 3.00
ROY24 Jamie Burke 1.25 3.00
ROY25 Mike Rabelo 1.25 3.00
ROY26 Elijah Dukes 2.00 5.00
ROY27 Travis Buck 1.25 3.00
ROY28 Kei Igawa 2.00 5.00
ROY29 Sean Henn 1.25 3.00
ROY30 American League Field 10.00 25.00
ROY31 National League Field 10.00 25.00
ROY32 Michael Bourn 1.25 3.00
ROY33 Alex Gordon 10.00 25.00
ROY34 Chase Wright 2.00 5.00
ROY35 Matt Chico 1.25 3.00
ROY36 Joe Smith 1.25 3.00
ROY37 Lee Gardner 1.25 3.00
ROY38 Gustavo Molina 1.25 3.00
ROY39 Jared Burton 1.25 3.00
ROY40 Jay Marshall 1.25 3.00
ROY41 Brandon Morrow 2.00 5.00
ROY42 Akinori Iwamura 4.00 10.00
ROY43 Delmon Young 2.00 5.00
ROY44 Juan Salas 1.25 3.00
ROY45 Zack Segovia 1.25 3.00
ROY46 Brian Stokes 1.25 3.00
ROY47 Joaquin Arias 1.25 3.00
ROY48 Hector Gimenez 1.25 3.00
ROY49 Ryan Z. Braun 1.25 3.00
ROY50 Juan Perez 1.25 3.00

2007 Upper Deck Star Power

COMMON CARD .40 1.00
SEMISTARS .60 1.50
UNLISTED STARS 1.00 2.50
STATED ODDS 2:1 FAT PACKS
AJ Andruw Jones .60 1.50
AP Albert Pujols 2.00 5.00
AR Alex Rodriguez 1.50 4.00
BR Brian Roberts .40 1.00
BZ Barry Zito .40 1.00
CA Chris Carpenter .40 1.00
CB Carlos Beltran .40 1.00
CC Carl Crawford .40 1.00
CJ Chipper Jones 1.00 2.50
CS Curt Schilling .60 1.50
CU Chase Utley 1.00 2.50
CZ Carlos Zambrano .40 1.00
DA Johnny Damon .60 1.50
DJ Derek Jeter 2.50 6.00
DO David Ortiz 1.00 2.50
DW Dontrelle Willis .40 1.00
FS Freddy Sanchez .40 1.00
FT Frank Thomas 1.00 2.50
HA Roy Halladay .40 1.00
HO Trevor Hoffman .40 1.00
IS Ichiro Suzuki 1.50 4.00
JB Jason Bay .40 1.00
JD Jermaine Dye .40 1.00
JM Joe Mauer .60 1.50
JP Jake Peavy .40 1.00
JR Jose Reyes .40 1.00
JS Johan Santana .60 1.50
JT Jim Thome .60 1.50
JU Justin Morneau .40 1.00
JV Justin Verlander 1.00 2.50
KG Ken Griffey Jr. 2.00 5.00
KR Kenny Rogers .40 1.00
LB Lance Berkman .40 1.00
MA Matt Cain .60 1.50
MC Miguel Cabrera .60 1.50
MH Matt Holliday .50 1.25
MO Magglio Ordonez .40 1.00
MR Manny Ramirez .60 1.50
MT Mark Teixeira .60 1.50
MY Michael Young .40 1.00
NG Nomar Garciaparra 1.00 2.50
NS Nick Swisher .40 1.00
PF Prince Fielder 1.00 2.50
RH Ryan Howard 1.50 4.00
RO Roy Oswalt .40 1.00
RZ Ryan Zimmerman 1.00 2.50
SM John Smoltz .60 1.50
TH Travis Hafner .40 1.00
VG Vladimir Guerrero 1.00 2.50
WR David Wright 1.50 4.00

2007 Upper Deck Star Rookies

SR1 Adam Lind .40 1.00
SR2 Akinori Iwamura 1.00 2.50
SR3 Alexi Casilla .60 1.50
SR4 Alex Gordon 1.25 3.00
SR5 Matt Chico .40 1.00
SR6 John Danks .60 1.50
SR7 Angel Sanchez .40 1.00
SR8 Elijah Dukes .60 1.50
SR9 Brian Burres .40 1.00
SR10 Gustavo Molina .40 1.00
SR11 Chris Stewart .40 1.00
SR12 Daisuke Matsuzaka 1.50 4.00
SR13 Joakim Soria .40 1.00
SR14 Delmon Young .60 1.50
SR15 Jay Marshall .40 1.00
SR16 Travis Buck .40 1.00
SR17 Doug Slaten .40 1.00
SR18 Don Kelly .40 1.00
SR19 Kevin Cameron .40 1.00
SR20 Glen Perkins .40 1.00
SR21 Hector Gimenez .40 1.00
SR22 Jeff Baker .40 1.00
SR23 Jared Burton .40 1.00
SR24 Kory Casto .40 1.00
SR25 Joe Smith .40 1.00
SR26 Joaquin Arias .40 1.00
SR27 Dallas Braden .40 1.00
SR28 Jon Knott .40 1.00
SR29 Jose Garcia .40 1.00
SR30 Jamie Burke .40 1.00
SR31 Zach Segovia .40 1.00
SR32 Felix Pie .40 1.00
SR33 Juan Salas .40 1.00
SR34 Kei Igawa 1.00 2.50
SR35 Philip Hughes 1.00 2.50
SR36 Kevin Kouzmanoff .40 1.00
SR37 Michael Bourn .60 1.50
SR38 Miguel Montero .40 1.00
SR39 Mike Rabelo .40 1.00
SR40 Josh Hamilton 1.25 3.00
SR41 Micah Owings .40 1.00
SR42 Alejandro De Aza .60 1.50
SR43 Brian Barden .40 1.00
SR44 Andy Gonzalez .40 1.00
SR45 Chase Wright 1.00 2.50
SR46 Sean Henn .40 1.00
SR47 Rick Vanden Hurk .40 1.00
SR48 Troy Tulowitzki 1.25 3.00
SR49 Rocky Cherry 1.00 2.50
SR50 Jesus Flores .40 1.00

2007 Upper Deck Star Signings

SER.1 ODDS 1:16 HOBBY, 1:960 RETAIL
SER.2 ODDS 1:16 HOBBY, 1:960 RETAIL
SP INFO PROVIDED BY UPPER DECK
EXCH DEADLINE 02/27/2010
AB Ambiorix Burgos 3.00 8.00
AB Adrian Beltre S2 SP 5.00 12.00
AC Alberto Callaspo S2 3.00 8.00
AC Aaron Cook 3.00 8.00
AG Alex Gordon S2 10.00 25.00
AH Aubrey Huff SP 5.00 12.00
AR Alex Rios 3.00 8.00
AS Angel Sanchez S2 3.00 8.00
BA Jeff Baker S2 3.00 8.00
BA Bobby Abreu 6.00 15.00
BB Brian Burres S2 3.00 8.00
BE Josh Beckett S2 SP 20.00 50.00
BL Joe Blanton 3.00 8.00
BO Jeremy Bonderman 6.00 15.00
BO Ben Broussard S2 4.00 10.00
BR Brandon Backe 3.00 8.00
BU B.J. Upton S2 SP 20.00 50.00
CB Craig Biggio S2 SP 15.00 40.00
CC Carl Crawford S2 SP 3.00 8.00
CJ Conor Jackson 6.00 15.00
CO Chad Cordero 3.00 8.00
CP Corey Patterson 3.00 8.00
CR Coco Crisp SP 5.00 12.00
CR Cal Ripken Jr. S2 SP 30.00 80.00
CS Chris Shelton 3.00 8.00
CY Chris Young SP 6.00 15.00
DC Daniel Cabrera SP 3.00 8.00
DH Danny Haren 4.00 10.00
DJ Derek Jeter 100.00 200.00
DJ Derek Jeter S2 SP 100.00 200.00
DL Derrek Lee SP 6.00 15.00
DU Chris Duffy 3.00 8.00
DY Delmon Young S2 SP 6.00 15.00
ED Elijah Dukes S2 6.00 15.00
FH Felix Hernandez S2 12.00 30.00
GA Garrett Atkins 3.00 8.00
GC Gustavo Chacin 3.00 8.00
HS Huston Street 3.00 8.00
HU Torii Hunter 6.00 15.00
IK Ian Kinsler S2 SP 3.00 8.00
IS Ian Snell S2 5.00 12.00
IS Ian Snell SP 5.00 12.00
JA Jeremy Accardo 3.00 8.00
JB Jason Bergmann SP 5.00 12.00
JD Joey Devine 3.00 8.00
JD J.D. Drew S2 SP 8.00 20.00
JG Jonny Gomes 3.00 8.00
JJ Jorge Julio 3.00 8.00
JK Jason Kubel 4.00 10.00
JM Justin Morneau 6.00 15.00
JN Joe Nathan 3.00 8.00
JS Jason Bay 3.00 8.00
JW Jake Westbrook 3.00 8.00
KF Keith Foulke 4.00 10.00
KG Ken Griffey Jr. 30.00 60.00
KG Ken Griffey Jr. S2 SP 30.00 60.00
KI Kei Igawa S2 SP 15.00 40.00
KJ Kelly Johnson S2 6.00 15.00
KM Kevin Mench 3.00 8.00
KS Kirk Saarloos 3.00 8.00
KY Kevin Youkilis 3.00 8.00
LN Laynce Nix SP 5.00 12.00
LO Lyle Overbay 3.00 8.00
MA Matt Cain SP 4.00 10.00
MH Matt Holliday 4.00 10.00
MK Mark Kotsay 4.00 10.00
MM Melvin Mora 4.00 10.00
MT Mark Teahen SP 5.00 12.00
NC Nelson Cruz S2 4.00 10.00
NM Nate McLouth SP 5.00 12.00
OP Oliver Perez S2 SP 15.00 40.00
RA Chris Ray S2 4.00 10.00
RC Ryan Church 3.00 8.00
RF Rafael Furcal SP 5.00 12.00
RG Ryan Garko 4.00 10.00
RI Juan Rivera SP 5.00 12.00
RJ Reed Johnson 3.00 8.00
RO Aaron Rowand SP 5.00 12.00
RU Carlos Ruiz 5.00 12.00
SA Juan Salas S2 3.00 8.00
SC Sean Casey SP 5.00 12.00
SD Stephen Drew 10.00 25.00
SH Sean Henn S2 3.00 8.00
SP Scott Podsednik SP 6.00 15.00
TI Tadahito Iguchi 6.00 15.00
VE Justin Verlander 20.00 50.00
WM Wily Mo Pena 6.00 15.00
XN Xavier Nady 4.00 10.00
YB Yuniesky Betancourt 10.00 25.00
YO Chris Young S2 5.00 12.00
ZS Zack Segovia S2 3.00 8.00

2007 Upper Deck Ticket to Stardom

STATED ODDS 1:4 TARGET PACKS
NO PRICING DUE TO LACK OF MARKET INFO
OVERALL PRINTING PLATE ODDS 1:96 HOBBY
PLATE PRINT RUN 1 SET PER COLOR
BLACK-CYAN-MAGENTA-YELLOW ISSUED
NO PLATE PRICING DUE TO SCARCITY
AD Alejandro De Aza .60 1.50
AG Alex Gordon 1.25 3.00
AI Akinori Iwamura 1.00 2.50
AS Angel Sanchez .40 1.00
BB Brian Barden .40 1.00
BI Joseph Bisenius .40 1.00
BM Brandon Morrow 2.00 5.00
BN Jared Burton .40 1.00

BU Jamie Burke	.40	1.00
CH Matt Chico	.40	1.00
CJ Cesar Jimenez	.40	1.00
CS Chris Stewart	.40	1.00
CW Chase Wright	1.00	2.50
DA John Danks	.60	1.50
DK Don Kelly	.40	1.00
DM Daisuke Matsuzaka	1.50	4.00
DS Doug Slaten	.40	1.00
DY Delmon Young	.60	1.50
ED Elijah Dukes	.60	1.50
FP Felix Pie	.40	1.00
GM Gustavo Molina	.40	1.00
HG Hector Gimenez	.40	1.00
HO Hideki Okajima	2.00	5.00
JA Joaquin Arias	.40	1.00
JB Jeff Baker	.40	1.00
JF Jesus Flores	.40	1.00
JG Jose Garcia	.40	1.00
JH Josh Hamilton	1.25	3.00
JM Jay Marshall	.40	1.00
JO Joe Smith	.40	1.00
JP Juan Perez	.40	1.00
KC Kevin Cameron	.40	1.00
KI Kei Igawa	1.00	2.50
KK Kevin Kouzmanoff	.40	1.00
KO Kory Casto	.40	1.00
LG Lee Gardner	.40	1.00
LS Levale Speigner	.40	1.00
MB Michael Bourn	.60	1.50
ML Matt Lindstrom	.40	1.00
MM Miguel Montero	.40	1.00
MO Micah Owings	.40	1.00
MR Mike Rabelo	.40	1.00
RB Ryan Z. Braun	.40	1.00
SA Juan Salas	.40	1.00
SH Sean Henn	.40	1.00
SO Joakim Soria	.40	1.00
ST Brian Stokes	.40	1.00
TB Travis Buck	.40	1.00
TT Troy Tulowitzki	1.25	3.00
ZS Zack Segovia	.40	1.00

2007 Upper Deck Triple Play Performers

COMPLETE SET	12.50	30.00
TPAP Albert Pujols	1.25	3.00
TPAR Alex Rodriguez	1.25	3.00
TPAS Alfonso Soriano	.60	1.50
TPCC Carl Crawford	.60	1.50
TPCJ Chipper Jones	1.00	2.50
TPDJ Derek Jeter	2.50	6.00
TPDL Derrek Lee	.40	1.00
TPDM Daisuke Matsuzaka	1.50	4.00
TPDO David Ortiz	1.00	2.50
TPDW David Wright	.75	2.00
TPGS Grady Sizemore	.60	1.50
TPHA Travis Hafner	.60	1.50
TPIS Ichiro Suzuki	1.25	3.00
TPJM Justin Morneau	.60	1.50
TPJP Jake Peavy	.40	1.00
TPJR Jose Reyes	.60	1.50
TPJS Johan Santana	.60	1.50
TPJT Jim Thome	.60	1.50
TPJV Justin Verlander	1.00	2.50
TPKG Ken Griffey	2.00	5.00
TPLB Lance Berkman	.60	1.50
TPMC Miguel Cabrera	1.00	2.50
TPMO Magglio Ordonez	.60	1.50
TPMT Mark Teixeira	.60	1.50
TPMT Miguel Tejada	.60	1.50
TPPF Prince Fielder	.60	1.50
TPRH Ryan Howard	.75	2.00
TPRJ Randy Johnson	1.00	2.50
TPTH Todd Helton	.40	1.00
TPVG Vladimir Guerrero	.60	1.50

2007 Upper Deck UD Game Materials

SER.1 STATED ODDS 1:8 H, 1:24 R
SER.2 STATED ODDS 1:8 H, 1:24 R

AB A.J. Burnett S2	3.00	8.00
AJ Andruw Jones Jsy S1	3.00	8.00
AP Albert Pujols Pants S1	6.00	15.00
AP Albert Pujols S2	6.00	15.00
AR Alex Rios S2	4.00	10.00
BA Bobby Abreu S2	3.00	8.00
BC Bartolo Colon S2	3.00	8.00
BE Josh Beckett Jsy S1	3.00	8.00
BJ Bobby Jenks S2	3.00	8.00
BR Brian Roberts Jsy S1	3.00	8.00
BS Ben Sheets Jsy S1	3.00	8.00
CA Chris Carpenter Jsy S1	3.00	8.00
CB Carlos Beltran Pants S1	4.00	10.00
CC Carl Crawford Pants S1	3.00	8.00
CC Carl Crawford S2	3.00	8.00
CD Carlos Delgado Jsy S1	3.00	8.00
CJ Chipper Jones S2	3.00	8.00
CL Carlos Lee Jsy S1	3.00	8.00
CP Corey Patterson Jsy S1	3.00	8.00
CS C.C. Sabathia Jsy S1	3.00	8.00
CS Curt Schilling S2	6.00	15.00
CU Chase Utley S2	4.00	10.00
DJ Derek Jeter S2	12.50	30.00
DJ Derek Jeter Pants S1	12.50	30.00
DO David Ortiz Jsy S1	4.00	10.00
DW Dontrelle Willis Jsy S1	3.00	8.00
EB Erik Bedard S2	4.00	10.00
EC Eric Chavez Jsy S1	3.00	8.00
EN Juan Encarnacion S2	3.00	8.00
FH Felix Hernandez Jsy S1	4.00	10.00
FR Jeff Francoeur S2	4.00	10.00
GS Gary Sheffield S2	3.00	8.00
HB Hank Blalock S2	3.00	8.00
HO Trevor Hoffman S2	3.00	8.00
HU Torii Hunter Jsy S1	3.00	8.00
IR Ivan Rodriguez Jsy S1	3.00	8.00
JB Jason Bay Jsy S1	3.00	8.00
JD Johnny Damon S2	3.00	8.00
JE Jim Edmonds S2	3.00	8.00
JF Jeff Francis S2	3.00	8.00
JG Jason Giambi Jsy S1	3.00	8.00
JM Joe Mauer Jsy S1	3.00	8.00
JR Jose Reyes Jsy S1	4.00	10.00
JS Johan Santana Jsy S1	3.00	8.00
JS John Smoltz S2	4.00	10.00
JT Jim Thome S2	3.00	8.00
JU Juan Uribe Jsy S1	3.00	8.00
JV Justin Verlander Jsy S1	6.00	15.00
JV Jose Vidro S2	3.00	8.00
KG Ken Griffey Jr. S2	6.00	15.00
KG Ken Griffey Jr. Pants S1	6.00	15.00
LB Lance Berkman S2	3.00	8.00
LG Luis Gonzalez S2	3.00	8.00
MC Miguel Cabrera Jsy S1	4.00	10.00
MH Matt Holliday Jsy S1	4.00	10.00
MM Melvin Mora Jsy S1	3.00	8.00
MO Justin Morneau Jsy S1	4.00	10.00
MR Manny Ramirez Jsy S1	4.00	10.00
MR Manny Ramirez S2	4.00	10.00
MS Mike Sweeney Jsy S1	3.00	8.00
MT Miguel Tejada Jsy S1	3.00	8.00
MT Mark Teixeira S2	3.00	8.00
MU Mike Mussina Jsy S1	4.00	10.00
OR Magglio Ordonez Jsy S1	3.00	8.00
PF Prince Fielder Jsy S1	4.00	10.00
RB Rocco Baldelli S2	3.00	8.00
RH Roy Halladay Jsy S1	3.00	8.00
RJ Randy Johnson S2	4.00	10.00
RN Ricky Nolasco S2	3.00	8.00
RO Roy Oswalt S2	3.00	8.00
RW Rickie Weeks S2	3.00	8.00
RZ Ryan Zimmerman Jsy S1	4.00	10.00
SD Stephen Drew S2	3.00	8.00
SK Scott Kazmir S2	3.00	8.00
SR Scott Rolen S2	3.00	8.00
SR Scott Rolen Jsy S1	4.00	10.00
TG Tom Glavine S2	4.00	10.00
TH Todd Helton S2	3.00	8.00
TH Tim Hudson Jsy S1	3.00	8.00
TN Trot Nixon S2	3.00	8.00
VG Vladimir Guerrero S2	4.00	10.00
VM Victor Martinez Jsy S1	3.00	8.00
ZD Zach Duke S2	3.00	8.00

2007 Upper Deck UD Game Patch

STATED ODDS 1:192 H, 1:2500 R

AJ Andruw Jones	15.00	40.00
AP Albert Pujols	40.00	80.00
BE Josh Beckett	10.00	25.00
BR Brian Roberts	10.00	25.00
BS Ben Sheets	10.00	25.00
CA Chris Carpenter	15.00	40.00
CB Carlos Beltran	15.00	40.00
CC Carl Crawford	10.00	25.00
CD Carlos Delgado	10.00	25.00
CL Carlos Lee	10.00	25.00
CP Corey Patterson	10.00	25.00
CS C.C. Sabathia	10.00	25.00
DJ Derek Jeter	40.00	80.00
DO David Ortiz	20.00	50.00
DW Dontrelle Willis	10.00	25.00
EC Eric Chavez	10.00	25.00
FH Felix Hernandez	15.00	40.00
HU Torii Hunter	15.00	40.00
IR Ivan Rodriguez	15.00	40.00
JB Jason Bay	15.00	40.00
JG Jason Giambi	15.00	40.00
JM Joe Mauer	15.00	40.00
JR Jose Reyes	20.00	50.00
JS Johan Santana	15.00	40.00
JU Juan Uribe	10.00	25.00
KG Ken Griffey Jr.	40.00	80.00
MC Miguel Cabrera	15.00	40.00
MH Matt Holliday	12.50	30.00
MM Melvin Mora	10.00	25.00
MO Justin Morneau	10.00	25.00
MR Manny Ramirez	20.00	50.00
MS Mike Sweeney	10.00	25.00
MT Miguel Tejada	10.00	25.00
MU Mike Mussina	10.00	25.00
OR Magglio Ordonez	10.00	25.00
PF Prince Fielder	15.00	40.00
RH Roy Halladay	10.00	25.00
RZ Ryan Zimmerman	20.00	50.00
SR Scott Rolen	20.00	50.00
TH Tim Hudson	10.00	25.00
VM Victor Martinez	15.00	40.00

2008 Upper Deck

COMPLETE SET (799)	50.00	100.00
COMP.SER.1 (1-400)	20.00	50.00
COMP.SER.2 (401-799)	20.00	50.00
COMMON CARD (1-799)	.15	.40
COMMON ROOKIE (1-799)	.40	1.00
1 Joe Saunders	.15	.40
2 Kelvim Escobar	.25	.60
3 Jered Weaver	.25	.60
4 Justin Speier	.25	.60
5 Scot Shields	.25	.60
6 Mike Napoli	.25	.60
7 Orlando Cabrera	.25	.60
8 Casey Kotchman	.15	.40
9 Vladimir Guerrero	.25	.60
10 Garret Anderson	.15	.40
11 Roy Oswalt	.25	.60
12 Wandy Rodriguez	.15	.40
13 Woody Williams	.25	.60
14 Chad Qualls	.15	.40
15 Brian Moehler	.15	.40
16 Mark Loretta	.25	.60
17 Brad Ausmus	.15	.40
18 Ty Wigginton	.25	.60
19 Carlos Lee	.15	.40
20 Hunter Pence	.25	.60
21 Dan Haren	.15	.40
22 Lenny DiNardo	.25	.60
23 Chad Gaudin	.25	.60
24 Huston Street	.25	.60
25 Andrew Brown	.15	.40
26 Mike Piazza	.40	1.00
27 Jack Cust	.15	.40
28 Mark Ellis	.15	.40
29 Shannon Stewart	.15	.40
30 Travis Buck	.25	.60
31 Shaun Marcum	.15	.40
32 A.J. Burnett	.15	.40
33 Jesse Litsch	.25	.60
34 Casey Janssen	.15	.40
35 Jeremy Accardo	.25	.60
36 Gregg Zaun	.15	.40
37 Aaron Hill	.15	.40
38 Frank Thomas	.40	1.00
39 Matt Stairs	.15	.40
40 Vernon Wells	.15	.40
41 Tim Hudson	.25	.60
42 Chuck James	.15	.40
43 Buddy Carlyle	.15	.40
44 Rafael Soriano	.15	.40
45 Peter Moylan	.15	.40
46 Brian McCann	.25	.60
47 Edgar Renteria	.15	.40
48 Mark Teixeira	.25	.60
49 Willie Harris	.15	.40
50 Andruw Jones	.15	.40
51 Ben Sheets	.15	.40
52 Dave Bush	.15	.40
53 Yovani Gallardo	.15	.40
54 Francisco Cordero	.15	.40
55 Matt Wise	.15	.40
56 Johnny Estrada	.15	.40
57 Prince Fielder	.25	.60
58 J.J. Hardy	.15	.40
59 Corey Hart	.15	.40
60 Geoff Jenkins	.15	.40
61 Adam Wainwright	.25	.60
62 Joel Pineiro	.15	.40
63 Brad Thompson	.15	.40
64 Jason Isringhausen	.15	.40
65 Troy Percival	.15	.40
66 Yadier Molina	.50	1.25
67 Albert Pujols	.50	1.25
68 David Eckstein	.15	.40
69 Jim Edmonds	.25	.60
70 Rick Ankiel	.15	.40
71 Ted Lilly	.15	.40
72 Rich Hill	.15	.40
73 Jason Marquis	.15	.40
74 Carlos Marmol	.25	.60
75 Ryan Dempster	.15	.40
76 Jason Kendall	.15	.40
77 Aramis Ramirez	.15	.40
78 Ryan Theriot	.15	.40
79 Alfonso Soriano	.25	.60
80 Jacque Jones	.15	.40
81 James Shields	.15	.40
82 Andy Sonnanstine	.15	.40
83 Scott Dohmann	.15	.40
84 Al Reyes	.15	.40
85 Dioner Navarro	.15	.40
86 B.J. Upton	.25	.60
87 Carlos Pena	.25	.60
88 Brendan Harris	.15	.40
89 Josh Wilson	.15	.40
90 Jonny Gomes	.15	.40
91 Brandon Webb	.25	.60
92 Micah Owings	.15	.40
93 Livan Hernandez	.15	.40
94 Doug Slaten	.15	.40
95 Brandon Lyon	.15	.40
96 Miguel Montero	.15	.40
97 Stephen Drew	.15	.40
98 Mark Reynolds	.15	.40
99 Conor Jackson	.15	.40
100 Chris B. Young	.15	.40
101 Chad Billingsley	.25	.60
102 Derek Lowe	.15	.40
103 Mark Hendrickson	.15	.40
104 Takashi Saito	.15	.40
105 Rudy Seanez	.15	.40
106 Russell Martin	.15	.40
107 Jeff Kent	.15	.40
108 Nomar Garciaparra	.25	.60
109 Matt Kemp	.30	.75
110 Juan Pierre	.15	.40
111 Matt Cain	.25	.60
112 Barry Zito	.25	.60
113 Kevin Correia	.15	.40
114 Brad Hennessey	.15	.40
115 Jack Taschner	.15	.40
116 Bengie Molina	.15	.40
117 Ryan Klesko	.15	.40
118 Omar Vizquel	.25	.60
119 Dave Roberts	.25	.60
120 Rajai Davis	.15	.40
121 Fausto Carmona	.15	.40
122 Jake Westbrook	.15	.40
123 Cliff Lee	.25	.60
124 Rafael Betancourt	.15	.40
125 Joe Borowski	.15	.40
126 Victor Martinez	.25	.60
127 Travis Hafner	.15	.40
128 Ryan Garko	.15	.40
129 Kenny Lofton	.15	.40
130 Franklin Gutierrez	.15	.40
131 Felix Hernandez	.25	.60
132 Jeff Weaver	.15	.40
133 J.J. Putz	.15	.40
134 Brandon Morrow	.15	.40
135 Sean Green	.15	.40
136 Kenji Johjima	.15	.40
137 Jose Vidro	.15	.40
138 Richie Sexson	.15	.40
139 Ichiro Suzuki	.50	1.25
140 Ben Broussard	.15	.40
141 Sergio Mitre	.15	.40
142 Scott Olsen	.15	.40
143 Rick Vanden Hurk	.15	.40
144 Justin Miller	.15	.40
145 Lee Gardner	.15	.40
146 Miguel Olivo	.15	.40
147 Hanley Ramirez	.25	.60
148 Mike Jacobs	.15	.40
149 Josh Willingham	.25	.60
150 Alfredo Amezaga	.15	.40
151 John Maine	.15	.40
152 Tom Glavine	.25	.60
153 Orlando Hernandez	.15	.40
154 Billy Wagner	.15	.40
155 Aaron Heilman	.15	.40
156 David Wright	.25	.60
157 Luis Castillo	.15	.40
158 Shawn Green	.15	.40
159 Damion Easley	.15	.40
160 Carlos Delgado	.15	.40
161 Shawn Hill	.15	.40
162 Mike Bacsik	.15	.40
163 John Lannan	.15	.40
164 Chad Cordero	.15	.40
165 Jon Rauch	.15	.40
166 Jesus Flores	.15	.40
167 Dmitri Young	.15	.40
168 Cristian Guzman	.15	.40
169 Austin Kearns	.15	.40
170 Nook Logan	.15	.40
171 Erik Bedard	.15	.40
172 Daniel Cabrera	.15	.40
173 Chris Ray	.15	.40
174 Danys Baez	.15	.40
175 Chad Bradford	.15	.40
176 Ramon Hernandez	.15	.40
177 Miguel Tejada	.25	.60
178 Freddie Bynum	.15	.40
179 Corey Patterson	.15	.40
180 Aubrey Huff	.15	.40
181 Chris Young	.15	.40
182 Greg Maddux	.50	1.25
183 Clay Hensley	.15	.40
184 Kevin Cameron	.15	.40
185 Doug Brocail	.15	.40
186 Josh Bard	.15	.40
187 Kevin Kouzmanoff	.15	.40
188 Geoff Blum	.15	.40
189 Milton Bradley	.15	.40
190 Brian Giles	.15	.40
191 Jamie Moyer	.15	.40
192 Kyle Kendrick	.15	.40
193 Kyle Lohse	.15	.40
194 Antonio Alfonseca	.15	.40
195 Ryan Madson	.15	.40
196 Chris Coste	.15	.40
197 Chase Utley	.25	.60
198 Tadahito Iguchi	.15	.40
199 Aaron Rowand	.15	.40
200 Shane Victorino	.15	.40
201 Paul Maholm	.15	.40
202 Ian Snell	.15	.40
203 Shane Youman	.15	.40
204 Damaso Marte	.15	.40
205 Shawn Chacon	.15	.40
206 Ronny Paulino	.15	.40
207 Jack Wilson	.15	.40
208 Adam LaRoche	.15	.40
209 Ryan Doumit	.15	.40
210 Xavier Nady	.15	.40
211 Kevin Millwood	.15	.40
212 Brandon McCarthy	.15	.40
213 Joaquin Benoit	.15	.40
214 Wes Littleton	.15	.40
215 Mike Wood	.15	.40
216 Gerald Laird	.15	.40
217 Hank Blalock	.15	.40
218 Ian Kinsler	.25	.60
219 Marlon Byrd	.15	.40
220 Brad Wilkerson	.15	.40
221 Tim Wakefield	.25	.60
222 Daisuke Matsuzaka	.25	.60
223 Julian Tavarez	.15	.40
224 Hideki Okajima	.15	.40
225 Manny Delcarmen	.15	.40
226 Doug Mirabelli	.15	.40
227 Dustin Pedroia	.40	1.00
228 Mike Lowell	.15	.40
229 Manny Ramirez	.40	1.00
230 Coco Crisp	.15	.40
231 Bronson Arroyo	.15	.40
232 Matt Belisle	.15	.40
233 Jared Burton	.15	.40
234 David Weathers	.15	.40
235 Mike Gosling	.15	.40
236 David Ross	.15	.40
237 Jeff Keppinger	.15	.40
238 Edwin Encarnacion	.40	1.00
239 Ken Griffey Jr.	.75	2.00
240 Adam Dunn	.25	.60
241 Jeff Francis	.15	.40
242 Jason Hirsh	.15	.40
243 Josh Fogg	.15	.40
244 Manny Corpas	.15	.40
245 Jeremy Affeldt	.15	.40
246 Yorvit Torrealba	.15	.40
247 Todd Helton	.25	.60
248 Kazuo Matsui	.15	.40
249 Brad Hawpe	.15	.40
250 Willy Taveras	.15	.40
251 Brian Bannister	.15	.40
252 Zack Greinke	.40	1.00
253 Kyle Davies	.15	.40
254 David Riske	.15	.40
255 Joel Peralta	.15	.40
256 John Buck	.15	.40
257 Mark Grudzielanek	.15	.40
258 Ross Gload	.15	.40
259 Billy Butler	.15	.40
260 David DeJesus	.15	.40
261 Jeremy Bonderman	.15	.40
262 Chad Durbin	.15	.40
263 Andrew Miller	.25	.60
264 Bobby Seay	.15	.40
265 Todd Jones	.15	.40
266 Brandon Inge	.15	.40
267 Sean Casey	.15	.40
268 Placido Polanco	.15	.40
269 Gary Sheffield	.15	.40
270 Magglio Ordonez	.25	.60
271 Matt Garza	.15	.40
272 Boof Bonser	.15	.40
273 Scott Baker	.15	.40
274 Joe Nathan	.15	.40
275 Dennys Reyes	.15	.40
276 Joe Mauer	.30	.75
277 Michael Cuddyer	.15	.40
278 Jason Bartlett	.15	.40
279 Torii Hunter	.15	.40
280 Jason Tyner	.15	.40
281 Mark Buehrle	.25	.60
282 Jon Garland	.15	.40
283 Jose Contreras	.15	.40
284 Matt Thornton	.15	.40
285 Ryan Bukvich	.15	.40
286 Juan Uribe	.15	.40
287 Jim Thome	.25	.60
288 Scott Podsednik	.15	.40
289 Jerry Owens	.15	.40
290 Jermaine Dye	.15	.40
291 Andy Pettitte	.25	.60
292 Phil Hughes	.15	.40
293 Mike Mussina	.25	.60
294 Joba Chamberlain	.15	.40
295 Brian Bruney	.15	.40
296 Jorge Posada	.25	.60
297 Derek Jeter	1.00	2.50
298 Jason Giambi	.15	.40
299 Johnny Damon	.25	.60
300 Melky Cabrera	.15	.40
301 Jonathan Albaladejo RC	.60	1.50
302 Josh Anderson (RC)	.40	1.00
303 Wladimir Balentien (RC)	.40	1.00
304 Josh Banks (RC)	.40	1.00
305 Daric Barton (RC)	.40	1.00
306 Jerry Blevins RC	.60	1.50
307 Emilio Bonifacio RC	1.00	2.50
308 Lance Broadway (RC)	.40	1.00
309 Clay Buchholz (RC)	.60	1.50
310 Billy Buckner (RC)	.40	1.00
311 Jeff Clement (RC)	.60	1.50
312 Willie Collazo RC	.60	1.50
313 Ross Detwiler RC	.60	1.50
314 Sam Fuld RC	1.25	3.00
315 Harvey Garcia (RC)	.40	1.00
316 Alberto Gonzalez RC	.60	1.50
317 Ryan Hanigan RC	.60	1.50
318 Kevin Hart (RC)	.40	1.00
319 Luke Hochevar RC	.60	1.50
320 Chin-Lung Hu (RC)	.40	1.00
321 Rob Johnson (RC)	.40	1.00
322 Radhames Liz RC	.60	1.50
323 Ian Kennedy RC	1.00	2.50
324 Joe Koshansky (RC)	.40	1.00
325 Donny Lucy (RC)	.40	1.00
326 Justin Maxwell RC	.40	1.00
327 Jonathan Meloan RC	.60	1.50
328 Luis Mendoza (RC)	.40	1.00
329 Jose Morales (RC)	.40	1.00
330 Nyjer Morgan (RC)	.40	1.00
331 Carlos Muniz RC	.60	1.50
332 Bill Murphy (RC)	.40	1.00
333 Josh Newman RC	.60	1.50
334 Ross Ohlendorf RC	.60	1.50
335 Troy Patton (RC)	.40	1.00
336 Felipe Paulino RC	.60	1.50
337 Steve Pearce RC	2.00	5.00
338 Heath Phillips RC	.60	1.50
339 Justin Ruggiano RC	.60	1.50
340 Clint Sammons (RC)	.40	1.00
341 Bronson Sardinha (RC)	.40	1.00
342 Chris Seddon (RC)	.40	1.00
343 Seth Smith (RC)	.40	1.00
344 Mitch Stetter RC	.60	1.50
345 Dave Davidson RC	.60	1.50
346 Rich Thompson RC	.60	1.50
347 J.R. Towles RC	.60	1.50
348 Eugenio Velez RC	.40	1.00
349 Joey Votto (RC)	3.00	8.00
350 Bill White RC	.40	1.00
351 Vladimir Guerrero CL	.25	.60
352 Lance Berkman CL	.25	.60
353 Dan Haren CL	.15	.40
354 Frank Thomas CL	.40	1.00
355 Chipper Jones CL	.40	1.00
356 Prince Fielder CL	.25	.60
357 Albert Pujols CL	.50	1.25
358 Alfonso Soriano CL	.25	.60
359 B.J. Upton CL	.25	.60
360 Eric Byrnes CL	.15	.40
361 Russell Martin CL	.15	.40
362 Tim Lincecum CL	.25	.60
363 Grady Sizemore CL	.25	.60
364 Ichiro Suzuki CL	.50	1.25
365 Hanley Ramirez CL	.25	.60
366 David Wright CL	.25	.60
367 Ryan Zimmerman CL	.25	.60
368 Nick Markakis CL	.30	.75
369 Jake Peavy CL	.15	.40
370 Ryan Howard CL	.25	.60
371 Freddy Sanchez CL	.15	.40
372 Michael Young CL	.15	.40
373 David Ortiz CL	.40	1.00
374 Ken Griffey Jr. CL	.75	2.00
375 Matt Holliday CL	.40	1.00
376 Brian Bannister CL	.15	.40
377 Magglio Ordonez CL	.25	.60
378 Johan Santana CL	.25	.60
379 Jim Thome CL	.25	.60
380 Alex Rodriguez CL	.50	1.25
381 Alex Rodriguez HL	.50	1.25
382 Brandon Webb HL	.25	.60
383 Chone Figgins HL	.15	.40
384 Clay Buchholz HL	.25	.60
385 Curtis Granderson HL	.25	.60
386 Frank Thomas HL	.40	1.00
387 Fred Lewis HL	.15	.40
388 Garret Anderson HL	.15	.40
389 J.R. Towles HL	.25	.60
390 Jake Peavy HL	.15	.40
391 Jim Thome HL	.25	.60
392 Jimmy Rollins HL	.25	.60
393 Johan Santana HL	.25	.60
394 Justin Verlander HL	.40	1.00
395 Mark Buehrle HL	.25	.60
396 Matt Holliday HL	.40	1.00
397 Jarrod Saltalamacchia HL	.15	.40
398 Sammy Sosa HL	.40	1.00
399 Tom Glavine HL	.25	.60
400 Trevor Hoffman HL	.25	.60
401 Dan Haren	.15	.40
402 Randy Johnson	.40	1.00
403 Chris Burke	.15	.40
404 Orlando Hudson	.15	.40
405 Justin Upton	.25	.60
406 Eric Byrnes	.15	.40
407 Doug Davis	.15	.40
408 Chad Tracy	.15	.40
409 Tom Glavine	.25	.60
410 Kelly Johnson	.15	.40
411 Chipper Jones	.40	1.00
412 Matt Diaz	.15	.40
413 Jeff Francoeur	.25	.60
414 Mark Kotsay	.15	.40
415 John Smoltz	.40	1.00
416 Tyler Yates	.15	.40
417 Yunel Escobar	.15	.40
418 Mike Hampton	.15	.40
419 Luke Scott	.15	.40
420 Adam Jones	.25	.60
421 Jeremy Guthrie	.15	.40
422 Nick Markakis	.30	.75
423 Jay Payton	.15	.40
424 Brian Roberts	.15	.40
425 Melvin Mora	.15	.40
426 Adam Loewen	.15	.40
427 Luis Hernandez	.15	.40
428 Steve Trachsel	.15	.40
429 Josh Beckett	.15	.40
430 Jon Lester	.25	.60
431 Curt Schilling	.25	.60
432 Jonathan Papelbon	.25	.60
433 Jason Varitek	.40	1.00
434 David Ortiz	.40	1.00
435 Jacoby Ellsbury	.30	.75
436 Julio Lugo	.15	.40
437 Sean Casey	.15	.40
438 Kevin Youkilis	.15	.40
439 J.D. Drew	.15	.40
440 Alex Cora	.25	.60
441 Derrek Lee	.15	.40
442 Carlos Zambrano	.25	.60
443 Sean Marshall	.15	.40
444 Matt Murton	.15	.40
445 Kerry Wood	.15	.40
446 Felix Pie	.15	.40
447 Mark DeRosa	.15	.40
448 Ronny Cedeno	.15	.40
449 Jon Lieber	.15	.40
450 Geovany Soto	.40	1.00
451 Gavin Floyd	.15	.40
452 Bobby Jenks	.15	.40
453 Scott Linebrink	.15	.40
454 Javier Vazquez	.15	.40
455 A.J. Pierzynski	.15	.40
456 Orlando Cabrera	.25	.60
457 Joe Crede	.15	.40
458 Josh Fields	.15	.40
459 Paul Konerko	.25	.60
460 Brian Anderson	.15	.40
461 Nick Swisher	.25	.60
462 Carlos Quentin	.15	.40
463 Homer Bailey	.25	.60
464 Francisco Cordero	.15	.40
465 Aaron Harang	.15	.40
466 Alex Gonzalez	.15	.40
467 Brandon Phillips	.15	.40
468 Ryan Freel	.15	.40
469 Scott Hatteberg	.15	.40
470 Juan Castro	.15	.40
471 Norris Hopper	.15	.40
472 Josh Barfield	.15	.40
473 Casey Blake	.15	.40
474 Paul Byrd	.15	.40
475 Grady Sizemore	.25	.60
476 Jason Michaels	.15	.40
477 Jhonny Peralta	.15	.40
478 Asdrubal Cabrera	.25	.60
479 David Dellucci	.15	.40
480 C.C. Sabathia	.25	.60
481 Andy Marte	.15	.40
482 Troy Tulowitzki	.40	1.00
483 Matt Holliday	.40	1.00
484 Garrett Atkins	.15	.40
485 Aaron Cook	.15	.40
486 Brian Fuentes	.15	.40
487 Ryan Spilborghs	.15	.40
488 Ubaldo Jimenez	.15	.40
489 Jayson Nix	.15	.40
490 Nate Robertson	.15	.40
491 Kenny Rogers	.15	.40
492 Justin Verlander	.40	1.00
493 Dontrelle Willis	.15	.40
494 Joel Zumaya	.15	.40
495 Ivan Rodriguez	.25	.60
496 Miguel Cabrera	.40	1.00
497 Carlos Guillen	.15	.40
498 Edgar Renteria	.15	.40
499 Curtis Granderson	.25	.60
500 Jacque Jones	.15	.40
501 Marcus Thames	.15	.40
502 Josh Johnson	.25	.60
503 Jeremy Hermida	.15	.40
504 Dan Uggla	.15	.40
505 Mark Hendrickson	.15	.40
506 Luis Gonzalez	.15	.40
507 Dallas McPherson	.15	.40
508 Cody Ross	.15	.40
509 Matt Treanor	.15	.40
510 Andrew Miller	.25	.60
511 Jorge Cantu	.15	.40
512 Kazuo Matsui	.15	.40
513 Lance Berkman	.25	.60
514 Darin Erstad	.15	.40
515 Miguel Tejada	.25	.60
516 Jose Valverde	.15	.40
517 Geoff Blum	.15	.40
518 Reggie Abercrombie	.15	.40
519 Brandon Backe	.15	.40
520 Michael Bourn	.15	.40
521 Gil Meche	.15	.40
522 Brett Tomko	.15	.40
523 Miguel Olivo	.15	.40
524 Shane Costa	.15	.40
525 Joey Gathright	.15	.40
526 Mark Teahen	.15	.40
527 Alex Gordon	.25	.60
528 Tony Pena	.15	.40
529 Jose Guillen	.15	.40
530 Torii Hunter	.15	.40
531 Ervin Santana	.15	.40
532 Francisco Rodriguez	.25	.60
533 Howie Kendrick	.15	.40
534 Reggie Willits	.15	.40
535 John Lackey	.25	.60
536 Gary Matthews	.15	.40
537 Jon Garland	.15	.40
538 Kendry Morales	.15	.40
539 Chone Figgins	.15	.40
540 Andruw Jones	.15	.40
541 Jason Schmidt	.15	.40
542 James Loney	.15	.40
543 Andre Ethier	.25	.60
544 Rafael Furcal	.15	.40
545 Brad Penny	.15	.40
546 Hong-Chih Kuo	.15	.40
547 Jonathan Broxton	.15	.40
548 Esteban Loaiza	.15	.40
549 Delwyn Young	.15	.40
550 Mike Cameron	.15	.40
551 Ryan Braun	.25	.60
552 Rickie Weeks	.15	.40
553 Bill Hall	.15	.40
554 Tony Gwynn Jr.	.15	.40
555 Eric Gagne	.15	.40
556 Jeff Suppan	.15	.40
557 Chris Capuano	.15	.40
558 Derrick Turnbow	.15	.40
559 Jason Kendall	.15	.40
560 Livan Hernandez	.15	.40
561 Philip Humber	.15	.40
562 Francisco Liriano	.15	.40
563 Pat Neshek	.25	.60
564 Adam Everett	.15	.40
565 Brendan Harris	.15	.40
566 Justin Morneau	.25	.60
567 Craig Monroe	.15	.40
568 Carlos Gomez	.15	.40
569 Delmon Young	.25	.60
570 Mike Lamb	.15	.40
571 Oliver Perez	.15	.40
572 Jose Reyes	.25	.60
573 Moises Alou	.15	.40
574 Carlos Beltran	.25	.60
575 Endy Chavez	.15	.40
576 Ryan Church	.15	.40
577 Pedro Martinez	.25	.60
578 Johan Santana	.25	.60
579 Mike Pelfrey	.15	.40
580 Brian Schneider	.15	.40
581 Joe Smith	.15	.40
582 Matt Wise	.15	.40
583 Duaner Sanchez	.15	.40
584 Ramon Castro	.15	.40
585 Kei Igawa	.15	.40
586 Mariano Rivera	.50	1.25
587 Chien-Ming Wang	.25	.60
588 Wilson Betemit	.15	.40
589 Robinson Cano	.25	.60
590 Alex Rodriguez	.50	1.25
591 Bobby Abreu	.15	.40
592 Shelley Duncan	.15	.40
593 Hideki Matsui	.40	1.00
594 Kyle Farnsworth	.15	.40
595 Joe Blanton	.15	.40
596 Bobby Crosby	.15	.40
597 Eric Chavez	.15	.40
598 Dan Johnson	.15	.40
599 Rich Harden	.15	.40
600 Justin Duchscherer	.15	.40
601 Kurt Suzuki	.15	.40
602 Chris Denorfia	.15	.40
603 Emil Brown	.15	.40
604 Ryan Howard	.25	.60
605 Jimmy Rollins	.25	.60
606 Pedro Feliz	.15	.40
607 Adam Eaton	.15	.40
608 Brad Lidge	.15	.40
609 Brett Myers	.15	.40
610 Pat Burrell	.15	.40
611 So Taguchi	.15	.40
612 Geoff Jenkins	.15	.40
613 Tom Gordon	.15	.40
614 Zach Duke	.15	.40
615 Matt Morris	.15	.40
616 Tom Gorzelanny	.15	.40
617 Jason Bay	.25	.60
618 Chris Duffy	.15	.40
619 Freddy Sanchez	.15	.40
620 Jose Bautista	.25	.60
621 Nyjer Morgan	.15	.40
622 Matt Capps	.15	.40
623 Paul Maholm	.15	.40
624 Tadahito Iguchi	.15	.40
625 Adrian Gonzalez	.25	.60
626 Jim Edmonds	.25	.60
627 Jake Peavy	.15	.40
628 Khalil Greene	.15	.40
629 Trevor Hoffman	.25	.60
630 Mark Prior	.25	.60
631 Randy Wolf	.15	.40
632 Michael Barrett	.15	.40
633 Scott Hairston	.15	.40
634 Tim Lincecum	.25	.60
635 Noah Lowry	.15	.40
636 Rich Aurilia	.15	.40
637 Aaron Rowand	.15	.40
638 Randy Winn	.15	.40
639 Daniel Ortmeier	.15	.40
640 Ray Durham	.15	.40
641 Brian Wilson	.40	1.00
642 Adrian Beltre	.40	1.00
643 Jeremy Reed	.15	.40
644 Jarrod Washburn	.15	.40
645 Yuniesky Betancourt	.15	.40
646 Jose Lopez	.15	.40
647 Raul Ibanez	.25	.60
648 Mike Morse	.15	.40
649 Erik Bedard	.15	.40
650 Brad Wilkerson	.15	.40
651 Chris Carpenter	.25	.60
652 Mark Mulder	.15	.40
653 Juan Encarnacion	.15	.40
654 Skip Schumaker	.15	.40
655 Troy Glaus	.25	.60
656 Anthony Reyes	.15	.40
657 Cesar Izturis	.15	.40
658 Adam Kennedy	.15	.40
659 Chris Duncan	.15	.40
660 Matt Clement	.15	.40
661 Scott Kazmir	.25	.60
662 Troy Percival	.15	.40
663 Akinori Iwamura	.15	.40
664 Carl Crawford	.25	.60
665 Cliff Floyd	.15	.40
666 Jason Bartlett	.15	.40
667 Rocco Baldelli	.15	.40
668 Matt Garza	.15	.40
669 Edwin Jackson	.15	.40
670 Vicente Padilla	.15	.40

671 Josh Hamilton .25 .60
672 Jason Botts .15 .40
673 Milton Bradley .15 .40
674 Michael Young .15 .40
675 Eddie Guardado .15 .40
676 David Murphy .15 .40
677 Ramon Vazquez .15 .40
678 Ben Broussard .15 .40
679 C.J. Wilson .15 .40
680 Jason Jennings .15 .40
681 Gustavo Chacin .15 .40
682 BJ Ryan .15 .40
683 David Eckstein .15 .40
684 Alex Rios .15 .40
685 John McDonald .15 .40
686 Rod Barajas .15 .40
687 Lyle Overbay .15 .40
688 Scott Rolen .25 .60
689 Reed Johnson .15 .40
690 Marco Scutaro .25 .60
691 Lastings Milledge .15 .40
692 Johnny Estrada .15 .40
693 Paul Lo Duca .15 .40
694 Ryan Zimmerman .25 .60
695 Odalis Perez .15 .40
696 Wily Mo Pena .15 .40
697 Elijah Dukes .15 .40
698 Aaron Boone .25 .60
699 Ronnie Belliard .15 .40
700 Nick Johnson .15 .40
701 Randor Bierd RC .40 1.00
702 Brian Barton RC .60 1.50
703 Brian Bass (RC) .40 1.00
704 Brian Bocock RC .40 1.00
705 Gregor Blanco (RC) .40 1.00
706 Callix Crabbe (RC) .40 1.00
707 Johnny Cueto RC 1.00 2.50
708 Kosuke Fukudome RC 4.00 10.00
708b K.Fukudome Japanese 40.00 80.00
709 Scott Kazmir SH .25 .60
710 Steve Holm RC .40 1.00
711 Fernando Hernandez RC .40 1.00
712 Elliot Johnson (RC) .40 1.00
713 Masahide Kobayashi RC .60 1.50
714 Hiroki Kuroda RC 1.00 2.50
715 Blake DeWitt (RC) .60 1.50
716 Kyle McClellan RC .40 1.00
717 Evan Meek RC .40 1.00
718 Denard Span (RC) .60 1.50
719 Darren O'Day RC .40 1.00
720 Alexei Ramirez RC 1.25 3.00
721 Alex Romero (RC) .60 1.50
722 Clete Thomas RC .60 1.50
723 Matt Tolbert RC .60 1.50
724 Ramon Troncoso RC .40 1.00
725 Matt Tupman RC .40 1.00
726 Rico Washington (RC) .40 1.00
727 Randy Wells RC .60 1.50
728 Wesley Wright RC .40 1.00
729 Yasuhiko Yabuta RC .60 1.50
730 Alex Rodriguez SH .50 1.25
731 Andruw Jones SH .15 .40
732 C.C. Sabathia SH .25 .60
733 Carlos Beltran SH .25 .60
734 David Wright SH .25 .60
735 Derrek Lee SH .15 .40
736 Dustin Pedroia SH .40 1.00
737 Grady Sizemore SH .25 .60
738 Greg Maddux SH .50 1.25
739 Ichiro Suzuki SH .50 1.25
740 Ivan Rodriguez SH .25 .60
741 Jake Peavy SH .15 .40
742 Jimmy Rollins SH .25 .60
743 Johan Santana SH .25 .60
744 Josh Beckett SH .25 .60
745 Kevin Youkilis SH .15 .40
746 Matt Holliday SH .40 1.00
747 Mike Lowell SH .15 .40
748 Ryan Braun SH .25 .60
749 Torii Hunter SH .15 .40
750 Alex Rodriguez SH .50 1.25
751 Torii Hunter CL .15 .40
752 Miguel Tejada CL .25 .60
753 Huston Street CL .15 .40
754 Scott Rolen CL .25 .60
755 Tom Glavine CL .25 .60
756 Ryan Braun CL .25 .60
757 Troy Glaus CL .15 .40
758 Carlos Zambrano CL .25 .60
759 Carl Crawford CL .25 .60
760 Dan Haren CL .15 .40
761 Andruw Jones CL .15 .40
762 Barry Zito CL .25 .60
763 Victor Martinez CL .25 .60
764 Erik Bedard CL .15 .40
765 Josh Willingham CL .15 .40
766 Johan Santana CL .25 .60
767 Dmitri Young CL .15 .40
768 Brian Roberts CL .15 .40
769 Jim Edmonds CL .25 .60
770 Jimmy Rollins CL .25 .60
771 Jason Bay CL .25 .60
772 Josh Hamilton CL .25 .60
773 Josh Beckett CL .15 .40
774 Aaron Harang CL .15 .40
775 Troy Tulowitzki CL .40 1.00
776 Jose Guillen CL .15 .40
777 Miguel Cabrera CL .40 1.00
778 Joe Mauer CL .30 .75
779 Nick Swisher CL .25 .60
780 Derek Jeter CL 1.00 2.50
781 Brandon Webb SH .25 .60
782 Brian Roberts SH .15 .40
783 C.C. Sabathia SH .25 .60
784 Carl Crawford SH .25 .60
785 Curtis Granderson SH .25 .60
786 David Ortiz SH .40 1.00
787 Ichiro Suzuki SH .50 1.25
788 Jake Peavy SH .15 .40
789 Jimmy Rollins SH .25 .60
790 Joe Borowski SH .15 .40
791 Johan Santana SH .25 .60
792 John Lackey SH .25 .60
793 Jose Reyes SH .25 .60
794 Jose Valverde SH .15 .40
795 Josh Beckett SH .15 .40
796 Juan Pierre SH .15 .40
797 Magglio Ordonez SH .25 .60
798 Matt Holliday SH .40 1.00
799 Prince Fielder SH .25 .60

2008 Upper Deck Gold

*GOLD VET: 4X TO 10X BASIC
*GOLD RC: 3X TO 8X BASIC
RANDOM INSERTS IN PACKS
STATED PRINT RUN 99 SER. #'d SETS
708 Kosuke Fukudome 50.00 100.00

2008 Upper Deck A Piece of History 500 Club

STATED ODDS 1:192 HOBBY
EXCHANGE DEADLINE 1/14/2010
FT Frank Thomas 15.00 40.00
JT Jim Thome 15.00 40.00

2008 Upper Deck All Rookie Team Signatures

STATED ODDS 1:80 H, 1:7500 R
AI Akinori Iwamura 10.00 25.00
AL Adam Lind 3.00 8.00
BB Billy Butler 5.00 12.00
BU Brian Burres 3.00 8.00
DY Delmon Young 6.00 15.00
HA Justin Hampson 3.00 8.00
JH Josh Hamilton 12.50 30.00
KC Kevin Cameron 3.00 8.00
KK Kyle Kendrick 6.00 15.00
MB Michael Bourn 3.00 8.00
MF Mike Fontenot 5.00 12.00
MO Micah Owings 5.00 12.00
RB Ryan Braun 10.00 25.00
SO Joakim Soria 3.00 8.00

2008 Upper Deck Derek Jeter O-Pee-Chee Reprints

STATED ODDS 1:6 TARGET
DJ1 Derek Jeter 1.50 4.00
DJ2 Derek Jeter 1.50 4.00
DJ3 Derek Jeter 1.50 4.00
DJ4 Derek Jeter 1.50 4.00
DJ5 Derek Jeter 1.50 4.00
DJ6 Derek Jeter 1.50 4.00
DJ7 Derek Jeter 1.50 4.00
DJ8 Derek Jeter 1.50 4.00
DJ9 Derek Jeter 1.50 4.00
DJ10 Derek Jeter 1.50 4.00
DJ11 Derek Jeter 1.50 4.00
DJ12 Derek Jeter 1.50 4.00
DJ13 Derek Jeter 1.50 4.00
DJ14 Derek Jeter 1.50 4.00
DJ15 Derek Jeter 1.50 4.00

2008 Upper Deck Diamond Collection

COMPLETE SET (20) 6.00 15.00
1 Adam LaRoche .40 1.00
2 Brian McCann .60 1.50
3 Bronson Arroyo .40 1.00
4 Chad Billingsley .60 1.50
5 Chin-Lung Hu .40 1.00
6 Felix Pie .40 1.00
7 Garrett Atkins .40 1.00
8 Homer Bailey .60 1.50
9 Ian Kennedy 1.00 2.50
10 James Shields .40 1.00
11 Jarrod Saltalamacchia .40 1.00
12 Manny Corpas .40 1.00
13 Mark Ellis .40 1.00
14 Micah Owings .40 1.00
15 Nick Swisher .60 1.50
16 Rich Hill .40 1.00
17 Russell Martin .40 1.00
18 Ryan Theriot .40 1.00
19 Steve Pearce 2.00 5.00
20 Victor Martinez .60 1.50

2008 Upper Deck Hit Brigade

HB1 Albert Pujols 1.25 3.00
HB2 Alex Rodriguez 1.25 3.00
HB3 David Ortiz 1.00 2.50
HB4 David Wright .60 1.50
HB5 Derek Jeter 2.50 6.00
HB6 Derrek Lee .40 1.00
HB7 Freddy Sanchez .40 1.00
HB8 Hanley Ramirez .60 1.50
HB9 Ichiro Suzuki 1.25 3.00
HB10 Joe Mauer .75 2.00
HB11 Magglio Ordonez .60 1.50
HB12 Matt Holliday 1.00 2.50
HB13 Miguel Cabrera 1.00 2.50
HB14 Todd Helton .60 1.50
HB15 Vladimir Guerrero .60 1.50

2008 Upper Deck Hot Commodities

COMPLETE SET (50) 8.00 20.00
STATED ODDS 2:1 WALMART/FAT PACKS
HC1 Miguel Tejada .60 1.50
HC2 Daisuke Matsuzaka .60 1.50
HC3 David Ortiz 1.00 2.50
HC4 Manny Ramirez 1.00 2.50
HC5 Alex Rodriguez 1.25 3.00
HC6 Derek Jeter 2.50 6.00
HC7 Carl Crawford .60 1.50
HC8 Alex Rios .40 1.00
HC9 Jim Thome .60 1.50
HC10 Grady Sizemore .60 1.50
HC11 Travis Hafner .40 1.00
HC12 Victor Martinez .60 1.50
HC13 Justin Verlander 1.00 2.50
HC14 Magglio Ordonez .60 1.50
HC15 Gary Sheffield .40 1.00
HC16 Alex Gordon .60 1.50
HC17 Justin Morneau .60 1.50
HC18 Johan Santana .60 1.50
HC19 Vladimir Guerrero .60 1.50
HC20 Dan Haren .40 1.00
HC21 Ichiro Suzuki 1.25 3.00
HC22 Mark Teixeira .60 1.50
HC23 Chipper Jones 1.00 2.50
HC24 John Smoltz 1.00 2.50
HC25 Miguel Cabrera 1.00 2.50
HC26 Hanley Ramirez .60 1.50
HC27 Jose Reyes .60 1.50
HC28 David Wright .60 1.50
HC29 Carlos Beltran .60 1.50
HC30 Ryan Howard .60 1.50
HC31 Chase Utley .60 1.50
HC32 Ryan Zimmerman .60 1.50
HC33 Aramis Ramirez .40 1.00
HC34 Derrek Lee .40 1.00
HC35 Alfonso Soriano .60 1.50
HC36 Ken Griffey Jr. 2.00 5.00
HC37 Adam Dunn .60 1.50
HC38 Carlos Lee .40 1.00
HC39 Lance Berkman .60 1.50
HC40 Prince Fielder .60 1.50
HC41 Ryan Braun .60 1.50
HC42 Jason Bay .60 1.50
HC43 Albert Pujols 1.25 3.00
HC44 Brandon Webb .60 1.50
HC45 Matt Holliday 1.00 2.50
HC46 Brad Penny .40 1.00
HC47 Russell Martin .40 1.00
HC48 Trevor Hoffman .60 1.50
HC49 Jake Peavy .40 1.00
HC50 Tim Lincecum .60 1.50

2008 Upper Deck Infield Power

RANDOM INSERTS IN RETAIL PACKS
AB Adrian Beltre .60 1.50
AG Alex Gordon .40 1.00
AP Albert Pujols .75 2.00
AR Aramis Ramirez .25 .60
BP Brandon Phillips .25 .60
BR Brian Roberts .25 .60
CJ Chipper Jones .60 1.50
CP Carlos Pena .40 1.00
CU Chase Utley .40 1.00
DJ Derek Jeter 1.50 4.00
DW David Wright .40 1.00
GA Garrett Atkins .25 .60
GO Adrian Gonzalez .40 1.00
HK Howie Kendrick .25 .60
HR Hanley Ramirez .40 1.00
JI Jimmy Rollins .40 1.00
JK Jeff Kent .25 .60
JM Justin Morneau .40 1.00
JR Jose Reyes .40 1.00
LB Lance Berkman .40 1.00
MC Miguel Cabrera .60 1.50
ML Mike Lowell .25 .60
MT Mark Teixeira .40 1.00
PF Prince Fielder .40 1.00
PK Paul Konerko .40 1.00
RG Ryan Garko .25 .60
RH Ryan Howard .40 1.00
RO Alex Rodriguez .75 2.00
RZ Ryan Zimmerman .40 1.00
TT Troy Tulowitzki .60 1.50

2008 Upper Deck Inkredible

STATED ODDS 1:80 H, 1:7500 R
AL Adam Lind 3.00 8.00
CP Corey Patterson 3.00 8.00
CR Cody Ross 6.00 15.00
DL Derrek Lee 6.00 15.00
EA Erick Aybar 3.00 8.00
IK Ian Kinsler 5.00 12.00
IR Ivan Rodriguez 20.00 50.00
JB Josh Barfield 5.00 12.00
JH Jason Hammel 3.00 8.00
JS James Shields 3.00 8.00
KE Ian Kennedy 5.00 12.00
LS Luke Scott 3.00 8.00
MJ Mike Jacobs 5.00 12.00
RC Ryan Church 3.00 8.00
RL Ruddy Lugo 3.00 8.00
RS Ryan Shealy 3.00 8.00
RT Ryan Theriot 6.00 15.00
SO Jorge Sosa 5.00 12.00
TB Taylor Buchholz 3.00 8.00

2008 Upper Deck Milestone Memorabilia

STATED ODDS 1:192 HOBBY
GS Gary Sheffield 4.00 10.00
KG Ken Griffey Jr. 6.00 15.00
TG Tom Glavine 6.00 15.00
TH Trevor Hoffman 4.00 10.00

2008 Upper Deck Mr. November

STATED ODDS 1:6 TARGET
1 Derek Jeter 1.50 4.00
2 Derek Jeter 1.50 4.00
3 Derek Jeter 1.50 4.00
4 Derek Jeter 1.50 4.00
5 Derek Jeter 1.50 4.00
6 Derek Jeter 1.50 4.00
7 Derek Jeter 1.50 4.00
8 Derek Jeter 1.50 4.00
9 Derek Jeter 1.50 4.00
10 Derek Jeter 1.50 4.00
11 Derek Jeter 1.50 4.00
12 Derek Jeter 1.50 4.00
13 Derek Jeter 1.50 4.00
14 Derek Jeter 1.50 4.00
15 Derek Jeter 1.50 4.00

2008 Upper Deck O-Pee-Chee

COMPLETE SET (50) 30.00 60.00
STATED ODDS 1:2 HOBBY
AG Alex Gordon .60 1.50
AP Albert Pujols 1.25 3.00
AR Alex Rodriguez 1.25 3.00
BP Brad Penny .40 1.00
BR Babe Ruth 2.50 6.00
BU B.J. Upton .60 1.50
BW Brandon Webb .60 1.50
CD Chris Duncan .40 1.00
CJ Chipper Jones 1.00 2.50
CL Carlos Lee .40 1.00
CP Carlos Pena .60 1.50
CU Chase Utley .60 1.50
CY Chris Young .60 1.50
DH Dan Haren .40 1.00
DJ Derek Jeter 2.50 6.00
DL Derrek Lee .40 1.00
DM Daisuke Matsuzaka .60 1.50
DO David Ortiz 1.00 2.50
DW David Wright .60 1.50
EB Erik Bedard .40 1.00
ER Edgar Renteria .40 1.00
GS Gary Sheffield .40 1.00
HP Hunter Pence .60 1.50
HR Hanley Ramirez .60 1.50
IS Ichiro Suzuki 1.25 3.00
JB Jason Bay .60 1.50
JJ J.J. Putz .40 1.00
JM Justin Morneau .60 1.50
JP Jake Peavy .40 1.00
JR Jose Reyes .60 1.50
JS Johan Santana .60 1.50
JT Jim Thome .60 1.50
JW Jered Weaver .60 1.50
KG Ken Griffey Jr. 2.00 5.00
MC Miguel Cabrera 1.00 2.50
MH Matt Holliday 1.00 2.50
MO Magglio Ordonez .60 1.50
MR Manny Ramirez 1.00 2.50
MT Mark Teixeira .60 1.50
NL Noah Lowry .40 1.00
PF Prince Fielder .60 1.50
PH Brandon Phillips .40 1.00
RA Aramis Ramirez .40 1.00
RB Ryan Braun .60 1.50
RH Ryan Howard .60 1.50
RM Russell Martin .40 1.00
RZ Ryan Zimmerman .60 1.50
TH Todd Helton .60 1.50
VG Vladimir Guerrero .60 1.50
VW Vernon Wells .40 1.00

2008 Upper Deck Presidential Predictors

COMP.SET w/o HILLARY (8) 15.00 40.00
STATED ODDS 1:6 H,1:6 R,1:10 WAL MART
PP1 Rudy Giuliani 2.00 5.00
PP2 John Edwards 2.00 5.00
PP3 John McCain 2.00 5.00
PP4 Barack Obama 4.00 10.00
PP5 Mitt Romney 2.00 5.00
PP6 Fred Thompson 2.00 5.00
PP7 Hillary Clinton SP 60.00 150.00
PP8 A.Gore/G.Bush 2.00 5.00
PP9 Wild Card 2.00 5.00
PV1 Barack Obama Victor 4.00 10.00
PP15 Sarah Palin 30.00 80.00
PP16 Joe Biden 75.00 200.00

2008 Upper Deck Presidential Running Mate Predictors

PP7B H.Clinton/B.Obama 10.00 25.00
PP7H H.Clinton/B.Obama 60.00 120.00
PP10 B.Obama/J.McCain 4.00 10.00
PP10A J.McCain/H.Clinton 4.00 10.00
PP11 B.Obama/J.McCain 4.00 10.00
PP11A J.McCain/H.Clinton 2.00 5.00
PP12 B.Obama/J.McCain 4.00 10.00
PP12A J.McCain/H.Clinton 2.00 5.00
PP13 B.Obama/J.McCain 4.00 10.00
PP13A J.McCain/H.Clinton 2.00 5.00
PP14 B.Obama/J.McCain 4.00 10.00
PP14A J.McCain/H.Clinton 2.00 5.00
PP15 B.Obama/J.McCain 150.00 300.00

2008 Upper Deck Rookie Debut

COMPLETE SET (30) 12.50 30.00
1 Emilio Bonafacio 1.00 2.50
2 Billy Buckner .40 1.00
3 Brandon Jones 1.00 2.50
4 Clay Buchholz .60 1.50
5 Lance Broadway .40 1.00
6 Joey Votto 3.00 8.00
7 Ryan Hanigan .60 1.50
8 Seth Smith .40 1.00
9 Joe Koshansky .40 1.00
10 Chris Seddon .40 1.00
11 J.R. Towles .60 1.50
12 Luke Hochevar .60 1.50
13 Chin-Lung Hu .40 1.00
14 Sam Fuld 1.25 3.00
15 Jose Morales .40 1.00
16 Carlos Muniz .60 1.50
17 Ian Kennedy 1.00 2.50
18 Alberto Gonzalez .60 1.50
19 Jonathan Albaladejo .60 1.50
20 Daric Barton .40 1.00
21 Jerry Blevins .60 1.50
22 Steve Pearce 2.00 5.00
23 Dave Davidson .60 1.50
24 Eugenio Velez .40 1.00
25 Erick Threets .40 1.00
26 Bronson Sardinha .40 1.00
27 Wladimir Balentien .40 1.00
28 Justin Ruggiano .60 1.50
29 Luis Mendoza .40 1.00
30 Justin Maxwell .40 1.00

2008 Upper Deck Season Highlights Signatures

STATED ODDS 1:80 H, 1:7500 R
BB Brian Bannister 6.00 15.00
BF Ben Francisco 3.00 8.00
CG Curtis Granderson 6.00 15.00
CS Curt Schilling 20.00 50.00
FL Fred Lewis 3.00 8.00
JS Jarrod Saltalamacchia 5.00 12.00
JW Josh Willingham 3.00 8.00
KK Kevin Kouzmanoff 3.00 8.00
MO Micah Owings 5.00 12.00
MR Mark Reynolds 6.00 15.00
MT Miguel Tejada 12.50 30.00
RB Ryan Braun 20.00 50.00
RS Ryan Spilborghs 6.00 15.00

2008 Upper Deck Signature Sensations

STATED ODDS 1:80 H, 1:7500 R
AE Andre Ethier 3.00 8.00
AK Austin Kearns 5.00 12.00
AM Aaron Miles 5.00 12.00
BB Boof Bonser 3.00 8.00
BH Brendan Harris 3.00 8.00
BM Brandon McCarthy 3.00 8.00
CB Cha-Seung Baek 3.00 8.00
DL Derrek Lee 6.00 15.00
IR Ivan Rodriguez 30.00 60.00
JP Joel Peralta 3.00 8.00
JS James Shields 3.00 8.00
JV John Van Benschoten 3.00 8.00
LS Luke Scott 3.00 8.00
MC Matt Cain 8.00 20.00
NS Nick Swisher 5.00 12.00
RA Reggie Abercrombie 3.00 8.00
SM Sean Marshall 3.00 8.00
YP Yusmeiro Petit 3.00 8.00

2008 Upper Deck Signs of History Cut Signatures

BH Benjamin Harrison/45 700.00 1000.00
GC Grover Cleveland/30 600.00 850.00
GF Gerald Ford/75 100.00 200.00
HT Harry Truman/47 400.00 700.00
JC Jimmy Carter/49 150.00 300.00
RH Rutherford B. Hayes/75 400.00 650.00
WT William H. Taft/50 500.00 750.00
NNO Exchange Card 700.00 1000.00

2008 Upper Deck Star Attractions

SA1 B.J. Upton .60 1.50
SA2 Carl Crawford .60 1.50
SA3 Chris B. Young .40 1.00
SA4 John Maine .40 1.00
SA5 Jonathan Papelbon .60 1.50
SA6 Nick Markakis .75 2.00
SA7 Prince Fielder .60 1.50
SA8 Takashi Saito .40 1.00
SA9 Tom Gorzelanny .40 1.00
SA10 Troy Tulowitzki 1.00 2.50

2008 Upper Deck StarQuest

SER.1 ODDS 1:1 RETAIL/TARGET
SER.1 ODDS 1:1 WAL MART
*UNCOMMON: .4X TO 1X COMMON
SER.1 UNC ODDS 1:4 RETAIL/TARGET
SER.1 UNC ODDS 1:6 WAL MART
*RARE: .6X TO 1.5X COMMON
SER.1 RARE ODDS 1:8 RETAIL/TARGET
SER.1 RARE ODDS 1:12 WAL MART
*SUPER: 1X TO 2.5X COMMON
SER.1 SUPER ODDS 1:16 RETAIL/TARGET
SER.1 SUPER ODDS 1:24 WAL MART
*ULTRA: 1.5X TO 4X BASIC
SER.1 ULTRA ODDS 1:24 RETAIL/TARGET
SER.1 ULTRA ODDS 1:36 WAL MART
1 Ichiro Suzuki 1.25 3.00
2 Ryan Braun .60 1.50
3 Prince Fielder .60 1.50
4 Ken Griffey Jr. 2.00 5.00
5 Vladimir Guerrero .60 1.50
6 Travis Hafner .40 1.00
7 Matt Holliday 1.00 2.50
8 Ryan Howard .60 1.50
9 Derek Jeter 2.50 6.00
10 Chipper Jones 1.00 2.50
11 Carlos Lee .40 1.00
12 Justin Morneau .60 1.50
13 Magglio Ordonez .60 1.50
14 David Ortiz 1.00 2.50
15 Jake Peavy .40 1.00
16 Albert Pujols 1.25 3.00
17 Hanley Ramirez .60 1.50
18 Manny Ramirez 1.00 2.50
19 Jose Reyes .60 1.50
20 Alex Rodriguez 1.25 3.00
21 Johan Santana .60 1.50
22 Grady Sizemore .60 1.50
23 Alfonso Soriano .60 1.50
24 Mark Teixeira .60 1.50
25 Frank Thomas 1.00 2.50
26 Jim Thome .60 1.50
27 Chase Utley .60 1.50
28 Brandon Webb .60 1.50
29 David Wright .60 1.50
30 Michael Young .40 1.00
31 Adam Dunn .60 1.50
32 Albert Pujols 1.25 3.00
33 Alex Rodriguez 1.25 3.00
34 B.J. Upton .60 1.50
35 C.C. Sabathia .60 1.50
36 Carlos Beltran .60 1.50
37 Carlos Pena .60 1.50
38 Cole Hamels .75 2.00
39 Curtis Granderson .60 1.50
40 Daisuke Matsuzaka .60 1.50
41 David Ortiz 1.00 2.50
42 Derek Jeter 2.50 6.00
43 Derrek Lee .40 1.00
44 Eric Byrnes .40 1.00
45 Felix Hernandez .60 1.50
46 Ichiro Suzuki 1.25 3.00
47 Jeff Francoeur .60 1.50
48 Jimmy Rollins .60 1.50
49 Joe Mauer .75 2.00
50 John Smoltz 1.00 2.50
51 Ken Griffey Jr. 2.00 5.00
52 Lance Berkman .60 1.50
53 Miguel Cabrera 1.00 2.50
54 Paul Konerko .60 1.50
55 Pedro Martinez .60 1.50
56 Randy Johnson 1.00 2.50
57 Russell Martin .40 1.00
58 Troy Tulowitzki 1.00 2.50
59 Vernon Wells .40 1.00
60 Vladimir Guerrero .60 1.50

2008 Upper Deck Superstar Scrapbooks

SS1 Albert Pujols 1.25 3.00
SS2 Alex Rodriguez 1.25 3.00
SS3 Chase Utley .60 1.50
SS4 Chipper Jones 1.00 2.50
SS5 David Ortiz 1.00 2.50
SS6 Derek Jeter 2.50 6.00
SS7 Ichiro Suzuki 1.25 3.00
SS8 Johan Santana .60 1.50
SS9 Jose Reyes .60 1.50
SS10 Ken Griffey Jr. 2.00 5.00
SS11 Manny Ramirez 1.00 2.50
SS12 Prince Fielder .60 1.50
SS13 Randy Johnson 1.00 2.50
SS14 Ryan Howard .60 1.50
SS15 Vladimir Guerrero .60 1.50

2008 Upper Deck The House That Ruth Built

STATED ODDS 1:4 WAL MART BLISTER
STATED ODDS 1:6 WAL MART BLASTER
SILVER INSERTED IN WAL MART PACKS
SILVER PRINT RUN 1 SER.#'d SET
NO SILVER PRICING DUE TO SCARCITY
HRB1 Babe Ruth 1.50 4.00
HRB2 Babe Ruth 1.50 4.00
HRB3 Babe Ruth 1.50 4.00
HRB4 Babe Ruth 1.50 4.00
HRB5 Babe Ruth 1.50 4.00
HRB6 Babe Ruth 1.50 4.00
HRB7 Babe Ruth 1.50 4.00
HRB8 Babe Ruth 1.50 4.00
HRB9 Babe Ruth 1.50 4.00
HRB10 Babe Ruth 1.50 4.00
HRB11 Babe Ruth 1.50 4.00
HRB12 Babe Ruth 1.50 4.00
HRB13 Babe Ruth 1.50 4.00
HRB14 Babe Ruth 1.50 4.00
HRB15 Babe Ruth 1.50 4.00
HRB16 Babe Ruth 1.50 4.00
HRB17 Babe Ruth 1.50 4.00
HRB18 Babe Ruth 1.50 4.00
HRB19 Babe Ruth 1.50 4.00
HRB20 Babe Ruth 1.50 4.00
HRB21 Babe Ruth 1.50 4.00
HRB22 Babe Ruth 1.50 4.00
HRB23 Babe Ruth 1.50 4.00
HRB24 Babe Ruth 1.50 4.00
HRB25 Babe Ruth 1.50 4.00

2008 Upper Deck UD Autographs

STATED ODDS 1:80 H, 1:7500 R
CD Chris Duffy 3.00 8.00
CS Curt Schilling 20.00 50.00
JK Jeff Karstens 3.00 8.00
JP Joel Peralta 3.00 8.00
JS Jorge Sosa 5.00 12.00
JV John Van Benschoten 3.00 8.00
KI Kei Igawa 6.00 15.00
KS Kelly Shoppach 3.00 8.00
LS Luke Scott 3.00 8.00
MC Manny Corpas 6.00 15.00
MP Mike Pelfrey 5.00 12.00
MT Miguel Tejada 12.50 30.00
NM Nate McLouth 6.00 15.00
RH Ramon Hernandez 5.00 12.00
SA Kirk Saarloos 3.00 8.00
SF Scott Feldman 4.00 10.00
SH James Shields 3.00 8.00
SR Saul Rivera 3.00 8.00
SS Skip Schumaker 8.00 20.00

2008 Upper Deck UD Game Materials

SER.1 ODDS 1:32 HOBBY,1:96 RETAIL
SER.1 ODDS 1:40 WAL MART BLASTER
SER.1 ODDS 1:96 TARGET/WM BLISTER
AJ Andruw Jones S2 3.00 8.00
AP Albert Pujols S2 6.00 15.00
BB Boof Bonser S2 3.00 8.00
BM Brandon McCarthy S2 3.00 8.00
BP Brandon Phillips S2 3.00 8.00
BR Brian Roberts 3.00 8.00
BU B.J. Upton S2 3.00 8.00
BZ Barry Zito S2 3.00 8.00
CA Matt Cain S2 3.00 8.00
CB Chris Burke S2 3.00 8.00
CB Carlos Beltran 3.00 8.00
CC Coco Crisp 3.00 8.00
CC Chris Carpenter S2 3.00 8.00
CD Chris Duncan S2 3.00 8.00
CG Carlos Guillen 3.00 8.00
CJ Conor Jackson S2 3.00 8.00
CL Cliff Lee S2 3.00 8.00
CQ Carlos Quentin S2 3.00 8.00
CU Michael Cuddyer S2 3.00 8.00
DC Daniel Cabrera 3.00 8.00
DJ Derek Jeter 8.00 20.00
DJ Derek Jeter S2 8.00 20.00
DL Derrek Lee S2 3.00 8.00
DO David Ortiz S2 4.00 10.00
DO David Ortiz 4.00 10.00
DW Dontrelle Willis 3.00 8.00
DW David Wells S2 3.00 8.00
EC Eric Chavez S2 3.00 8.00
EG Eric Gagne 3.00 8.00
ES Ervin Santana S2 3.00 8.00
FH Felix Hernandez S2 3.00 8.00
FL Francisco Liriano S2 3.00 8.00
FR Francisco Rodriguez S2 3.00 8.00
FS Freddy Sanchez S2 3.00 8.00
GA Garrett Atkins S2 3.00 8.00
GC Gustavo Chacin 1.50 4.00
GJ Geoff Jenkins 3.00 8.00
GL Troy Glaus S2 3.00 8.00
GM Gil Meche S2 3.00 8.00
GO Jonny Gomes S2 3.00 8.00
HR Hanley Ramirez S2 3.00 8.00
IR Ivan Rodriguez S2 3.00 8.00
JB Jeremy Bonderman S2 3.00 8.00
JB Jason Bay 3.00 8.00
JD Justin Duchscherer 3.00 8.00
JD Jermaine Dye S2 3.00 8.00
JG Jason Giambi S2 3.00 8.00
JH Jeremy Hermida S2 3.00 8.00
JJ Josh Johnson S2 3.00 8.00
JL James Loney S2 3.00 8.00
JP Jonathan Papelbon S2 4.00 10.00
JP Jake Peavy 4.00 10.00
JR Jeremy Reed S2 3.00 8.00
JS Jason Schmidt S2 3.00 8.00
JS Jeremy Sowers 3.00 8.00
JV Jason Varitek 4.00 10.00
JV Justin Verlander S2 3.00 8.00
JW Jered Weaver S2 3.00 8.00
KG Khalil Greene S2 3.00 8.00
KJ Kenji Johjima S2 3.00 8.00
KM Kazuo Matsui 3.00 8.00
KW Kerry Wood S2 3.00 8.00
MC Miguel Cabrera S2 4.00 10.00
ME Melky Cabrera S2 3.00 8.00
ME Morgan Ensberg 3.00 8.00
MG Marcus Giles S2 3.00 8.00
MJ Mike Jacobs S2 3.00 8.00
MK Masumi Kuwata 3.00 8.00
MM Melvin Mora 3.00 8.00
MN Mike Napoli S2 3.00 8.00
MP Mark Prior S2 3.00 8.00
MS Mike Sweeney 3.00 8.00
MY Michael Young 3.00 8.00
MY Brett Myers S2 3.00 8.00
OL Scott Olsen S2 3.00 8.00
PA Jonathan Papelbon 4.00 10.00
PE Mike Pelfrey S2 3.00 8.00
PF Prince Fielder S2 4.00 10.00
PK Paul Konerko S2 3.00 8.00
RC Ryan Church S2 3.00 8.00
RD Ray Durham S2 3.00 8.00
RF Ryan Freel S2 3.00 8.00
RH Roy Halladay 3.00 8.00
RJ Reed Johnson S2 3.00 8.00
RQ Robb Quinlan S2 3.00 8.00
RW Rickie Weeks S2 3.00 8.00
RZ Ryan Zimmerman S2 4.00 10.00
SK Scott Kazmir S2 3.00 8.00
SO Jeremy Sowers S2 3.00 8.00
TG Tom Glavine S2 3.00 8.00
TS Takashi Saito 3.00 8.00
VW Vernon Wells S2 3.00 8.00
WI Dontrelle Willis S2 3.00 8.00
YM Yadier Molina S2 3.00 8.00
ZD Zach Duke S2 3.00 8.00

2008 Upper Deck UD Game Patch

SER.1 ODDS 1:768 H,1:7500 R
AJ Andruw Jones S2 8.00 20.00
AP Albert Pujols S2 20.00 50.00
BB Boof Bonser S2 8.00 20.00
BM Brandon McCarthy S2 8.00 20.00
BP Brandon Phillips S2 8.00 20.00
BR Brian Roberts 8.00 20.00
BU B.J. Upton S2 8.00 20.00
BZ Barry Zito S2 8.00 20.00
CA Matt Cain S2 8.00 20.00
CB Chris Burke S2 8.00 20.00
CB Carlos Beltran 8.00 20.00
CC Coco Crisp 8.00 20.00
CC Chris Carpenter S2 8.00 20.00
CD Chris Duncan S2 8.00 20.00
CG Carlos Guillen 8.00 20.00
CJ Conor Jackson S2 8.00 20.00
CL Cliff Lee S2 8.00 20.00
CQ Carlos Quentin S2 8.00 20.00
CU Michael Cuddyer S2 8.00 20.00
DC Daniel Cabrera 8.00 20.00
DJ Derek Jeter 50.00 100.00
DJ Derek Jeter S2 50.00 100.00
DL Derrek Lee S2 8.00 20.00
DO David Ortiz S2 12.50 30.00
DO David Ortiz 12.50 30.00
DW Dontrelle Willis 8.00 20.00
DW David Wells S2 8.00 20.00
EC Eric Chavez S2 8.00 20.00
EG Eric Gagne 8.00 20.00
ES Ervin Santana S2 8.00 20.00
FH Felix Hernandez S2 8.00 20.00
FL Francisco Liriano S2 8.00 20.00
FR Francisco Rodriguez S2 8.00 20.00
FS Freddy Sanchez S2 8.00 20.00
GA Garrett Atkins S2 8.00 20.00
GC Gustavo Chacin 8.00 20.00
GJ Geoff Jenkins 8.00 20.00
GL Troy Glaus S2 8.00 20.00
GM Gil Meche S2 8.00 20.00
GO Jonny Gomes S2 8.00 20.00
HR Hanley Ramirez S2 8.00 20.00
IR Ivan Rodriguez S2 8.00 20.00
JB Jeremy Bonderman S2 8.00 20.00
JB Jason Bay 8.00 20.00
JD Justin Duchscherer 8.00 20.00
JD Jermaine Dye S2 8.00 20.00
JG Jason Giambi S2 8.00 20.00
JH Jeremy Hermida S2 8.00 20.00
JJ Josh Johnson S2 8.00 20.00
JL James Loney S2 8.00 20.00
JP Jonathan Papelbon S2 12.50 30.00
JP Jake Peavy 12.50 30.00
JR Jeremy Reed S2 8.00 20.00
JS Jason Schmidt S2 8.00 20.00
JS Jeremy Sowers 8.00 20.00
JV Jason Varitek 12.50 30.00
JV Justin Verlander S2 8.00 20.00
JW Jered Weaver S2 8.00 20.00
KG Khalil Greene S2 8.00 20.00
KJ Kenji Johjima S2 8.00 20.00
KM Kazuo Matsui 8.00 20.00
KW Kerry Wood S2 8.00 20.00
MC Miguel Cabrera S2 12.50 30.00
ME Melky Cabrera S2 8.00 20.00
ME Morgan Ensberg 8.00 20.00
MG Marcus Giles S2 8.00 20.00
MJ Mike Jacobs S2 8.00 20.00
MK Masumi Kuwata 8.00 20.00
MM Melvin Mora 8.00 20.00
MN Mike Napoli S2 8.00 20.00
MP Mark Prior S2 8.00 20.00
MS Mike Sweeney 8.00 20.00
MY Michael Young 8.00 20.00
MY Brett Myers S2 8.00 20.00
OL Scott Olsen S2 8.00 20.00
PA Jonathan Papelbon 12.50 30.00
PE Mike Pelfrey S2 8.00 20.00

PF Prince Fielder S2 12.50 30.00
PK Paul Konerko S2 8.00 20.00
RC Ryan Church S2 8.00 20.00
RD Ray Durham S2 8.00 20.00
RF Ryan Freel S2 8.00 20.00
RH Roy Halladay 8.00 20.00
RJ Reed Johnson S2 8.00 20.00
RQ Robb Quinlan S2 8.00 20.00
RW Rickie Weeks S2 8.00 20.00
RZ Ryan Zimmerman S2 12.50 30.00
SK Scott Kazmir S2 8.00 20.00
SO Jeremy Sowers S2 8.00 20.00
TG Tom Glavine S2 8.00 20.00
TS Takashi Saito 8.00 20.00
VW Vernon Wells S2 8.00 20.00
WI Dontrelle Willis S2 8.00 20.00
YM Yadier Molina S2 8.00 20.00
ZD Zach Duke S2 8.00 20.00

2008 Upper Deck UD Game Materials 1997

SER.1 ODDS 1:32 HOBBY,1:96 RETAIL
SER.1 ODDS 1:40 WAL MART BLASTER
SER.1 ODDS 1:96 TARGET/WM BLISTER
AP Albert Pujols 8.00 20.00
BC Bobby Crosby 3.00 8.00
BG Brian Giles 3.00 8.00
BR B.J. Ryan 3.00 8.00
BS Ben Sheets 3.00 8.00
CH Cole Hamels S2 3.00 8.00
CS Curt Schilling 4.00 10.00
DL Derek Lowe 3.00 8.00
DO David Ortiz 4.00 10.00
DO David Ortiz S2 4.00 10.00
DU Dan Uggla S2 3.00 8.00
GJ Geoff Jenkins 3.00 8.00
HK Hong-Chih Kuo 4.00 10.00
IR Ivan Rodriguez 4.00 10.00
JB Joe Blanton 3.00 8.00
JC Joe Crede 3.00 8.00
JJ Josh Johnson 3.00 8.00
JM Justin Morneau S2 3.00 8.00
JP Jonathan Papelbon S2 4.00 10.00
JS James Shields 3.00 8.00
JV Justin Verlander S2 3.00 8.00
JW Jake Westbrook 3.00 8.00
JZ Joel Zumaya S2 3.00 8.00
LM Lastings Milledge 3.00 8.00
MC Miguel Cabrera 4.00 10.00
MO Magglio Ordonez 4.00 10.00
NM Nick Markakis 4.00 10.00
PE Andy Pettitte 4.00 10.00
PF Prince Fielder S2 4.00 10.00
PO Jorge Posada S2 3.00 8.00
RB Rocco Baldelli 3.00 8.00
TH Todd Helton 4.00 10.00
VG Vladimir Guerrero S2 3.00 8.00
VM Victor Martinez 3.00 8.00
XN Xavier Nady 3.00 8.00

2008 Upper Deck UD Game Materials 1997 Patch

SER.1 ODDS 1:768 H,1:7500 R
AP Albert Pujols 15.00 40.00
BC Bobby Crosby 8.00 20.00
BG Brian Giles 8.00 20.00
BR BJ Ryan 8.00 20.00
BS Ben Sheets 8.00 20.00
CH Cole Hamels S2 8.00 20.00
CS Curt Schilling 12.50 30.00
DL Derek Lowe 8.00 20.00
DO David Ortiz 12.50 30.00
DO David Ortiz S2 12.50 30.00
DU Dan Uggla S2 8.00 20.00
GJ Geoff Jenkins 8.00 20.00
HK Hong-Chih Kuo 8.00 20.00
IR Ivan Rodriguez 12.50 30.00
JB Joe Blanton 8.00 20.00
JC Joe Crede 8.00 20.00
JJ Josh Johnson 8.00 20.00
JM Justin Morneau S2 8.00 20.00
JP Jonathan Papelbon S2 12.50 30.00
JS James Shields 8.00 20.00
JV Justin Verlander S2 8.00 20.00
JW Jake Westbrook 8.00 20.00
JZ Joel Zumaya S2 8.00 20.00
LM Lastings Milledge 8.00 20.00
MC Miguel Cabrera 12.50 30.00
MO Magglio Ordonez 12.50 30.00
NM Nick Markakis 12.50 30.00
PE Andy Pettitte 12.50 30.00
PF Prince Fielder S2 12.50 30.00
PO Jorge Posada S2 8.00 20.00
RB Rocco Baldelli 8.00 20.00
TH Todd Helton 12.50 30.00
VG Vladimir Guerrero S2 8.00 20.00
VM Victor Martinez 8.00 20.00
XN Xavier Nady 8.00 20.00

2008 Upper Deck UD Game Materials 1998

SER.1 ODDS 1:32 HOBBY,1:96 RETAIL
SER.1 ODDS 1:40 WAL MART BLASTER
SER.1 ODDS 1:96 TARGET/WM BLISTER
AJ Andruw Jones S2 3.00 8.00
BH Bill Hall 3.00 8.00
BS Ben Sheets 3.00 8.00
CD Chris Duncan S2 3.00 8.00
CF Chone Figgins 3.00 8.00
CZ Carlos Zambrano 3.00 8.00
DJ Derek Jeter S2 10.00 25.00
DL Derrek Lee S2 3.00 8.00
EG Eric Gagne 3.00 8.00
FC Fausto Carmona 3.00 8.00
FH Felix Hernandez 4.00 10.00
GM Greg Maddux S2 5.00 12.00
GS Grady Sizemore 4.00 10.00
HB Hank Blalock 3.00 8.00
IS Ian Snell 3.00 8.00
JE Johnny Estrada 3.00 8.00
JJ Jacque Jones 3.00 8.00
JK Jason Kendall 3.00 8.00
JS Johan Santana 4.00 10.00
KM Kevin Millwood 3.00 8.00
MB Mark Buehrle 3.00 8.00
MG Marcus Giles 3.00 8.00
NM Nick Markakis 4.00 10.00
PK Paul Konerko 3.00 8.00
RM Russell Martin S2 3.00 8.00
RO Roy Oswalt S2 3.00 8.00
TH Travis Hafner S2 3.00 8.00
VG Vladimir Guerrero S2 3.00 8.00
VM Victor Martinez S2 3.00 8.00
VM Victor Martinez 3.00 8.00

2008 Upper Deck UD Game Materials 1998 Patch

SER.1 ODDS 1:768 H,1:7500 R
AJ Andruw Jones S2 8.00 20.00
BH Bill Hall 8.00 20.00
BS Ben Sheets 8.00 20.00
CD Chris Duncan S2 8.00 20.00
CF Chone Figgins 8.00 20.00
CZ Carlos Zambrano 8.00 20.00
DJ Derek Jeter S2 20.00 50.00
DL Derrek Lee S2 8.00 20.00
EG Eric Gagne 8.00 20.00
FC Fausto Carmona 8.00 20.00
FH Felix Hernandez 12.50 30.00
GM Greg Maddux S2 12.50 30.00
GS Grady Sizemore 12.50 30.00
HB Hank Blalock 8.00 20.00
IS Ian Snell 8.00 20.00
JE Johnny Estrada 8.00 20.00
JJ Jacque Jones 8.00 20.00
JK Jason Kendall 8.00 20.00
JS Johan Santana 12.50 30.00
KM Kevin Millwood 8.00 20.00
MB Mark Buehrle 8.00 20.00
MG Marcus Giles 8.00 20.00
NM Nick Markakis 12.50 30.00
PK Paul Konerko 8.00 20.00
RM Russell Martin S2 8.00 20.00
RO Roy Oswalt S2 8.00 20.00
TH Travis Hafner S2 8.00 20.00
VG Vladimir Guerrero S2 8.00 20.00
VM Victor Martinez S2 8.00 20.00
VM Victor Martinez 8.00 20.00

2008 Upper Deck UD Game Materials 1999

SER.1 ODDS 1:32 HOBBY,1:96 RETAIL
SER.1 ODDS 1:40 WAL MART BLASTER
SER.1 ODDS 1:96 TARGET/WM BLISTER
BR Brian Roberts 3.00 8.00
BU B.J. Upton S2 3.00 8.00
BW Brandon Webb S2 3.00 8.00
CA Matt Cain S2 3.00 8.00
CD Chris Duffy 3.00 8.00
CJ Chipper Jones 4.00 10.00
CS C.C. Sabathia 3.00 8.00
DL Derrek Lee 3.00 8.00
DO David Ortiz S2 4.00 10.00
DW David Wells 3.00 8.00
EB Erik Bedard 3.00 8.00
FS Freddy Sanchez 3.00 8.00
HR Hanley Ramirez S2 3.00 8.00
JB Jason Bay 3.00 8.00
JD Johnny Damon 3.00 8.00
JG Jeremy Guthrie 3.00 8.00
JH J.J. Hardy 3.00 8.00
JK Jason Kubel 3.00 8.00
JM Joe Mauer S2 3.00 8.00
JP Jorge Posada 4.00 10.00
KG Khalil Greene S2 3.00 8.00
KJ Kenji Johjima 3.00 8.00
KM Kendry Morales 3.00 8.00
MC Miguel Cabrera S2 3.00 8.00
MT Mark Teixeira 4.00 10.00
NM Nick Markakis S2 3.00 8.00
RW Rickie Weeks 3.00 8.00
TE Miguel Tejada 3.00 8.00
TH Travis Hafner 3.00 8.00
TH Torii Hunter S2 3.00 8.00

2008 Upper Deck UD Game Materials 1999 Patch

SER.1 ODDS 1:768 H,1:7500 R
BR Brian Roberts 8.00 20.00
BU B.J. Upton S2 8.00 20.00
BW Brandon Webb S2 8.00 20.00
CA Matt Cain S2 8.00 20.00
CD Chris Duffy 8.00 20.00
CJ Chipper Jones 12.50 30.00
CS C.C. Sabathia 8.00 20.00
DL Derrek Lee 8.00 20.00
DO David Ortiz S2 12.50 30.00
DW David Wells 8.00 20.00
EB Erik Bedard 8.00 20.00
FS Freddy Sanchez 8.00 20.00
HR Hanley Ramirez S2 8.00 20.00
JB Jason Bay 8.00 20.00
JD Johnny Damon 8.00 20.00
JG Jeremy Guthrie 8.00 20.00
JH J.J. Hardy 8.00 20.00
JK Jason Kubel 8.00 20.00
JM Joe Mauer S2 8.00 20.00
JP Jorge Posada 12.50 30.00
KG Khalil Greene S2 8.00 20.00
KJ Kenji Johjima 8.00 20.00
KM Kendry Morales 8.00 20.00
MC Miguel Cabrera S2 8.00 20.00
MT Mark Teixeira 12.50 30.00
NM Nick Markakis S2 8.00 20.00
RW Rickie Weeks 8.00 20.00
TE Miguel Tejada 8.00 20.00
TH Travis Hafner 8.00 20.00
TH Torii Hunter S2 8.00 20.00

2008 Upper Deck Superstar

COMPLETE SET (10) 6.00 15.00
STATED ODDS 3:1 SUPER PACKS
9 Vladimir Guerrero .40 1.00
48 Mark Teixeira .40 1.00
57 Prince Fielder .40 1.00
67 Albert Pujols .75 2.00
139 Ichiro Suzuki .75 2.00
147 Hanley Ramirez .40 1.00
156 David Wright .40 1.00
239 Ken Griffey Jr. 1.25 3.00
270 Magglio Ordonez .40 1.00
297 Derek Jeter 1.50 4.00

2008 Upper Deck USA Junior National Team

USJR1 Eric Hosmer 6.00 15.00
USJR2 Garrison Lassiter 1.25 3.00
USJR3 Harold Martinez 1.25 3.00
USJR4 J.P. Ramirez 1.25 3.00
USJR5 Jeff Malm 2.00 5.00
USJR6 Jordan Swagerty 1.25 3.00
USJR7 Kyle Buchanan 1.25 3.00
USJR8 Kyle Skipworth 2.00 5.00
USJR9 L.J. Hoes 1.25 3.00
USJR10 Matthew Purke 1.25 3.00
USJR11 Mychal Givens 1.25 3.00
USJR12 Nick Maronde 1.25 3.00
USJR13 Riccio Torrez 1.25 3.00
USJR14 Robbie Grossman 2.00 5.00
USJR15 Ryan Weber 1.25 3.00
USJR16 T.J. House 1.25 3.00
USJR17 Tim Melville 1.25 3.00
USJR18 Tyler Hibbs 1.25 3.00
USJR19 Tyler Stovall 1.25 3.00
USJR20 Tyler Wilson 1.25 3.00

2008 Upper Deck USA Junior National Team Autographs

PRINT RUNS B/WN 133-500 COPIES PER
EH Eric Hosmer/238 5.00 12.00
GL Garrison Lassiter/375 4.00 10.00
HI Tyler Hibbs/375 4.00 10.00
HM Harold Martinez/237 4.00 10.00
JM Jeff Malm/375 4.00 10.00
JR J.P. Ramirez/239 4.00 10.00
JS Jordan Swagerty/350 4.00 10.00
KB Kyle Buchanan/375 4.00 10.00
KS Kyle Skipworth/177 4.00 10.00
LH L.J. Hoes/158 4.00 10.00
MG Mychal Givens/209 4.00 10.00
MP Matthew Purke/375 4.00 10.00
NM Nick Maronde/166 4.00 10.00
RG Robbie Grossman/155 4.00 10.00
RT Riccio Torrez/500 4.00 10.00
RW Ryan Weber/375 4.00 10.00
TH T.J. House/147 4.00 10.00
TM Tim Melville/133 4.00 10.00
TS Tyler Stovall/375 4.00 10.00
TW Tyler Wilson/375 4.00 10.00

2008 Upper Deck USA Junior National Team Autographs Blue

*BLUE AU: .4X TO 1X BASIC AU
PRINT RUNS B/WN 75-400 COPIES PER
EH Eric Hosmer/75 10.00 25.00
GL Garrison Lassiter/175 4.00 10.00
HI Tyler Hibbs/400 4.00 10.00
HM Harold Martinez/275 4.00 10.00
JM Jeff Malm/175 4.00 10.00
JR J.P. Ramirez/90 4.00 10.00
JS Jordan Swagerty/195 4.00 10.00
KB Kyle Buchanan/175 4.00 10.00
LH L.J. Hoes/300 4.00 10.00
MG Mychal Givens/309 4.00 10.00
MP Matthew Purke/390 4.00 10.00
NM Nick Maronde/100 4.00 10.00
RG Robbie Grossman/175 4.00 10.00
RT Riccio Torrez/400 4.00 10.00
RW Ryan Weber/392 4.00 10.00
TH T.J. House/75 4.00 10.00
TM Tim Melville/330 4.00 10.00
TS Tyler Stovall/186 4.00 10.00
TW Tyler Wilson/75 4.00 10.00

2008 Upper Deck USA Junior National Team Autographs Red

*RED AU: .5X TO 1.2X BASIC AU
PRINT RUNS B/WN 50-150 COPIES PER
EH Eric Hosmer/50 30.00 80.00

2008 Upper Deck USA Junior National Team Jerseys

EH Eric Hosmer 6.00 15.00
GL Garrison Lassiter 3.00 8.00
HI Tyler Hibbs 3.00 8.00
HM Harold Martinez 3.00 8.00
JM Jeff Malm 3.00 8.00
JR J.P. Ramirez 3.00 8.00
JS Jordan Swagerty 3.00 8.00
KB Kyle Buchanan 3.00 8.00
KS Kyle Skipworth 4.00 10.00
LH L.J. Hoes 3.00 8.00
MG Mychal Givens 3.00 8.00
MP Matthew Purke 3.00 8.00
NM Nick Maronde 3.00 8.00
RG Robbie Grossman 3.00 8.00
RT Riccio Torrez 3.00 8.00
RW Ryan Weber 3.00 8.00
TH T.J. House 3.00 8.00
TM Tim Melville 3.00 8.00
TS Tyler Stovall 3.00 8.00
TW Tyler Wilson 3.00 8.00

2008 Upper Deck USA Junior National Team Jerseys Autographs Black

PRINT RUNS B/WN 99-400 COPIES PER
EH Eric Hosmer/100 15.00 40.00
GL Garrison Lassiter/226 4.00 10.00
HI Tyler Hibbs/222 4.00 10.00
HM Harold Martinez/99 4.00 10.00
JM Jeff Malm/258 4.00 10.00
JR J.P. Ramirez/99 4.00 10.00
JS Jordan Swagerty/199 4.00 10.00
KB Kyle Buchanan/205 4.00 10.00
KS Kyle Skipworth/99 4.00 10.00
LH L.J. Hoes/150 4.00 10.00
MG Mychal Givens/99 4.00 10.00
MP Matthew Purke/209 4.00 10.00
NM Nick Maronde/99 4.00 10.00
RG Robbie Grossman/150 4.00 10.00
RT Riccio Torrez/400 4.00 10.00
RW Ryan Weber/222 4.00 10.00
TH T.J. House/149 4.00 10.00
TM Tim Melville/175 4.00 10.00
TS Tyler Stovall/199 4.00 10.00
TW Tyler Wilson/199 4.00 10.00

2008 Upper Deck USA Junior National Team Jerseys Autographs Blue

*JSY BLUE: .4X TO 1X JSY BLACK
PRINT RUNS B/WN 50-400 COPIES PER
EH Eric Hosmer/121 15.00 40.00
GL Garrison Lassiter/172 4.00 10.00
HI Tyler Hibbs/392 4.00 10.00
HM Harold Martinez/375 4.00 10.00
JM Jeff Malm/107 4.00 10.00
JR J.P. Ramirez/200 4.00 10.00
RW Ryan Weber/400 4.00 10.00

2008 Upper Deck USA Junior National Team Jerseys Autographs Red

*JSY RED: .5X TO 1.2X JSY BLACK
PRINT RUNS B/WN 25-150 COPIES PER
NO PRICING ON QTY 25 OR LESS
EH Eric Hosmer/50 20.00 50.00
GL Garrison Lassiter/50 5.00 12.00
HI Tyler Hibbs/75 5.00 12.00
HM Harold Martinez/50 5.00 12.00
JM Jeff Malm/75 5.00 12.00
JR J.P. Ramirez/50 5.00 12.00
JS Jordan Swagerty/60 5.00 12.00
KB Kyle Buchanan/85 5.00 21.00
LH L.J. Hoes/60 5.00 12.00
MG Mychal Givens/60 5.00 12.00
MP Matthew Purke/74 5.00 12.00
RG Robbie Grossman/50 5.00 12.00
RT Riccio Torrez/150 5.00 12.00
RW Ryan Weber/50 5.00 12.00
TH T.J. House/50 5.00 12.00
TM Tim Melville/50 5.00 12.00
TS Tyler Stovall/85 5.00 12.00
TW Tyler Wilson/85 5.00 12.00

2008 Upper Deck USA Junior National Team Patch

*PATCH 99: .5X TO 1.2X BASIC JSY
STATED PRINT RUN 99 SER.#'d SETS
EH Eric Hosmer 8.00 20.00
KS Kyle Skipworth 6.00 15.00

2008 Upper Deck USA Junior National Team Patch Autographs

STATED PRINT RUN 99 SER.#'d SETS
EH Eric Hosmer 20.00 50.00
GL Garrison Lassiter 6.00 15.00
HI Tyler Hibbs 6.00 15.00
HM Harold Martinez 6.00 15.00
JM Jeff Malm 6.00 15.00
JR J.P. Ramirez 6.00 15.00
JS Jordan Swagerty 6.00 15.00
KB Kyle Buchanan 6.00 15.00
KS Kyle Skipworth 10.00 25.00
LH L.J. Hoes 6.00 15.00
MG Mychal Givens 6.00 15.00
MP Matthew Purke 6.00 15.00
NM Nick Maronde 6.00 15.00
RG Robbie Grossman 6.00 15.00
RT Riccio Torrez 6.00 15.00
RW Ryan Weber 6.00 15.00
TH T.J. House 6.00 15.00
TM Tim Melville 6.00 15.00
TS Tyler Stovall 6.00 15.00
TW Tyler Wilson 6.00 15.00

2008 Upper Deck USA National Team

USA1 Brett Hunter 1.25 3.00
USA2 Brian Matusz 1.25 3.00
USA3 Brett Wallace 1.25 3.00
USA4 Cody Satterwhite 1.25 3.00
USA5 Danny Espinosa 1.25 3.00
USA6 Eric Surkamp 1.25 3.00
USA7 Jordan Danks 1.25 3.00
USA8 Jeremy Hamilton 1.25 3.00
USA9 Joe Kelly 1.25 3.00
USA10 Jordy Mercer 1.25 3.00
USA11 Josh Romanski 1.25 3.00
USA12 Justin Smoak 1.25 3.00
USA13 Jacob Thompson 1.25 3.00
USA14 Logan Forsythe 1.25 3.00
USA15 Lance Lynn 1.25 3.00
USA16 Mike Minor 1.25 3.00
USA17 Pedro Alvarez 1.25 3.00
USA18 Petey Paramore 1.25 3.00
USA19 Ryan Berry 1.25 3.00
USA20 Ryan Flaherty 1.25 3.00
USA21 Roger Kieschnick 1.25 3.00
USA22 Seth Frankoff 1.25 3.00
USA23 Scott Gorgen 1.25 3.00
USA24 Tommy Medica 1.25 3.00
USA25 Tyson Ross 1.25 3.00

2008 Upper Deck USA National Team Autographs

PRINT RUNS B/WN 183-500 COPIES PER
BH Brett Hunter/297 4.00 10.00
BM Brian Matusz/264 10.00 25.00
BW Brett Wallace/183 6.00 15.00
CS Cody Satterwhite/375 4.00 10.00
DE Danny Espinosa/311 12.50 30.00
JD Jordan Danks/311 4.00 10.00
JH Jeremy Hamilton/375 4.00 10.00
JK Joe Kelly/457 4.00 10.00
JM Jordy Mercer/375 4.00 10.00
JR Josh Romanski/375 4.00 10.00
JS Justin Smoak/345 10.00 25.00
JT Jacob Thompson/267 4.00 10.00
LF Logan Forsythe/201 5.00 12.00
LL Lance Lynn/425 4.00 10.00
MM Mike Minor/375 6.00 15.00
PA Pedro Alvarez/205 6.00 15.00
PP Petey Paramore/237 4.00 10.00
RB Ryan Berry/375 4.00 10.00
RF Ryan Flaherty/244 4.00 10.00
RK Roger Kieschnick/272 4.00 10.00
TM Tommy Medica/487 4.00 10.00
TR Tyson Ross/500 4.00 10.00

2008 Upper Deck USA National Team Autographs Blue

*BLUE AU: .4X TO 1X BASIC AU
PRINT RUNS B/WN 50-204 COPIES PER
BH Brett Hunter/129 4.00 10.00
BM Brian Matusz/50 15.00 40.00
BW Brett Wallace/75 6.00 15.00
CS Cody Satterwhite/131 4.00 10.00
DE Danny Espinosa/75 12.50 30.00
ES Eric Surkamp/117 4.00 10.00
JD Jordan Danks/75 6.00 15.00
JH Jeremy Hamilton/204 4.00 10.00
JK Joe Kelly/125 4.00 10.00
JM Jordy Mercer/175 4.00 10.00
JR Josh Romanski/175 4.00 10.00
JS Justin Smoak/60 20.00 50.00
JT Jacob Thompson/105 4.00 10.00
LF Logan Forsythe/75 5.00 12.00
MM Mike Minor/175 6.00 15.00
PA Pedro Alvarez/75 8.00 20.00
PP Petey Paramore/175 4.00 10.00
RB Ryan Berry/175 4.00 10.00
RF Ryan Flaherty/75 4.00 10.00
RK Roger Kieschnick/113 5.00 12.00
SF Seth Frankoff/175 4.00 10.00
SG Scott Gorgen/175 4.00 10.00
TM Tommy Medica/175 4.00 10.00
TR Tyson Ross/75 4.00 10.00

2008 Upper Deck USA National Team Autographs Red

*RED AU: .5X TO 1.2X BASIC AU
STATED PRINT RUN 50 SER.#'d SETS
BM Brian Matusz 15.00 40.00
BW Brett Wallace 6.00 15.00
JD Jordan Danks 6.00 15.00
LF Logan Forsythe 5.00 12.00
LL Lance Lynn 6.00 15.00
RF Ryan Flaherty 4.00 10.00
TR Tyson Ross 4.00 10.00

2008 Upper Deck USA National Team Highlights

H1 Game 1 1.00 2.50
H2 Game 2 1.00 2.50
H3 Game 3 1.00 2.50
H4 Game 4 1.00 2.50
H5 Game 5 1.00 2.50

2008 Upper Deck USA National Team Jerseys

BH Brett Hunter 3.00 8.00
BM Brian Matusz 3.00 8.00
BW Brett Wallace 3.00 8.00
CS Cody Satterwhite 3.00 8.00
DE Danny Espinosa 4.00 10.00
ES Eric Surkamp 3.00 8.00
JD Jordan Danks 3.00 8.00
JH Jeremy Hamilton 3.00 8.00
JK Joe Kelly 3.00 8.00
JM Jordy Mercer 3.00 8.00
JR Josh Romanski 3.00 8.00
JS Justin Smoak 5.00 12.00
JT Jacob Thompson 3.00 8.00
LF Logan Forsythe 3.00 8.00
LL Lance Lynn 3.00 8.00
MM Mike Minor 3.00 8.00
PA Pedro Alvarez 4.00 10.00
PP Petey Paramore 3.00 8.00
RB Ryan Berry 3.00 8.00
RF Ryan Flaherty 3.00 8.00
RK Roger Kieschnick 3.00 8.00
SF Seth Frankoff 3.00 8.00
SG Scott Gorgen 3.00 8.00
TM Tommy Medica 3.00 8.00
TR Tyson Ross 3.00 8.00

2008 Upper Deck USA National Team Jerseys Autographs Black

PRINT RUNS B/WN 99-400 COPIES PER
BH Brett Hunter/99 4.00 10.00
BM Brian Matusz/181 20.00 50.00
BW Brett Wallace/199 4.00 10.00
CS Cody Satterwhite/273 6.00 15.00
DE Danny Espinosa/130 10.00 25.00
JD Jordan Danks/99 6.00 15.00
JH Jeremy Hamilton/271 4.00 10.00
JK Joe Kelly/300 4.00 10.00
JM Jordy Mercer/287 4.00 10.00
JR Josh Romanski/311 4.00 10.00
JS Justin Smoak/199 12.50 30.00
JT Jacob Thompson/199 4.00 10.00
LF Logan Forsythe/199 4.00 10.00
LL Lance Lynn/149 4.00 10.00
MM Mike Minor/359 4.00 10.00
PA Pedro Alvarez/275 5.00 12.00
PP Petey Paramore/199 4.00 10.00
RB Ryan Berry/284 4.00 10.00
RF Ryan Flaherty/149 6.00 15.00
RK Roger Kieschnick/199 4.00 10.00
TM Tommy Medica/400 4.00 10.00
TR Tyson Ross/400 4.00 10.00

2008 Upper Deck USA National Team Jerseys Autographs Blue

*BLUE JSY AU: .4X TO 1X BLACK JSY AU
PRINT RUNS B/WN 69-292 COPIES PER
ES Eric Surkamp/200 4.00 10.00
SF Seth Frankoff/69 4.00 10.00
SG Scott Gorgen/247 4.00 10.00

2008 Upper Deck USA National Team Jerseys Autographs Red

*RED JSY AU: .5X TO 1.2X BASIC JSY AU
PRINT RUNS B/WN 50-182 COPIES PER
ES Eric Surkamp/50 5.00 12.00
LL Lance Lynn/50 5.00 12.00
PA Pedro Alvarez/50 8.00 20.00
SF Seth Frankoff/50 5.00 12.00
SG Scott Gorgen/50 5.00 12.00

2008 Upper Deck USA National Team Patch

*PATCH: .5X TO 1.2X BASIC JSY
STATED PRINT RUN 99 SER.#'d SETS
BM Brian Matusz 15.00 40.00
LL Lance Lynn 10.00 25.00
PA Pedro Alvarez 10.00 25.00

2008 Upper Deck USA National Team Patch Autographs

STATED PRINT RUN 99 SER.#'d SETS
BH Brett Hunter 6.00 15.00
BM Brian Matusz 30.00 60.00
BW Brett Wallace 12.50 30.00
CS Cody Satterwhite 15.00 40.00
DE Danny Espinosa 8.00 20.00
ES Eric Surkamp 6.00 15.00
JD Jordan Danks 8.00 20.00
JH Jeremy Hamilton 6.00 15.00
JK Joe Kelly 6.00 15.00
JM Jordy Mercer 6.00 15.00
JR Josh Romanski 6.00 15.00
JS Justin Smoak 10.00 25.00
JT Jacob Thompson 6.00 15.00
LF Logan Forsythe 6.00 15.00
LL Lance Lynn 10.00 25.00
MM Mike Minor 8.00 20.00
PA Pedro Alvarez 12.50 30.00
PP Petey Paramore 6.00 15.00
RB Ryan Berry 6.00 15.00
RF Ryan Flaherty 6.00 15.00
RK Roger Kieschnick 6.00 15.00
SF Seth Frankoff 6.00 15.00
SG Scott Gorgen 6.00 15.00
TM Tommy Medica 6.00 15.00
TR Tyson Ross 10.00 25.00

2008 Upper Deck Sportsfest

COMPLETE SET (12) 15.00 40.00
UNPRICED AUTO PRINT RUN 5 SETS
SF1 Ken Griffey Jr. 1.25 3.00
SF5 Daisuke Matsuzaka 1.00 2.50
SF9 Derek Jeter 1.50 4.00

2008 Upper Deck Yankee Stadium Legacy Collection

COMMON CLEMENS 1.50 4.00
COMMON DIMAGGIO 2.50 6.00
COMMON GEHRIG 2.50 6.00
COMMON JETER 3.00 8.00
COMMON MATTINGLY 2.50 6.00
COMMON RODRIGUEZ 1.50 4.00
COMMON RUTH 3.00 8.00
1-6661 ISSUED IN VARIOUS 08 UD PRODUCTS
6662-6742 ISSUED IN 2009 UD1
1 Babe Ruth 10.00 25.00

2008 Upper Deck Yankee Stadium Legacy Collection Historical Moments

473 Notre Dame v. Army 1.50 4.00
1198 Joe Louis 1.25 3.00
1288 Joe DiMaggio 2.00 5.00
2835 1958 NFL Championship 1.50 4.00
2946 Whitey Ford 1.50 4.00
3407 Pope Paul VI 1.25 3.00
4131 Muhammad Ali v. Ken Norton 2.00 5.00
4181 Reggie Jackson 1.50 4.00
5404 U2 1.25 3.00
6710 2008 MLB All Star Game 1.50 4.00

2008 Upper Deck Yankee Stadium Legacy Collection Memorabilia

AP Andy Pettitte 6.00 15.00
BD Bill Dickey 6.00 15.00
BM Billy Martin 10.00 25.00
BR Babe Ruth 200.00 500.00
CL Roger Clemens 6.00 15.00
CS Casey Stengel 10.00 25.00
CW Chien-Ming Wang 6.00 15.00
DE Bucky Dent 4.00 10.00
DJ Derek Jeter 12.00 30.00
DM Don Mattingly 10.00 25.00
DW Dave Winfield 6.00 15.00
EH Elston Howard 6.00 15.00
FC Frankie Crosetti 10.00 25.00
GG Goose Gossage 6.00 15.00
GM Gil McDougald 6.00 15.00
GN Graig Nettles 6.00 15.00
GS Gary Sheffield 4.00 10.00
JA Reggie Jackson 6.00 15.00
JC Joba Chamberlain 4.00 10.00
JD Joe DiMaggio 75.00 200.00
JG Jason Giambi 4.00 10.00
JP Joe Pepitone 10.00 25.00
LG Lou Gehrig 125.00 300.00
LP Lou Piniella 50.00 120.00
MC Melky Cabrera 4.00 10.00
MM Mike Mussina 6.00 15.00
MU Bobby Murcer 4.00 10.00
ON Paul O'Neill 6.00 15.00
PN Phil Niekro 6.00 15.00
PO Jorge Posada 6.00 15.00
RC Robinson Cano 6.00 15.00
RE Allie Reynolds 10.00 25.00
RG Ron Guidry 6.00 15.00
RJ Randy Johnson 6.00 15.00
RM Roger Maris 10.00 25.00
SL Sparky Lyle 4.00 10.00
TH Tommy Henrich 10.00 25.00
TM Thurman Munson 10.00 25.00
WB Wade Boggs 6.00 15.00
WF Whitey Ford 10.00 25.00
WR Willie Randolph 4.00 10.00
YB Yogi Berra 10.00 25.00

2009 Upper Deck

COMP.SER 1 SET w/o #0 (500) 40.00 80.00
COMP.SER 2 SET w/SP RC (506) 75.00 150.00
COMP.SER 2 SET w/o SP RC (500) 50.00 100.00
COMMON CARD (1-1000) .15 .40
COMMON RC (1-1000) .40 1.00
COMMON RC (1001-1006) 1.25 3.00
0 Joe DiMaggio SP 40.00 80.00
1 Randy Johnson .40 1.00
2 Conor Jackson .15 .40
3 Brandon Webb .25 .60
4 Dan Haren .15 .40
5 Orlando Hudson .15 .40
6 Stephen Drew .15 .40
7 Mark Reynolds .15 .40
8 Eric Byrnes .15 .40
9 Justin Upton .25 .60
10 Chris B. Young .15 .40
11 Max Scherzer .40 1.00
12 Alex Romero .15 .40
13 Chad Tracy .15 .40
14 Brandon Lyon .15 .40
15 Adam Dunn .25 .60
16 David Eckstein .15 .40
17 Jair Jurrjens .15 .40
18 Mike Hampton .15 .40
19 Brandon Jones .15 .40
20 Tom Glavine .25 .60
21 John Smoltz .40 1.00
22 Chipper Jones .40 1.00
23 Yunel Escobar .15 .40
24 Kelly Johnson .15 .40
25 Brian McCann .25 .60
26 Jeff Francoeur .25 .60
27 Tim Hudson .25 .60
28 Casey Kotchman .15 .40
29 Nick Markakis .30 .75
30 Brian Roberts .15 .40
31 Jeremy Guthrie .15 .40
32 Ramon Hernandez .15 .40
33 Adam Jones .25 .60
34 Luke Scott .15 .40
35 Aubrey Huff .15 .40
36 Daniel Cabrera .15 .40
37 George Sherrill .15 .40
38 Melvin Mora .15 .40
39 Jay Payton .15 .40
40 Mark Kotsay .15 .40
41 David Ortiz .40 1.00
42 Jacoby Ellsbury .30 .75
43 Coco Crisp .15 .40
44 J.D. Drew .15 .40
45 Daisuke Matsuzaka .25 .60
46 Josh Beckett .15 .40
47 Curt Schilling .25 .60
48 Clay Buchholz .15 .40
49 Dustin Pedroia .40 1.00
50 Julio Lugo .15 .40
51 Mike Lowell .15 .40
52 Jonathan Papelbon .25 .60
53 Jason Varitek .40 1.00
54 Hideki Okajima .15 .40
55 Jon Lester .25 .60
56 Tim Wakefield .25 .60
57 Kevin Youkilis .15 .40
58 Jason Bay .25 .60
59 Justin Masterson .15 .40
60 Jeff Samardzija .25 .60
61 Alfonso Soriano .25 .60
62 Derrek Lee .15 .40
63 Aramis Ramirez .15 .40
64 Kerry Wood .15 .40
65 Jim Edmonds .25 .60
66 Kosuke Fukudome .25 .60
67 Geovany Soto .25 .60
68 Ted Lilly .15 .40
69 Carlos Zambrano .25 .60
70 Ryan Theriot .15 .40
71 Mark DeRosa .25 .60
72 Ronny Cedeno .15 .40
73 Ryan Dempster .15 .40
74 Jon Lieber .15 .40
75 Rich Hill .15 .40
76 Rich Harden .15 .40
77 Alexei Ramirez .25 .60
78 Nick Swisher .25 .60
79 Carlos Quentin .15 .40
80 Jermaine Dye .15 .40
81 Paul Konerko .25 .60
82 Orlando Cabrera .15 .40
83 Joe Crede .25 .60
84 Jim Thome .25 .60
85 Gavin Floyd .15 .40
86 Javier Vazquez .15 .40
87 Mark Buehrle .25 .60
88 Bobby Jenks .15 .40
89 Brian Anderson .15 .40
90 A.J. Pierzynski .15 .40
91 Jose Contreras .15 .40
92 Juan Uribe .15 .40
93a Ken Griffey Jr. .75 2.00
93b K.Griffey Jr. SEA 20.00 50.00
94 Chris Dickerson .15 .40
95 Brandon Phillips .15 .40
96 Aaron Harang .15 .40
97 Bronson Arroyo .15 .40
98 Edinson Volquez .15 .40
99 Johnny Cueto .25 .60
100 Edwin Encarnacion .40 1.00
101 Jeff Keppinger .15 .40
102 Joey Votto .40 1.00
103 Jay Bruce .25 .60
104 Ryan Freel .15 .40
105 Travis Hafner .15 .40
106 Victor Martinez .25 .60
107 Grady Sizemore .25 .60
108 Cliff Lee .25 .60
109 Ryan Garko .15 .40
110 Jhonny Peralta .15 .40
111 Franklin Gutierrez .15 .40
112 Fausto Carmona .15 .40
113 Jeff Baker .15 .40
114 Troy Tulowitzki .40 1.00
115 Matt Holliday .40 1.00
116 Todd Helton .25 .60
117 Ubaldo Jimenez .15 .40
118 Brian Fuentes .15 .40
119 Willy Taveras .15 .40
120 Aaron Cook .15 .40
121 Jason Grilli .15 .40
122 Garrett Atkins .15 .40
123 Jeff Francis .15 .40
124 Ryan Spilborghs .15 .40
125 Armando Galarraga .15 .40
126 Miguel Cabrera .40 1.00
127 Placido Polanco .15 .40
128 Edgar Renteria .15 .40
129 Carlos Guillen .15 .40
130 Gary Sheffield .15 .40
131 Curtis Granderson .30 .75
132 Marcus Thames .15 .40
133 Magglio Ordonez .25 .60
134 Jeremy Bonderman .15 .40
135 Dontrelle Willis .15 .40
136 Kenny Rogers .15 .40
137 Justin Verlander .40 1.00
138 Nate Robertson .15 .40
139 Todd Jones .15 .40
140 Joel Zumaya .15 .40
141 Hanley Ramirez .25 .60
142 Jeremy Hermida .15 .40
143 Mike Jacobs .15 .40
144 Andrew Miller .25 .60
145 Josh Willingham .25 .60
146 Luis Gonzalez .15 .40
147 Dan Uggla .15 .40
148 Scott Olsen .15 .40
149 Josh Johnson .25 .60
150 Darin Erstad .15 .40

151 Hunter Pence .25 .60
152 Roy Oswalt .25 .60
153 Lance Berkman .25 .60
154 Carlos Lee .15 .40
155 Michael Bourn .15 .40
156 Kazuo Matsui .15 .40
157 Miguel Tejada .25 .60
158 Ty Wigginton .15 .40
159 Jose Valverde .15 .40
160 J.R. Towles .15 .40
161 Brandon Backe .15 .40
162 Randy Wolf .15 .40
163 Mike Aviles .15 .40
164 Brian Bannister .15 .40
165 Zack Greinke .40 1.00
166 Gil Meche .15 .40
167 Alex Gordon .25 .60
168 Tony Pena .15 .40
169 Luke Hochevar .15 .40
170 Mark Grudzielanek .15 .40
171 Jose Guillen .15 .40
172 Billy Butler .15 .40
173 David DeJesus .15 .40
174 Joey Gathright .15 .40
175 Mark Teahen .15 .40
176 Joakim Soria .15 .40
177 Mark Teixeira .25 .60
178 Vladimir Guerrero .25 .60
179 Torii Hunter .15 .40
180 Jered Weaver .25 .60
181 Chone Figgins .15 .40
182 Francisco Rodriguez .25 .60
183 Garret Anderson .15 .40
184 Howie Kendrick .15 .40
185 John Lackey .25 .60
186 Ervin Santana .15 .40
187 Joe Saunders .15 .40
188 Gary Matthews .15 .40
189 Jon Garland .15 .40
190 Nick Adenhart .15 .40
191 Manny Ramirez .40 1.00
192 Casey Blake .15 .40
193 Chad Billingsley .25 .60
194 Russell Martin .15 .40
195 Matt Kemp .30 .75
196 James Loney .15 .40
197 Jeff Kent .15 .40
198 Nomar Garciaparra .25 .60
199 Rafael Furcal .15 .40
200 Andruw Jones .15 .40
201 Andre Ethier .25 .60
202 Takashi Saito .15 .40
203 Brad Penny .15 .40
204 Hiroki Kuroda .15 .40
205 Jonathan Broxton .15 .40
206 Chin-Lung Hu .15 .40
207 Juan Pierre .15 .40
208 Blake DeWitt .15 .40
209 Derek Lowe .15 .40
210 Clayton Kershaw .60 1.50
211 Greg Maddux .50 1.25
212 CC Sabathia .25 .60
213 Yovani Gallardo .15 .40
214 Ryan Braun .25 .60
215 Prince Fielder .25 .60
216 Corey Hart .15 .40
217 Bill Hall .15 .40
218 Rickie Weeks .15 .40
219 Mike Cameron .15 .40
220 Ben Sheets .15 .40
221 Jason Kendall .15 .40
222 J.J. Hardy .15 .40
223 Jeff Suppan .15 .40
224 Ray Durham .15 .40
225 Denard Span .15 .40
226 Carlos Gomez .15 .40
227 Joe Mauer .30 .75
228 Justin Morneau .25 .60
229 Michael Cuddyer .15 .40
230 Joe Nathan .15 .40
231 Kevin Slowey .25 .60
232 Delmon Young .25 .60
233 Jason Kubel .15 .40
234 Craig Monroe .15 .40
235 Livan Hernandez .15 .40
236 Francisco Liriano .15 .40
237 Pat Neshek .25 .60
238 Boof Bonser .15 .40
239 Nick Blackburn .15 .40
240 Daniel Murphy RC 1.50 4.00
241 Nick Evans .15 .40
242 Jose Reyes .25 .60
243 David Wright .30 .75
244 Carlos Delgado .15 .40
245 Luis Castillo .15 .40
246 Ryan Church .15 .40
247 Carlos Beltran .25 .60
248 Moises Alou .15 .40
249 Pedro Martinez .25 .60
250 Johan Santana .25 .60
251 John Maine .15 .40
252 Endy Chavez .15 .40
253 Oliver Perez .15 .40
254 Brian Schneider .15 .40
255 Fernando Tatis .15 .40
256 Mike Pelfrey .15 .40
257 Billy Wagner .15 .40
258 Ramon Castro .15 .40
259 Ivan Rodriguez .25 .60
260 Alex Rodriguez .50 1.25
261 Derek Jeter 1.00 2.50
262 Robinson Cano .25 .60
263 Jason Giambi .15 .40
264 Bobby Abreu .15 .40
265 Johnny Damon .25 .60
266 Melky Cabrera .15 .40
267 Hideki Matsui .40 1.00
268 Jorge Posada .25 .60
269 Joba Chamberlain .15 .40
270 Ian Kennedy .15 .40
271 Mike Mussina .25 .60
272 Andy Pettitte .25 .60
273 Mariano Rivera .50 1.25
274 Chien-Ming Wang .25 .60
275 Phil Hughes .15 .40
276 Xavier Nady .15 .40
277 Richie Sexson .15 .40
278 Brad Ziegler .15 .40
279 Justin Duchscherer .15 .40
280 Eric Chavez .15 .40
281 Bobby Crosby .15 .40
282 Mark Ellis .15 .40
283 Daric Barton .15 .40
284 Frank Thomas .40 1.00
285 Emil Brown .15 .40
286 Huston Street .15 .40
287 Jack Cust .15 .40
288 Kurt Suzuki .15 .40
289 Joe Blanton .15 .40
290 Ryan Howard .30 .75
291 Chase Utley .25 .60
292 Jimmy Rollins .25 .60
293 Pedro Feliz .15 .40
294 Pat Burrell .15 .40
295 Geoff Jenkins .15 .40
296 Shane Victorino .15 .40
297 Brett Myers .15 .40
298 Brad Lidge .15 .40
299 Cole Hamels .30 .75
300 Jamie Moyer .15 .40
301 Adam Eaton .15 .40
302 Matt Stairs .15 .40
303 Nate McLouth .15 .40
304 Ian Snell .15 .40
305 Matt Capps .15 .40
306 Freddy Sanchez .15 .40
307 Ryan Doumit .15 .40
308 Adam LaRoche .15 .40
309 Jack Wilson .15 .40
310 Tom Gorzelanny .15 .40
311 Jody Gerut .15 .40
312 Jake Peavy .15 .40
313 Chris Young .15 .40
314 Trevor Hoffman .25 .60
315 Adrian Gonzalez .30 .75
316 Chase Headley .15 .40
317 Khalil Greene .15 .40
318 Kevin Kouzmanoff .15 .40
319 Brian Giles .15 .40
320 Josh Bard .15 .40
321 Scott Hairston .15 .40
322 Barry Zito .25 .60
323 Tim Lincecum .25 .60
324 Matt Cain .25 .60
325 Brian Wilson .40 1.00
326 Aaron Rowand .25 .60
327 Randy Winn .15 .40
328 Omar Vizquel .25 .60
329 Bengie Molina .15 .40
330 Fred Lewis .15 .40
331 Erik Bedard .15 .40
332 Felix Hernandez .25 .60
333 Ichiro Suzuki .50 1.25
334 J.J. Putz .15 .40
335 Raul Ibanez .25 .60
336 Adrian Beltre .40 1.00
337 Jose Vidro .15 .40
338 Jeff Clement .15 .40
339 Kenji Johjima .25 .60
340 Wladimir Balentien .15 .40
341 Jose Lopez .15 .40
342 Kyle Lohse .15 .40
343 Albert Pujols .50 1.25
344 Troy Glaus .15 .40
345 Chris Carpenter .25 .60
346 Adam Kennedy .15 .40
347 Rick Ankiel .15 .40
348 Adam Wainwright .25 .60
349 Jason Isringhausen .15 .40
350 Chris Duncan .15 .40
351 Skip Schumaker .15 .40
352 Mark Mulder .15 .40
353 Todd Wellemeyer .15 .40
354 Cesar Izturis .15 .40
355 Ryan Ludwick .25 .60
356 Yadier Molina .50 1.25
357 Braden Looper .15 .40
358 B.J. Upton .25 .60
359 Carl Crawford .25 .60
360 Evan Longoria .25 .60
361 James Shields .15 .40
362 Scott Kazmir .15 .40
363 Carlos Pena .25 .60
364 Akinori Iwamura .15 .40
365 Jonny Gomes .15 .40
366 Cliff Floyd .15 .40
367 Troy Percival .15 .40
368 Edwin Jackson .15 .40
369 Matt Garza .15 .40
370 Eric Hinske .15 .40
371 Rocco Baldelli .15 .40
372 Chris Davis .25 .60
373 Marlon Byrd .15 .40
374 Michael Young .15 .40
375 Ian Kinsler .25 .60
376 Josh Hamilton .25 .60
377 Hank Blalock .15 .40
378 Milton Bradley .15 .40
379 Kevin Millwood .15 .40
380 Vicente Padilla .15 .40
381 Jarrod Saltalamacchia .15 .40
382 Jesse Litsch .15 .40
383 Roy Halladay .25 .60
384 A.J. Burnett .15 .40
385 Dustin McGowan .15 .40
386 Scott Rolen .25 .60
387 Alex Rios .15 .40
388 Vernon Wells .15 .40
389 Shannon Stewart .15 .40
390 B.J. Ryan .15 .40
391 Lyle Overbay .15 .40
392 Elijah Dukes .15 .40
393 Lastings Milledge .15 .40
394 Chad Cordero .15 .40
395 Ryan Zimmerman .25 .60
396 Austin Kearns .15 .40
397 Wily Mo Pena .15 .40
398 Ronnie Belliard .15 .40
399 Cristian Guzman .15 .40
400 Jesus Flores .15 .40
401a David Price RC .75 2.00
401b David Price White Uni SP 50.00 100.00
402 Matt Antonelli RC .60 1.50
403 Jonathon Niese RC .60 1.50
404 Phil Coke RC .60 1.50
405 Jason Pridie (RC) .40 1.00
406 Mark Saccomanno RC .40 1.00
407 Freddy Sandoval (RC) .40 1.00
408 Travis Snider RC .60 1.50
409 Matt Tuiasosopo (RC) .40 1.00
410 Will Venable RC .40 1.00
411 Brad Nelson (RC) .40 1.00
412 Aaron Cunningham RC .40 1.00
413 Wilkin Castillo RC .40 1.00
414 Robert Parnell RC .60 1.50
415 Conor Gillaspie RC 1.00 2.50
416 Dexter Fowler (RC) .60 1.50
417 George Kottaras (RC) .40 1.00
418 Josh Roenicke RC .40 1.00
419 Luis Valbuena RC .60 1.50
420 Casey McGehee (RC) .40 1.00
421 Mat Gamel RC 1.00 2.50
422 Greg Golson (RC) .40 1.00
423 Alfredo Aceves RC .60 1.50
424 Michael Bowden (RC) .40 1.00
425 Kila Kaaihue (RC) .60 1.50
426 Josh Geer (RC) .40 1.00
427 James Parr (RC) .40 1.00
428 Chris Lambert (RC) .40 1.00
429 Fernando Perez (RC) .40 1.00
430 Josh Whitesell RC .60 1.50
431 Pedroia/Dice-K/Beckett TL .40 1.00
432 Howard/Hamels/Rollins TL .30 .75
433 Reyes/Wright/Delgado TL .30 .75
434 Rodriguez/Jeter/Mussina TL 1.00 2.50
435 Carlos Quentin/Gavin Floyd
Javier Vazquez TL .15 .40
436 Ludwick/Pujols/Wellem TL .50 1.25
437 Cabrera/Grand/Verlander .40 1.00
438 Adrian Gonzalez/Jake Peavy
Brian Giles TL .30 .75
439 Braun/Fielder/Sheets TL .25 .60
440 Cliff Lee/Grady Sizemore
Jhonny Peralta TL .25 .60
441 Josh Hamilton/Ian Kinsler
Vicente Padilla TL .25 .60
442 Jorge Cantu/Hanley Ramirez
Ricky Nolasco TL .25 .60
443 Carlos Pena/Akinori Iwamura
B.J. Upton TL .25 .60
444 Jack Cust/Dana Eveland
Kurt Suzuki TL .15 .40
445 Alfonso Soriano/Ryan Dempster
Aramis Ramirez TL .25 .60
446 Lance Berkman/Roy Oswalt
Miguel Tejada TL .25 .60
447 Matt Holliday/Aaron Cook
Willy Taveras TL .40 1.00
448 Nate McLouth .15 .40
Adam LaRoche
Paul Maholm TL
449 Brian Roberts/Aubrey Huff
Jeremy Guthrie TL .15 .40
450 Justin Morneau/Joe Mauer
Carlos Gomez TL .30 .75
451 Ibanez/Ichiro/King Felix TL .50 1.25
452 Chipper Jones
Jair Jurrjens/Brian McCann TL .40 1.00
453 Brandon Webb/Dan Haren
Stephen Drew TL .25 .60
454 Lincecum/Winn/Molina TL .25 .60
455 Roy Halladay/A.J. Burnett
Alex Rios TL .25 .60
456 Edinson Volquez
Brandon Phillips/Edwin Encarnacion TL .40 1.00
457 Chad Billingsley/Matt Kemp
James Loney TL .30 .75
458 Ervin Santana/Vladimir Guerrero
Francisco Rodriguez TL .25 .60
459 Zack Greinke/Gil Meche
David DeJesus TL .40 1.00
460 Tim Redding/Cristian Guzman
Lastings Milledge TL .15 .40
461 Carlos Zambrano HL .25 .60
462 Jon Lester HL .25 .60
463 Jim Thome HL .25 .60
464 Ken Griffey Jr. HL .75 2.00
465 Manny Ramirez HL .40 1.00
466 Derek Jeter HL 1.00 2.50
467 Josh Hamilton HL .25 .60
468 Francisco Rodriguez HL .25 .60
469 Alex Rodriguez HL .50 1.25
470 J.D. Drew HL .15 .40
471 David Wright CL .30 .75
472 Chase Utley CL .25 .60
473 Chipper Jones CL .40 1.00
474 Cristian Guzman CL .15 .40
475 Hanley Ramirez CL .25 .60
476 CC Sabathia CL .25 .60
477 Lance Berkman CL .25 .60
478 Alfonso Soriano CL .25 .60
479 Albert Pujols CL .50 1.25
480 Nate McLouth CL .15 .40
481 Brandon Phillips CL .15 .40
482 Adrian Gonzalez CL .30 .75
483 Brandon Webb CL .25 .60
484 Manny Ramirez CL .40 1.00
485 Tim Lincecum CL .25 .60
486 Matt Holliday CL .40 1.00
487 Dustin Pedroia CL .40 1.00
488 Alex Rodriguez CL .50 1.25
489 Evan Longoria CL .25 .60
490 Roy Halladay CL .25 .60
491 Nick Markakis CL .30 .75
492 Grady Sizemore CL .25 .60
493 Carlos Quentin CL .15 .40
494 Joakim Soria CL .15 .40
495 Miguel Cabrera CL .40 1.00
496 Joe Mauer CL .30 .75
497 Francisco Rodriguez CL .25 .60
498 Jack Cust CL .15 .40
499 Ichiro Suzuki CL .50 1.25
500 Josh Hamilton CL .25 .60
501 Brandon Webb .25 .60
502 Miguel Montero .15 .40
503 Tony Pena .15 .40
504 Jon Rauch .15 .40
505 Augie Ojeda .15 .40
506 Yusmeiro Petit .15 .40
507 Chris Snyder .15 .40
508 Chris B. Young .15 .40
509 Doug Slaten .15 .40
510 Tony Clark .15 .40
511 Justin Upton .25 .60
512 Chad Qualls .15 .40
513 Doug Davis .15 .40
514 Eric Byrnes .15 .40
515 Conor Jackson .15 .40
516 Mike Gonzalez .15 .40
517 Josh Anderson .15 .40
518 Tom Glavine .25 .60
519 Clint Sammons .15 .40
520 Martin Prado .15 .40
521 Jorge Campillo .15 .40
522 Omar Infante .15 .40
523 Javier Vazquez .15 .40
524 Jo Jo Reyes .15 .40
525 Gregor Blanco .15 .40
526 Rafael Soriano .15 .40
527 Manny Acosta .15 .40
528 Chipper Jones .40 1.00
529 Buddy Carlyle .15 .40
530 Radhames Liz .15 .40
531 Scott Moore .15 .40
532 Jim Johnson .15 .40
533 Oscar Salazar .15 .40
534 Nick Markakis .30 .75
535 Brian Roberts .15 .40
536 Jeremy Guthrie .15 .40
537 Adam Jones .25 .60
538 Chris Ray .15 .40
539 Aubrey Huff .15 .40
540 Ty Wigginton .15 .40
541 Dennis Sarfate .15 .40
542 Melvin Mora .15 .40
543 Chris Waters .15 .40
544 John Smoltz .40 1.00
545 Brad Penny .15 .40
546 Josh Bard .15 .40
547 Takashi Saito .15 .40
548 Jacoby Ellsbury .30 .75
549 Jeff Bailey .15 .40
550 Ramon Ramirez .15 .40
551 Daisuke Matsuzaka .25 .60
552 Josh Beckett .25 .60
553 Jed Lowrie .15 .40
554 Dustin Pedroia .40 1.00
555 David Ortiz .40 1.00
556 Jonathan Van Every .15 .40
557 Jonathan Papelbon .25 .60
558 Manny Delcarmen .15 .40
559 Hideki Okajima .15 .40
560 Jon Lester .25 .60
561 Javier Lopez .15 .40
562 Kevin Youkilis .15 .40
563 Jason Varitek .40 1.00
564 Milton Bradley .15 .40
565 Mike Fontenot .15 .40
566 Micah Hoffpauir .15 .40
567 Sean Marshall .15 .40
568 Alfonso Soriano .25 .60
569 Neal Cotts .15 .40
570 Kosuke Fukudome .25 .60
571 Reed Johnson .15 .40
572 Carlos Marmol .25 .60
573 Chad Gaudin .15 .40
574 Rich Harden .15 .40
575 Ted Lilly .15 .40
576 Carlos Zambrano .25 .60
577 Ryan Theriot .15 .40
578 Ryan Dempster .15 .40
579 Matt Thornton .15 .40
580 Jerry Owens .15 .40
581 Alexei Ramirez .25 .60
582 John Danks .15 .40
583 Carlos Quentin .15 .40
584 D.J. Carrasco .15 .40
585 Dewayne Wise .15 .40
586 Clayton Richard .15 .40
587 Brent Lillibridge .15 .40
588 Jim Thome .25 .60
589 Chris Getz .15 .40
590 Octavio Dotel .15 .40
591 Mark Buehrle .25 .60
592 Bobby Jenks .15 .40
593 Joey Votto .40 1.00
594 Jay Bruce .25 .60
595 David Weathers .15 .40
596 Bill Bray .15 .40
597 Mike Lincoln .15 .40
598 Norris Hopper .15 .40
599 Alex Gonzalez .15 .40
600 Jerry Hairston Jr. .15 .40
601 Brandon Phillips .15 .40
602 Aaron Harang .15 .40
603 Bronson Arroyo .15 .40
604 Edinson Volquez .15 .40
605 Ryan Hanigan .15 .40
606 Jared Burton .15 .40
607 Aaron Laffey .15 .40
608 Kerry Wood .15 .40
609 Shin-Soo Choo .25 .60
610 David Dellucci .15 .40
611 Mark DeRosa .25 .60
612 Masahide Kobayashi .15 .40
613 Rafael Perez .15 .40
614 Grady Sizemore .25 .60
615 Cliff Lee .25 .60
616 Ben Francisco .15 .40
617 Jensen Lewis .15 .40
618 Joe Smith .15 .40
619 Asdrubal Cabrera .25 .60
620 Brad Hawpe .15 .40
621 Chris Iannetta .15 .40
622 Clint Barmes .15 .40
623 Seth Smith .15 .40
624 Aaron Cook .15 .40
625 Troy Tulowitzki .40 1.00
626 Todd Helton .25 .60
627 Taylor Buchholz .15 .40
628 Jason Marquis .15 .40
629 Ian Stewart .15 .40
630 Ryan Speier .15 .40
631 Manny Corpas .15 .40
632 Yorvit Torrealba .15 .40
633 Fernando Rodney .15 .40
634 Justin Verlander .40 1.00
635 Bobby Seay .15 .40
636 Clete Thomas .15 .40
637 Placido Polanco .15 .40
638 Ramon Santiago .15 .40
639 Adam Everett .15 .40
640 Gary Sheffield .15 .40
641 Curtis Granderson .30 .75
642 Freddy Dolsi .15 .40
643 Magglio Ordonez .25 .60
644 Zach Miner .15 .40
645 Brandon Inge .15 .40
646 Dallas McPherson .15 .40
647 Anibal Sanchez .15 .40
648 Jorge Cantu .15 .40
649 John Baker .15 .40
650 Wes Helms .15 .40
651 Ricky Nolasco .15 .40
652 Chris Volstad .15 .40
653 Renyel Pinto .15 .40
654 Alfredo Amezaga .15 .40
655 Cameron Maybin .15 .40
656 Matt Lindstrom .15 .40
657 Cody Ross .15 .40
658 Logan Kensing .15 .40
659 Tim Byrdak .15 .40
660 Reggie Abercrombie .15 .40
661 Geoff Blum .15 .40
662 Humberto Quintero .15 .40
663 Doug Brocail .15 .40
664 Roy Oswalt .25 .60
665 Lance Berkman .25 .60
666 Carlos Lee .15 .40
667 Latroy Hawkins .15 .40
668 Geoff Geary .15 .40
669 Brian Moehler .15 .40
670 Wandy Rodriguez .15 .40
671 Esteban German .15 .40
672 Ross Gload .15 .40
673 Joakim Soria .15 .40
674 Kyle Farnsworth .15 .40
675 Ryan Shealy .15 .40
676 Mike Aviles .15 .40
677 John Buck .15 .40
678 Zack Greinke .40 1.00
679 John Bale .15 .40
680 Alex Gordon .25 .60
681 Coco Crisp .15 .40
682 Miguel Olivo .15 .40
683 Alberto Callaspo .15 .40
684 Kyle Davies .15 .40
685 Brandon Wood .15 .40
686 Erick Aybar .15 .40
687 Robb Quinlan .15 .40
688 Bobby Abreu .15 .40
689 Jose Arredondo .15 .40
690 Juan Rivera .15 .40
691 Kendry Morales .15 .40
692 Vladimir Guerrero .25 .60
693 Darren Oliver .15 .40
694 Jeff Mathis .15 .40
695 Maicer Izturis .15 .40
696 Mike Napoli .15 .40
697 Reggie Willits .15 .40
698 Scot Shields .15 .40
699 John Lackey .25 .60
700 Manny Ramirez .40 1.00
701 Danny Ardoin .15 .40
702 Orlando Hudson .15 .40
703 Hong-Chih Kuo .15 .40
704 Mark Loretta .15 .40
705 Cory Wade .15 .40
706 Casey Blake .15 .40
707 Eric Stults .15 .40
708 Jason Schmidt .15 .40
709 Chad Billingsley .25 .60
710 Russell Martin .15 .40
711 Matt Kemp .30 .75
712 James Loney .15 .40
713 Rafael Furcal .15 .40
714 Ramon Troncoso .15 .40
715 Jonathan Broxton .15 .40
716 Hiroki Kuroda .15 .40
717 Andre Ethier .25 .60
718 Corey Hart .15 .40
719 Mitch Stetter .15 .40
720 Manny Parra .15 .40
721 Dave Bush .15 .40
722 Trevor Hoffman .25 .60
723 Tony Gwynn .15 .40
724 Chris Duffy .15 .40
725 Seth McClung .15 .40
726 J.J. Hardy .15 .40
727 David Riske .15 .40
728 Todd Coffey .15 .40
729 Rickie Weeks .15 .40
730 Mike Rivera .15 .40
731 Carlos Villanueva .15 .40
732 Ryan Braun .25 .60
733 Nick Punto .15 .40
734 Francisco Liriano .15 .40
735 Craig Breslow .15 .40
736 Matt Macri .15 .40
737 Scott Baker .15 .40
738 Jesse Crain .15 .40
739 Brendan Harris .15 .40
740 Alexi Casilla .15 .40
741 Nick Blackburn .15 .40
742 Brian Buscher .15 .40
743 Denard Span .15 .40
744 Mike Redmond .15 .40
745 Joe Mauer .30 .75
746 Carlos Gomez .15 .40
747 Matt Guerrier .15 .40
748 Joe Nathan .15 .40
749 Livan Hernandez .15 .40
750 Ryan Church .15 .40
751 Carlos Beltran .25 .60
752 Jeremy Reed .15 .40
753 Oliver Perez .15 .40
754 Duaner Sanchez .15 .40
755 J.J. Putz .15 .40
756 Mike Pelfrey .15 .40
757 Brian Schneider .15 .40
758 Francisco Rodriguez .25 .60
759 John Maine .15 .40
760 Daniel Murphy .60 1.50
761 Johan Santana .25 .60
762 Jose Reyes .25 .60
763 David Wright .30 .75
764 Carlos Delgado .15 .40
765 Pedro Feliciano .15 .40
766 Derek Jeter 1.00 2.50
767 Brian Bruney .15 .40
768 A.J. Burnett .15 .40
769 Andy Pettitte .25 .60
770 Nick Swisher .25 .60
771 Damaso Marte .15 .40
772 Edwar Ramirez .15 .40
773 CC Sabathia .25 .60
774 Chien-Ming Wang .25 .60
775 Mariano Rivera .50 1.25
776 Mark Teixeira .25 .60
777 Joba Chamberlain .15 .40
778 Jose Veras .15 .40
779 Hideki Matsui .40 1.00
780 Jose Molina .15 .40
781 Alex Rodriguez .50 1.25
782 Michael Wuertz .15 .40
783 Orlando Cabrera .15 .40
784 Sean Gallagher .15 .40
785 Dallas Braden .15 .40
786 Gio Gonzalez .25 .60
787 Rajai Davis .15 .40
788 Brad Ziegler .15 .40
789 Matt Holliday .40 1.00
790 Jack Cust .15 .40
791 Santiago Casilla .15 .40
792 Jason Giambi .25 .60
793 Joey Devine .15 .40
794 Travis Buck .15 .40
795 Justin Duchscherer .15 .40
796 Rob Bowen .15 .40
797 Andrew Brown .15 .40
798 Ryan Sweeney .15 .40
799 Jimmy Rollins .25 .60
800 Chad Durbin .15 .40
801 Clay Condrey .15 .40
802 Chris Coste .15 .40
803 Ryan Madson .15 .40
804 Chan Ho Park .25 .60
805 Carlos Ruiz .15 .40
806 Kyle Kendrick .15 .40
807 Jayson Werth .25 .60
808 Cole Hamels .30 .75
809 Brad Lidge .15 .40
810 Greg Dobbs .15 .40
811 Scott Eyre .15 .40
812 Eric Bruntlett .15 .40
813 Ryan Howard .30 .75
814 Chase Utley .25 .60
815 Paul Maholm .15 .40
816 Andy LaRoche .15 .40
817 Brandon Moss .15 .40
818 Nyjer Morgan .15 .40
819 John Grabow .15 .40
820 Tom Gorzelanny .15 .40
821 Steve Pearce .40 1.00
822 Sean Burnett .15 .40
823 Tyler Yates .15 .40
824 Zach Duke .15 .40
825 Matt Capps .15 .40
826 Ross Ohlendorf .15 .40
827 Nate McLouth .15 .40
828 Adrian Gonzalez .30 .75
829 Heath Bell .15 .40
830 Luis Rodriguez .15 .40
831 Kevin Kouzmanoff .15 .40
832 Edgar Gonzalez .15 .40
833 Cha-Seung Baek .15 .40
834 Cla Meredith .15 .40
835 Justin Hampson .15 .40
836 Nick Hundley .15 .40
837 Mike Adams .15 .40
838 Jake Peavy .15 .40
839 Chris Young .15 .40
840 Brian Giles .15 .40
841 Steve Holm .15 .40
842 Dave Roberts .25 .60
843 Travis Ishikawa .15 .40
844 Pablo Sandoval .30 .75
845 Emmanuel Burriss .15 .40
846 Nate Schierholtz .15 .40
847 Randy Johnson .40 1.00
848 Kevin Frandsen .15 .40
849 Edgar Renteria .15 .40
850 Jack Taschner .15 .40
851 Tim Lincecum .25 .60
852 Alex Hinshaw .15 .40
853 Jonathan Sanchez .15 .40
854 Eugenio Velez .15 .40
855a K.Griffey Jr. 09 SEA .75 2.00
855b K.Griffey Jr. 89 SEA 12.00 30.00
855c K.Griffey Jr. 90 SEA 12.00 30.00
855d K.Griffey Jr. 91 SEA 12.00 30.00
855e K.Griffey Jr. 92 SEA 12.00 30.00
855f K.Griffey Jr. 93 SEA 12.00 30.00
855g K.Griffey Jr. 94 SEA 12.00 30.00
855h K.Griffey Jr. 95 SEA 12.00 30.00
855i K.Griffey Jr. 96 SEA 12.00 30.00
855j K.Griffey Jr. 97 SEA 12.00 30.00
855k K.Griffey Jr. 98 SEA 12.00 30.00
855l K.Griffey Jr. 99 SEA 12.00 30.00
855m K.Griffey Jr. 00 CIN 12.00 30.00
855n K.Griffey Jr. 01 CIN 12.00 30.00
855o K.Griffey Jr. 02 CIN 12.00 30.00
855p K.Griffey Jr. 03 CIN 12.00 30.00
855q K.Griffey Jr. 04 CIN 12.00 30.00
855r K.Griffey Jr. 05 CIN 12.00 30.00
855s K.Griffey Jr. 06 CIN 12.00 30.00
855t K.Griffey Jr. 07 CIN 12.00 30.00
855u K.Griffey Jr. 08 CHI 12.00 30.00
856 Garrett Olson .15 .40
857 Cesar Jimenez .15 .40
858 Bryan LaHair .40 1.00
859 Franklin Gutierrez .25 .60
860 Brandon Morrow .15 .40
861 Roy Corcoran .15 .40
862 Carlos Silva .15 .40
863 Kenji Johjima .25 .60
864 Jarrod Washburn .15 .40
865 Felix Hernandez .25 .60
866 Ichiro Suzuki .50 1.25
867 Miguel Batista .15 .40
868 Yuniesky Betancourt .15 .40
869 Adrian Beltre .40 1.00
870 Ryan Rowland-Smith .15 .40
871 Khalil Greene .15 .40
872 Kyle McClellan .15 .40
873 Ryan Franklin .25 .60
874 Brian Barton .15 .40
875 Josh Kinney .15 .40
876 Ryan Ludwick .25 .60
877 Brendan Ryan .15 .40
878 Albert Pujols .50 1.25
879 Troy Glaus .15 .40
880 Joel Pineiro .15 .40
881 Jason LaRue .15 .40
882 Yadier Molina .50 1.25
883 Adam Wainwright .25 .60
884 Chris Perez .15 .40
885 Adam Kennedy .15 .40
886 Akinori Iwamura .15 .40
887 J.P. Howell .15 .40
888 Ben Zobrist .25 .60
889 Gabe Gross .15 .40
890 Matt Joyce .15 .40
891 Dan Wheeler .15 .40
892 Willie Aybar .15 .40
893 Jason Bartlett .15 .40
894 Dioner Navarro .15 .40
895 Andy Sonnanstine .15 .40
896 B.J. Upton .25 .60
897 Chad Bradford .15 .40
898 Evan Longoria .25 .60
899 Shawn Riggans .15 .40
900 Scott Kazmir .15 .40
901 Grant Balfour .15 .40
902 Josh Hamilton .25 .60
903 Frank Francisco .15 .40
904 Frank Catalanotto .15 .40
905 German Duran .15 .40
906 Brandon Boggs .15 .40
907 Matt Harrison .15 .40
908 David Murphy .15 .40
909 Nelson Cruz .40 1.00
910 Joaquin Benoit .15 .40
911 Taylor Teagarden .15 .40
912 Joaquin Arias .15 .40
913 Kevin Millwood .15 .40
914 Ian Kinsler .25 .60
915 T.J. Beam .15 .40
916 Marco Scutaro .25 .60
917 Adam Lind .15 .40
918 John McDonald .15 .40
919 Scott Downs .15 .40
920 Rod Barajas .15 .40
921 Joe Inglett .15 .40
922 Alex Rios .15 .40
923 David Purcey .15 .40
924 Roy Halladay .25 .60
925 Jason Frasor .15 .40
926 Shaun Marcum .15 .40
927 Aaron Hill .15 .40
928 Adam Dunn .25 .60
929 Shawn Hill .15 .40
930 Steven Shell .15 .40
931 Saul Rivera .15 .40
932 Josh Willingham .25 .60
933 John Lannan .15 .40
934 Joel Hanrahan .25 .60
935 Daniel Cabrera .15 .40
936 Willie Harris .15 .40
937 Wil Nieves .15 .40
938 Nick Johnson .15 .40
939 Garrett Mock .15 .40
940 Anderson Hernandez .15 .40
941 Koji Uehara RC 1.00 2.50
942 Kenshin Kawakami RC .60 1.50
943 Jason Motte (RC) .60 1.50
944 Elvis Andrus RC 1.00 2.50
945 Rick Porcello RC 1.25 3.00
946 Colby Rasmus (RC) .60 1.50
947 Shairon Martis RC .60 1.50
948 Ricky Romero (RC) .60 1.50
949 Kevin Jepsen (RC) .40 1.00
950 James McDonald RC 1.00 2.50
951 Joe Mauer AW .30 .75
952 Carlos Pena AW .25 .60
953 Dustin Pedroia AW .40 1.00
954 Adrian Beltre AW .40 1.00
955 Michael Young AW .15 .40
956 Torii Hunter AW .15 .40
957 Grady Sizemore AW .25 .60
958 Ichiro Suzuki AW .50 1.25
959 Yadier Molina AW .50 1.25
960 Adrian Gonzalez AW .30 .75
961 Brandon Phillips AW .15 .40
962 David Wright AW .30 .75
963 Jimmy Rollins AW .25 .60
964 Nate McLouth AW .15 .40
965 Carlos Beltran AW .25 .60
966 Shane Victorino AW .15 .40
967 Cliff Lee AW .25 .60
968 Brad Lidge AW .15 .40
969 Evan Longoria AW .25 .60
970 Geovany Soto AW .25 .60
971 Francisco Rodriguez CL .25 .60
972 Raul Ibanez CL .25 .60
973 Derek Lowe CL .15 .40
974 Scott Olsen CL .15 .40
975 Josh Johnson CL .25 .60
976 Prince Fielder CL .25 .60
977 Mike Hampton CL .15 .40
978 Kevin Gregg CL .15 .40
979 Rick Ankiel CL .15 .40
980 Nate McLouth CL .15 .40
981 Ramon Hernandez CL .15 .40
982 David Eckstein CL .15 .40
983 Felipe Lopez CL .15 .40
984 Clayton Kershaw CL .60 1.50
985 Randy Johnson CL .40 1.00
986 Huston Street CL .15 .40
987 Rocco Baldelli CL .15 .40
988 Mark Teixeira CL .25 .60
989 Pat Burrell CL .15 .40
990 Vernon Wells CL .15 .40
991 Cesar Izturis CL .15 .40
992 Kerry Wood CL .15 .40
993 Wilson Betemit CL .15 .40
994 Mike Jacobs CL .15 .40
995 Gerald Laird CL .15 .40
996 Justin Morneau CL .25 .60
997 Brian Fuentes CL .15 .40
998 Jason Giambi CL .15 .40
999 Endy Chavez CL .15 .40
1000 Michael Young CL .15 .40
1001 Brett Anderson SP RC 2.00 5.00
1002 Trevor Cahill SP RC 3.00 8.00
1003 Jordan Schafer SP (RC) 2.00 5.00

1004 Trevor Crowe SP RC 1.25 3.00
1005 Everth Cabrera SP RC 2.00 5.00
1006 Ryan Perry SP RC 3.00 8.00
SP1 M.Buehrle PG SP 6.00 15.00
SP2 Obama/Pujols ASG SP 2.50 6.00
SP3 D.Jeter ATHK SP 12.50 30.00

2009 Upper Deck Gold
*GOLD VET: 5X TO 12X BASIC VET
*GOLD RC: 2X TO 5X BASIC RC
RANDOM INSERTS IN PACKS
STATED PRINT RUN 99 SER.#'d SETS

2009 Upper Deck 1989 Design
RANDOM INSERTS IN PACKS
801 Ken Griffey Jr. 25.00 60.00
802 Randy Johnson 6.00 15.00
803 Ronald Reagan 12.50 30.00
804 George H.W. Bush 30.00 60.00

2009 Upper Deck A Piece of History 500 Club
RANDOM INSERTS IN PACKS
MR Manny Ramirez 12.50 30.00

2009 Upper Deck A Piece of History 600 Club
RANDOM INSERTS IN PACKS
600KG Ken Griffey Jr. 12.00 30.00

2009 Upper Deck Derek Jeter 1993 Buyback Autograph
RANDOM INSERTS IN PACKS
STATED PRINT RUN 93 SER.#'d SETS
449 Derek Jeter/93 200.00 400.00

2009 Upper Deck Goodwin Champions Preview
RANDOM INSERTS IN PACKS
GCP1 Joe DiMaggio 5.00 12.00
GCP2 Tony Gwynn 3.00 8.00
GCP3 Cole Hamels 3.00 8.00
GCP4 Laird Hamilton 1.25 3.00
GCP5 Gordie Howe 6.00 15.00
GCP6 Ichiro Suzuki 3.00 8.00
GCP7 Derek Jeter 6.00 15.00
GCP8 Michael Jordan 6.00 15.00
GCP9 Barack Obama 6.00 15.00
GCP10 Albert Pujols 5.00 12.00
GCP11 Cal Ripken Jr. 10.00 25.00
GCP12 Bill Rodgers 1.25 3.00

2009 Upper Deck Griffey-Jordan
RANDOM INSERTS IN PACKS
KGMJ K.Griffey Jr./M.Jordan 20.00 50.00

2009 Upper Deck Historic Firsts
COMMON CARD .75 2.00
ODDS 1:4 HOB,1:6 RET,1:10 BLAST
HF1 Barack Obama 4.00 10.00
HF4 Republican Woman Runs As VP 2.00 5.00
HF11 Bo The First Puppy 10.00 25.00

2009 Upper Deck Historic Predictors
COMMON CARD .75 2.00
ODDS 1:4 HOB,1:6 RET,1:10 BLAST

2009 Upper Deck Inkredible
ODDS 1:17 HOB,1:1000 RET,1:1980 BLAST
EXCHANGE DEADLINE 1/12/2011
AC Aaron Cook 4.00 10.00
AE Andre Ethier 3.00 8.00
AG Alberto Gonzalez S2 3.00 8.00
AI Akinori Iwamura 6.00 15.00
AK Austin Kearns 3.00 8.00
AL Aaron Laffey 3.00 8.00
AR Bronson Arroyo 3.00 8.00
AR Alexei Ramirez S2 3.00 8.00
BA Burke Badenhop S2 3.00 8.00
BA Brian Bannister 3.00 8.00
BB Billy Butler 4.00 10.00
BB Brian Barton S2 3.00 8.00
BI Brian Bixler S2 3.00 8.00
BJ Jay Bruce S2 10.00 25.00
BK Bobby Korecky S2 4.00 10.00
BL Joe Blanton 6.00 15.00
BO Boof Bonser 3.00 8.00
BP Brandon Phillips 5.00 12.00
BR Brian Bruney 3.00 8.00
BR Brandon Jones S2 3.00 8.00
BW Billy Wagner 15.00 40.00
CA Chris Capuano 20.00 50.00
CB Craig Breslow 3.00 8.00
CC Chad Cordero 3.00 8.00
CD Chris Duffy 3.00 8.00
CG Carlos Gomez 8.00 20.00
CH Cole Hamels 50.00 100.00
CH Corey Hart S2 3.00 8.00
CR Chris Resop 3.00 8.00
CS Clint Sammons S2 3.00 8.00
CT Clete Thomas S2 10.00 25.00
DE David Eckstein 4.00 10.00
DL Derek Lowe 8.00 20.00
DM David Murphy 3.00 8.00
DP Dustin Pedroia S2 20.00 50.00
DU Dan Uggla 3.00 8.00
EA Erick Aybar 3.00 8.00
ED Elijah Dukes 3.00 8.00
ED Elijah Dukes S2 3.00 8.00
ET Elder Torres S2 5.00 12.00
EV Edinson Volquez 6.00 15.00
FC Fausto Carmona 4.00 10.00
FH Felix Hernandez 15.00 40.00
GA Garrett Atkins 4.00 10.00
GF Gavin Floyd 3.00 8.00
GP Glen Perkins 3.00 8.00
GP Gregorio Petit S2 3.00 8.00
GS Greg Smith S2 4.00 10.00
GW Tony Gwynn Mil 5.00 12.00
HA Brendan Harris 3.00 8.00
HE Jonathan Herrera S2 4.00 10.00
HI Hernan Iribarren S2 4.00 10.00
IK Ian Kennedy S2 6.00 15.00
IK Ian Kinsler 10.00 25.00
JA Joaquin Arias S2 3.00 8.00
JB Jason Bay S2 10.00 25.00
JB Jeff Baker 3.00 8.00
JC Jack Cust 3.00 8.00
JE Jeff Francoeur 3.00 8.00
JE Jeremy Hermida S2 4.00 10.00
JF Jeff Francis 4.00 10.00
JG Jeremy Guthrie 15.00 40.00
JH Josh Hamilton 30.00 60.00
JH J.A. Happ S2 3.00 8.00
JK Jeff Keppinger 4.00 10.00
JL James Loney 8.00 20.00
JL Jed Lowrie S2 3.00 8.00
JM John Maine S2 6.00 15.00
JM John Maine 30.00 60.00
JN Joe Nathan 3.00 8.00
JO Joey Gathright 3.00 8.00
JO Jonathan Albaladejo S2 4.00 10.00
JP Jonathan Papelbon 10.00 25.00
JS James Shields 4.00 10.00
JS Joe Smith S2 4.00 10.00
JW Jered Weaver 5.00 12.00
KG K.Griffey Jr. EXCH 100.00 200.00
KG Ken Griffey Jr. S2 100.00 200.00
KH Kevin Hart S2 4.00 10.00
KJ Kelly Johnson S2 3.00 8.00
KK Kevin Kouzmanoff 4.00 10.00
KM Kyle McClellan S2 4.00 10.00
KS Kevin Slowey S2 6.00 15.00
LA Adam LaRoche 6.00 15.00
LB Lance Broadway S2 3.00 8.00
LC Luke Carlin S2 5.00 12.00
LJ John Lackey 5.00 12.00
LM Luis Mendoza S2 3.00 8.00
LS Luke Scott 3.00 8.00
MA Matt Chico 3.00 8.00
MA Michael Aubrey S2 5.00 12.00
MB Mitchell Boggs S2 10.00 25.00
MB Marlon Byrd 3.00 8.00
MC Matt Cain 6.00 15.00
ME Mark Ellis 3.00 8.00
ME Mark Ellis S2 3.00 8.00
MI Michael Bourn 4.00 10.00
ML Matt Lindstrom S2 3.00 8.00
MO Dustin Moseley 3.00 8.00
MR Mike Rabelo S2 3.00 8.00
MT Mark Teahen 4.00 10.00
MU David Murphy S2 3.00 8.00
NB Nick Blackburn S2 3.00 8.00
NL Noah Lowry S2 3.00 8.00
NM Nyjer Morgan S2 4.00 10.00
NM Nick Markakis 10.00 25.00
NS Nick Swisher 6.00 15.00
OW Micah Owings 3.00 8.00
PA Mike Parisi S2 3.00 8.00
PF Prince Fielder 6.00 15.00
RB Ryan Braun 6.00 15.00
RG Ryan Garko 3.00 8.00
RH Ramon Hernandez 6.00 15.00
RH Ramon Hernandez S2 6.00 15.00
RM Russell Martin S2 3.00 8.00
RO Ross Ohlendorf S2 5.00 12.00
RT Ramon Troncoso S2 5.00 12.00
RT Ryan Theriot 6.00 15.00
SD Stephen Drew 4.00 10.00
SH Steve Holm S2 3.00 8.00
SM Sean Marshall 4.00 10.00
SO Andy Sonnanstine 3.00 8.00
TB Taylor Buchholz 4.00 10.00
TG Tom Gorzelanny 20.00 50.00
UJ Ubaldo Jimenez 5.00 12.00
VR Vinny Rottino S2 3.00 8.00
WI Josh Willingham 3.00 8.00
WW Wesley Wright S2 3.00 8.00
XN Xavier Nady 3.00 8.00
YE Yunel Escobar 6.00 15.00

2009 Upper Deck Ken Griffey Jr. 1989 Buyback Gold
RANDOM INSERTS IN PACKS
NNO Ken Griffey Jr. 15.00 40.00

2009 Upper Deck O-Pee-Chee
ODDS 1:6 HOB,1:30 RET,1:90 BLAST
*MINI: 1X TO 2.5X BASIC
MINI ODDS 1:48 HOB,1:240 RET,1:720 BLAST
OPC1 Albert Pujols 1.50 4.00
OPC2 Alex Rodriguez 1.50 4.00
OPC3 Alfonso Soriano .75 2.00
OPC4 B.J. Upton .75 2.00
OPC5 Brandon Webb .75 2.00
OPC6 CC Sabathia .75 2.00
OPC7 Carl Crawford .75 2.00
OPC8 Carlos Beltran .75 2.00
OPC9 Carlos Quentin .50 1.25
OPC10 Chase Utley .75 2.00
OPC11 Chien-Ming Wang .75 2.00
OPC12 Chipper Jones 1.25 3.00
OPC13 Daisuke Matsuzaka .75 2.00
OPC14 David Ortiz 1.25 3.00
OPC15 David Wright 1.00 2.50
OPC16 Derek Jeter 3.00 8.00
OPC17 Derrek Lee .50 1.25
OPC18 Evan Longoria 3.00 8.00
OPC19 Felix Hernandez .75 2.00
OPC20 Frank Thomas 1.25 3.00
OPC21 Grady Sizemore .75 2.00
OPC22 Greg Maddux 1.50 4.00
OPC23 Hanley Ramirez .75 2.00
OPC24 Ichiro Suzuki 1.50 4.00
OPC25 Jake Peavy .50 1.25
OPC26 Jimmy Rollins .75 2.00
OPC27 Joba Chamberlain .50 1.25
OPC28 Joe Mauer 1.00 2.50
OPC29 Johan Santana .75 2.00
OPC30 John Smoltz 1.25 3.00
OPC31 Jose Reyes .75 2.00
OPC32 Josh Beckett .50 1.25
OPC33 Josh Hamilton .75 2.00
OPC34 Ken Griffey Jr. 2.50 6.00
OPC35 Kosuke Fukudome .75 2.00
OPC36 Lance Berkman .75 2.00
OPC37 Magglio Ordonez .75 2.00
OPC38 Manny Ramirez 1.25 3.00
OPC39 Mark Teixeira .75 2.00
OPC40 Matt Holliday 1.25 3.00
OPC41 Matt Kemp 1.00 2.50
OPC42 Miguel Cabrera 1.25 3.00
OPC43 Prince Fielder .75 2.00
OPC44 Randy Johnson 1.25 3.00
OPC45 Rick Ankiel .50 1.25
OPC46 Russell Martin .50 1.25
OPC47 Ryan Braun .75 2.00
OPC48 Ryan Howard 1.00 2.50
OPC49 Travis Hafner .50 1.25
OPC50 Vladimir Guerrero .75 2.00

2009 Upper Deck O-Pee-Chee 1977 Preview
RANDOM INSERTS IN PACKS
OPC1 Prince Fielder .75 2.00
OPC2 Russell Martin .50 1.25
OPC3 Vladimir Guerrero .75 2.00
OPC4 Joe Mauer 1.00 2.50
OPC5 Justin Morneau .75 2.00
OPC6 Dustin Pedroia 1.25 3.00
OPC7 Mark Teixeira .75 2.00
OPC8 Tim Lincecum .75 2.00
OPC9 Jimmy Rollins .75 2.00
OPC10 Carlos Lee .50 1.25
OPC11 Hanley Ramirez .75 2.00
OPC12 Chipper Jones 1.25 3.00
OPC13 Matt Holliday 1.25 3.00
OPC14 Travis Hafner .50 1.25
OPC15 Magglio Ordonez .75 2.00
OPC16 Carlos Quentin .50 1.25
OPC17 Derrek Lee .50 1.25
OPC18 Aramis Ramirez .50 1.25
OPC19 Randy Johnson 1.25 3.00
OPC20 Brandon Webb .75 2.00
OPC21 Josh Hamilton .75 2.00
OPC22 CC Sabathia .75 2.00
OPC23 Carlos Beltran .75 2.00
OPC24 Adrian Gonzalez 1.00 2.50
OPC25 Jake Peavy .50 1.25
OPC26 Matt Kemp 1.00 2.50
OPC27 Joba Chamberlain .50 1.25
OPC28 Jonathan Papelbon .75 2.00
OPC29 Carlos Zambrano .75 2.00
OPC30 Jay Bruce .75 2.00
OPC31 Albert Pujols 1.50 4.00
OPC32 Alex Rodriguez 1.50 4.00
OPC33 Alfonso Soriano .75 2.00
OPC34 Chase Utley .75 2.00
OPC35 Daisuke Matsuzaka .75 2.00
OPC36 David Ortiz 1.25 3.00
OPC37 David Wright 1.00 2.50
OPC38 Derek Jeter 3.00 8.00
OPC39 Evan Longoria .75 2.00
OPC40 Grady Sizemore .75 2.00
OPC41 Ichiro Suzuki 1.50 4.00
OPC42 Johan Santana .75 2.00
OPC43 Jose Reyes .75 2.00
OPC44 Josh Beckett .50 1.25
OPC45 Ken Griffey Jr. 2.50 6.00
OPC46 Lance Berkman .75 2.00
OPC47 Manny Ramirez 1.25 3.00
OPC48 Miguel Cabrera 1.25 3.00
OPC49 Ryan Braun .75 2.00
OPC50 Ryan Howard 1.00 2.50

2009 Upper Deck Rivals
ODDS 1:12 HOB,1:50 RET,1:240 BLAST
R1 Jose Reyes/Jimmy Rollins .75 2.00
R2 D.Ortiz/D.Jeter 3.00 8.00
R3 A.Pujols/D.Lee 1.50 4.00
R4 Russell Martin/Bengie Molina .50 1.25
R5 Travis Hafner/Jim Thome .75 2.00
R6 Carlos Zambrano/CC Sabathia .75 2.00
R7 D.Wright/A.Rodriguez 1.50 4.00
R8 Josh Beckett/Scott Kazmir .50 1.25
R9 Vladimir Guerrero/Manny Ramirez 1.25 3.00
R10 Carlos Quentin/Alfonso Soriano .75 2.00
R11 L.Berkman/A.Pujols 1.50 4.00
R12 A.Rodriguez/E.Longoria 1.50 4.00
R13 Jake Peavy/Chad Billingsley .75 2.00
R14 Brandon Webb/Matt Kemp 1.00 2.50
R15 Johan Santana/Chipper Jones 1.25 3.00
R16 Jim Thome/Justin Morneau .75 2.00
R17 M.Cabrera/J.Mauer 1.25 3.00
R18 Hanley Ramirez/Jose Reyes .75 2.00
R19 R.Halladay/J.Chamberlain .75 2.00
R20 Josh Hamilton/Roy Oswalt .75 2.00
R21 T.Lincecum/J.Cust .75 2.00
R22 A.Pujols/P.Fielder 1.50 4.00
R23 F.Rodriguez/I.Suzuki 1.50 4.00
R24 D.Matsuzaka/N.Markakis 1.00 2.50
R25 Grady Sizemore/Jay Bruce .75 2.00

2009 Upper Deck Stars of the Game
ODDS 1:12 HOB,1:50 RET,1:240 BLAST
GGAP Albert Pujols 1.50 4.00
GGAR Alex Rodriguez 1.50 4.00
GGAS Alfonso Soriano .75 2.00
GGBW Brandon Webb .75 2.00
GGCJ Chipper Jones 1.25 3.00
GGCS CC Sabathia .75 2.00
GGCU Chase Utley .75 2.00
GGDJ Derek Jeter 3.00 8.00
GGDO David Ortiz 1.25 3.00
GGDP Dustin Pedroia 1.25 3.00
GGDW David Wright 1.00 2.50
GGEL Evan Longoria .75 2.00
GGGS Grady Sizemore .75 2.00
GGHR Hanley Ramirez .75 2.00
GGIS Ichiro Suzuki 1.50 4.00
GGJH Josh Hamilton .75 2.00
GGJR Jose Reyes .75 2.00
GGJS Johan Santana .75 2.00
GGLB Lance Berkman .75 2.00
GGMC Miguel Cabrera 1.25 3.00
GGMR Manny Ramirez 1.25 3.00
GGRB Ryan Braun .75 2.00
GGRH Ryan Howard 1.00 2.50
GGTL Tim Lincecum .75 2.00
GGVG Vladimir Guerrero .75 2.00

2009 Upper Deck StarQuest Common Purple
STATED ODDS 2:1 FAT PACK
*SILVER: .4X TO 1X PURPLE
SILVER ODDS 1:4 RETAIL,3:1 SUPER
*BLUE: .4X TO 1X PURPLE
BLUE ODDS 1:8 RET,1:32 BLAST,1:3 SUP
*GOLD: .5X TO 1.2X PURPLE
GLD ODDS 1:12 RET,1:48 BLAST,1:4 SUP
*EMERALD: .75X TO 2X PURPLE
EMLD ODDS 1:24 RET,1:96 BLAST,1:8 SUP
*BLACK: 1.2X TO 3X PURPLE
BLK ODDS 1:48 RET,1:192 BLAST,1:12 SUP
SQ1 Albert Pujols 1.50 4.00
SQ2 Alex Rodriguez 1.50 4.00
SQ3 Alfonso Soriano .75 2.00
SQ4 Chipper Jones 1.25 3.00
SQ5 Chase Utley .75 2.00
SQ6 Derek Jeter 3.00 8.00
SQ7 Daisuke Matsuzaka .75 2.00
SQ8 David Ortiz 1.25 3.00
SQ9 David Wright 1.00 2.50
SQ10 Grady Sizemore .75 2.00
SQ11 Hanley Ramirez .75 2.00
SQ12 Ichiro Suzuki 1.50 4.00
SQ13 Josh Beckett .50 1.25
SQ14 Jake Peavy .50 1.25
SQ15 Jose Reyes .75 2.00
SQ16 Johan Santana .75 2.00
SQ17 Ken Griffey Jr. 2.50 6.00
SQ18 Lance Berkman .75 2.00
SQ19 Miguel Cabrera 1.25 3.00
SQ20 Matt Holliday 1.25 3.00
SQ21 Manny Ramirez 1.25 3.00
SQ22 Prince Fielder .75 2.00
SQ23 Ryan Braun .75 2.00
SQ24 Ryan Howard 1.00 2.50
SQ25 Vladimir Guerrero .75 2.00
SQ26 B.J. Upton .75 2.00
SQ27 Brandon Phillips .50 1.25
SQ28 Brandon Webb .75 2.00
SQ29 Brian McCann .75 2.00
SQ30 Carl Crawford .75 2.00
SQ31 Carlos Beltran .75 2.00
SQ32 Carlos Quentin .50 1.25
SQ33 Chien-Ming Wang .75 2.00
SQ34 Cliff Lee .75 2.00
SQ35 Cole Hamels 1.00 2.50
SQ36 Curtis Granderson 1.00 2.50
SQ37 David Price 1.00 2.50
SQ38 Dustin Pedroia 1.25 3.00
SQ39 Evan Longoria .75 2.00
SQ40 Francisco Liriano .50 1.25
SQ41 Geovany Soto .75 2.00
SQ42 Ian Kinsler .75 2.00
SQ43 Jay Bruce .75 2.00
SQ44 Jimmy Rollins .75 2.00
SQ45 Jonathan Papelbon .75 2.00
SQ46 Josh Hamilton .75 2.00
SQ47 Justin Morneau .75 2.00
SQ48 Kevin Youkilis .50 1.25
SQ49 Nick Markakis 1.00 2.50
SQ50 Tim Lincecum .75 2.00

2009 Upper Deck StarQuest Turquoise
*TURQUOISE: .4X TO 1X PURPLE

2009 Upper Deck UD Game Jersey
STATED ODDS 1:19 HOB,1:24 RET,1:9 BLAST
GJAD Adam Dunn 2.50 6.00
GJAE Andre Ethier 2.50 6.00
GJAG Adrian Gonzalez 3.00 8.00
GJAH Aaron Harang 1.50 4.00
GJAI Akinori Iwamura 1.50 4.00
GJAN Rick Ankiel 1.50 4.00
GJAP Albert Pujols 5.00 12.00
GJAR Aaron Rowand 1.50 4.00
GJAS Alfonso Soriano 2.50 6.00
GJBA Rocco Baldelli Pants 1.50 4.00
GJBE Josh Beckett 1.50 4.00
GJBH Bill Hall 1.50 4.00
GJBM Brian McCann 2.50 6.00
GJBP Brandon Phillips 1.50 4.00
GJBR Brian Bass 1.50 4.00
GJBU B.J. Upton 2.50 6.00
GJBW Billy Wagner 1.50 4.00
GJCB Chad Billingsley 2.50 6.00
GJCD Chris Duncan 1.50 4.00
GJCH Chin-Lung Hu 1.50 4.00
GJCJ Chipper Jones 4.00 10.00
GJCL Clay Buchholz 1.50 4.00
GJCO Corey Hart 1.50 4.00
GJCS CC Sabathia 2.50 6.00
GJCT Clay Timpner 1.50 4.00
GJCW Chien-Ming Wang 2.50 6.00
GJDA Johnny Damon 2.50 6.00
GJDB Daric Barton 1.50 4.00
GJDH Dan Haren 1.50 4.00
GJDJ Derek Jeter 10.00 25.00
GJDL Derrek Lee 1.50 4.00
GJDM David Murphy 1.50 4.00
GJDO David Ortiz 4.00 10.00
GJDU Dan Uggla 1.50 4.00
GJGA Garrett Atkins 1.50 4.00
GJGM Greg Maddux 5.00 12.00
GJGO Alex Gordon 2.50 6.00
GJGR Curtis Granderson 3.00 8.00
GJGS Grady Sizemore 2.50 6.00
GJHA Cole Hamels 3.00 8.00
GJHI Aaron Hill 1.50 4.00
GJHJ Josh Hamilton 2.50 6.00
GJIK Ian Kennedy 1.50 4.00
GJJA Conor Jackson 1.50 4.00
GJJD J.D. Drew 1.50 4.00
GJJF Jeff Francis 1.50 4.00
GJJG Jeremy Guthrie 1.50 4.00
GJJH Jeremy Hermida 1.50 4.00
GJJJ Josh Johnson 2.50 6.00
GJJL James Loney 1.50 4.00
GJJM John Maine 1.50 4.00
GJJN Joe Nathan 1.50 4.00
GJJO John Lackey 2.50 6.00
GJJP Jake Peavy 1.50 4.00
GJJT J.R. Towles 1.50 4.00
GJJU Justin Upton 2.50 6.00
GJJV Jason Varitek 4.00 10.00
GJJW Josh Willingham 2.50 6.00
GJKG Ken Griffey Jr. 10.00 25.00
GJKI Ian Kinsler 2.50 6.00
GJKK Kevin Kouzmanoff 1.50 4.00
GJKY Kevin Youkilis 1.50 4.00
GJLA A.LaRoche UER 1.50 4.00
GJMC Matt Cain 2.50 6.00
GJMK Matt Kemp 3.00 8.00
GJMT Mark Teahen 1.50 4.00
GJNB Nick Blackburn 1.50 4.00
GJNM Nick Markakis 3.00 8.00
GJNS Nick Swisher 2.50 6.00
GJPA Jonathan Papelbon 2.50 6.00
GJPB Pat Burrell 1.50 4.00
GJPE Jhonny Peralta 1.50 4.00
GJPH Phil Hughes 1.50 4.00
GJPK Paul Konerko 2.50 6.00
GJRA Aramis Ramirez 1.50 4.00
GJRB Ryan Braun 2.50 6.00
GJRF Rafael Furcal 1.50 4.00
GJRH Rich Harden 1.50 4.00
GJRM Russell Martin 1.50 4.00
GJRO Roy Halladay 2.50 6.00
GJRW Rickie Weeks 1.50 4.00
GJRZ Ryan Zimmerman 2.50 6.00
GJSA Jarrod Saltalamacchia 1.50 4.00
GJSM Greg Smith 1.50 4.00
GJSO Joakim Soria 1.50 4.00
GJSP Scott Podsednik 1.50 4.00
GJTG Tom Glavine 2.50 6.00
GJTH Tim Hudson 2.50 6.00
GJTR Travis Hafner 1.50 4.00
GJTT Troy Tulowitzki 4.00 10.00
GJVM Victor Martinez 2.50 6.00
GJWE Jered Weaver 2.50 6.00

2009 Upper Deck UD Game Jersey Autographs
RANDOM INSERTS IN PACKS
PRINT RUNS B/WN 5-99 COPIES PER
NO PRICING ON QTY 25 OR LESS
GJAG Adrian Gonzalez/99 12.50 30.00
GJAH Aaron Harang/99 5.00 12.00
GJAK Austin Kearns/99 5.00 12.00
GJBM Brian McCann/99 10.00 25.00
GJBP Brandon Phillips/99 12.50 30.00
GJBR Brian Bass/99 5.00 12.00
GJBW Billy Wagner/35 10.00 25.00
GJCB Chad Billingsley/99 10.00 25.00
GJCD Chris Duncan/99 12.50 30.00
GJCH Chin-Lung Hu/99 12.50 30.00
GJCO Corey Hart/99 15.00 40.00
GJDB Daric Barton/99 6.00 15.00
GJGA Garrett Atkins/99 5.00 12.00
GJGO Alex Gordon/49 8.00 20.00
GJHJ Josh Hamilton/99 15.00 40.00
GJIK Ian Kennedy/35 5.00 12.00
GJJA Conor Jackson/49 8.00 20.00
GJJH Jeremy Hermida/99 6.00 15.00
GJJL James Loney/99 10.00 25.00
GJJN Joe Nathan/99 6.00 15.00
GJJO John Lackey/99 6.00 15.00
GJJT J.R. Towles/99 5.00 12.00
GJJW Josh Willingham/99 5.00 12.00
GJKG Ken Griffey Jr./99 50.00 100.00
GJKI Ian Kinsler/99 8.00 20.00
GJKK Kevin Kouzmanoff/99 5.00 12.00
GJKY Kevin Youkilis/99 20.00 50.00
GJLA Adam LaRoche/99 6.00 15.00
GJMC Matt Cain/99 15.00 40.00
GJMK Matt Kemp/25 20.00 50.00
GJMM Melvin Mora/99 5.00 12.00
GJMT Mark Teahen/99 6.00 15.00
GJNB Nick Blackburn/99 10.00 25.00
GJNM Nick Markakis/99 12.50 30.00
GJNS Nick Swisher/99 6.00 15.00
GJRM Russell Martin/35 10.00 25.00
GJRZ Ryan Zimmerman/50 12.50 30.00
GJSA Jarrod Saltalamacchia/99 5.00 12.00
GJSM Greg Smith/99 6.00 15.00
GJTR Travis Hafner/99 6.00 15.00
GJTT Troy Tulowitzki/99 6.00 15.00

2009 Upper Deck UD Game Jersey Dual
RANDOM INSERTS IN PACKS
PRINT RUNS B/WN 37-149 COPIES PER
GJAD Adam Dunn/149 4.00 10.00
GJAE Andre Ethier/149 4.00 10.00
GJAG Adrian Gonzalez/149 4.00 10.00
GJAH Aaron Harang/149 4.00 10.00
GJAI Akinori Iwamura/88 4.00 10.00
GJAN Rick Ankiel/149 5.00 12.00
GJAP Albert Pujols/149 10.00 25.00
GJAR Aaron Rowand/149 4.00 10.00
GJAS Alfonso Soriano/149 4.00 10.00
GJBA Rocco Baldelli/50 3.00 8.00
GJBM Brian McCann/149 4.00 10.00
GJBP Brandon Phillips/149 3.00 8.00
GJBR Brian Bass/149 3.00 8.00
GJBU B.J. Upton/149 3.00 8.00
GJBW Billy Wagner/149 5.00 12.00
GJCB Chad Billingsley/149 4.00 10.00
GJCC Carl Crawford/149 3.00 8.00
GJCD Chris Duncan/148 4.00 10.00
GJCH Chin-Lung Hu/149 4.00 10.00
GJCJ Chipper Jones/149 5.00 12.00
GJCL Clay Buchholz/149 4.00 10.00
GJCS CC Sabathia/149 3.00 8.00
GJCW Chien-Ming Wang/149 6.00 15.00
GJDB Daric Barton/149 4.00 10.00
GJDH Dan Haren/149 3.00 8.00
GJDJ Derek Jeter/139 12.50 30.00
GJDL Derrek Lee/149 3.00 8.00
GJDO David Ortiz/149 3.00 8.00
GJDU Dan Uggla/149 3.00 8.00
GJGO Alex Gordon/149 5.00 12.00
GJGR Curtis Granderson/149 4.00 10.00
GJHA Cole Hamels/149 6.00 15.00
GJHJ Josh Hamilton/149 10.00 25.00
GJIK Ian Kennedy/149 3.00 8.00
GJJA Conor Jackson/149 3.00 8.00
GJJD J.D. Drew/112 4.00 10.00
GJJF Jeff Francis/149 3.00 8.00
GJJG Jeremy Guthrie/149 3.00 8.00
GJJH Jeremy Hermida/149 3.00 8.00
GJJJ Josh Johnson/149 3.00 8.00
GJJL James Loney/149 5.00 12.00
GJJM John Maine/149 5.00 12.00
GJJN Joe Nathan/149 3.00 8.00
GJJO John Lackey/149 3.00 8.00
GJJT J.R. Towles/149 3.00 8.00
GJJU Justin Upton/149 5.00 12.00
GJJV Jason Varitek/149 5.00 12.00
GJJW Josh Willingham/149 3.00 8.00
GJKG Ken Griffey Jr./50 12.50 30.00
GJKI Ian Kinsler/75 3.00 8.00
GJKK Kevin Kouzmanoff/149 3.00 8.00
GJKY Kevin Youkilis/149 5.00 12.00
GJLA Adam LaRoche/75 5.00 12.00
GJMC Matt Cain/149 4.00 10.00
GJMK Matt Kemp/149 4.00 10.00
GJMM Melvin Mora/149 3.00 8.00
GJMT Mark Teahen/149 3.00 8.00
GJNB Nick Blackburn/149 3.00 8.00
GJNM Nick Markakis/149 4.00 10.00
GJPA Jonathan Papelbon/149 4.00 10.00
GJPB Pat Burrell/37 15.00 40.00
GJPE Jhonny Peralta/125 3.00 8.00
GJPH Phil Hughes/149 4.00 10.00
GJPK Paul Konerko/149 4.00 10.00
GJRA Aramis Ramirez/149 3.00 8.00
GJRB Ryan Braun/149 6.00 15.00
GJRF Rafael Furcal/149 4.00 10.00
GJRH Rich Harden/149 3.00 8.00
GJRM Russell Martin/149 5.00 12.00
GJRO Roy Halladay/50 6.00 15.00
GJRW Rickie Weeks/149 3.00 8.00
GJRZ Ryan Zimmerman/149 3.00 8.00
GJSO Joakim Soria/75 4.00 10.00
GJSP Scott Podsednik/149 3.00 8.00
GJTH Tim Hudson/149 5.00 12.00
GJTT Troy Tulowitzki/149 5.00 12.00
GJWE Jered Weaver/149 3.00 8.00

2009 Upper Deck UD Game Jersey Triple
RANDOM INSERTS IN PACKS
PRINT RUNS B/WN 15-100 COPIES PER
NO PRICING ON QTY 25 OR LESS
GJAD Adam Dunn/99 5.00 12.00
GJAG Adrian Gonzalez/99 5.00 12.00
GJAH Aaron Harang/99 5.00 12.00
GJAN Rick Ankiel/99 6.00 15.00
GJAP Albert Pujols/99 6.00 15.00
GJAS Alfonso Soriano/79 5.00 12.00
GJBH Bill Hall/73 4.00 10.00
GJBM Brian McCann/99 5.00 12.00
GJBR Brian Bass/65 4.00 10.00
GJBU B.J. Upton/99 4.00 10.00
GJCB Chad Billingsley/99 5.00 12.00
GJCC Carl Crawford/99 4.00 10.00
GJCD Chris Duncan/99 5.00 12.00
GJCH Chin-Lung Hu/99 5.00 12.00
GJCJ Chipper Jones/99 8.00 20.00
GJCO Corey Hart/63 5.00 12.00
GJCS CC Sabathia/99 6.00 15.00
GJCW Chien-Ming Wang/99 8.00 20.00
GJDB Daric Barton/99 5.00 12.00
GJDH Dan Haren/99 4.00 10.00
GJDJ Derek Jeter/69 15.00 40.00
GJDO David Ortiz/99 6.00 15.00
GJGA Garrett Atkins/99 4.00 10.00
GJGO Alex Gordon/99 6.00 15.00
GJGR Curtis Granderson/99 5.00 12.00
GJGS Grady Sizemore/99 5.00 12.00
GJHI Aaron Hill/44 5.00 12.00
GJHJ Josh Hamilton/83 12.50 30.00
GJIK Ian Kennedy/99 4.00 10.00
GJJA Conor Jackson/99 4.00 10.00
GJJD J.D. Drew/58 5.00 12.00
GJJF Jeff Francis/99 4.00 10.00
GJJG Jeremy Guthrie/99 4.00 10.00
GJJH Jeremy Hermida/99 4.00 10.00
GJJL James Loney/99 5.00 12.00
GJJM John Maine/99 6.00 15.00
GJJN Joe Nathan/99 4.00 10.00
GJJT J.R. Towles/99 4.00 10.00
GJJU Justin Upton/99 6.00 15.00
GJJV Jason Varitek/66 6.00 15.00
GJKI Ian Kinsler/43 4.00 10.00
GJKK Kevin Kouzmanoff/99 4.00 10.00
GJKY Kevin Youkilis/99 6.00 15.00
GJMC Matt Cain/99 5.00 12.00
GJMK Matt Kemp/99 5.00 12.00
GJMT Mark Teahen/99 4.00 10.00
GJNB Nick Blackburn/91 4.00 10.00
GJNM Nick Markakis/100 5.00 12.00
GJPA Jonathan Papelbon/100 5.00 12.00
GJPE Jhonny Peralta/53 4.00 10.00
GJPH Phil Hughes/66 5.00 12.00
GJPK Paul Konerko/83 5.00 12.00
GJRA Aramis Ramirez/99 4.00 10.00
GJRB Ryan Braun/99 8.00 20.00
GJRH Rich Harden/99 4.00 10.00
GJRM Russell Martin/99 6.00 15.00
GJRW Rickie Weeks/99 4.00 10.00
GJRZ Ryan Zimmerman/99 4.00 10.00
GJSM Greg Smith/66 4.00 10.00
GJSO Joakim Soria/50 5.00 12.00
GJSP Scott Podsednik/65 4.00 10.00
GJTH Tim Hudson/50 6.00 15.00
GJTR Travis Hafner/99 5.00 12.00
GJTT Troy Tulowitzki/99 6.00 15.00
GJWE Jered Weaver/66 4.00 10.00

2009 Upper Deck UD Game Materials
RANDOM INSERTS IN PACKS
GMAH Aaron Harang 3.00 8.00
GMAJ Andruw Jones 2.50 6.00
GMAP Albert Pujols 6.00 15.00
GMAR Alex Romero 2.50 6.00
GMBA Josh Barfield 2.50 6.00
GMBB Brian Bocock 2.50 6.00
GMBC Bartolo Colon 2.50 6.00
GMBH Bill Hall 2.50 6.00
GMBI Brandon Inge 2.50 6.00
GMBM Brian McCann 3.00 8.00
GMBP Brandon Phillips 3.00 8.00
GMCB Chris Burke 2.50 6.00
GMCD Carlos Delgado 3.00 8.00
GMCH Chin-Lung Hu 2.50 6.00
GMCL Carlos Lee 2.50 6.00
GMCM Colt Morton 2.50 6.00
GMCR Bobby Crosby 2.50 6.00
GMCY Chris Young 3.00 8.00
GMDB Daric Barton 2.50 6.00
GMDE Darin Erstad 2.50 6.00
GMDL Derrek Lee 2.50 6.00
GMDM Daisuke Matsuzaka 3.00 8.00
GMDU Chris Duncan 2.50 6.00
GMEC Eric Chavez 2.50 6.00
GMED Jim Edmonds 3.00 8.00
GMEG Eric Gagne 2.50 6.00
GMFH Felix Hernandez 4.00 10.00
GMFS Freddy Sanchez 2.50 6.00
GMHB Hank Blalock 2.50 6.00
GMHE Ramon Hernandez 2.50 6.00
GMHI Hernan Iribarren 2.50 6.00
GMHK Hong-Chih Kuo 2.50 6.00
GMIK Ian Kinsler 3.00 8.00
GMJB Jason Bay 4.00 10.00
GMJE Jeff Baker 2.50 6.00
GMJG Jason Giambi 3.00 8.00
GMJH Josh Hamilton 3.00 8.00
GMJK Jason Kubel 2.50 6.00
GMJP Jhonny Peralta 2.50 6.00
GMJW Jake Westbrook 2.50 6.00
GMKG Ken Griffey Jr. 6.00 15.00
GMKJ Kelly Johnson 2.50 6.00
GMKM Kendry Morales 2.50 6.00
GMLM Lastings Milledge 2.50 6.00
GMMK Matt Kemp 15.00 40.00
GMMM Melvin Mora 2.50 6.00
GMMP Mark Prior 2.50 6.00
GMMN Nyjer Morgan 2.50 6.00
GMPK Paul Konerko 2.50 6.00
GMRA Aramis Ramirez 3.00 8.00
GMRB Rocco Baldelli 2.50 6.00
GMRF Rafael Furcal 3.00 8.00
GMTG Troy Glaus 2.50 6.00
GMTT Troy Tulowitzki 2.50 6.00
GMTW Tim Wakefield 3.00 8.00
GMUG Dan Uggla 2.50 6.00
GMVM Victor Martinez 3.00 8.00
GMYE Yunel Escobar 2.50 6.00
GMYG Yovani Gallardo 2.50 6.00
GMZG Zack Greinke 4.00 10.00

2009 Upper Deck UD Game Materials Autographs
RANDOM INSERTS IN PACKS
PRINT RUNS B/WN 5-99 COPIES PER
GMAH Aaron Harang/76 5.00 12.00
GMAR Alex Romero/72 4.00 10.00
GMBA Josh Barfield/69 4.00 10.00
GMBB Brian Bocock/61 4.00 10.00
GMBH Bill Hall/99 6.00 15.00
GMBM Brian McCann/71 15.00 40.00
GMBP Brandon Phillips/99 8.00 20.00
GMCB Chad Billingsley/99 15.00 40.00
GMCH Chin-Lung Hu/99 5.00 12.00
GMCM Colt Morton/99 4.00 10.00
GMDB Daric Barton/99 6.00 15.00
GMDU Chris Duncan/99 6.00 15.00
GMJE Jeff Baker/99 4.00 10.00
GMJS Jarrod Saltalamacchia/99 4.00 10.00
GMKJ Kelly Johnson/99 6.00 15.00
GMMK Matt Kemp/99 10.00 25.00
GMMM Melvin Mora/99 6.00 15.00
GMNM Nyjer Morgan/99 4.00 10.00
GMYG Yovani Gallardo/99 10.00 25.00

2009 Upper Deck USA 18U National Team
ODDS 1:3 HOB,1:6 RET,1:200 BLAST
18UAA Andrew Aplin .75 2.00
18UAM Austin Maddox 1.25 3.00
18UCC Colton Cain 1.25 3.00
18UCG Cameron Garfield .75 2.00
18UCT Cecil Tanner .75 2.00
18UDN David Nick 1.25 3.00
18UDT Donavan Tate 1.25 3.00
18UFO Nolan Fontana 1.25 3.00
18UHM Harold Martinez 1.25 3.00
18UJB Jake Barrett .75 2.00
18UJM Jeff Malm .75 2.00
18UJT Jacob Turner 3.00 8.00
18UME Jonathan Meyer .75 2.00
18UMP Matthew Purke .75 2.00
18UMS Max Stassi 1.25 3.00
18UNF Nick Franklin 2.00 5.00
18URW Ryan Weber .75 2.00
18UWH Wes Hatton .75 2.00

2009 Upper Deck USA 18U National Team Jersey
STATED ODDS 1:96 HOB,1:1715 RET,1:3163 BLAST
18UAA Andrew Aplin 4.00 10.00
18UAM Austin Maddox 4.00 10.00
18UCC Colton Cain 2.50 6.00
18UCG Cameron Garfield 4.00 10.00
18UCT Cecil Tanner 2.50 6.00
18UDN David Nick 2.50 6.00
18UDT Donavan Tate 4.00 10.00
18UFO Nolan Fontana 4.00 10.00
18UHM Harold Martinez 4.00 10.00
18UJB Jake Barrett 2.50 6.00
18UJM Jeff Malm 2.50 6.00
18UJT Jacob Turner 4.00 10.00
18UME Jonathan Meyer 2.50 6.00
18UMP Matthew Purke 4.00 10.00
18UMS Max Stassi 4.00 10.00
18UNF Nick Franklin 2.50 6.00
18URW Ryan Weber 2.50 6.00
18UWH Wes Hatton 4.00 10.00

2009 Upper Deck USA National Team
RANDOM INSERTS IN PACKS
AG A.J. Griffin 1.25 3.00
AO Andrew Oliver .75 2.00
BS Blake Smith .75 2.00
CC Christian Colon 1.25 3.00
CH Chris Hernandez .75 2.00
DD Derek Dietrich 2.00 5.00
HM Hunter Morris .75 2.00
JC Jared Clark .75 2.00
JF Josh Fellhauer .75 2.00
KD Kentrail Davis 1.25 3.00
KG Kyle Gibson 2.00 5.00
KV Kendal Volz 1.25 3.00
MD Matt den Dekker 1.25 3.00
MG Micah Gibbs .75 2.00
ML Mike Leake 2.50 6.00
MM Mike Minor 1.25 3.00
RJ Ryan Jackson .75 2.00
RL Ryan Lipkin .75 2.00
SS Stephen Strasburg 4.00 10.00
SW Scott Woodward .75 2.00
TL Tyler Lyons 1.25 3.00
TM Tommy Mendonca .75 2.00

2009 Upper Deck USA National Team Autographs
RANDOM INSERTS IN PACKS

AG A.J. Griffin 3.00 8.00
AO Andrew Oliver 3.00 8.00
BS Blake Smith 3.00 8.00
CC Christian Colon 4.00 10.00
CH Chris Hernandez 3.00 8.00
DD Derek Dietrich 8.00 20.00
HM Hunter Morris 3.00 8.00
JF Josh Fellhauer 3.00 8.00
KD Kentrail Davis 4.00 10.00
KV Kendal Volz 3.00 8.00
MD Matt den Dekker 4.00 10.00
MG Micah Gibbs 4.00 10.00
ML Mike Leake 6.00 15.00
MM Mike Minor 4.00 10.00
RJ Ryan Jackson 3.00 8.00
RL Ryan Lipkin 3.00 8.00
TL Tyler Lyons 3.00 8.00

2009 Upper Deck USA National Team Jerseys

AG A.J. Griffin 3.00 8.00
AO Andrew Oliver 3.00 8.00
BS Blake Smith 3.00 8.00
CC Christian Colon 3.00 8.00
CH Chris Hernandez 3.00 8.00
DD Derek Dietrich 3.00 8.00
HM Hunter Morris 3.00 8.00
JF Josh Fellhauer 3.00 8.00
KD Kentrail Davis 3.00 8.00
KG Kyle Gibson 3.00 8.00
KR Kevin Rhoderick 3.00 8.00
KV Kendal Volz 3.00 8.00
MD Matt den Dekker 3.00 8.00
MG Micah Gibbs 3.00 8.00
ML Mike Leake 4.00 10.00
MM Mike Minor 3.00 8.00
RJ Ryan Jackson 3.00 8.00
RL Ryan Lipkin 3.00 8.00
SS Stephen Strasburg 5.00 12.00
TL Tyler Lyons 3.00 8.00

2009 Upper Deck USA National Team Jersey Autographs

RANDOM INSERTS IN PACKS
STATED PRINT RUN 225 SER.#'d SETS
AG A.J. Griffin 4.00 10.00
AO Andrew Oliver 4.00 10.00
BS Blake Smith 6.00 15.00
CC Christian Colon 8.00 20.00
CH Chris Hernandez 5.00 12.00
DD Derek Dietrich 8.00 20.00
HM Hunter Morris 5.00 12.00
JF Josh Fellhauer 5.00 12.00
KD Kentrail Davis 4.00 10.00
KG Kyle Gibson 15.00 40.00
KR Kevin Rhoderick 4.00 10.00
KV Kendal Volz 4.00 10.00
MD Matt den Dekker 4.00 10.00
MG Micah Gibbs 4.00 10.00
ML Mike Leake 4.00 10.00
MM Mike Minor 6.00 12.00
RJ Ryan Jackson 4.00 10.00
RL Ryan Lipkin 4.00 10.00
SS Stephen Strasburg 40.00 100.00
TL Tyler Lyons 4.00 10.00

2009 Upper Deck USA National Team Retrospective

ODDS 1:8 HOB,1:36 RET,1:108 BLAST
USA1 Matt Brown .75 2.00
USA2 Stephen Strasburg 4.00 10.00
USA3 Jayson Nix .75 2.00
USA4 Brian Duensing 1.25 3.00
USA5 Jake Arrieta 2.00 5.00
USA6 Dexter Fowler 1.25 3.00
USA7 Casey Weathers .75 2.00
USA8 Mike Koplove .75 2.00
USA9 Jason Donald .75 2.00
USA10 Taylor Teagarden .75 2.00
USA11 Kevin Jepsen .75 2.00
USA12 Matt LaPorta 1.25 3.00
USA13 Team USA Wins Bronze Medal .75 2.00
USA14 Team USA Wins Third Olympic Medal .75 2.00

2010 Upper Deck

COMPLETE SET (609) 25.00 60.00
COMMON CARD (2-40) .50 1.25
COMMON CARD (1/41-600) .15 .40
C EQUALS COMMON VARIATION
R EQUALS RARE VARIATION
S EQUALS SUPER RARE VARIATION
U EQUALS ULTRA RARE VARIATION
1 Star Rookie CL .15 .40
2 Daniel McCutchen RC .75 2.00
3 Eric Young Jr. (RC) .50 1.25
4 Michael Brantley RC .75 2.00
5 Brian Matusz RC 1.25 3.00
6 Ian Desmond (RC) .75 2.00
7 Carlos Carrasco (RC) 1.25 3.00
8 Dustin Richardson RC .50 1.25
9 Tyler Flowers RC .75 2.00
10 Drew Stubbs RC 1.25 3.00
11 Reid Gorecki (RC) .75 2.00
12 Tommy Manzella (RC) .50 1.25
13 Wade Davis (RC) .75 2.00
14 Esmil Rogers RC .50 1.25
15 Michael Dunn RC .50 1.25
16 Luis Durango RC .50 1.25
17 Juan Francisco RC .75 2.00
18 Ernesto Frieri RC .50 1.25
19 Tyler Colvin RC .75 2.00
20 Armando Gabino RC .50 1.25
21 Adam Moore RC .50 1.25
22 Cesar Ramos (RC) .50 1.25
23 Chris Johnson RC .75 2.00
24 Chris Pettit RC .50 1.25
25 Brandon Allen (RC) .50 1.25
26 Brad Kilby RC .50 1.25
27 Dusty Hughes RC .50 1.25
28 Buster Posey RC 4.00 10.00
29 Kevin Richardson (RC) .50 1.25
30 Josh Thole RC .75 2.00
31 John Hester RC .50 1.25
32 Kyle Phillips RC .50 1.25
33 Neil Walker (RC) .75 2.00
34 Matt Carson (RC) .50 1.25
35 Pedro Strop RC 1.25 3.00
36 Pedro Viola RC .50 1.25
37 Daniel Runzler RC .75 2.00
38 Henry Rodriguez RC .50 1.25
39 Justin Turner RC 4.00 10.00
40 Madison Bumgarner RC 5.00 12.00
41 Chris B. Young .15 .40
42A Justin Upton .25 .60
43 Conor Jackson .15 .40
44 Augie Ojeda .15 .40
45 Mark Reynolds .15 .40
46 Miguel Montero .15 .40
47 Max Scherzer .40 1.00
48 Doug Slaten .15 .40
49 Chad Qualls .15 .40
50 Dan Haren .15 .40
51 Juan Gutierrez .15 .40
52 Doug Davis .15 .40
53 Leo Rosales .15 .40
54 Chad Tracy .15 .40
55 Stephen Drew .15 .40
56 Jordan Schafer .15 .40
57 Rafael Soriano .15 .40
58 Javier Vazquez .15 .40
59 Brandon Jones .15 .40
60 Matt Diaz .15 .40
61 Jair Jurrjens .15 .40
62 Adam LaRoche .15 .40
63 Martin Prado .15 .40
64 Omar Infante .15 .40
65 Chipper Jones .40 1.00
66A Yunel Escobar .15 .40
67 David Ross .15 .40
68 Derek Lowe .15 .40
69 James Parr .15 .40
70 Kenshin Kawakami .25 .60
71 Kris Medlen .25 .60
72 Ryan Church .15 .40
73 Nate McLouth .15 .40
74 Adam Jones .25 .60
75 Luke Scott .15 .40
76 Nolan Reimold .15 .40
77 Felix Pie .15 .40
78 Lou Montanez .15 .40
79 Ty Wigginton .15 .40
80 Cesar Izturis .15 .40
81 Robert Andino .15 .40
82 Chad Moeller .15 .40
83A Koji Uehara .15 .40
84 Matt Wieters .40 1.00
85 Jim Johnson .15 .40
86 Chris Ray .15 .40
87 Danys Baez .15 .40
88 David Hernandez .15 .40
89 Jeremy Guthrie .15 .40
90 Rich Hill .15 .40
91 Dustin Pedroia .40 1.00
92 David Ortiz .40 1.00
93 J.D. Drew .15 .40
94 Jeff Bailey .15 .40
95 Kevin Youkilis .15 .40
96 Clay Buchholz .15 .40
97 Jed Lowrie .15 .40
98 Mike Lowell .15 .40
99 George Kottaras .15 .40
100 Takashi Saito .15 .40
101 Hideki Okajima .15 .40
102 Jason Varitek .40 1.00
103 Jon Lester .25 .60
104A Josh Beckett .15 .40
105 Daniel Bard .15 .40
106 Jonathan Papelbon .25 .60
107 Nick Green .15 .40
108 Kevin Gregg .15 .40
109A Ryan Theriot .15 .40
110A Kosuke Fukudome .25 .60
111 Derrek Lee .15 .40
112 Bobby Scales .15 .40
113 Aramis Ramirez .15 .40
114 Aaron Miles .15 .40
115 Mike Fontenot .15 .40
116 Koyie Hill .15 .40
117 Carlos Zambrano .25 .60
118 Jeff Samardzija .15 .40
119 Randy Wells .15 .40
120 Sean Marshall .15 .40
121 Carlos Marmol .25 .60
122 Ryan Dempster .15 .40
123 Reed Johnson .15 .40
124 Jake Fox .15 .40
125 Tony Pena .15 .40
126 Carlos Quentin .15 .40
127 A.J. Pierzynski .15 .40
128 Scott Podsednik .15 .40
129A Alexei Ramirez .25 .60
130 Paul Konerko .25 .60
131 Josh Fields .15 .40
132 Alex Rios .15 .40
133 Matt Thornton .15 .40
134 Mark Buehrle .25 .60
135 Scott Linebrink .15 .40
136 Freddy Garcia .15 .40
137 John Danks .15 .40
138 Bobby Jenks .15 .40
139 Gavin Floyd .15 .40
140 DJ Carrasco .15 .40
141 Jake Peavy .15 .40
142 Justin Lehr .15 .40
143 Wladimir Balentien .15 .40
144 Laynce Nix .15 .40
145 Chris Dickerson .15 .40
146A Joey Votto .40 1.00
147 Paul Janish .15 .40
148 Brandon Phillips .15 .40
149 Scott Rolen .25 .60
150 Ryan Hanigan .15 .40
151 Edinson Volquez .15 .40
152 Arthur Rhodes .15 .40
153 Micah Owings .15 .40
154 Ramon Hernandez .15 .40
155 Francisco Cordero .15 .40
156 Bronson Arroyo .15 .40
157 Jared Burton .15 .40
158 Homer Bailey .15 .40
159 Travis Hafner .15 .40
160 Grady Sizemore .25 .60
161 Matt LaPorta .15 .40
162 Jeremy Sowers .15 .40
163 Trevor Crowe .15 .40
164 Asdrubal Cabrera .25 .60
165A Shin-Soo Choo .25 .60
166 Kelly Shoppach .15 .40
167 Kerry Wood .15 .40
168 Jake Westbrook .15 .40
169 Fausto Carmona .15 .40
170 Aaron Laffey .15 .40
171 Justin Masterson .15 .40
172 Jhonny Peralta .15 .40
173 Jensen Lewis .15 .40
174 Luis Valbuena .15 .40
175 Jason Giambi .15 .40
176 Ryan Spilborghs .15 .40
177 Seth Smith .15 .40
178 Matt Murton .15 .40
179 Dexter Fowler .25 .60
180A Troy Tulowitzki .40 1.00
181 Ian Stewart .15 .40
182 Omar Quintanilla .15 .40
183 Clint Barmes .15 .40
184 Garrett Atkins .15 .40
185 Chris Iannetta .15 .40
186 Huston Street .15 .40
187 Franklin Morales .15 .40
188 Todd Helton .25 .60
189 Carlos Gonzalez .25 .60
190 Aaron Cook .15 .40
191 Jason Hammel .25 .60
192 Edwin Jackson .15 .40
193 Clete Thomas .15 .40
194 Marcus Thames .15 .40
195 Ryan Raburn .15 .40
196 Fernando Rodney .15 .40
197 Adam Everett .15 .40
198A Brandon Inge .25 .60
199 Miguel Cabrera .40 1.00
200 Gerald Laird .15 .40
201 Joel Zumaya .15 .40
202 Curtis Granderson .30 .75
203 Justin Verlander .40 1.00
204 Bobby Seay .15 .40
205 Nate Robertson .15 .40
206 Rick Porcello .25 .60
207 Ryan Perry .15 .40
208 Fu-Te Ni .25 .60
209 Cody Ross .15 .40
210 Jeremy Hermida .15 .40
211 Alfredo Amezaga .15 .40
212A Chris Coghlan .15 .40
213 Wes Helms .15 .40
214 Emilio Bonifacio .15 .40
215 Ricky Nolasco .15 .40
216 Anibal Sanchez .15 .40
217 Josh Johnson .25 .60
218 Burke Badenhop .15 .40
219 Kiko Calero .15 .40
220 Renyel Pinto .15 .40
221 Andrew Miller .25 .60
222 Hanley Ramirez .25 .60
223 Gaby Sanchez .15 .40
224 Hunter Pence .25 .60
225 Carlos Lee .15 .40
226A Michael Bourn .15 .40
227 Kazuo Matsui .15 .40
228 Darin Erstad .15 .40
229 Lance Berkman .25 .60
230 Humberto Quintero .15 .40
231 J.R. Towles .15 .40
232 Wesley Wright .15 .40
233 Jose Valverde .15 .40
234 Wandy Rodriguez .15 .40
235 Roy Oswalt .25 .60
236 Latroy Hawkins .15 .40
237 Bud Norris .15 .40
238 Alberto Arias .15 .40
239 Billy Butler .15 .40
240 Jose Guillen .15 .40
241 David DeJesus .15 .40
242 Willie Bloomquist .15 .40
243 Mike Aviles .15 .40
244 Alberto Callaspo .15 .40
245 John Buck .15 .40
246 Joakim Soria .15 .40
247 Zack Greinke .40 1.00
248 Miguel Olivo .15 .40
249 Kyle Davies .15 .40
250 Juan Cruz .15 .40
251 Luke Hochevar .15 .40
252 Brian Bannister .15 .40
253 Robinson Tejeda .15 .40
254 Kyle Farnsworth .15 .40
255 John Lackey .25 .60
256 Torii Hunter .15 .40
257 Chone Figgins .15 .40
258 Kevin Jepsen .15 .40
259 Reggie Willits .15 .40
260 Kendry Morales .15 .40
261 Howie Kendrick .15 .40
262 Erick Aybar .15 .40
263 Brandon Wood .15 .40
264 Maicer Izturis .15 .40
265 Mike Napoli .15 .40
266 Jeff Mathis .15 .40
267A Jered Weaver .25 .60
268 Joe Saunders .15 .40
269 Ervin Santana .15 .40
270 Brian Fuentes .15 .40
271 Jose Arredondo .15 .40
272 Chad Billingsley .25 .60
273 Juan Pierre .15 .40
274 Matt Kemp .30 .75
275 Randy Wolf .15 .40
276 Doug Mientkiewicz .15 .40
277 James Loney .15 .40
278 Casey Blake .15 .40
279 Rafael Furcal .15 .40
280 Blake DeWitt .15 .40
281 Russell Martin .15 .40
282 Jeff Weaver .15 .40
283 Cory Wade .15 .40
284 Eric Stults .15 .40
285 George Sherrill .15 .40
286 Hiroki Kuroda .15 .40
287 Hong-Chih Kuo .15 .40
288A Clayton Kershaw .60 1.50
289 Corey Hart .15 .40
290 Jody Gerut .15 .40
291A Ryan Braun .25 .60
292 Mike Cameron .15 .40
293 Casey McGehee .15 .40
294 Mat Gamel .15 .40
295 J.J. Hardy .15 .40
296 Braden Looper .15 .40
297 Yovani Gallardo .15 .40
298 Mike Rivera .15 .40
299 Carlos Villanueva .15 .40
300 Jeff Suppan .15 .40
301 Mitch Stetter .15 .40
302 David Riske .15 .40
303 Manny Parra .15 .40
304 Seth McClung .15 .40
305 Todd Coffey .15 .40
306 Joe Mauer .30 .75
307 Delmon Young .25 .60
308 Michael Cuddyer .15 .40
309 Matt Tolbert .15 .40
310 Nick Punto .15 .40
311 Jason Kubel .15 .40
312 Brendan Harris .15 .40
313 Brian Buscher .15 .40
314 Kevin Slowey .15 .40
315 Glen Perkins .15 .40
316 Joe Nathan .15 .40
317 Nick Blackburn .15 .40
318 Jesse Crain .15 .40
319 Matt Guerrier .15 .40
320 Scott Baker .15 .40
321 Anthony Swarzak .15 .40
322 Jon Rauch .15 .40
323A David Wright .30 .75
324 Jeremy Reed .15 .40
325 Angel Pagan .15 .40
326 Jose Reyes .25 .60
327 Jeff Francoeur .25 .60
328 Luis Castillo .15 .40
329 Daniel Murphy .30 .75
330 Omir Santos .15 .40
331 John Maine .15 .40
332 Brian Schneider .15 .40
333 Johan Santana .25 .60
334 Francisco Rodriguez .25 .60
335 Tim Redding .15 .40
336 Mike Pelfrey .15 .40
337 Bobby Parnell .15 .40
338 Pat Misch .15 .40
339 Pedro Feliciano .15 .40
340 Nick Swisher .25 .60
341 Melky Cabrera .15 .40
342 Mark Teixeira .25 .60
343 CC Sabathia .25 .60
344 Ramiro Pena .15 .40
345 Derek Jeter 1.00 2.50
346 Andy Pettitte .25 .60
347A Jorge Posada .25 .60
348 Francisco Cervelli .15 .40
349 Chien-Ming Wang .25 .60
350A Mariano Rivera .50 1.25
351 Phil Hughes .15 .40
352 Phil Coke .15 .40
353 A.J. Burnett .15 .40
354 Jose Molina .15 .40
355 Jonathan Albaladejo .15 .40
356 Ryan Sweeney .15 .40
357 Jack Cust .15 .40
358 Rajai Davis .15 .40
359 Andrew Bailey .15 .40
360 Aaron Cunningham .15 .40
361 Adam Kennedy .15 .40
362 Mark Ellis .15 .40
363 Daric Barton .15 .40
364 Kurt Suzuki .15 .40
365 Brad Ziegler .15 .40
366 Michael Wuertz .15 .40
367 Josh Outman .15 .40
368 Edgar Gonzalez .15 .40
369 Joey Devine .15 .40
370 Craig Breslow .15 .40
371 Trevor Cahill .15 .40
372 Brett Anderson .15 .40
373 Scott Hairston .15 .40
374 Jayson Werth .25 .60
375 Raul Ibanez .25 .60
376A Chase Utley .25 .60
377 Greg Dobbs .15 .40
378 Eric Bruntlett .15 .40
379 Shane Victorino .25 .60
380 Jimmy Rollins .25 .60
381 Jack Taschner .15 .40
382 Ryan Madson .15 .40
383 Brad Lidge .15 .40
384 J.A. Happ .25 .60
385 Cole Hamels .30 .75
386 Carlos Ruiz .15 .40
387 JC Romero .15 .40
388 Kyle Kendrick .15 .40
389 Chad Durbin .15 .40
390 Cliff Lee .25 .60
391 Delwyn Young .15 .40
392 Brandon Moss .15 .40
393 Ramon Vazquez .15 .40
394 Andy LaRoche .15 .40
395 Jason Jaramillo .15 .40
396 Ross Ohlendorf .15 .40
397 Paul Maholm .15 .40
398 Jeff Karstens .15 .40
399 Charlie Morton .40 1.00
400 Zach Duke .15 .40
401 Jesse Chavez .15 .40
402 Lastings Milledge .15 .40
403 Matt Capps .15 .40
404 Evan Meek .15 .40
405 Ryan Doumit .15 .40
406 Drew Macias .15 .40
407 Chase Headley .15 .40
408A Tony Gwynn Jr. .15 .40
409 Kevin Kouzmanoff .15 .40
410 Edgar Gonzalez .15 .40
411 David Eckstein .15 .40
412 Everth Cabrera .15 .40
413 Nick Hundley .15 .40
414 Chris Young .15 .40
415 Luis Perdomo .15 .40
416 Edward Mujica .15 .40
417 Clayton Richard .15 .40
418A Luke Gregerson .15 .40
419 Heath Bell .15 .40
420 Kevin Correia .15 .40
421 Cha-Seung Baek .15 .40
422 Joe Thatcher .15 .40
423 Luis Rodriguez .15 .40
424 Bengie Molina .15 .40
425 Ryan Garko .15 .40
426 Nate Schierholtz .15 .40
427 Aaron Rowand .15 .40
428 Eugenio Velez .15 .40
429 Pablo Sandoval .25 .60
430 Edgar Renteria .15 .40
431 Kevin Frandsen .15 .40
432 Rich Aurilia .15 .40
433 Jonathan Sanchez .15 .40
434 Barry Zito .25 .60
435 Brian Wilson .40 1.00
436 Merkin Valdez .15 .40
437 Juan Uribe .15 .40
438 Brandon Medders .15 .40
439 Noah Lowry .15 .40
440 Tim Lincecum .25 .60
441 Jeremy Affeldt .15 .40
442 Russell Branyan .15 .40
443 Ian Snell .15 .40
444 Franklin Gutierrez .15 .40
445 Ken Griffey Jr. .75 2.00
446 Matt Tuiasosopo .15 .40
447 Jose Lopez .15 .40
448 Michael Saunders .25 .60
449 Ryan Rowland-Smith .15 .40
450 Carlos Silva .15 .40
451A Ichiro Suzuki .50 1.25
452 Brandon Morrow .15 .40
453 Chris Jakubauskas .15 .40
454 Felix Hernandez .25 .60
455 David Aardsma .15 .40
456 Mark Lowe .15 .40
457 Rob Johnson .15 .40
458 Garrett Olson .15 .40
459 Ryan Ludwick .15 .40
460 Colby Rasmus .25 .60
461 Brendan Ryan .15 .40
462 Skip Schumaker .15 .40
463 Albert Pujols .50 1.25
464 Joe Thurston .15 .40
465 Julio Lugo .15 .40
466A Yadier Molina .50 1.25
467 Adam Wainwright .25 .60
468 Brad Thompson .15 .40
469 Dennys Reyes .15 .40
470 Mitchell Boggs .15 .40
471 Jason Motte .15 .40
472 Kyle McClellan .15 .40
473 Kyle Lohse .15 .40
474 Chris Carpenter .25 .60
475 Ryan Franklin .15 .40
476 Fernando Perez .15 .40
477 Ben Zobrist .25 .60
478 Evan Longoria .25 .60
479 Gabe Gross .15 .40
480 Pat Burrell .15 .40
481 Carlos Pena .25 .60
482 Jason Bartlett .15 .40
483 Willie Aybar .15 .40
484 Dioner Navarro .15 .40
485 Dan Wheeler .15 .40
486 Andy Sonnanstine .15 .40
487 James Shields .15 .40
488 Jeff Niemann .15 .40
489 J.P. Howell .15 .40
490 Grant Balfour .15 .40
491 David Price .30 .75
492 Matt Garza .15 .40
493 David Murphy .15 .40
494 Nelson Cruz .40 1.00
495 Michael Young .15 .40
496 Ian Kinsler .25 .60
497 Chris Davis .25 .60
498A Elvis Andrus .25 .60
499 Taylor Teagarden .15 .40
500 Jarrod Saltalamacchia .15 .40
501 CJ Wilson .15 .40
502 Derek Holland .15 .40
503 Darren O'Day .15 .40
504 Brandon McCarthy .15 .40
505 Scott Feldman .15 .40
506 Jason Jennings .15 .40
507 Eddie Guardado .15 .40
508 Frank Francisco .15 .40
509 Marlon Byrd .15 .40
510 Scott Downs .15 .40
511 Adam Lind .25 .60
512 Brett Cecil .15 .40
513 Travis Snider .15 .40
514 Ricky Romero .15 .40
515 Lyle Overbay .15 .40
516 Aaron Hill .15 .40
517 Jose Bautista .25 .60
518 Michael Barrett .15 .40
519 Roy Halladay .25 .60
520 Brian Tallet .15 .40
521 Marc Rzepczynski .15 .40
522 Robert Ray .15 .40
523 Dustin McGowan .15 .40
524 Shaun Marcum .15 .40
525 Jesse Litsch .15 .40
526 Josh Willingham .25 .60
527 Nyjer Morgan .15 .40
528 Adam Dunn .25 .60
529 Ryan Zimmerman .25 .60
530 Willie Harris .15 .40
531 Wil Nieves .15 .40
532 Ron Villone .15 .40
533 Livan Hernandez .15 .40
534 Austin Kearns .15 .40
535 Alberto Gonzalez .15 .40
536 Shairon Martis .15 .40
537 Ross Detwiler .15 .40
538 Garrett Mock .15 .40
539 Mike MacDougal .15 .40
540 Jason Bergmann .15 .40
541 Arizona Diamondbacks BP .15 .40
542 Atlanta Braves BP .15 .40
543 Baltimore Orioles BP .15 .40
544 Boston Red Sox BP .25 .60
545 Chicago Cubs BP .25 .60
546 Chicago White Sox BP .15 .40
547 Cincinnati Reds BP .15 .40
548 Cleveland Indians BP .15 .40
549 Colorado Rockies BP .15 .40
550 Detroit Tigers BP .15 .40
551 Florida Marlins BP .15 .40
552 Houston Astros BP .15 .40
553 Kansas City Royals BP .15 .40
554 Los Angeles Angels BP .15 .40
555 Los Angeles Dodgers BP .25 .60
556 Milwaukee Brewers BP .15 .40
557 Minnesota Twins BP .15 .40
558 New York Mets BP .25 .60
559 New York Yankees BP .40 1.00
560 Oakland Athletics BP .15 .40
561 Philadelphia Phillies .15 .40
562 Pittsburgh Pirates .15 .40
563 San Diego Padres .15 .40
564 San Francisco Giants .15 .40
565 St. Louis Cardinals .25 .60
566 Seattle Mariners .15 .40
567 Tampa Bay Rays .15 .40
568 Texas Rangers .15 .40
569 Toronto Blue Jays .15 .40
570 Washington Nationals .15 .40
571 Arizona Diamondbacks CL .15 .40
572 Atlanta Braves CL .15 .40
573 Baltimore Orioles CL .15 .40
574 Boston Red Sox CL .25 .60
575 Chicago Cubs CL .25 .60
576 Chicago White Sox CL .15 .40
577 Cincinnati Reds CL .15 .40
578 Cleveland Indians CL .15 .40
579 Colorado Rockies CL .15 .40
580 Detroit Tigers CL .15 .40
581 Florida Marlins CL .15 .40
582 Houston Astros CL .15 .40
583 Kansas City Royals CL .15 .40
584 Los Angeles Angels CL .15 .40
585 Los Angeles Dodgers CL .25 .60
586 Milwaukee Brewers CL .15 .40
587 Minnesota Twins CL .15 .40
588 New York Mets CL .25 .60
589 New York Yankees CL .40 1.00
590 Oakland Athletics CL .15 .40
591 Philadelphia Phillies CL .15 .40
592 Pittsburgh Pirates CL .15 .40
593 San Diego Padres CL .15 .40
594 San Francisco Giants CL .15 .40
595 St. Louis Cardinals CL .15 .40
596 Seattle Mariners CL .15 .40
597 Tampa Bay Rays CL .15 .40
598 Texas Rangers CL .15 .40
599 Toronto Blue Jays CL .15 .40
600 Washington Nationals CL .15 .40
R1 Pete Rose ATHK SP 12.50 30.00
R2 Pos/Jet/Riv/Pet SP 60.00 120.00
R3 Joe Jackson SP 20.00 50.00

2010 Upper Deck Gold

*GOLD 2-40: 4X TO 10X BASIC RC
*GOLD 1/41-600: 12X TO 30X BASIC VET
STATED PRINT RUN 99 SER.#'d SETS
28 Buster Posey 40.00 100.00

2010 Upper Deck 2000 Star Rookie Update

541 Mark Buehrle 3.00 8.00
542 Miguel Cabrera 5.00 12.00
543 Jorge Cantu 2.00 5.00
544 Carl Crawford 3.00 8.00
545 Adam Dunn 3.00 8.00
546 Adrian Gonzalez 4.00 10.00
547 Matt Holliday 5.00 12.00
548 Brandon Inge 3.00 8.00
549 Roy Oswalt 3.00 8.00
550 Carlos Pena 3.00 8.00
551 Brandon Phillips 2.00 5.00
552 Francisco Rodriguez 3.00 8.00
553 Jimmy Rollins 3.00 8.00
554 Aaron Rowand 2.00 5.00
555 CC Sabathia 3.00 8.00
556 Johan Santana 3.00 8.00
557 Grady Sizemore 3.00 8.00
558 Adam Wainwright 3.00 8.00
559 Michael Young 2.00 5.00
560 Carlos Zambrano 3.00 8.00

2010 Upper Deck A Piece of History 500 Club

GS Gary Sheffield 15.00 40.00

2010 Upper Deck All World

AW1 Albert Pujols 1.25 3.00
AW2 Carlos Beltran .60 1.50
AW3 Carlos Lee .40 1.00
AW4 Chien-Ming Wang .60 1.50
AW5 Daisuke Matsuzaka .60 1.50
AW6 Derek Jeter 2.50 6.00
AW7 Felix Hernandez .60 1.50
AW8 Hanley Ramirez .60 1.50
AW9 Ichiro Suzuki 1.25 3.00
AW10 Johan Santana .60 1.50
AW11 Justin Morneau .60 1.50
AW12 Kendry Morales .40 1.00
AW13 Magglio Ordonez .60 1.50
AW14 Russell Martin .40 1.00
AW15 Vladimir Guerrero .60 1.50

2010 Upper Deck Baseball Heroes

JD Joe DiMaggio 1.50 4.00
BH1 Joe DiMaggio 1.50 4.00
BH2 Joe DiMaggio 1.50 4.00
BH3 Joe DiMaggio 1.50 4.00
BH4 Joe DiMaggio 1.50 4.00
BH5 Joe DiMaggio 1.50 4.00
BH6 Joe DiMaggio 1.50 4.00
BH7 Joe DiMaggio 1.50 4.00
BH8 Joe DiMaggio 1.50 4.00

2010 Upper Deck Baseball Heroes 20th Anniversary Art

BHA1 Ken Griffey Jr. 2.00 5.00
BHA2 Derek Jeter 2.50 6.00
BHA3 Evan Longoria .60 1.50
BHA4 Hanley Ramirez .60 1.50
BHA5 David Price .75 2.00
BHA6 Jon Lester .60 1.50
BHA7 Nick Markakis .75 2.00
BHA8 Cole Hamels .75 2.00
BHA9 Jonathan Papelbon .60 1.50
BHA10 Chipper Jones 1.00 2.50

2010 Upper Deck Baseball Heroes 20th Anniversary Art Autographs

STATED PRINT RUN 90 SER.#'d SETS
BHA1 Ken Griffey Jr. 125.00 250.00
BHA2 Derek Jeter 100.00 200.00
BHA3 Evan Longoria 15.00 40.00
BHA5 David Price 12.50 30.00
BHA7 Nick Markakis 30.00 60.00
BHA8 Cole Hamels 20.00 50.00
BHA9 Jonathan Papelbon 6.00 15.00

2010 Upper Deck Baseball Heroes DiMaggio Cut Signature

STATED PRINT RUN 56 SER.#'d SETS
JD Joe DiMaggio 300.00 500.00

2010 Upper Deck Celebrity Predictors

CP1/CP2 Jennifer Aniston/John Mayer 1.50 4.00
CP3/CP4 Cameron Diaz Justin Timberlake 1.50 4.00
CP5/CP6 Megan Fox/Shia LaBeouf 1.50 4.00
CP7/CP8 Katie Holmes/Tom Cruise 1.50 4.00
CP11/CP12 Anna Kournikova Enrique Iglesias 1.50 4.00
CP13/CP14 Mariah Carey/Nick Cannon 1.50 4.00
CP15/CP16 Rob Pattinson/Kristen Stewart 1.50 4.00
CP17/CP18 A.Jolie/B.Pitt 6.00 15.00
CP19/CP20 C.Ronaldo/P.Hilton 6.00 15.00
CP9/CP10 Chris Martin/Gwyneth Paltrow 1.50 4.00

2010 Upper Deck Portraits

*GOLD: 1.5X TO 4X BASIC
GOLD PRINT RUN 99 SER.#'d SETS
SE1 Justin Upton .60 1.50
SE2 Dan Haren .40 1.00
SE3 Chipper Jones 1.00 2.50
SE4 Yunel Escobar .40 1.00
SE5 Derek Lowe .40 1.00
SE6 Nick Markakis .75 2.00
SE7 Brian Roberts .40 1.00
SE8 Koji Uehara .40 1.00
SE9 Josh Beckett .40 1.00
SE10 Jon Lester .60 1.50
SE11 David Ortiz 1.00 2.50
SE12 Jason Varitek 1.00 2.50
SE13 Carlos Zambrano .60 1.50
SE14 Kosuke Fukudome .60 1.50
SE15 Aramis Ramirez .40 1.00
SE16 Mark Buehrle .60 1.50
SE17 Paul Konerko .60 1.50
SE18 Carlos Quentin .40 1.00
SE19 Joey Votto 1.00 2.50
SE20 Brandon Phillips .40 1.00
SE21 Edinson Volquez .40 1.00
SE22 Shin-Soo Choo .60 1.50
SE23 Kerry Wood .40 1.00
SE24 Grady Sizemore .60 1.50
SE25 Troy Tulowitzki 1.00 2.50
SE26 Aaron Cook .40 1.00
SE27 Todd Helton .60 1.50
SE28 Justin Verlander 1.00 2.50
SE29 Miguel Cabrera 1.00 2.50
SE30 Rick Porcello .60 1.50
SE31 Chris Coghlan .40 1.00
SE32 Josh Johnson .60 1.50
SE33 Carlos Lee .40 1.00
SE34 Lance Berkman .60 1.50
SE35 Roy Oswalt .60 1.50
SE36 Zack Greinke 1.00 2.50
SE37 Billy Butler .40 1.00
SE38 Joakim Soria .40 1.00
SE39 Jered Weaver .60 1.50
SE40 Torii Hunter .40 1.00
SE41 Kendry Morales .40 1.00
SE42 Chone Figgins .40 1.00
SE43 Russell Martin .40 1.00
SE44 Clayton Kershaw 1.50 4.00
SE45 Matt Kemp .75 2.00
SE46 Hiroki Kuroda .40 1.00
SE47 Alcides Escobar .60 1.50
SE48 Yovani Gallardo .40 1.00
SE49 Ryan Braun .60 1.50
SE50 Justin Morneau .60 1.50
SE51 Joe Nathan .40 1.00
SE52 Michael Cuddyer .40 1.00
SE53 Johan Santana .60 1.50
SE54 David Wright .75 2.00
SE55 Jose Reyes .60 1.50
SE56 Francisco Rodriguez .60 1.50
SE57 Mark Teixeira .60 1.50
SE58 Derek Jeter 2.50 6.00
SE59 Mariano Rivera 1.25 3.00
SE60 A.J. Burnett .40 1.00
SE61 Jorge Posada .60 1.50
SE62 Jack Cust .40 1.00
SE63 Mark Ellis .40 1.00
SE64 Andrew Bailey .40 1.00
SE65 Chase Utley .60 1.50
SE66 Cole Hamels .75 2.00
SE67 Raul Ibanez .60 1.50
SE68 Jimmy Rollins .60 1.50
SE69 Ryan Doumit .40 1.00
SE70 Zach Duke .40 1.00
SE71 Tony Gwynn Jr. .40 1.00
SE72 Chris Young .40 1.00
SE73 Heath Bell .40 1.00
SE74 Barry Zito .60 1.50
SE75 Pablo Sandoval .60 1.50
SE76 Aaron Rowand .40 1.00
SE77 Tim Lincecum .60 1.50
SE78 Felix Hernandez .60 1.50
SE79 Ichiro Suzuki 1.25 3.00
SE80 Franklin Gutierrez .40 1.00
SE81 Albert Pujols 1.25 3.00
SE82 Adam Wainwright .60 1.50

SE83 Chris Carpenter .60 1.50
SE84 Colby Rasmus .60 1.50
SE85 Yadier Molina 1.25 3.00
SE86 Evan Longoria .60 1.50
SE87 Jeff Niemann .40 1.00
SE88 James Shields .40 1.00
SE89 Carlos Pena .60 1.50
SE90 Scott Feldman .40 1.00
SE91 Michael Young .40 1.00
SE92 Ian Kinsler .60 1.50
SE93 Elvis Andrus .60 1.50
SE94 Ricky Romero .40 1.00
SE95 Roy Halladay .60 1.50
SE96 Adam Lind .60 1.50
SE97 Aaron Hill .40 1.00
SE98 Ryan Zimmerman .60 1.50
SE99 Adam Dunn .60 1.50
SE100 Nyjer Morgan .40 1.00

2010 Upper Deck Portraits Gold

*GOLD: 1.5X TO 4X BASIC
STATED PRINT RUN 99 SER.#'d SETS

2010 Upper Deck Pure Heat

PH1 Adrian Gonzalez .75 2.00
PH2 Albert Pujols 1.25 3.00
PH3 Alex Rodriguez 1.25 3.00
PH4 Cole Hamels .75 2.00
PH5 CC Sabathia .60 1.50
PH6 Evan Longoria .60 1.50
PH7 Josh Beckett .40 1.00
PH8 Joe Mauer .75 2.00
PH9 Justin Verlander 1.00 2.50
PH10 Manny Ramirez 1.00 2.50
PH11 Mark Teixeira .60 1.50
PH12 Prince Fielder .60 1.50
PH13 Ryan Howard .75 2.00
PH14 Tim Lincecum .60 1.50
PH15 Troy Tulowitzki 1.00 2.50

2010 Upper Deck Season Biography

SB1 Derek Lowe .40 1.00
SB2 Johan Santana .60 1.50
SB3 Aaron Rowand .40 1.00
SB4 Koji Uehara .40 1.00
SB5 Everth Cabrera .40 1.00
SB6 Miguel Cabrera 1.00 2.50
SB7 Justin Verlander 1.00 2.50
SB8 Evan Longoria .60 1.50
SB9 Orlando Hudson .40 1.00
SB10 Zach Duke .40 1.00
SB11 Ken Griffey Jr. 2.00 5.00
SB12 Ian Kinsler .60 1.50
SB13 Tim Wakefield .60 1.50
SB14 Grady Sizemore .60 1.50
SB15 Gary Sheffield .40 1.00
SB16 Tim Lincecum .60 1.50
SB17 Randy Johnson 1.00 2.50
SB18 Dustin Pedroia 1.00 2.50
SB19 Ryan Braun .60 1.50
SB20 Dan Haren .40 1.00
SB21 Dave Bush .40 1.00
SB22 Carlos Pena .60 1.50
SB23 Albert Pujols 1.25 3.00
SB24 Jacoby Ellsbury .75 2.00
SB25 Dexter Fowler .60 1.50
SB26 Ryan Howard .75 2.00
SB27 Jorge Cantu .40 1.00
SB28 Yovani Gallardo .40 1.00
SB29 Evan Longoria .60 1.50
SB30 Matt Garza .40 1.00
SB31 Jake Peavy .40 1.00
SB32 Jason Marquis .40 1.00
SB33 Carl Crawford .60 1.50
SB34 Zack Greinke 1.00 2.50
SB35 Vicente Padilla .40 1.00
SB36 Manny Ramirez 1.00 2.50
SB37 Hanley Ramirez .60 1.50
SB38 Alex Rodriguez 1.25 3.00
SB39 Joe Saunders .40 1.00
SB40 Torii Hunter .40 1.00
SB41 Brett Cecil .40 1.00
SB42 Ryan Zimmerman .60 1.50
SB43 Derek Holland .40 1.00
SB44 Ryan Zimmerman .60 1.50
SB45 Torii Hunter .40 1.00
SB46 Jimmy Rollins .60 1.50
Barack Obama
SB47 Alex Rodriguez 1.25 3.00
SB48 Ivan Rodriguez .60 1.50
SB49 Clayton Kershaw 1.50 4.00
SB50 Jake Peavy .40 1.00
SB51 Jason Kendall .40 1.00
SB52 Mark Teixeira .60 1.50
SB53 David Ortiz 1.00 2.50
SB54 Joe Mauer .75 2.00
SB55 Raul Ibanez .60 1.50
SB56 Kenshin Kawakami .60 1.50
SB57 Nelson Cruz 1.00 2.50
SB58 Alex Gonzalez .40 1.00
SB59 Freddy Sanchez .40 1.00
SB60 Chris B. Young .40 1.00
SB61 Rick Porcello .60 1.50
SB62 Nolan Reimold .40 1.00
SB63 Scott Feldman .40 1.00
SB64 Ryan Howard .75 2.00
SB65 Ryan Dempster .40 1.00
SB66 Jamie Moyer .40 1.00
SB67 Jim Thome .60 1.50
SB68 Roy Halladay .60 1.50
SB69 Jeff Niemann .40 1.00
SB70 Randy Johnson 1.00 2.50
SB71 Jonathan Broxton .40 1.00
SB72 Carlos Zambrano .60 1.50
SB73 Jon Lester .60 1.50
SB74 Alfonso Soriano .60 1.50
SB75 Dan Haren .40 1.00
SB76 Vin Mazzaro .40 1.00
SB77 Sean West .40 1.00
SB78 Andre Ethier .60 1.50
SB79 Colby Rasmus .60 1.50
SB80 Jim Thome .60 1.50
SB81 Tim Lincecum .60 1.50
SB82 Miguel Tejada .60 1.50
SB83 Torii Hunter .40 1.00
SB84 Albert Pujols 1.25 3.00
SB85 Todd Helton .60 1.50
SB86 Jered Weaver .60 1.50
SB87 Prince Fielder .60 1.50
SB88 Robinson Cano .60 1.50
SB89 Ivan Rodriguez .60 1.50
SB90 Tommy Hanson .40 1.00
SB91 Kenshin Kawakami .60 1.50
SB92 Jeff Weaver .40 1.00
SB93 Albert Pujols 1.25 3.00
SB94 B.J. Upton .60 1.50
SB95 Trevor Cahill .40 1.00
SB96 Tim Lincecum .60 1.50
SB97 Troy Tulowitzki 1.00 2.50
SB98 Jermaine Dye .40 1.00
SB99 Lance Berkman .60 1.50
SB100 Hanley Ramirez .60 1.50
SB101 Alex Rodriguez 1.25 3.00
SB102 Albert Pujols 1.25 3.00
SB103 Tommy Hanson .40 1.00
SB104 Zack Greinke 1.00 2.50
SB105 Brandon Phillips .40 1.00
SB106 Dallas Braden .60 1.50
SB107 Joey Votto 1.00 2.50
SB108 Albert Pujols 1.25 3.00
SB109 Adam Dunn .60 1.50
SB110 Ricky Nolasco .40 1.00
SB111 Ted Lilly .40 1.00
SB112 Vladimir Guerrero .60 1.50
SB113 Ryan Spilborghs .40 1.00
SB114 Garrett Atkins .40 1.00
SB115 Jonathan Sanchez .40 1.00
SB116 Josh Beckett .40 1.00
SB117 Kurt Suzuki .40 1.00
SB118 Ichiro Suzuki 1.25 3.00
Barack Obama
SB119 Ryan Howard .75 2.00
SB120 Marc Rzepczynski .40 1.00
SB121 Clayton Kershaw 1.50 4.00
SB122 Roy Halladay .60 1.50
SB123 Jason Marquis .40 1.00
SB124 Manny Ramirez 1.00 2.50
SB125 Scott Hairston .40 1.00
SB126 A.J. Burnett .40 1.00
SB127 Mark Buehrle .60 1.50
SB128 Jeremy Sowers .40 1.00
SB129 Chone Figgins .40 1.00
SB130 Cliff Lee .60 1.50
SB131 Michael Young .40 1.00
SB132 Josh Willingham .60 1.50
SB133 Pablo Sandoval .60 1.50
SB134 Cliff Lee .60 1.50
SB135 Aaron Hill .40 1.00
SB136 Bud Norris .40 1.00
SB137 Neftali Feliz .40 1.00
SB138 Chase Utley .60 1.50
SB139 Fausto Carmona .40 1.00
SB140 Barry Zito .60 1.50
SB141 Jered Weaver .60 1.50
SB142 Roy Halladay .60 1.50
SB143 Wandy Rodriguez .40 1.00
SB144 Mark Teixeira .60 1.50
SB145 Vladimir Guerrero .60 1.50
SB146 Adrian Gonzalez .75 2.00
SB147 Tim Lincecum .60 1.50
SB148 Pedro Martinez .60 1.50
SB149 Felix Pie .40 1.00
SB150 Jim Thome .60 1.50
SB151 Derek Jeter 2.50 6.00
SB152 Gregg Zaun .40 1.00
SB153 Ian Kinsler .60 1.50
SB154 Brandon Inge .60 1.50
SB155 Hanley Ramirez .60 1.50
SB156 Russell Branyan .40 1.00
SB157 Pedro Martinez .60 1.50
SB158 Michael Cuddyer .40 1.00
SB159 Jake Fox .40 1.00
SB160 John Smoltz 1.00 2.50
SB161 Ryan Howard .75 2.00
SB162 Matt LaPorta .40 1.00
SB163 Joe Saunders .40 1.00
SB164 Tony Gwynn Jr. .40 1.00
SB165 Carlos Ruiz .40 1.00
SB166 Edgar Renteria .40 1.00
SB167 Josh Hamilton .60 1.50
SB168 Tim Hudson .60 1.50
SB169 Garrett Jones .40 1.00
SB170 Landon Powell .40 1.00
SB171 Casey McGehee .40 1.00
SB172 Ichiro Suzuki 1.25 3.00
SB173 Daniel Murphy .75 2.00
SB174 Jon Lester .60 1.50
SB175 Derrek Lee .40 1.00
SB176 Mark Buehrle .60 1.50
SB177 Mark Teixeira .60 1.50
SB178 Brad Penny .40 1.00
SB179 Wade LeBlanc .40 1.00
SB180 Micah Hoffpauir .40 1.00
SB181 Ian Desmond .60 1.50
SB182 Derek Jeter 2.50 6.00
SB183 Brian Matusz 1.00 2.50
SB184 Ichiro Suzuki 1.25 3.00
SB185 Josh Johnson .60 1.50
SB186 Luis Durango .40 1.00
SB187 Jody Gerut .40 1.00
SB188 Francisco Rodriguez .60 1.50
SB189 Jake Peavy .40 1.00
SB190 Mariano Rivera 1.25 3.00
SB191 Sonia Sotomayor .40 1.00
SB192 Willy Aybar .40 1.00
SB193 Wade Davis .60 1.50
SB194 Cesear Ramos .40 1.00
SB195 Kevin Millwood .40 1.00
SB196 Andres Torres .40 1.00
SB197 Willy Aybar .40 1.00
SB198 Clayton Kershaw 1.50 4.00
SB199 Justin Verlander 1.00 2.50
SB200 Alexi Casilla .40 1.00

2010 Upper Deck Signature Sensations

AA Aaron Rowand 8.00 20.00
AE Alcides Escobar 5.00 12.00
AH Aaron Harang 8.00 20.00
AI Akinori Iwamura 8.00 20.00
AL Andy LaRoche 6.00 15.00
AR Alex Romero 3.00 8.00
AS Anibal Sanchez 4.00 10.00
BA Burke Badenhop 3.00 8.00
BB Brian Bixler 5.00 12.00
BO Jeremy Bonderman 15.00 40.00
CB Clay Buchholz 6.00 15.00
CF Chone Figgins 4.00 10.00
CH Chase Headley 3.00 8.00
CK Clayton Kershaw 50.00 100.00
CL Carlos Lee 3.00 8.00
DE David Eckstein 5.00 12.00
DJ Derek Jeter 200.00 500.00
DO Darren O'Day 4.00 10.00
DP Dustin Pedroia 12.50 30.00
DS Denard Span 4.00 10.00
DU Dan Uggla 6.00 15.00
DV Donald Veal 5.00 12.00
EB Emilio Bonifacio 3.00 8.00
ED Elijah Dukes 3.00 8.00
EM Evan Meek 12.50 30.00
EV Eugenio Velez 4.00 10.00
FP Felix Pie 8.00 20.00
HE Jeremy Hermida 3.00 8.00
HJ Josh Hamilton 8.00 20.00
HP Hunter Pence 5.00 12.00
JA Jonathan Albaladejo 3.00 8.00
JC Johnny Cueto 4.00 10.00
JH J.A. Happ 8.00 20.00
JL Jesse Litsch 4.00 10.00
JM John Maine 3.00 8.00
JO Joaquin Arias 3.00 8.00
JP Jonathan Papelbon 8.00 20.00
JW Josh Willingham 3.00 8.00
KG Khalil Greene 6.00 15.00
KH Kevin Hart 4.00 10.00
KJ Kelly Johnson 3.00 8.00
KK Kevin Kouzmanoff 3.00 8.00
KS Kevin Slowey 6.00 15.00
KY Kevin Youkilis 10.00 25.00
MB Marlon Byrd 3.00 8.00
MG Mat Gamel 4.00 10.00
MO Micah Owings 4.00 10.00
MP Mike Pelfrey 5.00 12.00
NY Nyjer Morgan 4.00 10.00
PA Felipe Paulino 3.00 8.00
PF Prince Fielder 10.00 25.00
RA Alexei Ramirez 6.00 15.00
RH Roy Halladay 30.00 60.00
RM Russell Martin 6.00 15.00
RO Ross Ohlendorf 5.00 12.00
RT Ryan Theriot 10.00 25.00
SK Scott Kazmir 15.00 40.00
SM Sean Marshall 3.00 8.00
TE Miguel Tejada 3.00 8.00
TP Troy Patton 3.00 8.00
TR Ramon Troncoso 3.00 8.00
TS Takashi Saito 10.00 25.00
VO Edinson Volquez 4.00 10.00
WW Wesley Wright 3.00 8.00
YE Yunel Escobar 5.00 12.00
YG Yovani Gallardo 6.00 15.00
ZD Zach Duke 5.00 12.00

2010 Upper Deck Supreme Blue

*BLUE: 1.5X TO 4X BASIC
S37 Tim Lincecum 4.00 10.00

2010 Upper Deck Supreme Green

S1 Dan Haren .60 1.50
S2 Chipper Jones 1.50 4.00
S3 Tommy Hanson .60 1.50
S4 Adam Jones 1.00 2.50
S5 Jonathan Papelbon 1.00 2.50
S6 Dustin Pedroia 1.50 4.00
S7 Kevin Youkilis .60 1.50
S8 Jason Bay 1.00 2.50
S9 Alfonso Soriano 1.00 2.50
S10 Paul Konerko 1.00 2.50
S11 Mark Buehrle 1.00 2.50
S12 Joey Votto 1.50 4.00
S13 Grady Sizemore 1.00 2.50
S14 Travis Hafner .60 1.50
S15 Troy Tulowitzki 1.50 4.00
S16 Jason Marquis .60 1.50
S17 Brandon Inge 1.00 2.50
S18 Justin Verlander 1.50 4.00
S19 Josh Johnson 1.00 2.50
S20 Carlos Lee .60 1.50
S21 Billy Butler .60 1.50
S22 Vladimir Guerrero 1.00 2.50
S23 Torii Hunter .60 1.50
S24 Manny Ramirez 1.50 4.00
S25 Ryan Braun 1.00 2.50
S26 Michael Cuddyer .60 1.50
S27 Joe Mauer 1.25 3.00
S28 Carlos Beltran 1.00 2.50
S29 David Wright 1.25 3.00
S30 Hideki Matsui 1.50 4.00
S31 Derek Jeter 4.00 10.00
S32 CC Sabathia 1.00 2.50
S33 Kurt Suzuki .60 1.50
S34 Ryan Howard 1.25 3.00
S35 Cole Hamels 1.25 3.00
S36 Mat Latos 1.00 2.50
S37 Tim Lincecum 1.00 2.50
S38 Pablo Sandoval 1.00 2.50
S39 Ichiro Suzuki 2.00 5.00
S40 Matt Holliday 1.50 4.00
S41 Yadier Molina 2.00 5.00
S42 Colby Rasmus 1.00 2.50
S43 Evan Longoria 1.00 2.50
S44 Carlos Pena 1.00 2.50
S45 Carl Crawford 1.00 2.50
S46 Ian Kinsler 1.00 2.50
S47 Josh Hamilton 1.00 2.50
S48 Scott Feldman .60 1.50
S49 Roy Halladay 1.00 2.50
S50 Ryan Zimmerman 1.00 2.50
S51 Justin Upton 1.00 2.50
S52 Mark Reynolds .60 1.50
S53 Brian McCann 1.00 2.50
S54 Nick Markakis 1.25 3.00
S55 Matt Wieters 1.50 4.00
S56 Jacoby Ellsbury 1.25 3.00
S57 David Ortiz 1.50 4.00
S58 Josh Beckett .60 1.50
S59 Carlos Zambrano 1.00 2.50
S60 Gordon Beckham .60 1.50
S61 Jay Bruce 1.00 2.50
S62 Shin-Soo Choo 1.00 2.50
S63 Todd Helton 1.00 2.50
S64 Dexter Fowler 1.00 2.50
S65 Miguel Cabrera 1.50 4.00
S66 Curtis Granderson 1.25 3.00
S67 Hanley Ramirez 1.00 2.50
S68 Dan Uggla .60 1.50
S69 Lance Berkman 1.00 2.50
S70 Zack Greinke 1.50 4.00
S71 Chone Figgins .60 1.50
S72 John Lackey 1.00 2.50
S73 Russell Martin .60 1.50
S74 Matt Kemp 1.25 3.00
S75 Prince Fielder 1.00 2.50
S76 Yovani Gallardo .60 1.50
S77 Justin Morneau 1.00 2.50
S78 Jose Reyes 1.00 2.50
S79 Johan Santana 1.00 2.50
S80 Francisco Rodriguez 1.00 2.50
S81 Johnny Damon 1.00 2.50
S82 Mark Teixeira 1.00 2.50
S83 Mariano Rivera 2.00 5.00
S84 Alex Rodriguez 2.00 5.00
S85 Cliff Lee 1.00 2.50
S86 Chase Utley 1.00 2.50
S87 Shane Victorino 1.00 2.50
S88 Zach Duke .60 1.50
S89 Andrew McCutchen 1.50 4.00
S90 Adrian Gonzalez 1.25 3.00
S91 Matt Cain 1.00 2.50
S92 Ken Griffey Jr. 3.00 8.00
S93 Felix Hernandez 1.00 2.50
S94 Albert Pujols 2.00 5.00
S95 Adam Wainwright 1.00 2.50
S96 David Price 1.25 3.00
S97 B.J. Upton 1.00 2.50
S98 Michael Young .60 1.50
S99 Adam Lind 1.00 2.50
S100 Adam Dunn 1.00 2.50

2010 Upper Deck Tape Measure Shots

TMS1 Mark Reynolds .40 1.00
TMS2 Raul Ibanez .60 1.50
TMS3 Joey Votto 1.00 2.50
TMS4 Adam Dunn .60 1.50
TMS5 Josh Hamilton .60 1.50
TMS6 Adrian Gonzalez .75 2.00
TMS7 Miguel Montero .40 1.00
TMS8 Seth Smith .40 1.00
TMS9 Nelson Cruz 1.00 2.50
TMS10 Carlos Pena .60 1.50
TMS11 Albert Pujols 1.25 3.00
TMS12 Pablo Sandoval .60 1.50
TMS13 Josh Willingham .60 1.50
TMS14 Manny Ramirez 1.00 2.50
TMS15 Prince Fielder .60 1.50
TMS16 Jermaine Dye .40 1.00
TMS17 Brandon Inge .60 1.50
TMS18 Lance Berkman .60 1.50
TMS19 Kelly Shoppach .40 1.00
TMS20 Ian Stewart .40 1.00
TMS21 Magglio Ordonez .60 1.50
TMS22 Michael Cuddyer .40 1.00
TMS23 Ryan Howard .75 2.00
TMS24 Troy Tulowitzki 1.00 2.50
TMS25 Colby Rasmus .60 1.50

2010 Upper Deck UD Game Jersey

AE Andre Ethier 2.00 5.00
AG Alex Gordon 2.00 5.00
AJ Adam Jones 2.00 5.00
AP Albert Pujols 4.00 10.00
AR Aramis Ramirez 1.25 3.00
BE Josh Beckett 1.25 3.00
BI Brandon Inge 2.00 5.00
BM Brandon Morrow 1.25 3.00
BO John Bowker 1.25 3.00
BR Ryan Braun 2.00 5.00
BU B.J. Upton 2.00 5.00
BZ Barry Zito 2.00 5.00
CA Matt Cain 2.00 5.00
CB Clay Buchholz 1.25 3.00
CC Chris Carpenter 2.00 5.00
CF Chone Figgins 1.25 3.00
CG Curtis Granderson 2.50 6.00
CH Cole Hamels 2.50 6.00
CJ Chipper Jones 3.00 8.00
CR Carl Crawford 2.00 5.00
CU Chase Utley 2.00 5.00
CY Chris Young 1.25 3.00
DA Johnny Damon 2.00 5.00
DE David Eckstein 1.25 3.00
DH Dan Haren 1.25 3.00
DJ Derek Jeter 8.00 20.00
DL Derrek Lee 1.25 3.00
DO David Ortiz 3.00 8.00
EJ Edwin Jackson 1.25 3.00
EL Evan Longoria 2.00 5.00
EM Evan Meek 1.25 3.00
EV Eugenio Velez 1.25 3.00
FC Fausto Carmona 1.25 3.00
FH Felix Hernandez 2.00 5.00
FL Francisco Liriano 1.25 3.00
FN Fu-Te Ni 2.00 5.00
FR Fernando Rodney 1.25 3.00
GA Armando Galarraga 1.25 3.00
GO Adrian Gonzalez 2.50 6.00
GS Grady Sizemore 2.00 5.00
HB Hank Blalock 1.25 3.00
HE Chase Headley 1.25 3.00
HK Howie Kendrick 1.25 3.00
HR Hanley Ramirez 2.00 5.00
IK Ian Kinsler 2.00 5.00
JB Jeremy Bonderman 1.25 3.00
JD Jermaine Dye 1.25 3.00
JE Jacoby Ellsbury 2.50 6.00
JH Josh Hamilton 2.00 5.00
JN Jayson Nix 1.25 3.00
JP Jonathan Papelbon 2.00 5.00
JR Jimmy Rollins 2.00 5.00
JS Johan Santana 2.00 5.00
JU Justin Morneau 2.00 5.00
JV Jason Varitek 3.00 8.00
KE Kendry Morales 1.25 3.00
KF Kosuke Fukudome 2.00 5.00
KG Ken Griffey Jr. 6.00 15.00
KH Kevin Hart 1.25 3.00
KK Kevin Kouzmanoff 1.25 3.00
KM Kevin Millwood 1.25 3.00
KY Kevin Youkilis 1.25 3.00
MA Max Scherzer 3.00 8.00
MB Mark Buehrle 2.00 5.00
MC Michael Cuddyer 1.25 3.00
MI Miguel Cabrera 3.00 8.00
MK Matt Kemp 2.50 6.00
ML Matt LaPorta 1.25 3.00
MM Melvin Mora 1.25 3.00
MO Magglio Ordonez 2.00 5.00
MR Mariano Rivera 4.00 10.00
MT Matt Tolbert 1.25 3.00
MY Michael Young 1.25 3.00
NM Nick Markakis 2.50 6.00
PF Prince Fielder 2.00 5.00
PH Phil Hughes 1.25 3.00
PM Pedro Martinez 2.00 5.00
PO Jorge Posada 2.00 5.00
RC Robinson Cano 2.00 5.00
RE Jose Reyes 2.00 5.00
RH Roy Halladay 2.00 5.00
RI Raul Ibanez 2.00 5.00
RM Russell Martin 1.25 3.00
RO Alex Rodriguez 4.00 10.00
RT Ramon Troncoso 1.25 3.00
RW Randy Wells 1.25 3.00
RZ Ryan Zimmerman 2.00 5.00
SC Shin-Soo Choo 2.00 5.00
SD Stephen Drew 1.25 3.00
SK Scott Kazmir 1.25 3.00
TH Travis Hafner 1.25 3.00
TL Tim Lincecum 2.00 5.00
TO Todd Helton 2.00 5.00
TT Troy Tulowitzki 3.00 8.00
UP Justin Upton 2.00 5.00
VE Justin Verlander 3.00 8.00
VG Vladimir Guerrero 2.00 5.00
WW Wesley Wright 1.25 3.00
YY Yasuhiko Yabuta 1.25 3.00
ZG Zack Greinke 3.00 8.00

2011 Upper Deck National Convention

NSCC2 Ryne Sandberg 1.25 3.00
NSCC9 Greg Maddux 1.25 3.00
NSCC10 Bo Jackson .75 2.00
NSCC20 Matt Szczur 2.00 5.00

2011 Upper Deck National Convention Autographs

NSCCSZ Matt Szczur/35 20.00 50.00

2012 Upper Deck National Convention

NSCC5 Cody Buckel .30 .75
NSCC9 Don Mattingly 1.50 4.00
NSCC12 John Kruk .30 .75
NSCC18 Jack Morris .30 .75

2012 Upper Deck National Convention Autographs

STATED PRINT RUN 1-35

2013 Upper Deck National Convention

COMPLETE SET (20) 15.00 40.00
2 Mark McGwire
3 Troy Glaus
7 Tony Cingrani
9 Tony Gwynn
13 Reggie Jackson
14 Pete Incaviglia
15 Ken Griffey Jr.
17 Frank Thomas
19 Darryl Strawberry
20 Jim Abbott

2013 Upper Deck National Convention VIP

COMPLETE SET (6) 3.00 8.00
5 Frank Thomas

2015 Upper Deck National Convention

NSCC17 Ken Griffey Jr. .60 1.50

2008 Upper Deck 20th Anniversary

UD46 Ken Griffey Jr. 1.00 2.50
UD47 Derek Jeter 1.25 3.00
UD48 Ichiro Suzuki .75 2.00
UD49 Albert Pujols 1.25 3.00
UD50 Daisuke Matsuzaka .75 2.00
UD51 Babe Ruth 1.25 3.00
UD52 Joe DiMaggio 1.25 3.00
UD53 Alex Rodriguez .75 2.00
UD54 Cal Ripken Jr. 2.00 5.00
UD55 Frank Thomas .30 .75
UD56 Nolan Ryan 1.50 4.00
UD57 Roger Clemens .30 .75
UD58 Randy Johnson .30 .75
UD59 Greg Maddux .25 .60
UD60 Ryne Sandberg 1.00 2.50
UD76 Kosuke Fukudome .30 .75
UD77 Evan Longoria .75 2.00
UD78 Josh Hamilton .30 .75
UD79 Jay Bruce .30 .75
UD80 Clayton Kershaw .30 .75

2009 Upper Deck 20th Anniversary

CARDS ISSUED IN FIVE CARD RUNS
EACH PRICED EQUALLY WITHIN RUNS
1 Ken Griffey Jr. 1.00 2.50
2 Ken Griffey Jr. 1.00 2.50
3 Ken Griffey Jr. 1.00 2.50
4 Ken Griffey Jr. 1.00 2.50
5 Ken Griffey Jr. 1.00 2.50
11 Johnny Bench .40 1.00
12 Johnny Bench .40 1.00
13 Johnny Bench .40 1.00
14 Johnny Bench .40 1.00
15 Johnny Bench .40 1.00
16 Carl Yastrzemski .75 2.00
17 Carl Yastrzemski .75 2.00
18 Carl Yastrzemski .75 2.00
19 Carl Yastrzemski .75 2.00
20 Carl Yastrzemski .75 2.00
51 Ken Griffey Jr. 1.00 2.50
52 Ken Griffey Jr. 1.00 2.50
53 Ken Griffey Jr. 1.00 2.50
54 Ken Griffey Jr. 1.00 2.50
55 Ken Griffey Jr. 1.00 2.50
61 Mike Schmidt .75 2.00
62 Mike Schmidt .75 2.00
63 Mike Schmidt .75 2.00
64 Mike Schmidt .75 2.00
65 Mike Schmidt .75 2.00
66 Oakland Athletics .20 .50
67 Oakland Athletics .20 .50
68 Oakland Athletics .20 .50
69 Oakland Athletics .20 .50
70 Oakland Athletics .20 .50
71 Gary Sheffield .20 .50
72 Gary Sheffield .20 .50
73 Gary Sheffield .20 .50
74 Gary Sheffield .20 .50
75 Gary Sheffield .20 .50
126 Randy Johnson .40 1.00
127 Randy Johnson .40 1.00
128 Randy Johnson .40 1.00
129 Randy Johnson .40 1.00
130 Randy Johnson .40 1.00
131 John Smoltz .40 1.00
132 John Smoltz .40 1.00
133 John Smoltz .40 1.00
134 John Smoltz .40 1.00
135 John Smoltz .40 1.00
146 Oriole Park At Camden Yards .20 .50
147 Oriole Park At Camden Yards .20 .50
148 Oriole Park At Camden Yards .20 .50
149 Oriole Park At Camden Yards .20 .50
150 Oriole Park At Camden Yards .20 .50
151 Frank Thomas .40 1.00
152 Frank Thomas .40 1.00
153 Frank Thomas .40 1.00
154 Frank Thomas .40 1.00
155 Frank Thomas .40 1.00
201 Randy Johnson .40 1.00
202 Randy Johnson .40 1.00
203 Randy Johnson .40 1.00
204 Randy Johnson .40 1.00
205 Randy Johnson .40 1.00
206 Nolan Ryan 1.50 4.00
207 Nolan Ryan 1.50 4.00
208 Nolan Ryan 1.50 4.00
209 Nolan Ryan 1.50 4.00
210 Nolan Ryan 1.50 4.00
226 Nolan Ryan 1.50 4.00
227 Nolan Ryan 1.50 4.00
228 Nolan Ryan 1.50 4.00
229 Nolan Ryan 1.50 4.00
230 Nolan Ryan 1.50 4.00
236 K.Griffey Jr./K.Griffey Sr. 1.00 2.50
237 K.Griffey Jr./K.Griffey Sr. 1.00 2.50
238 K.Griffey Jr./K.Griffey Sr. 1.00 2.50
239 K.Griffey Jr./K.Griffey Sr. 1.00 2.50
240 K.Griffey Jr./K.Griffey Sr. 1.00 2.50
241 Comiskey Park .20 .50
242 Comiskey Park .20 .50
243 Comiskey Park .20 .50
244 Comiskey Park .20 .50
245 Comiskey Park .20 .50
246 Cincinnati Reds .20 .50
247 Cincinnati Reds .20 .50
248 Cincinnati Reds .20 .50
249 Cincinnati Reds .20 .50
250 Cincinnati Reds .20 .50
261 Gaylord Perry .20 .50
262 Gaylord Perry .20 .50
263 Gaylord Perry .20 .50
264 Gaylord Perry .20 .50
265 Gaylord Perry .20 .50
266 Jim Thome .25 .60
267 Jim Thome .25 .60
268 Jim Thome .25 .60
269 Jim Thome .25 .60
270 Jim Thome .25 .60
271 Don Mattingly 1.00 2.50
272 Don Mattingly 1.00 2.50
273 Don Mattingly 1.00 2.50
274 Don Mattingly 1.00 2.50
275 Don Mattingly 1.00 2.50
281 Nolan Ryan 1.50 4.00
282 Nolan Ryan 1.50 4.00
283 Nolan Ryan 1.50 4.00
284 Nolan Ryan 1.50 4.00
285 Nolan Ryan 1.50 4.00
286 Ivan Rodriguez .25 .60
287 Ivan Rodriguez .25 .60
288 Ivan Rodriguez .25 .60
289 Ivan Rodriguez .25 .60
290 Ivan Rodriguez .25 .60
321 Minnesota Twins .20 .50
322 Minnesota Twins .20 .50
323 Minnesota Twins .20 .50
324 Minnesota Twins .20 .50
325 Minnesota Twins .20 .50
391 Ken Griffey Jr. 1.00 2.50
392 Ken Griffey Jr. 1.00 2.50
393 Ken Griffey Jr. 1.00 2.50
394 Ken Griffey Jr. 1.00 2.50
395 Ken Griffey Jr. 1.00 2.50
396 Pedro Martinez .25 .60
397 Pedro Martinez .25 .60
398 Pedro Martinez .25 .60
399 Pedro Martinez .25 .60
400 Pedro Martinez .25 .60
416 Toronto Blue Jays .20 .50
417 Toronto Blue Jays .20 .50
418 Toronto Blue Jays .20 .50
419 Toronto Blue Jays .20 .50
420 Toronto Blue Jays .20 .50
431 Derek Jeter 1.25 3.00
432 Derek Jeter 1.25 3.00
433 Derek Jeter 1.25 3.00
434 Derek Jeter 1.25 3.00
435 Derek Jeter 1.25 3.00
461 Greg Maddux .50 1.25
462 Greg Maddux .50 1.25
463 Greg Maddux .50 1.25
464 Greg Maddux .50 1.25
465 Greg Maddux .50 1.25
466 Tim Wakefield .20 .50
467 Tim Wakefield .20 .50
468 Tim Wakefield .20 .50
469 Tim Wakefield .20 .50
470 Tim Wakefield .20 .50
481 Jeff Kent .20 .50
482 Jeff Kent .20 .50
483 Jeff Kent .20 .50
484 Jeff Kent .20 .50
485 Jeff Kent .20 .50
486 Dennis Eckersley .20 .50
487 Dennis Eckersley .20 .50
488 Dennis Eckersley .20 .50
489 Dennis Eckersley .20 .50
490 Dennis Eckersley .20 .50
491 Rollie Fingers .20 .50
492 Rollie Fingers .20 .50
493 Rollie Fingers .20 .50
494 Rollie Fingers .20 .50
495 Rollie Fingers .20 .50
506 Reggie Jackson .25 .60
507 Reggie Jackson .25 .60
508 Reggie Jackson .25 .60
509 Reggie Jackson .25 .60
510 Reggie Jackson .25 .60
511 Jim Edmonds .25 .60
512 Jim Edmonds .25 .60
513 Jim Edmonds .25 .60
514 Jim Edmonds .25 .60
515 Jim Edmonds .25 .60
516 Florida Marlins .20 .50
517 Florida Marlins .20 .50
518 Florida Marlins .20 .50
519 Florida Marlins .20 .50
520 Florida Marlins .20 .50
531 Ken Griffey Jr. 1.00 2.50
532 Ken Griffey Jr. 1.00 2.50
533 Ken Griffey Jr. 1.00 2.50
534 Ken Griffey Jr. 1.00 2.50
535 Ken Griffey Jr. 1.00 2.50
546 Derek Jeter 1.25 3.00
547 Derek Jeter 1.25 3.00
548 Derek Jeter 1.25 3.00
549 Derek Jeter 1.25 3.00
550 Derek Jeter 1.25 3.00
551 Ken Griffey Jr. 1.00 2.50
552 Ken Griffey Jr. 1.00 2.50
553 Ken Griffey Jr. 1.00 2.50
554 Ken Griffey Jr. 1.00 2.50
555 Ken Griffey Jr. 1.00 2.50
571 Nolan Ryan 1.50 4.00
572 Nolan Ryan 1.50 4.00
573 Nolan Ryan 1.50 4.00
574 Nolan Ryan 1.50 4.00
575 Nolan Ryan 1.50 4.00
586 Toronto Blue Jays/Molitor .20 .50
587 Toronto Blue Jays .20 .50
588 Toronto Blue Jays .20 .50
589 Toronto Blue Jays .20 .50
590 Toronto Blue Jays .20 .50
591 Frank Thomas .40 1.00
592 Frank Thomas .40 1.00
593 Frank Thomas .40 1.00
594 Frank Thomas .40 1.00
595 Frank Thomas .40 1.00
621 Manny Ramirez .40 1.00
622 Manny Ramirez .40 1.00
623 Manny Ramirez .40 1.00
624 Manny Ramirez .40 1.00
625 Manny Ramirez .40 1.00
626 Michael Jordan 4.00 10.00
627 Michael Jordan 4.00 10.00
628 Michael Jordan 4.00 10.00
629 Michael Jordan 4.00 10.00
630 Michael Jordan 4.00 10.00
636 Steve Carlton .20 .50
637 Steve Carlton .20 .50
638 Steve Carlton .20 .50
639 Steve Carlton .20 .50
640 Steve Carlton .20 .50
641 Tony Gwynn .40 1.00
642 Tony Gwynn .40 1.00
643 Tony Gwynn .40 1.00
644 Tony Gwynn .40 1.00
645 Tony Gwynn .40 1.00
661 Kenny Rogers .20 .50
662 Kenny Rogers .20 .50
663 Kenny Rogers .20 .50
664 Kenny Rogers .20 .50
665 Kenny Rogers .20 .50
671 Don Mattingly 1.00 2.50
672 Don Mattingly 1.00 2.50
673 Don Mattingly 1.00 2.50
674 Don Mattingly 1.00 2.50
675 Don Mattingly 1.00 2.50
676 Ken Griffey Jr. 1.00 2.50
677 Ken Griffey Jr. 1.00 2.50
678 Ken Griffey Jr. 1.00 2.50
679 Ken Griffey Jr. 1.00 2.50
680 Ken Griffey Jr. 1.00 2.50
701 Alex Rodriguez .75 2.00
702 Alex Rodriguez .75 2.00
703 Alex Rodriguez .75 2.00
704 Alex Rodriguez .75 2.00
705 Alex Rodriguez .75 2.00
716 Frank Thomas .40 1.00
717 Frank Thomas .40 1.00
718 Frank Thomas .40 1.00
719 Frank Thomas .40 1.00
720 Frank Thomas .40 1.00
756 Derek Jeter 1.25 3.00
757 Derek Jeter 1.25 3.00
758 Derek Jeter 1.25 3.00
759 Derek Jeter 1.25 3.00
760 Derek Jeter 1.25 3.00
761 Mike Schmidt .75 2.00
762 Mike Schmidt .75 2.00
763 Mike Schmidt .75 2.00
764 Mike Schmidt .75 2.00
765 Mike Schmidt .75 2.00
766 Mariano Rivera .40 1.00
767 Mariano Rivera .40 1.00
768 Mariano Rivera .40 1.00
769 Mariano Rivera .40 1.00
770 Mariano Rivera .40 1.00
776 Andy Pettitte .25 .60
777 Andy Pettitte .25 .60
778 Andy Pettitte .25 .60
779 Andy Pettitte .25 .60
780 Andy Pettitte .25 .60
806 Cal Ripken Jr. 2.00 5.00
807 Cal Ripken Jr. 2.00 5.00
808 Cal Ripken Jr. 2.00 5.00
809 Cal Ripken Jr. 2.00 5.00
810 Cal Ripken Jr. 2.00 5.00
811 Cal Ripken Jr. 2.00 5.00
812 Cal Ripken Jr. 2.00 5.00
813 Cal Ripken Jr. 2.00 5.00
814 Cal Ripken Jr. 2.00 5.00
815 Cal Ripken Jr. 2.00 5.00
816 Ozzie Smith .75 2.00

817 Ozzie Smith .75 2.00
818 Ozzie Smith .75 2.00
819 Ozzie Smith .75 2.00
820 Ozzie Smith .75 2.00
821 New York Yankees .40 1.00
822 New York Yankees .40 1.00
823 New York Yankees .40 1.00
824 New York Yankees .40 1.00
825 New York Yankees .40 1.00
831 Jorge Posada .25 .60
832 Jorge Posada .25 .60
833 Jorge Posada .25 .60
834 Jorge Posada .25 .60
835 Jorge Posada .25 .60
836 John Smoltz .40 1.00
837 John Smoltz .40 1.00
838 John Smoltz .40 1.00
839 John Smoltz .40 1.00
840 John Smoltz .40 1.00
861 Joe Torre .25 .60
862 Joe Torre .25 .60
863 Joe Torre .25 .60
864 Joe Torre .25 .60
865 Joe Torre .25 .60
871 Greg Maddux .50 1.25
872 Greg Maddux .50 1.25
873 Greg Maddux .50 1.25
874 Greg Maddux .50 1.25
875 Greg Maddux .50 1.25
876 Alex Rodriguez .75 2.00
877 Alex Rodriguez .75 2.00
878 Alex Rodriguez .75 2.00
879 Alex Rodriguez .75 2.00
880 Alex Rodriguez .75 2.00
891 Derek Jeter 1.25 3.00
892 Derek Jeter 1.25 3.00
893 Derek Jeter 1.25 3.00
894 Derek Jeter 1.25 3.00
895 Derek Jeter 1.25 3.00
906 Vladimir Guerrero .40 1.00
907 Vladimir Guerrero .40 1.00
908 Vladimir Guerrero .40 1.00
909 Vladimir Guerrero .40 1.00
910 Vladimir Guerrero .40 1.00
921 Nomar Garciaparra .40 1.00
922 Nomar Garciaparra .40 1.00
923 Nomar Garciaparra .40 1.00
924 Nomar Garciaparra .40 1.00
925 Nomar Garciaparra .40 1.00
951 New York Yankees .40 1.00
952 New York Yankees .40 1.00
953 New York Yankees .40 1.00
954 New York Yankees .40 1.00
955 New York Yankees .40 1.00
1011 First Year of Interleague Baseball .20 .50
1012 First Year of Interleague Baseball .20 .50
1013 First Year of Interleague Baseball .20 .50
1014 First Year of Interleague Baseball .20 .50
1015 First Year of Interleague Baseball .20 .50
1046 Don Mattingly 1.00 2.50
1047 Don Mattingly 1.00 2.50
1048 Don Mattingly 1.00 2.50
1049 Don Mattingly 1.00 2.50
1050 Don Mattingly 1.00 2.50
1061 Florida Marlins .20 .50
1062 Florida Marlins .20 .50
1063 Florida Marlins .20 .50
1064 Florida Marlins .20 .50
1065 Florida Marlins .20 .50
1066 Ken Griffey Jr. 1.00 2.50
1067 Ken Griffey Jr. 1.00 2.50
1068 Ken Griffey Jr. 1.00 2.50
1069 Ken Griffey Jr. 1.00 2.50
1070 Ken Griffey Jr. 1.00 2.50
1076 Pedro Martinez .25 .60
1077 Pedro Martinez .25 .60
1078 Pedro Martinez .25 .60
1079 Pedro Martinez .25 .60
1080 Pedro Martinez .25 .60
1081 Jason Varitek .40 1.00
1082 Jason Varitek .40 1.00
1083 Jason Varitek .40 1.00
1084 Jason Varitek .40 1.00
1085 Jason Varitek .40 1.00
1101 Derrek Lee .20 .50
1102 Derrek Lee .20 .50
1103 Derrek Lee .20 .50
1104 Derrek Lee .20 .50
1105 Derrek Lee .20 .50
1111 Nomar Garciaparra .40 1.00
1112 Nomar Garciaparra .40 1.00
1113 Nomar Garciaparra .40 1.00
1114 Nomar Garciaparra .40 1.00
1115 Nomar Garciaparra .40 1.00
1141 Tampa Bay Rays .20 .50
1142 Tampa Bay Rays .20 .50
1143 Tampa Bay Rays .20 .50
1144 Tampa Bay Rays .20 .50
1145 Tampa Bay Rays .20 .50
1156 New York Yankees .40 1.00
1157 New York Yankees .40 1.00
1158 New York Yankees .40 1.00
1159 New York Yankees .40 1.00
1160 New York Yankees .40 1.00
1166 Cal Ripken Jr. 2.00 5.00
1167 Cal Ripken Jr. 2.00 5.00
1168 Cal Ripken Jr. 2.00 5.00
1169 Cal Ripken Jr. 2.00 5.00
1170 Cal Ripken Jr. 2.00 5.00
1191 Kerry Wood .20 .50
1192 Kerry Wood .20 .50
1193 Kerry Wood .20 .50
1194 Kerry Wood .20 .50
1195 Kerry Wood .20 .50
1241 Carlos Beltran .20 .50
1242 Carlos Beltran .20 .50
1243 Carlos Beltran .20 .50
1244 Carlos Beltran .20 .50
1245 Carlos Beltran .20 .50
1246 New York Yankees .40 1.00
1247 New York Yankees .40 1.00
1248 New York Yankees .40 1.00
1249 New York Yankees .40 1.00
1250 New York Yankees .40 1.00
1256 Orlando Cepeda .20 .50
1257 Orlando Cepeda .20 .50
1258 Orlando Cepeda .20 .50
1259 Orlando Cepeda .20 .50
1260 Orlando Cepeda .20 .50
1276 New York Yankees .40 1.00
1277 New York Yankees .40 1.00
1278 New York Yankees .40 1.00
1279 New York Yankees .40 1.00
1280 New York Yankees .40 1.00
1281 Chipper Jones .50 1.25
1282 Chipper Jones .50 1.25
1283 Chipper Jones .50 1.25
1284 Chipper Jones .50 1.25
1285 Chipper Jones .50 1.25
1286 Pedro Martinez .25 .60
1287 Pedro Martinez .25 .60
1288 Pedro Martinez .25 .60
1289 Pedro Martinez .25 .60
1290 Pedro Martinez .25 .60
1291 Nolan Ryan 1.50 4.00
1292 Nolan Ryan 1.50 4.00
1293 Nolan Ryan 1.50 4.00
1294 Nolan Ryan 1.50 4.00
1295 Nolan Ryan 1.50 4.00
1296 Robin Yount .40 1.00
1297 Robin Yount .40 1.00
1298 Robin Yount .40 1.00
1299 Robin Yount .40 1.00
1300 Robin Yount .40 1.00
1301 Tony Gwynn .40 1.00
1302 Tony Gwynn .40 1.00
1303 Tony Gwynn .40 1.00
1304 Tony Gwynn .40 1.00
1305 Tony Gwynn .40 1.00
1306 Bob Gibson .25 .60
1307 Bob Gibson .25 .60
1308 Bob Gibson .25 .60
1309 Bob Gibson .25 .60
1310 Bob Gibson .25 .60
1311 Johnny Bench .40 1.00
1312 Johnny Bench .40 1.00
1313 Johnny Bench .40 1.00
1314 Johnny Bench .40 1.00
1315 Johnny Bench .40 1.00
1316 Yogi Berra .40 1.00
1317 Yogi Berra .40 1.00
1318 Yogi Berra .40 1.00
1319 Yogi Berra .40 1.00
1320 Yogi Berra .40 1.00
1321 Mike Schmidt .75 2.00
1322 Mike Schmidt .75 2.00
1323 Mike Schmidt .75 2.00
1324 Mike Schmidt .75 2.00
1325 Mike Schmidt .75 2.00
1326 Brooks Robinson .25 .60
1327 Brooks Robinson .25 .60
1328 Brooks Robinson .25 .60
1329 Brooks Robinson .25 .60
1330 Brooks Robinson .25 .60
1331 Cal Ripken Jr. 2.00 5.00
1332 Cal Ripken Jr. 2.00 5.00
1333 Cal Ripken Jr. 2.00 5.00
1334 Cal Ripken Jr. 2.00 5.00
1335 Cal Ripken Jr. 2.00 5.00
1336 Ernie Banks .40 1.00
1337 Ernie Banks .40 1.00
1338 Ernie Banks .40 1.00
1339 Ernie Banks .40 1.00
1340 Ernie Banks .40 1.00
1341 Ted Williams 1.25 3.00
1342 Ted Williams 1.25 3.00
1343 Ted Williams 1.25 3.00
1344 Ted Williams 1.25 3.00
1345 Ted Williams 1.25 3.00
1346 Joe DiMaggio 1.25 3.00
1347 Joe DiMaggio 1.25 3.00
1348 Joe DiMaggio 1.25 3.00
1349 Joe DiMaggio 1.25 3.00
1350 Joe DiMaggio 1.25 3.00
1351 Ken Griffey Jr. 1.00 2.50
1352 Ken Griffey Jr. 1.00 2.50
1353 Ken Griffey Jr. 1.00 2.50
1354 Ken Griffey Jr. 1.00 2.50
1355 Ken Griffey Jr. 1.00 2.50
1356 Alfonso Soriano .20 .50
1357 Alfonso Soriano .20 .50
1358 Alfonso Soriano .20 .50
1359 Alfonso Soriano .20 .50
1360 Alfonso Soriano .20 .50
1361 Lance Berkman .25 .60
1362 Lance Berkman .25 .60
1363 Lance Berkman .25 .60
1364 Lance Berkman .25 .60
1365 Lance Berkman .25 .60
1366 Rick Ankiel .25 .60
1367 Rick Ankiel .25 .60
1368 Rick Ankiel .25 .60
1369 Rick Ankiel .25 .60
1370 Rick Ankiel .25 .60
1386 Derek Jeter 1.25 3.00
1387 Derek Jeter 1.25 3.00
1388 Derek Jeter 1.25 3.00
1389 Derek Jeter 1.25 3.00
1390 Derek Jeter 1.25 3.00
1416 New York Yankees .40 1.00
1417 New York Yankees .40 1.00
1418 New York Yankees .40 1.00
1419 New York Yankees .40 1.00
1420 New York Yankees .40 1.00
1426 Derek Jeter 1.25 3.00
1427 Derek Jeter 1.25 3.00
1428 Derek Jeter 1.25 3.00
1429 Derek Jeter 1.25 3.00
1430 Derek Jeter 1.25 3.00
1441 Jimmy Rollins .25 .60
1442 Jimmy Rollins .25 .60
1443 Jimmy Rollins .25 .60
1444 Jimmy Rollins .25 .60
1445 Jimmy Rollins .25 .60
1446 Carlton Fisk .25 .60
1447 Carlton Fisk .25 .60
1448 Carlton Fisk .25 .60
1449 Carlton Fisk .25 .60
1450 Carlton Fisk .25 .60
1451 Ken Griffey Jr. 1.00 2.50
1452 Ken Griffey Jr. 1.00 2.50
1453 Ken Griffey Jr. 1.00 2.50
1454 Ken Griffey Jr. 1.00 2.50
1455 Ken Griffey Jr. 1.00 2.50
1456 Baseball Season Opens in Japan .20 .50
1457 Baseball Season Opens in Japan .20 .50
1458 Baseball Season Opens in Japan .20 .50
1459 Baseball Season Opens in Japan .20 .50
1460 Baseball Season Opens in Japan .20 .50
1461 Cal Ripken Jr. 2.00 5.00
1462 Cal Ripken Jr. 2.00 5.00
1463 Cal Ripken Jr. 2.00 5.00
1464 Cal Ripken Jr. 2.00 5.00
1465 Cal Ripken Jr. 2.00 5.00
1471 Michael Young .25 .60
1472 Michael Young .25 .60
1473 Michael Young .25 .60
1474 Michael Young .25 .60
1475 Michael Young .25 .60
1476 Pedro Martinez .25 .60
1477 Pedro Martinez .25 .60
1478 Pedro Martinez .25 .60
1479 Pedro Martinez .25 .60
1480 Pedro Martinez .25 .60
1496 Tony Perez .20 .50
1497 Tony Perez .20 .50
1498 Tony Perez .20 .50
1499 Tony Perez .20 .50
1500 Tony Perez .20 .50
1506 Josh Beckett .25 .60
1507 Josh Beckett .25 .60
1508 Josh Beckett .25 .60
1509 Josh Beckett .25 .60
1510 Josh Beckett .25 .60
1531 Arizona Diamondbacks .20 .50
1532 Arizona Diamondbacks .20 .50
1533 Arizona Diamondbacks .20 .50
1534 Arizona Diamondbacks .20 .50
1535 Arizona Diamondbacks .20 .50
1536 Willie Stargell .25 .60
1537 Willie Stargell .25 .60
1538 Willie Stargell .25 .60
1539 Willie Stargell .25 .60
1540 Willie Stargell .25 .60
1546 New York Mets Win
Emotional Post 9/11 Game .25 .60
1547 New York Mets Win
Emotional Post 9/11 Game .25 .60
1548 New York Mets Win
Emotional Post 9/11 Game .25 .60
1549 New York Mets Win
Emotional Post 9/11 Game .25 .60
1550 New York Mets Win
Emotional Post 9/11 Game .25 .60
1551 Ichiro Suzuki .75 2.00
1552 Ichiro Suzuki .75 2.00
1553 Ichiro Suzuki .75 2.00
1554 Ichiro Suzuki .75 2.00
1555 Ichiro Suzuki .75 2.00
1556 Albert Pujols 1.25 3.00
1557 Albert Pujols 1.25 3.00
1558 Albert Pujols 1.25 3.00
1559 Albert Pujols 1.25 3.00
1560 Albert Pujols 1.25 3.00
1566 Dave Winfield .20 .50
1567 Dave Winfield .20 .50
1568 Dave Winfield .20 .50
1569 Dave Winfield .20 .50
1570 Dave Winfield .20 .50
1571 Cal Ripken Jr. 2.00 5.00
1572 Cal Ripken Jr. 2.00 5.00
1573 Cal Ripken Jr. 2.00 5.00
1574 Cal Ripken Jr. 2.00 5.00
1575 Cal Ripken Jr. 2.00 5.00
1576 Tony Gwynn .40 1.00
1577 Tony Gwynn .40 1.00
1578 Tony Gwynn .40 1.00
1579 Tony Gwynn .40 1.00
1580 Tony Gwynn .40 1.00
1581 Bill Mazeroski .25 .60
1582 Bill Mazeroski .25 .60
1583 Bill Mazeroski .25 .60
1584 Bill Mazeroski .25 .60
1585 Bill Mazeroski .25 .60
1611 Ichiro Suzuki .75 2.00
1612 Ichiro Suzuki .75 2.00
1613 Ichiro Suzuki .75 2.00
1614 Ichiro Suzuki .75 2.00
1615 Ichiro Suzuki .75 2.00
1621 New York Yankees .40 1.00
1622 New York Yankees .40 1.00
1623 New York Yankees .40 1.00
1624 New York Yankees .40 1.00
1625 New York Yankees .40 1.00
1641 Anaheim Angels .20 .50
1642 Anaheim Angels .20 .50
1643 Anaheim Angels .20 .50
1644 Anaheim Angels .20 .50
1645 Anaheim Angels .20 .50
1646 Ted Williams 1.25 3.00
1647 Ted Williams 1.25 3.00
1648 Ted Williams 1.25 3.00
1649 Ted Williams 1.25 3.00
1650 Ted Williams 1.25 3.00
1661 Ozzie Smith .75 2.00
1662 Ozzie Smith .75 2.00
1663 Ozzie Smith .75 2.00
1664 Ozzie Smith .75 2.00
1665 Ozzie Smith .75 2.00
1696 Randy Johnson .40 1.00
1697 Randy Johnson .40 1.00
1698 Randy Johnson .40 1.00
1699 Randy Johnson .40 1.00
1700 Randy Johnson .40 1.00
1736 Francisco Rodriguez .20 .50
1737 Francisco Rodriguez .20 .50
1738 Francisco Rodriguez .20 .50
1739 Francisco Rodriguez .20 .50
1740 Francisco Rodriguez .20 .50
1756 Derek Jeter 1.25 3.00
1757 Derek Jeter 1.25 3.00
1758 Derek Jeter 1.25 3.00
1759 Derek Jeter 1.25 3.00
1760 Derek Jeter 1.25 3.00
1766 Chase Utley .40 1.00
1767 Chase Utley .40 1.00
1768 Chase Utley .40 1.00
1769 Chase Utley .40 1.00
1770 Chase Utley .40 1.00
1776 Hideki Matsui .40 1.00
1777 Hideki Matsui .40 1.00
1778 Hideki Matsui .40 1.00
1779 Hideki Matsui .40 1.00
1780 Hideki Matsui .40 1.00
1781 Florida Marlins .20 .50
1782 Florida Marlins .20 .50
1783 Florida Marlins .20 .50
1784 Florida Marlins .20 .50
1785 Florida Marlins .20 .50
1836 Eddie Murray .40 1.00
1837 Eddie Murray .40 1.00
1838 Eddie Murray .40 1.00
1839 Eddie Murray .40 1.00
1840 Eddie Murray .40 1.00
1881 Boston Red Sox .40 1.00
1882 Boston Red Sox .40 1.00
1883 Boston Red Sox .40 1.00
1884 Boston Red Sox .40 1.00
1885 Boston Red Sox .40 1.00
1931 Ryan Howard .50 1.25
1932 Ryan Howard .50 1.25
1933 Ryan Howard .50 1.25
1934 Ryan Howard .50 1.25
1935 Ryan Howard .50 1.25
1936 Boston Red Sox .40 1.00
1937 Boston Red Sox .40 1.00
1938 Boston Red Sox .40 1.00
1939 Boston Red Sox .40 1.00
1940 Boston Red Sox .40 1.00
1941 Ichiro Suzuki .75 2.00
1942 Ichiro Suzuki .75 2.00
1943 Ichiro Suzuki .75 2.00
1944 Ichiro Suzuki .75 2.00
1945 Ichiro Suzuki .75 2.00
1946 Montreal Expos .20 .50
1947 Montreal Expos .20 .50
1948 Montreal Expos .20 .50
1949 Montreal Expos .20 .50
1950 Montreal Expos .20 .50
1951 Alex Rodriguez .75 2.00
1952 Alex Rodriguez .75 2.00
1953 Alex Rodriguez .75 2.00
1954 Alex Rodriguez .75 2.00
1955 Alex Rodriguez .75 2.00
1956 David Wright .50 1.25
1957 David Wright .50 1.25
1958 David Wright .50 1.25
1959 David Wright .50 1.25
1960 David Wright .50 1.25
1961 Chipper Jones .50 1.25
1962 Chipper Jones .50 1.25
1963 Chipper Jones .50 1.25
1964 Chipper Jones .50 1.25
1965 Chipper Jones .50 1.25
1966 Ken Griffey Jr. 1.00 2.50
1967 Ken Griffey Jr. 1.00 2.50
1968 Ken Griffey Jr. 1.00 2.50
1969 Ken Griffey Jr. 1.00 2.50
1970 Ken Griffey Jr. 1.00 2.50
2016 Washington Nationals .20 .50
2017 Washington Nationals .20 .50
2018 Washington Nationals .20 .50
2019 Washington Nationals .20 .50
2020 Washington Nationals .20 .50
2066 Jonathan Papelbon .25 .60
2067 Jonathan Papelbon .25 .60
2068 Jonathan Papelbon .25 .60
2069 Jonathan Papelbon .25 .60
2070 Jonathan Papelbon .25 .60
2071 Chicago White Sox .20 .50
2072 Chicago White Sox .20 .50
2073 Chicago White Sox .20 .50
2074 Chicago White Sox .20 .50
2075 Chicago White Sox .20 .50
2076 Wade Boggs .25 .60
2077 Wade Boggs .25 .60
2078 Wade Boggs .25 .60
2079 Wade Boggs .25 .60
2080 Wade Boggs .25 .60
2081 Ryne Sandberg 1.00 2.50
2082 Ryne Sandberg 1.00 2.50
2083 Ryne Sandberg 1.00 2.50
2084 Ryne Sandberg 1.00 2.50
2085 Ryne Sandberg 1.00 2.50
2086 Albert Pujols 1.25 3.00
2087 Albert Pujols 1.25 3.00
2088 Albert Pujols 1.25 3.00
2089 Albert Pujols 1.25 3.00
2090 Albert Pujols 1.25 3.00
2116 Chien-Ming Wang .40 1.00
2117 Chien-Ming Wang .40 1.00
2118 Chien-Ming Wang .40 1.00
2119 Chien-Ming Wang .40 1.00
2120 Chien-Ming Wang .40 1.00
2151 St. Louis Cardinals .25 .60
2152 St. Louis Cardinals .25 .60
2153 St. Louis Cardinals .25 .60
2154 St. Louis Cardinals .25 .60
2155 St. Louis Cardinals .25 .60
2156 Daisuke Matsuzaka .75 2.00
2157 Daisuke Matsuzaka .75 2.00
2158 Daisuke Matsuzaka .75 2.00
2159 Daisuke Matsuzaka .75 2.00
2160 Daisuke Matsuzaka .75 2.00
2161 Dustin Pedroia .75 2.00
2162 Dustin Pedroia .75 2.00
2163 Dustin Pedroia .75 2.00
2164 Dustin Pedroia .75 2.00
2165 Dustin Pedroia .75 2.00
2176 Cole Hamels .40 1.00
2177 Cole Hamels .40 1.00
2178 Cole Hamels .40 1.00
2179 Cole Hamels .40 1.00
2180 Cole Hamels .40 1.00
2201 Ryan Howard .50 1.25
2202 Ryan Howard .50 1.25
2203 Ryan Howard .50 1.25
2204 Ryan Howard .50 1.25
2205 Ryan Howard .50 1.25
2206 Hanley Ramirez .40 1.00
2207 Hanley Ramirez .40 1.00
2208 Hanley Ramirez .40 1.00
2209 Hanley Ramirez .40 1.00
2210 Hanley Ramirez .40 1.00
2221 Joe Mauer .40 1.00
2222 Joe Mauer .40 1.00
2223 Joe Mauer .40 1.00
2224 Joe Mauer .40 1.00
2225 Joe Mauer .40 1.00
2226 Brandon Webb .25 .60
2227 Brandon Webb .25 .60
2228 Brandon Webb .25 .60
2229 Brandon Webb .25 .60
2230 Brandon Webb .25 .60
2256 Josh Hamilton .40 1.00
2257 Josh Hamilton .40 1.00
2258 Josh Hamilton .40 1.00
2259 Josh Hamilton .40 1.00
2260 Josh Hamilton .40 1.00
2261 Tom Glavine .25 .60
2262 Tom Glavine .25 .60
2263 Tom Glavine .25 .60
2264 Tom Glavine .25 .60
2265 Tom Glavine .25 .60
2266 Boston Red Sox .40 1.00
2267 Boston Red Sox .40 1.00
2268 Boston Red Sox .40 1.00
2269 Boston Red Sox .40 1.00
2270 Boston Red Sox .40 1.00
2291 Cal Ripken Jr. 2.00 5.00
2292 Cal Ripken Jr. 2.00 5.00
2293 Cal Ripken Jr. 2.00 5.00
2294 Cal Ripken Jr. 2.00 5.00
2295 Cal Ripken Jr. 2.00 5.00
2296 Tony Gwynn .40 1.00
2297 Tony Gwynn .40 1.00
2298 Tony Gwynn .40 1.00
2299 Tony Gwynn .40 1.00
2300 Tony Gwynn .40 1.00
2301 Ryan Braun .50 1.25
2302 Ryan Braun .50 1.25
2303 Ryan Braun .50 1.25
2304 Ryan Braun .50 1.25
2305 Ryan Braun .50 1.25
2306 Jimmy Rollins .25 .60
2307 Jimmy Rollins .25 .60
2308 Jimmy Rollins .25 .60
2309 Jimmy Rollins .25 .60
2310 Jimmy Rollins .25 .60
2311 Alex Rodriguez .75 2.00
2312 Alex Rodriguez .75 2.00
2313 Alex Rodriguez .75 2.00
2314 Alex Rodriguez .75 2.00
2315 Alex Rodriguez .75 2.00
2316 Ichiro Suzuki .75 2.00
2317 Ichiro Suzuki .75 2.00
2318 Ichiro Suzuki .75 2.00
2319 Ichiro Suzuki .75 2.00
2320 Ichiro Suzuki .75 2.00
2331 Joba Chamberlain .50 1.25
2332 Joba Chamberlain .50 1.25
2333 Joba Chamberlain .50 1.25
2334 Joba Chamberlain .50 1.25
2335 Joba Chamberlain .50 1.25
2366 Alex Rodriguez .75 2.00
2367 Alex Rodriguez .75 2.00
2368 Alex Rodriguez .75 2.00
2369 Alex Rodriguez .75 2.00
2370 Alex Rodriguez .75 2.00
2381 Manny Ramirez .40 1.00
2382 Manny Ramirez .40 1.00
2383 Manny Ramirez .40 1.00
2384 Manny Ramirez .40 1.00
2385 Manny Ramirez .40 1.00
2386 Ken Griffey Jr. 1.00 2.50
2387 Ken Griffey Jr. 1.00 2.50
2388 Ken Griffey Jr. 1.00 2.50
2389 Ken Griffey Jr. 1.00 2.50
2390 Ken Griffey Jr. 1.00 2.50
2401 Josh Hamilton .40 1.00
2402 Josh Hamilton .40 1.00
2403 Josh Hamilton .40 1.00
2404 Josh Hamilton .40 1.00
2405 Josh Hamilton .40 1.00
2451 Jay Bruce .40 1.00
2452 Jay Bruce .40 1.00
2453 Jay Bruce .40 1.00
2454 Jay Bruce .40 1.00
2455 Jay Bruce .40 1.00
2476 Philadelphia Phillies .20 .50
2477 Philadelphia Phillies .20 .50
2478 Philadelphia Phillies .20 .50
2479 Philadelphia Phillies .20 .50
2480 Philadelphia Phillies .20 .50
2481 Manny Ramirez .40 1.00
2482 Manny Ramirez .40 1.00
2483 Manny Ramirez .40 1.00
2484 Manny Ramirez .40 1.00
2485 Manny Ramirez .40 1.00
2486 Travis Snider .40 1.00
2487 Travis Snider .40 1.00
2488 Travis Snider .40 1.00
2489 Travis Snider .40 1.00
2490 Travis Snider .40 1.00
2491 Evan Longoria .75 2.00
2492 Evan Longoria .75 2.00
2493 Evan Longoria .75 2.00
2494 Evan Longoria .75 2.00
2495 Evan Longoria .75 2.00

2009 Upper Deck 20th Anniversary Memorabilia

MLBAP Andy Pettitte
MLBAR Aramis Ramirez 3.00 8.00
MLBBO Bo Jackson 8.00 20.00
MLBBS Ben Sheets 4.00 10.00
MLBBW Brandon Webb 10.00 25.00
MLBBZ Barry Zito 4.00 10.00
MLBCC Chris Carpenter 3.00 8.00
MLBCD Carlos Delgado 3.00 8.00
MLBCG Carlos Guillen 3.00 8.00
MLBCL Carlos Lee 3.00 8.00
MLBCR Cal Ripken Jr. 12.00 30.00
MLBCS Curt Schilling 3.00 8.00
MLBCY Chris B. Young 4.00 10.00
MLBDJ Derek Jeter 10.00 25.00
MLBDL Derrek Lee 4.00 10.00
MLBDO David Ortiz 10.00 25.00
MLBEG Eric Gagne 4.00 10.00
MLBFL Francisco Liriano 4.00 10.00
MLBFT Frank Thomas 30.00 60.00
MLBGL Tom Glavine 4.00 10.00
MLBGM Greg Maddux
MLBGS Gary Sheffield 3.00 8.00
MLBGT Garret Anderson 5.00 12.00
MLBHE Todd Helton 5.00 12.00
MLBIR Ivan Rodriguez 3.00 8.00
MLBJD Johnny Damon 5.00 12.00
MLBJE Jim Edmonds 3.00 8.00
MLBJG Jason Giambi 5.00 12.00
MLBJM Joe Mauer 6.00 15.00
MLBJO Jonathan Papelbon 5.00 12.00
MLBJP Jorge Posada 4.00 10.00
MLBJS Johan Santana 3.00 8.00
MLBJT Jim Thome 5.00 12.00
MLBJU Justin Verlander 3.00 8.00
MLBJV Jason Varitek 6.00 15.00
MLBKG Ken Griffey Jr. 5.00 12.00
MLBMH Matt Holliday 4.00 10.00
MLBMM Mike Mussina
MLBMO Magglio Ordonez 3.00 8.00
MLBMP Mark Prior 3.00 8.00
MLBMR Mariano Rivera
MLBMT Mark Teixeira 3.00 8.00
MLBPM Pedro Martinez 6.00 15.00
MLBRA Manny Ramirez 10.00 25.00
MLBRB Roy Halladay 4.00 10.00
MLBRC Roger Clemens 5.00 12.00
MLBRC2 Roger Clemens 5.00 12.00
MLBRC3 Roger Clemens 5.00 12.00
MLBRJ Randy Johnson 6.00 15.00
MLBRO Roy Oswalt 3.00 8.00
MLBSK Scott Kazmir 5.00 12.00
MLBTE Miguel Tejada 3.00 8.00
MLBTG Tony Gwynn 20.00 50.00
MLBTG2 Tony Gwynn 20.00 50.00
MLBTH Trevor Hoffman 3.00 8.00
MLBTI Tim Hudson 10.00 25.00
MLBTR Tim Raines 6.00 15.00
MLBVG Vladimir Guerrero 6.00 15.00
MLBWB Wade Boggs 8.00 20.00

2014 Upper Deck 25th Anniversary

24 Ken Griffey Jr. 1.00 2.50
37 Tony Gwynn .50 1.25
66 Bob Horner .30 .75
115 Corey Black .30 .75
116 Miguel Almonte .30 .75
117 Byron Buxton 1.00 2.50
120 Roberto Osuna .30 .75
122 Rodney Daal .30 .75
128 Eduardo Rodriguez .30 .75
137 Bryan Mitchell .30 .75
143 Joey Gallo 1.00 2.50
144 Jonathan Gray .40 1.00
145 Marten Gasparini .30 .75
147 Jacob May .30 .75
149 Jorge Alfaro .40 1.00

2014 Upper Deck 25th Anniversary Silver

*SILVER/250: 1.2X TO 3X BASIC CARDS

2014 Upper Deck 25th Anniversary Autographs

24 Ken Griffey Jr./25
27 Danica Patrick/25
37 Tony Gwynn/25
66 Bob Horner/125 5.00 12.00
117 Byron Buxton/25
120 Roberto Osuna/25
122 Rodney Daal/125 4.00 10.00
128 Eduardo Rodriguez/25
137 Bryan Mitchell/25
143 Joey Gallo/25
144 Jonathan Gray/25
147 Jacob May/25
149 Jorge Alfaro/25

2014 Upper Deck 25th Anniversary Promos

UD25KG Ken Griffey Jr 5.00 12.00

2002 Upper Deck 40-Man

COMPLETE SET (1182) 100.00 200.00
SUBSET CARDS HALF VALUE OF BASE CARDS
1 Darin Erstad .15 .40
2 Kevin Appier .15 .40
3 Scott Schoeneweis .15 .40
4 Ben Molina .15 .40
5 Troy Glaus .15 .40
6 Adam Kennedy .15 .40
7 Aaron Sele .15 .40
8 Garret Anderson .15 .40
9 Ramon Ortiz .15 .40
10 Dennis Cook .15 .40
11 Scott Spiezio .15 .40
12 Orlando Palmeiro .15 .40
13 Troy Percival .15 .40
14 David Eckstein .15 .40
15 Jarrod Washburn .15 .40
16 Nathan Haynes .15 .40
17 Benji Gil .15 .40
18 Alfredo Amezaga .15 .40
19 Ben Weber .15 .40
20 Al Levine .15 .40
21 Brad Fullmer .15 .40
22 Elpidio Guzman .15 .40
23 Tim Salmon .25 .60
24 Jose Nieves .15 .40
25 Shawn Wooten .15 .40
26 Lou Pote .15 .40
27 Mickey Callaway .15 .40
28 Steve Green .15 .40
29 John Lackey .15 .40
30 Mark Lukasiewicz .15 .40
31 Jorge Fabregas .15 .40
32 Jeff DaVanon .15 .40
33 Elvin Nina .15 .40
34 Donne Wall .15 .40
35 Eric Chavez .15 .40
36 Jermaine Dye .15 .40
37 Scott Hatteberg .15 .40
38 Mark Mulder .15 .40
39 Ramon Hernandez .15 .40
40 Jim Mecir .15 .40
41 Barry Zito .15 .40
42 Greg Myers .15 .40
43 David Justice .15 .40
44 Mike Magnante .15 .40
45 Terrence Long .15 .40
46 Tim Hudson .15 .40
47 Olmedo Saenz .15 .40
48 Billy Koch .15 .40
49 Carlos Pena .15 .40
50 Mike Venafro .15 .40
51 Mark Ellis .15 .40
52 Randy Velarde .15 .40
53 Jeremy Giambi .15 .40
54 Mike Colangelo .15 .40
55 Mike Holtz .15 .40
56 Chad Bradford .15 .40
57 Miguel Tejada .15 .40
58 Mike Fyhrie .15 .40
59 Erik Hiljus .15 .40
60 Juan Pena .15 .40
61 Mario Valdez .15 .40
62 Franklyn German RC .25 .60
63 Carlos Delgado .15 .40
64 Orlando Hudson .15 .40
65 Chris Carpenter .15 .40
66 Kelvim Escobar .15 .40
67 Felipe Lopez .15 .40
68 Brandon Lyon .15 .40
69 Jose Cruz Jr. .15 .40
70 Luke Prokopec .15 .40
71 Darrin Fletcher .15 .40
72 Bob File .15 .40
73 Felix Heredia .15 .40
74 Mike Sirotka .15 .40
75 Shannon Stewart .15 .40
76 Joe Lawrence .15 .40
77 Chris Woodward .15 .40
78 Dan Plesac .15 .40
79 Pedro Borbon .15 .40
80 Roy Halladay .15 .40
81 Raul Mondesi .15 .40
82 Steve Parris .15 .40
83 Homer Bush .15 .40
84 Esteban Loaiza .15 .40
85 Vernon Wells .15 .40
86 Justin Miller .15 .40
87 Scott Eyre .15 .40
88 Dave Berg .15 .40
89 Gustavo Chacin RC .60 1.50
90 Joe Orloski RC .25 .60
91 Corey Thurman RC .25 .60
92 Tom Wilson RC .25 .60
93 Eric Hinske .15 .40
94 Chris Baker RC .25 .60
95 Reed Johnson RC .60 1.50
96 Greg Vaughn .15 .40
97 Toby Hall .15 .40
98 Brent Abernathy .15 .40
99 Bobby Smith .15 .40
100 Tanyon Sturtze .15 .40
101 Chris Gomez .15 .40
102 Joe Kennedy .15 .40
103 Ben Grieve .15 .40
104 Aubrey Huff .15 .40
105 Jesus Colome .15 .40
106 Felix Escalona RC .25 .60
107 Paul Wilson .15 .40
108 Ryan Rupe .15 .40
109 Jason Tyner .15 .40
110 Esteban Yan .15 .40
111 Russ Johnson .15 .40
112 Randy Winn .15 .40
113 Wilson Alvarez .15 .40
114 Wilmy Caceres .15 .40
115 Steve Cox .15 .40
116 Dewon Brazelton .15 .40
117 Doug Creek .15 .40
118 Jason Conti .15 .40
119 John Flaherty .15 .40
120 Delvin James .15 .40
121 Steve Kent .15 .40
122 Kevin McGlinchy .15 .40
123 Travis Phelps .15 .40
124 Bobby Seay .15 .40
125 Travis Harper .15 .40
126 Victor Zambrano .15 .40
127 Jace Brewer .15 .40
128 Jason Smith .15 .40
129 Ramon Soler .15 .40
130 Brandon Backe RC .40 1.00
131 Jorge Sosa RC .40 1.00
132 Jim Thome .25 .60
133 Brady Anderson .15 .40
134 C.C. Sabathia .15 .40
135 Einar Diaz .15 .40
136 Ricky Gutierrez .15 .40
137 Danys Baez .15 .40
138 Bob Wickman .15 .40
139 Milton Bradley .15 .40
140 Bartolo Colon .15 .40
141 Jolbert Cabrera .15 .40
142 Eddie Taubensee .15 .40
143 Ellis Burks .15 .40
144 Omar Vizquel .25 .60
145 Eddie Perez .15 .40
146 Jaret Wright .15 .40
147 Chuck Finley .15 .40
148 Paul Shuey .15 .40
149 Travis Fryman .15 .40
150 Wil Cordero .15 .40
151 Ricardo Rincon .15 .40
152 Victor Martinez .40 1.00
153 Charles Nagy .15 .40
154 Alex Escobar .15 .40
155 Russell Branyan .15 .40
156 Matt Lawton .15 .40
157 Ryan Drese .15 .40
158 Jerrod Riggan .15 .40
159 David Riske .15 .40
160 Jake Westbrook .15 .40
161 Mark Wohlers .15 .40
162 John McDonald .15 .40
163 Ichiro Suzuki .75 2.00
164 Freddy Garcia .15 .40
165 Edgar Martinez .25 .60
166 Ben Davis .15 .40
167 Shigetoshi Hasegawa .15 .40
168 Carlos Guillen .15 .40
169 Ruben Sierra .15 .40
170 Joel Pineiro .15 .40

171 Norm Charlton .15 .40
172 Bret Boone .15 .40
173 Jamie Moyer .15 .40
174 Jeff Nelson .15 .40
175 Kazuhiro Sasaki .15 .40
176 Jeff Cirillo .15 .40
177 Mark McLemore .15 .40
178 Paul Abbott .15 .40
179 Mike Cameron .15 .40
180 Dan Wilson .15 .40
181 John Olerud .15 .40
182 Arthur Rhodes .15 .40
183 Desi Relaford .15 .40
184 John Halama .15 .40
185 Antonio Perez .15 .40
186 Ryan Anderson .15 .40
187 James Baldwin .15 .40
188 Ryan Franklin .15 .40
189 Justin Kaye .15 .40
190 J.J. Putz RC .25 .60
191 Allan Simpson RC .15 .40
192 Matt Thornton RC .25 .60
193 Luis Ugueto RC .25 .60
194 Chris Richard .15 .40
195 Sidney Ponson .15 .40
196 Brook Fordyce .15 .40
197 Luis Matos .15 .40
198 Josh Towers .15 .40
199 David Segui .15 .40
200 Chris Brock RC .15 .40
201 Tony Batista .15 .40
202 Erik Bedard .15 .40
203 Marty Cordova .15 .40
204 Jerry Hairston Jr. .15 .40
205 Jason Johnson .15 .40
206 Buddy Groom .15 .40
207 Mike Bordick .15 .40
208 Melvin Mora .15 .40
209 Calvin Maduro .15 .40
210 Jeff Conine .15 .40
211 Luis Rivera .15 .40
212 Jay Gibbons .15 .40
213 B.J. Ryan .15 .40
214 Sean Douglass .15 .40
215 Rodrigo Lopez .15 .40
216 Rick Bauer .15 .40
217 Scott Erickson .15 .40
218 Jorge Julio .15 .40
219 Willis Roberts .15 .40
220 John Stephens .15 .40
221 Geronimo Gil .15 .40
222 Chris Singleton .15 .40
223 Mike Paradis .15 .40
224 John Parrish .15 .40
225 Steve Bechler RC .25 .60
226 Mike Moriarty RC .15 .40
227 Luis Garcia RC .25 .60
228 Alex Rodriguez .50 1.50
229 Mark Teixeira .60 1.50
230 Chan Ho Park .15 .40
231 Todd Van Poppel .15 .40
232 Mike Young .40 1.00
233 Kenny Rogers .15 .40
234 Rusty Greer .15 .40
235 Rafael Palmeiro .25 .60
236 Francisco Cordero .15 .40
237 John Rocker .15 .40
238 Dave Burba .15 .40
239 Travis Hafner .15 .40
240 Kevin Mench .15 .40
241 Carl Everett .15 .40
242 Ivan Rodriguez .25 .60
243 Jeff Zimmerman .15 .40
244 Juan Gonzalez .15 .40
245 Herbert Perry .15 .40
246 Rob Bell .15 .40
247 Doug Davis .15 .40
248 Frank Catalanotto .15 .40
249 Jay Powell .15 .40
250 Gabe Kapler .15 .40
251 Joaquin Benoit .15 .40
252 Jovanny Cedeno .15 .40
253 Hideki Irabu .15 .40
254 Dan Miceli .15 .40
255 Danny Kolb .15 .40
256 Colby Lewis .15 .40
257 Rich Rodriguez .15 .40
258 Ismael Valdes .15 .40
259 Bill Haselman .15 .40
260 Jason Hart .15 .40
261 Rudy Seanez .15 .40
262 Travis Hughes RC .25 .60
263 Hank Blalock .40 1.00
264 Steve Woodard .15 .40
265 Nomar Garciaparra .60 1.50
266 Pedro Martinez .25 .60
267 Frank Castillo .15 .40
268 Johnny Damon Sox .25 .60
269 Doug Mirabelli .15 .40
270 Derek Lowe .15 .40
271 Shea Hillenbrand .15 .40
272 Paxton Crawford .15 .40
273 Tony Clark .15 .40
274 Dustin Hermanson .15 .40
275 Trot Nixon .15 .40
276 John Burkett .15 .40
277 Rich Garces .15 .40
278 Josh Hancock RC .30 .75
279 Michael Coleman .15 .40
280 Darren Oliver .15 .40
281 Jason Varitek .40 1.00
282 Jose Offerman .15 .40
283 Tim Wakefield .15 .40
284 Rolando Arrojo .15 .40
285 Rickey Henderson .40 1.00
286 Ugueth Urbina .15 .40
287 Casey Fossum .15 .40
288 Manny Ramirez .25 .60
289 Sun-Woo Kim .15 .40
290 Juan Diaz .15 .40
291 Willie Banks .15 .40
292 Jorge De La Rosa RC .25 .60
293 Juan Pena .15 .40
294 Jeff Wallace .15 .40
295 Calvin Pickering .15 .40
296 Anastacio Martinez RC .25 .60
297 Carlos Baerga .15 .40
298 Rey Sanchez .15 .40
299 Mike Sweeney .15 .40
300 Jeff Suppan .15 .40
301 Brent Mayne .15 .40
302 Chad Durbin .15 .40
303 Dan Reichert .15 .40
304 Raul Ibanez .15 .40
305 Joe Randa .15 .40
306 Chris George .15 .40
307 Michael Tucker .15 .40
308 Paul Byrd .15 .40
309 Kris Wilson .15 .40
310 Luis Alicea .15 .40
311 Neifi Perez .15 .40
312 Brian Shouse .15 .40
313 Chuck Knoblauch .15 .40
314 Dave McCarty .15 .40
315 Blake Stein .15 .40
316 Alexis Gomez .15 .40
317 Mark Quinn .15 .40
318 A.J. Hinch .15 .40
319 Carlos Febles .15 .40
320 Roberto Hernandez .15 .40
321 Brandon Berger .15 .40
322 Jeff Austin RC .25 .60
323 Cory Bailey .15 .40
324 Tony Cogan .15 .40
325 Nate Field RC .25 .60
326 Jason Grimsley .15 .40
327 Darrell May RC .15 .40
328 Donnie Sadler .15 .40
329 Carlos Beltran .15 .40
330 Miguel Asencio RC .25 .60
331 Jeff Weaver .15 .40
332 Bobby Higginson .15 .40
333 Mike Rivera .15 .40
334 Matt Anderson .15 .40
335 Craig Paquette .15 .40
336 Jose Lima .15 .40
337 Juan Acevedo .15 .40
338 Danny Patterson .15 .40
339 Andres Torres .15 .40
340 Dean Palmer .15 .40
341 Randall Simon .15 .40
342 Craig Monroe .15 .40
343 Damion Easley .15 .40
344 Robert Fick .15 .40
345 Steve Sparks .15 .40
346 Dmitri Young .15 .40
347 Nate Cornejo .15 .40
348 Matt Miller .15 .40
349 Wendell Magee .15 .40
350 Shane Halter .15 .40
351 Brian Moehler .15 .40
352 Mitch Meluskey .15 .40
353 Jose Macias .15 .40
354 Mark Redman .15 .40
355 Jeff Farnsworth .15 .40
356 Kris Keller .15 .40
357 Adam Pettyjohn .15 .40
358 Fernando Rodney .15 .40
359 Andy Van Hekken .15 .40
360 Damian Jackson .15 .40
361 Jose Paniagua .15 .40
362 Jacob Cruz .15 .40
363 Doug Mientkiewicz .15 .40
364 Torii Hunter .15 .40
365 Brad Radke .15 .40
366 Denny Hocking .15 .40
367 Mike Jackson .15 .40
368 Eddie Guardado .15 .40
369 Jacque Jones .15 .40
370 Joe Mays .15 .40
371 Matt Kinney .15 .40
372 Kyle Lohse .15 .40
373 David Ortiz .40 1.00
374 Luis Rivas .15 .40
375 Jay Canizaro .15 .40
376 Dustan Mohr .15 .40
377 LaTroy Hawkins .15 .40
378 Warren Morris .15 .40
379 A.J. Pierzynski .15 .40
380 Eric Milton .15 .40
381 Bob Wells .15 .40
382 Cristian Guzman .15 .40
383 Brian Buchanan .15 .40
384 Bobby Kielty .15 .40
385 Corey Koskie .15 .40
386 J.C. Romero .15 .40
387 Jack Cressend .15 .40
388 Mike Duvall .15 .40
389 Tony Fiore .15 .40
390 Tom Prince .15 .40
391 Todd Sears .15 .40
392 Kevin Frederick RC .25 .60
393 Frank Thomas .40 1.00
394 Mark Buehrle .15 .40
395 Jon Garland .15 .40
396 Jeff Liefer .15 .40
397 Magglio Ordonez .15 .40
398 Rocky Biddle .15 .40
399 Lorenzo Barcelo .15 .40
400 Ray Durham .15 .40
401 Bob Howry .15 .40
402 Aaron Rowand .15 .40
403 Keith Foulke .15 .40
404 Paul Konerko .15 .40
405 Sandy Alomar Jr. .15 .40
406 Mark Johnson .15 .40
407 Carlos Lee .15 .40
408 Jose Valentin .15 .40
409 Jon Rauch .15 .40
410 Royce Clayton .15 .40
411 Kenny Lofton .15 .40
412 Tony Graffanino .15 .40
413 Todd Ritchie .15 .40
414 Antonio Osuna .15 .40
415 Gary Glover .15 .40
416 Mike Porzio .15 .40
417 Danny Wright .15 .40
418 Kelly Wunsch .15 .40
419 Miguel Olivo .15 .40
420 Edwin Almonte RC .25 .60
421 Kyle Kane RC .15 .40
422 Mitch Wylie RC .25 .60
423 Derek Jeter 1.00 2.50
424 Jason Giambi .15 .40
425 Roger Clemens .75 2.00
426 Enrique Wilson .15 .40
427 David Wells .15 .40
428 Mike Mussina .25 .60
429 Bernie Williams .25 .60
430 Mike Stanton .15 .40
431 Sterling Hitchcock .15 .40
432 Alex Graman .15 .40
433 Robin Ventura .15 .40
434 Mariano Rivera .40 1.00
435 Jay Tessmer .15 .40
436 Andy Pettitte .25 .60
437 John Vander Wal .15 .40
438 Adrian Hernandez .15 .40
439 Alberto Castillo .15 .40
440 Steve Karsay .15 .40
441 Alfonso Soriano .15 .40
442 Rondell White .15 .40
443 Nick Johnson .15 .40
444 Jorge Posada .25 .60
445 Ramiro Mendoza .15 .40
446 Gerald Williams .15 .40
447 Orlando Hernandez .15 .40
448 Randy Choate .15 .40
449 Randy Keisler .15 .40
450 Ted Lilly .15 .40
451 Christian Parker .15 .40
452 Ron Coomer .15 .40
453 Marcus Thames .15 .40
454 Drew Henson .15 .40
455 Jeff Bagwell .25 .60
456 Wade Miller .15 .40
457 Lance Berkman .15 .40
458 Julio Lugo .15 .40
459 Roy Oswalt .15 .40
460 Nelson Cruz .15 .40
461 Morgan Ensberg .15 .40
462 Geoff Blum .15 .40
463 Ryan Jamison .15 .40
464 Billy Wagner .15 .40
465 Dave Mlicki .15 .40
466 Brad Ausmus .15 .40
467 Jose Vizcaino .15 .40
468 Craig Biggio .25 .60
469 Shane Reynolds .15 .40
470 Greg Zaun .15 .40
471 Octavio Dotel .15 .40
472 Carlos Hernandez .15 .40
473 Richard Hidalgo .15 .40
474 Daryle Ward .15 .40
475 Orlando Merced .15 .40
476 John Buck .15 .40
477 Adam Everett .15 .40
478 Doug Brocail .15 .40
479 Brad Lidge .15 .40
480 Scott Linebrink .15 .40
481 T.J. Mathews .15 .40
482 Greg Miller .15 .40
483 Hipolito Pichardo .15 .40
484 Brandon Puffer RC .25 .60
485 Ricky Stone RC .15 .40
486 Jason Lane .15 .40
487 Brian L. Hunter .15 .40
488 Rodrigo Rosario RC .25 .60
489 Tom Shearn RC .25 .60
490 Gary Sheffield .15 .40
491 Tom Glavine .25 .60
492 Mike Remlinger .15 .40
493 Henry Blanco .15 .40
494 Vinny Castilla .15 .40
495 Chris Hammond .15 .40
496 Kevin Millwood .15 .40
497 Darren Holmes .15 .40
498 Cory Aldridge .15 .40
499 Tim Spooneybarger .15 .40
500 Rafael Furcal .15 .40
501 Albie Lopez .15 .40
502 Javy Lopez .15 .40
503 Greg Maddux .60 1.50
504 Andruw Jones .25 .60
505 Steve Torrealba .15 .40
506 George Lombard .15 .40
507 B.J. Surhoff .15 .40
508 Marcus Giles .15 .40
509 Derrick Lewis .15 .40
510 Wes Helms .15 .40
511 John Smoltz .25 .60
512 Chipper Jones .40 1.00
513 Jason Marquis .15 .40
514 Mark DeRosa .15 .40
515 Jung Bong .15 .40
516 Kevin Gryboski RC .15 .40
517 Damian Moss .15 .40
518 Horacio Ramirez .15 .40
519 Scott Sobkowiak .15 .40
520 Billy Sylvester .15 .40
521 Nick Green .15 .40
522 Travis Wilson .15 .40
523 Ryan Langerhans .15 .40
524 John Ennis RC .25 .60
525 John Foster RC .25 .60
526 Keith Lockhart .15 .40
527 Julio Franco .15 .40
528 Richie Sexson .15 .40
529 Jeffrey Hammonds .15 .40
530 Ben Sheets .15 .40
531 Mike DeJean .15 .40
532 Mark Loretta .15 .40
533 Alex Ochoa .15 .40
534 Jamey Wright .15 .40
535 Jose Hernandez .15 .40
536 Glendon Rusch .15 .40
537 Geoff Jenkins .15 .40
538 Luis Lopez .15 .40
539 Curtis Leskanic .15 .40
540 Chad Fox .15 .40
541 Tyler Houston .15 .40
542 Nick Neugebauer .15 .40
543 Matt Stairs .15 .40
544 Paul Rigdon .15 .40
545 Bill Hall .15 .40
546 Luis Vizcaino .15 .40
547 Lenny Harris .15 .40
548 Alex Sanchez .15 .40
549 Raul Casanova .15 .40
550 Eric Young .15 .40
551 Jeff Deardorff .15 .40
552 Nelson Figueroa .15 .40
553 Ron Belliard .15 .40
554 Mike Buddie .15 .40
555 Jose Cabrera .15 .40
556 J.M. Gold .15 .40
557 Ray King .15 .40
558 Jose Mieses .15 .40
559 Takahito Nomura RC .25 .60
560 Ruben Quevedo .15 .40
561 Jackson Melian .15 .40
562 Cristian Guerrero .15 .40
563 Paul Bako .15 .40
564 Luis Martinez RC .25 .60
565 Brian Mallette RC .15 .40
566 Matt Morris .15 .40
567 Tino Martinez .25 .60
568 Fernando Vina .15 .40
569 Gene Stechschulte .15 .40
570 Andy Benes .15 .40
571 Placido Polanco .15 .40
572 Luis Garcia .15 .40
573 Jim Edmonds .15 .40
574 Bud Smith .15 .40
575 Mike Matheny .15 .40
576 Garrett Stephenson .15 .40
577 Miguel Cairo .15 .40
578 Darryl Kile .15 .40
579 Mike Timlin .15 .40
580 Rick Ankiel .15 .40
581 Jason Isringhausen .15 .40
582 Albert Pujols .75 2.00
583 Eli Marrero .15 .40
584 Steve Kline .15 .40
585 J.D. Drew .15 .40
586 Mike DiFelice .15 .40
587 Dave Veres .15 .40
588 Kerry Robinson .15 .40
589 Edgar Renteria .15 .40
590 Woody Williams .15 .40
591 Chance Caple .15 .40
592 Mike Crudale RC .25 .60
593 Luther Hackman .15 .40
594 Josh Pearce .15 .40
595 Kevin Joseph .15 .40
596 Jim Journell .15 .40
597 Jeremy Lambert RC .25 .60
598 Mike Matthews .15 .40
599 Les Walrond .15 .40
600 Keith McDonald .15 .40
601 William Ortega .15 .40
602 Scotty Layfield RC .25 .60
603 So Taguchi RC .40 1.00
604 Eduardo Perez .15 .40
605 Sammy Sosa .40 1.00
606 Kerry Wood .15 .40
607 Kyle Farnsworth .15 .40
608 Alex Gonzalez .15 .40
609 Tom Gordon .15 .40
610 Carlos Zambrano .15 .40
611 Roosevelt Brown .15 .40
612 Bill Mueller .15 .40
613 Mark Prior .40 1.00
614 Darren Lewis .15 .40
615 Joe Girardi .15 .40
616 Fred McGriff .25 .60
617 Jon Lieber .15 .40
618 Robert Machado .15 .40
619 Corey Patterson .15 .40
620 Joe Borowski .15 .40
621 Todd Hundley .15 .40
622 Jason Bere .15 .40
623 Moises Alou .15 .40
624 Jeff Fassero .15 .40
625 Jesus Sanchez .15 .40
626 Chris Stynes .15 .40
627 Delino DeShields .15 .40
628 Augie Ojeda .15 .40
629 Juan Cruz .15 .40
630 Ben Christensen .15 .40
631 Mike Meyers .15 .40
632 Will Ohman .15 .40
633 Steve Smyth .15 .40
634 Mark Bellhorn .15 .40
635 Nate Frese .15 .40
636 David Kelton .15 .40
637 Francis Beltran RC .25 .60
638 Antonio Alfonseca .15 .40
639 Donovan Osborne .15 .40
640 Shawn Sonnier .15 .40
641 Matt Clement .15 .40
642 Luis Gonzalez .15 .40
643 Brian Anderson .15 .40
644 Randy Johnson .40 1.00
645 Mark Grace .25 .60
646 Danny Bautista .15 .40
647 Junior Spivey .15 .40
648 Jay Bell .15 .40
649 Miguel Batista .15 .40
650 Tony Womack .15 .40
651 Byung-Hyun Kim .15 .40
652 Steve Finley .15 .40
653 Rick Helling .15 .40
654 Curt Schilling .15 .40
655 Erubiel Durazo .15 .40
656 Chris Donnels .15 .40
657 Greg Colbrunn .15 .40
658 Mike Morgan .15 .40
659 Jose Guillen .15 .40
660 Matt Williams .15 .40
661 Craig Counsell .15 .40
662 Greg Swindell .15 .40
663 Rod Barajas .15 .40
664 David Dellucci .15 .40
665 Todd Stottlemyre .15 .40
666 P.J. Bevis RC .25 .60
667 Mike Koplove .15 .40
668 Mike Myers .15 .40
669 John Patterson .15 .40
670 Bret Prinz .15 .40
671 Jeremy Ward RC .25 .60
672 Danny Klassen .15 .40
673 Luis Terrero .15 .40
674 Jose Valverde RC .25 .60
675 Doug Devore RC .25 .60
676 Quinton McCracken .15 .40
677 Paul LoDuca .15 .40
678 Mark Grudzielanek .15 .40
679 Kevin Brown .15 .40
680 Paul Quantrill .15 .40
681 Shawn Green .15 .40
682 Hideo Nomo .40 1.00
683 Eric Gagne .15 .40
684 Giovanni Carrara .15 .40
685 Marquis Grissom .15 .40
686 Hiram Bocachica .15 .40
687 Guillermo Mota .15 .40
688 Alex Cora .15 .40
689 Odalis Perez .15 .40
690 Brian Jordan .15 .40
691 Andy Ashby .15 .40
692 Eric Karros .15 .40
693 Chad Kreuter .15 .40
694 Dave Roberts .15 .40
695 Omar Daal .15 .40
696 Dave Hansen .15 .40
697 Adrian Beltre .15 .40
698 Terry Mulholland .15 .40
699 Cesar Izturis .15 .40
700 Steve Colyer .15 .40
701 Carlos Garcia .15 .40
702 Ricardo Rodriguez .15 .40
703 Darren Dreifort .15 .40
704 Jeff Reboulet .15 .40
705 Victor Alvarez RC .25 .60
706 Kazuhisa Ishii RC .40 1.00
707 Jose Vidro .15 .40
708 Henry Mateo .15 .40
709 Tony Armas Jr. .15 .40
710 Carl Pavano .15 .40
711 Peter Bergeron .15 .40
712 Bruce Chen .15 .40
713 Orlando Cabrera .15 .40
714 Britt Reames .15 .40
715 Masato Yoshii .15 .40
716 Fernando Tatis .15 .40
717 Graeme Lloyd .15 .40
718 Scott Stewart .15 .40
719 Lou Collier .15 .40
720 Michael Barrett .25 .60
721 Vladimir Guerrero .40 1.00
722 Troy Mattes .15 .40
723 Brian Schneider .15 .40
724 Lee Stevens .15 .40
725 Javier Vazquez .15 .40
726 Brad Wilkerson .15 .40
727 Zach Day .15 .40
728 Ed Vosberg .15 .40
729 Tomo Ohka .15 .40
730 Mike Mordecai .15 .40
731 Donnie Bridges .15 .40
732 Ron Chiavacci .15 .40
733 T.J. Tucker .15 .40
734 Scott Hodges .15 .40
735 Valentino Pascucci .15 .40
736 Andres Galarraga .15 .40
737 Scott Downs .15 .40
738 Eric Good RC .25 .60
739 Ron Calloway RC .25 .60
740 Jorge Nunez RC .25 .60
741 Henry Rodriguez .15 .40
742 Jeff Kent .15 .40
743 Russ Ortiz .15 .40
744 Felix Rodriguez .15 .40
745 Benito Santiago .15 .40
746 Tsuyoshi Shinjo .15 .40
747 Tim Worrell .15 .40
748 Marvin Benard .15 .40
749 Kurt Ainsworth .15 .40
750 Edwards Guzman .15 .40
751 J.T. Snow .15 .40
752 Jason Christiansen .15 .40
753 Robb Nen .15 .40
754 Barry Bonds 1.00 2.50
755 Shawon Dunston .15 .40
756 Chad Zerbe .15 .40
757 Ramon E. Martinez .15 .40
758 Calvin Murray .15 .40
759 Pedro Feliz .15 .40
760 Jason Schmidt .15 .40
761 Damon Minor .15 .40
762 Reggie Sanders .15 .40
763 Rich Aurilia .15 .40
764 Kirk Rueter .15 .40
765 David Bell .15 .40
766 Yorvit Torrealba .15 .40
767 Livan Hernandez .15 .40
768 Felix Diaz .15 .40
769 Aaron Fultz .15 .40
770 Ryan Jensen .15 .40
771 Arturo McDowell .15 .40
772 Carlos Valderrama .15 .40
773 Nelson Castro RC .25 .60
774 Jay Witasick .15 .40
775 Deivis Santos .15 .40
776 Josh Beckett .15 .40
777 Charles Johnson .15 .40
778 Derrek Lee .25 .60
779 A.J. Burnett .15 .40
780 Vic Darensbourg .15 .40
781 Cliff Floyd .15 .40
782 Jose Cueto .15 .40
783 Nate Teut .15 .40
784 Alex Gonzalez .15 .40
785 Brad Penny .15 .40
786 Kevin Olsen .15 .40
787 Mike Lowell .15 .40
788 Mike Redmond .15 .40
789 Braden Looper .15 .40
790 Eric Owens .15 .40
791 Andy Fox .15 .40
792 Vladimir Nunez .15 .40
793 Luis Castillo .15 .40
794 Ryan Dempster .15 .40
795 Armando Almanza .15 .40
796 Preston Wilson .15 .40
797 Pablo Ozuna .15 .40
798 Gary Knotts .15 .40
799 Ramon Castro .15 .40
800 Benito Baez .15 .40
801 Michael Tejera .15 .40
802 Claudio Vargas .15 .40
803 Chip Ambres .15 .40
804 Hansel Izquierdo RC .25 .60
805 Tim Raines Sr. .15 .40
806 Marty Malloy .15 .40
807 Julian Tavarez .15 .40
808 Roberto Alomar .25 .60
809 Al Leiter .15 .40
810 Jeromy Burnitz .15 .40
811 John Franco .15 .40
812 Edgardo Alfonzo .15 .40
813 Mike Piazza .60 1.50
814 Shawn Estes .15 .40
815 Joe McEwing .15 .40
816 David Weathers .15 .40
817 Pedro Astacio .15 .40
818 Timo Perez .15 .40
819 Grant Roberts .15 .40
820 Rey Ordonez .15 .40
821 Steve Trachsel .15 .40
822 Roger Cedeno .15 .40
823 Mark Johnson .15 .40
824 Armando Benitez .15 .40
825 Vance Wilson .15 .40
826 Jay Payton .15 .40
827 Mo Vaughn .15 .40
828 Scott Strickland .15 .40
829 Mark Guthrie .15 .40
830 Jeff D'Amico .15 .40
831 Mark Corey RC .25 .60
832 Kane Davis .15 .40
833 Jae Weong Seo .15 .40
834 Pat Strange .15 .40
835 Adam Walker RC .25 .60
836 Tyler Walker .15 .40
837 Gary Matthews Jr. .15 .40
838 Jaime Cerda RC .25 .60
839 Satoru Komiyama RC .25 .60
840 Tyler Yates RC .25 .60
841 John Valentin .15 .40
842 Ryan Klesko .15 .40
843 Wiki Gonzalez .15 .40
844 Trevor Hoffman .15 .40
845 Sean Burroughs .15 .40
846 Alan Embree .15 .40
847 Dennis Tankersley .15 .40
848 D'Angelo Jimenez .15 .40
849 Kevin Jarvis .15 .40
850 Mark Kotsay .15 .40
851 Phil Nevin .15 .40
852 Jeremy Fikac .15 .40
853 Brett Tomko .15 .40
854 Brian Lawrence .15 .40
855 Steve Reed .15 .40
856 Bubba Trammell .15 .40
857 Tom Davey .15 .40
858 Ramon Vazquez .15 .40
859 Tom Lampkin .15 .40
860 Bobby Jones .15 .40
861 Ray Lankford .15 .40
862 Mark Sweeney .15 .40
863 Adam Eaton .15 .40
864 Trenidad Hubbard .15 .40
865 Jason Boyd .15 .40
866 Javier Cardona .15 .40
867 Cliff Bartosh RC .25 .60
868 Mike Bynum .15 .40
869 Eric Cyr .15 .40
870 Jose Nunez .15 .40
871 Ron Gant .15 .40
872 Deivi Cruz .15 .40
873 Ben Howard RC .25 .60
874 Todd Donovan RC .25 .60
875 Andy Shibilo RC .25 .60
876 Scott Rolen .25 .60
877 Jose Mesa .15 .40
878 Rheal Cormier .15 .40
879 Travis Lee .15 .40
880 Mike Lieberthal .15 .40
881 Brandon Duckworth .15 .40
882 David Coggin .15 .40
883 Bob Abreu .15 .40
884 Turk Wendell .15 .40
885 Marlon Byrd .15 .40
886 Jason Michaels .15 .40
887 Robert Person .15 .40
888 Tomas Perez .15 .40
889 Jimmy Rollins .15 .40
890 Vicente Padilla .15 .40
891 Pat Burrell .15 .40
892 Dave Hollins .15 .40
893 Randy Wolf .15 .40
894 Jose Santiago .15 .40
895 Doug Glanville .15 .40
896 Cliff Politte .15 .40
897 Marlon Anderson .15 .40
898 Ricky Bottalico .15 .40
899 Terry Adams .15 .40
900 Brad Baisley .15 .40
901 Hector Mercado .15 .40
902 Elio Serrano RC .25 .60
903 Todd Pratt .15 .40
904 Pete Zamora RC .25 .60
905 Nick Punto .15 .40
906 Ricky Ledee .15 .40
907 Eric Junge RC .25 .60
908 Anderson Machado RC .25 .60
909 Jorge Padilla RC .25 .60
910 John Mabry .15 .40
911 Brian Giles .15 .40
912 Jason Kendall .15 .40
913 Jack Wilson .15 .40
914 Kris Benson .15 .40
915 Aramis Ramirez .15 .40
916 Mike Fetters .15 .40
917 Adrian Brown .15 .40
918 Pokey Reese .15 .40
919 Dave Williams .15 .40
920 Mike Benjamin .15 .40
921 Kip Wells .15 .40
922 Mike Williams .15 .40
923 Pat Meares .15 .40
924 Ron Villone .15 .40
925 Armando Rios .15 .40
926 Jimmy Anderson .15 .40
927 Rob Mackowiak .15 .40
928 Kevin Young .15 .40
929 Brian Boehringer .15 .40
930 Joe Beimel .15 .40
931 Chad Hermansen .15 .40
932 Scott Sauerbeck .15 .40
933 Josh Fogg .15 .40
934 Mike Gonzalez RC .25 .60
935 Mike Lincoln .15 .40
936 Sean Lowe .15 .40
937 Matt Guerrier .15 .40
938 Ryan Vogelsong .15 .40
939 J.R. House .15 .40
940 Craig Wilson .15 .40
941 Tony Alvarez .15 .40
942 J.J. Davis .15 .40
943 Abraham Nunez .15 .40
944 Adrian Burnside RC .25 .60
945 Ken Griffey Jr. .75 2.00
946 Jimmy Haynes .15 .40
947 Juan Castro .15 .40
948 Jose Rijo .15 .40
949 Corky Miller .15 .40
950 Elmer Dessens .15 .40
951 Aaron Boone .15 .40
952 Juan Encarnacion .15 .40
953 Chris Reitsma .15 .40
954 Wilton Guerrero .15 .40
955 Danny Graves .15 .40
956 Jim Brower .15 .40
957 Barry Larkin .25 .60
958 Todd Walker .15 .40
959 Gabe White .15 .40
960 Adam Dunn .15 .40
961 Jason LaRue .15 .40
962 Reggie Taylor .15 .40
963 Sean Casey .15 .40
964 Scott Williamson .15 .40
965 Austin Kearns .15 .40
966 Kelly Stinnett .15 .40
967 Jose Acevedo .15 .40
968 Gookie Dawkins .15 .40
969 Brady Clark .15 .40
970 Scott Sullivan .15 .40
971 Ricardo Aramboles .15 .40
972 Lance Davis .15 .40
973 Seth Etherton .15 .40
974 Luke Hudson .15 .40
975 Joey Hamilton .15 .40
976 Luis Pineda .15 .40
977 John Riedling .15 .40
978 Jose Silva .15 .40
979 Dane Sardinha .15 .40
980 Ben Broussard .15 .40
981 David Espinosa .15 .40
982 Ruben Mateo .15 .40
983 Larry Walker .15 .40
984 Juan Uribe .15 .40
985 Mike Hampton .15 .40
986 Aaron Cook RC .25 .60
987 Jose Ortiz .15 .40
988 Todd Jones .15 .40
989 Todd Helton .25 .60
990 Shawn Chacon .15 .40
991 Jason Jennings .15 .40
992 Todd Zeile .15 .40
993 Ben Petrick .15 .40
994 Denny Neagle .15 .40
995 Jose Jimenez .15 .40
996 Juan Pierre .15 .40
997 Todd Hollandsworth .15 .40
998 Kent Mercker .15 .40
999 Greg Norton .15 .40
1000 Terry Shumpert .15 .40
1001 Mark Little .15 .40
1002 Gary Bennett .15 .40
1003 Dennis Reyes .15 .40
1004 Justin Speier .15 .40
1005 John Thomson .15 .40
1006 Rick White .15 .40
1007 Colin Young RC .25 .60
1008 Cam Esslinger RC .25 .60
1009 Rene Reyes RC .25 .60
1010 Mike James .15 .40
1011 Morgan Ensberg NR .15 .40
1012 Adam Everett NR .15 .40
1013 Rodrigo Rosario NR .15 .40
1014 Carlos Pena NR .15 .40
1015 Eric Hinske NR .15 .40
1016 Orlando Hudson NR .15 .40
1017 Reed Johnson NR .30 .75
1018 Jung Bong NR .15 .40
1019 Bill Hall NR .15 .40
1020 Mark Prior NR .20 .50
1021 Francis Beltran NR .15 .40
1022 David Kelton NR .15 .40
1023 Felix Escalona NR .15 .40
1024 Jorge Sosa NR .20 .50
1025 Dewon Brazelton NR .15 .40
1026 Jose Valverde NR .15 .40
1027 Luis Terrero NR .15 .40
1028 Kazuhisa Ishii NR .20 .50
1029 Cesar Izturis NR .15 .40
1030 Ryan Jensen NR .15 .40
1031 Matt Thornton NR .15 .40
1032 Hansel Izquierdo NR .15 .40
1033 Jaime Cerda NR .15 .40
1034 Erik Bedard NR .15 .40
1035 Sean Burroughs NR .15 .40
1036 Ben Howard NR .15 .40
1037 Ramon Vazquez NR .15 .40
1038 Marlon Byrd NR .15 .40
1039 Josh Fogg NR .15 .40
1040 Hank Blalock NR .20 .50
1041 Mark Teixeira NR .30 .75
1042 Kevin Mench NR .15 .40
1043 Dane Sardinha NR .15 .40
1044 Austin Kearns NR .15 .40
1045 Anastacio Martinez NR .15 .40
1046 Eric Munson NR .15 .40
1047 Jon Rauch NR .15 .40
1048 Nick Johnson NR .15 .40
1049 Alex Graman NR .15 .40
1050 Drew Henson NR .15 .40
1051 Darin Erstad HM .15 .40
1052 Garret Anderson HM .15 .40
1053 Craig Biggio HM .15 .40
1054 Lance Berkman HM .15 .40
1055 Jeff Bagwell HM .15 .40
1056 Shannon Stewart HM .15 .40
1057 Chipper Jones HM .25 .60
1058 J.D. Drew HM .15 .40
1059 Moises Alou HM .15 .40
1060 Mark Grace HM .15 .40
1061 Jose Vidro HM .15 .40
1062 Vladimir Guerrero HM .25 .60
1063 Matt Lawton HM .15 .40
1064 Ichiro Suzuki HM .40 1.00
1065 Edgar Martinez HM .15 .40
1066 John Olerud HM .15 .40

1067 Jeff Cirillo HM .15 .40
1068 Mike Lowell HM .15 .40
1069 Mike Piazza HM .40 1.00
1070 Roberto Alomar HM .15 .40
1071 Bob Abreu HM .15 .40
1072 Jason Kendall HM .15 .40
1073 Brian Giles HM .15 .40
1074 Rafael Palmeiro HM .15 .40
1075 Ivan Rodriguez HM .15 .40
1076 Alex Rodriguez HM .30 .75
1077 Juan Gonzalez HM .15 .40
1078 Nomar Garciaparra HM .40 1.00
1079 Manny Ramirez HM .25 .60
1080 Sean Casey HM .15 .40
1081 Barry Larkin HM .15 .40
1082 Larry Walker HM .15 .40
1083 Carlos Beltran HM .15 .40
1084 Corey Koskie HM .15 .40
1085 Magglio Ordonez HM .15 .40
1086 Frank Thomas HM .25 .60
1087 Kenny Lofton HM .15 .40
1088 Derek Jeter HM .50 1.25
1089 Bernie Williams HM .15 .40
1090 Jason Giambi HM .15 .40
1091 Troy Glaus PC .15 .40
1092 Jeff Bagwell PC .15 .40
1093 Lance Berkman PC .15 .40
1094 David Justice PC .15 .40
1095 Eric Chavez PC .15 .40
1096 Carlos Delgado PC .15 .40
1097 Gary Sheffield PC .15 .40
1098 Chipper Jones PC .25 .60
1099 Andruw Jones PC .15 .40
1100 Richie Sexson PC .15 .40
1101 Albert Pujols PC .40 1.00
1102 Sammy Sosa PC .25 .60
1103 Fred McGriff PC .15 .40
1104 Greg Vaughn PC .15 .40
1105 Matt Williams PC .15 .40
1106 Luis Gonzalez PC .15 .40
1107 Shawn Green PC .15 .40
1108 Andres Galarraga PC .15 .40
1109 Vladimir Guerrero PC .25 .60
1110 Barry Bonds PC .50 1.25
1111 Rich Aurilia PC .15 .40
1112 Ellis Burks PC .15 .40
1113 Jim Thome PC .15 .40
1114 Bret Boone PC .15 .40
1115 Cliff Floyd PC .15 .40
1116 Mike Piazza PC .40 1.00
1117 Jeromy Burnitz PC .15 .40
1118 Phil Nevin PC .15 .40
1119 Brian Giles PC .15 .40
1120 Rafael Palmeiro PC .15 .40
1121 Juan Gonzalez PC .15 .40
1122 Alex Rodriguez PC .30 .75
1123 Manny Ramirez PC .25 .60
1124 Ken Griffey Jr. PC .50 1.25
1125 Larry Walker PC .15 .40
1126 Todd Helton PC .15 .40
1127 Mike Sweeney PC .15 .40
1128 Frank Thomas PC .25 .60
1129 Paul Konerko PC .15 .40
1130 Jason Giambi PC .15 .40
1131 Aaron Sele RT .15 .40
1132 Roy Oswalt RT .15 .40
1133 Wade Miller RT .15 .40
1134 Tim Hudson RT .15 .40
1135 Barry Zito RT .15 .40
1136 Mark Mulder RT .15 .40
1137 Greg Maddux RT .40 1.00
1138 Tom Glavine RT .15 .40
1139 Ben Sheets RT .15 .40
1140 Darryl Kile RT .15 .40
1141 Matt Morris RT .15 .40
1142 Kerry Wood RT .15 .40
1143 Jon Lieber RT .15 .40
1144 Juan Cruz RT .15 .40
1145 Randy Johnson RT .25 .60
1146 Curt Schilling RT .15 .40
1147 Kevin Brown RT .15 .40
1148 Javier Vazquez RT .15 .40
1149 Russ Ortiz RT .15 .40
1150 C.C. Sabathia RT .15 .40
1151 Bartolo Colon RT .15 .40
1152 Freddy Garcia RT .15 .40
1153 Jamie Moyer RT .15 .40
1154 Josh Beckett RT .15 .40
1155 Brad Penny RT .15 .40
1156 Al Leiter RT .15 .40
1157 Brandon Duckworth RT .15 .40
1158 Robert Person RT .15 .40
1159 Kris Benson RT .15 .40
1160 Chan Ho Park RT .15 .40
1161 Pedro Martinez RT .25 .60
1162 Mike Hampton RT .15 .40
1163 Jeff Weaver RT .15 .40
1164 Joe Mays RT .15 .40
1165 Brad Radke RT .15 .40
1166 Eric Milton RT .15 .40
1167 Roger Clemens RT .40 1.00
1168 Mike Mussina RT .15 .40
1169 Andy Pettitte RT .15 .40
1170 David Wells RT .15 .40
1171 Ken Griffey Jr. CL .50 1.25
1172 Ichiro Suzuki CL .40 1.00
1173 Jason Giambi CL .15 .40
1174 Alex Rodriguez CL .30 .75
1175 Sammy Sosa CL .25 .60
1176 Nomar Garciaparra CL .40 1.00
1177 Barry Bonds CL .50 1.25
1178 Mike Piazza CL .40 1.00
1179 Derek Jeter CL .50 1.25
1180 Randy Johnson CL .25 .60
1181 Jeff Bagwell CL .15 .40
1182 Albert Pujols CL .40 1.00

2002 Upper Deck 40-Man Electric

*ELECTRIC: 1.25X TO 3X BASIC
*ELECTRIC RC'S: .75X TO 2X BASIC
*ELECTRIC 1011-1050: 1.25X TO 3X BASIC
*ELECTRIC 1011-1050 RC's: .75X TO 2X BASIC
STATED ODDS 1:4

2002 Upper Deck 40-Man Electric Rainbow

*ELEC.RAIN: 10X TO 25X BASIC
*ELEC.RAIN RC'S: 5X TO 12X
*ELEC.RAIN 1011-1050: 10X TO 25X
*ELEC.RAIN 1011-1050 RC's: 5X TO 12X
RANDOM INSERTS IN HOBBY PACKS
STATED PRINT RUN 40 SERIAL #'d SETS

2002 Upper Deck 40-Man Gargantuan Gear

STATED ODDS 1:48 RETAIL
SP INFO PROVIDED BY UPPER DECK
*GOLD: .75X TO 2X BASIC
*GOLD: .6X TO 1.5X BASIC SP'S
GOLD RANDOM INSERTS IN RETAIL PACKS
GOLD PRINT RUN 100 SERIAL #'d SETS
GAJ Andruw Jones 6.00 15.00
GAP Andy Pettitte 6.00 15.00
GAR Alex Rodriguez 6.00 15.00
GAS Aaron Sele 4.00 10.00
GBC Bruce Chen 4.00 10.00
GBG Ben Grieve 4.00 10.00
GBR Brad Radke 4.00 10.00
GBW Bernie Williams 6.00 15.00
GBZ Barry Zito 4.00 10.00
GCS Curt Schilling 4.00 10.00
GDY Dmitri Young 4.00 10.00
GIS Ichiro Suzuki SP 20.00 50.00
GJB James Baldwin 4.00 10.00
GJB Jeromy Burnitz 4.00 10.00
GJD Jermaine Dye SP 6.00 15.00
GJG Juan Gonzalez 4.00 10.00
GJK Jeff Kent 4.00 10.00
GJO John Olerud 4.00 10.00
GJP Jorge Posada 6.00 15.00
GKG Ken Griffey Jr. 8.00 20.00
GLG Luis Gonzalez 4.00 10.00
GML Mike Lieberthal 4.00 10.00
GMO Magglio Ordonez 4.00 10.00
GMP Mike Piazza SP 10.00 25.00
GPM Pedro Martinez 6.00 15.00
GSR Scott Rolen 6.00 15.00
GSS Sammy Sosa 6.00 15.00
GTH Tim Hudson SP 6.00 15.00
GTM Tino Martinez 6.00 15.00
GTZ Todd Zeile 4.00 10.00

2002 Upper Deck 40-Man Looming Large Jerseys

STATED PRINT RUN 250 SERIAL #'d SETS
*GOLD: 1X TO 2.5X BASIC
GOLD PRINT RUN 40 SERIAL #'d SETS
LAL Al Leiter 4.00 10.00
LAR Alex Rodriguez 6.00 15.00
LBG Brian Giles 4.00 10.00
LBZ Barry Zito 4.00 10.00
LCE Carl Everett 4.00 10.00
LCF Chuck Finley 4.00 10.00
LCS Curt Schilling 4.00 10.00
LDK Darryl Kile 6.00 15.00
LEM Edgar Martinez 6.00 15.00
LFM Fred McGriff 6.00 15.00
LFT Frank Thomas 6.00 15.00
LGM Greg Maddux 6.00 15.00
LHN Hideo Nomo 10.00 25.00
LIV Ismael Valdes 4.00 10.00
LJBA Jeff Bagwell 6.00 15.00
LJBU John Burkett 4.00 10.00
LJC Jeff Cirillo 4.00 10.00
LJD J.D. Drew 4.00 10.00
LJGI Jason Giambi 4.00 10.00
LJGO Juan Gonzalez 4.00 10.00
LJP Jorge Posada 6.00 15.00
LJR Jimmy Rollins 4.00 10.00
LJS J.T. Snow 4.00 10.00
LKG Ken Griffey Jr. 10.00 25.00
LKL Kenny Lofton 4.00 10.00
LKS Kazuhiro Sasaki 4.00 10.00
LLB Lance Berkman 6.00 15.00
LML Mike Lieberthal 4.00 10.00
LMO Magglio Ordonez 4.00 10.00
LRC Roger Clemens 10.00 25.00
LRJ Randy Johnson 6.00 15.00
LRP Rafael Palmeiro 6.00 15.00
LRV Randy Velarde 4.00 10.00
LRV Ron Villone 4.00 10.00
LSC Sean Casey 4.00 10.00
LSR Shane Reynolds 4.00 10.00
LSS Sammy Sosa 6.00 15.00
LTC Tony Clark 4.00 10.00
LTF Travis Fryman 4.00 10.00
LTG Tom Glavine 6.00 15.00
LTH Todd Helton 6.00 15.00

2002 Upper Deck 40-Man Lumber Yard

COMPLETE SET (18) 250.00 400.00
STATED ODDS 1:168
LY1 Chipper Jones 6.00 15.00
LY2 Joe DiMaggio 12.00 30.00
LY3 Albert Pujols 10.00 25.00
LY4 Mark McGwire 15.00 40.00
LY5 Sammy Sosa 6.00 15.00
LY6 Vladimir Guerrero 6.00 15.00
LY7 Barry Bonds 12.50 30.00
LY8 Mickey Mantle 25.00 50.00
LY9 Mike Piazza 6.00 15.00
LY10 Alex Rodriguez 6.00 15.00
LY11 Nomar Garciaparra 8.00 20.00
LY12 Ken Griffey Jr. 10.00 25.00
LY13 Frank Thomas 6.00 15.00
LY14 Jason Giambi 6.00 15.00
LY15 Derek Jeter 12.50 30.00
LY16 Luis Gonzalez 6.00 15.00
LY17 Jeff Bagwell 6.00 15.00
LY18 Todd Helton 6.00 15.00

2002 Upper Deck 40-Man Mark McGwire Flashbacks

COMPLETE SET (40) 100.00 200.00
COMMON CARD (MM1-MM40) 3.00 8.00
STATED ODDS 1:24
MM1 Mark McGwire USA 4.00 10.00

2002 Upper Deck 40-Man Super Swatch

STATED PRINT RUN 250 SERIAL #'d SETS
*GOLD: 1X TO 2.5X BASIC
GOLD PRINT RUN 40 SERIAL #'d SETS
SAR Alex Rodriguez 10.00 25.00
SBS Ben Sheets 4.00 10.00
SCD Carlos Delgado 4.00 10.00
SCJ Chipper Jones 6.00 15.00
SCS Curt Schilling 4.00 10.00
SDE Darin Erstad 4.00 10.00
SDJ David Justice 4.00 10.00
SDW David Wells 4.00 10.00
SEA Edgardo Alfonzo 4.00 10.00
SEB Ellis Burks 4.00 10.00
SEM Eric Milton 4.00 10.00
SFT Frank Thomas 6.00 15.00
SGV Greg Vaughn 4.00 10.00
SHN Hideo Nomo 30.00 60.00
SIR Ivan Rodriguez 6.00 15.00
SIS Ichiro Suzuki 10.00 25.00
SJB Jeff Bagwell 6.00 15.00
SJG Juan Gonzalez Standing 4.00 10.00
SJGO Juan Gonzalez Batting 4.00 10.00
SJM Joe Mays 4.00 10.00
SJP Jorge Posada 6.00 15.00
SJV Jose Vidro 4.00 10.00
SKG Ken Griffey Jr. Batting 10.00 25.00
SKG Ken Griffey Jr. Fielding 10.00 25.00
SKL Kenny Lofton 4.00 10.00
SKS Kazuhiro Sasaki 4.00 10.00
SLB Lance Berkman 4.00 10.00
SMG Mark Grace 6.00 15.00
SMH Mike Hampton 4.00 10.00
SMM Matt Morris 4.00 10.00
SMR Manny Ramirez 6.00 15.00
SMR Mariano Rivera 6.00 15.00
SMS Mike Sweeney 4.00 10.00
SMY Masato Yoshii 4.00 10.00
SRA Rich Aurilia 4.00 10.00
SRC Roger Cedeno 4.00 10.00
SRD Ray Durham 4.00 10.00
SSC Sean Casey 4.00 10.00
SSG Shawn Green 4.00 10.00
SSS Sammy Sosa 6.00 15.00
STG Tony Gwynn 6.00 15.00
STH Trevor Hoffman 4.00 10.00

2003 Upper Deck 40-Man

COMPLETE SET (990) 50.00 100.00
COMMON CARD (1-990) .15 .40
COMMON NR (877-960) .15 .40
COMMON NR RC (877-960) .15 .40
1 Troy Glaus .15 .40
2 Darin Erstad .15 .40
3 Garret Anderson .15 .40
4 Aaron Sele .15 .40
5 Adam Kennedy .15 .40
6 Scott Spiezio .15 .40
7 Troy Percival .15 .40
8 David Eckstein .15 .40
9 Ramon Ortiz .15 .40
10 Bengie Molina .15 .40
11 Tim Salmon .15 .40
12 John Lackey .25 .60
13 Brad Fullmer .15 .40
14 Jarrod Washburn .15 .40
15 Shawn Wooten .15 .40
16 Kevin Appier .15 .40
17 Ben Weber .15 .40
18 Eric Owens .15 .40
19 Matt Wise .15 .40
20 Francisco Rodriguez .25 .60
21 Scot Shields .15 .40
22 Jose Molina .15 .40
23 Scott Schoeneweis .15 .40
24 Derrick Turnbow .15 .40
25 Benji Gil .15 .40
26 Julio Ramirez .15 .40
27 Mickey Callaway .15 .40
28 Barry Zito .25 .60
29 Tim Hudson .25 .60
30 Mark Mulder .15 .40
31 Eric Chavez .15 .40
32 Miguel Tejada .25 .60
33 Terrence Long .15 .40
34 Jermaine Dye .15 .40
35 Erubiel Durazo .15 .40
36 Scott Hatteberg .15 .40
37 Chris Singleton .15 .40
38 Keith Foulke .15 .40
39 John Halama .15 .40
40 Mark Ellis .15 .40
41 Ted Lilly .15 .40
42 Jim Mecir .15 .40
43 Adam Piatt .15 .40
44 Freddie Bynum .15 .40
45 Adam Morrissey .15 .40
46 Jeremy Fikac .15 .40
47 Ricardo Rincon .15 .40
48 Ramon Hernandez .15 .40
49 Micah Bowie .15 .40
50 Chad Bradford .15 .40
51 Eric Byrnes .15 .40
52 Ron Gant .15 .40
53 Jose Flores .15 .40
54 Mark Johnson .15 .40
55 Carlos Delgado .15 .40
56 Orlando Hudson .15 .40
57 Kelvim Escobar .15 .40
58 Eric Hinske .15 .40
59 Doug Creek .15 .40
60 Josh Phelps .15 .40
61 Shannon Stewart .15 .40
62 Roy Halladay .25 .60
63 Vernon Wells .15 .40
64 Mark Hendrickson .15 .40
65 Mike Bordick .15 .40
66 Jayson Werth .25 .60
67 Chris Woodward .15 .40
68 Ken Huckaby .15 .40
69 Frank Catalanotto .15 .40
70 Jason Kershner .15 .40
71 Greg Myers .15 .40
72 Tanyon Sturtze .15 .40
73 Trever Miller .15 .40
74 Pete Walker .15 .40
75 Alexis Rios .15 .40
76 Tom Wilson .15 .40
77 Dave Berg .15 .40
78 Doug Linton .15 .40
79 Cliff Politte .15 .40
80 Damion Easley .15 .40
81 Toby Hall .15 .40
82 George Lombard .15 .40
83 Ben Grieve .15 .40
84 Aubrey Huff .15 .40
85 Jesus Colome .15 .40
86 Dewon Brazelton .15 .40
87 Rey Ordonez .15 .40
88 Al Martin .15 .40
89 Carl Crawford .25 .60
90 Travis Lee .15 .40
91 Marlon Anderson .15 .40
92 Javier Valentin .15 .40
93 Joe Kennedy .15 .40
94 Jorge Sosa .15 .40
95 Travis Harper .15 .40
96 Bobby Seay .15 .40
97 Seth McClung .15 .40
98 Delvin James .15 .40
99 Victor Zambrano .15 .40
100 Terry Shumpert .15 .40
101 Josh Hamilton .25 .60
102 Jared Sandberg .15 .40
103 Steve Parris .15 .40
104 C.C. Sabathia .25 .60
105 Omar Vizquel .25 .60
106 Milton Bradley .15 .40
107 Ellis Burks .15 .40
108 Danys Baez .15 .40
109 Jason Davis .15 .40
110 Terry Mulholland .15 .40
111 Matt Lawton .15 .40
112 Alex Escobar .15 .40
113 Mark Wohlers .15 .40
114 Josh Bard .15 .40
115 Bill Selby .15 .40
116 Brandon Phillips .15 .40
117 Jason Bere .15 .40
118 Casey Blake .15 .40
119 Travis Hafner .15 .40
120 Brian Anderson .15 .40
121 David Riske .15 .40
122 Karim Garcia .15 .40
123 Ricardo Rodriguez .15 .40
124 Carl Sadler .15 .40
125 Jose Santiago .15 .40
126 Tim Laker .15 .40
127 John McDonald .15 .40
128 Jake Westbrook .15 .40
129 Ichiro Suzuki .50 1.25
130 Freddy Garcia .15 .40
131 Edgar Martinez .25 .60
132 Ben Davis .15 .40
133 Shigetoshi Hasegawa .15 .40
134 Carlos Guillen .15 .40
135 Randy Winn .15 .40
136 John Mabry .15 .40
137 Matt Thornton .15 .40
138 Bret Boone .15 .40
139 Jamie Moyer .15 .40
140 Giovanni Carrara .15 .40
141 Kazuhiro Sasaki .15 .40
142 Jeff Cirillo .15 .40
143 Mark McLemore .15 .40
144 Pat Borders .15 .40
145 Mike Cameron .15 .40
146 Dan Wilson .15 .40
147 John Olerud .15 .40
148 Arthur Rhodes .15 .40
149 Rafael Soriano .15 .40
150 Greg Colbrunn .15 .40
151 Ryan Franklin .15 .40
152 Joel Pineiro .15 .40
153 Jeff Nelson .15 .40
154 Jerry Hairston Jr. .15 .40
155 Rick Helling .15 .40
156 Gary Matthews Jr. .15 .40
157 Jeff Conine .15 .40
158 Sidney Ponson .15 .40
159 Tony Batista .15 .40
160 Jay Gibbons .15 .40
161 Marty Cordova .15 .40
162 Geronimo Gil .15 .40
163 Deivi Cruz .15 .40
164 B.J. Ryan .15 .40
165 Jason Johnson .15 .40
166 Buddy Groom .15 .40
167 Pat Hentgen .15 .40
168 Omar Daal .15 .40
169 Willis Roberts .15 .40
170 Scott Erickson .15 .40
171 David Segui .15 .40
172 Brook Fordyce .15 .40
173 Rodrigo Lopez .15 .40
174 Jose Leon .15 .40
175 Jose Morban .15 .40
176 Melvin Mora .15 .40
177 B.J. Surhoff .15 .40
178 Jorge Julio .15 .40
179 Alex Rodriguez .50 1.25
180 Mark Teixeira .25 .60
181 Chan Ho Park .25 .60
182 Todd Van Poppel .15 .40
183 Todd Greene .15 .40
184 Ismael Valdes .15 .40
185 Rusty Greer .15 .40
186 Rafael Palmeiro .25 .60
187 Francisco Cordero .15 .40
188 Einar Diaz .15 .40
189 Doug Glanville .15 .40
190 Michael Young .15 .40
191 Kevin Mench .15 .40
192 Carl Everett .15 .40
193 Herbert Perry .15 .40
194 Jeff Zimmerman .15 .40
195 Juan Gonzalez .15 .40
196 Ugueth Urbina .15 .40
197 Jermaine Clark .15 .40
198 John Thomson .15 .40
199 Hank Blalock .15 .40
200 Jay Powell .15 .40
201 Mike Lamb .15 .40
202 Aaron Fultz .15 .40
203 Esteban Yan .15 .40
204 Nomar Garciaparra .25 .60
205 Pedro Martinez .25 .60
206 John Burkett .15 .40
207 Johnny Damon .25 .60
208 Doug Mirabelli .15 .40
209 Derek Lowe .15 .40
210 Shea Hillenbrand .15 .40
211 Brandon Lyon .15 .40
212 Trot Nixon .15 .40
213 Jason Varitek .40 1.00
214 Tim Wakefield .25 .60
215 Manny Ramirez .40 1.00
216 Todd Walker .15 .40
217 Jeremy Giambi .15 .40
218 Ramiro Mendoza .15 .40
219 Bill Mueller .15 .40
220 David Ortiz .40 1.00
221 Mike Timlin .15 .40
222 Alan Embree .15 .40
223 Bob Howry .15 .40
224 Chad Fox .15 .40
225 Damian Jackson .15 .40
226 Casey Fossum .15 .40
227 Steve Woodard .15 .40
228 Freddy Sanchez .15 .40
229 Mike Sweeney .15 .40
230 Desi Relaford .15 .40
231 Brent Mayne .15 .40
232 Angel Berroa .15 .40
233 Albie Lopez .15 .40
234 Raul Ibanez .25 .60
235 Joe Randa .15 .40
236 Chris George .15 .40
237 Michael Tucker .15 .40
238 Mendy Lopez .15 .40
239 Kris Wilson .15 .40
240 Jason Grimsley .15 .40
241 Carlos Febles .15 .40
242 Runelvys Hernandez .15 .40
243 Mike MacDougal .15 .40
244 Carlos Beltran .25 .60
245 Brandon Berger .15 .40
246 Darrell May .15 .40
247 Miguel Asencio .15 .40
248 Ryan Bukvich .15 .40
249 Dee Brown .15 .40
250 Jeremy Hill .15 .40
251 Jeremy Affeldt .15 .40
252 Ken Harvey .15 .40
253 Bobby Higginson .15 .40
254 Matt Anderson .15 .40
255 Dmitri Young .15 .40
256 Gene Kingsale .15 .40
257 Craig Paquette .15 .40
258 Adam Bernero .15 .40
259 Andres Torres .15 .40
260 Carlos Pena .25 .60
261 Dean Palmer .15 .40
262 Eric Munson .15 .40
263 Omar Infante .15 .40
264 Shane Halter .15 .40
265 Jeremy Bonderman RC .60 1.50
266 Steve Sparks .15 .40
267 Gary Knotts .15 .40
268 Mike Maroth .15 .40
269 Nate Cornejo .15 .40
270 Matt Roney .15 .40
271 Franklyn German .15 .40
272 Matt Walbeck .15 .40
273 Brandon Inge .15 .40
274 Hiram Bocachica .15 .40
275 Chris Spurling .15 .40
276 Craig Monroe .15 .40
277 Ramon Santiago .15 .40
278 Doug Mientkiewicz .15 .40
279 Torii Hunter .15 .40
280 Brad Radke .15 .40
281 Denny Hocking .15 .40
282 Tom Prince .15 .40
283 Eddie Guardado .15 .40
284 Jacque Jones .15 .40
285 Joe Mays .15 .40
286 Mike Fetters .15 .40
287 LaTroy Hawkins .15 .40
288 A.J. Pierzynski .15 .40
289 Eric Milton .15 .40
290 Cristian Guzman .15 .40
291 Bobby Kielty .15 .40
292 Corey Koskie .15 .40
293 J.C. Romero .15 .40
294 Mike Cuddyer .15 .40
295 Luis Rivas .15 .40
296 Matt LeCroy .15 .40
297 Tony Fiore .15 .40
298 Dustan Mohr .15 .40
299 Chris Gomez .15 .40
300 Johan Santana .25 .60
301 Kyle Lohse .15 .40
302 Frank Thomas .40 1.00
303 Mark Buehrle .25 .60
304 Jon Garland .15 .40
305 Magglio Ordonez .25 .60
306 Paul Konerko .25 .60
307 Sandy Alomar Jr. .15 .40
308 Carlos Lee .15 .40
309 Jon Rauch .15 .40
310 Esteban Loaiza .15 .40
311 Danny Wright .15 .40
312 Kelly Wunsch .15 .40
313 Tony Graffanino .15 .40
314 Aaron Rowand .15 .40
315 Armando Rios .15 .40
316 Jose Valentin .15 .40
317 D'Angelo Jimenez .15 .40
318 Joe Crede .15 .40
319 Miguel Olivo .15 .40
320 Rick White .15 .40
321 Billy Koch .15 .40
322 Tom Gordon .15 .40
323 Bartolo Colon .15 .40
324 Josh Paul .15 .40
325 Joe Borchard .15 .40
326 Damaso Marte .15 .40
327 Derek Jeter 1.00 2.50
328 Jason Giambi .15 .40
329 Roger Clemens .50 1.25
330 Enrique Wilson .15 .40
331 David Wells .15 .40
332 Mike Mussina .25 .60
333 Bernie Williams .25 .60
334 Todd Zeile .15 .40
335 Sterling Hitchcock .15 .40
336 Juan Acevedo .15 .40
337 Robin Ventura .15 .40
338 Mariano Rivera .50 1.25
339 John Flaherty .15 .40
340 Andy Pettitte .25 .60
341 Antonio Osuna .15 .40
342 Erick Almonte .15 .40
343 Chris Hammond .15 .40
344 Steve Karsay .15 .40
345 Alfonso Soriano .25 .60
346 Bubba Trammell .15 .40
347 Nick Johnson .15 .40
348 Jorge Posada .25 .60
349 Jeff Weaver .15 .40
350 Raul Mondesi .15 .40
351 Randy Choate .15 .40
352 Drew Henson .15 .40
353 Jeff Bagwell .25 .60
354 Wade Miller .15 .40
355 Lance Berkman .25 .60
356 Julio Lugo .15 .40
357 Roy Oswalt .25 .60
358 Bruce Chen .15 .40
359 Morgan Ensberg .15 .40
360 Geoff Blum .15 .40
361 Brian Moehler .15 .40
362 Billy Wagner .15 .40
363 Pete Munro .15 .40
364 Brad Ausmus .15 .40
365 Jose Vizcaino .15 .40
366 Craig Biggio .25 .60
367 Tim Redding .15 .40
368 Gregg Zaun .15 .40
369 Octavio Dotel .15 .40
370 Carlos Hernandez .15 .40
371 Richard Hidalgo .15 .40
372 Jeriome Robertson .15 .40
373 Orlando Merced .15 .40
374 John Buck .15 .40
375 Adam Everett .15 .40
376 Raul Chavez .15 .40
377 Brad Lidge .15 .40
378 Jeff Kent .15 .40
379 Scott Linebrink .15 .40
380 Greg Miller .15 .40
381 Kirk Saarloos .15 .40
382 Brandon Puffer .15 .40
383 Ricky Stone .15 .40
384 Jason Lane .15 .40
385 Brian L. Hunter .15 .40
386 Rodrigo Rosario .15 .40
387 Horacio Ramirez .15 .40
388 Gary Sheffield .15 .40
389 Mike Hampton .15 .40
390 Robert Fick .15 .40
391 Henry Blanco .15 .40
392 Vinny Castilla .15 .40
393 Joe Dawley .15 .40
394 Jung Bong .15 .40
395 Rafael Furcal .15 .40
396 Javy Lopez .15 .40
397 Greg Maddux .50 1.25
398 Andruw Jones .15 .40
399 John Smoltz .40 1.00
400 Chipper Jones .40 1.00
401 Mark DeRosa .15 .40
402 Shane Reynolds .15 .40
403 Kevin Gryboski .15 .40
404 Russ Ortiz .15 .40
405 Roberto Hernandez .15 .40
406 Ray King .15 .40
407 Matt Franco .15 .40
408 Marcus Giles .15 .40
409 Trey Hodges .15 .40
410 Darren Holmes .15 .40
411 Julio Franco .15 .40
412 Darren Bragg .15 .40
413 Richie Sexson .15 .40
414 Jeffrey Hammonds .15 .40
415 Ben Sheets .15 .40
416 Mike DeJean .15 .40
417 Royce Clayton .15 .40
418 Wes Helms .15 .40
419 Valerio de Los Santos .15 .40
420 Brady Clark .15 .40
421 Glendon Rusch .15 .40
422 Geoff Jenkins .15 .40
423 John Foster .15 .40
424 Curtis Leskanic .15 .40
425 Todd Ritchie .15 .40
426 Enrique Cruz .15 .40
427 Wayne Franklin .15 .40
428 Matt Ford .15 .40
429 Matt Kinney .15 .40
430 Scott Podsednik .15 .40
431 Luis Vizcaino .15 .40
432 Shane Nance .15 .40
433 Alex Sanchez .15 .40
434 John Vander Wal .15 .40
435 Eric Young .15 .40
436 Eddie Perez .15 .40
437 Jason Conti .15 .40
438 Matt Morris .15 .40
439 Tino Martinez .15 .40
440 Fernando Vina .15 .40
441 Kiko Calero RC .15 .40
442 Cal Eldred .15 .40
443 Jimmy Journell .15 .40
444 Jim Edmonds .25 .60
445 Jeff Fassero .15 .40
446 Mike Matheny .15 .40
447 Garrett Stephenson .15 .40
448 Brett Tomko .15 .40
449 So Taguchi .15 .40
450 Eduardo Perez .15 .40
451 Lance Painter .15 .40
452 Jason Isringhausen .15 .40
453 Albert Pujols .50 1.25
454 Eli Marrero .15 .40
455 Jason Simontacchi .15 .40
456 J.D. Drew .15 .40
457 Scott Rolen .25 .60
458 Orlando Palmeiro .15 .40
459 Dustin Hermanson .15 .40
460 Edgar Renteria .15 .40
461 Woody Williams .15 .40
462 Chris Carpenter .25 .60
463 Sammy Sosa .40 1.00
464 Kerry Wood .15 .40
465 Kyle Farnsworth .15 .40
466 Alex Gonzalez .15 .40
467 Eric Karros .15 .40
468 Troy O'Leary .15 .40
469 Mark Grudzielanek .15 .40
470 Alan Benes .15 .40
471 Mark Prior .25 .60
472 Paul Bako .15 .40
473 Shawn Estes .15 .40
474 Matt Clement .15 .40
475 Ramon E. Martinez .15 .40
476 Tom Goodwin .15 .40
477 Corey Patterson .15 .40
478 Moises Alou .15 .40
479 Juan Cruz .15 .40
480 Bobby Hill .15 .40
481 Mark Bellhorn .15 .40
482 Mark Guthrie .15 .40
483 Mike Remlinger .15 .40
484 Lenny Harris .15 .40
485 Antonio Alfonseca .15 .40
486 Dave Veres .15 .40
487 Hee Seop Choi .15 .40
488 Luis Gonzalez .15 .40
489 Lyle Overbay .15 .40
490 Randy Johnson .40 1.00
491 Mark Grace .25 .60
492 Danny Bautista .15 .40
493 Junior Spivey .15 .40
494 Matt Williams .15 .40
495 Miguel Batista .15 .40
496 Tony Womack .15 .40
497 Byung-Hyun Kim .15 .40
498 Steve Finley .15 .40
499 Craig Counsell .15 .40
500 Curt Schilling .25 .60
501 Elmer Dessens .15 .40
502 Rod Barajas .15 .40
503 David Dellucci .15 .40
504 Mike Koplove .15 .40
505 Mike Myers .15 .40
506 Matt Mantei .15 .40
507 Stephen Randolph RC .15 .40
508 Chad Moeller .15 .40
509 Carlos Baerga .15 .40
510 Andrew Good .15 .40
511 Quinton McCracken .15 .40
512 Jason Romano .15 .40
513 Jolbert Cabrera .15 .40
514 Darren Dreifort .15 .40
515 Kevin Brown .15 .40
516 Paul Quantrill .15 .40
517 Shawn Green .15 .40
518 Hideo Nomo .40 1.00
519 Eric Gagne .15 .40
520 Troy Brohawn .15 .40
521 Kazuhisa Ishii .15 .40
522 Guillermo Mota .15 .40
523 Alex Cora .25 .60
524 Odalis Perez .15 .40
525 Brian Jordan .15 .40
526 Andy Ashby .15 .40
527 Fred McGriff .25 .60
528 Adrian Beltre .40 1.00
529 Daryle Ward .15 .40
530 Todd Hundley .15 .40
531 David Ross .15 .40
532 Paul Shuey .15 .40
533 Paul Lo Duca .15 .40
534 Dave Roberts .25 .60
535 Mike Kinkade .15 .40
536 Cesar Izturis .15 .40
537 Ron Coomer .15 .40
538 Jose Vidro .15 .40
539 Henry Mateo .15 .40
540 Tony Armas Jr. .15 .40
541 Joey Eischen .15 .40
542 Orlando Cabrera .15 .40
543 Jose Macias .15 .40
544 Fernando Tatis .15 .40
545 Jeff Liefer .15 .40
546 Michael Barrett .15 .40
547 Vladimir Guerrero .25 .60
548 Javier Vazquez .15 .40
549 Brad Wilkerson .15 .40
550 Zach Day .15 .40
551 Tomo Ohka .15 .40
552 Livan Hernandez .15 .40
553 Endy Chavez .15 .40
554 Dan Smith .15 .40
555 Scott Stewart .15 .40
556 T.J. Tucker .15 .40
557 Jamey Carroll .15 .40
558 Ron Calloway .15 .40
559 Brian Schneider .15 .40
560 Orlando Hernandez .15 .40
561 Wil Cordero .15 .40
562 Rocky Biddle .15 .40
563 Edgardo Alfonzo .15 .40
564 Andres Galarraga .25 .60
565 Felix Rodriguez .15 .40
566 Benito Santiago .15 .40
567 Jose Cruz Jr. .15 .40
568 Tim Worrell .15 .40
569 Marvin Benard .15 .40
570 Kurt Ainsworth .15 .40
571 Jim Brower .15 .40
572 J.T. Snow .15 .40
573 Scott Eyre .15 .40
574 Robb Nen .15 .40
575 Barry Bonds .60 1.50
576 Ray Durham .15 .40
577 Marquis Grissom .15 .40
578 Pedro Feliz .15 .40
579 Jason Schmidt .15 .40
580 Rich Aurilia .15 .40
581 Kirk Rueter .15 .40
582 Chad Zerbe .15 .40
583 Damian Moss .15 .40
584 Neifi Perez .15 .40
585 Joe Nathan .15 .40

586 Ruben Rivera .15 .40
587 Yorvit Torrealba .15 .40
588 Josh Beckett .15 .40
589 Todd Hollandsworth .15 .40
590 Derrek Lee .15 .40
591 A.J. Burnett .15 .40
592 Juan Pierre .15 .40
593 Mark Redman .15 .40
594 Blaine Neal .15 .40
595 Mike Mordecai .15 .40
596 Alex Gonzalez .15 .40
597 Brad Penny .15 .40
598 Tim Spooneybarger .15 .40
599 Mike Lowell .15 .40
600 Mike Redmond .15 .40
601 Braden Looper .15 .40
602 Ivan Rodriguez .25 .60
603 Andy Fox .15 .40
604 Vladimir Nunez .15 .40
605 Luis Castillo .15 .40
606 Juan Encarnacion .15 .40
607 Armando Almanza .15 .40
608 Gerald Williams .15 .40
609 Carl Pavano .15 .40
610 Michael Tejera .15 .40
611 Ramon Castro .15 .40
612 Brian Banks .15 .40
613 Roberto Alomar .25 .60
614 Al Leiter .15 .40
615 Jeromy Burnitz .15 .40
616 John Franco .15 .40
617 Tom Glavine .25 .60
618 Mike Piazza .40 1.00
619 Cliff Floyd .15 .40
620 Joe McEwing .15 .40
621 David Weathers .15 .40
622 Pedro Astacio .15 .40
623 Timo Perez .15 .40
624 Jason Phillips .15 .40
625 Ty Wigginton .15 .40
626 Steve Trachsel .15 .40
627 Roger Cedeno .15 .40
628 Tsuyoshi Shinjo .15 .40
629 Armando Benitez .15 .40
630 Vance Wilson .15 .40
631 Mike Stanton .15 .40
632 Mo Vaughn .15 .40
633 Scott Strickland .15 .40
634 Rey Sanchez .15 .40
635 Jay Bell .15 .40
636 David Cone .15 .40
637 Jae Weong Seo .15 .40
638 Ryan Klesko .15 .40
639 Wiki Gonzalez .15 .40
640 Trevor Hoffman .25 .60
641 Sean Burroughs .15 .40
642 Mike Bynum .15 .40
643 Clay Condrey .15 .40
644 Gary Bennett .15 .40
645 Kevin Jarvis .15 .40
646 Mark Kotsay .15 .40
647 Phil Nevin .15 .40
648 Dave Hansen .15 .40
649 Keith Lockhart .15 .40
650 Brian Lawrence .15 .40
651 Jay Witasick .15 .40
652 Rondell White .15 .40
653 Jaret Wright .15 .40
654 Luther Hackman .15 .40
655 Jake Peavy .15 .40
656 Brian Buchanan .15 .40
657 Mark Loretta .15 .40
658 Oliver Perez .15 .40
659 Adam Eaton .15 .40
660 Xavier Nady .15 .40
661 Jesse Orosco .15 .40
662 Ramon Vazquez .15 .40
663 Jim Thome .25 .60
664 Jose Mesa .15 .40
665 Rheal Cormier .15 .40
666 David Boll .15 .40
667 Mike Lieberthal .15 .40
668 Brandon Duckworth .15 .40
669 David Coggin .15 .40
670 Bobby Abreu .15 .40
671 Turk Wendell .15 .40
672 Marlon Byrd .15 .40
673 Jason Michaels .15 .40
674 Kevin Millwood .15 .40
675 Tomas Perez .15 .40
676 Jimmy Rollins .25 .60
677 Vicente Padilla .15 .40
678 Pat Burrell .15 .40
679 Tyler Houston .15 .40
680 Hector Mercado .15 .40
681 Carlos Silva .15 .40
682 Nick Punto .15 .40
683 Ricky Ledee .15 .40
684 Randy Wolf .15 .40
685 Todd Pratt .15 .40
686 Placido Polanco .15 .40
687 Chase Utley .25 .60
688 Brian Giles .15 .40
689 Jason Kendall .15 .40
690 Matt Stairs .15 .40
691 Kris Benson .15 .40
692 Julian Tavarez .15 .40
693 Reggie Sanders .15 .40
694 Jeff D'Amico .15 .40
695 Pokey Reese .15 .40
696 Kenny Lofton .15 .40
697 Mike Williams .15 .40
698 David Williams .15 .40
699 Kevin Young .15 .40
700 Brian Boehringer .15 .40
701 Scott Sauerbeck .15 .40
702 Josh Fogg .15 .40
703 Joe Beimel .15 .40
704 Dennis Reyes .15 .40
705 Jeff Suppan .15 .40
706 Salomon Torres .15 .40
707 Kip Wells .15 .40
708 Craig Wilson .15 .40
709 Jack Wilson .15 .40
710 Rob Mackowiak .15 .40
711 Abraham Nunez .15 .40
712 Randall Simon .15 .40
713 Josias Manzanillo .15 .40
714 Ken Griffey Jr. .75 2.00
715 Jimmy Haynes .15 .40
716 Felipe Lopez .15 .40
717 Jimmy Anderson .15 .40
718 Ryan Dempster .15 .40
719 Russell Branyan .15 .40
720 Aaron Boone .15 .40
721 Luke Prokopec .15 .40
722 Felix Heredia .15 .40
723 Scott Sullivan .15 .40
724 Danny Graves .15 .40
725 Kent Mercker .15 .40
726 Barry Larkin .25 .60
727 Jason LaRue .15 .40
728 Gabe White .15 .40
729 Adam Dunn .25 .60
730 Brandon Larson .15 .40
731 Reggie Taylor .15 .40
732 Sean Casey .15 .40
733 Scott Williamson .15 .40
734 Austin Kearns .15 .40
735 Kelly Stinnett .15 .40
736 Ruben Mateo .15 .40
737 Wily Mo Pena .15 .40
738 Larry Walker .25 .60
739 Juan Uribe .15 .40
740 Denny Neagle .15 .40
741 Darren Oliver .15 .40
742 Charles Johnson .15 .40
743 Todd Jones .15 .40
744 Todd Helton .25 .60
745 Shawn Chacon .15 .40
746 Jason Jennings .15 .40
747 Preston Wilson .15 .40
748 Chris Richard .15 .40
749 Chris Stynes .15 .40
750 Jose Jimenez .15 .40
751 Gabe Kapler .15 .40
752 Jay Payton .15 .40
753 Aaron Cook .15 .40
754 Greg Norton .15 .40
755 Scott Elarton .15 .40
756 Brian Fuentes .15 .40
757 Jose Hernandez .15 .40
758 Nelson Cruz .15 .40
759 Justin Speier .15 .40
760 Javier A. Lopez RC .15 .40
761 Garret Anderson AS .15 .40
762 Tony Batista AS .15 .40
763 Mark Buehrle AS .25 .60
764 Johnny Damon AS .25 .60
765 Freddy Garcia AS .15 .40
766 Nomar Garciaparra AS .25 .60
767 Jason Giambi AS .15 .40
768 Roy Halladay AS .25 .60
769 Shea Hillenbrand AS .15 .40
770 Torii Hunter AS .15 .40
771 Derek Jeter AS 1.00 2.50
772 Paul Konerko AS .25 .60
773 Derek Lowe AS .15 .40
774 Pedro Martinez AS .25 .60
775 A.J. Pierzynski AS .15 .40
776 Jorge Posada AS .25 .60
777 Manny Ramirez AS .40 1.00
778 Mariano Rivera AS .50 1.25
779 Alex Rodriguez AS .50 1.25
780 Kazuhiro Sasaki AS .15 .40
781 Alfonso Soriano AS .25 .60
782 Ichiro Suzuki AS .50 1.25
783 Mike Sweeney AS .15 .40
784 Miguel Tejada AS .25 .60
785 Ugueth Urbina AS .15 .40
786 Robin Ventura AS .15 .40
787 Omar Vizquel AS .25 .60
788 Randy Winn AS .15 .40
789 Barry Zito AS .25 .60
790 Lance Berkman AS .25 .60
791 Barry Bonds AS .60 1.50
792 Adam Dunn AS .25 .60
793 Tom Glavine AS .25 .60
794 Luis Gonzalez AS .15 .40
795 Shawn Green AS .15 .40
796 Vladimir Guerrero AS .25 .60
797 Todd Helton AS .25 .60
798 Trevor Hoffman AS .25 .60
799 Randy Johnson AS .40 1.00
800 Andruw Jones AS .15 .40
801 Byung-Hyun Kim AS .15 .40
802 Mike Lowell AS .15 .40
803 Eric Gagne AS .15 .40
804 Matt Morris AS .15 .40
805 Robb Nen AS .15 .40
806 Vicente Padilla AS .15 .40
807 Odalis Perez AS .15 .40
808 Mike Piazza AS .40 1.00
809 Mike Remlinger AS .15 .40
810 Scott Rolen AS .25 .60
811 Jimmy Rollins AS .25 .60
812 Benito Santiago AS .15 .40
813 Curt Schilling AS .25 .60
814 Richie Sexson AS .15 .40
815 John Smoltz AS .40 1.00
816 Sammy Sosa AS .40 1.00
817 Junior Spivey AS .15 .40
818 Jose Vidro AS .15 .40
819 Mike Williams AS .15 .40
820 Luis Castillo AS .15 .40
821 Jason Giambi HR Derby .15 .40
822 Luis Gonzalez HR Derby .15 .40
823 Sammy Sosa HR Derby .40 1.00
824 Ken Griffey Jr. HR Derby .75 2.00
825 Ken Griffey Jr. HR Derby .75 2.00
826 Tino Martinez HR Derby .15 .40
827 Barry Bonds HR Derby .60 1.50
828 Frank Thomas HR Derby .40 1.00
829 Ken Griffey Jr. HR Derby .75 2.00
830 Barry Bonds 02 WS .60 1.50
831 Tim Salmon 02 WS .15 .40
832 Troy Glaus 02 WS .15 .40
833 Robb Nen 02 WS .15 .40
834 Jeff Kent 02 WS .15 .40
835 Scott Spiezio 02 WS .15 .40
836 Darin Erstad 02 WS .15 .40
837 Randy Johnson T40 .40 1.00
838 Chipper Jones T40 .40 1.00
839 Greg Maddux T40 .50 1.25
840 Nomar Garciaparra T40 .25 .60
841 Manny Ramirez T40 .40 1.00
842 Pedro Martinez T40 .25 .60
843 Sammy Sosa T40 .40 1.00
844 Ken Griffey Jr. T40 .75 2.00
845 Jim Thome T40 .25 .60
846 Vladimir Guerrero T40 .25 .60
847 Mike Piazza T40 .40 1.00
848 Derek Jeter T40 1.00 2.50
849 Jason Giambi T40 .15 .40
850 Roger Clemens T40 .50 1.25
851 Alfonso Soriano T40 .25 .60
852 Hideki Matsui T40 .75 2.00
853 Barry Bonds T40 .60 1.50
854 Ichiro Suzuki T40 .50 1.25
855 Albert Pujols T40 .50 1.25
856 Alex Rodriguez T40 .50 1.25
857 Darin Erstad T40 .15 .40
858 Troy Glaus T40 .15 .40
859 Curt Schilling T40 .25 .60
860 Luis Gonzalez T40 .15 .40
861 Tom Glavine T40 .25 .60
862 Andruw Jones T40 .15 .40
863 Gary Sheffield T40 .15 .40
864 Frank Thomas T40 .40 1.00
865 Mark Prior T40 .25 .60
866 Ivan Rodriguez T40 .25 .60
867 Jeff Bagwell T40 .25 .60
868 Lance Berkman T40 .25 .60
869 Shawn Green T40 .15 .40
870 Hideo Nomo T40 .40 1.00
871 Torii Hunter T40 .15 .40
872 Bernie Williams T40 .25 .60
873 Barry Zito T40 .25 .60
874 Pat Burrell T40 .15 .40
875 Carlos Delgado T40 .15 .40
876 Miguel Tejada T40 .25 .60
877 Hideki Matsui NR RC .75 2.00
878 Jose Contreras NR RC .40 1.00
879 Jason Anderson NR .15 .40
880 Jason Shiell NR RC .15 .40
881 Kevin Tolar NR RC .15 .40
882 Michel Hernandez NR RC .15 .40
883 Arnie Munoz NR RC .15 .40
884 David Sanders NR RC .15 .40
885 Willie Eyre NR RC .15 .40
886 Brent Hoard NR RC .15 .40
887 Lew Ford NR RC .15 .40
888 Beau Kemp NR RC .15 .40
889 Jon Pridie NR RC .15 .40
890 Mike Ryan NR RC .15 .40
891 Richard Fischer NR RC .15 .40
892 Luis Ayala NR RC .15 .40
893 Mike Neu NR RC .15 .40
894 Joe Valentine NR RC .15 .40
895 Nate Bland NR RC .15 .40
896 Shane Bazzell NR RC .15 .40
897 Aquilino Lopez NR RC .15 .40
898 Diegomar Markwell NR RC .15 .40
899 Francisco Rosario NR RC .15 .40
900 Guillermo Quiroz NR RC .15 .40
901 Luis De Los Santos NR .15 .40
902 Fernando Cabrera NR RC .15 .40
903 Francisco Cruceta NR RC .15 .40
904 Jhonny Peralta NR .15 .40
905 Rett Johnson NR RC .15 .40
906 Aaron Looper NR RC .15 .40
907 Bobby Madritsch NR RC .15 .40
908 Luis Matos NR .15 .40
909 Jose Castillo NR .15 .40
910 Chris Waters NR RC .15 .40
911 Jeremy Guthrie NR .15 .40
912 Pedro Liriano NR .15 .40
913 Joe Borowski NR .15 .40
914 Felix Sanchez NR RC .15 .40
915 Jon Leicester NR RC .15 .40
916 Todd Wellemeyer NR RC .15 .40
917 Matt Bruback NR RC .15 .40
918 Chris Capuano NR RC .15 .40
919 Oscar Villarreal NR RC .15 .40
920 Matt Kata NR RC .15 .40
921 Robby Hammock NR RC .15 .40
922 Gerald Laird NR .15 .40
923 Brandon Webb NR RC .50 1.25
924 Tommy Whiteman NR .15 .40
925 Andrew Brown NR RC .15 .40
926 Alfredo Gonzalez NR RC .15 .40
927 Carlos Rivera NR .15 .40
928 Rick Roberts NR RC .15 .40
929 Termel Sledge NR RC .15 .40
930 Josh Willingham NR RC .50 1.25
931 Prentice Redman NR RC .15 .40
932 Jeff Duncan NR RC .15 .40
933 Craig Brazell NR RC .15 .40
934 Jeremy Griffiths NR RC .15 .40
935 Phil Seibel NR RC .15 .40
936 Heath Bell NR RC .25 .60
937 Bernie Castro NR RC .15 .40
938 Mike Nicolas NR RC .15 .40
939 Cory Stewart NR RC .15 .40
940 Shane Victorino NR RC .50 1.25
941 Brandon Villafuerte NR .15 .40
942 Jeremy Wedel NR RC .15 .40
943 Tommy Phelps NR .15 .40
944 Josh Hall NR RC .15 .40
945 Ryan Cameron NR RC .15 .40
946 Garrett Atkins NR .15 .40
947 Clint Barmes NR RC .40 1.00
948 Mike Hessman NR RC .15 .40
949 Brian Stokes NR RC .15 .40
950 Rocco Baldelli NR .15 .40
951 Hector Luna NR RC .15 .40
952 Jaime Cerda NR .15 .40
953 D.J. Carrasco NR RC .15 .40
954 Ian Ferguson NR RC .15 .40
955 Tim Olson NR RC .15 .40
956 Alejandro Machado NR RC .15 .40
957 Jorge Cordova NR RC .15 .40
958 Wilfredo Ledezma NR RC .15 .40
959 Nate Robertson NR RC .50 1.25
960 Nook Logan NR RC .15 .40
961 Anaheim Angels TC .15 .40
962 Baltimore Orioles TC .15 .40
963 Boston Red Sox TC .25 .60
964 Chicago White Sox TC .25 .60
965 Cleveland Indians TC .15 .40
966 Detroit Tigers TC .15 .40
967 Kansas City Royals TC .15 .40
968 Minnesota Twins TC .15 .40
969 New York Yankees TC .25 .60
970 Oakland Athletics TC .25 .60
971 Seattle Mariners TC .50 1.25
972 Tampa Bay Devil Rays TC .15 .40
973 Texas Rangers TC .50 1.25
974 Toronto Blue Jays TC .15 .40
975 Arizona Diamondbacks TC .25 .60
976 Atlanta Braves TC .15 .40
977 Chicago Cubs TC .15 .40
978 Cincinnati Reds TC .15 .40
979 Colorado Rockies TC .25 .60
980 Florida Marlins TC .25 .60
981 Houston Astros TC .25 .60
982 Los Angeles Dodgers TC .15 .40
983 Milwaukee Brewers TC .15 .40
984 Montreal Expos TC .25 .60
985 New York Mets TC .25 .60
986 Philadelphia Phillies TC .25 .60
987 Pittsburgh Pirates TC .15 .40
988 San Diego Padres TC .15 .40
989 San Francisco Giants TC .60 1.50
990 St. Louis Cardinals TC .50 1.25
KG Ken Griffey Jr. Sample .75 2.00

2003 Upper Deck 40-Man Rainbow

*RAINBOW: 10X TO 25X BASIC
*RAINBOW RC'S: 10X TO 25X BASIC
*RAINBOW NR: 10X TO 25X BASIC
*RAINBOW NR RC'S: 10X TO 25X BASIC
RANDOM INSERTS IN PACKS
STATED PRINT RUN 40 SERIAL #'d SETS

2003 Upper Deck 40-Man Red White and Blue

*RWB: 1.5X TO 4X BASIC
*RWB NR: 1.5X TO 4X BASIC
1-752 STATED ODDS 1:6
877-960 STATED ODDS 1:36

2003 Upper Deck 40-Man Endorsements Signatures

STATED ODDS 1:500
SERIAL #'d CARDS B/WN 10-50 COPIES PER
NO PRICING ON QTY OF 50 OR LESS
BD Ben Diggins 6.00 15.00
JL Jon Lieber 10.00 25.00
KGS Ken Griffey Sr. 10.00 25.00
RA Rick Ankiel 6.00 15.00
TO Tomo Ohka 15.00 40.00

2006 Upper Deck All-Star FanFest

1 Ken Griffey Jr. 2.50 6.00
2 Derek Jeter 3.00 8.00
3 Miguel Cabrera 1.25 3.00
4 Albert Pujols 1.50 4.00
5 Babe Ruth 3.00 8.00
6 Ty Cobb 2.00 5.00

2007 Upper Deck All-Star FanFest

COMPLETE SET (12) 3.00 8.00
1 Derek Jeter .50 1.25
2 Ken Griffey Jr. .40 1.00
3 Cal Ripken Jr. .60 1.50
4 Albert Pujols .25 .60
5 Barry Zito .12 .30
6 Ichiro Suzuki .25 .60
7 Daisuke Matsuzaka .30 .75
8 Kei Igawa .20 .50
9 Akinori Iwamura .20 .50
10 Josh Hamilton .25 .60
11 Phil Hughes .20 .50
12 Tim Lincecum .40 1.00

2009 Upper Deck All-Star FanFest

FF1 Albert Pujols .60 1.50
FF2 Bob Gibson .30 .75
FF3 Bruce Sutter .30 .75
FF4 Colby Rasmus .30 .75
FF5 Enos Slaughter .20 .50
FF6 Lou Brock .30 .75
FF7 Ozzie Smith .60 1.50
FF8 Red Schoendienst .30 .75
FF9 Rick Ankiel .20 .50
FF10 Stan Musial .75 2.00
FF11 Daisuke Matsuzaka .30 .75
FF12 Derek Jeter 1.25 3.00
FF13 Dustin Pedroia .50 1.25
FF14 Ichiro Suzuki .60 1.50
FF15 Joe DiMaggio 1.00 2.50
FF16 Josh Hamilton .30 .75
FF17 Ken Griffey Jr. 1.00 2.50
FF18 Zack Greinke .50 1.25
FF19 Ryan Braun .30 .75
FF20 Tim Lincecum .30 .75
STLOUIS Stan Musial 25.00 60.00
Albert Pujols
Lou Brock
Bob Gibson
Ozzie Smith/500

2012 Upper Deck All-Time Greats

STATED PRINT RUN 99 SER. #'d SETS
85 Pete Rose 4.00 10.00

2012 Upper Deck All-Time Greats Bronze

*BRONZE/65: .5X TO 1.2X BASIC CARDS

2012 Upper Deck All-Time Greats Silver

*SILVER/35: .6X TO 1.5X BASIC CARDS

2012 Upper Deck All-Time Greats Athletes of the Century Booklet Autographs

STATED PRINT RUN 5-35
ACPR Pete Rose/30 30.00 60.00

2012 Upper Deck All-Time Greats Letterman Autographs

PRINT RUN 7-140
LPR Pete Rose/80 15.00 40.00

2012 Upper Deck All-Time Greats Shining Moments Autographs

PRINT RUN 2-30
SMPR1 Pete Rose/20 10.00 25.00
SMPR2 Pete Rose/20 10.00 25.00
SMPR3 Pete Rose/20 10.00 25.00
SMPR4 Pete Rose/20 10.00 25.00

2012 Upper Deck All-Time Greats Signatures

PRINT RUN 3-70
GAPR1 Pete Rose/30 15.00 40.00
GAPR2 Pete Rose/30 15.00 40.00
GAPR3 Pete Rose/30 15.00 40.00
GAPR4 Pete Rose/30 15.00 40.00

2012 Upper Deck All-Time Greats Signatures Silver

*SILVER: X TO X BASIC CARDS
PRINT RUN 2-25

2012 Upper Deck All-Time Greats SPx All-Time Forces Autographs

PRINT RUN 1-30
ATFPR Pete Rose/30

2008 Upper Deck Ballpark Collection

COMMON CARD (1-100) .60 1.50
COMMON AU RC (101-150) 3.00 8.00
OVERALL AU ODDS 1:5 HOBBY
EXCHANGE DEADLINE 08/27/2010
COMMON 2X GU (151-200) 4.00 10.00
COMMON 4X GU (201-250) 4.00 10.00
COMMON 6X GU (251-295) 5.00 12.00
COMMON 8X GU (296-340) 6.00 15.00
OVERALL GU ODDS 2:1 HOBBY
1 Brandon Webb 1.00 2.50
2 Dan Haren .60 1.50
3 Chris B. Young .60 1.50
4 Randy Johnson 1.50 4.00
5 Mark Teixeira 1.00 2.50
6 John Smoltz 1.50 4.00
7 Tom Glavine 1.00 2.50
8 Brian McCann 1.00 2.50
9 Chipper Jones 1.50 4.00
10 Nick Markakis 1.25 3.00
11 Brian Roberts .60 1.50
12 Josh Beckett .60 1.50
13 David Ortiz 1.50 4.00
14 Manny Ramirez 1.50 4.00
15 Dustin Pedroia 1.50 4.00
16 Jonathan Papelbon 1.00 2.50
17 Daisuke Matsuzaka 1.00 2.50
18 Alfonso Soriano 1.00 2.50
19 Aramis Ramirez .60 1.50
20 Carlos Zambrano 1.00 2.50
21 Nick Swisher 1.00 2.50
22 Jim Thome 1.00 2.50
23 Ken Griffey Jr. 3.00 8.00
24 Adam Dunn 1.00 2.50
25 Grady Sizemore 1.00 2.50
26 Victor Martinez 1.00 2.50
27 Travis Hafner .60 1.50
28 C.C. Sabathia 1.00 2.50
29 Garrett Atkins .60 1.50
30 Matt Holliday 1.50 4.00
31 Troy Tulowitzki 1.50 4.00
32 Magglio Ordonez 1.00 2.50
33 Justin Verlander 1.50 4.00
34 Miguel Cabrera 1.50 4.00
35 Gary Sheffield .60 1.50
36 Ivan Rodriguez 1.00 2.50
37 Dontrelle Willis .60 1.50
38 Curtis Granderson 1.00 2.50
39 Hanley Ramirez 1.00 2.50
40 Dan Uggla .60 1.50
41 Lance Berkman 1.00 2.50
42 Roy Oswalt 1.00 2.50
43 Carlos Lee .60 1.50
44 Hunter Pence 1.00 2.50
45 Alex Gordon 1.00 2.50
46 Jose Guillen .60 1.50
47 Torii Hunter .60 1.50
48 Vladimir Guerrero 1.00 2.50
49 Andruw Jones .60 1.50
50 Matt Kemp 1.25 3.00
51 Russell Martin .60 1.50
52 Jeff Kent .60 1.50
53 Ryan Braun 1.00 2.50
54 Prince Fielder 1.00 2.50
55 Delmon Young 1.00 2.50
56 Joe Mauer 1.25 3.00
57 Justin Morneau 1.00 2.50
58 Jose Reyes 1.00 2.50
59 David Wright 1.00 2.50
60 Carlos Beltran 1.00 2.50
61 Johan Santana 1.00 2.50
62 Pedro Martinez 1.00 2.50
63 Alex Rodriguez 2.00 5.00
64 Derek Jeter 4.00 10.00
65 Hideki Matsui 1.50 4.00
66 Robinson Cano 1.00 2.50
67 Joba Chamberlain .60 1.50
68 Phil Hughes .60 1.50
69 Mariano Rivera 2.00 5.00
70 Eric Chavez .60 1.50
71 Bobby Crosby .60 1.50
72 Cole Hamels 1.25 3.00
73 Ryan Howard 1.00 2.50
74 Jimmy Rollins 1.00 2.50
75 Chase Utley 1.00 2.50
76 Jason Bay 1.00 2.50
77 Freddy Sanchez .60 1.50
78 Jake Peavy .60 1.50
79 Greg Maddux 2.00 5.00
80 Trevor Hoffman 1.00 2.50
81 Kosuke Fukudome RC 2.50 6.00
82 Barry Zito 1.00 2.50
83 Tim Lincecum 1.00 2.50
84 Erik Bedard .60 1.50
85 Felix Hernandez 1.00 2.50
86 Ichiro Suzuki 2.00 5.00
87 Troy Glaus 1.00 2.50
88 Albert Pujols 2.00 5.00
89 Chris Carpenter 1.00 2.50
90 Scott Kazmir 1.00 2.50
91 Carl Crawford 1.00 2.50
92 Michael Young .60 1.50
93 Hank Blalock .60 1.50
94 Roy Halladay 1.00 2.50
95 Vernon Wells .60 1.50
96 Alex Rios .60 1.50
97 Scott Rolen 1.00 2.50
98 Frank Thomas 1.50 4.00
99 Lastings Milledge .60 1.50
100 Ryan Zimmerman 1.00 2.50
101 Bobby Wilson AU RC 3.00 8.00
102 Alex Romero AU (RC) 4.00 10.00
104 Brandon Boggs AU (RC) 3.00 8.00
105 Brian Barton AU RC 4.00 10.00
106 B.Bass AU (RC) 6.00 15.00
107 Brian Bixler AU (RC) 3.00 8.00
108 Brian Bocock AU RC 3.00 8.00
109 Burke Badenhop AU RC 3.00 8.00
110 Callix Crabbe AU (RC) 3.00 8.00
111 C.Kershaw AU RC 50.00 100.00
112 C.Hu AU (RC) 12.50 30.00
113 C.Buchholz AU (RC) 6.00 15.00
114 E.Torres AU (RC) 5.00 12.00
115 Clete Thomas AU RC 3.00 8.00
116 Colt Morton AU RC 3.00 8.00
117 Daric Barton AU (RC) 3.00 8.00
118 C.Wade AU (RC) 5.00 12.00
119 Elliot Johnson AU (RC) 3.00 8.00
121 E.Longoria AU RC 40.00 80.00
122 Evan Meek AU RC 3.00 8.00
123 German Duran AU RC 3.00 8.00
124 Fernando Hernandez AU RC 3.00 8.00
125 Greg Smith AU RC 3.00 8.00
126 J.Bruce AU (RC) EXCH 20.00 50.00
127 Wladimir Balentien AU (RC) 4.00 10.00
128 Hernan Iribarren AU (RC) 3.00 8.00
129 J.Lowrie AU (RC) 6.00 15.00
130 I.Kennedy AU RC 3.00 8.00
131 J.Clement AU (RC) 8.00 20.00
132 J.Carlson AU RC 6.00 15.00
133 Jonathan Herrera AU RC 3.00 8.00
134 J.Cueto AU RC 6.00 15.00
135 Jonathan Albaladejo AU RC 4.00 10.00
136 Josh Newman AU RC 3.00 8.00
137 Kevin Hart AU (RC) 4.00 10.00
138 J.Masterson AU RC 15.00 40.00
140 Luis Mendoza AU (RC) 3.00 8.00
141 M.Tupman AU RC 8.00 20.00
143 N.Blackburn AU RC 12.50 30.00
144 N.Adenhart AU (RC) 6.00 15.00
145 R.Troncoso AU RC 5.00 12.00
146 Paul Janish AU (RC) 4.00 10.00
147 R.Bierd AU RC 15.00 40.00
148 Robinzon Diaz AU (RC) 3.00 8.00
149 Steve Holm AU RC 4.00 10.00
150 W.Wright AU RC 6.00 15.00
151 Jason Giambi 4.00 10.00
David Ortiz
152 J.Papelbon/M.Rivera 5.00 12.00
153 N.Ryan/J.Santana 6.00 15.00
154 M.Mussina/J.Posada 5.00 12.00
155 J.Papelbon/J.Varitek 5.00 12.00
156 Dan Uggla 4.00 10.00
Howie Kendrick
157 Kenji Johjima 4.00 10.00
Jason Varitek
158 Carlos Lee 4.00 10.00
Roy Oswalt
159 A.Pujols/D.Lee 5.00 12.00
160 A.Pujols/O.Smith 12.50 30.00
161 A.Soriano/C.Zambrano 6.00 15.00
162 Tony Gwynn 4.00 10.00
Trevor Hoffman
163 Cole Hamels 4.00 10.00
Johan Santana
164 David Ortiz 4.00 10.00
Kendry Morales
165 Curt Schilling 4.00 10.00
Randy Johnson
166 Curtis Granderson 4.00 10.00
B.J. Upton
167 C.Utley/R.Sandberg 12.50 30.00
168 Nick Markakis 4.00 10.00
Melvin Mora
169 Conor Jackson 4.00 10.00
Prince Fielder
170 Roy Halladay 4.00 10.00
Ben Sheets
171 Kerry Wood 4.00 10.00
Mark Mulder
172 A.Jones/K.Griffey Jr. 5.00 12.00
173 Troy Tulowitzki 4.00 10.00
J.J. Hardy
174 M.Cain/T.Lincecum 10.00 25.00
175 D.Jeter/O.Cabrera 5.00 12.00
176 A.Pujols/P.Fielder 5.00 12.00
177 F.Thomas/R.Halladay 6.00 15.00
178 Josh Beckett 4.00 10.00
Jason Varitek
179 M.Cabrera/M.Schmidt 5.00 12.00
180 A.Pujols/C.Duncan 5.00 12.00
181 C.C. Sabathia 4.00 10.00
Dontrelle Willis
182 Matt Holliday 4.00 10.00
Manny Ramirez
183 Roy Halladay 4.00 10.00
Zack Greinke
184 Nick Markakis 4.00 10.00
Vladimir Guerrero
185 Ben Sheets 4.00 10.00
Roy Halladay
186 A.Pujols/V.Guerrero 5.00 12.00
187 Johnny Damon 4.00 10.00
Manny Ramirez
188 Johan Santana 4.00 10.00
Chris Carpenter
191 C.Schilling/J.Papelbon 5.00 12.00
192 D.Jeter/C.Ripken Jr. 12.50 30.00
193 Jason Varitek 4.00 10.00
Wade Boggs
194 D.Lee/A.Soriano 5.00 12.00
196 Hong-Chih Kuo 4.00 10.00
Kenji Johjima
197 Kerry Wood 4.00 10.00
Alfonso Soriano
198 A.Pujols/C.Delgado 5.00 12.00
199 D.Mattingly/D.Jeter 12.50 30.00
200 D.Jeter/J.Damon 6.00 15.00
201 Field/Sheet/Kemp/Loney 6.00 15.00
202 Ortiz/Youk/Giambi/Jeter 8.00 20.00
203 Ripken/Jeter/Greene/Tulo 10.00 25.00
204 Yount/Prince/Weeks/Hardy 6.00 15.00
205 Vladimir Guerrero 4.00 10.00
Howie Kendrick
Casey Kotchman
Chone Figgins
206 Jason Varitek 4.00 10.00
Jorge Posada
Ivan Rodriguez
Kenji Johjima
207 Trevor Hoffman 4.00 10.00
Mariano Rivera
Eric Gagne
Joe Nathan
208 Carlos Guillen 4.00 10.00
Brandon Inge
Gary Sheffield
Ivan Rodriguez
209 Kazmir/Unit/Liriano/Johan 5.00 12.00
210 Johan/Wagner/Maine/Pedro 5.00 12.00
211 C.Jack/Prince/Pujols/D.Lee 10.00 25.00
212 Josh Beckett 4.00 10.00
Justin Verlander
Jered Weaver
Zack Greinke
213 Maddux/Peavy/Young/Hoffman 5.00 12.00
215 Maddux/Hoff/Greene/Gwynn 6.00 15.00
216 Griffey/Harang/Soriano/Zamb. 6.00 15.00
217 Maddux/Smoltz/Muss/Halla 6.00 15.00
218 Griffey/Thome/Big Hurt/Manny 10.00 25.00
220 Vlad/Manny/Pujols/Lee 6.00 15.00
221 Griffey/Soriano/C.Lee/Bay 6.00 15.00
223 D.Lee/Soriano/Jeter/Giambi 6.00 15.00
225 C.C. Sabathia 4.00 10.00
Randy Johnson
Scott Kazmir
Cole Hamels
226 Pujols/Ankiel/Carp/Ozzie 10.00 25.00
227 Schmidt/Pujols/Griffey/Papi 10.00 25.00
228 Grand/Furcal/Jeter/Weeks 5.00 12.00
229 Papi/Manny/Varitek/Boggs 6.00 15.00
230 Pett/Jeter/Peavy/Greene 6.00 15.00
231 Matt/Jeter/Manny/Papi 12.50 30.00
232 Smoltz/Chip/Johan/Delgad 5.00 12.00
233 Jeter/Giambi/Mora/Roberts 6.00 15.00
234 D.Lee/Aramis/Pujols/Dunc 6.00 15.00
235 Mulder/Pujols/Sheets/Prince 8.00 20.00
237 Manny/Vlad/Burrell/Pujols 6.00 15.00
238 Pett/Jeter/Pudge/Verland 8.00 20.00
239 Jason Varitek 5.00 12.00
Ivan Rodriguez
Jorge Posada
Kenji Johjima
240 Brian Roberts 4.00 10.00
Rickie Weeks
Chase Utley
Dan Uggla
241 Mulder/Pujols/Pudge/Ordon 6.00 15.00
242 Griffey/Prince/Papi/Markak 8.00 20.00
243 Jeter/Roberts/Young/Uggla 6.00 15.00
244 Manny/Papi/Ordon/Vlad 5.00 12.00
245 Randy Johnson 4.00 10.00
Conor Jackson
Chad Billingsley
James Loney
246 Manny Ramirez 4.00 10.00
Magglio Ordonez
Pat Burrell
Josh Willingham
247 Jeter/Giambi/Rivera/Wang 10.00 25.00
248 Carl Crawford 4.00 10.00
B.J. Upton
Hanley Ramirez
Dan Uggla
249 Pujols/Griffey/D.Lee/Prince 6.00 15.00
251 Chris Carpenter 5.00 12.00
Ben Sheets
Dan Haren
Josh Johnson
Jake Peavy
Cole Hamels
252 Vladimir Guerrero 6.00 15.00
Manny Ramirez
Curtis Granderson
Mark Teahen
Rocco Baldelli
Nick Markakis
253 Randy Johnson 5.00 12.00
Barry Zito
Johan Santana
Francisco Liriano
Mark Mulder
Scott Kazmir
255 CLE/LAA 10.00 25.00
256 NL First Basemen 10.00 25.00
257 Outfielders 12.50 30.00
260 NYY/NYM 12.50 30.00
262 Jered Weaver 5.00 12.00
Rickie Weeks
Zack Greinke
Khalil Greene
Scott Kazmir
Howie Kendrick
263 Mus/Pet/Smol/Unit/Hall/Glav 6.00 15.00
265 CHC/STL 10.00 25.00
266 LAD/LAA 5.00 12.00
267 Puj/Mul/Lee/Wood/Field/Sheet 8.00 20.00
268 Grif/Jet/Man/Vlad/Papi/Pujol 15.00 40.00
269 ATL/NYM/FLA 8.00 20.00
270 Hurt/Man/Vlad/Lee/Schm/Puj 6.00 15.00
271 Ivan Rodriguez 6.00 15.00
Jason Varitek
Jorge Posada
Joe Mauer
Brian McCann
Kenji Johjima
272 Manny Ramirez 5.00 12.00
Magglio Ordonez
Pat Burrell
Josh Willingham

Delmon Young
Nick Markakis
273 Miguel Tejada 6.00 15.00
Mark Loretta
Roy Oswalt
Kevin Millwood
Michael Young
Josh Hamilton
274 Johan Santana 10.00 25.00
Carlos Delgado
Moises Alou
Cole Hamels
Pat Burrell
Chase Utley
275 Chase Utley 5.00 12.00
Aaron Hill
Rickie Weeks
Chris Burke
Dan Uggla
Akinori Iwamura
276 CHC/ARI 10.00 25.00
277 DET/STL 8.00 20.00
278 Grif/Field/Jen/Papi/And/Marka 10.00 25.00
280 Man/Vlad/Mags/Papi/Aram/Ken 6.00 15.00
281 Jason Varitek 5.00 12.00
Jorge Posada
Kenji Johjima
Miguel Cabrera
Melvin Mora
Eric Chavez
282 Gr/Ca/Ba/Si/Te/Yo 12.50 30.00
284 BOS/DET 6.00 15.00
285 Prince Fielder 6.00 15.00
Mike Cameron
Rickie Weeks
Justin Morneau
Delmon Young
Francisco Liriano
286 Carl Crawford 5.00 12.00
Scott Kazmir
Akinori Iwamura
Luis Gonzalez
Josh Johnson
Dan Uggla
287 Mar/Ank/Ham/Nad/Dre/Dun 8.00 20.00
288 SD/COL/SF 5.00 12.00
290 Yankee Stars 15.00 40.00
291 Red Sox Stars 10.00 25.00
292 ARI/COL/LAD 5.00 12.00
294 Tigers Stars 10.00 25.00
295 Vladimir Guerrero 6.00 15.00
Garret Anderson
John Lackey
Chone Figgins
Jered Weaver
Casey Kotchman
296 W/G/L/C/N/Z/P/R 5.00 12.00
297 BOS/NYY 10.00 25.00
298 Vladimir Guerrero 8.00 20.00
John Lackey
Howie Kendrick
Kendry Morales
Travis Hafner
C.C. Sabathia
Victor Martinez
Grady Sizemore
299 P/F/B/L/T/D/G/L 12.50 30.00
300 H/L/W/B/G/B/D/C 8.00 20.00
301 Johan Santana 6.00 15.00
Carlos Delgado
Josh Johnson
Josh Willingham
John Smoltz
Chipper Jones
Cole Hamels
Pat Burrell
303 NYM/NYY 15.00 40.00
304 O/K/G/T/S/H/T/M 6.00 15.00
306 G/P/L/L/F/D/B/S 12.50 30.00
311 P/M/L/W/F/S/G/N 10.00 25.00
312 R/J/P/O/G/R/T/G 10.00 25.00
314 P/G/B/G/T/L/R/R 12.50 30.00
317 Manny Ramirez 6.00 15.00
Magglio Ordonez
Nick Markakis
RoC.C.o Baldelli
Moises Alou
Pat Burrell
Josh Willingham
Delmon Young
318 Michael Young 8.00 20.00
Kevin Millwood
Hank Blalock
Josh Hamilton
Carlos Lee
Roy Oswalt
Miguel Tejada
Mark Loretta
319 Chase Utley 8.00 20.00
Cole Hamels
Pat Burrell
Brad Lidge
Carlos Delgado
Johan Santana
Moises Alou
Billy Wagner
320 U/C/W/R/U/L/H/B 10.00 25.00
321 Randy Johnson 8.00 20.00
Chad Tracy
Chris Burke
Stephen Drew
Kerry Wood
Alfonso Soriano
Derrek Lee
Aramis Ramirez
322 DET/STL 12.50 30.00
323 David Ortiz 8.00 20.00
Manny Ramirez
Jonathan Papelbon
Jason Varitek
Matt Holliday
Troy Tulowitzki
Jeff Francis
Garrett Atkins
324 G/F/J/T/O/M/A/C 15.00 40.00
327 Johan Santana 6.00 15.00
Magglio Ordonez
Vladimir Guerrero
David Ortiz
Aramis Ramirez
Kendry Morales
Ivan Rodriguez
Manny Ramirez
329 G/C/D/B/O/S/Y/T 8.00 20.00
330 James Loney 6.00 15.00
Adam LaRoche
Mark Teixeira
Aaron Boone
Casey Kotchman
Kevin Youkilis
Jason Giambi
Aubrey Huff
331 Miguel Cabrera 6.00 15.00
Magglio Ordonez
Dontrelle Willis
Joel Zumaya
Manny Ramirez
David Ortiz
Jonathan Papelbon
Josh Beckett
333 Carl Crawford 6.00 15.00
Scott Kazmir
RoC.C.o Baldelli
B.J. Upton
Hanley Ramirez
Josh Johnson
Josh Willingham
Dan Uggla
334 Pat Burrell 8.00 20.00
Nick Markakis
Josh Willingham
Xavier Nady
J.D. Drew
Chris Duncan
Rick Ankiel
Josh Hamilton
335 Jake Peavy 8.00 20.00
Chris Young
Jeff Francis
Troy Tulowitzki
Randy Johnson
Chad Tracy
Tim Lincecum
Matt Cain
336 Yankee Stars 15.00 40.00
337 Red Sox Stars 12.50 30.00
338 G/H/L/Z/F/S/P/M 10.00 25.00
339 Aaron Harang 6.00 15.00
Dan Haren
Roy Oswalt
Chad Billingsley
Josh Johnson
Zack Greinke
A.J. Burnett
Jered Weaver

2008 Upper Deck Ballpark Collection Dual Memorabilia Autographs

OVERALL AU ODDS 1:5 HOBBY
NO PRICING DUE TO SCARCITY

2008 Upper Deck Ballpark Collection Jersey Autographs

OVERALL AU ODDS 1:5 HOBBY
1 Aaron Harang 4.00 10.00
2 Takashi Saito 4.00 10.00
3 Troy Tulowitzki 6.00 15.00
4 Adam LaRoche 5.00 12.00
5 Adrian Gonzalez 10.00 25.00
7 Andre Ethier 10.00 25.00
8 Joe Mauer 20.00 50.00
9 Justin Upton 12.00 30.00
10 Aramis Ramirez 6.00 15.00
11 Scott Baker 4.00 10.00
12 B.J. Upton 12.00 30.00
13 Bill Hall 5.00 12.00
14 Billy Wagner 30.00 60.00
15 Brandon Phillips 8.00 20.00
16 Brandon Webb 30.00 60.00
18 Brian McCann 8.00 20.00
19 Brian Roberts 6.00 15.00
20 Bronson Arroyo 5.00 12.00
21 Tim Lincecum 40.00 80.00
22 Mark Reynolds 5.00 12.00
23 Chad Billingsley 12.00 30.00
24 Chad Cordero 4.00 10.00
25 Chone Figgins 5.00 12.00
27 Chris B. Young 6.00 15.00
28 Tom Gorzelanny 4.00 10.00
29 Corey Hart 10.00 25.00
30 Dan Uggla 4.00 10.00
32 D.Jeter EXCH 75.00 150.00
33 Edinson Volquez 8.00 20.00
38 Xavier Nady 4.00 10.00
39 Felix Pie 4.00 10.00
42 Garrett Atkins 4.00 10.00
43 K.Griffey Jr. EXCH 40.00 80.00
44 D.Jeter EXCH 75.00 150.00
45 Hanley Ramirez 10.00 25.00
46 Hong-Chih Kuo 20.00 50.00
47 Ian Kinsler 6.00 15.00
49 Derek Lowe 6.00 15.00
50 Alfonso Soriano 20.00 50.00
51 Jeff Baker 4.00 10.00
52 Jeff Francis 4.00 10.00
53 Jeff Francoeur 4.00 25.00
54 Jered Weaver 6.00 15.00
55 Ben Sheets 10.00 25.00
56 Jeremy Guthrie 4.00 10.00
57 Jeremy Hermida 4.00 10.00
60 Joakim Soria 6.00 15.00
61 Joe Blanton 4.00 10.00
62 Joe Nathan 6.00 15.00
64 Chien-Ming Wang 60.00 120.00
65 Chris Young 4.00 10.00
66 Jon Lester 15.00 40.00
68 Cole Hamels 8.00 20.00
69 Josh Johnson 5.00 12.00
70 Josh Willingham 4.00 10.00
71 Kelly Johnson 4.00 10.00
72 K.Griffey Jr. EXCH 40.00 80.00
73 Kevin Kouzmanoff 4.00 10.00
74 Kevin Youkilis 12.00 30.00
75 Derrek Lee 6.00 15.00
76 James Shields 8.00 20.00
77 Jason Bay 8.00 20.00
78 Jason Varitek 20.00 50.00
81 Mark Teahen 4.00 10.00
83 Matt Cain 8.00 20.00
84 John Lackey 6.00 15.00
85 Matt Kemp 20.00 50.00
86 John Maine 5.00 12.00
88 Melvin Mora 5.00 12.00
91 Kerry Wood 8.00 20.00
92 Nick Markakis 12.00 30.00
93 Lance Berkman 8.00 20.00
94 Noah Lowry 4.00 10.00
95 Rickie Weeks 8.00 20.00
96 Prince Fielder 12.00 30.00
97 Roy Halladay 15.00 40.00
98 Tim Hudson 8.00 20.00
99 Grady Sizemore 20.00 50.00

2008 Upper Deck Ballpark Collection Jersey Buttons

OVERALL GU ODDS 2:1 HOBBY
PRINT RUNS B/WN 3-25 COPIES PER
NO PRICING DUE TO SCARCITY

2008 Upper Deck Ballpark Collection Jersey Laundry Tag

OVERALL GU ODDS 2:1 HOBBY
PRINT RUNS B/WN 2-15 COPIES PER
NO PRICING DUE TO SCARCITY

2008 Upper Deck Ballpark Collection Jersey MLB Logo

OVERALL GU ODDS 2:1 HOBBY
PRINT RUNS B/WN 1-5 COPIES PER
NO PRICING DUE TO SCARCITY

2009 Upper Deck Ballpark Collection

COMMON CARD (1-70) .60 1.50
COMMON AU RC (71-100) 3.00 8.00
OVERALL AU ODDS .5:1 HOBBY
AU PRINT RUN B/WN 75-500 COPIES PER
COMMON 2X GU (101-200) 3.00 8.00
2X PRINT RUNS B/WN 25-500 COPIES PER
NO 2X PRICING ON QTY 25 OR LESS
COMMON 4X GU (201-300) 3.00 8.00
4X PRINT RUNS B/WN 25-500 COPIES PER
NO 4X PRICING ON QTY 25 OR LESS
COMMON 6X GU (301-350) 4.00 10.00
6X PRINT RUNS B/WN 20-300 COPIES PER
NO 6X PRICING ON QTY 25 OR LESS
COMMON 8X GU (351-400) 4.00 10.00
OVERALL GU ODDS 2.5:1 HOBBY
8X PRINT RUNS B/WN 25-350 COPIES PER
NO 8X PRICING ON QTY 25 OR LESS
1 Adrian Beltre 1.50 4.00
2 Adrian Gonzalez 1.25 3.00
3 Akinori Iwamura .60 1.50
4 Albert Pujols 2.00 5.00
5 Alex Gordon 1.00 2.50
6 Alex Rodriguez 2.00 5.00
7 Alfonso Soriano 1.00 2.50
8 B.J. Upton 1.00 2.50
9 Brandon Webb 1.00 2.50
10 Brian McCann 1.00 2.50
11 Brian Roberts .60 1.50
12 Carl Crawford 1.00 2.50
13 Carlos Beltran 1.00 2.50
14 Carlos Zambrano 1.00 2.50
15 CC Sabathia 1.00 2.50
16 Chase Utley 1.00 2.50
17 Chien-Ming Wang 1.00 2.50
18 Chipper Jones 1.50 4.00
19 Cliff Lee 1.00 2.50
20 Cole Hamels 1.25 3.00
21 Daisuke Matsuzaka 1.00 2.50
22 David Ortiz 1.50 4.00
23 David Wright 1.25 3.00
24 Derek Jeter 4.00 10.00
25 Dustin Pedroia 1.50 4.00
26 Evan Longoria 1.00 2.50
27 Felix Hernandez 1.00 2.50
28 Francisco Liriano .60 1.50
29 Freddy Sanchez .60 1.50
30 Gary Sheffield .60 1.50
31 Grady Sizemore 1.00 2.50
32 Hanley Ramirez 1.00 2.50
33 Hideki Matsui 1.50 4.00
34 Ichiro Suzuki 2.00 5.00
35 Ivan Rodriguez 1.00 2.50
36 Jason Giambi .60 1.50
37 Jason Varitek 1.50 4.00
38 Jay Bruce 1.00 2.50
39 Jim Thome 1.00 2.50
40 Joba Chamberlain .60 1.50
41 Joe Mauer 1.25 3.00
42 Joe Nathan .60 1.50
43 Johan Santana 1.00 2.50
44 John Lackey 1.00 2.50
45 Jon Lester 1.00 2.50
46 Jorge Posada 1.00 2.50
47 Jose Reyes 1.00 2.50
48 Josh Beckett .60 1.50
49 Josh Hamilton 1.00 2.50
50 Justin Morneau 1.00 2.50
51 Ken Griffey Jr. 3.00 8.00
52 Kevin Youkilis .60 1.50
53 Lance Berkman 1.00 2.50
54 Manny Ramirez 1.50 4.00
55 Mariano Rivera 2.00 5.00
56 Mark Teixeira 1.00 2.50
57 Matt Kemp 1.25 3.00
58 Miguel Cabrera 1.50 4.00
59 Nick Markakis 1.25 3.00
60 Prince Fielder 1.00 2.50
61 Roy Halladay 1.00 2.50
62 Roy Oswalt 1.00 2.50
63 Ryan Braun 1.00 2.50
64 Ryan Howard 1.25 3.00
65 Ryan Zimmerman 1.00 2.50
66 Tim Hudson 1.00 2.50
67 Tim Lincecum 1.00 2.50
68 Todd Helton 1.00 2.50
69 Tom Glavine 1.00 2.50
70 Vladimir Guerrero 1.00 2.50
71 B.Parnell AU/500 RC 3.00 8.00
72 B.Anderson AU/200 RC 3.00 8.00
73 C.Rasmus AU/200 (RC) 20.00 50.00
74 D.Freese AU/100 RC 40.00 80.00
75 David Patton AU/500 RC 3.00 8.00
76 D.Price AU/150 RC 10.00 25.00
77 D.Fowler AU/500 (RC) 5.00 12.00
78 E.Andrus AU/200 RC 12.50 30.00
79 F.Martinez AU/375 RC 3.00 8.00
80 G.Kottaras AU/100 (RC) 12.50 30.00
81 G.Beckham AU/200 RC 5.00 12.00
82 James McDonald AU/500 RC 5.00 12.00
83 James Parr AU/500 (RC) 3.00 8.00
84 J.Motte AU/500 (RC) 6.00 15.00
85 J.Schafer AU/199 (RC) 3.00 8.00
86 J.Zimmermann AU/400 RC 6.00 15.00
87 K.Kawakami AU/200 RC 30.00 60.00
88 Kevin Jepsen AU/400 (RC) 3.00 8.00
89 K.Uehara AU/100 RC 50.00 100.00
90 M.Wieters AU/150 RC 15.00 40.00
91 N.Reimold AU/500 (RC) 3.00 8.00
92 P.Sandoval AU/300 (RC) 6.00 15.00
93 P.Coke AU/375 RC 3.00 8.00
94 R.Porcello AU/100 RC 6.00 15.00
95 R.Romero AU/75 (RC) 8.00 20.00
96 R.Perry AU/300 RC 5.00 12.00
97 Sharon Martis AU/500 RC 3.00 8.00
98 T.Hanson AU/125 RC 15.00 40.00
99 T.Snider AU/125 RC 5.00 12.00
100 T.Cahill AU/300 RC 4.00 10.00
101 David Murphy/Adam Jones/500 3.00 8.00
102 Kerry Wood/Travis Hafner/500 3.00 8.00
103 Hank Blalock/Prince Fielder/500 3.00 8.00
104 Chone Figgins/Juan Pierre/400 3.00 8.00
105 Randy Johnson/Carlos Delgado/400 4.00 10.00
106 John Smoltz/Jake Peavy/400 3.00 8.00
108 Yunel Escobar/Miguel Tejada/400 3.00 8.00
111 Justin Verlander/Josh Johnson/400 3.00 8.00
112 Hank Blalock/David Ortiz/500 3.00 8.00
113 Jake Peavy/Barry Zito/400 3.00 8.00
114 Jermaine Dye/Bobby Abreu/500 3.00 8.00
115 Chad Billingsley/Kerry Wood/400 3.00 8.00
116 Jorge Posada/Michael Young/400 3.00 8.00
118 David Murphy/Delmon Young/400 3.00 8.00
119 Jered Weaver/Aramis Ramirez/400 3.00 8.00
120 Francisco Liriano/Barry Zito/400 3.00 8.00
121 Francisco Liriano/Brandon Webb/400 4.00 10.00
122 C.Carpenter/Big Unit/400 5.00 12.00
123 Travis Hafner/Derrek Lee/500 3.00 8.00
125 Randy Johnson/Brandon Webb/400 3.00 8.00
126 Justin Verlander/Victor Martinez/400 3.00 8.00
127 Yunel Escobar/Chone Figgins/325 3.00 8.00
128 Prince Fielder/Jonathan Papelbon/300 3.00 8.00
129 Juan Rivera/Matt Kemp/400 5.00 12.00
130 B.J. Upton/Justin Upton/400 3.00 8.00
131 Clayton Kershaw/Jake Peavy/240 3.00 8.00
132 Chad Billingsley/Chris B. Young/500 3.00 8.00
133 James Shields/Josh Beckett/400 3.00 8.00
134 Ryan Zimmerman/Josh Fields/400 3.00 8.00
135 Dan Uggla/Kevin Youkilis/230 4.00 10.00
136 Robinson Cano/Yunel Escobar/335 3.00 8.00
137 Max Scherzer/Jered Weaver/400 3.00 8.00
139 Papelbon/DiceK/200 5.00 12.00
140 Grady Sizemore/Fausto Carmona/500 3.00 8.00
141 John Maine/Jose Reyes/400 4.00 10.00
142 Josh Beckett/A.J. Burnett/400 3.00 8.00
143 Michael Young/Josh Hamilton/200 4.00 10.00
145 Jorge Posada/Robinson Cano/400 3.00 8.00
147 CC Sabathia/Fausto Carmona/500 3.00 8.00
148 Ryan Braun/Prince Fielder/400 4.00 10.00
149 Kevin Youkilis/Josh Beckett/275 4.00 10.00
150 Francisco Liriano/Joe Mauer/400 4.00 10.00
151 Ross Ohlendorf/Robinson Cano/400 3.00 8.00
152 Curtis Granderson Justin Verlander/350 4.00 10.00
153 Kevin Youkilis Jonathan Papelbon/300 4.00 10.00
154 Jonathan Papelbon/Josh Beckett/400 4.00 10.00
155 Jason Varitek/Jonathan Papelbon/400 3.00 8.00
156 Jonathan Papelbon/Mike Lowell/375 3.00 8.00
157 Stephen Drew/Chris B. Young/350 3.00 8.00
159 Jorge Posada/Chien-Ming Wang/400 3.00 8.00
160 Prince Fielder/Bill Hall/500 3.00 8.00
161 Chris B. Young/Brandon Webb/500 3.00 8.00
162 R.Halladay/A.Rios/350 5.00 12.00
163 Ian Kinsler/David Murphy/400 3.00 8.00
164 Adam Lind/A.J. Burnett/340 3.00 8.00
165 C.Billingsley/J.Pierre/400 5.00 12.00
166 David Ortiz/Josh Beckett/400 3.00 8.00
167 Nick Markakis/Jeremy Guthrie/400 4.00 10.00
168 Jeff Francoeur/Kelly Johnson/500 3.00 8.00
169 Rich Aurilia/Omar Vizquel/400 3.00 8.00
170 J.Papelbon/J.Lester/400 5.00 12.00
172 Nate McLouth/Freddy Sanchez/400 3.00 8.00
173 Johnny Damon/Robinson Cano/400 6.00 15.00
174 Kerry Wood/Derrek Lee/400 3.00 8.00
175 Jesse Litsch/Roy Halladay/400 3.00 8.00
176 Juan Rivera/Jered Weaver/400 3.00 8.00
177 Derrek Lee/Kerry Wood/400 3.00 8.00
178 Melvin Mora/Nick Markakis/400 4.00 10.00
179 Carlos Delgado/Prince Fielder/350 3.00 8.00
180 Johnny Bench/Brian McCann/125 3.00 8.00
181 Michael Young/Miguel Cabrera/300 3.00 8.00
182 Brandon Webb/Jake Peavy/300 4.00 10.00
183 Kerry Wood/Justin Verlander/300 4.00 10.00
184 Michael Young/Robinson Cano/350 3.00 8.00
185 Kelly Johnson/Felipe Lopez/400 3.00 8.00
186 Carlos Guillen/Melvin Mora/390 4.00 10.00
187 Kerry Wood/Jonathan Papelbon/400 3.00 8.00
188 Jermaine Dye/CC Sabathia/350 3.00 8.00
189 Jon Lester/Manny Ramirez/250 4.00 10.00
190 Justin Verlander/Josh Beckett/300 3.00 8.00
191 Alfonso Soriano Vladimir Guerrero/400 3.00 8.00
192 Manny Ramirez/Johnny Damon/300 4.00 10.00
193 Fausto Carmona/Brandon Webb/400 3.00 8.00
195 Chad Billingsley/Bronson Arroyo/400 3.00 8.00
196 Magglio Ordonez Aramis Ramirez/350 3.00 8.00
197 Stephen Drew/J.D. Drew/400 3.00 8.00
198 Billy Wagner/Trevor Hoffman/225 3.00 8.00
199 Michael Young/Khalil Greene/350 3.00 8.00
200 Jorge Posada/Victor Martinez/350 3.00 8.00
201 Mark/Youn/Mau/Bra/400 6.00 15.00
202 Ver/Slo/Bil/Lit/400 5.00 12.00
203 Matt Holliday/Grady Sizemore Andruw Jones/Chris B. Young/400 3.00 8.00
205 Rey/Esc/Kin/Ram/500 5.00 12.00
206 Billy Wagner/Roy Halladay Josh Beckett Jonathan Papelbon/500 3.00 8.00
207 Verland/Mauer/Bill/Ram/400 10.00 25.00
208 James Shields/Jonathan Papelbon Josh Beckett/Brandon Morrow/400 3.00 8.00
209 Hil/Lin/Zit/Zam/400 5.00 12.00
210 Carlos Lee/Travis Hafner Carlos Delgado/Matt Holliday/500 3.00 8.00
212 Kur/Wan/Mat/Joh/500 5.00 12.00
213 Ian Kinsler/Joe Crede Bill Hall/Hanley Ramirez/385 3.00 8.00
214 Joe Mauer/Russell Martin Kenji Johjima/Victor Martinez/500 3.00 8.00
215 Chien-Ming Wang/Jonathan Papelbon Roy Halladay/Joe Nathan/400 3.00 8.00
216 Chad Billingsley/James Shields/Jonathan Papelbon/Chien-Ming Wang/400 3.00 8.00
217 Travis Hafner/Carlos Delgado/Alfonso Soriano/Manny Ramirez/400 3.00 8.00
218 Freddy Sanchez/Ian Kinsler Howie Kendrick/Yunel Escobar/400 3.00 8.00
220 Troy Glaus/Ian Kinsler/Howie Kendrick Melvin Mora/500 4.00 10.00
224 Fausto Carmona/Jonathan Albaladejo Kelly Johnson/Ross Ohlendorf/400 3.00 8.00
225 Michael Young/Matt Garza/Nick Markakis Fausto Carmona/500 4.00 10.00
226 Jonathan Papelbon/James Shields Chris B. Young/Hunter Pence/400 3.00 8.00
227 Joe Mauer/Russell Martin/Victor Martinez Kenji Johjima/500 4.00 10.00
229 Joe Mauer/Grady Sizemore/Chien-Ming Wang Nick Markakis/400 3.00 8.00
230 Chien-Ming Wang/Michael Young Chad Billingsley/Prince Fielder/400 3.00 8.00
231 Chris B. Young/Matt Kemp/Adam Jones Jeff Francoeur/400 4.00 10.00
232 Jesse Litsch/Yunel Escobar/Jonathan Albaladejo/Josh Willingham/400 3.00 8.00
233 Juan Rivera/Matt Holliday/Erik Bedard Rich Hill/400 4.00 10.00
235 Prince Fielder/Michael Young/Adam Jones Fausto Carmona/500 4.00 10.00
236 Jon/Mar/McL/Bra/400 5.00 12.00
237 Jeremy Hermida/Joe Mauer/Adam Jones Nick Markakis/500 4.00 10.00
238 Esc/Her/Lin/Fie/400 5.00 12.00
239 Ryan Braun/Josh Hamilton/Hiroki Kuroda Chien-Ming Wang/400 4.00 10.00
240 Cha/Car/Bil/Ver/400 6.00 15.00
242 Yunel Escobar/Kelly Johnson/Tom Glavine Brian McCann/400 4.00 10.00
244 Daisuke Matsuzaka/Jon Lester/David Ortiz Manny Ramirez/500 4.00 10.00
245 Gla/Rio/Del/Hal/500 5.00 12.00
247 Manny Ramirez/Jason Varitek/Mike Lowell Josh Beckett/490 4.00 10.00
248 Adam Jones/Nick Markakis/Jon Lester Daisuke Matsuzaka/400 3.00 8.00
249 Carlos Zambrano/Alfonso Soriano Aramis Ramirez/Derrek Lee/400 4.00 10.00
251 Bec/Ort/Les/Ram/400 5.00 12.00
253 Mor/Mar/Ver/Cab/400 5.00 12.00
254 Hal/Hof/Bra/Fie/400 5.00 12.00
256 Victor Martinez/Grady Sizemore/Nick Markakis/Adam Jones/400 3.00 8.00
258 Jonathan Papelbon/Nick Markakis Adam Jones/Josh Beckett/400 3.00 8.00
259 Andruw Jones/Matt Kemp/Chad Billingsley/Russell Martin/400 4.00 10.00
261 Josh Beckett/Jason Varitek/Jorge Posada Chien-Ming Wang/400 4.00 10.00
262 Jonathan Papelbon/Josh Beckett/Carlos Delgado John Maine/500 3.00 8.00
263 Grady Sizemore/Victor Martinez Cliff Lee/Travis Hafner/400 3.00 8.00
264 Can/Pos/Ber/Jet/400 15.00 40.00
265 Takashi Saito/Jonathan Albaladejo Mike Lowell/Ross Ohlendorf/400 3.00 8.00
266 Josh Beckett/Nick Markakis/Melvin Mora Jonathan Papelbon/400 4.00 10.00
267 Rip/Mor/Rob/Mar/400 10.00 25.00
268 Rich Hill/Kerry Wood/Aramis Ramirez Derrek Lee/400 4.00 10.00
269 Carlos Lee/Hunter Pence/Roy Oswalt Ivan Rodriguez/500 3.00 8.00
271 Torii Hunter/Matt Garza/Manny Ramirez Johnny Damon/500 4.00 10.00
272 Lir/Mau/Spa/Mor/500 6.00 15.00
274 Car/Gre/Puj/Lud400 8.00 20.00
275 Manny Ramirez/Jonathan Papelbon Travis Hafner/Victor Martinez/400 4.00 10.00
276 Ivan Rodriguez/Carlos Guillen/Magglio Ordonez Justin Verlander/400 4.00 10.00
277 Josh Hamilton/Hank Blalock/Victor Martinez Grady Sizemore/400 3.00 8.00
279 John Lackey/Vladimir Guerrero/Jered Weaver Troy Glaus/400 3.00 8.00
280 Cud/Nat/Slo/Hun/472 5.00 12.00
282 Jet/Mat/Wan/Bec/400 6.00 15.00
283 Josh Beckett/Jonathan Papelbon/Matt Garza James Shields/400 3.00 8.00
284 Troy Tulowitzki/Hank Blalock/Yunel Escobar Melvin Mora/500 4.00 10.00
285 Roy Halladay/Randy Johnson/Jake Peavy Carlos Zambrano/400 4.00 10.00
286 James Shields/Barry Zito/Daisuke Matsuzaka Roy Halladay/400 4.00 10.00
287 Jonathan Papelbon/Andy Pettitte/Jake Peavy Joe Nathan/500 4.00 10.00
288 Matt Garza/Trevor Hoffman/CC Sabathia Johan Santana/500 4.00 10.00
289 Mar/Ort/Gra/Cra/400 5.00 12.00
290 Torii Hunter/Andruw Jones/Mark Teixeira Jason Bay/400 3.00 8.00
291 Lin/Bec/Hal/Ver/400 6.00 15.00
292 Chris Carpenter/Josh Beckett/Chris Young Randy Johnson/500 4.00 10.00
293 Kerry Wood/Roy Halladay/Hank Blalock Aramis Ramirez/400 3.00 8.00
294 Derrek Lee/Miguel Cabrera/Jeremy Hermida Ian Kinsler/500 3.00 8.00
295 Chris B. Young/Ryan Braun/Nate McLouth Matt Holliday/400 4.00 10.00
296 Matt Holliday/Nick Markakis/Chris B. Young Josh Hamilton/400 3.00 8.00
297 Justin Verlander/Jered Weaver/Josh Beckett Roy Halladay/400 4.00 10.00
299 Troy Tulowitzki/Ian Kinsler/Prince Fielder Melvin Mora/400 4.00 10.00
300 Ich/Wan/Mat/Mat/100 30.00 60.00
301 Jon Lester/Prince Fielder/Chris B. Young James Shields/Troy Tulowitzki/Chad 4.00 10.00
302 Th/He/Sl/Ve/Yo/Wa/300 6.00 15.00
303 Ri/De/Je/Go/Sm/Th/30 50.00 100.00
304 Mi/Wa/Pa/Ma/Ha/Hu/200 10.00 25.00
305 Johan Santana/Jorge Posada/Randy Johnson Kerry Wood/Joe Mauer Ivan Rodrigue 4.00 10.00
308 Andruw Jones/Pat Burrell/Torii Hunter Gary Sheffield/Matt Holliday/J.D. Dre 5.00 12.00
309 Yo/Dy/Mc/Ca/Gr/Tu/205 12.50 30.00
311 Miguel Tejada/Troy Glaus/Matt Holliday/Nick Markakis/Josh Beckett/Fausto Ca 4.00 10.00
312 Brian McCann/Nate McLouth/Bronson Arroyo/Jered Weaver/Max Scherzer Miguel C 5.00 12.00
315 La/Fi/Mo/Pu/Gu/Ca/200 8.00 20.00
316 Wa/Ja/Je/Be/Va/Or/200 10.00 25.00
317 Je/Pe/Be/Ja/Wa/Ch/200 20.00 50.00
318 El/Le/Ma/Va/Or/Ya/200 8.00 20.00
319 Ha/Si/Ma/Li/Ma/200 6.00 15.00
320 Pu/Ca/Lu/Za/Le/Wo/300 8.00 20.00
321 Daisuke Matsuzaka/Kevin Youkilis/Josh Beckett Nick Markakis/Adam Jones/Bria 5.00 12.00
322 Ja/Ch/Hu/Ha/Bl/Te/150 15.00 40.00
323 Ja/Dr/We/Sc/Up/Jo/200 12.50 30.00
324 Dr/Te/Fr/Mc/Jo/Sm/170 8.00 20.00
325 John Smoltz/Mark Teixeira/A.J. Burnett/Xavier Nady/J.D. Drew/Rocco Baldelli 5.00 12.00
326 Dr/Wo/Sm/Sa/Fu/Jo/160 10.00 25.00
327 Mike Lowell/Josh Beckett/Rich Hill/Aubrey Huff Luke Scott/Jason Bay/200 4.00 10.00
328 Josh Beckett/Ivan Rodriguez/Derrek Lee/Miguel Cabrera/Hanley Ramirez/Jeremy 4.00 10.00
329 Va/Be/Or/Ma/Ri/Ro/200 15.00 40.00
330 Li/Lo/Zi/Ha/Ki/Bla/200 10.00 25.00
331 Ro/Be/Jo/Ma/Wa/De/200 8.00 20.00
332 Ch/Ca/Wa/Le/Ma/200 12.50 30.00
335 Pe/Je/Wa/Ki/Ha/Yo/200 8.00 20.00
337 Le/Or/Be/Va/Lo/Ra/300 6.00 15.00
338 Pu/Sm/Lu/Ra/Lo/Yo/200 12.50 30.00
339 Juan Pierre/Chad Billingsley/Hiroki Kuroda/Russell Martin/Matt Kemp Andruw 4.00 10.00
340 Bl/Fi/Br/Zi/Yo/Mo/160 6.00 15.00
341 Wi/Gr/Ja/Th/Ha/Mo/40 30.00 60.00
343 Be/Ha/Wa/Le/Ca/Sh/200 6.00 15.00
344 Carl Crawford/Curtis Granderson/Mike Cameron/Chris B. Young Delmon Young/Na 5.00 12.00
345 Jason Bay/Aaron Rowand/Delmon Young Manny Ramirez/Andruw Jones Mike Cameron 4.00 10.00
346 Ra/Vi/Ro/Je/Re/Ri/160 12.00 30.00
347 Be/Va/Mc/Jo/Po/Ma/160 10.00 25.00
348 Lu/Le/Ca/Yo/Fi/Br/200 8.00 20.00
350 Matt Holliday/Nate McLouth/Hunter Pence Alfonso Soriano/Curtis Granderson/C 4.00 10.00
352 J/J/S/W/Y/V/R/S/50 40.00 80.00
353 H/R/H/M/R/M/F/M/200 15.00 40.00
354 M/D/S/S/C/M/V/C/300 6.00 15.00
355 B/C/Y/M/L/P/D/F/300 8.00 20.00
356 G/P/L/O/L/Z/H/F/300 6.00 15.00
357 Bill Hall/Hanley Ramirez/Ian Kinsler/Yunel Escobar/Carlos Delgado/Melvin Mo 4.00 10.00
358 Jonathan Albaladejo/Andy Pettitte/Josh Beckett/Mike Lowell/Nick Markakis/Ad 4.00 10.00
361 J/I/S/M/M/W/I/K/75 40.00 80.00
363 Rich Hill/Josh Beckett/J.D. Drew/Kerry Wood Josh Willingham/Huston Street/M 4.00 10.00
364 Huston Street/B.J. Upton/Curtis Granderson Kerry Wood/Joba Chamberlain/Jona 4.00 10.00
365 Jeff Francoeur/Nick Markakis/Adam Jones Curtis Granderson/Chris B. Young/Ju 4.00 10.00
366 M/M/S/B/Y/W/G/L/175 12.50 30.00
368 T/K/B/K/L/H/J/M/75 12.50 30.00
369 R/B/E/P/U/C/R/U 10.00 25.00
370 Josh Hamilton/David Murphy/Troy Tulowitzki Prince Fielder/Jonathan Papelbon 8.00 20.00
371 Yunel Escobar/Adam Jones/Nick Markakis/Fausto Carmona/Bill Hall/Troy Tulowi 4.00 10.00
372 S/F/H/V/S/W/Y/L/150 8.00 20.00
373 R/P/P/J/C/W/C/J/200 20.00 50.00
374 A.J. Burnett/Josh Beckett/Mike Lowell/Josh Willingham/Hanley Ramirez/Dan Ug 4.00 10.00
375 John Lackey/Jered Weaver/Howie Kendrick/Juan Rivera/David Murphy/Ian Kinsle 5.00 12.00
376 Huston Street/Miguel Tejada/Dan Haren/Rich Harden/Tim Hudson/Travis Buck/Er 5.00 12.00
377 W/B/H/U/M/S/K/M/T/100 15.00 40.00
378 R/L/O/V/L/B/Y/P/300 6.00 15.00
379 M/K/B/K/R/K/W/L/200 6.00 15.00
382 LAD/BOS/50 30.00 60.00
383 BOS/ATL/275 8.00 20.00
384 HOU/DET/125 10.00 25.00
385 CHI/TEX/SD/50 30.00 60.00
387 E/J/M/J/B/F/C/V/300 6.00 15.00
388 V/K/B/K/B/M/C/H/300 6.00 15.00
389 Jake Peavy/Fausto Carmona/Tim Hudson/John Maine/Roy Halladay/Josh Beckett/S 5.00 12.00
390 J/F/R/G/M/Y/R/M/200 8.00 20.00
392 A/B/W/V/C/L/H/B/300 6.00 15.00
393 B/S/R/G/J/S/T/L/75 30.00 80.00
394 Carl Crawford/Bobby Abreu/Miguel Cabrera/Magglio Ordonez Curtis Granderson/ 4.00 10.00
395 Jake Peavy/Mariano Rivera/Kevin Youkilis Trevor Hoffman/Alfonso Soriano/Man 4.00 10.00
398 T/S/R/F/H/R/L/E/200 10.00 25.00
399 O/F/O/G/B/R/G/T/200 6.00 15.00

2009 Upper Deck Ballpark Collection 500 HR Club Dual Swatch

OVERALL MEM ODDS 2.5:1 HOBBY PACKS
STATED PRINT RUN 10 SER.#'d SETS
NO PRICING DUE TO SCARCITY

2009 Upper Deck Ballpark Collection 500 HR Club Dual Swatch Autographs

OVERALL AU ODDS .5:1 HOBBY
STATED PRINT RUN 10 SER.#'d SETS
NO PRICING DUE TO SCARCITY

2009 Upper Deck Ballpark Collection 500 HR Club Eight Swatch

OVERALL MEM ODDS 2.5:1 HOBBY PACKS
STATED PRINT RUN 10 SER.#'d SETS
NO PRICING DUE TO SCARCITY

2009 Upper Deck Ballpark Collection 500 HR Club Quad Swatch

OVERALL MEM ODDS 2.5:1 HOBBY PACKS
STATED PRINT RUN 15 SER.#'d SETS
NO PRICING DUE TO SCARCITY

2009 Upper Deck Ballpark Collection 500 HR Club Six Swatch

OVERALL MEM ODDS 2.5:1 HOBBY PACKS
STATED PRINT RUN 15 SER.#'d SETS
NO PRICING DUE TO SCARCITY

2009 Upper Deck Ballpark Collection 500 HR Club Triple Swatch

OVERALL MEM ODDS 2.5:1 HOBBY PACKS
STATED PRINT RUN 15 SER.#'d SETS
NO PRICING DUE TO SCARCITY

2009 Upper Deck Ballpark Collection Career Legacy Dual Swatch

OVERALL MEM ODDS 2.5:1 HOBBY PACKS
STATED PRINT RUN 25 SER.#'d SETS
NO PRICING DUE TO SCARCITY

2009 Upper Deck Ballpark Collection Career Legacy Quad Swatch

OVERALL MEM ODDS 2.5:1 HOBBY PACKS
STATED PRINT RUN 25 SER.#'d SETS
NO PRICING DUE TO SCARCITY

2009 Upper Deck Ballpark Collection Career Legacy Triple Swatch

OVERALL MEM ODDS 2.5:1 HOBBY PACKS
STATED PRINT RUN 25 SER.#'d SETS
NO PRICING DUE TO SCARCITY

2009 Upper Deck Ballpark Collection Jersey Autographs

OVERALL AUTO ODDS .5:1 HOBBY
AA Aaron Rowand 4.00 10.00
AE Andre Ethier 8.00 20.00
AL Andy LaRoche 3.00 8.00
AR Aramis Ramirez 5.00 12.00
BI Chad Billingsley 6.00 15.00
BM Brian McCann 8.00 20.00
BR Brian Roberts 12.50 30.00
BW Brandon Webb 15.00 40.00
CF Chone Figgins 5.00 12.00
CH Cole Hamels 8.00 20.00
CJ Chipper Jones 75.00 150.00
CL Carlos Lee 5.00 12.00
DJ Derek Jeter 100.00 250.00
DM David Murphy 3.00 8.00
DP Dustin Pedroia 10.00 25.00
DS Denard Span 8.00 20.00
DU Dan Uggla 4.00 10.00
EC Eric Chavez 8.00 20.00
FC Fausto Carmona 3.00 8.00
GA Garrett Atkins 3.00 8.00
HA Corey Hart 4.00 10.00
HR Hanley Ramirez 8.00 20.00
JA Jonathan Albaladejo 3.00 8.00
JB Jason Bay 10.00 25.00
JF Jeff Francoeur 6.00 15.00
JH Jeremy Hermida 3.00 8.00
JL Jon Lester 30.00 60.00
JM Joe Mauer 50.00 100.00
JN Joe Nathan 5.00 12.00
JO Josh Hamilton 6.00 15.00
JP Jonathan Papelbon 5.00 12.00
JS Jarrod Saltalamacchia 3.00 8.00
JW Josh Willingham 3.00 8.00
JZ Joel Zumaya 3.00 8.00
KG Ken Griffey Jr. 30.00 60.00
KJ Kelly Johnson 3.00 8.00
KY Kevin Youkilis 10.00 25.00
LE Cliff Lee 4.00 10.00
LI Adam Lind 5.00 12.00
MA John Maine 4.00 10.00
MD Daisuke Matsuzaka 20.00 50.00
MG Matt Garza 4.00 10.00
MH Matt Holliday 8.00 20.00
MK Matt Kemp 20.00 50.00
MT Miguel Tejada 3.00 8.00
NM Nick Markakis 12.50 30.00
NS Nick Swisher 6.00 15.00
NY Nyjer Morgan 3.00 8.00
PF Prince Fielder 12.50 30.00
PK Paul Konerko 4.00 10.00
RB Ryan Braun 20.00 50.00
RH Roy Halladay 12.50 30.00
RM Russell Martin 8.00 20.00
RO Ross Ohlendorf 3.00 8.00
RS Ryne Sandberg 75.00 150.00
RW Rickie Weeks 5.00 12.00
SH James Shields 4.00 10.00
SK Scott Kazmir 6.00 15.00
TH Travis Hafner 4.00 10.00
TT Troy Tulowitzki 10.00 25.00
VM Victor Martinez 6.00 15.00
ZG Zack Greinke 12.00 30.00

2009 Upper Deck Ballpark Collection Jersey Buttons

OVERALL MEM ODDS 2.5:1 HOBBY
PRINT RUNS B/WN 4-5 COPIES PER
NO PRICING DUE TO SCARCITY

2009 Upper Deck Ballpark Collection Laundry Tags

OVERALL MEM ODDS 2.5:1 HOBBY
PRINT RUNS B/WN 1-10 COPIES PER
NO PRICING DUE TO SCARCITY

2002 Upper Deck Ballpark Idols

COMP.SET w/o SP's (200) 15.00 40.00
COMMON CARD (1-200) .10 .30
COMMON CARD (201-245) 1.50 4.00
201-245 RANDOM INSERTS IN PACKS
201-245 PRINT RUN 1750 SERIAL #'d SETS
1 Troy Glaus .10 .30
2 Kevin Appier .10 .30
3 Darin Erstad .10 .30
4 Garret Anderson .10 .30
5 Brad Fullmer .10 .30
6 Tim Salmon .20 .50
7 Eric Chavez .10 .30
8 Tim Hudson .10 .30
9 David Justice .10 .30
10 Barry Zito .10 .30
11 Miguel Tejada .10 .30
12 Mark Mulder .10 .30
13 Jermaine Dye .10 .30
14 Carlos Delgado .10 .30
15 Jose Cruz Jr. .10 .30
16 Brandon Lyon .10 .30
17 Shannon Stewart .10 .30
18 Eric Hinske .10 .30
19 Chris Carpenter .10 .30
20 Greg Vaughn .10 .30
21 Tanyon Sturtze .10 .30
22 Jason Tyner .10 .30
23 Toby Hall .10 .30
24 Ben Grieve .10 .30
25 Jim Thome .20 .50
26 Omar Vizquel .20 .50
27 Ricky Gutierrez .10 .30
28 C.C. Sabathia .10 .30
29 Ellis Burks .10 .30
30 Matt Lawton .10 .30
31 Milton Bradley .10 .30
32 Edgar Martinez .20 .50
33 Ichiro Suzuki .60 1.50
34 Bret Boone .10 .30
35 Freddy Garcia .10 .30
36 Mike Cameron .10 .30
37 John Olerud .10 .30
38 Kazuhiro Sasaki .10 .30
39 Jeff Cirillo .10 .30
40 Jeff Conine .10 .30
41 Marty Cordova .10 .30
42 Tony Batista .10 .30
43 Jerry Hairston Jr. .10 .30
44 Jason Johnson .10 .30
45 David Segui .10 .30
46 Alex Rodriguez .40 1.00
47 Rafael Palmeiro .20 .50
48 Carl Everett .10 .30
49 Chan Ho Park .10 .30
50 Ivan Rodriguez .20 .50
51 Juan Gonzalez .10 .30
52 Hank Blalock .20 .50
53 Manny Ramirez .20 .50
54 Pedro Martinez .20 .50
55 Tony Clark .10 .30
56 Nomar Garciaparra .50 1.25
57 Johnny Damon Sox .20 .50
58 Trot Nixon .10 .30
59 Rickey Henderson .30 .75
60 Mike Sweeney .10 .30
61 Neifi Perez .10 .30
62 Joe Randa .10 .30
63 Carlos Beltran .10 .30
64 Chuck Knoblauch .10 .30
65 Michael Tucker .10 .30
66 Dean Palmer .10 .30
67 Bobby Higginson .10 .30
68 Dmitri Young .10 .30
69 Randall Simon .10 .30
70 Mitch Meluskey .10 .30
71 Damion Easley .10 .30
72 Joe Mays .10 .30
73 Doug Mientkiewicz .10 .30
74 Corey Koskie .10 .30
75 Brad Radke .10 .30
76 Cristian Guzman .10 .30
77 Torii Hunter .10 .30
78 Eric Milton .10 .30
79 Frank Thomas .30 .75
80 Paul Konerko .10 .30
81 Mark Buehrle .10 .30
82 Magglio Ordonez .10 .30
83 Carlos Lee .10 .30
84 Joe Crede .10 .30
85 Derek Jeter .75 2.00
86 Bernie Williams .20 .50
87 Mike Mussina .20 .50
88 Jorge Posada .20 .50
89 Roger Clemens .60 1.50
90 Jason Giambi .10 .30
91 Alfonso Soriano .10 .30
92 Rondell White .10 .30
93 Jeff Bagwell .20 .50
94 Lance Berkman .10 .30
95 Roy Oswalt .10 .30
96 Richard Hidalgo .10 .30
97 Wade Miller .10 .30
98 Craig Biggio .20 .50
99 Greg Maddux .50 1.25
100 Chipper Jones .30 .75
101 Gary Sheffield .10 .30
102 Rafael Furcal .10 .30
103 Andruw Jones .20 .50
104 Vinny Castilla .10 .30
105 Marcus Giles .10 .30
106 Tom Glavine .20 .50
107 Richie Sexson .10 .30
108 Geoff Jenkins .10 .30
109 Glendon Rusch .10 .30
110 Eric Young .10 .30
111 Ben Sheets .10 .30
112 Alex Sanchez .10 .30
113 Albert Pujols .60 1.50
114 J.D. Drew .10 .30
115 Matt Morris .10 .30
116 Jim Edmonds .10 .30
117 Tino Martinez .20 .50
118 Scott Rolen .20 .50
119 Edgar Renteria .10 .30
120 Sammy Sosa .30 .75
121 Kerry Wood .10 .30
122 Moises Alou .10 .30
123 Jon Lieber .10 .30
124 Fred McGriff .20 .50
125 Juan Cruz .10 .30
126 Alex Gonzalez .10 .30
127 Corey Patterson .10 .30
128 Randy Johnson .30 .75
129 Luis Gonzalez .10 .30
130 Steve Finley .10 .30
131 Matt Williams .10 .30
132 Curt Schilling .10 .30
133 Mark Grace .20 .50
134 Craig Counsell .10 .30
135 Shawn Green .10 .30
136 Kevin Brown .10 .30
137 Hideo Nomo .30 .75
138 Paul Lo Duca .10 .30
139 Brian Jordan .10 .30
140 Eric Karros .10 .30
141 Adrian Beltre .10 .30
142 Vladimir Guerrero .30 .75
143 Fernando Tatis .10 .30
144 Javier Vazquez .10 .30
145 Orlando Cabrera .10 .30
146 Tony Armas Jr. .10 .30
147 Jose Vidro .10 .30
148 Barry Bonds .75 2.00
149 Rich Aurilia .10 .30
150 Tsuyoshi Shinjo .10 .30
151 Jeff Kent .10 .30
152 Russ Ortiz .10 .30
153 Jason Schmidt .10 .30
154 Reggie Sanders .10 .30
155 Preston Wilson .10 .30
156 Luis Castillo .10 .30
157 Charles Johnson .10 .30
158 Josh Beckett .10 .30
159 Derrek Lee .20 .50
160 Mike Lowell .10 .30
161 Mike Piazza .50 1.25
162 Roberto Alomar .20 .50
163 Al Leiter .10 .30
164 Mo Vaughn .10 .30
165 Jeromy Burnitz .10 .30
166 Edgardo Alfonzo .10 .30
167 Roger Cedeno .10 .30
168 Ryan Klesko .10 .30
169 Brian Lawrence .10 .30
170 Sean Burroughs .10 .30
171 Phil Nevin .10 .30
172 Ramon Vazquez .10 .30
173 Mark Kotsay .10 .30
174 Marlon Anderson .10 .30
175 Mike Lieberthal .10 .30
176 Bobby Abreu .10 .30
177 Pat Burrell .10 .30
178 Robert Person .10 .30
179 Brandon Duckworth .10 .30
180 Jimmy Rollins .10 .30
181 Brian Giles .10 .30
182 Pokey Reese .10 .30
183 Kris Benson .10 .30
184 Aramis Ramirez .10 .30
185 Jason Kendall .10 .30
186 Kip Wells .10 .30
187 Ken Griffey Jr. .60 1.50
188 Adam Dunn .10 .30
189 Barry Larkin .20 .50
190 Sean Casey .10 .30
191 Austin Kearns .10 .30
192 Aaron Boone .10 .30
193 Todd Helton .20 .50
194 Juan Pierre .10 .30
195 Mike Hampton .10 .30
196 Jose Ortiz .10 .30
197 Larry Walker .10 .30
198 Juan Uribe .10 .30
199 Ichiro Suzuki CL .30 .75
200 Jason Giambi CL .10 .30
201 Franklyn German ROO RC 1.50 4.00
202 Rodrigo Rosario ROO RC 1.50 4.00
203 Brandon Puffer ROO RC 1.50 4.00
204 Kirk Saarloos ROO RC 1.50 4.00
205 Chris Baker ROO RC 1.50 4.00
206 John Ennis ROO RC 1.50 4.00
207 Luis Martinez ROO RC 1.50 4.00
208 So Taguchi ROO RC 2.00 5.00
209 Mike Crudale ROO RC 1.50 4.00
210 Francis Beltran ROO RC 1.50 4.00
211 Brandon Backe ROO RC 2.00 5.00
212 Felix Escalona ROO RC 1.50 4.00
213 Jose Valverde ROO RC 1.50 4.00
214 Doug Devore ROO RC 1.50 4.00
215 Kazuhisa Ishii ROO RC 2.00 5.00
216 Victor Alvarez ROO RC 1.50 4.00
217 Ron Calloway ROO RC 1.50 4.00
218 Eric Good ROO RC 1.50 4.00
219 Jorge Nunez ROO RC 1.50 4.00
220 Deivis Santos ROO 1.50 4.00
221 Nelson Castro ROO RC 1.50 4.00
222 Matt Thornton ROO RC 1.50 4.00
223 Jason Simontacchi ROO RC 1.50 4.00
224 Hansel Izquierdo ROO RC 1.50 4.00
225 Tyler Yates ROO RC 1.50 4.00
226 Jaime Cerda ROO RC 1.50 4.00
227 Satoru Komiyama ROO RC 1.50 4.00
228 Steve Bechler ROO RC 1.50 4.00
229 Ben Howard ROO RC 1.50 4.00
230 Todd Donovan ROO RC 1.50 4.00
231 Jorge Padilla ROO RC 1.50 4.00
232 Eric Junge ROO RC 1.50 4.00
233 Anderson Machado ROO RC 1.50 4.00
234 Adrian Burnside ROO RC 1.50 4.00
235 Mike Gonzalez ROO RC 1.50 4.00
236 Josh Hancock ROO RC 2.00 5.00
237 Anastacio Martinez ROO RC 1.50 4.00
238 Chris Booker ROO RC 1.50 4.00
239 Rene Reyes ROO RC 1.50 4.00
240 Cam Esslinger ROO RC 1.50 4.00
241 Oliver Perez ROO RC 2.00 5.00
242 Tim Kalita ROO RC 1.50 4.00
243 Kevin Frederick ROO RC 1.50 4.00
244 Mitch Wylie ROO RC 1.50 4.00
245 Edwin Almonte ROO RC 1.50 4.00

2002 Upper Deck Ballpark Idols Bronze

*BRONZE 1-200: 8X TO 20X BASIC CARDS
*BRONZE 201-245: 1X TO 2.5X BASIC
STATED PRINT RUN 100 SERIAL #'d SETS
204 Kirk Saarloos ROO 4.00 10.00
215 Kazuhisa Ishii ROO 5.00 12.00
223 Jason Simontacchi ROO 4.00 10.00
241 Oliver Perez ROO 5.00 12.00

2002 Upper Deck Ballpark Idols Bobbers

ONE PER SEALED BOX
SP INFO PROVIDED BY UPPER DECK
MANTLE/DIMAGGIO ARE NOT SERIAL #'d
MANTLE/DIMAGGIO INFO PROVIDED BY UD
NO SP PRICING DUE TO LACK OF MKT INFO
1 Roberto Alomar Away 6.00 15.00
3 Jeff Bagwell 6.00 15.00
4 Josh Beckett Away 4.00 10.00
6 Barry Bonds Away 15.00 40.00
8 Sean Burroughs Away 4.00 10.00
11 R.Clemens Yanks Away 12.50 30.00
13 Joe DiMaggio Away/555 15.00 40.00
15 Nomar Garciaparra Away 10.00 25.00
17 Jason Giambi Away 4.00 10.00
19 Luis Gonzalez Away 4.00 10.00
22 Ken Griffey Reds Away 12.50 30.00
24 Vladimir Guerrero 6.00 15.00
25 Kazuhisa Ishii Away 6.00 15.00
29 Randy Johnson D'Backs 6.00 15.00
30 Randy Johnson Expos 6.00 15.00
31 Chipper Jones 6.00 15.00
32 Greg Maddux 10.00 25.00
33 Mickey Mantle Away/777 20.00 50.00
34 Mickey Mantle Home/536 30.00 60.00
36 M.McGwire Cards Away 15.00 40.00
39 Mike Piazza Mets 10.00 25.00
40 Mark Prior Away 4.00 10.00
42 Albert Pujols Away 12.50 30.00
44 Alex Rodriguez Away 8.00 20.00
46 Ivan Rodriguez Away 6.00 15.00
48 Curt Schilling D'Backs 4.00 10.00
50 S.Sosa Cubs Away 6.00 15.00
55 Frank Thomas Away 6.00 15.00
57 Jim Thome Away 6.00 15.00

2002 Upper Deck Ballpark Idols Bobbers Gold

NO PRICING DUE TO SCARCITY

2002 Upper Deck Ballpark Idols Field Garb Jerseys

STATED ODDS 1:72
AR Alex Rodriguez 6.00 15.00
BG Brian Giles 4.00 10.00
BZ Barry Zito 4.00 10.00
IR Ivan Rodriguez 6.00 15.00
JK Jeff Kent 4.00 10.00
JO John Olerud 4.00 10.00
LW Larry Walker 4.00 10.00
MR Manny Ramirez 6.00 15.00
MS Mike Sweeney 4.00 10.00
RJ Randy Johnson 6.00 15.00
RV Robin Ventura 4.00 10.00
TB Tony Batista 4.00 10.00
TM Tino Martinez 6.00 15.00

2002 Upper Deck Ballpark Idols Figure-Heads

COMPLETE SET (10) 12.50 30.00
STATED ODDS 1:12
F1 Ichiro Suzuki 2.00 5.00
F2 Sammy Sosa 1.25 3.00
F3 Alex Rodriguez 1.25 3.00
F4 Jason Giambi 1.25 3.00
F5 Barry Bonds 2.50 6.00
F6 Chipper Jones 1.25 3.00
F7 Mike Piazza 1.50 4.00
F8 Derek Jeter 2.50 6.00
F9 Nomar Garciaparra 1.50 4.00
F10 Ken Griffey Jr. 2.00 5.00

2002 Upper Deck Ballpark Idols Player's Club Jerseys

STATED ODDS 1:72
SP INFO PROVIDED BY UPPER DECK
AJ Andruw Jones 4.00 10.00
CS Curt Schilling 4.00 10.00
DE Darin Erstad 4.00 10.00
HN Hideo Nomo 12.50 30.00
IS Ichiro Suzuki SP 20.00 50.00
JK Jason Kendall 4.00 10.00
JT Jim Thome 4.00 10.00
KB Kevin Brown 4.00 10.00
MM Mark McGwire SP 50.00 100.00
MO Magglio Ordonez 4.00 10.00
PN Phil Nevin 4.00 10.00
RF Rafael Furcal 4.00 10.00
TH Tim Hudson 4.00 10.00

2002 Upper Deck Ballpark Idols Playmakers

COMPLETE SET (20) 15.00 40.00
STATED ODDS 1:6
P1 Ken Griffey Jr. 1.50 4.00
P2 Alex Rodriguez 1.00 2.50
P3 Sammy Sosa .75 2.00
P4 Derek Jeter 2.00 5.00
P5 Mike Piazza 1.25 3.00
P6 Jason Giambi .60 1.50
P7 Barry Bonds 2.00 5.00
P8 Frank Thomas .75 2.00
P9 Randy Johnson .75 2.00
P10 Chipper Jones .75 2.00
P11 Jeff Bagwell .60 1.50
P12 Vladimir Guerrero .75 2.00
P13 Albert Pujols 1.50 4.00
P14 Nomar Garciaparra 1.25 3.00
P15 Ichiro Suzuki 1.50 4.00
P16 Troy Glaus .60 1.50
P17 Ivan Rodriguez .60 1.50
P18 Carlos Delgado .60 1.50
P19 Greg Maddux 1.25 3.00
P20 Todd Helton .60 1.50

2002 Upper Deck Ballpark Idols Uniform Sluggers Jerseys

STATED ODDS 1:72
SP INFO PROVIDED BY UPPER DECK
AR Alex Rodriguez 6.00 15.00
BW Bernie Williams 4.00 10.00
CJ Chipper Jones 6.00 15.00
JB Jeff Bagwell 4.00 10.00
KG Ken Griffey Jr. SP 10.00 25.00
MM Mickey Mantle SP 20.00 50.00
MP Mike Piazza 5.00 12.00
SG Shawn Green 4.00 10.00
TH Todd Helton 4.00 10.00
JGI Jason Giambi 4.00 10.00
JGO Juan Gonzalez 4.00 10.00

2005 Upper Deck Baseball Heroes

COMP.SET w/o SP's (100) 100.00 200.00
B.FELLER (1-5) 1.00 2.50
B.ROBINSON (6-10) 1.50 4.00
C.RIPKEN (11-15) 8.00 20.00
C.YASTRZEMSKI (16-20) 3.00 8.00
D.MATTINGLY (21-25) 5.00 12.00
T.SEAVER (26-30) 1.50 4.00
H.KILLEBREW (31-35) 2.50 6.00
J.PALMER (36-40) 1.00 2.50
M.SCHMIDT (41-45) 5.00 12.00
O.SMITH (46-50) 4.00 10.00
P.MOLITOR (51-55) 1.00 2.50
A.KALINE (56-60) 2.50 6.00
R.YOUNT (61-65) 2.50 6.00
R.SANDBERG (66-70) 5.00 12.00
S.MUSIAL (71-75) 4.00 10.00
S.CARLTON (76-80) 1.00 2.50
T.GWYNN (81-85) 3.00 8.00
W.BOGGS (86-90) 1.50 4.00
W.CLARK (91-95) 1.50 4.00
Y.BERRA (96-100) 2.50 6.00
B.RUTH (101-105) 6.00 15.00
R.MARIS (106-110) 2.50 6.00
D.DRYSDALE (111-115) 1.00 2.50
E.MATHEWS (116-120) 1.50 4.00
H.WAGNER (121-125) 1.50 4.00
J.ROBINSON (126-130) 1.50 4.00
J.FOXX (131-135) 1.50 4.00
J.DIMAGGIO (136-140) 3.00 8.00
J.MIZE (141-145) 1.50 4.00
L.GROVE (146-150) 1.00 2.50
L.GEHRIG (151-155) 2.50 6.00
M.OTT (156-160) 2.50 6.00
M.MANTLE (161-165) 8.00 20.00
R.CLEMENTE (166-170) 6.00 15.00
R.HORNSBY (171-175) 1.00 2.50
R.CAMPANELLA (176-180) 1.50 4.00
S.PAIGE (181-185) 1.50 4.00
T.WILLIAMS (186-190) 5.00 12.00
T.MUNSON (191-195) 1.50 4.00
T.COBB (196-200) 1.50 4.00
101-200 STATED ODDS ONE PER TIN
101-200 PRINT RUN 575 SERIAL #'d SETS

2005 Upper Deck Baseball Heroes Emerald

*EMERALD 1-100: .6 TO 1.5X BASIC
*EMERALD 101-200: .5X TO 1.2X BASIC
ONE PARALLEL CARD PER TIN
STATED PRINT RUN 199 SERIAL #'d SETS

2005 Upper Deck Baseball Heroes Red

*RED 1-100: .75X TO 2X BASIC
*RED 101-200: .75X TO 2X BASIC
ONE PARALLEL CARD PER TIN
STATED PRINT RUN 75 SERIAL #'d SETS

2005 Upper Deck Baseball Heroes Memorabilia

B.RUTH BAT (101-105) 150.00 300.00
R.MARIS JSY (106-110) 40.00 80.00
DRYSD PANTS (110-115) 10.00 25.00
E.MATHEWS JSY (116-120) 40.00 80.00
JACKIE PANTS (126-130) 40.00 80.00
J.FOXX BAT (131-135) 30.00 60.00
J.DIMAGGIO JSY (136-140) 60.00 120.00
J.MIZE PANTS (141-145) 10.00 25.00
L.GEHRIG BAT (151-155) 125.00 200.00
M.OTT JSY (156-160) 30.00 60.00
M.MANTLE JSY (161-165) 100.00 175.00
CLEMENTE JSY (166-170) 75.00 150.00
HORNSBY HAT (171-175) 30.00 60.00
R.CAMPY JSY (176-180) 30.00 60.00
S.PAIGE PANTS (181-185) 40.00 80.00
T.WILLIAMS JSY (186-190) 60.00 120.00
T.MUNSON JSY (191-195) 15.00 40.00
T.COBB BAT (196-200) 75.00 150.00
OVERALL GAME-USED ODDS 2:3 TINS
STATED PRINT RUN 10 SERIAL #'d SETS

2005 Upper Deck Baseball Heroes Memorabilia Blue

*BLUE: .4X TO 1X EMERALD
OVERALL GAME-USED ODDS 2:3 TINS
STATED PRINT RUN 99 SERIAL #'d SETS

2005 Upper Deck Baseball Heroes Memorabilia Bronze

*BRONZE: .5X TO 1.2X EMERALD
OVERALL GAME-USED ODDS 2:3 TINS
STATED PRINT RUN 50 SERIAL #'d SETS
11 Cal Ripken Jsy 15.00 40.00
12 Cal Ripken Jsy 15.00 40.00
13 Cal Ripken Jsy 15.00 40.00
14 Cal Ripken Jsy 15.00 40.00
15 Cal Ripken HDR Jsy 15.00 40.00

2005 Upper Deck Baseball Heroes Memorabilia Emerald

B.FELLER PANTS (1-5) 4.00 10.00
B.ROBINSON JSY (6-10) 4.00 10.00
C.RIPKEN JSY (11-15) 10.00 25.00
C.YAZ JSY (16-20) 6.00 15.00
D.MATTINGLY JSY (21-25) 8.00 20.00
T.SEAVER JSY (26-30) 4.00 10.00
H.KILLEBREW JSY (31-35) 6.00 15.00
J.PALMER JSY (36-40) 4.00 10.00
M.SCHMIDT JSY (41-45) 8.00 20.00
O.SMITH JSY (46-50) 6.00 15.00
P.MOLITOR JSY (51-55) 4.00 10.00
A.KALINE PANTS (56-60) 8.00 20.00
R.YOUNT JSY (61-65) 6.00 15.00
R.SANDBERG JSY (66-70) 8.00 20.00
S.MUSIAL PANTS (71-75) 6.00 15.00
S.CARLTON JSY (76-80) 4.00 10.00
T.GWYNN JSY (81-85) 6.00 15.00
W.BOGGS JSY (86-90) 4.00 10.00
W.CLARK JSY (91-95) 4.00 10.00
Y.BERRA PANTS (96-100) 6.00 15.00
OVERALL GAME-USED ODDS 2:3 TINS
STATED PRINT RUN 99 SERIAL #'d SETS

2005 Upper Deck Baseball Heroes Memorabilia Red

*RED: .4X TO 1X EMERALD
OVERALL GAME-USED ODDS 2:3 TINS
STATED PRINT RUN 99 SERIAL #'d SETS

2005 Upper Deck Baseball Heroes Memorabilia Silver

*SILVER: 1X TO 2.5X EMERALD
OVERALL GAME-USED ODDS 2:3 TINS
STATED PRINT RUN 15 SERIAL #'d SETS
11 Cal Ripken Jsy 40.00 80.00
12 Cal Ripken Jsy 40.00 80.00
13 Cal Ripken Jsy 40.00 80.00
14 Cal Ripken Jsy 40.00 80.00
15 Cal Ripken HDR Jsy 40.00 80.00

2005 Upper Deck Baseball Heroes Signature Blue

*BLUE: .6X TO 1.5X EMERALD
OVERALL AUTO ODDS 1:3 TINS
STATED PRINT RUN 20 SERIAL #'d SETS

2005 Upper Deck Baseball Heroes Signature Emerald

B.FELLER (1-5) 10.00 25.00
B.ROBINSON (6-10) 10.00 25.00
C.RIPKEN (11-15) 40.00 80.00
C.YASTRZEMSKI (16-20) 20.00 50.00
D.MATTINGLY (21-25) 30.00 60.00
T.SEAVER (26-30) 10.00 25.00
H.KILLEBREW (31-35) 15.00 40.00
J.PALMER (36-40) 8.00 20.00
M.SCHMIDT (41-45) 20.00 50.00
O.SMITH (46-50) 15.00 40.00
P.MOLITOR (51-55) 8.00 20.00
A.KALINE (56-60) 15.00 40.00
R.YOUNT (61-65) 15.00 40.00
R.SANDBERG (66-70) 20.00 50.00
S.MUSIAL (71-75) 40.00 80.00
S.CARLTON (76-80) 10.00 25.00
T.GWYNN (81-85) 15.00 40.00
W.BOGGS (86-90) 12.50 30.00
W.CLARK (91-95) 10.00 25.00
Y.BERRA (96-100) 30.00 60.00
OVERALL AUTO ODDS 1:3 TINS
STATED PRINT RUN 99 SERIAL #'d SETS

2005 Upper Deck Baseball Heroes Signature Red

*RED: .5X TO 1.2X EMERALD
OVERALL AUTO ODDS 1:3 TINS
STATED PRINT RUN 49 SERIAL #'d SETS

2005 Upper Deck Baseball Heroes Signature Memorabilia

*MEMORABILIA: .75X TO 2X EMERALD
OVERALL AUTO ODDS 1:3 TINS
STATED PRINT RUN 15 SERIAL #'d SETS

2005 Upper Deck Baseball Heroes Tins

COMPLETE SET (4)
1 Ty Cobb 1.50 4.00
2 Lou Gehrig 2.00 5.00
3 Babe Ruth 2.50 6.00
4 Ted Williams 2.00 5.00

2002 Upper Deck Collectors Club

COMP.FACT.SET (21) 12.00 30.00
COMPLETE SET (20) 8.00 20.00
MLB1 Alex Rodriguez .50 1.50
MLB2 Barry Bonds .60 1.50
MLB3 Ken Griffey Jr. .75 2.00
MLB4 Sammy Sosa .50 1.25
MLB5 Jason Giambi .30 .75
MLB6 Ichiro Suzuki 1.00 2.50
MLB7 Chipper Jones .60 1.50
MLB8 Derek Jeter 1.25 3.00
MLB9 Nomar Garciaparra .50 1.25
MLB10 Greg Maddux .60 1.50
MLB11 Mike Piazza .60 1.50
MLB12 Frank Thomas .40 1.00
MLB13 Albert Pujols 1.25 3.00
MLB14 Randy Johnson .50 1.25
MLB15 Pedro Martinez .50 1.25
MLB16 Todd Helton .40 1.00
MLB17 Vladimir Guerrero .50 1.25
MLB18 Jeff Bagwell .50 1.25
MLB19 Roger Clemens .60 1.50
MLB20 Shawn Green .30 .75

2002 Upper Deck Collectors Club Memorabilia

ARB Alex Rodriguez Bat 4.00 10.00
ARJ Alex Rodriguez Jsy 4.00 10.00
JRB Ken Griffey Jr Bat 6.00 15.00
JRJ Ken Griffey Jr Jsy 6.00 15.00
SSB Sammy Sosa Bat 3.00 8.00
SSJ Sammy Sosa Jsy 3.00 8.00

2000 Upper Deck Brooklyn Dodgers Master Collection

COMPLETE SET (15) 100.00 200.00
STATED PRINT RUN 250 SERIAL #'d SETS
BD1 Jackie Robinson 10.00 25.00
BD2 Duke Snider 6.00 15.00
BD3 Pee Wee Reese 6.00 15.00
BD4 Gil Hodges 6.00 15.00
BD5 Carl Furillo 4.00 10.00
BD6 Don Newcombe 4.00 10.00
BD7 Sandy Koufax 20.00 50.00
BD8 Roy Campanella 10.00 25.00
BD9 Jim Gilliam 4.00 10.00
BD10 Don Drysdale 6.00 15.00
BD11 Sandy Amoros 4.00 10.00
BD12 Joe Black 4.00 10.00
BD13 Carl Erskine 4.00 10.00
BD14 Johnny Podres 4.00 10.00
BD15 Zack Wheat 6.00 15.00
NNO Mini Bat Mail Out/750 2.00 5.00

2000 Upper Deck Brooklyn Dodgers Master Collection Legends of Flatbush

ONE SET PER MASTER COLLECTION BOX
STATED PRINT RUN 250 SERIAL #'d SETS
LOF1 Gil Hodges Bat 20.00 50.00
LOF2 Jackie Robinson Bat 40.00 80.00
LOF3 Pee Wee Reese Bat 12.00 30.00
LOF4 Jim Gilliam Bat 12.00 30.00
LOF5 Roy Campanella Bat 12.00 30.00
LOF6 Zach Wheat Bat 20.00 50.00
LOF7 Carl Furillo Bat 12.00 30.00
LOF8 Don Newcombe Bat AU 30.00 60.00
LOF9 Duke Snider Bat AU 40.00 80.00
LOF10 Don Drysdale Jsy 12.00 30.00
LOF11 Sandy Koufax Jsy AU 250.00 500.00

1999 Upper Deck Century Legends

This set was released in June, 1999 and was distributed in five card packs with an SRP of $4.99 per pack. The packs came 24 to a box. The first 47 card of the set feature an assortment of players honored from the Sporting News of 100 Greatest Players. The next 50 cards feature Upper Deck's choices of the best active players. The final cards are utilized for the following subsets: 21 CP (Cards numbered 101 through 120) and Memorablue Shots (Cards numbered 122 through 135.) Cards 11, 25, 26 and 126 do not exist. Due to contractual problems, Upper Deck had to pull the player's originally intended to be featured on these cards. Thus, though the set is numbered 1-135, it is complete at only 131 cards. A game-used bat from legendary slugger Jimmie Foxx was cut into approximately 350 pieces, incorporated into special A Piece of History 500 Club cards and randomly seeded into packs. Pricing for these scarce Foxx bat cards can be referenced under 1999 Upper Deck A Piece of History 500 Club. A Babe Ruth sample card was distributed to dealers and media several weeks prior to the product's national release. The card parallels Ruth's regular issue card except for the word "SAMPLE" running in red text diagonally across the card back.

COMPLETE SET (131) 20.00 50.00
CARDS 11, 25, 26 AND 126 DO NOT EXIST
FOXX BAT LISTED W/UD APH 500 CLUB
1 Babe Ruth 1.00 2.50
2 Willie Mays .60 1.50
3 Ty Cobb .50 1.25
4 Walter Johnson .30 .75
5 Hank Aaron .60 1.50
6 Lou Gehrig .60 1.50
7 Christy Mathewson .30 .75
8 Ted Williams .60 1.50
9 Rogers Hornsby .30 .75
10 Stan Musial .50 1.25
12 Grover Alexander .30 .75
13 Honus Wagner .30 .75
14 Cy Young .30 .75
15 Jimmie Foxx .30 .75
16 Johnny Bench .30 .75
17 Mickey Mantle 1.25 3.00
18 Josh Gibson .30 .75
19 Satchel Paige .30 .75
20 Roberto Clemente .60 1.50
21 Warren Spahn .20 .50
22 Frank Robinson .20 .50
23 Lefty Grove .30 .75
24 Eddie Collins .20 .50
27 Tris Speaker .30 .75
28 Mike Schmidt .60 1.50
29 Napoleon Lajoie .30 .75
30 Steve Carlton .15 .40
31 Bob Gibson .20 .50
32 Tom Seaver .20 .50
33 George Sisler .15 .40
34 Barry Bonds .75 2.00
35 Joe Jackson NNO UER .40 1.00
36 Bob Feller .15 .40
37 Hank Greenberg .30 .75
38 Ernie Banks .30 .75
39 Greg Maddux .50 1.25
40 Yogi Berra .30 .75
41 Nolan Ryan .75 2.00
42 Mel Ott .30 .75
43 Al Simmons .15 .40
44 Jackie Robinson .30 .75
45 Carl Hubbell .20 .50
46 Charley Gehringer .15 .40
47 Buck Leonard .15 .40
48 Reggie Jackson .20 .50
49 Tony Gwynn .40 1.00
50 Roy Campanella .30 .75
51 Ken Griffey Jr. .60 1.50
52 Barry Bonds .75 2.00
53 Roger Clemens .60 1.50
54 Tony Gwynn .40 1.00
55 Cal Ripken 1.00 2.50
56 Greg Maddux .50 1.25
57 Frank Thomas .30 .75
58 Mark McGwire .75 2.00
59 Mike Piazza .50 1.25
60 Wade Boggs .20 .50
61 Alex Rodriguez .50 1.25
62 Juan Gonzalez .15 .40
63 Mo Vaughn .15 .40
64 Albert Belle .15 .40
65 Sammy Sosa .30 .75
66 Nomar Garciaparra .50 1.25
67 Derek Jeter .75 2.00
68 Kevin Brown .20 .50
69 Jose Canseco .20 .50
70 Randy Johnson .30 .75
71 Tom Glavine .20 .50
72 Barry Larkin .20 .50
73 Curt Schilling .15 .40
74 Moises Alou .15 .40
75 Fred McGriff .20 .50
76 Pedro Martinez .20 .50
77 Andres Galarraga .15 .40
78 Will Clark .20 .50
79 Larry Walker .15 .40
80 Ivan Rodriguez .20 .50
81 Chipper Jones .30 .75
82 Jeff Bagwell .20 .50
83 Craig Biggio .20 .50
84 Kerry Wood .15 .40
85 Roberto Alomar .20 .50
86 Vinny Castilla .15 .40
87 Kenny Lofton .15 .40
88 Rafael Palmeiro .20 .50
89 Manny Ramirez .20 .50
90 David Wells .15 .40
91 Mark Grace .20 .50
92 Bernie Williams .20 .50
93 David Cone .15 .40
94 John Olerud .15 .40
95 John Smoltz .20 .50
96 Tino Martinez .20 .50
97 Raul Mondesi .15 .40
98 Gary Sheffield .15 .40
99 Orel Hershiser .15 .40
100 Rickey Henderson .30 .75
101 J.D. Drew 21CP .15 .40
102 Troy Glaus 21CP .20 .50
103 Nomar Garciaparra 21CP .50 1.25
104 Scott Rolen 21CP .15 .40
105 Ryan Minor 21CP .10 .30
106 Travis Lee 21CP .10 .30
107 Roy Halladay 21CP .40 1.00
108 Carlos Beltran 21CP .20 .50
109 Alex Rodriguez 21CP .50 1.25
110 Eric Chavez 21CP .15 .40
111 Vladimir Guerrero 21CP .30 .75
112 Ben Grieve 21CP .10 .30
113 Kerry Wood 21CP .15 .40
114 Alex Gonzalez 21CP .10 .30
115 Darin Erstad 21CP .15 .40
116 Derek Jeter 21CP .75 2.00
117 Jaret Wright 21CP .10 .30
118 Jose Cruz Jr. 21CP .10 .30
119 Chipper Jones 21CP .30 .75
120 Gabe Kapler 21CP .15 .40
121 Satchel Paige MEM .30 .75
122 Willie Mays MEM .60 1.50
123 Roberto Clemente MEM .60 1.50
124 Lou Gehrig MEM .60 1.50
125 Mark McGwire MEM .75 2.00
127 Bob Gibson MEM .20 .50
128 Johnny VanderMeer MEM .10 .30
129 Walter Johnson MEM .30 .75
130 Ty Cobb MEM .50 1.25
131 Don Larsen MEM .15 .40
132 Jackie Robinson MEM .30 .75
133 Tom Seaver MEM .15 .40
134 Johnny Bench MEM .20 .50
135 Frank Robinson MEM .20 .50
S1 Babe Ruth Sample .75 2.00

1999 Upper Deck Century Legends Century Collection

*ACTIVE STARS: 12X TO 30X BASIC
*POST-WAR STARS: 20X TO 50X BASIC
*PRE-WAR STARS: 10X TO 25X BASIC
*21ST CENT: 12X TO 30X BASIC
RANDOM INSERTS IN HOBBY PACKS
STATED PRINT RUN 100 SERIAL #'d SETS
67 Derek Jeter 125.00 250.00
116 Derek Jeter 21CP 125.00 250.00

1999 Upper Deck Century Legends All-Century Team

COMPLETE SET (10) 25.00 60.00
STATED ODDS 1:23
AC1 Babe Ruth 5.00 12.00
AC2 Ty Cobb 2.50 6.00
AC3 Willie Mays 3.00 8.00
AC4 Lou Gehrig 3.00 8.00
AC5 Jackie Robinson 1.50 4.00
AC6 Mike Schmidt 3.00 8.00
AC7 Ernie Banks 1.50 4.00
AC8 Johnny Bench 1.50 4.00
AC9 Cy Young 1.50 4.00
AC10 Lineup Sheet .60 1.50

1999 Upper Deck Century Legends Artifacts

1900 Ty Cobb Framed Cut
1910 Babe Ruth Framed Cut
1920 Rogers Hornsby Framed Cut
1930 Satchel Paige Framed Cut
1950 Aaron
Mays
Mantle AU Balls
1960 Banks
Gibson
Bench AU Balls
1970 Seaver
Schmidt
Carlton AU Balls
1980 N.Ryan
K.Griffey Jr. AU Balls
1990 Ken Griffey Jr. AU Jersey

1999 Upper Deck Century Legends Epic Milestones

COMPLETE SET (9) 15.00 40.00
STATED ODDS 1:12
CARD EM1 DOES NOT EXIST 1.00 2.50
EM2 Jackie Robinson 1.00 2.50
EM3 Nolan Ryan 2.50 6.00
EM4 Mark McGwire 2.50 6.00
EM5 Roger Clemens 2.00 5.00
EM6 Sammy Sosa 1.00 2.50
EM7 Cal Ripken 3.00 8.00
EM8 Rickey Henderson 1.00 2.50
EM9 Hank Aaron 2.00 5.00
EM10 Barry Bonds 2.50 6.00

1999 Upper Deck Century Legends Epic Signatures

STATED ODDS 1:24
EXCHANGE DEADLINE 12/31/99
AR Alex Rodriguez 125.00 300.00
BB Barry Bonds 100.00 250.00
BD Bucky Dent 8.00 20.00
BF Bob Feller 10.00 25.00
BG Bob Gibson 15.00 40.00
BM Bill Mazeroski 12.00 30.00
BT Bobby Thomson 6.00 15.00
CF Carlton Fisk 15.00 40.00
CFX Carlton Fisk EXCH 2.00 5.00
DL Don Larsen 10.00 25.00
EB Ernie Banks 25.00 60.00
EMA Eddie Mathews 15.00 40.00
FR Frank Robinson 20.00 50.00
FT Frank Thomas 60.00 150.00

GM Greg Maddux 150.00 300.00
HK Harmon Killebrew 15.00 40.00
JB Johnny Bench 25.00 60.00
JBX Johnny Bench EXCH 4.00 10.00
JG Juan Gonzalez 25.00 60.00
JR Ken Griffey Jr. 100.00 250.00
MS Mike Schmidt 25.00 60.00
NR Nolan Ryan 175.00 350.00
RJ Reggie Jackson 60.00 150.00
SC Steve Carlton 12.00 30.00
SM Stan Musial 50.00 120.00
SR Ken Griffey Sr. 6.00 15.00
TG Tony Gwynn 25.00 60.00
TS Tom Seaver 60.00 150.00
VG Vladimir Guerrero 15.00 40.00
WMC Willie McCovey 25.00 60.00
WMCX Willie McCovey EXCH 2.00 5.00
WS Warren Spahn 20.00 50.00
YB Yogi Berra 30.00 80.00
YBX Yogi Berra EXCH 4.00 10.00

1999 Upper Deck Century Legends Epic Signatures Century

RANDOM INSERTS IN PACKS
STATED PRINT RUN 100 SERIAL #'d SETS
EXCHANGE DEADLINE 12/31/99
AR Alex Rodriguez 200.00 500.00
BB Barry Bonds 150.00 400.00
BD Bucky Dent 30.00 80.00
BF Bob Feller 40.00 100.00
BG Bob Gibson 20.00 50.00
BM Bill Mazeroski 20.00 50.00
BT Bobby Thomson 20.00 50.00
CF Carlton Fisk 20.00 50.00
CFX Carlton Fisk EXCH
DL Don Larsen 30.00 80.00
EB Ernie Banks 100.00 250.00
EMA Eddie Mathews 60.00 150.00
FR Frank Robinson 25.00 60.00
FT Frank Thomas 75.00 200.00
GM Greg Maddux 175.00 300.00
HK Harmon Killebrew 20.00 50.00
JB Johnny Bench 60.00 150.00
JBX Johnny Bench EXCH
JG Juan Gonzalez 20.00 50.00
JR Ken Griffey Jr. 400.00 800.00
MS Mike Schmidt 125.00 200.00
NR Nolan Ryan 300.00 500.00
RJ Reggie Jackson 100.00 200.00
SC Steve Carlton 25.00 60.00
SM Stan Musial 125.00 250.00
SR Ken Griffey Sr. 20.00 50.00
TG Tony Gwynn 60.00 120.00
TS Tom Seaver 60.00 150.00
TW Ted Williams 1500.00 2000.00
VG Vladimir Guerrero 25.00 60.00
WM Willie Mays 700.00 900.00
WMC Willie McCovey 75.00 200.00
WMCX Willie McCovey EXCH
WS Warren Spahn 75.00 150.00
YB Yogi Berra 50.00 120.00
YBX Yogi Berra EXCH

1999 Upper Deck Century Legends Jerseys of the Century

STATED ODDS 1:418
DW Dave Winfield 6.00 15.00
EM Eddie Murray 6.00 15.00
GB George Brett 8.00 20.00
GM Greg Maddux 5.00 12.00
MS Mike Schmidt 6.00 15.00
NR Nolan Ryan 20.00 50.00
OZ Ozzie Smith 5.00 12.00
RC Roger Clemens 8.00 20.00
TG Tony Gwynn 6.00 15.00

1999 Upper Deck Century Legends Memorable Shots

COMPLETE SET (10) 12.50 30.00
STATED ODDS 1:12
HR1 Babe Ruth 4.00 10.00
HR2 Bobby Thomson .40 1.00
HR3 Kirk Gibson .40 1.00
HR4 Carlton Fisk .40 1.00
HR5 Bill Mazeroski .40 1.00
HR6 Bucky Dent .40 1.00
HR7 Mark McGwire 2.00 5.00
HR8 M.Mantle Stadium 4.00 10.00
HR9 Joe Carter .40 1.00
HR10 Mark McGwire 2.00 5.00

1999 Upper Deck Challengers for 70

This 90 card set was distributed in five card packs. The set is broken up into 45 regular player cards with the following themes: Power Corps, Rookie Power and Power Elite. The other 45 cards of the set feature Mark McGwire Home Run Highlight subset cards. A game-used bat from legendary slugger Harmon Killebrew was cut up and incorporated into approximately 350 A Piece of History 500 Club bat cards. In addition, Killebrew signed and numbered three copies (in concert with his jersey number). Pricing for these scarce bat cards can be referenced under 1999 Upper Deck A Piece of History 500 Club.

COMPLETE SET (90) 15.00 40.00
KILLEBREW BAT LISTED W/UD APH 500 CLUB
1 Mark McGwire .75 2.00
2 Sammy Sosa .30 .75
3 Ken Griffey Jr. .60 1.50
4 Alex Rodriguez .50 1.25
5 Albert Belle .10 .30
6 Mo Vaughn .10 .30
7 Mike Piazza .50 1.25
8 Frank Thomas .30 .75
9 Juan Gonzalez .10 .30
10 Barry Bonds .75 2.00
11 Rafael Palmeiro .20 .50
12 Jose Canseco .20 .50
13 Nomar Garciaparra .50 1.25
14 Carlos Delgado .10 .30
15 Brian Jordan .10 .30
16 Vladimir Guerrero .30 .75
17 Vinny Castilla .10 .30
18 Chipper Jones .30 .75
19 Jeff Bagwell .20 .50
20 Moises Alou .10 .30
21 Tony Clark .10 .30
22 Jim Thome .20 .50
23 Tino Martinez .20 .50
24 Greg Vaughn .10 .30
25 Javy Lopez .10 .30
26 Jeromy Burnitz .10 .30
27 Cal Ripken 1.00 2.50
28 Manny Ramirez .20 .50
29 Darin Erstad .10 .30
30 Ken Caminiti .10 .30
31 Edgar Martinez .20 .50
32 Ivan Rodriguez .20 .50
33 Larry Walker .10 .30
34 Todd Helton .20 .50
35 Andruw Jones .20 .50
36 Ray Lankford .10 .30
37 Travis Lee .10 .30
38 Raul Mondesi .10 .30
39 Scott Rolen .20 .50
40 Ben Grieve .10 .30
41 J.D. Drew .10 .30
42 Troy Glaus .20 .50
43 Eric Chavez .10 .30
44 Gabe Kapler .10 .30
45 Michael Barrett .10 .30
46 Mark McGwire HRH .40 1.00
47 Jose Canseco HRH .20 .50
48 Greg Vaughn HRH .10 .30
49 Albert Belle HRH .10 .30
50 Mark McGwire HRH .40 1.00
51 Vinny Castilla HRH .10 .30
52 Vladimir Guerrero HRH .20 .50
53 Andres Galarraga HRH .10 .30
54 Rafael Palmeiro HRH .10 .30
55 Juan Gonzalez HRH .10 .30
56 Ken Griffey Jr. HRH .40 1.00
57 Barry Bonds HRH .40 1.00
58 Mo Vaughn HRH .10 .30
59 Nomar Garciaparra HRH .30 .75
60 Tino Martinez HRH .10 .30
61 Mark McGwire HRH .40 1.00
62 Mark McGwire HRH .40 1.00
63 Mark McGwire HRH .40 1.00
64 Mark McGwire HRH .40 1.00
65 Mark McGwire HRH .40 1.00
66 Sammy Sosa HRH .20 .50
67 Mark McGwire HRH .40 1.00
68 Mark McGwire HRH .40 1.00
69 Mark McGwire HRH .40 1.00
70 Mark McGwire HRH .40 1.00
71 Mark McGwire HRH .40 1.00
72 Scott Brosius HRH .10 .30
73 Tony Gwynn HRH .20 .50
74 Chipper Jones HRH .20 .50
75 Jeff Bagwell HRH .10 .30
76 Moises Alou HRH .10 .30
77 Manny Ramirez HRH .10 .30
78 Carlos Delgado HRH .10 .30
79 Kerry Wood HRH .10 .30
80 Ken Griffey Jr. HRH .40 1.00
81 Cal Ripken HRH .50 1.25
82 Alex Rodriguez HRH .30 .75
83 Barry Bonds HRH .40 1.00
84 Ken Griffey Jr. HRH .40 1.00
85 Travis Lee HRH .10 .30
86 George Lombard HRH .10 .30
87 Michael Barrett HRH .10 .30
88 Jeremy Giambi HRH .10 .30
89 Troy Glaus HRH .10 .30
90 J.D. Drew HRH .10 .30

1999 Upper Deck Challengers for 70 Challengers Edition

COMPLETE SET (90) 400.00 800.00
*STARS: 5X TO 12X BASIC CARDS
RANDOM INSERTS IN PACKS
STATED PRINT RUN 600 SERIAL #'d SETS

1999 Upper Deck Challengers for 70 Challengers Inserts

COMPLETE SET (30) 10.00 25.00
ONE PER PACK
*PARALLEL: 20X TO 50X BASIC CHALL.INS.
PARALLEL: RANDOM INSERTS IN PACKS
PARALLEL PRINT RUN 70 SERIAL #'d SETS
C1 Mark McGwire .75 2.00
C2 Sammy Sosa .30 .75
C3 Ken Griffey Jr. .60 1.50
C4 Alex Rodriguez .50 1.25
C5 Albert Belle .10 .30
C6 Mo Vaughn .10 .30
C7 Mike Piazza .50 1.25
C8 Frank Thomas .30 .75
C9 Juan Gonzalez .10 .30
C10 Barry Bonds .75 2.00
C11 Rafael Palmeiro .20 .50
C12 Nomar Garciaparra .50 1.25
C13 Vladimir Guerrero .30 .75
C14 Vinny Castilla .10 .30
C15 Chipper Jones .30 .75
C16 Jeff Bagwell .20 .50
C17 Moises Alou .10 .30
C18 Tony Clark .10 .30
C19 Jim Thome .20 .50
C20 Tino Martinez .20 .50
C21 Greg Vaughn .10 .30
C22 Manny Ramirez .20 .50
C23 Darin Erstad .10 .30
C24 Ken Caminiti .10 .30
C25 Ivan Rodriguez .20 .50
C26 Andruw Jones .20 .50
C27 Travis Lee .10 .30
C28 Scott Rolen .20 .50
C29 Ben Grieve .10 .30
C30 J.D. Drew .10 .30

1999 Upper Deck Challengers for 70 Longball Legends

COMPLETE SET (30) 125.00 250.00
STATED ODDS 1:39
L1 Ken Griffey Jr. 6.00 15.00
L2 Mark McGwire 8.00 20.00
L3 Sammy Sosa 3.00 8.00
L4 Cal Ripken 10.00 25.00
L5 Barry Bonds 8.00 20.00
L6 Larry Walker 1.25 3.00
L7 Fred McGriff 2.00 5.00
L8 Alex Rodriguez 5.00 12.00
L9 Frank Thomas 3.00 8.00
L10 Juan Gonzalez 1.25 3.00
L11 Jeff Bagwell 2.00 5.00
L12 Mo Vaughn 1.25 3.00
L13 Albert Belle 1.25 3.00
L14 Mike Piazza 5.00 12.00
L15 Vladimir Guerrero 3.00 8.00
L16 Chipper Jones 3.00 8.00
L17 Ken Caminiti 1.25 3.00
L18 Rafael Palmeiro 2.00 5.00
L19 Nomar Garciaparra 5.00 12.00
L20 Jim Thome 2.00 5.00
L21 Edgar Martinez 2.00 5.00
L22 Ivan Rodriguez 2.00 5.00
L23 Andres Galarraga 1.25 3.00
L24 Scott Rolen 2.00 5.00
L25 Darin Erstad 1.25 3.00
L26 Moises Alou 1.25 3.00
L27 J.D. Drew 1.25 3.00
L28 Andruw Jones 2.00 5.00
L29 Manny Ramirez 2.00 5.00
L30 Tino Martinez 2.00 5.00

1999 Upper Deck Challengers for 70 Mark on History

COMPLETE SET (25) 40.00 100.00
COMMON CARD (M1-M25) 1.50 4.00
STATED ODDS 1:5
*PARALLEL HR 70: 6X TO 15X BASIC MARK
PARALLEL: RANDOM INSERTS IN PACKS
PARALLEL PRINT RUN 70 SERIAL #'d SETS

1999 Upper Deck Challengers for 70 Swinging for the Fences

COMPLETE SET (15) 25.00 60.00
STATED ODDS 1:19
S1 Ken Griffey Jr. 3.00 8.00
S2 Mark McGwire 4.00 10.00
S3 Sammy Sosa 1.50 4.00
S4 Alex Rodriguez 2.50 6.00
S5 Nomar Garciaparra 2.50 6.00
S6 J.D. Drew .60 1.50
S7 Vladimir Guerrero 1.50 4.00
S8 Ben Grieve .60 1.50
S9 Chipper Jones 1.50 4.00
S10 Gabe Kapler .60 1.50
S11 Travis Lee .60 1.50
S12 Todd Helton 1.00 2.50
S13 Juan Gonzalez .60 1.50
S14 Mike Piazza 2.50 6.00
S15 Mo Vaughn .60 1.50

1999 Upper Deck Challengers for 70 Swinging for the Fences Autograph

RANDOM INSERTS IN PACKS
2700 TOTAL CARDS SIGNED
AR Alex Rodriguez 50.00 100.00
GK Gabe Kapler 6.00 15.00
JR Ken Griffey Jr. 60.00 120.00
TH Todd Helton 6.00 15.00
TL Travis Lee 6.00 15.00
VG Vladimir Guerrero 15.00 40.00

2009-10 Upper Deck Champ's Hall of Legends Memorabilia

STATED ODDS 1:160
HLCR Cal Ripken Jr.
HLJA Bo Jackson 20.00 50.00
HLMS Mike Schmidt 20.00 50.00
HLNR Nolan Ryan 25.00 60.00

2009-10 Upper Deck Champ's Signatures

STATED ODDS 1:15
CSBF Bob Feller 25.00 60.00
CSCR Cal Ripken Jr. 125.00 200.00
CSMS Mike Schmidt 20.00 40.00
CSNR Nolan Ryan 125.00 200.00

2003 Upper Deck Classic Portraits

COMP.SET w/o SP's (100) 10.00 25.00
COMMON CARD (1-100) .15 .40
COMMON CARD (101-145) .60 1.50
COMMON RC (101-145) .60 1.50
101-145 STATED ODDS 1:4
COMMON CARD (146-190) .75 2.00
COMMON RC (146-190) .75 2.00
146-190 STATED ODDS 3 PER BOX
146-190 PRINT RUN 2003 SERIAL #'d SETS
COMMON ACTIVE (191-232) 1.00 2.50
COMMON RETIRED (191-232) 1.00 2.50
191-232 STATED ODDS 2 PER BOX
191-232 PRINT RUN 1200 SERIAL #'d SETS
1 Ken Griffey Jr. .75 2.00
2 Randy Johnson .40 1.00
3 Rafael Furcal .15 .40
4 Omar Vizquel .25 .60
5 Shawn Green .15 .40
6 Roy Oswalt .25 .60
7 Hideo Nomo .40 1.00
8 Jason Giambi .15 .40
9 Barry Bonds .60 1.50
10 Mike Piazza .40 1.00
11 Ichiro Suzuki .50 1.25
12 Carlos Delgado .15 .40
13 Preston Wilson .15 .40
14 Lance Berkman .25 .60
15 Magglio Ordonez .25 .60
16 Kerry Wood .15 .40
17 Ivan Rodriguez .25 .60
18 Chipper Jones .40 1.00
19 Adam Dunn .25 .60
20 C.C. Sabathia .25 .60
21 Mike MacDougal .15 .40
22 Torii Hunter .15 .40
23 Jim Thome .25 .60
24 Hank Blalock .15 .40
25 Johnny Damon .25 .60
26 Troy Glaus .15 .40
27 Manny Ramirez .40 1.00
28 Mark Prior .25 .60
29 Brent Mayne .15 .40
30 Derek Jeter 1.00 2.50
31 Tim Hudson .25 .60
32 Mike Cameron .15 .40
33 Mark Teixeira .25 .60
34 Shannon Stewart .15 .40
35 Tim Salmon .15 .40
36 Luis Gonzalez .15 .40
37 Jason Johnson .15 .40
38 Shea Hillenbrand .15 .40
39 Bartolo Colon .15 .40
40 Austin Kearns .15 .40
41 Vladimir Guerrero .25 .60
42 Tom Glavine .25 .60
43 Andres Galarraga .25 .60
44 Kazuhiro Sasaki .15 .40
45 Juan Gonzalez .15 .40
46 Vernon Wells .15 .40
47 Jeff Bagwell .25 .60
48 Mike Sweeney .15 .40
49 Carlos Beltran .25 .60
50 Dave Roberts .25 .60
51 Todd Helton .25 .60
52 Carlos Pena .25 .60
53 Darin Erstad .15 .40
54 Gary Sheffield .15 .40
55 Lyle Overbay .15 .40
56 Sammy Sosa .40 1.00
57 Mike Mussina .25 .60
58 Matt Morris .15 .40
59 Roberto Alomar .25 .60
60 Larry Walker .25 .60
61 Jacque Jones .15 .40
62 Josh Beckett .15 .40
63 Richie Sexson .15 .40
64 Derek Lowe .15 .40
65 Pedro Martinez .25 .60
66 Moises Alou .15 .40
67 Craig Biggio .25 .60
68 Curt Schilling .25 .60
69 Jesse Foppert .15 .40
70 Nomar Garciaparra .25 .60
71 Barry Zito .25 .60
72 Alfonso Soriano .25 .60
73 Miguel Tejada .25 .60
74 Rafael Palmeiro .25 .60
75 Albert Pujols .50 1.25
76 Mariano Rivera .50 1.25
77 Bobby Abreu .15 .40
78 Alex Rodriguez .50 1.25
79 Andruw Jones .15 .40
80 Frank Thomas .40 1.00
81 Greg Maddux .50 1.25
82 Jim Edmonds .25 .60
83 Bernie Williams .25 .60
84 Roger Clemens .50 1.25
85 Eric Chavez .15 .40
86 Scott Rolen .25 .60
87 Jorge Posada .25 .60
88 Bret Boone .15 .40
89 Ben Sheets .15 .40
90 John Olerud .15 .40
91 J.D. Drew .15 .40
92 Aaron Boone .15 .40
93 Corey Koskie .15 .40
94 Sean Casey .15 .40
95 Jose Cruz Jr. .15 .40
96 Pat Burrell .15 .40
97 Jose Guillen .15 .40
98 Mark Mulder .15 .40
99 Garret Anderson .15 .40
100 Kazuhisa Ishii .15 .40
101 David Matranga SP RC .60 1.50
102 Colin Porter SP RC .60 1.50
103 Jason Gilfillan SP RC .60 1.50
104 Carlos Mendez SP RC .60 1.50
105 Jason Shiell SP RC .60 1.50
106 Kevin Tolar SP RC .60 1.50
107 Termel Sledge SP RC .60 1.50
108 Craig Brazell SP RC .60 1.50
109 Bernie Castro SP RC .60 1.50
110 Tim Olson SP RC .60 1.50
111 Kevin Ohme SP RC .60 1.50
112 Pedro Liriano SP .60 1.50
113 Joe Borowski SP .60 1.50
114 Edgar Gonzalez SP RC .60 1.50
115 Joe Thurston SP .60 1.50
116 Bobby Hill SP .60 1.50
117 Michel Hernandez SP RC .60 1.50
118 Arnie Munoz SP RC .60 1.50
119 David Sanders SP RC .60 1.50
120 Willie Eyre SP RC .60 1.50
121 Brent Hoard SP RC .60 1.50
122 Lew Ford SP RC .60 1.50
123 Beau Kemp SP RC .60 1.50
124 Jon Pridie SP RC .60 1.50
125 Mike Ryan SP RC .60 1.50
126 Richard Fischer SP RC .60 1.50
127 Luis Ayala SP RC .60 1.50
128 Mike Neu SP RC .60 1.50
129 Joe Valentine SP RC .60 1.50
130 Nate Bland SP RC .60 1.50
131 Shane Bazzell SP RC .60 1.50
132 Jason Roach SP RC .60 1.50
133 Diegomar Markwell SP RC .60 1.50
134 Francisco Rosario SP RC .60 1.50
135 Guillermo Quiroz SP RC .60 1.50
136 Jerome Williams SP .60 1.50
137 Fernando Cabrera SP RC .60 1.50
138 Francisco Cruceta SP RC .60 1.50
139 Jhonny Peralta SP .60 1.50
140 Rett Johnson SP RC .60 1.50
141 Aaron Looper SP RC .60 1.50
142 Bobby Madritsch SP RC .60 1.50
143 Dan Haren SP RC 3.00 8.00
144 Jose Castillo SP .60 1.50
145 Chris Waters SP RC .60 1.50
146 Hideki Matsui MP RC 4.00 10.00
147 Jose Contreras MP RC 2.00 5.00
148 Felix Sanchez MP RC .75 2.00
149 Jon Leicester MP RC .75 2.00
150 Todd Wellemeyer MP RC .75 2.00
151 Matt Bruback MP RC .75 2.00
152 Chris Capuano MP RC .75 2.00
153 Oscar Villarreal MP RC .75 2.00
154 Matt Kata MP RC .75 2.00
155 Robby Hammock MP RC .75 2.00
156 Gerald Laird MP .75 2.00
157 Brandon Webb MP RC 2.50 6.00
158 Tommy Whiteman MP .75 2.00
159 Andrew Brown MP RC .75 2.00
160 Alfredo Gonzalez MP RC .75 2.00
161 Carlos Rivera MP .75 2.00
162 Rick Roberts MP RC .75 2.00
163 Dontrelle Willis MP .75 2.00
164 Josh Willingham MP RC 2.50 6.00
165 Prentice Redman MP RC .75 2.00
166 Jeff Duncan MP RC .75 2.00
167 Jose Reyes MP 2.00 5.00
168 Jeremy Griffiths MP RC .75 2.00
169 Phil Seibel MP RC .75 2.00
170 Heath Bell MP RC 1.25 3.00
171 Anthony Ferrari MP RC .75 2.00
172 Mike Nicolas MP RC .75 2.00
173 Cory Stewart MP RC .75 2.00
174 Miguel Ojeda MP RC .75 2.00
175 Rickie Weeks MP RC 2.50 6.00
176 Delmon Young MP RC 5.00 12.00
177 Tommy Phelps MP .75 2.00
178 Josh Hall MP RC .75 2.00
179 Ryan Cameron MP RC .75 2.00
180 Garrett Atkins MP .75 2.00
181 Clint Barmes MP RC 2.00 5.00
182 Mike Hessman MP RC .75 2.00
183 Chin-Hui Tsao MP .75 2.00
184 Rocco Baldelli MP .75 2.00
185 Bo Hart MP RC .75 2.00
186 Wilfredo Ledezma MP RC .75 2.00
187 Miguel Cabrera MP 10.00 25.00
188 Ian Ferguson MP RC .75 2.00
189 Michael Nakamura MP RC .75 2.00
190 Alejandro Machado MP RC .75 2.00
191 Mickey Mantle BBR 8.00 20.00
192 Ted Williams BBR 5.00 12.00
193 Mark Prior BBR 1.50 4.00
194 Stan Musial BBR 4.00 10.00
195 Phil Rizzuto BBR 1.50 4.00
196 Nolan Ryan BBR 8.00 20.00
197 Tom Seaver BBR 1.50 4.00
198 Robin Yount BBR 2.50 6.00
199 Yogi Berra BBR 2.50 6.00
200 Ernie Banks BBR 2.50 6.00
201 Willie McCovey BBR 1.50 4.00
202 Ralph Kiner BBR 1.50 4.00
203 Ken Griffey Jr. BBR 5.00 12.00
204 Sammy Sosa BBR 2.50 6.00
205 Derek Jeter BBR 6.00 15.00
206 Nomar Garciaparra BBR 1.50 4.00
207 Alex Rodriguez BBR 3.00 8.00
208 Ichiro Suzuki BBR 3.00 8.00
209 Mike Piazza BBR 2.50 6.00
210 Jackie Robinson BBR 2.50 6.00
211 Roberto Clemente BBR 6.00 15.00
212 Babe Ruth BBR 6.00 15.00
213 Duke Snider BBR 1.50 4.00
214 Greg Maddux BBR 3.00 8.00
215 Juan Marichal BBR 1.50 4.00
216 Joe Morgan BBR 1.50 4.00
217 Rollie Fingers BBR 1.50 4.00
218 Warren Spahn BBR 1.50 4.00
219 Pee Wee Reese BBR 1.50 4.00
220 Troy Glaus BBR 1.00 2.50
221 Jason Giambi BBR 1.00 2.50
222 Roger Clemens BBR 3.00 8.00
223 Pedro Martinez BBR 1.50 4.00
224 Chipper Jones BBR 2.50 6.00
225 Randy Johnson BBR 2.50 6.00
226 Jim Thome BBR 1.50 4.00
227 Barry Bonds BBR 4.00 10.00
228 Hideo Nomo BBR 2.50 6.00
229 Whitey Ford BBR 1.50 4.00
230 Bob Gibson BBR 1.50 4.00
231 Alfonso Soriano BBR 1.50 4.00
232 Richie Ashburn BBR 1.50 4.00

2003 Upper Deck Classic Portraits Gold

STATED PRINT RUN 25 SERIAL #'d SETS
NO PRICING DUE TO SCARCITY

2003 Upper Deck Classic Portraits Busts Bronze

STATED ODDS 1:2 BOXES
SP PRINT RUNS PROVIDED BY UD
SP'S ARE NOT SERIAL-NUMBERED
A IS AWAY UNIFORM, H IS HOME UNIFORM
AWAY ='s CITY NAME ACROSS BUST
HOME ='s TEAM NAME/LOGO ACROSS BUST
BGH Bob Gibson H 10.00 25.00
BRSH Babe Ruth Sox H/300 20.00 50.00
BRYA Babe Ruth Yanks A 25.00 60.00
BRYH Babe Ruth Yanks H 25.00 60.00
DSA Duke Snider A 30.00 60.00
DSH Duke Snider H 10.00 25.00
HMH Hideki Matsui H 12.50 30.00
ISH Ichiro Suzuki H/300 15.00 40.00
JGH Jason Giambi H 10.00 25.00
KGH Ken Griffey Jr. H/300 20.00 50.00
MMA Mickey Mantle A 50.00 100.00
MMH Mickey Mantle H 50.00 100.00
NGH Nomar Garciaparra H 15.00 40.00
NRAH Nolan Ryan Astros H/300 30.00 60.00
NRMA Nolan Ryan Mets A 15.00 40.00
NRMH Nolan Ryan Mets H 15.00 40.00
RCH Roberto Clemente H 15.00 40.00
SMH Stan Musial H 50.00 100.00
SSH Sammy Sosa H/300 10.00 25.00
TSMA Tom Seaver Mets A 10.00 25.00
TSMH Tom Seaver Mets H 10.00 25.00
TSRA Tom Seaver Reds A/300 10.00 25.00
TSRH Tom Seaver Reds H 10.00 25.00
TWA Ted Williams A 20.00 50.00
TWH Ted Williams H 20.00 50.00
YBA Yogi Berra A 10.00 25.00
YBH Yogi Berra H 10.00 25.00

2003 Upper Deck Classic Portraits Busts Marble

STATED ODDS 1:4 BOXES
PRINT RUNS B/WN 100-250 COPIES PER
PRINT RUNS PROVIDED BY UPPER DECK
BUSTS ARE NOT SERIAL-NUMBERED
BGH Bob Gibson H/250 10.00 25.00
BRSH Babe Ruth Sox H/250 25.00 60.00
BRYA Babe Ruth Yanks A/125 40.00 100.00
BRYH Babe Ruth Yanks H/250 30.00 80.00
DSA Duke Snider A/100 15.00 40.00
DSH Duke Snider H/250 10.00 25.00
HMH Hideki Matsui H/250 15.00 40.00
ISH Ichiro Suzuki H/250 20.00 50.00
JGH Jason Giambi H/250 10.00 25.00
KGH Ken Griffey Jr. H/250 25.00 60.00
MMA Mickey Mantle A/125 60.00 120.00
MMH Mickey Mantle H/250 50.00 100.00
NGH Nomar Garciaparra H/250 20.00 50.00
NRAH Nolan Ryan Astros H/250 25.00 60.00
NRMA Nolan Ryan Mets A/125 30.00 80.00
NRMH Nolan Ryan Mets H/250 25.00 60.00
RCH Roberto Clemente H/250 30.00 80.00
SMH Stan Musial H/250 25.00 60.00
SSH Sammy Sosa H/250 10.00 25.00
TSMA Tom Seaver Mets A/125 15.00 40.00
TSMH Tom Seaver Mets H/250 10.00 25.00
TSRA Tom Seaver Reds A/125 15.00 40.00
TSRH Tom Seaver Reds H/250 10.00 25.00
TWA Ted Williams A/125 30.00 80.00
TWH Ted Williams H/250 25.00 60.00
YBA Yogi Berra A/125 15.00 40.00
YBH Yogi Berra H/250 10.00 25.00

2003 Upper Deck Classic Portraits Busts Pewter

STATED ODDS 1:6 BOXES
PRINT RUNS B/WN 75-100 COPIES PER
PRINT RUNS PROVIDED BY UPPER DECK
BUSTS ARE NOT SERIAL-NUMBERED
BGH Bob Gibson H/100 15.00 40.00
BRSH Babe Ruth Sox H/100 40.00 100.00
BRYA Babe Ruth Yanks A/75 50.00 120.00
BRYH Babe Ruth Yanks H/100 50.00 120.00
DSA Duke Snider A/75 15.00 40.00
DSH Duke Snider H/100 15.00 40.00
HMH Hideki Matsui H/100 25.00 60.00
ISH Ichiro Suzuki H/100 30.00 80.00
JGH Jason Giambi H/100 15.00 40.00
KGH Ken Griffey Jr. H/100 40.00 100.00
MMA Mickey Mantle A/75 100.00 200.00
MMH Mickey Mantle H/100 100.00 200.00
NGH Nomar Garciaparra H/100 30.00 80.00
NRAH Nolan Ryan Astros H/100 40.00 100.00
NRMA Nolan Ryan Mets A/75 40.00 100.00
NRMH Nolan Ryan Mets H/100 40.00 100.00
RCH Roberto Clemente H/100 60.00 120.00
SMH Stan Musial H/100 25.00 60.00
SSH Sammy Sosa H/100 15.00 40.00
TSMA Tom Seaver Mets A/75 15.00 40.00
TSMH Tom Seaver Mets H/100 15.00 40.00
TSRA Tom Seaver Reds A/100 15.00 40.00
TSRH Tom Seaver Reds H/75 15.00 40.00
TWA Ted Williams A/75 40.00 100.00
TWH Ted Williams H/100 30.00 80.00
YBA Yogi Berra A/75 15.00 40.00
YBH Yogi Berra H/100 15.00 40.00

2003 Upper Deck Classic Portraits Busts Pewter Wood

PRINT RUNS B/WN 10-11 COPIES PER
PRINT RUNS PROVIDED BY UPPER DECK
BUSTS ARE NOT SERIAL-NUMBERED

2003 Upper Deck Classic Portraits Busts Autograph Bronze

OVERALL AUTO ODDS 1:12 BOXES
SP PRINT RUNS B/WN 1-106 COPIES PER
SP PRINT RUNS PROVIDED BY UPPER DECK
SP'S ARE NOT SERIAL-NUMBERED
NO PRICING ON QTY OF 14 OR LESS
A IS AWAY UNIFORM, H IS HOME UNIFORM
AWAY ='s CITY NAME ACROSS BUST
HOME ='s TEAM NAME/LOGO ACROSS BUST
BGH Bob Gibson H 40.00 80.00
DSH Duke Snider H 50.00 100.00
HMH Hideki Matsui H 175.00 300.00
ISH Ichiro Suzuki H/62 175.00 300.00
KGH Ken Griffey Jr. H 50.00 100.00
NGH N.Garciaparra H/106 60.00 120.00
SMH Stan Musial H/62 60.00 120.00
YBH Yogi Berra H 60.00 150.00

2003 Upper Deck Classic Portraits Busts Autograph Marble

OVERALL AUTO ODDS 1:12 BOXES
PRINT RUNS B/WN 1-26 COPIES PER
PRINT RUNS PROVIDED BY UPPER DECK
BUSTS ARE NOT SERIAL-NUMBERED
NO PRICING DUE TO SCARCITY
A IS AWAY UNIFORM, H IS HOME UNIFORM
AWAY ='s CITY NAME ACROSS BUST
HOME ='s TEAM NAME/LOGO ACROSS BUST

2003 Upper Deck Classic Portraits Busts Autograph Pewter

OVERALL AUTO ODDS 1:12 BOXES
PRINT RUNS B/WN 1-17 COPIES PER
PRINT RUNS PROVIDED BY UPPER DECK
BUSTS ARE NOT SERIAL-NUMBERED
NO PRICING DUE TO SCARCITY
A IS AWAY UNIFORM, H IS HOME UNIFORM
AWAY ='s CITY NAME ACROSS BUST
HOME ='s TEAM NAME/LOGO ACROSS BUST

2003 Upper Deck Classic Portraits Busts Autograph Pewter Wood

OVERALL AUTO ODDS 1:12 BOXES
PRINT RUNS B/WN 1-3 COPIES PER
PRINT RUNS PROVIDED BY UPPER DECK
BUSTS ARE NOT SERIAL-NUMBERED
NO PRICING DUE TO SCARCITY
A IS AWAY UNIFORM
AWAY ='s CITY NAME ACROSS BUST

2003 Upper Deck Classic Portraits Signs of Success

PRINT RUNS B/WN 9-299 COPIES PER
NO PRICING ON QTY OF 22 OR LESS
GOLD PRINT RUN 25 SERIAL #'d SETS
NO GOLD PRICING DUE TO SCARCITY
AG Alex Graman/215 4.00 10.00
AH Andy Van Hekken/299 4.00 10.00
BC Brad Cresse/121 4.00 10.00
BD Ben Diggins/299 4.00 10.00
BH Ben Howard/299 4.00 10.00
BP Brandon Phillips/131 4.00 10.00
BR Brandon Claussen/121 4.00 10.00
CC C.C. Sabathia/106 6.00 15.00
CM Corwin Malone/103 4.00 10.00
DB Dewon Brazelton/299 4.00 10.00
DH Drew Henson/246 4.00 10.00
DK David Kelton/102 4.00 10.00
HI Hansel Izquierdo/299 4.00 10.00
JB John Buck/98 4.00 10.00
JD Johnny Damon/297 6.00 15.00
JE Jerome Williams/103 4.00 10.00
JJ Jimmy Journell/98 4.00 10.00
JU Justin Wayne/299 4.00 10.00
JW Jayson Werth/299 6.00 15.00
KG Ken Griffey Jr./299 50.00 100.00
KL Kenny Lofton/296 10.00 25.00
MB Mark Buehrle/220 12.50 30.00
MI Milton Bradley/220 6.00 15.00
MT Mark Teixeira/280 10.00 25.00
TG Tony Gwynn/49 30.00 80.00
TH Matt Thornton/298 4.00 10.00

2003 Upper Deck Classic Portraits Stitches

STATED PRINT RUN 299 SERIAL #'d SETS
GOLD PRINT RUN 25 SERIAL #'d SETS
NO GOLD PRICING DUE TO SCARCITY
AD Adam Dunn 3.00 8.00
AJ Andruw Jones 4.00 10.00
AL Albert Pujols 8.00 20.00
AP Andy Pettitte 4.00 10.00
AR Alex Rodriguez 6.00 15.00
AS Alfonso Soriano 3.00 8.00
CJ Chipper Jones 4.00 10.00
CP Corey Patterson 3.00 8.00
CS Curt Schilling 3.00 8.00
DW Dontrelle Willis 4.00 10.00
GM Greg Maddux 4.00 10.00
GS Gary Sheffield 3.00 8.00
HB Hank Blalock 3.00 8.00
HC Hee Seop Choi 3.00 8.00
HM Hideki Matsui 12.50 30.00
HN Hideo Nomo 6.00 15.00
IR Ivan Rodriguez 4.00 10.00
IS Ichiro Suzuki 10.00 25.00
JB Jeff Bagwell 4.00 10.00
JD J.D. Drew 3.00 8.00
JE Jim Edmonds 3.00 8.00
JG Jason Giambi 3.00 8.00
JK Jeff Kent 3.00 8.00
JT Jim Thome 4.00 10.00
KG Ken Griffey Jr. 6.00 15.00
KW Kerry Wood 3.00 8.00
MI Mike Piazza 4.00 10.00
ML Mike Lowell 3.00 8.00
MM Matt Morris 3.00 8.00
MO Magglio Ordonez 3.00 8.00
MP Mark Prior 4.00 10.00
PM Pedro Martinez 4.00 10.00
RB Rocco Baldelli 3.00 8.00
RC Roger Clemens 6.00 15.00
RF Rafael Furcal 3.00 8.00
RJ Randy Johnson 4.00 10.00
RO Roy Oswalt 3.00 8.00
SG Shawn Green 3.00 8.00
SS Sammy Sosa 4.00 10.00
TG Troy Glaus 3.00 8.00
TH Torii Hunter 3.00 8.00
VG Vladimir Guerrero 4.00 10.00

2003 Upper Deck Classic Portraits Stitches Patch

STATED PRINT RUN 99 SERIAL #'d SETS
PATCH GOLD PRINT 10 SERIAL #'d SETS
NO PATCH GOLD PRICING DUE TO SCARCITY
AD Adam Dunn 6.00 15.00
AJ Andruw Jones 10.00 25.00
AL Albert Pujols 20.00 50.00
AP Andy Pettitte 10.00 25.00
AR Alex Rodriguez 12.50 30.00
AS Alfonso Soriano 6.00 15.00
CJ Chipper Jones 10.00 25.00
CP Corey Patterson 6.00 15.00
CS Curt Schilling 6.00 15.00
DW Dontrelle Willis 10.00 25.00
GM Greg Maddux 15.00 40.00
GS Gary Sheffield 6.00 15.00
HB Hank Blalock 6.00 15.00
HC Hee Seop Choi 6.00 15.00
HM Hideki Matsui 50.00 100.00
HN Hideo Nomo 40.00 80.00
IR Ivan Rodriguez 10.00 25.00
IS Ichiro Suzuki 40.00 100.00
JB Jeff Bagwell 10.00 25.00
JD J.D. Drew 6.00 15.00
JE Jim Edmonds 6.00 15.00
JG Jason Giambi 6.00 15.00
JK Jeff Kent 6.00 15.00
JT Jim Thome 10.00 25.00
KG Ken Griffey Jr. 15.00 40.00
KW Kerry Wood 6.00 15.00
MI Mike Piazza 20.00 50.00
ML Mike Lowell 6.00 15.00
MM Matt Morris 6.00 15.00
MO Magglio Ordonez 6.00 15.00
MP Mark Prior 10.00 25.00
PM Pedro Martinez 10.00 25.00
RB Rocco Baldelli 6.00 15.00
RC Roger Clemens 20.00 50.00
RF Rafael Furcal 6.00 15.00
RJ Randy Johnson 12.00 30.00
RO Roy Oswalt 6.00 15.00
SG Shawn Green 6.00 15.00
SS Sammy Sosa 10.00 25.00
TG Troy Glaus 6.00 15.00
TH Torii Hunter 6.00 15.00
VG Vladimir Guerrero 10.00 25.00

2005 Upper Deck Classics

COMP.SET w/o SP's (100) 10.00 25.00
COMMON CARD (1-100) .25 .60
COMMON CARD (101-130) .75 2.00
101-130 STATED ODDS 1:4 H/R
1 Al Kaline .60 1.50
2 Al Lopez .25 .60
3 Allie Reynolds .25 .60
4 Babe Herman .25 .60
5 Bill Mazeroski .40 1.00
6 Bill Russell .25 .60
7 Billy Herman .25 .60
8 Billy Williams .40 1.00
9 Bob Feller .40 1.00

10 Bob Gibson .40 1.00
11 Bob Lemon .40 1.00
12 Bobby Doerr .40 1.00
13 Boog Powell .25 .60
14 Ken Hubbs .25 .60
15 Brooks Robinson .40 1.00
16 Buck Leonard .25 .60
17 Cal Ripken 2.00 5.00
18 Carl Hubbell .40 1.00
19 Catfish Hunter .40 1.00
20 Johnny Hopp .25 .60
21 Charlie Gehringer .25 .60
22 Curt Flood .25 .60
23 Jimmie Foxx .40 1.00
24 Dave McNally .25 .60
25 Davey Lopes .25 .60
26 Don Drysdale .40 1.00
27 Don Sutton .40 1.00
28 Earl Weaver .40 1.00
29 Early Wynn .40 1.00
30 Edd Roush .40 1.00
31 Eddie Mathews .60 1.50
32 Enos Slaughter .40 1.00
33 Fergie Jenkins .40 1.00
34 Frank Howard .25 .60
35 Leon Wagner .25 .60
36 Frankie Crosetti .25 .60
37 Gaylord Perry .40 1.00
38 George Bell .25 .60
39 George Kell .40 1.00
40 Graig Nettles .25 .60
41 Hal Newhouser .40 1.00
42 Harmon Killebrew .60 1.50
43 Harvey Kuenn .25 .60
44 Howard Johnson .25 .60
45 Hoyt Wilhelm .40 1.00
46 Jack Clark .25 .60
47 Jack Morris .40 1.00
48 Jim Bunning .40 1.00
49 Jim Palmer .40 1.00
50 Joe Adcock .25 .60
51 Joe Carter .25 .60
52 Casey Stengel .40 1.00
53 Joe Morgan .40 1.00
54 Joe Sewell .40 1.00
55 Smokey Joe Wood .25 .60
56 Johnny Bench .60 1.50
57 Johnny Mize .40 1.00
58 Jose Canseco .40 1.00
59 Juan Marichal .40 1.00
60 Keith Hernandez .25 .60
61 Ken Griffey Sr. .25 .60
62 Kent Hrbek .25 .60
63 Kevin Mitchell .25 .60
64 Kirk Gibson .25 .60
65 Larry Doby .40 1.00
66 Lou Boudreau .40 1.00
67 Lou Brock .40 1.00
68 Luis Aparicio .40 1.00
69 Luke Appling .40 1.00
70 Monte Irvin .40 1.00
71 Nellie Fox .40 1.00
72 Norm Cash .25 .60
73 Orlando Cepeda .40 1.00
74 Pedro Guerrero .25 .60
75 Pee Wee Reese .40 1.00
76 Phil Niekro .40 1.00
77 Phil Rizzuto .40 1.00
78 Ralph Kiner .40 1.00
79 Ray Dandridge .25 .60
80 Red Schoendienst .40 1.00
81 Richie Ashburn .40 1.00
82 Rick Ferrell .25 .60
83 Robin Roberts .40 1.00
84 Rollie Fingers .40 1.00
85 Ron Cey .25 .60
86 Sparky Anderson .40 1.00
87 Stan Coveleski .40 1.00
88 Ted Kluszewski .40 1.00
89 Ted Lyons .25 .60
90 Tom Seaver .40 1.00
91 Tommie Agee .25 .60
92 Tommy Lasorda .40 1.00
93 Tony Perez .40 1.00
94 Vada Pinson .25 .60
95 Waite Hoyt .25 .60
96 Warren Spahn .40 1.00
97 Willie McCovey .40 1.00
98 Lyman Bostock .25 .60
99 Willie Stargell .40 1.00
100 Yogi Berra .60 1.50
101 Andre Dawson RSR 1.25 3.00
102 Andy Van Slyke RSR .75 2.00
103 Bret Saberhagen RSR .75 2.00
104 Carl Yastrzemski RSR 2.50 6.00
105 Carlton Fisk RSR 1.25 3.00
106 Dale Murphy RSR 2.00 5.00
107 Darryl Strawberry RSR .75 2.00
108 David Cone RSR .75 2.00
109 Dennis Eckersley RSR 1.25 3.00
110 Don Mattingly RSR 4.00 10.00
111 Dwight Gooden RSR .75 2.00
112 Eddie Murray RSR 1.25 3.00
113 Eric Davis RSR .75 2.00
114 Fred Lynn RSR .75 2.00
115 George Brett RSR 4.00 10.00
116 Jim Rice RSR 1.25 3.00
117 John Kruk RSR .75 2.00
118 Lenny Dykstra RSR .75 2.00
119 Mickey Mantle RSR 6.00 15.00
120 Mike Schmidt RSR 3.00 8.00
121 Nolan Ryan RSR 6.00 15.00
122 Ozzie Smith RSR 2.50 6.00
123 Paul Molitor RSR 2.00 5.00
124 Robin Yount RSR 2.00 5.00
125 Ryne Sandberg RSR 4.00 10.00
126 Steve Carlton RSR 1.25 3.00
127 Ted Williams RSR 4.00 10.00
128 Tony Gwynn RSR 2.50 6.00
129 Wade Boggs RSR 1.25 3.00
130 Will Clark RSR 1.25 3.00

2005 Upper Deck Classics Gold

*GOLD 1-100: 2X TO 5X BASIC
*GOLD 101-130: .6X TO 1.5X BASIC
OVERALL INSERT ODDS 1:7 H, 1:14 R
STATED PRINT RUN 199 SERIAL #'d SETS

2005 Upper Deck Classics Platinum

*PLATINUM 1-100: 4X TO 10X BASIC
*PLATINUM 101-130: 1.5X TO 4X BASIC
OVERALL INSERT ODDS 1:7
STATED PRINT RUN 25 SERIAL #'d SETS

2005 Upper Deck Classics Silver

*SILVER 1-100: 1.5X TO 4X BASIC
*SILVER 101-130: .5X TO 1.2X BASIC
OVERALL INSERT ODDS 1:7
STATED PRINT RUN 399 SERIAL #'d SETS

2005 Upper Deck Classics UD Promos

*PROMOS: .6X TO 1.5X BASIC

2005 Upper Deck Classics Counterparts

OVERALL INSERT ODDS 1:7 H, 1:14 R
STATED PRINT RUN 1999 SERIAL #'d SETS
CC W.Clark 1.00 2.50
J.Clark
CG D.Cone .60 1.50
D.Gooden
DS D.Strawberry .60 1.50
L.Dykstra
GB T.Gwynn 2.00 5.00
W.Boggs
GP T.Perez 1.00 2.50
K.Griffey Sr.
KD L.Dykstra .60 1.50
J.Kruk
KH J.Kruk .60 1.50
K.Hrbek
LR J.Rice 1.00 2.50
F.Lynn
MC K.Mitchell 1.00 2.50
W.Clark
MH D.Mattingly 3.00 8.00
K.Hernandez
MY P.Molitor 1.50 4.00
R.Yount
NC R.Cey .60 1.50
G.Nettles
PH B.Powell .60 1.50
F.Howard
RC N.Ryan 5.00 12.00
S.Carlton
RL B.Russell .60 1.50
D.Lopes
RS N.Ryan 5.00 12.00
T.Seaver
SD D.Strawberry .60 1.50
E.Davis
SG D.Strawberry .60 1.50
D.Gooden
SR C.Ripken 5.00 12.00
M.Schmidt
VC A.Van Slyke .60 1.50
J.Clark

2005 Upper Deck Classics Counterparts Materials

STATED ODDS 1:448 H, 1:1120 R
STATED PRINT RUN 84 SETS
CARDS ARE NOT SERIAL-NUMBERED
PRINT RUN INFO PROVIDED BY UD
CC W.Clark Jsy/J.Clark Jsy 10.00 25.00
CG Cone Jsy/Gooden Jsy 6.00 15.00
DS Strawberry Jsy/Dykstra Jsy 12.50 30.00
GB Gwynn Jsy/Boggs Jsy 10.00 25.00
GP Perez Jsy/Griffey Sr. Jsy 6.00 15.00
KD Dykstra Jsy/Kruk Bat 10.00 25.00
KH Kruk Bat/Hrbek Pants 10.00 25.00
LR Rice Pants/Lynn Jsy 6.00 15.00
MC Mitchell Jsy/W.Clark Jsy 10.00 25.00
MH Mattingly Jsy/K.Hern Jsy 12.50 30.00
MY Molitor Jsy/Yount Jsy 10.00 25.00
NC Cey Pants/Nettles Jsy 6.00 15.00
PH Powell Bat/Howard Jsy 6.00 15.00
RC Ryan Jsy/Carlton Pants 15.00 40.00
RL Russell Pants/Lopes Jsy 6.00 15.00
RS Ryan Jsy/Seaver Jsy 20.00 50.00
SD Strawberry Jsy/E.Davis Jsy 10.00 25.00
SG Straw Jsy/Gooden Pants 6.00 15.00
SR Ripken Jsy/Schmidt Jsy 30.00 60.00
VC Van Slyke Jsy/J.Clark Jsy 12.50 30.00

2005 Upper Deck Classics Counterparts Signatures

TIER 3 PRINT RUNS 105+ COPIES PER
TIER 2 PRINT RUNS B/WN 35-50 PER
TIER 1 PRINT RUNS B/WN 5-10 PER
NO TIER 1 OR 2 PRICING DUE TO SCARCITY
STATED ODDS 1:448 H
CARDS ARE NOT SERIAL-NUMBERED
PRINT RUN INFO PROVIDED BY UD
DS D.Strawberry/L.Dykstra T3 10.00 25.00
GP T.Perez/K.Griffey Sr. T3 10.00 25.00
KH J.Kruk/K.Hrbek T3 6.00 15.00
NC R.Cey/G.Nettles T3 10.00 25.00
PH B.Powell/F.Howard T3 10.00 25.00
RL B.Russell/D.Lopes T3 10.00 25.00

2005 Upper Deck Classics Fantasy Team

ONE CUT OR WOOD PER 448 HOBBY PACKS
STATED PRINT RUN 36 SETS
CARDS ARE NOT SERIAL-NUMBERED
PRINT RUN INFO PROVIDED BY UD
1 Nolan Ryan 25.00 60.00
2 Don Drysdale 5.00 12.00
3 Bob Feller 5.00 12.00
4 Bob Gibson 5.00 12.00
5 Tom Seaver 5.00 12.00
6 Dennis Eckersley 5.00 12.00
7 Johnny Bench 8.00 20.00
8 Yogi Berra 8.00 20.00
9 Harmon Killebrew 8.00 20.00
10 Joe Morgan 5.00 12.00
11 Ryne Sandberg 15.00 40.00
12 Mike Schmidt 12.00 30.00
13 George Brett 15.00 40.00
14 Cal Ripken 25.00 60.00
15 Mickey Mantle 25.00 60.00
16 Joe DiMaggio 15.00 40.00
17 Ted Williams 15.00 40.00
18 Carl Yastrzemski 10.00 25.00

2005 Upper Deck Classics League Leaders

OVERALL INSERT ODDS 1:7 H, 1:14 R
STATED PRINT RUN 999 SERIAL #'d SETS
AD Andre Dawson 1.25 3.00
AV Andy Van Slyke .75 2.00
DE Dennis Eckersley 1.25 3.00
DG Dwight Gooden .75 2.00
DM Dale Murphy 2.00 5.00
FH Frank Howard .75 2.00
GB George Bell .75 2.00
GG Goose Gossage 1.25 3.00
HJ Howard Johnson .75 2.00
JC Jack Clark .75 2.00
JR Jim Rice 1.25 3.00
KH Keith Hernandez .75 2.00
KM Kevin Mitchell .75 2.00
LD Lenny Dykstra .75 2.00
MA Don Mattingly 4.00 10.00
PG Pedro Guerrero .75 2.00
PM Paul Molitor 2.00 5.00
TG Tony Gwynn 2.50 6.00
WB Wade Boggs 1.25 3.00
WC Will Clark 1.25 3.00

2005 Upper Deck Classics League Leaders Materials

OVERALL GU ODDS 1:14 HOBBY
AD Andre Dawson Jsy 3.00 8.00
AV Andy Van Slyke Jsy 10.00 25.00
DE Dennis Eckersley Jsy 3.00 8.00
DG Dwight Gooden Pants 3.00 8.00
DM Dale Murphy Jsy 4.00 10.00
FH Frank Howard Jsy 4.00 10.00
GB George Bell Bat 3.00 8.00
GG Goose Gossage Jsy 3.00 8.00
HJ Howard Johnson Jsy 3.00 8.00
JC Jack Clark Jsy 3.00 8.00
JR Jim Rice Pants 3.00 8.00
KH Keith Hernandez Jsy 3.00 8.00
KM Kevin Mitchell Jsy 3.00 8.00
LD Lenny Dykstra Jsy 3.00 8.00
MA Don Mattingly Jsy 6.00 15.00
PG Pedro Guerrero Jsy 3.00 8.00
PM Paul Molitor Jsy 3.00 8.00
TG Tony Gwynn Jsy SP 6.00 15.00
WB Wade Boggs Jsy 4.00 10.00
WC Will Clark Pants 4.00 10.00

2005 Upper Deck Classics League Leaders Signatures

TIER 3 PRINT RUNS 250+ COPIES PER
TIER 2 PRINT RUNS B/WN 72-165 PER
TIER 1 PRINT RUNS B/WN 10-50 PER
NO TIER 1 PRICING DUE TO SCARCITY
OVERALL AU ODDS 1:28 H, 1:1800 R
CARDS ARE NOT SERIAL-NUMBERED
PRINT RUN INFO PROVIDED BY UD
DE Dennis Eckersley T2 6.00 15.00
DG Dwight Gooden T2 6.00 15.00
DM Dale Murphy T3 10.00 25.00
FH Frank Howard T3 6.00 15.00
GB George Bell T3 4.00 10.00
GG Goose Gossage T3 6.00 15.00
HJ Howard Johnson T3 4.00 10.00
JC Jack Clark T3 6.00 15.00
KH Keith Hernandez T2 6.00 15.00
KM Kevin Mitchell T3 4.00 10.00
PG Pedro Guerrero T3 6.00 15.00
PM Paul Molitor T2 6.00 15.00
WC Will Clark T2 15.00 40.00

2005 Upper Deck Classics Materials

STATED ODDS 1:28 HOBBY
OVERALL ODDS 1:28 RETAIL
SP INFO PROVIDED BY UD
AD Andre Dawson Cubs Jsy 3.00 8.00
AD1 Andre Dawson Expos Jsy 3.00 8.00
AV Andy Van Slyke Jsy 10.00 25.00
BP Boog Powell Bat SP 4.00 10.00
BR Bill Russell Pants 3.00 8.00
CA Jose Canseco Jsy 6.00 15.00
CR Cal Ripken Jsy 10.00 25.00
CY Carl Yastrzemski Jsy 6.00 15.00
DC David Cone Jsy 3.00 8.00
DE Dennis Eckersley Jsy 3.00 8.00
DG Dwight Gooden Pants 3.00 8.00
DL Davey Lopes Jsy 3.00 8.00
DM Dale Murphy Jsy 4.00 10.00
DS Darryl Strawberry Jsy 3.00 8.00
ED Eric Davis Jsy 4.00 10.00
FH Frank Howard Jsy 4.00 10.00
FI Carlton Fisk Jsy 4.00 10.00
FL Fred Lynn Jsy 3.00 8.00
GB George Brett Jsy 6.00 15.00
GG Goose Gossage Jsy 3.00 8.00
GI Kirk Gibson Jsy 3.00 8.00
GN Graig Nettles Jsy 3.00 8.00
HR Kent Hrbek Pants 3.00 8.00
JC Jack Clark Jsy 3.00 8.00
JM Jack Morris Jsy 3.00 8.00
JO Joe Carter Jsy 3.00 8.00
JR Jim Rice Pants 3.00 8.00
KG Ken Griffey Sr. Jsy 3.00 8.00
KH Keith Hernandez Jsy 3.00 8.00
LD Lenny Dykstra Jsy 3.00 8.00
MA Don Mattingly Jsy 6.00 15.00
MS Mike Schmidt Jsy 6.00 15.00
NR Nolan Ryan Jsy 8.00 20.00
PG Pedro Guerrero Jsy 3.00 8.00
PM Paul Molitor Brew Jsy 3.00 8.00
PM1 Paul Molitor Twins Jsy SP 4.00 10.00
RC Ron Cey Pants 3.00 8.00
RS Ryne Sandberg Jsy 6.00 15.00
RY Robin Yount Jsy 4.00 10.00
TG Tony Gwynn Jsy 4.00 10.00
WB Wade Boggs Jsy 4.00 10.00
WC Will Clark Pants 4.00 10.00

2005 Upper Deck Classics Moments

OVERALL INSERT ODDS 1:7 H, 1:14 R
STATED PRINT RUN 1999 SERIAL #'d SETS
BS Bret Saberhagen .60 1.50
CA Joe Carter .60 1.50
CR Cal Ripken 5.00 12.00
DS Don Sutton 1.00 2.50
FI Carlton Fisk 1.00 2.50
GP Gaylord Perry 1.00 2.50
JC Jack Clark .60 1.50
JM Jack Morris 1.00 2.50
KG Kirk Gibson .60 1.50
KM Kevin Mitchell .60 1.50
LD Lenny Dykstra .60 1.50
MS Mike Schmidt 2.50 6.00
NR Nolan Ryan 5.00 12.00
PM Paul Molitor 1.50 4.00
RS Ryne Sandberg 3.00 8.00
RY0 Robin Yount 1.50 4.00
SC Steve Carlton 1.00 2.50
TG Tony Gwynn 2.00 5.00
WB Wade Boggs 1.00 2.50
WJ Wally Joyner .60 1.50

2005 Upper Deck Classics Moments Materials

OVERALL GU ODDS 1:14 HOBBY
CA Joe Carter Jsy 3.00 8.00
CR Cal Ripken Jsy 10.00 25.00
DS Don Sutton Jsy 3.00 8.00
FI Carlton Fisk Jsy 4.00 10.00
GP Gaylord Perry Jsy 3.00 8.00
JC Jack Clark Jsy 3.00 8.00
JM Jack Morris Jsy 3.00 8.00
KG Kirk Gibson Jsy 3.00 8.00
KM Kevin Mitchell Jsy 3.00 8.00
LD Lenny Dykstra Jsy 3.00 8.00
MS Mike Schmidt Jsy 6.00 15.00
NR Nolan Ryan Jsy 8.00 20.00
PM Paul Molitor Jsy 3.00 8.00
RS Ryne Sandberg Jsy 6.00 15.00
RY Robin Yount Jsy 4.00 10.00
SC Steve Carlton Pants 3.00 8.00
TG Tony Gwynn Jsy 4.00 10.00
WB Wade Boggs Jsy 4.00 10.00
WJ Wally Joyner Jsy 6.00 15.00

2005 Upper Deck Classics Moments Signatures

TIER 3 PRINT RUNS 350+ COPIES PER
TIER 2 PRINT RUNS B/WN 96-299 PER
TIER 1 PRINT RUNS B/WN 10-50 PER
NO TIER 1 PRICING DUE TO SCARCITY
OVERALL AU ODDS 1:28 H, 1:1560 R
CARDS ARE NOT SERIAL-NUMBERED
PRINT RUN INFO PROVIDED BY UD
BS Bret Saberhagen T3 6.00 15.00
DS Don Sutton T2 6.00 15.00
GP Gaylord Perry T2 6.00 15.00
JC Jack Clark T3 6.00 15.00
JM Jack Morris T3 6.00 15.00
KG Kirk Gibson T2 6.00 15.00
KM Kevin Mitchell T3 4.00 10.00
LD Lenny Dykstra T3 6.00 15.00
MS Mike Schmidt T2 30.00 60.00
RY Robin Yount T2 15.00 40.00
SC Steve Carlton T2 6.00 15.00
TG Tony Gwynn T2 15.00 40.00
WJ Wally Joyner T2 10.00 25.00

2005 Upper Deck Classics Post Season Performers

OVERALL INSERT ODDS 1:7 H, 1:14 R
STATED PRINT RUN 999 SERIAL #'d SETS
BR Brooks Robinson 1.25 3.00
BS Bret Saberhagen .75 2.00
CA Joe Carter .75 2.00
CF Carlton Fisk 1.25 3.00
CR Cal Ripken 6.00 15.00
DC David Cone .75 2.00
DG Dwight Gooden .75 2.00
DS Darryl Strawberry .75 2.00
ED Eric Davis .75 2.00
JC Jack Clark .75 2.00
JK John Kruk .75 2.00
JM Jack Morris 1.25 3.00
JO Jose Canseco 1.25 3.00
KH Kent Hrbek .75 2.00
KM Kevin Mitchell .75 2.00
LD Lenny Dykstra .75 2.00
MS Mike Schmidt 3.00 8.00
PG Pedro Guerrero .75 2.00
PM Paul Molitor 2.00 5.00
WC Will Clark 1.25 3.00

2005 Upper Deck Classics Post Season Performers Materials

OVERALL GU ODDS 1:14 HOBBY
BR Brooks Robinson Pants 4.00 10.00
CA Joe Carter Jsy 3.00 8.00
CF Carlton Fisk Jsy 4.00 10.00
CR Cal Ripken Jsy SP 15.00 40.00
DC David Cone Jsy 3.00 8.00
DG Dwight Gooden Jsy 3.00 8.00
DS Darryl Strawberry Jsy 3.00 8.00
ED Eric Davis Jsy SP 6.00 15.00
JC Jack Clark Jsy SP 4.00 10.00
JK John Kruk Bat SP 6.00 15.00
JM Jack Morris Jsy 3.00 8.00
JO Jose Canseco Jsy 6.00 15.00
KH Kent Hrbek Pants 3.00 8.00
KM Kevin Mitchell Jsy 3.00 8.00
LD Lenny Dykstra Jsy SP 4.00 10.00
MS Mike Schmidt Bat 6.00 15.00
PG Pedro Guerrero Jsy 3.00 8.00
PM Paul Molitor Jsy SP 4.00 10.00
WC Will Clark Pants 4.00 10.00

2005 Upper Deck Classics Post Season Performers Signatures

TIER 3 PRINT RUNS 350+ COPIES PER
TIER 2 PRINT RUNS B/WN 96-299 PER
TIER 1 PRINT RUNS B/WN 10-50 PER
NO TIER 1 PRICING DUE TO SCARCITY
OVERALL AU ODDS 1:28 H, 1:1800 R
CARDS ARE NOT SERIAL-NUMBERED
PRINT RUN INFO PROVIDED BY UD
BS Bret Saberhagen T3 6.00 15.00
DC David Cone T2 6.00 15.00
DG Dwight Gooden T2 6.00 15.00
DS Darryl Strawberry T2 6.00 15.00
ED Eric Davis T2 10.00 25.00
JC Jack Clark T3 6.00 15.00
JK John Kruk T2 10.00 25.00
JM Jack Morris T2 6.00 15.00
KH Kent Hrbek T3 6.00 15.00
KM Kevin Mitchell T3 4.00 10.00
LD Lenny Dykstra T3 6.00 15.00
PG Pedro Guerrero T3 6.00 15.00

2005 Upper Deck Classics Seasons

OVERALL INSERT ODDS 1:7 H, 1:14 R
STATED PRINT RUN 1999 SERIAL #'d SETS
AD Andre Dawson 1.00 2.50
BE George Bell .60 1.50
BS Bret Saberhagen .60 1.50
CL Jack Clark .60 1.50
CR Cal Ripken 5.00 12.00
CY Carl Yastrzemski 2.00 5.00
DC David Cone .60 1.50
DG Dwight Gooden .60 1.50
DM Dale Murphy 1.50 4.00
ED Eric Davis .60 1.50
FL Fred Lynn .60 1.50
JC Jose Canseco 1.00 2.50
JR Jim Rice 1.00 2.50
KG Kirk Gibson .60 1.50
KM Kevin Mitchell .60 1.50
MA Don Mattingly 3.00 8.00
MS Mike Schmidt 2.50 6.00
NR Nolan Ryan 5.00 12.00
RS Ryne Sandberg 3.00 8.00
WC Will Clark 1.00 2.50

2005 Upper Deck Classics Seasons Materials

OVERALL GU ODDS 1:14 HOBBY
AD Andre Dawson Jsy 3.00 8.00
BE George Bell Bat 3.00 8.00
CL Jack Clark Jsy 3.00 8.00
CR Cal Ripken Jsy 6.00 15.00
CY Carl Yastrzemski Jsy 6.00 15.00
DC David Cone Jsy 3.00 8.00
DG Dwight Gooden Pants 3.00 8.00
DM Dale Murphy Jsy 4.00 10.00
ED Eric Davis Jsy SP 6.00 15.00
FL Fred Lynn Jsy 3.00 8.00
JC Jose Canseco Jsy 6.00 15.00
JR Jim Rice Pants 3.00 8.00
KG Kirk Gibson Jsy 3.00 8.00
KM Kevin Mitchell Jsy 3.00 8.00
MA Don Mattingly Jsy 6.00 15.00
MS Mike Schmidt Jsy 6.00 15.00
NR Nolan Ryan Jsy 8.00 20.00
RS Ryne Sandberg Jsy 6.00 15.00
WC Will Clark Pants 4.00 10.00

2005 Upper Deck Classics Seasons Signatures

TIER 3 PRINT RUNS 350+ COPIES PER
TIER 2 PRINT RUNS B/WN 150-175 PER
TIER 1 PRINT RUNS B/WN 10-60 PER
NO TIER 1 PRICING DUE TO SCARCITY
OVERALL AU ODDS 1:28 H, 1:1560 R
CARDS ARE NOT SERIAL-NUMBERED
PRINT RUN INFO PROVIDED BY UD
BE George Bell T3 6.00 15.00
BS Bret Saberhagen T3 6.00 15.00
CL Jack Clark T3 6.00 15.00
DC David Cone T3 6.00 15.00
DG Dwight Gooden T3 6.00 15.00
DM Dale Murphy T2 12.00 30.00
ED Eric Davis T3 8.00 20.00
FL Fred Lynn T2 6.00 15.00
KM Kevin Mitchell T3 6.00 15.00

2001 Upper Deck Coca Cola Ripken

COMPLETE SET (8) 3.00 8.00
1 Cal Ripken Jr. .60 1.50
Receives ROY award from GM Hank Peters
2 Cal Ripken Jr. .60 1.50
Going all out during 1991 AL MVP season
3 Cal Ripken Jr. .60 1.50
Diving to make a play during the 1991 Gold Glove season
4 Cal Ripken Jr. .60 1.50
The Iron Man salutes the crowd during 2131 9-6-95
5 Cal Ripken Jr. .60 1.50
Going deep for home run number 400 9-2-99
6 Cal Ripken Jr. .60 1.50
Connecting for 3000th career hit 4-15-00
7 Cal Ripken Jr. .60 1.50
Holding the 2001 All-Star MVP award 7-10-01
8 Cal Ripken Jr. .60 1.50
Future Hall-of-Famer announces retirement 6-19-01

2014 Upper Deck College Colors

COMPLETE SET (26)
2 Frank Thomas BB .60 1.50
7 Tony Gwynn BB .60 1.50

2001 Upper Deck Decade 1970's

COMPLETE SET (180) 15.00 40.00
1 Nolan Ryan 1.50 4.00
2 Don Baylor .25 .60
3 Bobby Grich .25 .60
4 Reggie Jackson .40 1.00
5 Catfish Hunter .40 1.00
6 Gene Tenace .25 .60
7 Rollie Fingers .25 .60
8 Sal Bando .25 .60
9 Bert Campaneris .25 .60
10 John Mayberry .15 .40
11 Rico Carty .15 .40
12 Gaylord Perry .25 .60
13 Andre Thornton .15 .40
14 Buddy Bell .25 .60
15 Dennis Eckersley .25 .60
16 Ruppert Jones .15 .40
17 Brooks Robinson .40 1.00
18 Tommy Davis .15 .40
19 Eddie Murray .60 1.50
20 Boog Powell .40 1.00
21 Al Oliver .25 .60
22 Jeff Burroughs .15 .40
23 Mike Hargrove .25 .60
24 Dwight Evans .40 1.00
25 Fred Lynn .25 .60
26 Rico Petrocelli .15 .40
27 Carlton Fisk .40 1.00
28 Luis Aparicio .25 .60
29 Amos Otis .15 .40
30 Hal McRae .25 .60
31 Jason Thompson .15 .40
32 Al Kaline .60 1.50
33 Jim Perry .25 .60
34 Bert Blyleven .25 .60
35 Harmon Killebrew .60 1.50
36 Wilbur Wood .25 .60
37 Jim Kaat .25 .60
38 Ron Guidry .25 .60
39 Thurman Munson .60 1.50
40 Graig Nettles .25 .60
41 Bobby Murcer .25 .60
42 Chris Chambliss .25 .60
43 Roy White .15 .40
44 J.R. Richard .25 .60
45 Jose Cruz .25 .60
46 Hank Aaron 1.25 3.00
47 Phil Niekro .25 .60
48 Bob Horner .15 .40
49 Darrell Evans .25 .60
50 Gorman Thomas .25 .60
51 Don Money .15 .40
52 Robin Yount .60 1.50
53 Joe Torre .25 .60
54 Tim McCarver .25 .60
55 Lou Brock .40 1.00
56 Keith Hernandez .25 .60
57 Bill Madlock .25 .60
58 Ron Santo .40 1.00
59 Billy Williams .25 .60
60 Ferguson Jenkins .25 .60
61 Steve Garvey .25 .60
62 Bill Russell .25 .60
63 Maury Wills .25 .60
64 Ron Cey .25 .60
65 Manny Mota .15 .40
66 Ron Fairly .15 .40
67 Steve Rogers .15 .40
68 Gary Carter .25 .60
69 Andre Dawson .25 .60
70 Bobby Bonds .25 .60
71 Jack Clark .25 .60
72 Willie McCovey .25 .60
73 Tom Seaver .40 1.00
74 Bud Harrelson .25 .60
75 Dave Kingman .25 .60
76 Jerry Koosman .25 .60
77 Jon Matlack .15 .40
78 Randy Jones .15 .40
79 Ozzie Smith 1.00 2.50
80 Garry Maddox .15 .40
81 Mike Schmidt 1.25 3.00
82 Greg Luzinski .25 .60
83 Tug McGraw .25 .60
84 Willie Stargell .40 1.00
85 Dave Parker .25 .60
86 Roberto Clemente 1.50 4.00
87 Johnny Bench .60 1.50
88 Joe Morgan .25 .60
89 George Foster .25 .60
90 Ken Griffey Sr. .25 .60
91 Carlton Fisk RF .40 1.00
92 Andre Dawson RF .25 .60
93 Fred Lynn RF .25 .60
94 Eddie Murray RF .60 1.50
95 Bob Horner RF .15 .40
96 Jon Matlack RF .15 .40
97 Mike Hargrove RF .25 .60
98 Robin Yount RF .60 1.50
99 Mike Schmidt RF .60 1.50
100 Gary Carter RF .25 .60
101 Ozzie Smith RF .60 1.50
102 Paul Molitor RF .25 .60
103 Dennis Eckersley RF .25 .60
104 Dale Murphy RF .40 1.00
105 Bert Blyleven RF .25 .60
106 Thurman Munson RF .60 1.50
107 Dave Parker RF .25 .60
108 Jack Clark RF .25 .60
109 Keith Hernandez RF .25 .60
110 Ron Cey RF .25 .60
111 Billy Williams DD .15 .40
112 Tom Seaver DD .25 .60
113 Reggie Jackson DD .25 .60
114 Bobby Bonds DD .15 .40
115 Willie Stargell DD .25 .60
116 Harmon Killebrew DD .60 1.50
117 Roberto Clemente DD .75 2.00
118 Wilbur Wood DD .15 .40
119 Billy Williams DD .15 .40
120 Nolan Ryan DD .75 2.00
121 Ron Blomberg DD .15 .40
122 Hank Aaron DD .60 1.50
123 Lou Brock DD .25 .60
124 Al Kaline DD .40 1.00
125 Brooks Robinson DD .25 .60
126 Bill Madlock DD .15 .40
127 Rennie Stennett DD .15 .40
128 Carlton Fisk DD .25 .60
129 Chris Chambliss DD .15 .40
130 Ruppert Jones DD .15 .40
131 Ron Fairly DD .15 .40
132 George Foster DD .15 .40
133 Reggie Jackson DD .25 .60
134 Ron Guidry DD .15 .40
135 Gaylord Perry DD .15 .40
136 Bucky Dent DD .15 .40
137 Dave Kingman DD .15 .40
138 Lou Brock DD .25 .60
139 Thurman Munson DD .40 1.00
140 Willie Stargell DD .25 .60
141 Johnny Bench AW .40 1.00
142 Boog Powell AW .25 .60
143 Jim Perry AW .15 .40
144 Joe Torre AW .15 .40
145 Chris Chambliss AW .15 .40
146 Ferguson Jenkins AW .15 .40
147 Carlton Fisk AW .25 .60
148 Gaylord Perry AW .25 .60
149 Johnny Bench AW .40 1.00
150 Reggie Jackson AW .25 .60
151 Tom Seaver AW .25 .60
152 Thurman Munson AW .40 1.00
153 Steve Garvey AW .15 .40
154 Catfish Hunter AW .25 .60
155 Mike Hargrove AW .15 .40
156 Joe Morgan AW .15 .40
157 Fred Lynn AW .15 .40
158 Tom Seaver AW .25 .60
159 Thurman Munson AW .40 1.00
160 Randy Jones AW .15 .40
161 Joe Morgan AW .15 .40
162 George Foster AW .15 .40
163 Eddie Murray AW .40 1.00
164 Andre Dawson AW .15 .40
165 Gaylord Perry AW .15 .40
166 Ron Guidry AW .15 .40
167 Dave Parker AW .15 .40
168 Don Baylor AW .15 .40
169 Bruce Sutter AW .15 .40
170 Willie Stargell AW .25 .60
171 Brooks Robinson WS .25 .60
172 Roberto Clemente WS .75 2.00
173 Gene Tenace WS .15 .40
174 Reggie Jackson WS .25 .60
175 Rollie Fingers WS .15 .40
176 Carlton Fisk WS .25 .60
177 Johnny Bench WS .40 1.00
178 Reggie Jackson WS .25 .60
179 Bucky Dent WS .15 .40
180 Willie Stargell WS .25 .60

2001 Upper Deck Decade 1970's Arms Race

COMPLETE SET (10) 10.00 25.00
STATED ODDS 1:14
AR1 Nolan Ryan 3.00 8.00
AR2 Ferguson Jenkins .50 1.25
AR3 Jim Hunter .75 2.00
AR4 Tom Seaver .75 2.00
AR5 Randy Jones .50 1.25
AR6 J.R. Richard .50 1.25
AR7 Rollie Fingers .50 1.25
AR8 Gaylord Perry .50 1.25
AR9 Ron Guidry .50 1.25
AR10 Phil Niekro .50 1.25

2001 Upper Deck Decade 1970's Bellbottomed Bashers

COMPLETE SET (10) 10.00 25.00
STATED ODDS 1:14
BB1 Reggie Jackson .75 2.00
BB2 Gorman Thomas .50 1.25
BB3 Willie McCovey .50 1.25
BB4 Willie Stargell .75 2.00
BB5 Mike Schmidt 2.50 6.00
BB6 George Foster .50 1.25
BB7 Johnny Bench 1.25 3.00
BB8 Dave Kingman .50 1.25
BB9 Graig Nettles .50 1.25
BB10 Steve Garvey .50 1.25

2001 Upper Deck Decade 1970's Disco Era Dandies

COMPLETE SET (6) 8.00 20.00
STATED ODDS 1:23
DE1 Mike Schmidt 2.50 6.00
DE2 Johnny Bench 1.25 3.00
DE3 Lou Brock .75 2.00
DE4 Reggie Jackson .75 2.00
DE5 Willie Stargell .75 2.00
DE6 Tom Seaver .75 2.00

2001 Upper Deck Decade 1970's Dynasties

COMPLETE SET (10) 10.00 25.00
STATED ODDS 1:14
D1 Boog Powell .50 1.25
D2 Johnny Bench 1.25 3.00
D3 Willie Stargell .75 2.00
D4 Jim Hunter .75 2.00
D5 Steve Garvey .50 1.25
D6 Carlton Fisk .75 2.00
D7 Mike Schmidt 2.50 6.00
D8 Hal McRae .50 1.25
D9 Tom Seaver .75 2.00
D10 Reggie Jackson .75 2.00

2001 Upper Deck Decade 1970's Game Bat

STATED ODDS 1:24 HOBBY, 1:48 RETAIL
SP PRINT RUNS PROVIDED BY UPPER DECK
SP'S ARE NOT SERIAL-NUMBERED
BAD Andre Dawson 4.00 10.00
BAO Al Oliver 4.00 10.00
BBB Bobby Bonds 4.00 10.00
BBG Bobby Grich 4.00 10.00
BBH Bud Harrelson SP/290 * 4.00 10.00
BBIM Bill Madlock 4.00 10.00
BBOM Bobby Murcer 15.00 40.00
BBP Boog Powell 6.00 15.00
BBR Bill Russell 4.00 10.00
BCF Carlton Fisk 6.00 15.00
BDAE Darrell Evans 4.00 10.00
BDB Don Baylor 4.00 10.00
BDC Dave Concepcion 4.00 10.00
BDP Dave Parker 4.00 10.00
BDW Dave Winfield 4.00 10.00
BDWE Dwight Evans 6.00 15.00
BEM Eddie Murray 6.00 15.00
BFL Fred Lynn 4.00 10.00
BGC Gary Carter 4.00 10.00
BGF George Foster 4.00 10.00
BGL Greg Luzinski 4.00 10.00
BGM Garry Maddox 4.00 10.00
BHA Hank Aaron 12.50 30.00
BHM Hal McRae 4.00 10.00
BJAC Jack Clark 4.00 10.00
BJM Joe Morgan 4.00 10.00
BJOC Jose Cruz 4.00 10.00
BKG Ken Griffey Sr. 4.00 10.00
BKH Keith Hernandez SP/243 * 10.00 25.00
BMM Manny Mota 4.00 10.00
BMW Maury Wills 4.00 10.00
BNR Nolan Ryan 10.00 25.00
BOS Ozzie Smith 6.00 15.00
BRAJ Randy Jones 4.00 10.00
BRC Roberto Clemente SP/243 * 12.50 30.00
BREJ Reggie Jackson 6.00 15.00
BRH Ron Hunt 4.00 10.00
BRM Rick Monday 4.00 10.00
BRS Ron Santo 6.00 15.00

BRW Roy White 4.00 10.00
BSG Steve Garvey 4.00 10.00
BTD Tommy Davis 4.00 10.00
BTIM Tim McCarver 4.00 10.00
BTOS Tom Seaver SP/121 * 15.00 40.00
BWM Willie Montanez 4.00 10.00
BWR Willie Randolph 4.00 10.00

2001 Upper Deck Decade 1970's Game Bat Combos

STATED ODDS 1:336
SP PRINT RUNS PROVIDED BY UPPER DECK
SP'S ARE NOT SERIAL-NUMBERED
LA Steve Garvey 10.00 25.00
Ron Cey
Bill Russell
Rick Monday
RD Fost/Morg/Cey/Russ 10.00 25.00
RY Cham/Reg/White/SP/238 * 40.00 80.00
WS72 Reg/Bert/Bench SP/97 30.00 60.00
WS73 Reggie/Bert/Seaver/Harr 15.00 40.00
WS74 Reggie/Bert/Garvey/Cey 15.00 40.00
WS75 Fisk/Lynn/Foster/Morg 15.00 40.00
WS76 Cha/Nett/Ben/Gril SP/97 * 40.00 80.00
WS77 Reggie/Nett/Garv/Cey 10.00 25.00
WS78 Net/Cha/Cey SP/238 * 15.00 40.00
BAT Hern/Madl/Lynn/Parker 10.00 25.00
CIN Bench/Fost/Grif/Morgan 30.00 60.00
GGA Fisk/Nettles/Grich/Lynn 15.00 40.00
GGN Bench/Clem/Conc/Mdx 30.00 60.00
NYM Seav/Harr/Hunt/McGr 10.00 25.00
NYY Reggie/Nett/Cham/White 10.00 25.00
ROY Dawson/Lynn/Fisk/Murray 15.00 40.00
ASMV Madl/Morg/Garv/Parker 10.00 25.00
MVPN Bench/Garv/Starg/Fost 20.00 50.00

2001 Upper Deck Decade 1970's Game Jersey

STATED ODDS 1:168
SP PRINT RUNS PROVIDED BY UPPER DECK
SP'S ARE NOT SERIAL-NUMBERED
JBH Burt Hooton 4.00 10.00
JBM Bobby Murcer 15.00 40.00
JBM Bill Madlock 4.00 10.00
JCF Carlton Fisk 6.00 15.00
JCH Catfish Hunter 6.00 15.00
JHA Hank Aaron 10.00 25.00
JJB Johnny Bench 6.00 15.00
JJKA Jim Kaat 4.00 10.00
JJKO Jerry Koosman 4.00 10.00
JJM Jon Matlack 4.00 10.00
JJP Jim Perry 4.00 10.00
JLA Luis Aparicio 4.00 10.00
JLP Lou Piniella 4.00 10.00
JMW Maury Wills 4.00 10.00
JNR Nolan Ryan SP/50 * 30.00 60.00
JRC Roberto Clemente 20.00 50.00
JRF Rollie Fingers 4.00 10.00
JRG Ron Guidry 4.00 10.00
JTM Tug McGraw 4.00 10.00
JTS Tom Seaver 6.00 15.00
JWD Willie Davis 4.00 10.00
JWR Willie Randolph 4.00 10.00
JWS Willie Stargell 6.00 15.00

2001 Upper Deck Decade 1970's Game Jersey Autograph

STATED ODDS 1:168 HOBBY, 1:480 RETAIL
SP PRINT RUNS PROVIDED BY UPPER DECK
SP'S ARE NOT SERIAL-NUMBERED
SJBH Burt Hooton 10.00 25.00
SJBM Bobby Murcer 10.00 25.00
SJBM Bill Madlock 10.00 25.00
SJCF Carlton Fisk SP/243 * 15.00 40.00
SJHA Hank Aaron SP/97 * 150.00 250.00
SJJB Johnny Bench 30.00 60.00
SJJKA Jim Kaat 6.00 15.00
SJJKO Jerry Koosman 6.00 15.00
SJKG Ken Griffey Sr. 6.00 15.00
SJLA Luis Aparicio 10.00 25.00
SJMW Maury Wills 10.00 25.00
SJNR Nolan Ryan SP/291 * 60.00 150.00
SJRF Rollie Fingers 6.00 15.00
SJRG Ron Guidry 10.00 25.00
SJRJ Reggie Jackson SP/291 * 50.00 100.00
SJRP Rico Petrocelli 6.00 15.00
SJSB Sal Bando 6.00 15.00
SJTM Tug McGraw 20.00 50.00

2001 Upper Deck Decade 1970's Super Powers

COMPLETE SET (6) 8.00 20.00
STATED ODDS 1:23
SP1 Reggie Jackson .75 2.00
SP2 Joe Morgan .75 2.00
SP3 Willie Stargell .75 2.00
SP4 Willie McCovey .75 2.00
SP5 Mike Schmidt 2.50 6.00
SP6 Nolan Ryan 3.00 8.00

2002 Upper Deck Diamond Connection

COMP.LOW w/o SP's (90) 10.00 25.00
COMP.UPDATE w/o SP's (30) 4.00 10.00
COMMON CARD (1-90) .15 .40
COMMON CARD (91-200) 1.50 4.00
91-200: TWO PER 7-PACK MINI BOX
91-200 PRINT RUN 1500 SERIAL #'d SETS
BAT/JSY: ONE PER 7-PACK MINI BOX
DC JSY 201-270/537-547 PRINT 775 #'d SETS
BLH JSY 271-320/548-550 PRINT 200 #'d SETS
HM JSY 321-353/551-552 PRINT 150 #'d SETS
FC JSY 354-368/553 PRINT 100 #'d SETS
DC BAT 369-438/554-564 PRINT 775 #'d SETS
BLH BAT 439-488/565-567 PRINT 200 #'d SETS
HM BAT 489-521/568-569 PRINT 150 #'d SETS
FC BAT 522-536/570 PRINT 100 #'d SETS
COMMON CARD (571-600) .25 .60
COMMON CARD (601-630) 2.00 5.00
601-630 RANDOM IN ROOKIE UPD.PACKS
601-630 PRINT RUN 1999 SERIAL #'d SETS
571-630 DISTRIBUTED IN ROOKIE UPD.PACKS
1 Troy Glaus .15 .40
2 Darin Erstad .15 .40
3 Barry Zito .15 .40
4 Eric Chavez .15 .40
5 Tim Hudson .15 .40
6 Miguel Tejada .15 .40
7 Carlos Delgado .15 .40
8 Shannon Stewart .15 .40
9 Greg Vaughn .15 .40
10 Jim Thome .25 .60
11 C.C. Sabathia .15 .40
12 Ichiro Suzuki .75 2.00
13 Edgar Martinez .25 .60
14 Bret Boone .15 .40
15 Freddy Garcia .15 .40
16 Jeff Conine .15 .40
17 Alex Rodriguez .50 1.50
18 Rafael Palmeiro .25 .60
19 Ivan Rodriguez .25 .60
20 Juan Gonzalez .15 .40
21 Pedro Martinez .25 .60
22 Nomar Garciaparra .60 1.50
23 Manny Ramirez .25 .60
24 Carlos Beltran .15 .40
25 Mike Sweeney .15 .40
26 Dmitri Young .15 .40
27 Bobby Higginson .15 .40
28 Corey Koskie .15 .40
29 Cristian Guzman .15 .40
30 Doug Mientkiewicz .15 .40
31 Torii Hunter .15 .40
32 Frank Thomas .40 1.00
33 Mark Buehrle .15 .40
34 Carlos Lee .15 .40
35 Magglio Ordonez .15 .40
36 Roger Clemens .75 2.00
37 Bernie Williams .25 .60
38 Jason Giambi .15 .40
39 Derek Jeter 1.00 2.50
40 Mike Mussina .25 .60
41 Jeff Bagwell .25 .60
42 Richard Hidalgo .15 .40
43 Lance Berkman .15 .40
44 Roy Oswalt .15 .40
45 Chipper Jones .40 1.00
46 Gary Sheffield .15 .40
47 Andruw Jones .25 .60
48 Greg Maddux .60 1.50
49 Geoff Jenkins .15 .40
50 Ben Sheets .15 .40
51 Richie Sexson .15 .40
52 Albert Pujols .75 2.00
53 Matt Morris .15 .40
54 J.D. Drew .15 .40
55 Tino Martinez .15 .40
56 Sammy Sosa .40 1.00
57 Kerry Wood .15 .40
58 Moises Alou .15 .40
59 Fred McGriff .25 .60
60 Randy Johnson .40 1.00
61 Luis Gonzalez .15 .40
62 Curt Schilling .15 .40
63 Kevin Brown .15 .40
64 Shawn Green .15 .40
65 Paul LoDuca .15 .40
66 Vladimir Guerrero .40 1.00
67 Jose Vidro .15 .40
68 Barry Bonds 1.00 2.50
69 Jeff Kent .15 .40
70 Rich Aurilia .15 .40
71 Preston Wilson .15 .40
72 Josh Beckett .15 .40
73 Cliff Floyd .15 .40
74 Mike Piazza .60 1.50
75 Mo Vaughn .15 .40
76 Roberto Alomar .25 .60
77 Jeromy Burnitz .15 .40
78 Phil Nevin .15 .40
79 Sean Burroughs .15 .40
80 Scott Rolen .25 .60
81 Bob Abreu .15 .40
82 Pat Burrell .15 .40
83 Brian Giles .15 .40
84 Jason Kendall .15 .40
85 Ken Griffey Jr. .75 2.00
86 Adam Dunn .15 .40
87 Aaron Boone .15 .40
88 Larry Walker .15 .40
89 Todd Helton .25 .60
90 Mike Hampton .15 .40
91 Brandon Puffer DC RC 1.50 4.00
92 Rodrigo Rosario DC RC 1.50 4.00
93 Tom Shearn DC RC 1.50 4.00
94 Morgan Ensberg DC 1.50 4.00
95 Jason Lane DC 1.50 4.00
96 Franklyn German DC RC 1.50 4.00
97 Carlos Pena DC 1.50 4.00
98 Joe Orloski DC RC 1.50 4.00
99 Reed Johnson DC RC 2.00 5.00
100 Chris Baker DC RC 1.50 4.00
101 Corey Thurman DC RC 1.50 4.00
102 Gustavo Chacin DC RC 2.00 5.00
103 Eric Hinske DC 1.50 4.00
104 John Foster DC RC 1.50 4.00
105 John Ennis DC RC 1.50 4.00
106 Kevin Gryboski DC RC 1.50 4.00
107 Jung Bong DC 1.50 4.00
108 Travis Wilson DC 1.50 4.00
109 Luis Martinez DC RC 1.50 4.00
110 Brian Mallette DC RC 1.50 4.00
111 Takahito Nomura DC RC 1.50 4.00
112 Bill Hall DC 1.50 4.00
113 Jeff Deardorff DC 1.50 4.00
114 Cristian Guerrero DC 1.50 4.00
115 Scotty Layfield DC RC 1.50 4.00
116 Mike Crudale DC RC 1.50 4.00
117 So Taguchi DC RC 2.00 5.00
118 Jeremy Lambert DC RC 1.50 4.00
119 Jim Journell DC 1.50 4.00
120 Francis Beltran DC RC 1.50 4.00
121 Mark Prior DC 2.00 5.00
122 Ben Christensen DC 1.50 4.00
123 Jorge Sosa DC RC 2.00 5.00
124 Brandon Backe DC RC 2.00 5.00
125 Steve Kent DC RC 1.50 4.00
126 Felix Escalona DC RC 1.50 4.00
127 P.J. Bevis DC RC 1.50 4.00
128 Jose Valverde DC RC 1.50 4.00
129 Doug Devore DC RC 1.50 4.00
130 Jeremy Ward DC RC 1.50 4.00
131 Mike Koplove DC 1.50 4.00
132 Luis Terrero DC 1.50 4.00
133 John Patterson DC 1.50 4.00
134 Victor Alvarez DC RC 1.50 4.00
135 Kirk Saarloos DC RC 1.50 4.00
136 Kazuhisa Ishii DC RC 2.00 5.00
137 Steve Colyer DC 1.50 4.00
138 Cesar Izturis DC 1.50 4.00
139 Ron Calloway DC RC 1.50 4.00
140 Eric Good DC RC 1.50 4.00
141 Jorge Nunez DC RC 1.50 4.00
142 Ron Chiavacci DC 1.50 4.00
143 Donnie Bridges DC 1.50 4.00
144 Nelson Castro DC RC 1.50 4.00
145 Deivis Santos DC 1.50 4.00
146 Kurt Ainsworth DC 1.50 4.00
147 Arturo McDowell DC 1.50 4.00
148 Allan Simpson DC RC 1.50 4.00
149 Matt Thornton DC RC 1.50 4.00
150 Luis Ugueto DC RC 1.50 4.00
151 J.J. Putz DC RC 1.50 4.00
152 Hansel Izquierdo DC RC 1.50 4.00
153 Oliver Perez DC RC 2.00 5.00
154 Jaime Cerda DC RC 1.50 4.00
155 Mark Corey DC RC 1.50 4.00
156 Tyler Yates DC RC 1.50 4.00
157 Satoru Komiyama DC RC 1.50 4.00
158 Adam Walker DC RC 1.50 4.00
159 Steve Bechler DC RC 1.50 4.00
160 Erik Bedard DC 1.50 4.00
161 Todd Donovan DC RC 1.50 4.00
162 Clifford Bartosh DC RC 1.50 4.00
163 Ben Howard DC RC 1.50 4.00
164 Andy Shibilo DC RC 1.50 4.00
165 Dennis Tankersley DC 1.50 4.00
166 Mike Bynum DC 1.50 4.00
167 Anderson Machado DC RC 1.50 4.00
168 Pete Zamora DC RC 1.50 4.00
169 Eric Junge DC RC 1.50 4.00
170 Elio Serrano DC RC 1.50 4.00
171 Jorge Padilla DC RC 1.50 4.00
172 Marlon Byrd DC 1.50 4.00
173 Adrian Burnside DC RC 1.50 4.00
174 Mike Gonzalez DC RC 1.50 4.00
175 J.R. House DC 1.50 4.00
176 Hank Blalock DC 2.00 5.00
177 Travis Hughes DC RC 1.50 4.00
178 Mark Teixeira DC 2.00 5.00
179 Josh Hancock DC RC 2.00 5.00
180 Anastacio Martinez DC RC 1.50 4.00
181 Jorge de la Rosa DC RC 1.50 4.00
182 Ben Broussard DC 1.50 4.00
183 Austin Kearns DC 1.50 4.00
184 Corky Miller DC 1.50 4.00
185 Colin Young DC RC 1.50 4.00
186 Cam Esslinger DC RC 1.50 4.00
187 Rene Reyes DC RC 1.50 4.00
188 Aaron Cook DC RC 1.50 4.00
189 Alexis Gomez DC 1.50 4.00
190 Nate Field DC RC 1.50 4.00
191 Miguel Asencio DC RC 1.50 4.00
192 Brandon Berger DC 1.50 4.00
193 Fernando Rodney DC 1.50 4.00
194 Andy Van Hekken DC 1.50 4.00
195 Kevin Frederick DC RC 1.50 4.00
196 Todd Sears DC 1.50 4.00
197 Edwin Almonte DC RC 1.50 4.00
198 Kyle Kane DC RC 1.50 4.00
199 Mitch Wylie DC RC 1.50 4.00
200 Mike Porzio DC 1.50 4.00
201 Darin Erstad DC Jsy 4.00 10.00
202 Tim Salmon DC Jsy 6.00 15.00
203 Jeff Bagwell DC Jsy 6.00 15.00
204 Lance Berkman DC Jsy 4.00 10.00
205 Eric Chavez DC Jsy 4.00 10.00
206 Tim Hudson DC Jsy 4.00 10.00
207 Carlos Delgado DC Jsy 4.00 10.00
208 Chipper Jones DC Jsy 6.00 15.00
209 Gary Sheffield DC Jsy 4.00 10.00
210 Greg Maddux DC Jsy 6.00 15.00
211 Tom Glavine DC Jsy 6.00 15.00
212 Mike Mussina DC Jsy 6.00 15.00
213 J.D. Drew DC Jsy 4.00 10.00
214 Rick Ankiel DC Jsy 4.00 10.00
215 Sammy Sosa DC Jsy 6.00 15.00
216 Mike Lieberthal DC Jsy 4.00 10.00
217 Fred McGriff DC Jsy 6.00 15.00
218 David Wells DC Jsy 4.00 10.00
219 Curt Schilling DC Jsy 4.00 10.00
220 Luis Gonzalez DC Jsy 4.00 10.00
221 Mark Grace DC Jsy 6.00 15.00
222 Kevin Brown DC Jsy 4.00 10.00
223 Hideo Nomo DC Jsy 10.00 25.00
224 Jose Vidro DC Jsy 4.00 10.00
225 Jeff Kent DC Jsy 4.00 10.00
226 Rich Aurilia DC Jsy 4.00 10.00
227 Kenny Lofton DC Jsy 4.00 10.00
228 C.C. Sabathia DC Jsy 4.00 10.00
229 Edgar Martinez DC Jsy 6.00 15.00
230 Freddy Garcia DC Jsy 4.00 10.00
231 Cliff Floyd DC Jsy 4.00 10.00
232 Preston Wilson DC Jsy 4.00 10.00
233 Mike Piazza DC Jsy 6.00 15.00
234 Roberto Alomar DC Jsy 6.00 15.00
235 Trevor Hoffman DC Jsy 4.00 10.00
236 Ryan Klesko DC Jsy 4.00 10.00
237 Sean Burroughs DC Jsy 4.00 10.00
238 Scott Rolen DC Jsy 6.00 15.00
239 Pat Burrell DC Jsy 4.00 10.00
240 Edgardo Alfonzo DC Jsy 4.00 10.00
241 Brian Giles DC Jsy 4.00 10.00
242 Jason Kendall DC Jsy 4.00 10.00
243 Alex Rodriguez DC Jsy 8.00 20.00
244 Juan Gonzalez DC Jsy 4.00 10.00
245 Ivan Rodriguez DC Jsy 6.00 15.00
246 Rafael Palmeiro DC Jsy 6.00 15.00
247 Ken Griffey Jr. DC Jsy 8.00 20.00
248 Adam Dunn DC Jsy 4.00 10.00
249 Barry Larkin DC Jsy 6.00 15.00
250 Manny Ramirez DC Jsy 6.00 15.00
251 Pedro Martinez DC Jsy 6.00 15.00
252 Todd Helton DC Jsy 6.00 15.00
253 Larry Walker DC Jsy 4.00 10.00
254 Randy Johnson DC Jsy 6.00 15.00
255 Mike Sweeney DC Jsy 4.00 10.00
256 Carlos Beltran DC Jsy 4.00 10.00
257 Dmitri Young DC Jsy SP/380 4.00 10.00
258 Joe Mays DC Jsy 4.00 10.00
259 Doug Mientkiewicz DC Jsy 4.00 10.00
260 Corey Koskie DC Jsy 4.00 10.00
261 Magglio Ordonez DC Jsy 4.00 10.00
262 Frank Thomas DC Jsy 6.00 15.00
263 Ray Durham DC Jsy 4.00 10.00
264 Jason Giambi DC Jsy 4.00 10.00
265 Bernie Williams DC Jsy 6.00 15.00
266 Roger Clemens DC Jsy 10.00 25.00
267 Mariano Rivera DC Jsy 6.00 15.00
268 Robin Ventura DC Jsy 4.00 10.00
269 Andy Pettitte DC Jsy 6.00 15.00
270 Jorge Posada DC Jsy 6.00 15.00
271 Mike Piazza BLH Jsy 8.00 20.00
272 Alex Rodriguez BLH Jsy 10.00 25.00
273 Ken Griffey Jr. BLH Jsy 10.00 25.00
274 Jason Giambi BLH Jsy 6.00 15.00
275 Frank Thomas BLH Jsy 8.00 20.00
276 Greg Maddux BLH Jsy 8.00 20.00
277 Sammy Sosa BLH Jsy 8.00 20.00
278 Roger Clemens BLH Jsy 12.50 30.00
279 Jeff Bagwell BLH Jsy 8.00 20.00
280 Todd Helton BLH Jsy 8.00 20.00
281 Ichiro Suzuki BLH Jsy 10.00 25.00
282 Randy Johnson BLH Jsy 8.00 20.00
283 Jim Thome BLH Jsy 8.00 20.00
284 Ivan Rodriguez BLH Jsy 8.00 20.00
285 Darin Erstad BLH Jsy 6.00 15.00
286 Eric Chavez BLH Jsy 6.00 15.00
287 Barry Zito BLH Jsy 6.00 15.00
288 Carlos Delgado BLH Jsy 6.00 15.00
289 Omar Vizquel BLH Jsy 8.00 20.00
290 Edgar Martinez BLH Jsy 8.00 20.00
291 Manny Ramirez BLH Jsy 8.00 20.00
292 Mike Sweeney BLH Jsy 6.00 15.00
293 Tom Glavine BLH Jsy 8.00 20.00
294 Joe Mays BLH Jsy 4.00 10.00
295 Eric Milton BLH Jsy 4.00 10.00
296 Magglio Ordonez BLH Jsy 6.00 15.00
297 Bernie Williams BLH Jsy 8.00 20.00
298 Trevor Hoffman BLH Jsy 6.00 15.00
299 Andruw Jones BLH Jsy 8.00 20.00
300 Aubrey Huff BLH Jsy 6.00 15.00
301 Jim Edmonds BLH Jsy 6.00 15.00
302 Kerry Wood BLH Jsy 6.00 15.00
303 Luis Gonzalez BLH Jsy 6.00 15.00
304 Shawn Green BLH Jsy 6.00 15.00
305 Jose Vidro BLH Jsy 4.00 10.00
306 Jeff Kent BLH Jsy 6.00 15.00
307 Edgardo Alfonzo BLH Jsy 4.00 10.00
308 Preston Wilson BLH Jsy 6.00 15.00
309 Roberto Alomar BLH Jsy 8.00 20.00
310 Jeromy Burnitz BLH Jsy 6.00 15.00
311 Phil Nevin BLH Jsy 6.00 15.00
312 Ryan Klesko BLH Jsy 6.00 15.00
313 Bob Abreu BLH Jsy 6.00 15.00
314 Scott Rolen BLH Jsy 8.00 20.00
315 Kazuhiro Sasaki BLH Jsy 6.00 15.00
316 Jason Kendall BLH Jsy 6.00 15.00
317 Sean Casey BLH Jsy 6.00 15.00
318 Larry Walker BLH Jsy 6.00 15.00
319 Mike Hampton BLH Jsy 6.00 15.00
320 Juan Gonzalez BLH Jsy 6.00 15.00
321 Darin Erstad HM Jsy 6.00 15.00
322 Tim Hudson HM Jsy 6.00 15.00
323 Carlos Delgado HM Jsy 6.00 15.00
324 Greg Vaughn HM Jsy 6.00 15.00
325 Jim Thome HM Jsy 8.00 20.00
326 Ichiro Suzuki HM Jsy 20.00 50.00
327 Rafael Palmeiro HM Jsy 8.00 20.00
328 Alex Rodriguez HM Jsy 10.00 25.00
329 Juan Gonzalez HM Jsy 6.00 15.00
330 Manny Ramirez HM Jsy 8.00 20.00
331 Carlos Beltran HM Jsy 6.00 15.00
332 Eric Milton HM Jsy 6.00 15.00
333 Frank Thomas HM Jsy 8.00 20.00
334 Roger Clemens HM Jsy 12.50 30.00
335 Jason Giambi HM Jsy 6.00 15.00
336 Lance Berkman HM Jsy 6.00 15.00
337 Greg Maddux HM Jsy 8.00 20.00
338 Chipper Jones HM Jsy 8.00 20.00
339 Sean Casey HM Jsy 6.00 15.00
340 Jim Edmonds HM Jsy 6.00 15.00
341 Kerry Wood HM Jsy 6.00 15.00
342 Sammy Sosa HM Jsy 8.00 20.00
343 Luis Gonzalez HM Jsy 6.00 15.00
344 Shawn Green HM Jsy 6.00 15.00
345 Jeff Kent HM Jsy 6.00 15.00
346 Preston Wilson HM Jsy 6.00 15.00
347 Roberto Alomar HM Jsy 8.00 20.00
348 Phil Nevin HM Jsy 6.00 15.00
349 Scott Rolen HM Jsy 8.00 20.00
350 Mike Sweeney HM Jsy 6.00 15.00
351 Ken Griffey Jr. HM Jsy 10.00 25.00
352 Todd Helton HM Jsy 8.00 20.00
353 Larry Walker HM Jsy 6.00 15.00
354 Alex Rodriguez FC Jsy 12.50 30.00
355 Pedro Martinez FC Jsy 10.00 25.00
356 Frank Thomas FC Jsy 10.00 25.00
357 Jason Giambi FC Jsy 8.00 20.00
358 Bernie Williams FC Jsy 10.00 25.00
359 Jeff Bagwell FC Jsy 10.00 25.00
360 Chipper Jones FC Jsy 10.00 25.00
361 Sammy Sosa FC Jsy 10.00 25.00
362 Randy Johnson FC Jsy 10.00 25.00
363 Shawn Green FC Jsy 8.00 20.00
364 Mike Piazza FC Jsy 10.00 25.00
365 Ichiro Suzuki FC Jsy 30.00 60.00
366 Ken Griffey Jr. FC Jsy 12.50 30.00
367 Larry Walker FC Jsy 8.00 20.00
368 Jim Edmonds FC Jsy 8.00 20.00
369 Darin Erstad DC Bat 4.00 10.00
370 Tim Salmon DC Bat 6.00 15.00
371 Mark Kotsay DC Bat 4.00 10.00
372 Craig Biggio DC Bat 6.00 15.00
373 Eric Chavez DC Bat 4.00 10.00
374 David Justice DC Bat 4.00 10.00
375 Carlos Delgado DC Bat 4.00 10.00
376 Chipper Jones DC Bat 6.00 15.00
377 Gary Sheffield DC Bat 4.00 10.00
378 Greg Maddux DC Bat 6.00 15.00
379 Eric Karros DC Bat 4.00 10.00
380 Fred McGriff DC Bat 6.00 15.00
381 J.D. Drew DC Bat 4.00 10.00
382 Rick Ankiel DC Bat 4.00 10.00
383 Sammy Sosa DC Bat 6.00 15.00
384 Moises Alou DC Bat 4.00 10.00
385 Ben Grieve DC Bat 4.00 10.00
386 Greg Vaughn DC Bat 4.00 10.00
387 Jay Payton DC Bat 4.00 10.00
388 Luis Gonzalez DC Bat 4.00 10.00
389 Ray Durham DC Bat 4.00 10.00
390 Shawn Green DC Bat 4.00 10.00
391 Hideo Nomo DC Bat 10.00 25.00
392 Jose Vidro DC Bat 4.00 10.00
393 Jeff Kent DC Bat 4.00 10.00
394 Adrian Beltre DC Bat 4.00 10.00
395 Jim Thome DC Bat 6.00 15.00
396 Bob Abreu DC Bat 4.00 10.00
397 Edgar Martinez DC Bat 6.00 15.00
398 Carl Everett DC Bat 4.00 10.00
399 Luis Castillo DC Bat 4.00 10.00
400 Preston Wilson DC Bat 4.00 10.00
401 Jermaine Dye DC Bat 4.00 10.00
402 Roberto Alomar DC Bat 6.00 15.00
403 Todd Hundley DC Bat 4.00 10.00
404 Ryan Klesko DC Bat 4.00 10.00
405 Phil Nevin DC Bat 4.00 10.00
406 Scott Rolen DC Bat 6.00 15.00
407 Rafael Furcal DC Bat 4.00 10.00
408 Miguel Tejada DC Bat 4.00 10.00
409 Brian Giles DC Bat 4.00 10.00
410 Jason Kendall DC Bat 4.00 10.00
411 Alex Rodriguez DC Bat 8.00 20.00
412 Juan Gonzalez DC Bat 4.00 10.00
413 Ivan Rodriguez DC Bat 6.00 15.00
414 Rafael Palmeiro DC Bat 6.00 15.00
415 Ken Griffey Jr. DC Bat 8.00 20.00
416 Edgardo Alfonzo DC Bat 4.00 10.00
417 Barry Larkin DC Bat 6.00 15.00
418 Manny Ramirez DC Bat 6.00 15.00
419 Pedro Martinez DC Bat 6.00 15.00
420 Todd Helton DC Bat 6.00 15.00
421 Larry Walker DC Bat 4.00 10.00
422 Garret Anderson DC Bat 4.00 10.00
423 Mike Sweeney DC Bat 4.00 10.00
424 Carlos Beltran DC Bat 4.00 10.00
425 Javier Lopez DC Bat 4.00 10.00
426 J.T. Snow DC Bat 4.00 10.00
427 Doug Mientkiewicz DC Bat 4.00 10.00
428 John Olerud DC Bat 4.00 10.00
429 Magglio Ordonez DC Bat 4.00 10.00
430 Frank Thomas DC Bat 6.00 15.00
431 Kenny Lofton DC Bat 4.00 10.00
432 Al Leiter DC Bat 4.00 10.00
433 Bernie Williams DC Bat 6.00 15.00
434 Roger Clemens DC Bat 10.00 25.00
435 Tom Glavine DC Bat 6.00 15.00
436 Robin Ventura DC Bat 4.00 10.00
437 Chan Ho Park DC Bat 4.00 10.00
438 Jorge Posada DC Bat 6.00 15.00
439 Charles Johnson BLH Bat 6.00 15.00
440 Alex Rodriguez BLH Bat 10.00 25.00
441 Ken Griffey Jr. BLH Bat 10.00 25.00
442 Mark Kotsay BLH Bat 6.00 15.00
443 Frank Thomas BLH Bat 8.00 20.00
444 Greg Maddux BLH Bat 8.00 20.00
445 Sammy Sosa BLH Bat 8.00 20.00
446 Tom Glavine BLH Bat 8.00 20.00
447 Chipper Jones BLH Bat 8.00 20.00
448 Todd Helton BLH Bat 8.00 20.00
449 Jeff Cirillo BLH Bat 4.00 10.00
450 Steve Finley BLH Bat 6.00 15.00
451 Jim Thome BLH Bat 8.00 20.00
452 Ivan Rodriguez BLH Bat 8.00 20.00
453 Darin Erstad BLH Bat 6.00 15.00
454 Eric Chavez BLH Bat 6.00 15.00
455 Miguel Tejada BLH Bat 6.00 15.00
456 Carlos Delgado BLH Bat 6.00 15.00
457 Omar Vizquel BLH Bat 8.00 20.00
458 Edgar Martinez BLH Bat 8.00 20.00
459 J.Damon Sox BLH Bat 6.00 15.00
460 Russell Branyan BLH Bat 4.00 10.00
461 Kenny Lofton BLH Bat 6.00 15.00
462 Jermaine Dye BLH Bat 6.00 15.00
463 Ellis Burks BLH Bat 6.00 15.00
464 Magglio Ordonez BLH Bat 6.00 15.00
465 Bernie Williams BLH Bat 8.00 20.00
466 Tim Salmon BLH Bat 8.00 20.00
467 Andruw Jones BLH Bat 8.00 20.00
468 Jeffrey Hammonds BLH Bat 4.00 10.00
469 Jim Edmonds BLH Bat 6.00 15.00
470 Kerry Wood BLH Bat 6.00 15.00
471 Luis Gonzalez BLH Bat 6.00 15.00
472 Shawn Green BLH Bat 6.00 15.00
473 Jose Vidro BLH Bat 4.00 10.00
474 Jeff Kent BLH Bat SP/189 6.00 15.00
475 Javier Lopez BLH Bat 6.00 15.00
476 Preston Wilson BLH Bat 6.00 15.00
477 Roberto Alomar BLH Bat 8.00 20.00
478 Robin Ventura BLH Bat 6.00 15.00
479 Phil Nevin BLH Bat 6.00 15.00
480 Ryan Klesko BLH Bat 6.00 15.00
481 Bob Abreu BLH Bat 6.00 15.00
482 Scott Rolen BLH Bat 8.00 20.00
483 Brian Giles BLH Bat 6.00 15.00
484 Jason Kendall BLH Bat 6.00 15.00
485 Tsuyoshi Shinjo BLH Bat 6.00 15.00
486 Larry Walker BLH Bat 6.00 15.00
487 Mike Lieberthal BLH Bat 6.00 15.00
488 Juan Gonzalez BLH Bat 6.00 15.00
489 Darin Erstad HM Bat 6.00 15.00
490 Tom Glavine HM Bat 8.00 20.00
491 Carlos Delgado HM Bat 6.00 15.00
492 Greg Vaughn HM Bat 6.00 15.00
493 Jim Thome HM Bat 8.00 20.00
494 Mark Grace HM Bat 8.00 20.00
495 Rafael Palmeiro HM Bat 8.00 20.00
496 Alex Rodriguez HM Bat 10.00 25.00
497 Juan Gonzalez HM Bat 6.00 15.00
498 Miguel Tejada HM Bat 6.00 15.00
499 Carlos Beltran HM Bat 6.00 15.00
500 Andruw Jones HM Bat 8.00 20.00
501 Frank Thomas HM Bat 8.00 20.00
502 Andres Galarraga HM Bat 6.00 15.00
503 Gary Sheffield HM Bat 6.00 15.00
504 Craig Biggio HM Bat 8.00 20.00
505 Greg Maddux HM Bat 8.00 20.00
506 Chipper Jones HM Bat 8.00 20.00
507 Pat Burrell HM Bat 6.00 15.00
508 Jim Edmonds HM Bat 6.00 15.00
509 Kerry Wood HM Bat 6.00 15.00
510 Sammy Sosa HM Bat 8.00 20.00
511 Luis Gonzalez HM Bat 6.00 15.00
512 Shawn Green HM Bat 6.00 15.00
513 Edgardo Alfonzo HM Bat 6.00 15.00
514 Preston Wilson HM Bat 6.00 15.00
515 Roberto Alomar HM Bat 8.00 20.00
516 Phil Nevin HM Bat 6.00 15.00
517 Scott Rolen HM Bat 8.00 20.00
518 Brian Giles HM Bat 6.00 15.00
519 Jorge Posada HM Bat 8.00 20.00
520 Todd Helton HM Bat 8.00 20.00
521 Larry Walker HM Bat 6.00 15.00
522 Alex Rodriguez FC Bat 12.50 30.00
523 Pedro Martinez FC Bat 10.00 25.00
524 Frank Thomas FC Bat 10.00 25.00
525 Jason Giambi FC Bat 8.00 20.00
526 Bernie Williams FC Bat 10.00 25.00
527 J.D. Drew FC Bat 8.00 20.00
528 Chipper Jones FC Bat 10.00 25.00
529 Sammy Sosa FC Bat 10.00 25.00
530 Randy Johnson FC Bat 10.00 25.00
531 Shawn Green FC Bat 8.00 20.00
532 Kevin Brown FC Bat 8.00 20.00
533 Brian Giles FC Bat 8.00 20.00
534 Ken Griffey Jr. FC Bat 12.50 30.00
535 Larry Walker FC Bat 8.00 20.00
536 Jim Edmonds FC Bat 8.00 20.00
537 Barry Zito DC Jsy 4.00 10.00
538 Bobby Abreu DC Jsy 4.00 10.00
539 Eric Karros DC Jsy 4.00 10.00
540 Sean Casey DC Jsy 4.00 10.00
541 Phil Nevin DC Jsy 4.00 10.00
542 Andruw Jones DC Jsy 6.00 15.00
543 Jim Thome DC Jsy 6.00 15.00
544 Jim Edmonds DC Jsy 4.00 10.00
545 Ichiro Suzuki DC Jsy 15.00 40.00
546 Kerry Wood DC Jsy 4.00 10.00
547 Eric Milton DC Jsy 4.00 10.00
548 Pat Burrell BLH Jsy 6.00 15.00
549 Adam Dunn BLH Jsy 6.00 15.00
550 Lance Berkman BLH Jsy 6.00 15.00
551 Lance Berkman HM Jsy 6.00 15.00
552 Barry Zito HM Jsy 6.00 15.00
553 Roger Clemens FC Jsy 10.00 25.00
554 Andres Galarraga DC Bat 4.00 10.00
555 J.Damon Sox DC Bat 6.00 15.00
556 Jose Cruz Jr. DC Bat 4.00 10.00
557 Charles Johnson DC Bat 4.00 10.00
558 Matt Williams DC Bat 4.00 10.00
559 Andruw Jones DC Bat 6.00 15.00
560 Tsuyoshi Shinjo DC Bat 4.00 10.00
561 Jim Thome DC Bat 6.00 15.00
562 Omar Vizquel DC Bat 6.00 15.00
563 Frank Thomas DC Bat 6.00 15.00
564 Corey Patterson DC Bat 4.00 10.00
565 Fred McGriff BLH Bat 8.00 20.00
566 Manny Ramirez BLH Bat 8.00 20.00
567 Gary Sheffield BLH Bat 6.00 15.00
568 Manny Ramirez HM Bat 8.00 20.00
569 Mike Sweeney HM Bat 6.00 15.00
570 Todd Helton FC Bat 10.00 25.00
571 Erubiel Durazo .25 .60
572 Geronimo Gil .25 .60
573 Shea Hillenbrand .25 .60
574 Cliff Floyd .25 .60
575 Corey Patterson .25 .60
576 Joe Borchard .25 .60
577 Austin Kearns .25 .60
578 Ryan Dempster .25 .60
579 Brandon Larson .25 .60
580 Luis Castillo .25 .60
581 Juan Encarnacion .25 .60
582 Chin-Feng Chen .25 .60
583 Hideo Nomo .60 1.50
584 Bartolo Colon .25 .60
585 Raul Mondesi .25 .60
586 Eric Munson .25 .60
587 Alfonso Soriano .25 .60
588 Ted Lilly .25 .60
589 Ray Durham .25 .60
590 Brett Myers .25 .60
591 Brandon Phillips .25 .60
592 Kenny Lofton .25 .60
593 Scott Rolen .40 1.00
594 Jim Edmonds .25 .60
595 Carl Crawford .25 .60
596 Hank Blalock .40 1.00
597 Kevin Mench .25 .60
598 Josh Phelps .25 .60
599 Orlando Hudson .25 .60
600 Eric Hinske .25 .60
601 Mike Mahoney DC 2.00 5.00
602 Jason Davis DC RC 2.00 5.00
603 Trey Hodges DC RC 2.00 5.00
604 Josh Bard DC RC 2.00 5.00
605 Jeriome Robertson DC RC 2.00 5.00
606 Jose Diaz DC RC 2.00 5.00
607 Jorge Nunez DC RC 2.00 5.00
608 Danny Mota DC RC 2.00 5.00
609 David Ross DC RC 2.00 5.00
610 Jayson Durocher DC RC 2.00 5.00
611 Freddy Sanchez DC RC 3.00 8.00
612 Julius Matos DC RC 2.00 5.00
613 Wil Nieves DC RC 2.00 5.00
614 Ben Kozlowski DC RC 2.00 5.00
615 Jason Simontacchi DC RC 2.00 5.00
616 Mike Coolbaugh DC RC 2.00 5.00
617 Travis Driskill DC RC 2.00 5.00
618 Howie Clark DC RC 2.00 5.00
619 Earl Snyder DC RC 2.00 5.00
620 Carl Sadler DC RC 2.00 5.00
621 Jason Beverlin DC RC 2.00 5.00
622 Terry Pearson DC RC 2.00 5.00
623 Eric Eckenstahler DC RC 2.00 5.00
624 Shawn Sedlacek DC RC 2.00 5.00
625 Aaron Guiel DC RC 2.00 5.00
626 Ryan Bukvich DC RC 2.00 5.00
627 Julio Mateo DC RC 2.00 5.00
628 Chris Snelling DC RC 2.50 6.00
629 Lance Carter DC RC 2.00 5.00
630 Scott Wiggins DC RC 2.00 5.00

2002 Upper Deck Diamond Connection Bat Around Quads

ONE EXCH.CARD PER REDEMPTION PACK
GOLD PRINT RUN 50 SERIAL #'d SETS
NO GOLD PRICING DUE TO SCARCITY
ABBV Roberto Alomar 3.00 8.00
Bret Boone
Craig Biggio
Jose Vidro
ALAE Moises Alou 2.00 5.00
Kenny Lofton
Garret Anderson
Carl Everett
DGVC Carlos Delgado 3.00 8.00
Andres Galarraga
Jose Vidro
Jose Cruz Jr.
DMGS Dimaggio/McG/Griffey/Sosa 10.00 25.00
DRME J.D. Drew 3.00 8.00
Scott Rolen
Tino Martinez
Jim Edmonds
FVRT Furc/Viz/Arod/Tej 6.00 15.00
GRPR Gonz/Irod/Palm/Arod 6.00 15.00
GSGB Grn/Sosa/Girffey/Burr 10.00 25.00
GSMJ Griffey/Sosa/Madd/Jhnsn 10.00 25.00
GSWG Shawn Green 5.00 12.00
Sammy Sosa
Larry Walker
Luis Gonzalez
HGSR Helt/Griffey/Sosa/Arod 6.00 15.00
INSH Kazuhisa Ishii 5.00 12.00
Hideo Nomo
Tsuyoshi Shinjo
Shigetoshi Hasegawa
JMEG David Justice 3.00 8.00
Edgar Martinez
Darin Erstad
Juan Gonzalez
JWGF Randy Johnson 5.00 12.00
Matt Williams
Luis Gonzalez
Steve Finley
KRLJ Jason Kendall 3.00 8.00
Ivan Rodriguez
Mike Lieberthal
Charles Johnson
MGMC Mart/Glav/Madd/Clem 8.00 20.00
MGSG McG/Griffey/Sosa/Giam 10.00 25.00
OSGA Maggio Ordonez 3.00 8.00
Tim Salmon
Shawn Green
Bobby Abreu
PBBD Corey Patterson 5.00 12.00
Adrian Beltre
Russell Branyan
Adam Dunn
PTMO Rafael Palmeiro 5.00 12.00
Frank Thomas
Doug Mientkiewicz
John Olerud
SAKS Gary Sheffield 5.00 12.00
Bobby Abreu
Ryan Klesko
Sammy Sosa
SGPM Sosa/Griffey/Palm/McG 10.00 25.00
SJJM Sheff/Jones/Jones/Madd 8.00 20.00
SMTT Mike Sweeney 5.00 12.00
Edgar Martinez
Jim Thome
Frank Thomas
TGTD Jim Thome 5.00 12.00
Juan Gonzalez
Frank Thomas
Carlos Delgado
TROJ Thome/Arod/Ord/Just 6.00 15.00
VRBA Vent/Rolen/Belt/Alfnzo 5.00 12.00
WGGH Preston Wilson 3.00 8.00
Brian Giles
Shawn Green
Todd Helton
WGPV Wllms/Giam/Pos/Vent 3.00 8.00
WLAV Bernie Williams 3.00 8.00
Al Leiter
Roberto Alomar
Robin Ventura

2002 Upper Deck Diamond Connection Great Connections

RANDOM INSERTS IN PACKS
STATED PRINT RUN 50 SERIAL #'d SETS
CARDS FEATURE BAT-JSY COMBOS
GR J.Giambi/B.Ruth 250.00 400.00
IG I.Suzuki/K.Griffey Jr. 100.00 200.00
MD M.Mantle/J.DiMaggio 250.00 400.00
MR M.McGwire/B.Ruth 300.00 500.00
MS M.McGwire/S.Sosa 75.00 150.00
RR A.Rodriguez/N.Ryan 40.00 80.00

2002 Upper Deck Diamond Connection Memorable Signatures Bat

RANDOM INSERTS IN PACKS
PRINT RUNS B/WN 3-145 COPIES PER
NO PRICING ON QTY OF 20 OR LESS
AR Alex Rodriguez/145 20.00 50.00
CR Cal Ripken/145 30.00 80.00
IS Ichiro Suzuki/99 500.00 700.00
JG Jason Giambi/49 10.00 25.00
JM Joe Morgan/99 30.00 60.00
KG Ken Griffey Jr./49 40.00 80.00
KP Kirby Puckett/145 100.00 250.00
MMC Mark McGwire/49 250.00 400.00
NR Nolan Ryan/99 50.00 120.00
SS Sammy Sosa/99 25.00 60.00

2002 Upper Deck Diamond Connection Memorable Signatures Jersey

PRINT RUNS B/WN 1-150 COPIES PER
NO PRICING ON QTY OF 20 OR LESS
*GOLD: .5X TO 1X BASIC
GOLD PRINT RUN 150 SERIAL #'d CARDS
AR Alex Rodriguez/145 20.00 50.00
CR Cal Ripken/145 30.00 60.00
EB Ernie Banks/150 30.00 80.00
IS Ichiro Suzuki/99 500.00 700.00
JM Joe Morgan/99 10.00 25.00
KG Ken Griffey Jr./49 60.00 150.00
MMC Mark McGwire/49 150.00 300.00
NR Nolan Ryan/99 30.00 80.00
SK Sandy Koufax/150 150.00 300.00
SS Sammy Sosa/99 50.00 100.00

2008 Upper Deck Documentary

COMMON CARD (1-4954)	.20	.50
SEMISTARS	.30	.75
UNLISTED STARS	.50	1.25

ALL PLAYER VARIATIONS PRICED SAME
4891-4954 ISSUED IN 2009 UD1
4891-4954 ODDS 1:4 H,1:10 R,1:72 BLAST

2008 Upper Deck Documentary Gold

*GOLD: .75X TO 2X BASIC
STATED ODDS 1:1

2008 Upper Deck Documentary All Star Game

STATED ODDS 1:4

AC Aaron Cook	.40	1.00
AG Adrian Gonzalez	.60	1.50
AP Albert Pujols	1.00	2.50
AR Alex Rodriguez	1.00	2.50
BM Brian McCann	.60	1.50
BS Ben Sheets	.40	1.00
BW Billy Wagner	.40	1.00
CG Carlos Guillen	.40	1.00
CJ Chipper Jones	.75	2.00
CL Cliff Lee	.60	1.50
CQ Carlos Quentin	.40	1.00
CU Chase Utley	.60	1.50
CZ Carlos Zambrano	.60	1.50
DH Dan Haren	.40	1.00
DJ Derek Jeter	2.00	5.00
DN Dioner Navarro	.40	1.00
DP Dustin Pedroia	.75	2.00
DU Dan Uggla	.40	1.00
DW David Wright	.50	1.25
EL Evan Longoria	1.50	4.00
EV Edinson Volquez	.40	1.00
FR Francisco Rodriguez	.60	1.50
GS Grady Sizemore	.60	1.50
GU Cristian Guzman	.40	1.00
HR Hanley Ramirez	.60	1.50
IK Ian Kinsler	.60	1.50
IS Ichiro Suzuki	1.00	2.50
JD J.D. Drew	.40	1.00
JH Josh Hamilton	.50	1.25
JM Justin Morneau	.60	1.50
JN Joe Nathan	.40	1.00
JO Joe Mauer	.75	2.00
JP Jonathan Papelbon	.60	1.50
JS Joakim Soria	.40	1.00
JU Justin Duchscherer	.40	1.00
KF Kosuke Fukudome	1.00	2.50
KY Kevin Youkilis	.40	1.00
LB Lance Berkman	.60	1.50
MB Milton Bradley	.40	1.00
MH Matt Holliday	1.00	2.50
MR Manny Ramirez	1.00	2.50
MT Miguel Tejada	.60	1.50
MY Michael Young	.40	1.00
NM Nate McLouth	.40	1.00
RB Ryan Braun	.50	1.25
RD Ryan Dempster	.40	1.00
RH Roy Halladay	.60	1.50
RI Mariano Rivera	1.25	3.00
RL Ryan Ludwick	.40	1.00
RM Russell Martin	.40	1.00
SH George Sherrill	.40	1.00
SK Scott Kazmir	.60	1.50
SO Geovany Soto	1.00	2.50
WE Brandon Webb	.60	1.50
WI Brian Wilson	1.00	2.50

2008 Upper Deck Documentary Home Run Derby

STATED ODDS 1:4

HRD1 Josh Hamilton	.50	1.25
HRD2 Josh Hamilton	.50	1.25
HRD3 Josh Hamilton	.50	1.25
HRD4 Josh Hamilton	.50	1.25
HRD5 Justin Morneau	.60	1.50

2008 Upper Deck Documentary Seasonal Signatures

STATED ODDS 1:24

AL Aaron Laffey	8.00	20.00
AR Alex Romero	3.00	8.00
BB Brandon Boggs	4.00	10.00
BL Brent Lillibridge	3.00	8.00
BO Brian Bocock	3.00	8.00
BR Brian Bass	5.00	12.00
BW Bobby Wilson	3.00	8.00
CC Callix Crabbe	3.00	8.00
CP Chris Perez	3.00	8.00
CS Chris Smith	3.00	8.00
CT Clay Timpner	4.00	10.00
DB Daric Barton	3.00	8.00
DM David Murphy	4.00	10.00
DP David Purcey	4.00	10.00
EJ Elliot Johnson	3.00	8.00
FC Fausto Carmona	4.00	10.00
FP Felipe Paulino	3.00	8.00
GD German Duran	3.00	8.00
GS Greg Smith	3.00	8.00
HG Harvey Garcia	3.00	8.00
HI Hernan Iribarren	3.00	8.00
JB Jerry Blevins	3.00	8.00
JK Joe Koshansky	3.00	8.00
KM Kyle McClellan	8.00	20.00
LB Lance Broadway	3.00	8.00
LC Luke Carlin	3.00	8.00
LI Adam Lind	4.00	10.00
MH Micah Hoffpauir	10.00	25.00
MJ Matt Joyce	3.00	8.00
MT Matt Tolbert	3.00	8.00
NM Nyjer Morgan	4.00	10.00
OH Ross Ohlendorf	4.00	10.00
RB Randor Bierd	3.00	8.00
RC Ryan Church	8.00	20.00
RD Robinzon Diaz	3.00	8.00
RO Alex Romero	3.00	8.00
RT Ramon Troncoso	3.00	8.00
SH Steve Holm	3.00	8.00
SP Steve Pearce	6.00	15.00
TU Matt Tupman	10.00	25.00
WW Wesley Wright	3.00	8.00

2009-10 Upper Deck Draft Edition Alma Mater

COMPLETE SET (24)	25.00	50.00

RANDOM INSERTS IN PACKS
*BLUE: .6X TO 1.5X BASE HI
BLUE PRINT RUN 99 SER.#'d SETS

AMDP Dustin Pedroia	1.25	3.00
AMFI Jennie Finch	2.50	6.00
AMFT Frank Thomas	1.00	2.50
AMJF Jennie Finch	2.50	6.00
AMLF Lisa Fernandez	1.00	2.50

2009-10 Upper Deck Draft Edition Alma Mater Green

*GREEN: .75X TO 2X BASE HI
GREEN PRINT RUN 50 SER.#'d SETS

2009-10 Upper Deck Draft Edition Alma Mater Red

*RED: 2X TO 5X BASE HI
RED PRINT RUN 25 SER.#'d SETS

2009-10 Upper Deck Draft Edition Alma Mater Autographs

STATED PRINT RUN 10 TO 99 SER.#'d SETS
SOME UNPRICED DUE TO SCARCITY

AMDP Dustin Pedroia/99	20.00	50.00
AMFI Jennie Finch/99	20.00	40.00
AMFT Frank Thomas/25	40.00	100.00
AMJF Jennie Finch/99	20.00	40.00
AMLF Lisa Fernandez/99	10.00	25.00

2007 Upper Deck Elements

COMMON CARD	.30	.75

CARDS 1-42 FOUND IN GRIFFEY PACKS
CARDS 43-84 FOUND IN RIPKEN PACKS
CARDS 85-126 FOUND IN JETER PACKS
ALL VETERAN VERSIONS EQUAL VALUE

COMMON RC (127-168)	.75	2.00

RC 127-168 FOUND IN GRIFFEY PACKS
RC 169-210 FOUND IN RIPKEN PACKS

COMMON RC (211-252)	.75	2.00

RC 211-252 FOUND IN JETER PACKS
ROOKIE PRINT RUN 550 SER.#'d SETS
PRINTING PLATES RANDOMLY INSERTED
PLATE PRINT RUN 1 SET PER COLOR
BLACK-CYAN-MAGENTA-YELLOW ISSUED
NO PLATE PRICING DUE TO SCARCITY
GIFT EXCH ODDS 1 PER CASE
GIFT EXCH DEADLINE 9/30/2007

1 Stephen Drew	.30	.75
2 Andruw Jones	.30	.75
3 Chipper Jones	.75	2.00
4 Miguel Tejada	.50	1.25
5 David Ortiz	.75	2.00
6 Manny Ramirez	.75	2.00
7 Derrek Lee	.30	.75
8 Alfonso Soriano	.50	1.25
9 Jermaine Dye	.30	.75
10 Jim Thome	.50	1.25
11 Ken Griffey Jr.	1.50	4.00
12 Adam Dunn	.50	1.25
13 Travis Hafner	.30	.75
14 Grady Sizemore	.50	1.25
15 Todd Helton	.50	1.25
16 Gary Sheffield	.30	.75
17 Miguel Cabrera	.75	2.00
18 Lance Berkman	.50	1.25
19 Mark Teahen	.30	.75
20 Vladimir Guerrero	.50	1.25
21 Jered Weaver	.50	1.25
22 Rafael Furcal	.30	.75
23 Prince Fielder	.50	1.25
24 Justin Morneau	.50	1.25
25 Johan Santana	.50	1.25
26 David Wright	.60	1.50
27 Jose Reyes	.50	1.25
28 Derek Jeter	2.00	5.00
29 Alex Rodriguez	1.00	2.50
30 Nick Swisher	.50	1.25
31 Ryan Howard	.60	1.50
32 Jason Bay	.50	1.25
33 Adrian Gonzalez	.60	1.50
34 Ray Durham	.30	.75
35 Ichiro Suzuki	1.00	2.50
36 Albert Pujols	1.00	2.50
37 Scott Rolen	.50	1.25
38 Carl Crawford	.50	1.25
39 Mark Teixeira	.50	1.25
40 Michael Young	.30	.75
41 Vernon Wells	.30	.75
42 Ryan Zimmerman	.50	1.25
43 Stephen Drew	.30	.75
44 Andruw Jones	.30	.75
45 Chipper Jones	.75	2.00
46 Miguel Tejada	.50	1.25
47 David Ortiz	.75	2.00
48 Manny Ramirez	.75	2.00
49 Derrek Lee	.30	.75
50 Alfonso Soriano	.50	1.25
51 Jermaine Dye	.30	.75
52 Jim Thome	.50	1.25
53 Ken Griffey Jr.	1.50	4.00
54 Adam Dunn	.50	1.25
55 Travis Hafner	.30	.75
56 Grady Sizemore	.50	1.25
57 Todd Helton	.50	1.25
58 Gary Sheffield	.30	.75
59 Miguel Cabrera	.75	2.00
60 Lance Berkman	.50	1.25
61 Mark Teahen	.30	.75
62 Vladimir Guerrero	.50	1.25
63 Jered Weaver	.50	1.25
64 Rafael Furcal	.30	.75
65 Prince Fielder	.50	1.25
66 Justin Morneau	.50	1.25
67 Johan Santana	.50	1.25
68 David Wright	.60	1.50
69 Jose Reyes	.50	1.25
70 Derek Jeter	2.00	5.00
71 Alex Rodriguez	1.00	2.50
72 Nick Swisher	.50	1.25
73 Ryan Howard	.60	1.50
74 Jason Bay	.50	1.25
75 Adrian Gonzalez	.60	1.50
76 Ray Durham	.30	.75
77 Ichiro Suzuki	1.00	2.50
78 Albert Pujols	1.00	2.50
79 Scott Rolen	.50	1.25
80 Carl Crawford	.50	1.25
81 Mark Teixeira	.50	1.25
82 Michael Young	.30	.75
83 Vernon Wells	.30	.75
84 Ryan Zimmerman	.50	1.25
85 Stephen Drew	.30	.75
86 Andruw Jones	.30	.75
87 Chipper Jones	.75	2.00
88 Miguel Tejada	.50	1.25
89 David Ortiz	.75	2.00
90 Manny Ramirez	.75	2.00
91 Derrek Lee	.30	.75
92 Alfonso Soriano	.50	1.25
93 Jermaine Dye	.30	.75
94 Jim Thome	.50	1.25
95 Ken Griffey Jr.	1.50	4.00
96 Adam Dunn	.50	1.25
97 Travis Hafner	.30	.75
98 Grady Sizemore	.50	1.25
99 Todd Helton	.50	1.25
100 Gary Sheffield	.30	.75
101 Miguel Cabrera	.75	2.00
102 Lance Berkman	.50	1.25
103 Mark Teahen	.30	.75
104 Vladimir Guerrero	.50	1.25
105 Jered Weaver	.50	1.25
106 Rafael Furcal	.30	.75
107 Prince Fielder	.50	1.25
108 Justin Morneau	.50	1.25
109 Johan Santana	.50	1.25
110 David Wright	.60	1.50
111 Jose Reyes	.50	1.25
112 Derek Jeter	2.00	5.00
113 Alex Rodriguez	1.00	2.50
114 Nick Swisher	.50	1.25
115 Ryan Howard	.60	1.50
116 Jason Bay	.50	1.25
117 Adrian Gonzalez	.60	1.50
118 Ray Durham	.30	.75
119 Ichiro Suzuki	1.00	2.50
120 Albert Pujols	1.00	2.50
121 Scott Rolen	.50	1.25
122 Carl Crawford	.50	1.25
123 Mark Teixeira	.50	1.25
124 Michael Young	.30	.75
125 Vernon Wells	.30	.75
126 Ryan Zimmerman	.50	1.25
127 Miguel Montero (RC)	.75	2.00
128 Doug Slaten RC	.75	2.00
129 Hunter Pence (RC)	2.50	6.00
130 Brian Burres (RC)	.75	2.00
131 Daisuke Matsuzaka RC	3.00	8.00
132 Hideki Okajima RC	4.00	10.00
133 Devern Hansack RC	.75	2.00
134 Felix Pie (RC)	.75	2.00
135 Ryan Sweeney (RC)	.75	2.00
136 Chris Stewart RC	.75	2.00
137 Jarrod Saltalamacchia (RC)	1.25	3.00
138 John Danks RC	1.25	3.00
139 Travis Buck (RC)	.75	2.00
140 Troy Tulowitzki (RC)	2.50	6.00
141 Chase Wright RC	2.00	5.00
142 Matt DeSalvo (RC)	.75	2.00
143 Micah Owings (RC)	.75	2.00
144 Jeff Baker (RC)	.75	2.00
145 Andy LaRoche (RC)	.75	2.00
146 Billy Butler (RC)	1.25	3.00
147 Jose Garcia RC	.75	2.00
148 Angel Sanchez RC	.75	2.00
149 Alex Gordon RC	2.50	6.00
150 Glen Perkins (RC)	.75	2.00
151 Alexi Casilla RC	1.25	3.00
152 Joe Smith RC	.75	2.00
153 Kei Igawa RC	2.00	5.00
154 Sean Henn (RC)	.75	2.00
155 Phil Hughes (RC)	2.00	5.00
156 Michael Bourn (RC)	1.25	3.00
157 Josh Hamilton (RC)	2.50	6.00
158 Kevin Kouzmanoff (RC)	.75	2.00
159 Tim Lincecum RC	4.00	10.00
160 Brandon Morrow RC	4.00	10.00
161 Brandon Wood (RC)	.75	2.00
162 Akinori Iwamura RC	2.00	5.00
163 Delmon Young (RC)	1.25	3.00
164 Juan Salas (RC)	.75	2.00
165 Elijah Dukes RC	1.25	3.00
166 Joaquin Arias (RC)	.75	2.00
167 Adam Lind (RC)	.75	2.00
168 Matt Chico (RC)	.75	2.00
169 Miguel Montero (RC)	.75	2.00
170 Doug Slaten RC	.75	2.00
171 Hunter Pence (RC)	2.50	6.00
172 Brian Burres (RC)	.75	2.00
173 Daisuke Matsuzaka RC	3.00	8.00
174 Hideki Okajima RC	4.00	10.00
175 Devern Hansack RC	.75	2.00
176 Felix Pie (RC)	.75	2.00
177 Ryan Sweeney (RC)	.75	2.00
178 Chris Stewart RC	.75	2.00
179 Jarrod Saltalamacchia (RC)	1.25	3.00
180 John Danks RC	1.25	3.00
181 Travis Buck (RC)	.75	2.00
182 Troy Tulowitzki (RC)	2.50	6.00
183 Chase Wright RC	2.00	5.00
184 Matt DeSalvo (RC)	.75	2.00
185 Micah Owings (RC)	.75	2.00
186 Jeff Baker (RC)	.75	2.00
187 Andy LaRoche (RC)	.75	2.00
188 Billy Butler (RC)	1.25	3.00
189 Jose Garcia RC	.75	2.00
190 Angel Sanchez RC	.75	2.00
191 Alex Gordon RC	2.50	6.00
192 Glen Perkins (RC)	.75	2.00
193 Alexi Casilla RC	1.25	3.00
194 Joe Smith RC	.75	2.00
195 Kei Igawa RC	2.00	5.00
196 Sean Henn (RC)	.75	2.00
197 Phil Hughes (RC)	2.00	5.00
198 Michael Bourn (RC)	1.25	3.00
199 Josh Hamilton (RC)	2.50	6.00
200 Kevin Kouzmanoff (RC)	.75	2.00
201 Tim Lincecum RC	4.00	10.00
202 Brandon Morrow RC	4.00	10.00
203 Brandon Wood (RC)	.75	2.00
204 Akinori Iwamura RC	2.00	5.00
205 Delmon Young (RC)	1.25	3.00
206 Juan Salas (RC)	.75	2.00
207 Elijah Dukes RC	1.25	3.00
208 Joaquin Arias (RC)	.75	2.00
209 Adam Lind (RC)	.75	2.00
210 Matt Chico (RC)	.75	2.00
211 Miguel Montero (RC)	.75	2.00
212 Doug Slaten RC	.75	2.00
213 Hunter Pence (RC)	2.50	6.00
214 Brian Burres (RC)	.75	2.00
215 Daisuke Matsuzaka RC	3.00	8.00
216 Hideki Okajima RC	4.00	10.00
217 Devern Hansack RC	.75	2.00
218 Felix Pie (RC)	.75	2.00
219 Ryan Sweeney (RC)	.75	2.00
220 Chris Stewart RC	.75	2.00
221 Jarrod Saltalamacchia (RC)	1.25	3.00
222 John Danks RC	1.25	3.00
223 Travis Buck (RC)	.75	2.00
224 Troy Tulowitzki (RC)	2.50	6.00
225 Chase Wright RC	2.00	5.00
226 Matt DeSalvo (RC)	.75	2.00
227 Micah Owings (RC)	.75	2.00
228 Jeff Baker (RC)	.75	2.00
229 Andy LaRoche (RC)	.75	2.00
230 Billy Butler (RC)	1.25	3.00
231 Jose Garcia RC	.75	2.00
232 Angel Sanchez RC	.75	2.00
233 Alex Gordon RC	2.50	6.00
234 Glen Perkins (RC)	.75	2.00
235 Alexi Casilla RC	1.25	3.00
236 Joe Smith RC	.75	2.00
237 Kei Igawa RC	2.00	5.00
238 Sean Henn (RC)	.75	2.00
239 Phil Hughes (RC)	2.00	5.00
240 Michael Bourn (RC)	1.25	3.00
241 Josh Hamilton (RC)	2.50	6.00
242 Kevin Kouzmanoff (RC)	.75	2.00
243 Tim Lincecum RC	4.00	10.00
244 Brandon Morrow RC	4.00	10.00
245 Brandon Wood (RC)	.75	2.00
246 Akinori Iwamura RC	2.00	5.00
247 Delmon Young (RC)	1.25	3.00
248 Juan Salas (RC)	.75	2.00
249 Elijah Dukes RC	1.25	3.00
250 Joaquin Arias (RC)	.75	2.00
251 Adam Lind (RC)	.75	2.00
252 Matt Chico (RC)	.75	2.00

2007 Upper Deck Elements Clear Cut Elements Bronze

RANDOM INSERTS IN PACKS
PRINT RUNS B/WN 149-350 COPIES PER
EXCH DEADLINE 7/14/2010

AH Aaron Harang	6.00	15.00
AK Austin Kearns/234	4.00	10.00
AS Alfonso Soriano/199	10.00	25.00
BB Brian Bannister	4.00	10.00
BR Brian Roberts	5.00	12.00
CA Matt Cain	5.00	12.00
CC Chris Carpenter	8.00	20.00
CP Corey Patterson	6.00	15.00
CR Cal Ripken Jr.	30.00	80.00
CL Carl Crawford	4.00	10.00
DJ Derek Jeter	125.00	300.00
DW Dontrelle Willis	6.00	15.00
FL Francisco Liriano	4.00	10.00
GR Ken Griffey Jr.	40.00	80.00
HR Hanley Ramirez/314	4.00	10.00
JB Jason Bay	4.00	10.00
JG Jonny Gomes	4.00	10.00
JH Jeremy Hermida	4.00	10.00
JP Jake Peavy	6.00	15.00
JT Jim Thome/199	30.00	80.00
JV Justin Verlander	15.00	40.00
JZ Joel Zumaya	6.00	15.00
KG Khalil Greene	4.00	10.00
KW Kerry Wood/199	6.00	15.00
MC Miguel Cabrera	20.00	50.00
MG Marcus Giles/290	4.00	10.00
MH Matt Holliday	4.00	10.00
ML Mark Loretta/199	4.00	10.00
MM Melvin Mora	4.00	10.00
MT Miguel Tejada/149	4.00	10.00
RH Rich Harden	4.00	10.00
RJ Reed Johnson	4.00	10.00
RZ Ryan Zimmerman	5.00	12.00
SA Johan Santana/299	8.00	20.00
SK Scott Kazmir	8.00	20.00
SR Scott Rolen/299	6.00	15.00
TH Travis Hafner	4.00	10.00
VM Victor Martinez	4.00	10.00

2007 Upper Deck Elements Clear Cut Elements Gold

RANDOM INSERTS IN PACKS
PRINT RUNS B/W 49-199 COPIES PER
EXCH DEADLINE 7/14/2010

AK Austin Kearns/99	5.00	12.00
AS Alfonso Soriano/99	12.00	30.00
BB Brian Bannister	5.00	12.00
BR Brian Roberts	6.00	15.00
CA Matt Cain	6.00	15.00
CC Chris Carpenter	10.00	25.00
CP Corey Patterson	8.00	20.00
CR Miguel Cabrera/149 EXCH	40.00	100.00
CL Carl Crawford	5.00	12.00
DJ Derek Jeter	150.00	400.00
DW Dontrelle Willis	8.00	20.00
FL Francisco Liriano	5.00	12.00
GS Khalil Greene	5.00	12.00
HR Hanley Ramirez	6.00	15.00
JB Jason Bay	5.00	12.00
JG Jonny Gomes	5.00	12.00
JH Jeremy Hermida	5.00	12.00
JP Jake Peavy	8.00	20.00
JV Justin Verlander	20.00	50.00
JZ Joel Zumaya	8.00	20.00
KG Ken Griffey Jr.	40.00	100.00
KW Kerry Wood/99	8.00	20.00
MC Miguel Cabrera/149	25.00	60.00
MG Marcus Giles/99	5.00	12.00
MH Matt Holliday	5.00	12.00
ML Mark Loretta/99	5.00	12.00
RC Johan Santana/99	15.00	40.00
RJ Reed Johnson	5.00	12.00
RO Melvin Mora	5.00	12.00
RZ Ryan Zimmerman	8.00	20.00
SK Scott Kazmir	10.00	25.00
SR Scott Rolen/99	8.00	20.00
TH Travis Hafner	5.00	12.00
VM Victor Martinez	5.00	12.00

2007 Upper Deck Elements Clear Cut Elements Silver

RANDOM INSERTS IN PACKS
PRINT RUNS B/WN 13-99 COPIES PER
NO PRICING ON QTY 13 OR LESS
EXCH DEADLINE 7/14/2010

AK Austin Kearns/49	6.00	15.00
AS Alfonso Soriano/49	12.00	30.00
BB Brian Bannister	6.00	15.00
BR Brian Roberts	8.00	20.00
CA Matt Cain/49	8.00	20.00
CC Chris Carpenter	12.00	30.00
CP Corey Patterson	10.00	25.00
CR Cal Ripken Jr.	50.00	120.00
CL Carl Crawford	6.00	15.00
DJ Derek Jeter	200.00	500.00
DW Dontrelle Willis	10.00	25.00
FL Francisco Liriano	6.00	15.00
HR Hanley Ramirez	8.00	20.00
JB Jason Bay	6.00	15.00
JG Jonny Gomes	6.00	15.00
JH Jeremy Hermida	6.00	15.00
JP Jake Peavy	10.00	25.00
JV Justin Verlander	25.00	60.00
JZ Joel Zumaya	10.00	25.00
KG Ken Griffey Jr.	50.00	120.00
KW Kerry Wood/49	10.00	25.00
MC Miguel Cabrera/49	25.00	60.00
MG Marcus Giles/49	6.00	15.00
MH Matt Holliday	6.00	15.00
RC Johan Santana/49	20.00	50.00
RJ Reed Johnson	6.00	15.00
RO Melvin Mora	6.00	15.00
RZ Ryan Zimmerman	6.00	15.00
SK Scott Kazmir	10.00	25.00
SR Scott Rolen/49	10.00	25.00
TH Travis Hafner	6.00	15.00
VM Victor Martinez	6.00	15.00

2007 Upper Deck Elements Dual Elements Dual Memorabilia

RANDOM INSERTS IN PACKS
STATED PRINT RUN 50 SER.#'d SETS

BB L.Berkman/C.Biggio	6.00	15.00
BM J.Beckett/D.Matsuzaka	30.00	60.00
BS J.Bay/F.Sanchez	6.00	15.00
CA C.Beltran/A.Soriano	6.00	15.00
CB C.Crawford/R.Baldelli	4.00	10.00
CM C.Carpenter/M.Mulder	8.00	20.00
DB C.Delgado/C.Beltran	4.00	10.00
DG A.Dunn/K.Griffey Jr./29	12.50	30.00
DJ J.Damon/D.Jeter	10.00	25.00
GG B.Giles/M.Giles	4.00	10.00
GJ K.Griffey Jr./D.Jeter	20.00	50.00
GM T.Glavine/P.Martinez	6.00	15.00
GS V.Guerrero/A.Soriano	6.00	15.00
GT K.Griffey Jr./F.Thomas	12.50	30.00
HB R.Halladay/A.Burnett	4.00	10.00
HU C.Hamels/C.Utley	6.00	15.00
JJ C.Jones/A.Jones	6.00	15.00
JR D.Jeter/J.Reyes	25.00	50.00
JT D.Jeter/M.Tejada	10.00	25.00
LP J.Lester/J.Papelbon	10.00	25.00
MM V.Martinez/J.Mauer	6.00	15.00
MS G.Maddux/J.Smoltz	30.00	60.00
MT J.Mauer/J.Morneau	6.00	15.00
OR D.Ortiz/M.Ramirez	10.00	25.00
PG A.Pujols/K.Griffey Jr.	15.00	40.00
PZ J.Papelbon/J.Zumaya	10.00	25.00
RH M.Rivera/T.Hoffman	6.00	15.00
RR J.Reyes/H.Ramirez	10.00	25.00
RW A.Rios/V.Wells	4.00	10.00
SB C.Schilling/J.Beckett	12.50	30.00
SH G.Sizemore/T.Hafner	6.00	15.00
SZ J.Santana/B.Zito	6.00	15.00
TH J.Thome/T.Hafner	6.00	15.00
TK J.Thome/P.Konerko	6.00	15.00
TM M.Teixeira/J.Morneau	4.00	10.00
TR M.Tejada/B.Roberts	4.00	10.00
TY M.Teixeira/M.Young	4.00	10.00
UU D.Uggla/C.Utley	6.00	15.00
VB J.Verlander/J.Bonderman	6.00	15.00
WH V.Wells/T.Hunter	6.00	15.00
WJ B.Webb/R.Johnson	6.00	15.00
WS B.Webb/J.Santana	6.00	15.00
ZR R.Zimmerman/S.Rolen	6.00	15.00

2007 Upper Deck Elements Elemental Autographs

RANDOM INSERTS IN PACKS

AI Akinori Iwamura	6.00	15.00
BA Bronson Arroyo	6.00	15.00
BH Bill Hall	4.00	10.00
BL Joe Blanton	3.00	8.00
BN Brendan Harris	3.00	8.00
BO Jeremy Bonderman	4.00	10.00
BR Jared Burton	12.00	30.00
BT Jason Bartlett	3.00	8.00
BU Brian Burres	3.00	8.00
BW Brandon Wood	4.00	10.00
CB Cha-Seung Baek	3.00	8.00
CO Jon Coutlangus	4.00	10.00
CR Cal Ripken Jr.	60.00	120.00
CU Chase Utley	15.00	40.00
CW Chase Wright	6.00	15.00
DB Denny Bautista	3.00	8.00
DC Daniel Cabrera	3.00	8.00
DJ Derek Jeter	75.00	200.00
DU Dan Uggla	4.00	10.00
FP Felix Pie	4.00	10.00
GA Garrett Atkins	3.00	8.00
GO Alex Gordon	12.00	30.00
GP Glen Perkins	3.00	8.00
HA Rich Harden	3.00	8.00
HE Sean Henn	3.00	8.00
HR Hanley Ramirez	6.00	15.00
IK Ian Kinsler	4.00	10.00
JA Joaquin Arias	3.00	8.00
JB Jason Bay	6.00	15.00
JC Jesse Crain	3.00	8.00
JG Jonny Gomes	3.00	8.00
JH Josh Hamilton	10.00	25.00
JK Jon Knott	3.00	8.00
JO Josh Willingham	3.00	8.00
JP Jake Peavy	3.00	8.00
JV Justin Verlander	20.00	50.00
JW Jayson Werth	6.00	15.00
KE Howie Kendrick	4.00	10.00
KI Kei Igawa	3.00	8.00
KM Kendry Morales	4.00	10.00
KY Kevin Youkilis	6.00	15.00
LA Andy LaRoche	4.00	10.00
LI Bobby Livingston	3.00	8.00
LS Luke Scott	4.00	10.00
PA Jonathan Papelbon	6.00	15.00
RH Rich Hill	6.00	15.00
RL Ruddy Lugo	3.00	8.00
RO Scott Rolen	6.00	15.00
RT Ryan Theriot	6.00	15.00
SD Stephen Drew	10.00	25.00
SK Scott Kazmir	5.00	12.00
SM John Smoltz	12.00	30.00
SS Skip Schumaker	6.00	15.00
ST Scott Thorman	3.00	8.00
TB Travis Buck	6.00	15.00
TH Travis Hafner	6.00	15.00
TI Tadahito Iguchi	6.00	15.00
VG Vladimir Guerrero	10.00	25.00
VM Victor Martinez	4.00	10.00
WO Jason Wood	3.00	8.00

2007 Upper Deck Elements Elemental Autographs Dual

RANDOM INSERTS IN PACKS
STATED PRINT RUN 15 SER.#'d SETS
NO PRICING DUE TO SCARCITY

2007 Upper Deck Elements Elemental Autographs Quad

RANDOM INSERTS IN PACKS
STATED PRINT RUN 1 SER.#'d SET
NO PRICING DUE TO SCARCITY

2007 Upper Deck Elements Elemental Autographs Triple

RANDOM INSERTS IN PACKS
STATED PRINT RUN 5 SER.#'d SETS
NO PRICING DUE TO SCARCITY

2007 Upper Deck Elements Essential Elements

RANDOM INSERTS IN PACKS

AB Adrian Beltre	3.00	8.00
AD Adam Dunn	3.00	8.00
AJ Andruw Jones	3.00	8.00
AP Andy Pettitte	4.00	10.00
AR Aramis Ramirez	3.00	8.00
AS Alfonso Soriano	3.00	8.00
BA Bobby Abreu	3.00	8.00
BC Bobby Crosby	3.00	8.00
BE Carlos Beltran	3.00	8.00
BG Brian Giles	3.00	8.00
BO Jeremy Bonderman	3.00	8.00
BR Brian Roberts	3.00	8.00
BU B.J. Upton	3.00	8.00
BW Billy Wagner	4.00	10.00
BZ Barry Zito	3.00	8.00
CA Miguel Cabrera	3.00	8.00
CB Craig Biggio	4.00	10.00
CC Carl Crawford	3.00	8.00
CH Cole Hamels	4.00	10.00
CJ Chipper Jones	4.00	10.00
CS Curt Schilling	4.00	10.00
CU Chase Utley	4.00	10.00
DA Johnny Damon	4.00	10.00
DM Daisuke Matsuzaka	10.00	25.00
DO David Ortiz	6.00	15.00
DR JD Drew	3.00	8.00
DU Dan Uggla	4.00	10.00
DW Dontrelle Willis	3.00	8.00
EC Eric Chavez	3.00	8.00
ED Jim Edmonds	3.00	8.00
FG Freddy Garcia	3.00	8.00
FH Felix Hernandez	3.00	8.00
FL Francisco Liriano	4.00	10.00
FT Frank Thomas	4.00	10.00
GA Garret Anderson	3.00	8.00
GJ Geoff Jenkins	3.00	8.00
GM Greg Maddux	10.00	25.00
GS Grady Sizemore	6.00	15.00
HA Rich Harden	3.00	8.00
HB Hank Blalock	3.00	8.00
HO Trevor Hoffman	3.00	8.00
HS Huston Street	3.00	8.00
HU Torii Hunter	3.00	8.00
IR Ivan Rodriguez	4.00	10.00
JA Jason Bay	3.00	8.00
JB Josh Beckett	3.00	8.00
JC Jorge Cantu	3.00	8.00
JD Jermaine Dye	3.00	8.00
JE Johnny Estrada	3.00	8.00
JF Jeff Francoeur	6.00	15.00
JG Jason Giambi	3.00	8.00
JJ Josh Johnson	3.00	8.00
JK Jeff Kent	3.00	8.00
JM Joe Mauer	4.00	10.00
JP Jake Peavy	3.00	8.00
JR Jimmy Rollins	3.00	8.00
JS Johan Santana	4.00	10.00
JT Jim Thome	4.00	10.00
JV Justin Verlander	4.00	10.00
KG Khalil Greene	4.00	10.00
LB Lance Berkman	3.00	8.00
LG Luis Gonzalez	3.00	8.00
MM Mike Mussina	4.00	10.00
MO Justin Morneau	4.00	10.00
MP Mike Piazza	6.00	15.00
MR Manny Ramirez	4.00	10.00
MT Mark Teixeira	4.00	10.00
MY Michael Young	3.00	8.00
OR Magglio Ordonez	4.00	10.00
PA Jonathan Papelbon	6.00	15.00
PB Pat Burrell	3.00	8.00
PE Jhonny Peralta	3.00	8.00
PF Prince Fielder	4.00	10.00
PO Jorge Posada	4.00	10.00
PU Albert Pujols	10.00	25.00
RE Jose Reyes	4.00	10.00
RH Roy Halladay	3.00	8.00
RI Mariano Rivera	6.00	15.00
RJ Randy Johnson	4.00	10.00
RO Roy Oswalt	3.00	8.00
RW Rickie Weeks	3.00	8.00
RZ Ryan Zimmerman	4.00	10.00
SK Scott Kazmir	3.00	8.00
SM John Smoltz	4.00	10.00
SR Scott Rolen	4.00	10.00
TE Miguel Tejada	3.00	8.00
TH Todd Helton	4.00	10.00
TI Tim Hudson	3.00	8.00
TR Travis Hafner	3.00	8.00
VG Vladimir Guerrero	4.00	10.00
VM Victor Martinez	3.00	8.00

2007 Upper Deck Elements Quad Memorabilia

RANDOM INSERTS IN PACKS
STATED PRINT RUN 10 SER.#'d SETS
NO PRICING DUE TO SCARCITY

2007 Upper Deck Elements Rare Elements Patches

RANDOM INSERTS IN PACKS
PRINT RUNS B/WN 4-35 COPIES PER
NO PRICING ON QTY 19 OR LESS

AB Adrian Beltre/35	6.00	15.00
AJ Andruw Jones/35	10.00	25.00
AP Andy Pettitte/35	8.00	20.00
AR Aramis Ramirez/35	6.00	15.00
BA Bobby Abreu/35	6.00	15.00
BC Bobby Crosby/35	10.00	25.00
BE Carlos Beltran/35	10.00	25.00
BG Brian Giles/35	6.00	15.00
BO Jeremy Bonderman/35	10.00	25.00
BR Brian Roberts/30	10.00	25.00
BW Billy Wagner/35	10.00	25.00
BZ Barry Zito/35	6.00	15.00
CA Miguel Cabrera/35	6.00	15.00
CB Craig Biggio/35	15.00	40.00
CC Carl Crawford/35	10.00	25.00
CJ Chipper Jones/35	20.00	50.00
CL Carlos Lee/35	10.00	25.00
CS Curt Schilling/35	10.00	25.00
DA Johnny Damon/28	10.00	25.00
DR JD Drew/35	6.00	15.00
DU Dan Uggla/35	10.00	25.00
DW Dontrelle Willis/35	6.00	15.00
EC Eric Chavez/35	6.00	15.00
ED Jim Edmonds/35	10.00	25.00
FG Freddy Garcia/35	6.00	15.00
FH Felix Hernandez/35	6.00	15.00
FL Francisco Liriano/35	8.00	20.00
FT Frank Thomas/35	15.00	40.00
GA Garret Anderson/35	6.00	15.00
GJ Geoff Jenkins/35	6.00	15.00
GM Greg Maddux/35	30.00	60.00
GR Ken Griffey Jr./35	40.00	80.00
GS Grady Sizemore/35	10.00	25.00
HA Rich Harden/35	6.00	15.00
HB Hank Blalock/35	6.00	15.00
HO Trevor Hoffman/35	6.00	15.00
HR Hanley Ramirez/35	10.00	25.00
HS Huston Street/35	6.00	15.00
HU Torii Hunter/35	6.00	15.00
IR Ivan Rodriguez/28	10.00	25.00
JA Jason Bay/35	10.00	25.00
JB Josh Beckett/35	15.00	40.00
JC Jorge Cantu/35	6.00	15.00
JD Jermaine Dye/35	6.00	15.00
JE Johnny Estrada/35	6.00	15.00
JF Jeff Francoeur/35	20.00	50.00
JG Jason Giambi/35	20.00	50.00
JJ Josh Johnson/29	6.00	15.00
JK Jeff Kent/35	10.00	25.00
JP Jake Peavy/35	6.00	15.00
JR Jimmy Rollins/35	10.00	25.00
JS Johan Santana/35	10.00	25.00
JT Jim Thome/35	10.00	25.00
KG Khalil Greene/35	10.00	25.00
LB Lance Berkman/35	6.00	15.00
LG Luis Gonzalez/35	6.00	15.00
MP Mike Piazza/35	12.00	30.00
MT Mark Teixeira/35	15.00	40.00
MY Michael Young/35	10.00	25.00
OR Maggio Ordonez/35	10.00	25.00
PB Pat Burrell/35	6.00	15.00
PE Jhonny Peralta/35	6.00	15.00
PO Jorge Posada/35	10.00	25.00
RC Roger Clemens/35	30.00	60.00
RE Jose Reyes/35	15.00	40.00
RH Roy Halladay/35	10.00	25.00
RI Mariano Rivera/35	15.00	40.00
RJ Randy Johnson/35	10.00	25.00
RO Roy Oswalt/35	6.00	15.00
SK Scott Kazmir/35	10.00	25.00
SM John Smoltz/35	20.00	50.00
SR Scott Rolen/35	10.00	25.00
TH Todd Helton/35	10.00	25.00
TI Tim Hudson/35	6.00	15.00
TR Travis Hafner/35	10.00	25.00
VA Jason Varitek/35	15.00	40.00
VG Vladimir Guerrero/35	15.00	40.00

2007 Upper Deck Elements Triple Memorabilia

RANDOM INSERTS IN PACKS
STATED PRINT RUN 25 SER.#'d SETS
NO PRICING DUE TO SCARCTIY

1999 Upper Deck Encore

The 1999 Upper Deck Encore set was issued in one series for a total of 180 cards and was distributed in six-card packs with a suggested retail price of $3.99. The set features 90 of the best cards from the 1999 Upper Deck set printed on rainbow-foil cards with three short-printed subsets: Star Rookies (91-135) with an insertion rate of 1:4, Homer Odyssey (136-165) inserted 1:6 packs, and Strokes of Genius (166-180) inserted 1:8 packs. Rookie Cards include Pat Burrell and Eric Munson.

COMPLETE SET (180)	100.00	200.00
COMP.SET w/o SP's (90)	8.00	20.00
COMMON CARD (1-90)	.15	.40
COMMON SR (91-135)	.40	1.00
SR STATED ODDS 1:4		
COMMON HO (136-165)	.30	.75
HO STATED ODDS 1:6		
COMMON SG (166-180)	.40	1.00
SG STATED ODDS 1:8		
1 Darin Erstad	.15	.40
2 Mo Vaughn	.15	.40

3 Travis Lee .15 .40
4 Randy Johnson .40 1.00
5 Matt Williams .15 .40
6 John Smoltz .25 .60
7 Greg Maddux .60 1.50
8 Chipper Jones .40 1.00
9 Tom Glavine .25 .60
10 Andruw Jones .25 .60
11 Cal Ripken 1.25 3.00
12 Mike Mussina .25 .60
13 Albert Belle .15 .40
14 Nomar Garciaparra .60 1.50
15 Jose Offerman .15 .40
16 Pedro Martinez .25 .60
17 Trot Nixon .15 .40
18 Kerry Wood .15 .40
19 Sammy Sosa .40 1.00
20 Frank Thomas .40 1.00
21 Paul Konerko .15 .40
22 Sean Casey .15 .40
23 Barry Larkin .25 .60
24 Greg Vaughn .15 .40
25 Travis Fryman .15 .40
26 Jaret Wright .15 .40
27 Jim Thome .25 .60
28 Manny Ramirez .25 .60
29 Roberto Alomar .25 .60
30 Kenny Lofton .15 .40
31 Todd Helton .25 .60
32 Larry Walker .15 .40
33 Vinny Castilla .15 .40
34 Dante Bichette .15 .40
35 Tony Clark .15 .40
36 Dean Palmer .15 .40
37 Gabe Kapler .15 .40
38 Juan Encarnacion .15 .40
39 Alex Gonzalez .15 .40
40 Preston Wilson .15 .40
41 Mark Kotsay .15 .40
42 Moises Alou .15 .40
43 Craig Biggio .25 .60
44 Ken Caminiti .15 .40
45 Jeff Bagwell .25 .60
46 Johnny Damon .25 .60
47 Gary Sheffield .15 .40
48 Kevin Brown .25 .60
49 Raul Mondesi .15 .40
50 Jeff Cirillo .15 .40
51 Jeromy Burnitz .15 .40
52 Todd Walker .15 .40
53 Corey Koskie .15 .40
54 Brad Fullmer .15 .40
55 Vladimir Guerrero .40 1.00
56 Mike Piazza .60 1.50
57 Robin Ventura .15 .40
58 Rickey Henderson .40 1.00
59 Derek Jeter 1.00 2.50
60 Paul O'Neill .25 .60
61 Bernie Williams .25 .60
62 Tino Martinez .25 .60
63 Roger Clemens .75 2.00
64 Ben Grieve .15 .40
65 Jason Giambi .15 .40
66 Bob Abreu .15 .40
67 Scott Rolen .25 .60
68 Curt Schilling .15 .40
69 Marlon Anderson .15 .40
70 Kevin Young .15 .40
71 Jason Kendall .15 .40
72 Brian Giles .15 .40
73 Mark McGwire 1.00 2.50
74 Fernando Tatis .15 .40
75 Eric Davis .15 .40
76 Trevor Hoffman .15 .40
77 Tony Gwynn .50 1.25
78 Matt Clement .15 .40
79 Robb Nen .15 .40
80 Barry Bonds 1.00 2.50
81 Ken Griffey Jr. .75 2.00
82 Alex Rodriguez .60 1.50
83 Wade Boggs .25 .60
84 Fred McGriff .25 .60
85 Jose Canseco .25 .60
86 Ivan Rodriguez .25 .60
87 Juan Gonzalez .15 .40
88 Rafael Palmeiro .25 .60
89 Carlos Delgado .15 .40
90 David Wells .15 .40
91 Troy Glaus SR .60 1.50
92 Adrian Beltre SR .40 1.00
93 Matt Anderson SR .40 1.00
94 Eric Chavez SR .40 1.00
95 Jeff Weaver SR RC .60 1.50
96 Warren Morris SR .40 1.00
97 George Lombard SR .40 1.00
98 Mike Kinkade SR .40 1.00
99 Kyle Farnsworth SR RC .40 1.00
100 J.D. Drew SR .40 1.00
101 Joe McEwing SR RC .40 1.00
102 Carlos Guillen SR .40 1.00
103 Kelly Dransfeldt SR RC .40 1.00
104 Eric Munson SR RC .40 1.00
105 Armando Rios SR .40 1.00
106 Ramon E.Martinez SR RC .40 1.00
107 Orlando Hernandez SR .40 1.00
108 Jeremy Giambi SR .40 1.00
109 Pat Burrell SR RC 2.00 5.00
110 Shea Hillenbrand SR RC 1.00 2.50
111 Billy Koch SR .40 1.00
112 Roy Halladay SR 1.00 2.50
113 Ruben Mateo SR .40 1.00
114 Bruce Chen SR .40 1.00
115 Angel Pena SR .40 1.00
116 Michael Barrett SR .40 1.00
117 Kevin Witt SR .40 1.00
118 Damon Minor SR .40 1.00
119 Ryan Minor SR .40 1.00
120 A.J. Pierzynski SR .40 1.00
121 A.J. Burnett SR RC 1.00 2.50
122 Cristian Guzman SR .40 1.00
123 Joe Lawrence SR .40 1.00
124 Derrick Gibson SR .40 1.00
125 Carlos Febles SR .40 1.00
126 Chris Haas SR .40 1.00
127 Cesar King SR .40 1.00
128 Calvin Pickering SR .40 1.00
129 Mitch Meluskey SR .40 1.00
130 Carlos Beltran SR .60 1.50
131 Ron Belliard SR .40 1.00
132 Jerry Hairston Jr. SR .40 1.00
133 Fernando Seguignol SR .40 1.00
134 Kris Benson SR .40 1.00
135 Chad Hutchinson SR RC .40 1.00
136 Ken Griffey Jr. HO 1.50 4.00
137 Mark McGwire HO 2.00 5.00
138 Sammy Sosa HO .75 2.00
139 Albert Belle HO .30 .75
140 Mo Vaughn HO .30 .75
141 Alex Rodriguez HO 1.25 3.00
142 Manny Ramirez HO .50 1.25
143 J.D. Drew HO .30 .75
144 Juan Gonzalez HO .30 .75
145 Vladimir Guerrero HO .75 2.00
146 Fernando Tatis HO .30 .75
147 Mike Piazza HO 1.25 3.00
148 Barry Bonds HO 2.00 5.00
149 Ivan Rodriguez HO .50 1.25
150 Jeff Bagwell HO .50 1.25
151 Raul Mondesi HO .30 .75
152 Nomar Garciaparra HO 1.25 3.00
153 Jose Canseco HO .50 1.25
154 Greg Vaughn HO .30 .75
155 Scott Rolen HO .50 1.25
156 Vinny Castilla HO .30 .75
157 Troy Glaus HO .50 1.25
158 Craig Biggio HO .50 1.25
159 Tino Martinez HO .50 1.25
160 Jim Thome HO .50 1.25
161 Frank Thomas HO .75 2.00
162 Tony Clark HO .30 .75
163 Ben Grieve HO .30 .75
164 Matt Williams HO .30 .75
165 Derek Jeter HO 2.00 5.00
166 Ken Griffey Jr. SG 1.25 3.00
167 Tony Gwynn SG .75 2.00
168 Mike Piazza SG 1.00 2.50
169 Mark McGwire SG 1.50 4.00
170 Sammy Sosa SG .60 1.50
171 Juan Gonzalez SG .40 1.00
172 Mo Vaughn SG .40 1.00
173 Derek Jeter SG 1.50 4.00
174 Bernie Williams SG .40 1.00
175 Ivan Rodriguez SG .40 1.00
176 Barry Bonds SG 1.50 4.00
177 Scott Rolen SG .40 1.00
178 Larry Walker SG .40 1.00
179 Chipper Jones SG .60 1.50
180 Alex Rodriguez SG 1.00 2.50

1999 Upper Deck Encore FX Gold

*STARS 1-90: 6X TO 15X BASIC 1-90
*SR 91-135: 1.5X TO 4X BASIC SR
*SR RC'S 91-135: 1.5X TO 4X BASIC SR RC
*HOMER ODYSSEY: 1.5X TO 4X BASIC HO
*STROKES OF GENIUS: 2X TO 5X BASIC SG
RANDOM INSERTS IN PACKS
STATED PRINT RUN 125 SERIAL #'d SETS

1999 Upper Deck Encore 2K Countdown

COMPLETE SET (10) 10.00 25.00
STATED ODDS 1:11
2K1 Ken Griffey Jr. 1.25 3.00
2K2 Derek Jeter 1.50 4.00
2K3 Mike Piazza 1.00 2.50
2K4 J.D. Drew .40 1.00
2K5 Vladimir Guerrero .60 1.50
2K6 Chipper Jones .60 1.50
2K7 Alex Rodriguez 1.00 2.50
2K8 Nomar Garciaparra 1.00 2.50
2K9 Mark McGwire 1.50 4.00
2K10 Sammy Sosa .60 1.50

1999 Upper Deck Encore Batting Practice Caps

STATED ODDS 1:750
CBB Barry Bonds 30.00 60.00
CBH Frank Thomas 10.00 25.00
CCB Carlos Beltran 10.00 25.00
CDP Dean Palmer 6.00 15.00
CEC Eric Chavez 6.00 15.00
CGK Gabe Kapler 6.00 15.00
CGV Greg Vaughn 4.00 10.00
CJD J.D. Drew 6.00 15.00
CJK Jason Kendall 6.00 15.00
CTC Tony Clark 4.00 10.00
CTG Tony Gwynn 12.50 30.00
CTH Todd Helton 10.00 25.00
CTW Todd Walker 4.00 10.00
CVC Vinny Castilla 6.00 15.00
CVG Vladimir Guerrero 10.00 25.00

1999 Upper Deck Encore Driving Forces

COMPLETE SET (15) 30.00 80.00
STATED ODDS 1:23
FX GOLD RANDOM INSERTS IN PACKS
FX GOLD PRINT RUN 10 SERIAL #'d SETS
FX GOLD NOT PRICED DUE TO SCARCITY
D1 Ken Griffey Jr. 3.00 8.00
D2 Mark McGwire 4.00 10.00
D3 Sammy Sosa 1.50 4.00
D4 Albert Belle .60 1.50
D5 Alex Rodriguez 2.50 6.00
D6 Mo Vaughn .60 1.50
D7 Juan Gonzalez .60 1.50
D8 Jeff Bagwell 1.00 2.50
D9 Mike Piazza 2.50 6.00
D10 Frank Thomas 1.50 4.00
D11 Barry Bonds 4.00 10.00
D12 Vladimir Guerrero 1.50 4.00
D13 Chipper Jones 1.50 4.00
D14 Tony Gwynn 2.00 5.00
D15 J.D. Drew .60 1.50

1999 Upper Deck Encore McGwired

COMPLETE SET (10) 30.00 80.00
STATED ODDS 1:23
*FX GOLD: 1X TO 2.5X BASIC MCGWIRED
FX GOLD RANDOM INSERTS IN PACKS
FX GOLD PRINT RUN 500 SERIAL #'d SETS
MC1 McGwire 4.00 10.00
C.Pavano
MC2 McGwire 3.00 8.00
M.Morgan
MC3 McGwire 3.00 8.00
S.Trachsel
MC4 McGwire 3.00 8.00
R.Martinez
MC5 McGwire 3.00 8.00
W.Blair
MC6 McGwire 3.00 8.00
S.Elarton
MC7 McGwire 3.00 8.00
J.Parque
MC8 McGwire 3.00 8.00
L.Hernandez
MC9 McGwire 3.00 8.00
R.Roque
MC10 McGwire 3.00 8.00
J.Wright

1999 Upper Deck Encore Pure Excitement

COMPLETE SET (30) 30.00 80.00
STATED ODDS 1:7
P1 Mo Vaughn .40 1.00
P2 Darin Erstad .40 1.00
P3 Travis Lee .40 1.00
P4 Chipper Jones 1.00 2.50
P5 Greg Maddux 1.50 4.00
P6 Gabe Kapler .40 1.00
P7 Cal Ripken 3.00 8.00
P8 Nomar Garciaparra 1.50 4.00
P9 Kerry Wood .40 1.00
P10 Frank Thomas 1.00 2.50
P11 Manny Ramirez .60 1.50
P12 Larry Walker .40 1.00
P13 Tony Clark .40 1.00
P14 Jeff Bagwell .60 1.50
P15 Craig Biggio .60 1.50
P16 Vladimir Guerrero 1.00 2.50
P17 Mike Piazza 1.50 4.00
P18 Bernie Williams .60 1.50
P19 Derek Jeter 2.50 6.00
P20 Ben Grieve .40 1.00
P21 Eric Chavez .40 1.00
P22 Scott Rolen .60 1.50
P23 Mark McGwire 2.50 6.00
P24 Tony Gwynn 1.25 3.00
P25 Barry Bonds 2.50 6.00
P26 Ken Griffey Jr. 2.00 5.00
P27 Alex Rodriguez 1.50 4.00
P28 J.D. Drew .40 1.00
P29 Juan Gonzalez .40 1.00
P30 Roger Clemens 2.00 5.00

1999 Upper Deck Encore Rookie Encore

COMPLETE SET (10) 6.00 15.00
STATED ODDS 1:23
*FX GOLD: 1.25X TO 3X BASIC ROOK.ENCORE
FX GOLD RANDOM INSERTS IN PACKS
FX GOLD PRINT RUN 500 SERIAL #'d SETS
R1 J.D. Drew .25 .60
R2 Eric Chavez .25 .60
R3 Gabe Kapler .60 1.50
R4 Bruce Chen .25 .60
R5 Carlos Beltran .40 1.00
R6 Troy Glaus .40 1.00
R7 Roy Halladay .60 1.50
R8 Adrian Beltre .25 .60
R9 Michael Barrett .25 .60
R10 Pat Burrell 1.50 4.00

1999 Upper Deck Encore UD Authentics

STATED ODDS 1:288
JD J.D. Drew 6.00 15.00
JR Ken Griffey Jr. 60.00 120.00
MB Michael Barrett 4.00 10.00
NG Nomar Garciaparra 15.00 40.00
PB Pat Burrell 10.00 25.00
TG Troy Glaus 10.00 25.00

1999 Upper Deck Encore Upper Realm

COMPLETE SET (15) 20.00 50.00
STATED ODDS 1:11
U1 Ken Griffey Jr. 1.50 4.00
U2 Mark McGwire 2.00 5.00
U3 Sammy Sosa .75 2.00
U4 Tony Gwynn 1.00 2.50
U5 Alex Rodriguez 1.25 3.00
U6 Juan Gonzalez .30 .75
U7 J.D. Drew .30 .75
U8 Roger Clemens 1.50 4.00
U9 Greg Maddux 1.25 3.00
U10 Randy Johnson .75 2.00
U11 Mo Vaughn .30 .75
U12 Derek Jeter 2.00 5.00
U13 Vladimir Guerrero .75 2.00
U14 Cal Ripken 2.50 6.00
U15 Nomar Garciaparra 1.25 3.00

2006 Upper Deck Epic

COMMON CARD (1-300) 2.00 5.00
COMMON ROOKIE 2.00 5.00
STATED PRINT RUN 450 SERIAL #'d SETS
1 Conor Jackson (RC) 1.25 3.00
2 Brandon Webb 1.25 3.00
3 Craig Counsell .75 2.00
4 Luis Gonzalez .75 2.00
5 Miguel Batista .75 2.00
6 Orlando Hudson .75 2.00
7 Russ Ortiz .75 2.00
8 Shawn Green .75 2.00
9 Andruw Jones .75 2.00
10 Chipper Jones 2.00 5.00
11 Edgar Renteria .75 2.00
12 Jeff Francoeur 2.00 5.00
13 John Smoltz 2.00 5.00
14 Marcus Giles .75 2.00
15 Mike Hampton .75 2.00
16 Tim Hudson 1.25 3.00
17 Erik Bedard .75 2.00
18 Brian Roberts .75 2.00
19 Javy Lopez .75 2.00
20 Jay Gibbons .75 2.00
21 Jeff Conine .75 2.00
22 Melvin Mora .75 2.00
23 Miguel Tejada 1.25 3.00
24 Daniel Cabrera .75 2.00
25 Rodrigo Lopez .75 2.00
26 Ramon Hernandez .75 2.00
27 Bronson Arroyo .75 2.00
28 Curt Schilling 1.25 3.00
29 David Ortiz 2.00 5.00
30 David Wells .75 2.00
31 Jason Varitek 2.00 5.00
32 Josh Beckett .75 2.00
33 Kevin Youkilis .75 2.00
34 Manny Ramirez 2.00 5.00
35 Matt Clement .75 2.00
36 Mike Lowell .75 2.00
37 Tim Wakefield 1.25 3.00
38 Trot Nixon .75 2.00
39 Aramis Ramirez .75 2.00
40 Carlos Zambrano 1.25 3.00
41 Derrek Lee .75 2.00
42 Greg Maddux 2.50 6.00
43 Juan Pierre .75 2.00
44 Kerry Wood .75 2.00
45 Mark Prior 1.25 3.00
46 Michael Barrett .75 2.00
47 Ryan Dempster .75 2.00
48 Todd Walker .75 2.00
49 Wade Miller .75 2.00
50 A.J. Pierzynski .75 2.00
51 Brian Anderson (RC) .75 2.00
52 Frank Thomas 2.00 5.00
53 Javier Vazquez .75 2.00
54 Jim Thome 1.25 3.00
55 Joe Crede .75 2.00
56 Jon Garland .75 2.00
57 Juan Uribe .75 2.00
58 Mark Buehrle 1.25 3.00
59 Paul Konerko 1.25 3.00
60 Scott Podsednik .75 2.00
61 Tadahito Iguchi .75 2.00
62 Aaron Harang .75 2.00
63 Adam Dunn 1.25 3.00
64 Austin Kearns .75 2.00
65 Edwin Encarnacion 2.00 5.00
66 Eric Milton .75 2.00
67 Felipe Lopez .75 2.00
68 Jason LaRue .75 2.00
69 Ken Griffey Jr. 4.00 10.00
70 Wily Mo Pena .75 2.00
71 Aaron Boone .75 2.00
72 Ben Broussard .75 2.00
73 C.C. Sabathia 1.25 3.00
74 Casey Blake .75 2.00
75 Cliff Lee 1.25 3.00
76 Grady Sizemore 1.25 3.00
3/17/1900 Jake Westbrook .75 2.00
78 Josh Bard .75 2.00
79 Travis Hafner .75 2.00
80 Victor Martinez 1.25 3.00
81 Chin-hui Tsao .75 2.00
82 Clint Barmes .75 2.00
83 Garrett Atkins .75 2.00
84 Josh Wilson (RC) .75 2.00
85 Luis Gonzalez .75 2.00
86 Matt Holliday 2.00 5.00
87 Todd Helton 1.25 3.00
88 Brandon Inge .75 2.00
89 Carlos Guillen .75 2.00
90 Chris Shelton .75 2.00
91 Craig Monroe .75 2.00
92 Dmitri Young .75 2.00
93 Ivan Rodriguez 1.25 3.00
94 Jeremy Bonderman .75 2.00
95 Magglio Ordonez 1.25 3.00
96 Alex Gonzalez .75 2.00
97 Brian Moehler .75 2.00
98 Dontrelle Willis .75 2.00
99 Jeremy Hermida (RC) .75 2.00
100 Jason Vargas .75 2.00
101 Miguel Cabrera 2.00 5.00
102 Adam Everett .75 2.00
103 Andy Pettitte 1.25 3.00
104 Brad Ausmus .75 2.00
105 Brad Lidge .75 2.00
106 Craig Biggio 1.25 3.00
107 Dan Wheeler .75 2.00
108 Jeff Bagwell 1.25 3.00
109 Lance Berkman 1.25 3.00
110 Morgan Ensberg .75 2.00
111 Preston Wilson .75 2.00
112 Roger Clemens 2.50 6.00
113 Roy Oswalt 1.25 3.00
114 Dave Gassner (RC) .75 2.00
115 Angel Berroa .75 2.00
116 Doug Mientkiewicz .75 2.00
117 Joe Mays .75 2.00
118 Mark Grudzielanek .75 2.00
119 Mike Sweeney .75 2.00
120 Reggie Sanders .75 2.00
121 Runelvys Hernandez .75 2.00
122 Scott Elarton .75 2.00
123 Brandon Watson (RC) .75 2.00
124 Zack Greinke 2.00 5.00
125 Brad Penny .75 2.00
126 Derek Lowe .75 2.00
127 Eric Gagne .75 2.00
128 J.D. Drew .75 2.00
129 Jayson Werth 1.25 3.00
130 Jeff Kent .75 2.00
131 Nomar Garciaparra 1.25 3.00
132 Olmedo Saenz .75 2.00
133 Rafael Furcal .75 2.00
134 Ben Sheets .75 2.00
135 Bill Hall .75 2.00
136 Carlos Lee .75 2.00
137 Geoff Jenkins .75 2.00
138 Prince Fielder (RC) 4.00 10.00
139 Rickie Weeks .75 2.00
140 Jose Capellan (RC) .75 2.00
141 Brad Radke .75 2.00
142 Joe Mauer 1.25 3.00
143 Joe Nathan .75 2.00
144 Johan Santana 1.25 3.00
145 Justin Morneau 1.25 3.00
146 Kyle Lohse .75 2.00
147 Lew Ford .75 2.00
148 Luis Castillo .75 2.00
149 Matt LeCroy .75 2.00
150 Michael Cuddyer .75 2.00
151 Shannon Stewart .75 2.00
152 Torii Hunter .75 2.00
153 Billy Wagner .75 2.00
154 Carlos Beltran 1.25 3.00
155 Carlos Delgado .75 2.00
156 Cliff Floyd .75 2.00
157 David Wright 1.50 4.00
158 Jose Reyes 1.25 3.00
159 Kazuo Matsui .75 2.00
160 Mike Piazza 2.00 5.00
161 Paul Lo Duca .75 2.00
162 Pedro Martinez 1.25 3.00
163 Tom Glavine 1.25 3.00
164 Victor Diaz .75 2.00
165 Alex Rodriguez 2.50 6.00
166 Bernie Williams 1.25 3.00
167 Carl Pavano .75 2.00
168 Chien-Ming Wang 1.25 3.00
169 Derek Jeter 5.00 12.00
170 Gary Sheffield .75 2.00
171 Hideki Matsui 2.00 5.00
172 Jason Giambi .75 2.00
173 Johnny Damon 1.25 3.00
174 Jorge Posada 1.25 3.00
175 Robinson Cano 1.25 3.00
176 Mariano Rivera 2.50 6.00
177 Mike Mussina 1.25 3.00
178 Randy Johnson 2.00 5.00
179 Miguel Cairo .75 2.00
180 Barry Zito 1.25 3.00
181 Bobby Crosby .75 2.00
182 Bobby Kielty .75 2.00
183 Eric Chavez .75 2.00
184 Josh Barfield (RC) .75 2.00
185 Esteban Loaiza .75 2.00
186 Huston Street .75 2.00
187 Jason Kendall .75 2.00
188 Nick Swisher 1.25 3.00
189 Aaron Rowand .75 2.00
190 Bobby Abreu .75 2.00
191 Chase Utley 1.25 3.00
192 Gavin Floyd .75 2.00
193 Jimmy Rollins 1.25 3.00
194 Mike Lieberthal .75 2.00
195 Pat Burrell .75 2.00
196 Ryan Howard 1.50 4.00
197 Craig Wilson .75 2.00
198 Jack Wilson .75 2.00
199 Jason Bay .75 2.00
200 Joe Randa .75 2.00
201 Josh Fogg .75 2.00
202 Kip Wells .75 2.00
203 Sean Casey .75 2.00
204 Zach Duke .75 2.00
205 Brian Giles .75 2.00
206 Dave Roberts 1.25 3.00
207 Jake Peavy .75 2.00
208 Khalil Greene .75 2.00
209 Mike Cameron .75 2.00
210 Ryan Klesko .75 2.00
211 Trevor Hoffman 1.25 3.00
212 Vinny Castilla .75 2.00
213 Armando Benitez .75 2.00
214 Jason Schmidt .75 2.00
215 Matt Morris .75 2.00
216 Moises Alou .75 2.00
217 Omar Vizquel 1.25 3.00
218 Ray Durham .75 2.00
219 Adrian Beltre 2.00 5.00
220 Carl Everett .75 2.00
221 Kenji Johjima RC 2.00 5.00
222 Felix Hernandez 1.25 3.00
223 Ichiro Suzuki 2.50 6.00
224 Jamie Moyer .75 2.00
225 Jeremy Reed .75 2.00
226 Joel Pineiro .75 2.00
227 Raul Ibanez 1.25 3.00
228 Richie Sexson .75 2.00
229 Albert Pujols 2.50 6.00
230 Chris Carpenter 1.25 3.00
231 David Eckstein .75 2.00
232 Jason Marquis .75 2.00
233 Jeff Suppan .75 2.00
234 Jim Edmonds 1.25 3.00
235 Yadier Molina 2.50 6.00
236 Mark Mulder .75 2.00
237 Scott Rolen 1.25 3.00
238 Alex Scott Gonzalez .75 2.00
239 Aubrey Huff .75 2.00
240 Carl Crawford 1.25 3.00
241 Casey Fossum .75 2.00
242 Joey Gathright .75 2.00
243 Scott Kazmir 1.25 3.00
244 Toby Hall .75 2.00
245 Travis Lee .75 2.00
246 Adam Eaton .75 2.00
247 Francisco Cordero .75 2.00
248 Hank Blalock .75 2.00
249 Kevin Mench .75 2.00
250 Kevin Millwood .75 2.00
251 Laynce Nix .75 2.00
252 Mark Teixeira 1.25 3.00
253 Michael Young .75 2.00
254 A.J. Burnett .75 2.00
255 Alex Rios .75 2.00
256 B.J. Ryan .75 2.00
257 Corey Koskie .75 2.00
258 Josh Towers .75 2.00
259 Lyle Overbay .75 2.00
260 Reed Johnson .75 2.00
261 Roy Halladay 1.25 3.00
262 Russ Adams .75 2.00
263 Troy Glaus .75 2.00
264 Vernon Wells .75 2.00
265 Alfonso Soriano 1.25 3.00
266 John Patterson .75 2.00
267 Damian Jackson .75 2.00
268 Jose Guillen .75 2.00
269 Jose Vidro .75 2.00
270 Livan Hernandez .75 2.00
271 Adam Kennedy .75 2.00
272 Bartolo Colon .75 2.00
273 Bengie Molina .75 2.00
274 Casey Kotchman .75 2.00
275 Chone Figgins .75 2.00
276 Matt Cain (RC) 5.00 12.00
277 Darin Erstad .75 2.00
278 Edgardo Alfonzo .75 2.00
279 Francisco Rodriguez 1.25 3.00
280 Garret Anderson .75 2.00
281 Vladimir Guerrero 1.25 3.00
282 Chris Denorfia (RC) .75 2.00
283 Joey Devine RC .75 2.00
284 Justin Verlander (RC) 6.00 15.00
285 Scott Feldman RC .75 2.00
286 Jason Bergmann RC .75 2.00
287 Jeremy Accardo RC .75 2.00
288 Adam Wainwright (RC) 1.25 3.00
289 Hanley Ramirez (RC) 1.25 3.00
290 Josh Johnson (RC) 2.00 5.00
291 Ryan Zimmerman (RC) 2.50 6.00
292 Anderson Hernandez (RC) .75 2.00
293 Francisco Liriano (RC) 2.00 5.00
294 Josh Willingham (RC) 1.25 3.00
295 Hong-Chih Kuo (RC) 2.00 5.00
296 Steve Stemle RC .75 2.00
297 Jeff Harris RC .75 2.00
298 John Van Benschoten (RC) .75 2.00
299 Jonathan Papelbon (RC) 4.00 10.00
300 Jason Kubel (RC) .75 2.00

2006 Upper Deck Epic Awesome 8 Materials

OVERALL GU ODDS ONE PER PACK
PRINT RUNS B/WN 1-10 COPIES PER
NO PRICING DUE TO SCARCITY

2006 Upper Deck Epic Endorsements

OVERALL AU ODDS ONE PER CASE
PRINT RUNS B/WN 10-45 COPIES PER
NO PRICING ON QTY OF 25 OR LESS
AD Adam Dunn/45 20.00 50.00
AJ Andruw Jones/30 20.00 50.00
AS Alfonso Soriano/30 20.00 50.00
BF1 Bob Feller/45 10.00 25.00
BF2 Bob Feller/45 10.00 25.00
BG Bob Gibson/30 30.00 60.00
BM Bill Mazeroski/30 30.00 60.00
BN Brian Roberts/45 12.50 30.00
BO Bo Jackson/30 30.00 60.00
BR1 Brooks Robinson/30 10.00 25.00
BR2 Brooks Robinson/30 10.00 25.00
BW Billy Williams/45 12.50 30.00
CB Craig Biggio/30 30.00 60.00
CF Carlton Fisk/30 30.00 60.00
CU Chase Utley/45 40.00 80.00
DJ1 Derek Jeter/30 150.00 250.00
DJ2 Derek Jeter/30 150.00 250.00
DJ3 Derek Jeter/30 150.00 250.00
DO David Ortiz/30 50.00 100.00
DS Don Sutton/30 12.50 30.00
DW1 Dontrelle Willis/30 20.00 50.00
DW2 Dontrelle Willis/30 20.00 50.00
EC Eric Chavez/30 12.50 30.00
FH1 Felix Hernandez/30 15.00 40.00
FH2 Felix Hernandez/30 15.00 40.00
FL Fred Lynn/45 12.50 30.00
FR Frank Robinson/30 20.00 50.00
JA Jake Peavy/45 12.50 30.00
JB Jason Bay/45 12.50 30.00
JH1 Jeremy Hermida/45 12.50 30.00
JH2 Jeremy Hermida/45 12.50 30.00
JI Jim Bunning/30 12.50 30.00
JP1 Jim Palmer/30 20.00 50.00
JP2 Jim Palmer/30 20.00 50.00
KG1 Ken Griffey Jr./30 60.00 150.00
KG2 Ken Griffey Jr./30 60.00 150.00
KG3 Ken Griffey Jr./30 60.00 150.00
LA Don Larsen/30 12.50 30.00
LB Lou Brock/30 40.00 80.00
MC1 Miguel Cabrera/30 30.00 60.00
MC2 Miguel Cabrera/30 30.00 60.00
MW Maury Wills/45 12.50 30.00
OS Ozzie Smith/30 40.00 80.00
PF Prince Fielder/44 40.00 80.00
PM1 Paul Molitor/30 20.00 50.00
PM2 Paul Molitor/30 20.00 50.00
RC Rod Carew/30 20.00 50.00
RH Ryan Howard/45 30.00 60.00
RO1 Roy Oswalt/45 6.00 15.00
RO2 Roy Oswalt/45 6.00 15.00
RZ1 Ryan Zimmerman/30 60.00 120.00
RZ2 Ryan Zimmerman/30 60.00 120.00
SC1 Steve Carlton/26 8.00 20.00
SC2 Steve Carlton/27 8.00 20.00
SG Steve Garvey/45 10.00 25.00
SM John Smoltz/30 100.00 200.00
TG Tony Gwynn/30 30.00 60.00
TO Tony Oliva/45 12.50 30.00
TP Tony Perez/45 20.00 50.00
TS Tom Seaver/30 30.00 80.00
WB Wade Boggs/30 20.00 50.00

2006 Upper Deck Epic Events

OVERALL ODDS 3:5 PACKS
STATED PRINT RUN 675 SERIAL #'d SETS
EE1 Ryan Howard 1.50 4.00
EE2 Tadahito Iguchi .75 2.00
EE3 Paul Konerko 1.25 3.00
EE4 Craig Biggio 1.25 3.00
EE5 Alex Rodriguez 2.50 6.00
EE6 Ichiro Suzuki 2.50 6.00
EE7 David Ortiz 2.00 5.00
EE8 Miguel Cabrera 2.00 5.00
EE9 Dontrelle Willis .75 2.00
EE10 Mark Teixeira 1.25 3.00
EE11 Hideki Matsui 2.00 5.00
EE12 Albert Pujols 2.50 6.00
EE13 Albert Pujols 2.50 6.00
EE14 Greg Maddux 2.50 6.00
EE15 Greg Maddux 2.50 6.00
EE16 Manny Ramirez 2.00 5.00
EE17 Mark Teixeira 1.25 3.00
EE18 Alex Rodriguez 2.50 6.00
EE19 Manny Ramirez 2.00 5.00
EE20 Randy Johnson 2.00 5.00
EE21 Jason Varitek 2.00 5.00
EE22 Vladimir Guerrero 1.25 3.00
EE23 Roger Clemens 2.50 6.00
EE24 Manny Ramirez 2.00 5.00
EE25 Curt Schilling 1.25 3.00
EE26 Johnny Damon 1.25 3.00
EE27 David Ortiz 2.00 5.00
EE28 David Wright 1.50 4.00
EE29 Ichiro Suzuki 2.50 6.00
EE30 Ichiro Suzuki 2.50 6.00
EE31 Adam Dunn 1.25 3.00
EE32 Adrian Beltre 2.00 5.00
EE33 Javy Lopez .75 2.00
EE34 Greg Maddux 2.50 6.00
EE35 Randy Johnson 2.00 5.00
EE36 Jim Thome 1.25 3.00
EE37 Adam Dunn 1.25 3.00
EE38 Bobby Abreu .75 2.00
EE39 Felix Hernandez 1.25 3.00
EE40 Greg Maddux 2.50 6.00
EE41 Ken Griffey Jr. 4.00 10.00
EE42 Randy Johnson 2.00 5.00
EE43 Johan Santana 1.25 3.00
EE44 Magglio Ordonez 1.25 3.00
EE45 Josh Beckett .75 2.00
EE46 Ivan Rodriguez 1.25 3.00
EE47 Alfonso Soriano 1.25 3.00
EE48 Eric Gagne .75 2.00
EE49 Hank Blalock .75 2.00
EE50 Roger Clemens 2.50 6.00
EE51 Derek Jeter 5.00 12.00
EE52 Derek Jeter 5.00 12.00
EE53 Barry Zito 1.25 3.00
EE54 Alex Rodriguez 2.50 6.00
EE55 Nomar Garciaparra 1.25 3.00
EE56 Torii Hunter .75 2.00
EE57 Ichiro Suzuki 2.50 6.00
EE58 Randy Johnson 2.00 5.00
EE59 Ichiro Suzuki 2.50 6.00
EE60 Albert Pujols 2.50 6.00
EE61 Albert Pujols 2.50 6.00
EE62 Ichiro Suzuki 2.50 6.00
EE63 Derek Jeter 5.00 12.00
EE64 Pedro Martinez 1.25 3.00
EE65 Chris Shelton .75 2.00
EE66 Ivan Rodriguez 1.25 3.00
EE67 Chipper Jones 2.00 5.00
EE68 Pedro Martinez 1.25 3.00
EE69 Ken Griffey Jr. 4.00 10.00
EE70 Jeff Bagwell 1.25 3.00
EE71 Nomar Garciaparra 1.25 3.00
EE72 Mark Prior 1.25 3.00
EE73 Kerry Wood .75 2.00
EE74 Andruw Jones .75 2.00
EE75 Derek Jeter 5.00 12.00
EE76 Cal Ripken 6.00 15.00
EE77 Ken Griffey Jr. 4.00 10.00
EE78 Ken Griffey Jr. 4.00 10.00
EE79 Mike Piazza 2.00 5.00
EE80 Nolan Ryan 6.00 15.00
EE81 Greg Maddux 2.50 6.00
EE82 Greg Maddux 2.50 6.00
EE83 Roger Clemens 2.50 6.00
EE84 Ozzie Smith 2.50 6.00
EE85 Tom Seaver 1.25 3.00
EE86 Thurman Munson 2.00 5.00
EE87 Reggie Jackson 1.25 3.00
EE88 Johnny Bench 2.00 5.00
EE89 Mike Schmidt 3.00 8.00
EE90 Carlton Fisk 1.25 3.00
EE91 Eddie Mathews 2.00 5.00
EE92 Roy Campanella 2.00 5.00
EE93 Jackie Robinson 2.00 5.00
EE94 Joe DiMaggio 4.00 10.00
EE95 Jimmie Foxx 2.00 5.00
EE96 Lou Gehrig 4.00 10.00
EE97 Babe Ruth 5.00 12.00
EE98 Ty Cobb 3.00 8.00
EE99 Honus Wagner 2.00 5.00
EE100 Cy Young 2.00 5.00

2006 Upper Deck Epic Four Barrel

OVERALL GU ODDS ONE PER PACK
STATED PRINT RUN 1 SERIAL #'d SET
NO PRICING DUE TO SCARCITY

2006 Upper Deck Epic Foursome Fabrics

OVERALL GU ODDS ONE PER PACK
PRINT RUNS B/WN 5-50 COPIES PER
NO PRICING ON QTY OF 30 OR LESS
GRSM Gibs/Ryan/Seav/Mari/50 30.00 60.00
PJGG Puj/Jeter/Grif/Vlad/50 75.00 150.00
RCJP Ryan/Clem/Rand/Pri/50 30.00 60.00
WYBS Will/Yaz/Bog/Schil/50 50.00 100.00

2006 Upper Deck Epic Materials Blue

*BLUE p/r 75-99: .5X TO 1.2X ORG p/r 125-185
*BLUE p/r 75-99: .4X TO 1X ORG p/r 75-99
*BLUE p/r 75-99: .3X TO .8X ORG p/r 39-52
*BLUE p/r 49-65: .6 TO 1.5X ORG p/r 125-185
*BLUE p/r 49-65: .4 TO 1X ORG p/r 39-52
*BLUE p/r 25-34: .75X TO 2X ORG p/r 125-185
*BLUE p/r 25-34: .6X TO 1.5X ORG p/r 125-185
*BLUE p/r 25-34: .5X TO 1.2X ORG p/r 39-52
*BLUE p/r 25-34: .4X TO 1X ORG p/r 35
*BLUE p/r 10: .6X TO 1.5X ORG p/r 39-52
*BLUE p/r 10: .4X TO 1X ORG p/r 10-16
OVERALL GU ODDS ONE PER PACK
PRINT RUNS B/WN 3-99 COPIES PER
NO WAGNER PRICING DUE TO SCARCITY
BR1 Babe Ruth Bat/3 300.00 500.00
BR2 Babe Ruth Bat/3 300.00 500.00
CL1 R.Clemente Pants/99 15.00 40.00
JD1 Joe DiMaggio Jsy/25 40.00 80.00
JD2 Joe DiMaggio Jsy/25 40.00 80.00
JD3 Joe DiMaggio Jsy/25 40.00 80.00
JR Jackie Robinson Bat/10 20.00 50.00
LG1 Lou Gehrig Bat/10 100.00 200.00
LG2 Lou Gehrig Bat/10 60.00 120.00
LG3 Lou Gehrig Bat/10 60.00 120.00
RH Rogers Hornsby Jkt/10 20.00 50.00
TW1 Ted Williams Jsy/25 30.00 60.00
TW2 Ted Williams Pants/25 30.00 60.00

2006 Upper Deck Epic Materials Dark Green

*DG p/r 50: .6X TO 1.5X ORG p/r 125-185
*DG p/r 50: .5X TO 1.2X ORG p/r 75-99
*DG p/r 50: .4X TO 1X ORG p/r 39-52
*DG p/r 10: 1X TO 2.5X ORG p/r 125-185
*DG p/r 10: .75X TO 2X ORG p/r 75-99
*DG p/r 10: .6X TO 1.5X ORG p/r 39-52

*DG p/r 10: .5X TO 1.2X ORG p/r 35
*DG p/r 10: .4X TO 1X ORG p/r 10-16
OVERALL GU ODDS ONE PER PACK
PRINT RUNS B/WN 3-50 COPIES PER
BR1 Babe Ruth Bat/3 300.00 500.00
BR2 Babe Ruth Bat/3 300.00 500.00
CL1 R.Clemente Pants/50 20.00 50.00
HW Honus Wagner Pants/15 50.00 100.00
JD1 Joe DiMaggioJsy/15 50.00 100.00
JD2 Joe DiMaggio Jsy/50 30.00 60.00
JD3 Joe DiMaggio Jsy/15 50.00 100.00
JR Jackie Robinson Bat/10 20.00 50.00
LG1 Lou Gehrig Bat/5 100.00 200.00
LG2 Lou Gehrig Bat/5 100.00 200.00
LG3 Lou Gehrig Bat/5 100.00 200.00
RH Rogers Hornsby Jkt/10 20.00 50.00
TW1 Ted Williams Jsy/50 20.00 50.00
TW2 Ted Williams Jsy/50 20.00 50.00

2006 Upper Deck Epic Materials Dark Orange

*DO p/r 119-185: .4X TO 1X ORG p/r 125-185
*DO p/r 119-185: .25X TO .6X ORG p/r 39-52
*DO p/r 75-99: .5X TO 1.2X ORG p/r 125-185
*DO p/r 75-99: .4X TO 1X ORG p/r 75-99
*DO p/r 39-65: .6X TO 1.5X ORG p/r 125-185
*DO p/r 39-65: .5X TO 1.2X ORG p/r 75-99
*DO p/r 39-65: .4X TO 1X ORG p/r 39-52
*DO p/r 25-35: .4X TO 1X ORG p/r 35
*DO p/r 25-35: .3X TO .8X ORG p/r 10-16
OVERALL GU ODDS ONE PER PACK
PRINT RUNS B/WN 5-185 COPIES PER
BR1 Babe Ruth Bat/5 300.00 500.00
BR2 Babe Ruth Bat/5 300.00 500.00
CL1 R.Clemente Pants/65 20.00 50.00
HW Honus Wagner Pants/25 40.00 80.00
JD1 Joe DiMaggioPants/65 30.00 60.00
JD2 Joe DiMaggio Pants/65 30.00 60.00
JD3 Joe DiMaggio Pants/65 30.00 60.00
JR Jackie Robinson Bat/11 20.00 50.00
LG1 Lou Gehrig Bat/15 60.00 120.00
LG2 Lou Gehrig Bat/15 60.00 120.00
LG3 Lou Gehrig Bat/15 60.00 120.00
RH Rogers Hornsby Jkt/50 12.50 30.00
TW1 Ted Williams Jsy/99 15.00 40.00
TW2 Ted Williams Pants/99 15.00 40.00

2006 Upper Deck Epic Materials Dark Purple

*DP p/r 102-185: .4X TO 1X ORG p/r 125-185
*DP p/r 102-185: .25X TO .6X ORG p/r 39-52
*DP p/r 75: .5X TO 1.2X ORG p/r 125-185
*DP p/r 75: .4X TO 1X ORG p/r 75-99
*DP p/r 39-50: .6X TO 1.5X ORG p/r 125-185
*DP p/r 39-50: .5X TO 1.2X ORG p/r 75-99
*DP p/r 39-50: .4X TO 1X ORG p/r 39-52
*DP p/r 25-50: .75X TO 2X ORG p/r 125-185
*DP p/r 25-50: .6X TO 1.5X ORG p/r 75-99
*DP p/r 25-50: .4X TO 1X ORG p/r 35
*DP p/r 25-50: .3X TO .8X ORG p/r 10-16
OVERALL GU ODDS ONE PER PACK
PRINT RUNS B/WN 3-185 COPIES PER
NO B.ROBINSON PRICING DUE TO SCARCITY
BR1 Babe Ruth Bat/3 300.00 500.00
BR2 Babe Ruth Bat/3 300.00 500.00
CL1 R.Clemente Pants/45 20.00 50.00
HW Honus Wagner Pants/25 40.00 80.00
JD1 Joe DiMaggio Jsy/25 40.00 80.00
JD2 Joe DiMaggio Jsy/35 30.00 60.00
JD3 Joe DiMaggio Jsy/35 30.00 60.00
JR Jackie Robinson Bat/11 20.00 50.00
LG1 Lou Gehrig Bat/15 60.00 120.00
LG2 Lou Gehrig Bat/15 60.00 120.00
LG3 Lou Gehrig Bat/15 60.00 120.00
RH Rogers Hornsby Jkt/50 12.50 30.00
TW1 Ted Williams Jsy/45 20.00 50.00
TW2 Ted Williams Jsy/45 20.00 50.00

2006 Upper Deck Epic Materials Gold

*GOLD p/r 24-25: .75X TO 2X ORG p/r 125-185
*GOLD p/r 24-25: .6X TO 1.5X ORG p/r 75-99
*GOLD p/r 24-25: .5X TO 1.2X ORG p/r 39-52
*GOLD p/r 10-19: 1X TO 2.5X ORG p/r 125-185
*GOLD p/r 10-19: .75X TO 2X ORG p/r 75-99
*GOLD p/r 10-19: .6X TO 1.5X ORG p/r 39-52
*GOLD p/r 10-19: .5X TO 1.2X ORG p/r 35
*GOLD p/r 10-19: .4X TO 1X ORG p/r 10-16
OVERALL GU ODDS ONE PER PACK
PRINT RUNS B/WN 1-25 COPIES PER
NO CLEMENTE PRICING DUE TO SCARCITY
NO GREENBERG PRICING DUE TO SCARCITY
NO MATHEWS PRICING DUE TO SCARCITY
NO RUTH PRICING DUE TO SCARCITY
HW Honus Wagner Pants/15 50.00 100.00
JD1 Joe DiMaggio Jsy/15 50.00 100.00
JD2 Joe DiMaggio Jsy/15 50.00 100.00
JD3 Joe DiMaggio Jsy/16 50.00 100.00
JR Jackie Robinson Bat/11 20.00 50.00
LG1 Lou Gehrig Bat/5 100.00 200.00
LG2 Lou Gehrig Bat/5 100.00 200.00
LG3 Lou Gehrig Bat/5 100.00 200.00
RH Rogers Hornsby Jkt/10 20.00 50.00
TW1 Ted Williams Jsy/24 30.00 60.00
TW2 Ted Williams Jsy/25 30.00 60.00

2006 Upper Deck Epic Materials Green

*GRN p/r 75: .5X TO 1.2X ORG p/r 125-185
*GRN p/r 75: .4X TO 1X ORG p/r 75-99
*GRN p/r 75: .3X TO .8X ORG p/r 39-52
*GRN p/r 20: .5X TO 1.2X ORG p/r 39-52
*GRN p/r 10-19: 1X TO 2.5X ORG p/r 125-185
*GRN p/r 10-19: .75X TO 2X ORG p/r 75-99
*GRN p/r 10-19: .6X TO 1.5X ORG p/r 39-52
*GRN p/r 10-19: .5X TO 1.2X ORG p/r 35
*GRN p/r 10-19: .4X TO 1X ORG p/r 10-16
OVERALL GU ODDS ONE PER PACK
PRINT RUNS B/WN 3-75 COPIES PER
NO J.ROBINSON PRICING DUE TO SCARCITY
BR1 Babe Ruth Bat/3 300.00 500.00
BR2 Babe Ruth Bat/3 300.00 500.00
CL1 R.Clemente Pants/75 15.00 40.00
HW Honus Wagner Pants/15 50.00 100.00
JD1 Joe DiMaggio Jsy/75 20.00 50.00
JD2 Joe DiMaggio Jsy/15 50.00 100.00
JD3 Joe DiMaggio Jsy/16 50.00 100.00
LG1 Lou Gehrig Bat/5 100.00 200.00
LG2 Lou Gehrig Bat/5 100.00 200.00
LG3 Lou Gehrig Bat/5 100.00 200.00
RH Rogers Hornsby Jkt/10 20.00 50.00
TW1 Ted Williams Jsy/75 15.00 40.00
TW2 Ted Williams Jsy/75 15.00 40.00

2006 Upper Deck Epic Materials Grey

*GREY p/r 40: .6X TO 1.5X ORG p/r 125-185
*GREY p/r 40: .5X TO 1.2X ORG p/r 75-99
*GREY p/r 40: .4X TO 1X ORG p/r 39-52
*GREY p/r 10-19: 1X TO 2.5X ORG p/r 125-185
*GREY p/r 10-19: .75X TO 2X ORG p/r 75-99
*GREY p/r 10-19: .6X TO 1.5X ORG p/r 39-52
*GREY p/r 10-19: .5X TO 1.2X ORG p/r 35
*GREY p/r 10-19: .4X TO 1X ORG p/r 10-16
OVERALL GU ODDS ONE PER PACK
PRINT RUNS B/WN 3-40 COPIES PER
NO GREENBERG PRICING DUE TO SCARCITY
NO J.ROBINSON PRICING DUE TO SCARCITY
BR1 Babe Ruth Bat/3 300.00 500.00
BR2 Babe Ruth Bat/3 300.00 500.00
CL1 R.Clemente Pants/40 20.00 50.00
HW Honus Wagner Pants/15 50.00 100.00
JD1 Joe DiMaggio Jsy/40 30.00 60.00
JD2 Joe DiMaggio Jsy/16 50.00 100.00
JD3 Joe DiMaggio Jsy/16 50.00 100.00
LG1 Lou Gehrig Bat/5 100.00 200.00
LG2 Lou Gehrig Bat/5 100.00 200.00
LG3 Lou Gehrig Bat/5 100.00 200.00
RH Rogers Hornsby Jkt/10 20.00 50.00
TW1 Ted Williams Jsy/40 20.00 50.00
TW2 Ted Williams Jsy/40 20.00 50.00

2006 Upper Deck Epic Materials Light Purple

*LP p/r 105-185: .4X TO 1X ORG p/r 125-185
*LP p/r 105-185: .25X TO .6X ORG p/r 39-52
*LP p/r 75: .5X TO 1.2X ORG p/r 125-185
*LP p/r 75: .4X TO 1X ORG p/r 75-99
*LP p/r 39-59: .6X TO 1.5X ORG p/r 125-185
*LP p/r 39-59: .5X TO 1.2X ORG p/r 75-99
*LP p/r 39-59: .4X TO 1X ORG p/r 39-52
*LP p/r 24-34: .75X TO 2X ORG p/r 125-185
*LP p/r 24-34: .4X TO 1X ORG p/r 35
*LP p/r 24-34: .3X TO .8X ORG p/r 10-16
OVERALL GU ODDS ONE PER PACK
PRINT RUNS B/WN 4-185 COPIES PER
NO SEAVER/15 PRICING DUE TO SCARCITY
BR1 Babe Ruth Bat/4 300.00 500.00
BR2 Babe Ruth Bat/4 300.00 500.00
CL1 R.Clemente Pants/50 20.00 50.00
HW Honus Wagner Pants/24 40.00 80.00
JD1 Joe DiMaggio Jsy/25 40.00 80.00
JD2 Joe DiMaggio Jsy/45 30.00 60.00
JD3 Joe DiMaggio Jsy/45 30.00 60.00
JR Jackie Robinson Bat/10 20.00 50.00
LG1 Lou Gehrig Bat/15 60.00 120.00
LG2 Lou Gehrig Bat/15 60.00 120.00
LG3 Lou Gehrig Bat/15 60.00 120.00
RH Rogers Hornsby Jkt/50 12.50 30.00
TW1 Ted Williams Jsy/55 20.00 50.00
TW2 Ted Williams Jsy/55 20.00 50.00

2006 Upper Deck Epic Materials Orange

OVERALL GU ODDS ONE PER PACK
PRINT RUNS B/WN 10-185 COPIES PER
NO COBB PRICING DUE TO SCARCITY
AP1 Albert Pujols Jsy/185 8.00 20.00
AP2 Albert Pujols Jsy/185 8.00 20.00
AP3 Albert Pujols Jsy/185 8.00 20.00
BG Bob Gibson Jsy/155 4.00 10.00
BG2 Bob Gibson Pants/155 4.00 10.00
BR1 Babe Ruth Bat/15 175.00 300.00
BR2 Babe Ruth Bat/15 175.00 300.00
CF Carlton Fisk Jsy/169 4.00 10.00
CF2 Carlton Fisk Jsy/185 4.00 10.00
CL1 R.Clemente Pants/50 20.00 50.00
CR1 Cal Ripken Jsy/185 8.00 20.00
CR2 Cal Ripken Jsy/177 8.00 20.00
CR3 Cal Ripken Jsy/155 8.00 20.00
CY1 Carl Yastrzemski Jsy/185 4.00 10.00
CY2 Carl Yastrzemski Jsy/185 4.00 10.00
CY3 Carl Yastrzemski Jsy/185 4.00 10.00
DJ1 Derek Jeter Jsy/185 12.50 30.00
DJ2 Derek Jeter Jsy/185 12.50 30.00
DJ3 Derek Jeter Jsy/185 12.50 30.00
DM1 Don Mattingly Jsy/185 6.00 15.00
DM2 Don Mattingly Jsy/185 6.00 15.00
EB Ernie Banks Jsy/155 5.00 12.00
ED Eddie Mathews Jsy/75 5.00 12.00
EM1 Eddie Murray Jsy/185 4.00 10.00
EM2 Eddie Murray Jsy/165 4.00 10.00
EM3 Eddie Murray Jsy/155 4.00 10.00
FR1 Frank Robinson Jsy/130 4.00 10.00
FR2 Frank Robinson Jsy/130 4.00 10.00
GH Gil Hodges Bat/39 10.00 25.00
HG Hank Greenberg Bat/50 10.00 25.00
HK H.Killebrew Pants/155 4.00 10.00
HW Honus Wagner Pants/16 50.00 100.00
JB1 Johnny Bench Jsy/155 4.00 10.00
JB2 Johnny Bench Jsy/155 4.00 10.00
JD1 Joe DiMaggio Pants/185 15.00 40.00
JD2 Joe DiMaggio Pants/173 15.00 40.00
JD3 Joe DiMaggio Pants/99 20.00 50.00
JM Juan Marichal Jsy/155 4.00 10.00
JO Joe Morgan Jsy/145 4.00 10.00
JO2 Joe Morgan Jsy/155 4.00 10.00
JR Jackie Robinson Bat/10 20.00 50.00
KG1 Ken Griffey Jr. Jsy/175 8.00 20.00
KG2 Ken Griffey Jr. Jsy/175 8.00 20.00
KG3 Ken Griffey Jr. Jsy/175 8.00 20.00
KP1 Kirby Puckett Jsy/155 10.00 25.00
KP2 Kirby Puckett Jsy/155 10.00 25.00
LB1 Lou Brock Pants/48 6.00 15.00
LB2 Lou Brock Pants/48 6.00 15.00
LG1 Lou Gehrig Bat/15 60.00 120.00
LG2 Lou Gehrig Bat/15 60.00 120.00
LG3 Lou Gehrig Bat/15 60.00 120.00
MA Mark Prior Jsy/185 4.00 10.00
MA2 Mark Prior Jsy/185 4.00 10.00
MP1 Mike Piazza Jsy/145 4.00 10.00
MP2 Mike Piazza Jsy/145 4.00 10.00
MS1 Mike Schmidt Jsy/185 5.00 12.00
MS2 Mike Schmidt Jsy/185 5.00 12.00
MS3 Mike Schmidt Jsy/185 5.00 12.00
NR1 Nolan Ryan Jsy/155 8.00 20.00
NR2 Nolan Ryan Jsy/155 8.00 20.00
NR3 Nolan Ryan Jsy/155 8.00 20.00
OS1 Ozzie Smith Bat/155 4.00 10.00
OS2 Ozzie Smith Jsy/185 4.00 10.00
PM1 Paul Molitor Jsy/155 4.00 10.00
PM2 Paul Molitor Jsy/155 4.00 10.00
PR1 Pee Wee Reese Jsy/145 4.00 10.00
PR2 Pee Wee Reese Jsy/145 4.00 10.00
RC1 Roger Clemens Pants/155 5.00 12.00
RC2 Roger Clemens Pants/155 5.00 12.00
RC3 Roger Clemens Pants/155 5.00 12.00
RE1 Reggie Jackson Jsy/52 6.00 15.00
RE2 Reggie Jackson Jsy/52 6.00 15.00
RE3 Reggie Jackson Jsy/52 6.00 15.00
RH Rogers Hornsby Jkt/50 12.50 30.00
RJ1 Randy Johnson Jsy/145 4.00 10.00
RJ2 Randy Johnson Jsy/145 4.00 10.00
RO Brooks Robinson Pants/49 6.00 15.00
RO2 Brooks Robinson Pants/99 5.00 12.00
RS1 Ryne Sandberg Jsy/155 4.00 10.00
RS2 Ryne Sandberg Jsy/155 4.00 10.00
RS3 Ryne Sandberg Jsy/155 4.00 10.00
RY1 Robin Yount Jsy/155 4.00 10.00
RY2 Robin Yount Jsy/155 4.00 10.00
SM1 Stan Musial Jsy/50 8.00 20.00
SM2 Stan Musial Jsy/75 6.00 15.00
TH1 T.Munson Pants/35 10.00 25.00
TH2 T.Munson Pants/35 10.00 25.00
TS Tom Seaver Jsy/155 4.00 10.00
TS2 Tom Seaver Jsy/155 4.00 10.00
TW1 Ted Williams Pants/125 15.00 40.00
TW2 Ted Williams Pants/125 15.00 40.00
VG Vladimir Guerrero Jsy/145 4.00 10.00
VG2 Vladimir Guerrero Jsy/145 4.00 10.00
WB1 Wade Boggs Jsy/185 4.00 10.00
WB2 Wade Boggs Jsy/185 4.00 10.00
WF Whitey Ford Pants/155 6.00 15.00
WM Willie McCovey Jsy/155 4.00 10.00
WM2 Willie McCovey Pants/155 4.00 10.00
WM3 Willie McCovey Pants/155 4.00 10.00

2006 Upper Deck Epic Materials Red

*RED p/r 105-185: .4X TO 1X ORG p/r 125-185
*RED p/r 105-185: .25X TO .6X ORG p/r 39-52
*RED p/r 69-99: .5X TO 1.2X ORG p/r 125-185
*RED p/r 69-99: .4X TO 1X ORG p/r 75-99
*RED p/r 69-99: .3X TO .8X ORG p/r 39-52
*RED p/r 49-65: .5X TO 1.2X ORG p/r 75-99
*RED p/r 49-65: .4X TO 1X ORG p/r 39-52
*RED p/r 25-34: .75X TO 2X ORG p/r 125-185
*RED p/r 25-34: .4X TO 1X ORG p/r 35
*RED p/r 25-34: .3X TO .8X ORG p/r 10-16
*RED p/r 10-19: .6X TO 1.5X ORG p/r 39-52
*RED p/r 10-19: .4X TO 1X ORG p/r 10-16
OVERALL GU ODDS ONE PER PACK
PRINT RUNS B/WN 10-185 COPIES PER
NO GEHRIG PRICING DUE TO SCARCITY
CL1 R.Clemente Pants/65 20.00 50.00
HW Honus Wagner Pants/25 40.00 80.00
JD1 Joe DiMaggio Jsy/25 40.00 80.00
JD2 Joe DiMaggio Jsy/55 30.00 60.00
JD3 Joe DiMaggio Jsy/55 30.00 60.00
JR Jackie Robinson Bat/10 20.00 50.00
LG1 Lou Gehrig Bat/15 60.00 120.00
LG2 Lou Gehrig Bat/15 60.00 120.00
LG3 Lou Gehrig Bat/15 60.00 120.00
RH Rogers Hornsby Jkt/50 12.50 30.00
TW1 Ted Williams Jsy/75 15.00 40.00
TW2 Ted Williams Jsy/75 15.00 40.00

2006 Upper Deck Epic Materials Teal

*TEAL p/r 99: .5X TO 1.2X ORG p/r 125-185
*TEAL p/r 99: .4X TO 1X ORG p/r 75-99
*TEAL p/r 99: .3X TO .8X ORG p/r 39-52
*TEAL p/r 65: .6X TO 1.5X ORG p/r 125-185
*TEAL p/r 21: .5X TO 1.2X ORG p/r 39-52
*TEAL p/r 10-19: 1X TO 2.5X ORG p/r 125-185
*TEAL p/r 10-19: .75X TO 2X ORG p/r 75-99
*TEAL p/r 10-19: .6X TO 1.5X ORG p/r 39-52
*TEAL p/r 10-19: .5X TO 1.2X ORG p/r 35
*TEAL p/r 10-19: .4X TO 1X ORG p/r 10-16
OVERALL GU ODDS ONE PER PACK
PRINT RUNS B/WN 5-99 COPIES PER
BR1 Babe Ruth Bat/5 300.00 500.00
BR2 Babe Ruth Bat/5 300.00 500.00
CL1 R.Clemente Pants/99 15.00 40.00
HW Honus Wagner Pants/15 50.00 100.00
JD1 Joe DiMaggio Jsy/16 50.00 100.00
JD2 Joe DiMaggio Jsy/16 50.00 100.00
JD3 Joe DiMaggio Jsy/16 50.00 100.00
JR Jackie Robinson Bat/15 20.00 50.00
LG1 Lou Gehrig Bat/5 100.00 200.00
LG2 Lou Gehrig Bat/5 100.00 200.00
LG3 Lou Gehrig Bat/5 100.00 200.00
RH Rogers Hornsby Jkt/10 20.00 50.00
TW1 Ted Williams Jsy/99 15.00 40.00
TW2 Ted Williams Jsy/99 15.00 40.00

2006 Upper Deck Epic Materials Signature

OVERALL AU ODDS ONE PER CASE
STATED PRINT RUN 5 SERIAL #'d SETS
NO PRICING DUE TO SCARCITY

2006 Upper Deck Epic Pairings

OVERALL GU ODDS ONE PER PACK
PRINT RUNS B/WN 5-99 COPIES PER
NO PRICING ON QTY OF 25 OR LESS
BB Boggs J/Brooks B/99 10.00 25.00
BM Bench J/Morgan J/99 10.00 25.00
BR Gibson J/Ryan J/99 15.00 40.00
BS Brock J/Ozzie J/99 10.00 25.00
BS2 Boggs J/Sandberg J/99 10.00 25.00
CJ Clemens P/Randy P/99 12.50 30.00
CR Clemens P/Ryan J/99 10.00 25.00
FB Fisk P/Bench J/99 10.00 25.00
FP Fisk P/Piazza J/99 10.00 25.00
GB Gibson J/Brock J/99 10.00 25.00
GG Griffey Jr. J/Vlad J/99 15.00 40.00
GP Griffey Jr. J/K.Puck J/99 20.00 50.00
GR Gehrig B/Ripken J/45 125.00 200.00
JD Jeter J/DiMaggio B/99 40.00 80.00
JG Jeter J/Griffey Jr. J/99 20.00 50.00
JJ Reggie J/Jeter J/99 12.50 30.00
JK Reggie J/Killebrew P/99 10.00 25.00
JM Jeter J/Mattingly J/99 40.00 80.00
JS Reggie J/Schmidt J/99 15.00 40.00
KP Killebrew P/Puck J/99 15.00 40.00
MB Munson P/Bench J/30 20.00 50.00
MM Marichal J/McCovey J/99 10.00 25.00
MM2 Mattingly J/Munson P/30 40.00 80.00
MR Mathews J/Brooks B/50 15.00 40.00
MS Mathews J/Schmidt J/50 30.00 60.00
MY Molitor J/Yount J/99 10.00 25.00
PH Pujols J/Hornsby JK/99 20.00 50.00
PM Pujols J/Musial J/99 15.00 40.00
RJ Reese J/Jeter J/99 10.00 25.00
RM Ripken J/Murray J/99 10.00 25.00
RR2 Brooks B/F.Rob J/99 10.00 25.00
RY F.Rob J/C.Yaz J/99 12.50 30.00
SB Sandberg J/Banks J/99 15.00 40.00
SM Sandberg J/J.Morgan J/99 10.00 25.00
SR Seaver J/Ryan J/99 20.00 50.00
SS Sandberg J/Ozzie J/99 15.00 40.00
WD T.Will J/DiMaggio B/45 60.00 120.00
WM T.Will J/Musial J/45 30.00 60.00
YW C.Yaz J/T.Williams J/50 40.00 80.00

2006 Upper Deck Epic Swatch

OVERALL GU ODDS ONE PER PACK
STATED PRINT RUN 50 SERIAL #'d SETS
AP Albert Pujols Jsy 10.00 25.00
CF Carlton Fisk Pants 8.00 20.00
CR Cal Ripken Jsy 20.00 50.00
CS Curt Schilling Jsy 8.00 20.00
CY Carl Yastrzemski Jsy 10.00 25.00
DJ1 Derek Jeter Jsy 30.00 60.00
DJ2 Derek Jeter Jsy 30.00 60.00
DO David Ortiz Jsy 8.00 20.00
DW Dontrelle Willis Jsy 6.00 15.00
EC Eric Chavez Jsy 6.00 15.00
IR Ivan Rodriguez Jsy 8.00 20.00
JB Jason Bay Jsy 6.00 15.00
JM Joe Morgan Jsy 6.00 15.00
JP Jake Peavy Jsy 6.00 15.00
JR Jose Reyes Jsy 6.00 15.00
JS Johan Santana Jsy 8.00 20.00
KG1 Ken Griffey Jr. Jsy 10.00 25.00
KG2 Ken Griffey Jr. Jsy 10.00 25.00
MI Miguel Tejada Jsy 6.00 15.00
MP Mark Prior Jsy 6.00 15.00
MR Manny Ramirez Jsy 8.00 20.00
MT Mark Teixeira Jsy 6.00 15.00
PM Pedro Martinez Jsy 8.00 20.00
RC Roger Clemens Pants 15.00 40.00
RJ Randy Johnson Jsy 8.00 20.00
RO Roy Oswalt Jsy 6.00 15.00
RZ Ryan Zimmerman Jsy 15.00 40.00
SR Scott Rolen Jsy 8.00 20.00
TG Tony Gwynn Jsy 10.00 25.00
VG Vladimir Guerrero Jsy 8.00 20.00

2006 Upper Deck Epic Triple Materials

OVERALL GU ODDS ONE PER PACK
PRINT RUNS B/WN 3-99 COPIES PER
NO PRICING ON QTY OF 25 OR LESS
BER Bench/Murr/Brooks/60 12.50 30.00
BMR Boggs/Moli/Brooks/99 12.50 30.00
BSP Banks/Ryno/Prior/99 12.50 30.00
FJJ Ford/Reggie/Jeter/99 20.00 50.00
FMJ Ford/Matt/Reggie/51 15.00 40.00
GJC Gibs/Rand/Clemens/99 12.00 30.00
GPS Gibson/Prior/Seav/99 12.50 30.00
GRM Griff/F.Rob/McCov/99 30.00 60.00
JGK Reggie/Vlad/Kill/99 12.50 30.00
JKR Reggie/Kill/F.Rob/99 12.50 30.00
JPG Jeter/Pujols/Griff/99 20.00 50.00
MBF Munson/Bench/Fisk/99 12.50 30.00
MBG Morgan/Bench/Griff/99 12.50 30.00
MFM Munson/Fisk/Murr/99 12.00 30.00
MMG Murr/Matt/Garv/49 15.00 40.00
MPS Murr/Piazza/Seav/99 12.50 30.00
MSY Moli/Ozzie/Yount/49 20.00 50.00
RBS Rip/Boggs/Schm/99 20.00 50.00
RCJ Ryan/Clemens/Randy/75 30.00 60.00
RJD Ruth/Reggie/DiMag/99 125.00 250.00
RRM Jackie/F.Rob/McCov/50 20.00 50.00
WSR Wagner/Ozzie/Reese/99 60.00 120.00
YRJ Yount/Ripken/Jeter/99 20.00 50.00

2005 Upper Deck ESPN

COMPLETE SET (90) 10.00 25.00
COMMON CARD (1-90) .10 .30
1 Garret Anderson .12 .30
2 Troy Glaus .12 .30
3 Vladimir Guerrero .20 .50
4 Luis Gonzalez .12 .30
5 Randy Johnson .30 .75
6 Andruw Jones .12 .30
7 Chipper Jones .30 .75
8 J.D. Drew .12 .30
9 John Smoltz .30 .75
10 Miguel Tejada .20 .50
11 Rafael Palmeiro .20 .50
12 Curt Schilling .20 .50
13 David Ortiz .30 .75
14 Manny Ramirez .30 .75
15 Pedro Martinez .20 .50
16 Carlos Zambrano .20 .50
17 Greg Maddux .40 1.00
18 Kerry Wood .12 .30
19 Mark Prior .20 .50
20 Nomar Garciaparra .20 .50
21 Sammy Sosa .30 .75
22 Carlos Lee .12 .30
23 Frank Thomas .30 .75
24 Magglio Ordonez .20 .50
25 Paul Konerko .20 .50
26 Adam Dunn .20 .50
27 Ken Griffey Jr. .60 1.50
28 Travis Hafner .12 .30
29 Victor Martinez .20 .50
30 Todd Helton .20 .50
31 Ivan Rodriguez .20 .50
32 Carl Pavano .12 .30
33 Josh Beckett .12 .30
34 Miguel Cabrera .30 .75
35 Mike Lowell .12 .30
36 Carlos Beltran .20 .50
37 Craig Biggio .20 .50
38 Jeff Bagwell .20 .50
39 Lance Berkman .20 .50
40 Roger Clemens .40 1.00
41 Roy Oswalt .20 .50
42 Mike Sweeney .12 .30
43 Adrian Beltre .30 .75
44 Brad Penny .12 .30
45 Eric Gagne .12 .30
46 Shawn Green .12 .30
47 Steve Finley .12 .30
48 Ben Sheets .12 .30
49 Scott Podsednik .12 .30
50 Joe Mauer .25 .60
51 Johan Santana .20 .50
52 Torii Hunter .12 .30
53 Jose Vidro .12 .30
54 Livan Hernandez .12 .30
55 Jose Reyes .20 .50
56 Mike Piazza .30 .75
57 Tom Glavine .20 .50
58 Alex Rodriguez .40 1.00
59 Bernie Williams .20 .50
60 Derek Jeter .75 2.00
61 Gary Sheffield .12 .30
62 Hideki Matsui .50 1.25
63 Kevin Brown .12 .30
64 Mike Mussina .20 .50
65 Eric Chavez .12 .30
66 Mark Mulder .12 .30
67 Tim Hudson .20 .50
68 Bobby Abreu .12 .30
69 Jim Thome .20 .50
70 Craig Wilson .12 .30
71 Jason Kendall .12 .30
72 Oliver Perez .12 .30
73 Brian Giles .12 .30
74 Jake Peavy .12 .30
75 Jason Schmidt .12 .30
76 Bret Boone .12 .30
77 Ichiro Suzuki .40 1.00
78 Albert Pujols .40 1.00
79 Jim Edmonds .20 .50
80 Larry Walker .20 .50
81 Scott Rolen .20 .50
82 Aubrey Huff .12 .30
83 Carl Crawford .20 .50
84 Alfonso Soriano .20 .50
85 Hank Blalock .12 .30
86 Mark Teixeira .20 .50
87 Michael Young .12 .30
88 Carlos Delgado .12 .30
89 Roy Halladay .20 .50
90 Vernon Wells .12 .30

2005 Upper Deck ESPN ESPY Award Winners

STATED ODDS 1:5
25TH ANN. RANDOM IN PACKS
25TH ANN. PRINT RUN 25 SERIAL #'d SETS
NO 25TH ANN PRICING DUE TO SCARCITY
AW1 Gary Sheffield .40 1.00
AW2 Greg Maddux 1.25 3.00
AW3 Mike Piazza 1.00 2.50
AW4 Jeff Bagwell .60 1.50
AW5 Kenny Rogers .40 1.00
AW6 Cal Ripken 3.00 8.00
AW7 Greg Maddux 1.25 3.00
AW8 Hideo Nomo 1.00 2.50
AW9 Javier Lopez .40 1.00
AW10 Jim Edmonds Angels .60 1.50
AW11 Ken Griffey Jr. 2.00 5.00
AW12 Larry Walker Rockies .60 1.50
AW13 Nomar Garciaparra .60 1.50
AW14 Roger Clemens 1.25 3.00
AW15 David Wells .40 1.00
AW16 Sammy Sosa 1.00 2.50
AW17 Pedro Martinez .60 1.50
AW18 Andres Galarraga .60 1.50
AW19 Derek Jeter 2.50 6.00
AW20 Alfonso Soriano .60 1.50

2005 Upper Deck ESPN Ink

OVERALL AUTO ODDS 1:480
SP INFO PROVIDED BY UPPER DECK
NO PRICING DUE TO SCARCITY
SS Stuart Scott 20.00 50.00

2005 Upper Deck ESPN Magazine Covers

STATED ODDS 1:5
25TH ANN. RANDOM IN PACKS
25TH ANN. PRINT RUN 25 SERIAL #'d SETS
NO 25TH ANN PRICING DUE TO SCARCITY
MC1 Roger Clemens 1.25 3.00
MC2 Derek Jeter 2.50 6.00
MC3 P.Martinez 1.00 2.50
R.Johnson
MC4 Nomar Garciaparra .60 1.50
MC5 Manny Ramirez 1.00 2.50
MC6 Ken Griffey Jr. 2.00 5.00
MC7 Mike Piazza 1.00 2.50
MC8 Ichiro Suzuki 1.25 3.00
MC9 Vladimir Guerrero .60 1.50
MC10 Randy Johnson 1.00 2.50
MC11 Torii .40 1.00
Jacque
A.J.
Mient
MC12 Jason Giambi .40 1.00
MC13 Jeff Kent .40 1.00
MC14 Albert Pujols 1.25 3.00
MC15 Kazuo Matsui .40 1.00
MC16 Miguel Cabrera 1.00 2.50
MC17 Alex Rodriguez 1.25 3.00
MC18 Ivan Rodriguez .60 1.50
MC19 Eric Gagne .40 1.00
MC20 Pujols 1.25 3.00
Edmonds
Rolen

2005 Upper Deck ESPN Sports Center Swatches

STATED ODDS 1:12
SP INFO PROVIDED BY UPPER DECK
NO SP PRICING DUE TO SCARCITY
AB Adrian Beltre 3.00 8.00
AD Adam Dunn 3.00 8.00
AH Aubrey Huff 3.00 8.00
AJ Andruw Jones 4.00 10.00
AP Albert Pujols 8.00 20.00
AS Alfonso Soriano 3.00 8.00
BB Bret Boone 3.00 8.00
BC Bartolo Colon 3.00 8.00
BI Craig Biggio 4.00 10.00
BS Ben Sheets 3.00 8.00
BU B.J. Upton 4.00 10.00
CB Carlos Beltran 3.00 8.00
CC Carl Crawford 3.00 8.00
CP Corey Patterson 3.00 8.00
DJ Derek Jeter Pants 10.00 25.00
DL Derrek Lee 4.00 10.00
EC Eric Chavez 3.00 8.00
EG Eric Gagne 3.00 8.00
GA Garret Anderson 3.00 8.00
HB Hank Blalock 3.00 8.00
IR Ivan Rodriguez 4.00 10.00
IS Ichiro Suzuki 15.00 40.00
JD J.D. Drew 3.00 8.00
JE Jim Edmonds 3.00 8.00
JK Jeff Kent 3.00 8.00
JS Jason Schmidt 3.00 8.00
JT Jim Thome 4.00 10.00
KG Ken Griffey Jr. 8.00 20.00
LB Lance Berkman 3.00 8.00
LO Derek Lowe 3.00 8.00
MC Miguel Cabrera 4.00 10.00
MM Mark Mulder 3.00 8.00
MS Mike Sweeney 3.00 8.00
MT Mark Teixeira 4.00 10.00
PK Paul Konerko Pants 3.00 8.00
RB Rocco Baldelli 3.00 8.00
SA Johan Santana 4.00 10.00
TG Troy Glaus 3.00 8.00
TH Tim Hudson 3.00 8.00
VW Vernon Wells 3.00 8.00

2005 Upper Deck ESPN Sports Century

STATED ODDS 1:5
25TH ANN. RANDOM IN PACKS
25TH ANN. PRINT RUN 25 SERIAL #'d SETS
NO 25TH ANN PRICING DUE TO SCARCITY
SC1 Babe Ruth 2.50 6.00
SC2 Jackie Robinson .60 1.50
SC4 Ty Cobb 1.50 4.00
SC5 Joe DiMaggio 2.00 5.00
SC6 Lou Gehrig 2.00 5.00
SC7 Mickey Mantle 3.00 8.00
SC8 Walter Johnson .60 1.50
SC9 Stan Musial 1.50 4.00
SC10 Satchel Paige 1.00 2.50
SC11 Bob Gibson .60 1.50
SC12 Roberto Clemente 2.50 6.00
SC13 Cy Young .60 1.50
SC14 Honus Wagner .60 1.50
SC15 Rogers Hornsby .40 1.00

2005 Upper Deck ESPN This Day in Baseball History

STATED ODDS 1:5
25TH ANN. RANDOM IN PACKS
25TH ANN. PRINT RUN 25 SERIAL #'d SETS
NO 25TH ANN PRICING DUE TO SCARCITY
BH1 Cal Ripken 3.00 8.00
BH2 Nolan Ryan 3.00 8.00
BH3 Nolan Ryan 3.00 8.00
BH4 Roger Clemens 1.25 3.00
BH5 Thurman Munson .60 1.50
BH6 Mickey Mantle 3.00 8.00
BH7 Ernie Banks 1.00 2.50
BH8 Roy Campanella .60 1.50
BH9 Yogi Berra 1.00 2.50
BH10 Mickey Mantle 3.00 8.00
BH11 Jackie Robinson .60 1.50
BH12 Joe DiMaggio 2.00 5.00
BH13 Bob Feller .60 1.50
BH14 Lou Gehrig 2.00 5.00
BH15 Ty Cobb 1.50 4.00
BH16 Babe Ruth 2.50 6.00
BH17 Walter Johnson .60 1.50
BH18 Rogers Hornsby .40 1.00
BH19 George Sisler .60 1.50
BH20 Cy Young .60 1.50
BH21 Mike Schmidt 1.50 4.00

2005 Upper Deck ESPN Web Gems

STATED ODDS 1:5
25TH ANN. RANDOM IN PACKS
25TH ANN. PRINT RUN 25 SERIAL #'d SETS
NO 25TH ANN PRICING DUE TO SCARCITY
WG1 Adrian Beltre 1.00 2.50
WG2 Alex Rodriguez 1.25 3.00
WG3 Andruw Jones .40 1.00
WG4 Bernie Williams .60 1.50
WG5 Bret Boone .40 1.00
WG6 Cesar Izturis .40 1.00
WG7 Darin Erstad .40 1.00
WG8 Derek Jeter 2.50 6.00
WG9 Derrek Lee .40 1.00
WG10 Eric Chavez .40 1.00
WG11 Greg Maddux 1.25 3.00
WG12 Ichiro Suzuki 1.25 3.00
WG13 Ivan Rodriguez .60 1.50
WG14 Jim Edmonds .60 1.50
WG15 Ken Griffey Jr. 2.00 5.00
WG16 Larry Walker .60 1.50
WG17 Miguel Tejada .60 1.50
WG18 Mike Mussina .60 1.50
WG19 Nomar Garciaparra .60 1.50
WG20 Scott Rolen .60 1.50
WG21 Steve Finley .40 1.00
WG22 Todd Helton .60 1.50
WG23 Torii Hunter .40 1.00
WG24 Vernon Wells .40 1.00
WG25 Vladimir Guerrero .60 1.50

2004 Upper Deck Etchings

COMP.SET w/o SP's (90) 10.00 25.00
COMMON CARD (1-90) .20 .50
COMMON CARD (91-120) .75 2.00
91-120 STATED ODDS 1:6
91-120 PRINT RUN 2004 SERIAL #'d SETS
COMMON AUTO (121-150) 3.00 8.00
121-150 OVERALL AU ODDS 1:4
121-150 PRINT RUN 700 SERIAL #'d SETS
1 Albert Pujols .60 1.50
2 Torii Hunter .20 .50
3 Jim Edmonds .30 .75
4 Alex Rodriguez .60 1.50
5 Rafael Palmeiro .30 .75
6 Ken Griffey Jr. 1.00 2.50
7 Adam Dunn .30 .75
8 Andruw Jones .20 .50
9 Carlos Lee .20 .50
10 Mike Piazza .50 1.25
11 Jeff Bagwell .30 .75
12 Hideki Matsui .75 2.00
13 Gary Sheffield .20 .50
14 Edgar Renteria .20 .50
15 Shawn Green .20 .50
16 Kerry Wood .20 .50
17 Ivan Rodriguez .30 .75
18 Josh Beckett .20 .50
19 Scott Rolen .30 .75
20 Brian Giles .20 .50
21 Derrek Lee .20 .50
22 Mike Lowell .20 .50
23 Mike Mussina .30 .75
24 Sammy Sosa .50 1.25
25 Brandon Webb .20 .50
26 Jacque Jones .20 .50
27 Randy Johnson .50 1.25
28 Luis Gonzalez .20 .50
29 Eric Chavez .20 .50
30 Carlos Delgado .20 .50
31 Phil Nevin .20 .50
32 Ichiro Suzuki .60 1.50
33 Roy Oswalt .30 .75
34 Tim Hudson .30 .75
35 Juan Gonzalez .20 .50
36 Frank Thomas .50 1.25
37 Mark Mulder .20 .50
38 Mark Teixeira .30 .75
39 Miguel Tejada .30 .75
40 Jeff Kent .20 .50
41 Andy Pettitte .30 .75
42 Barry Zito .30 .75
43 Roy Halladay .30 .75
44 Rocco Baldelli .20 .50
45 Derek Jeter 1.25 3.00
46 Corey Patterson .20 .50
47 Javy Lopez .20 .50
48 A.J. Burnett .20 .50
49 Chipper Jones .50 1.25
50 Curt Schilling .30 .75
51 Todd Helton .30 .75
52 Pedro Martinez .30 .75
53 Hideo Nomo .50 1.25
54 Jose Reyes .30 .75
55 Vernon Wells .20 .50
56 Geoff Jenkins .20 .50
57 Troy Glaus .20 .50
58 Greg Maddux .60 1.50
59 Jason Schmidt .20 .50
60 Preston Wilson .20 .50
61 Miguel Cabrera .50 1.25
62 Hank Blalock .20 .50
63 Rafael Furcal .20 .50
64 Vladimir Guerrero .30 .75
65 Lance Berkman .30 .75
66 Javier Vazquez .20 .50
67 Bret Boone .20 .50
68 Mark Prior .30 .75
69 Magglio Ordonez .30 .75
70 Dontrelle Willis .20 .50
71 Richie Sexson .20 .50
72 Alfonso Soriano .30 .75
73 Edwin Jackson .20 .50
74 Jose Vidro .20 .50
75 Jason Giambi .20 .50
76 Kevin Brown .20 .50
77 Orlando Cabrera .20 .50
78 Nomar Garciaparra .30 .75
79 Bobby Abreu .20 .50
80 Manny Ramirez .50 1.25
81 J.D. Drew .20 .50
82 Roger Clemens .60 1.50
83 Pat Burrell .20 .50
84 Ryan Klesko .20 .50
85 Garret Anderson .20 .50
86 Johan Santana .30 .75
87 Kevin Millwood .20 .50
88 Austin Kearns .20 .50
89 Jim Thome .30 .75
90 Carlos Beltran .30 .75
91 Kazuo Matsui FE RC 1.25 3.00
92 Jamie Brown FE RC .75 2.00
93 Brandon Medders FE RC .75 2.00
94 Carlos Vasquez FE RC .75 2.00
95 Chris Aguila FE RC .75 2.00
96 David Aardsma FE RC .75 2.00
97 Justin Leone FE RC .75 2.00
98 Mike Johnston FE RC .75 2.00
99 Tim Bittner FE RC .75 2.00
100 Mike Rouse FE RC .75 2.00
101 Dennis Sarfate FE RC .75 2.00
102 Jason Frasor FE RC .75 2.00
103 Jorge Vasquez FE RC .75 2.00
104 Mike Gosling FE RC .75 2.00
105 Jake Woods FE RC .75 2.00
106 Akinori Otsuka FE RC .75 2.00
107 Lincoln Holdzkom FE RC .75 2.00
108 Jesse Harper FE RC .75 2.00
109 Edwin Moreno FE RC .75 2.00
110 Shingo Takatsu FE RC .75 2.00
111 Ryan Meaux FE RC .75 2.00
112 Donnie Kelly FE RC 1.25 3.00
113 Jerome Gamble FE RC .75 2.00
114 Josh Labandeira FE RC .75 2.00
115 Ian Snell FE RC .75 2.00
116 Michael Wuertz FE RC .75 2.00
117 Greg Dobbs FE RC .75 2.00
118 Sean Henn FE RC .75 2.00
119 Dave Crouthers FE RC .75 2.00
120 Hector Gimenez FE RC .75 2.00
121 Renyel Pinto FE AU RC 3.00 8.00
122 Tim Hamulack FE AU RC 3.00 8.00
123 Chris Saenz FE AU RC 3.00 8.00
124 Carlos Hines FE AU RC 3.00 8.00
125 Justin Knoedler FE AU RC 3.00 8.00
126 Onil Joseph FE AU RC 3.00 8.00
127 Ryan Wing FE AU RC 3.00 8.00
128 Scott Proctor FE AU RC 3.00 8.00
129 Rusty Tucker FE AU RC 3.00 8.00
130 Fernando Nieve FE AU RC 3.00 8.00

131 Chad Bentz FE AU RC 3.00 8.00
132 Jerry Gil FE AU RC 3.00 8.00
133 Mariano Gomez FE AU RC 3.00 8.00
134 Justin Germano FE AU RC 3.00 8.00
135 Jason Bartlett FE AU RC 4.00 10.00
136 Ronald Belisario FE AU RC 3.00 8.00
137 E.Pacheco FE AU RC 3.00 8.00
138 Justin Hampson FE AU RC 3.00 8.00
139 Mike Vento FE AU RC 3.00 8.00
140 Merkin Valdez FE AU RC 3.00 8.00
141 Casey Daigle FE AU RC 3.00 8.00
142 Eddy Rodriguez FE AU RC 3.00 8.00
143 William Bergolla FE AU RC 3.00 8.00
144 Jose Capellan FE AU RC 3.00 8.00
145 Ronny Cedeno FE AU RC 4.00 10.00
146 F.Gracesqui FE AU RC 3.00 8.00
147 Roman Colon FE AU RC 3.00 8.00
148 Roberto Novoa FE AU RC 3.00 8.00
149 Ivan Ochoa FE AU RC 3.00 8.00
150 Shawn Hill FE AU RC 3.00 8.00

2004 Upper Deck Etchings Blue Ink

*BLUE INK: .6X TO 1.5X BLACK INK
OVERALL AU ODDS 1:4
STATED PRINT RUN 200 SERIAL #'d SETS

2004 Upper Deck Etchings Red Ink

OVERALL AU ODDS 1:4 PACKS
STATED PRINT RUN 25 SERIAL #'d SETS
NO PRICING DUE TO SCARCITY

2004 Upper Deck Etchings A Piece of History 500 Club

RANDOM INSERTS IN PACKS
STATED PRINT RUN 350 CARDS
KG Ken Griffey Jr. 100.00 200.00

2004 Upper Deck Etchings A Piece of History 500 Club Autograph

RANDOM INSERTS IN PACKS
STATED PRINT RUN 25 SERIAL #'d CARDS

2004 Upper Deck Etchings Combo Etching Autograph Copper Foil

OVERALL AU ODDS 1:4
PRINT RUNS B/WN 5-115 COPIES PER
NO PRICING ON QTY OF 10 OR LESS
EXCHANGE DEADLINE 08/06/07
AR A.Rod w Glasses/15 100.00 200.00
AR1 A.Rod Smile w o Glass/15 100.00 200.00
AR2 A.Rod Smile w Glass/115 40.00 80.00
CD C.Delgado Face Right/15 20.00 50.00
CD1 C.Delgado Face Left/15 20.00 50.00
CR Cal Ripken Smile/15 175.00 300.00
CR1 Cal Ripken No Smile/15 175.00 300.00
DJ Derek Jeter Look Ahead/15 250.00 500.00
DJ1 Derek Jeter Look Left/25 200.00 400.00
IS Ichiro Look Right/15 400.00 600.00
IS1 Ichiro Look Left/9 400.00 600.00
JB Josh Beckett/25 20.00 50.00
KG Ken Griffey Jr./100 50.00 100.00
KG1 K.Grif Jr. Look Right/25 50.00 100.00
KG2 K.Grif Jr. Look Left/90 50.00 100.00
KW Kerry Wood Face Right/20 20.00 50.00
KW1 K.Wood Right Smile/20 20.00 50.00
KW2 K.Wood Look Ahead/30 20.00 50.00
MC Miguel Cabrera Smile/23 30.00 60.00
MC1 M.Cabrera No Smile/22 30.00 60.00
MP Mark Prior Face Right/15 30.00 60.00
MP2 M.Prior Face Ahead/15 30.00 60.00
MR M.Ram Mouth Open/60 EX 40.00 80.00
MR1 M.Ram Mouth Close/60 EX 40.00 80.00
MT Miguel Tejada Smile/25 10.00 25.00
PI Mike Piazza Black Cap/15 100.00 200.00
PI1 Mike Piazza Blue Cap/15 100.00 200.00
VG Vladimir Guerrero/60 20.00 50.00

2004 Upper Deck Etchings Combo Etching Autograph Gold Foil

*GOLD p/r 50: .6X TO 1.2X CPR p/r 100
*GOLD p/r 15: .75X TO 1.5X CPR p/r 90
*GOLD p/r 15: .6X TO 1.2X CPR p/r 60
*GOLD p/r 15: .6X TO 1.2X CPR p/r 22-23
OVERALL AU ODDS 1:4
PRINT RUNS B/WN 1-50 COPIES PER
NO PRICING ON QTY OF 10 OR LESS
EXCHANGE DEADLINE 08/06/07
MP1 Mark Prior Face Left/15 30.00 60.00
MT1 M.Tejada Mouth Open/25 30.00 60.00

2004 Upper Deck Etchings Combo Etching Autograph Silver Foil

*SILVER p/r 50: .6X TO 1.2X CPR p/r 100
*SILVER p/r 25: .6X TO 1.2X CPR p/r 90-115
*SILVER p/r 25: .5X TO 1X CPR p/r 60
*SILVER p/r 25: .5X TO 1X CPR p/r 22-23
*SILVER p/r 15: .6X TO 1.2X CPR p/r 30
*SILVER p/r 15: .6X TO 1.2X CPR p/r 25
OVERALL AU ODDS 1:4
PRINT RUNS B/WN 4-50 COPIES PER
NO PRICING ON QTY OF 10 OR LESS
EXCHANGE DEADLINE 08/06/07
IS2 Ichiro Look Right Smile/15 400.00 600.00
MT1 M.Tejada Mouth Open/15 30.00 60.00

2004 Upper Deck Etchings Etched in Time Autograph Black

OVERALL AU ODDS 1:4
PRINT RUNS B/WN 100-1625 COPIES PER
EXCHANGE DEADLINE 08/06/07
AA Alfredo Amezaga/375 4.00 10.00
AB Angel Berroa/1325 3.00 8.00
AC Alex Cintron/375 4.00 10.00
AD Andre Dawson/375 6.00 15.00
AE Adam Everett/1325 3.00 8.00
AG Adrian Gonzalez/1325 4.00 10.00
AH Aaron Harang/375 6.00 15.00
AK Adam Kennedy/375 4.00 10.00
AL Adam Loewen/375 4.00 10.00
AT Alan Trammell/375 6.00 15.00
BA Dusty Baker/150 6.00 15.00
BB Bert Blyleven/375 8.00 20.00
BC Bobby Crosby/1325 5.00 12.00
BD Brandon Duckworth/375 4.00 10.00
BE Carlos Beltran/150 6.00 15.00
BG Brian Giles/375 6.00 15.00
BK Bobby Kielty/1325 3.00 8.00
BP Brad Penny/375 6.00 15.00
BR Brooks Robinson/375 8.00 20.00
BS Ben Sheets/375 6.00 15.00
CA Chris Capuano/375 12.50 30.00
CB Chris Bootcheck/375 4.00 10.00
CC Chad Cordero/375 6.00 15.00
CG Chad Gaudin/375 4.00 10.00
CL Brandon Claussen/375 4.00 10.00
CP Corey Patterson/375 4.00 10.00
CR Cal Ripken/100 40.00 80.00
CS Carlos Lee/325 6.00 15.00
CU Chase Utley/375 8.00 20.00
CZ Carlos Zambrano/375 4.00 10.00
DB Dewon Brazelton/375 4.00 10.00
DE Dwight Evans/375 6.00 15.00
DG Dwight Gooden/375 6.00 15.00
DJ Derek Jeter/100 75.00 200.00
DK Dave Kingman/375 6.00 15.00
DM Don Mattingly/150 20.00 60.00
DS Darryl Strawberry/150 6.00 15.00
DY Delmon Young/375 6.00 15.00
EC Eric Chavez/375 6.00 15.00
EJ Edwin Jackson/325 6.00 15.00
GB Geoff Blum/375 4.00 10.00
GK Graham Koonce/375 4.00 10.00
GO Jonny Gomes/325 6.00 15.00
GR Ken Griffey Sr./375 10.00 25.00
HA Rich Harden/1325 5.00 12.00
HB Hank Blalock/375 6.00 15.00
HE Ramon Hernandez/325 4.00 10.00
JB Jason Bay/375 6.00 15.00
JF Josh Fogg/325 4.00 10.00
JI Jim Rice/375 6.00 15.00
JJ Jacque Jones/375 6.00 15.00
JM Justin Miller/325 4.00 10.00
JP Jason Phillips/375 4.00 10.00
JR Jose Reyes/325 6.00 15.00
JW Jerome Williams/1325 3.00 8.00
KA Al Kaline/375 12.00 30.00
KF Kyle Farnsworth/1325 4.00 10.00
KG Ken Griffey Jr./1625 40.00 100.00
KW Kerry Wood/150 10.00 25.00
LA Adam LaRoche/1325 3.00 8.00
LE Cliff Lee/1325 6.00 15.00
LF Lew Ford/375 4.00 10.00
LM Luis Matos/325 4.00 10.00
LO Lyle Overbay/1325 3.00 8.00
LP Lou Piniella/150 6.00 15.00
LT Luis Tiant/375 4.00 10.00
MA Joe Mauer/375 12.50 30.00
MB Marlon Byrd/1025 3.00 8.00
MC Miguel Cabrera/1025 20.00 50.00
ME Morgan Ensberg/1325 5.00 12.00
MG Marcus Giles/325 6.00 15.00
MK Matt Kata/325 4.00 10.00
ML Mike Lowell/375 6.00 15.00
MM Mark Mulder/375 6.00 15.00
MN Mike Neu/325 4.00 10.00
MO Jack Morris/375 6.00 15.00
MP Mark Prior/150 4.00 10.00
MS Mike Scioscia/375 8.00 20.00
MT Mark Teixeira/325 6.00 15.00
MU Dale Murphy/375 12.00 30.00
MY Michael Young/1325 6.00 15.00
NG Nomar Garciaparra/100 25.00 100.00
PA Jim Palmer/375 6.00 15.00
PF Pedro Feliz/325 4.00 10.00
PO Boog Powell/375 6.00 15.00
RA Randy Winn/375 4.00 10.00
RF Rollie Fingers/375 4.00 10.00
RH Rob Hammock/325 4.00 10.00
RI Raul Ibanez/325 8.00 20.00
RO Roy Oswalt/375 6.00 15.00
RS Ryne Sandberg/150 15.00 60.00
RW Ryan Wagner/1325 3.00 8.00
SA Sparky Anderson/375 10.00 25.00
SH Scott Hairston/375 4.00 10.00
SO Ron Santo/375 15.00 40.00
SS Steve Sax/375 4.00 10.00
TA Tony Armas Jr./325 4.00 10.00
TG Tony Gwynn/150 25.00 60.00
TL Ted Lilly/325 10.00 25.00
TS Termel Sledge/325 4.00 10.00
WC Will Clark/150 10.00 25.00
WE Willie Eyre/375 4.00 10.00
WI Josh Willingham/1325 3.00 8.00

2004 Upper Deck Etchings Etched in Time Autograph Blue

*BLUE p/r 150-250: .5X TO 1.2X p/r 1025-1625
*BLUE p/r 150-250: .4X TO 1X p/r 325-375
*BLUE p/r 100: .4X TO 1X p/r 325-375
*BLUE p/r 50: .5X TO 1.2X p/r 150
*BLUE p/r 50: .5X TO 1.2X p/r 100
OVERALL AU ODDS 1:4
PRINT RUNS B/WN 50-250 COPIES PER
EXCHANGE DEADLINE 08/06/07
VG Vladimir Guerrero/50 20.00 50.00

2004 Upper Deck Etchings Etched in Time Autograph Red

*RED: 1X TO 2.5X BLACK p/r 1025-1625
*RED: .75X TO 2X BLACK p/r 325-375
*RED: .6X TO 1.5X BLACK p/r 150
*RED: .75X TO 1.5X BLACK p/r 100
OVERLL AU ODDS 1:4
STATED PRINT RUN 25 SERIAL #'d SETS
EXCHANGE DEADLINE 08/06/07
VG Vladimir Guerrero 30.00 60.00

2004 Upper Deck Etchings Game Bat Blue

OVERALL GU ODDS 1:4
SP'S ARE NOT SERIAL-NUMBERED
SP PRINT RUNS PROVIDED BY UD
AB Adrian Beltre 3.00 8.00
AD Adam Dunn 3.00 8.00
AJ Andruw Jones 4.00 10.00
AP Albert Pujols SP 8.00 20.00
AR Alex Rodriguez 6.00 15.00
AS Alfonso Soriano 3.00 8.00
BA Bobby Abreu 3.00 8.00
BB Bret Boone SP 3.00 8.00
BG Brian Giles 3.00 8.00
BW Bernie Williams SP 4.00 10.00
CB Carlos Beltran 3.00 8.00
CD Carlos Delgado 3.00 8.00
CF Cliff Floyd 3.00 8.00
CJ Chipper Jones 4.00 10.00
CS Curt Schilling 4.00 10.00
DJ Derek Jeter SP 10.00 25.00
EC Eric Chavez 3.00 8.00
FT Frank Thomas 4.00 10.00
GA Garret Anderson 3.00 8.00
GJ Geoff Jenkins SP/80 5.00 12.00
GS Gary Sheffield 3.00 8.00
HB Hank Blalock 3.00 8.00
HU Torii Hunter SP 3.00 8.00
IR Ivan Rodriguez 4.00 10.00
IS Ichiro Suzuki 10.00 25.00
JC Jose Cruz Jr. 3.00 8.00
JD J.D. Drew 3.00 8.00
JE Jim Edmonds SP/70 5.00 12.00
JG Jason Giambi 3.00 8.00
JL Javy Lopez 3.00 8.00
JP Jay Payton 3.00 8.00
JR Jose Reyes 3.00 8.00
JT Jim Thome 4.00 10.00
KG Ken Griffey Jr. 6.00 15.00
KM Kazuo Matsui 3.00 8.00
KW Kerry Wood SP 3.00 8.00
LB Lance Berkman 3.00 8.00
LG Luis Gonzalez SP 3.00 8.00
LW Larry Walker 3.00 8.00
ML Mike Lowell 3.00 8.00
MO Magglio Ordonez 3.00 8.00
MR Manny Ramirez 4.00 10.00
MT Mark Teixeira 4.00 10.00
NG Nomar Garciaparra 6.00 15.00
OV Omar Vizquel 4.00 10.00
PI Mike Piazza 6.00 15.00
RA Roberto Alomar 4.00 10.00
RF Rafael Furcal SP 3.00 8.00
RJ Randy Johnson 4.00 10.00
RP Rafael Palmeiro 4.00 10.00
SC Sean Casey 3.00 8.00
SG Shawn Green 3.00 8.00
SS Sammy Sosa 4.00 10.00
TE Miguel Tejada 3.00 8.00
TG Troy Glaus 3.00 8.00
TH Todd Helton 4.00 10.00
TS Tim Salmon 4.00 10.00
VG Vladimir Guerrero 4.00 10.00
VW Vernon Wells 3.00 8.00

2004 Upper Deck Etchings Game Bat Green

*GREEN: .6X TO 1.5X BLUE
*GREEN: 1X TO 2.5X BLUE RC YR
*GREEN: .6X TO 1.5X BLUE SP
*GREEN: .4X TO 1X BLUE SP/70-80
OVERALL GU ODDS 1:4
STATED PRINT RUN 50 SERIAL #'d SETS
SR Scott Rolen 6.00 15.00

2004 Upper Deck Etchings Game Bat Purple

*PURPLE: .6X TO 1.5X BLUE RC YR
*PURPLE: .4X TO 1X BLUE SP
*PURPLE: .25X TO .6X BLUE SP/70-80
OVERALL GU ODDS 1:4
STATED PRINT RUN 250 SERIAL #'d SETS
SR Scott Rolen 4.00 10.00

2004 Upper Deck Etchings Game Bat Red

*RED: .4X TO 1X BLUE
*RED: .6X TO 1.5X BLUE RC YR
*RED: .4X TO 1X BLUE SP
*RED: .25X TO .6X BLUE SP/70-80
OVERALL GU ODDS 1:4
STATED PRINT RUN 150 SERIAL #'d SETS

2004 Upper Deck Etchings Game Bat Dual

OVERALL GU ODDS 1:4
STATED PRINT RUN 150 SERIAL #'d SETS
MM H.Matsui/K.Matsui 15.00 40.00
MW M.Mantle/T.Williams 100.00 200.00
PG A.Pujols/V.Guerrero 15.00 40.00
RJ A.Rodriguez/D.Jeter 40.00 80.00
RP J.Reyes/M.Piazza 10.00 25.00
WP K.Wood/M.Prior 10.00 25.00

2004 Upper Deck Etchings Game Bat Triple

OVERALL GU ODDS 1:4
STATED PRINT RUN 50 SERIAL #'d SETS
DMW DiMaggio/Mantle/Ted 90.00 150.00
PER Pujols/Edmonds/Rolen 12.50 30.00
RJM A.Rod/Jeter/Hideki 25.00 60.00
SBT Soriano/Blalock/Teixeira 12.50 30.00
SRG Schilling/Manny/Nomar 20.00 50.00
WPS Wood/Prior/Sosa 12.55 30.00

2004 Upper Deck Etchings Master Etchings Autograph

OVERALL MASTER ODDS 1:30,000
STATED PRINT RUN 1 SERIAL #'d SET
NO PRICING DUE TO SCARCITY

2004 Upper Deck Etchings Master Etchings Game Bat

OVERALL MASTER ODDS 1:30,000
STATED PRINT RUN 1 SERIAL #'d SET
NO PRICING DUE TO SCARCITY

2004 Upper Deck Etchings Star Etchings Autograph

STATED ODDS 1:192
PRINT RUNS B/WN 10-50 COPIES PER
NO PRICING ON QTY OF 10 OR LESS
EXCHANGE DEADLINE 08/06/07
AD Adam Dunn/50 8.00 20.00
BB Bret Boone/50 10.00 25.00
BW Brandon Webb/50 6.00 15.00
CB Carlos Beltran/50 10.00 25.00
DL Derrek Lee/50 15.00 40.00
DW Dontrelle Willis/50 15.00 40.00
EC Eric Chavez/50 10.00 25.00
FT Frank Thomas/15 40.00 80.00
GA Garret Anderson/50 10.00 25.00
GJ Geoff Jenkins/50 10.00 25.00
HB Hank Blalock/50 10.00 25.00
HE Todd Helton/15 30.00 60.00
IR Ivan Rodriguez/15 40.00 80.00
JB Josh Beckett/50 15.00 40.00
JD J.D. Drew/50 10.00 25.00
JS Jason Schmidt/50 10.00 25.00
KG K.Grif Jr. w Glasses/50 50.00 100.00
KG1 K.Grif Jr.w o Glasses/50 50.00 100.00
KW Kerry Wood/50 15.00 40.00
LB Lance Berkman/15 15.00 40.00
MC Miguel Cabrera/50 20.00 50.00
MM Mike Mussina/15 30.00 60.00
MO Magglio Ordonez/50 10.00 25.00
MR Manny Ramirez/15 60.00 120.00
MT Mark Teixeira/50 10.00 25.00
MU Mark Mulder/50 10.00 25.00
NG Nomar Garciaparra/15 75.00 150.00
PR Mark Prior/50 12.50 30.00
RO Roy Oswalt/50 10.00 25.00
TE Miguel Tejada/15 30.00 60.00
TH Tim Hudson/50 10.00 25.00
VG Vladimir Guerrero/15 40.00 80.00

2001 Upper Deck Evolution

COMP.SET w/o SP's (90) 6.00 15.00
COMMON CARD (1-90) .10 .30
COMMON CARD (91-120) 1.50 4.00
91-120 RANDOM INSERTS IN PACKS
91-120 PRINT RUN 2250 SERIAL #'d SETS
1 Darin Erstad .10 .30
2 Troy Glaus .10 .30
3 Jason Giambi .10 .30
4 Tim Hudson .10 .30
5 Jermaine Dye .10 .30
6 Barry Zito .20 .50
7 Carlos Delgado .10 .30
8 Shannon Stewart .10 .30
9 Jose Cruz Jr. .10 .30
10 Greg Vaughn .10 .30
11 Juan Gonzalez .10 .30
12 Roberto Alomar .20 .50
13 Omar Vizquel .20 .50
14 Jim Thome .20 .50
15 Edgar Martinez .20 .50
16 John Olerud .10 .30
17 Kazuhiro Sasaki .10 .30
18 Cal Ripken 1.00 2.50
19 Alex Rodriguez .40 1.00
20 Ivan Rodriguez .20 .50
21 Rafael Palmeiro .20 .50
22 Pedro Martinez .20 .50
23 Nomar Garciaparra .50 1.25
24 Manny Ramirez Sox .20 .50
25 Carl Everett .10 .30
26 Mark Quinn .10 .30
27 Mike Sweeney .10 .30
28 Neifi Perez .10 .30
29 Tony Clark .10 .30
30 Eric Milton .10 .30
31 Doug Mientkiewicz .10 .30
32 Corey Koskie .10 .30
33 Frank Thomas .30 .75
34 David Wells .10 .30
35 Magglio Ordonez .10 .30
36 Derek Jeter .75 2.00
37 Mike Mussina .20 .50
38 Bernie Williams .20 .50
39 Roger Clemens .60 1.50
40 David Justice .10 .30
41 Jeff Bagwell .20 .50
42 Richard Hidalgo .10 .30
43 Wade Miller .10 .30
44 Chipper Jones .30 .75
45 Greg Maddux .50 1.25
46 Andruw Jones .20 .50
47 Rafael Furcal .10 .30
48 Geoff Jenkins .10 .30
49 Jeromy Burnitz .10 .30
50 Ben Sheets .20 .50
51 Richie Sexson .10 .30
52 Mark McGwire .75 2.00
53 Jim Edmonds .10 .30
54 Darryl Kile .10 .30
55 J.D. Drew .10 .30
56 Sammy Sosa .30 .75
57 Kerry Wood .10 .30
58 Randy Johnson .30 .75
59 Luis Gonzalez .10 .30
60 Matt Williams .10 .30
61 Kevin Brown .10 .30
62 Gary Sheffield .10 .30
63 Shawn Green .10 .30
64 Chan Ho Park .10 .30
65 Vladimir Guerrero .30 .75
66 Jose Vidro .10 .30
67 Fernando Tatis .10 .30
68 Barry Bonds .75 2.00
69 Jeff Kent .10 .30
70 Russ Ortiz .10 .30
71 Preston Wilson .10 .30
72 Ryan Dempster .10 .30
73 Charles Johnson .10 .30
74 Mike Piazza .50 1.25
75 Edgardo Alfonzo .10 .30
76 Robin Ventura .10 .30
77 Jay Payton .10 .30
78 Tony Gwynn .40 1.00
79 Phil Nevin .10 .30
80 Pat Burrell .10 .30
81 Scott Rolen .20 .50
82 Bob Abreu .10 .30
83 Brian Giles .10 .30
84 Jason Kendall .10 .30
85 Ken Griffey Jr. .60 1.50
86 Barry Larkin .20 .50
87 Sean Casey .10 .30
88 Todd Helton .20 .50
89 Larry Walker .10 .30
90 Mike Hampton .10 .30
91 Ichiro Suzuki PROS RC 12.00 30.00
92 Albert Pujols PROS RC 15.00 40.00
93 Wilson Betemit PROS RC 2.00 5.00
94 Jay Gibbons PROS RC 2.00 5.00
95 Juan Uribe PROS RC 2.00 5.00
96 Morgan Ensberg PROS RC 2.00 5.00
97 Christian Parker PROS RC 1.50 4.00
98 Tsuyoshi Shinjo PROS RC 2.00 5.00
99 Jack Wilson PROS RC 2.00 5.00
100 Donaldo Mendez PROS RC 1.50 4.00
101 Ryan Freel PROS RC 2.00 5.00
102 Juan Diaz PROS RC 1.50 4.00
103 Horacio Ramirez PROS RC 2.00 5.00
104 Ricardo Rodriguez PROS RC 1.50 4.00
105 Erick Almonte PROS RC 1.50 4.00
106 Josh Towers PROS RC 2.00 5.00
107 Adr Hernandez PROS RC 1.50 4.00
108 Bran.Duckworth PROS RC 1.50 4.00
109 Travis Hafner PROS RC 4.00 10.00
110 Martin Vargas PROS RC 1.50 4.00
111 Kris Keller PROS RC 1.50 4.00
112 Brian Lawrence PROS RC 1.50 4.00
113 Esix Snead PROS RC 1.50 4.00
114 Wilkin Ruan PROS RC 1.50 4.00
115 Jose Mieses PROS RC 1.50 4.00
116 Johnny Estrada PROS RC 2.00 5.00
117 Elpidio Guzman PROS RC 1.50 4.00
118 Sean Douglass PROS RC 1.50 4.00
119 Billy Sylvester PROS RC 1.50 4.00
120 Bret Prinz PROS RC 1.50 4.00

2001 Upper Deck Evolution e-Card Classics

COMPLETE SET (15) 15.00 40.00
STATED ODDS 1:4
WINNERS EVOLVE INTO GAME JERSEY CARD
PRICES BELOW ARE FOR UNSCRATCHED
EC1 Ken Griffey Jr. 89 2.50 6.00
EC2 Gary Sheffield 89 .40 1.00
EC3 Randy Johnson 89 1.00 2.50
EC4 Sammy Sosa 90 1.00 2.50
EC5 Carlos Delgado 93 .40 1.00
EC6 Ichiro Suzuki 01 8.00 20.00
EC7 Andruw Jones 97 .60 1.50
EC8 Chipper Jones 91 1.00 2.50
EC9 Kazuhiro Sasaki 00 .40 1.00
EC10 Shawn Green 92 .40 1.00
EC11 Alex Rodriguez 94 1.25 3.00
EC12 Brian Giles 97 .40 1.00
EC13 J.D. Drew 99 .40 1.00
EC14 Pat Burrell 99 .40 1.00
EC15 Ivan Rodriguez 91 .60 1.50

2001 Upper Deck Evolution e-Card Game Bat

STATED ODDS 1:120
WINNERS EVOLVE INTO BAT-JSY AU'S
PRICES BELOW ARE FOR UNSCRATCHED
BAJ Andruw Jones 6.00 15.00
BAR Alex Rodriguez 10.00 25.00
BCD Carlos Delgado 4.00 10.00
BGS Gary Sheffield 4.00 10.00
BJaG Jason Giambi 4.00 10.00
BJD J.D. Drew 4.00 10.00
BJK Jason Kendall 4.00 10.00
BKG Ken Griffey Jr. 8.00 20.00
BPB Pat Burrell 4.00 10.00
BRB Russell Branyan 4.00 10.00

2001 Upper Deck Evolution e-Card Game Bat-Jersey Autograph

STATED ODDS 1:480 EVOLVE UPGRADES
NO PRICING DUE TO SCARCITY

2001 Upper Deck Evolution Game Jersey

STATED ODDS 1:120
JJaG Jason Giambi 4.00 10.00
JAJ Andruw Jones 6.00 15.00
JAR Alex Rodriguez 10.00 25.00
JBG Brian Giles 4.00 10.00
JCJ Chipper Jones 6.00 15.00
JCR Cal Ripken 15.00 40.00
JGS Gary Sheffield 4.00 10.00
JJD J.D. Drew 4.00 10.00
JJK Jason Kendall 4.00 10.00
JKG Ken Griffey Jr. 8.00 20.00
JPB Pat Burrell 4.00 10.00
JRB Russell Branyan 4.00 10.00
JSG Shawn Green 4.00 10.00
JSS Sammy Sosa 6.00 15.00
JTG Troy Glaus 4.00 10.00

2001 Upper Deck Evolution Ichiro Suzuki All-Star Game

STATED PRINT RUNS LISTED BELOW
51B Ichiro Suzuki Bronze 5.00 12.00
51G Ichiro Suzuki Gold/51 30.00 80.00
51S Ichiro Suzuki Silver/2001 12.00 30.00

2003 Upper Deck Finite

COMMON CARD (1-100) .40 1.00
1-100 PRINT RUN 1999 SERIAL #'d SETS
COMMON CARD (101-150) .50 1.25
101-150 PRINT RUN 1599 SERIAL #'d SETS
COMMON CARD (151-180) .75 2.00
151-180 PRINT RUN 499 SERIAL #'d SETS
COMMON CARD (181-200) 1.00 2.50
181-200 PRINT RUN 299 SERIAL #'d SETS
1-200 STATED ODDS TWO PER PACK
COMMON CARD (201-300) .60 1.50
201-300 PRINT RUN 1299 SERIAL #'d SETS
COMMON CARD (301-330) .75 2.00
301-330 PRINT RUN 599 SERIAL #'d SETS
COMMON CARD (331-360) 1.00 2.50
331-360 PRINT RUN 299 SERIAL #'d SETS
COMMON CARD (361-380) 1.50 4.00
361-380 PRINT RUN 150 SERIAL #'d SETS
201-380/STARS 'N STRIPES ODDS 1:1
1 Darin Erstad .40 1.00
2 Garret Anderson .40 1.00
3 Tim Salmon .40 1.00
4 Troy Glaus .40 1.00
5 Luis Gonzalez .40 1.00
6 Randy Johnson 1.00 2.50
7 Curt Schilling .60 1.50
8 Andruw Jones .40 1.00
9 Gary Sheffield .40 1.00
10 Rafael Furcal .40 1.00
11 Greg Maddux 1.25 3.00
12 Chipper Jones 1.00 2.50
13 Tony Batista .40 1.00
14 Jay Gibbons .40 1.00
15 Johnny Damon .60 1.50
16 Derek Lowe .40 1.00
17 Nomar Garciaparra .60 1.50
18 Pedro Martinez .60 1.50
19 Manny Ramirez 1.00 2.50
20 Mark Prior .60 1.50
21 Kerry Wood .40 1.00
22 Corey Patterson .40 1.00
23 Sammy Sosa 1.00 2.50
24 Moises Alou .40 1.00
25 Magglio Ordonez .60 1.50
26 Frank Thomas 1.00 2.50
27 Paul Konerko .60 1.50
28 Bartolo Colon .40 1.00
29 Adam Dunn .60 1.50
30 Austin Kearns .40 1.00
31 Aaron Boone .40 1.00
32 Ken Griffey Jr. 2.00 5.00
33 Omar Vizquel .60 1.50
34 C.C. Sabathia .60 1.50
35 Brandon Phillips .40 1.00
36 Larry Walker .60 1.50
37 Preston Wilson .40 1.00
38 Todd Helton .60 1.50
39 Eric Munson .40 1.00
40 Ivan Rodriguez .60 1.50
41 Josh Beckett .40 1.00
42 Roy Oswalt .60 1.50
43 Craig Biggio .60 1.50
44 Jeff Bagwell .60 1.50
45 Dontrelle Willis .40 1.00
46 Carlos Beltran .60 1.50
47 Brent Mayne .40 1.00
48 Hideo Nomo 1.00 2.50
49 Rickey Henderson 1.00 2.50
50 Adrian Beltre 1.00 2.50
51 Miguel Cabrera 6.00 15.00
52 Kazuhisa Ishii .40 1.00
53 Richie Sexson .40 1.00
54 Torii Hunter .40 1.00
55 Jacque Jones .40 1.00
56 A.J. Pierzynski .40 1.00
57 Jose Vidro .40 1.00
58 Vladimir Guerrero .60 1.50
59 Tom Glavine .60 1.50
60 Jose Reyes 1.00 2.50
61 Mike Piazza 1.00 2.50
62 Jorge Posada .60 1.50
63 Mike Mussina .60 1.50
64 Robin Ventura .40 1.00
65 Mariano Rivera 1.25 3.00
66 Roger Clemens 1.25 3.00
67 Jason Giambi .40 1.00
68 Bernie Williams .60 1.50
69 Alfonso Soriano .60 1.50
70 Derek Jeter 2.50 6.00
71 Miguel Tejada .60 1.50
72 Eric Chavez .40 1.00
73 Tim Hudson .60 1.50
74 Barry Zito .60 1.50
75 Pat Burrell .40 1.00
76 Jim Thome .60 1.50
77 Bobby Abreu .40 1.00
78 Brian Giles .40 1.00
79 Reggie Sanders .40 1.00
80 Ryan Klesko .40 1.00
81 Edgardo Alfonzo .40 1.00
82 Rich Aurilia .40 1.00
83 Barry Bonds 1.50 4.00
84 Mike Cameron .40 1.00
85 Kazuhiro Sasaki .40 1.00
86 Bret Boone .40 1.00
87 Ichiro Suzuki 1.25 3.00
88 J.D. Drew .40 1.00
89 Jim Edmonds .60 1.50
90 Scott Rolen .60 1.50
91 Matt Morris .40 1.00
92 Tino Martinez .40 1.00
93 Albert Pujols 1.25 3.00
94 Rocco Baldelli .40 1.00
95 Hank Blalock .40 1.00
96 Alex Rodriguez 1.25 3.00
97 Rafael Palmeiro .60 1.50
98 Eric Hinske .40 1.00
99 Orlando Hudson .40 1.00
100 Carlos Delgado .40 1.00
101 Albert Pujols MF 1.50 4.00
102 Alex Rodriguez MF 1.50 4.00
103 Alfonso Soriano MF .75 2.00
104 Andruw Jones MF .50 1.25
105 Barry Zito MF .75 2.00
106 Bernie Williams MF .75 2.00
107 Carlos Delgado MF .50 1.25
108 Chipper Jones MF 1.25 3.00
109 Curt Schilling MF .75 2.00
110 Doug Mientkiewicz MF .50 1.25
111 Frank Thomas MF 1.25 3.00
112 Garret Anderson MF .50 1.25
113 Gary Sheffield MF .50 1.25
114 Greg Maddux MF 1.50 4.00
115 Hank Blalock MF .50 1.25
116 Hideki Matsui MF 2.50 6.00
117 Hideo Nomo MF 1.25 3.00
118 Ichiro Suzuki MF 1.50 4.00
119 Ivan Rodriguez MF .75 2.00
120 Jason Giambi MF .50 1.25
121 Jeff Bagwell MF .75 2.00
122 Jeff Kent MF .50 1.25
123 Jerome Williams MF .50 1.25
124 Jeromy Burnitz MF .50 1.25
125 Jim Thome MF .75 2.00
126 Jose Cruz Jr. MF .50 1.25
127 Ken Griffey Jr. MF 2.50 6.00
128 Kerry Wood MF .50 1.25
129 Lance Berkman MF .75 2.00
130 Luis Gonzalez MF .50 1.25
131 Manny Ramirez MF 1.25 3.00
132 Mark Prior MF .75 2.00
133 Miguel Cabrera MF 6.00 15.00
134 Miguel Tejada MF .75 2.00
135 Mike Piazza MF 1.25 3.00
136 Pat Burrell MF .50 1.25
137 Pedro Martinez MF .75 2.00
138 Rafael Furcal MF .50 1.25
139 Randy Johnson MF 1.25 3.00
140 Rich Harden MF .75 2.00
141 Rickey Henderson MF 1.25 3.00
142 Roberto Alomar MF .75 2.00
143 Roger Clemens MF 1.50 4.00
144 Sammy Sosa MF 1.25 3.00
145 Shawn Green MF .50 1.25
146 Todd Helton MF .75 2.00
147 Tom Glavine MF .75 2.00
148 Torii Hunter MF .50 1.25
149 Troy Glaus MF .50 1.25
150 Vladimir Guerrero MF .75 2.00
151 Adam Dunn PP 1.25 3.00
152 Albert Pujols PP 2.50 6.00
153 Alex Rodriguez PP 2.50 6.00
154 Alfonso Soriano PP 1.25 3.00
155 Andruw Jones PP .75 2.00
156 Barry Bonds PP 3.00 8.00
157 Carlos Delgado PP .75 2.00
158 Chipper Jones PP 2.00 5.00
159 Derek Jeter PP 5.00 12.00
160 Gary Sheffield PP .75 2.00
161 Hank Blalock PP .75 2.00
162 Hideki Matsui PP 4.00 10.00
163 Ichiro Suzuki PP 2.50 6.00
164 J.D. Drew PP .75 2.00
165 Jason Giambi PP .75 2.00
166 Jeff Bagwell PP 1.25 3.00
167 Jeff Kent PP .75 2.00
168 Jim Edmonds PP 1.25 3.00
169 Jim Thome PP 1.25 3.00
170 Ken Griffey Jr. PP 4.00 10.00
171 Luis Gonzalez PP .75 2.00
172 Magglio Ordonez PP 1.25 3.00
173 Manny Ramirez PP 2.00 5.00
174 Mike Lowell PP .75 2.00
175 Mike Piazza PP 2.00 5.00
176 Nomar Garciaparra PP 1.25 3.00
177 Rafael Palmeiro PP 1.25 3.00
178 Shawn Green PP .75 2.00
179 Troy Glaus PP .75 2.00
180 Vladimir Guerrero PP 1.25 3.00
181 Albert Pujols FC 3.00 8.00
182 Alex Rodriguez FC 3.00 8.00
183 Alfonso Soriano FC 1.50 4.00
184 Bernie Williams FC 1.50 4.00
185 Chipper Jones FC 2.50 6.00
186 Derek Jeter FC 6.00 15.00
187 Hideki Matsui FC 5.00 12.00
188 Ichiro Suzuki FC 3.00 8.00
189 Jim Thome FC 1.50 4.00
190 Joe DiMaggio FC 5.00 12.00
191 Ken Griffey Jr. FC 5.00 12.00
192 Mickey Mantle FC 8.00 20.00
193 Mike Piazza FC 2.50 6.00
194 Pedro Martinez FC 1.50 4.00
195 Randy Johnson FC 2.50 6.00
196 Roger Clemens FC 3.00 8.00
197 Sammy Sosa FC 2.50 6.00
198 Ted Williams FC 5.00 12.00
199 Troy Glaus FC 1.00 2.50
200 Vladimir Guerrero FC 1.50 4.00
201 Aaron Looper T1 RC .60 1.50
202 Alejandro Machado T1 RC .60 1.50
203 Alfredo Gonzalez T1 RC .60 1.50
204 Andrew Brown T1 RC .60 1.50
205 Anthony Ferrari T1 RC .60 1.50
206 Aquilino Lopez T1 RC .60 1.50
207 Beau Kemp T1 RC .60 1.50
208 Bernie Castro T1 RC .60 1.50
209 Bobby Madritsch T1 RC .60 1.50
210 Brandon Villafuerte T1 .60 1.50
211 Brent Hoard T1 RC .60 1.50
212 Brian Stokes T1 RC .60 1.50
213 Carlos Mendez T1 RC .60 1.50
214 Chris Capuano T1 RC .60 1.50
215 Chris Waters T1 RC .60 1.50
216 Clint Barmes T1 RC 1.50 4.00
217 Colin Porter T1 RC .60 1.50
218 Cory Stewart T1 RC .60 1.50
219 Craig Brazell T1 RC .60 1.50
220 D.J. Carrasco T1 RC .60 1.50
221 Daniel Cabrera T1 RC 1.00 2.50
222 David Matranga T1 RC .60 1.50
223 David Sanders T1 RC .60 1.50
224 Diegomar Markwell T1 RC .60 1.50
225 Edgar Gonzalez T1 RC .60 1.50
226 Felix Sanchez T1 RC .60 1.50
227 Fernando Cabrera T1 RC .60 1.50
228 Francisco Cruceta T1 RC .60 1.50
229 Francisco Rosario T1 RC .60 1.50
230 Garrett Atkins T1 .60 1.50
231 Gerald Laird T1 .60 1.50
232 Guillermo Quiroz T1 RC .60 1.50
233 Heath Bell T1 RC 1.00 2.50
234 Delmon Young T1 RC 4.00 10.00
235 Jason Shiell T1 RC .60 1.50
236 Jeremy Bonderman T1 RC 2.50 6.00
237 Jeremy Griffiths T1 RC .60 1.50
238 Jeremy Guthrie T1 .60 1.50
239 Jeremy Wedel T1 RC .60 1.50
240 Carlos Rivera T1 .60 1.50
241 Joe Valentine T1 RC .60 1.50
242 Jon Leicester T1 RC .60 1.50
243 Jon Pridie T1 RC .60 1.50
244 Jorge Cordova T1 RC .60 1.50
245 Jose Castillo T1 .60 1.50
246 Josh Hall T1 RC .60 1.50
247 Josh Stewart T1 RC .60 1.50
248 Josh Willingham T1 RC 2.00 5.00
249 Julio Manon T1 RC .60 1.50
250 Kevin Correia T1 RC .60 1.50
251 Kevin Ohme T1 RC .60 1.50
252 Kevin Tolar T1 RC .60 1.50
253 Luis De Los Santos T1 .60 1.50
254 Jermaine Clark T1 .60 1.50
255 Mark Malaska T1 RC .60 1.50
256 Juan Dominguez T1 .60 1.50
257 Michael Hessman T1 RC .60 1.50
258 Michael Nakamura T1 RC .60 1.50
259 Miguel Ojeda T1 RC .60 1.50
260 Mike Gallo T1 RC .60 1.50
261 Edwin Jackson T1 RC 1.00 2.50
262 Mike Ryan T1 RC .60 1.50
263 Nate Bland T1 RC .60 1.50
264 Nate Robertson T1 RC 2.00 5.00
265 Nook Logan T1 RC .60 1.50
266 Phil Seibel T1 RC .60 1.50
267 Prentice Redman T1 RC .60 1.50

268 Rafael Betancourt T1 RC .60 1.50
269 Rett Johnson T1 RC .60 1.50
270 Richard Fischer T1 RC .60 1.50
271 Rick Roberts T1 RC .60 1.50
272 Roger Deago T1 RC .60 1.50
273 Ryan Cameron T1 RC .60 1.50
274 Shane Bazzell T1 RC .60 1.50
275 Erasmo Ramirez T1 .60 1.50
276 Termel Sledge T1 RC .60 1.50
277 Tim Olson T1 RC .60 1.50
278 Tommy Phelps T1 .60 1.50
279 Tommy Whiteman T1 .60 1.50
280 Willie Eyre T1 RC .60 1.50
281 Alex Prieto T1 RC .60 1.50
282 Michel Hernandez T1 RC .60 1.50
283 Greg Jones T1 RC .60 1.50
284 Victor Martinez T1 1.00 2.50
285 Tom Gregorio T1 RC .60 1.50
286 Marcus Thames T1 .60 1.50
287 Jorge DePaula T1 .60 1.50
288 Aaron Miles T1 RC .60 1.50
289 Reynaldo Garcia T1 .60 1.50
290 Brian Sweeney T1 RC .60 1.50
291 Pete LaForest T1 RC .60 1.50
292 Pete Zoccolillo T1 RC .60 1.50
293 Danny Garcia T1 RC .60 1.50
294 Jonny Gomes T1 .60 1.50
295 Rosman Garcia T1 RC .60 1.50
296 Mike Edwards T1 .60 1.50
297 Marlon Byrd T1 .60 1.50
298 Khalil Greene T1 1.00 2.50
299 Jose Valverde T1 .60 1.50
300 Drew Henson T1 .60 1.50
301 Chris Bootcheck T2 .75 2.00
302 Matt Belisle T2 .75 2.00
303 Kevin Gregg T2 .75 2.00
304 Bobby Jenks T2 .75 2.00
305 Jason Young T2 .75 2.00
306 Laynce Nix T2 .75 2.00
307 Robb Quinlan T2 .75 2.00
308 Chase Utley T2 1.25 3.00
309 Humberto Quintero T2 RC .75 2.00
310 Tim Raines Jr. T2 .75 2.00
311 Stephen Smitherman T2 .75 2.00
312 Jason Anderson T2 .75 2.00
313 Joe Dawley T2 .75 2.00
314 Chad Cordero T2 RC .75 2.00
315 Victor Alvarez T2 .75 2.00
316 Jimmy Gobble T2 .75 2.00
317 Jared Fernandez T2 .75 2.00
318 Eric Bruntlett T2 .75 2.00
319 Neal Cotts T2 .75 2.00
320 Ryan Madson T2 .75 2.00
321 Rocco Baldelli T2 .75 2.00
322 Graham Koonce T2 RC .75 2.00
323 Bobby Crosby T2 .75 2.00
324 Mike Wood T2 .75 2.00
325 Jesse Garcia T2 .75 2.00
326 Noah Lowry T2 .75 2.00
327 Edwin Almonte T2 .75 2.00
328 Justin Morneau T2 1.25 3.00
329 Steve Colyer T2 .75 2.00
330 Vinnie Chulk T2 .75 2.00
331 Brian Schmack T3 RC 1.00 2.50
332 Stephen Randolph T3 RC 1.00 2.50
333 Pedro Feliciano T3 RC 1.00 2.50
334 Koyie Hill T3 1.00 2.50
335 Geoff Geary T3 RC 1.00 2.50
336 Jon Switzer T3 1.00 2.50
337 Xavier Nady T3 1.00 2.50
338 Rich Harden T3 1.50 4.00
339 Dontrelle Willis T3 1.00 2.50
340 Angel Berroa T3 1.00 2.50
341 Jerome Williams T3 1.00 2.50
342 Brandon Claussen T3 1.00 2.50
343 Kurt Ainsworth T3 1.00 2.50
344 Horacio Ramirez T3 1.00 2.50
345 Hee Seop Choi T3 1.00 2.50
346 Billy Traber T3 1.00 2.50
347 Brandon Phillips T3 1.00 2.50
348 Jody Gerut T3 1.00 2.50
349 Mark Teixeira T3 1.50 4.00
350 Javier A. Lopez T3 RC 1.00 2.50
351 Miguel Cabrera T3 12.00 30.00
352 Brad Lidge T3 1.00 2.50
353 Mike MacDougal T3 1.00 2.50
354 Ken Harvey T3 1.00 2.50
355 Chien-Ming Wang T3 RC 4.00 10.00
356 Aaron Heilman T3 1.00 2.50
357 Jason Phillips T3 1.00 2.50
358 Jason Bay T3 2.00 5.00
359 Arnie Munoz T3 RC 1.00 2.50
360 Ian Ferguson T3 RC 1.00 2.50
361 Ryan Wagner T4 RC 1.50 4.00
362 Rickie Weeks T4 RC 5.00 12.00
363 Chad Gaudin T4 RC 1.50 4.00
364 Jason Gilfillan T4 RC 1.50 4.00
365 Jason Roach T4 RC 1.50 4.00
366 Jhonny Peralta T4 1.50 4.00
367 Mike Neu T4 RC 1.50 4.00
368 Jose Contreras T4 RC 4.00 10.00
369 Wilfredo Ledezma T4 RC 1.50 4.00
370 Lew Ford T4 RC 1.50 4.00
371 Luis Ayala T4 RC 1.50 4.00
372 Bo Hart T4 RC 1.50 4.00
373 Brandon Webb T4 RC 5.00 12.00
374 Dan Haren T4 RC 8.00 20.00
375 Hideki Matsui T4 RC 8.00 20.00
376 Jeff Duncan T4 RC 1.50 4.00
377 Matt Kata T4 RC 1.50 4.00
378 Oscar Villarreal T4 RC 1.50 4.00
379 Rob Hammock T4 RC 1.50 4.00
380 Todd Wellemeyer T4 RC 1.50 4.00

2003 Upper Deck Finite Gold

*GOLD 1-100: 1.5X TO 4X BASIC
*GOLD 101-150: 1.25X TO 3X BASIC
*GOLD 151-180: .75X TO 2X BASIC
1-180 PRINT RUN 199 SERIAL #'d SETS
*GOLD 181-200 ACTIVE: .75X TO 2X BASIC
*GOLD 181-200 RETIRED: .75X TO 2X BASIC
181-200 PRINT RUN 99 SERIAL #'d SETS

2003 Upper Deck Finite Elements Game Jersey

OVERALL GU ODDS 1:3
SP INFO PROVIDED BY UPPER DECK
AD Adam Dunn 3.00 8.00
AL Albert Pujols 6.00 15.00
AP Andy Pettitte 4.00 10.00
AR Alex Rodriguez 4.00 10.00
AS Alfonso Soriano 3.00 8.00
CJ Chipper Jones 4.00 10.00
CP Corey Patterson 3.00 8.00
DW Dontrelle Willis 4.00 10.00
DY Delmon Young SP/100 10.00 25.00
GM Greg Maddux 4.00 10.00
HB Hank Blalock 3.00 8.00
HC Hee Seop Choi 3.00 8.00
HM Hideki Matsui 6.00 15.00
IS Ichiro Suzuki 10.00 25.00
JB Jeff Bagwell 4.00 10.00
JD J.D. Drew 3.00 8.00
JE Jim Edmonds 3.00 8.00
JK Jeff Kent 3.00 8.00
JT Jim Thome 4.00 10.00
KG Ken Griffey Jr. SP 10.00 25.00
KW Kerry Wood 3.00 8.00
MI Mike Piazza 4.00 10.00
ML Mike Lowell 3.00 8.00
MM Matt Morris 3.00 8.00
MP Mark Prior 4.00 10.00
RB Rocco Baldelli 3.00 8.00
RO Roy Oswalt 3.00 8.00
RW Rickie Weeks SP/100 6.00 15.00
SG Shawn Green 3.00 8.00
TH Torii Hunter 3.00 8.00

2003 Upper Deck Finite Elements Game Patch

STATED PRINT RUN 25 SERIAL #'d SETS
NO PRICING DUE TO SCARCITY

2003 Upper Deck Finite Elements Game Patch Gold

STATED PRINT RUN 10 SERIAL #'d SETS
NO PRICING DUE TO SCARCITY

2003 Upper Deck Finite First Class Game Jersey

OVERALL GU ODDS 1:3
SP INFO PROVIDED BY UPPER DECK
AP Albert Pujols 6.00 15.00
AR Alex Rodriguez 4.00 10.00
AS Alfonso Soriano 3.00 8.00
BW Bernie Williams 4.00 10.00
CJ Chipper Jones 4.00 10.00
HM Hideki Matsui 10.00 25.00
IS Ichiro Suzuki 10.00 25.00
JDO J DiMaggio Pants SP/200 25.00 60.00
JT Jim Thome 4.00 10.00
KG Ken Griffey Jr. 6.00 15.00
LG Luis Gonzalez 3.00 8.00
MMO M.Mantle Pants SP/100 60.00 120.00
MP Mike Piazza 4.00 10.00
PM Pedro Martinez 4.00 10.00
RC Roger Clemens 6.00 15.00
RJ Randy Johnson 4.00 10.00
SS Sammy Sosa 4.00 10.00
TG Troy Glaus 3.00 8.00
TWO T.Williams Pants SP/100 40.00 80.00
VG Vladimir Guerrero 4.00 10.00

2003 Upper Deck Finite Signatures

STATED ODDS 1:120
PRINT RUNS B/WN 25-355 COPIES PER
NO PRICING ON QTY OF 25 OR LESS
BH Bo Hart/150 4.00 10.00
BW Brandon Webb/150 6.00 15.00
CS C.C. Sabathia/50 30.00 60.00
DS David Sanders/150 4.00 10.00
DW Dontrelle Willis/50 10.00 25.00
DY Delmon Young/50 10.00 25.00
EA Erick Almonte/355 4.00 10.00
HM Hideki Matsui/99 200.00 350.00
JR Jose Reyes/100 20.00 50.00
JW Jerome Williams/150 4.00 10.00
MC Miguel Cabrera/100 30.00 60.00
MP Mark Prior/75 12.50 30.00
MT Mark Teixeira/200 10.00 25.00
NG Nomar Garciaparra/50 12.50 30.00
PS Phil Seibel/200 4.00 10.00
RC Roger Clemens/50 100.00 175.00
RK Rob Hammock/200 4.00 10.00
RN Rich Harden/150 10.00 25.00
SR Scott Rolen/100 6.00 15.00
SZ Shane Bazzell/250 4.00 10.00
WE Willie Eyre/200 4.00 10.00

2003 Upper Deck Finite Stars and Stripes

STRIPES/FINITE RC OVERALL ODDS 1:1
STATED PRINT RUN 299 SERIAL #'d SETS
1 Justin Orenduff 2.00 5.00
2 Micah Owings 1.25 3.00
3 Steven Register 1.25 3.00
4 Huston Street 2.00 5.00
5 Justin Verlander 10.00 25.00
6 Jered Weaver 5.00 12.00
7 Matt Campbell 1.25 3.00
8 Stephen Head 1.25 3.00
9 Mark Romanczuk 1.25 3.00
10 Jeff Clement 2.00 5.00
11 Mike Nickeas 1.25 3.00
12 Tyler Greene 1.25 3.00
13 Paul Janish 2.00 5.00
14 Jeff Larish 1.25 3.00
15 Eric Patterson 1.25 3.00
16 Dustin Pedroia 8.00 20.00
17 Michael Griffin 1.25 3.00
18 Brent Lillibridge 1.25 3.00
19 Danny Putnam 1.25 3.00
20 Seth Smith 2.00 5.00

2003 Upper Deck Finite Stars and Stripes Game Jersey

OVERALL GU ODDS 1:3
J1 Justin Orenduff 3.00 8.00
J2 Micah Owings 3.00 8.00
J3 Steven Register 2.00 5.00
J4 Huston Street 3.00 8.00
J5 Justin Verlander 12.50 30.00
J6 Jered Weaver 5.00 12.00
J7 Matt Campbell 2.00 5.00
J8 Stephen Head 3.00 8.00
J9 Mark Romanczuk 2.00 5.00
J10 Jeff Clement 5.00 12.00
J11 Mike Nickeas 3.00 8.00
J12 Tyler Greene 3.00 8.00
J13 Paul Janish 3.00 8.00
J14 Jeff Larish 3.00 8.00
J15 Eric Patterson 3.00 8.00
J16 Dustin Pedroia 4.00 10.00
J17 Michael Griffin 2.00 5.00
J18 Brent Lillibridge 2.00 5.00
J19 Danny Putnam 3.00 8.00
J20 Seth Smith 3.00 8.00

2007 Upper Deck First Edition

COMPLETE SET (300) 20.00 50.00
COMMON CARD (1-300) .12 .30
COMMON ROOKIE (1-310) .15 .40
PRINTING PLATE ODDS 1 PER CASE
PLATE PRINT RUN 1 SET PER COLOR
BLACK-CYAN-MAGENTA-YELLOW ISSUED
NO PLATE PRICING DUE TO SCARCITY
1 Doug Slaten RC .15 .40
2 Miguel Montero (RC) .15 .40
3 Brian Burres (RC) .15 .40
4 Devern Hansack RC .15 .40
5 David Murphy (RC) .15 .40
6 Jose Reyes RC .15 .40
7 Scott Moore (RC) .15 .40
8 Josh Fields (RC) .15 .40
9 Chris Stewart RC .15 .40
10 Jerry Owens (RC) .15 .40
11 Ryan Sweeney (RC) .15 .40
12 Kevin Kouzmanoff (RC) .15 .40
13 Jeff Baker (RC) .15 .40
14 Justin Hampson (RC) .15 .40
15 Jeff Salazar (RC) .15 .40
16 Alvin Colina RC .40 1.00
17 Troy Tulowitzki (RC) .50 1.25
18 Andrew Miller RC .60 1.50
19 Mike Rabelo RC .15 .40
20 Jose Diaz (RC) .15 .40
21 Angel Sanchez RC .15 .40
22 Ryan Braun RC .15 .40
23 Delwyn Young (RC) .15 .40
24 Drew Anderson RC .15 .40
25 Dennis Sarfate (RC) .15 .40
26 Vinny Rottino (RC) .15 .40
27 Glen Perkins (RC) .15 .40
28 Alexi Casilla RC .25 .60
29 Philip Humber (RC) .25 .60
30 Andy Cannizaro RC .15 .40
31 Jeremy Brown .12 .30
32 Sean Henn (RC) .15 .40
33 Brian Rogers (RC) .15 .40
34 Carlos Maldonado (RC) .15 .40
35 Juan Morillo (RC) .15 .40
36 Fred Lewis (RC) .15 .40
37 Patrick Misch (RC) .15 .40
38 Billy Sadler (RC) .15 .40
39 Ryan Feierabend (RC) .15 .40
40 Cesar Jimenez RC .15 .40
41 Oswaldo Navarro RC .15 .40
42 Travis Chick (RC) .15 .40
43 Delmon Young (RC) .40 1.00
44 Shawn Riggans (RC) .15 .40
45 Brian Stokes (RC) .15 .40
46 Juan Salas (RC) .15 .40
47 Joaquin Arias (RC) .15 .40
48 Adam Lind (RC) .15 .40
49 Beltran Perez (RC) .15 .40
50 Brett Campbell RC .15 .40
51 Miguel Tejada .20 .50
52 Brandon Fahey .12 .30
53 Jay Gibbons .12 .30
54 Nick Markakis .25 .60
55 Kris Benson .12 .30
56 Erik Bedard .12 .30
57 Chris Ray .12 .30
58 Chris Britton .12 .30
59 Manny Ramirez .30 .75
60 David Ortiz .30 .75
61 Alex Cora .20 .50
62 Trot Nixon .12 .30
63 Doug Mirabelli .12 .30
64 Curt Schilling .20 .50
65 Jonathan Papelbon .30 .75
66 Craig Hansen .12 .30
67 Jermaine Dye .12 .30
68 Jim Thome .20 .50
69 Rob Mackowiak .12 .30
70 Brian Anderson .12 .30
71 A.J. Pierzynski .12 .30
72 Alex Cintron .12 .30
73 Jose Contreras .12 .30
74 Bobby Jenks .12 .30
75 Mike MacDougal .12 .30
76 Travis Hafner .12 .30
77 Ryan Garko .12 .30
78 Victor Martinez .20 .50
79 Casey Blake .12 .30
80 Shin-Soo Choo .20 .50
81 Paul Byrd .12 .30
82 Jeremy Sowers .12 .30
83 Cliff Lee .20 .50
84 Sean Casey .12 .30
85 Brandon Inge .12 .30
86 Omar Infante .12 .30
87 Magglio Ordonez .20 .50
88 Marcus Thames .12 .30
89 Justin Verlander .30 .75
90 Todd Jones .12 .30
91 Joel Zumaya .12 .30
92 Nate Robertson .12 .30
93 Mark Teahen .12 .30
94 Ryan Shealy .12 .30
95 Mark Grudzielanek .12 .30
96 Shane Costa .12 .30
97 Reggie Sanders .12 .30
98 Mark Redman .12 .30
99 Todd Wellemeyer .12 .30
100 Ambiorix Burgos .12 .30
101 Joe Nelson .12 .30
102 Orlando Cabrera .12 .30
103 Maicer Izturis .12 .30
104 Vladimir Guerrero .20 .50
105 Juan Rivera .12 .30
106 Jered Weaver .20 .50
107 Joe Saunders .12 .30
108 Bartolo Colon .12 .30
109 Francisco Rodriguez .20 .50
110 Justin Morneau .20 .50
111 Luis Castillo .12 .30
112 Michael Cuddyer .12 .30
113 Joe Mauer .25 .60
114 Francisco Liriano .12 .30
115 Joe Nathan .12 .30
116 Brad Radke .12 .30
117 Juan Rincon .12 .30
118 Derek Jeter .75 2.00
119 Jason Giambi .12 .30
120 Bobby Abreu .12 .30
121 Gary Sheffield .12 .30
122 Melky Cabrera .12 .30
123 Chien-Ming Wang .20 .50
124 Mariano Rivera .40 1.00
125 Jaret Wright .12 .30
126 Kyle Farnsworth .12 .30
127 Frank Thomas .30 .75
128 Dan Johnson .12 .30
129 Marco Scutaro .20 .50
130 Jay Payton .12 .30
131 Joe Blanton .12 .30
132 Rich Harden .12 .30
133 Esteban Loaiza .12 .30
134 Chad Gaudin .12 .30
135 Yuniesky Betancourt .12 .30
136 Willie Bloomquist .12 .30
137 Ichiro Suzuki .40 1.00
138 Raul Ibanez .20 .50
139 Chris Snelling .12 .30
140 Cha-Seung Baek .12 .30
141 Julio Mateo .12 .30
142 Rafael Soriano .12 .30
143 Jorge Cantu .12 .30
144 B.J. Upton .12 .30
145 Dioner Navarro .12 .30
146 Carl Crawford .20 .50
147 Damon Hollins .12 .30
148 Casey Fossum .12 .30
149 Ruddy Lugo .12 .30
150 Tyler Walker .12 .30
151 Shawn Camp .12 .30
152 Ian Kinsler .20 .50
153 Jerry Hairston Jr. .12 .30
154 Gerald Laird .12 .30
155 Mark DeRosa .12 .30
156 Kip Wells .12 .30
157 Vicente Padilla .12 .30
158 John Koronka .12 .30
159 Wes Littleton .12 .30
160 Lyle Overbay .12 .30
161 Aaron Hill .12 .30
162 John McDonald .12 .30
163 Vernon Wells .12 .30
164 Frank Catalanotto .12 .30
165 Roy Halladay .20 .50
166 B.J. Ryan .12 .30
167 Casey Janssen .12 .30
168 Stephen Drew .12 .30
169 Conor Jackson .12 .30
170 Chad Tracy .12 .30
171 Johnny Estrada .12 .30
172 Eric Byrnes .12 .30
173 Carlos Quentin .12 .30
174 Brandon Webb .20 .50
175 Jorge Julio .12 .30
176 Luis Vizcaino .12 .30
177 Chipper Jones .30 .75
178 Adam LaRoche .12 .30
179 Brian McCann .12 .30
180 Ryan Langerhans .12 .30
181 Matt Diaz .12 .30
182 John Smoltz .30 .75
183 Oscar Villarreal .12 .30
184 Chad Paronto .12 .30
185 Derrek Lee .12 .30
186 Ryan Theriot .12 .30
187 Ronny Cedeno .12 .30
188 Juan Pierre .12 .30
189 Matt Murton .12 .30
190 Carlos Zambrano .20 .50
191 Mark Prior .20 .50
192 Ryan Dempster .12 .30
193 Ryan O'Malley .12 .30
194 Brandon Phillips .12 .30
195 Rich Aurilia .12 .30
196 Ken Griffey Jr. .60 1.50
197 Ryan Freel .12 .30
198 Aaron Harang .12 .30
199 Brandon Claussen .12 .30
200 David Weathers .12 .30
201 Eric Milton .12 .30
202 Kazuo Matsui .12 .30
203 Jamey Carroll .12 .30
204 Matt Holliday .30 .75
205 Brad Hawpe .12 .30
206 Jason Jennings .12 .30
207 Josh Fogg .12 .30
208 Aaron Cook .12 .30
209 Miguel Cabrera .30 .75
210 Dan Uggla .12 .30
211 Hanley Ramirez .20 .50
212 Jeremy Hermida .12 .30
213 Cody Ross .12 .30
214 Josh Willingham .20 .50
215 Anibal Sanchez .12 .30
216 Jose Garcia RC .15 .40
217 Taylor Tankersley .12 .30
218 Lance Berkman .20 .50
219 Craig Biggio .20 .50
220 Brad Ausmus .12 .30
221 Willy Taveras .12 .30
222 Chris Burke .12 .30
223 Roger Clemens .40 1.00
224 Brandon Backe .12 .30
225 Brad Lidge .12 .30
226 Dan Wheeler .12 .30
227 Wilson Betemit .12 .30
228 Julio Lugo .12 .30
229 Russell Martin .12 .30
230 Kenny Lofton .12 .30
231 Brad Penny .12 .30
232 Chad Billingsley .20 .50
233 Greg Maddux .40 1.00
234 Jonathan Broxton .12 .30
235 Rickie Weeks .12 .30
236 Bill Hall .12 .30
237 Tony Gwynn Jr. .12 .30
238 Corey Hart .12 .30
239 Laynce Nix .12 .30
240 Ben Sheets .12 .30
241 Dave Bush .12 .30
242 Francisco Cordero .12 .30
243 Jose Reyes .20 .50
244 Carlos Delgado .12 .30
245 Paul Lo Duca .12 .30
246 Carlos Beltran .20 .50
247 Lastings Milledge .20 .50
248 Pedro Martinez .20 .50
249 John Maine .12 .30
250 Steve Trachsel .12 .30
251 Ryan Howard .25 .60
252 Jimmy Rollins .20 .50
253 Chris Coste .12 .30
254 Jeff Conine .12 .30
255 David Dellucci .12 .30
256 Cole Hamels .25 .60
257 Ryan Madson .12 .30
258 Brett Myers .12 .30
259 Freddy Sanchez .12 .30
260 Xavier Nady .12 .30
261 Jose Castillo .12 .30
262 Jason Bay .20 .50
263 Jose Bautista .20 .50
264 Ronny Paulino .12 .30
265 Zach Duke .12 .30
266 Shane Youman RC .15 .40
267 Matt Capps .12 .30
268 Adrian Gonzalez .25 .60
269 Josh Barfield .12 .30
270 Mike Piazza .30 .75
271 Dave Roberts .20 .50
272 Geoff Blum .12 .30
273 Chris Young .12 .30
274 Woody Williams .12 .30
275 Cla Meredith .12 .30
276 Trevor Hoffman .20 .50
277 Ray Durham .12 .30
278 Mark Sweeney .12 .30
279 Eliezer Alfonzo .12 .30
280 Todd Linden .12 .30
281 Jason Schmidt .12 .30
282 Noah Lowry .12 .30
283 Brad Hennessey .12 .30
284 Jonathan Sanchez .12 .30
285 Albert Pujols .40 1.00
286 David Eckstein .12 .30
287 Jim Edmonds .20 .50
288 Chris Duncan .12 .30
289 Juan Encarnacion .12 .30
290 Jeff Suppan .12 .30
291 Jeff Weaver .12 .30
292 Braden Looper .12 .30
293 Ryan Zimmerman .20 .50
294 Nick Johnson .12 .30
295 Alfonso Soriano .20 .50
296 Austin Kearns .12 .30
297 Alex Escobar .12 .30
298 Tony Armas .12 .30
299 Chad Cordero .12 .30
300 Jon Rauch .12 .30
301 Daisuke Matsuzaka RC .60 1.50
302 Kei Igawa RC .40 1.00
303 Akinori Iwamura RC .40 1.00
304 Alex Gordon RC .50 1.25
305 Matt Chico (RC) .15 .40
306 John Danks RC .25 .60
307 Elijah Dukes RC .25 .60
308 Gustavo Molina RC .15 .40
309 Joakim Soria RC .15 .40
310 Jay Marshall RC .15 .40

2007 Upper Deck First Edition First Pitch Aces

COMPLETE SET (15) 6.00 15.00
STATED ODDS 1:6
BW Brandon Webb .40 1.00
CC Chris Carpenter .40 1.00
CS Curt Schilling .60 1.50
CZ Carlos Zambrano .40 1.00
DW Dontrelle Willis .40 1.00
FH Felix Hernandez .60 1.50
JS Johan Santana .60 1.50
JV Justin Verlander 1.00 2.50
PM Pedro Martinez .60 1.50
RC Roger Clemens 1.25 3.00
RH Roy Halladay .40 1.00
RJ Randy Johnson 1.00 2.50
SA C.C. Sabathia .40 1.00
SK Scott Kazmir .60 1.50
SM John Smoltz .60 1.50

2007 Upper Deck First Edition First Pitch Foundations

COMPLETE SET (20) 6.00 15.00
STATED ODDS 1:6
AL Adam Lind .40 1.00
AM Andrew Miller 1.50 4.00
DM David Murphy .40 1.00
DY Delmon Young .60 1.50
FL Fred Lewis .60 1.50
GP Glen Perkins .40 1.00
JA Joaquin Arias .40 1.00
JF Josh Fields .40 1.00
JO Jerry Owens .40 1.00
JS Jeff Salazar .40 1.00
MM Mitch Maier .40 1.00
MO Miguel Montero .40 1.00
PH Philip Humber .40 1.00
RB Ryan Braun .40 1.00
RS Ryan Sweeney .40 1.00
SM Scott Moore .40 1.00
SR Shawn Riggans .40 1.00
TC Travis Chick .40 1.00
TT Troy Tulowitzki 1.25 3.00
UJ Ubaldo Jimenez 1.25 3.00

2007 Upper Deck First Edition Leading Off

COMPLETE SET (15) 6.00 15.00
STATED ODDS 1:6
AS Alfonso Soriano .60 1.50
BR Brian Roberts .40 1.00
CF Chone Figgins .40 1.00
DR Dave Roberts .60 1.50
FR Ryan Freel .40 1.00
GS Grady Sizemore .60 1.50
HR Hanley Ramirez .60 1.50
IS Ichiro Suzuki 1.25 3.00
JD Johnny Damon .60 1.50
JP Juan Pierre .40 1.00
JR Jose Reyes .60 1.50
RF Rafael Furcal .40 1.00
RO Jimmy Rollins .60 1.50
SP Scott Podsednik .40 1.00
WT Willy Taveras .40 1.00

2007 Upper Deck First Edition Momentum Swing

COMPLETE SET (20) 6.00 15.00
STATED ODDS 1:6
AD Adam Dunn .60 1.50
AJ Andruw Jones .40 1.00
AP Albert Pujols 1.50 4.00
AR Alex Rodriguez 1.25 3.00
AS Alfonso Soriano .60 1.50
CB Carlos Beltran .60 1.50
CD Carlos Delgado .40 1.00
DL Derrek Lee .40 1.00
DO David Ortiz 1.00 2.50
JB Jason Bay .60 1.50
JD Jermaine Dye .40 1.00
JG Jason Giambi .40 1.00
JM Justin Morneau .60 1.50
JT Jim Thome .60 1.50
LB Lance Berkman .60 1.50
MC Miguel Cabrera 1.00 2.50
MT Mark Teixeira .60 1.50
RH Ryan Howard 1.25 3.00
TH Travis Hafner .40 1.00
VG Vladimir Guerrero .60 1.50

2007 Upper Deck First Edition Pennant Chasers

COMPLETE SET (30) 6.00 15.00
STATED ODDS 1:4
AR Aramis Ramirez .25 .60
CC Carl Crawford .25 .60
CG Carlos Guillen .25 .60
CJ Chipper Jones .60 1.50
CU Chase Utley .60 1.50
DA Johnny Damon .40 1.00
DU Dan Uggla .40 1.00
DW David Wright 1.00 2.50
FS Freddy Sanchez .25 .60
JM Joe Mauer .40 1.00
JR Juan Rivera .25 .60
KG Ken Griffey Jr. 1.25 3.00
MH Matt Holliday .30 .75
MR Manny Ramirez .40 1.00
MT Miguel Tejada .25 .60
MY Michael Young .25 .60
NG Nomar Garciaparra .60 1.50
NS Nick Swisher .25 .60
OH Orlando Hudson .25 .60
PF Prince Fielder .60 1.50
PK Paul Konerko .25 .60
RD Ray Durham .25 .60
RI Raul Ibanez .25 .60
RO Roy Oswalt .25 .60
RZ Ryan Zimmerman .60 1.50
SR Scott Rolen .40 1.00
TE Mark Teahen .25 .60
TH Trevor Hoffman .25 .60
VM Victor Martinez .25 .60
VW Vernon Wells .25 .60

2008 Upper Deck First Edition

COMPLETE SET (1-300) 10.00 25.00
COMP.UPD.SET (301-500) 10.00 25.00
COMMON CARD (1-250/301-500) .12 .30
COMMON RC (250-300/329/390) .20 .50
1 Joe Saunders .12 .30
2 Kelvim Escobar .20 .50
3 Jered Weaver .20 .50
4 Justin Speier .20 .50
5 Scot Shields .20 .50
6 Orlando Cabrera .20 .50
7 Casey Kotchman .12 .30
8 Vladimir Guerrero .20 .50
9 Garret Anderson .12 .30
10 Roy Oswalt .20 .50
11 Wandy Rodriguez .12 .30
12 Woody Williams .20 .50
13 Chad Qualls .12 .30
14 Mark Loretta .20 .50
15 Brad Ausmus .12 .30
16 Carlos Lee .12 .30
17 Hunter Pence .20 .50
18 Dan Haren .12 .30
19 Lenny DiNardo .20 .50
20 Chad Gaudin .20 .50
21 Huston Street .20 .50
22 Andrew Brown .12 .30
23 Mike Piazza .30 .75
24 Mark Ellis .12 .30
25 Shannon Stewart .12 .30
26 Shaun Marcum .12 .30
27 A.J. Burnett .12 .30
28 Casey Janssen .12 .30
29 Jeremy Accardo .20 .50
30 Aaron Hill .12 .30
31 Frank Thomas .30 .75
32 Matt Stairs .12 .30
33 Vernon Wells .12 .30
34 Tim Hudson .20 .50
35 Buddy Carlyle .12 .30
36 Rafael Soriano .12 .30
37 Brian McCann .20 .50
38 Edgar Renteria .12 .30
39 Mark Teixeira .20 .50
40 Willie Harris .12 .30
41 Andruw Jones .12 .30
42 Ben Sheets .12 .30
43 Dave Bush .12 .30
44 Yovani Gallardo .12 .30
45 Matt Wise .12 .30
46 Johnny Estrada .12 .30
47 Prince Fielder .20 .50
48 J.J. Hardy .12 .30
49 Corey Hart .12 .30
50 Adam Wainwright .20 .50
51 Joel Pineiro .12 .30
52 Jason Isringhausen .12 .30
53 Troy Percival .12 .30
54 Albert Pujols .40 1.00
55 David Eckstein .12 .30
56 Jim Edmonds .20 .50
57 Rick Ankiel .12 .30
58 Ted Lilly .12 .30
59 Rich Hill .12 .30
60 Jason Marquis .12 .30
61 Carlos Marmol .20 .50
62 Jason Kendall .12 .30
63 Aramis Ramirez .12 .30
64 Ryan Theriot .12 .30
65 Alfonso Soriano .20 .50
66 Jacque Jones .12 .30
67 James Shields .12 .30
68 Andy Sonnanstine .12 .30
69 Scott Dohmann .12 .30
70 Dioner Navarro .12 .30
71 B.J. Upton .20 .50
72 Carlos Pena .20 .50
73 Brendan Harris .12 .30
74 Josh Wilson .12 .30
75 Brandon Webb .20 .50
76 Micah Owings .12 .30
77 Doug Slaten .12 .30
78 Brandon Lyon .12 .30
79 Miguel Montero .12 .30
80 Stephen Drew .12 .30
81 Mark Reynolds .12 .30
82 Chris B. Young .12 .30
83 Chad Billingsley .20 .50
84 Derek Lowe .12 .30
85 Mark Hendrickson .12 .30
86 Takashi Saito .12 .30
87 Russell Martin .12 .30
88 Jeff Kent .12 .30
89 Matt Kemp .25 .60
90 Juan Pierre .12 .30
91 Matt Cain .20 .50
92 Barry Zito .20 .50
93 Kevin Correia .12 .30
94 Jack Taschner .12 .30
95 Bengie Molina .12 .30
96 Omar Vizquel .20 .50
97 Dave Roberts .20 .50
98 Rajai Davis .12 .30
99 Fausto Carmona .12 .30
100 Jake Westbrook .12 .30
101 Rafael Betancourt .12 .30
102 Joe Borowski .12 .30
103 Victor Martinez .20 .50
104 Travis Hafner .12 .30
105 Ryan Garko .12 .30
106 Kenny Lofton .12 .30
107 Franklin Gutierrez .12 .30
108 Felix Hernandez .20 .50
109 J.J. Putz .12 .30
110 Brandon Morrow .12 .30
111 Kenji Johjima .12 .30
112 Jose Vidro .12 .30
113 Richie Sexson .12 .30
114 Ichiro Suzuki .40 1.00
115 Ben Broussard .12 .30
116 Sergio Mitre .12 .30
117 Scott Olsen .12 .30
118 Rick Vanden Hurk .12 .30
119 Lee Gardner .12 .30
120 Miguel Olivo .12 .30
121 Hanley Ramirez .20 .50
122 Mike Jacobs .12 .30
123 Josh Willingham .20 .50
124 John Maine .12 .30
125 Tom Glavine .20 .50
126 Billy Wagner .12 .30
127 Aaron Heilman .12 .30
128 David Wright .20 .50
129 Luis Castillo .12 .30
130 Shawn Green .12 .30
131 Damion Easley .12 .30
132 Carlos Delgado .12 .30
133 Shawn Hill .12 .30
134 John Lannan .12 .30
135 Chad Cordero .12 .30
136 Jon Rauch .12 .30
137 Jesus Flores .12 .30
138 Dmitri Young .12 .30
139 Cristian Guzman .12 .30
140 Austin Kearns .12 .30
141 Nook Logan .12 .30
142 Erik Bedard .12 .30
143 Daniel Cabrera .12 .30
144 Chris Ray .12 .30
145 Chad Bradford .12 .30
146 Ramon Hernandez .12 .30
147 Miguel Tejada .20 .50
148 Freddie Bynum .12 .30
149 Corey Patterson .12 .30
150 Chris Young .12 .30
151 Greg Maddux .40 1.00
152 Kevin Cameron .12 .30
153 Doug Brocail .12 .30
154 Kevin Kouzmanoff .12 .30
155 Geoff Blum .12 .30
156 Milton Bradley .12 .30
157 Brian Giles .12 .30
158 Jamie Moyer .12 .30
159 Kyle Kendrick .12 .30
160 Kyle Lohse .12 .30
161 Antonio Alfonseca .12 .30
162 Chris Coste .12 .30
163 Chase Utley .20 .50
164 Tadahito Iguchi .12 .30
165 Aaron Rowand .12 .30
166 Shane Victorino .12 .30
167 Ian Snell .12 .30
168 Shane Youman .12 .30
169 Shawn Chacon .12 .30
170 Ronny Paulino .12 .30
171 Jack Wilson .12 .30
172 Adam LaRoche .12 .30
173 Ryan Doumit .12 .30
174 Xavier Nady .12 .30

175 Kevin Millwood .12 .30
176 Brandon McCarthy .12 .30
177 Wes Littleton .12 .30
178 Mike Wood .12 .30
179 Hank Blalock .12 .30
180 Ian Kinsler .20 .50
181 Marlon Byrd .12 .30
182 Brad Wilkerson .12 .30
183 Tim Wakefield .20 .50
184 Daisuke Matsuzaka .20 .50
185 Julian Tavarez .12 .30
186 Hideki Okajima .12 .30
187 Doug Mirabelli .12 .30
188 Dustin Pedroia .30 .75
189 Mike Lowell .12 .30
190 Manny Ramirez .30 .75
191 Coco Crisp .12 .30
192 Bronson Arroyo .12 .30
193 Matt Belisle .12 .30
194 Jared Burton .12 .30
195 Mike Gosling .12 .30
196 David Ross .12 .30
197 Edwin Encarnacion .30 .75
198 Ken Griffey Jr. .60 1.50
199 Adam Dunn .20 .50
200 Jeff Francis .12 .30
201 Jason Hirsh .12 .30
202 Manny Corpas .12 .30
203 Jeremy Affeldt .12 .30
204 Yorvit Torrealba .12 .30
205 Todd Helton .20 .50
206 Kazuo Matsui .12 .30
207 Brad Hawpe .12 .30
208 Willy Taveras .12 .30
209 Brian Bannister .12 .30
210 Zack Greinke .30 .75
211 Kyle Davies .12 .30
212 David Riske .12 .30
213 John Buck .12 .30
214 Mark Grudzielanek .12 .30
215 Billy Butler .12 .30
216 David DeJesus .12 .30
217 Jeremy Bonderman .12 .30
218 Chad Durbin .12 .30
219 Andrew Miller .20 .50
220 Todd Jones .12 .30
221 Brandon Inge .12 .30
222 Placido Polanco .12 .30
223 Gary Sheffield .12 .30
224 Magglio Ordonez .20 .50
225 Matt Garza .12 .30
226 Boof Bonser .12 .30
227 Joe Nathan .12 .30
228 Dennys Reyes .12 .30
229 Joe Mauer .25 .60
230 Michael Cuddyer .12 .30
231 Jason Bartlett .12 .30
232 Torii Hunter .12 .30
233 Jason Tyner .12 .30
234 Mark Buehrle .20 .50
235 Jon Garland .12 .30
236 Jose Contreras .12 .30
237 Matt Thornton .12 .30
238 Juan Uribe .12 .30
239 Jim Thome .20 .50
240 Jerry Owens .12 .30
241 Jermaine Dye .12 .30
242 Andy Pettitte .20 .50
243 Phil Hughes .12 .30
244 Mike Mussina .20 .50
245 Joba Chamberlain .12 .30
246 Brian Bruney .12 .30
247 Jorge Posada .20 .50
248 Derek Jeter .75 2.00
249 Jason Giambi .12 .30
250 Johnny Damon .20 .50
251 Jonathan Albaladejo RC .30 .75
252 Josh Anderson (RC) .20 .50
253 Wladimir Balentien (RC) .20 .50
254 Josh Banks (RC) .20 .50
255 Daric Barton (RC) .20 .50
256 Jerry Blevins RC .30 .75
257 Emilio Bonifacio RC .50 1.25
258 Lance Broadway (RC) .20 .50
259 Clay Buchholz (RC) .30 .75
260 Billy Buckner (RC) .20 .50
261 Jeff Clement (RC) .30 .75
262 Willie Collazo RC .30 .75
263 Ross Detwiler RC .30 .75
264 Sam Fuld RC .60 1.50
265 Harvey Garcia (RC) .20 .50
266 Alberto Gonzalez RC .30 .75
267 Ryan Hanigan RC .30 .75
268 Kevin Hart (RC) .20 .50
269 Luke Hochevar RC .30 .75
270 Chin-Lung Hu (RC) .20 .50
271 Rob Johnson (RC) .20 .50
272 Radhames Liz RC .30 .75
273 Ian Kennedy RC .50 1.25
274 Joe Koshansky (RC) .20 .50
275 Donny Lucy (RC) .20 .50
276 Justin Maxwell RC .30 .75
277 Jonathan Meloan RC .30 .75
278 Luis Mendoza (RC) .20 .50
279 Jose Morales (RC) .20 .50
280 Nyjer Morgan (RC) .20 .50
281 Carlos Muniz RC .30 .75
282 Bill Murphy (RC) .20 .50
283 Josh Newman RC .30 .75
284 Ross Ohlendorf RC .30 .75
285 Troy Patton (RC) .20 .50
286 Felipe Paulino RC .30 .75
287 Steve Pearce RC 1.00 2.50
288 Heath Phillips RC .30 .75
289 Justin Ruggiano RC .30 .75
290 Clint Sammons (RC) .20 .50
291 Bronson Sardinha (RC) .20 .50
292 Chris Seddon (RC) .20 .50
293 Seth Smith (RC) .20 .50
294 Mitch Stetter RC .30 .75
295 Dave Davidson RC .30 .75
296 Rich Thompson RC .30 .75
297 J.R. Towles RC .30 .75
298 Eugenio Velez RC .30 .75
299 Joey Votto (RC) 1.50 4.00
300 Bill White RC .20 .50
301 Dan Haren .12 .30
302 Randy Johnson .30 .75
303 Justin Upton .20 .50
304 Tom Glavine .20 .50
305 Chipper Jones .30 .75
306 Jeff Francoeur .20 .50
307 John Smoltz .30 .75
308 Yunel Escobar .12 .30
309 Adam Jones .20 .50
310 Jeremy Guthrie .12 .30
311 Nick Markakis .25 .60
312 Brian Roberts .12 .30
313 Melvin Mora .12 .30
314 Josh Beckett .12 .30
315 Jon Lester .20 .50
316 Curt Schilling .20 .50
317 Jonathan Papelbon .20 .50
318 Jason Varitek .30 .75
319 David Ortiz .30 .75
320 Jacoby Ellsbury .25 .60
321 Julio Lugo .12 .30
322 Sean Casey .12 .30
323 Kevin Youkilis .12 .30
324 J.D. Drew .12 .30
325 Derrek Lee .12 .30
326 Carlos Zambrano .20 .50
327 Kerry Wood .12 .30
328 Geovany Soto .30 .75
329 Kosuke Fukudome RC .60 1.50
330 Gavin Floyd .12 .30
331 Bobby Jenks .12 .30
332 Javier Vazquez .12 .30
333 A.J. Pierzynski .12 .30
334 Orlando Cabrera .20 .50
335 Joe Crede .12 .30
336 Paul Konerko .20 .50
337 Nick Swisher .20 .50
338 Carlos Quentin .12 .30
339 Alexei Ramirez .40 1.00
340 Johnny Cueto .30 .75
341 Aaron Harang .12 .30
342 Brandon Phillips .12 .30
343 Paul Byrd .12 .30
344 Grady Sizemore .20 .50
345 Jhonny Peralta .12 .30
346 Asdrubal Cabrera .20 .50
347 C.C. Sabathia .20 .50
348 Troy Tulowitzki .30 .75
349 Matt Holliday .30 .75
350 Garrett Atkins .12 .30
351 Ubaldo Jimenez .12 .30
352 Kenny Rogers .12 .30
353 Justin Verlander .30 .75
354 Dontrelle Willis .12 .30
355 Joel Zumaya .12 .30
356 Ivan Rodriguez .20 .50
357 Miguel Cabrera .30 .75
358 Carlos Guillen .12 .30
359 Edgar Renteria .12 .30
360 Curtis Granderson .20 .50
361 Jeremy Hermida .12 .30
362 Dan Uggla .12 .30
363 Luis Gonzalez .12 .30
364 Andrew Miller .20 .50
365 Jorge Cantu .12 .30
366 Kazuo Matsui .12 .30
367 Lance Berkman .20 .50
368 Miguel Tejada .20 .50
369 Jose Valverde .12 .30
370 Michael Bourn .12 .30
371 Gil Meche .12 .30
372 Joey Gathright .12 .30
373 Mark Teahen .12 .30
374 Alex Gordon .20 .50
375 Tony Pena .12 .30
376 Jose Guillen .12 .30
377 Torii Hunter .12 .30
378 Ervin Santana .12 .30
379 Francisco Rodriguez .20 .50
380 Howie Kendrick .12 .30
381 John Lackey .20 .50
382 Gary Matthews .12 .30
383 Jon Garland .12 .30
384 Chone Figgins .12 .30
385 Andruw Jones .12 .30
386 James Loney .12 .30
387 Andre Ethier .20 .50
388 Rafael Furcal .12 .30
389 Brad Penny .12 .30
390 Hiroki Kuroda RC .50 1.25
391 Blake DeWitt .20 .50
392 Mike Cameron .12 .30
393 Ryan Braun .20 .50
394 Rickie Weeks .12 .30
395 Bill Hall .12 .30
396 Tony Gwynn .12 .30
397 Eric Gagne .12 .30
398 Jeff Suppan .12 .30
399 Jason Kendall .12 .30
400 Livan Hernandez .12 .30
401 Francisco Liriano .12 .30
402 Pat Neshek .20 .50
403 Adam Everett .12 .30
404 Justin Morneau .20 .50
405 Craig Monroe .12 .30
406 Carlos Gomez .12 .30
407 Delmon Young .20 .50
408 Oliver Perez .12 .30
409 Jose Reyes .20 .50
410 Moises Alou .12 .30
411 Carlos Beltran .20 .50
412 Endy Chavez .12 .30
413 Ryan Church .12 .30
414 Pedro Martinez .20 .50
415 Johan Santana .20 .50
416 Mike Pelfrey .12 .30
417 Brian Schneider .12 .30
418 Ramon Castro .12 .30
419 Kei Igawa .12 .30
420 Mariano Rivera .40 1.00
421 Chien-Ming Wang .20 .50
422 Wilson Betemit .12 .30
423 Robinson Cano .20 .50
424 Alex Rodriguez .40 1.00
425 Bobby Abreu .12 .30
426 Shelley Duncan .12 .30
427 Hideki Matsui .30 .75
428 Joe Blanton .12 .30
429 Bobby Crosby .12 .30
430 Eric Chavez .12 .30
431 Dan Johnson .12 .30
432 Rich Harden .12 .30
433 Kurt Suzuki .12 .30
434 Ryan Howard .20 .50
435 Jimmy Rollins .20 .50
436 Pedro Feliz .12 .30
437 Adam Eaton .12 .30
438 Brad Lidge .12 .30
439 Brett Myers .12 .30
440 Pat Burrell .12 .30
441 Geoff Jenkins .12 .30
442 Zach Duke .12 .30
443 Matt Morris .12 .30
444 Tom Gorzelanny .12 .30
445 Jason Bay .20 .50
446 Freddy Sanchez .12 .30
447 Matt Capps .12 .30
448 Tadahito Iguchi .12 .30
449 Adrian Gonzalez .20 .50
450 Jim Edmonds .20 .50
451 Jake Peavy .12 .30
452 Khalil Greene .12 .30
453 Trevor Hoffman .20 .50
454 Mark Prior .20 .50
455 Randy Wolf .12 .30
456 Scott Hairston .12 .30
457 Tim Lincecum .20 .50
458 Noah Lowry .12 .30
459 Aaron Rowand .12 .30
460 Randy Winn .12 .30
461 Ray Durham .12 .30
462 Brian Wilson .30 .75
463 Adrian Beltre .30 .75
464 Jarrod Washburn .12 .30
465 Yuniesky Betancourt .12 .30
466 Jose Lopez .12 .30
467 Raul Ibanez .20 .50
468 Erik Bedard .12 .30
469 Brad Wilkerson .12 .30
470 Chris Carpenter .20 .50
471 Mark Mulder .12 .30
472 Skip Schumaker .12 .30
473 Troy Glaus .20 .50
474 Chris Duncan .12 .30
475 Scott Kazmir .20 .50
476 Troy Percival .12 .30
477 Akinori Iwamura .12 .30
478 Carl Crawford .20 .50
479 Cliff Floyd .12 .30
480 Matt Garza .12 .30
481 Edwin Jackson .12 .30
482 Vicente Padilla .12 .30
483 Josh Hamilton .20 .50
484 Milton Bradley .12 .30
485 Michael Young .12 .30
486 David Murphy .12 .30
487 Ben Broussard .12 .30
488 B.J. Ryan .12 .30
489 David Eckstein .12 .30
490 Alex Rios .12 .30
491 Lyle Overbay .12 .30
492 Scott Rolen .20 .50
493 Lastings Milledge .12 .30
494 Paul Lo Duca .12 .30
495 Ryan Zimmerman .20 .50
496 Odalis Perez .12 .30
497 Wily Mo Pena .12 .30
498 Elijah Dukes .12 .30
499 Ronnie Belliard .12 .30
500 Nick Johnson .12 .30

2008 Upper Deck First Edition Jerseys

ANNCD PRINT RUN 750 SER.#'d SETS
FEAB A.J. Burnett Jsy/750 * 1.50 4.00
FEAE Andre Ethier Jsy/750 * 2.50 6.00
FEAG Adrian Gonzalez Jsy/750 * 2.50 6.00
FEAH Aaron Harang Jsy/750 * 1.50 4.00
FEAP Albert Pujols Jsy/750 * 5.00 12.00
FEAR Aaron Rowand Jsy/750 * 1.50 4.00
FEAX Alex Rios Jsy/750 * 1.50 4.00
FEBA Bobby Abreu Jsy/750 * 1.50 4.00
FEBG Brian Giles Jsy/750 * 1.50 4.00
FEBO Aaron Boone Jsy/750 * 2.50 6.00
FEBU Clay Buchholz Jsy/750 * 2.50 6.00
FEBW Billy Wagner Jsy/750 * 1.50 4.00
FEBZ Barry Zito Jsy/750 * 2.50 6.00
FECA Mike Cameron Jsy/750 * 1.50 4.00
FECB Chad Billingsley Jsy/750 * 2.50 6.00
FECC Chris Carpenter Jsy/750 * 2.50 6.00
FECD Chris Duncan Jsy/750 * 1.50 4.00
FECF Chone Figgins Jsy/750 * 1.50 4.00
FECG Curtis Granderson Jsy/750 * 2.50 6.00
FECH Cole Hamels Jsy/750 * 3.00 8.00
FECJ Conor Jackson Jsy/750 * 1.50 4.00
FECL Carlos Lee Jsy/750 * 1.50 4.00
FECR Coco Crisp Jsy/750 * 1.50 4.00
FECS Curt Schilling Jsy/750 * 2.50 6.00
FECU Michael Cuddyer Jsy/750 * 1.50 4.00
FECY Chris Young Jsy/750 * 1.50 4.00
FEDA Johnny Damon Jsy/750 * 2.50 6.00
FEDH Dan Haren Jsy/750 * 1.50 4.00
FEDJ Derek Jeter Jsy/750 * 10.00 25.00
FEDL Derrek Lee Jsy/750 * 1.50 4.00
FEDO David Ortiz Jsy/750 * 4.00 10.00
FEDP Dustin Pedroia Jsy/750 * 4.00 10.00
FEDU Dan Uggla Jsy/750 * 1.50 4.00
FEDW Dontrelle Willis Jsy/750 * 1.50 4.00
FEDY Delmon Young Jsy/750 * 2.50 6.00
FEED Jim Edmonds Jsy/750 * 2.50 6.00
FEEG Eric Gagne Jsy/750 * 1.50 4.00
FEES Johnny Estrada Jsy/750 * 1.50 4.00
FEFH Felix Hernandez Jsy/750 * 2.50 6.00
FEFL Francisco Liriano Jsy/750 * 1.50 4.00
FEFS Freddy Sanchez Jsy/750 * 1.50 4.00
FEFT Frank Thomas Jsy/750 * 4.00 10.00
FEGJ Geoff Jenkins Jsy/750 * 1.50 4.00
FEGM Greg Maddux Jsy/750 * 5.00 12.00
FEGU Jeremy Guthrie Jsy/750 * 1.50 4.00
FEHB Hank Blalock Jsy/750 * 1.50 4.00
FEHI Aaron Hill Jsy/750 * 1.50 4.00
FEHR Hanley Ramirez Jsy/750 * 2.50 6.00
FEHS Huston Street Jsy/750 * 2.50 6.00
FEJA Jason Bay Jsy/750 * 2.50 6.00
FEJB Jeremy Bonderman Jsy/750 * 1.50 4.00
FEJC Joe Crede Jsy/750 * 1.50 4.00
FEJD J.D. Drew Jsy/750 * 1.50 4.00
FEJE Jermaine Dye Jsy/750 * 1.50 4.00
FEJF Jeff Francoeur Jsy/750 * 2.50 6.00
FEJG Jason Giambi Jsy/750 * 1.50 4.00
FEJH Jeremy Hermida Jsy/750 * 1.50 4.00
FEJK Jason Kendall Jsy/750 * 1.50 4.00
FEJM Joe Mauer Jsy/750 * 3.00 8.00
FEJO Josh Barfield Jsy/750 * 1.50 4.00
FEJP Jhonny Peralta Jsy/750 * 1.50 4.00
FEJQ Jacque Jones Jsy/750 * 1.50 4.00
FEJR Jimmy Rollins Jsy/750 * 2.50 6.00
FEJV Justin Verlander Jsy/750 * 4.00 10.00
FEJW Jered Weaver Jsy/750 * 2.50 6.00
FEKE Howie Kendrick Jsy/750 * 1.50 4.00
FEKG Ken Griffey Jr. Jsy/750 * 8.00 20.00
FEKJ Kenji Johjima Jsy/750 * 1.50 4.00
FEKM Kevin Millwood Jsy/750 * 1.50 4.00
FEKU Jason Kubel Jsy/750 * 1.50 4.00
FEKW Kerry Wood Jsy/750 * 1.50 4.00
FEKY Kevin Youkilis Jsy/750 * 1.50 4.00
FELM Lastings Milledge Jsy/750 * 1.50 4.00
FEMA Kazuo Matsui Jsy/750 * 1.50 4.00
FEMC Matt Cain Jsy/750 * 2.50 6.00
FEMG Matt Garza Jsy/750 * 1.50 4.00
FEMM Mark Mulder Jsy/750 * 1.50 4.00
FEMO Justin Morneau Jsy/750 * 2.50 6.00
FEMU Mike Mussina Jsy/750 * 2.50 6.00
FENM Nick Markakis Jsy/750 * 3.00 8.00
FENS Nick Swisher Jsy/750 * 2.50 6.00
FEPA Jonathan Papelbon Jsy/750 * 2.50 6.00
FEPI Juan Pierre Jsy/750 * 1.50 4.00
FEPO Jorge Posada Jsy/750 * 2.50 6.00
FERA Aramis Ramirez Jsy/750 * 1.50 4.00
FERF Rafael Furcal Jsy/750 * 1.50 4.00
FERH Rich Hill Jsy/750 * 1.50 4.00
FERJ Randy Johnson Jsy/750 * 4.00 10.00
FESC Sean Casey Jsy/750 * 1.50 4.00
FESP Scott Podsednik Jsy/750 * 1.50 4.00
FETG Tom Gorzelanny Jsy/750 * 1.50 4.00
FETH Trevor Hoffman Jsy/750 * 2.50 6.00
FETL Tim Lincecum Jsy/750 * 2.50 6.00
FETS Takashi Saito Jsy/750 * 1.50 4.00
FEVA Jason Varitek Jsy/750 * 4.00 10.00
FEVM Victor Martinez Jsy/750 * 2.50 6.00
FEWI Josh Willingham Jsy/750 * 2.50 6.00
FEWL Jack Wilson Jsy/750 * 1.50 4.00
FEXN Xavier Nady Jsy/750 * 1.50 4.00
FEZG Zack Greinke Jsy/750 * 4.00 10.00

2008 Upper Deck First Edition StarQuest

SQ1 Ichiro Suzuki 1.00 2.50
SQ2 Ryan Braun .50 1.25
SQ3 Prince Fielder .60 1.50
SQ4 Ken Griffey Jr. 1.50 4.00
SQ5 Vladimir Guerrero .60 1.50
SQ6 Travis Hafner .40 1.00
SQ7 Matt Holliday 1.00 2.50
SQ8 Ryan Howard .50 1.25
SQ9 Derek Jeter 2.00 5.00
SQ10 Chipper Jones 1.00 2.50
SQ11 Carlos Lee .40 1.00
SQ12 Justin Morneau .60 1.50
SQ13 Magglio Ordonez .60 1.50
SQ14 David Ortiz 1.00 2.50
SQ15 Jake Peavy .40 1.00
SQ16 Albert Pujols 1.00 2.50
SQ17 Hanley Ramirez .60 1.50
SQ18 Manny Ramirez 1.00 2.50
SQ19 Jose Reyes .60 1.50
SQ20 Alex Rodriguez 1.00 2.50
SQ21 Johan Santana .60 1.50
SQ22 Grady Sizemore .60 1.50
SQ23 Alfonso Soriano .60 1.50
SQ24 Mark Teixeira .60 1.50
SQ25 Frank Thomas 1.00 2.50
SQ26 Jim Thome .60 1.50
SQ27 Chase Utley .60 1.50
SQ28 Brandon Webb .60 1.50
SQ29 David Wright .50 1.25
SQ30 Michael Young .40 1.00
SQ31 Adam Dunn .60 1.50
SQ32 Albert Pujols 1.00 2.50
SQ33 Alex Rodriguez 1.00 2.50
SQ34 B.J. Upton .60 1.50
SQ35 CC Sabathia .60 1.50
SQ36 Carlos Beltran .60 1.50
SQ37 Carlos Pena .60 1.50
SQ38 Cole Hamels .75 2.00
SQ39 Curtis Granderson .60 1.50
SQ40 Daisuke Matsuzaka .50 1.25
SQ41 David Ortiz 1.00 2.50
SQ42 Derek Jeter 2.00 5.00
SQ43 Derrek Lee .40 1.00
SQ44 Eric Byrnes .40 1.00
SQ45 Felix Hernandez .60 1.50
SQ46 Ichiro Suzuki 1.00 2.50
SQ47 Jeff Francoeur .60 1.50
SQ48 Jimmy Rollins .60 1.50
SQ49 Joe Mauer .75 2.00
SQ50 John Smoltz 1.00 2.50
SQ51 Ken Griffey Jr. 1.50 4.00
SQ52 Lance Berkman .60 1.50
SQ53 Miguel Cabrera 1.00 2.50
SQ54 Paul Konerko .60 1.50
SQ55 Pedro Martinez .60 1.50
SQ56 Randy Johnson 1.00 2.50
SQ57 Russell Martin .40 1.00
SQ58 Troy Tulowitzki 1.00 2.50
SQ59 Vernon Wells .40 1.00
SQ60 Vladimir Guerrero .60 1.50

2009 Upper Deck First Edition

COMP.FACT.SET (400) 20.00 50.00
COMPLETE SET (300) 15.00 40.00
COMMON CARD (1-300) .12 .30
COMMON ROOKIE (1-300) .20 .50
COMMON CARD (301-384) .12 .30
COMMON RC (385-400) .20 .50
300-400 ISSUED IN FACT.SET ONLY
1 Randy Johnson .30 .75
2 Conor Jackson .12 .30
3 Brandon Webb .20 .50
4 Dan Haren .12 .30
5 Stephen Drew .12 .30
6 Mark Reynolds .12 .30
7 Eric Byrnes .12 .30
8 Justin Upton .20 .50
9 Chris B. Young .12 .30
10 Max Scherzer .30 .75
11 Adam Dunn .20 .50
12 David Eckstein .12 .30
13 Jair Jurrjens .12 .30
14 Brandon Jones .12 .30
15 Tom Glavine .20 .50
16 John Smoltz .30 .75
17 Chipper Jones .30 .75
18 Yunel Escobar .12 .30
19 Kelly Johnson .12 .30
20 Brian McCann .20 .50
21 Jeff Francoeur .20 .50
22 Tim Hudson .20 .50
23 Casey Kotchman .12 .30
24 James Parr (RC) .20 .50
25 Nick Markakis .25 .60
26 Brian Roberts .12 .30
27 Jeremy Guthrie .12 .30
28 Adam Jones .20 .50
29 Luke Scott .12 .30
30 Aubrey Huff .12 .30
31 Daniel Cabrera .12 .30
32 George Sherrill .12 .30
33 Melvin Mora .12 .30
34 David Ortiz .30 .75
35 Jacoby Ellsbury .25 .60
36 Coco Crisp .12 .30
37 J.D. Drew .12 .30
38 Daisuke Matsuzaka .20 .50
39 Josh Beckett .12 .30
40 Curt Schilling .20 .50
41 Clay Buchholz .12 .30
42 Dustin Pedroia .30 .75
43 Julio Lugo .12 .30
44 Mike Lowell .12 .30
45 Jonathan Papelbon .20 .50
46 Jason Varitek .30 .75
47 Hideki Okajima .12 .30
48 Jon Lester .20 .50
49 Tim Wakefield .20 .50
50 Kevin Youkilis .12 .30
51 Jason Bay .20 .50
52 Justin Masterson .12 .30
53 Jeff Samardzija .20 .50
54 Alfonso Soriano .20 .50
55 Derrek Lee .12 .30
56 Aramis Ramirez .12 .30
57 Kerry Wood .12 .30
58 Jim Edmonds .20 .50
59 Kosuke Fukudome .20 .50
60 Geovany Soto .20 .50
61 Ted Lilly .12 .30
62 Carlos Zambrano .20 .50
63 Ryan Theriot .20 .50
64 Mark DeRosa .20 .50
65 Ryan Dempster .12 .30
66 Rich Harden .12 .30
67 Alexei Ramirez .20 .50
68 Nick Swisher .20 .50
69 Carlos Quentin .12 .30
70 Jermaine Dye .12 .30
71 Paul Konerko .20 .50
72 Joe Crede .12 .30
73 Jim Thome .20 .50
74 Gavin Floyd .12 .30
75 Javier Vazquez .12 .30
76 Mark Buehrle .20 .50
77 Bobby Jenks .12 .30
78 Ken Griffey Jr. .60 1.50
79 Brandon Phillips .12 .30
80 Aaron Harang .12 .30
81 Edinson Volquez .12 .30
82 Johnny Cueto .20 .50
83 Edwin Encarnacion .30 .75
84 Joey Votto .30 .75
85 Jay Bruce .20 .50
86 Travis Hafner .12 .30
87 Victor Martinez .20 .50
88 Grady Sizemore .20 .50
89 Cliff Lee .20 .50
90 Ryan Garko .12 .30
91 Jhonny Peralta .12 .30
92 Fausto Carmona .12 .30
93 Troy Tulowitzki .30 .75
94 Matt Holliday .30 .75
95 Todd Helton .20 .50
96 Ubaldo Jimenez .12 .30
97 Brian Fuentes .12 .30
98 Willy Taveras .12 .30
99 Aaron Cook .12 .30
100 Garrett Atkins .12 .30
101 Jeff Francis .12 .30
102 Dexter Fowler (RC) .30 .75
103 Armando Galarraga .12 .30
104 Miguel Cabrera .30 .75
105 Carlos Guillen .12 .30
106 Gary Sheffield .12 .30
107 Curtis Granderson .25 .60
108 Magglio Ordonez .20 .50
109 Dontrelle Willis .12 .30
110 Kenny Rogers .12 .30
111 Justin Verlander .30 .75
112 Hanley Ramirez .20 .50
113 Jeremy Hermida .12 .30
114 Mike Jacobs .12 .30
115 Andrew Miller .20 .50
116 Josh Willingham .20 .50
117 Dan Uggla .12 .30
118 Josh Johnson .20 .50
119 Hunter Pence .20 .50
120 Roy Oswalt .20 .50
121 Lance Berkman .20 .50
122 Carlos Lee .12 .30
123 Michael Bourn .12 .30
124 Miguel Tejada .20 .50
125 Jose Valverde .12 .30
126 Mike Aviles .12 .30
127 Zack Greinke .30 .75
128 Gil Meche .12 .30
129 Alex Gordon .20 .50
130 Luke Hochevar .12 .30
131 Jose Guillen .12 .30
132 Billy Butler .12 .30
133 David DeJesus .12 .30
134 Mark Teahen .12 .30
135 Joakim Soria .12 .30
136 Mark Teixeira .20 .50
137 Vladimir Guerrero .20 .50
138 Torii Hunter .12 .30
139 Jered Weaver .20 .50
140 Chone Figgins .12 .30
141 Francisco Rodriguez .20 .50
142 Garret Anderson .12 .30
143 Howie Kendrick .12 .30
144 John Lackey .20 .50
145 Ervin Santana .12 .30
146 Joe Saunders .12 .30
147 Manny Ramirez .30 .75
148 Casey Blake .12 .30
149 Chad Billingsley .20 .50
150 Russell Martin .12 .30
151 Matt Kemp .25 .60
152 James Loney .12 .30
153 Jeff Kent .12 .30
154 Nomar Garciaparra .20 .50
155 Rafael Furcal .12 .30
156 Andruw Jones .12 .30
157 Andre Ethier .20 .50
158 Takashi Saito .12 .30
159 Brad Penny .12 .30
160 Hiroki Kuroda .12 .30
161 Jonathan Broxton .12 .30
162 Chin-Lung Hu .12 .30
163 Derek Lowe .12 .30
164 Clayton Kershaw .50 1.25
165 Greg Maddux .40 1.00
166 CC Sabathia .20 .50
167 Yovani Gallardo .12 .30
168 Ryan Braun .20 .50
169 Prince Fielder .20 .50
170 Corey Hart .12 .30
171 Bill Hall .12 .30
172 Rickie Weeks .12 .30
173 Mike Cameron .12 .30
174 Ben Sheets .12 .30
175 J.J. Hardy .12 .30
176 Mat Gamel RC .50 1.25
177 Denard Span .12 .30
178 Carlos Gomez .12 .30
179 Joe Mauer .25 .60
180 Justin Morneau .20 .50
181 Joe Nathan .12 .30
182 Delmon Young .20 .50
183 Francisco Liriano .12 .30
184 Nick Blackburn .12 .30
185 Daniel Murphy RC .50 1.25
186 Nick Evans .12 .30
187 Jose Reyes .20 .50
188 David Wright .25 .60
189 Carlos Delgado .12 .30
190 Ryan Church .12 .30
191 Carlos Beltran .20 .50
192 Pedro Martinez .20 .50
193 Johan Santana .20 .50
194 John Maine .12 .30
195 Endy Chavez .12 .30
196 Oliver Perez .12 .30
197 Mike Pelfrey .12 .30
198 Jonathon Niese RC .30 .75
199 Ivan Rodriguez .20 .50
200 Alex Rodriguez .40 1.00
201 Derek Jeter .75 2.00
202 Robinson Cano .20 .50
203 Jason Giambi .12 .30
204 Bobby Abreu .12 .30
205 Johnny Damon .20 .50
206 Hideki Matsui .30 .75
207 Jorge Posada .20 .50
208 Joba Chamberlain .12 .30
209 Ian Kennedy .12 .30
210 Mike Mussina .20 .50
211 Andy Pettitte .20 .50
212 Mariano Rivera .40 1.00
213 Chien-Ming Wang .20 .50
214 Phil Hughes .12 .30
215 Xavier Nady .12 .30
216 Justin Duchscherer .12 .30
217 Eric Chavez .12 .30
218 Bobby Crosby .12 .30
219 Mark Ellis .12 .30
220 Daric Barton .12 .30
221 Frank Thomas .30 .75
222 Huston Street .12 .30
223 Jack Cust .12 .30
224 Greg Golson (RC) .20 .50
225 Joe Blanton .12 .30
226 Ryan Howard .25 .60
227 Chase Utley .20 .50
228 Jimmy Rollins .20 .50
229 Pat Burrell .12 .30
230 Shane Victorino .12 .30
231 Brett Myers .12 .30
232 Brad Lidge .12 .30
233 Cole Hamels .25 .60
234 Nate McLouth .12 .30
235 Ian Snell .12 .30
236 Ryan Doumit .12 .30
237 Matt Antonelli RC .30 .75
238 Will Venable RC .20 .50
239 Jake Peavy .12 .30
240 Chris Young .12 .30
241 Trevor Hoffman .20 .50
242 Adrian Gonzalez .25 .60
243 Chase Headley .12 .30
244 Khalil Greene .12 .30
245 Kevin Kouzmanoff .12 .30
246 Brian Giles .12 .30
247 Barry Zito .20 .50
248 Tim Lincecum .20 .50
249 Matt Cain .20 .50
250 Brian Wilson .30 .75
251 Aaron Rowand .12 .30
252 Conor Gillaspie RC .50 1.25
253 Omar Vizquel .20 .50
254 Bengie Molina .12 .30
255 Erik Bedard .12 .30
256 Felix Hernandez .20 .50
257 Ichiro Suzuki .40 1.00
258 J.J. Putz .12 .30
259 Raul Ibanez .20 .50
260 Adrian Beltre .30 .75
261 Jeff Clement .12 .30
262 Kenji Johjima .20 .50
263 Jose Lopez .12 .30
264 Albert Pujols .40 1.00
265 Troy Glaus .12 .30
266 Chris Carpenter .20 .50
267 Rick Ankiel .12 .30
268 Adam Wainwright .20 .50
269 Chris Duncan .12 .30
270 Todd Wellemeyer .12 .30
271 Ryan Ludwick .20 .50
272 Yadier Molina .40 1.00
273 B.J. Upton .20 .50
274 Carl Crawford .20 .50
275 Evan Longoria .20 .50
276 James Shields .12 .30
277 Scott Kazmir .12 .30
278 Carlos Pena .20 .50
279 Akinori Iwamura .12 .30
280 David Price RC .40 1.00
281 Matt Garza .12 .30
282 Rocco Baldelli .12 .30
283 Michael Young .12 .30
284 Ian Kinsler .20 .50
285 Josh Hamilton .20 .50
286 Hank Blalock .12 .30
287 Milton Bradley .12 .30
288 Jarrod Saltalamacchia .12 .30
289 Roy Halladay .20 .50
290 A.J. Burnett .12 .30
291 Dustin McGowan .12 .30
292 Scott Rolen .20 .50
293 Alex Rios .12 .30
294 Vernon Wells .12 .30
295 B.J. Ryan .12 .30
296 Elijah Dukes .12 .30
297 Lastings Milledge .12 .30
298 Chad Cordero .12 .30
299 Ryan Zimmerman .20 .50
300 Cristian Guzman .12 .30
301 Brandon Webb .20 .50
302 Chris B. Young .12 .30
303 Justin Upton .20 .50
304 Conor Jackson .12 .30
305 Tom Glavine .20 .50
306 Javier Vazquez .12 .30
307 Chipper Jones .30 .75
308 Nick Markakis .25 .60
309 Brian Roberts .12 .30
310 Adam Jones .20 .50
311 Ty Wigginton .12 .30
312 John Smoltz .30 .75
313 Brad Penny .12 .30
314 Takashi Saito .12 .30
315 Josh Beckett .12 .30
316 Dustin Pedroia .30 .75
317 David Ortiz .30 .75
318 Jason Varitek .30 .75
319 Milton Bradley .12 .30
320 Alfonso Soriano .20 .50
321 Kosuke Fukudome .20 .50
322 Carlos Zambrano .20 .50
323 Jim Thome .20 .50
324 Chris Getz .12 .30
325 Octavio Dotel .12 .30
326 Joey Votto .30 .75
327 Jay Bruce .20 .50
328 Kerry Wood .12 .30
329 Mark DeRosa .20 .50
330 Grady Sizemore .20 .50
331 Troy Tulowitzki .30 .75
332 Todd Helton .20 .50
333 Adam Everett .12 .30
334 Cameron Maybin .12 .30
335 Roy Oswalt .20 .50
336 Lance Berkman .20 .50
337 Joakim Soria .12 .30
338 Alex Gordon .20 .50
339 Bobby Abreu .12 .30
340 Vladimir Guerrero .20 .50
341 Manny Ramirez .30 .75
342 Orlando Hudson .12 .30
343 Mark Loretta .12 .30
344 Russell Martin .12 .30
345 Trevor Hoffman .20 .50
346 Ryan Braun .20 .50
347 Francisco Liriano .12 .30
348 Joe Mauer .25 .60
349 Livan Hernandez .12 .30
350 Jeremy Reed .12 .30
351 J.J. Putz .12 .30
352 Francisco Rodriguez .20 .50
353 Johan Santana .20 .50
354 Jose Reyes .20 .50
355 David Wright .25 .60
356 Derek Jeter .75 2.00
357 A.J. Burnett .12 .30
358 Nick Swisher .20 .50
359 CC Sabathia .20 .50
360 Chien-Ming Wang .20 .50
361 Mark Teixeira .20 .50
362 Joba Chamberlain .12 .30
363 Alex Rodriguez .40 1.00
364 Orlando Cabrera .12 .30
365 Matt Holliday .30 .75
366 Jason Giambi .12 .30
367 Chan Ho Park .20 .50
368 Cole Hamels .25 .60
369 Ryan Howard .25 .60
370 Chase Utley .20 .50
371 Randy Johnson .30 .75
372 Edgar Renteria .12 .30
373 Ken Griffey Jr. .60 1.50
374 Ichiro Suzuki .40 1.00
375 Khalil Greene .12 .30
376 Albert Pujols .40 1.00
377 Akinori Iwamura .12 .30
378 B.J. Upton .20 .50
379 Evan Longoria .20 .50
380 Josh Hamilton .20 .50
381 Nelson Cruz .30 .75
382 Adam Dunn .20 .50
383 Josh Willingham .20 .50
384 Daniel Cabrera .12 .30

385 Koji Uehara RC .50 1.25
386 Kenshin Kawakami RC .30 .75
387 Jason Motte (RC) .30 .75
388 Elvis Andrus RC .50 1.25
389 Rick Porcello RC .60 1.50
390 Colby Rasmus (RC) .30 .75
391 Shairon Martis RC .30 .75
392 Ricky Romero (RC) .30 .75
393 Kevin Jepsen (RC) .20 .50
394 James McDonald RC .50 1.25
395 Brett Anderson RC .30 .75
396 Trevor Cahill RC .50 1.25
397 Jordan Schafer (RC) .30 .75
398 Trevor Crowe RC .20 .50
399 Everth Cabrera RC .30 .75
400 Ryan Perry RC .50 1.25

2009 Upper Deck First Edition StarQuest

SQ1 Albert Pujols .75 2.00
SQ2 Alex Rodriguez .75 2.00
SQ3 Alfonso Soriano .40 1.00
SQ4 Chipper Jones .60 1.50
SQ5 Chase Utley .40 1.00
SQ6 Derek Jeter 1.50 4.00
SQ7 Daisuke Matsuzaka .40 1.00
SQ8 David Ortiz .60 1.50
SQ9 David Wright .50 1.25
SQ10 Grady Sizemore .40 1.00
SQ11 Hanley Ramirez .40 1.00
SQ12 Ichiro Suzuki .75 2.00
SQ13 Josh Beckett .25 .60
SQ14 Jake Peavy .25 .60
SQ15 Jose Reyes .40 1.00
SQ16 Johan Santana .40 1.00
SQ17 Ken Griffey Jr. 1.25 3.00
SQ18 Lance Berkman .40 1.00
SQ19 Miguel Cabrera .60 1.50
SQ20 Matt Holliday .60 1.50
SQ21 Manny Ramirez .60 1.50
SQ22 Prince Fielder .40 1.00
SQ23 Ryan Braun .40 1.00
SQ24 Ryan Howard .50 1.25
SQ25 Vladimir Guerrero .40 1.00

2003 Upper Deck First Pitch

COMP.SET w/o SP's (270) 20.00 50.00
COMMON CARD (1-270) .12 .30
*FIRST PITCH 1-270: .4X TO 1X BASIC UD
COMMON CARD (271-283) .40 1.00
COMMON CARD (284-300) .40 1.00
271-300 STATED ODDS 1:4
271 Hideki Matsui SP RC 2.00 5.00
272 Jose Contreras SP RC 1.00 2.50
273 Robert Madritsch SP RC .40 1.00
274 Shane Bazzell SP RC .40 1.00
275 Felix Sanchez SP RC .40 1.00
276 Todd Wellemeyer SP RC .40 1.00
277 Lew Ford SP RC .40 1.00
278 Jeremy Griffiths SP RC .40 1.00
279 Oscar Villarreal SP RC .40 1.00
280 Brandon Webb SP RC 1.25 3.00
281 Delvis Lantigua SP RC .40 1.00
282 Josh Willingham SP RC 1.25 3.00
283 Mike Nicolas SP RC .40 1.00
284 Mike Hampton SP .40 1.00
285 Jim Thome SP .60 1.50
286 Bartolo Colon SP .40 1.00
287 Orlando Hernandez SP .40 1.00
288 Jeremy Giambi SP .40 1.00
289 Jeff Kent SP .40 1.00
290 Tom Glavine SP .60 1.50
291 Cliff Floyd SP .40 1.00
292 Tsuyoshi Shinjo SP .40 1.00
293 Jose Cruz Jr. SP .40 1.00
294 Edgardo Alfonzo SP .40 1.00
295 Andres Galarraga SP .60 1.50
296 Troy O'Leary SP .40 1.00
297 Eric Karros SP .40 1.00
298 Ivan Rodriguez SP .60 1.50
299 Fred McGriff SP .60 1.50
300 Preston Wilson SP .40 1.00

2004 Upper Deck First Pitch

COMP.SET w/o SP'S (270) 20.00 50.00
COMMON CARD (1-270) .10 .30
*FIRST PITCH 1-270: .4X TO 1X BASIC UD
COMMON CARD (271-300) .40 1.00
271-300 STATED ODDS 1:4
271 Rickie Weeks SP .40 1.00
272 Delmon Young SP .60 1.50
273 Chien-Ming Wang SP 1.50 4.00
274 Rich Harden SP .40 1.00
275 Edwin Jackson SP .40 1.00
276 Dan Haren SP .40 1.00
277 Todd Wellemeyer SP .40 1.00
278 Prentice Redman SP .40 1.00
279 Ryan Wagner SP .40 1.00
280 Aaron Looper SP .40 1.00
281 Rick Roberts SP .40 1.00
282 Josh Willingham SP .60 1.50
283 Dave Crouthers SP RC .40 1.00
284 Chris Capuano SP .40 1.00
285 Mike Gosling SP RC .40 1.00
286 Brian Sweeney SP .40 1.00
287 Donald Kelly SP RC .60 1.50
288 Ryan Meaux SP RC .40 1.00
289 Colin Porter SP .40 1.00
290 Jerome Gamble SP RC .40 1.00
291 Colby Miller SP RC .40 1.00
292 Ian Ferguson SP .40 1.00
293 Tim Bittner SP RC .40 1.00
294 Jason Frasor SP RC .40 1.00
295 Brandon Medders SP RC .40 1.00
296 Mike Johnston SP RC .40 1.00
297 Tim Bausher SP RC .40 1.00
298 Justin Leone SP RC .40 1.00
299 Sean Henn SP RC .40 1.00
300 Michel Hernandez SP .40 1.00

2004 Upper Deck First Pitch First and Foremost Jumbos

ONE PER BLASTER BOX
BW Brandon Webb 1.25 3.00
DH Dan Haren 1.25 3.00
DW Dontrelle Willis 1.25 3.00
EB Ernie Banks 3.00 8.00
GH George H.W. Bush 5.00 12.00
GW George W. Bush 5.00 12.00
HR Horacio Ramirez 1.25 3.00
JC Jose Contreras 1.25 3.00
JW Jerome Williams 1.25 3.00
LT Luis Tiant 1.25 3.00
MS Mike Schmidt 5.00 12.00
RH Rich Harden 1.25 3.00
RW Ryan Wagner 1.25 3.00
WF Whitey Ford 2.00 5.00

2005 Upper Deck First Pitch

COMP.SET w/o SP'S (300) 20.00 50.00
*1st PITCH 1-300: .4X TO 1X BASIC UD
301-320 STATED ODDS 1:4
COMMON CARD (321-330) .75 2.00
321-330 STATED ODDS 1:36
301 Guillermo Quiroz SR SP .40 1.00
302 Jeff Bajenaru SR SP .40 1.00
303 Bartolome Fortunato SR SP .40 1.00
304 Jason Alfaro SR SP .40 1.00
305 Mike Rose SR SP .40 1.00
306 Joe Hietpas SR SP .40 1.00
307 Kyle Denney SR SP .40 1.00
308 Rene Rivera SR SP .40 1.00
309 Kameron Loe SR SP .40 1.00
310 Rickie Weeks SR SP .40 1.00
311 Gustavo Chacin SR SP .40 1.00
312 Chris Burke SR SP .40 1.00
313 Yhency Brazoban SR SP .40 1.00
314 Brandon League SR SP .40 1.00
315 Jose Capellan SR SP .40 1.00
316 Russ Adams SR SP .40 1.00
317 Adrian Gonzalez SR SP .75 2.00
318 Jason DuBois SR SP .40 1.00
319 Abe Alvarez SR SP .40 1.00
320 Eric Crozier SR SP .40 1.00
321 B.Colon .75 2.00
B.Molina SOD
322 C.Sabathia 1.25 3.00
V Martinez SOD
323 J.Peavy .75 2.00
R.Hernandez SOD
324 J.Schmidt .75 2.00
A.Pierzynski SOD
325 J.Santana 1.50 4.00
J.Mauer SOD
326 M.Prior 1.25 3.00
M.Barrett SOD
327 M.Mussina 1.25 3.00
J.Posada SOD
328 R.Clemens 2.50 6.00
B.Ausmus SOD
329 R.Halladay 1.25 3.00
G.Quiroz SOD
330 T.Glavine 2.00 5.00
M.Piazza SOD

2005 Upper Deck First Pitch Fabric

STATED ODDS 1:180
SP INFO PROVIDED BY UPPER DECK
NO SP PRICING DUE TO SCARCITY
AJ Andruw Jones Jsy 4.00 10.00
AS Alfonso Soriano Jsy 3.00 8.00
BB Bret Boone Jsy 3.00 8.00
BE Josh Beckett Jsy 3.00 8.00
CJ Chipper Jones Jsy 4.00 10.00
CS Curt Schilling Jsy 4.00 10.00
DJ Derek Jeter Pants 10.00 25.00
EC Eric Chavez Jsy 3.00 8.00
EG Eric Gagne Jsy 3.00 8.00
JB Jeff Bagwell Jsy 4.00 10.00
JE Jim Edmonds Jsy 3.00 8.00
MM Mark Mulder Jsy 3.00 8.00
MO Magglio Ordonez Jsy 3.00 8.00
SR Scott Rolen Pants 4.00 10.00
SS Sammy Sosa Jsy 4.00 10.00
TG Troy Glaus Jsy 3.00 8.00
TH Torii Hunter Jsy 3.00 8.00

2005 Upper Deck First Pitch Jumbos

ISSUED ONLY IN BLASTER BOXES
FP1 Shingo Takatsu .40 1.00
FP2 Jeff Francis .40 1.00
FP3 Jesse Crain .40 1.00
FP4 Jose Capellan .40 1.00
FP5 Zack Greinke 1.25 3.00
FP6 Scott Proctor .40 1.00
FP7 Scott Kazmir 1.00 2.50
FP8 Gavin Floyd .40 1.00
FP9 Joe Blanton .40 1.00
FP10 Akinori Otsuka .40 1.00

2005 Upper Deck First Pitch Signature Stars

STATED ODDS 1:720
SP INFO PROVIDED BY UPPER DECK
NO SP PRICING DUE TO SCARCITY
DR Dave Roberts 20.00 50.00
JE Johnny Estrada 10.00 25.00
JW Jeff Weaver 15.00 40.00

2006 Upper Deck First Pitch

COMPLETE SET (220) 30.00 60.00
1 Chad Tracy .12 .30
2 Conor Jackson .20 .50
3 Craig Counsell .12 .30
4 Javier Vazquez .12 .30
5 Luis Gonzalez .12 .30
6 Shawn Green .12 .30
7 Troy Glaus .12 .30
8 Joey Devine RC .12 .30
9 Andruw Jones .12 .30
10 Chipper Jones .30 .75
11 John Smoltz .30 .75
12 Marcus Giles .12 .30
13 Jeff Francoeur .30 .75
14 Tim Hudson .20 .50
15 Brian Roberts .12 .30
16 Erik Bedard .12 .30
17 Javy Lopez .12 .30
18 Melvin Mora .12 .30
19 Miguel Tejada .20 .50
20 Alejandro Freire RC .12 .30
21 Sammy Sosa .30 .75
22 Craig Hansen RC .30 .75
23 Curt Schilling .20 .50
24 David Ortiz .30 .75
25 Edgar Renteria .12 .30
26 Johnny Damon .20 .50
27 Manny Ramirez .30 .75
28 Matt Clement .12 .30
29 Trot Nixon .12 .30
30 Aramis Ramirez .12 .30
31 Carlos Zambrano .20 .50
32 Derrek Lee .12 .30
33 Greg Maddux .40 1.00
34 Jeromy Burnitz .12 .30
35 Kerry Wood .12 .30
36 Mark Prior .20 .50
37 Nomar Garciaparra .20 .50
38 Aaron Rowand .12 .30
39 Chris DeMaria RC .12 .30
40 Jon Garland .12 .30
41 Mark Buehrle .20 .50
42 Paul Konerko .20 .50
43 Scott Podsednik .12 .30
44 Tadahito Iguchi .12 .30
45 Adam Dunn .20 .50
46 Austin Kearns .12 .30
47 Felipe Lopez .12 .30
48 Ken Griffey Jr. .60 1.50
49 Ryan Freel .12 .30
50 Sean Casey .12 .30
51 Wily Mo Pena .12 .30
52 C.C. Sabathia .20 .50
53 Cliff Lee .20 .50
54 Coco Crisp .12 .30
55 Grady Sizemore .20 .50
56 Jake Westbrook .12 .30
57 Travis Hafner .12 .30
58 Victor Martinez .20 .50
59 Aaron Miles .12 .30
60 Clint Barmes .12 .30
61 Garrett Atkins .12 .30
62 Jeff Baker .12 .30
63 Jeff Francis .12 .30
64 Matt Holliday .30 .75
65 Todd Helton .20 .50
66 Carlos Guillen .12 .30
67 Chris Shelton .12 .30
68 Dmitri Young .12 .30
69 Ivan Rodriguez .20 .50
70 Jeremy Bonderman .12 .30
71 Magglio Ordonez .20 .50
72 Placido Polanco .12 .30
73 A.J. Burnett .12 .30
74 Carlos Delgado .12 .30
75 Dontrelle Willis .12 .30
76 Josh Beckett .12 .30
77 Juan Pierre .12 .30
78 Ryan Jorgensen RC .12 .30
79 Miguel Cabrera .30 .75
80 Robert Andino RC .12 .30
81 Andy Pettitte .20 .50
82 Brad Lidge .12 .30
83 Craig Biggio .20 .50
84 Jeff Bagwell .20 .50
85 Lance Berkman .20 .50
86 Morgan Ensberg .12 .30
87 Roger Clemens .40 1.00
88 Roy Oswalt .20 .50
89 Angel Berroa .12 .30
90 David DeJesus .12 .30
91 Steve Stemle RC .12 .30
92 Jonah Bayliss RC .12 .30
93 Mike Sweeney .12 .30
94 Ryan Theriot RC .40 1.00
95 Zack Greinke .30 .75
96 Brad Penny .12 .30
97 Cesar Izturis .12 .30
98 Brian Myrow RC .12 .30
99 Eric Gagne .12 .30
100 J.D. Drew .12 .30
101 Jeff Kent .12 .30
102 Milton Bradley .12 .30
103 Odalis Perez .12 .30
104 Ben Sheets .12 .30
105 Brady Clark .12 .30
106 Carlos Lee .12 .30
107 Geoff Jenkins .12 .30
108 Lyle Overbay .12 .30
109 Prince Fielder .60 1.50
110 Rickie Weeks .12 .30
111 Jacque Jones .12 .30
112 Joe Mauer .20 .50
113 Joe Nathan .12 .30
114 Johan Santana .20 .50
115 Justin Morneau .20 .50
116 Chris Heintz RC .12 .30
117 Torii Hunter .12 .30
118 Carlos Beltran .20 .50
119 Cliff Floyd .12 .30
120 David Wright .25 .60
121 Jose Reyes .20 .50
122 Mike Cameron .12 .30
123 Mike Piazza .30 .75
124 Pedro Martinez .20 .50
125 Tom Glavine .20 .50
126 Alex Rodriguez .40 1.00
127 Derek Jeter .75 2.00
128 Gary Sheffield .12 .30
129 Hideki Matsui .30 .75
130 Jason Giambi .12 .30
131 Jorge Posada .20 .50
132 Mariano Rivera .40 1.00
133 Mike Mussina .20 .50
134 Randy Johnson .30 .75
135 Barry Zito .20 .50
136 Bobby Crosby .12 .30
137 Danny Haren .12 .30
138 Eric Chavez .12 .30
139 Huston Street .12 .30
140 Ron Flores RC .12 .30
141 Nick Swisher .20 .50
142 Rich Harden .12 .30
143 Bobby Abreu .12 .30
144 Danny Sandoval RC .12 .30
145 Chase Utley .20 .50
146 Jim Thome .20 .50
147 Jimmy Rollins .20 .50
148 Pat Burrell .12 .30
149 Ryan Howard .25 .60
150 Craig Wilson .12 .30
151 Jack Wilson .12 .30
152 Jason Bay .12 .30
153 Matt Lawton .12 .30
154 Oliver Perez .12 .30
155 Rob Mackowiak .12 .30
156 Zach Duke .12 .30
157 Brian Giles .12 .30
158 Jake Peavy .12 .30
159 Craig Breslow RC .12 .30
160 Khalil Greene .12 .30
161 Mark Loretta .12 .30
162 Ryan Klesko .12 .30
163 Trevor Hoffman .20 .50
164 J.T. Snow .12 .30
165 Jason Schmidt .12 .30
166 Marquis Grissom .12 .30
167 Moises Alou .12 .30
168 Omar Vizquel .20 .50
169 Pedro Feliz .12 .30
170 Jeremy Accardo RC .12 .30
171 Adrian Beltre .30 .75
172 Ichiro Suzuki .40 1.00
173 Felix Hernandez .20 .50
174 Jeff Harris RC .12 .30
175 Randy Winn .12 .30
176 Raul Ibanez .20 .50
177 Richie Sexson .12 .30
178 Albert Pujols .40 1.00
179 Chris Carpenter .20 .50
180 David Eckstein .12 .30
181 Jim Edmonds .20 .50
182 Larry Walker .20 .50
183 Matt Morris .12 .30
184 Reggie Sanders .12 .30
185 Scott Rolen .20 .50
186 Aubrey Huff .12 .30
187 Jonny Gomes .12 .30
188 Carl Crawford .20 .50
189 Tim Corcoran RC .12 .30
190 Julio Lugo .12 .30
191 Rocco Baldelli .12 .30
192 Scott Kazmir .20 .50
193 Alfonso Soriano .20 .50
194 Hank Blalock .12 .30
195 Kenny Rogers .12 .30
196 Scott Feldman RC .12 .30
197 Laynce Nix .12 .30
198 Mark Teixeira .20 .50
199 Michael Young .12 .30
200 Aaron Hill .12 .30
201 Alex Rios .12 .30
202 Eric Hinske .12 .30
203 Gustavo Chacin .12 .30
204 Roy Halladay .20 .50
205 Shea Hillenbrand .12 .30
206 Vernon Wells .12 .30
207 Brad Wilkerson .12 .30
208 Chad Cordero .12 .30
209 Jose Guillen .12 .30
210 Jose Vidro .12 .30
211 Livan Hernandez .12 .30
212 Preston Wilson .12 .30
213 Jason Bergmann RC .12 .30
214 Bartolo Colon .12 .30
215 Chone Figgins .12 .30
216 Darin Erstad .12 .30
217 Francisco Rodriguez .20 .50
218 Garret Anderson .12 .30
219 Steve Finley .12 .30
220 Vladimir Guerrero .20 .50

2006 Upper Deck First Pitch Diamond Stars

COMPLETE SET (35) 10.00 25.00
OVERALL INSERT ODDS ONE PER PACK
DS1 Luis Gonzalez .40 1.00
DS2 Andruw Jones .40 1.00
DS3 John Smoltz 1.00 2.50
DS4 Miguel Tejada .60 1.50
DS5 Johnny Damon .60 1.50
DS6 Manny Ramirez 1.00 2.50
DS7 Derrek Lee .40 1.00
DS8 Mark Prior .60 1.50
DS9 Mark Buehrle .60 1.50
DS10 Ken Griffey Jr. 2.00 5.00
DS11 Travis Hafner .40 1.00
DS12 Todd Helton .60 1.50
DS13 Ivan Rodriguez .60 1.50
DS14 Miguel Cabrera 1.00 2.50
DS15 Roger Clemens 1.25 3.00
DS16 Mike Sweeney .40 1.00
DS17 Jeff Kent .40 1.00
DS18 Carlos Lee .40 1.00
DS19 Johan Santana .60 1.50
DS20 Torii Hunter .40 1.00
DS21 Pedro Martinez .60 1.50
DS22 Alex Rodriguez 1.25 3.00
DS23 Derek Jeter 2.50 6.00
DS24 Eric Chavez .40 1.00
DS25 Bobby Abreu .40 1.00
DS26 Jason Bay .40 1.00
DS27 Jake Peavy .40 1.00
DS28 Moises Alou .40 1.00
DS29 Ichiro Suzuki 1.25 3.00
DS30 Albert Pujols 1.25 3.00
DS31 Carl Crawford .60 1.50
DS32 Mark Teixeira .60 1.50
DS33 Roy Halladay .60 1.50
DS34 Jose Guillen .40 1.00
DS35 Vladimir Guerrero .60 1.50

2006 Upper Deck First Pitch Goin Deep

COMPLETE SET (35) 10.00 25.00
OVERALL INSERT ODDS ONE PER PACK
GD1 Adam Dunn .60 1.50
GD2 Albert Pujols 1.25 3.00
GD3 Alex Rodriguez 1.25 3.00
GD4 Alfonso Soriano .60 1.50
GD5 Andruw Jones .40 1.00
GD6 Aramis Ramirez .40 1.00
GD7 Bobby Abreu .40 1.00
GD8 Brian Giles .40 1.00
GD9 Carlos Delgado .40 1.00
GD10 Carlos Lee .40 1.00
GD11 Chipper Jones 1.00 2.50
GD12 David Ortiz 1.00 2.50
GD13 David Wright .75 2.00
GD14 Derrek Lee .40 1.00
GD15 Eric Chavez .40 1.00
GD16 Gary Sheffield .40 1.00
GD17 Hideki Matsui 1.00 2.50
GD18 Jeff Kent .40 1.00
GD19 Jim Edmonds .60 1.50
GD20 Ken Griffey Jr. 2.00 5.00
GD21 Luis Gonzalez .40 1.00
GD22 Manny Ramirez 1.00 2.50
GD23 Mark Teixeira .60 1.50
GD24 Miguel Cabrera 1.00 2.50
GD25 Miguel Tejada .60 1.50
GD26 Moises Alou .40 1.00
GD27 Pat Burrell .40 1.00
GD28 Paul Konerko .60 1.50
GD29 Rafael Palmeiro .60 1.50
GD30 Richie Sexson .40 1.00
GD31 Todd Helton .60 1.50
GD32 Torii Hunter .40 1.00
GD33 Travis Hafner .40 1.00
GD34 Vernon Wells .40 1.00
GD35 Vladimir Guerrero .60 1.50

2006 Upper Deck First Pitch Hot Stove Headlines

COMPLETE SET (20) 6.00 15.00
OVERALL INSERT ODDS ONE PER PACK
HS1 Alex Rodriguez 1.25 3.00
HS2 Carlos Beltran .60 1.50
HS3 Carlos Delgado .40 1.00
HS4 Curt Schilling .60 1.50
HS5 Derrek Lee .40 1.00
HS6 Greg Maddux 1.25 3.00
HS7 Hideki Matsui 1.00 2.50
HS8 Ichiro Suzuki 1.25 3.00
HS9 Ivan Rodriguez .60 1.50
HS10 Jim Thome .60 1.50
HS11 Johnny Damon .60 1.50
HS12 Ken Griffey Jr. 2.00 5.00
HS13 Manny Ramirez 1.00 2.50
HS14 Miguel Tejada .60 1.50
HS15 Nomar Garciaparra .60 1.50
HS16 Pedro Martinez .60 1.50
HS17 Randy Johnson 1.00 2.50
HS18 Roger Clemens 1.25 3.00
HS19 Scott Rolen .60 1.50
HS20 Vladimir Guerrero .60 1.50

2006 Upper Deck First Pitch Signature Stars

OVERALL INSERT ODDS ONE PER PACK
SP INFO PROVIDED BY UPPER DECK
DR J.D. Drew 10.00 25.00
GQ Guillermo Quiroz 4.00 10.00
IS Ian Snell 4.00 10.00
JE Johnny Estrada 4.00 10.00
PL Paul LoDuca 6.00 15.00
RH Rich Harden 6.00 15.00
RI Juan Rivera 4.00 10.00
RW Ryan Wagner 4.00 10.00
VM Victor Martinez 6.00 15.00
YM Yadier Molina 20.00 50.00

2006 Upper Deck Future Stars

COMP.SET w/o AU's (75) 10.00 25.00
COMMON CARD (1-75) .15 .40
COMMON AU RC (76-159) 3.00 8.00
FIVE AU RC PER BOX ON AVERAGE
NO SP PRICING DUE TO SCARCITY
PRINTING PLATE ODDS 1:2 CASES
PLATE PRINT RUN 1 SET PER COLOR
BLACK-CYAN-MAGENTA-YELLOW ISSUED
NO PLATE PRICING DUE TO SCARCITY
1 Miguel Tejada .25 .60
2 Brian Roberts .15 .40
3 Brandon Webb .25 .60
4 Luis Gonzalez .15 .40
5 Andruw Jones .15 .40
6 Chipper Jones .40 1.00
7 John Smoltz .40 1.00
8 Curt Schilling .25 .60
9 Josh Beckett .15 .40
10 David Ortiz .40 1.00
11 Manny Ramirez .40 1.00
12 Jim Thome .25 .60
13 Paul Konerko .25 .60
14 Jermaine Dye .15 .40
15 Derrek Lee .15 .40
16 Greg Maddux .50 1.25
17 Ken Griffey Jr. .75 2.00
18 Adam Dunn .25 .60
19 Felipe Lopez .15 .40
20 Travis Hafner .15 .40
21 Victor Martinez .25 .60
22 Grady Sizemore .25 .60
23 Todd Helton .25 .60
24 Matt Holliday .40 1.00
25 Jeremy Bonderman .15 .40
26 Ivan Rodriguez .25 .60
27 Miguel Cabrera .40 1.00
28 Dontrelle Willis .15 .40
29 Roger Clemens .50 1.25
30 Roy Oswalt .25 .60
31 Lance Berkman .25 .60
32 Reggie Sanders .15 .40
33 Vladimir Guerrero .25 .60
34 Chone Figgins .15 .40
35 Jeff Kent .15 .40
36 Eric Gagne .15 .40
37 Carlos Lee .15 .40
38 Rickie Weeks .15 .40
39 Johan Santana .25 .60
40 Torii Hunter .15 .40
41 Alex Rodriguez .50 1.25
42 Derek Jeter 1.00 2.50
43 Randy Johnson .40 1.00
44 Hideki Matsui .40 1.00
45 Johnny Damon .25 .60
46 Pedro Martinez .25 .60
47 David Wright .30 .75
48 Carlos Beltran .25 .60
49 Rich Harden .15 .40
50 Eric Chavez .15 .40
51 Huston Street .15 .40
52 Ryan Howard .30 .75
53 Bobby Abreu .15 .40
54 Chase Utley .25 .60
55 Jason Bay .15 .40
56 Jake Peavy .15 .40
57 Brian Giles .15 .40
58 Trevor Hoffman .25 .60
59 Jason Schmidt .15 .40
60 Randy Winn .15 .40
61 Kenji Johjima RC .40 1.00
62 Ichiro Suzuki .50 1.25
63 Felix Hernandez .25 .60
64 Albert Pujols .50 1.25
65 Chris Carpenter .25 .60
66 Jim Edmonds .25 .60
67 Carl Crawford .25 .60
68 Scott Kazmir .25 .60
69 Jonny Gomes .15 .40
70 Mark Teixeira .25 .60
71 Michael Young .15 .40
72 Vernon Wells .15 .40
73 Roy Halladay .25 .60
74 Nick Johnson .15 .40
75 Alfonso Soriano .25 .60
76 A.Wainwright AU (RC) 6.00 15.00
77 A.Hernandez AU (RC) 3.00 8.00
78 A.Ethier AU SP (RC) 3.00 8.00
79 Colter Bean AU SP (RC) 4.00 10.00
80 Ben Johnson AU (RC) 3.00 8.00
81 Boof Bonser AU SP (RC) 5.00 12.00
82 Boone Logan AU RC 3.00 8.00
83 Brian Anderson AU (RC) 3.00 8.00
84 B.Bannister AU (RC) 5.00 12.00
85 C.Denorfia AU SP (RC) 4.00 10.00
86 C.Billingsley AU SP (RC) 8.00 20.00
87 Cody Ross AU (RC) 3.00 8.00
88 Cole Hamels AU SP (RC) 8.00 20.00
89 Conor Jackson AU (RC) 5.00 12.00
91 D.Gassner AU SP (RC) 3.00 8.00
92 Jordan Tata AU RC 3.00 8.00
93 Eric Reed AU (RC) 3.00 8.00
94 Fausto Carmona AU (RC) 5.00 12.00
96 F.Liriano AU SP (RC) 10.00 25.00
97 Freddie Bynum AU (RC) 3.00 8.00
98 H.Ramirez AU SP (RC) 3.00 8.00
99 H.Kuo AU SP (RC) 5.00 12.00
100 Ian Kinsler AU (RC) 4.00 10.00
101 N.Cruz AU SP (RC) 8.00 20.00
102 Ruddy Lugo AU (RC) 3.00 8.00
103 J.Kubel AU SP (RC) 3.00 8.00
104 Jeff Harris AU RC 3.00 8.00
105 S.Ramirez AU (RC) 3.00 8.00
106 Jer.Weaver AU SP (RC) 20.00 50.00
107 J.Accardo AU SP RC 3.00 8.00
108 J.Willingham AU SP (RC) 3.00 8.00
109 J.Zumaya AU SP (RC) 5.00 12.00
110 Joey Devine AU RC 3.00 8.00
111 John Koronka AU (RC) 3.00 8.00
112 J.Papelbon AU (RC) 8.00 20.00
113 Jose Capellan AU (RC) 3.00 8.00
114 Josh Johnson AU (RC) 8.00 20.00
115 Josh Rupe AU SP (RC) 3.00 8.00
116 J.Hermida AU SP (RC) 3.00 8.00
117 Josh Wilson AU (RC) 3.00 8.00
118 J.Verlander AU SP (RC) 30.00 60.00
119 K.Shoppach AU (RC) 3.00 8.00
120 K.Morales AU (RC) 5.00 12.00
121 Sean Tracey AU (RC) 3.00 8.00
122 Macay McBride AU (RC) 3.00 8.00
124 Matt Cain AU (RC) 6.00 15.00
125 R.Martin AU (RC) 3.00 8.00
126 T.Hamulack AU SP (RC) 3.00 8.00
127 M.Jacobs AU (RC) 5.00 12.00
128 B.Hendrickson AU (RC) 3.00 8.00
129 Jack Taschner AU (RC) 3.00 8.00
130 N.McLouth AU (RC) 6.00 15.00
131 J.Sowers AU SP (RC) 8.00 20.00
132 Paul Maholm AU (RC) 3.00 8.00
134 Jason Bergmann AU RC 3.00 8.00
135 Rich Hill AU SP (RC) 3.00 8.00
137 Scott Dunn AU (RC) 3.00 8.00
138 R.Zimmerman AU (RC) 6.00 15.00
139 A.Sanchez AU (RC) 3.00 8.00
140 Sean Marshall AU (RC) 5.00 12.00
142 T.Buchholz AU (RC) 3.00 8.00
143 C.Quentin AU SP (RC) 3.00 8.00
144 Matt Garza AU (RC) 3.00 8.00
145 Wil Nieves AU (RC) 3.00 8.00
146 Jamie Shields AU RC 3.00 8.00
147 Jon Lester AU SP RC 6.00 15.00
149 Aaron Rakers AU (RC) 3.00 8.00
150 B.Livingston AU (RC) 3.00 8.00
151 B.Harris AU (RC) 3.00 8.00
152 Alay Soler AU SP RC 3.00 8.00
153 Chris Britton AU RC 3.00 8.00
154 H.Kendrick AU SP (RC) 6.00 15.00
155 J.Van Buren AU (RC) 3.00 8.00
156 C.Freeman AU SP (RC) 3.00 8.00
157 Matt Capps AU (RC) 3.00 8.00
158 Peter Moylan AU RC 3.00 8.00
159 Ty Taubenheim AU RC 3.00 12.00

2006 Upper Deck Future Stars Black

*BLACK: 2.5X TO 6X BASIC
STATED PRINT RUN 50 SER.#'d SETS

2006 Upper Deck Future Stars Blue

*BLUE: 2X TO 5X BASIC
STATED PRINT RUN 99 SER.#'d SETS

2006 Upper Deck Future Stars Gold

*GOLD: 6X TO 15X BASIC
STATED PRINT RUN 25 SER.#'d SETS

2006 Upper Deck Future Stars Green

*GREEN: 1.5X TO 4X BASIC
STATED PRINT RUN 499 SER.#'d SETS

2006 Upper Deck Future Stars Purple

*PURPLE: 1.25X TO 3X BASIC
STATED PRINT RUN 1799 SER.#'d SETS

2006 Upper Deck Future Stars Red

*RED: 1.5X TO 4X BASIC
STATED PRINT RUN 299 SER.#'d SETS

2006 Upper Deck Future Stars Rookie Signatures Red

STATED PRINT RUN 35 SER.#'d SETS
NO PRICING DUE TO SCARCITY

2006 Upper Deck Future Stars Clear Path to History Triple Signatures

STATED ODDS 1:288
BSJ Bay/Soriano/Andruw 30.00 60.00
CPO Carpenter/Peavy/Oswalt 10.00 25.00
CUK Crawford/B.Upton/Kazmir 20.00 50.00
DRR S.Drew/Reyes/Hanley 50.00 100.00
GEH Gwynn Jr./Ethier/Hermida 20.00 50.00
JVW J.Johns/Verlan/Jer.Weav 40.00 80.00
KTZ Kend/Tulo/Zimmerman 10.00 25.00
MKW Morales/KendrJer.Weav 20.00 50.00
MLG Mauer/Liriano/Garza 30.00 60.00
MML Morneau/Mauer/Liriano 40.00 80.00
MOH Morneau/Overbay/Hafner 10.00 25.00
NHP Nathan/Hoffman/Papel 30.00 60.00
PSO Peavy/Sheets/Oswalt 20.00 50.00
PVW Papel/Verland/Weaver 60.00 120.00
SBH Soler/Billingsley/Hamels 10.00 25.00
SHL Sowers/Hamels/Liriano 12.50 30.00
TZU Tulo/Zimmerman/B.Upton 20.00 50.00
URB Utley/Roberts/Biggio 30.00 60.00
VBZ Verland/Bonde/Zumaya 10.00 25.00

2006 Upper Deck Future Stars World Future Stars

COMPLETE SET (25) 10.00 25.00
PRINTING PLATE ODDS 1:2 CASES
PLATE PRINT RUN 1 SET PER COLOR
BLACK-CYAN-MAGENTA-YELLOW ISSUED
NO PLATE PRICING DUE TO SCARCITY
BLACK PRINT RUN 50 SER.#'d SETS
BLUE PRINT RUN 99 SER.#'d SETS
GOLD PRINT RUN 25 SER.#'d SETS
NO GOLD PRICING DUE TO SCARCITY
GREEN PRINT RUN 499 SER.#'d SETS
PURPLE PRINT RUN 1799 SER.#'d SETS
RED PRINT RUN 299 SER.#'d SETS
1 Adam Loewen .30 .75
2 Nan Wang .30 .75
3 Yi Feng .30 .75
4 Chien-Ming Chang .50 1.25
5 Yung Chi Chen .50 1.25
6 Chin-Lung Hu .30 .75
7 Yadel Marti .30 .75
8 Frederich Cepeda .30 .75
9 Pedro Luis Lazo .50 1.25
10 Osmany Urrutia .30 .75
11 Yoandy Garlobo .30 .75
12 Nobuhiko Matsunaka .50 1.25
13 Daisuke Matsuzaka 1.00 2.50
14 Tsuyoshi Nishioka 2.00 5.00
15 Tomoya Satozaki .50 1.25
16 Koji Uehara 1.00 2.50
17 Shunsuke Watanabe .50 1.25
18 Jong Beom Lee .30 .75
19 Sidney de Jong .30 .75
20 Shairon Martis .30 .75
21 Len Pecota .30 .75
22 Dicky Gonzalez .30 .75
23 Nicholas Dempsey .30 .75
24 Brett Willemburg .30 .75
25 Chase Utley .50 1.25

2006 Upper Deck Future Stars World Future Stars Black

*BLACK: 3X TO 8X BASIC
COMMON TEAM CHINESE TAIPEI 12.50 30.00
COMMON TEAM JAPAN 12.50 30.00
STATED PRINT RUN 50 SER.#'d SETS

2006 Upper Deck Future Stars World Future Stars Blue

*BLUE: 2.5X TO 6X BASIC
COMMON TEAM CHINESE TAIPEI 5.00 12.00
COMMON TEAM JAPAN 5.00 12.00
STATED PRINT RUN 99 SER.#'d SETS

2006 Upper Deck Future Stars World Future Stars Green

*GREEN: 1.5X TO 4X BASIC
COMMON TEAM CHINESE TAIPEI 4.00 10.00
COMMON TEAM JAPAN 4.00 10.00
STATED PRINT RUN 499 SER.#'d SETS

2006 Upper Deck Future Stars World Future Stars Purple

*PURPLE: .75X TO 2X BASIC
STATED PRINT RUN 1799 SER.#'d SETS

2006 Upper Deck Future Stars World Future Stars Red

*RED: 2X TO 5X BASIC
COMMON TEAM CHINESE TAIPEI 4.00 10.00
COMMON TEAM JAPAN 4.00 10.00
STATED PRINT RUN 299 SER.#'d SETS

2007 Upper Deck Future Stars

COMP.SET w/o AU's (100) 10.00 25.00
COMMON CARD (1-100) .15 .40
COMMON AU RC (101-190) 2.50 6.00
101-190 ODDS 1:6 HOB,1:24 RET,1:350 WALMART
EXCHANGE DEADLINE 9/5/2009
1 Brandon Webb .25 .60
2 Conor Jackson .15 .40
3 Stephen Drew .15 .40
4 Chipper Jones .40 1.00
5 Andruw Jones .15 .40
6 Jeff Francoeur .40 1.00
7 John Smoltz .40 1.00
8 Miguel Tejada .25 .60
9 Nick Markakis .30 .75
10 Brian Roberts .15 .40
11 David Ortiz .40 1.00
12 Manny Ramirez .40 1.00
13 Josh Beckett .15 .40
14 Curt Schilling .25 .60
15 Derrek Lee .15 .40
16 Aramis Ramirez .15 .40
17 Carlos Zambrano .25 .60
18 Alfonso Soriano .25 .60
19 Jim Thome .25 .60
20 Paul Konerko .25 .60
21 Jon Garland .15 .40
22 Ken Griffey Jr. .75 2.00
23 Adam Dunn .25 .60
24 Aaron Harang .15 .40

25 Travis Hafner .15 .40
26 Victor Martinez .25 .60
27 Grady Sizemore .25 .60
28 C.C. Sabathia .25 .60
29 Todd Helton .25 .60
30 Matt Holliday .40 1.00
31 Garrett Atkins .15 .40
32 Ivan Rodriguez .25 .60
33 Magglio Ordonez .25 .60
34 Gary Sheffield .15 .40
35 Justin Verlander .40 1.00
36 Miguel Cabrera .40 1.00
37 Hanley Ramirez .25 .60
38 Dontrelle Willis .15 .40
39 Lance Berkman .25 .60
40 Roy Oswalt .25 .60
41 Carlos Lee .15 .40
42 Gil Meche .15 .40
43 Emil Brown .15 .40
44 Mark Teahen .15 .40
45 Vladimir Guerrero .25 .60
46 Jered Weaver .25 .60
47 Howie Kendrick .15 .40
48 Juan Pierre .15 .40
49 Nomar Garciaparra .25 .60
50 Rafael Furcal .15 .40
51 Jeff Kent .15 .40
52 Prince Fielder .25 .60
53 Ben Sheets .15 .40
54 Rickie Weeks .15 .40
55 Justin Morneau .25 .60
56 Joe Mauer .30 .75
57 Torii Hunter .15 .40
58 Johan Santana .25 .60
59 Jose Reyes .25 .60
60 David Wright .30 .75
61 Carlos Delgado .15 .40
62 Carlos Beltran .25 .60
63 Derek Jeter 1.00 2.50
64 Alex Rodriguez .50 1.25
65 Johnny Damon .25 .60
66 Jason Giambi .15 .40
67 Bobby Abreu .15 .40
68 Mike Piazza .40 1.00
69 Nick Swisher .25 .60
70 Eric Chavez .15 .40
71 Ryan Howard .30 .75
72 Chase Utley .25 .60
73 Jimmy Rollins .25 .60
74 Jason Bay .25 .60
75 Freddy Sanchez .15 .40
76 Zach Duke .15 .40
77 Greg Maddux .50 1.25
78 Adrian Gonzalez .30 .75
79 Jake Peavy .15 .40
80 Ray Durham .15 .40
81 Barry Zito .25 .60
82 Matt Cain .25 .60
83 Ichiro Suzuki .50 1.25
84 Felix Hernandez .25 .60
85 Richie Sexson .15 .40
86 Albert Pujols .50 1.25
87 Scott Rolen .25 .60
88 Chris Carpenter .25 .60
89 Chris Duncan .15 .40
90 Carl Crawford .25 .60
91 Rocco Baldelli .15 .40
92 Scott Kazmir .25 .60
93 Michael Young .15 .40
94 Mark Teixeira .25 .60
95 Ian Kinsler .25 .60
96 Troy Glaus .15 .40
97 Vernon Wells .15 .40
98 Roy Halladay .25 .60
99 Ryan Zimmerman .25 .60
100 Nick Johnson .15 .40
101 Zack Segovia AU (RC) 2.50 6.00
102 Joaquin Arias AU (RC) 2.50 6.00
104 Travis Buck AU (RC) 2.50 6.00
105 Mike Schultz AU RC 2.50 6.00
107 Sean Henn AU (RC) 2.50 6.00
108 Ryan Z. Braun AU RC 2.50 6.00
109 Rick Vanden Hurk AU RC 2.50 6.00
110 Carlos Gomez AU SP RC 8.00 20.00
111 Mike Rabelo AU RC 2.50 6.00
112 Felix Pie AU (RC) 2.50 6.00
113 Miguel Montero AU (RC) 2.50 6.00
114 Michael Bourn AU (RC) 4.00 10.00
116 Matt Lindstrom AU (RC) 2.50 6.00
117 Matt Chico AU (RC) 2.50 6.00
118 Levale Speigner AU RC 2.50 6.00
119 Lee Gardner AU (RC) 2.50 6.00
120 Kory Casto AU (RC) 2.50 6.00
121 Kevin Kouzmanoff AU (RC) 2.50 6.00
122 Kevin Cameron AU RC 2.50 6.00
124 Tyler Clippard AU (RC) 4.00 10.00
125 Juan Perez AU RC 2.50 6.00
126 Josh Hamilton AU SP (RC) 8.00 20.00
127 Joseph Bisenius AU RC 2.50 6.00
128 Jose Luis Garcia AU RC 2.50 6.00
129 Jon Knott AU RC 2.50 6.00
130 Jon Coutlangus AU (RC) 2.50 6.00
131 John Danks AU RC 4.00 10.00
132 Joe Smith AU RC 2.50 6.00
133 Matt Brown AU (RC) 2.50 6.00
134 Joakim Soria AU RC 2.50 6.00
135 Jesus Flores AU RC 2.50 6.00
136 Jeff Baker AU (RC) 2.50 6.00
137 Jay Marshall AU RC 2.50 6.00
138 Jared Burton AU RC 2.50 6.00
139 Jamie Vermilyea AU RC 2.50 6.00
140 Jamie Burke AU (RC) 2.50 6.00
141 Ryan Rowland-Smith AU RC 2.50 6.00
142 Connor Robertson AU RC 2.50 6.00
143 Hector Gimenez AU (RC) 2.50 6.00
144 Gustavo Molina AU RC 2.50 6.00
145 Glen Perkins AU (RC) 2.50 6.00
147 Doug Slaten AU RC 2.50 6.00
148 Ryan Braun AU (RC) 12.00 30.00
150 Garrett Jones AU (RC) 6.00 15.00
152 Cesar Jimenez AU RC 2.50 6.00
153 Brian Stokes AU (RC) 2.50 6.00
154 Brian Burres AU (RC) 2.50 6.00
156 Kyle Kendrick AU RC 6.00 15.00
157 Andrew Miller AU RC 10.00 25.00
158 Alexi Casilla AU RC 4.00 10.00
159 Alex Gordon AU SP RC 8.00 20.00
160 A.J. Murray AU RC 2.50 6.00
162 Adam Lind AU (RC) 2.50 6.00
163 Chase Wright AU RC 6.00 15.00
164 Dallas Braden AU RC 4.00 10.00
165 Rocky Cherry AU RC 6.00 15.00
166 Andy Gonzalez AU RC 2.50 6.00
167 Neal Musser AU RC 2.50 6.00
168 Mark Reynolds AU RC 8.00 20.00
169 Dennis Dove AU (RC) 2.50 6.00
170 Justin Hampson AU (RC) 2.50 6.00
172 Kelvin Jimenez AU RC 2.50 6.00
173 Hunter Pence AU SP (RC) 8.00 20.00
174 Brad Salmon AU RC 2.50 6.00
175 Ryan Sweeney AU (RC) 2.50 6.00
176 Brandon Wood AU (RC) 2.50 6.00
177 Billy Butler AU SP (RC) 4.00 10.00
178 Ben Francisco AU (RC) 2.50 6.00
180 Yoel Hernandez AU RC 2.50 6.00
181 Tim Lincecum AU SP RC 12.00 30.00
182 Danny Putnam AU (RC) 2.50 6.00
183 J.Salta AU SP (RC) 4.00 10.00
185 Matt DeSalvo AU (RC) 2.50 6.00
186 Fred Lewis AU (RC) 4.00 10.00
187 Anthony Lerew AU (RC) 2.50 6.00
188 Jesse Litsch AU RC 4.00 10.00
189a Daisuke Matsuzaka RC .60 1.50
189b Daisuke Matsuzaka AU SP 12.00 30.00

2007 Upper Deck Future Stars Gold

*GOLD: 2X TO 5X BASIC
RANDOM INSERTS IN PACKS
STATED PRINT RUN 99 SER.#'d SETS
83 Ichiro Suzuki 6.00 15.00
189 Daisuke Matsuzaka 6.00 15.00

2007 Upper Deck Future Stars Red

*RED: 1.5X TO 4X BASIC
RANDOM INSERTS IN PACKS
STATED PRINT RUN 199 SER.#'d SETS
83 Ichiro Suzuki 5.00 12.00
189 Daisuke Matsuzaka 8.00 20.00

2007 Upper Deck Future Stars All Star Futures

RANDOM INSERTS IN PACKS
STATED PRINT RUN 500 SER.#'d SETS
AD Alejandro De Aza .75 2.00
AG Alex Gordon 1.50 4.00
AI Akinori Iwamura 1.25 3.00
AL Adam Lind .50 1.25
AM Andrew Miller 2.00 5.00
BA Jeff Baker .50 1.25
BI Billy Butler .75 2.00
BM Brandon Morrow 2.50 6.00
BU B.J. Upton .50 1.25
BW Brandon Wood .50 1.25
CA Alexi Casilla .75 2.00
CG Carlos Gomez 1.00 2.50
CW Chase Wright 1.25 3.00
CY Chris Young .50 1.25
DM Daisuke Matsuzaka 2.00 5.00
DP Danny Putnam .50 1.25
DY Delmon Young .75 2.00
FL Fred Lewis .75 2.00
FP Felix Pie .50 1.25
GP Glen Perkins .50 1.25
HA Josh Hamilton 1.50 4.00
HK Howie Kendrick .50 1.25
HP Hunter Pence 1.50 4.00
IK Ian Kinsler .75 2.00
JA Joaquin Arias .50 1.25
JD John Danks .75 2.00
JS Jarrod Saltalamacchia .75 2.00
JV Justin Verlander 1.25 3.00
KC Kory Casto .50 1.25
KI Kei Igawa 1.25 3.00
KK Kevin Kouzmanoff .50 1.25
LA Andy LaRoche .50 1.25
MA Matt Chico .50 1.25
MB Michael Bourn .75 2.00
MC Matt Cain .75 2.00
MI Miguel Montero .50 1.25
ML Matt Lindstrom .50 1.25
MO Micah Owings .50 1.25
PF Prince Fielder .75 2.00
PH Phil Hughes 1.25 3.00
RB Ryan Braun 2.50 6.00
RS Ryan Sweeney .50 1.25
RZ Ryan Zimmerman .75 2.00
SD Stephen Drew .50 1.25
SM Joe Smith .50 1.25
SO Joakim Soria .50 1.25
TB Travis Buck .50 1.25
TL Tim Lincecum 2.50 6.00
TP Tony Pena .50 1.25
TT Troy Tulowitzki 1.50 4.00

2007 Upper Deck Future Stars All Star Futures Signatures

STATED ODDS 1:72 H,1:2500 R,1:2500 WALMART
NO SP PRICING DUE TO SCARCITY
EXCH DEADLINE 9/5/2009
AL Adam Lind 4.00 10.00
AM Andrew Miller 6.00 15.00
BA Jeff Baker 3.00 8.00
BU B.J. Upton 4.00 10.00
BW Brandon Wood 6.00 15.00
CA Alexi Casilla 3.00 8.00
CG Carlos Gomez 6.00 15.00
CW Chase Wright 5.00 12.00
CY Chris Young 10.00 25.00
DP Danny Putnam 4.00 10.00
FL Fred Lewis 3.00 8.00
FP Felix Pie 3.00 8.00
GP Glen Perkins 5.00 12.00
HA Josh Hamilton 15.00 40.00
HP Hunter Pence 30.00 60.00
IK Ian Kinsler 6.00 15.00
JA Joaquin Arias 3.00 8.00
JD John Danks 4.00 10.00
JS Jarrod Saltalamacchia 6.00 15.00
KC Kory Casto 3.00 8.00
KK Kevin Kouzmanoff 5.00 12.00
LA Andy LaRoche 4.00 10.00
MA Matt Chico 3.00 8.00
MC Matt Cain 5.00 12.00
MI Miguel Montero 3.00 8.00
ML Matt Lindstrom 3.00 8.00
RB Ryan Braun 40.00 80.00
RS Ryan Sweeney 4.00 10.00
SM Joe Smith 3.00 8.00
SO Joakim Soria 5.00 12.00
TB Travis Buck 5.00 12.00
TL Tim Lincecum 40.00 80.00
TP Tony Pena 5.00 12.00
TT Troy Tulowitzki 10.00 25.00

2007 Upper Deck Future Stars Clear Path to History Triple Signatures

STATED ODDS 1:288 HOB,1:5000 RET
NO SP PRICING DUE TO SCARCITY
CCH Crosby/Chavez/Harden 20.00 50.00
DMY S.Drew/ Montero/C.Young 6.00 15.00
FEG Furcal/Ethier/L.Gonzalez 10.00 25.00
HAT Holliday/Atkins/Tulo 6.00 15.00
HMS Hafner/V.Martinez/Sowers 30.00 60.00
KUC Kazmir/B.Upton/Crawford 10.00 25.00
KUK Kinsler/H.Kendrick/Uggla 6.00 15.00
MPM Mora/Markakis/Patterson 6.00 15.00
SWF Prince/Sheets/Weeks 20.00 50.00
VZR Hanley/Verlander/Zimmerman 40.00 80.00
YBP Delmon/Butler/Pie 15.00 40.00

2007 Upper Deck Future Stars Cy Young Futures

RANDOM INSERTS IN PACKS
STATED PRINT RUN 500 SER.#'d SETS
AL Anthony Lerew .50 1.25
AM Andrew Miller 2.00 5.00
BM Brandon Morrow 2.50 6.00
CH Cole Hamels 1.00 2.50
CW Chase Wright 1.25 3.00
DM Daisuke Matsuzaka 2.00 5.00
GP Glen Perkins .50 1.25
JD John Danks .75 2.00
JG Jose Garcia .50 1.25
JL Jon Lester .75 2.00
JS Jeremy Sowers .50 1.25
JV Justin Verlander 1.25 3.00
JZ Joel Zumaya .50 1.25
KI Kei Igawa 1.25 3.00
MA Matt Chico .50 1.25
MC Matt Cain .75 2.00
MO Micah Owings .50 1.25
PH Phil Hughes 1.25 3.00
RV Rick VandenHurk .50 1.25
SH Sean Henn .50 1.25
SK Scott Kazmir .75 2.00
SM Joe Smith .50 1.25
TC Tyler Clippard .75 2.00
TL Tim Lincecum 2.50 6.00
ZS Zack Segovia .50 1.25

2007 Upper Deck Future Stars Cy Young Futures Signatures

STATED ODDS 1:72 H,1:2500 R,1:2500 WALMART
NO SP PRICING DUE TO SCARCITY
EXCH DEADLINE 9/5/2009
AL Anthony Lerew 3.00 8.00
AM Andrew Miller 4.00 10.00
CH Cole Hamels 12.50 30.00
CW Chase Wright 3.00 8.00
GP Glen Perkins 5.00 12.00
JD John Danks 4.00 10.00
JG Jose Garcia 3.00 8.00
MA Matt Chico 3.00 8.00
MC Matt Cain 5.00 12.00
MO Micah Owings 6.00 15.00
RV Rick VandenHurk 3.00 8.00
SH Sean Henn 3.00 8.00
SM Joe Smith 3.00 8.00
TC Tyler Clippard 6.00 15.00
TL Tim Lincecum 30.00 60.00
ZS Zack Segovia 3.00 8.00

2007 Upper Deck Future Stars MVP Futures

RANDOM INSERTS IN PACKS
STATED PRINT RUN 500 SER.#'d SETS
AD Alejandro De Aza .75 2.00
AG Alex Gordon 1.50 4.00
AI Akinori Iwamura 1.25 3.00
AL Adam Lind .50 1.25
DM Daisuke Matsuzaka 2.00 5.00
DY Delmon Young .75 2.00
FP Felix Pie .50 1.25
HP Hunter Pence 1.50 4.00
IK Ian Kinsler .75 2.00
JA Joaquin Arias .50 1.25
JB Jeff Baker .50 1.25
JH Josh Hamilton 1.50 4.00
JS Jarrod Saltalamacchia .75 2.00
JV Justin Verlander 1.25 3.00
KI Kei Igawa 1.25 3.00
KK Kevin Kouzmanoff .50 1.25
LA Andy LaRoche .50 1.25
MB Michael Bourn .75 2.00
MM Miguel Montero .50 1.25
PF Prince Fielder .75 2.00
RB Ryan Braun 2.50 6.00
RS Ryan Sweeney .50 1.25
RZ Ryan Zimmerman .75 2.00
TB Travis Buck .50 1.25
TT Troy Tulowitzki 1.50 4.00

2007 Upper Deck Future Stars MVP Futures Signatures

STATED ODDS 1:72 H,1:2500 R,1:2500 WALMART
NO SP PRICING DUE TO SCARCITY
EXCH DEADLINE 9/5/2009
AL Adam Lind 4.00 10.00
FP Felix Pie 3.00 8.00
HP Hunter Pence 8.00 20.00
IK Ian Kinsler 6.00 15.00
JA Joaquin Arias 3.00 8.00
JB Jeff Baker 3.00 8.00
JH Josh Hamilton 8.00 20.00
JS Jarrod Saltalamacchia 6.00 15.00
KK Kevin Kouzmanoff 5.00 12.00
LA Andy LaRoche 4.00 10.00
MB Michael Bourn 3.00 8.00
MM Miguel Montero 3.00 8.00
PF Prince Fielder 25.00 50.00
RB Ryan Braun 6.00 15.00
RS Ryan Sweeney 4.00 10.00
TB Travis Buck 5.00 12.00

2007 Upper Deck Future Stars Rookie Dated Debut

RANDOM INSERTS IN PACKS
STATED PRINT RUN 999 SER.#'d SETS
AC Alexi Casilla .50 1.25
AD Alejandro De Aza .50 1.25
AG Alex Gordon 1.00 2.50
AI Akinori Iwamura .75 2.00
AL Adam Lind .30 .75
BA Jeff Baker .30 .75
BB Brian Barden .30 .75
BI Joseph Bisenius .30 .75
BM Brandon Morrow 1.50 4.00
BW Brandon Wood .30 .75
CA Kory Casto .30 .75
CG Carlos Gomez .60 1.50
CR Cal Ripken Jr. 2.50 6.00
CW Chase Wright .75 2.00
DA John Danks .50 1.25
DJ Derek Jeter 2.00 5.00
DM Daisuke Matsuzaka 1.25 3.00
DY Delmon Young .50 1.25
ED Elijah Dukes .50 1.25
FL Fred Lewis .50 1.25
FP Felix Pie .30 .75
GM Gustavo Molina .30 .75
GP Glen Perkins .30 .75
HO Hideki Okajima 1.50 4.00
HP Hunter Pence 1.00 2.50
JA Joaquin Arias .30 .75
JC Jon Coutlangus .30 .75
JF Jesus Flores .30 .75
JH Josh Hamilton 1.00 2.50
JM Jay Marshall .30 .75
JP Juan Perez .30 .75
JS Joakim Soria .30 .75
KC Kevin Cameron .30 .75
KG Ken Griffey Jr. 1.50 4.00
KI Kei Igawa .75 2.00
KK Kevin Kouzmanoff .30 .75
LA Andy LaRoche .30 .75
LG Lee Gardner .30 .75
MB Michael Bourn .50 1.25
MC Matt Chico .30 .75
MM Miguel Montero .30 .75
MO Micah Owings .30 .75
MR Mike Rabelo .30 .75
PH Phil Hughes .75 2.00
RS Ryan Sweeney .30 .75
SA Jarrod Saltalamacchia .50 1.25
SM Joe Smith .30 .75
TB Travis Buck .30 .75
TL Tim Lincecum 1.50 4.00
TT Troy Tulowitzki 1.00 2.50

2007 Upper Deck Future Stars Two for the Bigs

RANDOM INSERTS IN PACKS
STATED PRINT RUN 999 SER.#'d SETS
AS J.Arias/C.Stewart .30 .75
BB M.Bourn/J.Bisenius .50 1.25
BD T.Buck/E.Dukes .50 1.25
BG R.Braun/A.Gordon 1.50 4.00
BS R.Z. Braun/J.Soria .30 .75
BT TTulowitzki/J.Baker 1.00 2.50
CF K.Casto/J.Flores .30 .75
CL T.Lincecum/M.Chico 1.50 4.00
CP G.Perkins/A.Casilla .50 1.25
CS M.Chico/L.Speigner .30 .75
DG A.De Aza/L.Gardner .50 1.25
DK D.Matsuzaka/K.Igawa 1.25 3.00
DM J.Danks/G.Molina .50 1.25
DT T.Tulowitzki/S.Drew 1.00 2.50
DV A.De Aza/R.Vanden Hurk .50 1.25
DW M.DeSalvo/C.Wright .75 2.00
DY S.Drew/C.Young .30 .75
GB A.Gordon/B.Butler 1.00 2.50
GF J.Flores/H.Gimenez .30 .75
GI A.Gordon/A.Iwamura 1.00 2.50
GL A.Gordon/A.LaRoche 1.00 2.50
GM A.Gordon/D.Matsuzaka 1.25 3.00
GP H.Pence/H.Gimenez 1.00 2.50
HB J.Hamilton/J.Burton 1.00 2.50
HD J.Hamilton/A.De Aza 1.00 2.50
HL T.Lincecum/P.Hughes .75 2.00
HP H.Pence/J.Hamilton 1.00 2.50
II A.Iwamura/K.Igawa .75 2.00
KC K.Kouzmanoff/K.Cameron .30 .75
LG L.Gardner/M.Lindstrom .30 .75
LV A.Lind/J.Vermilyea .30 .75
MG M.Montero/H.Gimenez .30 .75
MI D.Matsuzaka/A.Iwamura 1.25 3.00
MO D.Matsuzaka/H.Okajima 1.50 4.00
MR M.Rabelo/G.Molina .30 .75
MW B.Morrow/S.White 1.50 4.00
OL T.Lincecum/M.Owings 1.50 4.00
OM M.Owings/M.Montero .30 .75
PB T.Buck/D.Putnam .30 .75
PD H.Pence/A.De Aza 1.00 2.50
PH F.Pie/J.Hamilton 1.00 2.50
PP H.Pence/F.Pie 1.00 2.50
RS M.Rabelo/C.Stewart .30 .75
SM J.Salta/M.Montero .50 1.25
ST T.Tulo/J.Salta 1.00 2.50
SW C.Wright/J.Smith .75 2.00
TB T.Buck/B.Butler .50 1.25
WH P.Hughes/C.Wright .75 2.00
YD D.Young/E.Dukes .50 1.25
YM D.Matsuzaka/D.Young 1.25 3.00

2003 Upper Deck Game Face UD Promos

*PROMOS: 1.25X TO 3X BASIC CARDS

2003 Upper Deck Game Face

COMP.SET w/o SP's (90) 10.00 25.00
COMMON CARD (1-120) .20 .50
COMMON SP (1-120) .75 2.00
SP 1-120 STATED ODDS 1:4
COMMON CARD (121-150) .75 2.00
121-150 STATED ODDS 1:8
COMMON CARD (151-171) 1.00 2.50
151-171 STATED ODDS 1:16
COMMON CARD (172-192) .75 2.00
172-192 STATED ODDS 1:8
COMMON CARD (193-217) 1.50 4.00
193-217 RANDOM IN FINITE BONUS PACKS
193-217 PRINT RUN 299 SERIAL #'d SETS
CARD 75 DOES NOT EXIST
JETER AND CLEMENS ARE BOTH CARD 79
1 Darin Erstad .20 .50
2 Garret Anderson .20 .50
3 Tim Salmon .20 .50
4 Jarrod Washburn .20 .50
5 Troy Glaus SP .75 2.00
6 Luis Gonzalez .20 .50
7 Junior Spivey .20 .50
8 Randy Johnson SP 2.00 5.00
9 Curt Schilling SP 1.25 3.00
10 Andruw Jones .20 .50
11 Gary Sheffield .20 .50
12 Rafael Furcal .20 .50
13 Greg Maddux SP 2.50 6.00
14 Chipper Jones SP 2.00 5.00
15 Tony Batista .20 .50
16 Rodrigo Lopez .20 .50
17 Jay Gibbons .20 .50
18 Shea Hillenbrand .20 .50
19 Johnny Damon .30 .75
20 Derek Lowe .20 .50
21 Nomar Garciaparra .30 .75
22 Pedro Martinez SP 1.25 3.00
23 Manny Ramirez SP 2.00 5.00
24 Mark Prior .30 .75
25 Kerry Wood .20 .50
26 Corey Patterson .20 .50
27 Sammy Sosa SP 2.00 5.00
28 Magglio Ordonez .30 .75
29 Frank Thomas .50 1.25
30 Paul Konerko .30 .75
31 Adam Dunn .30 .75
32 Austin Kearns .20 .50
33 Aaron Boone .20 .50
34 Ken Griffey Jr. SP 4.00 10.00
35 Omar Vizquel .30 .75
36 C.C. Sabathia .30 .75
37 Karim Garcia SP .75 2.00
38 Larry Walker .30 .75
39 Preston Wilson .20 .50
40 Jay Payton .20 .50
41 Todd Helton SP 1.25 3.00
42 Carlos Pena .30 .75
43 Eric Munson .20 .50
44 Mike Lowell .20 .50
45 Josh Beckett .20 .50
46 A.J. Burnett .20 .50
47 Roy Oswalt .30 .75
48 Craig Biggio .30 .75
49 Jeff Bagwell SP 1.25 3.00
50 Lance Berkman SP 1.25 3.00
51 Mike Sweeney .20 .50
52 Carlos Beltran .30 .75
53 Hideo Nomo .50 1.25
54 Odalis Perez .20 .50
55 Adrian Beltre .50 1.25
56 Shawn Green SP .75 2.00
57 Kazuhisa Ishii SP .75 2.00
58 Ben Sheets .20 .50
59 Richie Sexson .20 .50
60 Torii Hunter .20 .50
61 Jacque Jones .20 .50
62 Eric Milton .20 .50
63 Corey Koskie .20 .50
64 A.J. Pierzynski .20 .50
65 Jose Vidro .20 .50
66 Bartolo Colon .20 .50
67 Vladimir Guerrero SP 1.25 3.00
68 Tom Glavine .30 .75
69 Mike Piazza SP 2.00 5.00
70 Roberto Alomar SP 1.25 3.00
71 Jorge Posada .30 .75
72 Mike Mussina .30 .75
73 Robin Ventura .20 .50
74 Raul Mondesi .20 .50
76 Jason Giambi SP .75 2.00
77 Bernie Williams SP 1.25 3.00
78 Alfonso Soriano SP 1.25 3.00
79a Derek Jeter SP 5.00 12.00
79b Roger Clemens SP 2.50 6.00
80 Miguel Tejada .30 .75
81 Eric Chavez .20 .50
82 Tim Hudson .30 .75
83 Barry Zito .30 .75
84 Mark Mulder .20 .50
85 Pat Burrell .20 .50
86 Jim Thome .30 .75
87 Bobby Abreu .20 .50
88 Brian Giles .20 .50
89 Jason Kendall .20 .50
90 Aramis Ramirez .20 .50
91 Ryan Klesko .20 .50
92 Phil Nevin .20 .50
93 Sean Burroughs .20 .50
94 J.T. Snow .20 .50
95 Rich Aurilia .20 .50
96 Benito Santiago .20 .50
97 Barry Bonds SP 3.00 8.00
98 Edgar Martinez .30 .75
99 John Olerud .20 .50
100 Bret Boone .20 .50
101 Ichiro Suzuki SP 2.50 6.00
102 J.D. Drew .20 .50
103 Jim Edmonds .30 .75
104 Scott Rolen .30 .75
105 Matt Morris .20 .50
106 Tino Martinez .20 .50
107 Albert Pujols SP 2.50 6.00
108 Aubrey Huff .20 .50
109 Carl Crawford .30 .75
110 Rafael Palmeiro .30 .75
111 Hank Blalock .20 .50
112 Alex Rodriguez SP 2.50 6.00
113 Kevin Mench SP .75 2.00
114 Juan Gonzalez SP .75 2.00
115 Shannon Stewart .20 .50
116 Vernon Wells .20 .50
117 Josh Phelps .20 .50
118 Eric Hinske .20 .50
119 Orlando Hudson .20 .50
120 Carlos Delgado SP .75 2.00
121 David Sanders FF RC .75 2.00
122 Rob Hammock FF RC .75 2.00
123 Rett Johnson FF RC .75 2.00
124 Mike Nicolas FF RC .75 2.00
125 Termel Sledge FF RC .75 2.00
126 Ryan Cameron FF RC .75 2.00
127 Prentice Redman FF RC .75 2.00
128 Clint Barmes FF RC 2.00 5.00
129 Brent Hoard FF RC .75 2.00
130 Willie Eyre FF RC .75 2.00
131 Phil Seibel FF RC .75 2.00
132 Chris Capuano FF RC .75 2.00
133 Bobby Madritsch FF RC .75 2.00
134 Shane Bazzell FF RC .75 2.00
135 Jeremy Griffiths FF RC .75 2.00
136 Jon Leicester FF RC .75 2.00
137 Brandon Webb FF RC 2.50 6.00
138 Todd Wellemeyer FF RC .75 2.00
139 Jose Contreras FF RC 2.00 5.00
140 Felix Sanchez FF RC .75 2.00
141 Arnie Munoz FF RC .75 2.00
142 Delvis Lantigua FF RC .75 2.00
143 Francisco Cruceta FF RC .75 2.00
144 Josh Willingham FF RC 2.50 6.00
145 Oscar Villarreal FF RC .75 2.00
146 Ian Ferguson FF RC .75 2.00
147 Pedro Liriano FF .75 2.00
148 Lew Ford FF RC .75 2.00
149 Jeff Duncan FF RC .75 2.00
150 Rich Fischer FF RC .75 2.00
151 Troy Glaus GF 1.00 2.50
152 Randy Johnson GF 2.50 6.00
153 Hideki Matsui GF RC 5.00 12.00
154 Chipper Jones GF 2.50 6.00
155 Nomar Garciaparra GF 1.50 4.00
156 Pedro Martinez GF 1.50 4.00
157 Ted Williams GF 5.00 12.00
158 Sammy Sosa GF 2.50 6.00
159 Ken Griffey Jr. GF 5.00 12.00
160 Vladimir Guerrero GF 1.50 4.00
161 Mike Piazza GF 2.50 6.00
162 Mickey Mantle GF 8.00 20.00
163 Alfonso Soriano GF 1.50 4.00
164 Derek Jeter GF 6.00 15.00
165 Roger Clemens GF 3.00 8.00
166 Jason Giambi GF 1.00 2.50
167 Barry Bonds GF 4.00 10.00
168 Ichiro Suzuki GF 3.00 8.00
169 Albert Pujols GF 3.00 8.00
170 Mark McGwire GF 4.00 10.00
171 Alex Rodriguez GF 3.00 8.00
172 R.Oswalt 4.00 10.00
K.Griffey Jr.
173 B.Zito 1.25 3.00
T.Glaus
174 T.Hudson 2.50 6.00
I.Suzuki
175 M.Mulder 2.50 6.00
A.Rodriguez
176 T.Glavine 1.25 3.00
V.Guerrero
177 G.Maddux 2.50 6.00
M.Piazza
178 M.McGwire 3.00 8.00
S.Sosa
179 M.Prior 1.25 3.00
L.Berkman
180 K.Wood 2.50 6.00
A.Pujols
181 R.Johnson 2.00 5.00
J.Bagwell
182 C.Schilling 5.00 12.00
D.Jeter
183 H.Nomo 3.00 8.00
B.Bonds
184 K.Ishii 1.25 3.00
T.Helton
185 F.Garcia .75 2.00
E.Chavez
186 A.Leiter 2.00 5.00
C.Jones
187 T.Williams 4.00 10.00
N.Garciaparra
188 P.Martinez 4.00 10.00
H.Matsui
189 D.Lowe 1.25 3.00
B.Williams
190 R.Clemens 2.50 6.00
M.Piazza
191 M.Mussina 2.00 5.00
M.Ramirez
192 M.Mantle 6.00 15.00
J.Giambi
193 Aaron Looper FF RC 1.50 4.00
194 Alex Prieto FF RC 1.50 4.00
195 Bo Hart FF RC 1.50 4.00
196 Chad Gaudin FF RC 1.50 4.00
197 Colin Porter FF RC 1.50 4.00
198 D.J. Carrasco FF RC 1.50 4.00
199 Dan Haren FF RC 8.00 20.00
200 Delmon Young FF RC 10.00 25.00
201 Dontrelle Willis FF 1.50 4.00
202 Jon Switzer FF 1.50 4.00
203 Edwin Jackson FF RC 2.50 6.00
204 Fernando Cabrera FF RC 1.50 4.00
205 Garrett Atkins FF 1.50 4.00
206 Jeremy Bonderman FF RC 6.00 15.00
207 Kevin Ohme FF RC 1.50 4.00
208 Khalil Greene FF 2.50 6.00
209 Luis Ayala FF RC 1.50 4.00
210 Matt Kata FF RC 1.50 4.00
211 Noah Lowry FF 1.50 4.00
212 Rich Harden FF 2.50 6.00
213 Rickie Weeks FF RC 5.00 12.00
214 Rosman Garcia FF RC 1.50 4.00
215 Ryan Wagner FF RC 1.50 4.00
216 Tom Gregorio FF RC 1.50 4.00
217 Wilfredo Ledezma FF RC 1.50 4.00
NNO Ken Griffey Jr. Sample 2.00 5.00

2003 Upper Deck Game Face Autographs

STATED ODDS 1:576
GOLD RANDOM INSERTS IN PACKS
GOLD PRINT RUN 25 SERIAL #'d SETS
NO GOLD PRICING DUE TO SCARCITY
EXCHANGE DEADLINE 05/12/06
AJ Andruw Jones SP 30.00 60.00
BZ Barry Zito 6.00 15.00
HM H.Matsui Engl SP/55 125.00 300.00
IS Ichiro Suzuki SP 300.00 600.00
JG Jason Giambi 20.00 50.00
KG Ken Griffey Jr. 40.00 100.00
LB Lance Berkman SP 40.00 80.00
MM Mark McGwire SP 200.00 400.00
MP Mark Prior SP 30.00 60.00
SS Sammy Sosa 30.00 60.00
TH Todd Helton SP 30.00 60.00

2003 Upper Deck Game Face Gear

STATED ODDS 1:8
SP INFO PROVIDED BY UPPER DECK
AB Aaron Boone SP 6.00 15.00
AD Adam Dunn 4.00 10.00
AJ Andruw Jones 6.00 15.00
AK Austin Kearns 4.00 10.00
AR Alex Rodriguez Home 10.00 25.00
AR2 Alex Rodriguez Away 10.00 25.00
AS Alfonso Soriano 4.00 10.00
BA Bobby Abreu 4.00 10.00
BG Brian Giles 4.00 10.00
BW Bernie Williams 6.00 15.00
BZ Barry Zito Home 4.00 10.00
BZ2 Barry Zito Away 4.00 10.00
CB Carlos Beltran 4.00 10.00
CD Carlos Delgado 4.00 10.00
CJ Chipper Jones 6.00 15.00
CS Curt Schilling 4.00 10.00
DE Darin Erstad Home 4.00 10.00
DE2 Darin Erstad Away 4.00 10.00
DR J.D. Drew Home 4.00 10.00
DR2 J.D. Drew Away 4.00 10.00
EA Edgardo Alfonzo 4.00 10.00
EC Eric Chavez 4.00 10.00
EM Edgar Martinez 6.00 15.00
FT Frank Thomas 6.00 15.00
GM Greg Maddux Home 6.00 15.00
GM2 Greg Maddux Away 6.00 15.00
HN Hideo Nomo 10.00 25.00
HU Torii Hunter 4.00 10.00
IR Ivan Rodriguez 6.00 15.00
IS Ichiro Suzuki SP 40.00 80.00
JB Jeff Bagwell 6.00 15.00
JE Jim Edmonds 4.00 10.00
JG Jason Giambi 4.00 10.00
JG Juan Gonzalez 4.00 10.00
JJO J.Jones UER Guzman Image 4.00 10.00
JK Jason Kendall 4.00 10.00
JK Jeff Kent 4.00 10.00
JP Jorge Posada 6.00 15.00
JT Jim Thome 6.00 15.00
JV Jose Vidro 4.00 10.00
KG Ken Griffey Jr. SP 12.50 30.00
KI Kazuhisa Ishii 4.00 10.00
KW Kerry Wood 4.00 10.00
LB Lance Berkman 4.00 10.00
LG Luis Gonzalez Home 4.00 10.00
LG2 Luis Gonzalez Away 4.00 10.00
LW Larry Walker 4.00 10.00
ML Mike Lowell 4.00 10.00
MM Mike Mussina 6.00 15.00
MO Maggio Ordonez 4.00 10.00
MPI Mike Piazza 8.00 20.00
MPR Mark Prior 6.00 15.00
MR Manny Ramirez 6.00 15.00
MS Mike Sweeney 4.00 10.00
MT Miguel Tejada 4.00 10.00
OV Omar Vizquel 6.00 15.00
PB Pat Burrell 4.00 10.00
PM Pedro Martinez 6.00 15.00
PW Preston Wilson 4.00 10.00
RC Roger Clemens 8.00 20.00
RJ Randy Johnson 6.00 15.00
RK Ryan Klesko 4.00 10.00
RO Roy Oswalt 4.00 10.00
RP Rafael Palmeiro 6.00 15.00
RS Richie Sexson 4.00 10.00
SG Shawn Green 4.00 10.00
SR Scott Rolen 6.00 15.00
SS Sammy Sosa 6.00 15.00
TG Tom Glavine 6.00 15.00
TH Todd Helton SP 6.00 15.00
TI Tim Hudson 4.00 10.00

2003 Upper Deck Game Face Patch

RANDOM INSERTS IN PACKS
STATED PRINT RUN 100 SERIAL #'d SETS
AB Aaron Boone 10.00 25.00
AD Adam Dunn 10.00 25.00
AJ Andruw Jones 15.00 40.00
AK Austin Kearns 10.00 25.00
AR Alex Rodriguez Home 25.00 60.00
AR2 Alex Rodriguez Away 25.00 60.00
AS Alfonso Soriano 10.00 25.00
BA Bobby Abreu 10.00 25.00
BW Bernie Williams 15.00 40.00
BZ Barry Zito Home 10.00 25.00
BZ2 Barry Zito Away 10.00 25.00
CB Carlos Beltran 15.00 40.00
CD Carlos Delgado 10.00 25.00
CJ Chipper Jones 20.00 50.00
CS Curt Schilling 10.00 25.00
DE Darin Erstad Home 10.00 25.00
DE2 Darin Erstad Away 10.00 25.00
DR J.D. Drew Home 10.00 25.00
DR2 J.D. Drew Away 10.00 25.00
EA Edgardo Alfonzo 10.00 25.00
EC Eric Chavez 10.00 25.00
EM Edgar Martinez 15.00 40.00
FT Frank Thomas 20.00 50.00
GM Greg Maddux Home 40.00 100.00
GM2 Greg Maddux Away 40.00 100.00
HN Hideo Nomo 100.00 200.00
HU Torii Hunter 10.00 25.00
IR Ivan Rodriguez 15.00 40.00
IS Ichiro Suzuki 40.00 80.00
JB Jeff Bagwell 12.00 30.00
JE Jim Edmonds 10.00 25.00
JG Jason Giambi 10.00 25.00
JG Juan Gonzalez 15.00 40.00
JJ Jacque Jones 10.00 25.00
JK Jason Kendall 10.00 25.00
JK Jeff Kent 10.00 25.00
JP Jorge Posada 20.00 50.00
JT Jim Thome 15.00 40.00
JV Jose Vidro 10.00 25.00
KG Ken Griffey Jr. 30.00 80.00
KI Kazuhisa Ishii 10.00 25.00
KW Kerry Wood 10.00 25.00
LB Lance Berkman 10.00 25.00
LG Luis Gonzalez Home 10.00 25.00
LG2 Luis Gonzalez Away 10.00 25.00
LW Larry Walker 10.00 25.00

ML Mike Lowell 10.00 25.00
MMO Mike Mussina SP/81 15.00 40.00
MO Magglio Ordonez 10.00 25.00
MP Mike Piazza 40.00 100.00
MP Mark Prior 15.00 40.00
MR Manny Ramirez 15.00 40.00
MS Mike Sweeney 10.00 25.00
MT Miguel Tejada 10.00 25.00
OV Omar Vizquel 15.00 40.00
PB Pat Burrell 10.00 25.00
PM Pedro Martinez 15.00 40.00
PW Preston Wilson 10.00 25.00
RC Roger Clemens 40.00 100.00
RJ Randy Johnson 20.00 50.00
RK Ryan Klesko 10.00 25.00
RO Roy Oswalt 10.00 25.00
RP Rafael Palmeiro 15.00 40.00
RS Richie Sexson 10.00 25.00
SG Shawn Green 10.00 25.00
SR Scott Rolen 10.00 25.00
SS Sammy Sosa 20.00 50.00
TG Tom Glavine 15.00 40.00
TH Todd Helton 15.00 40.00
TI Tim Hudson 10.00 25.00

2001 Upper Deck Gold Glove

COMP.SET w/o SP'S (90) 6.00 15.00
COMMON CARD (1-90) .25 .60
COMMON CARD (91-129) 1.00 2.50
91-129 RANDOM INSERTS IN PACKS
91-129 PRINT RUN 1000 SERIAL #'d SETS
COMMON CARD (130-135) 2.00 5.00
130-135 RANDOM INSERTS IN PACKS
130-135 PRINT RUN 500 SERIAL #'d SETS
1 Troy Glaus .25 .60
2 Darin Erstad .25 .60
3 Jason Giambi .25 .60
4 Tim Hudson .25 .60
5 Jermaine Dye .25 .60
6 Raul Mondesi .25 .60
7 Carlos Delgado .25 .60
8 Shannon Stewart .25 .60
9 Greg Vaughn .25 .60
10 Aubrey Huff .25 .60
11 Juan Gonzalez .25 .60
12 Roberto Alomar .40 1.00
13 Omar Vizquel .40 1.00
14 Jim Thome .40 1.00
15 John Olerud .25 .60
16 Edgar Martinez .40 1.00
17 Kazuhiro Sasaki .25 .60
18 Aaron Sele .25 .60
19 Cal Ripken 2.00 5.00
20 Chris Richard .25 .60
21 Ivan Rodriguez .40 1.00
22 Rafael Palmeiro .40 1.00
23 Alex Rodriguez .75 2.00
24 Pedro Martinez .40 1.00
25 Nomar Garciaparra 1.00 2.50
26 Manny Ramirez Sox .40 1.00
27 Neifi Perez .25 .60
28 Mike Sweeney .25 .60
29 Bobby Higginson .25 .60
30 Dean Palmer .25 .60
31 Tony Clark .25 .60
32 Doug Mientkiewicz .25 .60
33 Brad Radke .25 .60
34 Joe Mays .25 .60
35 Frank Thomas .60 1.50
36 Magglio Ordonez .25 .60
37 Carlos Lee .25 .60
38 Bernie Williams .40 1.00
39 Mike Mussina .40 1.00
40 Derek Jeter 1.50 4.00
41 Roger Clemens 1.25 3.00
42 Craig Biggio .40 1.00
43 Jeff Bagwell .40 1.00
44 Lance Berkman .25 .60
45 Andruw Jones .40 1.00
46 Greg Maddux 1.00 2.50
47 Chipper Jones .60 1.50
48 Geoff Jenkins .25 .60
49 Ben Sheets .40 1.00
50 Jeromy Burnitz .25 .60
51 Jim Edmonds .25 .60
52 Mark McGwire 1.50 4.00
53 Mike Matheny .25 .60
54 J.D. Drew .25 .60
55 Sammy Sosa .60 1.50
56 Kerry Wood .25 .60
57 Fred McGriff .40 1.00
58 Randy Johnson .60 1.50
59 Steve Finley .25 .60
60 Mark Grace .40 1.00
61 Matt Williams .25 .60
62 Luis Gonzalez .25 .60
63 Shawn Green .25 .60
64 Kevin Brown .25 .60
65 Gary Sheffield .25 .60
66 Vladimir Guerrero .60 1.50
67 Tony Armas Jr. .25 .60
68 Barry Bonds 1.50 4.00
69 J.T. Snow .25 .60
70 Jeff Kent .25 .60
71 Charles Johnson .25 .60
72 Preston Wilson .25 .60
73 Cliff Floyd .25 .60
74 Robin Ventura .25 .60
75 Mike Piazza 1.00 2.50
76 Edgardo Alfonzo .25 .60
77 Tony Gwynn .75 2.00
78 Ryan Klesko .25 .60
79 Scott Rolen .40 1.00
80 Mike Lieberthal .25 .60
81 Pat Burrell .25 .60
82 Jason Kendall .25 .60
83 Brian Giles .25 .60
84 Ken Griffey Jr. 1.25 3.00
85 Barry Larkin .40 1.00
86 Pokey Reese .25 .60
87 Larry Walker .25 .60
88 Mike Hampton .25 .60
89 Juan Pierre .25 .60
90 Todd Helton .40 1.00
91 Mike Penney GD RC 1.00 2.50
92 Wilkin Ruan GD RC 1.00 2.50
93 Greg Miller GD RC 1.00 2.50
94 Johnny Estrada GD RC 1.50 4.00
95 Tsuyoshi Shinjo GD RC 1.50 4.00
96 Josh Towers GD RC 1.50 4.00
97 Horacio Ramirez GD RC 1.50 4.00
98 Ryan Freel GD RC 1.50 4.00
99 Morgan Ensberg GD RC 1.50 4.00
100 Adrian Hernandez GD RC 1.00 2.50
101 Juan Uribe GD RC 1.50 4.00
102 Jose Mieses GD RC 1.00 2.50
103 Jack Wilson GD RC 1.50 4.00
104 Cesar Crespo GD RC 1.00 2.50
105 Bud Smith GD RC 1.00 2.50
106 Erick Almonte GD RC 1.00 2.50
107 Elpidio Guzman GD RC 1.00 2.50
108 Brandon Duckworth GD RC 1.00 2.50
109 Juan Diaz GD RC 1.00 2.50
110 Kris Keller GD RC 1.00 2.50
111 Jason Michaels GD RC 1.00 2.50
112 Bret Prinz GD RC 1.00 2.50
113 Henry Mateo GD RC 1.00 2.50
114 Ricardo Rodriguez GD RC 1.00 2.50
115 Travis Hafner GD RC 2.50 6.00
116 Nate Teut GD RC 1.00 2.50
117 Alexis Gomez GD RC 1.00 2.50
118 Billy Sylvester GD RC 1.00 2.50
119 Adam Pettyjohn GD RC 1.00 2.50
120 Josh Fogg GD RC 1.00 2.50
121 Juan Cruz GD RC 1.00 2.50
122 Carlos Valderrama GD RC 1.00 2.50
123 Jay Gibbons GD RC 1.50 4.00
124 Donaldo Mendez GD RC 1.00 2.50
125 Bill Ortega GD RC 1.00 2.50
126 Sean Douglass GD RC 1.00 2.50
127 Christian Parker GD RC 1.00 2.50
128 Grant Balfour GD RC 1.00 2.50
129 Joe Kennedy GD RC 1.50 4.00
130 Albert Pujols GD RC 30.00 80.00
131 Wilson Betemit GD RC 3.00 8.00
132 Mark Teixeira GD RC 3.00 0.00
133 Mark Prior GD RC 5.00 12.00
134 Dewon Brazelton GD RC 2.00 5.00
135 Ichiro Suzuki GD RC 25.00 60.00

2001 Upper Deck Gold Glove Finite

*STARS 1-90: 8X TO 20X BASIC CARDS

2001 Upper Deck Gold Glove Limited

*STARS 1-90: 2.5X TO 6X BASIC CARDS
*DEBUT 91-129: .6X TO 1.5X BASIC
*DEBUT 130-135: .6X TO 1.5X BASIC
STATED PRINT RUN 100 SERIAL #'d SETS
130 Albert Pujols GD 125.00 300.00
135 Ichiro Suzuki GD 50.00 120.00

2001 Upper Deck Gold Glove Game Jersey

STATED ODDS 1:20
SP PRINT RUNS PROVIDED BY UPPER DECK
SP'S ARE NOT SERIAL NUMBERED
GOLD RANDOM INSERTS IN PACKS
GOLD PRINT RUN 25 SERIAL #'d SETS
GOLD NO PRICING DUE TO SCARCITY
GGAJ Andruw Jones 2.50 6.00
GGBB Barry Bonds 6.00 15.00
GGBR B.Richardson SP/274 * 10.00 25.00
GGBW Bernie Williams 2.50 6.00
GGCC Cesar Cedeno 1.50 4.00
GGCF Carlton Fisk 2.50 6.00
GGCR Cal Ripken 12.00 30.00
GGDE Darin Erstad 1.50 4.00
GGDM Don Mattingly 8.00 20.00
GGGC Gary Carter 2.50 6.00
GGGM Greg Maddux 6.00 15.00
GGIR Ivan Rodriguez 2.50 6.00
GGIS Ichiro Suzuki 20.00 50.00
GGJB Jeff Bagwell 2.50 6.00
GGJK Jim Kaat 1.50 4.00
GGKG Ken Griffey Jr. 8.00 20.00
GGLA Luis Aparicio 2.50 6.00
GGMG Mark Grace 2.50 6.00
GGMMA M.Mantle SP/264 * 40.00 80.00
GGMMU Mike Mussina 2.50 6.00
GGOS Ozzie Smith 5.00 12.00
GGOV Omar Vizquel 2.50 6.00
GGRG Ron Guidry 1.50 4.00
GGRM Roger Maris SP/265 12.50 30.00
GGRP Rafael Palmeiro 2.50 6.00
GGSG Shawn Green 1.50 4.00
GGTM T.Munson SP/204 * 40.00 80.00

2001 Upper Deck Gold Glove Leather Bound

STATED ODDS 1:60
STATED PRINT RUN 100 SETS
CARDS ARE NOT SERIAL-NUMBERED
GOLD RANDOM INSERTS IN PACKS
GOLD PRINT RUN 25 SERIAL #'d SETS
NO GOLD PRICING DUE TO SCARCITY
LBAG Alex Gonzalez 6.00 15.00
LBAR Alex Rodriguez 10.00 25.00
LBAS Aaron Sele 6.00 15.00
LBBB Barry Bonds 40.00 80.00
LBBG Ben Grieve 6.00 15.00
LBCB Craig Biggio 10.00 25.00
LBCF Cliff Floyd 6.00 15.00
LBCJ Chipper Jones 10.00 25.00
LBCL Carlos Lee 6.00 15.00
LBCP Chan Ho Park 10.00 25.00
LBDE Dock Ellis 6.00 15.00
LBDW Dave Winfield 6.00 15.00
LBEM Edgar Martinez 10.00 25.00
LBGC Gary Carter 6.00 15.00
LBGL Greg Luzinski 6.00 15.00
LBGS Gary Sheffield 6.00 15.00
LBHI Hideki Irabu 6.00 15.00
LBHK Harvey Kuenn 10.00 25.00
LBI Ichiro Suzuki 200.00 500.00
LBIR Ivan Rodriguez 10.00 25.00
LBJD Johnny Damon 10.00 25.00
LBJE Jim Edmonds 6.00 15.00
LBJL Javy Lopez 6.00 15.00
LBJO John Olerud 6.00 15.00
LBJBL Johnny Blanchard 20.00 50.00
LBJKA Jim Kaat 10.00 25.00
LBJKE Jason Kendall 6.00 15.00
LBKC Ken Caminiti 6.00 15.00
LBKG Ken Griffey Jr. 15.00 40.00
LBKL Kenny Lofton 10.00 25.00
LBLD Leon Day 75.00 150.00
LBLG Lefty Grove 150.00 250.00
LBMG Marquis Grissom 6.00 15.00
LBMP Mike Piazza 15.00 40.00
LBMR Manny Ramirez Sox 10.00 25.00
LBNF Nellie Fox 40.00 80.00
LBOD Octavio Dotel 6.00 15.00
LBOH Orlando Hernandez 6.00 15.00
LBOS Ozzie Smith 20.00 50.00
LBOV Omar Vizquel 10.00 25.00
LBPM Pedro Martinez 10.00 25.00
LBPO Paul O'Neill 10.00 25.00
LBRF Rafael Furcal 6.00 15.00
LBRJ Reggie Jackson 15.00 40.00
LBRK Ryan Klesko 6.00 15.00
LBRP Rafael Palmeiro 10.00 25.00
LBRCA Roy Campanella 125.00 200.00
LBSS Sammy Sosa 10.00 25.00
LBTS Tim Salmon 10.00 25.00
LBTHE Todd Helton 10.00 25.00
LBTHO Todd Hollandsworth 6.00 15.00

2001 Upper Deck Gold Glove Leather Bound Autograph

STATED ODDS 1:240
SP PRINT RUNS B/WN 29-68 COPIES PER
SP'S ARE NOT SERIAL-NUMBERED
SP PRINT RUNS PROVIDED BY UPPER DECK
SP'S NOT PRICED DUE TO SCARCITY
SLBCF Cliff Floyd 6.00 15.00
SLBDW Dave Winfield 15.00 40.00
SLBEM Edgar Martinez 50.00 100.00
SLBFR Frank Robinson 20.00 50.00
SLBFT Frank Thomas 50.00 100.00
SLBGL Greg Luzinski 20.00 50.00
SLBIR Ivan Rodriguez 50.00 100.00
SLBJD Johnny Damon 30.00 60.00
SLBJK Jim Kaat 20.00 50.00
SLBJK Jason Kendall 20.00 50.00
SLBJL Javy Lopez 20.00 50.00
SLBJO John Olerud 20.00 50.00
SLBKG Ken Griffey Jr. SP/49 100.00 250.00
SLBKL Kenny Lofton 40.00 80.00
SLBOS Ozzie Smith 75.00 150.00
SLBPO Paul O'Neill 40.00 80.00
SLBRF Rafael Furcal 6.00 15.00
SLBRJ Reggie Jackson SP/68 100.00 175.00
SLBRK Ryan Klesko 6.00 15.00

2001 Upper Deck Gold Glove Official Issue Game Ball

STATED ODDS 1:20
SP PRINT RUNS PROVIDED BY UPPER DECK
SP'S ARE NOT SERIAL-NUMBERED
NO PRICING ON QTY OF 25 OR LESS
OIAG R.Alomar J.Gonzalez 4.00 10.00
OIBA P.Burrell B.Abreu 4.00 10.00
OIBB J.Bagwell L.Berkman 6.00 15.00
OIBH L.Berkman R.Hidalgo 4.00 10.00
OIBK B.Bonds J.Kent 12.50 30.00
OIBS J.Burnitz R.Sexson 4.00 10.00
OIDM C.Delgado R.Mondesi 4.00 10.00
OIDP J.Drew A.Pujols 20.00 50.00
OIEA D.Erstad G.Anderson 4.00 10.00
OIFJ C.Floyd C.Johnson 4.00 10.00
OIGB S.Green A.Beltre 4.00 10.00
OIGC K.Griffey Jr. S.Casey 8.00 20.00
OIGE T.Glaus D.Erstad 4.00 10.00
OIGG L.Gonzalez M.Grace 6.00 15.00
OIGJ C.Guzman J.Jones SP/194 6.00 15.00
OIGK T.Gwynn R.Klesko 8.00 20.00
OIGR B.Giles A.Ramirez 4.00 10.00
OIGT J.Giambi M.Tejada 4.00 10.00
OIGV V.Guerrero J.Vidro 6.00 15.00
OIHC Higginson T.Clark SP/160 6.00 15.00
OIHH M.Hampton T.Helton 6.00 15.00
OIHW T.Helton L.Walker 6.00 15.00
OIIO I.Suzuki J.Olerud 12.00 30.00
OIJB G.Jenkins J.Burnitz 4.00 10.00
OIJF A.Jones R.Furcal 6.00 15.00
OIJG R.Johnson L.Gonzalez 6.00 15.00
OIJJ C.Jones A.Jones 6.00 15.00
OIKA J.Kent R.Aurilia 4.00 10.00
OIKG J.Kendall B.Giles 4.00 10.00
OILG B.Larkin K.Griffey Jr. 8.00 20.00
OIMG Mientk Guzman SP/194 6.00 15.00
OIMJ G.Maddux C.Jones 8.00 20.00
OIMO Edgar Olerud SP/160 10.00 25.00
OIMP M.McGwire A.Pujols 50.00 120.00
OINK P.Nevin R.Klesko 4.00 10.00
OIPE A.Pujols J.Edmonds 30.00 80.00
OIPR R.Palmeiro A.Rodriguez 10.00 25.00
OIPS M.Piazza T.Shinjo 6.00 15.00
OIRB C.Ripken T.Batista 15.00 40.00
OIRE M.Ramirez Sox C.Everett 6.00 15.00
OIRP I.Rodriguez R.Palmeiro 6.00 15.00
OIRR A.Rodriguez I.Rodriguez 10.00 25.00
OIRBU S.Rolen P.Burrell 6.00 15.00
OISB M.Sweeney C.Beltran 4.00 10.00
OISG G.Sheffield S.Green 4.00 10.00
OISV T.Shinjo R.Ventura 6.00 15.00
OISW S.Sosa R.White 6.00 15.00
OITC M.Tejada E.Chavez 4.00 10.00
OITO Thomas Magglio SP/160 10.00 25.00
OIVM G.Vaughn McGriff SP/170 10.00 25.00
OIVP R.Ventura M.Piazza 8.00 20.00
OIWF P.Wilson C.Floyd 4.00 10.00
OIWP L.Walker J.Pierre 4.00 10.00
OIWS K.Wood S.Sosa 6.00 15.00

2001 Upper Deck Gold Glove Slugger's Choice

STATED ODDS 1:20
SP PRINT RUNS PROVIDED BY UPPER DECK
SP'S ARE NOT SERIAL-NUMBERED
GOLD RANDOM INSERTS IN PACKS
GOLD PRINT RUN 25 SERIAL #'d SETS
NO GOLD PRICING DUE TO SCARCITY
SCAG Andres Galarraga 4.00 10.00
SCARM Alex Rodriguez M's 12.50 30.00
SCARR Alex Rodriguez Rangers 12.50 30.00
SCBA Bobby Abreu 4.00 10.00
SCBA Brady Anderson 4.00 10.00
SCBB Barry Bonds 10.00 25.00
SCCJ Chipper Jones 6.00 15.00
SCEM Edgar Martinez 6.00 15.00
SCFT Fernando Tatis SP/147 * 4.00 10.00
SCGS Gary Sheffield SP/201 * 4.00 10.00
SCHR Henry Rodriguez SP/185 * 4.00 10.00
SCIR Ivan Rodriguez 6.00 15.00
SCJC Jose Cruz Jr. SP/191 * 4.00 10.00
SCJG Juan Gonzalez 4.00 10.00
SCJI Jason Isringhausen 4.00 10.00
SCKGM Ken Griffey Jr. M's 6.00 15.00
SCKGR Ken Griffey Jr. Reds 6.00 15.00
SCMC Marty Cordova 4.00 10.00
SCMR Manny Ramirez Sox 6.00 15.00
SCMT Miguel Tejada 4.00 10.00
SCNP Neifi Perez 4.00 10.00
SCPO Paul O'Neill 6.00 15.00
SCRF Rafael Furcal 4.00 10.00
SCRP Rafael Palmeiro 6.00 15.00
SCSS Sammy Sosa 6.00 15.00
SCTB Tony Batista 4.00 10.00

2000 Upper Deck Gold Reserve

COMPLETE SET (300) 175.00 350.00
COMP.SET w/o SP's (270) 20.00 50.00
COMMON (1-267/298-300) .12 .30
COMMON CARD (268-297) 1.00 2.50
268-297 RANDOM INSERTS IN PACKS
268-297 PRINT RUN 2500 SERIAL #'d SETS
CARD 27 DOES NOT EXIST
R.HERNANDEZ & O'LEARY NUMBERED 73
1 Mo Vaughn .12 .30
2 Darin Erstad .12 .30
3 Garret Anderson .12 .30
4 Troy Glaus .12 .30
5 Troy Percival .12 .30
6 Kent Bottenfield .12 .30
7 Orlando Palmeiro .12 .30
8 Tim Salmon .12 .30
9 Jason Giambi .12 .30
10 Eric Chavez .12 .30
11 Matt Stairs .12 .30
12 Miguel Tejada .20 .50
13 Tim Hudson .20 .50
14 John Jaha .12 .30
15 Ben Grieve .12 .30
16 Kevin Appier .12 .30
17 David Wells .12 .30
18 Jose Cruz Jr. .12 .30
19 Homer Bush .12 .30
20 Shannon Stewart .12 .30
21 Carlos Delgado .12 .30
22 Roy Halladay .20 .50
23 Tony Batista .12 .30
24 Raul Mondesi .12 .30
25 Fred McGriff .20 .50
26 Jose Canseco .20 .50
27 Roberto Hernandez UER 73 .12 .30
28 Vinny Castilla .12 .30
29 Gerald Williams .12 .30
30 Ryan Rupe .12 .30
31 Greg Vaughn .12 .30
32 Miguel Cairo .12 .30
33 Roberto Alomar .20 .50
34 Jim Thome .20 .50
35 Bartolo Colon .12 .30
36 Omar Vizquel .20 .50
37 Manny Ramirez .30 .75
38 Chuck Finley .12 .30
39 Travis Fryman .12 .30
40 Kenny Lofton .12 .30
41 Richie Sexson .12 .30
42 Charles Nagy .12 .30
43 John Halama .12 .30
44 David Bell .12 .30
45 Jay Buhner .12 .30
46 Edgar Martinez .20 .50
47 Alex Rodriguez .40 1.00
48 Freddy Garcia .12 .30
49 Aaron Sele .12 .30
50 Jamie Moyer .12 .30
51 Mike Cameron .12 .30
52 Albert Belle .12 .30
53 Jerry Hairston Jr. .12 .30
54 Sidney Ponson .12 .30
55 Cal Ripken 1.00 2.50
56 Mike Mussina .20 .50
57 B.J. Surhoff .12 .30
58 Brady Anderson .12 .30
59 Mike Bordick .12 .30
60 Ivan Rodriguez .20 .50
61 Rusty Greer .12 .30
62 Rafael Palmeiro .20 .50
63 John Wetteland .12 .30
64 Ruben Mateo .12 .30
65 Gabe Kapler .12 .30
66 David Segui .12 .30
67 Justin Thompson .12 .30
68 Rick Helling .12 .30
69 Jose Offerman .12 .30
70 Trot Nixon .12 .30
71 Pedro Martinez .20 .50
72 Jason Varitek .30 .75
73 Troy O'Leary .12 .30
74 Nomar Garciaparra .20 .50
75 Carl Everett .12 .30
76 Wilton Veras .12 .30
77 Tim Wakefield .20 .50
78 Ramon Martinez .12 .30
79 Johnny Damon .20 .50
80 Mike Sweeney .12 .30
81 Rey Sanchez .12 .30
82 Carlos Beltran .20 .50
83 Carlos Febles .12 .30
84 Jermaine Dye .12 .30
85 Joe Randa .12 .30
86 Jose Rosado .12 .30
87 Jeff Suppan .12 .30
88 Juan Encarnacion .12 .30
89 Damion Easley .12 .30
90 Brad Ausmus .12 .30
91 Todd Jones .12 .30
92 Juan Gonzalez .12 .30
93 Bobby Higginson .12 .30
94 Tony Clark .12 .30
95 Brian Moehler .12 .30
96 Dean Palmer .12 .30
97 Joe Mays .12 .30
98 Eric Milton .12 .30
99 Corey Koskie .12 .30
100 Ron Coomer .12 .30
101 Brad Radke .12 .30
102 Todd Walker .12 .30
103 Butch Huskey .12 .30
104 Jacque Jones .12 .30
105 Frank Thomas .30 .75
106 Mike Sirotka .12 .30
107 Carlos Lee .12 .30
108 Ray Durham .12 .30
109 Bob Howry .12 .30
110 Magglio Ordonez .20 .50
111 Paul Konerko .12 .30
112 Chris Singleton .12 .30
113 James Baldwin .12 .30
114 Derek Jeter .75 2.00
115 Tino Martinez .12 .30
116 Orlando Hernandez .12 .30
117 Chuck Knoblauch .12 .30
118 Bernie Williams .20 .50
119 David Cone .12 .30
120 Paul O'Neill .20 .50
121 Roger Clemens .40 1.00
122 Mariano Rivera .40 1.00
123 Ricky Ledee .12 .30
124 Richard Hidalgo .12 .30
125 Jeff Bagwell .20 .50
126 Jose Lima .12 .30
127 Billy Wagner .12 .30
128 Shane Reynolds .12 .30
129 Moises Alou .12 .30
130 Craig Biggio .20 .50
131 Roger Cedeno .12 .30
132 Octavio Dotel .12 .30
133 Greg Maddux .40 1.00
134 Brian Jordan .12 .30
135 Kevin Millwood .12 .30
136 Javy Lopez .12 .30
137 Bruce Chen .12 .30
138 Chipper Jones .30 .75
139 Tom Glavine .20 .50
140 Andruw Jones .12 .30
141 Andres Galarraga .20 .50
142 Reggie Sanders .12 .30
143 Geoff Jenkins .12 .30
144 Jeromy Burnitz .12 .30
145 Ron Belliard .12 .30
146 Mark Loretta .12 .30
147 Steve Woodard .12 .30
148 Marquis Grissom .12 .30
149 Bob Wickman .12 .30
150 Mark McGwire .50 1.25
151 Fernando Tatis .12 .30
152 Edgar Renteria .12 .30
153 J.D. Drew .12 .30
154 Ray Lankford .12 .30
155 Fernando Vina .12 .30
156 Pat Hentgen .12 .30
157 Jim Edmonds .12 .30
158 Mark Grace .20 .50
159 Kerry Wood .12 .30
160 Eric Young .12 .30
161 Ismael Valdes .12 .30
162 Sammy Sosa .30 .75
163 Henry Rodriguez .12 .30
164 Kyle Farnsworth .12 .30
165 Glenallen Hill .12 .30
166 Jon Lieber .12 .30
167 Luis Gonzalez .12 .30
168 Tony Womack .12 .30
169 Omar Daal .12 .30
170 Randy Johnson .30 .75
171 Erubiel Durazo .12 .30
172 Jay Bell .12 .30
173 Steve Finley .12 .30
174 Travis Lee .12 .30
175 Matt Williams .12 .30
176 Matt Mantei .12 .30
177 Adrian Beltre .30 .75
178 Kevin Brown .12 .30
179 Chan Ho Park .20 .50
180 Mark Grudzielanek .12 .30
181 Jeff Shaw .12 .30
182 Shawn Green .12 .30
183 Gary Sheffield .12 .30
184 Todd Hundley .12 .30
185 Eric Karros .12 .30
186 Kevin Elster .12 .30
187 Vladimir Guerrero .20 .50
188 Michael Barrett .12 .30
189 Chris Widger .12 .30
190 Ugueth Urbina .12 .30
191 Dustin Hermanson .12 .30
192 Rondell White .12 .30
193 Jose Vidro .12 .30
194 Hideki Irabu .12 .30
195 Lee Stevens .12 .30
196 Livan Hernandez .12 .30
197 Ellis Burks .12 .30
198 J.T. Snow .12 .30
199 Jeff Kent .12 .30
200 Robb Nen .12 .30
201 Marvin Benard .12 .30
202 Barry Bonds .50 1.25
203 Russ Ortiz .12 .30
204 Rich Aurilia .12 .30
205 Joe Nathan .12 .30
206 Preston Wilson .12 .30
207 Cliff Floyd .12 .30
208 Mike Lowell .12 .30
209 Ryan Dempster .12 .30
210 Luis Castillo .12 .30
211 Alex Fernandez .12 .30
212 Mark Kotsay .12 .30
213 Brant Brown .12 .30
214 Edgardo Alfonzo .12 .30
215 Robin Ventura .12 .30
216 Rickey Henderson .30 .75
217 Mike Hampton .12 .30
218 Mike Piazza .30 .75
219 Al Leiter .12 .30
220 Derek Bell .12 .30
221 Armando Benitez .12 .30
222 Rey Ordonez .12 .30
223 Todd Zeile .12 .30
224 Tony Gwynn .30 .75
225 Eric Owens .12 .30
226 Damian Jackson .12 .30
227 Trevor Hoffman .20 .50
228 Ben Davis .12 .30
229 Sterling Hitchcock .12 .30
230 Ruben Rivera .12 .30
231 Ryan Klesko .12 .30
232 Phil Nevin .12 .30
233 Mike Lieberthal .12 .30
234 Bob Abreu .12 .30
235 Doug Glanville .12 .30
236 Rico Brogna .12 .30
237 Scott Rolen .20 .50
238 Andy Ashby .12 .30
239 Robert Person .12 .30
240 Curt Schilling .20 .50
241 Mike Jackson .12 .30
242 Warren Morris .12 .30
243 Kris Benson .12 .30
244 Kevin Young .12 .30
245 Brian Giles .12 .30
246 Jason Schmidt .12 .30
247 Jason Kendall .12 .30
248 Todd Ritchie .12 .30
249 Wil Cordero .12 .30
250 Aramis Ramirez .12 .30
251 Sean Casey .12 .30
252 Barry Larkin .20 .50
253 Pokey Reese .12 .30
254 Scott Williamson .12 .30
255 Aaron Boone .12 .30
256 Dante Bichette .12 .30
257 Ken Griffey Jr. .60 1.50
258 Denny Neagle .12 .30
259 Dmitri Young .12 .30
260 Todd Helton .20 .50
261 Larry Walker .20 .50
262 Pedro Astacio .12 .30
263 Neifi Perez .12 .30
264 Jeff Cirillo .12 .30
265 Jeffrey Hammonds .12 .30
266 Tom Goodwin .12 .30
267 Rolando Arrojo .12 .30
268 Rick Ankiel FF 1.50 4.00
269 Pat Burrell FF 1.00 2.50
270 Eric Munson FF 1.00 2.50
271 Rafael Furcal FF 1.50 4.00
272 Brad Penny FF 1.00 2.50
273 Adam Kennedy FF 1.00 2.50
274 Mike Lamb FF RC 1.00 2.50
275 Matt Riley FF 1.00 2.50
276 Eric Gagne FF 1.00 2.50
277 Kazuhiro Sasaki FF RC 2.50 6.00
278 Julio Lugo FF 1.00 2.50
279 Kip Wells FF 1.00 2.50
280 Danys Baez FF RC 1.00 2.50
281 Josh Beckett FF 2.00 5.00
282 Alfonso Soriano FF 2.50 6.00
283 Vernon Wells FF 1.00 2.50
284 Nick Johnson FF 1.00 2.50
285 Ramon Ortiz FF 1.00 2.50
286 Peter Bergeron FF 1.00 2.50
287 Wascar Serrano FF RC 1.00 2.50
288 Josh Paul FF 1.00 2.50
289 Mark Quinn FF 1.00 2.50
290 Jason Marquis FF 1.00 2.50
291 Rob Bell FF 1.00 2.50
292 Pablo Ozuna FF 1.00 2.50
293 Milton Bradley FF 1.00 2.50
294 Roosevelt Brown FF 1.00 2.50
295 Terrence Long FF 1.00 2.50
296 Chad Durbin FF RC 1.00 2.50
297 Matt LeCroy FF 1.00 2.50
298 Ken Griffey Jr. CL .60 1.50
299 Mark McGwire CL .50 1.25
300 Derek Jeter CL .75 2.00

2000 Upper Deck Gold Reserve 24-Karat Gems

COMPLETE SET 8.00 20.00
STATED ODDS 1:7
K1 Pedro Martinez .60 1.50
K2 Scott Rolen .60 1.50
K3 Jason Giambi .40 1.00
K4 Jeromy Burnitz .40 1.00
K5 Rafael Palmeiro .60 1.50
K6 Rick Ankiel .60 1.50
K7 Carlos Beltran .60 1.50
K8 Derek Jeter 2.50 6.00
K9 Jason Kendall .40 1.00
K10 Chipper Jones 1.00 2.50
K11 Carlos Delgado .40 1.00
K12 Alex Rodriguez 1.25 3.00
K13 Randy Johnson 1.00 2.50
K14 Tony Gwynn 1.00 2.50
K15 Shawn Green .40 1.00

2000 Upper Deck Gold Reserve Game Ball

STATED ODDS 1:480
BAJ Andruw Jones 10.00 25.00
BBB Barry Bonds 40.00 80.00
BBW Bernie Williams 10.00 25.00
BCJ Chipper Jones 10.00 25.00
BDJ Derek Jeter 10.00 25.00
BGM Greg Maddux 15.00 40.00
BGS Gary Sheffield 6.00 15.00
BKG Ken Griffey Jr. 15.00 40.00
BMM Mark McGwire 10.00 25.00
BMP Mike Piazza 15.00 40.00
BMR Manny Ramirez 10.00 25.00
BNG Nomar Garciaparra 15.00 40.00
BRC Roger Clemens 20.00 50.00
BSC Sean Casey 6.00 15.00
BSG Shawn Green 6.00 15.00
BSR Scott Rolen 10.00 25.00
BSS Sammy Sosa 10.00 25.00
BTG Tony Gwynn 15.00 40.00

2000 Upper Deck Gold Reserve Setting the Standard

COMPLETE SET (15) 15.00 40.00
STATED ODDS 1:11
S1 Tony Gwynn 1.00 2.50
S2 Manny Ramirez 1.00 2.50
S3 Derek Jeter 2.50 6.00
S4 Cal Ripken 3.00 8.00
S5 Mo Vaughn .40 1.00
S6 Jose Canseco .60 1.50
S7 Barry Bonds 1.50 4.00
S8 Nomar Garciaparra .60 1.50
S9 Juan Gonzalez .40 1.00
S10 Mark McGwire 1.50 4.00
S11 Alex Rodriguez 1.25 3.00
S12 Jeff Bagwell .60 1.50
S13 Ken Griffey Jr. 2.00 5.00
S14 Frank Thomas 1.00 2.50
S15 Sammy Sosa 1.00 2.50

2000 Upper Deck Gold Reserve Solid Gold Gallery

COMPLETE SET (12) 12.50 30.00
STATED ODDS 1:13
G1 Ken Griffey Jr. 2.00 5.00
G2 Alex Rodriguez 1.25 3.00
G3 Mike Piazza 1.00 2.50
G4 Sammy Sosa 1.00 2.50
G5 Derek Jeter 2.50 6.00
G6 Jeff Bagwell .60 1.50
G7 Mark McGwire 1.50 4.00
G8 Cal Ripken 3.00 8.00
G9 Pedro Martinez .60 1.50
G10 Chipper Jones 1.00 2.50
G11 Ivan Rodriguez .60 1.50
G12 Vladimir Guerrero .60 1.50

2000 Upper Deck Gold Reserve UD Authentics

STATED ODDS 1:480
GOLD RANDOM INSERTS IN PACKS
GOLD PRINT RUN 25 SERIAL #'d SETS
NO GOLD PRICING DUE TO SCARCITY
EXCHANGE DEADLINE 04/10/01
AR Alex Rodriguez 30.00 80.00
CB Carlos Beltran 6.00 15.00
CJ Chipper Jones 30.00 80.00
CR Cal Ripken 40.00 80.00
IR Ivan Rodriguez 15.00 40.00
JC Jose Canseco 10.00 25.00
KG Ken Griffey Jr. 60.00 120.00
MR Manny Ramirez 20.00 50.00
SG Shawn Green 15.00 40.00
TG Tony Gwynn 30.00 60.00

2009 Upper Deck Goodwin Champions

COMMON CARD (1-150) .15 .40
COMMON NIGHT 5.00 12.00
COMMON SP (151-190) 1.25 3.00
151-190 STATED ODDS 1:2 HOBBY
COMMON SUPER SP (191-210) 1.50 4.00
SUPER SP MINORS 1.50 4.00
SUPER SP SEMIS 1.50 4.00
SUPER SP UNLISTED 1.50 4.00
191-210 STATED ODDS 1:10 HOBBY
PLATES RANDOMLY INSERTED
PLATE PRINT RUN 1 SET PER COLOR
BLACK-CYAN-MAGENTA-YELLOW ISSUED
NO PLATE PRICING DUE TO SCARCITY
1a K.Griffey Jr. Day .75 2.00
1b K.Griffey Jr. Night SP 10.00 25.00
2 Derek Jeter 1.00 2.50
3 Jon Lester .25 .60
4 Jorge Posada .25 .60
5 Albert Pujols .50 1.25
6 Chipper Jones .40 1.00
7a R.Sandberg Day .75 2.00
7b R.Sandberg Night SP 6.00 15.00
8 Johnny Damon .25 .60
9 Carlos Delgado .15 .40
10 Vladimir Guerrero .25 .60

11 Johnny Bench .40 1.00
12 Matt Cain .25 .60
13 Bill Skowron CL .15 .40
14 Donovan Bailey .15 .40
15 Dick Allen CL .15 .40
16 Abraham Lincoln .25 .60
17 Rollie Fingers .25 .60
18 Bo Jackson CL .40 1.00
19 Scott Kazmir .15 .40
20a Grady Sizemore Day .25 .60
20b G.Sizemore Night SP 5.00 12.00
21 Ian Kinsler .25 .60
22 Jim Palmer .25 .60
23 Kevin Youkilis .15 .40
24 O.J. Mayo .20 .50
25 Hunter Pence .25 .60
26 Hiroki Kuroda .15 .40
27 Derrek Lee .15 .40
28 Brian McCann .25 .60
29 Carlos Quentin .15 .40
30 Al Kaline .40 1.00
31 Hanley Ramirez .25 .60
32 Josh Hamilton .25 .60
33 Jeff Samardzija .25 .60
34 Alexander Ovechkin 1.25 3.00
35 Clayton Kershaw .60 1.50
36 Lyndon Johnson .15 .40
37 Whitey Ford .25 .60
38 Carey Price 1.00 2.50
39 Jay Bruce .25 .60
40 Phil Niekro .25 .60
41 Ted Williams .75 2.00
42 Justin Upton .25 .60
43 Cole Hamels .30 .75
44a B.Obama Day .40 1.00
44b B.Obama Night SP 8.00 20.00
45 Peyton Manning .50 1.25
46 Jim Thome .25 .60
47 Nick Markakis .30 .75
48 Joe Carter CL .15 .40
49 Ryan Braun .25 .60
50 Mike Schmidt .60 1.50
51 Carlos Beltran .25 .60
52 Nolan Ryan 1.25 3.00
53 Anderson Silva .50 1.25
54 Kosuke Fukudome .25 .60
55 Chad Reed .15 .40
56a O.Smith Day .50 1.25
56b O.Smith Night SP 8.00 20.00
57 Eli Manning .40 1.00
58 CC Sabathia .25 .60
59 Evan Longoria .25 .60
60 Matt Garza .15 .40
61 Michael Beasley .40 1.00
62 Yogi Berra .40 1.00
63 Brian Roberts .15 .40
64 Alex Rodriguez .50 1.25
65a T.Woods Day 1.50 4.00
65b T.Woods Night SP 12.50 30.00
66 Buffalo Bill Cody .15 .40
67 Josh Beckett .15 .40
68 Matt Ryan .40 1.00
69a I.Suzuki Day .50 1.25
69b I.Suzuki Night SP 8.00 20.00
70 Chuck Liddell .50 1.25
71 Adrian Gonzalez .30 .75
72 David Wright .30 .75
73 LeBron James 1.50 4.00
74a G.Lopez Day .15 .40
74b G.Lopez Night SP 5.00 12.00
75 Carlton Fisk .25 .60
76 Joe Mauer .30 .75
77 Manny Ramirez .40 1.00
78 Jason Varitek .40 1.00
79 John Lackey .25 .60
80 Ivan Rodriguez .25 .60
81 Wayne Gretzky 2.00 5.00
82 Justin Morneau .25 .60
83 Akinori Iwamura .15 .40
84 Joe Lewis .25 .60
85 Lance Berkman .25 .60
86 Brooks Robinson .25 .60
87a A.Pettitte Day .25 .60
87b A.Pettitte Night SP 5.00 12.00
88 Peggy Fleming .15 .40
89 Joe DiMaggio .75 2.00
90 Jonathan Toews .60 1.50
91 Todd Helton .25 .60
92 Dennis Eckersley .25 .60
93 Daisuke Matsuzaka .25 .60
94 Adrian Peterson .60 1.50
95 Alfonso Soriano .25 .60
96 Paul Molitor .40 1.00
97 Johan Santana .25 .60
98 Jason Giambi .15 .40
99 Ben Roethlisberger .50 1.25
100 Chase Utley .25 .60
101a C.Ripken Jr. Day 1.25 3.00
101b C.Ripken Jr. Night SP 10.00 25.00
102 Curtis Granderson .30 .75
103 James Shields .15 .40
104 Nate McLouth .15 .40
105 Evelyn Ng .40 1.00
106a R.Howard Day .25 .60
106b R.Howard Night SP 6.00 15.00
107 Joe Nathan .15 .40
108 Tim Lincecum .25 .60
109 Chad Billingsley .25 .60
110 Matt Holliday .40 1.00
111 Kevin Garnett .60 1.50
112 Robin Roberts .25 .60
113 Jose Reyes .25 .60
114 Michael Jordan 8.00 20.00
115a S.Jones Day .25 .60
115b S.Jones Night SP 5.00 12.00
116 Kristi Yamaguchi .25 .60
117 Carlos Zambrano .25 .60
118 Bucky Dent CL .15 .40
119 Carl Yastrzemski .60 1.50
120 Stephen Drew .15 .40
121 Dustin Pedroia .40 1.00
122 Jonathan Papelbon .25 .60
123 B.J. Upton .25 .60
124 Steve Carlton .25 .60
125 Chris Johnson .40 1.00
126a T.Tulowitzki Day .40 1.00
126b T.Tulowitzki Night SP 5.00 12.00
127 Francisco Liriano .15 .40
128 Bill Rodgers .15 .40
129 Laird Hamilton .15 .40
130 Brandon Webb .25 .60
131 Miguel Cabrera .40 1.00
132a C.Wang Day .25 .60
132b C.Wang Night SP 5.00 12.00
133 Joba Chamberlain .15 .40
134 Felix Hernandez .25 .60
135 Tony Gwynn .40 1.00
136 Roy Oswalt .25 .60
137 Prince Fielder .25 .60
138 Gary Sheffield .15 .40
139 Koji Uehara RC .40 1.00
140a G.Howe Day 1.00 2.50
140b G.Howe Night SP 5.00 12.00
141 Bobby Orr 1.00 2.50
142 Zack Greinke .40 1.00
143 Derrick Rose .50 1.25
144 Cliff Lee .25 .60
145 Joey Votto .40 1.00
146 Phil Hellmuth .40 1.00
147 Mark Teixeira .25 .60
148 David Price RC .30 .75
149 Ryan Ludwick .25 .60
150 David Ortiz .40 1.00
151 Cory Wade SP 1.25 3.00
152 Roy White SP 1.25 3.00
153 Jed Lowrie SP .75 2.00
154 Gavin Floyd SP 1.25 3.00
155 Justin Masterson SP .75 2.00
156 Travis Hafner SP 1.25 3.00
157 Kelly Shoppach SP 1.25 3.00
158 David Purcey SP 1.25 3.00
159 Howie Kendrick SP 1.25 3.00
160 Mike Parsons SP 1.25 3.00
161 Jeremy Bloom SP 1.25 3.00
162 Dave Scott SP 1.25 3.00
163 Nyjer Morgan SP 1.25 3.00
164 Chris Volstad SP 1.25 3.00
165 Barry Zito SP 2.00 5.00
166 Adrian Beltre SP 3.00 8.00
167 Mark Zupan SP 1.25 3.00
168 Victor Martinez SP 1.25 3.00
169 Eric Chavez SP 1.25 3.00
170 Chris Perez SP 1.25 3.00
171 Jered Weaver SP 2.00 5.00
172 Justin Verlander SP 2.00 5.00
173 Adam Lind SP 1.25 3.00
174 Corky Carroll SP 1.25 3.00
175 Ryan Zimmerman SP 1.25 3.00
176 Josh Willingham SP 2.00 5.00
177 Graig Nettles SP 1.25 3.00
178 Jonathan Albaladejo SP 1.25 3.00
179 Ted Martin SP 1.25 3.00
180 Bill Hall SP 1.25 3.00
181 Brad Hawpe SP 1.25 3.00
182 John Maine SP 1.25 3.00
183 Tom Curren SP 1.25 3.00
184 Ken Griffey Sr. CL SP 1.25 3.00
185 Josh Johnson SP 2.00 5.00
186 Phil Hughes SP .75 2.00
187 Joe Alexander SP 1.25 3.00
188 Fausto Carmona SP 1.25 3.00
189 Daniel Murphy SP RC 2.00 5.00
190 Alex Hinshaw SP 1.25 3.00
191 Clayton Richard SP 1.50 4.00
192 Sparky Lyle CL SP 1.50 4.00
193 Don Gay SP 1.50 4.00
194 Aramis Ramirez SP 1.50 4.00
195 Gaylord Perry CL SP 2.50 6.00
196 Carlos Lee SP 1.50 4.00
197 Paul Konerko SP 2.50 6.00
198 Kent Hrbek CL SP 1.50 4.00
199 Chris B. Young SP 1.50 4.00
200 Roy Halladay SP 1.50 4.00
201 Geovany Soto SP 1.50 4.00
202 Chone Figgins SP 1.50 4.00
203 Joe Pepitone CL SP 1.50 4.00
204 Mark Allen SP 1.50 4.00
205 Garrett Atkins SP 1.50 4.00
206 Ken Shamrock SP 1.50 4.00
207 Jermaine Dye SP 1.50 4.00
208 Don Newcombe CL SP 1.50 4.00
209 Rick Cerone CL SP 1.50 4.00
210 Adam Jones SP 1.50 4.00

2009 Upper Deck Goodwin Champions Mini

COMPLETE SET (192) 75.00 150.00
*MINI 1-150: 1X TO 2.5X BASIC
APPX.MINI ODDS ONE PER PACK
PLATES RANDOMLY INSERTED
PLATE PRINT RUN 1 SET PER COLOR
BLACK-CYAN-MAGENTA-YELLOW ISSUED
NO PLATE PRICING DUE TO SCARCITY
211 Brian Giles EXT .60 1.50
212 Robinson Cano EXT 1.00 2.50
213 Erik Bedard EXT .60 1.50
214 James Loney EXT .60 1.50
215 Jimmy Rollins EXT 1.00 2.50
216 Joakim Soria EXT .60 1.50
217 Jeremy Guthrie EXT .60 1.50
218 Adam Wainwright EXT 1.00 2.50
219 B.J. Ryan EXT .60 1.50
220 Aaron Cook EXT .60 1.50
221 Aaron Harang EXT .60 1.50
222 Mariano Rivera EXT 2.00 5.00
223 Freddy Sanchez EXT .60 1.50
224 Ryan Dempster EXT .60 1.50
225 Jacoby Ellsbury EXT 1.25 3.00
226 Russell Martin EXT .60 1.50
227 Ervin Santana EXT .60 1.50
228 Nomar Garciaparra EXT 1.00 2.50
229 Chris Young EXT .60 1.50
230 Jair Jurrjens EXT .60 1.50
231 Francisco Cordero EXT .60 1.50
232 Bobby Crosby EXT .60 1.50
233 Rich Harden EXT .60 1.50
234 Cameron Maybin EXT .60 1.50
235 Conor Jackson EXT .60 1.50
236 Jake Peavy EXT .60 1.50
237 Brad Ziegler EXT .60 1.50
238 Aaron Rowand EXT .60 1.50
239 Carl Crawford EXT 1.00 2.50
240 Mark Buehrle EXT 1.00 2.50
241 Carlos Guillen EXT .60 1.50
242 Alex Rios EXT .60 1.50
243 Vernon Wells EXT .60 1.50
244 Bobby Jenks EXT .60 1.50
245 Rick Ankiel EXT .60 1.50
246 Alex Gordon EXT 1.00 2.50
247 Paul Maholm EXT .60 1.50
248 Carlos Gomez EXT .60 1.50
249 Brad Lidge EXT .60 1.50
250 Hideki Okajima EXT .60 1.50
251 Michael Bourn EXT .60 1.50
252 Jhonny Peralta EXT .60 1.50

2009 Upper Deck Goodwin Champions Mini Black Border

*MINI BLK 1-150: 1.5X TO 4X BASE
*MINI BLK 211-252: .75X TO 2X MINI
RANDOM INSERTS IN PACKS

2009 Upper Deck Goodwin Champions Mini Foil

*MINI FOIL 1-150: 3X TO 8X BASE
*MINI FOIL 211-252: 1.5X TO 4X MINI
RANDOM INSERTS IN PACKS
ANNCD PRINT RUN OF 88 TOTAL SETS

2009 Upper Deck Goodwin Champions Animal Series

RANDOM INSERTS IN PACKS
AS1 King Cobra 2.00 5.00
AS2 Dodo Bird 2.00 5.00
AS3 Tasmanian Devil 2.00 5.00
AS4 Komodo Dragon 2.00 5.00
AS5 Bald Eagle 2.00 5.00
AS6 Great White Shark 2.00 5.00
AS7 Gorilla 2.00 5.00
AS8 Bengal Tiger 2.00 5.00
AS9 Killer Whale 2.00 5.00
AS10 Giant Panda 2.00 5.00

2009 Upper Deck Goodwin Champions Autographs

STATED ODDS 1:20 HOBBY
EXCHANGE DEADLINE 8/31/2011
AG Adrian Gonzalez/45 * 10.00 25.00
AH Alex Hinshaw 4.00 10.00
AK Al Kaline/50 * 40.00 100.00
AL Jonathan Albaladejo 4.00 10.00
BD Bucky Dent 8.00 20.00
BL Jeremy Bloom 5.00 12.00
BO Bobby Orr/25 * 90.00 150.00
BR Bill Rodgers 4.00 10.00
BS Bill Skowron 10.00 25.00
CB Chad Billingsley 6.00 15.00
CC Corky Carroll 10.00 25.00
CE Rick Cerone 4.00 10.00
CF Chone Figgins 4.00 10.00
CJ Chipper Jones/25 * 100.00 200.00
CK Clayton Kershaw/50 * 30.00 60.00
CL Carlos Lee 4.00 10.00
CP Chris Perez 5.00 12.00
CR Clayton Richard 4.00 10.00
CV Chris Volstad 4.00 10.00
CW Cory Wade 4.00 10.00
DA Dick Allen 12.50 30.00
DE Dennis Eckersley/50 * 10.00 25.00
DG Don Gay 5.00 12.00
DJ Derek Jeter/25 * 175.00 300.00
DM Daniel Murphy 10.00 25.00
DN Don Newcombe 6.00 15.00
DO Donovan Bailey 10.00 25.00
DP Dustin Pedroia 12.50 30.00
DS Dave Scott 5.00 12.00
EC Eric Chavez/50 * 5.00 12.00
EL Evan Longoria/25 * 100.00 250.00
EN Evelyn Ng 5.00 12.00
FH F.Hernandez EXCH 15.00 40.00
GA Garrett Atkins 4.00 10.00
GF Gavin Floyd 4.00 10.00
GK Kevin Garnett/25 * 50.00 100.00
GS Sizemore/50 * 10.00 25.00
GY Ken Griffey Sr. 8.00 20.00
HP Hunter Pence/50 * 12.50 30.00
HR Hanley Ramirez 4.00 10.00
JA Joe Alexander 6.00 15.00
JB Jay Bruce 4.00 10.00
JC Joe Carter/45 * 15.00 40.00
JE Jed Lowrie 5.00 12.00
JJ Josh Johnson 8.00 20.00
JL Joe Lewis 4.00 10.00
JM John Maine 4.00 10.00
JO Jon Lester/25 * 60.00 120.00
JS James Shields 4.00 10.00
JU Justin Masterson 6.00 15.00
JW Josh Willingham 4.00 10.00
KH Kent Hrbek 15.00 40.00
KU Koji Uehara/25 * 50.00 100.00
KY Kevin Youkilis 8.00 20.00
LA Ryan Braun/50 * 30.00 60.00
LH Laird Hamilton 20.00 50.00
LO Gerry Lopez 10.00 25.00
MA Mark Allen 5.00 12.00
MC Matt Cain 5.00 12.00
MG Matt Garza 5.00 12.00
MJ Michael Jordan/23 * 500.00 700.00
MN Nate McLouth 4.00 10.00
MZ Mark Zupan 5.00 12.00
NM Nick Markakis 6.00 15.00
OS Ozzie Smith/50 * 40.00 80.00
PA Mike Parsons 6.00 15.00
PD David Price 8.00 20.00
PF Prince Fielder/50 * 8.00 20.00
PH Phil Hellmuth 6.00 15.00
PJ Jonathan Papelbon 4.00 10.00
PK Paul Konerko 10.00 25.00
PM Paul Molitor/50 * 10.00 25.00
PU David Purcey 4.00 10.00
RB Brooks Robinson/50 * 12.50 30.00
RC Chad Reed 10.00 25.00
RF Rollie Fingers/50 * 10.00 25.00
RH Roy Halladay/50 * 50.00 100.00
RW Roy White 4.00 10.00
SC Steve Carlton 10.00 25.00
SD Stephen Drew/50 * 8.00 20.00
SK Kelly Shoppach 4.00 10.00
SL Sparky Lyle 5.00 12.00
SO Geovany Soto 10.00 25.00
TC Tom Curren 12.50 30.00
TM Ted Martin 4.00 10.00
TT Troy Tulowitzki 10.00 25.00
WF Whitey Ford/25 * 75.00 150.00
YA Kristi Yamaguchi/49 * 50.00 100.00
ZG Zack Greinke/25 * 15.00 40.00

2009 Upper Deck Goodwin Champions Citizens of the Century

RANDOM INSERTS IN PACKS
CC1 Hillary Clinton 2.00 5.00
CC2 Bill Clinton 2.00 5.00
CC3 Tony Blair 2.00 5.00
CC4 Princess Diana 2.50 6.00
CC5 Barack Obama 3.00 8.00
CC6 Ronald Reagan 2.00 5.00
CC7 Mikhail Gorbachev 2.00 5.00
CC8 Al Gore 2.00 5.00
CC9 Pope John Paul II 2.00 5.00
CC10 Winston Churchill 2.00 5.00

2009 Upper Deck Goodwin Champions Citizens of the Day

RANDOM INSERTS IN PACKS
CD1 Susan B. Anthony 2.00 5.00
CD2 P.T. Barnum 2.00 5.00
CD3 Cap Anson 2.50 6.00
CD4 Theodore Roosevelt 2.00 5.00
CD5 John D. Rockefeller 2.00 5.00
CD6 King Kelly 2.50 6.00
CD7 Will Rogers 2.00 5.00
CD8 Grover Cleveland 2.00 5.00
CD9 Scott Joplin 2.00 5.00
CD10 Sitting Bull 2.00 5.00
CD11 Bram Stoker 2.00 5.00
CD12 Wyatt Earp 2.00 5.00
CD13 Claude Monet 2.00 5.00
CD14 Queen Victoria 2.00 5.00
CD15 Grigori Rasputin 2.00 5.00

2009 Upper Deck Goodwin Champions Entomology

RANDOM INSERTS IN PACKS
EXCHANGE DEADLINE 8/31/2011
ENT5 BD Butterfly EXCH 60.00 120.00
ENT14 Strawberry Bluff EXCH 90.00 150.00
NNO EXCH Card 75.00 150.00

2009 Upper Deck Goodwin Champions Landmarks

RANDOM INSERTS IN PACKS
EXCHANGE DEADLINE 8/31/2011
TT RMS Titanic Coal 75.00 150.00
NNO EXCH Card 60.00 120.00

2009 Upper Deck Goodwin Champions Memorabilia

STATED ODDS 1:10 HOBBY
EXCHANGE DEADLINE 8/31/2011
AB Adrian Beltre 3.00 8.00
AI Akinori Iwamura 1.25 3.00
AJ Adam Jones 2.00 5.00
BE Johnny Bench 3.00 8.00
BH Bill Hall 1.25 3.00
BJ Bo Jackson 3.00 8.00
BM Brian McCann 2.00 5.00
BR Brian Roberts 1.25 3.00
BW Brandon Webb 2.00 5.00
BZ Barry Zito 2.00 5.00
CB Chad Billingsley 2.00 5.00
CD Carlos Delgado 1.25 3.00
CF Carlton Fisk 2.00 5.00
CG Curtis Granderson 2.50 6.00
CH Cole Hamels 2.50 6.00
CJ Chipper Jones 3.00 8.00
CL Carlos Lee 1.25 3.00
CR Cal Ripken Jr. 10.00 25.00
CU Chase Utley/100 * 5.00 12.00
CW Chien-Ming Wang 2.00 5.00
CY Carl Yastrzemski 5.00 12.00
CZ Carlos Zambrano 2.00 5.00
DA Johnny Damon 2.00 5.00
DJ Derek Jeter 8.00 20.00
DL Derrek Lee 1.25 3.00
DM Daisuke Matsuzaka 2.00 5.00
DO David Ortiz 3.00 8.00
DR Derrick Rose 5.00 12.00
EC Eric Chavez 1.25 3.00
FC Fausto Carmona 1.25 3.00
FH Felix Hernandez 2.00 5.00
FI Chone Figgins 1.25 3.00
FL Francisco Liriano 1.25 3.00
GN Graig Nettles 1.25 3.00
GP Gaylord Perry 2.00 5.00
GR Ken Griffey Jr. 6.00 15.00
HA Brad Hawpe 1.25 3.00
HK Hiroki Kuroda 1.25 3.00
HP Hunter Pence 2.00 5.00
IK Ian Kinsler 2.00 5.00
JA James Shields 1.25 3.00
JB Josh Beckett 1.25 3.00
JD Jermaine Dye 1.25 3.00
JH Jonathan Albaladejo 1.25 3.00
JL John Lackey 2.00 5.00
JM Joe Mauer 2.50 6.00
JN Joe Nathan 1.25 3.00
JP Jim Palmer 2.00 5.00
JR Jose Reyes/100 * 4.00 10.00
JT Jim Thome 2.00 5.00
JU Justin Upton 2.00 5.00
JV Jason Varitek 3.00 8.00
JW Jered Weaver 2.00 5.00
KE Howie Kendrick 1.25 3.00
KF Kosuke Fukudome 2.00 5.00
KG Kevin Garnett 6.00 15.00
LE Cliff Lee 2.00 5.00
LJ LeBron James 15.00 40.00
MA John Maine 1.25 3.00
MB Michael Beasley 4.00 10.00
MC Miguel Cabrera 3.00 8.00
MJ Michael Jordan/50 * 30.00 60.00
MO Justin Morneau 2.00 5.00
MS Mike Schmidt 5.00 12.00
NM Nick Markakis 2.50 6.00
OM O.J. Mayo 2.00 5.00
PA Jonathan Papelbon 2.00 5.00
PF Prince Fielder 2.00 5.00
PH Phil Hughes 1.25 3.00
PK Paul Konerko 2.00 5.00
PO Jorge Posada 2.00 5.00
PU Albert Pujols 4.00 10.00
RA Aramis Ramirez 1.25 3.00
RB Ryan Braun 2.00 5.00
RH Roy Halladay 2.00 5.00
RO Roy Oswalt 2.00 5.00
RS Ryne Sandberg 6.00 15.00
RZ Manny Ramirez 3.00 8.00
SC Steve Carlton 2.00 5.00
SK Scott Kazmir 1.25 3.00
TG Tony Gwynn 3.00 8.00
TH Todd Helton 2.00 5.00
TL Tim Lincecum 2.00 5.00
TR Travis Hafner 1.25 3.00
TT Troy Tulowitzki 3.00 8.00
TW Ted Williams/40 * 20.00 50.00
VE Justin Verlander 3.00 8.00
VG Vladimir Guerrero 2.00 5.00
VM Victor Martinez 2.00 5.00
WD Tiger Woods 15.00 40.00
WF Whitey Ford 2.00 5.00
YB Yogi Berra 3.00 8.00
YO Chris B. Young 1.25 3.00
ZG Zack Greinke 3.00 8.00

2009 Upper Deck Goodwin Champions Thoroughbred Hair Cuts

RANDOM INSERTS IN PACKS
EXCHANGE DEADLINE 8/31/2011
AA1 Afleet Alex 20.00 50.00
AA2 Afleet Alex 20.00 50.00
FC1 Funny Cide 20.00 50.00
FC2 Funny Cide 20.00 50.00
SJ1 Smarty Jones 20.00 50.00
SJ2 Smarty Jones 20.00 50.00

2011 Upper Deck Goodwin Champions

COMP.SET w/o VAR (210) 40.00 80.00
COMP.SET w/o SP's (150) 10.00 25.00
COMMON SP (151-190) 1.00 2.50
151-190 SP ODDS 1:3 HOBBY
COMMON SP (191-210) 1.50 4.00
191-210 SP ODDS 1:12 HOBBY
COMMON VARIATION SP 4.00 10.00
1A King Kelly .15 .40
1B Kelly Lightning SP 4.00 10.00
11 Greg Maddux .30 .75
16 Don Mattingly .50 1.25
19A Lou Brock .20 .50
19B L.Brock/J.Carter SP 4.00 10.00
24 Miller Huggins .15 .40
25 Manny Machado .30 .75
38 Nolan Ryan .75 2.00
39 Addie Joss .15 .40
41 Whitey Ford .20 .50
43 Stan Musial .40 1.00
46 Ryne Sandberg .50 1.25
50 Steve Carlton .15 .40
56 Jim Rice .20 .50
64 Johnny Bench .25 .60
68 Hugh Jennings .15 .40
69 Wilbert Robinson .15 .40
94 Ozzie Smith .40 1.00
95 Willie Keeler .15 .40
103 Rube Waddell .15 .40
112 Mike Schmidt .40 1.00
116 John Lamb .15 .40
119 Cap Anson .20 .50
120 Tony Perez .15 .40
126 Jose Canseco .20 .50
128 Bob Gibson .20 .50
140 John McGraw .15 .40
146 Carlton Fisk .20 .50
152 Jack Chesbro SP 1.00 2.50
158 Charles Comiskey SP 1.00 2.50
163 Ed Delahanty SP 1.00 2.50
178 Dennis Oil Can Boyd SP 1.00 2.50
181 Buck Ewing SP 1.00 2.50
184 Dan Brouthers SP 1.00 2.50
189 Eddie Plank SP 1.00 2.50
194 Rube Foster SP 1.50 4.00
195 John Montgomery Ward SP 1.50 4.00
209 Albert Spalding SP 1.50 4.00
210 Abner Doubleday SP 1.50 4.00

2011 Upper Deck Goodwin Champions Mini

*1-150 MINI: 1X TO 2.5X BASIC
1-150 MINI ODDS 1:4 HOBBY
COMMON CARD (211-231) .60 1.50
211-231 MINI ODDS 1:13 HOBBY
PRINTING PLATES RANDOMLY INSERTED
PLATE PRINT RUN 1 SET PER COLOR
BLACK-CYAN-MAGENTA-YELLOW ISSUED
NO PLATE PRICING DUE TO SCARCITY
211 Matt Packer SP .60 1.50
212 Gary Brown SP 1.00 2.50
213 Ramon Morla SP .60 1.50
214 Aaron Crow SP .60 1.50
215 Ryan Lavarnaway SP .60 1.50
216 Michael Choice SP .60 1.50
217 Matt Lipka SP .60 1.50
218 Aaron Hicks SP .60 1.50
219 Peter Tago SP .60 1.50
220 Jurickson Profar SP .60 1.50
221 Cody Hawn SP .60 1.50
222 Carlos Perez SP .60 1.50
223 Robinson Yambati SP .60 1.50
224 Mike Olt SP .75 2.00
225 LeVon Washington SP .60 1.50
226 Kyle Parker SP .75 2.00
227 Jonathan Garcia SP .60 1.50
228 Yordano Ventura SP 2.00 5.00
229 Delino DeShields Jr. SP .75 2.00
230 Collin Cowgill SP .60 1.50
231 Kyle Skipworth SP .60 1.50

2011 Upper Deck Goodwin Champions Mini Black

*1-150 MINI BLACK: 1.2X TO 3X BASIC
1-150 MINI BLACK ODDS 1:13 HOBBY
*211-231 MINI BLK: .6X TO 1.5X BASIC MINI
211-231 MINI BLACK ODDS 1:46 HOBBY

2011 Upper Deck Goodwin Champions Mini Foil

*1-150 MINI FOIL: 2.5X TO 6X BASIC
1-150 ANNCD PRINT RUN OF 89
*211-231 MINI FOIL : 1X TO 2.5X BASIC MINI
211-231 ANNCD PRINT RUN OF 178
PRINT RUNS PROVIDED BY UD
38 Nolan Ryan 12.50 30.00

2011 Upper Deck Goodwin Champions Autographs

GROUP A ODDS 1:1577 HOBBY
GROUP B ODDS 1:729 HOBBY
GROUP C ODDS 1:339 HOBBY
GROUP D ODDS 1:246 HOBBY
GROUP E ODDS 1:72 HOBBY
GROUP F ODDS 1:35 HOBBY
OVERALL AUTO ODDS 1:20 HOBBY
EXCHANGE DEADLINE 6/7/2013
CA Steve Carlton C 10.00 25.00
CF Carlton Fisk B 12.00 30.00
CH Cody Hawn F 4.00 10.00
JB Johnny Bench A 40.00 80.00
JG Jonathan Garcia F 4.00 10.00
JL John Lamb F 4.00 10.00
JR Jim Rice D 8.00 20.00
KV Kolbrin Vitek F 4.00 10.00
LO Lou Brock B 20.00 50.00
LW LeVon Washington E 4.00 10.00
MM Manny Machado C 20.00 50.00
MO Mike Olt F 5.00 12.00
MU Stan Musial B 75.00 150.00
NR Nolan Ryan A
OC Dennis Oil Can Boyd E 6.00 15.00
PE Carlos Perez F 4.00 10.00
PT Peter Tago F 4.00 8.00
RL Ryan Lavarnway D 8.00 20.00
RM Ramon Morla F 4.00 10.00
RS Ryne Sandberg B 20.00 50.00
RY Robinson Yambati F 4.00 10.00
TP Tony Perez D 10.00 25.00
WF Whitey Ford B 15.00 40.00
YV Yordano Ventura F 8.00 20.00

2011 Upper Deck Goodwin Champions Figures of Sport

COMP.SET. w/o SP's (14) 10.00 25.00
COMMON CARD (1-14) .60 1.50
1-14 STATED ODDS 1:21 HOBBY
15-18 SP ODDS 1:300 HOBBY
FS11 Bo Jackson 1.25 3.00
FS12 Ozzie Smith 1.25 3.00
FS17 Nolan Ryan SP 5.00 12.00

2011 Upper Deck Goodwin Champions Memorabilia

GROUP A ODDS 1:14,613 HOBBY
GROUP B ODDS 1:179 HOBBY
GROUP C ODDS 1:31 HOBBY
GROUP D ODDS 1:22 HOBBY
KS Kyle Skipworth D 3.00 8.00
MC Michael Choice D 3.00 8.00
MM Manny Machado D 3.00 8.00
PT Peter Tago D 3.00 8.00

2011 Upper Deck Goodwin Champions Memorabilia Dual

GROUP A ODDS 1:67,680 HOBBY
GROUP B ODDS 1:8768 HOBBY
GROUP C ODDS 1:2923 HOBBY
GROUP D ODDS 1:877 HOBBY
GROUP E ODDS 1:585 HOBBY
NO GROUP A PRICING AVAILABLE
MM Manny Machado E 6.00 15.00

2012 Upper Deck Goodwin Champions

COMP.SET w/o VAR (210) 25.00 50.00
COMP.SET w/o SP's (150) 10.00 25.00
151-190 SP ODDS 1:3 HOBBY, BLASTER
191-210 SP ODDS 1:12 HOBBY, BLASTER
6 Carlton Fisk .20 .50
15 Billy Beane .15 .40
22 Greg Maddux .30 .75
25 Sam Thompson .15 .40
27 Mike Schmidt .40 1.00
29 Johnny Bench .25 .60
38 Billy Hamilton .15 .40
53A Lou Brock .20 .50
53B Lou Brock Horizontal SP 6.00 15.00
54 Al Kaline .25 .60
55B Kaline/Nixon/Palmer SP 6.00 15.00
75 Jack Morris .15 .40
81 Whitey Ford .20 .50
84 Don Mattingly .50 1.25
101 Ryne Sandberg .50 1.25
107A Ernie Banks .25 .60
107B Ernie Banks Horizontal SP 4.00 10.00
108 Nolan Ryan .75 2.00
109 John Kruk .15 .40
110 Jim O'Rourke .15 .40
113 Steve Carlton .20 .50
127A Dennis Eckersley .20 .50
127B Dennis Eckersley Horizontal SP 4.00 10.00
133 Bob Gibson .20 .50
139 Shoeless Joe Jackson .25 .60
145A Pete Rose .60 1.50
145B Pete Rose 8.00 20.00
w/Rolls Royce SP
152 Stan Musial SP 1.00 2.50
153 Ross Youngs SP 1.00 2.50
159 Ross Barnes SP 1.00 2.50
160 Pud Galvin SP 1.00 2.50
163 Ned Hanlon SP 1.00 2.50
164 Mike Donlin SP 1.00 2.50
171 Pat Moran SP 1.00 2.50
180 Ozzie Smith SP 1.00 2.50
182 Deacon White SP 1.00 2.50
183 Joe McGinnity SP 1.00 2.50
186 Ned Williamson SP 1.00 2.50
189 Kid Gleason SP 1.00 2.50
190 Sherry McGee SP 1.00 2.50
197 William Wrigley Jr. SP 1.50 4.00
204 Charles Ebbetts SP 1.50 4.00
205 Joe Start SP 1.50 4.00

2012 Upper Deck Goodwin Champions Mini

*1-150 MINI: 1X TO 2.5X BASIC
1-150 MINI STATED ODDS 1:2 HOBBY, BLASTER
211-231 MINI ODDS 1:2 HOBBY, BLASTER
211 Christian Yelich .60 1.50
212 Cesar Puello .60 1.50
213 Matthew Andriese .60 1.50
214 Matt Lipka .60 1.50
215 Gauntlett Eldemire .75 2.00
216 Nick Bucci .60 1.50
217 Jared Hoying .60 1.50
218 Zach Walters .60 1.50
219 Aaron Altherr .60 1.50
220 Marcell Ozuna .60 1.50
221 Wilin Rosario .60 1.50
222 Billy Hamilton 2.00 5.00
223 Reggie Golden .60 1.50
224 Matt Szczur 1.25 3.00
225 Jake Hager .60 1.50
226 Nick Kingham .60 1.50
227 Marcus Knecht .60 1.50
228 Michael Choice .75 2.00
229 Cody Buckel .60 1.50
230 Matt Packer .60 1.50
231 Will Swanner .60 1.50

2012 Upper Deck Goodwin Champions Mini Foil

*1-150 MINI FOIL: 2.5X TO 6X BASIC
1-150 MINI FOIL ANNCD. PRINT RUN 99
*211-231 MINI FOIL: 1X TO 2.5X BASIC MINI
211-231 MINI FOIL ANNCD. PRINT RUN 199

2012 Upper Deck Goodwin Champions Mini Green

*1-150 MINI GREEN: 1.25X TO 3X BASIC
*211-231 MINI GREEN: .6X TO 1.5X BASIC MINI
TWO MINI GREEN PER HOBBY BOX
ONE MINI GREEN PER BLASTER

2012 Upper Deck Goodwin Champions Mini Green Blank Back

UNPRICED DUE TO SCARCITY

2012 Upper Deck Goodwin Champions Autographs

GROUP A ODDS 1:1,977
GROUP B ODDS 1:353
GROUP C ODDS 1:264
GROUP D ODDS 1:185
GROUP E ODDS 1:82
GROUP F ODDS 1:36
OVERALL AUTO ODDS 1:20
EXCHANGE DEADLINE 7/12/2014
AAA Aaron Altherr F 4.00 10.00
ABH Billy Hamilton E 10.00 25.00
ACB Cody Buckel F 4.00 10.00
ACF Carlton Fisk B 8.00 20.00
ACH Michael Choice F 4.00 10.00
ACY Christian Yelich D 30.00 80.00
ADB Don Mattingly B 30.00 60.00
ADE Dennis Eckersley B 6.00 15.00
AEB Ernie Banks/Liz Banks 25.00 50.00
AGE Gauntlett Eldemire F 4.00 10.00
AHR Jake Hager F 4.00 10.00
AJH Jared Hoying E 4.00 10.00
AJM Jack Morris C 6.00 15.00
AMK Marcus Knecht F 4.00 10.00
AMO Marcell Ozuna E 4.00 10.00
AMP Matt Packer F 4.00 10.00
AMS Mike Schmidt B 12.50 30.00
ANK Nick Kingham F 4.00 10.00
ANR Nolan Ryan A 100.00 200.00
APR Pete Rose B 30.00 60.00
ARG Reggie Golden E 4.00 10.00
AWR Wilin Rosario E 4.00 10.00
AWS Will Swanner F 4.00 10.00

2012 Upper Deck Goodwin Champions Memorabilia

GROUP A ODDS 1:10,631
GROUP B ODDS 1:4,784
GROUP C ODDS 1:302
GROUP D ODDS 1:118
GROUP E ODDS 1:36
GROUP F ODDS 1:23
MJJ Shoeless Joe Jackson B 40.00 80.00

2012 Upper Deck Goodwin Champions Memorabilia Dual

GROUP A ODDS 1:95,680
GROUP B ODDS 1:31,893
GROUP C ODDS 1:2,514
GROUP D ODDS 1:1,306
GROUP E ODDS 1:520
NO PRICING ON GROUP A
M2JJ Shoeless Joe Jackson B 150.00 300.00

2013 Upper Deck Goodwin Champions

COMP. SET w/o VAR (210) 25.00 60.00
COMP. SET w/o SP's (150) 8.00 20.00
151-190 SP ODDS 1:3 HOBBY,BLASTER
191-210 SP ODDS 1:12 HOBBY,BLASTER
OVERALL VARIATION ODDS 1:320 H, 1:1,200 B
GROUP A ODDS 1:4,800
GROUP B ODDS 1:2,400
GROUP C ODDS 1:1,400
6 Ozzie Smith .25 .60
22 Andre Dawson .20 .50
27 Ernie Banks .25 .60
31 Reggie Jackson .30 .75
51 Pete Rose .60 1.50
71 Johnny Bench .30 .75
78 Jim Rice .25 .60
79 Darryl Strawberry .20 .50
85 Keith Hernandez .15 .40
90 Mark McGwire .40 1.00
91 Rafael Palmeiro .25 .60
95 Kent Hrbek .15 .40
96 Juan Gonzalez .20 .50
97 Jim Abbott .25 .60
99A Paul O'Neill .15 .40
99B P.O'Neill/O.Smith SP
101 Tony Gwynn .30 .75
111 Fred Lynn .20 .50
113 Steve Carlton .25 .60
115 Tim Salmon .20 .50
119 Jay Buhner .15 .40
124 Edgar Martinez .15 .40
126A Kenny Lofton .20 .50
126B K.Lofton/W.Moon SP 12.00 30.00
128 Frank Thomas .30 .75
136 John Olerud .25 .60
141 Nolan Ryan .75 2.00
142 Mike Schmidt .30 .75
151 Harry Stovey SP 1.00 2.50
152 John Clarkson SP 1.00 2.50
153 Mike Donovan SP 1.00 2.50
155 Ed Killian SP 1.00 2.50
157 Jake Beckley SP 1.00 2.50
158 Harry Wright SP 1.00 2.50
159 Mickey Welch SP 1.00 2.50
161 Tommy McCarthy SP 1.00 2.50
169 Tim Keefe SP 1.00 2.50
170 Jimmy Collins SP 1.00 2.50
178 George Wright SP 1.00 2.50

179 Amos Rusie SP 1.00 2.50
183 Bid McPhee SP 1.00 2.50
198 Jake Daubert SP 1.50 4.00
199 Lave Cross SP 1.50 4.00
209 Roger Connor SP 1.50 4.00

2013 Upper Deck Goodwin Champions Mini

*1-150 MINI: 1X TO 2.5X BASIC CARDS
7 MINIS PER HOBBY BOX, 4 MINIS PER BLASTER
211 Bobby Bundy .60 1.50
212 Nick Castellanos .60 1.50
214 Yao-Lin Wang .75 2.00
215 Matt Davidson .75 2.00
216 Zach Lee .75 2.00
217 Kevin Pillar .60 1.50
219 Kyle Parker .60 1.50
220 Nick Bucci .60 1.50
221 Clayton Blackburn .75 2.00
222 Matthew Andriese .60 1.50
224 Kolten Wong .75 2.00
225 Alen Hanson .75 2.00

2013 Upper Deck Goodwin Champions Mini Canvas

*1-150 MINI CANVAS: 2.5X TO 6X BASIC CARDS
1-150 MINI CANVAS ANNCD. PRINT RUN 99
*211-225 MINI CANVAS: 1X TO 2.5 BASIC MINI
211-225 MINI CANVAS ANNCD. PRINT RUN 198

2013 Upper Deck Goodwin Champions Mini Green

STATED ODDS 1:12 HOBBY, 1:15 BLASTER
STATED SP ODDS 1:60 HOBBY, 1:72 BLASTER

2013 Upper Deck Goodwin Champions Autographs

OVERALL ODDS 1:20
GROUP A ODDS 1:7,517
GROUP B ODDS 1:1,224
GROUP C ODDS 1:489
GROUP D ODDS 1:142
GROUP E ODDS 1:206
GROUP F ODDS 1:28
AAH Alen Hanson G 4.00 10.00
AAN Matthew Andriese F 4.00 10.00
AEM Edgar Martinez D 10.00 25.00
AGO Juan Gonzalez D 15.00 40.00
AJA Jim Abbott G 4.00 10.00
AJB Jay Buhner E 6.00 15.00
AJO John Olerud E 5.00 12.00
AJR Jim Rice D 6.00 15.00
AKH Kent Hrbek G 5.00 12.00
AKL Kenny Lofton D 6.00 15.00
AKW Kolten Wong G 5.00 12.00
AMD Matt Davidson G 4.00 10.00
AME Mark McGwire B 175.00 300.00
ANB Nick Bucci G 4.00 10.00
APL Kevin Pillar G 4.00 10.00
APO Paul O'Neill D 10.00 25.00
ARJ Reggie Jackson B 20.00 50.00
ARP Rafael Palmeiro D 12.00 30.00
ATG Tony Gwynn D 12.00 30.00
ATS Tim Salmon F 4.00 10.00
DJ Doc Jacobs/100 8.00 20.00

2013 Upper Deck Goodwin Champions Sport Royalty Autographs

OVERALL ODDS 1:1,161
GROUP A ODDS 1:7,473
GROUP B ODDS 1:4,171
GROUP C ODDS 1:2,050
SRANR Nolan Ryan A

2014 Upper Deck Goodwin Champions

COMPLETE SET w/o AU's(180) 40.00 100.00
COMPLETE SET w/o SP's(155) 12.00 30.00
131-155 SP ODDS 1:3 HOBBY,BLAST
156-180 SP ODDS 1:12 HOB/1:12 BLAST
AU ODDS 1:60 HOB/1:720 BLAST
NOLA AU ODDS 1:860 '15 PACKS
NOLA AU ISSUED IN '15 GOODWIN
1 Frank Thomas .25 .60
4 Ron Cey .15 .40
28 Troy Glaus .15 .40
66 Bob Horner .15 .40
69 Steve Garvey .15 .40
83 Robin Ventura .15 .40
89 Ken Griffey Jr. .50 1.25
93 Tony Gwynn .25 .60
108 Pete Rose .50 1.25
112 Roger Clemens .30 .75
115 Will Clark .20 .50
120B Kidd/Clemens SP 4.00 10.00
126 Nolan Ryan .75 2.00
129 Mark McGwire .50 1.25
133 Oyster Burns SP 1.00 2.50
137 Cristobal Torriente SP 1.00 2.50
143 King Kelly SP 1.00 2.50
146 Buck Ewing SP 1.00 2.50
148 Jose Mendez SP 1.00 2.50
149 Fred Dunlap SP 1.00 2.50
152 Tip O'Neill SP 1.00 2.50
156 Babe Siebert SP 1.50 4.00
157 Urban Shocker SP 1.50 4.00
158 Jim McCormick SP 1.50 4.00
161 Cap Anson SP 1.50 4.00
165 Pete Browning SP 1.50 4.00
171 Dan Brouthers SP 1.50 4.00
173 Miller Huggins SP 1.50 4.00
175 Jack Chesbro SP 1.50 4.00
178 Joe Kelley SP 1.50 4.00
180 George Davis SP 1.50 4.00
181 Byron Buxton AU 12.00 30.00
182 Miguel Sano AU 6.00 15.00
183 Chris Anderson AU 3.00 8.00
184 Travis Demeritte AU 3.00 8.00
185 Roberto Osuna AU 3.00 8.00
186 Raul Mondesi Jr. AU 6.00 15.00
187 Jorge Alfaro AU 3.00 8.00
188 Corey Black AU 3.00 8.00
189 Breyvic Valera AU 3.00 8.00
190 Jacob May AU 3.00 8.00
191 Jonathan Gray AU 3.00 8.00
192 Joey Gallo AU 10.00 25.00
193 Zach Bornstein AU 3.00 8.00
194 Bryan Mitchell AU 3.00 8.00
195 Joc Pederson AU 6.00 15.00
196 Nola AU Issued in '15 8.00 20.00
197 Miguel Almonte AU 3.00 8.00
198 Eduardo Rodriguez AU 3.00 8.00
199 Marten Gasparini AU 3.00 8.00
200 Micker Adolfo Zapata AU 6.00 15.00

2014 Upper Deck Goodwin Champions Mini

*1-130 MINI: .75X TO 2X BASIC
COMMON CARD (131-180) .50 1.25
7 MINIS PER HOBBY 4 PER BLASTER

2014 Upper Deck Goodwin Champions Mini Canvas

*1-130 MINI CANVAS: 2X TO 5X BASIC
COMMON CARD (131-180) 1.25 3.00
RANDOM INSERTS IN PACKS
1 Frank Thomas 3.00 8.00
89 Ken Griffey Jr. 12.00 30.00
93 Tony Gwynn 5.00 12.00
108 Pete Rose 4.00 10.00
126 Nolan Ryan 10.00 25.00
129 Mark McGwire 8.00 20.00

2014 Upper Deck Goodwin Champions Mini Green

*1-130 MINI GREEN: 1X TO 2.5X BASIC
COMMON CARD (131-180) .60 1.50
STATED ODDS 1:10 HOB/1:12 BLAST

2014 Upper Deck Goodwin Champions Autographs

GROUP A ODDS 1:54,400 HOBBY
GROUP B ODDS 1:6590 HOBBY
GROUP C ODDS 1:17,525 HOBBY
GROUP D ODDS 1:1280 HOBBY
GROUP E ODDS 1:410 HOBBY
GROUP F ODDS 1:135 HOBBY
GROUP G ODDS 1:42 HOBBY
'16 STATED ODDS 1:4352 HOBBY
AFT Frank Thomas D 40.00 80.00
AGA Steve Garvey F 6.00 15.00
AHO Bob Horner F 3.00 8.00
AKG Ken Griffey Jr. D 75.00 150.00
ANR Nolan Ryan C
ARC Roger Clemens
ARO Pete Rose C
ARV Robin Ventura F 5.00 12.00

2014 Upper Deck Goodwin Champions Goudey

COMPLETE SET (52) 25.00 60.00
BB ODDS 1:13 HOB/1:32 BLAST
BK ODDS 1:25 HOB/1:60 BLAST
FB ODDS 1:25 HOB/1:60 BLAST
HK ODDS 1:33 HOB/1:80 BLAST
GOLF ODDS 1:33 HOB/1:80 BLAST
MISC SPORT ODDS 1:100 HOB/1:240 BLAST
HISTORY ODDS 1:40 HOB/1:96 BLAST
1 Will Clark .50 1.25
2 Mark McGwire 1.25 3.00
3 Ken Griffey Jr. 1.25 3.00
4 Nolan Ryan 2.00 5.00
5 Johnny Bench .60 1.50
6 Reggie Jackson .50 1.25
7 Carlton Fisk .50 1.25
8 Mike Schmidt 1.00 2.50
9 Paul O'Neill .50 1.25
10 Edgar Martinez .50 1.25

2014 Upper Deck Goodwin Champions Goudey Autographs

GROUP A ODDS 1:7200 HOBBY
GROUP B ODDS 1:4800 HOBBY
GROUP C ODDS 1:1650 HOBBY
GROUP D ODDS 1:1200 HOBBY
'16 GROUP A ODDS 1:21,760 HOBBY
'16 GROUP B ODDS 1:8369 HOBBY
2 Mark McGwire C 100.00 200.00
3 Ken Griffey Jr. B 90.00 150.00
5 Johnny Bench C 20.00 50.00
6 Reggie Jackson C 15.00 40.00
7 Carlton Fisk D 12.00 30.00
8 Mike Schmidt C 20.00 50.00
9 Paul O'Neill D 12.00 30.00
10 Edgar Martinez D 20.00 50.00

2014 Upper Deck Goodwin Champions Memorabilia

GROUP A ODDS 1:5140
GROUP B ODDS 1:685
GROUP C ODDS 1:80
GROUP D ODDS 1:18
MGR Jonathan Gray D 2.50 6.00
MJG Joey Gallo D 2.50 6.00
MMZ Micker Adolfo Zapata D 4.00 10.00
MOS Roberto Osuna D 2.50 6.00
MPE Joc Pederson D 3.00 8.00

2014 Upper Deck Goodwin Champions Memorabilia Premium

*PREMIUM: .75X TO 2X BASIC
RANDOM INSERTS IN PACKS
PRINT RUNS B/WN 10-50 COPIES PER
NO PRICING ON QTY 15 OR LESS
MGR Jonathan Gray/50 5.00 12.00
MMG Marten Gasparini/50

2014 Upper Deck Goodwin Champions Sport Royalty Autographs

GROUP A ODDS 1:17,130 HOBBY
GROUP B ODDS 1:4670 HOBBY
GROUP C ODDS 1:2855 HOBBY
GROUP D ODDS 1:1070 HOBBY
'16 GROUP A ODDS 1:21,760 HOBBY
'16 GROUP B ODDS 1:5440 HOBBY
SRAKG Ken Griffey Jr. C 75.00 150.00
SRAMM Mark McGwire A

2015 Upper Deck Goodwin Champions

COMPLETE SET w/o AU's(150) 25.00 60.00
COMPLETE SET w/o SP's(100) 6.00 15.00
131-155 SP ODDS APPX. 1:3 PACKS
156-180 SP ODDS 1:8 PACKS
GROUP A AU ODDS 1:755 PACKS
GROUP B AU ODDS 1:65 PACKS
PRINTING PLATES RANDOMLY INSERTED
PLATE PRINT RUN 1 SET PER COLOR
BLACK-CYAN-MAGENTA-YELLOW ISSUED
NO PLATE PRICING DUE TO SCARCITY
EXCHNAGE DEADLINE 6/10/2017
3 John McGraw .15 .40
46 Kenesaw Landis .15 .40
47 Mark McGwire .50 1.25
48 Nolan Ryan .75 2.00
70 Candy Cummings .15 .40
82 Ken Griffey Jr. .50 1.25
93 Eddie Plank .15 .40
95 Roger Bresnahan .15 .40
119 Mark McGwire SP 1.50 4.00
129 Ken Griffey Jr. SP 2.00 5.00
137 Nolan Ryan SP 3.00 8.00
151 D.Dahl AU A EXCH 5.00 12.00
152 Michael Feliz AU B 2.50 6.00
153 Austin Meadows AU B 4.00 10.00
154 Colin Moran AU B 2.50 6.00
155 Sean Newcomb AU B 2.50 6.00
156 Jose Berrios AU B 3.00 8.00
157 Rob Kaminsky AU B 2.50 6.00
158 Blake Snell AU B 2.50 6.00
159 Raimel Tapia AU B 2.50 6.00
160 Matt Olson AU B 4.00 10.00
161 J.Thompson AU A EXCH 5.00 12.00
162 Jorge Mateo AU B 4.00 10.00
163 D.Garcia AU A EXCH 5.00 12.00
165 Bobby Bradley AU B 2.50 6.00

2015 Upper Deck Goodwin Champions Mini

*MINI 1-100: 1X TO 2.5X BASIC
*MINI 101-125: .3X TO .75X BASIC
*MINI 126-150: .25X TO .6X BASIC
STATED ODDS THREE PER BOX

2015 Upper Deck Goodwin Champions Mini Canvas

*CANVAS 1-100: 2X TO 5X BASIC
*CANVAS 101-125: .6X TO 1.5X BASIC
*CANVAS 126-150: .5X TO 1.2X BASIC
RANDOM INSERTS IN PACKS
ANNCD PRINT RUN OF 99 COPIES PER

2015 Upper Deck Goodwin Champions Mini Cloth Lady Luck

*LUCK 1-100: 2.5X TO 6X BASIC
*LUCK 101-125: .75X TO 2X BASIC
*LUCK 126-150: .6X TO 1.5X BASIC
RANDOM INSERTS IN PACKS
STATED PRINT RUN 50 SER.#'d SETS

2015 Upper Deck Goodwin Champions Mini Leather Magician

*MAGICIAN 1-100: 6X TO 15X BASIC
*MAGICIAN 101-125: 2X TO 5X BASIC
*MAGICIAN 126-150: 1.5X TO 4X BASIC
RANDOM INSERTS IN PACKS
STATED PRINT RUN 15 SER.#'d SETS

2015 Upper Deck Goodwin Champions Autographs

GROUP A ODDS 1:6830 PACKS
GROUP B ODDS 1:780 PACKS
GROUP C ODDS 1:685 PACKS
GROUP D ODDS 1:350 PACKS
GROUP E ODDS 1:150 PACKS
GROUP F ODDS 1:65 PACKS
'16 GROUP A ODDS 1:14,836 PACKS
'16 GROUP B ODDS 1:1106 PACKS
EXCHANGE DEADLINE 6/10/2017
ANR Nolan Ryan A EXCH

2015 Upper Deck Goodwin Champions Autographs Black and White

GROUP A ODDS 1:24,800 PACKS
GROUP B ODDS 1:7630 PACKS
GROUP C ODDS 1:5670 PACKS
GROUP D ODDS 1:6615 PACKS
OVERALL B/W ODDS 1:2000 PACKS
EXCHANGE DEADLINE 6/10/2017
126 Nolan Ryan A
142 Mark McGwire B

2015 Upper Deck Goodwin Champions Autographs Inscriptions

RANDOM INSERTS IN PACKS
PRINT RUNS B/WN 2-298 COPIES PER
NO PRICING ON QTY 16 OR LESS
EXCHANGE DEADLINE 6/10/2017

2015 Upper Deck Goodwin Champions Goudey

COMPLETE SET (60) 15.00 40.00
1-40 STATED ODDS 1:5 PACKS
41-60 STATED ODDS 1:20 PACKS
6 Ken Griffey Jr. 1.25 3.00

2015 Upper Deck Goodwin Champions Goudey Sport Royalty Autographs

GROUP A ODDS 1:1:24,960 PACKS
GROUP B ODDS 1:9985 PACKS
GROUP C ODDS 1:3995 PACKS
OVERALL GOUDEY ODDS 1:2560 PACKS
'16 STATED ODDS 1:32,640 HOBBY
EXCHANGE DEADLINE 6/10/2017
SRALB Larry Bird

2015 Upper Deck Goodwin Champions Memorabilia

GROUP A ODDS 1:1420 PACKS
GROUP B ODDS 1:175 PACKS
GROUP C ODDS 1:28 PACKS
MBE Jose Berrios Shirt C 2.50 6.00
MRT Raimel Tapia Shirt C 2.50 6.00

2015 Upper Deck Goodwin Champions Memorabilia Premium Series

*PREMIUM: .6X TO 1.5X BASIC
RANDOM INSERTS IN PACKS
PRINT RUNS B/WN 10-75 COPIES PER
NO PRICING ON QTY 15 OR LESS

2016 Upper Deck Goodwin Champions

COMPLETE SET w/o SP's(100) 6.00 15.00
101-150 SP ODDS 1:4 HOBBY
SP1 STATED ODDS 1:1280 HOBBY
PRINTING PLATES RANDOMLY INSERTED
PLATE PRINT RUN 1 SET PER COLOR
BLACK-CYAN-MAGENTA-YELLOW ISSUED
NO PLATE PRICING DUE TO SCARCITY
12 Tom Glavine .20 .50
62 Tom Glavine .20 .50
107 Tom Glavine BW SP .50 1.25

2016 Upper Deck Goodwin Champions Mini

*MINI 1-100: 1X TO 2.5X BASIC
*MINI BW 101-150: .4X TO 1X BASIC BW
STATED ODDS 1:4 HOBBY

2016 Upper Deck Goodwin Champions Mini Canvas

*CANVAS 1-100: 1.2X TO 3X BASIC
*CANVAS BW 101-150: .5X TO 1.2X BASIC BW
STATED ODDS 1:12 HOBBY

2016 Upper Deck Goodwin Champions Mini Cloth Lady Luck

*CLOTH 1-100: 5X TO 12X BASIC
*CLOTH BW 101-150: 2X TO 5X BASIC BW
RANDOM INSERTS IN PACKS
STATED PRINT RUN 25 SER.#'d SETS

2016 Upper Deck Goodwin Champions Goudey

COMPLETE SET (50) 12.00 30.00
STATED ODDS 1:4 PACKS
PRINTING PLATES RANDOMLY INSERTED
PLATE PRINT RUN 1 SET PER COLOR
BLACK-CYAN-MAGENTA-YELLOW ISSUED
NO PLATE PRICING DUE TO SCARCITY
35 Tom Glavine .40 1.00

2016 Upper Deck Goodwin Champions Goudey Autographs

GROUP A STATED ODDS 1:119,716 PACKS
GROUP B STATED ODDS 1:30,784 PACKS
GROUP C STATED ODDS 1:7280 PACKS
GROUP D STATED ODDS 1:1796 PACKS
GROUP E STATED ODDS 1:1247 PACKS
GROUP F STATED ODDS 1:630 PACKS
EXCHANGE DEADLINE 6/21/2018
GATG Tom Glavine D 10.00 25.00

2016 Upper Deck Goodwin Champions Goudey Sport Royalty Autographs

GROUP A STATED ODDS 1:200,192 PACKS
GROUP B STATED ODDS 1:52,682 PACKS
GROUP C STATED ODDS 1:19,627 PACKS
GROUP D STATED ODDS 1:3168 PACKS
EXCHANGE DEADLINE 6/21/2018
SRTG Tom Glavine D 12.00 30.00

2017 Upper Deck Goodwin Champions

COMPLETE SET w/o SP's(100) 6.00 15.00
101-150 SP ODDS 1:4 HOBBY
SP1 STATED ODDS 1:1280 HOBBY
PRINTING PLATES RANDOMLY INSERTED
PLATE PRINT RUN 1 SET PER COLOR
BLACK-CYAN-MAGENTA-YELLOW ISSUED
NO PLATE PRICING DUE TO SCARCITY
49 Kevin Maitan .25 1.00
99 Kevin Maitan .25 1.00
149 Kevin Maitan BW SP .60 1.50

2017 Upper Deck Goodwin Champions Mini

*MINI 1-100: .6X TO 1.5X BASIC
*MINI BW 101-150: .4X TO 1X BASIC BW
STATED ODDS 1:4 HOBBY

2017 Upper Deck Goodwin Champions Mini Canvas

*CANVAS 1-100: 1.2X TO 3X BASIC
*CANVAS BW 101-150: .75X TO 2X BASIC BW
RANDOM INSERTS IN PACKS

2017 Upper Deck Goodwin Champions Mini Cloth Lady Luck

*CLOTH 1-100: 5X TO 12X BASIC
*CLOTH BW 101-150: 3X TO 8X BASIC BW
RANDOM INSERTS IN PACKS
STATED PRINT RUN 25 SER.#'d SETS

2017 Upper Deck Goodwin Champions Autographs

GROUP A 1:25,933 HOBBY
GROUP B 1:4914 HOBBY
GROUP C 1:3154 HOBBY
GROUP D 1:546 HOBBY
GROUP E 1:419 HOBBY
GROUP F 1:99 HOBBY
AKM Kevin Maitan F 8.00 20.00

2017 Upper Deck Goodwin Champions Autographs Inscriptions

RANDOM INSERTS IN PACKS
PRINT RUNS B/WN 5-650 COPIES PER
NO PRICING ON QTY 15 OR LESS
AKM Kevin Maitan/50 15.00 40.00

2017 Upper Deck Goodwin Champions Goudey

COMPLETE SET (25) 10.00 25.00
STATED ODDS 1:8 PACKS
PRINTING PLATES RANDOMLY INSERTED
PLATE PRINT RUN 1 SET PER COLOR
BLACK-CYAN-MAGENTA-YELLOW ISSUED
NO PLATE PRICING DUE TO SCARCITY
G24 Kevin Maitan .75 2.00

2017 Upper Deck Goodwin Champions Goudey Memorabilia

STATED GROUP A ODDS 1:2,288 HOBBY
STATED GROUP B ODDS 1:161 HOBBY
*PREMIUM/35-65: .5X TO 1.2X BASIC
*PREMIUM/25: 1X TO 2.5X BASIC
GMKM Kevin Maitan B 2.50 6.00

2017 Upper Deck Goodwin Champions Memorabilia

STATED GROUP A ODDS 1:1,285 HOBBY
STATED GROUP B ODDS 1:1,573 HOBBY
STATED GROUP C ODDS 1:541 HOBBY
STATED GROUP D ODDS 1:198 HOBBY
STATED GROUP E ODDS 1:51 HOBBY
*PREMIUM/35-65: .5X TO 1.2X BASIC
*PREMIUM/25: 1X TO 2.5X BASIC
MKM Kevin Maitan E 2.50 6.00

2017 Upper Deck Goodwin Champions Memorabilia Dual Swatch

STATED GROUP A ODDS 1:4061 HOBBY
STATED GROUP B ODDS 1:1218 HOBBY
STATED GROUP C ODDS 1:1248 HOBBY
STATED GROUP D ODDS 1:435 HOBBY
*PREMIUM/25: 1X TO 2.5X BASIC
M2KM Kevin Maitan D 2.50 6.00

2018 Upper Deck Goodwin Champions Autographs

GROUP A 1:107,323 HOBBY
GROUP B 1:53,661 HOBBY
GROUP C 1:17,887 HOBBY
GROUP D 1:3960 HOBBY
GROUP E 1:1239 HOBBY
GROUP F 1:715 HOBBY
GROUP G 1:390 HOBBY
GROUP H 1:236 HOBBY
GROUP I 1:101 HOBBY
ASO Shohei Ohtani B 300.00 600.00

2018 Upper Deck Goodwin Champions Autographs Inscriptions

RANDOM INSERTS IN PACKS
PRINT RUNS B/WN 5-53 COPIES PER
NO PRICING ON QTY 15 OR LESS

2018 Upper Deck Goodwin Champions Goudey Autographs

GROUP A 1:110,880 HOBBY
GROUP B 1:20,921 HOBBY
GROUP C 1:11,314 HOBBY
GROUP D 1:1724 HOBBY
GROUP E 1:736 HOBBY
GASO Shohei Ohtani B 150.00 300.00

2018 Upper Deck Goodwin Champions Goudey Sport Royalty Autographs

GROUP A ODDS 1:116,880 HOBBY
GROUP B ODDS 1:8588 HOBBY
NO GROUP A PRICING DUE TO SCARCITY

2018 Upper Deck Goodwin Champions Splash of Color Autographs

GROUP A ODDS 1:211,200 HOBBY
GROUP B ODDS 1:15,304 HOBBY
GROUP C RANDOMLY INSERTED
GROUP D ODDS 1:10,667 HOBBY
GROUP E ODDS 1:8123 HOBBY
GROUP F ODDS 1:4735 HOBBY
GROUP G ODDS 1:3771 HOBBY
NO GROUP A PRICING DUE TO SCARCITY
SCASO Shohei Ohtani B 300.00 600.00

2019 Upper Deck Goodwin Champions

COMPLETE SET (150) 12.00 30.00
COMPLETE SET w/o SP's(100) 6.00 15.00
101-150 SP ODDS 1:4 HOBBY
PRINTING PLATES RANDOMLY INSERTED
PLATE PRINT RUN 1 SET PER COLOR
BLACK-CYAN-MAGENTA-YELLOW ISSUED
NO PLATE PRICING DUE TO SCARCITY
49 Victor Robles .30 .75
99 Victor Robles .30 .75
149 Victor Robles SP .50 1.25

2019 Upper Deck Goodwin Champions Goudey

COMPLETE SET (50) 10.00 25.00
STATED ODDS 1:4 HOBBY
PRINTING PLATES RANDOMLY INSERTED
PLATE PRINT RUN 1 SET PER COLOR
BLACK-CYAN-MAGENTA-YELLOW ISSUED
NO PLATE PRICING DUE TO SCARCITY
*MINI: .5X TO 1.2X BASIC
*MINI WOOD: .75X TO 2X BASIC
G47 Victor Robles .40 1.00

2019 Upper Deck Goodwin Champions Goudey Memorabilia

GMVR Victor Robles D

2019 Upper Deck Goodwin Champions Splash of Color Autographs

SCAVR Victor Robles

2019 Upper Deck Goodwin Champions Memorabilia

MVR Victor Robles C

2019 Upper Deck Goodwin Champions Mini

*MINI 1-100: .6X TO 1.5X BASIC
APPX. ODDS 1:4 HOBBY

2019 Upper Deck Goodwin Champions Mini Wood Lumberjack

*MINI WOOD 1-100: 1X TO 2.5X BASIC
APPX. ODDS 1:20 HOBBY, 1:20 EPACK

2019 Upper Deck Goodwin Champions Splash of Color 3D

LSVR Victor Robles T2

2019 Upper Deck Goodwin Champions Splash of Color Memorabilia

SMVR Victor Robles B

2020 Upper Deck Goodwin Champions

101-150 SP ODDS 1:4 HOBBY
PRINTING PLATES RANDOMLY INSERTED
PLATE PRINT RUN 1 SET PER COLOR
NO PLATE PRICING DUE TO SCARCITY
7 Casey Mize .60 1.50
30 Wander Franco 2.00 5.00
45 Jasson Dominguez 2.50 6.00
57 Casey Mize .60 1.50
80 Wander Franco 2.00 5.00
95 Jasson Dominguez 2.50 6.00
107 Casey Mize 1.00 2.50
130 Wander Franco 3.00 8.00
145 Jasson Dominguez 4.00 10.00

2020 Upper Deck Goodwin Champions '11 Goodwin Champions

RANDOM INSERTS IN PACKS
30 Wander Franco 10.00 25.00
45 Jasson Dominguez 25.00 60.00

2020 Upper Deck Goodwin Champions Autographs

GROUP A ODDS 1:35,401 HOBBY
GROUP B ODDS 1:25,287 HOBBY
GROUP C ODDS 1:6627 HOBBY
GROUP D ODDS 1:1535 HOBBY
GROUP E ODDS 1:981 HOBBY
GROUP F ODDS 1:284 HOBBY
GROUP G ODDS 1:146 HOBBY
GROUP H ODDS 1:129 HOBBY
EXCHANGE DEADLINE 12/31/22
ACM Casey Mize E 15.00 40.00
AJD Jasson Dominguez C 100.00 250.00
AWF Wander Franco D EXCH 40.00 100.00

2020 Upper Deck Goodwin Champions Autographs Inscriptions

INSCRIPTION/75-200: .6X TO 1.5X BASIC
INSCRIPTION/25: .75X TO 2X BASIC
RANDOM INSERTS IN PACKS
PRINT RUNS B/WN 25-200 COPIES PER
EXCHANGE DEADLINE 12/31/22
AJD Jasson Dominguez Martian/20 300.00 600.00

2020 Upper Deck Goodwin Champions Dual Swatch Memorabilia

STATED ODDS 1:300 HOBBY; 1:600 EPACK
M2CM Casey Mize 4.00 10.00

2020 Upper Deck Goodwin Champions Dual Swatch Memorabilia Premium

PREMIUM/35: .8X TO 2X BASIC
RANDOM INSERTS IN PACKS
STATED PRINT RUN 35 SER.#'d SETS

2020 Upper Deck Goodwin Champions Fanimation

STATED ODDS 1:2540 HOBBY; 1:2540 EPACK
F7 Wander Franco 40.00 100.00

2020 Upper Deck Goodwin Champions Goudey

STATED ODDS 1:4 HOBBY; 1:4 EPACK
*MINI 1-100: .5X TO 1.2X BASIC
*MINI WOOD 1-100: .75X TO 2X BASIC
G7 Casey Mize .75 2.00
G30 Wander Franco 2.50 6.00
G45 Jasson Dominguez 3.00 8.00

2020 Upper Deck Goodwin Champions Goudey Autographs

GROUP A ODDS 1:7842 HOBBY
GROUP B ODDS 1:1511 HOBBY
EXCHANGE DEADLINE 12/31/22
GAJD Jasson Dominguez A 100.00 250.00

2020 Upper Deck Goodwin Champions Goudey Memorabilia

STATED ODDS 1:300 HOBBY; 1:600 EPACK
GMCM Casey Mize 4.00 10.00
GMJD Jasson Dominguez 8.00 20.00
GMWF Wander Franco 8.00 20.00

2020 Upper Deck Goodwin Champions Goudey Memorabilia Premium

PREMIUM/50: .8X TO 2X BASIC
RANDOM INSERTS IN PACKS
STATED PRINT RUN 50 SER.#'d SETS
GMJD Jasson Dominguez 20.00 50.00

2020 Upper Deck Goodwin Champions Goudey Sport Royalty Dual Swatch Memorabilia

STATED ODDS 1:2880 HOBBY; 1:2880 EPACK
SRM2WF Wander Franco 8.00 20.00

2020 Upper Deck Goodwin Champions Goudey Sport Royalty Memorabilia

STATED ODDS 1:300 HOBBY; 1:600 EPACK
SRMWF Wander Franco 8.00 20.00

2020 Upper Deck Goodwin Champions Horizontal Autographs

GROUP A ODDS 1:20,295 HOBBY
GROUP B ODDS 1:4832 HOBBY
GROUP C ODDS 1:2585 HOBBY
GROUP D ODDS 1:1532 HOBBY
GROUP E ODDS 1:782 HOBBY
GROUP F ODDS 1:385 HOBBY
EXCHANGE DEADLINE 12/31/22
HACM Casey Mize D 15.00 40.00
HAJD Jasson Dominguez C 100.00 250.00
HAWF Wander Franco C EXCH 40.00 100.00

2020 Upper Deck Goodwin Champions Memorabilia

GROUP A ODDS 1:29211 EXCH
GROUP B ODDS 1:2434 EXCH
GROUP C ODDS 1:2921 EXCH
GROUP D ODDS 1:2142 EXCH
GROUP E ODDS 1:42 EXCH
MCM Casey Mize E 4.00 10.00
MDO Jasson Dominguez E 8.00 20.00
MWF Wander Franco E 6.00 15.00

2020 Upper Deck Goodwin Champions Memorabilia Premium

PREMIUM/25-65: .8X TO 2X BASIC
RANDOM INSERTS IN PACKS
PRINT RUNS B/WN 25-65 COPIES PER
MDO Jasson Dominguez/65 20.00 50.00

2020 Upper Deck Goodwin Champions Splash of Color Autographs

GROUP A ODDS 1:44,742 HOBBY
GROUP B ODDS 1:4873 HOBBY
GROUP C ODDS 1:1806 HOBBY
EXCHANGE DEADLINE 12/31/22
SCACM Casey Mize B 15.00 40.00
SCAJD Jasson Dominguez A 100.00 250.00
SCAWF Wander Franco B EXCH 40.00 100.00

2020 Upper Deck Goodwin Champions Splash of Color Memorabilia

GROUP A ODDS 1:3351 HOBBY
GROUP B ODDS 1:1510 HOBBY
GROUP C ODDS 1:1416 HOBBY
SMJD Jasson Dominguez B 8.00 20.00
SMWF Wander Franco C 8.00 20.00

2020 Upper Deck Goodwin Champions Splash of Color Memorabilia Premium

PREMIUM/25: .8X TO 2X BASIC
RANDOM INSERTS IN PACKS
STATED PRINT RUN 25 SER.#'d SETS
SMJD Jasson Dominguez 40.00 100.00

2007 Upper Deck Goudey

COMP.SET w/o SPs (200) 20.00 50.00
COMMON CARD (1-200) .20 .50
COMMON ROOKIE (1-200) .30 .75
COMMON SP (201-240) 2.00 5.00
SP ODDS 1:6 HOBBY,1:6 RETAIL
1933 ORIGINALS ODDS TWO PER CASE
SEE 1933 GOUDEY PRICING FOR ORIGINALS
1 A.J. Burnett .20 .50
2 Aaron Boone .20 .50
3 Aaron Rowand .20 .50
4 Adam Dunn .30 .75
5 Adrian Beltre .50 1.25
6 Albert Pujols .60 1.50
7 Ivan Rodriguez .30 .75
8 Alfonso Soriano .30 .75
9 Andruw Jones .20 .50
10 Andy Pettitte .30 .75
11 Aramis Ramirez .20 .50
12 B.J. Upton .20 .50
13 Barry Zito .30 .75
14 Bartolo Colon .20 .50
15 Ben Sheets .20 .50
16 Bobby Abreu .20 .50
17 Bobby Crosby .20 .50
18 Brian Giles .20 .50
19 Brian Roberts .20 .50
20 C.C. Sabathia .30 .75
21 Carlos Beltran .30 .75
22 Carlos Delgado .20 .50
23 Carlos Lee .20 .50
24 Carlos Zambrano .30 .75
25 Chad Cordero .20 .50
26 Chad Tracy .20 .50
27 Chipper Jones .50 1.25
28 Craig Biggio .30 .75
29 Curt Schilling .30 .75
30 Danny Haren .20 .50
31 Darin Erstad .20 .50
32 David Ortiz .50 1.25
33 Billy Wagner .20 .50
34 Derek Jeter 1.25 3.00
35 Derek Lee .20 .50
36 Dontrelle Willis .20 .50
37 Edgar Renteria .20 .50
38 Eric Chavez .20 .50
39 Felix Hernandez .30 .75
40 Garret Anderson .20 .50
41 Garrett Atkins .20 .50
42 Gary Sheffield .20 .50
43 Grady Sizemore .30 .75
44 Greg Maddux .60 1.50
45 Hank Blalock .20 .50
46 Hanley Ramirez .30 .75
47 J.D. Drew .20 .50
48 Jacque Jones .20 .50
49 Jake Peavy .20 .50
50 Jake Westbrook .20 .50
51 Jason Bay .30 .75
52 Jason Giambi .20 .50
53 Jason Schmidt .20 .50
54 Jason Varitek .50 1.25
55 Troy Tulowitzki (RC) 1.00 2.50
56 Jeff Francoeur .50 1.25
57 Jeff Kent .20 .50
58 Jeremy Bonderman .20 .50
59 Jim Edmonds .30 .75
60 Jim Thome .30 .75
61 Jimmy Rollins .30 .75
62 Joe Mauer .40 1.00
63 Johan Santana .30 .75
64 John Smoltz .50 1.25
65 Johnny Damon .30 .75
66 Jose Reyes .30 .75
67 Josh Beckett .20 .50
68 Justin Morneau .30 .75
69 Ken Griffey Jr. 1.00 2.50
70 Kerry Wood .20 .50
71 Khalil Greene .20 .50
72 Lance Berkman .30 .75
73 Livan Hernandez .20 .50
74 Manny Ramirez .50 1.25
75 Mark Mulder .20 .50
76 Chase Utley .30 .75
77 Mark Teixeira .30 .75
78 Miguel Tejada .30 .75
79 Miguel Cabrera .50 1.25
80 Mike Piazza .50 1.25
81 Pat Burrell .20 .50
82 Paul LoDuca .20 .50
83 Pedro Martinez .30 .75
84 Prince Fielder .30 .75
85 Rafael Furcal .20 .50
86 Randy Johnson .50 1.25
87 Richie Sexson .20 .50
88 Robinson Cano .30 .75
89 Roy Halladay .30 .75
90 Roy Oswalt .30 .75
91 Scott Rolen .30 .75
92 Tim Hudson .30 .75
93 Todd Helton .30 .75
94 Tom Glavine .30 .75
95 Torii Hunter .20 .50
96 Travis Hafner .20 .50
97 Trevor Hoffman .30 .75
98 Vernon Wells .20 .50
99 Vladimir Guerrero .30 .75
100 Zach Duke .20 .50
101 Alex Rodriguez .60 1.50

102 Ryan Howard .40 1.00
103 Michael Barrett .20 .50
104 Ichiro Suzuki .60 1.50
105 Hideki Matsui .50 1.25
106 Jered Weaver .30 .75
107 Dan Uggla .20 .50
108 Ryan Freel .20 .50
109 Bill Hall .20 .50
110 Ray Durham .20 .50
111 Morgan Ensberg .20 .50
112 Shawn Green .20 .50
113 Brandon Webb .30 .75
114 Frank Thomas .50 1.25
115 Corey Patterson .20 .50
116 Edwin Encarnacion .50 1.25
117 Mike Cameron .20 .50
118 Matt Holliday .50 1.25
119 Jhonny Peralta .20 .50
120 Nick Swisher .30 .75
121 Brad Penny .20 .50
122 Kenji Johjima .50 1.25
123 Francisco Rodriguez .30 .75
124 Mark Teahen .20 .50
125 Jonathan Papelbon .50 1.25
126 Carlos Guillen .20 .50
127 Freddy Sanchez .20 .50
128 Chien-Ming Wang .30 .75
129 Andre Ethier .30 .75
130 Matt Cain .30 .75
131 Austin Kearns .20 .50
132 Ramon Hernandez .20 .50
133 Chris Carpenter .30 .75
134 Michael Cuddyer .20 .50
135 Stephen Drew .20 .50
136 David Wright .40 1.00
137 David DeJesus .20 .50
138 Gary Matthews .20 .50
139 Brandon Phillips .20 .50
140 Josh Barfield .20 .50
141 Alex Gordon RC 1.00 2.50
142 Scott Kazmir .30 .75
143 Luis Gonzalez .20 .50
144 Mike Sweeney .20 .50
145 Luis Castillo .20 .50
146 Huston Street .20 .50
147 Phil Hughes (RC) .75 2.00
148 Adrian Gonzalez .40 1.00
149 Raul Ibanez .30 .75
150 Joe Crede .20 .50
151 Mark Loretta .20 .50
152 Adam LaRoche (RC) .30 .75
153 Troy Glaus .20 .50
154 Conor Jackson .20 .50
155 Michael Young .20 .50
156 Scott Podsednik .20 .50
157 David Eckstein .20 .50
158 Mike Jacobs .20 .50
159 Nomar Garciaparra .30 .75
160 Mariano Rivera .60 1.50
161 Pedro Feliz .20 .50
162 Josh Hamilton (RC) 1.00 2.50
163 Ryan Langerhans .20 .50
164 Willy Taveras .20 .50
165 Carl Crawford .30 .75
166 Melvin Mora .20 .50
167 Francisco Liriano .20 .50
168 Orlando Cabrera .20 .50
169 Chris Duncan .20 .50
170 Johnny Estrada .20 .50
171 Ryan Zimmerman .30 .75
172 Rickie Weeks .20 .50
173 Paul Konerko .30 .75
174 Jack Wilson .20 .50
175 Jorge Posada .30 .75
176 Magglio Ordonez .30 .75
177 Nick Johnson .20 .50
178 Geoff Jenkins .20 .50
179 Reggie Sanders .20 .50
180 Moises Alou .20 .50
181 Glen Perkins (RC) .30 .75
182 Brad Lidge .20 .50
183 Kevin Kouzmanoff (RC) .30 .75
184 Jorge Cantu .20 .50
185 Carlos Quentin .20 .50
186 Rich Harden .20 .50
187 Jose Vidro .20 .50
188 Aaron Harang .20 .50
189 Noah Lowry .20 .50
190 Jermaine Dye .20 .50
191 Victor Martinez .30 .75
192 Chone Figgins .20 .50
193 Aubrey Huff .20 .50
194 Jason Isringhausen .20 .50
195 Brian McCann .20 .50
196 Juan Pierre .20 .50
197 Delmon Young (RC) .50 1.25
198 Felipe Lopez .20 .50
199 Brad Hawpe .20 .50
200 Justin Verlander .50 1.25
201 Mike Schmidt SP 4.00 10.00
202 Nolan Ryan SP 5.00 12.00
203 Cal Ripken Jr. SP 4.00 10.00
204 Harmon Killebrew SP 2.50 6.00
205 Reggie Jackson SP 2.50 6.00
206 Johnny Bench SP 2.50 6.00
207 Carlton Fisk SP 2.50 6.00
208 Yogi Berra SP 2.50 6.00
209 Al Kaline SP 2.50 6.00
210 Alan Trammell SP 2.00 5.00
211 Bill Mazeroski SP 2.50 6.00
212 Bob Gibson SP 2.50 6.00
213 Brooks Robinson SP 2.50 6.00
214 Carl Yastrzemski SP 3.00 8.00
215 Don Mattingly SP 5.00 12.00
216 Fergie Jenkins SP 2.00 5.00
217 Jim Rice SP 2.00 5.00
218 Lou Brock SP 2.50 6.00
219 Rod Carew SP 2.50 6.00
220 Stan Musial SP 3.00 8.00
221 Tom Seaver SP 2.50 6.00
222 Tony Gwynn SP 2.50 6.00
223 Wade Boggs SP 2.50 6.00
224 Alex Rodriguez SP 3.00 8.00
225 David Wright SP 3.00 8.00
226 Ryan Howard SP 3.00 8.00
227 Ichiro Suzuki SP 3.00 8.00
228 Ken Griffey Jr. SP 4.00 10.00
229 Daisuke Matsuzaka SP RC 4.00 10.00
230 Kei Igawa SP RC 2.50 6.00
231 Akinori Iwamura SP RC 3.00 8.00
232 Derek Jeter SP 4.00 10.00
233 Albert Pujols SP 4.00 10.00
234 Greg Maddux SP 3.00 8.00
235 David Ortiz SP 2.50 6.00
236 Manny Ramirez SP 2.50 6.00
237 Johan Santana SP 2.50 6.00
238 Pedro Martinez SP 2.50 6.00
239 Roger Clemens SP 4.00 10.00
240 Vladimir Guerrero SP 2.50 6.00

2007 Upper Deck Goudey Red Backs

COMPLETE SET (240) 20.00 50.00
*RED: .4X TO 1X BASIC
APPX. FOUR PER PACK
CARDS 201-240 DO NOT EXIST

2007 Upper Deck Goudey Diamond Stars Autographs

RANDOM INSERTS IN PACKS
STATED PRINT RUN 1 SER.#'d SET
NO PRICING DUE TO SCARCITY

2007 Upper Deck Goudey Goudey Graphs

STATED ODDS 1:24 HOB, 1:2500 RET
EXCH DEADLINE 8/7/2010
SP INFO PROVIDED BY UPPER DECK
AC Alberto Callaspo 3.00 8.00
AH Aaron Harang 6.00 15.00
AM Andy Marte 3.00 8.00
AR Aaron Rowand 6.00 15.00
BA Brian Anderson 3.00 8.00
BB Brian Bannister 6.00 15.00
BO Boof Bonser 6.00 15.00
BU B.J. Upton 5.00 12.00
CC Carl Crawford 4.00 10.00
CL Cliff Lee 4.00 10.00
CO Coco Crisp 6.00 15.00
CY Chris Young 3.00 8.00
DJ Derek Jeter 125.00 250.00
FH Felix Hernandez 12.50 30.00
GA Garrett Atkins 5.00 12.00
GP Glen Perkins 3.00 8.00
HA Bill Hall 5.00 12.00
HI Rich Hill 3.00 8.00
HR Hanley Ramirez 3.00 8.00
JB Jason Bay 6.00 15.00
JM Joe Mauer 15.00 40.00
JW Jered Weaver 6.00 15.00
JZ Joel Zumaya 6.00 15.00
KG Ken Griffey Jr. 60.00 120.00
KJ Kelly Johnson 3.00 8.00
KK Kevin Kouzmanoff 3.00 8.00
LS Luke Scott 3.00 8.00
MJ Mike Jacobs 3.00 8.00
MO Justin Morneau 6.00 15.00
RA Reggie Abercrombie 3.00 8.00
RT Ryan Theriot 3.00 8.00
RZ Ryan Zimmerman 6.00 15.00
SA Anibal Sanchez 3.00 8.00
SK Scott Kazmir 8.00 20.00
TB Taylor Buchholz 3.00 8.00
VM Victor Martinez 3.00 8.00

2007 Upper Deck Goudey Heads Up

CARDS 1-24 ODDS 1:10 HOB, 1:10 RET
CARDS 25-48 ODDS 1:10 HOB, 1:10 RET
241 Ken Griffey Jr. 4.00 10.00
242 Derek Jeter 5.00 12.00
243 Ichiro Suzuki 3.00 8.00
244 Cal Ripken Jr. 5.00 12.00
245 Daisuke Matsuzaka 4.00 10.00
246 Kei Igawa 2.50 6.00
247 Joe Mauer 2.00 5.00
248 Babe Ruth 4.00 10.00
249 Johnny Bench 2.50 6.00
250 Reggie Jackson 2.50 6.00
251 Carlton Fisk 2.50 6.00
252 Albert Pujols 4.00 10.00
253 Nolan Ryan 5.00 12.00
254 Ryan Howard 3.00 8.00
255 Mike Schmidt 3.00 8.00
256 Brooks Robinson 2.50 6.00
257 Harmon Killebrew 2.50 6.00
258 Alex Rodriguez 3.00 8.00
259 David Ortiz 2.50 6.00
260 David Wright 3.00 8.00
261 Al Kaline 2.50 6.00
262 Justin Verlander 2.50 6.00
263 Chase Utley 2.50 6.00
264 Justin Morneau 2.00 5.00
265 Ken Griffey Jr. 4.00 10.00
266 Derek Jeter 5.00 12.00
267 Ichiro Suzuki 3.00 8.00
268 Cal Ripken Jr. 5.00 12.00
269 Daisuke Matsuzaka 4.00 10.00
270 Kei Igawa 2.50 6.00
271 Joe Mauer 2.00 5.00
272 Babe Ruth 4.00 10.00
273 Johnny Bench 2.50 6.00
274 Reggie Jackson 2.50 6.00
275 Carlton Fisk 2.50 6.00
276 Albert Pujols 4.00 10.00
277 Nolan Ryan 5.00 12.00
278 Ryan Howard 3.00 8.00
279 Mike Schmidt 3.00 8.00
280 Brooks Robinson 2.50 6.00
281 Harmon Killebrew 2.50 6.00
282 Alex Rodriguez 3.00 8.00
283 David Ortiz 2.50 6.00
284 David Wright 3.00 8.00
285 Al Kaline 2.50 6.00
286 Justin Verlander 2.50 6.00
287 Chase Utley 2.50 6.00
288 Justin Morneau 2.00 5.00

2007 Upper Deck Goudey Immortals Memorabilia

STATED ODDS 1:288 HOB,1:960 RET
IAD Adam Dunn 5.00 12.00
IAJ Andruw Jones 6.00 15.00
IAK Al Kaline 8.00 20.00
IAP Albert Pujols 15.00 40.00
IAS Alfonso Soriano 5.00 12.00
IBR Babe Ruth 250.00 400.00
ICD Carlos Delgado 5.00 12.00
ICF Carlton Fisk 6.00 15.00
ICJ Chipper Jones 8.00 20.00
ICL Roger Clemens 12.50 30.00
ICR Cal Ripken Jr. 20.00 50.00
ICS Curt Schilling 6.00 15.00
IDJ Derek Jeter 20.00 50.00
IDO David Ortiz 8.00 20.00
IDW Dontrelle Willis 5.00 12.00
IGL Tom Glavine 6.00 15.00
IGM Greg Maddux 12.50 30.00
IGS Gary Sheffield 5.00 12.00
IHE Todd Helton 6.00 15.00
IHK Harmon Killebrew 12.50 30.00
IIR Ivan Rodriguez 6.00 15.00
IJB Johnny Bench 8.00 20.00
IJD Joe DiMaggio 50.00 100.00
IJE Jim Edmonds 6.00 15.00
IJG Jason Giambi 5.00 12.00
IJM Justin Morneau 5.00 12.00
IJO Randy Johnson 6.00 15.00
IJR Jose Reyes 6.00 15.00
IJS John Smoltz 6.00 15.00
IJT Jim Thome 6.00 15.00
IKG Ken Griffey Jr. 30.00 60.00
ILB Lance Berkman 5.00 12.00
IMP Mike Piazza 8.00 20.00
IMR Manny Ramirez 6.00 15.00
IMS Mike Schmidt 15.00 40.00
INR Nolan Ryan 20.00 50.00
IPM Pedro Martinez 6.00 15.00
IRJ Reggie Jackson 6.00 15.00
ISA Johan Santana 6.00 15.00
ITH Trevor Hoffman 5.00 12.00
IVG Vladimir Guerrero 6.00 15.00
IYB Yogi Berra 15.00 40.00

2007 Upper Deck Goudey Memorabilia

STATED ODDS 1:24 HOBBY, 1:24 RETAIL
1 A.J. Burnett 1.25 3.00
2 Aaron Boone 1.25 3.00
3 Aaron Rowand 1.25 3.00
4 Adam Dunn 2.00 5.00
5 Adrian Beltre 3.00 8.00
6 Albert Pujols 4.00 10.00
7 Ivan Rodriguez 2.00 5.00
8 Alfonso Soriano 2.00 5.00
9 Andruw Jones 1.25 3.00
10 Andy Pettitte 2.00 5.00
11 Aramis Ramirez 1.25 3.00
12 B.J. Upton 1.25 3.00
13 Barry Zito 2.00 5.00
14 Bartolo Colon 1.25 3.00
15 Ben Sheets 1.25 3.00
16 Bobby Abreu 1.25 3.00
17 Bobby Crosby 1.25 3.00
18 Brian Giles 1.25 3.00
19 Brian Roberts 1.25 3.00
20 C.C. Sabathia 2.00 5.00
21 Carlos Beltran 2.00 5.00
22 Carlos Delgado 1.25 3.00
23 Carlos Lee 1.25 3.00
24 Carlos Zambrano 2.00 5.00
26 Chad Tracy 1.25 3.00
27 Chipper Jones 3.00 8.00
28 Craig Biggio 2.00 5.00
29 Curt Schilling 2.00 5.00
31 Darin Erstad 1.25 3.00
32 David Ortiz 3.00 8.00
33 Billy Wagner 1.25 3.00
34 Derek Jeter 8.00 20.00
35 Derek Lee 1.25 3.00
36 Dontrelle Willis 1.25 3.00
37 Edgar Renteria 1.25 3.00
38 Eric Chavez 1.25 3.00
39 Felix Hernandez 2.00 5.00
40 Garret Anderson 1.25 3.00
41 Garrett Atkins 1.25 3.00
42 Gary Sheffield 1.25 3.00
43 Grady Sizemore 2.00 5.00
44 Greg Maddux 4.00 10.00
45 Hank Blalock 1.25 3.00
46 Hanley Ramirez 2.00 5.00
47 J.D. Drew 1.25 3.00
49 Jake Peavy 1.25 3.00
50 Jake Westbrook 1.25 3.00
51 Jason Bay 2.00 5.00
52 Jason Giambi 1.25 3.00
54 Jason Varitek 3.00 8.00
56 Jeff Francoeur 3.00 8.00
57 Jeff Kent 1.25 3.00
58 Jeremy Bonderman 1.25 3.00
59 Jim Edmonds 2.00 5.00
60 Jim Thome 2.00 5.00
61 Jimmy Rollins 2.00 5.00
62 Joe Mauer 2.50 6.00
63 Johan Santana 2.00 5.00
64 John Smoltz 3.00 8.00
66 Jose Reyes 2.00 5.00
67 Josh Beckett 1.25 3.00
68 Justin Morneau 2.00 5.00
69 Ken Griffey Jr. 6.00 15.00
70 Kerry Wood 1.25 3.00
71 Khalil Greene 1.25 3.00
72 Lance Berkman 2.00 5.00
73 Livan Hernandez 1.25 3.00
74 Manny Ramirez 3.00 8.00
75 Mark Mulder 1.25 3.00
76 Chase Utley 2.00 5.00
77 Mark Teixeira 2.00 5.00
78 Miguel Tejada 2.00 5.00
79 Miguel Cabrera 3.00 8.00
80 Mike Piazza 3.00 8.00
81 Pat Burrell 1.25 3.00
82 Paul LoDuca 1.25 3.00
83 Pedro Martinez 2.00 5.00
84 Prince Fielder 2.00 5.00
85 Rafael Furcal 1.25 3.00
86 Randy Johnson 3.00 8.00
87 Richie Sexson 1.25 3.00
88 Robinson Cano 2.00 5.00
89 Roy Halladay 2.00 5.00
90 Roy Oswalt 2.00 5.00
91 Scott Rolen 2.00 5.00
92 Tim Hudson 2.00 5.00
93 Todd Helton 2.00 5.00
94 Tom Glavine 2.00 5.00
95 Torii Hunter 1.25 3.00
96 Travis Hafner 1.25 3.00
97 Trevor Hoffman 2.00 5.00
98 Vernon Wells 1.25 3.00
99 Vladimir Guerrero 2.00 5.00
100 Zach Duke 1.25 3.00

2007 Upper Deck Goudey Sport Royalty

ONE PER HOBBY BOX LOADER
AI Akinori Iwamura 5.00 12.00
AP Albert Pujols 5.00 12.00
AS Alfonso Soriano 4.00 10.00
CC Chris Carpenter 4.00 10.00
CR Cal Ripken Jr. 12.50 30.00
DJ Derek Jeter 10.00 25.00
DM Daisuke Matsuzaka 8.00 20.00
DO David Ortiz 4.00 10.00
DS Dean Smith 2.00 5.00
ES Emmitt Smith 4.00 10.00
GH Gordie Howe 12.50 30.00
GM Greg Maddux 3.00 8.00
HI Martina Hingis 3.00 8.00
HR Hanley Ramirez 3.00 8.00
JM Justin Morneau 2.00 5.00
JN Joe Namath 6.00 15.00
JV Justin Verlander 2.00 5.00
JW John Wooden 3.00 8.00
KB Kobe Bryant 6.00 15.00
KD Kevin Durant 15.00 40.00
KG Ken Griffey Jr. 6.00 15.00
KH Katie Hoff 3.00 8.00
KI Kei Igawa 3.00 8.00
LE Jeanette Lee 12.00 30.00
LJ LeBron James 15.00 40.00
LT LaDainian Tomlinson 3.00 8.00
MH Mia Hamm 10.00 25.00
MJ Michael Jordan 20.00 50.00
NR Nolan Ryan 15.00 40.00
PI Mike Piazza 5.00 12.00
PM Peyton Manning 5.00 12.00
RH Roy Halladay 2.00 5.00
RJ Randy Johnson 3.00 8.00
RL Ryan Lochte 4.00 10.00
SA Johan Santana 3.00 8.00
SC Sidney Crosby 12.50 30.00
TH Trevor Hoffman 3.00 8.00
TW Tiger Woods 30.00 60.00
VG Vladimir Guerrero 3.00 8.00

2007 Upper Deck Goudey Sport Royalty Autographs

STATED ODDS TWO PER CASE
FOUND IN HOBBY BOX LOADER PACKS
EXCH DEADLINE 8/8/2009
AI Akinori Iwamura 10.00 25.00
CR Cal Ripken Jr. 300.00 400.00
DJ Derek Jeter 200.00 400.00
DM Daisuke Matsuzaka 30.00 60.00
GH Gordie Howe 50.00 100.00
HI Martina Hingis 100.00 200.00
HR Hanley Ramirez 10.00 25.00
JM Justin Morneau 10.00 25.00
JV Justin Verlander 60.00 120.00
JW John Wooden 100.00 200.00
KD Kevin Durant 400.00 800.00
KG Ken Griffey Jr. 75.00 150.00
KH Katie Hoff 20.00 50.00
KI Kei Igawa 10.00 25.00
LE Jeanette Lee 60.00 120.00
LJ LeBron James 400.00 800.00
LT LaDainian Tomlinson 40.00 80.00
MH Mia Hamm 50.00 100.00
MJ Michael Jordan 2500.00 5000.00
PM Peyton Manning 100.00 175.00
RH Roy Halladay 30.00 60.00
RJ Randy Johnson 125.00 250.00
RL Ryan Lochte 100.00 175.00
SC Sidney Crosby 175.00 300.00

2008 Upper Deck Goudey

COMP.SET w/o HIGH #s (200) 20.00 50.00
COMMON CARD (1-200) .20 .50
COMMON ROOKIE (1-200) .30 .75
COMMON SP (201-230) 2.00 5.00
COMMON SP (231-250) 1.50 4.00
COMMON SP (251-270) 2.00 5.00
COMMON CARD (271-300) 2.00 5.00
COMMON CARD (301-330) 3.00 8.00
1 Eric Byrnes .20 .50
2 Randy Johnson .50 1.25
3 Brandon Webb .30 .75
4 Dan Haren .20 .50
5 Chris B. Young .20 .50
6 Max Scherzer RC 3.00 8.00
7 Mark Teixeira .30 .75
8 John Smoltz .50 1.25
9 Jeff Francoeur .30 .75
10 Phil Niekro .30 .75
11 Chipper Jones .50 1.25
12 Kelly Johnson .20 .50
13 Tom Glavine .30 .75
14 Yunel Escobar .20 .50
15 Erik Bedard .20 .50
16 Melvin Mora .20 .50
17 Brian Roberts .20 .50
18 Eddie Murray .30 .75
19 Jim Palmer .30 .75
20 Jeremy Guthrie .20 .50
21 Nick Markakis .40 1.00
22 David Ortiz .50 1.25
23 Manny Ramirez .50 1.25
24 Josh Beckett .20 .50
25 Dustin Pedroia .50 1.25
26 Bobby Doerr .30 .75
27 Clay Buchholz (RC) .50 1.25
28 Daisuke Matsuzaka .30 .75
29 Jonathan Papelbon .30 .75
30 Kevin Youkilis .20 .50
31 Pee Wee Reese .30 .75
32 Billy Williams .30 .75
33 Alfonso Soriano .30 .75
34 Derrek Lee .20 .50
35 Rich Hill .20 .50
36 Kosuke Fukudome RC 1.00 2.50
37 Aramis Ramirez .20 .50
38 Carlos Zambrano .30 .75
39 Luis Aparicio .30 .75
40 Mark Buehrle .30 .75
41 Orlando Cabrera .30 .75
42 Paul Konerko .30 .75
43 Jermaine Dye .20 .50
44 Jim Thome .30 .75
45 Nick Swisher .30 .75
46 Sparky Anderson .30 .75
47 Johnny Bench .50 1.25
48 Joe Morgan .30 .75
49 Tony Perez .30 .75
50 Adam Dunn .30 .75
51 Aaron Harang .20 .50
52 Brandon Phillips .20 .50
53 Edwin Encarnacion .50 1.25
54 Ken Griffey Jr. 1.00 2.50
55 Larry Doby .30 .75
56 Bob Feller .30 .75
57 C.C. Sabathia .30 .75
58 Travis Hafner .20 .50
59 Grady Sizemore .30 .75
60 Fausto Carmona .20 .50
61 Victor Martinez .30 .75
62 Brad Hawpe .20 .50
63 Todd Helton .30 .75
64 Garrett Atkins .20 .50
65 Troy Tulowitzki .50 1.25
66 Matt Holliday .50 1.25
67 Jeff Francis .20 .50
68 Justin Verlander .50 1.25
69 Curtis Granderson .30 .75
70 Miguel Cabrera .50 1.25
71 Gary Sheffield .20 .50
72 Magglio Ordonez .30 .75
73 Jack Morris .30 .75
74 Andrew Miller .30 .75
75 Clayton Kershaw RC 10.00 25.00
76 Dan Uggla .20 .50
77 Hanley Ramirez .30 .75
78 Jeremy Hermida .20 .50
79 Josh Willingham .30 .75
80 Lance Berkman .30 .75
81 Roy Oswalt .30 .75
82 Miguel Tejada .30 .75
83 Hunter Pence .30 .75
84 Carlos Lee .20 .50
85 J.R. Towles RC .50 1.25
86 Brian Bannister .20 .50
87 Luke Hochevar RC .50 1.25
88 Billy Butler .20 .50
89 Alex Gordon .30 .75
90 Kelvim Escobar .30 .75
91 John Lackey .30 .75
92 Chone Figgins .20 .50
93 Jered Weaver .30 .75
94 Torii Hunter .20 .50
95 Vladimir Guerrero .30 .75
96 Brad Penny .20 .50
97 James Loney .20 .50
98 Andruw Jones .20 .50
99 Chad Billingsley .30 .75
100 Chin-Lung Hu (RC) .30 .75
101 Russell Martin .20 .50
102 Eddie Mathews .50 1.25
103 Warren Spahn .30 .75
104 Prince Fielder .30 .75
105 Ryan Braun .30 .75
106 J.J. Hardy .20 .50
107 Ben Sheets .20 .50
108 Corey Hart .20 .50
109 Yovani Gallardo .20 .50
110 Joe Mauer .40 1.00
111 Delmon Young .30 .75
112 Johan Santana .30 .75
113 Glen Perkins .20 .50
114 Justin Morneau .30 .75
115 Carlos Beltran .30 .75
116 Jose Reyes .30 .75
117 David Wright .30 .75
118 Pedro Martinez .30 .75
119 Tom Seaver .30 .75
120 Billy Wagner .20 .50
121 John Maine .20 .50
122 Alex Rodriguez .60 1.50
123 Chien-Ming Wang .30 .75
124 Hideki Matsui .50 1.25
125 Jorge Posada .30 .75
126 Mariano Rivera .60 1.50
127 Phil Rizzuto .30 .75
128 Bucky Dent .20 .50
129 Derek Jeter 1.25 3.00
130 Graig Nettles .20 .50
131 Ian Kennedy RC .75 2.00
132 Don Larsen .20 .50
133 Joe Blanton .20 .50
134 Mark Ellis .20 .50
135 Dennis Eckersley .30 .75
136 Rollie Fingers .30 .75
137 Catfish Hunter .30 .75
138 Daric Barton (RC) .30 .75
139 Jack Cust .20 .50
140 Ryan Howard .30 .75
141 Jimmy Rollins .30 .75
142 Chase Utley .30 .75
143 Shane Victorino .20 .50
144 Cole Hamels .40 1.00
145 Richie Ashburn .30 .75
146 Jason Bay .30 .75
147 Freddy Sanchez .20 .50
148 Adam LaRoche .20 .50
149 Jack Wilson .20 .50
150 Ralph Kiner .30 .75
151 Bill Mazeroski .30 .75
152 Tom Gorzelanny .20 .50
153 Jay Bruce (RC) 1.00 2.50
154 Jake Peavy .20 .50
155 Chris Young .20 .50
156 Trevor Hoffman .30 .75
157 Khalil Greene .20 .50
158 Adrian Gonzalez .30 .75
159 Tim Lincecum .30 .75
160 Matt Cain .30 .75
161 Aaron Rowand .20 .50
162 Orlando Cepeda .30 .75
163 Juan Marichal .30 .75
164 Noah Lowry .20 .50
165 Ichiro Suzuki .60 1.50
166 Felix Hernandez .30 .75
167 J.J. Putz .20 .50
168 Jose Vidro .20 .50
169 Raul Ibanez .30 .75
170 Wladimir Balentien .20 .50
171 Albert Pujols .60 1.50
172 Scott Rolen .30 .75
173 Lou Brock .30 .75
174 Chris Duncan .20 .50
175 Vince Coleman .20 .50
176 B.J. Upton .30 .75
177 Carl Crawford .30 .75
178 Carlos Pena .30 .75
179 Scott Kazmir .30 .75
180 Akinori Iwamura .20 .50
181 James Shields .20 .50
182 Michael Young .20 .50
183 Jarrod Saltalamacchia .20 .50
184 Hank Blalock .20 .50
185 Ian Kinsler .30 .75
186 Josh Hamilton .30 .75
187 Marlon Byrd .20 .50
188 David Murphy .20 .50
189 Vernon Wells .20 .50
190 Roy Halladay .30 .75
191 Frank Thomas .50 1.25
192 Alex Rios .20 .50
193 Troy Glaus .30 .75
194 David Eckstein .20 .50
195 Ryan Zimmerman .30 .75
196 Dmitri Young .20 .50
197 Austin Kearns .20 .50
198 Chad Cordero .20 .50
199 Ryan Church .20 .50
200 Evan Longoria RC 1.50 4.00
201 Brooks Robinson SP 2.00 5.00
202 Cal Ripken Jr. SP 5.00 12.00
203 Frank Robinson SP 2.00 5.00
204 Carl Yastrzemski SP 3.00 8.00
205 Carlton Fisk SP 2.00 5.00
206 Fred Lynn SP 2.00 5.00
207 Wade Boggs SP 2.50 6.00
208 Nolan Ryan SP 5.00 12.00
209 Ernie Banks SP 2.50 6.00
210 Ryne Sandberg SP 4.00 10.00
211 Al Kaline SP 2.50 6.00
212 Bo Jackson SP 2.50 6.00
213 Paul Molitor SP 2.50 6.00
214 Robin Yount SP 2.50 6.00
215 Harmon Killebrew SP 2.50 6.00
216 Rod Carew SP 2.00 5.00
217 Bobby Thomson SP 2.00 5.00
218 Gaylord Perry SP 2.00 5.00
219 Dave Winfield SP 2.00 5.00
220 Don Mattingly SP 3.00 8.00
221 Reggie Jackson SP 2.00 5.00
222 Roger Clemens SP 3.00 8.00
223 Whitey Ford SP 2.00 5.00
224 Mike Schmidt SP 3.00 8.00
225 Steve Carlton SP 2.00 5.00
226 Tony Gwynn SP 2.00 5.00
227 Willie McCovey SP 2.00 5.00
228 Bob Gibson SP 2.00 5.00
229 Ozzie Smith SP 3.00 8.00
230 Stan Musial SP 3.00 8.00
231 George Washington SP 2.00 5.00
232 Thomas Jefferson SP 2.00 5.00
233 James Madison SP 1.50 4.00
234 James Monroe SP 1.50 4.00
235 Andrew Jackson SP 1.50 4.00
236 John Tyler SP 1.50 4.00
237 Abraham Lincoln SP 2.00 5.00
238 Ulysses S. Grant SP 1.50 4.00
239 Grover Cleveland SP 1.50 4.00
240 Theodore Roosevelt SP 1.50 4.00
241 Calvin Coolidge SP 1.50 4.00
242 John Adams SP 1.50 4.00
243 Martin Van Buren SP 1.50 4.00
244 William McKinley SP 1.50 4.00
245 Woodrow Wilson SP 1.50 4.00
246 James K. Polk SP 1.50 4.00
247 Rutherford B. Hayes SP 1.50 4.00
248 William H. Taft SP 1.50 4.00
249 Andrew Johnson SP 1.50 4.00
250 James Buchanan SP 1.50 4.00
251 A.Pujols 36 BW SP 3.00 8.00
252 A.Rodriguez 36 BW SP 3.00 8.00
253 Alfonso Soriano 36 BW SP 2.50 6.00
254 C.C. Sabathia 36 BW SP 2.00 5.00
255 Chase Utley 36 BW SP 2.50 6.00
256 David Ortiz 36 BW SP 2.50 6.00
257 D.Wright 36 BW SP 1.25 3.00
258 D.Jeter 36 BW SP 4.00 10.00
259 Hanley Ramirez 36 BW SP 2.50 6.00
260 I.Suzuki 36 BW SP 2.50 6.00
261 Jake Peavy 36 BW SP 2.50 6.00
262 Johan Santana 36 BW SP 2.50 6.00
263 Jose Reyes 36 BW SP 2.50 6.00
264 K.Griffey Jr. 36 BW SP 4.00 10.00
265 Magglio Ordonez 36 BW SP 2.50 6.00
266 Matt Holliday 36 BW SP 2.50 6.00
267 Prince Fielder 36 BW SP 2.50 6.00
268 R.Braun 36 BW SP 1.25 3.00
269 R.Howard 36 BW SP 1.25 3.00
270 Vladimir Guerrero 36 BW SP 2.50 6.00
271 Carl Yastrzemski SR SP 2.00 5.00
272 Albert Pujols SR SP 3.00 8.00
273 Amy Van Dyken SR SP 2.00 5.00
274 Tom Seaver SR SP 2.00 5.00
275 Brett Favre SR SP 4.00 10.00
276 Bruce Jenner SR SP 2.00 5.00
277 Bill Russell SR SP 3.00 8.00
278 Barry Sanders SR SP 3.00 8.00
279 Cynthia Cooper SR SP 2.00 5.00
280 Mike Schmidt SR SP 2.50 6.00
281 Chipper Jones SR SP 2.50 6.00
282 Cal Ripken Jr. SR SP 4.00 10.00
283 Cael Sanderson SR SP 2.00 5.00
284 Dan Gable SR SP 2.00 5.00
285 Derek Jeter SR SP 4.00 10.00
286 Andre Dawson SR SP 2.00 5.00
287 Dan O'Brien SR SP 2.00 5.00
288 Julius Erving SR SP 2.50 6.00
289 Emmitt Smith SR SP 3.00 8.00
290 Janet Evans SR SP 2.00 5.00
291 Chase Utley SR SP 2.00 5.00
292 Gary Hall Jr. SR SP 2.00 5.00
293 Gordie Howe SR SP 3.00 8.00
294 Josh Beckett SR SP 2.00 5.00
295 John Elway SR SP 3.00 8.00
296 Julie Foudy SR SP 2.00 5.00
297 Jackie Joyner-Kersee SR SP 2.00 5.00
298 Jack Nicklaus SR SP 4.00 10.00
299 Magic Johnson SR SP 3.00 8.00
300 Michael Jordan SR SP 3.00 8.00
301 Bo Jackson SR SP 4.00 10.00
302 Tom Brady SR SP 6.00 15.00
303 Wade Boggs SR SP 4.00 10.00
304 Dan Marino SR SP 6.00 15.00
305 Dave Winfield SR SP 3.00 8.00
306 Jenny Thompson SR SP 3.00 8.00
307 Kobe Bryant SR SP 5.00 12.00
308 Kevin Durant SR SP 5.00 12.00
309 Ken Griffey Jr. SR SP 6.00 15.00
310 Kerri Strug SR SP 4.00 10.00
311 Kerri Walsh SR SP 4.00 10.00
312 Larry Bird SR SP 6.00 15.00
313 LeBron James SR SP 6.00 15.00
314 Matt Biondi SR SP 3.00 8.00
315 Mark Messier SR SP 4.00 10.00
316 Michael Johnson SR SP 3.00 8.00
317 Misty May-Treanor SR SP 8.00 20.00
318 Bob Gibson SR SP 6.00 15.00
319 Nolan Ryan SR SP 6.00 15.00
320 Ozzie Smith SR SP 5.00 12.00
321 Prince Fielder SR SP 4.00 10.00
322 Rulon Gardner SR SP 3.00 8.00
323 Reggie Jackson SR SP 4.00 10.00
324 Ernie Banks SR SP 5.00 12.00
325 Sidney Crosby SR SP 10.00 25.00
326 Sanya Richards SR SP 3.00 8.00
327 Terry Bradshaw SR SP 4.00 10.00
328 Tony Gwynn SR SP 4.00 10.00
329 Stan Musial SR SP 6.00 15.00
330 Tiger Woods SR SP 20.00 40.00

2008 Upper Deck Goudey Mini Black Backs

*BLACK 1-200: .75X TO 2X GRN 1-200
*BLACK RC 1-200: .75X TO 2X GRN RC 1-200
*BLACK SP 201-250: .75X TO 2X GRN 201-250
*BLACK SP 251-270: .5X TO 1.2X GRN 251-270
*BLACK SR 271-330: .5X TO 1.2X GRN 271-330
RANDOM INSERTS IN PACKS
STATED PRINT RUN 34 SER.#'d SETS
11 Chipper Jones 10.00 25.00
36 Kosuke Fukudome 20.00 50.00
100 Chin-Lung Hu 10.00 25.00
129 Derek Jeter 10.00 25.00
142 Chase Utley 6.00 15.00
186 Josh Hamilton 10.00 25.00
200 Evan Longoria 20.00 50.00
278 Barry Sanders SR 10.00 25.00
281 Chipper Jones SR 15.00 40.00
282 Cal Ripken Jr. SR 40.00 80.00
300 Michael Jordan SR 20.00 50.00
307 Kobe Bryant 6.00 15.00
330 Tiger Woods 40.00 80.00

2008 Upper Deck Goudey Mini Blue Backs

*BLUE 1-200: 1.5X TO 4X BASIC 1-200
*BLUE RC 1-200: 1X TO 2.5X BASIC RC 1-200
*BLUE 201-270: .6X TO 1.5X BASIC SP 201-270
*BLUE 271-330: .6X TO 1.5X BASIC SR 201-270
RANDOM INSERTS IN PACKS
298 Jack Nicklaus SR 15.00 40.00
330 Tiger Woods 30.00 60.00

2008 Upper Deck Goudey Mini Green Backs

RANDOM INSERTS IN PACKS
STATED PRINT RUN 88 SER.#'d SETS
1 Eric Byrnes 1.00 2.50
2 Randy Johnson 2.50 6.00
3 Brandon Webb 1.50 4.00
4 Dan Haren 1.00 2.50
5 Chris B. Young 1.00 2.50
6 Max Scherzer 10.00 25.00
7 Mark Teixeira 1.50 4.00
8 John Smoltz 2.50 6.00
9 Jeff Francoeur 1.50 4.00
10 Phil Niekro 1.50 4.00
11 Chipper Jones 6.00 15.00
12 Kelly Johnson 1.00 2.50
13 Tom Glavine 1.50 4.00
14 Yunel Escobar 1.00 2.50
15 Erik Bedard 1.00 2.50
16 Melvin Mora 1.00 2.50
17 Brian Roberts 1.00 2.50
18 Eddie Murray 1.50 4.00
19 Jim Palmer 1.50 4.00
20 Jeremy Guthrie 1.00 2.50
21 Nick Markakis 2.00 5.00
22 David Ortiz 2.50 6.00
23 Manny Ramirez 2.50 6.00
24 Josh Beckett 1.00 2.50
25 Dustin Pedroia 2.50 6.00
26 Bobby Doerr 1.50 4.00
27 Clay Buchholz 1.50 4.00
28 Daisuke Matsuzaka 1.50 4.00
29 Jonathan Papelbon 1.50 4.00
30 Kevin Youkilis 1.00 2.50
31 Pee Wee Reese 1.50 4.00
32 Billy Williams 1.50 4.00
33 Alfonso Soriano 1.50 4.00
34 Derrek Lee 1.00 2.50
35 Rich Hill 1.00 2.50
36 Kosuke Fukudome 10.00 25.00
37 Aramis Ramirez 1.00 2.50
38 Carlos Zambrano 1.50 4.00
39 Luis Aparicio 1.50 4.00
40 Mark Buehrle 1.50 4.00
41 Orlando Cabrera 1.50 4.00
42 Paul Konerko 1.50 4.00
43 Jermaine Dye 1.00 2.50
44 Jim Thome 1.50 4.00
45 Nick Swisher 1.50 4.00
46 Sparky Anderson 1.50 4.00
47 Johnny Bench 2.50 6.00
48 Joe Morgan 1.50 4.00
49 Tony Perez 1.50 4.00

50 Adam Dunn	1.50	4.00
51 Aaron Harang	1.00	2.50
52 Brandon Phillips	1.00	2.50
53 Edwin Encarnacion	2.50	6.00
54 Ken Griffey Jr.	5.00	12.00
55 Larry Doby	1.50	4.00
56 Bob Feller	1.50	4.00
57 C.C. Sabathia	1.50	4.00
58 Travis Hafner	1.00	2.50
59 Grady Sizemore	1.50	4.00
60 Fausto Carmona	1.00	2.50
61 Victor Martinez	1.50	4.00
62 Brad Hawpe	1.00	2.50
63 Todd Helton	1.50	4.00
64 Garrett Atkins	1.00	2.50
65 Troy Tulowitzki	2.50	6.00
66 Matt Holliday	2.50	6.00
67 Jeff Francis	1.00	2.50
68 Justin Verlander	2.50	6.00
69 Curtis Granderson	1.50	4.00
70 Miguel Cabrera	2.50	6.00
71 Gary Sheffield	1.00	2.50
72 Magglio Ordonez	1.50	4.00
73 Jack Morris	1.50	4.00
74 Andrew Miller	1.50	4.00
75 Clayton Kershaw	30.00	80.00
76 Dan Uggla	1.00	2.50
77 Hanley Ramirez	1.50	4.00
78 Jeremy Hermida	1.00	2.50
79 Josh Willingham	1.50	4.00
80 Lance Berkman	1.50	4.00
81 Roy Oswalt	1.50	4.00
82 Miguel Tejada	1.50	4.00
83 Hunter Pence	1.50	4.00
84 Carlos Lee	1.00	2.50
85 J.R. Towles	1.50	4.00
86 Brian Bannister	1.00	2.50
87 Luke Hochevar	1.50	4.00
88 Billy Butler	1.00	2.50
90 Kelvim Escobar	1.50	4.00
91 John Lackey	1.50	4.00
92 Chone Figgins	1.00	2.50
93 Jered Weaver	1.50	4.00
94 Torii Hunter	1.00	2.50
95 Vladimir Guerrero	1.50	4.00
96 Brad Penny	1.00	2.50
97 James Loney	1.00	2.50
98 Andruw Jones	1.00	2.50
99 Chad Billingsley	1.50	4.00
100 Chin-Lung Hu	1.00	2.50
101 Russell Martin	1.00	2.50
102 Eddie Mathews	2.50	6.00
103 Warren Spahn	1.50	4.00
104 Prince Fielder	1.50	4.00
105 Ryan Braun	1.50	4.00
106 J.J. Hardy	1.00	2.50
107 Ben Sheets	1.00	2.50
108 Corey Hart	1.00	2.50
109 Yovani Gallardo	1.00	2.50
110 Joe Mauer	2.00	5.00
111 Delmon Young	1.50	4.00
112 Johan Santana	1.50	4.00
113 Glen Perkins	1.00	2.50
114 Justin Morneau	1.50	4.00
115 Carlos Beltran	1.50	4.00
116 Jose Reyes	1.50	4.00
117 David Wright	1.50	4.00
118 Pedro Martinez	1.50	4.00
119 Tom Seaver	1.50	4.00
120 Billy Wagner	1.00	2.50
121 John Maine	1.00	2.50
122 Alex Rodriguez	3.00	8.00
123 Chien-Ming Wang	1.50	4.00
124 Hideki Matsui	2.50	6.00
125 Jorge Posada	1.50	4.00
126 Mariano Rivera	3.00	8.00
127 Phil Rizzuto	1.50	4.00
128 Bucky Dent	1.00	2.50
129 Derek Jeter	6.00	15.00
130 Graig Nettles	1.00	2.50
131 Ian Kennedy	2.50	6.00
132 Don Larsen	1.00	2.50
133 Joe Blanton	1.00	2.50
134 Mark Ellis	1.00	2.50
135 Dennis Eckersley	1.50	4.00
136 Rollie Fingers	1.50	4.00
137 Catfish Hunter	1.50	4.00
138 Daric Barton	1.00	2.50
139 Jack Cust	1.00	2.50
140 Ryan Howard	1.50	4.00
141 Jimmy Rollins	1.50	4.00
142 Chase Utley	1.50	4.00
143 Shane Victorino	1.00	2.50
144 Cole Hamels	2.00	5.00
145 Richie Ashburn	1.50	4.00
146 Jason Bay	1.50	4.00
147 Freddy Sanchez	1.00	2.50
148 Adam LaRoche	1.00	2.50
149 Jack Wilson	1.00	2.50
150 Ralph Kiner	1.50	4.00
151 Bill Mazeroski	1.50	4.00
152 Tom Gorzelanny	1.00	2.50
153 Jay Bruce	3.00	8.00
154 Jake Peavy	1.00	2.50
155 Chris Young	1.00	2.50
156 Trevor Hoffman	1.50	4.00
157 Khalil Greene	1.00	2.50
158 Adrian Gonzalez	1.50	4.00
159 Tim Lincecum	1.50	4.00
160 Matt Cain	1.50	4.00
161 Aaron Rowand	1.00	2.50
162 Orlando Cepeda	1.50	4.00
163 Juan Marichal	1.50	4.00
164 Noah Lowry	1.00	2.50
165 Ichiro Suzuki	3.00	8.00
166 Felix Hernandez	1.50	4.00
167 J.J. Putz	1.00	2.50
168 Jose Vidro	1.00	2.50
169 Raul Ibanez	1.50	4.00
170 Wladimir Balentien	1.00	2.50
171 Albert Pujols	3.00	8.00
172 Scott Rolen	1.50	4.00
173 Lou Brock	1.50	4.00
174 Chris Duncan	1.00	2.50
175 Vince Coleman	1.00	2.50
176 B.J. Upton	1.50	4.00
177 Carl Crawford	1.50	4.00
178 Carlos Pena	1.50	4.00
179 Scott Kazmir	1.50	4.00
180 Akinori Iwamura	1.00	2.50
181 James Shields	1.00	2.50
182 Michael Young	1.00	2.50
183 Jarrod Saltalamacchia	1.00	2.50
184 Hank Blalock	1.00	2.50
185 Ian Kinsler	1.50	4.00
186 Josh Hamilton	1.50	4.00
187 Marlon Byrd	1.00	2.50
188 David Murphy	1.00	2.50
189 Vernon Wells	1.00	2.50
190 Roy Halladay	1.50	4.00
191 Frank Thomas	2.50	6.00
192 Alex Rios	1.00	2.50
193 Troy Glaus	1.50	4.00
194 David Eckstein	1.00	2.50
195 Ryan Zimmerman	1.50	4.00
196 Dmitri Young	1.00	2.50
197 Austin Kearns	1.00	2.50
198 Chad Cordero	1.00	2.50
199 Ryan Church	1.00	2.50
200 Evan Longoria	10.00	25.00
201 Brooks Robinson	2.50	6.00
203 Frank Robinson	2.50	6.00
204 Carl Yastrzemski	4.00	10.00
205 Carlton Fisk	2.50	6.00
206 Fred Lynn	2.50	6.00
207 Wade Boggs	3.00	8.00
208 Nolan Ryan	10.00	25.00
209 Ernie Banks	3.00	8.00
210 Ryne Sandberg	5.00	12.00
211 Al Kaline	3.00	8.00
212 Bo Jackson	3.00	8.00
213 Paul Molitor	3.00	8.00
214 Robin Yount	3.00	8.00
215 Harmon Killebrew	3.00	8.00
216 Rod Carew	2.50	6.00
217 Bobby Thomson	2.50	6.00
218 Gaylord Perry	2.50	6.00
219 Dave Winfield	2.50	6.00
220 Don Mattingly	4.00	10.00
221 Reggie Jackson	2.50	6.00
222 Roger Clemens	4.00	10.00
223 Whitey Ford	2.50	6.00
224 Mike Schmidt	4.00	10.00
225 Steve Carlton	2.50	6.00
226 Tony Gwynn	2.50	6.00
227 Willie McCovey	2.50	6.00
228 Bob Gibson	2.50	6.00
229 Ozzie Smith	4.00	10.00
230 Stan Musial	4.00	10.00
231 George Washington	2.50	6.00
232 Thomas Jefferson	2.50	6.00
233 James Madison	2.00	5.00
234 James Monroe	2.00	5.00
235 Andrew Jackson	2.00	5.00
236 John Tyler	2.00	5.00
237 Abraham Lincoln	2.50	6.00
238 Ulysses S. Grant	2.00	5.00
239 Grover Cleveland	2.00	5.00
240 Theodore Roosevelt	2.00	5.00
241 Calvin Coolidge	2.00	5.00
242 John Adams	2.00	5.00
243 Martin Van Buren	2.00	5.00
244 William McKinley	2.00	5.00
245 Woodrow Wilson	2.00	5.00
246 James K. Polk	2.00	5.00
247 Rutherford B. Hayes	2.00	5.00
248 William H. Taft	2.00	5.00
249 Andrew Johnson	2.00	5.00
250 James Buchanan	2.00	5.00
251 Albert Pujols 36 BW	5.00	12.00
252 Alex Rodriguez 36 BW	4.00	10.00
253 Alfonso Soriano 36 BW	3.00	8.00
254 C.C. Sabathia 36 BW	2.50	6.00
255 Chase Utley 36 BW	3.00	8.00
256 David Ortiz 36 BW	3.00	8.00
257 David Wright 36 BW	3.00	8.00
258 Derek Jeter 36 BW	6.00	15.00
259 Hanley Ramirez 36 BW	3.00	8.00
260 Ichiro Suzuki 36 BW	4.00	10.00
261 Jake Peavy 36 BW	3.00	8.00
262 Johan Santana 36 BW	3.00	8.00
263 Jose Reyes 36 BW	3.00	8.00
264 Ken Griffey Jr. 36 BW	5.00	12.00
265 Magglio Ordonez 36 BW	3.00	8.00
266 Matt Holliday 36 BW	3.00	8.00
267 Prince Fielder 36 BW	3.00	8.00
268 Ryan Braun 36 BW	3.00	8.00
269 Ryan Howard 36 BW	3.00	8.00
270 Vladimir Guerrero 36 BW	3.00	8.00
271 Carl Yastrzemski SR	2.50	6.00
272 Albert Pujols SR	5.00	12.00
273 Amy Van Dyken SR	2.50	6.00
274 Tom Seaver SR	2.50	6.00
275 Brett Favre SR	5.00	12.00
276 Bruce Jenner SR	2.50	6.00
277 Bill Russell SR	4.00	10.00
278 Barry Sanders SR	4.00	10.00
279 Cynthia Cooper SR	2.50	6.00
280 Mike Schmidt SR	3.00	8.00
281 Chipper Jones SR	3.00	8.00
282 Cal Ripken Jr. SR	10.00	25.00
283 Cael Sanderson SR	2.50	6.00
284 Dan Gable SR	2.50	6.00
285 Derek Jeter SR	6.00	15.00
286 Andre Dawson SR	2.50	6.00
287 Dan O'Brien SR	2.50	6.00
288 Julius Erving SR	3.00	8.00
289 Emmitt Smith SR	4.00	10.00
290 Janet Evans SR	2.50	6.00
291 Chase Utley SR	2.50	6.00
292 Gary Hall Jr. SR	2.50	6.00
293 Gordie Howe SR	4.00	10.00
294 Josh Beckett SR	2.50	6.00
295 John Elway SR	6.00	15.00
296 Julie Foudy SR	2.50	6.00
297 Jackie Joyner-Kersee SR	2.50	6.00
298 Jack Nicklaus SR	12.50	30.00
299 Magic Johnson SR	4.00	10.00
300 Michael Jordan SR	12.50	30.00
301 Bo Jackson	3.00	8.00
302 Tom Brady	10.00	25.00
303 Wade Boggs	3.00	8.00
304 Dan Marino	5.00	12.00
305 Dave Winfield	2.50	6.00
306 Jenny Thompson	2.50	6.00
307 Kobe Bryant	4.00	10.00
308 Kevin Durant	4.00	10.00
309 Ken Griffey Jr.	5.00	12.00
310 Kerri Strug	3.00	8.00
311 Kerri Walsh	3.00	8.00
312 Larry Bird	5.00	12.00
313 LeBron James	10.00	25.00
314 Matt Biondi	2.50	6.00
315 Mark Messier	3.00	8.00
316 Michael Johnson	2.50	6.00
317 Misty May-Treanor	3.00	8.00
318 Bob Gibson	2.50	6.00
319 Nolan Ryan	8.00	20.00
320 Ozzie Smith	4.00	10.00
321 Prince Fielder	3.00	8.00
322 Rulon Gardner	2.50	6.00
323 Reggie Jackson	3.00	8.00
324 Ernie Banks	4.00	10.00
325 Sidney Crosby	8.00	20.00
326 Sanya Richards	2.50	6.00
327 Terry Bradshaw	3.00	8.00
328 Tony Gwynn	3.00	8.00
329 Stan Musial	5.00	12.00
330 Tiger Woods	75.00	150.00

2008 Upper Deck Goudey Mini Red Backs

*RED 1-200: 1X TO 2.5X BASIC 1-200
*RED RC 1-200: .75X TO 2X BASIC RC 1-200
*RED 201-270: .5X TO 1.2X BASIC SP 201-270
*RED 271-330: .5X to 1.2X BASIC SR 271-330
RANDOM INSERTS IN PACKS

298 Jack Nicklaus SR	12.50	30.00
330 Tiger Woods	30.00	60.00

2008 Upper Deck Goudey Autographs

OVERALL AUTO ODDS 1:18 HOBBY
ASTERISK EQUALS PARTIAL EXCHANGE
EXCHANGE DEADLINE 7/17/2010

AH Aaron Harang	4.00	10.00
BB Billy Buckner	3.00	8.00
BD Bucky Dent	3.00	8.00
BP Brandon Phillips	5.00	12.00
BR Brooks Robinson	20.00	50.00
BT Bobby Thomson	10.00	25.00
BW Billy Wagner	4.00	10.00
CH Corey Hart	4.00	10.00
CJ Chipper Jones SP	30.00	60.00
CL Carlos Lee	8.00	20.00
DB Daric Barton	3.00	8.00
DE David Eckstein	6.00	15.00
DJ Derek Jeter	150.00	250.00
DL Derrek Lee	6.00	15.00
DM Daisuke Matsuzaka SP EXCH	75.00	150.00
EE Edwin Encarnacion	6.00	15.00
FC Fausto Carmona	4.00	10.00
FL Fred Lynn SP	15.00	40.00
GN Graig Nettles	4.00	10.00
GO Tom Gorzelanny	4.00	10.00
GP Glen Perkins	3.00	8.00
HR Hanley Ramirez SP	30.00	60.00
HU Chin-Lung Hu SP	20.00	50.00
IK Ian Kennedy	6.00	15.00
JB Johnny Bench SP	20.00	50.00
JC Jack Cust	3.00	8.00
JF Jeff Francis SP	5.00	12.00
JG Jeremy Guthrie	6.00	15.00
JH Jeremy Hermida	3.00	8.00
JO John Maine	4.00	10.00
JP Jonathan Papelbon	6.00	15.00
JT J.R. Towles	3.00	8.00
JW Josh Willingham	3.00	8.00
KG Ken Griffey Jr. SP	225.00	450.00
KJ Kelly Johnson	3.00	8.00
KY Kevin Youkilis SP	15.00	40.00
LA Don Larsen SP	15.00	40.00
MA Don Mattingly SP	60.00	120.00
MB Marlon Byrd	3.00	8.00
MO Jack Morris	6.00	15.00
MS Mike Schmidt SP	25.00	60.00
MU David Murphy	4.00	10.00
NL Noah Lowry	3.00	8.00
NM Nick Markakis	8.00	20.00
NS Nick Swisher	5.00	12.00
PM Paul Molitor	10.00	25.00
RM Russell Martin SP	20.00	50.00
SC Steve Carlton SP	40.00	80.00
SP Steve Pearce	6.00	15.00
TG Tom Glavine SP	20.00	50.00
VC Vince Coleman	6.00	15.00
YG Yovani Gallardo SP	4.00	10.00

2008 Upper Deck Goudey Hit Parade of Champions

RANDOM INSERTS IN PACKS

1 Albert Pujols	.75	2.00
2 Don Mattingly	1.25	3.00
3 Ben Roethlisberger	.75	2.00
4 Bill Russell	1.25	3.00
5 Bobby Orr	2.50	6.00
6 Cal Ripken Jr.	2.00	5.00
7 Carl Yastrzemski	1.00	2.50
8 Derek Jeter	1.50	4.00
9 Emmitt Smith	1.25	3.00
10 Gordie Howe	1.50	4.00
11 Joe Montana	1.25	3.00
12 Joe Namath	.75	2.00
13 Ken Griffey Jr.	1.25	3.00
14 Kobe Bryant	2.50	6.00
15 LaDainian Tomlinson	.75	2.00
16 Larry Bird	2.00	5.00
17 LeBron James	3.00	8.00
18 Magic Johnson	1.25	3.00
19 Mario Lemieux	2.50	6.00
20 Yogi Berra	.60	1.50
21 Michael Jordan	4.00	10.00
22 Nolan Ryan	2.00	5.00
23 Patrick Roy	1.50	4.00
24 Peyton Manning	.75	2.00
25 Reggie Jackson	.40	1.00
26 Roger Clemens	.75	2.00
27 Roger Staubach	.75	2.00
28 Manny Ramirez	.60	1.50
29 Tom Brady	1.00	2.50
30 Wayne Gretzky	4.00	10.00

2008 Upper Deck Goudey Memorabilia

OVERALL GU ODDS 1:18 HOBBY

AD Adam Dunn	3.00	8.00
AG Adrian Gonzalez	3.00	8.00
AH Aaron Harang	3.00	8.00
AI Akinori Iwamura	3.00	8.00
AJ Andruw Jones	3.00	8.00
AP Albert Pujols	6.00	15.00
AR Aaron Rowand	3.00	8.00
AS Alfonso Soriano	4.00	10.00
BB Billy Butler	3.00	8.00
BD Bucky Dent	3.00	8.00
BE Josh Beckett	3.00	8.00
BR Brian Roberts	3.00	8.00
BU B.J. Upton	3.00	8.00
BW Brandon Webb	3.00	8.00
CC Carl Crawford	3.00	8.00
CH Cole Hamels	4.00	10.00
CJ Chipper Jones	5.00	12.00
CL Carlos Lee	3.00	8.00
CR Cal Ripken Jr.	8.00	20.00
CU Chase Utley	4.00	10.00
CY Chris Young	3.00	8.00
CZ Carlos Zambrano	3.00	8.00
DJ Derek Jeter	8.00	20.00
DL Derrek Lee	3.00	8.00
DM Daisuke Matsuzaka	6.00	15.00
DO David Ortiz	4.00	10.00
DU Dan Uggla	3.00	8.00
DY Delmon Young	3.00	8.00
FH Felix Hernandez	3.00	8.00
FS Freddy Sanchez	3.00	8.00
GA Garrett Atkins	3.00	8.00
GR Khalil Greene	3.00	8.00
GS Gary Sheffield	3.00	8.00
HO Trevor Hoffman	3.00	8.00
HP Hunter Pence	3.00	8.00
HR Hanley Ramirez	4.00	10.00
HU Catfish Hunter	5.00	12.00
JB Jason Bay	3.00	8.00
JD Jermaine Dye	3.00	8.00
JF Jeff Francoeur	3.00	8.00
JM Joe Mauer	3.00	8.00
JP Jake Peavy	3.00	8.00
JR Jimmy Rollins	3.00	8.00
JV Justin Verlander	3.00	8.00
JW Jered Weaver	3.00	8.00
KG Ken Griffey Jr.	6.00	15.00
KY Kevin Youkilis	4.00	10.00
LB Lance Berkman	3.00	8.00
MA John Maine	3.00	8.00
MB Mark Buehrle	3.00	8.00
MC Matt Cain	3.00	8.00
MH Matt Holliday	3.00	8.00
MI Miguel Cabrera	3.00	8.00
MO Justin Morneau	3.00	8.00
MR Manny Ramirez	4.00	10.00
MT Mark Teixeira	3.00	8.00
NM Nick Markakis	3.00	8.00
OR Magglio Ordonez	3.00	8.00
PA Jonathan Papelbon	4.00	10.00
PF Prince Fielder	4.00	10.00
PM Pedro Martinez	3.00	8.00
PO Jorge Posada	3.00	8.00
RA Aramis Ramirez	3.00	8.00
RE Jose Reyes	3.00	8.00
RH Roy Halladay	3.00	8.00
RI Mariano Rivera	3.00	8.00
RJ Randy Johnson	3.00	8.00
RM Russell Martin	3.00	8.00
RO Roy Oswalt	3.00	8.00
RZ Ryan Zimmerman	3.00	8.00
SI Grady Sizemore	3.00	8.00
SM John Smoltz	3.00	8.00
TE Miguel Tejada	3.00	8.00
TH Travis Hafner	3.00	8.00
VG Vladimir Guerrero	3.00	8.00
VM Victor Martinez	3.00	8.00
VW Vernon Wells	3.00	8.00
WI Jack Wilson	3.00	8.00
WS Warren Spahn	10.00	25.00
YG Yovani Gallardo	3.00	8.00

2008 Upper Deck Goudey Sport Royalty Autographs

OVERALL AUTO ODDS 1:18 HOBBY
ASTERISK EQUALS PARTIAL EXCHANGE
EXCHANGE DEADLINE 7/17/2010

AV Amy Van Dyken	12.50	30.00
CC Cynthia Cooper	8.00	20.00
CS Cael Sanderson	15.00	40.00
DO Dan O'Brien	8.00	20.00
EV Janet Evans	12.50	30.00
FO Julie Foudy	10.00	25.00
GH Gary Hall Jr.	8.00	20.00
JE Bruce Jenner	8.00	15.00
JJ Jackie Joyner-Kersee	6.00	15.00
JT Jenny Thompson	8.00	20.00
KG Ken Griffey Jr. SP	75.00	150.00
KS Kerri Strug	8.00	20.00
KW Kerri Walsh	12.50	30.00
MA Misty May-Treanor	40.00	80.00
MB Matt Biondi	8.00	20.00
PD Phil Dalhausser	8.00	20.00
PF P.Fielder SP EXCH	50.00	100.00
RG Rulon Gardner	10.00	25.00
SR Sanya Richards	8.00	20.00
TB Terry Bradshaw SP	60.00	120.00
TR Todd Rogers	12.50	30.00

2009 Upper Deck Goudey

COMPLETE SET (300)	200.00	300.00
COMP.SET w/o SP's (200)	20.00	50.00
COMMON CARD (1-200)	.20	.50
COMMON RC (1-200)	.40	1.00
COMMON SP (201-300)	2.00	5.00
APPX.SP ODDS 201-220 1:9 HOBBY		
APPX.SP ODDS 221-260 1:6 HOBBY		
APPX.SP ODDS 261-300 1:6 HOBBY		
1 Adam Dunn	.30	.75
2 Max Scherzer	.50	1.25
3 Stephen Drew	.20	.50
4 Randy Johnson	.50	1.25
5 Brandon Webb	.30	.75
6 Dan Haren	.20	.50
7 Chris B. Young	.20	.50
8 Brian McCann	.30	.75
9 Jeff Francoeur	.30	.75
10 James Parr (RC)	.40	1.00
11 Tom Glavine	.30	.75
12 Tim Hudson	.30	.75
13 Chipper Jones	.50	1.25
14 Kelly Johnson	.20	.50
15 Adam Jones	.30	.75
16 Jeremy Guthrie	.20	.50
17 Brian Roberts	.20	.50
18 Nick Markakis	.40	1.00
19 Jed Lowrie	.20	.50
20 Cal Ripken Jr.	1.50	4.00
21 Melvin Mora	.20	.50
22 Jason Bay	.30	.75
23 Josh Beckett	.20	.50
24 Justin Masterson	.20	.50
25 Kevin Youkilis	.20	.50
26 Michael Bowden (RC)	.40	1.00
27 Dustin Pedroia	.50	1.25
28 Jacoby Ellsbury	.40	1.00
29 Jason Varitek	.50	1.25
30 Jonathan Papelbon	.30	.75
31 David Ortiz	.50	1.25
32 Daisuke Matsuzaka	.30	.75
33 J.D. Drew	.20	.50
34 Curt Schilling	.30	.75
35 Clay Buchholz	.20	.50
36 Wilkin Castillo RC	.40	1.00
37 Derrek Lee	.20	.50
38 Kosuke Fukudome	.30	.75
39 Aramis Ramirez	.20	.50
40 Alfonso Soriano	.30	.75
41 Kerry Wood	.20	.50
42 Carlos Zambrano	.30	.75
43 Rich Harden	.20	.50
44 Geovany Soto	.30	.75
45 Gavin Floyd	.20	.50
46 Ken Griffey Jr.	1.00	2.50
47 Nick Swisher	.30	.75
48 Jim Thome	.30	.75
49 Jermaine Dye	.20	.50
50 Alexei Ramirez	.30	.75
51 Carlos Quentin	.20	.50
52 Brandon Phillips	.20	.50
53 Johnny Cueto	.30	.75
54 Jay Bruce	.30	.75
55 Dave Concepcion	.20	.50
56 Joey Votto	.50	1.25
57 Aaron Harang	.20	.50
58 Edinson Volquez	.20	.50
59 Kelly Shoppach	.20	.50
60 Fausto Carmona	.20	.50
61 Grady Sizemore	.30	.75
62 Travis Hafner	.20	.50
63 Victor Martinez	.30	.75
64 Cliff Lee	.30	.75
65 Dexter Fowler (RC)	.60	1.50
66 Garrett Atkins	.20	.50
67 Troy Tulowitzki	.50	1.25
68 Matt Holliday	.50	1.25
69 Curtis Granderson	.40	1.00
70 Carlos Guillen	.20	.50
71 Gary Sheffield	.20	.50
72 Miguel Cabrera	.50	1.25
73 Magglio Ordonez	.30	.75
74 Justin Verlander	.50	1.25
75 Hanley Ramirez	.30	.75
76 Josh Willingham	.30	.75
77 Dan Uggla	.20	.50
78 Josh Johnson	.30	.75
79 Carlos Lee	.20	.50
80 Roy Oswalt	.30	.75
81 Miguel Tejada	.30	.75
82 Lance Berkman	.30	.75
83 Kila Ka'aihue (RC)	.60	1.50
84 Joakim Soria	.20	.50
85 Alex Gordon	.30	.75
86 Chone Figgins	.20	.50
87 John Lackey	.30	.75
88 Jered Weaver	.30	.75
89 Vladimir Guerrero	.30	.75
90 Mark Teixeira	.30	.75
91 Garret Anderson	.20	.50
92 Torii Hunter	.20	.50
93 Howie Kendrick	.20	.50
94 Clayton Kershaw	.75	2.00
95 Cory Wade	.20	.50
96 Matt Kemp	.40	1.00
97 Russell Martin	.20	.50
98 Scott Elbert (RC)	.40	1.00
99 Manny Ramirez	.50	1.25
100 Andre Ethier	.30	.75
101 Rafael Furcal	.20	.50
102 Brad Penny	.20	.50
103 Takashi Saito	.20	.50
104 Kirk Gibson	.20	.50
105 Alcides Escobar RC	.60	1.50
106 Bill Hall	.20	.50
107 Mat Gamel RC	1.00	2.50
108 Prince Fielder	.30	.75
109 Miguel Montero	.20	.50
110 Yovani Gallardo	.20	.50
111 Ben Sheets	.20	.50
112 CC Sabathia	.30	.75
113 Ryan Braun	.30	.75
114 J.J. Hardy	.20	.50
115 Denard Span	.20	.50
116 Joe Nathan	.20	.50
117 Nick Blackburn	.20	.50
118 Joe Mauer	.40	1.00
119 Justin Morneau	.30	.75
120 Francisco Liriano	.20	.50
121 Kevin Slowey	.30	.75
122 Delmon Young	.30	.75
123 John Maine	.20	.50
124 Jonathon Niese RC	.60	1.50
125 David Wright	.40	1.00
126 Jose Reyes	.30	.75
127 Carlos Beltran	.30	.75
128 Johan Santana	.30	.75
129 A.J. Burnett	.20	.50
130 Derek Jeter	1.25	3.00
131 Francisco Cervelli RC	1.00	2.50
132 Ian Kennedy	.20	.50
133 Phil Coke RC	.60	1.50
134 Phil Hughes	.20	.50
135 Alex Rodriguez	.60	1.50
136 Chien-Ming Wang	.30	.75
137 Mariano Rivera	.60	1.50
138 Joba Chamberlain	.20	.50
139 Jason Giambi	.20	.50
140 Andy Pettitte	.30	.75
141 Greg Smith	.20	.50
142 Marlon Byrd	.20	.50
143 Johnny Damon	.30	.75
144 Frank Thomas	.50	1.25
145 Carlos Gonzalez	.30	.75
146 Jeff Baisley RC	.40	1.00
147 Mark Teahen	.20	.50
148 Jack Cust	.20	.50
149 Kurt Suzuki	.20	.50
150 Bobby Crosby	.20	.50
151 Cole Hamels	.40	1.00
152 Lou Marson (RC)	.40	1.00
153 Chase Utley	.30	.75
154 Jimmy Rollins	.30	.75
155 Ryan Howard	.40	1.00
156 Greg Golson (RC)	.40	1.00
157 Pat Burrell	.20	.50
158 Shane Victorino	.20	.50
159 Brad Lidge	.20	.50
160 Edwin Encarnacion	.50	1.25
161 Nate McLouth	.20	.50
162 Ryan Doumit	.20	.50
163 Adrian Gonzalez	.40	1.00
164 Matt Antonelli RC	.60	1.50
165 Jake Peavy	.20	.50
166 Kevin Kouzmanoff	.20	.50
167 Chris Young	.20	.50
168 Trevor Hoffman	.30	.75
169 Conor Gillaspie RC	1.00	2.50
170 Wade LeBlanc RC	.60	1.50
171 Matt Cain	.30	.75
172 Tim Lincecum	.30	.75
173 Matt Tuiasosopo (RC)	.40	1.00
174 Ichiro Suzuki	.60	1.50
175 Felix Hernandez	.30	.75
176 Erik Bedard	.20	.50
177 Ryan Ludwick	.30	.75
178 Albert Pujols	.60	1.50
179 Rick Ankiel	.20	.50
180 Troy Glaus	.20	.50
181 Bob Gibson	.30	.75
182 B.J. Upton	.30	.75
183 David Price RC	.75	2.00
184 Evan Longoria	.30	.75
185 Carl Crawford	.30	.75
186 Scott Kazmir	.20	.50
187 Carlos Pena	.30	.75
188 James Shields	.20	.50
189 Josh Hamilton	.30	.75
190 Ian Kinsler	.30	.75
191 Michael Young	.20	.50
192 Mike Aviles	.20	.50
193 Roy Halladay	.30	.75
194 Travis Snider RC	.60	1.50
195 Vernon Wells	.20	.50
196 Alex Rios	.20	.50
197 Ryan Zimmerman	.30	.75
198 Shairon Martis RC	.60	1.50
199 Lastings Milledge	.20	.50
200 Cristian Guzman	.20	.50
201 Brooks Robinson SP	2.00	5.00
202 Carlton Fisk SP	2.00	5.00
203 Gaylord Perry SP	2.00	5.00
204 Jack Morris SP	2.00	5.00
205 Rollie Fingers SP	2.00	5.00
206 Ron Santo SP	2.00	5.00
207 Sparky Lyle SP	2.00	5.00
208 Nolan Ryan SP	5.00	12.00
209 Whitey Ford SP	2.50	6.00
210 Phil Niekro SP	2.00	5.00
211 Ryne Sandberg SP	3.00	8.00
212 Jim Palmer SP	2.50	6.00
213 Joe DiMaggio SP	5.00	12.00
214 Johnny Bench SP	3.00	8.00
215 Ted Williams SP	5.00	12.00
216 Robin Yount SP	3.00	8.00
217 Ozzie Smith SP	3.00	8.00
218 Reggie Jackson SP	2.50	6.00
219 Yogi Berra SP	3.00	8.00
220 Mike Schmidt SP	3.00	8.00
221 Cal Ripken Jr. SR SP	5.00	12.00
222 Ozzie Smith SR SP	3.00	8.00
223 Tony Gwynn SR SP	3.00	8.00
224 Don Mattingly SR SP	3.00	8.00
225 Steve Carlton SR SP	2.00	5.00
226 Reggie Jackson SR SP	2.50	6.00
227 Carl Yastrzemski SR SP	3.00	8.00
228 Johnny Bench SR SP	3.00	8.00
229 Mike Schmidt SR SP	3.00	8.00
230 Nolan Ryan SR SP	5.00	12.00
231 Ernie Banks SR SP	3.00	8.00
232 Stan Musial SR SP	4.00	10.00
233 Ryne Sandberg SR SP	3.00	8.00
234 Bob Gibson SR SP	3.00	8.00
235 Dennis Eckersley SR SP	2.00	5.00
236 Felix Hernandez SR SP	2.50	6.00
237 Jim Rice SR SP	2.50	6.00
238 Chien-Ming Wang SR SP	3.00	8.00
239 Jonathan Papelbon SR SP	2.50	6.00
240 Evan Longoria SR SP	3.00	8.00
241 Cole Hamels SR SP	2.50	6.00
242 Ken Griffey Jr. SR SP	5.00	12.00
243 Tiger Woods SR SP	15.00	40.00
244 B.J. Upton SR SP	2.50	6.00
245 Randy Johnson SR SP	3.00	8.00
246 Guy Lafleur SR SP	2.50	6.00
247 Nicklas Lidstrom SR SP	2.00	5.00
248 Mike Bossy SR SP	2.50	6.00
249 Bobby Orr SR SP	4.00	10.00
250 Patrick Roy SR SP	5.00	12.00
251 Adrian Peterson SR SP	4.00	10.00
252 Juan Marichal SR SP	2.00	5.00
253 Chipper Jones SR SP	3.00	8.00
254 Rollie Fingers SR SP	2.00	5.00
255 Al Kaline SR SP	3.00	8.00
256 Paul Pierce SR SP	3.00	8.00
257 Jerry West SR SP	3.00	8.00
258 Larry Bird SR SP	3.00	8.00
259 John Havlicek SR SP	2.50	6.00
260 Michael Jordan SR SP	5.00	12.00
261 Cal Ripken Jr. HU SP	5.00	12.00
262 Reggie Jackson HU SP	2.50	6.00
263 Nolan Ryan HU SP	5.00	12.00
264 Yogi Berra HU SP	3.00	8.00
265 Ernie Banks HU SP	3.00	8.00
266 Dave Winfield HU SP	2.50	6.00
267 Ozzie Smith HU SP	3.00	8.00
268 Stan Musial HU SP	4.00	10.00
269 Ichiro Suzuki HU SP	3.00	8.00
270 Albert Pujols HU SP	4.00	10.00
271 Alex Rodriguez HU SP	4.00	10.00
272 Jose Reyes HU SP	3.00	8.00
273 David Wright HU SP	3.00	8.00
274 Johan Santana HU SP	3.00	8.00
275 Josh Hamilton HU SP	3.00	8.00
276 David Ortiz HU SP	3.00	8.00
277 Josh Beckett HU SP	2.50	6.00
278 Manny Ramirez HU SP	3.00	8.00
279 Ryan Howard HU SP	3.00	8.00
280 Chase Utley HU SP	3.00	8.00
281 Jimmy Rollins HU SP	3.00	8.00
282 Hanley Ramirez HU SP	3.00	8.00
283 CC Sabathia HU SP	3.00	8.00
284 Ryan Braun HU SP	2.50	6.00
285 Evan Longoria HU SP	3.00	8.00
286 Grady Sizemore HU SP	2.50	6.00
287 Dustin Pedroia HU SP	3.00	8.00
288 Mark Teixeira HU SP	3.00	8.00
289 Ken Griffey Jr. HU SP	5.00	12.00
290 Lance Berkman HU SP	2.50	6.00
291 Alfonso Soriano HU SP	2.50	6.00
292 Derrek Lee HU SP	2.50	6.00
293 Brandon Webb HU SP	2.50	6.00
294 Derek Jeter HU SP	5.00	12.00
295 Daisuke Matsuzaka HU SP	3.00	8.00
296 Vladimir Guerrero HU SP	3.00	8.00
297 Jim Thome HU SP	2.50	6.00
298 Carlos Zambrano HU SP	2.00	5.00
299 Justin Morneau HU SP	2.50	6.00
300 Tim Lincecum HU SP	3.00	8.00

2009 Upper Deck Goudey Mini Green Back

*GREEN 1-200: 1.2X TO 3X BASIC
*GREEN RC 1-200: .6X TO 1.5X BASIC

COMMON CARD (201-300)	.75	2.00
APPROX.ODDS 1:6 HOBBY		
201 Brooks Robinson	1.25	3.00
202 Carlton Fisk	1.25	3.00
203 Gaylord Perry	1.25	3.00
204 Jack Morris	.75	2.00
205 Rollie Fingers	1.25	3.00
206 Ron Santo	1.25	3.00
207 Sparky Lyle	.75	2.00
208 Nolan Ryan	6.00	15.00
209 Whitey Ford	1.25	3.00
210 Phil Niekro	1.25	3.00
211 Ryne Sandberg	4.00	10.00
212 Jim Palmer	1.25	3.00
213 Joe DiMaggio	4.00	10.00
214 Johnny Bench	2.00	5.00
215 Ted Williams	4.00	10.00
216 Robin Yount	2.00	5.00
217 Ozzie Smith	2.50	6.00
218 Reggie Jackson	1.25	3.00
219 Yogi Berra	2.00	5.00
220 Mike Schmidt	3.00	8.00
221 Cal Ripken Jr. SR	6.00	15.00
222 Ozzie Smith SR	2.50	6.00
223 Tony Gwynn SR	2.00	5.00
224 Don Mattingly SR	4.00	10.00
225 Steve Carlton SR	1.25	3.00
226 Reggie Jackson SR	1.25	3.00
227 Carl Yastrzemski SR	3.00	8.00
228 Johnny Bench SR	2.00	5.00
229 Mike Schmidt SR	3.00	8.00
230 Nolan Ryan SR	6.00	15.00
231 Ernie Banks SR	2.00	5.00
232 Stan Musial SR	3.00	8.00
233 Ryne Sandberg SR	4.00	10.00
234 Bob Gibson SR	1.25	3.00
235 Dennis Eckersley SR	1.25	3.00
236 Felix Hernandez SR	1.25	3.00
237 Jim Rice SR	1.25	3.00
238 Chien-Ming Wang SR	1.25	3.00
239 Jonathan Papelbon SR	1.25	3.00
240 Evan Longoria SR	1.25	3.00
241 Cole Hamels SR	1.50	4.00
242 Ken Griffey Jr. SR	4.00	10.00
243 Tiger Woods SR	60.00	120.00
244 B.J. Upton SR	1.25	3.00
245 Randy Johnson SR	2.00	5.00
246 Guy Lafleur SR	4.00	10.00
247 Nicklas Lidstrom SR	2.00	5.00
248 Mike Bossy SR	2.00	5.00
249 Bobby Orr SR	6.00	15.00
250 Patrick Roy SR	6.00	15.00
251 Adrian Peterson SR	4.00	10.00
252 Juan Marichal SR	1.25	3.00
253 Chipper Jones SR	2.00	5.00
254 Rollie Fingers SR	1.25	3.00
255 Al Kaline SR	2.00	5.00
256 Paul Pierce SR	2.50	6.00
257 Jerry West SR	3.00	8.00
258 Larry Bird SR	5.00	12.00
259 John Havlicek SR	2.00	5.00
260 Michael Jordan SR	6.00	15.00
261 Cal Ripken Jr. HU	6.00	15.00
262 Reggie Jackson HU	1.25	3.00
263 Nolan Ryan HU	6.00	15.00
264 Yogi Berra HU	2.00	5.00
265 Ernie Banks HU	2.00	5.00
266 Dave Winfield HU	1.25	3.00
267 Ozzie Smith HU	2.50	6.00
268 Stan Musial HU	3.00	8.00
269 Ichiro Suzuki HU	2.50	6.00
270 Albert Pujols HU	2.50	6.00
271 Alex Rodriguez HU	2.50	6.00
272 Jose Reyes HU	1.25	3.00
273 David Wright HU	1.50	4.00
274 Johan Santana HU	1.25	3.00

275 Josh Hamilton HU 1.25 3.00
276 David Ortiz HU 2.00 5.00
277 Josh Beckett HU .75 2.00
278 Manny Ramirez HU 2.00 5.00
279 Ryan Howard HU 1.50 4.00
280 Chase Utley HU 1.25 3.00
281 Jimmy Rollins HU 1.25 3.00
282 Hanley Ramirez HU 1.25 3.00
283 CC Sabathia HU 1.25 3.00
284 Ryan Braun HU 1.25 3.00
285 Evan Longoria HU 1.25 3.00
286 Grady Sizemore HU 1.25 3.00
287 Dustin Pedroia HU 2.00 5.00
288 Mark Teixeira HU 1.25 3.00
289 Ken Griffey Jr. HU 4.00 10.00
290 Lance Berkman HU 1.25 3.00
291 Alfonso Soriano HU 1.25 3.00
292 Derrek Lee HU .75 2.00
293 Brandon Webb HU 1.25 3.00
294 Derek Jeter HU 5.00 12.00
295 Daisuke Matsuzaka HU 1.25 3.00
296 Vladimir Guerrero HU 1.25 3.00
297 Jim Thome HU 1.25 3.00
298 Carlos Zambrano HU 1.25 3.00
299 Justin Morneau HU 1.25 3.00
300 Tim Lincecum HU 1.25 3.00

2009 Upper Deck Goudey Mini Navy Blue Back

*BLUE 1-200: 1.5X TO 4X BASIC
*BLUE RC 1-200: .75X TO 2X BASIC
*BLUE: 201-300: .6X TO 1.5X MINI GREEN
APPROX.ODDS 1:9 HOBBY
243 Tiger Woods SR 100.00 175.00

2009 Upper Deck Goudey 4-In-1

APPX.ODDS 1:2 HOBBY
BLACK RANDOMLY INSERTED
BLACK PRINT RUN 21 SER.#'d SETS
NO BLACK PRICING AVAILABLE
*BLUE: .6X TO 1.5X BASIC
APPX.BLUE ODDS 1:9
*GREEN: .75X TO 2X BASIC
APPX.GREEN ODDS 1:18
1 Sparky Lyle/Phil Niekro/Johnny Bench
Reggie Jackson 1.25 3.00
2 Lud/Ozzie/Gibson/Pujols 1.50 4.00
3 Gib/Peav/Lince/Beckett .75 2.00
4 Jacoby Ellsbury/Jose Reyes
Carl Crawford/Brian Roberts 1.00 2.50
5 Jeter/Reg/Yogi/Ford 3.00 8.00
6 Ford/Jeter/ARod/Berra 3.00 8.00
7 Ford/ARod/Jeter/Wang 3.00 8.00
8 Brooks/Ichiro/Size/Hamilton 1.50 4.00
9 Carl Crawford/Alex Rios
Jacoby Ellsbury/Johnny Damon 1.00 2.50
10 Ryan/Kaz/Beckett/Kershaw 4.00 10.00
11 Elly/Gib/Martin/Kershaw 2.00 5.00
12 Schm/Manny/Grif/ARod 2.50 6.00
13 Dan Haren/Stephen Drew/Chris Young
Adrian Gonzalez 1.00 2.50
14 Gaylord Perry/Jack Morris/Jim Palmer
Rollie Fingers .75 2.00
15 Pap/Sor/Holt/Riv 1.50 4.00
16 Ryne Sandberg/Dan Uggla/Chase Utley
Ian Kinsler 2.50 6.00
17 Ron Santo/Billy Williams/Alfonso Soriano
Carlos Zambrano .75 2.00
18 Ripken/Smith/Han/Jeter 4.00 10.00
19 Rip/Palm/Mora/Markakis 4.00 10.00
20 Johnny Bench/Dave Concepcion
Brandon Phillips/Jay Bruce 1.25 3.00
21 Vict/Hamels/Schm/Howard 2.00 5.00
22 Ron Santo/Ryne Sandberg/Derrek Lee
Aramis Ramirez 2.50 6.00
23 Yount/Braun/Gall/Prince 1.25 3.00
24 Wang/Jeter/Johan/Reyes 3.00 8.00
25 Ripken/Smith/Jeter/Reyes 4.00 10.00
26 Brian McCann/Tim Hudson
Chipper Jones/Kelly Johnson 1.25 3.00
27 Johnny Bench/Yogi Berra/Joe Mauer
Brian McCann 1.25 3.00
28 Palmer/Ryan/Gibson/Perry 4.00 10.00
29 Schm/Howard/Yount/Prince 2.00 5.00
30 Pujols/Ankiel/Glaus/Lud 1.50 4.00
31 Holl/Braun/Quentin/Bay 1.25 3.00
32 Johan Santana/Cole Hamels
CC Sabathia/Scott Kazmir 1.00 2.50
33 Lince/Volq/Kersh/Harden 2.00 5.00
34 Ped/Roberts/Kend/Kinsler 1.25 3.00
35 Upton/Long/Pena/Crawford .75 2.00
36 Ham/Morn/Prince/Howard 1.00 2.50
37 Cabrera/Ordonez/Grand/Guillen 1.25 3.00
38 Jose Reyes/Jimmy Rollins/Hanley Ramirez
Cristian Guzman .75 2.00
39 Matt Kemp/Russell Martin/Rafael Furcal
Andre Ethier 1.00 2.50
40 Ichiro/Tuia/Felix/Bedard 1.50 4.00
41 Crosb/Cust/Lince/Cain .75 2.00
42 Reyes/Beltran/Wright/Johan 1.25 3.00
43 Hanley Ramirez/Dan Uggla/Jimmy Rollins
Chase Utley .75 2.00
44 Howie Kendrick/Vladimir Guerrero/Torii
Hunter/Chone Figgins .75 2.00
45 Kazmir/Shields/Long/Price 1.00 2.50
46 Pujols/Lee/Prince/Berk 1.50 4.00
47 Rollins/Utley/Howard/Hamels 1.00 2.50
48 Matsu/Beckett/Mast/Papel .75 2.00
49 Joakim Soria/Jonathan Papelbon
Brad Lidge/Kerry Wood .75 2.00
50 Ells/Ped/Ortiz/Youkilis 1.25 3.00
51 John Lackey/Jered Weaver
Felix Hernandez/Erik Bedard .75 2.00
52 Josh Hamilton/Ian Kinsler
Marlon Byrd/Michael Young .75 2.00
53 Grady Sizemore/Travis Hafner
Victor Martinez/Kelly Shoppach .75 2.00
54 Chipper Jones/Jeff Francoeur
Brian McCann/Kelly Johnson 1.25 3.00
55 Chip/Wright/Atkins/Aramis 1.25 3.00
56 Russell Martin/Brian McCann/Ryan
Doumit/Geovany Soto .75 2.00
57 Braun/Prince/Hardy/Hall .75 2.00
58 Jeff Baisley/Jack Cust/Bobby Crosby
Kurt Suzuki .50 1.25
59 Wang/Riv/Kenn/Joba 1.50 4.00
60 Joba/ Harden/Linc/Verland 1.25 3.00
61 Vlad/Lack/Eth/Kershaw 2.00 5.00
62 Wright/Zim/Upton/Maine 1.00 2.50
63 Ichiro/Size/Upton/Torii 1.50 4.00
64 Carlos Beltran/Lance Berkman/Jimmy Rollins
Chipper Jones 1.25 3.00
65 Halla/Snider/Wells/Rios .75 2.00
66 Carlos Zambrano/Rich Harden
Kosuke Fukudome/Geovany Soto .75 2.00
67 Ortiz/Howard/Prince/Giambi 1.25 3.00
68 Ken/Joba/Buch/Masterson .50 1.25
69 Jonathan Papelbon/Josh Beckett
Joe Nathan/Francisco Liriano .75 2.00
70 Long/Alexei/Soto/Bruce .75 2.00
71 How/Ham/Pujols/Cabrera 1.50 4.00
72 Young/Gonz/Kershaw/Furcal 2.00 5.00
73 Alfonso Soriano/Derrek Lee
Aramis Ramirez/Geovany Soto .75 2.00
74 Matsu/Wang/Fuku/Ichiro 1.50 4.00
75 Andy Pettitte/Curt Schilling/Tom Glavine
Randy Johnson 1.25 3.00
76 Grif/Dye/Quentin/Thome 2.50 6.00
77 Liri/Kersh/Price/Cole 2.00 5.00
78 Justin Morneau/Joe Mauer/Delmon Young
Denard Span 1.00 2.50
79 Carlos Beltran/Carlos Lee/Carlos Quentin
Carlos Guillen .75 2.00
80 Travis Hafner/Magglio Ordonez/Jermaine Dye
Manny Ramirez 1.25 3.00
81 Lee/Size/Felix/Ichiro 1.50 4.00
82 Jack Cust/Kurt Suzuki/Johnny Cueto
Jay Bruce .75 2.00
83 Denard Span/Adam Jones/Dexter Fowler
Alexei Ramirez .75 2.00
84 Buch/Master/Lowrie/Pedr 1.25 3.00
85 ARod/Wright/Aramis/Long 1.50 4.00
86 ARod/Grif/Manny/Thome 2.50 6.00
87 Brian McCann/Ryan Doumit/Russell Martin
Joe Mauer 1.00 2.50
88 Man/Nathan/Pujols/Lidge 1.50 4.00
89 Lance Berkman/Carlos Lee/Miguel Tejada
Roy Oswalt .75 2.00
90 ARod/Jeter/Joba/Rivera 3.00 8.00
91 Carlos Zambrano/Randy Johnson
Roy Halladay/Tim Hudson 1.25 3.00
92 Jim Thome/Jermaine Dye/Alexei Ramirez
Carlos Quentin .75 2.00
93 Nate McLouth/Jay Bruce/Rick Ankiel
Lance Berkman .75 2.00
94 Franc/Ankiel/Ichiro/Mark 1.50 4.00
95 B.J. Upton/Lastings Milledge
Chris B. Young/Matt Kemp 1.00 2.50
96 Ped/Lee/Pujols/Lince 1.50 4.00
97 Reyes/Wright/Jeter/ARod 3.00 8.00
98 Michael Young/Ian Kinsler
Hanley Ramirez/Dan Uggla .75 2.00
99 Fow/Snider/Anton/Bowden .75 2.00
100 Pedr/Papi/Fisk/Beckett 1.25 3.00

2009 Upper Deck Goudey 4-In-1 Blue

APPX.ODDS 1:9 HOBBY

2009 Upper Deck Goudey Autographs

OVERALL AUTO ODDS 1:18 HOBBY
EXCHANGE DEADLINE 4/1/2011
GGAG Adrian Gonzalez 6.00 15.00
GGAV Mike Aviles 10.00 25.00
GGBE Josh Beckett 30.00 60.00
GGBH Bill Hall 3.00 8.00
GGBM Brian McCann 8.00 20.00
GGBP Brandon Phillips 5.00 12.00
GGBR Brooks Robinson 15.00 40.00
GGBU B.J. Upton 5.00 12.00
GGBY Marlon Byrd 3.00 8.00
GGCF Carlton Fisk 30.00 60.00
GGCG Conor Gillaspie 6.00 15.00
GGCH Cole Hamels 12.50 30.00
GGCK Clayton Kershaw 50.00 120.00
GGCL Carlos Lee 6.00 15.00
GGCU Johnny Cueto 4.00 10.00
GGDF Dexter Fowler 6.00 15.00
GGDJ Derek Jeter 150.00 250.00
GGDP David Price 15.00 40.00
GGED Edgar Martinez 15.00 40.00
GGEE Edwin Encarnacion 3.00 8.00
GGEL Evan Longoria 150.00 250.00
GGFC Francisco Cervelli 6.00 15.00
GGFI Chone Figgins 4.00 10.00
GGGA Garrett Atkins 3.00 8.00
GGGP Gaylord Perry 6.00 15.00
GGGS Grady Sizemore 20.00 50.00
GGHR Hanley Ramirez 10.00 25.00
GGIK Ian Kennedy 4.00 10.00
GGJB Jeff Baisley 6.00 15.00
GGJC Joe Carter 5.00 12.00
GGJF Jeff Francoeur 6.00 15.00
GGJG Jeremy Guthrie 4.00 10.00
GGJP James Parr 3.00 8.00
GGJU Justin Masterson 10.00 25.00
GGKG K.Griffey Jr. EXCH 100.00 175.00
GGKK Kila Ka'aihue 6.00 15.00
GGKS Kelly Shoppach 3.00 8.00
GGKY Kevin Youkilis 10.00 25.00
GGLM Lou Marson 6.00 15.00
GGMA Matt Antonelli 3.00 8.00
GGMB Michael Bowden 10.00 25.00
GGMG Mat Gamel 8.00 20.00
GGMM Miguel Montero 3.00 8.00
GGMS Max Scherzer 40.00 100.00
GGMT Matt Tuiasosopo 6.00 15.00
GGNB Nick Blackburn 10.00 25.00
GGPC Phil Coke 5.00 12.00
GGPE Dustin Pedroia 12.50 30.00
GGPF Prince Fielder 12.50 30.00
GGRF Rollie Fingers 6.00 15.00
GGRH Roy Halladay 30.00 60.00
GGRS Ron Santo 15.00 40.00
GGSD Stephen Drew 5.00 12.00
GGSI Greg Smith 3.00 8.00
GGTG Tom Glavine 40.00 80.00
GGTR Tim Raines 12.50 30.00
GGTT Troy Tulowitzki 8.00 20.00
GGVM Victor Martinez 6.00 15.00
GGWF Whitey Ford 30.00 60.00
GGWL Wade LeBlanc 3.00 8.00
GGYG Yovani Gallardo 8.00 20.00

2009 Upper Deck Goudey Memorabilia

OVERALL AUTO ODDS 1:18 HOBBY
GMAB A.J. Burnett 3.00 8.00
GMAE Andre Ethier 5.00 12.00
GMAH Aaron Harang 3.00 8.00
GMAR Aramis Ramirez 3.00 8.00
GMBC Bobby Crosby 3.00 8.00
GMBE Carlos Beltran 3.00 8.00
GMBG Bob Gibson 4.00 10.00
GMBH Bill Hall 3.00 8.00
GMBM Brian McCann 4.00 10.00
GMBP Brandon Phillips 3.00 8.00
GMBR Brian Roberts 3.00 8.00
GMBS Ben Sheets 3.00 8.00
GMBW Billy Williams 3.00 8.00
GMCA Miguel Cabrera 4.00 10.00
GMCB Clay Buchholz 3.00 8.00
GMCG Carlos Guillen 3.00 8.00
GMCH Cole Hamels 5.00 12.00
GMCL Carlos Lee 3.00 8.00
GMCR Cal Ripken Jr. 10.00 25.00
GMCS Curt Schilling 3.00 8.00
GMCU Chase Utley 4.00 10.00
GMCY Chris Young 3.00 8.00
GMDJ Derek Jeter 6.00 15.00
GMDL Derrek Lee 3.00 8.00
GMDM Daisuke Matsuzaka 5.00 12.00
GMDO David Ortiz 3.00 8.00
GMDS Denard Span 3.00 8.00
GMDY Delmon Young 3.00 8.00
GMFH Felix Hernandez 4.00 10.00
GMFL Francisco Liriano 3.00 8.00
GMGA Garret Anderson 3.00 8.00
GMHK Howie Kendrick 3.00 8.00
GMHR Hanley Ramirez 3.00 8.00
GMHU Tim Hudson 3.00 8.00
GMJD Jermaine Dye 3.00 8.00
GMJE Jacoby Ellsbury 3.00 8.00
GMJF Jeff Francoeur 3.00 8.00
GMJG Jason Giambi 3.00 8.00
GMJH J.J. Hardy 3.00 8.00
GMJJ Josh Johnson 3.00 8.00
GMJM John Maine 3.00 8.00
GMJN Joe Nathan 3.00 8.00
GMJO Johnny Bench 10.00 25.00
GMJT Jim Thome 3.00 8.00
GMJV Jason Varitek 3.00 8.00
GMJW Jered Weaver 3.00 8.00
GMKJ Kelly Johnson 3.00 8.00
GMKS Kevin Slowey 3.00 8.00
GMKW Kerry Wood 3.00 8.00
GMKY Kevin Youkilis 3.00 8.00
GMLE Cliff Lee 3.00 8.00
GMMA Joe Mauer 3.00 8.00
GMME Melvin Mora 3.00 8.00
GMMK Matt Kemp 3.00 8.00
GMMS Mike Schmidt 12.50 30.00
GMMY Michael Young 3.00 8.00
GMNM Nick Markakis 4.00 10.00
GMNR Nolan Ryan 15.00 40.00
GMNS Nick Swisher 3.00 8.00
GMOS Ozzie Smith 12.50 30.00
GMPA Jonathan Papelbon 3.00 8.00
GMPE Brad Penny 3.00 8.00
GMPF Prince Fielder 3.00 8.00
GMPH Phil Hughes 3.00 8.00
GMPN Phil Niekro 10.00 25.00
GMRF Rafael Furcal 3.00 8.00
GMRO Roy Oswalt 3.00 8.00
GMRS Ryne Sandberg 10.00 25.00
GMRY Robin Yount 10.00 25.00
GMSH Gary Sheffield 4.00 10.00
GMTH Trevor Hoffman 3.00 8.00
GMTS Takashi Saito 3.00 8.00
GMTT Troy Tulowitzki 3.00 8.00
GMVM Victor Martinez 3.00 8.00
GMWI Josh Willingham 3.00 8.00
GMYG Yovani Gallardo 3.00 8.00

2009 Upper Deck Goudey Sport Royalty Autographs

OVERALL AUTO ODDS 1:18 HOBBY
EXCHANGE DEADLINE 4/1/2011
AK Al Kaline 30.00 80.00
BB Brooks Robinson 30.00 60.00
BF Bob Feller 50.00 100.00
BG Bob Gibson 40.00 80.00
BJ Bo Jackson 50.00 100.00
BR Lou Brock 60.00 120.00
BS Bill Sharman 15.00 40.00
BU B.J. Upton 75.00 150.00
CJ Chipper Jones 250.00 350.00
CK Clayton Kershaw 50.00 100.00
CW Chien-Ming Wang 100.00 200.00
DB Dennis Boyd 30.00 60.00
DE Dennis Eckersley 20.00 50.00
DM Don Mattingly 60.00 120.00
DP Dustin Pedroia 30.00 60.00
DS Don Sutton 15.00 40.00
EL Evan Longoria 100.00 200.00
EM Edgar Martinez 90.00 150.00
GP Gaylord Perry 15.00 40.00
GS Grady Sizemore 60.00 120.00
HM Cole Hamels 20.00 50.00
JB Johnny Bench 50.00 100.00
JC Joe Carter 20.00 50.00
JH John Havlicek 125.00 250.00
JO Michael Jordan 1000.00 2000.00
JP Jim Palmer 15.00 40.00
JW Jerry West 75.00 150.00
KG Ken Griffey Jr. 125.00 250.00
KH Kent Hrbek 15.00 40.00
KY Kevin Youkilis 75.00 150.00
LB Larry Bird 30.00 60.00
MI Mike Bossy 12.50 30.00
NL Nicklas Lidstrom 30.00 60.00
NR Nolan Ryan 200.00 300.00
OR Bobby Orr 100.00 200.00
PA Jonathan Papelbon 30.00 60.00
PM Paul Molitor 30.00 60.00
RF Rollie Fingers 15.00 40.00
RS Ron Santo 30.00 60.00
RY Ryne Sandberg 75.00 150.00
SM Stan Musial 125.00 250.00
WB Wade Boggs 40.00 80.00
YB Yogi Berra 30.00 80.00

2005 Upper Deck Hall of Fame

COMMON CARD (1-85) 1.00 2.50
COMMON CARD (86-100) 1.00 2.50
TWO BASIC AND/OR PARALLELS PER TIN
STATED PRINT RUN 550 SERIAL #'d SETS
1 Al Kaline 2.50 6.00
2 Al Lopez 1.00 2.50
3 Bill Mazeroski 1.50 4.00
4 Billy Williams 1.50 4.00
5 Bob Feller 1.50 4.00
6 Bob Gibson 1.50 4.00
7 Bob Lemon 1.50 4.00
8 Bobby Doerr 1.50 4.00
9 Brooks Robinson 1.50 4.00
10 Buck Leonard 1.00 2.50
11 Carl Yastrzemski 3.00 8.00
12 Carlton Fisk 1.50 4.00
13 Casey Stengel 1.50 4.00
14 Catfish Hunter 1.50 4.00
15 Dave Winfield 1.50 4.00
16 Dennis Eckersley 1.50 4.00
17 Dizzy Dean 1.50 4.00
18 Don Drysdale 1.50 4.00
19 Don Sutton 1.50 4.00
20 Duke Snider 1.50 4.00
21 Early Wynn 1.50 4.00
22 Eddie Mathews 2.50 6.00
23 Eddie Murray 1.50 4.00
24 Enos Slaughter 1.50 4.00
25 Ernie Banks 2.50 6.00
26 Fergie Jenkins 1.50 4.00
27 Frank Robinson 1.50 4.00
28 Gary Carter 1.50 4.00
29 Gaylord Perry 1.50 4.00
30 George Brett 5.00 12.00
31 George Kell 1.50 4.00
32 George Sisler 1.50 4.00
33 Hal Newhouser 1.50 4.00
34 Harmon Killebrew 2.50 6.00
35 Hoyt Wilhelm 1.50 4.00
36 Jackie Robinson 1.50 4.00
37 Jim Bunning 1.50 4.00
38 Jim Palmer 1.50 4.00
39 Jimmie Foxx 1.50 4.00
40 Joe Morgan 1.50 4.00
41 Johnny Bench 2.50 6.00
42 Johnny Mize 1.50 4.00
43 Juan Marichal 1.50 4.00
44 Kirby Puckett 2.50 6.00
45 Larry Doby 1.50 4.00
46 Lefty Grove 1.50 4.00
47 Lou Boudreau 1.50 4.00
48 Lou Brock 1.50 4.00
49 Luis Aparicio 1.50 4.00
50 Mel Ott 2.50 6.00
51 Mickey Cochrane 1.50 4.00
52 Monte Irvin 1.50 4.00
53 Orlando Cepeda 1.50 4.00
54 Ozzie Smith 3.00 8.00
55 Paul Molitor 2.50 6.00
56 Pee Wee Reese 1.50 4.00
57 Phil Niekro 1.50 4.00
58 Phil Rizzuto 1.50 4.00
59 Pie Traynor 1.50 4.00
60 Ralph Kiner 1.50 4.00
61 Red Schoendienst 1.50 4.00
62 Richie Ashburn 1.50 4.00
63 Rick Ferrell 1.00 2.50
64 Robin Roberts 1.50 4.00
65 Robin Yount 2.50 6.00
66 Rod Carew 1.50 4.00
67 Rogers Hornsby 1.00 2.50
68 Rollie Fingers 1.50 4.00
69 Roy Campanella 1.50 4.00
70 Steve Carlton 1.50 4.00
71 Tony Perez 1.50 4.00
72 Warren Spahn 1.50 4.00
73 Whitey Ford 1.50 4.00
74 Willie McCovey 1.50 4.00
75 Willie Stargell 1.50 4.00
76 Yogi Berra 2.50 6.00
77 Babe Ruth 6.00 15.00
78 Honus Wagner 1.50 4.00
79 Lou Gehrig 5.00 12.00
80 Mickey Mantle 8.00 20.00
81 Ty Cobb 4.00 10.00
82 Ryne Sandberg 5.00 12.00
83 Satchel Paige 2.50 6.00
84 Wade Boggs 1.50 4.00
85 Reggie Jackson 1.50 4.00
86 Babe Ruth PC 6.00 15.00
87 Christy Mathewson PC 2.50 6.00
88 Cy Young PC 1.50 4.00
89 Honus Wagner PC 1.50 4.00
90 Joe DiMaggio PC 5.00 12.00
91 Lou Gehrig PC 5.00 12.00
92 Mickey Mantle PC 8.00 20.00
93 Mike Schmidt PC 4.00 10.00
94 Nolan Ryan PC 8.00 20.00
95 Satchel Paige PC 2.50 6.00
96 Stan Musial PC 4.00 10.00
97 Ted Williams PC 5.00 12.00
98 Tom Seaver PC 1.50 4.00
99 Ty Cobb PC 4.00 10.00
100 Walter Johnson PC 1.50 4.00

2005 Upper Deck Hall of Fame Gold

*GOLD: 1X TO 2.5X BASIC
TWO BASIC AND/OR PARALLELS PER TIN
STATED PRINT RUN 25 SERIAL #'d SETS

2005 Upper Deck Hall of Fame Green

*GREEN: .6X TO 1.5X BASIC
TWO BASIC AND/OR PARALLELS PER TIN
STATED PRINT RUN 200 SERIAL #'d SETS

2005 Upper Deck Hall of Fame Silver

*SILVER: .75X TO 2X BASIC
TWO BASIC AND/OR PARALLELS PER TIN
STATED PRINT RUN 99 SERIAL #'d SETS

2005 Upper Deck Hall of Fame Class of Cooperstown

STATED PRINT RUN 50 SERIAL #'d SETS
GOLD PRINT RUN 5 SERIAL #'d SETS
NO GOLD PRICING DUE TO SCARCITY
RAINBOW PRINT RUN 1 SERIAL #'d SET
NO RAINBOW PRICING DUE TO SCARCITY
*SILVER: .6X TO 1.5X BASIC
SILVER PRINT RUN 15 SERIAL #'d SETS
OVERALL INSERT ODDS ONE PER TIN
AK1 Al Kaline Batting 2.50 6.00
AK2 Al Kaline Fielding 2.50 6.00
AK3 Al Kaline Portrait 2.50 6.00
BD1 Bobby Doerr Portrait 1.50 4.00
BD2 Bobby Doerr Fielding 1.50 4.00
BE1 Johnny Bench Batting 2.50 6.00
BE2 Johnny Bench Fielding 2.50 6.00
BF1 Bob Feller Pitching 1.50 4.00
BF2 Bob Feller Portrait 1.50 4.00
BG1 Bob Gibson Pitching 1.50 4.00
BG2 Bob Gibson Portrait 1.50 4.00
BM1 Bill Mazeroski 1.50 4.00
BR1 Brooks Robinson Batting 1.50 4.00
BR2 Brooks Robinson Fielding 1.50 4.00
BR3 Brooks Robinson Portrait 1.50 4.00
BW1 Billy Williams Batting 1.50 4.00
BW2 Billy Williams Fielding 1.50 4.00
BW3 Billy Williams Portrait 1.50 4.00
CF1 Carlton Fisk R.Sox 1.50 4.00
CF2 Carlton Fisk W.Sox 1.50 4.00
CY1 Carl Yastrzemski Batting 3.00 8.00
CY2 Carl Yastrzemski Fielding 3.00 8.00
DE1 Dennis Eckersley 1.50 4.00
DS1 Don Sutton 1.50 4.00
DW1 Dave Winfield Padres 1.50 4.00
DW2 Dave Winfield Yanks 1.50 4.00
EB1 Ernie Banks Batting 2.50 6.00
EB2 Ernie Banks Fielding 2.50 6.00
EM1 Eddie Murray 1.50 4.00
FJ1 Fergie Jenkins 1.50 4.00
FR1 Frank Robinson Reds 1.50 4.00
FR2 Frank Robinson O's 1.50 4.00
GB1 George Brett Batting 5.00 12.00
GB2 George Brett Fielding 5.00 12.00
GB3 George Brett Portrait 5.00 12.00
GC1 Gary Carter Mets 1.50 4.00
GC2 Gary Carter Expos 1.50 4.00
GK1 George Kell 1.50 4.00
GP1 Gaylord Perry Giants 1.50 4.00
GP2 Gaylord Perry Indians 1.50 4.00
HK1 H.Kill Senators Port 2.50 6.00
HK2 H.Kill Twins Batting 2.50 6.00
HK3 H.Kill Senators Run 2.50 6.00
HK4 H.Kill Twins Portrait 2.50 6.00
JB1 Jim Bunning Tigers 1.50 4.00
JB2 Jim Bunning Phils 1.50 4.00
JM1 Joe Morgan Astros 1.50 4.00
JM2 Joe Morgan Reds 1.50 4.00
JP1 Jim Palmer Pitching 1.50 4.00
JP2 Jim Palmer Portrait 1.50 4.00
KP1 Kirby Puckett 2.50 6.00
LA1 Luis Aparicio W.Sox 1.50 4.00
LA2 Luis Aparicio O's 1.50 4.00
LB1 Lou Brock 1.50 4.00
MA1 Juan Marichal Pitching 1.50 4.00
MA2 Juan Marichal Portrait 1.50 4.00
MI1 Monte Irvin Batting 1.50 4.00
MI2 Monte Irvin Fielding 1.50 4.00
MS1 Mike Schmidt Batting 4.00 10.00
MS2 Mike Schmidt Fielding 4.00 10.00
MS3 Mike Schmidt Portrait 4.00 10.00
NR1 Nolan Ryan Mets 8.00 20.00
NR2 Nolan Ryan Angels 8.00 20.00
NR3 Nolan Ryan Astros 8.00 20.00
NR4 Nolan Ryan Rgr 8.00 20.00
OC1 Orlando Cepeda 1.50 4.00
OS1 Ozzie Smith Padres 3.00 8.00
OS2 Ozzie Smith Cards 3.00 8.00
PM1 Paul Molitor Brew 2.50 6.00
PM2 Paul Molitor Jays 2.50 6.00
PM3 Paul Molitor Twins 2.50 6.00
PN1 Phil Niekro 1.50 4.00
RC1 Rod Carew Twins 1.50 4.00
RC2 Rod Carew Angels 1.50 4.00
RF1 Rollie Fingers 1.50 4.00
RJ1 Reggie Jackson A's 1.50 4.00
RJ2 Reggie Jackson Yanks 1.50 4.00
RJ3 Reggie Jackson Angels 1.50 4.00
RK1 Ralph Kiner Batting 1.50 4.00
RK2 Ralph Kiner Portrait 1.50 4.00
RR1 Robin Roberts 1.50 4.00
RS1 Red Schoendienst 1.50 4.00
RY1 Robin Yount Batting 2.50 6.00
RY2 Robin Yount Fielding 2.50 6.00
SC1 S.Carlton Cards Pitch 1.50 4.00
SC2 S.Carlton Phils Pitch 1.50 4.00
SC3 S.Carlton Cards Portrait 1.50 4.00
SC4 S.Carlton Phils Portrait 1.50 4.00
SM1 Stan Musial Batting 4.00 10.00
SM2 Stan Musial Portrait 4.00 10.00
SN1 Duke Snider 1.50 4.00
TP1 Tony Perez 1.50 4.00
TS1 Tom Seaver Mets 1.50 4.00
TS2 Tom Seaver Reds 1.50 4.00
WF1 Whitey Ford Pitching 1.50 4.00
WF2 Whitey Ford Portrait 1.50 4.00
WM1 Willie McCovey Batting 1.50 4.00
WM2 Willie McCovey Fielding 1.50 4.00
YB1 Yogi Berra Batting 2.50 6.00
YB2 Yogi Berra Fielding 2.50 6.00

2005 Upper Deck Hall of Fame Class of Cooperstown Autograph

STATED PRINT RUN 25 SERIAL #'d SETS
GOLD PRINT RUN 5 SERIAL #'d SETS
NO GOLD PRICING DUE TO SCARCITY
RAINBOW PRINT RUN 1 SERIAL #'d SET
NO RAINBOW PRICING DUE TO SCARCITY
*SILVER: .5X TO 1.2X BASIC
SILVER PRINT RUN 15 SERIAL #'d SETS
MATERIAL GOLD PRINT RUN 5 #'d SETS
NO MAT.GOLD PRICING DUE TO SCARCITY
MATERIAL RAINBOW PRINT RUN 1 #'d SET
NO MAT.RB PRICING DUE TO SCARCITY
*MAT.SILVER: .5X TO 1.2X BASIC
MATERIAL SILVER PRINT RUN 15 #'d SETS
PATCH GOLD PRINT 5 SERIAL #'d SETS
SM2 MUSIAL PATCH GOLD QTY 3 #'d CARDS
NO PATCH GOLD PRICING AVAILABLE
PATCH RAINBOW PRINT RUN 1 #'d SET
NO PATCH RAINBOW PRICING AVAILABLE
PATCH SILVER PRINT RUN 10 #'d SETS
NO PATCH SILVER PRICING AVAILABLE
OVERALL AUTO ODDS ONE PER TIN
AK1 Al Kaline Batting 15.00 40.00
AK2 Al Kaline Fielding 15.00 40.00
AK3 Al Kaline Portrait 15.00 40.00
BD1 Bobby Doerr Portrait 12.50 30.00
BD2 Bobby Doerr Fielding 12.50 30.00
BE1 Johnny Bench Batting 30.00 60.00
BE2 Johnny Bench Fielding 30.00 60.00
BF1 Bob Feller Pitching 10.00 25.00
BF2 Bob Feller Portrait 10.00 25.00
BG1 Bob Gibson Pitching 20.00 50.00
BG2 Bob Gibson Portrait 20.00 50.00
BM1 Bill Mazeroski 20.00 50.00
BR1 Brooks Robinson Batting 15.00 40.00
BR2 Brooks Robinson Fielding 15.00 40.00
BR3 Brooks Robinson Portrait 15.00 40.00
BW1 Billy Williams Batting 10.00 25.00
BW2 Billy Williams Fielding 10.00 25.00
BW3 Billy Williams Portrait 10.00 25.00
CF1 Carlton Fisk R.Sox 20.00 50.00
CF2 Carlton Fisk W.Sox 20.00 50.00
CY1 Carl Yastrzemski Batting 30.00 60.00
CY2 Carl Yastrzemski Fielding 30.00 60.00
DE1 Dennis Eckersley 10.00 25.00
DS1 Don Sutton 8.00 20.00
DW1 Dave Winfield Padres 15.00 40.00
DW2 Dave Winfield Yanks 15.00 40.00
EB1 Ernie Banks Batting 30.00 60.00
EB2 Ernie Banks Fielding 30.00 60.00
EM1 Eddie Murray 30.00 60.00
FJ1 Fergie Jenkins 8.00 20.00
FR1 Frank Robinson Reds 10.00 25.00
FR2 Frank Robinson O's 10.00 25.00
GB1 George Brett Batting 40.00 80.00
GB2 George Brett Fielding 40.00 80.00
GB3 George Brett Portrait 40.00 80.00
GC1 Gary Carter Mets 20.00 50.00
GC2 Gary Carter Expos 20.00 50.00
GK1 George Kell 10.00 25.00
GP1 Gaylord Perry Giants 8.00 20.00
GP2 Gaylord Perry Indians 8.00 20.00
HK1 H.Kill Senators Port 30.00 60.00
HK2 H.Kill Twins Batting 30.00 60.00
HK3 H.Kill Senators Run 30.00 60.00
HK4 H.Kill Twins Portrait 30.00 60.00
JB1 Jim Bunning Tigers 6.00 15.00
JB2 Jim Bunning Phils 6.00 15.00
JM1 Joe Morgan Astros 10.00 25.00
JM2 Joe Morgan Reds 10.00 25.00
JP1 Jim Palmer Pitching 10.00 25.00
JP2 Jim Palmer Portrait 10.00 25.00
KP1 Kirby Puckett 50.00 100.00
LA1 Luis Aparicio W.Sox 10.00 25.00
LA2 Luis Aparicio O's 10.00 25.00
LB1 Lou Brock 15.00 40.00
MA1 Juan Marichal Pitching 10.00 25.00
MA2 Juan Marichal Portrait 10.00 25.00
MI1 Monte Irvin Batting 10.00 25.00
MI2 Monte Irvin Fielding 10.00 25.00
MS1 Mike Schmidt Batting 30.00 60.00
MS2 Mike Schmidt Fielding 30.00 60.00
MS3 Mike Schmidt Portrait 30.00 60.00
NR1 Nolan Ryan Mets 50.00 100.00
NR2 Nolan Ryan Angels 50.00 100.00
NR3 Nolan Ryan Astros 50.00 100.00
NR4 Nolan Ryan Rgr 50.00 100.00
OC1 Orlando Cepeda 10.00 25.00
OS1 Ozzie Smith Padres 20.00 50.00
OS2 Ozzie Smith Cards 20.00 50.00
PM1 Paul Molitor Brew 10.00 25.00
PM2 Paul Molitor Jays 10.00 25.00
PM3 Paul Molitor Twins 10.00 25.00
PN1 Phil Niekro 8.00 20.00
RC1 Rod Carew Twins 15.00 40.00
RC2 Rod Carew Angels 15.00 40.00
RF1 Rollie Fingers 8.00 20.00
RJ1 Reggie Jackson A's 20.00 50.00
RJ2 Reggie Jackson Yanks 20.00 50.00
RJ3 Reggie Jackson Angels 20.00 50.00
RK1 Ralph Kiner Batting 20.00 50.00
RK2 Ralph Kiner Portrait 20.00 50.00
RR1 Robin Roberts 15.00 40.00
RS1 Red Schoendienst 10.00 25.00
RY1 Robin Yount Batting 20.00 50.00
RY2 Robin Yount Fielding 20.00 50.00
SC1 S.Carlton Cards Pitch 10.00 25.00
SC2 S.Carlton Phils Pitch 10.00 25.00
SC3 S.Carlton Cards Portrait 10.00 25.00
SC4 S.Carlton Phils Portrait 10.00 25.00
SM1 Stan Musial Batting 20.00 50.00
SM2 Stan Musial Portrait 20.00 50.00
SN1 Duke Snider 15.00 40.00
TP1 Tony Perez 6.00 15.00
TS1 Tom Seaver Mets 25.00 60.00
TS2 Tom Seaver Reds 25.00 60.00
WF1 Whitey Ford Pitching 15.00 40.00
WF2 Whitey Ford Portrait 15.00 40.00
WM1 Willie McCovey Batting 15.00 40.00
WM2 Willie McCovey Fielding 15.00 40.00
YB1 Yogi Berra Batting 30.00 80.00
YB2 Yogi Berra Fielding 30.00 80.00

2005 Upper Deck Hall of Fame Cooperstown Calling

STATED PRINT RUN 50 SERIAL #'d SETS
GOLD PRINT RUN 5 SERIAL #'d SETS
NO GOLD PRICING DUE TO SCARCITY
*GREEN: .5X TO 1.2X BASIC
GREEN PRINT RUN 25 SERIAL #'d SETS
RAINBOW PRINT RUN 1 SERIAL #'d SET
NO RAINBOW PRICING DUE TO SCARCITY
*SILVER: .5X TO 1.2X BASIC
SILVER PRINT RUN 15 SERIAL #'d SETS
OVERALL INSERT ODDS ONE PER TIN
AK1 Al Kaline Batting 2.50 6.00
AK2 Al Kaline Fielding 2.50 6.00
BD1 Bobby Doerr Batting 1.50 4.00
BD2 Bobby Doerr Fielding 1.50 4.00
BE1 Johnny Bench 2.50 6.00
BF1 Bob Feller Pitching 1.50 4.00
BF2 Bob Feller Portrait 1.50 4.00
BG1 Bob Gibson 1.50 4.00
BM1 Bill Mazeroski 1.50 4.00
BR1 Brooks Robinson Batting 1.50 4.00
BR2 Brooks Robinson Fielding 1.50 4.00
BR3 Brooks Robinson Portrait 1.50 4.00
BW1 Billy Williams Cubs 1.50 4.00
BW2 Billy Williams A's 1.50 4.00
CF1 Carlton Fisk W.Sox 1.50 4.00
CF2 Carlton Fisk R.Sox 1.50 4.00
CY1 Carl Yastrzemski Sleeves 3.00 8.00
CY2 C.Yastrzemski No Sleeves 3.00 8.00
DE1 Dennis Eckersley Sox 1.50 4.00
DE2 Dennis Eckersley A's 1.50 4.00
DS1 Don Sutton Dgr 1.50 4.00
DS2 Don Sutton Angels 1.50 4.00
DS3 Don Sutton Astros 1.50 4.00
DW1 Dave Winfield 1.50 4.00
EB1 Ernie Banks 2.50 6.00
EM1 Eddie Murray O's 1.50 4.00
EM2 Eddie Murray Dgr 1.50 4.00
FJ1 Fergie Jenkins Cubs 1.50 4.00
FJ2 Fergie Jenkins Rgr 1.50 4.00
FR1 Frank Robinson 1.50 4.00
GB1 George Brett Glove Up 5.00 12.00
GB2 George Brett Glove Down 5.00 12.00
GC1 Gary Carter Expos 1.50 4.00
GC2 Gary Carter Mets 1.50 4.00
GC3 Gary Carter Dgr 1.50 4.00
GK1 George Kell 1.50 4.00
GP1 Gaylord Perry Indians 1.50 4.00
GP2 Gaylord Perry Padres 1.50 4.00
HK1 H.Killebrew Senators 2.50 6.00
HK2 Harmon Killebrew Twins 2.50 6.00
JB1 Jim Bunning 1.50 4.00
JM1 Juan Marichal 1.50 4.00
JP1 Jim Palmer Pitching 1.50 4.00
JP2 Jim Palmer Portrait 1.50 4.00
KP1 Kirby Puckett 2.50 6.00
KP2 Kirby Puckett 2.50 6.00
LA1 Luis Aparicio W.Sox 1.50 4.00
LA2 Luis Aparicio O's 1.50 4.00
LB1 Lou Brock Cubs 1.50 4.00
LB2 Lou Brock Cards 1.50 4.00
MI1 Monte Irvin 1.50 4.00
MO1 Joe Morgan Astros 1.50 4.00
MO2 Joe Morgan Reds 1.50 4.00
MS1 Mike Schmidt Batting 4.00 10.00
MS2 Mike Schmidt Fielding 4.00 10.00
MS3 Mike Schmidt Portrait 4.00 10.00
NR1 Nolan Ryan Angels 8.00 20.00
NR2 Nolan Ryan Rgr 8.00 20.00
NR3 Nolan Ryan Mets 8.00 20.00
NR4 Nolan Ryan Astros 8.00 20.00
OC1 Orlando Cepeda Giants 1.50 4.00
OC2 Orlando Cepeda Braves 1.50 4.00
OS1 Ozzie Smith Padres 3.00 8.00
OS2 Ozzie Smith Cards 3.00 8.00
OS3 Ozzie Smith Cards 3.00 8.00
PM1 Paul Molitor Brew 2.50 6.00
PM2 Paul Molitor Jays 2.50 6.00
PM3 Paul Molitor Twins 2.50 6.00
PN1 Phil Niekro Braves 1.50 4.00
PN2 Phil Niekro Yanks 1.50 4.00
RC1 Rod Carew Twins 1.50 4.00
RC2 Rod Carew Angels 1.50 4.00
RF1 Rollie Fingers A's 1.50 4.00
RF2 Rollie Fingers Padres 1.50 4.00
RJ1 Reggie Jackson A's 1.50 4.00
RJ2 Reggie Jackson Yanks 1.50 4.00
RJ3 Reggie Jackson Angels 1.50 4.00
RK1 Ralph Kiner 1.50 4.00
RR1 Robin Roberts 1.50 4.00
RS1 Red Schoendienst 1.50 4.00
RY1 Robin Yount Batting 2.50 6.00
RY2 Robin Yount Fielding 2.50 6.00
RY3 Robin Yount Portrait 2.50 6.00
SA1 Ryne Sandberg Batting 5.00 12.00
SA2 Ryne Sandberg Fielding 5.00 12.00
SA3 Ryne Sandberg Portrait 5.00 12.00
SC1 Steve Carlton Cards 1.50 4.00
SC2 Steve Carlton Phils 1.50 4.00
SM1 Stan Musial B
W 4.00 10.00
SM2 Stan Musial Color 4.00 10.00
SN1 Duke Snider 1.50 4.00
TP1 Tony Perez Reds 1.50 4.00
TP2 Tony Perez Sox 1.50 4.00
TS1 Tom Seaver 1.50 4.00
WB1 Wade Boggs Sox 1.50 4.00
WB2 Wade Boggs Yanks 1.50 4.00
WB3 Wade Boggs Rays 1.50 4.00
WF1 Whitey Ford 1.50 4.00
WM1 Willie McCovey 1.50 4.00
YB1 Yogi Berra 2.50 6.00

2005 Upper Deck Hall of Fame Cooperstown Calling Autograph

STATED PRINT RUN 25 SERIAL #'d SETS
GOLD PRINT RUN 5 SERIAL #'d SETS
NO GOLD PRICING DUE TO SCARCITY
RAINBOW PRINT RUN 1 SERIAL #'d SET
NO RAINBOW PRICING DUE TO SCARCITY
*SILVER: .5X TO 1.2X BASIC
SILVER PRINT RUN 15 SERIAL #'d SETS
MATERIAL GOLD PRINT RUN 5 #'d SETS
NO MAT.GOLD PRICING DUE TO SCARCITY
MATERIAL RAINBOW PRINT RUN 1 #'d SET
NO MAT.RB PRICING DUE TO SCARCITY
*MAT.SILVER: .5X TO 1.2X BASIC
MATERIAL SILVER PRINT RUN 15 #'d SETS
PATCH GOLD PRINT RUN 5 #'d SETS
NO PATCH GOLD PRICING AVAILABLE
PATCH RAINBOW PRINT RUN 1 #'d SET
NO PATCH RAINBOW PRICING AVAILABLE
PATCH SILVER PRINT RUN 10 #'d SETS
NO PATCH SILVER PRICING AVAILABLE
OVERALL AUTO ODDS ONE PER TIN
EXCHANGE DEADLINE 07/18/08
AK1 Al Kaline Batting 30.00 80.00
AK2 Al Kaline Fielding 40.00 100.00
BD1 Bobby Doerr Batting 12.50 30.00
BD2 Bobby Doerr Fielding 12.50 30.00
BE1 Johnny Bench 20.00 50.00
BF1 Bob Feller Pitching 10.00 25.00
BF2 Bob Feller Portrait 10.00 25.00
BG1 Bob Gibson 15.00 40.00
BM1 Bill Mazeroski 10.00 25.00
BR1 Brooks Robinson Batting 15.00 40.00
BR2 Brooks Robinson Fielding 15.00 40.00
BR3 Brooks Robinson Portrait 15.00 40.00
BW1 Billy Williams Cubs 10.00 25.00
BW2 Billy Williams A's 10.00 25.00
CF1 Carlton Fisk W.Sox 15.00 40.00
CF2 Carlton Fisk R.Sox 15.00 40.00
CY2 C.Yaz No Sleeves 30.00 60.00
DE1 Dennis Eckersley Sox 10.00 25.00
DE2 Dennis Eckersley A's 10.00 25.00
DS1 Don Sutton Dgr 8.00 20.00
DS2 Don Sutton Angels 8.00 20.00
DS3 Don Sutton Astros 8.00 20.00
DW1 Dave Winfield 15.00 40.00
EB1 Ernie Banks 30.00 60.00
EM1 Eddie Murray O's 15.00 40.00

2005 Upper Deck Hall of Fame Cooperstown Calling Autograph

EM2 Eddie Murray Dgr 15.00 40.00
FJ1 Fergie Jenkins Cubs 8.00 20.00
FJ2 Fergie Jenkins Rgr 8.00 20.00
FR1 Frank Robinson 10.00 25.00
GB1 George Brett Glove Up 40.00 80.00
GB2 George Brett Glove Down 40.00 80.00
GC1 Gary Carter Expos 10.00 25.00
GC2 Gary Carter Mets 10.00 25.00
GC3 Gary Carter Dgr 10.00 25.00
GP1 Gaylord Perry Indians 8.00 20.00
GP2 Gaylord Perry Padres 8.00 20.00
HK2 Harmon Killebrew Twins 30.00 60.00
JB1 Jim Bunning 10.00 25.00
JM1 Juan Marichal 10.00 25.00
JP1 Jim Palmer Pitching 10.00 25.00
JP2 Jim Palmer Portrait 10.00 25.00
KP1 Kirby Puckett 100.00 200.00
KP2 Kirby Puckett 100.00 200.00
LA1 Luis Aparicio W.Sox 10.00 25.00
LA2 Luis Aparicio O's 10.00 25.00
LB1 Lou Brock Cubs 15.00 40.00
LB2 Lou Brock Cards 15.00 40.00
MO1 Joe Morgan Astros 10.00 25.00
MO2 Joe Morgan Reds 10.00 25.00
MS1 Mike Schmidt Batting 30.00 60.00
MS2 Mike Schmidt Fielding 30.00 60.00
MS3 Mike Schmidt Portrait 30.00 60.00
NR1 Nolan Ryan Angels 50.00 100.00
NR2 Nolan Ryan Rgr 50.00 100.00
NR3 Nolan Ryan Mets 50.00 100.00
NR4 Nolan Ryan Astros 50.00 100.00
OS1 Ozzie Smith Padres 20.00 50.00
OS2 Ozzie Smith Cards 20.00 50.00
OS3 Ozzie Smith Cards 20.00 50.00
PM1 Paul Molitor Brew 10.00 25.00
PM2 Paul Molitor Jays 10.00 25.00
PM3 Paul Molitor Twins 10.00 25.00
PN1 Phil Niekro Braves 10.00 25.00
PN2 Phil Niekro Yanks 10.00 25.00
RC1 Rod Carew Twins 15.00 40.00
RC2 Rod Carew Angels 10.00 25.00
RF1 Rollie Fingers A's 8.00 20.00
RF2 Rollie Fingers Padres 8.00 20.00
RJ1 Reggie Jackson A's 20.00 50.00
RJ2 Reggie Jackson Yanks 20.00 50.00
RJ3 Reggie Jackson Angels 20.00 50.00
RK1 Ralph Kiner 20.00 50.00
RR1 Robin Roberts 10.00 25.00
RS1 Red Schoendienst 10.00 25.00
RY1 Robin Yount Batting 20.00 50.00
RY2 Robin Yount Fielding 20.00 50.00
RY3 Robin Yount Portrait 20.00 50.00
SA1 Ryne Sandberg Batting 40.00 80.00
SA2 Ryne Sandberg Fielding 40.00 80.00
SA3 Ryne Sandberg Portrait 40.00 80.00
SC1 Steve Carlton Cards 12.50 30.00
SC2 Steve Carlton Phils 12.50 30.00
SM1 Stan Musial B/W 40.00 80.00
SM2 Stan Musial Color 40.00 80.00
SN1 Duke Snider 15.00 40.00
TP1 Tony Perez Reds 10.00 25.00
TP2 Tony Perez Sox 10.00 25.00
TS1 Tom Seaver 25.00 60.00
WB1 Wade Boggs Sox 15.00 40.00
WB2 Wade Boggs Yanks 15.00 40.00
WB3 Wade Boggs Rays 15.00 40.00
WF1 Whitey Ford 15.00 40.00
YB1 Yogi Berra 30.00 80.00

2005 Upper Deck Hall of Fame Essential Enshrinement

STATED PRINT RUN 50 SERIAL #'d SETS
GOLD PRINT RUN 5 SERIAL #'d SETS
NO GOLD PRICING DUE TO SCARCITY
RAINBOW PRINT RUN 1 SERIAL #'d SET
NO RAINBOW PRICING DUE TO SCARCITY
*SILVER: .6X TO 1.5X BASIC
SILVER PRINT RUN 15 SERIAL #'d SETS
OVERALL INSERT ODDS ONE PER TIN

AK1 Al Kaline Batting 2.50 6.00
AK2 Al Kaline Fielding 2.50 6.00
BD1 Bobby Doerr Batting 1.50 4.00
BD2 Bobby Doerr Fielding 1.50 4.00
BE1 Johnny Bench Batting 2.50 6.00
BE2 Johnny Bench Fielding 2.50 6.00
BF1 Bob Feller Pitching 1.50 4.00
BF2 Bob Feller Portrait 1.50 4.00
BG1 Bob Gibson Pitching 1.50 4.00
BG2 Bob Gibson Portrait 1.50 4.00
BM1 Bill Mazeroski 1.50 4.00
BR1 Brooks Robinson Batting 1.50 4.00
BR2 Brooks Robinson Fielding 1.50 4.00
BR3 Brooks Robinson Portrait 1.50 4.00
BW1 Billy Williams Cubs 1.50 4.00
BW2 Billy Williams A's 1.50 4.00
CF1 Carlton Fisk R.Sox 1.50 4.00
CF2 Carlton Fisk W.Sox 1.50 4.00
CY1 C.Yastrzemski Red Hand 3.00 8.00
CY2 C.Yaz Bare Hands 3.00 8.00
CY3 C.Yastrzemski Sleeves 3.00 8.00
DE1 Dennis Eckersley 1.50 4.00
DS1 Don Sutton Pitching 1.50 4.00
DS2 Don Sutton Portrait 1.50 4.00
DW1 Dave Winfield 1.50 4.00
EB1 Ernie Banks 2.50 6.00
EM1 Eddie Murray O's 1.50 4.00
EM2 Eddie Murray Dgr 1.50 4.00
FJ1 Fergie Jenkins Cubs 1.50 4.00
FJ2 Fergie Jenkins Rgr 1.50 4.00
FR1 Frank Robinson Reds 1.50 4.00
FR2 Frank Robinson O's 1.50 4.00
GB1 George Brett Batting 5.00 12.00
GB2 George Brett Fielding 5.00 12.00
GB3 George Brett Portrait 5.00 12.00
GC1 Gary Carter Mets 1.50 4.00
GC2 Gary Carter Expos 1.50 4.00
GK1 George Kell 1.50 4.00
GP1 Gaylord Perry Giants 1.50 4.00
GP2 Gaylord Perry Padres 1.50 4.00
HK1 H.Killebrew Senators 2.50 6.00
HK2 Harmon Killebrew Twins 2.50 6.00
JB1 Jim Bunning 1.50 4.00
JM1 Juan Marichal 1.50 4.00
JP1 Jim Palmer Pitching 1.50 4.00
JP2 Jim Palmer Portrait 1.50 4.00
KP1 Kirby Puckett 2.50 6.00
KP2 Kirby Puckett 2.50 6.00
LA1 Luis Aparicio 1.50 4.00
LB1 Lou Brock Cards 1.50 4.00
LB2 Lou Brock Cubs 1.50 4.00
MI1 Monte Irvin 1.50 4.00
MO1 Joe Morgan Astros 1.50 4.00
MO2 Joe Morgan Reds 1.50 4.00
MO3 Joe Morgan Giants 1.50 4.00
MS1 Mike Schmidt Batting 4.00 10.00
MS2 Mike Schmidt Fielding 4.00 10.00
NR1 Nolan Ryan Mets 8.00 20.00
NR2 Nolan Ryan Rgr 8.00 20.00
NR3 Nolan Ryan Astros 8.00 20.00
NR4 Nolan Ryan Angels 8.00 20.00
OC1 Orlando Cepeda 1.50 4.00
OS1 Ozzie Smith Padres 3.00 8.00
OS2 Ozzie Smith Cards 3.00 8.00
PM1 Paul Molitor Brew 2.50 6.00
PM2 Paul Molitor Twins 2.50 6.00
PM3 Paul Molitor Jays 2.50 6.00
PN1 Phil Niekro Braves 1.50 4.00
PN2 Phil Niekro Yanks 1.50 4.00
RC1 Rod Carew Twins 1.50 4.00
RC2 Rod Carew Angels 1.50 4.00
RF1 Rollie Fingers 1.50 4.00
RJ1 Reggie Jackson A's 1.50 4.00
RJ2 Reggie Jackson Yanks 1.50 4.00
RJ3 Reggie Jackson Angels 1.50 4.00
RK1 Ralph Kiner 1.50 4.00
RR1 Robin Roberts 1.50 4.00
RS1 Red Schoendienst 1.50 4.00
RY1 Robin Yount Batting 2.50 6.00
RY2 Robin Yount Fielding 2.50 6.00
RY3 Robin Yount Portrait 2.50 6.00
SA1 Ryne Sandberg Batting 5.00 12.00
SA2 Ryne Sandberg Fielding 5.00 12.00
SA3 Ryne Sandberg Portrait 5.00 12.00
SC1 Steve Carlton Cards 1.50 4.00
SC2 Steve Carlton Phils 1.50 4.00
SM1 Stan Musial B
W 4.00 10.00
SM2 Stan Musial Color 4.00 10.00
SN1 Duke Snider Brooklyn 1.50 4.00
SN2 Duke Snider LA 1.50 4.00
TP1 Tony Perez 1.50 4.00
TS1 Tom Seaver 1.50 4.00
WB1 Wade Boggs Sox 1.50 4.00
WB2 Wade Boggs Yanks 1.50 4.00
WB3 Wade Boggs Rays 1.50 4.00
WF1 Whitey Ford Fielding 1.50 4.00
WF2 Whitey Ford Portrait 1.50 4.00
WM1 Willie McCovey 1.50 4.00
YB1 Yogi Berra Batting 2.50 6.00
YB2 Yogi Berra Fielding 2.50 6.00

2005 Upper Deck Hall of Fame Essential Enshrinement Autograph

STATED PRINT RUN 25 SERIAL #'d SETS
GOLD PRINT RUN 5 SERIAL #'d SETS
NO GOLD PRICING DUE TO SCARCITY
RAINBOW PRINT RUN 1 SERIAL #'d SET
NO RAINBOW PRICING DUE TO SCARCITY
*SILVER: .5X TO 1.2X BASIC
SILVER PRINT RUN 15 SERIAL #'d SETS
MATERIAL GOLD PRINT RUN 5 #'d SETS
NO MAT.GOLD PRICING DUE TO SCARCITY
MATERIAL RAINBOW PRINT RUN 1 #'d SET
NO MAT.RB PRICING DUE TO SCARCITY
*MAT.SILVER: .5X TO 1.2X BASIC
MATERIAL SILVER PRINT RUN 15 #'d SETS
PATCH GOLD PRINT RUN 5 #'d SETS
NO PATCH GOLD PRICING AVAILABLE
PATCH RAINBOW PRINT RUN 1 #'d SET
NO PATCH RAINBOW PRICING AVAILABLE
PATCH SILVER PRINT RUN 10 #'d SETS
NO PATCH SILVER PRICING AVAILABLE
OVERALL AUTO ODDS ONE PER TIN
EXCHANGE DEADLINE 07/18/08

AK1 Al Kaline Batting 30.00 80.00
AK2 Al Kaline Fielding 30.00 80.00
BD1 Bobby Doerr Batting 8.00 20.00
BD2 Bobby Doerr Fielding 8.00 20.00
BE1 Johnny Bench Batting 20.00 50.00
BE2 Johnny Bench Fielding 20.00 50.00
BF1 Bob Feller Pitching 10.00 25.00
BF2 Bob Feller Portrait 10.00 25.00
BG1 Bob Gibson Pitching 15.00 40.00
BG2 Bob Gibson Portrait 15.00 40.00
BM1 Bill Mazeroski 20.00 50.00
BR1 Brooks Robinson Batting 15.00 40.00
BR2 Brooks Robinson Fielding 15.00 40.00
BR3 Brooks Robinson Portrait 15.00 40.00
BW1 Billy Williams Cubs 10.00 25.00
BW2 Billy Williams A's 10.00 25.00
CF1 Carlton Fisk R.Sox 10.00 25.00
CF2 Carlton Fisk W.Sox 10.00 25.00
CY1 C.Yastrzemski Red Hand 30.00 60.00
CY2 C.Yaz Bare Hands 30.00 60.00
CY3 C.Yastrzemski Sleeves 30.00 60.00
DE1 Dennis Eckersley 10.00 25.00
DS1 Don Sutton Pitching 8.00 20.00
DS2 Don Sutton Portrait 8.00 20.00
DW1 Dave Winfield 15.00 40.00
EB1 Ernie Banks 40.00 80.00
FJ1 Fergie Jenkins Cubs 8.00 20.00
FJ2 Fergie Jenkins Rgr 8.00 20.00
FR1 Frank Robinson Reds 10.00 25.00
FR2 Frank Robinson O's 10.00 25.00
GB3 George Brett Portrait 40.00 80.00
GC1 Gary Carter Mets 15.00 40.00
GC2 Gary Carter Expos 15.00 40.00
GK1 George Kell 10.00 25.00
GP1 Gaylord Perry Giants 8.00 20.00
GP2 Gaylord Perry Padres 8.00 20.00
HK1 H.Killebrew Senators 30.00 60.00
HK2 Harmon Killebrew Twins 30.00 60.00
JB1 Jim Bunning 10.00 25.00
JM1 Juan Marichal 10.00 25.00
JP1 Jim Palmer Pitching 10.00 25.00
JP2 Jim Palmer Portrait 10.00 25.00
KP1 Kirby Puckett 50.00 100.00
KP2 Kirby Puckett 50.00 100.00
LA1 Luis Aparicio 10.00 25.00
LB1 Lou Brock Cards 15.00 40.00
LB2 Lou Brock Cubs 15.00 40.00
MI1 Monte Irvin 10.00 25.00
MO1 Joe Morgan Astros 12.50 30.00
MO2 Joe Morgan Reds 12.50 30.00
MO3 Joe Morgan Giants 12.50 30.00
MS1 Mike Schmidt Batting 30.00 60.00
MS2 Mike Schmidt Fielding 30.00 60.00
NR1 Nolan Ryan Mets 50.00 100.00
NR2 Nolan Ryan Rgr 50.00 100.00
NR3 Nolan Ryan Astros 50.00 100.00
NR4 Nolan Ryan Angels 50.00 100.00
OC1 Orlando Cepeda 10.00 25.00
OS1 Ozzie Smith Padres 20.00 50.00
OS2 Ozzie Smith Cards 20.00 50.00
PM1 Paul Molitor Brew 10.00 25.00
PM2 Paul Molitor Twins 10.00 25.00
PM3 Paul Molitor Jays 10.00 25.00
PN1 Phil Niekro Braves 10.00 25.00
PN2 Phil Niekro Yanks 10.00 25.00
RC1 Rod Carew Twins 15.00 40.00
RC2 Rod Carew Angels 15.00 40.00
RF1 Rollie Fingers 8.00 20.00
RJ1 Reggie Jackson A's 30.00 60.00
RJ2 Reggie Jackson Yanks 30.00 60.00
RJ3 Reggie Jackson Angels 30.00 60.00
RK1 Ralph Kiner 10.00 25.00
RR1 Robin Roberts 15.00 40.00
RS1 Red Schoendienst 10.00 25.00
RY1 Robin Yount Batting 20.00 50.00
RY2 Robin Yount Fielding 20.00 50.00
RY3 Robin Yount Portrait 20.00 50.00
SA1 Ryne Sandberg Batting 15.00 40.00
SA2 Ryne Sandberg Fielding 15.00 40.00
SA3 Ryne Sandberg Portrait 15.00 40.00
SC1 Steve Carlton Cards 10.00 25.00
SC2 Steve Carlton Phils 10.00 25.00
SM1 Stan Musial B/W 40.00 80.00
SM2 Stan Musial Color 40.00 80.00
SN1 Duke Snider Brooklyn 15.00 40.00
SN2 Duke Snider LA 15.00 40.00
TP1 Tony Perez 15.00 40.00
TS1 Tom Seaver 40.00 100.00
WB1 Wade Boggs Sox 15.00 40.00
WB2 Wade Boggs Yanks 15.00 40.00
WB3 Wade Boggs Rays 15.00 40.00
WF1 Whitey Ford Fielding 15.00 40.00
WF2 Whitey Ford Portrait 15.00 40.00
WM1 Willie McCovey 15.00 40.00
YB1 Yogi Berra Batting 30.00 80.00
YB2 Yogi Berra Fielding 30.00 80.00

2005 Upper Deck Hall of Fame Hall Worthy

STATED PRINT RUN 50 SERIAL #'d SETS
GOLD PRINT RUN 5 SERIAL #'d SETS
NO GOLD PRICING DUE TO SCARCITY
RAINBOW PRINT RUN 1 SERIAL #'d SET
NO RAINBOW PRICING DUE TO SCARCITY
*SILVER: .6X TO 1.5X BASIC
SILVER PRINT RUN 15 SERIAL #'d SETS
OVERALL INSERT ODDS ONE PER TIN

AK1 Al Kaline Batting 2.50 6.00
AK2 Al Kaline Portrait 2.50 6.00
BD1 Bobby Doerr 1.50 4.00
BE1 Johnny Bench Batting 2.50 6.00
BE2 Johnny Bench Portrait 2.50 6.00
BF1 Bob Feller Color 1.50 4.00
BF2 Bob Feller B
W 1.50 4.00
BG1 Bob Gibson 1.50 4.00
BM1 Bill Mazeroski 1.50 4.00
BR1 Brooks Robinson Batting 1.50 4.00
BR2 Brooks Robinson Fielding 1.50 4.00
BW1 Billy Williams 1.50 4.00
CF1 Carlton Fisk R.Sox 1.50 4.00
CF2 Carlton Fisk W.Sox 1.50 4.00
CY1 Carl Yastrzemski Batting 3.00 8.00
CY2 Carl Yastrzemski Portrait 3.00 8.00
DE1 Dennis Eckersley Cubs 1.50 4.00
DE2 Dennis Eckersley A's 1.50 4.00
DE3 Dennis Eckersley Indians 1.50 4.00
DE4 Dennis Eckersley Sox 1.50 4.00
DS1 Don Sutton Dgr 1.50 4.00
DS2 Don Sutton Angels 1.50 4.00
DS3 Don Sutton Astros 1.50 4.00
DW1 Dave Winfield 1.50 4.00
EB1 Ernie Banks 2.50 6.00
EM1 Eddie Murray O's 1.50 4.00
EM2 Eddie Murray Dgr 1.50 4.00
EM3 Eddie Murray Mets 1.50 4.00
FJ1 Fergie Jenkins Cubs 1.50 4.00
FJ2 Fergie Jenkins Sox 1.50 4.00
FJ3 Fergie Jenkins Rgr 1.50 4.00
FR1 Frank Robinson Reds 1.50 4.00
FR2 Frank Robinson O's 1.50 4.00
GB1 George Brett Batting 5.00 12.00
GB2 George Brett Fielding 5.00 12.00
GB3 George Brett Portrait 5.00 12.00
GC1 Gary Carter Expos 1.50 4.00
GC2 Gary Carter Mets 1.50 4.00
GK1 George Kell 1.50 4.00
GP1 Gaylord Perry Giants 1.50 4.00
GP2 Gaylord Perry Indians 1.50 4.00
HK1 H.Killebrew Senators 2.50 6.00
HK2 Harmon Killebrew Twins 2.50 6.00
JB1 Jim Bunning 1.50 4.00
JM1 Juan Marichal 1.50 4.00
JP1 Jim Palmer Pitching 1.50 4.00
JP2 Jim Palmer Portrait 1.50 4.00
KP1 Kirby Puckett 2.50 6.00
LA1 Luis Aparicio 1.50 4.00
LB1 Lou Brock Cards 1.50 4.00
LB2 Lou Brock Cubs 1.50 4.00
MI1 Monte Irvin 1.50 4.00
MO1 Joe Morgan Reds 1.50 4.00
MO2 Joe Morgan Giants 1.50 4.00
MS1 Mike Schmidt Batting 4.00 10.00
MS2 Mike Schmidt Fielding 4.00 10.00
MS3 Mike Schmidt Portrait 4.00 10.00
NR1 Nolan Ryan Mets 8.00 20.00
NR2 Nolan Ryan Angels 8.00 20.00
NR3 Nolan Ryan Astros 8.00 20.00
NR4 Nolan Ryan Rgr 8.00 20.00
OC1 Orlando Cepeda Giants 1.50 4.00
OC2 Orlando Cepeda Braves 1.50 4.00
OS1 Ozzie Smith Padres 3.00 8.00
OS2 Ozzie Smith Cards 3.00 8.00
PM1 Paul Molitor Brew 2.50 6.00
PM2 Paul Molitor Twins 2.50 6.00
PN1 Phil Niekro Braves 1.50 4.00
PN2 Phil Niekro Yanks 1.50 4.00
RC1 Rod Carew Angels 1.50 4.00
RC2 Rod Carew Twins 1.50 4.00
RF1 Rollie Fingers A's 1.50 4.00
RF2 Rollie Fingers Brew 1.50 4.00
RJ1 Reggie Jackson A's 1.50 4.00
RJ2 Reggie Jackson O's 1.50 4.00
RJ3 Reggie Jackson Yanks 1.50 4.00
RJ4 Reggie Jackson Angels 1.50 4.00
RK1 Ralph Kiner 1.50 4.00
RR1 Robin Roberts 1.50 4.00
RS1 Red Schoendienst 1.50 4.00
RY1 Robin Yount Batting 2.50 6.00
RY2 Robin Yount Fielding 2.50 6.00
SA1 Ryne Sandberg Batting 5.00 12.00
SA2 Ryne Sandberg Fielding 5.00 12.00
SA3 Ryne Sandberg Portrait 5.00 12.00
SC1 Steve Carlton Cards 1.50 4.00
SC2 Steve Carlton Phils 1.50 4.00
SM1 Stan Musial 4.00 10.00
SN1 Duke Snider Brooklyn 1.50 4.00
SN2 Duke Snider LA 1.50 4.00
TP1 Tony Perez Reds 1.50 4.00
TP2 Tony Perez Sox 1.50 4.00
TS1 Tom Seaver Mets 1.50 4.00
TS2 Tom Seaver Reds 1.50 4.00
WB1 Wade Boggs Sox 1.50 4.00
WB2 Wade Boggs Yanks 1.50 4.00
WB3 Wade Boggs Rays 1.50 4.00
WF1 Whitey Ford 1.50 4.00
WM1 Willie McCovey 1.50 4.00
YB1 Yogi Berra 2.50 6.00

2005 Upper Deck Hall of Fame Hall Worthy Autograph

STATED PRINT RUN 25 SERIAL #'d SETS
GOLD PRINT RUN 5 SERIAL #'d SETS
NO GOLD PRICING DUE TO SCARCITY
RAINBOW PRINT RUN 1 SERIAL #'d SET
NO RAINBOW PRICING DUE TO SCARCITY
*SILVER: .5X TO 1.2X BASIC
SILVER PRINT RUN 15 SERIAL #'d SETS
MATERIAL GOLD PRINT RUN 5 #'d SETS
NO MAT.GOLD PRICING DUE TO SCARCITY
MATERIAL RAINBOW PRINT RUN 1 #'d SET
NO MAT.RB PRICING DUE TO SCARCITY
*MAT.SILVER: .5X TO 1.2X BASIC
MATERIAL SILVER PRINT RUN 15 #'d SETS
PATCH GOLD PRINT RUN 5 #'d SETS
NO PATCH GOLD PRICING AVAILABLE
PATCH RAINBOW PRINT RUN 1 #'d SET
NO PATCH RAINBOW PRICING AVAILABLE
PATCH SILVER PRINT RUN 10 #'d SETS
SM1 MUSIAL PATCH SILV.QTY 3 #'d CARDS
NO PATCH SILVER PRICING AVAILABLE
OVERALL AUTO ODDS ONE PER TIN
EXCHANGE DEADLINE 07/18/08

AK1 Al Kaline Batting 12.00 30.00
AK2 Al Kaline Portrait 12.00 30.00
BD1 Bobby Doerr 8.00 20.00
BE1 Johnny Bench Batting 20.00 50.00
BE2 Johnny Bench Portrait 20.00 50.00
BF1 Bob Feller Color 10.00 25.00
BF2 Bob Feller B
W 10.00 25.00
BG1 Bob Gibson 15.00 40.00
BM1 Bill Mazeroski 20.00 50.00
BR1 Brooks Robinson Batting 15.00 40.00
BR2 Brooks Robinson Fielding 15.00 40.00
BW1 Billy Williams 10.00 25.00
CF1 Carlton Fisk R.Sox 10.00 25.00
CF2 Carlton Fisk W.Sox 10.00 25.00
CY1 Carl Yastrzemski Batting 30.00 60.00
CY2 Carl Yastrzemski Portrait 30.00 60.00
DE1 Dennis Eckersley Cubs 10.00 25.00
DE2 Dennis Eckersley A's 10.00 25.00
DE3 Dennis Eckersley Indians 10.00 25.00
DE4 Dennis Eckersley Sox 10.00 25.00
DS1 Don Sutton Dgr 8.00 20.00
DS2 Don Sutton Angels 8.00 20.00
DS3 Don Sutton Astros 8.00 20.00
DW1 Dave Winfield 15.00 40.00
EB1 Ernie Banks 30.00 60.00
EM1 Eddie Murray O's 30.00 60.00
EM3 Eddie Murray Mets 30.00 60.00
FJ1 Fergie Jenkins Cubs 8.00 20.00
FJ2 Fergie Jenkins Sox 8.00 20.00
FJ3 Fergie Jenkins Rgr 8.00 20.00
FR1 Frank Robinson Reds 10.00 25.00
FR2 Frank Robinson O's 10.00 25.00
GB3 George Brett Portrait 40.00 80.00
GC1 Gary Carter Expos 10.00 25.00
GC2 Gary Carter Mets 10.00 25.00
GK1 George Kell 15.00 40.00
GP1 Gaylord Perry Giants 8.00 20.00
GP2 Gaylord Perry Indians 8.00 20.00
HK1 H.Killebrew Senators 30.00 60.00
HK2 Harmon Killebrew Twins 30.00 60.00
JB1 Jim Bunning 10.00 25.00
JM1 Juan Marichal 10.00 25.00
JP1 Jim Palmer Pitching 10.00 25.00
JP2 Jim Palmer Portrait 10.00 25.00
KP1 Kirby Puckett 100.00 200.00
LA1 Luis Aparicio 10.00 25.00
LB1 Lou Brock Cards 15.00 40.00
LB2 Lou Brock Cubs 15.00 40.00
MI1 Monte Irvin 10.00 25.00
MO1 Joe Morgan Reds 10.00 25.00
MO2 Joe Morgan Giants 10.00 25.00
MS1 Mike Schmidt Batting 30.00 60.00
MS2 Mike Schmidt Fielding 30.00 60.00
MS3 Mike Schmidt Portrait 30.00 60.00
NR1 Nolan Ryan Mets 50.00 100.00
NR2 Nolan Ryan Angels 50.00 100.00
NR3 Nolan Ryan Astros 50.00 100.00
NR4 Nolan Ryan Rgr 50.00 100.00
OC1 Orlando Cepeda Giants 10.00 25.00
OC2 Orlando Cepeda Braves 10.00 25.00
OS1 Ozzie Smith Padres 20.00 50.00
OS2 Ozzie Smith Cards 20.00 50.00
PM1 Paul Molitor Brew 10.00 25.00
PM2 Paul Molitor Twins 10.00 25.00
PN1 Phil Niekro Braves 10.00 25.00
PN2 Phil Niekro Yanks 10.00 25.00
RC1 Rod Carew Angels 15.00 40.00
RC2 Rod Carew Twins 15.00 40.00
RF1 Rollie Fingers A's 8.00 20.00
RF2 Rollie Fingers Brew 8.00 20.00
RJ1 Reggie Jackson A's 20.00 50.00
RJ2 Reggie Jackson O's 20.00 50.00
RJ3 Reggie Jackson Yanks 20.00 50.00
RJ4 Reggie Jackson Angels 20.00 50.00
RK1 Ralph Kiner 20.00 50.00
RR1 Robin Roberts 15.00 40.00
RS1 Red Schoendienst 15.00 40.00
RY1 Robin Yount Batting 20.00 50.00
RY2 Robin Yount Fielding 20.00 50.00
SA1 Ryne Sandberg Batting 40.00 80.00
SA2 Ryne Sandberg Fielding 40.00 80.00
SA3 Ryne Sandberg Portrait 40.00 80.00
SC1 Steve Carlton Cards 10.00 25.00
SC2 Steve Carlton Phils 10.00 25.00
SM1 Stan Musial 50.00 100.00
SN1 Duke Snider Brooklyn 15.00 40.00
SN2 Duke Snider LA 15.00 40.00
TP1 Tony Perez Reds 10.00 25.00
TP2 Tony Perez Sox 15.00 40.00
TS1 Tom Seaver Mets 30.00 80.00
TS2 Tom Seaver Reds 30.00 80.00
WB1 Wade Boggs Sox 15.00 40.00
WB2 Wade Boggs Yanks 15.00 40.00
WB3 Wade Boggs Rays 15.00 40.00
WF1 Whitey Ford 15.00 40.00
WM1 Willie McCovey 15.00 40.00
YB1 Yogi Berra 30.00 80.00

2005 Upper Deck Hall of Fame Materials

STATED PRINT RUN 25 SERIAL #'d SETS
GOLD PRINT RUN 5 SERIAL #'d SETS
NO GOLD PRICING DUE TO SCARCITY
GREEN PRINT RUN 10 SERIAL #'d SETS
NO GREEN PRICING DUE TO SCARCITY
RAINBOW PRINT RUN 1 SERIAL #'d SET
NO RAINBOW PRICING DUE TO SCARCITY
*SILVER: .5X TO 1.2X BASIC
SILVER PRINT RUN 15 SERIAL #'d SETS
OVERALL GAME-USED/CUT SIG ODDS 1:20

BR1 Babe Ruth Sox Bat 75.00 150.00
BR2 B.Ruth Yanks Btg Bat 150.00 250.00
BR3 B.Ruth Yanks Port Bat 150.00 250.00
DD1 Dizzy Dean Cards Jsy 50.00 100.00
DD2 Dizzy Dean Cubs Jsy 50.00 100.00
GS1 George Sisler Browns Bat 15.00 40.00
GS2 George Sisler Braves Bat 15.00 40.00
JD1 J.DiMaggio Btg Pants 60.00 120.00
JD2 J.DiMaggio Fldg Pants 60.00 120.00
JD3 J.DiMaggio Port Pants 60.00 120.00
JF1 Jimmie Foxx A's Bat 30.00 60.00
JF2 Jimmie Foxx Sox Bat 30.00 60.00
JM1 Johnny Mize Cards Pants 10.00 25.00
JM2 Johnny Mize Giants Pants 10.00 25.00
JM3 Johnny Mize Yanks Pants 10.00 25.00
JR1 J.Robinson Btg Pants 30.00 60.00
JR2 J.Robinson Port Pants 30.00 60.00
JR3 J.Robinson Fldg Pants 30.00 60.00
LG1 Lou Gehrig Batting Bat 50.00 100.00
LG2 Lou Gehrig Portrait Bat 50.00 100.00
LG3 Lou Gehrig Fielding Bat 50.00 100.00
MC1 Mickey Cochrane Bat 20.00 50.00
MM1 Mickey Mantle Btg Jsy 75.00 150.00
MM2 Mickey Mantle Fldg Jsy 75.00 150.00
MM3 Mickey Mantle Port Jsy 75.00 150.00
MO1 Mel Ott Black Cap Jsy 30.00 60.00
MO2 Mel Ott Pinstripe Jsy 30.00 60.00
RC1 R.Clemente Batting Jsy 60.00 120.00
RC2 R.Clemente Portrait Jsy 60.00 120.00
RC3 R.Clemente Fldg Jsy 60.00 120.00
RH1 Rogers Hornsby Jkt 50.00 100.00
SP1 S.Paige Indians Pants 30.00 60.00
SP2 S.Paige Brwn Pitch Pants 30.00 60.00
SP3 S.Paige Brwn Port Pants 30.00 60.00
TC1 Ty Cobb Tigers Btg Bat 60.00 120.00
TC2 Ty Cobb Tigers Port Bat 60.00 120.00
TC3 Ty Cobb A's Bat 60.00 120.00
TW1 Ted Williams Batting Jsy 20.00 50.00
TW2 Ted Williams Fielding Jsy 50.00 100.00
TW3 Ted Williams Portrait Jsy 50.00 100.00

2005 Upper Deck Hall of Fame Seasons

STATED PRINT RUN 50 SERIAL #'d SETS
GOLD PRINT RUN 5 SERIAL #'d SETS
NO GOLD PRICING DUE TO SCARCITY
RAINBOW PRINT RUN 1 SERIAL #'d SET
NO RAINBOW PRICING DUE TO SCARCITY
*SILVER: .6X TO 1.5X BASIC
SILVER PRINT RUN 15 SERIAL #'d SETS
OVERALL INSERT ODDS ONE PER TIN

AK1 Al Kaline Batting 2.50 6.00
AK2 Al Kaline Fielding 2.50 6.00
AK3 Al Kaline Portrait 2.50 6.00
BD1 Bobby Doerr 1.50 4.00
BE1 Johnny Bench Batting 2.50 6.00
BE2 Johnny Bench Fielding 2.50 6.00
BF1 Bob Feller Pitching 1.50 4.00
BF2 Bob Feller Portrait 1.50 4.00
BG1 Bob Gibson Pitching 1.50 4.00
BG2 Bob Gibson Portrait 1.50 4.00
BM1 Bill Mazeroski 1.50 4.00
BR1 Brooks Robinson Batting 1.50 4.00
BR2 Brooks Robinson Fielding 1.50 4.00
BR3 Brooks Robinson Portrait 1.50 4.00
BW1 Billy Williams Batting 1.50 4.00
BW2 Billy Williams Portrait 1.50 4.00
CF1 Carlton Fisk R.Sox 1.50 4.00
CF2 Carlton Fisk W.Sox 1.50 4.00
CY1 Carl Yastrzemski Batting 3.00 8.00
CY2 Carl Yastrzemski Fielding 3.00 8.00
DE1 Dennis Eckersley A's 92 1.50 4.00
DE2 Dennis Eckersley A's 88 1.50 4.00
DE3 Dennis Eckersley Sox 1.50 4.00
DS1 Don Sutton 76 1.50 4.00
DS2 Don Sutton 72 1.50 4.00
DW1 Dave Winfield 1.50 4.00
EB1 Ernie Banks 2.50 6.00
EM1 Eddie Murray 83 1.50 4.00
EM2 Eddie Murray 82 1.50 4.00
FJ1 Fergie Jenkins Cubs 1.50 4.00
FJ2 Fergie Jenkins Rgr 1.50 4.00
FR1 Frank Robinson Reds 1.50 4.00
FR2 Frank Robinson O's 1.50 4.00
GB1 George Brett 80 5.00 12.00
GB2 George Brett 85 5.00 12.00
GC1 Gary Carter 1.50 4.00
GK1 George Kell 1.50 4.00
GP1 Gaylord Perry Indians 1.50 4.00
GP2 Gaylord Perry Padres 1.50 4.00
HK1 H.Killebrew Senators 2.50 6.00
HK2 H.Kill Twins Batting 2.50 6.00
HK3 H.Kill Twins Fldg 2.50 6.00
JB1 Jim Bunning 1.50 4.00
JM1 Juan Marichal 1.50 4.00
JP1 Jim Palmer Windup 1.50 4.00
JP2 Jim Palmer Throwing 1.50 4.00
JP3 Jim Palmer Portrait 1.50 4.00
KP1 Kirby Puckett 88 2.50 6.00
KP2 Kirby Puckett 92 2.50 6.00
LA1 Luis Aparicio 1.50 4.00
LB1 Lou Brock 74 1.50 4.00
LB2 Lou Brock 67 1.50 4.00
MI1 Monte Irvin 1.50 4.00
MO1 Joe Morgan Astros 1.50 4.00
MO2 Joe Morgan Reds 1.50 4.00
MS1 Mike Schmidt Batting 4.00 10.00
MS2 Mike Schmidt Fielding 4.00 10.00
MS3 Mike Schmidt Portrait 4.00 10.00
NR1 Nolan Ryan Angels 8.00 20.00
NR2 Nolan Ryan Rgr 8.00 20.00
NR3 N.Ryan Astros Portrait 8.00 20.00
NR4 N.Ryan Astros Pitching 8.00 20.00
OC1 Orlando Cepeda 1.50 4.00
OS1 Ozzie Smith Padres 3.00 8.00
OS2 Ozzie Smith Cards 3.00 8.00
PM1 Paul Molitor Brew 2.50 6.00
PM2 Paul Molitor Jays 2.50 6.00
PM3 Paul Molitor Twins 2.50 6.00
PN1 Phil Niekro Braves 1.50 4.00
PN2 Phil Niekro Yanks 1.50 4.00
RC1 Rod Carew 77 1.50 4.00
RC2 Rod Carew 75 1.50 4.00
RF1 Rollie Fingers 1.50 4.00
RJ1 Reggie Jackson A's 1.50 4.00
RJ2 Reggie Jackson Yanks 1.50 4.00
RJ3 Reggie Jackson Angels 1.50 4.00
RK1 Ralph Kiner 1.50 4.00
RR1 Robin Roberts 1.50 4.00
RS1 Red Schoendienst 1.50 4.00
RY1 Robin Yount Batting 2.50 6.00
RY2 Robin Yount Fielding 2.50 6.00
SA1 Ryne Sandberg 90 5.00 12.00
SA2 Ryne Sandberg 84 5.00 12.00
SC1 Steve Carlton Cards 1.50 4.00
SC2 S.Carlton Phils Pitch 1.50 4.00
SC3 S.Carlton Phils Portrait 1.50 4.00
SM1 Stan Musial Batting 4.00 10.00
SM2 Stan Musial Fielding 4.00 10.00
SN1 Duke Snider 1.50 4.00
TP1 Tony Perez 1.50 4.00
TS1 Tom Seaver Mets 1.50 4.00
TS2 Tom Seaver Reds 1.50 4.00
WB1 Wade Boggs Sox Batting 1.50 4.00
WB2 Wade Boggs Sox Fielding 1.50 4.00
WB3 Wade Boggs Yanks 1.50 4.00
WF1 Whitey Ford Pitching 1.50 4.00
WF2 Whitey Ford Portrait 1.50 4.00
WM1 Willie McCovey 1.50 4.00
YB1 Yogi Berra Batting 2.50 6.00
YB2 Yogi Berra Fielding 2.50 6.00

2005 Upper Deck Hall of Fame Seasons Autograph

STATED PRINT RUN 25 SERIAL #'d SETS
GOLD PRINT RUN 5 SERIAL #'d SETS
NO GOLD PRICING DUE TO SCARCITY
RAINBOW PRINT RUN 1 SERIAL #'d SET
NO RAINBOW PRICING DUE TO SCARCITY
*SILVER: .5X TO 1.2X BASIC
SILVER PRINT RUN 15 SERIAL #'d SETS
MATERIAL GOLD PRINT RUN 5 #'d SETS
NO MAT.GOLD PRICING DUE TO SCARCITY
MATERIAL RAINBOW PRINT RUN 1 #'d SET
NO MAT.RB PRICING DUE TO SCARCITY
*MAT.SILVER: .5X TO 1.2X BASIC
MATERIAL SILVER PRINT RUN 15 #'d SETS
PATCH GOLD PRINT RUN 5 #'d SETS
NO PATCH GOLD PRICING AVAILABLE
PATCH RAINBOW PRINT RUN 1 #'d SET
NO PATCH RAINBOW PRICING AVAILABLE
PATCH SILVER PRINT RUN 10 #'d SETS
NO PATCH SILVER PRICING AVAILABLE
OVERALL AUTO ODDS ONE PER TIN
EXCHANGE DEADLINE 07/18/08

AK1 Al Kaline Batting 20.00 50.00
AK2 Al Kaline Fielding 20.00 50.00
AK3 Al Kaline Portrait 30.00 80.00
BD1 Bobby Doerr 8.00 20.00
BE1 Johnny Bench Batting 20.00 50.00
BE2 Johnny Bench Fielding 20.00 50.00
BF1 Bob Feller Pitching 10.00 25.00
BF2 Bob Feller Portrait 10.00 25.00
BG1 Bob Gibson Pitching 15.00 40.00
BG2 Bob Gibson Portrait 15.00 40.00
BM1 Bill Mazeroski 20.00 50.00
BR1 Brooks Robinson Batting 15.00 40.00
BR2 Brooks Robinson Fielding 15.00 40.00
BR3 Brooks Robinson Portrait 15.00 40.00
BW1 Billy Williams Batting 10.00 25.00
BW2 Billy Williams Portrait 10.00 25.00
CF1 Carlton Fisk R.Sox 10.00 25.00
CF2 Carlton Fisk W.Sox 10.00 25.00
CY1 Carl Yastrzemski Batting 30.00 60.00
CY2 Carl Yastrzemski Fielding 30.00 60.00
DE1 Dennis Eckersley A's 92 10.00 25.00
DE2 Dennis Eckersley A's 88 10.00 25.00
DE3 Dennis Eckersley Sox 10.00 25.00
DS1 Don Sutton 76 8.00 20.00
DS2 Don Sutton 72 8.00 20.00
DW1 Dave Winfield 15.00 40.00
EB1 Ernie Banks 30.00 60.00
EM1 Eddie Murray 83 30.00 60.00
EM2 Eddie Murray 82 30.00 60.00
FJ1 Fergie Jenkins Cubs 8.00 20.00
FJ2 Fergie Jenkins Rgr 8.00 20.00
FR1 Frank Robinson Reds 10.00 25.00
FR2 Frank Robinson O's 10.00 25.00
GB1 George Brett 80 50.00 100.00
GB2 George Brett 85 50.00 100.00
GC1 Gary Carter 20.00 50.00
GK1 George Kell 15.00 40.00
GP1 Gaylord Perry Indians 8.00 20.00
GP2 Gaylord Perry Padres 8.00 20.00
HK1 H.Killebrew Senators 30.00 60.00
HK2 H.Kill Twins Batting 30.00 60.00
HK3 H.Kill Twins Fldg 20.00 50.00
JB1 Jim Bunning 10.00 25.00
JM1 Juan Marichal 10.00 25.00
JP1 Jim Palmer Windup 10.00 25.00
JP2 Jim Palmer Throwing 10.00 25.00
JP3 Jim Palmer Portrait 10.00 25.00
KP1 Kirby Puckett 88 50.00 100.00
KP2 Kirby Puckett 92 50.00 100.00
LA1 Luis Aparicio 10.00 25.00
LB1 Lou Brock 74 15.00 40.00
LB2 Lou Brock 67 15.00 40.00
MI1 Monte Irvin 10.00 25.00
MO1 Joe Morgan Astros 10.00 25.00
MO2 Joe Morgan Reds 10.00 25.00
MS1 Mike Schmidt Batting 30.00 60.00
MS2 Mike Schmidt Fielding 30.00 60.00
MS3 Mike Schmidt Portrait 30.00 60.00
NR1 Nolan Ryan Angels 50.00 100.00
NR2 Nolan Ryan Rgr 50.00 100.00
NR3 N.Ryan Astros Portrait 50.00 100.00
NR4 N.Ryan Astros Pitching 50.00 100.00
OC1 Orlando Cepeda 10.00 25.00
OS1 Ozzie Smith Padres 20.00 50.00
OS2 Ozzie Smith Cards 20.00 50.00
PM1 Paul Molitor Brew 15.00 40.00
PM2 Paul Molitor Jays 15.00 40.00
PM3 Paul Molitor Twins 15.00 40.00
PN1 Phil Niekro Braves 10.00 25.00
PN2 Phil Niekro Yanks 10.00 25.00
RC1 Rod Carew 77 15.00 40.00
RC2 Rod Carew 75 15.00 40.00
RF1 Rollie Fingers 8.00 20.00
RJ1 Reggie Jackson A's 20.00 50.00
RJ2 Reggie Jackson Yanks 20.00 50.00
RJ3 Reggie Jackson Angels 20.00 50.00
RK1 Ralph Kiner 20.00 50.00
RR1 Robin Roberts 15.00 40.00
RS1 Red Schoendienst 10.00 25.00
RY1 Robin Yount Batting 20.00 50.00
RY2 Robin Yount Fielding 20.00 50.00
SA1 Ryne Sandberg 90 40.00 80.00
SA2 Ryne Sandberg 84 40.00 80.00
SC1 Steve Carlton Cards 20.00 50.00
SC2 S.Carlton Phils Pitch 20.00 50.00
SC3 S.Carlton Phils Portrait 20.00 50.00
SM1 Stan Musial Batting 50.00 100.00
SM2 Stan Musial Fielding 50.00 100.00
SN1 Duke Snider 15.00 40.00
TP1 Tony Perez 15.00 40.00
TS1 Tom Seaver Mets 25.00 60.00
TS2 Tom Seaver Reds 25.00 60.00
WB1 Wade Boggs Sox Batting 15.00 40.00
WB2 Wade Boggs Sox Fielding 15.00 40.00
WB3 Wade Boggs Yanks 15.00 40.00
WF1 Whitey Ford Pitching 15.00 40.00
WF2 Whitey Ford Portrait 15.00 40.00
WM1 Willie McCovey 15.00 40.00
YB1 Yogi Berra Batting 60.00 150.00
YB2 Yogi Berra Fielding 60.00 150.00

2005 Upper Deck Hall of Fame Signs of Cooperstown Duals

STATED PRINT RUN 50 SERIAL #'d SETS
GOLD PRINT RUN 5 SERIAL #'d SETS
NO GOLD PRICING DUE TO SCARCITY
RAINBOW PRINT RUN 1 SERIAL #'d SET
NO RAINBOW PRICING DUE TO SCARCITY
*SILVER: .6X TO 1.5X BASIC
SILVER PRINT RUN 15 SERIAL #'d SETS
OVERALL INSERT ODDS ONE PER TIN

AB L.Aparicio/E.Banks 2.50 6.00
AS L.Aparicio/O.Smith 3.00 8.00
BC J.Bunning/S.Carlton 1.50 4.00
BF B.Robinson/F.Robinson 1.50 4.00
BG B.Robinson/G.Brett 5.00 12.00
BM L.Brock/S.Musial 4.00 10.00
BR J.Bunning/R.Roberts 1.50 4.00
BS E.Banks/R.Sandberg 5.00 12.00
CM O.Cepeda/W.McCovey 1.50 4.00
CS T.Seaver/G.Carter 1.50 4.00
DB B.Doerr/W.Boggs 1.50 4.00
EF D.Eckersley/R.Fingers 1.50 4.00
FB C.Fisk/J.Bench 2.50 6.00
FC B.Feller/S.Carlton 1.50 4.00
FP B.Feller/G.Perry 1.50 4.00
GC B.Gibson/S.Carlton 1.50 4.00
GF B.Gibson/W.Ford 1.50 4.00
IM M.Irvin/W.McCovey 1.50 4.00
JJ J.Morgan/J.Bench 2.50 6.00
JM R.Jackson/W.McCovey 1.50 4.00
JW D.Winfield/R.Jackson 1.50 4.00
JY J.Bench/Y.Berra 2.50 6.00
KK A.Kaline/G.Bell 2.50 6.00
KP H.Killebrew/K.Puckett 2.50 6.00
LO L.Brock/O.Smith 3.00 8.00
MK B.Mazeroski/R.Kiner 1.50 4.00
MP J.Morgan/T.Perez 1.50 4.00
MY P.Molitor/R.Yount 2.50 6.00
NS N.Ryan/S.Carlton 8.00 20.00
PM G.Perry/J.Marichal 1.50 4.00
PN G.Perry/P.Niekro 1.50 4.00
PR P.Molitor/R.Carew 2.50 6.00
RC N.Ryan/R.Carew 8.00 20.00
RP B.Robinson/J.Palmer 1.50 4.00
RS N.Ryan/T.Seaver 8.00 20.00
RW R.Sandberg/W.Boggs 5.00 12.00
SB G.Brett/M.Schmidt 5.00 12.00
SC M.Schmidt/S.Carlton 4.00 10.00
SK D.Snider/R.Kiner 1.50 4.00
SM O.Smith/S.Musial 4.00 10.00
SP D.Sutton/G.Perry 1.50 4.00
SR B.Robinson/M.Schmidt 4.00 10.00
SS O.Smith/R.Schoendienst 3.00 8.00
SW R.Sandberg/B.Williams 5.00 12.00
WB B.Williams/E.Banks 2.50 6.00
WJ B.Williams/F.Jenkins 1.50 4.00
WS D.Winfield/O.Smith 3.00 8.00
WY W.Ford/Y.Berra 2.50 6.00
YF C.Yastrzemski/C.Fisk 3.00 8.00
YJ C.Yastrzemski/R.Jackson 3.00 8.00

2005 Upper Deck Hall of Fame Signs of Cooperstown Duals Autograph

STATED PRINT RUN 20 SERIAL #'d SETS

GOLD PRINT RUN 5 SERIAL #'d SETS
NO GOLD PRICING DUE TO SCARCITY
RAINBOW PRINT RUN 1 SERIAL #'d SET
NO RAINBOW PRICING DUE TO SCARCITY
SILVER PRINT RUN 10 SERIAL #'d SETS
NO SILVER PRICING DUE TO SCARCITY
OVERALL AUTO ODDS ONE PER TIN
AB L.Aparicio/E.Banks 50.00 100.00
AS L.Aparicio/O.Smith 40.00 80.00
BC J.Bunning/S.Carlton 20.00 50.00
BF B.Robinson/F.Robinson 40.00 80.00
BG B.Robinson/G.Brett 60.00 120.00
BM L.Brock/S.Musial 60.00 120.00
BR J.Bunning/R.Roberts 20.00 50.00
BS E.Banks/R.Sandberg 75.00 150.00
CM O.Cepeda/W.McCovey 30.00 60.00
CS T.Seaver/G.Carter 40.00 100.00
DB B.Doerr/W.Boggs 30.00 60.00
EF D.Eckersley/R.Fingers 20.00 50.00
FB C.Fisk/J.Bench 40.00 80.00
FC B.Feller/S.Carlton 20.00 50.00
FP B.Feller/G.Perry 20.00 50.00
GC B.Gibson/S.Carlton 30.00 60.00
GF B.Gibson/W.Ford 40.00 80.00
IM M.Irvin/W.McCovey 30.00 60.00
JJ J.Morgan/J.Bench 50.00 100.00
JM R.Jackson/W.McCovey 50.00 100.00
JW D.Winfield/R.Jackson 50.00 100.00
JY J.Bench/Y.Berra 75.00 200.00
KK A.Kaline/G.Bell 60.00 150.00
KP H.Killebrew/K.Puckett 75.00 150.00
LO L.Brock/O.Smith 20.00 50.00
MK B.Mazeroski/R.Kiner 40.00 80.00
MP J.Morgan/T.Perez 20.00 50.00
MY P.Molitor/R.Yount 50.00 100.00
NS N.Ryan/S.Carlton 75.00 150.00
PM G.Perry/J.Marichal 20.00 50.00
PN G.Perry/P.Niekro 20.00 50.00
PR P.Molitor/R.Carew 30.00 60.00
RC N.Ryan/R.Carew 75.00 150.00
RP B.Robinson/J.Palmer 30.00 60.00
RS N.Ryan/T.Seaver 100.00 250.00
RW R.Sandberg/W.Boggs 60.00 120.00
SB G.Brett/M.Schmidt 75.00 150.00
SC M.Schmidt/S.Carlton 50.00 100.00
SK D.Snider/R.Kiner 40.00 80.00
SM O.Smith/S.Musial 100.00 200.00
SP D.Sutton/G.Perry 20.00 50.00
SR B.Robinson/M.Schmidt 50.00 100.00
SS O.Smith/R.Schoendienst 40.00 80.00
SW R.Sandberg/B.Williams 50.00 100.00
WB B.Williams/E.Banks 50.00 100.00
WJ B.Williams/F.Jenkins 20.00 50.00
WS D.Winfield/O.Smith 40.00 80.00
WY W.Ford/Y.Berra 60.00 150.00
YF C.Yastrzemski/C.Fisk 60.00 120.00
YJ C.Yastrzemski/R.Jackson 60.00 120.00

2005 Upper Deck Hall of Fame Signs of Cooperstown Triples

STATED PRINT RUN 50 SERIAL #'d SETS
GOLD PRINT RUN 5 SERIAL #'d SETS
NO GOLD PRICING DUE TO SCARCITY
RAINBOW PRINT RUN 1 SERIAL #'d SET
NO RAINBOW PRICING DUE TO SCARCITY
*SILVER: .6X TO 1.5X BASIC
SILVER PRINT RUN 15 SERIAL #'d SETS
OVERALL INSERT ODDS ONE PER TIN
ASY Aparicio/Smith/Young 3.00 8.00
BFJ Robinson/Robinson/Palmer 1.50 4.00
BSB Brett/Schmidt/Boggs 5.00 12.00
BSY Banks/Smith/Young 3.00 8.00
CMI Cepeda/McCovey/Irvin 1.50 4.00
DFY Doerr/Fisk/Yaz 3.00 8.00
DYB Doerr/Yaz/Boggs 3.00 8.00
FPE Feller/Perry/Eckersley 1.50 4.00
FRC Feller/Ryan/Carlton 8.00 20.00
FSE Fingers/Sutton/Eckersley 1.50 4.00
GCE Gibson/Carlton/Eckersley 1.50 4.00
GSM Gibson/Smith/Musial 4.00 10.00
JFB Jackson/Ford/Berra 2.50 6.00
JPR Jenkins/Perry/Ryan 8.00 20.00
KKB Kaline/Kell/Bunning 2.50 6.00
KPC Killebrew/Puckett/Carew 2.50 6.00
KSR Kiner/Snider/Robinson 1.50 4.00
KWR Kaline/Winfield/Robinson 2.50 6.00
MBP Morgan/Bench/Perez 2.50 6.00
MCM Marichal/Cepeda/McCovey 1.50 4.00
MMS Mazeroski/Morgan/Schoend 1.50 4.00
MRJ Murray/Robinson/Jackson 1.50 4.00
MSC Morgan/Sandberg/Carew 5.00 12.00
MYF Molitor/Yount/Fingers 2.50 6.00
PMC Puckett/Molitor/Carew 2.50 6.00
RAP Robinson/Aparicio/Palmer 1.50 4.00
RBC Roberts/Bunning/Carlton 1.50 4.00
RBS Robinson/Brett/Schmidt 5.00 12.00
RSR Roberts/Sutton/Ryan 8.00 20.00
SRC Schmidt/Roberts/Carlton 4.00 10.00
WBI Williams/Brock/Irvin 1.50 4.00
WBJ Williams/Banks/Jenkins 2.50 6.00
WJB Winfield/Jackson/Boggs 1.50 4.00
WSP Winfield/Smith/Perry 3.00 8.00
YKM Yaz/Kiner/Musial 4.00 10.00

2005 Upper Deck Hall of Fame Signs of Cooperstown Triples Autograph

STATED PRINT RUN 20 SERIAL #'d SETS
GOLD PRINT RUN 5 SERIAL #'d SETS
NO GOLD PRICING DUE TO SCARCITY
RAINBOW PRINT RUN 1 SERIAL #'d SET
NO RAINBOW PRICING DUE TO SCARCITY
SILVER PRINT RUN 10 SERIAL #'d SETS
NO SILVER PRICING DUE TO SCARCITY
OVERALL AUTO ODDS ONE PER TIN
ASY Aparicio/Ozzie/Yount 75.00 150.00
BFJ Brooks/F.Rob/Palmer 60.00 120.00
BSB Brett/Schmidt/Boggs 150.00 250.00
BSY Banks/Ozzie/Yount 75.00 150.00
CMI Cepeda/McCovey/Irvin 50.00 100.00
DFY Doerr/Fisk/Yaz 75.00 150.00
DYB Doerr/Yaz/Boggs 75.00 150.00
FRC Feller/Ryan/Carlton 100.00 200.00
GSM Gibson/Ozzie/Musial 100.00 200.00
JFB Jackson/Whitey/Yogi 125.00 250.00
JPR Jenkins/Perry/Ryan 100.00 200.00
KPC Killebrew/Puckett/Carew 125.00 250.00
KSR Kiner/Snider/F.Rob 60.00 120.00
MBP Morgan/Bench/Perez 100.00 200.00
MCM Marichal/Cepeda/McCovey 60.00 120.00
MSC Morgan/Sandberg/Carew 75.00 150.00
MYF Molitor/Yount/Fingers 75.00 150.00
PMC Puckett/Molitor/Carew 150.00 300.00
RAP Brooks/Aparicio/Palmer 50.00 100.00
RBC Roberts/Bunning/Carlton 50.00 100.00
RBS Brooks/Brett/Schmidt 150.00 250.00
SRC Schmidt/Roberts/Carlton 75.00 150.00
WJB Winfield/Jackson/Boggs 60.00 120.00
WSP Winfield/Ozzie/Perry 40.00 80.00
YKM Yaz/Kiner/Musial 75.00 150.00

2005 Upper Deck Hall of Fame Signs of Cooperstown Quads

STATED PRINT RUN 50 SERIAL #'d SETS
GOLD PRINT RUN 5 SERIAL #'d SETS
NO GOLD PRICING DUE TO SCARCITY
RAINBOW PRINT RUN 1 SERIAL #'d SET
NO RAINBOW PRICING DUE TO SCARCITY
*SILVER: .6X TO 1.5X BASIC
SILVER PRINT RUN 15 SERIAL #'d SETS
OVERALL INSERT ODDS ONE PER TIN
BMYC Brett/Molitor/Yount/Carew 5.00 12.00
BSAY Banks/Ozzie/Aparicio/Yount 3.00 8.00
FCBB Fisk/Carter/Bench/Berra 2.50 6.00
FGRC Feller/Gibson/Ryan/Carlton 8.00 20.00
KCPM Killebrew/Cepeda/Perez/McCovey 2.50 6.00
KYBM Kaline/Yaz/Brock/Musial 4.00 10.00
MBKM Murray/Banks/Killebrew/McCovey 2.50 6.00
MDMC Maz/Doerr/Morgan/Carew 1.50 4.00
MRKS Murray/F.Rob/Killebrew/Schmidt 4.00 10.00
RBKS Brooks/Brett/Kell/Schmidt 5.00 12.00
SPNS Sutton/Perry/Niekro/Seaver 1.50 4.00
SPSF Sutton/Palmer/Seaver/Ford 1.50 4.00
SRCS Sutton/Ryan/Carlton/Seaver 8.00 20.00
WYKM B.Will/Yaz/Kiner/Musial 4.00 10.00
YWMM Yaz/Winfield/Murray/Musial 4.00 10.00

2005 Upper Deck Hall of Fame Tins

ISSUED AS COLLECTIBLE PACKAGING
MS Mike Schmidt 2.50 6.00
NR Nolan Ryan 5.00 12.00
SM Stan Musial 2.50 6.00
TC Ty Cobb 2.50 6.00

2001 Upper Deck Hall of Famers

COMPLETE SET (90) 8.00 20.00
1 Reggie Jackson .15 .40
2 Hank Aaron .50 1.25
3 Eddie Mathews .25 .60
4 Warren Spahn .15 .40
5 Robin Yount .25 .60
6 Lou Brock .15 .40
7 Dizzy Dean .25 .60
8 Bob Gibson .15 .40
9 Stan Musial .40 1.00
10 Enos Slaughter .08 .25
11 Rogers Hornsby .25 .60
12 Ernie Banks .25 .60
13 Fergie Jenkins .08 .25
14 Roy Campanella .25 .60
15 Pee Wee Reese .25 .60
16 Jackie Robinson .25 .60
17 Juan Marichal .08 .25
18 Christy Mathewson .25 .60
19 Willie Mays .50 1.25
20 Hoyt Wilhelm .08 .25
21 Buck Leonard .08 .25
22 Bob Feller .08 .25
23 Cy Young .25 .60
24 Satchel Paige .25 .60
25 Tom Seaver .15 .40
26 Brooks Robinson .15 .40
27 Mike Schmidt .50 1.25
28 Roberto Clemente .60 1.50
29 Ralph Kiner .08 .25
30 Willie Stargell .15 .40
31 Honus Wagner .30 .75
32 Josh Gibson .25 .60
33 Nolan Ryan .60 1.50
34 Carlton Fisk .15 .40
35 Jimmie Foxx .25 .60
36 Johnny Bench .25 .60
37 Joe Morgan .08 .25
38 George Brett .50 1.25
39 Walter Johnson .25 .60
40 Cool Papa Bell .08 .25
41 Ty Cobb .40 1.00
42 Al Kaline .25 .60
43 Harmon Killebrew .25 .60
44 Luis Aparicio .08 .25
45 Yogi Berra .25 .60
46 Joe DiMaggio .50 1.25
47 Whitey Ford .15 .40
48 Lou Gehrig .50 1.25
49 Mickey Mantle 1.00 2.50
50 Babe Ruth .75 2.00
51 Josh Gibson OG .15 .40
52 Honus Wagner OG .25 .60
53 Hoyt Wilhelm OG .08 .25
54 Cy Young OG .15 .40
55 Walter Johnson OG .15 .40
56 Satchel Paige OG .15 .40
57 Rogers Hornsby OG .15 .40
58 Christy Mathewson OG .15 .40
59 Tris Speaker OG .15 .40
60 Nap Lajoie OG .25 .60
61 Mickey Mantle NP .50 1.25
62 Jackie Robinson NP .25 .60
63 Nolan Ryan NP .40 1.00
64 Josh Gibson NP .15 .40
65 Yogi Berra NP .15 .40
66 Brooks Robinson NP .08 .25
67 Stan Musial NP .25 .60
68 Mike Schmidt NP .25 .60
69 Joe DiMaggio NP .25 .60
70 Ernie Banks NP .15 .40
71 Willie Stargell NP .08 .25
72 Johnny Bench NP .15 .40
73 Willie Mays NP .25 .60
74 Satchel Paige NP .15 .40
75 Bob Gibson NP .08 .25
76 Harmon Killebrew NP .25 .60
77 Al Kaline NP .15 .40
78 Carlton Fisk NP .08 .25
79 Tom Seaver NP .08 .25
80 Reggie Jackson NP .08 .25
81 Bob Gibson HR .08 .25
82 Nolan Ryan HR .40 1.00
83 Walter Johnson HR .15 .40
84 Stan Musial HR .25 .60
85 Josh Gibson HR .15 .40
86 Cy Young HR .15 .40
87 Joe DiMaggio HR .25 .60
88 Hoyt Wilhelm HR .08 .25
89 Lou Brock HR .08 .25
90 Mickey Mantle HR .50 1.25
w/Willie Mays
Hank Aaron

2001 Upper Deck Hall of Famers 20th Century Showcase

COMPLETE SET (11) 12.50 30.00
STATED ODDS 1:8
S1 Cy Young .75 2.00
S2 Joe DiMaggio 1.50 4.00
S3 Harmon Killebrew .75 2.00
S4 Stan Musial 1.25 3.00
S5 Mickey Mantle 3.00 8.00
S6 Satchel Paige .75 2.00
S7 Nolan Ryan 2.00 5.00
S8 Bob Gibson .60 1.50
S9 Ernie Banks .75 2.00
S10 Mike Schmidt 1.50 4.00
S11 Willie Mays 1.50 4.00

2001 Upper Deck Hall of Famers Class of '36

COMPLETE SET (5) 6.00 15.00
STATED ODDS 1:17
C1 Ty Cobb 1.25 3.00
C2 Babe Ruth 2.50 6.00
C3 Christy Mathewson .75 2.00
C4 Walter Johnson .75 2.00
C5 Honus Wagner 1.00 2.50

2001 Upper Deck Hall of Famers Endless Summer

COMPLETE SET (11) 12.50 30.00
STATED ODDS 1:8
ES1 Mickey Mantle 3.00 8.00
ES2 Yogi Berra .75 2.00
ES3 Mike Schmidt 1.50 4.00
ES4 Jackie Robinson .75 2.00
ES5 Johnny Bench .75 2.00
ES6 Tom Seaver .75 2.00
ES7 Ernie Banks .75 2.00
ES8 Harmon Killebrew .75 2.00
ES9 Joe DiMaggio 1.50 4.00
ES10 Willie Mays 1.50 4.00
ES11 Brooks Robinson .75 2.00

2001 Upper Deck Hall of Famers Gallery

COMPLETE SET (15) 15.00 40.00
STATED ODDS 1:6
G1 Reggie Jackson .50 1.25
G2 Tom Seaver .50 1.25
G3 Bob Gibson .50 1.25
G4 Jackie Robinson .75 2.00
G5 Joe DiMaggio 1.50 4.00
G6 Ernie Banks .75 2.00
G7 Mickey Mantle 3.00 8.00
G8 Willie Mays 1.50 4.00
G9 Cy Young .75 2.00
G10 Nolan Ryan 2.00 5.00
G11 Johnny Bench .75 2.00
G12 Yogi Berra .75 2.00
G13 Satchel Paige .75 2.00
G14 George Brett 1.50 4.00
G15 Stan Musial 1.25 3.00

2001 Upper Deck Hall of Famers Game Bat

STATED ODDS 1:24
SP PRINT RUNS PROVIDED BY UPPER DECK
SP'S ARE NOT SERIAL-NUMBERED
ASTERISKS PERCEIVED AS LARGER SUPPLY
BBR Babe Ruth 75.00 200.00
BBRO Brooks Robinson 3.00 8.00
BBW Billy Williams 3.00 8.00
BCF Carlton Fisk DP 3.00 8.00
BDD Don Drysdale 3.00 8.00
BDS Duke Snider 3.00 8.00
BEB Ernie Banks 5.00 12.00
BES Enos Slaughter 10.00 25.00
BEW Early Wynn 3.00 8.00
BFR Frank Robinson 3.00 8.00
BGB George Brett DP 6.00 15.00
BGK George Kell 3.00 8.00
BHA Hank Aaron DP 10.00 25.00
BHG Hank Greenberg 8.00 20.00
BJB Johnny Bench DP 5.00 12.00
BJBO Jim Bottomley 10.00 25.00
BJD Joe DiMaggio 15.00 40.00
BJF Jimmie Foxx 12.50 30.00
BJM Johnny Mize 3.00 8.00
BJMO Joe Morgan DP 3.00 8.00
BJP Jim Palmer SP/372 * 50.00 100.00
BJR Jackie Robinson SP/371 * 30.00 80.00
BLA Luis Aparicio 3.00 8.00
BMM Mickey Mantle 20.00 50.00
BMO Mel Ott 12.50 30.00
BNF Nellie Fox 3.00 8.00
BNR Nolan Ryan 8.00 20.00
BOC Orlando Cepeda 3.00 8.00
BRC R.Clemente SP/409 40.00 100.00
BRCA Roy Campanella 5.00 12.00
BRF Rollie Fingers 3.00 8.00
BRH Rogers Hornsby 10.00 25.00
BRJ Reggie Jackson DP 4.00 10.00
BRK Ralph Kiner 3.00 8.00
BRS Red Schoendienst 3.00 8.00
BRY Robin Yount DP 5.00 12.00
BTP Tony Perez 3.00 8.00
BWM Willie Mays DP 12.00 30.00
BWS Willie Stargell 3.00 8.00
BYB Yogi Berra 8.00 20.00

2001 Upper Deck Hall of Famers Game Jersey

STATED ODDS 1:168
SP PRINT RUNS PROVIDED BY UPPER DECK
SP'S ARE NOT SERIAL-NUMBERED
ASTERISKS PERCEIVED AS LARGER SUPPLY
JBR Brooks Robinson 10.00 25.00
JDS Duke Snider SP/267 * 20.00 50.00
JDSU Don Sutton 10.00 25.00
JFR Frank Robinson 10.00 25.00
JJD Joe DiMaggio 50.00 100.00
JJM Joe Morgan 6.00 15.00
JLA Luis Aparicio 6.00 15.00
JLG L.Gehrig Pants SP/194 * 100.00 200.00
JMM Mickey Mantle SP/216 * 75.00 150.00
JNR Nolan Ryan DP 6.00 15.00
JOC Orlando Cepeda 6.00 15.00
JPW Pee Wee Reese 6.00 15.00
JRC Roberto Clemente 20.00 50.00
JTP Tony Perez 10.00 25.00
JTS Tom Seaver 10.00 25.00
JWM Willie Mays 12.50 30.00
JWS Willie Stargell 10.00 25.00

2001 Upper Deck Hall of Famers Game Jersey Autograph

STATED ODDS 1:504
SJBR Brooks Robinson 15.00 40.00
SJDS Duke Snider 20.00 50.00
SJDSU Don Sutton 15.00 40.00
SJEB Ernie Banks 40.00 100.00
SJFR Frank Robinson 30.00 60.00
SJGB George Brett 75.00 150.00
SJJM Joe Morgan 15.00 40.00
SJLA Luis Aparicio 15.00 40.00
SJNR Nolan Ryan 40.00 100.00
SJOC Orlando Cepeda 15.00 40.00
SJRJ Reggie Jackson 50.00 100.00
SJTP Tony Perez 20.00 50.00
SJTS Tom Seaver 40.00 100.00

2006 Upper Deck Hawaii Trade Conference Signature Dual Jumbos

UNPRICED AUTO PRINT RUN 8-15

2006 Upper Deck Hawaii Trade Conference Signature Jumbos

UNPRICED AUTO PRINT RUN 9-15

2007 Upper Deck Hawaii Trade Conference

COMPLETE SET (13) 15.00 40.00
1 Daisuke Matsuzaka 1.25 3.00
2 Kei Igawa .40 1.00
3 Akinori Iwamura .40 1.00
4 Ken Griffey Jr. 2.00 5.00
5 Cal Ripken Jr. 4.00 10.00
6 Derek Jeter 2.50 6.00
7 Delmon Young .60 1.50
8 Joaquin Arias .40 1.00
9 Troy Tulowitzki .60 1.50

2008 Upper Deck Heroes

COMPLETE SET (200) 20.00 50.00
COMMON CARD (1-200) .20 .50
COMMON ROOKIE (1-200) .40 1.00
1 Brandon Webb .30 .75
2 Dan Haren .20 .50
3 Chris B. Young .20 .50
4 Justin Upton .30 .75
5 Randy Johnson .50 1.25
6 Chipper Jones .50 1.25
7 John Smoltz .50 1.25
8 Tom Glavine .30 .75
9 Mark Teixeira .30 .75
10 Brian McCann .30 .75
11 Jeff Francoeur .30 .75
12 Josh Hamilton .30 .75
13 Tim Hudson .30 .75
14 Nick Markakis .40 1.00
15 Brian Roberts .20 .50
16 Cal Ripken Jr. 1.50 4.00
17 John Maine .20 .50
18 Frank Robinson .20 .50
19 Mike Lowell .20 .50
20 Jason Varitek .50 1.25
21 David Ortiz .50 1.25
22 Manny Ramirez .50 1.25
23 Jonathan Papelbon .30 .75
24 Jacoby Ellsbury .40 1.00
25 Kevin Youkilis .20 .50
26 Curt Schilling .30 .75
27 Josh Beckett .20 .50
28 Daisuke Matsuzaka .30 .75
29 Clay Buchholz (RC) .60 1.50
30 Dustin Pedroia .50 1.25
31 Ryan Theriot .20 .50
32 Carlton Fisk .30 .75
33 Carl Yastrzemski .75 2.00
34 Wade Boggs .30 .75
35 Nolan Ryan 1.50 4.00
36 Alfonso Soriano .30 .75
37 Kosuke Fukudome RC 1.25 3.00
38 Derrek Lee .20 .50
39 Carlos Zambrano .30 .75
40 Aramis Ramirez .20 .50
41 Ernie Banks .50 1.25
42 Jim Thome .30 .75
43 Jermaine Dye .20 .50
44 Paul Konerko .30 .75
45 Nick Swisher .30 .75
46 Corey Hart .20 .50
47 Ken Griffey Jr. 1.00 2.50
48 Adam Dunn .30 .75
49 Aaron Harang .20 .50
50 Johnny Bench .50 1.25
51 Grady Sizemore .30 .75
52 Victor Martinez .30 .75
53 C.C. Sabathia .30 .75
54 Travis Hafner .20 .50
55 Jeff Francis .20 .50
56 Matt Holliday .50 1.25
57 Troy Tulowitzki .50 1.25
58 Garrett Atkins .20 .50
59 Todd Helton .30 .75
60 Curtis Granderson .30 .75
61 Dontrelle Willis .20 .50
62 Magglio Ordonez .30 .75
63 Gary Sheffield .20 .50
64 Miguel Cabrera .50 1.25
65 Justin Verlander .50 1.25
66 Ivan Rodriguez .30 .75
67 Al Kaline .50 1.25
68 Hanley Ramirez .30 .75
69 Edinson Volquez .20 .50
70 Dan Uggla .20 .50
71 Andrew Miller .30 .75
72 Josh Willingham .30 .75
73 J.R. Towles RC .60 1.50
74 Lance Berkman .30 .75
75 Carlos Lee .20 .50
76 Roy Oswalt .30 .75
77 Hunter Pence .30 .75
78 Luke Hochevar RC .60 1.50
79 Alex Gordon .30 .75
80 Matt Cain .30 .75
81 Bo Jackson .50 1.25
82 Vladimir Guerrero .30 .75
83 Torii Hunter .20 .50
84 Howie Kendrick .20 .50
85 John Lackey .30 .75
86 Chone Figgins .20 .50
87 Andruw Jones .20 .50
88 Brad Penny .20 .50
89 James Loney .20 .50
90 Matt Kemp .40 1.00
91 Nomar Garciaparra .30 .75
92 Jon Lester .30 .75
93 Chin-Lung Hu (RC) .40 1.00
94 Chad Billingsley .30 .75
95 Kelly Johnson .20 .50
96 Prince Fielder .30 .75
97 Ryan Braun .30 .75
98 Ben Sheets .20 .50
99 Robin Yount .50 1.25
100 Justin Morneau .30 .75
101 Joe Mauer .40 1.00
102 Delmon Young .30 .75
103 Rod Carew .30 .75
104 Carlos Beltran .30 .75
105 Jose Reyes .30 .75
106 Pedro Martinez .30 .75
107 David Wright .30 .75
108 Johan Santana .30 .75
109 Billy Wagner .20 .50
110 Carlos Delgado .20 .50
111 Mariano Rivera .60 1.50
112 Chien-Ming Wang .30 .75
113 Phil Hughes .30 .75
114 Derek Jeter 1.25 3.00
115 Alex Rodriguez .60 1.50
116 Robinson Cano .30 .75
117 Jorge Posada .30 .75
118 Hideki Matsui .50 1.25
119 Joba Chamberlain .20 .50
120 Ian Kennedy RC 1.00 2.50
121 Yogi Berra .50 1.25
122 Reggie Jackson .30 .75
123 Roger Clemens .60 1.50
124 Ozzie Smith .60 1.50
125 Don Mattingly 1.00 2.50
126 Dave Winfield .30 .75
127 Joe DiMaggio 1.00 2.50
128 Eric Chavez .20 .50
129 Bill Hall .20 .50
130 Rich Harden .20 .50
131 Andre Ethier .30 .75
132 Daric Barton (RC) .40 1.00
133 Ryan Howard .30 .75
134 Jimmy Rollins .30 .75
135 Chase Utley .30 .75
136 Cole Hamels .40 1.00
137 Pat Burrell .20 .50
138 Mike Schmidt .75 2.00
139 Steve Carlton .30 .75
140 Freddy Sanchez .20 .50
141 Joe Blanton .20 .50
142 Felix Pie .20 .50
143 Roberto Clemente 1.25 3.00
144 Jake Peavy .30 .75
145 Greg Maddux .60 1.50
146 Tom Gorzelanny .60 1.50
147 Tony Gwynn .50 1.25
148 Barry Zito .30 .75
149 Tim Lincecum .30 .75
150 Rich Hill .20 .50
151 Omar Vizquel .20 .50
152 Ichiro Suzuki .60 1.50
153 Felix Hernandez .50 1.25
154 Kenji Johjima .20 .50
155 Erik Bedard .20 .50
156 Albert Pujols .60 1.50
157 Troy Glaus .20 .50
158 Chris Carpenter .30 .75
159 Chris Duncan .30 .75
160 Mark Mulder .20 .50
161 Scott Rolen .30 .75
162 Stan Musial .75 2.00
163 Bob Gibson .30 .75
164 B.J. Upton .30 .75
165 Carl Crawford .30 .75
166 Scott Kazmir .30 .75
167 Michael Young .20 .50
168 Luke Scott .20 .50
169 Roy Halladay .30 .75
170 Vernon Wells .20 .50
171 Kevin Kouzmanoff .20 .50
172 Frank Thomas .50 1.25
173 Ryan Zimmerman .30 .75
174 Lastings Milledge .20 .50
175 Ian Kinsler .30 .75
176 D.Mattingly/W.Boggs 1.00 2.50
177 C.Fisk/C.Yastrzemski .75 2.00
178 A.Pujols/S.Musial .75 2.00
179 J.Reyes/D.Jeter 1.25 3.00
180 C.Ripken/T.Gwynn 1.50 4.00
181 Eddie Murray/Prince Fielder .30 .75
182 I.Suzuki/K.Fukudome .60 1.50
183 Steve Carlton/Johan Santana .30 .75
184 Bob Gibson/Jake Peavy .30 .75
185 Johnny Bench/Ivan Rodriguez .50 1.25
186 Vlad/Molitor/Manny .50 1.25
187 Yaz/Fisk/Boggs .75 2.00
188 ARod/Jeter/Cano 1.25 3.00
189 Chipper/Braun/Mig.Cabrera .50 1.25
190 Mattingly/Winfield/Reggie 1.00 2.50
191 Utley/Howard/Rollins .30 .75
192 Joe Mauer/Hanley Ramirez
Troy Tulowitzki .50 1.25
193 Ryan/Maddux/Unit 1.50 4.00
194 Webb/Verland/Hernand .50 1.25
195 Schmidt/Banks/F.Robinson .75 2.00
196 Jeter/Griffey/Ripken/Ichiro 1.50 4.00
197 Yogi/Reggie/Joe D/Jeter 1.25 3.00
198 Jonathan Papelbon/Manny Ramirez
Jason Varitek/David Ortiz .50 1.25
199 Griffey/Clemente/Vlad/Joe D 1.25 3.00
200 Pujols/Jeter/Prince/Papi 1.25 3.00

2008 Upper Deck Heroes Beige

*BEIGE VET: .75X TO 2X BASIC
*BEIGE RC: .5X TO 1.2X BASIC RC
RANDOM INSERTS IN PACKS
STATED PRINT RUN 299 SER.#'d SETS

2008 Upper Deck Heroes Black

*BLACK VET: .75X TO 2X BASIC
*BLACK RC: .5X TO 1.2X BASIC RC
RANDOM INSERTS IN PACKS

2008 Upper Deck Heroes Brown

*BROWN VET: 1X TO 2.5X BASIC
*BROWN RC: .6X TO 1.5X BASIC RC
RANDOM INSERTS IN PACKS
STATED PRINT RUN 149 SER.#'d SETS

2008 Upper Deck Heroes Charcoal

*CHARCOAL VET: .75X TO 2X BASIC
*CHARCOAL RC: .5X TO 1.2X BASIC RC
RANDOM INSERTS IN RETAIL PACKS
STATED PRINT RUN 399 SER.#'d SETS

2008 Upper Deck Heroes Emerald

*EMERALD VET: .75X TO 2X BASIC
*EMERALD RC: .5X TO 1.2X BASIC RC
RANDOM INSERTS IN PACKS
STATED PRINT RUN 499 SER.#'d SETS

2008 Upper Deck Heroes Light Blue

*LT.BLUE VET: 1.5X TO 4X BASIC
*LT.BLUE RC: 1X TO 2.5X BASIC RC
RANDOM INSERTS IN PACKS
STATED PRINT RUN 49 SER.#'d SETS

2008 Upper Deck Heroes Navy Blue

*NAVY VET: 1X TO 2.5X BASIC
*NAVY RC: .6X TO 1.5X BASIC RC
RANDOM INSERTS IN PACKS
STATED PRINT RUN 199 SER.#'d SETS

2008 Upper Deck Heroes Purple

RANDOM INSERTS IN PACKS
STATED PRINT RUN 25 SER.#'d SETS
NO PRICING DUE TO SCARCITY

2008 Upper Deck Heroes Red

*RED VET: 1X TO 2.5X BASIC
*RED RC: .6X TO 1.5X BASIC RC
RANDOM INSERTS IN PACKS
STATED PRINT RUN 249 SER.#'d SETS

2008 Upper Deck Heroes Sea Green

*SEA GREEN VET: 1.2X TO 3X BASIC
*SEA GREEN RC: .75X TO 2X BASIC RC
RANDOM INSERTS IN PACKS
STATED PRINT RUN 99 SER.#'d SETS

2008 Upper Deck Heroes Autographs Charcoal

RANDOM INSERTS IN BACKS
PRINT RUNS B/WN 11-150 COPIES PER
NO PRICING ON QTY 11 OR LESS
12 Josh Hamilton/150 30.00 60.00
14 Nick Markakis/50 10.00 25.00
29 Clay Buchholz/95 6.00 15.00
31 Ryan Theriot/150 4.00 10.00
45 Nick Swisher/150 5.00 12.00
46 Corey Hart/150 4.00 10.00
47 Ken Griffey Jr./75 40.00 80.00
49 Aaron Harang/150 4.00 10.00
69 Edinson Volquez/150 10.00 25.00
73 J.R. Towles/150 4.00 10.00
80 Matt Cain/150 4.00 10.00
86 Chone Figgins/150 4.00 10.00
90 Matt Kemp/150 5.00 12.00
93 Chin-Lung Hu/150 10.00 25.00
94 Chad Billingsley/150 4.00 10.00
95 Kelly Johnson/150 4.00 10.00
120 Ian Kennedy/95 6.00 15.00
131 Andre Ethier/150 6.00 15.00
132 Daric Barton/150 4.00 10.00
141 Joe Blanton/144 4.00 10.00
142 Felix Pie/150 4.00 10.00
146 Tom Gorzelanny/150 4.00 10.00
150 Rich Hill/100 4.00 10.00
168 Luke Scott/148 4.00 10.00
171 Kevin Kouzmanoff/150 4.00 10.00
175 Ian Kinsler/150 5.00 12.00

2008 Upper Deck Heroes Autographs Black

RANDOM INSERTS IN BACKS
PRINT RUNS B/WN 25-50 COPIES PER
NO PRICING ON QTY 25 OR LESS
10 Brian McCann/50 8.00 20.00
12 Josh Hamilton/50 40.00 80.00
17 John Maine/50 6.00 15.00
29 Clay Buchholz/35 8.00 20.00
31 Ryan Theriot/50 5.00 12.00
45 Nick Swisher/50 6.00 15.00
46 Corey Hart/50 5.00 12.00
49 Aaron Harang/50 5.00 12.00
69 Edinson Volquez/50 12.50 30.00
71 Andrew Miller/35 5.00 12.00
72 Josh Willingham/50 5.00 12.00
78 Luke Hochevar/50 6.00 15.00
86 Chone Figgins/50 5.00 12.00
90 Matt Kemp/50 5.00 12.00
93 Chin-Lung Hu/50 12.50 30.00
95 Kelly Johnson/50 5.00 12.00
120 Ian Kennedy/35 8.00 20.00
132 Daric Barton/50 5.00 12.00
141 Joe Blanton/50 5.00 12.00
146 Tom Gorzelanny/50 5.00 12.00
150 Rich Hill/50 5.00 12.00
168 Luke Scott/50 5.00 12.00
171 Kevin Kouzmanoff/50 5.00 12.00
175 Ian Kinsler/50 6.00 15.00

2008 Upper Deck Heroes Autographs Navy Blue

RANDOM INSERTS IN BACKS
PRINT RUNS B/WN 35-100 COPIES PER
12 Josh Hamilton/100 12.00 30.00
17 John Maine/100 5.00 12.00
29 Clay Buchholz/55 8.00 20.00
31 Ryan Theriot/100 4.00 10.00
45 Nick Swisher/100 5.00 12.00
46 Corey Hart/100 4.00 10.00
47 Ken Griffey Jr./35 50.00 100.00
49 Aaron Harang/100 4.00 10.00
69 Edinson Volquez/100 10.00 25.00
71 Andrew Miller/35 5.00 12.00
72 Josh Willingham/100 4.00 10.00
73 J.R. Towles/100 4.00 10.00
80 Matt Cain/100 4.00 10.00
85 John Lackey/65 4.00 10.00
90 Matt Kemp/100 5.00 12.00
93 Chin-Lung Hu/100 10.00 25.00
94 Chad Billingsley/100 4.00 10.00
95 Kelly Johnson/100 4.00 10.00
120 Ian Kennedy/55 6.00 15.00
131 Andre Ethier/100 6.00 15.00
132 Daric Barton/50 5.00 12.00
141 Joe Blanton/100 4.00 10.00
142 Felix Pie/100 4.00 10.00
146 Tom Gorzelanny/100 4.00 10.00
150 Rich Hill/50 5.00 12.00
168 Luke Scott/100 4.00 10.00
171 Kevin Kouzmanoff/100 4.00 10.00
175 Ian Kinsler/100 5.00 12.00

2008 Upper Deck Heroes Jersey Autograph Light Blue

RANDOM INSERTS IN PACKS
PRINT RUNS B/WN 5-75 COPIES PER
NO PRICING ON QTY 15 OR LESS
46 Corey Hart/75 8.00 20.00
47 Ken Griffey Jr./50 40.00 80.00
49 Aaron Harang/75 4.00 10.00
55 Jeff Francis/50 6.00 15.00
69 Edinson Volquez/75 10.00 25.00
90 Matt Kemp/75 10.00 25.00
93 Chin-Lung Hu/75 15.00 40.00
94 Chad Billingsley/75 20.00 50.00
114 Derek Jeter/35 150.00 250.00
141 Joe Blanton/75 4.00 10.00
142 Felix Pie/75 4.00 10.00
146 Tom Gorzelanny/75 4.00 10.00
175 Ian Kinsler/75 8.00 20.00

2008 Upper Deck Heroes Jersey Autograph Red

RANDOM INSERTS IN PACKS
PRINT RUNS B/WN 3-50 COPIES PER
NO PRICING ON QTY 25 OR LESS
46 Corey Hart/50 8.00 20.00
69 Edinson Volquez/50 12.50 30.00
80 Matt Cain/50 10.00 25.00
90 Matt Kemp/50 12.50 30.00
92 Jon Lester/35 20.00 50.00
93 Chin-Lung Hu/50 20.00 50.00
94 Chad Billingsley/50 12.50 30.00
95 Kelly Johnson/50 6.00 15.00
141 Joe Blanton/50 5.00 12.00
142 Felix Pie/50 5.00 12.00
146 Tom Gorzelanny/50 5.00 12.00
175 Ian Kinsler/50 10.00 25.00

2008 Upper Deck Heroes Jersey Light Blue

RANDOM INSERTS IN PACKS
STATED PRINT RUN 200 SER.#'d SETS
1 Brandon Webb 3.00 8.00
3 Chris B. Young 3.00 8.00
4 Justin Upton 4.00 10.00
5 Randy Johnson 4.00 10.00
6 Chipper Jones 5.00 12.00
7 John Smoltz 4.00 10.00
9 Mark Teixeira 4.00 10.00
10 Brian McCann 4.00 10.00
11 Jeff Francoeur 4.00 10.00
13 Tim Hudson 3.00 8.00
14 Nick Markakis 6.00 15.00
15 Brian Roberts 3.00 8.00
16 Cal Ripken Jr. 12.50 30.00
17 John Maine 3.00 8.00
18 Frank Robinson 3.00 8.00
19 Mike Lowell 4.00 10.00
20 Jason Varitek 4.00 10.00
21 David Ortiz 4.00 10.00
22 Manny Ramirez 4.00 10.00
23 Jonathan Papelbon 4.00 10.00
24 Jacoby Ellsbury 12.50 30.00
25 Kevin Youkilis 4.00 10.00
26 Curt Schilling 4.00 10.00
27 Josh Beckett 4.00 10.00
28 Daisuke Matsuzaka 6.00 15.00
29 Clay Buchholz 4.00 10.00
33 Carl Yastrzemski 5.00 12.00
34 Wade Boggs 3.00 8.00
35 Nolan Ryan 8.00 20.00
36 Alfonso Soriano 4.00 10.00
37 Kosuke Fukudome 12.50 30.00
38 Derrek Lee 4.00 10.00
39 Carlos Zambrano 3.00 8.00
40 Aramis Ramirez 3.00 8.00
41 Ernie Banks 5.00 12.00
42 Jim Thome 4.00 10.00
43 Jermaine Dye 3.00 8.00
44 Paul Konerko 3.00 8.00
46 Corey Hart 3.00 8.00
47 Ken Griffey Jr. 6.00 15.00
48 Adam Dunn 3.00 8.00
49 Aaron Harang 3.00 8.00
50 Johnny Bench 6.00 15.00
51 Grady Sizemore 4.00 10.00
52 Victor Martinez 3.00 8.00
53 C.C. Sabathia 3.00 8.00
54 Travis Hafner 3.00 8.00
55 Jeff Francis 3.00 8.00
56 Matt Holliday 4.00 10.00
57 Troy Tulowitzki 4.00 10.00
58 Garrett Atkins 3.00 8.00
59 Todd Helton 4.00 10.00

60 Curtis Granderson 4.00 10.00
62 Magglio Ordonez 4.00 10.00
65 Justin Verlander 4.00 10.00
66 Ivan Rodriguez 4.00 10.00
68 Hanley Ramirez 4.00 10.00
69 Edinson Volquez 3.00 8.00
70 Dan Uggla 4.00 10.00
71 Andrew Miller 4.00 10.00
72 Josh Willingham 3.00 8.00
74 Lance Berkman 4.00 10.00
75 Carlos Lee 3.00 8.00
76 Roy Oswalt 3.00 8.00
77 Hunter Pence 4.00 10.00
79 Alex Gordon 4.00 10.00
80 Matt Cain 3.00 8.00
81 Bo Jackson 4.00 10.00
82 Vladimir Guerrero 4.00 10.00
84 Howie Kendrick 3.00 8.00
85 John Lackey 3.00 8.00
86 Chone Figgins 3.00 8.00
88 Brad Penny 3.00 8.00
89 James Loney 4.00 10.00
90 Matt Kemp 3.00 8.00
93 Chin-Lung Hu 4.00 10.00
94 Chad Billingsley 3.00 8.00
95 Kelly Johnson 3.00 8.00
96 Prince Fielder 4.00 10.00
97 Ryan Braun 5.00 12.00
98 Ben Sheets 4.00 10.00
99 Robin Yount 4.00 10.00
100 Justin Morneau 4.00 10.00
101 Joe Mauer 4.00 10.00
103 Rod Carew 4.00 10.00
104 Carlos Beltran 3.00 8.00
106 Pedro Martinez 4.00 10.00
109 Billy Wagner 3.00 8.00
110 Carlos Delgado 3.00 8.00
111 Mariano Rivera 4.00 10.00
112 Chien-Ming Wang 6.00 15.00
113 Phil Hughes 4.00 10.00
114 Derek Jeter 10.00 25.00
115 Alex Rodriguez 8.00 20.00
116 Robinson Cano 4.00 10.00
117 Jorge Posada 4.00 10.00
120 Ian Kennedy 5.00 12.00
121 Yogi Berra 4.00 10.00
123 Roger Clemens 4.00 10.00
124 Ozzie Smith 6.00 15.00
125 Don Mattingly 6.00 15.00
126 Dave Winfield 3.00 8.00
128 Eric Chavez 3.00 8.00
129 Bill Hall 3.00 8.00
130 Rich Harden 3.00 8.00
131 Andre Ethier 4.00 10.00
134 Jimmy Rollins 4.00 10.00
135 Chase Utley 4.00 10.00
136 Cole Hamels 4.00 10.00
137 Pat Burrell 3.00 8.00
138 Mike Schmidt 6.00 15.00
139 Steve Carlton 3.00 8.00
140 Freddy Sanchez 3.00 8.00
142 Felix Pie 3.00 8.00
143 Roberto Clemente 12.50 30.00
144 Jake Peavy 3.00 8.00
145 Greg Maddux 5.00 12.00
146 Tom Gorzelanny 3.00 8.00
147 Tony Gwynn 5.00 12.00
148 Barry Zito 3.00 8.00
149 Tim Lincecum 4.00 10.00
150 Rich Hill 3.00 8.00
151 Omar Vizquel 3.00 8.00
153 Felix Hernandez 4.00 10.00
154 Kenji Johjima 3.00 8.00
156 Albert Pujols 8.00 20.00
157 Troy Glaus 4.00 10.00
158 Chris Carpenter 3.00 8.00
159 Chris Duncan 3.00 8.00
160 Mark Mulder 3.00 8.00
161 Scott Rolen 4.00 10.00
163 Bob Gibson 5.00 12.00
164 B.J. Upton 4.00 10.00
165 Carl Crawford 3.00 8.00
166 Scott Kazmir 4.00 10.00
167 Michael Young 3.00 8.00
169 Roy Halladay 3.00 8.00
170 Vernon Wells 3.00 8.00
171 Kevin Kouzmanoff 3.00 8.00
173 Ryan Zimmerman 4.00 10.00
175 Ian Kinsler 4.00 10.00
176 D.Mattingly/W.Boggs 8.00 20.00
179 J.Reyes/D.Jeter 8.00 20.00
180 C.Ripken Jr./T.Gwynn 15.00 40.00
181 Eddie Murray/Prince Fielder 4.00 10.00
184 Bob Gibson/Jake Peavy 4.00 10.00
185 J.Bench/I.Rodriguez 8.00 20.00
188 ARod/Jeter/Cano 15.00 40.00
190 Mattingly/Winfield/Reggie 12.50 30.00
192 Mauer/Hanley/Tulo 4.00 10.00
193 Ryan/Maddux/Unit 10.00 25.00
194 Webb/Verlander/King Felix 4.00 10.00
195 Schmidt/Banks/F.Robinson 10.00 25.00
197 Yogi/Reggie/Joe D/Jeter 30.00 60.00
198 Papel./Manny/Varitek/Papi 8.00 20.00
199 Griffey/Clemente/Vlad/Joe D 100.00 150.00
200 Pujols/Jeter/Prince/Papi 12.50 30.00

2008 Upper Deck Heroes Jersey Charcoal

RANDOM INSERTS IN RETAIL PACKS
NO PRICING DUE TO SCARCITY

2008 Upper Deck Heroes Jersey Black

*JSY BLK: .4X TO 1X JSY LT.BLUE
RANDOM INSERTS IN PACKS
STATED PRINT RUN 125 SER.#'d SETS

2008 Upper Deck Heroes Jersey Navy Blue

*JSY NAVY: .5X TO 1.2X JSY LT.BLUE
RANDOM INSERTS IN PACKS
STATED PRINT RUN 50 SER.#'d SETS

2008 Upper Deck Heroes Patch Autograph

RANDOM INSERTS IN PACKS
PRINT RUNS B/WN 4-50 COPIES PER
NO PRICING ON QTY 25 OR LESS
17 John Maine/50 10.00 25.00
46 Corey Hart/50 6.00 15.00
49 Aaron Harang/50 6.00 15.00
69 Edinson Volquez/50 20.00 50.00
94 Chad Billingsley/50 20.00 50.00
95 Kelly Johnson/50 10.00 25.00
141 Joe Blanton/50 6.00 15.00
142 Felix Pie/50 10.00 25.00
146 Tom Gorzelanny/50 10.00 25.00
150 Rich Hill/50 6.00 15.00

2000 Upper Deck Hitter's Club

COMPLETE SET (90) 10.00 25.00
COMMON CARD (1-90) .12 .30
1 Mo Vaughn .12 .30
2 Troy Glaus .12 .30
3 Jeff Bagwell .20 .50
4 Craig Biggio .20 .50
5 Jason Giambi .12 .30
6 Eric Chavez .12 .30
7 Carlos Delgado .12 .30
8 Chipper Jones .30 .75
9 Andruw Jones .12 .30
10 Andres Galarraga .20 .50
11 Jeromy Burnitz .12 .30
12 Mark McGwire .50 1.25
13 Mark Grace .20 .50
14 Sammy Sosa .30 .75
15 Jose Canseco .20 .50
16 Vinny Castilla .12 .30
17 Matt Williams .12 .30
18 Gary Sheffield .12 .30
19 Shawn Green .12 .30
20 Vladimir Guerrero .20 .50
21 Barry Bonds .50 1.25
22 Manny Ramirez .30 .75
23 Roberto Alomar .20 .50
24 Jim Thome .20 .50
25 Ken Griffey Jr. .60 1.50
26 Alex Rodriguez .40 1.00
27 Edgar Martinez .20 .50
28 Preston Wilson .12 .30
29 Mike Piazza .30 .75
30 Robin Ventura .12 .30
31 Albert Belle .12 .30
32 Cal Ripken 1.00 2.50
33 Tony Gwynn .30 .75
34 Scott Rolen .20 .50
35 Bob Abreu .12 .30
36 Brian Giles .12 .30
37 Ivan Rodriguez .20 .50
38 Rafael Palmeiro .20 .50
39 Nomar Garciaparra .20 .50
40 Sean Casey .12 .30
41 Larry Walker .20 .50
42 Todd Helton .20 .50
43 Carlos Beltran .20 .50
44 Dean Palmer .12 .30
45 Juan Gonzalez .12 .30
46 Corey Koskie .12 .30
47 Frank Thomas .30 .75
48 Magglio Ordonez .20 .50
49 Derek Jeter .75 2.00
50 Bernie Williams .20 .50
51 Paul Waner W3K .20 .50
52 Honus Wagner W3K .30 .75
53 Tris Speaker W3K .20 .50
54 Nap Lajoie W3K .30 .75
55 Eddie Collins W3K .20 .50
56 Roberto Clemente W3K .75 2.00
57 Ty Cobb W3K .50 1.25
58 Cap Anson W3K .20 .50
59 Robin Yount W3K .30 .75
60 Carl Yastrzemski W3K .50 1.25
61 Dave Winfield W3K .20 .50
62 Stan Musial W3K .50 1.25
63 Eddie Murray W3K .20 .50
64 Paul Molitor W3K .30 .75
65 Wille Mays W3K .60 1.50
66 Al Kaline W3K .30 .75
67 Tony Gwynn W3K .30 .75
68 Rod Carew W3K .20 .50
69 Lou Brock W3K .20 .50
70 George Brett W3K .60 1.50
71 Wade Boggs W3K .20 .50
72 Hank Aaron W3K .60 1.50
73 Jorge Toca HS .12 .30
74 J.D. Drew HS .12 .30
75 Pat Burrell HS .12 .30
76 Vernon Wells HS .12 .30
77 Julio Ramirez HS .12 .30
78 Gabe Kapler HS .12 .30
79 Erubiel Durazo HS .12 .30
80 Lance Berkman HS .20 .50
81 Peter Bergeron HS .12 .30
82 Alfonso Soriano HS .30 .75
83 Jacque Jones HS .12 .30
84 Ben Petrick HS .12 .30
85 Jerry Hairston Jr. HS .12 .30
86 Kevin Witt HS .12 .30
87 Dermal Brown HS .12 .30
88 Chad Hermansen HS .12 .30
89 Ruben Mateo HS .12 .30
90 Ken Griffey Jr. CL .60 1.50

2000 Upper Deck Hitter's Club Accolades

COMPLETE SET (10) 10.00 25.00
STATED ODDS 1:11
A1 Robin Yount 1.00 2.50
A2 Tony Gwynn 1.00 2.50
A3 Sammy Sosa 1.00 2.50
A4 Mike Piazza 1.00 2.50
A5 Cal Ripken 3.00 8.00
A6 Mark McGwire 1.50 4.00
A7 Barry Bonds 1.50 4.00
A8 Wade Boggs .60 1.50
A9 Ken Griffey Jr. 2.00 5.00
A10 Willie Mays 2.00 5.00

2000 Upper Deck Hitter's Club Autographs

STATED ODDS 1:215
AU EXCHANGE DEADLINE 9/13/00
AL Al Kaline 15.00 40.00
DW Dave Winfield 12.00 30.00
EM Eddie Murray 40.00 80.00
GB George Brett 60.00 150.00
HA Hank Aaron SP 150.00 250.00
LOU Lou Brock 12.00 30.00
MAN Stan Musial 40.00 80.00
PM Paul Molitor 10.00 25.00
ROD Rod Carew 10.00 25.00
RY Robin Yount 20.00 50.00
TG Tony Gwynn 30.00 80.00
WB Wade Boggs 12.00 30.00
WM Willie Mays 175.00 350.00
YAZ Carl Yastrzemski 30.00 60.00

2000 Upper Deck Hitter's Club Epic Performances

COMPLETE SET (10) 5.00 12.00
STATED ODDS 1:3
CARD NUMBER 2 DOES NOT EXIST
EP1 Mark McGwire .60 1.50
EP3 Sammy Sosa .40 1.00
EP4 Ken Griffey Jr. .75 2.00
EP5 Carl Yastrzemski .60 1.50
EP6 Tony Gwynn .40 1.00
EP7 Nomar Garciaparra .25 .60
EP8 Cal Ripken 1.25 3.00
EP9 George Brett .75 2.00
EP10 Hank Aaron .75 2.00
EP11 Wade Boggs .25 .60

2000 Upper Deck Hitter's Club Eternals

COMPLETE SET (10) 12.50 30.00
STATED ODDS 1:23
E1 Cal Ripken 3.00 8.00
E2 Mark McGwire 1.50 4.00
E3 Ken Griffey Jr. 2.00 5.00
E4 Nomar Garciaparra .60 1.50
E5 Tony Gwynn 1.00 2.50
E6 Derek Jeter 2.50 6.00
E7 Jose Canseco .60 1.50
E8 Mike Piazza 1.00 2.50
E9 Alex Rodriguez 1.25 3.00
E10 Barry Bonds 1.50 4.00

2000 Upper Deck Hitter's Club Generations of Excellence

COMPLETE SET (10) 8.00 20.00
STATED ODDS 1:6
GE1 C.Ripken E.Murray 2.00 5.00
GE2 V.Guerrero R.Clemente 1.50 4.00
GE3 G.Brett R.Yount 1.25 3.00
GE4 B.Bonds W.Mays 1.25 3.00
GE5 C.Jones H.Aaron 1.25 3.00
GE6 M.McGwire S.Sosa 1.00 2.50
GE7 T.Gwynn W.Boggs .60 1.50
GE8 R.Henderson L.Brock .60 1.50
GE9 D.Jeter N.Garciaparra 1.50 4.00
GE10 A.Rodriguez K.Griffey Jr. 1.25 3.00

2000 Upper Deck Hitter's Club Inserts

COMPLETE SET (10) 20.00 50.00
STATED ODDS 1:95
HC1 Rod Carew 1.50 4.00
HC2 Alex Rodriguez 3.00 8.00
HC3 Willie Mays 5.00 12.00
HC4 George Brett 5.00 12.00
HC5 Tony Gwynn 2.50 6.00
HC6 Stan Musial 4.00 10.00
HC7 Frank Thomas 2.50 6.00
HC8 Wade Boggs 1.50 4.00
HC9 Larry Walker 1.50 4.00
HC10 Nomar Garciaparra 1.50 4.00

2000 Upper Deck Hitter's Club On Target

COMPLETE SET (10) 6.00 15.00
STATED ODDS 1:23
OT1 Nomar Garciaparra .60 1.50
OT2 Sean Casey .40 1.00
OT3 Alex Rodriguez 1.25 3.00
OT4 Troy Glaus .40 1.00
OT5 Ivan Rodriguez .60 1.50
OT6 Chipper Jones 1.00 2.50
OT7 Manny Ramirez 1.00 2.50
OT8 Derek Jeter 2.50 6.00
OT9 Vladimir Guerrero .60 1.50
OT10 Scott Rolen .60 1.50

2007 Upper Deck Holiday Inn

COMPLETE SET (60) 8.00 20.00
1 Miguel Tejada .20 .50
2 David Ortiz .30 .75
3 Manny Ramirez .30 .75
4 Paul Konerko .20 .50
5 Jermaine Dye .12 .30
6 Grady Sizemore .20 .50
7 Travis Hafner .12 .30
8 Ivan Rodriguez .20 .50
9 Gary Sheffield .12 .30
10 Gil Meche .12 .30
11 Vladimir Guerrero .20 .50
12 Ervin Santana .12 .30
13 Joe Mauer .25 .60
14 Justin Morneau .20 .50
15 Johan Santana .20 .50
16 Derek Jeter .75 2.00
17 Alex Rodriguez .40 1.00
18 Nick Swisher .20 .50
19 Eric Chavez .12 .30
20 Kenji Johjima .30 .75
21 Felix Hernandez .20 .50
22 Brandon Webb .20 .50
23 Randy Johnson .30 .75
24 Chipper Jones .30 .75
25 Andruw Jones .12 .30
26 John Smoltz .30 .75
27 Alfonso Soriano .20 .50
28 Derrek Lee .12 .30
29 Ken Griffey Jr. .60 1.50
30 Adam Dunn .20 .50
31 Todd Helton .20 .50
32 Garrett Atkins .12 .30
33 Miguel Cabrera .30 .75
34 Dontrelle Willis .12 .30
35 Carlos Lee .12 .30
36 Roy Oswalt .20 .50
37 Jeff Kent .12 .30
38 Jason Schmidt .12 .30
39 Rickie Weeks .12 .30
40 Prince Fielder .20 .50
41 Jose Reyes .20 .50
42 David Wright .25 .60
43 Carlos Delgado .12 .30
44 Carl Crawford .20 .50
45 Delmon Young .20 .50
46 Michael Young .12 .30
47 Mark Teixeira .20 .50
48 Vernon Wells .12 .30
49 Roy Halladay .20 .50
50 Barry Zito .20 .50
51 Omar Vizquel .20 .50
52 Ryan Howard .25 .60
53 Chase Utley .20 .50
54 Jason Bay .20 .50
55 Freddy Sanchez .12 .30
56 Albert Pujols .40 1.00
57 Chris Carpenter .20 .50
58 Greg Maddux .40 1.00
59 Trevor Hoffman .20 .50
60 Ryan Zimmerman .20 .50

2007 Upper Deck Holiday Inn Cal Ripken

COMPLETE SET (5) 2.00 5.00
1 Cal Ripken .75 2.00
2 Cal Ripken .75 2.00
3 Cal Ripken .75 2.00
4 Cal Ripken .75 2.00
5 Cal Ripken .75 2.00

1999 Upper Deck HoloGrFX

Issued only through Retail outlets, this 60 card set was distributed in the summer of 1999. There were 36 packs in a box with three cards per pack at a SRP of $1.99 per pack. All the cards in this set featured a hi-tech holographic treatment. Notable Rookie Cards include Pat Burrell. Two separate A Piece of History 500 Club bat cards featuring legendary sluggers Eddie Mathews and Willie McCovey were randomly seeded into HoloGrFX packs. Approximately 350 of each card were made. In addition, 41 signed Mathews cards and 44 signed McCovey cards were also included in packs. Both players signed to their jersey numbers. Pricing for these APH 500 Club cards can be found under 1999 Upper Deck A Piece of History 500 Club. A Ken Griffey Jr. HoloGrFX sample card was distributed to dealers and hobby media several weeks prior to the product's national release. The card is similar to the basic HoloGrFX Griffey except for it's numbering (the basic Griffey is number 53, the sample is number 60) and the white text "SAMPLE" running diagonally across the card back.

COMPLETE SET (60) 10.00 25.00
MATHEWS BAT LISTED W/UD APH 500 CLUB
MCCOVEY BAT LISTED W/UD APH 500 CLUB
1 Mo Vaughn .15 .40
2 Troy Glaus .25 .60
3 Tim Salmon .25 .60
4 Randy Johnson .40 1.00
5 Travis Lee .15 .40
6 Chipper Jones .40 1.00
7 Greg Maddux .60 1.50
8 Andruw Jones .25 .60
9 Tom Glavine .25 .60
10 Cal Ripken 1.25 3.00
11 Albert Belle .15 .40
12 Nomar Garciaparra .60 1.50
13 Pedro Martinez .25 .60
14 Sammy Sosa .40 1.00
15 Frank Thomas .40 1.00
16 Greg Vaughn .15 .40
17 Kenny Lofton .15 .40
18 Jim Thome .25 .60
19 Manny Ramirez .25 .60
20 Todd Helton .25 .60
21 Larry Walker .15 .40
22 Tony Clark .15 .40
23 Juan Encarnacion .15 .40
24 Mark Kotsay .15 .40
25 Jeff Bagwell .25 .60
26 Craig Biggio .25 .60
27 Ken Caminiti .15 .40
28 Carlos Beltran .25 .60
29 Jeremy Giambi .15 .40
30 Raul Mondesi .15 .40
31 Kevin Brown .25 .60
32 Jeromy Burnitz .15 .40
33 Corey Koskie .15 .40
34 Todd Walker .15 .40
35 Vladimir Guerrero .40 1.00
36 Mike Piazza .60 1.50
37 Robin Ventura .15 .40
38 Derek Jeter 1.00 2.50
39 Roger Clemens .75 2.00
40 Bernie Williams .25 .60
41 Orlando Hernandez .15 .40
42 Ben Grieve .15 .40
43 Eric Chavez .15 .40
44 Scott Rolen .25 .60
45 Pat Burrell RC .75 2.00
46 Warren Morris .15 .40
47 Jason Kendall .15 .40
48 Mark McGwire 1.00 2.50
49 J.D. Drew .15 .40
50 Tony Gwynn .50 1.25
51 Trevor Hoffman .15 .40
52 Barry Bonds 1.00 2.50
53 Ken Griffey Jr. .75 2.00
54 Alex Rodriguez .60 1.50
55 Jose Canseco .25 .60
56 Juan Gonzalez .15 .40
57 Ivan Rodriguez .25 .60
58 Rafael Palmeiro .25 .60
59 David Wells .15 .40
60 Carlos Delgado .15 .40
S60 Ken Griffey Jr. Sample 1.00 2.50

1999 Upper Deck HoloGrFX AuSOME

COMPLETE SET (60) 75.00 150.00
*STARS: 2.5X TO 6X BASIC CARDS
*ROOKIES: 1.25X TO 3X BASIC CARDS
STATED ODDS 1:8

1999 Upper Deck HoloGrFX Future Fame

COMPLETE SET (6) 20.00 50.00
STATED ODDS 1:32
*GOLD: 6X TO 1.5X BASIC FUTURE FAME
GOLD STATED ODDS 1:432
F1 Tony Gwynn 2.00 5.00
F2 Cal Ripken 6.00 15.00
F3 Mark McGwire 3.00 8.00
F4 Ken Griffey Jr. 4.00 10.00
F5 Greg Maddux 2.50 6.00
F6 Roger Clemens 2.50 6.00

1999 Upper Deck HoloGrFX Launchers

COMPLETE SET (15) 12.50 30.00
STATED ODDS 1:4
*GOLD: 2.5X TO 6X BASIC LAUNCHERS
GOLD STATED ODDS 1:105
L1 Mark McGwire 1.50 4.00
L2 Ken Griffey Jr. 1.25 3.00
L3 Sammy Sosa .60 1.50
L4 J.D. Drew .25 .60
L5 Mo Vaughn .25 .60
L6 Juan Gonzalez .25 .60
L7 Mike Piazza 1.00 2.50
L8 Alex Rodriguez 1.00 2.50
L9 Chipper Jones .60 1.50
L10 Nomar Garciaparra 1.00 2.50
L11 Vladimir Guerrero .60 1.50
L12 Albert Belle .25 .60
L13 Barry Bonds 1.50 4.00
L14 Frank Thomas .60 1.50
L15 Jeff Bagwell .40 1.00

1999 Upper Deck HoloGrFX StarView

COMPLETE SET (9) 15.00 40.00
STATED ODDS 1:16
*GOLD: 2X TO 5X BASIC STARVIEW
GOLD STATED ODDS 1:210
S1 Mark McGwire 2.50 6.00
S2 Ken Griffey Jr. 2.00 5.00
S3 Sammy Sosa 1.00 2.50
S4 Nomar Garciaparra 1.50 4.00
S5 Roger Clemens 2.00 5.00
S6 Greg Maddux 1.50 4.00
S7 Mike Piazza 1.50 4.00
S8 Alex Rodriguez 1.50 4.00
S9 Chipper Jones 1.00 2.50

1999 Upper Deck HoloGrFX UD Authentics

STATED ODDS 1:431
AG Alex Gonzalez 4.00 10.00
BC Bruce Chen 4.00 10.00
CB Carlos Beltran 12.00 30.00
CJ Chipper Jones 40.00 80.00
CK Corey Koskie 6.00 15.00
GK Gabe Kapler 6.00 15.00
GL George Lombard 4.00 10.00
JD J.D. Drew 6.00 15.00
JR Ken Griffey Jr. 100.00 250.00
MK Mike Kinkade 4.00 10.00
RM Ryan Minor 4.00 10.00
SM Shane Monahan 4.00 10.00

2000 Upper Deck HoloGrFX

COMPLETE SET (90) 10.00 25.00
COMMON CARD (1-90) .15 .40
1 Mo Vaughn .15 .40
2 Troy Glaus .15 .40
3 Daryle Ward .15 .40
4 Jeff Bagwell .25 .60
5 Craig Biggio .25 .60
6 Jose Lima .15 .40
7 Jason Giambi .15 .40
8 Eric Chavez .15 .40
9 Tim Hudson .25 .60
10 Raul Mondesi .15 .40
11 Carlos Delgado .15 .40
12 David Wells .15 .40
13 Chipper Jones .40 1.00
14 Greg Maddux .50 1.25
15 Andruw Jones .15 .40
16 Brian Jordan .15 .40
17 Jeromy Burnitz .15 .40
18 Ron Belliard .15 .40
19 Mark McGwire .60 1.50
20 Fernando Tatis .15 .40
21 J.D. Drew .15 .40
22 Sammy Sosa .40 1.00
23 Mark Grace .25 .60
24 Greg Vaughn .15 .40
25 Jose Canseco .25 .60
26 Vinny Castilla .15 .40
27 Fred McGriff .25 .60
28 Matt Williams .15 .40
29 Randy Johnson .40 1.00
30 Erubiel Durazo .15 .40
31 Shawn Green .15 .40
32 Gary Sheffield .15 .40
33 Kevin Brown .15 .40
34 Vladimir Guerrero .25 .60
35 Michael Barrett .15 .40
36 Russ Ortiz .15 .40
37 Barry Bonds .60 1.50
38 Jeff Kent .15 .40
39 Kenny Lofton .15 .40
40 Manny Ramirez .40 1.00
41 Roberto Alomar .25 .60
42 Richie Sexson .15 .40
43 Edgar Martinez .25 .60
44 Alex Rodriguez .50 1.25
45 Freddy Garcia .15 .40
46 Preston Wilson .15 .40
47 Alex Gonzalez .15 .40
48 Mike Hampton .15 .40
49 Mike Piazza .40 1.00
50 Robin Ventura .15 .40
51 Edgardo Alfonzo .15 .40
52 Albert Belle .15 .40
53 Cal Ripken 1.25 3.00
54 B.J. Surhoff .15 .40
55 Tony Gwynn .40 1.00
56 Trevor Hoffman .25 .60
57 Mike Lieberthal .15 .40
58 Scott Rolen .25 .60
59 Bob Abreu .15 .40
60 Curt Schilling .25 .60
61 Jason Kendall .15 .40
62 Brian Giles .15 .40
63 Kris Benson .15 .40
64 Rafael Palmeiro .25 .60
65 Ivan Rodriguez .25 .60
66 Gabe Kapler .15 .40
67 Nomar Garciaparra .25 .60
68 Pedro Martinez .25 .60
69 Troy O'Leary .15 .40
70 Barry Larkin .25 .60
71 Dante Bichette .15 .40
72 Sean Casey .15 .40
73 Ken Griffey Jr. .75 2.00
74 Jeff Cirillo .15 .40
75 Todd Helton .25 .60
76 Larry Walker .25 .60
77 Carlos Beltran .25 .60
78 Jermaine Dye .15 .40
79 Juan Gonzalez .15 .40
80 Juan Encarnacion .15 .40
81 Dean Palmer .15 .40
82 Corey Koskie .15 .40
83 Eric Milton .15 .40
84 Frank Thomas .40 1.00
85 Magglio Ordonez .25 .60
86 Carlos Lee .15 .40
87 Derek Jeter 1.00 2.50
88 Tino Martinez .15 .40
89 Bernie Williams .25 .60
90 Roger Clemens .50 1.25

2000 Upper Deck HoloGrFX A Piece of the Series

STATED ODDS 1:431
CARD NUMBER 10 DOES NOT EXIST
PS1 Derek Jeter 10.00 25.00
PS2 Chipper Jones 10.00 25.00
PS3 Roger Clemens 8.00 20.00
PS4 Greg Maddux 10.00 25.00
PS5 Bernie Williams 10.00 25.00
PS6 Andruw Jones 10.00 25.00
PS7 Tino Martinez 10.00 25.00
PS8 Brian Jordan 6.00 15.00
PS9 Mariano Rivera 10.00 25.00
PS11 Paul O'Neill 10.00 25.00
PS12 Tom Glavine 10.00 25.00

2000 Upper Deck HoloGrFX A Piece of the Series Autographs

PRINT RUNS B/WN 24-47 COPIES PER
NO PRICING ON QTY OF 25 OR LESS
CARD NUMBERS 5, 9 AND 10 DO NOT EXIST
VARIATIONS EXIST FOR 7/8/11/12
PSA8A Brian Jordan/33 30.00 60.00
PSA12A Tom Glavine/47 75.00 150.00

2000 Upper Deck HoloGrFX Bomb Squad

COMPLETE SET (6) 6.00 15.00
STATED ODDS 1:34
BS1 Ken Griffey Jr. 2.00 5.00
BS2 Mark McGwire 1.50 4.00
BS3 Chipper Jones 1.00 2.50
BS4 Alex Rodriguez 1.25 3.00
BS5 Sammy Sosa 1.00 2.50
BS6 Barry Bonds 1.50 4.00

2000 Upper Deck HoloGrFX Future Fame

COMPLETE SET (6) 8.00 20.00
STATED ODDS 1:34
FF1 Cal Ripken 3.00 8.00
FF2 Mark McGwire 1.50 4.00
FF3 Greg Maddux 1.25 3.00
FF4 Tony Gwynn 1.00 2.50
FF5 Ken Griffey Jr. 2.00 5.00
FF6 Roger Clemens 1.25 3.00

2000 Upper Deck HoloGrFX Longball Legacy

COMPLETE SET (15) 8.00 20.00
STATED ODDS 1:6
LL1 Mike Piazza .75 2.00
LL2 Ivan Rodriguez .50 1.25
LL3 Jeff Bagwell .50 1.25
LL4 Alex Rodriguez 1.00 2.50
LL5 Jose Canseco .50 1.25
LL6 Mark McGwire 1.25 3.00
LL7 Scott Rolen .50 1.25
LL8 Carlos Delgado .30 .75
LL9 Mo Vaughn .30 .75
LL10 Manny Ramirez .75 2.00
LL11 Matt Williams .30 .75
LL12 Sammy Sosa .75 2.00
LL13 Ken Griffey Jr. 1.50 4.00
LL14 Nomar Garciaparra .50 1.25
LL15 Larry Walker .50 1.25

2000 Upper Deck HoloGrFX Stars of the System

COMPLETE SET (10) 3.00 8.00
STATED ODDS 1:8
SS1 Rick Ankiel .60 1.50
SS2 Alfonso Soriano 1.00 2.50
SS3 Vernon Wells .40 1.00
SS4 Ben Petrick .40 1.00
SS5 Francisco Cordero .40 1.00
SS6 Matt Riley .40 1.00
SS7 A.J. Burnett .40 1.00
SS8 Pat Burrell .40 1.00
SS9 Ed Yarnall .40 1.00
SS10 Dermal Brown .40 1.00

2000 Upper Deck HoloGrFX StarView

COMPLETE SET (8) 8.00 20.00
STATED ODDS 1:11
SV1 Ken Griffey Jr. 2.00 5.00
SV2 Nomar Garciaparra .60 1.50
SV3 Chipper Jones 1.00 2.50
SV4 Mark McGwire 1.50 4.00
SV5 Sammy Sosa 1.00 2.50
SV6 Derek Jeter 2.50 6.00
SV7 Mike Piazza 1.00 2.50
SV8 Alex Rodriguez 1.25 3.00

2002 Upper Deck Honor Roll

COMP.LOW SET (100) 10.00 25.00
COMP.UPDATE SET (90) 10.00 25.00
DUPE STARS 28-100 VALUED EQUALLY
COMMON CARD (101-130) .10 .30
101-190 ISSUED IN UD ROOKIE DEBUT PACKS
1 Randy Johnson NLD9 .20 .50
2 Mike Piazza NLD9 .30 .75
3 Albert Pujols NLD9 .40 1.00
4 Roberto Alomar NLD9 .10 .30
5 Chipper Jones NLD9 .20 .50
6 Rich Aurilia NLD9 .07 .20
7 Barry Bonds NLD9 .50 1.25
8 Ken Griffey Jr. NLD9 .40 1.00
9 Sammy Sosa NLD9 .30 .75
10 Roger Clemens ALD9 .40 1.00
11 Ivan Rodriguez ALD9 .10 .30
12 Jason Giambi ALD9 .07 .20
13 Bret Boone ALD9 .07 .20
14 Troy Glaus ALD9 .07 .20
15 Alex Rodriguez ALD9 .25 .60
16 Manny Ramirez ALD9 .10 .30
17 Bernie Williams ALD9 .10 .30
18 Ichiro Suzuki ALD9 .40 1.00
19 Matt Thornton PD9 RC .15 .40
20 Chris Baker PD9 RC .15 .40
21 Tyler Yates PD9 RC .15 .40
22 Jorge Nunez PD9 RC .15 .40
23 Rene Reyes PD9 RC .15 .40
24 Ben Howard PD9 RC .15 .40
25 Ron Calloway PD9 RC .15 .40
26 Dan Wright PD9 .15 .40
27 Reed Johnson PD9 RC .30 .75
28 Randy Johnson .20 .50
29 Randy Johnson .20 .50
30 Randy Johnson .20 .50
31 Randy Johnson .20 .50
32 Mike Piazza .30 .75
33 Mike Piazza .30 .75
34 Mike Piazza .30 .75
35 Mike Piazza .30 .75
36 Albert Pujols .40 1.00
37 Albert Pujols .40 1.00
38 Albert Pujols .40 1.00
39 Albert Pujols .40 1.00
40 Roberto Alomar .10 .30
41 Roberto Alomar .10 .30
42 Roberto Alomar .10 .30
43 Roberto Alomar .10 .30
44 Chipper Jones .20 .50
45 Chipper Jones .20 .50
46 Chipper Jones .20 .50
47 Chipper Jones .20 .50
48 Rich Aurilia .07 .20
49 Rich Aurilia .07 .20
50 Rich Aurilia .07 .20
51 Rich Aurilia .07 .20
52 Barry Bonds .50 1.25
53 Barry Bonds .50 1.25
54 Barry Bonds .50 1.25
55 Barry Bonds .50 1.25
56 Ken Griffey Jr. .40 1.00
57 Ken Griffey Jr. .40 1.00
58 Ken Griffey Jr. .40 1.00
59 Ken Griffey Jr. .40 1.00
60 Sammy Sosa .20 .50
61 Sammy Sosa .20 .50
62 Sammy Sosa .20 .50
63 Sammy Sosa .20 .50
64 Roger Clemens .40 1.00
65 Roger Clemens .40 1.00
66 Roger Clemens .40 1.00
67 Roger Clemens .40 1.00
68 Ivan Rodriguez .10 .30
69 Ivan Rodriguez .10 .30
70 Ivan Rodriguez .10 .30
71 Ivan Rodriguez .10 .30
72 Jason Giambi .07 .20
73 Jason Giambi .07 .20
74 Jason Giambi .07 .20
75 Jason Giambi .07 .20
76 Bret Boone .07 .20
77 Bret Boone .07 .20
78 Bret Boone .07 .20
79 Bret Boone .07 .20
80 Troy Glaus .07 .20
81 Troy Glaus .07 .20
82 Troy Glaus .07 .20
83 Troy Glaus .07 .20
84 Alex Rodriguez .25 .60
85 Alex Rodriguez .25 .60
86 Alex Rodriguez .25 .60
87 Alex Rodriguez .25 .60
88 Manny Ramirez .10 .30
89 Manny Ramirez .10 .30
90 Manny Ramirez .10 .30
91 Manny Ramirez .10 .30
92 Bernie Williams .10 .30
93 Bernie Williams .10 .30
94 Bernie Williams .10 .30
95 Bernie Williams .10 .30
96 Ichiro Suzuki .40 1.00
97 Ichiro Suzuki .40 1.00
98 Ichiro Suzuki .40 1.00
99 Ichiro Suzuki .40 1.00
100 Checklist .07 .20
101 Curt Schilling DM .10 .30
102 Geronimo Gil DM .10 .30
103 Cliff Floyd DM .10 .30
104 Derek Lowe DM .10 .30
105 Hee Seop Choi DM .10 .30
106 Mark Prior DM 2.00 5.00
107 Joe Borchard DM .10 .30
108 Austin Kearns DM .10 .30
109 Adam Dunn DM .10 .30

110 Brandon Phillips DM .10 .30
111 Carlos Pena DM .10 .30
112 Andy Van Hekken DM .10 .30
113 Juan Encarnacion DM .10 .30
114 Lance Berkman DM .10 .30
115 Torii Hunter DM .10 .30
116 Bartolo Colon DM .10 .30
117 Raul Mondesi DM .10 .30
118 Alfonso Soriano DM .10 .30
119 Miguel Tejada DM .10 .30
120 Ray Durham DM .10 .30
121 Eric Chavez DM .10 .30
122 Brett Myers DM .10 .30
123 Marlon Byrd DM .10 .30
124 Sean Burroughs DM .10 .30
125 Kenny Lofton DM .10 .30
126 Scott Rolen DM .20 .50
127 Carl Crawford DM .10 .30
128 Josh Phelps DM .10 .30
129 Eric Hinske DM .10 .30
130 Orlando Hudson DM .10 .30
131 Barry Wesson UDP RC .15 .40
132 Jose Valverde UDP RC .15 .40
133 Kevin Gryboski UDP RC .15 .40
134 Trey Hodges UDP RC .15 .40
135 Howie Clark UDP RC .15 .40
136 John Hancock UDP RC .15 .40
137 Freddy Sanchez UDP RC .75 2.00
138 Francis Beltran UDP RC .15 .40
139 Mike Mahoney UDP .15 .40
140 Brian Tallet UDP RC .15 .40
141 Jason Davis UDP RC .15 .40
142 Carl Sadler UDP RC .15 .40
143 Jason Beverlin UDP RC .15 .40
144 Josh Bard UDP RC .15 .40
145 Aaron Cook UDP RC .15 .40
146 Eric Eckenstahler UDP RC .15 .40
147 Tim Kalita UDP RC .15 .40
148 Franklyn German UDP RC .15 .40
149 Hansel Izquierdo UDP RC .15 .40
150 Brandon Puffer UDP RC .15 .40
151 Rodrigo Rosario UDP RC .15 .40
152 Kirk Saarloos UDP RC .15 .40
153 Jeriome Robertson UDP RC .15 .40
154 Jeremy Hill UDP RC .15 .40
155 Wes Obermueller UDP RC .15 .40
156 Aaron Guiel UDP RC .15 .40
157 Kazuhisa Ishii UDP RC .20 .50
158 David Ross UDP RC .25 .60
159 Jayson Durocher UDP RC .15 .40
160 Luis Martinez UDP RC .15 .40
161 Shane Nance UDP RC .15 .40
162 Eric Good UDP RC .15 .40
163 Jamey Carroll UDP RC .30 .75
164 Jaime Cerda UDP RC .15 .40
165 Satoru Komiyama UDP RC .15 .40
166 Adam Walker UDP RC .15 .40
167 Nate Field UDP RC .15 .40
168 Cody McKay UDP RC .15 .40
169 Jose Flores UDP RC .15 .40
170 Eric Junge UDP RC .15 .40
171 Jorge Padilla UDP RC .15 .40
172 Oliver Perez UDP RC .30 .75
173 Julius Matos UDP RC .15 .40
174 Wil Nieves UDP RC .15 .40
175 Clay Condrey UDP RC .15 .40
176 Mike Crudale UDP RC .15 .40
177 Jason Simontacchi UDP RC .15 .40
178 So Taguchi UDP RC .20 .50
179 Jose Rodriguez UDP RC .15 .40
180 Jorge Sosa UDP RC .20 .50
181 Felix Escalona UDP RC .15 .40
182 Lance Carter UDP RC .15 .40
183 Travis Hughes UDP RC .15 .40
184 Reynaldo Garcia UDP RC .15 .40
185 Mike Smith UDP RC .15 .40
186 Corey Thurman UDP RC .15 .40
187 Ken Huckaby UDP RC .15 .40
188 Reed Johnson UDP .20 .50
189 Kevin Cash UDP RC .15 .40
190 Scott Wiggins UDP RC .15 .40

2002 Upper Deck Honor Roll Gold

*GOLD 1-18/28-100: 25X TO 60X BASIC
*GOLD 101-130: 10X TO 25X BASIC
*GOLD 131-190: 6X TO 15X BASIC
1-100 PRINT RUN 25 SERIAL #'d SETS
101-190 PRINT RUN 50 SERIAL #'d SETS
CARDS 19-27 NOT PRICED DUE TO SCARCITY

2002 Upper Deck Honor Roll Silver

*SILVER 1-18/28-100: 6X TO 15X BASIC
*SILVER RC's 19-27: 4X TO 10X BASIC
RANDOM INSERTS IN PACKS
STATED PRINT RUN 100 SERIAL #'d SETS

2002 Upper Deck Honor Roll Batting Gloves

PRINT RUNS B/WN 46-250 COPIES PER
STATED PRINT RUNS LISTED BELOW
GAR Alex Rodriguez/250 12.50 30.00
GIR1 Ivan Rodriguez/250 10.00 25.00
GIR2 Ivan Rodriguez/250 10.00 25.00
GJG Jason Giambi/210 10.00 25.00
GKG Ken Griffey Jr./250 15.00 40.00
GSS Sammy Sosa/250 10.00 25.00

2002 Upper Deck Honor Roll Game Bats

RANDOM INSERTS IN PACKS
STATED PRINT RUN 99 SERIAL #'d SETS
BAR1 Alex Rodriguez Helmet 15.00 40.00
BAR2 Alex Rodriguez Hand 15.00 40.00
BAR3 Alex Rodriguez Cap 15.00 40.00
BAR4 Alex Rodriguez Shades 15.00 40.00
BBB1 Bret Boone Left 6.00 15.00
BBB2 Bret Boone w Cap Btg. 6.00 15.00
BBB3 Bret Boone Right 6.00 15.00
BCJ1 Chipper Jones Bat 10.00 25.00
BCJ2 Chipper Jones Look Up 10.00 25.00
BCJ3 Chipper Jones Run 10.00 25.00
BI1 Ichiro Suzuki Run 15.00 40.00
BI2 Ichiro Suzuki Profile 15.00 40.00
BI3 Ichiro Suzuki w Cap 15.00 40.00
BIR1 Ivan Rodriguez Look Up 10.00 25.00
BIR2 Ivan Rodriguez Hold Bat 10.00 25.00
BIR3 Ivan Rodriguez Field 10.00 25.00
BIR4 Ivan Rodriguez Red Hat 10.00 25.00
BJG1 Jason Giambi Field 6.00 15.00
BJG2 Jason Giambi Run 6.00 15.00
BJG3 Jason Giambi Studio 6.00 15.00
BKG1 Ken Griffey Jr. Bat 20.00 50.00
BKG2 Ken Griffey Jr. Walk 20.00 50.00
BKG3 Ken Griffey Jr. Look Up 20.00 50.00
BRC1 Roger Clemens Look Right 8.00 20.00
BRC2 Roger Clemens Motion 8.00 20.00
BRC3 Roger Clemens Glove 8.00 20.00
BSS1 Sammy Sosa Look Right 10.00 25.00
BSS2 Sammy Sosa Btg Action 10.00 25.00
BSS3 Sammy Sosa Btg Close 10.00 25.00
BSS4 Sammy Sosa w Cap 10.00 25.00

2002 Upper Deck Honor Roll Game Jersey

STATED ODDS 1:90
SP PRINT RUNS PROVIDED BY UPPER DECK
SP'S ARE NOT SERIAL-NUMBERED
JI1 Ichiro Suzuki Throw SP 20.00 50.00
JI2 Ichiro Suzuki Cap SP 20.00 50.00
JI3 Ichiro Suzuki Helmet SP 20.00 50.00
JAR1 Alex Rodriguez Helmet 6.00 15.00
JAR2 Alex Rodriguez Glasses 6.00 15.00
JAR3 Alex Rodriguez Cap 6.00 15.00
JAR4 Alex Rodriguez No Hat 6.00 15.00
JCJ1 Chipper Jones Helmet 6.00 15.00
JCJ2 Chipper Jones Right 6.00 15.00
JCJ3 Chipper Jones Earflap 6.00 15.00
JIR1 Ivan Rodriguez 6.00 15.00
JIR2 Ivan Rodriguez 6.00 15.00
JIR3 Ivan Rodriguez 6.00 15.00
JIR4 Ivan Rodriguez 6.00 15.00
JJG1 Jason Giambi Bat 4.00 10.00
JJG2 Jason Giambi Helmet 4.00 10.00
JJG3 Jason Giambi Cap 4.00 10.00
JKG1 Ken Griffey Jr. No Hat 8.00 20.00
JKG2 Ken Griffey Jr. Helmet 8.00 20.00
JKG3 Ken Griffey Jr. Cap 8.00 20.00
JRC1 Roger Clemens White 10.00 25.00
JRC2 Roger Clemens Right 10.00 25.00
JRC3 Roger Clemens Gray 10.00 25.00
JSS1 Sammy Sosa Glove SP 10.00 25.00
JSS2 Sammy Sosa Cap SP 10.00 25.00
JSS3 Sammy Sosa No Hat SP 10.00 25.00
JSS4 Sammy Sosa Field SP 10.00 25.00

2002 Upper Deck Honor Roll Star Swatches Game Jersey

STATED ODDS 1:90
SP PRINT RUNS PROVIDED BY UPPER DECK
SP'S ARE NOT SERIAL-NUMBERED
SSAR1 Alex Rodriguez Bat 6.00 15.00
SSAR2 Alex Rodriguez Field 6.00 15.00
SSAR3 Alex Rodriguez Throw 6.00 15.00
SSAR4 Alex Rodriguez Fist 6.00 15.00
SSCJ1 Chipper Jones Bat Left 6.00 15.00
SSCJ2 Chipper Jones Bat Right 6.00 15.00
SSCJ3 Chipper Jones Field 6.00 15.00
SSIR1 Ivan Rodriguez Throw 6.00 15.00
SSIR2 Ivan Rodriguez Run 6.00 15.00
SSIR3 Ivan Rodriguez Cap 6.00 15.00
SSIR4 Ivan Rodriguez Bat 6.00 15.00
SSI1 I.Suzuki White Jsy SP 20.00 50.00
SSI2 Ichiro Suzuki Helmet SP 20.00 50.00
SSI3 Ichiro Suzuki Gray Jsy SP 20.00 50.00
SSJG1 Jason Giambi Cap 4.00 10.00
SSJG2 Jason Giambi Bat 4.00 10.00
SSJG3 Jason Giambi Helmet 4.00 10.00
SSKG1 Ken Griffey Jr. Bat SP 12.50 30.00
SSKG2 Ken Griffey Red Hat SP 12.50 30.00
SSKG3 K.Griffey Jr. Blk Hat SP 12.50 30.00
SSSS1 Sammy Sosa White Jsy 6.00 15.00
SSSS2 Sammy Sosa Bat 6.00 15.00
SSSS3 Sammy Sosa Field 6.00 15.00
SSSS4 Sammy Sosa Blue Jsy 6.00 15.00

2002 Upper Deck Honor Roll Stitch of Nine Game Jersey

STATED ODDS 1:90
SP PRINT RUNS PROVIDED BY UPPER DECK
SP'S ARE NOT SERIAL-NUMBERED
S9I1 Ichiro Hat SP/85 10.00 25.00
S9I2 Ichiro Glasses SP/85 10.00 25.00
S9I3 Ichiro Helmet SP/85 10.00 25.00
S9AR1 Alex Rodriguez Left 6.00 15.00
S9AR2 Alex Rodriguez Hat 6.00 15.00
S9AR3 Alex Rodriguez No Hat 6.00 15.00
S9AR4 Alex Rodriguez Right 6.00 15.00
S9CJ1 Chipper Jones Cap 6.00 15.00
S9CJ2 Chipper Jones Helmet 6.00 15.00
S9CJ3 C.Jones Cap Right 6.00 15.00
S9IR1 Ivan Rodriguez Helmet 6.00 15.00
S9IR2 Ivan Rodriguez Hat 6.00 15.00
S9IR3 Ivan Rodriguez No Hat 6.00 15.00
S9IR4 Ivan Rodriguez Left 6.00 15.00
S9JG1 Jason Giambi Helmet SP 4.00 10.00
S9JG2 Jason Giambi Hat SP 4.00 10.00
S9JG3 Jason Giambi Left SP 4.00 10.00
S9KG1 Ken Griffey Jr. White 8.00 20.00
S9KG2 Ken Griffey Jr. Red 8.00 20.00
S9KG3 Ken Griffey Jr. Helmet 8.00 20.00
S9RC1 Roger Clemens Follow 10.00 25.00
S9RC2 Roger ClemensThrow 10.00 25.00
S9RC3 Roger Clemens Chin 10.00 25.00
S9SS1 Sammy Sosa Bat 6.00 15.00
S9SS2 Sammy Sosa Helmet 6.00 15.00
S9SS3 Sammy Sosa Left 6.00 15.00
S9SS4 Sammy Sosa Right 6.00 15.00

2002 Upper Deck Honor Roll Time Capsule Game Jersey

STATED ODDS 1:90
SP PRINT RUNS PROVIDED BY UPPER DECK
SP'S ARE NOT SERIAL-NUMBERED
TCAR1 Alex Rodriguez 96 6.00 15.00
TCAR2 Alex Rodriguez 98 6.00 15.00
TCAR3 Alex Rodriguez 00 6.00 15.00
TCAR4 Alex Rodriguez 01 6.00 15.00
TCCJ1 Chipper Jones 99 6.00 15.00
TCCJ2 Chipper Jones 00 6.00 15.00
TCCJ3 Chipper Jones 01 6.00 15.00
TCIR1 Ivan Rodriguez 92 SP 6.00 15.00
TCIR2 Ivan Rodriguez 98 SP 6.00 15.00
TCIR3 Ivan Rodriguez 00 SP 6.00 15.00
TCIR4 Ivan Rodriguez 01 SP 6.00 15.00
TCI1 Ichiro Suzuki 4-2-01 15.00 40.00
TCI2 Ichiro Suzuki 7-10-01 15.00 40.00
TCI3 Ichiro Suzuki 11-12-01 15.00 40.00
TCRC1 Roger Clemens 86 10.00 25.00
TCRC2 Roger Clemens 98 10.00 25.00
TCRC3 Roger Clemens 01 10.00 25.00
TCSS1 Sammy Sosa 93 6.00 15.00
TCSS2 Sammy Sosa 98 6.00 15.00
TCSS3 Sammy Sosa 00 6.00 15.00
TCSS4 Sammy Sosa 01 6.00 15.00

2003 Upper Deck Honor Roll

COMP SET w/o SP's (100) 10.00 25.00
COMMON CARD (1-130) .12 .30
COMMON EVEN (2-60) .50 1.25
2-60 EVEN #'s STATED ODDS 1:6
CARD 131 STATED PRINT RUN 1000 COPIES
COMMON CARD (132-161) .75 2.00
132-161 RANDOM INSERTS IN PACKS
132-161 PRINT RUN 2500 SERIAL #'d SETS
1 Derek Jeter .75 2.00
2 Derek Jeter SP 3.00 8.00
3 Alex Rodriguez .40 1.00
4 Alex Rodriguez SP 1.50 4.00
5 Roger Clemens .40 1.00
6 Roger Clemens SP 1.50 4.00
7 Mike Piazza .30 .75
8 Mike Piazza SP 1.25 3.00
9 Jeff Bagwell .20 .50
10 Jeff Bagwell SP .75 2.00
11 Vladimir Guerrero .20 .50
12 Vladimir Guerrero SP .75 2.00
13 Ken Griffey Jr. .60 1.50
14 Ken Griffey Jr. SP 2.50 6.00
15 Greg Maddux .40 1.00
16 Greg Maddux SP 1.50 4.00
17 Chipper Jones .30 .75
18 Chipper Jones SP 1.25 3.00
19 Randy Johnson .30 .75
20 Randy Johnson SP 1.25 3.00
21 Miguel Tejada .20 .50
22 Miguel Tejada SP .75 2.00
23 Nomar Garciaparra .20 .50
24 Nomar Garciaparra SP .75 2.00
25 Ichiro Suzuki .40 1.00
26 Ichiro Suzuki SP 1.50 4.00
27 Sammy Sosa .30 .75
28 Sammy Sosa SP 1.25 3.00
29 Albert Pujols .40 1.00
30 Albert Pujols SP 1.50 4.00
31 Alfonso Soriano .20 .50
32 Alfonso Soriano SP .75 2.00
33 Barry Bonds .50 1.25
34 Barry Bonds SP 2.00 5.00
35 Jeff Kent .12 .30
36 Jeff Kent SP .50 1.25
37 Jim Thome .20 .50
38 Jim Thome SP .75 2.00
39 Pedro Martinez .20 .50
40 Pedro Martinez SP .75 2.00
41 Todd Helton .20 .50
42 Todd Helton SP .75 2.00
43 Troy Glaus .12 .30
44 Troy Glaus SP .50 1.25
45 Mark Prior .20 .50
46 Mark Prior SP .75 2.00
47 Tom Glavine .20 .50
48 Tom Glavine SP .75 2.00
49 Pat Burrell .12 .30
50 Pat Burrell SP .50 1.25
51 Barry Zito .20 .50
52 Barry Zito SP .75 2.00
53 Bernie Williams .20 .50
54 Bernie Williams SP .75 2.00
55 Curt Schilling .20 .50
56 Curt Schilling SP .75 2.00
57 Darin Erstad .12 .30
58 Darin Erstad SP .50 1.25
59 Carlos Delgado .12 .30
60 Carlos Delgado SP .50 1.25
61 Gary Sheffield .12 .30
62 Gary Sheffield .12 .30
63 Frank Thomas .30 .75
64 Frank Thomas .30 .75
65 Lance Berkman .20 .50
66 Lance Berkman .20 .50
67 Shawn Green .12 .30
68 Shawn Green .12 .30
69 Hideo Nomo .30 .75
70 Hideo Nomo .30 .75
71 Torii Hunter .12 .30
72 Torii Hunter .12 .30
73 Roberto Alomar .20 .50
74 Roberto Alomar .20 .50
75 Andruw Jones .12 .30
76 Andruw Jones .12 .30
77 Scott Rolen .20 .50
78 Scott Rolen .20 .50
79 Eric Chavez .12 .30
80 Eric Chavez .12 .30
81 Rafael Palmeiro .20 .50
82 Rafael Palmeiro .20 .50
83 Bobby Abreu .12 .30
84 Bobby Abreu .12 .30
85 Craig Biggio .20 .50
86 Craig Biggio .20 .50
87 Rafael Furcal .12 .30
88 Rafael Furcal .12 .30
89 Jose Vidro .12 .30
90 Jose Vidro .12 .30
91 Luis Gonzalez .12 .30
92 Luis Gonzalez .12 .30
93 Roy Oswalt .20 .50
94 Roy Oswalt .20 .50
95 Cliff Floyd .12 .30
96 Cliff Floyd .12 .30
97 Larry Walker .20 .50
98 Larry Walker .20 .50
99 Jim Edmonds .20 .50
100 Jim Edmonds .20 .50
101 Adam Dunn .20 .50
102 Adam Dunn .20 .50
103 J.D. Drew .12 .30
104 J.D. Drew .12 .30
105 Josh Beckett .12 .30
106 Josh Beckett .12 .30
107 Brian Giles .12 .30
108 Brian Giles .12 .30
109 Magglio Ordonez .20 .50
110 Magglio Ordonez .20 .50
111 Edgardo Alfonzo .12 .30
112 Edgardo Alfonzo .12 .30
113 Bartolo Colon .12 .30
114 Bartolo Colon .12 .30
115 Roy Halladay .20 .50
116 Roy Halladay .20 .50
117 Joe Thurston .12 .30
118 Joe Thurston .12 .30
119 Brandon Phillips .12 .30
120 Brandon Phillips .12 .30
121 Kazuhisa Ishii .12 .30
122 Kazuhisa Ishii .12 .30
123 Mike Mussina .20 .50
124 Mike Mussina .20 .50
125 Tim Hudson .20 .50
126 Tim Hudson .20 .50
127 Mariano Rivera .40 1.00
128 Mariano Rivera .40 1.00
129 Travis Hafner .12 .30
130 Travis Hafner .12 .30
131 Hideki Matsui DL Jsy RC 3.00 8.00
132 Jose Contreras FC RC 2.00 5.00
133 Jason Anderson FC RC .75 2.00
134 Willie Eyre FC RC .75 2.00
135 Shane Bazzell FC RC .75 2.00
136 Guillermo Quiroz FC RC .75 2.00
137 Francisco Cruceta FC RC .75 2.00
138 Jhonny Peralta FC .75 2.00
139 Aaron Looper FC RC .75 2.00
140 Bobby Madritsch FC RC .75 2.00
141 Michael Hessman FC RC .75 2.00
142 Todd Wellemeyer FC RC .75 2.00
143 Matt Bruback FC RC .75 2.00
144 Chris Capuano FC RC .75 2.00
145 Oscar Villarreal FC RC .75 2.00
146 Prentice Redman FC RC .75 2.00
147 Jeff Duncan FC RC .75 2.00
148 Phil Seibel FC RC .75 2.00
149 Arnaldo Munoz FC RC .75 2.00
150 David Sanders FC RC .75 2.00
151 Rick Roberts FC RC .75 2.00
152 Termel Sledge FC RC .75 2.00
153 Franklin Perez FC RC .75 2.00
154 Jeremy Wedel FC RC .75 2.00
155 Ian Ferguson FC RC .75 2.00
156 Josh Hall FC RC .75 2.00
157 Rocco Baldelli FC .75 2.00
158 Alejandro Machado FC RC .75 2.00
159 Jorge Cordova FC RC .75 2.00
160 Wilfredo Ledezma FC RC .75 2.00
161 Luis Ayala FC RC .75 2.00

2003 Upper Deck Honor Roll Gold

STATED PRINT RUN 25 SERIAL #'d SETS
NO PRICING DUE TO SCARCITY
CARD 131 DOES NOT EXIST

2003 Upper Deck Honor Roll Silver

*SILVER 1-130: 5X TO 12X BASIC
*SILVER 2-60 EVEN: 1.25X TO 3X BASIC
*SILVER 132-161: .75X TO 2X BASIC
RANDOM INSERTS IN PACKS
STATED PRINT RUN 150 SERIAL #'d SETS
CARD 131 DOES NOT EXIST

2003 Upper Deck Honor Roll Dean's List Jerseys

STATED ODDS 1:24
AP Albert Pujols A 6.00 15.00
AP1 Albert Pujols P 6.00 15.00
AR Alex Rodriguez A 6.00 15.00
AR1 Alex Rodriguez R 6.00 15.00
CJ Chipper Jones C 5.00 12.00
CJ1 Chipper Jones J 5.00 12.00
HM Hideki Matsui H Pants 6.00 15.00
HM1 Hideki Matsui M Pants 6.00 15.00
HN Hideo Nomo H 5.00 12.00
HN1 Hideo Nomo N 5.00 12.00
IS Ichiro Suzuki I 6.00 15.00
IS1 Ichiro Suzuki S 6.00 15.00
JG Jason Giambi J 2.00 5.00
JG1 Jason Giambi G 2.00 5.00
KG Ken Griffey Jr. K 6.00 15.00
KG1 Ken Griffey Jr. G 6.00 15.00
MA Mark Prior M 3.00 8.00
MA1 Mark Prior P 3.00 8.00
MP Mike Piazza M 5.00 12.00
MP1 Mike Piazza P 5.00 12.00
NG Shawn Green S 2.00 5.00
NG1 Shawn Green G 2.00 5.00
RC Roger Clemens R 6.00 15.00
RC1 Roger Clemens C 6.00 15.00
SS Sammy Sosa S 5.00 12.00
TG Troy Glaus T 2.00 5.00
TG1 Troy Glaus G 2.00 5.00
VG Vladimir Guerrero V 3.00 8.00
VG1 Vladimir Guerrero G 3.00 8.00

2003 Upper Deck Honor Roll Grade A Batting Gloves

STATED ODDS 1:960
PRINT RUNS B/WN 25-70 COPIES PER
PRINT RUNS PROVIDED BY UPPER DECK
CARDS ARE NOT SERIAL-NUMBERED
NO PRICING DUE TO SCARCITY

2003 Upper Deck Honor Roll Leather of Distinction

STATED ODDS 1:960
PRINT RUNS B/WN 9-70 COPIES PER
PRINT RUNS PROVIDED BY UPPER DECK
CARDS ARE NOT SERIAL-NUMBERED
NO PRICING DUE TO SCARCITY

2009 Upper Deck Icons

COMP.SET w/o RC's (100) 12.50 30.00
COMMON CARD (1-100) .15 .40
COMMON RC (101-130) .75 2.00
RC 101-130 PRINT RUN 999 SER.#'d SETS
COMMON AU RC (131-160) 3.00 8.00
AU RC PRINT RUN B/WN 50-600 PER
OVERALL AU ODDS 1:10 HOBBY
EXCHANGE DEADLINE 6/11/2011
1 A.J. Burnett .15 .40
2 Adam Dunn .25 .60
3 Adrian Gonzalez .30 .75
4 Akinori Iwamura .15 .40
5 Albert Pujols .50 1.25
6 Alex Rodriguez .50 1.25
7 Alfonso Soriano .25 .60
8 Aramis Ramirez .15 .40
9 B.J. Upton .25 .60
10 Brandon Webb .25 .60
11 Brian Giles .15 .40
12 Brian McCann .25 .60
13 Brian Roberts .15 .40
14 Carlos Beltran .25 .60
15 Carlos Lee .15 .40
16 Carlos Quentin .15 .40
17 Carlos Zambrano .25 .60
18 CC Sabathia .25 .60
19 Chad Billingsley .25 .60
20 Chase Utley .25 .60
21 Chien-Ming Wang .25 .60
22 Chipper Jones .40 1.00
23 Chris B. Young .15 .40
24 Clayton Kershaw .60 1.50
25 Cliff Lee .25 .60
26 Cole Hamels .30 .75
27 Curtis Granderson .30 .75
28 Daisuke Matsuzaka .25 .60
29 Dan Haren .15 .40
30 Dan Uggla .15 .40
31 David Ortiz .40 1.00
32 David Wright .30 .75
33 Derek Jeter 1.00 2.50
34 Derrek Lee .15 .40
35 Dustin Pedroia .40 1.00
36 Edinson Volquez .15 .40
37 Ervin Santana .15 .40
38 Evan Longoria .25 .60
39 Felix Hernandez .25 .60
40 Francisco Rodriguez .25 .60
41 Garrett Atkins .15 .40
42 Grady Sizemore .25 .60
43 Hanley Ramirez .25 .60
44 Ian Kinsler .25 .60
45 Freddy Sanchez .15 .40
46 Ichiro Suzuki .50 1.25
47 Jason Varitek .40 1.00
48 Jake Peavy .15 .40
49 James Shields .15 .40
50 Jason Giambi .15 .40
51 Javier Vazquez .15 .40
52 Jay Bruce .25 .60
53 Jim Thome .25 .60
54 Jimmy Rollins .25 .60
55 Joakim Soria .15 .40
56 Joba Chamberlain .15 .40
57 Joe Mauer .30 .75
58 Joey Votto .40 1.00
59 Johan Santana .25 .60
60 John Lackey .25 .60
61 Jon Lester .25 .60
62 Jonathan Papelbon .25 .60
63 Jose Reyes .25 .60
64 Josh Beckett .15 .40
65 Josh Hamilton .25 .60
66 Justin Morneau .25 .60
67 Justin Verlander .40 1.00
68 Ken Griffey Jr. .75 2.00
69 Kerry Wood .15 .40
70 Kevin Youkilis .15 .40
71 Kosuke Fukudome .25 .60
72 Lance Berkman .25 .60
73 Magglio Ordonez .25 .60
74 Manny Ramirez .40 1.00
75 Mariano Rivera .50 1.25
76 Mark Teixeira .25 .60
77 Matt Holliday .40 1.00
78 Matt Kemp .30 .75
79 Michael Young .15 .40
80 Miguel Cabrera .40 1.00
81 Nate McLouth .15 .40
82 Nick Markakis .30 .75
83 Prince Fielder .25 .60
84 Randy Johnson .40 1.00
85 Rick Ankiel .15 .40
86 Roy Halladay .25 .60
87 Roy Oswalt .25 .60
88 Russell Martin .15 .40
89 Ryan Braun .25 .60
90 Ryan Dempster .15 .40
91 Ryan Howard .30 .75
92 Ryan Ludwick .25 .60
93 Ryan Zimmerman .25 .60
94 Scott Kazmir .15 .40
95 Stephen Drew .15 .40
96 Tim Hudson .25 .60
97 Tim Lincecum .25 .60
98 Troy Tulowitzki .40 1.00
99 Vernon Wells .15 .40
100 Vladimir Guerrero .25 .60
101 Koji Uehara RC 2.00 5.00
102 Rick Porcello RC 2.50 6.00
103 Jason Motte (RC) 1.25 3.00
104 Colby Rasmus (RC) 1.25 3.00
105 Brett Anderson RC 1.25 3.00
106 George Kottaras (RC) .75 2.00
107 Josh Outman RC 1.25 3.00
108 Travis Snider RC 1.25 3.00
109 Matt Tuiasosopo (RC) .75 2.00
110 Kevin Jepsen (RC) .75 2.00
111 Trevor Cahill RC 2.00 5.00
112 Elvis Andrus RC 2.00 5.00
113 Jordan Schafer (RC) 1.25 3.00
114 Matt LaPorta RC 1.25 3.00
115 Shairon Martis RC 1.25 3.00
116 Dexter Fowler (RC) 1.25 3.00
117 Scott Lewis (RC) .75 2.00
118 Everth Cabrera RC 1.25 3.00
119 James McDonald RC 2.00 5.00
120 David Freese RC 2.50 6.00
121 David Patton RC 1.25 3.00
122 Kenshin Kawakami RC 1.25 3.00
123 David Price RC 1.50 4.00
124 Phil Coke RC 1.25 3.00
125 Matt Wieters RC 2.50 6.00
126 Mike Hinckley (RC) .75 2.00
127 Ramiro Pena RC 1.25 3.00
128 Bobby Parnell RC 1.25 3.00
129 Ryan Perry RC 2.00 5.00
130 Ricky Romero (RC) 1.25 3.00
131a Uehara AU/90 * Eng. 10.00 25.00
132 Travis Snider AU/100 10.00 25.00
133 Dexter Fowler AU/400 5.00 12.00
134 Kevin Jepsen AU/600 5.00 12.00
135 David Freese AU/200 10.00 25.00
136 Jordan Schafer AU/400 6.00 15.00
137 Everth Cabrera AU/600 4.00 10.00
138 James McDonald AU/399 6.00 15.00
139 Shairon Martis AU/600 3.00 8.00
140 Josh Outman AU/200 3.00 8.00
141 Matt Tuiasosopo AU/400 3.00 8.00
142 Phil Coke AU/600 5.00 12.00
143 Matt Wieters AU/100 EXCH 30.00 60.00
144 Ricky Romero AU/600 3.00 8.00
145 George Kottaras AU/600 4.00 10.00
146 Elvis Andrus AU/300 10.00 25.00
147 David Patton AU/50 4.00 10.00
148 Brett Anderson AU/400 5.00 12.00
149 Trevor Cahill AU/300 5.00 12.00
150 T.Crowe AU/600 RC 3.00 8.00
151 Colby Rasmus AU/400 6.00 15.00
152 Kenshin Kawakami AU/400 10.00 25.00
153 David Price AU/150 6.00 15.00
154 Rick Porcello AU/100 8.00 20.00
155 B.Gardner AU/600 (RC) 8.00 20.00
156 Davis AU/50 (RC) EXCH
157 P.Sandoval AU/100 (RC) 10.00 25.00
158 Bobby Parnell AU/600 4.00 10.00
159 D.Holland AU/100 RC 6.00 15.00
160 M.Gamel AU/200 RC 6.00 15.00

2009 Upper Deck Icons Celebrity Lettermen

OVERALL LETTER ODDS 1:5 HOBBY
TOTAL PRINT RUNS LISTED BELOW
EN Evelyn Ng/440 * 4.00 10.00
GO Jeremy Piven/440 * 4.00 10.00
NE D.Negreanu/440 * 8.00 20.00
PH Phil Hellmuth/420 * 10.00 25.00

2009 Upper Deck Icons Celebrity Lettermen Autographs

OVERALL LETTER ODDS 1:5 HOBBY
TOTAL PRINT RUNS LISTED BELOW
GO Jeremy Piven/70 * 40.00 80.00

2009 Upper Deck Icons Future Foundations

RANDOM INSERTS IN PACKS
STATED PRINT RUN 999 SER.#'d SETS
*GRN: .6X TO 1.5X BASIC
GRN RANDOMLY INSERTED
GRN PRINT RUN 125 SER.#'d SETS
BM Brian McCann .75 2.00
CH Cole Hamels 1.00 2.50
DM Daisuke Matsuzaka .75 2.00
EL Evan Longoria .75 2.00
FC Fausto Carmona .50 1.25
FL Francisco Liriano .50 1.25
HR Hanley Ramirez .75 2.00
JM Joe Mauer 1.00 2.50
JP Jonathan Papelbon .75 2.00
MK Matt Kemp 1.00 2.50
NM Nick Markakis 1.00 2.50
PF Prince Fielder .75 2.00
RA Rick Ankiel .50 1.25
TT Troy Tulowitzki 1.25 3.00

2009 Upper Deck Icons Future Foundations Autographs

OVERALL AUTO ODDS 1:10 HOBBY
PRINT RUNS B/WN 25-199 COPIES PER
NO PRICING ON QTY 25 OR LESS
CH Cole Hamels/75 12.00 30.00
FC Fausto Carmona/199 3.00 8.00
HR Hanley Ramirez/75 6.00 15.00
JM Joe Mauer/75 15.00 40.00
JP J.Papelbon/99 8.00 20.00
MK Matt Kemp/199 8.00 20.00
NM Nick Markakis/199 6.00 15.00
PF Prince Fielder/75 10.00 25.00
TT T.Tulowitzki/199 4.00 10.00

2009 Upper Deck Icons Future Foundations Jerseys

OVERALL MEM ODDS 1:5 HOBBY
BM Brian McCann 3.00 8.00
CH Cole Hamels 3.00 8.00
DM Daisuke Matsuzaka 5.00 12.00
FC Fausto Carmona 3.00 8.00
FL Francisco Liriano 3.00 8.00
HR Hanley Ramirez 3.00 8.00
JM Joe Mauer 3.00 8.00
JP Jonathan Papelbon 3.00 8.00
MK Matt Kemp 3.00 8.00
NM Nick Markakis 3.00 8.00
PF Prince Fielder 3.00 8.00
RA Rick Ankiel 3.00 8.00
TT Troy Tulowitzki 3.00 8.00

2009 Upper Deck Icons Icons

RANDOM INSERTS IN PACKS
STATED PRINT RUN 999 SER.#'d SETS
*GRN: .6X TO 1.5X BASIC
GRN RANDOMLY INSERTED
GRN PRINT RUN 125 SER.#'d SETS
AE Andre Ethier .75 2.00
AG Alex Gordon .75 2.00
AL Adam Lind .50 1.25
AR Alex Rios .50 1.25
AS Alfonso Soriano .75 2.00
BE Josh Beckett .50 1.25
BH Bill Hall .50 1.25
BR Brian Roberts .50 1.25
BW Billy Wagner .50 1.25
CA Miguel Cabrera 1.25 3.00
CB Chad Billingsley .75 2.00
CC Chris Carpenter .75 2.00
CD Chris Duncan .50 1.25
CF Chone Figgins .50 1.25
CJ Chipper Jones 1.25 3.00
CL Carlos Lee .50 1.25
CR Carl Crawford .75 2.00
CT Corey Hart .50 1.25
CU Michael Cuddyer .50 1.25
CY Chris Young .50 1.25
CZ Carlos Zambrano .75 2.00
DJ Derek Jeter 3.00 8.00
DL Derrek Lee .50 1.25
DO David Ortiz 1.25 3.00
DY Delmon Young .75 2.00
FH Felix Hernandez .75 2.00
GU Carlos Guillen .50 1.25
HP Hunter Pence .75 2.00
JD Jermaine Dye .50 1.25
JF Jeff Francoeur .75 2.00
JG Jason Giambi .50 1.25
JH J.J. Hardy .50 1.25
JJ Josh Johnson .50 1.25
JL John Lackey .75 2.00
JM John Maine .50 1.25
JP Jake Peavy .50 1.25
JR Jimmy Rollins .75 2.00
JS James Shields .50 1.25
JT Jim Thome .75 2.00
JV Jason Varitek 1.25 3.00
JW Jake Westbrook .50 1.25
JZ Joel Zumaya .50 1.25
KF Kosuke Fukudome .75 2.00
KJ Kelly Johnson .50 1.25
KY Kevin Youkilis .50 1.25
MA Mike Aviles .50 1.25
MC Matt Cain .75 2.00
MH Matt Holliday 1.25 3.00
MY Michael Young .50 1.25
PE Jhonny Peralta .50 1.25
PK Paul Konerko .75 2.00
PO Jorge Posada .75 2.00
RA Aramis Ramirez .50 1.25
RF Rafael Furcal .50 1.25
RH Roy Halladay .75 2.00
RJ Randy Johnson 1.25 3.00
RL Ryan Ludwick .75 2.00
RO Roy Oswalt .75 2.00
RZ Ryan Zimmerman .75 2.00
SD Stephen Drew .50 1.25
SK Scott Kazmir .50 1.25
TG Tom Glavine .75 2.00
TH Travis Hafner .50 1.25
VE Justin Verlander 1.25 3.00
VM Victor Martinez .75 2.00
WB Brandon Webb .75 2.00
WE Jered Weaver .75 2.00

2009 Upper Deck Icons Icons Autographs

OVERALL AUTO ODDS 1:10 HOBBY
PRINT RUNS B/WN 5-99 COPIES PER
MANY NOT PRICED DUE TO LACK OF INFO
AE Andre Ethier/99 6.00 15.00
AL Adam Lind/99 15.00 40.00
CD Chris Duncan/99 6.00 15.00
FH Felix Hernandez/30 12.50 30.00
JJ Josh Johnson/35 8.00 20.00
JM John Maine/99 6.00 15.00
KJ Kelly Johnson/99 5.00 12.00
KY Kevin Youkilis/99 10.00 25.00
MA Mike Aviles/40 5.00 12.00
SK Scott Kazmir/99 12.50 30.00

2009 Upper Deck Icons Icons Jerseys

OVERALL MEM ODDS 1:5 HOBBY
AE Andre Ethier 3.00 8.00
AG Alex Gordon 3.00 8.00
AL Adam Lind 4.00 10.00
AR Alex Rios 4.00 10.00
AS Alfonso Soriano 3.00 8.00
BE Josh Beckett 3.00 8.00
BH Bill Hall 3.00 8.00
BR Brian Roberts 3.00 8.00
BW Billy Wagner 3.00 8.00
CA Miguel Cabrera 4.00 10.00
CB Chad Billingsley 3.00 8.00
CC Chris Carpenter 3.00 8.00
CD Chris Duncan 4.00 10.00
CF Chone Figgins 3.00 8.00
CJ Chipper Jones 4.00 10.00
CL Carlos Lee 3.00 8.00
CR Carl Crawford 3.00 8.00
CT Corey Hart 3.00 8.00
CU Michael Cuddyer 3.00 8.00
CY Chris Young 3.00 8.00
DJ Derek Jeter 6.00 15.00
DL Derrek Lee 3.00 8.00
DO David Ortiz 3.00 8.00
DY Delmon Young 3.00 8.00
FH Felix Hernandez 3.00 8.00
GU Carlos Guillen 3.00 8.00
HP Hunter Pence 3.00 8.00
JD Jermaine Dye 3.00 8.00
JF Jeff Francoeur 3.00 8.00
JH J.J. Hardy 3.00 8.00
JJ Josh Johnson 3.00 8.00
JL John Lackey 3.00 8.00
JM John Maine 3.00 8.00
JP Jake Peavy 3.00 8.00
JR Jimmy Rollins 4.00 10.00
JS James Shields 3.00 8.00
JT Jim Thome 3.00 8.00
JV Jason Varitek 4.00 10.00
JW Jake Westbrook 3.00 8.00
JZ Joel Zumaya 3.00 8.00
KJ Kelly Johnson 3.00 8.00
MC Matt Cain 3.00 8.00
MY Michael Young 3.00 8.00
PE Jhonny Peralta 3.00 8.00
PK Paul Konerko 3.00 8.00
PO Jorge Posada 3.00 8.00
RA Aramis Ramirez 3.00 8.00
RF Rafael Furcal 3.00 8.00
RH Roy Halladay 3.00 8.00
RJ Randy Johnson 4.00 10.00
RO Roy Oswalt 3.00 8.00
RZ Ryan Zimmerman 3.00 8.00
SD Stephen Drew 3.00 8.00
SK Scott Kazmir 3.00 8.00
TG Tom Glavine 3.00 8.00
TH Travis Hafner 3.00 8.00
VE Justin Verlander 3.00 8.00
VM Victor Martinez 3.00 8.00

WB Brandon Webb 3.00 8.00
WE Jered Weaver 3.00 8.00

2009 Upper Deck Icons Icons Jerseys Gold

OVERALL MEM ODDS 1:5 HOBBY
STATED PRINT RUN 25 SER.#'d SETS
NO PRICING DUE TO SCARCITY

2009 Upper Deck Icons Immortal Lettermen

OVERALL LETTER ODDS 1:5 HOBBY
TOTAL PRINT RUNS LISTED BELOW
AK A.Kaline/420 * 10.00 25.00
BJ B.Jackson/450 * 20.00 50.00
BS Bill Skowron/420 * 4.00 10.00
GF C.Fisk/405 * 12.00 30.00
DA D.Allen/405 * 5.00 12.00
DB Dennis Oil Can Boyd/400 * 6.00 15.00
DE Bucky Dent/405 * 4.00 10.00
DN D.Newcombe/440 * 5.00 12.00
GP G.Perry/420 * 10.00 25.00
JP Joe Pepitone/440 * 5.00 12.00
KH K.Hrbek/450 * 12.00 30.00
OS O.Smith/400 * 12.00 30.00
PM P.Molitor/440 * 12.00 30.00
RW Roy White/440 * 4.00 10.00
TG T.Gwynn/200 * 12.00 30.00
WF W.Ford/450 * 5.00 12.00
YB Y.Berra/405 * 8.00 20.00

2009 Upper Deck Icons Immortal Lettermen Autographs

OVERALL AUTO ODDS 1:10 HOBBY
PRINT RUNS B/WN 10-84 COPIES PER
TOTAL PRINT RUNS LISTED
SER.# ON CARDS ARE DIFFERENT
NO PRICING ON QTY 21 OR LESS
AK Al Kaline/28 * 50.00 120.00
BS Bill Skowron/36 * 20.00 50.00
DA Dick Allen/27 * 20.00 50.00
DB Oil Can Boyd/40 * 8.00 20.00
DE Bucky Dent/27 * 12.50 30.00
DN D.Newcombe/32 * 12.00 30.00
GP Gaylord Perry/36 * 12.00 30.00
KH Kent Hrbek/84 * 15.00 40.00
PM Paul Molitor/28 * 40.00 80.00

2009 Upper Deck Icons Legendary Icons

RANDOM INSERTS IN PACKS
STATED PRINT RUN 999 SER.#'d SETS
*GRN: .6X TO 1.5X BASIC
GRN RANDOMLY INSERTED
GRN PRINT RUN 125 SER.#'d SETS
BJ Bo Jackson 1.25 3.00
BS Bruce Sutter .75 2.00
CR Cal Ripken Jr. 4.00 10.00
JD Joe DiMaggio 2.50 6.00
MS Mike Schmidt 2.00 5.00
NR Nolan Ryan 4.00 10.00
OS Ozzie Smith 1.50 4.00
RJ Reggie Jackson .75 2.00
TG Tony Gwynn 1.25 3.00
WB Wade Boggs .75 2.00

2009 Upper Deck Icons Legendary Icons Jerseys

OVERALL MEM ODDS 1:5 HOBBY
BJ Bo Jackson 4.00 10.00
BS Bruce Sutter 3.00 8.00
CR Cal Ripken Jr. 6.00 15.00
JD Joe DiMaggio 20.00 50.00
MS Mike Schmidt 4.00 10.00
NR Nolan Ryan 8.00 20.00
OS Ozzie Smith 8.00 20.00
RJ Reggie Jackson 5.00 12.00
TG Tony Gwynn 4.00 10.00
WB Wade Boggs 3.00 8.00

2009 Upper Deck Icons Lettermen

OVERALL LETTER ODDS 1:5 HOBBY
TOTAL PRINT RUNS LISTED BELOW
AG Adrian Gonzalez/420 * 4.00 10.00
CH C.Hamels/450 * 5.00 12.00
CJ C.Jones/420 * 15.00 40.00
CK C.Kershaw/420 * 10.00 25.00
CL C.Lee/405 * 4.00 10.00
CM C.Wang/420 * 12.00 30.00
CP C.Perez/450 * 4.00 10.00
CV Chris Volstad/420 * 4.00 10.00
CW C.Wang/420 * 10.00 25.00
DJ D.Jeter/450 * 20.00 50.00
DP D.Pedroia/455 * 10.00 25.00
EC E.Chavez/450 * 4.00 10.00
EL E.Longoria/420 * 10.00 25.00
GF Gavin Floyd/450 * 4.00 10.00
GS G.Soto/440 * 5.00 12.00
HP Hunter Pence/450 * 5.00 12.00
HR H.Ramirez/455 * 6.00 15.00
IK I.Kinsler/300 * 5.00 12.00
JA J.Bruce/455 * 6.00 15.00
JL J.Lester/450 * 4.00 10.00
JM J.Masterson/450 * 4.00 10.00
JN J.Nathan/405 * 4.00 10.00
JR J.Reyes/315 * 4.00 10.00
JS J.Shields/420 * 4.00 10.00
JW J.Willingham/420 * 4.00 10.00
KG K.Griffey Jr./455 * 30.00 80.00
KS Kelly Shoppach/315 * 4.00 10.00
LO Jed Lowrie/450 * 4.00 10.00
MC M.Cain/440 * 10.00 25.00
MN N.McLouth/455 * 5.00 12.00
NM N.Markakis/420 * 4.00 10.00
SD Stephen Drew/440 * 4.00 10.00
TT T.Tulowitzki/350 * 8.00 20.00
ZG Z.Greinke/440 * 4.00 10.00

2009 Upper Deck Icons Lettermen Autographs

OVERALL AUTO ODDS 1:10 HOBBY
PRINT RUNS B/WN 7-100 COPIES PER
TOTAL PRINT RUNS LISTED
SER.# ON CARDS ARE DIFFERENT
NO PRICING ON QTY 24 OR LESS
AG A.Gonzalez/30 * 10.00 25.00
CH Cole Hamels/30 * 30.00 60.00
CK C.Kershaw/28 * 12.50 30.00
CL Carlos Lee/30 * 15.00 40.00
CM C.Wang/28 * 200.00 300.00
CV Chris Volstad/96 * 5.00 12.00
DP D.Pedroia/35 * 75.00 150.00
EC Eric Chavez/30 * 10.00 25.00
EL E.Longoria/24 * 125.00 250.00
GF Gavin Floyd/90 * 10.00 25.00
GS G.Soto/33 * 30.00 60.00
HR H.Ramirez/26 * 12.50 30.00
IK Ian Kinsler/100 * 20.00 50.00
JA Jay Bruce/91 * 12.00 30.00
JL Jon Lester/45 * 50.00 100.00
JM J.Masterson/90 * 10.00 25.00
JN Joe Nathan/45 * 10.00 25.00
JS James Shields/36 * 15.00 40.00
JW J.Willingham/99 * 6.00 15.00
KS K.Shoppach/80 * 10.00 25.00
LO Jed Lowrie/72 * 10.00 25.00
MC Matt Cain/40 * 12.00 30.00
MN N.McLouth/55 * 15.00 40.00
NM N.Markakis/36 * 50.00 100.00
TT T.Tulowitzki/40 * 15.00 40.00
ZG Zack Greinke/44 * 30.00 60.00

2009 Upper Deck Icons Retail Red

*RED: .4X TO 1X BASIC
AVAILABLE IN RETAIL PACKS

2012 Upper Deck Industry Summit Signature Icons Autographs

LAS VEGAS INDUSTRY SUMMIT EXCLUSIVE
LVRS Ryne Sandberg/20

2000 Upper Deck Legends

COMPLETE SET (135) 20.00 50.00
COMP.SET w/o SP'S (90) 6.00 15.00
COMMON CARD (1-90) .12 .30
COMMON CARD (91-105) .40 1.00
91-105 STATED ODDS 1:9
COMMON CARD (106-135) .40 1.00
106-135 STATED ODDS 1:5
1 Darin Erstad .12 .30
2 Troy Glaus .12 .30
3 Mo Vaughn .12 .30
4 Craig Biggio .20 .50
5 Jeff Bagwell .20 .50
6 Reggie Jackson .20 .50
7 Tim Hudson .20 .50
8 Jason Giambi .12 .30
9 Hank Aaron .60 1.50
10 Greg Maddux .40 1.00
11 Chipper Jones .30 .75
12 Andres Galarraga .20 .50
13 Robin Yount .30 .75
14 Jeromy Burnitz .12 .30
15 Paul Molitor .30 .75
16 David Wells .12 .30
17 Carlos Delgado .12 .30
18 Ernie Banks .30 .75
19 Sammy Sosa .30 .75
20 Kerry Wood .12 .30
21 Stan Musial .50 1.25
22 Bob Gibson .20 .50
23 Mark McGwire .50 1.25
24 Fernando Tatis .12 .30
25 Randy Johnson .30 .75
26 Matt Williams .12 .30
27 Jackie Robinson .30 .75
28 Sandy Koufax .60 1.50
29 Shawn Green .12 .30
30 Kevin Brown .12 .30
31 Gary Sheffield .12 .30
32 Greg Vaughn .12 .30
33 Jose Canseco .20 .50
34 Gary Carter .20 .50
35 Vladimir Guerrero .20 .50
36 Willie Mays .60 1.50
37 Barry Bonds .50 1.25
38 Jeff Kent .12 .30
39 Bob Feller .20 .50
40 Roberto Alomar .20 .50
41 Jim Thome .20 .50
42 Manny Ramirez .30 .75
43 Alex Rodriguez .40 1.00
44 Preston Wilson .12 .30
45 Tom Seaver .20 .50
46 Robin Ventura .12 .30
47 Mike Piazza .30 .75
48 Mike Hampton .12 .30
49 Brooks Robinson .20 .50
50 Frank Robinson .20 .50
51 Cal Ripken 1.00 2.50
52 Albert Belle .12 .30
53 Eddie Murray .20 .50
54 Tony Gwynn .30 .75
55 Roberto Clemente .75 2.00
56 Willie Stargell .20 .50
57 Brian Giles .12 .30
58 Jason Kendall .12 .30
59 Mike Schmidt .50 1.25
60 Bob Abreu .12 .30
61 Scott Rolen .20 .50
62 Curt Schilling .12 .30
63 Johnny Bench .30 .75
64 Sean Casey .12 .30
65 Barry Larkin .20 .50
66 Ken Griffey Jr. .60 1.50
67 George Brett .60 1.50
68 Carlos Beltran .20 .50
69 Nolan Ryan 1.00 2.50
70 Ivan Rodriguez .20 .50
71 Rafael Palmeiro .20 .50
72 Larry Walker .20 .50
73 Todd Helton .12 .30
74 Jeff Cirillo .12 .30
75 Carl Everett .12 .30
76 Nomar Garciaparra .20 .50
77 Pedro Martinez .20 .50
78 Harmon Killebrew .30 .75
79 Corey Koskie .12 .30
80 Ty Cobb .50 1.25
81 Dean Palmer .12 .30
82 Juan Gonzalez .12 .30
83 Carlton Fisk .20 .50
84 Frank Thomas .30 .75
85 Magglio Ordonez .20 .50
86 Lou Gehrig .60 1.50
87 Babe Ruth .75 2.00
88 Derek Jeter .75 2.00
89 Roger Clemens .40 1.00
90 Bernie Williams .20 .50
91 Rick Ankiel Y2K .60 1.50
92 Kip Wells Y2K .40 1.00
93 Pat Burrell Y2K .40 1.00
94 Mark Quinn Y2K .40 1.00
95 Ruben Mateo Y2K .40 1.00
96 Adam Kennedy Y2K .40 1.00
97 Brad Penny Y2K .40 1.00
98 Kazuhiro Sasaki Y2K RC 1.00 2.50
99 Peter Bergeron Y2K .40 1.00
100 Rafael Furcal Y2K .60 1.50
101 Eric Munson Y2K .40 1.00
102 Nick Johnson Y2K .60 1.50
103 Rob Bell Y2K .40 1.00
104 Vernon Wells Y2K .40 1.00
105 Ben Petrick Y2K .40 1.00
106 Babe Ruth 20C 2.50 6.00
107 Mark McGwire 20C 1.50 4.00
108 Nolan Ryan 20C 3.00 8.00
109 Hank Aaron 20C 2.00 5.00
110 Barry Bonds 20C 1.50 4.00
111 Nomar Garciaparra 20C .60 1.50
112 Roger Clemens 20C 1.25 3.00
113 Johnny Bench 20C 1.00 2.50
114 Alex Rodriguez 20C 1.25 3.00
115 Cal Ripken 20C 3.00 8.00
116 Willie Mays 20C 2.00 5.00
117 Mike Piazza 20C 1.00 2.50
118 Reggie Jackson 20C .60 1.50
119 Tony Gwynn 20C 1.00 2.50
120 Cy Young 20C 1.00 2.50
121 George Brett 20C 2.00 5.00
122 Greg Maddux 20C 1.25 3.00
123 Yogi Berra 20C 1.00 2.50
124 Sammy Sosa 20C 1.00 2.50
125 Randy Johnson 20C 1.00 2.50
126 Bob Gibson 20C .60 1.50
127 Lou Gehrig 20C 2.00 5.00
128 Ken Griffey Jr. 20C 2.00 5.00
129 Derek Jeter 20C 2.50 6.00
130 Mike Schmidt 20C 1.50 4.00
131 Pedro Martinez 20C .60 1.50
132 Jackie Robinson 20C 1.00 2.50
133 Jose Canseco 20C .60 1.50
134 Ty Cobb 20C 1.50 4.00
135 Stan Musial 20C 1.50 4.00

2000 Upper Deck Legends Commemorative Collection

*COMMEM.1-90: 10X TO 25X BASIC
*COMM.Y2K: 3X TO 8X BASIC Y2K
*COMM.20C: 3X TO 8X BASIC 20C
STATED PRINT RUN 100 SERIAL #'d SETS

2000 Upper Deck Legends Defining Moments

COMPLETE SET (10) 12.50 30.00
STATED ODDS 1:12
DM1 Reggie Jackson .60 1.50
DM2 Hank Aaron 2.00 5.00
DM3 Babe Ruth 2.50 6.00
DM4 Cal Ripken 3.00 8.00
DM5 Carlton Fisk .60 1.50
DM6 Ken Griffey Jr. 2.00 5.00
DM7 Nolan Ryan 3.00 8.00
DM8 Roger Clemens 1.25 3.00
DM9 Willie Mays 2.00 5.00
DM10 Mark McGwire 1.50 4.00

2000 Upper Deck Legends Eternal Glory

COMPLETE SET (6) 8.00 20.00
STATED ODDS 1:24
CARD NUMBER EG3 DOES NOT EXIST
EG1 Nolan Ryan 3.00 8.00
EG2 Ken Griffey Jr. 2.00 5.00
EG4 Sammy Sosa 1.00 2.50
EG5 Derek Jeter 2.50 6.00
EG6 Willie Mays 2.00 5.00
EG7 Roger Clemens 1.25 3.00

2000 Upper Deck Legends Legendary Game Jerseys

STATED ODDS 1:48
SP'S ARE NOT SERIAL-NUMBERED
SP INFO PROVIDED BY UPPER DECK
NO SP PRICING ON QTY OF 32 OR LESS
JAR Alex Rodriguez 8.00 20.00
JBAB Barry Bonds 6.00 15.00
JBG Bob Gibson Pants 6.00 15.00
JBM Bill Mazeroski 4.00 10.00
JBOB Bobby Bonds 4.00 10.00
JBR Brooks Robinson 6.00 15.00
JCJ Chipper Jones 6.00 15.00
JCR Cal Ripken 15.00 40.00
JDC Dave Concepcion 4.00 10.00
JDD Don Drysdale 4.00 10.00
JDJ Derek Jeter 20.00 50.00
JDM Dale Murphy 6.00 15.00
JDW Dave Winfield 6.00 15.00
JEM Eddie Mathews 8.00 20.00
JEW Earl Weaver 6.00 15.00
JFR Frank Robinson 4.00 10.00
JFT Frank Thomas 6.00 15.00
JGB George Brett 6.00 15.00
JGM Greg Maddux 6.00 15.00
JGP Gaylord Perry 4.00 10.00
JHA Hank Aaron 15.00 40.00
JJB Jeff Bagwell 6.00 15.00
JJB Johnny Bench 6.00 15.00
JJC Jose Canseco 6.00 15.00
JJP Jim Palmer 4.00 10.00
JJT Joe Torre 6.00 15.00
JKG Ken Griffey Jr. 10.00 25.00
JLB Lou Brock 6.00 15.00
JLG Lou Gehrig Pants 100.00 200.00
JMM Mickey Mantle 40.00 100.00
JMR Manny Ramirez 6.00 15.00
JMS Mike Schmidt 10.00 25.00
JMW Matt Williams 4.00 10.00
JMW Maury Wills 4.00 10.00
JNR Nolan Ryan 10.00 25.00
JOS Ozzie Smith 6.00 15.00
JRAJ Randy Johnson 6.00 15.00
JRC Roger Clemens 8.00 20.00
JRF Rollie Fingers 4.00 10.00
JRJ Reggie Jackson 6.00 15.00
JRM Roger Maris Pants 12.00 30.00
JSK Sandy Koufax SP/95 30.00 60.00
JSM Stan Musial SP/28 175.00 350.00
JTG Tony Gwynn 6.00 15.00
JTM Thurman Munson 15.00 40.00
JTS Tom Seaver 6.00 15.00
JWB Wade Boggs 6.00 15.00
JWM Willie Mays SP/29 175.00 350.00
JWMC Willie McCovey 4.00 10.00
JWS Willie Stargell 6.00 15.00

2000 Upper Deck Legends Legendary Signatures

STATED ODDS 1:24
EXCHANGE DEADLINE 04/22/01
SAD Andre Dawson 12.00 30.00
SAR Alex Rodriguez 40.00 100.00
SAT Alan Trammell 6.00 15.00
SBB Bobby Bonds 8.00 20.00
SCJ Chipper Jones 40.00 80.00
SCR Cal Ripken 50.00 100.00
SDC Dave Concepcion 12.00 30.00
SDJ Derek Jeter SP/61 500.00 700.00
SDM Dale Murphy 8.00 20.00
SFL Fred Lynn 8.00 20.00
SFT Frank Thomas 25.00 60.00
SGB George Brett 40.00 80.00
SGC Gary Carter 12.00 30.00
SHA Hank Aaron SP/94 400.00 1000.00
SHK Harmon Killebrew 20.00 50.00
SIR Ivan Rodriguez 20.00 50.00
SJB Johnny Bench 20.00 50.00
SJC Jose Canseco 12.00 30.00
SJP Jim Palmer 8.00 20.00
SKG Ken Griffey Jr. 60.00 120.00
SLB Lou Brock 10.00 25.00
SMP Mike Piazza 50.00 120.00
SMR Manny Ramirez SP/141 25.00 60.00
SMS Mike Schmidt 30.00 80.00
SMV Mo Vaughn 6.00 15.00
SMW Matt Williams 6.00 15.00
SNR Nolan Ryan 50.00 120.00
SOS Ozzie Smith 20.00 50.00
SPN Phil Niekro 6.00 15.00
SRC Roger Clemens 25.00 60.00
SRF Rollie Fingers 6.00 15.00
SRJ Reggie Jackson 20.00 50.00
SSC Sean Casey 6.00 15.00
SSM Stan Musial 25.00 60.00
STG Tony Gwynn 20.00 50.00
STS Tom Seaver 40.00 100.00
SVG Vladimir Guerrero 10.00 25.00
SWS Willie Stargell 15.00 40.00
SRAJ Randy Johnson 50.00 120.00

2000 Upper Deck Legends Legendary Signatures Gold

STATED PRINT RUN 50 SERIAL #'d SETS
EXCHANGE DEADLINE 04/22/01
SAD Andre Dawson 25.00 60.00
SAR Alex Rodriguez 100.00 175.00
SAT Alan Trammell 15.00 40.00
SBB Bobby Bonds 30.00 60.00
SCJ Chipper Jones 40.00 80.00
SCR Cal Ripken 100.00 175.00
SDC Dave Concepcion 25.00 60.00
SDM Dale Murphy 20.00 50.00
SFL Fred Lynn 15.00 40.00
SFT Frank Thomas 60.00 120.00
SGB George Brett 75.00 150.00
SGC Gary Carter 30.00 60.00
SHA Hank Aaron 500.00 1200.00
SHK Harmon Killebrew 30.00 80.00
SIR Ivan Rodriguez 50.00 120.00
SJB Johnny Bench 40.00 80.00
SJC Jose Canseco 30.00 80.00
SJP Jim Palmer 20.00 50.00
SKG Ken Griffey Jr. 125.00 250.00
SLB Lou Brock 20.00 50.00
SMP Mike Piazza 75.00 150.00
SMR Manny Ramirez 30.00 60.00
SMS Mike Schmidt 40.00 100.00
SMV Mo Vaughn 15.00 40.00
SMW Matt Williams 20.00 50.00
SNR Nolan Ryan 75.00 200.00
SOS Ozzie Smith 50.00 100.00
SPN Phil Niekro 15.00 40.00
SRC Roger Clemens 125.00 200.00
SRF Rollie Fingers 15.00 40.00
SRJ Reggie Jackson 40.00 80.00
SSC Sean Casey 15.00 40.00
SSM Stan Musial 50.00 100.00
STG Tony Gwynn 75.00 150.00
STS Tom Seaver 60.00 150.00
SVG Vladimir Guerrero 15.00 40.00
SWS Willie Stargell 40.00 80.00
SRAJ Randy Johnson 100.00 250.00

2000 Upper Deck Legends Millennium Team

COMPLETE SET (9) 4.00 10.00
STATED ODDS 1:4 HOBBY
UD1 Mark McGwire .50 1.25
UD2 Jackie Robinson .30 .75
UD3 Mike Schmidt .50 1.25
UD4 Cal Ripken 1.00 2.50
UD5 Babe Ruth .75 2.00
UD6 Ted Williams
UD7 Willie Mays .60 1.50
UD8 Johnny Bench .30 .75
UD9 Nolan Ryan 1.00 2.50
UD10 Ken Griffey Jr. .60 1.50

2000 Upper Deck Legends Ones for the Ages

COMPLETE SET (7) 10.00 25.00
STATED ODDS 1:24
O1 Ty Cobb 1.50 4.00
O2 Cal Ripken 3.00 8.00
O3 Babe Ruth 2.50 6.00
O4 Jackie Robinson 1.00 2.50
O5 Mark McGwire 1.50 4.00
O6 Alex Rodriguez 1.25 3.00
O7 Mike Piazza 1.00 2.50

2000 Upper Deck Legends Reflections in Time

COMPLETE SET (10) 12.50 30.00
STATED ODDS 1:12
R1 K.Griffey Jr. 2.00 5.00
H.Aaron
R2 S.Sosa 2.50 6.00
R.Clemente
R3 R.Clemens 3.00 8.00
N.Ryan
R4 I.Rodriguez 1.00 2.50
J.Bench
R5 A.Rodriguez 1.25 3.00
E.Banks
R6 T.Gwynn 1.50 4.00
S.Musial
R7 B.Bonds 2.00 5.00
W.Mays
R8 C.Ripken 3.00 8.00
L.Gehrig
R9 C.Jones 1.50 4.00
M.Schmidt
R10 M.McGwire 2.50 6.00
B.Ruth

2001 Upper Deck Legends

COMPLETE SET (90) 8.00 20.00
1 Darin Erstad .10 .30
2 Troy Glaus .10 .30
3 Nolan Ryan .75 2.00
4 Reggie Jackson .20 .50
5 Catfish Hunter .20 .50
6 Jason Giambi .10 .30
7 Tim Hudson .10 .30
8 Miguel Tejada .10 .30
9 Carlos Delgado .10 .30
10 Shannon Stewart .10 .30
11 Greg Vaughn .10 .30
12 Larry Doby .10 .30
13 Jim Thome .20 .50
14 Juan Gonzalez .10 .30
15 Roberto Alomar .20 .50
16 Edgar Martinez .20 .50
17 John Olerud .10 .30
18 Eddie Murray .30 .75
19 Cal Ripken 1.00 2.50
20 Alex Rodriguez .40 1.00
21 Ivan Rodriguez .20 .50
22 Rafael Palmeiro .20 .50
23 Jimmie Foxx .30 .75
24 Cy Young .30 .75
25 Manny Ramirez Sox .20 .50
26 Pedro Martinez .20 .50
27 Nomar Garciaparra .50 1.25
28 George Brett .60 1.50
29 Mike Sweeney .10 .30
30 Jermaine Dye .10 .30
31 Ty Cobb .50 1.25
32 Dean Palmer .10 .30
33 Harmon Killebrew .30 .75
34 Matt Lawton .10 .30
35 Luis Aparicio .10 .30
36 Frank Thomas .30 .75
37 Magglio Ordonez .10 .30
38 David Wells .10 .30
39 Mickey Mantle 1.25 3.00
40 Joe DiMaggio .60 1.50
41 Roger Maris .30 .75
42 Babe Ruth 1.00 2.50
43 Derek Jeter .75 2.00
44 Roger Clemens .60 1.50
45 Bernie Williams .20 .50
46 Jeff Bagwell .20 .50
47 Richard Hidalgo .10 .30
48 Warren Spahn .20 .50
49 Greg Maddux .50 1.25
50 Chipper Jones .30 .75
51 Andruw Jones .20 .50
52 Robin Yount .30 .75
53 Jeromy Burnitz .10 .30
54 Jeffrey Hammonds .10 .30
55 Ozzie Smith .50 1.25
56 Stan Musial .50 1.25
57 Mark McGwire .75 2.00
58 Jim Edmonds .10 .30
59 Sammy Sosa .30 .75
60 Ernie Banks .30 .75
61 Kerry Wood .10 .30
62 Randy Johnson .30 .75
63 Luis Gonzalez .10 .30
64 Don Drysdale .20 .50
65 Jackie Robinson .30 .75
66 Gary Sheffield .10 .30
67 Kevin Brown .10 .30
68 Vladimir Guerrero .30 .75
69 Willie Mays .60 1.50
70 Mel Ott .30 .75
71 Jeff Kent .10 .30
72 Barry Bonds .75 2.00
73 Preston Wilson .10 .30
74 Ryan Dempster .10 .30
75 Tom Seaver .20 .50
76 Mike Piazza .50 1.25
77 Robin Ventura .10 .30
78 Dave Winfield .10 .30
79 Tony Gwynn .40 1.00
80 Bob Abreu .10 .30
81 Scott Rolen .20 .50
82 Mike Schmidt .60 1.50
83 Roberto Clemente .75 2.00
84 Brian Giles .10 .30
85 Ken Griffey Jr. .60 1.50
86 Frank Robinson .20 .50
87 Johnny Bench .30 .75
88 Todd Helton .20 .50
89 Larry Walker .10 .30
90 Mike Hampton .10 .30

2001 Upper Deck Legends Fiorentino Collection

COMPLETE SET (14) 15.00 40.00
STATED ODDS 1:12
F1 Babe Ruth 3.00 8.00
F2 Satchel Paige 1.00 2.50
F3 Joe DiMaggio 2.00 5.00
F4 Willie Mays 2.00 5.00
F5 Ty Cobb 1.50 4.00
F6 Nolan Ryan 3.00 8.00
F7 Lou Gehrig 2.00 5.00
F8 Jackie Robinson 1.00 2.50
F9 Hank Aaron 2.00 5.00
F10 Roberto Clemente 2.00 5.00
F11 Stan Musial 1.25 3.00
F12 Johnny Bench 1.00 2.50
F13 Honus Wagner 1.00 2.50
F14 Reggie Jackson 1.00 2.50

2001 Upper Deck Legends Legendary Game Jersey

STATED ODDS 1:24
SP PRINT RUNS PROVIDED BY UPPER DECK
SP'S ARE NOT SERIAL-NUMBERED
ASTERISKS PERCEIVED AS LARGER SUPPLY
GOLD RANDOM INSERTS IN PACKS
GOLD PRINT RUN 25 SERIAL #'d SETS
NO GOLD PRICING DUE TO SCARCITY
JAR Alex Rodriguez 4.00 10.00
JBB Barry Bonds 5.00 12.00
JCJ Chipper Jones 3.00 8.00
JCR Cal Ripken DP 6.00 15.00
JDW Dave Winfield 2.00 5.00
JEB Ernie Banks Uni 3.00 8.00
JGM Greg Maddux 5.00 12.00
JGS Gary Sheffield 1.25 3.00
JHA Hank Aaron 15.00 40.00
JIR Ivan Rodriguez DP 2.00 5.00
JJB Jeff Bagwell 2.00 5.00
JJC Jose Canseco 2.00 5.00
JJD J.DiMaggio Uni SP/245 * 30.00 80.00
JKG Ken Griffey Jr. 6.00 15.00
JKS Kazuhiro Sasaki 1.25 3.00
JMM M.Mantle Uni SP/245 * 50.00 120.00
JMP Mike Piazza 3.00 8.00
JMR Manny Ramirez Sox 3.00 8.00
JNR Nolan Ryan 8.00 20.00
JOS Ozzie Smith DP 4.00 10.00
JPM Pedro Martinez 2.00 5.00
JRCL Roger Clemens 5.00 12.00
JRJA R.Jackson Uni 2.50 6.00
JRJO Randy Johnson DP 3.00 8.00
JRM Roger Maris SP/343 * 12.00 30.00
JROC R.Clemente SP/195 * 30.00 60.00
JRY Robin Yount 3.00 8.00
JSM S.Musial Uni SP/490 * 8.00 20.00
JSS Sammy Sosa 2.00 5.00
JTG Tony Gwynn Uni DP 3.00 8.00
JTS Tom Seaver 2.00 5.00
JWM Willie Mays 10.00 25.00
JYB Yogi Berra Uni 6.00 15.00

2001 Upper Deck Legends Legendary Game Jersey Autographs

STATED ODDS 1:288
SP PRINT RUNS PROVIDED BY UPPER DECK
SP'S ARE NOT SERIAL-NUMBERED
GOLD RANDOM INSERTS IN PACKS
GOLD PRINT RUN 25 SERIAL #'d SETS
NO GOLD PRICING DUE TO SCARCITY
SJAR Alex Rodriguez 30.00 80.00
SJEB Ernie Banks 40.00 100.00
SJKG Ken Griffey Jr. 60.00 150.00
SJNR Nolan Ryan 75.00 150.00
SJOS Ozzie Smith 15.00 40.00
SJRC Roger Clemens SP/211 * 30.00 80.00
SJRJ Reggie Jackson SP/224 * 20.00 50.00
SJSM Stan Musial SP/266 * 40.00 100.00
SJSS Sammy Sosa SP/91 * 40.00 80.00
SJTS Tom Seaver 20.00 50.00

2001 Upper Deck Legends Legendary Lumber

STATED ODDS 1:24
SP PRINT RUNS PROVIDED BY UPPER DECK
SP'S ARE NOT SERIAL-NUMBERED
ASTERISKS PERCEIVED AS LARGER SUPPLY
GOLD RANDOM INSERTS IN PACKS
GOLD PRINT RUN 25 SERIAL #'d SETS
NO GOLD PRICING DUE TO SCARCITY
LAJ Andruw Jones 3.00 8.00
LAP Albert Pujols 12.00 30.00
LAR Alex Rodriguez 6.00 15.00
LBB Barry Bonds DP 4.00 10.00
LCJ Chipper Jones 5.00 12.00
LCR Cal Ripken 10.00 25.00
LEB Ernie Banks SP/80 * 30.00 60.00
LEM Eddie Murray 3.00 8.00
LFR Frank Robinson 3.00 8.00
LGS Gary Sheffield DP
LHA Hank Aaron 12.00 30.00
LIR Ivan Rodriguez DP 3.00 8.00
LJB Johnny Bench 5.00 12.00
LJC Jose Canseco 3.00 8.00
LJD Joe DiMaggio 15.00 40.00
LJF Jimmie Foxx SP/351 * 15.00 40.00
LKG Ken Griffey Jr. 6.00 15.00
LLA Luis Aparicio 3.00 8.00
LMM Mickey Mantle 30.00 80.00
LMO Mel Ott SP/355 10.00 25.00
LMP Mike Piazza 5.00 12.00
LMR Manny Ramirez Sox 5.00 12.00
LOS Ozzie Smith 5.00 12.00
LRCA R.Campanella SP/335 * 6.00 15.00
LRCL Roger Clemens 5.00 12.00
LRJ Reggie Jackson 4.00 10.00
LRJ Randy Johnson 5.00 12.00
LRM Roger Maris 15.00 40.00
LROC R.Clemente SP/170 * 30.00 60.00
LSS Sammy Sosa DP 3.00 8.00
LTG Tony Gwynn 5.00 12.00
LWM Willie Mays DP 12.00 30.00

2001 Upper Deck Legends Legendary Lumber Autographs

STATED ODDS 1:288
SP PRINT RUNS PROVIDED BY UPPER DECK
SP'S ARE NOT SERIAL-NUMBERED
GOLD RANDOM INSERTS IN PACKS
GOLD PRINT RUN 25 SERIAL #'d SETS
NO GOLD PRICING DUE TO SCARCITY
SLAR Alex Rodriguez 30.00 60.00
SLEB Ernie Banks 30.00 80.00
SLEM Eddie Murray 30.00 60.00
SLKG Ken Griffey Jr. 50.00 120.00
SLLA Luis Aparicio 10.00 25.00
SLRC Roger Clemens SP/227 * 25.00 60.00
SLRJ Reggie Jackson SP/211 * 20.00 50.00
SLSS Sammy Sosa SP/66 * 30.00 80.00
SLTG Tony Gwynn 30.00 80.00

2001 Upper Deck Legends Reflections in Time

COMPLETE SET (10) 12.50 30.00
STATED ODDS 1:18
R1 B.Williams 4.00 10.00
M.Mantle
R2 P.Martinez .60 1.50
C.Young
R3 B.Bonds 3.00 8.00
W.Mays
R4 S.Rolen 2.00 5.00
M.Schmidt
R5 M.McGwire 2.50 6.00
S.Musial
R6 K.Griffey Jr. 2.00 5.00
F.Robinson
R7 S.Sosa 1.00 2.50
A.Dawson
R8 K.Brown .60 1.50
D.Drysdale
R9 J.Giambi .60 1.50
R.Jackson
R10 T.Hudson .60 1.50
C.Hunter

2001 Upper Deck Legends of NY

COMPLETE SET (200) 20.00 50.00
1 Billy Herman .20 .50
2 Carl Erskine .20 .50
3 Burleigh Grimes .20 .50
4 Don Newcombe .20 .50
5 Gil Hodges .50 1.25
6 Pee Wee Reese .50 1.25
7 Jackie Robinson .50 1.25
8 Duke Snider .30 .75
9 Jim Gilliam .20 .50
10 Roy Campanella .50 1.25
11 Carl Furillo .20 .50
12 Casey Stengel .30 .75
13 Casey Stengel DB .15 .40
14 Billy Herman DB .15 .40
15 Jackie Robinson DB .30 .75
16 Jackie Robinson DB .30 .75
17 Gil Hodges DB .50 1.25
18 Carl Furillo DB .15 .40
19 Roy Campanella DB .30 .75
20 Don Newcombe DB .15 .40
21 Duke Snider DB .20 .50
22 Casey Stengel BNS .20 .50
23 Burleigh Grimes BNS .15 .40
24 Pee Wee Reese BNS .30 .75
25 Jackie Robinson BNS .30 .75
26 Jackie Robinson BNS .30 .75
27 Carl Erskine BNS .15 .40
28 Roy Campanella BNS .30 .75
29 Duke Snider BNS .30 .75
30 Rube Marquard .20 .50
31 Ross Youngs .20 .50
32 Bobby Thomson .20 .50
33 Christy Mathewson .50 1.25
34 Carl Hubbell .50 1.25
35 Hoyt Wilhelm .20 .50
36 Johnny Mize .20 .50
37 John McGraw .30 .75
38 Monte Irvin .20 .50
39 Travis Jackson .20 .50
40 Mel Ott .50 1.25
41 Dusty Rhodes .15 .40
42 Leo Durocher .20 .50
43 John McGraw BG .20 .50
44 Christy Mathewson BG .30 .75
45 The Polo Grounds BG .15 .40
46 Travis Jackson BG .15 .40
47 Mel Ott BG .15 .40
48 Johnny Mize BG .15 .40
49 Leo Durocher BG .15 .40
50 Bobby Thomson BG .15 .40
51 Monte Irvin BG .15 .40
52 Bobby Thomson BG .15 .40
53 Christy Mathewson BNS .30 .75
54 Christy Mathewson BNS .30 .75
55 Christy Mathewson BNS .30 .75
56 John McGraw BNS .20 .50
57 John McGraw BNS .20 .50
58 John McGraw BNS .20 .50
59 Travis Jackson BNS .15 .40
60 Mel Ott BNS .20 .50
61 Mel Ott BNS .20 .50
62 Carl Hubbell BNS .20 .50
63 Bobby Thomson BNS .15 .40
64 Monte Irvin BNS .15 .40
65 Al Weis .15 .40
66 Donn Clendenon .15 .40
67 Ed Kranepool .15 .40
68 Gary Carter .20 .50
69 Tommie Agee .20 .50
70 Jon Matlack .15 .40
71 Ken Boswell .15 .40
72 Len Dykstra .20 .50
73 Nolan Ryan 1.25 3.00
74 Ray Sadecki .15 .40
75 Ron Darling .15 .40
76 Ron Swoboda .20 .50
77 Dwight Gooden .20 .50
78 Tom Seaver .30 .75
79 Wayne Garrett .15 .40
80 Casey Stengel MM .20 .50
81 Tom Seaver MM .20 .50
82 Tommie Agee MM .15 .40
83 Tom Seaver MM .20 .50
84 Yogi Berra MM .30 .75
85 Yogi Berra MM .30 .75
86 Tom Seaver MM .20 .50
87 Dwight Gooden MM .15 .40
88 Gary Carter MM .15 .40
89 Ron Darling MM .15 .40
90 Tommie Agee BNS .15 .40
91 Tom Seaver BNS .20 .50
92 Gary Carter BNS .15 .40
93 Len Dykstra BNS .15 .40
94 Babe Ruth 1.50 4.00
95 Bill Dickey .30 .75
96 Rich Gossage .20 .50

97 Casey Stengel .30 .75
98 Catfish Hunter .30 .75
99 Charlie Keller .15 .40
100 Chris Chambliss .20 .50
101 Don Larsen .20 .50
102 Dave Winfield .20 .50
103 Don Mattingly 1.00 2.50
104 Elston Howard .30 .75
105 Frankie Crosetti .20 .50
106 Hank Bauer .20 .50
107 Joe DiMaggio 1.00 2.50
108 Graig Nettles .20 .50
109 Lefty Gomez .30 .75
110 Phil Rizzuto .50 1.25
111 Lou Gehrig 1.00 2.50
112 Lou Piniella .20 .50
113 Mickey Mantle 2.00 5.00
114 Red Rolfe .20 .50
115 Reggie Jackson .30 .75
116 Roger Maris .50 1.25
117 Roy White .15 .40
118 Thurman Munson .50 1.25
119 Tom Tresh .20 .50
120 Tommy Henrich .20 .50
121 Waite Hoyt .20 .50
122 Willie Randolph .20 .50
123 Whitey Ford .30 .75
124 Yogi Berra .50 1.25
125 Babe Ruth BT .75 2.00
126 Babe Ruth BT .75 2.00
127 Lou Gehrig BT .50 1.25
128 Babe Ruth BT .75 2.00
129 Joe DiMaggio BT .50 1.25
130 Joe DiMaggio BT .50 1.25
131 Mickey Mantle BT 1.00 2.50
132 Roger Maris BT .30 .75
133 Mickey Mantle BT 1.00 2.50
134 Reggie Jackson BT .20 .50
135 Babe Ruth BNS .75 2.00
136 Babe Ruth BNS .75 2.00
137 Babe Ruth BNS .75 2.00
138 Lefty Gomez BNS .20 .50
139 Lou Gehrig BNS .50 1.25
140 Lou Gehrig BNS .50 1.25
141 Joe DiMaggio BNS .50 1.25
142 Joe DiMaggio BNS .50 1.25
143 Casey Stengel BNS .20 .50
144 Mickey Mantle BNS 1.00 2.50
145 Yogi Berra BNS .30 .75
146 Mickey Mantle BNS 1.00 2.50
147 Elston Howard BNS .20 .50
148 Whitey Ford BNS .20 .50
149 Reggie Jackson BNS .20 .50
150 Reggie Jackson BNS .20 .50
151 J.McGraw .75 2.00
B.Ruth
152 B.Ruth .75 2.00
J.McGraw
153 L.Gehrig .50 1.25
M.Ott
154 J.DiMaggio .50 1.25
M.Ott
155 J.DiMaggio .50 1.25
B.Herman
156 J.DiMaggio .50 1.25
J.Robinson
157 M.Mantle 1.00 2.50
B.Thomson
158 Y.Berra .30 .75
P.Reese
159 R.Campanella 1.00 2.50
M.Mantle
160 D.Larsen .20 .50
D.Snider
161 Christy Mathewson TT .30 .75
162 Christy Mathewson TT .30 .75
163 Rube Marquard TT .15 .40
164 Christy Mathewson TT .30 .75
165 John McGraw TT .20 .50
166 Burleigh Grimes TT .15 .40
167 Babe Ruth TT .75 2.00
168 Burleigh Grimes TT .15 .40
169 Babe Ruth TT .75 2.00
170 John McGraw TT .20 .50
171 Lou Gehrig TT .50 1.25
172 Babe Ruth TT .75 2.00
173 Babe Ruth TT .75 2.00
174 Carl Hubbell TT .20 .50
175 Joe DiMaggio TT .50 1.25
176 Lou Gehrig TT .50 1.25
177 Leo Durocher TT .15 .40
178 Mel Ott TT .30 .75
179 Joe DiMaggio TT .50 1.25
180 Jackie Robinson TT .30 .75
181 Babe Ruth TT .75 2.00
182 Bobby Thomson TT .15 .40
183 Joe DiMaggio TT .50 1.25
184 Mickey Mantle TT 1.00 2.50
185 Monte Irvin TT .15 .40
186 Roy Campanella TT .30 .75
187 Duke Snider TT .30 .75
188 Dusty Rhodes TT .15 .40
189 Yogi Berra TT .30 .75
190 Mickey Mantle TT 1.00 2.50
191 Mickey Mantle TT 1.00 2.50
192 Casey Stengel TT .20 .50
193 Tom Seaver TT .20 .50
194 Mickey Mantle TT 1.00 2.50
195 Tommie Agee TT .15 .40
196 Tom Seaver TT .20 .50
197 Chris Chambliss TT .15 .40
198 Reggie Jackson TT .20 .50
199 Reggie Jackson TT .20 .50
200 Gary Carter TT .15 .40

2001 Upper Deck Legends of NY Game Base

GOLD PRINT RUN 25 SERIAL #'d SETS
NO GOLD PRICING DUE TO SCARCITY
SILVER PRINT RUN 50 SERIAL #'d SETS
SILVER NO PRICING DUE TO SCARCITY

2001 Upper Deck Legends of NY Game Bat

ONE BAT OR JERSEY CARD PER BOX
SP PRINT RUNS PROVIDED BY UPPER DECK
SP'S ARE NOT SERIAL NUMBERED
SP PRINT RUNS LISTED BELOW
LDBBH Billy Herman 1.50 4.00
LDBDN Don Newcombe SP/67 10.00 25.00
LDBJG Jim Gilliam 1.50 4.00
LGBBTH Bobby Thomson 2.50 6.00
LMBAW Al Weis 1.50 4.00
LMBDC Donn Clendenon SP/60 20.00 50.00
LMBEK Ed Kranepool 1.50 4.00
LMBGC Gary Carter 2.50 6.00
LMBJM J.C. Martin 1.50 4.00
LMBKB Ken Boswell 1.50 4.00
LMBLD Len Dykstra 1.50 4.00
LMBNR Nolan Ryan 10.00 25.00
LMBRS Ron Swoboda 1.50 4.00
LMBTS Tom Seaver 2.50 6.00
LMBWG Wayne Garrett 1.50 4.00
LYBBD Bill Dickey 1.50 4.00
LYBBR Babe Ruth SP/107 125.00 200.00
LYBCC Chris Chambliss SP/130 50.00 120.00
LYBCK Charlie Keller 1.50 4.00
LYBDM Don Mattingly 8.00 20.00
LYBDW Dave Winfield 2.50 6.00
LYBEH Elston Howard 2.00 5.00
LYBHB Hank Bauer 1.50 4.00
LYBLP Lou Piniella 1.50 4.00
LYBMM Mickey Mantle SP/134 75.00 150.00
LYBMR Mickey Rivers 1.50 4.00
LYBRJ Reggie Jackson 3.00 8.00
LYBRM Roger Maris SP/60 12.00 30.00
LYBTH Tommy Henrich 1.50 4.00
LYBTM Thurman Munson 12.00 30.00
LYBTT Tom Tresh 1.50 4.00
LYBYB Yogi Berra 5.00 12.00

2001 Upper Deck Legends of NY Game Bat Autograph

STATED ODDS 1:336
SP PRINT RUNS PROVIDED BY UPPER DECK
SP'S ARE NOT SERIAL NUMBERED
SP PRINT RUNS LISTED BELOW
SDBDN Don Newcombe 10.00 25.00
SMBDC Donn Clendenon 20.00 50.00
SMBGC Gary Carter 20.00 50.00
SMBNR Nolan Ryan SP/129 * 75.00 150.00
SMBRS Ron Swoboda 10.00 25.00
SMBTS Tom Seaver SP/89 * 50.00 120.00
SYBCC Chris Chambliss 10.00 25.00
SYBDM Don Mattingly 40.00 80.00
SYBDW D.Winfield SP/167 * 30.00 60.00
SYBMR Mickey Rivers 10.00 25.00
SYBRJ R.Jackson SP/123 * 50.00 100.00
SYBRW Roy White 10.00 25.00
SYBYB Yogi Berra 40.00 100.00

2001 Upper Deck Legends of NY Game Jersey

ONE BAT OR JERSEY CARD PER BOX
SP PRINT RUNS PROVIDED BY UPPER DECK
SP'S ARE NOT SERIAL NUMBERED
SP PRINT RUNS LISTED BELOW
LDJCE Carl Erskine 4.00 10.00
LDJJR J.Rob Pants SP/126 * 40.00 80.00
LMJCS Casey Stengel 8.00 20.00
LMJJM Jon Matlack 4.00 10.00
LMJRD Ron Darling 6.00 15.00
LMJRS Ray Sadecki 4.00 10.00
LMJTS Tom Seaver 6.00 15.00
LYJBT Bob Turley 8.00 20.00
LYJCD Chuck Dressen 4.00 10.00
LYJCH Catfish Hunter 6.00 15.00
LYJCM C.Mathewson SP/63 * 250.00 400.00
LYJDM Duke Maas 4.00 10.00
LYJDW Dave Winfield 4.00 10.00
LYJEH Elston Howard 6.00 15.00
LYJFC Frank Crosetti 4.00 10.00
LYJGN Graig Nettles 4.00 10.00
LYJHB Hank Behrman 4.00 10.00
LYJHB Hank Bauer 4.00 10.00
LYJJD Joe DiMaggio SP/63 * 40.00 80.00
LYJJP Joe Pepitone 4.00 10.00
LYJJT Joe Torre 6.00 15.00
LYJLM Lindy McDaniel 6.00 15.00
LYJPN Phil Niekro 4.00 10.00
LYJRM Roger Maris SP/63 * 50.00 100.00
LYJRR Red Rolfe 10.00 25.00
LYJSJ Spider Jorgensen 4.00 10.00
LYJTH Tommy Henrich 6.00 15.00
LYJTM Thurman Munson 15.00 40.00
LYJWR Willie Randolph 8.00 20.00

2001 Upper Deck Legends of NY Game Jersey Autograph

STATED ODDS 1:336
SP PRINT RUNS PROVIDED BY UPPER DECK
SP'S ARE NOT SERIAL NUMBERED
SP PRINT RUNS LISTED BELOW
SDJCE Carl Erskine 12.50 30.00
SDJJP J.Podres SP/193 * 12.50 30.00
SMJCS Craig Swan 10.00 25.00
SMJGF George Foster SP/196 * 15.00 40.00
SYJBD Bucky Dent 10.00 25.00
SYJDL Don Larsen 10.00 25.00
SYJDM Don Mattingly SP/72 * 60.00 120.00
SYJDR Dave Righetti 15.00 40.00
SYJGN Graig Nettles 15.00 40.00
SYJHL Hector Lopez SP/195 * 15.00 40.00
SYJJP Joe Pepitone 15.00 40.00
SYJPN Phil Niekro SP/195 * 10.00 25.00
SYJSL Sparky Lyle 10.00 25.00
SYJTJ Tommy John 6.00 15.00
SYJWR Willie Randolph 15.00 40.00
SYJRIG Rich Gossage SP/145 * 15.00 40.00
SYJROG Ron Guidry 10.00 25.00

2001 Upper Deck Legends of NY Game Jersey Gold

PRINT RUNS ARE BETWEEN 125-500 COPIES
LDJCD Chuck Dressen/400 5.00 12.00
LDJCE Carl Erskine/400 5.00 12.00
LDJHB Hank Behrman/500 5.00 12.00
LDJSJ Spider Jorgensen/500 5.00 12.00
LMJJM Jon Matlack/400 5.00 12.00
LMJRD Ron Darling/400 5.00 12.00
LMJRS Ray Sadecki/400 5.00 12.00
LMJTS Tom Seaver/400 8.00 20.00
LYJBT Bob Turley/400 5.00 12.00
LYJCH Catfish Hunter/500 8.00 20.00
LYJDM Duke Maas/400 5.00 12.00
LYJDW Dave Winfield/250 6.00 15.00
LYJEH Elston Howard/400 8.00 20.00
LYJFC Frank Crosetti/400 5.00 12.00
LYJGN Graig Nettles/250 6.00 15.00
LYJHB Hank Bauer/400 5.00 12.00
LYJJP Joe Pepitone/250 6.00 15.00
LYJJT Joe Torre/250 10.00 25.00
LYJLM Lindy McDaniel/400 5.00 12.00
LYJPN Phil Niekro/125 8.00 20.00
LYJRR Red Rolfe/400 8.00 20.00
LYJTH Tommy Henrich/400 5.00 12.00
LYJTM Thurman Munson/400 20.00 50.00
LYJWR Willie Randolph/125 8.00 20.00

2001 Upper Deck Legends of NY Stadium Seat

STATED PRINT RUN 100 SERIAL #'d SETS
GOLD RANDOM INSERTS IN PACKS
GOLD PRINT RUN 25 SERIAL #'d SETS
GOLD NO PRICING DUE TO SCARCITY
SILVER RANDOM INSERTS IN PACKS
SILVER PRINT RUN 50 SERIAL #'d SETS
SILVER NO PRICING DUE TO SCARCITY
EFSJR Jackie Robinson 15.00 40.00
YSMM Mickey Mantle 60.00 120.00

2001 Upper Deck Legends of NY United We Stand

COMPLETE SET (15) 30.00 60.00
COMMON CARD (1-15) 2.00 5.00
STATED ODDS 1:12

1999 Upper Deck MVP Preview

COMPLETE SET (110) 10.00 25.00
3 Jack McDowell .02 .10
4 Troy Glaus .15 .40
5 Darin Erstad .15 .40
6 Tim Salmon .07 .20
10 Travis Lee .07 .20
11 Matt Williams .10 .30
13 Jay Bell .02 .10
15 Chipper Jones .40 1.00
16 Andruw Jones .25 .60
17 Greg Maddux .50 1.25
18 Tom Glavine .15 .40
19 Javy Lopez .10 .30
22 John Smoltz .10 .30
23 Cal Ripken .75 2.00
26 Brady Anderson .07 .20
27 Mike Mussina .15 .40
31 Nomar Garciaparra .40 1.00
32 Pedro Martinez .20 .50
34 Troy O'Leary .02 .10
37 John Valentin .02 .10
38 Kerry Wood .10 .30
39 Sammy Sosa .25 .60
40 Mark Grace .15 .40
41 Henry Rodriguez .02 .10
42 Rod Beck .07 .20
44 Kevin Tapani .02 .10
45 Frank Thomas .20 .50
47 Magglio Ordonez .07 .20
49 Ray Durham .07 .20
50 Jim Parque .02 .10
53 Pete Harnisch .02 .10
55 Sean Casey .10 .30
57 Barry Larkin .15 .40
58 Pokey Reese .02 .10
59 Sandy Alomar Jr. .07 .20
61 Bartolo Colon .15 .40
62 Kenny Lofton .07 .20
63 Omar Vizquel .07 .20
64 Travis Fryman .07 .20
65 Jim Thome .20 .50
66 Manny Ramirez .20 .50
67 Jaret Wright .02 .10
68 Darryl Kile .02 .10
69 Kirt Manwaring .02 .10
70 Vinny Castilla .02 .10
72 Dante Bichette .07 .20
73 Larry Walker .15 .40
77 Matt Anderson .02 .10
79 Damion Easley .02 .10
80 Tony Clark .02 .10
81 Juan Encarnacion .07 .20
82 Livan Hernandez .02 .10
83 Alex Gonzalez .02 .10
85 Derrek Lee .15 .40
86 Mark Kotsay .07 .20
87 Todd Dunwoody .02 .10
88 Cliff Floyd .07 .20
90 Jeff Bagwell .20 .50
91 Moises Alou .07 .20
92 Craig Biggio .15 .40
93 Billy Wagner .07 .20
95 Derek Bell .02 .10
97 Jeff King .02 .10
98 Carlos Beltran .30 .75
100 Larry Sutton .02 .10
101 Johnny Damon .25 .60
104 Chan Ho Park .02 .10
105 Raul Mondesi .02 .10
106 Eric Karros .07 .20
109 Gary Sheffield .20 .50
112 Marquis Grissom .07 .20
114 Jeff Cirillo .02 .10
115 Geoff Jenkins .07 .20
116 Jeromy Burnitz .07 .20
117 Brad Radke .07 .20
118 Eric Milton .02 .10
120 Todd Walker .02 .10
121 David Ortiz .30 .75
123 Vladimir Guerrero .30 .75
124 Rondell White .07 .20
125 Brad Fullmer .07 .20
127 Dustin Hermanson .02 .10
130 Mike Piazza .50 1.25
132 Rey Ordonez .02 .10
133 John Olerud .07 .20
135 Hideo Nomo .15 .40
137 Al Leiter .07 .20
138 Brian McRae .02 .10
139 Derek Jeter .75 2.00
140 Bernie Williams .15 .40
141 Paul O'Neill .15 .40
142 Scott Brosius .02 .10
143 Tino Martinez .07 .20
145 Orlando Hernandez .02 .10
148 A.J. Hinch .02 .10
149 Ben Grieve .02 .10
151 Miguel Tejada .20 .50
152 Matt Stairs .02 .10
154 Jason Giambi .10 .30
155 Curt Schilling .20 .50
156 Scott Rolen .20 .50
158 Doug Glanville .02 .10
159 Bobby Abreu .20 .50
160 Rico Brogna .02 .10
169 Mark McGwire .40 1.00
176 Tony Gwynn .40 1.00
183 Barry Bonds .40 1.00
190 Ken Griffey Jr. .50 1.25
191 Alex Rodriguez .50 1.25
204 Juan Gonzalez .15 .40

1999 Upper Deck MVP

This 220 card set was distributed in 10 cards packs with an SRP of $1.59 per pack. Cards numbered from 218 through 220 are checklist subsets. Approximately 350 Mike Schmidt A Piece of History 500 Home Run Game-Used bat cards were distributed in this product. In addition, 20 hand serial numbered versions of this card personally signed by Schmidt himself were also randomly seeded into packs. Pricing for these bat cards can be referenced under 1999 Upper Deck A Piece of History 500 Club. A Ken Griffey Jr. Sample card was distributed to dealers and hobby media several weeks prior to the product's national release. Unlike most Upper Deck promotional cards, this card does not have the word "SAMPLE" pasted across the back of the card. The card, however, is numbered "S3". It's believed that cards S1 and S2 were Upper Deck MVP football and basketball promo cards.

COMPLETE SET (220) 10.00 25.00
SCHMIDT BAT LISTED W/UD APH 500 CLUB
1 Mo Vaughn .07 .20
2 Tim Belcher .07 .20
3 Jack McDowell .07 .20
4 Troy Glaus .10 .30
5 Darin Erstad .07 .20
6 Tim Salmon .10 .30
7 Jim Edmonds .07 .20
8 Randy Johnson .20 .50
9 Steve Finley .07 .20
10 Travis Lee .07 .20
11 Matt Williams .07 .20
12 Todd Stottlemyre .07 .20
13 Jay Bell .07 .20
14 David Dellucci .07 .20
15 Chipper Jones .20 .50
16 Andruw Jones .10 .30
17 Greg Maddux .30 .75
18 Tom Glavine .10 .30
19 Javy Lopez .07 .20
20 Brian Jordan .07 .20
21 George Lombard .07 .20
22 John Smoltz .10 .30
23 Cal Ripken .60 1.50
24 Charles Johnson .07 .20
25 Albert Belle .07 .20
26 Brady Anderson .07 .20
27 Mike Mussina .10 .30
28 Calvin Pickering .07 .20
29 Ryan Minor .07 .20
30 Jerry Hairston Jr. .07 .20
31 Nomar Garciaparra .30 .75
32 Pedro Martinez .10 .30
33 Jason Varitek .20 .50
34 Troy O'Leary .07 .20
35 Donnie Sadler .07 .20
36 Mark Portugal .07 .20
37 John Valentin .07 .20
38 Kerry Wood .07 .20
39 Sammy Sosa .20 .50
40 Mark Grace .10 .30
41 Henry Rodriguez .07 .20
42 Rod Beck .07 .20
43 Benito Santiago .07 .20
44 Kevin Tapani .07 .20
45 Frank Thomas .20 .50
46 Mike Caruso .07 .20
47 Magglio Ordonez .07 .20
48 Paul Konerko .07 .20
49 Ray Durham .07 .20
50 Jim Parque .07 .20
51 Carlos Lee .07 .20
52 Denny Neagle .07 .20
53 Pete Harnisch .07 .20
54 Michael Tucker .07 .20
55 Sean Casey .07 .20
56 Eddie Taubensee .07 .20
57 Barry Larkin .10 .30
58 Pokey Reese .07 .20
59 Sandy Alomar Jr. .07 .20
60 Roberto Alomar .10 .30
61 Bartolo Colon .07 .20
62 Kenny Lofton .07 .20
63 Omar Vizquel .10 .30
64 Travis Fryman .07 .20
65 Jim Thome .10 .30
66 Manny Ramirez .10 .30
67 Jaret Wright .07 .20
68 Darryl Kile .07 .20
69 Kirt Manwaring .07 .20
70 Vinny Castilla .07 .20
71 Todd Helton .10 .30
72 Dante Bichette .07 .20
73 Larry Walker .07 .20
74 Derrick Gibson .07 .20
75 Gabe Kapler .07 .20
76 Dean Palmer .07 .20
77 Matt Anderson .07 .20
78 Bobby Higginson .07 .20
79 Damion Easley .07 .20
80 Tony Clark .07 .20
81 Juan Encarnacion .07 .20
82 Livan Hernandez .07 .20
83 Alex Gonzalez .07 .20
84 Preston Wilson .07 .20
85 Derrek Lee .10 .30
86 Mark Kotsay .07 .20
87 Todd Dunwoody .07 .20
88 Cliff Floyd .07 .20
89 Ken Caminiti .07 .20
90 Jeff Bagwell .10 .30
91 Moises Alou .07 .20
92 Craig Biggio .10 .30
93 Billy Wagner .07 .20
94 Richard Hidalgo .07 .20
95 Derek Bell .07 .20
96 Hipolito Pichardo .07 .20
97 Jeff King .07 .20
98 Carlos Beltran .10 .30
99 Jeremy Giambi .07 .20
100 Larry Sutton .07 .20
101 Johnny Damon .10 .30
102 Dee Brown .07 .20
103 Kevin Brown .10 .30
104 Chan Ho Park .07 .20
105 Raul Mondesi .07 .20
106 Eric Karros .07 .20
107 Adrian Beltre .07 .20
108 Devon White .07 .20
109 Gary Sheffield .07 .20
110 Sean Berry .07 .20
111 Alex Ochoa .07 .20
112 Marquis Grissom .07 .20
113 Fernando Vina .07 .20
114 Jeff Cirillo .07 .20
115 Geoff Jenkins .07 .20
116 Jeromy Burnitz .07 .20
117 Brad Radke .07 .20
118 Eric Milton .07 .20
119 A.J. Pierzynski .07 .20
120 Todd Walker .07 .20
121 David Ortiz .20 .50
122 Corey Koskie .07 .20
123 Vladimir Guerrero .20 .50
124 Rondell White .07 .20
125 Brad Fullmer .07 .20
126 Ugueth Urbina .07 .20
127 Dustin Hermanson .07 .20
128 Michael Barrett .07 .20
129 Fernando Seguignol .07 .20
130 Mike Piazza .30 .75
131 Rickey Henderson .20 .50
132 Rey Ordonez .07 .20
133 John Olerud .07 .20
134 Robin Ventura .07 .20
135 Hideo Nomo .20 .50
136 Mike Kinkade .07 .20
137 Al Leiter .07 .20
138 Brian McRae .07 .20
139 Derek Jeter .50 1.25
140 Bernie Williams .10 .30
141 Paul O'Neill .10 .30
142 Scott Brosius .07 .20
143 Tino Martinez .10 .30
144 Roger Clemens .40 1.00
145 Orlando Hernandez .07 .20
146 Mariano Rivera .20 .50
147 Ricky Ledee .07 .20
148 A.J. Hinch .07 .20
149 Ben Grieve .07 .20
150 Eric Chavez .07 .20
151 Miguel Tejada .07 .20
152 Matt Stairs .07 .20
153 Ryan Christenson .07 .20
154 Jason Giambi .07 .20
155 Curt Schilling .07 .20
156 Scott Rolen .10 .30
157 Pat Burrell RC .40 1.00
158 Doug Glanville .07 .20
159 Bobby Abreu .07 .20
160 Rico Brogna .07 .20
161 Ron Gant .07 .20
162 Jason Kendall .07 .20
163 Aramis Ramirez .07 .20
164 Jose Guillen .07 .20
165 Emil Brown .07 .20
166 Pat Meares .07 .20
167 Kevin Young .07 .20
168 Brian Giles .07 .20
169 Mark McGwire .50 1.25
170 J.D. Drew .07 .20
171 Edgar Renteria .07 .20
172 Fernando Tatis .07 .20
173 Matt Morris .07 .20
174 Eli Marrero .07 .20
175 Ray Lankford .07 .20
176 Tony Gwynn .25 .60
177 Sterling Hitchcock .07 .20
178 Ruben Rivera .07 .20
179 Wally Joyner .07 .20
180 Trevor Hoffman .07 .20
181 Jim Leyritz .07 .20
182 Carlos Hernandez .07 .20
183 Barry Bonds .60 1.50
184 Ellis Burks .07 .20
185 F.P. Santangelo .07 .20
186 J.T. Snow .07 .20
187 Ramon E.Martinez RC .07 .20
188 Jeff Kent .07 .20
189 Robb Nen .07 .20
190 Ken Griffey Jr. .40 1.00
191 Alex Rodriguez .30 .75
192 Shane Monahan .07 .20
193 Carlos Guillen .07 .20
194 Edgar Martinez .10 .30
195 David Segui .07 .20
196 Jose Mesa .07 .20
197 Jose Canseco .10 .30
198 Rolando Arrojo .07 .20
199 Wade Boggs .10 .30
200 Fred McGriff .10 .30
201 Quinton McCracken .07 .20
202 Bobby Smith .07 .20
203 Bubba Trammell .07 .20
204 Juan Gonzalez .07 .20
205 Ivan Rodriguez .10 .30
206 Rafael Palmeiro .10 .30
207 Royce Clayton .07 .20
208 Rick Helling .07 .20
209 Todd Zeile .07 .20
210 Rusty Greer .07 .20
211 David Wells .07 .20
212 Roy Halladay .20 .50
213 Carlos Delgado .07 .20
214 Darrin Fletcher .07 .20
215 Shawn Green .07 .20
216 Kevin Witt .07 .20
217 Jose Cruz Jr. .07 .20
218 Ken Griffey Jr. CL .25 .60
219 Sammy Sosa CL .10 .30
220 Mark McGwire CL .25 .60
S3 Ken Griffey Jr. Sample .50 1.25

1999 Upper Deck MVP Gold Script

*STARS: 12.5X TO 30X BASIC CARDS
*ROOKIES: 12.5X TO 30X BASIC CARDS
RANDOM INSERTS IN HOBBY PACKS
STATED PRINT RUN 100 SERIAL #'d SETS

1999 Upper Deck MVP Silver Script

*STARS: 1.5X TO 4X BASIC CARDS
*ROOKIES: 1.5X TO 4X BASIC CARDS
STATED ODDS 1:2
S3 Ken Griffey Jr. Sample 2.00 5.00

1999 Upper Deck MVP Super Script

*STARS: 30X TO 80X BASIC CARDS
RANDOM INSERTS IN HOBBY PACKS
STATED PRINT RUN 25 SERIAL #'d SETS
NO ROOKIE PRICING DUE TO SCARCITY

1999 Upper Deck MVP Dynamics

COMPLETE SET (15) 40.00 100.00
STATED ODDS 1:28
D1 Ken Griffey Jr. 3.00 8.00
D2 Alex Rodriguez 2.50 6.00
D3 Nomar Garciaparra 2.50 6.00
D4 Mike Piazza 2.50 6.00
D5 Mark McGwire 4.00 10.00
D6 Sammy Sosa 1.50 4.00
D7 Chipper Jones 1.50 4.00
D8 Mo Vaughn .60 1.50
D9 Tony Gwynn 2.00 5.00
D10 Vladimir Guerrero 1.50 4.00
D11 Derek Jeter 4.00 10.00
D12 Jeff Bagwell 1.00 2.50
D13 Cal Ripken 5.00 12.00
D14 Juan Gonzalez .60 1.50
D15 J.D. Drew .60 1.50

1999 Upper Deck MVP Game Used Souvenirs

STATED ODDS 1:144 HOBBY
GUBB Barry Bonds 10.00 25.00
GUCJ Chipper Jones 8.00 20.00
GUCR Cal Ripken 10.00 25.00
GUJB Jeff Bagwell 6.00 15.00
GUJD J.D. Drew 4.00 10.00
GUKG Ken Griffey Jr. 10.00 25.00
GUMP Mike Piazza 12.50 30.00
GUMV Mo Vaughn 4.00 10.00
GUSR Scott Rolen 6.00 15.00
GAKG Ken Griffey Jr. AU/24
GACJ Chipper Jones AU/10

1999 Upper Deck MVP Power Surge

COMPLETE SET (15) 10.00 25.00
STATED ODDS 1:9
P1 Mark McGwire 1.25 3.00
P2 Sammy Sosa .50 1.25
P3 Ken Griffey Jr. 1.00 2.50
P4 Alex Rodriguez .75 2.00
P5 Juan Gonzalez .20 .50
P6 Nomar Garciaparra .75 2.00
P7 Vladimir Guerrero .50 1.25
P8 Chipper Jones .50 1.25
P9 Albert Belle .20 .50
P10 Frank Thomas .50 1.25
P11 Mike Piazza .75 2.00
P12 Jeff Bagwell .30 .75
P13 Manny Ramirez .30 .75
P14 Mo Vaughn .20 .50
P15 Barry Bonds 1.50 4.00

1999 Upper Deck MVP ProSign

STATED ODDS 1:216 RETAIL
SP'S NOT CONFIRMED BY UPPER DECK
AG Alex Gonzalez 4.00 10.00
AN Abraham Nunez 4.00 10.00
BC Bruce Chen 4.00 10.00
BF Brad Fullmer 4.00 10.00
BG Ben Grieve 4.00 10.00
CB Carlos Beltran 8.00 20.00
CG Chris Gomez 4.00 10.00
CJ Chipper Jones SP 75.00 150.00
CK Corey Koskie 6.00 15.00
CP Calvin Pickering 4.00 10.00
DG Derrick Gibson 4.00 10.00
EC Eric Chavez 6.00 15.00
GK Gabe Kapler 6.00 15.00
GL George Lombard 4.00 10.00
IR Ivan Rodriguez SP 50.00 100.00
JG Jeremy Giambi 4.00 10.00
JP Jim Parque 4.00 10.00
JR Ken Griffey Jr. SP 250.00 350.00
JRA Jason Rakers 4.00 10.00
KW Kevin Witt 4.00 10.00
MA Matt Anderson 4.00 10.00
ML Mike Lincoln 4.00 10.00
MLO Mike Lowell 6.00 15.00
NG Nomar Garciaparra SP 75.00 150.00
RB Russ Branyan 4.00 10.00
RH Richard Hidalgo 4.00 10.00
RL Ricky Ledee 4.00 10.00
RM Ryan Minor 4.00 10.00
RR Ruben Rivera 4.00 10.00
SH Shea Hillenbrand 6.00 15.00
SK Scott Karl 4.00 10.00
SM Shane Monahan 4.00 10.00

1999 Upper Deck MVP Scout's Choice

COMPLETE SET (15) 5.00 12.00
STATED ODDS 1:9
SC1 J.D. Drew .25 .60
SC2 Ben Grieve .25 .60
SC3 Troy Glaus .40 1.00
SC4 Gabe Kapler .25 .60
SC5 Carlos Beltran .40 1.00
SC6 Aramis Ramirez .25 .60
SC7 Pat Burrell .50 1.25
SC8 Kerry Wood .25 .60
SC9 Ryan Minor .25 .60
SC10 Todd Helton .40 1.00
SC11 Eric Chavez .25 .60
SC12 Russ Branyan .25 .60
SC13 Travis Lee .25 .60
SC14 Ruben Mateo .25 .60
SC15 Roy Halladay .60 1.50

1999 Upper Deck MVP Super Tools

COMPLETE SET (15) 20.00 50.00
STATED ODDS 1:14
T1 Ken Griffey Jr. 2.00 5.00
T2 Alex Rodriguez 1.50 4.00
T3 Sammy Sosa 1.00 2.50
T4 Derek Jeter 2.50 6.00
T5 Vladimir Guerrero 1.00 2.50
T6 Ben Grieve .40 1.00
T7 Mike Piazza 1.50 4.00
T8 Kenny Lofton .40 1.00
T9 Barry Bonds 3.00 8.00
T10 Darin Erstad .40 1.00
T11 Nomar Garciaparra 1.50 4.00
T12 Cal Ripken 3.00 8.00
T13 J.D. Drew .40 1.00
T14 Larry Walker .40 1.00
T15 Chipper Jones 1.00 2.50

1999 Upper Deck MVP Swing Time

COMPLETE SET (12) 8.00 20.00
STATED ODDS 1:6
S1 Ken Griffey Jr. .75 2.00
S2 Mark McGwire 1.00 2.50
S3 Sammy Sosa .40 1.00
S4 Tony Gwynn .50 1.25
S5 Alex Rodriguez .60 1.50
S6 Nomar Garciaparra .60 1.50
S7 Barry Bonds 1.25 3.00
S8 Frank Thomas .40 1.00
S9 Chipper Jones .40 1.00
S10 Ivan Rodriguez .25 .60
S11 Mike Piazza .60 1.50
S12 Derek Jeter 1.00 2.50

1999 Upper Deck MVP FanFest

This 30 card standard-size set was issued by Upper Deck during the annual FanFest celebration. The cards were issued in three-card packs with 15,000 packs produced and distributed during the show. The cards have a silver All-Star Game logo on the lower right corner of the card and they are all numbered with an "AS" prefix. Ten of the cards were printed in smaller quantities then the other 20 cards, those cards are notated with an SP in the listings below

COMPLETE SET 25.00 60.00
COMMON CARD (AS1-AS30) .12 .30
COMMON SP .80 2.00
AS1 Mo Vaughn SP .75 2.00
AS2 Randy Johnson .30 .75
AS3 Chipper Jones .60 1.50
AS4 Greg Maddux SP 2.50 6.00
AS5 Cal Ripken 1.25 3.00
AS6 Albert Belle .10 .30
AS7 Nomar Garciaparra SP 2.50 6.00
AS8 Pedro Martinez .30 .75
AS9 Sammy Sosa .50 1.25
AS10 Frank Thomas .30 .75
AS11 Sean Casey .10 .30
AS12 Roberto Alomar .25 .60
AS13 Manny Ramirez .30 .75
AS14 Larry Walker .10 .30
AS15 Jeff Bagwell SP 1.25 3.00
AS16 Craig Biggio .25 .60
AS17 Raul Mondesi .10 .30
AS18 Vladimir Guerrero .30 .75
AS19 Mike Piazza SP 3.00 8.00
AS20 Derek Jeter SP 5.00 12.00
AS21 Roger Clemens SP 2.50 6.00
AS22 Scott Rolen .25 .60
AS23 Mark McGwire SP 3.00 8.00
AS24 Tony Gwynn .60 1.50
AS25 Barry Bonds .60 1.50
AS26 Ken Griffey Jr SP 3.00 8.00
AS27 Alex Rodriguez .60 1.50
AS28 Jose Canseco .30 .75
AS29 Juan Gonzalez .30 .75
AS30 Ivan Rodriguez .30 .75

2000 Upper Deck MVP

COMPLETE SET (220) 6.00 15.00
COMMON CARD (1-220) .07 .20
1 Garret Anderson .07 .20
2 Mo Vaughn .07 .20
3 Tim Salmon .07 .20
4 Ramon Ortiz .07 .20
5 Darin Erstad .07 .20
6 Troy Glaus .07 .20
7 Troy Percival .07 .20
8 Jeff Bagwell .12 .30
9 Ken Caminiti .07 .20
10 Daryle Ward .07 .20
11 Craig Biggio .12 .30
12 Jose Lima .07 .20
13 Moises Alou .07 .20
14 Octavio Dotel .07 .20
15 Ben Grieve .07 .20
16 Jason Giambi .07 .20
17 Tim Hudson .12 .30
18 Eric Chavez .07 .20
19 Matt Stairs .07 .20
20 Miguel Tejada .12 .30
21 John Jaha .07 .20
22 Chipper Jones .20 .50
23 Kevin Millwood .07 .20
24 Brian Jordan .07 .20
25 Andruw Jones .07 .20
26 Andres Galarraga .12 .30
27 Greg Maddux .25 .60
28 Reggie Sanders .07 .20
29 Javy Lopez .07 .20
30 Jeromy Burnitz .07 .20
31 Kevin Barker .07 .20
32 Jose Hernandez .07 .20
33 Ron Belliard .07 .20
34 Henry Blanco .07 .20
35 Marquis Grissom .07 .20
36 Geoff Jenkins .07 .20
37 Carlos Delgado .07 .20
38 Raul Mondesi .07 .20
39 Roy Halladay .12 .30
40 Tony Batista .07 .20

41 David Wells .07 .20
42 Shannon Stewart .07 .20
43 Vernon Wells .07 .20
44 Sammy Sosa .20 .50
45 Ismael Valdes .07 .20
46 Joe Girardi .12 .30
47 Mark Grace .12 .30
48 Henry Rodriguez .07 .20
49 Kerry Wood .07 .20
50 Eric Young .07 .20
51 Mark McGwire .30 .75
52 Darryl Kile .07 .20
53 Fernando Vina .07 .20
54 Ray Lankford .07 .20
55 J.D. Drew .07 .20
56 Fernando Tatis .07 .20
57 Rick Ankiel .12 .30
58 Matt Williams .07 .20
59 Erubiel Durazo .07 .20
60 Tony Womack .07 .20
61 Jay Bell .07 .20
62 Randy Johnson .20 .50
63 Steve Finley .07 .20
64 Matt Mantei .07 .20
65 Luis Gonzalez .07 .20
66 Gary Sheffield .07 .20
67 Eric Gagne .07 .20
68 Adrian Beltre .20 .50
69 Mark Grudzielanek .07 .20
70 Kevin Brown .07 .20
71 Chan Ho Park .12 .30
72 Shawn Green .07 .20
73 Vinny Castilla .07 .20
74 Fred McGriff .12 .30
75 Wilson Alvarez .07 .20
76 Greg Vaughn .07 .20
77 Gerald Williams .07 .20
78 Ryan Rupe .07 .20
79 Jose Canseco .12 .30
80 Vladimir Guerrero .12 .30
81 Dustin Hermanson .07 .20
82 Michael Barrett .07 .20
83 Rondell White .07 .20
84 Tony Armas Jr. .07 .20
85 Wilton Guerrero .07 .20
86 Jose Vidro .07 .20
87 Barry Bonds .30 .75
88 Russ Ortiz .07 .20
89 Ellis Burks .07 .20
90 Jeff Kent .07 .20
91 Russ Davis .07 .20
92 J.T. Snow .07 .20
93 Roberto Alomar .12 .30
94 Manny Ramirez .20 .50
95 Chuck Finley .07 .20
96 Kenny Lofton .07 .20
97 Jim Thome .12 .30
98 Bartolo Colon .07 .20
99 Omar Vizquel .12 .30
100 Richie Sexson .07 .20
101 Mike Cameron .07 .20
102 Brett Tomko .07 .20
103 Edgar Martinez .12 .30
104 Alex Rodriguez .25 .60
105 John Olerud .07 .20
106 Freddy Garcia .07 .20
107 Kazuhiro Sasaki RC .20 .50
108 Preston Wilson .07 .20
109 Luis Castillo .07 .20
110 A.J. Burnett .07 .20
111 Mike Lowell .07 .20
112 Cliff Floyd .07 .20
113 Brad Penny .07 .20
114 Alex Gonzalez .07 .20
115 Mike Piazza .20 .50
116 Derek Bell .07 .20
117 Edgardo Alfonzo .07 .20
118 Rickey Henderson .20 .50
119 Todd Zeile .07 .20
120 Mike Hampton .07 .20
121 Al Leiter .07 .20
122 Robin Ventura .07 .20
123 Cal Ripken .60 1.50
124 Mike Mussina .12 .30
125 B.J. Surhoff .07 .20
126 Jerry Hairston Jr. .07 .20
127 Brady Anderson .07 .20
128 Albert Belle .07 .20
129 Sidney Ponson .07 .20
130 Tony Gwynn .20 .50
131 Ryan Klesko .07 .20
132 Sterling Hitchcock .07 .20
133 Eric Owens .07 .20
134 Trevor Hoffman .12 .30
135 Al Martin .07 .20
136 Bret Boone .07 .20
137 Brian Giles .07 .20
138 Chad Hermansen .07 .20
139 Kevin Young .07 .20
140 Kris Benson .07 .20
141 Warren Morris .07 .20
142 Jason Kendall .07 .20
143 Wil Cordero .07 .20
144 Scott Rolen .12 .30
145 Curt Schilling .12 .30
146 Doug Glanville .07 .20
147 Mike Lieberthal .07 .20
148 Mike Jackson .07 .20
149 Rico Brogna .07 .20
150 Andy Ashby .07 .20
151 Bob Abreu .07 .20
152 Sean Casey .07 .20
153 Pete Harnisch .07 .20
154 Dante Bichette .07 .20
155 Pokey Reese .07 .20
156 Aaron Boone .07 .20
157 Ken Griffey Jr. .40 1.00
158 Barry Larkin .12 .30
159 Scott Williamson .07 .20
160 Carlos Beltran .12 .30
161 Jermaine Dye .07 .20
162 Jose Rosado .07 .20
163 Joe Randa .07 .20
164 Johnny Damon .12 .30
165 Mike Sweeney .07 .20
166 Mark Quinn .07 .20
167 Ivan Rodriguez .12 .30
168 Rusty Greer .07 .20
169 Ruben Mateo .07 .20
170 Doug Davis .07 .20
171 Gabe Kapler .07 .20
172 Justin Thompson .07 .20
173 Rafael Palmeiro .12 .30
174 Larry Walker .12 .30
175 Neifi Perez .07 .20
176 Rolando Arrojo .07 .20
177 Jeffrey Hammonds .07 .20
178 Todd Helton .12 .30
179 Pedro Astacio .07 .20
180 Jeff Cirillo .07 .20
181 Pedro Martinez .12 .30
182 Carl Everett .07 .20
183 Troy O'Leary .07 .20
184 Nomar Garciaparra .12 .30
185 Jose Offerman .07 .20
186 Bret Saberhagen .07 .20
187 Trot Nixon .07 .20
188 Jason Varitek .20 .50
189 Todd Walker .07 .20
190 Eric Milton .07 .20
191 Chad Allen .07 .20
192 Jacque Jones .07 .20
193 Brad Radke .07 .20
194 Corey Koskie .07 .20
195 Joe Mays .07 .20
196 Juan Gonzalez .07 .20
197 Jeff Weaver .07 .20
198 Juan Encarnacion .07 .20
199 Deivi Cruz .07 .20
200 Damion Easley .07 .20
201 Tony Clark .07 .20
202 Dean Palmer .07 .20
203 Frank Thomas .20 .50
204 Carlos Lee .07 .20
205 Mike Sirotka .07 .20
206 Kip Wells .07 .20
207 Magglio Ordonez .12 .30
208 Paul Konerko .07 .20
209 Chris Singleton .07 .20
210 Derek Jeter .50 1.25
211 Tino Martinez .07 .20
212 Mariano Rivera .25 .60
213 Roger Clemens .25 .60
214 Nick Johnson .07 .20
215 Paul O'Neill .12 .30
216 Bernie Williams .12 .30
217 David Cone .07 .20
218 Ken Griffey Jr. CL .40 1.00
219 Sammy Sosa CL .20 .50
220 Mark McGwire CL .30 .75

2000 Upper Deck MVP Gold Script

*STARS: 25X TO 60X BASIC CARDS
*ROOKIES: 25X TO 60X BASIC CARDS
STATED PRINT RUN 50 SERIAL #'d SETS

2000 Upper Deck MVP Silver Script

COMPLETE SET (220) 75.00 150.00
*STARS: 1.25X TO 3X BASIC CARDS
*ROOKIES: 1.25X TO 3X BASIC CARDS
STATED ODDS 1:2

2000 Upper Deck MVP Super Script

NO PRICING DUE TO SCARCITY

2000 Upper Deck MVP All Star Game

COMPLETE SET (30) 8.00 20.00
AS1 Mo Vaughn .15 .40
AS2 Jeff Bagwell .25 .60
AS3 Jason Giambi .15 .40
AS4 Chipper Jones .40 1.00
AS5 Greg Maddux .50 1.25
AS6 Tony Batista .15 .40
AS7 Sammy Sosa .40 1.00
AS8 Mark McGwire .60 1.50
AS9 Randy Johnson .40 1.00
AS10 Shawn Green .15 .40
AS11 Greg Vaughn .15 .40
AS12 Vladimir Guerrero .25 .60
AS13 Barry Bonds .60 1.50
AS14 Manny Ramirez .40 1.00
AS15 Alex Rodriguez .50 1.25
AS16 Preston Wilson .15 .40
AS17 Mike Piazza .40 1.00
AS18 Cal Ripken Jr. 1.25 3.00
AS19 Tony Gwynn .40 1.00
AS20 Scott Rolen .25 .60
AS21 Ken Griffey Jr. .75 2.00
AS22 Carlos Beltran .25 .60
AS23 Ivan Rodriguez .25 .60
AS24 Larry Walker .25 .60
AS25 Nomar Garciaparra .25 .60
AS26 Pedro Martinez .25 .60
AS27 Juan Gonzalez .15 .40
AS28 Frank Thomas .40 1.00
AS29 Derek Jeter 1.00 2.50
AS30 Bernie Williams .25 .60

2000 Upper Deck MVP Draw Your Own Card

COMPLETE SET (31) 10.00 25.00
STATED ODDS 1:6
DT1 Frank Thomas .40 1.00
DT2 Joe DiMaggio .75 2.00
DT3 Barry Bonds .60 1.50
DT4 Mark McGwire .60 1.50
DT5 Ken Griffey Jr. .75 2.00
DT6 Mark McGwire .60 1.50
DT7 Mike Stanley .15 .40
DT8 Nomar Garciaparra .25 .60
DT9 Mickey Mantle 1.25 3.00
DT10 Randy Johnson .40 1.00
DT11 Nolan Ryan 1.25 3.00
DT12 Chipper Jones .40 1.00
DT13 Ken Griffey Jr. .75 2.00
DT14 Troy Glaus .15 .40
DT15 Manny Ramirez .40 1.00
DT16 Mark McGwire .60 1.50
DT17 Ivan Rodriguez .25 .60
DT18 Mike Piazza .40 1.00
DT19 Sammy Sosa .40 1.00
DT20 Ken Griffey Jr. .75 2.00
DT21 Jeff Bagwell .25 .60
DT22 Ken Griffey Jr. .75 2.00
DT23 Kerry Wood .15 .40
DT24 Mark McGwire .60 1.50
DT25 Greg Maddux .50 1.25
DT26 Sandy Alomar Jr. .15 .40
DT27 Albert Belle .15 .40
DT28 Sammy Sosa .40 1.00
DT29 Alexandra Brunet .15 .40
DT30 Mark McGwire .60 1.50
DT31 Nomar Garciaparra .25 .60

2000 Upper Deck MVP Drawing Power

COMPLETE SET (7) 5.00 12.00
STATED ODDS 1:28
DP1 Mark McGwire 1.50 4.00
DP2 Ken Griffey Jr. 2.00 5.00
DP3 Mike Piazza 1.00 2.50
DP4 Chipper Jones 1.00 2.50
DP5 Nomar Garciaparra .60 1.50
DP6 Sammy Sosa 1.00 2.50
DP7 Jose Canseco .60 1.50

2000 Upper Deck MVP Game Used Souvenirs

STATED ODDS 1:130
ABG Albert Belle Glove 6.00 15.00
AFG Alex Fernandez Glove 4.00 10.00
AGG Alex Gonzalez Glove 4.00 10.00
ARB Alex Rodriguez Bat 6.00 15.00
ARG Alex Rodriguez Glove 20.00 50.00
BBB Barry Bonds Bat 10.00 25.00
BBG Barry Bonds Glove 15.00 40.00
BGG Ben Grieve Glove 4.00 10.00
BWG Bernie Williams Glove 10.00 25.00
CRG Cal Ripken Glove 12.50 30.00
IRB Ivan Rodriguez Bat 4.00 10.00
IRG Ivan Rodriguez Glove 10.00 25.00
JBG Jeff Bagwell Glove 15.00 40.00
JCB Jose Canseco Bat 4.00 10.00
KGB Ken Griffey Jr. Bat 6.00 15.00
KGG Ken Griffey Jr. Glove 15.00 40.00
KLG Kenny Lofton Glove 10.00 25.00
LWG Larry Walker Glove 6.00 15.00
MRB Manny Ramirez Bat 4.00 10.00
NRG Nolan Ryan Glove 15.00 40.00
POG Paul O'Neill Glove 10.00 25.00
RAG Roberto Alomar Glove 10.00 25.00
RMG Raul Mondesi Glove 6.00 15.00
RPG Rafael Palmeiro Glove 25.00 50.00
TGB Tony Gwynn Bat 6.00 15.00
TGG Tony Gwynn Glove 15.00 40.00
TSG Tim Salmon Glove 10.00 25.00
WCG Will Clark Glove 30.00 80.00

2000 Upper Deck MVP Prolifics

COMPLETE SET (7) 8.00 20.00
STATED ODDS 1:28
P1 Manny Ramirez 1.00 2.50
P2 Vladimir Guerrero .60 1.50
P3 Derek Jeter 2.50 6.00
P4 Pedro Martinez .60 1.50
P5 Shawn Green .40 1.00
P6 Alex Rodriguez 1.25 3.00
P7 Cal Ripken 3.00 8.00

2000 Upper Deck MVP ProSign

STATED ODDS 1:143
LIMITED RANDOM IN PACKS
LIMITED PRINT RUN 25 SERIAL #'d SETS
NO LTD PRICING DUE TO SCARCITY
BP Ben Petrick 4.00 10.00
BT Bubba Trammell 4.00 10.00
DD Doug Davis 6.00 15.00
EY Ed Yarnall 4.00 10.00
JM Jim Morris 6.00 15.00
JV Jose Vidro 4.00 10.00
JZ Jeff Zimmerman 4.00 10.00
KW Kevin Witt 4.00 10.00
MB Michael Barrett 4.00 10.00
MM Mike Meyers 6.00 15.00
MQ Mark Quinn 4.00 10.00
MS Mike Sweeney 6.00 15.00
PW Preston Wilson 6.00 15.00
RA Rick Ankiel 6.00 15.00
SW Scott Williamson 4.00 10.00
TH Tim Hudson 6.00 15.00
TN Trot Nixon 6.00 15.00
WM Warren Morris 4.00 10.00

2000 Upper Deck MVP Pure Grit

COMPLETE SET (10) 4.00 10.00
STATED ODDS 1:6
G1 Derek Jeter 1.25 3.00
G2 Kevin Brown .20 .50
G3 Craig Biggio .30 .75
G4 Ivan Rodriguez .30 .75
G5 Scott Rolen .30 .75
G6 Carlos Beltran .30 .75
G7 Ken Griffey Jr. 1.00 2.50
G8 Cal Ripken 1.50 4.00
G9 Nomar Garciaparra .30 .75
G10 Randy Johnson .50 1.25

2000 Upper Deck MVP Scout's Choice

COMPLETE SET (10) 3.00 8.00
STATED ODDS 1:14
SC1 Rick Ankiel .60 1.50
SC2 Vernon Wells .40 1.00
SC3 Pat Burrell .40 1.00
SC4 Travis Dawkins .40 1.00
SC5 Eric Munson .40 1.00
SC6 Nick Johnson .40 1.00
SC7 Dermal Brown .40 1.00
SC8 Alfonso Soriano 1.00 2.50
SC9 Ben Petrick .40 1.00
SC10 Adam Everett .40 1.00

2000 Upper Deck MVP Second Season Standouts

COMPLETE SET (10) 2.50 6.00
STATED ODDS 1:6
SS1 Pedro Martinez .30 .75
SS2 Mariano Rivera .60 1.50
SS3 Orlando Hernandez .20 .50
SS4 Ken Caminiti .20 .50
SS5 Bernie Williams .30 .75
SS6 Jim Thome .30 .75
SS7 Nomar Garciaparra .30 .75
SS8 Edgardo Alfonzo .20 .50
SS9 Derek Jeter 1.25 3.00
SS10 Kevin Millwood .20 .50

2001 Upper Deck MVP

COMPLETE SET (330) 15.00 40.00
1 Mo Vaughn .07 .20
2 Troy Percival .07 .20
3 Adam Kennedy .07 .20
4 Darin Erstad .07 .20
5 Tim Salmon .10 .30
6 Bengie Molina .07 .20
7 Troy Glaus .07 .20
8 Garret Anderson .07 .20
9 Ismael Valdes .07 .20
10 Glenallen Hill .07 .20
11 Tim Hudson .07 .20
12 Eric Chavez .07 .20
13 Johnny Damon .10 .30
14 Barry Zito .10 .30
15 Jason Giambi .07 .20
16 Terrence Long .07 .20
17 Jason Hart .07 .20
18 Jose Ortiz .07 .20
19 Miguel Tejada .07 .20
20 Jason Isringhausen .07 .20
21 Adam Piatt .07 .20
22 Jeremy Giambi .07 .20
23 Tony Batista .07 .20
24 Darrin Fletcher .07 .20
25 Mike Sirotka .07 .20
26 Carlos Delgado .07 .20
27 Billy Koch .07 .20
28 Shannon Stewart .07 .20
29 Raul Mondesi .07 .20
30 Brad Fullmer .07 .20
31 Jose Cruz Jr. .07 .20
32 Kelvim Escobar .07 .20
33 Greg Vaughn .07 .20
34 Aubrey Huff .07 .20
35 Albie Lopez .07 .20
36 Gerald Williams .07 .20
37 Ben Grieve .07 .20
38 John Flaherty .07 .20
39 Fred McGriff .10 .30
40 Ryan Rupe .07 .20
41 Travis Harper .07 .20
42 Steve Cox .07 .20
43 Roberto Alomar .10 .30
44 Jim Thome .10 .30
45 Russell Branyan .07 .20
46 Bartolo Colon .07 .20
47 Omar Vizquel .10 .30
48 Travis Fryman .07 .20
49 Kenny Lofton .07 .20
50 Chuck Finley .07 .20
51 Ellis Burks .07 .20
52 Eddie Taubensee .07 .20
53 Juan Gonzalez .07 .20
54 Edgar Martinez .10 .30
55 Aaron Sele .07 .20
56 John Olerud .07 .20
57 Jay Buhner .07 .20
58 Mike Cameron .07 .20
59 John Halama .07 .20
60 Ichiro Suzuki RC 8.00 20.00
61 David Bell .07 .20
62 Freddy Garcia .07 .20
63 Carlos Guillen .07 .20
64 Bret Boone .07 .20
65 Al Martin .07 .20
66 Cal Ripken .60 1.50
67 Delino DeShields .07 .20
68 Chris Richard .07 .20
69 Sean Douglass RC .20 .50
70 Melvin Mora .07 .20
71 Luis Matos .07 .20
72 Sidney Ponson .07 .20
73 Mike Bordick .07 .20
74 Brady Anderson .07 .20
75 David Segui .07 .20
76 Jeff Conine .07 .20
77 Alex Rodriguez .25 .60
78 Gabe Kapler .07 .20
79 Ivan Rodriguez .10 .30
80 Rick Helling .07 .20
81 Kenny Rogers .07 .20
82 Andres Galarraga .07 .20
83 Rusty Greer .07 .20
84 Justin Thompson .07 .20
85 Ken Caminiti .07 .20
86 Rafael Palmeiro .10 .30
87 Ruben Mateo .07 .20
88 Travis Hafner RC 1.25 3.00
89 Manny Ramirez Sox .10 .30
90 Pedro Martinez .10 .30
91 Carl Everett .07 .20
92 Dante Bichette .07 .20
93 Derek Lowe .07 .20
94 Jason Varitek .20 .50
95 Nomar Garciaparra .30 .75
96 David Cone .07 .20
97 Tomokazu Ohka .07 .20
98 Troy O'Leary .07 .20
99 Trot Nixon .07 .20
100 Jermaine Dye .07 .20
101 Joe Randa .07 .20
102 Jeff Suppan .07 .20
103 Roberto Hernandez .07 .20
104 Mike Sweeney .07 .20
105 Mac Suzuki .07 .20
106 Carlos Febles .07 .20
107 Jose Rosado .07 .20
108 Mark Quinn .07 .20
109 Carlos Beltran .07 .20
110 Dean Palmer .07 .20
111 Mitch Meluskey .07 .20
112 Bobby Higginson .07 .20
113 Brandon Inge .07 .20
114 Tony Clark .07 .20
115 Brian Moehler .07 .20
116 Juan Encarnacion .07 .20
117 Damion Easley .07 .20
118 Roger Cedeno .07 .20
119 Jeff Weaver .07 .20
120 Matt Lawton .07 .20
121 Jay Canizaro .07 .20
122 Eric Milton .07 .20
123 Corey Koskie .07 .20
124 Mark Redman .07 .20
125 Jacque Jones .07 .20
126 Brad Radke .07 .20
127 Cristian Guzman .07 .20
128 Joe Mays .07 .20
129 Denny Hocking .07 .20
130 Frank Thomas .20 .50
131 David Wells .07 .20
132 Ray Durham .07 .20
133 Paul Konerko .07 .20
134 Joe Crede .20 .50
135 Jim Parque .07 .20
136 Carlos Lee .07 .20
137 Magglio Ordonez .07 .20
138 Sandy Alomar Jr. .07 .20
139 Chris Singleton .07 .20
140 Jose Valentin .07 .20
141 Roger Clemens .40 1.00
142 Derek Jeter .50 1.25
143 Orlando Hernandez .07 .20
144 Tino Martinez .10 .30
145 Bernie Williams .10 .30
146 Jorge Posada .10 .30
147 Mariano Rivera .20 .50
148 David Justice .07 .20
149 Paul O'Neill .10 .30
150 Mike Mussina .10 .30
151 Christian Parker RC .20 .50
152 Andy Pettitte .10 .30
153 Alfonso Soriano .10 .30
154 Jeff Bagwell .10 .30
155 Morgan Ensberg RC .75 2.00
156 Daryle Ward .07 .20
157 Craig Biggio .10 .30
158 Richard Hidalgo .07 .20
159 Shane Reynolds .07 .20
160 Scott Elarton .07 .20
161 Julio Lugo .07 .20
162 Moises Alou .07 .20
163 Lance Berkman .07 .20
164 Chipper Jones .20 .50
165 Greg Maddux .30 .75
166 Javy Lopez .07 .20
167 Andruw Jones .10 .30
168 Rafael Furcal .07 .20
169 Brian Jordan .07 .20
170 Wes Helms .07 .20
171 Tom Glavine .10 .30
172 B.J. Surhoff .07 .20
173 John Smoltz .10 .30
174 Quilvio Veras .07 .20
175 Rico Brogna .07 .20
176 Jeromy Burnitz .07 .20
177 Jeff D'Amico .07 .20
178 Geoff Jenkins .07 .20
179 Henry Blanco .07 .20
180 Mark Loretta .07 .20
181 Richie Sexson .07 .20
182 Jimmy Haynes .07 .20
183 Jeffrey Hammonds .07 .20
184 Ron Belliard .07 .20
185 Tyler Houston .07 .20
186 Mark McGwire .50 1.25
187 Rick Ankiel .07 .20
188 Darryl Kile .07 .20
189 Jim Edmonds .07 .20
190 Mike Matheny .07 .20
191 Edgar Renteria .07 .20
192 Ray Lankford .07 .20
193 Garrett Stephenson .07 .20
194 J.D. Drew .07 .20
195 Fernando Vina .07 .20
196 Dustin Hermanson .07 .20
197 Sammy Sosa .20 .50
198 Corey Patterson .07 .20
199 Jon Lieber .07 .20
200 Kerry Wood .07 .20
201 Todd Hundley .07 .20
202 Kevin Tapani .07 .20
203 Rondell White .07 .20
204 Eric Young .07 .20
205 Matt Stairs .07 .20
206 Bill Mueller .07 .20
207 Randy Johnson .20 .50
208 Mark Grace .10 .30
209 Jay Bell .07 .20
210 Curt Schilling .07 .20
211 Erubiel Durazo .07 .20
212 Luis Gonzalez .07 .20
213 Steve Finley .07 .20
214 Matt Williams .07 .20
215 Reggie Sanders .07 .20
216 Tony Womack .07 .20
217 Gary Sheffield .07 .20
218 Kevin Brown .07 .20
219 Adrian Beltre .07 .20
220 Shawn Green .07 .20
221 Darren Dreifort .07 .20
222 Chan Ho Park .20 .50
223 Eric Karros .30 .75
224 Alex Cora .07 .20
225 Mark Grudzielanek .07 .20
226 Andy Ashby .07 .20
227 Vladimir Guerrero .20 .50
228 Tony Armas Jr. .07 .20
229 Fernando Tatis .07 .20
230 Jose Vidro .07 .20
231 Javier Vazquez .07 .20
232 Lee Stevens .07 .20
233 Milton Bradley .07 .20
234 Carl Pavano .07 .20
235 Peter Bergeron .07 .20
236 Wilton Guerrero .07 .20
237 Ugueth Urbina .07 .20
238 Barry Bonds .50 1.25
239 Livan Hernandez .07 .20
240 Jeff Kent .07 .20
241 Pedro Feliz .07 .20
242 Bobby Estalella .07 .20
243 J.T. Snow .07 .20
244 Shawn Estes .07 .20
245 Robb Nen .07 .20
246 Rich Aurilia .07 .20
247 Russ Ortiz .07 .20
248 Preston Wilson .07 .20
249 Brad Penny .07 .20
250 Cliff Floyd .07 .20
251 A.J. Burnett .07 .20
252 Mike Lowell .07 .20
253 Luis Castillo .07 .20
254 Ryan Dempster .07 .20
255 Derrek Lee .10 .30
256 Charles Johnson .07 .20
257 Pablo Ozuna .07 .20
258 Antonio Alfonseca .07 .20
259 Mike Piazza .30 .75
260 Robin Ventura .07 .20
261 Al Leiter .07 .20
262 Timo Perez .07 .20
263 Edgardo Alfonzo .07 .20
264 Jay Payton .07 .20
265 Tsuyoshi Shinjo RC .20 .50
266 Todd Zeile .07 .20
267 Armando Benitez .07 .20
268 Glendon Rusch .07 .20
269 Rey Ordonez .07 .20
270 Kevin Appier .07 .20
271 Tony Gwynn .25 .60
272 Phil Nevin .07 .20
273 Mark Kotsay .07 .20
274 Ryan Klesko .07 .20
275 Adam Eaton .07 .20
276 Mike Darr .07 .20
277 Damian Jackson .07 .20
278 Woody Williams .07 .20
279 Chris Gomez .07 .20
280 Trevor Hoffman .07 .20
281 Xavier Nady .07 .20
282 Scott Rolen .10 .30
283 Bruce Chen .07 .20
284 Pat Burrell .07 .20
285 Mike Lieberthal .07 .20
286 Brandon Duckworth RC .20 .50
287 Travis Lee .07 .20
288 Bobby Abreu .07 .20
289 Jimmy Rollins .07 .20
290 Robert Person .07 .20
291 Randy Wolf .07 .20
292 Jason Kendall .07 .20
293 Derek Bell .07 .20
294 Brian Giles .07 .20
295 Kris Benson .07 .20
296 John VanderWal .07 .20
297 Todd Ritchie .07 .20
298 Warren Morris .07 .20
299 Kevin Young .07 .20
300 Francisco Cordova .07 .20
301 Aramis Ramirez .07 .20
302 Ken Griffey Jr. .40 1.00
303 Pete Harnisch .07 .20
304 Aaron Boone .07 .20
305 Sean Casey .07 .20
306 Jackson Melian RC .20 .50
307 Rob Bell .07 .20
308 Barry Larkin .10 .30
309 Dmitri Young .07 .20
310 Danny Graves .07 .20
311 Pokey Reese .07 .20
312 Leo Estrella .07 .20
313 Todd Helton .10 .30
314 Mike Hampton .07 .20
315 Juan Pierre .07 .20
316 Brent Mayne .07 .20
317 Larry Walker .07 .20
318 Denny Neagle .07 .20
319 Jeff Cirillo .07 .20
320 Pedro Astacio .07 .20
321 Todd Hollandsworth .07 .20
322 Neifi Perez .07 .20
323 Ron Gant .07 .20
324 Todd Walker .07 .20
325 Alex Rodriguez CL .15 .40
326 Ken Griffey Jr. CL .25 .60
327 Mark McGwire CL .25 .60
328 Pedro Martinez CL .10 .30
329 Derek Jeter CL .25 .60
330 Mike Piazza CL .20 .50

2001 Upper Deck MVP Authentic Griffey

STATED ODDS 1:288
STATED PRINT RUNS LISTED BELOW
B Ken Griffey Jr. Bat 6.00 15.00
C Ken Griffey Jr. Cap 15.00 40.00
J Ken Griffey Jr. Jsy 6.00 15.00
S Ken Griffey Jr. AU 60.00 150.00
U Ken Griffey Jr. Uni 6.00 15.00
GB K.Griffey Jr. Gold Bat/30 60.00 120.00
GC K.Griffey Gold Cap/30 60.00 120.00
GJ K.Griffey Jr. Gold Jsy/30 60.00 120.00
GS K.Griffey Gold AU/30 125.00 200.00
CGR Griffey 20.00 50.00
A.Rod Jsy/100
CGS Griffey 15.00 40.00
Sosa Jsy/100
CGT Griffey/Thomas Jsy/100 15.00 40.00

2001 Upper Deck MVP Drawing Power

COMPLETE SET (10) 10.00 25.00
STATED ODDS 1:12
DP1 Mark McGwire 2.50 6.00
DP2 Vladimir Guerrero 1.00 2.50
DP3 Manny Ramirez Sox 1.00 2.50
DP4 Frank Thomas 1.00 2.50
DP5 Ken Griffey Jr. 2.00 5.00
DP6 Alex Rodriguez 1.25 3.00
DP7 Mike Piazza 1.50 4.00
DP8 Derek Jeter 2.50 6.00
DP9 Sammy Sosa 1.00 2.50
DP10 Todd Helton 1.00 2.50

2001 Upper Deck MVP Game Souvenirs Bat Duos

STATED ODDS 1:144
B3K T.Gwynn/C.Ripken 10.00 25.00
BDV C.Delgado/J.Vidro 1.25 3.00
BGS K.Griffey Jr./S.Sosa 6.00 15.00
BHR J.Canseco/K.Griffey Jr. 6.00 15.00
BJF C.Jones/R.Furcal 3.00 8.00
BJJ A.Jones/C.Jones 3.00 8.00
BOW P.O'Neill/B.Williams 2.00 5.00
BRM A.Rodriguez/E.Martinez 4.00 10.00
BRP I.Rodriguez/R.Palmeiro 2.00 5.00
BRR A.Rodriguez/I.Rodriguez 4.00 10.00
BTG J.Thome/K.Griffey Jr. 6.00 15.00
BTO F.Thomas/M.Ordonez 3.00 8.00
BTS F.Thomas/S.Sosa 3.00 8.00
BWA K.Wood/R.Ankiel 1.25 3.00

2001 Upper Deck MVP Game Souvenirs Batting Glove

STATED ODDS 1:96 HOBBY
SP PRINT RUNS PROVIDED BY UPPER DECK
SP'S ARE NOT SERIAL-NUMBERED
GAR Alex Rodriguez 10.00 25.00
GBB Barry Bonds 20.00 50.00
GCJ Chipper Jones 6.00 15.00
GCR Cal Ripken 10.00 25.00
GEM Edgar Martinez 6.00 15.00
GFM Fred McGriff 6.00 15.00
GFT Frank Thomas 6.00 15.00
GGM Greg Maddux SP/95 * 40.00 80.00
GIR Ivan Rodriguez 6.00 15.00
GJG Juan Gonzalez 4.00 10.00
GJL Javy Lopez 4.00 10.00
GKG Ken Griffey Jr. 10.00 25.00
GMT Miguel Tejada 4.00 10.00
GMV Mo Vaughn 4.00 10.00
GRP Rafael Palmeiro 6.00 15.00
GSS Sammy Sosa 6.00 15.00
GTOG Tony Gwynn SP/200 * 15.00 40.00
GTRG Troy Glaus 4.00 10.00

2001 Upper Deck MVP Super Tools

COMPLETE SET (20) 15.00 40.00
STATED ODDS 1:6
ST1 Ken Griffey Jr. 2.00 5.00
ST2 Carlos Delgado .40 1.00
ST3 Alex Rodriguez 1.25 3.00
ST4 Troy Glaus .40 1.00
ST5 Jeff Bagwell .60 1.50
ST6 Ichiro Suzuki 5.00 12.00
ST7 Derek Jeter 2.50 6.00
ST8 Jim Edmonds .40 1.00
ST9 Vladimir Guerrero 1.00 2.50
ST10 Jason Giambi .40 1.00
ST11 Todd Helton .60 1.50
ST12 Cal Ripken 3.00 8.00
ST13 Barry Bonds 2.50 6.00
ST14 Nomar Garciaparra 1.50 4.00
ST15 Randy Johnson 1.00 2.50
ST16 Jermaine Dye .40 1.00
ST17 Andruw Jones .60 1.50
ST18 Ivan Rodriguez .60 1.50
ST19 Sammy Sosa 1.00 2.50
ST20 Pedro Martinez .60 1.50

2002 Upper Deck MVP

COMPLETE SET (301) 15.00 40.00
1 Darin Erstad .07 .20
2 Ramon Ortiz .07 .20
3 Garret Anderson .07 .20
4 Jarrod Washburn .07 .20
5 Troy Glaus .07 .20
6 Brendan Donnelly RC .20 .50
7 Troy Percival .07 .20
8 Tim Salmon .10 .30
9 Aaron Sele .07 .20
10 Brad Fullmer .07 .20
11 Scott Hatteberg .07 .20
12 Barry Zito .07 .20
13 Tim Hudson .07 .20
14 Miguel Tejada .07 .20
15 Jermaine Dye .07 .20
16 Mark Mulder .07 .20
17 Eric Chavez .07 .20
18 Terrence Long .07 .20
19 Carlos Pena .07 .20
20 David Justice .07 .20
21 Jeremy Giambi .07 .20
22 Shannon Stewart .07 .20
23 Raul Mondesi .07 .20
24 Chris Carpenter .07 .20
25 Carlos Delgado .07 .20
26 Mike Sirotka .07 .20
27 Reed Johnson RC .30 .75
28 Darrin Fletcher .07 .20
29 Jose Cruz Jr. .07 .20
30 Vernon Wells .07 .20
31 Tanyon Sturtze .07 .20
32 Toby Hall .07 .20
33 Brent Abernathy .07 .20
34 Ben Grieve .07 .20
35 Joe Kennedy .07 .20
36 Dewon Brazelton .07 .20
37 Aubrey Huff .07 .20
38 Steve Cox .07 .20
39 Greg Vaughn .07 .20
40 Brady Anderson .07 .20
41 Chuck Finley .07 .20
42 Jim Thome .10 .30
43 Russell Branyan .07 .20
44 C.C. Sabathia .07 .20
45 Matt Lawton .07 .20
46 Omar Vizquel .10 .30
47 Bartolo Colon .07 .20
48 Alex Escobar .07 .20
49 Ellis Burks .07 .20
50 Bret Boone .07 .20
51 John Olerud .07 .20
52 Jeff Cirillo .07 .20
53 Ichiro Suzuki .40 1.00
54 Kazuhiro Sasaki .07 .20
55 Freddy Garcia .07 .20
56 Edgar Martinez .10 .30
57 Matt Thornton RC .20 .50
58 Mike Cameron .07 .20
59 Carlos Guillen .07 .20
60 Jeff Conine .07 .20
61 Tony Batista .07 .20
62 Jason Johnson .07 .20
63 Melvin Mora .07 .20
64 Brian Roberts .07 .20
65 Josh Towers .07 .20

66 Steve Bechler RC .20 .50
67 Jerry Hairston Jr. .07 .20
68 Chris Richard .07 .20
69 Alex Rodriguez .25 .60
70 Chan Ho Park .07 .20
71 Ivan Rodriguez .10 .30
72 Jeff Zimmerman .07 .20
73 Mark Teixeira .20 .50
74 Gabe Kapler .07 .20
75 Frank Catalanotto .07 .20
76 Rafael Palmeiro .10 .30
77 Doug Davis .07 .20
78 Carl Everett .07 .20
79 Pedro Martinez .10 .30
80 Nomar Garciaparra .30 .75
81 Tony Clark .07 .20
82 Trot Nixon .07 .20
83 Manny Ramirez .10 .30
84 Josh Hancock RC .25 .60
85 Johnny Damon Sox .10 .30
86 Jose Offerman .07 .20
87 Rich Garces .07 .20
88 Shea Hillenbrand .07 .20
89 Carlos Beltran .07 .20
90 Mike Sweeney .07 .20
91 Jeff Suppan .07 .20
92 Joe Randa .07 .20
93 Chuck Knoblauch .07 .20
94 Mark Quinn .07 .20
95 Neifi Perez .07 .20
96 Carlos Febles .07 .20
97 Miguel Asencio RC .20 .50
98 Michael Tucker .07 .20
99 Dean Palmer .07 .20
100 Jose Lima .07 .20
101 Craig Paquette .07 .20
102 Dmitri Young .07 .20
103 Bobby Higginson .07 .20
104 Jeff Weaver .07 .20
105 Matt Anderson .07 .20
106 Damion Easley .07 .20
107 Eric Milton .07 .20
108 Doug Mientkiewicz .07 .20
109 Cristian Guzman .07 .20
110 Brad Radke .07 .20
111 Torii Hunter .07 .20
112 Corey Koskie .07 .20
113 Joe Mays .07 .20
114 Jacque Jones .07 .20
115 David Ortiz .20 .50
116 Kevin Frederick RC .20 .50
117 Magglio Ordonez .07 .20
118 Ray Durham .07 .20
119 Mark Buehrle .07 .20
120 Jon Garland .07 .20
121 Paul Konerko .07 .20
122 Todd Ritchie .07 .20
123 Frank Thomas .20 .50
124 Edwin Almonte RC .20 .50
125 Carlos Lee .07 .20
126 Kenny Lofton .07 .20
127 Roger Clemens .40 1.00
128 Derek Jeter .50 1.25
129 Jorge Posada .10 .30
130 Bernie Williams .10 .30
131 Mike Mussina .10 .30
132 Alfonso Soriano .07 .20
133 Robin Ventura .07 .20
134 John Vander Wal .07 .20
135 Jason Giambi Yankees .07 .20
136 Mariano Rivera .20 .50
137 Rondell White .07 .20
138 Jeff Bagwell .10 .30
139 Wade Miller .07 .20
140 Richard Hidalgo .07 .20
141 Julio Lugo .07 .20
142 Roy Oswalt .07 .20
143 Rodrigo Rosario RC .20 .50
144 Lance Berkman .07 .20
145 Craig Biggio .10 .30
146 Shane Reynolds .07 .20
147 John Smoltz .10 .30
148 Chipper Jones .20 .50
149 Gary Sheffield .07 .20
150 Rafael Furcal .07 .20
151 Greg Maddux .30 .75
152 Tom Glavine .10 .30
153 Andruw Jones .10 .30
154 John Ennis RC .20 .50
155 Vinny Castilla .07 .20
156 Marcus Giles .07 .20
157 Javy Lopez .07 .20
158 Richie Sexson .07 .20
159 Geoff Jenkins .07 .20
160 Jeffrey Hammonds .07 .20
161 Alex Ochoa .07 .20
162 Ben Sheets .07 .20
163 Jose Hernandez .07 .20
164 Eric Young .07 .20
165 Luis Martinez RC .20 .50
166 Albert Pujols .40 1.00
167 Darryl Kile .07 .20
168 So Taguchi RC .20 .50
169 Jim Edmonds .07 .20
170 Fernando Vina .07 .20
171 Matt Morris .07 .20
172 J.D. Drew .07 .20
173 Bud Smith .07 .20
174 Edgar Renteria .07 .20
175 Placido Polanco .07 .20
176 Tino Martinez .10 .30
177 Sammy Sosa .20 .50
178 Moises Alou .07 .20
179 Kerry Wood .07 .20
180 Delino DeShields .07 .20
181 Alex Gonzalez .07 .20
182 Jon Lieber .07 .20
183 Fred McGriff .10 .30
184 Corey Patterson .07 .20
185 Mark Prior .10 .30
186 Tom Gordon .07 .20
187 Francis Beltran RC .20 .50
188 Randy Johnson .20 .50
189 Luis Gonzalez .07 .20
190 Matt Williams .07 .20
191 Mark Grace .10 .30
192 Curt Schilling .07 .20
193 Doug Devore RC .20 .50
194 Erubiel Durazo .07 .20
195 Steve Finley .07 .20
196 Craig Counsell .07 .20
197 Shawn Green .07 .20
198 Kevin Brown .07 .20
199 Paul LoDuca .07 .20
200 Brian Jordan .07 .20
201 Andy Ashby .07 .20
202 Darren Dreifort .07 .20
203 Adrian Beltre .07 .20
204 Victor Alvarez RC .20 .50
205 Eric Karros .07 .20
206 Hideo Nomo .20 .50
207 Vladimir Guerrero .20 .50
208 Javier Vazquez .07 .20
209 Michael Barrett .07 .20
210 Jose Vidro .07 .20
211 Brad Wilkerson .07 .20
212 Tony Armas Jr. .07 .20
213 Eric Good RC .20 .50
214 Orlando Cabrera .07 .20
215 Lee Stevens .07 .20
216 Jeff Kent .07 .20
217 Rich Aurilia .07 .20
218 Robb Nen .07 .20
219 Calvin Murray .07 .20
220 Russ Ortiz .07 .20
221 Deivis Santos .07 .20
222 Marvin Benard .07 .20
223 Jason Schmidt .07 .20
224 Reggie Sanders .07 .20
225 Barry Bonds .50 1.25
226 Brad Penny .07 .20
227 Cliff Floyd .07 .20
228 Mike Lowell .07 .20
229 Derrek Lee .10 .30
230 Ryan Dempster .07 .20
231 Josh Beckett .07 .20
232 Hansel Izquierdo RC .20 .50
233 Preston Wilson .07 .20
234 A.J. Burnett .07 .20
235 Charles Johnson .07 .20
236 Mike Piazza .30 .75
237 Al Leiter .07 .20
238 Jay Payton .07 .20
239 Roger Cedeno .07 .20
240 Jeromy Burnitz .07 .20
241 Roberto Alomar .10 .30
242 Mo Vaughn .07 .20
243 Shawn Estes .07 .20
244 Armando Benitez .07 .20
245 Tyler Yates RC .20 .50
246 Phil Nevin .07 .20
247 D'Angelo Jimenez .07 .20
248 Ramon Vazquez .07 .20
249 Bubba Trammell .07 .20
250 Trevor Hoffman .07 .20
251 Ben Howard RC .20 .50
252 Mark Kotsay .07 .20
253 Ray Lankford .07 .20
254 Ryan Klesko .07 .20
255 Scott Rolen .10 .30
256 Robert Person .07 .20
257 Jimmy Rollins .07 .20
258 Pat Burrell .07 .20
259 Anderson Machado RC .20 .50
260 Randy Wolf .07 .20
261 Travis Lee .07 .20
262 Mike Lieberthal .07 .20
263 Doug Glanville .07 .20
264 Bobby Abreu .07 .20
265 Brian Giles .07 .20
266 Kris Benson .07 .20
267 Aramis Ramirez .07 .20
268 Kevin Young .07 .20
269 Jack Wilson .07 .20
270 Mike Williams .07 .20
271 Jimmy Anderson .07 .20
272 Jason Kendall .07 .20
273 Pokey Reese .07 .20
274 Rob Mackowiak .07 .20
275 Sean Casey .07 .20
276 Juan Encarnacion .07 .20
277 Austin Kearns .07 .20
278 Danny Graves .07 .20
279 Ken Griffey Jr. .40 1.00
280 Barry Larkin .10 .30
281 Todd Walker .07 .20
282 Elmer Dessens .07 .20
283 Aaron Boone .07 .20
284 Adam Dunn .07 .20
285 Larry Walker .07 .20
286 Rene Reyes RC .20 .50
287 Juan Uribe .07 .20
288 Mike Hampton .07 .20
289 Todd Helton .10 .30
290 Juan Pierre .07 .20
291 Denny Neagle .07 .20
292 Jose Ortiz .07 .20
293 Todd Zeile .07 .20
294 Ben Petrick .07 .20
295 Ken Griffey Jr. CL .25 .60
296 Derek Jeter CL .25 .60
297 Sammy Sosa CL .10 .30
298 Ichiro Suzuki CL .20 .50
299 Barry Bonds CL .30 .75
300 Alex Rodriguez CL .15 .40
301 Kazuhisa Ishii RC .20 .50

2002 Upper Deck MVP Silver

*SILVER STARS: 12.5X TO 30X BASIC CARDS
*SILVER ROOKIES: 6X TO 15X BASIC
RANDOM INSERTS IN ALL PACKS
STATED PRINT RUN 100 SERIAL #'d SETS

2002 Upper Deck MVP Game Souvenirs Bat

STATED ODDS 1:144 HOBBY
BAR Alex Rodriguez 10.00 25.00
BBG Brian Giles 6.00 15.00
BBW Bernie Williams 8.00 20.00
BDM Doug Mientkiewicz 6.00 15.00
BEM Edgar Martinez 8.00 20.00
BGV Greg Vaughn 6.00 15.00
BIR Ivan Rodriguez 8.00 20.00
BJK Jeff Kent 6.00 15.00
BJT Jim Thome 8.00 20.00
BKG Ken Griffey Jr. 10.00 25.00
BLG Luis Gonzalez 6.00 15.00
BLW Larry Walker 6.00 15.00
BMO Magglio Ordonez 6.00 15.00
BRK Ryan Klesko 6.00 15.00
BSG Shawn Green 6.00 15.00
BSS Sammy Sosa 8.00 20.00

2002 Upper Deck MVP Game Souvenirs Bat Jersey Combos

STATED ODDS 1:144 HOBBY
GOLD RANDOM INSERTS IN PACKS
GOLD PRINT RUN 25 SERIAL #'d SETS
NO GOLD PRICING DUE TO SCARCITY
CAB Adrian Beltre 8.00 20.00
CAR Alex Rodriguez 20.00 50.00
CBG Brian Giles 8.00 20.00
CCD Carlos Delgado Bat-Pants 8.00 20.00
CCJ Chipper Jones 15.00 40.00
CDE Darin Erstad 8.00 20.00
CEA Edgardo Alfonzo 8.00 20.00
CIR Ivan Rodriguez 10.00 25.00
CJG Jason Giambi 8.00 20.00
CJK Jeff Kent 8.00 20.00
CJT Jim Thome 10.00 25.00
CKG Ken Griffey Jr. 20.00 50.00
CLG Luis Gonzalez 8.00 20.00
CMO Magglio Ordonez 8.00 20.00
CMP Mike Piazza 20.00 50.00
CRJ Randy Johnson 15.00 40.00
CRP Rafael Palmeiro 10.00 25.00
CRV Robin Ventura 8.00 20.00
CSG Shawn Green 8.00 20.00
CSR Scott Rolen 10.00 25.00
CSS Sammy Sosa 15.00 40.00
CTH Todd Helton 10.00 25.00
CTZ Todd Zeile 8.00 20.00

2002 Upper Deck MVP Game Souvenirs Jersey

STATED ODDS 1:48 HOBBY/RETAIL
ASTERISKS PERCEIVED AS LARGER SUPPLY
JAB Adrian Beltre 4.00 10.00
JAR Alex Rodriguez 6.00 15.00
JCD Carlos Delgado Pants 4.00 10.00
JDE Darin Erstad 4.00 10.00
JEM Edgar Martinez 6.00 15.00
JFT Frank Thomas 6.00 15.00
JGA Garret Anderson 4.00 10.00
JIR Ivan Rodriguez 6.00 15.00
JJB Jeff Bagwell Pants 6.00 15.00
JJB Jeromy Burnitz 4.00 10.00
JJG Juan Gonzalez 4.00 10.00
JJK Jeff Kent 4.00 10.00
JJP Jay Payton SP 6.00 15.00
JJT Jim Thome SP 10.00 25.00
JKL Kenny Lofton 4.00 10.00
JMK Mark Kotsay 4.00 10.00
JMP Mike Piazza 10.00 25.00
JOV Omar Vizquel Pants * 6.00 15.00
JPK Paul Konerko SP 6.00 15.00
JPW Preston Wilson 4.00 10.00
JRA Roberto Alomar Pants 6.00 15.00
JRC Roger Clemens 10.00 25.00
JRF Rafael Furcal 4.00 10.00
JRV Robin Ventura 4.00 10.00
JSR Scott Rolen 6.00 15.00
JTHO Trevor Hoffman 4.00 10.00
JTHU Tim Hudson 4.00 10.00
JTS Tim Salmon 6.00 15.00
JTZ Todd Zeile 4.00 10.00

2002 Upper Deck MVP Ichiro A Season to Remember

COMPLETE SET (10) 12.50 30.00
COMMON CARD (I1-I10) 1.25 3.00
STATED ODDS 1:12 HOBBY/RETAIL

2003 Upper Deck MVP

COMP.FACT.SET (330) 25.00 40.00
COMPLETE LO SET (220) 10.00 25.00
COMPLETE HI SET (110) 6.00 15.00
COMMON CARD (1-330) .07 .20
COMMON RC .25 .60
CARDS 221-330 DIST.IN FACTORY SETS
1 Troy Glaus .07 .20
2 Darin Erstad .07 .20
3 Jarrod Washburn .07 .20
4 Francisco Rodriguez .12 .30
5 Garret Anderson .07 .20
6 Tim Salmon .07 .20
7 Adam Kennedy .07 .20
8 Randy Johnson .20 .50
9 Luis Gonzalez .07 .20
10 Curt Schilling .12 .30
11 Junior Spivey .07 .20
12 Craig Counsell .07 .20
13 Mark Grace .12 .30
14 Steve Finley .07 .20
15 Javy Lopez .07 .20
16 Rafael Furcal .07 .20
17 John Smoltz .20 .50
18 Greg Maddux .25 .60
19 Chipper Jones .20 .50
20 Gary Sheffield .07 .20
21 Andruw Jones .07 .20
22 Tony Batista .07 .20
23 Geronimo Gil .07 .20
24 Jay Gibbons .07 .20
25 Rodrigo Lopez .07 .20
26 Chris Singleton .07 .20
27 Melvin Mora .07 .20
28 Jeff Conine .07 .20
29 Nomar Garciaparra .12 .30
30 Pedro Martinez .12 .30
31 Manny Ramirez .20 .50
32 Shea Hillenbrand .07 .20
33 Johnny Damon .12 .30
34 Jason Varitek .20 .50
35 Derek Lowe .07 .20
36 Trot Nixon .07 .20
37 Sammy Sosa .20 .50
38 Kerry Wood .07 .20
39 Mark Prior .12 .30
40 Moises Alou .07 .20
41 Corey Patterson .07 .20
42 Hee Seop Choi .07 .20
43 Mark Bellhorn .07 .20
44 Frank Thomas .20 .50
45 Mark Buehrle .12 .30
46 Magglio Ordonez .12 .30
47 Carlos Lee .07 .20
48 Paul Konerko .12 .30
49 Joe Borchard .07 .20
50 Joe Crede .07 .20
51 Ken Griffey Jr. .40 1.00
52 Adam Dunn .12 .30
53 Austin Kearns .07 .20
54 Aaron Boone .07 .20
55 Sean Casey .07 .20
56 Danny Graves .07 .20
57 Russell Branyan .07 .20
58 Matt Lawton .07 .20
59 C.C. Sabathia .12 .30
60 Omar Vizquel .12 .30
61 Brandon Phillips .07 .20
62 Karim Garcia .07 .20
63 Ellis Burks .07 .20
64 Cliff Lee .50 1.25
65 Todd Helton .12 .30
66 Larry Walker .12 .30
67 Jay Payton .07 .20
68 Brent Butler .07 .20
69 Juan Uribe .07 .20
70 Jason Jennings .07 .20
71 Denny Stark .07 .20
72 Dmitri Young .07 .20
73 Carlos Pena .12 .30
74 Andres Torres .07 .20
75 Andy Van Hekken .07 .20
76 George Lombard .07 .20
77 Eric Munson .07 .20
78 Bobby Higginson .07 .20
79 Luis Castillo .07 .20
80 A.J. Burnett .07 .20
81 Juan Encarnacion .07 .20
82 Ivan Rodriguez .12 .30
83 Mike Lowell .07 .20
84 Josh Beckett .07 .20
85 Brad Penny .07 .20
86 Craig Biggio .12 .30
87 Jeff Kent .07 .20
88 Morgan Ensberg .07 .20
89 Daryle Ward .07 .20
90 Jeff Bagwell .12 .30
91 Roy Oswalt .12 .30
92 Lance Berkman .12 .30
93 Mike Sweeney .07 .20
94 Carlos Beltran .12 .30
95 Raul Ibanez .12 .30
96 Carlos Febles .07 .20
97 Joe Randa .07 .20
98 Shawn Green .07 .20
99 Kevin Brown .07 .20
100 Paul Lo Duca .07 .20
101 Adrian Beltre .20 .50
102 Eric Gagne .07 .20
103 Kazuhisa Ishii .07 .20
104 Odalis Perez .07 .20
105 Brian Jordan .07 .20
106 Geoff Jenkins .07 .20
107 Richie Sexson .07 .20
108 Ben Sheets .07 .20
109 Alex Sanchez .07 .20
110 Eric Young .07 .20
111 Jose Hernandez .07 .20
112 Torii Hunter .07 .20
113 Eric Milton .07 .20
114 Corey Koskie .07 .20
115 Doug Mientkiewicz .07 .20
116 A.J. Pierzynski .07 .20
117 Jacque Jones .07 .20
118 Cristian Guzman .07 .20
119 Bartolo Colon .07 .20
120 Brad Wilkerson .07 .20
121 Michael Barrett .07 .20
122 Vladimir Guerrero .12 .30
123 Jose Vidro .07 .20
124 Javier Vazquez .07 .20
125 Endy Chavez .07 .20
126 Roberto Alomar .12 .30
127 Mike Piazza .20 .50
128 Jeromy Burnitz .07 .20
129 Mo Vaughn .07 .20
130 Tom Glavine .12 .30
131 Al Leiter .07 .20
132 Armando Benitez .07 .20
133 Timo Perez .07 .20
134 Roger Clemens .25 .60
135 Derek Jeter .50 1.25
136 Jason Giambi .07 .20
137 Alfonso Soriano .12 .30
138 Bernie Williams .12 .30
139 Mike Mussina .12 .30
140 Jorge Posada .12 .30
141 Hideki Matsui RC 1.25 3.00
142 Robin Ventura .07 .20
143 David Wells .07 .20
144 Nick Johnson .07 .20
145 Tim Hudson .12 .30
146 Eric Chavez .07 .20
147 Barry Zito .12 .30
148 Miguel Tejada .12 .30
149 Jermaine Dye .07 .20
150 Mark Mulder .07 .20
151 Terrence Long .07 .20
152 Scott Hatteberg .07 .20
153 Marlon Byrd .07 .20
154 Jim Thome .12 .30
155 Marlon Anderson .07 .20
156 Vicente Padilla .07 .20
157 Bobby Abreu .07 .20
158 Jimmy Rollins .12 .30
159 Pat Burrell .07 .20
160 Brian Giles .07 .20
161 Aramis Ramirez .07 .20
162 Jason Kendall .07 .20
163 Josh Fogg .07 .20
164 Kip Wells .07 .20
165 Pokey Reese .07 .20
166 Kris Benson .07 .20
167 Ryan Klesko .07 .20
168 Brian Lawrence .07 .20
169 Mark Kotsay .07 .20
170 Jake Peavy .07 .20
171 Phil Nevin .07 .20
172 Sean Burroughs .07 .20
173 Trevor Hoffman .12 .30
174 Jason Schmidt .07 .20
175 Kirk Rueter .07 .20
176 Barry Bonds .30 .75
177 Pedro Feliz .07 .20
178 Rich Aurilia .07 .20
179 Benito Santiago .07 .20
180 J.T. Snow .07 .20
181 Robb Nen .07 .20
182 Ichiro Suzuki .25 .60
183 Edgar Martinez .12 .30
184 Bret Boone .07 .20
185 Freddy Garcia .07 .20
186 John Olerud .07 .20
187 Mike Cameron .07 .20
188 Joel Piniero .07 .20
189 Albert Pujols .25 .60
190 Matt Morris .07 .20
191 J.D. Drew .07 .20
192 Scott Rolen .12 .30
193 Tino Martinez .07 .20
194 Jim Edmonds .12 .30
195 Edgar Renteria .07 .20
196 Fernando Vina .07 .20
197 Jason Isringhausen .07 .20
198 Ben Grieve .07 .20
199 Carl Crawford .12 .30
200 Dewon Brazelton .07 .20
201 Aubrey Huff .07 .20
202 Jared Sandberg .07 .20
203 Steve Cox .07 .20
204 Carl Everett .07 .20
205 Kevin Mench .07 .20
206 Alex Rodriguez .25 .60
207 Rafael Palmeiro .12 .30
208 Michael Young .07 .20
209 Hank Blalock .07 .20
210 Juan Gonzalez .07 .20
211 Carlos Delgado .07 .20
212 Eric Hinske .07 .20
213 Josh Phelps .07 .20
214 Mark Hendrickson .07 .20
215 Roy Halladay .12 .30
216 Orlando Hudson .07 .20
217 Shannon Stewart .07 .20
218 Vernon Wells .07 .20
219 Ichiro Suzuki CL .25 .60
220 Jason Giambi CL .07 .20
221 Scott Spiezio .07 .20
222 Rich Fischer RC .25 .60
223 Bengie Molina .07 .20
224 David Eckstein .07 .20
225 Brandon Webb RC .75 2.00
226 Oscar Villarreal RC .25 .60
227 Rob Hammock RC .25 .60
228 Matt Kata RC .25 .60
229 Lyle Overbay .07 .20
230 Chris Capuano RC .25 .60
231 Horacio Ramirez .07 .20
232 Shane Reynolds .07 .20
233 Russ Ortiz .07 .20
234 Mike Hampton .07 .20
235 Mike Hessman RC .25 .60
236 Byung-Hyun Kim .07 .20
237 Freddy Sanchez .07 .20
238 Jason Shiell RC .25 .60
239 Ryan Cameron RC .25 .60
240 Todd Wellemeyer RC .25 .60
241 Joe Borowski .07 .20
242 Alex Gonzalez .07 .20
243 Jon Leicester RC .25 .60
244 David Sanders RC .25 .60
245 Roberto Alomar .12 .30
246 Barry Larkin .12 .30
247 Jhonny Peralta .07 .20
248 Zach Sorensen .07 .20
249 Jason Davis .07 .20
250 Coco Crisp .07 .20
251 Greg Vaughn .07 .20
252 Preston Wilson .07 .20
253 Denny Neagle .07 .20
254 Clint Barmes RC .60 1.50
255 Jeremy Bonderman RC 1.00 2.50
256 Wilfredo Ledezma RC .25 .60
257 Dontrelle Willis .07 .20
258 Alex Gonzalez .07 .20
259 Tommy Phelps .07 .20
260 Kirk Saarloos .07 .20
261 Colin Porter RC .25 .60
262 Nate Bland RC .25 .60
263 Jason Gilfillan RC .25 .60
264 Mike MacDougal .07 .20
265 Ken Harvey .07 .20
266 Brent Mayne .07 .20
267 Miguel Cabrera 1.00 2.50
268 Hideo Nomo .20 .50
269 Dave Roberts .12 .30
270 Fred McGriff .12 .30
271 Joe Thurston .07 .20
272 Royce Clayton .07 .20
273 Michael Nakamura RC .25 .60
274 Brad Radke .07 .20
275 Joe Mays .07 .20
276 Lew Ford RC .25 .60
277 Michael Cuddyer .07 .20
278 Luis Ayala RC .25 .60
279 Julio Manon RC .25 .60
280 Anthony Ferrari RC .25 .60
281 Livan Hernandez .07 .20
282 Jae Weong Seo .07 .20
283 Jose Reyes .20 .50
284 Tony Clark .07 .20
285 Ty Wigginton .07 .20
286 Cliff Floyd .07 .20
287 Jeremy Griffiths RC .25 .60
288 Jason Roach RC .25 .60
289 Jeff Duncan RC .25 .60
290 Phil Seibel RC .25 .60
291 Prentice Redman RC .25 .60
292 Jose Contreras RC .60 1.50
293 Ruben Sierra .07 .20
294 Andy Pettitte .12 .30
295 Aaron Boone .07 .20
296 Mariano Rivera .25 .60
297 Michel Hernandez RC .25 .60
298 Mike Neu RC .25 .60
299 Erubiel Durazo .07 .20
300 Billy McMillon .07 .20
301 Rich Harden .12 .30
302 David Bell .07 .20
303 Kevin Millwood .07 .20
304 Mike Lieberthal .07 .20
305 Jeremy Wedel RC .25 .60
306 Kenny Lofton .07 .20
307 Reggie Sanders .07 .20
308 Randall Simon .07 .20
309 Xavier Nady .07 .20
310 Rod Beck .07 .20
311 Miguel Ojeda RC .25 .60
312 Mark Loretta .07 .20
313 Edgardo Alfonzo .07 .20
314 Andres Galarraga .12 .30
315 Jose Cruz Jr. .07 .20
316 Jesse Foppert .07 .20
317 Kurt Ainsworth .07 .20
318 Dan Wilson .07 .20
319 Ben Davis .07 .20
320 Rocco Baldelli .07 .20
321 Al Martin .07 .20
322 Runelvys Hernandez .07 .20
323 Dan Haren RC 1.25 3.00
324 Bo Hart RC .25 .60
325 Einar Diaz .07 .20
326 Mike Lamb .07 .20
327 Aquilino Lopez RC .25 .60
328 Reed Johnson .07 .20
329 Diegomar Markwell RC .25 .60
330 Hideki Matsui CL 1.25 3.00

2003 Upper Deck MVP Black

*BLACK: 15X TO 40X BASIC
*BLACK RC'S: 6X TO 15X BASIC
RANDOM INSERTS IN HOBBY PACKS
STATED PRINT RUN 50 SERIAL #'d SETS

2003 Upper Deck MVP Gold

*GOLD: 10X TO 25X BASIC
*GOLD RC'S: 3X TO 8X BASIC
RANDOM INSERTS IN HOBBY PACKS
STATED PRINT RUN 125 SERIAL #'d SETS

2003 Upper Deck MVP Silver

*SILVER: 3X TO 8X BASIC
*SILVER RC'S: 1X TO 2.5X BASIC
STATED ODDS 1:12
ERRONEOUS 1:2 ODDS ON WRAPPER

2003 Upper Deck MVP Base-to-Base

STATED ODDS 1:488
CP R.Clemens M.Piazza 10.00 25.00
IG I.Suzuki K.Griffey Jr. 10.00 25.00
IJ I.Suzuki D.Jeter 10.00 25.00
JW D.Jeter B.Williams 10.00 25.00
MB M.McGwire B.Bonds 10.00 25.00
RJ A.Rodriguez D.Jeter 10.00 25.00

2003 Upper Deck MVP Celebration

B/WN 1955 AND 2002 #'d OF EACH CARD
*GOLD: 1.25X TO 3X BASIC
GOLD PRINT RUN 75 SERIAL #'d SETS
1 Yogi Berra MVP/1955 1.50 4.00
2 Mickey Mantle MVP/1956 5.00 12.00
3 Mickey Mantle MVP/1957 5.00 12.00
4 Mickey Mantle MVP/1962 5.00 12.00
5 Roger Clemens MVP/1986 2.00 5.00
6 Rickey Henderson MVP/1990 1.50 4.00
7 Frank Thomas MVP/1993 1.50 4.00
8 Mo Vaughn MVP/1995 .60 1.50
9 Juan Gonzalez MVP/1996 .60 1.50
10 Ken Griffey Jr. MVP/1997 3.00 8.00
11 Juan Gonzalez MVP/1998 .60 1.50
12 Ivan Rodriguez MVP/1998 1.00 2.50
13 Jason Giambi MVP/2000 .60 1.50
14 Ichiro Suzuki MVP/2001 2.00 5.00
15 Miguel Tejada MVP/2002 1.00 2.50
16 Barry Bonds MVP/1990 2.50 6.00
17 Barry Bonds MVP/1992 2.50 6.00
18 Barry Bonds MVP/1993 2.50 6.00
19 Jeff Bagwell MVP/1994 1.00 2.50
20 Barry Larkin MVP/1995 1.00 2.50
21 Larry Walker MVP/1997 1.00 2.50
22 Sammy Sosa MVP/1998 1.50 4.00
23 Chipper Jones MVP/1999 1.50 4.00
24 Jeff Kent MVP/2000 .60 1.50
25 Barry Bonds MVP/2001 2.50 6.00
26 Barry Bonds MVP/2002 2.50 6.00
27 Ken Griffey Sr. AS/1980 .60 1.50
28 Roger Clemens AS/1986 2.00 5.00
29 Ken Griffey Jr. AS/1992 3.00 8.00
30 Fred McGriff AS/1994 1.00 2.50
31 Jeff Conine AS/1995 .60 1.50
32 Mike Piazza AS/1996 1.50 4.00
33 Sandy Alomar Jr. AS/1997 .60 1.50
34 Roberto Alomar AS/1998 1.00 2.50
35 Pedro Martinez AS/1999 1.00 2.50
36 Derek Jeter AS/2000 4.00 10.00
37 Rickey Henderson ALCS/1989 1.50 4.00
38 Roberto Alomar ALCS/1992 1.00 2.50
39 Bernie Williams ALCS/1996 1.00 2.50
40 Marquis Grissom ALCS/1997 .60 1.50
41 David Wells ALCS/1998 .60 1.50
42 Orlando Hernandez ALCS/1999 .60 1.50
43 David Justice ALCS/2000 .60 1.50
44 Andy Pettitte ALCS/2001 1.00 2.50
45 Adam Kennedy ALCS/2002 .60 1.50
46 John Smoltz NLCS/1992 1.50 4.00
47 Curt Schilling NLCS/1993 1.00 2.50
48 Javy Lopez NLCS/1996 .60 1.50
49 Livan Hernandez NLCS/1997 .60 1.50
50 Sterling Hitchcock NLCS/1998 .60 1.50
51 Mike Hampton NLCS/2000 .60 1.50
52 Craig Counsell NLCS/2001 .60 1.50
53 Benito Santiago NLCS/2002 .60 1.50
54 Tom Glavine WS/1995 1.00 2.50
55 Livan Hernandez WS/1997 .60 1.50
56 Mariano Rivera WS/1999 2.00 5.00
57 Derek Jeter WS/2000 4.00 10.00
58 Randy Johnson WS/2001 1.50 4.00
59 Curt Schilling WS/2001 1.00 2.50
60 Troy Glaus WS/2002 .60 1.50
61 Yogi Berra MM/1951 1.50 4.00
62 Yogi Berra MM/1955 1.50 4.00
63 Mickey Mantle MM/1956 5.00 12.00
64 Mickey Mantle MM/1957 5.00 12.00
65 Ken Griffey Sr. MM/1980 .60 1.50
66 Rickey Henderson MM/1989 1.50 4.00
67 Roberto Alomar MM/1992 1.00 2.50
68 Bernie Williams MM/1996 1.00 2.50
69 Livan Hernandez MM/1997 .60 1.50
70 Sammy Sosa MM/1998 1.50 4.00
71 Sterling Hitchcock MM/1998 .60 1.50
72 David Wells MM/1998 .60 1.50
73 Mariano Rivera MM/1999 2.00 5.00
74 Chipper Jones MM/1999 1.50 4.00
75 Ivan Rodriguez MM/1999 1.00 2.50
76 Derek Jeter MM/2000 4.00 10.00
77 Jason Giambi MM/2000 .60 1.50
78 Jeff Kent MM/2000 .60 1.50
79 Mike Hampton MM/2000 .60 1.50
80 Randy Johnson MM/2001 1.50 4.00
81 Curt Schilling MM/2001 1.00 2.50
82 Barry Bonds MM/2001 2.50 6.00
83 Ichiro Suzuki MM/2001 2.00 5.00
84 Ichiro Suzuki MM/2001 2.00 5.00
85 Adam Kennedy MM/2002 .60 1.50
86 Benito Santiago MM/2002 .60 1.50
87 Troy Glaus MM/2002 .60 1.50
88 Troy Glaus MM/2002 .60 1.50
89 Miguel Tejada MM/2002 1.00 2.50
90 Barry Bonds MM/2002 2.50 6.00

2003 Upper Deck MVP Covering the Bases

STATED ODDS 1:125
AR Alex Rodriguez 6.00 15.00
BB Barry Bonds 8.00 20.00
CD Carlos Delgado 3.00 8.00
DE Darin Erstad 3.00 8.00
DJ Derek Jeter 8.00 20.00
FT Frank Thomas 4.00 10.00
IR Ivan Rodriguez 4.00 10.00
IS Ichiro Suzuki 8.00 20.00
JD J.D. Drew 3.00 8.00
JT Jim Thome 4.00 10.00
LG Luis Gonzalez 3.00 8.00
MP Mike Piazza 6.00 15.00
MT Miguel Tejada 3.00 8.00
SG Shawn Green 3.00 8.00
TG Troy Glaus 3.00 8.00

2003 Upper Deck MVP Covering the Plate Game Bat

STATED ODDS 1:160
FM Fred McGriff 6.00 15.00
JT Jim Thome 6.00 15.00
MG Mark McGwire 10.00 25.00
RA Roberto Alomar 6.00 15.00
RF Rafael Furcal 4.00 10.00
VG Vladimir Guerrero 6.00 15.00

2003 Upper Deck MVP Dual Aces Game Base

STATED ODDS 1:488
BS K.Brown/C.Schilling 4.00 10.00
CJ R.Clemens/R.Johnson 8.00 20.00
CL R.Clemens/A.Leiter 6.00 15.00
ML M.Morris/A.Leiter 4.00 10.00
SJ C.Schilling/R.Johnson 4.00 10.00
SP C.Schilling/A.Pettitte 4.00 10.00

2003 Upper Deck MVP Express Delivery

STATED ODDS 1:12
ED1 Randy Johnson 1.00 2.50
ED2 Curt Schilling .60 1.50
ED3 Pedro Martinez .60 1.50
ED4 Kerry Wood .40 1.00
ED5 Mark Prior .60 1.50
ED6 A.J. Burnett .40 1.00
ED7 Josh Beckett .40 1.00
ED8 Roy Oswalt .60 1.50
ED9 Hideo Nomo 1.00 2.50
ED10 Ben Sheets .40 1.00
ED11 Bartolo Colon .40 1.00
ED12 Roger Clemens 1.25 3.00
ED13 Mike Mussina .60 1.50
ED14 Tim Hudson .60 1.50
ED15 Matt Morris .40 1.00

2003 Upper Deck MVP Pro View

ONE 2-CARD PACK PER SEALED BOX
*GOLD: .75X TO 2X BASIC PRO VIEW
ONE 2-CARD PACK PER 6 SEALED BOXES
PV1 Troy Glaus .50 1.25
PV2 Darin Erstad .50 1.25
PV3 Randy Johnson 1.25 3.00
PV4 Curt Schilling .75 2.00
PV5 Luis Gonzalez .50 1.25
PV6 Chipper Jones 1.25 3.00
PV7 Andruw Jones .50 1.25
PV8 Greg Maddux 1.50 4.00
PV9 Pedro Martinez .75 2.00
PV10 Manny Ramirez 1.25 3.00
PV11 Sammy Sosa 1.25 3.00
PV12 Mark Prior .75 2.00
PV13 Magglio Ordonez .75 2.00
PV14 Frank Thomas 1.25 3.00
PV15 Ken Griffey Jr. 2.50 6.00
PV16 Adam Dunn .75 2.00
PV17 Jim Thome .75 2.00
PV18 Todd Helton .75 2.00
PV19 Jeff Bagwell .75 2.00
PV20 Lance Berkman .75 2.00
PV21 Shawn Green .50 1.25
PV22 Hideo Nomo 1.25 3.00
PV23 Vladimir Guerrero .75 2.00
PV24 Roberto Alomar .75 2.00
PV25 Mike Piazza 1.25 3.00
PV26 Jason Giambi .50 1.25
PV27 Roger Clemens 1.50 4.00
PV28 Alfonso Soriano .75 2.00
PV29 Derek Jeter 3.00 8.00
PV30 Miguel Tejada .75 2.00
PV31 Eric Chavez .50 1.25
PV32 Barry Zito .75 2.00
PV33 Pat Burrell .50 1.25
PV34 Brian Giles .50 1.25
PV35 Barry Bonds 2.00 5.00
PV36 Ichiro Suzuki 1.50 4.00
PV37 Albert Pujols 1.50 4.00
PV38 Scott Rolen .75 2.00
PV39 J.D. Drew .50 1.25
PV40 Mark McGwire 2.00 5.00
PV41 Alex Rodriguez 1.50 4.00
PV42 Rafael Palmeiro .75 2.00

PV43 Juan Gonzalez .50 1.25
PV44 Eric Hinske .50 1.25
PV45 Carlos Delgado .50 1.25

2003 Upper Deck MVP SportsNut

STATED ODDS 1:3
SN1 Troy Glaus .40 1.00
SN2 Darin Erstad .40 1.00
SN3 Luis Gonzalez .40 1.00
SN4 Andruw Jones .40 1.00
SN5 Chipper Jones 1.00 2.50
SN6 Gary Sheffield .40 1.00
SN7 Jay Gibbons .40 1.00
SN8 Manny Ramirez 1.00 2.50
SN9 Shea Hillenbrand .40 1.00
SN10 Johnny Damon .60 1.50
SN11 Nomar Garciaparra .60 1.50
SN12 Sammy Sosa 1.00 2.50
SN13 Magglio Ordonez .60 1.50
SN14 Frank Thomas 1.00 2.50
SN15 Ken Griffey Jr. 2.00 5.00
SN16 Adam Dunn .60 1.50
SN17 Matt Lawton .40 1.00
SN18 Larry Walker .60 1.50
SN19 Todd Helton .60 1.50
SN20 Carlos Pena .60 1.50
SN21 Mike Lowell .40 1.00
SN22 Jeff Bagwell .60 1.50
SN23 Lance Berkman .60 1.50
SN24 Mike Sweeney .40 1.00
SN25 Carlos Beltran .60 1.50
SN26 Shawn Green .40 1.00
SN27 Richie Sexson .40 1.00
SN28 Torii Hunter .40 1.00
SN29 Jacque Jones .40 1.00
SN30 Vladimir Guerrero .60 1.50
SN31 Jose Vidro .40 1.00
SN32 Roberto Alomar .60 1.50
SN33 Mike Piazza 1.00 2.50
SN34 Alfonso Soriano .60 1.50
SN35 Derek Jeter 2.50 6.00
SN36 Jason Giambi .40 1.00
SN37 Bernie Williams .60 1.50
SN38 Eric Chavez .40 1.00
SN39 Miguel Tejada .60 1.50
SN40 Jim Thome .60 1.50
SN41 Pat Burrell .40 1.00
SN42 Bobby Abreu .40 1.00
SN43 Brian Giles .40 1.00
SN44 Jason Kendall .40 1.00
SN45 Ryan Klesko .40 1.00
SN46 Phil Nevin .40 1.00
SN47 Barry Bonds 1.50 4.00
SN48 Rich Aurilia .40 1.00
SN49 Ichiro Suzuki 1.25 3.00
SN50 Bret Boone .40 1.00
SN51 J.D. Drew .40 1.00
SN52 Jim Edmonds .60 1.50
SN53 Albert Pujols 1.25 3.00
SN54 Scott Rolen .60 1.50
SN55 Ben Grieve .40 1.00
SN56 Alex Rodriguez 1.25 3.00
SN57 Rafael Palmeiro .60 1.50
SN58 Juan Gonzalez .40 1.00
SN59 Carlos Delgado .40 1.00
SN60 Josh Phelps .40 1.00
SN61 Jarrod Washburn .40 1.00
SN62 Randy Johnson 1.00 2.50
SN63 Curt Schilling .60 1.50
SN64 Greg Maddux 1.25 3.00
SN65 Mike Hampton .40 1.00
SN66 Rodrigo Lopez .40 1.00
SN67 Pedro Martinez .60 1.50
SN68 Derek Lowe .40 1.00
SN69 Mark Prior .60 1.50
SN70 Kerry Wood .40 1.00
SN71 Mark Buehrle .60 1.50
SN72 Roy Oswalt .60 1.50
SN73 Wade Miller .40 1.00
SN74 Odalis Perez .40 1.00
SN75 Hideo Nomo 1.00 2.50
SN76 Ben Sheets .40 1.00
SN77 Eric Milton .40 1.00
SN78 Bartolo Colon .40 1.00
SN79 Tom Glavine .60 1.50
SN80 Al Leiter .40 1.00
SN81 Roger Clemens 1.25 3.00
SN82 Mike Mussina .60 1.50
SN83 Tim Hudson .60 1.50
SN84 Barry Zito .60 1.50
SN85 Mark Mulder .40 1.00
SN86 Vicente Padilla .40 1.00
SN87 Jason Schmidt .40 1.00
SN88 Freddy Garcia .40 1.00
SN89 Matt Morris .40 1.00
SN90 Roy Halladay .60 1.50

2003 Upper Deck MVP Talk of the Town

STATED ODDS 1:12
TT1 Hideki Matsui 2.00 5.00
TT2 Chipper Jones 1.00 2.50
TT3 Manny Ramirez 1.00 2.50
TT4 Sammy Sosa 1.00 2.50
TT5 Ken Griffey Jr. 2.00 5.00
TT6 Lance Berkman .60 1.50
TT7 Shawn Green .40 1.00
TT8 Vladimir Guerrero .60 1.50
TT9 Mike Piazza 1.00 2.50
TT10 Jason Giambi .40 1.00
TT11 Alfonso Soriano .60 1.50
TT12 Ichiro Suzuki 1.25 3.00
TT13 Albert Pujols 1.25 3.00
TT14 Alex Rodriguez 1.25 3.00
TT15 Eric Hinske .40 1.00

2003 Upper Deck MVP Three Bagger Game Base

STATED ODDS 1:488
BMP Bonds/McGwire/Piazza 10.00 25.00
GIB Griffey/Suzuki/Bonds 10.00 25.00
GTD Glaus/Thomas/Delgado 6.00 15.00
IBJ Suzuki/Bonds/Jeter 12.00 30.00
JWP Jeter/Williams/Posada 15.00 40.00
SCB Schilling/Clemens/Brown 10.00 25.00

2003 Upper Deck MVP Total Bases

RANDOM INSERTS IN PACKS
STATED PRINT RUN 150 SERIAL #'d SETS
NO PRICING DUE TO LACK OF MARKET INFO
AR Alex Rodriguez 10.00 25.00
BB Barry Bonds 15.00 40.00
DJ Derek Jeter 15.00 40.00
IS Ichiro Suzuki 15.00 40.00
KG Ken Griffey Jr. 10.00 25.00
MM Mark McGwire 20.00 50.00
MP Mike Piazza 10.00 25.00
RC Roger Clemens 10.00 25.00
TG Troy Glaus 4.00 10.00

2005 Upper Deck MVP

COMPLETE SET (90) 10.00 25.00
COMMON CARD (1-90) .08 .25
1 Adam Dunn .15 .40
2 Adrian Beltre .25 .60
3 Albert Pujols .30 .75
4 Alex Rodriguez .30 .75
5 Alfonso Soriano .15 .40
6 Andruw Jones .10 .25
7 Aubrey Huff .10 .25
8 Barry Zito .15 .40
9 Ben Sheets .10 .25
10 Bobby Abreu .10 .25
11 Bobby Crosby .10 .25
12 Bret Boone .10 .25
13 Brian Giles .10 .25
14 Carlos Beltran .15 .40
15 Carlos Delgado .10 .25
16 Carlos Lee .10 .25
17 Chipper Jones .25 .60
18 Craig Biggio .15 .40
19 Curt Schilling .15 .40
20 Dallas McPherson .10 .25
21 David Ortiz .25 .60
22 David Wright .20 .50
23 Derek Jeter .60 1.50
24 Derek Lowe .10 .25
25 Eric Chavez .10 .25
26 Eric Gagne .10 .25
27 Frank Thomas .25 .60
28 Garret Anderson .10 .25
29 Gary Sheffield .10 .25
30 Greg Maddux .30 .75
31 Hank Blalock .10 .25
32 Hideki Matsui .40 1.00
33 Ichiro Suzuki .30 .75
34 Ivan Rodriguez .15 .40
35 J.D. Drew .10 .25
36 Jake Peavy .10 .25
37 Jason Bay .10 .25
38 Jason Giambi .10 .25
39 Jason Schmidt .10 .25
40 Jeff Bagwell .15 .40
41 Jeff Kent .10 .25
42 Jim Edmonds .15 .40
43 Jim Thome .15 .40
44 Joe Mauer .20 .50
45 Johan Santana .15 .40
46 John Smoltz .25 .60
47 Johnny Damon .15 .40
48 Jorge Posada .15 .40
49 Jose Vidro .10 .25
50 Josh Beckett .10 .25
51 Kazuo Matsui .10 .25
52 Ken Griffey Jr. .50 1.25
53 Kerry Wood .10 .25
54 Khalil Greene .10 .25
55 Lance Berkman .15 .40
56 Livan Hernandez .10 .25
57 Luis Gonzalez .10 .25
58 Magglio Ordonez .15 .40
59 Manny Ramirez .25 .60
60 Mark Mulder .10 .25
61 Mark Prior .15 .40
62 Mark Teixeira .15 .40
63 Miguel Cabrera .25 .60
64 Miguel Tejada .15 .40
65 Mike Mussina .15 .40
66 Mike Piazza .25 .60
67 Mike Sweeney .10 .25
68 Moises Alou .10 .25
69 Nomar Garciaparra .15 .40
70 Oliver Perez .10 .25
71 Paul Konerko .15 .40
72 Pedro Martinez .15 .40
73 Rafael Palmeiro .15 .40
74 Randy Johnson .25 .60
75 Richie Sexson .10 .25
76 Roger Clemens .30 .75
77 Roy Halladay .15 .40
78 Roy Oswalt .15 .40
79 Sammy Sosa .25 .60
80 Scott Rolen .15 .40
81 Shawn Green .10 .25
82 Steve Finley .10 .25
83 Tim Hudson .15 .40
84 Todd Helton .15 .40
85 Tom Glavine .15 .40
86 Torii Hunter .10 .25
87 Travis Hafner .10 .25
88 Troy Glaus .10 .25
89 Victor Martinez .15 .40
90 Vladimir Guerrero .15 .40

2005 Upper Deck MVP Batter Up!

COMPLETE SET (42) 15.00 40.00
ONE PER PACK
1 Al Kaline 1.00 2.50
2 Bill Mazeroski .60 1.50
3 Billy Williams .60 1.50
4 Bob Feller .60 1.50
5 Bob Gibson .60 1.50
6 Bob Lemon .60 1.50
7 Brooks Robinson .60 1.50
8 Carlton Fisk .60 1.50
9 Catfish Hunter .60 1.50
10 Dennis Eckersley .60 1.50
11 Eddie Mathews 1.00 2.50
12 Eddie Murray .60 1.50
13 Fergie Jenkins .60 1.50
14 Gaylord Perry .60 1.50
15 Harmon Killebrew 1.00 2.50
16 Jim Bunning .60 1.50
17 Jim Palmer .60 1.50
18 Joe DiMaggio 2.00 5.00
19 Joe Morgan .60 1.50
20 Johnny Bench 1.00 2.50
21 Juan Marichal .60 1.50
22 Lou Brock .60 1.50
23 Luis Aparicio .60 1.50
24 Mike Schmidt 1.50 4.00
25 Monte Irvin .60 1.50
26 Nolan Ryan 3.00 8.00
27 Orlando Cepeda .60 1.50
28 Ozzie Smith 1.25 3.00
29 Pee Wee Reese .60 1.50
30 Phil Niekro .60 1.50
31 Phil Rizzuto .60 1.50
32 Ralph Kiner .60 1.50
33 Richie Ashburn .60 1.50
34 Robin Roberts .60 1.50
35 Robin Yount 1.00 2.50
36 Rollie Fingers .60 1.50
37 Tom Seaver .60 1.50
38 Tony Perez .60 1.50
39 Warren Spahn .60 1.50
40 Willie McCovey .60 1.50
41 Willie Stargell .60 1.50
42 Yogi Berra 1.00 2.50

2005 Upper Deck MVP Jersey

STATED ODDS 1:24
AB Adrian Beltre 4.00 10.00
AP Albert Pujols 5.00 12.00
AS Alfonso Soriano 2.50 6.00
CB Carlos Beltran 2.50 6.00
CJ Chipper Jones 4.00 10.00
CS Curt Schilling 2.50 6.00
DJ Derek Jeter 10.00 25.00
EC Eric Chavez 1.50 4.00
EG Eric Gagne 1.50 4.00
GM Greg Maddux 5.00 12.00
HB Hank Blalock 1.50 4.00
IR Ivan Rodriguez 2.50 6.00
JS Johan Santana 2.50 6.00
JT Jim Thome 2.50 6.00
KG Ken Griffey Jr. 8.00 20.00
KW Kerry Wood 1.50 4.00
MC Miguel Cabrera 4.00 10.00
MP Mark Prior 2.50 6.00
MR Manny Ramirez 4.00 10.00
MT Mark Teixeira 2.50 6.00
PI Mike Piazza 4.00 10.00
RJ Randy Johnson 4.00 10.00
SB Sean Burroughs 1.50 4.00
SR Scott Rolen 2.50 6.00
SS Sammy Sosa 4.00 10.00
TE Miguel Tejada 2.50 6.00
TH Todd Helton 2.50 6.00
VG Vladimir Guerrero 2.50 6.00

2006 Upper Deck National Baseball Card Day

COMPLETE SET (5) 2.00 5.00
UD6 Derek Jeter .75 2.00
UD7 Ken Griffey Jr. .60 1.50
UD8 Dontrelle Willis .12 .30
UD9 David Ortiz .30 .75
UD10 Paul Konerko .20 .50

2006 Upper Deck National Baseball Card Day National Pastime

COMPLETE SET (3) 1.50 4.00
ONE PER NBCD PACK
IS Ichiro Suzuki .40 1.00
KJ Kenji Johjima .30 .75
NG Nomar Garciaparra .20 .50

2008 Upper Deck National Baseball Card Day

COMPLETE SET (8) 2.50 6.00
UD9 Ken Griffey Jr. 1.00 2.50
UD10 Derek Jeter 1.25 3.00
UD11 Albert Pujols .60 1.50
UD12 Ichiro Suzuki .60 1.50
UD13 Prince Fielder .30 .75
UD14 Ian Kennedy .50 1.25
UD15 Chin-Lung Hu .20 .50
UD16 Luke Hochevar .30 .75

2002 Upper Deck National Convention

N1 Mark McGwire 1.00 2.50
N2 Sammy Sosa .50 1.25
N3 Jason Giambi .30 .75
N4 Ichiro Suzuki .75 2.00
N5 Ken Griffey Jr. 1.00 2.50

2004 Upper Deck National Convention

STATED PRINT RUN 500 SER.#'d SETS
TN4 Ken Griffey Jr. 1.25 3.00
TN5 Ichiro Suzuki 1.25 3.00
TN6 Derek Jeter 2.00 5.00
TN7 Mickey Mantle 2.00 5.00
TN8 Joe DiMaggio 1.50 4.00

2004 Upper Deck National Convention VIP

VIP3 Derek Jeter 5.00 12.00

2005 Upper Deck National Convention

STATED PRINT RUN 750 SER.#'d SETS
UNPRICED AUTO PRINT RUN 5
CL1 Ernie Banks 1.50 4.00
CL2 Ryne Sandberg 1.50 4.00

2006 Upper Deck National MLB

MLB1 Ken Griffey Jr. 2.00 5.00
MLB2 Derek Jeter 2.50 6.00
MLB3 Albert Pujols 1.25 3.00
MLB4 Miguel Cabrera 1.00 2.50
MLB5 David Wright .75 2.00
MLB6 David Ortiz 1.00 2.50

2006 Upper Deck National MLB VIP

1 Lou Gehrig 1.00 2.50
2 Babe Ruth 1.25 3.00
3 Scott Podsednik .20 .50
4 Derrek Lee .20 .50
5 Ken Griffey Jr. 1.00 2.50
6 Derek Jeter 1.25 3.00

2006 Upper Deck National Southern California

COMPLETE SET (6) 5.00 12.00
SoCal5 Vladimir Guerrero .60 1.50
SoCal6 Nomar Garciaparra .60 1.50

2007 Upper Deck National Convention

NTL1 Derek Jeter 1.25 3.00
NTL2 Ken Griffey Jr. 1.25 3.00
NTL3 Kei Igawa .75 2.00
NTL4 Cal Ripken Jr. 1.50 4.00
NTL16 Daisuke Matsuzaka 1.00 2.50

2007 Upper Deck National Convention VIP

VIP1 Derek Jeter 2.00 5.00
VIP2 Ken Griffey Jr. 1.50 4.00
VIP3 Kei Igawa 1.00 2.50
VIP4 Cal Ripken Jr. 2.00 5.00
VIP16 Daisuke Matsuzaka 1.25 3.00

2008 Upper Deck National Convention

NAT1 Derek Jeter 1.25 3.00
NAT5 Ken Griffey Jr. 1.00 2.50
NAT11 Kosuke Fukudome .20 .50
NAT15 Joe DiMaggio 1.25 3.00
NAT17 Derrek Lee .30 .75
NAT20 Daisuke Matsuzaka .30 .75
NAT22 Alfonso Soriano .30 .75
NAT23 Ichiro Suzuki .75 2.00

2008 Upper Deck National Convention VIP

CARDS FEATURE VIP LOGO ON FRONT
NAT1 Derek Jeter 4.00 10.00
NAT5 Ken Griffey Jr. 3.00 8.00
NAT11 Kosuke Fukudome .60 1.50
NAT15 Joe DiMaggio 4.00 10.00
NAT17 Derrek Lee .60 1.50
NAT20 Daisuke Matsuzaka 1.00 2.50
NAT22 Alfonso Soriano 1.00 2.50
NAT23 Ichiro Suzuki 2.50 6.00

2009 Upper Deck National Convention

NC1 Bob Feller .20 .50
NC3 Cliff Lee .30 .75
NC4 Grady Sizemore .30 .75
NC5 Kerry Wood .30 .75
NC12 Derek Jeter 1.25 3.00
NC16 Joe DiMaggio 1.25 3.00
NC17 Ken Griffey Jr. 1.00 2.50

2009 Upper Deck National Convention VIP

VIP1 Bob Feller .60 1.50
VIP2 Grady Sizemore 1.00 2.50
VIP4 Derek Jeter 4.00 10.00
VIP6 Joe DiMaggio 4.00 10.00
VIP7 Ken Griffey Jr. 3.00 8.00

1999 Upper Deck Ovation

This 90-card set was distributed in five-card packs with a suggested retail price of $3.99. The cards feature action color player images printed on game-ball stock for the look and feel of an actual baseball. The set contains the following subsets: World Premiere (61-80) with an insertion rate of one in every 3.5 packs, and Superstar Spotlight (81-90) inserted at a rate of one in six packs. In addition, 350 Mickey Mantle A Piece of History 500 Home Run bat cards were randomly seeded into packs. In addition, one special Mantle card was created by Upper Deck featuring both a chip of wood from a game used Mantle bat plus an authentic Mantle signature cut. Only one copy was produced and the design harkens from the popular 1999 A Piece of History Club cards except that much of the card front is devoted to a window to house the cut signature. Pricing and checklisting for these scarce bat cards can be referenced under 1999 Upper Deck A Piece of History 500 Club.

COMPLETE SET (90) 10.00 25.00
COMP.SET w/o SP's (60) 10.00 25.00
COMMON CARD (1-60) .15 .40
COMMON WP (61-80) .75 2.00
WP STATED ODDS 1:3.5
COMMON SS (81-90) 1.00 2.50
SS STATED ODDS 1:6
MANTLE BAT LISTED W/UD APH 500 CLUB
MANTLE BAT-AU RANDOM IN PACKS
MANTLE BAT-AU PRINT RUN 1 #'d CARD
NO MANTLE BAT-AU PRICING AVAILABLE
1 Ken Griffey Jr. .75 2.00
2 Rondell White .15 .40
3 Tony Clark .15 .40
4 Barry Bonds 1.00 2.50
5 Larry Walker .15 .40
6 Greg Vaughn .15 .40
7 Mark Grace .25 .60
8 John Olerud .15 .40
9 Matt Williams .15 .40
10 Craig Biggio .25 .60
11 Quinton McCracken .15 .40
12 Kerry Wood .15 .40
13 Derek Jeter 1.00 2.50
14 Frank Thomas .40 1.00
15 Tino Martinez .25 .60
16 Albert Belle .15 .40
17 Ben Grieve .15 .40
18 Cal Ripken 1.25 3.00
19 Johnny Damon .25 .60
20 Jose Cruz Jr. .15 .40
21 Barry Larkin .25 .60
22 Jason Giambi .15 .40
23 Sean Casey .15 .40
24 Scott Rolen .25 .60
25 Jim Thome .25 .60
26 Curt Schilling .15 .40
27 Moises Alou .15 .40
28 Alex Rodriguez .60 1.50
29 Mark Kotsay .15 .40
30 Darin Erstad .15 .40
31 Mike Mussina .25 .60
32 Todd Walker .15 .40
33 Nomar Garciaparra .60 1.50
34 Vladimir Guerrero .40 1.00
35 Jeff Bagwell .25 .60
36 Mark McGwire 1.00 2.50
37 Travis Lee .15 .40
38 Dean Palmer .15 .40
39 Fred McGriff .25 .60
40 Sammy Sosa .40 1.00
41 Mike Piazza .60 1.50
42 Andres Galarraga .15 .40
43 Pedro Martinez .25 .60
44 Juan Gonzalez .15 .40
45 Greg Maddux .60 1.50
46 Jeromy Burnitz .15 .40
47 Roger Clemens .75 2.00
48 Vinny Castilla .15 .40
49 Kevin Brown .25 .60
50 Mo Vaughn .15 .40
51 Raul Mondesi .15 .40
52 Randy Johnson .40 1.00
53 Ray Lankford .15 .40
54 Jaret Wright .15 .40
55 Tony Gwynn .50 1.25
56 Chipper Jones .40 1.00
57 Gary Sheffield .15 .40
58 Ivan Rodriguez .25 .60
59 Kenny Lofton .15 .40
60 Jason Kendall .15 .40
61 J.D. Drew WP .75 2.00
62 Gabe Kapler WP .75 2.00
63 Adrian Beltre WP .75 2.00
64 Carlos Beltran WP 1.00 2.50
65 Eric Chavez WP .75 2.00
66 Mike Lowell WP .75 2.00
67 Troy Glaus WP 1.00 2.50
68 George Lombard WP .75 2.00
69 Alex Gonzalez WP .75 2.00
70 Mike Kinkade WP .75 2.00
71 Jeremy Giambi WP .75 2.00
72 Bruce Chen WP .75 2.00
73 Preston Wilson WP .75 2.00
74 Kevin Witt WP .75 2.00
75 Carlos Guillen WP .75 2.00
76 Ryan Minor WP .75 2.00
77 Corey Koskie WP .75 2.00
78 Robert Fick WP 1.00 2.50
79 Michael Barrett WP .75 2.00
80 Calvin Pickering WP .75 2.00
81 Ken Griffey Jr. SS 2.00 5.00
82 Mark McGwire SS 2.50 6.00
83 Cal Ripken SS 3.00 8.00
84 Derek Jeter SS 2.50 6.00
85 Chipper Jones SS 1.00 2.50
86 Nomar Garciaparra SS 1.50 4.00
87 Sammy Sosa SS 1.00 2.50
88 Juan Gonzalez SS 1.00 2.50
89 Mike Piazza SS 1.50 4.00
90 Alex Rodriguez SS 1.50 4.00

1999 Upper Deck Ovation Standing Ovation

*STARS 1-60: 5X TO 12X BASIC 1-60
*WP CARDS 61-80: 1X TO 2.5X BASIC WP
*SS CARDS 81-90: 2X TO 5X BASIC SS
RANDOM INSERTS IN PACKS
STATED PRINT RUN 500 SERIAL #'d SETS
1 Ken Griffey Jr. 25.00 50.00

1999 Upper Deck Ovation A Piece of History

STATED ODDS 1:247
AR Alex Rodriguez 8.00 20.00
BB Barry Bonds 10.00 25.00
BG Ben Grieve 4.00 10.00
BW Bernie Williams 5.00 12.00
CJ Chipper Jones 5.00 12.00
CR Cal Ripken 15.00 40.00
DJ Derek Jeter 10.00 25.00
JG Juan Gonzalez 4.00 10.00
MP Mike Piazza 12.50 30.00
NG Nomar Garciaparra 8.00 20.00
SS Sammy Sosa 5.00 12.00
TG Tony Gwynn 5.00 12.00
VG Vladimir Guerrero 5.00 12.00
KGJ Ken Griffey Jr. 8.00 20.00
BGAU Ben Grieve Bat AU/25
KWAU K.Wood Ball AU/25

1999 Upper Deck Ovation Curtain Calls

COMPLETE SET (20) 30.00 80.00
STATED ODDS 1:8
R1 Mark McGwire 3.00 8.00
R2 Sammy Sosa 1.25 3.00
R3 Ken Griffey Jr. 2.50 6.00
R4 Alex Rodriguez 2.00 5.00
R5 Roger Clemens 2.50 6.00
R6 Cal Ripken 4.00 10.00
R7 Barry Bonds 3.00 8.00
R8 Kerry Wood .50 1.25
R9 Nomar Garciaparra 2.00 5.00
R10 Derek Jeter 3.00 8.00
R11 Juan Gonzalez .50 1.25
R12 Greg Maddux 2.00 5.00
R13 Pedro Martinez .75 2.00
R14 David Wells .50 1.25
R15 Moises Alou .50 1.25
R16 Tony Gwynn 1.50 4.00
R17 Albert Belle .50 1.25
R18 Mike Piazza 2.00 5.00
R19 Ivan Rodriguez .75 2.00
R20 Randy Johnson 1.25 3.00

1999 Upper Deck Ovation Major Production

COMPLETE SET (20) 200.00 400.00
STATED ODDS 1:45
S1 Mike Piazza 8.00 20.00
S2 Mark McGwire 12.50 30.00
S3 Chipper Jones 5.00 12.00
S4 Cal Ripken 15.00 40.00
S5 Ken Griffey Jr. 10.00 25.00
S6 Barry Bonds 12.50 30.00
S7 Tony Gwynn 6.00 15.00
S8 Randy Johnson 5.00 12.00
S9 Ivan Rodriguez 3.00 8.00
S10 Frank Thomas 5.00 12.00
S11 Alex Rodriguez 4.00 10.00
S12 Albert Belle 2.00 5.00
S13 Juan Gonzalez 2.00 5.00
S14 Greg Maddux 8.00 20.00
S15 Jeff Bagwell 3.00 8.00
S16 Derek Jeter 12.50 30.00
S17 Matt Williams 2.00 5.00
S18 Kenny Lofton 2.00 5.00
S19 Sammy Sosa 5.00 12.00
S20 Roger Clemens 10.00 25.00

1999 Upper Deck Ovation ReMarkable Moments

COMPLETE SET (15) 12.50 30.00
COMMON CARD (1-5) 1.00 2.50
CARDS 1-5 STATED ODDS 1:9
COMMON CARD (6-10) 1.25 3.00
CARDS 6-10 STATED ODDS 1:25
COMMON CARD (11-15) 2.00 5.00
CARDS 11-15 STATED ODDS 1:99

2000 Upper Deck Ovation

COMPLETE SET (89) 30.00 80.00
COMP.SET w/o SP's (60) 8.00 20.00
COMMON CARD (1-60) .15 .40
COMMON WP (61-80) .40 1.00
WP STATED ODDS 1:3
COMMON SS (81-90) .40 1.00
SS STATED ODDS 1:6
CARD 70 NOT MEANT FOR PUBLIC RELEASE
COMP.SET DOESN'T INCLUDE CARD 70
1 Mo Vaughn .15 .40
2 Troy Glaus .15 .40
3 Jeff Bagwell .25 .60
4 Craig Biggio .25 .60
5 Mike Hampton .15 .40
6 Jason Giambi .15 .40
7 Tim Hudson .25 .60
8 Chipper Jones .40 1.00
9 Greg Maddux .50 1.25
10 Kevin Millwood .15 .40
11 Brian Jordan .15 .40
12 Jeromy Burnitz .15 .40
13 David Wells .15 .40
14 Carlos Delgado .15 .40
15 Sammy Sosa .40 1.00
16 Mark McGwire .60 1.50
17 Matt Williams .15 .40
18 Randy Johnson .40 1.00
19 Erubiel Durazo .15 .40
20 Kevin Brown .15 .40
21 Shawn Green .15 .40
22 Gary Sheffield .15 .40
23 Jose Canseco .25 .60
24 Vladimir Guerrero .25 .60
25 Barry Bonds .60 1.50
26 Manny Ramirez .40 1.00
27 Roberto Alomar .25 .60
28 Richie Sexson .15 .40
29 Jim Thome .25 .60
30 Alex Rodriguez .50 1.25
31 Ken Griffey Jr. .75 2.00
32 Preston Wilson .15 .40
33 Mike Piazza .40 1.00
34 Al Leiter .15 .40
35 Robin Ventura .15 .40
36 Cal Ripken 1.25 3.00
37 Albert Belle .15 .40
38 Tony Gwynn .40 1.00
39 Brian Giles .15 .40
40 Jason Kendall .15 .40
41 Scott Rolen .25 .60
42 Bob Abreu .15 .40
43 Ken Griffey Jr. Reds .75 2.00
44 Sean Casey .15 .40
45 Carlos Beltran .25 .60
46 Gabe Kapler .15 .40
47 Ivan Rodriguez .25 .60
48 Rafael Palmeiro .25 .60
49 Larry Walker .25 .60
50 Nomar Garciaparra .25 .60
51 Pedro Martinez .25 .60
52 Eric Milton .15 .40
53 Juan Gonzalez .15 .40
54 Tony Clark .15 .40
55 Frank Thomas .40 1.00
56 Magglio Ordonez .25 .60
57 Roger Clemens .50 1.25
58 Derek Jeter 1.00 2.50
59 Bernie Williams .25 .60
60 Orlando Hernandez .15 .40
61 Rick Ankiel WP .60 1.50
62 Josh Beckett WP .75 2.00
63 Vernon Wells WP .40 1.00
64 Alfonso Soriano WP 1.00 2.50
65 Pat Burrell WP .40 1.00
66 Eric Munson WP .40 1.00
67 Chad Hutchinson WP .40 1.00
68 Eric Gagne WP .40 1.00
69 Peter Bergeron WP .40 1.00
70 Ryan Anderson WP SP 30.00 60.00
71 A.J. Burnett WP .40 1.00
72 Jorge Toca WP .40 1.00
73 Matt Riley WP .40 1.00
74 Chad Hermansen WP .40 1.00
75 Doug Davis WP .40 1.00
76 Jim Morris WP 1.00 2.50
77 Ben Petrick WP .40 1.00
78 Mark Quinn WP .40 1.00
79 Ed Yarnall WP .40 1.00
80 Ramon Ortiz WP .40 1.00
81 Ken Griffey Jr. SS 2.00 5.00
82 Mark McGwire SS 1.50 4.00
83 Derek Jeter SS 2.50 6.00
84 Jeff Bagwell SS .60 1.50
85 Nomar Garciaparra SS .60 1.50
86 Sammy Sosa SS 1.00 2.50
87 Mike Piazza SS 1.00 2.50
88 Alex Rodriguez SS 1.25 3.00
89 Cal Ripken SS 3.00 8.00
90 Pedro Martinez SS .60 1.50

2000 Upper Deck Ovation Standing Ovation

*STANDING O: 10X TO 25X BASIC
*WORLD PREM: 4X TO 10X BASIC WP
*SPOTLIGHT: 4X TO 10X BASIC SS
STATED PRINT RUN 50 SERIAL #'d SETS
CARD NUMBER 70 DOES NOT EXIST

2000 Upper Deck Ovation A Piece of History

STATED PRINT RUN 400 SETS
AR Alex Rodriguez/400* 8.00 20.00
CJ Chipper Jones/400* 8.00 20.00
CR Cal Ripken/400* 10.00 25.00
DJ Derek Jeter/400* 20.00 50.00
IR Ivan Rodriguez/400* 6.00 15.00
JC Jose Canseco/400* 12.50 30.00
KG Ken Griffey Jr./400* 15.00 40.00
MR Manny Ramirez/400* 6.00 15.00
PB Pat Burrell/400* 6.00 15.00
SR Scott Rolen/400* 6.00 15.00
TG Tony Gwynn/400* 10.00 25.00
VG Vladimir Guerrero/400* 8.00 20.00

2000 Upper Deck Ovation Center Stage Silver

COMPLETE SET (10) 10.00 25.00
STATED ODDS 1:9
*GOLD: .75X TO 2X CENTER SILVER
GOLD STATED ODDS 1:39
*RAINBOW: 1.5X TO 4X CENTER SILVER
RAINBOW STATED ODDS 1:99
CS1 Jeff Bagwell .60 1.50
CS2 Ken Griffey Jr. 2.00 5.00
CS3 Nomar Garciaparra .60 1.50
CS4 Mike Piazza 1.00 2.50
CS5 Mark McGwire 1.50 4.00
CS6 Alex Rodriguez 1.25 3.00
CS7 Cal Ripken 3.00 8.00
CS8 Derek Jeter 2.50 6.00
CS9 Chipper Jones 1.00 2.50
CS10 Sammy Sosa 1.00 2.50

2000 Upper Deck Ovation Curtain Calls

COMPLETE SET (20) 10.00 25.00
STATED ODDS 1:3
CC1 David Cone .30 .75
CC2 Mark McGwire 1.25 3.00
CC3 Sammy Sosa .75 2.00
CC4 Eric Milton .30 .75
CC5 Bernie Williams .50 1.25
CC6 Tony Gwynn .75 2.00
CC7 Nomar Garciaparra .50 1.25
CC8 Manny Ramirez .75 2.00
CC9 Wade Boggs .50 1.25
CC10 Randy Johnson .75 2.00
CC11 Cal Ripken 2.50 6.00
CC12 Pedro Martinez .50 1.25
CC13 Alex Rodriguez 1.00 2.50
CC14 Fernando Tatis .30 .75
CC15 Vladimir Guerrero .50 1.25
CC16 Robin Ventura .30 .75
CC17 Larry Walker .50 1.25
CC18 Carlos Beltran .50 1.25
CC19 Jose Canseco .50 1.25
CC20 Ken Griffey Jr. 1.50 4.00

2000 Upper Deck Ovation Diamond Futures

COMPLETE SET (10) 3.00 8.00
STATED ODDS 1:6
DM1 J.D. Drew .40 1.00
DM2 Alfonso Soriano 1.00 2.50
DM3 Preston Wilson .40 1.00
DM4 Erubiel Durazo .40 1.00
DM5 Rick Ankiel .60 1.50
DM6 Octavio Dotel .40 1.00
DM7 A.J. Burnett .40 1.00
DM8 Carlos Beltran .60 1.50
DM9 Vernon Wells .40 1.00
DM10 Troy Glaus .40 1.00

2000 Upper Deck Ovation Lead Performers

COMPLETE SET (10) 10.00 25.00
STATED ODDS 1:19
LP1 Mark McGwire 1.50 4.00
LP2 Derek Jeter 2.50 6.00
LP3 Vladimir Guerrero .60 1.50
LP4 Mike Piazza 1.00 2.50
LP5 Cal Ripken 3.00 8.00
LP6 Sammy Sosa 1.00 2.50
LP7 Jeff Bagwell .60 1.50
LP8 Nomar Garciaparra .60 1.50
LP9 Chipper Jones 1.00 2.50
LP10 Ken Griffey Jr. 2.00 5.00

2000 Upper Deck Ovation Super Signatures

SILVER PRINT RUN 100 SERIAL #'d SETS
GOLD PRINT RUN 50 SERIAL #'d SETS
RAINBOW PRINT RUN 10 SERIAL #'d SETS
NO RAINBOW PRICING DUE TO SCARCITY
PIAZZA EXCH.DEADLINE 12/09/00
SSKGG K.Griffey Gold/50 75.00 150.00
SSKGS K.Griffey Silver/100 125.00 250.00
SSMPG M.Piazza Gold/50 150.00 250.00
SSMPS M.Piazza Silver/100 60.00 120.00

2000 Upper Deck Ovation Superstar Theatre

COMPLETE SET (20) 10.00 25.00
STATED ODDS 1:19
ST1 Ivan Rodriguez .60 1.50
ST2 Brian Giles .40 1.00
ST3 Bernie Williams .60 1.50
ST4 Greg Maddux 1.25 3.00
ST5 Frank Thomas 1.00 2.50
ST6 Sean Casey .40 1.00
ST7 Mo Vaughn .40 1.00
ST8 Carlos Delgado .40 1.00
ST9 Tony Gwynn 1.00 2.50
ST10 Pedro Martinez .60 1.50
ST11 Scott Rolen .60 1.50
ST12 Mark McGwire 1.50 4.00
ST13 Manny Ramirez 1.00 2.50
ST14 Rafael Palmeiro .60 1.50
ST15 Jose Canseco .60 1.50
ST16 Randy Johnson 1.00 2.50
ST17 Gary Sheffield .40 1.00
ST18 Larry Walker .60 1.50
ST19 Barry Bonds 1.50 4.00
ST20 Roger Clemens 1.25 3.00

2001 Upper Deck Ovation

COMP.SET w/o SP'S (60) 8.00 20.00
COMMON CARD (1-60) .15 .40
COMMON WP (61-90) 2.00 5.00

WP RANDOM INSERTS IN PACKS
WP PRINT RUN 2000 SERIAL #'d SETS
1 Troy Glaus .15 .40
2 Darin Erstad .15 .40
3 Jason Giambi .15 .40
4 Tim Hudson .15 .40
5 Eric Chavez .15 .40
6 Carlos Delgado .15 .40
7 David Wells .15 .40
8 Greg Vaughn .15 .40
9 Omar Vizquel UER .25 .60
10 Jim Thome .25 .60
11 Roberto Alomar .25 .60
12 John Olerud .15 .40
13 Edgar Martinez .25 .60
14 Cal Ripken 1.25 3.00
15 Alex Rodriguez .50 1.25
16 Ivan Rodriguez .25 .60
17 Manny Ramirez Sox .25 .60
18 Nomar Garciaparra .60 1.50
19 Pedro Martinez .25 .60
20 Jermaine Dye .15 .40
21 Juan Gonzalez .15 .40
22 Matt Lawton .15 .40
23 Frank Thomas .40 1.00
24 Magglio Ordonez .15 .40
25 Bernie Williams .25 .60
26 Derek Jeter 1.00 2.50
27 Roger Clemens .75 2.00
28 Jeff Bagwell .25 .60
29 Richard Hidalgo .15 .40
30 Chipper Jones .40 1.00
31 Greg Maddux .60 1.50
32 Andruw Jones .25 .60
33 Jeromy Burnitz .15 .40
34 Mark McGwire 1.00 2.50
35 Jim Edmonds .25 .60
36 Sammy Sosa .40 1.00
37 Kerry Wood .15 .40
38 Randy Johnson .40 1.00
39 Steve Finley .15 .40
40 Gary Sheffield .15 .40
41 Kevin Brown .15 .40
42 Shawn Green .15 .40
43 Vladimir Guerrero .40 1.00
44 Jose Vidro .15 .40
45 Barry Bonds 1.00 2.50
46 Jeff Kent .15 .40
47 Preston Wilson .15 .40
48 Luis Castillo .15 .40
49 Mike Piazza .60 1.50
50 Edgardo Alfonzo .15 .40
51 Tony Gwynn .50 1.25
52 Ryan Klesko .15 .40
53 Scott Rolen .25 .60
54 Bob Abreu .15 .40
55 Jason Kendall .15 .40
56 Brian Giles .15 .40
57 Ken Griffey Jr. .75 2.00
58 Barry Larkin .25 .60
59 Todd Helton .25 .60
60 Mike Hampton .15 .40
61 Corey Patterson WP 2.00 5.00
62 Timo Perez WP 2.00 5.00
63 Toby Hall WP 2.00 5.00
64 Brandon Inge WP 2.00 5.00
65 Joe Crede WP 3.00 8.00
66 Xavier Nady WP 2.00 5.00
67 Adam Pettyjohn WP RC 2.00 5.00
68 Keith Ginter WP 2.00 5.00
69 Brian Cole WP 2.00 5.00
70 Tyler Walker WP RC 2.00 5.00
71 Juan Uribe WP RC 2.00 5.00
72 Alex Hernandez WP 2.00 5.00
73 Leo Estrella WP 2.00 5.00
74 Joey Nation WP 2.00 5.00
75 Aubrey Huff WP 2.00 5.00
76 Ichiro Suzuki WP RC 15.00 40.00
77 Jay Spurgeon WP 2.00 5.00
78 Sun Woo Kim WP 2.00 5.00
79 Pedro Feliz WP 2.00 5.00
80 Pablo Ozuna WP 2.00 5.00
81 Hiram Bocachica WP 2.00 5.00
82 Brad Wilkerson WP 2.00 5.00
83 Rocky Biddle WP 2.00 5.00
84 Aaron McNeal WP 2.00 5.00
85 Adam Bernero WP 2.00 5.00
86 Danys Baez WP 2.00 5.00
87 Dee Brown WP 2.00 5.00
88 Jimmy Rollins WP 2.00 5.00
89 Jason Hart WP 2.00 5.00
90 Ross Gload WP 2.00 5.00

2001 Upper Deck Ovation A Piece of History

COMMON RETIRED 6.00 15.00
STATED ODDS 1:40
AJ Andruw Jones 6.00 15.00
AR Alex Rodriguez 6.00 15.00
BB Barry Bonds 10.00 25.00
BR Brooks Robinson 10.00 25.00
BW Bernie Williams 6.00 15.00
CD Carlos Delgado 4.00 10.00
CF Carlton Fisk 10.00 25.00
CJ Chipper Jones 6.00 15.00
CR Cal Ripken 12.50 30.00
DC David Cone 4.00 10.00
DD Don Drysdale 6.00 15.00
DE Darin Erstad 4.00 10.00
EW Early Wynn 6.00 15.00
FT Frank Thomas 6.00 15.00
GM Greg Maddux 6.00 15.00
GS Gary Sheffield 4.00 10.00
IR Ivan Rodriguez 6.00 15.00
JB Johnny Bench 10.00 25.00
JC Jose Canseco 6.00 15.00
JD Joe DiMaggio 10.00 25.00
JE Jim Edmonds 4.00 10.00
JP Jim Palmer 6.00 15.00
KG Ken Griffey Jr. 6.00 15.00
KGS Ken Griffey Sr. 4.00 10.00
KKB Kevin Brown 4.00 10.00
MH Mike Hampton 4.00 10.00
MM Mickey Mantle 30.00 60.00
MW Matt Williams 4.00 10.00
NR Nolan Ryan SP 20.00 50.00
OS Ozzie Smith 6.00 15.00
RA Rick Ankiel 4.00 10.00
RC Roger Clemens 6.00 15.00
RF Rollie Fingers 6.00 15.00
RF Rafael Furcal 4.00 10.00
RJ Randy Johnson 6.00 15.00
SG Shawn Green 4.00 10.00
SS Sammy Sosa 6.00 15.00
TG Tom Glavine 6.00 15.00
TRG Troy Glaus 4.00 10.00
TS Tom Seaver 10.00 25.00

2001 Upper Deck Ovation A Piece of History Autographs

STATED PRINT RUNS LISTED BELOW
NO PRICING ON QTY OF 25 OR LESS
SKG Ken Griffey Jr./30 200.00 400.00

2001 Upper Deck Ovation Curtain Calls

COMPLETE SET (10) 8.00 20.00
STATED ODDS 1:7
CC1 Sammy Sosa .75 2.00
CC2 Darin Erstad .50 1.25
CC3 Barry Bonds 2.00 5.00
CC4 Todd Helton .50 1.25
CC5 Mike Piazza 1.25 3.00
CC6 Ken Griffey Jr. 1.50 4.00
CC7 Nomar Garciaparra 1.25 3.00
CC8 Carlos Delgado .50 1.25
CC9 Jason Giambi .50 1.25
CC10 Alex Rodriguez 1.00 2.50

2001 Upper Deck Ovation Lead Performers

COMPLETE SET (11) 12.50 30.00
STATED ODDS 1:12
LP1 Mark McGwire 2.50 6.00
LP2 Derek Jeter 2.50 6.00
LP3 Alex Rodriguez 1.25 3.00
LP4 Frank Thomas 1.00 2.50
LP5 Sammy Sosa 1.00 2.50
LP6 Mike Piazza 1.50 4.00
LP7 Vladimir Guerrero 1.00 2.50
LP8 Pedro Martinez .60 1.50
LP9 Carlos Delgado .60 1.50
LP10 Ken Griffey Jr. 2.00 5.00
LP11 Jeff Bagwell .60 1.50

2001 Upper Deck Ovation Superstar Theatre

COMPLETE SET (11) 12.50 30.00
STATED ODDS 1:12
ST1 Nomar Garciaparra 1.50 4.00
ST2 Ken Griffey Jr. 2.00 5.00
ST3 Frank Thomas 1.00 2.50
ST4 Derek Jeter 2.50 6.00
ST5 Mike Piazza 1.50 4.00
ST6 Sammy Sosa 1.00 2.50
ST7 Barry Bonds 2.50 6.00
ST8 Alex Rodriguez 1.25 3.00
ST9 Todd Helton 1.00 2.50
ST10 Mark McGwire 2.50 6.00
ST11 Jason Giambi 1.00 2.50

2002 Upper Deck Ovation

COMP.LOW w/o SP's (90) 10.00 25.00
COMP.UPDATE w/o SP's (30) 6.00 15.00
COMMON CARD (1-60) .15 .40
COMMON (61-89/120/151-180) 1.50 4.00
61-89/120 RANDOM IN OVATION PACKS
151-180 RANDOM IN UD ROOK.DEBUT PACKS
61-89/120/151-180 PRINT RUN 2002 #'d SETS
COMMON CARD (90-119) .20 .50
DUPE STARS 90-119 VALUED EQUALLY
COMMON CARD (121-150) .25 .60
121-150 DIST.IN UD ROOK.DEBUT PACKS
1 Troy Glaus .15 .40
2 David Justice .15 .40
3 Tim Hudson .15 .40
4 Jermaine Dye .15 .40
5 Carlos Delgado .15 .40
6 Greg Vaughn .15 .40
7 Jim Thome .25 .60
8 C.C. Sabathia .15 .40
9 Ichiro Suzuki .75 2.00
10 Edgar Martinez .25 .60
11 Chris Richard .15 .40
12 Rafael Palmeiro .25 .60
13 Alex Rodriguez .50 1.50
14 Ivan Rodriguez .25 .60
15 Nomar Garciaparra .60 1.50
16 Manny Ramirez .25 .60
17 Pedro Martinez .25 .60
18 Mike Sweeney .15 .40
19 Dmitri Young .15 .40
20 Doug Mientkiewicz .15 .40
21 Brad Radke .15 .40
22 Cristian Guzman .15 .40
23 Frank Thomas .40 1.00
24 Magglio Ordonez .15 .40
25 Bernie Williams .25 .60
26 Derek Jeter 1.00 2.50
27 Jason Giambi .15 .40
28 Roger Clemens .75 2.00
29 Jeff Bagwell .25 .60
30 Lance Berkman .15 .40
31 Chipper Jones .40 1.00
32 Gary Sheffield .15 .40
33 Greg Maddux .60 1.50
34 Richie Sexson .15 .40
35 Albert Pujols .75 2.00
36 Tino Martinez .25 .60
37 J.D. Drew .15 .40
38 Sammy Sosa .40 1.00
39 Moises Alou .15 .40
40 Randy Johnson .40 1.00
41 Luis Gonzalez .15 .40
42 Shawn Green .15 .40
43 Kevin Brown .15 .40
44 Vladimir Guerrero .40 1.00
45 Barry Bonds 1.00 2.50
46 Jeff Kent .15 .40
47 Cliff Floyd .15 .40
48 Josh Beckett .15 .40
49 Mike Piazza .60 1.50
50 Mo Vaughn .15 .40
51 Jeromy Burnitz .15 .40
52 Roberto Alomar .25 .60
53 Phil Nevin .15 .40
54 Scott Rolen .25 .60
55 Jimmy Rollins .15 .40
56 Brian Giles .15 .40
57 Ken Griffey Jr. .75 2.00
58 Sean Casey .15 .40
59 Larry Walker .15 .40
60 Todd Helton .25 .60
61 Rodrigo Rosario WP RC 1.50 4.00
62 Reed Johnson WP RC 2.00 5.00
63 John Ennis WP RC 1.50 4.00
64 Luis Martinez WP RC 1.50 4.00
65 So Taguchi WP RC 2.00 5.00
66 Brandon Backe WP RC 2.00 5.00
67 Doug Devore WP RC 1.50 4.00
68 Victor Alvarez WP RC 1.50 4.00
69 Kazuhisa Ishii WP RC 2.00 5.00
70 Eric Good WP RC 1.50 4.00
71 Deivis Santos WP 1.50 4.00
72 Matt Thornton WP RC 1.50 4.00
73 Hansel Izquierdo WP RC 1.50 4.00
74 Tyler Yates WP RC 1.50 4.00
75 Jaime Cerda WP RC 1.50 4.00
76 Satoru Komiyama WP RC 1.50 4.00
77 Steve Bechler WP RC 1.50 4.00
78 Ben Howard WP RC 1.50 4.00
79 Jorge Padilla WP RC 1.50 4.00
80 Eric Junge WP RC 1.50 4.00
81 Anderson Machado WP RC 1.50 4.00
82 Adrian Burnside WP RC 1.50 4.00
83 Josh Hancock WP RC 2.00 5.00
84 Anastacio Martinez WP RC 1.50 4.00
85 Rene Reyes WP RC 1.50 4.00
86 Nate Field WP RC 1.50 4.00
87 Tim Kalita WP RC 1.50 4.00
88 Kevin Frederick WP RC 1.50 4.00
89 Edwin Almonte WP RC 1.50 4.00
90 Ichiro Suzuki SS .40 1.00
91 Ichiro Suzuki SS .40 1.00
92 Ichiro Suzuki SS .40 1.00
93 Ichiro Suzuki SS .40 1.00
94 Ichiro Suzuki SS .40 1.00
95 Ken Griffey Jr. SS .40 1.00
96 Ken Griffey Jr. SS .40 1.00
97 Ken Griffey Jr. SS .40 1.00
98 Ken Griffey Jr. SS .40 1.00
99 Ken Griffey Jr. SS .40 1.00
100 Jason Giambi A's SS .20 .50
101 Jason Giambi A's SS .20 .50
102 Jason Giambi A's SS .20 .50
103 Jason Giambi Yankees SS .25 .60
104 Jason Giambi Yankees SS .25 .60
105 Sammy Sosa SS .25 .60
106 Sammy Sosa SS .25 .60
107 Sammy Sosa SS .25 .60
108 Sammy Sosa SS .25 .60
109 Sammy Sosa SS .25 .60
110 Alex Rodriguez SS .25 .60
111 Alex Rodriguez SS .25 .60
112 Alex Rodriguez SS .25 .60
113 Alex Rodriguez SS .25 .60
114 Alex Rodriguez SS .25 .60
115 Mark McGwire SS .50 1.25
116 Mark McGwire SS .50 1.25
117 Mark McGwire SS .50 1.25
118 Mark McGwire SS .50 1.25
119 Mark McGwire SS .50 1.25
120 Six Spokesmen SP/2002 10.00 25.00
121 Curt Schilling .25 .60
122 Cliff Floyd .25 .60
123 Derek Lowe .25 .60
124 Hee Seop Choi .25 .60
125 Mark Prior .40 1.00
126 Joe Borchard .25 .60
127 Austin Kearns .25 .60
128 Adam Dunn .25 .60
129 Jay Payton .25 .60
130 Carlos Pena .25 .60
131 Andy Van Hekken .25 .60
132 Andres Torres .25 .60
133 Ben Diggins .25 .60
134 Torii Hunter .25 .60
135 Bartolo Colon .25 .60
136 Raul Mondesi .25 .60
137 Alfonso Soriano .25 .60
138 Miguel Tejada .25 .60
139 Ray Durham .25 .60
140 Eric Chavez .25 .60
141 Marlon Byrd .25 .60
142 Brett Myers .25 .60
143 Jason Burroughs .25 .60
144 Kenny Lofton .25 .60
145 Scott Rolen .40 1.00
146 Carl Crawford .25 .60
147 Jayson Werth .25 .60
148 Josh Phelps .25 .60
149 Eric Hinske .25 .60
150 Orlando Hudson .25 .60
151 Jose Valverde WP RC 1.50 4.00
152 Trey Hodges WP RC 1.50 4.00
153 Joey Dawley WP RC 1.50 4.00
154 Travis Driskill WP RC 1.50 4.00
155 Howie Clark WP RC 1.50 4.00
156 Jorge De La Rosa WP RC 1.50 4.00
157 Freddy Sanchez WP RC 2.00 5.00
158 Earl Snyder WP RC 1.50 4.00
159 Cliff Lee WP RC 3.00 8.00
160 Josh Bard WP RC 1.50 4.00
161 Aaron Cook WP RC 1.50 4.00
162 Franklyn German WP RC 1.50 4.00
163 Brandon Puffer WP RC 1.50 4.00
164 Kirk Saarloos WP RC 1.50 4.00
165 Jeriome Robertson WP RC 1.50 4.00
166 Miguel Asencio WP RC 1.50 4.00
167 Shawn Sedlacek WP RC 1.50 4.00
168 Jayson Durocher WP RC 1.50 4.00
169 Shane Nance WP RC 1.50 4.00
170 Jamey Carroll WP RC 2.00 5.00
171 Oliver Perez WP RC 2.00 5.00
172 Wil Nieves WP RC 1.50 4.00
173 Clay Condrey WP RC 1.50 4.00
174 Chris Snelling WP RC 1.50 4.00
175 Mike Crudale WP RC 1.50 4.00
176 Jason Simontacchi WP RC 1.50 4.00
177 Felix Escalona WP RC 1.50 4.00
178 Lance Carter WP RC 1.50 4.00
179 Scott Wiggins WP RC 1.50 4.00
180 Kevin Cash WP RC 1.50 4.00

2002 Upper Deck Ovation Silver

*SILVER 1-60: 1.25X TO 3X BASIC
*SILVER 61-89/120: .5X TO 1.2X BASIC
*SILVER 61-119: 2.5X TO 6X BASIC
1-60/90-119 APPROXIMATE ODDS 1:4
61-89/120 RANDOM INSERTS IN PACKS
61-89/120 PRINT RUN 100 SERIAL #'d SETS

2002 Upper Deck Ovation Standing Ovation

*STANDING O 151-180: 1.5X TO 4X BASIC
RANDOM IN UD ROOKIE DEBUT PACKS
STATED PRINT RUN 50 SERIAL #'d SETS

2002 Upper Deck Ovation Authentic McGwire

RANDOM INSERTS IN PACKS
STATED PRINT RUNS 70 SERIAL #'d SETS
AMB Mark McGwire Bat 30.00 60.00
AMJ Mark McGwire Jsy 30.00 60.00

2002 Upper Deck Ovation Authentic McGwire Gold

RANDOM INSERTS IN PACKS
STATED PRINT RUN 50 SERIAL #'d SETS
AMBG Mark McGwire Bat 60.00 120.00
AMJG Mark McGwire Jsy 60.00 120.00

2002 Upper Deck Ovation Diamond Futures Jerseys

STATED ODDS 1:72
GOLD RANDOM INSERTS IN PACKS
GOLD PRINT RUN 25 SERIAL #'d SETS
NO GOLD PRICING DUE TO SCARCITY
DFBZ Barry Zito 4.00 10.00
DFFG Freddy Garcia 4.00 10.00
DFIR Ivan Rodriguez 6.00 15.00
DFJK Jason Kendall 4.00 10.00
DFJP Jorge Posada 6.00 15.00
DFJR Jimmy Rollins 4.00 10.00
DFJV Jose Vidro 4.00 10.00
DFKS Kazuhiro Sasaki 4.00 10.00
DFLB Lance Berkman 4.00 10.00
DFPB Pat Burrell 4.00 10.00
DFRB Russell Branyan 4.00 10.00
DFTH Tim Hudson 4.00 10.00

2002 Upper Deck Ovation Lead Performer Jerseys

STATED ODDS 1:72
SP INFO PROVIDED BY UPPER DECK
GOLD RANDOM INSERTS IN PACKS
GOLD PRINT RUN 25 SERIAL #'d SETS
NO GOLD PRICING DUE TO SCARCITY
LPAR Alex Rodriguez 6.00 15.00
LPCD Carlos Delgado 4.00 10.00
LPFT Frank Thomas 6.00 15.00
LPIR Ivan Rodriguez 6.00 15.00
LPIS Ichiro Suzuki Shirt 20.00 50.00
LPJB Jeff Bagwell 6.00 15.00
LPJG Jason Giambi 4.00 10.00
LPJG Juan Gonzalez 4.00 10.00
LPKG Ken Griffey Jr. SP 10.00 25.00
LPLG Luis Gonzalez 4.00 10.00
LPMP Mike Piazza 6.00 15.00
LPSS Sammy Sosa SP 6.00 15.00

2002 Upper Deck Ovation Swatches

STATED ODDS 1:72
GOLD RANDOM INSERTS IN PACKS
GOLD PRINT RUN 25 SERIAL #'d SETS
NO GOLD PRICING DUE TO SCARCITY
OAR Alex Rodriguez 5.00 12.00
OBW Bernie Williams 2.50 6.00
OCD Carlos Delgado 1.50 4.00
OCJ Chipper Jones 4.00 10.00
ODE Darin Erstad 1.50 4.00
OEB Ellis Burks 1.50 4.00
OEC Eric Chavez 1.50 4.00
OGM Greg Maddux 6.00 15.00
OJB Jeromy Burnitz 1.50 4.00
OMG Mark Grace 2.50 6.00
OPM Pedro Martinez 2.50 6.00
ORA Roberto Alomar SP 2.50 6.00

2006 Upper Deck Ovation

COMP.SET w/o RC's (84) 10.00 25.00
COMMON CARD (1-84) .20 .50
COMMON ROOKIE (85-126) .75 2.00
85-126 STATED ODDS 1:18
85-126 PRINT RUN 999 SERIAL #'d SETS
EXQUISITE EXCH ODDS 1:144
EXQUISITE EXCH DEADLINE 07/27/07
1 Vladimir Guerrero .30 .75
2 Bartolo Colon .20 .50
3 Chone Figgins .20 .50
4 Lance Berkman .30 .75
5 Roy Oswalt .30 .75
6 Craig Biggio .30 .75
7 Rich Harden .20 .50
8 Eric Chavez .20 .50
9 Huston Street .20 .50
10 Vernon Wells .20 .50
11 Roy Halladay .30 .75
12 Troy Glaus .20 .50
13 Andruw Jones .20 .50
14 Chipper Jones .50 1.25
15 John Smoltz .50 1.25
16 Carlos Lee .20 .50
17 Rickie Weeks .20 .50
18 J.J. Hardy .20 .50
19 Albert Pujols .60 1.50
20 Chris Carpenter .30 .75
21 Scott Rolen .30 .75
22 Derrek Lee .20 .50
23 Mark Prior .30 .75
24 Aramis Ramirez .20 .50
25 Carl Crawford .30 .75
26 Scott Kazmir .30 .75
27 Luis Gonzalez .20 .50
28 Brandon Webb .30 .75
29 Chad Tracy .20 .50
30 Jeff Kent .20 .50
31 J.D. Drew .20 .50
32 Jason Schmidt .20 .50
33 Randy Winn .20 .50
34 Travis Hafner .20 .50
35 Victor Martinez .30 .75
36 Grady Sizemore .30 .75
37 Ichiro Suzuki .60 1.50
38 Felix Hernandez .30 .75
39 Adrian Beltre .50 1.25
40 Miguel Cabrera .50 1.25
41 Dontrelle Willis .20 .50
42 David Wright .40 1.00
43 Jose Reyes .30 .75
44 Pedro Martinez .30 .75
45 Carlos Beltran .30 .75
46 Alfonso Soriano .30 .75
47 Livan Hernandez .20 .50
48 Jose Guillen .20 .50
49 Miguel Tejada .30 .75
50 Brian Roberts .20 .50
51 Melvin Mora .20 .50
52 Jake Peavy .20 .50
53 Brian Giles .20 .50
54 Khalil Greene .20 .50
55 Bobby Abreu .20 .50
56 Ryan Howard .40 1.00
57 Chase Utley .30 .75
58 Jason Bay .20 .50
59 Sean Casey .20 .50
60 Mark Teixeira .30 .75
61 Michael Young .20 .50
62 Hank Blalock .20 .50
63 Manny Ramirez .50 1.25
64 David Ortiz .50 1.25
65 Josh Beckett .20 .50
66 Jason Varitek .50 1.25
67 Ken Griffey Jr. 1.00 2.50
68 Adam Dunn .30 .75
69 Todd Helton .30 .75
70 Garrett Atkins .20 .50
71 Reggie Sanders .20 .50
72 Mike Sweeney .20 .50
73 Chris Shelton .20 .50
74 Ivan Rodriguez .30 .75
75 Johan Santana .30 .75
76 Torii Hunter .20 .50
77 Justin Morneau .30 .75
78 Jim Thome .30 .75
79 Paul Konerko .30 .75
80 Scott Podsednik .20 .50
81 Derek Jeter 1.25 3.00
82 Hideki Matsui .50 1.25
83 Johnny Damon .30 .75
84 Alex Rodriguez .60 1.50
85 Conor Jackson (RC) 1.25 3.00
86 Joey Devine RC .75 2.00
87 Jonathan Papelbon (RC) 4.00 10.00
88 Freddie Bynum (RC) .75 2.00
89 Chris Denorfia (RC) .75 2.00
90 Ryan Shealy (RC) .75 2.00
91 Josh Wilson (RC) .75 2.00
92 Brian Anderson (RC) .75 2.00
93 Justin Verlander (RC) 6.00 15.00
94 Jeremy Hermida (RC) .75 2.00
95 Mike Jacobs (RC) .75 2.00
96 Josh Johnson (RC) 2.00 5.00
97 Hanley Ramirez (RC) 2.00 5.00
98 Josh Willingham (RC) 1.25 3.00
99 Cole Hamels (RC) 2.50 6.00
100 Hong-Chih Kuo (RC) 2.00 5.00
101 Cody Ross (RC) 2.00 5.00
102 Jose Capellan (RC) .75 2.00
103 Prince Fielder (RC) 4.00 10.00
104 David Gassner (RC) .75 2.00
105 Jason Kubel (RC) .75 2.00
106 Francisco Liriano (RC) 2.00 5.00
107 Anderson Hernandez (RC) .75 2.00
108 Boof Bonser (RC) 1.25 3.00
109 Jered Weaver (RC) 2.50 6.00
110 Ben Johnson (RC) .75 2.00
111 Jeff Harris RC .75 2.00
112 Stephen Drew (RC) 1.50 4.00
113 Matt Cain (RC) 5.00 12.00
114 Skip Schumaker (RC) .75 2.00
115 Adam Wainwright (RC) 1.25 3.00
116 Jeremy Sowers (RC) .75 2.00
117 Jason Bergmann RC .75 2.00
118 Chad Billingsley (RC) 1.25 3.00
119 Ryan Zimmerman (RC) 2.50 6.00
120 Macay McBride (RC) .75 2.00
121 Aaron Rakers (RC) .75 2.00
122 Alay Soler RC .75 2.00
123 Melky Cabrera (RC) 1.25 3.00
124 Tim Hamulack (RC) .75 2.00
125 Andre Ethier (RC) 2.50 6.00
126 Kenji Johjima RC 2.00 5.00

2006 Upper Deck Ovation Gold

*GOLD: 2.5X TO 6X BASIC
STATED ODDS 1:18
STATED PRINT RUN 499 SERIAL #'d SETS

2006 Upper Deck Ovation Gold Rookie Autographs

OVERALL AU ODDS 1:18
STATED PRINT RUN 99 SERIAL #'d SETS
EXCH DEADLINE 10/06/08
85 Conor Jackson 8.00 20.00
86 Joey Devine 5.00 12.00
87 Jonathan Papelbon 40.00 80.00
88 Freddie Bynum 5.00 12.00
89 Chris Denorfia 5.00 12.00
90 Ryan Shealy 5.00 12.00
92 Brian Anderson 5.00 12.00
93 Justin Verlander 25.00 60.00
94 Jeremy Hermida 8.00 20.00
95 Mike Jacobs 5.00 12.00
96 Josh Johnson 8.00 20.00
97 Hanley Ramirez 10.00 25.00
99 Cole Hamels 20.00 50.00
102 Jose Capellan 5.00 12.00
104 David Gassner 5.00 12.00
105 Jason Kubel 5.00 12.00
106 Francisco Liriano 20.00 50.00
107 Anderson Hernandez 5.00 12.00
108 Boof Bonser 5.00 12.00
109 Jered Weaver 10.00 25.00
110 Ben Johnson 5.00 12.00
111 Jeff Harris 5.00 12.00
113 Matt Cain 15.00 40.00
114 Skip Schumaker 6.00 15.00
115 Adam Wainwright 15.00 40.00
117 Jason Bergmann 5.00 12.00
118 Chad Billingsley 12.00 30.00
119 Ryan Zimmerman 20.00 50.00
120 Macay McBride 5.00 12.00
121 Aaron Rakers 5.00 12.00
124 Tim Hamulack 5.00 12.00
125 Andre Ethier 40.00 80.00

2006 Upper Deck Ovation Apparel

STATED ODDS 1:18
AB A.J. Burnett Jsy 3.00 8.00
AO Akinori Otsuka Jsy 3.00 8.00
AP Albert Pujols Jsy 8.00 20.00
BA Jason Bay Jsy 3.00 8.00
CC Carl Crawford Jsy 3.00 8.00
CF Chone Figgins Jsy 3.00 8.00
CL Carlos Lee Jsy 3.00 8.00
CS Chris Shelton Jsy 3.00 8.00
DJ Derek Jeter Pants 10.00 25.00
DO David Ortiz Jsy 4.00 10.00
DW David Wright Jsy 6.00 15.00
EC Eric Chavez Jsy 3.00 8.00
FH Felix Hernandez Jsy 4.00 10.00
GR Ken Griffey Jr. Jsy 6.00 15.00
GS Grady Sizemore Jsy 4.00 10.00
HA Travis Hafner Jsy 3.00 8.00
HE Todd Helton Jsy 4.00 10.00
HS Huston Street Jsy 3.00 8.00
HU Torii Hunter Jsy 3.00 8.00
JB Jeremy Bonderman Jsy 3.00 8.00
JE Jim Edmonds Jsy 4.00 10.00
JF Jeff Francoeur Jsy 4.00 10.00
JG Jonny Gomes Jsy 3.00 8.00
JH J.J. Hardy Jsy 3.00 8.00
JK Jeff Kent Jsy 3.00 8.00
JM Joe Mauer Jsy 4.00 10.00
KG Khalil Greene Jsy 4.00 10.00
LB Lance Berkman Jsy 3.00 8.00
MP Mark Prior Jsy 4.00 10.00
MR Manny Ramirez Jsy 4.00 10.00
MT Mark Teixeira Jsy 4.00 10.00
PF Prince Fielder Jsy 4.00 10.00
RH Ryan Howard Jsy 6.00 15.00
RK Ryan Klesko Jsy 3.00 8.00
RO Roy Oswalt Jsy 3.00 8.00
RZ Ryan Zimmerman Jsy SP 8.00 20.00
SR Scott Rolen Jsy 4.00 10.00
TH Trevor Hoffman Jsy 3.00 8.00
TN Trot Nixon Jsy 3.00 8.00
VG Vladimir Guerrero Jsy 4.00 10.00
VM Victor Martinez Jsy 3.00 8.00
VW Vernon Wells Jsy 3.00 8.00

2006 Upper Deck Ovation Center Stage

STATED ODDS 1:11
AC Aaron Cook .50 1.25
AP Albert Pujols 1.50 4.00
BC Bobby Crosby .50 1.25
CA Miguel Cabrera 1.25 3.00
CS Chris Shelton .50 1.25
CW Chien-Ming Wang .75 2.00
DC Daniel Cabrera .50 1.25
DD David DeJesus .50 1.25
DJ Derek Jeter 3.00 8.00
DL Derrek Lee .50 1.25
DW David Wright 1.00 2.50
FH Felix Hernandez .75 2.00
FS Freddy Sanchez .50 1.25
IS Ian Snell .50 1.25
JB Josh Beckett .50 1.25
JC Jose Contreras .50 1.25
JF Jason Frasor .50 1.25
KG Ken Griffey Jr. 2.50 6.00
MC Michael Cuddyer .50 1.25
MP Mark Prior .75 2.00
MT Mark Teixeira .75 2.00
RH Runelvys Hernandez .50 1.25
SD Stephen Drew 1.00 2.50
VG Vladimir Guerrero .75 2.00
YM Yadier Molina 1.50 4.00

2006 Upper Deck Ovation Curtain Calls

STATED ODDS 1:14
BC Bobby Crosby .50 1.25
CS Chris Shelton .50 1.25
CW Chien-Ming Wang .75 2.00
DC Daniel Cabrera .50 1.25
DD David DeJesus .50 1.25
EC Eric Chavez .50 1.25
FS Freddy Sanchez .50 1.25
HE Runelvys Hernandez .50 1.25
HR Horacio Ramirez .50 1.25
JC Jose Contreras .50 1.25
JE Jered Weaver 1.50 4.00
JW Josh Willingham .75 2.00
KG1 Ken Griffey Jr. 2.50 6.00
KG2 Ken Griffey Jr. 2.50 6.00
MP Mark Prior .75 2.00
MT Miguel Tejada .75 2.00
MY Michael Young .50 1.25
RH Rich Harden .50 1.25
TO Tomo Ohka .50 1.25
YM Yadier Molina 1.50 4.00

2006 Upper Deck Ovation Nation

STATED ODDS 1:19
AJ Andruw Jones .50 1.25
AP Albert Pujols 1.50 4.00
DC Daniel Cabrera .50 1.25
DJ Derek Jeter 3.00 8.00
DM Daisuke Matsuzaka 1.50 4.00
FC Frederich Cepeda .50 1.25
JA Jae Seo .50 1.25
JB Jason Bay .50 1.25
JS Johan Santana .75 2.00
KG Ken Griffey Jr. 2.50 6.00
MC Miguel Cabrera 1.25 3.00
MT Miguel Tejada .75 2.00
NM Nobuhiko Matsunaka .75 2.00
SL Seung Yeop Lee .75 2.00
YG Yoandy Garlobo .50 1.25

2006 Upper Deck Ovation Spotlight Signatures

OVERALL AU ODDS 1:18
AC Aaron Cook 4.00 10.00
AG Andy Green 4.00 10.00
BC Bobby Crosby 4.00 10.00
CA Miguel Cabrera 15.00 40.00
CS Chris Shelton 4.00 10.00
CW Chien-Ming Wang 12.50 30.00
DC Daniel Cabrera 4.00 10.00
DD David DeJesus 4.00 10.00
DR David Ross 20.00 50.00
EC Eric Chavez SP 6.00 15.00
EJ Edwin Jackson 4.00 10.00
FG Franklyn German 4.00 10.00
FN Fernando Nieve 4.00 10.00
FS Freddy Sanchez 6.00 15.00
HA Rich Harden SP 4.00 10.00
HR Horacio Ramirez SP 4.00 10.00
JB Josh Beckett SP 15.00 40.00
JC Jose Contreras 6.00 15.00
JD Jorge De La Rosa 4.00 10.00
JF Jason Frasor 4.00 10.00
JW Josh Willingham SP 6.00 15.00
KG1 Ken Griffey Jr. 30.00 60.00
KG2 Ken Griffey Jr. 30.00 60.00
KS Kirk Saarloos 4.00 10.00
LC Lance Cormier 4.00 10.00
MC Michael Cuddyer SP 6.00 15.00
MG Mike Gonzalez 4.00 10.00
MP Mark Prior 6.00 15.00
MT Matt Thornton 4.00 10.00
MW Michael Wuertz 4.00 10.00
MY Michael Young 6.00 15.00
RH Runelvys Hernandez 4.00 10.00
RW Ryan Wagner 4.00 10.00
SC Shawn Camp 4.00 10.00
TE Miguel Tejada SP 10.00 25.00
TO Tomo Ohka 10.00 25.00
TR Matt Treanor 4.00 10.00
YM Yadier Molina 30.00 80.00

2006 Upper Deck Ovation Superstar Theatre

STATED ODDS 1:9
AJ Andruw Jones .50 1.25
AP Albert Pujols 1.50 4.00
AR Alex Rodriguez 1.50 4.00
BA Jason Bay .50 1.25
BC Bobby Crosby .50 1.25
CC Chris Carpenter .75 2.00
CS Chris Shelton .50 1.25
CW Chien-Ming Wang .75 2.00
DC Daniel Cabrera .50 1.25
DD David DeJesus .50 1.25
DJ Derek Jeter 3.00 8.00
DL Derrek Lee .50 1.25
DO David Ortiz 1.25 3.00
HM Hideki Matsui 1.25 3.00
IS Ichiro Suzuki 1.50 4.00
JB Josh Beckett .50 1.25
JC Jose Contreras .50 1.25
KG1 Ken Griffey Jr. 2.50 6.00
KG2 Ken Griffey Jr. 2.50 6.00
MC Miguel Cabrera 1.25 3.00
MP Mark Prior .75 2.00
MR Manny Ramirez 1.25 3.00
MT Miguel Tejada .75 2.00
MY Michael Young .50 1.25
PM Pedro Martinez .75 2.00
RH Rich Harden .50 1.25
TE Mark Teixeira .75 2.00
TH Travis Hafner .50 1.25
TO Tomo Ohka .50 1.25
YM Yadier Molina 1.50 4.00

2003 Upper Deck Play Ball UD Promos

*PROMOS: 1.25X TO 3X BASIC CARDS

2003 Upper Deck Play Ball

COMP.SET w/o SP's (74) 15.00 40.00
COMMON CARD (1-73) .12 .30
COMMON CARD (74-88) .75 2.00
74-88 STATED ODDS 1:24
COMMON T.WILLIAMS (89-103) 4.00 10.00
89-103 STATED ODDS 1:24
CARD 104 IS NOT AN SP
1 Troy Glaus .12 .30
2 Darin Erstad .12 .30
3 Randy Johnson .30 .75
4 Luis Gonzalez .12 .30
5 Curt Schilling .20 .50
6 Tom Glavine .20 .50
7 Chipper Jones .30 .75
8 Greg Maddux .40 1.00
9 Andruw Jones .12 .30
10 Pedro Martinez .20 .50
11 Manny Ramirez .30 .75
12 Nomar Garciaparra .20 .50
13 Billy Williams .20 .50
14 Sammy Sosa .30 .75
15 Kerry Wood .12 .30
16 Mark Prior .20 .50
17 Ernie Banks .30 .75
18 Frank Thomas .30 .75
19 Joe Morgan .20 .50
20 Ken Griffey Jr. .60 1.50
21 Adam Dunn .20 .50
22 Jim Thome .20 .50
23 Todd Helton .20 .50
24 Larry Walker .20 .50
25 Lance Berkman .20 .50
26 Roy Oswalt .20 .50
27 Jeff Bagwell .20 .50
28 Nolan Ryan 1.00 2.50
29 Mike Sweeney .12 .30
30 Shawn Green .12 .30
31 Hideo Nomo .30 .75
32 Kazuhisa Ishii .12 .30
33 Richie Sexson .12 .30
34 Robin Yount .30 .75
35 Harmon Killebrew .30 .75
36 Torii Hunter .12 .30
37 Vladimir Guerrero .20 .50
38 Roberto Alomar .20 .50
39 Mike Piazza .30 .75
40 Tom Seaver .20 .50
41 Phil Rizzuto .20 .50

42 Yogi Berra .30 .75
43 Mike Mussina .20 .50
44 Roger Clemens .40 1.00
45 Derek Jeter .75 2.00
46 Jason Giambi .12 .30
47 Bernie Williams .20 .50
48 Alfonso Soriano .20 .50
49 Catfish Hunter .20 .50
50 Barry Zito .20 .50
51 Eric Chavez .12 .30
52 Tim Hudson .20 .50
53 Rollie Fingers .20 .50
54 Miguel Tejada .20 .50
55 Pat Burrell .12 .30
56 Brian Giles .12 .30
57 Willie Stargell .20 .50
58 Phil Nevin .12 .30
59 Orlando Cepeda .20 .50
60 Barry Bonds .50 1.25
61 Jeff Kent .12 .30
62 Willie McCovey .20 .50
63 Ichiro Suzuki .40 1.00
64 Stan Musial .50 1.25
65 Albert Pujols .40 1.00
66 J.D. Drew .12 .30
67 Scott Rolen .20 .50
68 Mark McGwire .50 1.25
69 Alex Rodriguez .40 1.00
70 Juan Gonzalez .12 .30
71 Ivan Rodriguez .20 .50
72 Rafael Palmeiro .20 .50
73 Carlos Delgado .12 .30
74 Ted Williams S41 4.00 10.00
75 Hank Greenberg S41 2.00 5.00
76 Joe DiMaggio S41 4.00 10.00
77 Lefty Gomez S41 .75 2.00
78 Tommy Henrich S41 .75 2.00
79 Pee Wee Reese S41 1.25 3.00
80 Mel Ott S41 2.00 5.00
81 Carl Hubbell S41 1.25 3.00
82 Jimmie Foxx S41 2.00 5.00
83 Joe Cronin S41 .75 2.00
84 Charlie Gehringer S41 .75 2.00
85 Frank Hayes S41 .75 2.00
86 Babe Dahlgren S41 .75 2.00
87 Dolph Camilli S41 .75 2.00
88 Johnny VanderMeer S41 .75 2.00
89 Ted Williams TRIB 3.00 8.00
90 Ted Williams TRIB 3.00 8.00
91 Ted Williams TRIB 3.00 8.00
92 Ted Williams TRIB 3.00 8.00
93 Ted Williams TRIB 3.00 8.00
94 Ted Williams TRIB 3.00 8.00
95 Ted Williams TRIB 3.00 8.00
96 Ted Williams TRIB 3.00 8.00
97 Ted Williams TRIB 3.00 8.00
98 Ted Williams TRIB 3.00 8.00
99 Ted Williams TRIB 3.00 8.00
100 Ted Williams TRIB 3.00 8.00
101 Ted Williams TRIB 3.00 8.00
102 Ted Williams TRIB 3.00 8.00
103 Ted Williams TRIB 3.00 8.00
104 Hideki Matsui RC 1.25 3.00
MM1 Mark McGwire Sample .50 1.25

2003 Upper Deck Play Ball 1941 Series

*1941 ACTIVE: 1.25X TO 3X BASIC
*1941 RETIRED: 1.25X TO 3X BASIC
STATED ODDS 1:2

2003 Upper Deck Play Ball Red Backs

*RED BACK ACTIVE 1-73: .75X TO 2X BASIC
*RED BACK RETIRED 1-73: .75X TO 2X BASIC
*RED BACK 74-88: .6X TO 1.5X BASIC
*RED BACK 89-103: .6X TO 1.5X BASIC
*RED BACK 104: 1X TO 2.5X BASIC
1-73/104 STATED ODDS 1:1
74-103 STATED ODDS 1:96

2003 Upper Deck Play Ball 1941 Reprints

COMPLETE SET (25) 12.50 30.00
STATED ODDS 1:2
R1 Ted Williams 2.00 5.00
R2 Hank Greenberg 1.00 2.50
R3 Joe DiMaggio 2.00 5.00
R4 Lefty Gomez .40 1.00
R5 Tommy Henrich .40 1.00
R6 Pee Wee Reese .60 1.50
R7 Mel Ott 1.00 2.50
R8 Carl Hubbell .60 1.50
R9 Jimmie Foxx 1.00 2.50
R10 Joe Cronin .40 1.00
R11 Charley Gehringer .40 1.00
R12 Frank Hayes .40 1.00
R13 Babe Dahlgren .40 1.00
R14 Dolph Camilli .40 1.00
R15 Johnny VanderMeer .40 1.00
R16 Bucky Walters .40 1.00
R17 Red Ruffing .40 1.00
R18 Charlie Keller .40 1.00
R19 Indian Bob Johnson .40 1.00
R20 Dutch Leonard .40 1.00
R21 Barney McCosky .40 1.00
R22 Soupy Campbell .40 1.00
R23 Stormy Weatherly .40 1.00
R24 Bobby Doerr .60 1.50
R25 Bill Dickey .60 1.50

2003 Upper Deck Play Ball Game Used Memorabilia Tier 1

STATED ODDS 1:82
GOLD RANDOM INSERTS IN PACKS
GOLD PRINT RUN 25 SERIAL #'d SETS
NO GOLD PRICING DUE TO SCARCITY
AD1 Adam Dunn Jsy 3.00 8.00
AS1 Alfonso Soriano Jsy 3.00 8.00
BW1 Bernie Williams Jsy 4.00 10.00
CD1 Carlos Delgado Jsy 3.00 8.00
CJ1 Chipper Jones Jsy 4.00 10.00
CS1 Curt Schilling Jsy 3.00 8.00
DR1 J.D. Drew Jsy 3.00 8.00
IR1 Ivan Rodriguez Jsy 4.00 10.00
IS1 Ichiro Suzuki Jsy 15.00 40.00
JG1 Jason Giambi Jsy 3.00 8.00
KG1 Ken Griffey Jr. Jsy 10.00 25.00
KI1 Kazuhisa Ishii Jsy 3.00 8.00
LG1 Luis Gonzalez Jsy 3.00 8.00
MM1 Mark McGwire Jsy 10.00 25.00
MP1 Mike Piazza Jsy 6.00 15.00
MS1 Mike Sweeney Jsy 3.00 8.00
PR1 Mark Prior Jsy 4.00 10.00
RC1 Roger Clemens Jsy 8.00 20.00
RP1 Rafael Palmeiro Jsy 4.00 10.00
SS1 Sammy Sosa Jsy 4.00 10.00
TH1 Tommy Henrich Pants 3.00 8.00

2003 Upper Deck Play Ball Game Used Memorabilia Tier 2

RANDOM INSERTS IN PACKS
STATED PRINT RUN 150 SERIAL #'d SETS
AJ2 Andruw Jones Jsy 6.00 15.00
AR2 Alex Rodriguez Jsy 10.00 25.00
CJ2 Chipper Jones Jsy 8.00 20.00
CS2 Curt Schilling Jsy 4.00 10.00
DE2 Darin Erstad Jsy 4.00 10.00
GM2 Greg Maddux Jsy 6.00 15.00
IS2 Ichiro Suzuki Jsy 40.00 80.00
JB2 Jeff Bagwell Jsy 6.00 15.00
JD2 Joe DiMaggio Jsy 30.00 80.00
JG2 Jason Giambi Jsy 4.00 10.00
JT2 Jim Thome Jsy 6.00 15.00
KG2 Ken Griffey Jr. Jsy 10.00 25.00
KW2 Kerry Wood Jsy 4.00 10.00
LB2 Lance Berkman Jsy 4.00 10.00
MM2 Mark McGwire Jsy 15.00 40.00
MP2 Mike Piazza Jsy 6.00 15.00
MR2 Manny Ramirez Jsy 6.00 15.00
PM2 Pedro Martinez Jsy 6.00 15.00
RJ2 Randy Johnson Jsy 8.00 20.00
SG2 Shawn Green Jsy 4.00 10.00
SS2 Sammy Sosa Jsy 8.00 20.00

2003 Upper Deck Play Ball Game Used Memorabilia Tier 2 Signatures

RANDOM INSERTS IN PACKS
STATED PRINT RUN 50 SERIAL #'d SETS
ALL MCGWIRE'S INSCRIBED ALL CENTURY
AJ2 Andruw Jones Jsy 50.00 100.00
AR2 Alex Rodriguez Jsy/285 20.00 50.00
CS2 Curt Schilling Jsy 50.00 100.00
DE2 Darin Erstad Jsy 40.00 80.00
IS2 Ichiro Suzuki Jsy 1000.00 2000.00
JB2 Jeff Bagwell Jsy 60.00 120.00
JG2 Jason Giambi Jsy 8.00 20.00
JT2 Jim Thome Jsy 50.00 100.00
KG2 Ken Griffey Jr. Jsy 75.00 150.00
KW2 Kerry Wood Jsy 10.00 25.00
LB2 Lance Berkman Jsy 50.00 100.00
MM2 Mark McGwire Jsy 100.00 200.00
SS2 Sammy Sosa Jsy 50.00 100.00

2003 Upper Deck Play Ball Yankee Clipper 1941 Streak

COMMON CARD (1-41) 3.00 8.00
COMMON CARD (42-56) 3.00 8.00
1-41 STATED ODDS 1:12
42-56 STATED ODDS 1:24

2003 Upper Deck Play Ball Hawaii

COMPLETE SET (10) 60.00 150.00
KY1 Sammy Sosa 6.00 15.00
KY2 Ken Griffey Jr. 12.00 30.00
KY3 Jason Giambi 2.50 6.00
KY4 Ichiro Suzuki 8.00 20.00
KY5 Mark McGwire 10.00 25.00
KY6 Troy Glaus 2.50 6.00
KY7 Derek Jeter 15.00 40.00
KY8 Barry Bonds 10.00 25.00
KY9 Alex Rodriguez 8.00 20.00
KY10 Nomar Garciaparra 4.00 10.00

2003 Upper Deck Play Ball Hawaii Autographs

JG Jason Giambi 15.00 30.00

2004 Upper Deck Play Ball

COMP.SET w/o SP's (132) 10.00 25.00
COMP.UPDATE SET (50) 8.00 20.00
COMMON ACTIVE (1-132) .10 .30
COMMON RETIRED (1-132) .10 .30
COMMON CARD (133-162) .60 1.50
133-162 STATED ODDS 1:16
133-162 PRINT RUN 2004 SERIAL #'d SETS
COMMON CARD (163-183) .60 1.50
163-183 STATED ODDS 1:24
163-183 PRINT RUN 1999 SERIAL #'d SETS
COMMON CARD (183-232) .25 .60
ONE UPDATE SET PER 4 UD2 HOBBY BOXES
1 Hideo Nomo .30 .75
2 Curt Schilling .20 .50
3 Barry Zito .20 .50
4 Nomar Garciaparra .20 .50
5 Yogi Berra .30 .75
6 Randy Johnson .30 .75
7 Jason Giambi .12 .30
8 Sammy Sosa .30 .75
9 David Ortiz .30 .75
10 Derek Jeter .75 2.00
11 Warren Spahn .20 .50
12 Mark Prior .20 .50
13 Roger Clemens .40 1.00
14 Mike Piazza .30 .75
15 Nolan Ryan 1.00 2.50
16 Joe DiMaggio .60 1.50
17 Alfonso Soriano .20 .50
18 Brandon Webb .12 .30
19 Shawn Green .12 .30
20 Bob Feller .20 .50
21 Mike Schmidt .50 1.25
22 Mark Teixeira .20 .50
23 Pedro Martinez .20 .50
24 Vladimir Guerrero .20 .50
25 Rafael Furcal .12 .30
26 Derrek Lee .12 .30
27 Carlos Delgado .12 .30
28 Mickey Mantle 1.00 2.50
29 Dontrelle Willis .12 .30
30 Ted Williams .60 1.50
31 Vernon Wells .12 .30
32 Alex Rodriguez Yanks .40 1.00
33 Brooks Robinson .20 .50
34 Tom Seaver .20 .50
35 Ernie Banks .30 .75
36 Bob Gibson .20 .50
37 Jim Thome .20 .50
38 Mike Mussina .20 .50
39 Eric Chavez .12 .30
40 Roy Halladay .20 .50
41 Eric Gagne .12 .30
42 Jose Reyes .20 .50
43 Jeff Bagwell .20 .50
44 Rich Harden .12 .30
45 Jeff Kent .12 .30
46 Lance Berkman .20 .50
47 Adam Dunn .20 .50
48 Richie Sexson .12 .30
49 Andruw Jones .12 .30
50 Ichiro Suzuki .40 1.00
51 Edgar Renteria .12 .30
52 Rocco Baldelli .12 .30
53 Jim Edmonds .20 .50
54 Magglio Ordonez .20 .50
55 Austin Kearns .12 .30
56 Garret Anderson .12 .30
57 Manny Ramirez .30 .75
58 Roy Oswalt .20 .50
59 Gary Sheffield .12 .30
60 Mark Mulder .12 .30
61 Ben Sheets .12 .30
62 Scott Rolen .20 .50
63 Greg Maddux .40 1.00
64 Jose Contreras .12 .30
65 Miguel Cabrera .30 .75
66 Hank Blalock .12 .30
67 Miguel Tejada .20 .50
68 Albert Pujols .40 1.00
69 Hideki Matsui .50 1.25
70 Mike Lowell .12 .30
71 Tim Hudson .20 .50
72 Bret Boone .12 .30
73 Ivan Rodriguez .20 .50
74 Josh Beckett .12 .30
75 Todd Helton .20 .50
76 Brian Giles .12 .30
77 Orlando Cabrera .12 .30
78 Carlos Beltran .20 .50
79 Jason Schmidt .12 .30
80 Kerry Wood .12 .30
81 Preston Wilson .12 .30
82 Troy Glaus .12 .30
83 Kevin Brown .12 .30
84 Rafael Palmeiro .20 .50
85 Chipper Jones .30 .75
86 Reggie Sanders .12 .30
87 Cliff Floyd .12 .30
88 Corey Patterson .12 .30
89 Kevin Millwood .12 .30
90 Aaron Boone .12 .30
91 Darin Erstad .12 .30
92 Richard Hidalgo .12 .30
93 Dmitri Young .12 .30
94 Jeremy Bonderman .12 .30
95 Larry Walker .20 .50
96 Edgar Martinez .20 .50
97 Jerome Williams .12 .30
98 Luis Gonzalez .12 .30
99 Roberto Alomar .20 .50
100 Jerry Hairston Jr. .12 .30
101 Luis Matos .12 .30
102 Andy Pettitte .20 .50
103 Frank Thomas .30 .75
104 Rondell White .12 .30
105 Jody Gerut .12 .30
106 Bartolo Colon .12 .30
107 Johnny Damon .20 .50
108 Ryan Klesko .12 .30
109 Geoff Jenkins .12 .30
110 Jorge Posada .20 .50
111 Melvin Mora .12 .30
112 Bernie Williams .20 .50
113 Shannon Stewart .12 .30
114 Bobby Abreu .12 .30
115 Jose Guillen .12 .30
116 Brandon Phillips .12 .30
117 Jose Vidro .12 .30
118 Mike Sweeney .12 .30
119 Jacque Jones .12 .30
120 Josh Phelps .12 .30
121 Milton Bradley .12 .30
122 Torii Hunter .12 .30
123 Carl Crawford .20 .50
124 Javier Vazquez .12 .30
125 Juan Gonzalez .12 .30
126 Travis Hafner .12 .30
127 Ken Griffey Jr. .60 1.50
128 Phil Nevin .12 .30
129 Trot Nixon .12 .30
130 Carlos Lee .12 .30
131 Javy Lopez .12 .30
132 Jay Gibbons .12 .30
133 Brandon Medders RP RC .60 1.50
134 Colby Miller RP RC .60 1.50
135 Dave Crouthers RP RC .60 1.50
136 Dennis Sarfate RP RC .60 1.50
137 Donald Kelly RP RC 1.00 2.50
138 Frank Brooks RP RC .60 1.50
139 Chris Aguila RP RC .60 1.50
140 Greg Dobbs RP RC .60 1.50
141 Ian Snell RP RC .60 1.50
142 Jake Woods RP RC .60 1.50
143 Jamie Brown RP RC .60 1.50
144 Jason Frasor RP RC .60 1.50
145 Jerome Gamble RP RC .60 1.50
146 Jesse Harper RP RC .60 1.50
147 Josh Labandeira RP RC .60 1.50
148 Justin Hampson RP RC .60 1.50
149 Justin Huisman RP RC .60 1.50
150 Justin Leone RP RC .60 1.50
151 Lincoln Holdzkom RP RC .60 1.50
152 Mike Bumatay RP RC .60 1.50
153 Mike Gosling RP RC .60 1.50
154 Mike Johnston RP RC .60 1.50
155 Mike Rouse RP RC .60 1.50
156 Nick Regilio RP RC .60 1.50
157 Ryan Meaux RP RC .60 1.50
158 Scott Dohmann RP RC .60 1.50
159 Sean Henn RP RC .60 1.50
160 Tim Bausher RP RC .60 1.50
161 Tim Bittner RP RC .60 1.50
162 Alec Zumwalt RP RC .60 1.50
163 Boone 1.00 2.50
Jenk
Prior
Zito CC
164 Pujols 2.00 5.00
Renteria
A.Rod CC
165 A.Soriano 1.50 4.00
S.Sosa CC
166 B.Abreu 1.00 2.50
J.Thome CC
167 Boone 2.00 5.00
Olerud
Ichiro CC
168 D.Jeter 4.00 10.00
A.Soriano CC
169 E.Chavez 1.00 2.50
M.Tejada CC
170 Garret 1.00 2.50
Edmonds
Glaus CC
171 H.Blalock 2.00 5.00
A.Rodriguez CC
172 A.Rod 2.00 5.00
Teix
Young
Raffy CC
173 I.Rodriguez 1.00 2.50
D.Willis CC
174 J.Giambi 4.00 10.00
D.Jeter CC
175 J.DiMaggio 5.00 12.00
M.Mantle CC
176 DiMaggio 5.00 12.00
Mantle
T.Will CC
177 J.DiMaggio 3.00 8.00
T.Williams CC
178 N.Garciaparra 1.00 2.50
A.Soriano CC
179 N.Garciaparra 1.00 2.50
J.Giambi CC
180 P.LoDuca 1.50 4.00
H.Nomo CC
181 Raffy 2.00 5.00
A.Rod
Young CC
182 R.Kiner 3.00 8.00
T.Williams CC
183A A.Boone 4.00 10.00
D.Jeter CC
183B Kazuo Matsui RC .40 1.00
184 Jerry Gil RC .25 .60
185 Jose Capellan RC .25 .60
186 Tim Hamulack RC .25 .60
187 Renyel Pinto RC .25 .60
188 Carlos Vasquez RC .25 .60
189 Enemencio Pacheco RC .25 .60
190 Ronny Cedeno RC .25 .60
191 Mariano Gomez RC .25 .60
192 Carlos Hines RC .25 .60
193 Mike Vento RC .25 .60
194 David Aardsma RC .25 .60
195 Hector Gimenez RC .25 .60
196 Fernando Nieve RC .25 .60
197 Chris Saenz RC .25 .60
198 Shawn Hill RC .25 .60
199 Angel Chavez RC .25 .60
200 Scott Proctor RC .25 .60
201 William Bergolla RC .25 .60
202 Justin Germano RC .25 .60
203 Onil Joseph RC .25 .60
204 Rusty Tucker RC .25 .60
205 Justin Knoedler RC .25 .60
206 Casey Daigle RC .25 .60
207 Edwin Moreno RC .25 .60
208 Chad Bentz RC .25 .60
209 Ryan Wing RC .25 .60
210 Shawn Camp RC .25 .60
211 Eddy Rodriguez RC .25 .60
212 Roman Colon RC .25 .60
213 Jason Bartlett RC .75 2.00
214 Jorge Vasquez RC .25 .60
215 Ivan Ochoa RC .25 .60
216 Akinori Otsuka RC .25 .60
217 Merkin Valdez RC .25 .60
218 Shingo Takatsu RC .25 .60
219 Chris Oxspring RC .25 .60
220 Kevin Cave RC .25 .60
221 Ramon Ramirez RC .25 .60
222 Orlando Rodriguez RC .25 .60
223 Lino Urdaneta RC .25 .60
224 Franklyn Gracesqui RC .25 .60
225 Michael Wuertz RC .25 .60
226 Jorge Sequea RC .25 .60
227 Luis A. Gonzalez RC .25 .60
228 Jason Szuminski RC .25 .60
229 John Gall RC .25 .60
230 Freddy Guzman RC .25 .60
231 Jeff Bennett RC .25 .60
232 Roberto Novoa RC .25 .60

2004 Upper Deck Play Ball Blue

*BLUE ACTIVE: 1.5X TO 4X BASIC
*BLUE RETIRED: 1.5X TO 4X BASIC
STATED ODDS 1:6

2004 Upper Deck Play Ball Parallel 175

*PAR.175 ACTIVE: 2.5X TO 6X BASIC
*PAR.175 RETIRED: 2.5X TO 6X BASIC
RANDOM INSERTS IN PACKS
STATED PRINT RUN 175 SERIAL #'d SETS
1-42 FEATURE THICK RED BORDERS
43-132 FEATURE DIE-CUT SILVER BORDERS

2004 Upper Deck Play Ball Apparel Collection

STATED ODDS 1:24
SP INFO PROVIDED BY UPPER DECK
AD Adam Dunn 3.00 8.00
AP Albert Pujols 6.00 15.00
AR Alex Rodriguez SP 6.00 15.00
AS Alfonso Soriano 3.00 8.00
BE Josh Beckett 3.00 8.00
BH Bo Hart 3.00 8.00
BW Bernie Williams 4.00 10.00
BZ Barry Zito SP 4.00 10.00
CD Carlos Delgado 3.00 8.00
CJ Chipper Jones 4.00 10.00
CS Curt Schilling 3.00 8.00
DJ Derek Jeter 8.00 20.00
DW Dontrelle Willis 4.00 10.00
HA Roy Halladay 3.00 8.00
HM Hideki Matsui 10.00 25.00
HN Hideo Nomo 4.00 10.00
IS Ichiro Suzuki 10.00 25.00
JB Jeff Bagwell 4.00 10.00
JD Joe DiMaggio SP/150 30.00 60.00
JG Jason Giambi 3.00 8.00
JP Jorge Posada 4.00 10.00
JT Jim Thome 4.00 10.00
KG Ken Griffey Jr. 6.00 15.00
KW Kerry Wood 3.00 8.00
LB Lance Berkman 3.00 8.00
ML Mike Lowell SP 4.00 10.00
MM Mickey Mantle SP/150 60.00 120.00
MP Mark Prior 4.00 10.00
MR Manny Ramirez 4.00 10.00
MU Mike Mussina 4.00 10.00
PI Mike Piazza 4.00 10.00
PM Pedro Martinez SP 6.00 15.00
RB Rocco Baldelli 3.00 8.00
RF Rafael Furcal 3.00 8.00
RH Rich Harden SP 4.00 10.00
RJ Randy Johnson 4.00 10.00
RO Roy Oswalt 3.00 8.00
RP Rafael Palmeiro 4.00 10.00
SS Sammy Sosa 4.00 10.00
TG Troy Glaus 3.00 8.00
TH Torii Hunter 3.00 8.00
TW Ted Williams SP/150 30.00 60.00

2004 Upper Deck Play Ball Artist's Touch Jersey

STATED PRINT RUN 250 SERIAL #'d SETS
*JERSEY 50: .6X TO 1.5X BASIC
JERSEY 50 PRINT 50 SERIAL #'d SETS
RANDOM INSERTS IN PACKS
AP Albert Pujols 6.00 15.00
AR Alex Rodriguez 4.00 10.00
AS Alfonso Soriano 3.00 8.00
BH Bo Hart 3.00 8.00
BW Bernie Williams 4.00 10.00
BZ Barry Zito 3.00 8.00
CD Carlos Delgado 3.00 8.00
CJ Chipper Jones 4.00 10.00
DJ Derek Jeter 8.00 20.00
DW Dontrelle Willis 4.00 10.00
HA Roy Halladay 3.00 8.00
HM Hideki Matsui 10.00 25.00
HN Hideo Nomo 4.00 10.00
IS Ichiro Suzuki 10.00 25.00
JB Josh Beckett 3.00 8.00
JG Jason Giambi 3.00 8.00
JP Jorge Posada 4.00 10.00
JT Jim Thome 4.00 10.00
KG Ken Griffey Jr. 6.00 15.00
KW Kerry Wood 3.00 8.00
LB Lance Berkman 3.00 8.00
MM Mike Mussina 4.00 10.00
MP Mark Prior 4.00 10.00
MR Manny Ramirez 4.00 10.00
PI Mike Piazza 5.00 12.00
PM Pedro Martinez 4.00 10.00
RB Rocco Baldelli 3.00 8.00
RF Rafael Furcal 3.00 8.00
RJ Randy Johnson 4.00 10.00
RO Roy Oswalt 3.00 8.00
RP Rafael Palmeiro 4.00 10.00
SS Sammy Sosa 4.00 10.00
TG Troy Glaus 3.00 8.00
TH Torii Hunter 3.00 8.00

2004 Upper Deck Play Ball Home Run Heroics

STATED ODDS 1:24
AB Aaron Boone Walk-Off .60 1.50
AR Alex Rodriguez M's 40th 2.00 5.00
AR1 Alex Rodriguez Rgr 57th 2.00 5.00
AS Alfonso Soriano 13th Lead 1.00 2.50
BM Bill Mueller 2 Slams .60 1.50
CD Carlos Delgado 4 HR's .60 1.50
CR Cal Ripken 9-6-95 5.00 12.00
CR1 Cal Ripken 9-5-95 5.00 12.00
EB Ernie Banks 500th 1.50 4.00
EM Eddie Mathews 500th 1.50 4.00
FR Frank Robinson AS 1.00 2.50
HB Hank Blalock AS .60 1.50
HK Harmon Killebrew 500th 1.50 4.00
HM Hideki Matsui Slam 2.50 6.00
HM1 Hideki Matsui WS 2.50 6.00
JD Joe DiMaggio 361st 3.00 8.00
JD1 Joe DiMaggio 1st 3.00 8.00
JG Jason Giambi Slam .60 1.50
KG Ken Griffey Jr. M's 1st 3.00 8.00
KG1 Ken Griffey Jr. M's 8th Cons. 3.00 8.00
MC Miguel Cabrera Walk-Off 1.50 4.00
MM Mickey Mantle 1st 5.00 12.00
MM1 Mickey Mantle WS 5.00 12.00
MM2 Mickey Mantle 500th 5.00 12.00
MS Mike Schmidt 500th 2.50 6.00
RH Rickey Henderson 81st Lead 1.50 4.00
RJ Randy Johnson 1st 1.50 4.00
RP Rafael Palmeiro 500th 1.00 2.50
RS Red Schoendienst 14th Inn 1.00 2.50
SG Shawn Green 7 HR's .60 1.50
SM Stan Musial Walk-Off 2.50 6.00
SS Sammy Sosa Rgr 1st 1.50 4.00
SS1 Sammy Sosa Cubs June 1.50 4.00
SS2 Sammy Sosa Cubs 66th 1.50 4.00
SS3 Sammy Sosa Cubs 500th 1.50 4.00
TW Ted Williams AS 3.00 8.00
TW1 Ted Williams 500th 3.00 8.00
TW2 Ted Williams Final AB 3.00 8.00
TW3 Ted Williams 1st Ever 3.00 8.00
WM Willie McCovey 500th 1.00 2.50

2004 Upper Deck Play Ball Rookie Portfolio Signature

STATED ODDS 1:30
AZ Alec Zumwalt 3.00 8.00
BI Tim Bittner 3.00 8.00
BM Brandon Medders 3.00 8.00
CA Chris Aguila 3.00 8.00
CM Colby Miller 3.00 8.00
DC Dave Crouthers 3.00 8.00
DK Donald Kelly 3.00 8.00
DS Dennis Sarfate 3.00 8.00
FB Frank Brooks 3.00 8.00
GD Greg Dobbs 3.00 8.00
HA Justin Hampson 3.00 8.00
HU Justin Huisman 3.00 8.00
IS Ian Snell 6.00 15.00
JB Jamie Brown 3.00 8.00
JF Jason Frasor 3.00 8.00
JG Jerome Gamble 3.00 8.00
JH Jesse Harper 3.00 8.00
JL Josh Labandeira 3.00 8.00
JW Jake Woods 3.00 8.00
LE Justin Leone 4.00 10.00
LH Lincoln Holdzkom 3.00 8.00
MB Mike Bumatay 3.00 8.00
MG Mike Gosling 3.00 8.00
MJ Mike Johnston 3.00 8.00
MR Mike Rouse 3.00 8.00
NR Nick Regilio 3.00 8.00
RM Ryan Meaux 3.00 8.00
SD Scott Dohmann 3.00 8.00
SH Sean Henn 3.00 8.00
TB Tim Bausher 3.00 8.00

2004 Upper Deck Play Ball Signature Portfolio Black 100

STATED PRINT RUN 100 SERIAL #'d SETS
BLACK 10 PRINT RUN 10 SERIAL #'d SETS
NO BLACK 10 PRICING DUE TO SCARCITY
BLUE 25 PRINT RUN 25 SERIAL #'d SETS
NO BLUE 25 PRICING DUE TO SCARCITY
BLUE 5 PRINT RUN 5 SERIAL #'d SETS
NO BLUE 5 PRICING DUE TO SCARCITY
RED 10 PRINT RUN 10 SERIAL #'d SETS
NO RED 10 PRICING DUE TO SCARCITY
RED 1 PRINT RUN 1 SERIAL #'d SET
NO RED 1 PRICING DUE TO SCARCITY
BZ Barry Zito 6.00 15.00
CR Cal Ripken 50.00 100.00
CZ Carl Yastrzemski 40.00 80.00
HM Hideki Matsui 175.00 300.00
KG Ken Griffey Jr. 50.00 100.00
TS Tom Seaver 25.00 60.00

2004 Upper Deck Play Ball Tools of the Stars Bat

STATED ODDS 1:48
TOOLS 25 RANDOM INSERTS IN PACKS
TOOLS 25 PRINT RUN 25 SERIAL #'d SETS
NO TOOLS 25 PRICING DUE TO SCARCITY
*TOOLS 250: .4X TO 1X BASIC
TOOLS 250 RANDOM INSERTS IN PACKS
TOOLS 250 PRINT RUN 250 SERIAL #'d SETS
AP Albert Pujols 6.00 15.00
AR Alex Rodriguez 4.00 10.00
AS Alfonso Soriano 3.00 8.00
CD Carlos Delgado 3.00 8.00
CJ Chipper Jones 4.00 10.00
DJ Derek Jeter 8.00 20.00
HM Hideki Matsui 10.00 25.00
HN Hideo Nomo 4.00 10.00
IS Ichiro Suzuki 10.00 25.00
JB Josh Beckett 3.00 8.00
JT Jim Thome 4.00 10.00
KG Ken Griffey Jr. 6.00 15.00
KW Kerry Wood 3.00 8.00
PI Mike Piazza 4.00 10.00

2004 Upper Deck Power Up

COMPLETE SET (100) 10.00 25.00
COMMON CARD (1-100) .08 .25
BASIC CARDS WORTH 10 POINTS EACH
1 Austin Kearns .10 .25
2 Rafael Furcal .10 .25
3 Larry Walker .15 .40
4 Jeremy Bonderman .10 .25
5 Scott Rolen .15 .40
6 Nomar Garciaparra .15 .40
7 Jody Gerut .10 .25
8 Troy Glaus .10 .25
9 Roy Halladay .15 .40
10 Barry Zito .15 .40
11 Gary Sheffield .10 .25
12 Ichiro Suzuki .30 .75
13 Juan Gonzalez .10 .25
14 Jim Edmonds .15 .40
15 Hank Blalock .10 .25
16 Roy Oswalt .15 .40
17 Magglio Ordonez .15 .40
18 Garret Anderson .10 .25
19 Mark Teixeira .15 .40
20 Mike Sweeney .10 .25
21 Reggie Sanders .10 .25
22 Rafael Palmeiro .15 .40
23 Orlando Cabrera .10 .25
24 Edgar Renteria .10 .25
25 Ryan Klesko .10 .25
26 Torii Hunter .10 .25
27 Bret Boone .10 .25
28 Roberto Alomar .15 .40
29 Frank Thomas .25 .60
30 Chipper Jones .25 .60
31 Eric Chavez .10 .25
32 Miguel Tejada .15 .40
33 Carlos Beltran .15 .40
34 Geoff Jenkins .10 .25
35 Hideki Matsui .40 1.00
36 Jason Kendall .10 .25
37 Adam Dunn .15 .40
38 Jay Gibbons .10 .25
39 Ivan Rodriguez .15 .40
40 Sidney Ponson .10 .25
41 Albert Pujols .30 .75
42 Bartolo Colon .10 .25
43 Lance Berkman .15 .40
44 Brandon Webb .10 .25
45 Shannon Stewart .10 .25
46 Josh Beckett .10 .25
47 Jason Schmidt .10 .25
48 Luis Gonzalez .10 .25
49 Jacque Jones .10 .25
50 Andruw Jones .10 .25
51 Todd Helton .15 .40
52 Javier Vazquez .10 .25
53 Alfonso Soriano .15 .40
54 Manny Ramirez .25 .60
55 Bobby Abreu .10 .25
56 Rocco Baldelli .10 .25
57 Kerry Wood .10 .25
58 Derek Jeter .60 1.50
59 Phil Nevin .10 .25
60 Jeff Bagwell .15 .40
61 Sammy Sosa .25 .60
62 Tom Glavine .15 .40
63 Miguel Cabrera .25 .60
64 Shawn Green .10 .25
65 Mark Prior .15 .40
66 Jose Reyes .15 .40
67 Curt Schilling .15 .40
68 Hideo Nomo .25 .60
69 Mike Lowell .10 .25
70 Randy Johnson .25 .60
71 Edgar Martinez .15 .40
72 Dontrelle Willis .10 .25
73 Milton Bradley .10 .25
74 Preston Wilson .10 .25
75 Mike Piazza .25 .60
76 Mike Mussina .15 .40
77 Darin Erstad .10 .25
78 Greg Maddux .30 .75
79 Tim Hudson .15 .40
80 Kevin Millwood .10 .25
81 Dmitri Young .10 .25
82 Ben Sheets .10 .25
83 Alex Rodriguez .30 .75
84 Johan Santana .15 .40
85 Jeff Kent .10 .25
86 Pedro Martinez .15 .40
87 Carlos Delgado .10 .25
88 Jim Thome .15 .40
89 Aubrey Huff .10 .25
90 Ken Griffey Jr. .50 1.25
91 Kevin Brown .10 .25
92 Tony Batista .10 .25
93 Richie Sexson .10 .25
94 Cliff Floyd .10 .25
95 Jose Vidro .10 .25
96 Brian Giles .10 .25
97 Jorge Posada .15 .40
98 Vernon Wells .10 .25
99 Vladimir Guerrero .15 .40
100 Jason Giambi .10 .25

2004 Upper Deck Power Up Lavender

*LAVENDER: 6X TO 15X BASIC
STATED ODDS 1:96
LAVENDER WORTH 500 POINTS EACH
ALSO REFERRED TO AS SUPER RARE

2004 Upper Deck Power Up Orange

*ORANGE: 2.5X TO 6X BASIC
STATED ODDS 1:6
ORANGE WORTH 100 POINTS EACH
ALSO REFERRED TO AS RARE

2004 Upper Deck Power Up Purple

*PURPLE: 4X TO 10X BASIC
STATED ODDS 1:24
PURPLE WORTH 250 POINTS EACH
ALSO REFERRED TO AS ULTRA RARE

2004 Upper Deck Power Up Shining Through

STATED ODDS 1:1
SHINING WORTH 50 POINTS EACH
1 Hideo Nomo .75 2.00
2 Mark Prior .50 1.25
3 Scott Rolen .50 1.25
4 Luis Gonzalez .30 .75
5 Miguel Tejada .50 1.25
6 Richie Sexson .30 .75
7 Jim Edmonds .50 1.25
8 Carlos Beltran .50 1.25
9 Manny Ramirez .75 2.00
10 Torii Hunter .30 .75
11 Garret Anderson .30 .75
12 Eric Chavez .30 .75
13 Juan Gonzalez .30 .75
14 Albert Pujols 1.00 2.50
15 Tim Hudson .50 1.25
16 Roy Halladay .50 1.25
17 Roy Oswalt .50 1.25
18 Andruw Jones .30 .75
19 Gary Sheffield .30 .75
20 Magglio Ordonez .50 1.25
21 Jason Giambi .30 .75
22 Brian Giles .30 .75
23 Barry Zito .50 1.25
24 Todd Helton .50 1.25
25 Randy Johnson .75 2.00
26 Pedro Martinez .50 1.25
27 Vernon Wells .30 .75
28 Lance Berkman .50 1.25
29 Mike Mussina .50 1.25
30 Carlos Delgado .30 .75
31 Ivan Rodriguez .50 1.25
32 Kevin Brown .30 .75
33 Kerry Wood .30 .75
34 Mark Teixeira .50 1.25
35 Hideki Matsui 1.25 3.00
36 Troy Glaus .30 .75
37 Mike Piazza .75 2.00
38 Nomar Garciaparra .50 1.25
39 Vladimir Guerrero .50 1.25
40 Derek Jeter 2.00 5.00
41 Jason Schmidt .30 .75
42 Alex Rodriguez Yanks 1.00 2.50
43 Jeff Bagwell .50 1.25
44 Shawn Green .30 .75
45 Sammy Sosa .75 2.00
46 Josh Beckett .30 .75
47 Bret Boone .30 .75
48 Ichiro Suzuki 1.00 2.50
49 Jeff Kent .30 .75
50 Rafael Palmeiro .50 1.25
51 Curt Schilling .50 1.25
52 Greg Maddux 1.00 2.50
53 Mike Lowell .30 .75
54 Dontrelle Willis .30 .75
55 Alfonso Soriano .50 1.25
56 Preston Wilson .30 .75
57 Jorge Posada .50 1.25
58 Frank Thomas .75 2.00
59 Jim Thome .50 1.25
60 Ken Griffey Jr. 1.50 4.00
61 Rocco Baldelli .30 .75
62 Jose Vidro .30 .75
63 Austin Kearns .30 .75
64 Cliff Floyd .30 .75
65 Phil Nevin .30 .75
66 Darin Erstad .30 .75
67 Johan Santana .50 1.25
68 Chipper Jones .75 2.00

69 Brandon Webb .30 .75
70 Hank Blalock .30 .75
71 Adam Dunn .50 1.25
72 Javier Vazquez .30 .75
73 Jacque Jones .30 .75
74 Bobby Abreu .30 .75
75 Edgar Renteria .30 .75
76 Roger Clemens 1.00 2.50
77 Rafael Furcal .30 .75
78 Mike Sweeney .30 .75
79 Geoff Jenkins .30 .75
80 Orlando Cabrera .30 .75
81 Ben Sheets .30 .75
82 Shannon Stewart .30 .75
83 Ryan Klesko .30 .75
84 Edgar Martinez .50 1.25
85 Kevin Millwood .30 .75
86 Bartolo Colon .30 .75
87 Larry Walker .50 1.25
88 Tom Glavine .50 1.25
89 Miguel Cabrera .75 2.00
90 Jose Reyes .50 1.25

2004 Upper Deck Power Up Stickers

STATED ODDS 1:6
1 Hideo Nomo 1.50 4.00
2 Mark Prior 1.00 2.50
3 Scott Rolen 1.00 2.50
4 Luis Gonzalez .60 1.50
5 Miguel Tejada 1.00 2.50
6 Richie Sexson .60 1.50
7 Jim Edmonds 1.00 2.50
8 Carlos Beltran 1.00 2.50
9 Manny Ramirez 1.50 4.00
10 Torii Hunter .60 1.50
11 Garret Anderson .60 1.50
12 Eric Chavez .60 1.50
13 Juan Gonzalez .60 1.50
14 Albert Pujols 2.00 5.00
15 Tim Hudson 1.00 2.50
16 Roy Halladay 1.00 2.50
17 Roy Oswalt 1.00 2.50
18 Andruw Jones .60 1.50
19 Gary Sheffield .60 1.50
20 Magglio Ordonez 1.00 2.50
21 Jason Giambi .60 1.50
22 Brian Giles .60 1.50
23 Barry Zito 1.00 2.50
24 Todd Helton 1.00 2.50
25 Randy Johnson 1.50 4.00
26 Pedro Martinez 1.00 2.50
27 Vernon Wells .60 1.50
28 Lance Berkman 1.00 2.50
29 Mike Mussina 1.00 2.50
30 Carlos Delgado .60 1.50
31 Ivan Rodriguez 1.00 2.50
32 Kevin Brown .60 1.50
33 Kerry Wood .60 1.50
34 Mark Teixeira 1.00 2.50
35 Hideki Matsui 2.50 6.00
36 Troy Glaus .60 1.50
37 Mike Piazza 1.50 4.00
38 Nomar Garciaparra 1.00 2.50
39 Vladimir Guerrero 1.00 2.50
40 Derek Jeter 4.00 10.00
41 Jason Schmidt .60 1.50
42 Alex Rodriguez 2.00 5.00
43 Jeff Bagwell 1.00 2.50
44 Shawn Green .60 1.50
45 Sammy Sosa 1.50 4.00
46 Josh Beckett .60 1.50
47 Bret Boone .60 1.50
48 Ichiro Suzuki 2.00 5.00
49 Jeff Kent .60 1.50
50 Rafael Palmeiro 1.00 2.50
51 Curt Schilling 1.00 2.50
52 Greg Maddux 2.00 5.00
53 Mike Lowell .60 1.50
54 Dontrelle Willis .60 1.50
55 Alfonso Soriano 1.00 2.50
56 Preston Wilson .60 1.50
57 Jorge Posada 1.00 2.50
58 Frank Thomas 1.50 4.00
59 Jim Thome 1.00 2.50
60 Ken Griffey Jr. 3.00 8.00
61 Rocco Baldelli .60 1.50
62 Jose Vidro .60 1.50
63 Austin Kearns .60 1.50
64 Phil Nevin .60 1.50
65 Darin Erstad .60 1.50
66 Johan Santana 1.00 2.50
67 Chipper Jones 1.50 4.00
68 Brandon Webb .60 1.50
69 Hank Blalock .60 1.50
70 Adam Dunn 1.00 2.50
71 Javier Vazquez .60 1.50
72 Jacque Jones .60 1.50
73 Bobby Abreu .60 1.50
74 Edgar Renteria .60 1.50
75 Rafael Furcal .60 1.50
76 Mike Sweeney .60 1.50
77 Geoff Jenkins .60 1.50
78 Shannon Stewart .60 1.50
79 Ryan Klesko .60 1.50
80 Edgar Martinez 1.00 2.50
81 Kevin Millwood .60 1.50
82 Bartolo Colon .60 1.50
83 Tom Glavine 1.00 2.50
84 Miguel Cabrera 1.50 4.00
85 Jose Reyes 1.00 2.50
86 Padres .60 1.50
Astros
A's
Angels
Cubs
D-Rays
87 Pirates .60 1.50
M's
Expos
Twins
Reds
Phils
88 Royals .60 1.50
O's
W.Sox
Dodgers
Marlins
Yanks
89 Giants .60 1.50
Mets
Cards
Indians
Braves
Rangers
90 Tigers .60 1.50
R.Sox
Rockies
D-Backs
Brewers
Jays

1999 Upper Deck PowerDeck

The Upper Deck Power Deck set featured both digital CD trading cards as well as more standard "paper" cards issued in three card packs. These packs which guaranteed having a digital card retailed for $4.99 per pack. Each digital card has game clips, sounds, photos and career highlights of the featured players. These cards can be played on almost any computer.

COMPLETE SET (25) 20.00 50.00
1 Ken Griffey Jr. 1.50 4.00
2 Mark McGwire 2.00 5.00
3 Cal Ripken 2.50 6.00
4 Sammy Sosa .75 2.00
5 Derek Jeter 2.00 5.00
6 Mike Piazza 1.25 3.00
7 Nomar Garciaparra 1.25 3.00
8 Greg Maddux 1.25 3.00
9 Tony Gwynn 1.00 2.50
10 Roger Clemens 1.50 4.00
11 Scott Rolen .50 1.25
12 Alex Rodriguez 1.25 3.00
13 Manny Ramirez .50 1.25
14 Chipper Jones .75 2.00
15 Juan Gonzalez .40 1.00
16 Ivan Rodriguez .50 1.25
17 Frank Thomas .75 2.00
18 Mo Vaughn .40 1.00
19 Barry Bonds 2.00 5.00
20 Vladimir Guerrero .75 2.00
21 Jose Canseco .50 1.25
22 Jeff Bagwell .50 1.25
23 Pedro Martinez .50 1.25
24 Gabe Kapler .40 1.00
25 J.D. Drew .40 1.00

1999 Upper Deck PowerDeck Auxiliary

COMPLETE SET (25) 8.00 20.00
*AUXILIARY: 20% OF BASIC CD'S
APPROXIMATELY TWO PER PACK

1999 Upper Deck PowerDeck Auxiliary Gold

COMMON CARD (AUX1-AUX25)
RANDOM INSERTS IN PACKS

1999 Upper Deck PowerDeck A Season To Remember

COMPLETE SET (1) 3.00 8.00
1 Mark McGwire 4.00 10.00

1999 Upper Deck PowerDeck Most Valuable Performances

COMPLETE SET (7) 125.00 250.00
STATED ODDS 1:287
*AUXILIARY: .3X TO .8X BASIC MVP CD
AUXILIARY STATED ODDS 1:287
1 OF 1 AUXILIARY GOLD CARDS EXIST
1 OF 1 AUX.GOLD TOO SCARCE TO PRICE
M1 Sammy Sosa 4.00 10.00
M2 Barry Bonds 10.00 25.00
M3 Cal Ripken 12.50 30.00
M4 Juan Gonzalez 2.00 5.00
M5 Ken Griffey Jr. 8.00 20.00
M6 Roger Clemens 8.00 20.00
M7 Mark McGwire 10.00 25.00

1999 Upper Deck PowerDeck Powerful Moments

COMPLETE SET (6) 20.00 50.00
STATED ODDS 1:7
*AUXILIARY: .3X TO .8X BASIC POW.MOM
AUXILIARY STATED ODDS 1:7
1 OF 1 AUXILIARY GOLD CARDS EXIST
1 OF 1 AUX.GOLD TOO SCARCE TO PRICE
P1 Mark McGwire 2.00 5.00
P2 Sammy Sosa .75 2.00
P3 Cal Ripken 2.50 6.00
P4 Ken Griffey Jr. 1.50 4.00
P5 Derek Jeter 2.00 5.00
P6 Alex Rodriguez 1.25 3.00

1999 Upper Deck PowerDeck Time Capsule

COMPLETE SET (6) 25.00 60.00
STATED ODDS 1:23
*AUXILIARY: .3X TO .8X BASIC TIME CAP.
AUXILIARY STATED ODDS 1:23
1 OF 1 AUXILIARY GOLD CARDS EXIST
1 OF 1 AUX.GOLD TOO SCARCE TO PRICE
R1 Ken Griffey Jr. 2.50 6.00
R2 Mike Piazza 2.00 5.00
R3 Mark McGwire 3.00 8.00
R4 Derek Jeter 3.00 8.00
R5 Jose Canseco .75 2.00
R6 Nomar Garciaparra 2.00 5.00

1999 Upper Deck PowerDeck Athletes of the Century

These CD-Rom cards featuring four of the most prominent athletes of the 20th century were issued by Upper Deck in one boxed set. The cards are inserted into a computer and display various highlights of the player's career and his stats and other information.

COMPLETE SET (4) 8.00 20.00
1 Babe Ruth 3.00 8.00

2000 Upper Deck PowerDeck

COMPLETE SET (12) 12.50 30.00
ONE CARD PER PACK
1 Sammy Sosa 1.00 2.50
2 Ken Griffey Jr. 2.00 5.00
3 Mark McGwire 1.50 4.00
4 Derek Jeter 2.50 6.00
5 Alex Rodriguez 1.25 3.00
6 Nomar Garciaparra .60 1.50
7 Mike Piazza 1.00 2.50
8 Cal Ripken 3.00 8.00
9 Ivan Rodriguez .60 1.50
10 Chipper Jones 1.00 2.50
11 Pedro Martinez .60 1.50
12 Manny Ramirez 1.00 2.50

2000 Upper Deck PowerDeck Magical Moments

COMPLETE SET (2) 6.00 15.00
STATED ODDS 1:10 HOBBY
CR Cal Ripken 4.00 10.00
KG Ken Griffey Jr. 2.50 6.00

2000 Upper Deck PowerDeck Magical Moments Autographs

STATED PRINT RUN 50 SERIAL #'d SETS
CR Cal Ripken 75.00 150.00
KG Ken Griffey Jr. 75.00 150.00

2000 Upper Deck PowerDeck Power Trio

COMPLETE SET (3) 4.00 10.00
STATED ODDS 1:7
PT1 Derek Jeter 2.50 6.00
PT2 Ken Griffey Jr. 2.00 5.00
PT3 Mark McGwire 1.50 4.00

2007 Upper Deck Premier

COMMON CARD (1-200) 2.00 5.00
BASE CARD ODDS ONE PER PACK
1-200 STATED PRINT RUN 99 SER.#'d SETS
COMMON ROOKIE (201-244) 2.00 5.00
RC ODDS ONE PER PACK
201-244 STATED PRINT RUN 199 SER.#'d SETS
PRINT.PLATES RANDOM INSERTS IN PACKS
PLATE PRINT RUN 1 SET PER COLOR
BLACK-CYAN-MAGENTA-YELLOW ISSUED
NO PLATE PRICING DUE TO SCARCITY
1 Roy Campanella 4.00 10.00
2 Ty Cobb 5.00 12.00
3 Mickey Cochrane 2.00 5.00
4 Dizzy Dean 3.00 8.00
5 Don Drysdale 3.00 8.00
6 Jimmie Foxx 4.00 10.00
7 Lou Gehrig 6.00 15.00
8 Lefty Grove 2.00 5.00
9 Rogers Hornsby 4.00 10.00
10 Walter Johnson 4.00 10.00
11 Eddie Mathews 4.00 10.00
12 Christy Mathewson 4.00 10.00
13 Johnny Mize 3.00 8.00
14 Thurman Munson 5.00 12.00
15 Mel Ott 3.00 8.00
16 Satchel Paige 4.00 10.00
17 Jackie Robinson 5.00 12.00
18 Babe Ruth 8.00 20.00
19 George Sisler 2.00 5.00
20 Honus Wagner 4.00 10.00
21 Cy Young 4.00 10.00
22 Luis Aparicio 2.00 5.00
23 Johnny Bench 4.00 10.00
24 Yogi Berra 4.00 10.00
25 Rod Carew 3.00 8.00
26 Orlando Cepeda 2.00 5.00
27 Bob Feller 3.00 8.00
28 Carlton Fisk 3.00 8.00
29 Bob Gibson 3.00 8.00
30 Catfish Hunter 2.00 5.00
31 Reggie Jackson 3.00 8.00
32 Al Kaline 4.00 10.00
33 Harmon Killebrew 4.00 10.00
34 Buck Leonard 2.00 5.00
35 Juan Marichal 2.00 5.00
36 Bill Mazeroski 3.00 8.00
37 Willie McCovey 3.00 8.00
38 Joe Morgan 3.00 8.00
39 Eddie Murray 4.00 10.00
40 Jim Palmer 3.00 8.00
41 Tony Perez 3.00 8.00
42 Pee Wee Reese 3.00 8.00
43 Brooks Robinson 4.00 10.00
44 Nolan Ryan 8.00 20.00
45 Mike Schmidt 4.00 10.00
46 Tom Seaver 3.00 8.00
47 Enos Slaughter 2.00 5.00
48 Willie Stargell 3.00 8.00
49 Early Wynn 2.00 5.00
50 Robin Yount 4.00 10.00
51 Tony Gwynn 4.00 10.00
52 Cal Ripken Jr. 10.00 25.00
53 Ernie Banks 4.00 10.00
54 Wade Boggs 3.00 8.00
55 Steve Carlton 2.00 5.00
56 Will Clark 3.00 8.00
57 Fergie Jenkins 2.00 5.00
58 Bo Jackson 4.00 10.00
59 Don Mattingly 6.00 15.00
60 Stan Musial 5.00 12.00
61 Frank Robinson 2.00 5.00
62 Ryne Sandberg 5.00 12.00
63 Ozzie Smith 6.00 15.00
64 Carl Yastrzemski 5.00 12.00
65 Dave Winfield 3.00 8.00
66 Paul Molitor 2.00 5.00
67 Jason Bay 2.00 5.00
68 Freddy Sanchez 2.00 5.00
69 Josh Beckett 2.00 5.00
70 Carlos Beltran 2.00 5.00
71 Craig Biggio 4.00 10.00
72 Matt Holliday 2.50 6.00
73 A.J. Burnett 2.00 5.00
74 Miguel Cabrera 3.00 8.00
75 Dontrelle Willis 2.00 5.00
76 Chris Carpenter 3.00 8.00
77 Roger Clemens 6.00 15.00
78 Johnny Damon 3.00 8.00
79 Jermaine Dye 2.00 5.00
80 Jim Thome 3.00 8.00
81 Vladimir Guerrero 4.00 10.00
82 Travis Hafner 2.00 5.00
83 Victor Martinez 2.00 5.00
84 Trevor Hoffman 2.00 5.00
85 Derek Jeter 8.00 20.00
86 Ken Griffey Jr. 6.00 15.00
87 Randy Johnson 4.00 10.00
88 Andruw Jones 3.00 8.00
89 Derrek Lee 2.00 5.00
90 Greg Maddux 5.00 12.00
91 Magglio Ordonez 3.00 8.00
92 David Ortiz 4.00 10.00
93 Jake Peavy 2.00 5.00
94 Roy Oswalt 2.00 5.00
95 Mike Piazza 4.00 10.00
96 Jose Reyes 4.00 10.00
97 Ivan Rodriguez 4.00 10.00
98 Johan Santana 3.00 8.00
99 Scott Rolen 3.00 8.00
100 Curt Schilling 3.00 8.00
101 John Smoltz 3.00 8.00
102 Alfonso Soriano 2.00 5.00
103 Miguel Tejada 3.00 8.00
104 Frank Thomas 5.00 12.00
105 Chase Utley 4.00 10.00
106 Joe Mauer 3.00 8.00
107 Alex Rodriguez 6.00 15.00
108 Alex Rios 3.00 8.00
109 Justin Verlander 4.00 10.00
110 Ryan Howard 5.00 12.00
111 Jered Weaver 3.00 8.00
112 Francisco Liriano 4.00 10.00
113 David Wright 5.00 12.00
114 Felix Hernandez 3.00 8.00
115 Jeremy Sowers 3.00 8.00
116 Cole Hamels 3.00 8.00
117 B.J. Upton 2.00 5.00
118 Chien-Ming Wang 20.00 50.00
119 Justin Morneau 3.00 8.00
120 Jonny Gomes 2.00 5.00
121 Adrian Gonzalez 2.00 5.00
122 Bill Hall 3.00 8.00
123 Rich Harden 3.00 8.00
124 Rich Hill 2.00 5.00
125 Tadahito Iguchi 2.00 5.00
126 Scott Kazmir 3.00 8.00
127 Howie Kendrick 3.00 8.00
128 Dan Uggla 3.00 8.00
129 Hanley Ramirez 3.00 8.00
130 Josh Willingham 2.00 5.00
131 Nick Markakis 3.00 8.00
132 Grady Sizemore 4.00 10.00
133 Ian Kinsler 3.00 8.00
134 Jonathan Papelbon 5.00 12.00
135 Ryan Zimmerman 4.00 10.00
136 Stephen Drew 3.00 8.00
137 Adam Wainwright 2.00 5.00
138 Joel Zumaya 3.00 8.00
139 Prince Fielder 4.00 10.00
140 Carl Crawford 3.00 8.00
141 Huston Street 2.00 5.00
142 Matt Cain 3.00 8.00
143 Andre Ethier 3.00 8.00
144 Brian McCann 3.00 8.00
145 Josh Barfield 2.00 5.00
146 Anibal Sanchez 2.00 5.00
147 Brian Roberts 3.00 8.00
148 Brandon Webb 2.00 5.00
149 Chipper Jones 4.00 10.00
150 Tim Hudson 3.00 8.00
151 Adam LaRoche 2.00 5.00
152 Jeff Francoeur 4.00 10.00
153 Marcus Giles 2.00 5.00
154 Jason Varitek 5.00 12.00
155 Coco Crisp 3.00 8.00
156 Manny Ramirez 3.00 8.00
157 Trot Nixon 3.00 8.00
158 Carlos Zambrano 2.00 5.00
159 Mark Prior 3.00 8.00
160 Aramis Ramirez 2.00 5.00
161 Mark Buehrle 2.00 5.00
162 Paul Konerko 2.00 5.00
163 Adam Dunn 3.00 8.00
164 C.C. Sabathia 2.00 5.00
165 Todd Helton 3.00 8.00
166 Garrett Atkins 3.00 8.00
167 Jeremy Bonderman 4.00 10.00
168 Curtis Granderson 3.00 8.00
169 Sean Casey 3.00 8.00
170 Lance Berkman 3.00 8.00
171 Brad Lidge 2.00 5.00
172 Reggie Sanders 2.00 5.00
173 Brad Penny 2.00 5.00
174 Nomar Garciaparra 5.00 12.00
175 Jeff Kent 2.00 5.00
176 Chone Figgins 2.00 5.00
177 Ben Sheets 3.00 8.00
178 Rickie Weeks 3.00 8.00
179 Joe Nathan 3.00 8.00
180 Torii Hunter 3.00 8.00
181 Carlos Delgado 3.00 8.00
182 Tom Glavine 4.00 10.00
183 Paul Lo Duca 2.00 5.00
184 Mariano Rivera 5.00 12.00
185 Robinson Cano 4.00 10.00
186 Bobby Abreu 3.00 8.00
187 Hideki Matsui 5.00 12.00
188 Barry Zito 2.00 5.00
189 Eric Chavez 3.00 8.00
190 Jimmy Rollins 3.00 8.00
191 Khalil Greene 4.00 10.00
192 Brian Giles 2.00 5.00
193 Jason Schmidt 2.00 5.00
194 Ichiro Suzuki 12.50 30.00
195 David Eckstein 4.00 10.00
196 Jim Edmonds 3.00 8.00
197 Mark Teixeira 3.00 8.00
198 Michael Young 2.00 5.00
199 Vernon Wells 3.00 8.00
200 Roy Halladay 3.00 8.00
201 Delmon Young (RC) 3.00 8.00
202 Andrew Miller RC 8.00 20.00
203 Troy Tulowitzki (RC) 3.00 8.00
204 Jeff Fiorentino (RC) 2.00 5.00
205 David Murphy (RC) 2.00 5.00
206 Jeff Baker (RC) 2.00 5.00
207 Kevin Hooper (RC) 2.00 5.00
208 Kevin Kouzmanoff (RC) 2.00 5.00
209 Adam Lind (RC) 3.00 8.00
210 Mike Rabelo RC 3.00 8.00
211 John Nelson (RC) 2.00 5.00
212 Mitch Maier RC 2.00 5.00
213 Ryan Braun RC 2.00 5.00
214 Vinny Rottino (RC) 2.00 5.00
215 Drew Anderson RC 2.00 5.00
216 Alexi Casilla RC 3.00 8.00
217 Glen Perkins (RC) 2.00 5.00
218 Cesar Jimenez RC 2.00 5.00
219 Tim Gradoville RC 2.00 5.00
220 Shane Youman RC 2.00 5.00
221 Billy Sadler (RC) 2.00 5.00
222 Patrick Misch (RC) 2.00 5.00
223 Juan Salas (RC) 2.00 5.00
224 Beltran Perez (RC) 2.00 5.00
225 Hector Gimenez (RC) 2.00 5.00
226 Philip Humber (RC) 3.00 8.00
227 Eric Stults RC 2.00 5.00
228 Dennis Sarfate (RC) 2.00 5.00
229 Andy Cannizaro RC 3.00 8.00
230 Juan Morillo (RC) 2.00 5.00
231 Fred Lewis (RC) 2.00 5.00
232 Ryan Sweeney (RC) 2.00 5.00
233 Chris Narveson (RC) 2.00 5.00
234 Michael Bourn (RC) 2.00 5.00
235 Joaquin Arias (RC) 2.00 5.00
236 Carlos Maldonado (RC) 2.00 5.00
237 Alvin Colina RC 2.00 5.00
238 Jon Knott (RC) 2.00 5.00
239 Justin Hampson (RC) 2.00 5.00
240 Jeff Salazar (RC) 2.00 5.00
241 Josh Fields (RC) 2.00 5.00
242 Delwyn Young (RC) 2.00 5.00
243 Daisuke Matsuzaka RC 15.00 40.00
244 Kei Igawa RC 8.00 20.00

2007 Upper Deck Premier Autograph Parallel

OVERALL AUTO ODDS 1 PER PACK
PRINT RUNS B/WN 15-73 COPIES PER
NO PRICING ON QTY OF 25 OR LESS
244 Kei Igawa/73 150.00 200.00

2007 Upper Deck Premier Bronze

*BRONZE: .5X TO 1.2X BASIC
BRONZE RANDOMLY INSERTED IN PACKS
STATED PRINT RUN 75 SER.#'d SETS
243 Daisuke Matsuzaka 15.00 40.00

2007 Upper Deck Premier Gold

*GOLD: .6X TO 1.5X BASIC
GOLD RANDOMLY INSERTED IN PACKS
STATED PRINT RUN 49 SER.#'d SETS
243 Daisuke Matsuzaka 20.00 50.00

2007 Upper Deck Premier Platinum

PLATINUM RANDOMLY INSERTED IN PACKS
STATED PRINT RUN 1 SER.#'d SET
NO PRICING DUE TO SCARCITY

2007 Upper Deck Premier Silver

*SILVER: .5X TO 1.2X BASIC
SILVER RANDOMLY INSERTED IN PACKS
STATED PRINT RUN 99 SER.#'d SETS
243 Daisuke Matsuzaka 15.00 40.00

2007 Upper Deck Premier Emerging Stars Autographs Dual

STATED PRINT RUN 50 SER.#'d SETS
BRONZE PRINT RUN 25 SER.#'d SETS
NO BRONZE PRICING DUE TO SCARCITY
GOLD PRINT RUN 10 SER.#'d SETS
NO GOLD PRICING DUE TO SCARCITY
PLATINUM PRINT RUN 1 SER.#'d SET
NO PLATINUM PRICING DUE TO SCARCITY
OVERALL AUTO ODDS ONE PER PACK
EXCHANGE DEADLINE 04/26/10
BU J.Barfield/D.Uggla 10.00 25.00
BV J.Bonderman/J.Verlander 12.50 30.00
CA C.Crawford/A.Rios 10.00 25.00
FJ F.Hernandez/Jer.Weaver 30.00 60.00
GB A.Gonzalez/J.Barfield 10.00 25.00
GC J.Gomes/C.Crawford 10.00 25.00
HP P.Humber/M.Pelfrey 30.00 60.00
HS R.Harden/H.Street 10.00 25.00
HV R.Harden/J.Verlander 15.00 40.00
IK T.Iguchi/I.Kinsler 20.00 50.00
KL S.Kazmir/F.Liriano 20.00 50.00
KS S.Kazmir/J.Sowers 10.00 25.00
LH J.Lester/C.Hansen 20.00 50.00
MB J.Mauer/J.Brown 20.00 50.00
MG J.Morneau/A.Gonzalez 10.00 25.00
MH A.Miller/C.Hamels 12.50 30.00
MZ A.Miller/J.Zumaya 30.00 60.00
PH J.Papelbon/C.Hansen 10.00 25.00
PW J.Papelbon/A.Wainwright 20.00 50.00
QD C.Quentin/S.Drew 12.50 30.00
RB R.Weeks/B.Hall 10.00 25.00
RD J.Reyes/S.Drew 30.00 60.00
RR J.Reyes/H.Ramirez 40.00 80.00
RY A.Rios/D.Young 20.00 50.00
SH J.Sowers/C.Hamels 10.00 25.00
SJ A.Sanchez/J.Johnson 10.00 25.00
TR T.Tulowitzki/H.Ramirez 15.00 40.00
UG B.Upton/J.Gomes 10.00 25.00
UR D.Uggla/H.Ramirez 20.00 50.00
UU C.Utley/D.Uggla 12.50 30.00
VH J.Verlander/F.Hernandez 50.00 100.00
VM J.Verlander/A.Miller 12.00 30.00
WK Jer.Weaver/H.Kendrick 10.00 25.00
WL Jer.Weaver/F.Liriano 20.00 50.00
YT D.Young/T.Tulowitzki 12.50 30.00
ZW J.Zumaya/A.Wainwright 10.00 25.00

2007 Upper Deck Premier Emerging Stars Autographs Triple

STATED PRINT RUN 50 SER.#'d SETS
BRONZE PRINT RUN 25 SER.#'d SETS
NO BRONZE PRICING DUE TO SCARCITY
GOLD PRINT RUN 10 SER.#'d SETS
NO GOLD PRICING DUE TO SCARCITY
PLATINUM PRINT RUN 1 SER.#'d SET
NO PLATINUM PRICING DUE TO SCARCITY
OVERALL AUTO ODDS ONE PER PACK
EXCHANGE DEADLINE 04/26/10
ELS Ethier/Loney/Saito 30.00 60.00
HHL Hill/Hamels/Liriano EXCH 10.00 25.00
HQE Holl/Quen/Ethier EXCH 10.00 25.00
KUK Kendrick/Uggla/Kinsler 10.00 25.00
LBG Liriano/Bonser/Garza 10.00 25.00
MHL A.Miller/Hamels/Liriano 30.00 60.00
MKL Morneau/Kubel/Liriano 10.00 25.00
MSK A.Miller/Sowers/Kazmir 10.00 25.00
MVB A.Miller/Verland/Bonder 30.00 60.00
MYE Markakis/Delmon/Ethier 50.00 100.00
PSW Papelbon/Street/Wain 20.00 50.00
QEY Quentin/Ethier/Delmon EXCH 10.00 25.00
RRD J.Reyes/Hanley/S.Drew 20.00 50.00
SHK Sowers/Hamels/Kazmir 20.00 50.00
TDR Tulo/S.Drew/Hanley 10.00 25.00
THA Tulo/Holliday/Atkins 10.00 25.00
UKW Utley/Kendrick/Weeks 10.00 25.00
UUW Utley/Uggla/Weeks 10.00 25.00
UYK B.Upton/Delmon/Kazmir 20.00 50.00
VMZ Verland/A.Miller/Zumaya 20.00 50.00
WHV Jer.Weaver/Felix/Verlan 40.00 80.00
WZS Wain/Zum/Saito EXCH 20.00 50.00
YER Delmon/Ethier/Rios 10.00 25.00

2007 Upper Deck Premier Hallmarks Autographs

PRINT RUNS B/WN 5-57 COPIES PER
NO PRICING ON QTY 25 OR LESS
GOLD PRINT RUN 25 SER.#'d SETS
NO GOLD PRICING DUE TO SCARCITY
PLATINUM PRINT RUN 1 SER.#'d SET
NO PLATINUM PRICING DUE TO SCARCITY
OVERALL AUTO ODDS ONE PER PACK
EXCHANGE DEADLINE 04/26/10
LA Luis Aparicio/57 20.00 50.00
MS Mike Schmidt/48 20.00 50.00
OS Ozzie Smith/57 20.00 50.00
PM Paul Molitor/39 10.00 25.00
RJ Reggie Jackson/47 20.00 50.00
RS Ryne Sandberg/40 30.00 60.00
RY Robin Yount/46 20.00 50.00
SC Steve Carlton/27 12.50 30.00
WM Willie McCovey/45 20.00 50.00

2007 Upper Deck Premier Insignias Autographs

STATED PRINT RUN 50 SER.#'d SETS
GOLD PRINT RUN 25 SER.#'d SETS
NO GOLD PRICING DUE TO SCARCITY
PLATINUM PRINT RUN 1 SER.#'d SET
NO PLATINUM PRICING DUE TO SCARCTIY
OVERALL AUTO ODDS ONE PER PACK
EXCHANGE DEADLINE 04/26/10
AK Al Kaline 20.00 50.00
AM Andrew Miller 10.00 25.00
BU B.J. Upton 10.00 25.00
CR Cal Ripken Jr. 60.00 120.00
DJ Derek Jeter 125.00 300.00
DL Derrek Lee 15.00 40.00
DM Don Mattingly 25.00 60.00
DY Delmon Young 20.00 50.00
FH Felix Hernandez 12.00 30.00
JM Joe Mauer 15.00 40.00
JP Jake Peavy 10.00 25.00
JR Jose Reyes 40.00 80.00
JT Jim Thome 30.00 60.00
JW Jered Weaver 10.00 25.00
KG Ken Griffey Jr. 50.00 100.00
MO Justin Morneau 10.00 25.00
OS Ozzie Smith 20.00 50.00
PA Jim Palmer 10.00 25.00
TT Troy Tulowitzki 10.00 25.00
WC Will Clark 10.00 25.00

2007 Upper Deck Premier Noteworthy Autographs

PRINT RUN B/WN 1-86 COPIES PER
NO PRICING ON QTY 25 OR LESS
GOLD PRINT RUN 25 SER.#'d SETS
NO GOLD PRICING DUE TO SCARCITY
PLATINUM PRINT RUN 1 SER.#'d SET
NO PLATINUM PRICING DUE TO SCARCITY
OVERALL AUTO ODDS ONE PER PACK
EXCHANGE DEADLINE 04/26/10
AD Andre Dawson/50 10.00 25.00
AK Al Kaline/50 15.00 40.00
AP Albert Pujols/49 100.00 175.00
AS Alfonso Soriano/35 12.50 30.00
BA Jeff Bagwell/75 20.00 50.00
BE Josh Beckett/50 6.00 15.00
BF Bob Feller/62 12.50 30.00
BJ Bo Jackson/35 40.00 80.00
BR Brooks Robinson/35 20.00 50.00
CB Craig Biggio/65 20.00 50.00
CC Chris Carpenter/50 15.00 40.00
CF Carlton Fisk/37 20.00 50.00
DE Dennis Eckersley/75 6.00 15.00
DM Don Mattingly/35 40.00 80.00
DS Don Sutton/50 6.00 15.00
FJ Fergie Jenkins/74 6.00 15.00
FR Frank Robinson/31 15.00 40.00
GS Gary Sheffield/86 15.00 40.00
HR Hanley Ramirez/51 12.50 30.00
JB Jim Bunning/54 12.50 30.00
JB Johnny Bench/45 20.00 50.00
JC Jack Clark/75 6.00 15.00
JM Juan Marichal/65 6.00 15.00
JM Joe Mauer/36 30.00 60.00
JP Jim Palmer/65 10.00 25.00
JS Johan Santana/65 20.00 50.00
JT Jim Thome/52 20.00 50.00
KG Ken Griffey Jr./56 40.00 80.00
KW Kerry Wood/35 10.00 25.00
LA Luis Aparicio/35 6.00 15.00
MM Mark Mulder/35 6.00 15.00
MO Justin Morneau/50 10.00 25.00
MT Miguel Tejada/50 12.50 30.00
PE Jake Peavy/55 8.00 20.00
PM Paul Molitor/40 10.00 25.00
RS Ryne Sandberg/45 20.00 50.00
RY Robin Yount/29 20.00 50.00
TG Tom Glavine/47 20.00 50.00
TG Tony Gwynn/56 25.00 60.00
TH Torii Hunter/26 12.50 30.00
WB Wade Boggs/45 12.50 30.00

2007 Upper Deck Premier Patches Dual

PRINT RUNS B/WN 1-75 COPIES PER
NO PRICING ON QTY 22 OR LESS
PLAT.PRINT RUNS B/WN 5-10 COPIES PER
NO PLATINUM PRICING DUE TO SCARCITY
MASTERPIECE PRINT RUN 1 SER.#'d SET
NO MASTERPIECE PRICING DUE TO SCARCITY
OVERALL PATCH ODDS ONE PER PACK
AD Adam Dunn 10.00 25.00
AD Adam Dunn 10.00 25.00
AP Albert Pujols 30.00 60.00
AP Albert Pujols 30.00 60.00
AS Alfonso Soriano 10.00 25.00
AS Alfonso Soriano 10.00 25.00
BU B.J. Upton 8.00 20.00
BU B.J. Upton 8.00 20.00
CH Cole Hamels 10.00 25.00
CH Cole Hamels 10.00 25.00
CR Cal Ripken Jr. 30.00 60.00
CR Cal Ripken Jr. 30.00 60.00
CU Chase Utley 10.00 25.00
CU Chase Utley 10.00 25.00
DJ Derek Jeter 20.00 50.00
DJ Derek Jeter 20.00 50.00
DJ2 Derek Jeter 20.00 50.00
DJ2 Derek Jeter 20.00 50.00
DM Don Mattingly 20.00 50.00
DM Don Mattingly 20.00 50.00
ED Jim Edmonds 10.00 25.00
ED Jim Edmonds 10.00 25.00
FL Francisco Liriano 8.00 20.00
FL Francisco Liriano 8.00 20.00
GM Greg Maddux 12.50 30.00
GM Greg Maddux 12.50 30.00
IR Ivan Rodriguez 10.00 25.00
IR Ivan Rodriguez 10.00 25.00
JB Johnny Bench 10.00 25.00
JB Johnny Bench 10.00 25.00
JG Jason Giambi 8.00 20.00
JG Jason Giambi 8.00 20.00
JM Joe Mauer 12.50 30.00
JM Joe Mauer 12.50 30.00
JO Randy Johnson 8.00 20.00
JO Randy Johnson 8.00 20.00
JP Jake Peavy 6.00 15.00
JP Jake Peavy 6.00 15.00
JR Jose Reyes 30.00 60.00
JR Jose Reyes 30.00 60.00
JT Jim Thome 8.00 20.00
JT Jim Thome 8.00 20.00
JT2 Jim Thome 8.00 20.00
JT2 Jim Thome 8.00 20.00
JV Justin Verlander 12.50 30.00
JV Justin Verlander/42 15.00 40.00
JW Jered Weaver 8.00 20.00
JW Jered Weaver 8.00 20.00
KG Ken Griffey Jr. 12.50 30.00
KG Ken Griffey Jr. 12.50 30.00
KG2 Ken Griffey Jr. 12.50 30.00
KG2 Ken Griffey Jr. 12.50 30.00
KM Kendry Morales 6.00 15.00
KM Kendry Morales 6.00 15.00
LB Lance Berkman 10.00 25.00
LB Lance Berkman 10.00 25.00
MC Miguel Cabrera 12.00 30.00
MC Miguel Cabrera 12.00 30.00
MR Manny Ramirez 10.00 25.00
MR Manny Ramirez 10.00 25.00
MS Mike Schmidt 12.50 30.00
MS Mike Schmidt 12.50 30.00
MT Mark Teixeira 10.00 25.00
MT Mark Teixeira 10.00 25.00
NR Nolan Ryan 15.00 40.00
NR Nolan Ryan 15.00 40.00
PF Prince Fielder 12.50 30.00
PF Prince Fielder/63 12.50 30.00
PM Pedro Martinez 12.50 30.00
PM Pedro Martinez 12.50 30.00
RJ Reggie Jackson 10.00 25.00
RJ Reggie Jackson 10.00 25.00
RS Ryne Sandberg 20.00 50.00
RS Ryne Sandberg 20.00 50.00
RZ Ryan Zimmerman 20.00 50.00
RZ Ryan Zimmerman 20.00 50.00
SA Johan Santana 12.50 30.00
SA Johan Santana 12.50 30.00
TE Miguel Tejada 6.00 15.00
TE Miguel Tejada 6.00 15.00
TG Tony Gwynn 12.50 30.00
TG Tony Gwynn 12.50 30.00
TO Tom Glavine 12.50 30.00
TO Tom Glavine 12.50 30.00
VG Vladimir Guerrero 10.00 25.00
VG Vladimir Guerrero 10.00 25.00
VG2 Vladimir Guerrero 10.00 25.00
VG2 Vladimir Guerrero 10.00 25.00

2007 Upper Deck Premier Patches Dual Gold

*GOLD: .4X to 1X BASIC
OVERALL PATCH ODDS ONE PER PACK
PRINT RUNS B/WN 6-58 COPIES PER
NO PRICING ON QTY 24 OR LESS
BR Brooks Robinson/28 15.00 40.00
DO David Ortiz/54 15.00 40.00
JS Jeremy Sowers/35 10.00 25.00

2007 Upper Deck Premier Patches Triple

PRINT RUNS B/WN 1-99 COPIES PER
NO PRICING ON QTY 10 OR LESS
MASTERPIECE PRINT RUN 1 SER.#'d SET
NO MASTERPIECE PRICING DUE TO SCARCITY
PLATINUM PRINT RUN 5 SER.#'d SETS
NO PLATINUM PRICING DUE TO SCARCITY
OVERALL PATCH ODDS ONE PER PACK
AJ Andruw Jones/97 12.50 30.00
AJ Andruw Jones/97 12.50 30.00
CC Chris Carpenter/97 12.50 30.00
CC Chris Carpenter/97 12.50 30.00
CD Carlos Delgado/94 10.00 25.00
CD Carlos Delgado/94 10.00 25.00
CJ Chipper Jones/95 20.00 50.00
CJ Chipper Jones/95 20.00 50.00
CL Carlos Lee/99 8.00 20.00
CL Carlos Lee/99 8.00 20.00
CR Cal Ripken Jr./82 40.00 80.00
CR Cal Ripken Jr./82 40.00 80.00
CS Curt Schilling/90 12.50 30.00
CS Curt Schilling/90 12.50 30.00
EM Eddie Murray/77 12.50 30.00
EM Eddie Murray/77 12.50 30.00
FR Frank Robinson/56 12.50 40.00
FR Frank Robinson/56 12.50 30.00
FT Frank Thomas/90 15.00 40.00
FT Frank Thomas/90 15.00 40.00
GM Greg Maddux/87 20.00 50.00
GM Greg Maddux/87 20.00 50.00

JT Jim Thome/91 8.00 20.00
JT Jim Thome/91 8.00 20.00
JT2 Jim Thome/91 8.00 20.00
JT2 Jim Thome/91 8.00 20.00
KG Ken Griffey Jr./89 20.00 50.00
KG Ken Griffey Jr./89 20.00 50.00
KG2 Ken Griffey Jr./89 20.00 50.00
KG2 Ken Griffey Jr./89 20.00 50.00
MR Manny Ramirez/94 10.00 25.00
MR Manny Ramirez/94 10.00 25.00
OS Ozzie Smith/78 20.00 50.00
OS Ozzie Smith/78 20.00 50.00
RJ Randy Johnson/89 10.00 25.00
RJ Randy Johnson/89 10.00 25.00
RO Roy Halladay/99 12.50 30.00
RO Roy Halladay/66 12.50 30.00
TE Miguel Tejada/98 10.00 25.00
TE Miguel Tejada/98 10.00 25.00
TG Tony Gwynn/82 15.00 40.00
TG Tony Gwynn/82 15.00 40.00
TS Tom Seaver/67 15.00 40.00
TS Tom Seaver/67 15.00 40.00
VG Vladimir Guerrero/97 12.50 30.00
VG Vladimir Guerrero/97 12.50 30.00
WB Wade Boggs/82 10.00 25.00
WB Wade Boggs/82 10.00 25.00

2007 Upper Deck Premier Patches Triple Gold

*GOLD: .4X TO 1X BASIC
OVERALL PATCH ODDS ONE PER PACK
PRINT RUNS B/WN 1-57 COPIES PER
NO PRICING ON QTY 25 OR LESS
CH Cole Hamels/35 15.00 40.00
CU Chase Utley/26 12.50 30.00
DO David Ortiz/34 20.00 50.00
FL Francisco Liriano/47 15.00 40.00
FT Frank Thomas/35 40.00 80.00
HA Travis Hafner/48 15.00 40.00
JS Jeremy Sowers/26 10.00 25.00
JV Justin Verlander/35 20.00 50.00
LB Lance Berkman/35 15.00 40.00
MO Justin Morneau/33 15.00 40.00
RW Rickie Weeks/47 15.00 40.00
RY Roy Oswalt/50 10.00 25.00
SA Johan Santana/57 20.00 50.00
VM Victor Martinez/41 12.50 30.00

2007 Upper Deck Premier Patches Triple Autographs

OVERALL AUTO ODDS ONE PER PACK
STATED PRINT RUN 15 SER.#'d SETS
NO PRICING DUE TO SCARCITY
EXCHANGE DEADLINE 04/26/10

2007 Upper Deck Premier Penmanship Autographs

PRINT RUNS B/WN 1-98 COPIES PER
NO PRICING ON QTY 10 OR LESS
MASTERPIECE PRINT RUN 1 SER.#'d SET
NO MASTERPIECE PRICING DUE TO SCARCITY
OVERALL AUTO ODDS ONE PER PACK
EXCHANGE DEADLINE 04/26/10
AK Al Kaline/53 20.00 50.00
BJ Bo Jackson/86 25.00 60.00
BR Brooks Robinson/57 15.00 40.00
CB Craig Biggio/88 10.00 25.00
CC Chris Carpenter/97 10.00 25.00
CF Carlton Fisk/72 10.00 25.00
CR Cal Ripken Jr./82 40.00 80.00
CR2 Cal Ripken Jr./82 40.00 80.00
CY Carl Yastrzemski/61 30.00 60.00
DJ Derek Jeter/96 100.00 200.00
DJ2 Derek Jeter/96 100.00 200.00
DL Derrek Lee/97 10.00 25.00
DM Don Mattingly/83 20.00 50.00
DM2 Don Mattingly/83 20.00 50.00
EB Ernie Banks/54 30.00 60.00
GM Greg Maddux/87 30.00 80.00
IR Ivan Rodriguez/91 10.00 25.00
JB Johnny Bench/68 20.00 50.00
JI Jim Palmer/65 10.00 25.00
JS John Smoltz/88 20.00 50.00
JT Jim Thome/91 30.00 60.00
KG Ken Griffey Jr./89 40.00 100.00
KG2 Ken Griffey Jr./89 40.00 100.00
LA Luis Aparicio/56 12.50 30.00
MS Mike Schmidt/73 20.00 50.00
NR Nolan Ryan/68 40.00 80.00
OZ Ozzie Smith/78 20.00 50.00
PM Paul Molitor/78 10.00 25.00
PM2 Paul Molitor/78 10.00 25.00
RA Randy Johnson/89 25.00 60.00
RC Roger Clemens/84 20.00 50.00
RJ Reggie Jackson/68 30.00 60.00
RS Ryne Sandberg/82 20.00 50.00
RY Robin Yount/74 30.00 60.00
SC Steve Carlton/67 12.50 30.00
SM Stan Musial/42 40.00 80.00
SR Scott Rolen/97 10.00 25.00
TE Miguel Tejada/98 10.00 25.00
TG Tony Gwynn/82 20.00 50.00
TG2 Tony Gwynn/82 20.00 50.00
TP Tony Perez/65 10.00 25.00
TT Troy Tulowitzki/28 10.00 25.00
VG Vladimir Guerrero/97 10.00 25.00
WB Wade Boggs/82 15.00 40.00
WC Will Clark/86 10.00 25.00
WF Whitey Ford/50 20.00 50.00
WM Willie McCovey/59 20.00 50.00
YB Yogi Berra/47 25.00 60.00

2007 Upper Deck Premier Penmanship Autographs Jersey Number

OVERALL AUTO ODDS ONE PER PACK
PRINT RUNS B/WN 1-58 COPIES PER
NO PRICING ON QTY 25 OR LESS
EXCHANGE DEADLINE 04/26/10
AM Andrew Miller/50 10.00 25.00
AM2 Andrew Miller/50 10.00 25.00
BA Jason Bay/38 10.00 25.00
BA2 Jason Bay/38 10.00 25.00
CC Chris Carpenter/29 10.00 25.00
CF Carlton Fisk/27 20.00 50.00
CH Cole Hamels/35 12.50 30.00
CZ Carlos Zambrano/38 10.00 25.00
DW Dontrelle Willis/35 15.00 40.00
DY Delmon Young/35 15.00 40.00
DY2 Delmon Young/35 15.00 40.00
FH Felix Hernandez/34 30.00 60.00
FL Francisco Liriano/47 12.50 30.00
GM Greg Maddux/36 50.00 100.00
JP Jake Peavy/44 10.00 25.00
JS John Smoltz/29 40.00 80.00
JV Justin Verlander/35 30.00 60.00
JW Jered Weaver/56 10.00 25.00
JZ Joel Zumaya/54 15.00 40.00
MO Justin Morneau/33 10.00 25.00
MO2 Justin Morneau/33 10.00 25.00
NR Nolan Ryan/34 60.00 120.00
PA Jonathan Papelbon/58 30.00 60.00
RA Randy Johnson/41 30.00 60.00
RO Roy Oswalt/45 12.50 30.00
RO2 Roy Oswalt/45 12.50 30.00
SA Johan Santana/57 10.00 25.00
SC Steve Carlton/32 10.00 25.00
SR Scott Rolen/27 10.00 25.00
VG Vladimir Guerrero/27 10.00 25.00
VM Victor Martinez/41 10.00 25.00
WB Wade Boggs/26 10.00 25.00
WM Willie McCovey/44 15.00 40.00

2007 Upper Deck Premier Preeminence Autographs

STATED PRINT RUN 50 SER.#'d SETS
GOLD PRINT RUN 25 SER.#'d SETS
NO GOLD PRICING DUE TO SCARCITY
PLATINUM PRINT RUN 1 SER.#'d SET
NO PLATINUM PRICING DUE TO SCARCTIY
OVERALL AUTO ODDS ONE PER PACK
EXCHANGE DEADLINE 04/26/10
AP Albert Pujols 50.00 100.00
BJ Bo Jackson 30.00 80.00
BR Brooks Robinson 10.00 25.00
CC Chris Carpenter 10.00 25.00
CR Cal Ripken Jr. 40.00 100.00
CY Carl Yastrzemski 30.00 60.00
GM Greg Maddux 60.00 120.00
JB Johnny Bench 20.00 50.00
JM Joe Mauer 40.00 80.00
JT Jim Thome 30.00 60.00
JV Justin Verlander 30.00 60.00
KG Ken Griffey Jr. 40.00 80.00
MS Mike Schmidt 15.00 40.00
NR Nolan Ryan 50.00 100.00
RC Roger Clemens 20.00 50.00
RJ Reggie Jackson 30.00 60.00
RS Ryne Sandberg 12.50 30.00
SM Stan Musial 40.00 80.00
TG Tony Gwynn 15.00 40.00
VG Vladimir Guerrero 20.00 50.00

2007 Upper Deck Premier Rare Patches Dual

STATED PRINT RUN 50 SER.#'d SETS
GOLD PRINT RUN 25 SER.#'d SETS
NO GOLD PRICING DUE TO SCARCITY
MASTERPIECE PRINT RUN 1 SER.#'d SET
NO MASTERPIECE PRICING DUE TO SCARCITY
PLATINUM PRINT RUN 10 SER.#'d SETS
NO PLATINUM PRICING DUE TO SCARCITY
OVERALL PATCH ODDS ONE PER PACK
BM J.Bench/J.Mauer 20.00 50.00
BR B.Roberts/R.Cano 12.50 30.00
BS A.Burnett/A.Sanchez 10.00 25.00
CP C.Carpenter/J.Peavy 12.50 30.00
CW Mig.Cabrera/D.Willis 12.50 30.00
DB C.Delgado/C.Beltran 20.00 50.00
DT S.Drew/M.Tejada 10.00 25.00
ER J.Edmonds/S.Rolen 20.00 50.00
FM P.Fielder/J.Morneau 12.50 30.00
FW P.Fielder/R.Weeks 15.00 40.00
GP K.Griffey Jr./A.Pujols 40.00 80.00
HR T.Hoffman/M.Rivera 15.00 40.00
HS C.Hamels/J.Sowers 10.00 25.00
JG D.Jeter/K.Griffey Jr. 40.00 80.00
JJ A.Jones/C.Jones 20.00 50.00
MG G.Maddux/T.Glavine 15.00 40.00
MH V.Martinez/T.Hafner 15.00 40.00
MJ D.Mattingly/D.Jeter 30.00 60.00
OT D.Ortiz/J.Thome 12.50 30.00
PO J.Peavy/R.Oswalt 10.00 25.00
PS J.Papelbon/C.Schilling 10.00 25.00
RC N.Ryan/R.Clemens 30.00 60.00
RD R.Jackson/D.Jeter 20.00 50.00
RG C.Ripken Jr./T.Gwynn 40.00 80.00
RJ R.Halladay/J.Santana 12.50 30.00
RU J.Rollins/C.Utley 20.00 50.00
SG A.Soriano/V.Guerrero 20.00 50.00
SH J.Santana/F.Hernandez 20.00 50.00
SM R.Sandberg/J.Morgan 20.00 50.00
SR M.Schmidt/B.Robinson 20.00 50.00
TR M.Tejada/J.Reyes 15.00 40.00
TT F.Thomas/J.Thome 20.00 50.00
UC B.Upton/C.Crawford 15.00 40.00
WJ D.Willis/J.Johnson 10.00 25.00
WL Jer.Weaver/F.Liriano 10.00 25.00
YM R.Yount/P.Molitor 20.00 50.00
ZU R.Zimmerman/B.Upton 10.00 25.00

2007 Upper Deck Premier Rare Remnants Triple

STATED PRINT RUN 50 SER.#'d SETS
GOLD PRINT RUN 25 SER.#'d SETS
NO GOLD PRICING DUE TO SCARCITY
MASTERPIECE PRINT RUN 1 SER.#'d SET
NO MASTERPIECE PRICING DUE TO SCARCITY
PLATINUM PRINT RUN 10 SER.#'d SETS
NO PLATINUM PRICING DUE TO SCARCITY
OVERALL PATCH ODDS ONE PER PACK
BMP Bench/Morgan/Perez 15.00 40.00
BZV Bonderman/Zumaya/Verlander 10.00 25.00
CBF RipkenBrooks/F.Robinson 30.00 60.00
CFY Cronin/Foxx/Yaz 30.00 60.00
CMK Clemente/Mazeroski/Kiner 50.00 100.00
CPR Carpenter/Pujols/Rolen 15.00 40.00
DMP Dickey/Munson/Posada 30.00 60.00
DMR Delgado/Pedro/J.Reyes 20.00 50.00
DRB Delgado/J.Reyes/Beltran 15.00 40.00
FBM Fisk/Bench/Munson 20.00 50.00
FGG Foxx/Gehrig/Greenberg 150.00 250.00
FMT Prince/Morneau/Teixeira 10.00 25.00
GGJ Griffey Jr./Vlad/Andruw 10.00 25.00
JCM Unit/Clemens/Maddux 20.00 50.00
JJR Unit/Jeter/Rivera 30.00 60.00
JMM Reggie/Mattingly/Munson 40.00 80.00
KUC Kazmir/B.Upton/Crawford 10.00 25.00
KVJ Johjima/V.Martinez/Mauer 10.00 25.00
LMS Liriano/Mauer/Santana 10.00 25.00
LSH Liriano/Sowers/Hamels 10.00 25.00
OPS Oswalt/Peavy/Sheets 10.00 25.00
OTB Ortiz/Thome/Berkman 10.00 25.00
PJG Pujols/Jeter/Griffey Jr. 15.00 40.00
PMH Pujols/Musial/Hornsby 50.00 100.00
RCD Ryan/Clemens/Drysdale 20.00 50.00
RDG Ruth/DiMaggio/Gehrig 300.00 500.00
RFS Rivera/Fingers/Sutter 10.00 25.00
RRR Ryan/Ryan/Ryan 40.00 80.00
RWH Ryan/Jer.Weaver/King Felix 20.00 50.00
RYS RipkenYount/Ozzie 10.00 25.00
SGA Soriano/Vlad/Abreu 10.00 25.00
SHM Sandberg/Hornsby/Morgan 12.00 30.00
SJZ Santana/Unit/Zito 10.00 25.00
SRB Schmidt/Brooks/Boggs 20.00 50.00
TJY Tejada/Jeter/Young 10.00 25.00
TTH Thome/Teixeira/Helton 10.00 25.00
VWJ Verland/Jer.Weaver/J.Johnson 10.00 25.00
YBM Yount/Boggs/Molitor 15.00 40.00

2007 Upper Deck Premier Remnants Triple

PRINT RUNS B/WN 21-75 COPIES PER
NO PRICING ON QTY 21 OR LESS
PLATINUM PRINT RUN 10 SER.#'d SETS
NO PLATINUM PRICING DUE TO SCARCITY
MASTERPIECE PRINT RUN 1 SER.#'d SET
NO MASTERPIECE PRICING DUE TO SCARCITY
OVERALL TRIPLE GU ODDS ONE PER PACK
AP Albert Pujols 12.50 30.00
AP Albert Pujols 12.50 30.00
AP2 Albert Pujols 12.50 30.00
AP2 Albert Pujols 12.50 30.00
AS Alfonso Soriano 6.00 15.00
AS Alfonso Soriano 6.00 15.00
BM Bill Mazeroski 10.00 25.00
BM Bill Mazeroski 10.00 25.00
BR Babe Ruth 200.00 400.00
BR Babe Ruth 200.00 400.00
CA Roy Campanella 15.00 40.00
CA Roy Campanella 15.00 40.00
CF Carlton Fisk 6.00 15.00
CF Carlton Fisk 6.00 15.00
CJ Chipper Jones 10.00 25.00
CJ Chipper Jones 10.00 25.00
CL Roger Clemens 10.00 25.00
CL Roger Clemens 10.00 25.00
CR Cal Ripken Jr. 15.00 40.00
CR Cal Ripken Jr. 15.00 40.00
CS Curt Schilling 6.00 15.00
CS Curt Schilling 6.00 15.00
CU Chase Utley 10.00 25.00
CU Chase Utley 10.00 25.00
CY Carl Yastrzemski 10.00 25.00
DD Don Drysdale/73 15.00 40.00
DJ Derek Jeter 20.00 50.00
DJ Derek Jeter 20.00 50.00
DJ2 Derek Jeter 20.00 50.00
DJ2 Derek Jeter 20.00 50.00
DM Don Mattingly 20.00 50.00
DM Don Mattingly 20.00 50.00
DO David Ortiz 6.00 15.00
DO David Ortiz 6.00 15.00
EM Eddie Mathews 8.00 20.00
EM Eddie Mathews 8.00 20.00
FR Frank Robinson 6.00 15.00
FR Frank Robinson 6.00 15.00
HO Rogers Hornsby 8.00 20.00
HO Rogers Hornsby 8.00 20.00
JB Johnny Bench 10.00 25.00
JB Johnny Bench 10.00 25.00
JD Joe DiMaggio 75.00 150.00
JD Joe DiMaggio 75.00 150.00
JO Jose Reyes 15.00 40.00
JO Jose Reyes 15.00 40.00
JR Jackie Robinson 15.00 40.00
JR Jackie Robinson 15.00 40.00
JT Jim Thome 6.00 15.00
JT Jim Thome 6.00 15.00
KG Ken Griffey Jr. 10.00 25.00
KG Ken Griffey Jr. 10.00 25.00
KG2 Ken Griffey Jr. 10.00 25.00
KG2 Ken Griffey Jr. 10.00 25.00
MO Mel Ott 20.00 50.00
MO Mel Ott 20.00 50.00
MR Manny Ramirez 6.00 15.00
MR Manny Ramirez 6.00 15.00
MS Mike Schmidt 10.00 25.00
MS Mike Schmidt 10.00 25.00
NR Nolan Ryan 15.00 40.00
NR Nolan Ryan 15.00 40.00
PM Paul Molitor 6.00 15.00
PM Paul Molitor 6.00 15.00
PR Pee Wee Reese 15.00 40.00
PR Pee Wee Reese 15.00 40.00
RC Roberto Clemente 50.00 100.00
RC Roberto Clemente 50.00 100.00
RJ Reggie Jackson 10.00 25.00
RJ Reggie Jackson 10.00 25.00
RO Brooks Robinson 10.00 25.00
RO Brooks Robinson 10.00 25.00
RS Ryne Sandberg 10.00 25.00
RS Ryne Sandberg 10.00 25.00
RY Robin Yount 10.00 25.00
RY Robin Yount 10.00 25.00
SM Stan Musial 15.00 40.00
SM Stan Musial 15.00 40.00
TG Tony Gwynn 10.00 25.00
TG Tony Gwynn 10.00 25.00
TM Thurman Munson 15.00 40.00
TM Thurman Munson 15.00 40.00
VG Vladimir Guerrero 6.00 15.00
VG Vladimir Guerrero 6.00 15.00

2007 Upper Deck Premier Remnants Triple Gold

*GOLD: .5X TO 1.2X BASIC
OVERALL TRIPLE GU ODDS ONE PER PACK
PRINT RUNS B/WN 6-60 COPIES PER
NO PRICING ON QTY 19 OR LESS
BR Babe Ruth/60 250.00 500.00
CL Roger Clemens/24 15.00 40.00
DJ Derek Jeter/24 20.00 50.00
DJ2 Derek Jeter/24 20.00 50.00
LG Lou Gehrig/40 125.00 250.00
RC Roberto Clemente/29 75.00 150.00
TC Ty Cobb/47 75.00 150.00
TM Thurman Munson/20 30.00 60.00

2007 Upper Deck Premier Remnants Quad

PRINT RUNS B/WN 1-96 COPIES PER
NO PRICING ON QTY 25 OR LESS
PLATINUM PRINT RUN 5 SER.#'d SETS
NO PLATINUM PRICING DUE TO SCARCITY
MASTERPIECE PRINT RUN 1 SER.#'d SET
NO MASTERPIECE PRICING DUE TO SCARCITY
OVERALL QUAD GU ODDS ONE PER PACK
AK Al Kaline/53 15.00 40.00
AK Al Kaline/53 15.00 40.00
BM Bill Mazeroski/56 12.50 30.00
BM Bill Mazeroski/56 12.50 30.00
CL Roberto Clemente/55 40.00 80.00
CL Roberto Clemente/55 40.00 80.00
CR Cal Ripken Jr./82 20.00 50.00
CR Cal Ripken Jr./82 20.00 50.00
DJ Derek Jeter/96 20.00 50.00
DJ Derek Jeter/96 20.00 50.00
DM Don Mattingly/83 15.00 40.00
DM Don Mattingly/83 15.00 40.00
EM Eddie Mathews/52 15.00 40.00
EM Eddie Mathews/52 15.00 40.00
HK Harmon Killebrew/55 20.00 50.00
HK Harmon Killebrew/55 20.00 50.00
JB Johnny Bench/68 12.50 30.00
JB Johnny Bench/68 12.50 30.00
JD Joe DiMaggio/36 40.00 80.00
JD Joe DiMaggio/36 40.00 80.00
JF Jimmie Foxx/27 60.00 120.00
JF Jimmie Foxx/27 60.00 120.00
JR Jackie Robinson/47 60.00 120.00
JR Jackie Robinson/47 60.00 120.00
JT Jim Thome/91 6.00 15.00
JT Jim Thome/91 6.00 15.00
KG Ken Griffey Jr./89 12.50 30.00
KG Ken Griffey Jr./89 12.50 30.00
LG Lou Gehrig/25 350.00 450.00
LG Lou Gehrig/25 350.00 450.00
MI Johnny Mize/36 20.00 50.00
MI Johnny Mize/36 20.00 50.00
MS Mike Schmidt/73 12.50 30.00
MS Mike Schmidt/73 12.50 30.00
NR Nolan Ryan/68 40.00 80.00
NR Nolan Ryan/68 40.00 80.00
RC Roger Clemens/84 12.50 30.00
RC Roger Clemens/84 12.50 30.00
RJ Reggie Jackson/68 10.00 25.00
RJ Reggie Jackson/68 10.00 25.00
RN Brooks Robinson/57 10.00 25.00
RN Brooks Robinson/48 10.00 25.00
RO Roy Campanella/48 15.00 40.00
RO Roy Campanella/48 15.00 40.00
SM Stan Musial/42 10.00 25.00
SM Stan Musial/42 10.00 25.00
TM Thurman Munson/70 20.00 50.00
TM Thurman Munson/70 20.00 50.00

2007 Upper Deck Premier Remnants Quad Gold

*GOLD: .5X TO 1.2X BASIC
OVERALL TRIPLE GU ODDS ONE PER PACK
PRINT RUNS B/WN 2-57 COPIES PER
NO PRICING ON QTY 25 OR LESS
CF Chone Figgins/47 4.00 10.00
CH Cole Hamels/35 12.50 30.00
CU Chase Utley/26 20.00 50.00
FL Francisco Liriano/47 10.00 25.00
HO Rogers Hornsby/50 20.00 50.00
JS Jeremy Sowers/45 4.00 10.00
JV Justin Verlander/35 10.00 25.00
JW Jered Weaver/56 6.00 15.00
MI Johnny Mize/50 20.00 50.00
MO Justin Morneau/33 6.00 15.00
NR Nolan Ryan/34 40.00 80.00
SA Johan Santana/57 10.00 25.00
TG Tom Glavine/50 12.50 30.00

2007 Upper Deck Premier Remnants Quad Autographs

OVERALL AUTO ODDS ONE PER PACK
STATED PRINT RUN 15 SER.#'d SETS
NO PRICING DUE TO SCARCITY
EXCHANGE DEADLINE 04/26/10

2007 Upper Deck Premier Stitchings

STATED PRINT RUN 50 SER.#'d SETS
*STITCHINGS 35: .4X TO 1X BASIC
STITCHINGS 35 PRINT RUN 35 SER.#'d SETS
STITCHINGS 10 PRINT RUN 10 SER.#'d SETS
OVERALL STITCHINGS ODDS ONE PER PACK
1 Babe Ruth 15.00 40.00
1 Babe Ruth 15.00 40.00
2 Babe Ruth 15.00 40.00
2 Babe Ruth 15.00 40.00
3 Babe Ruth 15.00 40.00
3 Babe Ruth 15.00 40.00
4 Ty Cobb 10.00 25.00
4 Ty Cobb 10.00 25.00
5 Ty Cobb 10.00 25.00
5 Ty Cobb 10.00 25.00
6 Lou Gehrig 12.50 30.00
7 Lou Gehrig 12.50 30.00
7 Lou Gehrig 12.50 30.00
8 Joe DiMaggio 12.50 30.00
8 Joe DiMaggio 12.50 30.00
9 Joe DiMaggio 12.50 30.00
9 Joe DiMaggio 12.50 30.00
12 Roberto Clemente 15.00 40.00
12 Roberto Clemente 15.00 40.00
13 Roberto Clemente 15.00 40.00
13 Roberto Clemente 15.00 40.00
14 Jackie Robinson 12.50 30.00
14 Jackie Robinson 12.50 30.00
15 Jackie Robinson 12.50 30.00
15 Jackie Robinson 12.50 30.00
16 Cy Young 6.00 15.00
16 Cy Young 6.00 15.00
17 Cy Young 6.00 15.00
17 Cy Young 6.00 15.00
18 Nolan Ryan 15.00 40.00
18 Nolan Ryan 15.00 40.00
19 Nolan Ryan 15.00 40.00
19 Nolan Ryan 15.00 40.00
20 Reggie Jackson 6.00 15.00
20 Reggie Jackson 6.00 15.00
21 Reggie Jackson 6.00 15.00
21 Reggie Jackson 6.00 15.00
22 Ken Griffey Jr. 15.00 40.00
22 Ken Griffey Jr. 15.00 40.00
23 Ken Griffey Jr. 15.00 40.00
23 Ken Griffey Jr. 15.00 40.00
24 Derek Jeter 15.00 40.00
24 Derek Jeter 15.00 40.00
25 Derek Jeter 15.00 40.00
25 Derek Jeter 15.00 40.00
26 Jimmie Foxx 6.00 15.00
26 Jimmie Foxx 6.00 15.00
27 Jimmie Foxx 6.00 15.00
27 Jimmie Foxx 6.00 15.00
28 Rogers Hornsby 6.00 15.00
28 Rogers Hornsby 6.00 15.00
30 Walter Johnson 12.50 30.00
30 Walter Johnson 12.50 30.00
31 Walter Johnson 12.50 30.00
31 Walter Johnson 12.50 30.00
32 Ernie Banks 10.00 25.00
32 Ernie Banks 10.00 25.00
33 Ernie Banks 10.00 25.00
33 Ernie Banks 10.00 25.00
34 Christy Mathewson 6.00 15.00
34 Christy Mathewson 6.00 15.00
35 Johnny Mize 6.00 15.00
35 Johnny Mize 6.00 15.00
36 Thurman Munson 12.50 30.00
36 Thurman Munson 12.50 30.00
37 Thurman Munson 12.50 30.00
37 Thurman Munson 12.50 30.00
38 Mel Ott 6.00 15.00
38 Mel Ott 6.00 15.00
39 Satchel Paige 10.00 25.00
39 Satchel Paige 10.00 25.00
40 George Sisler 6.00 15.00
40 George Sisler 6.00 15.00
41 Casey Stengel 6.00 15.00
41 Casey Stengel 6.00 15.00
42 Honus Wagner 10.00 25.00
42 Honus Wagner 10.00 25.00
43 Honus Wagner 10.00 25.00
43 Honus Wagner 10.00 25.00
44 Roy Campanella 6.00 15.00
44 Roy Campanella 6.00 15.00
45 Mickey Cochrane 6.00 15.00
45 Mickey Cochrane 6.00 15.00
46 Dizzy Dean 6.00 15.00
46 Dizzy Dean 6.00 15.00
47 Don Drysdale 6.00 15.00
47 Don Drysdale 6.00 15.00
48 Lefty Grove 6.00 15.00
48 Lefty Grove 6.00 15.00
49 Roger Clemens 10.00 25.00
49 Roger Clemens 10.00 25.00
50 Roger Clemens 10.00 25.00
50 Roger Clemens 10.00 25.00
51 Cal Ripken Jr. 20.00 50.00
51 Cal Ripken Jr. 20.00 50.00
52 Cal Ripken Jr. 20.00 50.00
52 Cal Ripken Jr. 20.00 50.00
53 Tony Gwynn 10.00 25.00
53 Tony Gwynn 10.00 25.00
54 Tony Gwynn 10.00 25.00
54 Tony Gwynn 10.00 25.00
55 Johnny Bench 6.00 15.00
55 Johnny Bench 6.00 15.00
56 Yogi Berra 6.00 15.00
56 Yogi Berra 6.00 15.00
57 Carlton Fisk 6.00 15.00
57 Carlton Fisk 6.00 15.00
58 Joe Morgan 6.00 15.00
58 Joe Morgan 6.00 15.00
59 Brooks Robinson 6.00 15.00
59 Brooks Robinson 6.00 15.00
60 Mike Schmidt 10.00 25.00
60 Mike Schmidt 10.00 25.00
61 Willie Stargell 6.00 15.00
61 Willie Stargell 6.00 15.00
62 Tom Seaver 10.00 25.00
62 Tom Seaver 10.00 25.00
63 Ozzie Smith 12.50 30.00
63 Ozzie Smith 12.50 30.00
64 Albert Pujols 12.50 30.00
64 Albert Pujols 12.50 30.00
65 Albert Pujols 12.50 30.00
65 Albert Pujols 12.50 30.00
66 Ryan Howard 10.00 25.00
66 Ryan Howard 10.00 25.00
67 David Ortiz 10.00 25.00
67 David Ortiz 10.00 25.00
68 Randy Johnson 6.00 15.00
68 Randy Johnson 6.00 15.00
69 Greg Maddux 10.00 25.00
69 Greg Maddux 10.00 25.00
70 Greg Maddux 10.00 25.00
70 Greg Maddux 10.00 25.00
71 Johan Santana 6.00 15.00
71 Johan Santana 6.00 15.00
72 Al Kaline 6.00 15.00
72 Al Kaline 6.00 15.00
73 Ryne Sandberg 10.00 25.00
73 Ryne Sandberg 10.00 25.00
74 Robin Yount 10.00 25.00
74 Robin Yount 10.00 25.00
75 Frank Robinson 6.00 15.00
75 Frank Robinson 6.00 15.00
76 Frank Robinson 6.00 15.00
76 Frank Robinson 6.00 15.00
78 Stan Musial 10.00 25.00
78 Stan Musial 10.00 25.00
79 Carl Yastrzemski 10.00 25.00
79 Carl Yastrzemski 10.00 25.00
80 Don Mattingly 20.00 50.00
80 Don Mattingly 20.00 50.00
81 Ichiro Suzuki 20.00 50.00
81 Ichiro Suzuki 20.00 50.00
82 Yogi Berra 6.00 15.00
82 Yogi Berra 6.00 15.00
83 C.Fisk 10.00 25.00
J.Bench
83 C.Fisk 10.00 25.00
J.Bench
84 T.Munson 10.00 25.00
J.Bench
84 T.Munson 10.00 25.00
J.Bench
85 B.Ruth 30.00 60.00
L.Gehrig
85 B.Ruth 30.00 60.00
L.Gehrig
86 W.Ford 10.00 25.00
Y.Berra
86 W.Ford 10.00 25.00
Y.Berra
87 D.Larsen 10.00 25.00
Y.Berra
87 D.Larsen 10.00 25.00
Y.Berra
88 K.Gibson 6.00 15.00
D.Eckersley
88 K.Gibson 6.00 15.00
D.Eckersley
90 J.Robinson 10.00 25.00
P.Reese
90 J.Robinson 10.00 25.00
P.Reese
91 J.Robinson 10.00 25.00
S.Paige
91 J.Robinson 10.00 25.00
S.Paige
92 L.Gehrig 15.00 40.00
C.Ripken Jr.
92 L.Gehrig 15.00 40.00
C.Ripken Jr.
93 I.Suzuki 20.00 50.00
G.Sisler
93 I.Suzuki 20.00 50.00
G.Sisler
94 Clemens 15.00 40.00
Ryan
Big Unit
Carlton
94 Clemens 15.00 40.00
Ryan
Big Unit
Carlton
95 Bench 10.00 25.00
Morgan
Perez
Concepcion
95 Bench 10.00 25.00
Morgan
Perez
Concepcion
96 Ruth 15.00 40.00
Foxx
Ott
Mathews
96 Ruth 15.00 40.00
Foxx
Ott
Mathews
97 Clemens 15.00 40.00
Maddux
Seaver
Ryan
97 Clemens 15.00 40.00
Maddux
Seaver
Ryan
98 Clemente 15.00 40.00
Gwynn
RipkenMusial
98 Clemente 15.00 40.00
Gwynn
RipkenMusial
99 John F. Kennedy 12.50 30.00
99 John F. Kennedy 12.50 30.00
100 Dwight Eisenhower 6.00 15.00
100 Dwight Eisenhower 6.00 15.00
DM Daisuke Matsuzaka 10.00 25.00
KI Kei Igawa 12.50 30.00
MI D.Matsuzaka 10.00 25.00
K.Igawa

2007 Upper Deck Premier Stitchings 10

OVERALL STITCHINGS ODDS ONE PER PACK
STATED PRINT RUN 10 SER.#'d SETS
NO PRICING ON MOST DUE TO SCARCITY
1 Babe Ruth 30.00 60.00
2 Babe Ruth 30.00 60.00
3 Babe Ruth 30.00 60.00
4 Ty Cobb 15.00 40.00
5 Ty Cobb 15.00 40.00
12 Roberto Clemente 40.00 80.00
13 Roberto Clemente 40.00 80.00
16 Cy Young 12.50 30.00
17 Cy Young 12.50 30.00
18 Nolan Ryan 40.00 80.00
19 Nolan Ryan 40.00 80.00
22 Ken Griffey Jr. 40.00 100.00
23 Ken Griffey Jr. 40.00 100.00
24 Derek Jeter 30.00 60.00
25 Derek Jeter 30.00 60.00
26 Jimmie Foxx 10.00 25.00
27 Jimmie Foxx 10.00 25.00
30 Walter Johnson 20.00 50.00
31 Walter Johnson 20.00 50.00
32 Ernie Banks 10.00 25.00
33 Ernie Banks 10.00 25.00
34 Christy Mathewson 10.00 25.00
36 Thurman Munson 30.00 60.00
37 Thurman Munson 30.00 60.00
39 Satchel Paige 15.00 40.00
40 George Sisler 10.00 25.00
41 Casey Stengel 10.00 25.00
51 Cal Ripken Jr. 40.00 80.00
52 Cal Ripken Jr. 40.00 80.00
53 Tony Gwynn 15.00 40.00
54 Tony Gwynn 15.00 40.00
64 Albert Pujols 30.00 60.00
65 Albert Pujols 30.00 60.00
67 David Ortiz 15.00 40.00
69 Greg Maddux 15.00 40.00
70 Greg Maddux 15.00 40.00
73 Ryne Sandberg 15.00 40.00
74 Robin Yount 20.00 50.00

2008 Upper Deck Premier

COMMON CARD (1-178) 2.00 5.00
COMMON RET (179-200) 1.25 3.00
ONE BASE CARD PER PACK
1-200 STATED PRINT RUN 99 SER.#'d SETS
COMMON AU RC p/r 299 (201-241) 4.00 10.00
COMMON AU RC p/r 99 (201-241) 5.00 12.00
OVERALL RC AUTO ONE PER PACK
201-241 PRINT RUNS b/w 99-299 SER.#'d SETS
EXCHANGE DEADLINE 3/13/2010
1 Chipper Jones 5.00 12.00
2 Andruw Jones 2.00 5.00
3 John Smoltz 5.00 12.00
4 Mark Teixeira 3.00 8.00
5 Edgar Renteria 2.00 5.00
6 Jeff Francoeur 3.00 8.00
7 Tim Hudson 3.00 8.00
8 Miguel Cabrera 5.00 12.00
9 Hanley Ramirez 3.00 8.00
10 Dan Uggla 2.00 5.00
11 Dontrelle Willis 2.00 5.00
12 Josh Willingham 3.00 8.00
13 Pedro Martinez 3.00 8.00
14 Carlos Delgado 2.00 5.00
15 Carlos Beltran 3.00 8.00
16 David Wright 3.00 8.00
17 Tom Glavine 3.00 8.00
18 Jose Reyes 3.00 8.00
19 Paul Lo Duca 2.00 5.00
20 John Maine 2.00 5.00
21 Chase Utley 3.00 8.00
22 Cole Hamels 4.00 10.00
23 Jimmy Rollins 3.00 8.00
24 Shane Victorino 2.00 5.00
25 Ryan Howard 3.00 8.00
26 Pat Burrell 2.00 5.00
27 Aaron Rowand 2.00 5.00
28 Ryan Zimmerman 3.00 8.00
29 Ryan Church 2.00 5.00
30 Matt Chico 2.00 5.00
31 Dmitri Young 2.00 5.00
32 Derrek Lee 2.00 5.00
33 Aramis Ramirez 2.00 5.00
34 Carlos Zambrano 3.00 8.00
35 Rich Hill 2.00 5.00
36 Alfonso Soriano 3.00 8.00
37 Kerry Wood 2.00 5.00
38 Ted Lilly 2.00 5.00
39 Ryan Theriot 2.00 5.00
40 Ken Griffey Jr. 10.00 25.00
41 Adam Dunn 3.00 8.00
42 Homer Bailey 3.00 8.00
43 Aaron Harang 2.00 5.00
44 Brandon Phillips 2.00 5.00
45 Josh Hamilton 3.00 8.00
46 Lance Berkman 3.00 8.00
47 Carlos Lee 2.00 5.00
48 Hunter Pence 3.00 8.00
49 Mark Loretta 3.00 8.00
50 Roy Oswalt 3.00 8.00
51 Prince Fielder 3.00 8.00
52 Ryan Braun 3.00 8.00
53 J.J. Hardy 2.00 5.00
54 Ben Sheets 2.00 5.00
55 Rickie Weeks 2.00 5.00
56 Corey Hart 2.00 5.00
57 Johnny Estrada 2.00 5.00
58 Jason Bay 3.00 8.00
59 Freddy Sanchez 2.00 5.00
60 Adam LaRoche 2.00 5.00
61 Ian Snell 2.00 5.00
62 Xavier Nady 2.00 5.00
63 Tom Gorzelanny 2.00 5.00
64 Scott Rolen 3.00 8.00
65 Albert Pujols 6.00 15.00
66 Jim Edmonds 3.00 8.00
67 Chris Duncan 2.00 5.00
68 Adam Wainwright 3.00 8.00
69 Brandon Webb 3.00 8.00
70 Orlando Hudson 2.00 5.00
71 Chris B. Young 2.00 5.00
72 Stephen Drew 2.00 5.00
73 Matt Holliday 5.00 12.00
74 Jeff Francis 2.00 5.00
75 Brad Hawpe 2.00 5.00
76 Todd Helton 3.00 8.00
77 Troy Tulowitzki 5.00 12.00
78 Russell Martin 2.00 5.00
79 Nomar Garciaparra 3.00 8.00
80 James Loney 2.00 5.00
81 Andre Ethier 3.00 8.00
82 Brad Penny 2.00 5.00
83 Rafael Furcal 2.00 5.00
84 Jeff Kent 2.00 5.00
85 Greg Maddux 6.00 15.00
86 Chris Young 2.00 5.00
87 Khalil Greene 2.00 5.00
88 Trevor Hoffman 3.00 8.00
89 Adrian Gonzalez 3.00 8.00
90 Jake Peavy 2.00 5.00
91 Noah Lowry 2.00 5.00
92 Omar Vizquel 3.00 8.00
93 Tim Lincecum 3.00 8.00
94 Matt Cain 3.00 8.00
95 Randy Winn 2.00 5.00
96 Miguel Tejada 3.00 8.00
97 Brian Roberts 2.00 5.00
98 Nick Markakis 4.00 10.00
99 Erik Bedard 2.00 5.00
100 Melvin Mora 2.00 5.00
101 David Ortiz 5.00 12.00
102 Manny Ramirez 5.00 12.00
103 Josh Beckett 2.00 5.00
104 Jonathan Papelbon 3.00 8.00
105 Curt Schilling 3.00 8.00
106 Daisuke Matsuzaka 3.00 8.00
107 Jason Varitek 5.00 12.00
108 Kevin Youkilis 2.00 5.00
109 Derek Jeter 12.00 30.00
110 Hideki Matsui 5.00 12.00
111 Alex Rodriguez 6.00 15.00
112 Johnny Damon 3.00 8.00
113 Robinson Cano 3.00 8.00
114 Jorge Posada 3.00 8.00
115 Mariano Rivera 6.00 15.00
116 Roger Clemens 6.00 15.00
117 Chien-Ming Wang 3.00 8.00
118 Carl Crawford 3.00 8.00
119 Delmon Young 3.00 8.00
120 B.J. Upton 3.00 8.00
121 Akinori Iwamura 2.00 5.00
122 Scott Kazmir 3.00 8.00
123 Alex Rios 2.00 5.00
124 Frank Thomas 5.00 12.00
125 Roy Halladay 3.00 8.00
126 Vernon Wells 2.00 5.00
127 Troy Glaus 3.00 8.00

128 Jeremy Accardo 3.00 8.00
129 A.J. Burnett 2.00 5.00
130 Paul Konerko 3.00 8.00
131 Jim Thome 3.00 8.00
132 Jermaine Dye 2.00 5.00
133 Mark Buehrle 3.00 8.00
134 Javier Vazquez 2.00 5.00
135 Grady Sizemore 3.00 8.00
136 Travis Hafner 2.00 5.00
137 Victor Martinez 3.00 8.00
138 C.C. Sabathia 3.00 8.00
139 Ryan Garko 2.00 5.00
140 Fausto Carmona 2.00 5.00
141 Justin Verlander 5.00 12.00
142 Jeremy Bonderman 2.00 5.00
143 Magglio Ordonez 3.00 8.00
144 Gary Sheffield 2.00 5.00
145 Carlos Guillen 2.00 5.00
146 Ivan Rodriguez 3.00 8.00
147 Curtis Granderson 3.00 8.00
148 Alex Gordon 3.00 8.00
149 Mark Teahen 2.00 5.00
150 Brian Bannister 2.00 5.00
151 Billy Butler 2.00 5.00
152 Johan Santana 3.00 8.00
153 Torii Hunter 2.00 5.00
154 Joe Mauer 4.00 10.00
155 Justin Morneau 3.00 8.00
156 Vladimir Guerrero 3.00 8.00
157 Chone Figgins 2.00 5.00
158 Jered Weaver 3.00 8.00
159 Kelvim Escobar 3.00 8.00
160 John Lackey 3.00 8.00
161 Dan Haren 2.00 5.00
162 Mike Piazza 5.00 12.00
163 Nick Swisher 3.00 8.00
164 Eric Chavez 2.00 5.00
165 Huston Street 3.00 8.00
166 Joe Blanton 2.00 5.00
167 Kenji Johjima 2.00 5.00
168 J.J. Putz 2.00 5.00
169 Felix Hernandez 3.00 8.00
170 Jose Guillen 2.00 5.00
171 Adrian Beltre 5.00 12.00
172 Ichiro 6.00 15.00
173 Marlon Byrd 2.00 5.00
174 Hank Blalock 2.00 5.00
175 Michael Young 2.00 5.00
176 Ian Kinsler 3.00 8.00
177 Sammy Sosa 5.00 12.00
178 Kevin Millwood 2.00 5.00
179 Luis Aparicio 2.00 5.00
180 Johnny Bench 3.00 8.00
181 Yogi Berra 3.00 8.00
182 Lou Brock 2.00 5.00
183 Jim Bunning 2.00 5.00
184 Rod Carew 2.00 5.00
185 Orlando Cepeda 2.00 5.00
186 Bobby Doerr 2.00 5.00
187 Bob Feller 2.00 5.00
188 Dennis Eckersley 2.00 5.00
189 Carlton Fisk 2.00 5.00
190 Monte Irvin 2.00 5.00
191 Rollie Fingers 2.00 5.00
192 Al Kaline 3.00 8.00
193 Nolan Ryan 10.00 25.00
194 Mike Schmidt 5.00 12.00
195 Ryne Sandberg 6.00 15.00
196 Robin Yount 3.00 8.00
197 Brooks Robinson 2.00 5.00
198 Bill Mazeroski 2.00 5.00
199 Reggie Jackson 2.00 5.00
200 Babe Ruth 8.00 20.00
201 Ian Kennedy AU RC/299 6.00 15.00
202 Jonathan Albaladejo AU RC/299 5.00 12.00
203 Josh Anderson AU (RC)/299 4.00 10.00
204 Wladimir Balentien AU (RC)/299 5.00 12.00
205 Daric Barton AU (RC)/299 5.00 12.00
206 Jerry Blevins AU RC/99 5.00 12.00
207 Emilio Bonifacio AU RC/99 6.00 15.00
208 Lance Broadway AU (RC)/299 4.00 10.00
209 Clay Buchholz AU (RC)/299 6.00 15.00
210 Billy Buckner AU (RC)/299 4.00 10.00
212 Ross Detwiler AU RC/299 5.00 12.00
213 Harvey Garcia AU (RC)/99 5.00 12.00
214 Alberto Gonzalez AU RC/99 12.50 30.00
215 Ryan Hanigan AU RC/99 5.00 12.00
216 Kevin Hart AU (RC)/299 4.00 10.00
217 Luke Hochevar AU RC/299 6.00 15.00
218 Chin-Lung Hu AU (RC)/299 6.00 15.00
219 Rob Johnson AU (RC)/99 5.00 12.00
220 Brandon Jones AU RC/299 6.00 15.00
221 Joe Koshansky AU (RC)/299 4.00 10.00
222 Donny Lucy AU (RC)/299 4.00 10.00
223 Justin Maxwell AU RC/299 6.00 15.00
224 Jonathan Meloan AU RC/299 4.00 10.00
225 Luis Mendoza AU (RC)/299 4.00 10.00
226 Jose Morales AU (RC)/299 4.00 10.00
227 Nyjer Morgan AU (RC)/99 5.00 12.00
228 Bill Murphy AU (RC)/99 5.00 12.00
229 Josh Newman AU RC/99 5.00 12.00
230 Ross Ohlendorf AU RC/299 5.00 12.00
231 Troy Patton AU (RC)/299 4.00 10.00
232 Felipe Paulino AU RC/99 EXCH 5.00 12.00
233 Steve Pearce AU RC/299 12.00 30.00
234 Justin Ruggiano AU RC/99 5.00 12.00
235 Clint Sammons AU (RC)/299 4.00 10.00
236 Bronson Sardinha AU (RC)/299 4.00 10.00
237 Chris Seddon AU (RC)/99 5.00 12.00
238 Seth Smith AU (RC)/299 4.00 10.00
239 J.R. Towles AU RC/299 5.00 12.00
240 Eugenio Velez AU RC/99 15.00 40.00
241 Joey Votto AU (RC)/299 15.00 40.00
242 Bill White AU RC/99 5.00 12.00

2008 Upper Deck Premier Blue

1-200 RANDOMLY INSERTED
1-200 PRINT RUN 15 SER.#'d SETS
NO 1-200 PRICING DUE TO SCARCITY
*BLUE AU p/r 99: .5X TO 1.2X BASIC p/r 299
*BLUE AU p/r 50: .4X TO 1X BASIC p/r 99
OVERALL RC AUTO ONE PER PACK
201-240 PRINT RUNS b/wn 50-99 COPIES PER
EXCHANGE DEADLINE 3/13/2010

2008 Upper Deck Premier Gold

1-200 RANDOMLY INSERTED
1-200 PRINT RUN 1 SER.#'d SET
NO 1-200 PRICING DUE TO SCARCITY
*GOLD AU p/r 50: .6X TO 1.5X BASIC p/r 299
OVERALL RC AUTO ONE PER PACK
201-240 PRINT RUNS b/wn 10-50 COPIES PER
NO PRICING ON QTY 10 OR LESS
EXCHANGE DEADLINE 3/13/2010

2008 Upper Deck Premier Silver

1-200 RANDOMLY INSERTED
1-200 PRINT RUN 5 SER.#'d SETS
NO 1-200 PRICING DUE TO SCARCITY
*SILVER AU p/r 75: .6X TO 1.5X BASIC p/r 299
OVERALL RC AUTO ONE PER PACK
201-240 PRINT RUNS 25-75 COPIES PER
NO PRICING ON QTY 25 OR LESS
EXCHANGE DEADLINE 3/13/2010

2008 Upper Deck Premier Rookie Autographs Jersey Number

OVERALL RC AUTO ONE PER PACK
PRINT RUNS B/WN 5-65 COPIES PER
NO PRICING ON QTY 25 OR LESS
EXCHANGE DEADLINE 3/13/2010
201 Ian Kennedy AU/36 6.00 15.00
202 Jonathan Albaladejo AU/53 8.00 20.00
204 Wladimir Balentien AU/50 8.00 20.00
208 Lance Broadway AU/41 6.00 15.00
209 Clay Buchholz AU/61 8.00 20.00
210 Billy Buckner AU/38 6.00 15.00
212 Ross Detwiler AU/29 8.00 20.00
216 Kevin Hart AU/55 6.00 15.00
217 Luke Hochevar AU/44 10.00 25.00
218 Chin-Lung Hu AU/60 30.00 60.00
220 Brandon Jones AU/28 10.00 25.00
221 Joe Koshansky AU/47 6.00 15.00
222 Donny Lucy AU/55 6.00 15.00
224 Jonathan Meloan AU/63 6.00 15.00
225 Luis Mendoza AU/32 6.00 15.00
226 Jose Morales AU/58 6.00 15.00
230 Ross Ohlendorf AU/60 8.00 20.00
231 Troy Patton AU/65 6.00 15.00
236 Bronson Sardinha AU/64 6.00 15.00
239 J.R. Towles AU/46 8.00 20.00
241 Joey Votto AU/60 30.00 60.00

2008 Upper Deck Premier Combos Memorablia

OVERALL GU ODDS TWO PER PACK
STATED PRINT RUN 50 SER.#'d SETS
GOLD PRINT RUN 25 SER.#'d SETS
NO GOLD PRICING DUE TO SCARCITY
PLATINUM PRINT RUN 5 SER.#'d SETS
NO PLATINUM PRICING AVAILABLE
BF R.Braun/P.Fielder/50 12.50 30.00
BY R.Braun/R.Yount/50 12.50 30.00
CZ Miguel Cabrera/Ryan Zimmerman/50 5.00 12.00
FO Prince Fielder/David Ortiz/50 6.00 15.00
FV Carlton Fisk/Jason Varitek/50 6.00 15.00
GC T.Gwynn/R.Carew/50 10.00 25.00
GD K.Griffey Jr./A.Dunn/50 10.00 25.00
GJ K.Griffey Jr./D.Jeter/50 15.00 40.00
GM Tom Glavine/Pedro Martinez/50 4.00 10.00
GR Vladimir Guerrero/Manny Ramirez/50 4.00 10.00
HH Matt Holliday/Todd Helton/50 5.00 12.00
JH Andruw Jones/Torii Hunter/50 4.00 10.00
JR D.Jeter/C.Ripken/50 20.00 50.00
LR T.Lazzeri/P.Rizzuto/50 10.00 25.00
MJ T.Munson/R.Jackson/50 20.00 50.00
MM Victor Martinez/Joe Mauer/50 4.00 10.00
MU Joe Morgan/Chase Utley/50 4.00 10.00
MY S.Musial/C.Yaz/50 12.50 30.00
OH David Ortiz/Travis Hafner/50 5.00 12.00
OK M.Ordonez/A.Kaline/50 20.00 50.00
OR David Ortiz/Manny Ramirez/50 6.00 15.00
OY David Ortiz/Kevin Youkilis/50 6.00 15.00
PB H.Pence/R.Braun/50 10.00 25.00
PM A.Pujols/S.Musial/50 12.00 30.00
PO A.Pujols/D.Ortiz/50 12.50 30.00
PY Jake Peavy/Chris Young/50 5.00 12.00
RB Jose Reyes/Carlos Beltran/50 4.00 10.00
RC J.Robinson/R.Camp/50 30.00 60.00
RG C.Ripken/K.Griffey/50 20.00 50.00
RJ H.Ramirez/D.Jeter/50 10.00 25.00
SC J.Santana/R.Clemens/50 6.00 15.00
SH Grady Sizemore/Travis Hafner/50 4.00 10.00
SM J.Smoltz/G.Maddux/50 10.00 25.00
TG F.Thomas/K.Griffey/50 20.00 50.00
UH C.Utley/C.Hamels/50 10.00 25.00
VM Jason Varitek/Victor Martinez/50 6.00 15.00
VR J.Verlander/N.Ryan/50 15.00 40.00
WH C.Wang/P.Hughes/50 15.00 40.00

2008 Upper Deck Premier Combos Patch

OVERALL GU ODDS TWO PER PACK
PRINT RUNS B/WN 10-50 COPIES PER
NO PRICING ON QTY 10 OR LESS
GOLD PRINT RUN 25 SER.#'d SETS
NO GOLD PRICING DUE TO SCARCITY
MASTERPIECE PRINT RUN 1 SER.#'d SET
NO MASTERPIECE PRICING AVAILABLE
PLATINUM PRINT RUN 10 SER.#'d SETS
NO PLATINUM PRICING AVAILABLE
BD Ben Sheets/Dan Haren/50 6.00 15.00
BP J.Bench/A.Pujols/50 20.00 50.00
BR R.Braun/C.Ripken Jr./50 30.00 60.00
BS E.Bedard/C.Sabathia/50 6.00 15.00
BZ J.Bonderman/C.Zambrano/50 6.00 15.00
CR M.Cabrera/M.Ramirez/50 12.50 30.00
CV C.Fisk/V.Guerrero/50 6.00 15.00
FG J.Francoeur/A.Gordon/50 12.50 30.00
FM J.Francoeur/J.Mauer/50 10.00 25.00
GR K.Griffey Jr./C.Ripken Jr./50 25.00 60.00
GY T.Gwynn/R.Yount/50 20.00 50.00
HG J.Hardy/A.Gordon/50 10.00 25.00
HH M.Holliday/T.Helton/50 12.50 30.00
HM C.Hamels/A.Miller/50 6.00 15.00
HR F.Hernandez/N.Ryan/50 20.00 50.00
HW C.Hamels/D.Willis/50 6.00 15.00
JD R.Jackson/A.Dunn/50 6.00 15.00
JH A.Jones/T.Hunter/50 6.00 15.00
JJ J.Reyes/J.Mauer/50 12.50 30.00
LC N.Lowry/M.Cain/50 6.00 15.00
LK D.Lee/P.Konerko/50 12.50 30.00
LT L.Berkman/T.Helton/50 6.00 15.00
MB N.Markakis/J.Bay/50 10.00 25.00
MM R.Martin/G.Meche/50 6.00 15.00
OR D.Ortiz/M.Ramirez/50 20.00 50.00
PO J.Peavy/R.Oswalt/50 10.00 25.00
PR T.Perez/M.Ramirez/50 10.00 25.00
RI B.Roberts/A.Iwamura/50 6.00 15.00
RJ R.Martin/J.Loney/50 10.00 25.00
RM A.Ramirez/B.McCann/50 10.00 25.00
RO M.Ramirez/M.Ordonez/50 10.00 25.00
RT H.Ramirez/T.Tulowitzki/50 12.50 30.00
SB C.Schilling/J.Bonderman/50 10.00 25.00
SH J.Santana/C.Hamels/50 12.50 30.00
SJ C.Sabathia/R.Johnson/50 12.50 30.00
TH F.Thomas/T.Hafner/50 8.00 20.00
TK T.Hunter/K.Griffey Jr./50 15.00 40.00
TT T.Hunter/T.Hafner/50 10.00 25.00
UU C.Utley/D.Uggla/50 20.00 50.00
UY C.Utley/D.Young/50 6.00 15.00
VH J.Verlander/C.Hamels/50 12.50 30.00
VR J.Verlander/N.Ryan/50 20.00 50.00
WJ V.Wells/C.Jones/50 10.00 25.00
YH R.Yount/J.Hardy/50 12.50 30.00
ZJ R.Zimmerman/C.Jones/50 10.00 25.00
ZR R.Zimmerman/J.Rollins/50 10.00 25.00

2008 Upper Deck Premier Emerging Stars Autographs

OVERALL AU ODDS THREE PER PACK
STATED PRINT RUN 35 SER.#'d SETS
GOLD PRINT RUN 15 SER.#'d SETS
NO GOLD PRICING DUE TO SCARCITY
MASTERPIECE PRINT RUN 1 SER.#'d SET
NO MASTERPIECE PRICING AVAILABLE
EXCHANGE DEADLINE 3/13/2010
BB D.Barton/T.Buck 10.00 25.00
BG B.Butler/A.Gordon 30.00 60.00
BH R.Braun/C.Hart 10.00 25.00
BM Chad Billingsley/Jonathan Meloan 6.00 15.00
BP C.Buchholz/J.Papelbon 8.00 20.00
BV H.Bailey/J.Votto 8.00 20.00
BW B.Butler/B.Wood 10.00 25.00
CL M.Cain/N.Lowry 12.50 30.00
CT C.Hart/T.Buck 6.00 20.00
FB Josh Fields/Lance Broadway 6.00 15.00
FO Josh Fields/Jerry Owens 6.00 15.00
GH A.Gordon/L.Hochevar 15.00 40.00
GL C.Granderson/F.Lewis 10.00 25.00
GM C.Gomez/D.Murphy 10.00 25.00
HB P.Hughes/H.Bailey 8.00 20.00
HK C.Hamels/S.Kazmir 15.00 40.00
HL C.Hu/J.Loney 8.00 20.00
HS D.Haren/H.Street 6.00 15.00
HV J.Hamilton/J.Votto 60.00 120.00
HW C.Hart/R.Weeks 10.00 25.00
KB Kevin Kouzmanoff/Brandon Wood 6.00 15.00
KH I.Kennedy/P.Hughes 15.00 40.00
KU Howie Kendrick/Dan Uggla 6.00 15.00
KW H.Kendrick/J.Weaver 15.00 40.00
LE J.Loney/A.Ethier 12.50 30.00
LL A.LaRoche/J.Loney 4.00 10.00
MB John Maine/Chad Billingsley 6.00 15.00
MC John Maine/Matt Cain 6.00 15.00
ME B.McCann/Y.Escobar 8.00 20.00
MG J.Maine/C.Gomez 10.00 25.00
MH N.Markakis/J.Hermida 8.00 20.00
ML R.Martin/J.Loney 30.00 60.00
MM B.McCann/R.Martin 12.50 30.00
MP N.Markakis/S.Pearce 10.00 25.00
MS B.McCann/J.Saltala 12.50 30.00
MT R.Martin/J.Towles 12.50 30.00
NJ N.Markakis/J.Hamilton 8.00 20.00
PL J.Papelbon/J.Lester 30.00 60.00
PZ J.Papelbon/J.Zumaya 6.00 15.00
SB James Shields/Scott Baker 6.00 15.00
TA T.Tulowitzki/G.Atkins 20.00 50.00
TG T.Tulowitzki/A.Gordon 15.00 40.00
UR D.Uggla/H.Ramirez 8.00 20.00
UY B.Upton/D.Young 12.50 30.00
VH J.Verlander/D.Haren 15.00 40.00

2008 Upper Deck Premier Legendary Remnants Triple

OVERALL GU ODDS TWO PER PACK
PRINT RUNS B/WN 15-50 COPIES PER
NO PRICING ON QTY 15 OR LESS
BRONZE B/WN 10-25 COPIES PER
NO BRONZE PRICING DUE TO SCARCITY
GOLD B/WN 5-10 COPIES PER
NO GOLD PRICING DUE TO SCARCITY
MASTERPIECE PRINT RUN 1 SER.#'d SET
NO MASTERPIECE PRICING AVAILABLE
HG Hank Greenberg/50 10.00 25.00
JD Joe DiMaggio/50 60.00 120.00
JR Jackie Robinson/50 40.00 80.00
LG Lou Gehrig/50 150.00 250.00
MO Mel Ott/50 40.00 80.00
RC Roberto Clemente/50 40.00 80.00
RM Roger Maris/50 12.50 30.00
WS Willie Stargell/50 8.00 20.00

2008 Upper Deck Premier Legendary Remnants Triple Gold Milestones

OVERALL GU ODDS TWO PER PACK
PRINT RUNS B/WN 7-61 COPIES PER
NO PRICING ON QTY 23 OR LESS
HG Hank Greenberg/36 50.00 100.00
RM Roger Maris/61 12.50 30.00

2008 Upper Deck Premier Legendary Remnants Triple Silver

OVERALL GU ODDS TWO PER PACK
PRINT RUNS B/WN 10-30 COPIES PER
NO PRICING ON QTY 10 OR LESS
JD Joe DiMaggio/30 75.00 150.00
JR Jackie Robinson/30 12.00 30.00
LG Lou Gehrig/30 200.00 300.00
MO Mel Ott/30 50.00 100.00
RC Roberto Clemente/30 50.00 100.00
RM Roger Maris/30 15.00 40.00
WS Willie Stargell/30 10.00 25.00

2008 Upper Deck Premier Memorabilia Triple

OVERALL GU ODDS TWO PER PACK
PRINT RUNS B/WN 25-50 COPIES PER
GOLD PRINT RUN 3 SER.#'d SETS
NO GOLD PRICING DUE TO SCARCITY
AP Albert Pujols/75 10.00 25.00
AP2 Albert Pujols/75 10.00 25.00
BE Johnny Bench/50 10.00 25.00
DJ Derek Jeter/75 12.50 30.00
DM Daisuke Matsuzaka/75 12.50 30.00
DO David Ortiz/50 5.00 12.00
GM Greg Maddux/50 6.00 15.00
JD Joe DiMaggio/75 50.00 100.00
KG Ken Griffey Jr./50 10.00 25.00
MA Don Mattingly/50 10.00 25.00
MS Mike Schmidt/50 12.50 30.00
NR Nolan Ryan/75 12.50 30.00
OS Ozzie Smith/75 10.00 25.00
RJ Reggie Jackson/75 6.00 15.00
SM Stan Musial/75 12.50 30.00
TS Tom Seaver/75 10.00 25.00
WB Wade Boggs/50 5.00 12.00
WS Warren Spahn/75 10.00 25.00

2008 Upper Deck Premier Memorabilia Quad

OVERALL GU ODDS TWO PER PACK
PRINT RUNS B/WN 15-40 COPIES PER
NO RUTH PRICING DUE TO SCARCITY
GOLD STATED PRINT RUN 4 SER.#'d SETS
NO GOLD PRICING DUE TO SCARCITY
AS Alfonso Soriano/40 6.00 15.00
CC Chris Carpenter/40 5.00 12.00
CH Cole Hamels/40 5.00 12.00
CL Roger Clemens/40 6.00 15.00
CS Curt Schilling/40 5.00 12.00
CU Chase Utley/40 5.00 12.00
CW Chien-Ming Wang/40 20.00 50.00
CY Carl Yastrzemski/40 6.00 15.00
DJ Derek Jeter/40 20.00 50.00
DL Derrek Lee/40 4.00 10.00
DM Don Mattingly/40 12.50 30.00
DO David Ortiz/40 6.00 15.00
DO2 David Ortiz/40 6.00 15.00
DP Dave Parker/40 6.00 15.00
DW Dontrelle Willis/40 4.00 10.00
EM Eddie Mathews/40 20.00 50.00
HP Hunter Pence/40 6.00 15.00
JM Joe Mauer/40 5.00 12.00
JR Jackie Robinson/40 40.00 80.00
JS Johan Santana/40 6.00 15.00
JV Justin Verlander/40 10.00 25.00
MA Russell Martin/40 10.00 25.00
MO Justin Morneau/40 4.00 10.00
MS Mike Schmidt/40 10.00 25.00
MT Mark Teixeira/40 10.00 25.00
NM Nick Markakis/40 6.00 15.00
NR Nolan Ryan/40 15.00 40.00
OR Magglio Ordonez/40 5.00 12.00
PF Prince Fielder/40 6.00 15.00
PH Phil Hughes/40 12.50 30.00
PW Pee Wee Reese/40 10.00 25.00
RB Ryan Braun/40 10.00 25.00
RC Roberto Clemente/40 40.00 80.00
RE Jose Reyes/40 6.00 15.00
RH Rogers Hornsby/40 30.00 60.00
RJ Reggie Jackson/40 10.00 25.00
RM Roger Maris/40 30.00 60.00
RY Robin Yount/40 15.00 40.00
SM Stan Musial/40 12.50 30.00
TM Thurman Munson/40 20.00 50.00
TP Tony Perez/40 10.00 25.00
VG Vladimir Guerrero/40 6.00 15.00
VM Victor Martinez/40 4.00 10.00

2008 Upper Deck Premier Patches

OVERALL GU ODDS TWO PER PACK
PRINT RUNS B/WN 55-75 COPIES PER
*GOLD: .4X TO 1X BASIC PATCH
GOLD B/WN 25-50 COPIES PER
NO GOLD PRICING ON QTY 25 OR LESS
SILVER PRINT RUN 10 SER.#'d SETS
NO SILVER PRICING DUE TO SCARCITY
AI Akinori Iwamura 10.00 25.00
AJ Andruw Jones 6.00 15.00
AL Adam LaRoche 6.00 15.00
BR Brian Roberts 6.00 15.00
CB Carlos Beltran 6.00 15.00
CJ Chipper Jones 15.00 40.00
CR Cal Ripken Jr. 30.00 60.00
CU Chase Utley 15.00 40.00
CW Chien-Ming Wang 20.00 50.00
DM Daisuke Matsuzaka/55 30.00 60.00
DO David Ortiz 12.50 30.00
DW Dontrelle Willis 6.00 15.00
EB Erik Bedard 6.00 15.00
FT Frank Thomas 10.00 25.00
GS Grady Sizemore 12.50 30.00
HA Travis Hafner 6.00 15.00
HK Hong-Chih Kuo 12.50 30.00
HP Hunter Pence 12.50 30.00
HR Hanley Ramirez 12.50 30.00
HU Torii Hunter 6.00 15.00
IR Ivan Rodriguez 12.50 30.00
JB Jeremy Bonderman 10.00 25.00
JF Jeff Francoeur 15.00 40.00
JM Justin Morneau 10.00 25.00
JP Jake Peavy 12.50 30.00
JR Jose Reyes 12.50 30.00
JS Johan Santana 10.00 25.00
JV Jason Varitek/65 20.00 50.00
MA Don Mattingly/74 12.50 30.00
MC Miguel Cabrera 12.50 30.00
MO Magglio Ordonez 6.00 15.00
NM Nick Markakis 10.00 25.00
NR Nolan Ryan 15.00 40.00
RB Ryan Braun 20.00 50.00
RJ Randy Johnson/57 12.50 30.00
RO Roy Oswalt 6.00 15.00
RW Rickie Weeks 6.00 15.00
RZ Ryan Zimmerman 12.50 30.00
SM Stan Musial 15.00 40.00
TG Tony Gwynn 20.00 50.00
TH Todd Helton 10.00 25.00
TL Tim Lincecum 10.00 25.00
TS Takashi Saito/65 10.00 25.00
VE Justin Verlander 10.00 25.00
WB Wade Boggs 6.00 15.00

2008 Upper Deck Premier Patches Gold Milestones

OVERALL GU ODDS TWO PER PACK
PRINT RUNS B/WN 10-33 COPIES PER
NO PRICING ON QTY 25 OR LESS
CJ Chipper Jones/26 15.00 40.00
CU Chase Utley/32 15.00 40.00
GS Grady Sizemore/28 12.50 30.00
HA Travis Hafner/33 6.00 15.00
HK Hong-Chih Kuo/27 12.50 30.00
HU Torii Hunter/31 6.00 15.00
MC Miguel Cabrera/26 12.50 30.00

2008 Upper Deck Premier Patches Gold Milestones Jersey Number

OVERALL GU ODDS TWO PER PACK
PRINT RUNS B/WN 1-57 COPIES PER
NO PRICING ON QTY 25 OR LESS
CU Chase Utley/26 15.00 40.00
CW Chien-Ming Wang/40 20.00 50.00
DO David Ortiz/34 12.50 30.00
DW Dontrelle Willis/35 6.00 15.00
EB Erik Bedard/45 6.00 15.00
FT Frank Thomas/35 30.00 60.00
HA Travis Hafner/48 6.00 15.00
HK Hong-Chih Kuo/56 12.50 30.00
HU Torii Hunter/48 6.00 15.00
JA Reggie Jackson/44 10.00 25.00
JB Jeremy Bonderman/38 10.00 25.00
JM Justin Morneau/33 10.00 25.00
JP Jake Peavy/44 12.50 30.00
JS Johan Santana/57 10.00 25.00
JV Jason Varitek/33 20.00 50.00
MO Magglio Ordonez/30 6.00 15.00
NR Nolan Ryan/30 30.00 60.00
RJ Randy Johnson/51 12.50 30.00
RO Roy Oswalt/44 6.00 15.00
TL Tim Lincecum/55 10.00 25.00
TS Takashi Saito/44 10.00 25.00
VE Justin Verlander/35 10.00 25.00
WB Wade Boggs/26 6.00 15.00

2008 Upper Deck Premier Patches Autographs

OVERALL AU ODDS THREE PER PACK
STATED PRINT RUN 15 SER.#'d SETS
NO PRICING DUE TO SCARCITY
EXCHANGE DEADLINE 3/13/2010

2008 Upper Deck Premier Penmanship Autographs

OVERALL AU ODDS THREE PER PACK
PRINT RUNS B/WN 15-50 COPIES PER
NO PRICING ON QTY 20 OR LESS
GOLD B/WN 3-5 COPIES PER
NO GOLD PRICING DUE TO SCARCITY
MASTERPIECE PRINT RUN 1 SER.#'d SET
NO MASTERPIECE PRICING AVAILABLE
EXCHANGE DEADLINE 3/13/2010
AK Al Kaline/50 20.00 50.00
BB Billy Butler/50 4.00 10.00
BE Johnny Bench/50 20.00 50.00
BL Joe Blanton/50 4.00 10.00
BT Bobby Thomson/50 10.00 25.00
CB Chad Billingsley/50 4.00 10.00
CC Carl Crawford/50 6.00 15.00
CF Carlton Fisk/50 10.00 25.00
CH Cole Hamels/50 10.00 25.00
CJ Chipper Jones/50 40.00 80.00
CR Cal Ripken Jr./50 50.00 100.00
CW Chien-Ming Wang/50 100.00 150.00
FC Fausto Carmona/50 6.00 15.00
FH Felix Hernandez/50 15.00 40.00
FT Frank Thomas/50 40.00 80.00
GP Gaylord Perry/50 4.00 10.00
HK Howie Kendrick/50 4.00 10.00
HP Hunter Pence/50 12.50 30.00
IK Ian Kennedy/50 30.00 60.00
IR Ivan Rodriguez/50 12.00 30.00
JB Jeremy Bonderman/50 6.00 15.00
JL John Lackey/50 4.00 10.00
JM John Maine/50 6.00 15.00
JP Jim Palmer/50 6.00 15.00
JV Justin Verlander/50 15.00 40.00
JW Josh Willingham/50 4.00 10.00
KW Kerry Wood/50 4.00 10.00
LA Luis Aparicio/40 8.00 20.00
MS Mike Schmidt/50 20.00 50.00
NM Nick Markakis/50 12.50 30.00
NR Nolan Ryan/50 40.00 80.00
PA Jonathan Papelbon/50 12.50 30.00
RB Ryan Braun/50 20.00 50.00
RC Rod Carew/50 10.00 25.00
RH Ramon Hernandez/50 4.00 10.00
RM Russell Martin/50 3.00 8.00
RZ Ryan Zimmerman/50 10.00 25.00
TH Travis Hafner/50 6.00 15.00
TT Troy Tulowitzki/50 6.00 15.00
VM Victor Martinez/50 4.00 10.00

2008 Upper Deck Premier Remnants Triple Blue-Gold

OVERALL GU ODDS TWO PER PACK
PRINT RUNS B/WN 25-75 COPIES PER
NO PRICING ON QTY 25
*BLUE-SILVER: .4X TO 1X BASIC
B-S PRINT RUNS B/WN 25-75 PER
NO B-S PRICING ON QTY 25
*BRONZE: .4X TO 1X BASIC
BRONZE PRINT RUNS B/WN 25-75 PER
NO BRONZE PRICING ON QTY 25
MASTERPIECE PRINT RUN 1 SER.#'d SET
NO MASTERPIECE PRICING AVAILABLE
AP A.Pujols STL/75 10.00 25.00
CY Carl Yastrzemski YAZ/50 5.00 12.00
DJ D.Jeter NYY/75 12.50 30.00
DM D.Matsu JPN/75 12.50 30.00
DO David Ortiz BOS/50 5.00 12.00
KG K.Griffey OF3/50 10.00 25.00
MS M.Schmidt PHI/50 12.50 30.00
NR N.Ryan TEX/75 12.50 30.00
RJ R.Jackson NYY/75 6.00 15.00
RY R.Yount MVP/50 12.50 30.00
WB Wade Boggs BOS/50 5.00 12.00

2008 Upper Deck Premier Remnants Triple Gold

OVERALL GU ODDS TWO PER PACK
PRINT RUNS B/WN 2-44 COPIES PER
NO PRICING ON QTY 23 OR LESS
DO David Ortiz/34 5.00 12.00
MS Mike Schmidt/33 12.50 30.00
NR Nolan Ryan/34 12.50 30.00
RJ Reggie Jackson/44 6.00 15.00
VG Vladimir Guerrero/27 5.00 12.00
WB Wade Boggs/26 5.00 12.00

2008 Upper Deck Premier Remnants Triple Gold Milestones

OVERALL GU ODDS TWO PER PACK
PRINT RUNS B/WN 5-50 COPIES PER
NO PRICING ON QTY 25 OR LESS
AP Albert Pujols/50 10.00 25.00

2000 Upper Deck Yankees Master Collection

COMPLETE SET (25) 150.00 300.00
COMMON CARD (1-25) 2.50 6.00
ONE SET PER MASTER COLLECTION BOX
STATED PRINT RUN 500 SERIAL #'d SETS
NYY1 Babe Ruth 23 15.00 40.00
NYY2 Lou Gehrig 27 12.00 30.00
NYY3 Tony Lazzeri 28 4.00 10.00
NYY4 Babe Ruth 32 15.00 40.00
NYY5 Lou Gehrig 36 12.00 30.00
NYY6 Lefty Gomez 37 2.50 6.00
NYY7 Bill Dickey 38 2.50 6.00
NYY8 Bill Dickey 39 2.50 6.00
NYY9 Tommy Henrich 41 2.50 6.00
NYY10 Spud Chandler 43 2.50 6.00
NYY11 Tommy Henrich '47 2.50 6.00
NYY12 Phil Rizzuto 49 4.00 10.00
NYY13 Whitey Ford 50 4.00 10.00
NYY14 Yogi Berra 51 6.00 15.00
NYY15 Casey Stengel 52 4.00 10.00
NYY16 Billy Martin 53 4.00 10.00
NYY17 Don Larsen 56 2.50 6.00
NYY18 Elston Howard 58 2.50 6.00
NYY19 Roger Maris 61 6.00 15.00
NYY20 Mickey Mantle 62 20.00 50.00
NYY21 Reggie Jackson '77 4.00 10.00
NYY22 Bucky Dent 78 2.50 6.00
NYY23 Derek Jeter 96 15.00 40.00
NYY24 Derek Jeter 98 15.00 40.00
NYY25 Derek Jeter 99 15.00 40.00

2000 Upper Deck Yankees Master Collection All-Time Yankees Game Bats

ONE SET PER MASTER COLLECTION BOX
STATED PRINT RUN 500 SERIAL #'d SETS
ATY1 Babe Ruth 75.00 150.00
ATY2 Mickey Mantle 75.00 150.00
ATY3 Reggie Jackson 10.00 25.00
ATY4 Don Mattingly 15.00 40.00
ATY5 Billy Martin 10.00 25.00
ATY6 Graig Nettles 10.00 25.00
ATY7 Derek Jeter 50.00 100.00
ATY8 Yogi Berra 15.00 40.00
ATY9 Thurman Munson 40.00 80.00
ATY10 Whitey Ford 10.00 25.00
ATY11 Lou Gehrig COMM 10.00 25.00

2000 Upper Deck Yankees Master Collection Mystery Pack Inserts

ONE MYSTERY PACK PER MAST.COLL.BOX
PRINT RUNS B/WN 2-100 COPIES PER
NO PRICING ON QTY OF 25 OR LESS
DJB Derek Jeter Bat AU/100 250.00 400.00
DJJ Derek Jeter Jsy AU/100 300.00 500.00
RJB Reggie Jackson Bat AU/100 120.00 200.00
WFJ Whitey Ford Bat AU/100 75.00 150.00
YBB Yogi Berra Bat AU/80 120.00 200.00

2008 Upper Deck Premier Remnants Quad

OVERALL GU ODDS TWO PER PACK
PRINT RUNS15-50 COPIES PER
NO PRICING ON QTY 15 OR LESS
BRONZE PRINT RUN 25 SER.#'d SETS
NO BRONZE PRICING DUE TO SCARCITY
GOLD B/WN 5-10 COPIES PER
NO GOLD PRICING DUE TO SCARCITY
MASTERPIECE PRINT RUN 1 SER.#'d SET
NO MASTERPIECE PRICING AVAILABLE
AD Adam Dunn DUNN/50 3.00 8.00
AD Adam Dunn REDS/50 3.00 8.00
BE Carlos Beltran METS/50 3.00 8.00
BE Carlos Beltran HITS/50 3.00 8.00
BR Brooks Robinson 16GG/50 4.00 10.00
BS Ben Sheets WINS/50 3.00 8.00
BS Ben Sheets 2001/50 3.00 8.00
CF Carlton Fisk FISK/50 4.00 10.00
CF Carlton Fisk HITS/50 4.00 10.00
CH Cole Hamels COLE/50 4.00 10.00
CH Cole Hamels WINS/50 4.00 10.00
CL Roger Clemens ALCY/50 6.00 15.00
CL Roger Clemens WINS/50 6.00 15.00
CR C.Ripken CAL8/50 20.00 50.00
CR C.Ripken 2632/50 20.00 50.00
CS Curt Schilling SOCK/50 4.00 10.00
CS Curt Schilling CURT/50 4.00 10.00
CW C.Wang WANG/50 20.00 50.00
CW C.Wang WINS/50 20.00 50.00
DJ D.Jeter CAPT/50 20.00 50.00
DJ D.Jeter SS#2/50 20.00 50.00
DL Derrek Lee CUBS/50 3.00 8.00
DL Derrek Lee RUNS/50 3.00 8.00
DM D.Mattingly1985/50 10.00 25.00
DM D.Mattingly CAPT/50 10.00 25.00
DO David Ortiz PAPI/50 6.00 15.00
DO David Ortiz 2004/50 6.00 15.00
FH Felix Hernandez KING/50 6.00 15.00
FH Felix Hernandez WINS/50 6.00 15.00
HK Hong-Chih Kuo HONG/50 6.00 15.00
HK Hong-Chih Kuo WINS/50 6.00 15.00
HR Hanley Ramirez SS#2/50 4.00 10.00
HR Hanley Ramirez HITS/50 4.00 10.00
JB Johnny Bench 1972/50 6.00 15.00
JB Johnny Bench REDS/50 6.00 15.00
JH J.J. Hardy SS#7/50 4.00 10.00
JH J.J. Hardy 2007/50 4.00 10.00
JP Jake Peavy JAKE/50 4.00 10.00
JP Jake Peavy WINS/50 4.00 10.00
JR Jim Rice RICE/50 4.00 10.00
JR Jim Rice1978/50 4.00 10.00
JS John Smoltz WINS/50 4.00 10.00
JS John Smoltz 1996/50 4.00 10.00
KG K.Griffey REDS/50 10.00 25.00
KG K.Griffey OF#3/50 10.00 25.00
MH Matt Holliday MATT/50 4.00 10.00
MH Matt Holliday OF#5/50 4.00 10.00
NR N.Ryan RYAN/50 20.00 50.00
NR N.Ryan 383K/50 20.00 50.00
NR2 N.Ryan 5714/50 20.00 50.00
NR2 N.Ryan WINS/50 20.00 50.00
PF Prince Fielder RUNS/50 6.00 15.00
PF Prince Fielder HITS/50 6.00 15.00
PR P.Rizzuto NYSS/50 10.00 25.00
PR P.Rizzuto1950/50 10.00 25.00
RC Rod Carew 3000/50 4.00 10.00
RC Rod Carew 1977/50 4.00 10.00
RE J.Reyes METS/50 10.00 25.00
RE J.Reyes JOSE/50 10.00 25.00
RJ Reggie Jackson NYRF/50 6.00 15.00
RJ Reggie Jackson1977/50 6.00 15.00
RS R.Sandberg CUBS/50 10.00 25.00
RS R.Sandberg RYNO/50 10.00 25.00
RZ R.Zimm WASH/50 10.00 25.00
RZ R.Zimm RYAN/50 10.00 25.00
SM S.Musial STAN/50 15.00 40.00
SM S.Musial 3MVP/50 15.00 40.00
TG T.Gwynn 3000/50 12.50 30.00
TG T.Gwynn TONY/50 12.50 30.00
TM T.Munson CAPT/50 15.00 40.00
TM T.Munson 1976/50 15.00 40.00
TR Tim Raines ROCK/50 3.00 8.00
TR Tim Raines RUNS/50 3.00 8.00
TS T.Seaver METS/50 10.00 25.00
TS T.Seaver 1969/50 10.00 25.00
VG Vladimir Guerrero VLAD/50 4.00 10.00
VG Vladimir Guerrero STAR/50 4.00 10.00
WB W.Boggs 3000/50 10.00 25.00
WB W.Boggs WADE/50 10.00 25.00

2008 Upper Deck Premier Remnants Quad Gold Milestones

OVERALL GU ODDS TWO PER PACK
PRINT RUNS B/WN 2-77 COPIES PER
NO PRICING ON QTY 24 OR LESS
AD Adam Dunn/46 3.00 8.00
BE Carlos Beltran/41 3.00 8.00
CF Carlton Fisk/37 4.00 10.00
CR Cal Ripken Jr./34 20.00 50.00
CW Chien-Ming Wang/47 20.00 50.00
DL Derrek Lee/46 3.00 8.00
DM Don Mattingly/35 10.00 25.00
DO David Ortiz/54 6.00 15.00
FH Felix Hernandez/77 6.00 15.00
HK Hong-Chih Kuo/71 6.00 15.00
HR Hanley Ramirez/51 4.00 10.00
JB Johnny Bench/45 6.00 15.00
JR Jim Rice/46 4.00 10.00
MH Matt Holliday/36 4.00 10.00
PF Prince Fielder/50 6.00 15.00
PR Phil Rizzuto/38 10.00 25.00
RC Rod Carew/49 4.00 10.00
RE Jose Reyes/60 10.00 25.00
RS Ryne Sandberg/40 10.00 25.00
TG Tony Gwynn/33 12.50 30.00
TR Tim Raines/50 3.00 8.00
VG Vladimir Guerrero/39 4.00 10.00

2008 Upper Deck Premier Signature Premier

OVERALL AU ODDS THREE PER PACK
PRINT RUNS B/WN 5-45 COPIES PER
NO PRICING ON QTY 25 OR LESS
BRONZE B/WN 1-25 COPIES PER
NO BRONZE PRICING AVAILABLE
GOLD B/WN 1-15 COPIES PER
NO GOLD PRICING DUE TO SCARCITY
MASTERPIECE PRINT RUN 1 SER.#'d SET
NO MASTERPIECE PRICING AVAILABLE
INK CHANGE PRINT RUN 1 SER.#'d SET
NO INK CHANGE PRICING AVAILABLE
EXCHANGE DEADLINE 3/13/2010
AE Andre Ethier 10.00 25.00
AG Adrian Gonzalez 10.00 25.00
AI Akinori Iwamura 10.00 25.00
AM Andrew Miller 4.00 10.00
AR Aramis Ramirez 6.00 15.00
BB Billy Buckner 4.00 10.00
BE Johnny Bench 20.00 50.00
BI Chad Billingsley 4.00 10.00
BJ B.J. Upton 6.00 15.00
BM Brian McCann 6.00 15.00
BO Jeremy Bonderman 6.00 15.00
BS Bronson Sardinha 4.00 10.00
BU Billy Butler 6.00 15.00
CA Matt Cain 4.00 10.00
CB Clay Buchholz 6.00 15.00
CC Chris Carpenter 10.00 25.00
CF Carlton Fisk 10.00 25.00
CR Cal Ripken Jr. 30.00 80.00
DB Daric Barton 4.00 10.00
DH Dan Haren 4.00 10.00
DL Derrek Lee 6.00 15.00
DM Don Mattingly 15.00 40.00
EB Ernie Banks/37 15.00 40.00
EM Edgar Martinez 15.00 40.00
FC Fausto Carmona 6.00 15.00
GA Garret Anderson 6.00 15.00
GO Alex Gordon 10.00 25.00
GP Gaylord Perry 8.00 20.00
HK Howie Kendrick 4.00 10.00
HR Harold Reynolds 4.00 10.00
HU Chin-Lung Hu 6.00 15.00
JB Jim Bunning 6.00 15.00
JL John Lackey 4.00 10.00
JM John Maine 6.00 15.00
JP Jim Palmer 6.00 15.00
JT J.R. Towles 4.00 10.00
JV Joey Votto 30.00 60.00
JW Josh Willingham 4.00 10.00
JZ Joel Zumaya 4.00 10.00
KE Ian Kennedy 10.00 25.00
KI Ian Kinsler 6.00 15.00
KY Kevin Youkilis 6.00 15.00
LA Luis Aparicio 6.00 15.00
LE Jon Lester 12.50 30.00
LH Luke Hochevar 6.00 15.00
MS Mike Schmidt 20.00 50.00
MT Miguel Tejada 6.00 15.00
MU Stan Musial 50.00 100.00
NL Noah Lowry 4.00 10.00
NM Nick Markakis 12.50 30.00
NR Nolan Ryan 40.00 80.00
NS Nick Swisher 4.00 10.00
OH Ross Ohlendorf 6.00 15.00
OW Micah Owings 6.00 15.00
PF Prince Fielder 10.00 25.00
PH Phil Hughes 8.00 20.00
PM Pedro Martinez 15.00 40.00
RB Ryan Braun 20.00 50.00
RC Rod Carew 15.00 40.00
RD Ross Detwiler 4.00 10.00
RH Rich Hill 4.00 10.00
RJ Reggie Jackson 20.00 50.00

RO Roger Clemens 40.00 80.00
RT Ryan Theriot 10.00 25.00
RY Ryne Sandberg 20.00 50.00
SA Jarrod Saltalamacchia 4.00 10.00
SD Stephen Drew 4.00 10.00
SK Scott Kazmir 5.00 12.00
TB Travis Buck 4.00 10.00
TG Tony Gwynn 20.00 50.00
TH Travis Hafner 6.00 15.00
TM Tino Martinez 10.00 25.00
TP Tony Perez 10.00 25.00
WB Wladimir Balentien 6.00 15.00
WF Whitey Ford 20.00 50.00
YE Yunel Escobar 10.00 25.00

2008 Upper Deck Premier Signature Premier Gold Jersey Number

OVERALL AU ODDS THREE PER PACK
PRINT RUNS B/WN 1-65 COPIES PER
NO PRICING ON QTY 25 OR LESS
EXCHANGE DEADLINE 3/13/2010
AM Andrew Miller/48 4.00 10.00
BB Billy Buckner/38 4.00 10.00
BI Chad Billingsley/58 4.00 10.00
BO Jeremy Bonderman/38 6.00 15.00
BS Bronson Sardinha/64 4.00 10.00
CB Clay Buchholz/61 4.00 10.00
CC Chris Carpenter/29 10.00 25.00
CF Carlton Fisk/27 10.00 25.00
FC Fausto Carmona/55 6.00 15.00
GP Gaylord Perry/36 8.00 20.00
HK Howie Kendrick/47 4.00 10.00
HU Chin-Lung Hu/60 6.00 15.00
JL John Lackey/41 4.00 10.00
JM John Maine/33 6.00 15.00
JT J.R. Towles/46 4.00 10.00
JV Joey Votto/60 50.00 100.00
JZ Joel Zumaya/54 4.00 10.00
KE Ian Kennedy/36 10.00 25.00
LE Jon Lester/31 12.50 30.00
LH Luke Hochevar/44 6.00 15.00
NL Noah Lowry/51 4.00 10.00
NR Nolan Ryan/30 40.00 80.00
NS Nick Swisher/33 4.00 10.00
OH Ross Ohlendorf/60 6.00 15.00
OW Micah Owings/44 6.00 15.00
PF Prince Fielder/28 10.00 25.00
PH Phil Hughes/65 6.00 15.00
PM Pedro Martinez/45 15.00 40.00
RC Rod Carew/29 10.00 25.00
RD Ross Detwiler/29 4.00 10.00
RH Rich Hill/53 4.00 10.00
RJ Reggie Jackson/44 20.00 50.00
TH Travis Hafner/48 6.00 15.00
WB Wladimir Balentien/50 6.00 15.00

2008 Upper Deck Premier Stitchings

OVERALL STITCHINGS ONE PER PACK
PRINT RUNS B/WN 50-75 COPIES PER
GOLD B/WN 15-25 COPIES PER
NO GOLD PRICING DUE TO SCARCITY
MASTERPIECE PRINT RUN 1 SER.#'d SET
NO MASTERPIECE PRICING AVAILABLE
SILVER B/WN 5-10 COPIES PER
NO SILVER PRICING DUE TO SCARCITY
AG Alex Gordon/75 10.00 25.00
AG Alex Gordon/50 10.00 25.00
AK Al Kaline/75 10.00 25.00
AK Al Kaline/50 10.00 25.00
AP Albert Pujols/75 12.50 30.00
AP Albert Pujols/50 12.50 30.00
AR Alex Rodriguez/75 12.50 30.00
AR Alex Rodriguez/50 12.50 30.00
AS Alfonso Soriano/75 5.00 12.00
AS Alfonso Soriano/50 5.00 12.00
BD Bobby Doerr/75 2.00 5.00
BD Bobby Doerr/50 2.00 5.00
BE Johnny Bench/75 12.50 30.00
BE Johnny Bench/50 12.50 30.00
BF Bob Feller/75 10.00 25.00
BF Bob Feller/50 10.00 25.00
BG Bob Gibson/75 5.00 12.00
BG Bob Gibson/50 5.00 12.00
BM Bill Mazeroski/75 3.00 8.00
BM Bill Mazeroski/50 3.00 8.00
BR Babe Ruth/75 15.00 40.00
BR Babe Ruth/50 15.00 40.00
CA Miguel Cabrera/75 3.00 8.00
CA Miguel Cabrera/50 3.00 8.00
CB Craig Biggio/50 3.00 8.00
CB Craig Biggio/75 3.00 8.00
CF Carlton Fisk/75 10.00 25.00
CF Carlton Fisk/50 10.00 25.00
CJ Chipper Jones/75 6.00 15.00
CJ Chipper Jones/50 6.00 15.00
CR Cal Ripken Jr./75 20.00 50.00
CR Cal Ripken Jr./50 20.00 50.00
CS Rod Carew/Tom Seaver/75 5.00 12.00
CS Tom Seaver/Rod Carew/50 5.00 12.00
CU Chase Utley/75 5.00 12.00
CU Chase Utley/50 5.00 12.00
CW C.Wang/75 12.50 30.00
CW C.Wang/50 12.50 30.00
CY C.Yastrzemski/75 10.00 25.00
CY C.Yastrzemski/50 10.00 25.00
DJ Derek Jeter/75 20.00 50.00
DJ Derek Jeter/50 20.00 50.00
DL Derrek Lee/75 2.00 5.00
DL Derrek Lee/50 2.00 5.00
DM D.Matsuzaka/75 10.00 25.00
DM D.Matsuzaka/50 10.00 25.00
DY Delmon Young/75 3.00 8.00
DY Delmon Young/50 3.00 8.00
EM Eddie Murray/75 6.00 15.00
EM Eddie Murray/50 6.00 15.00
FA N.Fox/L.Aparicio/75 6.00 15.00
FA N.Fox/L.Aparicio/50 6.00 15.00
FH Felix Hernandez/75 6.00 15.00
FH Felix Hernandez/50 6.00 15.00
FJ Fergie Jenkins/75 2.00 5.00
FJ Fergie Jenkins/50 2.00 5.00
FT Frank Thomas/75 10.00 25.00
FT Frank Thomas/50 10.00 25.00
FT2 Frank Thomas/75 10.00 25.00
FT2 Frank Thomas/50 10.00 25.00
GR L.Gehrig/B.Ruth/75 12.50 30.00
GR L.Gehrig/B.Ruth/50 12.50 30.00
GS Grady Sizemore/75 3.00 8.00
GS Grady Sizemore/50 3.00 8.00
GW Tony Gwynn/75 10.00 25.00
GW Tony Gwynn/50 10.00 25.00
HA Travis Hafner/75 5.00 12.00
HA Travis Hafner/50 5.00 12.00
HP Hunter Pence/75 5.00 12.00
HP Hunter Pence/50 5.00 12.00
HR Hanley Ramirez/75 3.00 8.00
HR Hanley Ramirez/50 3.00 8.00
HU Torii Hunter/75 2.00 5.00
HU Torii Hunter/50 2.00 5.00
JB Jason Bay/75 2.00 5.00
JB Jason Bay/50 2.00 5.00
JD Joe DiMaggio/75 15.00 40.00
JD Joe DiMaggio/50 15.00 40.00
JE Jim Edmonds/75 2.00 5.00
JE Jim Edmonds/50 2.00 5.00
JH Josh Hamilton/75 6.00 15.00
JH Josh Hamilton/50 6.00 15.00
JM Joe Mauer/75 3.00 8.00
JM Joe Mauer/50 3.00 8.00
JO Jonathan Papelbon/75 3.00 8.00
JO Jonathan Papelbon/50 3.00 8.00
JP Jake Peavy/75 3.00 8.00
JP Jake Peavy/50 3.00 8.00
JR J.Robinson/R.Camp/75 6.00 15.00
JR J.Robinson/R.Camp/50 6.00 15.00
JS Johan Santana/75 5.00 12.00
JS Johan Santana/50 5.00 12.00
JU Justin Morneau/75 2.00 5.00
JU Justin Morneau/50 2.00 5.00
JV Justin Verlander/75 6.00 15.00
JV Justin Verlander/50 6.00 15.00
JZ Joel Zumaya/75 2.00 5.00
JZ Joel Zumaya/50 2.00 5.00
KG Ken Griffey Jr./75 15.00 40.00
KG Ken Griffey Jr./50 15.00 40.00
KG2 Ken Griffey Jr./75 15.00 40.00
KG2 Ken Griffey Jr./50 15.00 40.00
KG3 Ken Griffey Jr./75 15.00 40.00
KG3 Ken Griffey Jr./50 15.00 40.00
KW Kerry Wood/75 2.00 5.00
KW Kerry Wood/50 2.00 5.00
LA Luis Aparicio/75 5.00 12.00
LA Luis Aparicio/50 5.00 12.00
LB Lou Brock/75 6.00 15.00
LB Lou Brock/50 6.00 15.00
LI Tim Lincecum/75 5.00 12.00
LI Tim Lincecum/50 5.00 12.00
MA Juan Marichal/75 5.00 12.00
MA Juan Marichal/50 5.00 12.00
MC Brian McCann/75 2.00 5.00
MC Brian McCann/50 2.00 5.00
MH Matt Holliday/75 3.00 8.00
MH Matt Holliday/50 3.00 8.00
MH2 Matt Holliday/75 3.00 8.00
MH2 Matt Holliday/50 3.00 8.00
MI Monte Irvin/75 5.00 12.00
MI Monte Irvin/50 5.00 12.00
MJ H.Matsui/D.Jeter/75 12.50 30.00
MJ H.Matsui/D.Jeter/50 12.50 30.00
MO Joe Morgan/75 5.00 12.00
MO Joe Morgan/50 5.00 12.00
MP Mike Piazza/75 5.00 12.00
MP Mike Piazza/50 5.00 12.00
MR Manny Ramirez/75 5.00 12.00
MR Manny Ramirez/50 5.00 12.00
MS Mike Schmidt/75 8.00 20.00
MS Mike Schmidt/50 8.00 20.00
NR Nolan Ryan/75 15.00 40.00
NR Nolan Ryan/50 15.00 40.00
OC Orlando Cepeda/75 5.00 12.00
OC Orlando Cepeda/50 5.00 12.00
OM H.Okajima/D.Mats/75 10.00 25.00
OM H.Okajima/D.Mats/50 10.00 25.00
OR D.Ortiz/M.Ramirez/75 10.00 25.00
OR D.Ortiz/M.Ramirez/50 10.00 25.00
PA Jim Palmer/75 3.00 8.00
PA Jim Palmer/50 3.00 8.00
PF Prince Fielder/75 5.00 12.00
PF Prince Fielder/50 5.00 12.00
PH Phil Hughes/75 6.00 15.00
PH Phil Hughes/50 6.00 15.00
PN Phil Niekro/75 3.00 8.00
PN Phil Niekro/50 3.00 8.00
RA Richie Ashburn/75 10.00 25.00
RA Richie Ashburn/50 10.00 25.00
RB Ryan Braun/75 6.00 15.00
RB Ryan Braun/50 6.00 15.00
RC Rod Carew/75 5.00 12.00
RC Rod Carew/50 5.00 12.00
RF Rollie Fingers/75 3.00 8.00
RF Rollie Fingers/50 3.00 8.00
RH Roy Halladay/75 3.00 8.00
RH Roy Halladay/50 3.00 8.00
RI Mariano Rivera/75 5.00 12.00
RI Mariano Rivera/50 5.00 12.00
RJ Reggie Jackson/75 3.00 8.00
RJ Reggie Jackson/50 3.00 8.00
RK Ralph Kiner/75 3.00 8.00
RK Ralph Kiner/50 3.00 8.00
RM Russell Martin/75 3.00 8.00
RM Russell Martin/50 3.00 8.00
RO Brooks Robinson/75 5.00 12.00
RO Brooks Robinson/50 5.00 12.00
RS Ryne Sandberg/75 10.00 25.00
RS Ryne Sandberg/50 10.00 25.00
RY Ryan Howard/75 6.00 15.00
RY Ryan Howard/50 6.00 15.00
RZ Ryan Zimmerman/75 5.00 12.00
RZ Ryan Zimmerman/50 5.00 12.00
SJ Ichiro/K. Johjima/75 8.00 20.00
SJ K.Johjima/Ichiro/50 8.00 20.00
SS Sammy Sosa/75 10.00 25.00
SS Sammy Sosa/50 10.00 25.00
SV Shane Victorino/75 2.00 5.00
SV Shane Victorino/50 2.00 5.00
TG Tom Glavine/75 3.00 8.00
TG Tom Glavine/50 3.00 8.00
TH Trevor Hoffman/75 3.00 8.00
TH Trevor Hoffman/50 3.00 8.00
TL Tommy Lasorda/75 5.00 12.00
TL Tommy Lasorda/50 5.00 12.00
TS Tom Seaver/75 5.00 12.00
TS Tom Seaver/50 5.00 12.00
TT Troy Tulowitzki/75 5.00 12.00
TT Troy Tulowitzki/50 5.00 12.00
VG Vladimir Guerrero/75 3.00 8.00
VG Vladimir Guerrero/50 3.00 8.00
VM Victor Martinez/75 2.00 5.00
VM Victor Martinez/50 2.00 5.00
WM Willie McCovey/75 5.00 12.00
WM Willie McCovey/50 5.00 12.00

2008 Upper Deck Premier Swatches

OVERALL GU ODDS TWO PER PACK
STATED PRINT RUN 50 SER.#'d SETS
GOLD 25 PRINT RUN 25 SER.#'d SETS
NO GOLD 25 PRICING AVAILABLE
GOLD 20 PRINT RUN 20 SER.#'d SETS
NO GOLD 20 PRICING AVAILABLE
SILVER PRINT RUN 10 SER.#'d SETS
NO SILVER PRICING DUE TO SCARCITY
AP Albert Pujols 12.50 30.00
AR Aramis Ramirez 5.00 12.00
AS Alfonso Soriano 8.00 20.00
BR Brian Roberts 5.00 12.00
BS Ben Sheets 5.00 12.00
CD Carlos Delgado 5.00 12.00
CH Cole Hamels 10.00 25.00
CS C.C. Sabathia 8.00 20.00
CY Carl Yastrzemski 20.00 50.00
CZ Carlos Zambrano 8.00 20.00
DH Dan Haren 5.00 12.00
DL Derrek Lee 5.00 12.00
EM Eddie Murray 8.00 20.00
FH Felix Hernandez 15.00 40.00
FS Freddy Sanchez 5.00 12.00
GM Greg Maddux 15.00 40.00
GP Gaylord Perry 8.00 20.00
GS Grady Sizemore 8.00 20.00
HK Howie Kendrick 5.00 12.00
JB Jason Bay 8.00 20.00
JL James Loney 5.00 12.00
JM Joe Mauer 10.00 25.00
JS John Smoltz 12.00 30.00
JT Jim Thome 8.00 20.00
KG Ken Griffey Jr. 25.00 60.00
KI Harmon Killebrew 12.00 30.00
KW Kerry Wood 5.00 12.00
LB Lance Berkman 8.00 20.00
MO Joe Morgan 8.00 20.00
MR Manny Ramirez 12.00 30.00
MS Mike Schmidt 20.00 50.00
MT Miguel Tejada 8.00 20.00
NM Nick Markakis 10.00 25.00
NS Nick Swisher 8.00 20.00
OR Magglio Ordonez 8.00 20.00
PM Pedro Martinez 8.00 20.00
RH Rich Hill 5.00 12.00
RM Russell Martin 8.00 20.00
RS Ryne Sandberg 25.00 60.00
RY Robin Yount 12.00 30.00
SC Curt Schilling 8.00 20.00
TG Tom Glavine 8.00 20.00
TH Trevor Hoffman 8.00 20.00
VG Vladimir Guerrero 8.00 20.00
VM Victor Martinez 8.00 20.00
VW Vernon Wells 5.00 12.00

2008 Upper Deck Premier Swatches Jersey Number

OVERALL GU ODDS TWO PER PACK
PRINT RUNS B/WN 1-76 COPIES PER
NO PRICING ON QTY 25 OR LESS
CH Cole Hamels/35 12.00 30.00
CS C.C. Sabathia/53 10.00 25.00
CZ Carlos Zambrano/76 10.00 25.00
EM Eddie Murray/33 10.00 25.00
FH Felix Hernandez/34 40.00 80.00
GM Greg Maddux/31 20.00 50.00
GP Gaylord Perry/34 10.00 25.00
HK Howie Kendrick/48 6.00 15.00
JB Jason Bay/38 10.00 25.00
JM Joe Mauer/29 25.00 60.00
JT Jim Thome/50 10.00 25.00
KW Kerry Wood/36 6.00 15.00
NS Nick Swisher/33 10.00 25.00
OR Magglio Ordonez/30 10.00 25.00
PM Pedro Martinez/45 10.00 25.00
RH Rich Hill/53 6.00 15.00
RM Russell Martin/55 6.00 15.00
SC Curt Schilling/38 10.00 25.00
TG Tom Glavine/47 10.00 25.00
TH Trevor Hoffman/51 10.00 25.00
VG Vladimir Guerrero/27 10.00 25.00
VM Victor Martinez/41 10.00 25.00

2008 Upper Deck Premier Swatches Autographs

OVERALL AU ODDS THREE PER PACK
PRINT RUNS B/WN 3-10 COPIES PER
NO PRICING DUE TO SCARCITY
EXCHANGE DEADLINE 3/13/2010

2008 Upper Deck Premier Teams Memorabilia

OVERALL GU ODDS TWO PER PACK
PRINT RUNS B/WN 20-50 COPIES PER
NO PRICING ON QTY 20 OR LESS
SILVER PRINT RUN 3 SER.#'d SETS
NO SILVER PRICING DUE TO SCARCITY
BFS Braun/Prince/Sheets/50 20.00 50.00
BMP Bench/Morgan/Perez/50 15.00 40.00
CMW Clemens/Mussina/Wang/50 15.00 40.00
CPB Clemente/Parker/Bay/50 30.00 60.00
CRJ Clemens/Rivera/Jeter/50 15.00 40.00
CRR Campy/Reese/Robinson/50 30.00 60.00
GDH Ken Griffey Jr./Adam Dunn
Josh Hamilton/50 12.50 30.00
JJF Chipper Jones/Andruw Jones
Jeff Francoeur/50 12.50 30.00
JWD Randy Johnson/Brandon Webb
Stephen Drew/50 12.50 30.00
MJJ Don Mattingly/Reggie Jackson
Derek Jeter/50 12.50 30.00
MPB Musial/Pujols/Brock/50 20.00 50.00
MSB Mats/Schilling/Beckett/50 15.00 40.00
OBY David Ortiz/Wade Boggs
Kevin Youkilis/50 10.00 25.00
ORY David Ortiz/Manny Ramirez
Kevin Youkilis/50 10.00 25.00
PCR Albert Pujols/Chris Carpenter
Scott Rolen/50 12.50 30.00
PMH Peavy/Maddux/Hoffman/50 15.00 40.00
SBW Sandberg/Banks/Williams/50 20.00 50.00
USH Utley/Schmidt/Hamels/50 10.00 25.00

2008 Upper Deck Premier Teams Memorabilia Gold

OVERALL GU ODDS TWO PER PACK
PRINT RUNS B/WN 9-33 COPIES PER
NO PRICING ON QTY 15 OR LESS
BFS Braun/Prince/Sheets/33 20.00 50.00
BMP Bench/Morgan/Perez/33 15.00 40.00
CMW Clemens/Mussina/Wang/33 15.00 40.00
CPB Clemente/Parker/Bay/33 30.00 60.00
CRJ Clemens/Rivera/Jeter/33 15.00 40.00
CRR Campy/Reese/Robinson/33 30.00 60.00
GDH Ken Griffey Jr./Adam Dunn
Josh Hamilton/33 40.00 80.00
JJF Chipper Jones/Andruw Jones
Jeff Francoeur/33 12.50 30.00
JWD Randy Johnson/Brandon Webb
Stephen Drew/33 12.50 30.00
MJJ Don Mattingly/Reggie Jackson
Derek Jeter/33 12.50 30.00
MPB Musial/Pujols/Brock/33 20.00 50.00
MSB Mats/Schilling/Beckett/33 15.00 40.00
OBY David Ortiz/Wade Boggs
Kevin Youkilis/33 10.00 25.00
ORY David Ortiz/Manny Ramirez
Kevin Youkilis/33 10.00 25.00
PCR Albert Pujols/Chris Carpenter
Scott Rolen/33 12.50 30.00
PMH Peavy/Maddux/Hoffman/33 15.00 40.00
SBW Sandberg/Banks/Williams/33 10.00 25.00
USH Utley/Schmidt/Hamels/33 20.00 50.00

2008 Upper Deck Premier Trios Memorabilia

OVERALL GU ODDS TWO PER PACK
PRINT RUNS B/WN 25-50 COPIES PER
NO PRICING ON QTY 25 OR LESS
SILVER PRINT RUN 3 SER.#'d SETS
NO SILVER PRICING AVAILABLE
BFB Bench/Fisk/Berra/50 12.50 30.00
BPG Bay/Pujols/Griffey/50 12.50 30.00
BRD Carlos Beltran/Jose Reyes
Carlos Delgado/50 6.00 15.00
BZJ Ryan Braun/Ryan Zimmerman
Chipper Jones/50 6.00 15.00
CMM Michael Cuddyer/Justin Morneau
Joe Mauer/50 6.00 15.00
DOF Adam Dunn/David Ortiz
Prince Fielder/50 10.00 25.00
GTP Griffey/Thomas/Pujols/50 12.00 30.00
GWK Vladimir Guerrero
Jered Weaver/Howie Kendrick/50 6.00 15.00
HAT Matt Holliday/Garrett Atkins
Troy Tulowitzki/50 10.00 25.00
HMS Travis Hafner/Victor Martinez
Grady Sizemore/50 6.00 15.00
HSS Dan Haren/Nick Swisher
Huston Street/50 6.00 15.00
JFS Chipper/Francoeur/Smoltz/50 8.00 20.00
JTR Derek Jeter/Troy Tulowitzki
Hanley Ramirez/50 10.00 25.00
JWP Jeter/Wang/Pettitte/50 20.00 50.00
LRS Derrek Lee/Aramis Ramirez
Alfonso Soriano/50 6.00 15.00
MCG Maddux/Clemens/Glavine/50 12.50 30.00
MMS Joe Mauer/Justin Morneau
Johan Santana/50 6.00 15.00
ORY David Ortiz/Manny Ramirez
Kevin Youkilis/50 10.00 25.00
OVB Magglio Ordonez
Justin Verlander/Jeremy Bonderman/50 10.00 25.00
PBO Hunter Pence/Lance Berkman
Roy Oswalt/50 10.00 25.00
PLM Albert Pujols/Derrek Lee
Justin Morneau/50 10.00 25.00
RCS Jose Reyes/Carl Crawford
Grady Sizemore/50 6.00 15.00
RPV Manny/Papelbon/Varitek/50 12.50 30.00
RSB Brooks/Schmidt/Boggs/50 15.00 40.00
SRB Schmidt/Ripken/Boggs/50 15.00 40.00
SWB Sandberg/Williams/Banks/50 20.00 50.00
TOT Jim Thome/David Ortiz
Frank Thomas/50 10.00 25.00
TWH Frank Thomas/Vernon Wells
Roy Halladay/50 10.00 25.00
UHR Chase Utley/Cole Hamels
Jimmy Rollins/50 10.00 25.00
URU Chase Utley/Brian Roberts
Dan Uggla/50 6.00 15.00
YMC Yaz/Musial/Carew/50 15.00 40.00

2008 Upper Deck Premier Trios Memorabilia Gold

OVERALL GU ODDS TWO PER PACK
PRINT RUNS B/WN 10-33 COPIES PER
NO PRICING ON QTY 10 OR LESS
BFB Bench/Fisk/Berra/33 12.50 30.00
BPG Bay/Pujols/Griffey/33 12.50 30.00
BRD Carlos Beltran/Jose Reyes
Carlos Delgado/33 6.00 15.00
BZJ Ryan Braun/Ryan Zimmerman
Chipper Jones/33 6.00 15.00
CMM Michael Cuddyer/Justin Morneau
Joe Mauer/33 6.00 15.00
DOF Adam Dunn/David Ortiz
Prince Fielder/33 10.00 25.00
GTP Griffey/Thomas/Pujols/33 12.00 30.00
GWK Vladimir Guerrero/Jered Weave
/Howie Kendrick/33 6.00 15.00
HAT Matt Holliday/Garrett Atkins
Troy Tulowitzki/33 10.00 25.00
HMS Travis Hafner/Victor Martinez
Grady Sizemore/33 6.00 15.00
HSS Dan Haren/Nick Swisher
Huston Street/33 6.00 15.00
JFS Chipper/Francoeur/Smoltz/33 30.00 60.00
JTR Derek Jeter/Troy Tulowitzki
Hanley Ramirez/33 10.00 25.00
JWP Jeter/Wang/Pettitte/33 20.00 50.00
LRS Derrek Lee/Aramis Ramirez
Alfonso Soriano/33 6.00 15.00
MCG Maddux/Clemens/Glavine/33 12.50 30.00
MMS Joe Mauer/Justin Morneau
Johan Santana/33 6.00 15.00
ORY David Ortiz/Manny Ramirez
Kevin Youkilis/33 10.00 25.00
OVB Magglio Ordonez/Justin Verlander
Jeremy Bonderman/33 10.00 25.00
PBO Hunter Pence/Lance Berkman
Roy Oswalt/33 10.00 25.00
PLM Albert Pujols/Derrek Lee
Justin Morneau/33 10.00 25.00
RCS Jose Reyes/Carl Crawford
Grady Sizemore/33 6.00 15.00
RPV Manny/Papelbon/Varitek/33 12.50 30.00
RSB Brooks/Schmidt/Boggs/33 15.00 40.00
SRB Schmidt/Ripken/Boggs/33 15.00 40.00
SWB Sandberg/Williams/Banks/33 15.00 40.00
TOT Jim Thome/David Ortiz
Frank Thomas/33 10.00 25.00
TWH Frank Thomas/Vernon Wells
Roy Halladay/33 10.00 25.00
UHR Chase Utley/Cole Hamels
Jimmy Rollins/33 10.00 25.00
URU Chase Utley/Brian Roberts
Dan Uggla/33 6.00 15.00
YMC Yaz/Musial/Carew/33 15.00 40.00

2008 Upper Deck Premier Trios Patches

OVERALL GU ODDS TWO PER PACK
STATED PRINT RUN 30 SER.#'d SETS
GOLD PRINT RUN 15 SER.#'d SETS
NO GOLD PRICING DUE TO SCARCITY
PLATINUM PRINT RUN 3 SER.#'d SETS
NO PLATINUM PRICING AVAILABLE
MASTERPIECE PRINT RUN 1 SER.#'d SET
NO MASTERPIECE PRICING AVAILABLE
AER Rick Ankiel/Jim Edmonds
Scott Rolen 20.00 50.00
BNS Jason Bay/Xavier Nady
Freddy Sanchez 12.50 30.00
BPG Bay/Pujols/Griffey 30.00 60.00
CRS Miguel Cabrera/Manny Ramirez
Grady Sizemore 20.00 50.00
DZV Ray Durham/Barry Zito/Omar Vizquel 12.50 30.00
GKW Vladimir Guerrero/Howie Kendrick
Jered Weaver 20.00 50.00
JCZ Chipper Jones/Eric Chavez
Ryan Zimmerman 20.00 50.00
JJF Chipper Jones/Andruw Jones
Jeff Francoeur 20.00 50.00
JTR Jeter/Tulo/Hanley 60.00 120.00
LMS James Loney/Russell Martin
Takashi Saito 20.00 50.00
LRS Derrek Lee/Aramis Ramirez
Alfonso Soriano 20.00 50.00
MJD Willie McCovey/Reggie Jackson
Adam Dunn 20.00 50.00
MMM Victor Martinez/Joe Mauer
Russell Martin 20.00 50.00
MMR Brian McCann/Russell Martin
Ivan Rodriguez 20.00 50.00
MWM Pedro Martinez/Billy Wagner
John Maine 20.00 50.00
ORY Ortiz/Manny/Youkilis 20.00 50.00
PRB Jonathan Papelbon
Manny Ramirez/Josh Beckett 20.00 50.00
SCM Tom Seaver/Steve Carlton
Greg Maddux 30.00 60.00
SHC Nick Swisher/Dan Haren/Eric Chavez 12.50 30.00
SZB Curt Schilling/Carlos Zambrano
Jeremy Bonderman 20.00 50.00
TKB Jim Thome/Paul Konerko
Mark Buehrle 20.00 50.00
UHR Chase Utley/Cole Hamels
Jimmy Rollins 20.00 50.00
UUK Chase Utley/Dan Uggla/Jeff Kent 20.00 50.00

2009 Upper Deck Prominent Cuts

COMPLETE SET (60) 30.00 60.00
53 Dinesh Kumar Patel .60 1.50
57 Rinku Singh .60 1.50

2005 Upper Deck Pro Sigs

COMPLETE SET (132) 20.00 50.00
COMMON CARD (1-90) .10 .30
COMMON CARD (91-132) .25 .60
91-132 ACTUAL ODDS TWO PER PACK
91-132 WRAPPER ODDS OF 1:4 IS WRONG
1 Dallas McPherson .12 .30
2 Garret Anderson .12 .30
3 Steve Finley .12 .30
4 Vladimir Guerrero .20 .50
5 Luis Gonzalez .12 .30
6 Shawn Green .12 .30
7 Troy Glaus .12 .30
8 Andruw Jones .12 .30
9 Chipper Jones .30 .75
10 John Smoltz .30 .75
11 Tim Hudson .20 .50
12 Miguel Tejada .20 .50
13 Rafael Palmeiro .20 .50
14 Sammy Sosa .30 .75
15 Curt Schilling .20 .50
16 David Ortiz .30 .75
17 Johnny Damon .20 .50
18 Manny Ramirez .30 .75
19 Greg Maddux .40 1.00
20 Kerry Wood .12 .30
21 Mark Prior .20 .50
22 Nomar Garciaparra .20 .50
23 Frank Thomas .30 .75
24 Paul Konerko .20 .50
25 Adam Dunn .20 .50
26 Ken Griffey Jr. .60 1.50
27 Travis Hafner .12 .30
28 Victor Martinez .20 .50
29 Todd Helton .20 .50
30 Ivan Rodriguez .20 .50
31 Magglio Ordonez .20 .50
32 Carlos Delgado .12 .30
33 Josh Beckett .12 .30
34 Miguel Cabrera .30 .75
35 Craig Biggio .20 .50
36 Jeff Bagwell .20 .50
37 Lance Berkman .20 .50
38 Roger Clemens .40 1.00
39 Roy Oswalt .20 .50
40 Mike Sweeney .12 .30
41 Derek Lowe .12 .30
42 Eric Gagne .12 .30
43 J.D. Drew .12 .30
44 Jeff Kent .12 .30
45 Ben Sheets .12 .30
46 Carlos Lee .12 .30
47 Joe Mauer .25 .60
48 Johan Santana .20 .50
49 Torii Hunter .12 .30
50 Carlos Beltran .20 .50
51 David Wright .25 .60
52 Kazuo Matsui .12 .30
53 Mike Piazza .30 .75
54 Pedro Martinez .20 .50
55 Tom Glavine .20 .50
56 Alex Rodriguez .40 1.00
57 Derek Jeter .75 2.00
58 Gary Sheffield .12 .30
59 Hideki Matsui .50 1.25
60 Jason Giambi .12 .30
61 Jorge Posada .20 .50
62 Mike Mussina .20 .50
63 Randy Johnson .30 .75
64 Barry Zito .20 .50
65 Bobby Crosby .12 .30
66 Eric Chavez .12 .30
67 Bobby Abreu .12 .30
68 Jim Thome .20 .50
69 Jason Bay .12 .30
70 Oliver Perez .12 .30
71 Brian Giles .12 .30
72 Jake Peavy .12 .30
73 Khalil Greene .12 .30
74 Jason Schmidt .12 .30
75 Moises Alou .12 .30
76 Adrian Beltre .30 .75
77 Bret Boone .12 .30
78 Ichiro Suzuki .40 1.00
79 Richie Sexson .12 .30
80 Albert Pujols .40 1.00
81 Jim Edmonds .20 .50
82 Mark Mulder .12 .30
83 Scott Rolen .20 .50
84 Aubrey Huff .12 .30
85 Alfonso Soriano .20 .50
86 Hank Blalock .12 .30
87 Mark Teixeira .20 .50
88 Roy Halladay .20 .50
89 Jose Vidro .12 .30
90 Livan Hernandez .12 .30
91 Tony Pena FC RC .25 .60
92 Luis Hernandez FC RC .25 .60
93 Pete Orr FC RC .40 1.00
94 Anibal Sanchez FC RC 1.00 2.50
95 Luis Mendoza FC RC .25 .60
96 Stephen Drew FC RC .75 2.00
97 Russ Rohlicek FC RC .25 .60
98 Casey Rogowski FC RC .40 1.00
99 Pedro Lopez FC RC .25 .60
100 Tadahito Iguchi FC RC .40 1.00
101 Daylan Childress FC RC .25 .60
102 Juan Morillo FC RC .25 .60
103 Marcos Carvajal FC RC .25 .60
104 Ubaldo Jimenez FC RC .60 1.50
105 Justin Verlander FC RC 5.00 12.00
106 Chris Resop FC RC .25 .60
107 Yorman Bazardo FC RC .25 .60
108 Jared Gothreaux FC RC .25 .60
109 Luke Scott FC RC .60 1.50
110 Ambiorix Burgos FC RC .25 .60
111 Prince Fielder FC RC 1.25 3.00
112 Dennis Houlton FC RC .25 .60
113 Franquelis Osoria FC RC .25 .60
114 Norihiro Nakamura FC RC .25 .60
115 Oscar Robles FC RC .25 .60
116 Steve Schmoll FC RC .25 .60
117 Luis Pena FC RC .25 .60
118 Dave Gassner FC RC .25 .60
119 Ambiorix Concepcion FC RC .25 .60
120 Dae-Sung Koo FC RC .25 .60
121 Matthew Lindstrom FC RC .25 .60
122 Colter Bean FC RC .25 .60
123 Keiichi Yabu FC RC .25 .60
124 Philip Humber FC RC .60 1.50
125 Wladimir Balentien FC RC .40 1.00
126 Tony Giarratano FC RC .25 .60
127 Shane Costa FC RC .25 .60
128 Jeff Niemann FC RC .60 1.50
129 Nick Masset FC RC .25 .60
130 Ismael Ramirez FC RC .25 .60
131 John Hattig FC RC .25 .60
132 Brandon McCarthy FC RC .40 1.00

2005 Upper Deck Pro Sigs Gold

*GOLD: 2X TO 5X BASIC
OVERALL PARALLEL ODDS 1:5
STATED PRINT RUN 350 SERIAL #'d SETS

2005 Upper Deck Pro Sigs Silver

*SILVER: 1.25X TO 3X BASIC
OVERALL PARALLEL ODDS 1:5

2005 Upper Deck Pro Sigs Signature Sensations

OVERALL AU ODDS 1:24
TIER INFO PROVIDED BY UPPER DECK
NO TIER 1 PRICING DUE TO SCARCITY
EXCHANGE DEADLINE 12/05/08
AA Abe Alvarez T3 4.00 10.00
AM Aaron Miles T4 4.00 10.00
AR Aaron Rowand T4 15.00 40.00
BA Bronson Arroyo T4 15.00 40.00
BD Brandon Duckworth T3 4.00 10.00
BT Brett Tomko T3 4.00 10.00
CC Chad Cordero T3 6.00 15.00
CS Cory Sullivan T3 4.00 10.00
DB Denny Bautista T3 4.00 10.00
DJ Derek Jeter T2 100.00 250.00
DW David Wright T2 10.00 25.00
GA Garrett Atkins T4 4.00 10.00
HR Horacio Ramirez T2 6.00 15.00
JC Juan Cruz T3 4.00 10.00
JE Johnny Estrada T3 4.00 10.00
JJ Jorge Julio T3 4.00 10.00
JS Jeff Suppan T4 4.00 10.00
KC Kiko Calero T4 4.00 10.00
KH Keith Hernandez T2 10.00 25.00
LF Lew Ford T2 6.00 15.00
MC Miguel Cabrera T2 30.00 60.00
MV Merkin Valdez T3 4.00 10.00
NP Nick Punto T4 4.00 10.00
OH Orlando Hernandez T2 10.00 25.00
OI Omar Infante T3 4.00 10.00
RB Russell Branyan T3 4.00 10.00
RN Roberto Novoa T3 4.00 10.00
TH Travis Hafner T3 6.00 15.00
YM Yadier Molina T4 25.00 60.00

2005 Upper Deck Pro Sigs Signature Sensations Silver

*SILVER: .6X TO 1.5X T4
*SILVER: .6X TO 1.5X T3
*SILVER: .4X TO 1X T2
STATED PRINT RUN 50 SERIAL #'d SETS
*GOLD PRINT RUN 5 SERIAL #'d SETS
NO GOLD PRICING DUE TO SCARCITY
OVERALL AU ODDS 1:24
EXCHANGE DEADLINE 12/05/08
CT Chad Tracy 6.00 15.00
DJ Derek Jeter 100.00 250.00
JB Josh Bard 6.00 15.00
JF Jesse Foppert 6.00 15.00
JW Jerome Williams 10.00 25.00
KT Kazuhito Tadano 10.00 25.00
MT Mark Teixeira 15.00 40.00
PL Paul Lo Duca 10.00 25.00

2000 Upper Deck Pros and Prospects

COMP.BASIC w/o SP's (90) 8.00 20.00
COMP.UPDATE w/o SP's (30) 4.00 10.00
COMMON CARD (1-90) .15 .40
COMMON PS (91-120) .60 1.50
91-120 RANDOM INSERTS IN PACKS
91-120 PRINT RUN 1350 SERIAL #'d SETS
COMMON PF (121-132) .40 1.00
121-132 RANDOM INSERTS IN PACKS
121-132 PRINT RUN 1000 SERIAL #'d SETS
COMMON PS (133-162) .60 1.50
133-162 PRINT RUN 1600 SERIAL #'d SETS
COMMON CARD (163-192) .25 .60
133-192 DISTRIBUTED IN ROOKIE UPD.PACKS
1 Darin Erstad .15 .40
2 Troy Glaus .15 .40
3 Mo Vaughn .15 .40
4 Jason Giambi .15 .40
5 Tim Hudson .25 .60
6 Ben Grieve .15 .40
7 Eric Chavez .15 .40
8 Shannon Stewart .15 .40
9 Raul Mondesi .15 .40
10 Carlos Delgado .15 .40
11 Jose Canseco .25 .60
12 Fred McGriff .25 .60
13 Greg Vaughn .15 .40
14 Manny Ramirez .40 1.00
15 Roberto Alomar .25 .60
16 Jim Thome .25 .60
17 Alex Rodriguez .50 1.25
18 Freddy Garcia .15 .40
19 John Olerud .15 .40
20 Cal Ripken 1.25 3.00
21 Albert Belle .15 .40
22 Mike Mussina .25 .60
23 Ivan Rodriguez .25 .60
24 Rafael Palmeiro .25 .60
25 Ruben Mateo .15 .40
26 Gabe Kapler .15 .40
27 Pedro Martinez .25 .60
28 Nomar Garciaparra .25 .60
29 Carl Everett .15 .40
30 Carlos Beltran .25 .60
31 Jermaine Dye .15 .40
32 J.Damon UER Randa Photo .25 .60
33 Juan Gonzalez .15 .40
34 Juan Encarnacion .15 .40
35 Dean Palmer .15 .40
36 Jacque Jones .15 .40
37 Matt Lawton .15 .40
38 Frank Thomas .40 1.00
39 Paul Konerko .15 .40
40 Magglio Ordonez .25 .60
41 Derek Jeter 1.00 2.50
42 Bernie Williams .25 .60
43 Mariano Rivera .50 1.25
44 Roger Clemens .50 1.25
45 Jeff Bagwell .25 .60
46 Craig Biggio .25 .60
47 Richard Hidalgo .15 .40
48 Chipper Jones .40 1.00
49 Andres Galarraga .25 .60
50 Andruw Jones .15 .40
51 Greg Maddux .50 1.25
52 Jeromy Burnitz .15 .40
53 Geoff Jenkins .15 .40
54 Mark McGwire .60 1.50
55 Jim Edmonds .15 .40
56 Fernando Tatis .15 .40
57 J.D. Drew .15 .40
58 Sammy Sosa .40 1.00
59 Kerry Wood .15 .40
60 Randy Johnson .40 1.00
61 Matt Williams .15 .40
62 Erubiel Durazo .15 .40
63 Shawn Green .15 .40
64 Kevin Brown .15 .40
65 Gary Sheffield .15 .40
66 Adrian Beltre .40 1.00
67 Vladimir Guerrero .25 .60
68 Jose Vidro .15 .40
69 Barry Bonds .60 1.50
70 Jeff Kent .15 .40
71 Preston Wilson .15 .40
72 Ryan Dempster .15 .40
73 Mike Lowell .15 .40
74 Mike Piazza .40 1.00
75 Robin Ventura .15 .40
76 Edgardo Alfonzo .15 .40
77 Derek Bell .15 .40
78 Tony Gwynn .40 1.00
79 Matt Clement .15 .40
80 Scott Rolen .25 .60
81 Bobby Abreu .15 .40
82 Curt Schilling .25 .60

83 Brian Giles .15 .40
84 Jason Kendall .15 .40
85 Kris Benson .15 .40
86 Ken Griffey Jr. .75 2.00
87 Sean Casey .15 .40
88 Pokey Reese .15 .40
89 Larry Walker .25 .60
90 Todd Helton .25 .60
91 Rick Ankiel PS 1.00 2.50
92 Milton Bradley PS .60 1.50
93 Vernon Wells PS .60 1.50
94 Rafael Furcal PS 1.00 2.50
95 Kazuhiro Sasaki PS RC 1.50 4.00
96 Joe Torres PS RC .60 1.50
97 Adam Kennedy PS .60 1.50
98 Adam Piatt PS .60 1.50
99 Matt Wheatland PS RC .60 1.50
100 Alex Cabrera PS RC .60 1.50
101 Barry Zito PS RC 5.00 12.00
102 Mike Lamb PS RC .60 1.50
103 Scott Heard PS RC .60 1.50
104 Danys Baez PS RC .60 1.50
105 Matt Riley PS .60 1.50
106 Mark Mulder PS .60 1.50
107 Wilfredo Rodriguez PS RC .60 1.50
108 Luis Matos PS RC .60 1.50
109 Alfonso Soriano PS 1.50 4.00
110 Pat Burrell PS .60 1.50
111 Mike Tonis PS RC .60 1.50
112 Aaron McNeal PS RC .60 1.50
113 Dave Krynzel PS RC .60 1.50
114 Josh Beckett PS 1.25 3.00
115 Sean Burnett PS RC .60 1.50
116 Eric Munson PS .60 1.50
117 Scott Downs PS RC .60 1.50
118 Brian Tollberg PS RC .60 1.50
119 Nick Johnson PS .60 1.50
120 Leo Estrella PS RC .60 1.50
121 Ken Griffey Jr. PF 2.00 5.00
122 Frank Thomas PF 1.00 2.50
123 Cal Ripken PF 3.00 8.00
124 Ivan Rodriguez PF .60 1.50
125 Derek Jeter PF 2.50 6.00
126 Mark McGwire PF 1.50 4.00
127 Pedro Martinez PF .60 1.50
128 Chipper Jones PF 1.00 2.50
129 Sammy Sosa PF 1.00 2.50
130 Alex Rodriguez PF 1.25 3.00
131 Vladimir Guerrero PF .60 1.50
132 Jeff Bagwell PF .60 1.50
133 Dane Artman PS RC .60 1.50
134 Juan Pierre PS RC 3.00 8.00
135 Jace Brewer PS RC .60 1.50
136 Sun Woo Kim PS RC .60 1.50
137 Jon Rauch PS RC .60 1.50
138 Juan Guzman PS RC .60 1.50
139 Daylan Holt PS RC .60 1.50
140 Rico Washington PS RC .60 1.50
141 Ben Diggins PS RC .60 1.50
142 Mike Meyers PS RC 1.00 2.50
143 Chris Wakeland PS RC .60 1.50
144 Cory Vance PS RC .60 1.50
145 Keith Ginter PS RC .60 1.50
146 Koyie Hill PS RC .60 1.50
147 Julio Zuleta PS RC .60 1.50
148 Geraldo Guzman PS RC .60 1.50
149 Jay Spurgeon PS RC .60 1.50
150 Ross Gload PS RC .60 1.50
151 Ben Sheets PS RC 1.50 4.00
152 Josh Kalinowski PS RC .60 1.50
153 Kurt Ainsworth PS RC .60 1.50
154 Paxton Crawford PS RC .60 1.50
155 Xavier Nady PS RC 1.50 4.00
156 Brad Wilkerson PS RC 1.50 4.00
157 Kris Wilson PS RC .60 1.50
158 Paul Rigdon PS RC .60 1.50
159 Ryan Kohlmeier PS RC .60 1.50
160 Dane Sardinha PS RC .60 1.50
161 Javier Cardona PS RC .60 1.50
162 Brad Cresse PS RC .60 1.50
163 Ron Gant .25 .60
164 Mark Mulder .25 .60
165 David Wells .25 .60
166 Jason Tyner .25 .60
167 David Segui .25 .60
168 Al Martin .25 .60
169 Melvin Mora .25 .60
170 Ricky Ledee .25 .60
171 Rolando Arrojo .25 .60
172 Mike Sweeney .25 .60
173 Bobby Higginson .25 .60
174 Eric Milton .25 .60
175 Charles Johnson .25 .60
176 David Justice .25 .60
177 Moises Alou .25 .60
178 Andy Ashby .25 .60
179 Richie Sexson .25 .60
180 Will Clark .40 1.00
181 Rondell White .25 .60
182 Curt Schilling .40 1.00
183 Tom Goodwin .25 .60
184 Lee Stevens .25 .60
185 Ellis Burks .25 .60
186 Henry Rodriguez .25 .60
187 Mike Bordick .25 .60
188 Ryan Klesko .25 .60
189 Travis Lee .25 .60
190 Kevin Young .25 .60
191 Barry Larkin .40 1.00
192 Jeff Cirillo .25 .60

2000 Upper Deck Pros and Prospects Best in the Bigs

COMPLETE SET (10) 10.00 25.00
STATED ODDS 1:12
B1 Sammy Sosa 1.00 2.50
B2 Tony Gwynn 1.00 2.50
B3 Pedro Martinez .60 1.50
B4 Mark McGwire 1.50 4.00
B5 Chipper Jones 1.00 2.50
B6 Derek Jeter 2.50 6.00
B7 Ken Griffey Jr. 2.00 5.00
B8 Cal Ripken 3.00 8.00
B9 Greg Maddux 1.25 3.00
B10 Ivan Rodriguez .60 1.50

2000 Upper Deck Pros and Prospects Future Forces

COMPLETE SET (10) 4.00 10.00
STATED ODDS 1:6
F1 Pat Burrell .40 1.00
F2 Brad Penny .40 1.00
F3 Rick Ankiel .40 1.00
F4 Adam Kennedy .40 1.00
F5 Eric Munson .40 1.00
F6 Rafael Furcal .40 1.00
F7 Mark Mulder .40 1.00
F8 Vernon Wells .40 1.00
F9 Matt Riley .40 1.00
F10 Nick Johnson .40 1.00

2000 Upper Deck Pros and Prospects Game Jersey Autograph

STATED ODDS 1:96
EXCHANGE DEADLINE 07/05/01
CANSECO-GLAVINE EXCH.GOT VAUGHN AU
AR Alex Rodriguez 60.00 120.00
BB Barry Bonds 60.00 120.00
CJ Chipper Jones 40.00 80.00
CR Cal Ripken 60.00 120.00
DJ Derek Jeter SP 1400.00 2000.00
FT Frank Thomas 40.00 100.00
GS Gary Sheffield 6.00 15.00
IR Ivan Rodriguez 20.00 50.00
JC Jose Canseco 12.00 30.00
JD J.D. Drew 8.00 20.00
KG Ken Griffey Jr. 75.00 150.00
KL Kenny Lofton 12.50 30.00
LG Luis Gonzalez 6.00 15.00
MV Mo Vaughn 6.00 15.00
MW Matt Williams 6.00 15.00
PW Preston Wilson 6.00 15.00
RJ Randy Johnson 50.00 100.00
RV Robin Ventura 6.00 15.00
SR Scott Rolen 6.00 15.00
TGL Tom Glavine 20.00 50.00
TGW Tony Gwynn 25.00 60.00

2000 Upper Deck Pros and Prospects Game Jersey Autograph Gold

PRINT RUNS B/WN 2-51 COPIES PER
NO PRICING ON QTY OF 25 OR LESS
EXCHANGE DEADLINE 07/05/01
FT Frank Thomas/35 50.00 120.00
KG Ken Griffey Jr./30 150.00 300.00
MV Mo Vaughn/42 12.50 30.00
PW Preston Wilson/44 15.00 40.00
RJ Randy Johnson/51 100.00 175.00
TGL Tom Glavine/47 40.00 100.00

2000 Upper Deck Pros and Prospects ProMotion

COMPLETE SET (10) 5.00 12.00
STATED ODDS 1:6
P1 Derek Jeter 1.50 4.00
P2 Mike Piazza .60 1.50
P3 Mark McGwire 1.00 2.50
P4 Ivan Rodriguez .40 1.00
P5 Kerry Wood .25 .60
P6 Nomar Garciaparra .40 1.00
P7 Sammy Sosa .60 1.50
P8 Alex Rodriguez .75 2.00
P9 Ken Griffey Jr. 1.25 3.00
P10 Vladimir Guerrero .40 1.00

2000 Upper Deck Pros and Prospects Rare Breed

COMPLETE SET (12) 15.00 40.00
STATED ODDS 1:12
R1 Mark McGwire 1.50 4.00
R2 Frank Thomas 1.00 2.50
R3 Mike Piazza 1.00 2.50
R4 Barry Bonds 1.50 4.00
R5 Manny Ramirez 1.00 2.50
R6 Ken Griffey Jr. 2.00 5.00
R7 Nomar Garciaparra .60 1.50
R8 Randy Johnson 1.00 2.50
R9 Vladimir Guerrero .60 1.50
R10 Jeff Bagwell .60 1.50
R11 Rick Ankiel .60 1.50
R12 Alex Rodriguez 1.25 3.00

2001 Upper Deck Pros and Prospects

COMP.SET w/o SP's (90) 6.00 15.00
COMMON CARD (1-90) .15 .40
COMMON CARD (91-135) 2.00 5.00
91-135 RANDOM INSERTS IN PACKS
91-135 PRINT RUN 1250 SERIAL #'d SETS
COMMON CARD (136-141) 8.00 20.00
136-141 RANDOM INSERTS IN PACKS
136-141 PRINT RUN 500 SERIAL #'d SETS
1 Troy Glaus .15 .40
2 Darin Erstad .15 .40
3 Tim Hudson .15 .40
4 Jason Giambi .15 .40
5 Jermaine Dye .15 .40
6 Barry Zito .25 .60
7 Carlos Delgado .15 .40
8 Shannon Stewart .15 .40
9 Raul Mondesi .15 .40
10 Greg Vaughn .15 .40
11 Ben Grieve .15 .40
12 Roberto Alomar .25 .60
13 Juan Gonzalez .15 .40
14 Jim Thome .25 .60
15 C.C. Sabathia .15 .40
16 Edgar Martinez .25 .60
17 Kazuhiro Sasaki .15 .40
18 Aaron Sele .15 .40
19 John Olerud .15 .40
20 Cal Ripken 1.25 3.00
21 Rafael Palmeiro .25 .60
22 Ivan Rodriguez .25 .60
23 Alex Rodriguez .50 1.25
24 Manny Ramirez Sox .40 1.00
25 Pedro Martinez .25 .60
26 Carl Everett .15 .40
27 Nomar Garciaparra .60 1.50
28 Neifi Perez .15 .40
29 Mike Sweeney .15 .40
30 Bobby Higginson .15 .40
31 Tony Clark .15 .40
32 Doug Mientkiewicz .15 .40
33 Cristian Guzman .15 .40
34 Brad Radke .15 .40
35 Magglio Ordonez .15 .40
36 Carlos Lee .15 .40
37 Frank Thomas .40 1.00
38 Roger Clemens .75 2.00
39 Bernie Williams .25 .60
40 Derek Jeter 1.00 2.50
41 Tino Martinez .25 .60
42 Wade Miller .15 .40
43 Jeff Bagwell .25 .60
44 Lance Berkman .15 .40
45 Richard Hidalgo .15 .40
46 Greg Maddux .60 1.50
47 Andruw Jones .25 .60
48 Chipper Jones .40 1.00
49 Rafael Furcal .15 .40
50 Jeromy Burnitz .15 .40
51 Geoff Jenkins .15 .40
52 Ben Sheets .25 .60
53 Mark McGwire 1.00 2.50
54 Jim Edmonds .15 .40
55 J.D. Drew .15 .40
56 Fred McGriff .25 .60
57 Sammy Sosa .40 1.00
58 Kerry Wood .15 .40
59 Randy Johnson .40 1.00
60 Luis Gonzalez .15 .40
61 Curt Schilling .15 .40
62 Kevin Brown .15 .40
63 Shawn Green .15 .40
64 Gary Sheffield .15 .40
65 Vladimir Guerrero .40 1.00
66 Jose Vidro .15 .40
67 Barry Bonds 1.00 2.50
68 Jeff Kent .15 .40
69 Rich Aurilia .15 .40
70 Preston Wilson .15 .40
71 Charles Johnson .15 .40
72 Cliff Floyd .15 .40
73 Mike Piazza .60 1.50
74 Al Leiter .15 .40
75 Matt Lawton .15 .40
76 Tony Gwynn .50 1.25
77 Ryan Klesko .15 .40
78 Phil Nevin .15 .40
79 Scott Rolen .25 .60
80 Pat Burrell .15 .40
81 Jimmy Rollins .15 .40
82 Jason Kendall .15 .40
83 Brian Giles .15 .40
84 Aramis Ramirez .15 .40
85 Ken Griffey Jr. .75 2.00
86 Barry Larkin .25 .60
87 Sean Casey .15 .40
88 Larry Walker .15 .40
89 Todd Helton .25 .60
90 Mike Hampton .15 .40
91 Juan Cruz PS RC 2.00 5.00
92 Brian Lawrence PS RC 2.00 5.00
93 Brandon Lyon PS RC 2.00 5.00
94 Adrian Hernandez PS RC 2.00 5.00
95 Jose Mieses PS RC 2.00 5.00
96 Juan Uribe PS RC 2.00 5.00
97 Morgan Ensberg PS RC 3.00 8.00
98 Wilson Betemit PS RC 3.00 8.00
99 Ryan Freel PS RC 3.00 8.00
100 Jack Wilson PS RC 2.00 5.00
101 Cesar Crespo PS RC 2.00 5.00
102 Bret Prinz PS RC 2.00 5.00
103 Horacio Ramirez PS RC 2.00 5.00
104 Elpidio Guzman PS RC 2.00 5.00
105 Josh Towers PS RC 2.00 5.00
106 Brandon Duckworth PS RC 2.00 5.00
107 Esix Snead PS RC 2.00 5.00
108 Billy Sylvester PS RC 2.00 5.00
109 Alexis Gomez PS RC 2.00 5.00
110 Johnny Estrada PS RC 2.00 5.00
111 Joe Kennedy PS RC 2.00 5.00
112 Travis Hafner PS RC 4.00 10.00
113 Martin Vargas PS RC 2.00 5.00
114 Jay Gibbons PS RC 2.00 5.00
115 Andres Torres PS RC 2.00 5.00
116 Sean Douglass PS RC 2.00 5.00
117 Juan Diaz PS RC 2.00 5.00
118 Greg Miller PS RC 2.00 5.00
119 Carlos Valderrama PS RC 2.00 5.00
120 Bill Ortega PS RC 2.00 5.00
121 Josh Fogg PS RC 2.00 5.00
122 Wilken Ruan PS RC 2.00 5.00
123 Kris Keller PS RC 2.00 5.00
124 Erick Almonte PS RC 2.00 5.00
125 Ricardo Rodriguez PS RC 2.00 5.00
126 Grant Balfour PS RC 2.00 5.00
127 Nick Maness PS RC 2.00 5.00
128 Jeremy Owens PS RC 2.00 5.00
129 Doug Nickle PS RC 2.00 5.00
130 Bert Snow PS RC 2.00 5.00
131 Jason Smith PS RC 2.00 5.00
132 Henry Mateo PS RC 2.00 5.00
133 Mike Penney PS RC 2.00 5.00
134 Bud Smith PS RC 2.00 5.00
135 Junior Spivey PS RC 2.00 5.00
136 Ichiro Suzuki JSY RC 30.00 80.00
137 Albert Pujols JSY RC 100.00 250.00
138 Mark Teixeira JSY RC 30.00 60.00
139 Dewon Brazelton JSY RC 6.00 15.00
140 Mark Prior JSY RC 20.00 50.00
141 Tsuyoshi Shinjo JSY RC 10.00 25.00

2001 Upper Deck Pros and Prospects Franchise Building Blocks

COMPLETE SET (30) 20.00 50.00
STATED ODDS 1:6
F1 D.Erstad .40 1.00
E.Guzman
F2 J.Giambi .40 1.00
J.Hart
F3 C.Delgado .40 1.00
V.Wells
F4 G.Vaughn .40 1.00
A.Huff
F5 J.Thome .40 1.00
C.Sabathia
F6 E.Martinez 2.50 6.00
I.Suzuki
F7 C.Ripken 2.00 5.00
J.Towers
F8 I.Rodriguez .40 1.00
C.Pena
F9 N.Garciaparra 1.00 2.50
D.Stenson
F10 M.Sweeney .40 1.00
D.Brown
F11 B.Higginson .40 1.00
B.Inge
F12 B.Radke .40 1.00
A.Johnson
F13 F.Thomas .60 1.50
J.Crede
F14 D.Jeter 1.50 4.00
N.Johnson
F15 J.Bagwell 1.00 2.50
M.Ensberg
F16 C.Jones 1.00 2.50
W.Betemit
F17 J.Burnitz .40 1.00
B.Sheets
F18 M.McGwire 12.00 30.00
A.Pujols
F19 S.Sosa .60 1.50
C.Patterson
F20 L.Gonzalez .40 1.00
J.Cust
F21 K.Brown .40 1.00
L.Prokopec
F22 V.Guerrero .60 1.50
W.Ruan
F23 B.Bonds 1.50 4.00
C.Valderrama
F24 P.Wilson .40 1.00
A.Nunez
F25 M.Piazza 1.00 2.50
A.Escobar
F26 T.Gwynn .75 2.00
X.Nady
F27 S.Rolen .40 1.00
J.Rollins
F28 J.Kendall .40 1.00
J.Wilson
F29 K.Griffey Jr. 1.25 3.00
A.Dunn
F30 T.Helton .40 1.00
J.Uribe

2001 Upper Deck Pros and Prospects Game-Used Dual Bat

STATED ODDS 1:24
GOLD RANDOM INSERTS IN PACKS
GOLD PRINT RUN 25 SERIAL #'d SETS
NO GOLD PRICING DUE TO SCARCITY
PPBT J.Bagwell/F.Thomas 6.00 15.00
PPGBO K.Griffey Jr./B.Bonds 10.00 25.00
PPGBU S.Green/J.Burnitz 4.00 10.00
PPJL A.Jones/K.Lofton 6.00 15.00
PPJP C.Jones/A.Pujols 12.00 30.00
PPKA J.Kent/R.Alomar 6.00 15.00
PPMJ G.Maddux/R.Johnson 6.00 15.00
PPPT R.Palmeiro/J.Thome 6.00 15.00
PPRF A.Rodriguez/R.Furcal 6.00 15.00
PPRG M.Ramirez Sox/J.Gonzalez 6.00 15.00
PPRP I.Rodriguez/M.Piazza 6.00 15.00
PPSG S.Sosa/L.Gonzalez 6.00 15.00
PPWI B.Williams/I.Suzuki 20.00 50.00

2001 Upper Deck Pros and Prospects Ichiro World Tour

COMPLETE SET (15) 40.00 100.00
COMMON CARD (WT1-WT15) 3.00 8.00
STATED ODDS 1:12

2001 Upper Deck Pros and Prospects Legends Game Bat

STATED ODDS 1:216
GOLD RANDOM INSERTS IN PACKS
GOLD PRINT RUN 25 SERIAL #'d SETS
NO GOLD PRICING DUE TO SCARCITY
PLBY J.Burnitz/R.Yount 10.00 25.00
PLRF M.Ramirez Sox/C.Fisk 10.00 25.00
PLRG C.Ripken/T.Gwynn 12.50 30.00
PLWJ B.Williams/R.Jackson 10.00 25.00

2001 Upper Deck Pros and Prospects Specialty Game Jersey

STATED ODDS 1:24
GOLD RANDOM INSERTS IN PACKS
GOLD PRINT RUN 25 SERIAL #'d SETS
NO GOLD PRICING DUE TO SCARCITY
SI Ichiro Suzuki 12.00 30.00
SAR Alex Rodriguez 4.00 10.00
SBB Barry Bonds 5.00 12.00
SCR Cal Ripken 6.00 15.00
SJE Jim Edmonds 2.00 5.00
SJG Juan Gonzalez 1.25 3.00
SJT Jim Thome 2.00 5.00
SLW Larry Walker 2.00 5.00
SRA Roberto Alomar 2.00 5.00
SRJ Randy Johnson 3.00 8.00
SSG Shawn Green 1.25 3.00
SSR Scott Rolen 2.00 5.00
SSS Sammy Sosa 2.00 5.00
STG Tony Gwynn 3.00 8.00

2001 Upper Deck Pros and Prospects Then and Now Game Jersey

STATED ODDS 1:24
GOLD RANDOM INSERTS IN PACKS
GOLD PRINT RUN 25 SERIAL #'d SETS
NO GOLD PRICING DUE TO SCARCITY
ALL EXCEPT RYAN ARE DUAL JSY CARDS
NOLAN RYAN IS A TRIPLE JSY CARD
TNAR Alex Rodriguez 4.00 10.00
TNB Barry Bonds 5.00 12.00
TNCS Curt Schilling 1.25 3.00
TNFG Freddy Garcia 1.25 3.00
TNGM Greg Maddux 5.00 12.00
TNGS Gary Sheffield 1.25 3.00
TNJE Jim Edmonds 2.00 5.00
TNJG Jason Giambi 1.25 3.00
TNJG Juan Gonzalez 1.25 3.00
TNKB Kevin Brown 1.25 3.00
TNKG Ken Griffey Jr. 6.00 15.00
TNMP Mike Piazza 3.00 8.00
TNMR Manny Ramirez Sox 3.00 8.00
TNNR Nolan Ryan 10.00 25.00
Triple Jsy
TNPM Pedro Martinez 2.00 5.00
TNPN Phil Nevin 1.25 3.00
TNRA Rick Ankiel 1.25 3.00
TNRC Roger Clemens 5.00 12.00
TNRJ Randy Johnson 3.00 8.00
TNRV Robin Ventura 1.25 3.00
TNXN Xavier Nady 1.25 3.00

2005 Upper Deck Pros and Prospects

COMP.SET w/o SP's (100) 10.00 25.00
COMMON CARD (1-100) .10 .30
COMMON CARD (101-150) .60 1.50
101-150 PRINT RUN 999 SERIAL #'d SETS
COMMON CARD (151-175) .75 2.00
151-175 PRINT RUN 499 SERIAL #'d SETS
COMMON CARD (176-200) 1.00 2.50
176-200 PRINT RUN 199 SERIAL #'d SETS
101-200 OVERALL ODDS 1:8
1 Adam Dunn .20 .50
2 Aramis Ramirez .12 .30
3 Bobby Abreu .12 .30
4 Mike Lowell .12 .30
5 Josh Beckett .12 .30
6 Derek Jeter .75 2.00
7 Alex Rodriguez .40 1.00
8 Andruw Jones .12 .30
9 Brian Giles .12 .30
10 Ivan Rodriguez .20 .50
11 Aubrey Huff .12 .30
12 Jake Peavy .12 .30
13 Hank Blalock .12 .30
14 Curt Schilling .20 .50
15 Carlos Zambrano .20 .50
16 Mike Mussina .20 .50
17 Travis Hafner .12 .30
18 Scott Rolen .20 .50
19 Luis Gonzalez .12 .30
20 Torii Hunter .12 .30
21 Greg Maddux .40 1.00
22 J.D. Drew .12 .30
23 Kevin Brown .12 .30
24 Carl Pavano .12 .30
25 David Ortiz .30 .75
26 Jose Reyes .20 .50
27 Johan Santana .20 .50
28 Todd Helton .20 .50
29 Jason Kendall .12 .30
30 Pedro Martinez .20 .50
31 Chipper Jones .30 .75
32 Ben Sheets .12 .30
33 Garret Anderson .12 .30
34 Carl Crawford .20 .50
35 Jason Schmidt .12 .30
36 Johnny Damon .20 .50
37 Richie Sexson .12 .30
38 Brad Penny .12 .30
39 Carlos Delgado .12 .30
40 Gary Sheffield .12 .30
41 John Smoltz .30 .75
42 Eric Chavez .12 .30
43 Carlos Guillen .12 .30
44 Jeff Kent .12 .30
45 Miguel Tejada .20 .50
46 Shawn Green .12 .30
47 Vernon Wells .12 .30
48 Albert Pujols .40 1.00
49 Alfonso Soriano .20 .50
50 Eric Gagne .12 .30
51 Mark Prior .20 .50
52 Rafael Furcal .12 .30
53 Preston Wilson .12 .30
54 Barry Larkin .20 .50
55 Randy Johnson .30 .75
56 Craig Wilson .12 .30
57 Victor Martinez .20 .50
58 Jim Thome .20 .50
59 Paul Konerko .20 .50
60 Jeff Bagwell .20 .50
61 Lyle Overbay .12 .30
62 Miguel Cabrera .30 .75
63 Melvin Mora .12 .30
64 Scott Podsednik .12 .30
65 Mark Mulder .12 .30
66 Mark Teixeira .20 .50
67 Tom Glavine .20 .50
68 Frank Thomas .30 .75
69 Livan Hernandez .12 .30
70 Kazuo Matsui .12 .30
71 Jose Vidro .12 .30
72 Ichiro Suzuki .40 1.00
73 Roger Clemens .40 1.00
74 Manny Ramirez .30 .75
75 Michael Young .12 .30
76 Rafael Palmeiro .20 .50
77 Steve Finley .12 .30
78 Andy Pettitte .20 .50
79 Lance Berkman .20 .50
80 Adrian Beltre .30 .75
81 Carlos Lee .12 .30
82 Bret Boone .12 .30
83 Magglio Ordonez .20 .50
84 Sammy Sosa .30 .75
85 Tim Hudson .20 .50
86 Vladimir Guerrero .20 .50
87 Carlos Beltran .20 .50
88 Kerry Wood .12 .30
89 Jim Edmonds .20 .50
90 Mike Sweeney .12 .30
91 Nomar Garciaparra .30 .75
92 Mike Piazza .30 .75
93 Roy Halladay .20 .50
94 Troy Glaus .12 .30
95 Bernie Williams .20 .50
96 Larry Walker .20 .50
97 Craig Biggio .20 .50
98 Roy Oswalt .20 .50
99 Ken Griffey Jr. .50 1.25
100 Hideki Matsui .50 1.25
101 Bucky Jacobsen T1 .60 1.50
102 J.D. Closser T1 .60 1.50
103 Antonio Perez T1 .60 1.50
104 Chris Shelton T1 .60 1.50
105 David Aardsma T1 .60 1.50
106 Jake Woods T1 .60 1.50
107 Jung Bong T1 .60 1.50
108 Kazuhito Tadano T1 .60 1.50
109 John Van Benschoten T1 .60 1.50
110 Jesse Foppert T1 .60 1.50
111 Jose Borchard T1 .60 1.50
112 Brandon Phillips T1 .60 1.50
113 J.D. Durbin T1 .60 1.50
114 Brandon Claussen T1 .60 1.50
115 Robb Quinlan T1 .60 1.50
116 Aaron Harang T1 .60 1.50
117 Chris Burke T1 .60 1.50
118 Sergio Mitre T1 .60 1.50
119 David DeJesus T1 .60 1.50
120 Gustavo Chacin T1 .60 1.50
121 Xavier Nady T1 .60 1.50
122 Garrett Atkins T1 .60 1.50
123 Jimmy Gobble T1 .60 1.50
124 Yhency Brazoban T1 .60 1.50
125 David Kelton T1 .60 1.50
126 Dewon Brazelton T1 .60 1.50
127 Koyie Hill T1 .60 1.50
128 Roman Colon T1 .60 1.50
129 Daniel Cabrera T1 .60 1.50
130 Chris Bootcheck T1 .60 1.50
131 Brad Halsey T1 .60 1.50
132 Bobby Madritsch T1 .60 1.50
133 Grady Sizemore T1 1.00 2.50
134 Akinori Otsuka T1 .60 1.50
135 Wilfredo Ledezma T1 .60 1.50
136 Russ Adams T1 .60 1.50
137 Joe Crede T1 .60 1.50
138 Chad Cordero T1 .60 1.50
139 Willie Harris T1 .60 1.50
140 Joey Gathright T1 .60 1.50
141 Logan Kensing T1 .60 1.50
142 Jon Leicester T1 .60 1.50
143 Freddy Guzman T1 .60 1.50
144 Jonny Gomes T1 .60 1.50
145 Jeff Bajenaru T1 .60 1.50
146 Andres Blanco T1 .60 1.50
147 Jhonny Peralta T1 .60 1.50
148 Jayson Werth T1 1.00 2.50
149 Bill Hall T1 .60 1.50
150 Jason Davis T1 .60 1.50
151 Gabe Gross T2 .75 2.00
152 Abe Alvarez T2 .75 2.00
153 Josh Willingham T2 1.25 3.00
154 Merkin Valdez T2 .75 2.00
155 Jeff Niemann T2 RC 2.00 5.00
156 Yadier Molina T2 8.00 20.00
157 Guillermo Quiroz T2 .75 2.00
158 Ian Snell T2 .75 2.00
159 Dan Meyer T2 .75 2.00
160 Jason Lane T2 .75 2.00
161 Adrian Gonzalez T2 1.50 4.00
162 Eddy Rodriguez T2 .75 2.00
163 Jason DuBois T2 .75 2.00
164 Juan Rincon T2 .75 2.00
165 Ryan Wagner T2 .75 2.00
166 Nick Swisher T2 1.25 3.00
167 Chad Tracy T2 .75 2.00
168 Dioner Navarro T2 .75 2.00
169 Gerald Laird T2 .75 2.00
170 Alexis Rios T2 .75 2.00
171 Aaron Rowand T2 .75 2.00
172 Adam LaRoche T2 .75 2.00
173 Kevin Youkilis T2 .75 2.00
174 Philip Humber T2 RC 2.00 5.00
175 Chin-Hui Tsao T2 .75 2.00
176 Jeff Francis T3 1.00 2.50
177 Chase Utley T3 1.50 4.00
178 Gavin Floyd T3 1.00 2.50
179 David Wright T3 2.00 5.00
180 B.J. Upton T3 1.50 4.00
181 Laynce Nix T3 1.00 2.50
182 Joe Mauer T3 2.00 5.00
183 Justin Morneau T3 1.50 4.00
184 Zack Greinke T3 3.00 8.00
185 Jose Capellan T3 1.00 2.50
186 Khalil Greene T3 1.00 2.50
187 Oliver Perez T3 1.00 2.50
188 Joe Blanton T3 1.00 2.50
189 Wily Mo Pena T3 1.00 2.50
190 Dallas McPherson T3 1.00 2.50
191 Edwin Jackson T3 1.00 2.50
192 Casey Kotchman T3 1.00 2.50
193 Jesse Crain T3 1.00 2.50
194 Ryan Howard T3 2.00 5.00
195 Bobby Crosby T3 1.00 2.50
196 Jason Bay T3 1.00 2.50
197 Rickie Weeks T3 1.00 2.50
198 Scott Proctor T3 1.00 2.50
199 Danny Haren T3 1.00 2.50
200 Scott Kazmir T3 2.50 6.00

2005 Upper Deck Pros and Prospects Gold

*GOLD 1-100: 4X TO 10X BASIC
1-100 PRINT RUN 125 SERIAL #'d SETS
*GOLD 101-150: .5X TO 1.2X BASIC
101-150 PRINT RUN 150 SERIAL #'d SETS
*GOLD 151-175: .5X TO 1.2X BASIC
151-175 PRINT RUN 99 SERIAL #'d SETS
176-200 PRINT RUN 25 SERIAL #'d SETS
176-200 NO PRICING DUE TO SCARCITY
OVERALL PARALLEL ODDS 1:8

2005 Upper Deck Pros and Prospects Future Fabrics

*GOLD: .6X TO 1.5X BASIC
GOLD PRINT RUN 75 SERIAL #'d SETS
OVERALL GAME USED ODDS 1:24
AK Adam Kennedy 2.00 5.00
BC Bobby Crosby 2.00 5.00
BU B.J. Upton 2.00 5.00
CK Casey Kotchman 2.00 5.00
CS C.C. Sabathia 2.00 5.00
DM Dallas McPherson 2.00 5.00
DW David Wright 6.00 15.00
EH Eric Hinske 2.00 5.00
JJ Jacque Jones 2.00 5.00
JM Joe Mauer 3.00 8.00
JR Jose Reyes 2.00 5.00
JW Jayson Werth 2.00 5.00
KE Austin Kearns 2.00 5.00
KG Khalil Greene 3.00 8.00
KM Kazuo Matsui 2.00 5.00
MC Miguel Cabrera 2.00 5.00
RH Rich Harden 2.00 5.00
SP Sidney Ponson 2.00 5.00
SS Shannon Stewart 2.00 5.00
TN Trot Nixon 2.00 5.00
VM Victor Martinez 2.00 5.00

2005 Upper Deck Pros and Prospects Pro Material

*GOLD: .6X TO 1.5X BASIC
GOLD PRINT RUN 50 SERIAL #'d SETS
OVERALL GAME USED ODDS 1:24
AB Adrian Beltre 3.00 8.00
AP Albert Pujols 6.00 15.00
CB Carlos Beltran 3.00 8.00
CJ Chipper Jones 4.00 10.00
CS Curt Schilling 4.00 10.00
DJ Derek Jeter 8.00 20.00
EC Eric Chavez 3.00 8.00
HB Hank Blalock 3.00 8.00
IS Ichiro Suzuki 10.00 25.00
JB Jeff Bagwell 4.00 10.00
JT Jim Thome 4.00 10.00
KG Ken Griffey Jr. 6.00 15.00
MP Mark Prior 4.00 10.00
MR Manny Ramirez 4.00 10.00
MT Miguel Tejada 3.00 8.00
PI Mike Piazza 4.00 10.00
RJ Randy Johnson 4.00 10.00
SR Scott Rolen 4.00 10.00
SS Sammy Sosa 4.00 10.00
TH Todd Helton 4.00 10.00
VG Vladimir Guerrero 4.00 10.00

2005 Upper Deck Pros and Prospects Signs of Stardom

TIER 3 PRINT RUNS 713 OR MORE PER
TIER 2 PRINT RUNS B/WN 247-557 PER
TIER 1 PRINT RUNS B/WN 147-202 PER
OVERALL AUTO ODDS 1:24
CARDS ARE NOT SERIAL-NUMBERED
PRINT RUN INFO PROVIDED BY UD
AB Angel Berroa T1 4.00 10.00
AE Adam Eaton T1 4.00 10.00
AO Akinori Otsuka T3 6.00 15.00
BC Bobby Crosby T1 6.00 15.00
BS Ben Sheets T1 6.00 15.00
CC Chad Cordero T1 6.00 15.00
CK Casey Kotchman T1 6.00 15.00
CL Cliff Lee T2 6.00 15.00
CP Corey Patterson T1 4.00 10.00
DW Dontrelle Willis T1 6.00 15.00
FF Frank Francisco T2 4.00 10.00
GA John Gall T2 4.00 10.00
GR Khalil Greene T1 10.00 25.00
HB Hank Blalock T1 6.00 15.00
HR Horacio Ramirez T3 4.00 10.00
JB Josh Beckett T1 10.00 25.00
JF Jason Frasor T2 4.00 10.00
JK Jeff Keppinger T2 4.00 10.00
JL Justin Leone T3 4.00 10.00
JR Jose Reyes T1 6.00 15.00
JW Jerome Williams T1 4.00 10.00
KT Kazuhito Tadano T3 6.00 15.00
LO Lyle Overbay T1 4.00 10.00
MA Joe Mauer T1 20.00 50.00
MC Miguel Cabrera T2 15.00 40.00
MG Marcus Giles T1 6.00 15.00
MJ Mike Johnston T3 4.00 10.00
MR Mike Rouse T3 4.00 10.00
MT Mark Teixeira T1 10.00 25.00
OP Oliver Perez T3 4.00 10.00
PE Jake Peavy T1 8.00 20.00
RB Rocco Baldelli T2 6.00 15.00
RH Rich Harden T3 6.00 15.00
RW Rickie Weeks T1 6.00 15.00
SB Sean Burroughs T1 4.00 10.00
SK Scott Kazmir T2 8.00 20.00
SP Scott Podsednik T1 10.00 25.00
ST Shingo Takatsu T2 4.00 10.00
TS Termel Sledge T3 4.00 10.00
WA Ryan Wagner T3 4.00 10.00
WE Brandon Webb T1 4.00 10.00

2005 Upper Deck Pros and Prospects Stardom Signatures

OVERALL AUTO ODDS 1:24
PRINT RUNS B/WN 50-240 COPIES PER
AK Al Kaline/99 25.00 50.00
BE Josh Beckett/50 12.50 30.00
BL Hank Blalock/50 10.00 25.00
EB Ernie Banks/240 30.00 60.00
JG Jason Giambi/100 10.00 25.00
JM Joe Morgan/194 10.00 25.00
KG Ken Griffey Jr./198 40.00 80.00
KP Kirby Puckett/156 75.00 150.00

2001 Upper Deck Prospect Premieres

COMP.SET w/o SP's (90) 20.00 50.00
COMMON CARD (1-90) .15 .40
COMMON AUTO (91-102) 6.00 15.00
91-102 RANDOM INSERTS IN PACKS
91-102 PRINT RUN 1000 SERIAL #'d SETS
1 Jeff Mathis XRC .20 .50
2 Jake Woods XRC .15 .40
3 Dallas McPherson XRC .40 1.00
4 Steven Shell XRC .15 .40
5 Ryan Budde XRC .15 .40
6 Kirk Saarloos XRC .15 .40
7 Ryan Stegall XRC .15 .40
8 Bobby Crosby XRC 1.25 3.00
9 J.T. Stotts XRC .15 .40
10 Neal Cotts XRC .40 1.00
11 Jeremy Bonderman XRC 1.50 4.00
12 Brandon League XRC .15 .40
13 Tyrell Godwin XRC .15 .40
14 Gabe Gross XRC .20 .50
15 Chris Neylan XRC .15 .40
16 Macay McBride XRC .30 .75
17 Josh Burrus XRC .15 .40
18 Adam Stern XRC .15 .40
19 Richard Lewis XRC .15 .40
20 Cole Barthel XRC .15 .40
21 Mike Jones XRC .20 .50
22 J.J. Hardy XRC 2.50 6.00
23 Jon Steitz XRC .15 .40
24 Brad Nelson XRC .15 .40
25 Justin Pope XRC .15 .40
26 Dan Haren XRC .75 2.00
27 Andy Sisco XRC .15 .40
28 Ryan Theriot XRC 1.25 3.00
29 Ricky Nolasco XRC .75 2.00
30 Jon Switzer XRC .15 .40
31 Justin Wechsler XRC .15 .40
32 Mike Gosling XRC .15 .40
33 Scott Hairston XRC .20 .50
34 Brian Pilkington XRC .15 .40
35 Kole Strayhorn XRC .15 .40
36 David Taylor XRC .15 .40
37 Donald Levinski XRC .15 .40
38 Mike Hinckley XRC .20 .50
39 Nick Long XRC .15 .40

Card	Low	High
40 Brad Hennessey XRC	.20	.50
41 Noah Lowry XRC	.75	2.00
42 Josh Cram XRC	.15	.40
43 Jesse Foppert XRC	.20	.50
44 Julian Benavidez XRC	.15	.40
45 Dan Denham XRC	.15	.40
46 Travis Foley XRC	.15	.40
47 Mike Conroy XRC	.15	.40
48 Jake Dittler XRC	.15	.40
49 Rene Rivera XRC	.15	.40
50 John Cole XRC	.15	.40
51 Lazaro Abreu XRC	.15	.40
52 David Wright XRC	3.00	8.00
53 Aaron Heilman XRC	.20	.50
54 Len DiNardo XRC	.15	.40
55 Alhaji Turay XRC	.15	.40
56 Chris Smith XRC	.15	.40
57 Rommie Lewis XRC	.15	.40
58 Bryan Bass XRC	.15	.40
59 David Crouthers XRC	.15	.40
60 Josh Barfield XRC	1.25	3.00
61 Jake Peavy XRC	1.25	3.00
62 Ryan Howard XRC	4.00	10.00
63 Gavin Floyd XRC	.40	1.00
64 Michael Floyd XRC	.15	.40
65 Stefan Bailie XRC	.15	.40
66 Jon DeVries XRC	.15	.40
67 Steve Kelly XRC	.15	.40
68 Alan Moye XRC	.15	.40
69 Justin Gillman XRC	.15	.40
70 Jayson Nix XRC	.15	.40
71 John Draper XRC	.15	.40
72 Kenny Baugh XRC	.15	.40
73 Michael Woods XRC	.15	.40
74 Preston Larrison XRC	.20	.50
75 Matt Coenen XRC	.15	.40
76 Scott Tyler XRC	.20	.50
77 Jose Morales XRC	.15	.40
78 Corwin Malone XRC	.15	.40
79 Dennis Ulacia XRC	.15	.40
80 Andy Gonzalez XRC	.15	.40
81 Kris Honel XRC	.15	.40
82 Wyatt Allen XRC	.15	.40
83 Ryan Wing XRC	.15	.40
84 Sean Henn XRC	.15	.40
85 John-Ford Griffin XRC	.15	.40
86 Bronson Sardinha XRC	.15	.40
87 Jon Skaggs XRC	.15	.40
88 Shelley Duncan XRC	1.50	4.00
89 Jason Arnold XRC	.15	.40
90 Aaron Rifkin XRC	.15	.40
91 Colt Griffin AU XRC	6.00	15.00
92 J.D. Martin AU XRC	6.00	15.00
93 Justin Wayne AU XRC	6.00	15.00
94 J.VanBenschoten AU XRC	6.00	15.00
95 Chris Burke AU XRC	10.00	25.00
96 Casey Kotchman AU XRC	6.00	15.00
97 Michael Garciaparra AU XRC	6.00	15.00
98 Jake Gautreau AU XRC	6.00	15.00
99 Jerome Williams AU XRC	6.00	15.00
100 Toe Nash AU XRC	6.00	15.00
101 Joe Borchard AU XRC	6.00	15.00
102 Mark Prior AU XRC	12.50	30.00

2001 Upper Deck Prospect Premieres Heroes of Baseball Game Bat

STATED ODDS 1:18

Card	Low	High
BAO Al Oliver	3.00	8.00
BBB Bill Buckner	3.00	8.00
BBM Bill Madlock	3.00	8.00
BDB Don Baylor	3.00	8.00
BDE Dwight Evans	4.00	10.00
BDL Davey Lopes	3.00	8.00
BDP Dave Parker	3.00	8.00
BDW Dave Winfield	3.00	8.00
BEM Eddie Murray	4.00	10.00
BFL Fred Lynn	3.00	8.00
BGC Gary Carter	3.00	8.00
BGM Gary Matthews	3.00	8.00
BJM Joe Morgan	3.00	8.00
BKEG Ken Griffey Sr.	3.00	8.00
BKIG Kirk Gibson	3.00	8.00
BKP Kirby Puckett	4.00	10.00
BMM Manny Mota	3.00	8.00
BOS Ozzie Smith	4.00	10.00
BRJ Reggie Jackson	4.00	10.00
BSG Steve Garvey	3.00	8.00
BTM Tim McCarver	3.00	8.00
BTP Tony Perez	3.00	8.00
BWB Wade Boggs	4.00	10.00

2001 Upper Deck Prospect Premieres Heroes of Baseball Game Jersey Duos

STATED ODDS 1:144

Card	Low	High
JBH B.Bass/J.Hardy	5.00	12.00
JDG S.Duncan/T.Godwin	10.00	25.00
JGS S.Garvey/R.Smith	3.00	8.00
JHB A.Heilman/J.Bonderman	3.00	8.00
JJJ M.Jordan/M.Jordan	20.00	50.00
JSG J.Switzer/M.Gosling	3.00	8.00
JWP D.Winfield/K.Puckett	10.00	25.00

2001 Upper Deck Prospect Premieres Heroes of Baseball Game Jersey Trios

STATED ODDS 1:144

Card	Low	High
BBC Burke/Bass/Crosby	4.00	10.00
CGS Crosby/Garciaparra/Sard	4.00	10.00
GGH Gautreau/Godwin/Heilman	3.00	8.00
GKB Gross/Kotchman/Baugh	3.00	8.00
GMS Griffin/Martin/Switzer	3.00	8.00
JMD Jordan/Mantle/DiMag	150.00	250.00
JPW Jordan/Puckett/Winfield	30.00	60.00
MMD Maris/Mant/DiMag SP	250.00	400.00
VPJ VanBen/Prior/Jones	4.00	10.00

2001 Upper Deck Prospect Premieres MJ Grandslam Game Bat

Card	Low	High
COMMON CARD (MJ1-MJ4)	10.00	25.00
MJ5 Michael Jordan SP	12.50	30.00

2001 Upper Deck Prospect Premieres Tribute to 42

STATED ODDS 1:750
NO AUTO PRICING DUE TO SCARCITY

Card	Low	High
B J.Robinson Bat	20.00	50.00
J J.Robinson Pants	20.00	50.00
GB J.Robinson Gold Bat/42	30.00	60.00
GJ J.Robinson Pants Gold/42	30.00	60.00

2002 Upper Deck Prospect Premieres

Card	Low	High
COMP.SET w/o SP's (72)	25.00	40.00
COMMON CARD (1-60)	.15	.40
COMMON CARD (61-85)	2.00	5.00
61-85 JSY STATED ODDS 1:18		
COMMON CARD (86-97)	3.00	8.00
86-97 AU STATED ODDS 1:18		
COMMON RIPKEN (98-99)	.75	2.00
COMMON MCGWIRE (100-105)	.75	2.00
COMMON DIMAGGIO (106-109)	.60	1.50
PENDER COR AVAIL.VIA MAIL EXCHANGE		
1 Josh Rupe XRC	.15	.40
2 Blair Johnson XRC	.15	.40
3 Jason Pridie XRC	.15	.40
4 Tim Gilhooly XRC	.15	.40
5 Kennard Jones XRC	.15	.40
6 Darrell Rasner XRC	.15	.40
7 Adam Donachie XRC	.15	.40
8 Josh Murray XRC	.15	.40
9 Brian Dopirak XRC	.40	1.00
10 Jason Cooper XRC	.15	.40
11 Zach Hammes XRC	.15	.40
12 Jon Lester XRC	5.00	12.00
13 Kevin Jepsen XRC	.20	.50
14 Curtis Granderson XRC	3.00	8.00
15 David Bush XRC	.40	1.00
16 Joel Guzman	.30	.75
17A M.Pender UER Granderson	.60	1.50
17B Matt Pender COR	.40	1.00
18 Derick Grigsby XRC	.15	.40
19 Jeremy Reed XRC	.40	1.00
20 Jonathan Broxton XRC	.40	1.00
21 Jesse Crain XRC	.30	.75
22 Justin Jones XRC	.20	.50
23 Brian Slocum XRC	.15	.40
24 Brian McCann XRC	3.00	8.00
25 Francisco Liriano XRC	3.00	8.00
26 Fred Lewis XRC	.15	.40
27 Steve Stanley XRC	.15	.40
28 Chris Snyder XRC	.20	.50
29 Dan Cevette XRC	.15	.40
30 Kiel Fisher XRC	.20	.50
31 Brandon Weeden XRC	1.00	2.50
32 Pat Osborn XRC	.15	.40
33 Taber Lee XRC	.15	.40
34 Dan Ortmeier XRC	.20	.50
35 Josh Johnson XRC	1.50	4.00
36 Val Majewski XRC	.15	.40
37 Larry Broadway XRC	.15	.40
38 Joey Gomes XRC	.15	.40
39 Eric Thomas XRC	.15	.40
40 James Loney XRC	2.00	5.00
41 Charlie Morton XRC	2.00	5.00
42 Mark McLemore XRC	.15	.40
43 Matt Craig XRC	.20	.50
44 Ryan Rodriguez XRC	.15	.40
45 Rich Hill XRC	1.25	3.00
46 Bob Malek XRC	.15	.40
47 Justin Maureau XRC	.15	.40
48 Randy Braun XRC	.15	.40
49 Brian Grant XRC	.15	.40
50 Tyler Davidson XRC	.20	.50
51 Travis Hanson XRC	.20	.50
52 Kyle Boyer XRC	.15	.40
53 James Holcomb XRC	.15	.40
54 Ryan Williams XRC	.15	.40
55 Ben Crockett XRC	.15	.40
56 Adam Greenberg XRC	1.25	3.00
57 John Baker XRC	.15	.40
58 Matt Carson XRC	.15	.40
59 Jonathan George XRC	.15	.40
60 David Jensen XRC	.15	.40
61 Nick Swisher JSY XRC	4.00	10.00
62 Brent Clevlen JSY UER XRC	3.00	8.00
63 Royce Ring JSY XRC	2.00	5.00
64 Mike Nixon JSY XRC	2.00	5.00
65 Ricky Barrett JSY XRC	2.00	5.00
66 Russ Adams JSY XRC	2.00	5.00
67 Joe Mauer JSY XRC	12.00	30.00
68 Jeff Francoeur JSY XRC	5.00	12.00
69 Joe Blanton JSY XRC	3.00	8.00
70 Micah Schilling JSY XRC	2.00	5.00
71 John McCurdy JSY XRC	2.00	5.00
72 Sergio Santos JSY XRC	3.00	8.00
73 Josh Womack JSY XRC	2.00	5.00
74 Jared Doyle JSY XRC	2.00	5.00
75 Ben Fritz JSY XRC	2.00	5.00
76 Greg Miller JSY XRC	2.00	5.00
77 Luke Hagerty JSY XRC	2.00	5.00
78 Matt Whitney JSY XRC	2.00	5.00
79 Dan Meyer JSY XRC	3.00	8.00
80 Bill Murphy JSY XRC	2.00	5.00
81 Zach Segovia JSY XRC	2.00	5.00
82 Steve Obenchain JSY XRC	2.00	5.00
83 Matt Clanton JSY XRC	2.00	5.00
84 Mark Teahen JSY XRC	3.00	8.00
85 Kyle Pawelczyk JSY XRC	2.00	5.00
86 Khalil Greene AU XRC	3.00	8.00
87 Joe Saunders AU XRC	3.00	8.00
88 Jeremy Hermida AU XRC	3.00	8.00
89 Drew Meyer AU XRC	3.00	8.00
90 Jeff Francis AU XRC	6.00	15.00
91 Scott Moore AU XRC	3.00	8.00
92 Prince Fielder AU XRC	10.00	25.00
93 Zack Greinke AU XRC	125.00	300.00
94 Chris Gruler AU XRC	3.00	8.00
95 Scott Kazmir AU XRC	5.00	12.00
96 B.J. Upton AU XRC	5.00	12.00
97 Clint Everts AU XRC	3.00	8.00
98 Cal Ripken TRIB	.75	2.00
99 Cal Ripken TRIB	.75	2.00
100 Mark McGwire TRIB	.75	2.00
101 Mark McGwire TRIB	.75	2.00
102 Mark McGwire TRIB	.75	2.00
103 Mark McGwire TRIB	.75	2.00
104 Mark McGwire TRIB	.75	2.00
105 Joe DiMaggio TRIB	.60	1.50
106 Joe DiMaggio TRIB	.60	1.50
107 Joe DiMaggio TRIB	.60	1.50
108 Joe DiMaggio TRIB	.60	1.50
109 Joe DiMaggio TRIB	.60	1.50

2002 Upper Deck Prospect Premieres Future Gems Quads

ONE PER SEALED BOX
STATED PRINT RUN 600 SERIAL #'d SETS
LISTED ALPHABETICAL BY TOP LEFT CARD

Card	Low	High
1 David Bush	3.00	8.00
Matt Craig		
Josh Johnson		
Brian McCann		
2 Jason Cooper	3.00	8.00
Jonathan George		
Larry Broadway		
Joel Guzman		
3 Matt Craig	3.00	8.00
Josh Murray		
Brian McCann		
Jason Pridie		
4 Jesse Crain	3.00	8.00
Brian Grant		
Curtis Granderson		
Joey Gomes		
5 Tyler Davidson	3.00	8.00
Val Majewski		
Justin Jones		
Daniel Cevette		
6 Dim/Lest/McG/McL	8.00	20.00
7 Jonathan George	3.00	8.00
Jeremy Reed		
Adam Donachie		
Matt Carson		
8 Jonathan George	3.00	8.00
Eric Thomas		
Joel Guzman		
Kiel Fisher		
9 Tim Gilhooly	3.00	8.00
Brandon Weeden		
Brian Slocum		
Brian Dopirak		
10 Grant/Hull/Gom/Dim	4.00	10.00
11 Grig/Mal/Loney/Lewis	5.00	12.00
12 Zach Hammes	3.00	8.00
James Holcomb		
Cal Ripken		
Kennard Jones		
13 Hill/McG/Grant/Carson	5.00	12.00
14 James Holcomb	3.00	8.00
David Jensen		
Kennard Jones		
Ryan Williams		
15 Jens/Lir/Will/Hans	5.00	12.00
16 Josh Johnson	3.00	8.00
Jesse Crain		
Adam Greenberg		
Curtis Granderson		
17 Lest/Grge/McL/Don	8.00	20.00
18 Lir/McG/Han/Lee	5.00	12.00
19 Val Majewski	3.00	8.00
Charlie Morton		
Daniel Cevette		
Joey Gomes		
20 Bob Malek	3.00	8.00
Zach Hammes		
Fred Lewis		
Cal Ripken		
21 Justin Maureau	3.00	8.00
Joe DiMaggio		
Chris Snyder		
Mark McGwire		
22 Mark McGwire	3.00	8.00
Bob Malek		
Joe DiMaggio		
Kyle Boyer		
23 Charlie Morton	3.00	8.00
David Bush#Joey Gomes		
Josh Johnson		
24 Josh Murray	3.00	8.00
Mark McGwire		
Jason Pridie		
Joe DiMaggio		
25 Matt Pender UER	3.00	8.00
Mark McGwire		
Mark McLemore		
Ryan Rodriguez		
26 Jason Pridie	3.00	8.00
Josh Murray		
Matt Craig		
Brian McCann		
27 Jeremy Reed	3.00	8.00
Josh Johnson		
Matt Carson		
Adam Greenberg		
28 Cal Ripken	3.00	8.00
Jason Cooper		
Matt Carson		
Larry Broadway		
29 Ryan Rodriguez	3.00	8.00
Eric Thomas		
Pat Osborn		
Randy Braun		
30 Josh Rupe	3.00	8.00
Tyler Davidson		
John Baker		
Justin Jones		
31 Thom/Grig/Brau/Lon	5.00	12.00
32 Eric Thomas	3.00	8.00
Matt Pender UER		
Kiel Fisher		
Mark McLemore		
33 Weed/Hill/Dop/Grnt	5.00	12.00

2002 Upper Deck Prospect Premieres Heroes of Baseball

Card	Low	High
COMP.RIPKEN SET (10)	8.00	20.00
COMMON RIPKEN (CR1-HDR)	1.00	2.50
COMP.DIMAGGIO SET (10)	4.00	10.00
COMMON DIMAGGIO (JD1-HDR)	.50	1.25
COMP.MORGAN SET (10)	2.00	5.00
COMMON MORGAN (JM1-HDR)	.30	.75
COMP.MCGWIRE SET (10)	8.00	20.00
COMMON MCGWIRE (MC1-HDR)	1.00	2.50
COMP.MANTLE SET (10)	10.00	25.00
COMMON MANTLE (MM1-HDR)	1.25	3.00
COMP.OZZIE SET (10)	6.00	15.00
COMMON OZZIE (OS1-HDR)	.75	2.00
COMP.GWYNN SET (10)	6.00	15.00
COMMON GWYNN (TG1-HDR)	.75	2.00
COMP.SEAVER SET (10)	4.00	10.00
COMMON SEAVER (TS1-HDR)	.50	1.25
COMP.STARGELL SET (10)	.20	5.00
COMMON STARGELL (WS1-HDR)	.30	.75
STATED ODDS 1:1		

2002 Upper Deck Prospect Premieres Heroes of Baseball 85 Quads

Card	Low	High
1 DiMaggio	4.00	10.00
Gwynn		
Gwy		
DiMag		
2 Joe DiMaggio	6.00	15.00
Tony Gwynn		
Cal Ripken		
Cal Ripken		
3 Joe DiMaggio Hdr	6.00	15.00
Mickey Mantle		
Willie Stargell Hdr		
Mickey Mantle		
4 Tony Gwynn	4.00	10.00
Tony Gwynn		
Ozzie Smith		
Willie Stargell		
5 Tony Gwynn	4.00	10.00
Willie Stargell		
Joe DiMaggio		
Joe Morgan		
6 Tony Gwynn	4.00	10.00
Willie Stargell		
Cal Ripken		
Ozzie Smith		
7 Mickey Mantle	6.00	15.00
Mark McGwire		
Joe Morgan		
Tom Seaver		
8 Mickey Mantle	6.00	15.00
Tom Seaver		
Mickey Mantle		
Tom Seaver		
9 Mark McGwire	6.00	15.00
Joe Morgan		
Mark McGwire		
Joe Morgan		
10 Mark McGwire Hdr	6.00	15.00
Cal Ripken		
Tony Gwynn		
Joe DiMaggio		
11 Mark McGwire	4.00	10.00
Tom Seaver		
Joe Morgan		
Ozzie Smith		
12 Joe Morgan	4.00	10.00
Tony Gwynn		
Joe Morgan		
Tony Gwynn		
13 Joe Morgan	6.00	15.00
Joe DiMaggio		
Mickey Mantle		
Cal Ripken		
14 Joe Morgan	4.00	10.00
Joe DiMaggio		
Willie Stargell		
Tony Gwynn		
15 Ozzie Smith	4.00	10.00
Joe DiMaggio		
Ozzie Smith		
Willie Stargell		
16 Ozzie Smith	4.00	10.00
Mark McGwire		
Willie Stargell		
Tony Gwynn		
17 Ozzie Smith	4.00	10.00
Tom Seaver		
Tom Seaver		
Mark McGwire		
18 Cal Ripken	6.00	15.00
Mickey Mantle		
Joe DiMaggio		
Joe Morgan		
19 Cal Ripken	6.00	15.00
Mark McGwire		
Cal Ripken		
Mark McGwire		
20 Tom Seaver	4.00	10.00
Joe DiMaggio		
Tom Seaver		
Joe DiMaggio		
21 Tom Seaver	4.00	10.00
Joe Morgan		
Ozzie Smith		
Willie Stargell		
22 Tom Seaver	6.00	15.00
Cal Ripken		
Mark McGwire		
Mickey Mantle		
23 Willie Stargell	4.00	10.00
Ozzie Smith		
Ozzie Smith		
Willie Stargell		
24 Willie Stargell	4.00	10.00
Ozzie Smith		
Tom Seaver		
Joe Morgan		

2003 Upper Deck Prospect Premieres

Card	Low	High
COMPLETE SET (90)	20.00	40.00
1 Bryan Opdyke XRC	.20	.50
2 Gabriel Sosa XRC	.20	.50
3 Tila Reynolds XRC	.20	.50
4 Aaron Hill XRC	.60	1.50
5 Aaron Marsden XRC	.20	.50
6 Abe Alvarez XRC	.20	.50
7 Adam Jones XRC	5.00	12.00
8 Adam Miller XRC	.75	2.00
9 Andre Ethier XRC	2.50	6.00
10 Anthony Gwynn XRC	.20	.50
11 Brad Snyder XRC	.20	.50
12 Brad Sullivan XRC	.20	.50
13 Brian Anderson XRC	.20	.50
14 Brian Buscher XRC	.20	.50
15 Brian Snyder XRC	.20	.50
16 Carlos Quentin XRC	1.00	2.50
17 Chad Billingsley XRC	1.00	2.50
18 Fraser Dizard XRC	.20	.50
19 Chris Durbin XRC	.20	.50
20 Chris Ray XRC	.30	.75
21 Conor Jackson XRC	1.00	2.50
22 Kory Casto XRC	.20	.50
23 Craig Whitaker XRC	.20	.50
24 Daniel Moore XRC	.20	.50
25 Daric Barton XRC	.30	.75
26 Darin Downs XRC	.20	.50
27 David Murphy XRC	.50	1.25
28 Dustin Majewski XRC	.20	.50
29 Edgardo Baez XRC	.20	.50
30 Jake Fox XRC	.60	1.50
31 Jake Stevens XRC	.20	.50
32 Jamie D'Antona XRC	.20	.50
33 James Houser XRC	.20	.50
34 Jarrod Saltalamacchia XRC	1.00	2.50
35 Jason Hirsh XRC	.20	.50
36 Javi Herrera XRC	.20	.50
37 Jeff Allison XRC	.20	.50
38 John Hudgins XRC	.20	.50
39 Jo Jo Reyes XRC	.20	.50
40 Justin James XRC	.20	.50
41 Kurt Isenberg XRC	.20	.50
42 Kyle Boyer XRC	.20	.50
43 Lastings Milledge XRC	.60	1.50
44 Luis Atilano XRC	.20	.50
45 Matt Murton XRC	.20	.50
46 Matt Moses XRC	.50	1.25
47 Matt Harrison XRC	.75	2.00
48 Michael Bourn XRC	.60	1.50
49 Miguel Vega XRC	.20	.50
50 Mitch Maier XRC	.20	.50
51 Omar Quintanilla XRC	.20	.50
52 Ryan Sweeney XRC	.50	1.25
53 Scott Baker XRC	.50	1.25
54 Sean Rodriguez XRC	.30	.75
55 Steve Lerud XRC	.20	.50
56 Thomas Pauly XRC	.20	.50
57 Tom Gorzelanny XRC	.30	.75
58 Tim Moss XRC	.30	.75
59 Robbie Wooley XRC	.20	.50
60 Trey Webb XRC	.20	.50
61 Wes Littleton XRC	.20	.50
62 Beau Vaughan XRC	.20	.50
63 Willy Jo Ronda XRC	.20	.50
64 Chris Lubanski XRC	.20	.50
65 Ian Stewart XRC	.60	1.50
66 John Danks XRC	.50	1.25
67 Kyle Sleeth XRC	.20	.50
68 Michael Aubrey XRC	.50	1.25
69 Kevin Kouzmanoff XRC	1.50	4.00
70 Ryan Harvey XRC	.20	.50
71 Tim Stauffer XRC	.50	1.25
72 Tony Richie XRC	.20	.50
73 Brandon Wood XRC	1.25	3.00
74 David Aardsma XRC	.20	.50
75 David Shinskie XRC	.20	.50
76 Dennis Dove XRC	.20	.50
77 Eric Sultemeier XRC	.20	.50
78 Jay Sborz XRC	.20	.50
79 Jimmy Barthmaier XRC	.20	.50
80 Josh Whitesell XRC	.20	.50
81 Josh Anderson XRC	.20	.50
82 Kenny Lewis XRC	.20	.50
83 Mateo Miramontes XRC	.20	.50
84 Nick Markakis XRC	1.50	4.00
85 Paul Bacot XRC	.20	.50
86 Peter Stonard XRC	.20	.50
87 Reggie Willits XRC	.75	2.00
88 Shane Costa XRC	.20	.50
89 Billy Sadler XRC	.20	.50
90 Delmon Young XRC	1.25	3.00

2003 Upper Deck Prospect Premieres Autographs

STATED ODDS 1:9
CARDS 18/28/47/54/59/69 DO NOT EXIST

Card	Low	High
P1 Bryan Opdyke	4.00	10.00
P2 Gabriel Sosa	4.00	10.00
P3 Tila Reynolds	4.00	10.00
P4 Aaron Hill	6.00	15.00
P5 Aaron Marsden	4.00	10.00
P6 Abe Alvarez	6.00	15.00
P7 Adam Jones	40.00	80.00
P8 Adam Miller	4.00	10.00
P9 Andre Ethier	8.00	20.00
P10 Anthony Gwynn	4.00	10.00
P11 Brad Snyder	6.00	15.00
P12 Brad Sullivan	4.00	10.00
P13 Brian Anderson	15.00	30.00
P14 Brian Buscher	6.00	15.00
P15 Brian Snyder	4.00	10.00
P16 Carlos Quentin	4.00	10.00
P17 Chad Billingsley	5.00	12.00
P19 Chris Durbin	4.00	10.00
P20 Chris Ray	6.00	15.00
P21 Conor Jackson	4.00	10.00
P22 Kory Casto	6.00	15.00
P23 Craig Whitaker	6.00	15.00
P24 Daniel Moore	4.00	10.00
P25 Daric Barton	4.00	10.00
P26 Darin Downs	6.00	15.00
P27 David Murphy	4.00	10.00
P29 Edgardo Baez	6.00	15.00
P30 Jake Fox	10.00	25.00
P31 Jake Stevens	6.00	15.00
P32 Jamie D'Antona	6.00	15.00
P33 James Houser	4.00	10.00
P34 Jarrod Saltalamacchia	6.00	15.00
P35 Jason Hirsh	4.00	10.00
P36 Javi Herrera	4.00	10.00
P37 Jeff Allison	4.00	10.00
P38 John Hudgins	4.00	10.00
P39 Jo Jo Reyes	4.00	10.00
P40 Justin James	4.00	10.00
P41 Kurt Isenberg	4.00	10.00
P42 Kyle Boyer	4.00	10.00
P43 Lastings Milledge	6.00	15.00
P44 Luis Atilano	4.00	10.00
P45 Matt Murton	4.00	10.00
P46 Matt Moses	8.00	20.00
P48 Michael Bourn	8.00	20.00
P49 Miguel Vega	4.00	10.00
P50 Mitch Maier	6.00	15.00
P51 Omar Quintanilla	6.00	15.00
P52 Ryan Sweeney	5.00	12.00
P53 Scott Baker	4.00	10.00
P55 Steve Lerud	6.00	15.00
P56 Thomas Pauly	4.00	10.00
P57 Tom Gorzelanny	4.00	10.00
P58 Tim Moss	6.00	15.00
P60 Trey Webb	4.00	10.00
P61 Wes Littleton	6.00	15.00
P62 Beau Vaughan	6.00	15.00
P63 Willy Jo Ronda	6.00	15.00
P64 Chris Lubanski	8.00	20.00
P65 Ian Stewart	8.00	20.00
P66 John Danks	8.00	20.00
P67 Kyle Sleeth	6.00	15.00
P68 Michael Aubrey	4.00	10.00
P70 Ryan Harvey	10.00	25.00
P71 Tim Stauffer	4.00	10.00

2003 Upper Deck Prospect Premieres Game Jersey

STATED ODDS 1:18
CARD 90 DOES NOT EXIST

Card	Low	High
P72 Tony Richie	2.00	5.00
P73 Brandon Wood	6.00	15.00
P74 David Aardsma	3.00	8.00
P75 David Shinskie	2.00	5.00
P76 Dennis Dove	3.00	8.00
P77 Eric Sultimeier	2.00	5.00
P78 Jay Sborz	2.00	5.00
P79 Jimmy Barthmaier	3.00	8.00
P80 Josh Whitesell	2.00	5.00
P81 Josh Anderson	3.00	8.00
P82 Kenny Lewis	3.00	8.00
P83 Mateo Miramontes	2.00	5.00
P84 Nick Markakis	15.00	40.00
P85 Paul Bacot	3.00	8.00
P86 Peter Stonard	2.00	5.00
P87 Reggie Willits	10.00	25.00
P88 Shane Costa	2.00	5.00
P89 Billy Sadler	2.00	5.00
P91 Kyle Sleeth	3.00	8.00
P92 Ian Stewart	6.00	15.00
P93 Fraser Dizard	2.00	5.00
P94 Abe Alvarez	3.00	8.00
P95 Adam Jones	12.50	30.00
P96 Brian Anderson	3.00	8.00
P97 Chris Durbin	2.00	5.00
P98 Craig Whitaker	3.00	8.00
P99 Jake Fox	5.00	12.00
P100 Kurt Isenberg	2.00	5.00
P101 Luis Atilano	2.00	5.00
P102 Miguel Vega	2.00	5.00
P103 Mitch Maier	3.00	8.00
P104 Ryan Sweeney	4.00	10.00
P105 Scott Baker	3.00	8.00
P106 Sean Rodriguez	4.00	10.00
P108 Trey Webb	2.00	5.00
P109 Willy Jo Ronda	3.00	8.00
P110 John Danks	3.00	8.00
P111 Michael Aubrey	3.00	8.00
P112 Lastings Milledge	6.00	15.00
P113 Chris Lubanski	3.00	8.00

2004 Upper Deck r-class

Card	Low	High
COMPLETE SET (180)	50.00	100.00
COMP.SET w/o SP'S (90)	8.00	20.00
COMMON CARD (1-90)	.10	.30
COMMON CARD (91-180)	.40	1.00
91-180 STATED ODDS 1:2		
1 Adam Dunn	.20	.50
2 Jose Vidro	.12	.30
3 Vladimir Guerrero	.20	.50
4 Hideo Nomo	.30	.75
5 Eric Chavez	.12	.30
6 Carlos Delgado	.12	.30
7 Javy Lopez	.12	.30
8 Javier Vazquez	.12	.30
9 Miguel Cabrera	.30	.75
10 Manny Ramirez	.30	.75
11 Scott Rolen	.20	.50
12 Rafael Furcal	.12	.30
13 Jim Thome	.20	.50
14 Edgar Renteria	.12	.30
15 Jason Kendall	.12	.30
16 Alfonso Soriano	.20	.50
17 Troy Glaus	.12	.30
18 Vernon Wells	.12	.30
19 Todd Helton	.20	.50
20 Mark Mulder	.12	.30
21 Albert Pujols	.40	1.00
22 Andy Pettitte	.20	.50
23 Kevin Millwood	.12	.30
24 Bret Boone	.12	.30
25 Ken Griffey Jr.	.60	1.50
26 Kevin Brown	.12	.30
27 J.D. Drew	.12	.30
28 Corey Patterson	.12	.30
29 Jason Giambi	.12	.30
30 Jason Schmidt	.12	.30
31 Jose Reyes	.20	.50
32 Torii Hunter	.12	.30
33 Brian Giles	.12	.30
34 Garret Anderson	.12	.30
35 Mark Teixeira	.20	.50
36 Sammy Sosa	.30	.75
37 Rocco Baldelli	.12	.30
38 Jeff Bagwell	.20	.50
39 Rafael Palmeiro	.20	.50
40 Derrek Lee	.12	.30
41 Randy Johnson	.30	.75
42 Roger Clemens	.40	1.00
43 Austin Kearns	.12	.30
44 Dontrelle Willis	.12	.30
45 Lance Berkman	.20	.50
46 Juan Gonzalez	.12	.30
47 Ichiro Suzuki	.40	1.00
48 Pat Burrell	.12	.30
49 Miguel Tejada	.20	.50
50 Mike Piazza	.30	.75
51 Mark Prior	.20	.50
52 C.C. Sabathia	.20	.50
53 Jacque Jones	.12	.30
54 Carlos Beltran	.20	.50
55 Mike Mussina	.20	.50
56 Mike Lowell	.12	.30
57 Phil Nevin	.12	.30
58 Andruw Jones	.12	.30
59 Barry Zito	.20	.50
60 Magglio Ordonez	.20	.50
61 Carlos Lee	.12	.30
62 Nomar Garciaparra	.20	.50
63 Kerry Wood	.12	.30
64 Luis Gonzalez	.12	.30
65 Derek Jeter	.75	2.00
66 Preston Wilson	.12	.30
67 Greg Maddux	.40	1.00
68 Pedro Martinez	.20	.50
69 Richie Sexson	.12	.30
70 Hank Blalock	.12	.30
71 Chipper Jones	.30	.75
72 Ivan Rodriguez	.20	.50
73 Roy Halladay	.20	.50
74 Tim Hudson	.20	.50
75 Ryan Klesko	.12	.30
76 Hideki Matsui	.50	1.25
77 Josh Beckett	.12	.30
78 Brandon Webb	.12	.30
79 Alex Rodriguez	.40	1.00
80 Jim Edmonds	.20	.50
81 Jeff Kent	.12	.30
82 Bobby Abreu	.12	.30
83 Curt Schilling	.20	.50
84 Roy Oswalt	.20	.50
85 Orlando Cabrera	.12	.30
86 Johan Santana	.20	.50
87 Geoff Jenkins	.12	.30
88 Gary Sheffield	.12	.30
89 Shawn Green	.12	.30
90 Frank Thomas	.30	.75
91 Tim Hamulack TC RC	.40	1.00
92 Shingo Takatsu TC RC	.40	1.00
93 Justin Huisman TC RC	.40	1.00
94 Sean Henn TC RC	.40	1.00
95 Jamie Brown TC RC	.40	1.00
96 Dennis Sarfate TC RC	.40	1.00
97 Lincoln Holdzkom TC RC	.40	1.00
98 Roman Colon TC RC	.40	1.00
99 Scott Dohmann TC RC	.40	1.00
100 Ivan Ochoa TC RC	.40	1.00
101 Akinori Otsuka TC RC	.40	1.00
102 Fernando Nieve TC RC	.40	1.00
103 Mike Johnston TC RC	.40	1.00
104 Mariano Gomez TC RC	.40	1.00
105 Justin Leone TC RC	.40	1.00
106 Evan Rust TC RC	.40	1.00
107 Mike Rouse TC RC	.40	1.00
108 Ian Snell TC RC	.40	1.00
109 Jason Bartlett TC RC	1.25	3.00
110 Ryan Wing TC RC	.40	1.00
111 Nick Regilio TC RC	.40	1.00
112 Merkin Valdez TC RC	.40	1.00
113 Josh Labandeira TC RC	.40	1.00
114 David Aardsma TC RC	.40	1.00
115 Justin Knoedler TC RC	.40	1.00
116 Shawn Hill TC RC	.40	1.00
117 Casey Daigle TC RC	.40	1.00
118 Donnie Kelly TC RC	.60	1.50
119 Justin Germano TC RC	.40	1.00
120 Eddy Rodriguez TC RC	.40	1.00
121 Onil Joseph TC RC	.40	1.00
122 Michael Wuertz TC RC	.40	1.00
123 Roberto Novoa TC RC	.40	1.00
124 Jerome Gamble TC RC	.40	1.00
125 Justin Hampson TC RC	.40	1.00
126 Ronald Belisario TC RC	.40	1.00
127 Tim Bausher TC RC	.40	1.00
128 Chris Saenz TC RC	.40	1.00
129 Hector Gimenez TC RC	.40	1.00
130 Ronny Cedeno TC RC	.40	1.00
131 Jason Frasor TC RC	.40	1.00
132 Kazuo Matsui TC RC	.60	1.50
133 Mike Gosling TC RC	.40	1.00
134 Jerry Gil TC RC	.40	1.00
135 Orlando Rodriguez TC RC	.40	1.00
136 Jorge Vasquez TC RC	.40	1.00
137 Chris Aguila TC RC	.40	1.00
138 Tim Bittner TC RC	.40	1.00
139 Jake Woods TC RC	.40	1.00
140 Enemencio Pacheco TC RC	.40	1.00
141 Dave Crouthers TC RC	.40	1.00
142 Jose Capellan TC RC	.40	1.00
143 Chad Bentz TC RC	.40	1.00
144 Mike Vento TC RC	.40	1.00
145 Scott Proctor TC RC	.40	1.00
146 Edwin Moreno TC RC	.40	1.00
147 Brandon Medders TC RC	.40	1.00
148 Renyel Pinto TC RC	.40	1.00
149 Rusty Tucker TC RC	.40	1.00
150 Ryan Meaux TC RC	.40	1.00
151 William Bergolla TC RC	.40	1.00
152 Angel Chavez TC RC	.40	1.00
153 Colby Miller TC RC	.40	1.00
154 John Gall TC RC	.40	1.00
155 Carlos Hines TC RC	.40	1.00
156 Carlos Vasquez TC RC	.40	1.00
157 Justin Lehr TC RC	.40	1.00
158 Kevin Cave TC RC	.40	1.00
159 Jeff Bennett TC RC	.40	1.00
160 Greg Dobbs TC RC	.40	1.00
161 Jorge Sequea TC RC	.40	1.00
162 Chris Oxspring TC RC	.40	1.00
163 Franklyn Gracesqui TC RC	.40	1.00
164 Shawn Camp TC RC	.40	1.00
165 Lino Urdaneta TC RC	.40	1.00
166 Luis A. Gonzalez TC RC	.40	1.00
167 Ramon Ramirez TC RC	.40	1.00
168 Freddy Guzman TC RC	.40	1.00
169 Chris Shelton TC RC	.40	1.00
170 Andres Blanco TC RC	.40	1.00
171 Aarom Baldiris TC RC	.40	1.00
172 Kazuhito Tadano TC RC	.40	1.00
173 Brian Dallimore TC RC	.40	1.00
174 Eduardo Villacis TC RC	.40	1.00
175 Frank Francisco TC RC	.40	1.00
176 Edwin Jackson TC	.40	1.00
177 Bobby Crosby TC	.40	1.00
178 Joe Mauer TC	.75	2.00
179 Rickie Weeks TC	.40	1.00
180 Delmon Young TC	.60	1.50

2004 Upper Deck r-class First Class Autograph Black

STATED ODDS 1:2880
BLUE RANDOM IN BLISTER BOXES
BLUE PRINT RUN 3 SERIAL #'d SETS
NO BLUE PRICING DUE TO SCARCITY

Card	Low	High
BL Barry Larkin	30.00	60.00

CD Carlos Delgado 15.00 40.00
DW Dontrelle Willis 20.00 50.00
EG Eric Gagne 20.00 50.00
EM Edgar Martinez 20.00 50.00
HR Horacio Ramirez 10.00 25.00
KG Ken Griffey Jr. 60.00 120.00
MC Miguel Cabrera 30.00 60.00
MP Mark Prior 15.00 40.00
PB Pat Burrell 15.00 40.00
PL Paul LoDuca 15.00 40.00
SA Sandy Alomar 10.00 25.00
TH Trevor Hoffman 15.00 40.00

2004 Upper Deck r-class Jersey

STATED ODDS 1:12
AJ Andruw Jones 3.00 8.00
AP Albert Pujols 6.00 15.00
AS Alfonso Soriano 2.00 5.00
BA Jeff Bagwell 3.00 8.00
BB Bret Boone 2.00 5.00
BW Bernie Williams 3.00 8.00
CD Carlos Delgado 2.00 5.00
CJ Chipper Jones 4.00 10.00
CS Curt Schilling 3.00 8.00
DJ Derek Jeter 8.00 20.00
DW Dontrelle Willis 3.00 8.00
EC Eric Chavez 2.00 5.00
EM Edgar Martinez 3.00 8.00
GL Troy Glaus 2.00 5.00
GS Gary Sheffield 2.00 5.00
HB Hank Blalock 2.00 5.00
HM Hideki Matsui 10.00 25.00
HN Hideo Nomo 4.00 10.00
HU Torii Hunter 2.00 5.00
IR Ivan Rodriguez 3.00 8.00
IS Ichiro Suzuki 10.00 25.00
JB Josh Beckett 2.00 5.00
JG Jason Giambi 2.00 5.00
KB Kevin Brown 2.00 5.00
KG Ken Griffey Jr. 5.00 12.00
KM Kazuo Matsui 3.00 8.00
KW Kerry Wood 2.00 5.00
MP Mark Prior 3.00 8.00
MR Manny Ramirez 3.00 8.00
MT Miguel Tejada 2.00 5.00
PI Mike Piazza 5.00 12.00
PM Pedro Martinez 3.00 8.00
RA Roberto Alomar 3.00 8.00
RB Rocco Baldelli 2.00 5.00
RC Roger Clemens 5.00 12.00
RI Mariano Rivera 4.00 10.00
RJ Randy Johnson 4.00 10.00
SR Scott Rolen 3.00 8.00
SS Sammy Sosa 4.00 10.00
TG Tom Glavine 3.00 8.00
TH Todd Helton 3.00 8.00
VG Vladimir Guerrero 4.00 10.00

2004 Upper Deck r-class Taking Over!

1-20 PRINT RUN 650 SERIAL #'d SETS
21-30 PRINT RUN 150 SERIAL #'d SETS
RANDOM INSERTS IN BLISTER BOXES
1 L.Overbay .75 2.00
R.Sexson
2 J.Phillips 2.00 5.00
M.Piazza
3 W.Bergolla 1.25 3.00
B.Larkin
4 J.DuBois .75 2.00
M.Alou
5 N.Logan .75 2.00
A.Sanchez
6 M.Valdez .75 2.00
R.Nen
7 F.Rodriguez 1.25 3.00
T.Percival
8 D.DeJesus 1.25 3.00
C.Beltran
9 M.Young 2.50 6.00
A.Rodriguez
10 A.Rios .75 2.00
V.Wells
11 G.Sizemore 1.25 3.00
M.Lawton
12 R.Wagner .75 2.00
D.Graves
13 M.Cabrera 2.00 5.00
J.Conine
14 J.Willingham 1.25 3.00
R.Castro
15 R.Weeks .75 2.00
J.Spivey
16 G.Quiroz .75 2.00
G.Myers
17 G.Koonce .75 2.00
S.Hatteberg
18 R.Reyes 1.25 3.00
L.Walker
19 K.Greene 1.25 3.00
R.Vazquez
20 O.Dotel .75 2.00
B.Wagner
21 J.Mauer 3.00 8.00
A.Pierzynski
22 J.Vazquez 5.00 12.00
R.Clemens
23 B.Webb 2.50 6.00
C.Schilling
24 D.Young 2.50 6.00
J.Cruz Jr.
25 V.Guerrero 2.50 6.00
T.Salmon
26 J.Drew 1.50 4.00
G.Sheffield
27 B.Crosby 2.50 6.00
M.Tejada
28 E.Jackson 1.50 4.00
K.Brown
29 K.Matsui 2.50 6.00
J.Reyes
30 W.Pena 8.00 20.00
K.Griffey Jr.

1998 Upper Deck Retro

The 1998 Upper Deck Retro set contains 129 standard size cards. The six-card packs retailed for $4.99 each. The set contains the subset: Futurama (101-130). The fronts feature current superstars as well as some retired legends surrounded by a four-sided white border and printed on super-thick, uncoated 24-pt stock card. The featured player's name lines the bottom border of the card. Card number 82 (originally slated to be Stan Musial) does not exist. Rookie Cards include Troy Glaus.

COMPLETE SET (129) 15.00 40.00
CARD NUMBER 82 DOES NOT EXIST
1 Jim Edmonds .15 .40
2 Darin Erstad .15 .40
3 Tim Salmon .25 .60
4 Jay Bell .15 .40
5 Matt Williams .15 .40
6 Andres Galarraga .15 .40
7 Andruw Jones .25 .60
8 Chipper Jones .40 1.00
9 Greg Maddux .60 1.50
10 Rafael Palmeiro .25 .60
11 Cal Ripken 1.25 3.00
12 Brooks Robinson .25 .60
13 Nomar Garciaparra .60 1.50
14 Pedro Martinez .25 .60
15 Mo Vaughn .15 .40
16 Ernie Banks .40 1.00
17 Mark Grace .25 .60
18 Gary Matthews Sr. .15 .40
19 Sammy Sosa .40 1.00
20 Albert Belle .15 .40
21 Carlton Fisk .25 .60
22 Frank Thomas .40 1.00
23 Ken Griffey Sr. .15 .40
24 Paul Konerko .15 .40
25 Barry Larkin .25 .60
26 Sean Casey .15 .40
27 Tony Perez .15 .40
28 Bob Feller .15 .40
29 Kenny Lofton .15 .40
30 Manny Ramirez .25 .60
31 Jim Thome .25 .60
32 Omar Vizquel .25 .60
33 Dante Bichette .15 .40
34 Larry Walker .15 .40
35 Tony Clark .15 .40
36 Damion Easley .15 .40
37 Cliff Floyd .15 .40
38 Livan Hernandez .15 .40
39 Jeff Bagwell .25 .60
40 Craig Biggio .25 .60
41 Al Kaline .40 1.00
42 Johnny Damon .25 .60
43 Dean Palmer .15 .40
44 Charles Johnson .15 .40
45 Eric Karros .15 .40
46 Gaylord Perry .15 .40
47 Raul Mondesi .15 .40
48 Gary Sheffield .15 .40
49 Eddie Mathews .40 1.00
50 Warren Spahn .25 .60
51 Jeromy Burnitz .15 .40
52 Jeff Cirillo .15 .40
53 Marquis Grissom .15 .40
54 Paul Molitor .15 .40
55 Kirby Puckett .40 1.00
56 Brad Radke .15 .40
57 Todd Walker .15 .40
58 Vladimir Guerrero .40 1.00
59 Brad Fullmer .15 .40
60 Rondell White .15 .40
61 Bobby Jones .15 .40
62 Hideo Nomo .40 1.00
63 Mike Piazza .60 1.50
64 Tom Seaver .25 .60
65 Frank Thomas .15 .40
66 Yogi Berra .40 1.00
67 Derek Jeter 1.00 2.50
68 Tino Martinez .25 .60
69 Paul O'Neill .25 .60
70 Andy Pettitte .25 .60
71 Rollie Fingers .15 .40
72 Rickey Henderson .40 1.00
73 Matt Stairs .15 .40
74 Scott Rolen .25 .60
75 Curt Schilling .15 .40
76 Jose Guillen .15 .40
77 Jason Kendall .15 .40
78 Lou Brock .25 .60
79 Bob Gibson .25 .60
80 Ray Lankford .15 .40
81 Mark McGwire 1.00 2.50
83 Kevin Brown .25 .60
84 Ken Caminiti .15 .40
85 Tony Gwynn .50 1.25
86 Greg Vaughn .15 .40
87 Barry Bonds 1.00 2.50
88 Willie Stargell .25 .60
89 Willie McCovey .15 .40
90 Ken Griffey Jr. .75 2.00
91 Randy Johnson .40 1.00
92 Alex Rodriguez .60 1.50
93 Quinton McCracken .15 .40
94 Fred McGriff .25 .60
95 Juan Gonzalez .15 .40
96 Ivan Rodriguez .25 .60
97 Nolan Ryan 1.00 2.50
98 Jose Canseco .25 .60
99 Roger Clemens .75 2.00
100 Jose Cruz Jr. .15 .40
101 Justin Baughman FUT RC .15 .40
102 Dave Dellucci FUT RC .30 .75
103 Travis Lee FUT .15 .40
104 Troy Glaus FUT RC .75 2.00
105 Kerry Wood FUT .20 .50
106 Mike Caruso FUT .15 .40
107 Jim Parque FUT RC .15 .40
108 Brett Tomko FUT .15 .40
109 Russell Branyan FUT .15 .40
110 Jaret Wright FUT .15 .40
111 Todd Helton FUT .25 .60
112 Gabe Alvarez FUT .15 .40
113 Matt Anderson FUT RC .15 .40
114 Alex Gonzalez FUT .15 .40
115 Mark Kotsay FUT .15 .40
116 Derrek Lee FUT .25 .60
117 Richard Hidalgo FUT .15 .40
118 Adrian Beltre FUT .15 .40
119 Geoff Jenkins FUT .15 .40
120 Eric Milton FUT .15 .40
121 Brad Fullmer FUT .15 .40
122 Vladimir Guerrero FUT .40 1.00
123 Carl Pavano FUT .15 .40
124 Orlando Hernandez FUT RC .60 1.50
125 Ben Grieve FUT .15 .40
126 A.J. Hinch FUT .15 .40
127 Matt Clement FUT .15 .40
128 Gary Matthews Jr. FUT RC .30 .75
129 Aramis Ramirez FUT .15 .40
130 Rolando Arrojo FUT RC .20 .50

1998 Upper Deck Retro Big Boppers

COMPLETE SET (30) 200.00 400.00
RANDOM INSERTS IN PACKS
STATED PRINT RUN 500 SERIAL #'d SETS
BB1 Darin Erstad 1.50 4.00
BB2 Rafael Palmeiro 2.50 6.00
BB3 Cal Ripken 12.50 30.00
BB4 Nomar Garciaparra 6.00 15.00
BB5 Mo Vaughn 1.50 4.00
BB6 Frank Thomas 4.00 10.00
BB7 Albert Belle 1.50 4.00
BB8 Jim Thome 2.50 6.00
BB9 Manny Ramirez 2.50 6.00
BB10 Tony Clark 1.50 4.00
BB11 Tino Martinez 2.50 6.00
BB12 Ben Grieve 1.50 4.00
BB13 Ken Griffey Jr. 8.00 20.00
BB14 Alex Rodriguez 6.00 15.00
BB15 Jay Buhner 1.50 4.00
BB16 Juan Gonzalez 1.50 4.00
BB17 Jose Cruz Jr. 1.50 4.00
BB18 Jose Canseco 2.50 6.00
BB19 Travis Lee 1.50 4.00
BB20 Chipper Jones 4.00 10.00
BB21 Andres Galarraga 1.50 4.00
BB22 Andruw Jones 2.50 6.00
BB23 Sammy Sosa 4.00 10.00
BB24 Vinny Castilla 1.50 4.00
BB25 Larry Walker 1.50 4.00
BB26 Jeff Bagwell 2.50 6.00
BB27 Gary Sheffield 1.50 4.00
BB28 Mike Piazza 6.00 15.00
BB29 Mark McGwire 10.00 25.00
BB30 Barry Bonds 10.00 25.00

1998 Upper Deck Retro Groovy Kind of Glove

COMPLETE SET (30) 60.00 120.00
STATED ODDS 1:7
G1 Roberto Alomar 2.00 5.00
G2 Cal Ripken 6.00 15.00
G3 Nomar Garciaparra 3.00 8.00
G4 Frank Thomas 2.00 5.00
G5 Robin Ventura .75 2.00
G6 Omar Vizquel 1.25 3.00
G7 Kenny Lofton .75 2.00
G8 Ben Grieve .75 2.00
G9 Alex Rodriguez 3.00 8.00
G10 Ken Griffey Jr. 4.00 10.00
G11 Ivan Rodriguez 1.25 3.00
G12 Travis Lee .75 2.00
G13 Matt Williams .75 2.00
G14 Greg Maddux 3.00 8.00
G15 Andres Galarraga .75 2.00
G16 Andruw Jones 1.25 3.00
G17 Kerry Wood 1.00 2.50
G18 Mark Grace 1.25 3.00
G19 Craig Biggio 1.25 3.00
G20 Charles Johnson .75 2.00
G21 Raul Mondesi .75 2.00
G22 Mike Piazza 3.00 8.00
G23 Rey Ordonez .75 2.00
G24 Derek Jeter 5.00 12.00
G25 Scott Rolen 1.25 3.00
G26 Mark McGwire 5.00 12.00
G27 Ken Caminiti .75 2.00
G28 Tony Gwynn 2.50 6.00
G29 J.T. Snow .75 2.00
G30 Barry Bonds 5.00 12.00

1998 Upper Deck Retro Lunchboxes

COMPLETE SET (6) 15.00 40.00
COLLECTIBLE BOX ISSUED AS PACKAGING
1 Nomar Garciaparra 3.00 8.00
2 Ken Griffey Jr. 4.00 10.00
3 Chipper Jones 2.00 5.00
4 Travis Lee .75 2.00
5 Mark McGwire 5.00 12.00
6 Cal Ripken 6.00 15.00

1998 Upper Deck Retro New Frontier

COMPLETE SET (30) 40.00 100.00
RANDOM INSERTS IN PACKS
STATED PRINT RUN 1000 SERIAL #'d SETS
NF1 Justin Baughman 1.25 3.00
NF2 David Dellucci 2.00 5.00
NF3 Travis Lee 1.25 3.00
NF4 Troy Glaus 4.00 10.00
NF5 Mike Caruso 1.25 3.00
NF6 Jim Parque 1.25 3.00
NF7 Kerry Wood 1.50 4.00
NF8 Brett Tomko 1.25 3.00
NF9 Russell Branyan 1.25 3.00
NF10 Jaret Wright 1.25 3.00
NF11 Todd Helton 2.00 5.00
NF12 Gabe Alvarez 1.25 3.00
NF13 Matt Anderson 1.25 3.00
NF14 Alex Gonzalez 1.25 3.00
NF15 Mark Kotsay 1.25 3.00
NF16 Derrek Lee 2.00 5.00
NF17 Richard Hidalgo 1.25 3.00
NF18 Adrian Beltre 1.25 3.00
NF19 Geoff Jenkins 1.25 3.00
NF20 Eric Milton 1.25 3.00
NF21 Brad Fullmer 1.25 3.00
NF22 Vladimir Guerrero 3.00 8.00
NF23 Carl Pavano 1.25 3.00
NF24 Orlando Hernandez 4.00 10.00
NF25 Ben Grieve 1.25 3.00
NF26 A.J. Hinch 1.25 3.00
NF27 Matt Clement 1.25 3.00
NF28 Gary Matthews Jr. 2.00 5.00
NF29 Aramis Ramirez 1.25 3.00
NF30 Rolando Arrojo 1.25 3.00

1998 Upper Deck Retro Quantum Leap

RANDOM INSERTS IN PACKS
STATED PRINT RUN 50 SERIAL #'d SETS
Q1 Darin Erstad 8.00 20.00
Q2 Cal Ripken 60.00 150.00
Q3 Nomar Garciaparra 30.00 80.00
Q4 Frank Thomas 20.00 50.00
Q5 Kenny Lofton 8.00 20.00
Q6 Ben Grieve 8.00 20.00
Q7 Ken Griffey Jr. 40.00 100.00
Q8 Alex Rodriguez 30.00 80.00
Q9 Juan Gonzalez 8.00 20.00
Q10 Jose Cruz Jr. 8.00 20.00
Q11 Roger Clemens 40.00 100.00
Q12 Travis Lee 8.00 20.00
Q13 Chipper Jones 20.00 50.00
Q14 Greg Maddux 30.00 80.00
Q15 Kerry Wood 10.00 25.00
Q16 Jeff Bagwell 12.50 30.00
Q17 Mike Piazza 30.00 80.00
Q18 Scott Rolen 12.50 30.00
Q19 Mark McGwire 50.00 120.00
Q20 Tony Gwynn 30.00 80.00
Q21 Larry Walker 8.00 20.00
Q22 Derek Jeter 50.00 120.00
Q23 Sammy Sosa 20.00 50.00
Q24 Barry Bonds 50.00 120.00
Q25 Mo Vaughn 8.00 20.00
Q26 Roberto Alomar 12.50 30.00
Q27 Todd Helton 12.50 30.00
Q28 Ivan Rodriguez 12.50 30.00
Q29 Vladimir Guerrero 20.00 50.00
Q30 Albert Belle 8.00 20.00

1998 Upper Deck Retro Sign of the Times

STATED ODDS 1:36
PRINT RUNS B/WN 100-1000 COPIES PER
AK Al Kaline/600 20.00 50.00
BF Bob Feller/600 10.00 25.00
BGI Bob Gibson/300 15.00 40.00
BGR Ben Grieve/300 4.00 10.00
BR Brooks Robinson/300 15.00 40.00
CF Carlton Fisk/600 15.00 40.00
EB Ernie Banks/300 25.00 60.00
EM Eddie Mathews/600 20.00 50.00
FT Frank Thomas/600 6.00 15.00
GMJ Gary Matthews Jr./750 5.00 12.00
GMS Gary Matthews Sr./600 6.00 15.00
GP Gaylord Perry/1000 6.00 15.00
JC Jose Cruz Jr./300 6.00 15.00
KGJ Ken Griffey Jr./100 250.00 350.00
KGS Ken Griffey Sr./600 6.00 15.00
KP Kirby Puckett/450 125.00 250.00
KW Kerry Wood/200 8.00 20.00
LB Lou Brock/300 10.00 25.00
NR Nolan Ryan/500 40.00 80.00
PK Paul Konerko/750 6.00 15.00
RB Russell Branyan/750 4.00 10.00
RF Rollie Fingers/600 6.00 15.00
SR Scott Rolen/300 10.00 25.00
TG Tony Gwynn/200 60.00 150.00
TLE Travis Lee/300 4.00 10.00
TP Tony Perez/600 10.00 25.00
TS Tom Seaver/300 20.00 50.00
WIS Willie Stargell/600 12.50 30.00
WM Willie McCovey/600 15.00 40.00
WS Warren Spahn/600 12.50 30.00
YB Yogi Berra/150 40.00 100.00

1998 Upper Deck Retro Time Capsule

COMPLETE SET (50) 60.00 120.00
STATED ODDS 1:2
TC1 Mike Mussina 1.25 3.00
TC2 Rafael Palmeiro .75 2.00
TC3 Cal Ripken 4.00 10.00
TC4 Nomar Garciaparra 2.00 5.00
TC5 Pedro Martinez .75 2.00
TC6 Mo Vaughn .50 1.25
TC7 Albert Belle .50 1.25
TC8 Frank Thomas 1.25 3.00
TC9 David Justice .50 1.25
TC10 Kenny Lofton .50 1.25
TC11 Manny Ramirez .75 2.00
TC12 Jim Thome .75 2.00
TC13 Derek Jeter 3.00 8.00
TC14 Tino Martinez .75 2.00
TC15 Ben Grieve .50 1.25
TC16 Rickey Henderson 1.25 3.00
TC17 Ken Griffey Jr. 2.50 6.00
TC18 Randy Johnson 1.25 3.00
TC19 Alex Rodriguez 2.00 5.00
TC20 Wade Boggs .75 2.00
TC21 Fred McGriff .75 2.00
TC22 Juan Gonzalez .50 1.25
TC23 Ivan Rodriguez .75 2.00
TC24 Nolan Ryan 3.00 8.00
TC25 Jose Canseco .75 2.00
TC26 Roger Clemens 2.50 6.00
TC27 Jose Cruz Jr. .50 1.25
TC28 Travis Lee .50 1.25
TC29 Matt Williams .50 1.25
TC30 Andres Galarraga .50 1.25
TC31 Andruw Jones .75 2.00
TC32 Chipper Jones 1.25 3.00
TC33 Greg Maddux 2.00 5.00
TC34 Kerry Wood 1.00 2.50
TC35 Barry Larkin .75 2.00
TC36 Dante Bichette .50 1.25
TC37 Larry Walker .50 1.25
TC38 Livan Hernandez .50 1.25
TC39 Jeff Bagwell .75 2.00
TC40 Craig Biggio .75 2.00
TC41 Charles Johnson .50 1.25
TC42 Gary Sheffield .50 1.25
TC43 Marquis Grissom .50 1.25
TC44 Mike Piazza 2.00 5.00
TC45 Scott Rolen .75 2.00
TC46 Curt Schilling .50 1.25
TC47 Mark McGwire 3.00 8.00
TC48 Ken Caminiti .50 1.25
TC49 Tony Gwynn 1.50 4.00
TC50 Barry Bonds 3.00 8.00

1999 Upper Deck Retro

This 110 card set features a mix of active stars and retired superstars. Similar to the 1998 Upper Deck Retro set, these cards were issued in special "Lunchboxes" which were designed to give the packaging a vintage. The lunchboxes had six cards per pack, 24 packs per box and 12 boxes per case at a SRP of $4.99 each. 350 Ted Williams A Piece of History 500 Club bat cards were randomly seeded into packs. In addition, Williams signed and numbered nine copies. Pricing for these bat cards can be referenced under 1999 Upper Deck A Piece of History 500 Club.

COMPLETE SET (110) 10.00 25.00
T.WILLIAMS BAT LISTED W/UD APH 500 CLUB
1 Mo Vaughn .10 .30
2 Troy Glaus .20 .50
3 Tim Salmon .20 .50
4 Randy Johnson .30 .75
5 Travis Lee .10 .30
6 Matt Williams .10 .30
7 Greg Maddux .50 1.25
8 Chipper Jones .30 .75
9 Andruw Jones .20 .50
10 Tom Glavine .20 .50
11 Javy Lopez .10 .30
12 Albert Belle .10 .30
13 Cal Ripken 1.00 2.50
14 Brady Anderson .10 .30
15 Nomar Garciaparra .50 1.25
16 Pedro Martinez .20 .50
17 Sammy Sosa .30 .75
18 Mark Grace .20 .50
19 Frank Thomas .30 .75
20 Ray Durham .10 .30
21 Sean Casey .10 .30
22 Greg Vaughn .10 .30
23 Barry Larkin .20 .50
24 Manny Ramirez .20 .50
25 Jim Thome .20 .50
26 Jaret Wright .10 .30
27 Kenny Lofton .10 .30
28 Larry Walker .10 .30
29 Todd Helton .20 .50
30 Vinny Castilla .10 .30
31 Tony Clark .10 .30
32 Juan Encarnacion .10 .30
33 Dean Palmer .10 .30
34 Mark Kotsay .10 .30
35 Alex Gonzalez .10 .30
36 Shane Reynolds .10 .30
37 Ken Caminiti .10 .30
38 Jeff Bagwell .20 .50
39 Craig Biggio .20 .50
40 Carlos Febles .10 .30
41 Carlos Beltran .20 .50
42 Jeremy Giambi .10 .30
43 Raul Mondesi .10 .30
44 Adrian Beltre .10 .30
45 Kevin Brown .20 .50
46 Jeromy Burnitz .10 .30
47 Jeff Cirillo .10 .30
48 Corey Koskie .10 .30
49 Todd Walker .10 .30
50 Vladimir Guerrero .30 .75
51 Michael Barrett .10 .30
52 Mike Piazza .50 1.25
53 Robin Ventura .10 .30
54 Edgardo Alfonzo .10 .30
55 Derek Jeter .75 2.00
56 Roger Clemens .60 1.50
57 Tino Martinez .20 .50
58 Orlando Hernandez .10 .30
59 Chuck Knoblauch .10 .30
60 Bernie Williams .20 .50
61 Eric Chavez .10 .30
62 Ben Grieve .10 .30
63 Jason Giambi .10 .30
64 Scott Rolen .20 .50
65 Curt Schilling .10 .30
66 Bobby Abreu .10 .30
67 Jason Kendall .10 .30
68 Kevin Young .10 .30
69 Mark McGwire .75 2.00
70 J.D. Drew .10 .30
71 Eric Davis .10 .30
72 Tony Gwynn .40 1.00
73 Trevor Hoffman .10 .30
74 Barry Bonds .75 2.00
75 Robb Nen .10 .30
76 Ken Griffey Jr. .60 1.50
77 Alex Rodriguez .50 1.25
78 Jay Buhner .10 .30
79 Carlos Guillen .10 .30
80 Jose Canseco .20 .50
81 Bobby Smith .10 .30
82 Juan Gonzalez .10 .30
83 Ivan Rodriguez .20 .50
84 Rafael Palmeiro .20 .50
85 Rick Helling .10 .30
86 Jose Cruz Jr. .10 .30
87 David Wells .10 .30
88 Carlos Delgado .10 .30
89 Nolan Ryan 1.25 3.00
90 George Brett .75 2.00
91 Robin Yount .50 1.25
92 Paul Molitor .10 .30
93 Dave Winfield .10 .30
94 Steve Garvey .10 .30
95 Ozzie Smith .50 1.25
96 Ted Williams .75 2.00
97 Don Mattingly .75 2.00
98 Mickey Mantle 1.25 3.00
99 Harmon Killebrew .30 .75
100 Rollie Fingers .10 .30
101 Kirk Gibson .10 .30
102 Bucky Dent .10 .30
103 Willie Mays .60 1.50
104 Babe Ruth 1.00 2.50
105 Gary Carter .10 .30
106 Reggie Jackson .20 .50
107 Frank Robinson .20 .50
108 Ernie Banks .30 .75
109 Eddie Murray .30 .75
110 Mike Schmidt .60 1.50

1999 Upper Deck Retro Gold

*ACTIVE STARS 1-88: 6X TO 15X BASIC
*RETIRED STARS 89-110: 10X TO 25X BASIC
RANDOM INSERTS IN PACKS
STATED PRINT RUN 250 SERIAL #'d SETS

1999 Upper Deck Retro Distant Replay

COMPLETE SET (15) 25.00 60.00
STATED ODDS 1:8
*LEVEL 2: 2.5X TO 6X BASIC DIST.REPLAY
LEVEL 2 RANDOM INSERTS IN PACKS
LEVEL 2 PRINT RUN 100 SERIAL #'d SETS
D1 Ken Griffey Jr. 2.00 5.00
D2 Mark McGwire 2.50 6.00
D3 Cal Ripken 3.00 8.00
D4 Greg Maddux 1.50 4.00
D5 Nomar Garciaparra 1.50 4.00
D6 Roger Clemens 2.00 5.00
D7 Alex Rodriguez 1.50 4.00
D8 Frank Thomas 1.00 2.50
D9 Mike Piazza 1.50 4.00
D10 Chipper Jones 1.00 2.50
D11 Juan Gonzalez .40 1.00
D12 Tony Gwynn 1.25 3.00
D13 Barry Bonds 2.50 6.00
D14 Ivan Rodriguez .60 1.50
D15 Derek Jeter 2.50 6.00

1999 Upper Deck Retro Inkredible

STATED ODDS 1:24
EXCHANGE DEADLINE 04/15/00
AP Angel Pena 4.00 10.00
BD Bucky Dent 6.00 15.00
BW Bernie Williams 15.00 40.00
CBE Carlos Beltran 4.00 10.00
CJ Chipper Jones 20.00 50.00
DE Darin Erstad 6.00 15.00
DM Don Mattingly 15.00 40.00
DW Dave Winfield 10.00 25.00
EM Eddie Murray SP 40.00 80.00
FL Fred Lynn 6.00 15.00
GB George Brett SP 60.00 120.00
GK Gabe Kapler 4.00 10.00
HK Harmon Killebrew 15.00 40.00
IR Ivan Rodriguez 10.00 25.00
JR Ken Griffey Jr. 60.00 120.00
KG Kirk Gibson 20.00 50.00
MR Manny Ramirez 15.00 40.00
NR Nolan Ryan 25.00 60.00
OZ Ozzie Smith 12.50 30.00
PB Pat Burrell 6.00 15.00
PM Paul Molitor 10.00 25.00
PO Paul O'Neill 8.00 20.00
RF Rollie Fingers 6.00 15.00
RG Rusty Greer 6.00 15.00
RY Robin Yount 15.00 40.00
SC Sean Casey 6.00 15.00
SG Steve Garvey 6.00 15.00
TC Tony Clark 4.00 10.00
TG Tony Gwynn 15.00 40.00

1999 Upper Deck Retro Inkredible Level 2

RANDOM INSERTS IN PACKS
PRINT RUNS B/WN 1-76 COPIES PER
NO PRICING ON QTY OF 25 OR LESS
EXCHANGE DEADLINE 04/15/00
AP Angel Pena/36 10.00 25.00
BD Bucky Dent/20
BW Bernie Williams/51 50.00 100.00
CBE Carlos Beltran/36 30.00 60.00
CJ Chipper Jones/10
DE Darin Erstad/17
DM Don Mattingly/23
DW Dave Winfield/31 30.00 60.00
EM Eddie Murray/33 75.00 150.00
FL Fred Lynn/19
GB George Brett/5
GK Gabe Kapler/23
HK Harmon Killebrew/3
IR Ivan Rodriguez/7
JR Ken Griffey Jr./24
KG Kirk Gibson/23
MR Manny Ramirez/24
NR Nolan Ryan/34 150.00 300.00
OZ Ozzie Smith/1
PB Pat Burrell/76 30.00 60.00
PM Paul Molitor/4
PO Paul O'Neill/21
RF Rollie Fingers/34 15.00 40.00
RG Rusty Greer/29 15.00 40.00
RY Robin Yount/19
SC Sean Casey/21
SG Steve Garvey/6
TC Tony Clark/17
TG Tony Gwynn/19

1999 Upper Deck Retro Lunchboxes

COMPLETE SET (17) 100.00 200.00
ONE DUAL PLAYER BOX PER 12-CT CASE
1 Roger Clemens 5.00 12.00
2 Ken Griffey Jr. 12.50 30.00
3 Mickey Mantle 10.00 25.00
4 Mark McGwire 10.00 25.00
5 Mike Piazza 6.00 15.00
6 Alex Rodriguez 6.00 15.00
7 Babe Ruth 10.00 25.00
8 Sammy Sosa 5.00 12.00
9 Ted Williams 8.00 20.00
10 K.Griffey Jr. 8.00 20.00
M.Mantle
11 K.Griffey Jr. 8.00 20.00
M.McGwire
12 K.Griffey Jr. 8.00 20.00
B.Ruth
13 K.Griffey Jr. 8.00 20.00
T.Williams
14 M.Mantle 6.00 15.00
B.Ruth
15 M.McGwire 6.00 15.00
M.Mantle
16 M.McGwire 6.00 15.00
B.Ruth
17 M.McGwire 6.00 15.00
T.Williams

1999 Upper Deck Retro Old School/New School

COMPLETE SET (30) 100.00 200.00
STATED PRINT RUN 1000 SERIAL #'d SETS
*LEVEL 2 STARS: 1.25X TO 3X BASIC SCHOOL
*LEVEL 2 ROOKIES: .75X TO 2X BASIC SCHOOL
STATED PRINT RUN 50 SERIAL #'d SETS
RANDOM INSERTS IN PACKS 2.50 6.00
S1 Ken Griffey Jr. 5.00 12.00
S2 Alex Rodriguez 4.00 10.00
S3 Frank Thomas 2.50 6.00
S4 Cal Ripken 8.00 20.00
S5 Chipper Jones 2.50 6.00
S6 Craig Biggio 1.50 4.00
S7 Greg Maddux 4.00 10.00
S8 Jeff Bagwell 1.50 4.00
S9 Juan Gonzalez 1.00 2.50
S10 Mark McGwire 6.00 15.00
S11 Mike Piazza 4.00 10.00
S12 Mo Vaughn 1.00 2.50
S13 Roger Clemens 5.00 12.00
S14 Sammy Sosa 2.50 6.00
S15 Tony Gwynn 3.00 8.00
S16 Gabe Kapler 1.00 2.50
S17 J.D. Drew 1.00 2.50
S18 Pat Burrell 2.50 6.00
S19 Roy Halladay 2.50 6.00
S20 Jeff Weaver 1.50 4.00
S21 Troy Glaus 1.50 4.00
S22 Vladimir Guerrero 2.50 6.00
S23 Michael Barrett 1.00 2.50
S24 Carlos Beltran 1.50 4.00
S25 Scott Rolen 1.50 4.00
S26 Nomar Garciaparra 4.00 10.00
S27 Warren Morris 1.00 2.50
S28 Alex Gonzalez 1.00 2.50
S29 Kyle Farnsworth 1.00 2.50
S30 Derek Jeter 6.00 15.00

1999 Upper Deck Retro Throwback Attack

COMPLETE SET (15) 15.00 40.00
STATED ODDS 1:5
*LEVEL 2: 1.25X TO 3X BASIC THROWBACK
LEVEL 2 RANDOM INSERTS IN PACKS
LEVEL 2 PRINT RUN 500 SERIAL #'d SETS
T1 Ken Griffey Jr. 1.50 4.00
T2 Mark McGwire 2.00 5.00
T3 Sammy Sosa .75 2.00
T4 Roger Clemens 1.50 4.00
T5 J.D. Drew .30 .75
T6 Alex Rodriguez 1.25 3.00
T7 Greg Maddux 1.25 3.00
T8 Mike Piazza 1.25 3.00
T9 Juan Gonzalez .30 .75
T10 Mo Vaughn .30 .75
T11 Cal Ripken 2.50 6.00
T12 Frank Thomas .75 2.00
T13 Nomar Garciaparra 1.25 3.00
T14 Vladimir Guerrero .75 2.00
T15 Tony Gwynn 1.00 2.50

1992 Upper Deck Richard McWilliam

FD1 Richard McWilliam

2007 Upper Deck Ripken Gwynn Road to the Hall

COMPLETE SET (50) 75.00 150.00
COMMON CARD 2.00 5.00

2002 Upper Deck Rookie Debut Solid Contact

STATED ODDS 1:24
AR Alex Rodriguez 6.00 15.00
BA Bobby Abreu 4.00 10.00
BG Brian Giles 4.00 10.00
BL Barry Larkin 6.00 15.00
BW Bernie Williams 6.00 15.00
CD Carlos Delgado SP 6.00 15.00
CE Carl Everett 4.00 10.00
DM Doug Mientkiewicz 6.00 15.00
EA Edgardo Alfonzo 4.00 10.00
EM Edgar Martinez 6.00 15.00
FM Fred McGriff 6.00 15.00
FT Frank Thomas 6.00 15.00
GS Gary Sheffield 4.00 10.00
IR Ivan Rodriguez 6.00 15.00
JC Jose Cruz Jr. 4.00 10.00
JE Jim Edmonds 4.00 10.00
JG Jason Giambi SP/50 6.00 15.00
JK Jason Kendall 4.00 10.00
JO John Olerud 4.00 10.00
JP Jorge Posada 6.00 15.00
JT Jim Thome 6.00 15.00
KG Ken Griffey Jr. 8.00 20.00
MA Moises Alou 4.00 10.00
MO Maggio Ordonez 4.00 10.00
MW Matt Williams 4.00 10.00
OV Omar Vizquel 6.00 15.00
RA Roberto Alomar 6.00 15.00
SS Sammy Sosa 6.00 15.00
TA Fernando Tatis 4.00 10.00
TH Todd Helton 6.00 15.00

2001 Upper Deck Rookie Update Ichiro Tribute

COMPLETE SET (51) 30.00 60.00
COMMON CARD (1-51) .75 2.00
DISTRIBUTED IN ICHIRO TRIBUTE PACKS
*GOLD: 5X TO 12X BASIC ICHIRO TRIB.
GOLD PRINT RUN 100 SERIAL #'d SETS
*PLATINUM: 12.5X TO 30X BASIC TRIB
PLATINUM PRINT RUN 25 SERIAL #'d SETS

2001 Upper Deck Rookie Update Ichiro Tribute Game Bat

COMMON CARD (B-I1-B-I12) 20.00 50.00
B-I1-B-I12 PRINT 100 SERIAL #'d SETS
COMMON BLUE (B-I13-B-I17) 40.00 80.00
B-I13-B-I17 BLUE PRINT 50 SERIAL #'d SETS
COMMON TEAL (B-I18-B-I19) 75.00 150.00
B-I18-B-I19 TEAL PRINT 25 SERIAL #'d SETS
BI-20 GOLD PRINT RUN 1 SERIAL #'d SET
BI-20 GOLD NO PRICING DUE TO SCARCITY

2001 Upper Deck Rookie Update Ichiro Tribute Game Pants

COMMON CARD (J-I1-J-I12) 20.00 50.00
J-I1-J-I12 PRINT 100 SERIAL #'d SETS
COMMON BLUE (J-I13-J-I17) 40.00 80.00
J-I13-J-I17 BLUE PRINT 50 SERIAL #'d SETS
COMMON TEAL (J-I18-J-I19) 75.00 150.00
J-I18-J-I19 TEAL PRINT 25 SERIAL #'d SETS
JI-20 GOLD PRINT RUN 1 SERIAL #'d SET
JI-20 GOLD NO PRICING DUE TO SCARCITY

2001 Upper Deck Rookie Update USA Touch of Gold Autographs

STATED PRINT RUN 500 SERIAL #'d SETS
AE Adam Everett 4.00 10.00
AS Anthony Sanders 4.00 10.00
BA Brent Abernathy 4.00 10.00
BW Brad Wilkerson 6.00 15.00
CG Chris George 4.00 10.00
DM Doug Mientkiewicz 6.00 15.00
EY Ernie Young 4.00 10.00
JC John Cotton 4.00 10.00
JR Jon Rauch 4.00 10.00
KU Kurt Ainsworth 4.00 10.00
MJ Marcus Jensen 4.00 10.00
MK Mike Kinkade 4.00 10.00
MN Mike Neill 4.00 10.00
PB Pat Borders 4.00 10.00
RF Ryan Franklin 4.00 10.00
RK Rick Krivda 4.00 10.00
RO Roy Oswalt 8.00 20.00
SB Sean Burroughs 4.00 10.00
SH Shane Heams 4.00 10.00
TD Gookie Dawkins 4.00 10.00
TW Todd Williams 4.00 10.00
TY Tim Young 4.00 10.00
BSE Bobby Seay 4.00 10.00
BSH Ben Sheets 10.00 25.00

2002 Upper Deck Rookie Update Star Tributes

STATED ODDS 1:15
AD Adam Dunn 3.00 8.00
AR Alex Rodriguez 6.00 15.00
AS Alfonso Soriano 3.00 8.00
CD Carlos Delgado 3.00 8.00
CJ Chipper Jones 4.00 10.00
CS Curt Schilling 3.00 8.00
FT Frank Thomas 4.00 10.00
IR Ivan Rodriguez 4.00 10.00
JB Josh Beckett 3.00 8.00
JD Joe DiMaggio SP 20.00 50.00
JG Jason Giambi 3.00 8.00
KG Ken Griffey Jr. 6.00 15.00
KI Kazuhisa Ishii 4.00 10.00
KS Kazuhiro Sasaki 3.00 8.00
LB Lance Berkman 3.00 8.00
LG Luis Gonzalez SP 4.00 10.00
MM Mark McGwire SP 30.00 60.00
MPI Mike Piazza 5.00 12.00
MPR Mark Prior 3.00 8.00
MS Mike Sweeney 3.00 8.00
PM Pedro Martinez 4.00 10.00
RC Roger Clemens 6.00 15.00
RJ Randy Johnson 4.00 10.00
RP Rafael Palmeiro 4.00 10.00
SG Shawn Green 3.00 8.00
SS Sammy Sosa 4.00 10.00
TG Tom Glavine 4.00 10.00
TS Tsuyoshi Shinjo 3.00 8.00

2002 Upper Deck Rookie Update USA Future Watch Swatches

STATED ODDS 1:15
COPPER PRINT RUN 25 SERIAL #'d SETS
NO COPPER PRICING DUE TO SCARCITY
GOLD PRINT RUN 5 SERIAL #'d SETS
NO GOLD PRICING DUE TO SCARCITY
RED PRINT RUN 50 SERIAL #'d SETS
NO RED PRICING DUE TO LACK OF INFO
SILVER PRINT RUN 25 SERIAL #'d SETS
NO SILVER PRICING DUE TO SCARCITY
AA Abe Alvarez 3.00 8.00
AH Aaron Hill 3.00 8.00
BS Brad Sullivan 3.00 8.00
BZ Bob Zimmermann 2.00 5.00
CC Chad Cordero 3.00 8.00
CJ Conor Jackson 4.00 10.00
CQ Carlos Quentin 6.00 15.00
CS Clint Sammons 3.00 8.00
DP Dustin Pedroia 15.00 40.00
EP Eric Patterson 3.00 8.00
GJ Grant Johnson 3.00 8.00
HS Huston Street 3.00 8.00
KB Kyle Bakker 2.00 5.00
KS Kyle Sleeth 3.00 8.00
LP Landon Powell 3.00 8.00
MA Michael Aubrey 3.00 8.00
MJ Mark Jurich 2.00 5.00
PH Philip Humber 3.00 8.00
RW Rickie Weeks 4.00 10.00
SC Shane Costa 2.00 5.00
SF Sam Fuld 2.00 5.00
WL Wes Littleton 3.00 8.00

2009 Upper Deck Signature Stars

COMMON CARD (1-100) .20 .50
COMMON CARD (101-120) 1.25 3.00
COMMON AU (121-210) 3.00 8.00
OVERALL AU/MEM ODDS 1:5 HOBBY
1 Aaron Harang .20 .50
2 Aaron Rowand .20 .50
3 Adam Dunn .30 .75
4 Adam Lind .20 .50
5 Adam Wainwright .30 .75
6 Adrian Gonzalez .40 1.00
7 Akinori Iwamura .20 .50
8 Albert Pujols .60 1.50
9 Alex Gordon .30 .75
10 Alfonso Soriano .30 .75
11 Andruw Jones .20 .50
12 Aramis Ramirez .20 .50
13 B.J. Upton .30 .75
14 Bill Hall .20 .50
15 Billy Wagner .20 .50
16 Brandon Phillips .20 .50
17 Brandon Webb .30 .75
18 Brian Giles .20 .50
19 Brian McCann .30 .75
20 Brian Roberts .20 .50
21 Carl Crawford .30 .75
22 Carlos Gomez .20 .50
23 Carlos Zambrano .30 .75
24 Chien-Ming Wang .30 .75
25 Chipper Jones .50 1.25
26 Chone Figgins .20 .50
27 Chris Carpenter .30 .75
28 Chris Duncan .20 .50
29 Chris Young .20 .50
30 Clayton Kershaw .75 2.00
31 Cole Hamels .40 1.00
32 Curtis Granderson .40 1.00
33 Daisuke Matsuzaka .30 .75
34 Dan Haren .20 .50
35 Dan Uggla .20 .50
36 Delmon Young .30 .75
37 Derek Jeter 1.25 3.00
38 Derek Lowe .20 .50
39 Dontrelle Willis .20 .50
40 Dustin Pedroia .50 1.25
41 Eric Chavez .20 .50
42 Evan Longoria .30 .75
43 Felix Hernandez .30 .75
44 Garret Anderson .20 .50
45 Garrett Atkins .20 .50
46 Grady Sizemore .30 .75
47 Hanley Ramirez .30 .75
48 Ivan Rodriguez .30 .75
49 Jake Peavy .20 .50
50 James Loney .20 .50
51 Jason Bay .30 .75
52 Jason Kubel .20 .50
53 Jason Varitek .50 1.25
54 Jay Bruce .30 .75
55 Jeff Francoeur .30 .75
56 Jered Weaver .30 .75
57 Jeremy Bonderman .20 .50
58 Jim Thome .30 .75
59 Joe Mauer .40 1.00
60 Joel Zumaya .20 .50
61 John Lackey .30 .75
62 Johnny Cueto .30 .75
63 Jon Lester .30 .75
64 Jonathan Papelbon .30 .75
65 Josh Beckett .20 .50
66 Josh Johnson .30 .75
67 Justin Verlander .50 1.25
68 Kelly Johnson .20 .50
69 Ken Griffey Jr. 1.00 2.50
70 Kerry Wood .20 .50
71 Kevin Kouzmanoff .20 .50
72 Kevin Slowey .30 .75
73 Kevin Youkilis .20 .50
74 Khalil Greene .20 .50
75 Lance Berkman .30 .75
76 Mark Teixeira .30 .75
77 Matt Holliday .50 1.25
78 Melvin Mora .20 .50
79 Miguel Cabrera .50 1.25
80 Miguel Tejada .30 .75
81 Nick Markakis .40 1.00
82 Nick Swisher .30 .75
83 Pablo Sandoval .40 1.00
84 Paul Konerko .30 .75
85 Randy Johnson .50 1.25
86 Rich Harden .20 .50
87 Roy Halladay .30 .75
88 Roy Oswalt .30 .75
89 Ryan Braun .30 .75
90 Ryan Garko .20 .50
91 Scott Kazmir .20 .50
92 Scott Rolen .30 .75
93 Takashi Saito .20 .50
94 Tim Hudson .30 .75
95 Tim Lincecum .30 .75
96 Torii Hunter .20 .50
97 Troy Tulowilzki .50 1.25
98 Vernon Wells .20 .50
99 Vladimir Guerrero .30 .75
100 Yunel Escobar .20 .50
101 Brett Anderson RC 2.00 5.00
102 Elvis Andrus RC 3.00 8.00
103 Gordon Beckham RC 2.00 5.00
104 Brad Bergesen (RC) 1.25 3.00
105 Trevor Cahill RC 3.00 8.00
106 Brett Cecil RC 1.25 3.00
107 Alcides Escobar RC 2.00 5.00
108 Mat Gamel RC 3.00 8.00
109 Tommy Hanson RC 3.00 8.00
110 Andrew McCutchen (RC) 6.00 15.00
111 Alex Avila RC 4.00 10.00
112 Sean O'Sullivan RC 1.25 3.00
113 Gerardo Parra RC 2.00 5.00
114 Ryan Perry RC 3.00 8.00
115 Aaron Poreda RC 1.25 3.00
116 Nolan Reimold (RC) 1.25 3.00
117 Ricky Romero (RC) 2.00 5.00
118 Neftali Feliz RC 2.00 5.00
119 Tommy Hunter RC 2.00 5.00
120 Sean West (RC) 1.50 4.00
121 Scott Baker AU 3.00 8.00
122 Wladimir Balentien AU 3.00 8.00
124 Nick Blackburn AU 3.00 8.00
125 Joe Blanton AU 5.00 12.00
126 Billy Butler AU 6.00 15.00
127 Matt Cain AU 10.00 25.00
128 Chris Capuano AU 3.00 8.00
129 Fausto Carmona AU 4.00 10.00
130 John Danks AU 4.00 10.00
131 Chris Davis AU 30.00 60.00
132 Ross Detwiler AU 3.00 8.00
134 Scott Feldman AU 3.00 8.00
135 Prince Fielder AU 4.00 10.00
137 Yovani Gallardo AU 3.00 8.00
138 Matt Garza AU 4.00 10.00
139 Alberto Gonzalez AU 3.00 8.00
140 Carlos Gonzalez AU 6.00 15.00
143 Jason Hammel AU 3.00 8.00
144 J.A. Happ AU 10.00 25.00
145 Corey Hart AU 5.00 12.00
146 Phil Hughes AU 6.00 15.00
147 Ramon Hernandez AU 3.00 8.00
148 Micah Hoffpauir AU 3.00 8.00
149 Travis Ishikawa AU 3.00 8.00
150 Matt Kemp AU 15.00 40.00
152 Derrek Lee AU 4.00 10.00
153 Noah Lowry AU 10.00 25.00
154 Jed Lowrie AU 4.00 10.00
157 Andrew Miller AU 3.00 8.00
158 Miguel Montero AU 6.00 15.00
159 David Murphy AU 4.00 10.00
160 Joe Nathan AU 3.00 8.00
161 Micah Owings AU 4.00 10.00
162 Felipe Paulino AU 3.00 8.00
163 Glen Perkins AU 6.00 15.00
164 Felix Pie AU 5.00 12.00
165 Alexei Ramirez AU 5.00 12.00
166 Jarrod Saltalamacchia AU 4.00 10.00
167 Luke Scott AU 3.00 8.00
170 Geovany Soto AU 6.00 15.00
173 Mark Teahen AU 4.00 10.00
174 Matt Tolbert AU 3.00 8.00
175 J.R. Towles AU 3.00 8.00
176 Edinson Volquez AU 3.00 8.00
177 Dewayne Wise AU 3.00 8.00
178 Chris B. Young AU 10.00 25.00
179 Ryan Zimmerman AU 6.00 15.00
181 Kyle Blanks AU RC 8.00 20.00
182 Michael Bowden AU RC 4.00 10.00
183 Everth Cabrera AU RC 3.00 8.00
184 Drew Carpenter AU RC 3.00 8.00
185 Francisco Cervelli AU RC 5.00 12.00
186 Jhoulys Chacin AU RC 3.00 8.00
188 David Freese AU RC 8.00 20.00
189 Derek Holland AU RC 4.00 10.00
191 Mat Latos AU RC 5.00 12.00
192 Lou Marson AU (RC) 4.00 10.00
194 Shairon Martis AU RC 3.00 8.00
195 James McDonald AU RC 3.00 8.00
196 Fu-Te Ni AU RC 5.00 12.00
197 Sean O'Sullivan AU RC 5.00 12.00
198 James Parr AU (RC) 3.00 8.00
199 David Patton AU RC 3.00 8.00
200 Rick Porcello AU RC 12.50 30.00
201 David Price AU RC 10.00 25.00
202 Josh Reddick AU RC 5.00 12.00
203 Michael Saunders AU RC 8.00 20.00
204 Jordan Schafer AU (RC) 4.00 10.00
205 Travis Snider AU RC 5.00 12.00
206 Matt Tuiasosopo AU (RC) 3.00 8.00
207 Koji Uehara AU RC 20.00 50.00
208 Chris Tillman AU RC 5.00 12.00
209 Matt Wieters AU RC 10.00 25.00
210 Jordan Zimmermann AU RC 6.00 15.00

2009 Upper Deck Signature Stars Gold Signatures

OVERAL AU/MEM ODDS 1:5 HOBBY
PRINT RUNS B/WN 5-100 COPIES PER
NO PRICING ON QTY 25 OR LESS
1 Aaron Harang/50 4.00 10.00
6 Adrian Gonzalez/50 10.00 25.00
13 B.J. Upton/35 4.00 10.00
35 Dan Uggla/100 4.00 10.00
37 Derek Jeter/100 100.00 200.00
40 Dustin Pedroia/100 20.00 50.00
46 Grady Sizemore/50 5.00 12.00
47 Hanley Ramirez/100 6.00 15.00
49 Jake Peavy/75 12.50 30.00
64 Jonathan Papelbon/100 8.00 20.00
69 Ken Griffey Jr./100 30.00 60.00
73 Kevin Youkilis/35 6.00 15.00
75 Lance Berkman/35 8.00 20.00
87 Roy Halladay/100 10.00 25.00
93 Takashi Saito/100 6.00 15.00

2009 Upper Deck Signature Stars Impressions Signatures

OVERALL AU/MEM ODDS 1:5 HOBBY
AC Drew Carpenter 3.00 8.00
AH Anderson Hernandez 3.00
AR Alexei Ramirez 5.00 12.00
BC Brett Carroll 3.00 8.00
BL Brent Lillibridge 3.00 8.00
CB Chad Billingsley 6.00 15.00
CH Corey Hart 3.00 8.00
CJ Chipper Jones 30.00 60.00
CT Clete Thomas 4.00 10.00
CW Cory Wade 3.00 8.00
DJ Derek Jeter 100.00 200.00
DM David Murphy 3.00 8.00
DU Dan Uggla 5.00 12.00
DW Dewayne Wise 3.00 8.00
FP Felipe Paulino 3.00 8.00
GP Glen Perkins 3.00 0.00
JA Jonathan Albaladejo 3.00
JB Josh Banks 3.00 8.00
JC Jorge Campillo 3.00 8.00
JH J.A. Happ 20.00 50.00
JL Jed Lowrie 3.00 8.00
JN Joe Nathan 3.00 8.00
JT J.R. Towles 3.00 8.00
KG Ken Griffey Jr. 40.00 80.00
KM Kyle McClellan 3.00 8.00
LB Lance Broadway 5.00 12.00
LR Luis Rodriguez 6.00 15.00
MI Mitch Maier 3.00 8.00
MJ Matt Joyce 3.00 8.00
MK Matt Kemp 6.00 15.00
ML Matt Lindstrom 3.00 8.00
MM Miguel Montero 3.00 8.00
MO Micah Owings 3.00 8.00
MT Matt Tolbert 3.00 8.00
MU Daniel Murphy 12.00 30.00
NB Nick Blackburn 3.00 8.00
NL Noah Lowry 5.00 12.00
PE Fernando Perez 3.00 8.00
PF Prince Fielder 10.00 25.00
PI Felix Pie 4.00 10.00
RD Robinzon Diaz 3.00 8.00
RM Russell Martin 3.00 8.00
RO Ross Ohlendorf 3.00 8.00
RZ Ryan Zimmerman 8.00 20.00
TG Tom Gorzelanny 3.00 8.00
WB Wladimir Balentien 3.00 8.00
YG Yovani Gallardo 3.00 8.00

2009 Upper Deck Signature Stars Signature Quads

OVERAL AU/MEM ODDS 1:5 HOBBY
PRINT RUNS B/WN 5-35 COPIES PER
NO PRICING ON QTY 25 OR LESS
MKBS Kub/Mau/Bla/Spa/35 20.00 50.00
MMRP Mar/Rob/Mor/Pie/35 10.00 25.00

2009 Upper Deck Signature Stars Signature Skills

RANDOM INSERTS IN PACKS
SS1 Grady Sizemore .75 2.00
SS2 Ryan Howard 1.00 2.50
SS3 Felix Hernandez .75 2.00
SS4 Johan Santana .75 2.00
SS5 Tim Lincecum .75 2.00
SS6 Francisco Rodriguez .75 2.00
SS7 Tim Wakefield .75 2.00
SS8 Carl Crawford .75 2.00
SS9 Ichiro Suzuki 1.50 4.00
SS10 Yadier Molina 1.50 4.00
SS11 David Ortiz 1.25 3.00
SS12 Trevor Hoffman .75 2.00
SS13 Torii Hunter .50 1.25
SS14 Jimmy Rollins .75 2.00
SS15 Derek Jeter 3.00 8.00
SS16 Todd Helton .75 2.00

2009 Upper Deck Signature Stars Signature Trios

OVERAL AU/MEM ODDS 1:5 HOBBY
PRINT RUNS B/WN 5-35 COPIES PER
NO PRICING ON QTY 25 OR LESS
CSI Ish/Cain/Sand/30 30.00 60.00
HSF Feld/Salt/Hamilton/35 10.00 25.00
RRS K.Suz/Rowand/Romero/30 10.00 25.00

2009 Upper Deck Signature Stars Signed Sealed and Delivered

RANDOM INSERTS IN PACKS
SSD1 Matt Holliday 1.25 3.00
SSD2 Mark Teixeira .75 2.00
SSD3 CC Sabathia .75 2.00
SSD4 Manny Ramirez 1.25 3.00
SSD5 John Smoltz 1.25 3.00
SSD6 Cliff Lee .75 2.00
SSD7 Adam Dunn .75 2.00
SSD8 Pedro Martinez .75 2.00

2009 Upper Deck Signature Stars Superstar Portraits Signatures

OVERAL AU/MEM ODDS 1:5 HOBBY
PRINT RUNS B/WN 5-35 COPIES PER
NO PRICING FOR QTY 25 OR LESS
SP16 Derek Jeter/35
SP18 Chipper Jones/35 75.00 150.00
SP19 Derrek Lee/35 10.00 25.00
SP25 Joe Mauer/35 20.00 50.00

2009 Upper Deck Signature Stars Trophy Winners

RANDOM INSERTS IN PACKS
TW1 Albert Pujols 1.50 4.00
TW2 Dustin Pedroia 1.25 3.00
TW3 Tim Lincecum .75 2.00
TW4 Cliff Lee .75 2.00
TW5 Chipper Jones 1.25 3.00
TW6 Joe Mauer 1.00 2.50
TW7 Ryan Howard 1.00 2.50
TW8 Miguel Cabrera 1.25 3.00

2009 Upper Deck Signature Stars UD Black Pride of a Nation

OVERALL AU/MEM ODDS 1:5 HOBBY
PRINT RUN B/WN 10-99 COPIES PER
NO PRICING ON QTY OF 25 OR LESS
22 Dexter Fowler/99 10.00 25.00
23 Tommy Hanson/99 10.00 25.00
24 Kenshin Kawakami/99 6.00 15.00
26 Rick Porcello/99 12.00 30.00
27 David Price/99 10.00 25.00
28 Neftali Feliz/99 10.00 25.00
30 Koji Uehara/99 30.00 60.00
32 Fu-Te Ni/99 40.00 80.00
33 J.Zimmermann/99 10.00 25.00
35 Matt LaPorta/99 6.00 15.00
36 Ricky Romero/99 6.00 15.00

2009 Upper Deck Signature Stars USA By the Letter Autographs

OVERALL AU/MEM ODDS 1:5 HOBBY
STATED PRINT RUN 100 SER.#'d SETS
AV AJ Vanegas 4.00 10.00
AW Andy Wilkins 6.00 15.00
BB Bryce Brentz 5.00 12.00
BE Chad Bettis 4.00 10.00
BF Blake Forsythe 4.00 10.00
BH Bryce Harper 100.00 200.00
BM Brad Miller 8.00 20.00
BR Brian Ragira 4.00 12.00
CB Cody Buckel 8.00 20.00
CC Christian Colon 5.00 12.00
CM Connor Mason 4.00 10.00
CO Gerrit Cole 15.00 40.00
CW Cody Wheeler 10.00 25.00
DP Drew Pomeranz 8.00 20.00
GC Garin Cecchini 6.00 15.00
JT Jameson Taillon 5.00 12.00
KG Kevin Gausman 8.00 20.00
KK Kavin Keyes 6.00 15.00
KW Karsten Whitson 8.00 20.00
MI Michael Choice 6.00 15.00
MM Manny Machado 40.00 100.00
NC Nick Castellanos 10.00 25.00
ND Nicky Delmonico 6.00 15.00
PP Phillip Pfeifer 6.00 15.00
RH Rick Hague 5.00 12.00
RR Robbie Ray 10.00 25.00
SC Sean Coyle 6.00 15.00
SG Sonny Gray 10.00 25.00
TB Trevor Bauer 15.00 40.00
TH Tyler Holt 4.00 10.00
TW Tony Wolters 6.00 15.00
WA T.J. Walz 10.00 25.00
WO Kolten Wong 10.00 25.00
YG Yasmani Grandal 6.00 15.00

2009 Upper Deck Signature Stars USA Flashback Fabrics Dual Jersey

OVERALL AU/MEM ODDS 1:5 HOBBY
EL Evan Longoria 6.00 15.00
JM Joe Mauer 5.00 12.00

2009 Upper Deck Signature Stars USA National Team Future Watch Jersey Autographs

OVERALL AU/MEM ODDS 1:5 HOBBY
PRINT RUNS B/WN 493-999 COPIES PER
1 Trevor Bauer/799 15.00 40.00
2 Christian Colon/799 6.00 15.00
4 Chad Bettis/799 4.00 10.00
5 Bryce Brentz/799 5.00 12.00
7 Michael Choice/799 6.00 15.00
8 Gerrit Cole/799 10.00 25.00
9 Sonny Gray/799 10.00 25.00
10 Tyler Holt/799 4.00 10.00
11 T.J. Walz/799 4.00 10.00
12 Rick Hague/799 4.00 10.00
13 Drew Pomeranz/799 5.00 12.00
14 Blake Forsythe/799 4.00 10.00
15 Matt Newman/799 4.00 10.00
16 Casey McGrew/799 4.00 10.00
17 Brad Miller/799 10.00 25.00
18 Yasmani Grandal/799 6.00 15.00
19 Kolten Wong/799 6.00 15.00
20 Tony Zych/799 4.00 10.00
21 Andy Wilkins/799 4.00 10.00
22 Asher Wojciechowski/799 4.00 10.00
23 Cody Buckel/899 5.00 12.00
24 Nick Castellanos/799 8.00 20.00
25 Garin Cecchini/899 6.00 15.00
26 Sean Coyle/899 6.00 15.00
27 Nicky Delmonico/493 4.00 10.00
28 Kevin Gausman/899 10.00 25.00
29 Cory Hahn/899 6.00 15.00
30 Bryce Harper/899 100.00 250.00
31 Kavin Keyes/899 4.00 10.00
32 Manny Machado/899 40.00 100.00
33 Connor Mason/899 4.00 10.00
34 Ladson Montgomery/899 4.00 10.00
36 Brian Ragira/899 4.00 10.00
37 Robbie Ray/899 4.00 10.00
38 Kyle Ryan/999 4.00 10.00
39 Jameson Taillon/899 6.00 15.00
40 AJ Vanegas/899 5.00 12.00
41 Karsten Whitson/899 4.00 10.00

2009 Upper Deck Signature Stars USA National Team Future Watch Patch Autographs

*PATCH: .6X TO 1.5X BASIC
OVERALL AU/MEM ODDS 1:5 HOBBY
STATED PRINT RUN 50 SER.#'d SETS
1 Trevor Bauer 25.00 60.00
2 Christian Colon 10.00 25.00
4 Chad Bettis 6.00 15.00
7 Michael Choice 10.00 25.00
9 Sonny Gray 12.00 30.00
10 Tyler Holt 6.00 15.00
11 T.J. Walz 6.00 15.00
12 Rick Hague 6.00 15.00
13 Drew Pomeranz 8.00 20.00
14 Blake Forsythe 6.00 15.00
15 Matt Newman 6.00 15.00
16 Casey McGrew 6.00 15.00
17 Brad Miller 6.00 15.00
18 Yasmani Grandal 6.00 15.00
20 Tony Zych 6.00 15.00
21 Andy Wilkins 6.00 15.00
22 Asher Wojciechowski 6.00 15.00
23 Cody Buckel 10.00 25.00
24 Nick Castellanos 40.00 80.00
25 Garin Cecchini 6.00 15.00
26 Sean Coyle 8.00 20.00
27 Nicky Delmonico 6.00 15.00
29 Cory Hahn 6.00 15.00
30 Bryce Harper 250.00 500.00
31 Kavin Keyes 6.00 15.00
32 Manny Machado 50.00 100.00
33 Connor Mason 6.00 15.00
34 Ladson Montgomery 6.00 15.00
36 Brian Ragira 12.50 30.00
37 Robbie Ray 6.00 15.00
38 Kyle Ryan 6.00 15.00
39 Jameson Taillon 6.00 15.00
40 AJ Vanegas 6.00 15.00
41 Karsten Whitson 12.50 30.00

2009 Upper Deck Signature Stars USA Star Prospects

RANDOM INSERTS IN PACKS
USA1 Cody Buckel .60 1.50
USA2 Nick Castellanos 2.00 5.00
USA3 Garin Cecchini 1.25 3.00
USA4 Sean Coyle .40 1.00
USA5 Nicky Delmonico .40 1.00
USA6 Kevin Gausman 2.00 5.00
USA7 Cory Hahn .40 1.00
USA8 Bryce Harper 5.00 12.00
USA9 Kavin Keyes .40 1.00
USA10 Manny Machado 2.50 6.00
USA11 Connor Mason .40 1.00
USA12 Ladson Montgomery .40 1.00
USA13 Phillip Pfeifer .40 1.00
USA14 Brian Ragira .60 1.50
USA15 Robbie Ray .40 1.00
USA16 Kyle Ryan .40 1.00
USA17 Jameson Taillon .60 1.50
USA18 AJ Vanegas .40 1.00
USA19 Karsten Whitson .60 1.50
USA20 Tony Wolters .40 1.00
USA21 Trevor Bauer 4.00 10.00
USA22 Chad Bettis .40 1.00
USA23 Bryce Brentz 1.00 2.50
USA24 Michael Choice .60 1.50
USA25 Gerrit Cole 4.00 10.00
USA26 Christian Colon .60 1.50
USA27 Blake Forsythe .40 1.00
USA28 Yasmani Grandal .60 1.50
USA29 Sonny Gray 1.00 2.50
USA30 Rick Hague .40 1.00
USA31 Tyler Holt .40 1.00
USA32 Casey McGrew .40 1.00
USA33 Brad Miller 1.00 2.50
USA34 Matt Newman .40 1.00
USA35 Nick Pepitone .40 1.00
USA36 Drew Pomeranz 1.25 3.00
USA37 T.J. Walz .40 1.00
USA38 Cody Wheeler .40 1.00
USA39 Andy Wilkins .40 1.00
USA40 Asher Wojciechowski .60 1.50
USA41 Kolten Wong .60 1.50
USA42 Tony Zych .40 1.00

2009 Upper Deck Signature Stars USA Star Prospects Jersey Autographs

OVERALL AU/MEM ODDS 1:5 HOBBY
STATED PRINT RUN 399 SER.#'d SETS
AS Asher Wojciechowski 4.00 10.00
AV AJ Vanegas 4.00 10.00
BB Bryce Brentz 3.00 8.00
BF Blake Forsythe 4.00 10.00
BH Bryce Harper 100.00 250.00
BM Brad Miller 6.00 15.00
BR Brian Ragira 4.00 10.00
CA Casey McGrew 4.00 10.00
CB Cody Buckel 5.00 12.00
CC Christian Colon 5.00 12.00
CH Cory Hahn 4.00 10.00
CM Connor Mason 8.00 20.00
CO Gerrit Cole 20.00 50.00
CW Cody Wheeler 5.00 12.00
DP Drew Pomeranz 6.00 15.00
GC Garin Cecchini 3.00 8.00
JT Jameson Taillon 5.00 12.00
KG Kevin Gausman 12.50 30.00
KK Kavin Keyes 4.00 10.00
KR Kyle Ryan 4.00 10.00
KW Karsten Whitson 8.00 20.00
MC Michael Choice 5.00 12.00
MM Manny Machado 20.00 50.00
MN Matt Newman 4.00 10.00
NC Nick Castellanos 10.00 25.00
ND Nicky Delmonico 5.00 12.00
NP Nick Pepitone 4.00 10.00
RH Rick Hague 4.00 10.00
RR Robbie Ray 4.00 10.00
SC Sean Coyle 6.00 15.00
SG Sonny Gray 6.00 15.00
TB Trevor Bauer 12.00 30.00
TH Tyler Holt 4.00 10.00
TW Tony Wolters 3.00 8.00
WO Kolten Wong 8.00 20.00
YG Yasmani Grandal 5.00 12.00

2009 Upper Deck Signature Stars USA Star Prospects Jerseys

OVERALL AU/MEM ODDS 1:5 HOBBY
1 Cody Buckel 4.00 10.00
2 Nick Castellanos 3.00 8.00
3 Garin Cecchini 3.00 8.00
4 Sean Coyle 3.00 8.00
5 Nicky Delmonico 3.00 8.00
6 Kevin Gausman 3.00 8.00
7 Cory Hahn 3.00 8.00
8 Bryce Harper 10.00 25.00
9 Kavin Keyes 3.00 8.00
10 Manny Machado 5.00 12.00
11 Connor Mason 3.00 8.00
12 Ladson Montgomery 3.00 8.00
13 Phillip Pfeifer 3.00 8.00
14 Brian Ragira 3.00 8.00
15 Robbie Ray 3.00 8.00
16 Kyle Ryan 3.00 8.00
17 Jameson Taillon 4.00 10.00
18 AJ Vanegas 3.00 8.00
19 Karsten Whitson 3.00 8.00
20 Tony Wolters 3.00 8.00
21 Trevor Bauer 6.00 15.00
22 Chad Bettis 3.00 8.00
23 Bryce Brentz 3.00 8.00
24 Michael Choice 3.00 8.00
25 Gerrit Cole 4.00 10.00
26 Christian Colon 3.00 8.00
27 Blake Forsythe 3.00 8.00
28 Yasmani Grandal 3.00 8.00
29 Sonny Gray 3.00 8.00
30 Rick Hague 3.00 8.00
31 Tyler Holt 3.00 8.00
32 Casey McGrew 3.00 8.00
33 Brad Miller 3.00 8.00
34 Matt Newman 3.00 8.00
35 Nick Pepitone 3.00 8.00
36 Drew Pomeranz 3.00 8.00
37 T.J. Walz 3.00 8.00
38 Cody Wheeler 3.00 8.00
39 Andy Wilkins 3.00 8.00
40 Asher Wojciechowski 3.00 8.00
41 Kolten Wong 3.00 8.00
42 Tony Zych 3.00 8.00

2009 Upper Deck Signature Stars USA Star Prospects Signatures

OVERALL AU/MEM ODDS 1:5 HOBBY
NO PRICING ON MOST DUE TO LACK OF SALES
USA1 Cody Buckel 6.00 15.00
USA2 Nick Castellanos 10.00 25.00
USA3 Garin Cecchini 4.00 10.00
USA5 Nicky Delmonico 8.00 20.00
USA6 Kevin Gausman 6.00 15.00
USA7 Cory Hahn 3.00 8.00
USA8 Bryce Harper 125.00 250.00
USA9 Kavin Keyes 10.00 25.00
USA10 Manny Machado 20.00 50.00
USA11 Connor Mason 8.00 20.00
USA13 Phillip Pfeifer 8.00 20.00
USA14 Brian Ragira 5.00 12.00
USA15 Robbie Ray 5.00 12.00
USA16 Kyle Ryan 4.00 10.00
USA17 Jameson Taillon 6.00 15.00
USA19 Karsten Whitson 5.00 12.00
USA20 Tony Wolters 8.00 20.00
USA21 Trevor Bauer 12.00 30.00
USA22 Chad Bettis 4.00 10.00
USA23 Bryce Brentz 15.00 40.00
USA24 Michael Choice 4.00 10.00
USA25 Gerrit Cole 20.00 50.00
USA26 Christian Colon 4.00 10.00
USA28 Yasmani Grandal 6.00 15.00
USA29 Sonny Gray 6.00 15.00
USA33 Brad Miller 8.00 20.00
USA35 Nick Pepitone 3.00 8.00
USA36 Drew Pomeranz 8.00 20.00
USA37 T.J. Walz 6.00 15.00
USA39 Andy Wilkins 4.00 10.00
USA41 Kolten Wong 8.00 20.00

2009 Upper Deck Signature Stars USA Winning Materials

OVERALL AU/MEM ODDS 1:5 HOBBY
STATED PRINT RUN 499 SER.#'d SETS
1 Cody Buckel 2.50 6.00
2 Nick Castellanos 5.00 12.00
3 Garin Cecchini 5.00 12.00
4 Sean Coyle 1.50 4.00
5 Nicky Delmonico 1.50 4.00
6 Kevin Gausman 8.00 20.00
7 Cory Hahn 1.50 4.00
8 Bryce Harper 12.00 30.00
9 Kavin Keyes 1.50 4.00
10 Manny Machado 10.00 25.00
11 Connor Mason 1.50 4.00
12 Ladson Montgomery 1.50 4.00
13 Phillip Pfeifer 1.50 4.00
14 Brian Ragira 2.50 6.00
15 Robbie Ray 1.50 4.00
16 Kyle Ryan 1.50 4.00
17 Jameson Taillon 2.50 6.00
18 AJ Vanegas 1.50 4.00
19 Karsten Whitson 2.50 6.00
20 Tony Wolters 1.50 4.00
21 Trevor Bauer 15.00 40.00
22 Christian Colon 2.50 6.00
23 Cody Wheeler 1.50 4.00
24 Chad Bettis 1.50 4.00
25 Bryce Brentz 4.00 10.00
26 Nick Pepitone 1.50 4.00
27 Michael Choice 2.50 6.00
28 Gerrit Cole 15.00 40.00
29 Sonny Gray 4.00 10.00
30 Tyler Holt 1.50 4.00
31 T.J. Walz 1.50 4.00
32 Rick Hague 1.50 4.00
33 Drew Pomeranz 5.00 12.00
34 Blake Forsythe 1.50 4.00
35 Matt Newman 1.50 4.00
36 Casey McGrew 1.50 4.00
37 Brad Miller 4.00 10.00
38 Yasmani Grandal 2.50 6.00
39 Kolten Wong 5.00 12.00
40 Tony Zych 1.50 4.00
41 Andy Wilkins 1.50 4.00
42 Asher Wojciechowski 2.50 6.00

1998 Upper Deck Special F/X

The 1998 Upper Deck Special F/X set was issued in one series totalling 150 cards. Distributed exclusively in retail outlets, six-card packs carried a $2.97 suggested retail price. The set contains a selection of the top 150 cards from the basic issue 1998 Upper Deck first series set including the topical subsets Griffey's Hot List (1-10) and Star Rookies (136-150). Each Special F/X card features a special foil treatment on the card fronts and is printed on sturdy 20 pt. stock.

COMPLETE SET (150) 15.00 40.00
1 Ken Griffey Jr. GHL 1.00 2.50
2 Mark McGwire GHL 1.25 3.00
3 Alex Rodriguez GHL .75 2.00
4 Larry Walker GHL .20 .50
5 Tino Martinez GHL .30 .75
6 Mike Piazza GHL .75 2.00
7 Jose Cruz Jr. GHL .20 .50
8 Greg Maddux GHL .75 2.00
9 Tony Gwynn GHL .60 1.50
10 Roger Clemens GHL 1.00 2.50
11 Jason Dickson .20 .50
12 Darin Erstad .20 .50
13 Chuck Finley .20 .50
14 Dave Hollins .20 .50
15 Garret Anderson .20 .50
16 Michael Tucker .20 .50
17 Javier Lopez .20 .50
18 John Smoltz .30 .75
19 Mark Wohlers .20 .50
20 Greg Maddux .75 2.00
21 Scott Erickson .20 .50
22 Jimmy Key .20 .50
23 B.J. Surhoff .20 .50
24 Eric Davis .20 .50
25 Rafael Palmeiro .30 .75
26 Tim Naehring .20 .50
27 Darren Bragg .20 .50
28 Troy O'Leary .20 .50
29 John Valentin .20 .50
30 Mo Vaughn .20 .50
31 Mark Grace .30 .75
32 Kevin Foster .20 .50
33 Kevin Tapani .20 .50
34 Kevin Orie .20 .50
35 Albert Belle .20 .50
36 Ray Durham .20 .50
37 Jaime Navarro .20 .50
38 Mike Cameron .20 .50
39 Eddie Taubensee .20 .50
40 Barry Larkin .30 .75
41 Willie Greene .20 .50
42 Jeff Shaw .20 .50
43 Omar Vizquel .30 .75
44 Brian Giles .20 .50
45 Jim Thome .30 .75
46 David Justice .20 .50
47 Sandy Alomar Jr. .20 .50
48 Neifi Perez .20 .50
49 Dante Bichette .20 .50
50 Vinny Castilla .20 .50
51 John Thomson .20 .50
52 Damion Easley .20 .50
53 Justin Thompson .20 .50
54 Bobby Higginson .20 .50
55 Tony Clark .20 .50
56 Charles Johnson .20 .50
57 Edgar Renteria .20 .50
58 Alex Fernandez .20 .50
59 Gary Sheffield .20 .50
60 Livan Hernandez .20 .50
61 Craig Biggio .30 .75
62 Chris Holt .20 .50
63 Billy Wagner .20 .50
64 Brad Ausmus .20 .50
65 Dean Palmer .20 .50
66 Tim Belcher .20 .50
67 Jeff King .20 .50
68 Jose Rosado .20 .50
69 Chan Ho Park .20 .50
70 Raul Mondesi .20 .50
71 Hideo Nomo .50 1.25
72 Todd Zeile .20 .50
73 Eric Karros .20 .50
74 Cal Eldred .20 .50
75 Jeff D'Amico .20 .50
76 Doug Jones .20 .50

77 Dave Nilsson	.20	.50
78 Todd Walker	.20	.50
79 Rick Aguilera	.20	.50
80 Paul Molitor	.20	.50
81 Brad Radke	.20	.50
82 Vladimir Guerrero	.50	1.25
83 Carlos Perez	.20	.50
84 F.P. Santangelo	.20	.50
85 Rondell White	.20	.50
86 Butch Huskey	.20	.50
87 Edgardo Alfonzo	.20	.50
88 John Franco	.20	.50
89 John Olerud	.20	.50
90 Todd Hundley	.20	.50
91 Bernie Williams	.30	.75
92 Andy Pettitte	.30	.75
93 Paul O'Neill	.30	.75
94 David Cone	.20	.50
95 Jason Giambi	.20	.50
96 Damon Mashore	.20	.50
97 Scott Spiezio	.20	.50
98 Ariel Prieto	.20	.50
99 Rico Brogna	.20	.50
100 Mike Lieberthal	.20	.50
101 Garrett Stephenson	.20	.50
102 Ricky Bottalico	.20	.50
103 Kevin Polcovich	.20	.50
104 Jon Lieber	.20	.50
105 Kevin Young	.20	.50
106 Tony Womack	.20	.50
107 Gary Gaetti	.20	.50
108 Alan Benes	.20	.50
109 Willie McGee	.20	.50
110 Mark McGwire	1.25	3.00
111 Ron Gant	.20	.50
112 Andy Ashby	.20	.50
113 Steve Finley	.20	.50
114 Quilvio Veras	.20	.50
115 Ken Caminiti	.20	.50
116 Joey Hamilton	.20	.50
117 Bill Mueller	.20	.50
118 Mark Gardner	.20	.50
119 Shawn Estes	.20	.50
120 J.T. Snow	.20	.50
121 Dante Powell	.20	.50
122 Jeff Kent	.20	.50
123 Jamie Moyer	.20	.50
124 Joey Cora	.20	.50
125 Ken Griffey Jr.	1.00	2.50
126 Jeff Fassero	.20	.50
127 Edgar Martinez	.30	.75
128 Will Clark	.30	.75
129 Lee Stevens	.20	.50
130 Ivan Rodriguez	.30	.75
131 Rusty Greer	.20	.50
132 Ed Sprague	.20	.50
133 Pat Hentgen	.20	.50
134 Shannon Stewart	.20	.50
135 Carlos Delgado	.20	.50
136 Brett Tomko	.20	.50
137 Jose Guillen	.20	.50
138 Eli Marrero	.20	.50
139 Dennis Reyes	.20	.50
140 Mark Kotsay	.20	.50
141 Richie Sexson	.20	.50
142 Todd Helton	.30	.75
143 Jeremi Gonzalez	.20	.50
144 Jeff Abbott	.20	.50
145 Matt Morris	.20	.50
146 Aaron Boone	.20	.50
147 Todd Dunwoody	.20	.50
148 Mario Valdez	.20	.50
149 Fernando Tatis	.20	.50
150 Jaret Wright	.20	.50

1998 Upper Deck Special F/X Power Zone

COMPLETE SET (20)	20.00	50.00
STATED ODDS 1:7		
PZ1 Jose Cruz Jr.	.50	1.25
PZ2 Frank Thomas	1.25	3.00
PZ3 Juan Gonzalez	.50	1.25
PZ4 Mike Piazza	2.00	5.00
PZ5 Mark McGwire	3.00	8.00
PZ6 Barry Bonds	3.00	8.00
PZ7 Greg Maddux	2.00	5.00
PZ8 Alex Rodriguez	2.00	5.00
PZ9 Nomar Garciaparra	2.00	5.00
PZ10 Ken Griffey Jr.	2.50	6.00
PZ11 John Smoltz	.75	2.00
PZ12 Andruw Jones	.75	2.00
PZ13 Sandy Alomar Jr.	.50	1.25
PZ14 Roberto Alomar	.75	2.00
PZ15 Chipper Jones	1.25	3.00
PZ16 Kenny Lofton	.50	1.25
PZ17 Larry Walker	.50	1.25
PZ18 Jeff Bagwell	.75	2.00
PZ19 Mo Vaughn	.50	1.25
PZ20 Tom Glavine	.75	2.00

1998 Upper Deck Special F/X Power Zone OctoberBest

COMPLETE SET (15)	60.00	120.00
STATED ODDS 1:34		
PZ1 Frank Thomas	4.00	10.00
PZ2 Juan Gonzalez	1.50	4.00
PZ3 Mike Piazza	6.00	15.00
PZ4 Mark McGwire	10.00	25.00
PZ5 Jeff Bagwell	2.50	6.00
PZ6 Barry Bonds	10.00	25.00
PZ7 Ken Griffey Jr.	8.00	20.00
PZ8 John Smoltz	2.50	6.00
PZ9 Andruw Jones	2.50	6.00
PZ10 Greg Maddux	6.00	15.00
PZ11 Sandy Alomar Jr.	1.50	4.00
PZ12 Roberto Alomar	2.50	6.00
PZ13 Chipper Jones	4.00	10.00
PZ14 Kenny Lofton	1.50	4.00
PZ15 Tom Glavine	2.50	6.00

1998 Upper Deck Special F/X Power Zone Power Driven

COMPLETE SET (10)	60.00	120.00
STATED ODDS 1:69 SPECIAL F/X		
PZ1 Frank Thomas	5.00	12.00
PZ2 Juan Gonzalez	2.00	5.00
PZ3 Mike Piazza	8.00	20.00
PZ4 Larry Walker	2.00	5.00
PZ5 Mark McGwire	12.50	30.00
PZ6 Jeff Bagwell	3.00	8.00
PZ7 Mo Vaughn	2.00	5.00
PZ8 Barry Bonds	12.50	30.00
PZ9 Tino Martinez	3.00	8.00
PZ10 Ken Griffey Jr.	10.00	25.00

1998 Upper Deck Special F/X Power Zone Superstar Xcitement

COMPLETE SET (10)	125.00	250.00
RANDOM INSERTS IN SPECIAL F/X PACKS		
STATED PRINT RUN 250 SERIAL #'d SETS		
PZ1 Jose Cruz Jr.	3.00	8.00
PZ2 Frank Thomas	8.00	20.00
PZ3 Juan Gonzalez	3.00	8.00
PZ4 Mike Piazza	12.50	30.00
PZ5 Mark McGwire	10.00	25.00
PZ6 Barry Bonds	10.00	25.00
PZ7 Greg Maddux	12.50	30.00
PZ8 Alex Rodriguez	12.50	30.00
PZ9 Nomar Garciaparra	12.50	30.00
PZ10 Ken Griffey Jr.	15.00	40.00

2006 Upper Deck Special F/X

COMMON CARD (1-900)	.30	.75
COMMON RC (901-1025)	.50	1.25
1 Adam Kennedy	.30	.75
2 Bartolo Colon	.30	.75
3 Bengie Molina	.30	.75
4 Casey Kotchman	.30	.75
5 Chone Figgins	.30	.75
6 Dallas McPherson	.30	.75
7 Darin Erstad	.30	.75
8 Ervin Santana	.30	.75
9 Francisco Rodriguez	.50	1.25
10 Garret Anderson	.30	.75
11 Jarrod Washburn	.30	.75
12 John Lackey	.50	1.25
13 Juan Rivera	.30	.75
14 Orlando Cabrera	.30	.75
15 Paul Byrd	.30	.75
16 Steve Finley	.30	.75
17 Vladimir Guerrero	.50	1.25
18 Alex Cintron	.30	.75
19 Brandon Lyon	.30	.75
20 Brandon Webb	.50	1.25
21 Chad Tracy	.30	.75
22 Chris Snyder	.30	.75
23 Claudio Vargas	.30	.75
24 Conor Jackson	.50	1.25
25 Craig Counsell	.30	.75
26 Javier Vazquez	.30	.75
27 Jose Valverde	.30	.75
28 Luis Gonzalez	.30	.75
29 Royce Clayton	.30	.75
30 Russ Ortiz	.30	.75
31 Shawn Green	.30	.75
32 Dustin Nippert (RC)	.50	1.25
33 Tony Clark	.30	.75
34 Troy Glaus	.30	.75
35 Adam LaRoche	.30	.75
36 Andruw Jones	.30	.75
37 Craig Hansen RC	1.25	3.00
38 Chipper Jones	.75	2.00
39 Horacio Ramirez	.30	.75
40 Jeff Francoeur	.75	2.00
41 John Smoltz	.75	2.00
42 Joey Devine RC	.50	1.25
43 Johnny Estrada	.30	.75
44 Anthony Lerew (RC)	.50	1.25
45 Julio Franco	.30	.75
46 Kyle Farnsworth	.30	.75
47 Marcus Giles	.30	.75
48 Mike Hampton	.30	.75
49 Rafael Furcal	.30	.75
50 Chuck James (RC)	.50	1.25
51 Tim Hudson	.50	1.25
52 B.J. Ryan	.30	.75
53 Bernie Castro (RC)	.50	1.25
54 Brian Roberts	.30	.75
55 Luis Figueroa RC	.50	1.25
56 Daniel Cabrera	.30	.75
57 Eric Byrnes	.30	.75
58 Emiliano Fruto RC	.50	1.25
59 Erik Bedard	.30	.75
60 Javy Lopez	.30	.75
61 Jay Gibbons	.30	.75
62 Jorge Julio	.30	.75
63 Luis Matos	.30	.75
64 Melvin Mora	.30	.75
65 Miguel Tejada	.50	1.25
66 Rafael Palmeiro	.50	1.25
67 Rodrigo Lopez	.30	.75
68 Sammy Sosa	.75	2.00
69 Clay Hensley (RC)	.50	1.25
70 Bill Mueller	.30	.75
71 Bronson Arroyo	.30	.75
72 Curt Schilling	.50	1.25
73 David Ortiz	.75	2.00
74 David Wells	.30	.75
75 Edgar Renteria	.30	.75
76 Zach Jackson (RC)	.50	1.25
77 Jason Varitek	.75	2.00
78 Johnny Damon	.50	1.25
79 Keith Foulke	.30	.75
80 Kevin Youkilis	.30	.75
81 Manny Ramirez	.75	2.00
82 Matt Clement	.30	.75
83 Hanley Ramirez (RC)	.75	2.00
84 Tim Wakefield	.50	1.25
85 Trot Nixon	.30	.75
86 Wade Miller	.30	.75
87 Aramis Ramirez	.30	.75
88 Carlos Zambrano	.50	1.25
89 Corey Patterson	.30	.75
90 Derrek Lee	.30	.75
91 Geovany Soto (RC)	1.25	3.00
92 Greg Maddux	1.00	2.50
93 Jeromy Burnitz	.30	.75
94 Jerry Hairston Jr.	.30	.75
95 Kerry Wood	.30	.75
96 Mark Prior	.50	1.25
97 Matt Murton	.30	.75
98 Michael Barrett	.30	.75
99 Neifi Perez	.30	.75
100 Nomar Garciaparra	.50	1.25
101 Rich Hill	.75	2.00
102 Ryan Dempster	.30	.75
103 Todd Walker	.30	.75
104 A.J. Pierzynski	.30	.75
105 Aaron Rowand	.30	.75
106 Bobby Jenks	.30	.75
107 Carl Everett	.30	.75
108 Dustin Hermanson	.30	.75
109 Frank Thomas	.75	2.00
110 Freddy Garcia	.30	.75
111 Jermaine Dye	.30	.75
112 Joe Crede	.30	.75
113 Jon Garland	.30	.75
114 Jose Contreras	.30	.75
115 Juan Uribe	.30	.75
116 Mark Buehrle	.50	1.25
117 Orlando Hernandez	.30	.75
118 Paul Konerko	.50	1.25
119 Scott Podsednik	.30	.75
120 Tadahito Iguchi	.30	.75
121 Aaron Harang	.30	.75
122 Adam Dunn	.50	1.25
123 Austin Kearns	.30	.75
124 Brandon Claussen	.30	.75
125 Chris Denorfia (RC)	.50	1.25
126 Edwin Encarnacion	.75	2.00
127 Miguel Perez (RC)	.50	1.25
128 Felipe Lopez	.30	.75
129 Jason LaRue	.30	.75
130 Ken Griffey Jr.	1.50	4.00
131 Chris Booker (RC)	.50	1.25
132 Luke Hudson	.30	.75
133 Jason Bergmann RC	.50	1.25
134 Ryan Freel	.30	.75
135 Sean Casey	.30	.75
136 Wily Mo Pena	.30	.75
137 Aaron Boone	.30	.75
138 Ben Broussard	.30	.75
139 Ryan Garko (RC)	.50	1.25
140 C.C. Sabathia	.50	1.25
141 Casey Blake	.30	.75
142 Cliff Lee	.50	1.25
143 Coco Crisp	.30	.75
144 David Riske	.30	.75
145 Grady Sizemore	.50	1.25
146 Jake Westbrook	.30	.75
147 Jhonny Peralta	.30	.75
148 Josh Bard	.30	.75
149 Kevin Millwood	.30	.75
150 Ronnie Belliard	.30	.75
151 Scott Elarton	.30	.75
152 Travis Hafner	.30	.75
153 Victor Martinez	.50	1.25
154 Aaron Cook	.30	.75
155 Aaron Miles	.30	.75
156 Brad Hawpe	.30	.75
157 Bobby Keppel (RC)	.50	1.25
158 Chin-Hui Tsao	.30	.75
159 Clint Barmes	.30	.75
160 Cory Sullivan	.30	.75
161 Garrett Atkins	.30	.75
162 J.D. Closser	.30	.75
163 Jason Jennings	.30	.75
164 Jeff Baker	.30	.75
165 Jeff Francis	.30	.75
166 Luis Gonzalez	.30	.75
167 Matt Holliday	.75	2.00
168 Todd Helton	.50	1.25
169 Brandon Inge	.30	.75
170 Carlos Guillen	.30	.75
171 Carlos Pena	.50	1.25
172 Chris Shelton	.30	.75
173 Craig Monroe	.30	.75
174 Curtis Granderson	.60	1.50
175 Dmitri Young	.30	.75
176 Ivan Rodriguez	.50	1.25
177 Jason Johnson		
178 Jeremy Bonderman	.30	.75
179 Magglio Ordonez	.50	1.25
180 Mark Woodyard (RC)	.50	1.25
181 Russell Martin (RC)	.50	1.25
182 Omar Infante	.30	.75
183 Placido Polanco	.30	.75
184 Chris Heintz RC	.50	1.25
185 A.J. Burnett	.30	.75
186 Alex Gonzalez	.30	.75
187 Josh Johnson (RC)	1.25	3.00
188 Carlos Delgado	.30	.75
189 Dontrelle Willis	.30	.75
190 Josh Wilson (RC)	.50	1.25
191 Jason Vargas	.30	.75
192 Jeff Conine	.30	.75
193 Jeremy Hermida	.30	.75
194 Josh Beckett	.30	.75
195 Juan Encarnacion	.30	.75
196 Juan Pierre	.30	.75
197 Luis Castillo	.30	.75
198 Miguel Cabrera	.75	2.00
199 Mike Lowell	.30	.75
200 Paul Lo Duca	.30	.75
201 Todd Jones	.30	.75
202 Adam Everett	.30	.75
203 Andy Pettitte	.30	.75
204 Brad Ausmus	.30	.75
205 Brad Lidge	.30	.75
206 Brandon Backe	.30	.75
207 Charlton Jimerson (RC)	.50	1.25
208 Chris Burke	.30	.75
209 Craig Biggio	.50	1.25
210 Dan Wheeler	.30	.75
211 Jason Lane	.30	.75
212 Jeff Bagwell	.50	1.25
213 Lance Berkman	.50	1.25
214 Luke Scott	.30	.75
215 Morgan Ensberg	.30	.75
216 Roger Clemens	1.00	2.50
217 Roy Oswalt	.50	1.25
218 Willy Taveras	.30	.75
219 Andres Blanco	.30	.75
220 Angel Berroa	.30	.75
221 Ken Ray (RC)	.30	.75
222 David DeJesus	.30	.75
223 Emil Brown	.30	.75
224 J.P. Howell	.30	.75
225 Jeremy Affeldt	.30	.75
226 Jimmy Gobble	.30	.75
227 John Buck	.30	.75
228 Jose Lima	.30	.75
229 Mark Teahen	.30	.75
230 Matt Stairs	.30	.75
231 Mike MacDougal	.30	.75
232 Mike Sweeney	.30	.75
233 Runelvys Hernandez	.30	.75
234 Terrence Long	.30	.75
235 Zack Greinke	.75	2.00
236 Ron Flores RC	.50	1.25
237 Brad Penny	.30	.75
238 Cesar Izturis	.30	.75
239 D.J. Houlton	.30	.75
240 Derek Lowe	.30	.75
241 Eric Gagne	.30	.75
242 Hee Seop Choi	.30	.75
243 J.D. Drew	.30	.75
244 Jason Phillips	.30	.75
245 Jason Repko	.30	.75
246 Jayson Werth	.50	1.25
247 Jeff Kent	.30	.75
248 Jeff Weaver	.30	.75
249 Milton Bradley	.30	.75
250 Odalis Perez	.30	.75
251 Hong-Chih Kuo (RC)	1.25	3.00
252 Oscar Robles	.30	.75
253 Ben Sheets	.30	.75
254 Bill Hall	.30	.75
255 Brady Clark	.30	.75
256 Carlos Lee	.30	.75
257 Chris Capuano	.30	.75
258 Nelson Cruz (RC)	2.00	5.00
259 Derrick Turnbow	.30	.75
260 Doug Davis	.30	.75
261 Geoff Jenkins	.30	.75
262 J.J. Hardy	.30	.75
263 Lyle Overbay	.30	.75
264 Prince Fielder	1.50	4.00
265 Rickie Weeks	.30	.75
266 Russell Branyan	.30	.75
267 Tomo Ohka	.30	.75
268 Jonah Bayliss (RC)	.50	1.25
269 Brad Radke	.30	.75
270 Carlos Silva	.30	.75
271 Francisco Liriano (RC)	1.25	3.00
272 Jacque Jones	.30	.75
273 Joe Mauer	.50	1.25
274 Travis Bowyer (RC)	.50	1.25
275 Joe Nathan	.30	.75
276 Johan Santana	.50	1.25
277 Justin Morneau	.50	1.25
278 Kyle Lohse	.30	.75
279 Lew Ford	.30	.75
280 Matthew LeCroy	.30	.75
281 Michael Cuddyer	.30	.75
282 Nick Punto	.30	.75
283 Scott Baker	.30	.75
284 Shannon Stewart	.30	.75
285 Torii Hunter	.30	.75
286 Braden Looper	.30	.75
287 Carlos Beltran	.50	1.25
288 Cliff Floyd	.30	.75
289 David Wright	.60	1.50
290 Doug Mientkiewicz	.30	.75
291 Anderson Hernandez (RC)	.50	1.25
292 Jose Reyes	.50	1.25
293 Kazuo Matsui	.30	.75
294 Kris Benson	.30	.75
295 Miguel Cairo	.30	.75
296 Mike Cameron	.30	.75
297 Robert Andino RC	.50	1.25
298 Mike Piazza	.75	2.00
299 Pedro Martinez	.50	1.25
300 Tom Glavine	.50	1.25
301 Victor Diaz	.30	.75
302 Tim Hamulack (RC)	.50	1.25
303 Alex Rodriguez	1.00	2.50
304 Bernie Williams	.50	1.25
305 Carl Pavano	.30	.75
306 Chien-Ming Wang	.50	1.25
307 Derek Jeter	2.00	5.00
308 Gary Sheffield	.30	.75
309 Hideki Matsui	.75	2.00
310 Jason Giambi	.30	.75
311 Jorge Posada	.50	1.25
312 Kevin Brown	.30	.75
313 Mariano Rivera	1.00	2.50
314 Matt Lawton	.30	.75
315 Mike Mussina	.50	1.25
316 Randy Johnson	.75	2.00
317 Robinson Cano	.50	1.25
318 Mike Vento (RC)	.50	1.25
319 Stephen Andrade (RC)	.50	1.25
320 Tony Womack	.30	.75
321 Barry Zito	.50	1.25
322 Bobby Crosby	.30	.75
323 Bobby Kielty	.30	.75
324 Dan Johnson	.30	.75
325 Danny Haren	.30	.75
326 Eric Chavez	.30	.75
327 Erubiel Durazo	.30	.75
328 Huston Street	.30	.75
329 Jason Kendall	.30	.75
330 Jay Payton	.30	.75
331 Joe Blanton	.30	.75
332 Joe Kennedy	.30	.75
333 Kirk Saarloos	.30	.75
334 Mark Kotsay	.30	.75
335 Nick Swisher	.50	1.25
336 Rich Harden	.30	.75
337 Scott Hatteberg	.30	.75
338 Billy Wagner	.30	.75
339 Bobby Abreu	.30	.75
340 Brett Myers	.30	.75
341 Chase Utley	.50	1.25
342 Danny Sandoval RC	.50	1.25
343 David Bell	.30	.75
344 Gavin Floyd	.30	.75
345 Jim Thome	.50	1.25
346 Jimmy Rollins	.50	1.25
347 Jon Lieber	.30	.75
348 Kenny Lofton	.30	.75
349 Mike Lieberthal	.30	.75
350 Pat Burrell	.30	.75
351 Randy Wolf	.30	.75
352 Ryan Howard	.60	1.50
353 Vicente Padilla	.30	.75
354 Bryan Bullington (RC)	.50	1.25
355 J.J. Furmaniak (RC)	.50	1.25
356 Craig Wilson	.30	.75
357 Matt Capps (RC)	.50	1.25
358 Tom Gorzelanny (RC)	.50	1.25
359 Jack Wilson	.30	.75
360 Jason Bay	.30	.75
361 Jose Mesa	.30	.75
362 Josh Fogg	.30	.75
363 Kip Wells	.30	.75
364 Steve Stemle RC	.50	1.25
365 Oliver Perez	.30	.75
366 Rob Mackowiak	.30	.75
367 Ronny Paulino (RC)	.50	1.25
368 Joe Nelson (RC)	.30	.75
369 Zach Duke	.30	.75
370 Adam Eaton	.30	.75
371 Scott Feldman (RC)	.50	1.25
372 Brian Giles	.30	.75
373 Brian Lawrence	.30	.75
374 Damian Jackson	.30	.75
375 Dave Roberts	.50	1.25
376 Jake Peavy	.30	.75
377 Joe Randa	.30	.75
378 Khalil Greene	.30	.75
379 Mark Loretta	.30	.75
380 Ramon Hernandez	.30	.75
381 Robert Fick	.30	.75
382 Ryan Klesko	.30	.75
383 Trevor Hoffman	.50	1.25
384 Woody Williams	.30	.75
385 Xavier Nady	.30	.75
386 Armando Benitez	.30	.75
387 Brad Hennessey	.30	.75
388 Brian Myrow RC	.50	1.25
389 Edgardo Alfonzo	.30	.75
390 J.T. Snow	.30	.75
391 Jeremy Accardo RC	.50	1.25
392 Jason Schmidt	.30	.75
393 Lance Niekro	.30	.75
394 Matt Cain	2.00	5.00
395 Daniel Ortmeier (RC)	.50	1.25
396 Moises Alou	.30	.75
397 Doug Clark (RC)	.50	1.25
398 Omar Vizquel	.50	1.25
399 Pedro Feliz	.30	.75
400 Randy Winn	.30	.75
401 Ray Durham	.30	.75
402 Adrian Beltre	.75	2.00
403 Eddie Guardado	.30	.75
404 Felix Hernandez	.50	1.25
405 Gil Meche	.30	.75
406 Ichiro Suzuki	1.00	2.50
407 Jamie Moyer	.30	.75
408 Jeff Nelson	.30	.75
409 Jeremy Reed	.30	.75
410 Joel Pineiro	.30	.75
411 Chris Bootcheck (RC)	.50	1.25
412 Raul Ibanez	.50	1.25
413 Richie Sexson	.30	.75
414 Ryan Franklin	.30	.75
415 Willie Bloomquist	.30	.75
416 Yorvit Torrealba	.30	.75
417 Yuniesky Betancourt	.30	.75
418 Jeff Harris RC	.50	1.25
419 Albert Pujols	1.00	2.50
420 Chris Carpenter	.50	1.25
421 David Eckstein	.30	.75
422 Jason Isringhausen	.30	.75
423 Jason Marquis	.30	.75
424 Adam Wainwright (RC)	.75	2.00
425 Jim Edmonds	.50	1.25
426 Ryan Theriot RC	1.50	4.00
427 Chris Duncan (RC)	.75	2.00
428 Mark Grudzielanek	.30	.75
429 Mark Mulder	.30	.75
430 Matt Morris	.30	.75
431 Reggie Sanders	.30	.75
432 Scott Rolen	.50	1.25
433 Tyler Johnson (RC)	.50	1.25
434 Yadier Molina	1.00	2.50
435 Alex Gonzalez	.30	.75
436 Aubrey Huff	.30	.75
437 Tim Corcoran RC	.50	1.25
438 Carl Crawford	.50	1.25
439 Casey Fossum	.30	.75
440 Danys Baez	.30	.75
441 Edwin Jackson	.30	.75
442 Joey Gathright	.30	.75
443 Jonny Gomes	.30	.75
444 Jorge Cantu	.30	.75
445 Julio Lugo	.30	.75
446 Nick Green	.30	.75
447 Rocco Baldelli	.30	.75
448 Scott Kazmir	.50	1.25
449 Seth McClung	.30	.75
450 Toby Hall	.30	.75
451 Travis Lee	.30	.75
452 Craig Breslow RC	.50	1.25
453 Alfonso Soriano	.50	1.25
454 Chris R. Young	.30	.75
455 David Dellucci	.30	.75
456 Francisco Cordero	.30	.75
457 Gary Matthews	.30	.75
458 Hank Blalock	.30	.75
459 Juan Dominguez	.30	.75
460 Josh Rupe (RC)	.50	1.25
461 Kenny Rogers	.30	.75
462 Kevin Mench	.30	.75
463 Laynce Nix	.30	.75
464 Mark Teixeira	.50	1.25
465 Michael Young	.30	.75
466 Richard Hidalgo	.30	.75
467 Jason Botts (RC)	.50	1.25
468 Aaron Hill	.30	.75
469 Alex Rios	.30	.75
470 Corey Koskie	.30	.75
471 Chris Demaria RC	.50	1.25
472 Eric Hinske	.30	.75
473 Frank Catalanotto	.30	.75
474 Jason Childers RC	.50	1.25
475 Gustavo Chacin	.30	.75
476 Josh Towers	.30	.75
477 Miguel Batista	.30	.75
478 Orlando Hudson	.30	.75
479 Reed Johnson	.30	.75
480 Roy Halladay	.50	1.25
481 Shaun Marcum (RC)	.50	1.25
482 Shea Hillenbrand	.30	.75
483 Ted Lilly	.30	.75
484 Vernon Wells	.30	.75
485 Brad Wilkerson	.30	.75
486 Darrell Rasner (RC)	.50	1.25
487 Chad Cordero	.30	.75
488 Cristian Guzman	.30	.75
489 Esteban Loaiza	.30	.75
490 John Patterson	.30	.75
491 Jose Guillen	.30	.75
492 Jose Vidro	.30	.75
493 Livan Hernandez	.30	.75
494 Marlon Byrd	.30	.75
495 Nick Johnson	.30	.75
496 Preston Wilson	.30	.75
497 Ryan Church	.30	.75
498 Ryan Zimmerman (RC)	1.50	4.00
499 Tony Armas	.30	.75
500 Vinny Castilla	.30	.75
501 Andy Green	.30	.75
502 Damion Easley	.30	.75
503 Eric Byrnes	.30	.75
504 Jason Grimsley	.30	.75
505 Jeff DaVanon	.30	.75
506 Johnny Estrada	.30	.75
507 Luis Vizcaino	.30	.75
508 Miguel Batista	.30	.75
509 Orlando Hernandez	.30	.75
510 Orlando Hudson	.30	.75
511 Terry Mulholland	.30	.75
512 Chris Reitsma	.30	.75
513 Edgar Renteria	.30	.75
514 John Thomson	.30	.75
515 Jorge Sosa	.30	.75
516 Oscar Villarreal	.30	.75
517 Pete Orr	.30	.75
518 Ryan Langerhans	.30	.75
519 Todd Pratt	.30	.75
520 Wilson Betemit	.30	.75
521 Brian Jordan	.30	.75
522 Lance Cormier	.30	.75
523 Matt Diaz	.30	.75
524 Mike Remlinger	.30	.75
525 Bruce Chen	.30	.75
526 Chris Gomez	.30	.75
527 Chris Ray	.30	.75
528 Corey Patterson	.30	.75
529 David Newhan	.30	.75
530 Ed Rogers (RC)	.50	1.25
531 John Halama	.30	.75
532 Kris Benson	.30	.75
533 LaTroy Hawkins	.30	.75
534 Raul Chavez	.30	.75
535 Alex Cora	.50	1.25
536 Alex Gonzalez	.30	.75
537 Coco Crisp	.30	.75
538 David Riske	.30	.75
539 Doug Mirabelli	.30	.75
540 Josh Beckett	.30	.75
541 J.T. Snow	.30	.75
542 Mike Timlin	.30	.75
543 Julian Tavarez	.30	.75
544 Rudy Seanez	.30	.75
545 Wily Mo Pena	.30	.75
546 Bob Howry	.30	.75
547 Glendon Rusch	.30	.75
548 Henry Blanco	.30	.75
549 Jacque Jones	.30	.75
550 Jerome Williams	.30	.75
551 John Mabry	.30	.75
552 Juan Pierre	.30	.75
553 Scott Eyre	.30	.75
554 Scott Williamson	.30	.75
555 Wade Miller	.30	.75
556 Will Ohman	.30	.75
557 Alex Cintron	.30	.75
558 Rob Mackowiak	.30	.75
559 Brandon McCarthy	.30	.75
560 Chris Widger	.30	.75
561 Cliff Politte	.30	.75
562 Javier Vazquez	.30	.75
563 Jim Thome	.50	1.25
564 Matt Thornton	.30	.75
565 Neal Cotts	.30	.75
566 Pablo Ozuna	.30	.75
567 Ross Gload	.30	.75
568 Brandon Phillips	.30	.75
569 Bronson Arroyo	.30	.75
570 Dave Williams	.30	.75
571 David Ross	.30	.75
572 David Weathers	.30	.75
573 Eric Milton	.30	.75
574 Javier Valentin	.30	.75
575 Kent Mercker	.30	.75
576 Matt Belisle	.30	.75
577 Paul Wilson	.30	.75
578 Rich Aurilia	.30	.75
579 Rick White	.30	.75
580 Scott Hatteberg	.30	.75
581 Todd Coffey	.30	.75
582 Bob Wickman	.30	.75
583 Danny Graves	.30	.75
584 Eduardo Perez	.30	.75
585 Guillermo Mota	.30	.75
586 Jason Davis	.30	.75
587 Jason Johnson	.30	.75
588 Jason Michaels	.30	.75
589 Rafael Betancourt	.30	.75
590 Ramon Vazquez	.30	.75
591 Scott Sauerbeck	.30	.75
592 Todd Hollandsworth	.30	.75
593 Brian Fuentes	.30	.75
594 Danny Ardoin	.30	.75
595 David Cortes	.30	.75
596 Eli Marrero	.30	.75
597 Jamey Carroll	.30	.75
598 Jason Smith	.30	.75
599 Josh Fogg	.30	.75
600 Miguel Ojeda	.30	.75
601 Mike DeJean	.30	.75
602 Ray King	.30	.75
603 Omar Quintanilla (RC)	.50	1.25
604 Zach Day	.30	.75
605 Fernando Rodney	.30	.75
606 Kenny Rogers	.30	.75
607 Mike Maroth	.30	.75
608 Nate Robertson	.30	.75
609 Todd Jones	.30	.75
610 Vance Wilson	.30	.75
611 Bobby Seay	.30	.75
612 Chris Spurling	.30	.75
613 Roman Colon	.30	.75
614 Jason Grilli	.30	.75
615 Marcus Thames	.30	.75
616 Ramon Santiago	.30	.75
617 Alfredo Amezaga	.30	.75
618 Brian Moehler	.30	.75
619 Chris Aguila	.30	.75
620 Franklyn German	.30	.75
621 Joe Borowski	.30	.75
622 Logan Kensing (RC)	.50	1.25
623 Matt Treanor	.30	.75
624 Miguel Olivo	.30	.75
625 Sergio Mitre	.30	.75
626 Todd Wellemeyer	.30	.75
627 Wes Helms	.30	.75
628 Chad Qualls	.30	.75
629 Eric Bruntlett	.30	.75
630 Mike Gallo	.30	.75
631 Mike Lamb	.30	.75
632 Orlando Palmeiro	.30	.75
633 Russ Springer	.30	.75
634 Dan Wheeler	.30	.75
635 Eric Munson	.30	.75
636 Preston Wilson	.30	.75
637 Trever Miller	.30	.75
638 Ambiorix Burgos	.30	.75
639 Andy Sisco	.30	.75
640 Denny Bautista	.30	.75
641 Doug Mientkiewicz	.30	.75
642 Elmer Dessens	.30	.75
643 Esteban German	.30	.75
644 Joe Nelson (RC)	.50	1.25
645 Mark Grudzielanek	.30	.75
646 Mark Redman	.30	.75
647 Mike Wood	.30	.75
648 Paul Bako	.30	.75
649 Reggie Sanders	.30	.75
650 Scott Elarton	.30	.75
651 Shane Costa	.30	.75
652 Tony Graffanino	.30	.75
653 Jason Bulger (RC)	.50	1.25
654 Chris Bootcheck (RC)	.50	1.25
655 Esteban Yan	.30	.75
656 Hector Carrasco	.30	.75
657 J.C. Romero	.30	.75
658 Jeff Weaver	.30	.75
659 Jose Molina	.30	.75
660 Kelvim Escobar	.30	.75
661 Maicer Izturis	.30	.75
662 Robb Quinlan	.30	.75
663 Scot Shields	.30	.75
664 Tim Salmon	.30	.75
665 Bill Mueller	.30	.75
666 Brett Tomko	.30	.75
667 Dioner Navarro	.30	.75
668 Jae Seo	.30	.75
669 Jose Cruz	.30	.75
670 Kenny Lofton	.30	.75
671 Lance Carter	.30	.75
672 Nomar Garciaparra	.50	1.25
673 Olmedo Saenz	.30	.75
674 Rafael Furcal	.30	.75
675 Ramon Martinez	.30	.75
676 Ricky Ledee	.30	.75
677 Sandy Alomar	.30	.75
678 Yhency Brazoban	.30	.75
679 Corey Koskie	.30	.75
680 Dan Kolb	.30	.75
681 Gabe Gross	.30	.75
682 Jeff Cirillo	.30	.75
683 Matt Wise	.30	.75
684 Rick Helling	.30	.75
685 Chad Moeller	.30	.75
686 Dave Bush	.30	.75
687 Jorge De La Rosa	.30	.75
688 Justin Lehr	.30	.75
689 Jason Bartlett	.30	.75
690 Jesse Crain	.30	.75
691 Juan Rincon	.30	.75
692 Luis Castillo	.30	.75
693 Mike Redmond	.30	.75
694 Rondell White	.30	.75
695 Tony Batista	.30	.75
696 Juan Castro	.30	.75
697 Luis Rodriguez	.30	.75
698 Matt Guerrier	.30	.75
699 Willie Eyre (RC)	.50	1.25
700 Aaron Heilman	.30	.75
701 Billy Wagner	.30	.75
702 Carlos Delgado	.30	.75
703 Chad Bradford	.30	.75
704 Chris Woodward	.30	.75
705 Darren Oliver	.30	.75
706 Duaner Sanchez	.30	.75
707 Endy Chavez	.30	.75
708 Jorge Julio	.30	.75
709 Jose Valentin	.30	.75
710 Julio Franco	.30	.75
711 Paul Lo Duca	.30	.75
712 Ramon Castro	.30	.75
713 Steve Trachsel	.30	.75
714 Victor Zambrano	.30	.75
715 Xavier Nady	.30	.75
716 Andy Phillips	.30	.75
717 Bubba Crosby	.30	.75
718 Jaret Wright	.30	.75
719 Kelly Stinnett	.30	.75
720 Kyle Farnsworth	.30	.75
721 Mike Meyers	.30	.75
722 Octavio Dotel	.30	.75
723 Ron Villone	.30	.75
724 Scott Proctor	.30	.75
725 Shawn Chacon	.30	.75
726 Tanyon Sturtze	.30	.75
727 Adam Melhuse	.30	.75
728 Brad Halsey	.30	.75
729 Esteban Loaiza	.30	.75
730 Frank Thomas	.75	2.00
731 Jay Witasick	.30	.75
732 Justin Duchscherer	.30	.75
733 Kiko Calero	.30	.75
734 Marco Scutaro	.50	1.25
735 Mark Ellis	.30	.75
736 Milton Bradley	.30	.75
737 Aaron Fultz	.30	.75
738 Aaron Rowand	.30	.75
739 Geoff Geary	.30	.75
740 Arthur Rhodes	.30	.75
741 Chris Coste RC	1.25	3.00
742 Rheal Cormier	.30	.75
743 Ryan Franklin	.30	.75
744 Ryan Madson	.30	.75

745 Sal Fasano .30 .75
746 Tom Gordon .30 .75
747 Abraham Nunez .30 .75
748 David Dellucci .30 .75
749 Julio Santana .30 .75
750 Shane Victorino .30 .75
751 Damaso Marte .30 .75
752 Freddy Sanchez .30 .75
753 Humberto Cota .30 .75
754 Jeromy Burnitz .30 .75
755 Joe Randa .30 .75
756 Jose Castillo .30 .75
757 Mike Gonzalez .30 .75
758 Ryan Doumit .30 .75
759 Sean Burnett .30 .75
760 Sean Casey .30 .75
761 Ian Snell .30 .75
762 John Grabow .30 .75
763 Jose Hernandez .30 .75
764 Roberto Hernandez .30 .75
765 Ryan Vogelsong .30 .75
766 Victor Sanchez .30 .75
767 Adrian Gonzalez .60 1.50
768 Alan Embree .30 .75
769 Brian Sweeney (RC) .50 1.25
770 Chan Ho Park .50 1.25
771 Clay Hensley .30 .75
772 Dewon Brazelton .30 .75
773 Doug Brocail .30 .75
774 Eric Young .30 .75
775 Geoff Blum .30 .75
776 Josh Bard .30 .75
777 Mark Bellhorn .30 .75
778 Mike Cameron .30 .75
779 Mike Piazza .75 2.00
780 Rob Bowen .30 .75
781 Scott Cassidy .30 .75
782 Scott Linebrink .30 .75
783 Shawn Estes .30 .75
784 Termel Sledge .30 .75
785 Vinny Castilla .30 .75
786 Jeff Fassero .30 .75
787 Jose Vizcaino .30 .75
788 Mark Sweeney .30 .75
789 Matt Morris .30 .75
790 Steve Finley .30 .75
791 Tim Worrell .30 .75
792 Jamey Wright .30 .75
793 Jason Ellison .30 .75
794 Noah Lowry .30 .75
795 Steve Kline .30 .75
796 Todd Greene .30 .75
797 Carl Everett .30 .75
798 George Sherrill .30 .75
799 J.J. Putz .30 .75
800 Jake Woods .30 .75
801 Jose Lopez .30 .75
802 Julio Mateo .30 .75
803 Mike Morse .30 .75
804 Rafael Soriano .30 .75
805 Roberto Petagine .30 .75
806 Aaron Miles .30 .75
807 Braden Looper .30 .75
808 Gary Bennett .30 .75
809 Hector Luna .30 .75
810 Jeff Suppan .30 .75
811 John Rodriguez .30 .75
812 Josh Hancock .30 .75
813 Juan Encarnacion .30 .75
814 Larry Bigbie .30 .75
815 Scott Spiezio .30 .75
816 Sidney Ponson .30 .75
817 So Taguchi .30 .75
818 Brian Meadows .30 .75
819 Damon Hollins .30 .75
820 Dan Miceli .30 .75
821 Doug Waechter .30 .75
822 Jason Childers RC .50 1.25
823 Josh Paul .30 .75
824 Julio Lugo .30 .75
825 Mark Hendrickson .30 .75
826 Sean Burroughs .30 .75
827 Shawn Camp .30 .75
828 Travis Harper .30 .75
829 Ty Wigginton .30 .75
830 Adam Eaton .30 .75
831 Adrian Brown .30 .75
832 Akinori Otsuka .30 .75
833 Antonio Alfonseca .30 .75
834 Brad Wilkerson .30 .75
835 D'Angelo Jimenez .30 .75
836 Gerald Laird .30 .75
837 Joaquin Benoit .30 .75
838 Kameron Loe .30 .75
839 Kevin Millwood .30 .75
840 Mark DeRosa .30 .75
841 Phil Nevin .30 .75
842 Rod Barajas .30 .75
843 Vicente Padilla .30 .75
844 A.J. Burnett .30 .75
845 Bengie Molina .30 .75
846 Gregg Zaun .30 .75
847 John McDonald .30 .75
848 Lyle Overbay .30 .75
849 Russ Adams .30 .75
850 Troy Glaus .30 .75
851 Vinnie Chulk .30 .75
852 B.J. Ryan .30 .75
853 Justin Speier .30 .75
854 Pete Walker .30 .75
855 Scott Downs .30 .75
856 Scott Schoeneweis .30 .75
857 Alfonso Soriano .50 1.25
858 Brian Schneider .30 .75
859 Daryle Ward .30 .75
860 Felix Rodriguez .30 .75
861 Gary Majewski .30 .75
862 Joey Eischen .30 .75
863 Jon Rauch .30 .75
864 Marlon Anderson .30 .75
865 Matt LeCroy .30 .75
866 Mike Stanton .30 .75
867 Ramon Ortiz .30 .75
868 Robert Fick .30 .75
869 Royce Clayton .30 .75
870 Ryan Drese .30 .75
871 Vladimir Guerrero CL .50 1.25
872 Craig Biggio CL .50 1.25
873 Barry Zito CL .50 1.25
874 Vernon Wells CL .30 .75
875 Chipper Jones CL .75 2.00
876 Prince Fielder CL 1.50 4.00
877 Albert Pujols CL 1.00 2.50
878 Greg Maddux CL 1.00 2.50
879 Carl Crawford CL .50 1.25
880 Brandon Webb CL .50 1.25
881 J.D. Drew CL .30 .75
882 Jason Schmidt CL .30 .75
883 Victor Martinez CL .50 1.25
884 Ichiro Suzuki CL 1.00 2.50
885 Miguel Cabrera CL .75 2.00
886 David Wright CL .60 1.50
887 Alfonso Soriano CL .50 1.25
888 Miguel Tejada CL .50 1.25
889 Khalil Greene CL .30 .75
890 Ryan Howard CL .60 1.50
891 Jason Bay CL .30 .75
892 Mark Teixeira CL .50 1.25
893 Manny Ramirez CL .75 2.00
894 Ken Griffey Jr. CL 1.50 4.00
895 Todd Helton CL .50 1.25
896 Angel Berroa CL .30 .75
897 Ivan Rodriguez CL .50 1.25
898 Johan Santana CL .50 1.25
899 Paul Konerko CL .50 1.25
900 Derek Jeter CL 2.00 5.00
901 Macay McBride (RC) .50 1.25
902 Tony Pena Jr. (RC) .50 1.25
903 Peter Moylan RC .50 1.25
904 Aaron Rakers (RC) .50 1.25
905 Chris Britton RC .50 1.25
906 Nick Markakis (RC) 1.00 2.50
907 Sendy Rleal RC .50 1.25
908 Val Majewski (RC) .50 1.25
909 Jermaine Van Buren (RC) .50 1.25
910 Jonathan Papelbon (RC) 2.50 6.00
911 Angel Pagan (RC) .50 1.25
912 David Aardsma (RC) .50 1.25
913 Sean Marshall (RC) .50 1.25
914 Brian Anderson (RC) .50 1.25
915 Freddie Bynum (RC) .50 1.25
916 Fausto Carmona (RC) .50 1.25
917 Kelly Shoppach (RC) .50 1.25
918 Choo Freeman (RC) .50 1.25
919 Ryan Shealy (RC) .50 1.25
920 Joel Zumaya (RC) 1.25 3.00
921 Jordan Tata RC .50 1.25
922 Justin Verlander (RC) 4.00 10.00
923 Carlos Martinez RC .50 1.25
924 Chris Resop (RC) .50 1.25
925 Dan Uggla (RC) .75 2.00
926 Eric Reed (RC) .50 1.25
927 Hanley Ramirez (RC) .75 2.00
928 Yusmeiro Petit (RC) .50 1.25
929 Josh Willingham (RC) .75 2.00
930 Mike Jacobs (RC) .50 1.25
931 Reggie Abercrombie (RC) .50 1.25
932 Ricky Nolasco (RC) .50 1.25
933 Scott Olsen (RC) .50 1.25
934 Fernando Nieve (RC) .50 1.25
935 Taylor Buchholz (RC) .50 1.25
936 Cody Ross (RC) 1.25 3.00
937 James Loney (RC) .75 2.00
938 Takashi Saito RC .75 2.00
939 Tim Hamulack (RC) .50 1.25
940 Chris Demaria RC .50 1.25
941 Jose Capellan (RC) .50 1.25
942 David Gassner (RC) .50 1.25
943 Jason Kubel (RC) .50 1.25
944 Brian Bannister (RC) .50 1.25
945 Mike Thompson RC .50 1.25
946 Cole Hamels (RC) 1.50 4.00
947 Paul Maholm (RC) .50 1.25
948 John Van Benschoten (RC) .50 1.25
949 Nate McLouth (RC) .50 1.25
950 Ben Johnson (RC) .50 1.25
951 Josh Barfield (RC) .50 1.25
952 Travis Ishikawa (RC) .75 2.00
953 Jack Taschner (RC) .50 1.25
954 Kenji Johjima RC 1.25 3.00
955 Skip Schumaker (RC) .50 1.25
956 Ruddy Lugo (RC) .50 1.25
957 Jason Hammel (RC) 1.25 3.00
958 Chris Roberson (RC) .50 1.25
959 Fabio Castro RC .50 1.25
960 Ian Kinsler (RC) 1.50 4.00
961 John Koronka (RC) .50 1.25
962 Brandon Watson (RC) .50 1.25
963 Jon Lester RC 2.00 5.00
964 Ben Hendrickson (RC) .50 1.25
965 Martin Prado (RC) .75 2.00
966 Erick Aybar (RC) .50 1.25
967 Bobby Livingston (RC) .50 1.25
968 Ryan Spilborghs (RC) .50 1.25
969 Tommy Murphy (RC) .50 1.25
970 Howie Kendrick (RC) 1.00 2.50
971 Casey Janssen RC .50 1.25
972 Michael O'Connor RC .50 1.25
973 Conor Jackson (RC) .75 2.00
974 Jeremy Hermida (RC) .50 1.25
975 Renyel Pinto (RC) .50 1.25
976 Prince Fielder (RC) 2.50 6.00
977 Kevin Frandsen (RC) .50 1.25
978 Ty Taubenheim RC .75 2.00
979 Rich Hill (RC) 1.25 3.00
980 Jonathan Broxton (RC) .50 1.25
981 James Shields RC 1.50 4.00
982 Carlos Villanueva RC .50 1.25
983 Boone Logan RC .50 1.25
984 Brian Wilson RC 8.00 20.00
985 Andre Ethier (RC) 1.50 4.00
986 Mike Napoli RC .75 2.00
987 Agustin Montero (RC) .50 1.25
988 Jack Hannahan RC .50 1.25
989 Boof Bonser (RC) .75 2.00
990 Carlos Ruiz (RC) .50 1.25
991 Jason Botts (RC) .50 1.25
992 Kendry Morales (RC) 1.25 3.00
993 Alay Soler RC .50 1.25
994 Santiago Ramirez (RC) .50 1.25
995 Saul Rivera (RC) .50 1.25
996 Anthony Reyes (RC) .50 1.25
997 Matt Kemp (RC) 1.25 3.00
998 Jae Kuk Ryu RC .50 1.25
999 Lastings Milledge (RC) .50 1.25
1000 Jered Weaver (RC) 1.50 4.00
1001 Jeremy Sowers (RC) .50 1.25
1002 Chad Billingsley (RC) .75 2.00
1003 Stephen Drew (RC) 1.00 2.50
1004 Tony Gwynn Jr. (RC) .50 1.25
1005 Melky Cabrera (RC) .75 2.00
1006 Eliezer Alfonzo RC .50 1.25
1007 Dana Eveland (RC) .50 1.25
1008 Luis Figueroa RC .50 1.25
1009 Emiliano Fruto RC .50 1.25
1010 Clay Hensley (RC) .50 1.25
1011 Zach Jackson (RC) .50 1.25
1012 Bob Keppel (RC) .50 1.25
1013 Carlos Marmol RC 1.50 4.00
1014 Russell Martin (RC) .75 2.00
1015 Leo Nunez (RC) .50 1.25
1016 Ken Ray (RC) .50 1.25
1017 Mike Rouse (RC) .50 1.25
1018 Kevin Thompson (RC) .50 1.25
1019 C.J. Wilson (RC) .75 2.00
1021 Ed Rogers (RC) .50 1.25
1022 Joe Nelson (RC) .50 1.25
1023 Omar Quintanilla (RC) .50 1.25
1024 Chris Bootcheck (RC) .50 1.25
1025 Jason Childers RC .50 1.25
1088 Stephen Andrade (RC) .50 1.25

2006 Upper Deck Special F/X Blue

*BLUE: .5X TO 1.2X BASIC
*BLUE RC: .5X TO 1.2X BASIC RC
STATED ODDS 1:4

2006 Upper Deck Special F/X Green

*GREEN: 1X TO 2.5X BASIC
*GREEN RC: .75X TO 2X BASIC RC
STATED PRINT RUN 99 SER.#'d SETS

2006 Upper Deck Special F/X Purple

*PURPLE: .75X TO 2X BASIC
*PURPLE RC: .6X TO 1.5X BASIC RC
STATED PRINT RUN 150 SER.#'d SETS

2006 Upper Deck Special F/X Red

*RED: 1.25X TO 3X BASIC
*RED RC: 1X TO 2.5X BASIC RC
STATED PRINT RUN 50 SER.#'d SETS

2006 Upper Deck Special F/X Materials

STATED ODDS 1:8
AD Adam Dunn Jsy 2.50 6.00
AJ Andruw Jones Jsy 3.00 8.00
AP Albert Pujols Jsy 6.00 15.00
AS Alfonso Soriano Jsy 2.50 6.00
CA Chris Carpenter Jsy 3.00 8.00
CC Carl Crawford Jsy 2.50 6.00
CH Cole Hamels Jsy 5.00 12.00
CR Coco Crisp Jsy 2.50 6.00
CU Chase Utley Jsy 4.00 10.00
DJ Derek Jeter Jsy 8.00 20.00
DL Derrek Lee Jsy 3.00 8.00
DO David Ortiz Jsy 4.00 10.00
FH Felix Hernandez Jsy 3.00 8.00
FL Francisco Liriano Jsy 5.00 12.00
GS Grady Sizemore Jsy 3.00 8.00
HA Roy Halladay Jsy 2.50 6.00
HR Hanley Ramirez Jsy 3.00 8.00
IK Ian Kinsler Jsy 3.00 8.00
JB Jason Bay Jsy 2.50 6.00
JG Jason Giambi Jsy 2.50 6.00
JH Jeremy Hermida Jsy 2.50 6.00
JM Joe Mauer Jsy 3.00 8.00
JP Jonathan Papelbon Jsy 5.00 12.00
JR Jose Reyes Jsy 3.00 8.00
JS Johan Santana Jsy 3.00 8.00
JT Jim Thome Jsy 3.00 8.00
JV Justin Verlander Jsy 5.00 12.00
JW Josh Willingham Jsy 2.50 6.00
KG Ken Griffey Jr. Jsy 5.00 12.00
KJ Kenji Johjima Jsy 5.00 12.00
KM Kendry Morales Jsy 3.00 8.00
LB Lance Berkman Jsy 2.50 6.00
LM Lastings Milledge Jsy 3.00 8.00
MA Matt Cain Jsy 3.00 8.00
MC Miguel Cabrera Jsy 3.00 8.00
MT Mark Teixeira Jsy 3.00 8.00
PF Prince Fielder Jsy 4.00 10.00
PM Pedro Martinez Jsy 4.00 10.00
RF Rafael Furcal Jsy 2.50 6.00
RH Ryan Howard Jsy 6.00 15.00
RW Rickie Weeks Jsy 2.50 6.00
RZ Ryan Zimmerman Jsy 5.00 12.00
SK Scott Kazmir Jsy 3.00 8.00
TE Miguel Tejada Jsy 2.50 6.00
TG Troy Glaus Jsy 2.50 6.00
TH Travis Hafner Jsy 2.50 6.00
VG Vladimir Guerrero Jsy 3.00 8.00
VM Victor Martinez Jsy 2.50 6.00
WE Jered Weaver Jsy 4.00 10.00

2006 Upper Deck Special F/X Player Highlights

STATED ODDS 1:3
1 Andruw Jones .40 1.00
2 Manny Ramirez 1.00 2.50
3 Travis Hafner .40 1.00
4 Johnny Damon .60 1.50
5 Miguel Cabrera 1.00 2.50
6 Chris Carpenter .60 1.50
7 Derrek Lee .40 1.00
8 Jason Bay .40 1.00
9 Jason Varitek 1.00 2.50
10 Ryan Howard .75 2.00
11 Mark Teixeira .60 1.50
12 Carlos Delgado .40 1.00
13 Bartolo Colon .40 1.00
14 David Wright .75 2.00
15 Miguel Tejada .60 1.50
16 Mike Piazza 1.00 2.50
17 Paul Konerko .60 1.50
18 Jermaine Dye .40 1.00
19 Ichiro Suzuki 1.25 3.00
20 Brad Wilkerson .40 1.00
21 Hideki Matsui 1.00 2.50
22 Albert Pujols 1.25 3.00
23 Chris Burke .40 1.00
24 Derek Jeter 2.50 6.00
25 Brian Roberts .40 1.00
26 David Ortiz 1.00 2.50
27 Alex Rodriguez 1.25 3.00
28 Ken Griffey Jr. 2.00 5.00
29 Prince Fielder 2.00 5.00
30 Bobby Abreu .40 1.00
31 Vladimir Guerrero .60 1.50
32 Tadahito Iguchi .40 1.00
33 Jose Reyes .60 1.50
34 Scott Podsednik .40 1.00
35 Gary Sheffield .40 1.00

2006 Upper Deck Special F/X Run Producers

STATED ODDS 1:3
1 Ty Cobb 1.50 4.00
2 Derrek Lee .40 1.00
3 Andruw Jones .40 1.00
4 David Ortiz 1.00 2.50
5 Lou Gehrig 2.00 5.00
6 Ken Griffey Jr. 2.00 5.00
7 Albert Pujols 1.25 3.00
8 Derek Jeter 2.50 6.00
9 Manny Ramirez 1.00 2.50
10 Alex Rodriguez 1.25 3.00
11 Gary Sheffield .40 1.00
12 Miguel Cabrera 1.00 2.50
13 Hideki Matsui 1.00 2.50
14 Vladimir Guerrero .60 1.50
15 David Wright .75 2.00
16 Mike Schmidt 1.50 4.00
17 Mark Teixeira .60 1.50
18 Babe Ruth 2.50 6.00
19 Jimmie Foxx 1.00 2.50
20 Honus Wagner 1.00 2.50

2006 Upper Deck Special F/X Special Endorsements

STATED ODDS 1:16
EXCH DEADLINE 12/14/09
ASTERISK = PARTIAL EXCH
AA Aaron Rakers 3.00 8.00
AC Jeremy Accardo 3.00 8.00
AE Andre Ethier 6.00 15.00
AH Anderson Hernandez SP 3.00 8.00
AN Robert Andino 3.00 8.00
AW Adam Wainwright 5.00 12.00
BA Brian Anderson 3.00 8.00
BH Brendan Harris 3.00 8.00
BJ Ben Johnson 3.00 8.00
BL Boone Logan 3.00 8.00
BR Brian Bannister 3.00 8.00
BW Craig Breslow 3.00 8.00
CB Chris Britton 3.00 8.00
CH Cole Hamels 12.00 30.00
CM Matt Capps 3.00 8.00
CU Chase Utley 8.00 20.00
DE Chris Denorfia 3.00 8.00
DG Dave Gassner 3.00 8.00
DJ Derek Jeter 75.00 150.00
DU Dan Uggla 6.00 15.00
DW Dontrelle Willis 4.00 10.00
EV Dana Eveland 3.00 8.00
FB Freddie Bynum 3.00 8.00
FC Fausto Carmona 8.00 20.00
FL Francisco Liriano 10.00 25.00
FN Fernando Nieve 3.00 8.00
GS Geovany Soto 12.50 30.00
HK Hong-Chih Kuo 6.00 15.00
HR Hanley Ramirez 6.00 15.00
IK Ian Kinsler 6.00 15.00
JA Conor Jackson 5.00 12.00
JB Jason Bay 5.00 12.00
JC Jose Capellan SP 3.00 8.00
JD Joey Devine 3.00 8.00
JJ Josh Johnson 5.00 12.00
JK Jason Kubel 3.00 8.00
JO Josh Wilson 3.00 8.00
JP Jonathan Papelbon 10.00 25.00
JS James Shields 8.00 20.00
JU Justin Huber 3.00 8.00
JV John Van Benschoten 3.00 8.00
JW Jered Weaver 5.00 12.00
JZ Joel Zumaya 5.00 12.00
KE Howie Kendrick 6.00 15.00
KF Kevin Frandsen 3.00 8.00
KG Ken Griffey Jr. 40.00 100.00
KM Kendry Morales 4.00 10.00
KO John Koronka 3.00 8.00
KS Kelly Shoppach 3.00 8.00
MC Matt Cain 6.00 15.00
MI Miguel Cabrera 20.00 50.00
MJ Mike Jacobs 3.00 8.00
MS Matt Smith 3.00 8.00
NI Nick Masset 3.00 8.00
NM Nate McLouth 5.00 12.00
PE Peter Moylan 3.00 8.00
PM Paul Maholm 3.00 8.00
RA Reggie Abercrombie 3.00 8.00
RB Chris Roberson 3.00 8.00
RC Carlos Ruiz 8.00 20.00
RE Chris Resop 3.00 8.00
RF Ron Flores 3.00 8.00
RL Ruddy Lugo 3.00 8.00
RS Ryan Shealy 4.00 10.00
RU Josh Rupe 3.00 8.00
RW Rickie Weeks 4.00 10.00
RZ Ryan Zimmerman SP 10.00 25.00
SM Sean Marshall 5.00 12.00
TB Taylor Buchholz 3.00 8.00
TC Tim Corcoran 3.00 8.00
TH Travis Hafner 5.00 12.00
TS Takashi Saito 6.00 15.00
VE Justin Verlander 15.00 40.00
WI Josh Willingham 3.00 8.00
WN Wil Nieves 3.00 8.00

2006 Upper Deck Special F/X Star Attractions

STATED ODDS 1:8
AJ Andruw Jones .40 1.00
AS Alfonso Soriano .60 1.50
BA Bobby Abreu .40 1.00
CB Carlos Beltran .60 1.50
CD Carlos Delgado .40 1.00
CJ Chipper Jones 1.00 2.50
CS Curt Schilling .60 1.50
DJ Derek Jeter 2.50 6.00
DL Derrek Lee .40 1.00
DO David Ortiz 1.00 2.50
DW Dontrelle Willis .40 1.00
GM Greg Maddux 1.25 3.00
JB Josh Beckett .40 1.00
JC Jose Contreras .40 1.00
JD Johnny Damon .60 1.50
JE Jim Edmonds .60 1.50
JG Jason Giambi .40 1.00
JM Joe Mauer .60 1.50
JR Jose Reyes .60 1.50
JS Jason Schmidt .40 1.00
KG Ken Griffey Jr. 2.00 5.00
LB Lance Berkman .60 1.50
MO Magglio Ordonez .60 1.50
MR Manny Ramirez 1.00 2.50
MT Mark Teixeira .60 1.50
PM Pedro Martinez .60 1.50
PU Albert Pujols 1.25 3.00
RH Rich Harden .40 1.00
SM John Smoltz 1.00 2.50
WR David Wright .75 2.00

2006 Upper Deck Special F/X WBC Counterparts

STATED ODDS 1:6
1 Y. Gourriel/D.Matsuzaka 2.00 5.00
2 K.Griffey Jr./Y.Garlobo 3.00 8.00
3 K.Griffey Jr./I.Suzuki 3.00 8.00
4 D.Jeter/C.Hu 4.00 10.00
5 F.Cepeda/J.Lee .60 1.50
6 N.Matsunaka/S.Lee 1.00 2.50
7 T.Nishioka/G.Liu 4.00 10.00
8 I.Suzuki/O.Urrutia 2.00 5.00
9 D.Matsuzaka/R.Clemens 2.00 5.00
10 Y.Marti/C.Park 1.00 2.50
11 K.Uehara/J.Seo 2.00 5.00
12 S.Watanabe/B.Colon 1.00 2.50
13 D.Matsuzaka/J.Santana 2.00 5.00
14 P.Lazo/F.Garcia .60 1.50
15 K.Uehara/R.Clemens 2.00 5.00

2007 Upper Deck Spectrum

COMP.SET w/o RCs (100) 10.00 25.00
COMMON CARD (1-100) .15 .40
COMMON AU RC (101-149) 3.00 8.00
AU RC STATED ODDS 1:18 HOBBY
COMMON ROOKIE EXCH (151-170) 10.00 25.00
EXCHANGE DEADLINE 3/19/2010
1 Miguel Tejada .25 .60
2 Brian Roberts .15 .40
3 Melvin Mora .15 .40
4 David Ortiz .40 1.00
5 Manny Ramirez .40 1.00
6 Jason Varitek .40 1.00
7 Curt Schilling .25 .60
8 Jim Thome .25 .60
9 Paul Konerko .25 .60
10 Jermaine Dye .15 .40
11 Travis Hafner .15 .40
12 Victor Martinez .25 .60
13 Grady Sizemore .25 .60
14 C.C. Sabathia .25 .60
15 Ivan Rodriguez .25 .60
16 Magglio Ordonez .25 .60
17 Carlos Guillen .15 .40
18 Justin Verlander .40 1.00
19 Shane Costa .15 .40
20 Emil Brown .15 .40
21 Mark Teahen .15 .40
22 Vladimir Guerrero .25 .60
23 Jered Weaver .25 .60
24 Juan Rivera .15 .40
25 Justin Morneau .25 .60
26 Joe Mauer .30 .75
27 Torii Hunter .15 .40
28 Johan Santana .25 .60
29 Derek Jeter 1.00 2.50
30 Alex Rodriguez .50 1.25
31 Johnny Damon .25 .60
32 Jason Giambi .15 .40
33 Frank Thomas .40 1.00
34 Nick Swisher .25 .60
35 Eric Chavez .15 .40
36 Ichiro Suzuki .50 1.25
37 Raul Ibanez .25 .60
38 Richie Sexson .15 .40
39 Carl Crawford .25 .60
40 Rocco Baldelli .15 .40
41 Scott Kazmir .25 .60
42 Michael Young .15 .40
43 Mark Teixeira .25 .60
44 Carlos Lee .15 .40
45 Gary Matthews .15 .40
46 Vernon Wells .15 .40
47 Roy Halladay .25 .60
48 Lyle Overbay .15 .40
49 Brandon Webb .25 .60
50 Conor Jackson .15 .40
51 Stephen Drew .15 .40
52 Chipper Jones .40 1.00
53 Andruw Jones .15 .40
54 Adam LaRoche .15 .40
55 John Smoltz .40 1.00
56 Derrek Lee .15 .40
57 Aramis Ramirez .15 .40
58 Carlos Zambrano .25 .60
59 Ken Griffey Jr. .75 2.00
60 Adam Dunn .25 .60
61 Aaron Harang .15 .40
62 Todd Helton .25 .60
63 Matt Holliday .40 1.00
64 Garrett Atkins .15 .40
65 Miguel Cabrera .40 1.00
66 Hanley Ramirez .25 .60
67 Dontrelle Willis .15 .40
68 Lance Berkman .25 .60
69 Roy Oswalt .25 .60
70 Roger Clemens .50 1.25
71 J.D. Drew .15 .40
72 Nomar Garciaparra .25 .60
73 Rafael Furcal .15 .40
74 Jeff Kent .15 .40
75 Prince Fielder .25 .60
76 Bill Hall .15 .40
77 Rickie Weeks .15 .40
78 Jose Reyes .25 .60
79 David Wright .30 .75
80 Carlos Delgado .15 .40
81 Carlos Beltran .25 .60
82 Ryan Howard .30 .75
83 Chase Utley .25 .60
84 Jimmy Rollins .25 .60
85 Jason Bay .25 .60
86 Freddy Sanchez .15 .40
87 Zach Duke .15 .40
88 Trevor Hoffman .25 .60
89 Adrian Gonzalez .30 .75
90 Mike Piazza .40 1.00
91 Ray Durham .15 .40
92 Omar Vizquel .25 .60
93 Jason Schmidt .15 .40
94 Albert Pujols .50 1.25
95 Scott Rolen .25 .60
96 Jim Edmonds .25 .60
97 Chris Carpenter .25 .60
98 Alfonso Soriano .25 .60
99 Ryan Zimmerman .25 .60
100 Nick Johnson .15 .40
101 Adam Lind AU (RC) 4.00 10.00
103 Andrew Miller AU RC 15.00 40.00
104 Andy Cannizaro AU RC 4.00 10.00
106 Brian Stokes AU (RC) 3.00 8.00
108 Cesar Jimenez AU RC 3.00 8.00
109 Chris Stewart AU RC 3.00 8.00
111 David Murphy AU (RC) 3.00 8.00
112 Delmon Young AU (RC) 12.50 30.00
113 Delwyn Young AU (RC) 3.00 8.00
114 Dennis Sarfate AU (RC) 3.00 8.00
116 Drew Anderson AU RC 3.00 8.00
117 Fred Lewis AU (RC) 3.00 8.00
118 Glen Perkins AU (RC) 4.00 10.00
120 Jeff Baker AU (RC) 3.00 8.00
121 Jeff Fiorentino AU (RC) 3.00 8.00
122 Jeff Salazar AU (RC) 3.00 8.00
124 Joaquin Arias AU (RC) 3.00 8.00
125 Jon Knott AU (RC) 3.00 8.00
128 Juan Morillo AU (RC) 3.00 8.00
130 Juan Salas AU (RC) 3.00 8.00
131 Justin Hampson AU (RC) 3.00 8.00
132 Kevin Hooper AU (RC) 6.00 15.00
133 Kevin Kouzmanoff AU (RC) 4.00 10.00
134 Michael Bourn AU (RC) 4.00 10.00
135 Miguel Montero AU (RC) 3.00 8.00
137 Mitch Maier AU RC 3.00 8.00
139 Patrick Misch AU (RC) 3.00 8.00
140 Philip Humber AU (RC) 6.00 15.00
141 Ryan Braun AU RC 5.00 12.00
143 Ryan Sweeney AU (RC) 3.00 8.00
144 Scott Moore AU (RC) 3.00 8.00
145 Sean Henn AU (RC) 4.00 10.00
146 Shawn Riggans AU (RC) 3.00 8.00
148 Troy Tulowitzki AU (RC) 6.00 15.00
149 Ubaldo Jimenez AU (RC) 5.00 12.00
157 Elijah Dukes RC 10.00 25.00

2007 Upper Deck Spectrum Die Cut Gold

*GOLD 1-100: 2.5X TO 6X BASIC
GOLD 1-100 PRINT RUN 99 SER.#'d SETS
*GOLD AU 101-149: .75X TO 2X BASIC
GOLD 101-149 PRINT RUN 50 SER.#'d SETS
RANDOM INSERTS IN PACKS
101 Adam Lind AU 20.00 50.00
112 Delmon Young AU 20.00 50.00
134 Michael Bourn AU 8.00 20.00
145 Sean Henn AU 10.00 25.00

2007 Upper Deck Spectrum Die Cut Red

*RED: 2.5X TO 6X BASIC
RANDOM INSERTS IN PACKS
STATED PRINT RUN 99 SER.#'d SETS

2007 Upper Deck Spectrum Die Cut Blue Jersey Number

*JSY NUMBER p/r 26-57: 8X TO 20X BASIC
RANDOM INSERTS IN PACKS
PRINT RUNS B/WN 1-57 COPIES PER
NO PRICING ON QTY 25 OR LESS

2007 Upper Deck Spectrum Aligning the Stars

OVERALL GAME-USED ODDS 1:10
STATED PRINT RUN 99 SER.#'d SETS
BPO Berkman/Pujols/Papi 10.00 25.00
CJM Maddux/Clemens/Big Unit 10.00 25.00
CRR Cabrera/Aramis/Rolen 6.00 15.00
DBF Berkman/Delgado/Prince 6.00 15.00
GRS Sheffield/Manny/Griffey 10.00 25.00
HRW Hoffman/Rivera/Wagner 10.00 25.00
HTT Big Hurt/Hafner/Thome 10.00 25.00
JDB Dunn/Andruw/Beltran 10.00 25.00
JGC Jeter/Giambi/Cano 15.00 40.00
JTY Jeter/Tejada/Young 10.00 25.00
LHP Helton/Pujols/D.Lee 10.00 25.00
LVP Verlander/Liriano/Papelbon 10.00 25.00
MKT Morneau/Teixeira/Konerko 6.00 15.00
MOW Oswalt/Pedro/Willis 6.00 15.00
RFR Reyes/Rollins/Furcal 6.00 15.00
RMM V.Martinez/Mauer/Pudge 6.00 15.00
RSV Schilling/Manny/Varitek 10.00 25.00
SBA Abreu/Beltran/Soriano 6.00 15.00
SCF Figgins/Crawford/Sizemore 6.00 15.00
SHS Sabathia/Santana/Halladay 6.00 15.00
WGD Wells/Damon/Vlad 6.00 15.00

2007 Upper Deck Spectrum Cal Ripken Road to the Hall

COMMON CARD 2.00 5.00
STATED ODDS 1:10 HOBBY, 1:20 RETAIL
GOLD: .6X TO 1.5X BASIC
GOLD RANDOMLY INSERTED IN PACKS
GOLD PRINT RUN 99 SER.#'d SETS

2007 Upper Deck Spectrum Cal Ripken Road to the Hall Signatures

COMMON CARD 100.00 175.00
RANDOM INSERTS IN PACKS
STATED PRINT RUN 5 SER.#'d SETS

2007 Upper Deck Spectrum Grand Slamarama

STATED ODDS 1:280 HOBBY
AD Adam Dunn 3.00 8.00
AP Albert Pujols 6.00 15.00
AR Alex Rodriguez 6.00 15.00
BA Bobby Abreu 2.00 5.00
BG Brian Giles 2.00 5.00
CD Carlos Delgado 2.00 5.00
CJ Chipper Jones 5.00 12.00
DA Johnny Damon 3.00 8.00
DO David Ortiz 5.00 12.00
DW David Wright 4.00 10.00
HA Travis Hafner 2.00 5.00
JD Jermaine Dye 2.00 5.00
JM Justin Morneau 3.00 8.00
JT Jim Thome 3.00 8.00
KG Ken Griffey Jr. 10.00 25.00
MR Manny Ramirez 5.00 12.00
NG Nomar Garciaparra 3.00 8.00
RH Ryan Howard 4.00 10.00
RS Richie Sexson 2.00 5.00
VG Vladimir Guerrero 3.00 8.00

2007 Upper Deck Spectrum Rookie Retrospectrum

STATED ODDS 1:10 HOBBY, 1:20 RETAIL
RED: .6X TO 1.5X BASIC
RED RANDOMLY INSERTED IN PACKS
RED PRINT RUN 99 SER.#'d SETS
AE Andre Ethier .60 1.50
AW Adam Wainwright .40 1.00
BA Josh Barfield .40 1.00
BB Boof Bonser .40 1.00
BO Jason Botts .40 1.00
CA Matt Capps .40 1.00
CB Chad Billingsley .40 1.00
CD Chris Demaria .40 1.00
CF Choo Freeman .40 1.00
CH Clay Hensley .40 1.00
CQ Carlos Quentin .40 1.00
DE Chris Denorfia .40 1.00
DU Dan Uggla .60 1.50
FC Fausto Carmona .40 1.00
FL Francisco Liriano 1.00 2.50
HA Cole Hamels .60 1.50
HK Howie Kendrick .40 1.00
HR Hanley Ramirez .60 1.50
JA Jeremy Accardo .40 1.00
JB Jason Bergmann .40 1.00
JC Jose Capellan .40 1.00
JD Joey Devine .40 1.00
JH Jeremy Hermida .40 1.00
JK Jason Kubel .40 1.00
JL Jon Lester .60 1.50
JP Jonathan Papelbon 1.00 2.50
JV Justin Verlander 1.00 2.50
JW Jered Weaver .60 1.50
JZ Joel Zumaya .60 1.50
KM Kendry Morales .60 1.50
LM Lastings Milledge .60 1.50
MA Nick Markakis .60 1.50
MC Matt Cain .60 1.50
ME Melky Cabrera .40 1.00
MG Matt Garza .40 1.00
MJ Mike Jacobs .40 1.00
MM Matt Murton .40 1.00
NM Nate McLouth .40 1.00
PF Prince Fielder 1.00 2.50
RA Reggie Abercrombie .40 1.00
RG Ryan Garko .40 1.00
RM Russell Martin .40 1.00
RP Ronny Paulino .40 1.00
RS Ryan Shealy .40 1.00
RZ Ryan Zimmerman 1.00 2.50
SD Stephen Drew .60 1.50
TB Taylor Buchholz .40 1.00
TG Tony Gwynn Jr. .40 1.00
TS Takashi Saito .40 1.00
WI Josh Willingham .40 1.00

2007 Upper Deck Spectrum Rookie Retrospectrum Signatures

RANDOM INSERTS IN PACKS
PRINT RUNS B/WN 32-199 COPIES PER
EXCHANGE DEADLINE 3/19/2010
BB Boof Bonser 4.00 10.00
BO Jason Botts 4.00 10.00
CA Matt Capps 4.00 10.00
CD Chris Demaria 4.00 10.00
CF Choo Freeman 4.00 10.00
CH Clay Hensley 4.00 10.00
CQ Carlos Quentin 4.00 10.00
DU Dan Uggla 6.00 15.00
FC Fausto Carmona/158 4.00 10.00
FL Francisco Liriano 4.00 10.00
HK Howie Kendrick 10.00 25.00
HR Hanley Ramirez 4.00 10.00
JA Jeremy Accardo/32 6.00 15.00
JC Jose Capellan 4.00 10.00
JD Joey Devine 4.00 10.00
JH Jeremy Hermida 4.00 10.00
JK Jason Kubel 4.00 10.00
JP Jonathan Papelbon 8.00 20.00
JW Jered Weaver 10.00 25.00
JZ Joel Zumaya 10.00 25.00
KM Kendry Morales 4.00 10.00
MG Matt Garza 6.00 15.00
MJ Mike Jacobs 4.00 10.00
RA Reggie Abercrombie 4.00 10.00
RG Ryan Garko 6.00 15.00
RM Russell Martin 4.00 10.00
RS Ryan Shealy 4.00 10.00
SD Stephen Drew 5.00 12.00
TB Taylor Buchholz 4.00 10.00
TS Takashi Saito 10.00 25.00
WI Josh Willingham 4.00 10.00

2007 Upper Deck Spectrum Season Retrospectrum

STATED ODDS 1:10 HOBBY, 1:20 RETAIL
RED: .6X TO 1.5X BASIC
RED RANDOMLY INSERTED IN PACKS
RED PRINT RUN 99 SER.#'d SETS
AH Aaron Harang .40 1.00
AP Albert Pujols 1.25 3.00

AR Aramis Ramirez	.40	1.00
AS Alfonso Soriano	.60	1.50
BA Bobby Abreu	.40	1.00
BH Bill Hall	.40	1.00
BL Joe Blanton	.40	1.00
CA Miguel Cabrera	1.00	2.50
CB Carlos Beltran	.60	1.50
CC Chris Carpenter	.60	1.50
CD Carlos Delgado	.40	1.00
CO Jose Contreras	.40	1.00
CU Chase Utley	.60	1.50
CW Chien-Ming Wang	.60	1.50
CY Chris Young	.40	1.00
CZ Carlos Zambrano	.60	1.50
DJ Derek Jeter	2.50	6.00
DO David Ortiz	1.00	2.50
FS Freddy Sanchez	.40	1.00
FT Frank Thomas	1.00	2.50
GM Greg Maddux	1.25	3.00
GS Grady Sizemore	.60	1.50
HO Trevor Hoffman	.60	1.50
HR Hanley Ramirez	.60	1.50
JB Jason Bay	.60	1.50
JC Joe Crede	.40	1.00
JD Johnny Damon	.60	1.50
JM Joe Mauer	.75	2.00
JR Jose Reyes	.60	1.50
JS Jeff Suppan	.40	1.00
JT Jim Thome	.60	1.50
KG Ken Griffey Jr.	2.00	5.00
MC Michael Cuddyer	.40	1.00
MH Matt Holliday	1.00	2.50
ML Mark Loretta	.40	1.00
MO Justin Morneau	.60	1.50
MY Michael Young	.40	1.00
NG Nomar Garciaparra	.60	1.50
OR Magglio Ordonez	.60	1.50
OV Omar Vizquel	.60	1.50
RC Roger Clemens	1.25	3.00
RF Rafael Furcal	.40	1.00
RH Ryan Howard	.75	2.00
SA Johan Santana	.60	1.50
SK Scott Kazmir	.60	1.50
TH Travis Hafner	.40	1.00
TI Tadahito Iguchi	.40	1.00
VG Vladimir Guerrero	.60	1.50
VW Vernon Wells	.40	1.00
WT Willy Taveras	.40	1.00

2007 Upper Deck Spectrum Shining Star Signatures

RANDOM INSERTS IN PACKS
PRINT RUNS B/WN 50-99 COPIES PER
EXCHANGE DEADLINE 3/19/2010

AD Adam Dunn/99	6.00	15.00
AG Adrian Gonzalez/99	8.00	20.00
AP Albert Pujols/50	90.00	150.00
CJ Conor Jackson/54	6.00	15.00
CZ Carlos Zambrano/99	10.00	25.00
DJ Derek Jeter/54	150.00	200.00
DL Derrek Lee/99	10.00	25.00
DO David Ortiz/99	30.00	60.00
GA Garrett Atkins/99	6.00	15.00
HR Hanley Ramirez/99	6.00	15.00
JB Jason Bay/99	6.00	15.00
JM Joe Mauer/99	20.00	50.00
JR Jose Reyes/99	6.00	15.00
JS Johan Santana/99	20.00	50.00
KG Ken Griffey Jr./99	75.00	150.00
KY Kevin Youkilis/99	6.00	15.00
MH Matt Holliday/99	6.00	15.00
MO Justin Morneau/99	6.00	15.00
TH Travis Hafner/99	10.00	25.00

2007 Upper Deck Spectrum Spectrum of Stars Signatures

STATED ODDS 1:100 HOB, 1:460 RET
PRINT RUNS B/WN 3-160 COPIES PER
NO PRINT RUNS FOR #'s: DB, EB, FE
CARDS ARE NOT SERIAL-NUMBERED.
PRINT RUNS PROVIDED BY UPPER DECK
INSCRIPTIONS PROVIDED BE UPPER DECK
MYSTERY EXCH CL: DB/E01/E02/E03
MYSTERY EXCH CL: EB/FE/KS1/KS2/KS3
MYSTERY EXCH CL: KS4/MM1/MM2/MM3
NO PRICING ON QTY 24 OR LESS
EXCHANGE DEADLINE 3/19/2010

AH1 A.Hall Black/65 *	15.00	40.00
BL2 B.Ledford Whistler/30 *	20.00	50.00
BU1 T.Burton Black/120 *	6.00	15.00
BW1 B.Williams Black/155 *	12.50	30.00
CB1 C.Bach Black/155 *	20.00	50.00
CF1 C.Feldman Black/95 *	10.00	25.00
CF3 C.Feldman Goonies/30 *	30.00	60.00
DF1 D.Faustino Black/160 *	15.00	40.00
DF2 D.Faustino Blue Bud Bundy/30 *	30.00	60.00
GO1 L.Gossett Jr. Black/60 *	15.00	40.00
JC1 J.Conaway Black/150 *	10.00	25.00
JC2 J.Conaway Taxi/30 *	20.00	50.00
JD2 J.Duhamel Transformers/36 *	30.00	60.00
KM1 K.McNichol Black/150 *	30.00	60.00
KM2 K.McNichol Family/30 *	30.00	60.00
KM3 K.McNichol Little Darlings/25 *	30.00	60.00
LB1 L.Blair Black/150 *	12.50	30.00
LB2 L.Blair Regan/30 *	30.00	60.00
LG1 L.Garrett Black/60 *	12.50	30.00
LG2 L.Garrett Blue/30 *	20.00	50.00
LP1 L.Petty Black/150 *	10.00	25.00
LP2 L.Petty KIT/30 *	20.00	50.00
MS1 M.St. John Black/60 *	12.50	30.00
TB1 T.Bridges Black/60 *	8.00	20.00
TB2 T.Bridges Blue/30 *	12.50	30.00
TI1 Tiffany Black/155 *	20.00	50.00
NNO Mystery Redemption	100.00	200.00

2007 Upper Deck Spectrum Super Swatches

OVERALL GAME-USED ODDS 1:10
STATED PRINT RUN 50 SER.#'d SETS

AD Adam Dunn	5.00	12.00
AJ Andruw Jones	6.00	15.00
AP Albert Pujols	15.00	40.00
AR Aramis Ramirez	5.00	12.00
BA Bobby Abreu	5.00	12.00
BC Bobby Crosby	5.00	12.00
BE Josh Beckett	5.00	12.00
BU B.J. Upton	5.00	12.00
BZ Barry Zito	5.00	12.00
CB Carlos Beltran	5.00	12.00
CC Carl Crawford	5.00	12.00
CD Carlos Delgado	5.00	12.00
CJ Chipper Jones	6.00	15.00
CL Roger Clemens	12.50	30.00
CS Curt Schilling	6.00	15.00
CU Chase Utley	6.00	15.00
DA Johnny Damon	6.00	15.00
DJ Derek Jeter	20.00	50.00
DL Derrek Lee	5.00	12.00
DO David Ortiz	6.00	15.00
FT Frank Thomas	15.00	40.00
GS Gary Sheffield	5.00	12.00
HA Travis Hafner	5.00	12.00
HR Hanley Ramirez	6.00	15.00
JB Jeremy Bonderman	5.00	12.00
JD J.D. Drew	5.00	12.00
JR Jose Reyes	10.00	25.00
JS Johan Santana	6.00	15.00
JT Jim Thome	6.00	15.00
JV Jason Varitek	6.00	15.00
JW Jered Weaver	6.00	15.00
KG Ken Griffey Jr.	15.00	40.00
KJ Kenji Johjima	6.00	15.00
LB Lance Berkman	5.00	12.00
MT Miguel Tejada	5.00	12.00
PE Andy Pettitte	6.00	15.00
PF Prince Fielder	6.00	15.00
PK Paul Konerko	5.00	12.00
RB Rocco Baldelli	5.00	12.00
RC Robinson Cano	10.00	25.00
RH Roy Halladay	5.00	12.00
RJ Randy Johnson	6.00	15.00
RS Richie Sexson	5.00	12.00
SR Scott Rolen	6.00	15.00
TH Todd Helton	6.00	15.00
VE Justin Verlander	6.00	15.00
VG Vladimir Guerrero	6.00	15.00
VW Vernon Wells	5.00	12.00

2007 Upper Deck Spectrum Swatches

STATED PRINT RUN 199 SER.#'d SETS
GOLD: .5X TO 1.2X BASIC
OVERALL GAME-USED ODDS 1:10
GOLD PRINT RUN 75 SER.#'d SETS

AB Adrian Beltre	3.00	8.00
AG Adrian Gonzalez	3.00	8.00
AH Aaron Hill	3.00	8.00
AK Austin Kearns	3.00	8.00
AP Albert Pujols	8.00	20.00
AR Aaron Rowand	3.00	8.00
AS Alfonso Soriano	3.00	8.00
BA Bobby Abreu	3.00	8.00
BC Bartolo Colon	3.00	8.00
BG Brian Giles	3.00	8.00
BI Brandon Inge	3.00	8.00
BJ B.J. Upton	3.00	8.00
BL Joe Blanton	3.00	8.00
BR B.J. Ryan	3.00	8.00
BS Ben Sheets	3.00	8.00
BW Billy Wagner	3.00	8.00
CA Jorge Cantu	3.00	8.00
CB Clint Barmes	3.00	8.00
CC Chad Cordero	3.00	8.00
CD Chris Duffy	3.00	8.00
CG Carlos Guillen	3.00	8.00
CK Casey Kotchman	3.00	8.00
CO Coco Crisp	3.00	8.00
CR Bobby Crosby	3.00	8.00
CS C.C. Sabathia	3.00	8.00
CU Chase Utley	3.00	8.00
CY Chris Young	3.00	8.00
CZ Carlos Zambrano	3.00	8.00
DA Johnny Damon	4.00	10.00
DC Daniel Cabrera	3.00	8.00
DH Danny Haren	3.00	8.00
DJ Derek Jeter	10.00	25.00
DL Derrek Lee	3.00	8.00
DM Dallas McPherson	3.00	8.00
DO David Ortiz	4.00	10.00
DU Dan Uggla	4.00	10.00
DW Dontrelle Willis	3.00	8.00
ES Johnny Estrada	3.00	8.00
FG Freddy Garcia	3.00	8.00
FL Francisco Liriano	3.00	8.00
FS Freddy Sanchez	3.00	8.00
GA Garrett Atkins	3.00	8.00
GC Gustavo Chacin	3.00	8.00
GR Curtis Granderson	3.00	8.00
GS Grady Sizemore	3.00	8.00
HR Hanley Ramirez	4.00	10.00
HS Huston Street	3.00	8.00
HU Aubrey Huff	3.00	8.00
IS Ian Snell	3.00	8.00
JB Jeremy Bonderman	3.00	8.00
JC Joe Crede	3.00	8.00
JD J.D. Drew	3.00	8.00
JE Jermaine Dye	3.00	8.00
JF Jeff Francoeur	4.00	10.00
JH J.J. Hardy	3.00	8.00
JM Joe Mauer	4.00	10.00
JN Joe Nathan	3.00	8.00
JP Jake Peavy	3.00	8.00
JR Jose Reyes	3.00	8.00
JT Jim Thome	3.00	8.00
JU Justin Duchscherer	3.00	8.00
JW Jake Westbrook	3.00	8.00
KG Ken Griffey Jr.	6.00	15.00
KH Khalil Greene	4.00	10.00
LN Laynce Nix	3.00	8.00
MA Matt Cain	4.00	10.00
MB Mark Buehrle	3.00	8.00
MC Mike Cameron	3.00	8.00
ME Morgan Ensberg	3.00	8.00
MH Matt Holliday	4.00	10.00
MI Michael Cuddyer	3.00	8.00
MM Melvin Mora	3.00	8.00
MO Justin Morneau	3.00	8.00
MT Miguel Tejada	3.00	8.00
NL Noah Lowry	3.00	8.00
NS Nick Swisher	3.00	8.00
OR Magglio Ordonez	3.00	8.00
PA Jonathan Papelbon	6.00	15.00
PE Jhonny Peralta	3.00	8.00
PF Prince Fielder	4.00	10.00
PL Paul Lo Duca	3.00	8.00
RA Aramis Ramirez	3.00	8.00
RF Rafael Furcal	3.00	8.00
RH Rich Harden	3.00	8.00
RJ Reed Johnson	3.00	8.00
RO Brian Roberts	3.00	8.00
RQ Robb Quinlan	3.00	8.00
RW Rickie Weeks	3.00	8.00
RZ Ryan Zimmerman	4.00	10.00
SC Sean Casey	3.00	8.00
SK Scott Kazmir	4.00	10.00
TH Torii Hunter	3.00	8.00
TI Tadahito Iguchi	3.00	8.00
TN Trot Nixon	3.00	8.00
VM Victor Martinez	3.00	8.00
WT Willy Taveras	3.00	8.00
YM Yadier Molina	3.00	8.00
ZD Zach Duke	3.00	8.00
ZG Zack Greinke	3.00	8.00

2007 Upper Deck Spectrum Swatches Patches

OVERALL GAME-USED ODDS 1:10
STATED PRINT RUN 50 SER.#'d SETS

AB Adrian Beltre	6.00	15.00
AG Adrian Gonzalez	6.00	15.00
AH Aaron Hill	6.00	15.00
AK Austin Kearns	6.00	15.00
AP Albert Pujols	20.00	50.00
AR Aaron Rowand	6.00	15.00
AS Alfonso Soriano	12.00	30.00
BA Bobby Abreu	8.00	20.00
BC Bartolo Colon	6.00	15.00
BG Brian Giles	6.00	15.00
BI Brandon Inge	6.00	15.00
BJ B.J. Upton	6.00	15.00
BL Joe Blanton	6.00	15.00
BR B.J. Ryan	6.00	15.00
BS Ben Sheets	6.00	15.00
BW Billy Wagner	8.00	20.00
CA Jorge Cantu	6.00	15.00
CB Clint Barmes	6.00	15.00
CC Chad Cordero	6.00	15.00
CD Chris Duffy	6.00	15.00
CG Carlos Guillen	6.00	15.00
CK Casey Kotchman	6.00	15.00
CO Coco Crisp	6.00	15.00
CR Bobby Crosby	6.00	15.00
CS C.C. Sabathia	6.00	15.00
CY Chris Young	6.00	15.00
CZ Carlos Zambrano	6.00	15.00
DA Johnny Damon	8.00	20.00
DC Daniel Cabrera	6.00	15.00
DH Danny Haren	6.00	15.00
DL Derrek Lee	6.00	15.00
DM Dallas McPherson	6.00	15.00
DO David Ortiz	12.00	30.00
DU Dan Uggla	8.00	20.00
DW Dontrelle Willis	6.00	15.00
ES Johnny Estrada	6.00	15.00
FG Freddy Garcia	6.00	15.00
FL Francisco Liriano	8.00	20.00
FS Freddy Sanchez	6.00	15.00
GA Garrett Atkins	6.00	15.00
GC Gustavo Chacin	6.00	15.00
GR Curtis Granderson	6.00	15.00
GS Grady Sizemore	12.00	30.00
HR Hanley Ramirez	8.00	20.00
HS Huston Street	6.00	15.00
HU Aubrey Huff	6.00	15.00
IS Ian Snell	6.00	15.00
JB Jeremy Bonderman	12.00	30.00
JC Joe Crede	6.00	15.00
JD J.D. Drew	6.00	15.00
JE Jermaine Dye	6.00	15.00
JF Jeff Francoeur	12.00	30.00
JH J.J. Hardy	6.00	15.00
JM Joe Mauer	12.00	30.00
JN Joe Nathan	6.00	15.00
JP Jake Peavy	6.00	15.00
JR Jose Reyes	12.00	30.00
JT Jim Thome	8.00	20.00
JU Justin Duchscherer	6.00	15.00
JW Jake Westbrook	8.00	20.00
KG Ken Griffey Jr.	30.00	60.00
KH Khalil Greene	8.00	20.00
LN Laynce Nix	6.00	15.00
MA Matt Cain	8.00	20.00
MB Mark Buehrle	6.00	15.00
MC Mike Cameron	6.00	15.00
ME Morgan Ensberg	6.00	15.00
MH Matt Holliday	8.00	20.00
MI Michael Cuddyer	6.00	15.00
MM Melvin Mora	6.00	15.00
MO Justin Morneau	6.00	15.00
MT Miguel Tejada	6.00	15.00
NL Noah Lowry	8.00	20.00
NS Nick Swisher	6.00	15.00
OR Magglio Ordonez	6.00	15.00
PA Jonathan Papelbon	10.00	25.00
PE Jhonny Peralta	6.00	15.00
PF Prince Fielder	12.00	30.00
PL Paul Lo Duca	8.00	20.00
RA Aramis Ramirez	8.00	20.00
RF Rafael Furcal	6.00	15.00
RH Rich Harden	6.00	15.00
RJ Reed Johnson	12.00	30.00
RO Brian Roberts	6.00	15.00
RQ Robb Quinlan	6.00	15.00
RZ Ryan Zimmerman	12.00	30.00
SC Sean Casey	6.00	15.00
SK Scott Kazmir	6.00	15.00
TH Torii Hunter	8.00	20.00
TI Tadahito Iguchi	6.00	15.00
TN Trot Nixon	6.00	15.00
VM Victor Martinez	6.00	15.00
WT Willy Taveras	6.00	15.00
YM Yadier Molina	6.00	15.00
ZD Zach Duke	6.00	15.00
ZG Zack Greinke	6.00	15.00

2008 Upper Deck Spectrum

COMP.SET w/o AUs (100)	10.00	25.00
COMMON CARD	.20	.50
COMMOM AU RC	3.00	8.00

OVERALL AUTO ODDS 1:10
PRINTING PLATES RANDOMLY INSERTED
PLATE PRINT RUN 1 SET PER COLOR
BLACK-CYAN-MAGENTA-YELLOW ISSUED
NO PLATE PRICING DUE TO SCARCITY

1 Chris B. Young	.20	.50
2 Brandon Webb	.30	.75
3 Eric Byrnes	.20	.50
4 John Smoltz	.50	1.25
5 Chipper Jones	.50	1.25
6 Jeff Francoeur	.30	.75
7 Mark Teixeira	.30	.75
8 Brian Roberts	.20	.50
9 Erik Bedard	.20	.50
10 Miguel Tejada	.30	.75
11 Nick Markakis	.40	1.00
12 David Ortiz	.50	1.25
13 Daisuke Matsuzaka	.30	.75
14 Manny Ramirez	.50	1.25
15 Jonathan Papelbon	.30	.75
16 Josh Beckett	.20	.50
17 Alfonso Soriano	.30	.75
18 Carlos Zambrano	.30	.75
19 Derrek Lee	.20	.50
20 Aramis Ramirez	.20	.50
21 Paul Konerko	.30	.75
22 Jermaine Dye	.20	.50
23 Jim Thome	.30	.75
24 Ken Griffey Jr.	1.00	2.50
25 Brandon Phillips	.20	.50
26 Adam Dunn	.30	.75
27 Grady Sizemore	.30	.75
28 Fausto Carmona	.20	.50
29 Victor Martinez	.30	.75
30 Travis Hafner	.20	.50
31 Matt Holliday	.50	1.25
32 Troy Tulowitzki	.50	1.25
33 Todd Helton	.30	.75
34 Magglio Ordonez	.30	.75
35 Justin Verlander	.50	1.25
36 Gary Sheffield	.20	.50
37 Miguel Cabrera	.50	1.25
38 Hanley Ramirez	.30	.75
39 Dan Uggla	.20	.50
40 Carlos Lee	.20	.50
41 Roy Oswalt	.30	.75
42 Lance Berkman	.30	.75
43 Hunter Pence	.30	.75
44 Alex Gordon	.30	.75
45 David DeJesus	.20	.50
46 Vladimir Guerrero	.30	.75
47 Kelvim Escobar	.30	.75
48 Chone Figgins	.20	.50
49 Brad Penny	.20	.50
50 Takashi Saito	.20	.50
51 Russell Martin	.20	.50
52 Prince Fielder	.30	.75
53 Ryan Braun	.30	.75
54 JJ Hardy	.20	.50
55 Johan Santana	.30	.75
56 Justin Morneau	.30	.75
57 Torii Hunter	.20	.50
58 Joe Mauer	.40	1.00
59 Carlos Beltran	.30	.75
60 David Wright	.30	.75
61 Carlos Delgado	.20	.50
62 Jose Reyes	.30	.75
63 Derek Jeter	1.25	3.00
64 Alex Rodriguez	.60	1.50
65 Robinson Cano	.30	.75
66 Hideki Matsui	.50	1.25
67 Mariano Rivera	.60	1.50
68 Dan Haren	.20	.50
69 Nick Swisher	.30	.75
70 Eric Chavez	.20	.50
71 Jimmy Rollins	.30	.75
72 Ryan Howard	.30	.75
73 Cole Hamels	.40	1.00
74 Chase Utley	.30	.75
75 Freddy Sanchez	.20	.50
76 Jason Bay	.30	.75
77 Ian Snell	.20	.50
78 Greg Maddux	.60	1.50
79 Jake Peavy	.20	.50
80 Chris Young	.20	.50
81 Barry Zito	.30	.75
82 Tim Lincecum	.30	.75
83 Omar Vizquel	.30	.75
84 Felix Hernandez	.30	.75
85 Ichiro Suzuki	.60	1.50
86 Richie Sexson	.20	.50
87 Albert Pujols	.60	1.50
88 Scott Rolen	.30	.75
89 Chris Carpenter	.30	.75
90 Delmon Young	.30	.75
91 Carl Crawford	.30	.75
92 B.J. Upton	.30	.75
93 Michael Young	.20	.50
94 Hank Blalock	.20	.50
95 Sammy Sosa	.50	1.25
96 Roy Halladay	.30	.75
97 Alex Rios	.20	.50
98 Vernon Wells	.20	.50
99 Ryan Zimmerman	.30	.75
100 Dmitri Young	.20	.50
101 Alberto Gonzalez AU RC	10.00	25.00
102 Bill Murphy AU (RC)	3.00	8.00
103 Bill White AU RC	3.00	8.00
104 Billy Buckner AU (RC)	3.00	8.00
105 Brandon Jones AU RC	3.00	8.00
106 Bronson Sardinha AU (RC)	3.00	8.00
107 Chin-Lung Hu AU (RC)	10.00	25.00
108 Chris Seddon AU (RC)	3.00	8.00
109 Clay Buchholz AU (RC)	10.00	25.00
110 Clint Sammons AU (RC)	3.00	8.00
111 Daric Barton AU (RC)	4.00	10.00
112 Dave Davidson AU RC	4.00	10.00
113 Donny Lucy AU (RC)	3.00	8.00
114 Emilio Bonifacio AU RC	4.00	10.00
115 Eugenio Velez AU RC	4.00	10.00
117 Harvey Garcia AU (RC)	3.00	8.00
118 Ian Kennedy AU RC	6.00	15.00
119 J.R. Towles AU RC	6.00	15.00
121 Jerry Blevins AU RC	3.00	8.00
122 Joe Koshansky AU (RC)	3.00	8.00
123 Joey Votto AU (RC)	20.00	50.00
124 Jonathan Albaladejo AU RC	4.00	10.00
125 Jonathan Meloan AU RC	3.00	8.00
126 Jose Morales AU (RC)	3.00	8.00
127 Josh Anderson AU (RC)	3.00	8.00
128 Josh Newman AU RC	3.00	8.00
129 Justin Maxwell AU RC	4.00	10.00
130 Justin Ruggiano AU RC	3.00	8.00
131 Kevin Hart AU (RC)	3.00	8.00
132 Lance Broadway AU (RC)	3.00	8.00
133 Luis Mendoza AU (RC)	3.00	8.00
134 Luke Hochevar AU RC	6.00	15.00
135 Nyjer Morgan AU (RC)	3.00	8.00
136 Rob Johnson AU (RC)	3.00	8.00
137 Ross Detwiler AU RC	3.00	8.00
138 Ross Ohlendorf AU RC	4.00	10.00
139 Ryan Hanigan AU RC	3.00	8.00
140 Seth Smith AU (RC)	3.00	8.00
141 Steve Pearce AU RC	12.00	30.00
142 Troy Patton AU (RC)	3.00	8.00
143 Wladimir Balentien AU (RC)	4.00	10.00
144 Colt Morton AU RC	3.00	8.00

2008 Upper Deck Spectrum Green

*1-100 GRN: .75X TO 2X BASIC
RANDOM INSERTS IN PACKS
1-100 PRINT RUN 199 SER.#'d SETS
OVERALL AUTO ODDS 1:10
GREEN AUTOS ARE NOT SER.#'d
NO GREEN AU PRICING AVAILABLE

2008 Upper Deck Spectrum Orange

*ORANGE: .6X TO 1.5X BASIC
RANDOM INSERTS IN PACKS
STATED PRINT RUN 399 SER.#'d SETS

2008 Upper Deck Spectrum Red

*RED: 1X TO 2.5X BASIC
RANDOM INSERTS IN PACKS
STATED PRINT RUN 99 SER.#'d SETS

2008 Upper Deck Spectrum Buyback Autographs

OVERALL AUTO ODDS 1:10
PRINT RUNS B/WN 2-69 COPIES PER
NO PRICING ON MOST DUE TO SCARCITY

JR1 Jose Reyes 04 UD/70	20.00	50.00
KG1 Ken Griffey Jr. 03 UD Patch/50	40.00	80.00
KG2 Ken Griffey Jr. 03 UD 40-Man/50	40.00	80.00
KG3 Ken Griffey Jr. 03 Sweet Spot/49	40.00	80.00
KG4 Ken Griffey Jr. 04 Vintage/50	40.00	80.00
KG5 Ken Griffey Jr. 03 SPx/49	40.00	80.00
KG6 Ken Griffey Jr. 03 UDAuth/50	40.00	80.00
KG7 Ken Griffey Jr. 04 UD ASL/50	40.00	80.00
KG8 Ken Griffey Jr. 03 UD HR/50	40.00	80.00
KG9 Ken Griffey Jr. 03 UD ClasPort/49	40.00	80.00
RA3 Roberto Alomar 03 Sweet Spot/50	8.00	20.00
RA5 Roberto Alomar 03 UD HR/30	8.00	20.00
RA6 Roberto Alomar 03 UD Auth/50	8.00	20.00

2008 Upper Deck Spectrum Derek Jeter Retrospectrum

COMMON CARD	1.50	4.00

RANDOM INSERTS IN PACKS
PRINTING PLATES RANDOMLY INSERTED
PLATE PRINT RUN 1 SET PER COLOR
BLACK-CYAN-MAGENTA-YELLOW ISSUED
NO PLATE PRICING DUE TO SCARCITY
*RED: 1X TO 2.5X BASIC
RED RANDOMLY INSERTED
RED PRINT RUN 99 SER.#'d SETS

DJ1 Derek Jeter	1.50	4.00
DJ2 Derek Jeter	1.50	4.00
DJ3 Derek Jeter	1.50	4.00
DJ4 Derek Jeter	1.50	4.00
DJ5 Derek Jeter	1.50	4.00
DJ6 Derek Jeter	1.50	4.00
DJ7 Derek Jeter	1.50	4.00
DJ8 Derek Jeter	1.50	4.00
DJ9 Derek Jeter	1.50	4.00
DJ10 Derek Jeter	1.50	4.00
DJ11 Derek Jeter	1.50	4.00
DJ12 Derek Jeter	1.50	4.00
DJ13 Derek Jeter	1.50	4.00
DJ14 Derek Jeter	1.50	4.00
DJ15 Derek Jeter	1.50	4.00
DJ16 Derek Jeter	1.50	4.00
DJ17 Derek Jeter	1.50	4.00
DJ18 Derek Jeter	1.50	4.00
DJ19 Derek Jeter	1.50	4.00
DJ20 Derek Jeter	1.50	4.00
DJ21 Derek Jeter	1.50	4.00
DJ22 Derek Jeter	1.50	4.00
DJ23 Derek Jeter	1.50	4.00
DJ24 Derek Jeter	1.50	4.00
DJ25 Derek Jeter	1.50	4.00
DJ26 Derek Jeter	1.50	4.00
DJ27 Derek Jeter	1.50	4.00
DJ28 Derek Jeter	1.50	4.00
DJ29 Derek Jeter	1.50	4.00
DJ30 Derek Jeter	1.50	4.00
DJ31 Derek Jeter	1.50	4.00
DJ32 Derek Jeter	1.50	4.00
DJ33 Derek Jeter	1.50	4.00
DJ34 Derek Jeter	1.50	4.00
DJ35 Derek Jeter	1.50	4.00
DJ36 Derek Jeter	1.50	4.00
DJ37 Derek Jeter	1.50	4.00
DJ38 Derek Jeter	1.50	4.00
DJ39 Derek Jeter	1.50	4.00
DJ40 Derek Jeter	1.50	4.00
DJ41 Derek Jeter	1.50	4.00
DJ42 Derek Jeter	1.50	4.00
DJ43 Derek Jeter	1.50	4.00
DJ44 Derek Jeter	1.50	4.00
DJ45 Derek Jeter	1.50	4.00
DJ46 Derek Jeter	1.50	4.00
DJ47 Derek Jeter	1.50	4.00
DJ48 Derek Jeter	1.50	4.00
DJ49 Derek Jeter	1.50	4.00
DJ50 Derek Jeter	1.50	4.00
DJ51 Derek Jeter	1.50	4.00
DJ52 Derek Jeter	1.50	4.00
DJ53 Derek Jeter	1.50	4.00
DJ54 Derek Jeter	1.50	4.00
DJ55 Derek Jeter	1.50	4.00
DJ56 Derek Jeter	1.50	4.00
DJ57 Derek Jeter	1.50	4.00
DJ58 Derek Jeter	1.50	4.00
DJ59 Derek Jeter	1.50	4.00
DJ60 Derek Jeter	1.50	4.00
DJ61 Derek Jeter	1.50	4.00
DJ62 Derek Jeter	1.50	4.00
DJ63 Derek Jeter	1.50	4.00
DJ64 Derek Jeter	1.50	4.00
DJ65 Derek Jeter	1.50	4.00
DJ66 Derek Jeter	1.50	4.00
DJ67 Derek Jeter	1.50	4.00
DJ68 Derek Jeter	1.50	4.00
DJ69 Derek Jeter	1.50	4.00
DJ70 Derek Jeter	1.50	4.00
DJ71 Derek Jeter	1.50	4.00
DJ72 Derek Jeter	1.50	4.00
DJ73 Derek Jeter	1.50	4.00
DJ74 Derek Jeter	1.50	4.00
DJ75 Derek Jeter	1.50	4.00
DJ76 Derek Jeter	1.50	4.00
DJ77 Derek Jeter	1.50	4.00
DJ78 Derek Jeter	1.50	4.00
DJ79 Derek Jeter	1.50	4.00
DJ80 Derek Jeter	1.50	4.00
DJ81 Derek Jeter	1.50	4.00
DJ82 Derek Jeter	1.50	4.00
DJ83 Derek Jeter	1.50	4.00
DJ84 Derek Jeter	1.50	4.00
DJ85 Derek Jeter	1.50	4.00
DJ86 Derek Jeter	1.50	4.00
DJ87 Derek Jeter	1.50	4.00
DJ88 Derek Jeter	1.50	4.00
DJ89 Derek Jeter	1.50	4.00
DJ90 Derek Jeter	1.50	4.00
DJ91 Derek Jeter	1.50	4.00
DJ92 Derek Jeter	1.50	4.00
DJ93 Derek Jeter	1.50	4.00
DJ94 Derek Jeter	1.50	4.00
DJ95 Derek Jeter	1.50	4.00
DJ96 Derek Jeter	1.50	4.00
DJ97 Derek Jeter	1.50	4.00
DJ98 Derek Jeter	1.50	4.00
DJ99 Derek Jeter	1.50	4.00
DJ100 Derek Jeter	1.50	4.00

2008 Upper Deck Spectrum Derek Jeter Retrospectrum Autographs

COMMON CARD	300.00	400.00

OVERAL AUTO ODDS 1:10
STATED PRINT RUN 2 SER.#'d SETS

2008 Upper Deck Spectrum Retrospectrum Swatches

OVERALL MEM ODDS 1:10

AB1 Aaron Boone	2.50	6.00
AB2 Aaron Boone	2.50	6.00
AG1 Adrian Gonzalez	2.50	6.00
AG2 Adrian Gonzalez	2.50	6.00
AH1 Aubrey Huff	2.50	6.00
AH2 Aubrey Huff	2.50	6.00
AJ1 A.J. Burnett	2.50	6.00
AJ2 A.J. Burnett	2.50	6.00
AK Adam Kennedy	2.50	6.00
AK1 Austin Kearns	2.50	6.00
AK2 Austin Kearns	2.50	6.00
AL1 Adam LaRoche	2.50	6.00
AL2 Adam LaRoche	2.50	6.00
AP Albert Pujols	6.00	15.00
AP1 Andy Pettitte	3.00	8.00
AP2 Andy Pettitte	3.00	8.00
AR1 Aaron Rowand	2.50	6.00
AR2 Aaron Rowand	2.50	6.00
AS1 Alfonso Soriano	3.00	8.00
AS2 Alfonso Soriano	3.00	8.00
AS3 Alfonso Soriano	3.00	8.00
BA1 Bobby Abreu	2.50	6.00
BA2 Bobby Abreu	2.50	6.00
BC1 Bartolo Colon	2.50	6.00
BC2 Bartolo Colon	2.50	6.00
BE1 Adrian Beltre	2.50	6.00
BE2 Adrian Beltre	2.50	6.00
BG1 Brian Giles	2.50	6.00
BG2 Brian Giles	2.50	6.00
BZ1 Barry Zito	2.50	6.00
BZ2 Barry Zito	2.50	6.00
CA1 Sean Casey	2.50	6.00
CA2 Sean Casey	2.50	6.00
CC1 Coco Crisp	2.50	6.00
CC2 Coco Crisp	2.50	6.00
CD1 Carlos Delgado	2.50	6.00
CD2 Carlos Delgado	2.50	6.00
CL1 Carlos Lee	2.50	6.00
CL2 Carlos Lee	2.50	6.00
CY1 Chris Young	2.50	6.00
CY2 Chris Young	2.50	6.00
DJ Derek Jeter	8.00	20.00
DW1 David Wells	2.50	6.00
DW2 David Wells	2.50	6.00
EG1 Eric Gagne	2.50	6.00
EG2 Eric Gagne	2.50	6.00
ER1 Edgar Renteria	2.50	6.00
ER2 Edgar Renteria	2.50	6.00
FG1 Freddy Garcia	2.50	6.00
FG2 Freddy Garcia	2.50	6.00
FT1 Frank Thomas	5.00	12.00
FT2 Frank Thomas	5.00	12.00
GM1 Greg Maddux	5.00	12.00
GM2 Greg Maddux	5.00	12.00
GS1 Gary Sheffield	2.50	6.00
GS2 Gary Sheffield	2.50	6.00
IR1 Ivan Rodriguez	3.00	8.00
IR2 Ivan Rodriguez	3.00	8.00
JB1 Josh Barfield	2.50	6.00
JB2 Josh Barfield	2.50	6.00
JD1 J.D. Drew	2.50	6.00
JD2 J.D. Drew	2.50	6.00
JE Johnny Estrada	2.50	6.00
JJ1 Jacque Jones	2.50	6.00
JJ2 Jacque Jones	2.50	6.00
JO1 Josh Beckett	3.00	8.00
JO2 Josh Beckett	3.00	8.00
JS1 Jason Schmidt	2.50	6.00
JS2 Jason Schmidt	2.50	6.00
JT1 Jim Thome	3.00	8.00
JT2 Jim Thome	3.00	8.00
KM Kevin Millwood	2.50	6.00
LG1 Luis Gonzalez	2.50	6.00
LG2 Luis Gonzalez	2.50	6.00
LH Livan Hernandez	2.50	6.00
MA1 Moises Alou	2.50	6.00
MA2 Moises Alou	2.50	6.00
ME1 Morgan Ensberg	2.50	6.00
ME2 Morgan Ensberg	2.50	6.00
MG1 Marcus Giles	2.50	6.00
MG2 Marcus Giles	2.50	6.00
ML1 Mark Loretta	2.50	6.00
ML2 Mark Loretta	2.50	6.00
MP1 Mike Piazza	5.00	12.00
MP2 Mike Piazza	5.00	12.00
MT1 Mark Teixeira	3.00	8.00
MT2 Mark Teixeira	3.00	8.00
OV1 Omar Vizquel	2.50	6.00
OV2 Omar Vizquel	2.50	6.00
RF1 Rafael Furcal	2.50	6.00
RF2 Rafael Furcal	2.50	6.00
RJ1 Randy Johnson	5.00	12.00
RJ2 Randy Johnson	5.00	12.00
RK Ryan Klesko	2.50	6.00
SS1 Shannon Stewart	2.50	6.00
SS2 Shannon Stewart	2.50	6.00
TI1 Tadahito Iguchi	2.50	6.00
TI2 Tadahito Iguchi	2.50	6.00
WT1 Willy Taveras	2.50	6.00
WT2 Willy Taveras	2.50	6.00

2008 Upper Deck Spectrum Retrospectrum Swatches Red

*RED: .6X TO 1.5X BASIC
OVERALL MEM ODDS 1:10
STATED PRINT RUN 45 SER.#'d SETS

2008 Upper Deck Spectrum Spectrum of Stars Signatures

OVERALL SOS AUTO ODDS 1:20
EXCHANGE DEADLINE 3/17/2010

AP A.J. Pero	15.00	40.00
BP Butch Patrick	12.50	30.00
CM Christopher McDonald	12.50	30.00
DA Taylor Dayne	12.50	30.00
DD Don Dokken	6.00	15.00
EM Erin Moran	20.00	50.00
EO Eddie Ojeda	4.00	10.00
ER Eric Roberts	12.50	30.00
ET Erik Turner	4.00	10.00
FS Frank Stallone	6.00	15.00
HW Henry Winkler	20.00	50.00
JA Joey Allen	6.00	15.00
JD Jerry Dixon	6.00	15.00
JF Jay Jay French	4.00	10.00
JG Joe Gannascoli	15.00	40.00
JL Jani Lane	20.00	50.00
KO Martin Kove	10.00	25.00
LH Larry Hagman	20.00	50.00
LT Larry Thomas	10.00	25.00
MA Miljenko Matijevic	6.00	15.00
MB Michael Biehn	15.00	40.00
MK Margot Kidder	20.00	50.00
MM Mark Mendoza	4.00	10.00
PP Pat Priest	12.50	30.00
PS P.J. Soles	12.50	30.00
RF Robert Funaro	12.50	30.00
SB Sebastian Bach	10.00	25.00
SN Dee Snider	10.00	25.00
SP Stephen Pearcy	6.00	15.00
SS Steven Sweet	4.00	10.00
TB Tom Bosley	15.00	40.00
TR Mike Tramp	6.00	15.00
VN Vince Neil	6.00	15.00
NNO Random EXCH	200.00	300.00

2008 Upper Deck Spectrum Spectrum Swatches

OVERALL MEM ODDS 1:10
STATED PRINT RUN 99 SER.#'d SETS

AB A.J. Burnett	3.00	8.00
AH Aaron Harang	3.00	8.00
AJ Andruw Jones	3.00	8.00
AP Albert Pujols	8.00	20.00
BB Boof Bonser	3.00	8.00
BC Bartolo Colon	3.00	8.00
BE Adrian Beltre	3.00	8.00
BG Brian Giles	3.00	8.00
BM Brian McCann	3.00	8.00
BS Ben Sheets	3.00	8.00
BU B.J. Upton	3.00	8.00
BW Billy Wagner	3.00	8.00
CA Chris Carpenter	3.00	8.00
CB Carlos Beltran	3.00	8.00
CC Carl Crawford	3.00	8.00
CG Carlos Guillen	3.00	8.00
CH Cole Hamels	4.00	10.00
CJ Chipper Jones	4.00	10.00
CS Curt Schilling	4.00	10.00
CU Chase Utley	4.00	10.00
CZ Carlos Zambrano	3.00	8.00
DH Dan Haren	3.00	8.00
DJ Derek Jeter	10.00	25.00
DL Derrek Lee	3.00	8.00
DM Daisuke Matsuzaka	8.00	20.00
DO David Ortiz	5.00	12.00
DO2 David Ortiz	5.00	12.00
DU Dan Uggla	3.00	8.00
DW Dontrelle Willis	3.00	8.00
EC Eric Chavez	3.00	8.00
FH Felix Hernandez	4.00	10.00
FS Freddy Sanchez	3.00	8.00
GA Garrett Atkins	3.00	8.00
GJ Geoff Jenkins	3.00	8.00
GM Greg Maddux	6.00	15.00
GR Curtis Granderson	4.00	10.00
GS Grady Sizemore	4.00	10.00
HA Travis Hafner	3.00	8.00
HB Hank Blalock	3.00	8.00
HO Trevor Hoffman	3.00	8.00
HP Hunter Pence	5.00	12.00
HR Hanley Ramirez	4.00	10.00
HU Torii Hunter	3.00	8.00
IK Ian Kinsler	3.00	8.00
IR Ivan Rodriguez	4.00	10.00
JA Conor Jackson	3.00	8.00
JB Josh Beckett	4.00	10.00
JC Joba Chamberlain	5.00	12.00
JD Jermaine Dye	3.00	8.00
JE Jim Edmonds	3.00	8.00
JF Jeff Francoeur	4.00	10.00
JG Jason Giambi	4.00	10.00
JH J.J. Hardy	3.00	8.00
JK Jeff Kent	3.00	8.00
JM Joe Mauer	4.00	10.00

Card	Low	High
JP Jhonny Peralta	3.00	8.00
JR Jose Reyes	4.00	10.00
JS Johan Santana	5.00	12.00
JT Jim Thome	4.00	10.00
JV Jason Varitek	5.00	12.00
JW Jered Weaver	3.00	8.00
KG Ken Griffey Jr.	8.00	20.00
KJ Kenji Johjima	3.00	8.00
KY Kevin Youkilis	3.00	8.00
LB Lance Berkman	3.00	8.00
MC Miguel Cabrera	4.00	10.00
MG Matt Garza	3.00	8.00
MH Matt Holliday	4.00	10.00
MO Justin Morneau	3.00	8.00
MP Mike Piazza	5.00	12.00
MR Manny Ramirez	4.00	10.00
MT Miguel Tejada	3.00	8.00
MY Michael Young	3.00	8.00
OR Magglio Ordonez	4.00	10.00
OS Roy Oswalt	3.00	8.00
PA Jonathan Papelbon	4.00	10.00
PE Jake Peavy	4.00	10.00
PF Prince Fielder	5.00	12.00
PI Juan Pierre	3.00	8.00
PM Pedro Martinez	4.00	10.00
PO Jorge Posada	4.00	10.00
RA Aramis Ramirez	3.00	8.00
RB Ryan Braun	6.00	15.00
RC Robinson Cano	4.00	10.00
RF Rafael Furcal	3.00	8.00
RH Roy Halladay	3.00	8.00
RJ Randy Johnson	5.00	12.00
RM Russell Martin	3.00	8.00
RS Richie Sexson	3.00	8.00
RZ Ryan Zimmerman	4.00	10.00
SM John Smoltz	4.00	10.00
SO Jeremy Sowers	3.00	8.00
SR Scott Rolen	4.00	10.00
TH Tim Hudson	3.00	8.00
TW Tim Wakefield	3.00	8.00
VE Justin Verlander	4.00	10.00
VG Vladimir Guerrero	4.00	10.00
VM Victor Martinez	3.00	8.00
VW Vernon Wells	3.00	8.00
VW2 Vernon Wells	3.00	8.00

2008 Upper Deck Spectrum Spectrum Swatches Green

*GREEN: .5X TO 1.2X BASIC
OVERALL MEM ODDS 1:10
STATED PRINT RUN 50 SER.#'d SETS

2008 Upper Deck Spectrum Spectrum Swatches Orange

*ORANGE: .4X TO 1X BASIC
OVERALL MEM ODDS 1:10
STATED PRINT RUN 75 SER.#'d SETS

2008 Upper Deck Spectrum Spectrum Swatches Purple

OVERALL MEM ODDS 1:10
PRINT RUNS B/WN 2-58 COPIES PER
NO PRICING ON QTY 25 OR LESS

Card	Low	High
AB A.J. Burnett/34	5.00	12.00
AH Aaron Harang/39	5.00	12.00
BB Boof Bonser/26	5.00	12.00
BC Bartolo Colon/40	5.00	12.00
BE Adrian Beltre/29	5.00	12.00
CA Chris Carpenter/29	5.00	12.00
CH Cole Hamels/35	6.00	15.00
CS Curt Schilling/38	6.00	15.00
CU Chase Utley/26	6.00	15.00
CZ Carlos Zambrano/38	5.00	12.00
DO David Ortiz/34	8.00	20.00
DU Dan Uggla/35	5.00	12.00
EC Eric Chavez/34	5.00	12.00
FS Freddy Sanchez/27	5.00	12.00
GA Garrett Atkins/27	5.00	12.00
GJ Geoff Jenkins/30	5.00	12.00
GM Greg Maddux/28	10.00	25.00
GS Grady Sizemore/48	6.00	15.00
HB Hank Blalock/51	5.00	12.00
HR Hanley Ramirez/48	6.00	15.00
JR Jose Reyes/57	6.00	15.00
JT Jim Thome/33	6.00	15.00
JV Jason Varitek/36	8.00	20.00
MH Matt Holliday/33	6.00	15.00
MO Justin Morneau/31	5.00	12.00
MY Michael Young/30	5.00	12.00
OR Magglio Ordonez/44	6.00	15.00
OS Roy Oswalt/58	5.00	12.00
PA Jonathan Papelbon/44	6.00	15.00
PE Jake Peavy/28	6.00	15.00
PI Juan Pierre/45	5.00	12.00
RF Rafael Furcal/32	5.00	12.00
RH Roy Halladay/51	5.00	12.00
RJ Randy Johnson/55	8.00	20.00
RM Russell Martin/44	5.00	12.00
RZ Ryan Zimmerman/29	6.00	15.00
SM John Smoltz/45	6.00	15.00
SO Jeremy Sowers/27	5.00	12.00
TH Tim Hudson/49	5.00	12.00
TW Tim Wakefield/35	5.00	12.00
VE Justin Verlander/27	6.00	15.00
VG Vladimir Guerrero/41	6.00	15.00
VW Vernon Wells/34	5.00	12.00

2008 Upper Deck Spectrum Spectrum Swatches Red

*RED: .6X TO 1.5X BASIC
OVERALL MEM ODDS 1:10
STATED PRINT RUN 35 SER.#'d SETS

2008 Upper Deck Spectrum Spectrum Swatches Autographs

OVERALL AUTO ODDS 1:10
PRINT RUNS B/WN 5-30 COPIES PER
NO PRICING ON MOST DUE TO SCARCITY

Card	Low	High
AH Aaron Harang/30	8.00	20.00
BB Boof Bonser/30	8.00	20.00
BG Brian Giles/30	8.00	20.00
BM Brian McCann/30	15.00	40.00
BS Ben Sheets/30	12.00	30.00
BU B.J. Upton/30	12.00	30.00
CC Carl Crawford/30	8.00	20.00
CH Cole Hamels/30	15.00	40.00
CJ Chipper Jones/30	60.00	120.00
DH Dan Haren/30	8.00	20.00
DL Derrek Lee/30	10.00	25.00
DM Daisuke Matsuzaka/30	75.00	150.00
DU Dan Uggla/30	8.00	20.00
DW Dontrelle Willis/30	8.00	20.00
FH Felix Hernandez/30	20.00	50.00
GA Garrett Atkins/30	8.00	20.00
GR Curtis Granderson/30	15.00	40.00
HA Travis Hafner/30	8.00	20.00
HP Hunter Pence/30	15.00	40.00
HR Hanley Ramirez/30	8.00	20.00
HU Torii Hunter/30	8.00	20.00
IK Ian Kinsler/30	8.00	20.00
JM Joe Mauer/30	15.00	40.00
JS Johan Santana/30	12.00	30.00
JV Jason Varitek/30	20.00	50.00
JW Jered Weaver/30	10.00	25.00
KY Kevin Youkilis/30	15.00	40.00
LB Lance Berkman/30	10.00	25.00
MC Miguel Cabrera/30	30.00	60.00
MG Matt Garza/30	8.00	20.00
MH Matt Holliday/30	12.50	30.00
MO Justin Morneau/30	8.00	20.00
MT Miguel Tejada/30	10.00	25.00
OS Roy Oswalt/30	10.00	25.00
PA Jonathan Papelbon/30	8.00	20.00
PF Prince Fielder/30	10.00	25.00
RA Aramis Ramirez/30	12.50	30.00
RB Ryan Braun/30	30.00	60.00
RM Russell Martin/30	20.00	50.00
RZ Ryan Zimmerman/30	10.00	25.00
SO Jeremy Sowers/30	10.00	25.00
TH Tim Hudson/30	10.00	25.00
VE Justin Verlander/30	30.00	60.00
VG Vladimir Guerrero/30	20.00	50.00
VM Victor Martinez/30	15.00	40.00

2008 Upper Deck Spectrum Spectrum Swatches Dual

OVERALL MEM ODDS 1:10
STATED PRINT RUN 99 SER.#'d SETS

Card	Low	High
AP Aaron Rowand	4.00	10.00
Pat Burrell		
BM J.Beckett/D.Matsuzaka	12.50	30.00
BP R.Braun/H.Pence	8.00	20.00
CL Matt Cain	4.00	10.00
Noah Lowry		
CT Curt Schilling	5.00	12.00
Tim Wakefield		
CW Miguel Cabrera	5.00	12.00
Dontrelle Willis		
CY Carl Crawford	5.00	12.00
Delmon Young		
DC D.Jeter/J.Chamberlain	30.00	60.00
FB P.Fielder/R.Braun	10.00	25.00
FD Felix Hernandez	5.00	12.00
Dan Haren		
FK Rafael Furcal	4.00	10.00
Jeff Kent		
FM Jeff Francoeur	5.00	12.00
Brian McCann		
GC Vladimir Guerrero	4.00	10.00
Bartolo Colon		
GD K.Griffey/A.Dunn	10.00	25.00
GG Adrian Gonzalez	5.00	12.00
Brian Giles		
GM T.Glavine/G.Maddux	10.00	25.00
GO V.Guerrero/M.Ordonez	10.00	25.00
GP Jason Giambi	5.00	12.00
Jorge Posada		
GV Grady Sizemore	5.00	12.00
Victor Martinez		
HB Roy Halladay	4.00	10.00
A.J. Burnett		
HC Torii Hunter	4.00	10.00
Mike Cameron		
HF Matt Holliday	5.00	12.00
Jeff Francoeur		
HH Matt Holliday	6.00	15.00
Todd Helton		
HJ Felix Hernandez	6.00	15.00
Kenji Johjima		
HS Rich Harden	4.00	10.00
Huston Street		
JC D.Jeter/R.Cano	12.50	30.00
JF Andruw Jones	5.00	12.00
Jeff Francoeur		
JP D.Jeter/A.Pujols	15.00	40.00
JR D.Jeter/J.Reyes	12.50	30.00
JT John Smoltz	6.00	15.00
Tim Hudson		
JW Randy Johnson	6.00	15.00
Brandon Webb		
MH Justin Morneau	4.00	10.00
Torii Hunter		
ML Brett Myers	4.00	10.00
Brad Lidge		
MP Russell Martin	5.00	12.00
Juan Pierre		
MR Victor Martinez	5.00	12.00
Ivan Rodriguez		
MW P.Martinez/B.Wagner	10.00	25.00
OB Roy Oswalt	5.00	12.00
Lance Berkman		
OG Magglio Ordonez	5.00	12.00
Curtis Granderson		
OP D.Ortiz/A.Pujols	10.00	25.00
OR D.Ortiz/M.Ramirez	10.00	25.00
PE A.Pujols/J.Edmonds	8.00	20.00
PJ Prince Fielder	6.00	15.00
Justin Morneau		
PM Jake Peavy	6.00	15.00
Greg Maddux		
PS A.Pujols/A.Soriano	10.00	25.00
PW Jake Peavy	5.00	12.00
Brandon Webb		
RB Jose Reyes	5.00	12.00
Carlos Beltran		
RC Gary Sheffield	5.00	12.00
Miguel Cabrera		
RF Jose Reyes	5.00	12.00
Rafael Furcal		
RH Hanley Ramirez	5.00	12.00
J.J. Hardy		
RR Jose Reyes	5.00	12.00
Jimmy Rollins		
RU Hanley Ramirez	5.00	12.00
Dan Uggla		
SB Richie Sexson	4.00	10.00
Adrian Beltre		
SH Ben Sheets	4.00	10.00
J.J. Hardy		
SL Alfonso Soriano	5.00	12.00
Derrek Lee		
SM Johan Santana	5.00	12.00
Joe Mauer		
SW Johan Santana	5.00	12.00
Dontrelle Willis		
TD Jim Thome	4.00	10.00
Jermaine Dye		
TM Miguel Tejada	4.00	10.00
Nick Markakis		
UH C.Utley/C.Hamels	8.00	20.00
VB J.Verlander/J.Bonderman	10.00	25.00
VR J.Verlander/I.Rodriguez	10.00	25.00
VY Jason Varitek	6.00	15.00
Kevin Youkilis		
WR Vernon Wells	4.00	10.00
Alex Rios		
YK Michael Young	4.00	10.00
Ian Kinsler		
ZL Carlos Zambrano	4.00	10.00
Derrek Lee		

2008 Upper Deck Spectrum Three Star Swatches

OVERALL MEM ODDS 1:10
STATED PRINT RUN 75 SER.#'d SETS

Card	Low	High
GDH Griffey/Dunn/Harang	6.00	15.00
HBK Cole Hamels/Erik Bedard		
Scott Kazmir	4.00	10.00
JCC Jeter/Joba/Cano	10.00	25.00
JPG Jeter/Pujols/Griffey	20.00	50.00
KHS Ian Kinsler/Aaron Hill		
Freddy Sanchez	4.00	10.00
MGS Maddux/Glavine/Smoltz	12.50	30.00
MJS Pedro Martinez/Randy Johnson		
Curt Schilling	10.00	25.00
MRM Victor Martinez/Ivan Rodriguez		
Joe Mauer	4.00	10.00
OBP Roy Oswalt/Lance Berkman		
Hunter Pence	6.00	15.00
OVS Magglio Ordonez/Justin Verlander		
Gary Sheffield	10.00	25.00
PER Pujols/Edmonds/Rolen	10.00	25.00
PSB Jake Peavy/Johan Santana		
Josh Beckett	6.00	15.00
RBM Reyes/Beltran/Pedro	10.00	25.00
RUH Jimmy Rollins/Chase Utley		
Cole Hamels	6.00	15.00
SBH Grady Sizemore/Carlos Beltran		
Torii Hunter	4.00	10.00
SCG Alfonso Soriano/Miguel Cabrera		
Vladimir Guerrero	4.00	10.00
SJT John Smoltz/Chipper Jones		
Mark Teixeira	6.00	15.00
SMH Grady Sizemore/Victor Martinez		
Travis Hafner	6.00	15.00
SMM Johan Santana/Justin Morneau		
Joe Mauer	6.00	15.00
ZSL Zambrano/Soriano/Lee	10.00	25.00

2009 Upper Deck Spectrum

Card	Low	High
COMP.SET w/o AU's (100)	8.00	20.00
COMMON CARD	.15	.40
COMMON AU RC	3.00	8.00

OVERALL AUTO ODDS 1:7
EXCHANGE DEADLINE 1/29/2011
PRINTING PLATES RANDOMLY INSERTED
PLATE PRINT RUN 1 SET PER COLOR
BLACK-CYAN-MAGENTA-YELLOW ISSUED
NO PLATE PRICING DUE TO SCARCITY

Card	Low	High
1 Brandon Webb	.25	.60
2 Randy Johnson	.40	1.00
3 Chris B. Young	.15	.40
4 Dan Haren	.15	.40
5 Adam Dunn	.25	.60
6 Chipper Jones	.40	1.00
7 Tim Hudson	.25	.60
8 John Smoltz	.40	1.00
9 Brian Roberts	.15	.40
10 Nick Markakis	.30	.75
11 Josh Beckett	.15	.40
12 David Ortiz	.40	1.00
13 Daisuke Matsuzaka	.25	.60
14 J.D. Drew	.15	.40
15 Jonathan Papelbon	.25	.60
16 Mike Lowell	.15	.40
17 Alfonso Soriano	.25	.60
18 Derrek Lee	.15	.40
19 Kosuke Fukudome	.25	.60
20 Carlos Zambrano	.25	.60
21 Aramis Ramirez	.15	.40
22 Rich Harden	.15	.40
23 Carlos Quentin	.15	.40
24 Jim Thome	.25	.60
25 Ken Griffey Jr.	.75	2.00
26 Jay Bruce	.25	.60
27 Edinson Volquez	.15	.40
28 Brandon Phillips	.15	.40
29 Victor Martinez	.25	.60
30 Grady Sizemore	.25	.60
31 Travis Hafner	.15	.40
32 Matt Holliday	.40	1.00
33 Troy Tulowitzki	.40	1.00
34 Garrett Atkins	.15	.40
35 Miguel Cabrera	.40	1.00
36 Magglio Ordonez	.25	.60
37 Justin Verlander	.40	1.00
38 Hanley Ramirez	.25	.60
39 Dan Uggla	.15	.40
40 Lance Berkman	.25	.60
41 Carlos Lee	.15	.40
42 Roy Oswalt	.25	.60
43 Miguel Tejada	.25	.60
44 Joakim Soria	.15	.40
45 Alex Gordon	.25	.60
46 Mark Teixeira	.25	.60
47 Vladimir Guerrero	.25	.60
48 Torii Hunter	.15	.40
49 John Lackey	.25	.60
50 Manny Ramirez	.40	1.00
51 Russell Martin	.15	.40
52 Matt Kemp	.30	.75
53 Clayton Kershaw	.60	1.50
54 CC Sabathia	.25	.60
55 Prince Fielder	.25	.60
56 Ryan Braun	.25	.60
57 Joe Mauer	.30	.75
58 Justin Morneau	.25	.60
59 Jose Reyes	.25	.60
60 David Wright	.30	.75
61 Johan Santana	.25	.60
62 Carlos Beltran	.25	.60
63 Ivan Rodriguez	.25	.60
64 Alex Rodriguez	.50	1.25
65 Derek Jeter	1.00	2.50
66 Chien-Ming Wang	.25	.60
67 Jason Giambi	.15	.40
68 Joba Chamberlain	.15	.40
69 Mariano Rivera	.50	1.25
70 Xavier Nady	.15	.40
71 Frank Thomas	.40	1.00
72 Carlos Gonzalez	.25	.60
73 Chase Utley	.25	.60
74 Ryan Howard	.30	.75
75 Jimmy Rollins	.25	.60
76 Andy LaRoche	.15	.40
77 Nate McLouth	.15	.40
78 Adrian Gonzalez	.30	.75
79 Greg Maddux	.50	1.25
80 Jake Peavy	.15	.40
81 Trevor Hoffman	.25	.60
82 Tim Lincecum	.25	.60
83 Aaron Rowand	.15	.40
84 Felix Hernandez	.25	.60
85 Ichiro Suzuki	.50	1.25
86 Erik Bedard	.15	.40
87 Albert Pujols	.50	1.25
88 Troy Glaus	.15	.40
89 Rick Ankiel	.15	.40
90 B.J. Upton	.25	.60
91 Evan Longoria	.25	.60
92 Scott Kazmir	.15	.40
93 Carl Crawford	.25	.60
94 Josh Hamilton	.25	.60
95 Ian Kinsler	.25	.60
96 Michael Young	.15	.40
97 Roy Halladay	.25	.60
98 Vernon Wells	.15	.40
99 Ryan Zimmerman	.25	.60
100 Lastings Milledge	.15	.40
101 David Price AU RC	6.00	15.00
102 Conor Gillaspie AU RC	3.00	8.00
103 Jeff Baisley AU RC	3.00	8.00
104 Angel Salome AU (RC)	3.00	8.00
105 Aaron Cunningham AU RC	3.00	8.00
106 Lou Marson AU (RC)	3.00	8.00
107 Matt Antonelli AU RC	3.00	8.00
108 M.Bowden AU (RC)	3.00	8.00
109 F.Cervelli AU RC	6.00	15.00
110 Phil Coke AU RC	3.00	8.00
111 Josh Outman AU RC	3.00	8.00
112 Shairon Martis AU RC	4.00	10.00
113 Mat Gamel AU RC	3.00	8.00
114 Josh Geer AU (RC)	3.00	8.00
115 Greg Golson AU (RC)	3.00	8.00
116 Kila Ka'aihue AU (RC)	3.00	8.00
117 Wade LeBlanc AU RC	3.00	8.00
118 Chris Lambert AU (RC)	3.00	8.00
119 James Parr AU (RC)	3.00	8.00
120 Tuiasosopo AU (RC)	3.00	8.00

2009 Upper Deck Spectrum Black

*BLK: 4X TO 10X BASIC CARDS
RANDOM INSERTS IN PACKS
STATED PRINT RUN 50 SER.#'d SETS

2009 Upper Deck Spectrum Blue

RANDOM INSERTS IN RETAIL PACKS
NO PRICING DUE TO LACK OF MKT INFO

2009 Upper Deck Spectrum Gold Jersey

OVERALL MEM ODDS 1:7
STATED PRINT RUN 99 SER.#'d SETS

Card	Low	High
1 Brandon Webb Jsy	8.00	20.00
2 Randy Johnson Jsy	4.00	10.00
4 Dan Haren Jsy	3.00	8.00
5 Adam Dunn Jsy	3.00	8.00
6 Chipper Jones Jsy	4.00	10.00
7 Tim Hudson Jsy	3.00	8.00
8 John Smoltz Jsy	3.00	8.00
9 Brian Roberts Jsy	4.00	10.00
10 Nick Markakis Jsy	4.00	10.00
11 Josh Beckett Jsy	3.00	8.00
12 David Ortiz Jsy	3.00	8.00
13 Daisuke Matsuzaka Jsy	6.00	15.00
14 J.D. Drew Jsy/54	3.00	8.00
15 Jonathan Papelbon Jsy	3.00	8.00
16 Mike Lowell Jsy	4.00	10.00
17 Alfonso Soriano Jsy	3.00	8.00
18 Derrek Lee Jsy	3.00	8.00
19 Kosuke Fukudome Jsy	5.00	12.00
20 Carlos Zambrano Jsy	3.00	8.00
21 Aramis Ramirez Jsy	5.00	12.00
24 Jim Thome Jsy	3.00	8.00
25 Ken Griffey Jr. Jsy	6.00	15.00
26 Jay Bruce Jsy	8.00	20.00
27 Edinson Volquez Jsy	3.00	8.00
28 Brandon Phillips Jsy	3.00	8.00
29 Victor Martinez Jsy	3.00	8.00
30 Grady Sizemore Jsy	3.00	8.00
31 Travis Hafner Jsy	3.00	8.00
32 Matt Holliday Jsy	3.00	8.00
33 Troy Tulowitzki Jsy	3.00	8.00
34 Garrett Atkins Jsy	3.00	8.00
35 Miguel Cabrera Jsy	3.00	8.00
36 Magglio Ordonez Jsy	3.00	8.00
37 Justin Verlander Jsy	3.00	8.00
38 Hanley Ramirez Jsy	3.00	8.00
39 Dan Uggla Jsy	3.00	8.00
40 Lance Berkman Jsy	3.00	8.00
41 Carlos Lee Jsy	4.00	10.00
42 Roy Oswalt Jsy	3.00	8.00
43 Miguel Tejada Jsy	3.00	8.00
44 Joakim Soria Jsy	3.00	8.00
45 Alex Gordon Jsy	5.00	12.00
46 Mark Teixeira Jsy	4.00	10.00
47 Vladimir Guerrero Jsy	3.00	8.00
49 John Lackey Jsy	3.00	8.00
50 Manny Ramirez Jsy	4.00	10.00
51 Russell Martin Jsy	3.00	8.00
52 Matt Kemp Jsy	3.00	8.00
53 Clayton Kershaw Jsy	4.00	10.00
54 CC Sabathia Jsy	3.00	8.00
55 Prince Fielder Jsy	3.00	8.00
56 Ryan Braun Jsy	5.00	12.00
57 Joe Mauer Jsy	3.00	8.00
58 Justin Morneau Jsy	4.00	10.00
59 Jose Reyes Jsy	4.00	10.00
61 Johan Santana Jsy	5.00	12.00
62 Carlos Beltran Jsy	4.00	10.00
63 Ivan Rodriguez Jsy	3.00	8.00
65 Derek Jeter Jsy	10.00	25.00
66 Chien-Ming Wang Jsy	5.00	12.00
67 Jason Giambi Jsy	3.00	8.00
68 Joba Chamberlain Jsy	5.00	12.00
69 Mariano Rivera Jsy	4.00	10.00
70 Xavier Nady Jsy/80	3.00	8.00
71 Frank Thomas Jsy	8.00	20.00
72 Carlos Gonzalez Jsy	4.00	10.00
73 Chase Utley Jsy	6.00	15.00
78 Adrian Gonzalez Jsy	3.00	8.00
79 Greg Maddux Jsy	15.00	40.00
80 Jake Peavy Jsy	3.00	8.00
81 Trevor Hoffman Jsy	3.00	8.00
82 Tim Lincecum Jsy	5.00	12.00
84 Felix Hernandez Jsy	3.00	8.00
86 Erik Bedard Jsy	3.00	8.00
87 Albert Pujols Jsy	10.00	25.00
88 Troy Glaus Jsy	3.00	8.00
89 Rick Ankiel Jsy	5.00	12.00
90 B.J. Upton Jsy	3.00	8.00
91 Evan Longoria Jsy	6.00	15.00
92 Scott Kazmir Jsy	3.00	8.00
93 Carl Crawford Jsy	3.00	8.00
95 Ian Kinsler Jsy	3.00	8.00
96 Michael Young Jsy	3.00	8.00
97 Roy Halladay Jsy	3.00	8.00
98 Vernon Wells Jsy	3.00	8.00
99 Ryan Zimmerman Jsy	4.00	10.00
100 Lastings Milledge Jsy	3.00	8.00

2009 Upper Deck Spectrum Green

*GRN: 1.5X TO 4X BASIC CARDS
RANDOM INSERTS IN PACKS
STATED PRINT RUN 99 SER.#'d SETS

2009 Upper Deck Spectrum Red

*RED: .75X TO 2X BASIC CARDS
RANDOM INSERTS IN PACKS
STATED PRINT RUN 250 SER.#'d SETS

2009 Upper Deck Spectrum Turquoise

*TURQ: 4X TO 10X BASIC CARDS
RANDOM INSERTS IN PACKS
STATED PRINT RUN 25 SER.#'d SETS

2009 Upper Deck Spectrum Celebrity Cut Signatures

OVERALL AUTO ODDS 1:7
STATED PRINT RUN 1 SER.#'d SET
NO PRICING DUE TO SCARCITY

2009 Upper Deck Spectrum Spectrum of Stars Autographs

OVERALL AUTO ODDS 1:7
PRINTING PLATES RANDOMLY INSERTED
PLATE PRINT RUN 1 SET PER COLOR
BLACK-CYAN-MAGENTA-YELLOW ISSUED
NO PLATE PRICING DUE TO SCARCITY

Card	Low	High
BL B-Real	5.00	12.00
BT Brutus Beefcake	4.00	10.00
BU Burt Reynolds	15.00	40.00
CE Cheech Marin	20.00	50.00
CF Corey Feldman	6.00	15.00
EE Erika Eleniak	6.00	15.00
EO Ed O'Neill	12.50	30.00
FU Fabiana Udenio	5.00	12.00
HH Henry Hill	10.00	25.00
IS Ian Somerhalder	8.00	20.00
KI Kim Kardashian	60.00	120.00
KW Kendra Wilkinson	12.50	30.00
LE Leslie Nielsen	10.00	25.00
LF Lita Ford	6.00	15.00
LH Linda Hamilton	5.00	12.00
I P Lanny Poffo	5.00	12.00
LS Larry Storch	4.00	10.00
MK Martin Klebba	4.00	10.00
PR Matt Prokop	4.00	10.00
SF Susie Feldman	5.00	12.00
TC Tommy Chong	15.00	40.00
TR Terri Runnels	5.00	12.00

2009 Upper Deck Spectrum Spectrum of Stars Autographs Die Cut

*DIE CUT: .5X TO 1.2X BASIC INSERTS
OVERALL AUTO ODDS 1:7
STATED PRINT RUN 50 SER.#'d SETS

2009 Upper Deck Spectrum Spectrum Swatches Autographs

OVERALL AUTO ODDS 1:7
STATED PRINT RUN 3-99 SER.#'d SETS
NO PRICING ON QTY 25 OR LESS

Card	Low	High
SSAG A.Gonzalez/99	4.00	20.00
SSAM Andrew Miller/99	4.00	10.00
SSBI C.Billingsley/35	10.00	25.00
SSBJ B.J. Upton/50	10.00	25.00
SSBP Brandon Phillips/99	8.00	20.00
SSBS Ben Sheets/35	6.00	15.00
SSBW Brandon Webb/35	12.50	30.00
SSBZ Clay Buchholz/99	6.00	15.00
SSCC Carl Crawford/75	6.00	15.00
SSCK C.Kershaw/45	30.00	60.00
SSCL Carlos Lee/99	4.00	10.00
SSCY Chris Young/99	4.00	10.00
SSDH Dan Haren/35	5.00	12.00
SSDL Derrek Lee/35	8.00	20.00
SSDP Dustin Pedroia/50	15.00	40.00
SSDU Dan Uggla/99	5.00	12.00
SSDY Delmon Young/52	5.00	12.00
SSEV Edinson Volquez/35	6.00	15.00
SSFH Felix Hernandez/75	12.50	30.00
SSGA Garrett Atkins/99	4.00	10.00
SSGR Ken Griffey Jr./75	50.00	100.00
SSGT Garret Anderson/99	5.00	12.00
SSHA Corey Hart/99	3.00	8.00
SSHI Rich Hill/99	4.00	10.00
SSHR Hanley Ramirez/35	6.00	15.00
SSJM Joe Mauer/50	15.00	40.00
SSKG Ken Griffey Jr./75	60.00	120.00
SSKY Kevin Youkilis/99	12.50	30.00
SSMC Matt Cain/99	12.50	30.00
SSMK Matt Kemp/35	12.50	30.00
SSMO Justin Morneau/75	12.50	30.00
SSNI Nick Markakis/99	6.00	15.00
SSNS Nick Swisher/99	4.00	10.00
SSPA J.Papelbon/58	10.00	25.00
SSPK Paul Konerko/99	12.50	30.00
SSRB Ryan Braun/35	30.00	60.00
SSRH Roy Halladay/50	10.00	25.00
SSRM Russell Martin/50	15.00	40.00
SSRZ R.Zimmerman/99	10.00	25.00
SSSK Scott Kazmir/35	10.00	25.00
SSTL Tim Lincecum/50	50.00	100.00
SSTT Troy Tulowitzki/50	10.00	25.00
SSVW Vernon Wells/75	5.00	12.00

2009 Upper Deck Spectrum Spectrum Swatches Blue

OVERALL MEM ODDS ONE PER BOX
PRINTING PLATES RANDOMLY INSERTED
PLATE PRINT RUN 1 SET PER COLOR
BLACK-CYAN-MAGENTA-YELLOW ISSUED
NO PLATE PRICING DUE TO SCARCITY

Card	Low	High
SSAB Adrian Beltre	3.00	8.00
SSAG Adrian Gonzalez	2.50	6.00
SSAM Andrew Miller	2.00	5.00
SSAN Rick Ankiel	1.25	3.00
SSAP Albert Pujols	4.00	10.00
SSAR Alex Rios	1.25	3.00
SSAS Alfonso Soriano	2.00	5.00
SSBE Josh Beckett	1.25	3.00
SSBI Chad Billingsley	2.00	5.00
SSBJ B.J. Upton	2.00	5.00
SSBP Brandon Phillips	1.25	3.00
SSBS Ben Sheets	1.25	3.00
SSBW Brandon Webb	2.00	5.00
SSBZ Clay Buchholz	1.25	3.00
SSCA Miguel Cabrera	3.00	8.00
SSCB Carlos Beltran	2.00	5.00
SSCC Carl Crawford	2.00	5.00
SSCH Chin-Lung Hu	1.25	3.00
SSCJ Chipper Jones	3.00	8.00
SSCK Clayton Kershaw	5.00	12.00
SSCL Carlos Lee	1.25	3.00
SSCS CC Sabathia	2.00	5.00
SSCU Chase Utley	2.00	5.00
SSCW Chien-Ming Wang	2.00	5.00
SSCY Chris Young	1.25	3.00
SSDA David Ortiz	3.00	8.00
SSDH Dan Haren	1.25	3.00
SSDJ Derek Jeter	8.00	20.00
SSDL Derrek Lee	1.25	3.00
SSDM Daisuke Matsuzaka	2.00	5.00
SSDO David Ortiz	3.00	8.00
SSDP Dustin Pedroia	3.00	8.00
SSDU Dan Uggla	1.25	3.00
SSDY Delmon Young	2.00	5.00
SSEL Evan Longoria	2.00	5.00
SSEV Edinson Volquez	1.25	3.00
SSFH Felix Hernandez	2.00	5.00
SSGA Garrett Atkins	1.25	3.00
SSGL Troy Glaus	1.25	3.00
SSGM Greg Maddux	4.00	10.00
SSGO Alex Gordon	2.00	5.00
SSGR Ken Griffey Jr.	6.00	15.00
SSGS Grady Sizemore	2.00	5.00
SSGT Garret Anderson	1.25	3.00
SSHA Corey Hart	1.25	3.00
SSHI Rich Hill	1.25	3.00
SSHR Hanley Ramirez	2.00	5.00
SSIK Ian Kinsler	2.00	5.00
SSJA Jacoby Ellsbury	2.50	6.00
SSJC Joba Chamberlain	1.25	3.00
SSJE Derek Jeter	8.00	20.00
SSJH Josh Hamilton	2.00	5.00
SSJL James Loney	1.25	3.00
SSJM Joe Mauer	2.50	6.00
SSJO Josh Hamilton	2.00	5.00
SSJP Jake Peavy	1.25	3.00
SSJT Jim Thome	2.00	5.00
SSJU Justin Upton	2.00	5.00
SSKF Kosuke Fukudome	2.00	5.00
SSKG Ken Griffey Jr.	6.00	15.00
SSKY Kevin Youkilis	1.25	3.00
SSLB Lance Berkman	2.00	5.00
SSLO Evan Longoria	2.00	5.00
SSMA Manny Ramirez	3.00	8.00
SSMC Matt Cain	2.00	5.00
SSMH Matt Holliday	3.00	8.00
SSMK Matt Kemp	2.50	6.00
SSMO Justin Morneau	2.00	5.00
SSMR Manny Ramirez	3.00	8.00
SSMT Mark Teixeira	2.00	5.00
SSMY Michael Young	1.25	3.00
SSNI Nick Markakis	2.50	6.00
SSNS Nick Swisher	2.00	5.00
SSOR Magglio Ordonez	2.00	5.00
SSPA Jonathan Papelbon	2.00	5.00
SSPB Pat Burrell	1.25	3.00
SSPF Prince Fielder	2.00	5.00
SSPK Paul Konerko	2.00	5.00
SSPM Pedro Martinez	2.00	5.00
SSPU Albert Pujols	4.00	10.00
SSRB Ryan Braun	2.00	5.00
SSRE Jose Reyes	2.00	5.00
SSRH Roy Halladay	2.00	5.00
SSRJ Randy Johnson	3.00	8.00
SSRM Russell Martin	1.25	3.00
SSRZ Ryan Zimmerman	2.00	5.00
SSSA Johan Santana	2.00	5.00
SSSK Scott Kazmir	1.25	3.00
SSSO Alfonso Soriano	2.00	5.00
SSTG Tom Glavine	2.00	5.00
SSTH Tim Hudson	2.00	5.00
SSTL Tim Lincecum	2.00	5.00
SSTT Troy Tulowitzki	3.00	8.00
SSTW Tim Wakefield	2.00	5.00
SSVG Vladimir Guerrero	2.00	5.00
SSVW Vernon Wells	1.25	3.00

2009 Upper Deck Spectrum Spectrum Swatches Light Blue

OVERALL MEM ODDS 1:7
STATED PRINT RUN 99 SER.#'d SETS

Card	Low	High
SSAB Adrian Beltre	5.00	12.00
SSAG Adrian Gonzalez	4.00	10.00
SSAM Andrew Miller	3.00	8.00
SSAN Rick Ankiel	2.00	5.00
SSAP Albert Pujols	6.00	15.00
SSAR Alex Rios	2.00	5.00
SSAS Alfonso Soriano	3.00	8.00
SSBE Josh Beckett	2.00	5.00
SSBI Chad Billingsley	3.00	8.00
SSBJ B.J. Upton	3.00	8.00
SSBP Brandon Phillips	2.00	5.00
SSBS Ben Sheets	2.00	5.00
SSBW Brandon Webb	3.00	8.00
SSBZ Clay Buchholz	2.00	5.00
SSCA Miguel Cabrera	5.00	12.00
SSCB Carlos Beltran	3.00	8.00
SSCC Carl Crawford	3.00	8.00
SSCH Chin-Lung Hu	2.00	5.00
SSCJ Chipper Jones	5.00	12.00
SSCK Clayton Kershaw	8.00	20.00
SSCL Carlos Lee	2.00	5.00
SSCS CC Sabathia	3.00	8.00
SSCU Chase Utley	3.00	8.00
SSCW Chien-Ming Wang	3.00	8.00
SSCY Chris Young	2.00	5.00
SSDA David Ortiz	5.00	12.00
SSDH Dan Haren	2.00	5.00
SSDJ Derek Jeter	12.00	30.00
SSDL Derrek Lee	2.00	5.00
SSDM Daisuke Matsuzaka	3.00	8.00
SSDO David Ortiz	5.00	12.00
SSDP Dustin Pedroia	5.00	12.00
SSDU Dan Uggla	2.00	5.00
SSDY Delmon Young	3.00	8.00
SSEL Evan Longoria	3.00	8.00
SSEV Edinson Volquez	2.00	5.00
SSFH Felix Hernandez	3.00	8.00
SSGA Garrett Atkins	2.00	5.00
SSGL Troy Glaus	2.00	5.00
SSGM Greg Maddux	6.00	15.00
SSGO Alex Gordon	3.00	8.00
SSGR Ken Griffey Jr.	10.00	25.00
SSGS Grady Sizemore	3.00	8.00
SSGT Garret Anderson	2.00	5.00
SSHA Corey Hart	2.00	5.00
SSHI Rich Hill	2.00	5.00
SSHR Hanley Ramirez	3.00	8.00
SSIK Ian Kinsler	3.00	8.00
SSJA Jacoby Ellsbury	4.00	10.00
SSJC Joba Chamberlain	2.00	5.00
SSJE Derek Jeter	12.00	30.00
SSJH Josh Hamilton	3.00	8.00
SSJL James Loney	2.00	5.00
SSJM Joe Mauer	4.00	10.00
SSJO Josh Hamilton	3.00	8.00
SSJP Jake Peavy	2.00	5.00
SSJT Jim Thome	3.00	8.00
SSJU Justin Upton	3.00	8.00
SSKF Kosuke Fukudome	3.00	8.00
SSKG Ken Griffey Jr.	10.00	25.00
SSKY Kevin Youkilis	2.00	5.00
SSLB Lance Berkman	3.00	8.00
SSLO Evan Longoria	3.00	8.00
SSMA Manny Ramirez	5.00	12.00
SSMC Matt Cain	3.00	8.00
SSMH Matt Holliday	5.00	12.00
SSMK Matt Kemp	4.00	10.00
SSMO Justin Morneau	3.00	8.00
SSMR Manny Ramirez	5.00	12.00
SSMT Mark Teixeira	3.00	8.00
SSMY Michael Young	2.00	5.00
SSNI Nick Markakis	4.00	10.00
SSNS Nick Swisher	3.00	8.00
SSOR Magglio Ordonez	3.00	8.00
SSPA Jonathan Papelbon	3.00	8.00
SSPB Pat Burrell	2.00	5.00
SSPF Prince Fielder	3.00	8.00
SSPK Paul Konerko	3.00	8.00
SSPM Pedro Martinez	3.00	8.00
SSPU Albert Pujols	6.00	15.00
SSRB Ryan Braun	3.00	8.00
SSRE Jose Reyes	3.00	8.00
SSRH Roy Halladay	3.00	8.00
SSRJ Randy Johnson	5.00	12.00
SSRM Russell Martin	2.00	5.00
SSRZ Ryan Zimmerman	3.00	8.00
SSSA Johan Santana	3.00	8.00
SSSK Scott Kazmir	2.00	5.00
SSSO Alfonso Soriano	3.00	8.00
SSTG Tom Glavine	3.00	8.00
SSTH Tim Hudson	3.00	8.00
SSTL Tim Lincecum	3.00	8.00
SSTT Troy Tulowitzki	5.00	12.00
SSTW Tim Wakefield	3.00	8.00
SSVG Vladimir Guerrero	3.00	8.00
SSVW Vernon Wells	2.00	5.00

2003 Upper Deck Standing O

Card	Low	High
COMP.SET w/o SP's (84)	6.00	15.00
COMMON CARD (1-84)	.10	.30
COMMON CARD (85-126)	.75	2.00

85-126 STATED ODDS 1:4

Card	Low	High
1 Darin Erstad	.12	.30
2 Troy Glaus	.12	.30
3 Tim Salmon	.12	.30
4 Luis Gonzalez	.12	.30
5 Randy Johnson	.30	.75
6 Curt Schilling	.20	.50
7 Andruw Jones	.12	.30
8 Greg Maddux	.40	1.00
9 Chipper Jones	.30	.75
10 Gary Sheffield	.12	.30
11 Rodrigo Lopez	.12	.30
12 Geronimo Gil	.12	.30
13 Nomar Garciaparra	.20	.50
14 Pedro Martinez	.20	.50
15 Manny Ramirez	.30	.75
16 Mark Prior	.20	.50
17 Kerry Wood	.12	.30
18 Sammy Sosa	.30	.75
19 Magglio Ordonez	.20	.50
20 Frank Thomas	.30	.75
21 Adam Dunn	.20	.50
22 Ken Griffey Jr.	.60	1.50
23 Sean Casey	.12	.30
24 Omar Vizquel	.20	.50
25 C.C. Sabathia	.20	.50
26 Larry Walker	.20	.50
27 Todd Helton	.20	.50
28 Ivan Rodriguez	.20	.50
29 Josh Beckett	.12	.30
30 Roy Oswalt	.20	.50
31 Jeff Kent	.12	.30
32 Jeff Bagwell	.20	.50
33 Lance Berkman	.20	.50
34 Mike Sweeney	.12	.30
35 Carlos Beltran	.20	.50
36 Hideo Nomo	.30	.75
37 Shawn Green	.12	.30
38 Kazuhisa Ishii	.12	.30

39 Geoff Jenkins .12 .30
40 Richie Sexson .12 .30
41 Torii Hunter .12 .30
42 Jacque Jones .12 .30
43 Jose Vidro .12 .30
44 Vladimir Guerrero .20 .50
45 Cliff Floyd .12 .30
46 Al Leiter .12 .30
47 Mike Piazza .30 .75
48 Tom Glavine .20 .50
49 Roberto Alomar .20 .50
50 Roger Clemens .40 1.00
51 Jason Giambi .12 .30
52 Bernie Williams .20 .50
53 Alfonso Soriano .20 .50
54 Derek Jeter .75 2.00
55 Miguel Tejada .20 .50
56 Eric Chavez .12 .30
57 Barry Zito .20 .50
58 Pat Burrell .12 .30
59 Jim Thome .20 .50
60 Brian Giles .12 .30
61 Jason Kendall .12 .30
62 Ryan Klesko .12 .30
63 Phil Nevin .12 .30
64 Sean Burroughs .12 .30
65 Jason Schmidt .12 .30
66 Rich Aurilia .12 .30
67 Barry Bonds .50 1.25
68 Randy Winn .12 .30
69 Freddy Garcia .12 .30
70 Ichiro Suzuki .40 1.00
71 J.D. Drew .12 .30
72 Jim Edmonds .20 .50
73 Scott Rolen .20 .50
74 Matt Morris .12 .30
75 Albert Pujols .40 1.00
76 Tino Martinez .12 .30
77 Rey Ordonez .12 .30
78 Carl Crawford .20 .50
79 Rafael Palmeiro .20 .50
80 Kevin Mench .12 .30
81 Alex Rodriguez .40 1.00
82 Juan Gonzalez .12 .30
83 Carlos Delgado .12 .30
84 Eric Hinske .12 .30
85 Rich Fischer WP RC .75 2.00
86 Brandon Webb WP RC 2.50 6.00
87 Rob Hammock WP RC .75 2.00
88 Matt Kata WP RC .75 2.00
89 Tim Olson WP RC .75 2.00
90 Oscar Villarreal WP RC .75 2.00
91 Michael Hessman WP RC .75 2.00
92 Daniel Cabrera WP RC 1.25 3.00
93 Jon Leicester WP RC .75 2.00
94 Todd Wellemeyer WP RC .75 2.00
95 Felix Sanchez WP RC .75 2.00
96 David Sanders WP RC .75 2.00
97 Josh Stewart WP RC .75 2.00
98 Arnie Munoz WP RC .75 2.00
99 Ryan Cameron WP RC .75 2.00
100 Clint Barmes WP RC 2.00 5.00
101 Josh Willingham WP RC 2.50 6.00
103 Willie Eyre WP RC .75 2.00
104 Brent Hoard WP RC .75 2.00
105 Termel Sledge WP RC .75 2.00
106 Phil Seibel WP RC .75 2.00
107 Craig Brazell WP RC .75 2.00
108 Jeff Duncan WP RC .75 2.00
110 Bernie Castro WP RC .75 2.00
111 Mike Nicolas WP RC .75 2.00
112 Rett Johnson WP RC .75 2.00
113 Bobby Madritsch WP RC .75 2.00
114 Luis Ayala WP RC .75 2.00
115 Hideki Matsui WP RC 4.00 10.00
116 Jose Contreras WP RC 2.00 5.00
117 Lew Ford WP RC .75 2.00
118 Jeremy Griffiths WP RC .75 2.00
119 Guillermo Quiroz WP RC .75 2.00
120 Alejandro Machado WP RC .75 2.00
121 Francisco Cruceta WP RC .75 2.00
122 Prentice Redman WP RC .75 2.00
123 Shane Bazzell WP RC .75 2.00
124 Jason Anderson WP .75 2.00
125 Ian Ferguson WP RC .75 2.00
126 Nook Logan WP RC .75 2.00

2003 Upper Deck Standing O Die Cuts

*DIE CUTS 1-84:1.25X TO 3X BASIC
1-84 STATED ODDS 1:1
*DIE CUTS 85-126: .75X TO 2X BASIC
85-126 STATED ODDS 1:48

2003 Upper Deck Standing O Starring Role Game Jersey

STATED ODDS 1:240

2008 Upper Deck Timeline

COMMON CARD (1-50) .15 .40
COMMON RC (51-100) .25 .60
COMMON CARD (101-130) .25 .60
COMMON CARD (131-180) .25 .60
COMMON CARD (181-210) .25 .60
COMMON CARD (211-310) .25 .60
COMMON CARD (311-335) .40 1.00
COMMON CARD (336-360) .40 1.00
COMMON CARD (361-385) .75 2.00
1 Jose Reyes .25 .60
2 David Wright .25 .60
3 Carlos Beltran .25 .60
4 Pedro Martinez .25 .60
5 Johan Santana .25 .60
6 Hanley Ramirez .25 .60
7 John Smoltz .40 1.00
8 Chipper Jones .40 1.00
9 Mark Teixeira .25 .60
10 Chase Utley .25 .60
11 Ryan Howard .25 .60
12 Jimmy Rollins .25 .60
13 Alfonso Soriano .25 .60
14 Derrek Lee .15 .40
15 Jason Bay .25 .60
16 Lance Berkman .25 .60
17 Ken Griffey Jr. .75 2.00
18 Ryan Braun .25 .60
19 Prince Fielder .25 .60
20 Albert Pujols .50 1.25
21 Tim Lincecum .25 .60
22 Jake Peavy .15 .40
23 Matt Kemp .30 .75
24 Matt Holliday .40 1.00
25 Brandon Webb .25 .60
26 Randy Johnson .40 1.00
27 Alex Rodriguez .50 1.25
28 Derek Jeter 1.00 2.50
29 Chien-Ming Wang .25 .60
30 David Ortiz .40 1.00
31 Manny Ramirez .40 1.00
32 Daisuke Matsuzaka .25 .60
33 B.J. Upton .25 .60
34 Nick Markakis .30 .75
35 Roy Halladay .25 .60
36 Jim Thome .25 .60
37 Grady Sizemore .25 .60
38 Travis Hafner .15 .40
39 C.C. Sabathia .25 .60
40 Miguel Cabrera .40 1.00
41 Justin Verlander .40 1.00
42 Joe Mauer .30 .75
43 Alex Gordon .25 .60
44 Frank Thomas .40 1.00
45 Vladimir Guerrero .25 .60
46 Torii Hunter .15 .40
47 Josh Hamilton .25 .60
48 Ichiro Suzuki .50 1.25
49 Felix Hernandez .25 .60
50 Erik Bedard .15 .40
51 Daric Barton (RC) .25 .60
52 John Bowker (RC) .25 .60
53 Clay Buchholz (RC) .40 1.00
54 Jeff Clement (RC) .40 1.00
55 Johnny Cueto RC .60 1.50
56 Blake DeWitt (RC) .40 1.00
57 German Duran RC .40 1.00
58 Kosuke Fukudome RC .75 2.00
59 Alberto Gonzalez RC .40 1.00
60 Luke Hochevar RC .40 1.00
61 Chin-Lung Hu (RC) .25 .60
62 Ian Kennedy RC .60 1.50
63 Masahide Kobayashi RC .40 1.00
64 Hiroki Kuroda RC .60 1.50
65 Evan Longoria RC 1.25 3.00
66 Jed Lowrie (RC) .25 .60
67 Justin Masterson RC .60 1.50
68 Nick Blackburn RC .40 1.00
69 Micah Hoffpauir RC .75 2.00
70 Jeff Niemann (RC) .25 .60
71 Ross Ohlendorf RC .40 1.00
72 Jonathan Van Every RC .25 .60
73 Alexei Ramirez RC .75 2.00
74 Justin Ruggiano RC .40 1.00
75 Max Scherzer RC 2.50 6.00
76 Greg Smith RC .25 .60
77 Denard Span (RC) .40 1.00
78 Clete Thomas RC .40 1.00
79 Josh Banks (RC) .25 .60
80 Clay Timpner (RC) .25 .60
81 Matt Tolbert RC .40 1.00
82 J.R. Towles RC .40 1.00
83 Eugenio Velez RC .25 .60
84 Joey Votto (RC) 2.00 5.00
85 Rico Washington (RC) .25 .60
86 Jay Bruce (RC) .75 2.00
87 Wladimir Balentien (RC) .25 .60
88 Burke Badenhop RC .40 1.00
89 Brian Barton RC .40 1.00
90 Brian Bocock RC .25 .60
91 Brandon Boggs (RC) .40 1.00
92 Robinzon Diaz (RC) .25 .60
93 Hernan Iribarren (RC) .40 1.00
94 Brent Lillibridge (RC) .25 .60
95 Yasuhiko Yabuta RC .40 1.00
96 Jeff Samardzija RC .75 2.00
97 Carlos Gonzalez (RC) .60 1.50
98 Clayton Kershaw RC 8.00 20.00
99 Jonathan Albaladejo RC .40 1.00
100 Nick Adenhart (RC) .25 .60
101 Bobby Wilson 92 ML RC .25 .60
102 Brandon Phillips 92 ML .25 .60
103 Chad Billingsley 92 ML .40 1.00
104 Chris Duncan 92 ML .25 .60
105 Clay Timpner 92 ML (RC) .25 .60
106 Clete Thomas 92 ML RC .40 1.00
107 Corey Hart 92 ML .25 .60
108 Craig Breslow 92 ML .25 .60
109 David Murphy 92 ML .25 .60
110 Edinson Volquez 92 ML .25 .60
111 Elijah Dukes 92 ML .25 .60
112 Emmanuel Burriss 92 ML RC .40 1.00
113 Evan Longoria 92 ML RC 1.25 3.00
114 Fred Lewis 92 ML .25 .60
115 Felix Pie 92 ML .25 .60
116 German Duran 92 ML RC .40 1.00
117 Greg Smith 92 ML RC .25 .60
118 Hernan Iribarren 92 ML (RC) .40 1.00
119 Joey Votto 92 ML (RC) 2.00 5.00
120 Jonathan Van Every 92 ML RC .25 .60
121 Kosuke Fukudome 92 ML RC .75 2.00
122 Matt Joyce 92 ML RC .60 1.50
123 Max Scherzer 92 ML RC 2.50 6.00
124 Nick Swisher 92 ML .40 1.00
125 Paul Janish 92 ML (RC) .25 .60
126 Reed Johnson 92 ML .25 .60
127 Rico Washington 92 ML (RC) .25 .60
128 Russell Martin 92 ML .25 .60
129 Scott Kazmir 92 ML .40 1.00
130 Tyler Clippard 92 ML .25 .60
131 Randy Johnson 94 ATH .60 1.50
132 Frank Thomas 94 ATH .60 1.50
133 Greg Maddux 94 ATH .75 2.00
134 Vladimir Guerrero 94 ATH .40 1.00
135 Ryan Braun 94 ATH .40 1.00
136 David Ortiz 94 ATH .60 1.50
137 Jake Peavy 94 ATH .25 .60
138 Mark Teixeira 94 ATH .40 1.00
139 Jose Reyes 94 ATH .40 1.00
140 Chien-Ming Wang 94 ATH .40 1.00
141 Prince Fielder 94 ATH .40 1.00
142 Albert Pujols 94 ATH .75 2.00
143 Johan Santana 94 ATH .40 1.00
144 Josh Beckett 94 ATH .25 .60
145 Alex Rodriguez 94 ATH .75 2.00
146 Felix Hernandez 94 ATH .40 1.00
147 Brandon Webb 94 ATH .40 1.00
148 Chase Utley 94 ATH .40 1.00
149 Derek Jeter 94 ATH 1.50 4.00
150 Grady Sizemore 94 ATH .40 1.00
151 B.J. Upton 94 ATH .40 1.00
152 Carlos Beltran 94 ATH .40 1.00
153 Hanley Ramirez 94 ATH .40 1.00
154 Magglio Ordonez 94 ATH .40 1.00
155 Carlos Zambrano 94 ATH .40 1.00
156 Manny Ramirez 94 ATH .60 1.50
157 Travis Hafner 94 ATH .25 .60
158 David Wright 94 ATH .40 1.00
159 Jimmy Rollins 94 ATH .40 1.00
160 Matt Holliday 94 ATH .60 1.50
161 Ken Griffey Jr. 94 ATH 1.25 3.00
162 C.C. Sabathia 94 ATH .40 1.00
163 Joe Mauer 94 ATH .50 1.25
164 Derrek Lee 94 ATH .25 .60
165 Miguel Cabrera 94 ATH .60 1.50
166 Alfonso Soriano 94 ATH .40 1.00
167 Ichiro Suzuki 94 ATH .75 2.00
168 Daisuke Matsuzaka 94 ATH .40 1.00
169 Lance Berkman 94 ATH .40 1.00
170 Ryan Howard 94 ATH .40 1.00
171 J.R. Towles 94 ATH RC .40 1.00
172 Max Scherzer 94 ATH RC 2.50 6.00
173 Chin-Lung Hu 94 ATH .25 .60
174 Daric Barton 94 ATH .25 .60
175 Ian Kennedy 94 ATH .60 1.50
176 Clay Buchholz 94 ATH .40 1.00
177 Joey Votto 94 ATH (RC) 2.00 5.00
178 Kosuke Fukudome 94 ATH RC .75 2.00
179 Johnny Cueto 94 ATH .60 1.50
180 Evan Longoria 94 ATH 1.25 3.00
181 Brandon Boggs 95 STP (RC) .40 1.00
182 Brian Bocock 95 STP RC .25 .60
183 Burke Badenhop 95 STP RC .40 1.00
184 Callix Crabbe 95 STP (RC) .25 .60
185 Cha-Seung Baek 95 STP .25 .60
186 Chris Smith 95 STP (RC) .25 .60
187 Clayton Kershaw 95 STP RC 8.00 20.00
188 Felipe Paulino 95 STP RC .40 1.00
189 Glen Perkins 95 STP .25 .60
190 Homer Bailey 95 STP .40 1.00
191 James Loney 95 STP .25 .60
192 Jay Bruce 95 STP (RC) .75 2.00
193 Jeff Baker 95 STP .25 .60
194 Jeff Keppinger 95 STP .25 .60
195 Jesus Flores 95 STP .25 .60
196 Joakim Soria 95 STP .25 .60
197 Joey Votto 95 STP (RC) 2.00 5.00
198 Josh Hamilton 95 STP .40 1.00
199 Kosuke Fukudome 95 STP RC .75 2.00
200 Micah Hoffpauir 95 STP RC .75 2.00
201 Nick Blackburn 95 STP RC .40 1.00
202 Nyjer Morgan 95 STP (RC) .25 .60
203 Randor Bierd 95 STP RC .25 .60
204 Rich Hill 95 STP .25 .60
205 Ross Ohlendorf 95 STP RC .40 1.00
206 Russell Martin 95 STP .25 .60
207 Ryan Garko 95 STP .25 .60
208 Seth Smith 95 STP .25 .60
209 Steve Holm 95 STP RC .25 .60
210 Travis Hafner 95 STP .25 .60
211 Brandon Webb 04 TT .40 1.00
212 Randy Johnson 04 TT .60 1.50
213 Max Scherzer 04 TT RC 2.50 6.00
214 Chris B. Young 04 TT .25 .60
215 Justin Upton 04 TT .40 1.00
216 John Smoltz 04 TT .60 1.50
217 Chipper Jones 04 TT .60 1.50
218 Mark Teixeira 04 TT .40 1.00
219 Jeff Francoeur 04 TT .40 1.00
220 Adrian Gonzalez 04 TT .40 1.00
221 Nick Markakis 04 TT .50 1.25
222 Jacoby Ellsbury 04 TT .50 1.25
223 David Ortiz 04 TT .60 1.50
224 Manny Ramirez 04 TT .60 1.50
225 Daisuke Matsuzaka 04 TT .40 1.00
226 Clay Buchholz 04 TT (RC) .40 1.00
227 Jed Lowrie 04 TT (RC) .25 .60
228 Justin Masterson 04 TT RC .60 1.50
229 Geovany Soto 04 TT .60 1.50
230 Alfonso Soriano 04 TT .40 1.00
231 Derrek Lee 04 TT .25 .60
232 Kosuke Fukudome 04 TT RC .75 2.00
233 Jim Thome 04 TT .40 1.00
234 Alexei Ramirez 04 TT RC .75 2.00
235 Ken Griffey Jr. 04 TT 1.25 3.00
236 Johnny Cueto 04 TT RC .60 1.50
237 Joey Votto 04 TT (RC) 2.00 5.00
238 Brandon Phillips 04 TT .25 .60
239 Edinson Volquez 04 TT .25 .60
240 Grady Sizemore 04 TT .40 1.00
241 Travis Hafner 04 TT .25 .60
242 C.C. Sabathia 04 TT .40 1.00
243 Matt Holliday 04 TT .60 1.50
244 Troy Tulowitzki 04 TT .60 1.50
245 Miguel Cabrera 04 TT .60 1.50
246 Justin Verlander 04 TT .60 1.50
247 Matt Tolbert 04 TT RC .40 1.00
248 Hanley Ramirez 04 TT .40 1.00
249 Jeremy Hermida 04 TT .25 .60
250 Lance Berkman 04 TT .40 1.00
251 J.R. Towles 04 TT RC .40 1.00
252 Alex Gordon 04 TT .40 1.00
253 Luke Hochevar 04 TT RC .40 1.00
254 Vladimir Guerrero 04 TT .40 1.00
255 Torii Hunter 04 TT .25 .60
256 Nick Adenhart 04 TT (RC) .25 .60
257 Garrett Atkins 04 TT .25 .60
258 Blake DeWitt 04 TT (RC) .40 1.00
259 Chin-Lung Hu 04 TT (RC) .25 .60
260 Hiroki Kuroda 04 TT RC .60 1.50
261 Matt Kemp 04 TT .50 1.25
262 James Loney 04 TT .25 .60
263 Justin Morneau 04 TT .40 1.00
264 Dan Haren 04 TT .25 .60
265 Ryan Braun 04 TT .40 1.00
266 Corey Hart 04 TT .25 .60
267 Rickie Weeks 04 TT .25 .60
268 Prince Fielder 04 TT .40 1.00
269 Carlos Gomez 04 TT .25 .60
270 Joe Mauer 04 TT .50 1.25
271 Jose Reyes 04 TT .40 1.00
272 David Wright 04 TT .40 1.00
273 Carlos Beltran 04 TT .40 1.00
274 Pedro Martinez 04 TT .40 1.00
275 Hideki Matsui 04 TT .60 1.50
276 Alex Rodriguez 04 TT .75 2.00
277 Derek Jeter 04 TT 1.50 4.00
278 Chien-Ming Wang 04 TT .40 1.00
279 Ian Kennedy 04 TT RC .60 1.50
280 Phil Hughes 04 TT .25 .60
281 Frank Thomas 04 TT .60 1.50
282 Daric Barton 04 TT (RC) .25 .60
283 Greg Smith 04 TT RC .25 .60
284 Cole Hamels 04 TT .50 1.25
285 Chase Utley 04 TT .40 1.00
286 Ryan Howard 04 TT .40 1.00
287 Jimmy Rollins 04 TT .40 1.00
288 Jason Bay 04 TT .40 1.00
289 Jake Peavy 04 TT .25 .60
290 Brian McCann 04 TT .40 1.00
291 Tim Lincecum 04 TT .40 1.00
292 Justin Ruggiano 04 TT RC .40 1.00
293 Jay Bruce 04 TT (RC) .75 2.00
294 Brian Bocock 04 TT RC .25 .60
295 Ichiro Suzuki 04 TT .75 2.00
296 Adam Dunn 04 TT .40 1.00
297 Erik Bedard 04 TT .25 .60
298 Jeff Clement 04 TT (RC) .40 1.00
299 Felix Hernandez 04 TT .40 1.00
300 Albert Pujols 04 TT .75 2.00
301 Rick Ankiel 04 TT .25 .60
302 B.J. Upton 04 TT .40 1.00
303 Evan Longoria 04 TT RC 1.25 3.00
304 Clayton Kershaw 04 TT RC 8.00 20.00
305 Carl Crawford 04 TT .40 1.00
306 Russell Martin 04 TT .25 .60
307 Brandon Boggs 04 TT (RC) .40 1.00
308 Josh Hamilton 04 TT .40 1.00
309 Roy Halladay 04 TT .40 1.00
310 Ryan Zimmerman 04 TT .40 1.00
311 Evan Longoria 93 SP 2.00 5.00
312 Johnny Cueto 93 SP 1.00 2.50
313 Kosuke Fukudome 93 SP 1.25 3.00
314 Joey Votto 93 SP 3.00 8.00
315 Clay Buchholz 93 SP .60 1.50
316 Ian Kennedy 93 SP 1.00 2.50
317 Daric Barton 93 SP .40 1.00
318 Chin-Lung Hu 93 SP .40 1.00
319 Max Scherzer 93 SP 4.00 10.00
320 J.R. Towles 93 SP .60 1.50
321 Nick Adenhart 93 SP .40 1.00
322 Wladimir Balentien 93 SP .40 1.00
323 Brian Barton 93 SP .60 1.50
324 Brian Bocock 93 SP .40 1.00
325 Jonathan Herrera 93 SP RC .60 1.50
326 Jesse Carlson 93 SP RC .60 1.50
327 Jeff Clement 93 SP .60 1.50
328 Brandon Jones 93 SP RC 1.00 2.50
329 German Duran 93 SP .60 1.50
330 Alex Romero 93 SP (RC) .60 1.50
331 Jay Bruce 93 SP 1.25 3.00
332 Luke Hochevar 93 SP .60 1.50
333 Clayton Kershaw 93 SP 10.00 25.00
334 Nick Blackburn 93 SP .60 1.50
335 Jed Lowrie 93 SP .40 1.00
336 Evan Longoria 94 SP 2.00 5.00
337 Johnny Cueto 94 SP 1.00 2.50
338 Kosuke Fukudome 94 SP 1.25 3.00
339 Joey Votto 94 SP 3.00 8.00
340 Clay Buchholz 94 SP .60 1.50
341 Ian Kennedy 94 SP 1.00 2.50
342 Daric Barton 94 SP .40 1.00
343 Chin-Lung Hu 94 SP .40 1.00
344 Max Scherzer 94 SP 4.00 10.00
345 J.R. Towles 94 SP .60 1.50
346 Justin Masterson 94 SP 1.00 2.50
347 Kyle McClellan 94 SP RC .40 1.00
348 Evan Meek 94 SP RC .40 1.00
349 Nyjer Morgan 94 SP .40 1.00
350 Colt Morton 94 SP RC .60 1.50
351 Luke Carlin 94 SP RC .40 1.00
352 Emmanuel Burriss 94 SP .60 1.50
353 Clint Sammons 94 SP (RC) .40 1.00
354 Ross Ohlendorf 94 SP .60 1.50
355 Jay Bruce 94 SP 1.25 3.00
356 Felipe Paulino 94 SP .60 1.50
357 Alexei Ramirez 94 SP 1.25 3.00
358 Clayton Kershaw 94 SP 12.00 30.00
359 Cory Wade 94 SP (RC) .40 1.00
360 Greg Smith 94 SP .40 1.00
361 Evan Longoria 95 SP 3.00 8.00
362 Johnny Cueto 95 SP 2.00 5.00
363 Kosuke Fukudome 95 SP 2.00 5.00
364 Joey Votto 95 SP 6.00 15.00
365 Clay Buchholz 95 SP 1.25 3.00
366 Ian Kennedy 95 SP 2.00 5.00
367 Daric Barton 95 SP .75 2.00
368 Chin-Lung Hu 95 SP .75 2.00
369 Max Scherzer 95 SP 8.00 20.00
370 J.R. Towles 95 SP 1.25 3.00
371 Mitchell Boggs 95 SP (RC) .75 2.00
372 Jay Bruce 95 SP 2.50 6.00
373 Alberto Gonzalez 95 SP 1.25 3.00
374 Rich Thompson 95 SP RC 1.25 3.00
375 Robinzon Diaz 95 SP .75 2.00
376 Clay Timpner 95 SP .75 2.00
377 Eider Torres 95 SP (RC) 1.25 3.00
378 Ramon Troncoso 95 SP RC .75 2.00
379 Clayton Kershaw 95 SP 25.00 60.00
380 Rico Washington 95 SP .75 2.00
381 Brandon Jones 95 SP 2.00 5.00
382 Bobby Wilson 95 SP .75 2.00
383 Wesley Wright 95 SP RC .75 2.00
384 Mike Parisi 95 SP RC 1.25 3.00
385 Jonathan Van Every 95 SP .75 2.00

2008 Upper Deck Timeline Gold

*VET 1-50: 1X TO 2.5X BASIC
*RC 51-100: .6X TO 1.5X BASIC
VET ODDS 1:6 HOBBY, 1:24 RETAIL
RC ODDS 1:12 HOBBY, 1:48 RETAIL

2008 Upper Deck Timeline 1992 UD Minor League Autographs

STATED ODDS 1:27 HOB., 1:144 RET.
101 Bobby Wilson 3.00 8.00
105 Clay Timpner 3.00 8.00
106 Clete Thomas 3.00 8.00
108 Craig Breslow 4.00 10.00
111 Elijah Dukes 5.00 12.00
116 German Duran 3.00 8.00
117 Greg Smith 3.00 8.00
118 Hernan Iribarren 3.00 8.00
120 Jonathan Van Every 3.00 8.00
122 Matt Joyce 3.00 8.00
125 Paul Janish 3.00 8.00
126 Reed Johnson 3.00 8.00
127 Rico Washington 3.00 8.00
130 Tyler Clippard 3.00 8.00

2008 Upper Deck Timeline 1993 SP Autographs

OVERALL AU ODDS 1:9 HOBBY
STATED PRINT RUN 93 SER.#'d SETS
312 Johnny Cueto 10.00 25.00
315 Clay Buchholz 10.00 25.00
318 Chin-Lung Hu 20.00 50.00
322 Wladimir Balentien 6.00 15.00
324 Brian Bocock 3.00 8.00
327 Jeff Clement 10.00 25.00
328 Brandon Jones 6.00 15.00
329 German Duran 3.00 8.00
331 Jay Bruce 10.00 25.00
332 Luke Hochevar 4.00 10.00
333 Clayton Kershaw 75.00 150.00

2008 Upper Deck Timeline 1994 All-Time Heroes 20th Anniversary

STATED ODDS 1:9 HOB.,1:72 RET.
131 Randy Johnson 1.00 2.50
132 Frank Thomas 1.00 2.50
133 Greg Maddux 1.25 3.00
134 Vladimir Guerrero .60 1.50
135 Ryan Braun .60 1.50
136 David Ortiz 1.00 2.50
137 Jake Peavy .40 1.00
138 Mark Teixeira .60 1.50
139 Jose Reyes .60 1.50
140 Chien-Ming Wang .60 1.50
141 Prince Fielder .60 1.50
142 Albert Pujols 1.25 3.00
143 Johan Santana .60 1.50
144 Josh Beckett .40 1.00
145 Alex Rodriguez 1.25 3.00
146 Felix Hernandez .60 1.50
147 Brandon Webb .60 1.50
148 Chase Utley .60 1.50
149 Derek Jeter 2.50 6.00
150 Grady Sizemore .60 1.50
151 B.J. Upton .60 1.50
152 Carlos Beltran .60 1.50
153 Hanley Ramirez .60 1.50
154 Magglio Ordonez .60 1.50
155 Carlos Zambrano .60 1.50
156 Manny Ramirez 1.00 2.50
157 Travis Hafner .40 1.00
158 David Wright .60 1.50
159 Jimmy Rollins .60 1.50
160 Matt Holliday 1.00 2.50
161 Ken Griffey Jr. 2.00 5.00
162 C.C. Sabathia .60 1.50
163 Joe Mauer .75 2.00
164 Derrek Lee .40 1.00
165 Miguel Cabrera 1.00 2.50
166 Alfonso Soriano .60 1.50
167 Ichiro Suzuki 1.25 3.00
168 Daisuke Matsuzaka .60 1.50
169 Lance Berkman .60 1.50
170 Ryan Howard .60 1.50
171 J.R. Towles .60 1.50
172 Max Scherzer 4.00 10.00
173 Chin-Lung Hu .40 1.00
174 Daric Barton .40 1.00
175 Ian Kennedy 1.00 2.50
176 Clay Buchholz .60 1.50
177 Joey Votto 3.00 8.00
178 Kosuke Fukudome 1.25 3.00
179 Johnny Cueto 1.00 2.50
180 Evan Longoria 2.00 5.00

2008 Upper Deck Timeline 1994 All-Time Heroes Autographs

OVERALL AU ODDS 1:9 HOBBY
PRINT RUNS B/WN 5-99 COPIES PER
NO PRICING ON QTY 25 OR LESS
149 Derek Jeter/99 100.00 250.00
171 J.R. Towles/99 4.00 10.00
173 Chin-Lung Hu/99 20.00 50.00
176 Clay Buchholz/50 12.50 30.00

2008 Upper Deck Timeline 1994 SP Autographs

OVERALL AU ODDS 1:9 HOBBY
STATED PRINT RUN 94 SER.#'d SETS
336 Evan Longoria 75.00 150.00
342 Daric Barton 3.00 8.00
346 Justin Masterson 60.00 120.00
347 Kyle McClellan 10.00 25.00
354 Ross Ohlendorf 3.00 8.00
356 Felipe Paulino 3.00 8.00
357 Alexei Ramirez 10.00 25.00
358 Clayton Kershaw 75.00 150.00
359 Cory Wade 6.00 15.00
360 Greg Smith 5.00 12.00

2008 Upper Deck Timeline 1995 SP Autographs

OVERALL AU ODDS 1:9 HOBBY
STATED PRINT RUN 95 SER.#'d SETS
361 Evan Longoria 40.00 80.00
362 Johnny Cueto 10.00 25.00
365 Clay Buchholz 6.00 15.00
367 Daric Barton 5.00 12.00
370 J.R. Towles 4.00 10.00
371 Mitchell Boggs 5.00 12.00
375 Robinzon Diaz 4.00 10.00
376 Clay Timpner 3.00 8.00
379 Clayton Kershaw 75.00 150.00
382 Bobby Wilson 3.00 8.00

2008 Upper Deck Timeline 1995 SP Top Prospects Autographs

STATED ODDS 1:27 HOB.,1:144 RET.
181 Brandon Boggs 3.00 8.00
182 Brian Bocock 3.00 8.00
183 Burke Badenhop 3.00 8.00
186 Chris Smith 4.00 10.00
188 Felipe Paulino 3.00 8.00
190 Homer Bailey 4.00 10.00
191 James Loney 3.00 8.00
193 Jeff Baker 3.00 8.00
194 Jeff Keppinger 3.00 8.00
195 Jesus Flores 3.00 8.00
196 Joakim Soria 4.00 10.00
198 Josh Hamilton 12.50 30.00
200 Micah Hoffpauir 3.00 8.00
201 Nick Blackburn 6.00 15.00
202 Nyjer Morgan 3.00 8.00
203 Randor Bierd 3.00 8.00
208 Seth Smith 4.00 10.00
209 Steve Holm 3.00 8.00

2008 Upper Deck Timeline 2004 UD Timeless Teams Autographs

OVERALL AU ODDS 1:9 HOBBY
PRINT RUNS B/WN 5-99 COPIES PER
NO PRICING ON QTY 10 OR LESS
238 Brandon Phillips/99 5.00 12.00
239 Edinson Volquez/99 10.00 25.00
247 Matt Tolbert/99 6.00 15.00
269 Carlos Gomez/99 15.00 40.00
282 Daric Barton/99 5.00 12.00
283 Greg Smith/99 5.00 12.00
288 Jason Bay/99 12.50 30.00
298 Jeff Clement/99 10.00 25.00
307 Brandon Boggs/99 3.00 8.00

2008 Upper Deck Timeline 2004 UD Timeless Teams Gold

RANDOM INSERTS IN PACKS
STATED PRINT RUN 100 SER.#'d SETS
211 Brandon Webb 2.50 6.00
212 Randy Johnson 4.00 10.00
213 Max Scherzer 15.00 40.00
214 Chris B. Young 1.50 4.00
215 Justin Upton 2.50 6.00
216 John Smoltz 4.00 10.00
217 Chipper Jones 4.00 10.00
218 Mark Teixeira 2.50 6.00
219 Jeff Francoeur 2.50 6.00
220 Adrian Gonzalez 2.50 6.00
221 Nick Markakis 3.00 8.00
222 Jacoby Ellsbury 3.00 8.00
223 David Ortiz 4.00 10.00
224 Manny Ramirez 4.00 10.00
225 Daisuke Matsuzaka 2.50 6.00
226 Clay Buchholz 2.50 6.00
227 Jed Lowrie 1.50 4.00
228 Justin Masterson 4.00 10.00
229 Geovany Soto 4.00 10.00
230 Alfonso Soriano 2.50 6.00
231 Derrek Lee 1.50 4.00
232 Kosuke Fukudome 5.00 12.00
233 Jim Thome 2.50 6.00
234 Alexei Ramirez 5.00 12.00
235 Ken Griffey Jr. 8.00 20.00
236 Johnny Cueto 4.00 10.00
237 Joey Votto 12.00 30.00
238 Brandon Phillips 1.50 4.00
239 Edinson Volquez 1.50 4.00
240 Grady Sizemore 2.50 6.00
241 Travis Hafner 1.50 4.00
242 C.C. Sabathia 2.50 6.00
243 Matt Holliday 4.00 10.00
244 Troy Tulowitzki 4.00 10.00
245 Miguel Cabrera 4.00 10.00
246 Justin Verlander 4.00 10.00
247 Matt Tolbert 2.50 6.00
248 Hanley Ramirez 2.50 6.00
249 Jeremy Hermida 1.50 4.00
250 Lance Berkman 2.50 6.00
251 J.R. Towles 2.50 6.00
252 Alex Gordon 2.50 6.00
253 Luke Hochevar 2.50 6.00
254 Vladimir Guerrero 2.50 6.00
255 Torii Hunter 1.50 4.00
256 Nick Adenhart 1.50 4.00
257 Garrett Atkins 1.50 4.00
258 Blake DeWitt 2.50 6.00
259 Chin-Lung Hu 1.50 4.00
260 Hiroki Kuroda 4.00 10.00
261 Matt Kemp 3.00 8.00
262 James Loney 1.50 4.00
263 Justin Morneau 2.50 6.00
264 Dan Haren 1.50 4.00
265 Ryan Braun 2.50 6.00
266 Corey Hart 1.50 4.00
267 Rickie Weeks 1.50 4.00
268 Prince Fielder 2.50 6.00
269 Carlos Gomez 1.50 4.00
270 Joe Mauer 3.00 8.00
271 Jose Reyes 2.50 6.00
272 David Wright 2.50 6.00
273 Carlos Beltran 2.50 6.00
274 Pedro Martinez 2.50 6.00
275 Hideki Matsui 4.00 10.00
276 Alex Rodriguez 5.00 12.00
277 Derek Jeter 10.00 25.00
278 Chien-Ming Wang 2.50 6.00
279 Ian Kennedy 4.00 10.00
280 Phil Hughes 1.50 4.00
281 Frank Thomas 4.00 10.00
282 Daric Barton 1.50 4.00
283 Greg Smith 1.50 4.00
284 Cole Hamels 3.00 8.00
285 Chase Utley 2.50 6.00
286 Ryan Howard 2.50 6.00
287 Jimmy Rollins 2.50 6.00
288 Jason Bay 2.50 6.00
289 Jake Peavy 1.50 4.00
290 Brian McCann 2.50 6.00
291 Tim Lincecum 2.50 6.00
292 Justin Ruggiano 2.50 6.00
293 Jay Bruce 5.00 12.00
294 Brian Bocock 1.50 4.00
295 Ichiro Suzuki 5.00 12.00
296 Adam Dunn 2.50 6.00
297 Erik Bedard 1.50 4.00
298 Jeff Clement 2.50 6.00
299 Felix Hernandez 2.50 6.00
300 Albert Pujols 5.00 12.00
301 Rick Ankiel 1.50 4.00
302 B.J. Upton 2.50 6.00
303 Evan Longoria 8.00 20.00
304 Clayton Kershaw 50.00 120.00
305 Carl Crawford 2.50 6.00
306 Russell Martin 1.50 4.00
307 Brandon Boggs 2.50 6.00
308 Josh Hamilton 2.50 6.00
309 Roy Halladay 2.50 6.00
310 Ryan Zimmerman 2.50 6.00

2008 Upper Deck Timeline Cut Signatures

OVERALL AU ODDS 1:9 HOBBY
NNO Mystery Exchange 90.00 150.00

2008 Upper Deck Timeline Memorabilia

ONE PER TARGET/WM BLASTER
AB A.J. Burnett 3.00 8.00
AD Adrian Beltre 3.00 8.00
AE Andre Ethier 4.00 10.00
AG Adrian Gonzalez 4.00 10.00
AJ Andruw Jones 3.00 8.00
AM Andrew Miller 4.00 10.00
AP Albert Pujols 6.00 15.00
AR Aaron Rowand 3.00 8.00
BC Bartolo Colon 3.00 8.00
BE Adrian Beltre 3.00 8.00
BG Brian Giles 3.00 8.00
BM Brian McCann 4.00 10.00
BO Bobby Crosby 3.00 8.00
BR B.J. Ryan 3.00 8.00
BS Ben Sheets 4.00 10.00
BU A.J. Burnett 3.00 8.00
BZ Barry Zito 3.00 8.00
CB Chad Billingsley 3.00 8.00
CC Carl Crawford 3.00 8.00
CD Carlos Delgado 3.00 8.00
CG Curtis Granderson 4.00 10.00
CJ Chipper Jones 5.00 12.00
CQ Carlos Quentin 3.00 8.00
CR Bobby Crosby 3.00 8.00
CZ Carlos Zambrano 3.00 8.00
DA Johnny Damon 4.00 10.00
DE Carlos Delgado 3.00 8.00
DJ Derek Jeter 8.00 20.00
DL Derek Lowe 3.00 8.00
DO David Ortiz 4.00 10.00
DW Dontrelle Willis 3.00 8.00
ED Jim Edmonds 4.00 10.00
FR Ryan Freel 3.00 8.00
FS Freddy Sanchez 3.00 8.00
GA Garrett Atkins 3.00 8.00
GI Brian Giles 3.00 8.00
GJ Geoff Jenkins 3.00 8.00
GL Troy Glaus 4.00 10.00
GM Greg Maddux 5.00 12.00
GO Adrian Gonzalez 4.00 10.00
GT Troy Glaus 4.00 10.00
HA Josh Hamilton 5.00 12.00
HM Hideki Matsui 4.00 10.00
HO Trevor Hoffman 3.00 8.00
HT Travis Hafner 3.00 8.00
HU Torii Hunter 3.00 8.00
IS Ian Snell 3.00 8.00
JD Jermaine Dye 3.00 8.00
JE Jim Edmonds 4.00 10.00
JF Jeff Francoeur 4.00 10.00
JG Jeremy Guthrie 3.00 8.00
JH JJ Hardy 3.00 8.00
JL Jon Lester 4.00 10.00
JM Joe Mauer 4.00 10.00
JO Chipper Jones 5.00 12.00
JP Jorge Posada 4.00 10.00
JS Jeremy Sowers 3.00 8.00
KG Ken Griffey Jr. 6.00 15.00
KY Kevin Youkilis 4.00 10.00
MA Greg Maddux 5.00 12.00
MC Miguel Cabrera 4.00 10.00
MG Matt Garza 3.00 8.00
MO Justin Morneau 4.00 10.00
MS Mike Sweeney 3.00 8.00
MT Miguel Tejada 3.00 8.00
MY Michael Young 3.00 8.00
NS Nick Swisher 3.00 8.00
OR David Ortiz 4.00 10.00
OV Omar Vizquel 3.00 8.00
PE Andy Pettitte 4.00 10.00
PF Prince Fielder 4.00 10.00
PK Paul Konerko 3.00 8.00
PM Pedro Martinez 4.00 10.00
PU Albert Pujols 6.00 15.00
RA Aramis Ramirez 3.00 8.00
RB Ryan Braun 5.00 12.00
RC Robinson Cano 4.00 10.00
RF Rafael Furcal 3.00 8.00
RG Ryan Garko 3.00 8.00
RH Rich Harden 3.00 8.00
RJ Randy Johnson 4.00 10.00
RM Russell Martin 3.00 8.00
RO Roy Halladay 3.00 8.00
RS Richie Sexson 3.00 8.00
RZ Ryan Zimmerman 4.00 10.00
SA Johan Santana 4.00 10.00
SC Scott Rolen 4.00 10.00
SK Scott Kazmir 4.00 10.00
SP Scott Podsednik 3.00 8.00
SR Scott Rolen 4.00 10.00
TB Travis Buck 3.00 8.00
TG Tom Glavine 4.00 10.00
TH Tim Hudson 3.00 8.00
TL Tim Lincecum 4.00 10.00
TR Travis Hafner 3.00 8.00
TW Tim Wakefield 3.00 8.00
VG Vladimir Guerrero 4.00 10.00
VM Victor Martinez 3.00 8.00
WT Willy Taveras 3.00 8.00
ZD Zach Duke 3.00 8.00

2008 Upper Deck Timeline Team USA Signatures

STATED ODDS 1:41 HOBBY
AG A.J. Griffin 3.00 8.00
AO Andrew Oliver 5.00 12.00
BH Brett Hunter 3.00 8.00
BS Blake Smith 6.00 15.00
CC Christian Colon 8.00 20.00
CH Chris Hernandez 8.00 20.00
DD Derek Dietrich 8.00 20.00
HM Hunter Morris 4.00 10.00
JF Josh Fellhauer 6.00 15.00
KD Kentrail Davis 10.00 25.00
KG Kyle Gibson 10.00 25.00
KR Kevin Rhoderick 3.00 8.00
KV Kendal Volz 5.00 12.00
MD Matt den Dekker 4.00 10.00

MG Micah Gibbs 3.00 8.00
ML Mike Leake 8.00 20.00
MM Mike Minor 4.00 10.00
RJ Ryan Jackson 6.00 15.00
RL Ryan Lipkin 3.00 10.00
SS Stephen Strasburg 25.00 60.00
TL Tyler Lyons 3.00 8.00
TM Tommy Mendonca 10.00 25.00

2005 Upper Deck Trilogy

COMPLETE SET (100) 20.00 50.00
COMMON CARD (1-100) .40 1.00
COMMON RC (1-100) .40 1.00
1 A.J. Burnett .40 1.00
2 Adam Dunn .60 1.50
3 Adrian Beltre 1.00 2.50
4 Albert Pujols 1.25 3.00
5 Alex Rodriguez 1.25 3.00
6 Alfonso Soriano .60 1.50
7 Andruw Jones .40 1.00
8 Aramis Ramirez .40 1.00
9 Ben Sheets .40 1.00
10 Bobby Abreu .40 1.00
11 Bobby Crosby .40 1.00
12 Ryan Zimmerman RC 2.00 5.00
13 Brian Giles .40 1.00
14 Brian Roberts .40 1.00
15 Carl Crawford .60 1.50
16 Carlos Beltran .60 1.50
17 Carlos Delgado .40 1.00
18 Carlos Zambrano .60 1.50
19 Chipper Jones 1.00 2.50
20 Corey Patterson .40 1.00
21 Craig Biggio .60 1.50
22 Curt Schilling .60 1.50
23 Dallas McPherson .40 1.00
24 David Ortiz 1.00 2.50
25 David Wright .75 2.00
26 Delmon Young 1.00 2.50
27 Derek Jeter 2.50 6.00
28 Derrek Lee .40 1.00
29 Dontrelle Willis .40 1.00
30 Eric Chavez .40 1.00
31 Eric Gagne .40 1.00
32 Francisco Rodriguez .60 1.50
33 Gary Sheffield .40 1.00
34 Greg Maddux 1.25 3.00
35 Hank Blalock .40 1.00
36 Hideki Matsui 1.50 4.00
37 Ichiro Suzuki 1.25 3.00
38 Ivan Rodriguez .60 1.50
39 J.D. Drew .40 1.00
40 Jake Peavy .40 1.00
41 Jason Bay .40 1.00
42 Jason Schmidt .40 1.00
43 Jeff Bagwell .60 1.50
44 Jeff Kent .40 1.00
45 Jeff Niemann RC 1.00 2.50
46 Jeremy Bonderman .40 1.00
47 Jim Edmonds .60 1.50
48 Jim Thome .60 1.50
49 Joe Mauer .75 2.00
50 Johan Santana .60 1.50
51 John Smoltz 1.00 2.50
52 Johnny Damon .60 1.50
53 Jose Reyes .60 1.50
54 Jose Vidro .40 1.00
55 Josh Beckett .40 1.00
56 Justin Morneau .60 1.50
57 Justin Verlander RC 8.00 20.00
58 Ken Griffey Jr. 2.00 5.00
59 Kendry Morales RC 1.00 2.50
60 Kerry Wood .40 1.00
61 Khalil Greene .40 1.00
62 Lance Berkman .60 1.50
63 Luis Gonzalez .40 1.00
64 Manny Ramirez 1.00 2.50
65 Mark Buehrle .60 1.50
66 Mark Mulder .40 1.00
67 Mark Prior .60 1.50
68 Mark Teixeira .60 1.50
69 Michael Young .40 1.00
70 Miguel Cabrera 1.00 2.50
71 Miguel Tejada .60 1.50
72 Mike Mussina .60 1.50
73 Mike Piazza 1.00 2.50
74 Nomar Garciaparra .60 1.50
75 Pat Burrell .40 1.00
76 Paul Konerko .60 1.50
77 Pedro Martinez .60 1.50
78 Philip Humber RC 1.00 2.50
79 Prince Fielder RC 2.00 5.00
80 Randy Johnson 1.00 2.50
81 Richie Sexson .40 1.00
82 Rickie Weeks .40 1.00
83 Roger Clemens 1.25 3.00
84 Roy Halladay .60 1.50
85 Roy Oswalt .60 1.50
86 Sammy Sosa 1.00 2.50
87 Scott Kazmir 1.00 2.50
88 Scott Rolen .60 1.50
89 Stephen Drew RC 1.25 3.00
90 Tadahito Iguchi RC .60 1.50
91 Tim Hudson .60 1.50
92 Todd Helton .60 1.50
93 Tom Glavine .60 1.50
94 Torii Hunter .40 1.00
95 Travis Hafner .40 1.00
96 Troy Glaus .40 1.00
97 Vernon Wells .40 1.00
98 Victor Martinez .60 1.50
99 Vladimir Guerrero .60 1.50
100 Zack Greinke 1.25 3.00

2005 Upper Deck Trilogy Generations Future Lumber Silver

*LUMBER: .4X TO 1X MATERIAL
LUMBER PRINT RUN 100 SERIAL #'d SETS
*GOLD: .5X TO 1.2X SILVER
GOLD PRINT RUN 60 SERIAL #'d SETS
OVERALL LUMBER ODDS 1:3

2005 Upper Deck Trilogy Generations Future Materials Silver

STATED PRINT RUN 120 SERIAL #'d SETS
*GOLD: .5X TO 1.2X BASIC
GOLD PRINT RUN 75 SERIAL #'d SETS
OVERALL MATERIAL ODDS 1:3
AG Adrian Gonzalez Jsy 2.00 5.00
AH Aaron Hill Jsy 2.00 5.00
AM Aaron Miles Jsy 2.00 5.00
AR Alex Rios Jsy 3.00 8.00
BA Bronson Arroyo Jsy 3.00 8.00
BH Brad Halsey Jsy 2.00 5.00
BJ B.J. Upton Jsy 3.00 8.00
BL Joe Blanton Jsy 2.00 5.00
CA Jorge Cantu Jsy 3.00 8.00
CB Chris Burke Jsy 2.00 5.00
CL Clint Barmes Jsy 3.00 8.00
CT Chad Tracy Jsy 2.00 5.00
CU Chase Utley Jsy 5.00 12.00
DB Dewon Brazelton Jsy 2.00 5.00
DC Daniel Cabrera Jsy 2.00 5.00
DD David DeJesus Jsy 2.00 5.00
DH Danny Haren Jsy 2.00 5.00
DK Dae-Sung Koo Jsy 2.00 5.00
DM Dallas McPherson Jsy 2.00 5.00
DU Jason DuBois Jsy 2.00 5.00
EJ Edwin Jackson Jsy 2.00 5.00
ES Ervin Santana Jsy 3.00 8.00
GA Garrett Atkins Jsy 2.00 5.00
GC Gustavo Chacin Jsy 2.00 5.00
GF Gavin Floyd Jsy 2.00 5.00
HO D.J. Houlton Jsy 2.00 5.00
HS Huston Street Jsy 5.00 12.00
JB Jason Bartlett Pants 2.00 5.00
JD J.D. Closser Jsy 2.00 5.00
JE Jeff Baker Jsy 2.00 5.00
JF Jeff Francis Jsy 2.00 5.00
JJ J.J. Hardy Jsy 2.00 5.00
JL Jason Lane Jsy 2.00 5.00
JP Jhonny Peralta Jsy 3.00 8.00
JR Jeremy Reed Jsy 2.00 5.00
JW Jayson Werth Jsy 2.00 5.00
KO Casey Kotchman Jsy 3.00 8.00
KY Keiichi Yabu Jsy 2.00 5.00
LN Laynce Nix Jsy 2.00 5.00
LS Luke Scott Jsy 4.00 10.00
MT Mark Teahen Jsy 2.00 5.00
MY Brett Myers Jsy 2.00 5.00
NS Nick Swisher Jsy 3.00 8.00
RC Robinson Cano Jsy 10.00 25.00
RH Ryan Howard Jsy 6.00 15.00
RI Juan Rivera Jsy 2.00 5.00
RQ Robb Quinlan Jsy 2.00 5.00
RW Rickie Weeks Jsy 3.00 8.00
SI Grady Sizemore Jsy 5.00 12.00
SS Steve Schmoll Jsy 2.00 5.00
TH Charles Thomas Jsy 2.00 5.00
TI Tadahito Iguchi Jsy 6.00 15.00
WA Ryan Wagner Jsy 2.00 5.00
WT Willy Taveras Jsy 3.00 8.00
XN Xavier Nady Jsy 2.00 5.00
YB Yhency Brazoban Jsy 2.00 5.00
YM Yadier Molina Jsy 2.00 5.00
YO Kevin Youkilis Jsy 3.00 8.00

2005 Upper Deck Trilogy Generations Future Signatures Bronze

*BRONZE: .6X TO 1.5X SILVER p/r 150-199
*BRONZE: .6X TO 1.5X SILVER p/r 75-99
*BRONZE: .5X TO 1.2X SILVER p/r 50-60
OVERALL AUTO ODDS 1:3
STATED PRINT RUN 35 SERIAL #'d SETS
EXCHANGE DEADLINE 11/30/06
FH Felix Hernandez 50.00 100.00
JJ J.J. Hardy 6.00 15.00
JN Jeff Niemann 12.50 30.00
RM Russell Martin 40.00 80.00
RZ Ryan Zimmerman 75.00 150.00
TI Tadahito Iguchi 100.00 175.00

2005 Upper Deck Trilogy Generations Future Signatures Silver

OVERALL AUTO ODDS 1:3
PRINT RUNS B/WN 50-199 COPIES PER
EXCHANGE DEADLINE 11/30/06
AB Ambiorix Burgos/199 EXCH 4.00 10.00
AC Ambiorix Concepcion/199 4.00 10.00
AG Adrian Gonzalez/99 12.50 30.00
AR Alex Rios/99 6.00 15.00
BE Colter Bean/199 6.00 15.00
BJ B.J. Upton/50 8.00 20.00
BL Joe Blanton/99 6.00 15.00
CB Chris Burke/199 4.00 10.00
CR Casey Rogowski/199 6.00 15.00
CU Chase Utley/50 12.50 30.00
DC Daniel Cabrera/199 4.00 10.00
DD David DeJesus/99 4.00 10.00
DU Jason DuBois/99 4.00 10.00
DY Delmon Young/50 12.50 30.00
EJ Edwin Jackson/99 6.00 15.00
FH Felix Hernandez/60 30.00 60.00
GA Garrett Atkins/199 4.00 10.00
GF Gavin Floyd/99 4.00 10.00
GG Gabe Gross/99 4.00 10.00
HO D.J. Houlton/199 4.00 10.00
JB Jason Bartlett/199 4.00 10.00
JD J.D. Closser/99 4.00 10.00
JF Jeff Francis/99 4.00 10.00
JG Jared Gothreaux/199 4.00 10.00
JH John Hattig/199 4.00 10.00
JJ J.J. Hardy/199 4.00 10.00
JL Jason Lane/99 4.00 10.00
JN Jeff Niemann/75 8.00 20.00
JO Jose Capellan/199 4.00 10.00
JV Justin Verlander/75 20.00 50.00
JW Jayson Werth/99 4.00 10.00
KM Kendry Morales/199 15.00 40.00
KO Casey Kotchman/99 6.00 15.00
KY Keiichi Yabu/199 10.00 25.00
LS Luke Scott/199 15.00 40.00
ML Matthew Lindstrom/199 4.00 10.00
MT Mark Teahen/199 4.00 10.00
NS Nick Swisher/99 EXCH 5.00 12.00
PF Prince Fielder/75 10.00 25.00
PH Philip Humber/75 10.00 25.00
PL Pedro Lopez/199 4.00 10.00
PO Pete Orr/199 4.00 10.00
RH Ryan Howard/99 5.00 12.00
RM Russell Martin/199 10.00 25.00
RQ Robb Quinlan/199 4.00 10.00
RR Russ Rohlicek/199 4.00 10.00
RW Rickie Weeks/50 8.00 20.00
RZ Ryan Zimmerman/150 20.00 50.00
SD Stephen Drew/75 10.00 25.00
SS Steve Schmoll/199 4.00 10.00
TH Charles Thomas/199 4.00 10.00
TI Tadahito Iguchi/75 75.00 150.00
TP Tony Pena/199 4.00 10.00
TS Tim Stauffer/199 4.00 10.00
YB Yhency Brazoban/199 4.00 10.00
YO Kevin Youkilis/99 4.00 10.00

2005 Upper Deck Trilogy Generations Past Lumber Silver

*LUMBER p/r 115: .4X TO 1X MATL p/r 99
*LUMBER p/r 115: .4X TO 1X MATL p/r 75
PRINT RUNS B/WN 99-115 COPIES PER
*GOLD p/r 75: .4X TO 1X SILVER p/r 115
*GOLD p/r 25: .5X TO 1.2X SILVER p/r 99
GOLD PRINT RUNS B/WN 25-75 PER
OVERALL LUMBER ODDS 1:3
AT Alan Trammell/115 3.00 8.00
BB Bill Buckner/115 3.00 8.00
BD Bobby Doerr/115 3.00 8.00
BR Babe Ruth/99 40.00 100.00
FM Fred McGriff/115 4.00 10.00
FR Bill Freehan/115 3.00 8.00
GF George Foster/115 3.00 8.00
GK George Kell/115 4.00 10.00
GR Lefty Grove/99 15.00 40.00
JD Joe DiMaggio/99 30.00 60.00
JF Jimmie Foxx/99 15.00 40.00
JR Jackie Robinson/99 20.00 50.00
LG Lou Gehrig/99 30.00 60.00
MC Mickey Cochrane/99 20.00 50.00
RH Rogers Hornsby/99 20.00 50.00
RS Ron Santo/115 4.00 10.00
SI George Sisler/115 10.00 25.00
SK Bill Skowron/115 3.00 8.00
TC Ty Cobb/99 20.00 50.00

2005 Upper Deck Trilogy Generations Past Materials Silver

PRINT RUNS B/WN 75-99 COPIES PER
*GOLD: .6X TO 1.5X BASIC p/r 99
*GOLD: .5X TO 1.2X BASIC p/r 75
GOLD PRINT RUN 25 SERIAL #'d SETS
OVERALL MATERIAL ODDS 1:3
AD Andre Dawson Pants/99 3.00 8.00
AR Al Rosen Pants/99 6.00 15.00
AV Andy Van Slyke Jsy/99 6.00 15.00
BF Bob Feller Jsy/99 6.00 15.00
BJ Bo Jackson Jsy/99 6.00 15.00
BL Barry Larkin Jsy/99 4.00 10.00
RM Bill Madlock Jsy/99 3.00 8.00
BP Boog Powell Jsy/99 6.00 15.00
BU Jim Bunning Jsy/99 4.00 10.00
CA Rod Carew Jsy/99 4.00 10.00
CF Carlton Fisk Jsy/99 4.00 10.00
CM C.Mathewson Pants/75 75.00 150.00
CR Cal Ripken Jsy/99 12.50 30.00
CY Ron Cey Pants/99 3.00 8.00
DB Dusty Baker Jsy/99 3.00 8.00
DC David Cone Jsy/99 3.00 8.00
DD Dizzy Dean Jsy/75 12.00 30.00
DE Dwight Evans Jsy/99 4.00 10.00
DG Dwight Gooden Jsy/99 3.00 8.00
DL Davey Lopes Pants/99 3.00 8.00
DM Dale Murphy Jsy/99 4.00 10.00
DR Don Drysdale Jsy/99 6.00 15.00
DS Darryl Strawberry Jsy/99 3.00 8.00
ED Eric Davis Jsy/99 4.00 10.00
EM Eddie Mathews Pants/75 10.00 25.00
FH Frank Howard Jsy/99 4.00 10.00
FW Frank White Jsy/99 3.00 8.00
GC Gary Carter Jsy/99 3.00 8.00
GN Graig Nettles Jsy/99 3.00 8.00
GP Gaylord Perry Jsy/99 3.00 8.00
HB Harold Baines Jsy/99 3.00 8.00
HR Kent Hrbek Jsy/99 3.00 8.00
JA Jack Morris Jsy/99 3.00 8.00
JB Johnny Bench Jsy/99 6.00 15.00
JC Jack Clark Jsy/99 3.00 8.00
JD Joe DiMaggio Jsy/75 30.00 80.00
JK John Kruk Jsy/99 3.00 8.00
JM Johnny Mize Pants/99 4.00 10.00
JO Wally Joyner Jsy/99 3.00 8.00
JP Jim Palmer Jsy/99 3.00 8.00
KH Keith Hernandez Jsy/99 3.00 8.00
LA Luis Aparicio Jsy/99 3.00 8.00
LD Lenny Dykstra Jsy/99 3.00 8.00
LG Lou Gehrig Pants/75 100.00 175.00
MA Don Mattingly Jsy/99 8.00 20.00
MO Mel Ott Jsy/75 12.50 30.00
MS Mike Schmidt Jsy/99 8.00 20.00
MU Bobby Murcer Jsy/99 6.00 15.00
MY Eddie Murray Jsy/99 6.00 15.00
NR Nolan Ryan Pants/99 10.00 25.00
OC Orlando Cepeda Jsy/99 3.00 8.00
OS Ozzie Smith Jsy/99 6.00 15.00
RC Roy Campanella Pants/99 10.00 25.00
RG Ron Guidry Jsy/99 4.00 10.00
RH Rogers Hornsby Jsy/75 10.00 25.00
RI Jim Rice Jsy/99 3.00 8.00
RJ Reggie Jackson Jsy/99 4.00 10.00
RO Brooks Robinson Jsy/99 4.00 10.00
RP Rico Petrocelli Pants/99 3.00 8.00
SA Ryne Sandberg Jsy/99 8.00 20.00
SC Steve Carlton Pants/99 3.00 8.00
SM Stan Musial Jsy/99 8.00 20.00
SN Duke Snider Jsy/99 4.00 10.00
SP Satchel Paige Pants/75 20.00 50.00
TG Tony Gwynn Jsy/99 6.00 15.00
TM Thurman Munson Pants/99 8.00 20.00
TO Tony Oliva Jsy/99 3.00 8.00
TP Tony Perez Jsy/99 3.00 8.00
TR Tim Raines Jsy/99 3.00 8.00
WB Wade Boggs Pants/99 4.00 10.00
WC Will Clark Jsy/99 4.00 10.00
WW Willie Wilson Jsy/99 3.00 8.00
YA Carl Yastrzemski Jsy/99 6.00 15.00

2005 Upper Deck Trilogy Generations Past Signatures Bronze

*BRZ p/r 35: .6X TO 1.5X SILV p/r 199
*BRZ p/r 35: .6X TO 1.5X SILV p/r 99
*BRZ p/r 35: .5X TO 1.2X SILV p/r 50
OVERALL AUTO ODDS 1:3
PRINT RUNS B/WN 10-35 COPIES PER
NO PRICING ON QTY OF 10
EXCHANGE DEADLINE 11/30/06

2005 Upper Deck Trilogy Generations Past Signatures Silver

OVERALL AUTO ODDS 1:3
PRINT RUNS B/WN 24-199 COPIES PER
EXCHANGE DEADLINE 11/30/06
AD Andre Dawson/99 6.00 15.00
AR Al Rosen/199 6.00 15.00
AT Alan Trammell/50 8.00 20.00
AV Andy Van Slyke/199 10.00 25.00
BB Bill Buckner/50 10.00 25.00
BD Bobby Doerr/199 6.00 15.00
BF Bob Feller/99 10.00 25.00
BJ Bo Jackson/50 30.00 80.00
BL Barry Larkin/99 25.00 60.00
BM Bill Madlock/199 6.00 15.00
BP Boog Powell/199 6.00 15.00
BU Jim Bunning/99 10.00 25.00
CA Rod Carew/25 15.00 40.00
CR Cal Ripken/24 50.00 120.00
CY Ron Cey/199 6.00 15.00
DC David Cone/99 6.00 15.00
DE Dwight Evans/50 8.00 20.00
DG Dwight Gooden/199 6.00 15.00
DL Davey Lopes/199 4.00 10.00
DM Dale Murphy/99 10.00 25.00
DS Darryl Strawberry/99 6.00 15.00
ED Eric Davis/199 6.00 15.00
FH Frank Howard/199 6.00 15.00
FR Bill Freehan/199 6.00 15.00
FW Frank White/199 6.00 15.00
GF George Foster/199 4.00 10.00
GK George Kell/199 6.00 15.00
GN Graig Nettles/199 6.00 15.00
GP Gaylord Perry/199 6.00 15.00
HB Harold Baines/199 6.00 15.00
HR Kent Hrbek/199 6.00 15.00
JA Jack Morris/199 6.00 15.00
JC Jack Clark/199 6.00 15.00
JK John Kruk/199 6.00 15.00
JO Wally Joyner/199 6.00 15.00
JP Jim Palmer/50 8.00 20.00
KH Keith Hernandez/199 6.00 15.00
LA Luis Aparicio/50 8.00 20.00
LD Lenny Dykstra/199 6.00 15.00
MA Don Mattingly/25 40.00 80.00
MS Mike Schmidt/25 30.00 60.00
MU Bobby Murcer/199 15.00 40.00
NR Nolan Ryan/25 50.00 100.00
OS Ozzie Smith/25 20.00 50.00
RG Ron Guidry/199 6.00 15.00
RI Jim Rice/99 10.00 25.00
RJ Reggie Jackson/25 20.00 50.00
RO Brooks Robinson/50 12.50 30.00
RS Ron Santo/199 12.50 30.00
SA Ryne Sandberg/50 30.00 60.00
SC Steve Carlton/25 10.00 25.00
SK Bill Skowron/199 6.00 15.00
SM Stan Musial/25 40.00 80.00
TO Tony Oliva/99 6.00 15.00
TP Tony Perez/25 15.00 40.00
TR Tim Raines/199 10.00 25.00
WB Wade Boggs/50 12.50 30.00
WC Will Clark/25 15.00 40.00
WW Willie Wilson/199 6.00 15.00

2005 Upper Deck Trilogy Generations Present Lumber Silver

*LUMBER: .4X TO 1X MATERIAL
LUMBER PRINT RUN 115 SERIAL #'d SETS
*GOLD: .5X TO 1.2X SILVER
GOLD PRINT RUN 75 SERIAL #'d SETS
OVERALL LUMBER ODDS 1:3

2005 Upper Deck Trilogy Generations Present Materials Silver

STATED PRINT RUN 99 SERIAL #'d SETS
*GOLD: .6X TO 1.5X BASIC
GOLD PRINT RUN 25 SERIAL #'d SETS
OVERALL MATERIAL ODDS 1:3
AB Adrian Beltre Jsy 2.00 5.00
AD Adam Dunn Jsy 2.00 5.00
AH Aubrey Huff Jsy 2.00 5.00
AJ A.J. Burnett Jsy 2.00 5.00
AP Albert Pujols Jsy 8.00 20.00
AR Aramis Ramirez Jsy 2.00 5.00
AS Alfonso Soriano Jsy 2.00 5.00
BA Bobby Abreu Jsy 2.00 5.00
BC Bobby Crosby Jsy 2.00 5.00
BG Brian Giles Jsy 2.00 5.00
BI Craig Biggio Jsy 3.00 8.00
BL Brad Lidge Jsy 2.00 5.00
BM Bill Mueller Jsy 2.00 5.00
BO Jeremy Bonderman Jsy 2.00 5.00
BR Brian Roberts Jsy 2.00 5.00
BS Ben Sheets Jsy 2.00 5.00
BW Bernie Williams Jsy 3.00 8.00
CB Carlos Beltran Jsy 2.00 5.00
CC Carl Crawford Jsy 2.00 5.00
CD Carlos Delgado Jsy 2.00 5.00
CJ Chipper Jones Jsy 4.00 10.00
CS Curt Schilling Jsy 3.00 8.00
CZ Carlos Zambrano Jsy 2.00 5.00
DA Johnny Damon Jsy 3.00 8.00
DJ Derek Jeter Jsy 10.00 25.00
DL Derrek Lee Jsy 3.00 8.00
DO David Ortiz Jsy 4.00 10.00
DW David Wright Jsy 6.00 15.00
EC Eric Chavez Jsy 2.00 5.00
FT Frank Thomas Jsy 4.00 10.00
GA Garret Anderson Jsy 2.00 5.00
GM Greg Maddux Jsy 6.00 15.00
GR Khalil Greene Jsy 3.00 8.00
GS Gary Sheffield Jsy 2.00 5.00
HA Travis Hafner Jsy 2.00 5.00
HB Hank Blalock Jsy 2.00 5.00
HU Torii Hunter Jsy 2.00 5.00
IR Ivan Rodriguez Jsy 3.00 8.00
JB Jason Bay Jsy 2.00 5.00
JD J.D. Drew Jsy 2.00 5.00
JE Jeff Bagwell Jsy 3.00 8.00
JG Jason Giambi Jsy 2.00 5.00
JK Jeff Kent Jsy 2.00 5.00
JM Joe Mauer Jsy 4.00 10.00
JO Andruw Jones Pants 3.00 8.00
JP Jake Peavy Jsy 2.00 5.00
JR Jimmy Rollins Jsy 2.00 5.00
JS Johan Santana Jsy 4.00 10.00
JT Jim Thome Jsy 3.00 8.00
JV Jason Varitek Jsy 4.00 10.00
KG1 Ken Griffey Jr. Reds Jsy 8.00 20.00
KG2 Ken Griffey Jr. M's Jsy 8.00 20.00
KG3 Ken Griffey Jr. AS Jsy 8.00 20.00
KW Kerry Wood Jsy 2.00 5.00
LB Lance Berkman Jsy 2.00 5.00
MC Miguel Cabrera Jsy 3.00 8.00
ME Melvin Mora Jsy 2.00 5.00
MG Marcus Giles Jsy 2.00 5.00
ML Mark Loretta Jsy 2.00 5.00
MM Mark Mulder Jsy 2.00 5.00
MO Justin Morneau Jsy 2.00 5.00
MP Mark Prior Jsy 3.00 8.00
MR Manny Ramirez Jsy 3.00 8.00
MT Mark Teixeira Jsy 3.00 8.00
MY Michael Young Jsy 2.00 5.00
PA Corey Patterson Jsy 2.00 5.00
PB Pat Burrell Jsy 2.00 5.00
PI Mike Piazza Jsy 4.00 10.00
PM Pedro Martinez Jsy 3.00 8.00
RC Roger Clemens Pants 6.00 15.00
RE Jose Reyes Jsy 2.00 5.00
RF Rafael Furcal Jsy 2.00 5.00
RH Rich Harden Jsy 2.00 5.00
RJ Randy Johnson Jsy 4.00 10.00
RO Roy Oswalt Jsy 2.00 5.00
SC Sean Casey Jsy 2.00 5.00
SK Scott Kazmir Jsy 2.00 5.00
SM John Smoltz Jsy 3.00 8.00
SP Scott Podsednik Jsy 2.00 5.00
SR Scott Rolen Jsy 3.00 8.00
SS Sammy Sosa Jsy 4.00 10.00
TE Miguel Tejada Jsy 2.00 5.00
TG Troy Glaus Jsy 2.00 5.00
TH Todd Helton Jsy 3.00 8.00
VG Vladimir Guerrero Jsy 4.00 10.00
VI Jose Vidro Jsy 2.00 5.00
VM Victor Martinez Jsy 2.00 5.00
WI Dontrelle Willis Jsy 2.00 5.00
WM Wily Mo Pena Jsy 2.00 5.00
ZG Zack Greinke Jsy 2.00 5.00

2005 Upper Deck Trilogy Generations Present Signatures Bronze

*BRZ p/r 35: .6X TO 1.5X SILVER p/r 135-199
*BRZ p/r 35: .6X TO 1.5X SILVER p/r 95-99
*BRZ p/r 35: .5X TO 1.2X SILVER p/r 50
OVERALL AUTO ODDS 1:3
PRINT RUNS B/WN 10-35 COPIES PER
NO PRICING ON QTY OF 10
EXCHANGE DEADLINE 11/30/06
DJ Derek Jeter/35 125.00 200.00

2005 Upper Deck Trilogy Generations Present Signatures Silver

OVERALL AUTO ODDS 1:3
PRINT RUNS B/WN 25 199 COPIES PER
EXCHANGE DEADLINE 11/30/06
AB A.J. Burnett/199 6.00 15.00
AD Adam Dunn/95 10.00 25.00
AH Aubrey Huff/199 6.00 15.00
AR Aramis Ramirez/99 6.00 15.00
BC Bobby Crosby/99 6.00 15.00
BG Brian Giles/99 6.00 15.00
BL Brad Lidge/99 12.50 30.00
BO Jeremy Bonderman/199 6.00 15.00
BR Brian Roberts/99 6.00 15.00
CC Carl Crawford/99 6.00 15.00
DJ Derek Jeter/99 75.00 150.00
DL Derrek Lee/25 15.00 40.00
DO David Ortiz/25 25.00 60.00
DW David Wright/135 12.50 30.00
FT Frank Thomas/25 30.00 60.00
GA Garret Anderson/25 10.00 25.00
GR Khalil Greene/135 10.00 25.00
GS Gary Sheffield/25 15.00 40.00
HA Travis Hafner/99 6.00 15.00
HU Torii Hunter/25 10.00 25.00
JB Jason Bay/199 6.00 15.00
JM Joe Mauer/25 30.00 60.00
KG1 Ken Griffey Jr. Reds/199 30.00 60.00
KG2 Ken Griffey Jr. M's/199 30.00 60.00
KG3 Ken Griffey Jr. AS/199 30.00 60.00
MC Miguel Cabrera/25 20.00 50.00
ME Melvin Mora/199 6.00 15.00
MG Marcus Giles/199 6.00 15.00
ML Mark Loretta/99 4.00 10.00
MM Mark Mulder/99 6.00 15.00
MO Justin Morneau/99 6.00 15.00
MP Mark Prior/25 12.50 30.00
MT Mark Teixeira/25 15.00 40.00
MY Michael Young/199 6.00 15.00
RF Rafael Furcal/99 6.00 15.00
RH Rich Harden/199 6.00 15.00
RO Roy Oswalt/25 10.00 25.00
SC Sean Casey/50 8.00 20.00
SM John Smoltz/25 30.00 60.00
SP Scott Podsednik/99 10.00 25.00
TE Miguel Tejada/25 15.00 40.00
VI Jose Vidro/99 6.00 15.00
VM Victor Martinez/99 6.00 15.00
WI Dontrelle Willis/25 15.00 40.00
WM Wily Mo Pena/199 6.00 15.00
ZG Zack Greinke/199 12.50 30.00

2005 Upper Deck Trilogy Generations of Lumber Triple

*LUMBER: .3X TO .8X MATERIAL
OVERALL LUMBER ODDS 1:3
STATED PRINT RUN 85 SERIAL #'d SETS
SMR Santo/Madlock/Aramis 8.00 20.00
SSP Santo/Sandberg/Patterson 12.50 30.00

2005 Upper Deck Trilogy Generations of Materials Triple

OVERALL MATERIAL ODDS 1:3
STATED PRINT RUN 50 SERIAL #'d SETS
ALL ARE TRIPLE JERSEYS UNLESS NOTED
AAD Rosen Pants/Ram/McPh 6.00 15.00
AFB Apar/Furc/Bartlett Pants 6.00 15.00
API Aparicio/Pods/Iguchi 10.00 25.00
ARU Aparicio/Rollins/Upton 6.00 15.00
BCU Boggs Pants/Craw/Upt 6.00 15.00
BHH Baines/Hafner/R.How 10.00 25.00
BLS Biggio/Lane/Scott 10.00 25.00
BMY Boggs Pants/Mue/Youk 10.00 25.00
CCC Cepeda/J.Clark/W.Clark 10.00 25.00
CCK W.Clark/Casey/Kotch 10.00 25.00
CMG W.Clark/Morn/A.Gonz 10.00 25.00
CTG W.Clark/Teix/A.Gonz 10.00 25.00
DAR E.Davis/Abreu/Rios 10.00 25.00
DBS Dykstra/Bay/Swisher 6.00 15.00
DGL Daws Pants/Grit/Lane 10.00 25.00
DHL Dykstra/Hunter/Lane 6.00 15.00
DPD Daws Pants/Patt/DuBois 6.00 15.00
DPT Dykstra/Pods/Taveras 10.00 25.00
EDY Evans/Damon/Youkilis 10.00 25.00
GAS Gwynn/Abreu/Swisher 10.00 25.00
GDP Griffey Jr./Dunn/W.Pena 15.00 40.00
GGC Gwynn/Griffey Jr./Cabrera 15.00 40.00
GWJ Gooden/Willis/E.Jackson 10.00 25.00
HDH F.Howard/Dunn/R.How 15.00 40.00
HOH F.Howard/Ortiz/R.How 15.00 40.00
JGU Bo/Griffey Jr./Upton 15.00 40.00
JHR Bo/Hunter/Rios 10.00 25.00
JMK Joyner/McPh/Kotch 6.00 15.00
JSP Bo/Sheffield/W.Pena 10.00 25.00
KBH Kruk/Burrell/R.Howard 10.00 25.00
KBU Kruk/Burrell/Utley 10.00 25.00
LJU Larkin/Jeter/Upton 15.00 40.00
LYU Larkin/Young/Upton 10.00 25.00
MBS Murphy Pants/Burr/Swish 10.00 25.00
MCG Mattingly/Casey/A.Gonz 12.50 30.00
MDW Murphy Pants/Dunn/Werth 10.00 25.00
MMJ Murcer/Mattingly/Jeter 50.00 100.00
MOH Murray/Ortiz/R.Howard 15.00 40.00
NBW Nettles/Beltre/Wright 10.00 25.00
OAR Oliva/Abreu/Rios 6.00 15.00
PDP T.Perez/E.Davis/W.Pena 10.00 25.00
PGD T.Perez/B.Giles/DuBois 6.00 15.00
PGP T.Perez/Grif Jr./W.Pena 10.00 25.00
RBT Brooks/Beltre/Teahen 10.00 25.00
RCD Raines/Craw/DeJesus 6.00 15.00
RJC Ripken/Jeter/Crosby 30.00 60.00
ROY Rice/Ortiz/Youkilis 10.00 25.00
RRM Brooks/Ripken/Mora 10.00 25.00
RRT Brooks/Ripken/Tejada 10.00 25.00
SBM Schmidt/Beltre/McPh 12.50 30.00
SBW Schmidt/Beltre/Wright 15.00 40.00
SDW Snider/Drew/Werth 10.00 25.00
SGU Sandberg/M.Giles/Utley 10.00 25.00
SMR Santo/Madlock/A.Ramirez 10.00 25.00
SRU Schmidt/Rollins/Utley 15.00 40.00
SRW Sandberg/Roberts/Weeks 12.50 30.00
SSP Ryno/Santo/Patterson 15.00 40.00
VGB Van Slyke/B.Giles/Bay 10.00 25.00
VPD Van Slyke/Patt/DeJesus 10.00 25.00
WBI F.White/Biggio/Iguchi 10.00 25.00
WCT W.Wils/Craw/Taveras 6.00 15.00

2005 Upper Deck Trilogy Generations of Signatures Triple

OVERALL AUTO ODDS 1:3
STATED PRINT RUN 35 SERIAL #'d SETS
ALL BUT JKM AND LJU ARE REDEMPTIONS
EXCHANGE DEADLINE 11/30/06
AYU Aparicio/Young/Upton 10.00 25.00
BPN Bunning/Peavy/Niem 10.00 25.00
CTG W.Clark/Teix/A.Gonz 30.00 60.00
DBU Doerr/Biggio/Utley 20.00 50.00
DGL Dawson/Griffey Jr./Lane 60.00 120.00
DGU Doerr/Giles/Utley 20.00 50.00
DLB Doerr/Loretta/Burke 10.00 25.00
FPH Feller/Prior/Harden 10.00 25.00
GDP Griffey Jr./Dunn/W.Pena 60.00 120.00
HDG F.Howard/Dunn/Gross 10.00 25.00
JHR Bo/Hunter/Rios 50.00 100.00
JKM Joyner/Kotch/Morales 30.00 60.00
LJU Larkin/Jeter/Upton 150.00 300.00
MBV Morris/Bonder/Verl 40.00 80.00
MMJ Murcer/Mattingly/Jeter 175.00 300.00
NBW Nettles/Beltre/Wright 30.00 60.00
OHM Oliva/Hrbek/Morneau 30.00 60.00
PBF Perry/Bonderman/Floyd 10.00 25.00
PGP T.Perez/Grif Jr./W.Pena 60.00 120.00
PPH Palmer/Peavy/Humber 10.00 25.00
PPS Perry/Peavy/Stauffer 10.00 25.00
RCD Raines/Craw/DeJesus 10.00 25.00
RJC Ripken/Jeter/Crosby 250.00 400.00
RRM Brooks/Ripken/Mora 125.00 200.00
RSH Ryan/Smoltz/Humber 125.00 200.00
SBT Santo/Beltre/Teahen 20.00 50.00
SBW Schmidt/Beltre/Wright 40.00 80.00
SGH Ozzie/Khalil/Hardy 10.00 25.00
SMR Santo/Madlock/Aramis 20.00 50.00
SRW Sandberg/Roberts/Weeks 50.00 100.00
VGB Van Slyke/B.Giles/Bay 20.00 50.00

2005 Upper Deck Trilogy Signature Materials Dual

OVERALL AUTO ODDS 1:3
STATED PRINT RUN 75 SERIAL #'d SETS
EXCHANGE DEADLINE 11/30/06
AB Adrian Beltre Bat-Jsy 15.00 40.00
AD Andre Dawson Bat-Pants 15.00 40.00
AH Aubrey Huff Bat-Jsy 10.00 25.00
AP Albert Pujols Bat-Jsy 100.00 250.00
AV Andy Van Slyke Bat-Jsy 10.00 25.00
BC Bobby Crosby Bat-Jsy 15.00 40.00
BG Brian Giles Bat-Jsy 10.00 25.00
BL Barry Larkin Bat-Jsy 30.00 60.00
BR Brooks Robinson Bat-Jsy 12.00 30.00
BU B.J. Upton Bat-Jsy 15.00 40.00
CC Carl Crawford Bat-Jsy 10.00 25.00
CP Corey Patterson Bat-Jsy 10.00 25.00
CR Cal Ripken Bat-Jsy 60.00 120.00
DJ Derek Jeter Bat-Jsy 250.00 400.00
DM Don Mattingly Bat-Jsy 50.00 100.00
DU Adam Dunn Bat-Jsy 10.00 25.00
DW David Wright Bat-Jsy 50.00 100.00
FH Frank Howard Bat-Jsy 15.00 40.00
GI Marcus Giles Bat-Jsy 10.00 25.00
GN Graig Nettles Bat-Jsy 15.00 40.00
HB Harold Baines Bat-Jsy 10.00 25.00
HU Torii Hunter Bat-Jsy 10.00 25.00
JV Jose Vidro Bat-Jsy 10.00 25.00
JW Jayson Werth Bat-Jsy 10.00 25.00
KG Ken Griffey Jr. Bat-Jsy 100.00 175.00
KH Kent Hrbek Bat-Jsy 15.00 40.00
KY Kevin Youkilis Bat-Jsy 10.00 25.00
MA Bill Madlock Bat-Jsy 15.00 40.00
MC Miguel Cabrera Bat-Jsy 30.00 80.00
MS Mike Schmidt Bat-Jsy 40.00 80.00
MT Mark Teixeira Bat-Jsy 12.50 30.00
MU Dale Murphy Bat-Jsy 20.00 50.00
RA Aramis Ramirez Bat-Jsy 15.00 40.00
RE Jose Reyes Bat-Jsy 20.00 50.00
RH Ryan Howard Bat-Jsy 20.00 50.00
RI Jim Rice Bat-Jsy 15.00 40.00
RS Ryne Sandberg Bat-Jsy 40.00 80.00
SC Sean Casey Bat-Jsy 6.00 15.00
SP Scott Podsednik Bat-Jsy 20.00 50.00
TG Tony Gwynn Bat-Jsy 30.00 60.00
TH Travis Hafner Bat-Jsy 15.00 40.00
TO Tony Oliva Bat-Jsy 10.00 25.00
TP Tony Perez Bat-Jsy 20.00 50.00
TR Tim Raines Bat-Jsy 15.00 40.00
WB Wade Boggs Bat-Pants 20.00 50.00
WJ Wally Joyner Bat-Jsy 20.00 50.00
WP Wily Mo Pena Bat-Jsy 15.00 40.00

2005 Upper Deck Update

COMP.SET w/o SP's (100) 8.00 20.00
COMMON CARD (1-100) .10 .30
1-100 ONE PER PACK
COMMON CARD (101-177) .75 2.00
101-177: ONE #'d CARD OR AU PER PACK
101-177 PRINT RUN 599 SERIAL #'d SETS
COMMON AUTO (178-186) 6.00 15.00
178-186: OVERALL AU ODDS APPX 1:8
178-186 PRINT RUN 75 SERIAL #'d SETS
1 A.J. Burnett .12 .30
2 Adam Dunn .20 .50
3 Adrian Beltre .30 .75
4 Albert Pujols .40 1.00
5 Alex Rodriguez .40 1.00
6 Alfonso Soriano .20 .50
7 Andruw Jones .12 .30
8 Aramis Ramirez .12 .30
9 Barry Zito .20 .50
10 Bartolo Colon .12 .30
11 Ben Sheets .12 .30
12 Bobby Abreu .12 .30
13 Bobby Crosby .12 .30
14 Michael Cuddyer .12 .30
15 Brian Giles .12 .30
16 Brian Roberts .12 .30
17 Carl Crawford .20 .50
18 Carlos Beltran .20 .50
19 Carlos Delgado .12 .30
20 Carlos Lee .12 .30
21 Carlos Zambrano .20 .50
22 Chase Utley .20 .50
23 Chipper Jones .30 .75
24 Chris Carpenter .20 .50
25 Craig Biggio .20 .50
26 Curt Schilling .20 .50
27 David Ortiz .30 .75
28 David Wright .25 .60
29 Derek Jeter .75 2.00
30 Derrek Lee .12 .30
31 Dontrelle Willis .12 .30
32 Eric Chavez .12 .30
33 Eric Gagne .12 .30
34 Francisco Rodriguez .20 .50
35 Gary Sheffield .12 .30
36 Greg Maddux .40 1.00
37 Hank Blalock .12 .30
38 Hideki Matsui .50 1.25
39 Ichiro Suzuki .40 1.00
40 Ivan Rodriguez .20 .50
41 J.D. Drew .12 .30
42 Jake Peavy .12 .30
43 Jason Bay .12 .30
44 Jason Schmidt .12 .30
45 Jeff Bagwell .20 .50
46 Jeff Kent .12 .30
47 Jeremy Bonderman .12 .30
48 Jim Edmonds .20 .50
49 Jim Thome .20 .50
50 Joe Mauer .25 .60
51 Johan Santana .20 .50
52 John Smoltz .30 .75
53 Johnny Damon .20 .50
54 Jose Reyes .20 .50
55 Jose Vidro .12 .30
56 Josh Beckett .12 .30
57 Justin Morneau .20 .50
58 Ken Griffey Jr. .60 1.50
59 Kenny Rogers .12 .30
60 Kerry Wood .12 .30
61 Khalil Greene .12 .30
62 Lance Berkman .20 .50
63 Livan Hernandez .12 .30
64 Luis Gonzalez .12 .30
65 Manny Ramirez .30 .75
66 Mark Buehrle .20 .50
67 Mark Mulder .12 .30
68 Mark Prior .20 .50
69 Mark Teixeira .20 .50
70 Michael Young .12 .30
71 Miguel Cabrera .30 .75
72 Miguel Tejada .20 .50
73 Mike Mussina .20 .50
74 Mike Piazza .30 .75
75 Moises Alou .12 .30
76 Morgan Ensberg .12 .30
77 Nomar Garciaparra .20 .50
78 Pat Burrell .12 .30
79 Paul Konerko .20 .50
80 Pedro Martinez .20 .50
81 Randy Johnson .30 .75
82 Rich Harden .12 .30
83 Richie Sexson .12 .30
84 Rickie Weeks .12 .30
85 Robinson Cano .40 1.00
86 Roger Clemens .40 1.00

87 Roy Halladay .20 .50
88 Roy Oswalt .20 .50
89 Sammy Sosa .30 .75
90 Scott Kazmir .30 .75
91 Scott Rolen .20 .50
92 Shawn Green .12 .30
93 Tim Hudson .20 .50
94 Todd Helton .20 .50
95 Tom Glavine .20 .50
96 Torii Hunter .12 .30
97 Travis Hafner .12 .30
98 Troy Glaus .12 .30
99 Vernon Wells .12 .30
100 Vladimir Guerrero .20 .50
101 Adam Shabala PR RC .75 2.00
102 Ambiorix Burgos PR RC .75 2.00
103 Anibal Sanchez PR RC 3.00 8.00
104 Bill McCarthy PR RC .75 2.00
105 Brandon McCarthy PR RC 1.25 3.00
106 Brian Burres PR RC .75 2.00
107 Carlos Ruiz PR RC 1.25 3.00
108 Casey Rogowski PR RC 1.25 3.00
109 Chad Orvella PR RC .75 2.00
110 Chris Resop PR RC .75 2.00
111 Chris Roberson PR RC .75 2.00
112 Chris Seddon PR RC .75 2.00
113 Colter Bean PR RC .75 2.00
114 Dae-Sung Koo PR RC .75 2.00
115 Dave Gassner PR RC .75 2.00
116 Brian Anderson PR RC 1.25 3.00
117 D.J. Houlton PR RC .75 2.00
118 Derek Wathan PR RC .75 2.00
119 Devon Lowery PR RC .75 2.00
120 Enrique Gonzalez PR RC .75 2.00
121 Eude Brito PR RC .75 2.00
122 Francisco Butto PR RC .75 2.00
123 Franquelis Osoria PR RC .75 2.00
124 Garrett Jones PR RC 1.25 3.00
125 Geovany Soto PR RC 4.00 10.00
126 Hayden Penn PR RC .75 2.00
127 Ismael Ramirez PR RC .75 2.00
128 Jared Gothreaux PR RC .75 2.00
129 Jason Hammel PR RC 2.00 5.00
130 Jeff Miller PR RC .75 2.00
131 Joel Peralta PR RC .75 2.00
132 John Hattig PR RC .75 2.00
133 Jorge Campillo PR RC .75 2.00
134 Juan Morillo PR RC .75 2.00
135 Ryan Garko PR RC .75 2.00
136 Keiichi Yabu PR RC .75 2.00
137 Luis Hernandez PR RC .75 2.00
138 Luis Pena PR RC .75 2.00
139 Luis O.Rodriguez PR RC .75 2.00
140 Luke Scott PR RC 2.00 5.00
141 Marcos Carvajal PR RC .75 2.00
142 Mark Woodyard PR RC .75 2.00
143 Matt A.Smith PR RC .75 2.00
144 Matthew Lindstrom PR RC .75 2.00
145 Miguel Negron PR RC 1.25 3.00
146 Mike Morse PR RC 2.50 6.00
147 Nate McLouth PR RC 1.25 3.00
148 Nelson Cruz PR RC 10.00 25.00
149 Nick Masset PR RC .75 2.00
150 Oscar Robles PR RC .75 2.00
151 Paulino Reynoso PR RC .75 2.00
152 Pedro Lopez PR RC .75 2.00
153 Pete Orr PR RC 1.25 3.00
154 Randy Messenger PR RC .75 2.00
155 Randy Williams PR RC .75 2.00
156 Raul Tablado PR RC .75 2.00
157 Ronny Paulino PR RC 1.25 3.00
158 Russ Rohlicek PR RC .75 2.00
159 Russell Martin PR RC 2.50 6.00
160 Scott Baker PR RC 1.25 3.00
161 Scott Munter PR RC .75 2.00
162 Sean Thompson PR RC .75 2.00
163 Sean Tracey PR RC .75 2.00
164 Shane Costa PR RC .75 2.00
165 Steve Schmoll PR RC .75 2.00
166 Tony Giarratano PR RC .75 2.00
167 Tony Pena PR RC .75 2.00
168 Travis Bowyer PR RC .75 2.00
169 Ubaldo Jimenez PR RC 2.00 5.00
170 Wladimir Balentien PR RC 1.25 3.00
171 Yorman Bazardo PR RC .75 2.00
172 Yuniesky Betancourt PR RC 3.00 8.00
173 Chris Denorfia PR RC .75 2.00
174 Dana Eveland PR RC .75 2.00
175 Jermaine Van Buren PR .75 2.00
176 Mark McLemore PR RC .75 2.00
177 Ryan Spilborghs PR RC 2.00 5.00
178 Ambiorix Concepcion AU RC 6.00 15.00
179 Jeff Niemann AU RC 6.00 15.00
180 Justin Verlander AU RC 125.00 250.00
181 Kendry Morales AU RC 6.00 15.00
182 Philip Humber AU RC 6.00 15.00
183 Prince Fielder AU RC 50.00 100.00
184 Stephen Drew AU RC 10.00 25.00
185 Tadahito Iguchi AU RC 40.00 80.00
186 Ryan Zimmerman AU RC 100.00 175.00

2005 Upper Deck Update Gold

*GOLD 101-177: .6X TO 1.5X BASIC
101-177: ONE #'d CARD OR AU PER PACK
101-177 PRINT RUN 150 SERIAL #'d SETS
178-186: OVERALL AU ODDS APPX 1:8
178-186 AU PRINT RUN 10 SERIAL #'d SETS
178-186 AU NO PRICING DUE TO SCARCITY

2005 Upper Deck Update Silver

*SILVER 101-177: .4X TO 1X BASIC
101-177: ONE #'d CARD OR AU PER PACK
101-177 PRINT RUN 450 SERIAL #'d SETS
178-186: OVERALL AU ODDS APPX 1:8
178-186 AU PRINT RUN 25 SERIAL #'d SETS
178-186 AU NO PRICING DUE TO SCARCITY

2005 Upper Deck Update Link to the Future Dual Autographs

OVERALL AU ODDS APPX 1:8
STATED PRINT RUN 35 SERIAL #'d SETS
BR W.Balentien/J.Reed 15.00 40.00
BW Y.Bazardo/D.Willis 15.00 40.00
CD S.Costa/D.DeJesus 10.00 25.00
DD S.Drew/J.Drew 75.00 150.00
DJ S.Drew/D.Jeter 100.00 200.00
FO P.Fielder/L.Overbay 40.00 80.00
FT P.Fielder/M.Teixeira 30.00 60.00
FW P.Fielder/R.Weeks 15.00 40.00
GO J.Gothreaux/R.Oswalt 15.00 40.00
HF L.Hernandez/R.Furcal 10.00 25.00
HG P.Humber/T.Glavine 30.00 60.00
MB N.McLouth/J.Bay 15.00 40.00
MK K.Morales/C.Kotchman 15.00 40.00
NK J.Niemann/S.Kazmir 10.00 25.00
NW M.Negron/V.Wells 15.00 40.00
OB F.Osoria/Y.Brazoban 10.00 25.00
OG P.Orr/M.Giles 10.00 25.00
PV T.Pena/J.Vazquez 10.00 25.00
RH I.Ramirez/R.Halladay 15.00 40.00
SK C.Seddon/S.Kazmir 15.00 40.00
SL L.Scott/J.Lane 20.00 50.00
VB J.Verlander/J.Bonderman 30.00 60.00
VC J.Verlander/R.Clemens 60.00 120.00
ZC R.Zimmerman/C.Cordero 60.00 120.00

2005 Upper Deck Update Link to the Past Dual Autographs

OVERALL AU ODDS APPX 1:8
STATED PRINT RUN 25 SERIAL #'d SETS
BC E.Brito/S.Carlton 20.00 50.00
BM B.Burres/J.Marichal 15.00 40.00
CS A.Concepcion/D.Strawberry 15.00 40.00
GT T.Giarratano/A.Trammell 15.00 40.00
HG P.Humber/D.Gooden 10.00 25.00
HS P.Humber/T.Seaver 30.00 80.00
IA T.Iguchi/L.Aparicio 60.00 120.00
IC T.Iguchi/R.Carew 60.00 120.00
JH G.Jones/K.Hrbek 15.00 40.00
JJ J.Verlander/J.Morris 100.00 175.00
MC K.Morales/R.Carew 20.00 50.00
MJ K.Morales/W.Joyner 15.00 40.00
MV N.McLouth/A.Van Slyke 20.00 50.00
NB M.Negron/G.Bell 15.00 40.00
NR J.Niemann/N.Ryan 60.00 120.00
PP H.Penn/J.Palmer 15.00 40.00
RD C.Roberson/L.Dykstra 15.00 40.00
TP S.Thompson/G.Perry 10.00 25.00
VM J.Verlander/D.McLain 50.00 100.00

2009 Upper Deck Update

COMMON CARD (1-50) .15 .40
COMMON ROOKIE (1-50) .60 1.50
INSERTED IN COMBO FAT BACKS
U1 Barack Obama .50 1.25
U2 Garret Anderson .15 .40
U3 Nate McLouth .15 .40
U4 Wilkin Ramirez RC .60 1.50
U5 Kyle Blanks RC 1.00 2.50
U6 Aaron Poreda RC .60 1.50
U7 Bartolo Colon .15 .40
U8 Lou Marson (RC) .60 1.50
U9 Julio Borbon RC .60 1.50
U10 Pedro Martinez .25 .60
U11 Ivan Rodriguez .25 .60
U12 Gerardo Parra RC 1.00 2.50
U13 Brad Ausmus .15 .40
U14 Brad Mills RC .60 1.50
U15 Gary Sheffield .15 .40
U16 Nomar Garciaparra .25 .60
U17 Miguel Cairo .15 .40
U18 Sean O'Sullivan RC .60 1.50
U19 Eric Hinske .15 .40
U20 Sean West (RC) 1.00 2.50
U21 Mat Latos RC 2.00 5.00
U22 Daniel Bard RC .60 1.50
U23 David Huff RC .60 1.50
U24 Tony Gwynn Jr. .15 .40
U25 Vin Mazzaro RC .60 1.50
U26 Russell Branyan .15 .40
U27 Gabe Kapler .15 .40
U28 Andruw Jones .15 .40
U29 Marc Rzepczynski RC 1.00 2.50
U30 Jhoulys Chacin RC 1.00 2.50
U31 Daniel Schlereth RC .60 1.50
U32 Tommy Hanson RC 1.50 4.00
U33 Brad Bergesen (RC) .60 1.50
U34 Nolan Reimold (RC) .60 1.50
U35 Matt Wieters RC 10.00 25.00
U36 Gordon Beckham RC 1.00 2.50
U37 Matt LaPorta RC 1.00 2.50
U38 Anthony Swarzak (RC) .60 1.50
U39 Fu-Te Ni RC 1.00 2.50
U40 Fernando Martinez RC 1.50 4.00
U41 Francisco Cervelli RC 1.50 4.00
U42 Ramiro Pena RC 1.00 2.50
U43 Mark Melancon RC .60 1.50
U44 Andrew Bailey RC 1.50 4.00
U45 Drew Carpenter RC 1.00 2.50
U46 Antonio Bastardo RC .60 1.50
U47 Andrew McCutchen (RC) 3.00 8.00
U48 Derek Holland RC 1.00 2.50
U49 Brett Cecil RC .60 1.50
U50 Jordan Zimmermann RC 1.50 4.00

2009 Upper Deck Update Gold

*GOLD VET: 12X TO 30X BASIC VET
*GOLD RC: 3X TO 8X BASIC RC
INSERTED IN COMBO FAT PACKS
STATED PRINT RUN 99 SER.#'d SETS

2009 Upper Deck Update Generation Now

INSERTED IN COMBO FAT PACKS
*GOLD: 3X TO 8X BASIC
GOLD FOUND IN COMBO FAT PACKS
GOLD PRINT RUN 99 SER.#'d SETS
GN1 A.J. Burnett .40 1.00
GN2 Adam Dunn .60 1.50
GN3 Adrian Gonzalez .75 2.00
GN4 Albert Pujols 1.25 3.00
GN5 Alex Rodriguez 1.25 3.00
GN6 Alfonso Soriano .60 1.50
GN7 Aramis Ramirez .40 1.00
GN8 B.J. Upton .60 1.50
GN9 Brian McCann .60 1.50
GN10 Carlos Beltran .60 1.50
GN11 Carlos Quentin .40 1.00
GN12 CC Sabathia .60 1.50
GN13 Chase Utley .60 1.50
GN14 Chipper Jones 1.00 2.50
GN15 Chris Iannetta .40 1.00
GN16 Cole Hamels .75 2.00
GN17 David Wright .75 2.00
GN18 Derek Jeter 2.50 6.00
GN19 Dustin Pedroia 1.00 2.50
GN20 Evan Longoria .60 1.50
GN21 Grady Sizemore .60 1.50
GN22 Hanley Ramirez .60 1.50
GN23 Hunter Pence .60 1.50
GN24 Ian Kinsler .60 1.50
GN25 Jay Bruce .60 1.50
GN26 Jimmy Rollins .60 1.50
GN27 Joba Chamberlain .40 1.00
GN28 Joe Mauer .75 2.00
GN29 Joey Votto 1.00 2.50
GN30 Johan Santana .60 1.50
GN31 Jon Lester .60 1.50
GN32 Jose Reyes .60 1.50
GN33 Josh Beckett .40 1.00
GN34 Josh Hamilton .60 1.50
GN35 Justin Upton .60 1.50
GN36 Ken Griffey Jr. 2.00 5.00
GN37 Lance Berkman .60 1.50
GN38 Manny Ramirez 1.00 2.50
GN39 Mark Teixeira .60 1.50
GN40 Matt Holliday 1.00 2.50
GN41 Miguel Cabrera 1.00 2.50
GN42 Nick Markakis .75 2.00
GN43 Prince Fielder .60 1.50
GN44 Russell Martin .40 1.00
GN45 Ryan Braun .60 1.50
GN46 Ryan Howard .75 2.00
GN47 Ryan Zimmerman .60 1.50
GN48 Stephen Drew .40 1.00
GN49 Tim Lincecum .60 1.50
GN50 Zack Greinke 1.00 2.50

1996 Upper Deck U.S. Olympic

This multisport product was issued in June 1996, prior to the Centennial Olympic Games in Atlanta. Packs of 10 standard-size cards had a suggested retail price of $1.99. The set contains the following subsets: U.S. Olympic Moments (1-90), Future Champions (91-120) and Passing the Torch (121-135).

COMPLETE SET (135) 8.00 20.00
51 Will Clark .25 .60
52 Jim Abbott .10 .25

1999 Upper Deck Victory

This 470 standard-size set was issued in 12 card packs with 39 packs per box and 12 boxes per case. The SRP on these packs was only 99 cents and no insert cards were made for this product. The Subsets include 50 cards featuring 1999 rookies, 20 Rookie Flashback cards (451-470), 15 Power Trip cards, 10 History in the Making cards, 30 Team Checklist cards and 30 Mark McGwire Magic cards (421-450). Unless noted the subset cards are interspersed throughout the set. Also, through an internet-oriented contest, 10 autographed Ken Griffey Jr. jerseys were available through a contest which was entered through the Upper Deck website.

COMPLETE SET (470) 30.00 80.00
COMMON CARD (1-470) .07 .20
COMMON MCGWIRE (421-450) .30 .75
ONE MCGWIRE 421-450 PER PACK
SUBSET CARDS HALF VALUE OF BASE CARDS
1 Anaheim Angels TC .07 .20
2 Mark Harriger RC .07 .20
3 Mo Vaughn PT .07 .20
4 Darin Erstad BP .07 .20
5 Troy Glaus .10 .30
6 Tim Salmon .10 .30
7 Mo Vaughn .07 .20
8 Darin Erstad .07 .20
9 Garret Anderson .07 .20
10 Todd Greene .07 .20
11 Troy Percival .07 .20
12 Chuck Finley .07 .20
13 Jason Dickson .07 .20
14 Jim Edmonds .07 .20
15 Arizona Diamondbacks TC .07 .20
16 Randy Johnson .20 .50
17 Matt Williams .07 .20
18 Travis Lee .07 .20
19 Jay Bell .07 .20
20 Tony Womack .07 .20
21 Steve Finley .07 .20
22 Bernard Gilkey .07 .20
23 Tony Batista .07 .20
24 Todd Stottlemyre .07 .20
25 Omar Daal .07 .20
26 Atlanta Braves TC .07 .20
27 Bruce Chen .07 .20
28 George Lombard .07 .20
29 Chipper Jones PT .10 .30
30 Chipper Jones BP .10 .30
31 Greg Maddux .30 .75
32 Chipper Jones .20 .50
33 Javy Lopez .07 .20
34 Tom Glavine .10 .30
35 John Smoltz .10 .30
36 Andruw Jones .10 .30
37 Brian Jordan .07 .20
38 Walt Weiss .07 .20
39 Bret Boone .07 .20
40 Andres Galarraga .07 .20
41 Baltimore Orioles TC .07 .20
42 Ryan Minor .07 .20
43 Jerry Hairston Jr. .07 .20
44 Calvin Pickering .07 .20
45 Cal Ripken HM .30 .75
46 Cal Ripken .60 1.50
47 Charles Johnson .07 .20
48 Albert Belle .07 .20
49 Delino DeShields .07 .20
50 Mike Mussina .10 .30
51 Scott Erickson .07 .20
52 Brady Anderson .07 .20
53 B.J. Surhoff .07 .20
54 Harold Baines .07 .20
55 Will Clark .10 .30
56 Boston Red Sox TC .07 .20
57 Shea Hillenbrand RC .30 .75
58 Trot Nixon .07 .20
59 Jin Ho Cho .07 .20
60 Nomar Garciaparra PT .20 .50
61 Nomar Garciaparra BP .20 .50
62 Pedro Martinez .10 .30
63 Nomar Garciaparra .30 .75
64 Jose Offerman .07 .20
65 Jason Varitek .20 .50
66 Darren Lewis .07 .20
67 Troy O'Leary .07 .20
68 Donnie Sadler .07 .20
69 John Valentin .07 .20
70 Tim Wakefield .07 .20
71 Bret Saberhagen .07 .20
72 Chicago Cubs TC .07 .20
73 Kyle Farnsworth RC .10 .30
74 Sammy Sosa PT .10 .30
75 Sammy Sosa BP .10 .30
76 Sammy Sosa HM .10 .30
77 Kerry Wood HM .07 .20
78 Sammy Sosa .20 .50
79 Mark Grace .10 .30
80 Kerry Wood .07 .20
81 Kevin Tapani .07 .20
82 Benito Santiago .07 .20
83 Gary Gaetti .07 .20
84 Mickey Morandini .07 .20
85 Glenallen Hill .07 .20
86 Henry Rodriguez .07 .20
87 Rod Beck .07 .20
88 Chicago White Sox TC .07 .20
89 Carlos Lee .07 .20
90 Mark Johnson .07 .20
91 Frank Thomas PT .10 .30
92 Frank Thomas .20 .50
93 Jim Parque .07 .20
94 Mike Sirotka .07 .20
95 Mike Caruso .07 .20
96 Ray Durham .07 .20
97 Magglio Ordonez .07 .20
98 Paul Konerko .07 .20
99 Bob Howry .07 .20
100 Brian Simmons .07 .20
101 Jaime Navarro .07 .20
102 Cincinnati Reds TC .07 .20
103 Denny Neagle .07 .20
104 Pete Harnisch .07 .20
105 Greg Vaughn .07 .20
106 Brett Tomko .07 .20
107 Mike Cameron .07 .20
108 Sean Casey .07 .20
109 Aaron Boone .07 .20
110 Michael Tucker .07 .20
111 Dmitri Young .07 .20
112 Barry Larkin .10 .30
113 Cleveland Indians TC .07 .20
114 Russ Branyan .07 .20
115 Jim Thome PT .07 .20
116 Manny Ramirez PT .07 .20
117 Manny Ramirez .10 .30
118 Jim Thome .10 .30
119 David Justice .07 .20
120 Sandy Alomar Jr. .07 .20
121 Roberto Alomar .10 .30
122 Jaret Wright .07 .20
123 Bartolo Colon .07 .20
124 Travis Fryman .07 .20
125 Kenny Lofton .07 .20
126 Omar Vizquel .10 .30
127 Colorado Rockies TC .07 .20
128 Derrick Gibson .07 .20
129 Larry Walker BP .07 .20
130 Larry Walker .07 .20
131 Dante Bichette .07 .20
132 Todd Helton .10 .30
133 Neifi Perez .07 .20
134 Vinny Castilla .07 .20
135 Darryl Kile .07 .20
136 Pedro Astacio .07 .20
137 Darryl Hamilton .07 .20
138 Mike Lansing .07 .20
139 Kirt Manwaring .07 .20
140 Detroit Tigers TC .07 .20
141 Jeff Weaver RC .20 .50
142 Gabe Kapler .07 .20
143 Tony Clark PT .07 .20
144 Tony Clark .07 .20
145 Juan Encarnacion .07 .20
146 Dean Palmer .07 .20
147 Damion Easley .07 .20
148 Bobby Higginson .07 .20
149 Karim Garcia .07 .20
150 Justin Thompson .07 .20
151 Matt Anderson .07 .20
152 Willie Blair .07 .20
153 Brian Hunter .07 .20
154 Florida Marlins TC .07 .20
155 Alex Gonzalez .07 .20
156 Mark Kotsay .07 .20
157 Livan Hernandez .07 .20
158 Cliff Floyd .07 .20
159 Todd Dunwoody .07 .20
160 Alex Fernandez .07 .20
161 Matt Mantei .07 .20
162 Derrek Lee .10 .30
163 Kevin Orie .07 .20
164 Craig Counsell .07 .20
165 Rafael Medina .07 .20
166 Houston Astros TC .07 .20
167 Daryle Ward .07 .20
168 Mitch Meluskey .07 .20
169 Jeff Bagwell PT .07 .20
170 Jeff Bagwell .10 .30
171 Ken Caminiti .07 .20
172 Craig Biggio .10 .30
173 Derek Bell .07 .20
174 Moises Alou .07 .20
175 Billy Wagner .07 .20
176 Shane Reynolds .07 .20
177 Carl Everett .07 .20
178 Scott Elarton .07 .20
179 Richard Hidalgo .07 .20
180 Kansas City Royals TC .07 .20
181 Carlos Beltran .10 .30
182 Carlos Febles .07 .20
183 Jeremy Giambi .07 .20
184 Johnny Damon .10 .30
185 Joe Randa .07 .20
186 Jeff King .07 .20
187 Hipolito Pichardo .07 .20
188 Kevin Appier .07 .20
189 Chad Kreuter .07 .20
190 Rey Sanchez .07 .20
191 Larry Sutton .07 .20
192 Jeff Montgomery .07 .20
193 Jermaine Dye .07 .20
194 Los Angeles Dodgers TC .07 .20
195 Adam Riggs .07 .20
196 Angel Pena .07 .20
197 Todd Hundley .07 .20
198 Kevin Brown .10 .30
199 Ismael Valdes .07 .20
200 Chan Ho Park .07 .20
201 Adrian Beltre .07 .20
202 Mark Grudzielanek .07 .20
203 Raul Mondesi .07 .20
204 Gary Sheffield .07 .20
205 Eric Karros .07 .20
206 Devon White .07 .20
207 Milwaukee Brewers TC .07 .20
208 Ron Belliard .07 .20
209 Rafael Roque RC .07 .20
210 Jeromy Burnitz .07 .20
211 Fernando Vina .07 .20
212 Scott Karl .07 .20
213 Jim Abbott .10 .30
214 Sean Berry .07 .20
215 Marquis Grissom .07 .20
216 Geoff Jenkins .07 .20
217 Jeff Cirillo .07 .20
218 Dave Nilsson .07 .20
219 Jose Valentin .07 .20
220 Minnesota Twins TC .07 .20
221 Corey Koskie .07 .20
222 Cristian Guzman .07 .20
223 A.J. Pierzynski .07 .20
224 David Ortiz .20 .50
225 Brad Radke .07 .20
226 Todd Walker .07 .20
227 Matt Lawton .07 .20
228 Rick Aguilera .07 .20
229 Eric Milton .07 .20
230 Marty Cordova .07 .20
231 Torii Hunter .07 .20
232 Ron Coomer .07 .20
233 LaTroy Hawkins .07 .20
234 Montreal Expos TC .07 .20
235 Fernando Seguignol .07 .20
236 Michael Barrett .07 .20
237 Vladimir Guerrero BP .10 .30
238 Vladimir Guerrero .20 .50
239 Brad Fullmer .07 .20
240 Rondell White .07 .20
241 Ugueth Urbina .07 .20
242 Dustin Hermanson .07 .20
243 Orlando Cabrera .07 .20
244 Wilton Guerrero .07 .20
245 Carl Pavano .07 .20
246 Javier Vazquez .07 .20
247 Chris Widger .07 .20
248 New York Mets TC .07 .20
249 Mike Kinkade .07 .20
250 Octavio Dotel .07 .20
251 Mike Piazza PT .20 .50
252 Mike Piazza .30 .75
253 Rickey Henderson .20 .50
254 Edgardo Alfonzo .07 .20
255 Robin Ventura .07 .20
256 Al Leiter .07 .20
257 Brian McRae .07 .20
258 Rey Ordonez .07 .20
259 Bobby Bonilla .07 .20
260 Orel Hershiser .07 .20
261 John Olerud .07 .20
262 New York Yankees TC .07 .20
263 Ricky Ledee .07 .20
264 Bernie Williams BP .07 .20
265 Derek Jeter BP .25 .60
266 Scott Brosius HM .07 .20
267 Derek Jeter .50 1.25
268 Roger Clemens .40 1.00
269 Orlando Hernandez .07 .20
270 Scott Brosius .07 .20
271 Paul O'Neill .10 .30
272 Bernie Williams .10 .30
273 Chuck Knoblauch .07 .20
274 Tino Martinez .10 .30
275 Mariano Rivera .20 .50
276 Jorge Posada .10 .30
277 Oakland Athletics TC .07 .20
278 Eric Chavez .07 .20
279 Ben Grieve HM .07 .20
280 Jason Giambi .07 .20
281 John Jaha .07 .20
282 Miguel Tejada .07 .20
283 Ben Grieve .07 .20
284 Matt Stairs .07 .20
285 Ryan Christenson .07 .20
286 A.J. Hinch .07 .20
287 Kenny Rogers .07 .20
288 Tom Candiotti .07 .20
289 Scott Spiezio .07 .20
290 Philadelphia Phillies TC .07 .20
291 Pat Burrell RC .60 1.50
292 Marlon Anderson .07 .20
293 Scott Rolen BP .07 .20
294 Scott Rolen .10 .30
295 Doug Glanville .07 .20
296 Rico Brogna .07 .20
297 Ron Gant .07 .20
298 Bobby Abreu .07 .20
299 Desi Relaford .07 .20
300 Curt Schilling .07 .20
301 Chad Ogea .07 .20
302 Kevin Jordan .07 .20
303 Carlton Loewer .07 .20
304 Pittsburgh Pirates TC .07 .20
305 Kris Benson .07 .20
306 Brian Giles .07 .20
307 Jason Kendall .07 .20
308 Jose Guillen .07 .20
309 Pat Meares .07 .20
310 Brant Brown .07 .20
311 Kevin Young .07 .20
312 Ed Sprague .07 .20
313 Francisco Cordova .07 .20
314 Aramis Ramirez .07 .20
315 Freddy Adrian Garcia .07 .20
316 St. Louis Cardinals TC .07 .20
317 J.D. Drew .07 .20
318 Chad Hutchinson RC .10 .30
319 Mark McGwire PT .25 .60
320 J.D. Drew PT .07 .20
321 Mark McGwire BP .25 .60
322 Mark McGwire HM .25 .60
323 Mark McGwire .50 1.25
324 Fernando Tatis .07 .20
325 Edgar Renteria .07 .20
326 Ray Lankford .07 .20
327 Willie McGee .07 .20
328 Ricky Bottalico .07 .20
329 Eli Marrero .07 .20
330 Matt Morris .07 .20
331 Eric Davis .07 .20
332 Darren Bragg .07 .20
333 San Diego Padres TC .07 .20
334 Matt Clement .07 .20
335 Ben Davis .07 .20
336 Gary Matthews Jr. .07 .20
337 Tony Gwynn BP .10 .30
338 Tony Gwynn HM .10 .30
339 Tony Gwynn .25 .60
340 Reggie Sanders .07 .20
341 Ruben Rivera .07 .20
342 Wally Joyner .07 .20
343 Sterling Hitchcock .07 .20
344 Carlos Hernandez .07 .20
345 Andy Ashby .07 .20
346 Trevor Hoffman .07 .20
347 Chris Gomez .07 .20
348 Jim Leyritz .07 .20
349 San Francisco Giants TC .07 .20
350 Armando Rios .07 .20
351 Barry Bonds PT .30 .75
352 Barry Bonds BP .30 .75
353 Barry Bonds HM .30 .75
354 Robb Nen .07 .20
355 Bill Mueller .07 .20
356 Barry Bonds .60 1.50
357 Jeff Kent .07 .20
358 J.T. Snow .07 .20
359 Ellis Burks .07 .20
360 F.P. Santangelo .07 .20
361 Marvin Benard .07 .20
362 Stan Javier .07 .20
363 Shawn Estes .07 .20
364 Seattle Mariners TC .07 .20
365 Carlos Guillen .07 .20
366 Ken Griffey Jr. PT .25 .60
367 Alex Rodriguez PT .20 .50
368 Ken Griffey Jr. BP .25 .60
369 Alex Rodriguez BP .20 .50
370 Ken Griffey Jr. HM .25 .60
371 Alex Rodriguez HM .20 .50
372 Ken Griffey Jr. .40 1.00
373 Alex Rodriguez .30 .75
374 Jay Buhner .07 .20
375 Edgar Martinez .10 .30
376 Jeff Fassero .07 .20
377 David Bell .07 .20
378 David Segui .07 .20
379 Russ Davis .07 .20
380 Dan Wilson .07 .20
381 Jamie Moyer .07 .20
382 Tampa Bay Devil Rays TC .07 .20
383 Roberto Hernandez .07 .20
384 Bobby Smith .07 .20
385 Wade Boggs .10 .30
386 Fred McGriff .10 .30
387 Rolando Arrojo .07 .20
388 Jose Canseco .10 .30
389 Wilson Alvarez .07 .20
390 Kevin Stocker .07 .20
391 Miguel Cairo .07 .20
392 Quinton McCracken .07 .20
393 Texas Rangers TC .07 .20
394 Ruben Mateo .07 .20
395 Cesar King .07 .20
396 Juan Gonzalez PT .07 .20
397 Juan Gonzalez BP .07 .20
398 Ivan Rodriguez .10 .30
399 Juan Gonzalez .07 .20
400 Rafael Palmeiro .10 .30
401 Rick Helling .07 .20
402 Aaron Sele .07 .20
403 John Wetteland .07 .20
404 Rusty Greer .07 .20
405 Todd Zeile .07 .20
406 Royce Clayton .07 .20
407 Tom Goodwin .07 .20
408 Toronto Blue Jays TC .07 .20
409 Kevin Witt .07 .20
410 Roy Halladay 3.00 8.00
411 Jose Cruz Jr. .07 .20
412 Carlos Delgado .07 .20
413 Willie Greene .07 .20
414 Shawn Green .07 .20
415 Homer Bush .07 .20
416 Shannon Stewart .07 .20
417 David Wells .07 .20
418 Kelvim Escobar .07 .20
419 Joey Hamilton .07 .20
420 Alex Gonzalez .07 .20
421 Mark McGwire MM .30 .75
422 Mark McGwire MM .30 .75
423 Mark McGwire MM .30 .75
424 Mark McGwire MM .30 .75
425 Mark McGwire MM .30 .75
426 Mark McGwire MM .30 .75
427 Mark McGwire MM .30 .75
428 Mark McGwire MM .30 .75
429 Mark McGwire MM .30 .75
430 Mark McGwire MM .30 .75
431 Mark McGwire MM .30 .75
432 Mark McGwire MM .30 .75
433 Mark McGwire MM .30 .75
434 Mark McGwire MM .30 .75
435 Mark McGwire MM .30 .75
436 Mark McGwire MM .30 .75
437 Mark McGwire MM .30 .75
438 Mark McGwire MM .30 .75
439 Mark McGwire MM .30 .75
440 Mark McGwire MM .30 .75
441 Mark McGwire MM .30 .75
442 Mark McGwire MM .30 .75
443 Mark McGwire MM .30 .75
444 Mark McGwire MM .30 .75
445 Mark McGwire MM .30 .75
446 Mark McGwire MM .30 .75
447 Mark McGwire MM .30 .75
448 Mark McGwire MM .30 .75
449 Mark McGwire MM .30 .75
450 Mark McGwire MM .30 .75
451 Chipper Jones RF .10 .30
452 Cal Ripken RF .30 .75
453 Roger Clemens RF .20 .50
454 Wade Boggs RF .07 .20
455 Greg Maddux RF .20 .50
456 Frank Thomas RF .10 .30
457 Jeff Bagwell RF .07 .20
458 Mike Piazza RF .20 .50
459 Randy Johnson RF .10 .30
460 Mo Vaughn RF .07 .20
461 Mark McGwire RF .25 .60
462 Rickey Henderson RF .10 .30
463 Barry Bonds RF .30 .75
464 Tony Gwynn RF .10 .30
465 Ken Griffey Jr. RF .25 .60
466 Alex Rodriguez RF .20 .50
467 Sammy Sosa RF .10 .30
468 Juan Gonzalez RF .07 .20
469 Kevin Brown RF .07 .20
470 Fred McGriff RF .07 .20

2000 Upper Deck Victory

COMPLETE SET (440) 6.00 15.00
COMP.FACT.SET (466) 12.50 30.00
COMMON CARD (1-390) .07 .20
COMMON GRIFFEY (391-440) .30 .75
COMMON USA (441-466) .12 .30
441-466 AVAIL.ONLY IN FACTORY SETS
1 Mo Vaughn .07 .20
2 Garret Anderson .07 .20
3 Tim Salmon .07 .20
4 Troy Percival .07 .20
5 Orlando Palmeiro .07 .20
6 Darin Erstad .07 .20
7 Ramon Ortiz .07 .20
8 Ben Molina .07 .20
9 Troy Glaus .07 .20
10 Jim Edmonds .07 .20
11 M.Vaughn .07 .20
T.Percival CL
12 Craig Biggio .12 .30
13 Roger Cedeno .07 .20
14 Shane Reynolds .07 .20
15 Jeff Bagwell .12 .30
16 Octavio Dotel .07 .20
17 Moises Alou .07 .20
18 Jose Lima .07 .20
19 Ken Caminiti .07 .20
20 Richard Hidalgo .07 .20
21 Billy Wagner .07 .20
22 Lance Berkman .12 .30
23 J.Bagwell .12 .30
J.Lima CL
24 Jason Giambi .07 .20
25 Randy Velarde .07 .20
26 Miguel Tejada .12 .30
27 Matt Stairs .07 .20
28 A.J. Hinch .07 .20
29 Olmedo Saenz .07 .20
30 Ben Grieve .07 .20
31 Ryan Christenson .07 .20
32 Eric Chavez .07 .20
33 Tim Hudson .12 .30
34 John Jaha .07 .20
35 J.Giambi .07 .20
M.Stairs CL
36 Raul Mondesi .07 .20
37 Tony Batista .07 .20
38 David Wells .07 .20
39 Homer Bush .07 .20
40 Carlos Delgado .07 .20
41 Billy Koch .07 .20
42 Darrin Fletcher .07 .20
43 Tony Fernandez .07 .20
44 Shannon Stewart .07 .20
45 Roy Halladay .12 .30
46 Chris Carpenter .12 .30
47 C.Delgado .07 .20
D.Wells CL
48 Chipper Jones .20 .50
49 Greg Maddux .25 .60
50 Andruw Jones .07 .20
51 Andres Galarraga .12 .30
52 Tom Glavine .12 .30
53 Brian Jordan .07 .20
54 John Smoltz .20 .50
55 John Rocker .07 .20
56 Javy Lopez .07 .20
57 Eddie Perez .07 .20
58 Kevin Millwood .07 .20
59 C.Jones .25 .60
G.Maddux CL
60 Jeromy Burnitz .07 .20
61 Steve Woodard .07 .20
62 Ron Belliard .07 .20
63 Geoff Jenkins .07 .20
64 Bob Wickman .07 .20
65 Marquis Grissom .07 .20
66 Henry Blanco .07 .20
67 Mark Loretta .07 .20
68 Alex Ochoa .07 .20
69 M.Grissom .07 .20
J.Burnitz CL
70 Mark McGwire .30 .75
71 Edgar Renteria .07 .20
72 Dave Veres .07 .20
73 Eli Marrero .07 .20
74 Fernando Tatis .07 .20
75 J.D. Drew .07 .20
76 Ray Lankford .07 .20
77 Darryl Kile .07 .20
78 Kent Bottenfield .07 .20
79 Joe McEwing .07 .20
80 M.McGwire .30 .75
R.Lankford CL
81 Sammy Sosa .20 .50
82 Jose Nieves .07 .20
83 Jon Lieber .07 .20
84 Henry Rodriguez .07 .20
85 Mark Grace .12 .30
86 Eric Young .07 .20
87 Kerry Wood .07 .20

88 Ismael Valdes .07 .20
89 Glenallen Hill .07 .20
90 S.Sosa .20 .50
M.Grace CL
91 Greg Vaughn .07 .20
92 Fred McGriff .12 .30
93 Ryan Rupe .07 .20
94 Bubba Trammell .07 .20
95 Miguel Cairo .07 .20
96 Roberto Hernandez .07 .20
97 Jose Canseco .12 .30
98 Wilson Alvarez .07 .20
99 John Flaherty .07 .20
100 Vinny Castilla .07 .20
101 J.Canseco .12 .30
R.Hernandez CL
102 Randy Johnson .20 .50
103 Matt Williams .07 .20
104 Matt Mantei .07 .20
105 Steve Finley .07 .20
106 Luis Gonzalez .07 .20
107 Travis Lee .07 .20
108 Omar Daal .07 .20
109 Jay Bell .07 .20
110 Erubiel Durazo .07 .20
111 Tony Womack .07 .20
112 Todd Stottlemyre .07 .20
113 R.Johnson .20 .50
M.Williams CL
114 Gary Sheffield .07 .20
115 Adrian Beltre .20 .50
116 Kevin Brown .07 .20
117 Todd Hundley .07 .20
118 Eric Karros .07 .20
119 Shawn Green .07 .20
120 Chan Ho Park .12 .30
121 Mark Grudzielanek .07 .20
122 Todd Hollandsworth .07 .20
123 Jeff Shaw .07 .20
124 Darren Dreifort .07 .20
125 G.Sheffield .07 .20
K.Brown CL
126 Vladimir Guerrero .12 .30
127 Michael Barrett .07 .20
128 Dustin Hermanson .07 .20
129 Jose Vidro .07 .20
130 Chris Widger .07 .20
131 Mike Thurman .07 .20
132 Wilton Guerrero .07 .20
133 Brad Fullmer .07 .20
134 Rondell White .07 .20
135 Ugueth Urbina .07 .20
136 V.Guerrero .12 .30
R.White CL
137 Barry Bonds .30 .75
138 Russ Ortiz .07 .20
139 J.T. Snow .07 .20
140 Joe Nathan .07 .20
141 Rich Aurilia .07 .20
142 Jeff Kent .07 .20
143 Armando Rios .07 .20
144 Ellis Burks .07 .20
145 Robb Nen .07 .20
146 Marvin Benard .07 .20
147 B.Bonds .30 .75
R.Ortiz CL
148 Manny Ramirez .20 .50
149 Bartolo Colon .07 .20
150 Kenny Lofton .07 .20
151 Sandy Alomar Jr. .07 .20
152 Travis Fryman .07 .20
153 Omar Vizquel .12 .30
154 Roberto Alomar .12 .30
155 Richie Sexson .07 .20
156 David Justice .07 .20
157 Jim Thome .12 .30
158 M.Ramirez .20 .50
R.Alomar CL
159 Ken Griffey Jr. .40 1.00
160 Edgar Martinez .12 .30
161 Freddy Garcia .07 .20
162 Alex Rodriguez .25 .60
163 John Halama .07 .20
164 Russ Davis .07 .20
165 David Bell .07 .20
166 Gil Meche .07 .20
167 Jamie Moyer .07 .20
168 John Olerud .07 .20
169 K.Griffey Jr. .40 1.00
F.Garcia CL
170 Preston Wilson .07 .20
171 Antonio Alfonseca .07 .20
172 A.J. Burnett .07 .20
173 Luis Castillo .07 .20
174 Mike Lowell .07 .20
175 Alex Fernandez .07 .20
176 Mike Redmond .07 .20
177 Alex Gonzalez .07 .20
178 Vladimir Nunez .07 .20
179 Mark Kotsay .07 .20
180 P.Wilson .07 .20
L.Castillo CL
181 Mike Piazza .20 .50
182 Darryl Hamilton .07 .20
183 Al Leiter .07 .20
184 Robin Ventura .07 .20
185 Rickey Henderson .20 .50
186 Rey Ordonez .07 .20
187 Edgardo Alfonzo .07 .20
188 Derek Bell .07 .20
189 Mike Hampton .07 .20
190 Armando Benitez .07 .20
191 M.Piazza .20 .50
R.Henderson CL
192 Cal Ripken .60 1.50
193 B.J. Surhoff .07 .20
194 Mike Mussina .12 .30
195 Albert Belle .07 .20
196 Jerry Hairston Jr. .07 .20
197 Will Clark .12 .30
198 Sidney Ponson .07 .20
199 Brady Anderson .07 .20
200 Scott Erickson .07 .20
201 Ryan Minor .07 .20
202 C.Ripken .60 1.50
A.Belle CL
203 Tony Gwynn .20 .50
204 Bret Boone .07 .20
205 Ryan Klesko .07 .20
206 Ben Davis .07 .20
207 Matt Clement .07 .20
208 Eric Owens .07 .20
209 Trevor Hoffman .12 .30
210 Sterling Hitchcock .07 .20
211 Phil Nevin .07 .20
212 T.Gwynn .20 .50
T.Hoffman CL
213 Scott Rolen .12 .30
214 Bob Abreu .07 .20
215 Curt Schilling .12 .30
216 Rico Brogna .07 .20
217 Robert Person .07 .20
218 Doug Glanville .07 .20
219 Mike Lieberthal .07 .20
220 Andy Ashby .07 .20
221 Randy Wolf .07 .20
222 B.Abreu .12 .30
C.Schilling CL
223 Brian Giles .07 .20
224 Jason Kendall .07 .20
225 Kris Benson .07 .20
226 Warren Morris .07 .20
227 Kevin Young .07 .20
228 Al Martin .07 .20
229 Wil Cordero .07 .20
230 Bruce Aven .07 .20
231 Todd Ritchie .07 .20
232 J.Kendall .07 .20
B.Giles CL
233 Ivan Rodriguez .12 .30
234 Rusty Greer .07 .20
235 Ruben Mateo .07 .20
236 Justin Thompson .07 .20
237 Rafael Palmeiro .12 .30
238 Chad Curtis .07 .20
239 Royce Clayton .07 .20
240 Gabe Kapler .07 .20
241 Jeff Zimmerman .07 .20
242 John Wetteland .07 .20
243 I.Rodriguez .12 .30
R.Palmeiro CL
244 Nomar Garciaparra .12 .30
245 Pedro Martinez .12 .30
246 Jose Offerman .07 .20
247 Jason Varitek .20 .50
248 Troy O'Leary .07 .20
249 John Valentin .07 .20
250 Trot Nixon .07 .20
251 Carl Everett .07 .20
252 Wilton Veras .07 .20
253 Bret Saberhagen .07 .20
254 N.Garciaparra .12 .30
P.Martinez CL
255 Sean Casey .07 .20
256 Barry Larkin .12 .30
257 Pokey Reese .07 .20
258 Pete Harnisch .07 .20
259 Aaron Boone .07 .20
260 Dante Bichette .07 .20
261 Scott Williamson .07 .20
262 Steve Parris .07 .20
263 Dmitri Young .07 .20
264 Mike Cameron .07 .20
265 S.Casey .07 .20
S.Williamson CL
266 Larry Walker .12 .30
267 Rolando Arrojo .07 .20
268 Pedro Astacio .07 .20
269 Todd Helton .12 .30
270 Jeff Cirillo .07 .20
271 Neifi Perez .07 .20
272 Brian Bohanon .07 .20
273 Jeffrey Hammonds .07 .20
274 Tom Goodwin .07 .20
275 L.Walker .12 .30
T.Helton CL
276 Carlos Beltran .12 .30
277 Jermaine Dye .07 .20
278 Mike Sweeney .07 .20
279 Joe Randa .07 .20
280 Jose Rosado .07 .20
281 Carlos Febles .07 .20
282 Jeff Suppan .07 .20
283 Johnny Damon .12 .30
284 Jeremy Giambi .07 .20
285 M.Sweeney .12 .30
C.Beltran CL
286 Tony Clark .07 .20
287 Damion Easley .07 .20
288 Jeff Weaver .07 .20
289 Dean Palmer .07 .20
290 Juan Gonzalez .07 .20
291 Juan Encarnacion .07 .20
292 Todd Jones .07 .20
293 Karim Garcia .07 .20
294 Deivi Cruz .07 .20
295 D.Palmer .07 .20
J.Encarnacion CL
296 Corey Koskie .07 .20
297 Brad Radke .07 .20
298 Doug Mientkiewicz .07 .20
299 Ron Coomer .07 .20
300 Joe Mays .07 .20
301 Eric Milton .07 .20
302 Jacque Jones .07 .20
303 Chad Allen .07 .20
304 Cristian Guzman .07 .20
305 Jason Ryan .07 .20
306 Todd Walker .07 .20
307 C.Koskie .07 .20
E.Milton CL
308 Frank Thomas .20 .50
309 Paul Konerko .07 .20
310 Mike Sirotka .07 .20
311 Jim Parque .07 .20
312 Magglio Ordonez .12 .30
313 Bob Howry .07 .20
314 Carlos Lee .07 .20
315 Ray Durham .07 .20
316 Chris Singleton .07 .20
317 Brook Fordyce .07 .20
318 F.Thomas .20 .50
M.Ordonez CL
319 Derek Jeter .50 1.25
320 Roger Clemens .25 .60
321 Paul O'Neill .07 .20
322 Bernie Williams .12 .30
323 Mariano Rivera .25 .60
324 Tino Martinez .07 .20
325 David Cone .07 .20
326 Chuck Knoblauch .07 .20
327 Darryl Strawberry .07 .20
328 Orlando Hernandez .07 .20
329 Ricky Ledee .07 .20
330 D.Jeter .50 1.25
B.Williams CL
331 Pat Burrell .07 .20
332 Alfonso Soriano .20 .50
333 Josh Beckett .15 .40
334 Matt Riley .07 .20
335 Brian Cooper .07 .20
336 Eric Munson .07 .20
337 Vernon Wells .07 .20
338 Juan Pena .07 .20
339 Mark DeRosa .07 .20
340 Kip Wells .07 .20
341 Roosevelt Brown .07 .20
342 Jason LaRue .07 .20
343 Ben Petrick .07 .20
344 Mark Quinn .07 .20
345 Julio Ramirez .07 .20
346 Rod Barajas .07 .20
347 Robert Fick .07 .20
348 David Newhan .07 .20
349 Eric Gagne .07 .20
350 Jorge Toca .07 .20
351 Mitch Meluskey .07 .20
352 Ed Yarnall .07 .20
353 Chad Hermansen .07 .20
354 Peter Bergeron .07 .20
355 Dernal Brown .07 .20
356 Adam Kennedy .07 .20
357 Kevin Barker .07 .20
358 Francisco Cordero .07 .20
359 Travis Dawkins .07 .20
360 Jeff Williams RC .07 .20
361 Chad Hutchinson .07 .20
362 D'Angelo Jimenez .07 .20
363 Derrick Gibson .07 .20
364 Calvin Murray .07 .20
365 Doug Davis .07 .20
366 Rob Ramsay .07 .20
367 Mark Redman .07 .20
368 Rick Ankiel .12 .30
369 Domingo Guzman RC .07 .20
370 Eugene Kingsale .07 .20
371 Nomar Garciaparra BPM .12 .30
372 Ken Griffey Jr. BPM .40 1.00
373 Randy Johnson BPM .20 .50
374 Jeff Bagwell BPM .12 .30
375 Ivan Rodriguez BPM .12 .30
376 Derek Jeter BPM .50 1.25
377 Carlos Beltran BPM .12 .30
378 Vladimir Guerrero BPM .12 .30
379 Sammy Sosa BPM .20 .50
380 Barry Bonds BPM .30 .75
381 Pedro Martinez BPM .12 .30
382 Chipper Jones BPM .20 .50
383 Mo Vaughn BPM .07 .20
384 Mike Piazza BPM .20 .50
385 Alex Rodriguez BPM .25 .60
386 Manny Ramirez BPM .20 .50
387 Mark McGwire BPM .30 .75
388 Tony Gwynn BPM .20 .50
389 Sean Casey BPM .07 .20
390 Cal Ripken BPM .60 1.50
391 Ken Griffey Jr. JC .40 1.00
392 Ken Griffey Jr. JC .40 1.00
393 Ken Griffey Jr. JC .40 1.00
394 Ken Griffey Jr. JC .40 1.00
395 Ken Griffey Jr. JC .40 1.00
396 Ken Griffey Jr. JC .40 1.00
397 Ken Griffey Jr. JC .40 1.00
398 Ken Griffey Jr. JC .40 1.00
399 Ken Griffey Jr. JC .40 1.00
400 Ken Griffey Jr. JC .40 1.00
401 Ken Griffey Jr. JC .40 1.00
402 Ken Griffey Jr. JC .40 1.00
403 Ken Griffey Jr. JC .40 1.00
404 Ken Griffey Jr. JC .40 1.00
405 Ken Griffey Jr. JC .40 1.00
406 Ken Griffey Jr. JC .40 1.00
407 Ken Griffey Jr. JC .40 1.00
408 Ken Griffey Jr. JC .40 1.00
409 Ken Griffey Jr. JC .40 1.00
410 Ken Griffey Jr. JC .40 1.00
411 Ken Griffey Jr. JC .40 1.00
412 Ken Griffey Jr. JC .40 1.00
413 Ken Griffey Jr. JC .40 1.00
414 Ken Griffey Jr. JC .40 1.00
415 Ken Griffey Jr. JC .40 1.00
416 Ken Griffey Jr. JC .40 1.00
417 Ken Griffey Jr. JC .40 1.00
418 Ken Griffey Jr. JC .40 1.00
419 Ken Griffey Jr. JC .40 1.00
420 Ken Griffey Jr. JC .40 1.00
421 Ken Griffey Jr. JC .40 1.00
422 Ken Griffey Jr. JC .40 1.00
423 Ken Griffey Jr. JC .40 1.00
424 Ken Griffey Jr. JC .40 1.00
425 Ken Griffey Jr. JC .40 1.00
426 Ken Griffey Jr. JC .40 1.00
427 Ken Griffey Jr. JC .40 1.00
428 Ken Griffey Jr. JC .40 1.00
429 Ken Griffey Jr. JC .40 1.00
430 Ken Griffey Jr. JC .40 1.00
431 Ken Griffey Jr. JC .40 1.00
432 Ken Griffey Jr. JC .40 1.00
433 Ken Griffey Jr. JC .40 1.00
434 Ken Griffey Jr. JC .40 1.00
435 Ken Griffey Jr. JC .40 1.00
436 Ken Griffey Jr. JC .40 1.00
437 Ken Griffey Jr. JC .40 1.00
438 Ken Griffey Jr. JC .40 1.00
439 Ken Griffey Jr. JC .40 1.00
440 Ken Griffey Jr. JC .40 1.00
441 Tommy Lasorda USA MG .20 .50
442 Sean Burroughs USA .12 .30
443 Rick Krivda USA .12 .30
444 Ben Sheets USA RC .30 .75
445 Pat Borders USA .12 .30
446 Brent Abernathy USA RC .12 .30
447 Tim Young USA .12 .30
448 Adam Everett USA .12 .30
449 Anthony Sanders USA .12 .30
450 Ernie Young USA .12 .30
451 Brad Wilkerson USA RC .30 .75
452 Kurt Ainsworth USA RC .12 .30
453 Ryan Franklin USA RC .12 .30
454 Todd Williams USA .12 .30
455 Jon Rauch USA RC .12 .30
456 Roy Oswalt USA RC 2.00 5.00
457 Shane Heams USA RC .12 .30
458 Chris George USA .12 .30
459 Bobby Seay USA .12 .30
460 Mike Kinkade USA .12 .30
461 Marcus Jensen USA .12 .30
462 Travis Dawkins USA .12 .30
463 Doug Mientkiewicz USA .12 .30
464 John Cotton USA RC .12 .30
465 Mike Neill USA .12 .30
466 Team Photo USA .40 1.00

2001 Upper Deck Victory

COMPLETE SET (660) 20.00 50.00
VICTORY'S BEST ODDS 1:1
1 Troy Glaus .07 .20
2 Scott Spiezio .07 .20
3 Gary DiSarcina .07 .20
4 Darin Erstad .07 .20
5 Tim Salmon .10 .30
6 Troy Percival .07 .20
7 Ramon Ortiz .07 .20
8 Orlando Palmeiro .07 .20
9 Tim Belcher .07 .20
10 Mo Vaughn .07 .20
11 Bengie Molina .07 .20
12 Benji Gil .07 .20
13 Scott Schoeneweis .07 .20
14 Garret Anderson .07 .20
15 Matt Wise .07 .20
16 Adam Kennedy .07 .20
17 Jarrod Washburn .07 .20
18 D.Erstad .07 .20
T.Percival CL
19 Jason Giambi .07 .20
20 Tim Hudson .07 .20
21 Ramon Hernandez .07 .20
22 Eric Chavez .07 .20
23 Gil Heredia .07 .20
24 Jason Isringhausen .07 .20
25 Jeremy Giambi .07 .20
26 Miguel Tejada .07 .20
27 Barry Zito .10 .30
28 Terrence Long .07 .20
29 Ryan Christenson .07 .20
30 Mark Mulder .07 .20
31 Olmedo Saenz .07 .20
32 Adam Piatt .07 .20
33 Ben Grieve .07 .20
34 Omar Olivares .07 .20
35 John Jaha .07 .20
36 J.Giambi .07 .20
T.Hudson CL
37 Carlos Delgado .07 .20
38 Esteban Loaiza .07 .20
39 Brad Fullmer .07 .20
40 David Wells .07 .20
41 Chris Woodward .07 .20
42 Billy Koch .07 .20
43 Shannon Stewart .07 .20
44 Chris Carpenter .07 .20
45 Steve Parris .07 .20
46 Darrin Fletcher .07 .20
47 Joey Hamilton .07 .20
48 Jose Cruz Jr. .07 .20
49 Vernon Wells .07 .20
50 Raul Mondesi .07 .20
51 Kelvim Escobar .07 .20
52 Tony Batista .07 .20
53 Alex Gonzalez .07 .20
54 C.Delgado .07 .20
D.Wells CL
55 Greg Vaughn .07 .20
56 Albie Lopez .07 .20
57 Randy Winn .07 .20
58 Ryan Rupe .07 .20
59 Steve Cox .07 .20
60 Vinny Castilla .07 .20
61 Jose Guillen .07 .20
62 Wilson Alvarez .07 .20
63 Bryan Rekar .07 .20
64 Gerald Williams .07 .20
65 Esteban Yan .07 .20
66 Felix Martinez .07 .20
67 Fred McGriff .10 .30
68 John Flaherty .07 .20
69 Jason Tyner .07 .20
70 Russ Johnson .07 .20
71 Roberto Hernandez .07 .20
72 G.Vaughn .07 .20
A.Lopez CL
73 Eddie Taubensee .07 .20
74 Bob Wickman .07 .20
75 Ellis Burks .07 .20
76 Kenny Lofton .07 .20
77 Einar Diaz .07 .20
78 Travis Fryman .07 .20
79 Omar Vizquel .10 .30
80 Jason Bere .07 .20
81 Bartolo Colon .07 .20
82 Jim Thome .10 .30
83 Roberto Alomar .10 .30
84 Chuck Finley .07 .20
85 Steve Woodard .07 .20
86 Russ Branyan .07 .20
87 Dave Burba .07 .20
88 Jaret Wright .07 .20
89 Jacob Cruz .07 .20
90 Steve Karsay .07 .20
91 M.Ramirez .07 .20
B.Colon CL
92 Raul Ibanez .07 .20
93 Freddy Garcia .07 .20
94 Edgar Martinez .10 .30
95 Jay Buhner .07 .20
96 Jamie Moyer .07 .20
97 John Olerud .07 .20
98 Aaron Sele .07 .20
99 Kazuhiro Sasaki .07 .20
100 Mike Cameron .07 .20
101 John Halama .07 .20
102 David Bell .07 .20
103 Gil Meche .07 .20
104 Carlos Guillen .07 .20
105 Mark McLemore .07 .20
106 Stan Javier .07 .20
107 Al Martin .07 .20
108 Dan Wilson .07 .20
109 A.Rodriguez .15 .40
K.Sasaki CL
110 Cal Ripken .60 1.50
111 Delino DeShields .07 .20
112 Sidney Ponson .07 .20
113 Albert Belle .07 .20
114 Jose Mercedes .07 .20
115 Scott Erickson .07 .20
116 Jerry Hairston Jr. .07 .20
117 Brook Fordyce .07 .20
118 Luis Matos .07 .20
119 Eugene Kingsale .07 .20
120 Jeff Conine .07 .20
121 Chris Richard .07 .20
122 Fernando Lunar .07 .20
123 John Parrish .07 .20
124 Brady Anderson .07 .20
125 Ryan Kohlmeier .07 .20
126 Melvin Mora .07 .20
127 A.Belle .07 .20
J.Mercedes CL
128 Ivan Rodriguez .10 .30
129 Justin Thompson .07 .20
130 Kenny Rogers .07 .20
131 Rafael Palmeiro .10 .30
132 Rusty Greer .07 .20
133 Gabe Kapler .07 .20
134 John Wetteland .07 .20
135 Mike Lamb .07 .20
136 Doug Davis .07 .20
137 Ruben Mateo .07 .20
138 Alex Rodriguez Rangers .50 1.25
139 Chad Curtis .07 .20
140 Rick Helling .07 .20
141 Ryan Glynn .07 .20
142 Andres Galarraga .07 .20
143 Ricky Ledee .07 .20
144 Frank Catalanotto .07 .20
145 R.Palmeiro .07 .20
R.Helling CL
146 Pedro Martinez .10 .30
147 Wilton Veras .07 .20
148 Manny Ramirez .10 .30
149 Rolando Arrojo .07 .20
150 Nomar Garciaparra .30 .75
151 Darren Lewis .07 .20
152 Troy O'Leary .07 .20
153 Tomokazu Ohka .07 .20
154 Carl Everett .07 .20
155 Jason Varitek .20 .50
156 Frank Castillo .07 .20
157 Pete Schourek .07 .20
158 Jose Offerman .07 .20
159 Derek Lowe .07 .20
160 John Valentin .07 .20
161 Dante Bichette .07 .20
162 Trot Nixon .07 .20
163 N.Garciaparra .20 .50
P.Martinez CL
164 Jermaine Dye .07 .20
165 Dave McCarty .07 .20
166 Jose Rosado .07 .20
167 Mike Sweeney .07 .20
168 Rey Sanchez .07 .20
169 Jeff Suppan .07 .20
170 Chad Durbin .07 .20
171 Carlos Beltran .07 .20
172 Brian Meadows .07 .20
173 Todd Dunwoody .07 .20
174 Johnny Damon .10 .30
175 Blake Stein .07 .20
176 Carlos Febles .07 .20
177 Joe Randa .07 .20
178 Mac Suzuki .07 .20
179 Mark Quinn .07 .20
180 Gregg Zaun .07 .20
181 M.Sweeney .07 .20
J.Suppan CL
182 Juan Gonzalez .07 .20
183 Dean Palmer .07 .20
184 Wendell Magee .07 .20
185 Todd Jones .07 .20
186 Bobby Higginson .07 .20
187 Brian Moehler .07 .20
188 Juan Encarnacion .07 .20
189 Tony Clark .07 .20
190 Rich Becker .07 .20
191 Roger Cedeno .07 .20
192 Mitch Meluskey .07 .20
193 Shane Halter .07 .20
194 Jeff Weaver .07 .20
195 Deivi Cruz .07 .20
196 Damion Easley .07 .20
197 Robert Fick .07 .20
198 Matt Anderson .07 .20
199 B.Higginson .07 .20
B.Moehler CL
200 Brad Radke .07 .20
201 Mark Redman .07 .20
202 Corey Koskie .07 .20
203 Matt Lawton .07 .20
204 Eric Milton .07 .20
205 Chad Moeller .07 .20
206 Jacque Jones .07 .20
207 Matt Kinney .07 .20
208 Jay Canizaro .07 .20
209 Torii Hunter .07 .20
210 Ron Coomer .07 .20
211 Chad Allen .07 .20
212 Denny Hocking .07 .20
213 Cristian Guzman .07 .20
214 LaTroy Hawkins .07 .20
215 Joe Mays .07 .20
216 David Ortiz .20 .50
217 M.Lawton .07 .20
E.Milton CL
218 Frank Thomas .20 .50
219 Jose Valentin .07 .20
220 Mike Sirotka .07 .20
221 Kip Wells .07 .20
222 Magglio Ordonez .07 .20
223 Herbert Perry .07 .20
224 James Baldwin .07 .20
225 Jon Garland .07 .20
226 Sandy Alomar Jr. .07 .20
227 Chris Singleton .07 .20
228 Keith Foulke .07 .20
229 Paul Konerko .07 .20
230 Jim Parque .07 .20
231 Greg Norton .07 .20
232 Carlos Lee .07 .20
233 Cal Eldred .07 .20
234 Ray Durham .07 .20
235 Jeff Abbott .07 .20
236 F.Thomas .10 .30
M.Sirotka CL
237 Derek Jeter .50 1.25
238 Glenallen Hill .07 .20
239 Roger Clemens .40 1.00
240 Bernie Williams .10 .30
241 David Justice .07 .20
242 Luis Sojo .07 .20
243 Orlando Hernandez .07 .20
244 Mike Mussina .10 .30
245 Jorge Posada .10 .30
246 Andy Pettitte .10 .30
247 Paul O'Neill .10 .30
248 Scott Brosius .07 .20
249 Alfonso Soriano .10 .30
250 Mariano Rivera .20 .50
251 Chuck Knoblauch .07 .20
252 Ramiro Mendoza .07 .20
253 Tino Martinez .10 .30
254 David Cone .07 .20
255 D.Jeter .25 .60
A.Pettitte CL
256 Jeff Bagwell .10 .30
257 Lance Berkman .07 .20
258 Craig Biggio .10 .30
259 Scott Elarton .07 .20
260 Bill Spiers .07 .20
261 Moises Alou .07 .20
262 Billy Wagner .07 .20
263 Shane Reynolds .07 .20
264 Tony Eusebio .07 .20
265 Julio Lugo .07 .20
266 Jose Lima .07 .20
267 Octavio Dotel .07 .20
268 Brad Ausmus .07 .20
269 Daryle Ward .07 .20
270 Glen Barker .07 .20
271 Wade Miller .07 .20
272 Richard Hidalgo .07 .20
273 Chris Truby .07 .20
274 J.Bagwell .07 .20
S.Elarton CL
275 Greg Maddux .30 .75
276 Chipper Jones .20 .50
277 Tom Glavine .10 .30
278 Brian Jordan .07 .20
279 Andruw Jones .10 .30
280 Kevin Millwood .07 .20
281 Rico Brogna .07 .20
282 George Lombard .07 .20
283 Reggie Sanders .07 .20
284 John Rocker .07 .20
285 Rafael Furcal .07 .20
286 John Smoltz .10 .30
287 Javy Lopez .07 .20
288 Walt Weiss .07 .20
289 Quilvio Veras .07 .20
290 Eddie Perez .07 .20
291 B.J. Surhoff .07 .20
292 C.Jones .10 .30
T.Glavine CL
293 Jeromy Burnitz .07 .20
294 Charlie Hayes .07 .20
295 Jeff D'Amico .07 .20
296 Jose Hernandez .07 .20
297 Richie Sexson .07 .20
298 Tyler Houston .07 .20
299 Paul Rigdon .07 .20
300 Jamey Wright .07 .20
301 Mark Loretta .07 .20
302 Geoff Jenkins .07 .20
303 Luis Lopez .07 .20
304 John Snyder .07 .20
305 Henry Blanco .07 .20
306 Curtis Leskanic .07 .20
307 Ron Belliard .07 .20
308 Jimmy Haynes .07 .20
309 Marquis Grissom .07 .20
310 G.Jenkins .07 .20
J.D'Amico CL
311 Mark McGwire .50 1.25
312 Rick Ankiel .07 .20
313 Dave Veres .07 .20
314 Carlos Hernandez .07 .20
315 Jim Edmonds .07 .20
316 Andy Benes .07 .20
317 Garrett Stephenson .07 .20
318 Ray Lankford .07 .20
319 Dustin Hermanson .07 .20
320 Steve Kline .07 .20
321 Mike Matheny .07 .20
322 Edgar Renteria .07 .20
323 J.D. Drew .07 .20
324 Craig Paquette .07 .20
325 Darryl Kile .07 .20
326 Fernando Vina .07 .20
327 Eric Davis .07 .20
328 Placido Polanco .07 .20
329 J.Edmonds .07 .20
D.Kile CL
330 Sammy Sosa .20 .50
331 Rick Aguilera .07 .20
332 Willie Greene .07 .20
333 Kerry Wood .07 .20
334 Todd Hundley .07 .20
335 Rondell White .07 .20
336 Julio Zuleta .07 .20
337 Jon Lieber .07 .20
338 Joe Girardi .07 .20
339 Damon Buford .07 .20
340 Kevin Tapani .07 .20
341 Ricky Gutierrez .07 .20
342 Bill Mueller .07 .20
343 Ruben Quevedo .07 .20
344 Eric Young .07 .20
345 Gary Matthews Jr. .07 .20
346 Daniel Garibay .07 .20
347 S.Sosa .10 .30
J.Lieber CL
348 Randy Johnson .20 .50
349 Matt Williams .07 .20
350 Kelly Stinnett .07 .20
351 Brian Anderson .07 .20
352 Steve Finley .07 .20
353 Curt Schilling .07 .20
354 Erubiel Durazo .07 .20
355 Todd Stottlemyre .07 .20
356 Mark Grace .10 .30
357 Luis Gonzalez .07 .20
358 Danny Bautista .07 .20
359 Matt Mantei .07 .20
360 Tony Womack .07 .20
361 Armando Reynoso .07 .20
362 Greg Colbrunn .07 .20
363 Jay Bell .07 .20
364 Byung-Hyun Kim .07 .20
365 L.Gonzalez .10 .30
R.Johnson CL
366 Gary Sheffield .07 .20
367 Eric Karros .07 .20
368 Jeff Shaw .07 .20
369 Jim Leyritz .07 .20
370 Kevin Brown .07 .20
371 Alex Cora .07 .20
372 Andy Ashby .07 .20
373 Eric Gagne .07 .20
374 Chan Ho Park .07 .20
375 Shawn Green .07 .20
376 Kevin Elster .07 .20
377 Mark Grudzielanek .07 .20
378 Darren Dreifort .07 .20
379 Dave Hansen .07 .20
380 Bruce Aven .07 .20
381 Adrian Beltre .07 .20
382 Tom Goodwin .07 .20
383 G.Sheffield .07 .20
C.Park CL
384 Vladimir Guerrero .20 .50
385 Ugueth Urbina .07 .20
386 Michael Barrett .07 .20
387 Geoff Blum .07 .20
388 Fernando Tatis .07 .20
389 Carl Pavano .07 .20
390 Jose Vidro .07 .20
391 Orlando Cabrera .07 .20
392 Terry Jones .07 .20
393 Mike Thurman .07 .20
394 Lee Stevens .07 .20
395 Tony Armas Jr. .07 .20
396 Wilton Guerrero .07 .20
397 Peter Bergeron .07 .20
398 Milton Bradley .07 .20
399 Javier Vazquez .07 .20
400 Fernando Seguignol .07 .20
401 V.Guerrero .10 .30
D.Hermanson CL
402 Barry Bonds .50 1.25
403 Russ Ortiz .07 .20
404 Calvin Murray .07 .20
405 Armando Rios .07 .20
406 Livan Hernandez .07 .20
407 Jeff Kent .07 .20
408 Bobby Estalella .07 .20
409 Felipe Crespo .07 .20
410 Shawn Estes .07 .20
411 J.T. Snow .07 .20
412 Marvin Benard .07 .20
413 Joe Nathan .07 .20
414 Robb Nen .07 .20
415 Shawon Dunston .07 .20
416 Mark Gardner .07 .20
417 Kirk Rueter .07 .20
418 Rich Aurilia .07 .20
419 Doug Mirabelli .07 .20
420 Russ Davis .07 .20
421 B.Bonds .30 .75
L.Hernandez CL
422 Cliff Floyd .07 .20
423 Luis Castillo .07 .20
424 Antonio Alfonseca .07 .20
425 Preston Wilson .07 .20
426 Ryan Dempster .07 .20
427 Jesus Sanchez .07 .20
428 Derrek Lee .10 .30
429 Brad Penny .07 .20
430 Mark Kotsay .07 .20
431 Alex Fernandez .07 .20
432 Mike Lowell .07 .20
433 Chuck Smith .07 .20
434 Alex Gonzalez .07 .20
435 Dave Berg .07 .20
436 A.J. Burnett .07 .20
437 Charles Johnson .07 .20
438 Reid Cornelius .07 .20
439 Mike Redmond .07 .20
440 P.Wilson .07 .20
R.Dempster CL
441 Mike Piazza .30 .75
442 Kevin Appier .07 .20
443 Jay Payton .07 .20
444 Steve Trachsel .07 .20
445 Al Leiter .07 .20
446 Joe McEwing .07 .20
447 Armando Benitez .07 .20
448 Edgardo Alfonzo .07 .20
449 Glendon Rusch .07 .20
450 Mike Bordick .07 .20
451 Lenny Harris .07 .20
452 Matt Franco .07 .20
453 Darryl Hamilton .07 .20
454 Bobby Jones .07 .20

455 Robin Ventura .07 .20
456 Todd Zeile .07 .20
457 John Franco .07 .20
458 M.Piazza .20 .50
A.Leiter CL
459 Tony Gwynn .25 .60
460 John Mabry .07 .20
461 Trevor Hoffman .07 .20
462 Phil Nevin .07 .20
463 Ryan Klesko .07 .20
464 Wiki Gonzalez .07 .20
465 Matt Clement .07 .20
466 Alex Arias .07 .20
467 Woody Williams .07 .20
468 Ruben Rivera .07 .20
469 Sterling Hitchcock .07 .20
470 Ben Davis .07 .20
471 Bubba Trammell .07 .20
472 Jay Witasick .07 .20
473 Eric Owens .07 .20
474 Damian Jackson .07 .20
475 Adam Eaton .07 .20
476 Mike Darr .07 .20
477 P.Nevin .07 .20
T.Hoffman CL
478 Scott Rolen .10 .30
479 Robert Person .07 .20
480 Mike Lieberthal .07 .20
481 Reggie Taylor .07 .20
482 Paul Byrd .07 .20
483 Bruce Chen .07 .20
484 Pat Burrell .07 .20
485 Kevin Jordan .07 .20
486 Bobby Abreu .07 .20
487 Randy Wolf .07 .20
488 Kevin Sefcik .07 .20
489 Brian Hunter .07 .20
490 Doug Glanville .07 .20
491 Kent Bottenfield .07 .20
492 Travis Lee .07 .20
493 Jeff Brantley .07 .20
494 Omar Daal .07 .20
495 B.Abreu .07 .20
R.Wolf CL
496 Jason Kendall .07 .20
497 Adrian Brown .07 .20
498 Warren Morris .07 .20
499 Brian Giles .07 .20
500 Jimmy Anderson .07 .20
501 John VanderWal .07 .20
502 Mike Williams .07 .20
503 Aramis Ramirez .07 .20
504 Pat Meares .07 .20
505 Jason Schmidt .07 .20
506 Todd Ritchie .07 .20
507 Abraham Nunez .07 .20
508 Jose Silva .07 .20
509 Francisco Cordova .07 .20
510 Kevin Young .07 .20
511 Derek Bell .07 .20
512 Kris Benson .07 .20
513 B.Giles .07 .20
J.Silva CL
514 Ken Griffey Jr. .40 1.00
515 Scott Williamson .07 .20
516 Dmitri Young .07 .20
517 Sean Casey .07 .20
518 Barry Larkin .10 .30
519 Juan Castro .07 .20
520 Danny Graves .07 .20
521 Aaron Boone .07 .20
522 Pokey Reese .07 .20
523 Elmer Dessens .07 .20
524 Michael Tucker .07 .20
525 Benito Santiago .07 .20
526 Pete Harnisch .07 .20
527 Alex Ochoa .07 .20
528 Gookie Dawkins .07 .20
529 Seth Etherton .07 .20
530 Rob Bell .07 .20
531 K.Griffey Jr. .25 .60
S.Parris CL
532 Todd Helton .10 .30
533 Jose Jimenez .07 .20
534 Todd Walker .07 .20
535 Ron Gant .07 .20
536 Neifi Perez .07 .20
537 Butch Huskey .07 .20
538 Pedro Astacio .07 .20
539 Juan Pierre .07 .20
540 Jeff Cirillo .07 .20
541 Ben Petrick .07 .20
542 Brian Bohanon .07 .20
543 Larry Walker .07 .20
544 Masato Yoshii .07 .20
545 Denny Neagle .07 .20
546 Brent Mayne .07 .20
547 Mike Hampton .07 .20
548 Todd Hollandsworth .07 .20
549 Brian Rose .07 .20
550 T.Helton .07 .20
P.Astacio CL
551 Jason Hart .07 .20
552 Joe Crede .20 .50
553 Timo Perez .07 .20
554 Brady Clark .07 .20
555 Adam Pettyjohn RC .07 .20
556 Jason Grilli .07 .20
557 Paxton Crawford .07 .20
558 Jay Spurgeon .07 .20
559 Hector Ortiz .07 .20
560 Vernon Wells .07 .20
561 Aubrey Huff .07 .20
562 Xavier Nady .07 .20
563 Billy McMillon .07 .20
564 Ichiro Suzuki RC 3.00 8.00
565 Tomas De La Rosa .07 .20
566 Matt Ginter .07 .20
567 Sun Woo Kim .07 .20
568 Nick Johnson .07 .20
569 Pablo Ozuna .07 .20
570 Tike Redman .07 .20
571 Brian Cole .07 .20
572 Ross Gload .07 .20
573 Dee Brown .07 .20
574 Tony McKnight .07 .20
575 Allen Levrault .07 .20
576 Lesli Brea .07 .20
577 Adam Bernero .07 .20
578 Tom Davey .07 .20
579 Morgan Burkhart .07 .20
580 Britt Reames .07 .20
581 Dave Coggin .07 .20
582 Trey Moore .07 .20
583 Matt Kinney .07 .20
584 Pedro Feliz .07 .20
585 Brandon Inge .07 .20
586 Alex Hernandez .07 .20
587 Toby Hall .07 .20
588 Grant Roberts .07 .20
589 Brian Sikorski .07 .20
590 Aaron Myette .07 .20
591 Derek Jeter PM .50 1.25
592 Ivan Rodriguez PM .07 .20
593 Alex Rodriguez PM .25 .60
594 Carlos Delgado PM .07 .20
595 Mark McGwire PM .50 1.25
596 Troy Glaus PM .07 .20
597 Sammy Sosa PM .10 .30
598 Vladimir Guerrero PM .20 .50
599 Manny Ramirez PM .07 .20
600 Pedro Martinez PM .10 .30
601 Chipper Jones PM .10 .30
602 Jason Giambi PM .07 .20
603 Frank Thomas PM .10 .30
604 Ken Griffey Jr. PM .40 1.00
605 Nomar Garciaparra PM .30 .75
606 Randy Johnson PM .10 .30
607 Mike Piazza PM .30 .75
608 Barry Bonds PM .50 1.25
609 Todd Helton PM .07 .20
610 Jeff Bagwell PM .07 .20
611 Ken Griffey Jr. VB .40 1.00
612 Carlos Delgado VB .07 .20
613 Jeff Bagwell VB .07 .20
614 Jason Giambi VB .07 .20
615 Cal Ripken VB .60 1.50
616 Brian Giles VB .07 .20
617 Bernie Williams VB .07 .20
618 Greg Maddux VB .30 .75
619 Troy Glaus VB .07 .20
620 Greg Vaughn VB .07 .20
621 Sammy Sosa VB .10 .30
622 Pat Burrell VB .07 .20
623 Ivan Rodriguez VB .07 .20
624 Chipper Jones VB .10 .30
625 Barry Bonds VB .50 1.25
626 Roger Clemens VB .40 1.00
627 Jim Edmonds VB .07 .20
628 Nomar Garciaparra VB .30 .75
629 Frank Thomas VB .10 .30
630 Mike Piazza VB .30 .75
631 Randy Johnson VB .10 .30
632 Andruw Jones VB .07 .20
633 David Wells VB .07 .20
634 Manny Ramirez VB .07 .20
635 Preston Wilson VB .07 .20
636 Todd Helton VB .07 .20
637 Kerry Wood VB .07 .20
638 Albert Belle VB .07 .20
639 Juan Gonzalez VB .07 .20
640 Vladimir Guerrero VB .20 .50
641 Gary Sheffield VB .07 .20
642 Larry Walker VB .07 .20
643 Magglio Ordonez VB .07 .20
644 Jermaine Dye VB .07 .20
645 Scott Rolen VB .07 .20
646 Tony Gwynn VB .25 .60
647 Shawn Green VB .07 .20
648 Roberto Alomar VB .07 .20
649 Eric Milton VB .07 .20
650 Mark McGwire VB .50 1.25
651 Tim Hudson VB .07 .20
652 Jose Canseco VB .07 .20
653 Tom Glavine VB .07 .20
654 Derek Jeter VB .50 1.25
655 Alex Rodriguez VB .25 .60
656 Darin Erstad VB .07 .20
657 Jason Kendall VB .07 .20
658 Pedro Martinez VB .10 .30
659 Richie Sexson VB .07 .20
660 Rafael Palmeiro VB .07 .20

2002 Upper Deck Victory

COMPLETE SET (660) 35.00 75.00
COMP.LOW SET (550) 25.00 50.00
COMP.UPDATE SET (110) 10.00 25.00
COMMON (1-490/531-550) .07 .20
COMMON CARD (491-530) .08 .25
COMMON CARD (551-605) .15 .40
COMMON CARD (606-660) .15 .40
551-660 DIST.IN UD ROOKIE DEBUT PACKS
1 Troy Glaus .07 .20
2 Tim Salmon .10 .30
3 Troy Percival .07 .20
4 Darin Erstad .07 .20
5 Adam Kennedy .07 .20
6 Scott Spiezio .07 .20
7 Ramon Ortiz .07 .20
8 Ismael Valdes .07 .20
9 Jarrod Washburn .07 .20
10 Garrett Anderson .07 .20
11 David Eckstein .07 .20
12 Mo Vaughn .07 .20
13 Benji Gil .07 .20
14 Bengie Molina .07 .20
15 Scott Schoeneweis .07 .20
16 T.Glaus .07 .20
R.Ortiz
17 David Justice .07 .20
18 Jermaine Dye .07 .20
19 Eric Chavez .07 .20
20 Jeremy Giambi .07 .20
21 Terrence Long .07 .20
22 Miguel Tejada .07 .20
23 Johnny Damon .10 .30
24 Jason Hart .07 .20
25 Adam Piatt .07 .20
26 Billy Koch .07 .20
27 Ramon Hernandez .07 .20
28 Eric Byrnes .07 .20
29 Olmedo Saenz .07 .20
30 Barry Zito .07 .20
31 Tim Hudson .07 .20
32 Mark Mulder .07 .20
33 J.Giambi .07 .20
M.Mulder
34 Carlos Delgado .07 .20
35 Shannon Stewart .07 .20
36 Vernon Wells .07 .20
37 Homer Bush .07 .20
38 Brad Fullmer .07 .20
39 Jose Cruz Jr. .07 .20
40 Felipe Lopez .07 .20
41 Raul Mondesi .07 .20
42 Esteban Loaiza .07 .20
43 Darrin Fletcher .07 .20
44 Mike Sirotka .07 .20
45 Luke Prokopec .07 .20
46 Chris Carpenter .07 .20
47 Roy Halladay .07 .20
48 Kelvim Escobar .07 .20
49 C.Delgado .07 .20
B.Koch
50 Nick Bierbrodt .07 .20
51 Greg Vaughn .07 .20
52 Ben Grieve .07 .20
53 Damian Rolls .07 .20
54 Russ Johnson .07 .20
55 Brent Abernathy .07 .20
56 Steve Cox .07 .20
57 Aubrey Huff .07 .20
58 Randy Winn .07 .20
59 Jason Tyner .07 .20
60 Tanyon Sturtze .07 .20
61 Joe Kennedy .07 .20
62 Jared Sandberg .07 .20
63 Esteban Yan .07 .20
64 Ryan Rupe .07 .20
65 Toby Hall .07 .20
66 G.Vaughn .07 .20
T.Sturtze
67 Matt Lawton .07 .20
68 Juan Gonzalez .07 .20
69 Jim Thome .10 .30
70 Einar Diaz .07 .20
71 Ellis Burks .07 .20
72 Kenny Lofton .07 .20
73 Omar Vizquel .10 .30
74 Russell Branyan .07 .20
75 Brady Anderson .07 .20
76 John Rocker .07 .20
77 Travis Fryman .07 .20
78 Wil Cordero .07 .20
79 Chuck Finley .07 .20
80 C.C. Sabathia .07 .20
81 Bartolo Colon .07 .20
82 Bob Wickman .07 .20
83 R.Alomar .07 .20
C.Sabathia
84 Ichiro Suzuki .40 1.00
85 Edgar Martinez .10 .30
86 Aaron Sele .07 .20
87 Carlos Guillen .07 .20
88 Bret Boone .07 .20
89 John Olerud .07 .20
90 Jamie Moyer .07 .20
91 Ben Davis .07 .20
92 Dan Wilson .07 .20
93 Jeff Cirillo .07 .20
94 John Halama .07 .20
95 Freddy Garcia .07 .20
96 Kazuhiro Sasaki .07 .20
97 Mike Cameron .07 .20
98 Paul Abbott .07 .20
99 Mark McLemore .07 .20
100 I.Suzuki .20 .50
F.Garcia
101 Jeff Conine .07 .20
102 David Segui .07 .20
103 Marty Cordova .07 .20
104 Tony Batista .07 .20
105 Chris Richard .07 .20
106 Willis Roberts .07 .20
107 Melvin Mora .07 .20
108 Mike Bordick .07 .20
109 Jay Gibbons .07 .20
110 Mike Kinkade .07 .20
111 Brian Roberts .07 .20
112 Jerry Hairston Jr. .07 .20
113 Jason Johnson .07 .20
114 Josh Towers .07 .20
115 Calvin Maduro .07 .20
116 Sidney Ponson .07 .20
117 J.Conine .07 .20
J.Johnson
118 Alex Rodriguez .25 .60
119 Ivan Rodriguez .10 .30
120 Frank Catalanotto .07 .20
121 Mike Lamb .07 .20
122 Ruben Sierra .07 .20
123 Rusty Greer .07 .20
124 Rafael Palmeiro .10 .30
125 Gabe Kapler .07 .20
126 Aaron Myette .07 .20
127 Kenny Rogers .07 .20
128 Carl Everett .07 .20
129 Rick Helling .07 .20
130 Ricky Ledee .07 .20
131 Michael Young .20 .50
132 Doug Davis .07 .20
133 Jeff Zimmerman .07 .20
134 A.Rodriguez .15 .40
R.Helling
135 Manny Ramirez .10 .30
136 Nomar Garciaparra .30 .75
137 Jason Varitek .20 .50
138 Dante Bichette .07 .20
139 Tony Clark .07 .20
140 Scott Hatteberg .07 .20
141 Trot Nixon .10 .30
142 Hideo Nomo .20 .50
143 Dustin Hermanson .07 .20
144 Chris Stynes .07 .20
145 Jose Offerman .07 .20
146 Pedro Martinez .10 .30
147 Shea Hillenbrand .07 .20
148 Tim Wakefield .07 .20
149 Troy O'Leary .07 .20
150 Ugueth Urbina .07 .20
151 M.Ramirez .20 .50
H.Nomo
152 Carlos Beltran .07 .20
153 Dee Brown .07 .20
154 Mike Sweeney .07 .20
155 Luis Alicea .07 .20
156 Raul Ibanez .07 .20
157 Mark Quinn .07 .20
158 Joe Randa .07 .20
159 Roberto Hernandez .07 .20
160 Neifi Perez .07 .20
161 Carlos Febles .07 .20
162 Jeff Suppan .07 .20
163 Dave McCarty .07 .20
164 Blake Stein .07 .20
165 Chad Durbin .07 .20
166 Paul Byrd .07 .20
167 C.Beltran .07 .20
J.Suppan
168 Craig Paquette .07 .20
169 Dean Palmer .07 .20
170 Shane Halter .07 .20
171 Bobby Higginson .07 .20
172 Robert Fick .07 .20
173 Jose Macias .07 .20
174 Deivi Cruz .07 .20
175 Damion Easley .07 .20
176 Brandon Inge .07 .20
177 Mark Redman .07 .20
178 Dmitri Young .07 .20
179 Steve Sparks .07 .20
180 Jeff Weaver .07 .20
181 Victor Santos .07 .20
182 Jose Lima .07 .20
183 Matt Anderson .07 .20
184 R.Cedeno .07 .20
S.Sparks
185 Doug Mientkiewicz .07 .20
186 Cristian Guzman .07 .20
187 Torii Hunter .07 .20
188 Matt LeCroy .07 .20
189 Corey Koskie .07 .20
190 Jacque Jones .07 .20
191 Luis Rivas .07 .20
192 David Ortiz .20 .50
193 A.J. Pierzynski .07 .20
194 Brian Buchanan .07 .20
195 Joe Mays .07 .20
196 Brad Radke .07 .20
197 Denny Hocking .07 .20
198 Eric Milton .07 .20
199 LaTroy Hawkins .07 .20
200 D.Mientkiewicz .07 .20
J.Mays
201 Magglio Ordonez .07 .20
202 Jose Valentin .07 .20
203 Chris Singleton .07 .20
204 Aaron Rowand .07 .20
205 Paul Konerko .07 .20
206 Carlos Lee .07 .20
207 Ray Durham .07 .20
208 Keith Foulke .07 .20
209 Todd Ritchie .07 .20
210 Royce Clayton .07 .20
211 Jose Canseco .10 .30
212 Frank Thomas .20 .50
213 David Wells .07 .20
214 Mark Buehrle .07 .20
215 Jon Garland .07 .20
216 M.Ordonez .07 .20
M.Buehrle
217 Derek Jeter .50 1.25
218 Bernie Williams .10 .30
219 Rondell White .07 .20
220 Jorge Posada .10 .30
221 Alfonso Soriano .07 .20
222 Ramiro Mendoza .07 .20
223 Jason Giambi Yankees .50 1.25
224 John Vander Wal .07 .20
225 Steve Karsay .07 .20
226 Nick Johnson .07 .20
227 Mariano Rivera .20 .50
228 Orlando Hernandez .07 .20
229 Andy Pettitte .10 .30
230 Robin Ventura .07 .20
231 Roger Clemens .40 1.00
232 Mike Mussina .10 .30
233 D.Jeter .25 .60
R.Clemens
234 Moises Alou .07 .20
235 Lance Berkman .07 .20
236 Craig Biggio .10 .30
237 Octavio Dotel .07 .20
238 Jeff Bagwell .10 .30
239 Richard Hidalgo .07 .20
240 Morgan Ensberg .07 .20
241 Julio Lugo .07 .20
242 Daryle Ward .07 .20
243 Roy Oswalt .07 .20
244 Billy Wagner .07 .20
245 Brad Ausmus .07 .20
246 Jose Vizcaino .07 .20
247 Wade Miller .07 .20
248 Shane Reynolds .07 .20
249 J.Bagwell .07 .20
W.Miller
250 Chipper Jones .20 .50
251 Brian Jordan .07 .20
252 B.J. Surhoff .07 .20
253 Rafael Furcal .07 .20
254 Julio Franco .07 .20
255 Javy Lopez .07 .20
256 John Burkett .07 .20
257 Andruw Jones .10 .30
258 Marcus Giles .07 .20
259 Wes Helms .07 .20
260 Greg Maddux .30 .75
261 John Smoltz .10 .30
262 Tom Glavine .10 .30
263 Vinny Castilla .07 .20
264 Kevin Millwood .07 .20
265 Jason Marquis .07 .20
266 C.Jones .10 .30
G.Maddux
267 Tyler Houston .07 .20
268 Mark Loretta .07 .20
269 Richie Sexson .07 .20
270 Jeromy Burnitz .07 .20
271 Jimmy Haynes .07 .20
272 Geoff Jenkins .07 .20
273 Ron Belliard .07 .20
274 Jose Hernandez .07 .20
275 Jeffrey Hammonds .07 .20
276 Curtis Leskanic .07 .20
277 Devon White .07 .20
278 Ben Sheets .07 .20
279 Henry Blanco .07 .20
280 Jamey Wright .07 .20
281 Allen Levrault .07 .20
282 Jeff D'Amico .07 .20
283 R.Sexson .07 .20
J.Haynes
284 Albert Pujols .40 1.00
285 Jason Isringhausen .07 .20
286 J.D. Drew .07 .20
287 Placido Polanco .07 .20
288 Jim Edmonds .07 .20
289 Fernando Vina .07 .20
290 Edgar Renteria .07 .20
291 Mike Matheny .07 .20
292 Bud Smith .07 .20
293 Mike DiFelice .07 .20
294 Woody Williams .07 .20
295 Eli Marrero .07 .20
296 Matt Morris .07 .20
297 Darryl Kile .07 .20
298 Kerry Robinson .07 .20
299 Luis Saturria .07 .20
300 A.Pujols .20 .50
M.Morris
301 Sammy Sosa .20 .50
302 Michael Tucker .07 .20
303 Bill Mueller .07 .20
304 Ricky Gutierrez .07 .20
305 Fred McGriff .10 .30
306 Eric Young .07 .20
307 Corey Patterson .07 .20
308 Alex Gonzalez .07 .20
309 Ron Coomer .07 .20
310 Kerry Wood .07 .20
311 Delino DeShields .07 .20
312 Jon Lieber .07 .20
313 Tom Gordon .07 .20
314 Todd Hundley .07 .20
315 Jason Bere .07 .20
316 Kevin Tapani .07 .20
317 S.Sosa .10 .30
J.Lieber
318 Steve Finley .07 .20
319 Luis Gonzalez .07 .20
320 Mark Grace .10 .30
321 Craig Counsell .07 .20
322 Matt Williams .07 .20
323 Tony Womack .07 .20
324 Junior Spivey .07 .20
325 David Dellucci .07 .20
326 Jay Bell .07 .20
327 Curt Schilling .07 .20
328 Randy Johnson .20 .50
329 Danny Bautista .07 .20
330 Miguel Batista .07 .20
331 Erubiel Durazo .07 .20
332 Brian Anderson .07 .20
333 Byung-Hyun Kim .07 .20
334 L.Gonzalez .07 .20
C.Schilling
335 Paul LoDuca .07 .20
336 Gary Sheffield .07 .20
337 Shawn Green .07 .20
338 Adrian Beltre .07 .20
339 Darren Dreifort .07 .20
340 Mark Grudzielanek .07 .20
341 Eric Karros .07 .20
342 Cesar Izturis .07 .20
343 Tom Goodwin .07 .20
344 Marquis Grissom .07 .20
345 Kevin Brown .07 .20
346 James Baldwin .07 .20
347 Terry Adams .07 .20
348 Alex Cora .07 .20
349 Andy Ashby .07 .20
350 Chan Ho Park .07 .20
351 S.Green .07 .20
C.Park
352 Jose Vidro .07 .20
353 Vladimir Guerrero .20 .50
354 Orlando Cabrera .07 .20
355 Fernando Tatis .07 .20
356 Michael Barrett .07 .20
357 Lee Stevens .07 .20
358 Geoff Blum .07 .20
359 Brad Wilkerson .07 .20
360 Peter Bergeron .07 .20
361 Javier Vazquez .07 .20
362 Tony Armas Jr. .07 .20
363 Tomo Ohka .07 .20
364 Scott Strickland .07 .20
365 V.Guerrero .07 .20
J.Vazquez
366 Barry Bonds .50 1.25
367 Rich Aurilia .07 .20
368 Jeff Kent .07 .20
369 Andres Galarraga .07 .20
370 Desi Relaford .07 .20
371 Shawon Dunston .07 .20
372 Benito Santiago .07 .20
373 Tsuyoshi Shinjo .07 .20
374 Calvin Murray .07 .20
375 Marvin Benard .07 .20
376 J.T. Snow .07 .20
377 Livan Hernandez .07 .20
378 Russ Ortiz .07 .20
379 Robb Nen .07 .20
380 Jason Schmidt .07 .20
381 B.Bonds .30 .75
R.Ortiz
382 Cliff Floyd .07 .20
383 Antonio Alfonseca .07 .20
384 Mike Redmond .07 .20
385 Mike Lowell .07 .20
386 Derrek Lee .10 .30
387 Preston Wilson .07 .20
388 Luis Castillo .07 .20
389 Charles Johnson .07 .20
390 Eric Owens .07 .20
391 Alex Gonzalez .07 .20
392 Josh Beckett .07 .20
393 Brad Penny .07 .20
394 Ryan Dempster .07 .20
395 Matt Clement .07 .20
396 A.J. Burnett .07 .20
397 C.Floyd .07 .20
R.Dempster
398 Mike Piazza .30 .75
399 Joe McEwing .07 .20
400 Todd Zeile .07 .20
401 Jay Payton .07 .20
402 Robert Cedeno .07 .20
403 Rey Ordonez .07 .20
404 Edgardo Alfonzo .07 .20
405 Roberto Alomar .10 .30
406 Glendon Rusch .07 .20
407 Timo Perez .07 .20
408 Al Leiter .07 .20
409 Lenny Harris .07 .20
410 Shawn Estes .07 .20
411 Armando Benitez .07 .20
412 Kevin Appier .07 .20
413 Bruce Chen .07 .20
414 M.Piazza .10 .30
A.Leiter
415 Phil Nevin .07 .20
416 Ryan Klesko .07 .20
417 Mark Kotsay .07 .20
418 Ray Lankford .07 .20
419 Mike Darr .07 .20
420 D'Angelo Jimenez .07 .20
421 Bubba Trammell .07 .20
422 Adam Eaton .07 .20
423 Ramon Vazquez .07 .20
424 Cesar Crespo .07 .20
425 Trevor Hoffman .07 .20
426 Kevin Jarvis .07 .20
427 Wiki Gonzalez .07 .20
428 Damian Jackson .07 .20
429 Brian Lawrence .07 .20
430 P.Nevin .07 .20
T.Hoffman
431 Scott Rolen .10 .30
432 Marlon Anderson .07 .20
433 Bobby Abreu .07 .20
434 Jimmy Rollins .07 .20
435 Doug Glanville .07 .20
436 Travis Lee .07 .20
437 Brandon Duckworth .07 .20
438 Pat Burrell .07 .20
439 Kevin Jordan .07 .20
440 Robert Person .07 .20
441 Johnny Estrada .07 .20
442 Randy Wolf .07 .20
443 Jose Mesa .07 .20
444 Mike Lieberthal .07 .20
445 B.Abreu .07 .20
R.Person
446 Brian Giles .07 .20
447 Jason Kendall .07 .20
448 Aramis Ramirez .07 .20
449 Rob Mackowiak .07 .20
450 Abraham Nunez .07 .20
451 Pat Meares .07 .20
452 Craig Wilson .07 .20
453 Jack Wilson .07 .20
454 Gary Matthews Jr. .07 .20
455 Kevin Young .07 .20
456 Derek Bell .07 .20
457 Kip Wells .07 .20
458 Jimmy Anderson .07 .20
459 Kris Benson .07 .20
460 B.Giles .07 .20
T.Ritchie
461 Sean Casey .07 .20
462 Wilton Guerrero .07 .20
463 Jason LaRue .07 .20
464 Juan Encarnacion .07 .20
465 Todd Walker .07 .20
466 Aaron Boone .07 .20
467 Pete Harnisch .07 .20
468 Ken Griffey Jr. .40 1.00
469 Adam Dunn .07 .20
470 Barry Larkin .10 .30
471 Kelly Stinnett .07 .20
472 Pokey Reese .07 .20
473 Brady Clark .07 .20
474 Scott Williamson .07 .20
475 Danny Graves .07 .20
476 K.Griffey Jr. .25 .60
E.Dessens
477 Larry Walker .07 .20
478 Todd Helton .10 .30
479 Juan Pierre .07 .20
480 Juan Uribe .07 .20
481 Mario Encarnacion .07 .20
482 Jose Ortiz .07 .20
483 Todd Hollandsworth .07 .20
484 Alex Ochoa .07 .20
485 Mike Hampton .07 .20
486 Terry Shumpert .07 .20
487 Denny Neagle .07 .20
488 Jose Jimenez .07 .20
489 Jason Jennings .07 .20
490 T.Helton .07 .20
M.Hampton
491 Tim Redding ROO .08 .25
492 Mark Teixeira ROO .40 1.00
493 Alex Cintron ROO .08 .25
494 Tim Raines Jr. ROO .08 .25
495 Juan Cruz ROO .08 .25
496 Joe Crede ROO .15 .40
497 Steve Green ROO .08 .25
498 Mike Rivera ROO .08 .25
499 Mark Prior ROO .20 .50
500 Ken Harvey ROO .08 .25
501 Tim Spooneybarger ROO .08 .25
502 Adam Everett ROO .08 .25
503 Jason Standridge ROO .08 .25
504 Nick Neugebauer ROO .08 .25
505 Adam Johnson ROO .08 .25
506 Sean Douglass ROO .08 .25
507 Brandon Berger ROO .08 .25
508 Alex Escobar ROO .08 .25
509 Doug Nickle ROO .08 .25
510 Jason Middlebrook ROO .08 .25
511 Dewon Brazelton ROO .08 .25
512 Yorvit Torrealba ROO .08 .25
513 Henry Mateo ROO .08 .25
514 Dennis Tankersley ROO .08 .25
515 Marlon Byrd ROO .08 .25
516 Andy Barkett ROO .08 .25
517 Orlando Hudson ROO .08 .25
518 Josh Fogg ROO .08 .25
519 Ryan Drese ROO .08 .25
520 Mike MacDougal ROO .08 .25
521 Luis Pineda ROO .08 .25
522 Jack Cust ROO .08 .25
523 Kurt Ainsworth ROO .08 .25
524 Bart Miadich ROO .08 .25
525 Dernell Stenson ROO .08 .25
526 Carlos Zambrano ROO .15 .40
527 Austin Kearns ROO .08 .25
528 Larry Barnes ROO .08 .25
529 Mike Cuddyer ROO .08 .25
530 Carlos Pena ROO .08 .25
531 Derek Jeter BPM .25 .60
532 Ken Griffey Jr. BPM .25 .60
533 Manny Ramirez BPM .10 .30
534 Luis Gonzalez BPM .07 .20
535 Sammy Sosa BPM .10 .30
536 Roger Clemens BPM .20 .50
537 Phil Nevin BPM .07 .20
538 Mike Piazza BPM .20 .50
539 Alex Rodriguez BPM .15 .40
540 Jason Giambi Yankees BPM .25 .60
541 Randy Johnson BPM .10 .30
542 Albert Pujols BPM .20 .50
543 Jeff Bagwell BPM .07 .20
544 Shawn Green BPM .07 .20
545 Carlos Delgado BPM .07 .20
546 Pedro Martinez BPM .10 .30
547 Todd Helton BPM .07 .20
548 Roberto Alomar BPM .07 .20
549 Barry Bonds BPM .30 .75
550 Ichiro Suzuki BPM .20 .50
551 John Lackey .15 .40
552 Francisco Rodriguez .07 .20
553 Cliff Floyd .15 .40
554 Derek Lowe .15 .40
555 Mark Bellhorn .15 .40
556 Matt Clement .15 .40
557 Hee Seop Choi .15 .40
558 Joe Borchard .15 .40
559 Ryan Dempster .15 .40
560 Russell Branyan .15 .40
561 Brandon Larson .15 .40
562 Coco Crisp .40 1.00
563 Karim Garcia .15 .40
564 Brandon Phillips .15 .40
565 Jay Payton .15 .40
566 Gabe Kapler .15 .40
567 Carlos Pena .15 .40
568 George Lombard .15 .40
569 Andy Van Hekken .15 .40
570 Andres Torres .15 .40
571 Justin Wayne .15 .40
572 Juan Encarnacion .15 .40
573 Abraham Nunez .15 .40
574 Peter Munro .15 .40
575 Jason Lane .15 .40
576 Dave Roberts .15 .40
577 Eric Gagne .15 .40
578 Alex Sanchez .15 .40
579 Jim Rushford RC .15 .40
580 Ben Diggins .15 .40
581 Eddie Guardado .15 .40
582 Bartolo Colon .15 .40
583 Endy Chavez .15 .40
584 Raul Mondesi .15 .40
585 Jeff Weaver .15 .40
586 Marcus Thames .15 .40
587 Ted Lilly .15 .40
588 Ray Durham .15 .40
589 Jeremy Giambi .15 .40
590 Vicente Padilla .15 .40
591 Brett Myers .15 .40
592 Josh Fogg .15 .40
593 Tony Alvarez .15 .40
594 Jake Peavy .20 .50
595 Dennis Tankersley .15 .40
596 Sean Burroughs .15 .40
597 Kenny Lofton .15 .40
598 Scott Rolen .20 .50
599 Chuck Finley .15 .40
600 Carl Crawford .15 .40
601 Kevin Mench .15 .40
602 Juan Gonzalez .15 .40
603 Jayson Werth .15 .40
604 Eric Hinske .15 .40
605 Josh Phelps .15 .40
606 Jose Valverde ROO RC .15 .40
607 John Ennis ROO RC .15 .40
608 Trey Hodges ROO RC .15 .40
609 Kevin Gryboski ROO RC .15 .40
610 Travis Driskill ROO RC .15 .40
611 Howie Clark ROO RC .15 .40
612 Freddy Sanchez ROO RC .75 2.00
613 Josh Hancock ROO RC .20 .50
614 Jorge De La Rosa ROO RC .15 .40
615 Mike Mahoney ROO .15 .40
616 Jason Davis ROO RC .15 .40
617 Josh Bard ROO RC .15 .40
618 Jason Beverlin ROO RC .15 .40
619 Carl Sadler ROO RC .15 .40
620 Earl Snyder ROO RC .15 .40
621 Aaron Cook ROO RC .15 .40
622 Eric Eckenstahler ROO RC .15 .40
623 Franklyn German ROO RC .15 .40
624 Kirk Saarloos ROO RC .15 .40
625 Rodrigo Rosario ROO RC .15 .40
626 Jeriome Robertson ROO RC .15 .40
627 Brandon Puffer ROO RC .15 .40
628 Miguel Asencio ROO RC .15 .40
629 Aaron Guiel ROO RC .15 .40
630 Ryan Bukvich ROO RC .15 .40
631 Jeremy Hill ROO RC .15 .40
632 Kazuhisa Ishii ROO RC .20 .50
633 Jayson Durocher ROO RC .15 .40
634 Shane Nance ROO RC .15 .40
635 Eric Good ROO RC .15 .40
636 Jamey Carroll ROO RC .30 .75
637 Jaime Cerda ROO RC .15 .40
638 Nate Field ROO RC .15 .40
639 Cody McKay ROO RC .15 .40
640 Jose Flores ROO RC .15 .40
641 Jorge Padilla ROO RC .15 .40
642 Anderson Machado ROO RC .15 .40
643 Eric Junge ROO RC .15 .40
644 Oliver Perez ROO RC .30 .75
645 Julius Matos ROO RC .15 .40

646 Ben Howard ROO RC .15 .40
647 Julio Mateo ROO RC .15 .40
648 Matt Thornton ROO RC .15 .40
649 Chris Snelling ROO RC .25 .60
650 Jason Simontacchi ROO RC .15 .40
651 So Taguchi ROO RC .20 .50
652 Mike Crudale ROO RC .15 .40
653 Mike Coolbaugh ROO RC .15 .40
654 Felix Escalona ROO RC .15 .40
655 Jorge Sosa ROO RC .20 .50
656 Lance Carter ROO RC .15 .40
657 Reynaldo Garcia ROO RC .15 .40
658 Kevin Cash ROO RC .15 .40
659 Ken Huckaby ROO RC .15 .40
660 Scott Wiggins ROO RC .15 .40

2002 Upper Deck Victory Gold

COMMON CARD (1-550) .40 1.00
*GOLD 1-490/531-550: 4X TO 10X BASIC
*GOLD 491-530: 3X TO 8X BASIC
STATED ODDS 1:2

2003 Upper Deck Victory

COMPLETE SET (200) 30.00 80.00
COMP.SET w/o SP's (100) 10.00 25.00
COMMON CARD (1-100) .10 .30
COMMON CARD (101-200) .25 .60
101-128 STATED ODDS 1:4
129-168 STATED ODDS 1:5
169-188 STATED ODDS 1:10
189-200 STATED ODDS 1:20
1 Troy Glaus .12 .30
2 Garret Anderson .12 .30
3 Tim Salmon .12 .30
4 Darin Erstad .12 .30
5 Luis Gonzalez .12 .30
6 Curt Schilling .20 .50
7 Randy Johnson .30 .75
8 Junior Spivey .12 .30
9 Andruw Jones .12 .30
10 Greg Maddux .40 1.00
11 Chipper Jones .30 .75
12 Gary Sheffield .12 .30
13 John Smoltz .30 .75
14 Geronimo Gil .12 .30
15 Tony Batista .12 .30
16 Trot Nixon .12 .30
17 Manny Ramirez .30 .75
18 Pedro Martinez .20 .50
19 Nomar Garciaparra .20 .50
20 Derek Lowe .12 .30
21 Shea Hillenbrand .12 .30
22 Sammy Sosa .30 .75
23 Kerry Wood .12 .30
24 Mark Prior .20 .50
25 Magglio Ordonez .20 .50
26 Frank Thomas .30 .75
27 Mark Buehrle .20 .50
28 Paul Konerko .20 .50
29 Adam Dunn .20 .50
30 Ken Griffey Jr. .60 1.50
31 Austin Kearns .12 .30
32 Matt Lawton .12 .30
33 Larry Walker .20 .50
34 Todd Helton .20 .50
35 Jeff Bagwell .20 .50
36 Roy Oswalt .20 .50
37 Lance Berkman .20 .50
38 Mike Sweeney .12 .30
39 Carlos Beltran .20 .50
40 Kazuhisa Ishii .12 .30
41 Shawn Green .12 .30
42 Hideo Nomo .30 .75
43 Adrian Beltre .30 .75
44 Richie Sexson .12 .30
45 Ben Sheets .12 .30
46 Torii Hunter .12 .30
47 Jacque Jones .12 .30
48 Corey Koskie .12 .30
49 Vladimir Guerrero .20 .50
50 Jose Vidro .12 .30
51 Mo Vaughn .12 .30
52 Mike Piazza .30 .75
53 Roberto Alomar .20 .50
54 Derek Jeter .75 2.00
55 Alfonso Soriano .20 .50
56 Jason Giambi .12 .30
57 Roger Clemens .40 1.00
58 Mike Mussina .20 .50
59 Bernie Williams .20 .50
60 Jorge Posada .20 .50
61 Nick Johnson .12 .30
62 Hideki Matsui RC .60 1.50
63 Eric Chavez .12 .30
64 Barry Zito .20 .50
65 Miguel Tejada .20 .50
66 Tim Hudson .20 .50
67 Pat Burrell .12 .30
68 Bobby Abreu .12 .30
69 Jimmy Rollins .20 .50
70 Brett Myers .12 .30
71 Jim Thome .20 .50
72 Jason Kendall .12 .30
73 Brian Giles .12 .30
74 Aramis Ramirez .12 .30
75 Sean Burroughs .12 .30
76 Ryan Klesko .12 .30
77 Phil Nevin .12 .30
78 Barry Bonds .50 1.25
79 J.T.Snow .12 .30
80 Rich Aurilia .12 .30
81 Ichiro Suzuki .40 1.00
82 Edgar Martinez .20 .50
83 Freddy Garcia .12 .30
84 Jim Edmonds .20 .50
85 J.D. Drew .12 .30
86 Scott Rolen .20 .50
87 Albert Pujols .40 1.00
88 Mark McGwire .50 1.25
89 Matt Morris .12 .30
90 Ben Grieve .12 .30
91 Carl Crawford .20 .50
92 Alex Rodriguez .40 1.00
93 Carl Everett .12 .30
94 Juan Gonzalez .12 .30
95 Rafael Palmeiro .20 .50
96 Hank Blalock .12 .30
97 Carlos Delgado .12 .30
98 Josh Phelps .12 .30
99 Eric Hinske .12 .30
100 Shannon Stewart .12 .30
101 Albert Pujols SH .75 2.00
102 Alex Rodriguez SH .75 2.00
103 Alfonso Soriano SH .40 1.00
104 Barry Bonds SH 1.00 2.50
105 Bernie Williams SH .40 1.00
106 Brian Giles SH .25 .60
107 Chipper Jones SH .60 1.50
108 Darin Erstad SH .25 .60
109 Derek Jeter SH 1.50 4.00
110 Eric Chavez SH .25 .60
111 Miguel Tejada SH .40 1.00
112 Ichiro Suzuki SH .75 2.00
113 Rafael Palmeiro SH .40 1.00
114 Jason Giambi SH .25 .60
115 Jeff Bagwell SH .40 1.00
116 Jim Thome SH .40 1.00
117 Ken Griffey Jr. SH 1.25 3.00
118 Lance Berkman SH .40 1.00
119 Luis Gonzalez SH .25 .60
120 Manny Ramirez SH .60 1.50
121 Mike Piazza SH .60 1.50
122 J.D. Drew SH .25 .60
123 Sammy Sosa SH .60 1.50
124 Scott Rolen SH .40 1.00
125 Shawn Green SH .25 .60
126 Todd Helton SH .40 1.00
127 Troy Glaus SH .25 .60
128 Vladimir Guerrero SH .40 1.00
129 Albert Pujols CP .75 2.00
130 Brian Giles CP .25 .60
131 Carlos Delgado CP .25 .60
132 Curt Schilling CP .40 1.00
133 Derek Jeter CP 1.50 4.00
134 Frank Thomas CP .60 1.50
135 Greg Maddux CP .75 2.00
136 Jeff Bagwell CP .40 1.00
137 Jim Thome CP .40 1.00
138 Jorge Posada CP .40 1.00
139 Kazuhisa Ishii CP .25 .60
140 Larry Walker CP .40 1.00
141 Luis Gonzalez CP .25 .60
142 Miguel Tejada CP .40 1.00
143 Pat Burrell CP .25 .60
144 Pedro Martinez CP .40 1.00
145 Rafael Palmeiro CP .40 1.00
146 Roger Clemens CP .75 2.00
147 Tim Hudson CP .40 1.00
148 Troy Glaus CP .25 .60
149 Alfonso Soriano LL .40 1.00
150 Andruw Jones LL .25 .60
151 Barry Zito LL .40 1.00
152 Darin Erstad LL .25 .60
153 Eric Chavez LL .25 .60
154 Alex Rodriguez LL .75 2.00
155 J.D. Drew LL .25 .60
156 Jason Giambi LL .25 .60
157 Jason Kendall LL .25 .60
158 Ken Griffey Jr. LL 1.25 3.00
159 Lance Berkman LL .40 1.00
160 Mike Mussina LL .40 1.00
161 Mike Piazza LL .60 1.50
162 Nomar Garciaparra LL .40 1.00
163 Randy Johnson LL .60 1.50
164 Roberto Alomar LL .40 1.00
165 Scott Rolen LL .40 1.00
166 Shawn Green LL .25 .60
167 Torii Hunter LL .25 .60
168 Vladimir Guerrero LL .40 1.00
169 Alex Rodriguez TG .75 2.00
170 Andruw Jones TG .25 .60
171 Bernie Williams TG .40 1.00
172 Ichiro Suzuki TG .75 2.00
173 Miguel Tejada TG .40 1.00
174 Nomar Garciaparra TG .40 1.00
175 Pedro Martinez TG .40 1.00
176 Randy Johnson TG .60 1.50
177 Todd Helton TG .40 1.00
178 Vladimir Guerrero TG .40 1.00
179 Barry Bonds RP 1.00 2.50
180 Carlos Delgado RP .25 .60
181 Chipper Jones RP .60 1.50
182 Frank Thomas RP .60 1.50
183 Lance Berkman RP .40 1.00
184 Larry Walker RP .40 1.00
185 Manny Ramirez RP .60 1.50
186 Mike Piazza RP .60 1.50
187 Sammy Sosa RP .60 1.50
188 Shawn Green RP .25 .60
189 Chipper Jones DM .60 1.50
190 Curt Schilling DM .40 1.00
191 Derek Jeter DM 1.50 4.00
192 Ken Griffey Jr. DM 1.25 3.00
193 Sammy Sosa DM .60 1.50
194 Vladimir Guerrero DM .40 1.00
195 Alex Rodriguez WF .75 2.00
196 Barry Bonds WF 1.00 2.50
197 Greg Maddux WF .75 2.00
198 Ichiro Suzuki WF .75 2.00
199 Jason Giambi WF .25 .60
200 Mike Piazza WF .60 1.50

2003 Upper Deck Victory Tier 1 Green

COMPLETE SET (100) 20.00 50.00
*GREEN: 1X TO 2.5X BASIC
*GREEN MATSUI: 1X TO 2.5X BASIC
STATED ODDS 1:1

2003 Upper Deck Victory Tier 2 Orange

COMPLETE SET (100) 30.00 80.00
*ORANGE: 2X TO 5X BASIC
*ORANGE MATSUI: 2X TO 5X BASIC
STATED ODDS 1:8

2003 Upper Deck Victory Tier 3 Blue

*BLUE: 4X TO 10X BASIC
RANDOM INSERTS IN PACKS
STATED PRINT RUN 650 SERIAL #'d SETS

2003 Upper Deck Victory Tier 4 Purple

*PURPLE: 12.5X TO 30X BASIC
RANDOM INSERTS IN PACKS
STATED PRINT RUN 50 SERIAL #'d SETS

2001 Upper Deck Vintage

COMPLETE SET (400) 20.00 50.00
COMMON (1-340/371-400) .10 .30
COMMON CARD (341-370) .20 .50
1 Darin Erstad .10 .30
2 Seth Etherton .10 .30
3 Troy Glaus .10 .30
4 Bengie Molina .10 .30
5 Mo Vaughn .10 .30
6 Tim Salmon .20 .50
7 Ramon Ortiz .10 .30
8 Adam Kennedy .10 .30
9 Garret Anderson .10 .30
10 Troy Percival .10 .30
11 California Angels CL .10 .30
12 Jason Giambi .10 .30
13 Tim Hudson .10 .30
14 Adam Piatt .10 .30
15 Miguel Tejada .10 .30
16 Mark Mulder .10 .30
17 Eric Chavez .10 .30
18 Ramon Hernandez .10 .30
19 Terrence Long .10 .30
20 Jason Isringhausen .10 .30
21 Barry Zito .20 .50
22 Ben Grieve .10 .30
23 Oakland Athletics CL .10 .30
24 David Wells .10 .30
25 Raul Mondesi .10 .30
26 Darrin Fletcher .10 .30
27 Shannon Stewart .10 .30
28 Kelvim Escobar .10 .30
29 Tony Batista .10 .30
30 Carlos Delgado .10 .30
31 Brad Fullmer .10 .30
32 Billy Koch .10 .30
33 Jose Cruz Jr. .10 .30
34 Toronto Blue Jays CL .10 .30
35 Greg Vaughn .10 .30
36 Roberto Hernandez .10 .30
37 Vinny Castilla .10 .30
38 Gerald Williams .10 .30
39 Aubrey Huff .10 .30
40 Bryan Rekar .10 .30
41 Albie Lopez .10 .30
42 Fred McGriff .20 .50
43 Miguel Cairo .10 .30
44 Ryan Rupe .10 .30
45 Tampa Bay Devil Rays CL .10 .30
46 Jim Thome .20 .50
47 Roberto Alomar .20 .50
48 Bartolo Colon .10 .30
49 Omar Vizquel .20 .50
50 Travis Fryman .10 .30
51 Manny Ramirez UER .20 .50
52 Dave Burba .10 .30
53 Chuck Finley .10 .30
54 Russ Branyan .10 .30
55 Kenny Lofton .10 .30
56 Cleveland Indians CL UER .10 .30
57 Alex Rodriguez .40 1.00
58 Jay Buhner .10 .30
59 Aaron Sele .10 .30
60 Kazuhiro Sasaki .10 .30
61 Edgar Martinez .20 .50
62 John Halama .10 .30
63 Mike Cameron .10 .30
64 Freddy Garcia .10 .30
65 John Olerud .08 .25
66 Jamie Moyer .10 .30
67 Gil Meche .10 .30
68 Seattle Mariners CL .10 .30
69 Cal Ripken 1.00 2.50
70 Sidney Ponson .10 .30
71 Chris Richard .10 .30
72 Jose Mercedes .10 .30
73 Albert Belle .10 .30
74 Mike Mussina .20 .50
75 Brady Anderson .10 .30
76 Delino DeShields .10 .30
77 Melvin Mora .10 .30
78 Luis Matos .10 .30
79 Brook Fordyce .10 .30
80 Baltimore Orioles CL .10 .30
81 Rafael Palmeiro .20 .50
82 Rick Helling .10 .30
83 Ruben Mateo .10 .30
84 Rusty Greer .10 .30
85 Ivan Rodriguez .20 .50
86 Doug Davis .10 .30
87 Gabe Kapler .10 .30
88 Mike Lamb .10 .30
89 Alex Rodriguez Rangers 1.00 2.50
90 Kenny Rogers .10 .30
91 Texas Rangers CL .20 .50
92 Nomar Garciaparra .50 1.25
93 Trot Nixon .10 .30
94 Tomokazu Ohka .10 .30
95 Pedro Martinez .20 .50
96 Dante Bichette .10 .30
97 Jason Varitek .30 .75
98 Rolando Arrojo .10 .30
99 Carl Everett .10 .30
100 Derek Lowe .10 .30
101 Troy O'Leary .10 .30
102 Tim Wakefield .10 .30
103 Boston Red Sox CL .20 .50
104 Mike Sweeney .10 .30
105 Carlos Febles .10 .30
106 Joe Randa .10 .30
107 Jeff Suppan .10 .30
108 Mac Suzuki .10 .30
109 Jermaine Dye .10 .30
110 Carlos Beltran .10 .30
111 Mark Quinn .10 .30
112 Johnny Damon .20 .50
113 Kansas City Royals CL .10 .30
114 Tony Clark .10 .30
115 Dean Palmer .10 .30
116 Brian Moehler .10 .30
117 Brad Ausmus .10 .30
118 Juan Gonzalez .10 .30
119 Juan Encarnacion .10 .30
120 Jeff Weaver .10 .30
121 Bobby Higginson .10 .30
122 Todd Jones .10 .30
123 Deivi Cruz .10 .30
124 Detroit Tigers CL .10 .30
125 Corey Koskie .10 .30
126 Matt Lawton .10 .30
127 Mark Redman .10 .30
128 David Ortiz .30 .75
129 Jay Canizaro .10 .30
130 Eric Milton .10 .30
131 Jacque Jones .10 .30
132 J.C. Romero .10 .30
133 Ron Coomer .10 .30
134 Brad Radke .10 .30
135 Minnesota Twins CL .20 .50
136 Carlos Lee .10 .30
137 Frank Thomas .30 .75
138 Mike Sirotka .10 .30
139 Charles Johnson .10 .30
140 James Baldwin .10 .30
141 Magglio Ordonez .10 .30
142 Jon Garland .10 .30
143 Paul Konerko .10 .30
144 Ray Durham .10 .30
145 Keith Foulke .10 .30
146 Chris Singleton .10 .30
147 Chicago White Sox CL .20 .50
148 Bernie Williams .20 .50
149 Orlando Hernandez .10 .30
150 David Justice .10 .30
151 Andy Pettitte .20 .50
152 Mariano Rivera .30 .75
153 Derek Jeter .75 2.00
154 Jorge Posada .20 .50
155 Jose Canseco .20 .50
156 Glenallen Hill .10 .30
157 Paul O'Neill .20 .50
158 Denny Neagle .10 .30
159 Chuck Knoblauch .10 .30
160 Roger Clemens .60 1.50
161 New York Yankees CL .30 .75
162 Jeff Bagwell .20 .50
163 Moises Alou .10 .30
164 Lance Berkman .10 .30
165 Shane Reynolds .10 .30
166 Ken Caminiti .10 .30
167 Craig Biggio .20 .50
168 Jose Lima .10 .30
169 Octavio Dotel .10 .30
170 Richard Hidalgo .10 .30
171 Scott Elarton .10 .30
172 Houston Astros CL .20 .50
173 Rafael Furcal .10 .30
174 Greg Maddux .50 1.25
175 Quilvio Veras .10 .30
176 Chipper Jones .30 .75
177 Andres Galarraga .10 .30
178 Brian Jordan .10 .30
179 Tom Glavine .20 .50
180 Kevin Millwood .10 .30
181 Javier Lopez .10 .30
182 B.J. Surhoff .10 .30
183 Andruw Jones .20 .50
184 Andy Ashby .10 .30
185 Atlanta Braves CL .20 .50
186 Richie Sexson .10 .30
187 Jeff D'Amico .10 .30
188 Ron Belliard .10 .30
189 Jeromy Burnitz .10 .30
190 Jimmy Haynes .10 .30
191 Marquis Grissom .10 .30
192 Jose Hernandez .10 .30
193 Geoff Jenkins .10 .30
194 Jamey Wright .10 .30
195 Mark Loretta .10 .30
196 Milwaukee Brewers CL .10 .30
197 Rick Ankiel .10 .30
198 Mark McGwire .75 2.00
199 Fernando Vina .10 .30
200 Edgar Renteria .10 .30
201 Darryl Kile .10 .30
202 Jim Edmonds .10 .30
203 Ray Lankford .10 .30
204 Garrett Stephenson .10 .30
205 Fernando Tatis .10 .30
206 Will Clark .20 .50
207 J.D. Drew .10 .30
208 St. Louis Cardinals CL .10 .30
209 Mark Grace .20 .50
210 Eric Young .10 .30
211 Sammy Sosa .30 .75
212 Jon Lieber .10 .30
213 Joe Girardi .10 .30
214 Kevin Tapani .10 .30
215 Ricky Gutierrez .10 .30
216 Kerry Wood .10 .30
217 Rondell White .10 .30
218 Damon Buford .10 .30
219 Chicago Cubs CL .10 .30
220 Luis Gonzalez .10 .30
221 Randy Johnson .30 .75
222 Jay Bell .10 .30
223 Erubiel Durazo .10 .30
224 Matt Williams .10 .30
225 Steve Finley .10 .30
226 Curt Schilling .10 .30
227 Todd Stottlemyre .10 .30
228 Tony Womack .10 .30
229 Brian Anderson .10 .30
230 Arizona Diamondbacks CL .10 .30
231 Gary Sheffield .10 .30
232 Adrian Beltre .10 .30
233 Todd Hundley .10 .30
234 Chan Ho Park .10 .30
235 Shawn Green .10 .30
236 Kevin Brown .10 .30
237 Tom Goodwin .10 .30
238 Mark Grudzielanek .10 .30
239 Ismael Valdes .10 .30
240 Eric Karros .10 .30
241 Los Angeles Dodgers CL .10 .30
242 Jose Vidro .10 .30
243 Javier Vazquez .10 .30
244 Orlando Cabrera .10 .30
245 Peter Bergeron .10 .30
246 Vladimir Guerrero .30 .75
247 Dustin Hermanson .10 .30
248 Tony Armas Jr. .10 .30
249 Lee Stevens .10 .30
250 Milton Bradley .10 .30
251 Carl Pavano .10 .30
252 Montreal Expos CL .10 .30
253 Ellis Burks .10 .30
254 Robb Nen .10 .30
255 J.T. Snow .10 .30
256 Barry Bonds .75 2.00
257 Shawn Estes .10 .30
258 Jeff Kent .10 .30
259 Kirk Rueter .10 .30
260 Bill Mueller .10 .30
261 Livan Hernandez .10 .30
262 Rich Aurilia .10 .30
263 San Francisco Giants CL .10 .30
264 Ryan Dempster .10 .30
265 Cliff Floyd .10 .30
266 Mike Lowell .10 .30
267 A.J. Burnett .10 .30
268 Preston Wilson .10 .30
269 Luis Castillo .10 .30
270 Henry Rodriguez .10 .30
271 Antonio Alfonseca .10 .30
272 Derrek Lee .20 .50
273 Mark Kotsay .10 .30
274 Brad Penny .10 .30
275 Florida Marlins CL .20 .50
276 Mike Piazza .50 1.25
277 Jay Payton .10 .30
278 Al Leiter .10 .30
279 Mike Bordick .10 .30
280 Armando Benitez .10 .30
281 Todd Zeile .10 .30
282 Mike Hampton .10 .30
283 Edgardo Alfonzo .10 .30
284 Derek Bell .10 .30
285 Robin Ventura .10 .30
286 New York Mets CL .10 .30
287 Tony Gwynn .40 1.00
288 Trevor Hoffman .10 .30
289 Ryan Klesko .10 .30
290 Phil Nevin .10 .30
291 Matt Clement .10 .30
292 Ben Davis .10 .30
293 Ruben Rivera .10 .30
294 Bret Boone .10 .30
295 Adam Eaton .10 .30
296 Eric Owens .10 .30
297 San Diego Padres CL .10 .30
298 Bob Abreu .10 .30
299 Mike Lieberthal .10 .30
300 Robert Person .10 .30
301 Scott Rolen .20 .50
302 Randy Wolf .10 .30
303 Bruce Chen .10 .30
304 Travis Lee .10 .30
305 Kent Bottenfield .10 .30
306 Pat Burrell .10 .30
307 Doug Glanville .10 .30
308 Philadelphia Phillies CL .10 .30
309 Brian Giles .10 .30
310 Todd Ritchie .10 .30
311 Warren Morris .10 .30
312 John VanderWal .10 .30
313 Kris Benson .10 .30
314 Jason Kendall .10 .30
315 Kevin Young .10 .30
316 Francisco Cordova .10 .30
317 Jimmy Anderson .10 .30
318 Pittsburgh Pirates CL .10 .30
319 Ken Griffey Jr. .60 1.50
320 Pokey Reese .10 .30
321 Chris Stynes .10 .30
322 Barry Larkin .20 .50
323 Steve Parris .10 .30
324 Michael Tucker .10 .30
325 Dmitri Young .10 .30
326 Pete Harnisch .10 .30
327 Danny Graves .10 .30
328 Aaron Boone .10 .30
329 Sean Casey .10 .30
330 Cincinnati Reds CL .15 .40
331 Todd Helton .20 .50
332 Pedro Astacio .10 .30
333 Larry Walker .10 .30
334 Ben Petrick .10 .30
335 Brian Bohanon .10 .30
336 Juan Pierre .10 .30
337 Jeffrey Hammonds .10 .30
338 Jeff Cirillo .10 .30
339 Todd Hollandsworth .10 .30
340 Colorado Rockies CL .10 .30
341 M.Wise .20 .50
K.Luuloa
D.Turnbow
342 J.Hart .20 .50
J.Ortiz
343 Josh Phelps .20 .50
344 T.Harper .20 .50
K.Kelley
T.Hall
345 Martin Vargas RC .20 .50
346 Ichiro Suzuki RC 3.00 8.00
347 J.Spurgeon .20 .50
L.Brea
C.Casimiro
348 Waszgis .20 .50
Sikorski
Benoit
349 S.Kim .20 .50
P.Crawford
S.Lomasney
350 K.Wilson .20 .50
O.Moreno
D.Brown
351 M.Johnson .20 .50
B.Inge
A.Bernero
352 D.Ardoin .20 .50
M.Kinney
J.Ryan
353 Biddle .40 1.00
Crede
Paul
354 N.Johnson .20 .50
D.Jimenez
W.Pena
355 T.McKnight .20 .50
A.McNeal
K.Ginter
356 M.DeRosa .10 .30
J.Marquis
W.Helms
357 A.Levrault .20 .50
H.Estrada
S.Perez
358 L.Saturria .20 .50
G.Stechschulte
B.Reames
359 Corey Patterson .20 .50
360 A.Cabrera .20 .50
G.Guzman
N.Figuero
361 H.Bocachica .20 .50
M.Judd
L.Prokopec
362 T.de la Rosa .20 .50
Y.Valera
T.Nunnari
363 R.Vogelsong .20 .50
J.Melo
C.Zerbe
364 J.Grilli .20 .50
P.Ozuna
R.Castro
365 T.Perez .20 .50
G.Roberts
B.Cole
366 X.Nady .20 .50
D.Maurer RC
367 J.Rollins .20 .50
M.Brownson
R.Taylor
368 A.Hernandez .20 .50
A.Hyzdu
T.Redman
369 B.Clark .20 .50
J.Riedling
M.Bell
370 G.Carrara .20 .50
J.Kalinowski
C.House
371 Jim Edmonds SH .10 .30
372 Edgar Martinez SH .10 .30
373 Rickey Henderson SH .30 .75
374 Barry Zito SH .20 .50
375 Tino Martinez SH .20 .50
376 J.T. Snow SH .10 .30
377 Bobby Jones SH .10 .30
378 Alex Rodriguez SH .25 .60
379 Mike Hampton SH .10 .30
380 Roger Clemens SH .30 .75
381 Jay Payton SH .10 .30
382 John Olerud SH .10 .30
383 David Justice SH .10 .30
384 Mike Hampton SH .10 .30
385 New York Yankees SH .30 .75
386 Jose Vizcaino SH .10 .30
387 Roger Clemens SH .30 .75
388 Todd Zeile SH .10 .30
389 Derek Jeter SH .40 1.00
390 New York Yankees SH .30 .75
391 Nomar .30 .75
Jeter
Manny LL
392 T.Helton .20 .50
V.Guerrero LL
393 Glaus .25 .60
Thom
A-Rod
Giam LL
394 Sammy Sosa LL .20 .50
395 Giambi .10 .30
Edgar
Thomas LL
396 Helton .10 .30
Sosa
Bagw LL
397 Pedro .20 .50
Clem
Muss LL
398 Brown .10 .30
Johnson
Maddux LL
399 Hud .10 .30
Pett
Pedro LL
400 Glav .20 .50
Randy
Maddux LL
S30 Ken Griffey Jr. Sample .60 1.50

2001 Upper Deck Vintage All-Star Tributes

COMPLETE SET (10) 20.00 40.00
STATED ODDS 1:23
AS1 Derek Jeter 2.50 6.00
AS2 Mike Piazza 1.50 4.00
AS3 Carlos Delgado .60 1.50
AS4 Pedro Martinez .60 1.50
AS5 Vladimir Guerrero 1.00 2.50
AS6 Mark McGwire 2.50 6.00
AS7 Alex Rodriguez 1.25 3.00
AS8 Barry Bonds 2.50 6.00
AS9 Chipper Jones 1.00 2.50
AS10 Sammy Sosa 1.00 2.50

2001 Upper Deck Vintage Glory Days

COMPLETE SET (15) 15.00 40.00
STATED ODDS 1:15
G1 Jermaine Dye .60 1.50
G2 Chipper Jones 1.00 2.50
G3 Todd Helton .60 1.50
G4 Magglio Ordonez .60 1.50
G5 Tony Gwynn 1.25 3.00
G6 Jim Edmonds .60 1.50
G7 Rafael Palmeiro .60 1.50
G8 Barry Bonds 2.50 6.00
G9 Carl Everett .60 1.50
G10 Mike Piazza 1.50 4.00
G11 Brian Giles .60 1.50
G12 Tony Batista .60 1.50
G13 Jeff Bagwell .60 1.50
G14 Ken Griffey Jr. 2.00 5.00
G15 Troy Glaus .60 1.50

2001 Upper Deck Vintage Matinee Idols

COMPLETE SET (20) 10.00 25.00
STATED ODDS 1:4
M1 Ken Griffey Jr. 1.00 2.50
M2 Derek Jeter 1.25 3.00
M3 Barry Bonds 1.25 3.00
M4 Chipper Jones .50 1.25
M5 Mike Piazza .75 2.00
M6 Todd Helton .30 .75
M7 Randy Johnson .50 1.25
M8 Alex Rodriguez .60 1.50
M9 Sammy Sosa .50 1.25
M10 Cal Ripken 1.50 4.00
M11 Nomar Garciaparra .75 2.00
M12 Carlos Delgado .30 .75
M13 Jason Giambi .30 .75
M14 Ivan Rodriguez .30 .75
M15 Vladimir Guerrero .50 1.25
M16 Gary Sheffield .30 .75
M17 Frank Thomas .50 1.25
M18 Jeff Bagwell .30 .75
M19 Pedro Martinez .30 .75
M20 Mark McGwire 1.25 3.00

2001 Upper Deck Vintage Retro Rules

COMPLETE SET (15) 20.00 40.00
STATED ODDS 1:15
R1 Nomar Garciaparra 1.50 4.00
R2 Frank Thomas 1.00 2.50
R3 Jeff Bagwell .60 1.50
R4 Sammy Sosa 1.00 2.50
R5 Derek Jeter 2.50 6.00
R6 David Wells .60 1.50
R7 Vladimir Guerrero 1.00 2.50
R8 Jim Thome .60 1.50
R9 Mark McGwire 2.50 6.00
R10 Todd Helton .60 1.50
R11 Tony Gwynn 1.25 3.00
R12 Bernie Williams .60 1.50
R13 Cal Ripken 3.00 8.00
R14 Brian Giles .60 1.50
R15 Jason Giambi .60 1.50

2001 Upper Deck Vintage Timeless Teams

STATED BAT ODDS 1:72
STATED JERSEY ODDS 1:288
CI2JB Johnny Bench Bat 6.00 15.00
CI2JM Joe Morgan Bat 6.00 15.00
CI2KG Ken Griffey Sr. Bat 10.00 25.00
CI2TP Tony Perez Bat 6.00 15.00
BABP Boog Powell Bat 10.00 25.00
BABR Brooks Robinson Bat 6.00 15.00
BAFR Frank Robinson Bat 10.00 25.00
BAMB Mark Belanger Bat 6.00 15.00
BKDN Don Newcombe Bat 10.00 25.00
BKGH Gil Hodges Bat 10.00 25.00
BKJR Jackie Robinson Bat 10.00 25.00
BKRC Roy Campanella Bat 10.00 25.00
CIDC Dave Concepcion Jsy 6.00 15.00
CIJM Joe Morgan Jsy 6.00 15.00
CIKG Ken Griffey Sr. Jsy 10.00 25.00
CITP Tony Perez Jsy 6.00 15.00
LABR Bill Russell Bat 6.00 15.00
LADB Dusty Baker Bat 6.00 15.00
LARC Ron Cey Bat 6.00 15.00
LASG Steve Garvey Bat 6.00 15.00
NYMFK Ed Kranepool Bat 6.00 15.00
NYMNR Nolan Ryan Bat 10.00 25.00
NYMRS Ron Swoboda Bat 6.00 15.00
NYMTA Tommie Agee Bat 6.00 15.00
NYYBD Bill Dickey Bat 10.00 25.00
NYYBR Bobby Richardson Jsy 6.00 15.00
NYYCK Charlie Keller Bat 6.00 15.00
NYYJD Joe DiMaggio Bat 20.00 50.00
NYYMM Mickey Mantle Jsy 50.00 100.00
NYYRM Roger Maris Jsy 12.00 30.00
NYYTH Tommy Henrich Bat 6.00 15.00
OAGT Gene Tenace Bat 6.00 15.00
OAJR Joe Rudi Bat 6.00 15.00
OARJ Reggie Jackson Bat 6.00 15.00
OASB Sal Bando Bat 6.00 15.00
PIAO Al Oliver Bat 6.00 15.00
PIMS Manny Sanguillen Bat 6.00 15.00
PIRC Roberto Clemente Bat 12.00 30.00
PIWS Willie Stargell Bat 6.00 25.00

2001 Upper Deck Vintage Timeless Teams Combos

STATED PRINT RUN 100 SERIAL #'d SETS
LA81 1981 Dodgers 20.00 50.00
BAL70 1970 Orioles 40.00 80.00
BKN55 1955 Dodgers 150.00 250.00
CIN75B 1975 Reds Bat 40.00 80.00
CIN75J 1975 Reds Jsy 20.00 50.00
NYM69 1969 Mets 75.00 150.00
NYY41 1941 Yankees 125.00 200.00
NYY61 1961 Yankees 175.00 300.00
OAK72 1972 A's 40.00 80.00
PIT71 1971 Pirates 100.00 200.00

2002 Upper Deck Vintage

COMPLETE SET (300) 20.00 50.00
SET PRICE DOESN'T INCLUDE ERROR 274A
1 Darin Erstad .15 .40
2 Mo Vaughn .15 .40
3 Ramon Ortiz .15 .40
4 Garret Anderson .15 .40
5 Troy Glaus .15 .40
6 Troy Percival .15 .40
7 Tim Salmon .20 .50
8 W.Caceres .15 .40
E.Guzman
9 Ramon Ortiz TC .15 .40
10 Jason Giambi .15 .40
11 Mark Mulder .15 .40
12 Jermaine Dye .15 .40
13 Miguel Tejada .15 .40
14 Tim Hudson .15 .40
15 Eric Chavez .15 .40
16 Barry Zito .15 .40
17 O.Salazar .15 .40
J.Pena
18 M.Tejada .15 .40
J.Giambi TC
19 Carlos Delgado .15 .40
20 Raul Mondesi .15 .40
21 Chris Carpenter .15 .40
22 Jose Cruz Jr. .15 .40
23 Alex Gonzalez .15 .40
24 Brad Fullmer .15 .40
25 Shannon Stewart .15 .40
26 B.Lyon .15 .40

V.Wells
27 Carlos Delgado TC .15 .40
28 Greg Vaughn .15 .40
29 Toby Hall .15 .40
30 Ben Grieve .15 .40
31 Aubrey Huff .15 .40
32 Tanyon Sturtze .15 .40
33 Brent Abernathy .15 .40
34 D.Brazelton .15 .40
D.James
35 G.Vaughn .15 .40
F.McGriff TC
36 Roberto Alomar .20 .50
37 Juan Gonzalez .15 .40
38 Bartolo Colon .15 .40
39 C.C. Sabathia .15 .40
40 Jim Thome .20 .50
41 Omar Vizquel .20 .50
42 Russell Branyan .15 .40
43 R.Drese .15 .40
R.Smith
44 C.C. Sabathia TC .15 .40
45 Edgar Martinez .20 .50
46 Bret Boone .15 .40
47 Freddy Garcia .15 .40
48 John Olerud .15 .40
49 Kazuhiro Sasaki .15 .40
50 Ichiro Suzuki .60 1.50
51 Mike Cameron .15 .40
52 R.Soriano .15 .40
D.Stark
53 Jamie Moyer TC .15 .40
54 Tony Batista .15 .40
55 Jeff Conine .15 .40
56 Jason Johnson .15 .40
57 Jay Gibbons .15 .40
58 Chris Richard .15 .40
59 Josh Towers .15 .40
60 Jerry Hairston Jr. .15 .40
61 S.Douglass .15 .40
T.Raines Jr.
62 Cal Ripken TC .50 1.25
63 Alex Rodriguez .40 1.00
64 Ruben Sierra .15 .40
65 Ivan Rodriguez .20 .50
66 Gabe Kapler .15 .40
67 Rafael Palmeiro .20 .50
68 Frank Catalanotto .15 .40
69 M.Teixeira .40 1.00
C.Pena
70 Alex Rodriguez TC .25 .60
71 Nomar Garciaparra .50 1.25
72 Pedro Martinez .20 .50
73 Trot Nixon .15 .40
74 Dante Bichette .15 .40
75 Manny Ramirez .20 .50
76 Carl Everett .15 .40
77 Hideo Nomo .30 .75
78 D.Stenson .15 .40
J.Diaz
79 Manny Ramirez TC .20 .50
80 Mike Sweeney .15 .40
81 Carlos Febles .15 .40
82 Dee Brown .15 .40
83 Neifi Perez .15 .40
84 Mark Quinn .15 .40
85 Carlos Beltran .15 .40
86 Joe Randa .15 .40
87 K.Harvey .15 .40
M.MacDougal
88 Mike Sweeney TC .15 .40
89 Dean Palmer .15 .40
90 Jeff Weaver .15 .40
91 Jose Lima .15 .40
92 Tony Clark .15 .40
93 Damion Easley .15 .40
94 Bobby Higginson .15 .40
95 Robert Fick .15 .40
96 P.Santana .15 .40
M.Rivera
97 J.Encarnacion .15 .40
R.Cedeno TC
98 Doug Mientkiewicz .15 .40
99 David Ortiz .20 .50
100 Joe Mays .15 .40
101 Corey Koskie .15 .40
102 Eric Milton .15 .40
103 Cristian Guzman .15 .40
104 Brad Radke .15 .40
105 A.Johnson .15 .40
J.Rincon
106 Corey Koskie TC .15 .40
107 Frank Thomas .30 .75
108 Carlos Lee .15 .40
109 Mark Buehrle .15 .40
110 Jose Canseco .20 .50
111 Magglio Ordonez .15 .40
112 Jon Garland .15 .40
113 Ray Durham .15 .40
114 J.Crede .15 .40
J.Fogg
115 Carlos Lee TC .15 .40
116 Derek Jeter .75 2.00
117 Roger Clemens .60 1.50
118 Alfonso Soriano .15 .40
119 Paul O'Neill .20 .50
120 Jorge Posada .20 .50
121 Bernie Williams .20 .50
122 Mariano Rivera .30 .75
123 Tino Martinez .20 .50
124 Mike Mussina .20 .50
125 N.Johnson .15 .40
E.Almonte
126 Posada .30 .75
Justice
Brosius TC
127 Jeff Bagwell .20 .50
128 Wade Miller .15 .40
129 Lance Berkman .15 .40
130 Moises Alou .15 .40
131 Craig Biggio .20 .50
132 Roy Oswalt .15 .40
133 Richard Hidalgo .15 .40
134 M.Ensberg .15 .40
T.Redding
135 L.Berkman .15 .40
R.Hidalgo TC
136 Greg Maddux .50 1.25
137 Chipper Jones .30 .75
138 Brian Jordan .15 .40
139 Marcus Giles .15 .40
140 Andruw Jones .20 .50
141 Tom Glavine .20 .50
142 Rafael Furcal .15 .40
143 W.Betemit .15 .40
H.Ramirez
144 C.Jones .20 .50
B.Jordan TC
145 Jeromy Burnitz .15 .40
146 Ben Sheets .15 .40
147 Geoff Jenkins .15 .40
148 Devon White .15 .40
149 Jimmy Haynes .15 .40
150 Richie Sexson .15 .40
151 Jose Hernandez .15 .40
152 J.Mieses .15 .40
A.Sanchez
153 Richie Sexson TC .15 .40
154 Mark McGwire .75 2.00
155 Albert Pujols .60 1.50
156 Matt Morris .15 .40
157 J.D. Drew .15 .40
158 Jim Edmonds .15 .40
159 Bud Smith .15 .40
160 Darryl Kile .15 .40
161 B.Ortega .15 .40
L.Saturria
162 A.Pujols .60 1.50
M.McGwire TC
163 Sammy Sosa .30 .75
164 Jon Lieber .15 .40
165 Eric Young .15 .40
166 Kerry Wood .15 .40
167 Fred McGriff .20 .50
168 Corey Patterson .15 .40
169 Rondell White .15 .40
170 J.Cruz .25 .60
M.Prior
171 Sammy Sosa TC .20 .50
172 Luis Gonzalez .15 .40
173 Randy Johnson .30 .75
174 Matt Williams .15 .40
175 Mark Grace .20 .50
176 Steve Finley .15 .40
177 Reggie Sanders .15 .40
178 Curt Schilling .15 .40
179 A.Cintron .15 .40
J.Cust
180 Arizona Diamondbacks TC .30 .75
181 Gary Sheffield .15 .40
182 Paul LoDuca .15 .40
183 Chan Ho Park .15 .40
184 Shawn Green .15 .40
185 Eric Karros .15 .40
186 Adrian Beltre .15 .40
187 Kevin Brown .15 .40
188 R.Rodriguez .15 .40
C.Garcia
189 S.Green .15 .40
G.Sheffield TC
190 Vladimir Guerrero .30 .75
191 Javier Vazquez .15 .40
192 Jose Vidro .15 .40
193 Fernando Tatis .15 .40
194 Orlando Cabrera .15 .40
195 Lee Stevens .15 .40
196 Tony Armas Jr. .15 .40
197 D.Bridges .15 .40
H.Mateo
198 V.Guerrero .20 .50
J.Vidro TC
199 Barry Bonds .75 2.00
200 Rich Aurilia .15 .40
201 Russ Ortiz .15 .40
202 Jeff Kent .15 .40
203 Jason Schmidt .15 .40
204 John Vander Wal .15 .40
205 Robb Nen .15 .40
206 Y.Torrealba .15 .40
K.Ainsworth
207 Barry Bonds TC .40 1.00
208 Preston Wilson .15 .40
209 Brad Penny .15 .40
210 Cliff Floyd .15 .40
211 Luis Castillo .15 .40
212 Ryan Dempster .15 .40
213 Charles Johnson .15 .40
214 A.J. Burnett .15 .40
215 A.Nunez .15 .40
J.Beckett
216 Cliff Floyd TC .15 .40
217 Mike Piazza .50 1.25
218 Al Leiter .15 .40
219 Edgardo Alfonzo .15 .40
220 Tsuyoshi Shinjo .15 .40
221 Matt Lawton .15 .40
222 Robin Ventura .15 .40
223 Jay Payton .15 .40
224 A.Escobar .15 .40
J.Seo
225 M.Piazza .30 .75
R.Ventura TC
226 Ryan Klesko .15 .40
227 D'Angelo Jimenez .15 .40
228 Trevor Hoffman .15 .40
229 Phil Nevin .15 .40
230 Mark Kotsay .15 .40
231 Brian Lawrence .15 .40
232 Bubba Trammell .15 .40
233 J.Middlebrook .15 .40
X.Nady
234 Tony Gwynn TC .20 .50
235 Scott Rolen .20 .50
236 Jimmy Rollins .15 .40
237 Mike Lieberthal .15 .40
238 Bobby Abreu .15 .40
239 Brandon Duckworth .15 .40
240 Robert Person .15 .40
241 Pat Burrell .15 .40
242 N.Punto .15 .40
C.Silva
243 Mike Lieberthal TC .15 .40
244 Brian Giles .15 .40
245 Jack Wilson .15 .40
246 Kris Benson .15 .40
247 Jason Kendall .15 .40
248 Aramis Ramirez .15 .40
249 Todd Ritchie .15 .40
250 Rob Mackowiak .15 .40
251 J.Grabow .15 .40
H.Cota
252 Brian Giles TC .15 .40
253 Ken Griffey Jr. .60 1.50
254 Barry Larkin .20 .50
255 Sean Casey .15 .40
256 Aaron Boone .15 .40
257 Dmitri Young .15 .40
258 Pokey Reese .15 .40
259 Adam Dunn .15 .40
260 D.Espinosa .15 .40
D.Sardinha
261 Ken Griffey TC .40 1.00
262 Todd Helton .20 .50
263 Mike Hampton .15 .40
264 Juan Pierre .15 .40
265 Larry Walker .15 .40
266 Juan Uribe .15 .40
267 Jose Ortiz .15 .40
268 Jeff Cirillo .15 .40
269 J.Jennings .15 .40
L.Hudson
270 Larry Walker TC .15 .40
271 Ichiro .30 .75
Giambi
Alomar LL
272 Walker .15 .40
Helton
Alou LL
273 A.Rod .15 .40
Thome
Palmeiro LL
274 Bonds .40 1.00
Sosa
L.Gonz LL
274A Bonds 1.25 3.00
Sosa
L.Gonz LL ERR
275 Mulder .20 .50
Clemens
Moyer LL
276 Schilling .20 .50
Morris
R.John LL
277 Garcia .15 .40
Mussina
Mays LL
278 R.John .20 .50
Schill
Burkett LL
279 Rivera .20 .50
Sasaki
Foulke LL
280 Nen .15 .40
Benitez
Hoffman LL
281 Jason Giambi PS .15 .40
282 Jorge Posada PS .15 .40
283 J.Thome .20 .50
J.Gonzalez PS
284 Edgar Martinez PS .15 .40
285 Andruw Jones PS .15 .40
286 Chipper Jones PS .20 .50
287 Matt Williams PS .15 .40
288 Curt Schilling PS .15 .40
289 Derek Jeter PS .40 1.00
290 Mike Mussina PS .15 .40
291 Bret Boone PS .15 .40
292 Alfonso Soriano PS .15 .40
293 Randy Johnson PS .20 .50
294 Tom Glavine PS .15 .40
295 Curt Schilling PS .15 .40
296 Randy Johnson PS .20 .50
297 Derek Jeter PS .40 1.00
298 Tino Martinez PS .15 .40
299 Curt Schilling PS .15 .40
300 Luis Gonzalez PS .15 .40

2002 Upper Deck Vintage Aces Game Jersey

STATED ODDS 1:144 HOBBY, 1:210 RETAIL
AFJ Ferguson Jenkins 2.00 5.00
AGM Greg Maddux 10.00 25.00
AHN Hideo Nomo 15.00 40.00
AJD John Denny 1.25 3.00
AJM Juan Marichal 2.00 5.00
AJS Johnny Sain 1.25 3.00
AMMA Mike Marshall 1.25 3.00
AMMU Mike Mussina 2.00 5.00
AMT Mike Torrez 1.25 3.00
ANR Nolan Ryan 20.00 50.00
APM Pedro Martinez 2.00 5.00
ARC Roger Clemens SP 10.00 25.00
ARJ Randy Johnson 3.00 8.00
ATH Tim Hudson 2.00 5.00

2002 Upper Deck Vintage Day At The Park

COMPLETE SET (6) 8.00 20.00
STATED ODDS 1:23
DP1 Ichiro Suzuki 2.00 5.00
DP2 Derek Jeter 2.50 6.00
DP3 Alex Rodriguez 1.25 3.00
DP4 Mark McGwire 2.50 6.00
DP5 Barry Bonds 2.50 6.00
DP6 Sammy Sosa 1.50 4.00

2002 Upper Deck Vintage Night Gamers

COMPLETE SET (12) 6.00 15.00
STATED ODDS 1:11
NG1 Todd Helton .40 1.00
NG2 Manny Ramirez .40 1.00
NG3 Ivan Rodriguez .40 1.00
NG4 Albert Pujols 1.25 3.00
NG5 Greg Maddux 1.00 2.50
NG6 Carlos Delgado .40 1.00
NG7 Frank Thomas .60 1.50
NG8 Derek Jeter 1.50 4.00
NG9 Troy Glaus .40 1.00
NG10 Jeff Bagwell .40 1.00
NG11 Juan Gonzalez .40 1.00
NG12 Randy Johnson .60 1.50

2002 Upper Deck Vintage Sandlot Stars

COMPLETE SET (12) 8.00 20.00
STATED ODDS 1:11
SS1 Ken Griffey Jr. 1.25 3.00
SS2 Derek Jeter 1.50 4.00
SS3 Ichiro Suzuki 1.25 3.00
SS4 Nomar Garciaparra 1.00 2.50
SS5 Sammy Sosa .60 1.50
SS6 Chipper Jones .60 1.50
SS7 Jason Giambi .60 1.50
SS8 Alex Rodriguez .75 2.00
SS9 Mark McGwire 1.50 4.00
SS10 Barry Bonds 1.50 4.00
SS11 Mike Piazza 1.00 2.50
SS12 Vladimir Guerrero .60 1.50

2002 Upper Deck Vintage Signature Combos

RANDOM INSERTS IN PACKS
STATED PRINT RUN 100 SERIAL #'d SETS
VSAT R.Alomar/J.Thome 50.00 100.00
VSBB Y.Berra/J.Bench 75.00 200.00
VSBR S.Bando/J.Rudi 20.00 50.00
VSEL D.Evans/F.Lynn 40.00 80.00
VSFB C.Fisk/J.Bench 60.00 120.00
VSGR K.Griffey Jr./A.Rod 200.00 400.00
VSJM R.Jackson/W.McCovey 75.00 200.00
VSJO E.Martinez/J.Olerud 40.00 80.00
VSSD R.Sandberg/A.Dawson 75.00 150.00

2002 Upper Deck Vintage Special Collection Game Jersey

STATED ODDS 1:144 HOBBY, 1:210 RETAIL
SAD Andre Dawson Pants 6.00 15.00
SBC Bert Campaneris Jsy 6.00 15.00
SBW Billy Williams Jsy 6.00 15.00
SFJ Fergie Jenkins Pants SP 8.00 20.00
SJR Joe Rudi Jsy 6.00 15.00
SMG Mark Grace Jsy 8.00 20.00
SMH Mike Hegan Jsy 4.00 10.00
SPL Paul Lindblad Jsy 4.00 10.00
SRF Rollie Fingers Jsy 6.00 15.00
SRJ Reggie Jackson Jsy SP 8.00 20.00
SRS Ryne Sandberg Jsy 25.00 50.00
SSAB Sal Bando Jsy 6.00 15.00
SSS Sammy Sosa Jsy 10.00 25.00
SSTB Stan Bahnsen Jsy 4.00 10.00

2002 Upper Deck Vintage Timeless Teams Game Bat Quads

STATED ODDS 1:288 HOBBY, 1:480 RETAIL
B G'berg/McCov/Thom/Murr 10.00 25.00
OF2 Griff Jr./Bon/Hend/Gwynn 30.00 60.00
ATL Gla/Madd/Chipper/Andruw 12.50 30.00
CLE Gonz/Thome/Alomar/Lofton 15.00 40.00
NYY Rivera/William/O'Neill/Pos 10.00 25.00
OAK Parker/Cans/Hend/Baylor 10.00 25.00
SEA Ichiro/Edgar/Olerud/Boone 20.00 50.00

2002 Upper Deck Vintage Timeless Teams Game Jersey

STATED ODDS 1:144 HOBBY, 1:210 RETAIL
JAJ Andruw Jones Jsy 8.00 20.00
JCH Catfish Hunter Jsy 8.00 20.00
JCJ Chipper Jones Jsy 8.00 20.00
JDE Dwight Evans Jsy 8.00 20.00
JEMA Edgar Martinez Jsy 8.00 20.00
JEMU Eddie Murray Jsy 10.00 25.00
JFL Fred Lynn Jsy 8.00 20.00
JJB Johnny Bench Jsy 10.00 25.00
JKS Kazuhiro Sasaki Jsy 6.00 15.00
JRF Rollie Fingers Jsy 10.00 25.00
JRJ Reggie Jackson Jsy 8.00 20.00
JWM Willie McCovey Pants 8.00 20.00

2002 Upper Deck Vintage Timeless Teams Game Jersey Combos

STATED ODDS 1:288 HOBBY
ATL Maddux/Chipper/Andruw 10.00 25.00
NYY Clemens/Rivera/B.Williams 10.00 25.00
OAK Fingers/Hunter/Reggie 10.00 25.00

2003 Upper Deck Vintage

COMP.SET w/o SP's (200) 20.00 50.00
COMP.UPDATE SET (60) 6.00 15.00
COMMON ACTIVE (1-280) .12 .30
COMMON RETIRED .12 .30
COMMON SP (1-220) 1.00 2.50
SP 1-220 STATED ODDS 1:20
COMMON TR1 SP 1.00 2.50
TR1 SP STATED ODDS 1:20
COMMON TR2 SP 1.00 2.50
TR2 SP STATED ODDS 1:40
COMMON CARD (223-232) .60 1.50
223-232 STATED ODDS 1:7
COMMON CARD (233-247) .60 1.50
233-247 STATED ODDS 1:5
COMMON CARD (248-277) 1.50 4.00
248-277 STATED ODDS 1:48
COMMON CARD (281-341) .15 .40
COMMON RC (281-341) .15 .40
281-341 ONE PER 2003 UD 40-MAN PACK
1 Troy Glaus .12 .30
2 Darin Erstad .12 .30
3 Garret Anderson .12 .30
4 Jarrod Washburn .12 .30
5 Nolan Ryan 1.00 2.50
6 Tim Salmon .12 .30
7 Troy Percival .12 .30
8 Alex Ochoa TR1 SP 1.00 2.50
9 Daryle Ward .12 .30
10 Jeff Bagwell .20 .50
11 Roy Oswalt .20 .50
12 Lance Berkman .20 .50
13 Craig Biggio .20 .50
14 Richard Hidalgo .12 .30
15 Tim Hudson .20 .50
16 Eric Chavez .12 .30
17 Barry Zito .20 .50
18 Miguel Tejada .20 .50
19 Mark Mulder .12 .30
20 Rollie Fingers .20 .50
21 Catfish Hunter .20 .50
22 Jermaine Dye .12 .30
23 Ray Durham TR2 SP 1.00 2.50
24 Carlos Delgado .12 .30
25 Eric Hinske .12 .30
26 Josh Phelps .12 .30
27 Shannon Stewart .12 .30
28 Vernon Wells .12 .30
29 John Smoltz .30 .75
30 Greg Maddux .40 1.00
31 Chipper Jones .30 .75
32 Gary Sheffield .12 .30
33 Andruw Jones .12 .30
34 Tom Glavine .20 .50
35 Rafael Furcal .12 .30
36 Phil Niekro .20 .50
37 Eddie Mathews UER 376 .30 .75
38 Robin Yount .30 .75
39 Richie Sexson .12 .30
40 Ben Sheets .12 .30
41 Geoff Jenkins .12 .30
42 Alex Sanchez .12 .30
43 Jason Isringhausen .12 .30
44 Albert Pujols .40 1.00
45 Matt Morris .12 .30
46 J.D. Drew .12 .30
47 Jim Edmonds .20 .50
48 Stan Musial .50 1.25
49 Red Schoendienst .20 .50
50 Edgar Renteria .12 .30
51 Mark McGwire SP 4.00 10.00
52 Scott Rolen TR2 SP 1.50 4.00
53 Mark Bellhorn .12 .30
54 Kerry Wood .12 .30
55 Mark Prior .20 .50
56 Moises Alou .12 .30
57 Corey Patterson .12 .30
58 Ernie Banks .30 .75
59 Hee Seop Choi .12 .30
60 Billy Williams .20 .50
61 Sammy Sosa SP 2.50 6.00
62 Ben Grieve .12 .30
63 Jared Sandberg .12 .30
64 Carl Crawford .20 .50
65 Randy Johnson .30 .75
66 Luis Gonzalez .12 .30
67 Steve Finley .12 .30
68 Junior Spivey .12 .30
69 Erubiel Durazo .12 .30
70 Curt Schilling SP 1.50 4.00
71 Al Lopez .12 .30
72 Pee Wee Reese .20 .50
73 Eric Gagne .12 .30
74 Shawn Green .12 .30
75 Kevin Brown .12 .30
76 Paul Lo Duca .12 .30
77 Adrian Beltre .30 .75
78 Hideo Nomo .30 .75
79 Eric Karros .12 .30
80 Odalis Perez .12 .30
81 Kazuhisa Ishii SP 1.00 2.50
82 Tommy Lasorda .20 .50
83 Fernando Tatis .12 .30
84 Vladimir Guerrero .20 .50
85 Jose Vidro .12 .30
86 Javier Vazquez .12 .30
87 Brad Wilkerson .12 .30
88 Bartolo Colon TR1 SP 1.00 2.50
89 Monte Irvin .20 .50
90 Robb Nen .12 .30
91 Reggie Sanders .12 .30
92 Jeff Kent .12 .30
93 Rich Aurilia .12 .30
94 Orlando Cepeda .20 .50
95 Juan Marichal .20 .50
96 Willie McCovey .20 .50
97 David Bell .12 .30
98 Barry Bonds SP 4.00 10.00
99 Kenny Lofton TR2 SP 1.00 2.50
100 Jim Thome .20 .50
101 C.C. Sabathia .20 .50
102 Omar Vizquel .20 .50
103 Lou Boudreau .20 .50
104 Larry Doby .20 .50
105 Bob Lemon .20 .50
106 John Olerud .12 .30
107 Edgar Martinez .20 .50
108 Bret Boone .12 .30
109 Freddy Garcia .12 .30
110 Mike Cameron .12 .30
111 Kazuhiro Sasaki .12 .30
112 Ichiro Suzuki SP 3.00 8.00
113 Mike Lowell .12 .30
114 Josh Beckett .12 .30
115 A.J. Burnett .12 .30
116 Juan Pierre .12 .30
117 Derrek Lee .12 .30
118 Luis Castillo .12 .30
119 Juan Encarnacion TR1 SP 1.00 2.50
120 Roberto Alomar .20 .50
121 Edgardo Alfonzo .12 .30
122 Jeromy Burnitz .12 .30
123 Mo Vaughn .12 .30
124 Tom Seaver .20 .50
125 Al Leiter .12 .30
126 Mike Piazza SP 2.50 6.00
127 Tony Batista .12 .30
128 Geronimo Gil .12 .30
129 Chris Singleton .12 .30
130 Rodrigo Lopez .12 .30
131 Jay Gibbons .12 .30
132 Melvin Mora .12 .30
133 Earl Weaver .20 .50
134 Trevor Hoffman .20 .50
135 Phil Nevin .12 .30
136 Sean Burroughs .12 .30
137 Ryan Klesko .12 .30
138 Mark Kotsay .12 .30
139 Mike Lieberthal .12 .30
140 Bobby Abreu .12 .30
141 Jimmy Rollins .20 .50
142 Pat Burrell .12 .30
143 Vicente Padilla .12 .30
144 Richie Ashburn .20 .50
145 Jeremy Giambi TR1 SP 1.00 2.50
146 Josh Fogg .12 .30
147 Brian Giles .12 .30
148 Aramis Ramirez .12 .30
149 Jason Kendall .12 .30
150 Ralph Kiner .20 .50
151 Willie Stargell .20 .50
152 Kevin Mench .12 .30
153 Rafael Palmeiro .20 .50
154 Ivan Rodriguez .20 .50
155 Hank Blalock .12 .30
156 Juan Gonzalez .12 .30
157 Carl Everett .12 .30
158 Alex Rodriguez SP 3.00 8.00
159 Nomar Garciaparra .20 .50
160 Derek Lowe .12 .30
161 Manny Ramirez .30 .75
162 Shea Hillenbrand .12 .30
163 Bobby Doerr .20 .50
164 Johnny Damon .20 .50
165 Jason Varitek .30 .75
166 Pedro Martinez SP 1.50 4.00
167 Cliff Floyd TR2 SP 1.00 2.50
168 Ken Griffey Jr. .60 1.50
169 Adam Dunn .20 .50
170 Austin Kearns .12 .30
171 Aaron Boone .12 .30
172 Joe Morgan .20 .50
173 Sean Casey .12 .30
174 Todd Walker .12 .30
175 Ryan Dempster TR1 SP 1.00 2.50
176 Shawn Estes TR1 SP 1.00 2.50
177 Gabe Kapler TR1 SP 1.00 2.50
178 Jason Jennings .12 .30
179 Todd Helton .20 .50
180 Larry Walker .20 .50
181 Preston Wilson .12 .30
182 Jay Payton TR1 SP 1.00 2.50
183 Mike Sweeney .12 .30
184 Carlos Beltran .20 .50
185 Paul Byrd .12 .30
186 Raul Ibanez .20 .50
187 Rick Ferrell .12 .30
188 Early Wynn .20 .50
189 Dmitri Young .12 .30
190 Jim Bunning .20 .50
191 George Kell .20 .50
192 Hal Newhouser .20 .50
193 Bobby Higginson .12 .30
194 Carlos Pena TR1 SP 1.50 4.00
195 Sparky Anderson .20 .50
196 Torii Hunter .12 .30
197 Eric Milton .12 .30
198 Corey Koskie .12 .30
199 Jacque Jones .12 .30
200 Harmon Killebrew .30 .75
201 Doug Mientkiewicz .12 .30
202 Frank Thomas .30 .75
203 Mark Buehrle .20 .50
204 Magglio Ordonez .20 .50
205 Paul Konerko .20 .50
206 Joe Borchard .12 .30
207 Hoyt Wilhelm .20 .50
208 Carlos Lee .12 .30
209 Roger Clemens .40 1.00
210 Nick Johnson .12 .30
211 Jason Giambi .12 .30
212 Alfonso Soriano .20 .50
213 Bernie Williams .20 .50
214 Robin Ventura .12 .30
215 Jorge Posada .20 .50
216 Mike Mussina .20 .50
217 Yogi Berra .30 .75
218 Phil Rizzuto .20 .50
219 Mariano Rivera .40 1.00
220 Derek Jeter SP 6.00 15.00
221 Jeff Weaver TR1 SP 1.00 2.50
222 Raul Mondesi TR2 SP 1.00 2.50
223 F.Sanchez .60 1.50
J.Hancock
224 J.Borchard .60 1.50
M.Olivo
225 B.Phillips .60 1.50
J.Bard
226 A.Van Hekken .60 1.50
A.Torres
227 J.Lane .60 1.50
J.Robertson
228 C.Chen .60 1.50
J.Thurston
229 E.Chavez .60 1.50
J.Carroll
230 D.Henson .60 1.50
A.Graman
231 D.Brazelton .60 1.50
L.Carter
232 J.Werth 1.00 2.50
K.Cash
233 Johnson 1.50 4.00
Schilling
Zito
234 Pedro 1.50 4.00
Johnson
Lowe
235 Johnson 1.50 4.00
Schilling
Pedro
236 Smoltz 1.50 4.00
Gagne
Williams
237 Johnson 1.50 4.00
Colon
Burnett
238 Soriano 2.00 5.00
Suzuki
Guerrero
239 A-Rod 2.00 5.00
Thome
Sosa
240 Bonds 2.50 6.00
Ramirez
Sweeney
241 Soriano 4.00 10.00
A-Rod
Jeter
242 A-Rod 2.00 5.00
Magglio
Tejada
243 Castillo 1.00 2.50
Pierre
Roberts
244 Nomar 1.00 2.50
Anderson
Soriano
245 Damon 1.00 2.50
Rollins
Lofton
246 Bonds 2.50 6.00
Thome
Ramirez
247 Bonds 2.50 6.00
Giles
Ramirez
248 Troy Glaus 3D 1.50 4.00
249 Luis Gonzalez 3D 1.50 4.00
250 Chipper Jones 3D 4.00 10.00
251 Nomar Garciaparra 3D 2.50 6.00
252 Manny Ramirez 3D 4.00 10.00
253 Sammy Sosa 3D 4.00 10.00
254 Frank Thomas 3D 4.00 10.00
255 Maggio Ordonez 3D 2.50 6.00
256 Adam Dunn 3D 2.50 6.00
257 Ken Griffey Jr. 3D 8.00 20.00
258 Jim Thome 3D 2.50 6.00
259 Todd Helton 3D 2.50 6.00
260 Larry Walker 3D 2.50 6.00
261 Lance Berkman 3D 2.50 6.00
262 Jeff Bagwell 3D 2.50 6.00
263 Mike Sweeney 3D 1.50 4.00
264 Shawn Green 3D 1.50 4.00
265 Vladimir Guerrero 3D 2.50 6.00
266 Mike Piazza 3D 4.00 10.00
267 Jason Giambi 3D 1.50 4.00
268 Pat Burrell 3D 1.50 4.00
269 Barry Bonds 3D 6.00 15.00
270 Mark McGwire 3D 6.00 15.00
271 Alex Rodriguez 3D 5.00 12.00
272 Carlos Delgado 3D 1.50 4.00
273 Richie Sexson 3D 1.50 4.00
274 Andruw Jones 3D 1.50 4.00
275 Derek Jeter 3D 10.00 25.00
276 Juan Gonzalez 3D 1.50 4.00
277 Albert Pujols 3D 5.00 12.00
278 Jason Giambi CL .12 .30
279 Sammy Sosa CL .30 .75
280 Ichiro Suzuki CL .40 1.00
281 Tom Glavine .25 .60
282 Josh Stewart RC .15 .40
283 Aquilino Lopez RC .15 .40
284 Horacio Ramirez .15 .40
285 Brandon Phillips .15 .40
286 Kirk Saarloos .15 .40
287 Runelvys Hernandez .15 .40
288 Hideki Matsui RC .75 2.00
289 Jeremy Bonderman RC .60 1.50
290 Russ Ortiz .15 .40
291 Ken Harvey .15 .40
292 Edgardo Alfonzo .15 .40
293 Oscar Villareal RC .15 .40
294 Marlon Byrd .15 .40
295 Josh Bard .15 .40
296 David Cone .15 .40
297 Mike Neu RC .15 .40
298 Cliff Floyd .15 .40
299 Travis Lee .15 .40
300 Jeff Kent .15 .40
301 Ron Calloway .15 .40
302 Bartolo Colon .15 .40
303 Jose Contreras RC .40 1.00
304 Mark Teixeira .25 .60
305 Ivan Rodriguez .25 .60
306 Jim Thome .25 .60
307 Shane Reynolds .15 .40
308 Luis Ayala RC .15 .40
309 Lyle Overbay .15 .40
310 Travis Hafner .15 .40
311 Wilfredo Ledezma RC .15 .40
312 Rocco Baldelli .15 .40
313 Jason Anderson .15 .40
314 Kenny Lofton .15 .40
315 Brandon Larson .15 .40
316 Ty Wigginton .15 .40
317 Fred McGriff .25 .60
318 Antonio Osuna .15 .40
319 Corey Patterson .15 .40
320 Erubiel Durazo .15 .40
321 Mike MacDougal .15 .40
322 Sammy Sosa .40 1.00
323 Mike Hampton .15 .40
324 Ramiro Mendoza .15 .40
325 Kevin Millwood .15 .40
326 Dave Roberts .25 .60
327 Todd Zeile .15 .40
328 Reggie Sanders .15 .40
329 Billy Koch .15 .40
330 Mike Stanton .15 .40
331 Orlando Hernandez .15 .40
332 Tony Clark .15 .40
333 Chris Hammond .15 .40
334 Michael Cuddyer .15 .40
335 Sandy Alomar Jr. .15 .40
336 Jose Cruz Jr. .15 .40
337 Omar Daal .15 .40
338 Robert Fick .15 .40
339 Daryle Ward .15 .40
340 David Bell .15 .40
341 Checklist .15 .40

2003 Upper Deck Vintage All Caps

RANDOM INSERTS IN PACKS
STATED PRINT RUN 250 SERIAL #'d SETS
CP Chan Ho Park 6.00 15.00
DE Darin Erstad 6.00 15.00
GM Greg Maddux 10.00 25.00
JB Jeff Bagwell 8.00 20.00
JG Juan Gonzalez 6.00 15.00
KS Kazuhiro Sasaki 6.00 15.00
LB Lance Berkman 6.00 15.00
LG Luis Gonzalez 6.00 15.00
MP Mike Piazza 15.00 40.00
MV Mo Vaughn 6.00 15.00
RF Rafael Furcal 6.00 15.00
RP Rafael Palmeiro 8.00 20.00

RV Robin Ventura 6.00 15.00
TG Tony Gwynn 10.00 25.00
TH Tim Hudson 6.00 15.00

2003 Upper Deck Vintage Capping the Action

RANDOM INSERTS IN PACKS
B/WN 91-125 #'d COPIES OF EACH CARD
AR Alex Rodriguez/101 15.00 40.00
AS Alfonso Soriano/109 8.00 20.00
CD Carlos Delgado/91 8.00 20.00
HM Hideo Nomo/117 30.00 60.00
IR Ivan Rodriguez/125 10.00 25.00
JG Juan Gonzalez/99 8.00 20.00
KG Ken Griffey Jr./102 15.00 40.00
MM Mike Mussina/109 20.00 50.00
PM Pedro Martinez/125 10.00 25.00
RA Roberto Alomar/101 10.00 25.00
RP Rafael Palmeiro/125 10.00 25.00
SG Shawn Green/125 8.00 20.00
SR Scott Rolen/109 10.00 25.00
SS Sammy Sosa/125 10.00 25.00
TH Todd Helton/99 10.00 25.00

2003 Upper Deck Vintage Cracking the Lumber

GOLD PRINT RUN 5 SERIAL #'d SETS
NO PRICING DUE TO SCARCITY

2003 Upper Deck Vintage Dropping the Hammer

STATED ODDS 1:130
*GOLD: .75X TO 2X BASIC HAMMER
GOLD RANDOM INSERTS IN PACKS
GOLD PRINT RUN 100 SERIAL #'d SETS
AJ Andruw Jones 6.00 15.00
AR Alex Rodriguez 8.00 20.00
BA Bobby Abreu 4.00 10.00
DJ David Justice 4.00 10.00
FM Fred McGriff 6.00 15.00
FT Frank Thomas 6.00 15.00
JG Jason Giambi 4.00 10.00
JT Jim Thome 6.00 15.00
KG Ken Griffey Jr. 8.00 20.00
KL Kenny Lofton 4.00 10.00
LB Lance Berkman 4.00 10.00
LW Larry Walker 4.00 10.00
MO Magglio Ordonez 4.00 10.00
MP Mike Piazza 10.00 25.00
MT Miguel Tejada 4.00 10.00
OV Omar Vizquel 6.00 15.00
PW Preston Wilson 4.00 10.00
RA Roberto Alomar 6.00 15.00
RF Rafael Furcal 4.00 10.00
RP Rafael Palmeiro 6.00 15.00
RV Robin Ventura 4.00 10.00
SG Shawn Green 4.00 10.00
SS Sammy Sosa 6.00 15.00
TA Fernando Tatis 4.00 10.00
TH Todd Helton 6.00 15.00

2003 Upper Deck Vintage Hitmen

STATED PRINT RUN 150 SERIAL #'d SETS
GOLD PRINT RUN 10 SERIAL #'d SETS
NO GOLD PRICING DUE TO SCARCITY
IS Ichiro Suzuki 40.00 80.00
JG Jason Giambi 6.00 15.00
KG Ken Griffey Jr. 15.00 40.00
MM Mark McGwire 40.00 80.00

2003 Upper Deck Vintage Hitmen Double Signed

GOLD PRINT RUN 5 SERIAL #'d CARDS
NO GOLD PRICING DUE TO SCARCITY
MS M.McGwire/S.Sosa 300.00 450.00

2003 Upper Deck Vintage Men with Hats

STATED ODDS 1:285
MHAD Adam Dunn 6.00 15.00
MHAJ Andruw Jones 8.00 20.00
MHAR Alex Rodriguez 10.00 25.00
MHBW Bernie Williams 8.00 20.00
MHEC Eric Chavez 6.00 15.00
MHFT Frank Thomas 8.00 20.00
MHHU Tim Hudson 6.00 15.00
MHJD Johnny Damon 8.00 20.00
MHJG Jason Giambi 6.00 15.00
MHJK Jason Kendall 6.00 15.00
MHKL Kenny Lofton 6.00 15.00
MHMT Miguel Tejada 6.00 15.00
MHTH Todd Helton 8.00 20.00
MHTW Todd Walker 6.00 15.00
MHVC Vinny Castilla 6.00 15.00

2003 Upper Deck Vintage Slugfest

STATED PRINT RUN 200 SERIAL #'d SETS
*GOLD: .75X TO 2X BASIC SLUGFEST
GOLD PRINT RUN 50 SERIAL #'d SETS
SAJ Andruw Jones 6.00 15.00
SAR Alex Rodriguez 10.00 25.00
SBW Bernie Williams 6.00 15.00
SCD Carlos Delgado 4.00 10.00
SFT Frank Thomas 6.00 15.00
SJT Jim Thome 6.00 15.00
SLW Larry Walker 4.00 10.00
SMP Mike Piazza 12.50 30.00
SRP Rafael Palmeiro 6.00 15.00
SSG Shawn Green 4.00 10.00

2003 Upper Deck Vintage Timeless Teams Bat Quads

RANDOM INSERTS IN HOBBY PACKS
STATED PRINT RUN 175 SERIAL #'d SETS
BLAR Burrell/Lieb/Abreu/Roll 10.00 25.00
CTDJ Chavez/Tejada/Dye/Just 10.00 25.00
DEMR Drew/Edm/Tino/Rolen 15.00 40.00
DGCL Dunn/Grif/Casey/Lark 15.00 40.00
GNBL Green/Nomo/Belt/LoDu 15.00 40.00
GPMS Giam/Posa/Mond/A.Sor 15.00 40.00
GWVS Giam/Bernie/Vent/A.Sor 15.00 40.00
HWPZ Helton/Walker/Pier/Zeile 15.00 40.00
IMBC Ichiro/Edgar/Boone/Cam 15.00 40.00
JGSW Randy/Gonz/Schill/Will 10.00 25.00
JJSF Chip/Andruw/Shef/Furc 15.00 40.00
KNKB Klesko/Nevin/Kots/Burr 10.00 25.00
MGLJ Maddux/Glav/Javy/Chip 20.00 50.00
OTLK Magglio/Thom/Lee/Kon 15.00 40.00
PVAA Piazza/Mo/Alom/Alfonzo 30.00 60.00
RGRP A-Rod/Gonz/I-Rod/Raffy 20.00 50.00
RMHN Manny/Pedro/Shea/Nixon 15.00 40.00
SMAP Sosa/McGriff/Alou/Patt 15.00 40.00

2003 Upper Deck Vintage UD Giants

ONE SEALED GIANT PACK PER BOX
AD Adam Dunn .75 2.00
AJ Andruw Jones .50 1.25
AP Albert Pujols 1.50 4.00
AR Alex Rodriguez 1.50 4.00
BB Barry Bonds 2.00 5.00
BG Brian Giles .50 1.25
BW Bernie Williams .75 2.00
CD Carlos Delgado .50 1.25
CJ Chipper Jones 1.25 3.00
CS Curt Schilling .75 2.00
FT Frank Thomas 1.25 3.00
GM Greg Maddux 1.50 4.00
GO Juan Gonzalez .50 1.25
HN Hideo Nomo 1.25 3.00
IR Ivan Rodriguez .75 2.00
IS Ichiro Suzuki 1.50 4.00
JB Jeff Bagwell .75 2.00
JD J.D. Drew .50 1.25
JG Jason Giambi .50 1.25
JT Jim Thome .75 2.00
KG Ken Griffey Jr. 2.50 6.00
KI Kazuhisa Ishii .50 1.25
KW Kerry Wood .50 1.25
LB Lance Berkman .75 2.00
LG Luis Gonzalez .50 1.25
MM Mike Mussina .75 2.00
MO Magglio Ordonez .75 2.00
MP Mike Piazza 1.25 3.00
MR Manny Ramirez 1.25 3.00
NG Nomar Garciaparra .75 2.00
PB Pat Burrell .50 1.25
PM Pedro Martinez .75 2.00
PR Mark Prior .75 2.00
RA Roberto Alomar .75 2.00
RC Roger Clemens 1.50 4.00
RJ Randy Johnson 1.25 3.00
RP Rafael Palmeiro .75 2.00
SG Shawn Green .50 1.25
SR Scott Rolen .75 2.00
SS Sammy Sosa 1.25 3.00
TH Todd Helton .75 2.00
VG Vladimir Guerrero .75 2.00

2004 Upper Deck Vintage

COMP.SET w/o SP's (300) 30.00 60.00
COMP.UPDATE SET (50) 6.00 15.00
COMMON CARD (1-300) .10 .30
COMMON CARD (301-315) .40 1.00
301-315 STATED ODDS 1:5
COMMON CARD (316-325) .40 1.00
316-325 STATED ODDS 1:7
COMMON CARD (326-350) .75 2.00
326-350 STATED ODDS 1:5
COMMON CARD (351-440) 1.25 3.00
351-440 STATED ODDS 1:12
COMMON CARD (441-450) .75 2.00
441-450 DIST.IN OLD JUDGE HOBBY PACKS
ONE 3-CARD OJ PACK PER HOBBY BOX
COMMON CARD (451-465) .10 .30
COMMON CARD (466-500) .20 .50
ONE UPDATE SET PER 1.5 UD2 HOB.BOXES
1 Albert Pujols .40 1.00
2 Carlos Delgado .12 .30
3 Todd Helton .20 .50
4 Nomar Garciaparra .20 .50
5 Vladimir Guerrero .20 .50
6 Alfonso Soriano .20 .50
7 Alex Rodriguez .40 1.00
8 Jason Giambi .12 .30
9 Derek Jeter .75 2.00
10 Pedro Martinez .20 .50
11 Ivan Rodriguez .20 .50
12 Mark Prior .20 .50
13 Marquis Grissom .12 .30
14 Barry Zito .20 .50
15 Alex Cintron .12 .30
16 Wade Miller .12 .30
17 Eric Chavez .12 .30
18 Matt Clement .12 .30
19 Orlando Cabrera .12 .30
20 Odalis Perez .12 .30
21 Lance Berkman .20 .50
22 Keith Foulke .12 .30
23 Shawn Green .12 .30
24 Byung-Hyun Kim .12 .30
25 Geoff Jenkins .12 .30
26 Torii Hunter .12 .30
27 Richard Hidalgo .12 .30
28 Edgar Martinez .20 .50
29 Placido Polanco .12 .30
30 Brad Lidge .12 .30
31 Alex Escobar .12 .30
32 Garret Anderson .12 .30
33 Larry Walker .20 .50
34 Ken Griffey Jr. .60 1.50
35 Junior Spivey .12 .30
36 Carlos Beltran .20 .50
37 Bartolo Colon .12 .30
38 Ichiro Suzuki .40 1.00
39 Ramon Ortiz .12 .30
40 Roy Oswalt .20 .50
41 Mike Piazza .30 .75
42 Benito Santiago .12 .30
43 Mike Mussina .20 .50
44 Jeff Kent .12 .30
45 Curt Schilling .20 .50
46 Adam Dunn .20 .50
47 Mike Sweeney .12 .30
48 Chipper Jones .30 .75
49 Frank Thomas .30 .75
50 Kerry Wood .12 .30
51 Rod Beck .12 .30
52 Brian Giles .12 .30
53 Hank Blalock .12 .30
54 Andruw Jones .12 .30
55 Dmitri Young .12 .30
56 Juan Pierre .12 .30
57 Jacque Jones .12 .30
58 Phil Nevin .12 .30
59 Rocco Baldelli .12 .30
60 Greg Maddux .40 1.00
61 Eric Gagne .12 .30
62 Tim Hudson .20 .50
63 Brian Lawrence .12 .30
64 Sammy Sosa .30 .75
65 Corey Koskie .12 .30
66 Bobby Abreu .12 .30
67 Preston Wilson .12 .30
68 Jay Gibbons .12 .30
69 Dontrelle Willis .12 .30
70 Richie Sexson .12 .30
71 Kevin Millwood .12 .30
72 Randy Johnson .30 .75
73 Jack Cust .12 .30
74 Randy Wolf .12 .30
75 Johan Santana .20 .50
76 Magglio Ordonez .20 .50
77 Sean Casey .12 .30
78 Billy Wagner .12 .30
79 Javier Vazquez .12 .30
80 Jorge Posada .20 .50
81 Jason Schmidt .12 .30
82 Bret Boone .12 .30
83 Jeff Bagwell .20 .50
84 Rickie Weeks .12 .30
85 Troy Percival .12 .30
86 Jose Vidro .12 .30
87 Freddy Garcia .12 .30
88 Manny Ramirez .30 .75
89 John Smoltz .30 .75
90 Moises Alou .12 .30
91 Ugueth Urbina .12 .30
92 Bobby Hill .12 .30
93 Marcus Giles .12 .30
94 Aramis Ramirez .12 .30
95 Brad Wilkerson .12 .30
96 Ray Durham .12 .30
97 David Wells .12 .30
98 Paul Lo Duca .12 .30
99 Danny Graves .12 .30
100 Jason Kendall .12 .30
101 Carlos Lee .12 .30
102 Rafael Furcal .12 .30
103 Mike Lowell .12 .30
104 Kevin Brown .12 .30
105 Vicente Padilla .12 .30
106 Miguel Tejada .20 .50
107 Bernie Williams .20 .50
108 Octavio Dotel .12 .30
109 Steve Finley .12 .30
110 Lyle Overbay .12 .30
111 Delmon Young .20 .50
112 Bo Hart .12 .30
113 Jason Lane .12 .30
114 Matt Roney .12 .30
115 Brian Roberts .12 .30
116 Tom Glavine .20 .50
117 Rich Aurilia .12 .30
118 Adam Kennedy .12 .30
119 Hee Seop Choi .12 .30
120 Trot Nixon .12 .30
121 Gary Sheffield .12 .30
122 Jay Payton .12 .30
123 Brad Penny .12 .30
124 Garrett Atkins .12 .30
125 Aubrey Huff .12 .30
126 Juan Gonzalez .12 .30
127 Jason Jennings .12 .30
128 Luis Gonzalez .12 .30
129 Vinny Castilla .12 .30
130 Esteban Loaiza .12 .30
131 Erubiel Durazo .12 .30
132 Eric Hinske .12 .30
133 Scott Rolen .20 .50
134 Craig Biggio .20 .50
135 Tim Wakefield .20 .50
136 Darin Erstad .12 .30
137 Denny Stark .12 .30
138 Ben Sheets .12 .30
139 Hideo Nomo .30 .75
140 Derrek Lee .12 .30
141 Matt Mantei .12 .30
142 Reggie Sanders .12 .30
143 Jose Guillen .12 .30
144 Joe Mays .12 .30
145 Jimmy Rollins .20 .50
146 Juan Encarnacion .12 .30
147 Joe Crede .12 .30
148 Aaron Guiel .12 .30
149 Mark Mulder .12 .30
150 Travis Lee .12 .30
151 Josh Phelps .12 .30
152 Michael Young .12 .30
153 Paul Konerko .20 .50
154 John Lackey .20 .50
155 Damian Moss .12 .30
156 Javy Lopez .12 .30
157 Joe Borowski .12 .30
158 Jose Cruz Jr. .12 .30
159 Ramon Hernandez .12 .30
160 Raul Ibanez .20 .50
161 Adrian Beltre .30 .75
162 Bobby Higginson .12 .30
163 Jorge Julio .12 .30
164 Miguel Batista .12 .30
165 Luis Castillo .12 .30
166 Aaron Harang .12 .30
167 Ken Harvey .12 .30
168 Rocky Biddle .12 .30
169 Mariano Rivera .40 1.00
170 Matt Morris .12 .30
171 Laynce Nix .12 .30
172 Mike Maroth .12 .30
173 Francisco Rodriguez .20 .50
174 Livan Hernandez .12 .30
175 Aaron Heilman .12 .30
176 Nick Johnson .12 .30
177 Woody Williams .12 .30
178 Joe Kennedy .12 .30
179 Jesse Foppert .12 .30
180 Ryan Franklin .12 .30
181 Endy Chavez .12 .30
182 Chin-Hui Tsao .12 .30
183 Todd Walker .12 .30
184 Edgardo Alfonzo .12 .30
185 Edgar Renteria .12 .30
186 Matt LeCroy .12 .30
187 Carl Everett .12 .30
188 Jeff Conine .12 .30
189 Jason Varitek .30 .75
190 Russ Ortiz .12 .30
191 Melvin Mora .12 .30
192 Mark Buehrle .20 .50
193 Bill Mueller .12 .30
194 Miguel Cabrera .30 .75
195 Carlos Zambrano .20 .50
196 Jose Valverde .12 .30
197 Danys Baez .12 .30
198 Mike MacDougal .12 .30
199 Zach Day .12 .30
200 Roy Halladay .20 .50
201 Jerome Williams .12 .30
202 Josh Fogg .12 .30
203 Mark Kotsay .12 .30
204 Pat Burrell .12 .30
205 A.J. Pierzynski .12 .30
206 Fred McGriff .12 .30
207 Brandon Larson .12 .30
208 Robb Quinlan .12 .30
209 David Ortiz .30 .75
210 A.J. Burnett .12 .30
211 John Vander Wal .12 .30
212 Jim Thome .20 .50
213 Matt Kata .12 .30
214 Kip Wells .12 .30
215 Scott Podsednik .12 .30
216 Rickey Henderson .30 .75
217 Travis Hafner .12 .30
218 Tony Batista .12 .30
219 Robert Fick .12 .30
220 Derek Lowe .12 .30
221 Ryan Klesko .12 .30
222 Joe Beimel .12 .30
223 Doug Mientkiewicz .12 .30
224 Angel Berroa .12 .30
225 Adam Eaton .12 .30
226 C.C. Sabathia .20 .50
227 Wilfredo Ledezma .12 .30
228 Jason Johnson .12 .30
229 Ryan Wagner .12 .30
230 Al Leiter .12 .30
231 Joel Pineiro .12 .30
232 Jason Isringhausen .12 .30
233 John Olerud .12 .30
234 Ron Calloway .12 .30
235 Jose Reyes .20 .50
236 J.D. Drew .12 .30
237 Jared Sandberg .12 .30
238 Gil Meche .12 .30
239 Jose Contreras .12 .30
240 Eric Milton .12 .30
241 Jason Phillips .12 .30
242 Luis Ayala .12 .30
243 Bobby Kielty .12 .30
244 Jose Lima .12 .30
245 Brooks Kieschnick .12 .30
246 Xavier Nady .12 .30
247 Danny Haren .12 .30
248 Victor Zambrano .12 .30
249 Kelvim Escobar .12 .30
250 Oliver Perez .12 .30
251 Jamie Moyer .12 .30
252 Orlando Hudson .12 .30
253 Danny Kolb .12 .30
254 Jake Peavy .12 .30
255 Kris Benson .12 .30
256 Roger Clemens .40 1.00
257 Jim Edmonds .20 .50
258 Rafael Palmeiro .20 .50
259 Jae Weong Seo .12 .30
260 Chase Utley .20 .50
261 Rich Harden .12 .30
262 Mark Teixeira .20 .50
263 Johnny Damon .20 .50
264 Luis Matos .12 .30
265 Shigetoshi Hasegawa .12 .30
266 Alfredo Amezaga .12 .30
267 Tim Worrell .12 .30
268 Kazuhisa Ishii .12 .30
269 Miguel Ojeda .12 .30
270 Kazuhiro Sasaki .12 .30
271 Hideki Matsui .50 1.25
272 Troy Glaus .12 .30
273 Michael Tucker .12 .30
274 Lew Ford .12 .30
275 Brian Jordan .12 .30
276 David Eckstein .12 .30
277 Robby Hammock .12 .30
278 Corey Patterson .12 .30
279 Wes Helms .12 .30
280 Jermaine Dye .12 .30
281 Cliff Floyd .12 .30
282 Dustan Mohr .12 .30
283 Kevin Mench .12 .30
284 Ellis Burks .12 .30
285 Jerry Hairston Jr. .12 .30
286 Tim Salmon .12 .30
287 Omar Vizquel .20 .50
288 Andy Pettitte .20 .50
289 Guillermo Mota .12 .30
290 Tino Martinez .20 .50
291 Lance Carter .12 .30
292 Francisco Cordero .12 .30
293 Robb Nen .12 .30
294 Mike Cameron .12 .30
295 Jhonny Peralta .12 .30
296 Braden Looper .12 .30
297 Jarrod Washburn .12 .30
298 Mark Prior CL .20 .50
299 Alfonso Soriano CL .20 .50
300 Rocco Baldelli CL .12 .30
301 Pedro Martinez PBP .60 1.50
302 Mark Prior PBP .60 1.50
303 Barry Zito PBP .60 1.50
304 Roger Clemens PBP 1.25 3.00
305 Randy Johnson PBP 1.00 2.50
306 Roy Halladay PBP .60 1.50
307 Hideo Nomo PBP 1.00 2.50
308 Roy Oswalt PBP .60 1.50
309 Kerry Wood PBP .40 1.00
310 Dontrelle Willis PBP .40 1.00
311 Mark Mulder PBP .40 1.00
312 Brandon Webb PBP .40 1.00
313 Mike Mussina PBP .60 1.50
314 Curt Schilling PBP .60 1.50
315 Tim Hudson PBP .60 1.50
316 Dontrelle Willis WSH .40 1.00
317 Juan Pierre WSH .40 1.00
318 Hideki Matsui WSH 1.50 4.00
319 Andy Pettitte WSH .60 1.50
320 Mike Mussina WSH .60 1.50
321 Roger Clemens WSH 1.25 3.00
322 Alex Gonzalez WSH .40 1.00
323 Brad Penny WSH .40 1.00
324 Ivan Rodriguez WSH .60 1.50
325 Josh Beckett WSH .40 1.00
326 Aaron Boone TR .75 2.00
327 Jeff Suppan TR .75 2.00
328 Shea Hillenbrand TR .75 2.00
329 Jeromy Burnitz TR .75 2.00
330 Sidney Ponson TR .75 2.00
331 Rondell White TR .75 2.00
332 Shannon Stewart TR .75 2.00
333 Armando Benitez TR .75 2.00
334 Roberto Alomar TR 1.25 3.00
335 Raul Mondesi TR .75 2.00
336 Morgan Ensberg SP1 .75 2.00
337 Milton Bradley SP1 .75 2.00
338 Brandon Webb SP1 .75 2.00
339 Marlon Byrd SP1 .75 2.00
340 Carlos Pena SP1 1.25 3.00
341 Brandon Phillips SP1 .75 2.00
342 Josh Beckett SP1 .75 2.00
343 Eric Munson SP1 .75 2.00
344 Brett Myers SP1 .75 2.00
345 Austin Kearns SP1 .75 2.00
346 Jody Gerut SP2 .75 2.00
347 Vernon Wells SP2 .75 2.00
348 Jeff Duncan SP2 .75 2.00
349 Sean Burroughs SP2 .75 2.00
350 Jeremy Bonderman SP2 .75 2.00
351 Hideki Matsui 3D 6.00 15.00
352 Jason Giambi 3D 1.25 3.00
353 Alfonso Soriano 3D 2.00 5.00
354 Derek Jeter 3D 8.00 20.00
355 Aaron Boone 3D 1.25 3.00
356 Jorge Posada 3D 2.00 5.00
357 Bernie Williams 3D 2.00 5.00
358 Manny Ramirez 3D 3.00 8.00
359 Nomar Garciaparra 3D 2.00 5.00
360 Johnny Damon 3D 2.00 5.00
361 Jason Varitek 3D 3.00 8.00
362 Carlos Delgado 3D 1.25 3.00
363 Vernon Wells 3D 1.25 3.00
364 Jay Gibbons 3D 1.25 3.00
365 Tony Batista 3D 1.25 3.00
366 Rocco Baldelli 3D 1.25 3.00
367 Aubrey Huff 3D 1.25 3.00
368 Carlos Beltran 3D 2.00 5.00
369 Mike Sweeney 3D 1.25 3.00
370 Maggio Ordonez 3D 2.00 5.00
371 Frank Thomas 3D 3.00 8.00
372 Carlos Lee 3D 1.25 3.00
373 Roberto Alomar 3D 2.00 5.00
374 Jacque Jones 3D 1.25 3.00
375 Torii Hunter 3D 1.25 3.00
376 Milton Bradley 3D 1.25 3.00
377 Travis Hafner 3D 1.25 3.00
378 Jody Gerut 3D 1.25 3.00
379 Dmitri Young 3D 1.25 3.00
380 Carlos Pena 3D 2.00 5.00
381 Ichiro Suzuki 3D 4.00 10.00
382 Bret Boone 3D 1.25 3.00
383 Edgar Martinez 3D 2.00 5.00
384 Eric Chavez 3D 1.25 3.00
385 Miguel Tejada 3D 2.00 5.00
386 Erubiel Durazo 3D 1.25 3.00
387 Jose Guillen 3D 1.25 3.00
388 Garret Anderson 3D 1.25 3.00
389 Troy Glaus 3D 1.25 3.00
390 Alex Rodriguez 3D 4.00 10.00
391 Rafael Palmeiro 3D 2.00 5.00
392 Hank Blalock 3D 1.25 3.00
393 Mark Teixeira 3D 2.00 5.00
394 Gary Sheffield 3D 1.25 3.00
395 Andruw Jones 3D 1.25 3.00
396 Chipper Jones 3D 3.00 8.00
397 Javy Lopez 3D 1.25 3.00
398 Marcus Giles 3D 1.25 3.00
399 Rafael Furcal 3D 1.25 3.00
400 Jim Thome 3D 2.00 5.00
401 Bobby Abreu 3D 1.25 3.00
402 Pat Burrell 3D 1.25 3.00
403 Mike Lowell 3D 1.25 3.00
404 Ivan Rodriguez 3D 2.00 5.00
405 Derrek Lee 3D 1.25 3.00
406 Miguel Cabrera 3D 3.00 8.00
407 Vladimir Guerrero 3D 2.00 5.00
408 Orlando Cabrera 3D 1.25 3.00
409 Jose Vidro 3D 1.25 3.00
410 Mike Piazza 3D 3.00 8.00
411 Cliff Floyd 3D 1.25 3.00
412 Albert Pujols 3D 4.00 10.00
413 Scott Rolen 3D 2.00 5.00
414 Jim Edmonds 3D 2.00 5.00
415 Edgar Renteria 3D 1.25 3.00
416 Lance Berkman 3D 2.00 5.00
417 Jeff Bagwell 3D 2.00 5.00
418 Jeff Kent 3D 1.25 3.00
419 Richard Hidalgo 3D 1.25 3.00
420 Morgan Ensberg 3D 1.25 3.00
421 Sammy Sosa 3D 3.00 8.00
422 Moises Alou 3D 1.25 3.00
423 Ken Griffey Jr. 3D 6.00 15.00
424 Adam Dunn 3D 2.00 5.00
425 Austin Kearns 3D 1.25 3.00
426 Richie Sexson 3D 1.25 3.00
427 Geoff Jenkins 3D 1.25 3.00
428 Brian Giles 3D 1.25 3.00
429 Reggie Sanders 3D 1.25 3.00
430 Rich Aurilia 3D 1.25 3.00
431 Jose Cruz Jr. 3D 1.25 3.00
432 Shawn Green 3D 1.25 3.00
433 Jeromy Burnitz 3D 1.25 3.00
434 Luis Gonzalez 3D 1.25 3.00
435 Todd Helton 3D 2.00 5.00
436 Preston Wilson 3D 1.25 3.00
437 Larry Walker 3D 2.00 5.00
438 Ryan Klesko 3D 1.25 3.00
439 Phil Nevin 3D 1.25 3.00
440 Sean Burroughs 3D 1.25 3.00
441 Sammy Sosa OJ 2.00 5.00
442 Albert Pujols OJ 2.50 6.00
443 Magglio Ordonez OJ 1.25 3.00
444 Vladimir Guerrero OJ 1.25 3.00
445 Todd Helton OJ 1.25 3.00
446 Jason Giambi OJ .75 2.00
447 Ichiro Suzuki OJ 2.50 6.00
448 Alex Rodriguez OJ 2.50 6.00
449 Carlos Delgado OJ .75 2.00
450 Manny Ramirez OJ 2.00 5.00
451 Alex Rodriguez 4.00 10.00
452 Javy Lopez 1.25 3.00
453 Alfonso Soriano 2.00 5.00
454 Vladimir Guerrero 2.00 5.00
455 Rafael Palmeiro 2.00 5.00
456 Gary Sheffield 1.25 3.00
457 Curt Schilling 2.00 5.00
458 Miguel Tejada 2.00 5.00
459 Kevin Brown 1.25 3.00
460 Richie Sexson 1.25 3.00
461 Roger Clemens 4.00 10.00
462 Javier Vazquez 1.25 3.00
463 Bartolo Colon 1.25 3.00
464 Ivan Rodriguez 2.00 5.00
465 Greg Maddux 4.00 10.00
466 Jamie Brown RC 2.00 5.00
467 Dave Crouthers RC 2.00 5.00
468 Jason Frasor RC 2.00 5.00
469 Greg Dobbs RC 2.00 5.00
470 Jesse Harper RC 2.00 5.00
471 Nick Regilio RC 2.00 5.00
472 Ryan Wing RC 2.00 5.00
473 Akinori Otsuka RC 2.00 5.00
474 Shingo Takatsu RC 2.00 5.00
475 Kazuo Matsui RC 3.00 8.00
476 Mike Vento RC 2.00 5.00
477 Mike Gosling RC 2.00 5.00
478 Justin Huisman RC 2.00 5.00
479 Justin Hampson RC 2.00 5.00
480 Dennis Sarfate RC 2.00 5.00
481 Ian Snell RC 2.00 5.00
482 Tim Bausher RC 2.00 5.00
483 Donnie Kelly RC 3.00 8.00
484 Jerome Gamble RC 2.00 5.00
485 Mike Rouse RC 2.00 5.00
486 Merkin Valdez RC 2.00 5.00
487 Lincoln Holdzkom RC 2.00 5.00
488 Justin Leone RC 2.00 5.00
489 Sean Henn RC 2.00 5.00
490 Brandon Medders RC 2.00 5.00
491 Mike Johnston RC 2.00 5.00
492 Tim Bittner RC 2.00 5.00
493 Michael Wuertz RC 2.00 5.00
494 Chad Bentz RC 2.00 5.00
495 Ryan Meaux RC 2.00 5.00
496 Chris Aguila RC 2.00 5.00
497 Jake Woods RC 2.00 5.00
498 Scott Dohmann RC 2.00 5.00
499 Colby Miller RC 2.00 5.00
500 Josh Labandeira RC 2.00 5.00

2004 Upper Deck Vintage Black and White

*B/W 1-300: 3X TO 8X BASIC
1-300 STATED ODDS 1:6
*B/W 301-315: 1.25X TO 3X BASIC
301-315 STATED ODDS 1:24
*B/W 316-325: 1.25X TO 3X BASIC
316-325 STATED ODDS 1:24
*B/W 326-350: .75X TO 2X BASIC
326-350 STATED ODDS 1:20

2004 Upper Deck Vintage Black and White Color Variation

*B/W COLOR: 5X TO 12X BASIC
STATED ODDS 1:48

2004 Upper Deck Vintage Old Judge Subset Blue Back

*OJ BLUE BACK 441-450: .6X TO 1.5X BASIC
STATED ODD 1:4 OJ HOBBY PACKS
ONE 3-CARD OJ PACK PER HOBBY BOX

2004 Upper Deck Vintage Old Judge Subset Red Back

*OJ RED BACK 441-450: 1X TO 2.5X BASIC OJ
STATED ODDS 1:12 OJ HOBBY PACKS
ONE 3-CARD OJ PACK PER HOBBY BOX

2004 Upper Deck Vintage Old Judge

DISTRIBUTED IN OLD JUDGE HOBBY PACKS
ONE 3-CARD OJ PACK PER HOBBY BOX
*OJ BLUE BACK 11-30: .6X TO 1.5X BASIC
OJ BLUE BACK ODDS 1:4 OJ HOBBY PACKS
*OJ RED BACK 11-30: 1X TO 2.5X BASIC
OJ RED BACK ODDS 1:12 OJ HOBBY PACKS
11 Randy Johnson 2.00 5.00
12 Pedro Martinez 1.25 3.00
13 Mark Prior 1.25 3.00
14 Barry Zito 1.25 3.00
15 Roy Oswalt 1.25 3.00
16 Roy Halladay 1.25 3.00
17 Curt Schilling 1.25 3.00
18 Mike Mussina 1.25 3.00
19 Kevin Brown .75 2.00
20 Roger Clemens 2.50 6.00
21 Eric Gagne .75 2.00
22 Mariano Rivera 2.50 6.00
23 Mike Piazza 2.00 5.00
24 Jorge Posada 1.25 3.00
25 Jeff Kent .75 2.00
26 Alfonso Soriano 1.25 3.00
27 Scott Rolen 1.25 3.00
28 Eric Chavez .75 2.00
29 Edgar Renteria .75 2.00
30 Hideki Matsui 3.00 8.00

2004 Upper Deck Vintage Stellar Signatures

STATED ODDS 1:600
STATED PRINT RUN 150 SERIAL #'d SETS
EXCHANGE DEADLINE 01/27/07
AR Alex Rodriguez 30.00 80.00
BZ Barry Zito 6.00 15.00
CY Carl Yastrzemski 30.00 80.00
HM Hideki Matsui 100.00 200.00
IS Ichiro Suzuki 200.00 400.00
MP Mike Piazza 75.00 150.00
TS Tom Seaver 30.00 80.00

2004 Upper Deck Vintage Stellar Stat Men Jerseys

STATED ODDS 1:24
SP PRINT RUNS PROVIDED BY UPPER DECK
SP'S ARE NOT SERIAL-NUMBERED
1 Jose Reyes 3.00 8.00
2 Bo Hart 3.00 8.00
3 Hideki Matsui Pants 10.00 25.00
4 Dontrelle Willis 4.00 10.00
5 Rocco Baldelli 3.00 8.00
6 Ichiro Suzuki 12.50 30.00
7 Mike Lowell 3.00 8.00
8 Derek Jeter 12.50 30.00
9 Ken Griffey Jr. 6.00 15.00
10 Sammy Sosa 4.00 10.00
11 Kerry Wood 3.00 8.00
12 Chipper Jones 4.00 10.00
13 Alfonso Soriano 3.00 8.00
14 Khalil Greene 4.00 10.00
15 Jim Thome 4.00 10.00
16 Rafael Furcal 3.00 8.00
17 Andrew Brown 3.00 8.00
18 Mark Prior 4.00 10.00
19 Barry Zito 3.00 8.00
20 Al Leiter 3.00 8.00
21 Carlos Delgado 3.00 8.00
22 Pedro Martinez 4.00 10.00
23 Alex Rodriguez 6.00 15.00
24 Lance Berkman 3.00 8.00
25 Jeff Bagwell 4.00 10.00
26 Bernie Williams 4.00 10.00
27 Hideo Nomo 6.00 15.00
28 Randy Johnson 4.00 10.00
29 Curt Schilling 3.00 8.00
30 Mike Piazza 6.00 15.00
31 Albert Pujols 6.00 15.00
32 J.DiMaggio Pants SP/300 20.00 50.00
33 Ted Williams Pants SP/300 12.50 30.00
34 M.Mantle Pants SP/300 30.00 60.00
35 Mike Mussina 4.00 10.00
36 Rich Harden 3.00 8.00
37 Roy Oswalt 3.00 8.00
38 Torii Hunter 3.00 8.00
39 Jorge Posada 4.00 10.00
40 Troy Glaus 3.00 8.00
41 Manny Ramirez 4.00 10.00
42 Roy Halladay 3.00 8.00

2004 Upper Deck Vintage Timeless Teams Quad Bats

STATED ODDS 1:400
STATED PRINT RUN 175 SERIAL #'d SETS
CARD NUMBER 3 DOES NOT EXIST
TT1 Soriano/Jeter/Matsui/Giam 60.00 120.00
TT2 L.Gonz/Schill/Randy/Finley 10.00 25.00
TT4 Manny/Nomar/Trot/Damon 20.00 50.00
TT5 A.Rod/Raffy/Teix/Blalock 15.00 40.00
TT6 Maggio/Thomas/Alom/Ever 15.00 40.00
TT7 Jacque/Torii/Mient/Stewart 10.00 25.00
TT8 Edm/Rolen/Drew/Pujols 20.00 50.00
TT9 Ichiro/Olerud/Boone/Cam 15.00 40.00
TT10 Kent/Bagwell/Biggio/Berk 10.00 25.00
TT11 Glaus/Erst/Garret/Salmon 15.00 40.00
TT12 Bernie/Posa/Matsui/A.Sor 40.00 80.00
TT13 Tuck/Beltran/Sween/Mayne 10.00 25.00
TT14 Thome/Byrd/Lieb/Abreu 10.00 25.00
TT15 Cabr/I.Rod/Encar/Lowell 10.00 25.00
TT16 Sosa/Corey/Alou/Wood 10.00 25.00
TT17 Cruz/Alfonzo/Aurilia/Gala 10.00 25.00
TT18 A.Sor/Jeter/Matsui/Bernie 20.00 50.00

2010 Upper Deck World of Sports

COMPLETE SET (375) 100.00 150.00
COMP.SET w/o SPs (300) 30.00 60.00
121 Brett Hunter .15 .40
122 Collin Cowgill .15 .40
123 Bobby Lanigan .15 .40
124 Andrew Liebel .15 .40
125 Casey Kelly .40 1.00
126 Jason Castro .25 .60
127 David Cooper .15 .40
128 Daniel Schlereth .15 .40
129 Jemile Weeks .15 .40
130 Joshua Fields .15 .40
131 Brad Holt .15 .40
132 Aaron Hicks .25 .60
133 Jeremy Bleich .15 .40
134 Justin Bristow .15 .40
135 Danny Espinosa .15 .40
136 Zach Putnam .15 .40
137 Allan Dykstra .15 .40
138 Tim Federowicz .15 .40
139 J.P. Ramirez .15 .40
140 Beamer Weems .15 .40
141 Eric Berger .15 .40
142 Jeremy Farrell .15 .40
143 T.J. Steele .15 .40
144 Reese Havens .15 .40
145 Jeremy Beckham .15 .40
146 Dustin Coleman .15 .40
147 Casper Wells .15 .40
148 Ryan Flaherty .15 .40
149 Robbie Weinhardt .15 .40
150 Kyle Skipworth .15 .40
151 Aaron Crow .15 .40
152 Garrison Lassiter .15 .40
153 Stephen Fife .15 .40
154 Chris Smith .15 .40
155 Tim Melville .15 .40
156 D.J. Mitchell .15 .40
157 Jordan Danks .25 .60
158 David Adams .15 .40
341 Bo Jackson SP 1.00 2.50
342 Lou Brock SP 1.00 2.50
343 Jose Canseco SP 1.00 2.50

2010 Upper Deck World of Sports Athletes of the World Autographs

OVERALL AUTO ODDS TWO PER BOX
AW1 Chris Perez
AW2 Derrek Lee 5.00 12.00
AW3 Jeff Clement 4.00 10.00

AW4 Phil Hughes 6.00 15.00
AW13 Stephen Strasburg 15.00 40.00
AW48 Pedro Alvarez 15.00 30.00
AW49 Justin Smoak 8.00 20.00
AW90 Cal Ripken Jr.
AW99 Fu-Te Ni 4.00 10.00
AW100 Jim Palmer 8.00 20.00

2010 Upper Deck World of Sports Autographs

OVERALL AUTO ODDS TWO PER BOX
121 Brett Hunter 5.00 12.00
122 Collin Cowgill 5.00 12.00
123 Bobby Lanigan 5.00 12.00
124 Andrew Liebel 5.00 12.00
125 Casey Kelly 6.00 15.00
126 Jason Castro 5.00 12.00
127 David Cooper 5.00 12.00
128 Daniel Schlereth 5.00 12.00
129 Jemile Weeks 5.00 12.00
130 Joshua Fields 5.00 12.00
131 Brad Holt
132 Aaron Hicks 5.00 12.00
133 Jeremy Bleich 5.00 12.00
134 Justin Bristow 5.00 12.00
135 Danny Espinosa 5.00 12.00
136 Zach Putnam 5.00 12.00
137 Allan Dykstra 5.00 12.00
138 Tim Federowicz 6.00 15.00
139 J.P. Ramirez
140 Beamer Weems 5.00 12.00
141 Eric Berger 5.00 12.00
142 Jeremy Farrell
143 T.J. Steele 5.00 12.00
144 Reese Havens 5.00 12.00
145 Jeremy Beckham 5.00 12.00
146 Dustin Coleman
147 Casper Wells 6.00 15.00
148 Ryan Flaherty 5.00 12.00
149 Robbie Weinhardt 5.00 12.00
150 Kyle Skipworth 5.00 12.00
151 Aaron Crow 5.00 12.00
152 Garrison Lassiter 5.00 12.00
153 Stephen Fife 5.00 12.00
154 Chris Smith 5.00 12.00
155 Tim Melville 5.00 12.00
156 D.J. Mitchell 5.00 12.00
157 Jordan Danks 5.00 12.00
158 David Adams 5.00 12.00
341 Bo Jackson
342 Lou Brock 10.00 25.00
343 Jose Canseco

2010 Upper Deck World of Sports Clear Competitors

STATED ODDS ONE PER BOX
STATED PRINT RUN 550 SER.#'d SETS
CC14 Bo Jackson 4.00 10.00

2011 Upper Deck World of Sports

COMPLETE SET (400) 75.00 150.00
COMP.SET w/o SPs (300) 25.00 60.00
1 Ozzie Smith .25 .60
2 Mike Schmidt .25 .60
3 Matt Szczur .25 .60
4 Delino DeShields .15 .40
5 Jurickson Profar .15 .40
6 Jared Hoying .15 .40
7 Peter Tago .25 .60
8 Cody Hawn .15 .40
9 LeVon Washington .15 .40
10 Gary Brown .15 .40
11 Johnny Bench .25 .60
12 Kolbrin Vitek .15 .40
13 Jonathan Garcia .15 .40
14 Carlos Perez .15 .40
15 John Lamb .25 .60
16 Yordano Ventura .40 1.00
17 Robinson Yambati .15 .40
18 Reggie Golden .15 .40
19 Ryan Lavarnway .25 .60
20 Mike Olt .15 .40
21 Michael Choice .40 1.00
22 Matt Lipka .15 .40
23 Christian Yelich .25 .60
24 Aaron Altherr .15 .40
25 Ramon Morla .15 .40
26 Whitey Ford .25 .60
27 Carlton Fisk .25 .60
28 Zach Walters .25 .60
29 Dennis Oil Can Boyd .15 .40
30 Gauntlett Eldemire .15 .40
31 Kyle Parker .15 .40
32 Matt Packer .15 .40
301 Manny Machado SP 1.00 2.50
302 Greg Maddux SP 1.00 2.50
303 Ryne Sandberg SP 1.00 2.50
304 Nolan Ryan SP 1.25 3.00
305 Jose Canseco SP 1.00 2.50
306 Steve Carlton SP 1.00 2.50
307 Don Mattingly SP 1.00 2.50
308 Bob Gibson SP 1.00 2.50
309 Lou Brock SP 1.00 2.50

2011 Upper Deck World of Sports All-Sport Apparel Memorabilia

OVERALL AUTO/MEM ODDS 3 PER BOX
ASMC Michael Choice 3.00 8.00
ASMM Manny Machado 4.00 10.00
ASPT Peter Tago 3.00 8.00

2011 Upper Deck World of Sports All-Sport Apparel Memorabilia Autographs

ASMC Michael Choice/20

2011 Upper Deck World of Sports Athletes of the World Autographs

OVERALL AUTO/MEM ODDS 3 PER BOX
AWAH Aaron Hicks 4.00 10.00
AWBH Bryce Harper 60.00 120.00
AWBL Brett Lawrie 15.00 40.00
AWEH Eric Hosmer 12.00 30.00
AWEL Evan Longoria 12.00 30.00
AWFI Jennie Finch 10.00 25.00
AWJC Jason Castro 4.00 10.00
AWJF Jeff Francoeur 4.00 10.00
AWJL Jordan Lyles 5.00 12.00
AWJS Justin Smoak 5.00 12.00
AWLF Lisa Fernandez 5.00 12.00
AWLI Che-Hsuan Lin 5.00 12.00
AWMA Brian Matusz 4.00 10.00
AWPA Pedro Alvarez 4.00 10.00
AWRW Ryan Westmoreland 4.00 10.00
AWSS Stephen Strasburg
AWYR Yorman Rodriguez 4.00 10.00

2011 Upper Deck World of Sports Autographs

1 Ozzie Smith A
2 Mike Schmidt A
3 Matt Szczur B
4 Delino DeShields C 4.00 10.00
8 Cody Hawn C 4.00 10.00
12 Kolbrin Vitek C 4.00 10.00
13 Jonathan Garcia C 4.00 10.00
14 Carlos Perez C 4.00 10.00
15 John Lamb C 5.00 12.00
16 Yordano Ventura C 8.00 20.00
17 Robinson Yambati C 4.00 10.00
18 Reggie Golden C 4.00 10.00
20 Mike Olt C 5.00 12.00
21 Michael Choice C 6.00 15.00
22 Matt Lipka C 4.00 10.00
23 Christian Yelich C 30.00 80.00
24 Aaron Altherr C 4.00 10.00
26 Whitey Ford B
27 Carlton Fisk B
28 Zach Walters C 6.00 15.00
29 Dennis Oil Can Boyd B
30 Gauntlett Eldemire C 4.00 10.00
31 Kyle Parker C 4.00 10.00
32 Matt Packer C 4.00 10.00
301 Manny Machado B 20.00 50.00
303 Ryne Sandberg B 40.00 80.00
304 Nolan Ryan A
305 Jose Canseco B 12.50 30.00
306 Steve Carlton B 10.00 25.00
307 Don Mattingly B 20.00 50.00
308 Bob Gibson A 12.00 30.00
309 Lou Brock A 8.00 20.00

2011 Upper Deck World of Sports Sports Nation Autographs Dual

STATED PRINT RUN 10-25
SNLY C.Yelch/J.Lamb/15

2002 Upper Deck World Series Heroes

COMP.SET w/o SP's (90) 8.00 20.00
COMMON CARD (1-90) .10 .30
COMMON CARD (91-135) 1.25 3.00
91-135 STATED ODDS 1:10
COMMON CARD (136-180) 1.50 4.00
136-180 STATED ODDS 1:10
1 Catfish Hunter .20 .50
2 Jimmie Foxx .30 .75
3 Mark McGwire .75 2.00
4 Rollie Fingers .10 .30
5 Rickey Henderson .30 .75
6 Joe Carter .10 .30
7 John Olerud .10 .30
8 Roberto Alomar .20 .50
9 Pat Hentgen .10 .30
10 Devon White .10 .30
11 Eddie Mathews .30 .75
12 Greg Maddux .50 1.25
13 Chipper Jones .30 .75
14 Tom Glavine .20 .50
15 Andruw Jones .20 .50
16 Dave Justice .10 .30
17 Fred McGriff .20 .50
18 Ryan Klesko .10 .30
19 John Smoltz .20 .50
20 Javy Lopez .10 .30
21 Marquis Grissom .10 .30
22 Robin Yount .30 .75
23 Ozzie Smith .50 1.25
24 Frankie Frisch .20 .50
25 Stan Musial .50 1.25
26 Randy Johnson .30 .75
27 Luis Gonzalez .10 .30
28 Matt Williams .10 .30
29 Steve Finley .10 .30
30 Sandy Koufax .75 2.00
31 Duke Snider .20 .50
32 Kirk Gibson .10 .30
33 Steve Garvey .10 .30
34 Jackie Robinson .30 .75
35 Don Drysdale .20 .50
36 Juan Marichal .10 .30
37 Mel Ott .30 .75
38 Orlando Cepeda .10 .30
39 Jim Thome .20 .50
40 Manny Ramirez .20 .50
41 Omar Vizquel .20 .50
42 Lou Boudreau .10 .30
43 Gary Sheffield .10 .30
44 Moises Alou .10 .30
45 Livan Hernandez .10 .30
46 Edgar Renteria .10 .30
47 Al Leiter .10 .30
48 Tom Seaver .20 .50
49 Gary Carter .10 .30
50 Mike Piazza .50 1.25
51 Nolan Ryan .75 2.00
52 Robin Ventura .10 .30
53 Mike Hampton .10 .30
54 Jesse Orosco .10 .30
55 Cal Ripken 1.00 2.50
56 Brooks Robinson .20 .50
57 Tony Gwynn .40 1.00
58 Kevin Brown .10 .30
59 Curt Schilling .10 .30
60 Cy Young .30 .75
61 Honus Wagner .50 1.25
62 Willie Stargell .20 .50
63 Wade Boggs .20 .50
64 Carlton Fisk .20 .50
65 Ken Griffey Sr. .10 .30
66 Joe Morgan .10 .30
67 Johnny Bench .30 .75
68 Barry Larkin .20 .50
69 Jose Rijo .10 .30
70 Ty Cobb .50 1.25
71 Kirby Puckett .30 .75
72 Chuck Knoblauch .10 .30
73 Harmon Killebrew .30 .75
74 Mickey Mantle 1.25 3.00
75 Joe DiMaggio .60 1.50
76 Don Larsen .10 .30
77 Thurman Munson .30 .75
78 Roger Maris .30 .75
79 Phil Rizzuto .20 .50
80 Babe Ruth 1.00 2.50
81 Lou Gehrig .60 1.50
82 Billy Martin .20 .50
83 Derek Jeter .75 2.00
84 Roger Clemens .60 1.50
85 Tino Martinez .20 .50
86 Bernie Williams .20 .50
87 Mariano Rivera .30 .75
88 Andy Pettitte .20 .50
89 David Wells .10 .30
90 Jorge Posada .20 .50
91 Rodrigo Rosario PH RC 1.25 3.00
92 Brandon Puffer PH RC 1.25 3.00
93 Franklyn German PH RC 1.25 3.00
94 Reed Johnson PH RC 2.00 5.00
95 Chris Baker PH RC 1.25 3.00
96 John Ennis PH RC 1.25 3.00
97 Luis Martinez PH RC 1.25 3.00
98 Takaki Nomura PH RC 1.25 3.00
99 So Taguchi PH RC 2.00 5.00
100 Michael Crudale PH RC 1.25 3.00
101 Francis Beltran PH RC 1.25 3.00
102 Steve Kent PH RC 1.25 3.00
103 Jorge Sosa PH RC 2.00 5.00
104 Felix Escalona PH RC 1.25 3.00
105 Jose Valverde PH RC 1.25 3.00
106 Doug Devore PH RC 1.25 3.00
107 Kazuhisa Ishii PH RC 2.00 5.00
108 Victor Alvarez PH RC 1.25 3.00
109 Eric Good PH RC 1.25 3.00
110 Jorge Nunez PH RC 1.25 3.00
111 Ron Calloway PH RC 1.25 3.00
112 Nelson Castro PH RC 1.25 3.00
113 Matt Thornton PH RC 1.25 3.00
114 Luis Ugueto PH RC 1.25 3.00
115 Hansel Izquierdo PH RC 1.25 3.00
116 Jaime Cerda PH RC 1.25 3.00
117 Mark Corey PH RC 1.25 3.00
118 Tyler Yates PH RC 1.25 3.00
119 Satoru Komiyama PH RC 1.25 3.00
120 Steve Bechler PH RC 1.25 3.00
121 Ben Howard PH RC 1.25 3.00
122 Anderson Machado PH RC 1.25 3.00
123 Jorge Padilla PH RC 1.25 3.00
124 Eric Junge PH RC 1.25 3.00
125 Adrian Burnside PH RC 1.25 3.00
126 Mike Gonzalez PH RC 1.25 3.00
127 Anastacio Martinez PH RC 1.25 3.00
128 Josh Hancock PH RC 1.50 4.00
129 Rene Reyes PH RC 1.25 3.00
130 Aaron Cook PH RC 1.25 3.00
131 Cam Esslinger PH RC 1.25 3.00
132 Juan Brito PH RC 1.25 3.00
133 Miguel Asencio PH RC 1.25 3.00
134 Kevin Frederick PH RC 1.25 3.00
135 Edwin Almonte PH RC 1.25 3.00
136 Troy Glaus FWS 1.50 4.00
137 Darin Erstad FWS 1.50 4.00
138 Jeff Bagwell FWS 1.50 4.00
139 Lance Berkman FWS 1.50 4.00
140 Tim Hudson FWS 1.50 4.00
141 Eric Chavez FWS 1.50 4.00
142 Barry Zito FWS 1.50 4.00
143 Carlos Delgado FWS 1.50 4.00
144 Richie Sexson FWS 1.50 4.00
145 Albert Pujols FWS 5.00 12.00
146 Sammy Sosa FWS 2.50 6.00
147 Kerry Wood FWS 1.50 4.00
148 Greg Vaughn FWS 1.50 4.00
149 Shawn Green FWS 1.50 4.00
150 Vladimir Guerrero FWS 2.50 6.00
151 Barry Bonds FWS 6.00 15.00
152 C.C. Sabathia FWS 1.50 4.00
153 Ichiro Suzuki FWS 5.00 12.00
154 Freddy Garcia FWS 1.50 4.00
155 Edgar Martinez FWS 1.50 4.00
156 Josh Beckett FWS 1.50 4.00
157 Cliff Floyd FWS 1.50 4.00
158 Mo Vaughn FWS 1.50 4.00
159 Jeromy Burnitz FWS 1.50 4.00
160 Sean Burroughs FWS 1.50 4.00
161 Phil Nevin FWS 1.50 4.00
162 Scott Rolen FWS 1.50 4.00
163 Brian Giles FWS 1.50 4.00
164 Alex Rodriguez FWS 3.00 8.00
165 Ivan Rodriguez FWS 1.50 4.00
166 Juan Gonzalez FWS 1.50 4.00
167 Rafael Palmeiro FWS 1.50 4.00
168 Nomar Garciaparra FWS 4.00 10.00
169 Pedro Martinez FWS 1.50 4.00
170 Ken Griffey Jr. FWS 5.00 12.00
171 Adam Dunn FWS 1.50 4.00
172 Todd Helton FWS 1.50 4.00
173 Mike Sweeney FWS 1.50 4.00
174 Carlos Beltran FWS 1.50 4.00
175 Dmitri Young FWS 1.50 4.00
176 Doug Mientkiewicz FWS 1.50 4.00
177 Torii Hunter FWS 1.50 4.00
178 Frank Thomas FWS 2.50 6.00
179 Magglio Ordonez FWS 1.50 4.00
180 Jason Giambi FWS 1.50 4.00

2002 Upper Deck World Series Heroes Classic Match-Ups Memorabilia

STATED ODDS 1:24
SP INFO PROVIDED BY UPPER DECK
SP'S ARE NOT SERIAL-NUMBERED
SWATCH IS ONLY FOR 1ST PLAYER LISTED
MU M.Piazza Jsy Clemens 6.00 15.00
MUa A.Pettitte Pants Piazza 6.00 15.00
MUb A.Leiter Jsy Jeter 4.00 10.00
MUc R.Ventura Jsy Clemens 4.00 10.00
MUd E.Alfonzo Jsy Rivera 4.00 10.00
MUe J.Franco Jsy Jeter 4.00 10.00
MU1 M.Rivera Jsy Gonzalez 6.00 15.00
MU1a P.O'Neill Pants Schilling 6.00 15.00
MU1b B.Williams Pants Randy 4.00 10.00
MU1c D.Justice Jsy Schilling 4.00 10.00
MU1d R.Johnson Jsy Williams 6.00 15.00
MU1e C.Schilling Jsy Martinez 4.00 10.00
MU1f R.Clemens Jsy Gonzalez 6.00 15.00
MU1g P.O'Neill Pants Kim 6.00 15.00
MU1h L.Gonz Jsy MRiv SP/97 6.00 15.00
MU3 H.Wagner Pants Young 40.00 80.00
MU9 T.Cobb Pants Wag SP 60.00 120.00
MU30 J.Foxx Pants Frisch 8.00 20.00
MU36 J.DiMag Pants Ott SP 15.00 40.00
MU49 D.Snider Jsy DiMaggio 10.00 25.00
MU53 J.Robinson Pants Martin 15.00 40.00
MU55 M.Mantle Pants Jackie 30.00 60.00
MU56 D.Larsen Pants Snider 10.00 25.00
MU56a D.Larsen Pants Jackie 10.00 25.00
MU57 E.Mathews Jsy Berra 10.00 25.00
MU58 Y.Berra Jsy Mathews 10.00 25.00
MU62 R.Maris Pants Marichal 20.00 50.00
MU63 S.Koufax Jsy Mantle 25.00 60.00
MU66 D.Drysdale Jsy Brooks SP 20.00 50.00
MU69 N.Ryan Jsy Brooks 20.00 50.00
MU72 J.Morgan Jsy Hunter 4.00 10.00
MU72a R.Fingers Jsy Bench 4.00 10.00
MU73 T.Seaver Pants Hunter 6.00 15.00
MU74 C.Hunter Jsy Garvey 6.00 15.00
MU74a D.Lopes Jsy Hunter 4.00 10.00
MU76 K.Griffey Sr. Jsy Munson 4.00 10.00
MU76a T.Munson Pants Bench 10.00 25.00
MU78 T.Munson Pants Garvey 10.00 25.00
MU78a B.Russell Jsy Munson 4.00 10.00
MU81 S.Garvey Jsy Winfield 4.00 10.00
MU82 R.Yount Jsy Smith 6.00 15.00
MU83 C.Ripken Pants Morgan 12.50 30.00
MU84 J.Morris Jsy Gwynn 4.00 10.00
MU86 J.Orosco Jsy Clemens 4.00 10.00
MU87 O.Smith Jsy Puckett 8.00 20.00
MU88 M.McGwire Jsy Gibs SP 12.50 30.00
MU90 B.Larkin Jsy McGwire SP 8.00 20.00
MU91 T.Glavine Jsy Puckett 6.00 15.00
MU93 J.Carter Jsy Schilling 4.00 10.00
MU95 D.Martinez Jsy Justice 4.00 10.00
MU95a K.Lofton Jsy Smoltz 6.00 15.00
MU96 A.Jones Jsy Pettitte 6.00 15.00
MU96a T.Raines Pants Glavine 4.00 10.00
MU96b K.Rogers Jsy Jones 4.00 10.00
MU97 J.Thome Jsy Brown 6.00 15.00
MU98 T.Gwynn Pants BWill. 6.00 15.00
MU98a T.Hoffman Jsy BWill SP 6.00 15.00
MU99 J.Posada Jsy Maddux 6.00 15.00
MU99a G.Maddux Jsy Jeter 6.00 15.00
MU99b P.O'Neill Pants Smoltz 6.00 15.00
MU99c C.Jones Jsy Rivera 6.00 15.00

2002 Upper Deck World Series Heroes Patch Collection

COMMON PATCH 8.00 20.00
ONE PER HOBBY JUMBO PACK
EXCHANGE CARDS 1:24 RETAIL
STATED PRINT RUN 298 SETS
WS3 1903 World Series 10.00 25.00
WS12 1912 World Series 10.00 25.00
WS18 1918 World Series 10.00 25.00
WS19 1919 World Series 12.50 30.00
WS27 1927 World Series 12.50 30.00
WS32 1932 World Series 10.00 25.00
WS34 1934 World Series 10.00 25.00
WS55 1955 World Series 15.00 40.00
WS56 1956 World Series 10.00 25.00
WS60 1960 World Series 10.00 25.00
WS61 1961 World Series 15.00 40.00
WS69 1969 World Series 15.00 40.00
WS75 1975 World Series 12.50 30.00
WS77 1977 World Series 10.00 25.00
WS88 1988 World Series 10.00 25.00
WS96 1996 World Series 10.00 25.00
WS2000 2000 World Series 10.00 25.00

2002 Upper Deck World Series Heroes Patch Collection Signatures

STATED ODDS 1:24 JUMBO PACKS
WS55 Duke Snider 40.00 100.00
WS56 Don Larsen 15.00 40.00
WS65 Sandy Koufax 150.00 300.00
WS69 Nolan Ryan 75.00 200.00
WS70 Brooks Robinson 15.00 40.00
WS73 Tom Seaver 20.00 50.00
WS74 Rollie Fingers 15.00 40.00
WS75 Carlton Fisk 40.00 100.00
WS76 Joe Morgan 15.00 40.00
WS81 Steve Garvey 15.00 40.00
WS82 Ozzie Smith 25.00 60.00
WS83 Cal Ripken 75.00 250.00
WS89 Mark McGwire 150.00 300.00
WS91 Kirby Puckett 60.00 150.00
WS93 Joe Carter 15.00 40.00
WS99 Roger Clemens 50.00 120.00

2008 Upper Deck X

COMPLETE SET (100) 12.50 30.00
COMMON CARD (1-100) .15 .40
COMMON ROOKIE (1-100) .25 .60
PRINTING PLATES RANDOMLY INSERTED
PLATE PRINT RUN 1 SET PER COLOR
BLACK-CYAN-MAGENTA-YELLOW ISSUED
NO PLATE PRICING DUE TO SCARCITY
1 Randy Johnson .40 1.00
2 Conor Jackson .15 .40
3 Brandon Webb .25 .60
4 Justin Upton .25 .60
5 Dan Haren .15 .40
6 John Smoltz .40 1.00
7 Chipper Jones .40 1.00
8 Mark Teixeira .25 .60
9 Brian Roberts .15 .40
10 Nick Markakis .30 .75
11 Daisuke Matsuzaka .25 .60
12 David Ortiz .40 1.00
13 Manny Ramirez .40 1.00
14 Jonathan Papelbon .25 .60
15 Josh Beckett .15 .40
16 Clay Buchholz (RC) .40 1.00
17 Carlos Zambrano .25 .60
18 Derrek Lee .15 .40
19 Aramis Ramirez .15 .40
20 Kerry Wood .15 .40
21 Alfonso Soriano .25 .60
22 Kosuke Fukudome RC .75 2.00
23 Geovany Soto .40 1.00
24 Paul Konerko .25 .60
25 Jermaine Dye .15 .40
26 Carlos Quentin .15 .40
27 Jim Thome .25 .60
28 Ken Griffey Jr. .75 2.00
29 Adam Dunn .25 .60
30 Brandon Phillips .15 .40
31 Edinson Volquez .15 .40
32 Victor Martinez .25 .60
33 Travis Hafner .15 .40
34 CC Sabathia .25 .60
35 Grady Sizemore .25 .60
36 Garrett Atkins .15 .40
37 Matt Holliday .40 1.00
38 Troy Tulowitzki .40 1.00
39 Justin Verlander .40 1.00
40 Miguel Cabrera .40 1.00
41 Gary Sheffield .15 .40
42 Magglio Ordonez .25 .60
43 Hanley Ramirez .25 .60
44 Jeremy Hermida .15 .40
45 Carlos Lee .15 .40
46 Lance Berkman .25 .60
47 Roy Oswalt .25 .60
48 Alex Gordon .25 .60
49 Zack Greinke .40 1.00
50 Howie Kendrick .15 .40
51 Torii Hunter .15 .40
52 Vladimir Guerrero .25 .60
53 Matt Kemp .30 .75
54 Russell Martin .15 .40
55 Rafael Furcal .15 .40
56 Ryan Braun .25 .60
57 Prince Fielder .25 .60
58 Corey Hart .15 .40
59 Justin Morneau .25 .60
60 Joe Mauer .30 .75
61 Jose Reyes .25 .60
62 David Wright .25 .60
63 Carlos Beltran .25 .60
64 Johan Santana .25 .60
65 Pedro Martinez .25 .60
66 Ian Kennedy RC .60 1.50
67 Hideki Matsui .40 1.00
68 Alex Rodriguez .50 1.25
69 Chien-Ming Wang .25 .60
70 Derek Jeter 1.00 2.50
71 Robinson Cano .25 .60
72 Eric Chavez .15 .40
73 Frank Thomas .40 1.00
74 Cole Hamels .30 .75
75 Jimmy Rollins .25 .60
76 Ryan Howard .25 .60
77 Chase Utley .25 .60
78 Nate McLouth .15 .40
79 Jason Bay .25 .60
80 Adrian Gonzalez .25 .60
81 Khalil Greene .15 .40
82 Jake Peavy .15 .40
83 Greg Maddux .50 1.25
84 Trevor Hoffman .25 .60
85 Aaron Rowand .15 .40
86 Tim Lincecum .25 .60
87 Ichiro Suzuki .50 1.25
88 Felix Hernandez .25 .60
89 Erik Bedard .15 .40
90 Rick Ankiel .15 .40
91 Albert Pujols .50 1.25
92 B.J. Upton .25 .60
93 Carl Crawford .25 .60
94 Evan Longoria RC 1.25 3.00
95 Josh Hamilton .25 .60
96 Michael Young .15 .40
97 Vernon Wells .15 .40
98 Alex Rios .15 .40
99 Ryan Zimmerman .25 .60
100 Lastings Milledge .15 .40

2008 Upper Deck X Die Cut

*VETERAN 1-100: 1X TO 2.5X BASIC
*ROOKIE 1-100: .75X TO 2X BASIC RC
STATED ODDS ONE PER PACK

2008 Upper Deck X Die Cut Gold

*VETERAN GLD 1-100: 2.5X TO 6X BASIC
*ROOKIE GLD 1-100: 1.5X TO 4X BASIC RC
RANDOM INSERTS IN PACKS

2008 Upper Deck X Memorabilia

AA Aaron Harang 3.00 8.00
AE Andre Ethier 3.00 8.00
AG Adrian Gonzalez 3.00 8.00
AH Aubrey Huff 3.00 8.00
AK Austin Kearns 3.00 8.00
AR Alex Rodriguez 5.00 12.00
BG Brian Giles 3.00 8.00
BJ Brandon Jones 3.00 8.00
BM Brian McCann 3.00 8.00
BO Jeremy Bonderman 3.00 8.00
BP Brad Penny 3.00 8.00
BR Brian Roberts 3.00 8.00
BU A.J. Burnett 3.00 8.00
CA Melky Cabrera 3.00 8.00
CD Carlos Delgado 3.00 8.00
CJ Conor Jackson 3.00 8.00
CL Carlos Lee 3.00 8.00
CR Joe Crede 3.00 8.00
CS Curt Schilling 3.00 8.00
CZ Carlos Zambrano 3.00 8.00
DL Derrek Lee 3.00 8.00
DO David Ortiz 3.00 8.00
DR J.D. Drew 3.00 8.00
DU Dan Uggla 3.00 8.00
DY Jermaine Dye 3.00 8.00
FS Freddy Sanchez 3.00 8.00
GJ Geoff Jenkins 3.00 8.00
GM Greg Maddux 4.00 10.00
GS Grady Sizemore 3.00 8.00
HP Hunter Pence 3.00 8.00
HR Hanley Ramirez 3.00 8.00
HS Huston Street 3.00 8.00
HU Torii Hunter 3.00 8.00
IK Ian Kinsler 3.00 8.00
JF Jeff Francoeur 3.00 8.00
JG Jeremy Guthrie 3.00 8.00
JH J.J. Hardy 3.00 8.00
JK Jeff Kent 3.00 8.00
JS James Shields 3.00 8.00
KE Kelly Johnson 3.00 8.00
KJ Kenji Johjima 3.00 8.00
KU Jason Kubel 3.00 8.00
KW Kerry Wood 3.00 8.00
LG Luis Gonzalez 3.00 8.00
MG Matt Garza 3.00 8.00
MK Kendry Morales 3.00 8.00
MO Justin Morneau 3.00 8.00
NS Nick Swisher 3.00 8.00
PA Jonathan Papelbon 4.00 10.00
PO Jorge Posada 3.00 8.00
RA Aramis Ramirez 3.00 8.00
RF Rafael Furcal 3.00 8.00
RH Rich Hill 3.00 8.00
SA Johan Santana 3.00 8.00
TH Tim Hudson 3.00 8.00
TL Tim Lincecum 5.00 12.00
TT Troy Tulowitzki 3.00 8.00
TW Tim Wakefield 3.00 8.00
UP B.J. Upton 3.00 8.00
VE Justin Verlander 3.00 8.00

2008 Upper Deck X Sample

COMPLETE SET (1) 5.00 12.00
DJ Derek Jeter 5.00 12.00

2008 Upper Deck X Signatures

STATED ODDS 1:10 HOBBY
EXCHANGE DEADLINE 8/18/2010
BB Brian Bass 4.00 10.00
BI Brian Bixler 3.00 8.00
CA Jesse Carlson 3.00 8.00
CB Clay Buchholz 10.00 25.00
CC Callix Crabbe 3.00 8.00
CM Colt Morton 3.00 8.00
CT Clete Thomas 3.00 8.00
DJ Derek Jeter 75.00 150.00
EM Evan Meek 3.00 8.00
FC Frank Catalanotto 3.00 8.00
JA Jonathan Albaladejo 3.00 8.00
JK Jeff Keppinger 3.00 8.00
JN Josh Newman 3.00 8.00
JT J.R. Towles 4.00 10.00
KG Ken Griffey Jr. 50.00 100.00
KH Kevin Hart 3.00 8.00
LM Luis Mendoza 3.00 8.00
MB Marlon Byrd 3.00 8.00
RO Ross Ohlendorf 3.00 8.00
RT Rich Thompson 3.00 8.00
SH Steve Holm 3.00 8.00
TI Clay Timpner 3.00 8.00
TR Ramon Troncoso 3.00 8.00

2008 Upper Deck X Xponential

STATED ODDS 1:2 HOBBY
PRINTING PLATES RANDOMLY INSERTED
PLATE PRINT RUN 1 SET PER COLOR
BLACK-CYAN-MAGENTA-YELLOW ISSUED
NO PLATE PRICING DUE TO SCARCITY
AD Adam Dunn .50 1.25
AG Adrian Gonzalez .50 1.25
AJ Andruw Jones .30 .75
AL Alex Rodriguez 1.00 2.50
AP Albert Pujols 1.00 2.50
AR Aramis Ramirez .30 .75
AS Alfonso Soriano .50 1.25
BA Bobby Abreu .30 .75
BP Brandon Phillips .30 .75
BR Brian Roberts .30 .75
BU B.J. Upton .50 1.25
BW Brandon Webb .50 1.25
CB Carlos Beltran .50 1.25
CC Carl Crawford .50 1.25
CG Curtis Granderson .50 1.25
CH Corey Hart .30 .75
CJ Conor Jackson .30 .75
CL Carlos Lee .30 .75
CP Carlos Pena .50 1.25
CS CC Sabathia .50 1.25
CU Chase Utley .50 1.25
CW Chien-Ming Wang .50 1.25
CY Chris B. Young .30 .75
CZ Carlos Zambrano .50 1.25
DJ Derek Jeter 2.00 5.00
DL Derrek Lee .30 .75
DM Daisuke Matsuzaka .50 1.25
DO David Ortiz .75 2.00
DW Dontrelle Willis .30 .75
EB Erik Bedard .30 .75
FH Felix Hernandez .50 1.25
FT Frank Thomas .75 2.00
GA Garrett Atkins .30 .75
GM Greg Maddux 1.00 2.50
GR Khalil Greene .30 .75
GS Grady Sizemore .50 1.25
GU Carlos Guillen .30 .75
HE Todd Helton .50 1.25
HM Hideki Matsui .75 2.00
HO Trevor Hoffman .50 1.25
HR Hanley Ramirez .50 1.25
HU Torii Hunter .30 .75
IR Ivan Rodriguez .50 1.25
IS Ichiro Suzuki 1.00 2.50
JA Jason Bay .50 1.25
JB Josh Beckett .30 .75
JC Joba Chamberlain .30 .75
JF Jeff Francoeur .50 1.25
JH Josh Hamilton .50 1.25
JI Jimmy Rollins .50 1.25
JK Jeff Kent .30 .75
JM Justin Morneau .50 1.25
JO Chipper Jones .75 2.00
JP Jonathan Papelbon .50 1.25
JR Jose Reyes .50 1.25
JS John Smoltz .75 2.00
JT Jim Thome .50 1.25
JV Jason Varitek .75 2.00
KG Ken Griffey Jr. 1.50 4.00
LB Lance Berkman .50 1.25
MA Joe Mauer .60 1.50
MC Miguel Cabrera .75 2.00
MH Matt Holliday .75 2.00
MO Magglio Ordonez .50 1.25
MR Manny Ramirez .75 2.00
MT Mark Teixeira .50 1.25
NM Nick Markakis .60 1.50
NS Nick Swisher .50 1.25
PB Pat Burrell .30 .75
PE Jake Peavy .30 .75
PF Prince Fielder .50 1.25
PK Paul Konerko .50 1.25
PM Pedro Martinez .50 1.25
RA Rick Ankiel .30 .75
RB Ryan Braun .50 1.25
RH Ryan Howard .50 1.25
RI Mariano Rivera 1.00 2.50
RJ Randy Johnson .75 2.00
RM Russell Martin .30 .75
RO Roy Oswalt .50 1.25
RW Rickie Weeks .30 .75
RZ Ryan Zimmerman .50 1.25
SA Johan Santana .50 1.25
SH Gary Sheffield .30 .75
TE Miguel Tejada .50 1.25
TH Travis Hafner .30 .75
TT Troy Tulowitzki .75 2.00
VG Vladimir Guerrero .50 1.25
VM Victor Martinez .50 1.25
WR David Wright .50 1.25

2008 Upper Deck X Xponential 2

*X2: .5X TO 1.2X BASIC XPONENTIAL
APPX.ODDS 1:3 HOBBY
PRINTING PLATES RANDOMLY INSERTED
PLATE PRINT RUN 1 SET PER COLOR
BLACK-CYAN-MAGENTA-YELLOW ISSUED
NO PLATE PRICING DUE TO SCARCITY

2008 Upper Deck X Xponential 3

*X3: .75X TO 2X BASIC XPONENTIAL
STATED ODDS 1:10 HOBBY
PRINTING PLATES RANDOMLY INSERTED
PLATE PRINT RUN 1 SET PER COLOR
BLACK-CYAN-MAGENTA-YELLOW ISSUED
NO PLATE PRICING DUE TO SCARCITY

2008 Upper Deck X Xponential 4

*X4: 1X TO 2.5X BASIC XPONENTIAL
STATED ODDS 1:10 HOBBY
PRINTING PLATES RANDOMLY INSERTED
PLATE PRINT RUN 1 SET PER COLOR
BLACK-CYAN-MAGENTA-YELLOW ISSUED
NO PLATE PRICING DUE TO SCARCITY

2009 Upper Deck X

COMPLETE SET (100) 15.00 40.00
COMMON CARD (1-95) .15 .40
COMMON ROOKIE (96-100) .50 1.25
PRINTING PLATES RANDOMLY INSERTED
PLATE PRINT RUN 1 SET PER COLOR
BLACK-CYAN-MAGENTA-YELLOW ISSUED
NO PLATE PRICING DUE TO SCARCITY
1 Dan Haren .15 .40
2 Chris B. Young .15 .40
3 Brandon Webb .25 .60
4 Chipper Jones .40 1.00
5 Brian McCann .25 .60
6 Nick Markakis .30 .75
7 Brian Roberts .15 .40
8 Kevin Youkilis .15 .40
9 Josh Beckett .15 .40
10 Jonathan Papelbon .25 .60
11 Jacoby Ellsbury .30 .75

12 Dustin Pedroia .40 1.00
13 David Ortiz .40 1.00
14 Daisuke Matsuzaka .25 .60
15 Rich Harden .15 .40
16 Alfonso Soriano .25 .60
17 Derrek Lee .15 .40
18 Carlos Zambrano .25 .60
19 Aramis Ramirez .15 .40
20 Paul Konerko .25 .60
21 Jermaine Dye .15 .40
22 Carlos Quentin .15 .40
23 Jay Bruce .25 .60
24 Edinson Volquez .15 .40
25 Brandon Phillips .15 .40
26 Victor Martinez .25 .60
27 Travis Hafner .15 .40
28 Kerry Wood .15 .40
29 Grady Sizemore .25 .60
30 Cliff Lee .25 .60
31 Garrett Atkins .15 .40
32 Miguel Cabrera .40 1.00
33 Magglio Ordonez .25 .60
34 Carlos Guillen .15 .40
35 Hanley Ramirez .25 .60
36 Dan Uggla .15 .40
37 Miguel Tejada .25 .60
38 Lance Berkman .25 .60
39 Carlos Lee .15 .40
40 Jose Guillen .15 .40
41 Alex Gordon .25 .60
42 Vladimir Guerrero .25 .60
43 Torii Hunter .15 .40
44 Bobby Abreu .15 .40
45 Russell Martin .15 .40
46 Matt Kemp .30 .75
47 Manny Ramirez .40 1.00
48 Ryan Braun .25 .60
49 Prince Fielder .25 .60
50 Corey Hart .15 .40
51 Joe Nathan .15 .40
52 Justin Morneau .25 .60
53 Joe Mauer .30 .75
54 Jose Reyes .25 .60
55 Johan Santana .25 .60
56 Francisco Rodriguez .25 .60
57 David Wright .30 .75
58 Carlos Beltran .25 .60
59 Mark Teixeira .25 .60
60 Andy Pettitte .25 .60
61 Joba Chamberlain .15 .40
62 Derek Jeter 1.00 2.50
63 Chien-Ming Wang .25 .60
64 CC Sabathia .25 .60
65 Alex Rodriguez .50 1.25
66 Matt Holliday .40 1.00
67 Jason Giambi .15 .40
68 Jack Cust .15 .40
69 Ryan Howard .30 .75
70 Jimmy Rollins .25 .60
71 Chase Utley .25 .60
72 Nate McLouth .15 .40
73 Ryan Doumit .15 .40
74 Jake Peavy .15 .40
75 Adrian Gonzalez .30 .75
76 Tim Lincecum .25 .60
77 Aaron Rowand .15 .40
78 Randy Johnson .40 1.00
79 Ken Griffey Jr. .75 2.00
80 Ichiro Suzuki .50 1.25
81 Felix Hernandez .25 .60
82 Ryan Ludwick .25 .60
83 Rick Ankiel .15 .40
84 Albert Pujols .50 1.25
85 Scott Kazmir .15 .40
86 Evan Longoria .25 .60
87 Carl Crawford .25 .60
88 B.J. Upton .25 .60
89 Josh Hamilton .25 .60
90 Ian Kinsler .25 .60
91 Vernon Wells .15 .40
92 Roy Halladay .25 .60
93 Alex Rios .15 .40
94 Adam Dunn .25 .60
95 Ryan Zimmerman .25 .60
96 Rick Porcello RC 1.25 3.00
97 Colby Rasmus (RC) .60 1.50
98 James McDonald RC 1.00 2.50
99 Koji Uehara RC 1.00 2.50
100 Derek Holland RC .60 1.50

2009 Upper Deck X Die Cut

*VETERAN 1-100: 1X TO 2.5X BASIC
*ROOKIE 1-100: .5X TO 1.2X BASIC RC
RANDOM INSERTS IN PACKS

2009 Upper Deck X Icons Michael Jackson

MJ1 Michael Jackson 4.00 10.00
MJ2 Michael Jackson 4.00 10.00
MJ3 Michael Jackson 4.00 10.00
MJ4 Michael Jackson 4.00 10.00

2009 Upper Deck X Memorabilia

RANDOM INSERTS IN PACKS
NO PRICING AVAILABLE ON MOST
AE Andre Ethier 3.00 8.00
AN Rick Ankiel SP 3.00 8.00
BD Blake DeWitt 3.00 8.00
BE Josh Beckett 3.00 8.00
BP Brad Penny 3.00 8.00
BZ Barry Zito 3.00 8.00
CA Chris Carpenter 3.00 8.00
CD Carlos Delgado 3.00 8.00
CJ Conor Jackson 3.00 8.00
CL Carlos Lee 3.00 8.00
CU Michael Cuddyer 3.00 8.00
DH Dan Haren 3.00 8.00
DJ Derek Jeter 10.00 25.00
DO David Ortiz 3.00 8.00
DY Delmon Young 3.00 8.00
EC Eric Chavez 3.00 8.00
EL Evan Longoria 4.00 10.00
FP Felipe Paulino 3.00 8.00
GA Garrett Atkins 3.00 8.00
GR Curtis Granderson 3.00 8.00
HA Corey Hart 3.00 8.00
HO Trevor Hoffman 3.00 8.00
JB Jeff Baker 3.00 8.00
JC Joba Chamberlain 3.00 8.00
JD Jermaine Dye 3.00 8.00
JF Jeff Francoeur 3.00 8.00
JG Jeremy Guthrie 3.00 8.00
JH Jeremy Hermida 3.00 8.00
JJ Josh Johnson 3.00 8.00
JK Jason Kubel 3.00 8.00
JL James Loney 3.00 8.00
JM Joe Mauer 4.00 10.00
JN Joe Nathan 3.00 8.00
JO Josh Barfield 3.00 8.00
JP Jake Peavy 3.00 8.00
JT Jim Thome 3.00 8.00
JU Justin Upton 3.00 8.00
JW Jered Weaver 4.00 10.00
JZ Joel Zumaya 3.00 8.00
KJ Kelly Johnson 3.00 8.00
KK Kevin Kouzmanoff 3.00 8.00
KM Kendry Morales 3.00 8.00
MH Matt Holliday 3.00 8.00
MI Kevin Millwood 3.00 8.00
MK Matt Kemp 3.00 8.00
ML Mike Lowell 3.00 8.00
MO Justin Morneau 3.00 8.00
MR Manny Ramirez 4.00 10.00
MY Michael Young 3.00 8.00
OR Magglio Ordonez 4.00 10.00
PE Jhonny Peralta 3.00 8.00
PH Phil Hughes 3.00 8.00
PK Paul Konerko 3.00 8.00
RB Ryan Braun 3.00 8.00
RF Rafael Furcal 3.00 8.00
RH Rich Hill 3.00 8.00
RM Russell Martin 3.00 8.00
RO Roy Oswalt 3.00 8.00
RT Ramon Troncoso 3.00 8.00
SR Scott Rolen 3.00 8.00
TG Troy Glaus 3.00 8.00
TR Travis Hafner 5.00 12.00
WI Josh Willingham 3.00 8.00

2009 Upper Deck X Signatures

RANDOM INSERTS IN PACKS
23 Jay Bruce 4.00 10.00
24 Edinson Volquez 6.00 15.00
50 Corey Hart 6.00 15.00
98 James McDonald 4.00 10.00

2009 Upper Deck X Xponential

RANDOM INSERTS IN PACKS
PRINTING PLATES RANDOMLY INSERTED
PLATE PRINT RUN 1 SET PER COLOR
BLACK-CYAN-MAGENTA-YELLOW ISSUED
NO PLATE PRICING DUE TO SCARCITY
AB A.J. Burnett .30 .75
AG Adrian Gonzalez .60 1.50
AP Albert Pujols 1.00 2.50
AR Alex Rodriguez 1.00 2.50
AS Alfonso Soriano .50 1.25
AZ Aramis Ramirez .30 .75
BA Bobby Abreu .30 .75
BE Josh Beckett .30 .75
BM Brian McCann .50 1.25
BP Brandon Phillips .30 .75
BU B.J. Upton .50 1.25
BW Brandon Webb .50 1.25
CB Carlos Beltran .50 1.25
CC Carl Crawford .50 1.25
CH Cole Hamels .60 1.50
CJ Chipper Jones .75 2.00
CL Carlos Lee .30 .75
CQ Carlos Quentin .30 .75
CS CC Sabathia .50 1.25
CU Chase Utley .50 1.25
CW Chien-Ming Wang .50 1.25
CZ Carlos Zambrano .50 1.25
DH Dan Haren .30 .75
DJ Derek Jeter 2.00 5.00
DL Derrek Lee .30 .75
DM Daisuke Matsuzaka .50 1.25
DO David Ortiz .75 2.00
DP Dustin Pedroia .75 2.00
DU Dan Uggla .30 .75
DW David Wright .60 1.50
EL Evan Longoria .50 1.25
EV Edinson Volquez .30 .75
FH Felix Hernandez .50 1.25
FR Francisco Rodriguez .50 1.25
GE Geovany Soto .50 1.25
GS Grady Sizemore .50 1.25
HA Travis Hafner .30 .75
HO Ryan Howard .60 1.50
HR Hanley Ramirez .50 1.25
IK Ian Kinsler .50 1.25
IS Ichiro Suzuki 1.00 2.50
JB Jay Bruce .50 1.25
JD Jermaine Dye .30 .75
JE Jacoby Ellsbury .60 1.50
JG Jason Giambi .30 .75
JH Josh Hamilton .50 1.25
JM Joe Mauer .60 1.50
JP Jake Peavy .30 .75
JR Jimmy Rollins .50 1.25
JS Johan Santana .50 1.25
KG Ken Griffey Jr. 1.50 4.00
KY Kevin Youkilis .30 .75
LB Lance Berkman .50 1.25
MA Nick Markakis .60 1.50
MC Miguel Cabrera .75 2.00
MH Matt Holliday .75 2.00
ML Mike Lowell .30 .75
MO Magglio Ordonez .50 1.25
MR Manny Ramirez .75 2.00
MT Mark Teixeira .50 1.25
PA Jonathan Papelbon .50 1.25
PF Prince Fielder .50 1.25
RA Rick Ankiel .30 .75
RB Ryan Braun .50 1.25
RE Jose Reyes .50 1.25
RH Roy Halladay .50 1.25
RJ Randy Johnson .75 2.00
RM Russell Martin .30 .75
RZ Ryan Zimmerman .50 1.25
SK Scott Kazmir .30 .75
TE Miguel Tejada .50 1.25
TH Torii Hunter .30 .75
TL Tim Lincecum .50 1.25
VG Vladimir Guerrero .50 1.25
VW Vernon Wells .30 .75

2009 Upper Deck X Xponential 2

*X2: .5X TO 1.2X BASIC XPONENTIAL
RANDOM INSERTS IN PACKS
PRINTING PLATES RANDOMLY INSERTED
PLATE PRINT RUN 1 SET PER COLOR
BLACK-CYAN-MAGENTA-YELLOW ISSUED
NO PLATE PRICING DUE TO SCARCITY
AG Adrian Gonzalez .75 2.00
AP Albert Pujols 1.25 3.00
AR Alex Rodriguez 1.25 3.00
AS Alfonso Soriano .60 1.50
AZ Aramis Ramirez .40 1.00
BU B.J. Upton .60 1.50
BW Brandon Webb .60 1.50
CB Carlos Beltran .60 1.50
CC Carl Crawford .60 1.50
CJ Chipper Jones 1.00 2.50
CS CC Sabathia .60 1.50
CU Chase Utley .60 1.50
CZ Carlos Zambrano .60 1.50
DJ Derek Jeter 2.50 6.00
DL Derrek Lee .40 1.00
DO David Ortiz 1.00 2.50
DW David Wright .75 2.00
EV Edinson Volquez .40 1.00
GS Grady Sizemore .60 1.50
HR Hanley Ramirez .60 1.50
IK Ian Kinsler .60 1.50
IS Ichiro Suzuki 1.25 3.00
JB Josh Beckett .40 1.00
JD Jermaine Dye .40 1.00
JH Josh Hamilton .60 1.50
JM Joe Mauer .75 2.00
JP Jonathan Papelbon .60 1.50
JR Jimmy Rollins .60 1.50
JS Johan Santana .60 1.50
KG Ken Griffey Jr. 2.00 5.00
LB Lance Berkman .60 1.50
MC Miguel Cabrera 1.00 2.50
MH Matt Holliday 1.00 2.50
MO Magglio Ordonez .60 1.50
MR Manny Ramirez 1.00 2.50
MT Mark Teixeira .60 1.50
PE Jake Peavy .40 1.00
PF Prince Fielder .60 1.50
RA Rick Ankiel .40 1.00
RB Ryan Braun .60 1.50
RE Jose Reyes .60 1.50
RH Ryan Howard .75 2.00
RJ Randy Johnson 1.00 2.50
RM Russell Martin .40 1.00
VG Vladimir Guerrero .60 1.50

2009 Upper Deck X Xponential 3

*X3: .5X TO 1.2X BASIC XPONENTIAL
RANDOM INSERTS IN PACKS
PRINTING PLATES RANDOMLY INSERTED
PLATE PRINT RUN 1 SET PER COLOR
BLACK-CYAN-MAGENTA-YELLOW ISSUED
NO PLATE PRICING DUE TO SCARCITY
AG Adrian Gonzalez .75 2.00
AP Albert Pujols 1.25 3.00
AR Alex Rodriguez 1.25 3.00
AS Alfonso Soriano .60 1.50
AZ Aramis Ramirez .40 1.00
BU B.J. Upton .60 1.50
BW Brandon Webb .60 1.50
CB Carlos Beltran .60 1.50
CJ Chipper Jones 1.00 2.50
CU Chase Utley .60 1.50
DJ Derek Jeter 2.50 6.00
DL Derrek Lee .40 1.00
DO David Ortiz 1.00 2.50
DW David Wright .75 2.00
GS Grady Sizemore .60 1.50
HO Ryan Howard .75 2.00
HR Hanley Ramirez .60 1.50
IS Ichiro Suzuki 1.25 3.00
JB Josh Beckett .40 1.00
JD Jermaine Dye .40 1.00
JH Josh Hamilton .60 1.50
JP Jake Peavy .40 1.00
JR Jimmy Rollins .60 1.50
JS Johan Santana .60 1.50
KG Ken Griffey Jr. 2.00 5.00
LB Lance Berkman .60 1.50
MC Miguel Cabrera 1.00 2.50
MH Matt Holliday 1.00 2.50
MR Manny Ramirez 1.00 2.50
MT Mark Teixeira .60 1.50
PF Prince Fielder .60 1.50
RB Ryan Braun .60 1.50
RE Jose Reyes .60 1.50
RJ Randy Johnson 1.00 2.50
VG Vladimir Guerrero .60 1.50

2009 Upper Deck X Xponential 4

*X4: .6X TO 1.5X BASIC XPONENTIAL
RANDOM INSERTS IN PACKS
PRINTING PLATES RANDOMLY INSERTED
PLATE PRINT RUN 1 SET PER COLOR
BLACK-CYAN-MAGENTA-YELLOW ISSUED
NO PLATE PRICING DUE TO SCARCITY
AP Albert Pujols 1.50 4.00
AR Alex Rodriguez 1.50 4.00
AS Alfonso Soriano .75 2.00
CB Carlos Beltran .75 2.00
CU Chase Utley .75 2.00
DJ Derek Jeter 3.00 8.00
DO David Ortiz 1.25 3.00
DW David Wright 1.00 2.50
GS Grady Sizemore .75 2.00
HR Hanley Ramirez .75 2.00
IS Ichiro Suzuki 1.50 4.00
JB Josh Beckett .50 1.25
JH Josh Hamilton .75 2.00
JP Jake Peavy .50 1.25
JR Jose Reyes .75 2.00
JS Johan Santana .75 2.00
KG Ken Griffey Jr. 2.50 6.00
MH Matt Holliday 1.25 3.00
MR Manny Ramirez 1.25 3.00
MT Mark Teixeira .75 2.00
PF Prince Fielder .75 2.00
RB Ryan Braun .75 2.00
RH Ryan Howard 1.00 2.50
RJ Randy Johnson 1.25 3.00
VG Vladimir Guerrero .75 2.00

2009 Upper Deck X Xponential 5

*X5: .6X TO 1.5X BASIC XPONENTIAL
RANDOM INSERTS IN PACKS
PRINTING PLATES RANDOMLY INSERTED
PLATE PRINT RUN 1 SET PER COLOR
BLACK-CYAN-MAGENTA-YELLOW ISSUED
NO PLATE PRICING DUE TO SCARCITY
AP Albert Pujols 1.50 4.00
AR Alex Rodriguez 1.50 4.00
AS Alfonso Soriano .75 2.00
CU Chase Utley .75 2.00
DJ Derek Jeter 3.00 8.00
DO David Ortiz 1.25 3.00
DW David Wright 1.00 2.50
IS Ichiro Suzuki 1.50 4.00
JP Jake Peavy .50 1.25
JR Jose Reyes .75 2.00
KG Ken Griffey Jr. 2.50 6.00
MR Manny Ramirez 1.25 3.00
RB Ryan Braun .75 2.00
RH Ryan Howard 1.00 2.50
RJ Randy Johnson 1.25 3.00

2009 Upper Deck X Xponential 6

*X6: 1X TO 2.5X BASIC XPONENTIAL
RANDOM INSERTS IN PACKS
PRINTING PLATES RANDOMLY INSERTED
PLATE PRINT RUN 1 SET PER COLOR
BLACK-CYAN-MAGENTA-YELLOW ISSUED
NO PLATE PRICING DUE TO SCARCITY
AP Albert Pujols 2.50 6.00
AR Alex Rodriguez 2.50 6.00
DJ Derek Jeter 5.00 12.00
KG Ken Griffey Jr. 4.00 10.00
RJ Randy Johnson 2.00 5.00

2008 Upper Deck Yankee Stadium Legacy Collection Box Set

COMPLETE SET (100) 8.00 20.00
1 Babe Ruth .60 1.50
2 Mickey Mantle .75 2.00
3 Lou Gehrig .50 1.25
4 Wally Pipp .10 .25
5 Waite Hoyt .10 .25
6 Bob Meusel .10 .25
7 Herb Pennock .15 .40
8 Earle Combs .10 .25
9 Urban Shocker .10 .25
10 George Pipgras .10 .25
11 Bill Dickey .10 .25
12 Red Ruffing .10 .25
13 Joe McCarthy .10 .25
14 Frankie Crosetti .10 .25
15 Red Rolfe .10 .25
16 Joe DiMaggio .50 1.25
17 Joe Gordon .10 .25
18 Tommy Henrich .10 .25
19 Spud Chandler .10 .25
20 Phil Rizzuto .15 .40
21 Phil Rizzuto .15 .40
22 Joe DiMaggio .50 1.25
23 Charlie Keller .10 .25
24 Yogi Berra .25 .60
25 Allie Reynolds .10 .25
26 Vic Raschi .10 .25
27 Yogi Berra .25 .60
28 Billy Martin .15 .40
29 Billy Martin .15 .40
30 Hank Bauer .10 .25
31 Gil McDougald .10 .25
32 Whitey Ford .15 .40
33 Whitey Ford .15 .40
34 Don Larsen .10 .25
35 Moose Skowron .10 .25
36 Tony Kubek .10 .25
37 Elston Howard .10 .25
38 Roger Maris .25 .60
39 Roger Maris .25 .60
40 Clete Boyer .10 .25
41 Bobby Richardson .10 .25
42 Joe Pepitone .10 .25
43 Bobby Murcer .10 .25
44 Roy White .10 .25
45 Sparky Lyle .10 .25
46 Sparky Lyle .10 .25
47 Graig Nettles .10 .25
48 Graig Nettles .10 .25
49 Chris Chambliss .10 .25
50 Chris Chambliss .10 .25
51 Reggie Jackson .15 .40
52 Reggie Jackson .15 .40
53 Ron Guidry .10 .25
54 Bucky Dent .10 .25
55 Bucky Dent .10 .25
56 Goose Gossage .15 .40
57 Goose Gossage .15 .40
58 Ron Guidry .10 .25
59 Lou Piniella .10 .25
60 Lou Piniella .10 .25
61 Rick Cerone .10 .25
62 Tommy John .10 .25
63 Dave Winfield .15 .40
64 Dave Winfield .15 .40
65 Dave Righetti .10 .25
66 Dave Righetti .10 .25
67 Don Baylor .10 .25
68 Willie Randolph .10 .25
69 Don Mattingly .50 1.25
70 Don Mattingly .50 1.25
71 Jim Leyritz .10 .25
72 Bernie Williams .15 .40
73 Bernie Williams .15 .40
74 Wade Boggs .15 .40
75 Wade Boggs .15 .40
76 John Wetteland .10 .25
77 Joe Torre .15 .40
78 Joe Torre .15 .40
79 Tino Martinez .10 .25
80 Tino Martinez .10 .25
81 David Wells .10 .25
82 David Wells .10 .25
83 Derek Jeter .60 1.50
84 Derek Jeter .60 1.50
85 Paul O'Neill .15 .40
86 Paul O'Neill .15 .40
87 Andy Pettitte .15 .40
88 Andy Pettitte .15 .40
89 Roger Clemens .30 .75
90 Roger Clemens .30 .75
91 Mariano Rivera .30 .75
92 Hideki Matsui .25 .60
93 Hideki Matsui .25 .60
94 Jorge Posada .15 .40
95 Jorge Posada .15 .40
96 Alex Rodriguez .30 .75
97 Randy Johnson .25 .60
98 Randy Johnson .25 .60
99 Alex Rodriguez .30 .75
100 Mariano Rivera .30 .75
NNO Yankee Stadium Bat
NNO Yankee Stadium Jersey

2003 Upper Deck Yankees 100th Anniversary

COMP.FACT SET (30) 10.00 20.00
DISTRIBUTED IN TIN FACTORY SET
1 Babe Ruth 23 1.25 3.00
2 Tony Lazzeri 27 .15 .40
3 Lou Gehrig 28 1.00 2.50
4 Lou Gehrig 32 1.00 2.50
5 Red Rolfe 36 .15 .40
6 Lou Gehrig 37 1.00 2.50
7 Bill Dickey 38 .25 .60
8 Joe DiMaggio 39 1.00 2.50
9 Charlie Keller 41 .15 .40
10 Frank Crosetti 43 .15 .40
11 Phil Rizzuto 47 .25 .60
12 Joe DiMaggio 49 1.00 2.50
13 Joe DiMaggio 50 1.00 2.50
14 Phil Rizzuto 51 .25 .60
15 Mickey Mantle 52 1.50 4.00
16 Yogi Berra 53 .40 1.00
17 Yogi Berra 56 .40 1.00
18 Mickey Mantle 58 1.50 4.00
19 Whitey Ford 61 .25 .60
20 Mickey Mantle 62 1.50 4.00
21 Thurman Munson 77 .50 1.25
22 Thurman Munson 78 .50 1.25
23 Bernie Williams 96 .25 .60
24 Jorge Posada 98 .25 .60
25 Mariano Rivera 99 .25 .60
26 Derek Jeter 00 1.00 2.50
27 Hideki Matsui RH 03 HR 2.00 5.00
28 Hideki Matsui RH 03 AS 2.00 5.00
29 Roger Clemens 300th Win .75 2.00
30 Yankee Stadium CL .15 .40

2000 Upper Deck Yankees Legends

COMPLETE SET (90) 10.00 25.00
COMMON CARD (1-90) .15 .40
WINFIELD 3K LISTED W/UD 3000 CLUB
1 Babe Ruth 1.00 2.50
2 Mickey Mantle 1.25 3.00
3 Lou Gehrig .75 2.00
4 Joe DiMaggio .75 2.00
5 Yogi Berra .40 1.00
6 Don Mattingly .75 2.00
7 Reggie Jackson .25 .60
8 Dave Winfield .25 .60
9 Bill Skowron .15 .40
10 Willie Randolph .15 .40
11 Phil Rizzuto .25 .60
12 Tony Kubek .15 .40
13 Thurman Munson .40 1.00
14 Roger Maris .40 1.00
15 Billy Martin .25 .60
16 Elston Howard .15 .40
17 Graig Nettles .15 .40
18 Whitey Ford .25 .60
19 Earle Combs .15 .40
20 Tony Lazzeri .25 .60
21 Bob Meusel .15 .40
22 Joe Gordon .15 .40
23 Jerry Coleman .15 .40
24 Joe Torre .25 .60
25 Bucky Dent .15 .40
26 Don Larsen .15 .40
27 Bobby Richardson .15 .40
28 Ron Guidry .15 .40
29 Bobby Murcer .15 .40
30 Tommy Henrich .15 .40
31 Hank Bauer .15 .40
32 Joe Pepitone .15 .40
33 Clete Boyer .15 .40
34 Chris Chambliss .15 .40
35 Tommy John .15 .40
36 Goose Gossage .25 .60
37 Red Ruffing .15 .40
38 Charlie Keller .15 .40
39 Billy Gardner .15 .40
40 Hector Lopez .15 .40
41 Cliff Johnson .15 .40
42 Oscar Gamble .15 .40
43 Allie Reynolds .15 .40
44 Mickey Rivers .15 .40
45 Bill Dickey .15 .40
46 Dave Righetti .15 .40
47 Mel Stottlemyre .15 .40
48 Waite Hoyt .15 .40
49 Lefty Gomez .15 .40
50 Wade Boggs .25 .60
51 Billy Martin MN .25 .60
52 Babe Ruth MN 1.00 2.50
53 Lou Gehrig MN .75 2.00
54 Joe DiMaggio MN .75 2.00
55 Mickey Mantle MN 1.25 3.00
56 Yogi Berra MN .40 1.00
57 Bill Dickey MN .15 .40
58 Roger Maris MN .40 1.00
59 Phil Rizzuto MN .25 .60
60 Thurman Munson MN .40 1.00
61 Whitey Ford MN .25 .60
62 Don Mattingly MN .75 2.00
63 Elston Howard MN .15 .40
64 Casey Stengel MN .25 .60
65 Reggie Jackson MN .25 .60
66 Babe Ruth '23 TCY 1.00 2.50
67 Lou Gehrig '27 TCY .75 2.00
68 Tony Lazzeri '28 TCY .25 .60
69 Babe Ruth '32 TCY 1.00 2.50
70 Lou Gehrig '36 TCY .75 2.00
71 Lefty Gomez '37 TCY .15 .40
72 Bill Dickey '38 TCY .15 .40
73 Tommy Henrich '39 TCY .15 .40
74 Joe DiMaggio '41 TCY .75 2.00
75 Spud Chandler '43 TCY .15 .40
76 Tommy Henrich '47 TCY .15 .40
77 Phil Rizzuto '49 TCY .25 .60
78 Whitey Ford '50 TCY .25 .60
79 Yogi Berra '51 TCY .40 1.00
80 Casey Stengel '52 TCY .25 .60
81 Billy Martin '53 TCY .25 .60
82 Don Larsen '56 TCY .15 .40
83 Elston Howard '58 TCY .15 .40
84 Roger Maris '61 TCY .40 1.00
85 Mickey Mantle '62 TCY 1.25 3.00
86 Reggie Jackson '77 TCY .25 .60
87 Bucky Dent '78 TCY .15 .40
88 Wade Boggs '96 TCY .25 .60
89 Joe Torre '98 TCY .25 .60
90 Joe Torre '99 TCY .25 .60
NNO Mickey Mantle Promo 1.25 3.00

2000 Upper Deck Yankees Legends DiMaggio Memorabilia

BAT-AUTO CUT PRINT RUN 5 #'d CARDS
BAT-AUTO CUT PRICING NOT AVAILABLE
GOLD BAT PRINT RUN 56 #'d CARDS
YLBJD J.DiMaggio Bat 15.00 40.00
YLGJD DiMag Gold Bat/56 40.00 80.00

2000 Upper Deck Yankees Legends Golden Years

COMPLETE SET (10) 8.00 20.00
STATED ODDS 1:11
GY1 Joe DiMaggio 2.00 5.00
GY2 Phil Rizzuto .60 1.50
GY3 Yogi Berra 1.00 2.50
GY4 Billy Martin .60 1.50
GY5 Whitey Ford .60 1.50
GY6 Roger Maris 1.00 2.50
GY7 Mickey Mantle 3.00 8.00
GY8 Elston Howard .40 1.00
GY9 Tommy Henrich .40 1.00
GY10 Joe Gordon .40 1.00

2000 Upper Deck Yankees Legends Legendary Lumber

*GOLD HOLO: .5X TO 1X SILVER HOLO.
GOLD HOLO RANDOM INSERTS IN PACKS
BASIC CARDS HAVE WOOD NY
GOLD HOLO HAVE WOOD FRAME
STATED ODDS 1:23
BDLL Bucky Dent 4.00 10.00
BGLL Billy Gardner 6.00 15.00
BMLL Bobby Murcer 6.00 15.00
BRLL Babe Ruth 75.00 200.00
CBLL Clete Boyer 4.00 10.00
CCLL Chris Chambliss 4.00 10.00
CJLL Cliff Johnson 4.00 10.00
CKLL Charlie Keller 6.00 15.00
DMLL Don Mattingly 6.00 15.00
DWLL Dave Winfield 4.00 10.00
EHLL Elston Howard 4.00 10.00
GNLL Graig Nettles 4.00 10.00
HBLL Hank Bauer 6.00 15.00
HLLL Hector Lopez 6.00 15.00
JCLL Joe Collins 4.00 10.00
JPLL Joe Pepitone 6.00 15.00
MMLL Mickey Mantle 40.00 100.00
MRLL Mickey Rivers 4.00 10.00
MSLL Moose Skowron 6.00 15.00
OGLL Oscar Gamble 4.00 10.00
PBLL Paul Blair 4.00 10.00
RHLL Ralph Houk 6.00 15.00
RJLL Reggie Jackson 6.00 15.00
RMLL Roger Maris 20.00 50.00
THLL Tommy Henrich 6.00 15.00
TJLL Tommy John 6.00 15.00
TKLL Tony Kubek 6.00 15.00
TMLL Thurman Munson 12.00 30.00
WRLL Willie Randolph 4.00 10.00
YBLL Yogi Berra 6.00 15.00

2000 Upper Deck Yankees Legends Legendary Lumber Signature Cut

NO PRICING DUE TO SCARCITY

2000 Upper Deck Yankees Legends Legendary Pinstripes

STATED ODDS 1:144
ARLP Allie Reynolds 20.00 50.00
BDLP Bucky Dent 12.00 30.00
BMLP Billy Martin 12.00 30.00
BRLP Bobby Richardson 10.00 25.00
DMLP Don Mattingly 20.00 50.00
DWLP Dave Winfield 6.00 15.00
EHLP Elston Howard 10.00 25.00
GGLP Goose Gossage 6.00 15.00
GMLP Gil McDougald 6.00 15.00
HLLP Hector Lopez 6.00 15.00
JPLP Joe Pepitone 6.00 15.00
LGLP Lou Gehrig Pants 150.00 300.00
MMLP Mickey Mantle 75.00 150.00
PRLP Phil Rizzuto 10.00 25.00
RGLP Ron Guidry 10.00 25.00
RJLP Reggie Jackson 10.00 25.00
RMLP Roger Maris 10.00 25.00
THLP Tommy Henrich 10.00 25.00
TMLP Thurman Munson 30.00 60.00
WFLP Whitey Ford 15.00 40.00

2000 Upper Deck Yankees Legends Legendary Pinstripes Autograph

STATED ODDS 1:287
EXCH.DEADLINE 07/18/01
BDA Bucky Dent 15.00 40.00
DMA Don Mattingly 60.00 150.00
DWA Dave Winfield 30.00 60.00
GGA Goose Gossage 20.00 50.00
GMA Gil McDougald 15.00 40.00
JPA Joe Pepitone 15.00 40.00
PRA Phil Rizzuto 50.00 100.00
RGA Ron Guidry 15.00 40.00
THA Tommy Henrich 20.00 50.00
WFA Whitey Ford 25.00 60.00

2000 Upper Deck Yankees Legends Monument Park

COMPLETE SET (6) 8.00 20.00
STATED ODDS 1:23
MP1 Lou Gehrig 2.00 5.00
MP2 Babe Ruth 2.50 6.00
MP3 Mickey Mantle 3.00 8.00
MP4 Joe DiMaggio 2.00 5.00
MP5 Thurman Munson 1.00 2.50
MP6 Elston Howard .40 1.00

2000 Upper Deck Yankees Legends Murderer's Row

COMPLETE SET (10) 5.00 12.00
STATED ODDS 1:11
MR1 Tony Lazzeri .60 1.50
MR2 Babe Ruth 2.50 6.00
MR3 Bob Meusel .40 1.00
MR4 Lou Gehrig 2.00 5.00
MR5 Joe Dugan .40 1.00
MR6 Bill Dickey .40 1.00
MR7 Waite Hoyt .40 1.00
MR8 Red Ruffing .40 1.00
MR9 Earle Combs .40 1.00
MR10 Lefty Gomez .40 1.00

2000 Upper Deck Yankees Legends New Dynasty

COMPLETE SET (10) 5.00 12.00
STATED ODDS 1:11
ND1 Reggie Jackson .60 1.50
ND2 Graig Nettles .40 1.00
ND3 Don Mattingly 2.00 5.00
ND4 Goose Gossage .60 1.50
ND5 Dave Winfield .60 1.50
ND6 Chris Chambliss .40 1.00
ND7 Thurman Munson 1.00 2.50
ND8 Willie Randolph .40 1.00
ND9 Ron Guidry .40 1.00
ND10 Bucky Dent .40 1.00

2000 Upper Deck Yankees Legends Pride of the Pinstripes

COMPLETE SET (6) 10.00 25.00
STATED ODDS 1:23
PP1 Babe Ruth 3.00 8.00
PP2 Mickey Mantle 4.00 10.00
PP3 Joe DiMaggio 2.50 6.00
PP4 Lou Gehrig 2.50 6.00
PP5 Reggie Jackson .75 2.00
PP6 Yogi Berra 1.25 3.00

2003 Upper Deck Yankees Signature

COMPLETE SET (90) 20.00 50.00
1 Al Downing .40 1.00
2 Al Gettel .40 1.00
3 Art Ditmar .40 1.00
4 Babe Ruth 2.50 6.00
5 Bill Virdon MG .40 1.00
6 Billy Martin .60 1.50
7 Bob Cerv .40 1.00
8 Bob Turley .40 1.00
9 Bobby Cox .40 1.00
10 Bobby Richardson .40 1.00
11 Bobby Shantz .40 1.00
12 Bucky Dent .40 1.00
13 Bud Metheny XRC .40 1.00
14 Casey Stengel .60 1.50
15 Charlie Hayes .40 1.00
16 Charlie Silvera .40 1.00
17 Chris Chambliss .40 1.00
18 Danny Cater .40 1.00
19 Dave Kingman .40 1.00
20 Dave Righetti .40 1.00
21 Dave Winfield .60 1.50
22 David Cone .40 1.00
23 Dick Tidrow .40 1.00
24 Doc Medich .40 1.00
25 Dock Ellis .40 1.00
26 Don Gullett .40 1.00
27 Don Mattingly 2.00 5.00
28 Dwight Gooden .40 1.00
29 Eddie Robinson .40 1.00
30 Felipe Alou .40 1.00
31 Fred Sanford .40 1.00
32 Fred Stanley .40 1.00
33 Gene Michael .40 1.00
34 Hank Bauer .40 1.00
35 Hector Lopez .40 1.00
36 Horace Clarke .40 1.00
37 Jake Gibbs .40 1.00
38 Jerry Coleman .40 1.00
39 Jerry Lumpe .40 1.00
40 Jim Bouton .40 1.00
41 Jim Kaat .40 1.00
42 Jim Mason .40 1.00
43 Jimmy Key .40 1.00
44 Joe DiMaggio 2.00 5.00
45 Joe Torre .60 1.50
46 John Montefusco .40 1.00
47 Johnny Blanchard .40 1.00
48 Johnny Callison .40 1.00
49 Lew Burdette .40 1.00
50 Johnny Kucks .40 1.00
51 Steve Balboni .40 1.00
52 Ken Singleton ANC .40 1.00
53 Lee Mazzilli .40 1.00
54 Lou Gehrig 2.00 5.00
55 Lou Piniella .40 1.00
56 Luis Tiant .40 1.00
57 Marius Russo XRC .40 1.00
58 Mel Stottlemyre .40 1.00
59 Mickey Mantle 3.00 8.00
60 Mike Pagliarulo .40 1.00
61 Mike Torrez .40 1.00
62 Miller Huggins MG .40 1.00
63 Norm Siebern .40 1.00
64 Paul O'Neill .60 1.50
65 Phil Niekro .60 1.50
66 Phil Rizzuto .60 1.50
67 Ralph Branca .40 1.00
68 Ralph Houk .40 1.00
69 Ralph Terry .40 1.00
70 Randy Gumpert .40 1.00
71 Roger Maris 1.00 2.50

Card	Low	High
72 Ron Blomberg	.40	1.00
73 Ron Guidry	.40	1.00
74 Ruben Amaro	.40	1.00
75 Ryne Duren	.40	1.00
76 Sam McDowell	.40	1.00
77 Sparky Lyle	.40	1.00
78 Thurman Munson	1.00	2.50
79 Tom Sturdivant	.40	1.00
80 Tom Tresh	.40	1.00
81 Tommy Byrne	.40	1.00
82 Tommy Henrich	.40	1.00
83 Tommy John	.40	1.00
84 Tony Kubek	.40	1.00
85 Tony Lazzeri	.60	1.50
86 Virgil Trucks	.40	1.00
87 Wade Boggs	.60	1.50
88 Whitey Ford	.60	1.50
89 Willie Randolph	.40	1.00
90 Yogi Berra	1.00	2.50

2003 Upper Deck Yankees Signature Monumental Cuts

B/WN 1-9 COPIES OF EACH CARD
NO PRICING DUE TO SCARCITY

2003 Upper Deck Yankees Signature Pinstripe Excellence Autographs

RANDOM INSERTS IN PACKS
STATED PRINT RUN 125 SERIAL #'d SETS

Card	Low	High
AA F.Alou/R.Amaro	20.00	50.00
BA H.Bauer/F.Alou	10.00	25.00
BP W.Boggs/M.Pagliarulo	20.00	50.00
BR1 H.Bauer/P.Rizzuto	50.00	100.00
BR2 T.Byrne/M.Russo	15.00	40.00
BT J.Bouton/R.Terry	20.00	50.00
CK C.Chambliss/D.Kingman	10.00	25.00
DC B.Dent/C.Chambliss	20.00	50.00
DR B.Dent/W.Randolph	20.00	50.00
DS R.Duren/T.Sturdivant	10.00	25.00
FB W.Ford/Y.Berra	75.00	200.00
GB J.Gibbs/J.Blanchard	12.00	30.00
GM R.Guidry/J.Montefusco	10.00	25.00
GR R.Guidry/W.Randolph	20.00	50.00
JK T.John/J.Kaat	20.00	50.00
LG S.Lyle/R.Guidry	10.00	25.00
LM J.Lumpe/J.Mason	10.00	25.00
MC J.Montefusco/C.Chambliss	10.00	25.00
MK G.Michael/T.Kubek	20.00	50.00
ML S.McDowell/S.Lyle	20.00	50.00
MR D.Mattingly/D.Righetti	60.00	120.00
NT P.Niekro/L.Tiant	20.00	50.00
RB B.Richardson/H.Bauer	20.00	50.00
RC B.Richardson/J.Coleman	20.00	50.00
SC K.Singleton/J.Coleman	20.00	50.00
ST T.Sturdivant/B.Turley	10.00	25.00
TK L.Tiant/J.Kaat	10.00	25.00
TM M.Torrez/L.Mazzilli	10.00	25.00

2003 Upper Deck Yankees Signature Pride of New York Autographs

STATED ODDS 1:1
SP PRINT RUNS PROVIDED BY UPPER DECK

Card	Low	High
AD Al Downing	4.00	10.00
AG Al Gettel	6.00	15.00
BD Brian Doyle	5.00	12.00
BL Johnny Blanchard	4.00	10.00
BR Bobby Richardson	6.00	15.00
BS Bobby Shantz	4.00	10.00
BT Bob Turley	8.00	20.00
BV Bill Virdon	6.00	15.00
CA1 Johnny Callison	6.00	15.00
CA2 Brian Cashman SP/100	400.00	800.00
CC Chris Chambliss	4.00	10.00
CE Bob Cerv	4.00	10.00
CH Charlie Hayes	4.00	10.00
CO David Cone	8.00	20.00
CS Charlie Silvera	4.00	10.00
CX Bobby Cox	15.00	40.00
DC Danny Cater	5.00	12.00
DE Bucky Dent	6.00	15.00
DG Don Gullett	5.00	12.00
DI Art Ditmar	5.00	12.00
DK Dave Kingman	5.00	12.00
DM Doc Medich	4.00	10.00
DR Dave Righetti	6.00	15.00
DT Dick Tidrow	4.00	10.00
DW Dave Winfield SP/350	20.00	50.00
DZ Don Zimmer	15.00	40.00
EL Dock Ellis	8.00	20.00
ER Eddie Robinson	6.00	15.00
FA Felipe Alou	4.00	10.00
FS Fred Sanford	4.00	10.00
GM Gene Michael	4.00	10.00
GO Dwight Gooden	6.00	15.00
HB Hank Bauer	6.00	15.00
HC Horace Clarke	4.00	10.00
HL Hector Lopez	4.00	10.00
HR Hal Reniff	5.00	12.00
JA Jason Alexander SP/50	400.00	800.00
JB Jim Bouton	4.00	10.00
JC Jerry Coleman	4.00	10.00
JG1 Jake Gibbs	4.00	10.00
JG2 John Goodman SP/100	400.00	800.00
JK Jim Kaat	6.00	15.00
JL Jerry Lumpe	4.00	10.00
JM Jim Mason	4.00	10.00
JT Joe Torre	30.00	80.00
JW Jim Wynn	4.00	10.00
KE Jimmy Key	6.00	15.00
KS Ken Singleton	4.00	10.00
KU Johnny Kucks	6.00	15.00
LB Lew Burdette	5.00	12.00
LM Lee Mazzilli	5.00	12.00
LP Lou Piniella SP/542	6.00	15.00
LT Luis Tiant	4.00	10.00
MA Don Mattingly	40.00	100.00
MO John Montefusco	4.00	10.00
MP Mike Pagliarulo	4.00	10.00
MR Marius Russo	5.00	12.00
MS Mel Stottlemyre	10.00	25.00
MT Mike Torrez	6.00	15.00
NS Norm Siebern	4.00	10.00
PN Phil Niekro	10.00	25.00
PO Paul O'Neill SP/500	6.00	15.00
PR Phil Rizzuto	20.00	50.00
RA Ruben Amaro	4.00	10.00
RB1 Ron Blomberg	4.00	10.00
RB2 Ralph Branca	10.00	25.00
RD Ryne Duren	5.00	12.00
RG1 Ron Guidry	10.00	25.00
RG2 Randy Gumpert	4.00	10.00
RH Ralph Houk	6.00	15.00
RT Ralph Terry	4.00	10.00
SB Steve Balboni	6.00	15.00
SL Sparky Lyle	4.00	10.00
SM Sam McDowell	4.00	10.00
ST Fred Stanley	6.00	15.00
TB Tommy Byrne	4.00	10.00
TC Tom Carroll	6.00	15.00
TH Tommy Henrich	10.00	25.00
TJ Tommy John	6.00	15.00
TK Tony Kubek	20.00	50.00
TS Tom Sturdivant	4.00	10.00
TT Tom Tresh	5.00	12.00
VT Virgil Trucks	4.00	10.00
WB Wade Boggs	15.00	40.00
WF Whitey Ford	20.00	50.00
WR Willie Randolph SP/283	12.00	30.00
YB Yogi Berra	30.00	80.00

2003 Upper Deck Yankees Signature Yankees Forever Autographs

RANDOM INSERTS IN PACKS
STATED PRINT RUN 50 SERIAL #'d SETS
EXCHANGE DEADLINE 03/27/06

Card	Low	High
ALB Alou/Lopez/Bauer	75.00	150.00
AOM Alou/O'Neill/Mazzilli	30.00	60.00
BSB Berra/Shantz/Bauer	150.00	300.00
DFB Downing/Ford/Berra	175.00	350.00
DRC Dent/Rand/Chamb	30.00	60.00
EMG Ellis/Medich/Gullett	75.00	150.00
FKB Ford/Kucks/Bouton	40.00	80.00
GCK Good/Cone/Key	75.00	150.00
GRJ Guidry/Righ/John	75.00	150.00
HMC Houk/Michael/Cox	75.00	150.00
HRB Henrich/Rizzuto/Branca	100.00	200.00
JKL John/Kaat/Lyle	75.00	150.00
KCC King/Chamb/Cater	75.00	150.00
KGT Kaat/Gullet/Torrez	75.00	150.00
KJB Kaat/John/Bouton	30.00	60.00
MTT Monte/Torrez/Tid	75.00	150.00
OBK O'Neill/Boggs/Key	60.00	120.00
PTV Piniella/Torre/Virdon	40.00	80.00
RBC Rizzuto/Berra/Coleman	75.00	200.00
RKD Rizzuto/Kubek/Dent	100.00	200.00
RRC Rich/Rand/Coleman	40.00	80.00
RSB Russo/Sturdivant/Byrne	75.00	150.00
SSB Stanley/Silv/Blanch	30.00	60.00
STE Stottlemyre/Tiant/Ellis	30.00	60.00
TCO Torre/Cone/O'Neill	100.00	200.00
TLN Tiant/Lyle/Niekro	40.00	80.00
TMT Tiant/McDowell/Terry	30.00	60.00
WHM Winfield/Henrich/Maz	30.00	60.00
WMG Winf/Matt/Guid	50.00	100.00
WPC Winf/Pin/Chamb	40.00	80.00

1989 USPS Legends Stamp Cards

The 1989 USPS Legends Stamp Cards set includes four cards each measuring 2 1/2" by 3 9/16". On the fronts, the cards depict the four baseball-related stamp designs which featured actual players. The outer front borders are white; the inner front borders are orange and purple. The vertically oriented backs are beige and pink. These cards were sold by the U.S. Postal Service as a set (kit) for $7.95 along with the actual stamps, an attractive booklet, and other materials. The first printing of the set was sold out and so a second printing was made. The first printing cards did not have the USPS copyright logo. All the stamps in the set are drawings; for example, the Gehrig stamp was painted by noted sports artist, Bart Forbes. All of the stamps except Gehrig (25 cents) are 20-cent stamps.

Card	Low	High
COMPLETE SET (4)	10.00	25.00
1 Roberto Clemente Issued August 17, 1984	2.50	6.00
2 Lou Gehrig Issued June 10, 1989	2.50	6.00
3 Jackie Robinson Issued August 2, 1982	2.50	6.00
4 Babe Ruth Issued July 6, 1983	3.00	7.50

2000 USPS Legends of Baseball Postcards

Card	Low	High
COMPLETE SET (20)	2.40	6.00
1 Roberto Clemente	.40	1.00
2 Ty Cobb	.30	.75
3 Mickey Cochrane	.10	.25
4 Eddie Collins	.10	.25
5 Dizzy Dean	.10	.25
6 Jimmie Foxx	.20	.50
7 Lou Gehrig	.50	1.25
8 Josh Gibson	.30	.75
9 Lefty Grove	.20	.50
10 Rogers Hornsby	.20	.50
11 Walter Johnson	.30	.75
12 Christy Mathewson	.30	.75
13 Satchel Paige	.20	.50
14 Jackie Robinson	.40	1.00
15 Babe Ruth	.60	1.50
16 George Sisler	.10	.25
17 Tris Speaker	.10	.25
18 Pie Traynor	.10	.25
19 Honus Wagner	.30	.75
20 Cy Young	.20	.50

2000 USPS Legends of Baseball Stamps

Card	Low	High
COMPLETE SET (20)	2.64	6.60
1 Roberto Clemente	.13	.33
2 Ty Cobb	.13	.33
3 Mickey Cochrane	.13	.33
4 Eddie Collins	.13	.33
5 Dizzy Dean	.13	.33
6 Jimmie Foxx	.13	.33
7 Lou Gehrig	.13	.33
8 Josh Gibson	.13	.33
9 Lefty Grove	.13	.33
10 Rogers Hornsby	.13	.33
11 Walter Johnson	.13	.33
12 Christy Mathewson	.13	.33
13 Satchel Paige	.13	.33
14 Jackie Robinson	.13	.33
15 Babe Ruth	.13	.33
16 George Sisler	.13	.33
17 Tris Speaker	.13	.33
18 Pie Traynor	.13	.33
19 Honus Wagner	.13	.33
20 Cy Young	.13	.33

2000 Vanguard

Card	Low	High
COMPLETE SET (100)	10.00	25.00
COMMON CARD (1-100)	.12	.30
1 Troy Glaus	.12	.30
2 Tim Salmon	.12	.30
3 Mo Vaughn	.12	.30
4 Albert Belle	.12	.30
5 Mike Mussina	.20	.50
6 Cal Ripken	1.00	2.50
7 Nomar Garciaparra	.20	.50
8 Pedro Martinez	.20	.50
9 Troy O'Leary	.12	.30
10 Wilton Veras	.12	.30
11 Magglio Ordonez	.20	.50
12 Chris Singleton	.12	.30
13 Frank Thomas	.30	.75
14 Roberto Alomar	.20	.50
15 Russell Branyan	.12	.30
16 Manny Ramirez	.30	.75
17 Jim Thome	.20	.50
18 Omar Vizquel	.20	.50
19 Tony Clark	.12	.30
20 Juan Gonzalez	.12	.30
21 Dean Palmer	.12	.30
22 Carlos Beltran	.20	.50
23 Johnny Damon	.20	.50
24 Jermaine Dye	.12	.30
25 Mark Quinn	.12	.30
26 Jacque Jones	.12	.30
27 Corey Koskie	.12	.30
28 Brad Radke	.12	.30
29 Roger Clemens	.40	1.00
30 Derek Jeter	.75	2.00
31 Alfonso Soriano	.30	.75
32 Bernie Williams	.20	.50
33 Eric Chavez	.12	.30
34 Jason Giambi	.12	.30
35 Ben Grieve	.12	.30
36 Tim Hudson	.20	.50
37 Mike Cameron	.12	.30
38 Freddy Garcia	.12	.30
39 Edgar Martinez	.20	.50
40 Alex Rodriguez	.40	1.00
41 Jose Canseco	.20	.50
42 Vinny Castilla	.12	.30
43 Fred McGriff	.20	.50
44 Rusty Greer	.12	.30
45 Ruben Mateo	.12	.30
46 Rafael Palmeiro	.20	.50
47 Ivan Rodriguez	.20	.50
48 Carlos Delgado	.12	.30
49 Shannon Stewart	.12	.30
50 Vernon Wells	.12	.30
51 Erubiel Durazo	.12	.30
52 Randy Johnson	.30	.75
53 Matt Williams	.12	.30
54 Andruw Jones	.12	.30
55 Chipper Jones	.30	.75
56 Greg Maddux	.40	1.00
57 Mark Grace	.20	.50
58 Sammy Sosa	.30	.75
59 Kerry Wood	.12	.30
60 Sean Casey	.12	.30
61 Ken Griffey Jr.	.60	1.50
62 Barry Larkin	.20	.50
63 Todd Helton	.20	.50
64 Ben Petrick	.12	.30
65 Larry Walker	.20	.50
66 Luis Castillo	.12	.30
67 Alex Gonzalez	.12	.30
68 Preston Wilson	.12	.30
69 Jeff Bagwell	.20	.50
70 Craig Biggio	.20	.50
71 Billy Wagner	.12	.30
72 Kevin Brown	.12	.30
73 Shawn Green	.12	.30
74 Gary Sheffield	.12	.30
75 Kevin Barker	.12	.30
76 Ron Belliard	.12	.30
77 Jeromy Burnitz	.12	.30
78 Michael Barrett	.12	.30
79 Peter Bergeron	.12	.30
80 Vladimir Guerrero	.20	.50
81 Edgardo Alfonzo	.12	.30
82 Rey Ordonez	.12	.30
83 Mike Piazza	.30	.75
84 Robin Ventura	.12	.30
85 Bobby Abreu	.12	.30
86 Mike Lieberthal	.12	.30
87 Scott Rolen	.20	.50
88 Brian Giles	.12	.30
89 Chad Hermansen	.12	.30
90 Jason Kendall	.12	.30
91 Rick Ankiel	.20	.50
92 J.D. Drew	.12	.30
93 Mark McGwire	.50	1.25
94 Fernando Tatis	.12	.30
95 Ben Davis	.12	.30
96 Tony Gwynn	.30	.75
97 Trevor Hoffman	.20	.50
98 Barry Bonds	.50	1.25
99 Ellis Burks	.12	.30
100 Jeff Kent	.12	.30
SAMP Tony Gwynn	.50	1.25

2000 Vanguard Holographic Gold

*AL STARS 1-50: 4X TO 10X BASIC
A.L. STATED PRINT RUN 199 SERIAL #'d SETS
*NL STARS 51-100: 6X TO 15X BASIC
N.L. STATED PRINT RUN 99 SERIAL #'d SETS
RANDOM INSERTS IN RETAIL PACKS

2000 Vanguard Green

*AL STARS 1-50: 4X TO 10X BASIC
A.L. STATED PRINT RUN 99 SERIAL #'d SETS
*NL STARS 51-100: 2.5X TO 6X BASIC
N.L. STATED PRINT RUN 199 SERIAL #'d SETS
RANDOM INSERTS IN HOBBY PACKS

2000 Vanguard Premiere Date

*STARS: 4X TO 10X BASIC CARDS
STATED ODDS 1:25 HOBBY
STATED PRINT RUN 135 SERIAL #'d SETS

2000 Vanguard Cosmic Force

Card	Low	High
COMPLETE SET (10)	12.50	30.00
STATED ODDS 1:73		
1 Chipper Jones	1.25	3.00
2 Cal Ripken	4.00	10.00
3 Nomar Garciaparra	.75	2.00
4 Sammy Sosa	1.25	3.00
5 Ken Griffey Jr.	2.00	5.00
6 Mike Piazza	1.25	3.00
7 Derek Jeter	3.00	8.00
8 Mark McGwire	2.00	5.00
9 Tony Gwynn	1.25	3.00
10 Alex Rodriguez	1.50	4.00

2000 Vanguard Diamond Architects

Card	Low	High
COMPLETE SET (20)	15.00	40.00
STATED ODDS 1:25		
1 Chipper Jones	1.00	2.50
2 Greg Maddux	1.25	3.00
3 Cal Ripken	3.00	8.00
4 Nomar Garciaparra	.60	1.50
5 Sammy Sosa	1.00	2.50
6 Ken Griffey Jr.	2.00	5.00
7 Manny Ramirez	1.00	2.50
8 Larry Walker	.60	1.50
9 Jeff Bagwell	.60	1.50
10 Vladimir Guerrero	.60	1.50
11 Mike Piazza	1.00	2.50
12 Roger Clemens	1.25	3.00
13 Derek Jeter	2.50	6.00
14 Bernie Williams	.60	1.50
15 Scott Rolen	.60	1.50
16 Mark McGwire	1.50	4.00
17 Tony Gwynn	1.00	2.50
18 Alex Rodriguez	1.25	3.00
19 Rafael Palmeiro	.60	1.50
20 Ivan Rodriguez	.60	1.50

2000 Vanguard Game-Worn Jerseys

Card	Low	High
STATED ODDS 1:120		
1 Chipper Jones	6.00	15.00
2 Greg Maddux	10.00	25.00
3 Frank Thomas	6.00	15.00
4 Tony Gwynn	8.00	20.00
5 Alex Rodriguez	10.00	25.00

2000 Vanguard High Voltage

COMPLETE SET (36) 6.00 15.00
ONE PER PACK
BASIC CARDS HAVE TEAL BLUE FOIL
*GOLD: 5X TO 12X BASIC VOLTAGE
GOLD PRINT RUN 199 SERIAL #'d SETS
*GREEN: 8X TO 20X BASIC VOLTAGE
GREEN PRINT RUN 99 SERIAL #'d SETS
HOLO.SILVER PRINT RUN 10 SERIAL #'d SETS
HOLO.SILVER NOT PRICED DUE TO SCARCITY
*RED: 3X TO 8X BASIC VOLTAGE
RED PRINT RUN 299 SERIAL #'d SETS

Card	Low	High
1 Mo Vaughn	.10	.25
2 Erubiel Durazo	.10	.25
3 Randy Johnson	.25	.60
4 Andruw Jones	.10	.25
5 Chipper Jones	.25	.60
6 Greg Maddux	.30	.75
7 Cal Ripken	.75	2.00
8 Nomar Garciaparra	.15	.40
9 Pedro Martinez	.15	.40
10 Sammy Sosa	.25	.60
11 Frank Thomas	.25	.60
12 Sean Casey	.10	.25
13 Ken Griffey Jr.	.50	1.25
14 Barry Larkin	.15	.40
15 Manny Ramirez	.25	.60
16 Jim Thome	.15	.40
17 Larry Walker	.15	.40
18 Jeff Bagwell	.15	.40
19 Craig Biggio	.15	.40
20 Carlos Beltran	.15	.40
21 Shawn Green	.10	.25
22 Vladimir Guerrero	.15	.40
23 Edgardo Alfonzo	.10	.25
24 Mike Piazza	.25	.60
25 Roger Clemens	.30	.75
26 Derek Jeter	.60	1.50
27 Bernie Williams	.15	.40
28 Scott Rolen	.15	.40
29 Brian Giles	.10	.25
30 Rick Ankiel	.15	.40
31 Mark McGwire	.40	1.00
32 Tony Gwynn	.25	.60
33 Barry Bonds	.40	1.00
34 Alex Rodriguez	.30	.75
35 Rafael Palmeiro	.15	.40
36 Ivan Rodriguez	.15	.40

2000 Vanguard Press

Card	Low	High
COMPLETE A.L. SET (10)	5.00	12.00
COMPLETE N.L. SET (10)	5.00	12.00
STATED ODDS 2:25		
A1 Cal Ripken	1.50	4.00
A2 Nomar Garciaparra	.30	.75
A3 Pedro Martinez	.30	.75
A4 Manny Ramirez	.50	1.25
A5 Carlos Beltran	.30	.75
A6 Roger Clemens	.60	1.50
A7 Derek Jeter	1.25	3.00
A8 Alex Rodriguez	.60	1.50
A9 Rafael Palmeiro	.30	.75
A10 Ivan Rodriguez	.30	.75
N1 Chipper Jones	.50	1.25
N2 Greg Maddux	.60	1.50
N3 Sammy Sosa	.50	1.25
N4 Ken Griffey Jr.	1.00	2.50
N5 Larry Walker	.30	.75
N6 Jeff Bagwell	.30	.75
N7 Vladimir Guerrero	.30	.75
N8 Mike Piazza	.50	1.25
N9 Mark McGwire	.75	2.00
N10 Tony Gwynn	.50	1.25

1912 Vassar Sweaters

This oversized set measures approximately 4" by 6 1/2" and features black-and-white photos of players in sweaters with white borders. The only known players in the set are listed below in alphabetical order. Other cards may exist and any confirmed additions are welcomed.

Card	Low	High
COMPLETE SET	1250.00	2500.00
1 Ty Cobb	2000.00	4000.00
2 Sam Crawford	600.00	1200.00
3 Walter Johnson	1250.00	2500.00
4 Larry Lajoie	1250.00	2500.00
5 Smokey Joe Wood	500.00	1000.00

1915 Victory T214

The cards in this set measure 1 1/2" by 2 5/8". The set is easily distinguished by the presence of the reference to Victory Tobacco on the card backs. The players in this unnumbered set have been alphabetized and numbered for reference in the checklist below. The set can be dated to 1915 with Chief Bender's appearence as a Baltimore Federal.

Card	Low	High
1 Red Ames	1500.00	2500.00
2 Chief Bender	3000.00	5000.00
3 Roger Bresnahan	3000.00	5000.00
4 Al Bridwell	1500.00	2500.00
5 Howie Camnitz	1500.00	2500.00
6 Hal Chase Portrait	1500.00	2500.00
7 Hal Chase Throwing	1500.00	2500.00
8 Ty Cobb	8000.00	12000.00
9 Doc Crandall	1500.00	2500.00
10 Birdie Cree	1500.00	2500.00
11 Josh Devore	1500.00	2500.00
12 Ray Demmitt	1500.00	2500.00
13 Mickey Doolan	1500.00	2500.00
14 Mike Donlin	1500.00	2500.00
15 Tom Downey	1500.00	2500.00
16 Larry Doyle	1500.00	2500.00
17 Kid Elberfeld	1500.00	2500.00
18 Johnny Evers	3000.00	5000.00
19 Russ Ford	1500.00	2500.00
20 Art Fromme	1500.00	2500.00
21 Chick Gandil	1500.00	2500.00
22 Rube Geyer	1500.00	2500.00
23 Clark Griffith MG	3000.00	5000.00
24 Bob Groom	1500.00	2500.00
25 Buck Herzog	1500.00	2500.00
26 Hugh Jennings MG	3000.00	5000.00
27 Walter Johnson	5000.00	8000.00
28 Joe Kelley	3000.00	5000.00
29 Ed Konetchy	1500.00	2500.00
30 Nap Lajoie	3000.00	5000.00
31 Ed Lennox	1500.00	2500.00
32 Sherry Magee	1500.00	2500.00
33 Rube Marquard	1500.00	2500.00
34 John McGraw MG	3000.00	5000.00
35 George McQuillan	1500.00	2500.00
36 Chief Meyers Catching	1500.00	2500.00
37 Chief Meyers Portrait	1500.00	2500.00
38 George Mullin	1500.00	2500.00
39 Red Murray	1500.00	2500.00
40 Tom Needham	1500.00	2500.00
41 Rebel Oakes	1500.00	2500.00
42 Dode Paskert	1500.00	2500.00
43 Jack Quinn	1500.00	2500.00
44 Nap Rucker	1500.00	2500.00
45 Germany Schaefer	1500.00	2500.00
46 Frank Schulte	1500.00	2500.00
47 Frank Smith	1500.00	2500.00
48 Tris Speaker	3500.00	6000.00
49 George Stovall	1500.00	2500.00
50 Ed Summers	1500.00	2500.00
51 Bill Sweeney	1500.00	2500.00
52 Ed Sweeney	1500.00	2500.00
53 Ira Thomas	1500.00	2500.00
54 Joe Tinker	3000.00	5000.00
55 Heinie Wagner	1500.00	2500.00
56 Zack Wheat	3000.00	5000.00
57 Kaiser Wilhelm	1500.00	2500.00
58 Hooks Wiltse	1500.00	2500.00

1909 W.W. Smith Postcards

In 1909 W.W. Smith of Pittsburgh produced a set of Postcards for the 1909 World Series between the Pittsburgh Pirates and Detroit Tigers. One card is titled "World's Series Souvenir" titled two of a kind featuring the stars of each team, Ty Cobb of the Tigers and Honus Wagner of the Pirates featuring caracitures of the two stars. The other known card titled "The Mighty Honus" shows a caraciture of Wagner. It is possible that a caraciture of Cobb exists as well as some of the other prominent players from both teams but they have yet to be identified.

Card	Low	High
COMPLETE SET (2)	350.00	700.00
1 T.Cobb/H.Wagner WS Souvenir	500.00	1000.00
2 Honus Wagner The Mighty Honus	250.00	500.00

1922 W501

This 120-card set, referenced by the catalog designation W501, measures approximately 1 15/16" by 3 1/2". The cards have white borders which frame a posed black and white photo. The cards are blank backed and have the number in the upper right hand corner. The cards are thought to have been issued about 1922. All these pictures are the same as the ones in E-121. All photos are all identified by a G-4-22, which is the best guess to how the set is dated as 1922.

Card	Low	High
COMPLETE SET (120)	2000.00	4000.00
1 Ed Rommel	25.00	50.00
2 Urban Shocker	30.00	60.00
3 Frank Davis	50.00	100.00
4 George Sisler	100.00	200.00
5 Bobby Veach	25.00	50.00
6 Harry Heilmann	75.00	150.00
7 Ira Flagstead	25.00	50.00
8 Ty Cobb	300.00	600.00
9 Oscar Vitt	25.00	50.00
10 Muddy Ruel	25.00	50.00
11 Del Pratt	25.00	50.00
12 Joe Gharrity	25.00	50.00
13 Joe Judge	30.00	60.00
14 Sam Rice	50.00	100.00
15 Clyde Milan	30.00	60.00
16 Joe Sewell	50.00	100.00
17 Walter Johnson	200.00	400.00
18 Stuffy McInnis	30.00	60.00
19 Tris Speaker	125.00	250.00
20 Jim Bagby	25.00	50.00
21 Stan Coveleski	50.00	100.00
22 Bill Wambsganss	30.00	60.00
23 John Mails	25.00	50.00
24 Larry Gardner	25.00	50.00
25 Aaron Ward	25.00	50.00
26 Miller Huggins MG	50.00	100.00
27 Wally Schang	30.00	60.00
28 Thomas Rogers	25.00	50.00
29 Carl Mays	30.00	60.00
30 Everett Scott	25.00	50.00
31 Bob Shawkey	30.00	60.00
32 Waite Hoyt	75.00	150.00
33 Mike McNally	25.00	50.00
34 Joe Bush	25.00	50.00
35 Bob Meusel	40.00	80.00
36 Irish Meusel	25.00	50.00
37 Dickie Kerr	25.00	50.00
38 Eddie Collins	75.00	150.00
39 Kid Gleason MG	30.00	60.00
40 Johnny Mostil	25.00	50.00
41 Bibb Falk	25.00	50.00
42 Clarence Hodge	25.00	50.00
43 Ray Schalk	50.00	100.00
44 Amos Strunk	25.00	50.00
45 Edward Mulligan	25.00	50.00
46 Earl Sheely	25.00	50.00
47 Harry Hooper	75.00	150.00
48 Red Faber	50.00	100.00
49 Babe Ruth	500.00	1000.00
50 Ivy Wingo	25.00	50.00
51 Greasy Neale	30.00	60.00
52 Jake Daubert	25.00	50.00
53 Edd Roush	75.00	150.00
54 Eppa Rixey	50.00	100.00
55 Speed Martin	25.00	50.00
56 Bill Killifer	25.00	50.00
57 Charlie Hollocher	25.00	50.00
58 Zeb Terry	25.00	50.00
59 Grover Alexander	100.00	200.00
60 Turner Barber	25.00	50.00
61 Johnny Rawlings	25.00	50.00
62 Frankie Frisch	125.00	250.00
63 Red Shea	25.00	50.00
64 Dave Bancroft	50.00	100.00
65 Red Causey	25.00	50.00
66 Pancho Snyder	25.00	50.00
67 Heinie Groh	30.00	60.00
68 Ross Youngs	50.00	100.00
69 Fred Toney	25.00	50.00
70 Art Nehf	25.00	50.00
71 Earl Smith	25.00	50.00
72 George Kelly	50.00	100.00
73 John McGraw MG	75.00	150.00
74 Phil Douglas	25.00	50.00
75 Rosy Ryan	25.00	50.00
76 Jesse Haines	50.00	100.00
77 Milt Stock	25.00	50.00
78 Bill Doak	25.00	50.00
79 Specs Toporcer	25.00	50.00
80 Wilbur Cooper	25.00	50.00
81 Possum Whitted	25.00	50.00
82 Charlie Grimm	30.00	60.00
83 Rabbit Maranville	50.00	100.00
84 Babe Adams	30.00	60.00
85 Carson Bigbee	25.00	50.00
86 Max Carey	75.00	150.00
87 Whitey Glazner	25.00	50.00
88 George Gibson	25.00	50.00
89 Billy Southworth	30.00	60.00
90 Hank Gowdy	25.00	50.00
91 Walter Holke	25.00	50.00
92 Joe Oeschger	25.00	50.00
93 Pete Kilduff	25.00	50.00
94 Chief Meyers	30.00	60.00
95 Otto Miller	25.00	50.00
96 Wilbert Robinson MG	50.00	100.00
97 Zack Wheat	50.00	100.00
98 Dutch Ruether	25.00	50.00
99 Tilly Walker	25.00	50.00
100 Cy Williams	30.00	60.00
101 Dave Danforth	25.00	50.00
102 Ed Rommell	25.00	50.00
103 John McGraw MG	75.00	150.00
104 Frank Frisch	75.00	150.00
105 Al DeVormer	25.00	50.00
106 Tommy Griffith	25.00	50.00
107 George Harper	25.00	50.00
108 Doc Lavan	25.00	50.00
109 Elmer Smith	25.00	50.00
110 Hooks Dauss	25.00	50.00
111 Alex Gaston	25.00	50.00
112 Jack Graney	25.00	50.00
113 Irish Meusel	25.00	50.00
114 Rogers Hornsby	125.00	250.00
115 Les Nunamaker	25.00	50.00
116 Steve O'Neill	30.00	60.00
117 Max Flack	25.00	50.00
118 Billy Southworth	25.00	50.00
119 Art Nehf	25.00	50.00
120 Chick Fewster	25.00	50.00

1928 W502

This 60-card set, referenced by the catalog designation W502, measures approximately 1 5 /16" by 2 1/2". The photo is a black and white action-posed photo, while the back reads "One Bagger. Hold what you've got." The cards are thought to have been issued about 1928.

Card	Low	High
COMPLETE SET (60)	3000.00	6000.00
1 Burleigh Grimes	50.00	100.00
2 Walter Reuther	25.00	50.00
3 Joe Dugan	30.00	60.00
4 Red Faber	50.00	100.00
5 Gabby Hartnett	50.00	100.00
6 Babe Ruth	400.00	800.00
7 Bob Meusel	40.00	80.00
8 Herb Pennock	50.00	100.00
9 George Burns	25.00	50.00
10 Joe Sewell	50.00	100.00
11 George Uhle	25.00	50.00
12 Bob O'Farrell	25.00	50.00
13 Rogers Hornsby	100.00	200.00
14 Pie Traynor	50.00	100.00
15 Clarence Mitchell	25.00	50.00
16 Eppa Rixey	50.00	100.00
17 Carl Mays	25.00	50.00
18 Adolfo Luque	30.00	60.00
19 Dave Bancroft	50.00	100.00
20 George Kelly	50.00	100.00
21 Earle Combs	50.00	100.00
22 Harry Heilmann	50.00	100.00
23 Ray W. Schalk	50.00	100.00
24 Johnny Mostil	25.00	50.00
25 Hack Wilson	50.00	100.00
26 Lou Gehrig	250.00	500.00
27 Ty Cobb	250.00	500.00
28 Tris Speaker	100.00	200.00
29 Tony Lazzeri	50.00	100.00
30 Waite Hoyt	50.00	100.00
31 Sherwood Smith	25.00	50.00
32 Max Carey	50.00	100.00
33 Eugene Hargrave	25.00	50.00
34 Miguel J. Gonzalez	25.00	50.00
35 Joe Judge	30.00	60.00
36 E.C. (Sam) Rice	50.00	100.00
37 Earl Sheely	25.00	50.00
38 Sam Jones	25.00	50.00
39 Bob A. Falk	25.00	50.00
40 Willie Kamm	30.00	60.00
41 Bucky Harris	50.00	100.00
42 John J. McGraw	50.00	100.00
43 Artie Nehf	25.00	50.00
44 Grover Alexander	100.00	200.00
45 Paul Waner	50.00	100.00
46 William H. Terry	50.00	100.00
47 Glenn Wright	25.00	50.00
48 Earl Smith	25.00	50.00
49 Leon (Goose) Goslin	50.00	100.00
50 Frank Frisch	50.00	100.00
51 Joe Harris	25.00	50.00
52 Fred (Cy) Wiliams	30.00	60.00
53 Ed Roush	50.00	100.00
54 George Sisler	50.00	100.00
55 Ed Rommel	25.00	50.00
56 Roger Peckinpaugh	25.00	50.00
57 Stanley Coveleski	50.00	100.00
58 Lester Bell	25.00	50.00
59 Lloyd Waner	50.00	100.00
60 John P. McInnis	30.00	60.00

1923 W503

This 64-card set, referenced by the catalog designation W503, measures approximately 1 3/4" by 2 3/4". The cards have white borders which frame a black-and-white player portrait or action photo and the card number. The backs are blank, and there is no evidence of a manufacturer. The set is thought to have been issued in early 1923.

Card	Low	High
COMPLETE SET (64)	15000.00	30000.00
1 Joe Bush	200.00	400.00
2 Wally Schang	200.00	400.00
3 Dave Robertson	150.00	300.00
4 Wally Pipp	150.00	300.00
5 Bill Ryan	150.00	300.00
6 George Kelly	300.00	600.00
7 Frank Snyder	150.00	300.00
8 Jimmy O'Connell	150.00	300.00
9 Bill Cunningham	150.00	300.00
10 Norman McMillan	150.00	300.00
11 Waite Hoyt	300.00	600.00
12 Art Nehf	150.00	300.00
13 George Sisler	400.00	800.00
14 Al Devormer	150.00	300.00
15 Casey Stengel	500.00	1000.00
16 Ken Williams	200.00	400.00
17 Joe Dugan	200.00	400.00
18 Irish Muesel	150.00	300.00
19 Bob Meusel	250.00	500.00
20 Carl Mays	150.00	300.00
21 Frank Frisch	300.00	600.00
22 Jess Barnes	150.00	300.00
23 Walter Johnson	600.00	1200.00
24 Claude Jonnard	150.00	300.00
25 Dave Bancroft	300.00	600.00
26 Johnny Rawlings	150.00	300.00
27 Pep Young	150.00	300.00
28 Earl Smith	150.00	300.00
29 Willie Kamm	150.00	300.00
30 Art Fletcher	150.00	300.00
31 Kid Gleason	150.00	300.00
32 Babe Ruth	2000.00	4000.00
33 Guy Morton	150.00	300.00
34 Heinie Groh	150.00	300.00
35 Leon Cadore	150.00	300.00
36 Joe Tobin	150.00	300.00
37 Rube Marquard	150.00	300.00
38 Grover Alexander	500.00	1000.00
39 George Burns	150.00	300.00
40 Joe Oeschger	150.00	300.00
41 Chick Shorten	150.00	300.00
42 Roger Hornsby UER misspelled Rogers	600.00	1200.00
43 Adolfo Luque	200.00	400.00
44 Zack Wheat	300.00	600.00
45 Her Pruett UER misspelled Hub	150.00	300.00
46 Rabbit Maranville	300.00	600.00
47 Jimmy Ring	150.00	300.00
48 Sherrod Smith	150.00	300.00
49 Lea Meadows UER misspelled Lee	150.00	300.00
50 Aaron Ward	150.00	300.00
51 Herb Pennock	300.00	600.00
52 Carlson Bigbee UER misspelled Carson	150.00	300.00
53 Max Carey	300.00	600.00
54 Charels Robertson	150.00	300.00
55 Urban Shocker	200.00	400.00
56 Dutch Ruether	150.00	300.00
57 Jake Daubert	200.00	400.00
58 Louis Guisto	150.00	300.00
59 Ivy Wingo	150.00	300.00
60 Bill Pertica	150.00	300.00
61 Luke Sewell	150.00	300.00
62 Hank Gowdy	150.00	300.00
63 Jack Scott	150.00	300.00
64 Stan Coveleskie UER misspelled Coveleski	300.00	600.00

1926-27 W512

This set, referenced by the catalog designation W512, measures approximately 1 3/16" by 2 3/16" and features crude color drawings of the noted athlete. The cards are blank backed and the set includes actors and actresses as well as some of the athletes that made the 1920s "The Golden Age of Sports," Babe Ruth, Bill

Tilden, Johnny Weismuller, Walter Hagen, and Jack Dempsey. The cards are thought to have been issued between 1926-1927 and are often referred to as strip cards since they were commonly issued in panels or strips of multiple cards. The set is sometimes titled as "Athletes, Aviators, Movie Stars and Boxers."

COMPLETE SET (50) 187.50 375.00
1 Dave Bancroft 7.50 15.00
2 Grover Alexander 15.00 30.00
3 Ty Cobb 30.00 60.00
4 Tris Speaker 15.00 30.00
5 Glenn Wright 4.00 8.00
6 Babe Ruth 60.00 120.00
7 Everett Scott 5.00 10.00
8 Frank Frisch 7.50 15.00
9 Rogers Hornsby 15.00 30.00
10 Dazzy Vance 7.50 15.00

1928 W513

This set, referenced by the catalog designation W513, continues the numbering sequence started with W512. This set contains drawings and the cards which measure approximately 1 3/16" by 2 3/16" are blank backed. The most famous athletes outside the baseball players are Jack Sharkey, the heavyweight champion and Rene LaCoste, the famed tennis player and entrepeneur. The cards are thought to have been issued about 1928. The set is sometimes titled as "Athletes, Aviators, Movie Stars and Boxers."

COMPLETE SET (42) 2250.00 4500.00
61 Eddie Roush 10.00 20.00
62 Waite Hoyt 10.00 20.00
63 Gink Hundrick 5.00 10.00
64 Jumbo Elliott 5.00 10.00
65 John Miljus 5.00 10.00
66 Jumping Joe Dugan 5.00 10.00
67 Smiling Bill Terry 10.00 20.00
68 Herb Pennock 10.00 20.00
69 Rube Benton 5.00 10.00
70 Paul Waner 10.00 20.00
71 Adolfo Luque 5.00 10.00
72 Burleigh Grimes 10.00 20.00
73 Lloyd Waner 10.00 20.00
74 Hack Wilson 10.00 20.00
75 Hal Carlson 5.00 10.00
76 L. Grantham 5.00 10.00
77 Wilcey Moore 5.00 10.00
78 Jess Haines 10.00 20.00
79 Tony Lazzeri 10.00 20.00
80 Al DeVormer 5.00 10.00
81 Joe Harris 5.00 10.00
82 Pie Traynor 10.00 20.00
83 Mark Koenig 5.00 10.00
84 Babe Herman 6.00 12.00
85 George Harper 5.00 10.00
86 Earle Combs 10.00 20.00
92 Babe Herman 4.00 8.00

1919-21 W514

This 120-card set measures approximately 1 7/16" by 2 1/2" and are numbered in the lower right. The cards portray drawings of the athletes portrayed. The cards are thought to have been issued about 1919. Variations on team names are known to exist. This might suggest that these cards were actually issued over a period of years. Any further information on this fact would be appreciated.

COMPLETE SET (120) 4000.00 8000.00
1 Ira Flagstead 25.00 50.00
2 Babe Ruth 500.00 1000.00
3 Happy Felsch 50.00 100.00
4 Doc Lavan 25.00 50.00
5 Phil Douglas 25.00 50.00
6 Earl Neale 30.00 60.00
7 Leslie Nunamaker 25.00 50.00
8 Sam Jones 30.00 60.00
9 Claude Hendrix 25.00 50.00
10 Frank Schulte 25.00 50.00
11 Cactus Cravath 25.00 50.00
12 Pat Moran 25.00 50.00
13 Dick Rudolph 25.00 50.00
14 Arthur Fletcher 25.00 50.00
15 Joe Jackson 750.00 1500.00
16 Bill Southworth 30.00 60.00
17 Ad Luque 30.00 60.00
18 Charlie Deal 25.00 50.00
19 Al Mamaux 25.00 50.00
20 Stuffy McInnis 30.00 60.00
21 Rabbit Maranville 50.00 100.00
22 Max Carey 50.00 100.00
23 Dick Kerr 30.00 60.00
24 George Burns 25.00 50.00
25 Eddie Collins 50.00 100.00
26 Steve O'Neil 25.00 50.00
27 Bill Fisher 25.00 50.00
28 Rube Bressler 25.00 50.00
29 Bob Shawkey 30.00 60.00
30 Donie Bush 25.00 50.00
31 Chick Gandil 50.00 100.00
32 Ollie Zeider 25.00 50.00
33 Vean Gregg 25.00 50.00
34 Miller Huggins 50.00 100.00
35 Lefty Williams 50.00 100.00
36 Tub Spencer 25.00 50.00
37 Lew McCarthy 25.00 50.00
38 Hod Eller 25.00 50.00
39 Joe Gedeon 25.00 50.00
40 Dave Bancroft 50.00 100.00
41 Clark Griffith 50.00 100.00
42 Wilbur Cooper 25.00 50.00
43 Ty Cobb 250.00 500.00
44 Roger Peckinpaugh 30.00 60.00
45 Nic Carter 25.00 50.00
46 Heinie Groh 25.00 50.00
47 Bob Roth 25.00 50.00
48 Frank Davis 25.00 50.00
49 Leslie Mann 25.00 50.00
50 Fielder Jones 25.00 50.00
51 Bill Doak 25.00 50.00
52 John J. McGraw MG 50.00 100.00
53 Charles Hollocher 25.00 50.00
54 Babe Adams 30.00 60.00
55 Dode Paskert 25.00 50.00
56 Rogers Hornsby 100.00 200.00
57 Max Rath 25.00 50.00
58 Jeff Pfeffer 25.00 50.00
59 Nick Cullop 25.00 50.00
60 Ray Schalk 50.00 100.00
61 Bill Jacobson 25.00 50.00
62 Nap Lajoie 50.00 100.00
63 George Gibson MG 25.00 50.00
64 Harry Hooper 50.00 100.00
65 Grover Alexander 50.00 100.00
66 Ping Bodie 25.00 50.00
67 Hank Gowdy 25.00 50.00
68 Jake Daubert 30.00 60.00
69 Red Faber 50.00 100.00
70 Ivan Olson 25.00 50.00
71 Pickles Dilhoefer 25.00 50.00
72 Christy Mathewson 100.00 200.00
73 Ira Wingo 25.00 50.00
74 Fred Merkle 30.00 60.00
75 Frank Baker 50.00 100.00
76 Bert Gallia 25.00 50.00
77 Milton Watson 25.00 50.00
78 Bert Shotten 25.00 50.00
79 Sam Rice 50.00 100.00
80 Dan Greiner 25.00 50.00
81 Larry Doyle 30.00 60.00
82 Eddie Cicotte 50.00 100.00
83 Hugo Bezdek MG 25.00 50.00
84 Wally Pipp 30.00 60.00
85 Eddie Roush 50.00 100.00
86 Slim Sallee 25.00 50.00
87 Bill Killifer 25.00 50.00
88 Bob Veach 25.00 50.00
89 Jim Burke 25.00 50.00
90 Everett Scott 25.00 50.00
91 Buck Weaver 50.00 100.00
92 George Whitted 25.00 50.00
93 Ed Konetchy 25.00 50.00
94 Walter Johnson 100.00 200.00
95 Sam Crawford 50.00 100.00
96 Fred Mitchell 25.00 50.00
97 Ira Thomas 25.00 50.00
98 Jimmy Ring 25.00 50.00
99 Wally Schang 25.00 50.00
100 Benny Kauff 25.00 50.00
101 George Sisler 50.00 100.00
102 Tris Speaker 50.00 100.00
103 Carl Mays 25.00 50.00
104 Buck Herzog 25.00 50.00
105 Swede Risberg 50.00 100.00
106 Hugh Jennings CO 50.00 100.00
107 Pep Young 25.00 50.00
108 Walter Reuther 25.00 50.00
109 Joe Gharrity 25.00 50.00
110 Zack Wheat 50.00 100.00
111 Jim Vaughn 25.00 50.00
112 Kid Gleason MG 40.00 80.00
113 Casey Stengel 100.00 200.00
114 Hal Chase 30.00 60.00
115 Oscar Stanage 25.00 50.00
116 Larry Shean 25.00 50.00
117 Steve Pendergast 25.00 50.00
118 Larry Kopf 25.00 50.00
119 Charles Whiteman 25.00 50.00
120 Jesse Barnes 25.00 50.00

1923 W515-1

This 60-card set, referenced by the catalog designation W515, measures approximately 1 5/16" by 2 3/16". The cards are blank backed and feature drawings on the front with the name of the player, his position, and his team on the bottom of the card.

COMPLETE SET (60) 600.00 1200.00
1 Bill Cunningham 20.00 40.00
2 Al Mamauz 20.00 40.00
3 Babe Ruth 400.00 800.00
4 Dave Bancroft 40.00 80.00
5 Ed Rommell 20.00 40.00
6 Babe Adams 25.00 50.00
7 Clarence Walker 20.00 40.00
8 Waite Hoyt 40.00 80.00
9 Bob Shawkey 25.00 50.00
10 Ty Cobb 200.00 400.00
11 George Sisler 60.00 120.00
12 Jack Bentley 20.00 40.00
13 Jim O'Connell 20.00 40.00
14 Frank Frisch 60.00 120.00
15 Frank Baker 40.00 80.00
16 Burleigh Grimes 40.00 80.00
17 Wally Schang 25.00 50.00
18 Harry Heilman 40.00 80.00
19 Aaron Ward 20.00 40.00
20 Carl Mays 20.00 40.00
21 The Meusel Bros. 30.00 60.00
22 Arthur Nehf 20.00 40.00
23 Lee Meadows 20.00 40.00
24 Casey Stengel 100.00 200.00
25 Jack Scott 20.00 40.00
26 Kenneth Williams 25.00 50.00
27 Joe Bush 20.00 40.00
28 Tris Speaker 60.00 120.00
29 Ross Youngs 40.00 80.00
30 Joe Dugan 25.00 50.00
31 The Barnes Bros. 25.00 50.00
32 George Kelly 40.00 80.00
33 Hugh McQuillen 20.00 40.00
34 Hugh Jennings MG 40.00 80.00
35 Tom Griffith 20.00 40.00
36 Miller Huggins MG 40.00 80.00
37 Whitey Witt 20.00 40.00
38 Walter Johnson 100.00 200.00
39 Wally Pipp 25.00 50.00
40 Dutch Reuther 20.00 40.00
41 Jim Johnston 20.00 40.00
42 Willie Kamm 25.00 50.00
43 Sam Jones 20.00 40.00
44 Frank Snyder 20.00 40.00
45 John McGraw MG 40.00 80.00
46 Everett Scott 20.00 40.00
47 Babe Ruth 400.00 800.00
48 Urban Shocker 25.00 50.00
49 Grover Alexander 60.00 120.00
50 Rabbit Maranville 40.00 80.00
51 Ray Schalk 40.00 80.00
52 Heinie Groh 25.00 50.00
53 Wilbert Robinson MG 40.00 80.00
54 George Burns 20.00 40.00
55 Rogers Hornsby 100.00 200.00
56 Zack Wheat 40.00 80.00
57 Eddie Roush 40.00 80.00
58 Eddie Collins 40.00 80.00
59 Charlie Hollocher 20.00 40.00
60 Red Faber 40.00 80.00

1920 W516-1

This 30-card set, referenced by the catalog designation W516, measures approximately 1 7/16" by 2 5/16". The cards have colorful photos with a blank back. The copyright is reversed on the front of the card. There is also the name of the player and position on the bottom of the card.

COMPLETE SET (30) 3000.00 6000.00
1 Babe Ruth 750.00 1500.00
2 Heine Groh 60.00 120.00
3 Ping Bodie 50.00 100.00
4 Ray Shalk (Schalk) 100.00 200.00
5 Tris Speaker 200.00 400.00
6 Ty Cobb 400.00 800.00
7 Roger Hornsby (Rogers) 300.00 600.00
8 Walter Johnson 300.00 600.00
9 Grover Alexander 200.00 400.00
10 George Burns 50.00 100.00
11 Jimmy Ring 50.00 100.00
12 Jess Barnes 50.00 100.00
13 Larry Doyle 60.00 120.00
14 Arty Fletcher 50.00 100.00
15 Dick Rudolph 50.00 100.00
16 Benny Kauf (Kauff) 50.00 100.00
17 Art Nehf 50.00 100.00
18 Babe Adams 60.00 120.00
19 Will Cooper 50.00 100.00
20 R.Peckingpaugh 50.00 100.00
21 Eddie Cicotte 100.00 200.00
22 Hank Gowdy 50.00 100.00
23 Eddie Collins 100.00 200.00
24 Christy Mathewson 300.00 600.00
25 Clyde Milan 60.00 120.00
26 M. Kelley (G.) 50.00 100.00
27 Ed Hooper (Harry) 50.00 100.00
28 Pep Young 100.00 200.00
29 Eddie Rousch (Roush) 100.00 200.00
30 George Bancroft (Dave) 50.00 100.00

1921 W516-2-1

1 George Burns
2 Grover Alexander
3 Walter Johnson
4 Roger Hornsby (Rogers)
5 Ty Cobb
6 Tris Speaker
7 Ray Shalk (Schalk)
8 Ping Bodie
9 Heinie Groh
10 Babe Ruth
11 R.Peckingpaugh
12 Will Cooper
13 Babe Adams
14 Art Nehf
15 Benny Kauf (Kauff)
16 Dick Rudolph
17 Arty Fletcher
18 Larry Doyle
19 Jess Barnes
20 Jimmy Ring
21 George Bancroft (Dave)
22 Eddie Rousch (Roush)
23 Pep Young
24 Ed Hooper (Harry)
25 M. Kelly (G.)
26 Clyde Milan
27 Christy Mathewson
28 Eddie Collins
29 Hank Gowdy
30 Eddie Cicotte

1931 W517

The cards in this 54-card set measure approximately 3" by 4". This 1931 set of numbered, blank-backed cards was placed in the "W~ category in the original American Card Catalog because (1) its producer was unknown and (2) it was issued in strips of three. The photo is black and white but the entire obverse of each card is generally found tinted in tones of sepia, blue, green, yellow, rose, black or gray. The cards are numbered in a small circle on the front. A solid dark line at one end of a card entitled the purchaser to another piece of candy as a prize. There are two different cards of both Babe Ruth and Mickey Cochrane. There may be other variations in this set: such as cards without numbers (e.g., Paul Waner and Dazzy Vance) as well as Chalmer Cissell with both Chicago and Cleveland, Chick Hafey with both the Cardinals and Cincinnati, and George Kelly and Lefty O'Doul with Brooklyn.

COMPLETE SET (54) 3750.00 7500.00
1 Earle Combs 40.00 80.00
2 Pie Traynor 50.00 100.00
3 Eddie Roush/(Wearing Cincinnati 50.00 100.00
uniform& but lis
4 Babe Ruth/(Throwing) 750.00 1500.00
5 Chalmer Cissell 20.00 40.00
6 Bill Sherdel 20.00 40.00
7 Bill Shore 20.00 40.00
8 George Earnshaw 20.00 40.00
9 Bucky Harris 40.00 80.00
10 Chuck Klein 50.00 100.00
11 George Kelly 40.00 80.00
12 Travis Jackson 40.00 80.00
13 Willie Kamm 20.00 40.00
14 Harry Heilmann 50.00 100.00
15 Grover Alexander 75.00 150.00
16 Frank Frisch 50.00 100.00
17 Jack Quinn 30.00 60.00
18 Cy Williams 30.00 60.00
19 Kiki Cuyler 40.00 80.00
20 Babe Ruth/(Portrait) 1000.00 2000.00
21 Jimmy Foxx 125.00 250.00
(Jimmie)
22 Jimmy Dykes 30.00 60.00
23 Bill Terry 60.00 120.00
24 Freddy Lindstrom 40.00 80.00
25 Hugh Critz 20.00 40.00
26 Pete Donahue 20.00 40.00
27 Tony Lazzeri 50.00 100.00
28 Heinie Manush 40.00 80.00
29 Chick Hafey 40.00 80.00
St.Louis
30 Melvin Ott 100.00 200.00
31 Bing Miller 20.00 40.00
32 Mule Haas 20.00 40.00
33 Lefty O'Doul 30.00 60.00
34 Paul Waner 40.00 80.00
35 Lou Gehrig 500.00 1000.00
36 Dazzy Vance 40.00 80.00
37 Mickey Cochrane/(Catching pose) 50.00 100.00
38 Rogers Hornsby 125.00 250.00
39 Lefty Grove 100.00 200.00
40 Al Simmons 50.00 100.00
41 Rube Walberg 20.00 40.00
42 Hack Wilson 50.00 100.00
43 Art Shires 20.00 40.00
44 Sammy Hale 20.00 40.00
45 Ted Lyons 40.00 80.00
46 Joe Sewell 40.00 80.00
47 Goose Goslin, 40.00 80.00
48 Lou Fonseca 20.00 40.00
49 Bob Meusel 30.00 60.00
50 Lu Blue 20.00 40.00
51 Earl Averill 40.00 80.00
52 Eddie Collins 50.00 100.00
53 Joe Judge 20.00 40.00
54 Mickey Cochrane/(Portrait) 50.00 100.00

1920 W519 Un-Numbered

This 10-card unnumbered blank-backed strip-card set has a blue photo of the featured player along with his name on the bottom in block letters. Since these cards are unnumbered, we have sequenced them in alphabetical order.

COMPLETE SET 500.00 1000.00
1 Eddie Cicotte 60.00 120.00
2 Eddie Collins 60.00 120.00
3 Gavvy Cravath 40.00 80.00
4 Frank Frisch 30.00 60.00
5 Kid Gleason MG 40.00 80.00
6 Ernie Krueger 20.00 40.00
7 Rube Marquard 30.00 60.00
8 Guy Morton 20.00 40.00
9 Joe Murphy 20.00 40.00
10 Babe Ruth 400.00 800.00

1920 W519 Numbered

Apparently some of the W519 cards were issued with numbers on the side. This list is far from complete and any further information is appreciated.

COMPLETE SET 25.00 50.00

1920 W520

These cards which measure 1 3/** by 2 1/4" are numbered in the lower right hand corner. For some unexplicable reason, there are two Mike Gonzales cards in this set.

COMPLETE SET (20) 400.00 800.00
1 Dave Bancroft 50.00 100.00
2 Christy Mathewson 200.00 400.00
3 Larry Doyle 30.00 60.00
4 Jess Barnes 25.00 50.00
5 Art Fletcher 25.00 50.00
6 Wilbur Cooper 25.00 50.00
7 Mike Gonzalez 25.00 50.00
8 Zach Wheat 50.00 100.00
9 Tris Speaker 125.00 250.00
10 Benny Kauff 25.00 50.00
11 Zach Wheat 50.00 100.00
12 Phil Douglas 25.00 50.00
13 Babe Ruth 400.00 800.00
14 Stan Coveleski 50.00 100.00
Spelled Koveleski
15 Goldie Rapp 25.00 50.00
16 Pol Perritt 25.00 50.00
17 Otto Miller 25.00 50.00
18 George Kelly 50.00 100.00
19 Mike Gonzalez 25.00 50.00
20 Les Nunamaker 25.00 50.00

1921 W551

This 10-card set features color drawings of players that measure approximately 1 3/8" by 3 1/4" and were printed in strips. The players name and team name are printed in the bottom margin. The backs are blank. The cards are unnumbered and checklisted below in alphabetical order.

COMPLETE SET (10) 500.00 1000.00
1 Frank Baker 75.00 150.00
2 Dave Bancroft 50.00 100.00
3 Jess Barnes 25.00 50.00
4 Ty Cobb 400.00 800.00
5 Walter Johnson 300.00 600.00
6 Wally Pipp 25.00 50.00
7 Babe Ruth 500.00 1000.00
8 George Sisler 125.00 250.00
9 Tris Speaker 200.00 400.00
10 Casey Stengel 200.00 400.00

1929 W553

These cards, which measure 1 3/4" by 2 3/4", are very obscure and feature star players from the late 1920's. These blank-backed cards are known to exist in either green, red or B&W. The photos are framed with ornate picture frame style borders. Verified cards are listed below and more may exsist so any additions to this checklist are appreciated.

COMPLETE SET 1000.00 4000.00
1 Lu Blue 50.00 100.00
2 Mickey Cochrane 125.00 250.00
3 Jimmy Foxx 300.00
(Jimmie)
4 Frank Frisch 125.00 250.00
5 Lou Gehrig 250.00 500.00
6 Goose Goslin 125.00 250.00
7 Burleigh Grimes 125.00 250.00
8 Lefty Grove 150.00 300.00
9 Rogers Hornsby 150.00 300.00
10 Rabbit Maranville 125.00 250.00
11 Bing Miller 75.00 150.00
12 Lefty O'Doul 75.00 150.00
13 Babe Ruth 400.00 800.00
14 Al Simmons 125.00 250.00
15 Pie Traynor 125.00 250.00

1930 W554

This set corresponds to the poses in R316 and R306. The cards measure 5" by 7" and are reasonably available within the Hobby.

COMPLETE SET (18) 150.00 300.00
1 Gordon S. (Mickey) 40.00 80.00
Cochrane
2 Lewis A. Fonseca 25.00 50.00
3 Jimmy Foxx 75.00 150.00
(Jimmie)
4 Lou Gehrig 250.00 500.00
5 Burleigh Grimes 50.00 100.00
6 Robert M. Grove 60.00 120.00
7 Waite Hoyt 50.00 100.00
8 Joe Judge 30.00 60.00
9 Charles(Chuck)Klein 50.00 100.00
10 Douglas McWeeny 25.00 50.00
11 Frank O'Doul 30.00 60.00
12 Melvin Ott 75.00 150.00
13 Herbert Pennock 50.00 100.00
14 Eddie Rommel 30.00 60.00
15 Babe Ruth 400.00 800.00
16 Al Simmons 60.00 120.00
17 Lloyd Waner 50.00 100.00
18 Hack Wilson 50.00 100.00

1910 W555

This 66 card set measures 1 1/8" by 1 3/16" and have sepia pictures surrounded by a black border, which is framed by a white line. Eight cards: Bates, Bescher, Byrne, Collins, Crawford, Devlin, Lake and Mowery are frequently found on want lists. The Eddie Cicotte card was the most recent discovery and is also assumed to be one of the tougher cards. A recent discovery shows that these cards were included in box tops from the Jay S Meyer company in which a child could pretend he was taking the photo to match the actual photo on the box top. These cards came four to a box and were all in seperate parts of the cover.

COMPLETE SET (66) 5500.00 11000.00
1 Red Ames 50.00 100.00
2 Jimmy Austin 50.00 100.00
3 Johnny Bates 50.00 100.00
4 Chief Bender 125.00 250.00
5 Bob Bescher 50.00 100.00
6 Joe Birmingham 50.00 100.00
7 Bill Bradley 50.00 100.00
8 Kitty Bransfield 50.00 100.00
9 Mordecai Brown 125.00 250.00
10 Bobby Byrne 50.00 100.00
11 Frank Chance 125.00 250.00
12 Hal Chase 75.00 150.00
13 Eddie Cicotte 125.00 250.00
14 Fred Clarke 125.00 250.00
15 Ty Cobb 750.00 1500.00
16 Eddie Collins 250.00 500.00
dark uniform
17 Eddie Collins 250.00 500.00
light uniform
18 Harry Covelskie 50.00 100.00
19 Sam Crawford 125.00 250.00
20 Harry Davis 50.00 100.00
21 Jim Delahanty 50.00 100.00
22 Art Devlin 50.00 100.00
23 Josh Devore 50.00 100.00
24 Bill Donovan 50.00 100.00
25 Red Dooin 50.00 100.00
26 Mickey Doolan 50.00 100.00
27 Bull Durham 50.00 100.00
28 Jimmy Dygert 50.00 100.00
29 Johnny Evers 125.00 250.00
30 Russ Ford 50.00 100.00
31 George Gibson 50.00 100.00
32 Clark Griffith 125.00 250.00
33 Topsy Hartsell 50.00 100.00
34 Bill Hinchman 50.00 100.00
Sic, Heinchman
35 Charlie Hemphill 50.00 100.00
36 Hugh Jennings MG 125.00 250.00
37 Davy Jones 50.00 100.00
38 Addie Joss 150.00 300.00
39 Willie Keeler 125.00 250.00
40 Red Kleinow 50.00 100.00
41 Nap Lajoie 250.00 500.00
42 Joe Lake 50.00 100.00
43 Tommy Leach 50.00 100.00
44 Sherry Magee 50.00 100.00
45 Christy Mathewson 250.00 500.00
46 Ambrose McConnell 50.00 100.00
47 John McGraw MG 125.00 250.00
48 Chief Meyers 50.00 100.00
49 Earl Moore 50.00 100.00
50 Mike Mowrey 50.00 100.00
51 George Mullin 50.00 100.00
52 Red Murray 50.00 100.00
53 Simon Nicholls 50.00 100.00
54 Jim Pastorius 50.00 100.00
55 Deacon Phillipe 50.00 100.00
56 Eddie Plank 150.00 300.00
57 Fred Snodgrass 50.00 100.00
58 Harry Steinfeldt 50.00 100.00
59 Joe Tinker 125.00 250.00
60 Hippo Vaughn 50.00 100.00
61 Honus Wagner 500.00 1000.00
62 Rube Waddell 125.00 250.00
63 Hoooks Wiltse 50.00 100.00
64 Cy Young 300.00 600.00
Cleveland Amer.
65 Cy Young 300.00 600.00
Same pose as E93
66 Cy Young 300.00 600.00
Same pose as E97-8

1927 W560 Black

Cards in this set feature athletes from baseball and college football, along with an assortment of other sports and non-sports. The cards were issued in strips and full sheets and follow a standard playing card design. Quite a few Joker cards were produced. We've numbered the cards below according to the suit and playing card number (face cards were assigned numbers as well). It is thought there were at least three different printings and that the baseball and football players were added in the second printing replacing other subjects. All are baseball players below unless otherwise noted. Many cards were printed in a single color red, single color black, and a black/red dual color printing, thereby creating up to three versions. The full set, with just one of each different subject, contains 88-different cards. It is thought that the two-color cards are slightly tougher to find than the single color version.

COMPLETE SET (63) 900.00 1500.00
*RED: .4X TO 1X BLACK
*BLACK/RED: .5X TO 1.2X BLACK
C1 Kiki Cuyler 20.00 40.00
C2 Fred McGuire 4.00 8.00
C3 Lou Gehrig 250.00 400.00
C4 Max Bishop 4.00 8.00
C5 Jim Bottomley 12.50 25.00
C6 Buddy Myer 4.00 8.00
C7 Taylor Douthit 4.00 8.00
C8 Bill Sherdel 4.00 8.00
C9 Remy Kremer 4.00 8.00
C10 Goose Goslin 12.50 25.00
C11 Al Simmons 25.00 50.00
C12 Vic Aldridge 4.00 8.00
C13 Lefty Grove 30.00 60.00
D3 Paul Waner 20.00 40.00
D5 George Uhle 4.00 8.00
D8 Fred Lindstrom 12.50 25.00
D9 Larry Benton 4.00 8.00
D11 Cy Williams 4.00 8.00
D12 Lloyd Waner 12.50 25.00
D13 Fred Fitzsimmons 7.50 15.00
H1 Watty Clark 4.00 8.00
H2 Hugh Critz 4.00 8.00
H3 Willie Kamm 4.00 8.00
H4 Rogers Hornsby 40.00 75.00
H5 Luke Sewell 5.00 10.00
H7 Babe Herman 7.50 15.00
H10 Sam Gray 4.00 8.00
H11 Waite Hoyt 12.50 25.00
H13 Andy Cohen 4.00 8.00
S1 Glen Wright 4.00 8.00
S2 Walter Johnson 50.00 100.00
S3 Flint Rhem 4.00 8.00
S4 George Pipgras 4.00 8.00
S5 Jim Wilson 4.00 8.00
S6 Dazzy Vance 20.00 40.00
S7 Fred Marberry 4.00 8.00
S8 Thomas Thevenow 4.00 8.00
S9 Fresco Thompson 4.00 8.00
S10 Jesse Haines 12.50 25.00
S11 Guy Bush 4.00 8.00
S12 Johnny Mostil 4.00 8.00
S13 Del Bissonette 4.00 8.00
JOK Lester Bell 4.00 8.00
JOK Mickey Cochrane 20.00 40.00
JOK Jimmie Foxx 60.00 120.00
JOK Henry Johnson 4.00 8.00
JOK Herb Pennock 7.50 15.00
JOK Babe Ruth 175.00 300.00
JOK Rube Walberg 5.00 10.00

1922 W572

This 119-card set was issued in 1922 in ten-card strips along with strips of boxer cards. The cards measure approximately 1 5/16" by 2 1/2" and are blank backed. Most of the player photos on the fronts are black and white, although a few photos are sepia-toned. The pictures are the same ones used in the E120 set, but they have been cropped to fit on the smaller format. The player's signature and team appear at the bottom of the pictures, along with an IFS (International Feature Service) copyright notice. The cards are unnumbered and checklisted below in alphabetical order.

COMPLETE SET (119) 2500.00 5000.00
1 Eddie Ainsmith 20.00 40.00
2 Vic Aldridge 20.00 40.00
3 Grover C. Alexander 125.00 250.00
4 Dave Bancroft 40.00 80.00
5 Jesse Barnes 20.00 40.00
6 John Bassler 20.00 40.00
7 Lu Blue 20.00 40.00
8 Norm Boeckel 20.00 40.00
9 George Burns 20.00 40.00
10 Joe Bush 25.00 50.00
11 Leon Cadore 20.00 40.00
12 Virgil Cheevers 20.00 40.00
13 Ty Cobb 600.00 1200.00
14 Eddie Collins 50.00 100.00
15 John Collins 20.00 40.00
16 Wilbur Cooper 20.00 40.00
17 Stanley Coveleski 40.00 80.00
18 Walton Cruise 20.00 40.00
19 Dave Danforth 20.00 40.00
20 Jake Daubert 25.00 50.00
21 Hank DeBerry 20.00 40.00
22 Lou DeVormer 20.00 40.00
23 Bill Doak 20.00 40.00
24 Pete Donohue 20.00 40.00
25 Pat Duncan 20.00 40.00
26 Jimmy Dykes 25.00 50.00
27 Urban Faber 40.00 80.00
28 Bibb Falk 20.00 40.00
29 Frank Frisch 60.00 120.00
30 Chick Galloway 20.00 40.00
31 Ed Gharrity 20.00 40.00
32 Charles Glazner 20.00 40.00
33 Hank Gowdy 25.00 50.00
34 Tom Griffith 20.00 40.00
35 Burleigh Grimes 40.00 80.00
36 Ray Grimes 20.00 40.00
37 Heinie Groh 25.00 50.00
38 Joe Harris 20.00 40.00
39 Bucky Harris 40.00 80.00
40 Joe Hauser 20.00 40.00
41 Harry Heilmann 40.00 80.00
42 Walter Henline 20.00 40.00
43 Charles Hollocher 20.00 40.00
44 Harry Hooper 40.00 80.00
45 Rogers Hornsby 150.00 300.00
46 Waite Hoyt 40.00 80.00
47 Wilbur Hubbell 20.00 40.00
48 William Jacobson 20.00 40.00
49 Charles Jamieson 20.00 40.00
50 Syl Johnson 20.00 40.00
51 Walter Johnson 250.00 500.00
52 Jimmy Johnston 20.00 40.00
53 Joe Judge 25.00 50.00
54 George Kelly 40.00 80.00
55 Lee King 20.00 40.00
56 Larry Kopf 20.00 40.00
57 George Leverette 20.00 40.00
58 Al Mamaux 20.00 40.00
59 Rabbit Maranville 40.00 80.00
60 Rube Marquard 40.00 80.00
61 Martin McManus 20.00 40.00
62 Lee Meadows 20.00 40.00
63 Mike Menosky 20.00 40.00
64 Bob Meusel 30.00 60.00
65 Emil Meusel 20.00 40.00
66 George Mogridge 20.00 40.00
67 John Morrison 20.00 40.00
68 Johnny Mostil 20.00 40.00
69 Roleine Naylor 20.00 40.00
70 Art Nehf 20.00 40.00
71 Joe Oeschger 20.00 40.00
72 Bob O'Farrell 20.00 40.00
73 Steve O'Neill 25.00 50.00
74 Frank Parkinson 20.00 40.00
75 Ralph Perkins 20.00 40.00
76 Herman Pillette 20.00 40.00
77 Babe Pinelli 25.00 50.00
78 Wallie Pipp 30.00 60.00
79 Ray Powell 20.00 40.00
80 Jack Quinn 20.00 40.00
81 Goldie Rapp 20.00 40.00
82 Walt Reuther 20.00 40.00
83 Sam Rice 40.00 80.00
84 Emory Rigney 20.00 40.00
85 Eppa Rixey 40.00 80.00
86 Ed Rommel 25.00 50.00
87 Eddie Roush 60.00 120.00
88 Babe Ruth 1250.00 2500.00
89 Ray Schalk 40.00 80.00
90 Wally Schang 25.00 50.00
91 Walter Schmidt 20.00 40.00
92 Joe Schultz 20.00 40.00
93 Hank Severeid 20.00 40.00
94 Joe Sewell 40.00 80.00
95 Bob Shawkey 25.00 50.00
96 Earl Sheely 20.00 40.00
97 Will Sherdel 20.00 40.00
98 Urban Shocker 25.00 50.00
99 George Sisler 100.00 200.00
100 Earl Smith 20.00 40.00
101 Elmer Smith 20.00 40.00
102 Jack Smith 20.00 40.00
103 Bill Southworth 25.00 50.00
104 Tris Speaker 125.00 250.00
105 Jigger Statz 20.00 40.00
106 Milton Stock 20.00 40.00
107 Jim Tierney 20.00 40.00
108 Harold Traynor 50.00 100.00
109 George Uhle 20.00 40.00
110 Bob Veach 20.00 40.00
111 Clarence Walker 20.00 40.00
112 Curtis Walker 20.00 40.00
113 Bill Wambsganss 25.00 50.00
114 Aaron Ward 20.00 40.00
115 Zach Wheat 40.00 80.00
116 Fred Williams 20.00 40.00
117 Ken Williams 30.00 60.00
118 Ivy Wingo 20.00 40.00
119 Joe Wood 30.00 60.00
120 Tom Zachary 20.00 40.00

1922 W573

This set's design is similiar to the E120 American Caramel set. The backs are blank. These cards have been described as a "small strip card type of E120. Albums for these cards exist. They are made of black construction paper and the inside has pages for each team and specific places for each player.

COMPLETE SET (143) 1500.00 3000.00
1 Babe Adams 30.00 60.00
2 Eddie Ainsmith 25.00 50.00
3 Vic Aldridge 25.00 50.00
4 Grover C. Alexander 150.00 300.00
5 Frank Baker 50.00 100.00
6 Dave Bancroft 50.00 100.00
7 Turner Barber 25.00 50.00
8 Jesse Barnes 25.00 50.00
9 Johnny Bassler 25.00 50.00
10 Carson Bigbee 25.00 50.00
11 Lu Blue 25.00 50.00
12 Tony Boeckel 25.00 50.00
13 George H. Burns 25.00 50.00
14 George J. Burns 25.00 50.00
15 Marty Callaghan 25.00 50.00
16 Max Carey 50.00 100.00
17 Ike Caveney 25.00 50.00
18 Virgil Cheeves 25.00 50.00
19 Verne Clemons 25.00 50.00
20 Ty Cobb 300.00 600.00
21 Al Cole 25.00 50.00
22 Eddie Collins 50.00 100.00
23 Pat Collins 25.00 50.00
24 Wilbur Cooper 25.00 50.00
25 Dick Cox 25.00 50.00
26 Bill Cunningham 25.00 50.00
27 George Cutshaw 25.00 50.00
28 Dave Danforth 25.00 50.00
29 Hooks Dauss 25.00 50.00
30 Dixie Davis 25.00 50.00
31 Hank DeBerry 25.00 50.00
32 Al DeVormer 25.00 50.00
33 Bill Doak 25.00 50.00
34 Joe Dugan 30.00 60.00
35 Howard Ehmke 30.00 60.00
36 Frank Ellerbe 25.00 50.00
37 Red Faber 50.00 100.00
38 Bibb Falk 25.00 50.00
39 Max Flack 25.00 50.00
40 Ira Flagstead 25.00 50.00
41 Art Fletcher 25.00 50.00
42 Hod Ford 25.00 50.00
43 Jacques Fournier 25.00 50.00
44 Frank Frisch 75.00 150.00
45 Ollie Fuhrman 25.00 50.00
46 Chick Galloway 25.00 50.00
47 Wally Gerber 25.00 50.00
48 Patsy Gharrity 25.00 50.00
49 Whitey Glazner 25.00 50.00
50 Goose Goslin 50.00 100.00
51 Hank Gowdy 30.00 60.00
52 Jack Graney 25.00 50.00
53 Burleigh Grimes 50.00 100.00
54 Heinie Groh 30.00 60.00
55 Jesse Haines 50.00 100.00
56 Bubbles Hargrave 25.00 50.00
57 Joe Harris 25.00 50.00
58 Earl Hamilton 25.00 50.00
59 Cliff Heathcote 25.00 50.00
60 Harry Heilmann 50.00 100.00

61 Clarence Hodge 25.00 50.00
62 Charlie Hollocher 25.00 50.00
63 Harry Hooper 50.00 100.00
64 Rogers Hornsby 150.00 300.00
65 Waite Hoyt 50.00 100.00
66 Ernie Johnson 25.00 50.00
67 Syl Johnson 25.00 50.00
68 Walter Johnson 150.00 300.00
69 Paul Johnson 25.00 50.00
70 Sam Jones 30.00 60.00
71 Benjamin Karr 25.00 50.00
72 Doc Lavan 25.00 50.00
73 Dixie Levrette 25.00 50.00
74 Rabbit Maranville 50.00 100.00
75 Cliff Markle 25.00 50.00
76 Carl Mays 25.00 50.00
77 Harvey McClellan 25.00 50.00
78 Marty McManus 25.00 50.00
79 Lee Meadows 25.00 50.00
80 Mike Menosky 25.00 50.00
81 Irish Meusel 25.00 50.00
82 Clyde Milan 30.00 60.00
83 Bing Miller 25.00 50.00
84 Elmer Miller 25.00 50.00
85 Ralph Miller 25.00 50.00
86 Hack Miller 25.00 50.00
87 Clarence Mitchell 25.00 50.00
88 George Mogridge 25.00 50.00
89 John Morrison 25.00 50.00
90 Johnny Mostil 25.00 50.00
91 Elmer Myers 25.00 50.00
92 Roleine Naylor 25.00 50.00
93 Les Nunamaker 25.00 50.00
94 Bob O'Farrell 25.00 50.00
95 Steve O'Neill 30.00 60.00
96 Herb Pennock 50.00 100.00
97 Cy Perkins 25.00 50.00
98 Thomas Phillips 25.00 50.00
99 Val Picinich 25.00 50.00
100 Herman Pillette 25.00 50.00
101 Babe Pinelli 25.00 50.00
102 Wally Pipp 30.00 60.00
103 Clark Pittenger 25.00 50.00
104 Del Pratt 25.00 50.00
105 Goldie Rapp 25.00 50.00
106 Johnny Rawlings 25.00 50.00
107 Topper Rigney 25.00 50.00
108 Charlie Robertson 25.00 50.00
109 Ed Rommel 25.00 50.00
110 Muddy Ruel 25.00 50.00
111 Dutch Ruether 25.00 50.00
112 Babe Ruth 500.00 1000.00
113 Ray Schalk 50.00 100.00
114 Wally Schang 30.00 60.00
115 Ray Schmandt 25.00 50.00
116 Walter Schmidt 25.00 50.00
117 Germany Schultz 25.00 50.00
118 Henry Severeid 25.00 50.00
119 Joe Sewell 50.00 100.00
120 Bob Shawkey 40.00 80.00
121 Earl Sheely 25.00 50.00
122 Ralph Shinners 25.00 50.00
123 Urban Shocker 25.00 50.00
124 George Sisler 75.00 150.00
125 Earl L. Smith 25.00 50.00
126 Earl S. Smith 25.00 50.00
127 Jack Smith 25.00 50.00
128 Allen Sothoron 25.00 50.00
129 Tris Speaker 125.00 250.00
130 Amos Strunk 25.00 50.00
131 Cotton Tierney 25.00 50.00
132 Jack Tobin 25.00 50.00
133 Specs Toporcer 25.00 50.00
134 George Uhle 25.00 50.00
135 Bobby Veach 25.00 50.00
136 John Watson 25.00 50.00
137 Zack Wheat 50.00 100.00
138 Ken Williams 30.00 60.00
139 Cy Williams 25.00 50.00
140 Charles Woodall 25.00 50.00
141 Russell Wrightstone 25.00 50.00
142 Ross Youngs 50.00 100.00
143 Tom Zachary 25.00 50.00

1932 W574

This white-bordered blank-backed set, which measures approximately 2 1/8" by 2 3/4" and features a black and white photo with the player's name on the side and the team name on the bottom. Since these cards are unnumbered, we have sequenced them in alphabetical order.

COMPLETE SET (29) 600.00 1200.00
1 Dale Alexander 25.00 50.00
2 Paul Andrews 25.00 50.00
3 Luke Appling 50.00 100.00
4 Earl Averill 50.00 100.00
5 Irving Burns 25.00 50.00
6 George Blaeholder 25.00 50.00
7 Pat Caraway 25.00 50.00
8 Bud Cissell 25.00 50.00
9 Harry Davis 25.00 50.00
10 Jimmy Dykes 25.00 50.00
11 George Earnshaw 30.00 60.00
12 Red Faber 50.00 100.00
13 Lew Fonseca 25.00 50.00
14 Jimmie Foxx 125.00 250.00
15 Vic Frasier 25.00 50.00
16 Lefty Grove 100.00 200.00
17 Frank Grube 25.00 50.00
18 Bump Hadley 25.00 50.00
19 Willie Kamm 25.00 50.00
20 Bill Killefer 25.00 50.00
21 Red Kress 25.00 50.00
22 Firpo Marberry 25.00 50.00
23 Roger Peckinpaugh 30.00 60.00
24 Frank Reiber 25.00 50.00
25 Carl Reynolds 25.00 50.00
26 Al Simmons 75.00 150.00
27 Joe Vosmik 25.00 50.00
28 Gee Walker 25.00 50.00
29 Whit Wyatt 25.00 50.00

1922 W575

This 154-card set, referenced by the catalog designation W575, measures approximately 1 15/16" by 3 3/16". The cards have a black and white action posed photo are blank backed. The players name and position are under the photo on the front. Cards that are part of the "autograph on shoulder" series are marked with an asterisk in the checklist below and are worth a little more.

COMPLETE SET (154) 2000.00 4000.00
1 Babe Adams 25.00 50.00
2 Grover C. Alexander (2) 100.00 200.00
3 Jim Bagby 25.00 50.00
4 Frank Baker 50.00 100.00
5 Dave Bancroft (2) 100.00 200.00
6 Jesse Barnes 25.00 50.00
7 Johnny Bassler 40.00 80.00
8 Joe Berry 25.00 50.00
9 Carson Bigbee 25.00 50.00
10 Ping Bodie 25.00 50.00
11 Eddie Brown 25.00 50.00
12 Jesse Burkett CO 50.00 100.00
13 George H. Burns 25.00 50.00
14 Donie Bush 40.00 80.00
15 Joe Bush 25.00 50.00
16 Max Carey (2) 50.00 100.00
17 Ty Cobb 300.00 600.00
18 Eddie Collins* 50.00 100.00
19 Rip Collins 25.00 50.00
20 Stan Coveleski* 50.00 100.00
21 Bill Cunningham 25.00 50.00
22 Jake Daubert 40.00 80.00
23 Hooks Dauss (2) 25.00 50.00
24 Dixie Davis 25.00 50.00
25 Charlie Deal (2) 25.00 50.00
26 Al Devormer 25.00 50.00
27 Bill Doak 25.00 50.00
28 Bill Donovan MG 25.00 50.00
29 Phil Douglas 25.00 50.00
30 Joe Dugan 40.00 80.00
31 Johnny Evers MG (2) 50.00 100.00
32 Red Faber 50.00 100.00
33 Bibb Falk 25.00 50.00
34 Alex Ferguson 25.00 50.00
35 Chick Fewster 25.00 50.00
36 Eddie Foster 25.00 50.00
37 Frank Frisch 100.00 200.00
38 Larry Gardner 25.00 50.00
39 Alex Gaston 25.00 50.00
40 Wally Gerber 40.00 80.00
41 Patsy Gharrity 25.00 50.00
42 Whitey Glazner 25.00 50.00
43 Kid Gleason MG 30.00 60.00
44 Mike Gonzales 25.00 50.00
45 Hank Gowdy 30.00 60.00
46 Jack Graney (2) 25.00 50.00
47 Tommy Griffith 25.00 50.00
48 Charlie Grimm 30.00 60.00
49 Heinie Groh 30.00 60.00
New York NL
50 Henie Groh 30.00 60.00
Cincinnati NL
51 Jesse Haines 50.00 100.00
52 Harry Harper 25.00 50.00
53 Chicken Hawks 25.00 50.00
54 Harry Heilmann 50.00 100.00
55 Fred Hoffman 25.00 50.00
56 Walter Holke (3) 25.00 50.00
57 Charlie Hollocher (2) 25.00 50.00
58 Harry Hooper 50.00 100.00
59 Rogers Hornsby 100.00 200.00
60 Waite Hoyt 50.00 100.00
61 Miller Huggins MG 50.00 100.00
62 Baby Doll Jacobson 25.00 50.00
63 Hugh Jennings CO 50.00 100.00
64 Walter Johnson (2) 200.00 400.00
65 Jimmy Johnston 25.00 50.00
66 Joe Judge 40.00 80.00
67 George Kelly (2) 50.00 100.00
68 Dickie Kerr 30.00 60.00
69 Pete Kilduff 25.00 50.00
70 Doc Lavan 25.00 50.00
71 Nemo Leibold 25.00 50.00
72 Duffy Lewis 30.00 60.00
73 Al Mamaux 25.00 50.00
74 Rabbit Maranville* 50.00 100.00
75 Rube Marquard 50.00 100.00
76 Carl Mays (2) 30.00 60.00
77 John McGraw MG 100.00 200.00
78 Stuffy McInnis 30.00 60.00
79 Mike McNally 25.00 50.00
80 Bob Meusel 40.00 80.00
81 Irish Meusel 25.00 50.00
82 Clyde Milan 30.00 60.00
83 Elmer Miller 25.00 50.00
84 Otto Miller 25.00 50.00
85 Johnny Mitchell 25.00 50.00
86 Guy Morton 40.00 80.00
87 Eddie Mulligan 25.00 50.00
88 Eddie Murphy 25.00 50.00
89 Hy Myers (3) 25.00 50.00
90 Greasy Neale 30.00 60.00
91 Art Nehf 40.00 80.00
92 Joe Oeschger 25.00 50.00
93 Charley O'Leary CO 25.00 50.00
94 Steve O'Neill 30.00 60.00
95 Roger Peckinpaugh (2) 30.00 60.00
96 Bill Piercy 25.00 50.00
97 Jeff Pfeffer 25.00 50.00
Brook. NL
98 Jeff Pfeffer 25.00 50.00
St. L. NL
99 Wally Pipp 30.00 60.00
100 Jack Quinn 25.00 50.00
101 Johnny Rawlings (2) 25.00 50.00
102 Sam Rice (2) 50.00 100.00
103 Jimmy Ring 40.00 80.00
104 Eppa Rixey 50.00 100.00
105 Charlie Robertson* 40.00 80.00
106 Wilbert Robinson MG 50.00 100.00
107 Tom Rogers 25.00 50.00
108 Ed Rommel#(sic.Rounnel 40.00 80.00
109 Braggo Roth 25.00 50.00
110 Edd Roush (2) 50.00 100.00
111 Muddy Ruel 25.00 50.00
112 Babe Ruth (2) 500.00 1000.00
113 Rosy Ryan (2) 25.00 50.00
114 Slim Sallee (2) 25.00 50.00
115 Ray Schalk (2) 50.00 100.00
116 Wally Schang* (2) 40.00 80.00
117 Ferd Schupp (2) 25.00 50.00
118 Everett Scott 40.00 80.00
Boston AL
119 Everett Scott 25.00 50.00
New York AL
120 Hank Severeid 40.00 80.00
121 Joe Sewell* 50.00 100.00
122 Bob Shawkey 40.00 80.00
123 Red Shea 25.00 50.00
124 Earl Sheely 25.00 50.00
125 Urban Shocker 30.00 60.00
126 George Sisler* (2) 100.00 200.00
127 Elmer Smith 25.00 50.00
128 Earl Smith 25.00 50.00
129 Pancho Snyder 25.00 50.00
130 Tris Speaker* (2) 100.00 200.00
131 Casey Stengel 100.00 200.00
New York NL
132 Casey Stengel 100.00 200.00
Phila. NL
133 Riggs Stephenson 40.00 80.00
134 Milt Stock 25.00 50.00
135 Amos Strunk (2) 25.00 50.00
136 Zeb Terry 25.00 50.00
137 Pinch Thomas 25.00 50.00
138 Fred Toney (2) 25.00 50.00
139 Specs Torporcer 25.00 50.00
140 Lefty Tyler 25.00 50.00
141 Hippo Vaughn (2) 30.00 60.00
142 Bobby Veach (3) 40.00 80.00
143 Ossie Vitt 25.00 50.00
144 Frank Walker 40.00 80.00
145 Curt Walker 40.00 80.00
146 Bill Wambsganss (2) 30.00 60.00
147 Zack Wheat 50.00 100.00
148 Possum Whitted 25.00 50.00
149 Williams 40.00 80.00
Chicago AL *
150 Cy Williams 25.00 50.00
151 Ivy Wingo 25.00 50.00
152 Joe Wood 40.00 80.00
153 Ralph Young 25.00 50.00
154 Ross Youngs 100.00 200.00

1925-31 W590 Athletes

Issued over a period of years, this set (which measure approximately 1 3/8" by 2 1/2") features some of the leading athletes from the 1920's. The fronts have a B&W photo with the players name, position and team on the bottom for the baseball players and sport and additional short bio info on the other athletes. The backs are blank and as these cards are unnumbered we have sequenced them in alphabetical order within sport. They were initally issued in strips and panels and can often be found intact. A number of the baseball players were re-issued from year-to-year with updated team information.

1 Grover Cleveland Alexander 100.00 200.00
2 Dave Bancroft 40.00 80.00
3 Jess Barnes 20.00 40.00
4 Ray Blades 20.00 40.00
5 Ozzie Bluege 20.00 40.00
6A George Burns 25.00 50.00
NY NL
6B George Burns 25.00 50.00
Phi NL
6C George Burns 25.00 50.00
Cleveland
7 Max Carey 40.00 80.00
8 Jimmy Caveney 20.00 40.00
9 Ty Cobb 150.00 300.00
10 Eddie Collins 100.00 200.00
11 George Dauss 20.00 40.00
12 Red Faber 40.00 80.00
13 Frankie Frisch 60.00 120.00
14 Lou Gehrig 200.00 400.00
15 Sam Gray 20.00 40.00
16 Hank Gowdy 20.00 40.00
17 Charley Grimm 25.00 50.00
18 Bucky Harris 40.00 80.00
19A Rogers Hornsby St Louis 125.00 250.00
19B Rogers Hornsby Boston 125.00 250.00
20 Travis Jackson 40.00 80.00
21 Walter Johnson 125.00 250.00
22 George Kelly 25.00 50.00
23 Fred Lindstrom 40.00 80.00
24 Rabbit Maranville 40.00 80.00
25 Bob Meusel 30.00 60.00
26 Jack Quinn 25.00 50.00
27 Eppa Rixey 25.00 50.00
28 Ed Rommel 20.00 40.00
29 Babe Ruth 300.00 600.00
30 Heinie Sand 20.00 40.00
31 George Sissler UER 40.00 80.00
Sisler
32 Earl Smith 20.00 40.00
33 Tris Speaker 100.00 200.00
34 Roy Spencer 20.00 40.00
35 Milt Stock 20.00 40.00
36A Phil Todt 20.00 40.00
Phi AL
36B Phil Todt 20.00 40.00
Bos AL
37 Dazzy Vance 40.00 80.00
38 Zack Wheat 40.00 80.00
39A Ken Williams 25.00 50.00
St Louis AL
39B Ken Williams 25.00 50.00
Bos.AL
40A Ross Youngs 40.00 80.00
Right Fielder
40B Ross Youngs 40.00 80.00
Former Right Fielder

1921 W9316

1 Bobby Veach
2 Frank Baker
3 Wilbert Robinson MG
4 Tommy Griffith
5 Jimmie Johnston
6 Wally Schang
7 Leon Cadore
8 George Sisler
9 Ray Schalk
10 Jesse Barnes

2016 Wacky Packages MLB

COMPLETE SET (90) 8.00 20.00
UNOPENED BOX (24 PACKS)
UNOPENED PACK (10 STICKERS)
COMMON CARD (1-90) .20 .50
*GRASS: .6X TO 1.5X BASIC CARDS
*SEPIA: 1.5X TO 4X BASIC CARDS
*SILVER: 2.5X TO 6X BASIC CARDS
*BASEBALL LACE: X TO X BASIC CARDS
*BLACK LUDLOW: X TO X BASIC CARDS
*GREEN LUDLOW/50: X TO X BASIC CARDS
*GOLD/25: X TO X BASIC CARDS
*LUMBER/15: UNPRICED DUE TO SCARCITY
*RED LUDLOW/10: UNPRICED DUE TO SCARCITY
*LEATHER/3: UNPRICED DUE TO SCARCITY
*P.P.BLACK/1: UNPRICED DUE TO SCARCITY
*P.P.CYAN/1: UNPRICED DUE TO SCARCITY
*P.P.MAGENTA/1: UNPRICED DUE TO SCARCITY
*P.P.YELLOW/1: UNPRICED DUE TO SCARCITY

1963 Wagner Otto Milk Carton

This is the only baseball player featured in this set which honored promiment Western Pennsylvanians. The side panel of the milk carton inlcuded a drawing of Wagner as well as some brief biographical informaion as well as a biography.

1 Honus Wagner 40.00 80.00

1995 Wagner T-206 Reprint IMT

This one card reprint was issued as part of the promotion which celebrated the contest in which one very lucky collector could win a real T206 Wagner. This card resembles the original but has the information about who the producer is as well as who allowed the usage of Wagner's picture on the card.

1 Honus Wagner .40 1.00

1924 Walter Mails WG7

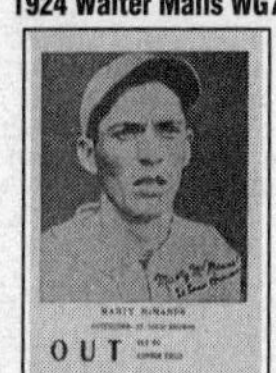

These cards were distributed as part of a baseball game produced in 1924. The cards each measure approximately 2 5/16" by 3 1/4" and have rounded corners. The card fronts show a black and white photo of the player, his name, position, his team, and the game outcome associated with that particular card. The card backs are all the same, each showing an ornate red and white design with "Walter Mails" inside a red circle in the middle all surrounded by a thin white outer border. Since the cards are unnumbered, they are listed below in alphabetical order.

COMPLETE SET 1800.00 3500.00
1 Buzz Arlett 50.00 100.00
2 Jim Bagby 50.00 100.00
3 Dave Bancroft 125.00 250.00
4 Johnny Bassler 50.00 100.00
Sic, Basseler
5 Jack Bentley 50.00 100.00
6 Rube Benton 50.00 100.00
7 George Burns 50.00 100.00
8 Joe Bush 50.00 100.00
9 Harold P. Chavez 50.00 100.00
10 Hugh Critz 50.00 100.00
11 Jake Daubert 100.00 200.00
12 Wheezer Dell 50.00 100.00
13 Joe Dugan 75.00 150.00
14 Pat Duncan 50.00 100.00
15 Howard Ehmke 50.00 100.00
16 Lew Fonseca 50.00 100.00
17 Ray French 50.00 100.00
18 Ed Gharity 50.00 100.00
Sic, Gharitty
19 Heinie Groh 75.00 150.00
20 George Grove 50.00 100.00
21 Bubbles Hargrave 50.00 100.00
22 Elmer Jacobs 50.00 100.00
23 Walter Johnson 500.00 1000.00
24 Duke Kenworthy 50.00 100.00
25 Harry Krause 50.00 100.00
26 Ray Kremer 50.00 100.00
27 Walter Mails 50.00 100.00
28 Rabbit Maranville 125.00 250.00
29 Stuffy McInnis 75.00 150.00
30 Marty McManus 50.00 100.00
31 Bob Meusel 100.00 200.00
32 Hack Miller 50.00 100.00
33 Pat J. Moran 75.00 150.00
34 Guy Morton 50.00 100.00
35 Johnny Mostil 50.00 100.00
36 Red Murphy 50.00 100.00
37 Jimmy O'Connell 50.00 100.00
38 Joe Oeschger 50.00 100.00
39 Steve O'Neil 75.00 150.00
40 Roger Peckinpaugh 75.00 150.00
41 Babe Pinelli 50.00 100.00
42 Wally Pipp 100.00 200.00
43 Elmer Ponder 50.00 100.00
44 Sam Rice 125.00 250.00
45 Ed Rommell 50.00 100.00
46 Walter Schmidt 50.00 100.00
47 Joe Sewell 125.00 250.00
48 Pat Shea 50.00 100.00
49 Wilford Shupe 50.00 100.00
50 Paddy Siglin 50.00 100.00
51 George Sisler 150.00 300.00
52 Bill Skiff 50.00 100.00
53 Jack Smith 50.00 100.00
54 Suds Sutherland 50.00 100.00
55 Cotton Tierney 50.00 100.00
56 George Uhle 50.00 100.00

1910 Washington Times

This very rare and obscure issue was apparently a supplement for the Washington Times newspaper. The cards measure approximately 2 1/2" by 3 1/2" and feature black-and-white player photos with blank backs. The cards are unnumbered and checklisted below in alphabetical order. The Walter Johnson card is rumored as being in the set. The checklist is probably incomplete and any confirmed additions are welcomed.

1 Ty Cobb 5000.00 10000.00
2 Eddie Collins 1500.00 3000.00
3 Wid Conroy 500.00 1000.00
4 Sam Crawford 1500.00 3000.00
5 Walter Johnson 2500.00 5000.00
6 Nap Lajoie 1500.00 3000.00
7 George McBride 500.00 1000.00
8 Clyde Milan 600.00 1200.00
9 Frank Oberlin 500.00 1000.00
10 Jack O'Connor 500.00 1000.00
11 Gabby Street 500.00 1000.00
12 Lee Tannehill 500.00 1000.00
13 Bob Unglaub 500.00 1000.00
14 Dixie Walker 500.00 1000.00
15 Ed Walsh 1000.00 2000.00
16 Joe Wood 750.00 1500.00
17 Cy Young 2500.00 5000.00

1987 Weis Market Discs

These discs are a parallel issue to the 1987 MSA Iced Tea Discs. They say Weis on the front and are valued the same as the MSA Discs.

COMPLETE SET (20) 3.00 8.00
1 Darryl Strawberry .07 .20
2 Roger Clemens .60 1.50
3 Ron Darling .02 .10
4 Keith Hernandez .07 .20
5 Tony Pena .02 .10
6 Don Mattingly .60 1.50
7 Eric Davis .07 .20
8 Gary Carter .30 .75
9 Dave Winfield .30 .75
10 Wally Joyner .25 .60
11 Mike Schmidt .30 .75
12 Robby Thompson .02 .10
13 Wade Boggs .30 .75
14 Cal Ripken 1.25 3.00
15 Dale Murphy .15 .40
16 Tony Gwynn .60 1.50
17 Jose Canseco .30 .75
18 Rickey Henderson .30 1.00
19 Lance Parrish .02 .10
20 Dave Righetti .02 .10

1988 Weis Market Discs

For the second year, Weis Markets was one of the distributors of these MSA Baseball Superstar Discs. These discs are valued the same as the MSA Iced Tea Discs.

COMPLETE SET (20) 4.00 10.00
1 Wade Boggs .40 1.00
2 Ellis Burks .40 1.00
3 Don Mattingly .75 2.00
4 Mark McGwire .75 2.00
5 Matt Nokes .02 .10
6 Kirby Puckett .50 1.25
7 Billy Ripken .02 .10
8 Kevin Seitzer .02 .10
9 Roger Clemens .75 2.00
10 Will Clark .30 .75
11 Vince Coleman .02 .10
12 Eric Davis .08 .25
13 Dave Magadan .02 .10
14 Dale Murphy .20 .50
15 Benito Santiago .08 .25
16 Mike Schmidt .30 1.00
17 Darryl Strawberry .08 .25
18 Steve Bedrosian .02 .10
19 Dwight Gooden .08 .25
20 Fernando Valenzuela .08 .25

1989 Weis Market Discs

For the third year, the MSA Iced Tea Discs were issued under the Weis Market name. They are valued the same as the regular MSA Iced Tea Discs.

COMPLETE SET (20) 12.50 30.00
1 Don Mattingly 2.50 6.00
2 Dave Cone .40 1.00
(David)
3 Mark McGwire 2.50 6.00
4 Will Clark 1.00 2.50
5 Darryl Strawberry .60 1.50
6 Dwight Gooden .60 1.50
7 Wade Boggs 1.50 4.00
8 Roger Clemens 2.50 6.00
9 Benito Santiago .60 1.50
10 Orel Hershiser .60 1.50
11 Eric Davis .60 1.50
12 Kirby Puckett 1.50 4.00
13 Dave Winfield 1.25 3.00
14 Andre Dawson 1.00 2.50
15 Steve Bedrosian .40 1.00
16 Cal Ripken 5.00 12.00
17 Andy Van Slyke .40 1.00
18 Jose Canseco 1.25 3.00
19 Jose Oquendo .40 1.00
20 Dale Murphy .75 2.00

1888 WG1 Card Game

These cards were distributed as part of a baseball game. The cards each measure approximately 2 1/2" by 3 1/2" and have rounded corners. The card fronts show a color drawing of the player, his name, his position, and the game outcome associated with that particular card. The card backs are all the same, each showing a geometric graphic design in blue. Since the cards are unnumbered, they are listed below in alphabetical order within each of the eight teams. The box features a photo of King Kelly on the front along with the words, "Patented Feb. 28, 1888".

COMPLETE SET (72) 25000.00 50000.00
1 Tom Brown 300.00 600.00
2 John Clarkson 750.00 1500.00
3 Joe Hornung 300.00 600.00
4 Dick Johnston 300.00 600.00
5 King Kelly 1250.00 2500.00
6 John Morrill 300.00 600.00
7 Billy Nash 300.00 600.00
8 Ezra Sutton 300.00 600.00
9 Sam Wise 300.00 600.00
10 Cap Anson 2500.00 5000.00
11 Tom Burns 300.00 600.00
12 Silver Flint 300.00 600.00
13 Bob Pettit 300.00 600.00
14 Fred Pfeffer 300.00 600.00
15 Jimmy Ryan 300.00 600.00
16 Marty Sullivan 600.00 1200.00
17 George Van Haltren 300.00 600.00
18 Ned Williamson 400.00 800.00
19 Charlie Bennett 400.00 800.00
20 Dan Brouthers 1000.00 2000.00
21 Charlie Getzein 300.00 600.00
22 Ned Hanlon 600.00 1200.00
23 Hardy Richardson 300.00 600.00
24 Jack Rowet 300.00 600.00
25 Sam Thompson 600.00 1200.00
26 Larry Twitchell 300.00 600.00
27 Deacon White 400.00 800.00
28 Charley Bassett 300.00 600.00
29 Henry Boyle 300.00 600.00
30 Jerry Denny 300.00 600.00
31 Dude Esterbrook 300.00 600.00
32 Jack Glasscock 600.00 1200.00
33 Paul Hines 300.00 600.00
34 George Meyers 300.00 600.00
35 Emmett Seery 300.00 600.00
36 Jumbo Shoeneck 300.00 600.00
37 Roger Connor 600.00 1200.00
38 Buck Ewing 1000.00 2000.00
39 Elmer Foster 300.00 600.00
40 George Gore 300.00 600.00
41 Tim Keefe 600.00 1200.00
42 Jim O'Rourke 600.00 1200.00
43 Danny Richardson 300.00 600.00
44 Mike Tiernan 300.00 600.00
45 John Ward 1000.00 2000.00
46 Ed Andrews 300.00 600.00
47 Charlie Bastian 300.00 600.00
48 Don Casey 300.00 600.00
49 Jack Clements 300.00 600.00
50 Sid Farrar 400.00 800.00
51 Jim Fogarty 300.00 600.00
52 Arthur Irwin 300.00 600.00
53 Joe Mulvey 300.00 600.00
54 George Wood 300.00 600.00
55 Fred Carroll 300.00 600.00
56 John Coleman 300.00 600.00
57 Abner Dalrymple 300.00 600.00
58 Fred Dunlap 300.00 600.00
59 Pud Galvin 600.00 1200.00
60 Willie Kuehne 300.00 600.00
61 Al Maul 300.00 600.00
62 Pop Smith 300.00 600.00
63 Billy Sunday 600.00 1200.00
64 Jim Donelly 300.00 600.00
65 Dummy Hoy 600.00 1200.00
66 John Irwin 300.00 600.00
67 Connie Mack 1500.00 3000.00
68 Al Myers 300.00 600.00
69 Billy O'Brien 300.00 600.00
70 George Shoch 300.00 600.00
71 Jim Whitney 300.00 600.00
72 Walt Wilmot 300.00 600.00

1935 Wheaties BB1

This set is referred to as "Fancy Frame with Script Signature". These cards (which made up the back of the Wheaties cereal box) measure 6" by 6 1/4" with the frame and about 5" by 5 1/2" if the frame is trimmed off. The player photo appears in blue on a blue-tinted field with a solid orange background behind the player. The player's facsimile autograph is displayed at the bottom of the card.

COMPLETE SET (27) 750.00 1500.00
1 Jack Armstrong 15.00 30.00
batting pose
fictional character
2 Jack Armstrong 15.00 30.00
throwing
your friend
fictional character
3 Wally Berger 15.00 30.00
batting follow
through
Sincerely Yours
4 Tommy Bridges 15.00 30.00
pitching
5A Mickey Cochrane 30.00 60.00
squatting wearing
black hat and uniform
with stripes
5B Mickey Cochrane 100.00 200.00
squatting wearing
white hat and uniform
with no stripes
6 James Rip Collins 15.00 30.00
jumping
7 Dizzy Dean 60.00 120.00
pitching follow
through
8 Dizzy Dean and 40.00 80.00
Paul Dean
squatting
9 Paul Dean 20.00 40.00
pitching
10 William Delancey 15.00 30.00
catching
11 Jimmie Foxx 50.00 100.00
facing camera
knee up
12 Frank Frisch 30.00 60.00
stooping to field
13 Lou Gehrig 200.00 400.00
batting follow
through
14 Goose Goslin 30.00 60.00
batting
15 Lefty Grove 50.00 100.00
holding trophy
16 Carl Hubbell 30.00 60.00
pitching
17 Travis C. Jackson 20.00 40.00
stooping to field
18 Chuck Klein 30.00 60.00
with four bats
19 Gus Mancuso 15.00 30.00
catching
20A Pepper Martin 15.00 30.00
batting
20B Pepper Martin 15.00 30.00
portrait
Sincerely Yours
21 Joe Medwick 30.00 60.00
batting follow
through
22 Mel Ott 50.00 100.00
batting follow
through
23 Harold Schumacher 15.00 30.00
pitching
24 Al Simmons 30.00 60.00
batting follow
through
Sincerely Yours
25 Jo Jo White 15.00 30.00
batting follow
through

1936 Wheaties BB3

This set is referred to as "Fancy Frame with Printed Name and Data." These cards (which made up the back of the Wheaties cereal box) measure 6" by 6 1/4" with the frame and about 5" by 5 1/2" if the frame is trimmed off. This set is distinguished from BB1 (above) in that this set also shows the player's name and some fact about him. The player's facsimile autograph is displayed at the bottom of the card. In the checklist below, the first few words of the printed data found on the card is also provided.

COMPLETE SET (12) 350.00 700.00
1 Earl Averill 25.00 50.00
batting
Star Outfielder
2 Mickey Cochrane 40.00 80.00
catching
Manager World
Champion Detroit
3 Jimmie Foxx 50.00 100.00
batting
All Around Star
4 Lou Gehrig 150.00 300.00
stooping to field
Iron Man
5 Hank Greenberg 40.00 80.00
jumping
Home Run Champion
6 Gabby Hartnett 30.00 60.00
squatting
Catcher Voted
Most Valuable
7 Carl Hubbell 30.00 60.00
ready to throw
Star Pitcher
8 Pepper Martin 15.00 30.00
jumping
Heavy Hitter
9 Van L. Mungo 15.00 30.00
pitching
Star Pitcher
10 Buck Newsom 15.00 30.00
pitching
Star Pitcher
11 Arky Vaughan 25.00 50.00
batting
Batting Champion
12 Jimmy Wilson 15.00 30.00
squatting
Manager and
Star Catcher

1936 Wheaties BB4

This set is refered to as the "Thin Orange Border / Figures in Border." These unnumbered cards (which made up the back of the Wheaties cereal box) mwasure 6" by 8 1/2". The set is the first in this larger size. The figures in the border include drawings of men and women competing baseball, football, hockey, track, golf, tennis, skiing and swimming. A train and an airplane also appear. The rectangular photo of the player appears in a box above an endorsment for Wheaties. The player's name is in script below the endorsment, A printed name, team and other information is near the top in the solid orange background.

COMPLETE SET (12) 300.00 600.00
1 Curt Davis 15.00 30.00
Philadelphia Phillies
2 Lou Gehrig 150.00 300.00
New York Yankees
3 Charlie Gehringer 30.00 60.00
Detroit Tigers
4 Lefty Grove 40.00 80.00
Boston Red Sox
5 Rollie Hemsley 15.00 30.00
St. Louis Browns
6 Billy Herman 25.00 50.00
Chicago Cubs
7 Joe Medwick 30.00 60.00
St. Louis Cardinals
8 Mel Ott 40.00 80.00
New York Giants
9 Schoolboy Rowe 15.00 30.00
Detroit Tigers
10 Arky Vaughan 25.00 50.00
Detroit Tigers
11 Joe Vosmik 15.00 30.00
Cleveland Indians
12 Lon Warneke 15.00 30.00
Chicago Cubs

1936 Wheaties BB5

This set is referred to as "How to Play Winning Baseball." These cards, which made up the back of the Wheaties box. measure 6" X 8 1/2" These panels combine a photo of the player with a series of blue and white drawings illustrating playing instructions. All of the players are shown in full length poses, except Earl Averill, who is pictured to the thighs. The players appear against a solid orange background. In addition to the numbers 1 thru 12, these panels are also found with a small number 28 combined with captial letters "A" thru "L." However, panels are know without these letter-number combinations. This set is sometimes refered to as the "28 Series."

COMPLETE SET (13) 250.00 500.00
1 Lefty Gomez 25.00 50.00
2 Billy Herman 20.00 40.00
3 Luke Appling 20.00 40.00
4 Jimmie Foxx 30.00 60.00
5 Joe Medwick 25.00 50.00
6 Charlie Gehringer 30.00 60.00
7A Mel Ott (large figure) 30.00 60.00
7B Mel Ott (small figure) 30.00 60.00
8 Odell Hale 15.00 30.00
9 Bill Dickey 30.00 60.00
10 Lefty Grove 30.00 60.00
11 Carl Hubbell 25.00 50.00
12 Earl Averill 20.00 40.00

1937 Wheaties BB6

This set is refered to as "How to Star in Baseball." These numbered cards, which made up the back of the cereal box, measure 6" X 8 1/4". This series is very similar to BB5. Both are instructional series' and the text and drawings used to illuatrate the tips are similar and in some cases identical. Each panel is a full length photo, The players name, team and script signature also appears on the card.

COMPLETE SET (12) 350.00 700.00
1 Bill Dickey 40.00 80.00
How to Catch
2 Red Ruffing 25.00 50.00
Pitching the
Fast Ball
3 Zeke Bonura 15.00 30.00
First Base - Make
More Outs
4 Charlie Gehringer/Second Base as the 40.00 80.00
Stars Pla
5 Arky Vaughan 25.00 50.00
Shortstop, Play
It Right
6 Carl Hubbell 30.00 60.00
Pitching the
Slow Ball
7 John Lewis 15.00 30.00
Third Base, Field
Those Hot Ones
8 Heinie Manush 25.00 50.00
Fielding for
Extra Outs
9 Lefty Grove 40.00 80.00
Pitching the
Outdrop Ball
10 Billy Herman 25.00 50.00
How to Score/(baserunning)
11 Joe DiMaggio 150.00 300.00
Bat Like a
Home Run King
12 Joe Medwick 25.00 50.00
Batting for
Extra Bases

1937 Wheaties BB7

This set is refered to as the "29 Series" These numbered cards which make up the back of the box measure 6" X 8 1/4". The players name, position, team and some information about him are printed near the top. His signature appears on the lower part of the panel near a printed endorsment for the cereal. This set contains several different card designs. One design shows the player outlined aganist an orange (nearly red) background. A two or three line endorsment is at the bottom. DiMaggio, Bonura and Bridges appear in this form. Another design shows a player against a solid white background , but the panel is rimmed by a red, white and blue border. Players shown in this fashion are Moore, Radcliff and Martin. A third style offers a panel with an orange border and a large orange circle behind the player. The rest of the background is white. Lombardi, Travis and Mungo appear in this design. The final style is a titled, orange background picture of the player with white and blue framing the photo. Trosky, Demaree and Vaughan show up in this design. The set also has three known Pacific Coast League players. One number, 29N, which could be a PCL player, is unknown.

COMPLETE SET (15) 400.00 800.00
29A Zeke Bonura/(batting) 15.00 30.00
29B Cecil Travis/(reaching left) 15.00 30.00
29C Frank Demaree/(batting) 15.00 30.00
29D Joe Moore/(batting) 15.00 30.00
29E Ernie Lombardi/(crouch) 25.00 50.00
29F Pepper Martin/(reaching) 15.00 30.00
29G Harold Trosky/(batting) 15.00 30.00
29H Ray Radcliff/(batting) 15.00 30.00
29I Joe DiMaggio/(batting) 150.00 300.00
29J Tommy Bridges/(hands over head) 15.00 30.00
29K Van L. Mungo/(pitching) 15.00 30.00
29L Arky Vaughan/(batting) 25.00 50.00
29M Arnold Statz (PCL) 60.00 120.00
29N Unknown
29O Fred Muller (PCL) 60.00 120.00
29P Gene Lillard (PCL) 60.00 120.00

1937 Wheaties BB8

This set is refered to as the "Speckled Orange, White and Blue Series." These unnumbered cards which made up the back of the Wheaties box measure 6" X 8 1/2". The set contains several different card designs. One design (DiMaggio and Feller) shows the player surrounded by orange spreckles on a white backgroung with a group of four blue and white drawings of players in action along the panel's right side. Another design shows the panel divided into four rectangles -- white at upper right and lower left and orange on the other two. -- with the players (Appling and Averill) leaping to catch the ball. Blue circles surrounded by orange and white speckles appear on the pictures of Hubbel and Grove. Medwick and Gehringer appear on white panels with a cloud of orange speckles behind them. The player's name in script style appears along with printed data about his 1936 season and a brief endorsement for the cereal.

COMPLETE SET (8) 450.00 900.00
1 Luke Appling/(reaching) 30.00 60.00
2 Earl Averill/(reaching) 30.00 60.00
3 Joe DiMaggio/(batting) 250.00 500.00
4 Bob Feller/(throwing) 75.00 150.00
5 Charlie Gehringer/(batting) 60.00 120.00
6 Lefty Grove/(throwing) 60.00 120.00
7 Carl Hubbell/(throwing) 60.00 120.00
8 Joe Medwick/(fielding) 30.00 60.00

1937 Wheaties BB9

This set is refered to as the "Color Series." These unnumbered cards measure 6" X 8 1/2" Photos of the players appear in circles. "V" shapes and rectangles, and stars among others. A player from every major League team is included. The player's name is in script with the team name below. The name , endorsment and player's 1936 highlights are printed near the bottom. John Moore and Harland Cliff have been reported on paper stock. Whether they were part of a store display is unknown.

COMPLETE SET (16) 400.00 800.00
1 Zeke Bonura 15.00 30.00
Chicago White Sox
fielding crossed
bats glove ball
at upper left
2 Tom Bridges 15.00 30.00
Detroit Tigers
pitching figure in
large orange circle
3 Harland Clift 15.00 30.00
St. Louis Browns
batting large
baseball behind him
4 Kiki Cuyler 25.00 50.00
Cincinnati Reds
batting on
green background
5 Joe DiMaggio 150.00 300.00
New York Yankees
leaping green and
white circle behind
6 Bob Feller 50.00 100.00
Cleveland Indians
pitching blue
circle on left knee
7 Lefty Grove 40.00 80.00
Boston Red Sox
pitching red
orange home plate
8 Billy Herman 25.00 50.00
Chicago Cubs
throwing yellow
star behind him
9 Carl Hubbell 30.00 60.00
New York Giants
pitching orange
yellow V's behind
10 Buck Jordan 15.00 30.00
Boston Bees
batting dark orange
rectangle blue sides
11 Pepper Martin 20.00 40.00
St. Louis Cardinals
reaching orange
rectangle
12 John Moore 15.00 30.00
Philadelphia Phillies
batting blue
background stands
on green
13 Wally Moses 15.00 30.00
Philadelphia A's
leaping dark orange
background yellow
and blue
14 Van L. Mungo 20.00 40.00
Brooklyn Dodgers
pitching green
background orange
and blue
15 Cecil Travis 15.00 30.00
Washington Senators
batting orange
lightning
16 Arky Vaughan 25.00 50.00
Pittsburgh Pirates
batting blue
diamond green frame

1937 Wheaties BB14

This set is referred to as the "Small Panels with Orange Background Series." These numbered (and unnumbered) cards, which made up the back of the Wheaties individual serving cereal box, measure about 2 5/8" by 3 7/8". These small panels have orange backgrounds and some, but not all, use poses that appear in some of the regular sized panels. Joe DiMaggio, for example, is the same pose as in the large Wheaties BB7 set and the Mel Ott is similar to the BB5 pose, but cropped a little differently. Some panels have been seen with and without the number 29 in combination with a letter, so apparently there were several printings. The player's name is in all capitals with his position and team in smaller caps. A printed block of data about him is on the main part of the card with a Wheaties endorsement in a white strip at the bottom.

COMPLETE SET (17) 700.00 1400.00
1 Zeke Bonura 29A 40.00 80.00
Led all A.L.
First Basemen
BB7 pose
2 Tommy Bridges 29J 40.00 80.00
Struck Out Most
Batters 173 ...
not BB7 pose
3 Dolph Camilli 50.00 100.00
Most Put Outs
1446 ...
unnumbered
4 Frank Demaree 40.00 80.00
5 Joe DiMaggio 29I 250.00 500.00
Outstanding
Rookie 1936 ...
BB7 pose
6 Billy Herman 60.00 120.00
Lifetime .300
Hitter ...
unnumbered
7 Carl Hubbell 100.00 200.00
Won Most Games
26 ...
unnumbered
8 Ernie Lombardi 60.00 120.00
9 Pepper Martin 50.00 100.00
10 Joe Moore 40.00 80.00
11 Van L. Mungo 50.00 100.00
12 Mel Ott 100.00 200.00
13 Raymond Radcliff 29H 40.00 80.00
most one-base hits
BB7 pose
14 Cecil Travis 29B 40.00 80.00
One of the Leading
Bats in ...
BB7 pose
15 Harold Trosky 40.00 80.00
16A Arky Vaughan 75.00 150.00
unnumbered
16B Arky Vaughan 29L 75.00 150.00
Lifetime .300
Hitter who ...
BB7 pose

1938 Wheaties BB10

This set is refered to as the "Biggest Thrills in Baseball." These numbered cards which make up the back of the cereal box measure 6" X 8 1/2." A player from every Major League team is included. Each panel describes the player's greatest thrill playing the game. The thrill is announced in large banner headline type and described in a block of copy over the players script signature, His team name and position are printed below the name. All sixteen are known to exist on both paper stock as well as heavy cardboard.

COMPLETE SET (16) 500.00 1000.00
1 Bob Feller 75.00 150.00
Cleveland Indians/(Two Hits in One
I
2 Cecil Travis 20.00 50.00
Washington Nationals/(Clicks in Fir
3 Joe Medwick 40.00 80.00
St. Louis Cardinals/(Goes on Batting
4 Gerald Walker 20.00 50.00
Chicago White Sox/(World Series Ga
5 Carl Hubbell 50.00 100.00
New York Giants/(Strikes Out
Murde
6 Bob Johnson 20.00 50.00
Philadelphia A's/(Setting New
A.L.
7 Beau Bell 20.00 50.00
St. Louis Browns/(Smacks First Major/
8 Ernie Lombardi 30.00 60.00
Cincinnati Reds/(Sold to Majors)
9 Lefty Grove 60.00 120.00
Boston Red Sox/(Fans Babe Ruth)
10 Lou Fette 20.00 50.00
Boston Bees/(Wins 20 Games)
11 Joe DiMaggio 200.00 400.00
New York Yankees/(Home Run King Get
12 Pinky Whitney 20.00 50.00
Philadelphia Phillies/(Hits Three
13 Dizzy Dean 60.00 120.00
Chicago Cubs/(11-0 Victory
Clinches
14 Charlie Gehringer 50.00 100.00
Detroit Tigers/(Homers Off
Di
15 Paul Waner 40.00 80.00
Pittsburgh Pirates/(Four Perfect Sixe
16 Dolph Camilli 30.00 60.00

1938 Wheaties BB11

This set is refered to as the "Dress Clothes or Civies Series." The cards are unnumbered and measure 6" 8 1/4" The panels feature the players and their friends in blue photos. The remainder of the panel uses the traditional orange, blue and white Wheaties colors.

COMPLETE SET (8) 150.00 300.00
1 Lou Fette/(pouring milk 15.00 30.00
over his Wheaties)
2 Jimmie Foxx/(slices banana for 30.00 60.00
his son's Wheatie
3 Charlie Gehringer/(and his young fan) 25.00 50.00
4 Lefty Grove/(watches waitress 25.00 50.00
pour Wheaties)
5 Hank Greenberg 30.00 60.00
and Roxie Lawson/(eat breakfast)
6 Ernie Lombardi 15.00 30.00
and Lee Grissom/(prepare to eat)
7 Joe Medwick/(pours milk 20.00 40.00
over cereal)
8 Lon Warneke/(smiles in anticip- 15.00 30.00
ation of Wheatie

1938 Wheaties BB15

This set is referred to as the "Small Panels with Orange, Blue and White Background Series." These numbered (and unnumbered) cards, which made up the back of the Wheaties individual serving cereal box, measure about 2 5/8" by 3 7/8". These small panels have orange, blue and white backgrounds and some, but not all, use poses that appear in some of the regular, larger-sized panels. Greenberg and Lewis are featured with a horizontal (HOR) pose.

COMPLETE SET (11) 500.00 1000.00
1 Zeke Bonura/(batted .345) 25.00 50.00
2 Joe DiMaggio/(46 home runs) 200.00 400.00
3A Charlie Gehringer (Leaping) 50.00 100.00
3B Charlie Gehringer (batting) 50.00 100.00
4 Hank Greenberg HOR/(second in home 60.00120.00
runs)
5 Lefty Grove/(17-9 won-lost 60.00 120.00
record)
6 Carl Hubbell/(star pitcher,/1937 Giants) 50.00100.00
7 John (Buddy) Lewis/(batted .314) HOR 25.00 50.00
8 Heinie Manush/(batted .332) 40.00 80.00
9 Joe Medwick 40.00 80.00
10 Arky Vaughan 40.00 80.00

1939 Wheaties BB12

This set is referred to as the "Personal Pointers Series." These numbered cards measure 6" X 8 1/4'. The panels feature an instructional format similar to both the BB5 and BB6 Wheaties sets. Drawings again illustrate the tips on batting and pitching. The colors are orange, blue and white and the players appear in photographs.

COMPLETE SET (9) 250.00 500.00
1 Ernie Lombardi 30.00 60.00
How to Place Hits
For Scores
2 Johnny Allen 20.00 40.00
It's Windup That
Counts
3 Lefty Gomez 40.00 80.00
Delivery That
Keeps 'Em Guessing
4 Bill Lee 20.00 40.00
Follow Through
For Stops
5 Jimmie Foxx 50.00 100.00
Stance Helps
Sluggers
6 Joe Medwick 30.00 60.00
Power-Drive Grip
7 Hank Greenberg 50.00 100.00
Smooth Swing
8 Mel Ott 40.00 80.00
Study That
Pitcher
9 Arky Vaughan 30.00 60.00
Beat 'Em With
Bunts

1939 Wheaties BB13

This set is referred to as the "100 Years of Baseball or Baseball Centennial Series." These numbered cards which make up the back of the Wheaties box measure 6" X 6 3/4". Each panel has a drawing that depicts various aspects and events in baseball in the traditional orange, blue and white Wheaties colors.

COMPLETE SET (8) 100.00 200.00
1 Design of First 25.00 50.00
Diamond with
Picture of Abner
D
2 Lincoln Gets News 25.00 50.00
3 Crowd Boos First 15.00 30.00
Baseball Glove/(pictures of
gl
4 Curve Ball 15.00 30.00
5 Fencer's Mask 15.00 30.00
6 Baseball Gets Dressed Up 15.00 30.00
7 Modern Bludgeon 15.00 30.00
Enters Game/(pictures of
bats)
8 Casey at the Bat 25.00 50.00

1940 Wheaties M4

This set is referred to as the "Champs in the USA" The cards measure about 6" 8 1'4" and are numbered. The drawing portion (inside the dotted lines) measures approximately 6" X 6". There is a Baseball player on each card and they are joined by football players, football coaches, race car drivers, airline pilots, a circus clown, ice skater, hockey star and golfers. Each athlete appears in what looks like a stamp with a serrated edge. The stamps appear one above the other with a brief block of copy describing his or her achievements. There appears to have been three printings, resulting in some variation panels. The full panels tell the cereal buyer to look for either 27, 39, or 63 champ stamps. The first nine panels apparently were printed more than once, since all the unknown variations occur with those numbers.

COMPLETE SET (20) 400.00 800.00
1A R. Ruffing/B. Feller 40.00 80.00
1B R. Ruffing/L. Durocher 30.00 50.00
2A J. DiMaggio/H. Greenberg 100.00 200.00
2B J. DiMaggio/M. Ott 100.00 200.00
3 J. Foxx/B. Dickey 35.00 60.00
5 Joe Medwick 15.00 25.00
Matty Bell
Ab Jenkins
6A J. Mize/D. O'Brien/Ralph Guldahl
(27 stamp 15.00 25.00
6B Mize/Feller/York/(39 stamp series 40.00 80.00
6C G. Hartnett/D. O'Brien
Ralph Guldahl/(unk 15.00 25.00
7A J. Cronin/Byron Nelson/(27 stamp 15.00 25.00
7B J. Cronin/H. Greenberg 25.00 50.00
7C P. Derringer/Byron Nelson/(unkno 15.00 25.00
8A J. Manders/E. Lombardi
George I. Myers/(27 15.00 25.00
8B P. Derringer/E. Lombardi
George I. Myers/(15.00 25.00
10 A. Inge/B. Herman 15.00 25.00
11 Dolph Camilli 15.00 25.00
Antoinette Concello
Wallace Wade
12 L. Appling/S. Hack 15.00 25.00
13 F. Adler/H. Trosky/Mabel Vinson 15.00 25.00

1941 Wheaties M5

This set is also referred to as "Champs of the U.S.A." These numbered cards made up the back of the Wheaties box; the whole panel measures 6" X 8 1/4" but the drawing portion (inside the dotted lines) is apparently 6" X 6". Each athlete appears in what looks like a stamp with a serrated edge. The stamps appear one above the other with a brief block of copy describing his or her achievements. The format is the same as the previous M4 set -- even the numbering system continues where the M4 set stops.

COMPLETE SET (8) 175.00 350.00
14 Jimmie Foxx 25.00 50.00
Felix Adler
Capt. R.G. Hanson
15 B. Bierman/B. Feller/Jessie McLeod 20.00 40.00
16 Hank Greenberg 20.00 40.00
Lowell Red Dawson
J.W. Stoker
17 J. DiMaggio/B. Nelson
Antoniette Concello 100.00 200.00
18 Pee Wee Reese 25.00 50.00
20 B. Walters/Barney McCosky 12.50 25.00
21 J. Gordon/S. Hack 12.50 25.00

1951 Wheaties

The cards in this six-card set measure approximately 2 1/2" by 3 1/4". Cards of the 1951 Wheaties set are actually the backs of small individual boxes of Wheaties. The cards are waxed and depict three baseball players, one football player, one basketball player, and one golfer. They are occasionally found as complete boxes, which are worth 50 percent more than the prices listed below. The catalog designation for this set is F272-3. The cards are blank-backed and unnumbered; they are numbered below in alphabetical order for convenience.

COMPLETE SET (6) 300.00 600.00
1 Bob Feller 40.00 80.00
4 Stan Musial 60.00 120.00
6 Ted Williams 75.00 150.00

1952 Wheaties

The cards in this 60-card set measure 2" by 2 3/4". The 1952 Wheaties set of orange, blue and white, unnumbered cards was issued in panels of eight or ten cards on the backs of Wheaties cereal boxes. Each player appears in an action pose, designated in the checklist with an "A", and as a portrait, listed in the checklist with a "B". The catalog designation is F272-4. The cards are blank-backed and unnumbered, but have been assigned numbers below using a sport prefix (BB- baseball, BK- basketball, FB- football, G-Golf, OT- other).

COMPLETE SET (60) 600.00 1000.00
BB1A Yogi Berra 20.00 40.00
Action
BB1B Yogi Berra 20.00 40.00
Portrait
BB2A Roy Campanella 25.00 50.00
Action
BB2B Roy Campanella 25.00 50.00
Portrait
BB3A Bob Feller 20.00 40.00
Action
BB3B Bob Feller 20.00 40.00
Portrait
BB4A George Kell 12.50 25.00
Action
BB4B George Kell 12.50 25.00
Portrait
BB5A Ralph Kiner 12.50 25.00
Action
BB5B Ralph Kiner 12.50 25.00
Portrait
BB6A Bob Lemon 12.50 25.00
Action
BB6B Bob Lemon 12.50 25.00
Portrait
BB7A Stan Musial 40.00 80.00
Action
BB7B Stan Musial 40.00 80.00
Portrait
BB8A Phil Rizzuto 15.00 30.00
Action
BB8B Phil Rizzuto 15.00 30.00
Portrait
BB9A Preacher Roe 5.00 10.00
Action
BB9B Preacher Roe 5.00 10.00
Portrait
BB10A Ted Williams 50.00 100.00
Action
BB10B Ted Williams 50.00 100.00
Portrait

1964 Wheaties Stamps

In 1964 General Mills issued the Wheaties Major League All-Star Baseball Player Stamp Album. The album is orange, blue and white and measures approximately 8 3/8" by 11"; it contains 48 pages with places for one or two stamps per page. The individual stamps are in full color with a thick white border and measure approximately 2 9/16" by 2 3/4". The stamps are unnumbered so they listed below in alphabetical order.

COMPLETE SET (50) 250.00 500.00
1 Hank Aaron 20.00 50.00
2 Bob Allison 1.50 4.00
3 Luis Aparicio 5.00 12.00
4 Ed Bailey 1.50 4.00
5 Steve Barber 1.50 4.00
6 Earl Battey 1.50 4.00
7 Jim Bouton 1.50 4.00
8 Ken Boyer 2.00 5.00
9 Jim Bunning 5.00 12.00
10 Orlando Cepeda 5.00 12.00
11 Roberto Clemente 40.00 80.00
12 Ray Culp 1.50 4.00
13 Tommy Davis 1.50 4.00
14 John Edwards 1.50 4.00
15 Whitey Ford 8.00 20.00
16 Nelson Fox 5.00 12.00
17 Bob Friend 1.50 4.00
18 Jim Gilliam 2.00 5.00
19 Jim Grant 1.50 4.00
20 Dick Groat 1.50 4.00
21 Elston Howard 2.00 5.00
22 Larry Jackson 1.50 4.00
23 Julian Javier 1.50 4.00
24 Al Kaline 10.00 25.00
25 Harmon Killebrew 8.00 20.00
26 Don Leppert 1.50 4.00
27 Frank Malzone 1.50 4.00
28 Juan Marichal 6.00 15.00
29 Willie Mays 20.00 50.00
30 Ken McBride 1.50 4.00
31 Willie McCovey 6.00 15.00
32 Jim O'Toole 1.50 4.00
33 Albie Pearson 1.50 4.00
34 Joe Pepitone 1.50 4.00
35 Ron Perranoski 1.50 4.00
36 Juan Pizarro 1.50 4.00
37 Dick Radatz 1.50 4.00
38 Bobby Richardson 2.50 6.00
39 Brooks Robinson 10.00 25.00
40 Ron Santo 2.50 6.00
41 Norm Siebern 1.50 4.00
42 Duke Snider 10.00 25.00
43 Warren Spahn 10.00 25.00
44 Joe Torre 2.50 6.00
45 Tom Tresh 1.50 4.00
46 Zoilo Versalles 1.50 4.00
47 Leon Wagner 1.50 4.00
48 Bill White 1.50 4.00
49 Hal Woodeshick 1.50 4.00
50 Carl Yastrzemski 8.00 20.00

1907 White Sox George W. Hull

This 12 card set measures 3 1/2" by 5 1/2" and contains World Champion White Sox players only. Each postcard contains club president Charles Comiskey's picture in a circle on the lower left on the front; assorted White Sox players pictures in ovals on socks in a clothesline; and the subject player's picture on the right side of the card. The George W. Hall identification is also pictured on the front.

COMPLETE SET (12) 800.00 1600.00
1 Nick Altrock 300.00 600.00
2 George Davis 500.00 1000.00
3 Jiggs Donohue 250.00 500.00
4 Pat Dougherty 250.00 500.00
5 Eddie Hahn 250.00 500.00
6 Frank Isbell 250.00 500.00
7 Fielder Jones 250.00 500.00
8 Ed McFarland 250.00 500.00
9 Frank Owens 250.00 500.00
10 Ray Patterson 250.00 500.00
11 George Rohe 250.00 500.00
12 Frank Smith 250.00 500.00
13 Billy Sullivan 250.00 500.00
14 Lee Tannehill 250.00 500.00
15 Ed Walsh 500.00 1000.00
16 Doc White 250.00 500.00

1917 White Sox Team Issue

These cards which measure 1 3/4" by 2 3/4" were issued in a box labeled "Davis Printing Works". The fronts feature clear photos and glossy photographs. The cards are unnumbered and we have sequenced them in alphabetical order.

COMPLETE SET (25) 14000.00 28000.00
1 Charles Comiskey OWN 600.00 1200.00
2 Joe Benz 200.00 400.00
3 Eddie Cicotte 1000.00 2000.00
4 Eddie Collins 1000.00 2000.00
5 Shano Collins 200.00 400.00
6 Dave Danforth 200.00 400.00
7 Red Faber 600.00 1200.00
8 Happy Felsch 600.00 1200.00
9 Chick Gandil 600.00 1200.00
10 Kid Gleason CO 400.00 800.00
11 Joe Jackson 4000.00 8000.00
12 Joe Jenkins 200.00 400.00
13 Ted Jourdan 200.00 400.00
14 Nemo Leibold 200.00 400.00
15 Byrd Lynn 200.00 400.00
16 Fred McMullen 400.00 800.00
17 Eddie Murphy 200.00 400.00
18 Swede Risberg 400.00 800.00
19 Pants Rowland MG 200.00 400.00
20 Reb Russell 200.00 400.00
21 Ray Schalk 1000.00 2000.00
22 James Scott 200.00 400.00
23 Buck Weaver 1000.00 2000.00
24 Claude Williams 600.00 1200.00
25 Meldon Wolfgang 200.00 400.00

1930 White Sox Blue Ribbon Malt

In addition to the smaller photos which were cut out of the team panorama, Blue Ribbon Malt also issued larger sized photos of members of the 1930 Chicago White Sox. These photos measure approximately 5" by 7" and are attached to grey mounts in a similar fashion to the Cubs issue. This checklist is probably incomplete and any additions are welcome.

COMPLETE SET 30.00 60.00
1 Jimmie Burke 25.00 50.00
2 Donie Bush MG 25.00 50.00
3 Bill Cissell 25.00 50.00
4 Red Faber 50.00 100.00
5 Lew Fonseca 25.00 50.00
6 Vic Frasier 25.00 50.00
7 Smead Jolley 30.00 60.00
8 Willie Kamm 30.00 60.00
9 Ted Lyons 60.00 120.00
10 Carl Reynolds 25.00 50.00
11 Art Shires 25.00 50.00
12 Tommy Thomas 25.00 50.00
13 Hal Totten ANN 25.00 50.00
14 Johnny Watwood 25.00 50.00

1930 White Sox Team Issue

These cards, which measure between 1 7/16 to 2 7/8" by 3 1/2" are actually photos cut out of a 1930 White Sox Team Panorama, which originally measured 11" by 37", and was issued by Blue Ribbon Malt.

COMPLETE SET (27) 150.00 300.00
1 Chick Autry 7.50 15.00
2 Red Barnes 7.50 15.00
3 Moe Berg 20.00 40.00
4 Garland Braxton 7.50 15.00
5 Donie Bush MG 10.00 20.00
6 Pat Caraway 7.50 15.00
7 Bill Cissell 7.50 15.00
8 Bud Clancy 7.50 15.00
9 Clyde Crouse 7.50 15.00
10 Red Faber 20.00 40.00
11 Bob Fothergill 10.00 20.00
12 Dutch Henry 7.50 15.00
13 Smead Jolley 10.00 20.00
14 Willie Kamm 10.00 20.00
15 Mike Kelly 7.50 15.00
16 Johnny Kerr 7.50 15.00
17 Ted Lyons 20.00 40.00
18 Harold McKain 7.50 15.00
19 Jim Moore 7.50 15.00
20 Greg Mulleavy 7.50 15.00
21 Carl Reynolds 10.00 20.00
22 Blondy Ryan 7.50 15.00
23 Benny Tate 7.50 15.00
24 Tommy Thomas 7.50 15.00
25 Ed Walsh Jr. 10.00 20.00
26 Johnny Watwood 7.50 15.00
27 Bob Weiland 7.50 15.00

1939 White Sox Team Issue

These 23 photos measure approximately 5 1/4" by 6 3/4". They feature player photos and a fascimile autograph. The backs are blank and we have sequenced them in alphabetical order.

COMPLETE SET (23) 200.00 400.00
1 Pete Appleton 7.50 15.00
2 Luke Appling 25.00 50.00
3 Clint Brown 7.50 15.00
4 Bill Dietrich 7.50 15.00
5 Mule Haas 7.50 15.00
6 Jack Hayes 7.50 15.00
7 Bob Kennedy 7.50 15.00
8 Jack Knott 7.50 15.00
9 Mike Kreevich 7.50 15.00
10 Joe Kuhel 7.50 15.00
11 Thornton Lee 15.00 30.00
12 Ted Lyons 25.00 50.00
13 Eric McNair 7.50 15.00
14 John Rigney 7.50 15.00
15 Larry Rosenthal 7.50 15.00
16 Ken Silvestri 7.50 15.00
17 Eddie Smith 7.50 15.00
18 Moose Solters 7.50 15.00
19 Monty Stratton 15.00 30.00
20 Mike Tresh 7.50 15.00
21 Skeeter Webb 7.50 15.00
22 Ed Weiland 7.50 15.00
23 Taft Wright 7.50 15.00

1948 White Sox Team Issue

These 30 photos represent members of the 1948 Chicago White Sox. They measure approximately 6 1/2" by 9" are black and white and have blank backs. We have sequenced this set in alphabetical order.

COMPLETE SET (30) 200.00 400.00
1 Luke Appling 20.00 40.00
2 Floyd Baker 5.00 10.00
3 Fred Bradley 5.00 10.00
4 Earl Caldwell 5.00 10.00
5 Red Faber CO 15.00 30.00
6 Bob Gillespie 5.00 10.00
7 Jim Goodwin 5.00 10.00
8 Orval Grove 5.00 10.00
9 Earl Harrist 5.00 10.00
10 Joe Haynes 5.00 10.00
11 Ralph Hodgin 5.00 10.00
12 Howie Judson 5.00 10.00
13 Bob Kennedy 6.00 12.00
14 Don Kolloway 5.00 10.00
15 Tony Lupien 5.00 10.00
16 Ted Lyons MG 15.00 30.00
17 Cass Michaels 5.00 10.00
18 Bing Miller CO 5.00 10.00
19 Buster Mills CO 5.00 10.00
20 Glen Moulder 5.00 10.00
21 Frank Papish 5.00 10.00
22 Ike Pearson 5.00 10.00
23 Dave Philley 5.00 10.00
24 Aaron Robinson 5.00 10.00
25 Mike Tresh 5.00 10.00
26 Jack Wallaesa 5.00 10.00
27 Ralph Weigel 5.00 10.00
28 Bill Wight 5.00 10.00
29 Taft Wright 5.00 10.00
30 Team Photo 25.00 50.00

1958 White Sox Jay Publishing

This 12-card set of the Chicago White Sox measures approximately 5" by 7" and features black-and-white player photos in a white border. These cards were packaged 12 to a packet. The backs are blank. The cards are unnumbered and checklisted below in alphabetical order.

COMPLETE SET (12) 25.00 50.00
1 Luis Aparicio 5.00 10.00
2 Dick Donovan 1.50 3.00
3 Nelson Fox 5.00 10.00
4 Tito Francona 1.50 3.00
5 Bill Goodman 1.50 3.00
6 Sherman Lollar 1.50 3.00
7 Ray Moore 1.50 3.00
8 Billy Pierce 2.50 5.00
9 Jim Rivera 1.50 3.00
10 Al Smith 1.50 3.00
11 Jim Wilson 1.50 3.00
12 Early Wynn 5.00 10.00

1959 White Sox Jay Publishing

This 12-card set of the Chicago White Sox measures approximately 5" by 7" and features black-and-white player photos in a white border. These cards were packaged 12 to a packet. The backs are blank. The cards are unnumbered and checklisted below in alphabetical order.

COMPLETE SET 30.00 60.00
1 Luis Aparicio 5.00 10.00
2 Johnny Callison 3.00 6.00
3 Dick Donovan 1.50 3.00
4 Nellie Fox 5.00 10.00
5 Billy Goodman 2.00 4.00
6 Jim Landis 1.50 3.00
7 Sherm Lollar 1.50 3.00
8 Al Lopez MG 3.00 6.00
9 Bubba Phillips 1.50 3.00
10 Billy Pierce 3.00 6.00
11 Al Smith 1.50 3.00
12 Early Wynn 5.00 10.00

1960 White Sox Jay Publishing

This 12-card set of the Chicago White Sox measures approximately 5" by 7" and features black-and-white player photos in a white border. These cards were packaged 12 to a packet. The backs are blank. The cards are unnumbered and checklisted below in alphabetical order.

COMPLETE SET (12) 20.00 50.00
1 Luis Aparicio 4.00 10.00
2 Nelson Fox 4.00 10.00
3 Gene Freese .75 2.00
4 Ted Kluszewski 1.50 4.00
5 Jim Landis .75 2.00
6 Sherman Lollar .75 2.00
7 Al Lopez MG 1.50 4.00
8 Minnie Minoso 1.50 4.00
9 Bob Shaw .75 2.00
10 Roy Sievers 1.00 2.50
11 Al Smith .75 2.00
12 Early Wynn 4.00 10.00

1960 White Sox Ticket Stubs

This set was the brainchild of famed owner Bill Veeck. Player's photos were put on a ticket stub so they could be collected. The players marked UNC below in the checklist are unconfirmed at this time and may not exist. These tickets come in mulitple colors. No extra value is attached for any color.

COMPLETE SET 50.00 100.00
1 Luis Aparicio 3.00 8.00
2 Earl Battey UNC 1.50 4.00
3 Frank Baumann 1.50 4.00
4 Dick Donovan 1.50 4.00
5 Nelson Fox 6.00 15.00
6 Gene Freese 1.50 4.00
7 Billy Goodman UNC 1.50 4.00
8 Ted Kluzewski 3.00 8.00
9 Jim Landis 1.50 4.00
10 Barry Latman 1.50 4.00
11 Sherman Lollar 1.50 4.00
12 Al Lopez MG 2.50 6.00
13 Turk Lown 1.50 4.00
14 Minnie Minoso 3.00 8.00
15 Billy Pierce 2.50 6.00
16 Jim Rivera 1.50 4.00
17 Bob Shaw 1.50 4.00
18 Roy Sievers 2.00 5.00
19 Al Smith 1.50 4.00
20 Gerry Staley 1.50 4.00
21 Earl Torgeson UNC 1.50 4.00
22 Early Wynn 3.00 8.00

1961 White Sox Jay Publishing

This 12-card set of the Chicago White Sox measures approximately 5" by 7". The fronts feature black-and-white posed player photos with the player's and team name printed below in the white border. These cards were packaged 12 in a packet. The backs are blank. The cards are unnumbered and checklisted below in alphabetical order.

COMPLETE SET (12) 4.00 10.00

1 Luis Aparicio 2.00 5.00
2 Frank Baumann .60 1.50
3 Nellie Fox 2.00 5.00
4 Jim Landis .60 1.50
5 Al Lopez MG 1.25 3.00
6 Sherm Lollar .60 1.50
7 Minnie Minoso 1.25 3.00
8 Billy Pierce 1.00 2.50
9 Roy Sievers .75 2.00
10 Al Smith .60 1.50
11 Gerry Staley .60 1.50
12 Early Wynn 2.00 5.00

1961 White Sox Rainbow Orchard Laundry Cleaners

This Pizzaro card is assumed to be part of a 20 card set. When unfolded the card measures 19 1/2" by 2 1/2" and has the player's photo on it as well as the 1961 White Sox home schedule. Since it is assumed this is part of a set any additions to this checklist is appreciated.

9 Juan Pizzaro 20.00 50.00

1961 White Sox Ticket Stubs

For the second year, the White Sox placed player photos on ticket stubs to promote interest in their players.

COMPLETE SET 40.00 80.00
1 Luis Aparicio 2.50 6.00
2 Frank Baumann 1.25 3.00
3 Cam Carreon 1.25 3.00
4 Sam Esposito 1.25 3.00
5 Nelson Fox 4.00 10.00
6 Jim Landis 1.25 3.00
7 Sherm Lollar 1.25 3.00
8 Al Lopez MG 2.00 5.00
9 Cal McLish 1.25 3.00
10 J.C. Martin 1.25 3.00
11 Minnie Minoso 2.50 6.00
12 Billy Pierce 2.00 5.00
13 Juan Pizarro 1.25 3.00
14 Bob Roselli 1.25 3.00
15 Herb Score 2.00 5.00
16 Bob Shaw 1.25 3.00
17 Roy Sievers 1.50 4.00
18 Al Smith 1.25 3.00
19 Gerry Staley 1.25 3.00
20 Early Wynn 3.00 8.00

1962 White Sox Jay Publishing

This 12-card set of the Chicago White Sox measures approximately 5" by 7". The fronts feature black-and-white posed player photos with the player's and team name printed below in the white border. These cards were packaged 12 to a packet. The backs are blank. The cards are unnumbered and checklisted below in alphabetical order.

COMPLETE SET (12) 20.00 50.00
1 Luis Aparicio 4.00 10.00
2 Frank Baumann 1.00 2.50
3 Nellie Fox 4.00 10.00
4 Russ Kemmerer 1.00 2.50
5 Jim Landis 1.00 2.50
6 Sherm Lollar 1.00 2.50
7 Al Lopez MG 2.00 5.00
8 Joe Martin 1.00 2.50
9 Juan Pizarro 1.00 2.50
10 Floyd Robinson 1.00 2.50
11 Al Smith 1.00 2.50
12 Early Wynn 4.00 10.00

1962 White Sox Ticket Stubs

This stubs featured White Sox players. The stubs had the player photo imprinted so fans could have more keepsakes of their favorite players.

COMPLETE SET 50.00 100.00
1 Luis Aparicio 3.00 8.00
2 Frank Baumann 1.50 4.00
3 John Buzhardt 1.50 4.00
4 Camilo Carreon 1.50 4.00
5 Joe Cunningham 2.00 5.00
6 Bob Farley 1.50 4.00
7 Eddie Fisher 1.50 4.00
8 Nelson Fox 3.00 8.00
9 Jim Landis 1.50 4.00
10 Sherm Lollar 2.00 5.00
11 Al Lopez MG 2.50 6.00
12 Turk Lown 1.50 4.00
13 J.C. Martin 1.50 4.00
14 Cal McLish 1.50 4.00
15 Gary Peters 2.00 5.00
16 Juan Pizarro 1.50 4.00
17 Floyd Robinson 1.50 4.00
18 Bob Roselli 1.50 4.00
19 Herb Score 2.50 6.00
20 Al Smith 1.50 4.00
21 Charles Smith 1.50 4.00
22 Early Wynn 3.00 8.00

1963 White Sox Jay Publishing

This 12-card set of the Chicago White Sox measures approximately 5" by 7". The fronts feature black-and-white posed player photos with the player's and team name printed below in the white border. These cards were packaged 12 to a packet. The backs are blank. The cards are unnumbered and checklisted below in alphabetical order.

COMPLETE SET (12) 12.50 30.00
1 Frank Baumann .75 2.00
2 Camilio Carreon .75 2.00
3 Joe Cunningham .75 2.00
4 Sam Esposito .75 2.00
5 Nellie Fox 3.00 8.00
6 Ray Herbert .75 2.00
7 Joel Horlen 1.00 2.50
8 Jim Landis .75 2.00
9 Sherm Lollar .75 2.00
10 Al Lopez MG 1.50 4.00
11 Juan Pizarro .75 2.00
12 Floyd Robinson .75 2.00

1963 White Sox Ticket Stubs

Again, the White Sox featured player photos on their ticket stubs. These photos were originally the idea of Hall of Famer Bill Veeck, but the promotion continued even after he had sold all his interest in the White Sox.

COMPLETE SET 40.00 80.00
1 Frank Baumann 1.25 3.00
2 John Buzhardt 1.25 3.00
3 Camilo Carreon 1.25 3.00
4 Joe Cunningham 1.50 4.00
5 Dave DeBusschere 2.00 5.00
6 Eddie Fisher 1.25 3.00
7 Nelson Fox 4.00 10.00
8 Ron Hansen 1.25 3.00
9 Ray Herbert 1.25 3.00
10 Mike Hershberger 1.25 3.00
11 Joel Horlen 1.50 4.00
12 Grover Jones 1.25 3.00
13 Mike Joyce 1.25 3.00
14 Frank Kreutzer 1.25 3.00
15 Jim Landis 1.25 3.00
16 Sherm Lollar 1.25 3.00
17 Al Lopez MG 2.50 6.00
18 J.C. Martin 1.25 3.00
19 Charlie Maxwell 1.25 3.00
20 Dave Nicholson 1.25 3.00
21 Juan Pizarro 1.25 3.00
22 Floyd Robinson 1.25 3.00
23 Charlie Smith 1.25 3.00
24 Pete Ward 1.25 3.00
25 Al Weis 1.25 3.00
26 Hoyt Wilhelm 4.00 10.00
27 Dom Zanni 1.25 3.00

1964 White Sox Iron-Ons

This 27-card set of the Chicago White Sox features head player drawings that could be ironed on various items and articles of clothing. The set was distributed in packages of three sheets with nine players to a sheet. One sheet displayed blue heads, another red, and another black. The cards are unnumbered and checklisted below in alphabetical order.

COMPLETE SET (27) 10.00 25.00
1 Fritz Ackley .40 1.00
2 Frank Bauman .40 1.00
3 Jim Brosnan .75 2.00
4 Don Buford .40 1.00
5 John Buzhardt .40 1.00
6 Camilo Carreon .40 1.00
7 Joe Cunningham .40 1.00
8 Dave DeBusschere 1.50 4.00
9 Ed Fisher .40 1.00
10 Jim Golden .40 1.00
11 Ron Hansen .40 1.00
12 Ray Herbert .40 1.00
13 Mike Hershberger .40 1.00
14 Joel Horlen .40 1.00
15 Mike Joyce .40 1.00
16 Jim Landis .40 1.00
17 J.C. Martin .40 1.00
18 Charlie Maxwell .40 1.00
19 Tom McGraw .40 1.00
20 Dave Nicholson .40 1.00
21 Gary Peters .40 1.00
22 Floyd Robinson .40 1.00
23 Gene Stephens .40 1.00
24 Pete Ward .40 1.00
25 Al Weis .40 1.00
26 Hoyt Wilhelm 2.50 6.00
27 Team Logo .40 1.00

1964 White Sox Jay Publishing

This 12-card set of the Chicago White Sox measures approximately 5" by 7". The fronts feature black-and-white posed player photos with the player's and team name printed below in the white border. These cards were packaged 12 to a packet. The backs are blank. The cards are unnumbered and checklisted below in alphabetical order.

COMPLETE SET (12) 15.00 40.00
1 Camilio Carreon 1.00 2.50
2 Joe Cunningham 1.25 3.00
3 Ron Hansen 1.00 2.50
4 Ray Herbert 1.00 2.50
5 Mike Hershberger 1.00 2.50
6 Joel Horlen 1.00 2.50
7 Jim Landis 1.25 3.00
8 Al Lopez MG 2.00 5.00
9 Dave Nicholson 1.00 2.50
10 Gary Peters 1.25 3.00
11 Juan Pizarro 1.25 3.00
12 Pete Ward 1.00 2.50

1964 White Sox Ticket Stubs

For the fifth consecutive year, White Sox players were featured on these collector strips. These stubs were issued so fans could have another way of collecting memorabilia of their favorite players.

COMPLETE SET 40.00 80.00
1 Fritz Ackley 1.25 3.00
2 Frank Baumann 1.25 3.00
3 Don Buford 1.25 3.00
4 John Buzhardt 1.25 3.00
5 Camilo Carreon 1.25 3.00
6 Joe Cunningham 1.25 3.00
7 Dave DeBusschere 2.00 5.00
8 Eddie Fisher 1.25 3.00
9 Jim Golden 1.25 3.00
10 Ron Hansen 1.25 3.00
11 Ray Herbert 1.25 3.00
12 Mike Hershberger 1.25 3.00
13 Joe Horlen 1.25 3.00
14 Jim Landis 1.25 3.00
15 Al Lopez MG 2.50 6.00
16 J.C. Martin 1.25 3.00
17 Dave Nicholson 1.25 3.00
18 Gary Peters 1.50 4.00
19 Juan Pizarro 1.25 3.00
20 Floyd Robinson 1.25 3.00
21 Gene Stephens 1.25 3.00
22 Pete Ward 1.50 4.00
23 Hoyt Wilhelm 3.00 8.00

1965 White Sox Jay Publishing

This 12-card set of the Chicago White Sox measures approximately 5" by 7". The fronts feature black-and-white posed player photos with the player's and team name printed below in the white border. These cards were packaged 12 to a packet. The backs are blank. The cards are unnumbered and checklisted below in alphabetical order.

COMPLETE SET (12) 15.00 40.00
1 Ron Hansen 1.00 2.50
2 Al Lopez MG 2.00 5.00
3 J.C. Martin 1.00 2.50
4 Tom McCraw 1.00 2.50
5 Dave Nicholson 1.00 2.50
6 Gary Peters 1.00 2.50
7 Juan Pizarro 1.00 2.50
8 Floyd Robinson 1.00 2.50
9 John Romano 1.00 2.50
10 Bill Skowron 1.25 3.00
11 Pete Ward 1.00 2.50
12 Hoyt Wilhelm 4.00 10.00

1966 White Sox Team Issue

This 12-card set of the Chicago White Sox measures 4 7/8" by 7" and features black-and-white player photos in a white border with blank backs. These cards were originally packaged 12 to a packet. The cards are unnumbered and checklisted below in alphabetical order.

COMPLETE SET (12) 10.00 25.00
1 Tommy Agee 1.00 2.50
2 John Buzhardt .75 2.00
3 Don Buford .75 2.00
4 Joel Horlen .75 2.00
5 Tommy John 1.50 4.00
6 Bob Locker .75 2.00
7 Gary Peters .75 2.00
8 Juan Pizarro .75 2.00
9 Floyd Robinson .75 2.00
10 Johnny Romano .75 2.00
11 Bill Skowron 1.25 3.00
12 Eddie Stanky MG .75 2.00

1967 White Sox Team Issue

This 12-card set of the Chicago White Sox measures 4 7/8" by 7" and features black-and-white player photos in a white border with blank backs. These cards were originally packaged 12 to a packet. The cards are unnumbered and checklisted below in alphabetical order.

COMPLETE SET (12) 10.00 25.00
1 Jerry Adair .75 2.00
2 Tom Agee .75 2.00
3 Ken Berry .75 2.00
4 Don Buford .75 2.00
5 Ron Hansen .75 2.00
6 Joe Horlen .75 2.00
7 Tommy John 1.50 4.00
8 Duane Josephson .75 2.00
9 Tom McCraw .75 2.00
10 Gary Peters .75 2.00
11 Ed Stanky MG .75 2.00
12 Pete Ward .75 2.00

1969 White Sox Team Issue Black and White

This 12-card set of the Chicago White Sox measures approximately 4 1/4" by 7". The fronts display black-and-white player portraits bordered in white. The player's name and team are printed in the top margin. The backs are blank. The cards are unnumbered and checklisted below in alphabetical order.

COMPLETE SET (12) 8.00 20.00
1 Sandy Alomar .75 2.00
2 Luis Aparicio 1.50 4.00
3 Ken Berry .60 1.50
4 Charles Bradford .60 1.50
5 Joe Horlen .60 1.50
6 Tommy John 1.00 2.50
7 Duane Josephson .60 1.50
8 Al Lopez 1.25 3.00
9 Carlos May .60 1.50
10 Bill Melton .60 1.50
11 Gary Peters .75 2.00
12 Pete Ward .60 1.50

1969 White Sox Team Issue Color

Similar to the Jewel food store issues, these color photos measure approximately 5" by 7" and feature members of the 1969 Chicago White Sox. Since these are unnumbered, we have sequenced them in alphabetical order.

COMPLETE SET 12.50 30.00
1 Luis Aparicio 2.50 6.00
2 Ken Berry .75 2.00
3 Buddy Bradford .75 2.00
4 Kerby Farrell CO .75 2.00
5 Don Gutteridge MG .75 2.00
6 Ed Herrmann .75 2.00
7 Gail Hopkins .75 2.00
8 Joel Horlen .75 2.00
9 Tommy John 1.50 4.00
10 Duane Josephson .75 2.00
11 Carlos May .75 2.00
12 Rich Morales .75 2.00
13 Bill Melton .75 2.00
14 Dan Osinski .75 2.00
15 Gary Peters 1.00 2.50
16 Wilbur Wood 1.00 2.50

1970 White Sox Team Issue

This 12-card set of the Chicago White Sox measures approximately 4 1/4" by 7" and features black-and-white player photos in a white border. Packaged 12 to a packet with blank backs, the cards are unnumbered and checklisted below in alphabetical order.

COMPLETE SET (12) 10.00 25.00
1 Luis Aparicio 2.50 6.00
2 Ken Berry .75 2.00
3 Charles Bradford .75 2.00
4 Don Gutteridge MG .75 2.00
5 Gail Hopkins .75 2.00
6 Joe Horlen .75 2.00
7 Tommy John 1.50 4.00
8 Duane Josephson .75 2.00
9 Bobby Knoop .75 2.00
10 Carlos May .75 2.00
11 Bill Melton .75 2.00
12 Walter Williams .75 2.00

1972 White Sox

The 1972 Chicago White Sox are featured in this set of 12 approximately 7 1/2" by 9 3/8" glossy color player photos. The photos are bordered in white, and the player's name is given below the picture. The backs are blank and the photos are checklisted below in alphabetical order.

COMPLETE SET (12) 15.00 40.00
1 Dick Allen 2.00 5.00
2 Stan Bahnsen 1.25 3.00
3 Terry Forster 1.50 4.00
4 Ken Henderson 1.25 3.00
5 Ed Herrmann 1.25 3.00
6 Pat Kelly 1.25 3.00
7 Eddie Leon 1.25 3.00
8 Carlos May 1.25 3.00
9 Bill Melton 1.50 4.00
10 Jorge Orta 1.25 3.00
11 Steve Stone 1.50 4.00
12 Wilbur Wood 1.50 4.00

1972 White Sox Chi-Foursome

These drawings feature members of the Chicago White Sox. These drawings measure 11" by 14" and also have the player's fascimile signature. The backs are blank and we have sequenced this set in alphabetical order.

COMPLETE SET (7) 15.00 40.00
1 Mike Andrews 2.00 5.00
2 Ed Herrmann 2.00 5.00
3 Pat Kelly 2.00 5.00
4 Carlos May 2.50 6.00
5 Bill Melton 2.50 6.00
6 Chuck Tanner MG 2.50 6.00
7 Wilbur Wood 3.00 8.00

1972 White Sox Durochrome Stickers

These stickers measure 3 1/2" by 4 1/2". They are unnumbered and we have sequenced them in alphabetical order.

COMPLETE SET (6) 5.00 12.00
1 Dick Allen 1.50 4.00
2 Ed Herrmann .60 1.50
3 Bart Johnson .60 1.50
4 Carlos May .60 1.50
5 Bill Melton .75 2.00
6 Wilbur Wood 1.25 3.00

1972 White Sox Team Issue

These cards measure 4 1/4" by 7" and were issued in groups of 12. The fronts feature a player photo against a white border along with the player's name and team on the bottom. The backs are blank. These cards were issued continually throughout the year so there is not an exact number divisible by 12.

COMPLETE SET 20.00 50.00
1 Dick Allen 2.50 6.00
2 Mike Andrews 1.25 3.00
3 Stan Bahnsen 1.50 4.00
4 Tom Bradley 1.25 3.00
5 Tom Egan 1.25 3.00
6 Terry Forster 1.50 4.00
7 Ed Herrmann 1.25 3.00
8 Jay Johnstone 1.50 4.00
9 Pat Kelly 1.25 3.00
10 Carlos May 1.25 3.00
10 Rick Reichardt 1.25 3.00
11 Bill Melton 1.50 4.00
12 Jorge Orta 1.25 3.00
13 Chuck Tanner MG 1.25 3.00
14 Walt Williams 1.25 3.00
15A Wilbur Wood UER/(Says Wilber on card) 2.00 5.00
15B Wilbur Wood COR 2.00 5.00

1973 White Sox Jewel

These 6 1/2" by 9 1/2" blank-backed, white bordered, full-color photos were issued as a premium by Jewel Foods. The photos have a fascimile autograph and since they are unnumbered we have sequenced them in alphabetical order.

COMPLETE SET 8.00 20.00
1 Dick Allen 1.25 3.00
2 Mike Andrews .60 1.50
3 Stan Bahnsen .60 1.50
4 Eddie Fisher .60 1.50
5 Terry Forster .60 1.50
6 Ken Henderson .60 1.50
7 Ed Herrmann .60 1.50
8 Johnny Jeter .60 1.50
9 Pat Kelly .60 1.50
10 Eddie Leon .60 1.50
11 Carlos May .60 1.50
12 Bill Melton .60 1.50
13 Tony Muser .60 1.50
14 Jorge Orta .60 1.50
15 Rick Reichardt .60 1.50
16 Wilbur Wood .75 2.00

1973 White Sox Team Issue

Measuring approximately 7" by 8 3/4" these blank-backed photos were issued to promote some of the leading players of the White Sox. The full-color photos are surrounded by white borders with the player's name and team on the bottom. Since these photos are unnumbered, we have sequenced them in alphabetical order.

COMPLETE SET 4.00 10.00
1 Dick Allen 1.25 3.00
2 Stan Bahnsen .60 1.50
3 Pat Kelly .60 1.50
4 Carlos May .60 1.50
5 Bill Melton .60 1.50
6 Wilbur Wood UER .75 2.00
Spelled Wilber

1975 White Sox 1919 TCMA

This 28-card set features the 1919 Chicago White Sox Team. The fronts display black-and-white player photos while the backs carry player statistics. The set includes one team picture jumbo card which measures approximately 3 1/2" by 4 3/4". The cards are unnumbered and checklisted below in alphabetical order.

COMPLETE SET (28) 10.00 25.00
1 Joe Benz .20 .50
2 Eddie Cicotte .75 2.00
3 Eddie Collins 1.25 3.00
4 Shano Collins .20 .50
5 Dave Danforth .20 .50
6 Red Faber .75 2.00
7 Happy Felsch .60 1.50
8 Charles Chick Gandil .60 1.50
9 Kid Gleason MG .60 1.50
10 Joe Jackson 2.00 5.00
11 Bill James .20 .50
12 Dickie Kerr .40 1.00
13 Nemo Leibold .20 .50
14 Byrd Lynn .20 .50
15 Erskine Mayer .20 .50
16 Harvey McClellan .20 .50
17 Fred McMullin .40 1.00
18 Eddie Murphy .20 .50
19 Pat Ragan .20 .50
20 Swede Risberg .40 1.00
21 Charlie Robertson .20 .50
22 Red Russell .20 .50
23 Ray Schalk .75 2.00
24 Frank Shellenback .20 .50
Grover Lowdermilk
25 Buck Weaver .75 2.00
26 Roy Wilkinson .20 .50
27 Lefty Williams .60 1.50
28 Team Picture .40 1.00

1976 White Sox TCMA All-Time Greats

This 12-card set of the All-Time Chicago White Sox Team features black-and-white player photos bordered in white with the player's name and position printed in red in the bottom margin. The white backs carry the roster of the team. The cards are unnumbered and checklisted below in alphabetical order.

COMPLETE SET (12) 4.00 10.00
1 Luke Appling .40 1.00
2 Eddie Collins .60 1.50
3 Harry Hooper .40 1.00
4 Willie Kamm .20 .50
5 Al Lopez MG .30 .75
6 Ted Lyons .40 1.00
7 Johnny Mostil .20 .50
8 Billy Pierce .30 .75
9 Eddie Robinson .20 .50
10 Ray Schalk .30 .75
11 Al Simmons .60 1.50
12 Gerry Staley .20 .50

1977 White Sox Jewel Tea

This 16-card set of the Chicago White Sox measures approximately 5 7/8" by 9". The white-bordered fronts feature color player head photos with a facsimile autograph below. The backs are blank. The cards are unnumbered and checklisted below in alphabetical order.

COMPLETE SET (16) 6.00 15.00
1 Alan Bannister .40 1.00
2 Francisco Barrios .40 1.00
3 Jim Essian .40 1.00
4 Oscar Gamble .60 1.50
5 Ralph Garr .60 1.50
6 Lamar Johnson .40 1.00
7 Chris Knapp .40 1.00
8 Ken Kravec .40 1.00
9 Lerrin LaGrow .40 1.00
10 Chet Lemon .60 1.50
11 Jorge Orta .40 1.00
12 Eric Soderholm .40 1.00
13 Jim Spencer .40 1.00
14 Steve Stone .60 1.50
15 Wilbur Wood .40 1.00
16 Richie Zisk .60 1.50

1977 White Sox Tribune

These portraits were issued as inserts in the Chicago Tribune newspaper and were issued two at a time. One player pictured was a Chicago Cub and another was a Chicago White Sox. The photos are black and white and are posed head shots, the bottom of the photo features statistics up to that time. The photos are unnumbered so we have sequenced them in alphabetical order.

COMPLETE SET 10.00 25.00
1 Alan Bannister .40 1.00
2 Francisco Barrios .40 1.00
3 Kevin Bell .40 1.00
4 Jack Brohamer .40 1.00
5 Bruce Dal Canton .40 1.00
6 Brian Downing .60 1.50
7 Jim Essian .40 1.00
8 Oscar Gamble .60 1.50
9 Ralph Garr .40 1.00
10 Dave Hamilton .40 1.00
11 Bart Johnson .40 1.00
12 Lamar Johnson .40 1.00
13 Don Kirkwood .40 1.00
14 Chris Knapp .40 1.00
15 Ken Kravec .40 1.00
16 Jack Kucek .40 1.00
17 Lerrin LaGrow .40 1.00
18 Chet Lemon .40 1.00
19 Tim Nordbrook .40 1.00
20 Wayne Nordhagen .40 1.00
21 Jorge Orta .40 1.00
22 Eric Soderholm .40 1.00
23 Jim Spencer .40 1.00
24 Royle Stillman .40 1.00
25 Steve Stone .60 1.50
26 Wilbur Wood .60 1.50
27 Richie Zisk .40 1.00

1980 White Sox Greats TCMA

This 12-card standard-size set features various all-time White Sox greats. The fronts display a player photo, while the backs carry information about the player.

COMPLETE SET (12) 2.00 5.00
1 Ted Lyons .30 .75
2 Eddie Collins .40 1.00
3 Al Lopez MG .20 .50
4 Luke Appling .40 1.00
5 Billy Pierce .20 .50
6 Willie Kamm .08 .25
7 Johnny Mostil .08 .25
8 Al Simmons .30 .75
9 Ray Schalk .30 .75
10 Gerry Staley .08 .25
11 Harry Hooper .30 .75
12 Eddie Robinson .08 .25

1981 White Sox 1959 TCMA

This 45-card set features photos of the 1959 American League champion Chicago White Sox team in blue borders. The backs carry player information.

COMPLETE SET (45) 10.00 25.00
1 Earl Torgeson .08 .25
2 Nellie Fox .60 1.50
3 Luis Aparicio .60 1.50
4 Bubba Phillips .08 .25
5 Jim McAnany .08 .25
6 Jim Landis .08 .25
7 Al Smith .08 .25
8 Sherman Lollar .20 .50
9 Billy Goodman .08 .25
10 Jim Rivera .08 .25
11 Sammy Esposito .08 .25
12 Norm Cash .30 .75
13 Johnny Romano .08 .25
14 Johnny Callison .20 .50
15 Harry Simpson .08 .25
16 Ted Kluszewski .40 1.00
17 Del Ennis .20 .50
18 Earl Battey .08 .25
19 Larry Doby .60 1.50
20 Ron Jackson .08 .25
21 Ray Boone .08 .25
22 Lou Skizas .08 .25
23 Joe Hicks .08 .25
24 Don Mueller .08 .25
25 J.C. Martin .08 .25
26 Cam Carreon .08 .25
27 Early Wynn .60 1.50
28 Bob Shaw .08 .25
29 Billy Pierce .20 .50
30 Turk Lown .08 .25
31 Dick Donovan .08 .25
32 Gerry Staley .08 .25
33 Barry Latman .08 .25
34 Ray Moore .08 .25
35 Rudy Arias .08 .25
36 Joe Stanka .08 .25
37 Ken McBride .08 .25
38 Don Rudolph .08 .25
39 Claude Raymond .08 .25
40 Gary Peters .08 .25
41 Al Lopez MG .30 .75
42 Don Gutteridge CO .08 .25
43 Ray Berres CO .08 .25
44 Tony Cuccinello CO .08 .25
45 John Cooney CO .08 .25

1983 White Sox True Value

This 23-card set was sponsored by True Value Hardware Stores and features full-color (approximately 2 5/8" by 4 1/4") cards of the Chicago White Sox. Most of the set was intended for distribution two cards per game at selected White Sox Tuesday night home games. The cards are unnumbered except for uniform number given in the lower right corner of the obverse. The card backs contain statistical information in basic black and white. The cards of Harold Baines, Salome Barojas, and Marc Hill were not issued at the park; hence they are more difficult to obtain than the other 20 cards and are marked SP in the checklist below.

COMPLETE SET (23) 15.00 40.00
COMMON SP 5.00
1 Scott Fletcher .20 .50
3 Harold Baines SP 3.00 8.00
5 Vance Law .20 .50
7 Marc Hill SP 2.00 5.00
10 Tony LaRussa MG .60 1.50
11 Rudy Law .20 .50
14 Tony Bernazard .20 .50
17 Jerry Hairston .20 .50
19 Greg Luzinski .40 1.00
24 Floyd Bannister .20 .50
25 Mike Squires .20 .50
30 Salome Barojas SP 2.00 5.00
31 LaMarr Hoyt .30 .75
34 Richard Dotson .20 .50
36 Jerry Koosman .40 1.00
40 Britt Burns .20 .50
41 Dick Tidrow .20 .50
42 Ron Kittle .60 1.50
44 Tom Paciorek .20 .50
45 Kevin Hickey .20 .50
53 Dennis Lamp .20 .50
67 Jim Kern .20 .50
72 Carlton Fisk 3.00 8.00

1984 White Sox Jewel

These 16 blank backed cards feature members of the 1984 Chicago White Sox. The fronts have the players photo against a blue background with a fascimile autograph on the bottom and the MLBPA logo in the upper left. These cards are unnumbered so we have sequenced them in alphabetical order.

COMPLETE SET (16) 6.00 15.00
1 Harold Baines .60 1.50
2 Floyd Bannister .20 .50
3 Julio Cruz .20 .50
4 Rich Dotson .20 .50
5 Jerry Dybzinski .20 .50
6 Carlton Fisk 1.25 3.00
7 Scott Fletcher .20 .50
8 Lamarr Hoyt .30 .75
9 Rudy Law .20 .50
10 Vance Law .20 .50
11 Greg Luzinski .40 1.00
12 Ron Kittle .30 .75
13 Tom Paciorek .20 .50
14 Tom Seaver 2.00 5.00
15 Mike Squires .20 .50
16 Greg Walker .20 .50

1984 White Sox True Value

This 30-card set features full color (approximately 2 1/2" by 4") cards of the Chicago White Sox. Most of the set was distributed two cards per game at selected White Sox Tuesday home games. Faust and Minoso were not given out although their cards were available through direct (promotional) contact with them. Brennan and Hulett were not released directly since they were sent down to the minors. The cards are unnumbered except for uniform number given in the lower right corner of the obverse; they are arbitrarily listed below in alphabetical order. The card backs contain statistical information in basic black and white.

COMPLETE SET (30) 10.00 25.00
COMMON SP 3.00
1 Juan Agosto .20 .50
2 Luis Aparicio 1.25 3.00
3 Harold Baines .60 1.50
4 Floyd Bannister .20 .50
5 Salome Barojas .20 .50
6 Tom Brennan SP 1.25 3.00
7 Britt Burns .20 .50
8 Coaching Staff/(Blank back) .30 .75
9 Julio Cruz .20 .50
10 Richard Dotson .20 .50
11 Jerry Dybzinski .20 .50
12 Nancy Faust ORG/(Blank back) .60 1.50
13 Carlton Fisk 2.50 6.00
14 Scott Fletcher .20 .50
15 Jerry Hairston .20 .50
16 Marc Hill .20 .50
17 LaMarr Hoyt .20 .50
18 Tim Hulett SP 1.25 3.00
19 Ron Kittle .30 .75
20 Tony LaRussa MG .60 1.50
21 Rudy Law .20 .50
22 Vance Law .20 .50
23 Greg Luzinski .40 1.00
24 Minnie Minoso 1.25 3.00
25 Tom Paciorek .20 .50
26 Ron Reed .20 .50
27 Tom Seaver 2.50 6.00
28 Dave Stegman .20 .50
29 Mike Squires .20 .50
30 Greg Walker .30 .75

1985 White Sox Coke

This 30-card set features present and past Chicago White Sox players and personnel. Cards measure approximately 2 5/8" by 4 1/8" and feature a red band at the bottom of the card. Within the red band are the White Sox logo, the player's name, position, uniform number, and a small oval portrait of an all-time White Sox Great at a similar position. The cards were available two at a time at Tuesday night White Sox home games or as a complete set through membership in the Coca-Cola White Sox Fan Club. The cards below are numbered by uniform number; the last three cards are unnumbered.

COMPLETE SET (30) 5.00 12.00
NNO Oscar Gamble .08 .25
Zeke Bonura
1 Scott Fletcher .40 1.00
Luke Appling
3 Harold Baines .30 .75
Bill Melton
5 Luis Salazar .08 .25
Chico Carrasquel
7 Marc Hill .08 .25
Sherm Lollar
8 Daryl Boston .08 .25
Jim Landis
10 Tony LaRussa MG .40 1.00
Al Lopez MG
12 Julio Cruz .40 1.00
Nellie Fox
13 Ozzie Guillen 2.00 5.00
Luis Aparicio
17 Jerry Hairston .08 .25
Smoky Burgess
20 Joe DeSa .08 .25
Carlos May
22 Joel Skinner .08 .25
J.C. Martin
23 Rudy Law .08 .25
Bill Skowron
24 Floyd Bannister .20 .50
Red Faber
29 Greg Walker .30 .75
Dick Allen
30 Gene Nelson .40 1.00
Early Wynn
32 Tim Hulett .08 .25
Pete Ward
34 Richard Dotson .20 .50
Ed Walsh
37 Dan Spillner .08 .25
Thornton Lee
40 Britt Burns .08 .25
Gary Peters
41 Tom Seaver 1.00 2.50
Ted Lyons
42 Ron Kittle .40 1.00
Minnie Minoso
43 Bob James .08 .25
Hoyt Wilhelm
44 Tom Paciorek .40 1.00
Eddie Collins
46 Tim Lollar .20 .50
Billy Pierce
50 Juan Agosto .08 .25
Wilbur Wood
72 Carlton Fisk 1.00 2.50
Ray Schalk
NNO Comiskey Park .08 .25
NNO Nancy Faust ORG .08 .25
NNO Ribbie and Roobarb .08 .25

1986 White Sox Coke

This colorful 30-card set features a borderless photo on top of a blue-on-white name, position, and uniform number. Card backs provide complete major and minor season-by-season career statistical information. Since the cards are unnumbered, they are numbered below according to uniform number. The cards measure approximately 2 5/8" by 4". The five unnumbered non-player cards are listed at the end of the checklist below.

COMPLETE SET (30) 5.00 12.00
1 Wayne Tolleson .08 .25
3 Harold Baines .40 1.00
7 Marc Hill .08 .25
8 Daryl Boston .08 .25
12 Julio Cruz .08 .25
13 Ozzie Guillen 1.00 2.50
17 Jerry Hairston .08 .25
19 Floyd Bannister .08 .25
20 Reid Nichols .08 .25
22 Joel Skinner .08 .25
24 Dave Schmidt .08 .25
26 Bobby Bonilla 1.00 2.50
29 Greg Walker .08 .25
30 Gene Nelson .08 .25
32 Tim Hulett .08 .25
33 Neil Allen .08 .25
34 Richard Dotson .08 .25
40 Joe Cowley .08 .25
41 Tom Seaver 1.25 3.00
42 Ron Kittle .20 .50
43 Bob James .08 .25
44 John Cangelosi .08 .25
50 Juan Agosto .08 .25
52 Joel Davis .08 .25
72 Carlton Fisk .60 1.50

NNO Nancy Faust ORG .08 .25
NNO Ken(Hawk) Harrelson GM .20 .50
NNO Tony LaRussa MG .30 .75
NNO Minnie Minoso CO .30 .75
NNO Ribbie and Roobarb .08 .25

1987 White Sox Coke

This colorful 30-card set features a card front with a blue-bordered photo and name, position, and uniform number. Card backs provide complete major and minor season-by-season career statistical information. Since the cards are unnumbered, they are numbered below in alphabetical order. The cards measure approximately 2 5/8" by 4". The card set, sponsored by Coca-Cola, is an exclusive for fan club members who join (for 10.00) in 1987.

COMPLETE SET (30) 5.00 12.00
1 Neil Allen .08 .25
2 Harold Baines .60 1.50
3 Floyd Bannister .08 .25
4 Daryl Boston .08 .25
5 Ivan Calderon .08 .25
6 Joel Davis .08 .25
7 Jose DeLeon .08 .25
8 Richard Dotson .08 .25
9 Nancy Faust ORG .08 .25
10 Carlton Fisk 1.25 3.00
11 Jim Fregosi MG .08 .25
12 Ozzie Guillen .60 1.50
13 Jerry Hairston .08 .25
14 Ron Hassey .08 .25
15 Donnie Hill .08 .25
16 Tim Hulett .08 .25
17 Bob James .08 .25
18 Ron Karkovice .20 .50
19 Steve Lyons .20 .50
20 Fred Manrique .08 .25
21 Joel McKeon .08 .25
22 Minnie Minoso .40 1.00
23 Russ Morman .08 .25
24 Gary Redus .08 .25
25 Ribbie and Roobarb .08 .25
26 Jerry Royster .08 .25
27 Ray Searage .08 .25
28 Bobby Thigpen .20 .50
29 Greg Walker .08 .25
30 Jim Winn .08 .25

1988 White Sox Coke

This colorful 30-card set features a card front with a red-bordered photo and name and position. Card backs provide a narrative without any statistical tables. Since the cards are unnumbered, they are numbered below in alphabetical order according to the subject's name or card's title. The cards measure approximately 2 5/8" by 3 1/2". The card set, sponsored by Coca-Cola, was for fan club members who join (for 10.00) in 1988. The cards were also given out at the May 22nd game at Comiskey Park. These cards do not even list the player's uniform number anywhere on the card. Card backs are printed in black and gray on thin white card stock.

COMPLETE SET (30) 3.00 8.00
1 Harold Baines .40 1.00
2 Daryl Boston .08 .25
3 Ivan Calderon .08 .25
4 Comiskey Park .08 .25
5 John Davis .08 .25
6 Nancy Faust ORG .08 .25
7 Jim Fregosi MG .08 .25
8 Carlton Fisk .75 2.00
9 Ozzie Guillen .60 1.50
10 Donnie Hill .08 .25
11 Ricky Horton .08 .25
12 Lance Johnson .75 2.00
13 Dave LaPoint .08 .25
14 Bill Long .08 .25
15 Steve Lyons .20 .50
16 Jack McDowell 1.00 2.50
17 Fred Manrique .08 .25
18 Minnie Minoso .40 1.00
19 Dan Pasqua .08 .25
20 John Pawlowski .08 .25
21 Melido Perez .08 .25
22 Billy Pierce .20 .50
23 Jerry Reuss .20 .50
24 Gary Redus .08 .25
25 Ribbie and Roobarb .08 .25
26 Mark Salas .08 .25
27 Jose Segura .08 .25
28 Bobby Thigpen .20 .50
29 Greg Walker .08 .25
30 Kenny Williams .50 1.25

1988 White Sox Kodak

This five-card, approximately 8" by 11 1/2" set was issued by Kodak including members of the 1988 Chicago White Sox. The cards are borderless and say "1988 Kodak Collectible Series" on top with the player's photo dominating the middle of the photo. Underneath the photo is a facsimile autograph and on the bottom left of the photo is an advertisment for Kodak and the bottom right of the card the White Sox logo is featured.

COMPLETE SET (5) 3.00 8.00
1 Ozzie Guillen 1.25 3.00
2 Carlton Fisk 1.25 3.00
3 Rick Horton .60 1.50
4 Ivan Calderon .60 1.50
5 Harold Baines .75 2.00

1989 White Sox Coke

The 1989 Coke Chicago White Sox set contains 30 cards measuring approximately 2 5/8" by 3 1/2". The players in the set represent the White Sox opening day roster. The fronts are blue. The horizontally oriented backs are gray and white, and feature biographical information. The set was a promotional give-away August 10, 1989 at the Baseball Card Night game against the Oakland A's to the first 15,000 fans. The set includes a special "New Comiskey Park, 1991" card. The complete set was also available with (10.00) membership in the Chi-Sox Fan Club. The cards in the set are numbered on the backs in the lower right corner in very small print.

COMPLETE SET (30) 3.00 8.00
1 New Comiskey Park 1991 .08 .25
2 Comiskey Park .08 .25
3 Jeff Torborg MG .08 .25
4 Coaching Staff .08 .25
5 Harold Baines .30 .75
6 Daryl Boston .08 .25
7 Ivan Calderon .08 .25
8 Carlton Fisk .60 1.50
9 Dave Gallagher .08 .25
10 Ozzie Guillen .60 1.50
11 Shawn Hillegas .08 .25
12 Barry Jones .08 .25
13 Ron Karkovice .08 .25
14 Eric King .08 .25
15 Ron Kittle .08 .25
16 Bill Long .08 .25
17 Steve Lyons .20 .50
18 Donn Pall .08 .25
19 Dan Pasqua .08 .25
20 Ken Patterson .08 .25
21 Melido Perez .08 .25
22 Jerry Reuss .20 .50
23 Billy Joe Robidoux .08 .25
24 Steve Rosenberg .08 .25
25 Jeff Schaefer .08 .25
26 Bobby Thigpen .08 .25
27 Greg Walker .08 .25
28 Eddie Williams .08 .25
29 Nancy Faust ORG .08 .25
30 Minnie Minoso .40 1.00

1989 White Sox Kodak

For the second consecutive year Kodak in conjunction with the Chicago White Sox issued a set about the White Sox. The 1989 set was marked by a color photo of the active star dominating the upper right half of the card with the bottom half of the card depicting two other famous White Sox players at the same position that the current star played. This six-card, approximately 8" by 11 1/2", set was given away at various games at Comiskey Park.

COMPLETE SET (6) 3.00 8.00
1 Greg Walker .60 1.50
Dick Allen
Ted Kluszewski
2 Steve Lyons .75 2.00
Eddie Collins
Nellie Fox
3 Carlton Fisk 1.25 3.00
Sherm Lollar
Ray Schalk
4 Harold Baines .60 1.50
Minnie Minoso
Jim Landis
5 Bobby Thigpen .60 1.50
Gerry Staley
Hoyt Wilhelm
6 Ozzie Guillen 1.25 3.00
Luke Appling
Luis Aparicio

1990 White Sox Coke

The 1990 Coca Cola White Sox set contains 30 cards. The set is a beautiful full-color set commemorating the 1990 White Sox who were celebrating the eightieth and last season played in old Comiskey Park. This (approximately) 2 5/8" by 3 1/2" set has a Comiskey Park logo on the front with 1989 statistics and a brief biography on the back. The set is checklisted alphabetically. The set features early cards of Sammy Sosa and Frank Thomas.

COMPLETE SET (30) 10.00 25.00
1 Ivan Calderon .20 .50
2 Wayne Edwards .20 .50
3 Carlton Fisk .75 2.00
4 Scott Fletcher .20 .50
5 Dave Gallagher .20 .50
6 Craig Grebeck .20 .50
7 Ozzie Guillen .60 1.50
8 Greg Hibbard .20 .50
9 Lance Johnson .20 .50
10 Barry Jones .20 .50
11 Ron Karkovice .20 .50
12 Eric King .20 .50
13 Ron Kittle .20 .50
14 Jerry Kutzler .20 .50
15 Steve Lyons .20 .50
16 Carlos Martinez .20 .50
17 Jack McDowell .50 1.25
18 Donn Pall .20 .50
19 Dan Pasqua .20 .50
20 Ken Patterson .20 .50
21 Melido Perez .20 .50
22 Scott Radinsky .20 .50
23 Sammy Sosa 4.00 10.00
24 Bobby Thigpen .20 .50
25 Frank Thomas 8.00 20.00
26 Jeff Torborg MG .20 .50
27 Robin Ventura 1.25 3.00
28 Rookies .50 1.25
R.Ventura
29 Captains: Ozzie .20 .50
Guillen and
Carlton Fisk
30 Coaches: Barry Foote .20 .50
Sammy Ellis
Walt Hriniak
T

1990 White Sox Kodak

In 1990 Kodak again in conjunction with the Chicago White Sox issued a beautiful six-card set about some key members of the 1990 White Sox. This was slightly reduced in size (from the previous two years) to be approximately 7" by 11" and featured a full-color picture with an advertisement for Kodak on the lower left corner of the front of the card and the White Sox logo in the lower right hand corner. The cards were again borderless and blank-backed.

COMPLETE SET (6) 4.00 10.00
1 Carlton Fisk 1.50 4.00
2 Melido Perez .50 1.25
3 Ozzie Guillen 1.00 2.50
4 Ron Kittle .50 1.25
5 Scott Fletcher .50 1.25
6 Comiskey Park .50 1.25

1991 White Sox Kodak

This 28-card set was sponsored by Kodak and measures approximately 2 5/8" by 3 1/2". The cards are skip-numbered by uniform number and checklisted below accordingly, with the unnumbered cards listed at the end.

COMPLETE SET (28) 12.50 30.00
1 Lance Johnson .08 .25
5 Matt Merullo .08 .25
7 Scott Fletcher .08 .25
8 Bo Jackson .40 1.00
10 Jeff Torborg MG .08 .25
13 Ozzie Guillen .40 1.00
14 Craig Grebeck .08 .25
20 Ron Karkovice .08 .25
21 Joey Cora .08 .25
22 Donn Pall .08 .25
23 Robin Ventura .75 2.00
25 Sammy Sosa 5.00 12.00
27 Greg Hibbard .08 .25
28 Cory Snyder .08 .25
29 Jack McDowell .30 .75
30 Tim Raines .20 .50
31 Scott Radinsky .08 .25
32 Alex Fernandez .08 .25
33 Melido Perez .08 .25
34 Ken Patterson .08 .25
35 Frank Thomas 3.00 8.00
37 Bobby Thigpen .08 .25
44 Dan Pasqua .08 .25
45 Wayne Edwards .08 .25
49 Charlie Hough .20 .50
50 Brian Drahman .08 .25
72 Carlton Fisk 1.00 2.50
NNO First Draft Choices 2.00 5.00
Jack McDowell
Robin Ventura#
NNO 1991 Co-Captains .30 .75
Carlton Fisk and
Ozzie Guillen
NNO 1991 Coaching Staff .08 .25
Walt Hriniak
Sammy Ellis
Te

1992 White Sox Kodak

This 30-card set was sponsored by Kodak and measures slightly larger (2 5/8" by 3 1/2") than standard size. The set was distributed at a White Sox vs. Milwaukee four-game series at Comiskey Park. The cards are skip-numbered on the front by uniform number and checklisted below accordingly.

COMPLETE SET (30) 6.00 15.00
NNO Waldo the Wolf .08 .25
1 Lance Johnson .08 .25
5 Matt Merullo .08 .25
7 Steve Sax .08 .25
12 Mike Huff .08 .25
13 Ozzie Guillen .40 1.00
14 Craig Grebeck .08 .25
20 Ron Karkovice .08 .25
21 George Bell .20 .50
22 Donn Pall .08 .25
23 Robin Ventura .75 2.00
24 Warren Newson .08 .25
25 Kirk McCaskill .08 .25
27 Greg Hibbard .08 .25
28 Joey Cora .08 .25
29 Jack McDowell .30 .75
30 Tim Raines .20 .50
31 Scott Radinsky .08 .25
32 Alex Fernandez .08 .25
33 Gene Lamont MG .08 .25
34 Terry Leach .08 .25
35 Frank Thomas 2.00 5.00
37 Bobby Thigpen .08 .25
39 Roberto Hernandez 1.00 2.50
40 Wilson Alvarez .40 1.00
44 Dan Pasqua .08 .25
45 Shawn Abner .08 .25
49 Charlie Hough .20 .50
72 Carlton Fisk 1.25 3.00
NNO Coaching Staff .08 .25
Walt Hriniak
Doug Mansolino
Dave

1993 White Sox Kodak

This 30-card set measures approximately 2 5/8" by 3 1/2" and features color player action photos on the fronts. The cards are unnumbered and checklisted below in alphabetical order.

COMPLETE SET (30) 5.00 12.00
1 Wilson Alvarez .08 .25
2 George Bell .20 .50
3 Jason Bere .08 .25
4 Rod Bolton .08 .25
5 Ellis Burks .40 1.00
6 Chuck Cary .08 .25
7 Joey Cora .08 .25
8 Alex Fernandez .08 .25
9 Craig Grebeck .08 .25
10 Ozzie Guillen .40 1.00
11 Roberto Hernandez .20 .50
12 Mike Huff .08 .25
13 Bo Jackson .40 1.00
14 Lance Johnson .08 .25
15 Ron Karkovice .08 .25
16 Gene Lamont MG .08 .25
17 Mike LaValliere .08 .25
18 Terry Leach .08 .25
19 Kirk McCaskill .08 .25
20 Jack McDowell .20 .50
21 Donn Pall .08 .25
22 Dan Pasqua .08 .25
23 Scott Radinsky .08 .25
24 Tim Raines .30 .75
25 Steve Sax .08 .25
26 Jeff Schwarz .08 .25
27 Bobby Thigpen .08 .25
28 Frank Thomas 1.50 4.00
29 Robin Ventura .60 1.50
30 Coaching Staff .08 .25
Jose Antigua
Terry Bevington
Jac

1993 White Sox Stadium Club

This 30-card standard-size set features the 1993 Chicago White Sox. The set was issued in hobby (plastic box) and retail (blister) form.

COMP. FACT SET (30) 3.00 8.00
1 Frank Thomas .60 1.50
2 Bo Jackson .30 .75
3 Rod Bolton .02 .10
4 Dave Stieb .08 .25
5 Tim Raines .08 .25
6 Joey Cora .02 .10
7 Warren Newson .02 .10
8 Roberto Hernandez .08 .25
9 Brandon Wilson .02 .10
10 Wilson Alvarez .08 .25
11 Dan Pasqua .02 .10
12 Ozzie Guillen .30 .75
13 Robin Ventura .30 .75
14 Craig Grebeck .02 .10
15 Lance Johnson .08 .25
16 Carlton Fisk .40 1.00
17 Ron Karkovice .02 .10
18 Jack McDowell .08 .25
19 Scott Radinsky .02 .10
20 Bobby Thigpen .08 .25
21 Donn Pall .02 .10
22 George Bell .08 .25
23 Alex Fernandez .02 .10
24 Mike Huff .02 .10
25 Jason Bere .08 .25
26 Johnny Ruffin .02 .10
27 Ellis Burks .30 .75
28 Kirk McCaskill .02 .10
29 Terry Leach .02 .10
30 Shawn Gilbert .02 .10

1994 White Sox Kodak

These 30 cards measure 2 5/8" by 3 1/2" and feature borderless color player action shots on their fronts. The cards are unnumbered and checklisted below in alphabetical order.

COMPLETE SET (30) 5.00 12.00
1 Wilson Alvarez .20 .50
2 Paul Assenmacher .08 .25
3 Jason Bere .08 .25
4 Dennis Cook .08 .25
5 Joey Cora .08 .25
6 Jose DeLeon .08 .25
7 Alex Fernandez .08 .25
8 Julio Franco .20 .50
9 Craig Grebeck .08 .25
10 Ozzie Guillen .40 1.00
11 Joe Hall .08 .25
12 Roberto Hernandez .20 .50
13 Dann Howitt .08 .25
14 Darrin Jackson .08 .25
15 Dane Johnson .08 .25
16 Lance Johnson .08 .25
17 Ron Karkovice .08 .25
18 Gene Lamont MG .08 .25
19 Mike LaValliere .08 .25
20 Norberto Martin .08 .25
21 Kirk McCaskill .08 .25
22 Jack McDowell .30 .75
23 Warren Newson .08 .25
24 Dan Pasqua .08 .25
25 Tim Raines .30 .75
26 Scott Sanderson .20 .50
27 Frank Thomas 1.50 4.00
28 Robin Ventura .75 2.00
29 Bob Zupcic .08 .25
30 Coaches Card .08 .25
Doug Mansolino
Rick Peterson
Roly

1995 White Sox Kodak

Sponsored by Kodak, this 31-card set commemorates the 95th anniversary of the Chicago White Sox. The cards measure 2 5/8" by 3 1/2". The cards are unnumbered and checklisted below in alphabetical order.

COMPLETE SET (31) 5.00 12.00
1 Jim Abbott .20 .50
2 Wilson Alvarez .20 .50
3 Jason Bere .08 .25
4 Terry Bevington MG .08 .25
5 Jose DeLeon .08 .25
6 Mike Devereaux .08 .25
7 Rob Dibble .08 .25
8 Ray Durham .60 1.50
9 Alex Fernandez .08 .25
10 Tim Fortugno .08 .25
11 Craig Grebeck .08 .25
12 Ozzie Guillen .40 1.00
13 Roberto Hernandez .30 .75
14 Lance Johnson .08 .25
15 Ron Karkovice .08 .25
16 Brian Keyser .08 .25
17 John Kruk .20 .50
18 Mike LaValliere .08 .25
19 Norberto Martin .08 .25
20 Dave Martinez .08 .25
21 Kirk McCaskill .08 .25
22 Warren Newson .08 .25
24 Steve Odgers .08 .25
Dir. of Conditioning
25 Scott Radinsky .08 .25
26 Tim Raines .30 .75
27 Herm Schneider TR .08 .25
Mark Anderson TR
28 Frank Thomas 1.25 3.00
29 Frank Thomas AS .60 1.50
30 Robin Ventura .60 1.50
31 Coaching Staff .08 .25
Terry Bevington
Don Cooper
Walt

1996 White Sox Dannon

These 30 cards were issued in conjunction with Dannon Yogurt and were given away at a special night at Comiskey Park. The cards are unnumbered so we have sequenced them in alphabetical order.

COMPLETE SET (30) 5.00 12.00
1 Wilson Alvarez .20 .50
2 James Baldwin .08 .25
3 Harold Baines .40 1.00
4 Jason Bere .08 .25
5 Terry Bevington MG .08 .25
6 Ray Durham .40 1.00
7 Alex Fernandez .08 .25
8 Ozzie Guillen .40 1.00
9 Roberto Hernandez .30 .75
10 Ron Karkovice .08 .25
11 Brian Keyser .08 .25
12 Matt Karchner .08 .25
13 Chad Kreuter .08 .25
14 Darren Lewis .08 .25
15 Joe Magrane .08 .25
16 Norberto Martin .08 .25
17 Dave Martinez .08 .25
18 Kirk McCaskill .08 .25
19 Lyle Mouton .08 .25
20 Jose Munoz .08 .25
21 Tony Philips .08 .25
22 Bill Simas .08 .25
23 Chris Snopek .08 .25
24 Kevin Tapani .08 .25
25 Dannny Tartabull .20 .50
26 Frank Thomas .75 2.00
27 Larry Thomas .08 .25
28 Robin Ventura .60 1.50
29 White Sox Infield .60 1.50
Frank Thomas
Ray Durham
Robin
30 White Sox Coaches .08 .25
Mark Salas
Bill Buckner
Mike

1996 White Sox Fleer

These 20 standard-size cards have the same design as the regular Fleer issue, except they are UV coated, they use silver foil and they are numbered "x of 20". The team set packs were available at retail locations and hobby shops in 10-card packs for a suggested price of $1.99.

COMPLETE SET (20) 1.50 3.00
1 Wilson Alvarez .07 .20
2 Harold Baines .15 .40
3 Jason Bere .02 .10
4 Ray Durham .15 .40
5 Alex Fernandez .02 .10
6 Ozzie Guillen .15 .40
7 Roberto Hernandez .07 .20
8 Matt Karchner .02 .10
9 Ron Karkovice .02 .10
10 Darren Lewis .02 .10
11 Dave Martinez .02 .10
12 Lyle Mouton .02 .10
13 Tony Phillips .02 .10
14 Chris Snopek .02 .10
15 Kevin Tapani .02 .10
16 Danny Tartabull .02 .10
17 Frank Thomas .40 1.00
18 Robin Ventura .20 .50
19 Logo card .02 .10
20 Checklist .02 .10

1997 White Sox Coke Magnet

This four-card set distributed by Coca-Cola features action color player photos printed on die-cut magnets. The magnets are unnumbered and checklisted below in alphabetical order.

COMPLETE SET (4) 3.00 8.00
1 Mike Cameron 1.50 4.00
2 Ray Durham 1.25 3.00
3 Jorge Fabregas .75 2.00
4 Lyle Mouton .75 2.00

1997 White Sox Score

This 15-card set of the Chicago White Sox was issued in five-card packs with a suggested retail price of $1.30 each. The fronts feature color player photos with special team specific color foil stamping. The backs carry player information. Only 100 cases were made for each team. Platinum parallel cards were inserted at a rate of 1:6, Premier parallel cards at a rate of 1:31.

COMPLETE SET (15) 2.00 5.00
*PLATINUM: 4X BASIC CARDS
*PREMIER: 20X BASIC CARDS
1 Frank Thomas .60 1.50
2 James Baldwin .08 .25
3 Danny Tartabull .08 .25
4 Jeff Darwin .08 .25
5 Harold Baines .40 1.00
6 Roberto Hernandez .15 .40
7 Ray Durham .40 1.00
8 Robin Ventura .40 1.00
9 Wilson Alvarez .15 .40
10 Lyle Mouton .08 .25
11 Alex Fernandez .08 .25
12 Ron Karkovice .08 .25
13 Kevin Tapani .08 .25
14 Tony Phillips .08 .25
15 Mike Cameron .40 1.00

1997 White Sox Team Issue

This 30-card set of the Chicago White Sox features color action player photos in white borders. The backs carry player information and career statistics.

COMPLETE SET (30) 5.00 12.00
2 Nellie Fox .40 1.00
3 Harold Baines .40 1.00
5 Ray Durham .30 .75
7 Norberto Martin .08 .25
8 Albert Belle .20 .50
10 Darren Lewis .08 .25
12 Jorge Fabregas .08 .25
13 Ozzie Guillen .40 1.00
14 Dave Martinez .08 .25
15 Doug Drabek .08 .25
18 Terry Bevington MG .08 .25
20 Ron Karkovice .08 .25
23 Robin Ventura .40 1.00
24 Mike Cameron .40 1.00
26 Chuck McElroy .08 .25
27 Chris Snopek .08 .25
28 Lyle Mouton .08 .25
29 Tony Pena .08 .25
35 Frank Thomas 1.25 3.00
37 James Baldwin .08 .25
38 Jaime Navarro .08 .25
39 Roberto Hernandez .30 .75
40 Wilson Alvarez .20 .50
41 Bill Simas .08 .25
43 Carlos Castillo .08 .25
44 Danny Darwin .08 .25
47 Matt Karchner .08 .25
49 Tony Castillo .08 .25
NNO White Sox Training Staff .08 .25
NNO White Sox Coaches Trivia .08 .25

1998 White Sox Lemon Chill

This 30-card standard-size set features members of the 1998 Chicago White Sox. The full bleed borders feature a player photos set up by a design on the left and the players name on the bottom. The horizontal backs have vital statistics, 1997 statistics and a blurb about the players 1997 season. Since the cards are unnumbered we have sequenced them in alphabetical order. Please note that Magglio Ordonez appears in his Rookie Card year.

COMPLETE SET (30) 5.00 12.00
1 Jeff Abbott .08 .25
2 James Baldwin .08 .25
3 Albert Belle .20 .50
4 Mike Cameron .30 .75
5 Mike Caruso .08 .25
6 Carlos Castillo .08 .25
7 Wil Cordero .08 .25
8 Ray Durham .40 1.00
9 Scott Eyre .08 .25
10 Keith Foulke .60 1.50
11 Bob Howry .08 .25
12 Matt Karchner .08 .25
13 Chad Krueter .08 .25
14 Jerry Manuel MG .08 .25
15 Jaime Navarro .08 .25
16 Greg Norton .08 .25
17 Charlie O'Brien .08 .25
18 Magglio Ordonez 1.25 3.00
19 Jim Parque .08 .25
20 Bill Simas .08 .25
21 Mike Sirotka .08 .25
22 Chris Snopek .08 .25
23 John Snyder .08 .25
24 Frank Thomas .60 1.50
25 Robin Ventura .40 1.00
26 Bryan Ward .08 .25
27 Nardi Contreras CO .08 .25
Von Joshua CO
28 Wallace Johnson CO .08 .25
Bryan Little CO
29 Joe Nossek CO .08 .25
Art Kusnyer CO
30 Mark Salas CO .08 .25
Steve Odgers COND
Herm Schneider T

1998 White Sox Score

This 15-card set was issued in special retail packs and features color photos of the Chicago White Sox team. The backs carry player information. A special platinum parallel set was also issued and randomly inserted in packs.

COMPLETE SET (15) 2.00 5.00
*PLATINUM: 5X BASIC CARDS
1 Albert Belle .20 .50
2 Chuck McElroy .08 .25
3 Mike Cameron .30 .75
4 Ozzie Guillen .40 1.00
5 Jaime Navarro .08 .25
6 Chris Clemons .08 .25
7 Lyle Mouton .08 .25
8 Frank Thomas .50 1.25
9 Doug Drabek .08 .25
10 Robin Ventura .40 1.00
11 Dave Martinez .08 .25
12 Ray Durham .30 .75
13 Chris Snopek .08 .25
14 James Baldwin .08 .25
15 Jorge Fabregas .08 .25

1999 White Sox Sheldon

These eight small cards (approximately 2" by 2 3/8") feature special art baseballs drawn by Monty Sheldon and feature members of the 1919 White Sox on the 80th anniversary of the Black Sox Scandal. The fronts feature a photo of the ball while the backs promote the artwork of Sheldon. Since these cards are unnumbered, we have sequenced them in alphabetical order.

COMPLETE SET (8) 6.00 15.00
1 Eddie Cicotte 1.00 2.50
2 Happy Felsch .60 1.50
3 Chick Gandil .75 2.00
4 Joe Jackson 2.00 5.00
5 Fred McMullin .40 1.00
6 Swede Risberg .40 1.00
7 Buck Weaver 1.00 2.50
8 Lefty Williams .60 1.50

2005 White Sox Donruss Team Heroes National

COMPLETE SET (6)
1 Frank Thomas 1.00 2.50
2 Shingo Takatsu .50 1.25
3 Aaron Rowand .60 1.50
4 Paul Konerko .75 2.00
5 Jermaine Dye .40 1.00
6 Mark Buehrle .50 1.25

2005 White Sox Topps World Series Champions

1 Mark Buehrle .15 .40
2 A.J. Pierzynski .10 .25
3 Juan Uribe .10 .25
4 Tadahito Iguchi .15 .40
5 Paul Konerko .15 .40
6 Frank Thomas .25 .60
7 Jermaine Dye .10 .25
8 Aaron Rowand .10 .25
9 Timo Perez .10 .25
10 Jose Contreras .10 .25
11 Carl Everett .10 .25
12 Pablo Ozuna .10 .25
13 Geoff Blum .10 .25
14 Cliff Politte .10 .25
15 Freddy Garcia .10 .25
16 Bobby Jenks .10 .25
17 Dustin Hermanson .10 .25
18 Neal Cotts .10 .25
19 Chris Widger .10 .25
20 Jon Garland .10 .25
21 Luis Vizcaino .10 .25
22 Damaso Marte .10 .25
23 Scott Podsednik .10 .25
24 Willie Harris .10 .25
25 Orlando Hernandez .10 .25
26 Joe Crede .10 .25
27 Ross Gload .10 .25
28 Brian Anderson .15 .40
29 Brandon McCarthy .15 .40
30 Ozzie Guillen MG .10 .25
31 White Sox Team Card .10 .25
32 Mark Buehrle 49 Straight HL .15 .40
33 White Sox Win 99 HL .10 .25
34 Mark Buehrle AL Starter HL .15 .40
35 Scott Podsednik Steals 59 HL .10 .25
36 Paul Konerko 40-100 HL .15 .40
37 A.J. Pierzynski ALDS .10 .25
38 Tadahito Iguchi ALDS .15 .40
39 Paul Konerko ALDS .15 .40
40 A.J. Pierzynski ALCS .10 .25
41 Paul Konerko ALCS .15 .40
42 South Side Series ALCS .10 .25
43 Mark Buehrle ALCS .15 .40
44 Jon Garland ALCS .10 .25
45 Freddy Garcia ALCS .10 .25
46 Jose Contreras ALCS .10 .25
47 Joe Crede .10 .25
Bobby Jenks WS
48 P.Konerko .15 .40
S.Podsednik WS
49 Geoff Blum WS .10 .25
50 ChiSox Sweep WS .10 .25
51 Freddy Garcia .10 .25
Juan Uribe WS
52 Astros Get Swept WS .10 .25
53 Scott Podsednik .15 .40
Jermaine Dye
Tadahito Iguchi PS
54 Paul Konerko ALCS MVP .15 .40
55 Jermaine Dye WS MVP .10 .25

2005 White Sox Topps World Series Champions Jumbo

NNO White Sox Team Photo .40 1.00

2006 White Sox Topps

COMPLETE SET (14) 3.00 8.00
CWS1 Jermaine Dye .12 .30
CWS2 Joe Crede .12 .30
CWS3 A.J. Pierzynski .12 .30
CWS4 Tadahito Iguchi .12 .30
CWS5 Scott Podsednik .12 .30
CWS6 Juan Uribe .12 .30
CWS7 Jim Thome .20 .50
CWS8 Mark Buehrle .20 .50
CWS9 Freddy Garcia .12 .30
CWS10 Bobby Jenks .12 .30
CWS11 Jon Garland .12 .30
CWS12 Jose Contreras .12 .30
CWS13 Rob Mackowiak .12 .30
CWS14 Paul Konerko .20 .50

2007 White Sox Topps

COMPLETE SET (14) 3.00 8.00
CHW1 Paul Konerko .20 .50
CHW2 Scott Podsednik .12 .30
CHW3 Tadahito Iguchi .12 .30
CHW4 Javier Vazquez .12 .30
CHW5 Jon Garland .12 .30
CHW6 Rob Mackowiak .12 .30
CHW7 Josh Fields .12 .30
CHW8 Juan Uribe .12 .30
CHW9 Ryan Sweeney .12 .30
CHW10 Jim Thome .20 .50
CHW11 Mark Buehrle .20 .50
CHW12 Jose Contreras .12 .30
CHW13 Bobby Jenks .12 .30
CHW14 Jermaine Dye .12 .30

2008 White Sox Topps

COMPLETE SET (14) 3.00 8.00
CHW1 Nick Swisher .20 .50
CHW2 Paul Konerko .20 .50
CHW3 Carlos Quentin .12 .30
CHW4 Javier Vazquez .12 .30
CHW5 Orlando Cabrera .20 .50
CHW6 Joe Crede .12 .30
CHW7 Josh Fields .12 .30
CHW8 A.J. Pierzynski .12 .30
CHW9 Jerry Owens .12 .30
CHW10 Jim Thome .20 .50
CHW11 Mark Buehrle .20 .50
CHW12 Jose Contreras .12 .30
CHW13 Bobby Jenks .12 .30
CHW14 Jermaine Dye .12 .30

2009 White Sox Topps

CWS1 Carlos Quentin .15 .40
CWS2 John Danks .15 .40
CWS3 Brian Anderson .15 .40
CWS4 Gavin Floyd .15 .40
CWS5 Paul Konerko .25 .60
CWS6 Mark Buehrle .25 .60
CWS7 Orlando Cabrera .15 .40
CWS8 Brent Lillibridge .15 .40
CWS9 Jermaine Dye .15 .40
CWS10 Bobby Jenks .15 .40
CWS11 Jim Thome .25 .60
CWS12 Jose Contreras .15 .40
CWS13 A.J. Pierzynski .15 .40
CWS14 Ozzie Guillen .15 .40
CWS15 Barack Obama .50 1.25

2010 White Sox Topps

CWS1 Gordon Beckham .15 .40
CWS2 Alexei Ramirez .25 .60
CWS3 Bobby Jenks .15 .40
CWS4 Alex Rios .15 .40
CWS5 Juan Pierre .15 .40
CWS6 Tyler Flowers .25 .60
CWS7 Mark Teahen .15 .40
CWS8 Daniel Hudson .25 .60
CWS9 Mark Buehrle .25 .60
CWS10 Gavin Floyd .15 .40
CWS11 Jake Peavy .15 .40
CWS12 A.J. Pierzynski .15 .40
CWS13 Paul Konerko .25 .60
CWS14 John Danks .15 .40
CWS15 Carlos Quentin .15 .40
CWS16 Omar Vizquel .25 .60
CWS17 Andruw Jones .15 .40

2011 White Sox Topps

CWS1 Adam Dunn .25 .60
CWS2 Gavin Floyd .15 .40
CWS3 Chris Sale 1.25 3.00
CWS4 Carlos Quentin .15 .40
CWS5 Juan Pierre .15 .40
CWS6 Jake Peavy .15 .40
CWS7 John Danks .15 .40
CWS8 Matt Thornton .15 .40
CWS9 Dayan Viciedo .15 .40
CWS10 Edwin Jackson .15 .40
CWS11 Omar Vizquel .25 .60
CWS12 Gordon Beckham .15 .40
CWS13 Alexei Ramirez .25 .60
CWS14 Alex Rios .15 .40
CWS15 A.J. Pierzynski .15 .40
CWS16 Paul Konerko .25 .60
CWS17 U.S. Cellular Field .15 .40

2012 White Sox Topps

CWS1 Paul Konerko .25 .60
CWS2 Jake Peavy .25 .60
CWS3 Matt Thornton .25 .60
CWS4 Gordon Beckham .25 .60
CWS5 Brent Morel .25 .60
CWS6 A.J. Pierzynski .25 .60
CWS7 Alex Rios .30 .75
CWS8 Dayan Viciedo .25 .60
CWS9 Alexei Ramirez .30 .75
CWS10 Adam Dunn .30 .75
CWS11 Brent Lillibridge .25 .60
CWS12 Alejandro De Aza .25 .60
CWS13 Chris Sale .40 1.00
CWS14 John Danks .25 .60
CWS15 Gavin Floyd .25 .60
CWS16 Philip Humber .25 .60
CWS17 U.S. Cellular Field .15 .40

2013 White Sox Topps

COMPLETE SET (17) 3.00 8.00
CHW1 Chris Sale .25 .60
CHW2 Paul Konerko .25 .60
CHW3 Jake Peavy .25 .60
CHW4 Adam Dunn .20 .50
CHW5 Addison Reed .15 .40
CHW6 Alejandro De Aza .15 .40
CHW7 Alex Rios .20 .50
CHW8 John Danks .15 .40
CHW9 Alexei Ramirez .30 .75
CHW10 Gavin Floyd .25 .60
CHW11 Jeff Keppinger .15 .40
CHW12 Matt Thornton .15 .40
CHW13 Dayan Viciedo .25 .60
CHW14 Gordon Beckham .15 .40
CHW15 Jose Quintana .15 .40
CHW16 Tyler Flowers .15 .40
CHW17 U.S. Cellular Field .25 .60

2014 White Sox Topps

COMPLETE SET (17) 3.00 8.00
CHW1 Chris Sale .25 .60
CHW2 Paul Konerko .20 .50
CHW3 Avisail Garcia .20 .50
CHW4 Adam Dunn .20 .50
CHW5 Tyler Flowers .15 .40
CHW6 Alejandro De Aza .15 .40
CHW7 Andre Rienzo .15 .40
CHW8 John Danks .15 .40
CHW9 Alexei Ramirez .20 .50
CHW10 Jordan Danks .15 .40
CHW11 Matt Davidson .20 .50
CHW12 Erik Johnson .15 .40
CHW13 Dayan Viciedo .15 .40
CHW14 Gordon Beckham .15 .40
CHW15 Jose Quintana .15 .40
CHW16 Adam Eaton .15 .40
CHW17 U.S. Cellular Field .15 .40

2015 White Sox Topps

COMPLETE SET (17) 3.00 8.00
CWS1 Jose Abreu .25 .60
CWS2 Tyler Flowers .15 .40
CWS3 Conor Gillaspie .20 .50
CWS4 Alexei Ramirez .20 .50
CWS5 Adam Eaton .15 .40
CWS6 Zach Duke .15 .40
CWS7 Avisail Garcia .20 .50
CWS8 Melky Cabrera .15 .40
CWS9 Adam LaRoche .15 .40
CWS10 Chris Sale .25 .60
CWS11 Jeff Samardzija .15 .40
CWS12 David Robertson .20 .50
CWS13 Jose Quintana .15 .40
CWS14 John Danks .15 .40
CWS15 Gordon Beckham .15 .40
CWS16 Emilio Bonifacio .15 .40
CWS17 Javy Guerra .15 .40

2016 White Sox Topps

COMPLETE SET (17) 3.00 8.00
CHW1 Chris Sale .25 .60
CHW2 Jose Abreu .25 .60
CHW3 Todd Frazier .15 .40
CHW4 Melky Cabrera .15 .40
CHW5 Adam Eaton .15 .40
CHW6 Avisail Garcia .20 .50
CHW7 Adam LaRoche .15 .40
CHW8 Brett Lawrie .20 .50
CHW9 David Robertson .15 .40
CHW10 Jose Quintana .15 .40
CHW11 John Danks .15 .40
CHW12 Carlos Rodon .25 .60
CHW13 Alex Avila .20 .50
CHW14 Zach Duke .15 .40
CHW15 Dioner Navarro .15 .40
CHW16 Jake Petricka .15 .40
CHW17 Nate Jones .15 .40

2017 White Sox Topps

COMPLETE SET (17) 3.00 8.00
CHW1 Jose Abreu .25 .60
CHW2 Carlos Sanchez .15 .40
CHW3 Carlos Rodon .25 .60
CHW4 Charlie Tilson .15 .40
CHW5 Tim Anderson .25 .60
CHW6 James Shields .15 .40
CHW7 Derek Holland .15 .40
CHW8 Guaranteed Rate Field .15 .40
CHW9 Melky Cabrera .15 .40
CHW10 Todd Frazier .15 .40
CHW11 Brett Lawrie .20 .50
CHW12 Nate Jones .15 .40
CHW13 Avisail Garcia .20 .50
CHW14 Miguel Gonzalez .15 .40
CHW15 Tyler Saladino .15 .40
CHW16 Zach Putnam .15 .40
CHW17 Yoan Moncada .50 1.25

2018 White Sox Topps

COMPLETE SET (17) 2.00 5.00
WS1 Jose Abreu .25 .60
WS2 Matt Davidson .20 .50
WS3 Avisail Garcia .20 .50
WS4 Yoan Moncada .25 .60
WS5 Tim Anderson .25 .60
WS6 Gregory Infante .15 .40
WS7 Nicky Delmonico .15 .40
WS8 Nate Jones .15 .40
WS9 Juan Minaya .15 .40
WS10 Leury Garcia .15 .40
WS11 Lucas Giolito .20 .50
WS12 Carson Fulmer .15 .40
WS13 James Shields .15 .40
WS14 Carlos Rodon .25 .60
WS15 Danny Farquhar .15 .40
WS16 Welington Castillo .15 .40
WS17 Reynaldo Lopez .20 .50

2019 White Sox Topps

COMPLETE SET (17) 2.00 5.00
WS1 Jose Abreu .25 .60
WS2 Yoan Moncada .25 .60
WS3 Tim Anderson .25 .60
WS4 James McCann .20 .50
WS5 Adam Engel .15 .40
WS6 Nicky Delmonico .15 .40
WS7 Yolmer Sanchez .15 .40
WS8 Lucas Giolito .20 .50
WS9 Reynaldo Lopez .20 .50
WS10 Carlos Rodon .25 .60
WS11 Daniel Palka .15 .40
WS12 Welington Castillo .15 .40
WS13 Dylan Covey .15 .40
WS14 Michael Kopech .50 1.25
WS15 Yonder Alonso .15 .40
WS16 Nate Jones
WS17 Ivan Nova .20 .50

2020 White Sox Topps

CWS1 Tim Anderson .25 .60
CWS2 Jose Abreu .25 .60
CWS3 Eloy Jimenez .50 1.25
CWS4 Lucas Giolito .20 .50
CWS5 Yasmani Grandal .15 .40
CWS6 Yoan Moncada .25 .60
CWS7 Alex Colome .15 .40
CWS8 Reynaldo Lopez .20 .50
CWS9 Dylan Cease .25 .60
CWS10 Kelvin Herrera .15 .40
CWS11 Leury Garcia .15 .40
CWS12 Michael Kopech .30 .75
CWS13 James McCann .20 .50
CWS14 Zack Collins .20 .50
CWS15 Dallas Keuchel .20 .50
CWS16 Carlos Rodon .25 .60
CWS17 Danny Mendick .20 .50

2017 White Sox Topps National Baseball Card Day

COMPLETE SET (10) 6.00 15.00
CWS1 Jose Abreu 1.00 2.50
CWS2 Nate Jones .60 1.50
CWS3 Yoan Moncada 2.00 5.00
CWS4 Carlos Rodon 1.00 2.50
CWS5 James Shields .60 1.50
CWS6 Tim Anderson 1.00 2.50
CWS7 Zach Putnam .60 1.50
CWS8 Avisail Garcia .75 2.00
CWS9 Tyler Saladino .60 1.50
CWS10 Frank Thomas 1.00 2.50

1992 Whitehall Prototypes

This five-card standard-size set features color close-up photos inside a tan inner border and a white outer border. By a process known as Photonix, old photographs from the National Baseball Library underwent extensive pixel value recomputation to restore contrast, resolution, and light balance. The cards are stamped "Prototype" across the text. The cards are unnumbered and checklisted below in alphabetical order.

COMPLETE SET (5) 5.00 12.00
1 Ty Cobb 1.50 4.00
2 Lou Gehrig 1.50 4.00
3 Babe Ruth 2.50 6.00
4 Honus Wagner 1.25 3.00
5 Cy Young .75 2.00

1992 Whitehall Legends to Life

This five-card hologram set from the Whitehall Collection, which measures the standard size, features hologram images created from actual photographs on the card fronts. The cards are unnumbered and checklisted below in alphabetical order.

COMPLETE SET (5) 5.00 12.00
1 Ty Cobb 1.50 4.00
2 Lou Gehrig 1.50 4.00
3 Babe Ruth 2.50 6.00
4 Honus Wagner 1.25 3.00
5 Cy Young .75 2.00

1978 Wiffle Ball Discs

These discs were on the side of Wiffle Ball boxes. Even though the copyright date on the discs are 1976, the player selection implies that this set was issued early in 1978. For some reason, Thurman Munson discs seem to be available in significantly higher quantities and we have labeled Munson as a DP. These discs are unnumbered and we have sequenced this set in alphabetical order.

COMPLETE SET 175.00 350.00
COMMON PLAYER .75 2.00
1 Sal Bando 1.00 2.50
2 Buddy Bell 1.25 3.00
3 Johnny Bench 3.00 8.00
4 Vida Blue 1.00 2.50
5 Bert Blyleven 1.25 3.00
6 Bobby Bonds 1.00 2.50
7 George Brett 10.00 25.00
8 Lou Brock 2.50 6.00
9 Bill Buckner 1.00 2.50
10 Ray Burris .75 2.00
11 Jeff Burroughs .75 2.00
12 Campy Campaneris 1.00 2.50
13 Rod Carew 2.50 6.00
14 Steve Carlton 2.50 6.00
15 Dave Cash .75 2.00
16 Cesar Cedeno 1.00 2.50
17 Ron Cey 1.25 3.00
18 Chris Chambliss .75 2.00
19 Dave Concepcion 1.25 3.00
20 Dennis Eckersley 2.50 6.00
21 Mark Fidrych 2.00 5.00
22 Rollie Fingers 2.50 6.00
23 Carlton Fisk 4.00 10.00
24 George Foster 1.00 2.50
25 Wayne Garland .75 2.00
26 Ralph Garr .75 2.00
27 Steve Garvey 2.00 5.00
28 Don Gullett .75 2.00
29 Larry Hisle .75 2.00
30 Al Hrabosky .75 2.00
31 Catfish Hunter 2.50 6.00
32 Reggie Jackson 5.00 12.00
33 Randy Jones .75 2.00
34 Dave Kingman 1.50 4.00
35 Jerry Koosman 1.25 3.00
36 Ed Kranepool .75 2.00
37 Ron LeFlore 1.00 2.50
38 Sixto Lezcano .75 2.00
39 Davey Lopes 1.00 2.50
40 Greg Luzinski 1.25 3.00
41 Fred Lynn 1.00 2.50
42 Garry Maddox .75 2.00
43 Jon Matlack .75 2.00
44 Gary Matthews 1.00 2.50
45 Lee May 1.00 2.50
46 John Mayberry .75 2.00
47 Bake McBride .75 2.00
48 Tug McGraw 1.25 3.00
49 Hal McRae 1.00 2.50
50 Andy Messersmith .75 2.00
51 Randy Moffitt .75 2.00
52 John Montefusco .75 2.00
53 Joe Morgan 2.50 6.00
54 Thurman Munson DP 4.00 10.00
55 Graig Nettles 1.25 3.00
56 Al Oliver 1.00 2.50
57 Jorge Orta .75 2.00
58 Jim Palmer 2.50 6.00
59 Dave Parker 1.50 4.00
60 Tony Perez 2.00 5.00
61 Gaylord Perry 2.50 6.00
62 Jim Rice 1.50 4.00
63 Steve Rogers .75 2.00
64 Pete Rose 15.00 40.00
65 Joe Rudi .75 2.00
66 Nolan Ryan 15.00 40.00
67 Manny Sanguillen .75 2.00
68 Mike Schmidt 5.00 12.00
69 Tom Seaver 5.00 12.00
70 Ted Simmons 1.25 3.00
71 Reggie Smith 1.00 2.50
72 Willie Stargell 5.00 12.00
73 Rusty Staub 1.25 3.00
74 Rennie Stennett .75 2.00
75 Don Sutton 2.00 5.00
76 Gene Tenace .75 2.00
77 Luis Tiant 1.25 3.00
78 Manny Trillo .75 2.00
79 Bob Watson 1.00 2.50
80 Carl Yastrzemski 8.00 20.00
81 Richie Zisk .75 2.00

1963 Wilhelm Motel

This one card postcard set was issued on November 2, 1963 to commemorate the opening of a motel in Georgia that Wilhelm had a stake in. The front of the postcard shows a photo of Wilhelm warming up in front of the White Sox dugout while the back has an ad for the motel.

1 Hoyt Wilhelm 4.00 10.00

1923 Willard's Chocolates V100

Issued in Canada by Willards Chocolates, these 180 blank-backed cards measure approximately 2" by 3 1/4". The catalog designation for this set is V100. The white-bordered fronts feature sepia-toned player photos. The player's facsimile autograph appears on the card face. The cards are unnumbered and checklisted below in alphabetical order.

COMPLETE SET (180) 5250.00 10500.00
1 Babe Adams 40.00 80.00
2 Grover C. Alexander 100.00 200.00
3 James Austin MG 30.00 60.00
4 Jim Bagby 30.00 60.00
5 Frank Baker 60.00 120.00
6 Dave Bancroft 60.00 120.00
7 Turner Barber 30.00 60.00
8 Jesse L. Barnes 30.00 60.00
9 John Bassler 30.00 60.00
10 Lu Blue 30.00 60.00
11 Norman Boeckel 30.00 60.00
12 Frank Brazill 30.00 60.00
13 George H. Burns 30.00 60.00
14 George J. Burns 30.00 60.00
15 Leon Cadore 40.00 80.00
16 Max Carey 60.00 120.00
17 Harold G. Carlson 30.00 60.00
18 Lloyd Christenberry 30.00 60.00
19 Vernon J. Clemons 30.00 60.00
20 Ty Cobb 500.00 1000.00
21 Bert Cole 30.00 60.00
22 John F. Collins 30.00 60.00
23 Stan Coveleski 60.00 120.00
24 Walton E. Cruise 30.00 60.00
25 George W. Cutshaw 30.00 60.00
26 Jake Daubert 40.00 80.00
27 George Dauss 30.00 60.00
28 Frank Davis 30.00 60.00
29 Charles A. Deal 30.00 60.00
30 William L. Doak 30.00 60.00
31 Wild Bill Donovan MG 30.00 60.00
32 Hugh Duffy MG 60.00 120.00
33 Joe Dugan 40.00 80.00
34 Louis B. Duncan 30.00 60.00
35 Jimmy Dykes 40.00 80.00
36 Howard Ehmke 40.00 80.00
37 Francis R. Ellerbe 30.00 60.00
38 Eric G. Erickson 30.00 60.00
39 Johnny Evers MG 60.00 120.00
40 Urban Faber 60.00 120.00
41 Bibb Falk 30.00 60.00
42 Max Flack 30.00 60.00
43 Lee Fohl MG 30.00 60.00
44 Jack Fournier 30.00 60.00
45 Frank Frisch 60.00 120.00
46 C.E. Galloway 30.00 60.00
47 Billy Gardner 30.00 60.00
48 Edward Gharrity 30.00 60.00
49 George Gibson 30.00 60.00
50 Kid Gleason MG 50.00 100.00
51 William Gleason 30.00 60.00
52 Hank Gowdy 40.00 80.00
53 I.M. Griffin 30.00 60.00
54 Thomas Griffith 30.00 60.00
55 Burleigh Grimes 60.00 120.00
56 Charlie Grimm 40.00 80.00
57 Jesse Haines 60.00 120.00
58 Bill Harris 30.00 60.00
59 Bucky Harris 60.00 120.00
60 Robert Hasty 30.00 60.00
61 Harry Heilmann 60.00 120.00
62 Walter Henline 30.00 60.00
63 Walter Holke 30.00 60.00
64 Charles Hollocher 30.00 60.00
65 Harry Hooper 60.00 120.00
66 Rogers Hornsby 150.00 300.00
67 Waite Hoyt 60.00 120.00
68 Miller Huggins MG 60.00 120.00
69 W.C. Jacobson 30.00 60.00
70 Charlie Jamieson 30.00 60.00
71 E. Johnson 30.00 60.00
72 Walter Johnson 250.00 500.00
73 James H. Johnston 30.00 60.00
74 Bob Jones 30.00 60.00
75 Sam Jones 40.00 80.00
76 Joe Judge 40.00 80.00
77 James W. Keenan 30.00 60.00
78 Geo. L. Kelly 60.00 120.00
79 Peter J. Kilduff 30.00 60.00
80 William Killefer 30.00 60.00
81 Lee King 30.00 60.00
82 Ray Kolp 30.00 60.00
83 John Lavan 30.00 60.00
84 Nemo Leibold 30.00 60.00
85 Connie Mack MG 100.00 200.00
86 Duster Mails 30.00 60.00
87 Walter Maranville 60.00 120.00
88 Richard W. Marquard 60.00 120.00
89 Carl W. Mays 40.00 80.00
90 Geo. F. McBride 30.00 60.00
91 Harvey McClellan 30.00 60.00
92 John J. McGraw MG 75.00 150.00
93 Austin B. McHenry 30.00 60.00
94 Snuffy McInnis 40.00 80.00
95 Douglas McWeeny 30.00 60.00
96 Mike Menosky 30.00 60.00
97 Emil F. Meusel 30.00 60.00
98 Bob Meusel 40.00 80.00
99 Henry W. Meyers 30.00 60.00
100 Clyde Milan MG 40.00 80.00
101 John K. Miljus 30.00 60.00
102 Edmund J. Miller 30.00 60.00
103 Elmer Miller 30.00 60.00
104 Otto L. Miller 30.00 60.00
105 Fred Mitchell MG 30.00 60.00
106 Geo. Mogridge 30.00 60.00
107 Patrick J. Moran MG 30.00 60.00
108 John D. Morrison 30.00 60.00
109 Johnny Mostil 30.00 60.00
110 Clarence F. Mueller 30.00 60.00
111 Greasy Neale 50.00 100.00
112 Joseph Oeschger 30.00 60.00
113 Robert J. O'Farrell 30.00 60.00
114 John Oldham 30.00 60.00
115 Ivy Olson 30.00 60.00
116 Geo. M. O'Neil 30.00 60.00
117 Steve O'Neill 30.00 60.00
118 Frank J. Parkinson 30.00 60.00
119 Dode Paskert 30.00 60.00
120 Roger Peckinpaugh 40.00 80.00
121 Herb Pennock 60.00 120.00
122 Ralph Perkins 30.00 60.00
123 Jeff Pfeffer 30.00 60.00
124 Wally Pipp 40.00 80.00
125 Charles Ponder 30.00 60.00
126 Raymond R. Powell 30.00 60.00
127 Del Pratt 30.00 60.00
128 Joseph Rapp 30.00 60.00
129 John H. Rawlings 30.00 60.00
130 Edgar Rice 60.00 120.00
131 Branch Rickey MG 75.00 150.00
132 James J. Ring 30.00 60.00
133 Eppa J. Rixey 60.00 120.00
134 Davis A. Robertson 30.00 60.00
135 Edwin Rommel 40.00 80.00
136 Edd J. Roush 60.00 120.00
137 Harold Ruel 30.00 60.00
138 Allen Russell 30.00 60.00
139 Babe Ruth 750.00 1500.00
140 Wilfred D. Ryan 30.00 60.00
141 Henry F. Sallee 30.00 60.00
142 Wally Schang 40.00 80.00
143 Raymond H. Schmandt 30.00 60.00
144 Everett Scott 40.00 80.00
145 Henry Severeid 30.00 60.00
146 Joseph W. Sewell 60.00 120.00
147 Howard S. Shanks 30.00 60.00
148 Earl Sheely 30.00 60.00
149 Ralph Shinners 30.00 60.00
150 Urban J. Shocker 40.00 80.00
151 George H. Sisler 75.00 150.00
152 Earl L. Smith 30.00 60.00
153 Earl S. Smith 30.00 60.00
154 George A. Smith 30.00 60.00
155 John Smith 30.00 60.00
156 Tris Speaker MG 100.00 200.00
157 Arnold Staatz 30.00 60.00
158 Riggs Stephenson 50.00 100.00
159 Milton J. Stock 30.00 60.00
160 John L. Sullivan 30.00 60.00
161 Herb Thormahlen 30.00 60.00
162 James A. Tierney 30.00 60.00
163 John Tobin 30.00 60.00
164 James L. Vaughn 30.00 60.00
165 Bobby Veach 30.00 60.00
166 Tilly Walker 30.00 60.00
167 Aaron Ward 30.00 60.00
168 Zack D. Wheat 60.00 120.00
169 George B. Whitted 30.00 60.00
170 Irvin K. Wilhelm 30.00 60.00
171 Roy H. Wilkinson 30.00 60.00
172 Fred C. Williams 40.00 80.00
173 Ken Williams 40.00 80.00
174 Samuel W. Wilson 30.00 60.00
175 Ivy B. Wingo 30.00 60.00
176 Whitey Witt 40.00 80.00
177 Joseph Wood 50.00 100.00
178 Clarence Yaryan 30.00 60.00
179 Ralph Young 30.00 60.00
180 Ross Youngs 60.00 120.00

1924 Willard's Chocolates Sports Champions V122

2 Eddie Collins
5 Babe Ruth
39 Ty Cobb

1922 William Paterson V89

This 50-card set was inserted in packages of caramel candy. The cards measure approximately 2" by 3 1/4". the fronts feature sepia-toned player photos framed by white borders. The following information appears in the bottom border beneath the picture: card number, player's name, team name and imprint information (Wm. Paterson, Limited; Brantford, Canada). The backs are blank.

COMPLETE SET (50) 3000.00 6000.00
1 Ed Roush 200.00 400.00
2 Rube Marquard 200.00 400.00
3 Del Gainer 100.00 200.00
4 George Sisler 200.00 400.00
5 Joe Bush 125.00 250.00
6 Joe Oeschger 100.00 200.00
7 Willie Kamm 100.00 200.00
8 John Watson 100.00 200.00
9 Adolfo Luque 125.00 250.00
10 Miller Huggins MG 200.00 400.00
11 Wally Schang 125.00 250.00
12 Bob Shawkey 125.00 250.00
13 Tris Speaker MG 200.00 400.00
14 Hugh McQuillen 100.00 200.00
15 George Kelly 200.00 400.00
16 Ray Schalk 200.00 400.00
17 Sam Jones 125.00 250.00
18 Grover Alexander 400.00 800.00
19 Bob Meusel 150.00 300.00
20 Emil Meusel 100.00 200.00
21 Rogers Hornsby 500.00 1000.00
22 Harry Heilmann 200.00 400.00
23 Heinie Groh 125.00 250.00
24 Frankie Frisch 200.00 400.00
25 Babe Ruth 3000.00 6000.00
26 Jack Bentley 100.00 200.00
27 Everett Scott 100.00 200.00
28 Max Carey 200.00 400.00
29 Chick Fewster 100.00 200.00
30 Cy Williams 125.00 250.00
31 Burleigh Grimes 200.00 400.00
32 Waite Hoyt 200.00 400.00
33 Frank Snyder 100.00 200.00
34 Clyde Milan MG 125.00 250.00
35 Eddie Collins 200.00 400.00
36 Travis Jackson 200.00 400.00
37 Ken Williams 125.00 250.00
38 Dave Bancroft 200.00 400.00
39 Mike McNally 100.00 200.00
40 John McGraw MG 400.00 800.00
41 Art Nehf 125.00 250.00
42 Rabbit Maranville 200.00 400.00
43 Charlie Grimm 125.00 250.00
44 Joe Judge 125.00 250.00
45 Wally Pipp 125.00 250.00
46 Ty Cobb 1500.00 3000.00
47 Walter Johnson 600.00 1200.00
48 Jake Daubert 100.00 200.00
49 Zach Wheat 200.00 400.00
50 Herb Pennock 200.00 400.00

1910 Williams Caramel E103

The cards in this 30-card set measure 1 1/2" by 2 3/4". E103 is distinctive for its black and white player portraits set onto a solid red background. Player names and teams are listed below each photo, with "Williams", the manufacturer's name, in the line below. Printed on thin cardboard, the blank back Williams set was released to the public about 1910. Since the cards are unnumbered, they are ordered below alphabetically.

COMPLETE SET (30) 60000.00 120000.00
1 Chas. Bender 2000.00 4000.00
2 Roger Bresnahan 2000.00 4000.00
3 Mordecai Brown 2000.00 4000.00
4 Frank Chance 2000.00 4000.00
5 Hal Chase 1500.00 3000.00
6 Ty Cobb 15000.00 30000.00
7 Eddie Collins 2500.00 5000.00
8 Sam Crawford 2000.00 4000.00
9 Harry Davis 1000.00 2000.00
10 Arthur Devlin 1000.00 2000.00
11 William Donovan 1000.00 2000.00
12 Chas. Dooin 1000.00 2000.00
13 Larry Doyle 1500.00 3000.00
14 John Ewing 1000.00 2000.00
15 George Gibson 1000.00 2000.00
16 Hugh Jennings 2000.00 4000.00
17 David Jones 1000.00 2000.00
18 Tim Jordon 1000.00 2000.00
19 Nap Lajoie 4000.00 8000.00
20 Thomas Leach 1000.00 2000.00
21 Harry Lord 1000.00 2000.00
22 Christy Mathewson 6000.00 12000.00
23 John McLean 1000.00 2000.00
24 George McQuillan 1000.00 2000.00
25 Jim Pastorious 1000.00 2000.00
26 Nap Rucker 1250.00 2500.00
27 Fred Tenney 1000.00 2000.00
28 Ira Thomas 1000.00 2000.00
29 Honus Wagner 7500.00 15000.00
30 Robert Wood 1500.00 3000.00

1912 Gus Williams Lemon Drop

Measuring approximately 2 1/4" by 4" this card feature a photo of Gus Williams taken by Johnston and Co. The front has a photo of Williams in street clothes while the back has the words "Compliments of W.T. Crane's Lemon Drop Package". It is possible that other players were created for this set.

1 Gus Williams 60.00 120.00

1989 Ted Williams Museum Postcards

These postcards, which measure 3 1/2" by 5 1/2" feature a mix of then active and retired players as well as a mix of superstars and noted people in baseball. Each postcard has a drawing on the front while the horizontal postcard back gives the player's name and states that it was approved by Ted Williams with each drawing copyrighted by "Thumper Inc" in 1989. Since these are not numbered, we have sequenced them in alphabetical order.

COMPLETE SET 60.00 120.00
1 Vida Blue 1.00 2.50
Posed shot
2 Vida Blue 1.00 2.50
In Windup
3 Lou Boudreau 1.50 4.00
4 Lou Brock 1.50 4.00
Running
5 Lou Brock 1.50 4.00
Fielding
6 Happy Chandler 1.00 2.50
7 Steve Carlton 2.00 5.00
8 Lou Dials 1.00 2.50
9 Larry Doby 1.50 4.00
10 Bill Doran 1.00 2.50
11 Walt Dropo 1.00 2.50
12 Dwight Evans 1.25 3.00
13 Bob Feller 2.00 5.00
14 Rick Ferrell 1.00 2.50
15 Charlie Gehringer 1.50 4.00
16 Billy Herman 1.50 4.00
17 Catfish Hunter 1.50 4.00
18 Monte Irvin 1.50 4.00
19 Bo Jackson 2.00 5.00
20 Howard Johnson 1.00 2.50
21 Al Kaline 2.00 5.00
22 Ralph Kiner 2.00 5.00
23 Hal Lanier 1.00 2.50
Posed Shot
24 Hal Lanier 1.00 2.50
Throwing
25 Max Lanier 1.00 2.50
26 Bob Lemon 1.50 4.00
27 Bill Madlock 1.25 3.00
28 Willie McCovey 2.00 5.00
29 Johnny Mize 1.50 4.00
30 Don Newcombe 1.25 3.00
31 Johnny Pesky 1.25 3.00
32 Johnny Podres 1.25 3.00
33 Pee Wee Reese 2.00 5.00
34 Red Schoendienst 1.50 4.00
35 Enos Slaughter 1.50 4.00
36 Willie Stargell 1.50 4.00
37 Hoyt Wilhelm 1.50 4.00
38 Ted Williams 4.00 10.00

2001 Ted Williams Museum

1 Ted Williams 4.00 10.00

1995 Ted Williams Tunnel

These twelve cards were issued to honor the opening of the "Ted Williams Tunnel" in Boston. The set was issued by Choice Marketing Inc. except for one of the card number 9's which was issued by Topps.

COMPLETE SET (12) 20.00 50.00
COMMON CARD (1-12) .40 1.00
9A Ted Williams 20.00 50.00
Topps Header Card

1929 Hack Wilson All-Weather Tire

This one card blank-backed photo set, measuring approximately 7" by 9" features Cub slugger Hack Wilson as a promotion for All-Weather Tire Co. on July 2, 1929.

1 Hack Wilson 100.00

1954 Wilson Franks

The cards in this 20-card set measure approximately 2 5/8" by 3 3/4". The 1954 "Wilson Wieners" set contains 20 full color, unnumbered cards. The obverse design of a package of hot dogs appearing to fly through the air is a distinctive feature of this set. Uncut sheets have been seen. Cards are numbered below alphabetically by player's name.

COMPLETE SET (20) 7500.00 15000.00
1 Roy Campanella 750.00 1500.00
2 Del Ennis 200.00 400.00
3 Carl Erskine 250.00 500.00
4 Ferris Fain 150.00 300.00
5 Bob Feller 600.00 1200.00
6 Nellie Fox 300.00 600.00
7 Johnny Groth 150.00 300.00
8 Stan Hack MG 150.00 300.00
9 Gil Hodges 300.00 600.00
10 Ray Jablonski 150.00 300.00
11 Harvey Kuenn 200.00 400.00
12 Roy McMillan 150.00 300.00
13 Andy Pafko 150.00 300.00
14 Paul Richards MG 150.00 300.00
15 Hank Sauer 150.00 300.00
16 Red Schoendienst 300.00 600.00
17 Enos Slaughter 300.00 600.00
18 Vern Stephens 150.00 300.00
19 Sammy White 150.00 300.00
20 Ted Williams 3000.00 6000.00

1959-61 Wilson Sporting Goods

This seven-card set measures approximately 8" by 10" and features white-bordered black-and-white player photos with a facsimile autograph. The player's and sponsor's names are printed in the bottom margin. The backs are blank. The cards are unnumbered and checklisted below in alphabetical order.

COMPLETE SET (8) 100.00 200.00
1 Luis Aparicio 12.50 25.00
2 Ernie Banks 40.00 80.00
3 Nellie Fox 40.00 80.00
4 Harmon Killebrew 40.00 80.00
5 Billy Pierce 7.50 15.00
6 Pete Runnels 5.00 10.00
7 Larry Sherry 5.00 10.00
8 Early Wynn 10.00 20.00

1961 Wilson Sporting Goods H828

This three-card set features black-and-white player images on a gray background with a black border and looks as if the cards were cut from boxes. A player facsimile autograph is printed at the bottom. The cards measure approximately 1 7/8" by 5 1/4" and the catalog number is H828. The cards are unnumbered and checklisted below in alphabetical order.

COMPLETE SET (3) 150.00 300.00
1 Don Hoak 50.00 100.00
2 Harvey Kuenn 50.00 100.00
3 Jim Piersall 50.00 100.00

1961 Wilson Sporting Goods H828-1

This six card set measures approximately 2 1/4" by 4" and features black and white blank backed photos containing a blue facsimile autograph and "Member - Advisory Staff Wilson Sporting Goods Co." across the bottom of the card. According to old hobby experts, this set may very well have more than six players. All additions to this checklist are appreciated. The catalog designation for this set is H828-1.

COMPLETE SET (6) 30.00 60.00
1 Dick Ellsworth 4.00 10.00
2 Don Hoak 4.00 10.00
3 Harvey Kuenn 4.00 10.00
4 Roy McMillan 4.00 10.00
5 Jim Piersall 6.00 15.00
6 Ron Santo 8.00 20.00

1990 Windwalker Discs

This nine-disc set features 1990 American League All-Stars. The discs measure approximately 3 13/16" in diameter. Inside a pale yellow outer border with red baseball stitching, the fronts have a color action player photo. A facsimile autograph is inscribed across the picture. The player's name and the words "1990 All-Star" appear below the picture. The reverse of each disc features a different player. The discs are unnumbered; they are listed below in alphabetical order according to the player on one of the sides.

COMPLETE SET (9) 10.00 25.00
1 Sandy Alomar Jr. .60 1.50
Dave Parker
2 Wade Boggs 2.50 6.00
Kirby Puckett
3 Roger Clemens 1.00 2.50
Bob Welch
4 Cecil Fielder .60 1.50
Bret Saberhagen
5 Chuck Finley .40 1.00
Kelly Gruber
6 Julio Franco .40 1.00
George Bell
7 Ken Griffey Jr. 4.00 10.00
Steve Sax
8 Rickey Henderson 2.00 5.00
Jose Canseco
9 Cal Ripken Jr. 2.50 6.00
Ozzie Guillen

1993 Winfield Rainbow Foods

This ten-card standard-size set was sponsored by Rainbow Foods, with a portion of the sales proceeds donated to the Minnesota Twins Rookie League youth baseball program. The blue-bordered fronts contain color and sepia photos of Winfield beginning with his college years and following him through his career in the major leagues. Winfield's name in red script is displayed on a gold stripe under the picture. The Rainbow Foods logo appears in the lower right. The horizontal backs contain a close-up picture on the left and the appropriate statistics and career summary on the right side. Cards 9 and 10 have vertical backs. The cards are numbered on the back. The cards originally sold in five-card packs for 99 cents. Each pack contained four blue-bordered cards and one gold-bordered card. The gold-bordered set is otherwise identical to the blue-bordered set but due to its relative scarcity sells for two to three times the values listed below.

COMPLETE SET (10) 2.50 6.00
COMMON PLAYER (1-10) .30 .75

1993 Winfield Rainbow Foods Gold

*GOLD: 1.5X TO 4X BASIC

1951-53 Wisconsin Hall of Fame Postcards

These 12 postcards were issued by the Wisconsin Hall of Fame and feature some of the leading athletes out of Milwaukee. The sepia illustrations have a relief of the player as well as some information about them. Since these cards are unnumbered, we have sequenced them in alphabetical order.

COMPLETE SET (12) 175.00 350.00
1 Addie Joss BB 30.00 60.00
4 George McBride BB 7.50 15.00
7 Kid Nichols BB 25.00 50.00
10 Al Simmons BB 30.00 60.00
11 Billy Sullivan BB 10.00 20.00

1990 Wonder Bread Stars

The 1990 Wonder Bread set was issued in 1990 by MSA (Michael Schechter Associates) in conjunction with Wonder Bread. One card was issued inside each specially marked package of Wonder Bread. Cards were available in grocery stores through June 15, 1990. The card was sealed in a pouch in the bread wrapper. This standard-size card set was issued without logos like many of the sets produced by MSA. Cards were printed on thin stock and hence were easily creased during bread handling making the set more difficult to put together one card at a time for condition-conscious collectors. Cards are numbered on the back in the lower right corner. Wonder Bread also offered sets in uncut sheet form to collectors mailing in with 3.00 and five proofs of purchase.

COMPLETE SET (20) 12.50 30.00
1 Bo Jackson .60 1.50
2 Roger Clemens 2.00 5.00
3 Jim Abbott .40 1.00
4 Orel Hershiser .30 .75
5 Ozzie Smith 1.25 3.00

6 Don Mattingly 2.00 5.00
7 Kevin Mitchell .20 .50
8 Jerome Walton .20 .50
9 Kirby Puckett 1.25 3.00
10 Darryl Strawberry .30 .75
11 Robin Yount 1.00 2.50
12 Tony Gwynn 2.00 5.00
13 Alan Trammell .40 1.00
14 Jose Canseco .75 2.00
15 Greg Swindell .20 .50
16 Nolan Ryan 4.00 10.00
17 Howard Johnson .20 .50
18 Ken Griffey Jr. 3.00 8.00
19 Will Clark .60 1.50
20 Ryne Sandberg 1.00 2.50

1985 Woolworth's Topps

This 44-card standard-size set features color as well as black and white cards of All Time Record Holders. The cards are printed with blue ink on an orange and white back. The set was produced for Woolworth's by Topps and was packaged in a colorful box which contained a checklist of the cards in the set on the back panel. The numerical order of the cards coincides alphabetically with the player's name.

COMPLETE SET (44) 2.50 6.00
1 Hank Aaron .30 .75
2 Grover C. Alexander .07 .20
3 Ernie Banks .07 .20
4 Yogi Berra .07 .20
5 Lou Brock .05 .15
6 Steve Carlton .07 .20
7 Jack Chesbro .01 .05
8 Ty Cobb .30 .75
9 Sam Crawford .05 .15
10 Rollie Fingers .05 .15
11 Whitey Ford .07 .20
12 John Frederick .01 .05
13 Frankie Frisch .05 .15
14 Lou Gehrig .30 .75
15 Jim Gentile .01 .05
16 Dwight Gooden .20 .50
17 Rickey Henderson .15 .40
18 Rogers Hornsby .07 .20
19 Frank Howard .02 .10
20 Cliff Johnson .01 .05
21 Walter Johnson .07 .20
22 Hub Leonard .01 .05
23 Mickey Mantle .40 1.00
24 Roger Maris .20 .50
25 Christy Mathewson .07 .20
26 Willie Mays .30 .75
27 Stan Musial .20 .50
28 Dan Quisenberry .01 .05
29 Frank Robinson .07 .20
30 Pete Rose .20 .50
31 Babe Ruth .40 1.00
32 Nolan Ryan .40 1.00
33 George Sisler .07 .20
34 Tris Speaker .07 .20
35 Ed Walsh .05 .15
36 Lloyd Waner .05 .15
37 Earl Webb .01 .05
38 Ted Williams .30 .75
39 Maury Wills .02 .10
40 Hack Wilson .05 .15
41 Owen Wilson .01 .05
42 Willie Wilson .01 .05
43 Rudy York .01 .05
44 Cy Young .07 .20

1986 Woolworth's Topps

This boxed set of 33 standard-size cards was produced by Topps for Woolworth's variety stores. The set features players who hold or have held hitting, home run or RBI titles. The cards have a glossy finish. The card fronts are bordered in yellow with the subtitle "Topps Collectors' Series" across the top. The card backs are printed in green and blue ink on white card stock. The custom box gives the set checklist on the back.

COMPLETE SET (33) 2.50 6.00
1 Tony Armas .01 .05
2 Don Baylor .02 .10
3 Wade Boggs .20 .50
4 George Brett .50 1.25
5 Bill Buckner .01 .05
6 Rod Carew .15 .40
7 Gary Carter .20 .50
8 Cecil Cooper .02 .10
9 Darrell Evans .01 .05
10 Dwight Evans .02 .10
11 George Foster .02 .10
12 Bob Grich .01 .05
13 Tony Gwynn .40 1.00
14 Keith Hernandez .02 .10
15 Reggie Jackson .20 .50
16 Dave Kingman .01 .05
17 Carney Lansford .01 .05
18 Fred Lynn .02 .10
19 Bill Madlock .01 .05
20 Don Mattingly .60 1.50
21 Willie McGee .02 .10
22 Hal McRae .01 .05
23 Dale Murphy .07 .20
24 Eddie Murray .20 .50
25 Ben Oglivie .01 .05
26 Al Oliver .01 .05
27 Dave Parker .02 .10
28 Jim Rice .02 .10
29 Pete Rose .30 .75
30 Mike Schmidt .30 .75
31 Gorman Thomas .01 .05
32 Willie Wilson .01 .05
33 Dave Winfield .20 .50

1987 Woolworth's Topps

Topps produced this 33-card standard-size set for Woolworth's stores. The set is subtitled "Topps Collectors Series Baseball Highlights" and consists of high gloss card fronts with full-color photos. The cards show and describe highlights of the previous season. The card backs are printed in gold and purple and are numbered. The set was sold nationally in Woolworth's for a 1.99 suggested retail price.

COMPLETE SET (33) 2.00 5.00
1 Steve Carlton .15 .40
2 Cecil Cooper .02 .10
3 Rickey Henderson .20 .50
4 Reggie Jackson .15 .40
5 Jim Rice .02 .10
6 Don Sutton .15 .40
7 Roger Clemens .40 1.00
8 Mike Schmidt .20 .50
9 Jesse Barfield .01 .05
10 Wade Boggs .15 .40
11 Tim Raines .02 .10
12 Jose Canseco .15 .40
13 Todd Worrell .02 .10
14 Dave Righetti .01 .05
15 Don Mattingly .40 1.00
16 Tony Gwynn .40 1.00
17 Marty Barrett .01 .05
18 Mike Scott .01 .05
19 Bruce Hurst .01 .05
20 Calvin Schiraldi .01 .05
21 Dwight Evans .02 .10
22 Dave Henderson .01 .05
23 Len Dykstra .05 .15
24 Bob Ojeda .01 .05
25 Gary Carter .15 .40
26 Ron Darling .01 .05
27 Jim Rice .02 .10
28 Bruce Hurst .01 .05
29 Darryl Strawberry .02 .10
30 Ray Knight .01 .05
31 Keith Hernandez .02 .10
32 Mets Celebration .01 .05
33 Ray Knight .01 .05

1988 Woolworth's Topps

Topps produced this 33-card standard-size set for Woolworth's stores. The set is subtitled "Topps Collectors' Series Baseball Highlights" and consists of high gloss card fronts with full-color photos. The cards show and describe highlights of the previous season. Cards 19-33 commemorate the World Series with highlights and key players of each game in the series. The card backs are printed in red and blue on white card stock and are numbered. The set was sold nationally in Woolworth's for a 1.99 suggested retail price.

COMPLETE SET (33) 2.00 5.00
1 Don Baylor .02 .10
2 Vince Coleman .01 .05
3 Darrell Evans .02 .10
4 Don Mattingly .40 1.00
5 Eddie Murray .15 .40
6 Nolan Ryan .75 2.00
7 Mike Schmidt .20 .50
8 Andre Dawson .07 .20
9 George Bell .01 .05
10 Steve Bedrosian .01 .05
11 Roger Clemens .40 1.00
12 Tony Gwynn .40 1.00
13 Wade Boggs .15 .40
14 Benito Santiago .02 .10
15 Mark McGwire UER/(Referenced on card .40
1.00
back as NL
16 Dave Righetti .01 .05
17 Jeffrey Leonard .01 .05
18 Gary Gaetti .02 .10
19 Frank Viola WS1 .01 .05
20 Dan Gladden WS1 .01 .05
21 Bert Blyleven WS2 .02 .10
22 Gary Gaetti WS2 .02 .10
23 John Tudor WS3 .01 .05
24 Todd Worrell WS3 .02 .10
25 Tom Lawless WS4 .01 .05
26 Willie McGee WS4 .02 .10
27 Danny Cox WS5 .01 .05
28 Curt Ford WS5 .01 .05
29 Don Baylor WS6 .02 .10
30 Kent Hrbek WS6 .02 .10
31 Kirby Puckett WS7 .20 .50
32 Greg Gagne WS7 .01 .05
33 Frank Viola WS-MVP .01 .05

1989 Woolworth's Topps

The 1989 Woolworth's Highlights set contains 33 standard-size glossy cards. The fronts have red and white borders. The vertically oriented backs are yellow and red, and describe highlights from the 1988 season including the World Series. The cards were distributed through Woolworth stores as a boxed set.

COMP.FACT SET (33) 2.00 5.00
1 Jose Canseco MVP .10 .30
2 Kirk Gibson MVP .05 .15
3 Frank Viola CY .01 .05
4 Orel Hershiser CY .02 .10
5 Walt Weiss ROY .01 .05
6 Chris Sabo ROY .01 .05
7 George Bell .01 .05
8 Wade Boggs .15 .40
9 Tom Browning .01 .05
10 Gary Carter .15 .40
11 Andre Dawson .07 .20
12 John Franco .02 .10
13 Randy Johnson 1.00 2.50
14 Doug Jones .01 .05
15 Kevin McReynolds .01 .05
16 Gene Nelson .01 .05
17 Jeff Reardon .02 .10
18 Pat Tabler .01 .05
19 Tim Belcher .01 .05
20 Dennis Eckersley .15 .40
21 Orel Hershiser .02 .10
22 Gregg Jefferies .01 .05
23 Jose Canseco .20 .50
24 Kirk Gibson .02 .10
25 Orel Hershiser .02 .10
26 Mike Marshall .01 .05
27 Mark McGwire .40 1.00
28 Rick Honeycutt .01 .05
29 Tim Belcher .01 .05
30 Jay Howell .01 .05
31 Mickey Hatcher .01 .05
32 Mike Davis .01 .05
33 Orel Hershiser .02 .10

1990 Woolworth's Topps

The 1990 Woolworth set is a 33-card standard-size set highlighting some of the more important events of the 1989 season. This set is broken down between major award winners, career highlights, and post-season heroes. The first six cards of the set feature the award winners while the last 11 cards of the set feature post-season heroes.

COMPLETE SET (33) 2.50 6.00
1 Robin Yount MVP .20 .50
2 Kevin Mitchell MVP .01 .05
3 Bret Saberhagen CY .02 .10
4 Mark Davis CY .01 .05
5 Gregg Olson ROY .01 .05
6 Jerome Walton ROY .01 .05
7 Bert Blyleven .02 .10
8 Wade Boggs .20 .50
9 George Brett .40 1.00
10 Vince Coleman .01 .05
11 Andre Dawson .07 .20
12 Dwight Evans .02 .10
13 Carlton Fisk .15 .40
14 Rickey Henderson .20 .50
15 Dale Murphy .07 .20
16 Eddie Murray .15 .40
17 Jeff Reardon .02 .10
18 Rick Reuschel .01 .05
19 Cal Ripken .75 2.00
20 Nolan Ryan .75 2.00
21 Ryne Sandberg .30 .75
22 Robin Yount .20 .50
23 Rickey Henderson .20 .50
24 Will Clark .07 .20
25 Dave Stewart .02 .10
26 Walt Weiss .01 .05
27 Mike Moore .01 .05
28 Terry Steinbach .01 .05
29 Dave Henderson .01 .05
30 Matt Williams .07 .20
31 Rickey Henderson .25 .60
32 Kevin Mitchell .01 .05
33 Dave Stewart .02 .10

1991 Woolworth's Topps

Topps produced this 33-card boxed standard-size set for Woolworth stores. The cards feature glossy color player photos on the fronts, with yellow borders on a white card face. The backs are printed in red, black, and white, and commemorate outstanding achievements of the players featured on the cards. The set can be subdivided as follows: MVPs (1-2), Cy Young winners (3-4), ROYs (5-6), '90 highlights in alphabetical order (7-22), playoff MVPs (23-24), and World Series action in chronological order (25-33).

COMPLETE SET (33) 2.00 5.00
1 Barry Bonds .40 1.00
2 Rickey Henderson/(Bat on shoulder) .20 .50
3 Doug Drabek .01 .05
4 Bob Welch .01 .05
5 David Justice .07 .20
6 Sandy Alomar Jr. .02 .10
7 Bert Blyleven .02 .10
8 George Brett .40 1.00
9 Andre Dawson .07 .20
10 Dwight Evans .02 .10
11 Alex Fernandez .01 .05
12 Carlton Fisk .20 .50
13 Kevin Maas .01 .05
14 Dale Murphy .20 .50
15 Eddie Murray .07 .20
16 Dave Parker .02 .10
17 Jeff Reardon .02 .10
18 Cal Ripken .75 2.00
19 Nolan Ryan .75 2.00
20 Ryne Sandberg .30 .75
21 Bobby Thigpen .01 .05
22 Robin Yount .20 .50
23 Rob Dibble and .01 .05
Randy Myers
24 Dave Stewart .02 .10
25 Eric Davis .05 .15
26 Rickey Henderson/(Running bases) .20 .50
27 Billy Hatcher .01 .05
28 Joe Oliver .01 .05
29 Chris Sabo .01 .05
30 Barry Larkin .07 .20
31 Jose Rijo/(Pitching Game 4) .01 .05
32 Reds Celebrate
(1990 World Champions) .01 .05
33 Jose Rijo .01 .05
World Series MVP

1910 World Series Photo Pack

These 12 pictures, which measure 4 1/2" by 6" are blank-backed and may have been cut from a larger album which featured all these cards. Since these cards are unnumbered, we are listing them in alphabetical order.

COMPLETE SET 1000.00 2000.00
1 Harry Davis 150.00 300.00
Eddie Collins
2 Rube Oldring 50.00 100.00
Topsy Hartsell
3 Lew Richie 50.00 100.00
Harry McIntyre
4 Ginger Beaumont 50.00 100.00
Solly Hofman
5 King Cole 50.00 100.00
Jimmy Archer
6 Frank Chance 200.00 400.00
Johnny Evers
7 John Kane 50.00 100.00
Ed Reulbach
8 Joe Tinker 125.00 250.00
Harry Steinfeldt
9 Orvie Overall 50.00 100.00
Tom Needham
10 Mordecai Brown 150.00 300.00
Johnny Kling
11 Frank Schulte 50.00 100.00
Jimmy Sheckard
12 Jack Pfeister 75.00 150.00
Heinie Zimmerman

1936 World Wide Gum

The cards in this 135-card set measure approximately 2 1/2" by 3". The 1936 Canadian Goudey set was issued by World Wide Gum Company and contains black and white cards. This issue is the most difficult to obtain of the Canadian Goudeys. The fronts feature player photos with white borders. The bilingual (French and English) backs carry player biography and career highlights. The World Wide Gum Company has its location listed as Granby, Quebec on these cards (as opposed to Montreal on earlier issues). The cards are numbered on both sides. The Phil Weintraub card (number 135) is very scarce and on many collectors wantlists.

COMPLETE SET (135) 10000.00 20000.00
1 Jimmy Dykes 60.00 120.00
2 Paul Waner 100.00 200.00
3 Cy Blanton 50.00 100.00
4 Sam Leslie 50.00 100.00
5 Johnny Vergez 50.00 100.00
6 Arky Vaughan 100.00 200.00
7 Bill Terry 100.00 200.00
8 Joe Moore 50.00 100.00
9 Gus Mancuso 50.00 100.00
10 Fred Marberry 50.00 100.00
11 George Selkirk 60.00 120.00
12 Spud Davis 50.00 100.00
13 Chuck Klein 100.00 200.00
14 Fred Fitzsimmons 60.00 120.00
15 Bill DeLancey 50.00 100.00
16 Billy Herman 100.00 200.00
17 George Davis 50.00 100.00
18 Rip Collins 50.00 100.00
19 Dizzy Dean 500.00
20 Roy Parmelee 50.00 100.00
21 Vic Sorrell 50.00 100.00
22 Harry Danning 50.00 100.00
23 Hal Schumacher 60.00 120.00
24 Cy Perkins 50.00 100.00
25 Leo Durocher 300.00
26 Glenn Myatt 50.00 100.00
27 Bob Seeds 50.00 100.00
28 Jimmy Ripple 50.00 100.00
29 Al Schacht 60.00 120.00
30 Pete Fox 50.00 100.00
31 Del Baker 50.00 100.00
32 Herman(Flea) Clifton 50.00 100.00
33 Tommy Bridges 60.00 120.00
34 Bill Dickey 300.00
35 Wally Berger 60.00 120.00
36 Slick Castleman 50.00 100.00
37 Dick Bartell 60.00 120.00
38 Red Rolfe 60.00 120.00
39 Waite Hoyt 100.00 200.00
40 Wes Ferrell 75.00 150.00
41 Hank Greenberg 300.00
42 Charlie Gehringer 100.00 200.00
43 Goose Goslin 100.00 200.00
44 Schoolboy Rowe 60.00 120.00
45 Mickey Cochrane MG 100.00 200.00
46 Joe Cronin 100.00 200.00
47 Jimmie Foxx 500.00
48 Jerry Walker 50.00 100.00
49 Charlie Gelbert 50.00 100.00
50 Ray Hayworth 50.00 100.00
51 Joe DiMaggio 5000.00
52 Billy Rogell 50.00 100.00
53 John McCarthy 50.00 100.00
54 Phil Cavarretta 60.00 120.00
55 KiKi Cuyler 100.00 200.00
56 Lefty Gomez 100.00 200.00
57 Gabby Hartnett 100.00 200.00
58 John Marcum 50.00 100.00
59 Burgess Whitehead 50.00 100.00
60 Whitey Whitehill 50.00 100.00
61 Bucky Walters 60.00 120.00
62 Luke Sewell 60.00 120.00
63 Joe Kuhel 50.00 100.00
64 Lou Finney 50.00 100.00
65 Fred Lindstrom 100.00 200.00
66 Paul Derringer 60.00 120.00
67 Steve O'Neill MG 60.00 120.00
68 Mule Haas 50.00 100.00
69 Marv Owen 50.00 100.00
70 Bill Hallahan 50.00 100.00
71 Billy Urbanski 50.00 100.00
72 Dan Taylor 50.00 100.00
73 Heinie Manush 100.00 200.00
74 Jo Jo White 50.00 100.00
75 Joe Medwick 100.00 200.00
76 Joe Vosmik 50.00 100.00
77 Al Simmons 100.00 200.00
78 Frank Shaughnessy 50.00 100.00
79 Harry Smythe 50.00 100.00
80 Bennie Tate 50.00 100.00
81 Billy Rheil 50.00 100.00
82 Lauri Myllykangas 50.00 100.00
83 Ben Sankey 50.00 100.00
84 Crip Polli 50.00 100.00
85 Jim Bottomley 100.00 200.00
86 Watson Clark 50.00 100.00
87 Ossie Bluege 60.00 120.00
88 Lefty Grove 300.00
89 Charlie Grimm MG 60.00 120.00
90 Ben Chapman 60.00 120.00
91 Frank Crosetti 75.00 150.00
Not him pictured on card
92 John Pomorski 50.00 100.00
93 Jess Haines 100.00 200.00
94 Chick Hafey 100.00 200.00
95 Tony Piet 50.00 100.00
96 Lou Gehrig 2000.00 4000.00
97 Billy Jurges 60.00 120.00
98 Smead Jolley 60.00 120.00
99 Jimmy Wilson 60.00 120.00
100 Lon Warneke 60.00 120.00
101 Vito Tamulis 50.00 100.00
102 Red Ruffing 100.00 200.00
103 Earl Grace 50.00 100.00
104 Rox Lawson 50.00 100.00
105 Stan Hack 60.00 120.00
106 Augie Galan 50.00 100.00
107 Frank Frisch MG 100.00 200.00
108 Bill McKechnie MG 100.00 200.00
109 Bill Lee 60.00 120.00
110 Connie Mack MG 100.00 200.00
111 Frank Reiber 50.00 100.00
112 Zeke Bonura 60.00 120.00
113 Luke Appling 100.00 200.00
114 Monte Pearson 50.00 100.00
115 Bob O'Farrell 60.00 120.00
116 Marvin Duke 50.00 100.00
117 Paul Florence 50.00 100.00
118 John Berley 50.00 100.00
119 Tom Oliver 50.00 100.00
120 Norman Kies 50.00 100.00
121 Hal King 50.00 100.00
122 Tom Abernathy 50.00 100.00
123 Phil Hensich 50.00 100.00
124 Ray Schalk 100.00 200.00
125 Paul Dunlap 50.00 100.00
126 Benny Bates 50.00 100.00
127 George Puccinelli 50.00 100.00
128 Stevie Stevenson 50.00 100.00
129 Rabbit Maranville MG 100.00 200.00
130 Bucky Harris MG 100.00 200.00
131 Al Lopez 100.00 200.00
132 Buddy Myer 60.00 120.00
133 Cliff Bolton 50.00 100.00
134 Estel Crabtree 50.00 100.00
135 Phil Weintraub 400.00 800.00

1939 World Wide Gum V351A

These 25 photos measure approximately 4" by 5 3/4" and feature on their fronts white-bordered sepia-toned posed player photos. The player's facsimile autograph appears across the picture. The backs carry tips printed in brown ink on how to play baseball. The photos are unnumbered and checklisted below in alphabetical order.

COMPLETE SET (25) 2000.00 4000.00
1 Morris Arnovich 30.00 60.00
2 Sam Bell 30.00 60.00
3 Zeke Bonura 40.00 80.00
4 Earl Caldwell 30.00 60.00
5 Flea Clifton 30.00 60.00
6 Frank Crosetti 50.00 100.00
7 Harry Danning 30.00 60.00
8 Dizzy Dean 150.00 300.00
9 Emile De Jonghe 30.00 60.00
10 Paul Derringer 30.00 60.00
11 Joe DiMaggio 600.00 1200.00
12 Vince DiMaggio 60.00 120.00
13 Charles Gehringer 150.00 300.00
14 Gene Hasson 30.00 60.00
15 Tommy Henrich 60.00 120.00
16 Fred Hutchinson 50.00 100.00
17 Phil Marchildon 40.00 80.00
18 Mike Meola 30.00 60.00
19 Arnold Moser 30.00 60.00
20 Frank Pytlak 30.00 60.00
21 Frank Reiber 30.00 60.00
22 Lee Rogers 30.00 60.00
23 Cecil Travis 40.00 80.00
24 Hal Trosky 40.00 80.00
25 Ted Williams 600.00 1200.00

1939 World Wide Gum Trimmed Premiums V351B

These 48 photos measure approximately 4" by 5 3/4" and feature on their fronts white-bordered sepia-toned posed player photos. The set is essentially a re-issue of the R303A set. The white borders at the top and bottom were trimmed (during the manufacturing process) to the same size as the Series A photos. The player's facsimile autograph appears across the photo. The backs carry tips printed in brown ink on how to play baseball. The photos are unnumbered and checklisted below in alphabetical order.

COMPLETE SET (48) 2500.00 5000.00
1 Luke Appling 60.00 120.00
2 Earl Averill 60.00 120.00
3 Wally Berger 40.00 80.00
4 Darrell Blanton 30.00 60.00
5 Zeke Bonura 40.00 80.00
6 Mace Brown 30.00 60.00
7 George Case 40.00 80.00
8 Ben Chapman 30.00 60.00
9 Joe Cronin 60.00 120.00
10 Frank Crosetti 50.00 100.00
11 Paul Derringer 40.00 80.00
12 Bill Dickey 60.00 120.00
13 Joe DiMaggio 400.00 800.00
14 Bob Feller 125.00 250.00
15 Jimmy Foxx 100.00 200.00
(Jimmie)
16 Charlie Gehringer 60.00 120.00
17 Lefty Gomez 60.00 120.00
18 Ival Goodman 30.00 60.00
19 Joe Gordon 50.00 100.00
20 Hank Greenberg 60.00 120.00
21 Buddy Hassett 30.00 60.00
22 Jeff Heath 30.00 60.00
23 Tommy Henrich 50.00 100.00
24 Billy Herman 60.00 120.00
25 Frank Higgins 30.00 60.00
26 Fred Hutchinson 40.00 80.00
27 Bob Johnson 40.00 80.00
28 Ken Keltner 40.00 80.00
29 Mike Kreevich 30.00 60.00
30 Ernie Lombardi 60.00 120.00
31 Gus Mancuso 30.00 60.00
32 Eric McNair 30.00 60.00
33 Van Mungo 40.00 80.00
34 Buck Newsom 40.00 80.00
35 Mel Ott 60.00 120.00
36 Marvin Owen 30.00 60.00
37 Frankie Pytlak 30.00 60.00
38 Woody Rich 30.00 60.00
39 Charlie Root 40.00 80.00
40 Al Simmons 60.00 120.00
41 Jim Tabor 30.00 60.00
42 Cecil Travis 30.00 60.00
43 Hal Trosky 30.00 60.00
44 Arky Vaughan 60.00 120.00
45 Joe Vosmik 30.00 60.00
46 Lon Warneke 30.00 60.00
47 Ted Williams 400.00 800.00
48 Rudy York 40.00 80.00

1933 Worch Cigar

These 3 7/16" by 5 7/16" photos were issued by Worch Cigars. They feature both major and minor leaguers and according to documentation issued by Worch in 1933 the players issued were the players they figured to be in the most demand and had negatives on hand to make. Interesting to note that just as many minor leaguers as major leaguers were produced.

COMPLETE SET 3000.00 6000.00
1 Sparky Adams 25.00 50.00
2 Dale Alexander 25.00 50.00
3 Ivy Paul Andrews 25.00 50.00
4 Earl Averill 50.00 100.00
Name at left)
5 Earl Averill 50.00 100.00
Name at right)
6 Richard Bartell 30.00 60.00
7 Walter Berger 30.00 60.00
Bos NL
8 Walter Berger 30.00 60.00
No team name
9 Huck Betts 25.00 50.00
10 Max Bishop 25.00 50.00
11 Jim Bottomley 50.00 100.00
12 Tom Bridges 25.00 50.00
13 Clint Brown 25.00 50.00
14 Max Carey 50.00 100.00
15 Tex Carleton 25.00 50.00
16 Ben Chapman 25.00 50.00
Name not in box
17 Ben Chapman 25.00 50.00
Name in box
18 Chalmer Cissell 25.00 50.00
19 Mickey Cochrane 75.00 150.00
20 Mickey Cochrane 75.00 150.00
Name spelled Cochran
21 Earle Combs 50.00 100.00
22 Rip Collins 25.00 50.00
23 Adam Comorosky 25.00 50.00
24 Crabtree 25.00 50.00
25 Roger Cramer 30.00 60.00
26 Pat Crawford 25.00 50.00
27 Hugh Critz 25.00 50.00
28 Joe Cronin 75.00 150.00
29 Frank Crosetti 40.00 80.00
30 Alvin Crowder 25.00 50.00
31 Tony Cuccinello 25.00 50.00
32 Kiki Cuyler 50.00 100.00
33 Geo. Davis 25.00 50.00
34 Dizzy Dean 125.00 250.00
35 Bill Dickey 100.00 200.00
Name not in box
36 Bill Dickey 100.00 200.00
Name in Box
37 Leo Durocher 100.00 200.00
38 James Dykes 40.00 80.00
39 George Earnshaw 25.00 50.00
40 Woody English 30.00 60.00
41 Richard Ferrel 50.00 100.00
Name Spelled incorrectly
42 Richard Ferrell 50.00 100.00
43 Wesley Ferrell 30.00 60.00
44 James Foxx 250.00 500.00
(Jimmie)
45 Fred Frankhouse 25.00 50.00
46 Frank Frisch 20.00 40.00
Large cropping)
47 Frank Frisch 20.00 40.00
Small cropping)
48 George Gantham 25.00 50.00
49 Lou Gehrig 750.00 1500.00
Box on Card
50 Lou Gehrig 750.00 1500.00
No Box on Card
51 Charlie Gehringer 100.00 200.00
52 Geo. Gibson MG 25.00 50.00
53 Lefty Gomez 125.00 250.00
No Box
54 Vernon Gomez 125.00 250.00
Box on Card
55 Leon Goslin 50.00 100.00
Name spelled Gaslin
56 Leon Goslin 50.00 100.00
Name correctly spelled
57 Charlie Grimm 40.00 80.00
58 Robert Grove 125.00 250.00
Name in box
59 Robert Grove 125.00 250.00
Name not in box
60 Chic Hafey 50.00 100.00
No Background on card
61 Chic Hafey 50.00 100.00
Photo Background on Card
62 Bill Hallahan 30.00 60.00
63 Mel Harder 30.00 60.00
64 Gabby Hartnett 50.00 100.00
65 Dutch Henry 25.00 50.00
66 Babe Herman 40.00 80.00
67 Bill Herman 50.00 100.00
68 Oral Hildebrand 25.00 50.00
Box on Card
69 Oral Hildebrand 25.00 50.00
No Box on Card
70 Rogers Hornsby 125.00 250.00
St Louis AL
71 Rogers Hornsby 125.00 250.00
St Louis Cards NL
72 Carl Hubbell 100.00 200.00
73 Travis Jackson 50.00 100.00
New York N.L.
74 Travis Jackson 50.00 100.00
No team name
75 Charles Klein 50.00 100.00
Philadelphia N.L., No Background
76 Chuck Klein 50.00 100.00
Chicago NL, no background
77 Chuck Klein 50.00 100.00
Philadelphia NL, background
78 Joe Kuhel 25.00 50.00
79 Tony Lazzeri 50.00 100.00
New York A.L.
80 Tony Lazzeri 50.00 100.00
N.Y. A.L.
81 Ernie Lombardi 50.00 100.00
82 Al Lopez 50.00 100.00
83 Red Lucas 25.00 50.00
84 Henry Manush 50.00 100.00
85 Fred Marberry 25.00 50.00
86 Pepper Martin 30.00 60.00
Has Background
87 Pepper Martin 30.00 60.00
No background
88 Joe Medwick 50.00 100.00
89 Joe Moore 25.00 50.00
90 Van Mungo 30.00 60.00
91 Buddy Myer 25.00 50.00
92 Bob O'Farrell 25.00 50.00
93 Lefty O'Doul 40.00 80.00
New York N.L>
94 Lefty O'Doul 40.00 80.00
No team name)
95 Ernie Orsatti 25.00 50.00
standing)
96 Ernie Orsatti 25.00 50.00
batting)
97 Melvin Ott 75.00 150.00
98 Homer Peel 25.00 50.00
99 Charles Ruffing 50.00 100.00
100 Jack Russell 25.00 50.00
101 Babe Ruth 1250.00 2500.00
Box on Card
102 Babe Ruth 1250.00 2500.00
No Box on Card
103 Blondy Ryan 25.00 50.00
104 Wilfred Ryan 25.00 50.00
105 Hal Schumacher 25.00 50.00
106 Luke Sewel 25.00 50.00
107 Luke Sewell 25.00 50.00
No Box Around Name
108 Al Simmons 75.00 150.00
Name at left)
109 Al Simmons 75.00 150.00
Name at right)
110 Ray Spencer 25.00 50.00
111 Gus Suhr 25.00 50.00
112 Bill Terry 75.00 150.00
113 Pie Traynor 100.00 200.00
114 Dazzy Vance 50.00 100.00
115 Gerald Walker 25.00 50.00
116 Lloyd Waner 50.00 100.00
With background)
117 Lloyd Waner 50.00 100.00
Without background)
118 Paul Waner 60.00 120.00
With background)
119 Paul Waner 60.00 120.00
Without background)
120 Lon Warneke 25.00 50.00
Brown background)
121 Lon Warneke 25.00 50.00
White background)
122 Monte Weaver 25.00 50.00
123 Sam West 25.00 50.00
124 Burgess Whitehead 25.00 50.00
125 Hack Wilson 50.00 100.00
126 Jimmy Wilson 25.00 50.00

1993 World University Games

This 10-card set features borderless photos of various sporting events at the World University Games in Buffalo in 1993. The backs display two different ways the collector could win prizes in two different scratch-off games. The cards are unnumbered and checklisted below alphabetically according to the sport pictured on the card front.

COMPLETE SET (10) 1.20 3.00
1 Baseball .40 1.00

1992 Vincentown Button Proofs

These proofs, which measure roughly 2" by 2" when cleanly cut, were issued to Carol Wright to promote their products. The phrase M.L.B.P.A. Baseball Buttons Vincentown, N.J, 1992 appears below each player image. They were intended to be cut and attached to a button and each proof had an announced print run of 1500. Since these cards are not numbered, we have listed this set in alphabetical order. Numbers 1-20 feature "hitters", while numbers 21-40 feature pitchers. The top half of the hitters "cards" are red, while the bottom half is yellow. The top half of the pitchers "cards" are yellow, while the bottom half is red.

COMPLETE SET 12.50 30.00
1 Craig Biggio .60 1.50
2 Wade Boggs .60 1.50
3 Barry Bonds 1.50 4.00
4 Bobby Bonilla .40 1.00
5 Jose Canseco .60 1.50
6 Joe Carter .40 1.00
7 Will Clark .60 1.50
8 Len Dykstra .40 1.00
9 Cecil Fielder .40 1.00
10 Ken Griffey Jr. 2.00 5.00
11 Tony Gwynn 1.00 2.50
12 Don Mattingly 2.00 5.00
13 Kirby Puckett 1.00 2.50
14 Cal Ripken Jr. 3.00 8.00
15 Chris Sabo .40 1.00
16 Ryne Sandberg 2.00 5.00
17 Ozzie Smith 1.25 3.00
18 Darryl Strawberry .40 1.00
19 Frank Thomas 1.00 2.50
20 Robin Yount 1.00 2.50
21 Jim Abbot .40 1.00
22 Steve Avery .40 1.00
23 Tom Browning .40 1.00
24 Roger Clemens 1.25 3.00
25 Mark Davis .40 1.00
26 Rob Dibble .40 1.00
27 Doug Drabek .40 1.00
28 Dwight Gooden .40 1.00
29 Orel Hershiser .40 1.00
30 Bruce Hurst .40 1.00
31 Ramon Martinez .40 1.00
32 Jack McDowell .40 1.00
33 Jack Morris .60 1.50
34 Charles Nagy .40 1.00
35 Dan Plesac .40 1.00
36 Jose Rijo .40 1.00
37 Nolan Ryan 3.00 8.00
38 Lee Smith .40 1.00
39 Rick Sutcliffe .40 1.00
40 Frank Viola .40 1.00

1993 XXV Jogos Olimpicos

This 84-card set commemorates medal winners from the 1992 XXV Olympics in Barcelona. The cards measure 2 11/16" by 3 7/8", have rounded corners, and are printed on thin cardboard stock. The fronts feature full-bleed color action photos, with the event, player's name, and country in one of the corners. The back is divided into two registers. The top register consists of a 1993 calendar, while the bottom lists the three medal winners' names, countries, and their winning scores or times. All text is in Portuguese. NBA stars Scottie Pippen (77) and Magic Johnson (78) are featured in this set.

COMPLETE SET (84) 25.00 60.00
82 Baseball (Cuba) .20 .50

1944 Yankees Stamps

This stamp set commemorates the New York Yankees and their World Series victory in 1943. The stamps were perforated together in a sheet with five rows of six stamps across. The stamps are ordered alphabetically on the stamp sheet left to right. Each stamp measures approximately 1 3/4" by 2 3/8" and is in full color. The player's name is printed in white on a red background at the bottom of each stamp. An album for the set was issued but it is more difficult to find than the stamps. The catalog designation for this set is ST101.

COMPLETE SET (30) 40.00 80.00
1 Ernie Bonham 2.50 5.00
2 Hank Borowy 2.50 5.00
3 Marvin Breuer 2.00 4.00
4 Tommy Byrne 2.50 5.00
5 Spud Chandler 3.00 6.00
6 Earle Combs CO 3.00 5.00
7 Frank Crosetti 3.00 6.00
8 Bill Dickey 10.00 20.00
9 Atley Donald 2.00 4.00
10 Nick Etten 2.00 4.00
11 Art Fletcher CO 2.00 4.00
12 Joe Gordon 3.00 6.00
13 Oscar Grimes 2.00 4.00
14 Rollie Hemsley 2.00 4.00
15 Bill Johnson 2.00 4.00
16 Charlie Keller 3.00 6.00
17 John Lindell 2.50 5.00
18 Joe McCarthy MG 5.00 10.00
19 Bud Metheny 2.00 4.00
20 Johnny Murphy 2.50 5.00
21 Pat O'Dougherty 2.00 4.00
22 Marius Russo 2.00 4.00
23 John Schulte 2.00 4.00
24 Ken Sears 2.00 4.00
25 Tuck Stainback 2.00 4.00
26 George Stirnweiss 2.50 5.00
27 Jim Turner 2.50 5.00
28 Roy Weatherly 2.00 4.00
29 Charley Wensloff 2.00 4.00
30 Bill Zuber 2.00 4.00
NNO Album 20.00 50.00

1947 Yankees Team Issue

This 25-card set of the New York Yankees measures approximately 6 1/2" by 9" and features black-and-white player portraits with white borders and facsimile autographs. The backs are blank. The cards are unnumbered and checklisted below in alphabetical order. This set was available from the Yankees at time of issue for 50 cents.

COMPLETE SET (25) 100.00 250.00
1 Yogi Berra 10.00 50.00
2 Bill Bevans 2.50 5.00
3 Bobby Brown 5.00 10.00
4 Spud Chandler 2.50 5.00
5 Gerry Coleman 2.50 5.00
6 John Corriden CO 2.50 5.00
7 Frank Crosetti 2.50 5.00
8 Joe DiMaggio 40.00 80.00
9 Chuck Dressen CO 4.00 8.00
10 Randy Gumpert 2.50 5.00
11 Bucky Harris MG 5.00 10.00
12 Tommy Henrich 4.00 8.00
13 Ralph Houk 3.00 6.00
14 Don Johnson 2.50 5.00
15 Bill Johnson 2.50 5.00
16 Charlie Keller 2.50 5.00
17 John Lindell 2.50 5.00
18 George McQuinn 2.50 5.00
19 Joe Page 2.50 5.00
20 Allie Reynolds 4.00 8.00
21 Phil Rizzuto 10.00 20.00
22 Aaron Robinson 2.50 5.00
23 Frank Shea 2.50 5.00
24 Ken Silvestri 2.50 5.00
25 George Stirnweiss 2.50 5.00

1948 Yankees Team Issue

These 26 photos measure approximately 6 1/2" by 9". They feature members of the 1948 New York Yankees. These black and white photos also feature a facsimile signature and are framed by white borders. The photos are unnumbered and we have sequenced them in alphabetical order.

COMPLETE SET (26) 137.50 275.00
1 Mel Allen ANN 5.00 10.00
2 Yogi Berra 15.00 40.00
3 Bobby Brown 3.00 6.00
4 Red Corriden CO 2.50 5.00
5 Frank Crosetti 4.00 8.00
6 Joe DiMaggio 40.00 80.00
7 Chuck Dressen CO 3.00 6.00
8 Karl Drews 2.50 5.00
9 Red Embree 2.50 5.00
10 Randy Gumpert 2.50 5.00
11 Bucky Harris MG 5.00 10.00
12 Tommy Henrich 4.00 8.00
13 Frank Hiller 2.50 5.00
14 Bill Johnson 2.50 5.00
15 Charlie Keller 3.00 6.00
16 Ed Lopat 4.00 8.00
17 John Lindell 2.50 5.00
18 Cliff Mapes 2.50 5.00
19 Gus Niarhos 2.50 5.00
20 George McQuinn 2.50 5.00
21 Joe Page 3.00 6.00
22 Vic Raschi 4.00 8.00
23 Allie Reynolds 4.00 8.00
24 Phil Rizzuto 12.50 30.00
25 Frank Shea 2.50 5.00
26 Snuffy Stirnweiss 3.00 6.00

1949 Yankees Team Issue

This 25-card set of the New York Yankees measures approximately 6 1/2" by 9" and features black-and-white player portraits with white borders. The backs are blank. The cards are unnumbered and checklisted below in alphabetical order.

COMPLETE SET (25) 150.00 300.00
1 Mel Allen ANN 5.00 10.00
2 Larry Berra 12.50 40.00
3 Bobby Brown 5.00 10.00
4 Tommy Byrne 2.50 5.00
5 Jerry Coleman 4.00 8.00
6 Frank Crosetti CO 4.00 8.00
7 Bill Dickey CO 10.00 20.00
8 Joe DiMaggio 40.00 80.00
9 Tom Henrich 4.00 8.00
10 Bill Johnson 2.50 5.00
11 Charlie Keller 2.50 5.00
12 John Lindell 2.50 5.00
13 Ed Lopat 4.00 8.00
14 Gus Niarhos 2.50 5.00
15 Joe Page 2.50 5.00
16 Bob Porterfield 2.50 5.00
17 Vic Raschi 4.00 8.00
18 Allie Reynolds 4.00 8.00
19 Phil Rizzuto 10.00 30.00
20 Fred Sanford 2.50 5.00
21 Frank Shea 2.50 5.00
22 Casey Stengel MG 10.00 25.00
23 George Stirnweiss 2.50 5.00
24 Jim Turner CO 2.50 5.00
25 Gene Woodling 3.00 6.00

1950 Yankees Team Issue

This 25-card set of the New York Yankees measures approximately 6 1/2" by 9" and features black-and-white player portraits with white borders. The backs are blank. The cards are unnumbered and checklisted below in alphabetical order.

COMPLETE SET (25) 150.00 300.00
1 Mel Allen ANN 5.00 10.00
2 Hank Bauer 5.00 10.00
3 Larry Berra 10.00 40.00
4 Bobby Brown 5.00 10.00
5 Tommy Byrne 2.50 5.00
6 Jerry Coleman 4.00 8.00
7 Frank Crosetti CO 4.00 8.00
8 Bill Dickey CO 10.00 20.00
9 Joe DiMaggio 40.00 80.00
10 Tom Henrich 4.00 8.00
11 Jack Jensen 7.50 20.00
12 Bill Johnson 2.50 5.00
13 Ed Lopat 2.50 5.00
14 Cliff Mapes 2.50 5.00
15 Joe Page 2.50 5.00
16 Bob Porterfield 2.50 5.00
17 Vic Raschi 4.00 8.00
18 Allie Reynolds 4.00 8.00
19 Phil Rizzuto 10.00 30.00
20 Fred Sanford 2.50 5.00
21 Charlie Silvera 2.50 5.00
22 Casey Stengel MG 10.00 25.00
23 George Stirnweiss 2.50 5.00
24 Jim Turner CO 2.50 5.00
25 Gene Woodling 3.00 6.00

1953 Yankees Photos

Issued by one of the "stores" across the street from Yankee Stadium, these photos feature portrait photos of the Yankees on the front and the backs have the name, address and phone number of the store used to distribute the photos. It is possible that there might be more photos so any additions are appreciated. Since the cards are unnumbered, we have sequenced them in alphabetical order.

COMPLETE SET 50.00 100.00
1 Hank Bauer 5.00 10.00
2 Yogi Berra 10.00 20.00
3 Joe Collins 2.50 5.00
4 Whitey Ford 10.00 20.00
5 Billy Martin 7.50 15.00
6 Gil McDougald 4.00 8.00
7 Johnny Mize 6.00 12.00
8 Vic Raschi 4.00 8.00
9 Phil Rizzuto 7.50 15.00
10 Gene Woodling 3.00 6.00

1956 Yankees Jay Publishing

This 12-card set of the New York Yankees measures approximately 5 1/8" by 7". The fronts feature black-and-white posed player photos with the player's and team name printed below in the white border. These cards were packaged 12 to a packet and originally sold for 25 cents. The backs are blank. The cards are unnumbered and checklisted below in alphabetical order.

COMPLETE SET (12) 60.00 120.00
1 Hank Bauer 3.00 6.00
2 Larry Berra 7.50 15.00
3 Tommy Byrne 2.00 4.00
4 Andy Carey 2.00 4.00
5 Joe Collins 2.00 4.00
6 Whitey Ford 7.50 15.00
7 Elston Howard 4.00 8.00
8 Mickey Mantle 20.00 50.00
9 Billy Martin 6.00 12.00
10 Gil McDougald 3.00 6.00
11 Casey Stengel MG 7.50 15.00
12 Bob Turley 2.00 4.00

1956 Yankees Team Issue

This 24-card set of the New York Yankees features black-and-white player photos measuring approximately 6" by 9" with the player's name printed at the bottom. The cards are unnumbered and checklisted below in alphabetical order.

COMPLETE SET (24) 125.00 250.00
1 Hank Bauer 6.00 12.00
2 Yogi Berra 10.00 20.00
3 Tommy Byrne 4.00 8.00
4 Andy Carey 4.00 8.00
5 Bob Cerv 4.00 8.00
6 Gerry Coleman 4.00 8.00
7 Joe Collins 4.00 8.00
8 Whitey Ford 10.00 20.00
9 Bob Grim 4.00 8.00
10 Elston Howard 7.50 15.00
11 Johnny Kucks 4.00 8.00
12 Don Larsen 6.00 12.00
13 Jerry Lumpe 4.00 8.00
14 Mickey Mantle 25.00 50.00
15 Billy Martin 7.50 15.00
16 Mickey McDermott 4.00 8.00
17 Gil McDougald 5.00 10.00
18 Tom Morgan 4.00 8.00
19 Irv Noren 4.00 8.00
20 Phil Rizzuto 10.00 20.00
21 Eddie Robinson 4.00 8.00
22 Charley Silvera 4.00 8.00
23 Bill Skowron 6.00 12.00
24 Bob Turley 5.00 10.00

1957 Yankees Jay Publishing

This 16-card set of the New York Yankees measures approximately 5" X 7". Since personnel changes were made during the season, there were more than just 12 cards issued. The fronts feature black-and-white posed player photos with the player's and team name printed below in the white border. These cards were packaged 12 to a packet and originally sold for 25 cents. The backs are blank. The cards are unnumbered and checklisted below in alphabetical order.

COMPLETE SET (12) 87.50 175.00
1 Hank Bauer 3.00 6.00
2 Larry Berra 12.50 25.00
3 Tommy Byrne 2.00 4.00
4 Jerry Coleman 2.00 4.00
5 Ed (Whitey) Ford 12.50 25.00
6 Elston Howard 4.00 8.00
7 Johnny Kucks 2.00 4.00
8 Don Larsen 2.50 5.00
9 Sal Maglie 2.50 5.00
10 Mickey Mantle 25.00 50.00
11 Billy Martin 4.00 8.00
12 Gil McDougald 2.50 5.00
13 Bill Skowron 3.00 6.00
14 Enos Slaughter 5.00 10.00
15 Casey Stengel MG 7.50 15.00
16 Tom Sturdivant 2.00 4.00

1957 Yankee Team Issue

These photos, which measure approximately 7 1/2" by 10" feature members of the 1957 New York Yankees. Since these photos are unnumbered, we have sequenced them in alphabetical order.

COMPLETE SET 100.00 200.00
1 Hank Bauer 8.00 15.00
2 Yogi Berra 10.00 20.00
3 Andy Carey 4.00 8.00
4 Joe Collins 4.00 8.00
5 Whitey Ford 10.00 20.00
6 Elston Howard 8.00 15.00
7 Don Larsen 5.00 10.00
8 Mickey Mantle 25.00 50.00
9 Gil McDougald 5.00 10.00
10 Bill Skowron 8.00 15.00
11 Casey Stengel MG 10.00 20.00
12 Bob Turley 5.00 10.00

1958 Yankees Jay Publishing

This 16-card set of the New York Yankees measures approximately 5" by 7" and features black-and-white player photos in a white border. These cards were packaged 12 to a packet. The backs are blank. The cards are unnumbered and checklisted below in alphabetical order. More than 12 cards are included in this set as they were released at different times during the season

COMPLETE SET 37.50 150.00
1 Hank Bauer 3.00 6.00
2 Yogi Berra 6.00 15.00
3 Andy Carey 2.00 4.00
4 Whitey Ford 6.00 15.00
5 Elston Howard 4.00 8.00
6 Tony Kubek 4.00 8.00
7 Don Larsen 2.50 5.00
8 Jerry Lumpe 2.00 4.00
9 Mickey Mantle 12.50 50.00
10 Gil McDougald 2.00 4.00
11 Bobby Shantz 2.50 5.00
12 Bill Skowron 3.00 6.00
13 Casey Stengel MG 15.00
14 Tom Sturdivant 2.00 4.00
15 Bob Turley 2.00 4.00
16 Jim Turner CO 4.00 8.00
Bill Dickey CO
Frank Crosetti CO/

1959 Yankees Team Issue

These 12 black and white blank-backed photos measure 8" by 10" and feature a photo surrounded by white borders with the player's name printed in the lower left hand corner. As the photos are unnumbered, we have sequenced them in alphabetical order.

COMPLETE SET 60.00 120.00
1 Yogi Berra 5.00 15.00
2 Ryne Duren 2.00 4.00
3 Whitey Ford 5.00 15.00
4 Elston Howard 4.00 8.00
5 Tony Kubek 4.00 8.00
6 Mickey Mantle 12.50 50.00
7 Gil McDougald 2.50 5.00
8 Bobby Richardson 4.00 8.00
9 Bobby Shantz 2.00 4.00
10 Bill Skowron 3.00 6.00
11 Casey Stengel MG 4.00 10.00
12 Bob Turley 2.50 5.00

1959 Yankees Yoo-Hoo

These cards are black and white, with no printing on the back. They feature New York Yankee ballplayers, and were distributed as a premium in the New York area with a six-pack of Yoo-Hoo. There were six cards issued in the set. A facsimile signature of the player, along with the phrase "Me for Yoo-Hoo" appears on the front. The cards have a 15/16" tab at the bottom. The cards measure approximately 2 7/16" by 3 9/16" without the tab and 2 7/16" by 4 1/2" with the tab. The cards are valued below as being with tabs intact. The Mantle card is actually an advertising piece for Yoo-Hoo and is blank-backed. Cards without tabs are valued between 50 and 75 percent of the full card.

COMPLETE SET (6) 2000.00 4000.00
1 Yogi Berra 500.00 1000.00
2 Whitey Ford 200.00 400.00
3 Tony Kubek 125.00 250.00
4 Mickey Mantle SP 1000.00 2000.00
5 Gil McDougald 100.00 200.00
6 Moose Skowron 125.00 250.00

1960 Yankees Jay Publishing

This 12-card set of the New York Yankees measures approximately 5" by 7" and features black-and-white player photos in a white border. These cards were packaged 12 to a packet. The backs are blank. The cards are unnumbered and checklisted below in alphabetical order.

COMPLETE SET (12) 50.00 100.00
1 Yogi Berra 6.00 15.00
2 Andy Carey 1.00 2.50
3 Whitey Ford 6.00 15.00
4 Elston Howard 2.00 5.00
5 Tony Kubek 2.00 5.00
6 Hector Lopez 1.00 2.50
7 Mickey Mantle 15.00 40.00
8 Roger Maris 5.00 12.00
9 Gil McDougald 1.00 2.50
10 Bill Skowron 1.25 3.00
11 Casey Stengel MG 4.00 10.00
12 Bob Turley 1.00 2.50

1960 Yankees Team Issue

These black and white cards, which measure approximately 6" by 8 1/2" featured members of the 1960 New York Yankees. Since these cards are unnumbered, we have sequenced them in alphabetical order.

COMPLETE SET 75.00 150.00
1 Yogi Berra 8.00 20.00
2 Andy Carey 2.00 5.00
3 Art Ditmar 2.00 5.00
4 Ryne Duren 2.00 5.00
5 Whitey Ford 8.00 20.00
6 Elston Howard 4.00 10.00
7 Tony Kubek 4.00 10.00
8 Mickey Mantle 15.00 40.00
9 Gil McDougald 2.50 6.00
10 Bobby Richardson 4.00 10.00
11 Bobby Shantz 2.00 5.00
12 Bill Skowron 4.00 10.00
13 Casey Stengel MG 5.00 12.00
14 Bob Turley 2.50 6.00

1961 Yankees Jay Publishing

This 12-card set of the New York Yankees measures approximately 5" by 7". The fronts feature black-and-white posed player photos with the player's and team name printed below in the white border. These cards were packaged 12 to a packet. The backs are blank. The cards are unnumbered and checklisted below in alphabetical order.

COMPLETE SET (12) 60.00 120.00
1 Yogi Berra 8.00 20.00
2 Clete Boyer 1.50 4.00
3 Art Ditmar 1.00 2.50
4 Whitey Ford 8.00 20.00
5 Ralph Houk MG 1.25 3.00
6 Elston Howard 2.00 5.00
7 Tony Kubek 2.00 5.00
8 Mickey Mantle 15.00 40.00
9 Roger Maris 8.00 20.00
10 Bobby Richardson 2.00 5.00
11 Bill Skowron 1.50 4.00
12 Bob Turley 1.00 2.50

1961 Yankees Team Issue

These 8" by 10" photos were issued to members of the press by the New York Yankees. These photos feature the player photo surrounded by white borders. Since these cards are not numbered, we have checklisted these cards in alphabetical order.

COMPLETE SET 75.00 150.00
1 Luis Arroyo 2.00 5.00
2 Yogi Berra 8.00 20.00
3 Jim Coates 2.00 5.00
4 Joe DeMaestri 2.00 5.00
5 Art Ditmar 2.00 5.00
6 Whitey Ford 8.00 20.00
7 Jesse Gonder 2.00 5.00
8 Ralph Houk MG 2.50 6.00
9 Deron Johnson 2.00 5.00
10 Tony Kubek 4.00 10.00
11 Mickey Mantle 15.00 40.00
12 Roger Maris 12.50 30.00
13 Bobby Richardson 4.00 10.00
14 Bill Skowron 3.00 8.00
15 Ralph Terry 2.00 5.00
16 Bob Turley 2.00 5.00

1962 Yankees Jay Publishing

This 12-card set of the New York Yankees measures approximately 5" by 7". The fronts feature black-and-white posed player photos with the player's and team name printed below in the white border. These cards were packaged 12 to a packet. The backs are blank. The cards are unnumbered and checklisted below in alphabetical order.

COMPLETE SET (12) 50.00 100.00
1 Luis Arroyo 1.00 2.50
2 Yogi Berra 8.00 20.00
3 John Blanchard 1.00 2.50
4 Cletis Boyer 1.50 4.00
5 Bud Daley 1.00 2.50
6 Whitey Ford 8.00 20.00
7 Ralph Houk MG 1.25 3.00
8 Elston Howard 2.00 5.00
9 Mickey Mantle 15.00 40.00
10 Roger Maris 8.00 20.00
11 Bobby Richardson 2.00 5.00
12 Bill Skowron 1.50 4.00

1962 Yankees Team Issue

These 5" by 7" blank backed photos feature members of the 1962 New York Yankees. The fronts feature black and white photos along with the players name printed in blank ink on the bottom. Since these photos are unnumbered we have sequenced them in alphabetical order

COMPLETE SET 60.00 120.00
1 Luis Arroyo 1.50 4.00
2 Yogi Berra 6.00 15.00
3 John Blanchard 1.50 4.00
4 Clete Boyer 2.00 5.00
5 Bob Cerv 1.50 4.00
6 Whitey Ford 6.00 15.00
7 Elston Howard 3.00 8.00
8 Tony Kubek 3.00 8.00
9 Hector Lopez 1.50 4.00
10 Mickey Mantle 15.00 40.00
11 Roger Maris 8.00 20.00
12 Bobby Richardson 3.00 8.00
13 Bill Skowron 2.00 5.00
14 Bob Turley 1.50 4.00

1963 Yankee Emblems

These seven patches which measure 3 1/2" by 4 1/2" feature members of the early 1960's Yankees. These patches have a player photo on the front and were issued in plastic-wrapped cardboard displays. Since these are unnumbered, we have sequenced them in alphabetical order.

COMPLETE SET 125.00 250.00
1 Yogi Berra 20.00 50.00
2 Clete Boyer 6.00 15.00
3 Elston Howard 12.50 30.00
4 Tony Kubek 12.50 30.00
5 Mickey Mantle 50.00 100.00
6 Roger Maris 40.00 80.00
7 Joe Pepitone 8.00 20.00
8 Bobby Richardson 12.50 30.00

1963 Yankees Jay Publishing

This 12-card set of the New York Yankees measures approximately 5" by 7". The fronts feature black-and-white posed player photos with the player's and team name printed below in the white border. These cards were packaged 12 to a packet. The backs are blank. The cards are unnumbered and checklisted below in alphabetical order.

COMPLETE SET (12) 50.00 100.00
1 Yogi Berra 6.00 15.00
2 Clete Boyer 1.50 4.00
3 Whitey Ford 6.00 15.00
4 Ralph Houk MG 1.25 3.00
5 Elston Howard 2.00 5.00
6 Tony Kubek 2.00 5.00
7 Mickey Mantle 15.00 40.00
8 Roger Maris 8.00 20.00
9 Joe Pepitone 2.00 5.00
10 Bobby Richardson 2.00 5.00
11 Ralph Terry 1.00 2.50
12 Tom Tresh 2.00 5.00

1963-67 Yankees Requena K Postcards

Issued over a period of several years this set features New York Yankee players only.The set features two types -- one in color, the other in black and white. Bridges only appears in black and white. We have sequenced this set in alphabetical order. Similar to the Dormand and Bill and Bob postcard, Requena postcards feature a K in the lower left of the reverse.

COMPLETE SET 250.00 500.00
1 Steve Barber 6.00 15.00
2A Yogi Berra 20.00 50.00
Fascimile sig at top
2B Yogi Berra 20.00 50.00
Facsimile Sig at bottom
2C Yogi Berra 20.00 50.00
No signature
3 Johnny Blanchard 6.00 15.00
4 Jim Bouton 10.00 25.00
5 Clete Boyer 8.00 20.00
6 Marshall Bridges 6.00 15.00
7 Whitey Ford (2) 20.00 50.00
8 Elston Howard 12.50 30.00
9 Tony Kubek 12.50 30.00
10 Phil Linz 6.00 15.00
11 Fritz Peterson 6.00 15.00
12 Joe Pepitone 10.00 25.00
13 Pedro Ramos 6.00 15.00
14 Bobby Richardson 12.50 30.00
15 Bill Stafford 6.00 15.00
16 Mel Stottlemyre 10.00 25.00
18 Ralph Terry 6.00 15.00
19 Tom Tresh (2) 8.00 20.00

1964 Yankees Jay Publishing

This 12-card set of the New York Yankees measures approximately 5" by 7". The fronts feature black-and-white posed player photos with the player's and team name printed below in the white border. These cards were packaged 12 to a packet. The backs are blank. The cards are unnumbered and checklisted below in alphabetical order.

COMPLETE SET (12) 50.00 100.00
1 Yogi Berra MG 6.00 15.00
2 Clete Boyer 1.25 3.00
3 Al Downing 1.00 2.50
4 Whitey Ford 3.00 8.00
5 Elston Howard 2.00 5.00
6 Tony Kubek 2.00 5.00
7 Mickey Mantle 15.00 40.00
8 Roger Maris 8.00 20.00
9 Joe Pepitone 1.50 4.00
10 Bobby Richardson 2.00 5.00
11 Ralph Terry 1.00 2.50
12 Tom Tresh 1.50 4.00

1965 Yankees Jay Publishing

This 12-card set of the New York Yankees measures approximately 5" by 7". The fronts feature black-and-white posed player photos with the player's and team name printed below in the white border. These cards were packaged 12 to a packet. The backs are blank. The cards are unnumbered and checklisted below in alphabetical order.

COMPLETE SET (12) 50.00 100.00
1 Jim Bouton 2.00 5.00
2 Clete Boyer 1.50 4.00
3 Al Downing 1.00 2.50
4 Whitey Ford 6.00 15.00
5 Elston Howard 2.00 5.00
6 Tony Kubek 2.00 5.00
7 Mickey Mantle 15.00 40.00
8 Roger Maris 8.00 20.00
9 Joe Pepitone 1.50 4.00
10 Bobby Richardson 2.00 5.00
11 Mel Stottlemyre 1.50 4.00
12 Tom Tresh 1.50 4.00

1966 Yankees Team Issue

This 12-card set of the New York Yankees measures 4 7/8" by 7" and features black-and-white player photos in a white border with blank backs. These cards were originally packaged 12 to a packet with a price of 25 cents. The cards are unnumbered and checklisted below in alphabetical order. Changes in personnel are responsible for this checklist having more than 12 names.

COMPLETE SET (12) 40.00 80.00
1 Jim Bouton 1.50 4.00
2 Clete Boyer 1.25 3.00
3 Al Downing .75 2.00
4 Whitey Ford 6.00 15.00
5 Ralph Houk MG .75 2.00
6 Elston Howard 2.00 5.00
7 Johnny Keane MG .75 2.00
8 Hector Lopez .75 2.00
9 Mickey Mantle 12.50 30.00
10 Roger Maris 6.00 15.00
11 Joe Pepitone 1.50 4.00
12 Bobby Richardson 2.00 5.00
13 Mel Stottlemyre 1.50 4.00
14 Tom Tresh 1.50 4.00

1967 Yankees Photos SCFC

This 12-card set of the New York Yankees measures approximately 4" by 5" and features black-and-white player photos with white borders. The cards are listed below according to the numbers stamped on their white backs.

COMPLETE SET (12) 8.00 20.00
88 Team Photo 1.50 4.00
89 Ruben Amaro .75 2.00
90 Steve Barber .75 2.00
91 Steve Hamilton .75 2.00
92 Bill Monbouquette .75 2.00
93 Hal Reniff .75 2.00
94 Tom Shopay .75 2.00
95 Charlie Smith .75 2.00
96 Thad Tillotson .75 2.00
97 Dooley Womack .75 2.00
98 Yankee Stadium 1.50 4.00
99 Jerry Coleman ANN 1.00 2.50

1968 Yankees Photos SCFC

This 29-card set of the New York Yankees measures approximately 4" by 5" and features black-and-white player photos with white borders. The cards are listed below according to the numbers stamped on their white backs.

COMPLETE SET (29) 30.00 60.00
59 Ruben Amaro .75 2.00
60 Stan Bahnsen .75 2.00
61 Steve Barber .75 2.00
62 Horace Clarke .75 2.00
63 Rocky Colavito 4.00 10.00
64 Al Downing .75 2.00
65 Frank Fernandez .75 2.00
66 Jake Gibbs .75 2.00
67 Steve Hamilton .75 2.00
68 Dick Howser .75 2.00
69 Andy Kosco .75 2.00
70 Lindy McDaniel .75 2.00
71 Gene Michael .75 2.00
72 Bill Monbouquette .75 2.00
73 Joe Pepitone 1.25 3.00
74 Fritz Peterson/(Autographed) .75 2.00
75 Fritz Peterson/(Closer Portrait) .75 2.00
76 Bill Robinson .75 2.00
77 Charlie Smith .75 2.00
78 Fred Talbot .75 2.00
79 Joe Verbanic .75 2.00
80 Steve Whitaker .75 2.00
81 Roy White 1.25 3.00
82 Dooley Womack .75 2.00
83 Bobby Cox 3.00 8.00
84 Bill Dickey CO 1.50 4.00
85 Frank Fernandez .75 2.00
86 Tom Tresh 1.25 3.00
87 Jim Turner CO 1.25 3.00

1969 Yankees Malanga

This 12-card set was issued in four strips of three cards each measuring approximately 8 1/2" by 3 3/4" and could be obtained from the artist. The fronts carry very crude black-and-white drawings of New York Yankee players by Rocco Malanga. The backs are blank. The cards are unnumbered and checklisted below in alphabetical order.

COMPLETE SET (12) 8.00 20.00
1 Horace Clarke .60 1.50
2 Jake Gibbs .60 1.50
3 Steve Hamiltom UER/(misspelled Hamilton) .60
1.50
4 Ralph Houk MG .75 2.00
5 Mickey Mantle 4.00 10.00
6 Joe Pepitone 1.00 2.50
7 Bill Robinson .60 1.50
8 Mel Stottemyre UER/(misspelled Stottlemyre) 1.00
2.50
9 Fred Talbot .60 1.50
10 Tom Tresh 1.00 2.50
11 Joe Verbanic .60 1.50
12 Roy White 1.00 2.50

1969 Yankees Photos SCFC

This 22-card set of the New York Yankees measures approximately 4" by 5" and features black-and-white player photos with white borders. The cards are listed below according to the numbers stamped on their white backs.

COMPLETE SET (22) 40.00 80.00
37 Len Boehmer 1.25 3.00
38 Bill Burbach 1.25 3.00
39 Bobby Cox 2.50 6.00
40 Jimmie Hall 1.25 3.00
41 Steve Hamilton 1.25 3.00
42 Jack Kennedy 1.25 3.00
43 Jerry Kenney 1.25 3.00
44 Lindy McDaniel 1.25 3.00
45 Bobby Murcer 2.50 6.00
46 Joe Pepitone 2.00 5.00
47 Fritz Peterson 1.25 3.00
48 Bill Robinson 1.25 3.00
49 Dick Simpson 1.25 3.00
50 Mel Stottlemyre 2.00 5.00
51 Fred Talbot 1.25 3.00
52 Joe Verbanic 1.25 3.00
53 Ron Woods 1.25 3.00
54 Jack Aker 1.25 3.00
55 Horace Clarke 1.25 3.00
56 Billy Cowan 1.25 3.00
57 John Ellis 1.25 3.00
58 Mike Kekich 1.25 3.00

1970 Yankees Clinic Day Postcards

During the 1970 season, The New York Yankees had a promotion where fans could meet their favorite players before a game. These postcards were issued so the fans could have something to sign. These cards are sequenced in order of the player's appearance. Some cards are known to be in much shorter supply. The card of Roy White is extremely difficult since the game was rained out. The Murcer card was issued early in the season is difficult as well. Both cards are noted with a SP in the listings.

COMPLETE SET 20.00 50.00
COMMON PLAYER .40 1.00
COMMON SP 2.00 5.00
1 Bobby Murcer SP 2.00 5.00
2 Roy White SP 10.00 25.00
3 Curt Blefary .40 1.00
4 Fritz Peterson .40 1.00
5 Danny Cater .40 1.00
6 Horace Clarke .40 1.00
7 Gene Michael .40 1.00
8 Stan Bahnsen .40 1.00
9 Thurman Munson 4.00 10.00
10 John Ellis .40 1.00
11 Jerry Kenney .40 1.00
12 Mel Stottlemyre .60 1.50
13 Joe DiMaggio 4.00 10.00
Mickey Mantle

1970 Yankees Photos SCFC

This 36-card set of the New York Yankees measures approximately 4" by 5" and features black-and-white player photos with white borders. The cards are listed below according to the numbers stamped on their white backs.

COMPLETE SET (36) 20.00 50.00
1 Jack Aker .60 1.50
2 Stan Bahnsen .60 1.50
3 Frank Baker .60 1.50
4 Curt Blefary .60 1.50
5 Ron Blomberg .60 1.50
6 Bill Burbach .60 1.50
7 Danny Cater .60 1.50
8 Horace Clarke .60 1.50
9 John Cumberland .60 1.50
10 John Ellis .60 1.50
11 Jake Gibbs .60 1.50
12 Steve Hamilton .60 1.50
13 Ron Hansen .60 1.50
14 Mike Hegan .60 1.50
15 Ralph Houk MG .60 1.50
16 Elston Howard CO 1.00 2.50
17 Dick Howser CO .60 1.50
18 Mike Kekich .60 1.50
19 Jerry Kenney .60 1.50
20 Ron Klimkowski .60 1.50
21 Steve Kline .60 1.50
22 Jim Lyttle .60 1.50
23 Mickey Mantle CO 4.00 10.00
24 Mike McCormick .60 1.50
25 Lindy McDaniel .60 1.50
26 Gene Michael .75 2.00
27 Thurman Munson 2.00 5.00
28 Bobby Murcer 1.00 2.50
29 Fritz Peterson .60 1.50
30 Mel Stottlemyre 1.00 2.50
31 Frank Tepedino .75 2.00
32 Joe Verbanic .60 1.50
33 Pete Ward .60 1.50
34 Gary Waslewski .60 1.50
35 Roy White .75 2.00
36 Ron Woods .60 1.50

1971 Yankees Arco Oil

Sponsored by Arco Oil, these 12 pictures of the 1971 New York Yankees measure approximately 8" by 10" and feature on their fronts white-bordered posed color player photos. The player's name is shown in black lettering within the white margin below the photo. His facsimile autograph appears across the picture. The white back carries the team's and player's names at the top, followed below by position, biography, career highlights, and statistics. An ad at the bottom for picture frames rounds out the back. The cards are unnumbered and checklisted below in alphabetical order.

COMPLETE SET (12) 30.00 60.00
1 Jack Aker 1.50 4.00
2 Stan Bahnsen 1.50 4.00
3 Frank Baker 1.50 4.00
4 Danny Cater 1.50 4.00
5 Horace Clarke 2.50 6.00
6 John Ellis 1.50 4.00
7 Gene Michael 2.50 6.00
8 Thurman Munson 5.00 12.00
9 Bobby Murcer 3.00 8.00
10 Fritz Peterson 1.50 4.00
11 Mel Stottlemyre 3.00 8.00
12 Roy White 2.50 6.00

1971 Yankees Clinic Day Postcards

Similar to the 1970 promotion, the New York Yankees again had days where the fans could meet their favorite players before selected home games. These cards were issued so fans could have an item for the player to sign. We have sequenced this set in alphabetical order. These postcards were produced by Dexter Press.

COMPLETE SET (16) 20.00 50.00
1 Stan Bahnsen .40 1.00
2 Curt Blefary .40 1.00
3 Danny Cater .40 1.00
4 Horace Clarke .40 1.00
Gene Michael
5 John Ellis .40 1.00
6 Jake Gibbs .40 1.00
7 Ralph Houk MG .40 1.00
8 Jerry Kenney .40 1.00
Frank Baker
9 Jim Lyttle .40 1.00
Felipe Alou
10 Mickey Mantle 10.00 25.00
11 Lindy McDaniel .40 1.00
12 Thurman Munson 4.00 10.00
13 Bobby Murcer 1.25 3.00
14 Fritz Peterson .40 1.00
15 Mel Stottlemyre .75 2.00
16 Roy White 1.25 3.00

1972 Yankees Schedules

This eight card set was issued in very limited quantities. These cards have 1972 Yankees schedules on the back and are very difficult to obtain. These cards are unnumbered and we have sequenced them in alphabetical order.

COMPLETE SET (8) 300.00 600.00

1 Felipe Alou 50.00 100.00
2 Ron Blomberg 10.00 25.00
3 Thurman Munson 100.00 200.00
4 Bobby Murcer 50.00 100.00
5 Mel Stottlemyre 40.00 80.00
6 Ron Swoboda 20.00 50.00
7 Roy White 40.00 80.00
8 Bill White ANN 50.00 100.00
Phil Rizzuto
Frank Messer

1972 Yankees Team Issue

This six-card set of the 1972 New York Yankees measures approximately 4" by 6" and features color player photos with white borders. The backs are blank. The cards are unnumbered and checklisted below in alphabetical order.

COMPLETE SET (6) 10.00 25.00
1 Danny Cater 1.25 3.00
2 John Ellis 1.25 3.00
3 Thurman Munson 4.00 10.00
4 Bobby Murcer 2.00 5.00
5 Fritz Peterson 1.25 3.00
6 Roy White 2.00 5.00

1973 Yankees TCMA All-Time Team

These cards measure 3.5 x 5.5 and feature black and white photos of twelve Yankee greats. The player's name appears on the front of the card beneath their photo, while the cardbacks lists the checklist. The unnumbered cards have been checklisted alphabetically.

COMPLETE SET (12) 12.50 30.00
1 Bill Dickey .60 1.50
2 Joe DiMaggio 4.00 10.00
3 Whitey Ford 1.00 2.50
4 Lou Gehrig 2.50 6.00
5 Tony Lazzeri .40 1.00
6 Mickey Mantle 2.50 6.00
7 Johnny Murphy .40 1.00
8 Phil Rizzuto .60 1.50
9 Red Rolfe .40 1.00
10 Red Ruffing .40 1.00
11 Babe Ruth 4.00 10.00
12 Casey Stengel MG 1.00 2.50

1973 Yankees Team Issue

This six-card set of the New York Yankees measures approximately 7" by 8 3/4" and features color player photos in a white border. The player's name and team are printed in the wide bottom margin. The backs are blank. The cards are unnumbered and checklisted in alphabetical order.

COMPLETE SET (6) 10.00 25.00
1 Ron Blomberg 1.25 3.00
2 Sparky Lyle 2.00 5.00
3 Bobby Murcer 2.00 5.00
4 Graig Nettles 2.00 5.00
5 Fritz Peterson 1.25 3.00
6 Roy White 1.50 4.00

1975 Yankees 1927 TCMA

This 30-card set of the 1927 New York Yankees features black-and-white player photos in white borders. The backs carry player information and statistics. The cards are unnumbered and checklisted below in alphabetical order.

COMPLETE SET (30) 20.00 50.00
1 Walter Beall .40 1.00
2 Benny Bengough .60 1.50
3 Pat Collins .40 1.00
4 Earle Combs 1.00 2.50
5 Joe Dugan .40 1.00
6 Cedric Durst .40 1.00
7 Mike Gazella .40 1.00
8 Lou Gehrig 2.00 5.00
9 Joe Giard .40 1.00
10 Johnny Grabowski .40 1.00
11 Waite Hoyt 1.00 2.50
12 Miller Huggins MG 1.00 2.50
13 Mark Koenig .60 1.50
14 Tony Lazzeri 1.00 2.50
15 Bob Meusel .75 2.00
16 Wiley Moore .40 1.00
17 Ray Morehart .40 1.00
18 Ben Paschal .40 1.00
19 Herb Pennock 1.00 2.50
20 George Pipgras .40 1.00
21 Dutch Ruether .40 1.00
22 Jacob Ruppert OWN .60 1.50
23 Babe Ruth 3.00 8.00
24 Bob Shawkey .60 1.50
25 Urban Shocker .40 1.00
26 Myles Thomas .40 1.00
27 Julie Wera .40 1.00
28 Yankee Stadium .40 1.00
29 Miller Huggins MG .60 1.50
Charlie O'Leary CO
Art Fletche
30 Lou Gehrig 1.25 3.00
Tony Lazzeri
Mark Koenig
Joe Dugan/

1975 Yankees All-Time Team TCMA

This 12-card set features two different photo variations of all-time great New York Yankees: blue-and-white and black and white. The cards measure approximately 2 1/2" by 3 3/4". The cardbacks carry the checklist of the set. The cards are unnumbered and checklisted below in alphabetical order.

COMPLETE SET (12) 10.00 25.00
1 Bill Dickey 1.00 2.50
2 Joe DiMaggio 2.00 5.00
3 Whitey Ford 1.00 2.50
4 Lou Gehrig 2.00 5.00
5 Tony Lazzeri 1.00 2.50
6 Mickey Mantle 2.00 5.00
7 Johnny Murphy .40 1.00
8 Phil Rizzuto 1.00 2.50
9 Red Rolfe .40 1.00
10 Red Ruffing .75 2.00
11 Babe Ruth 3.00 8.00
12 Casey Stengel MG 1.00 2.50

1975 Yankees Dynasty 1936-39 TCMA

The first 49 cards in this set measure 2 3/4" by 4" and feature black-and-white player photos with white borders. The final five cards are 4" by 5 1/2" and feature photos of Yankees from 1936-39. The player's name and position are printed in blue below the picture. The phrase "1936-1939 Yankee Dynasty" is at the top except for card numbers 50-53, which have "World Champions -- 19XX" printed at the top. The backs carry statistics printed in blue. The cards are unnumbered and checklisted below in alphabetical order. This set can be distinguished from the 1983 reprint by two major characteristics: The first one is the printing of these cards in blue and the second one is that neither Joe Gallagher or Lee Stine is in the 1975 set.

COMPLETE SET (54) 15.00 40.00
1 Ivy Paul Andrews .20 .50
2 Joe Beggs .20 .50
3 Marv Breuer .20 .50
4 Johnny Broaca .20 .50
5 Jumbo Brown .20 .50
6 Spud Chandler .30 .75
7 Ben Chapman .20 .50
8 Earl Combs CO .60 1.50
9 Frankie Crosetti .40 1.00
10 Babe Dahlgren .20 .50
11 Joe DiMaggio 2.50 6.00
12 Bill Dickey .60 1.50
13 Atley Donald .20 .50
14 Wes Farrell .30 .75
15 Artie Fletcher CO .20 .50
16 Lou Gehrig 2.50 6.00
17 Joe Glenn .20 .50
18 Lefty Gomez .60 1.50
19 Joe Gordon .40 1.00
20 Bump Hadley .20 .50
21 Don Heffner .20 .50
22 Tommy Henrich .40 1.00
23 Oral Hildebrand .20 .50
24 Myril Hoag .20 .50
25 Roy Johnson .20 .50
26 Art Jorgens .20 .50
27 Charlie Keller .30 .75
28 Ted Kleinhans .20 .50
29 Billy Knickerbocker .20 .50
30 Tony Lazzeri .60 1.50
31 Frank Makosky .20 .50
32 Pat Malone .20 .50
33 Joe McCarthy MG .40 1.00
Jacob Ruppert OWN
34 Johnny Murphy .30 .75
35 Monty Pearson .20 .50
36 Jake Powell .20 .50
37 Red Rolfe .30 .75
38 Buddy Rosar .20 .50
39 Red Ruffing .60 1.50
40 Marius Russo .20 .50
41 Jack Saltzgaver .20 .50
42 Paul Schreiber .20 .50
43 Johnny Schulte .20 .50
44 Bob Seeds .20 .50
45 Twinkletoes Selkirk .30 .75
46 Steve Sundra .20 .50
47 Sandy Vance .20 .50
48 Dixie Walker .30 .75
49 Kemp Wicker .20 .50
50 World Champions 1936
(Team celebrating) 1.50 4.00
51 World Champions 1937 1.50 4.00
Joe DiMaggio
Frankie Croset
52 World Champions 1938 .60 1.50
Red Rolfe
Tony Lazzeri
Lou
53 World Champions 1939 1.50 4.00
Lou Gehrig
Joe DiMaggio
54 Lou Gehrig Hits Another 1.50 4.00

1975 Yankees SSPC

This 23-card standard-size set of New York Yankees features white-bordered posed color player photos on their fronts, which are free of any other markings. The white back carries the player's name in red lettering above his blue-lettered biography and career highlights. The cards are numbered on the back within a circle formed by the player's team name. A similar set of New York Mets was produced at the same time. This set is dated 1975 because that was Ed Brinkman's only season with the Yankees.

COMPLETE SET (23) 8.00 20.00
1 Jim Hunter 1.50 4.00
2 Bobby Bonds .40 1.00
3 Ed Brinkman .10 .25
4 Ron Blomberg .20 .50
5 Thurman Munson 2.00 5.00
6 Roy White .30 .75
7 Larry Gura .10 .25
8 Ed Herrmann .10 .25
9 Bill Virdon MG .20 .50
10 Elliott Maddox .20 .50
11 Lou Piniella .40 1.00
12 Rick Dempsey .30 .75
13 Fred Stanley .10 .25
14 Chris Chambliss .40 1.00
15 George Medich .10 .25
16 Pat Dobson .20 .50
17 Alex Johnson .20 .50
18 Jim Mason .10 .25
19 Sandy Alomar .10 .25
20 Graig Nettles .40 1.00
21 Walt Williams .10 .25
22 Sparky Lyle .30 .75
23 Dick Tidrow .10 .25

1977 Yankees Burger King

The cards in this 24-card set measure 2 1/2" by 3 1/2". The cards in this set marked with an asterisk have different poses than those cards in the regular 1977 Topps set. The checklist card is unnumbered and the Piniella card was issued subsequent to the original printing. The complete set price below refers to all 24 cards listed, including Piniella.

COMPLETE SET (24) 15.00 40.00
1 Yankees Team .40 1.00
Billy Martin MG
2 Thurman Munson * UER
(Facsimile autograph 3.00 8.00
misspe
3 Fran Healy .10 .25
4 Jim Hunter 1.00 2.50
5 Ed Figueroa .10 .25
6 Don Gullett */(Mouth closed) .20 .50
7 Mike Torrez */(Shown as A's .20 .50
in 1977 Topps)
8 Ken Holtzman .20 .50
9 Dick Tidrow .10 .25
10 Sparky Lyle .20 .50
11 Ron Guidry .30 .75
12 Chris Chambliss .20 .50
13 Willie Randolph* .30 .75
No rookie trophy
14 Bucky Dent* .20 .50
Shown as White Sox
in 1977 Topps
15 Graig Nettles */(Closer photo than .40 1.00
in 1977 Topps
16 Fred Stanley .10 .25
17 Reggie Jackson* 5.00 12.00
Looking up with bat
18 Mickey Rivers .30 .75
19 Roy White .20 .50
20 Jim Wynn* .30 .75
Shown as Brave
in 1977 Topps
21 Paul Blair* .30 .75
Shown as Oriole
in 1977 Topps
22 Carlos May */(Shown as White Sox .20 .50
in 1977 Topps)
23 Lou Piniella SP 8.00 20.00
NNO Checklist Card TP .10 .25

1978 Yankees Burger King

The cards in this 23-card set measure 2 1/2" by 3 1/2". These cards were distributed in packs of three players plus a checklist at Burger King's New York area outlets. Cards with an asterisk have different poses than those in the Topps regular issue.

COMPLETE SET (23) 6.00 15.00
1 Billy Martin MG .40 1.00
2 Thurman Munson 1.50 4.00
3 Cliff Johnson .10 .25
4 Ron Guidry* .40 1.00
5 Ed Figueroa .10 .25
6 Dick Tidrow .10 .25
7 Jim Hunter 1.00 2.50
8 Don Gullett .10 .25
9 Sparky Lyle .30 .75
10 Goose Gossage * .40 1.00
11 Rawly Eastwick * .10 .25
12 Chris Chambliss .30 .75
13 Willie Randolph .30 .75
14 Graig Nettles .40 1.00
15 Bucky Dent .30 .75
16 Jim Spencer * .10 .25
17 Fred Stanley .10 .25
18 Lou Piniella .40 1.00
19 Roy White .30 .75
20 Mickey Rivers .30 .75
21 Reggie Jackson 1.50 4.00
22 Paul Blair .10 .25
NNO Checklist Card TP .08 .20

1978 Yankees Photo Album

This 27-card set of the New York Yankees measures approximately 8" square and features a color player portrait in a white border with a facsimile autograph. The backs are blank. The cards are unnumbered and checklisted below in alphabetical order.

COMPLETE SET (27) 6.00 15.00
1 Jim Beattie .10 .25
Brian Doyle
Paul Lindblad
Larry McC
2 Yogi Berra .40 1.00
Art Fowler
Elston Howard
Dick Howser
3 Paul Blair .10 .25
4 Chris Chambliss .30 .75
5 Kenny Clay .10 .25
6 Bucky Dent .30 .75
7 Ed Figueroa .10 .25
8 Goose(Rich) Gossage .40 1.00
9 Ron Guidry .40 1.00
10 Don Gullett .20 .50
11 Mike Heath .10 .25
12 Catfish(Jim) Hunter .60 1.50
13 Reggie Jackson 1.50 4.00
14 Cliff Johnson .10 .25
15 Jay Johnstone .20 .50
16 Bob Lemon MG .40 1.00
17 Sparky Lyle .20 .50
18 Thurman Munson .75 2.00
19 Graig Nettles .40 1.00
20 Lou Piniella .40 1.00
21 Willie Randolph .30 .75
22 Mickey Rivers .20 .50
23 Jim Spencer .10 .25
24 Fred Stanley .10 .25
25 Gary Thomasson .10 .25
26 Dick Tidrow .10 .25
27 Roy White .20 .50

1978 Yankees SSPC Diary

This 27 card standard-size set was inserted into the 1978 Yankees Yearbook and Diary of a Champion Yankee. These cards are full bleed and the backs have 1977 seasonal highlights.

COMPLETE SET (27) 4.00 10.00
1 Thurman Munson 1.25 3.00
2 Cliff Johnson .08 .20
3 Lou Piniella .30 .75
4 Dell Alston .08 .20
5 Yankee Stadium .08 .20
6 Ken Holtzman .08 .20
7 Chris Chambliss .10 .25
8 Roy White .08 .20
9 Ed Figueroa .08 .20
10 Dick Tidrow .08 .20
11 Sparky Lyle .10 .25
12 Fred Stanley .08 .20
13 Mickey Rivers .08 .20
14 Billy Martin MG .10 .25
15 George Zeber .08 .20
16 Ken Clay .08 .20
17 Ron Guidry .30 .75
18 Don Gullett .08 .20
19 Fran Healy .08 .20
20 Paul Blair .08 .20
21 Mickey Klutts .08 .20
22 Yankee Team .08 .20
23 Catfish Hunter .75 2.00
24 Bucky Dent .10 .25
25 Graig Nettles .30 .75
26 Reggie Jackson 1.25 3.00
27 Willie Randolph .30 .75

1979 Yankees Burger King

The cards in this 23-card set measure 2 1/2" by 3 1/2". There are 22 numbered cards and one unnumbered checklist in the 1979 Burger King Yankee set. The poses of Guidry, Tiant, John and Beniquez, each marked with an asterisk below, are different from their poses appearing in the regular Topps issue. The team card has the team leaders noted on the back.

COMPLETE SET (23) 5.00 12.00
1 Yankees Team: .40 1.00
Bob Lemon MG
2 Thurman Munson 1.50 4.00
3 Cliff Johnson .10 .25
4 Ron Guidry * .30 .75
5 Jay Johnstone .20 .50
6 Jim Hunter 1.00 2.50
7 Jim Beattie .20 .50
8 Luis Tiant */(Shown as Red Sox .40 1.00
in 1979 Topps)
9 Tommy John */(Shown as Dodgers .40 1.00
in 1979 Topps)
10 Goose Gossage .40 1.00
11 Ed Figueroa .10 .25
12 Chris Chambliss .30 .75
13 Willie Randolph .40 1.00
14 Bucky Dent .30 .75
15 Graig Nettles .40 1.00
16 Fred Stanley .10 .25
17 Jim Spencer .10 .25
18 Lou Piniella .40 1.00
19 Roy White .30 .75
20 Mickey Rivers .30 .75
21 Reggie Jackson 1.50 4.00
22 Juan Beniquez * .20 .50
NNO Checklist Card TP .08 .15

1979 Yankees 1927 TCMA

This 32-card set features sepia tone pictures of the 1927 New York Yankees team. The fronts feature the player photo while the back has information about the featured player.

COMPLETE SET (32) 8.00 20.00
1 Babe Ruth 3.00 8.00
2 Lou Gehrig 2.00 5.00
3 Tony Lazzeri .40 1.00
4 Mark Koenig .20 .50
5 Julie Wera .10 .25
6 Ray Morehart .10 .25
7 Art Fletcher CO .10 .25
8 Joe Dugan .20 .50
9 Charlie O'Leary CO .10 .25
10 Bob Meusel .30 .75
11 Earle Combs .40 1.00
12 Cedric Durst .10 .25
13 John Grabowski .10 .25
14 Mike Gazella .10 .25
15 Pat Collins .10 .25
16 Waite Hoyt .40 1.00
17 Myles Thomas .10 .25
18 Benny Bengough .20 .50
19 Herb Pennock .40 1.00
20 Wilcy Moore .10 .25
21 Urban Shocker .10 .25
22 Dutch Reuther .10 .25
23 George Pipgras .10 .25
24 Jacob Ruppert OWN .20 .50
25 Eddie Bennett BB .10 .25
26 Ed Barrow GM .20 .50
27 Ben Paschal .10 .25
28 Miller Huggins MG .40 1.00
29 Joe Giard .10 .25
30 Bob Shawkey .20 .50
31 Walter Beall .10 .25
32 Don Miller .10 .25

1979 Yankees Picture Album

This 32-page Picture Album of the 1979 New York Yankees measures approximately 8" by 8" and features posed color player photos in white borders with a facsimile autograph across the bottom. The backs are blank. The cards are unnumbered and checklisted below in alphabetical order. This set was issued late during the 1979 season as Thurman Munson is memoralized in his photo.

COMPLETE SET (34) 8.00 20.00
1 Jim Beattie .20 .50
2 Juan Beniquez .10 .25
3 Yogi Berra CO .75 2.00
4 Bobby Brown .10 .25
5 Ray Burris .10 .25
6 Chris Chambliss .20 .50
7 Ken Clay .10 .25
8 Ron Davis .10 .25
9 Bucky Dent .20 .50
10 Brian Doyle .10 .25
11 Mike Ferraro .10 .25
12 Ed Figueroa .10 .25
13 Art Fowler CO .10 .25
14 Goose Gossage .40 1.00
15 Ron Guidry .40 1.00
16 Don Gullett .10 .25
17 Jim Hegan CO .10 .25
18 Don Hood .10 .25
19 Jim Hunter .50 1.25
20 Reggie Jackson 1.25 3.00
21 Tommy John .40 1.00
22 Jim Kaat .30 .75
23 Charley Lau CO .10 .25
24 Billy Martin MG .40 1.00
25 Thurman Munson .75 2.00
26 Bobby Murcer .30 .75
27 Jerry Narron .10 .25
28 Graig Nettles .40 1.00
29 Lou Piniella .30 .75
30 Willie Randolph .40 1.00
31 Jim Spencer .10 .25
32 Fred Stanley .10 .25
33 Luis Tiant .30 .75
34 Roy White .20 .50

1980 Yankees Greats TCMA

These 12 standard-size cards feature all-time Yankee greats. The fronts have a player photo and the backs display a checklist of who is in the set.

COMPLETE SET (12) 4.00 10.00
1 Lou Gehrig 1.25 3.00
2 Tony Lazzeri .30 .75
3 Red Rolfe .20 .50
4 Phil Rizzuto .60 1.50
5 Babe Ruth 1.50 4.00
6 Mickey Mantle 1.50 4.00
7 Joe DiMaggio 1.25 3.00
8 Bill Dickey .40 1.00
9 Red Ruffing .40 1.00
10 Whitey Ford .60 1.50
11 Johnny Murphy .20 .50
12 Casey Stengel MG .40 1.00

1980 Yankees Photo Album

This 27-card set of the New York Yankees was distributed in a booklet measuring approximately 8" by 7 7/8". The fronts feature a color player portrait in a white border with a facsimile autograph. The backs are blank. The cards are unnumbered and checklisted below in alphabetical order.

COMPLETE SET (27) 5.00 12.00
1 Yogi Berra .40 1.00
Mike Ferraro
Jim Hegan
Charley Lau/
2 Bobby Brown .08 .25
3 Rick Cerone .08 .25
4 Ron Davis .08 .25
5 Bucky Dent .30 .75
6 Ed Figueroa .08 .25
7 Oscar Gamble .20 .50
8 Goose(Rich) Gossage .40 1.00
9 Ron Guidry .40 1.00
10 Don Gullett .08 .25
Johnny Oates
11 Dick Howser MG .08 .25
12 Reggie Jackson .75 2.00
13 Tommy John .40 1.00
14 Ruppert Jones .08 .25
15 Joe Lefebvre .08 .25
16 Rudy May .08 .25
17 Bobby Murcer .40 1.00
18 Graig Nettles .40 1.00
19 Lou Piniella .40 1.00
20 Willie Randolph .40 1.00
21 Eric Soderholm .08 .25
22 Jim Spencer .08 .25
23 Fred Stanley .08 .25
24 Luis Tiant .20 .50
25 Tom Underwood .08 .25
26 Bob Watson .20 .50
27 Dennis Werth .08 .25

1981 Yankees Photo Album

This 26-card set of the New York Yankees was distributed in a booklet measuring approximately 8" square. The fronts feature a color player portrait in a white border with a facsimile autograph. The backs are blank. The cards are unnumbered and checklisted below in alphabetical order.

COMPLETE SET (26) 6.00 15.00
1 Joe Altobetti .40 1.00
Yogi Berra
Mike Ferraro
Clyde Kin
2 Bobby Brown .08 .25
3 Ron Davis .08 .25
4 Bucky Dent .30 .75
5 Barry Foote .08 .25
6 Oscar Gamble .20 .50
7 Goose(Rich) Gossage .40 1.00
8 Ron Guidry .40 1.00
9 Reggie Jackson 1.00 2.50
10 Tommy John .40 1.00
11 Dave Laroche .08 .25
12 Rudy May .08 .25
13 Gene Michael MG .08 .25
14 Larry Milbourne .08 .25
15 Jerry Mumphrey .08 .25
16 Bobby Murcer .40 1.00
17 Gene Nelson .08 .25
18 Graig Nettles .40 1.00
19 Lou Piniella .40 1.00
20 Willie Randolph .40 1.00
21 Rick Reuschel .20 .50
22 Dave Revering .08 .25
23 Dave Righetti 1.00 2.50
24 Aurelio Rodriguez .08 .25
25 Bob Watson .20 .50
26 Dave Winfield 1.00 2.50

1982 Yankees 1961 Black and White

This 30-card set features black-and-white photos of the 1961 World Champion New York Yankees in white borders. The backs carry player information and career statistics. The last four cards are unnumbered and display photos of coaches. When placed together, the backs of these four cards form a blue-and-white photo of this championship team.

COMPLETE SET (30) 3.00 8.00
1 Roger Maris .75 2.00
2 Bobby Richardson .20 .50
3 Tony Kubek .20 .50
4 Elston Howard .20 .50
5 Bill Skowron .20 .50
6 Clete Boyer .12 .30
7 Mickey Mantle 1.50 4.00
8 Yogi Berra .60 1.50
9 Johnny Blanchard .07 .20
10 Hector Lopez .07 .20
11 Whitey Ford .75 2.00
12 Ralph Terry .07 .20
13 Bill Stafford .02 .10
14 Bud Daley .02 .10
15 Billy Gardner .02 .10
16 Jim Coates .02 .10
17 Luis Arroyo .02 .10
18 Tex Clevenger .02 .10
19 Bob Cerv .02 .10
20 Art Ditmar .02 .10
21 Bob Turley .07 .20
22 Joe DeMaestri .02 .10
23 Rollie Sheldon .02 .10
24 Earl Torgeson .02 .10
25 Hal Reniff .02 .10
26 Ralph Houk MG .07 .20
NNO Jim Hegan CO .02 .10
NNO Wally Moses CO .02 .10
NNO Frank Crosetti CO .07 .20
NNO Johnny Sain CO .07 .20

1982 Yankees 1961 Color

In addition to the black and white Yankees set Renata Galasso issued, they also issued a 37 card standard-size color set. The fronts have a player photo with the players name and position on the bottom and these are surrounded by white borders. The backs have some brief biographical information as well as an informational blurb and 1961 and career statistics.

COMPLETE SET (37) 8.00 20.00
1 Roger Maris .75 2.00
2 Yogi Berra .60 1.50
3 Whitey Ford .75 2.00
4 Hector Lopez .20 .50
5 Bob Turley .20 .50
6 Frank Crosetti CO .20 .50
7 Bob Cerv .08 .25
8 Jack Reed .08 .25
9 Luis Arroyo .08 .25
10 Danny McDevitt .08 .25
11 Duke Maas .08 .25
12 Jesse Gonder .08 .25
13 Ralph Terry .20 .50
14 Deron Johnson .08 .25
15 John Blanchard .08 .25
16 Bill Stafford .08 .25
17 Earl Torgeson .08 .25
18 Tony Kubek .30 .75
19 Rollie Sheldon .08 .25
20 Tex Clevenger .08 .25
21 Art Ditmar .08 .25
22 Bud Daley .08 .25
23 Jim Coates .08 .25
24 Al Downing .08 .25
25 Johnny Sain CO .08 .25
26 Jim Hegan CO .08 .25
27 Wally Moses CO .08 .25
28 Ralph Houk MG .08 .25
29 Bill Skowron .30 .75
30 Bobby Richardson .40 1.00
31 Johnny James .08 .25
32 Hal Reniff .08 .25
33 Mickey Mantle 1.50 4.00
34 Clete Boyer .20 .50
35 Elston Howard .40 1.00
36 Joe DeMaestri .08 .25
37 Billy Gardner .08 .25

1982 Yankees Photo Album

This 27-card set of the New York Yankees was distributed in a booklet measuring approximately 7 7/8" square. The fronts feature a color player portrait in a white border with a facsimile autograph. The backs are blank. The cards are unnumbered and checklisted below in alphabetical order.

COMPLETE SET (27) 5.00 12.00
1 Doyle Alexander .08 .25
Roger Erickson
Barry Foote
Dave
2 Joe Altobelli .40 1.00
Yogi Berra
Mike Ferraro
Clyde Kin
3 Rick Cerone .08 .25
4 Dave Collins .08 .25
5 Bucky Dent .30 .75
6 George Frazier .08 .25
7 Oscar Gamble .20 .50
8 Goose(Rich) Gossage .40 1.00
9 Ken Griffey .20 .50
10 Ron Guidry .40 1.00
11 Butch Hobson .08 .25
12 Tommy John .40 1.00
13 Ruby May .08 .25
14 John Mayberry .20 .50
15 Gene Michael MG .08 .25
16 Mike Morgan .08 .25
17 Jerry Mumphrey .08 .25
18 Bobby Murcer .40 1.00
19 Graig Nettles .40 1.00
20 Lou Piniella .40 1.00
21 Willie Randolph .30 .75
22 Shane Rawley .08 .25
23 Dave Righetti .40 1.00
24 Andre Robertson .08 .25
25 Roy Smalley .08 .25
26 Dave Winfield .75 2.00
27 Butch Wynegar .08 .25

1983 Yankees A-S Fifty Years

With the great New York Yankee tradition, this set commemorates the first 50 years of Yankee All-Stars. Other than the Mickey Mantle checklist card, this set is sequenced in alphabetical order.

COMPLETE SET (50) 8.00 20.00
1 Mickey Mantle CL .40 1.00
2 Luis Arroyo .02 .10
3 Hank Bauer .08 .25
4 Yogi Berra .30 .75
5 Tommy Byrne .02 .10
6 Spud Chandler .02 .10
7 Ben Chapman .02 .10
8 Jim Coates .02 .10
9 Bill Dickey .30 .75
10 Joe DiMaggio .75 2.00
11 Al Downing .02 .10
12 Ryne Duren .02 .10
13 Whitey Ford PORT .30 .75
14 Whitey Ford PIT .30 .75
15 Lou Gehrig .75 2.00
16 Lefty Gomez .30 .75
17 Bob Grim .02 .10
18 Tommy Henrich .20 .50
19 Elston Howard
20 Catfish Hunter .30 .75
21 Billy Johnson .02 .10
22 Charlie Keller .08 .25
23 Johnny Kucks .02 .10
24 Eddie Lopat .08 .25
25 Sparky Lyle .08 .25
26 Mickey Mantle 1.00 2.50
27 Roger Maris .60 1.50
28 Billy Martin .30 .75
29 Johnny Mize .30 .75
30 Bobby Murcer .20 .50
31 Irv Noren .02 .10
32 Joe Pepitone .20 .50
33 Fritz Peterson .02 .10
34 Vic Raschi .02 .10
35 Allie Reynolds .08 .25
36 Bobby Richardson .20 .50
37 Phil Rizzuto .30 .75
38 Marius Russo .02 .10
39 Babe Ruth .40 1.00
40 Johnny Sain .20 .50
41 George Selkirk .02 .10
42 Bobby Shantz .02 .10
43 Spec Shea .02 .10
44 Moose Skowron .20 .50
45 Casey Stengel .30 .75
46 Mel Stottlemyre .08 .25
47 Ralph Terry .02 .10
48 Tom Tresh .02 .10
49 Bob Turley .02 .10
50 Roy White .02 .10

1983 Yankees Photo Album

This 27-card set of the New York Yankees was sponsored by the New York Bus Service, the Bronx-Manhattan Express, and was distributed in a booklet measuring approximately 7 7/8" square. The fronts feature color player portraits in white borders with a facsimile autograph. The backs are blank. The cards are unnumbered and checklisted below in alphabetical order. This set is highlighted by a pre-Rookie Card Don Mattingly.

COMPLETE SET (27) 5.00 12.00
1 Steve Balboni 1.50 4.00
Ray Fontenot
Don Mattingly
Bobby
2 Don Baylor .20 .50
3 Yogi Berra .40 1.00
Sam Ellis
Jeff Torborg
Lee Walls
Ro
4 Bert Campaneris .20 .50
5 Rick Cerone .08 .25
6 George Frazier .08 .25
7 Oscar Gamble .20 .50
8 Goose Gossage .40 1.00
9 Ken Griffey .20 .50
10 Ron Guidry .40 1.00
11 Jay Howell .08 .25
12 Steve Kemp .08 .25
13 Matt Keough .08 .25
14 Billy Martin MG .30 .75
15 Rudy May .08 .25
16 Jerry Mumphrey .08 .25
17 Dale Murray .08 .25
18 Graig Nettles .40 1.00
19 Lou Piniella .40 1.00
20 Willie Randolph .40 1.00
21 Shane Rawley .08 .25
22 Dave Righetti .30 .75
23 Andre Robertson .08 .25
24 Bob Shirley .08 .25
25 Roy Smalley .08 .25
26 David Winfield .60 1.50
27 Butch Wynegar .08 .25

1983 Yankee Yearbook Insert TCMA

YOGI BERRA

Subtitled Baseball Picture Cards, this uncut sheet produced by TCMA features 18 American League players of the past (nine Yankees and nine from other AL teams) and measures approximately 16 1/2" by 10 7/8". If cut into singles, each card would measure the standard size. The fronts feature white-bordered color drawings of the players. The player's name appears in white lettering within a black rectangle near the bottom. The back carries the player's name in red lettering at the top, followed below by biography and career highlights.

COMPLETE SET (18) 4.00 10.00
1 Joe DiMaggio 1.00 2.50
2 Billy Pierce .20 .50
3 Phil Rizzuto .40 1.00
4 Ted Williams 1.00 2.50
5 Billy Martin .30 .75
6 Mel Parnell .08 .25
7 Harmon Killebrew .40 1.00
8 Yogi Berra .40 1.00
9 Roy Sievers .08 .25
10 Bill Dickey .30 .75
11 Hank Greenberg .30 .75
12 Allie Reynolds .20 .50
13 Joe Sewell .30 .75
14 Virgil Trucks .08 .25
15 Mickey Mantle 1.25 3.00
16 Boog Powell .20 .50
17 Whitey Ford .60 1.50
18 Lou Boudreau .30 .75

1984 Yankees 1927 Galasso

This 30-card set features replicas of oil paintings of the 1927 New York Yankees in blue borders by artist Ron Lewis. The backs carry player information and career statistics.

COMPLETE SET (30) 3.00 8.00
1 Lou Gehrig 1.00 2.50
2 Babe Ruth 1.50 4.00
3 Earle Combs .20 .50
4 Ed Barrow GM .07 .20
5 Bob Shawkey .10 .30
6 Bob Meusel .10 .30
7 Urban Shocker .07 .20
8 Ben Paschal .02 .10
9 John Grabowski .02 .10
10 Jacob Ruppert .07 .20
11 Herb Pennock .20 .50
12 Miller Huggins .20 .50
13 Wiley Moore .07 .20
14 Walter Beall .02 .10
15 Cedric Durst .02 .10
16 Tony Lazzeri .20 .50
17 Mark Koenig .07 .20
18 Waite Hoyt .20 .50
19 Myles Thomas .02 .10
20 Joe Dugan .10 .30
21 Art Fletcher .02 .10
22 Charlie O'Leary .02 .10
23 Ray Morehart .02 .10
24 Benny Bengough .07 .20
25 Pat Collins .02 .10
26 Dutch Ruether .02 .10
27 George Pipgras .02 .10
28 Mike Gazella .02 .10
29 Julian Wera .02 .10
30 Joe Giard .02 .10

1984 Yankees Photo Album

This 27-card set of the New York Yankees was distributed in a booklet measuring approximately 7 7/8" square. The fronts feature color player portraits in white borders with a facsimile autograph. The backs are blank. The cards are unnumbered and checklisted below in alphabetical order.

COMPLETE SET (27) 10.00 25.00
1 Yogi Berra MG 1.00 2.50
2 Holmquist/Michael/Connor/Torborg/Piniella .50
1.00
3 Don Baylor .75 2.00
4 Rick Cerone .20 .50
5 Tim Foli .20 .50
6 Ray Fontenot .20 .50
7 Oscar Gamble .20 .50
8 Ken Griffey Sr. .50 1.00
9 Ron Guidry .75 2.00
10 Toby Harrah .20 .50
11 Jay Howell .20 .50
12 Steve Kemp .20 .50
13 Don Mattingly 2.50 6.00
14 Bobby Meacham .20 .50
15 John Montefusco .20 .50
16 Omar Moreno .20 .50
17 Dale Murray .20 .50
18 Phil Niekro 1.00 2.50
19 Willie Randolph .75 2.00
20 Dave Righetti .60 1.50
21 Jose Rijo .75 2.00
22 Andre Robertson .20 .50
23 Bob Shirley .20 .50
24 Roy Smalley Jr. .20 .50
25 Dave Winfield 1.00 2.50
26 Butch Wynegar .20 .50
27 Armstrong/Christiansen/Dayett/O'Berry/Rasmussen
.20 .50

1985 Yankees TCMA Postcards

This 40-card set features color photos of the New York Yankees printed on postcard-size cards.

COMPLETE SET (40) 4.00 10.00
1 Mike Connor CO .02 .10
2 Yogi Berra MG .30 .75
3 Stump Merrill CO .02 .10
4 Gene Michael CO .02 .10
5 Lou Piniella CO .08 .25
6 Jeff Torborg CO .02 .10
7 Mike Armstrong .02 .10
8 Rich Bordi .02 .10
9 Clay Christiansen .04 .10
10 Joe Cowley .02 .10
11 Jim Deshaies .02 .10
12 Ron Guidry .20 .50
13 John Montefusco .02 .10
14 Dale Murray .02 .10
15 Phil Niekro .30 1.00
16 Alfonso Pulido .02 .10
17 Dennis Rasmussen .02 .10
18 Dave Righetti .08 .25
19 Bob Shirley .02 .10
20 Ed Whitson .02 .10
21 Scott Bradley .02 .10
22 Ron Hassey .02 .10
23 Butch Wynegar .02 .10
24 Dale Berra .02 .10
25 Billy Sample .02 .10
26 Rex Hudler .08 .25
27 Don Mattingly 1.25 3.00
28 Bobby Meacham .02 .10
29 Mike Pagliarulo .02 .10
30 Willie Randolph .30 .75
31 Andre Robertson .02 .10
32 Henry Cotto .02 .10
33 Don Baylor .20 .50
34 Ken Griffey .20 .50
35 Rickey Henderson .75 2.00
36 Vic Mata .02 .10
37 Omar Moreno .02 .10
38 Dan Pasqua .02 .10
39 Dave Winfield .60 1.50
40 Brian Fisher .02 .10

1986 Yankees TCMA

This 3 1/2" by 5 1/2" postcard set features members of the 1986 Yankees. The set has full-bleed color photographs. The backs have the players name and usually 1985 stats. The cards are numbered in the upper right corner with a "NYY86" prefix.

COMPLETE SET (40) 5.00 12.00
1 Tommy John .30 .75
2 Brad Arnsberg UER .08 .25
Name spelled Arnsburg
3 Al Holland UER .08 .25
Name spelled All
4 Mike Armstrong .08 .25
5 Marty Bystrom .08 .25
6 Doug Drabek .30 .75
7 Brian Fisher .08 .25
8 Stump Merrill CO .08 .25
9 Ron Guidry .30 .75
10 Joe Niekro .20 .50
12 Dennis Rasmussen .08 .25
13 Dave Righetti .20 .50
14 Rod Scurry .08 .25
15 Bob Shirley .08 .25
16 Bob Tewksbury .08 .25
17 Ed Whitson .08 .25
18 Britt Burns .08 .25
18 Gene Michael CO .08 .25
19 Butch Wynegar .08 .25
20 Ron Hassey .08 .25
21 Dale Berra .08 .25
22 Jeff Torborg CO .08 .25
23 Mike Fischlin .08 .25
24 Don Mattingly 1.50 4.00
25 Bobby Meacham .08 .25
26 Mike Pagliarulo .08 .25
27 Willie Randolph .40 1.00
28 Andre Robertson .08 .25
29 Roy White CO .20 .50
31 Henry Cotto .08 .25
32 Ken Griffey .30 .75
33 Rickey Henderson .60 1.50
34 Vic Mata .08 .25
35 Dan Pasqua .08 .25
36 Dave Winfield .40 1.25
37 Gary Roenicke .08 .25
38 Lou Piniella MG .30 .75
39 Joe Altobelli CO .08 .25
40 Sammy Ellis CO .08 .25
45 Mike Easler .08 .25

1987 Yankees 1927 TCMA

This nine-card standard-size set features key members of the 1927 Yankees. This team which had the famed "Murderers Row", is considered one of the all-time teams. The fronts feature black and white photographs. The backs have player information as well as stats from the 27 season.

COMPLETE SET (9) 2.50 6.00
1 Miller Huggins MG .20 .50
2 Herb Pennock .30 .75
3 Tony Lazzeri .30 .75
4 Waite Hoyt .30 .75
5 Wilcy Moore .08 .25
6 Earle Combs .30 .75
7 Bob Meusel .20 .50
8 Lou Gehrig .75 2.00
9 Babe Ruth 1.00 2.50

1987 Yankees 1961 TCMA

This nine-card standard-size set features members of the 1961 Yankees. This team set a major league record with 240 homers in a season and was led by Roger Maris and Mickey Mantle who combined for 115 of those blasts. The fronts display color photos, the player's name and position. The backs carry player information as well as more details about the 1961 season.

COMPLETE SET (9) 2.50 6.00
1 Bill Skowron .20 .50
2 Mickey Mantle 1.00 2.50
3 Bobby Richardson .30 .75
4 Tony Kubek .20 .50
5 Elston Howard .30 .75
6 Yogi Berra .40 1.00
7 Whitey Ford .40 1.00
8 Roger Maris .40 1.00
9 Ralph Houk MG .08 .25

1988 Yankees Donruss Team Book

The 1988 Donruss Yankees Team Book set features 27 cards (three pages with nine cards on each page) plus a large full-page puzzle of Stan Musial. Cards are in full color and are standard size. The set was distributed as a four-page book; although the puzzle page was perforated, the card pages were not. The cover of the "Team Collection" book is primarily bright red. Card fronts are very similar in design to the 1988 Donruss regular issue. The card numbers on the backs are the same for those players that are the same as in the regular Donruss set; the new players pictured are numbered on the back as "NEW." The book is usually sold intact. When cut from the book into individual cards, these cards are distinguishable from the regular 1988 Donruss cards since these have a 1988 copyright on the back whereas the regular issue has a 1987 copyright on the back.

COMPLETE SET (27) 1.50 4.00
43 Al Leiter RR .40 1.00
93 Dave Righetti .08 .25
105 Mike Pagliarulo .02 .10
128 Rick Rhoden .02 .10
175 Ron Guidry .02 .10
217 Don Mattingly .75 2.00
228 Willie Randolph .30 .75
251 Gary Ward .02 .10
277 Rickey Henderson .60 1.50
278 Dave Winfield .40 1.00
340 Claudell Washington .02 .10
374 Charles Hudson .02 .10
401 Tommy John .20 .50
474 Joel Skinner .02 .10
497 Tim Stoddard .02 .10
545 Jay Buhner .30 .75
616 Bobby Meacham .02 .10
635 Roberto Kelly .08 .25
NEW John Candelaria .02 .10
NEW Jack Clark .08 .25
NEW Jose Cruz .08 .25
NEW Richard Dotson .02 .10
NEW Cecilio Guante .02 .10
NEW Lee Guetterman .02 .10
NEW Rafael Santana .02 .10
NEW Steve Shields .02 .10
NEW Don Slaught .02 .10

1989 Yankee Citgo All-Time Greats

These six cards feature great New York Yankees. Since the cards are unnumbered we have checklisted them below in alphabetical order.

COMPLETE SET (6) 8.00 20.00
1 Whitey Ford 1.25 3.00
2 Lou Gehrig 2.00 5.00
3 Lefty Gomez 1.00 2.50
4 Phil Rizzuto 1.00 2.50
5 Babe Ruth 3.00 8.00
6 Casey Stengel .60 1.50

1989 Yankees Score Nat West

The 1989 Score National Westminster Bank New York Yankees set features 33 standard-size cards. The fronts and backs are navy; the backs have color mug shots, 1988 and career stats. The set was given away at a 1989 Yankees' home game.

COMPLETE SET (33) 8.00 20.00
1 Don Mattingly 3.00 8.00
2 Steve Sax .20 .50
3 Alvaro Espinoza .08 .25
4 Luis Polonia .08 .25
5 Jesse Barfield .08 .25
6 Dave Righetti .20 .50
7 Dave Winfield 1.50 4.00
8 John Candelaria .08 .25
9 Wayne Tolleson .08 .25
10 Ken Phelps .08 .25
11 Rafael Santana .08 .25
12 Don Slaught .08 .25
13 Mike Pagliarulo .08 .25
14 Lance McCullers .08 .25
15 Dave LaPoint .08 .25
16 Dale Mohorcic .08 .25
17 Steve Balboni .08 .25
18 Roberto Kelly .20 .50
19 Andy Hawkins .08 .25
20 Mel Hall .08 .25
21 Tom Brookens .08 .25
22 Deion Sanders 2.00 5.00
23 Richard Dotson .08 .25
24 Lee Guetterman .08 .25
25 Bob Geren .08 .25
26 Jimmy Jones .08 .25
27 Chuck Cary .08 .25
28 Ron Guidry .40 1.00
29 Hal Morris .20 .50
30 Clay Parker .08 .25
31 Dallas Green MG .20 .50
32 Thurman Munson MEM 2.00 5.00
33 Yankees Team Card .20 .50

1990 Yankees Crown

This nine-card standard size set featuring Yankee greats was issued by Crown and is titled on the back "Jack Marcus favorite Yankee collection". The fronts have a player photo as well as a description about the photo while the back just mentions what the front is titled again.

COMPLETE SET 8.00 20.00
1 Mickey Mantle 1.25 3.00
2 Yogi Berra .40 1.00
3 Phil Rizzuto .08 .25
4 Babe Ruth 1.25 3.00
Warren G Harding
At the Polo Grounds,
5 Babe Ruth 1.50 4.00
At the White house
6 Babe Ruth 1.25 3.00
William Bendix/1948
7 Babe Ruth 1.25 3.00
At Yankee Stadium, 1924
8 Babe Ruth 1.25 3.00
Sammy Vick
Ping Bodie/1920
9 Lou Gehrig .75 2.00

1990 Yankees Monument Park Rini Postcards

This set of 12 postcards measures 3 1/2" by 5 1/2". The fronts feature color drawings by Susan Rini.

COMPLETE SET (12) 2.00 5.00
1 Lou Gehrig .75 2.00
2 Babe Ruth 1.00 2.50
3 Thurman Munson .30 .75
4 Elston Howard .08 .25
5 Phil Rizzuto .30 .75
6 Mickey Mantle 1.00 2.50
7 Bill Dickey .30 .75
8 Lefty Gomez .20 .50
9 Pope Paul VI .40 1.00
10 Jacob Ruppert .08 .25
11 Roger Maris .40 1.00
12 Joe DiMaggio .75 2.00

1990 Yankees Score Nat West

1990 Score National Westminster Bank Yankees is a 32-card, standard-size set featuring members of the 1990 New York Yankees. This set also has a special Billy Martin memorial card which honored the late Yankee manager who died in a truck accident on 12/25/89.

COMPLETE SET (32) 6.00 15.00
1 Stump Merrill MG .08 .25
2 Don Mattingly 3.00 8.00
3 Steve Sax .20 .50
4 Alvaro Espinoza .08 .25
5 Jesse Barfield .20 .50
6 Roberto Kelly .20 .50
7 Mel Hall .08 .25
8 Claudell Washington .08 .25
9 Bob Geren .08 .25
10 Jim Leyritz .40 1.00
11 Pascual Perez .08 .25
12 Dave LaPoint .08 .25
13 Tim Leary .08 .25
14 Mike Witt .08 .25
15 Chuck Cary .08 .25
16 Dave Righetti .20 .50
17 Lee Guetterman .08 .25
18 Andy Hawkins .08 .25
19 Greg Cadaret .08 .25
20 Eric Plunk .08 .25
21 Jimmy Jones .08 .25
22 Deion Sanders 1.00 2.50
23 Jeff D. Robinson .08 .25
24 Matt Nokes .08 .25
25 Steve Balboni .08 .25
26 Wayne Tolleson .08 .25
27 Randy Velarde .40 1.00
28 Rick Cerone .08 .25
29 Alan Mills .08 .25
30 Billy Martin MEM 1.00 2.50
31 Stadium Card .20 .50
32 All-Time Yankee Record .20 .50

1990 Yankees 61 Ron Lewis

These 42 oversized cards feature members of the 1961 New York Yankees. The fronts feature artwork by noted sports artist Ron Lewis.

COMPLETE SET (42) 10.00 25.00
1 Team Photo .40 1.00
2 Bobby Richardson .60 1.50
3 Roger Maris 1.00 2.50
4 Elston Howard .60 1.50
5 Bill Skowron .60 1.50
6 Clete Boyer .40 1.00
7 Mickey Mantle 2.00 5.00
8 Yogi Berra 1.00 2.50
9 Johnny Blanchard .20 .50
10 Hector Lopez .20 .50
11 Whitey Ford 1.00 2.50
12 Ralph Terry .20 .50
13 Bill Stafford .20 .50
14 Bud Daley .20 .50
15 Billy Gardner .20 .50
16 Jim Coates .20 .50
17 Luis Arroyo .20 .50
18 Tex Clevenger .20 .50
19 Bob Cerv .20 .50
20 Art Ditmar .20 .50
21 Bob Turley .40 1.00
22 Joe DeMaestri .20 .50
23 Rollie Sheldon .20 .50
24 Earl Torgeson .20 .50
25 Hal Reniff .20 .50
26 Ralph Houk MG .40 1.00
27 Johnny James .20 .50
28 Bob Hale .20 .50
29 Danny McDevitt .20 .50
30 Duke Maas .20 .50
31 Jim Hegan CO .20 .50
32 Wally Moses CO .20 .50
33 Frank Crosetti CO .40 1.00
34 Lee Thomas .20 .50
35 Al Downing .20 .50
36 Jack Reed .20 .50
37 Ryne Duren .20 .50
38 Tom Tresh .40 1.00
39 Johnny Sain CO .40 1.00
40 Jesse Gonder .20 .50
41 Deron Johnson .20 .50
42 Tony Kubek .60 1.50

1990 Yankees Topps TV

This Yankees team set contains 66 standard-size cards. Cards numbered 1-34 were with the parent club, while cards 35-66 were in the farm system. An early card of Deion Sanders is featured in this set.

COMPLETE FACT. SET (66) 40.00 80.00
1 Bucky Dent MG .20 .50
2 Mark Connor CO .08 .25
3 Billy Connors CO .08 .25
4 Mike Ferraro CO .08 .25
5 Joe Sparks CO .08 .25
6 Champ Summers CO .08 .25
7 Greg Cadaret .08 .25
8 Chuck Cary .08 .25
9 Lee Guetterman .08 .25
10 Andy Hawkins .08 .25
11 Dave LaPoint .08 .25
12 Tim Leary .08 .25
13 Lance McCullers .08 .25
14 Alan Mills .08 .25
15 Clay Parker .08 .25
16 Pascual Perez .08 .25
17 Eric Plunk .08 .25
18 Dave Righetti .20 .50
19 Jeff D. Robinson .08 .25
20 Rick Cerone .08 .25
21 Bob Geren .08 .25
22 Steve Balboni .08 .25
23 Mike Blowers .20 .50
24 Alvaro Espinoza .08 .25
25 Don Mattingly 25.00 60.00
26 Steve Sax .20 .50
27 Wayne Tolleson .08 .25
28 Randy Velarde .20 .50
29 Jesse Barfield .20 .50
30 Mel Hall .08 .25
31 Roberto Kelly .20 .50
32 Luis Polonia .08 .25
33 Deion Sanders 6.00 15.00
34 Dave Winfield 6.00 15.00
35 Steve Adkins .10 .25
36 Oscar Azocar .08 .25
37 Bob Brower .08 .25
38 Britt Burns .08 .25
39 Bob Davidson .08 .25
40 Brian Dorsett .08 .25
41 Dave Eiland .08 .25
42 John Fishel .08 .25
43 Andy Fox .08 .25
44 John Habyan .08 .25
45 Cullen Hartzog .08 .25
46 Sterling Hitchcock .60 1.50
47 Brian Johnson .20 .50
48 Jimmy Jones .08 .25
49 Scott Kamieniecki .20 .50
50 Mark Leiter .08 .25
51 Jim Leyritz .60 1.50
52 Jason Maas .08 .25
53 Kevin Maas .20 .50
54 Hensley Meulens .08 .25
55 Kevin Mmahat .08 .25
56 Rich Monteleone .08 .25
57 Vince Phillips .08 .25
58 Carlos Rodriguez .08 .25
59 Dave Sax .08 .25
60 Willie Smith .08 .25
61 Van Snider .08 .25
62 Andy Stankiewicz .08 .25
63 Wade Taylor .08 .25
64 Ricky Torres .08 .25
65 Jim Walewander .08 .25
66 Bernie Williams 15.00 40.00

1991 Yankees Photo Album

These 30 blank back photos were issued to honor the 1991 New York Yankees. Each color photo, which is surrounded by white borders, has a picture of the player along with a facsimile autograph near the bottom. Other than the manager and the coaches at the beginning and the prospects at the end; these photos are sequenced in alphabetical order. The album is sponsored by NatWest Bank.

COMPLETE SET (28) 6.00 15.00
1 Stump Merrill MG .20 .50
2 Ferraro/Hill/Connor .20 .50
3 Nettles/Showalter/Howard .40 1.00
4 Jesse Barfield .30 .75
5 Greg Cadaret .20 .50
6 Alvaro Espinoza .20 .50
7 Steve Farr .20 .50
8 Bob Geren .30 .75
9 Lee Guetterman .20 .50
10 John Habyan .20 .50
11 Mel Hall .20 .50
12 Steve Howe .20 .50
13 Pat Kelly .20 .50
14 Roberto Kelly .30 .75
15 Tim Leary .20 .50
16 Kevin Maas .20 .50
17 Don Mattingly 1.25 3.00
18 Hensley Meulens .20 .50
19 Matt Nokes .20 .50
20 Pascual Perez .20 .50
21 Eric Plunk .20 .50
22 Scott Sanderson .20 .50
23 Steve Sax .20 .50
24 Pat Sheridan .20 .50
25 Randy Velarde .20 .50
26 Mike Witt .20 .50
27 Taylor/Kamieniecki/Johnson .20 .50
28 C.Rodriguez/B.Williams 1.00 2.50

1991 Yankees Rini Postcards 1961 1

This set of 12 postcards measures 3 1/2" by 5 1/2" and showcases the 1961 New York Yankees. On a white background with blue stripes, the horizontal fronts feature color drawings by Susan Rini. The cards are numbered on the back as "X of 12."

COMPLETE SET (12) 2.00 5.00
1 Yogi Berra .40 1.00
2 Tom Tresh .20 .50
3 Bill Skowron .20 .50
4 Al Downing .08 .25
5 Jim Coates .08 .25
6 Luis Arroyo .08 .25
7 Johnny Blanchard .08 .25
8 Hector Lopez .08 .25
9 Tony Kubek .30 .75
10 Ralph Houk MG .08 .25
11 Bobby Richardson .30 .75
12 Clete Boyer .20 .50

1991 Yankees Rini Postcards 1961 2

This set of 12 postcards measures 3 1/2" by 5 1/2" and showcases the 1961 New York Yankees. On a white background with blue stripes, the horizontal fronts feature color drawings by Susan Rini. The cards are numbered on the back as "X of 12."

COMPLETE SET (12) 2.00 5.00
1 Roger Maris .40 1.00
2 Jesse Gonder .08 .25
3 Danny McDevitt .08 .25
4 Lee Thomas .08 .25
5 Billy Gardner .20 .50
6 Ralph Terry .20 .50
7 Hal Reniff .08 .25
8 Earl Torgeson .08 .25
9 Art Ditmar .08 .25
10 Jack Reed .08 .25
11 Johnny James .08 .25
12 Elston Howard .30 .75

1991 Yankees Rini Postcards 1961 3

This set of 12 postcards measures 3 1/2" by 5 1/2" and showcases the 1961 New York Yankees. On a white background with blue stripes, the horizontal fronts feature color drawings by Susan Rini. The cards are numbered on the back as "X of 12."

COMPLETE SET (12) 2.00 5.00
1 Mickey Mantle .75 2.00
2 Deron Johnson .08 .25
3 Bob Hale .08 .25
4 Bill Stafford .08 .25
5 Duke Maas .08 .25
6 Bob Cerv .08 .25
7 Roland Sheldon .08 .25
8 Ryne Duren .20 .50
9 Bob Turley .20 .50
10 Whitey Ford .40 1.00
11 Bud Daley .08 .25
12 Joe DeMaestri .08 .25

1992 Yankees WIZ 50s

1 Loren Babe
2 Hank Bauer
3 Zeke Bella
4 Lou Berberet
5 Yogi Berra
6 Ewell Blackwell
7 Johnny Blanchard
8 Gary Blaylock
9 Don Bollweg
10 Clete Boyer
11 Ralph Branca
12 Fritzie Brickell
13 Jim Brideweser
14 Jim Bronstad
15 Bobby Brown
16 Lew Burdette
17 Harry Byrd
18 Tommy Byrne
19 Andy Carey
20 Tommy Carroll
21 Bob Cerv
22 Al Cicotte
23 Jim Coates
24 Jerry Coleman
25 Rip Coleman
26 Joe Collins
27 Clint Courtney
28 Bobby Del Greco
29 Jim Delsing
30 Murry Dickson
31 Joe DiMaggio
32 Art Ditmar
33 Sonny Dixon
34 Ryne Duren
35 Tom Ferrick
36 Whitey Ford
37 Mark Freeman
38 Tom Gorman
39 Ted Gray
40 Eli Grba
41 Bob Grim
42 Woodie Held
43 Tommy Henrich
44 Johnny Hopp
45 Ralph Houk
46 Elston Howard
47 Ken Hunt
48 Billy Hunter
49 Johnny James
50 Jackie Jensen
51 Billy Johnson
52 Darrell Johnson
53 Charlie Keller
54 Jim Konstanty
55 Steve Kraly
56 Jack Kramer
57 Tony Kubek
58 Johnny Kucks
59 Bob Kuzava
60 Don Larsen
61 Frank Leja
62 Johnny Lindell
63 Ed Lopat
64 Hector Lopez
65 Jerry Lumpe
66 Duke Maas
67 David Madison
68 Sal Maglee
69 Mickey Mantle
70 Cliff Mapes
71 Billy Martin
72 Mickey McDermott
73 Jim McDonald
74 Gil McDougald
75 Bill Miller
76 Willie Miranda
77 Johnny Mize
78 Zack Monroe
79 Tom Morgan
80 Bob Muncrief
81 Ernie Nevel
82 Irv Noren
83 Joe Ostrowski
84 Stubby Overmire
85 Joe Page
86 Duane Pillette
87 Jim Pisoni
88 Bob Porterfield
89 Vic Raschi
90 Bill Renna
91 Allie Reynolds
92 Bobby Richardson
93 Phil Rizzuto
94 Eddie Robinson
95 Johnny Sain
96 Fred Sanford
97 Ray Scarborough
98 Harry Schaeffer
99 Art Schallock
100 Johnny Schmitz
101 Art Schult
102 Kal Segrist
103 Bobby Shantz
104 Spec Shea
105 Norm Siebern
106 Charlie Silvera
107 Harry Simpson
108 Lou Skizas
109 Bill Skowron
110 Enos Slaughter
111 Gerry Staley
112 Snuffy Stirnweiss
113 Marlin Stuart
114 Tom Sturdivant
115 Ralph Terry
116 Dick Tettelbach
117 Marv Throneberry
118 Gus Triandos
119 Virgil Trucks
120 Bob Turley
121 Frank Verdi
122 Dick Wakefield
123 Bob Wiesler
124 Archie Wilson
125 George Wilson
126 Gordie Windhorn
127 Gene Woodling
128 Hank Workman

1992 Yankees WIZ 60s

This 140-card set was sponsored by WIZ Home Entertainment Centers and American Express. The set was issued on 10" by 9" perforated sheets yielding cards measuring approximately 2" by 3". The cards are unnumbered and checklisted in alphabetical order.

COMPLETE SET (140) 12.50 30.00
1 Jack Aker .02 .10
2 Ruben Amaro .02 .10
3 Luis Arroyo .02 .10
4 Stan Bahnsen .02 .10
5 Steve Barber .02 .10
6 Ray Barker .02 .10
7 Rich Beck .02 .10
8 Yogi Berra 1.50 4.00
9 Johnny Blanchard .08 .25
10 Gil Blanco .02 .10
11 Ron Blomberg .02 .10
12 Len Boehmer .02 .10
13 Jim Bouton .20 .50
14 Clete Boyer .08 .25
15 Jim Brenneman .02 .10
16 Marshall Bridges .02 .10
17 Harry Bright .02 .10
18 Hal Brown .02 .10
19 Billy Bryan .02 .10
20 Bill Burbach .02 .10
21 Andy Carey .08 .25
22 Duke Carmel .02 .10
23 Bob Cerv .08 .25
24 Horace Clarke .02 .10
25 Tex Clevenger .02 .10
26 Lu Clinton .02 .10
27 Jim Coates .02 .10
28 Rocky Colavito .75 2.00
29 Billy Cowan .02 .10
30 Bobby Cox .30 .75
31 Jack Cullen .02 .10
32 John Cumberland .02 .10
33 Bud Daley .02 .10
34 Joe DeMaestri .02 .10
35 Art Ditmar .02 .10
36 Al Downing .08 .25
37 Ryne Duren .08 .25
38 Doc Edwards .02 .10
39 John Ellis .02 .10
40 Frank Fernandez .02 .10
41 Mike Ferraro .02 .10
42 Whitey Ford 1.50 4.00
43 Bob Friend .08 .25
44 John Gabler .02 .10
45 Billy Gardner .02 .10
46 Jake Gibbs .08 .25
47 Jesse Gonder .02 .10
48 Pedro Gonzalez .02 .10
49 Eli Grba .02 .10
50 Kent Hadley .02 .10
51 Bob Hale .02 .10
52 Jimmie Hall .02 .10
53 Steve Hamilton .02 .10
54 Mike Hegan .02 .10
55 Bill Henry .02 .10
56 Elston Howard .30 .75
57 Dick Howser .08 .25
58 Ken Hunt .02 .10
59 Johnny James .02 .10
60 Deron Johnson .08 .25
61 Ken Johnson .02 .10
62 Elvio Jimenez .02 .10
63 Mike Jurewicz .02 .10
64 Mike Kekich .02 .10
65 John Kennedy .02 .10
66 Jerry Kenney .02 .10
67 Fred Kipp .02 .10
68 Ron Klimkowski .02 .10
69 Andy Kosco .02 .10
70 Tony Kubek .30 .75
71 Bill Kunkel .02 .10
72 Phil Linz .08 .25
73 Dale Long .08 .25
74 Art Lopez .02 .10
75 Hector Lopez .08 .25
76 Jim Lyttle .02 .10
77 Duke Maas .02 .10
78 Mickey Mantle 4.00 10.00
79 Roger Maris 1.50 4.00
80 Lindy McDaniel .08 .25
81 Danny McDevitt .02 .10
82 Dave McDonald .02 .10
83 Gil McDougald .20 .50
84 Tom Metcalf .02 .10
85 Bob Meyer .02 .10
86 Gene Michael .08 .25
87 Pete Mikkelsen .02 .10
88 John Miller .02 .10
89 Bill Monbouquette .02 .10
90 Archie Moore .02 .10
91 Ross Moschitto .02 .10
92 Thurman Munson .75 2.00
93 Bobby Murcer .20 .50
94 Don Nottebart .02 .10
95 Nate Oliver .02 .10
96 Joe Pepitone .08 .25
97 Cecil Perkins .02 .10
98 Fritz Peterson .02 .10
99 Jim Pisoni .02 .10
100 Pedro Ramos .02 .10
101 Jack Reed .02 .10
102 Hal Reniff .02 .10
103 Roger Repoz .02 .10
104 Bobby Richardson .30 .75
105 Dale Roberts .02 .10
106 Bill Robinson .08 .25
107 Ellie Rodriguez .02 .10
108 Charlie Sands .02 .10
109 Bob Schmidt .02 .10
110 Dick Schofield .02 .10
111 Billy Shantz .02 .10
112 Bobby Shantz .08 .25
113 Rollie Sheldon .02 .10
114 Tom Shopay .02 .10
115 Bill Short .02 .10
116 Dick Simpson .02 .10
117 Bill Skowron .20 .50
118 Charley Smith .02 .10
119 Tony Solaita .02 .10
120 Bill Stafford .02 .10
121 Mel Stottlemyre .20 .50
122 Hal Stowe .02 .10
123 Fred Talbot .02 .10
124 Frank Tepedino .08 .25
125 Ralph Terry .08 .25
126 Lee Thomas .02 .10
127 Bobby Tiefenauer .02 .10
128 Bob Tillman .02 .10
129 Thad Tillotson .02 .10
130 Earl Torgeson .02 .10
131 Tom Tresh .08 .25
132 Bob Turley .08 .25
133 Elmer Valo .02 .10
134 Joe Verbanic .02 .10
135 Steve Whitaker .02 .10
136 Roy White .08 .25
137 Stan Williams .02 .10
138 Dooley Womack .02 .10
139 Ron Woods .02 .10
140 John Wyatt .02 .10

1992 Yankees WIZ 70s

This 172-card set was sponsored by WIZ Home Entertainment Centers and Fisher. The set was issued on 10" by 9" perforated sheets yielding cards measuring approximately 2" by 3". The cards are unnumbered and checklisted in alphabetical order.

COMPLETE SET (172) 12.50 30.00
1 Jack Aker .02 .10
2 Doyle Alexander .02 .10
3 Bernie Allen .02 .10
4 Sandy Alomar .08 .25
5 Felipe Alou .30 .75
6 Matty Alou .08 .25
7 Dell Alston .02 .10
8 Rick Anderson .02 .10
9 Stan Bahnsen .02 .10
10 Frank Baker .02 .10
11 Jim Beattie .08 .25
12 Fred Beene .02 .10
13 Juan Beniquez .02 .10
14 Dave Bergman .02 .10
15 Juan Bernhardt .02 .10
16 Rick Bladt .02 .10
17 Paul Blair .08 .25
18 Wade Blasingame .02 .10
19 Steve Blateric .02 .10
20 Curt Blefary .02 .10
21 Ron Blomberg .08 .25
22 Len Boehmer .02 .10
23 Bobby Bonds .30 .75
24 Ken Brett .02 .10
25 Ed Brinkman .02 .10
26 Bobby Brown .02 .10
27 Bill Burbach .02 .10
28 Ray Burris .02 .10
29 Tom Buskey .02 .10
30 Johnny Callison .08 .25
31 Danny Cater .02 .10
32 Chris Chambliss .20 .50
33 Horace Clarke .02 .10
34 Ken Clay .02 .10
35 Al Closter .02 .10
36 Rich Coggins .02 .10
37 Loyd Colson .02 .10
38 Casey Cox .02 .10
39 John Cumberland .02 .10
40 Ron Davis .02 .10
41 Jim Deidel .02 .10
42 Rick Dempsey .10 .25
43 Bucky Dent .20 .50
44 Kerry Dineen .02 .10
45 Pat Dobson .02 .10
46 Brian Doyle .02 .10
47 Rawly Eastwick .02 .10
48 Dock Ellis .02 .10
49 John Ellis .02 .10
50 Ed Figueroa .02 .10
51 Oscar Gamble .08 .25
52 Damaso Garcia .02 .10
53 Rob Gardner .02 .10
54 Jake Gibbs .08 .25
55 Fernando Gonzalez .02 .10
56 Rich Gossage .30 .75
57 Larry Gowell .02 .10
58 Wayne Granger .02 .10
59 Mike Griffin .02 .10
60 Ron Guidry .20 .50
61 Brad Gulden .02 .10
62 Don Gullett .08 .25
63 Larry Gura .02 .10
64 Roger Hambright .02 .10
65 Steve Hamilton .02 .10
66 Ron Hansen .02 .10
67 Jim Hardin .02 .10
68 Jim Ray Hart .02 .10
69 Fran Healy .02 .10
70 Mike Heath .02 .10
71 Mike Hegan .02 .10
72 Elrod Hendricks .02 .10
73 Ed Herrmann .02 .10
74 Rich Hinton .02 .10
75 Ken Holtzman .08 .25
76 Don Hood .02 .10
77 Catfish Hunter .60 1.50
78 Grant Jackson .02 .10
79 Reggie Jackson 2.00 5.00
80 Tommy John .30 .75
81 Alex Johnson .02 .10
82 Cliff Johnson .08 .25
83 Jay Johnstone .20 .50
84 Darryl Jones .02 .10
85 Gary Jones .02 .10
86 Jim Kaat .30 .75
87 Bob Kammeyer .02 .10
88 Mike Kekich .02 .10
89 Jerry Kenney .02 .10
90 Dave Kingman .30 .75
91 Ron Klimkowski .02 .10
92 Steve Kline .02 .10
93 Mickey Klutts .02 .10
94 Hal Lanier .02 .10
95 Eddie Leon .02 .10
96 Terry Ley .02 .10
97 Paul Lindblad .02 .10
98 Gene Locklear .02 .10
99 Sparky Lyle .20 .50
100 Jim Lyttle .02 .10
101 Elliott Maddox .02 .10
102 Jim Magnuson .02 .10
103 Tippy Martinez .08 .25
104 Jim Mason .02 .10
105 Carlos May .02 .10
106 Rudy May .02 .10
107 Larry McCall .02 .10
108 Mike McCormick .02 .10
109 Lindy McDaniel .08 .25
110 Sam McDowell .08 .25
111 Rich McKinney .02 .10
112 George Medich .02 .10
113 Andy Messersmith .02 .10
114 Gene Michael .08 .25
115 Paul Mirabella .02 .10
116 Bobby Mitchell .02 .10
117 Gerry Moses .02 .10
118 Thurman Munson 1.00 2.50
119 Bobby Murcer .30 .75
120 Larry Murray .02 .10
121 Jerry Narron .02 .10
122 Graig Nettles .30 .75
123 Bob Oliver .02 .10
124 Dave Pagan .02 .10
125 Gil Patterson .02 .10
126 Marty Perez .02 .10
127 Fritz Peterson .08 .25
128 Lou Piniella .20 .50
129 Dave Rajsich .02 .10
130 Domingo Ramos .02 .10
131 Lenny Randle .02 .10
132 Willie Randolph .30 .75
133 Dave Righetti .20 .50
134 Mickey Rivers .20 .50
135 Bruce Robinson .02 .10
136 Jim Roland .02 .10
137 Celerino Sanchez .02 .10
138 Rick Sawyer .02 .10
139 George Scott .08 .25
140 Duke Sims .02 .10
141 Roger Slagle .02 .10
142 Jim Spencer .02 .10
143 Charlie Spikes .02 .10
144 Roy Staiger .02 .10
145 Fred Stanley .02 .10
146 Bill Sudakis .02 .10
147 Ron Swoboda .08 .25
148 Frank Tepedino .08 .25
149 Stan Thomas .02 .10
150 Gary Thomasson .02 .10
151 Luis Tiant .30 .75
152 Dick Tidrow .02 .10
153 Rusty Torres .02 .10
154 Mike Torrez .02 .10
155 Cesar Tovar .02 .10
156 Cecil Upshaw .02 .10
157 Otto Velez .02 .10
158 Joe Verbanic .02 .10
159 Mike Wallace .02 .10
160 Danny Walton .02 .10
161 Pete Ward .02 .10
162 Gary Waslewski .02 .10
163 Dennis Werth .02 .10
164 Roy White .08 .25
165 Terry Whitfield .02 .10
166 Walt Williams .02 .10
167 Ron Woods .02 .10
168 Dick Woodson .02 .10
169 Ken Wright .02 .10
170 Jimmy Wynn .08 .25
171 Jim York .02 .10
172 George Zeber .02 .10

1992 Yankees WIZ 80s

This 206-card set was sponsored by WIZ Home Entertainment Centers and Minolta. The set was issued on 10" by 9" perforated sheets yielding cards measuring approximately 2" by 3". The cards are unnumbered and checklisted in alphabetical order.

COMPLETE SET (206) 12.50 30.00
1 Luis Aguayo .02 .10
2 Doyle Alexander .08 .25
3 Neil Allen .02 .10
4 Mike Armstrong .02 .10
5 Brad Arnsberg .02 .10
6 Tucker Ashford .02 .10
7 Steve Balboni .02 .10
8 Jesse Barfield .08 .25
9 Don Baylor .20 .50
10 Dale Berra .02 .10
11 Doug Bird .02 .10
12 Paul Blair .08 .25
13 Mike Blowers .02 .10
14 Juan Bonilla .02 .10
15 Rick Bordi .02 .10
16 Scott Bradley .02 .10
17 Marshall Brant .02 .10
18 Tom Brookens .02 .10
19 Bob Brower .02 .10
20 Bobby Brown .02 .10
21 Curt Brown .02 .10
22 Jay Buhner .75 2.00
23 Marty Bystrom .02 .10
24 Greg Cadaret .02 .10
25 Bert Campaneris .08 .25
26 John Candelaria .08 .25
27 Chuck Cary .02 .10
28 Bill Castro .02 .10
29 Rick Cerone .02 .10
30 Chris Chambliss .08 .25
31 Clay Christiansen .02 .10
32 Jack Clark .08 .25
33 Pat Clements .02 .10
34 Dave Collins .02 .10
35 Don Cooper .02 .10
36 Henry Cotto .02 .10
37 Joe Cowley .02 .10
38 Jose Cruz .08 .25
39 Bobby Davidson .02 .10
40 Ron Davis .02 .10
41 Brian Dayett .02 .10
42 Ivan DeJesus .02 .10
43 Bucky Dent .08 .25
44 Jim Deshaies .02 .10
45 Orestes Destrade .02 .10
46 Brian Dorsett .02 .10
47 Richard Dotson .02 .10
48 Brian Doyle .02 .10
49 Doug Drabek .08 .25
50 Mike Easler .02 .10
51 Dave Eiland .02 .10
52 Roger Erickson .02 .10
53 Juan Espino .02 .10
54 Alvaro Espinoza .02 .10
55 Barry Evans .02 .10
56 Ed Figueroa .02 .10
57 Pete Filson .02 .10
58 Mike Fischlin .02 .10
59 Brian Fisher .02 .10
60 Tim Foli .02 .10
61 Ray Fontenot .02 .10
62 Barry Foote .02 .10
63 George Frazier .02 .10
64 Bill Fulton .02 .10
65 Oscar Gamble .08 .25
66 Bob Geren .02 .10
67 Rich Gossage .30 .75
68 Mike Griffin .02 .10
69 Ken Griffey .20 .50
70 Cecilio Guante .02 .10
71 Lee Guetterman .02 .10
72 Ron Guidry .20 .50
73 Brad Gulden .02 .10
74 Don Gullett .08 .25
75 Bill Gullickson .02 .10
76 Mel Hall .02 .10
77 Toby Harrah .02 .10
78 Ron Hassey .02 .10
79 Andy Hawkins .02 .10
80 Rickey Henderson 1.25 3.00
81 Leo Hernandez .02 .10
82 Butch Hobson .02 .10
83 Al Holland .02 .10
84 Roger Holt .02 .10
85 Jay Howell .02 .10
86 Rex Hudler .08 .25
87 Charles Hudson .02 .10
88 Keith Hughes .02 .10
89 Reggie Jackson 1.25 3.00
90 Stan Javier .02 .10
91 Stan Jefferson .02 .10
92 Tommy John .20 .50
93 Jimmy Jones .02 .10
94 Ruppert Jones .02 .10
95 Jim Kaat .30 .75
96 Curt Kaufman .02 .10
97 Roberto Kelly .20 .50
98 Steve Kemp .02 .10
99 Matt Keough .02 .10
100 Steve Kiefer .02 .10
101 Ron Kittle .02 .10
102 Dave LaPoint .02 .10
103 Marcus Lawton .02 .10
104 Joe Lefebvre .02 .10
105 Al Leiter .30 .75
106 Jim Lewis .02 .10
107 Bryan Little .02 .10
108 Tim Lollar .02 .10
109 Phil Lombardi .02 .10
110 Vic Mata .02 .10
111 Don Mattingly 10.00 25.00
112 Rudy May .02 .10
113 John Mayberry .08 .25
114 Lee Mazzilli .02 .10
115 Lance McCullers .02 .10
116 Andy McGaffigan .02 .10
117 Lynn McGlothen .02 .10
118 Bobby Meacham .02 .10
119 Hensley Meulens .02 .10
120 Larry Milbourne .02 .10
121 Kevin Mmahat .02 .10
122 Dale Mohorcic .02 .10
123 John Montefusco .02 .10
124 Omar Moreno .02 .10
125 Mike Morgan .02 .10
126 Jeff Moronko .02 .10
127 Hal Morris .02 .10
128 Jerry Mumphrey .02 .10
129 Bobby Murcer .20 .50
130 Dale Murray .02 .10
131 Gene Nelson .02 .10
132 Joe Niekro .08 .25
133 Phil Niekro .30 .75
134 Scott Nielsen .02 .10
135 Otis Nixon .02 .10
136 Johnny Oates .02 .10
137 Mike O'Berry .02 .10
138 Rowland Office .02 .10
139 John Pacella .02 .10
140 Mike Pagliarulo .08 .25
141 Clay Parker .02 .10
142 Dan Pasqua .02 .10
143 Mike Patterson .02 .10
144 Hipolito Pena .02 .10
145 Gaylord Perry .30 .75
146 Ken Phelps .02 .10
147 Lou Piniella .30 .75
148 Eric Plunk .02 .10
149 Luis Polonia .20 .50
150 Alfonso Pulido .02 .10
151 Jamie Quirk .02 .10
152 Bobby Ramos .02 .10
153 Willie Randolph .30 .75
154 Dennis Rasmussen .02 .10
155 Shane Rawley .02 .10
156 Rick Reuschel .08 .25
157 Dave Revering .02 .10
158 Rick Rhoden .02 .10
159 Dave Righetti .08 .25
160 Jose Rijo .02 .10
161 Andre Robertson .02 .10
162 Bruce Robinson .02 .10
163 Aurelio Rodriguez .02 .10
164 Edwin Rodriguez .02 .10
165 Gary Roenicke .02 .10
166 Jerry Royster .02 .10
167 Lenn Sakata .02 .10
168 Mark Salas .02 .10
169 Billy Sample .02 .10
170 Deion Sanders 1.25 3.00
171 Rafael Santana .02 .10
172 Steve Sax .08 .25
173 Don Schulze .02 .10
174 Rodney Scott .02 .10
175 Rod Scurry .02 .10
176 Dennis Sherrill .02 .10
177 Steve Shields .02 .10
179 Bob Shirley .02 .10
180 Joel Skinner .02 .10
181 Don Slaught .08 .25
182 Roy Smalley .08 .25
183 Keith Smith .02 .10
184 Eric Soderholm .02 .10
185 Jim Spencer .02 .10
186 Fred Stanley .02 .10
187 Dave Stegman .02 .10
188 Tim Stoddard .02 .10
189 Walt Terrell .02 .10
190 Bob Tewksbury .02 .10
191 Luis Tiant .20 .50
192 Wayne Tolleson .02 .10
193 Steve Trout .02 .10
194 Tom Underwood .02 .10
195 Randy Velarde .02 .10
196 Gary Ward .02 .10
197 Claudell Washington .08 .25
198 Bob Watson .20 .50
199 Dave Wehrmeister .02 .10
200 Dennis Werth .02 .10
201 Stefan Wever .02 .10
202 Ed Whitson .02 .10
203 Ted Wilborn .02 .10
204 Dave Winfield 1.25 3.00
205 Butch Wynegar .02 .10
206 Paul Zuvella .02 .10

1992 Yankees WIZ All-Stars

This 86-card set was sponsored by WIZ Home Entertainment Centers and American Express. The set was issued on five 15-card sheets and one 11-card title sheet, all measuring approximately 10" by 9". The perforated sheets yielded cards measuring approximately 2" by 3". The cards are unnumbered and checklisted in alphabetical order.

COMPLETE SET (86) 12.50 30.00
1 Luis Arroyo .02 .10
2 Hank Bauer .08 .25
3 Yogi Berra .75 2.00
4 Bobby Bonds .20 .50
5 Ernie Bonham .02 .10
6 Hank Borowy .02 .10
7 Jim Bouton .20 .50
8 Tommy Byrne .02 .10
9 Chris Chambliss .08 .25
10 Spud Chandler .08 .25
11 Ben Chapman .02 .10
12 Jim Coates .02 .10
13 Jerry Coleman .02 .10
14 Frank Crosetti .08 .25
15 Ron Davis .02 .10
16 Bucky Dent .08 .25
17 Bill Dickey .30 .75
18 Joe DiMaggio 2.00 5.00
19 Al Downing .02 .10
20 Ryne Duren .08 .25
21 Whitey Ford .75 2.00
22 Lou Gehrig 2.00 5.00
23 Lefty Gomez .30 .75
24 Joe Gordon .08 .25
25 Rich Gossage .20 .50
26 Bob Grim .02 .10
27 Ron Guidry .20 .50
28 Rollie Hemsley .02 .10
29 Rickey Henderson .60 1.50
30 Tommy Henrich .20 .50
31 Elston Howard .20 .50
32 Catfish Hunter .30 .75
33 Reggie Jackson .75 2.00
34 Tommy John .20 .50
35 Billy Johnson .02 .10
36 Charlie Keller .08 .25
37 Tony Kubek .08 .25
38 Johnny Kucks .02 .10
39 Tony Lazzeri .30 .75
40 Johnny Lindell .02 .10
41 Ed Lopat .20 .50
42 Sparky Lyle .08 .25
43 Mickey Mantle 3.00 8.00
44 Roger Maris .75 2.00
45 Billy Martin .30 .75
46 Don Mattingly 6.00 15.00
47 Gil McDougald .08 .25
48 George McQuinn .02 .10
49 Johnny Mize .30 .75
50 Thurman Munson .60 1.50
51 Bobby Murcer .08 .25
52 Johnny Murphy .02 .10
53 Graig Nettles .20 .50
54 Phil Niekro .30 .75
55 Irv Noren .02 .10
56 Joe Page .02 .10
57 Monte Pearson .02 .10
58 Joe Pepitone .08 .25
59 Fritz Peterson .02 .10
60 Willie Randolph .08 .25
61 Vic Raschi .08 .25
62 Allie Reynolds .20 .50
63 Bobby Richardson .20 .50
64 Dave Righetti .08 .25
65 Mickey Rivers .08 .25
66 Phil Rizzuto .60 1.50
67 Aaron Robinson .02 .10
68 Red Rolfe .02 .10
69 Buddy Rosar .02 .10
70 Red Ruffing .30 .75
71 Marius Russo .02 .10
72 Babe Ruth 3.00 8.00
73 Johnny Sain .20 .50
74 Scott Sanderson .02 .10
75 Steve Sax .08 .25
76 George Selkirk .02 .10
77 Bobby Shantz .08 .25
78 Spec Shea .02 .10
79 Bill Skowron .08 .25
80 Snuffy Stirnweiss .02 .10
81 Mel Stottlemyre .08 .25
82 Ralph Terry .02 .10
83 Tom Tresh .08 .25
84 Bob Turley .08 .25
85 Roy White .08 .25
86 Dave Winfield .75 2.00

1992 Yankees WIZ HOF

This 35-card set was sponsored by WIZ Home Entertainment Centers and Aiwa. The set was issued on two 15-card sheets and one five-card title sheet, all measuring approximately 10" by 9". The perforated sheets yielded cards measuring approximately 2" by 3". The cards are unnumbered and checklisted in alphabetical order.

COMPLETE SET (35) 8.00 20.00
1 Home Run Baker .08 .25
2 Edward G. Barrow .08 .25
3 Yogi Berra .75 2.00
4 Frank Chance .08 .25
5 Jack Chesbro .08 .25
6 Earle Combs .08 .25
7 Stan Coveleski .08 .25
8 Bill Dickey .30 .75
9 Joe DiMaggio 2.00 5.00
10 Whitey Ford .75 2.00
11 Lou Gehrig 1.50 4.00
12 Lefty Gomez .20 .50
13 Clark C. Griffith .08 .25
14 Burleigh Grimes .08 .25
15 Bucky Harris .08 .25
16 Waite Hoyt .08 .25
17 Miller Huggins .08 .25
18 Catfish Hunter .20 .50
19 Willie Keeler .08 .25
20 Tony Lazzeri .08 .25
21 Larry MacPhail .08 .25
22 Mickey Mantle 2.00 5.00
23 Joe McCarthy MG .08 .25
24 Johnny Mize .20 .50
25 Herb Pennock .08 .25
26 Gaylord Perry .20 .50
27 Branch Rickey .08 .25
28 Red Ruffing .08 .25
29 Babe Ruth 2.00 5.00
30 Joe Sewell .08 .25
31 Enos Slaughter .20 .50
32 Casey Stengel .30 .75
33 Dazzy Vance .08 .25
34 Paul Waner .08 .25
35 George M. Weiss GM .08 .25

1993 Yankees Stadium Club

This 30-card standard-size set features the 1993 New York Yankees. The set was issued in hobby (plastic box) and retail (blister) form.

COMP. FACT SET (30) 2.50 6.00
1 Don Mattingly .75 2.00
2 Jim Abbott .08 .25
3 Matt Nokes .02 .10
4 Danny Tartabull .02 .10
5 Wade Boggs .40 1.00
6 Melido Perez .02 .10
7 Steve Farr .02 .10
8 Kevin Maas .02 .10
9 Randy Velarde .02 .10
10 Mike Humphreys .02 .10
11 Mike Gallego .02 .10
12 Mike Stanley .02 .10
13 Jimmy Key .08 .25
14 Paul O'Neill .20 .50
15 Spike Owen .02 .10
16 Pat Kelly .02 .10
17 Sterling Hitchcock .02 .10
18 Mike Witt .02 .10
19 Scott Kamieniecki .02 .10
20 John Habyan .02 .10
21 Bernie Williams .30 .75
22 Brien Taylor .02 .10
23 Rick Monteleone .02 .10
24 Mark Hutton .02 .10
25 Robert Eenhoorn .02 .10
26 Gerald Williams .02 .10
27 Sam Militello .02 .10
28 Bob Wickman .30 .75
29 Andy Stankiewicz .02 .10
30 Domingo Jean .02 .10

1997 Yankees Score

This 15-card set of the New York Yankees was issued in five-card packs with a suggested retail price of $1.30 each. The fronts feature color player photos with special team specific color foil stamping. The backs carry player information. Only 100 cases were made for each team. Platinum parallel cards were inserted at a rate of 1:6, Premier parallel cards at a rate of 1:31.

COMPLETE SET (15) 3.00 8.00
*PLATINUM: 4X BASIC CARDS
*PREMIER: 20X BASIC CARDS
1 Bernie Williams .30 .75
2 Cecil Fielder .15 .40
3 Derek Jeter 1.50 4.00
4 Darryl Strawberry .15 .40
5 Andy Pettitte .40 1.00
6 Ruben Rivera .08 .25
7 Mariano Rivera .40 1.00
8 John Wetteland .15 .40
9 Paul O'Neill .30 .75
10 Wade Boggs .40 1.00
11 Dwight Gooden .15 .40
12 David Cone .25 .60
13 Tino Martinez .25 .60
14 Kenny Rogers .15 .40
15 Andy Fox .08 .25

1998 Yankees Kodak Wells

This one-card set measuring approximately 5" by 3 3/4" was produced by Kodak commemorating the perfect game pitched by New York Yankees David Wells against the Minnesota Twins on May 17, 1998. The front features an action photo of the final strike for the final out printed on a lenticular card. The back is blank.

1 David Wells 4.00 10.00

1998 Yankees Score

This 15-card set was issued in special retail packs and features color photos of the New York Yankees team. The backs carry player information. A special platinum parallel set was also issued and randomly inserted in packs.

COMPLETE SET (15) 2.50 8.00
*PLATINUM: 5X BASIC CARDS
1 Hideki Irabu .08 .25
2 Derek Jeter 1.50 4.00
3 Tino Martinez .25 .60
4 David Cone .25 .60
5 Andy Pettitte .40 1.00
6 Bernie Williams .30 .75
7 Charlie Hayes .08 .25
8 Pat Kelly .08 .25
9 Mariano Rivera .40 1.00
10 Paul O'Neill .30 .75
11 Chad Curtis .08 .25
12 David Wells .30 .75
13 Cecil Fielder .15 .40
14 Wade Boggs .40 1.00
15 Jorge Posada .30 .75

1998 Yankees 75th Anniversary

These 12 cards were issued by the New York Yankees and featured some of the stars of the team which celebrated the platinum anniversary since their move into Yankee stadium. The fronts have a player photo against the background of the big ball orchard in the Bronx. The back has an action photo and seasonal and career statistics. These cards were inserted into Yankee scorecards during the regular season.

COMPLETE SET (12) 4.00 10.00
1 David Cone .20 .50
2 Derek Jeter 1.25 3.00
3 Chili Davis .20 .50
4 Joe Girardi .30 .75
5 Hideki Irabu .20 .50
6 Chuck Knoblauch .20 .50
7 Tino Martinez .20 .50
8 Paul O'Neill .30 .75
9 Andy Pettitte .30 .75
10 Mariano Rivera .30 .75
11 David Wells .30 .75
12 Bernie Williams .30 .75

1998 Yankees Upper Deck

This 15-card set features 3 1/2" by 5" reproductions of Upper Deck's regular cards for the players of the 1998 New York Yankees. The fronts feature action color player photos and a silver foil Yankees logo with the backs displaying player information and career statistics. Only 10,000 of this set were produced. The cards are listed below according to their numbers in the regular 1998 Upper Deck set.

COMPLETE FACT. SET (15) 6.00 15.00
169 Bernie Williams .60 1.50
170 Andy Pettitte .75 2.00
172 Paul O'Neill .60 1.50
175 David Cone .60 1.50
176 Hideki Irabu .20 .50
449 Tim Raines .30 .75
450 Derek Jeter 3.00 8.00
460 Tino Martinez .50 1.25
461 Chad Curtis .20 .50
462 Ramiro Mendoza .20 .50
464 David Wells .60 1.50
465 Mariano Rivera .75 2.00
703 Chili Davis .30 .75
704 Scott Brosius .30 .75
705 Chuck Knoblauch .30 .75

1998 Yankees Upper Deck WS Commemorative

This one-card limited edition set commemorates the New York Yankees winning the 1998 World Series and has a suggested retail price of $19.95. The card features color action images of seven Yankees players on a die-cut card with a pin-striped background. Three players appear on the card front and four on the back. Only 9,800 of this card were produced and are sequentially numbered. The players are checklisted below as they appear on the card from left to right, front to back.

1 Paul O'Neill 8.00 20.00
Tino Martinez
Derek Jeter
David We

1999 Yankees Fleer

This 27-card set of the New York Yankees was distributed on three commemorative sheets each containing nine player cards, a title/checklist card, a sponsor card, and a 1999 Yankees schedule card. Each perforated sheet measures approximately 12 1/2" by 10 1/2".

COMPLETE SET (30) 3.00 8.00
1 Derek Jeter .75 2.00
2 Paul O'Neill .15 .40
3 Scott Brosius .07 .20
4 Mariano Rivera .20 .50
5 Chuck Knoblauch .07 .20
6 Graeme Lloyd .02 .10
7 Joe Girardi .07 .20
8 Orlando Hernandez .07 .20
9 Tim Raines .07 .20
10 Bernie Williams .15 .40
11 Tino Martinez .10 .30
12 Andy Pettitte .20 .50
13 Hideki Irabu .02 .10
14 Ramiro Mendoza .02 .10
15 Jeff Nelson .02 .10
16 Homer Bush .02 .10
17 Darren Holmes .02 .10
18 Yankees History .02 .10
19 David Cone .07 .20
20 David Wells .15 .40
21 Chili Davis .07 .20
22 Darryl Strawberry .07 .20
23 Ricky Ledee .02 .10
24 Jorge Posada .15 .40
25 Luis Sojo .02 .10
26 Chad Curtis .02 .10
27 Mike Stanton .02 .10
S1 Commemorative Sheet 1 2.00 5.00
S2 Commemorative Sheet 2 1.50 4.00
S3 Commemorative Sheet 3 1.50 4.00
NNO Sponsor Card .02 .10
NNO 1999 Schedule Card .02 .10
NNO Title Card CL .02 .10

2000 Yankees Star Ledger

COMPLETE SET (24) 24.00 60.00
1 Clay Bellinger .60 1.50
2 Scott Brosius .80 2.00
3 Randy Choate .60 1.50
4 Roger Clemens 3.20 8.00
5 David Conc 1.00 2.50
6 Dwight Gooden .80 2.00
7 Jason Grimsley .60 1.50
8 Orlando Hernandez .60 1.50
9 Glenallen Hill .60 1.50
10 Derek Jeter 6.00 15.00
11 Chuck Knoblauch .80 2.00
12 Ramiro Mendoza .60 1.50
13 Jeff Nelson .60 1.50
14 Paul O'Neill 1.20 3.00
15 Andy Pettitte 1.50 4.00
16 Jorge Posada 1.20 3.00
17 Luis Rivera .60 1.50
18 Mariano Rivera 1.50 4.00
19 Luis Sojo .60 1.50
20 Mike Stanton .60 1.50
21 Joe Torre MG 1.20 3.00
22 Chris Turner .60 1.50
23 Jose Vizcaino .60 1.50
24 Bernie Williams 1.20 3.00

2002 Yankees Starting Five Fleer

COMPLETE SET 4.00 10.00
UNLISTED STARS 1.00 2.50
1 Roger Clemens 2.00 5.00
2 David Wells 1.00 2.50
3 Mike Mussina 1.00 2.50
4 Orlando Hernandez .40 1.00
5 Andy Pettitte 1.00 2.50

2003 Yankees French Donruss

COMPLETE SET 6.00 15.00
1 Derek Jeter 5.00 10.00
2 Alfonso Soriano 1.00 2.50
3 Jorge Posada 1.00 2.50
4 Jose Contreras 1.00 2.50
5 Jeff Weaver .75 2.00
6 Steve Karsay .40 1.00
NNO Hot Dog Info Card .20 .50

2003 Yankees Greats Poland Springs

COMPLETE SET 2.00 5.00
1 Yogi Berra .60 1.50
2 Whitey Ford .60 1.50
3 Phil Rizzuto .60 1.50
4 Reggie Jackson .60 1.50
NNO Poland Springs Card .10 .25

2003 Yankees McDonald's Upper Deck

COMPLETE SET 6.00 15.00
1 Juan Acevedo .20 .50
2 Roger Clemens .60 1.50
3 John Flaherty .20 .50
4 Jason Giambi .20 .50
5 Chris Hammond .20 .50
6 Sterling Hitchcock .20 .50
7 Derek Jeter 1.25 3.00
8 Nick Johnson .20 .50
9 Steve Karsay .20 .50
10 Hideki Matsui 1.00 2.50
11 Raul Mondesi .20 .50
12 Mike Mussina .30 .75
13 Antonio Osuna .20 .50
14 Andy Pettitte .30 .75
15 Jorge Posada .30 .75
16 Mariano Rivera .60 1.50
17 Alfonso Soriano .30 .75
18 Bubba Trammell .20 .50
19 Robin Ventura .20 .50
20 Jeff Weaver .20 .50
21 David Wells .20 .50
22 Bernie Williams .30 .75
23 Enrique Wilson .20 .50
24 Todd Zeile .20 .50
XX Contest Card .20 .50

2004 Yankees Fleer Daily News

COMPLETE SET 2.50 6.00
1 Jason Giambi .15 .40
2 Hideki Matsui .40 1.00
3 Mariano Rivera .20 .50
4 Gary Sheffield .20 .50
5 Derek Jeter .75 2.00
6 Kenny Lofton .07 .20
7 Bernie Williams .15 .40
8 Jorge Posada .15 .40
9 Mike Mussina .15 .40
10 Alex Rodriguez .30 .75

2004 Yankees Poland Spring

COMPLETE SET (4) 2.00 5.00
1 Goose Gossage .40 1.00
2 Ron Guidry .40 1.00
3 Don Mattingly 1.00 2.50
4 Don Larsen .20 .50
XX Poland Spring Water .10 .25

2005 Yankees New York Post The Immortals Medallion Collection

CARDS LISTED ALPHABETAICALLY

2006 Yankees Topps

COMPLETE SET (14) 3.00 8.00
NYY1 Alex Rodriguez .40 1.00
NYY2 Derek Jeter .75 2.00
NYY3 Jason Giambi .12 .30
NYY4 Hideki Matsui .30 .75
NYY5 Jorge Posada .20 .50
NYY6 Robinson Cano .20 .50
NYY7 Gary Sheffield .12 .30
NYY8 Mariano Rivera .40 1.00
NYY9 Randy Johnson .30 .75
NYY10 Shawn Chacon .12 .30
NYY11 Mike Mussina .20 .50
NYY12 Chien-Ming Wang .20 .50
NYY13 Carl Pavano .12 .30
NYY14 Johnny Damon .20 .50

2007 Yankees Topps

COMPLETE SET (14) 3.00 8.00
NYY1 Derek Jeter .75 2.00
NYY2 Bobby Abreu .12 .30
NYY3 Jason Giambi .12 .30
NYY4 Andy Pettitte .20 .50
NYY5 Chien-Ming Wang .20 .50
NYY6 Melky Cabrera .12 .30
NYY7 Hideki Matsui .30 .75
NYY8 Mike Mussina .20 .50
NYY9 Robinson Cano .20 .50
NYY10 Doug Mientkiewicz .12 .30
NYY11 Johnny Damon .20 .50
NYY12 Mariano Rivera .40 1.00
NYY13 Jorge Posada .20 .50
NYY14 Alex Rodriguez .40 1.00

2007 Yankees Topps Gift Set

COMPLETE SET 12.50 30.00
NYY1 Roger Clemens .50 1.25
NYY2 Tyler Clippard .25 .60
NYY3 Brian Bruney .15 .40
NYY4 Kyle Farnsworth .15 .40
NYY5 Sean Henn .15 .40
NYY6 Phil Hughes .40 1.00
NYY7 Kei Igawa .40 1.00
NYY8 Mike Mussina .25 .60
NYY9 Andy Pettitte .25 .60

NYY10 Joba Chamberlain .25 .60
NYY11 Mariano Rivera .50 1.25
NYY12 Chien-Ming Wang .25 .60
NYY13 Luis Vizcaino .15 .40
NYY14 Jorge Posada .25 .60
NYY15 Miguel Cairo .15 .40
NYY16 Robinson Cano .25 .60
NYY17 Derek Jeter 1.00 2.50
NYY18 Doug Mientkiewicz .15 .40
NYY19 Josh Phelps .15 .40
NYY20 Alex Rodriguez .50 1.25
NYY21 Bobby Abreu .15 .40
NYY22 Melky Cabrera .15 .40
NYY23 Johnny Damon .25 .60
NYY24 Hideki Matsui .40 1.00
NYY25 Jason Giambi .15 .40
NYY26 Joe Torre MG .25 .60
NYY27 Don Mattingly CO .75 2.00
NYY28 Tony Pena CO .15 .40
NYY29 Larry Bowa CO .15 .40
NYY30 Kevin Long CO .15 .40
NYY31 Ron Guidry CO .15 .40
NYY32 Robinson Cano .25 .60
NYY33 Derek Jeter 1.00 2.50
NYY34 Jason Giambi .15 .40
NYY35 Robinson Cano .25 .60
NYY36 Alex Rodriguez .50 1.25
NYY37 Mike Mussina .25 .60
NYY38 Mariano Rivera .50 1.25
NYY39 Chien-Ming Wang .25 .60
NYY40 Scott Proctor .15 .40
NYY41 Rivera/Posada .50 1.25
NYY42 Jeter/Posada 1.00 2.50
NYY43 Phelps/Jeter/Rodriguez/Posada 1.00 2.50
NYY44 Alex Rodriguez .50 1.25
NYY45 Hideki Matsui .40 1.00
NYY46 Roger Clemens .50 1.25
NYY47 Derek Jeter 1.00 2.50
NYY48 Jason Giambi .15 .40
NYY49 Jorge Posada .25 .60
NYY50 Melky Cabrera .15 .40
NYY51 Bobby Abreu .15 .40
NYY52 Johnny Damon .25 .60
NYY53 Chien-Ming Wang .25 .60
NYY54 Andy Pettitte .25 .60
NYY55 Phil Hughes .40 1.00

2008 Yankees Topps

COMPLETE SET (14) 3.00 8.00
NYY1 Alex Rodriguez .40 1.00
NYY2 Bobby Abreu .12 .30
NYY3 Phil Hughes .12 .30
NYY4 Andy Pettitte .20 .50
NYY5 Chien-Ming Wang .20 .50
NYY6 Melky Cabrera .12 .30
NYY7 Hideki Matsui .30 .75
NYY8 Jason Giambi .12 .30
NYY9 Robinson Cano .20 .50
NYY10 Joba Chamberlain .12 .30
NYY11 Johnny Damon .20 .50
NYY12 Mariano Rivera .40 1.00
NYY13 Jorge Posada .20 .50
NYY14 Derek Jeter .75 2.00

2008 Yankees Topps Gift Set

1 Joe Girardi MG .25 .60
2 Alex Rodriguez 500 HR .50 1.25
3 Alex Rodriguez .50 1.25
4 Alex Rodriguez/Hideki Matsui
Jorge Posada .50 1.25
5 Andy Pettitte .25 .60
6 Derek Jeter 1.00 2.50
7 Chien-Ming Wang .25 .60
8 Robinson Cano .25 .60
9 Andy Pettitte 200th Win .25 .60
10 Chien-Ming Wang/Andy Pettitte .25 .60
11 Phil Hughes .15 .40
12 Johnny Damon .25 .60
13 Shelley Duncan 21 .15 .40
14 Mike Mussina .25 .60
15 Rob Thomson CO .15 .40
16 Alex Rodriguez HR Record .50 1.25
17 Hideki Matsui .40 1.00
18 Joba Chamberlain .15 .40
19 Andy Pettitte/Chien-Ming Wang
Mike Mussina .25 .60
20 Melky Cabrera .15 .40
21 Robinson Cano/Bobby Abreu .25 .60
22 Mariano Rivera .50 1.25
23 Jorge Posada/Derek Jeter
Alex Rodriguez 1.00 2.50
24 Chien-Ming Wang Wins 19 .25 .60
25 Bobby Abreu .15 .40
26 Tony Pena CO .15 .40
27 Kyle Farnsworth .15 .40
28 Yankees Clinch Wild Card .15 .40
29 Jason Giambi .15 .40
30 Chris Britton .15 .40
31 Chien-Ming Wang/Andy Pettitte
Mike Mussina .25 .60
32 Jorge Posada .25 .60
33 Edwar Ramirez .15 .40
34 Bobby Meacham CO .15 .40
35 Joba Chamberlain Mania .15 .40
36 Jose Molina .15 .40
37 Ross Ohlendorf .25 .60
38 Derek Jeter/Robinson Cano
Alex Rodriguez 1.00 2.50
39 Wilson Betemit .15 .40
40 Latroy Hawkins .15 .40
41 Dave Eiland CO .15 .40
42 Alex Rodriguez Grand Slam .50 1.25
43 Shelley Duncan .15 .40
44 Brian Bruney .15 .40
45 Andy Pettitte/Chien-Ming Wang
Mike Mussina .25 .60
46 Jorge Posada/Derek Jeter
Alex Rodriguez 1.00 2.50
47 Alex Rodriguez/Hideki Matsui
Bobby Abreu .50 1.25
48 Jonathan Albaladejo .25 .60
49 M.Rivera/J.Posada .50 1.25
50 Kei Igawa .15 .40
51 Kevin Long CO .15 .40
52 Derek Jeter/Alex Rodriguez 1.00 2.50
53 Jorge Posada/Derek Jeter
Alex Rodriguez 1.00 2.50
54 Jeff Karstens .15 .40
55 Yankee Stadium .15 .40

2009 Yankees Topps

NYY1 CC Sabathia .25 .60
NYY2 Mariano Rivera .50 1.25
NYY3 Derek Jeter 1.00 2.50
NYY4 Chien-Ming Wang .25 .60
NYY5 Hideki Matsui .40 1.00
NYY6 Joba Chamberlain .15 .40
NYY7 Jorge Posada .25 .60
NYY8 A.J. Burnett .15 .40
NYY9 Robinson Cano .25 .60
NYY10 Xavier Nady .15 .40
NYY11 Johnny Damon .25 .60
NYY12 Mark Teixeira .25 .60
NYY13 Alex Rodriguez .50 1.25
NYY14 Nick Swisher .25 .60
NYY15 Mickey Mantle 1.25 3.00

2010 Yankees Topps

NYY1 Mark Teixeira .25 .60
NYY2 Javier Vazquez .15 .40
NYY3 CC Sabathia .25 .60
NYY4 Phil Hughes .15 .40
NYY5 Brett Gardner .25 .60
NYY6 Andy Pettitte .25 .60
NYY7 Mickey Mantle 1.25 3.00
NYY8 Nick Swisher .25 .60
NYY9 Robinson Cano .25 .60
NYY10 A.J. Burnett .15 .40
NYY11 Joba Chamberlain .15 .40
NYY12 Mariano Rivera .50 1.25
NYY13 Jorge Posada .25 .60
NYY14 Derek Jeter 1.00 2.50
NYY15 Alex Rodriguez .50 1.25
NYY16 Curtis Granderson .30 .75
NYY17 Nick Johnson .15 .40

2011 Yankees Topps

NYY1 Derek Jeter 1.00 2.50
NYY2 Mariano Rivera .50 1.25
NYY3 Alex Rodriguez .50 1.25
NYY4 CC Sabathia .25 .60
NYY5 Nick Swisher .25 .60
NYY6 Mark Teixeira .25 .60
NYY7 Mickey Mantle 1.25 3.00
NYY8 Jorge Posada .25 .60
NYY9 Russell Martin .15 .40
NYY10 Ivan Nova .25 .60
NYY11 Phil Hughes .15 .40
NYY12 Curtis Granderson .30 .75
NYY13 Brett Gardner .25 .60
NYY14 Joba Chamberlain .15 .40
NYY15 A.J. Burnett .15 .40
NYY16 Robinson Cano .25 .60
NYY17 Yankee Stadium .15 .40

2012 Yankees Topps

NYY1 Derek Jeter 1.00 2.50
NYY2 Alex Rodriguez .50 1.25
NYY3 Brett Gardner .30 .75
NYY4 Russell Martin .25 .60
NYY5 Michael Pineda .25 .60
NYY6 CC Sabathia .30 .75
NYY7 Curtis Granderson .30 .75
NYY8 Eduardo Nunez .25 .60
NYY9 Mark Teixeira .30 .75
NYY10 Hiroki Kuroda .25 .60
NYY11 Ivan Nova .30 .75
NYY12 Nick Swisher .30 .75
NYY13 Robinson Cano .30 .75
NYY14 Freddy Garcia .25 .60
NYY15 Mariano Rivera .50 1.25
NYY16 Phil Hughes .25 .60
NYY17 Yankee Stadium .15 .40

2013 Yankees Topps

COMPLETE SET (17) 3.00 8.00
NYY1 Derek Jeter 1.00 2.50
NYY2 Robinson Cano .20 .50
NYY3 Alex Rodriguez .30 .75
NYY4 CC Sabathia .20 .50
NYY5 Mark Teixeira .30 .75
NYY6 Brett Gardner .20 .50
NYY7 Curtis Granderson .30 .75
NYY8 Mariano Rivera .50 1.25
NYY9 Hiroki Kuroda .25 .60
NYY10 Andy Pettitte .30 .75
NYY11 Phil Hughes .25 .60
NYY12 Ivan Nova .30 .75
NYY13 Francisco Cervelli .15 .40
NYY14 Kevin Youkilis .15 .40
NYY15 David Robertson .15 .40
NYY16 Eduardo Nunez .15 .40
NYY17 Yankee Stadium .15 .40

2014 Yankees Topps

COMPLETE SET (17) 3.00 .80
NYY1 Derek Jeter .60 1.50
NYY2 Jacoby Ellsbury .20 .50
NYY3 Alex Rodriguez .30 .75
NYY4 CC Sabathia .20 .50
NYY5 Mark Teixeira .20 .50
NYY6 Brett Gardner .20 .50
NYY7 Carlos Beltran .20 .50
NYY8 Alfonso Soriano .20 .50
NYY9 Hiroki Kuroda .15 .40
NYY10 Brian McCann .20 .50
NYY11 Eduardo Nunez .15 .40
NYY12 Ivan Nova .20 .50
NYY13 Kelly Johnson .15 .40
NYY14 Michael Pineda .15 .40
NYY15 David Robertson .15 .40
NYY16 Brian Roberts .15 .40
NYY17 Yankee Stadium .15 .40

2015 Yankees Topps

COMPLETE SET (17) 3.00 8.00
NYY1 Masahiro Tanaka .20 .50
NYY2 Jacoby Ellsbury .20 .50
NYY3 Brett Gardner .20 .50
NYY4 Dellin Betances .20 .50
NYY5 Carlos Beltran .20 .50
NYY6 Stephen Drew .15 .40
NYY7 Brian McCann .20 .50
NYY8 Garrett Jones .15 .40
NYY9 Michael Pineda .15 .40
NYY10 Jose Pirela .15 .40
NYY11 Mark Teixeira .20 .50
NYY12 Bryan Mitchell .15 .40
NYY13 CC Sabathia .20 .50
NYY14 Nathan Eovaldi .20 .50
NYY15 Alex Rodriguez .30 .75
NYY16 Didi Gregorius .20 .50
NYY17 Chase Headley .15 .40

2016 Yankees Topps

COMPLETE SET (17) 3.00 8.00
NYY1 Masahiro Tanaka .20 .50
NYY2 Brian McCann .20 .50
NYY3 Mark Teixeira .20 .50
NYY4 Starlin Castro .15 .40
NYY5 Didi Gregorius .20 .50
NYY6 Chase Headley .15 .40
NYY7 Brett Gardner .20 .50
NYY8 Jacoby Ellsbury .20 .50
NYY9 Greg Bird .20 .50
NYY10 Carlos Beltran .20 .50
NYY11 Alex Rodriguez .30 .75
NYY12 CC Sabathia .20 .50
NYY13 Michael Pineda .15 .40
NYY14 Andrew Miller .20 .50
NYY15 Dellin Betances .20 .50
NYY16 Aroldis Chapman .25 .60
NYY17 Ivan Nova .20 .50

2017 Yankees Topps

COMPLETE SET (17) 3.00 8.00
NYY1 Derek Jeter .60 1.50
NYY2 Jacoby Ellsbury .20 .50
NYY3 Matt Holliday .25 .60
NYY4 Luis Severino .20 .50
NYY5 Dellin Betances .20 .50
NYY6 Masahiro Tanaka .20 .50
NYY7 Greg Bird .20 .50
NYY8 Didi Gregorius .20 .50
NYY9 Aroldis Chapman .25 .60
NYY10 CC Sabathia .20 .50
NYY11 Brett Gardner .20 .50
NYY12 Tyler Austin .20 .50
NYY13 Gary Sanchez .25 .60
NYY14 Starlin Castro .15 .40
NYY15 Chase Headley .15 .40
NYY16 Aaron Judge 2.00 5.00
NYY17 Michael Pineda .15 .40

2018 Yankees Topps

COMPLETE SET (17) 3.00 8.00
NY1 Aaron Judge .60 1.50
NY2 Brett Gardner .20 .50
NY3 Giancarlo Stanton .25 .60
NY4 Aroldis Chapman .25 .60
NY5 Gary Sanchez .25 .60
NY6 Masahiro Tanaka .20 .50
NY7 Dellin Betances .20 .50
NY8 CC Sabathia .20 .50
NY9 Jordan Montgomery .15 .40
NY10 Luis Severino .20 .50
NY11 David Robertson .15 .40
NY12 Sonny Gray .20 .50
NY13 Jacoby Ellsbury .20 .50
NY14 Didi Gregorius .20 .50
NY15 Aaron Hicks .20 .50
NY16 Greg Bird .20 .50
NY17 Clint Frazier .30 .75

2019 Yankees Topps

COMPLETE SET (17) 4.00 10.00
NY1 Aaron Judge .60 1.50
NY2 Giancarlo Stanton .25 .60
NY3 Gleyber Torres .50 1.25
NY4 Luis Severino .20 .50
NY5 James Paxton .20 .50
NY6 Miguel Andujar .25 .60
NY7 Didi Gregorius .20 .50
NY8 Masahiro Tanaka .20 .50
NY9 CC Sabathia .20 .50
NY10 Sonny Gray .20 .50
NY11 Aroldis Chapman .25 .60
NY12 Troy Tulowitzki .25 .60
NY13 Gary Sanchez .25 .60
NY14 Luke Voit .40 1.00
NY15 Greg Bird .20 .50
NY16 Aaron Hicks .20 .50
NY17 Brett Gardner .20 .50

2020 Yankees Topps

NYY1 Aaron Judge .60 1.50
NYY2 Gleyber Torres .50 1.25
NYY3 Masahiro Tanaka .25 .60
NYY4 Gary Sanchez .25 .60
NYY5 Tommy Kahnle .15 .40
NYY6 DJ LeMahieu .25 .60
NYY7 Gio Urshela .25 .60
NYY8 Chad Green .15 .40
NYY9 Giancarlo Stanton .25 .60
NYY10 Gerrit Cole .40 1.00
NYY11 Aroldis Chapman .25 .60
NYY12 Luis Severino .20 .50
NYY13 James Paxton .20 .50
NYY14 Mike Tauchman .25 .60
NYY15 Aaron Hicks .20 .50
NYY16 Adam Ottavino .20 .50
NYY17 J.A. Happ .20 .50

2017 Yankees Topps National Baseball Card Day

COMPLETE SET (10) 12.00 30.00
NYY1 Dellin Betances .75 2.00
NYY2 Aaron Judge 8.00 20.00
NYY3 Starlin Castro .60 1.50
NYY4 Jacoby Ellsbury .75 2.00
NYY5 Masahiro Tanaka .75 2.00
NYY6 Gary Sanchez 1.00 2.50
NYY7 Matt Holliday 1.00 2.50
NYY8 Didi Gregorius .75 2.00
NYY9 Brett Gardner .75 2.00
NYY10 Babe Ruth 2.50 6.00

2010 Yankees Topps 27 World Championships

COMPLETE SET (27) 8.00 20.00
1 Babe Ruth 52T 2.00 5.00
2 Lou Gehrig 52T 1.50 4.00
3 Leo Durocher 52T .30 .75
4 Lefty Gomez 52T .30 .75
5 Tony Lazzeri 52T .50 1.25
6 Bill Dickey 52T .30 .75
7 Red Ruffing 52T .30 .75
8 Red Rolfe 52T .30 .75
9 Phil Rizzuto 52T .50 1.25
10 Charlie Keller 52T .30 .75
11 Yogi Berra 52T .75 2.00
12 Johnny Mize 52T .50 1.25
13 Hank Bauer 52T .30 .75
14 Mickey Mantle 51T 2.50 6.00
15 Mickey Mantle 52T 2.50 6.00
16 Mickey Mantle 53T 2.50 6.00
17 Don Larsen 56T .30 .75
18 Enos Slaughter 58T .50 1.25
19 Roger Maris 61T .75 2.00
20 Elston Howard 62T .30 .75
21 Thurman Munson 77T .75 2.00
22 Reggie Jackson 78T .50 1.25
23 Andy Pettitte 96T .50 1.25
24 Derek Jeter 98T 2.00 5.00
25 Jorge Posada 99T .50 1.25
26 Mariano Rivera 00T 1.00 2.50
27 Alex Rodriguez 09T 1.00 2.50

2009 Yankees Topps World Series Champions

COMPLETE SET (27) 6.00 15.00
COMMON CARD .20 .50
NYY1 CC Sabathia .30 .75
NYY2 Mark Teixeira .30 .75
NYY3 Phil Hughes .20 .50
NYY4 Hideki Matsui .50 1.25
NYY5 Andy Pettitte .30 .75
NYY6 Jorge Posada .30 .75
NYY7 Nick Swisher .30 .75
NYY8 A.J. Burnett .20 .50
NYY9 Joba Chamberlain .20 .50
NYY10 Phil Coke .30 .75
NYY11 Brett Gardner .30 .75
NYY12 Alfredo Aceves .30 .75
NYY13 Johnny Damon .30 .75
NYY14 Melky Cabrera .20 .50
NYY15 Mariano Rivera .60 1.50
NYY16 Alex Rodriguez .60 1.50
NYY17 David Robertson .20 .50
NYY18 Derek Jeter 1.25 3.00
NYY19 Robinson Cano .30 .75
NYY20 Jose Molina .20 .50
NYY21 Mark Teixeira HL .30 .75
NYY22 Mariano Rivera HL .60 1.50
NYY23 CC Sabathia HL .30 .75
NYY24 Andy Pettitte HL .30 .75
NYY26 Andy Pettitte HL .30 .75
NYY27 Joe Girardi MG .30 .75

1958 Yoo-Hoo Match Book Covers

This yellow match book cover was issued by the Yoo-Hoo chocolate drink company and featured a photo of Yogi Berra on the back. The sepia, head shot photo is encircled with a bottle cap design and above and below the cap are the words "Me for Yoo-Hoo". Yogi Berra's name is printed on the lower portion of the picture. The inner portion of the match book cover carries an offer to mail in the empty cover with $2.50 and receive a book entitled "The Story of Yogi Berra". A matchbook was also made of Yankee great Mickey Mantle and that had offers inside for memorabilia from assorted New York Yankee.

COMPLETE SET 62.50 125.00
1 Yogi Berra 12.50 25.00
2 Mickey Mantle 50.00 100.00

1993 Yoo-Hoo

This standard-size 20-card set was issued by Yoo-Hoo Chocolate Beverage Corporation and celebrates some of baseball's legends. The cards are unnumbered and checklisted below in alphabetical order.

COMPLETE SET (20) 4.00 10.00
1 Johnny Bench .40 1.00
2 Yogi Berra .60 1.50
3 Lou Brock .40 1.00
4 Rod Carew .40 1.00
5 Bob Feller .60 1.50
6 Whitey Ford .40 1.00
7 Steve Garvey .20 .50
8 Al Kaline .60 1.50
9 Willie McCovey .30 .75
10 Joe Morgan .30 .75
11 Stan Musial .60 1.50
12 Gaylord Perry .30 .75
13 Graig Nettles .20 .50
14 Jim Rice .20 .50
15 Phil Rizzuto .40 1.00
16 Brooks Robinson .60 1.50
17 Pete Rose .60 1.50
18 Tom Seaver .60 1.50
19 Duke Snider .60 1.50
20 Willie Stargell .30 .75

1994 Yoo-Hoo

Issued in conjunction with Rawlings in two ten-card sets, each set consisting of eight player cards and two fact cards, this 20-card set features past winners of Rawlings Gold Glove Award. The first series was introduced in May, while the second series was released in August. The entire set could be received for proofs-of-purchase as well as postage and handling; a toll free number on Yoo-Hoo products could be called to obtain the details of the offer. The Fact Cards are numbered 1-4 on their fronts and backs, and have been arbitrarily assigned an "F" prefix below to distinguish them from the player cards. Interestingly, Don Mattingly appeared in this set although he was still active at time of issue. Some packs were sent out with Carl Yastrzemski's autographs. There is no certified mark or other way to verify that the card was specifically autographed.

COMPLETE SET (20) 15.00 40.00
1 Luis Aparicio .75 2.00
2 Bobby Bonds .40 1.00
3 Bob Boone .40 1.00
4 Steve Carlton .75 2.00
5 Roberto Clemente 4.00 10.00
6 Bob Gibson .75 2.00
7 Keith Hernandez .60 1.50
8 Jim Kaat .60 1.50
9 Roger Maris 2.00 5.00
10 Don Mattingly 3.00 8.00
11 Thurman Munson .75 2.00
12 Phil Rizzuto 1.25 3.00
13 Brooks Robinson 1.25 3.00
14 Ryne Sandberg 3.00 8.00
15 Mike Schmidt 2.00 5.00
16 Carl Yastrzemski 1.25 3.00
16A Carl Yastrzemski AU 8.00 20.00
F1 Fact Card 1 .08 .25
F2 Fact Card 2 .08 .25
F3 Fact Card 3 .08 .25
F4 Fact Card 4 .08 .25

1927 York Caramel Type 1 E210

The cards in this 60-card set measure 1 3/8" by 2 1/2". This set contains numbered cards with black and white photos of baseball players in the series of "most prominent baseball stars" issued by the York Caramel Company. They were released to the public in 1927. Number 12 has been found with two spellings; number 58 appears with either Bell or Galloway; and numbers 9, 25, 31 and 46 have incorrect photos of players with the same last names. An interesting feature is the caption which appears under the players's name on back, e.g., Burleigh Grimes is dubbed "A Sterling National League Pitcher." The complete set price includes all variation cards listed in the checklist below.

COMPLETE SET (64) 20000.00 40000.00
1 Burleigh Grimes 250.00 500.00
2 Walter Reuther/(sic& Ruether) 150.00 300.00
3A Joe Duggan ERR/(sic& Dugan) 200.00 400.00
3B Joe Dugan COR 200.00 400.00
4 Red Faber 250.00 500.00
5 Gabby Hartnett 300.00 600.00
6 Babe Ruth 4000.00 8000.00
7 Bob Meusel 200.00 400.00
8 Herb Pennock 250.00 500.00
9 George (H.) Burns/(photo actually 150.00 300.00
George J. Burn
10 Joe Sewell 250.00 500.00
11 George Uhle 150.00 300.00
12A Bob O'Farrel ERR 200.00 400.00
12B Bob O'Farrell COR 200.00 400.00
13 Rogers Hornsby 750.00 1500.00
14 Pie Traynor 300.00 600.00
15 Clarence Mitchell 150.00 300.00
16 Eppa Rixey 250.00 500.00
17 Carl Mays 200.00 400.00
18 Dolf Luque 150.00 300.00
19 Dave Bancroft 250.00 500.00
20 George Kelly 250.00 500.00
21 Ira Flagstead 150.00 300.00
22 Harry Heilmann 300.00 600.00
23 Ray Schalk 250.00 500.00
24 Johnny Mostil 150.00 300.00
25 Hack Wilson/(photo actually 500.00 1000.00
Art Wilson)
26 Tom Zachary 150.00 300.00
27 Ty Cobb 2500.00 5000.00
28 Tris Speaker 750.00 1500.00
29 Ralph Perkins 150.00 300.00
30 Jess Haines/(sic& Jesse) 250.00 500.00
31 Sherwood Smith/(photo actually 150.00 300.00
Jack Coombs)
32 Max Carey 250.00 500.00
33 Eugene Hargraves 150.00 300.00
34 Miguel L. Gonzales 150.00 300.00
35A Clifton Heathcot ERR 200.00 400.00
35B Clifton Heathcote COR 200.00 400.00
36 Sam Rice 250.00 500.00
37 Earl Sheely 150.00 300.00
38 Emory E. Rigney 150.00 300.00
39 Bib Falk 150.00 300.00
40 Nick Altrock 150.00 300.00
41 Bucky Harris 250.00 500.00
42 John J. McGraw MG 500.00 1000.00
43 Wilbert Robinson MG 300.00 600.00
44 Grover C. Alexander 750.00 1500.00
45 Walter Johnson 1000.00 2000.00
46 William H. Terry/(photo actually 300.00 600.00
Zeb Terry)
47 Eddie Collins 300.00 600.00
48 Marty McManus 150.00 300.00
49 Goose Goslin 300.00 600.00
50 Frankie Frisch 500.00 1000.00
51 Jimmy Dykes 200.00 400.00
52 Cy Williams 200.00 400.00
53 Ed Roush 300.00 600.00
54 George Sisler 500.00 1000.00
55 Ed Rommel 200.00 400.00
56 Rogers Peckinpaugh/(sic& Roger) 200.00 400.00
57 Stan Coveleskie 250.00 500.00
58A Clarence Galloway 200.00 400.00
58B Lester Bell 200.00 400.00
59 Bob Shawkey 200.00 400.00
60 John P. McInnis 200.00 400.00

1974 Cy Young Museum Postcard

This one card postcard set was issued by TCMA to promote the Cy Young Museum in Newcomerstown, Ohio. The front has a picture of Young surrounded by the words "Cy Young Museum" on top and its location on the bottom. The back has some information about Young's career.

1 Cy Young 2.00 5.00

1994 Yount Ameritech

This credit card-sized (3 3/8" by 2 1/8") card was issued to fans at Milwaukee County Stadium on Robin Yount Tribute Day, May 29, 1994, to commemorate the retirement of his jersey number (19). It has rounded corners and features on its front a horizontal borderless color action shot of Yount. The card carries a value of 50 cents worth of pay telephone calls. The white back carries instructions for use and the production number out of 63,000 produced.

1 Robin Yount 1.25 3.00
50 Cents

1928 Yuengling's Ice Cream

The cards in this 60-card set measure approximately 1 3/8" by 2 9/16". This black and white, numbered set contains many Hall of Famers. The card backs are the same as those found in sets of E210 and W502. The Paul Waner card, number 45, actually contains a picture of Clyde Barnhardt. Each back contains an offer to redeem pictures of Babe Ruth for ice cream. The catalog designation for this set is F50.

COMPLETE SET (60) 1500.00 3000.00
1 Burleigh Grimes 50.00 100.00
2 Walter Reuther 20.00 50.00
3 Joe Dugan 30.00 60.00
4 Red Faber 50.00 100.00
5 Gabby Hartnett 50.00 100.00
6 Babe Ruth 1250.00 2500.00
7 Bob Meusel 40.00 80.00
8 Herb Pennock 50.00 100.00
9 George Burns 20.00 50.00
10 Joe Sewell 50.00 100.00
11 George Uhle 20.00 50.00
12 Bob O'Farrell 7.50 15.00
13 Rogers Hornsby 150.00 300.00
14 Pie Traynor 50.00 100.00
15 Clarence Mitchell 20.00 50.00
16 Eppa Rixey 50.00 100.00
17 Carl Mays 30.00 60.00
18 Adolfo Luque 30.00 60.00
19 Dave Bancroft 50.00 100.00
20 George Kelly 50.00 100.00
21 Earle Combs 50.00 100.00
22 Harry Heilmann 50.00 100.00
23 Ray Schalk 50.00 100.00
24 John Mostil 20.00 50.00
25 Hack Wilson 75.00 150.00
26 Lou Gehrig 750.00 1500.00
27 Ty Cobb 750.00 1500.00
28 Tris Speaker 125.00 250.00
29 Tony Lazzeri 50.00 100.00
30 Waite Hoyt 50.00 100.00
31 Sherwood Smith 20.00 50.00
32 Max Carey 50.00 100.00
33 Gene Hargrave 20.00 50.00
34 Miguel Gonzalez 30.00 60.00
35 Joe Judge 30.00 60.00
36 Sam Rice 50.00 100.00
37 Earl Sheely 20.00 50.00
38 Sam Jones 30.00 60.00
39 Bibb Falk 20.00 50.00
40 Willie Kamm 20.00 50.00
41 Bucky Harris 50.00 100.00
42 John McGraw MG 75.00 150.00
43 Art Nehf 30.00 60.00
44 Grover C. Alexander 150.00 300.00
45 Paul Waner 50.00 100.00
46 Bill Terry 100.00 200.00
47 Glenn Wright 20.00 50.00
48 Earl Smith 20.00 50.00
49 Goose Goslin 50.00 100.00
50 Frank Frisch 75.00 150.00
51 Joe Harris 20.00 50.00
52 Cy Williams 30.00 60.00
53 Eddie Roush 50.00 100.00
54 George Sisler 100.00 200.00
55 Ed Rommel 30.00 60.00
56 Roger Peckinpaugh 30.00 60.00
57 Stanley Coveleskie 50.00 100.00
58 Lester Bell 20.00 50.00
59 Lloyd Waner 50.00 100.00
60 John McInnis 30.00 60.00

1995 Zenith Samples

COMPLETE SET (9) 4.00 10.00
12 Cal Ripken 1.25 3.00
20 Dante Bichette .07 .20
51 Jim Thome .40 1.00
70 Mark Grace .30 .75
97 Ryan Klesko .15 .40
111 Chipper Jones .60 1.50
113 Curtis Goodwin .07 .20
R7 Hideo Nomo 1.25 3.00
NNO Information Card .07 .20

1995 Zenith

The complete 1995 Zenith set consists of 150 standard-size cards. The cards are made of thick stock and are borderless. Included is a subset of 50 Rookies (111-150). The regular issued cards are in alphabetical order by first name. Rookie Cards in this set include Bobby Higginson and Hideo Nomo.

COMPLETE SET (150) 15.00 40.00
1 Albert Belle .15 .40
2 Alex Fernandez .07 .20
3 Andy Benes .07 .20
4 Barry Larkin .25 .60
5 Barry Bonds 1.00 2.50
6 Ben McDonald .07 .20
7 Bernard Gilkey .07 .20
8 Billy Ashley .07 .20
9 Bobby Bonilla .15 .40
10 Bret Saberhagen .15 .40
11 Brian Jordan .15 .40
12 Cal Ripken 1.25 3.00
13 Carlos Baerga .07 .20
14 Carlos Delgado .15 .40
15 Cecil Fielder .15 .40
16 Chili Davis .15 .40
17 Chuck Knoblauch .15 .40
18 Craig Biggio .25 .60
19 Danny Tartabull .07 .20
20 Dante Bichette .15 .40
21 Darren Daulton .15 .40
22 David Justice .15 .40
23 Dave Winfield .15 .40
24 David Cone .15 .40
25 Dean Palmer .15 .40
26 Deion Sanders .25 .60
27 Dennis Eckersley .15 .40
28 Derek Bell .07 .20
29 Don Mattingly 1.00 2.50
30 Edgar Martinez .25 .60
31 Eric Karros .15 .40
32 James Mouton .07 .20
33 Frank Thomas .40 1.00
34 Fred McGriff .25 .60
35 Gary Sheffield .15 .40
36 Gary Gaetti .15 .40
37 Greg Maddux .60 1.50
38 Gregg Jefferies .07 .20
39 Ivan Rodriguez .25 .60
40 Kenny Rogers .15 .40
41 J.T. Snow .15 .40
42 Hal Morris .07 .20
43 Eddie Murray 3000th Hit .25 .60
44 Javier Lopez .15 .40
45 Jay Bell .15 .40
46 Jeff Conine .15 .40
47 Jeff Bagwell .25 .60
48 Hideo Nomo Japanese 1.00 2.50
49 Jeff Kent .15 .40
50 Jeff King .07 .20
51 Jim Thome .25 .60
52 Jimmy Key .15 .40
53 Joe Carter .15 .40
54 John Valentin .07 .20
55 John Olerud .15 .40
56 Jose Canseco .25 .60
57 Jose Rijo .07 .20
58 Jose Offerman .07 .20
59 Juan Gonzalez .15 .40
60 Ken Caminiti .15 .40
61 Ken Griffey Jr. .75 2.00
62 Kenny Lofton .15 .40
63 Kevin Appier .15 .40
64 Kevin Seitzer .07 .20
65 Kirby Puckett .40 1.00
66 Kirk Gibson .15 .40
67 Larry Walker .15 .40
68 Lenny Dykstra .15 .40
69 Manny Ramirez .25 .60
70 Mark Grace .25 .60
71 Mark McGwire 1.00 2.50
72 Marquis Grissom .15 .40
73 Jim Edmonds .25 .60
74 Matt Williams .15 .40
75 Mike Mussina .25 .60
76 Mike Piazza .60 1.50
77 Mo Vaughn .15 .40
78 Moises Alou .15 .40
79 Ozzie Smith .60 1.50
80 Paul O'Neill .25 .60
81 Paul Molitor .15 .40
82 Rafael Palmeiro .25 .60
83 Randy Johnson .40 1.00
84 Raul Mondesi .15 .40
85 Ray Lankford .15 .40
86 Reggie Sanders .15 .40
87 Rickey Henderson .40 1.00
88 Rico Brogna .07 .20
89 Roberto Alomar .25 .60
90 Robin Ventura .15 .40
91 Roger Clemens .75 2.00
92 Ron Gant .15 .40
93 Rondell White .15 .40
94 Royce Clayton .07 .20
95 Ruben Sierra .15 .40
96 Rusty Greer .15 .40
97 Ryan Klesko .15 .40
98 Sammy Sosa .40 1.00
99 Shawon Dunston .07 .20
100 Steve Ontiveros .07 .20
101 Tim Naehring .07 .20
102 Tim Salmon .25 .60
103 Tino Martinez .25 .60
104 Tony Gwynn .50 1.25
105 Travis Fryman .15 .40
106 Vinny Castilla .15 .40
107 Wade Boggs .25 .60
108 Wally Joyner .15 .40
109 Wil Cordero .07 .20
110 Will Clark .25 .60
111 Chipper Jones .40 1.00
112 Armando Benitez .07 .20
113 Curtis Goodwin .07 .20
114 Gabe White .07 .20
115 Vaughn Eshelman .07 .20
116 Marty Cordova .07 .20
117 Dustin Hermanson .07 .20
118 Rich Becker .07 .20
119 Ray Durham .15 .40
120 Shane Andrews .07 .20
121 Scott Ruffcorn .07 .20
122 Mark Grudzielanek RC .25 .60
123 James Baldwin .07 .20
124 Carlos Perez RC .15 .40
125 Julian Tavarez .07 .20
126 Joe Vitiello .07 .20
127 Jason Bates .07 .20
128 Edgardo Alfonzo .07 .20
129 Juan Acevedo RC .07 .20
130 Bill Pulsipher .07 .20
131 Bob Higginson RC .25 .60
132 Russ Davis .07 .20
133 Charles Johnson .15 .40
134 Derek Jeter 1.00 2.50
135 Orlando Miller .07 .20
136 LaTroy Hawkins .07 .20
137 Brian L.Hunter .07 .20
138 Roberto Petagine .07 .20
139 Midre Cummings .07 .20
140 Garret Anderson .15 .40
141 Ugueth Urbina .07 .20
142 Antonio Osuna .07 .20
143 Michael Tucker .07 .20
144 Benji Gil .07 .20
145 Jon Nunnally .07 .20
146 Alex Rodriguez 1.00 2.50
147 Todd Hollandsworth .07 .20
148 Alex Gonzalez .07 .20
149 Hideo Nomo RC 1.00 2.50
150 Shawn Green .15 .40

1995 Zenith All-Star Salute

COMPLETE SET (18) 15.00 40.00
STATED ODDS 1:6
1 Cal Ripken 2.50 6.00
2 Frank Thomas .75 2.00
3 Mike Piazza 1.25 3.00
4 Kirby Puckett .75 2.00
5 Manny Ramirez .50 1.25
6 Tony Gwynn 1.00 2.50
7 Hideo Nomo 1.50 4.00
8 Matt Williams .30 .75
9 Randy Johnson .75 2.00
10 Raul Mondesi .30 .75
11 Albert Belle .30 .75
12 Ivan Rodriguez .50 1.25
13 Barry Bonds 2.00 5.00
14 Carlos Baerga .15 .40
15 Ken Griffey Jr. 1.50 4.00
16 Jeff Conine .30 .75
17 Frank Thomas .75 2.00
18 C.Ripken 2.50 6.00
B.Bonds

1995 Zenith Rookie Roll Call

COMPLETE SET (18) 20.00 50.00
STATED ODDS 1:24
1 Alex Rodriguez 4.00 10.00
2 Derek Jeter 15.00 40.00
3 Chipper Jones 1.50 4.00
4 Shawn Green .60 1.50
5 Todd Hollandsworth .40 1.00
6 Bill Pulsipher .40 1.00
7 Hideo Nomo 2.00 5.00
8 Ray Durham .60 1.50
9 Curtis Goodwin .40 1.00
10 Brian L.Hunter .40 1.00
11 Julian Tavarez .40 1.00
12 Marty Cordova .40 1.00
13 Michael Tucker .40 1.00
14 Edgardo Alfonzo .40 1.00
15 LaTroy Hawkins .40 1.00
16 Carlos Perez .60 1.50
17 Charles Johnson .60 1.50
18 Benji Gil .40 1.00

1995 Zenith Z-Team

STATED ODDS 1:72
1 Cal Ripken 12.50 30.00
2 Ken Griffey Jr. 12.50 30.00
3 Frank Thomas 4.00 10.00
4 Matt Williams 1.50 4.00
5 Mike Piazza 6.00 15.00
6 Barry Bonds 10.00 25.00
7 Raul Mondesi 1.50 4.00
8 Greg Maddux 6.00 15.00
9 Jeff Bagwell 2.50 6.00
10 Manny Ramirez 2.50 6.00
11 Larry Walker 1.50 4.00
12 Tony Gwynn 5.00 12.00
13 Will Clark 2.50 6.00
14 Albert Belle 1.50 4.00
15 Kenny Lofton 1.50 4.00
16 Rafael Palmeiro 2.50 6.00
17 Don Mattingly 10.00 25.00
18 Carlos Baerga .75 2.00

1996 Zenith

This 1996 Zenith set was issued in one series totalling 150 cards. The six-card packs retailed for $3.99 each. The set contains the subset: Honor Roll (131-150). The fronts feature a color player cutout over an arrangement of baseball bats on a black background. The backs carry a hit location chart and player statistics. Rookie Card include Darin Erstad.

COMPLETE SET (150) 12.50 30.00
1 Ken Griffey Jr. .60 1.50
2 Ozzie Smith .50 1.25
3 Greg Maddux .50 1.25
4 Rondell White .10 .30
5 Mark McGwire .75 2.00
6 Jim Thome .20 .50
7 Ivan Rodriguez .20 .50
8 Marc Newfield .10 .30
9 Travis Fryman .10 .30
10 Fred McGriff .20 .50
11 Shawn Green .10 .30
12 Mike Piazza .50 1.25
13 Dante Bichette .10 .30
14 Tino Martinez .20 .50
15 Sterling Hitchcock .10 .30
16 Ryne Sandberg .50 1.25
17 Rico Brogna .10 .30
18 Roberto Alomar .20 .50
19 Barry Larkin .20 .50
20 Bernie Williams .20 .50
21 Gary Sheffield .10 .30
22 Frank Thomas .30 .75
23 Gregg Jefferies .10 .30
24 Jeff Bagwell .20 .50
25 Marty Cordova .10 .30
26 Jim Edmonds .10 .30
27 Jay Bell .10 .30
28 Ben McDonald .10 .30
29 Barry Bonds .75 2.00
30 Mo Vaughn .10 .30
31 Johnny Damon .20 .50
32 Dean Palmer .10 .30
33 Ismael Valdes .10 .30
34 Manny Ramirez .20 .50
35 Edgar Martinez .20 .50
36 Cecil Fielder .10 .30
37 Ryan Klesko .10 .30
38 Ray Lankford .10 .30
39 Tim Salmon .20 .50
40 Joe Carter .10 .30
41 Jason Isringhausen .10 .30
42 Rickey Henderson .30 .75
43 Lenny Dykstra .10 .30
44 Andre Dawson .10 .30
45 Paul O'Neill .20 .50
46 Ray Durham .10 .30
47 Raul Mondesi .10 .30
48 Jay Buhner .10 .30
49 Eddie Murray .30 .75
50 Henry Rodriguez .10 .30
51 Hal Morris .10 .30
52 Mike Mussina .20 .50
53 Wally Joyner .10 .30
54 Will Clark .20 .50
55 Chipper Jones .30 .75
56 Brian Jordan .10 .30
57 Larry Walker .10 .30
58 Wade Boggs .20 .50
59 Melvin Nieves .10 .30
60 Charles Johnson .10 .30
61 Juan Gonzalez .10 .30
62 Carlos Delgado .10 .30
63 Reggie Sanders .10 .30
64 Brian L.Hunter .10 .30
65 Edgardo Alfonzo .10 .30
66 Kenny Lofton .10 .30
67 Paul Molitor .10 .30
68 Mike Bordick .10 .30
69 Garret Anderson .10 .30
70 Orlando Merced .10 .30
71 Craig Biggio .20 .50
72 Chuck Knoblauch .10 .30
73 Mark Grace .20 .50
74 Jack McDowell .10 .30
75 Randy Johnson .30 .75
76 Cal Ripken 1.00 2.50
77 Matt Williams .10 .30
78 Benji Gil .10 .30
79 Moises Alou .10 .30
80 Robin Ventura .10 .30
81 Greg Vaughn .10 .30
82 Carlos Baerga .10 .30
83 Roger Clemens .60 1.50
84 Hideo Nomo .30 .75
85 Pedro Martinez .20 .50
86 John Valentin .10 .30
87 Andres Galarraga .10 .30
88 Andy Pettitte .20 .50
89 Derek Bell .10 .30
90 Kirby Puckett .30 .75
91 Tony Gwynn .40 1.00
92 Brady Anderson .10 .30
93 Derek Jeter .75 2.00
94 Michael Tucker .10 .30
95 Albert Belle .10 .30
96 David Cone .10 .30
97 J.T. Snow .10 .30
98 Tom Glavine .20 .50
99 Alex Rodriguez .60 1.50
100 Sammy Sosa .30 .75
101 Karim Garcia .10 .30
102 Alan Benes .10 .30
103 Chad Mottola .10 .30
104 Robin Jennings .10 .30
105 Bob Abreu .30 .75
106 Tony Clark .10 .30
107 George Arias .10 .30
108 Jermaine Dye .10 .30
109 Jeff Suppan .10 .30
110 Ralph Milliard RC .10 .30
111 Ruben Rivera .10 .30
112 Billy Wagner .10 .30
113 Jason Kendall .10 .30
114 Mike Grace RC .10 .30
115 Edgar Renteria .10 .30
116 Jason Schmidt .20 .50
117 Paul Wilson .10 .30
118 Rey Ordonez .10 .30
119 Rocky Coppinger RC .10 .30
120 Wilton Guerrero RC .10 .30
121 Brooks Kieschnick .10 .30
122 Raul Casanova .10 .30
123 Alex Ochoa .10 .30
124 Chan Ho Park .10 .30
125 John Wasdin .10 .30
126 Eric Owens .10 .30
127 Justin Thompson .10 .30
128 Chris Snopek .10 .30
129 Terrell Wade .10 .30
130 Darin Erstad RC .75 2.00
131 Albert Belle HON .10 .30
132 Cal Ripken HON .50 1.25
133 Frank Thomas HON .20 .50
134 Greg Maddux HON .30 .75
135 Ken Griffey Jr. HON .40 1.00
136 Mo Vaughn HON .10 .30
137 Chipper Jones HON .20 .50
138 Mike Piazza HON .30 .75
139 Ryan Klesko HON .10 .30
140 Hideo Nomo HON .20 .50
141 Roberto Alomar HON .10 .30
142 Manny Ramirez HON .10 .30
143 Gary Sheffield HON .10 .30
144 Barry Bonds HON .40 1.00
145 Matt Williams HON .10 .30
146 Jim Edmonds HON .10 .30
147 Derek Jeter HON .40 1.00
148 Sammy Sosa HON .20 .50
149 Kirby Puckett HON .20 .50
150 Tony Gwynn HON .20 .50

1996 Zenith Artist's Proofs

COMPLETE SET (150) 1500.00 2500.00
*STARS: 10X TO 25X BASIC CARDS
*ROOKIES: 4X TO 10X BASIC CARDS
STATED ODDS 1:35
76 Cal Ripken 15.00 40.00

1996 Zenith Diamond Club

COMPLETE SET (20) 60.00 120.00
STATED ODDS 1:24
*REAL DIAMOND: 2X TO 5X BASIC DIAMOND
REAL DIAMOND STATED ODDS 1:350
1 Albert Belle 1.00 2.50
2 Mo Vaughn 1.00 2.50
3 Ken Griffey Jr. 5.00 12.00
4 Mike Piazza 4.00 10.00
5 Cal Ripken 8.00 20.00
6 Jermaine Dye 1.00 2.50
7 Jeff Bagwell 1.50 4.00
8 Frank Thomas 2.50 6.00
9 Alex Rodriguez 5.00 12.00
10 Ryan Klesko 1.00 2.50
11 Roberto Alomar 1.50 4.00
12 Sammy Sosa 2.50 6.00
13 Matt Williams 1.00 2.50
14 Gary Sheffield 1.00 2.50
15 Ruben Rivera 1.00 2.50
16 Darin Erstad 2.00 5.00
17 Randy Johnson 2.50 6.00
18 Greg Maddux 4.00 10.00
19 Karim Garcia 1.00 2.50
20 Chipper Jones 2.50 6.00

1996 Zenith Mozaics

COMPLETE SET (25) 30.00 80.00
STATED ODDS 1:10
1 Maddux 2.50 6.00
Jones
Klesko
2 Gonzalez 1.00 2.50
Clark
Rodriguez
3 Thomas 1.50 4.00
Ventura
Durham
4 Bonds 4.00 10.00
Williams
Fernandez
5 Griffey 3.00 8.00
Johnson
Rodriguez
6 Sosa 1.50 4.00
Sandberg
Grace
7 Edmonds .60 1.50
Salmon
Anderson
8 Ripken 5.00 12.00
Alomar
Mussina
9 Clemens 3.00 8.00
Vaughn
Valentin
10 Larkin 1.00 2.50
Sanders
Morris
11 Lankford 2.50 6.00
Jordan
Smith
12 Bichette .60 1.50
Walker
Galarraga
13 Piazza 2.50 6.00
Nomo
Mondesi
14 McDonald .60 1.50
Vaughn
Seitzer
15 Carter .60 1.50
Delgado
Gonzalez
16 Sheffield .60 1.50
Johnson
Conine
17 White .60 1.50
Alou
Rodriguez
18 Ramirez 1.00 2.50
Belle
Baerga
19 Puckett 1.50 4.00
Molitor
Knoblauch
20 Gwynn 2.00 5.00
Henderson
Joyner
21 McGwire 4.00 10.00
Bordick
Brosius
22 Boggs 1.00 2.50
B.Williams
O'Neill
23 Bell .60 1.50
Merced
Kendall
24 Brogna .60 1.50
Wilson
Isringhausen
25 Bagwell 1.00 2.50
Biggio
Bell

1996 Zenith Z-Team

COMPLETE SET (18) 25.00 60.00
STATED ODDS 1:72
1 Ken Griffey Jr. 4.00 10.00
2 Albert Belle .75 2.00
3 Cal Ripken 6.00 15.00
4 Frank Thomas 2.00 5.00
5 Greg Maddux 3.00 8.00
6 Mo Vaughn .75 2.00
7 Chipper Jones 2.00 5.00
8 Mike Piazza 2.00 5.00
9 Ryan Klesko .75 2.00
10 Hideo Nomo 2.00 5.00
11 Roberto Alomar 1.25 3.00
12 Manny Ramirez 1.25 3.00
13 Gary Sheffield .75 2.00
14 Barry Bonds 3.00 8.00
15 Matt Williams .75 2.00
16 Jim Edmonds .75 2.00
17 Kirby Puckett 2.00 5.00
18 Sammy Sosa 2.00 5.00

1996 Zenith Z-Team Samples

1 Ken Griffey Jr. 5.00 12.00
2 Albert Belle 1.00 2.50
3 Cal Ripken 8.00 20.00
4 Frank Thomas 2.50 6.00
5 Greg Maddux 4.00 10.00
6 Mo Vaughn 1.00 2.50
7 Chipper Jones 2.50 6.00
8 Mike Piazza 2.50 6.00
9 Ryan Klesko 1.00 2.50
10 Hideo Nomo 2.50 6.00
11 Roberto Alomar 1.50 4.00
12 Manny Ramirez 1.50 4.00
13 Gary Sheffield 1.00 2.50
14 Barry Bonds 4.00 10.00
15 Matt Williams 1.00 2.50
16 Jim Edmonds 1.00 2.50
17 Kirby Puckett 2.50 6.00
18 Sammy Sosa 2.50 6.00

1997 Zenith Samples

S1 Ken Griffey Jr. 3.00 8.00
S2 Chuck Knoblauch .60 1.50
S3 Deion Sanders 1.00 2.50
S4 David Justice .60 1.50
S5 Derek Jeter 4.00 10.00
S6 Kenny Lofton .60 1.50

1997 Zenith

The 1997 Zenith set was issued in one series totalling 50 cards and was distributed in packs containing five standard-size cards and two 8" by 10" cards with a suggested retail price of $9.99. The fronts feature borderless color action player photos. The backs carry a black-and-white player photo with career statistics. The set contains 42 established player cards and eight rookie cards (43-50).

COMPLETE SET (50) 10.00 25.00
1 Frank Thomas .40 1.00
2 Tony Gwynn .50 1.25
3 Jeff Bagwell .25 .60
4 Paul Molitor .15 .40
5 Roberto Alomar .25 .60
6 Mike Piazza .60 1.50
7 Albert Belle .15 .40
8 Greg Maddux .60 1.50
9 Barry Larkin .25 .60
10 Tony Clark .15 .40
11 Larry Walker .15 .40
12 Chipper Jones .40 1.00
13 Juan Gonzalez .15 .40
14 Barry Bonds 1.00 2.50
15 Ivan Rodriguez .25 .60
16 Sammy Sosa .40 1.00
17 Derek Jeter 1.00 2.50
18 Hideo Nomo .40 1.00
19 Roger Clemens .75 2.00
20 Ken Griffey Jr. .75 2.00
21 Andy Pettitte .25 .60
22 Alex Rodriguez .60 1.50
23 Tino Martinez .25 .60
24 Bernie Williams .25 .60
25 Ken Caminiti .15 .40
26 John Smoltz .25 .60
27 Javier Lopez .15 .40
28 Mark McGwire 1.00 2.50
29 Gary Sheffield .15 .40
30 David Justice .15 .40
31 Randy Johnson .40 1.00
32 Chuck Knoblauch .15 .40
33 Mike Mussina .25 .60
34 Deion Sanders .25 .60
35 Cal Ripken 1.25 3.00
36 Darin Erstad .15 .40
37 Kenny Lofton .15 .40
38 Jay Buhner .15 .40
39 Brady Anderson .15 .40
40 Edgar Martinez .25 .60
41 Mo Vaughn .15 .40
42 Ryne Sandberg .60 1.50
43 Andruw Jones .25 .60
44 Nomar Garciaparra .60 1.50
45 Hideki Irabu RC .30 .75
46 Wilton Guerrero .15 .40
47 Jose Cruz Jr. RC .30 .75
48 Vladimir Guerrero .40 1.00
49 Scott Rolen .25 .60
50 Jose Guillen .15 .40

1997 Zenith 8 x 10

COMPLETE SET (24) 10.00 25.00
ONE PER PACK
*DUFEX : 1X TO 2.5X BASIC 8 X 10
ONE DUFEX PER PACK
1 Frank Thomas .50 1.25
2 Tony Gwynn .60 1.50
3 Jeff Bagwell .30 .75
4 Ken Griffey Jr. 1.00 2.50
5 Mike Piazza .75 2.00
6 Greg Maddux .75 2.00
7 Ken Caminiti .20 .50
8 Albert Belle .20 .50
9 Ivan Rodriguez .30 .75
10 Sammy Sosa .50 1.25
11 Mark McGwire 1.25 3.00
12 Roger Clemens 1.00 2.50
13 Alex Rodriguez .75 2.00
14 Chipper Jones .50 1.25
15 Juan Gonzalez .20 .50
16 Barry Bonds 1.25 3.00
17 Derek Jeter 1.25 3.00
18 Hideo Nomo .50 1.25
19 Cal Ripken 1.50 4.00
20 Hideki Irabu .40 1.00
21 Andruw Jones .30 .75
22 Nomar Garciaparra .75 2.00
23 Vladimir Guerrero .50 1.25
24 Scott Rolen .30 .75

1997 Zenith 8 x 10 Dufex Samples

13 Alex Rodriguez 2.00 5.00

1997 Zenith the Big Picture

1 Frank Thomas 2.50 6.00
4 Ken Griffey Jr. 4.00 10.00
5 Mike Piazza 4.00 10.00
13 Alex Rodriguez 4.00 10.00
17 Derek Jeter 6.00 15.00
19 Cal Ripken Jr. 6.00 15.00

1997 Zenith V-2

COMPLETE SET (8) 75.00 150.00
STATED ODDS 1:47
1 Ken Griffey Jr. 10.00 25.00
2 Andruw Jones 3.00 8.00
3 Frank Thomas 5.00 12.00
4 Mike Piazza 8.00 20.00
5 Alex Rodriguez 8.00 20.00
6 Cal Ripken 15.00 40.00
7 Derek Jeter 12.50 30.00
8 Vladimir Guerrero 5.00 12.00

1997 Zenith Z-Team

COMPLETE SET (9) 75.00 150.00
1 Ken Griffey Jr. 10.00 25.00
2 Larry Walker 2.00 5.00
3 Frank Thomas 5.00 12.00
4 Alex Rodriguez 8.00 20.00
5 Mike Piazza 8.00 20.00
6 Cal Ripken 15.00 40.00
7 Derek Jeter 12.50 30.00
8 Andruw Jones 3.00 8.00
9 Roger Clemens 10.00 25.00

1998 Zenith Samples Large

COMPLETE SET (9) 10.00 25.00
Z1 Nomar Garciaparra 1.25 3.00
Z3 Greg Maddux 1.25 3.00
Z4 Frank Thomas .60 1.50
Z9 Andruw Jones .50 1.25
Z15 Derek Jeter 2.50 6.00
Z21 Mike Piazza 1.50 4.00
Z22 Tony Gwynn 1.25 3.00
Z35 Ivan Rodriguez .60 1.50
Z40 Ken Griffey Jr. 1.50 4.00

1998 Zenith Samples Small

COMPLETE SET (6) 6.00 15.00
2 Ken Griffey Jr. 1.50 4.00
12 Greg Maddux 1.25 3.00
14 Mike Piazza 1.25 3.00
17 Derek Jeter 2.50 6.00
18 Nomar Garciaparra 1.25 3.00
19 Ivan Rodriguez .60 1.50

1998 Zenith

The 1998 Zenith set was issued in one series totalling 100 cards. The packs retailed for $5.99 each and contained three 5x7 Zenith cards each with one standard size card inside. The standard-size cards listed here had to be removed from the inside of the jumbo packs by tearing the large cards in half. This ill-conceived concept was entitled "Dare to Tear", thus collectors were faced with the dilemma of having to choose between the standard size card of the jumbo 5" by 7" card. Ultimately, collectors by and large chose to carefully slice the back of the jumbo cards and remove the small card. The fronts feature color action player photos. The backs carry player information and career statistic.

COMPLETE SET (100) 20.00 50.00
1 Larry Walker .20 .50
2 Ken Griffey Jr. 1.00 2.50
3 Cal Ripken 1.50 4.00
4 Sammy Sosa .50 1.25
5 Andruw Jones .30 .75
6 Frank Thomas .50 1.25
7 Tony Gwynn .60 1.50
8 Rafael Palmeiro .30 .75
9 Tim Salmon .30 .75
10 Randy Johnson .50 1.25
11 Juan Gonzalez .20 .50
12 Greg Maddux .75 2.00
13 Vladimir Guerrero .50 1.25
14 Mike Piazza .75 2.00
15 Andres Galarraga .20 .50
16 Alex Rodriguez .75 2.00
17 Derek Jeter 1.25 3.00
18 Nomar Garciaparra .75 2.00
19 Ivan Rodriguez .30 .75
20 Chipper Jones .50 1.25
21 Barry Larkin .30 .75
22 Mo Vaughn .20 .50
23 Albert Belle .20 .50
24 Scott Rolen .30 .75
25 Sandy Alomar Jr. .20 .50
26 Roberto Alomar .30 .75
27 Andy Pettitte .30 .75
28 Chuck Knoblauch .20 .50
29 Jeff Bagwell .30 .75
30 Mike Mussina .30 .75
31 Fred McGriff .30 .75
32 Roger Clemens 1.00 2.50
33 Rusty Greer .20 .50
34 Edgar Martinez .30 .75
35 Paul Molitor .20 .50
36 Mark Grace .30 .75
37 Darin Erstad .20 .50
38 Kenny Lofton .20 .50
39 Tom Glavine .30 .75
40 Javier Lopez .20 .50
41 Will Clark .30 .75
42 Tino Martinez .30 .75
43 Raul Mondesi .20 .50
44 Brady Anderson .20 .50
45 Chan Ho Park .20 .50
46 Jason Giambi .20 .50
47 Manny Ramirez .30 .75
48 Jay Buhner .20 .50
49 Dante Bichette .20 .50
50 Jose Cruz Jr. .20 .50
51 Charles Johnson .20 .50
52 Bernard Gilkey .20 .50
53 Johnny Damon .30 .75
54 David Justice .20 .50
55 Justin Thompson .20 .50
56 Bobby Higginson .20 .50
57 Todd Hundley .20 .50
58 Gary Sheffield .20 .50
59 Barry Bonds 1.25 3.00
60 Mark McGwire 1.25 3.00
61 John Smoltz .30 .75
62 Tony Clark .20 .50
63 Brian Jordan .20 .50
64 Jason Kendall .20 .50
65 Mariano Rivera .50 1.25
66 Pedro Martinez .30 .75
67 Jim Thome .30 .75
68 Neifi Perez .20 .50
69 Kevin Brown .30 .75
70 Hideo Nomo .50 1.25
71 Craig Biggio .30 .75
72 Bernie Williams .30 .75
73 Jose Guillen .20 .50
74 Ken Caminiti .20 .50
75 Livan Hernandez .20 .50
76 Ray Lankford .20 .50
77 Jim Edmonds .20 .50
78 Matt Williams .20 .50
79 Mark Kotsay .20 .50
80 Moises Alou .20 .50
81 Antone Williamson .20 .50
82 Jaret Wright .20 .50
83 Jacob Cruz .20 .50
84 Abraham Nunez .20 .50
85 Raul Ibanez .20 .50
86 Miguel Tejada .50 1.25
87 Derrek Lee .30 .75
88 Juan Encarnacion .20 .50
89 Todd Helton .30 .75
90 Travis Lee .20 .50
91 Ben Grieve .20 .50
92 Ryan McGuire .20 .50
93 Richard Hidalgo .20 .50
94 Paul Konerko .20 .50
95 Shannon Stewart .20 .50
96 Homer Bush .20 .50
97 Lou Collier .20 .50
98 Jeff Abbott .20 .50
99 Brett Tomko .20 .50
100 Fernando Tatis .20 .50

1998 Zenith Z-Gold

*STARS: 6X TO 15X BASIC CARDS
RANDOM INSERTS IN PACKS
STATED PRINT RUN 100 SERIAL #'d SETS

1998 Zenith Z-Silver

COMPLETE SET (100) 250.00 500.00
*STARS: 2X TO 5X BASIC CARDS
STATED ODDS 1:7

1998 Zenith 5 x 7

COMPLETE SET (80) 30.00 80.00
THREE CARDS PER PACK
*IMPULSE: 2X TO 5X BASIC 5 X 7
*IMPULSE SLIT-BACKS: .5X TO 1.25X BASIC
IMPULSE STATED ODDS 1:7
*IMP.GOLD: 8X TO 20X BASIC 5 X 7
IMPULSE GOLD STATED ODDS 1:35
GOLD PRINT RUN 100 SERIAL #'d SETS
CONDITION SENSITIVE SET
PRICES BELOW ARE FOR MT UNCUT CARDS
SLIT MUST BE CLEAN RAZOR CUT BACK
1 Nomar Garciaparra 1.00 2.50
2 Andres Galarraga .25 .60
3 Greg Maddux 1.00 2.50
4 Frank Thomas .60 1.50
5 Mark McGwire 1.50 4.00
6 Rafael Palmeiro .40 1.00
7 John Smoltz .40 1.00
8 Jeff Bagwell .40 1.00
9 Andruw Jones .40 1.00
10 Rusty Greer .25 .60
11 Paul Molitor .25 .60
12 Bernie Williams .40 1.00
13 Kenny Lofton .25 .60
14 Alex Rodriguez 1.00 2.50
15 Derek Jeter 1.50 4.00
16 Scott Rolen .40 1.00
17 Albert Belle .25 .60
18 Mo Vaughn .25 .60
19 Chipper Jones .60 1.50
20 Chuck Knoblauch .25 .60
21 Mike Piazza 1.00 2.50
22 Tony Gwynn .75 2.00
23 Juan Gonzalez .25 .60
24 Andy Pettitte .40 1.00
25 Tim Salmon .40 1.00
26 Brady Anderson .25 .60
27 Mike Mussina .40 1.00
28 Edgar Martinez .40 1.00
29 Jose Guillen .25 .60
30 Hideo Nomo .60 1.50
31 Jim Thome .40 1.00
32 Mark Grace .40 1.00
33 Darin Erstad .25 .60
34 Bobby Higginson .25 .60
35 Ivan Rodriguez .40 1.00
36 Todd Hundley .25 .60
37 Sandy Alomar Jr. .25 .60
38 Gary Sheffield .25 .60
39 David Justice .25 .60
40 Ken Griffey Jr. 1.25 3.00
41 Vladimir Guerrero .60 1.50
42 Larry Walker .25 .60
43 Barry Bonds 1.50 4.00
44 Randy Johnson .60 1.50
45 Roger Clemens 1.25 3.00
46 Raul Mondesi .25 .60
47 Tino Martinez .40 1.00
48 Jason Giambi .25 .60
49 Matt Williams .25 .60
50 Cal Ripken 2.00 5.00
51 Barry Larkin .40 1.00
52 Jim Edmonds .25 .60
53 Ken Caminiti .25 .60
54 Sammy Sosa .60 1.50
55 Tony Clark .25 .60
56 Manny Ramirez .40 1.00
57 Bernard Gilkey .25 .60
58 Jose Cruz Jr. .25 .60
59 Brian Jordan .25 .60
60 Kevin Brown .40 1.00
61 Craig Biggio .40 1.00
62 Javier Lopez .25 .60
63 Jay Buhner .25 .60
64 Roberto Alomar .40 1.00
65 Justin Thompson .25 .60
66 Todd Helton .40 1.00
67 Travis Lee .25 .60
68 Paul Konerko .25 .60
69 Jaret Wright .25 .60
70 Ben Grieve .25 .60
71 Juan Encarnacion .25 .60
72 Ryan McGuire .25 .60
73 Derrek Lee .40 1.00
74 Abraham Nunez .25 .60
75 Richard Hidalgo .25 .60
76 Miguel Tejada .60 1.50
77 Jacob Cruz .25 .60
78 Homer Bush .25 .60
79 Jeff Abbott .25 .60
80 Lou Collier .25 .60

1998 Zenith Raising the Bar

COMPLETE SET (15) 10.00 25.00
STATED ODDS 1:25
1 Ken Griffey Jr. 2.00 5.00
2 Frank Thomas 1.00 2.50
3 Alex Rodriguez 1.25 3.00
4 Tony Gwynn 1.00 2.50
5 Mike Piazza 1.00 2.50
6 Ivan Rodriguez .60 1.50
7 Cal Ripken 3.00 8.00
8 Greg Maddux 1.25 3.00
9 Hideo Nomo 1.00 2.50
10 Mark McGwire 1.50 4.00
11 Juan Gonzalez .40 1.00
12 Andruw Jones .40 1.00
13 Jeff Bagwell .60 1.50
14 Chipper Jones 1.00 2.50
15 Nomar Garciaparra .60 1.50

1998 Zenith Rookie Thrills

COMPLETE SET (15) 10.00 25.00
STATED ODDS 1:25
1 Travis Lee .75 2.00
2 Juan Encarnacion .75 2.00
3 Derrek Lee 1.25 3.00
4 Raul Ibanez .75 2.00
5 Ryan McGuire .75 2.00
6 Todd Helton 1.25 3.00
7 Jacob Cruz .75 2.00
8 Abraham Nunez .75 2.00
9 Paul Konerko .75 2.00
10 Ben Grieve .75 2.00
11 Jeff Abbott .75 2.00
12 Richard Hidalgo .75 2.00
13 Jaret Wright .75 2.00
14 Lou Collier .75 2.00
15 Miguel Tejada 2.00 5.00

1998 Zenith Z-Team

COMPLETE SET (18) 60.00 120.00
CARDS 1-9 STATED ODDS 1:35
CARDS 10-18 STATED ODDS 1:58
*5 x 7 STARS: .6X TO 1.5X BASIC Z-TEAM
5 x 7 STATED ODDS 1:35
*GOLD: 1.25X TO 3X BASIC Z-TEAM
GOLD STATED ODDS 1:175
1 Frank Thomas 3.00 8.00
2 Ken Griffey Jr. 6.00 15.00
3 Mike Piazza 5.00 12.00
4 Cal Ripken 10.00 25.00
5 Alex Rodriguez 5.00 12.00
6 Greg Maddux 5.00 12.00
7 Derek Jeter 8.00 20.00
8 Chipper Jones 3.00 8.00
9 Roger Clemens 6.00 15.00
10 Ben Grieve 1.25 3.00
11 Derrek Lee 2.00 5.00
12 Jose Cruz Jr. 1.25 3.00
13 Nomar Garciaparra 5.00 12.00
14 Travis Lee 1.25 3.00
15 Todd Helton 2.00 5.00
16 Paul Konerko 1.25 3.00
17 Miguel Tejada 3.00 8.00
18 Scott Rolen 2.00 5.00

2005 Zenith Promo Koufax

NNO Sandy Koufax 1.25 3.00

2005 Zenith

COMPLETE SET (250) 40.00 60.00
COMMON CARD (1-230) .15 .40
COMMON RC (1-230) .20 .50
COMMON CARD (231-250) .20 .50
1 Curt Schilling .25 .60
2 Jim Edmonds .25 .60
3 Ichiro Suzuki .50 1.25
4 Jody Gerut .15 .40
5 Carlos Beltran .25 .60
6 Miguel Tejada .25 .60
7 Ted Lilly .15 .40
8 Bobby Abreu .15 .40
9 Mark Teixeira .25 .60
10 Manny Ramirez .40 1.00
11 Eric Gagne .15 .40
12 Adrian Beltre .40 1.00
13 Dmitri Young .15 .40
14 Alfonso Soriano .25 .60
15 Vladimir Guerrero .25 .60
16 Carl Crawford .25 .60
17 David Ortiz .40 1.00
18 Jose Guillen .15 .40
19 Miguel Cabrera .40 1.00
20 Alex Rodriguez .50 1.25
21 Brad Lidge .15 .40
22 Francisco Rodriguez .25 .60
23 Carlos Lee .15 .40
24 Ben Sheets .15 .40
25 Jason Schmidt .15 .40
26 Cesar Izturis .15 .40
27 Corey Patterson .15 .40
28 Marcus Giles .15 .40
29 Melvin Mora .15 .40
30 Yadier Molina 1.50 4.00
31 Juan Pierre .15 .40
32 Aubrey Huff .15 .40
33 Rafael Furcal .15 .40
34 David Dellucci .15 .40
35 Jake Peavy .15 .40
36 Aramis Ramirez .15 .40
37 Javy Lopez .15 .40
38 Aaron Rowand .15 .40
39 Raul Ibanez .25 .60
40 Jason Bay .15 .40
41 Michael Young .15 .40
42 Ivan Rodriguez .25 .60
43 Derrek Lee .15 .40
44 Adam Dunn .25 .60
45 Eric Chavez .15 .40
46 Pedro Martinez .25 .60
47 Roy Oswalt .25 .60
48 Kevin Millwood .15 .40
49 Carlos Delgado .15 .40
50 Derek Jeter 1.00 2.50
51 Johnny Damon .25 .60
52 Richie Sexson .15 .40
53 Nomar Garciaparra .25 .60
54 Edgar Renteria .15 .40
55 Carl Pavano .15 .40
56 Tim Wakefield .25 .60
57 Michael Barrett .15 .40
58 Johnny Estrada .15 .40
59 Jeff Kent .15 .40
60 Mark Loretta .15 .40
61 Greg Maddux .50 1.25
62 Hank Blalock .15 .40
63 Moises Alou .15 .40
64 Brad Radke .15 .40
65 Brad Wilkerson .15 .40
66 Sean Casey .15 .40
67 Oliver Perez .15 .40
68 Scott Hatteberg .15 .40
69 Mike Lowell .15 .40
70 Kazuo Matsui .15 .40
71 Mark Prior .25 .60
72 Hideki Matsui .60 1.50
73 Geoff Jenkins .15 .40
74 Gary Sheffield .15 .40
75 A.J. Burnett .15 .40
76 Vernon Wells .15 .40
77 Kenny Rogers .15 .40
78 Jose Reyes .25 .60
79 Victor Martinez .25 .60
80 Jorge Posada .25 .60
81 Rich Harden .15 .40
82 Travis Hafner .15 .40
83 Bret Boone .15 .40
84 Chipper Jones .40 1.00

85 Bartolo Colon .15 .40
86 Scott Podsednik .15 .40
87 Coco Crisp .15 .40
88 Luis Castillo .15 .40
89 John Smoltz .40 1.00
90 Andruw Jones .15 .40
91 Milton Bradley .15 .40
92 Torii Hunter .15 .40
93 Shawn Green .15 .40
94 Paul Konerko .25 .60
95 David Wells .15 .40
96 Scott Rolen .25 .60
97 Rodrigo Lopez .15 .40
98 Garret Anderson .15 .40
99 Tim Hudson .25 .60
100 Sammy Sosa .40 1.00
101 Jason Varitek .40 1.00
102 Lance Berkman .25 .60
103 Troy Glaus .15 .40
104 Carlos Guillen .15 .40
105 Jeff Bagwell .25 .60
106 Phil Nevin .15 .40
107 Freddy Garcia .15 .40
108 Jake Westbrook .15 .40
109 Marquis Grissom .15 .40
110 Johan Santana .25 .60
111 Kerry Wood .15 .40
112 Jose Vidro .15 .40
113 Mike Mussina .25 .60
114 Josh Beckett .15 .40
115 Matt Lawton .15 .40
116 Craig Biggio .25 .60
117 Reggie Sanders .15 .40
118 Jason Kendall .15 .40
119 Larry Walker .25 .60
120 Roger Clemens .50 1.25
121 C.C. Sabathia .25 .60
122 Javier Vazquez .15 .40
123 Barry Zito .25 .60
124 Jon Lieber .15 .40
125 Kris Benson .15 .40
126 Jacque Jones .15 .40
127 Ray Durham .15 .40
128 Mark Kotsay .15 .40
129 Jack Wilson .15 .40
130 Bobby Crosby .15 .40
131 Todd Helton .25 .60
132 Lyle Overbay .15 .40
133 Jon Garland .15 .40
134 Roy Halladay .25 .60
135 Orlando Cabrera .15 .40
136 Danny Kolb .15 .40
137 Austin Kearns .15 .40
138 Paul Lo Duca .15 .40
139 Magglio Ordonez .25 .60
140 Rafael Palmeiro .25 .60
141 Omar Vizquel .25 .60
142 Mike Piazza .40 1.00
143 Mark Mulder .15 .40
144 Dontrelle Willis .15 .40
145 Tom Glavine .25 .60
146 Khalil Greene .15 .40
147 Ken Griffey Jr. .75 2.00
148 Mike Sweeney .15 .40
149 Trot Nixon .15 .40
150 Randy Johnson .40 1.00
151 Doug Mientkiewicz .15 .40
152 Jeromy Burnitz .15 .40
153 Brandon Webb .25 .60
154 Kevin Brown .15 .40
155 Carlos Zambrano .25 .60
156 Shingo Takatsu .15 .40
157 Erubiel Durazo .15 .40
158 Jason Isringhausen .15 .40
159 Corey Koskie .15 .40
160 Aaron Boone .15 .40
161 Joe Nathan .15 .40
162 Nick Johnson .15 .40
163 Michael Tucker .15 .40
164 Chris Carpenter .25 .60
165 Preston Wilson .15 .40
166 J.T. Snow .15 .40
167 Hideo Nomo .40 1.00
168 Miguel Olivo .15 .40
169 Jarrod Washburn .15 .40
170 Derek Lowe .15 .40
171 Eric Milton .15 .40
172 Andy Pettitte .25 .60
173 Jason Giambi .15 .40
174 Richard Hidalgo .15 .40
175 Jayson Werth .25 .60
176 Juan Gonzalez .15 .40
177 Rocco Baldelli .15 .40
178 Steve Finley .15 .40
179 Frank Thomas .40 1.00
180 Kenny Lofton .15 .40
181 Randy Winn .15 .40
182 Brandon McCarthy RC .30 .75
183 Lew Ford .15 .40
184 Mike Cameron .15 .40
185 Carlos Pena .25 .60
186 Brian Roberts .15 .40
187 Jeremy Bonderman .15 .40
188 Luis Gonzalez .15 .40
189 J.D. Drew .15 .40
190 Frank Catalanotto .15 .40
191 John Buck .15 .40
192 Pat Burrell .15 .40
193 Ryan Klesko .15 .40
194 Jermaine Dye .15 .40
195 Mariano Rivera .50 1.25
196 Angel Berroa .15 .40
197 Victor Zambrano .15 .40
198 Joel Pineiro .15 .40
199 Jay Gibbons .15 .40
200 Albert Pujols .50 1.25
201 Billy Wagner .15 .40
202 Darin Erstad .15 .40
203 Jim Thome .25 .60
204 Adam LaRoche .15 .40
205 Cliff Floyd .15 .40
206 Grady Sizemore .25 .60
207 Garrett Atkins .15 .40
208 Phil Humber RC .50 1.25
209 Zack Greinke .50 1.25
210 Wladimir Balentien RC .30 .75
211 Ubaldo Jimenez RC .50 1.25
212 Dallas McPherson .15 .40
213 Justin Verlander RC 4.00 10.00
214 Justin Morneau .25 .60
215 Chase Utley .25 .60
216 Casey Kotchman .15 .40
217 Tadahito Iguchi RC .30 .75
218 Hanley Ramirez .25 .60
219 Scott Kazmir .40 1.00
220 J.J. Hardy .15 .40
221 Ambiorix Concepcion RC .20 .50
222 Jeff Niemann RC .50 1.25
223 David Wright .30 .75
224 Joe Mauer .30 .75
225 Rickie Weeks .15 .40
226 Yuniesky Betancourt RC .75 2.00
227 Brady Clark .15 .40
228 Keiichi Yabu RC .20 .50
229 Delmon Young .40 1.00
230 Nick Swisher .25 .60
231 George Brett 1.00 2.50
232 Ryne Sandberg 1.00 2.50
233 Mike Schmidt .75 2.00
234 Tony Gwynn .60 1.50
235 Rickey Henderson .50 1.25
236 Ozzie Smith .60 1.50
237 Reggie Jackson .30 .75
238 Steve Carlton .30 .75
239 Robin Yount .50 1.25
240 Tom Seaver .30 .75
241 Ted Williams 1.00 2.50
242 Don Mattingly 1.00 2.50
243 Mark Grace .30 .75
244 Rod Carew .30 .75
245 Willie Mays 1.00 2.50
246 Gary Carter .30 .75
247 Wade Boggs .30 .75
248 Dale Murphy .50 1.25
249 Nolan Ryan 1.50 4.00
250 Cal Ripken 1.50 4.00

2005 Zenith Artist's Proofs Gold

*GOLD AP 1-230: 6X TO 15X BASIC
*GOLD AP 1-230: 3X TO 8X BASIC RC
*GOLD AP 231-250: 5X TO 12X BASIC
OVERALL INSERT ODDS ONE PER PACK
STATED PRINT RUN 50 SERIAL #'d SETS

2005 Zenith Artist's Proofs Silver

*AP 1-230: 3X TO 8X BASIC
*AP 1-230: 1.5X TO 4X BASIC RC
*AP 231-250: 3X TO 8X BASIC
STATED ODDS 1:16

2005 Zenith Museum Collection

*MUSEUM 1-230: 1.5X TO 4X BASIC
*MUSEUM 1-230: .75X TO 2X BASIC RC
*MUSEUM 231-250: 1.5X TO 4X BASIC
STATED ODDS 1:3

2005 Zenith Z-Gold

*GOLD 1-230: 4X TO 10X BASIC
*GOLD 1-230: 3X TO 8X BASIC RC
*GOLD 231-250: 3X TO 8X BASIC
STATED ODDS 1:18 RETAIL

2005 Zenith Z-Silver

*SILVER 1-230: 1.25X TO 3X BASIC
*SILVER 1-230: 1X TO 2.5X BASIC RC
*SILVER 231-250: 1X TO 2.5X BASIC
STATED ODDS 1:2 RETAIL

2005 Zenith Epix Orange Play

STATED PRINT RUN 750 SERIAL #'d SETS
*BLACK GAME: 1X TO 2.5X BASIC
BLACK GAME PRINT RUN 75 #'d SETS
*BLACK MOMENT: 1.5X TO 4X BASIC
BLACK MOMENT PRINT RUN 25 #'d SETS
*BLACK PLAY: .75X TO 2X BASIC
BLACK PLAY PRINT RUN 100 #'d SETS
*BLACK SEASON: 1.25X TO 3X BASIC
BLACK SEASON PRINT RUN 50 #'d SETS
*BLUE GAME: .6X TO 1.5X BASIC
BLUE GAME PRINT RUN 350 #'d SETS
*BLUE MOMENT: .75X TO 2X BASIC
BLUE MOMENT PRINT RUN 150 #'d SETS
*BLUE PLAY: .5X TO 1.2X BASIC
BLUE PLAY PRINT RUN 500 #'d SETS
*BLUE SEASON: .6X TO 1.5X BASIC
BLUE SEASON PRINT RUN 250 #'d SETS
*EMERALD GAME: .75X TO 2X BASIC
EMERALD GAME PRINT RUN 100 #'d SETS
*EMERALD MOMENT: 1.25X TO 3X BASIC
EMERALD MOMENT PRINT RUN 50 #'d SETS
*EMERALD PLAY: .75X TO 2X BASIC
EMERALD PLAY PRINT RUN 150 #'d SETS
*EMERALD SEASON: 1X TO 2.5X BASIC
EMERALD SEASON PRINT RUN 75 #'d SETS
*ORANGE GAME: .5X TO 1.2X BASIC
ORANGE GAME PRINT RUN 500 #'d SETS
*ORANGE MOMENT: .6X TO 1.5X BASIC
ORANGE MOMENT PRINT RUN 250 #'d SETS
*ORANGE SEASON: .6X TO 1.5X BASIC
ORANGE SEASON PRINT RUN 350 #'d SETS
*PURPLE GAME: .6X TO 1.5X BASIC
PURPLE GAME PRINT RUN 250 #'d SETS
*PURPLE MOMENT: .75X TO 2X BASIC
PURPLE MOMENT PRINT RUN 100 #'d SETS
*PURPLE PLAY: .6X TO 1.5X BASIC
PURPLE PLAY PRINT RUN 350 #'d SETS
*PURPLE SEASON: .75X TO 2X BASIC
PURPLE SEASON PRINT RUN 150 #'d SETS
*RED GAME: .75X TO 2X BASIC
RED GAME PRINT RUN 150 #'d SETS
*RED MOMENT: 1.25X TO 3X BASIC
RED MOMENT PRINT RUN 50 #'d SETS
*RED PLAY: .6X TO 1.5X BASIC
RED PLAY PRINT RUN 250 #'d SETS
*RED SEASON: .75X TO 2X BASIC
RED SEASON PRINT RUN 100 #'d SETS
OVERALL EPIX ODDS 2:9
1 Vladimir Guerrero 1.25 3.00
2 Alex Rodriguez 2.50 6.00
3 Johan Santana 1.25 3.00
4 Todd Helton 1.25 3.00
5 Mark Teixeira 1.25 3.00
6 Manny Ramirez 2.00 5.00
7 Scott Rolen 1.25 3.00
8 Gary Sheffield .75 2.00
9 Miguel Cabrera 2.00 5.00
10 Jim Thome 1.25 3.00
11 Eric Chavez .75 2.00
12 Roger Clemens 2.50 6.00
13 Pedro Martinez 1.25 3.00
14 Roy Oswalt 1.25 3.00
15 Carlos Delgado .75 2.00
16 Nomar Garciaparra 1.25 3.00
17 Hideki Matsui 3.00 8.00
18 Shawn Green .75 2.00
19 Greg Maddux 2.50 6.00
20 Ted Williams 4.00 10.00
21 Don Mattingly 4.00 10.00
22 Cal Ripken 6.00 15.00
23 George Brett 4.00 10.00
24 Nolan Ryan 6.00 15.00
25 Willie Mays 4.00 10.00

2005 Zenith Mozaics

STATED ODDS 1:8
1 Pedro .60 1.50
Beltran
Glavine
2 Pujols 1.25 3.00
Edmonds
Mulder
3 Sosa 1.00 2.50
Tejada
Palmeiro
4 Teixeira .60 1.50
Blalock
M.Young
5 Andruw .40 1.00
Furcal
Estrada
6 Crosby .60 1.50
Chavez
Zito
7 S.Green .40 1.00
Glaus
L.Gonzalez
8 Kearns .60 1.50
Dunn
Casey
9 Thome .60 1.50
Abreu
Burrell
10 Berkman .60 1.50
Bagwell
Biggio
11 O.Cabrera .40 1.00
Finley
Erstad
12 Drew .40 1.00
Kent
Bradley
13 Willis .40 1.00
Lowell
Burnett
14 Beltre 1.00 2.50
Reed
Sexson
15 Mauer .75 2.00
Morneau
Jacque
16 Sheffield 1.50 4.00
Matsui
Mussina

2005 Zenith Mozaics Materials Single

OVERALL GU ODDS 1:9
1 Pedro Martinez Jsy 2.50 6.00
2 Albert Pujols Bat 6.00 15.00
3 Miguel Tejada Jsy 2.00 5.00
4 Mark Teixeira Bat 2.50 6.00
5 Andruw Jones Bat 2.50 6.00
7 Luis Gonzalez Jsy 2.00 5.00
8 Adam Dunn Bat 2.00 5.00
9 Bobby Abreu Jsy 2.00 5.00
10 Craig Biggio Bat 2.50 6.00
11 Darin Erstad Bat 2.00 5.00
12 J.D. Drew Bat 2.00 5.00
13 A.J. Burnett Bat 2.00 5.00
14 Richie Sexson Bat 2.00 5.00
15 Jacque Jones Bat 2.00 5.00
16 Gary Sheffield Fld Glv 2.50 6.00

2005 Zenith Mozaics Materials Triple Jerseys

PRINT RUNS B/WN 5-100 COPIES PER
NO PRICING ON QTY OF 5
PRIME PRINT RUNS B/WN 5-10 PER
NO PRIME PRICING DUE TO SCARCITY
OVERALL GU ODDS 1:9
4 Teixeira/Blal/Young/100 5.00 12.00
6 Crosby/Chavez/Zito/25 6.00 15.00
8 Kearns/Dunn/Casey/100 4.00 10.00
9 Thome/Abreu/Burrell/100 5.00 12.00
10 Berk/Bagwell/Biggio/100 6.00 15.00
16 Sheff/Matsui/Mussina/50 10.00 25.00

2005 Zenith Positions

STATED ODDS 1:21
1 Randy 1.25 3.00
Prior
Clemens
2 Pudge 1.00 2.50
Piazza
V.Martinez
3 Pujols 1.25 3.00
Helton
Ortiz
4 M.Giles .40 1.00
Loretta
Boone
5 Rolen 1.00 2.50
A.Ramirez
Chipper
6 K.Matsui .60 1.50
Tejada
M.Young
7 B.Giles 1.00 2.50
Manny
Stewart
8 Rocco .40 1.00
Andruw
V.Wells
9 M.Cabrera 1.00 2.50
Berkman
Vlad

2005 Zenith Positions Materials Singl

OVERALL GU ODDS 1:9
1 Mark Prior Bat 2.50 6.00
2 Ivan Rodriguez Bat 2.50 6.00
3 Albert Pujols Bat 6.00 15.00
4 Bret Boone Jsy 2.00 5.00
5 Chipper Jones Bat 3.00 8.00
6 Kazuo Matsui Jsy 2.00 5.00
7 Manny Ramirez Bat 2.50 6.00
8 Andruw Jones Bat 2.50 6.00
9 Lance Berkman Bat 2.00 5.00

2005 Zenith Positions Materials Triple Jersey

OVERALL GU ODDS 1:9
PRINT RUNS B/WN 5-100 COPIES PER
NO PRICING ON QTY OF 5
2 Pudge/Piazza/V.Mart/50 8.00 20.00
3 Pujols/Helton/Ortiz/50 8.00 20.00
5 Rolen/A.Ramirez/Chip/100 6.00 15.00
6 K.Matsui/Tejada/Young/75 4.00 10.00
8 Rocco/Andruw/Wells/100 5.00 12.00
9 M.Cabrera/Berk/Vlad/100 6.00 15.00

2005 Zenith Positions Materials Triple Jersey Prime

*PRIME p/r 25: 1X TO 2.5X BASIC p/r 75-100
*PRIME p/r 25: .75X TO 2X BASIC p/r 50
OVERALL GU ODDS 1:9
PRINT RUNS B/WN 5-25 COPIES PER
NO PRICING ON QTY OF 5
7 B.Giles/Manny/Stewart/25 12.50 30.00

2005 Zenith Red Hot

STATED ODDS 1:16
*WHITE HOT: .6X TO 1.5X BASIC
WHITE HOT ODDS 1:65
1 Scott Rolen .60 1.50
2 Johan Santana .60 1.50
3 Josh Beckett .40 1.00
4 Aubrey Huff .40 1.00
5 Alfonso Soriano .60 1.50
6 Jeff Bagwell .60 1.50
7 Ted Williams 2.00 5.00
8 Mark Prior .60 1.50
9 Todd Helton .60 1.50
10 Vladimir Guerrero .60 1.50

2005 Zenith Red Hot Bats

*BAT p/r 150: .4X TO 1X JSY p/r 150-300
*BAT p/r 150: .2X TO .5X JSY p/r 25
*BAT p/r 50: .3X TO .8X JSY p/r 25
OVERALL GU ODDS 1:9
STATED PRINT RUN 150 SERIAL #'d SETS

2005 Zenith Red Hot Jerseys

OVERALL GU ODDS 1:9
PRINT RUNS B/WN 25-300 COPIES PER
1 Scott Rolen/150 2.50 6.00
2 Johan Santana/150 3.00 8.00
3 Josh Beckett/300 2.00 5.00
4 Aubrey Huff/25 4.00 10.00
5 Alfonso Soriano/150 2.00 5.00
6 Jeff Bagwell/300 2.50 6.00
7 Ted Williams/25 30.00 60.00
8 Mark Prior/250 2.50 6.00
9 Todd Helton/165 2.50 6.00
10 Vladimir Guerrero/150 3.00 8.00

2005 Zenith Red Hot Jerseys Prime

*PRIME p/r 25: 1.25X TO 3X JSY p/r 150-300
*PRIME p/r 25: .6X TO 1.5X JSY p/r 25
OVERALL GU ODDS 1:9
PRINT RUNS B/WN 1-25 COPIES PER
NO PRICING ON QTY OF 1

2005 Zenith Roll Call Autographs

STATED ODDS 1:24
TIER INFO PROVIDED BY DONRUSS
TIER 1 IS SCARCEST
SEE BECKETT.COM FOR TIER/SP INFO
1 Hanley Ramirez T3 6.00 15.00
2 Sean Tracey T2 3.00 8.00
3 Justin Wechsler T2 3.00 8.00
4 Matt Lindstrom T2 3.00 8.00
5 Garrett Jones T2 10.00 25.00
6 Ambiorix Concepcion T3 3.00 8.00
7 Casey Rogowski T2 4.00 10.00
8 Kelly Shoppach T2 6.00 15.00
9 Sean Thompson T1 3.00 8.00
10 Jeff Miller T3 3.00 8.00
11 Chris Resop T2 4.00 10.00
12 Justin Verlander T1 40.00 80.00
13 Geovany Soto T2 6.00 15.00
14 Paulino Reynoso T3 3.00 8.00
15 Chris Roberson T2 3.00 8.00
16 Justin Leone T3 3.00 8.00
17 Jeff Niemann T1 6.00 15.00
18 Mark Woodyard T3 3.00 8.00
19 Raul Tablado T1 3.00 8.00
20 Norihiro Nakamura T1 15.00 40.00
21 Tony Pena T1 3.00 8.00
22 Wladimir Balentien T2 3.00 8.00
23 Miguel Negron T2 4.00 10.00
24 Eude Brito T2 4.00 10.00
25 Ubaldo Jimenez T3 6.00 15.00
26 Mike Morse T2 10.00 25.00
27 Devon Lowery T2 3.00 8.00
28 Phil Humber T1 6.00 15.00
29 Nate McLouth T1 6.00 15.00
30 Jason Hammel T2 6.00 15.00

2005 Zenith Spellbound

COMMON MADDUX (1-4) 1.25 3.00
COMMON CLEMENS (5-9) 1.00 2.50
COMMON A.ROD (10-13) 1.25 3.00
COMMON PUJOLS (14-19) 2.00 5.00
STATED ODDS 1:11

2005 Zenith Spellbound Jerseys

COMMON MADDUX (1-4) 6.00 15.00
MADDUX PRINT RUN 150 #'d SETS
COMMON CLEMENS (5-9) 6.00 15.00
CLEMENS PRINT RUN 150 #'d SETS
COMMON PUJOLS (14-19) 6.00 15.00
PUJOLS PRINT RUN 250 #'d SETS
OVERALL GU ODDS 1:9

2005 Zenith Team Zenith

STATED ODDS 1:31
*GOLD: 1X TO 2.5X BASIC
GOLD RANDOM INSERTS IN PACKS
GOLD PRINT RUN 100 SERIAL #'d SETS
1 Ichiro Suzuki 1.25 3.00
2 Jim Edmonds .60 1.50
3 Hideki Matsui 1.50 4.00
4 Alex Rodriguez 1.25 3.00
5 Derek Jeter 2.50 6.00
6 Alfonso Soriano .60 1.50
7 Jim Thome .60 1.50
8 Jorge Posada .60 1.50
9 Barry Zito .60 1.50
10 Curt Schilling .60 1.50
11 Willie Mays 2.00 5.00

2005 Zenith Team Zenith Bats

*BAT p/r 150: .4X TO 1X JSY p/r 150-300
*BAT p/r 50: .6X TO 1.5X JSY p/r 150-300
*BAT p/r 25: .75X TO 2X JSY p/r 150-300
OVERALL GU ODDS 1:9
PRINT RUNS B/WN 5-150 COPIES PER
NO PRICING ON QTY OF 10 OR LESS

2005 Zenith Team Zenith Jerseys

OVERALL GU ODDS 1:9
PRINT RUNS B/WN 15-300 COPIES PER
NO PRICING ON QTY OF 15
3 Hideki Matsui/165 8.00 20.00
7 Jim Thome/175 2.50 6.00
8 Jorge Posada/300 2.50 6.00
9 Barry Zito/150 2.00 5.00
10 Curt Schilling/150 2.50 6.00
11 Willie Mays/175 15.00 40.00

2005 Zenith Team Zenith Jerseys Prime

*JSY PRIME: 1.25X TO 3X JSY p/r 150-300
OVERALL GU ODDS 1:9
STATED PRINT RUN 25 SERIAL #'d SETS
2 Jim Edmonds/25 6.00 15.00
6 Alfonso Soriano/25 6.00 15.00

2005 Zenith White Hot

STATED ODDS 1:65

2005 Zenith White Hot Bats

*BAT: .6X TO 1.5X RED JSY p/r 150-300
*BAT: .3X TO .8X RED JSY p/r 25
OVERALL GU ODDS 1:9
STATED PRINT RUN 50 SERIAL #'d SETS

2005 Zenith White Hot Jerseys

*JSYp/r151-200: .4XTO1X RED JSYp/r150-300
*JSYp/r 50: .6X TO 1.5X RED JSYp/r150-300
PRINT RUNS B/WN 1-200 COPIES PER
NO PRICING ON QTY OF 9 OR LESS
PRIME PRINT RUNS B/WN 1-10 PER
NO PRIME PRICING DUE TO SCARCITY
OVERALL GU ODDS 1:9

2005 Zenith Z-Bats

*BAT T3: .4X TO 1X JSY T2
*BAT T3: .3X TO .8X JSY T1
*BAT T2: .4X TO 1X JSY T2
*BAT T1: .5X TO 1.2X JSY T2
*BAT T1: .4X TO 1X JSY T1
*BAT SP: .6X TO 1.5X JSY T2
*BAT SP: .5X TO 1.2X JSY T1
OVERALL GU ODDS 1:9
TIER AND SP INFO PROVIDED BY DONRUSS
SEE BECKETT.COM FOR TIER/SP INFO
8 Adam LaRoche SP 3.00 8.00
9 Nick Johnson T3 2.00 5.00
12 Kenny Lofton T3 2.50 6.00
15 Morgan Ensberg SP 3.00 8.00
24 Angel Berroa T3 2.00 5.00
26 Brandon Webb T1 2.50 6.00
31 Johnny Estrada T3 2.00 5.00
76 Brad Wilkerson T2 2.00 5.00

2005 Zenith Z-Combos

*COMBO p/r 100-150: .6X TO 1.5X JSY T2
*COMBO p/r 50: .75X TO 2X JSY T2
*COMBO p/r 50: .6X TO 1.5X JSY T1
*COMBO p/r 25: 1X TO 2.5X JSY T2
OVERALL GU ODDS 1:9
PRINT RUNS B/WN 1-150 COPIES PER
NO PRICING ON QTY OF 10 OR LESS
24 Angel Berroa Bat-Pants/100 3.00 8.00
26 B.Webb Bat-Pants/100 3.00 8.00

2005 Zenith Z-Combos Prime

*PRIME p/r 25: 1.25X TO 3X JSY T2
*PRIME p/r 25: 1X TO 2.5X JSY T1
OVERALL GU ODDS 1:9
PRINT RUNS B/WN 1-25 COPIES PER
NO PRICING ON QTY OF 10 OR LESS

2005 Zenith Z-Jerseys

OVERALL GU ODDS 1:9
TIER INFO PROVIDED BY DONRUSS
TIER 1 IS SCARCEST
SEE BECKETT.COM FOR TIER/SP INFO
1 Dan Haren T1 2.50 6.00
3 Rickey Henderson T2 4.00 10.00
4 Andy Pettitte T2 2.50 6.00
5 Jeremy Bonderman T2 2.00 5.00
6 Pat Burrell T2 2.00 5.00
7 Craig Wilson T2 2.00 5.00
10 Bernie Williams T2 2.50 6.00
11 Dontrelle Willis T2 2.00 5.00
13 Tom Glavine T2 2.50 6.00
14 Kazuo Matsui T2 2.00 5.00
16 Mike Piazza T2 3.00 8.00
17 Trot Nixon T2 2.00 5.00
18 Ryan Klesko T2 2.00 5.00
19 B.J. Upton T2 2.00 5.00
20 Brian Roberts T2 2.00 5.00
21 Omar Vizquel T2 2.50 6.00
22 Shannon Stewart T1 2.50 6.00
23 Preston Wilson T2 2.00 5.00
25 Garrett Atkins T2 2.00 5.00
27 Rafael Palmeiro T2 2.50 6.00
28 Mike Sweeney T2 2.00 5.00
29 Magglio Ordonez T1 2.50 6.00
30 Cal Ripken T2 10.00 25.00
32 Austin Kearns T2 2.00 5.00
33 Nolan Ryan T2 8.00 20.00
34 Orlando Cabrera T2 2.00 5.00
35 Roy Oswalt T2 2.00 5.00
36 Roy Halladay T2 2.00 5.00
37 Lyle Overbay T2 2.00 5.00
39 Jack Wilson T1 2.50 6.00
40 Jacque Jones T2 2.00 5.00
41 Eric Byrnes T1 2.50 6.00
42 Barry Zito T2 2.00 5.00
43 C.C. Sabathia T2 2.00 5.00
44 Tony Gwynn T2 4.00 10.00
45 Mike Cameron T2 2.00 5.00
46 Geoff Jenkins T2 2.00 5.00
47 Bo Jackson T2 4.00 10.00
48 Luis Gonzalez T2 2.00 5.00
49 Johnny Damon T2 2.50 6.00
50 Craig Biggio T2 2.50 6.00
51 Josh Beckett T2 2.00 5.00
52 Paul Molitor T2 2.50 6.00
53 Kerry Wood T2 2.00 5.00
54 Lew Ford T2 2.00 5.00
55 Ryne Sandberg T2 6.00 15.00
56 Jeff Bagwell T2 2.50 6.00
57 Casey Kotchman T1 2.50 6.00
58 Chipper Jones T2 3.00 8.00
59 Chone Figgins T2 2.00 5.00
60 Paul Konerko T2 2.00 5.00
61 Kevin Mench T2 2.00 5.00
62 David Wright T2 4.00 10.00
64 Andruw Jones T2 2.50 6.00
65 Garret Anderson T2 2.00 5.00
66 Jorge Posada T2 2.50 6.00
68 Travis Hafner T2 2.00 5.00
69 Victor Martinez T2 2.00 5.00
70 Vernon Wells T2 2.00 5.00
71 A.J. Burnett T2 2.00 5.00
72 Francisco Rodriguez T2 2.00 5.00
73 Mark Prior T2 2.50 6.00
74 Mike Lowell T2 2.00 5.00
75 Sean Casey T2 2.00 5.00
77 Carlos Zambrano T2 2.00 5.00
78 Brad Radke T2 2.00 5.00
79 Moises Alou T2 2.00 5.00
80 Livan Hernandez T2 2.00 5.00
81 Hank Blalock T2 2.00 5.00
82 J.D. Drew T2 2.00 5.00
83 Reggie Jackson T2 3.00 8.00
84 Mark Buehrle T1 2.50 6.00
86 Edgar Renteria T2 2.00 5.00
87 Adam Dunn T2 2.00 5.00
88 Derrek Lee T2 2.50 6.00
90 Michael Young T2 2.00 5.00
91 Dale Murphy T2 3.00 8.00
92 Aramis Ramirez T2 2.00 5.00
93 Francisco Cordero T2 2.00 5.00
95 Aubrey Huff T2 2.00 5.00
96 Ben Sheets T2 2.00 5.00
97 Carlos Lee T2 2.00 5.00
98 Miguel Cabrera T2 5.00 12.00
99 Mark Teixeira T1 3.00 8.00
100 Albert Pujols T2 6.00 15.00

2005 Zenith Z-Jerseys Prime

*PRIME p/r 100-150: .75X TO 2X JSY T2
*PRIME p/r 100-150: .6X TO 1.5X JSY T1
*PRIME p/r 50-70: 1X TO 2.5X JSY T2
*PRIME p/r 50-70: .75X TO 2X JSY T1
*PRIME p/r 25: 1.25X TO 3X JSY T2
OVERALL GU ODDS 1:9
PRINT RUNS B/WN 1-150 COPIES PER
NO PRICING ON QTY OF 10 OR LESS
31 Johnny Estrada/100 4.00 10.00

2005 Zenith Z-Graphs

OVERALL AU ODDS 1:18
PRINT RUNS B/WN 1-250 COPIES PER
1 Dan Haren/250 6.00 15.00
2 Dallas McPherson/250 4.00 10.00
5 Jeremy Bonderman/200 6.00 15.00
7 Craig Wilson/250 4.00 10.00
8 Adam LaRoche/250 6.00 15.00
9 Nick Johnson/250 6.00 15.00
11 Dontrelle Willis/25 15.00 40.00
15 Morgan Ensberg/250 6.00 15.00
17 Trot Nixon/100 10.00 25.00
19 B.J. Upton/50 8.00 20.00
20 Brian Roberts/250 6.00 15.00
21 Omar Vizquel/100 10.00 25.00
22 Shannon Stewart/100 6.00 15.00
24 Angel Berroa/100 4.00 10.00
26 Brandon Webb/100 4.00 10.00
29 Magglio Ordonez/100 6.00 15.00
30 Cal Ripken/100 60.00 120.00
31 Johnny Estrada/50 5.00 12.00
32 Austin Kearns/100 4.00 10.00
33 Nolan Ryan/34 50.00 100.00
34 Orlando Cabrera/250 6.00 15.00
35 Roy Oswalt/100 6.00 15.00
36 Roy Halladay/50 12.50 30.00
38 Bobby Crosby/50 8.00 20.00
39 Jack Wilson/25 6.00 15.00
40 Jacque Jones/100 6.00 15.00
41 Eric Byrnes/250 4.00 10.00
44 Tony Gwynn/25 25.00 60.00
52 Paul Molitor/25 10.00 25.00
55 Ryne Sandberg/25 15.00 40.00
57 Casey Kotchman/100 6.00 15.00
60 Paul Konerko/100 10.00 25.00
62 David Wright/100 15.00 40.00
63 Milton Bradley/100 6.00 15.00
67 Rich Harden/250 6.00 15.00
68 Travis Hafner/250 6.00 15.00
69 Victor Martinez/25 10.00 25.00
70 Vernon Wells/25 10.00 25.00
72 Francisco Rodriguez/100 10.00 25.00
73 Mark Prior/25 6.00 15.00
75 Sean Casey/50 8.00 20.00
77 Carlos Zambrano/50 8.00 20.00
80 Livan Hernandez/100 6.00 15.00
84 Mark Buehrle/100 8.00 20.00
85 Keith Foulke/100 10.00 25.00
86 Edgar Renteria/50 8.00 20.00
88 Derrek Lee/100 10.00 25.00
89 Joe Nathan/100 6.00 15.00
90 Michael Young/50 8.00 20.00
91 Dale Murphy/100 10.00 25.00
93 Francisco Cordero/100 4.00 10.00
94 Jake Peavy/100 10.00 25.00
95 Aubrey Huff/100 6.00 15.00
96 Ben Sheets/50 8.00 20.00
97 Carlos Lee/25 10.00 25.00
98 Miguel Cabrera/25 20.00 50.00
99 Mark Teixeira/25 15.00 40.00

2005 Zenith Z-Batgraphs

*BAT p/r 100: .6X TO 1.5X AU p/r 200-250
*BAT p/r 100: .5X TO 1.2X AU p/r 100
*BAT p/r 100: .4X TO 1X AU p/r 50
*BAT p/r 50: .6X TO 1.5X AU p/r 100
*BAT p/r 50: .4X TO 1X AU p/r 25-34
*BAT p/r 20-25: .6X TO 1.5X AU p/r 50
*BAT p/r 20-25: .5X TO 1.2X AU p/r 25-34
OVERALL AU ODDS 1:18
PRINT RUNS B/WN 1-100 COPIES PER
NO PRICING ON QTY OF 10 OR LESS
59 Chone Figgins/50 10.00 25.00

2005 Zenith Z-Jerseygraphs

*JSY p/r 100: .6X TO 1.5X AU p/r 200-250
*JSY p/r 100: .5X TO 1.2X AU p/r 100
*JSY p/r 100: .4X TO 1X AU p/r 50
*JSY p/r 50: .75X TO 2X AU p/r 200-250
*JSY p/r 50: .6X TO 1.5X AU p/r 100
*JSY p/r 50: .5X TO 1.2X AU p/r 50
*JSY p/r 20-25: 1X TO 2.5X AU p/r 200-250
*JSY p/r 20-25: .75X TO 2X AU p/r 100
*JSY p/r 20-25: .6X TO 1.5X AU p/r 34-50
*JSY p/r 20-25: .5X TO 1.2X AU p/r 25
OVERALL AU ODDS 1:18
PRINT RUNS B/WN 1-100 COPIES PER
NO PRICING ON QTY OF 10 OR LESS
37 Lyle Overbay/25 8.00 20.00
59 Chone Figgins/50 10.00 25.00

2005 Zenith Z-Jerseygraphs Prime

*PRIME p/r 20-25: 1.25X TO 3X AUp/r200-250
*PRIME p/r 20-25: 1X TO 2.5X AU p/r 100
*PRIME p/r 20-25: .75X TO 2X AU p/r 50
*PRIME p/r 20-25: .6X TO 1.5X AU p/r 25-34
OVERALL AU ODDS 1:18
PRINT RUNS B/WN 1-25 COPIES PER
NO PRICING ON QTY OF 15 OR LESS
37 Lyle Overbay/20 10.00 25.00

2005 Zenith Z-Team

STATED ODDS 1:11
*GOLD: 1X TO 2.5X BASIC
GOLD RANDOM INSERTS IN PACKS
GOLD PRINT RUN 100 SERIAL #'d SETS
1 Albert Pujols 1.25 3.00
2 Carlos Beltran .60 1.50
3 Randy Johnson 1.00 2.50
4 Miguel Tejada .60 1.50
5 Ichiro Suzuki 1.25 3.00
6 Eric Gagne .40 1.00
7 Adrian Beltre 1.00 2.50
8 Alfonso Soriano .60 1.50
9 Jim Edmonds .60 1.50
10 David Ortiz 1.00 2.50
11 Curt Schilling .60 1.50
12 Mariano Rivera 1.25 3.00
13 Derek Jeter 2.50 6.00
14 Ivan Rodriguez .60 1.50
15 Johnny Damon .60 1.50
16 Mark Prior .60 1.50
17 Vernon Wells .40 1.00
18 Chipper Jones 1.00 2.50
19 Torii Hunter .40 1.00
20 Tim Hudson .60 1.50
21 Lance Berkman .60 1.50
22 Troy Glaus .40 1.00
23 Mike Piazza 1.00 2.50
24 Mark Mulder .40 1.00
25 Ken Griffey Jr. 2.00 5.00

1992 Ziploc

This 11-card standard-size set features posed player photos of many of the game's all-time greats. The set was available via a mail-in offer for 50 cents and two UPC's from Ziploc sandwich bags. Individual cards were found one per specially marked package.

COMPLETE SET (11) 4.00 10.00
1 Warren Spahn .40 1.00
2 Bob Gibson .40 1.00
3 Rollie Fingers .20 .50
4 Carl Yastrzemski .40 1.00
5 Brooks Robinson .60 1.50
6 Pee Wee Reese .40 1.00
7 Willie McCovey .40 1.00
8 Willie Mays .75 2.00
9 Nellie Fox .20 .50
10 Yogi Berra .60 1.50
11 Hank Aaron .75 2.00

1960 Bill Zuber Restaurant

These items features retired Yankee Bill Zuber. The postcard is black-and-white borderless portrait in his New York Yankees uniform with a facsimile autograph. The back displays a postcard format with an advertisement for his restaurant in Homestead, Iowa. The matchbook has a small photo of Zuber and then complete informaiton about the restaurant as well as some details about his career.

COMPLETE SET (2) 12.50 30.00
1 Bill Zuber Postcard 6.00 15.00
2 Bill Zuber Matchbook 6.00 15.00

ACKNOWLEDGEMENTS

Each year, we refine the process of developing the most accurate and up-to-date information for this book. We believe this year's Almanac is our best yet. Thanks again to all the contributors nationwide (listed below) as well as our staff here in Dallas.

Those who have worked closely with us on this and many other books have again proven themselves invaluable: Ed Allan, Frank and Vivian Barning, Levi Bleam and Jim Fleck (707 Sportscards), T. Scott Brandon, Peter Brennan, Ray Bright, Card Collectors Co., Dwight Chapin, Theo Chen, Barry Colla, Dick DeCourcy, Bill and Diane Dodge, Brett Domue, Ben Ecklar, Dan Even, David Festberg, Gean Paul Figari, Steve Freedman, Gervise Ford, Larry and Jeff Fritsch, Tony Galovich, Dick Gilkeson, Steve Gold (AU Sports), Bill Goodwin, Mike and Howard Gordon, George Grauer, Steve Green (STB Sports), John Greenwald, Wayne Grove, Bill Henderson, Jerry and Etta Hersh, Mike Hersh, Dan Hitt, Neil Hoppenworth, Keith Hower, Hunt Auction, Mike Jaspersen, Steven Judd, Jay and Mary Kasper (Jay's Emporium), Jerry Katz, Eddie Kelly, Pete Kennedy, Rich Klein, David Kohler (SportsCards Plus), Terry Knouse (Tik and Tik), Tom Layberger, Tom Leon, Robert Lifson (Robert Edward Auctions), Lew Lipset (Four Base Hits), Mike Livingston, Leon Luckey, Mark Macrae, Bill Madden, Bill Mastro, Doug Allen and Ron Oser (Mastro Auctions), Dr.William McAvoy, Michael McDonald, Mid-Atlantic Sports Cards (Bill Bossert), Gary Mills, Ernie Montella, Brian Morris, Mike Mosier (Columbia City Collectibles Co.), B.A. Murry, Ralph Nozaki, Oldies and Goodies (Nigel Spill), Oregon Trail Auctions, Jack Pollard, David Porter, Jeff Prillaman, Pat Quinn, Jerald Reichstein, Gavin Riley, Clifton Rouse, John Rumierz, Grant Sandground, Pat Blandford, Lonn Passon and Kevin Savage (Sports Gallery), Gary Sawatski and Jim Justus (The Wizards of Odd), Mike Schechter, Bill and Darlene Shafer, Dave Sliepka, Barry Sloate, John E. Spalding, Phil Spector, Rob Springs, Ted Taylor, Lee Temanson, Topps (Clay Luraschi), Tim Trout, Ed Twombly, Upper Deck (Don Williams and Chris Carlin), Wayne Varner, Bill Vizas, Waukesha Sportscards, Dave Weber, Brian and Mike Wentz (BMWCards), Bill Wesslund (Portland Sports Card Co.), Kit Young, Rick Young, Ted Zanidakis, Robert Zanze (Z-Cards and Sports), Bill Zimpleman and Dean Zindler. Finally we give a special acknowledgment to the late Dennis W. Eckes, "Mr. Sport Americana." The success of the Beckett Price Guides has always been the result of a team effort.

It is very difficult to be "accurate" - one can only do one's best. But this job is especially difficult since we're shooting at a moving target: Prices are fluctuating all the time. Having several full-time pricing experts has definitely proven to be better than just one, and I thank all of them for working together to provide you, our readers, with the most accurate prices possible.

Many people have provided price input, illustrative material, checklist verifications, errata, and/or background information. We should like to individually thank AbD Cards (Dale Wesolewski), Action Card Sales, Jerry Adamic, Johnny and Sandy Adams, Mehdi Ahlei, Alex's MVP Cards & Comics, Will Allison, Dennis Anderson, Ed Anderson, Shane Anderson, Ellis Anmuth, Alan Applegate, Ric Apter, Clyde Archer, Randy Archer, Burl Armstrong, Neil Armstrong, Barry Arnold, Carlos Ayala, B and J Sportscards, Jeremy Bachman, Dave Bailey, Ball Four Cards (Frank and Steve Pemper), Bob Bartosz, Jay Behrens, Bubba Bennett, Carl Berg, David Berman, Beulah Sports (Jeff Blatt), B.J. Sportscollectables, Al Blumkin, David Boedicker (The Wild Pitch Inc.), Louis Bollman, Tim Bond, Terry Boyd, Dan Brandenberry, Jeff Breitenfield, John Brigandi, Scott Brockleman, John Broggi, D.Bruce Brown, Virgil Burns, Greg Bussineau, David Byer, California Card Co., Capital Cards, Danny Cariseo, Carl Carlson (C.T.S.), Jim Carr, Brian Cataquet, Ira Cetron, Sandy Chan, Ric Chandgie, Ray Cherry, Bigg Wayne Christian, Ryan Christoff (Thanks for the help with Cuban Cards), Josh Chidester, Michael and Abe Citron, Dr. Jeffrey Clair, Michael Cohen, Tom Cohoon (Cardboard Dreams), Gary Collett, Jay Conti, Brian Coppola, Rick Cosmen (RC Card Co.), Lou Costanzo (Champion Sports), Mike Coyne, Tony Craig (T.C. Card Co.), Solomon Cramer, Kevin Crane, Taylor Crane, Chad Cripe, Scott Crump, Allen Custer, Dave Dame, Scott Dantio, Dee's Baseball Cards (Dee Robinson), Joe Delgrippo, Mike DeLuca, Ken Dinerman (California Cruizers), Rob DiSalvatore, Cliff Dolgins, Discount Dorothy, Richard Dolloff, Darren Duet, Joe Donato, Jerry Dong, Pat Dorsey, Double Play Baseball Cards, Joe Drelich, Richard Duglin (Baseball Cards-N-More), The Dugout, Ken Edick (Home Plate of Utah), Brad Englehardt, Terry Falkner, Mike and Chris Fanning, David Fela, Linda Ferrigno and Mark Mezzardi, Jay Finglass, A.J. Firestone, Scott Flatto, Bob Flitter, Fremont Fong, Paul Franzetti, Ron Frasier, Tom Freeman, Bob Frye, Bill Fusaro, Chris Gala, David Garza, David Gaumer, Georgetown Card Exchange, David Giove, Dick Goddard, Jeff Goldstein, Ron Gomez, Rich Gove, Paul Griggs, Jay and Jan Grinsby, Bob Grissett, Gerry Guenther, Neil Gubitz, Hall's Nostalgia, Gregg Hara, Lyman and Brett Hardeman (OldCardboard.com), Todd Harrell, Robert Harrison, Steve Hart, Floyd Haynes (H and H Baseball Cards), Kevin Heffner, Joel Hellman, Peter Henrici, Ron Hetrick, Hit and Run Cards (Jon, David, and Kirk Peterson), Vinny Ho, Paul Holstein, Johnny Hustle Card Co., John Inouye, Vern Isenberg, Dale Jackson, Marshall Jackson, Mike Jardina, Paul Jastrzembski, Jeff's Sports Cards, Donn Jennings Cards, George Johnson, Craig Jones, Chuck Juliana, Nick Kardoulias, Scott Kashner, Frank and Rose Katen, Steven J Kerno, Kevin's Kards, Kingdom Collectibles, Inc., John Klassnik, Steve Kluback, Don Knutsen, Gregg Kohn, Mike Kohlhas, Bob & Bryan Kornfield, Josh Krasner, Carl and Maryanne Laron, Bill Larsen, Howard Lau, Richard S. Lawrence, William Lawrence, Brent Lee, Morley Leeking, Irv Lerner, Larry and Sally Levine, Simeon Lipman, Larry Loeschen (A and J Sportscards), Neil Lopez, Kendall Loyd (Orlando Sportscards South), Steve Lowe, Leon Luckey, Ray Luurs, Jim Macie, Peter Maltin, Paul Marchant, Brian Marcy, Scott Martinez, James S. Maxwell Jr., McDag Productions Inc., Bob McDonald, Tony McLaughlin, Mendal Mearkle, Carlos Medina, Ken Melanson, William Mendel, Blake Meyer (Lone Star Sportscards), Tim Meyer, Joe Michalowicz, Lee Milazzo, Cary S. Miller, George Miller, Wayne Miller, Dick Millerd, Frank Mineo, Mitchell's Baseball Cards, John Morales, Paul Moss, William Munn, Mark Murphy, Robert Nappe, National Sportscard Exchange, Roger Neufeldt, Steve Novella, Bud Obermeyer, John O'Hara, Glenn Olson, Scott Olson, Luther Owen, Earle Parrish, Clay Pasternack, Michael Perrotta, Bobby Plapinger, Tom Pfirrmann, Don Phlong, Loran Pulver, Bob Ragonese, Bryan Rappaport, Don and Tom Ras, Robert M. Ray, Phil Regli, Rob Resnick, Dave Reynolds, David Ring, Carson Ritchey, Bill Rodman, Craig Roehrig, Mike Sablow, Terry Sack, Thomas Salem, Barry Sanders, Jon Sands, Tony Scarpa, John Schad, Dave Schau (Baseball Cards), Marc Scully, Masa Shinohara, Eddie Silard, Mike Slepcevic, Sam Sliheet, Art Smith, Cary Smith, Jerry Smolin, Lynn and Todd Solt, Jerry Sorice, Don Spagnolo, Sports Card Fan-Attic, The Sport Hobbyist, Norm Stapleton, Bill Steinberg, Lisa Stellato (Never Enough Cards), Rob Stenzel, Jason Stern, Andy Stoltz, Rob Stenzel, Bill Stone, Ted Straka, Tim Strandberg (East Texas Sports Cards), Edward Strauss, Strike Three, Richard Strobino, Kevin Struss, Superior Sport Card, Dr. Richard Swales, Steve Taft, George Tahinos, Ian Taylor, The Thirdhand Shoppe, Dick Thompson, Brent Thornton, Paul Thornton, Jim and Sally Thurtell, Bud Tompkins (Minnesota Connection), Philip J. Tremont, Ralph Triplette, Umpire's Choice Inc., Eric Unglaub, David Vargha, Hoyt Vanderpool, Steven Wagman, T. Wall, Gary A. Walter, Adam Warshaw, Dave Weber, Joe and John Weisenburger (The Wise Guys), Richard West, Mike Wheat, Louise and Richard Wiercinski, Don Williams (Robin's Nest of Dolls), Jeff Williams, John Williams, Kent Williams, Craig Williamson, Richard Wong, Rich Wojtasick, John Wolf Jr., Jay Wolt (Cavalcade of Sports), Eric Wu, Joe Yanello, Peter Yee, Tom Zocco, Mark Zubrensky and Tim Zwick.

Every year we make active solicitations for expert input. We are particularly appreciative of help (however extensive or cursory) provided for this volume. We receive many inquiries, comments and questions regarding material within this book. In fact, each and every one is read and digested. Time constraints, however, prevent us from personally replying. But keep sharing your knowledge. Your letters and input are part of the "big picture" of hobby information we can pass along to readers in our books and magazines. Even though we cannot respond to each letter or email, you are making significant contributions to the hobby through your interest and comments.

The effort to continually refine and improve this book also involves a growing number of people and types of expertise on our home team. Our company boasts a substantial Collectibles Data Group, which strengthens our ability to provide comprehensive analysis of the marketplace. CDG capably handled numerous technical details and provided able assistance in the preparation of this edition.

The Beckett baseball specialists are Brian Fleischer (Senior Market Analyst) and Sam Zimmer (Market Analyst). Their pricing analysis and careful proofreading were key contributions to the accuracy of this annual. They were ably assisted by the rest of the Market Analysts: Jeff Camay, Lloyd Almonguera, Kristian Redulla, Justin Grunert, Matt Bible, Eric Norton, Steve Dalton, Adrian Saba, Angelou Talle, and Rex Pastrana. Daniel Moscoso is in charge of our Digital Studio.

The price gathering and analytical talents of this fine group of hobbyists have helped make our Beckett team stronger, while making this guide and its companion monthly Price Guide more widely recognized as the hobby's most reliable and relied upon sources of pricing information. Surajpal Singh Bisht, Hemant Tiwari, Hritik Godara and Aman Kumar were responsible for layout of the book. The reason this book looks as good as it does is due to their hard work and expertise.

In the years since this guide debuted, Beckett Media has grown beyond any rational expectation. Many talented and hardworking individuals have been instrumental in this growth and success. Our whole team is to be congratulated for what we have accomplished.